Additional Content Online or on CD

Paragraph numbers in the main text marked with a "+", together with a symbol in the margin, denote content available only on *White Book on Westlaw UK* and the *Civil Procedure CD*.

See page v and the list of content available online and on CD on page xiii for further details.

# CIVIL PROCEDURE

2010

# CIVIL PROCEDURE

## Volume 2

The Civil Procedure Rules and Practice Directions contained in this volume are up-to-date generally to April 6, 2010. For further updates, see http://www.sweetandmaxwell.co.uk/whitebook.

**White Book Updating Service—Password**

To access the White Book Civil Procedure Rules and Forms Updating Service and to register for the Alerter services, you will need to enter the following password:

WB2010

SWEET & MAXWELL THOMSON REUTERS

Published in 2010 by Thomson Reuters (Legal) Limited
(Registered in England & Wales, Company No 1679046.
Registered Office and address for service:
100 Avenue Road, London, NW3 3PF) trading as Sweet & Maxwell.
Table of International and European Legislation and Additional Content Online and On CD Contents typeset by Hobbs the Printers Ltd, Totton, Hampshire. All other typesetting by Sweet & Maxwell electronic publishing system.
Printed by L.E.G.O. S.p.A., Lavis (TN), Italy.
For further information on our products and services, visit
http://www.sweetandmaxwell.co.uk.

*No natural forests were destroyed to make this product; only farmed timber was used and replanted.*

**British Library Cataloguing in Publication Data**
A catalogue record for this book is available from the British Library

ISBN 978-0-41404-259-9

## ADDITIONAL CONTENT ONLINE AND ON CD

A selection of existing content, together with brand new content, is available only on *White Book on Westlaw UK* and the *Civil Procedure CD*. This process has been started principally with Vol.2. We welcome any feedback—please email *whitebook@sweetandmaxwell.co.uk*

Please refer to the separate Additional Content Online and on CD list on page xiii for a detailed list of this material.

In order to assist navigation and to draw your attention to the relocated material, a symbol is placed in the margin of the main text.

In tandem with the symbol a system of cross-references is used. References to the relocated material are placed at the beginning of statutes or sections to flag that some or all of the content is online or and on CD only. References also appear within statutes or sections where a selection of material has been relocated. The latter alerts readers to relocated paragraph numbers and statutory sections (and relevant commentary).

Paragraph numbers marked with a "+" appear in the tables and index. The "+" denotes electronic content. Similar paragraph numbers appear in the cross-references mentioned above and within the statutory arrangement of sections.

On *White Book on Westlaw UK* and the *Civil Procedure CD*, the "+" paragraph numbers appear in their correct places, with the additional content remaining inline.

# CONTENTS



***See page xiii for a list of additional content online and on CD.***

***See page xiii for a list of additional content online and on CD.***

*See page xiii for a list of additional content online and on CD.*

*See page xiii for a list of additional content online and on CD.*

*See page xiii for a list of additional content online and on CD.*

# ADDITIONAL CONTENT ONLINE AND ON CD

This is a list of content and associated commentary available **only** on **White Book on Westlaw UK** or the **Civil Procedure CD**. This list does not refer to print content (please see the previous print contents on page vii).

We welcome any feedback—please email *whitebook@sweetandmaxwell.co.uk*.

## VOLUME ONE



## VOLUME TWO

**Section 3—Other Proceedings**

**3A Housing**



**3E Insolvency Proceedings**



**3F Personal Injury**



**3H Consumer Credit and Consumer Law**

**9B Other Statutes and Regulations**

**Section 10—Court Fees**



**Appendix 1—Courts Directory**

# SERVICE INFORMATION

### *The White Book Service 2010*

During 2009 we undertook a range of research with subscribers in order to help steer the continuing development of *The White Book Service*. As in previous years, we received a good response to our annual subscriber survey, which was followed up by a number of one-to-one interviews. Thank you to all who participated. A reminder that we welcome feedback from subscribers throughout the year—please email *whitebook@sweetandmaxwell.co.uk*.

### *Additional Content Online and on CD*

A selection of existing content, together with brand new content, is available only on *White Book on Westlaw UK* and the *Civil Procedure CD*. We have started this process principally with Vol.2. Please refer to the Additional Content Online and on CD on page xiii for a detailed list.

In order to assist navigation and to draw your attention to the relocated material, a symbol is placed in the margin of the text.

In tandem with the symbol, a system of cross-references is used. References to relocated material are placed at the beginning of statutes or sections to flag that some or all of the content is online and on CD only. References also appear within statutes or sections where a selection of material has been relocated. The latter alerts readers to relocated paragraph numbers and statutory sections (and relevant commentary).

Paragraph numbers marked with a "+" symbol appear in the tables and index. The "+" symbol denotes electronic content. Similar paragraph numbers appear in the cross-references mentioned above and within the statutory arrangement of sections.

On *White Book on Westlaw UK* and the *Civil Procedure CD*, the "+" paragraph numbers appear in their correct places, with the additional content online and on CD remaining inline.

### *Up-to-date to April 6, 2010*

*Civil Procedure* published on March 31, 2010. The Rules and Practice Directions have been updated to include changes introduced by the Civil Procedure (Amendment) Rules 2009 (SI 2009/2092) and TSO Update 50, in force generally October 1, 2009, and Civil Procedure (Amendment No.2) Rules 2009 (SI 2009/3390) and TSO Update 51, in force generally April 6, 2010, as well as the Civil Jurisdiction and Judgments Regulations 2009 (SI 2009/3131). Further amendments will be published in updating supplements. Notes have been included to indicate the in-force date of changes where necessary.

For further updates see **http://www.sweetandmaxwell.co.uk/whitebook** and click on "White Book Updating Service". You will need to enter your subscriber password: **WB2010**. This site contains the latest Civil Procedure Rules and Practice Directions. Changes which have been introduced since *The White Book* published in April are highlighted in red.

Every effort has been made to ensure that the commentary and case law is as stated at January 22, 2010. *Civil Procedure News* and the two updating supplements will keep you abreast of developments through the subscription year.

### *Forms*

The Forms Volume is no longer automatically included in *The White Book Service* (for new subscribers). New subscribers may order the Forms Volume separately. However, all subscribers will continue to be updated with the latest forms by way of receiving the Forms Release. We do ask that you keep your Forms Volume from one year to the next and update by way of filing the releases supplied, particularly as we cross-refer from the text of the CPR to forms in the Forms Volume and Forms CD. We avoid the duplication of forms in both the main volumes and the Forms Volume. This includes Practice Direction forms.

The Forms Release is nominally published three times a year. We will not publish a paper forms release with the supplements unless the number of new or amended forms released by the MOJ demands it (we will continue to release the Forms CD as normal). You will find a paper forms release released with the main volumes, which is the twenty-fifth release.

### *Forms on CD-ROM and Adobe forms*

Electronic forms on the Forms and the White Book CDs are available in two formats—RTF/Word and PDF.

As a basic requirement, all 600-odd court forms and notes are available in RTF/Word format. All are also available as interactive PDFs, many of which are able to be edited and saved using Adobe functionality. Please refer to the accompanying Quick Reference Card for full details.

### *Email alerters*

You may wish to sign up to receive our Forms email alerter service. An email notice is sent to you when new court forms are published by the Court Service. You can also download forms via our website: **http://www.sweetandmaxwell.co.uk/whitebook**. Click on "White Book Updating Service", enter the password: **WB2010** and click on "What's New".

You may also wish to sign up to receive our email alerter service to notify you of changes to the Civil Procedure Rules as they are introduced by Statutory Instrument and as the changes come into force. This service is also available via **http://www.sweetandmaxwell.co.uk/whitebook**.

*How to use Civil Procedure 2010*

As ever, we have endeavoured to ensure that the content of *The White Book* is presented logically. The Civil Procedure Rules are reproduced in bold type to ensure they are easily distinguished from editorial comment and Practice Directions. Notes have been added to provide a full record of the changes to the Civil Procedure Rules. CPR Part numbers have been added to the thumb tabs at the side of each page.

Please refer to your User Guide which walks you through the navigational features and various components of *The White Book Service*, including the new cross-references to the additional content online and on CD.

*Volume 1*

The Civil Procedure Rules and Practice Directions (including Schs 1 and 2 containing those RSC and CCR still in force) are contained in Vol.1 with the following exceptions:

- *CPR on Specialist lists*—CPR Pts 58–63 (dealing with the Commercial Court, the Mercantile Courts, the Technology and Construction Court, Admiralty Claims and Arbitrations, and Patents and Other Intellectual Property Claims) are set out in Vol.2, Section 2.

- *CPR Pt 49—Specialist proceedings*—the proceedings dealt with under the Practice Direction to Pt 49 (Proceedings under the Companies Acts) are set out in Vol.2, Section 2.

Miscellaneous Practice Directions, Pre-Action Protocols, procedural guides and a guide to time limits are also reproduced in Vol.1.

*Volume 2*

The main elements of Vol.2 are the specialist areas of practice and procedure: the specialist lists dealt with by CPR Pts 58–63 and the specialist proceedings under CPR Pt 49, other specialist proceedings (e.g. Housing and Consumer) and procedural legislation. Volume 2 also includes Litigation and Procedural Topics such as Interim Remedies and Alternative Dispute Resolution.

A quick guide to finding key materials is set out below. See the separate User Guide for further information.

**How to find ...**

***... CPR Rules and Supplementary Practice Directions (Vol.1, Section A)***

The Civil Procedure Rules and Practice Directions are contained in Section A, which adopts the following paragraph system.

| | |
|---|---|
| Part 3, r.1 | para.**3.1** |
| Commentary to Part 3, r.1 | para.3.1.**1**, (3.1.**2** etc.) |
| Practice Direction supplementing Part 3 | para.3**PD**.1 |
| Second Practice Direction supplementing Part 3 | para.3**B**PD.1 |

The paragraph numbers appear at the top outside corner of each page.

***... Rules of the Supreme Court, County Court Rules and Supplementary Practice Directions***

Section A also contains the re-enacted Rules of the Supreme Court and County Court Rules, with all supplementary Practice Directions. The following paragraph system is used:

| | |
|---|---|
| RSC Order 52, r.1 | para.**sc**52.1 |
| Commentary to RSC Order 52.1 | para.sc52.1.**1**, (sc52.1.**2** etc.) |
| Practice Direction supplementing Order 52 | para.sc**pd**52.1 |
| CCR Order 1, r.6 | para.**cc**1.6 |
| Commentary to CCR Order 1, r.6 | para.cc1.6.**1** |

***... Miscellaneous Practice Direction (Vol.1, Section B)***

Practice Directions which are not supplementary to a rule (e.g. the Practice Direction on Insolvency Proceedings) are contained in Section B, which adopts the following paragraph system.

| | |
|---|---|
| Practice Direction Insolvency Proceedings, etc. | para.B1 001 |

***... Pre-Action Protocols (Vol.1, Section C)***

The Pre-Action Protocols are contained in Section C, which adopts the following paragraph system:

| | |
|---|---|
| Practice Direction—Protocols | para.C**0**–001 |
| Pre-Action Protocol for Personal Injury Claims | para.C**1**–001 |

***... Chancery Guide***

The Chancery Guide Appears in Section 1 of Vol.2 and is numbered para.1–1 onwards.

***... Specialist Practice Directions under CPR Parts 58-63 and Specialist Court Guides, Applications under the Companies Act***

Specialist Proceedings under CPR Parts 58-63 and Specialist Court Guides, Applications under the Companies Act appear in Section 2 of Vol.2 as follows:

| | |
|---|---|
| CPR 58 | Commercial Court |
| CPR 59 | Mercantile Courts |
| CPR 60 | Technology and Construction Courts |
| CPR 61 | Admiralty Claims |
| CPR 62 | Arbitration Claims |
| CPR 63 | Patents and other Intellectual Property Claims |
| Practice Direction to CPR 49 | Applications Under the Companies Act |

***... Forms***

The forms are located in the Civil Procedure Forms Volume and on the Forms CD.

***... Litigation and Procedural Topics***

These are located at the end of Vol.2 in Sections 11 to 15.

### *Service Elements*

*The White Book Service* allows you to choose a customised product to suit your requirements.

**Civil Procedure CD and Print Service**
Annual subscription includes:
CD (includes all content in Vols 1 and 2 and the Forms Volume and additional research materials)
Civil Procedure 2010 Vol.1
Civil Procedure 2010 Vol.2
Civil Procedure Forms Updates
Civil Procedure Forms Volume (on request to new subscribers)
Cumulative paper supplements
Civil Procedure News (10 issues a year)
Internet-based primary law updating
Forms email Alerter Service
Rules email Alerter Service
Subscription price: £539 plus VAT

**Civil Procedure Volumes 1 and 2**
Annual subscription includes:
Civil Procedure 2010 Vol.1
Civil Procedure 2010 Vol.2
Civil Procedure Forms CD
Civil Procedure Forms Updates
Civil Procedure Forms Volume (on request to new subscribers)
Cumulative paper supplements
Civil Procedure News (10 issues a year)
Internet-based primary law updating
Forms email Alerter Service
Rules email Alerter Service
Subscription price: £465 plus VAT

**Civil Procedure Volume 1**
Annual subscription includes:
Civil Procedure 2010 Vol.1
Civil Procedure Forms CD
Civil Procedure Forms Updates
Civil Procedure Forms Volume (on request to new subscribers)
Cumulative paper supplements
Civil Procedure News (10 issues a year)
Internet-based primary law updating
Forms email Alerter Service
Rules email Alerter Service
Subscription price: £360 plus VAT

### *White Book on Westlaw UK*

Please contact our Westlaw UK helpdesk for further information on 0800 028 2200.

### *Customer Services*

If you have a query relating to your subscription or you wish to purchase extra copies of Civil Procedure 2010, please call our

Customer Services team on:

UK direct customers: 0845 600 9355

UK trade customers: 0845 082 1032

International customers: +44 (0) 1264 388560

Or you can write to:

Customer Services
Sweet & Maxwell
Freepost
PO Box 2000
Andover
SP10 9AH
United Kingdom
Website: *http://www.sweetandmaxwell.co.uk*
Email: *sweetandmaxwell.customer.services@thomson.com*

### *Comments and feedback*

We are always pleased to receive comments and suggestions from customers. Address correspondence to: Publishing Editor, The White Book Service, Sweet & Maxwell, 100 Avenue Road, London, NW3 3PF or email *whitebook@sweetandmaxwell.co.uk*

The White Book Team
March 2010

# CIVIL PROCEDURE RULES

# SECTION 1

## COURT GUIDES

# 1A COURT GUIDES

1A–0.0



## 1A CHANCERY GUIDE

### Editorial introduction

1A–0
Litigants in the Chancery Division and in Chancery District Registries will need to make careful reference to the latest Chancery Guide. Particular attention is directed in the Guide to administrative matters; separate parts deal with hearings before High Court Judges, Masters and Registrars and the preparation for such hearings, including time limits for filing bundles and skeleton arguments. Careful attention should be paid to the need for accurate time estimates for hearings and the likely costs consequences of inaccurate estimates. The Guide emphasises that time estimates must include time for pre-reading, as well as the time for the hearing, including time for judgment and any costs assessment.

An email protocol permits the filing of skeleton arguments, chronologies and draft orders by email but not authorities. Chapter 14 of the Guide deals with the use of information technology. A Practice Direction will deal with electronic filing of claims and subsequent steps from April 1, 2010 as part of a 24 hours a day all year round Electronic Working Scheme. This will enable claims to be issued and documents filed in electronic format.

As with previous editions it was issued after detailed consideration by the Chancellor, the judges, Masters and Registrars of the Division.

Practitioners should be aware that the Chancery Guide is from time to time updated on the HMCS website. Such changes are reflected in the Chancery Guide as printed in *Civil Procedure*.

### Case Management

1A–0.1
Of particular value is Appendix 3 to the Guide. Parties preparing draft directions for attachment to allocation questionnaires for consideration at case management conferences in the Chancery Division or in District Registries of the Division should follow the suggested form of directions. Parties should in every case discuss and seek to agree procedural directions in the form set out in Appendix 3 and submit them with their allocation questionnaires. This responsible practice assists the court in managing the claim effectively and expeditiously. The Guide makes clear in Ch.3.6 that it is not acceptable practice for the parties in their allocation questionnaires to indicate that they have not suggested or agreed draft directions. If, at the time of filing allocation questionnaires, draft directions are still the subject of discussion, the Master should be alerted to this. If an unusual or non-routine order is sought a brief explanation for the court should be provided with the allocation questionnaire and similarly if permission to adduce expert evidence is sought by the parties and if the reason is not obvious an agreed explanation of the parties for use by the court is appropriate.

# Chancery Guide

1A–1
Abbreviations used in this Guide:

| | |
|---|---|
| Civil Procedure Rules | CPR |
| HM Courts Service | HMCS |

***Paragraph numbers marked with a "+" can be found online and on CD.***

| | |
|---|---|
| Practice Direction supplementing a Civil Procedure Rule | PD |
| Rules of the Supreme Court 1965 | RSC |
| Pre-trial review | PTR |

Part 1 means CPR Part 1

rule 1.1 means CPR Part 1 rule 1.1

PD 52 means the PD supplementing CPR Part 52

The Civil Procedure Rules (comprising Rules, Practice Directions, Pre-Action Protocols and Forms) are published by the Stationery Office. They are also published on the Ministry of Justice website: *www.justice.gov.uk*. This Guide will also be found on the Chancery Division section of the Courts Service website: *www.hmcourts-service.gov.uk*.

**Preface**

1A–2 This, the sixth, edition of the Chancery Guide is published four years after its predecessor. In the intervening period much has changed either in relation to the substantive law, for example the Companies Act 2006, the practice of the court, for example the procedure for paper applications in trust cases introduced by the new rule 64.8A and the working of the court, for example the Electronic Pilot Scheme. What has not changed is the purpose and function of this guide. It is to explain how the substantive law, rules and practice directions are applied in the Chancery Division; it cannot affect their proper interpretation or effect, see *Secretary of State for Communities and Local Government v Bovale Ltd* [2009] EWCA Civ 171.

This edition has been produced under the supervision of Sir Kim Lewison. I am most grateful to him for undertaking the task in addition to his normal duties as a judge of the Chancery Division, the Chancery Supervising judge for Wales and the Midland and Western Circuits; author of Lewison on The Interpretation of Contracts and editor of Woodfall on Landlord and Tenant. He has been assisted with regard to various topics by a number of High Court and Specialist Chancery Circuit judges, Chief Master Winegarten, Master Bragge and Registrar Derrett from the judiciary; Mrs VC Bell from HMCS and Malcolm Davis-White QC and Katherine McQuail for the Chancery Bar Association. To all of them, named or unnamed, I send my thanks.

If all goes according to the present plan the Chancery Division will move to the Rolls Building in the summer of 2011. In that location it will, we are assured, have access to greatly improved IT systems. These events are bound to lead to substantial changes in the practices and working of the court thereby necessitating the seventh edition of the Chancery Guide in 2012. I hope and believe that this edition will be of considerable use to all who, in whatever capacity, have occasion to participate in litigation in the Chancery Division before the move occurs and will remain of some historical interest thereafter.

**Andrew Morritt**
**Chancellor of the High Court**
**October 2009**

## CHAPTER 1

## INTRODUCTORY

### About the Chancery Division

1A–3 1.1 The Chancery Division is one of the three parts, or Divisions, of the High Court of Justice The other two are the Queen's Bench Division and the Family Division. The head of the Chancery Division is the Chancellor of the High Court ("the Chancellor"). There are currently seventeen High Court judges attached to the Division. In addition, in the Royal Courts of Justice in London, there are six judges who are referred to as Masters (one of whom is the Chief Master), and six judges who are referred to as Bankruptcy Registrars (one of whom is the Chief Registrar). In the District Registries (see Chapter 12) the work done by Masters in London is performed by District Judges. References in this Guide to a Master include, in the case of proceedings in a District Registry, references to a District Judge. Deputies sit on a regular basis for both judges and Masters. Any reference to a judge or Master in the Guide includes a reference to a person sitting as a deputy.

***Paragraph numbers marked with a "+" can be found online and on CD.***

1.2 The Chancery Division undertakes civil work of many kinds, including specialist work such as companies, patents and contentious probate. The range of cases heard in the Chancery Division is wide and varied. The major part of the case-load today involves business or property disputes of one kind or another. Often these are complex and involve substantial sums of money.

1.3 Judges of the Chancery Division also sit as judges of the Court of Protection; in the Upper Tier Tribunal and in the Competition Appeal Tribunal. This Guide does not cover any of those courts or tribunals.

1.4 In many types of case (e.g. claims for professional negligence against solicitors, accountants, valuers or other professionals) the claimant has a choice whether to bring the claim in the Chancery Division or elsewhere in the High Court. But there are other types of case which, in the High Court, must be brought in the Chancery Division including claims (other than claims in the Commercial Court) relating to the application of Articles 81 and 82 of the EC Treaty and the equivalent provisions in the Competition Act 1998. The specialist work of the Chancery Division is dealt with in Section B of this Guide. There are also certain claims which must be started in the Chancery Division either in the High Court or in a District Registry where there is a Chancery District Registry or in the Central London Trial Centre (Chancery List).

### About this Guide

1.5 The aim of this Guide is to provide additional practical information not already **1A–4**
contained in the CPR or the Practice Directions supplementing them. Litigants and their advisers are expected to be familiar with the CPR and the PDs. This Guide should be used in conjunction with them. It is not the function of this Guide to summarise the CPR or the PDs, nor should it be regarded as a substitute for them.

1.6 This Guide does not have the status of a Practice Direction. So it does not have the force of law. But failure to comply with this Guide may influence the way in which the court exercises its powers under the CPR, including the making of adverse costs orders. In case of any conflict between this Guide and a rule or Practice Direction, the rule or Practice Direction prevails.

1.7 This Guide is published as part of a series of Guides to various civil courts. Where information is more readily available in another guide, this Guide may simply refer to it. A separate book contains Practice Forms for use in the Chancery Division and in the Queen's Bench Division. Some of the forms most commonly used in the Chancery Division are found in the Appendices to this Guide. Forms may also be downloaded from the HMCS website and may be found in the main procedural reference books.

1.8 Section A of this Guide is concerned with general civil work. Section B deals with specialist work. Some subjects are covered in more detail in the Appendices, and Appendix 1 sets out some contact details which may be useful.

1.9 Material which used to be contained in the Chancery Division Practice Directions and which remains relevant has been incorporated into either Section A or Section B of this Guide, as appropriate.

1.10 A reference in this Guide to a Part is to that Part of the CPR, to a rule is to the relevant rule in the CPR, unless otherwise stated, and to PD [number] is to the PD supplementing the Part so numbered, the title being given if necessary to distinguish one from another. The PD about costs, supplementing Parts 43 to 48, is called the Costs PD.

1.11 This Guide states the position as at September 2009. During the currency of the Guide, and even in some cases before publication, there are likely to be changes in matters covered in the text, including room numbers and other contact details; these should be checked as necessary. The Guide will be kept under review in the light of practical experience and of changes to the rules and practice directions. Any comments on the text of the Guide are welcome and should be addressed to the clerk to the Chancellor.

***Paragraph numbers marked with a "+" can be found online and on CD.***

1.12 The text of the Guide is also to be found, together with other Court Guides and other useful information concerning the administration of justice in the Chancery Division and elsewhere, on the HMCS website. Amendments will appear on the Guide on the website as appropriate: *www.hmcourts-service.gov.uk*. The Guide is also printed in the main procedural reference books.

## SECTION A GENERAL CIVIL WORK

### CHAPTER 2

### STARTING PROCEEDINGS, ALLOCATION AND STATEMENTS OF CASE

***Key Rules: CPR Parts 7, 8, 9, 10, 15, 16, 18, 20 and 26 and CPR Schedule 1***

**Before starting a claim**

1A–5 2.1 Before issuing a claim parties should consider the PD on Pre-Action Conduct. The PD applies only to claims begun as a Part 7 or Part 8 claim. It does not therefore apply to claims which are started by some other means (e.g. petition). The court will not expect the PD to be complied with where:

(1) telling the other potential party in advance would defeat the purpose of the application (e.g an application for a freezing order);
(2) the application involves the making of representation orders so that non-parties could be bound by the outcome (e.g. pension cases);
(3) there is no other party for the applicant to engage with (e.g. an application to the Court by trustees for directions);
(4) the application results from agreement following negotiation (e.g a variation of trust);
(4) the urgency of the application is such that it is not practicable to comply; or
(5) the claimant follows a statutory or other formal pre- action procedure.

2.2 In other cases the court will consider the extent to which the PD has been complied with.

**How to start a claim**

1A–6 2.3 Claims are issued out of the High Court of Justice, Chancery Division, either in the Royal Courts of Justice (Chancery Chambers) or in a District Registry. There is no Production Centre for Chancery claims. It is expected that the Electronic Working Pilot Scheme will apply to claims started in the Chancery Division as from October 1, 2009 (see PD (Electronic Working Pilot Scheme) supplementing rule 5.5 of the CPR).

2.4 The claim form must be issued either as a Part 7 claim under Part 7, or as a Part 8 claim under the alternative procedure for claims in Part 8.

2.5 When issuing proceedings, the general rule is that the title of the claim should contain only the names of the parties to the proceedings. There are five exceptions to this: (a) proceedings relating to the administration of an estate, which should be entitled "In the estate of AB deceased" (some cases relating to the estates of deceased Lloyd's names require additional wording: see paragraph 26.53 below); (b) contentious probate proceedings, which should be entitled "In the estate of AB deceased (probate)"; (c) proceedings under the Inheritance (Provision for Family and Dependants) Act 1975, which should be entitled "In the Matter of the Inheritance (Provision for Family and Dependants) Act 1975"; (d) proceedings relating to pension schemes, which may be entitled "In the Matter of the [] Pension Scheme"; and (e) proceedings in the Companies Court are entitled in the matter of the relevant company or other person and of the relevant legislation: see paragraph 20.5.

**Service**

1A–7 2.6 Part 6 applies to the service of documents, including claim forms. Unless the claimant notifies the court that he or she wishes to serve the claim form, or the court directs otherwise, it will be served by the court. Many solicitors, however, will prefer to serve the claim form themselves and will notify the court that they wish to do so.



### Allocation

2.7 The vast majority of claims issued, and all those retained, in the Chancery Division will be either expressly allocated to the multi-track or in the case of Part 8 claims, deemed to be allocated to that track. Chapter 13 deals with transfer to county courts. **1A–8**

### Statements of case

2.8 In addition to the matters which PD 16 requires to be set out specifically in the particulars of claim, a party must set out in any statement of case: **1A–9**

(1) full particulars of any allegation of fraud, dishonesty, malice or illegality;

(2) where any inference of fraud or dishonesty is alleged, the facts on the basis of which the inference is alleged.

2.9 A party should not set out allegations of fraud or dishonesty unless there is credible material to support the contentions made. Setting out such matters without such material being available may result in the particular allegations being struck out and may result in wasted costs orders being made against the legal advisers responsible.

2.10 In the preparation of statements of case, the guidelines in Appendix 2 should be followed.

2.11 The guidelines apply to: the claim form (unless no particulars are given in it); particulars of claim; defence; additional claims under Part 20; reply to a defence; and a response to a request for further information under Part 18.

2.12 Parties should not attach copies of documents or any expert's report to their statement of case if they are bulky.

2.13 Claimants should if possible serve any reply before they file their allocation questionnaire. This will enable other parties to consider the reply before they file their allocation questionnaire. However, the deadline for filing the questionnaire is that in rule 15.8.

### Part 8 claims

2.14 This procedure is appropriate in particular where there is no substantial dispute of fact, such as where the case raises only questions of the construction of a document or a statute. Additionally, PD 8 Section B lists a large number of particular claims which must be brought under Part 8. Other rules also require the Part 8 procedure to be used. Of particular relevance will be applications to enforce charging orders by sale, claims under the Inheritance (Provision for Family and Dependants) Act 1975, proceedings relating to solicitors and certain proceedings under the Companies Act 2006 (PD 49 para 5). Subject to jurisdiction, applications to enforce charging orders are now issued in the court in which the charging order was made. Proceedings to enforce charging orders made in any division of the High Court and the Court of Appeal are issued in the Chancery Division. **1A–10**

2.15 Part 8 also provides for a claim form to be issued without naming a defendant with the permission of the court. No separate application for permission is required where personal representatives seek permission to distribute the estate of a deceased Lloyd's name nor for applications under section 48 of the Administration of Justice Act 1985 (see further Chapter 26—Trusts). Where permission is needed, it is to be sought by application notice under Part 23. The application should be listed before a Master.

2.16 Part 8 claims will generally be disposed of on written evidence. The features of the Part 8 procedure are:

(1) no particulars of claim
(2) no defence
(3) no allocation questionnaire
(4) no judgment in default
(5) normally no oral evidence.

2.17 Defendants who wish to contest a Part 8 claim or to take part in the proceedings should complete and file the acknowledgment of service in form N210. Alternatively the information required to be contained in the acknowledgment of service can be provided by letter. Any objection to the use of the Part 8 procedure must be made at that time. A party who does not wish to contest a claim should indicate that fact on the form acknowledging service or by letter.

2.18 Claimants must file the written evidence, namely evidence by witness statement, on which they intend to rely with the claim form. Defendants are required to file and serve their evidence when they file their acknowledgment of service, namely within 14 days after service of the claim form (rule 8.5(3)). By paragraph 7.5 of PD 8 a defendant's time for filing evidence may be extended by written agreement for not more than 14 days from the filing of the acknowledgment of service. Any such agreement must be filed with the court by the defendant at the same time as he or she files an acknowledgment of service. The claimant has 14 days for filing evidence in reply but this period may be extended by written agreement for not more than 28 days from service of the defendant's evidence. Again, any such agreement must be filed with the court. Any longer extension either for the defendant or the claimant requires an application to the court. It is recognised that in substantial matters the provisions in Part 8 may be burdensome upon defendants and in such matters the court will readily grant an extension. If the parties are in agreement that such an extension should be granted the application should be made in writing by letter. The parties should at all times act co-operatively.

2.19 Defendants who acknowledge service but do not intend to file evidence should notify the court in writing when they file their acknowledgment of service that they do not intend to file evidence. This enables the court to know what each defendant's intention is when it considers the file.

2.20 The general rule is that the court file will be considered by the court after the time for acknowledgment of service has expired, or, if the time for serving the defendant's evidence has been extended, after the expiry of that period. There are exceptions to this rule (including some claims under the Variations of Trusts Act 1958 and cases where a party has applied for summary judgment).

2.21 In some cases if the papers are in order the court will not require any oral hearing, but will be able to deal with the matter on paper by making a final order. In other cases the court will direct that the Part 8 claim is listed either for a disposal hearing or for a case management conference.

## CHAPTER 3

## THE COURT'S CASE MANAGEMENT POWERS

***Key Rules: CPR rule 1.4, and Parts 3, 18, 19, 26, 29, 31, 39***

**1A–11** 3.1 A key feature of the CPR is that cases are closely monitored by the court. Case management by the court includes: identifying disputed issues at an early stage; fixing timetables; dealing with as many aspects of the case as possible on the same occasion; controlling costs; disposing of cases summarily where they disclose no case or defence; dealing with the case without the parties having to attend court; and giving directions to ensure that the trial of a case proceeds quickly and efficiently.

3.2 The rules require the parties themselves to help the court to further the overriding objective. Accordingly the court will expect the parties to co-operate with each other. Failure to do so may attract adverse costs consequences.

***Paragraph numbers marked with a "+" can be found online and on CD.***

3.3 Where appropriate the court will encourage the parties to use alternative dispute resolution (on which see Chapter 17) or otherwise help them settle the case. In particular, the court will readily grant a short stay at allocation or at any other stage to accommodate mediation or any other form of settlement negotiations. The court will not, however, normally, grant an open-ended stay for such purposes and if, for any reason, a lengthy stay is granted it will be on terms that the parties report to the court on a regular basis in respect of their negotiations.

3.4 In the Chancery Division case management is normally carried out by the Masters, but a judge may be nominated by the Chancellor to hear the case and to deal with the case management where it is appropriate due to the size or complexity of the case or for other reasons. A request by any or all parties for such a nomination should be addressed to the clerk to the Chancellor.

### Directions

3.5 It is expected that parties and their advisers will try to agree proposals for management of the case at the allocation stage in accordance with rule 29.4 and paragraphs 4.6 to 4.8 of PD 29. In particular, the parties must act co-operatively and seek to agree directions and a list of the issues to be tried. The court will approve the parties' proposals, if they are suitable, and give directions accordingly without a hearing. If it does not approve the agreed directions it may give modified directions or its own directions or, more usually, direct a case management conference. If the parties cannot agree directions then each party should put forward its own proposals for the future management of the case for consideration by the court. Digital copies should be available so that any necessary changes can be made quickly. Draft orders commonly made by the Masters on allocation and at case management conferences are set out at Appendix 3, and parties drafting proposed directions for submission to a Master on allocation or at a case management conference should have regard to and make use, as appropriate, of those draft orders. **1A–12**

3.6 If parties do not, at the allocation stage, agree or attempt to agree directions and if, in consequence, the court is unable to give directions without ordering a case management conference, the parties should not expect to recover any costs in respect of such a case management conference. It will not generally be acceptable for the parties in their Allocation questionnaires to indicate that they have not suggested or agreed draft directions (using the form at Appendix 3). If by the time limited for the filing of Allocation Questionnaires directions are still the subject of discussion, the Master should be alerted to this in the Allocation Questionnaire and given a time by which draft directions will be filed. If a party seeks an unusual or non-routine order he should provide a short explanation for the court with the Allocation Questionnaire. Similarly if the parties seek permission to adduce expert evidence and the reason for this is not obvious they should provide an agreed explanation for use by the court.

3.7 In many claims the court will give directions without holding a case management conference.

3.8 Any party who considers that a case management conference should be held before any directions are given should so state in his or her allocation questionnaire (or, in the case of a Part 8 claim, inform the court in writing) and give reasons why he or she considers that a case management conference is required. When sending out allocation questionnaires the court will also send out a questionnaire inviting the parties to give their time estimate for any case management conference and to specify any dates or times inconvenient for the holding of a case management conference.

3.9 Wherever possible, the advocate(s) instructed or expected to be instructed to appear at the trial should attend any hearing at which case management directions are likely to be given. To this end the court when ordering a case management conference, otherwise than upon allocation, will normally send out questionnaires to the parties in respect of their availability. Parties must not, however, expect that a case management conference will be delayed for a substantial length of time in order to accommodate the advocates' convenience.

3.10 Case management conferences are intended to deal with the general management of the case. They are not an opportunity to make controversial interim applications without appropriate notice to the opposing party. Accordingly, as provided by paragraph 5.8(1) of PD 29, where a party wishes to obtain an order not routinely made at a case management conference (such as an order for specific disclosure or summary disposal) such application should be made by separate Part 23 application to be heard at the case management conference and the case management conference should be listed for a sufficient period of time to allow the application to be heard. Where parties fail to comply with this paragraph it is highly unlikely that the court will entertain, other than by consent, an application which is not of a routine nature. It is the obligation of the parties to ensure that a realistic time estimate for any hearing is given to the court.

3.11 Even where routine orders are sought (i.e. orders falling within the topics set out in paragraph 5.3 of PD 29) care should be taken to ensure that the opposing party is given notice of the orders intended to be sought.

### Case management bundle

**1A-13** 3.12 Parties should consider the compiling of a permanent case management bundle containing a neutral case summary, the statements of case and court orders, updated as necessary during the progress of the case. The court may direct the compiling of such a bundle in an appropriate case.

### Applications for information and disclosure

**1A-14** 3.13 Before a party applies to the court for an order that another party provides him or her with any further information or specific disclosure of documents he or she must communicate directly with the other party in an attempt to reach agreement or narrow the issues before the matter is raised with the court. If not satisfied that the parties have taken steps to reach agreement or narrow the issues, the court will normally require such steps to be taken before hearing the application.

### Preliminary issues

**1A-15** 3.14 Costs can sometimes be saved by identifying decisive issues, or potentially decisive issues, and ordering that they are tried first. The decision of one issue, although not itself decisive of the whole case, may enable the parties to settle the remainder of the dispute. In such cases a preliminary issue may be appropriate.

3.15 At the allocation stage, at any case management conference and again at any PTR, consideration will be given to the possibility of the trial of preliminary issues the resolution of which is likely to shorten proceedings. The court may suggest the trial of a preliminary issue, but it will rarely make an order without the concurrence of at least one of the parties.

### Group Litigation Orders

**1A-16** 3. 16 Under rule 19.11, where there are likely to be a number of claims giving rise to common or related issues of fact or law, the court may make a Group Litigation Order ("GLO") for their case management. Such orders may be appropriate in chancery proceedings and there are a number in existence. A list of GLOs is published on the HMCS website. An application for a GLO is made under Part 23. The procedure is set out in PD 19 Group Litigation, which provides that the application should be made to the Chief Master, except for claims in a specialist list (such as the business of the Patents Court), when the application should be made to the senior judge of that list.

3.17 Claimants wishing to join in group litigation should issue proceedings in the normal way and should then apply (by letter) to be entered on the Group Register set up by a GLO. In the Chancery Division the Register is usually kept by the court and is maintained by the lead solicitors, as specified in the GLO. Where the Register is kept in the Chancery Division at the Royal Courts of Justice, it is kept by Mrs VC Bell, Chancery Lawyer (Room TM5.06, tel. 020 7947 6080). Any initial enquiries regarding GLOs may be addressed to her.

**Trial timetable**

3.18 The judge at trial, or sometimes at the PTR, may determine the timetable for the trial. The advocates for the parties should be ready to assist the court in this respect if so required. The time estimate given for the trial should have been based on an approximate forecast of the trial timetable (including any time needed for pre-reading by the trial judge) and must be reviewed by each party at the stage of the PTR and as preparation for trial proceeds thereafter. If that review requires a change in the estimate the other parties' advocates and the court must be informed. **1A–17**

3.19 When a trial timetable is set by the court, it will ordinarily fix the time for the oral submissions and factual and expert evidence, and it may do so in greater or lesser detail. Trial timetables are always subject to any further order by the trial judge.

**Pre-Trial Review**

3.20 The court has power to direct that a PTR be held (see rule 29.7). This power will normally be exercised in cases estimated to take more than 10 days and in other cases where the circumstances warrant it. **1A–18**

3.21 Such a PTR will normally be heard by a judge. The date and time should be fixed with the Chancery Judges' Listing Officer. If the trial judge has already been nominated, the application will if possible be heard by that judge. The advocates' clerks must attend the Chancery Judges' Listing Officer in sufficient time so that the PTR can be fixed between four and eight weeks before the trial date.

3.22 A PTR should be attended by advocates who are to represent the parties at the trial. Any unrepresented party should also attend.

3.23 Not less than 7 days before the date fixed for the PTR the claimant, or another party if so directed by the court, must circulate a list of matters to be considered at the PTR, including proposals as to how the case should be tried, to the other parties, who must respond with their comments at least 2 days before the PTR.

3.24 The claimant, or another party if so directed by the court, should deliver a bundle containing the lists of matters to be considered and proposals served by the parties on each other and the trial timetable, together with the results of the discussions between the parties as to those matters, and any other documents the court is likely to need in order to deal with the PTR, to the Chancery Judges' Listing Office by 10am on the day before the day fixed for the hearing of the PTR.

3.25 At the PTR the court will review the state of preparation of the case, and deal with outstanding procedural matters, not limited to those apparent from the lists of matters lodged by the parties. The court may give directions as to how the case is to be tried, including directions as to the order in which witnesses are to be called (for example all witnesses of fact before all expert witnesses) or as to the time to be allowed for particular stages in the trial.

## CHAPTER 4

## DISCLOSURE OF DOCUMENTS AND EXPERT EVIDENCE

***Key Rules: CPR Parts 18, 29, 31 and 35; PDs supplementing Parts 31 and 35***

4.1 As part of its management of a case, the court will give directions about the disclosure of documents and any expert evidence. An application for specific **1A–19** disclosure should be made by a specific Part 23 application and is not to be regarded as a matter routinely dealt with at a case management conference.

4.2 Although applications for disclosure pursuant to *Norwich Pharmacal v Customs and Excise Commissioners* [1974] AC 133 [1973] 2 All ER 943 HL may be made under Part 7 or Part 8 (as the case may be), nevertheless if the application is or is thought likely to be uncontested the court may entertain in the alternative an application under Part 23 supported by evidence.

**Disclosure of Documents**

1A–20 4.3 Under the CPR, the normal order for disclosure is an order for standard disclosure, which requires disclosure of

(1) *a party's own documents*—that is, the documents on which a party relies;
(2) *adverse documents*—that is, documents which adversely affect his or her own or another party's case or support another party's case; and
(3) *required documents*—that is, documents which a practice direction requires him or her to disclose.

4.4 Since disclosure can be very expensive, the parties should consider methods by which the expense can be limited. In the case of disclosure of documents stored digitally, this may include agreement on key words to be used in searching.

4.5 The court may also make an order for specific disclosure going beyond the limits of standard disclosure if it is satisfied that standard disclosure is inadequate.

4.6 The court will not make such an order readily. One of the clear principles underlying the CPR is that the burden and cost of disclosure should be reduced. The court will, therefore, seek to ensure that any specific disclosure ordered is proportionate in the sense that its cost does not outweigh the likely benefits to be obtained from such disclosure. The court will, accordingly, seek to tailor the order for disclosure to the requirements of the particular case. The financial position of the parties, the importance of the case and the complexity of the issues will be taken into account when considering whether more than standard disclosure should be ordered.

4.7 If specific disclosure is sought, the parties should give careful thought to the ways in which such disclosure can be limited, for example by requiring disclosure in stages or by requiring disclosure simply of sufficient documents to show a specified matter and so on. They should also consider whether the need for disclosure could be avoided by requiring a party to provide information under Part 18.

**Expert Evidence**

*General*

1A–21 4.8 Part 35 contains particular provisions designed to limit the amount of expert evidence to be placed before the court and to reinforce the obligation of impartiality which is imposed upon an expert witness. The key question now in relation to expert evidence is the question as to what added value such evidence will provide to the court in its determination of a given case.

4.9 Fundamentally, Part 35 states that expert evidence must be restricted to what is reasonably required to resolve the proceedings and makes provision for the court to direct that expert evidence is given by a single joint expert. The parties should consider from the outset of the proceedings whether appointment of a single joint expert is appropriate.

*Duties of an expert*

1A–22 4.10 It is the duty of an expert to help the court on the matters within his or her expertise; this duty overrides any obligation to the person from whom the expert has received instructions or by whom he or she is paid (rule 35.3). Attention is drawn to

PD 35 and the Protocol for the Instruction of Experts which sets out the duties of an expert and the form and contents of an expert's report.

*Single joint expert*

4.11 The introduction to PD 35 states that, where possible, matters requiring expert evidence should be dealt with by a single expert. **1A–23**

4.12 In very many cases it is possible for the question of expert evidence to be dealt with by a single expert. Single experts are, for example, often appropriate to deal with questions of quantum in cases where the primary issues are as to liability. Likewise, where expert evidence is required in order to acquaint the court with matters of expert fact, as opposed to opinion, a single expert will usually be appropriate. There remains, however, a substantial body of cases where liability will turn upon expert opinion evidence or where quantum is a primary issue and where it will be appropriate for the parties to instruct their own experts. For example, in cases where the issue for determination is as to whether a party acted in accordance with proper professional standards, it will often be of value to the court to hear the opinions of more than one expert as to the proper standard in order that the court becomes acquainted with the range of views existing upon the question and in order that the evidence can be tested in cross-examination.

4.13 It is not necessarily a sufficient objection to the making by the court of an order for a single joint expert that the parties have already appointed their own experts. An order for a single joint expert does not prevent a party from having his or her own expert to advise him or her, but he or she may well be unable to recover the cost of employing his or her own expert from the other party. The duty of an expert who is called to give evidence is to help the court.

4.14 When the use of a single joint expert is contemplated the court will expect the parties to co-operate in developing, and agreeing to the greatest possible extent, terms of reference for the expert. In most cases the terms of reference will (in particular) detail what the expert is asked to do, identify any documentary material he or she is asked to consider and specify any assumptions he or she is asked to make.

*More than one expert—exchange of reports*

4.15 In an appropriate case the court will direct that experts' reports are delivered sequentially. Sequential reports may, for example, be appropriate if the service of the first expert's report would help to define and limit the issues on which such evidence may be relevant. **1A–24**

*Discussion between experts*

4.16 The court will normally direct discussion between experts before trial. Sometimes it may be useful for there to be further discussions during the trial itself. The purpose of these discussions is to give the experts the opportunity: **1A–25**

(1) to discuss the expert issues; and
(2) to identify the expert issues on which they share the same opinion and those on which there remains a difference of opinion between them (and what that difference is).

4.17 Unless the court otherwise directs, the procedure to be adopted at these discussions is a matter for the experts. It may be sufficient if the discussion takes place by telephone.

4.18 Parties must not seek to restrict their expert's participation in any discussion directed by the court, but they are not bound by any agreement on any issue reached by their expert unless they expressly so agree.

*Written questions to experts*

4.19 It is emphasised that this procedure is only for the purpose (generally) of seeking clarification of an expert's report where the other party is unable to **1A–26**

***Paragraph numbers marked with a "+" can be found online and on CD.***

understand it. Written questions going beyond this can only be put with the agreement of the parties or with the permission of the court. The procedure of putting written questions to experts is not intended to interfere with the procedure for an exchange of professional opinion in discussions between experts or to inhibit that exchange of professional opinion. If questions that are oppressive in number or content are put or questions are put without permission for any purpose other than clarification of an expert's report, the court will not hesitate to disallow the questions and to make an appropriate order for costs against the party putting them.

*Request by an expert to the court for directions*

**1A–27** 4.20 An expert may file with the court a written request for directions to assist him or her in carrying out his or her function as expert: rule 35.14. Copies of any such request must be provided to the parties in accordance with rule 35.14(2) save where the court orders otherwise. The expert should guard against accidentally informing the court about, or about matters connected with, communications or potential communications between the parties that are without prejudice or privileged. The expert may properly be privy to the content of these communications because he or she has been asked to assist the party instructing him or her to evaluate them.

*Assessors*

**1A–28** 4.21 Under rule 35.15 the court may appoint an assessor to assist it in relation to any matter in which the assessor has skill and experience. The report of the assessor is made available to the parties. The remuneration of the assessor is determined by the court and forms part of the costs of the proceedings.

## CHAPTER 5

## APPLICATIONS

### *Key Rules: CPR Parts 23 and 25, PDs 23 and 25*

**1A–29** 5.1 This Chapter deals with applications to a judge, including applications for interim remedies, and applications to a Master. As regards the practical arrangements for making, listing and adjourning applications, the Chapter is primarily concerned with hearings at the Royal Courts of Justice. Hearings before Chancery judges and District Registrars outside London are dealt with in Chapter 12.

5.2 It is most important that only applications which need to be heard by a judge (e.g. most applications for an injunction) should be made to a judge. Any procedural application (e.g. for directions) should be made to a Master unless there is some special reason for making it to a judge. If an application is to be made to a judge, the application notice should state that it is a judge's application. If an application which should have been made to a Master is made to a judge, the judge may refuse to hear it.

5.3 Part 23 contains rules as to how an application may be made. In some circumstances it may be dealt with without a hearing, or by a telephone hearing.

**Applications without notice**

**1A–30** 5.4 Generally it is wrong to make an application without giving prior notice to the respondent. There are, however, three classes of exceptions.

(1) First, there are cases where the giving of notice might frustrate the order (e.g. a search order) or where there is such urgency that there has not been time to give notice. Even in an urgent case, however, the applicant should notify the respondent informally of the application if possible, unless secrecy is essential.

(2) Second, there are some procedural applications normally made without notice relating to such matters as service out of the jurisdiction, service, extension of the validity of claim forms, permission to issue writs of possession etc. All of these are properly made without notice but will be subjected by the rules to an

express provision in any order made that the absent party will be entitled to apply to set aside or vary the order provided that application is so made within a given number of days of service of the order.

(3) Third, there are cases in which the respondent can only be identified by description and not by name.

An application made without giving notice which does not fall within the classes of cases where absence of notice is justified may be dismissed or adjourned until proper notice has been given.

**Applications without a hearing**

5.5 Part 23 makes provision for applications to be dealt with without a hearing. This is a useful provision in a case where the parties consent to the terms of the order sought or agree that a hearing is not necessary (often putting in written representations by letter or otherwise). It is also a useful provision in a case where, although the parties have not agreed to dispense with a hearing and the order is not consented to, the order sought by the application is, essentially, non-contentious. In the latter case, the order made will be treated as being made on the court's own initiative and will set out the right of any party affected by the application who has not been heard to apply to vary or set aside the order. **1A–31**

5.6 These provisions should not be used to deal with contentious matters without notice to the opposing party and without a hearing. Usually, this will result in delay since the court will simply order a hearing. It may also give rise to adverse costs orders. It will normally be wrong to seek an order which imposes sanctions in the event of non-compliance without notice and without a hearing. An application seeking such an order may well be dismissed.

**Applications to a judge**

5.7 If an application is made to a judge in existing proceedings, e.g. for an injunction, it should be made by application notice. This is called an Interim Application. Normally three clear days' notice to the other party is required but in an emergency or for other good reason the application can be made without giving notice, or the full 3 days' notice, to the other side. Permission to serve on short notice may be obtained on application without notice to the Interim Applications judge. Such permission will not be given by the Master. Except in an emergency a party notifies the court of his or her wish to bring an application by delivering the requisite documents to the Chancery Judges' Listing Office (Room WG4) and paying the appropriate fee. He or she should at the same time deliver a completed "Judge's Application Information Form" in the form set out in Part 1 of Appendix 4. An application will only be listed if (1) two copies of the claim form and (2) two copies of the application notice (one stamped with the appropriate fee) are lodged in the Chancery Judges' Listing Office before 12 noon on the working day before the date for which notice of the application has been given. **1A–32**

5.8 The current practice is that one judge combines the functions of Interim Applications judge and Companies judge. The judge's name will be found in the Daily Cause List.

5.9 The Interim Applications judge is available to hear applications each working day in term and an application notice can be served for any working day in term except the last. If the volume of applications requires it, any other judge who is available to assist with Interim Applications will hear such applications as the Interim Applications judge may direct. Special arrangements are made for hearing applications out of hours and in vacation, for which see paragraphs 5.41 to 5.47 below.

5.10 An application should not be listed before the Interim Applications Judge if it is suitable for hearing by a Master or Registrar. The mere fact that it is urgent is not enough, because both Masters and Registrars are available to hear urgent applications. If an application which should be heard by a Master or Registrar is listed before the Interim Applications Judge, the judge may refuse to hear it.

***Paragraph numbers marked with a "+" can be found online and on CD.***

5.11 **An application should not be listed before the Interim Applications Judge unless the overall time required to deal with the application is two hours or less. The two hour maximum includes the judge's pre-reading time, time in court and time for judgment.**

5.12 If the overall time required to deal with an application is likely to exceed two hours the application should be heard as an application by order (see paragraphs 5.14 and 5.20). If an application is listed before the Interim Applications Judge and it becomes apparent (either on the day of the hearing or beforehand) that the overall time required to deal with it is likely to exceed two hours the Chancery Judges' Listing Officer (or, in appropriate cases, the clerk to the Interim Applications Judge) must be notified immediately.

5.13 Every skeleton argument must begin with an estimate of the time required for pre-reading and an estimate of the time required in court (including time for judgment).

5.14 At the beginning of each day's hearing the Interim Applications Judge calls on each of the applications to be made that day in turn. This enables the judge to establish the identity of the parties, their state of readiness, their estimates of the duration of the hearing, and where relevant the degree of urgency of the case. On completion of this process, the judge decides the order in which the applications will be heard and gives any other directions that may be necessary. Sometimes cases are released to other judges at this point. If a case is likely to take 2 hours or more (including pre-reading and oral delivery of judgment), the judge will usually order that it is given a subsequent fixed date for hearing and hear any application for a court order to last until the application is heard fully.

5.15 Where an application is to be heard as an application by order the solicitors or the clerks to counsel concerned should apply to the Chancery Judges' Listing Officer for a date for the hearing. Before so doing there must be lodged with the Chancery Judges' Listing Office a certificate signed by the advocate stating the estimated length of the hearing.

5.16 Parties and their representatives should arrive at least ten minutes before the court sits. This will assist the usher to take a note of the names of those proposing to address the court and any revised estimate of the hearing time. This information is given to the judge before he or she sits. Parties should also allow time before the court sits to agree any form of order with any other party if this has not already been done. If the form of the order is not agreed before the court sits, the parties may have to wait until there is a convenient break in the list before they can ask the court to make any agreed order. If an application, not being an Interim Application by Order, is adjourned the Associate in attendance will notify the Chancery Judges' Listing Office of the date to which it has been adjourned so that it may be relisted for the new date.

5.17 If an application is adjourned to a later date the applicant must:

(1) remove all bundles for the current hearing from the court unless otherwise directed by the Judge.

(2) ensure that all papers required for the adjourned hearing (including bundles and skeleton arguments) are lodged with the Chancery Listing Office in Room WG04, Royal Courts of Justice no later than two working days before it is due to come back before the Judge.

(3) ensure that the adjourned hearing has been re-listed on the correct day when the papers are re-lodged with the Listing Office.

5.18 Without Notice Applications If a return date is given on an interim injunction (or any other remedy granted by the Judge) the applicant must ensure that an application is issued and served on the other parties (normally 3 working days before the return date); and that the necessary bundles and written submissions are lodged as indicated in paragraph 5.17 above.

***Paragraph numbers marked with a "+" can be found online and on CD.***

**Agreed Adjournment of Interim Applications**

5.19 If all parties to an Interim Application agree, it can be adjourned for not more than 14 days by counsel's clerks or solicitors attending the Chancery Judges' Listing Officer in Room WG4 at any time before 4pm on the day before the hearing of the application and producing consents signed by solicitors or counsel for all parties agreeing to the adjournment. A litigant in person must attend before the Chancery Judges' Listing Officer as well as signing a consent. This procedure may not be used for more than three successive adjournments and no adjournment may be made by this procedure to the last two days of any term. **1A-33**

**Interim Applications by Order by agreement**

5.20 This procedure should also be used where the parties agree that the application will take two hours or more and that, in consequence, the application should be adjourned to be heard as an Interim Application by Order. In that event, the consents set out above should also contain an agreed timetable for the filing of evidence or confirmation that no further evidence is to be filed. Any application arising from the failure of a party to abide by the timetable and any application to extend the timetable must be made to the judge. Interim Applications by Order will, initially at least, enter the Interim Hearings warned list on the first Monday after close of evidence. **1A-34**

5.21 Undertakings given to the court may be continued unchanged over any adjournment. If, however, on an adjournment an undertaking is to be varied or a new undertaking given then that must be dealt with by the court.

**Applications without notice**

5.22 On all applications made in the absence of the respondent the applicant and his or her legal representatives owe a duty to the court to disclose all matters relevant to the application. This includes matters of fact or law which are or may be adverse to the applicant. If made orally, the disclosure must be confirmed by witness statement or affidavit. The applicant or his or her legal representatives must specifically direct the court to passages in the evidence which disclose matters adverse to the application. This duty also applies to litigants in person. If there is a failure to comply with this duty and an order is made, the court may subsequently set aside the order on this ground alone. **1A-35**

5.23 A party wishing to apply urgently to a judge for remedies without notice to the respondent must notify the clerk to the Interim Applications Judge by telephone. Where such an urgent application is made, two copies of the order sought and a completed judge's Application Information Form in the form in Part 1 of Appendix 4 should, where possible, be included with the papers handed to the judge's clerk. Where an application is very urgent and the Interim Applications Judge is unable to hear it promptly, it may be heard by any judge who is available, though the request for this must be made to the clerk to the Interim Applications Judge, or, in default, to the Chancery Judges' Listing Officer. Every effort should be made to issue the claim form before the application is made. If this is not practicable, the party making the application must give an undertaking to the court to issue the claim form forthwith even if the court makes no order, unless the court orders otherwise. A party making an urgent application must ensure that all necessary fees are paid.

5.24 A party wishing to make an application without notice should give as much advance warning to the court as possible. If the overall time required to deal with the application (including pre-reading) is likely to exceed two hours arrangements for the listing of the application should be made with the Chancery Judges' Listing Officer.

**Freezing Injunctions and Search Orders**

5.25 The grant of freezing injunctions (both domestic and world-wide) and search orders is a staple feature of the work of the Chancery Division. Applications for such **1A-36** orders are invariably made without notice in the first instance; and in a proper case the court will sit in private in order to hear them. Where such an application is to be listed, two copies of the order sought, together with the application notice, should be lodged with the Chancery Judges' Listing Office. If the application is to be made in private, it will be listed as 'Application without notice' without naming the parties. The judge will consider, in each case, whether publicity might defeat the object of the hearing and, if so, may hear the application in private.

**Period for which an injunction or an order appointing a receiver is granted if the application was without notice**

**1A-37** 5.26 When an application for an injunction is heard without notice, and the judge decides that an injunction should be granted, it will normally be granted for a limited period only—usually not more than seven days. The same applies to an interim order appointing a receiver. The applicant will be required to give the respondent notice of his or her intention to apply to the court at the expiration of that period for the order to be continued. In the meantime the respondent will be entitled to apply, though generally only after giving notice to the applicant, for the order to be varied or discharged.

**Opposed applications without notice**

**1A-38** 5.27 These are applications of which proper notice has not been given to the respondents but which are made in the presence of both parties in advance of a full hearing of the application. The judge may impose time limits on the parties if, having regard to the pressure of business or for any other reason, he or she considers it appropriate to do so. On these applications, the judge may, in an appropriate case, make an order which will have effect until trial or further order as if proper notice had been given.

**Implied cross-undertakings in damages**

**1A-39** 5.28 Often the party against whom an injunction is sought gives to the court an undertaking which avoids the need for the court to grant the injunction. In these cases, there is an implied undertaking in damages by the party applying for the injunction in favour of the other. The position is less clear where the party applying for the injunction also gives an undertaking to the court. The parties should consider and, if necessary, raise with the judge whether the party in whose favour the undertaking is given must give a cross-undertaking in damages in those circumstances. Consideration should also be given to the question whether a cross-undertaking should be given in favour of a person who is not a respondent to the application.

**Orders on applications**

**1A-40** 5.29 The judge may direct the parties to agree, sign and deliver to the court a statement of the terms of the order made by the court (commonly still referred to as a minute of order), particularly where complex undertakings are given.

**Form of order when continuing an injunction**

**1A-41** 5.30 An order ("the new order"), the effect of which is to continue an injunction granted by an earlier order ("the original order"), may be drawn up in either of the following ways:

a. by writing out in full in the new order the terms of the injunction granted by the original order, amended to give effect to a new expiry date or event;
b. by ordering in the new order that the injunction contained (in a specific paragraph or paragraphs) in the annexed original order is to continue until the new expiry date or event (and annexing the original order);

5.31 In general, the best practice is that indicated in 5.30 (a) above, as it expresses in the clearest possible way by reference to a single document exactly what it is that the party restrained is prevented from doing in the period of the continuation.

5.32 The practice indicated in 5.30 (b) is also acceptable, but can be cumbersome, particularly where an order is continued several times or where the original order is itself bulky and much of it no longer relevant.

5.33 Whilst it is also possible, in principle, to continue an injunction simply by ordering in the new order that the injunction contained (in a specific paragraph or paragraphs) of the original order is to continue until the new expiry date or event (without annexing the original order), this practice has the disadvantage that it is not possible for the party restrained and third parties to see what activities are prevented without cross-referring to another document (which may or may not have been served). This may also give rise to difficulties of enforcement. It is particularly inadvisable to use this form where a litigant in person is involved.

5.34 In drafting the new order, consideration should always be given to whether a penal notice should be included.

5.35 Care should be taken not to "continue" paragraphs which do not need to be continued because they have been carried out or are no longer appropriate, such as orders requiring information or documents to be disclosed.

5.36 It is good practice to recite in the new order that the original order has been made.

**Consents by parties not attending hearing**

5.37 It is commonly the case that on an interim application the respondent does not appear either in person or by solicitors or counsel but the applicant seeks a consent order based upon a letter of consent from the respondent or his or her solicitors or a draft statement of agreed terms signed by the respondent's solicitors. This causes no difficulty where the agreed relief falls wholly within the relief claimed in the application notice. **1A–42**

5.38 If, however, the agreed relief goes outside that which is claimed in the application notice or even in the claim form or when undertakings are offered then difficulties can arise. A procedure has been established for this purpose to be applied to all applications in the Chancery Division.

5.39 Subject always to the discretion of the court, no order will be made in such cases unless a consent signed by or on behalf of the respondent to an application is put before the court in accordance with the following provisions:

(1) Where there are solicitors on the record for the respondent the court will normally accept as sufficient a written consent signed by those solicitors on their headed notepaper.

(2) Where there are solicitors for the respondent who are not on the record, the court will normally accept as sufficient a written consent signed by those solicitors on their headed notepaper only if in the consent (or some other document) the solicitors certify that they have fully explained to the respondent the effect of the order and that the respondent appeared to have understood the explanation.

(3) Where there is a written consent signed by a respondent acting in person the court will not normally accept it as sufficient unless the court is satisfied that the respondent understands the effect of the order either by reason of the circumstances (for example the respondent is himself a solicitor or barrister) or by means of other material (for example, the respondent's consent is given in reply to a letter explaining in simple terms the effect of the order).

(4) Where the respondent offers any undertaking to the court (a) the document containing the undertaking must be signed by the respondent personally, (b) solicitors must certify on their headed notepaper that the signature is that of the respondent and (c) if the case falls within (2) or (3) above, solicitors must certify that they have explained to the respondent the consequences of giving the undertaking and that the respondent appeared to understand the explanation.

**Bundles and Skeleton Arguments**

1A–43 5.40 See Chapter 7 below.

**Out of hours emergency arrangements**

1A–44 5.41 An application should not be made out of hours unless it is essential. An explanation will be required as to why it was not made or could not be made during normal court hours. Applications made during legal vacations must also constitute vacation business.

5.42 There is always a Duty Chancery Judge available to hear urgent out of hours applications. The following is a summary of the procedure:

(1) All requests for the Duty Chancery Judge to hear urgent matters are to be made through the judge's clerk. There may be occasions when the Duty Chancery Judge is not immediately available. The clerk will be able to inform the applicant of the judge's likely availability.

(2) Initial contact should be through the Royal Courts of Justice (tel: 020 7947 6000), who should be requested to contact the Duty Chancery Judge's clerk. The applicant must give a telephone number for the return call.

(3) When the clerk contacts the applicant, he or she will need to know:

   (a) the name of the party on whose behalf the application is to be made;

   (b) the name of the person who is to make the application and his or her status (counsel or solicitor);

   (c) the nature of the application;

   (d) the degree of urgency;

   (e) contact telephone numbers for the persons involved in the application.

(4) The Duty Judge will indicate to his or her clerk whether he or she is prepared to deal with the matter by telephone or whether it will be necessary for the matter to be dealt with by a hearing, in court or elsewhere. The clerk will inform the applicant and make the necessary arrangements. The Duty Judge will also indicate how any necessary papers are to be delivered (whether physically or by fax or e-mail)

(5) Applications for interim injunctions will only be heard by telephone where the applicant is represented by counsel or solicitors (PD 25, Interim Injunctions, paragraph 4.5 (5)).

5.43 Which judge will, in appropriate cases, hear an out of hours application varies according to when the application is made.

(1) Weekdays. Out of hours duty, during term time, is the responsibility of the Interim Applications Judge. The judge is normally available from 4.15pm until 10.15am Monday to Thursday.

(2) Weekends. A Duty Chancery Judge is nominated by rota for weekends, commencing 4.15pm Friday until 10.15am Monday.

(3) Vacation. The Vacation Judge also undertakes out of hours applications.

5.44 Sealing orders out of hours. In normal circumstances it is not possible to issue a sealed order out of hours. The judge may direct the applicant to lodge a draft of the order made at Chancery Chambers Registry by 10am on the following working day.

5.45 County court matters and matters proceeding out of London. Similar arrangements exist for making urgent applications out of hours in county court matters in certain parts of England and Wales and High Court matters proceeding in Chancery District Registries. The pager numbers for regional Urgent Business Officers are given in Appendix 1 to this Guide. Contact with the Circuit judge on duty for the London County Courts can be made through the Royal Courts of Justice.

**Vacation arrangements**

1A–45 5.46 There is a Chancery judge available to hear applications in vacation.

***Paragraph numbers marked with a "+" can be found online and on CD.***

Applications must generally constitute vacation business in that, in particular, they require to be immediately or promptly heard.

5.47 In the Long Vacation, two Vacation judges sit each day to hear vacation business. In other vacations there is one Vacation judge. Mondays and Thursdays are made available for urgent Interim Applications on notice. The judge is available on the remaining days for urgent business.



### Applications to a Master

5.48 Applications to a Master should be made by application notice. Application notices are issued by the Masters' Appointments section in Room TM7.09. It is important that application notices are lodged at or addressed to Masters' Appointments, Room TM 7.09 Royal Courts of Justice, Strand, London WC2A 2LL and not to a more generalised address such as "Chancery Division, Royal Courts of Justice" otherwise the listing of the application may delayed or the application may be wrongly listed before a judge. If the Master has already directed a case management conference the parties should ensure that all applications in the proceedings are properly issued and listed to be heard at the case management conference. If the available listed time is likely to be insufficient to give directions and hear any application the parties should co-operate and invite the court to arrange a longer appointment. It is the duty of the parties to seek to agree directions if possible and to provide a draft of the order for consideration by the Master. **1A-46**

5.49 Applications to a Master estimated to last in excess of two hours will require serious co-operation between the parties and will require the Master's directions before they are listed. The Master will normally give his permission to list such an application on condition that there is compliance with directions given by the Master.

5.50 Those directions are likely to require:

(1) that the applicant agrees the time estimate (see below) with his opponent;
(2) that, if the time allowed subsequently becomes insufficient, the court is informed and a new and longer appointment given;
(3) that the parties agree an appropriate timetable for filing evidence such that the hearing will be effective on the date listed;
(4) that positive confirmation is to be given to the Master five working days before the hearing date that the hearing remains effective; and
(5) that, in the event of settlement, the Master be informed of that fact as soon as possible.

5.51 The agreed time estimate must identify separately the time for the Master to pre-read any documents required to be pre-read; the hearing time of the application and also time to give any judgment at the conclusion of the hearing. The time for judgment should also take into account any further time that may be required for the Master to assess costs, and for any application for permission to appeal.

5.52 Failure to comply with the Master's directions given in respect of the listing of an appointment in excess of two hours may result, depending upon the circumstances, in the application not being heard or in adverse costs orders being made.

5.53 On any matter of substance, the Master is likely to require a bundle and skeleton arguments to be provided before the hearing, as detailed in paragraphs 7.40 to 7.50 below. Where directions are given in respect of an application to which paragraph 5.49 applies, the provision of a bundle and skeleton arguments should form part of the agreed timetable.

5.54 The Masters may also allow applications to be made to them informally. The Masters are normally available to hear oral applications without notice between 2.15pm and 2.45pm (see paragraph 6.32 below). Such applications should not be used in place of a formal Part 23 application and care must be taken to notify in appropriate cases parties likely to be affected by any order made on the application. Letters should not be used in place of a Part 23 application, and parties should be particularly careful to keep any correspondence with the Masters to a minimum and to ensure that opposing parties receive copies of any correspondence. Failure in this regard will mean that the Master will refuse to deal with the correspondence. Correspondence should state that it has been copied to the other parties (or should state why it has not been copied). Unless the matter is one of urgency correspondence and any other documents should be sent by post. If, in a case of real urgency, a letter is sent by fax, it should not be followed by a hard copy, unless it contains an original document which needs to be filed. Further guidance is set out in the Chief Master's Practice Note reproduced at Appendix 5.

5.55 There is no distinction between term time and vacation so far as business before the Chancery Masters is concerned. They will deal with all types of business throughout the year. When a Master is on holiday, his or her list will normally be taken by a deputy Master.

#### Applications for payment out of court

**1A–47** 5.56 Applications under PD 37 for payment out of money held in court must be made by Part 23 Application Notice (Form N244). The required documents should be sent to Room TM5.04. The following must be included:

(1) the reasons why the payment should be made (in Part C of the application notice)
(2) any relevant documents such as birth, marriage or death certificate, title deeds etc. (exhibited to the application notice)
(3) a statement whether or not anyone else has any claim to the money (in the Statement of Truth)
(4) bank details, ie the name and address of the relevant bank/building society branch, its Sort Code, and the Account Title and Number
(5) the Court fee.

5. 57 If there is a dispute as to entitlement to money in court, the Master may order the matter to proceed by Part 8 claim (see paragraph 2.14 above). In all other cases the Master will consider the file without a hearing and make an order for payment and/or sign the appropriate payment schedule.

## CHAPTER 6

## LISTING ARRANGEMENTS

***Key Rules: CPR Parts 29 and 39***

**1A–48** 6.1 This Chapter deals with listing arrangements for hearings before judges and Masters in the Royal Courts of Justice.

#### Hearings before Judges

*Responsibility for listing*

**1A–49** 6.2 Subject to the direction of the Chancellor, the Clerk of the Lists (Room WG3, Royal Courts of Justice) has overall responsibility for listing. Day by day management of Chancery listing is dealt with by the Chancery Judges' Listing Officer (Room WG4). All applications relating to listing should, in the first instance, be made to the Chancery Judges' Listing Officer, who will refer matters, as necessary, to the Clerk of the Lists. Any party dissatisfied with any decision of the Clerk of the Lists may, on one clear day's notice to all other parties, apply to the Interim Applications Judge. Any such application should be made within seven days of the decision of the Clerk of the Lists and be arranged through the Chancery Judges' Listing Office.

6.3 There are three main lists in the Chancery Division: the Trial List, the Interim Hearings List and the General List. In addition there is a separate Patents List which is also controlled on a day-to-day basis by the Chancery Judges' Listing Officer in Room WG4 (see Chapter 23).

*The Trial List*

6.4 This comprises a list of all trials to be heard with witnesses. **1A–50**

*The Interim Hearings List*

6.5 This list comprises interim applications and appeals from Masters. **1A–51**

*The General List*

6.6 This list comprises other matters including bankruptcy and pension appeals, Part 8 proceedings, applications for judgment and all company matters. **1A–52**

6.7 The procedure for listing Chancery cases to be heard in the Royal Courts of Justice and listed in the Trial List is that at an early stage in the claim the court will give directions with a view to fixing the period during which the case will be heard. In a Part 7 claim that period (the Trial Window) will be determined by the court either when the case is allocated or subsequently at a case management conference or other directions hearing. In a Part 8 claim covered by this procedure, that is to say a Part 8 claim to be heard with witnesses, similar directions will be given when the Part 8 claim is listed for preliminary directions or for a case management conference. It is only in a small minority of Part 8 claims that the claim is tried by a judge in the Trial List and the Trial Window procedure applies. The bulk of Part 8 claims are heard on written evidence either by the Master or by the judge. Additionally, many Part 8 claims, even where oral evidence is to be called, will be heard by the Master pursuant to the jurisdiction set out in paragraph 4.1 of PD 2B—Allocation of Cases to Levels of Judiciary.

*Allocation of Cases to Levels of Judiciary*

6.8 In determining the Trial Window the court will have regard to the listing constraints created by the existing court list and will determine a Trial Window which provides the parties with enough time to complete their preparations for trial. A Trial Window, once fixed, will not readily be altered. A list of current trial windows is published on the HMCS website. When determining the Trial Window the court will direct that one party, normally the claimant, makes an appointment to attend on the Chancery Judges' Listing Officer (Room WG4) to fix a trial date within the Trial Window, by such date as may be specified in the order and gives notice of that appointment to all other parties. It is to be understood that an order to attend on the Chancery Judges' Listing Officer imposes a strict obligation of compliance, without which the Trial Window that has been given may be lost. **1A–53**

6.9 At the listing appointment, the Chancery Judges' Listing Officer will take account, insofar as it is practical to do so, of any difficulties the parties may have as to the availability of counsel, experts and witnesses. The Chancery Judges' Listing Officer will, nevertheless, try to ensure the speedy disposal of the trial by arranging a firm trial date as soon as possible within the Trial Window. If a Case Summary has been prepared (see PD 29 paragraphs 5.6 and 5.7) the claimant must produce a copy at the listing appointment together with a copy of the particulars of claim and any orders relevant to the fixing of the trial date. If, exceptionally, at the listing appointment, it appears to the Chancery Judges' Listing Officer that a trial date cannot be provided by the court within the trial window, he may fix the trial date outside the trial window at the first available date.

6.10 A party wishing to appeal a date allocated by the Chancery Judge's Listing Officer must, within 7 days of the allocation, make an application to the Interim Applications judge. The application notice should be filed in the Chancery Judges' Listing Office and served, giving one clear day's notice to the other parties.

6.11 A trial date once fixed will, like a Trial Window, only rarely be altered or vacated. An application to adjourn a trial date will normally be made to the Interim

Applications judge (see further paragraph 7.39). A contested application may however be entertained by the Master if, for example, on the hearing of an interim application or case management conference it becomes clear that the trial date cannot stand without injustice to one or both parties.

*Warned List—General and Interim Hearings Lists*

**1A-54** 6.12 On each Friday of term and on such other days as may be appropriate, the Chancery Judges' Listing Officer will publish a Warned List, showing the matters that are liable to be heard in the following week. Any matters for which no date has been arranged will be liable to appear in the list for hearing with no warning save that given by the next day's list of cases, posted each afternoon outside Room WG4. Where a case is listed in the Warned List, the parties may agree to offer the case for a specified date, in accordance with the statement of Chancery Judges' Listing Office practice on offering cases issued by the Clerk of the Lists.

*Estimate of duration*

**1A-55** 6.13 If after a case is listed the estimated length of the hearing is varied, or if the case is settled, withdrawn or discontinued, the solicitors for the parties must forthwith inform the Chancery Judges Listing Officer in writing. Failure so to do may result in an adverse costs order being made. If the case is settled but the parties wish the Master to make a consent order, the solicitor must notify the Chancery Judges' Listing Officer in writing, whereupon he or she will take the case out of the list and notify the Master. The Master may then make the consent order.

6.14 Seven days before the date for the hearing, the claimant's solicitors must inform the Chancery Judges' Listing Officer whether there is any variation in the estimate of duration, and, in particular, whether the case is likely to be disposed of in some summary way. If the claimant is a litigant in person, this must be done by the solicitor for the first-named defendant who has instructed a solicitor. If a summary disposal is likely, the solicitor must keep the Chancery Listing Officer informed of any developments as soon as they occur.

*Applications after listing for hearing*

**1A-56** 6.15 Where a case has been listed for hearing and because of the timing of the hearing an application needs to be made as a matter of urgency, parties should first consult the Masters' clerks (Room TM7.09) as to the availability of the assigned Master or, in an appropriate case, applying to the Master himself. Provision can be made for urgent applications to be dealt with by the Chief Master or a deputy (see further paragraph 6.28). Parties should not list an application before the Interim Applications judge without first consulting the Masters' clerks. If (and only if) a Master cannot hear the application in good time, the application may be made to the Interim Applications judge.

*Appeals*

**1A-57** 6.16 All appeals for hearing by High Court judges in the Division are issued by the Clerk of the Lists, High Court Appeals Office (Room WG8). Enquiries relating to such appeals are to be made in the first instance to that office, except as provided by paragraph 6.18 below.

*Daily list of cases*

**1A-58** 6.17 This list, known as the Daily Cause List, is available on the Courts Service website: *www.hmcourts-service.gov.uk*.

*Listing of Particular Business*

**1A-59** 6.18 Appeals from Masters

(1) Appeals from Masters, where permission has been given, will appear in the

***Paragraph numbers marked with a "+" can be found online and on CD.***

Appeals Warned List. Such appeals (stamped with the appropriate fee) must be filed with the Clerk of the Lists' Office in Room WG7. When an appeal is filed an appeal number will be allocated and any future order will bear both the original claim number and the appeal number. On being satisfied that the case has been placed in the Warned List, solicitors should forthwith inform the Chancery Judges' Listing Officer whether they intend to instruct counsel and, if so, the name or names of counsel.

(2) Any order made on appeal from a Master will be placed on the court file. However, practitioners should co-operate by ensuring that a copy of any relevant order is available to the Master at any subsequent hearing.

6.19 Applications for permission to appeal from Masters

Applications for permission to appeal from a decision of a Master (stamped with the appropriate fee) must be lodged in the clerk of the Lists' Office in Room WG7. If permission to appeal is granted the appeal will appear in the Interim Hearings List and the procedure set out above will apply.

6.20 Bankruptcy Appeals

Notice of appeal from the decision of a Registrar or of a county court should be lodged in the Clerk of the Lists' Office, Room WG7. The appeal will be entered in the Appeals Warned List, usually with a fixed date. The date of the hearing will be fixed by the Chancery Judges' Listing Officer in the usual way.

6.21 Bankruptcy Applications

All originating applications to the judge should be lodged with the Deputy Court Manager in Bankruptcy. Urgent applications without notice for (i) the committal of any person to prison for contempt or (ii) injunctions or the modification or discharge of injunctions will be passed directly to the clerk to the Interim Applications Judge for hearing by that judge. All applications on notice for (i) and (ii) above, and applications referred to the judge by the Registrar, will be listed by the Chancery Judges' Listing Officer. Applications estimated not to exceed two hours will be heard by the Interim Applications judge. The Chancery Judges' Listing Officer is to give at least three clear days' notice of the hearing to the applicant and to any respondent who attended before the Registrar. Applications over two hours will be placed in the General List and listed accordingly.

6.22 Companies Court

Matters for hearing before the Companies judge, such as applications for an administration order, applications for approval by the court of schemes of arrangement and applications for the appointment of provisional liquidators, may be issued for hearing on any working day in term time (other than the last day of each term). Unopposed applications for the approval of schemes of arrangement will sometimes be heard by a judge before the start of normal sittings. Other applications may be dealt with by the Interim Applications judge as Companies judge. Applications or petitions which are estimated to exceed two hours are liable to be stood over to a date to be fixed by the Chancery Judges' Listing Officer. Urgent applications will also be dealt with by the Interim Applications judge. Applications and petitions referred to the judge by the Registrar will be placed in the General List and listed accordingly.

6.23 Applications referred to the judge

Applications referred by the Master to the judge will be added to the Interim Hearings List. The power to refer applications made to the Master and in respect of which the Master has jurisdiction is now very sparingly exercised. The proper use of judicial resources dictates that where the Master has jurisdiction in respect of an interlocutory matter he should ordinarily exercise that jurisdiction. The same principles apply to Registrars.

***Paragraph numbers marked with a "+" can be found online and on CD.***

6.24 Judge's Applications

Reference should be made to Chapter 5.

6.25 Short Applications

An application for judgment in default made to a judge (because the Master has no jurisdiction) should be made to the Interim Applications Judge.

6.26 Summary Judgment

Where an application for summary judgment includes an application for an injunction or a declaration, it usually has to be made to a judge because in most cases the Master cannot grant an injunction or make a declaration save in terms agreed by the parties. In such cases the application should be made returnable before the judge instead of the Master and will be listed in the General List. The return date to be inserted in the application notice should be a Monday at least 14 clear days after the application notice has been served. The application notice should be issued in the Chancery Judges' Listing Office (Room WG4) when there must be lodged two copies of the application notice and the witness statements or affidavits in support together with their exhibits. On the return date the application will normally be adjourned to a date to be fixed if the hearing is likely to take longer than thirty minutes. The adjourned date will be fixed in the usual way through the Chancery Judges' Listing Officer, and a certificate signed by an advocate as to the estimated length of the hearing must be lodged with the Chancery Judges' Listing Officer.

If the applicant informs the Chancery Judges' Listing Officer at the time of issue of an application notice for summary judgment returnable before a judge that directions have been agreed, or are not necessary, the application will be listed for a substantive hearing without being listed for directions.

If, subsequent to issue, the parties agree directions the Chancery Judges' Listing Officer will, on application, re-list the application for a substantive hearing and any directions hearing will be vacated. Time estimates should be agreed.

6.27 Variation of Trusts: Application to a judge

Applications under the Variation of Trusts Act 1958 for a hearing before the judge may be listed for hearing in the General List without any direction by a Master on the lodgment in Room WG4 of a certificate signed by advocates for all the parties, stating (i) that the evidence is complete and has been filed; (ii) that the application is ready for hearing; and (iii) the estimated length of the hearing.

**Hearings before Masters**

*Assignment of cases before Masters*

**1A-60** 6.28 The general rule is that cases are assigned to the Masters in accordance with the last digit of the claim number. At present cases are allocated as follows:

| | | | |
|---|---|---|---|
| 0 and 1 | Master Bragge | 6 and 7 | Master Price |
| 2 and 3 | Master Teverson | 8 and 9 | Master Mon-caster |
| 4 and 5 | Master Bowles | | |

In view of administrative responsibilities, the Chief Master does not have assigned cases. He will take individual cases or classes of case in his own discretion and arrangements will be made accordingly through the Court Manager. Where an application is required to be heard at short notice or is urgent but the assigned Master's list cannot accommodate an early date for the length of hearing necessary, arrangements can often be made for it to be listed before the Chief Master. Application should first be made to the assigned Master, who will determine whether

*Paragraph numbers marked with a "+" can be found online and on CD.*

the case is one which it is appropriate to release to the Chief Master. In that event arrangements are made by the Deputy Court Manager (Room TM 5.05)

Applications by the Official Solicitor under rule 21.12 to be appointed a guardian of a minor's estate are normally dealt with by the Chief Master. All applications for a Group Litigation Order in the Chancery Division have to be made to the Chief Master: see paragraph 3.13.

6.29 An important exception to the general rule is that all registered trade mark claims are assigned to Master Bragge. Practitioners must, therefore, ensure, both at the date of issue of proceedings and when any application is to be made, that the court staff are aware that the claim is a registered trade mark claim and that, irrespective of the claim number, the claim and any application in the claim is assigned to and should be listed before Master Bragge. Each month in term time a day or more is usually set aside in Master Bragge's list specifically for trade mark applications and practitioners should, if possible, seek to have applications listed on that day. If the provisions of this paragraph are ignored and an application in a registered trade mark claim is listed other than before Master Bragge, it is likely that the Master before whom it is listed will refuse to hear it. If Master Bragge is away it is to be expected that the claim will be heard by the Deputy sitting for him.

6.30 In addition, from time to time, the Chief Master assigns particular classes of case to particular Masters. This will normally relate to managed litigation where the particular parties will be aware that their cases have been specifically assigned.

*Urgent or oral applications to the Masters*

6.31 Masters are normally available to hear short oral applications without notice between 2.15pm and 2.45pm on working days. Notice should be given to the Master's Appointments section in Room TM7.09, or by telephone or fax, by 4.30pm on the previous working day (except in cases of real emergency when notice may be given at any time) so that the file will be before the Master. If this procedure is not followed the Master will be likely to refuse to deal with the application. The Master will expect notice of such an application to have been given in an appropriate case to the other party. Applications without Notice time must not be used as a substitute for cases where the issue and service of an Application Notice is appropriate. (See paragraph 5.41 above). **1A–61**

6.32 If the assigned Master is not available on any particular day, the applicant will be informed and (except in cases of emergency) asked to come when the assigned Master is next available. Applications will only be heard by another Master in cases of emergency or when the assigned Master is on vacation.

6.33 See also Chapter 5, paragraphs 5.48 to 5.55 (Applications to Masters).

## CHAPTER 7

## PREPARATION FOR HEARINGS

### *Key Rules: CPR Parts 29 and 39*

7.1 This Chapter contains guidance on the preparation of cases for hearings before judges and Masters. Guidelines about the conduct of trials are given in Chapter 8 of this Guide. When an affidavit or witness statement (or other document) is filed in Chancery Chambers in preparation for a hearing or for any other purpose, it should be accompanied by a written evidence lodgment form as set out in Part 2 of Appendix 4, unless it accompanies an application notice. The preparation of witness statements is covered in Chapter 8. **1A–62**

**Hearings before Judges**

7.2 To ensure court time is used efficiently there must be adequate preparation of cases prior to the hearing. This covers, among other things, the preparation and **1A–63** exchange of skeleton arguments, compiling bundles of documents and dealing out of court with queries which need not concern the court. The parties should also use their best endeavours to agree before any hearing what are the issues or the main issues.

*Estimates*

**1A-64** 7.3 Realistic estimates of the length of time a hearing is expected to take must be given.

7.4 In estimating the length of a hearing, sufficient time must be allowed for pre-reading any documents required to be read, the length of the speeches, the time required to examine witnesses (if any), and, if appropriate, an immediate judgment, together with the summary assessment of costs, in cases where that may arise, and any application for permission to appeal.

7.5 Except as mentioned below, a written estimate signed by the advocates for all the parties is required in the case of any hearing before a judge. This should be delivered to the Chancery Judges' Listing Officer:

(1) in the case of a trial, on the application to fix the trial date; and
(2) in any other case, as soon as possible after the application notice or case papers have been lodged with the Chancery Judges' Listing Office.

7.6 If the estimate given in the application notice for an application to the Interim Applications Judge (other than applications by order) or for an application listed before the Companies judge requires to be revised, the revised estimate should be given to the court as soon as practicable; and in any event orally when the application is called on.

*Changes in Estimate*

**1A-65** 7.7 The parties must inform the court immediately of any material change in a time estimate. They should keep each other informed of any such change. In any event a further time estimate signed by the advocates to the parties must be lodged when bundles are lodged (see paragraph 7.30 below).

*Inaccurate estimates*

**1A-66** 7.8 Where estimates prove inaccurate, a hearing may have to be adjourned to a later date and the party responsible for the adjournment is likely to be ordered to pay the costs thrown away.

*Bundles*

**1A-67** 7.9 Bundles of documents for use in court will generally be required for all hearings if more than 25 pages are involved (and may be appropriate even if fewer pages are involved). The efficient preparation of bundles of documents is very important. Where bundles have been properly prepared, the case will be easier to understand and present, and time and costs are likely to be saved. Where documents are copied unnecessarily or bundled incompetently the cost may be disallowed.

7.10 Where the provisions of this Guide as to the preparation or delivery of bundles are not followed, the bundle may be rejected by the court or be made the subject of a special costs order.

7.11 The claimant or applicant (as the case may be) should begin preparation of the bundles in sufficient time to enable:

(1) the bundles to be agreed with the other parties (so far as possible);
(2) references to the bundles to be used in skeleton arguments; and
(3) the bundles to be delivered to the court at the required time.

7.12 The representatives for all parties involved must co-operate in agreeing bundles

***Paragraph numbers marked with a "+" can be found online and on CD.***

for use in court. The court and the advocates should all have exactly the same bundles.

7.13 When agreeing bundles for trial, the parties should establish through their legal representatives, and record in correspondence, whether the agreement of bundles:

(1) extends no further than agreement of the composition and preparation of the bundles; or
(2) includes agreement that the documents in the bundles are authentic (see rule 32.19); or
(3) includes agreement that the documents may be treated as evidence of the facts stated in them.

The court will normally expect parties to agree that the documents, or at any rate the great majority of them, may be treated as evidence of the facts stated in them. A party not willing to agree should, when the trial bundles are lodged, write a letter to the court (with a copy to all other parties) stating that it is not willing to agree, and explaining why.

7.14 Detailed guidelines on the preparation of bundles are set out in Appendix 6, in addition to those in PD 39, Miscellaneous Provisions relating to Hearings, paragraph 3. These must always be followed unless there is good reason not to do so. Particular attention is drawn to the need to consider the preparation of a core bundle.

7.15 The general rule is that the claimant/applicant must ensure that one copy of a properly prepared bundle is delivered at the Chancery Judges' Listing Office not less than three clear days (and not more than seven days) before a trial or application by order. However, the court may direct the delivery of bundles earlier than this. Where oral evidence is to be given an additional copy of the bundle must be available in court for the use of the witnesses. In the case of bundles to be used on judge's Applications (other than applications by order) the bundles must be delivered to the clerk to the Interim Applications Judge by 10am on the morning preceding the day of the hearing unless the court directs otherwise. A bundle delivered to the court should always be in final form and parties should not make a request to alter the bundle after it has been delivered to the court save for good reason.

7.16 If the case is one which does not require the preparation of a bundle, the advocate should check before the hearing starts that all the documents to which he or she wishes to refer and which ought to have been filed have been filed, and, if possible, indicate to the associate which they are.

7.17 Bundles provided for the use of the court should be removed promptly after the conclusion of the hearing unless the court directs otherwise.

*Skeleton Arguments*

7.18 The general rule is that for the purpose of all hearings before a judge skeleton arguments should be prepared. The exceptions to this general rule are where the application does not warrant one, for example because it is likely to be short, or where the application is so urgent that preparation of a skeleton argument is impracticable or where an application is ineffective and the order is agreed by all parties (see also paragraphs 26.26 and 26.33). **1A–68**

7.19 In an appropriate case the court may direct sequential rather than simultaneous delivery of skeleton arguments.

*Time for delivery of skeleton arguments*

7.20 **In the more substantial matters (e.g. trials and applications by order)**—subject to any contrary direction not less than two clear days before the date or first date on which the application or trial is due to come on for hearing; or, if earlier, one clear day before the trial judge is due to begin pre-reading. **1A–69**

7.21 **On judge's applications without notice**—with the papers which the judge is asked to read on the application.

***Paragraph numbers marked with a "+" can be found online and on CD.***

7.22 **On all other applications to a judge, including interim applications**—as soon as possible and not later than 10am on the day **preceding** the hearing. If a skeleton argument is delivered on the day of the hearing, the judge may not have time to read it before the hearing.

7.23 Where a case is liable to be placed in the Warned List, consideration should be given to the preparation of skeleton arguments as soon as the case is placed in the Warned List, so that the skeleton arguments are ready to be delivered to the court on time. Preparation of skeleton arguments should not be left until notice is given that the case is to be heard. Notice may be given that the case is to be heard the next day.

*Place to which skeleton arguments should be delivered*

**1A–70** 7.24 If the name of the judge is not known, or the judge is a Deputy Judge, skeleton arguments should be delivered to the Chancery Judges' Listing Office (Room WG4).

7.25 If the name of the judge (other than a Deputy Judge) is known, skeleton arguments should be delivered to the judge's clerk.

7.26 Parties should always ask the judge's clerk whether the judge wishes to receive a digital copy of the skeleton argument by e-mail and, if so, the e-mail address to which the skeleton argument should be sent.

*Content of skeleton arguments*

**1A–71** 7.27 Appendix 7 contains guidelines which should be followed on the content of skeleton arguments and chronologies, as well as indices and reading lists.

7.28 In most cases before a judge, a list of the persons involved in the facts of the case, a chronology and a list of issues will also be required. The chronology and list of issues should be agreed where possible. The claimant/applicant is responsible for preparing the list of persons involved and the chronology, and he or she should deliver these and his or her list of issues (if required) to the court with his or her skeleton argument.

7.29 Unless the court gives any other direction, the parties shall, as between themselves, arrange for the delivery, exchange, or sequential service of skeleton arguments and any list of persons involved, list of issues or chronology. Where there are no such arrangements, all such documents should, where possible, be given to the other parties (if any) in sufficient time before the hearing to enable them properly to consider them.

*Reading lists and time estimates*

**1A–72** 7.30 When lodging the agreed bundles, or as soon as practicable thereafter, there should also be lodged a further agreed time estimate, together with an agreed reading list and an agreed time estimate in respect of that reading list. The time estimates and reading list must be signed by the advocates for the parties. Failing agreement as to the time estimates or reading list then separate reading lists and time estimates must be submitted signed by the appropriate advocate. See Appendix 7 as to reading lists.

*Failure to lodge bundles or skeleton arguments on time*

**1A–73** 7.31 Failure to lodge skeleton arguments and bundles in accordance with this Guide may result in:

(1) the matter not being heard on the date in question;
(2) the costs of preparation being disallowed; and
(3) an adverse costs order being made.

7.32 In the Royal Courts of Justice, a log will be maintained of all late skeletons and bundles. The log will regularly be inspected by the Chancellor who will consider such

***Paragraph numbers marked with a "+" can be found online and on CD.***

further action as appropriate in relation to any recurrent failure by any chambers, barrister, or solicitors firm to comply with the requirements of the CPR and the Guide.

*Authorities*

7.33 Authorities are usually supplied as photocopies. Photocopies of authorities should be full size; and not reduced size. Unless photocopies of authorities are provided, lists of authorities should be supplied to the usher by 9am on the first day of the hearing. Delivery of skeleton arguments does not relieve a party of his or her duty to deliver his or her list of authorities to the usher by the time stated. **1A–74**

7.34 Advocates should exchange lists of authorities by 4pm on the day before the hearing. Any failure in this regard which has the effect of increasing the length of a hearing or of giving rise to delay in the hearing of an application may give rise to an adverse costs order.

7.35 Excessive citation of authority should be avoided and practitioners must have full regard to the matters contained in *Practice Note (citation of cases: restrictions and rules)* [2001] 1 WLR 1001. In particular, the citation of authority should be restricted to the expression of legal principle rather than the application of such principle to particular facts. Practitioners must also, when citing authority, seek to ensure that their citations comply with *Practice Direction (Judgments: Neutral Citations)* [2002] 1 WLR 346.

*Oral Argument*

7.36 The court may indicate the issues on which it wishes to be addressed and those on which it wishes to be addressed only briefly. **1A–75**

*Documents and Authorities*

7.37 Only the key part of any document or authority should be read aloud in court. **1A–76**

7.38 At any hearing, handing in written material designed to reduce or remove the need for the court to take a manuscript note will assist the court and save time. Any such material should also be available for the judge in digital form.

*Adjournments*

7.39 As a timetable for the case will have been fixed at an early stage, applications for adjournment of a trial should only be necessary where there has been a change of circumstances not known when the timetable was fixed. Once a trial has been fixed it will rarely be adjourned. **1A–77**

When to apply

(1) A party who seeks to have a hearing before a judge adjourned must inform the Chancery Judges' Listing Officer of his or her application as soon as possible.

(2) Applications for an adjournment immediately before a hearing begins should be avoided as they take up valuable time which could be used for dealing with effective business and, if successful, they may result in a loss of court time altogether.

How to apply

(3) If the application is agreed, the parties should, in writing, apply to the Chancery Judges' Listing Officer. The Officer will consult the judge nominated for such matters. The judge may grant the application on conditions and give directions as to a new hearing date. But the judge may direct that the application be listed for a hearing and that all parties attend.

(4) If the adjournment is opposed the party asking for it should apply to the judge nominated for such matters or to the judge to whom the mat-

***Paragraph numbers marked with a "+" can be found online and on CD.***

ter has been allocated. A hearing should be arranged, at the first opportunity, through the Chancery Judges' Listing Office.

(5) A short summary of the reasons for the adjournment should be delivered to the Chancery Judges' Listing Office, where possible by 12 noon on the day before the application is made. Where an application for an adjournment is made on medical grounds, the court will normally require a witness statement and/or medical evidence. The medical evidence should at least take the form of a medical certificate or doctor's letter. In other cases a witness statement may not be required.

(6) The party requesting an adjournment will, in general, be expected to show that he or she has conducted his or her own case diligently. Parties should take all reasonable steps to ensure that their cases are adequately prepared in sufficient time to enable a hearing before the court to proceed. Likewise, they should take reasonable steps to prepare and serve any document (including any written evidence) required to be served on any other party in sufficient time to enable the other party similarly to be adequately prepared.

(7) If a failure to take reasonable steps necessitates an adjournment, the court may disallow costs as between solicitor and client, or order the person responsible to pay the costs under rule 48.7, or dismiss the application, or make any other order (including an order for the payment of costs on an indemnity basis).

(8) A trial date may, on occasion, also be vacated by the Master in the circumstances envisaged in paragraph 6.11.

### Hearings before Masters and Registrars

**1A–78** 7.40 As in the case of hearings before judges, there must be adequate preparation of cases prior to a hearing before the Masters and Registrars. Parties must ensure when issuing applications to be heard by the Masters and Registrars that time estimates are realistic and make proper allowance for the time taken to pre-read any documents required to be read, give judgment and deal with the summary assessment of costs and any application for permission to appeal. The parties must inform the court and all other parties immediately of any material change in a time estimate. Where estimates prove inaccurate, the hearing may have to be adjourned to a later date and the party responsible for the adjournment is likely to be ordered to pay the costs thrown away.

7.41 In the case of a hearing before a Master or Registrar which is listed for one hour or more and in any other hearing before a Master or Registrar such as a case management conference, where a bundle would assist, a bundle should be provided.

7.42 Bundles must be provided for a trial or equivalent hearing (such as an account or inquiry or a Part 8 claim with oral evidence) which is listed before a Master or a Registrar. Such bundles must comply with Appendix 6 and contain or be accompanied by a reading list and an estimate of reading time as set out in paragraph 7.30 above.

7.43 Parties should always ask whether the Master or Registrar wishes to receive a digital copy of the skeleton argument by e-mail and, if so, the e-mail address to which the skeleton argument should be sent.

7.44 Bundles provided for the use of the Master and Registrars should be removed promptly after the conclusion of the hearing unless the Master or Registrar directs otherwise.

7.45 Delivery of Bundles for hearings before Masters

(1) Bundles should be delivered to Masters' Appointments, Room TM7.09, not less than 2 (and not more than 7) clear working days before the hearing. They should be clearly marked "For hearing on ..*[date]* before Master ...." They must <u>not</u> be taken to the Registry (Room TM5.04) or the Chancery Judges' Listing

Office, and no document required for any hearing must be taken to the RCJ post room. Documents delivered to the wrong place are unlikely to reach the Master in time for the hearing, resulting in probable postponement and the party responsible for the adjournment is likely to be ordered to pay the costs thrown away.

(2) Detailed guidance on where to deliver documents in Chancery Chambers is at Appendix 8.

(3) Where no bundle is provided for the use of the Master, but a party intends to rely on the exhibits to a witness statement or affidavit, that party must ensure that those documents are filed with the court in sufficient time to be available to be read by the Master in advance of the hearing. Documents filed less than 10 days before a hearing must be taken to Masters' Appointments, Room TM7.09, for filing and marked "For hearing on . . .*[date]* before Master . . . . . ." (Documents filed before that time should be filed in the Registry, Room TM5.04, in the normal way). Exhibits should not be placed in lever arch files but should be fastened securely, for example by treasury tags.

7.46 Delivery of bundles for hearings before Bankruptcy Registrars

Bundles should be delivered to Room TM1.10 not less than 2 (and not more than 7) clear working days before the hearing. The should be clearly marked "For hearing on . . . . . . . . . . . . .*[date]* before Registrar . . . . . . . . . . . . . . . . . . . . . . . . . . . . . . . . . . . . . . . . . . ."

7.47 Delivery of bundles for hearings before Companies Court Registrars

Bundles should be delivered to Room TM4.04 not less than 2 (and not more than 7) clear working days before the hearing. They should be clearly marked "For hearing on . . . . . . . . . . . . .*[date]* before Registrar . . . . . . . . . . . . . . . . . . . . . . . . . . . . . . . . . . . . . . . . . . ."

7.48 Late delivery of bundles for hearings before Masters and Registrars

Parties delivering bundles should note that a log will be kept recording the time of their delivery to Rooms TM1.10, TM4.04 and TM7.09. Any failure to comply with these requirements which results in the postponement of a hearing may render that party liable to pay the costs occasioned by the adjournment.

**Note:**Bundles for hearings before a Chancery judge must be delivered to the Chancery Judges' Listing Office (Room WG4).

*Skeleton arguments*

7.49 Skeleton arguments should normally be prepared in respect of any application before the Master or Registrar of one or more hours' duration and certainly for any trial or similar hearing. They are to be delivered to the same place and at the same time as bundles. The contents of the skeleton argument should be in accordance with Appendix 7. **1A–79**

7.50 Where a skeleton argument is required, photocopies of any authorities to be relied upon should accompany the skeleton argument.

7.51 If pursuant to the e-mail protocol for communications with the Chancery Division (paragraph 14.8 below), a skeleton argument is sent electronically, then the provisions of the protocol as well as the time limits set out above must be followed. In particular, any authorities relied on should not be attached to the electronic version of the skeleton argument; but should be delivered in hard form and, where it would assist, be accompanied by a copy of the skeleton argument in hard form.

7.52 Failure to deliver skeleton arguments or bundles in accordance with this Guide is likely to result in the matter not being heard on the date fixed, the costs of preparation being disallowed and an adverse costs order being made.

*Compromise or settlement of hearings*

7.53 When hearings before Masters are compromised or settled, Masters' Appointments (Room TM7.09) should be informed in writing immediately and in any **1A–80** event no later than 4pm on the day preceding the hearing. In the case of substantial hearings involving pre-reading Masters' Appointments should be informed immediately if it appears likely that a hearing will be ineffective, with a request that the Master is immediately notified. Written notification must be given to Room TM1.10 for Bankruptcy hearings and Room TM4.04 for Companies hearings. Failure to notify and consequent waste of court time may result in an adverse costs order being made.

## CHAPTER 8

## CONDUCT OF A TRIAL

***Key Rules: CPR Parts 32 and 39***

**1A–81** 8.1 An important aim of all concerned must be to ensure that at trial court time is used as efficiently as possible. Thorough preparation of the case prior to trial is the key to this.

8.2 Chapter 7 of this Guide applies to preparation for a trial as well as for other hearings in court. This Chapter contains matters which principally affect trials.

### Time limits

**1A–82** 8.3 The court may, either at the outset of the trial or at any time thereafter, fix time limits for oral submissions, and the examination and cross-examination of witnesses. (See paragraphs 3.18–3.19.)

### Oral submissions

**1A–83** 8.4 In general, and subject to any direction to the contrary by the trial judge, there should be a short opening statement on behalf of the claimant, at the conclusion of which the judge may invite short opening statements on behalf of the other parties.

8.5 Unless notified otherwise, advocates should assume that the judge will have read their skeleton arguments and the principal documents referred to in the reading list lodged in advance of the hearing (see paragraph 7.30). The judge will state at an early stage how much he or she has read and what arrangements are to be made about reading any documents not already read, for which an adjournment of the trial after opening speeches may be appropriate. If the judge needs to read any documents additional to those mentioned in the reading list lodged in advance of the hearing, a list should be provided during the opening.

8.6 It is normally convenient for any outstanding procedural matters to be dealt with in the course of, or immediately after, the opening statements.

8.7 After the evidence is concluded, and subject to any direction to the contrary by the trial judge, oral closing submissions will be made on behalf of the claimant first, followed by the defendant(s) in the order in which they appear on the claim form, followed by a reply on behalf of the claimant. In a lengthy and complex case each party should provide written summaries of their closing submissions.

8.8 The court may require the written summaries to set out the principal findings of fact for which a party contends.

### Witness Statements

**1A–84** 8.9 In the preparation of witness statements for use at trial, the guidelines in Appendix 9 should be followed.

8.10 If a witness wishes to deal with matters not dealt with in the original witness statement a supplementary witness statement should be prepared and served on the other parties, as soon as possible Permission is required to adduce a supplementary witness statement at trial if any other party objects to it. This need not be sought

***Paragraph numbers marked with a "+" can be found online and on CD.***

before service; it can be sought at a case management conference if convenient or, if need be, at trial.

8.11 Witnesses are expected to have re-read their witness statements shortly before they are called to give evidence.

8.12 Where a party decides not to call a witness whose witness statement has been served to give oral evidence at trial, prompt notice of this decision should be given to all other parties. The party should make plain when he or she gives this notice whether he or she proposes to put, or seek to put, the witness statement in as hearsay evidence. If he or she does not put the witness statement in as hearsay evidence, rule 32.5(5) allows any other party to put it in as hearsay evidence.

8.13 Facilities may be available to assist parties or witnesses with special needs, whether as regards access to the court, or audibility in court, or otherwise. The Chancery Judges' Listing Office should be notified of any such needs prior to the hearing. The Customer Service Officer (tel 020 7947 7731) can also assist with parking, access etc. Similar facilities may be available at courts outside the Royal Courts of Justice.

### Expert Evidence

8.14 The trial judge may disallow expert evidence which either is not relevant for any reason, or which he or she regards as excessive and disproportionate in all the circumstances, even though permission for the evidence has been given. **1A–85**

8.15 The evidence of experts (or of the experts on a particular topic) is commonly taken together at the same time and after the factual evidence has been given. If this is to be done it should be agreed by the parties before the trial and should be raised with the judge at the PTR, if there is one, or otherwise at the start of the trial. Expert evidence should as far as possible be given by reference to the reports exchanged.

### Physical exhibits

8.16 Some cases involve a number of physical exhibits. The parties should try to agree the exhibits in advance and their system of labelling. Where it would be desirable, they should agree a scheme of display (e.g. on a board with labels readable from a distance). Where witness statements refer to these, a note in the margin (which can be handwritten) of the exhibit number should be added. **1A–86**

## CHAPTER 9

## JUDGMENTS, ORDERS AND PROCEEDINGS AFTER JUDGMENT

***Key Rules: CPR Part 40, and PDs 40, 40B, 40D and 40E***

### Judgments

9.1 Where judgment is reserved, the judge will normally deliver his or her judgment by handing down the written text without reading it out in open court. Where this course is adopted, the advocates will be supplied with the full text of the draft judgment in advance of delivery. In such cases, the advocates should familiarise themselves with the text of the judgment and be ready to deal with any points which may arise when judgment is delivered. The parties should seek to agree any consequential orders: see paragraph 3.1 of PD 40E. **1A–87**

9.2 The text may be shown, in confidence, to the parties, but only for the purpose of obtaining instructions and on the strict understanding that the judgment, or its effect, is not to be disclosed to any other person, or used in the public domain, and that no action is taken (other than internally) in response to the judgment. Advocates should notify the judge's clerk of any obvious errors or omissions.

9.3 The judgment does not take effect until formally delivered in court, when, if requested and so far as practicable, it will be made available to the law reporters and the press. The judge will normally direct that the written judgment may be used for all purposes as the text of the judgment, and that no transcript of the judgment need be made. Where such a direction is made, copies of a judgment delivered in the Royal Courts of Justice may be obtained from the Mechanical Recording Department. Elsewhere, the court will supply a copy.

9.4 If the parties have agreed the form of the order and any consequential orders, and have supplied the judge with a draft, judgment may be handed down without the need for an attendance.

**Orders**

**1A–88** 9.5 It may often be possible for the court to prepare and seal an order more quickly if a draft of the order is handed in. Speed may be particularly important where the order involves the grant of an interim injunction or the appointment of a receiver without notice. In all but the most simple cases a draft order should be prepared and brought to the hearing.

9.6 The court may direct the parties to agree and sign a draft order. Where the proceedings are in the Royal Courts of Justice, the draft order should, when agreed and signed, be delivered (if it is a judge's order) to the relevant judge's clerk or (if it is a Master's order) to the Master's clerk in Room TM 7.09. In the case of any dispute or difficulty as to the contents of the order, the parties should mention the matter to the judge or Master who heard the application and should do so with expedition.

9.7 Where a draft or an agreed statement of the terms of an order exists in electronic form, it is often helpful if the draft or agreed statement is provided to the court by e-mail or on a digital storage device as well as in hard copy, particularly if the order needs to be drawn quickly. Any digital storage device supplied for this purpose must be new and newly-formatted before writing the material on it so as to minimise the risk of transferring a computer virus. The current word processing system used by the Chancery Associates is Microsoft Windows 2003. Enquiries regarding the provision of digital storage devices should be made of the associate responsible for drawing the order in question.

9.8 Further guidance on the drafting of orders by the parties may be found in Appendix 14.

**Drafting and Service of Orders**

**1A–89** 9.9 Orders will be drawn up by the court, unless the judge or Master directs that no order be drawn. Unless a contrary order is made, or the party concerned has asked to serve the order, a sealed order will be sent by the court to each party.

9.10 Where a particular order is required to be served personally, the party concerned (see above) will be responsible for service.

**Forms of Order**

**1A–90** 9.11 Recitals will be kept to a minimum and the body of the order will be confined to setting out the decision of the court and the directions required to give effect to it. If upon receipt of an order any party is of the view that it is not drawn up in such a way as to give effect to the decision of the court, prompt notice must be given to the Chancery Chambers Registry in Room TM5.04 and to all other parties setting out the reasons for dissatisfaction. If the differences cannot be resolved, the objecting party may apply on notice for the order to be amended and should do so promptly.

**Copies of Orders**

**1A–91** 9.12 Copies of orders may be obtained from Room TM5.04 upon payment of the appropriate fee.

**Consent Orders**

9.13 All consent orders filed in Chancery Chambers and in respect of which a fee has been paid are referred to the Master for approval before the order is sealed. Such orders should be delivered to Room TM 7.09. **1A–92**

**Consents by parties not attending the hearing**

9.14 This is covered in paragraphs 5.37–5.39 above. **1A–93**

**Tomlin Orders**

9.15 Where proceedings are to be stayed on agreed terms to be scheduled to the order, the draft order should be drawn so as to read, with any appropriate provision in respect of costs, as follows: **1A–94**

> "And the parties having agreed to the terms set out in the attached schedule
> IT IS BY CONSENT ORDERED
> That all further proceedings in this claim be stayed except for the purpose of carrying such terms into effect
> AND for that purpose the parties have permission to apply"

Any direction for:

(1) payment of money out of court, or
(2) payment and assessment of costs

should be contained in the body of the order and not in the schedule.

This form of order is called a "Tomlin Order". If the order refers to a confidential schedule or agreement, this must be filed with the order but with a prominent request that it be treated as a confidential document not open to inspection to be retained in a sealed envelope on the court file and marked "Not to be inspected without the permission of the Master or judge".

**Proceedings after judgment**

9.16 Proceedings under judgments and orders in the Chancery Division are now regulated by PD 40 Accounts, Inquiries etc., PD 40B Judgments and Orders, and PD 40D Court's Powers in Relation to Land etc. **1A–95**

**Directions**

9.17 Where a judgment or order directs further proceedings or steps, such as accounts or inquiries, it will often give directions as to how the accounts and inquiries are to be conducted, for example: **1A–96**

<u>for accounts</u>

(1) who is to lodge the account and within what period;
(2) within what period objection is to be made; and
(3) arrangements for inspection of vouchers or other relevant documents;

<u>for inquiries</u>

(4) whether the inquiry is to proceed on written evidence or with statements of case;
(5) directions for service of such evidence or statements; and
(6) directions as to disclosure.

9.18 If directions are not given in the judgment or order an application should be made to the assigned Master as soon as possible asking for such directions. The application notice should specify the directions sought. Before making the application, applicants should write to the other parties setting out the directions they seek and inviting their response within 14 days. The application to the court should not be made until after the expiry of that period unless there is some special urgency.

The application must state that the other parties have been consulted and have attached to it copies of the applicant's letter to the other parties and of any response from them. The Master will then consider what directions are appropriate. In complex cases he or she may direct a case management conference.

9.19 If any inquiry is estimated to last more than two days and involves very large sums of money or strongly contested issues of fact or difficult points of law, the Master may direct that it be heard by a judge. The parties are under an obligation to consider whether in any particular case the inquiry is more suitable to be heard by a judge and should assist the Master in this. Accounts, however long they are estimated to take, will normally be heard by the Master. The Master is likely to want to give detailed directions in connection with the account and the form of it.

**Registration of judgments**

**1A–97** 9.20 Under the Register of Judgments, Orders and Fines Regulations 2005, money judgments in claims commenced in the High Court after 6th April 2006 (unless exempt) are registered with the Registrar of Judgments, Orders and Fines. Returns are sent to the Registrar by the court. In non-contested cases (judgments in default or on admission) registration is immediate. In contested cases the judgment is not registered unless steps are taken to enforce it under Part 70 or Part 71.

9.21 Judgments which are the subject of an appeal under Part 52 are not registered until the appeal has been determined. The court officer responsible for returns (Malcolm Dann, Room TM 5.07, 020 7947 6531) should be informed if permission to appeal is granted after a judgment has been registered, and he should also be informed when an application is made under Part 70 or Part 71.

9.22 If the judgment debt is satisfied, the judgment has been set aside or reversed, or the amount of the debt increases as a result of the issue of a final costs certificate or an increase in the amount of the debt as a consequence of enforcement proceedings, the court officer responsible for returns (as above) should be notified.

## CHAPTER 10

## APPEALS

***Key Rules: CPR Part 52 and PD 52; PD Insolvency Proceedings, Part 4, paragraph 17: Appeals; PD Directors' Disqualification Para. 35***

**General**

**1A–98** 10.1 This Chapter is concerned with the following appeals affecting the Chancery Division:

(1) Appeals within the ordinary work of the Division, from Masters to High Court judges;
(2) Insolvency appeals from High Court Registrars and from county courts to High Court judges;
(3) Appeals to High Court judges in the Chancery Division from orders in claims proceeding in a county court;
(4) Statutory appeals to the Chancery Division.

Proceedings under the Companies Acts are specialist proceedings for the purposes of rule 49(2) and therefore as regards the destination of appeals. In those cases appeals from final decisions by a Registrar of the Companies Court go direct to the Court of Appeal. Such appeals are not covered in this Chapter. Most appeals from tribunals are now dealt with by the Upper Tier Tribunal, which is not covered by this Guide. Appeals from some other bodies (e.g. the Comptroller of Patents) still lie to the court.

10.2 This Chapter does not deal with appeals from High Court judges of the Division, except as regards permission to appeal, and as to giving notice to the court

***Paragraph numbers marked with a "+" can be found online and on CD.***

of an appeal in a contempt case. It does not deal with appeals in the course of the detailed assessment of costs.

10.3 The detailed procedure for appeals is set out in Part 52 and in PD 52, and in the PD relating to Insolvency Proceedings, to which reference should be made. This Chapter only refers to some of the salient points.

**Permission to appeal**

10.4 Permission to appeal is required in all cases except: (a) appeals against committal orders, (b) certain statutory appeals. Permission to appeal will only be given where the court considers that the appeal would have a real prospect of success or there is some other compelling reason why the appeal should be heard (rule 52.3(6)). An application for permission to appeal may be made to the lower court, but only if it is made at the hearing at which the decision to be appealed was made. However, the court has power to adjourn that hearing for the purpose of considering any application for permission to appeal. If the lower court refuses permission, or permission is not applied for to the lower court, an application may be made to the appeal court by Appellant's Notice. **1A–99**

10.5 An application to the appeal court for permission may be dealt with without a hearing, but if refused without a hearing the applicant may request that it be reconsidered at a hearing. Notice of the hearing is often given to the respondent; the respondent may submit written representations or attend the hearing but will not usually be awarded any costs of so doing even if permission to appeal is refused. The judge who hears the oral application will usually be the same judge who dealt with the application on the papers.

10.6 Guidance for litigants in relation to appeals to the High Court is available by way of a Practice Statement which may be obtained from the High Court Appeals Office at the Royal Courts of Justice (Room WG4).

10.7 If a party who wishes to appeal to the High Court cannot lodge all the documents which are required at the time when the appellant's notice is issued, the Appeals Office is able to allow some further time by way of an extension, but beyond this any further extension has to be allowed by a judge, who will consider the case on paper. If there is a delay in obtaining a transcript of the judgment to be appealed, the appellant should try to obtain a note of the judgment, which the lawyers representing any party at the hearing below ought to be able to provide, at least as an interim measure before a transcript is obtained.

10.8 If the documents required for consideration of an application for permission to appeal to the High Court have not been lodged, despite any extension which has been allowed, the case may be listed for oral hearing in the Dismissal List, for the appellant to show cause why the case should not be dismissed. The respondent will not normally be notified of such a hearing.

**Stay**

10.9 Unless the lower court or the appeal court orders otherwise, an appeal does not operate as a stay of any order or decision of the lower court. A stay of execution may be applied for in the appellant's notice. If it is, it may be dealt with on paper. If the stay is required as a matter of great urgency, or before the appellant's notice can be filed, an application should be made to the Interim Applications Judge. **1A–100**

**Appeals from Masters in cases proceeding in the Chancery Division**

10.10 If permitted, an appeal from a decision of a Master in a case proceeding in the Chancery Division usually lies to a High Court judge of the Division. An appeal from a final decision of a Master in a Part 7 claim allocated to the multi-track lies direct to the Court of Appeal. **1A–101**

**Insolvency appeals**

10.11 An appeal lies from a county court (Circuit or District Judge) or a High Court **1A–102**

*Paragraph numbers marked with a "+" can be found online and on CD.*

Registrar in bankruptcy or company insolvency matters to a High Court judge of the Chancery Division,. Permission to appeal is required.

10.12 Appeals in proceedings under the Company Directors Disqualification Act 1986 are treated as being in insolvency proceedings.

**Appeals from orders made in county court claims**

**1A–103** 10.13 An appeal against a decision of a circuit judge in a claim proceeding in a county court lies to the High Court, unless, either, the decision is a final decision in a claim allocated to the multi-track or in specialist proceedings to which rule 49(2) applies, or the decision is itself on an appeal. In either of these cases the appeal lies direct to the Court of Appeal. This does not apply, however, where the allocation to the multi-track is deemed, rather than the result of a specific order, so that in cases begun by a Part 8 claim form, even though they are deemed to be so allocated, appeals lie to the High Court. The general rules as to the requirement for permission described above apply to these appeals.

**Statutory appeals**

**1A–104** 10.14 The Chancery Division hears a variety of appeals and cases stated under statute from decisions of tribunals and other persons. Some of these are listed or referred to in PD 52, but this is not exhaustive. However, most appeals from tribunals are now dealt with by the Upper Tier Tribunal.

**Appeals to the Court of Appeal: permission to appeal**

**1A–105** 10.15 An appeal lies from a judgment of a High Court judge of the Division to the Court of Appeal (unless an enactment makes it final and unappealable), but permission is required in all cases except where the order is for committal. Permission may be granted by the High Court judge, if applied to at the hearing at which the decision to be appealed was made, unless the order of the High Court judge was itself on an appeal (other than an appeal from the Comptroller of Patents), in which case permission may only be granted by the Court of Appeal.

**Appeals in cases of contempt of court**

**1A–106** 10.16 Appellant's notices which by paragraph 21.4 of PD 52 are required to be served on "the court from whose order or decision the appeal is brought" may be served, in the case of appeals from the Chancery Division, on the Chief Master of the Chancery Division; service may be effected by leaving a copy of the notice of appeal with the clerk of the Lists in Room WG4, Royal Courts of Justice, Strand, London WC2A 2LL.

**Dismissal by consent**

**1A–107** 10.17 The practice is as set out in paragraph 12 of PD 52, for all appeals except first appeals in insolvency matters. Where the appeal is proceeding in the High Court a document signed by solicitors for all parties must be lodged with the High Court Appeals Office (Room WG7), Royal Courts of Justice, Strand, London WC2A 2LL, requesting dismissal of the appeal. The appeal can be dismissed without any hearing by an order made in the name of the Chancellor. Any orders with directions as to costs will be drawn by the Chancery Associates. In the case of a first appeal in an insolvency matter, reference should be made to paragraph 17.22(8) of the PD Insolvency Proceedings.

## CHAPTER 11

## COSTS

### *Key Rules: CPR Parts 43 to 48 and the PD supplementing them*

**1A–108** 11.1 This Chapter does not set out to do more than refer to some salient points on costs relevant to proceedings in the Chancery Division. In particular it does not deal with the processes of detailed assessment or appeals in relation to such assessments. In this Chapter the "paying party" is the party by whom the costs are to be paid; and the "receiving party" is the party to whom the costs are to be paid.

11.2 A number of provisions in respect of costs in the CPR and in the PD supplementing Parts 43 to 48 (Costs PD) are likely to be relevant to Chancery proceedings:

(1) *Informing the client of costs orders:* Solicitors have a duty to tell their clients, within 7 days, if an order for costs is made against them and they were not present at the hearing. Solicitors must also tell anyone else who has instructed them to act on the case or who is liable to pay their fees. They must inform these persons how the order came to be made (rule 44.2; Costs PD, paragraph 7.1).

(2) *Providing the court with estimates of costs:* The court can order a party to file an estimate of costs and to serve it on the other parties. (Costs PD, paragraph 6.3). This is to assist the court in deciding what case management orders to make and also to inform other parties as to their potential liability for costs. In addition parties must file estimates of costs when they file their allocation questionnaire or any listing questionnaire (Costs PD, paragraph 6.4).

(3) *Summary assessment of costs:* An outline of these provisions is given below. Their effect is that in the majority of contested hearings lasting no more than a day the court will decide, at the end of the hearing, not only who is to pay the costs but also how much those costs should be, and will order them to be paid, usually within 14 days. As a result the paying party will have to pay the costs at an early stage.

(4) *Interim orders for costs*: Where the court decides immediately who is to pay particular costs, but does not assess the costs summarily, for example after a trial lasting more than a day, so that the final amount of costs payable has to be fixed by a detailed assessment, the court may (and usually will) order the paying party to pay a sum or sums on account of the ultimate liability for costs.

(5) *Interest on costs*: The court has power to award interest on costs from a date before the date of the order, so compensating the receiving party for the delay between incurring the costs and receiving a payment in respect of them from the paying party.

**Summary Assessment**

11.3 The court will generally make a summary assessment of costs whenever the hearing lasts for less than one day. The judge or Master who heard the application or other hearing (which will include a trial, or the hearing of a Part 8 Claim, lasting less than a day) carries out the summary assessment. The court may decide not to assess costs summarily either because it orders the costs to be "costs in the case" or because it considers the case to be otherwise inappropriate for summary assessment, typically because substantial issues arise as to the amount of the costs claimed. Costs payable to a party funded by the Legal Services Commission cannot be assessed summarily. **1A–109**

11.4 In order that the court can assess costs summarily at the end of the hearing each party who intends to claim costs must, no later than 24 hours before the time fixed for the hearing, serve on the other party, and file with the court, his or her statement of costs. Paragraph 13.5 of the Costs PD contains requirements about the information to be included in this statement, and the form of the statement. Failure by a party to file and serve his or her statement of costs as required by paragraph 13.5 of the Costs PD will be taken into account by the court in deciding what order to make about costs and could result in a reduced assessment, in no order being made as to costs, or in the party being penalised in respect of the costs of any further hearing or detailed assessment hearing which may be required as a result of the party's failure.

11.5 Where the receiving party is funded by the Legal Services Commission the court cannot assess costs summarily. It is not, however, prevented from assessing costs summarily by the fact that the paying party is so funded. A summary assessment of costs payable by a person funded by the Legal Services Commission is not by itself a determination of the amount of those costs which the funded party is to pay (as to which see section 11 of the Access to Justice Act 1999 and regulation 10 of the Community Legal Services (Costs) Regulations 2000). Ordinarily, where costs are summarily assessed and ordered to be paid by a funded person the order will provide that the determination of any amount which the person who is or was in receipt of services funded by the Legal Services Commission is to pay shall be dealt with in accordance with regulation 10 of the Regulations.

11.6 The amount of costs to be paid by one person to another can be determined on the standard basis or the indemnity basis. The basis to be used is determined when the court decides that a person should pay the costs of another. The usual basis is the standard basis and this is the basis that will apply if the order does not specify the basis of assessment. Costs that are unreasonably incurred or are unreasonable in amount are not allowed on either basis.

11.7 On the standard basis the court only allows costs which are proportionate to the matters in issue. If it has any doubt as to whether the costs were reasonably incurred or reasonable and proportionate in amount, it resolves the doubt in favour of the paying party. The concept of proportionality will always require the court to consider whether the costs which have been incurred were warranted having regard to the issues involved. A successful party who incurs costs which are disproportionate to the issues involved and upon which he or she has succeeded will only recover an amount of costs which the court considers to have been proportionate to those issues.

11.8 On the indemnity basis the court resolves any doubt it may have as to whether the costs were reasonably incurred or were reasonable in amount in favour of the receiving party.

11.9 The court must take into account all the circumstances, including the parties' conduct and the other matters mentioned in rule 44.5. Indemnity costs are not confined to cases of improper or reprehensible conduct. They may be awarded where something takes the case out of the norm. They will not, however, usually be awarded unless there has been conduct by the paying party which the court regards as unreasonable or unless the case falls within rule 48.4 (see paragraph 11.13 below).

11.10 A party must normally pay costs which are awarded against him or her and summarily assessed within 14 days of the assessment. But the court can extend that time (rules 44.8, 3.1(2)(a)). The court may therefore direct payment by instalments, or defer the liability to pay costs until the end of the proceedings so that the costs can then be set against any costs or judgment to which the paying party then becomes entitled.

11.11 If the parties have agreed the amount of costs, they do not need to file a statement of the costs, and summary assessment is unnecessary. If the parties to an application are able to agree an order by consent without the parties attending they should also agree a figure for costs to be inserted in the order or agree that there should be no order as to costs. If the costs position cannot be agreed then the parties will have to attend on the appointment but unless good reason can be shown for the failure of the parties to deal with costs as set out above no costs will be allowed for that attendance. The court finds it most unsatisfactory if parties agree the terms of a consent order but not the provision for costs. Depending on the facts and circumstances, the court may not be able to decide on the question of costs without hearing the application fully, but it is not likely to be consistent with the overriding objective to allow the necessary amount of court time to the dispute on costs in such a case. The court may then have to decide the costs issue on a broad brush approach, making an order against one party or the other only if it is clear, without spending too much time on it, that such an order would be appropriate, and otherwise making no order as to the costs.

### Funding arrangements

**1A–110** 11.12 Funding arrangements are defined in CPR 43.2. If a claimant has entered into a funding arrangement before starting proceedings he must file notice of the

*Paragraph numbers marked with a "+" can be found online and on CD.*

arrangement when he issues the claim form or, if the court is to serve the claim form, file sufficient copies of the notice for service by the court. A claimant who enters into a funding arrangement on or after starting the proceedings must file and serve notice within seven days of entering the funding arrangement.

11.13 The court should be informed, on any application for the payment of costs, if any party has entered into a funding arrangement. The court can then consider whether, in the light of that arrangement, to stay the payment of any costs which have been summarily assessed until the end of the action, or to decline to order the payment of costs on account under rule 44.3(8).

### Other provisions

11.14 Parts 45 to 48, and the Costs PD, contain provisions regarding: **1A–111**

(1) special cases in which costs are payable;
(2) wasted costs;
(3) fixed costs (these are payable for instance if judgment for a sum of money is given in default); and
(d) detailed assessment.

In the context of Chancery litigation attention is drawn to rule 48.2 (Costs orders in favour of or against non-parties); rule 48.3 (Amount of costs where costs are payable pursuant to a contract) (see further Costs PD paragraph 50 and see also Chapter 21—Mortgage Claims); and rule 48.4 and Costs PD paragraph 50A (Limitations on court's power to award costs in favour of trustee or personal representative). Reference may also be made to Chapter 26 as regards costs orders in trust litigation.

## CHAPTER 12

## CHANCERY BUSINESS OUTSIDE LONDON

### General

12.1 Many Chancery cases are heard outside London. There are ten Chancery District Registries: Birmingham, Bristol, Caernarfon, Cardiff, Leeds, Liverpool, Manchester, Mold, Newcastle-upon-Tyne, and Preston. Chancery judges with jurisdiction to hear High Court cases sit regularly at these centres. **1A–112**

12.2 Outside London, county courts have exclusive jurisdiction in bankruptcy, and proceedings in bankruptcy must therefore be brought in the relevant county court which has bankruptcy jurisdiction rather than in the District Registries.

### Judges

12.3 Two Chancery judges supervise the arrangements for the hearing of Chancery cases out of London. Mr Justice Kitchin is the Chancery Supervising Judge for the Western, Wales, and Midland Circuits. Mr Justice David Richards, as Vice-Chancellor of the County Palatine of Lancaster, is the Chancery Supervising Judge for the Northern Circuit (which now includes Chester) and the North Eastern Circuit. Both these judges regularly take substantial Chancery matters for hearing outside London. Mr Justice Kitchin sits regularly in Birmingham, Bristol and Cardiff, but if appropriate will sit elsewhere on the relevant circuits. Mr Justice David Richards sits regularly in Manchester, Liverpool, Leeds and Newcastle, and may sit in Preston or in other court centres on either circuit (e.g. Carlisle or Sheffield) if business so requires. **1A–113**

12.4 There are also Specialist Circuit judges who have the authority to exercise the powers of a judge of the Chancery Division (under section 9 of the Senior Courts Act 1981, therefore known as section 9 judges) and who normally sit out of London. They exercise a general Chancery jurisdiction, subject to exceptions. Those exceptions are proceedings directly concerning revenue, and proceedings before the Patents Court constituted as part of the Chancery Division under section 96 of the Patents Act 1977.

*Paragraph numbers marked with a "+" can be found online and on CD.*

12.5 Currently the Circuit judges who sit regularly in Chancery matters out of London are:

Judge McCahill QC (Bristol)
Judge Purle QC (Birmingham)
Judge David Cooke (Birmingham)
Judge Jarman QC (Cardiff)
Judge Pelling QC (Manchester, Liverpool and Preston)
Judge Behrens (Leeds and Newcastle)
Judge Kaye QC (Leeds and Newcastle)
Judge Hodge QC (Manchester, Liverpool and Preston)

Judges Hegarty QC and Waksman QC (who are the local Mercantile judges based in Manchester and Liverpool) and Judges Raynor QC and Stephen Davies also assist in the disposal of Chancery business on the Northern Circuit. So also, on the North-Eastern Circuit, does Judge Langan QC who is the Mercantile judge for Leeds and Newcastle. The Chancery, Mercantile and TCC judges assist each other in Birmingham, Bristol and Cardiff as well. Judge Havelock-Allan QC, the Mercantile Judge in Bristol, is also authorised to sit as a Chancery Judge. All the judges who sit at the Cardiff Civil Justice Centre (Judges Masterman, Chambers QC and Seys-Llewellyn QC) are authorised to sit as Chancery judges.

12.6 In addition certain other Circuit judges and some Recorders or Queen's Counsel are authorised to take Chancery cases on the same basis.

### Trials

**1A–114** 12.7 If a Chancery case is proceeding in any District Registry other than a Chancery District Registry, the case should normally be transferred to the appropriate Chancery District Registry upon the first occasion the case comes before the court. Guidelines about transfer of cases are contained in Appendix 13.

12.8 The venue of a Chancery trial out of London will normally be one of the centres mentioned above. However in appropriate circumstances (e.g. because of the number or age of local witnesses, the need for a site visit, or travel problems) arrangements can be made for a Chancery judge to sit elsewhere. On the Northern circuit (which now includes Chester) there is a presumption that Chancery cases issued in the Liverpool District Registry will be tried in Liverpool. All other Chancery cases on the Northern Circuit will be heard in Manchester, although, exceptionally, and for good reason, Chancery cases may be listed for trial in Chester or Preston. In Wales Chancery cases are normally heard in Cardiff or Swansea, although arrangements can be made for trials at other venues.

12.9 In cases of great difficulty or importance the trial may be by a High Court judge. Arrangements can also be made in exceptional circumstances for a High Court judge to deal with any of the matters excepted from the jurisdiction of an authorised Circuit judge. Such a judge may be one of the Chancery judges other than Kitchin or David Richards JJ.

12.10 Where it is desired that a case be heard by a specialist Chancery judge outside one of the normal Chancery Centres, or be taken by a High Court judge, inquiries should normally be made in the first instance to the Listing Officer for the nearest Chancery District Registry on the relevant circuit. If the need arises, inquiries can also be made to the clerk to Mr Justice Kitchin or the clerk to Mr Justice David Richards, as the case may be. If no relevant clerk is available, inquiries should be made to the Chancery Listing Officer at the Royal Courts of Justice in London. The clerks' contact numbers are in Appendix 1.

### Applications

**1A–115** 12.11 Subject to the following paragraphs any application should normally be made to a District Judge (unless it relates to a matter which a District Judge does not have power to hear).

12.12 A District Judge may of his or her own initiative (for instance because of the complexity of the matter or the need for specialist attention) direct that an application be referred to a High Court judge or an authorised Circuit Judge.

12.13 If all or any of the parties consider that the matter should be dealt with by a judge (High Court or Circuit), the parties or any of them may arrange that the matter be listed on one of the ordinary application days (see paragraph 12.14 below). The District Judges, who will consult where necessary with one of the Chancery judges (High Court or Circuit), are usually available by post or telephone to give guidance on procedural matters, for example the court before which the matter should come or whether the matter may be dealt with in writing.



**Application Days before a judge**

12.14 Applications days are listed regularly before a judge, when applications and short appeals, including all interim matters are heard. Normally all matters will be called into court at the commencement of the day in order to work out a running order unless a specific time for the application has been given. Matters will be heard without the court going into private session unless good reason is shown. Rights of audience are unaffected. **1A–116**

12.15 Applications days are: Monday and Friday in Birmingham, Friday in Bristol and Friday in Cardiff. Short urgent applications in Birmingham can be accommodated at other times. On the Northern circuit application days are on Friday of each week in Manchester, although there are special arrangements for appropriate Liverpool applications to be listed before the Specialist Chancery District Judges in Liverpool. In Leeds and Newcastle Chancery and Mercantile application days are combined. In Leeds applications are heard most Fridays. In Newcastle there is at least one application day each month, on a Friday. An application which needs to be heard urgently may be made, by telephone or in person, on a day other than the regular applications day: the Listing Officer for the relevant centre should be approached as soon as possible when the need for an urgent hearing arises.

**Applications out of hours and telephone applications**

12.16 These are governed by the general rules, save that in the case of applications out of hours, the party applying should contact the relevant court office. The main relevant contact numbers are set out in Appendix 1. In case of difficulty, contact the Royal Courts of Justice, on the number given in Appendix 1. **1A–117**

**Agreed interim orders**

12.17 Normally a hearing will not be necessary. The procedure is as in the general rules. **1A–118**

12.18 A judge is unlikely to agree to more than two consent adjournments of an interim application. Applications to vacate a trial date will require substantial justification and a hearing, normally before the trial judge.

**Local Listing Arrangements**

12.19 Listing arrangements may vary at different centres, depending on availability of judges and courtrooms. The current details are described below. **1A–119**

**Birmingham: Listing**

12.20 There is a flexible arrangement whereby any of the specialist judges may direct that a particular case in their own list (normally not one involving complex specialist issues of law) is suitable for trial before any specialist judge, whatever his or her primary field. Parties may be asked for their views on this at a CMC, and are free to volunteer such views at any time. This may result in an earlier hearing date. An alternative in the Chancery list (normally only for cases of 3 days or less) is that with **1A–120** the agreement of the parties, the court may allocate a case both a first fixture and an earlier date on which it is listed as second fixture, to be called on if the case first fixed for that date settles. In such cases the court will give as much notice as possible, normally not less than seven days, if the second fixture is to be called on, and expects the parties to be prepared for trial

**Bristol: Listing**

**1A–121** 12.21 All cases are allocated a fixed starting date. No reserve list is operated. However, every case listed for trial will have a pre-trial review at least 6 weeks before the trial date. This review often identifies cases likely to settle. Parties in other cases which are ready for trial in the same period are then contacted and given the opportunity to take up any time made available by the settlement. Any discussions concerning listing should be with the Chancery Listing clerk in Bristol

**Cardiff: Reserve Listing**

**1A–122** 12.22 Judge Jarman QC sits both as a Chancery judge and a judge of the Technology and Construction Court. His list contains both categories of case. All cases are allocated a fixed starting date but some are first and some reserve fixtures. Other judges are called upon in the event of both first and reserve fixtures being effective. Any discussions concerning listing should be with the Chancery Listing clerk in Cardiff.

**Manchester, Liverpool and Preston**

**1A–123** 12.23 The Shared List

When sitting at the same court centre, Judge Hodge QC and Judge Pelling QC will assist each other in the disposal of their respective daily lists. If necessary and if they are available at the relevant court centre, Judge Hegarty QC and Judge Waksman QC (who are the local Mercantile judges), and other circuit judges will assist in the disposal of business. Listing for all Chancery matters in Manchester, Liverpool and Preston is dealt with from Manchester.

Second Fixtures

Given the very high settlement rate, most cases will be given a second fixture date as well as a first fixture date. Parties to second fixtures are notified in advance of the hearing date if the case will not be reached on that date. The amount of notice depends on the circumstances of the case. In some cases it may not be until the previous working day but it is usually further ahead, and longer may be guaranteed in the case of particular difficulties.

**Leeds and Newcastle**

**1A–124** 12.24 When sitting at the same time in Leeds or Newcastle Judge Behrens, Judge Langan QC and Judge Kaye QC will assist each other in the disposal of their respective daily lists. The Chancery and Mercantile Court lists are run on a shared basis in both Leeds and Newcastle. Second fixtures are used in the same way as on the Northern Circuit, and on the same basis.

## CHAPTER 13

## COUNTY COURTS

### *Key Rules: CPR Part 30; PD 7, paragraph 2*

**Unified procedure**

**1A–125** 13.1 A key feature of the civil justice reforms is the introduction of a unified procedure for the High Court and for county courts. The procedure to be followed in both courts is therefore the same.

***Paragraph numbers marked with a "+" can be found online and on CD.***

**Chancery cases brought in the county court**

13.2 Any county court has jurisdiction to hear a Chancery case, subject to three principal exceptions: (1) a probate claim in a county court must be brought in a county court where there is a Chancery District Registry: CPR part 57.2(3); (2) an intellectual property claim must be brought in any such county court or in the Patents County Court: CPR Part 63.13 and PD 63 paragraph 16. Claims relating to patents, registered designs, semiconductor topography rights and plant varieties may only be brought in the Patents County Court; (3) insolvency proceedings may only be brought in a county court which has insolvency jurisdiction. **1A–126**

13.3 If a case of a Chancery nature is brought in any county court, the claim form should be marked "Chancery business" in the top left hand corner: CPR Part 7, PD 2.5.

13.4 If a Chancery case is brought in a county court which does not coincide with a Chancery District Registry, consideration ought to be given at an early stage to whether it needs to have specialist case management or a specialist trial judge, because of the nature of the issues. If it needs either, then it may be necessary to transfer the case to a county court at a Chancery District Registry. If there are good reasons against such a transfer, for example because of the distance involved and the convenience of parties or witnesses, then it may be possible, with enough notice, to arrange that the trial is heard by a recorder with Chancery experience or even by a Chancery circuit judge. Guidance has been given to District Judges by the Chancery supervising judges as to the circumstances and types of case in respect of which either a transfer or a special arrangement for trial by a judge or recorder with specialist experience may be appropriate. These guidelines are reprinted in Appendix 13.

**Transfer to a county court**

13.5 Any Chancery case which does not require to be heard by a High Court judge, and falls within the jurisdiction of the county courts, may be transferred to a county court. Parties should expect that either the Master or the judge will consider whether a claim started in the High Court should be transferred to a county court. The High Court has power to transfer a case to a county court even where that court would not otherwise have had jurisdiction. The criteria for transfer are set out in CPR rule 30.3 (2). The Master will in particular consider whether proceedings seeking an order for sale of property outside Greater London should be transferred to the local county court. Where a case has been so transferred, the papers must be marked "Chancery Business" so as to ensure, so far as possible, suitable listing. **1A–127**

13.6 If the case is one of a specifically Chancery nature a transfer from the High Court will ordinarily be to the Central London County Court (Chancery List) ("the CLCC") where cases are heard by specialist Chancery Circuit judges or recorders and a continuous Chancery List is maintained, unless the parties prefer a transfer to a local county court which coincides with a Chancery District Registry.

13.7 If a claim is transferred to a county court at the allocation stage no other directions will usually be given and all case management will be left to the county court.

13.8 The Chancery List at the CLCC is managed by the Business Chancery and Patents Section at 26 Park Crescent, London W1 4HT. The telephone number of the section manager is set out in Appendix 1. A guide to the Chancery List may be obtained from the section manager.

13.9 As an alternative to starting the case in the Chancery Division and transferring to the CLCC a case (if appropriate to be started there) may be started at the CLCC and a request made there for it to be transferred to the Chancery List. The request will receive judicial consideration and a transfer will be made if appropriate.

13.10 It should be noted that only in very limited circumstances may freezing orders or search orders be granted in the county court. If necessary, an application may be made in the High Court in aid of the county court proceedings if such an order is to be sought in a case where it cannot be granted in the county court.

13.11 Practitioners should continue to take care that Chancery cases requiring chancery expertise are dealt with in a county court with a Chancery District Registry.

**Patents County Court**

1A-128 13.12 See Chapter 23 below.

## CHAPTER 14

## USE OF INFORMATION TECHNOLOGY

***Key Rules: CPR rule 1.4, PD 5B; Part 6; PD 6, PD 32, Annex 3***

**General**

1A-129 14.1 The CPR contain certain provisions about the use of information technology in the conduct of cases. PD 5B sets out the circumstances in which documents may be filed by e-mail. The PD on the Electronic Working Pilot Scheme does not yet apply to the Chancery Division but is expected to be extended to the Division in due course., Apart from these provisions, no standard practice has evolved or been prescribed for the use of information technology in civil cases, but it is possible to identify certain areas in which electronic techniques may be used which should encourage the efficient and economical conduct of litigation.

14.2 It must be remembered, however, that it is unlikely that the number of litigants in person will diminish, and the number may well increase, in the future and that not all solicitors have available sophisticated IT facilities. Use of IT (otherwise than in cases where the rules or Practice Directions permit it) is acceptable only if no party to the case will be unfairly prejudiced and its use will save time or money.

14.3 A number of specific applications of information technology have been well developed in recent years. The use of fax, the provision of skeleton arguments by e-mail or on digital storage devices, and daily transcripts on digital storage devices (with or without appropriate software) have become commonplace. Short applications may be economically heard by a conference telephone call, provided that the parties ensure that the judge or Master has the relevant documents and a draft order. Taking evidence by video link has become more common, and the available technology has improved considerably. There is still little experience of the intensive use of information technology in the ordinary course of the trial by, for example, providing documents as images to be displayed.

14.4 In any case in which it is proposed to use information technology in the preparation, management and presentation of a case in a manner which is not provided for by the CPR, it may be necessary for directions to be given by the judge who is to hear the case. It is unlikely to be satisfactory for parties and their solicitors to agree to a particular application of information technology (for example, using imaging techniques to deal either with disclosure or with the preparation of documents for use in court, in effect by way of electronic bundles) without the agreement of the judge. Accordingly it is likely, particularly in heavy cases, that it will be desirable for a judge to be nominated to conduct the case. Where a nomination is desired, application should be made to the Chancellor in writing by letter addressed to his clerk for a judge to be nominated.

14.5 In every case in which it is proposed to use information technology, the first step will be for the solicitors for all parties to determine whether it is possible to establish a common protocol for the electronic exchange and management of information. It is recommended that the protocol provided by the Technology and Construction Solicitors' Association ("TeCSA") be used. The TeCSA protocol has enjoyed success and is available from TeCSA's website at *http://www.tecsa.org.uk/ it_protocol-1345.htm.*

The CPR's underlying policy of co-operation and collaboration is particularly important in this context. In a large case the parties must facilitate the task of the judge by providing any additional help and IT know-how, including, for example, demonstrations, which he or she requires in order to control the case properly.

14.6 The judges of the Chancery Division and their clerks are equipped with IBM compatible computers running Windows (usually XP but in some cases another version) and Microsoft Office 2003 (including Word 2003). To avoid compatibility problems it is preferable that text files to be provided for use by a judge or clerk be provided either in a format compatible with Word 2003 or in .pdf text readable form or in Rich Text Format (RTF). Although the judges' computers can read the newer DocX format, it is inconvenient to have documents submitted in that format and documents should be submitted in .doc format (or equivalent for the other Office programmes).

**Provision of information on digital storage devices: Skeleton arguments etc**

14.7 Skeleton arguments, chronologies, witness statements, experts' reports and other documents (if available in digital form) should be provided on digital storage devices (or by e-mail) if the judge requests it. Enquiry should be made of the judge's clerk for this purpose. Where the complexity of the case justifies it, attention must be given to providing the judge with versions of the documents containing links to enable cross-references to be followed up in a convenient manner. Digital storage devices provided to judges must be checked for virus contamination and be clean. **1A–130**

**E-mail communications with the Chancery Division**

14.8 A protocol for e-mail communications with the Chancery Division sets out how parties may communicate by e-mail on certain matters, and can be found at *www.hmcourts-service.gov.uk*. The protocol applies PD 5B on electronic communication and filing of documents in respect of specified documents: skeleton arguments, chronologies, reading lists, lists of issues, lists of authorities (but not the authorities themselves) and lists of *dramatis personae* sent in advance of a hearing. The protocol sets out the relevant e-mail addresses, which are also to be found in Appendix 1. The clerk to the judge concerned should be contacted to find out whether the judge will accept other documents by e-mail and whether documents should be sent by e-mail direct to the judge's clerk's e-mail address. **1A–131**

**Transcripts**

14.9 The various shorthand writers provide a number of different transcript services. These range from an immediately displayed transcript which follows the evidence as it is given (usually with about 10 seconds delay) to provision of transcripts of a day's proceedings one or two days in arrears. The use of transcripts is always of assistance if they can be justified on the ground of cost and in long cases they are a considerable advantage. If an instantaneous service is proposed, inquiries should be made of the judge's clerk, and sufficient time for the installation of the equipment necessary and for any familiarisation on the part of the judge with the system should be found. If special transcript-handling software is to be used by the parties, consideration should be given to making the software available to the judge. **1A–132**

14.10 If the shorthand writers make transcripts available in digital form (and nearly all do) the judge should be provided with digitally stored transcripts as they appear if he or she requires them.

**Fax communications**

14.11 The use of fax in the service of documents is now authorised by rule 5.5 (1)(a) and 5PD paragraph 5. It should be noted in particular that were a party files a document by fax he must not send a hard copy in addition; and that faxes should not be used to send letters or documents of a routine or non-urgent nature. **1A–133**

14.12 Each of the judges sitting in the Chancery Division may be reached by fax if the occasion warrants it. The respective judges' clerks' telephone and fax numbers

***Paragraph numbers marked with a "+" can be found online and on CD.***

are set out in Appendix 1. Where the name of the judge is not known, short documents may be sent to the Chancery Judges' Listing Office, whose fax number is also given in Appendix 1. Written evidence should not be sent by fax to this number. All fax messages should have a cover sheet setting out the name of the case, the case number and the judge's name, if known.

**Telephone hearings**

**1A–134** 14.13 Applications may be heard by telephone, if the court so orders, but normally only if all parties entitled to be given notice agree, and none of them intends to be present in person. Special provisions apply where the applicant or another party is in person: see paragraph 6.3 of PD 23 and paragraph 4.5 of PD 25 Interim Injunctions. Guidance on other aspects of telephone hearings, and in particular how to set them up, is contained in paragraph 6.9 of PD 23. When putting that guidance into practice once an order has been made for a hearing to take place by a telephone conference call, the following points may be useful:

(1) A telephone hearing may be set up by calling the BT Legal Call Centre on 0800 028 4194. The caller's name and EB account number will have to be given. Other telecommunications providers may also be able to offer the same facility.
(2) The names and telephone numbers of the participants in the hearing including the judge must be provided.
(3) The co-ordinator should be told the date, time and likely approximate duration of the hearing.
(4) The name and address of the court and the court case reference should be given, for delivery of the tape of the hearing.
(5) Then tell the court that the hearing has been arranged.

It is necessary to ensure that all participants in the hearing have all documents that it may be necessary for any of them to refer to by the time the hearing begins. In all but the simplest applications a paginated bundle will normally be required.

**Video-conferencing**

**1A–135** 14.14 The court may allow evidence to be taken using video-conferencing facilities: rule 32.3. Experience has shown that normally taking evidence by this means is comparatively straightforward, but its suitability may depend on the particular witness, and the case, and on such matters as the volume and nature of documents which need to be referred to in the course of the evidence.

14.15 A video-link may also be used for an application, or otherwise in the course of any hearing.

14.16 Annex 3 to PD 32 (Video Conferencing Guidance) provides further detail on the manner in which video-conferencing facilities are to be used in civil proceedings.

14.17 Video-conferencing facilities are available at the Royal Courts of Justice in Court 38. It is convenient that these facilities should be used if at all possible in relation to proceedings which are under way in the Royal Courts of Justice. Attention is drawn to the following matters:

(1) Permission to use video conferencing during a hearing should be obtained as early as possible in the proceedings. If all parties are agreed that the use of video conferencing is appropriate, then a hearing may not be necessary to obtain such permission.
(2) Before an order fixing the appointment for the use of the facilities at the Royal Courts of Justice is obtained their availability must be ascertained from the video managers (Roger Little/Norman Muller, tel. 020 7947 7609, fax 020 7947 6357). When the order is made the video managers must be informed immediately so as to ensure that all necessary arrangements can be made well in advance of the hearing.
(3) If it is necessary for other facilities to be used, whether because the Royal

Courts of Justice facilities are unavailable or for any other reason, consideration should be given to using the facilities available at the Bar Council or the Law Society. The party seeking to use the facilities will be responsible for making all the necessary arrangements.

(4) If the use of facilities other than those at the Royal Courts of Justice, the Bar Council or the Law Society is proposed, the court's approval must first be obtained to the use of the particular facilities even if the parties are agreed.

# CHAPTER 15

## MISCELLANEOUS MATTERS

***Key Rules: CPR Part 39; PD—Miscellaneous Provisions relating to Hearings supplementing CPR Part 39***

### Litigants in person

15.1 The provisions of this Guide in general apply to litigants in person. Thus, for example, litigants in person should: **1A–136**

(1) prepare a written summary of their argument in the same circumstances as those in which a represented party is required to produce a skeleton argument;

(2) prepare a bundle of documents in the same way that a represented party is required to produce a bundle of documents;

(3) be prepared to put forward their argument within a limited time if they are directed to do so by the court; and

(4) if making an application in the absence of the respondent, comply with the duty of full and frank disclosure (see para 5.22).

15.2 This means that litigants in person should identify in advance of the hearing those points which they consider to be their strongest points, and that they should put those points at the forefront of their oral and written submissions to the court.

15.3 It is not the function of court officials to give legal advice. However, subject to that, they will do their best to assist any litigant. Litigants in person who need further assistance should contact the Community Legal Service (CLS) through their Information Points. The CLS is developing local networks of people giving legal assistance such as law centres, local solicitors or the Citizens' Advice Bureaux. CLS Information Points are being set up in libraries and other public places. Litigants can telephone the CLS to find their nearest CLS Information Point on 0845 608 1122 or can log on to the CLS website at *www.justask.org.uk* for the CLS directory and for legal information.

15.4 The Royal Courts of Justice Advice Bureau off the Main Hall at the Royal Courts of Justice is open from Monday to Friday from 10am to 1pm and from 2pm to 5pm. The Bureau is run by lawyers in conjunction with the Citizens' Advice Bureau and is independent of the court. The Bureau operates on a "first come first served" basis, or telephone advice is available on 0845 120 3715 (or 020 7947 6880) from Monday to Friday between 11am and 12 noon and between 3 and 4pm. The Bureau also operates a Bankruptcy Court Advice Desk on Monday and Wednesday mornings (10am—1pm) in the Consultation Room, 1st Floor, Thomas More Building. In appropriate cases the Bureau may be able to refer a case to the Bar Pro Bono Unit (*www.barprobono.org.uk*) which also administers the Personal Insolvency Litigation Advice and Representation Scheme ('PILARS').

15.5 Where a litigant in person is the applicant, the court may ask one of the represented parties to open the matter briefly and impartially, and to summarise the issues.

15.6 It is the duty of an advocate to ensure that the court is informed of all relevant decisions and enactments of which the advocate is aware (whether favourable or not to his or her case) and to draw the court's attention to any material irregularity.

15.7 Representatives for other parties must treat litigants in person with consideration. Before the case starts they should where possible be given photocopies of any authorities which are to be cited in addition to the skeleton argument. They should be asked to give their names to the usher if they have not already done so. Representatives for other parties should explain the court's order after the hearing if the litigant in person does not appear to understand it.

15.8 If a litigant in person wishes to give oral evidence he or she will generally be required to do so from the witness box in the same manner as any other witness of fact.

15.9 A litigant in person must give an address for service in England or Wales. If he or she is a claimant, the address will be in the claim form or other document by which the proceedings are brought. If he or she is a defendant, it will be in the acknowledgment of service form which he or she must send to the court on being served with the proceedings. It is essential that any change of address should be notified in writing to Chancery Chambers and to all other parties to the case.

15.10 Notice of hearing dates will be given by post to litigants at the address shown in the court file. A litigant in person will generally be given a fixed date for trial on application. A litigant in person who wishes to apply for a fixed date should ask the Chancery Judges' Listing Office for a copy of its Guidance Notes for Litigants in Person.

### Assistance to litigants in person

**1A–137** 15.11 A litigant who is acting in person may be assisted at a hearing by another person, often referred to as a McKenzie friend (see *McKenzie v. McKenzie* [1971] P 33). The litigant must be present at the hearing. If the hearing is in private, it is a matter of discretion for the court whether such an assistant is allowed to attend the hearing. That may depend, among other things, on the nature of the proceedings.

15.12 The McKenzie friend is allowed to help by taking notes, quietly prompting the litigant and offering advice and suggestions to the litigant. The court can, and sometimes does, permit the McKenzie friend to address the court on behalf of the litigant, by making an order to that effect under section 27(2)(c) of the Courts and Legal Services Act 1990 (to be replaced by Sched 3 para 2 of the Legal Services Act 2007). Although applications are considered on a case by case basis, the Chancery Division will usually follow the practice of the Family Division summarised in *Practice Note (Family Courts: Mackenzie Friends) (No 2)* [2008] 1 W.L.R. 2757 (*www.hmcourts-service.gov.uk/cms/files/mckenzie_friends_note.pdf*). Different considerations may apply where the person seeking the right of audience is acting for remuneration and any applicant should be prepared to disclose whether he or she is acting for remuneration and if so how the remuneration is calculated.

15.13 The Personal Support Unit (Room M104) offers personal support for litigants in person, witnesses and others. The PSU will sometimes be able to accompany litigants into court to provide emotional support and give other guidance, but it does not give legal advice.

### Representation on behalf of companies

**1A–138** 15.14 Rule 39.6 allows a company or other corporation to be represented at trial by an employee if the employee has been authorised by the company or corporation to appear on its behalf and the court gives permission. Paragraph 5 of PD 39 describes what is needed to obtain permission from the court for this purpose and mentions some of the considerations relevant to the grant or refusal of permission.

### Robed and unrobed hearings

**1A–139** 15.15 Judges wear robes for all hearings. Robes are not worn at hearings before Masters unless the Cause List is marked otherwise. Robes are worn at the following hearings before Bankruptcy and Companies Court Registrars: public examinations of bankrupts and of directors or other officers of companies; applications for discharge from bankruptcy or for suspension of such discharge; all proceedings under the Company Directors Disqualification Act 1986; petitions to wind up companies; final hearings of petitions for the reduction of capital of companies. District judges wear robes for trials and winding up petitions. Barristers wear robes for all trials and appeals and in any case where the liberty of the subject is at stake. Current guidance for barristers may be found on the Bar Council's website at *www.barcouncil.org.uk*.

#### Solicitors' rights of audience

15.16 At hearings in chambers before 26 April 1999 solicitors had general rights of audience. The fact that a matter which would then have been heard in chambers is now heard in public under Part 39 does not affect rights of audience, so in such matters as would have been heard in chambers previously, the general right of audience for solicitors continues to apply. Such cases included appeals from Masters, applications for summary judgment, and those concerned with pleadings, security for costs and the like, pre-trial reviews, and applications concerned with the administration of a deceased person's estate, a trust or a charity. They did not include applications in what is now the Interim Applications List or the Companies Court, nor appeals from county courts or insolvency appeals. Solicitors do, however, have general rights of audience in personal insolvency matters; this is not affected by whether the hearing is in public or private. **1A–140**

15.17 If a solicitor who does not have the appropriate special right of audience wishes to be heard in a case which is not one which, before 26 April 1999, would have been heard in chambers nor a personal insolvency case, an application may be made for the grant of a special right of audience before the particular court and for the particular proceedings under the Courts and Legal Services Act 1990, section 27(2)(c) (to be replaced by Schedule 3 paragraph 2 of the Legal Services Act 2007).

#### Recording at hearings

15.18 In the Royal Courts of Justice it is normal to record all oral evidence and any judgment delivered during a hearing before a judge. If any party wishes a recording to be made of any other part of the proceedings, this should be mentioned in advance or at the time of the hearing. **1A–141**

15.19 At hearings before Masters, it is not normally practicable to record anything other than any oral evidence and the judgment, but these will be recorded.

15.20 No party or member of the public may use recording equipment without the court's permission.

## CHAPTER 16

## SUGGESTIONS FOR IMPROVEMENT AND COURT USERS' COMMITTEES

16.1 Suggestions for improvements in this Guide or in the practice or procedure of the Chancery Division are welcome. Unless they fall within the remit of the committees mentioned at paras. 16.3 to 16.7 below, they should be sent to the clerk to the Chancellor. **1A–142**

#### Chancery Division Court Users' Committee

16.2 The Chancery Division Court Users' Committee's function is to review, as may from time to time be required, the practice and procedure of all courts forming part of the Chancery Division, to ensure that they continue to provide a just, economical and expeditious system for the resolution of disputes. The Chancellor is the chairman. Its membership includes judges, a Master, barristers, solicitors and other representatives of court staff and users. Meetings are held three times a year, and more often if necessary. Suggestions for points to be considered by the Committee should be sent to the clerk to the Chancellor. **1A–143**

**Insolvency Court Users' Committee**

**1A–144** 16.3 Proposals for change in insolvency matters fall within the remit of the Insolvency Court Users' Committee unless they relate to the Insolvency Rules 1986. The members of the Insolvency Court Users' Committee include members of the Bar, the Law Society, the Insolvency Service and the Society of Practitioners of Insolvency. Meetings are held three times a year, and more often if necessary. Suggestions for points to be considered by the Committee should be sent to the clerk to the Chancellor.

**Insolvency Rules Committee**

**1A–145** 16.4 The Insolvency Rules Committee must be consulted before any changes to the Insolvency Rules 1986 are made. The Chairman of the Insolvency Rules Committee is Mr Justice David Richards. Proposals for changes in the Rules should be sent to The Insolvency Service, Room 502, PO Box 203, 21 Bloomsbury Street, London WC1B 3QW, with a copy to the clerk to Mr Justice David Richards.

**Intellectual Property Court Users' Committee**

**1A–146** 16.5 This considers the problems and concerns of intellectual property litigation generally. Membership of the committee includes the Patent judges, a representative of each of the Patent Bar Association, the Intellectual Property Lawyers Association, the Chartered Institute of Patent Attorneys, the Institute of Trade Mark Attorneys and the Trade Marks Designs and Patents Federation. It will also include one or more other Chancery judges. The Chairman is Mr Justice Kitchin. Anyone having views concerning the improvement of intellectual property litigation is invited to make his or her views known to the committee, preferably through the relevant professional representative on the committee.

**Pension Litigation Court Users' Committee**

**1A–147** 16.6 This consists of a judge and a Master, two barristers and two solicitors. Its Chairman is Mr Justice Warren. Any suggestions for consideration by the committee should be sent to the clerk to Mr Justice Warren.

**Court Users' Committees outside London**

**1A–148** 16.7 There are several Court Users' Committees relating to Chancery work on circuit. They are as follows:

(1) *The Northern Circuit and the North-Eastern Circuit Court Users Committees*: the Northern Circuit Chancery Court Users' Committee, which meets in Manchester; the Leeds Chancery and Mercantile Court Users' Committee; and the Newcastle Joint Chancery Mercantile and TCC Court Users' Committee. Each of these meets two or three times a year, and has a membership including judges, court staff, barristers and solicitors. The Vice-Chancellor of the County Palatine of Lancaster chairs these three Committees, and the Vice-Chancellor's clerk acts as secretary to each Committee. All communications should be to the clerk.

(2) *The Western Circuit, Wales & Chester and Midland Circuits Court User Committees*: the circuit committees normally meet three or four times per year. They have a membership including judges, court staff, barristers and solicitors.

   (a) *Western Circuit*: Judge McCahill QC chairs the committee in Bristol (or Mr Justice Kitchin when there), Mrs Liz Bodman acts as secretary. All communications should be addressed to her at Chancery Listing Section, Bristol Crown Court, Small Street, Bristol.

   (b) *Wales & Chester Circuit*: Judge Jarman QC chairs the committee in Cardiff (or Mr Justice Kitchin when there), the Diary Manager, Annette Parsons acts as secretary. All communications should be addressed to her at Cardiff Civil Justice Centre, 2 Park Street, Cardiff.

   (c) *Midland Circuit*: Judge Purle QC chairs the committee in Birmingham (or Mr Justice Kitchin when there), the Chancery Listing Officer, acts as secretary. All communications should be addressed to him at Chancery Listing Section, Birmingham Civil Justice Centre, 33 Bull Street, Birmingham.

## CHAPTER 17

## ALTERNATIVE DISPUTE RESOLUTION

***Key Rules: CPR rules 3.1 and 26.4***

17.1 While emphasising the primary role of the court as a forum for deciding cases, the court encourages parties to consider the use of ADR (such as, but not confined to, mediation and conciliation) as a possible means of resolving disputes or particular issues. **1A–149**

17.2 The settlement of disputes by means of ADR can:

(1) significantly help litigants to save costs;
(2) save litigants the delay of litigation in reaching finality in their disputes;
(3) enable litigants to achieve settlement of their disputes while preserving their existing commercial relationships and market reputation;
(4) provide litigants with a wider range of solutions than those offered by litigation; and
(5) make a substantial contribution to the more efficient use of judicial resources.

17.3 The court will in an appropriate case invite the parties to consider whether their dispute, or particular issues in it, could be resolved through ADR. In particular, it is to be expected that the judge or Master at any case management conference will inquire what steps can usefully be taken to resolve the dispute by settlement discussion, alternative dispute resolution or other means. The parties should be in a position to tell the court what steps have been taken or are proposed to be taken. The court may also adjourn the case for a specified period of time to encourage and enable the parties to use ADR and for this purpose extend the time for compliance by the parties or any of them with any requirement under the CPR or this Guide or any order of the court. The court may make such order as to the costs that the parties may incur by reason of the adjournment or their using or attempting to use ADR as may in all the circumstances seem appropriate.

17.4 Legal representatives in all cases should consider with their clients and the other parties concerned the possibility of attempting to resolve the dispute or particular issues by ADR and they should ensure that their clients are fully informed as to the most cost effective means of resolving their dispute.

17.5 Parties who consider that ADR might be an appropriate means of resolving their dispute, or particular issues in the dispute, may apply for directions at any stage.

17.6 The clerk to the Commercial Court keeps some published information as to individuals and bodies that offer ADR services. (The list also includes individuals and bodies that offer arbitration services.) If the parties are unable to agree upon a neutral individual, or panel of individuals, for ADR, they may refer to the judge for assistance, though the court will not recommend any particular body or individual to act as mediator or arbitrator.

# SECTION B SPECIALIST WORK

## CHAPTER 18

## INTRODUCTION TO THE SPECIALIST WORK OF THE CHANCERY DIVISION

18.1 As explained in Chapter 1 of this Guide, some proceedings in the High Court must be brought in the Chancery Division. These matters include: **1A–150**

(1) claims for the sale, exchange or partition of land, or the raising of charges on land;

***Paragraph numbers marked with a "+" can be found online and on CD.***

(2) mortgage claims;
(3) claims relating to the execution of trusts;
(4) claims relating to the administration of the estates of deceased persons;
(5) bankruptcy matters;
(6) claims for the dissolution of partnerships or the taking of partnership or other accounts;
(7) claims for the rectification, setting aside or cancellation of deeds or other instruments in writing;
(8) contentious probate business;
(9) claims relating to patents, trade marks, registered designs, copyright or design right;
(10) claims for the appointment of a guardian of a minor's estate;
(11) jurisdiction under the Companies Act 2006 and the Insolvency Act 1986 relating to companies;
(12) some revenue matters;
(13) claims relating to charities;
(14) some proceedings under the Solicitors Act 1974;
(15) proceedings under the Landlord and Tenant Acts 1927 (Part I), 1954 (Part II) and 1987 and the Leasehold Reform Act 1967;
(16) proceedings (other than those in the Commercial Court) relating to the application of Articles 81 and 82 of the EC Treaty and the equivalent provisions of the Competition Act 1998.
(17) proceedings under other miscellaneous statutory jurisdictions.

18.2 There is concurrent jurisdiction with the Family Division under the Inheritance (Provision for Family and Dependants) Act 1975.

18.3 Certain appeals lie to the Chancery Division under statute. These are dealt with in paragraph 10.19. Intellectual property appeals are covered in Chapters 23.

18.4 The Chancery judges are among the nominated judges of the Court of Protection but this Guide does not deal with the Court of Protection. Chancery judges also sit in the Upper Tier Tribunal and the Competition Appeal Tribunal; but this Guide does not deal with those.

## CHAPTER 19

## THE BANKRUPTCY COURT

### *Key Rules: PD—Insolvency Proceedings; Insolvency Rules 1986*

**1A–151** 19.1 The Bankruptcy Court is part of the Chancery Division and disposes of proceedings relating to insolvent individuals arising under Parts VIII to XI of the Insolvency Act 1986 and related legislation. These include applications for interim orders to support an individual voluntary arrangement, applications to set aside a statutory demand, bankruptcy petitions and various applications concerned with the realisation and distribution of the assets of individuals who have been adjudged bankrupt, as well as proceedings concerning the administration in bankruptcy of the insolvent estate of a deceased person. The procedure in the Bankruptcy Court is governed by the Insolvency Rules and the PD—Insolvency Proceedings. Appeals in bankruptcy matters are covered in Chapter 10.

19.2 Proceedings in the Bankruptcy Court are issued in the Bankruptcy Issue and Search Room and are dealt with by the Registrars in Bankruptcy, not the Masters. Proceedings under Parts VIII to XI of the Insolvency Act 1986 should be entitled "IN BANKRUPTCY". All insolvency proceedings are allocated to the multi-track.

19.3 Certain matters, such as applications for injunctions or for committal for contempt, are heard by a judge. They are listed in *Practice Note on the Hearing of Insolvency Proceedings* 23 May 2005. A judge is available to hear such matters each day in term time and applications may be listed for any such day. The judge will normally also be hearing the interim applications list for the day, but one or more other judges may be available to assist if necessary.

19.4 The Registrar may refer or adjourn proceedings to the judge, having regard to such matters as the complexity of the proceedings, whether the proceedings raise new or controversial points of law, the likely date and length of the hearing, public interest in the proceedings, and the availability of relevant specialist expertise. When proceedings have been referred or adjourned to the judge, interim applications and applications for directions or case management will be listed before a judge, except where liberty to apply to the Registrar has been given.

19.5 There are prescribed forms for use in connection with all types of statutory demand and of petitions for bankruptcy orders. Every other type of application is either an originating application in Form 7.1 (meaning an application to the court which is not an application in pending proceedings before the court) or an ordinary application in Form 7.2 (meaning any other application to the court).

### Statutory demands

19.6 All applications to set aside a statutory demand are referred initially to a Registrar. The application may be dismissed by the court without a hearing if it fails to disclose sufficient grounds (see paragraph 12.4 of PD—Insolvency Proceedings and Insolvency Rules, r. 6.5(4). If it is not dismissed summarily, it will be allocated a hearing date when the Registrar may either dispose of it summarily or give directions for its disposal at a later date. Such directions will commonly include an order for the filing and service of written evidence and a listing certificate of compliance (see paragraph 19.13 below). **1A–152**

### Bankruptcy petitions

19.7 The court will not normally allow more than one bankruptcy petition to be presented against an individual at any one time. **1A–153**

19.8 In cases where the statutory demand relied on has not been personally served on the debtor or where execution of the debt has been returned unsatisfied in whole or in part, the permission of the Registrar is required before a petition may be presented to the court. For service of statutory demands see paragraphs 10–11 and 13 of PD—Insolvency Proceedings.

19.9 On presentation to the court a bankruptcy petition is given a distinctive number. The details of the name and address of the petitioner, of his solicitors and of the debtor are entered on a computerised record which may be searched by attendance at the Issue and Search Room. It will also be endorsed with a hearing date which may be extended on application without notice if the petitioner has been unable to serve the petition on the debtor before the hearing date (see paragraph 14 of PD—Insolvency Proceedings).

19.10 A debtor who intends to oppose the making of a bankruptcy order should file and serve a written notice in the prescribed form stating his grounds for opposing the petition not less than seven days before the hearing date. The court may give such further directions as to the filing of evidence and of listing certificates (see paragraph 19.13 below) as it considers appropriate to the disposal of the petition.

### Other applications

19.11 Many different types of application may be made to the court for the purpose of the administration of the estate and affairs of a bankrupt individual or insolvent person who is subject to an individual voluntary arrangement (IVA). These may involve such matters as the examination of the bankrupt or of persons having knowledge of his affairs, the realisation of assets in his estate and the determination of disputes regarding the validity of a creditor's claim to dividend or entitlement to vote at a creditors' meeting. Such applications will be given a hearing date when the **1A–154**

Registrar will give such directions as are appropriate to the type of case, which may include directions for the filing and service of written evidence, for the cross-examination of witnesses and for the filing of certificates of compliance (see paragraph 19.13 below).

**Orders without attendance**

**1A–155** 19.12 In suitable cases the court will normally be prepared to make orders under Part VIII of the Act (interim orders for IVAs) and consent orders without attendance by the parties. Details of these types of order are set out in paragraph 16 of the PD—Insolvency Proceedings.

**Listing certificates**

**1A–156** 19.13 In order to prevent waste of the court's time each party to insolvency proceedings may be required by the court to file a listing certificate in which he will be required to certify whether the directions previously given by the court have been complied with, whether and by whom he will be represented at the final hearing, his estimate of the time required for such hearing and his and his representative's dates to avoid. On the filing of the certificates in any particular case the court will fix a date for the final hearing of the case and notify the parties.

**Preparation for hearings before the Registrars**

**1A–157** 19.14 Paragraphs 7.40 to 7.52 apply to hearings before the Bankruptcy Registrars. Skeleton arguments and bundles should be delivered to the Bankruptcy Registry.

**General information**

**1A–158** 19.15 Inspection of the court's record and court file in any insolvency proceedings is governed by Insolvency Rules, rr. 7.28 and 7.31.

19.16 The following publications regarding practice and procedure in the Bankruptcy Court are available free from the Bankruptcy Issue and Search Room and from Room TM1.10 Thomas More Building, Royal Courts of Justice:

(1) Current Practice Direction and Practice Notes
(2) Bankruptcy Court Guide
(3) "I want to set aside my statutory demand—what do I do?"
(4) "I have a petition against me—what do I do?"
(5) "I wish to apply for my Certificate of Discharge from Bankruptcy—what do I do?"
(6) Dealing with debt—how to make someone bankrupt
(7) Dealing with debt—how to petition for your own bankruptcy.

## CHAPTER 20

## THE COMPANIES COURT

***Key Rules: PD 49—Applications under the Companies Acts and related legislation; PD—Insolvency; Insolvency Rules 1986; Insolvent Companies (Disqualification of Unfit Directors) Proceedings Rules 1987; PD—Directors Disqualification Proceedings***

**1A–159** 20.1 The Companies Court is a part of the Chancery Division. Applications in the High Court under the Companies Act 2006,, the Financial Services and Markets Act 2002, the Insolvency Act 1986 in relation to companies registered in England and Wales, and the Company Directors Disqualification Act 1986, must be commenced in the Companies Court. Proceedings concerning insolvent partnerships, under the Insolvent Partnerships Order 1994, are also brought in the Companies Court (unlike proceedings against partners separately, which, if the partner is an individual, are brought in bankruptcy). Many other kinds of application are brought in the Companies Court. Appeals in Companies Court matters are dealt with in Chapter 10.

***Paragraph numbers marked with a "+" can be found online and on CD.***

20.2 Applications, other than in insolvency, are governed by the Civil Procedure Rules and PD 49—Applications under the Companies Acts and related legislation.

20.3 Applications in insolvency relating to companies (and to insolvent partnerships) are governed by the Insolvency Rules and PD—Insolvency Proceedings.

20.4 Proceedings under the Company Directors Disqualification Act 1986 are governed by the Insolvent Companies (Disqualification of Unfit Directors) Proceedings Rules 1987 and the PD—Directors Disqualification Proceedings.

20.5 Proceedings in the Companies Court under a particular statute should be entitled accordingly, thus:

"In the matter of [name and registration number of the company] And in the matter of the Companies Act 2006 [and of any other statute as appropriate]"

"In the matter of [name of the relevant company] And in the matter of the Company Directors Disqualification Act 1986"

"In the matter of [name of the debtor] And in the matter of the Insolvency Act 1986 [and of any appropriate order, such as the Insolvent Partnerships Order 1994]"

20.6 The Companies Court has a separate administrative procedure. Proceedings are issued in the Companies Court General Office, and they are dealt with by the Registrars.

20.7 Petitions for winding up, petitions for confirmation by the court of reduction of capital, and interim applications for directions in proceedings by shareholders are among the principal matters heard by the Registrars. A Registrar may direct that any case be heard by a judge even if it is a kind of application which would normally be heard by a Registrar.

20.8 Certain matters such as applications for an administration order under Part II of the Insolvency Act 1986, applications for approval by the court of schemes of arrangement and applications for the appointment of provisional liquidators are heard by a judge. A judge is available to hear companies matters each day in term time, and applications to be heard by that judge may be listed for any such day. Unopposed applications for the approval of schemes of arrangement will sometimes be heard by a judge before the start of normal sittings. Other applications may be dealt with by the Interim Applications Judge as Companies judge. The Registrar may refer or adjourn proceedings to the judge in accordance with the criteria set out in paragraph 19.4 above.

**Preparation for hearings before the Registrars**

20.9 Paragraphs 7.40 to 7.52 apply to hearings before the Registrars of the Companies Court. Skeleton arguments and bundles should be delivered to the Companies Court Issue Section. **1A–160**

**Companies entering Administration**

20.10 The statutory regime for administrations commencing on or after 15 September 2003, with certain exceptions, is found in the Insolvency Act 1986, schedule B1, which should be read with the new Part 2 of the Insolvency Rules 1986. Administrations commenced before 15 September 2003 and administrations of certain bodies (building societies, insolvent partnerships, limited liability partnerships, certain insurers, and public utility companies listed in section 249(1)(a)–(d) of the Enterprise Act 2002) continue to be governed by Part II of the Insolvency Act 1986 (or enacted before the introduction of Schedule B1) and the former Part 2 of the Insolvency Rules 1986. Administration creates a statutory moratorium and allows the affairs, business and property of the company to be managed by an administrator. **1A–161**

*Court Order*

20.11 An application to the court must be commenced by the prescribed form of application (Form 2.1B) and must be supported by an affidavit or witness statement. **1A–162**

***Paragraph numbers marked with a "+" can be found online and on CD.***

The Act and Rules specify the information which must be included in the affidavit. The application may be made by the company, its directors, one or more creditors, the justices' chief executive for a magistrates' court (in relation to a fine) or any combination of the above. The application will be listed before a judge.

20.12 Where a pre-arranged sale of the business is envisaged consideration should be given to the extent of the information to be provided to the court on the making of the application. Attention is drawn in this respect to Statement of Insolvency Practice 16, issued under procedures agreed between the insolvency regulatory authorities acting through the Joint Insolvency Committee (JIC).

*Out of court*

**1A–163** 20.13 The holder of a qualifying floating charge, the company or its directors, may appoint an administrator without going through the court process. The appointment becomes effective when a notice of appointment in the prescribed form accompanied by the administrators' consent to act and a statement by him that in his opinion the purpose of the administration is likely to be achieved has been filed with the court. Rule 2.19 makes special provision for filing notice of appointment by fax out of business hours. (Form 2.7B). The fax number for filing notice in the Royal Courts of Justice is 020 7947 6607.

*Extension of administration order*

**1A–164** 20.14 Where it is necessary to apply to court for an extension of an administration order, the application should be made in good time so that it can be dealt with on paper. Failure to do so may result in any additional costs being disallowed as an expense of the administration.

**Schemes of arrangement**

**1A–165** 20.15 A scheme under Part 26 of the Companies Act 2006 can be proposed whether or not a company is in liquidation. It is necessary to obtain the sanction of the court to a scheme which has been approved by the requisite majority of members or creditors of each class at separately convened meetings directed by the court. If the company is insolvent the objective of the scheme may be more simply and economically achieved by a company voluntary arrangement under Part I of the Act. However, a scheme under Part 26 has the advantage that the court may approve the distribution of assets otherwise than in accordance with creditors' strict legal rights.

20.16 The application for an order to convene meetings of members or creditors under section 896 is made by a CPR Part 8 claim form. The application will usually be heard by a Registrar, unless it is thought that issues of difficulty may arise, in which case it can be heard by a judge. The relevant practice is set out in *Practice Statement (Companies: Schemes of Arrangements)* [2002] 1 WLR 1345.

20.17 The application to sanction a scheme of arrangement, once approved by members or creditors by the statutory majority, is made by the original claim form. The hearing of the application at which the sanction of the court is sought will be before a judge. If the application also seeks confirmation of a reduction of capital, there will first be an application to the Registrar for directions. In other cases the application will go straight to a judge.

**Winding up petitions**

**1A–166** 20.18 Proceedings to wind up a company are commenced by presenting a petition to the court. The presentation of a winding up petition can cause substantial damage to a company. A winding up petition should not be presented when it is known that there is a real dispute about the debt. Practitioners should make reasonable enquiries from their client as to the existence of any such dispute. The court may order a petitioner to pay the company's costs of a petition based on a disputed debt on the indemnity basis.

***Paragraph numbers marked with a "+" can be found online and on CD.***

20.19 When a winding up petition is presented to either the Companies Court, a Chancery District Registry or a county court having jurisdiction, particulars including the name of the company and the petitioner's solicitors are entered in a computerised register. This is called the Central Registry of Winding Up Petitions. It may be searched by personal attendance at the Companies Court General Office, or by telephone on 020 7947 7328.

20.20 The requirement to advertise the petition (Insolvency Rules, r. 4.11(2)(b)) is mandatory, and designed to ensure that the class remedy of winding up by the court is made available to all creditors, and is not used simply as a means of putting pressure on the company to pay the petitioner's debt. Failure to comply with the rule, without good reason accepted by the court, may lead to the summary dismissal of the petition on the return date (Insolvency Rules, r. 4.11(5)). If the court, in its discretion, grants an adjournment, this will be on condition that the petition is advertised in due time for the adjourned hearing. No further adjournment for the purpose of advertisement will normally be granted.

20.21 If an order is made restraining advertisement while an application is made to the court to stop the proceedings, the case is listed in the Daily Cause List by number only so that the name of the company is not given.

**Proceedings for relief from unfairly prejudicial conduct under the Companies Act 2006, section 994**

20.22 Petitions under the Companies Act 2006, section 994, are liable to involve extensive factual enquiry and many of the measures summarised in Section A of this Guide which are designed to avoid unnecessary cost and delay are particularly relevant to them. Procedure is governed by the Companies (Unfair Prejudice Applications) Proceedings Rules 1986 (SI 1986/2000). **1A–167**

20.23 Where applications are brought in the Companies Court and in a related case in the Chancery Division at the same time, special arrangements can be made on request to the Chancery Judges' Listing Officer for the applications to be heard by the same judge.

**Applications for leave to act as director of a company with a prohibited name**

20.24 Section 216 of the Insolvency Act 1986 restricts the use of a company name by any person who was a director or shadow director of the company in the 12 month period ending with the day upon which it went into insolvent liquidation—except with the leave of the court: section 216(3). **1A–168**

20.25 The application for leave is governed by the Insolvency Rules 1986, rr. 4.226 to 4.230. These rules provide for certain exceptions to the prohibition. The application for leave is by originating application supported by written evidence.

20.26 By r. 4.227 the court may call upon the liquidator for a report of the circumstances in which the company became insolvent and the extent of the applicant's apparent responsibility. However if the liquidator consents to the application it is helpful if his views are put before the court at the outset. The Registrar who then hears the application may be prepared to grant it at the first hearing.

20.27 Notice should be given to the Secretary of State and/or the Official Receiver.

**General**

20.28 Inspection of the court's records and the court file in any insolvency proceedings is governed by Insolvency Rules, rr. 7.28 to 7.31. **1A–169**

20.29 The following leaflets are available from the Companies Court Office:

(1) Current Practice Directions and Practice Notes

(2) "I want to wind up a company which owes me money: what do I do?"
(3) Treasury Solicitors'—A Guide to company restoration
(4) "I want to apply to extend time for registration of a charge or to rectify a misstatement or omission (in the registered particulars of a charge or of a memorandum of satisfaction): what do I do?"
(5) Dealing with debt. How to wind up your own company
(6) Dealing with debt. How to wind up a company that owes you money.

## CHAPTER 21

## MORTGAGE CLAIMS

### *Key Rules: CPR Parts 55 and 73 and the PDs supplementing them*

**1A-170** 21.1 Under Part 55 mortgage possession claims commenced since 15 October 2001, whether in respect of residential or commercial property, are generally heard in the county courts. The only exceptions to this are (a) a relatively small number of cases where either the county court has no jurisdiction or where the claimant can certify, verified by a statement of truth, exceptional reasons for bringing the claim in the High Court and (b) any remaining transitional cases, i.e. mortgage possession claims commenced before 15 October 2001, and proceedings to enforce charging orders commenced prior to 25 March 2002, as to which directions should be sought from the assigned Master.

21.2 Attention is drawn to the Pre-Action Protocol for Possession Claims based on Mortgage or Home Purchase Plan Arrears in Respect of Residential Property. Parties should be able, if requested by the court, to explain the actions that they have taken to comply with this protocol. Form N 123 contains a Mortgage Protocol Pre-action Checklist.

21.3 PD 55 emphasises that High Court possession claims are to be regarded as exceptional and that while the value of the property and the size of the claim may well be relevant circumstances they will not, taken alone, normally justify the issue of proceedings in the High Court. High Court proceedings may, however, be justified where there are complicated disputes of fact or where a claim gives rise to points of law of general importance; or where the County Court has no jurisdiction in respect of particular relief sought. Where a mortgage possession claim is issued in the High Court it is assigned to the Chancery Division. The provisions of Part 55 will apply to it.

21.4 The most common instance where, notwithstanding Part 55, the Chancery Division will retain jurisdiction in a mortgage possession case is where proceedings are brought seeking an order for sale under an equitable charge, ordinarily that created by a charging order, but where part of the relief claimed ancillary to the order for sale is an order for possession. Although rule 73.10 now provides that proceedings to enforce charging orders by sale should be made in the court in which the charging order was made, that provision is expressly subject to that court having jurisdiction. Except in cases which have been transferred from the High Court to the county court the jurisdiction of a county court to enforce a charge is confined to those cases where the amount secured by the charge falls within the relevant county court limit (currently £30,000) and it follows that in many cases where judgments have been obtained in county courts and charging orders made enforcement will nonetheless require proceedings in the High Court.

21.5 Such proceedings, as well as proceedings to enforce charging orders made in other divisions of the High Court, are assigned to the Chancery Division. The evidence required in support of such proceedings is that set out in paragraph 4.3 of PD 73.

21.6 The Chancery Division retains its jurisdiction in respect of redemption and foreclosure of mortgages and kindred matters.

21.7 Rule 48.3 and paragraph 50 of the Costs PD (Amount of costs where costs are payable under a contract) are of particular relevance to mortgage claims.

## CHAPTER 22

### PARTNERSHIP CLAIMS AND RECEIVERS

***Key Rules: CPR Part 69, PDs 24 and 40***

**Partnership Claims**

22.1 In claims for or arising out of the dissolution of a partnership often the only matters in dispute between the partners are matters of accounting. In such cases there will be no trial. The court will, if appropriate, make a summary order under paragraph 6 of PD 24 for the taking of an account. This will be taken before the Master. **1A–171**

22.2 Only if there is a dispute as to the existence of a partnership (whether it is claimed that there never was a partnership or that the partnership is still continuing and has not been dissolved) or if there is a material dispute as to the terms of the partnership (e.g. as to the profit sharing ratios) will there be a trial, at which the judge will decide those issues. In such cases there will be a two stage procedure with the judge deciding these issues at the trial and ordering the winding up of the partnership which will involve the taking of the partnership accounts by the Master (see PD 40 Accounts, Inquiries etc.).

22.3 In some cases and in order to reduce costs, it may be appropriate for the parties to invite the Master to determine factual issues as a preliminary to the account, eg issues as to terms of the partnership or assets comprised in it. At any case management conference it will be particularly important to identify the issues to be determined before an effective account or inquiry can be made. The court will not simply order accounts and inquiries without identifying the issues.

22.4 The expense of taking an account in court is usually wholly disproportionate to the amount at stake. Parties are strongly encouraged to refer disputes on accounts to a jointly instructed accountant for determination or mediation.

22.5 The functions of a receiver in a partnership action are limited. Unlike the liquidator of a company it is not his or her duty to wind up the partnership. His or her primary function is to get in the debts and preserve the assets pending winding up by the court and he or she has no power of sale without the permission of the court.

**Receivers**

22.6 The procedure for the appointment of receivers by the court is comprehensively governed by Part 69 and its PD. A new Guide for receivers in the Chancery Division is available. Copies of the Guide can be obtained from an associate or from the Court Manager, Chancery Chambers. The Guide is also reproduced at Appendix 10. Particular attention should be paid to the question of the receiver's remuneration and the fact that it must be authorised on the basis specified in an order of the court. **1A–172**

## CHAPTER 23

### THE PATENTS COURT AND INTELLECTUAL PROPERTY CLAIMS ETC.

***Key Rules: CPR Part 63 and PD 63—Patents, etc***

23.1 The matters assigned to the Patents Court are essentially all those concerned with patents, registered designs, semiconductor topography rights and plant varieties. CPR Part 63 and PD 63 deal with its particular procedures, and other intellectual property claims. Appeals in patent, design and trade mark cases are governed by Part 52 (see CPR 63.16); reference should be made to Chapter 10 for the general procedure as regards such appeals. **1A–173**

23.2 The principal Patent judges are Mr Justice Kitchin, Mr Justice Floyd and Mr Justice Arnold. The other assigned Patents judges currently nominated are:

Mr Justice Lewison
Mr Justice Mann
Mr Justice Warren
Mr Justice Morgan
Mr Justice Norris

Several senior practitioners have also been appointed to sit as Deputy High Court judges to hear Patent Court matters.

23.3 Mr Justice Kitchin is the judge in charge of the Patents List.

23.4 In cases of great urgency, when a nominated judge or Deputy Judge is not available an application can be made to any other judge of the High Court, preferably a judge of the Chancery Division.

23.5 The procedure of the Patents Court is broadly that of the Chancery Division as a whole, but there are important differences.

23.6 The Patents Court has its own Court Guide which is available on the Patents Court website (*www.hmcourts-service.gov.uk/infoabout/patents/index.htm*) and can also be found in Section 2F of Volume 2 of the White Book. That Guide must be consulted for guidance as to the procedure in the Patents Court.

23.7 The Court's diary can be accessed on its website. The Patents Court will endeavour, if the parties so desire and the case is urgent, to sit in September.

### Patents County Court

**1A–174** 23.8 Special provisions relate to the transfer of cases between the Patents Court and the Patents County Court. The Patents Court has no power to order the transfer to it of cases commenced in the Patents County Court which fall within the latter court's special jurisdiction (i.e. matters relating to patents and designs). On the other hand it does have the power to transfer cases commenced in the High Court to the Patents County Court.

### Registered trademarks and other intellectual property rights

**1A–175** 23.9 CPR 63.13 and paragraphs 16 to 24 of PD 63 apply to claims relating to matters arising out of the Trade Marks Act 1994 and other intellectual property rights (such as copyright, passing off, design rights, etc.) as set out in paragraph 16 of PD 63. Claims under the Trade Marks Act 1994 must be brought in the Chancery Division. Among the Chancery Masters trade mark cases are assigned to Master Bragge. Cases not specifically assigned to the Patents Court may be heard by any judge of the Division, and may also be heard in certain Chancery District Registries (see PD 63 paragraphs 16 and 21.1).

23.10 Appeals from decisions of the Registrar of Trade Marks are brought to the Chancery Division as a whole, not the Patents Court. Permission to appeal is not required.

## CHAPTER 24

## PROBATE AND INHERITANCE CLAIMS

***Key Rules: CPR Part 57 and PD 57***

### Probate

**1A–176** 24.1 In general, contentious probate proceedings follow the same pattern as an ordinary claim but there are important differences and Part 57 and PD 57 should be carefully studied. All probate claims are allocated to the multi-track. Particular regard should be had to the following:

***Paragraph numbers marked with a "+" can be found online and on CD.***

(1) The claim form must be issued out of Chancery Chambers or out of the Chancery District Registries, or if the claim is suitable to be heard in the county court, a county court where there is also a Chancery District Registry, or the Central London County Court.

(2) A defendant must file an acknowledgment of service. An additional 14 days is provided for doing so.

(3) Save where the court orders otherwise, the parties must at the outset of proceedings lodge all testamentary documents in their possession and control with the court. At the same time parties must file written evidence describing any testamentary document of the deceased of which they have knowledge, stating, if any such document is not in the party's possession or control, the name and address, if known, of the person in whose possession or under whose control the document is. In the case of a claimant, these materials must be lodged at the time when the claim form is issued. In the case of a defendant, these materials must be lodged when service is acknowledged. If these requirements are not complied with it is likely that the claim will not be issued and, correspondingly, that the acknowledgment of service will not be permitted to be lodged.

(4) The court will generally ensure that all persons with any potential interest in the proceedings are joined as parties or served with notice under Part 19.8A.

(5) A default judgment cannot be obtained in a probate claim. Where, however, no defendant acknowledges service or files a defence, the claimant may apply for an order that the claim proceed to trial and seek a direction that the claim be tried on written evidence.

(6) If an order pronouncing for a will in solemn form is sought under Part 24, the evidence in support must include written evidence proving due execution of the will. In such a case, if a defendant has given notice under rule 57.7(5) that he raises no positive case but requires that the will be proved in solemn form and that, to that end, he wishes to cross examine the attesting witnesses, then the claimant's application for summary judgment is subject to the right of such a defendant to require the attesting witnesses to attend for cross examination.

(7) A defendant who wishes to do more than test the validity of the will by cross examining the attesting witnesses must set up by counterclaim his positive case in order to enable the court to make an appropriate finding or declaration as to which is the valid will, or whether a person died intestate or as the case may be.

(8) The proceedings may not be discontinued without permission. Even if they are compromised, it will usually be necessary to have an order stating to whom the grant is to be made, either under rule 57.11 (leading to a grant in common form), or after a trial on written evidence under paragraph 6.1(1) of PD 57 (leading to a grant in solemn form) or under section 49 of the Administration of Justice Act 1985 and paragraph 6.1(3) of PD 57 (again leading to a grant in solemn form). Practitioners should refer to PF38CH and adapt as appropriate.

24.2 When the court orders trial of a contentious probate claim on written evidence, or where the court is asked to pronounce in solemn form under Part 24, it is normally necessary for an attesting witness to sign a witness statement or swear an affidavit of due execution of any will or codicil sought to be admitted to probate. The will or codicil is at that stage in the court's possession and cannot be handed out of court for use as an exhibit to the witness statement or affidavit, so that the attesting witness has to attend at the Royal Courts of Justice or the District Registry at which the documents are lodged.

24.3 Where an attesting witness is unable to attend the Royal Courts of Justice or the appropriate District Registry in order to sign his or her witness statement or swear his or her affidavit in the presence of an officer of the court, the solicitor concerned may request from Room TM7.09 or the District Registry, a photographic copy of the will or codicil in question. This will be certified as authentic by the court and may be exhibited to the witness statement or affidavit of due execution in lieu of the original. The witness statement or affidavit must in that case state that the exhibited document is an authenticated copy of the document signed in the witness' presence.

24.4 When a probate claim started in the Royal Courts of Justice is transferred to or listed for trial outside London, the solicitor for the party responsible for preparing the court bundle must write to Room TM7.09 and request that the testamentary documents be forwarded to the appropriate District Registry.

24.5 If a disputed will is required for forensic examination an application should be made under Part 23. The court will require to be satisfied that the examiner is suitably qualified and can give undertakings for the safe-keeping and preservation of the will, and that the proposed methods of examination will not damage the will.

### Inheritance (Provision for Family and Dependants) Act 1975

**1A–177** 24.6 Claims under the Inheritance (Provision for Family and Dependants) Act 1975 in the Chancery Division will be allocated to the Multi-Track and are issued by way of a Part 8 claim. Ordinarily they will be tried by the Master unless an order is made transferring the claim to a county court for trial. They are governed by Part 57 and PD 57.

24.7 The written evidence filed by the claimant with the claim form must exhibit an official copy of the grant of probate or letters of administration together with every testamentary document in respect of which probate or letters of administration was granted.

24.8 A defendant must file and serve acknowledgment of service not later than 21 days after service of the Part 8 claim form. Any written evidence (subject to any extension agreed or directed) must likewise be served and filed no later than 21 days after service.

24.9 The personal representatives of the deceased are necessary defendants to a claim under the 1975 Act and the written evidence filed by a defendant who is a personal representative must comply with paragraph 16 of PD 57.

24.10 On the hearing of a claim under the 1975 Act, the personal representatives must produce the original grant of representation to the deceased's estate. If the court makes an order under the Act, the original grant together with a sealed copy of the order must, under paragraph 18.2 of PD 57, be sent to the Principal Registry of the Family Division, First Avenue House, 42-49 High Holborn, London WC1V 6NP for a memorandum of the order to be endorsed on or permanently annexed to the grant.

24.11 Where claims under the 1975 Act are compromised the consent order filed must comply with paragraph 9.15 of this Guide.

## CHAPTER 25

## TRUSTS

***Key Rules: CPR Part 8; Part 19; Part 64 and PD 64***

### Introduction

**1A–178** 25.1 This Chapter contains material about a number of aspects of proceedings concerning trusts, the estates of deceased persons (other than probate claims) and charities.

25.2 The topics covered in this Chapter are (a) applications by trustees for directions and related matters; (b) the Variation of Trusts Act 1958; (c) section 48 of the Administration of Justice Act 1985; (d) vesting orders as regards property in Scotland; (e) trustees under a disability; (f) lodgment of funds; (g) the estates of deceased Lloyd's Names; and (h) judicial trustees.

### Trustees' applications for directions

**1A–179** 25.3 Applications to the court by trustees for directions in relation to the administration of a trust or charity, or by personal representatives in relation to a

*Paragraph numbers marked with a "+" can be found online and on CD.*

deceased person's estate, are to be brought by Part 8 claim form, and are governed by Part 64, and its PDs; rule 8.2A is also relevant. This Guide does not repeat what is in the PDs, which must be carefully studied.

25.4 Where the remedy sought is the approval of a sale, purchase, compromise or other transaction by a trustee, the claim form may be issued under rule 8.2A without naming a defendant. In all other cases, permission to issue the claim form under rule 8.2A is required. Case management directions will be given where the court grants an application to issue the claim form under rule 8.2A.

**Proceeding without a hearing**

25.5 The court will always consider whether it is possible to deal with the application on paper without a hearing. **1A–180**

25.6 Cases in which the directions can be given without a hearing include those where personal representatives apply to be allowed to distribute the estate of a deceased Lloyd's name, following the decision in *Re Yorke (deceased)* [1997] 4 All ER 907 (see paragraphs 25.50–55 below), as well as applications under section 48 of the Administration of Justice Act 1985 (see paragraphs 25.15–20 below).

**Representation Orders**

25.7 It is not necessary to make representation orders under rule 19.7 on an application for directions, and sometimes it would not be possible, for lack of separate representatives among the parties of all relevant classes of beneficiaries, but such orders can be useful in an appropriate case and they are sometimes made. **1A–181**

**Costs**

25.8 Normally the trustees' costs of a proper application will be allowed out of the trust fund, on an indemnity basis, as will the assessed (or agreed) costs of beneficiaries joined as defendants, subject to their conduct of the proceedings having been proper and reasonable. **1A–182**

**Prospective costs orders**

25.9 In proceedings brought by one or more beneficiaries against trustees, the court has power to direct that the beneficiaries be indemnified out of the trust fund in any event for any costs incurred by them and any costs which they may be ordered to pay to any other party, known as a prospective costs order: see *McDonald v. Horn* [1995] 1 All ER 961. Such an order may provide for payments out of the trust fund from time to time on account of the indemnity so that the beneficiaries' costs may be paid on an interim basis. Applications for prospective costs orders should be made on notice to the trustees. The court will require to be satisfied that there are matters which need to be investigated. How far the court will wish to go into that question, and in what way it should be done, will depend on the circumstances of the particular case. The order may be expressed to cover costs incurred only up to a particular stage in the proceedings, so that the application has to be renewed, if necessary, in the light of what has occurred in the proceedings in the meantime: See paragraph 6 of PD 64, to which is annexed a model form of order. **1A–183**

**Charity trustees' applications for permission to bring proceedings**

25.10 In the case of a charitable trust, if the Charity Commissioners refuse their consent to the trustees applying to the court for directions, under Charities Act 1993 section 33(2), and also refuse to give the trustees the directions under their own powers, under sections 26 or 29, the trustees may apply to the court under section 33(5). On such an application, which may be dealt with on paper, the judge may call for a statement from the Charity Commissioners of their reasons for refusing permission, if not already apparent from the papers. The court may require the trustees to attend before deciding whether to grant permission for the proceedings. It **1A–184** is possible to require notice of the hearing to be given to the Attorney-General, but this would not normally be appropriate.

**Variation of Trusts Act 1958**

**1A–185** 25.11 An application under the Variation of Trusts Act 1958 should be made by a Part 8 claim form. As to listing of such applications see paragraph 6.27. The Master will not consider the file without an application. Evidence is dealt with by PD 64 para 4.

25.12 Where any children or unborn beneficiaries will be affected by an arrangement under the Variation of Trusts Act 1958, evidence must normally be before the court which shows that their litigation friends or the trustees support the arrangements as being in the interests of the children or unborn beneficiaries, and exhibits a written opinion to this effect. In complicated cases a written opinion is usually essential to the understanding of the litigation friends and the trustees, and to the consideration by the court of the merits and fiscal consequences of the arrangement. If the written opinion was given on formal instructions, those instructions must be exhibited. Otherwise the opinion must state fully the basis on which it was given. The opinion must be given by the advocate who will appear on the hearing of the application. A skeleton argument may not be needed where a written opinion has been put in evidence and no matters not appearing from the instructions or the opinion are to be relied on.

25.13 Where the interests of two or more children, or two or more of the children and unborn beneficiaries, are similar, a single written opinion will suffice; and no written opinion is required in respect of those who fall within the proviso to section 1(1) of the Act (discretionary interests under protective trusts). Further, in proper cases the requirement of a written opinion may at any stage be dispensed with by the Master or the judge.

25.14 Where parties are represented by the same solicitors and counsel from the same Chambers the court is unlikely to assess costs summarily unless either the case is a clear one or the value of the trust fund is such that a detailed assessment of costs would be disproportionate.

**Applications under section 48 of the Administration of Justice Act 1985**

**1A–186** 25.15 Applications under section 48 of the Administration of Justice Act 1985 should be made by Part 8 Claim Form without naming a defendant, under rule 8.2A. No separate application for permission under rule 8.2A need be made. The claim should be supported by a witness statement or affidavit to which are exhibited: (a) copies of all relevant documents; (b) instructions to a person with a 10-year High Court qualification within the meaning of the Courts and Legal Services Act 1990 ("the qualified person"); (c) the qualified person's opinion; and (d) draft terms of the desired order. The application should not seek a decision of the court on the construction of any instrument.

25.16 The witness statement or affidavit (or exhibits thereto) should state: (a) the reason for the application (b) the names of all persons who are, or may be, affected by the order sought; (c) all surrounding circumstances admissible and relevant in construing the document; (d) the date of qualification of the qualified person and his or her experience in the construction of trust documents; (e) the approximate value of the fund or property in question; (f) whether it is known to the applicant that a dispute exists and, if so, details of such dispute and (g) what steps are proposed to be taken in reliance on the opinion.

25.17 When the file is placed before the Master he will consider whether the evidence is complete and if it is send the file to the judge.

25.18 The judge will consider the papers and, if necessary, direct service of notices under rule 19.8A or request such further information as he or she may desire. If the judge is satisfied that the order sought is appropriate, the order will be made and sent to the claimant.

25.19 If following service of notices under rule 19.8A any acknowledgment of service is received, the claimant must apply to the Master (on notice to the parties who have so acknowledged service) for directions. If the claimant desires to pursue the application to the court, in the ordinary case the Master will direct that the case proceeds as a Part 8 claim.

25.20 If on the hearing of the claim the judge is of the opinion that any party who entered an acknowledgment of service has no reasonably tenable argument contrary to the qualified person's opinion, in the exercise of his or her discretion he or she may order such party to pay any costs thrown away, or part thereof.

### Vesting orders—property in Scotland

25.21 In applications for vesting orders under the Trustee Act 1925 any investments or property situate in Scotland should be set out in a separate schedule to the claim form, and the claim form should ask that the trustees may have permission to apply for a vesting order in Scotland in respect thereto. **1A–187**

25.22 The form of the order to be made in such cases will (with any necessary variation) be as follows:

> "It is ordered that the [ ] as Trustees have permission to take all steps that may be necessary to obtain a vesting order in Scotland relating to [the securities] specified in the schedule herein."

### Disability of Trustee

25.23 There must be medical evidence showing incapacity to act as a trustee at the date of issue of the claim form and that the incapacity is continuing at the date of signing the witness statement or swearing the affidavit. The witness statement or affidavit should also show incapacity to execute transfers, where a vesting order of stocks and shares is asked for. **1A–188**

25.24 The trustee under disability should be made a defendant to the claim but need not be served unless he or she is sole trustee or has a beneficial interest.

### Lodgment of Funds

25.25 Mortgagees wishing to lodge surplus proceeds of sale in court under s.63 of the Trustee Act 1925 must in their witness statement or affidavit, and in addition to the matters set out in 37PD 6.1, set out the steps they have taken to fulfil their obligation under s.105 of the Law of Property Act 1925 to pay other incumbrancers (if any) and the mortgagor and why those steps have not been successful. Failure to do so will usually result in their application being rejected by the court. **1A–189**

### Estates of Deceased Lloyd's Names

25.26 The procedure concerning the estates of deceased Lloyd's names is governed by a *Practice Statement* [2001] 3 All ER 765. **1A–190**

25.27 Personal representatives who wish to apply to the court for permission to distribute the estate of a deceased Lloyd's Name following *Re Yorke (deceased)* [1997] 4 All ER 907, or trustees who wish to administer any will trusts arising in such an estate, may, until further notice and if appropriate in the particular estate, adopt the following procedure.

25.28 The procedure will be appropriate where:

(1) the only, or only substantial, reason for delaying distribution of the estate is the possibility of personal liability to Lloyd's creditors; and

(2) all liabilities of the estate in respect of syndicates of which the Name was a

member have for the years 1992 and earlier (if any) been reinsured (whether directly or indirectly) into the Equitas group; and

(3) all liabilities of the estate in respect of syndicates of which the Name was a member have for the years 1993 and later (if any) arise in respect of syndicates which have closed by reinsurance in the usual way or are protected by the terms of an Estate Protection Plan issued by Centrewrite Limited or are protected by the terms of EXEAT insurance cover provided by Centrewrite Limited.

25.29 In these circumstances personal representatives (and, if applicable, trustees) may apply by a Part 8 Claim Form headed "In the Matter of the Estate of [.........] deceased (a Lloyd's Estate) and In the Matter of the Practice Direction dated May 25 2001" for permission to distribute the estate (and, if applicable, to administer the will trusts) on the footing that no or no further provision need be made for Lloyd's creditors. Ordinarily, the claim form need not name any other party. It may be issued in this form without a separate application for permission under rule 8.2A.

25.30 The claim should be supported by a witness statement or an affidavit substantially in the form set out in Appendix 11 adapted as necessary to the particular circumstances and accompanied by a draft of the desired order substantially in the form also set out in Appendix 11. If the amount of costs has been agreed with the residuary beneficiaries (or, if the costs are not to be taken from residue, with the beneficiaries affected) their signed consent to those costs should also be submitted. If the Claimants are inviting the court to make a summary assessment they should submit a statement of costs in the form specified in the Costs PD. If in his discretion the Master (or outside London the District Judge) thinks fit, he will summarily assess the costs but with permission for the paying party to apply within 14 days of service of the order on him to vary or discharge the summary assessment. Subject to the foregoing, the order will provide for a detailed assessment unless subsequently agreed.

25.31 The application will be considered in the first instance by the Master who, if satisfied that the order should be made, may make the order without requiring the attendance of the applicants, and the court will send it to them. If not so satisfied, the Master may give directions for the further disposal of the application.

#### Judicial Trustees

**1A–191** 25.32 Judicial trustees are appointed by the court under the Judicial Trustees Act 1896, in accordance with the Judicial Trustee Rules 1983. An application for the appointment of a judicial trustee should be made by Part 8 claim (or, if in an existing claim, by an application notice in that claim) which must be served (subject to any directions by the court) on every existing trustee who is not an applicant and on such of the beneficiaries as the applicant thinks fit. Once appointed, a judicial trustee may obtain non-contentious directions from the assigned Master informally by letter, without the need for a Part 23 application (unless the court directs otherwise). Applications for directions can be sought from the court as to the trust or its administration by rule 8 of the Judicial Trustee Rules.

25.33 Where it is proposed to appoint the Official Solicitor as judicial trustee, inquiries must first be made to his office for confirmation that he is prepared to act if appointed. The Official Solicitor will not be required to give security.

25.34 A judicial trustee is entitled under rule 11 of the 1983 rules to such remuneration as is reasonable in respect of work reasonably performed. Applications for payment by the trustee must be by letter to the court, submitted with the accounts. A Practice Note issued by the Chief Chancery Master, with the authority of the Vice-Chancellor, on 1 July 2003 sets out the best practice to be followed in determining the amount of remuneration. The Practice Note mirrors the position regarding receivers' remuneration under CPR rule 69.7 and is reproduced at Appendix 12.

# APPENDICES

## APPENDIX 1

## ADDRESSES AND OTHER CONTACT DETAILS

### 1. Clerks to the Chancery Judges

*(all numbers to be preceded by 020 and by 7947, except where indicated)* **1A–192**

| Clerk to: | telephone | fax |
|---|---|---|
| The Chancellor | 6412 | 6572 |
| Mr Justice Peter Smith | 6183 | 6133 |
| Mr Justice Lewison | 6039 | 6894 |
| Mr Justice David Richards | 7419 | 6743 |
| Mr Justice Mann | 7964 | 6739 |
| Mr Justice Warren | 7260 | 7740 |
| Mr Justice Kitchin | 6518 | 6439 |
| Mr Justice Briggs | 6741 | 6196 |
| Mr Justice Henderson | 6669 | 7298 |
| Mr Justice Morgan | 6419 | 6062 |
| Mr Justice Norris | 7073 1728 | 6649 |
| Mr Justice Barling | 6238 | 6684 |
| Mr Justice Floyd | 7073 1740 | 6593 |
| Mr Justice Sales | 6657 | 7185 |
| Mrs Justice Proudman | 6671 | 6291 |
| Mr Justice Arnold | 7073 1789 | 6719 |
| Mr Justice Roth | 6589 | 7379 |
| Mr Justice Vos | 7606 | 6165 |

### 2. E-Mail Communications

The e-mail protocol sets out how parties may communicate by e-mail on certain matters with the Chancery Division, and can be found at: *www.hmcourts-service.gov.uk/infoabout/email_guidance/email_guidance_chancery.htm* **1A–193**

The relevant e-mail addresses are:

(a) For skeleton arguments, chronologies, reading lists, list of issues, lists of authorities (but not the authorities themselves) and lists of the persons involved in the facts of the case sent in advance of a hearing:

**Judge:**
rcjchancery.judgeslisting@hmcourts-service.gsi.gov.uk
[**Note:** The clerk to the judge concerned should be contacted to find out whether other documents will be accepted by e-mail, and whether documents should be sent direct to the judge's clerk's e-mail address.]

**Chancery Master:**
rcjchancery.mastersappointments@hmcourts-service.gsi.gov.uk

**Bankruptcy Registrar:**
rcjbankruptcy.registrarshearings@hmcourts-service.gsi.gov.uk

**Companies Court Registrar:**
rcjcompanies.orders@hmcourts-service.gsi.gov.uk

(b) For the agreed terms of an Order which is ready to be sealed following the conclusion of a hearing:

**Judge:**
rcjchancery.ordersandaccounts@hmcourts-service.gsi.gov.uk

**Chancery Master:**
rcjchancery.ordersandaccounts@hmcourts-service.gsi.gov.uk

***Paragraph numbers marked with a "+" can be found online and on CD.***

**Bankruptcy Registrar:**

rcjbankruptcy.registrarshearings@hmcourts-service.gsi.gov.uk

**Companies Court Registrar:**

rcjcompanies.orders@hmcourts-service.gsi.gov.uk

**3. At the Royal Courts of Justice, Thomas More Building**

1A–194 *(All telephone extension numbers and fax numbers should be prefixed by 020 7947 unless otherwise specified)*

| | |
|---|---|
| 1ST FLOOR | |
| TM1.10 | Bankruptcy Registrars' Clerks, applications without notice, Registrars' hearings and orders (6187/7387 ) |
| | Bankruptcy Registrars' Chambers (6444/7387) |
| | Bankruptcy Court fax number (6378) |
| 2ND FLOOR | |
| TM2.04 | Bankruptcy Operational Manager (6812) |
| TM2.05 | Companies Schemes and Reduction of Capital (6727) |
| TM2.07 | Court Manager, Companies, Bankruptcy and Chancery Chambers Courts (6870). |
| TM2.09 | Companies Court General Office: issue of all winding-up petitions and all other Companies Court applications; filing of documents for winding up procedure (6294); |
| | Central Index (7328) |
| TM2.11 | Bankruptcy Issue and Search Room; issue of all petitions presented by creditors and debtors and applications to set aside statutory demand and applications for interim orders; search room (6448); Companies Court Fax number (6958) |
| 3RD FLOOR | |
| TM3.08 | Bankruptcy and Companies Registry. Filing affidavits, witness statements and documents and requesting bankruptcy and company files for applications without notice to be made in Chambers; requests for office copies, lodging applications for certificates of discharge in bankruptcy (6441) |
| 4TH FLOOR | |
| TM4.05 | Companies Orders Section: Registrars' Orders and disqualification of directors (6822) |
| TM4.10 | Companies Operational Manager (7472) |
| 5TH FLOOR | |
| TM5.04 | Chancery Chambers Registry and Issue Section: issue and amendment of all Chancery process, filing affidavits and witness statements (save those lodged within two days of a hearing before a Master which are to be filed in Room TM7.09); filing acknowledgements of service, searches of cause book; applications for office copy documents, including orders; transfers in and out (6148/6167) |
| TM5.05 | Deputy Court Manager, Chancery Chambers. Certification of documents for use abroad (6754) |
| TM5.06 | Lawyer, Chancery Chambers (6080). |
| TM5.07 | Orders and Accounts Section. Associates: preparation of all Chancery Orders and Companies and Bankruptcy Court Orders; small payments; bills of costs for assessment; settlement of payment and lodgment schedules; accounts of receivers, judicial trustees, guardians and administrators; applications relating to security set by the court; matters arising out of accounts and inquiries ordered by the court (6855); Chancery Orders and Accounts Fax number: (7049) |

| | |
|---|---|
| 6TH FLOOR | |
| TM6.04 | Chancery Masters' Library |
| TM6.05 | Master Price |
| TM6.07 | Master Bowles |
| TM6.08 | Secretary to Masters (6777) |
| TM6.09 | Master Bragge |
| 7TH FLOOR | |
| TM7.05 | Mater Teverson |
| TM7.06 | Master Moncaster |
| TM7.08 | Chief Master Winegarten |
| TM7.09 | Masters' Appointments. Issue of Masters' applications, including applications without notice to Masters; filing affidavits and witness statements in proceedings before Masters (only if filed within two working days of hearing before the Master); applications to serve out of jurisdiction; filing stop notices; filing testamentary documents in contested probate cases; filing grants lodged under PArt57; filing affidavits relating to funds paid into court under the Trustee Act 1925, Compulsory Purchase Act 1965 and the Lands Clauses Consolidation Act 1845. Manager (6095); Clerks to Chancery Masters (6702/7391);<br>Masters' Appointments Fax no: (7422) |

**4. At the Royal Courts of Justice but Outside Thomas More Building**

(Prefaced by 020 7947 unless otherwise specified). **1A–195**

RCJ Switchboard (6000)

RCJ Security Office (6260)

Fees Office (Room E01) (6527)

Clerk of the Lists, Room WG3 (6318)

Chancery Judges' Listing Office, Room WG4 (6778/6690)

High Court Appeals Office, Room WG7 (7518)

Chancery Judges' Listing Office Fax number*: (0870 739 5869) (**See paragraph 14.12)*

Officer in charge of mechanical recording (Room WB.14) (6154)

Head Usher (6356, fax 6668)

Customer Service Officer (7731)

Video-conferencing managers (6581, fax 6613)

RCJ Advice Bureau (0845 120 3715, or 020 7947 6880, fax 020 7947 7167)

Personal Support Unit (Room M104). (7701/7703 fax 7702)

**5. London, Outside the Royal Courts of Justice**

Central London County Court **1A–196**

Civil Trial Centre, Chancery List, 26-29 Park Crescent, London W1N 4HT

DX 97325 Regents Park 2

Business Chancery and Patents section (020 7917 7821/7887)

Fax 0207 917 7935/7940

**6. Outside London**

The following are the Court addresses, telephone and fax numbers for the courts at which there are regular Chancery sittings outside London: **1A–197**

| | |
|---|---|
| Birmingham: | The Priory Courts, 33 Bull Street, Birmingham B4 6DS.<br>Telephone: 0121-681-3033. Fax: 0121-681-3121 |
| Bristol: | The Law Courts, Small Street, Bristol BS1 1DA.<br>Telephone: 0117-976-3098. Fax: 0117-976-3074 |

| | |
|---|---|
| | Bristol County Court<br>Lewins Place<br>Lewins Mead<br>Bristol<br>BS1 2NR<br>Telephone: 0117 9106706 (Chancery Listing Officer)<br>Fax: 0117 9106727 (Chancery Business)<br>Urgent Court Business Pager: 07795302944 |
| Cardiff: | The Civil Justice Centre, 2 Park Street, Cardiff CF1 1ET.<br>Telephone: 02920-376402. Fax: 02920-376470<br>Email: hearings@cardiffcountycourt.gsi.gov.uk |
| Leeds: | The Court House, 1 Oxford Row, Leeds LS1 3BG.<br>Telephone: 0113-283-0040. Fax: 0113-244-8507. |
| Liverpool: | 35 Vernon Street<br>Liverpool Merseyside<br>L2 2BX<br>DX 702600 Liverpool<br>Tel: 0151 296 2514 or 0151 296 2449 |
| Manchester: | Manchester Civil Justice Centre<br>1 Bridge Street West<br>Manchester Greater Manchester<br>M60 9DJ<br>DX 724783 Manchester 44<br>Tel: 0161 240 5307 or main switchboard 0161 240 5000<br>Email:<br>highcourtspecialhearings@manchester.countycourt.gsi.gov.uk |
| Newcastle: | The Law Courts, Quayside, Newcastle-upon-Tyne NE1 3LB.<br>Telephone: 0191-201-2000. Fax: 0191-201-2001 |
| Preston: | The Law Courts, Openshaw Place, Ringway, Preston PR1 2LL. Telephone: 01772-832300. Fax: 01772-832476. |

In some centres resources do not permit the listing telephone numbers to be attended personally at all times. In cases of urgency, solicitors, counsel and counsel's clerks may come into the Chancery Court and leave messages with the member of staff sitting in Court.

Urgent Court business officer pager numbers for out of hours applications:

| | | |
|---|---|---|
| Birmingham (Midland Circuit): | | |
| | West Side: | 07699-618079 |
| | East Side: | 07699-618078 |
| Bristol: | | 07699-618088 |
| Cardiff: | | 07699-618086 |
| Manchester and Liverpool: | | 07699-618080 |
| Preston | | 07699-618081 |
| Newcastle | | 01399-618083 |
| Leeds and Bradford | | 01399-618082 |

In case of difficulty out of hours, contact the Royal Courts of Justice on 020 7947 6260.

## APPENDIX 2

## GUIDELINES ON STATEMENTS OF CASE

1A–198 1. The document must be as brief and concise as possible.

2. The document must be set out in separate consecutively numbered paragraphs and sub-paragraphs.

3. So far as possible each paragraph or sub-paragraph should contain no more than one allegation.

4. The document should deal with the case on a point by point basis, to allow a point by point response.

5. Where the CPR require a party to give particulars of an allegation or reasons for a denial (see rule 16.5(2)), the allegation or denial should be stated first and then the particulars or reasons listed one by one in separate numbered sub-paragraphs.

6. A party wishing to advance a positive case must identify that case in the document; a simple denial is not sufficient.

7. Any matter which if not stated might take another party by surprise should be stated.

8. Where they will assist, headings, abbreviations and definitions should be used and a glossary annexed.

9. Contentious headings, abbreviations, paraphrasing and definitions should not be used; every effort should be made to ensure that headings, abbreviations and definitions are in a form that will enable them to be adopted without issue by the other parties.

10. Particulars of primary allegations should be stated as particulars and not as primary allegations.

11. Schedules or appendices should be used if this would be helpful, for example where lengthy particulars are necessary.

12. The names of any witness to be called may be given, and necessary documents (including an expert's report) can be attached or served contemporaneously if not bulky (PD 16; Guide paragraph 2.11). Otherwise evidence should not be included.

13. A response to particulars stated in a schedule should be stated in a corresponding schedule.

14. A party should not set out lengthy extracts from a document in his or her statement of case. If an extract has to be included, it should be placed in a schedule.

15. The document must be signed by the individual person or persons who drafted it not, in the case of a solicitor, in the name of the firm only. It must be accompanied by a Statement of Truth.

## APPENDIX 3

## CASE MANAGEMENT DIRECTIONS

DRAFT ORDERS FOR USE ON ALLOCATION OR AT CASE MANAGEMENT CONFERENCES **1A–199**

*Claim No.*

IT IS ORDERED

1. Allocation to multi-track

( ) that this claim is allocated to the multi-track.

2. Transfer of claims, including transfer from Part 8

( ) that the claim be transferred to:

(a) the Division of the High Court;

(b) the District Registry;

(c) the [Central London] County Court [Chancery List].

( ) that the issue(s) *(define issue(s))* be transferred to *(one of (a) to (c) above)* for determination.

***Paragraph numbers marked with a "+" can be found online and on CD.***

( ) that the (*party*) apply by (*date*) to a Judge of the Technology and Construction Court [*or other Specialist List*] for an Order to transfer the claim to that Court.

( ) that the claim (*title and claim number*) commenced in [the County Court][the District Registry of ], be transferred from that Court to the Chancery Division of the High Court.

( ) that this claim shall continue as if commenced under Part 7 and shall be allocated to the multi-track.

3. Alternative dispute resolution

This claim be stayed until [*one month*] for the parties to try to settle the dispute by alternative dispute resolution or other means. The parties shall notify the Court in writing at the end of that period whether settlement has been reached. The parties shall at the same time lodge *either*:

(a) (if a settlement has been reached) a draft consent Order signed by all parties; *or*

(b) (if no settlement has been reached) a statement of agreed directions signed by all parties or (in the absence of agreed directions) statements of the parties' respective proposed directions.

4. Probate cases only

( ) that the [*party*] file [his][her] witness statement or affidavit of testamentary scripts and lodge any testamentary script at Room TM7.09, Thomas More Building, Royal Courts of Justice, Strand, London WC2A 2LL [ District Registry] by (*date*).

5. Case summary

( )that [each party][the (*party*)] by (*date*) prepare and serve a case summary [not exceeding words] on all other parties, to be agreed by (*date*) and filed by (*date*) and if it is not agreed by that date the parties shall file their own case summaries.

6. Trial date

( ) that the trial of the claim/issue(s) take place between (*date*) and (*date*) ("the trial window").

6. Trial date

( ) that the (*party*) shall make an appointment to attend on the Listing Officer (Room WG4, Royal Courts of Justice, Strand, London WC2A 2LL; Tel. 020 7947 6816; Fax No. 0870 739 5869; email rcjchancery.judgeslisting@hmcourts-service.gsi.gov.uk) to fix a trial date within the trial window, such appointment to be not later than (*date*) and give notice of the appointment to all other parties.

( ) that

(i) the claim be entered in the [Trial List][General List], with a listing category of [A][B][C] (*to be decided by the Master with reference to the substance and difficulty of the case*), with a time estimate of days/weeks

(ii) the trial take place in London (*or* identify venue).

7. Pre Trial Review

( ) [the trial being estimated to last more than 10 days] that there be a Pre Trial Review on a date to be arranged by the Listing Officer [in conjunction with the parties] [to take place shortly before the trial and, if possible, in front of the Judge who will be conducting the trial] at which, except for urgent matters in the meantime, the Court will hear any further applications for Orders.

8. All directions agreed.

( ) The parties having agreed directions it is by consent ordered:—

[Set out all the directions by reference to parties' draft Order on file].

9. Some directions agreed

( ) The parties having agreed the following directions it is by consent ordered:

[Set out the agreed directions by reference to parties' draft Order on file as above, and any further directions to be given at this stage].

***Paragraph numbers marked with a "+" can be found online and on CD.***

10. Case management conference etc.

( ) that there be a [further] case management conference before the Master in Room TM ..., Thomas More Building, Royal Courts of Justice, Strand, London WC2A 2LL on (*date*) at o'clock (of hours/minutes duration).

( ) that there shall be a case management conference (of hours/ minutes duration). In order for the Court to fix a date the parties are to complete the accompanying questionnaire and file it by (*date*).

( ) that the (*party*) apply for an appointment for a [further] case management conference by (*date*).

( ) At the case management conference, except for urgent matters in the meantime, the Court will hear any further applications for Orders and any party must file an Application Notice for any such Orders and serve it and supporting evidence (if any) by (*date*).

11. Failure to file allocation questionnaire

( ) that, ***no allocation questionnaire having been received from [the Claimant-][the Defendant]***, if [the Claimant][the Defendant] [does not file [his][her] allocation questionnaire within 3 days after service of this Order upon [him-][her], the [claim] [counterclaim] shall be struck out without further Order *[or as the case may be]*. [Add Order as to costs].

12. Amendments to statement of case

( ) that the (*party*) has permission to amend [his][her] statement of case as in the copy on the Court file [initialled by the Master].

( ) that the amended statement of case be verified by a statement of truth.

( ) that the amended statement of case be filed by (*date*).

( ) that [the amended statement of case be served by (*date*).] [service of the amended statement of case be dispensed with].

( ) that any consequential amendments to other statements of case be filed and served by (*date*)

( ) that the costs of and consequential to the amendment to the statement of case [shall be paid by (*party*) in any event] [are assessed in the sum of £ and are to be paid by (*party*)][within (*time*)].

13. Addition of parties etc.

( ) that the (*party*) has permission:

(a) to [add][substitute][remove] (*name of party*) as a (*party*) and

(b) to amend [his][her] statement of case in accordance with the copy on the Court file [initialled by the Master].

and that the amended statement of case be verified by a statement of truth.

( ) that the amended statement of case be:

(a) filed by (*date*);

(b) served on (*new party, existing parties or removed party, as appropriate*), by (*date*).

( ) that a copy of this Order be served on (*new party, existing parties or removed party, as appropriate*), by (*date*).

( ) that any consequential amendments to other statements of case be filed and served by (*date*).

( ) that the costs of and consequential to the amendment to the statement of case [shall be paid by the (*party*) in any event] [are assessed in the sum of £ and are to be paid by the (*party*)].

14. Consolidation

( ) that this claim be consolidated with claim number (*number and title of claim*), the lead claim to be claim number . [The title to the consolidated case shall be as set out in the Schedule to this Order].

15. Trial of issue

( ) that the issue of (*define issue*) be tried as follows:

(a) with the consent of the parties, before a Master

(i) on (*date*) in Room TM Thomas More Build-

***Paragraph numbers marked with a "+" can be found online and on CD.***

ing, Royal Courts of Justice, Strand, London WC2A 2LL;

(ii) with a time estimate of (hours),

(iii) with the filing of listing questionnaires dispensed with, *or*

(b) before a Judge

(i) with the trial of the issue to take place between (*date*) and (*date*) ("the trial window")

(ii) with the (*party*) to make an appointment to attend on the Listing Officer (Room WG4, Royal Courts of Justice, Strand, London WC2A 2LL; Tel. 020 7947 6778/6690; Fax No. 020 7947 7345) to fix a trial date within the trial window, such appointment to be not later than (*date*) and to give notice of the appointment to all other parties.

(iii) with the issue to be entered in the [Trial List][General List], with a listing category of [A][B][C] (*to be decided by the Master with reference to the substance and difficulty of the case*, and a time estimate of days/ weeks and to take place in London (*or* identify venue).

16. Further information

( ) that the (*party*) provide by (*date*) the [further information][clarification] sought in the request dated (*date*) [initialled by the Master].

( ) that any request for [further information][clarification] shall be served by [*date*].

17. Disclosure of documents

( ) that each party give by (*date*) standard disclosure to every other party by list [by categories].

( ) that the (*party/parties*) give specific disclosure of documents [limited to the issues of ] described in the Schedule to this Order [initialled by the Master] by list [by categories] by (*date*).

( ) that the (*party*) give by (*date*) standard disclosure by list [by categories] to (*party*) of documents limited to the issue(s) of (*define issues*) by list.

18. Inspection of documents

( ) that any requests for inspection or copies of disclosed documents shall be made within days after service of the list.

19. Preservation of property

( ) that the (*party*) preserve (*give details of relevant property*) until trial of the claim or further Order *or other remedy under* rule 25.1(1).

20. Witness statements

( ) that each party serve on every other party the witness statement of the oral evidence which the party serving the statement intends to rely on in relation to [any issues of fact][the following issues of fact (*define issues*)] to be decided at the trial, those statements [and any notices of intention to rely on hearsay evidence] to be

(a) exchanged by (*date*) or

(b) served by (*party*) by (*date*) and by (*party*) by (*date*)

provided that before exchange the parties shall liaise with a view to agreeing a method of identification of any documents referred to in any such witness statement.

( ) that the (*party*) has permission to serve a witness summary relating to the evidence of (*name*) of (*address*) [on every other party by][to be served on (*party*)/exchanged at the same time as exchange of witness statements].

21. No expert evidence

( ) no expert evidence being necessary, that [no party has permission to call or rely on expert evidence][permission to call or rely on expert evidence is refused].

22. Single expert

( ) that evidence be given by the report of a single expert in the field of (*define field*) instructed jointly by the parties, on the issue of (*define issue*) [and [his][her] fees shall be limited to £ ].

( ) that if the parties are unable to agree [by (*date*)] who that expert is to be and about the payment of [his][her] fees any party may apply for further directions.

( ) that unless the parties agree in writing or the Court orders otherwise, the fees and expenses of the single expert shall be paid to [him][her] by the parties equally.

( ) that each party give [his][her] instructions to the single expert by (*date*).

( ) that the report of the single expert be filed and served by [him][her] on the parties by (*date*).

( ) that no party may recover from another party more than £ for the fees and expenses of the expert.

( ) that the evidence of the expert be given at the trial by [written report][oral evidence] of the expert.

23. Separate Experts

( ) that each party has permission to adduce [oral] expert evidence in the field of (*specify*) [limited to expert(s) [per party][on each side].

( ) that the experts' reports shall be exchanged by (*date*).

( ) that the experts shall hold a discussion for the purpose of:

(a) identifying the issues, if any, between them; and

(b) where possible, reaching agreement on those issues.

( ) that the experts shall by [*specify date after discussion*] prepare and file a statement for the Court showing:

(a) those issues on which they are agreed; and

(b) those issues on which they disagree and a summary of their reasons for disagreeing.

( ) No party shall be entitled to recover by way of costs from any other party more than £ for the fees or expenses of an expert.

24. Definition and reduction of issues.

( ) that by (*date*) the parties list and discuss the issues in the claim [including the experts' reports and statements] and attempt to define and narrow the issues [including those issues the subject of discussion by the experts].

25. Trial bundle and skeleton arguments.

( ) that not earlier than 7 days or later than 3 days before the date fixed for trial or of the claim entering the Warned List the Claimant shall file with the Chancery Listing Office a trial bundle for the use of the Judge in accordance with Appendix 6 of the Chancery Guide.

( ) that skeleton arguments and chronologies shall be filed not less than 2 clear days before the date fixed for trial or of the claim entering the Warned List, in accordance with Appendix 7 of the Chancery Guide.

26. Settlement

( ) that if the claim or part of the claim is settled the parties must immediately inform the Court, whether or not it is then possible to file a draft Consent Order to give effect to the settlement.

27. Compliance with Directions

( ) that the parties shall by (*date*) notify the Court in writing that they have fully complied with all directions or state:

(a) with which directions they have not complied;

(b) why they have not complied; and

(c) what steps they are taking to comply with the outstanding directions in time for the trial.

If the Court does not receive such notification or if the steps proposed to comply with outstanding directions are considered by the Court unsatisfactory, the Court may order a hearing (and may make appropriate orders as to costs against a party in default).

28. Costs

( ) that the costs of this application be:

(a) costs in the case;

(b) summarily assessed at £ and paid by *(party)*; *or*

(c) the [party/parties]'[s] in any event, to be subject to detailed assessment.

[] NOTE 1

The attention of the parties is drawn to the importance of seeking to agree at an early stage directions for the management of the case as emphasised in the Practice Direction to Part 29 of the Civil Procedure Rules.

[] NOTE 2

The parties may, subject to any agreement being in accordance with the provisions of the Civil Procedure Rules, agree to extend the time periods given in the directions above provided this does not affect the date given for any case management conference or pre-trial review or the date of the trial or trial period.

[] NOTE 3

If you fail to attend a hearing that has been ordered, the Court may order you to pay the costs of the other party, or parties, that do attend. Failure to pay those costs within the time stated may lead to your statement of case (claim or defence) being struck out.

[] NOTE 4

If you do not comply with these directions, any other party to the claim will be entitled to apply to the Court for an order that your statement of case (claim or defence) be struck out.

## APPENDIX 4

1A–200 **Part 1: Judge's Application Information Form**

Title as in claim form

Application Information

1. [DATE APPLICATION TO BE HEARD]
2. DETAILS OF SOLICITOR/PARTY LODGING THE APPLICATION
   a. [Name]
   b. [Address]
   c. [Telephone No.]
   d. [Reference]
   e. [Acting for Claimant(s)/Defendant(s)]
3. DETAILS OF COUNSEL/OR OTHER ADVOCATE
   a. [Name]
   b. [Address of Chambers/Firm]
   c. [Telephone No.]
4. DETAILS OF OTHER PART(Y'S)(IES') SOLICITORS
   a. [Name]
   b. [Address]
   c. [Telephone No.]
   d. [Reference]

[Acting for Claimant(s)/Defendant(s)]

**Part 2: Written Evidence Lodgment Form**

**CHANCERY CHAMBERS**

TO FILING SECTION—ROOM TM5.04

CLAIM NO:

SHORT TITLE:

Herewith Affidavit or witness statement of ..................................................

/or if other document specify ..................................................

filed in respect of:—

| | Tick |
|---|---|
| 1. Application before Judge on .................................................. | |
| 2. Application before Master on .................................................. | |
| 3. Charging Order | |
| 4. Garnishee Order | |
| 5. Permission to issue claim for possession | |
| 6. Service by alternative method | |
| 7. Service out of Jurisdiction | |
| 8. Evidence | |
| 9. Oral examination of debtor | |
| 10. To enable a Master's order to be drawn | |
| 11. Other (Specify) .................................................. | |

Signed

Solicitors for Claimant/Defendant

other (please specify)

Telephone No:

Ref:

## APPENDIX 5

### CORRESPONDENCE WITH CHANCERY MASTERS—PRACTICE NOTE

1. One of the consequences of the new Rules and Practice Directions has been a significant increase in letters to the Court from parties and their solicitors. This imposes a heavy extra burden on the staff and Masters. It also means that court files have to be moved more often, which itself gives rise to problems. It would therefore be greatly appreciated if parties and solicitors involved in litigation before the Chancery Masters had regard to the following points. **1A–201**

2. When corresponding, please consider carefully (a) whether your letter is really necessary and (b) if it is who the correct addressee should be. Only address letters to the Master if the letter needs to be seen by him. If not address the letter to his clerk.

3. Faxes should not be used to send letters or documents of a routine or non-urgent nature. Where a party files a document by fax he must not send a hard copy in addition. (If, exceptionally, a fax has included a document the original of which

*Paragraph numbers marked with a "+" can be found online and on CD.*

needs to go on the court file, then a hard copy enclosing the original may be sent and it should be marked clearly "confirmation of fax").

4. As a general rule all correspondence, whether letter or fax, must be copied to the other parties. Correspondence should therefore state that it has been copied to the other parties (or else it should state that it has not been and explain why).

5. Correspondence should not be used in place of a Part 23 application (which requires payment of a fee, a draft order and a statement of truth).

J Winegarten

Chief Chancery Master

July 2009

## APPENDIX 6

## GUIDELINES ON BUNDLES

1A-202 Bundles of documents must comply with paragraph 3 of PD 39 Miscellaneous Provisions relating to Hearings. These guidelines are additional to those requirements, and they should be followed wherever possible.

1. The preparation of bundles requires co-operation between the legal representatives for all parties, and in many cases a high level of co-operation. It is the duty of all legal representatives to co-operate to the necessary level. Where a party is acting in person it is also that party's duty to co-operate as necessary with the other parties' legal representatives.

2. Bundles should be prepared in accordance with the following guidance.

### Avoidance of duplication

1A-203 3. No more than one copy of any one document should be included, unless there is good reason for doing otherwise. One such reason may be the use of a separate core bundle.

4. If the same document is included in the chronological bundles and is also an exhibit to an affidavit or witness statement, it should be included in the chronological bundle and where it would otherwise appear as an exhibit a sheet should instead be inserted. This sheet should state the page and bundle number in the chronological bundles where the document can be found.

5. Where the court considers that costs have been wasted by copying unnecessary documents, a special costs order may be made against the relevant person. In no circumstances should rival bundles be presented to the court.

### Chronological order and organisation

1A-204 6. In general documents should be arranged in date order starting with the earliest document.

7. If a contract or other transactional document is central to the case it may be included in a separate place provided that a page is inserted in the chronological run of documents to indicate where it would have appeared chronologically and where it is to be found instead. Alternatively transactional documents may be placed in a separate bundle as a category.

### Pagination

1A-205 8. This is covered by paragraph 3 of the PD, but it is permissible, instead of numbering the whole bundle, to number documents separately within tabs. An exception to consecutive page numbering arises in the case of the core bundle. For this it may be preferable to retain the original numbering with each bundle represented by a separate divider.

9. Page numbers should be inserted in bold figures, at the bottom of the page and in a form that can clearly be distinguished from any other pagination on the document.

#### Format and presentation

10. Where possible, the documents should be in A4 format. Where a document has to be read across rather than down the page, it should so be placed in the bundle as to ensure that the top of the text starts nearest the spine. **1A–206**

11. Where any marking or writing in colour on a document is important, for example on a conveyancing plan, the document must be copied in colour or marked up correctly in colour.

12. Documents in manuscript, or not easily legible, should be transcribed; the transcription should be marked and placed adjacent to the document transcribed.

13. Documents in a foreign language should be translated; the translation should be marked and placed adjacent to the document translated; the translation should be agreed or, if it cannot be agreed, each party's proposed translation should be included.

14. The size of any bundle should be tailored to its contents. There is no point having a large lever-arch file with just a few pages inside. On the other hand bundles should not be overloaded as they tend to break. **No bundle should contain more than 300 pages.**

15. Binders and files must be strong enough to withstand heavy use.

16. Large documents, such as plans, should be placed in an easily accessible file. If they will need to be opened up often, it may be sensible for the file to be larger than A4 size.

#### Indices and labels

17. Indices should, if possible, be on a single sheet. It is not necessary to waste space with the full heading of the action. Documents should be identified briefly but properly, e.g. "AGS3—Defendants Accounts". **1A–207**

18. Outer labels should use large lettering, e.g. "A. Pleadings." The full title of the action and solicitors' names and addresses should be omitted. A label should be used on the front as well as on the spine.

19. A label should also be stuck on to the front inside cover of a file at the top left, in such a way that it can be seen even when the file is open.

#### Staples etc.

20. All staples, heavy metal clips etc. should be removed. **1A–208**

#### Statements of case

21. Statements of case should be assembled in 'chapter' form, i.e. claim form followed by particulars of claim, followed by further information, irrespective of date. **1A–209**

22. Redundant documents, e.g. particulars of claim overtaken by amendments, requests for further information recited in the answers given, should generally be excluded. Backsheets to statements of case should also be omitted.

#### Witness statements, affidavits and expert reports

23. Where there are witness statements, affidavits and/or expert reports from two or more parties, each party's witness statements etc. should, in large cases, be contained in separate bundles. **1A–210**

***Paragraph numbers marked with a "+" can be found online and on CD.***

24. The copies of the witness statements, affidavits and expert reports in the bundles should have written on them, next to the reference to any document, the reference to that document in the bundles. This can be done in manuscript.

25. Documents referred to in, or exhibited to, witness statements, affidavits and expert reports should be put in a separate bundle and not placed behind the statement concerned, so that the reader can see both the text of the statement and the document referred to at the same time.

26. Backsheets to affidavits and witness statements should be omitted.

#### New Documents

1A–211 27. Before a new document is introduced into bundles which have already been delivered to the court—indeed before it is copied—steps should be taken to ensure that it carries an appropriate bundle/page number, so that it can be added to the court documents. It should not be stapled, and it should be prepared with punch holes for immediate inclusion in the binders in use.

28. If it is expected that a large number of miscellaneous new documents will from time to time be introduced, there should be a special tabbed empty loose-leaf file for that purpose. It is conventional to label this file "X". An index should be produced for this file, updated as necessary.

#### Inter-Solicitor Correspondence

1A–212 29. It is seldom that all inter-solicitor correspondence is required. Only those letters which are likely to be referred to should be copied. They should normally be placed in a separate bundle.

#### Core bundle

1A–213 30. Where the volume of documents needed to be included in the bundles, and the nature of the case, makes it sensible, a separate core bundle should be prepared for the trial, containing those documents likely to be referred to most frequently.

#### Basis of agreement of bundles

1A–214 31. See Chapter 7, paragraph 13.

#### Photocopy authorities

1A–215 32. If authorities, extracts from text-books etc. are photocopied for convenience for use in court, the photocopies should be placed in a separate bundle with an index and dividers. Reduced size copies (i.e. 2 pages of original to each A4 sheet) should not be used. Where only a short passage from a long case is needed, the headnote and key pages only should be copied and the usher should be asked to have the full volume in court. Whenever possible the parties' advocates should liaise about these bundles in order to avoid duplication of copies.

## APPENDIX 7

## GUIDELINES ON SKELETON ARGUMENTS, CHRONOLOGIES, INDICES AND READING LISTS

#### Skeleton arguments

1A–216 1. A skeleton argument is intended to identify both for the parties and the court those points which are, and those that are not, in issue, and the nature of the argument in relation to those points which are in issue. It is not a substitute for oral argument.

2. Every skeleton argument should therefore:

(1) identify concisely:
 (a) the nature of the case generally, and the background facts insofar as they are relevant to the matter before the court;
 (b) the propositions of law relied on with references to the relevant authorities;
 (c) the submissions of fact to be made with reference to the evidence;
(2) be as brief as the nature of the issues allows—it should not normally exceed 20 pages of double-spaced A4 paper and in many cases it should be much shorter than this;
(3) be in numbered paragraphs and state the name (and contact details) of the advocate(s) who prepared it;
(4) avoid arguing the case at length;
(5) avoid formality and make use of abbreviations, e.g. C for Claimant, A/345 for bundle A page 345, 1.1.95 for 1st January 1995 etc.

3. Paragraph 1 also applies to written summaries of opening speeches and final speeches. Even though in a large case these may necessarily be longer, they should still be as brief as the case allows.

**Reading lists**

4. The documents which the Judge should if possible read before the hearing may be identified in a skeleton argument, but must in any event be listed in a separate reading list, if possible agreed between the advocates, which must be lodged with the agreed bundles, together with an estimate, if possible agreed, of the time required for the reading. **1A–217**

**Chronologies and indices**

5. Chronologies and indices should be non-contentious and agreed with the other parties if possible. If there is a material dispute about any event stated in the chronology, that should be stated in neutral terms and the competing versions shortly stated. **1A–218**

6. If time and circumstances allow its preparation, a chronology or index to which all parties have contributed and agreed can be invaluable.

7. Chronologies and indices once prepared can be easily updated and may be of continuing usefulness throughout the case.

## APPENDIX 8

## DELIVERY OF DOCUMENTS IN CHANCERY CHAMBERS

1. ***Delivery of documents for Masters' hearings*** **1A–219**
 (a) Deliver bundles and skeletons (if required) to Masters' Appointments, Room TM7.09, 2 clear working days (not more than 7) before the hearing.
 (b) Mark clearly "for hearing on ............*(date)* before Master ............
 (c) Insert a reading list and estimate of reading time if appropriate.
 (d) Bundles may be presented in ring binders or lever arch files, or as appropriate.
 (e) Documents for Masters' hearings should not be taken direct to the Master's room unless in any particular case the Master has directed otherwise.
 (f) Documents required for Masters' hearings should never be taken to (i) the Registry (Room TM5.04); (ii) the Chancery Judges' Listing Office (Room WG 4) or (iii) the RCJ Post Room)—if they are they may well not reach the Master in time.

**Note:**

Documents required for hearings before a Chancery judge must not be delivered to

Chancery Chambers. They must be delivered to the Chancery Judges' Listing Office (Room WG 4).

2. ***Filing of documents***

(a) Take or send documents required to be filed (i.e. placed on the Court file, either under the CPR or under an Order of the Court (e.g. statements of case, defences, allocation questionnaires, some witness statements)) to the Chancery Registry, Room TM5.04 for filing.

(b) But documents (e.g. witness statements, exhibits) required to be filed which are needed for a Masters' hearing within 10 working days must be delivered for filing to Masters' Appointments, Room 7.09 not the Registry.

(c) If bulky, use treasury tags, not files or ring binders.

## APPENDIX 9

## GUIDELINES ON WITNESS STATEMENTS

**1A–220** 1. The function of a witness statement is to set out in writing the evidence in chief of the maker of the statement. Accordingly witness statements should, so far as possible, be expressed in the witness's own words. This guideline applies unless the perception or recollection of the witness of the events in question is not in issue.

2. Witness statements should be as concise as the circumstances of the case allow. They should be written in consecutively numbered paragraphs. They should present the evidence in an orderly and readily comprehensible manner. They must be signed by the witness, and contain a statement that he or she believes that the facts stated in his or her witness statement are true. They must indicate which of the statements made are made from the witness' own knowledge and which are made on information and belief, giving the source of the information or basis for the belief.

3. Inadmissible material should not be included. Irrelevant material should likewise not be included.

4. Any party on whom a witness statement is served who objects to the relevance or admissibility of material contained in a witness statement should notify the other party of his or her objection within 28 days after service of the witness statement in question and the parties concerned should attempt to resolve the matter as soon as possible. If it is not possible to resolve the matter, the party who objects should make an appropriate application, normally at the PTR, if there is one, or otherwise at trial.

5. It is incumbent on solicitors and counsel not to allow the costs of preparation of witness statements to be unnecessarily increased by over-elaboration of the statements. Any unnecessary elaboration may be the subject of a special order as to costs.

6. Witness statements must contain the truth, the whole truth and nothing but the truth on the issues covered. Great care must be taken in the preparation of witness statements. No pressure of any kind should be placed on a witness to give other than a true and complete account of his or her evidence. It is improper to serve a witness statement which is known to be false or which the maker does not in all respects actually believe to be true. In addition, a professional adviser may be under an obligation to check where practicable the truth of facts stated in a witness statement if he or she is put on enquiry as to their truth. If a party discovers that a witness statement which he or she has served is incorrect he or she must inform the other parties immediately.

7. A witness statement should simply cover those issues, but only those issues, on which the party serving the statement wishes that witness to give evidence in chief. Thus it is not, for example, the function of a witness statement to provide a commentary on the documents in the trial bundle, nor to set out quotations from such documents, nor to engage in matters of argument. Witness statements should not deal with other matters merely because they may arise in the course of the trial.

8. Witness statements very often refer to documents. If there could be any doubt as to what document is being referred to, or if the document has not previously been made available on disclosure, it may be helpful for the document to be exhibited to the witness statement. If, to assist reference to the documents, the documents referred to are exhibited to the witness statement, they should nevertheless not be included in trial bundles in that form: see Appendix 6, paragraph 4. If (as is normally preferable) the documents referred to in the witness statement are not exhibited, care should be taken in identifying them, for example by reference to the lists of documents exchanged on disclosure. In preparation for trial, it will be necessary to insert cross-references to the trial bundles so as to identify the documents: see Appendix 6, paragraph 24.

9. If a witness is not sufficiently fluent in English to give his or her evidence in English, the witness statement should be in the witness' own language and a translation provided. If a witness is not fluent in English but can make himself or herself understood in broken English and can understand written English, the statement need not be in his or her own words provided that these matters are indicated in the statement itself. It must however be written so as to express as accurately as possible the substance of his or her evidence.

## APPENDIX 10

## A GUIDE FOR RECEIVERS IN THE CHANCERY DIVISION

1. This guide sets out brief notes on the procedure to be followed after an order has been made appointing a receiver in the Chancery Division. The procedure is now governed by CPR Part 69 and its PD. **1A–221**

2. Appendix C contains notes on the main powers and duties of a receiver and a copy should be passed to the receiver.

### Action on the Appointment of a Receiver (Rule 69.6; PD 6&8)

3. Where an order has been made appointing a receiver, it is generally necessary to apply for directions, by application notice under Part 23. Part 69 PD 6 lists the matters on which directions will usually be given. A draft order should normally be submitted with the Application Notice. **1A–222**

4. The application for directions should normally be made immediately after the making of the order appointing the receiver, especially where security has to be given within a limited time (see below). Only if the order appointing the receiver appoints him or her by name and gives full directions as to accounts and security will an application for directions not be necessary.

5. The receiver may of course apply to the Master at any time for other directions as necessary. Where the directions are unlikely to be contentious or important to the parties this may be done by letter (see Part 69 PD 8).

### Giving Security (Rule 69.5; PD 7)

6. The order appointing a receiver will normally include directions in relation to security, and will specify the date by which security is to be given. It is therefore important to obtain an early date for the directions hearing. If security is not completed within the time specified the receivership may be terminated and it will then be necessary for an application to be made to renew it. To avoid this, if it seems likely that security will not be given in time an application should be made at the directions hearing for an extension of time to give security. **1A–223**

7. When the amount of the security has been settled, a guarantee in Form PF 30 CH (Appendix A) must (unless the receiver is a licensed insolvency practitioner covered by bond, which has been extended to cover the appointment) be prepared and entered into with one of the four main clearing banks or the insurance company listed in Appendix B.

8. The guarantee must then be engrossed and executed, i.e. signed by the receiver and signed and sealed by the bank or insurance company. It should then be lodged in Chancery Chambers, Room TM7.09, Royal Courts of Justice, Strand London WC2A 2LL. It will then be signed by the Master and endorsed with a certificate of completion of security and placed on the court file. Where security is given by bond, written evidence of the extended bond and the sufficiency of its cover must be filed in Room 7.09 in accordance with the requirements of Part 69 PD 7.3(1).

9. If the amount of the security given is subsequently increased or decreased, an endorsement is made to the original guarantee.

**Receiver's Remuneration (Rule 69.7; PD9)**

1A–224 10. A receiver may only charge for his services if the court permits it and specifies the basis on which the receiver is to be remunerated. Unless the court directs the remuneration to be fixed by reference to some fixed scale, or percentage of rents collected, it will determine the amount in accordance with the criteria set out in rule 69.7(4).

**Receiver's Accounts (Rule 69.8; PD 10)**

1A–225 11. If directions as to the receiver's accounts have not been given in the order appointing the receiver, such directions must be obtained at the directions hearing.

12. Normally accounts are prepared half-yearly and must be delivered within a month of the end of the accounting period.

13. Generally accounts need only be presented to the court if any party receiving them serves notice on the receiver, under rule 69.8(3), that he objects to any item in the accounts.

**Discharge of Receiver and Cancellation of Security (Rule 69.10 & 11)**

1A–226 14. When a receiver has completed his duties, the receiver or any party should apply for an order discharging the receiver and cancelling the security.

15. When an order for cancellation of a receiver's security has been made, any guarantee and the duplicate order appointing the receiver are endorsed to that effect.

16. The endorsed guarantee and duplicate order should then be taken to the bank or insurance company by the solicitors for cancellation and return of any outstanding premium.

Appendix A *to Guide for Receivers*

**Guarantee for receiver's acts and defaults**[1]

IN THE HIGH COURT OF JUSTICE

CHANCERY DIVISION

[TITLE]

I, ..(*Name*). of ..(*address*), the Receiver [and manager] appointed by Order dated..(*date*) (*or* proposed to be appointed) in this claim hereby undertake to the Court duly to account for all money and property received by me as such Receiver [and manager] at such times and in such manner in all respects as the Court directs.

[1] Adapted from Form PF 30CH.

And we ..(*name*(s) *of surety or sureties*) hereby [jointly and severally[1]] undertake with the Court and guarantee to be answerable for any default by .....(*name*) as such Receiver [and manager] and upon such default to pay to any person or persons or otherwise as the Court directs any sum or sums not exceeding £ ..in total that may from time to time be certified by [a Master of the Supreme Court][a District Judge] to be due from .......(*name*) as Receiver [and manager] and we submit to the jurisdiction of the Court in this action to determine any claim made under this undertaking.

DATED this ..........................day of ..........................20.........

Signed sealed and delivered by the above named ................in the presence of

or

The Common Seal of ..................was hereunto affixed in the presence of:—

(*Signature of receiver*)

(*Seal of surety with appropriate signature or signatures*)

Appendix B **to Guide for Receivers**

**Guarantees for Personal Applicants**

The insurance company detailed below is willing to act as surety

| Name of company | Address to be shown on and for correspondence |
|---|---|
| Zurich GSG Limited | Hawthorn Hall<br>Hall Road<br>Wilmslow<br>Cheshire SK9 5BZ |

Appendix C ***to Guide for Receivers***

**The Powers and Duties of a Receiver**

1. The main function of a receiver appointed by the court is to protect the assets received by him pending the court proceedings. The following notes set out some of the more important powers and duties a receiver should be aware of.
2. A receiver must obtain the permission of the court (which may be contained in the order appointing him) before he can:
   (a) bring, defend or compromise legal proceedings
   (b) pay a debt (other than in a partnership claim)
   (c) compromise a claim
   (d) purchase or sell assets other than in the normal course of business
   (e) grant obtain or surrender a lease or purchase or sell real property (even in the course of managing a business); since the appointment of a receiver is an equitable remedy it does not confer on him any title to land: unless the legal owner is prepared to join in the conveyance or lease the receiver would in any case have to obtain a vesting order under section 47 or section 50 of the Trustee Act 1925.
   (f) borrow money
   (g) carry on or close down or sell a business
   (h) employ additional staff in the course of managing a business
   (i) carry out repairs to property costing more than £1000 in any one accounting year
3. Receivers should ensure that they have insurance (if any) transferred into their own names and should consider the adequacy of the insurance cover.

[1] Omit these words in the case of a guarantee or other company.

***Paragraph numbers marked with a "+" can be found online and on CD.***

4. Receivers are not entitled to instruct their own solicitors without the express permission of the court.
5. Receivers should seek the court's directions on any question of doubt which arises in the course of the receivership.
6. Receivers should bear in mind that their function as receiver does not include the preparation of partnership accounts and they cannot include fees for such work in their remuneration as receiver.
7. Unless expressly authorised by the court (whether in the Order appointing him or otherwise) the receiver must not part with assets in his hands, whether to the person appointing him or otherwise. If he has completed his functions as receiver before the disputes between the parties have been resolved in the proceedings, the receiver should normally apply to be discharged on lodging into court the money he is holding.

## APPENDIX 11

## LLOYD'S NAMES' ESTATE APPLICATIONS: FORMS

### FORM OF WITNESS STATEMENT

**1A–227** **[Heading as in claim form]**

1. We are the personal representatives of the estate of the above-named Deceased ("the Deceased") who died on [ ]. We obtained [a grant of probate][letters of administration] out of the [ ] Registry on [ ] and a copy of the grant [and the Deceased's will dated [ ]] is now produced and shown to us marked " . 1". We make this witness statement in support of our application for permission to distribute the Deceased's estate [and to administer the will trusts of which we will be the Trustees following administration.]. This witness statement contains facts and matters which, unless otherwise stated, are within our own knowledge obtained in acting in the administration of the estate. We believe them to be true.

2. The Deceased was before his death an underwriting member of Lloyd's of London whose underwriting activities are treated as having ceased on [ ]. The estate was sworn for probate purposes at £[ ]. We are now in a position to complete the administration of the estate and to distribute it to the beneficiaries but we do not wish to do so [or to constitute the will trusts] without the authority of the Court because of the existence of possible contingent claims arising out of the Deceased's underwriting liabilities for which we might be liable.

3. The position concerning the Deceased's Lloyd's liabilities is as follows:

[3.1 The Deceased's liabilities in respect of the years of account 1992 and earlier were reinsured into Equitas as part of the Lloyd's settlement. There is now produced and shown to us marked " .2" a copy of the certificate or statement of reinsurance into Equitas].

3.2 [The syndicates in which the Deceased participated in the years of account 1993 and later have [closed by reinsurance in the usual way] [are the subject of an Estate Protection Plan issued to the Deceased by Centrewrite Limited][are protected by an EXEAT policy obtained by the Claimants from Centrewrite Limited].

4. There is now produced and shown to us marked " .3" a copy of a letter dated [ ] from the estate's Lloyd's agents confirming that [all] the syndicates have been reinsured to close [with the exception of [ ] which syndicate is protected by [the Estate Protection Plan][the EXEAT policy]] and confirming that in the case of failure of a reinsuring syndicate to honour its obligations, the primary liability to a creditor will fall on Lloyd's Central Fund. [A copy of the [Estate Protection Plan and Annual Certificate] [EXEAT policy] is now produced and shown to us marked " .4".]

5. The Claimants believe that the interests of any Lloyd's claimant are reasonably

secured by virtue of the fact that all the Lloyd's syndicates in which the Deceased participated have either been closed ultimately by reinsurance to close (in respect of any open years prior to 1992 into the Equitas group) or, in respect of subsequent years [have all closed by reinsurance] [are protected by the Estate Protection Plan][are protected by the EXEAT policy.] Equitas remains licensed to conduct insurance business and there is presently no reason to doubt its solvency. A copy of the latest report and accounts of Equitas Holdings Limited is now produced and shown to us marked " .5". [The [Estate Protection Plan] [EXEAT policy] is provided by Centrewrite Limited which is a wholly-owned subsidiary of Lloyd's and the beneficiary of an undertaking by Lloyd's to maintain its solvency. We have no reason to doubt the solvency of Centrewrite. A copy of the latest report and accounts of Centrewrite Limited is now produced and shown to us marked " . 6".]

6. As appears from the schedule now produced and shown to us marked " .7" in which we summarise the assets and liabilities of the estate, we have paid all the debts of the Deceased known to us (apart from the costs and expenses associated with the final administration of the estate) and we have also advertised for and dealt with all claimants in accordance with s.27 of the Trustee Act 1925 [or if not explain why].

7. We know of no special reason or circumstance which might give rise to doubt whether the provision described above can reasonably be regarded as adequate provision for potential claims against the estate and we ask for permission to distribute accordingly.

## FORM OF ORDER

**[Heading as in claim form]**

ON THE APPLICATION of the Claimants by Part 8 Claim Form dated [ ] **1A–228**
UPON READING the documents recorded on the Court file as having been read
IT IS ORDERED THAT:

1. the Claimants as [the personal representatives of the estate ("the Estate") of the above named deceased ("the Deceased")] [and] [the trustees of the trusts of the Deceased's will dated [ ]("the Will")] have permission to [distribute the Estate] [and] [administer the trusts of the Will and distribute capital and income in accordance with such trusts] without making any retention or further provision in respect of any contract of insurance or reinsurance underwritten by the Deceased in the course of his business as an underwriting member of Lloyd's of London
2. the costs of the Claimants of this application [either in the agreed sum of £ ] [or summarily assessed in the sum of £ [assessed in the sum of £..] (with permission to [the residuary beneficiaries][name beneficiaries] to apply within 14 days after service of this order on them for the variation or discharge of this summary assessment] [or subject to detailed assessment on the indemnity basis if not agreed by or on behalf of [the residuary beneficiaries] name beneficiaries]] be raised and paid or retained out of the Estate in due course of administration.

## APPENDIX 12

## PRACTICE NOTE: REMUNERATION OF JUDICIAL TRUSTEES

1. When dealing with the assignment of remuneration to a judicial trustee under section 1(5) of the Judicial Trustees Act 1896 and rule 11 of the Judicial Trustee Rules 1983 the court will consider directions as to remuneration based on the common form of order set out below, subject to such modifications as may be required in any particular case. **1A–229**

2. In general the court when considering reasonable remuneration for the purposes of rule 11(1)(a) will need to be satisfied as to the basis upon which the remuneration is claimed, that it is justified and that the amount is reasonable and proportionate

and within the limit of 15% of the capital value of the trust property specified in the rule.

3. The court may, before determining the amount of remuneration, require the judicial trustee to provide further information, alternatively refer the matter to a costs judge for him to assess remuneration.

4. When an application is made to the court for the appointment of a judicial trustee or when the court gives directions under rule 8 practitioners should produce to the court a draft order which should take account of the common form of order

**Draft Paragraphs of Order**

1A-230 [IT IS ORDERED]

...that the remuneration of the Judicial Trustee shall be in such amount as may be approved from time to time by this court upon application for payment on examination of his accounts

...that the Judicial Trustees accounts shall be endorsed by him with a certificate of the approximate capital value of the trust property at the commencement of the year of account

... that every application for payment by the Judicial Trustee shall be in the form of a letter to the court (with a copy to the beneficiaries) which shall (a) set out the basis of the claim to remuneration, the scales or rates of any professional charges, the work done and time spent, any information concerning the complexity of the trusteeship that may be relied on and any other matters which the court shall be invited by the Judicial Trustee to take into account and (b) certify that he considers that the claim for remuneration is reasonable and proportionate

J. Winegarten
Chief Chancery Master
With the authority of the Vice-Chancellor

1st July 2003

## APPENDIX 13

## TRANSFER OF CASES TO CHANCERY TRIAL CENTRES

1A-231 1. **Matters that ought normally to be transferred to a Chancery trial centre. Careful consideration should be given to whether the case should be transferred to a District Registry or a county court or whether arrangements should simply be made for the case to be heard in a different trial centre.**

Proceedings under the Companies Acts;

Other disputes among company shareholders;

Corporate insolvency proceedings (except for winding up petitions by creditors);

Personal insolvency proceedings (except for bankruptcy petitions, interim orders and applications to set aside statutory demands);

Directors' disqualification proceedings (but note that the transferee court must have jurisdiction under the Company Directors Disqualification Act 1986);

Claims within CPR Part 56 (Landlord and Tenant Claims and Miscellaneous Provisions about Land) other than applications under section 24 or section 38(4) of the Landlord and Tenant Act 1954 or under the Access to Neighbouring Land Act 1992;

Probate claims, or claims for the rectification of wills, substitution and removal of personal representatives within CPR Part 57 (probate claims ought not to be started outside a Chancery county court in any event);

Proceedings relating to the estate of a deceased person, to trusts or to charities within CPR Part 64;

Proceedings under section 14 of the Trusts of Land and Appointment of Trustees Act 1996 (though a simple case of a joint property dispute, where there is little or no dispute as to the beneficial shares, may best be dealt with at the home county court);

Proceedings relating to intellectual property, including passing-off;

Proceedings relating to land, easements, covenants or contracts relating to land where an injunction, specific performance or declaration is sought or where there are substantial or complex issues (though not all injunction cases are appropriate for transfer, e.g. housing disrepair cases and many neighbour disputes);

Proceedings for breach of a restrictive covenant, breach of trust or breach of fiduciary duty where an injunction is sought or where there are substantial or complex issues;

Claims for rescission on the grounds of undue influence or other equitable grounds, or for rectification of a document;

Claims relating to membership of, exclusion from, or dissolution of, a club or other unincorporated association;

Other claims—for instance for professional negligence or for breach of contract—which involve issues of trust, company, intellectual property, land or conveyancing law or procedure;

Claims for the dissolution of partnerships or the taking of partnership accounts;

Matters other than those listed above, where an account is one of the remedies sought and the issues likely to arise on the account are substantial or complex.

2. **Matters which ought not normally to be transferred**

Proceedings relating to residential tenancies;

Proceedings relating to residential mortgages (unless a serious issue arises, for example, as to the occupation rights of a third party and as to whether the mortgagee's rights prevail over those of such a third party);

Claims to enforce a charging order;

Applications under section 24 of the Landlord and Tenant Act 1954;

Applications under section 38(4) of the Landlord and Tenant Act 1954;

Applications under the Access to Neighbouring Land Act 1992;

Proceedings under the Inheritance (Provision for Family and Dependants) Act 1975.

## APPENDIX 14

## GUIDELINES ON DRAFTING ORDERS

### Title and Parties

In the heading to the title the name and judicial title of the Judge should appear followed by the date of the Order immediately below the words "Chancery Division". If the Judge sat in private the words "sitting in private" should be added after the Judge's name. **1A–232**

Normally all the parties should be listed. Apart from the exceptions set out in Paragraph 2.3 of the Chancery Guide there is no need to recite Statutes, deeds etc in the Title.

### Recitals

The Order should begin with a recital as to how the matter got before the Court (e.g. Upon the Application of ..................by Notice dated ..................) **1A–233**

***Paragraph numbers marked with a "+" can be found online and on CD.***

There should be a recital as to who the Court heard.

There may be a recital that the Court "read the written evidence filed". The words "And upon reading the evidence recorded on the Court File as having been read" are no longer relevant since nothing is now recorded on the Court File as having been read. On an Application without notice there should be a recital of the evidence before the Court—this would usually be in a Schedule.

**Consent orders**

1A-234 If the order is an order made by consent it must bear the words "By consent".

**Order**

1A-235 The paragraphs should be consecutively numbered.

If a Minute of Order directs a Payment into or out of Court after the direction the words "as directed in the attached Payment/Lodgment Schedule" should appear. It would be as well to attach a note drawing attention to this. In such a Case a Payment or Lodgment Schedule should be drawn by the Associate.

If a party applied for permission to appeal at the hearing the order must state—

(a) whether or not the judgment or order is final;

(b) whether an appeal lies from the judgment or order and, if so, to which appeal court;

(c) whether the court gave permission to appeal; and

(d) if not, the appropriate appeal court to which any further application for permission to appeal may be made.

If the Applicant wishes to serve the Order, it would be helpful for a clause to be included in the Order to that effect. This will cut out the need to secure an undertaking to serve when the Order is collected after it is entered.

**Backsheet**

1A-236 All Orders should have backsheets which should—

- Show the name of the Judge and date of the Order immediately below the words Chancery Division as in the title.
- Give the Claim Number

There is no need to recite all parties on the backsheet. It suffices to give the name of the First Claimant and the First Defendant

The backsheet should record how the Order is to be served. If it is intended that the Court should serve the Order the words "The Court sent sealed copies of this Order to" should appear under the word Order and the names, addresses (including DX address) and references of the Solicitors or litigants in person to whom it is to be sent given. If it is intended that one of the parties should serve then under the word Order the words "The Court sent this Order and sealed copies for service to" followed by the name and address etc of the party who is to effect service should appear.

**Further guidance**

1A-237 Further guidance is contained in PD 40B.

## APPENDIX 15

## CHANCERY BUSINESS AT CENTRAL LONDON CIVIL JUSTICE CENTRE

1A-238 February 2009

**Chancery Business Contact Details – at a glance**

| | |
|---|---|
| Addresses | (1) For County Court Offices, District Judges and all fee remittances: (NB This is the Court's official postal address)<br>**13-14 Park Crescent London W1B 1HT**<br>(2) For Trial Centre, Circuit Judges, and Chancery Section office:<br>**26 Park Crescent London W1N 4HT** |
| DX | **97325 Regents Park 2** |

***Paragraph numbers marked with a "+" can be found online and on CD.***

| | |
|---|---|
| FAX | **08703 305717** (All general Chancery List and Trial Centre matters)<br>020 7917 5014 (ONLY for District Judge hearings at 13-14 Park Crescent)<br>020 7917 7940 (ONLY for skeleton arguments for hearings at 26 Park Crescent) |
| TEL | **020 7917 7821** or<br>**020 7917 7889** Chancery Section (for all general matters)<br>020 7917 7938 (ONLY for transcripts of Trial Centre hearings)<br>020 7917 5107 (ONLY for transcripts of DJ hearings) |
| E-MAIL | chance.clerk@hmcourts-service.gsi.uk (All general enquiries and communications)<br>clondctyla@hmcourts-service.gsi.gov.uk (ONLY for listing appointments, as directed)<br>CentralLondonCJSKEL@hmcourts-service.gsi.gov.uk (ONLY for skeleton arguments for Circuit Judge hearings) |
| Contacts | Clerk to HH Judge Hazel Marshall QC (Senior Chancery Judge)<br>**Mr Pio Fernandes**<br>Pio.Fernandes@hmcourts-service.gsi.gov.uk<br>Clerk to HH Judge Marc Dight (Second Senior Chancery Judge)<br>**Mrs Birgit Bock**<br>Birgit.Bock@hmcourts-service.gsi.gov.uk<br>Chancery Section Manager<br>**Mr Mark Peacock**<br>Trial Centre Office Manager<br>**Miss Michelle Bayley** |

### Introduction

The High Court transfers an increasing number of Chancery cases to the Central London Civil Justice Centre ("CLCJC") at 26 Park Crescent, London W1. Two specialist Chancery Senior Circuit Judges have been appointed to maintain CLCJC as a centre for Chancery business. CLCJC therefore handles not only Chancery cases commenced in the County Court, but also cases commenced in the High Court but regarded as suitable for conduct at CLCJC, either by agreement of the parties (see s 23 County Courts Act 1984) or by the High Court, which may decide to transfer the matter to CLCJC on its own initiative under Section 40(2) of that Act. **1A–239**

In addition, any significant Chancery case in a County Court in the London area will be transferred to CLCJC Chancery List for trial, and any lengthy or complex cases from any County Court on the South Eastern Circuit or elsewhere may also be transferred. Litigants may wish to consider commencing such cases at CLCJC in the first place.

Suitable High Court cases may also be tried by one of the specialist Chancery Senior Circuit Judges sitting at CLCJC as a High Court judge under s. 9 Senior Courts Act 1981.

### 1. The Chancery List at Central London

1.1 The business of the Chancery List at CLCJC now comprises business from the three sources mentioned above ie,: **1A–240**

1.1.1 cases transferred from the Chancery Division of the High Court; cases are often transferred at a very early stage.

1.1.2 cases transferred from other county courts on the SE Circuit, because of complexity or length (an estimated trial of two days or more); and

1.1.3 Chancery claims issued in the Central London County Court.

1.2 All business of the Chancery List is identified by a unique case number currently starting "CHY".

1.3 A list of the kinds of case which are suitable for the Chancery List appears at Annex A. The following should be noted.

1.3.1 Since 2001 the court has had original jurisdiction in contentious probate matters pursuant to CPR Part 57.2.

1.3.2 The court has only limited original jurisdiction in matters relating to companies. However where CLCJC has no original jurisdiction, appropriate

***Paragraph numbers marked with a "+" can be found online and on CD.***

cases can, by arrangement, be directed by the High Court to be heard at CLCJC by one of the Specialist Chancery Judges sitting as a High Court Judge, authorised under s 9 of the Senior Courts Act 1981.

1.3.3 The court's original jurisdiction in trust, equity and partnership matters is currently technically limited to £30,000 under the County Courts Act 1984. However it is commonplace for higher value cases to be transferred to CLCJC from the High Court, or for the parties to agree to confer extended jurisdiction (see Paragraph 1.5 below).

1.4 Claims may be issued in the Chancery List if the Claimant thinks it appropriate. The claim form must be clearly marked "Chancery Business". If it later appears that the case is unsuitable for the Chancery List it will be transferred back to the General List by a judge. Otherwise, cases from the above sources may be identified as suitable for the Chancery List at any stage. At this point they will be transferred into the Chancery List, (subject to the approval of a Chancery judge if the transfer order is not made by a specialist Chancery judge), and allocated a "CHY" number.

1.5 It is open to parties to increase the court's jurisdiction beyond the current limits under the County Courts Act 1984 by filing a signed joint memorandum of consent pursuant to s 23 of the Act. This can be a useful way of obtaining an earlier hearing in an urgent case which is suitable for trial by a specialist Circuit Judge.

**2. The Court House**

**1A–241** 2.1 CLCJC is located in two buildings in Park Crescent, London W1.

2.2 The Trial Centre is at 26 Park Crescent London W1N 4HT, at the western end of Park Crescent, (ie nearest to the London Clinic and Harley Street). Trials and applications before Circuit Judges take place here.

2.3 The County Court Offices and the District Judges' Chambers, are on the eastern side of Park Crescent, at 13–14 Park Crescent. London W1B 1HT (which is the court's official postal address). Applications and hearings before District Judges may be heard either here, or at 26 Park Crescent (see Paragraph 3.6 below).

2.4 The nearest Underground stations are Regents Park (on the Bakerloo Line: 2 minutes) and Great Portland Street (on the Metropolitan, Hammersmith and City, and Circle Lines: 5 minutes). Warren Street (Northern Line: 10 minutes) and Baker Street (Jubilee line:10 minutes) are also within walking distance.

**3. The Judiciary**

**1A–242** 3.1 The senior specialist Chancery Circuit Judge is Her Honour Judge Hazel Marshall QC, who is also authorised to sit as a Deputy Judge of the High Court under s 9 of the Senior Courts Act 1981. Any communications for her attention should be addressed to her clerk:

Mr Pio Fernandes
Clerk to the Senior Chancery Judge
E-Mail: Pio.Fernandes@hmcourts-service.gsi.gov.uk.

3.2 The second senior specialist Chancery Circuit Judge is His Honour Judge Marc Dight, who is similarly authorised in respect of High Court business. His clerk is Mrs Birgit Bock (Birgit.Bock@hmcourts-service.gsi.gov.uk).

3.3 Four other resident and visiting Circuit Judges are generally authorised to hear any Chancery List cases ("Category 2" business). These are HH Judge Peter Cowell, HH Judge Edward Bailey, HH Judge Robert Wakefield, and HH Judge Daniel Serota QC.

3.4 In addition there is a panel of Recorders drawn from the Chancery Bar and approved by the Chancellor of the High Court. The Recorders are asked to sit from time to time if the Chancery Circuit Judges are not available, or to relieve pressure on the list. References in this Guide to a "Circuit Judge" include a Recorder unless the context suggests otherwise.

3.5 There are two designated specialist Chancery District Judges: District Judge Margaret Langley and District Judge Barry Lightman. They are based at 13–14 Park Crescent. In addition, District Judge Ruth Fine is authorised to deal with Chancery cases if the state of the lists requires.

3.6 The Chancery District Judges normally deal with Chancery applications and case management in the District Judges' Chancery List, which is heard on Fridays at 13–14 Park Crescent. However, hearings may take place at other times, or at 26 Park Crescent, according to the state of the list. Litigants should always check the location on the court hearing list. Appointments before Chancery District Judges are made through the Chancery Section in the same way as appointments before Chancery Circuit Judges.

3.7 It is the policy of the court to ensure that all Chancery List matters are dealt with by a judge of suitable experience. Although not Chancery specialists, a number of the Resident Judges at the court have considerable experience in some Chancery areas (e.g. landlord and tenant matters). If, at case management, the Senior Chancery Judge considers that because of its nature, a particular case could be efficiently heard by any such other Resident Judge, the case will be marked accordingly ("Category 3" business), and may subsequently be listed before either a Chancery Judge or any other Judge so nominated.

3.8 A party who considers it appropriate, on the grounds of the particular nature, importance or value of the case, may apply to the Senior Chancery Judge (through her clerk) for the case to be reserved to the Senior Chancery Judges' List ("Category 1" business).

#### 4. The Chancery Section and communicating with the Court

4.1 The Chancery List is administered by the Chancery and Specialist Section. Their offices are on the fourth floor at 26 Park Crescent. Queries and applications can be presented in person at the reception desk on the fourth floor, so long as they do **not** involve the payment of fees (but note Paragraph 6.6 below with regard to obtaining expedition.) **1A–243**

4.2 All enquiries and correspondence concerned with the Chancery List should be addressed by post to the postal address of the court:—

THE CHANCERY SECTION
Central London Civil Justice Centre
13-14 Park Crescent
London
W1B 1HT

or sent through the DX system to
DX 97325 Regents Park 2

4.3 The following numbers are dedicated numbers for use of the Chancery List business:

| | | | |
|---|---|---|---|
| Tel: | 020 7917 7821 | Fax: | 08703 305 717 |
| | 020 7917 7889 | | |
| | E-mail: chance.clerk@hmcourts-service.gsi.gov.uk | | |

Please note the special fax number. These contact details go directly to Chancery Section personnel. **Chancery List communications should not be sent to any other numbers.**

4.4 The Chancery Section Manager is **Mr Mark Peacock**.

Communications should be addressed to THE CHANCERY SECTION MANAGER, at the above address.

4.5 For administrative reasons, all post to CLCJC is received at 13–14 Park Crescent. After sorting, Chancery List post is transferred to the Chancery Section Office at 26 Park Crescent.

4.6 All applications requiring a fee to be paid **must** be initiated at 13–14 Park Crescent, whether made by post or in person. After fee processing, Chancery applications are then transferred to the Chancery Section Office, as soon as possible.

4.7 To assist Chancery Section staff to deal correctly and quickly with letters and applications, it is important that **the case's "CHY" number, names of the parties and the date of the next fixed hearing are stated prominently on the first page of the letter or application**. If the matter is regarded as urgent this may also be stated: see further Paragraph 6.4 below.

4.8 Communications to the court may be made, and **short** documents (12 pages maximum and not involving payment of fees) may be filed, with the Chancery Section by email to the email address given above. The subject line **must** include the CHY number, the parties' names (abbreviated if necessary), the nature of the document, and the date and time of any forthcoming hearing (see also general guidance in CPR PD 5B supplemental to Rule 5.5).

4.9 Faxed documents (other than skeleton arguments: see (Paragraph 9.3 below) for any CHY list hearings taking place at 26 Park Crescent must be faxed to **08703 305 717** to ensure that they reach the Judges' hearing rooms in time.

Faxed Documents for hearings at 13/14 Park Crescent must be faxed to 0207 917 5014.

**It is likely that your document will not reach the Judge in time if faxed to the wrong number**.

### 5. Case management

1A–244 5.1 Subject to the protocols set out in this Guide and to any specific requirements of the Civil Procedure Rules, the Chancery List at CLCJC will follow the practice set out in the Chancery Guide (see Volume II of the White Book).

5.2 When a case is transferred to Central London Chancery List from either a county court or the High Court, directions will usually be given at the transferring court to continue progress towards trial during the transfer period. However, the transferring court cannot make any order fixing a trial date or window at CLCJC. When the file is received at CLCJC, it will be immediately placed before one of the senior Chancery Judges, who will review the existing case management directions (if any), and either give appropriate directions on paper for the further conduct of the matter (which may include giving a listing appointment for trial) or direct an immediate case management conference.

5.3 Case management hearings before a District Judge will usually be held on Fridays, or by telephone under CPR Pt 23. Case management hearings and applications before a Circuit Judge will usually also be heard on Fridays at 10 a.m. or 2 pm, at 26 Park Crescent, or by telephone under CPR Pt 23.

5.4 The judge may have a telephone list in the morning (at 10 am) or the afternoon (at 2 pm) but not both. Telephone appointments are dealt with strictly by time allocated.

A Note setting out the procedure for arranging a telephone hearing will, where applicable, be attached to the Notice of Hearing issued by the Court. The parties and their advisers should refer to this.

5.5 Matters in the list for attended hearings are dealt with in a convenient order, according to urgency and time estimate.

5.6 Appeals from a Chancery District Judge will normally be listed before one of the specialist Chancery Circuit Judges as part of the normal weekday Chancery List. If a trial is imminent, appropriate time arrangements will be made.

5.7 It is essential that the parties provide accurate time estimates for applications and case management conferences. If hearings overrun their allocated time, telephone hearings will, and attended hearings may, be adjourned, with possible sanctions in costs.

5.8 Parties will usually be asked to provide an agreed minute of case management directions ordered at a hearing, and they can often avoid the need for a hearing by drafting or agreeing proposed directions beforehand. To assist litigants, a form of standard model directions frequently given in CHY cases (Form MT3(CHY) ) is at Annex B. Attention is draw in particular to the procedure for fixing trial dates—see paragraph 7.2 below.

### 6. Applications

*Normal business*

6.1 Chancery applications before Circuit Judges are normally heard with case management business, which is listed every Friday. In exceptional cases of urgency (for example an urgent injunction) an appointment may be given for another day and time. Longer hearings (2 hours or more) may be listed in the normal daily trial lists. **1A–245**

6.2 Any routine application in a CHY case should be made to the Court Office at 13–14 Park Crescent by leaving or posting copies of the Application Notice (one more than the number of parties involved), and the required fee. After issue by the office, the application will be delivered to the Chancery Section, either on the same day or the following morning, and will be dealt with as follows (subject to Paragraphs 6.4 and 6.5) below:

- 6.2.1 Where a hearing is requested, the Chancery Section clerk will list it for hearing before a judge of the appropriate level (Circuit or District) on the first convenient Friday (or other listing day) at least two weeks after the day when the application is processed. The court will notify the parties of the date and time of the appointment.
- 6.2.2 Where the applicant requests that the application be dealt with without a hearing, the Application Notice will be placed before a judge of the appropriate level. If the judge is of the view that a hearing is required, he or she will direct a hearing within an appropriate timescale. The Chancery Section clerk will then list the matter and notify the parties of the date and time.
- 6.2.3 If the judge deals with the matter on paper, he or she will make such order as is considered appropriate in the circumstances. This will not necessarily be the order requested in the application. The court will then notify the parties of the application and of the order which has been made. Any such order will always contain a provision that any party may apply to the court, as provided in the order (usually within 7 days) to have the order set aside or varied.

6.3 The Chancery Section will endeavour to deal with Chancery Application Notices as set out above, within five working days of their receipt.

*Urgent business*

Certified urgent business

6.4 Any party making an application which is considered urgent may certify it "**URGENT**" and give brief reasons in a covering letter. The Chancery Section clerk will then give the application such priority as it appears to warrant, and is likely to **1A–246** put it before a Circuit Judge immediately for directions. Parties should note that any abuse of the "urgent" certification may have the result that costs will be disallowed.

Applications within four weeks of trial

6.5 Any application received by the Chancery Section within four weeks before the date fixed for trial will automatically be treated as urgent business. Regardless of the nature of the application or the level of judge which may be suggested by the applicant, the application will be placed immediately before a Circuit Judge for directions. The Judge will then make such order as is considered appropriate to the circumstances.

Voluntary expedited procedure

6.6 Any party wishing to obtain an early appointment for the hearing of an application may use the following procedure.

6.6.1 The applicant should take the Application Notice (and copies) and fee, in person to the Court Office at 13–14 Park Crescent for immediate issue, wait whilst the issue is processed and receive back the issued Application Notice and copies.

6.6.2 The issued Application Notice should then be taken in person to the Chancery Section Office on the fourth floor of 26 Park Crescent.

6.6.3 The Chancery Section clerk will then immediately list the application for hearing whilst the applicant waits, and will list it for hearing on the immediately following Friday if requested by the applicant. Such applications will be listed before a Circuit Judge.

6.6.4 The applicant will then be responsible for service of notice of the appointment on the responding party or parties.

When using this procedure, applicants are reminded that **at least three clear days' notice** to any other party (ie before close of business on Monday) are required if an application is to be heard "with notice" on a Friday. If insufficient notice is given the hearing can, and normally will, take place as an application made "without notice", whether or not the responding party attends. The Judge will make such order as is appropriate in the circumstances.

*Extreme urgency*

**1A–247** 6.7 During normal working hours, emergency applications (ie applications where even the expedited timetable above would be inadequate) can and should be made directly to one of the Senior Chancery Judges. Contact should be made through their clerks (see Paragraphs 3.1 and 3.2) who will make special arrangements appropriate to the circumstances... There is <u>no</u> facility at the court for dealing with "out of hours" emergency applications. In any such case, litigants should use the emergency "out of hours" service at the Royal Courts of Justice in the Strand (Tel: 020 7947 6000/6260).

### 7. Listing and Trials

**1A–248** 7.1 Fast track Chancery trials will usually be heard by one of the Chancery District Judges. Fast track trials take place on Thursdays, and the Chancery District Judges list their own cases for hearing.

7.2 Multi-track Chancery trials will be given fixed dates in accordance with the usual practice of the CLCJC for multi-track cases. Under the present system, the trial date is set by a telephone listing appointment,

7.2.1 This will be given for a **precise time,** usually on a Thursday.

7.2.2 Prior to the appointment, the court will ascertain (or estimate, if such information has not been given) the likely trial length, and will specify an appropriate trial window.

7.2.3 The parties will be directed to keep the listing appointment, with dates to avoid during the trial window, by telephone either by setting up a telephone conference appointment as under CPR Pt 23, or, if the parties can agree a

***Paragraph numbers marked with a "+" can be found online and on CD.***

combined list of dates to avoid, one party may telephone at the relevant time in the usual way.

7.2.4 The trial date will be fixed by the court officer over the telephone, on the basis of the information then available. If the telephone appointment is not set up and the required information is not received by the time stated, the court will proceed to list in any event. No telephone call after the appointment date and time will be considered or otherwise dealt with unless directed by the Court.

7.25 In either case a formal notice of hearing will also be sent by post or DX. Thereafter, the hearing date will not be altered except on application on notice to a Circuit Judge.

When drafting case management orders, solicitors and counsel should note that the above is now the usual procedure, and expressions such as "first open date after ..." are obsolete. The court's standard form listing direction can be found in Annex B.

7.3 Parties should note that the practice in the Chancery List is to give listing appointments at an early stage, as soon as the likely witnesses and trial length can be known. The court is able to fix an appropriate window well in advance to take account of likely trial preparation time, and the early fixing of a trial date has been shown to improve efficient trial management.

7.4 Subject to absences, there are three or four Chancery Circuit Judges available to sit at all times. It is therefore the practice of the Chancery Section to list five cases to be heard in parallel at any time, in the confident expectation that, with settlements and the flexibility of listing arrangements, there will be a Chancery List Judge available to hear all listed CHY cases. There remains, however the risk that all cases will stand up. In such a situation, every effort is made (including, where possible, the use of a Recorder or of another Resident Judge with appropriate experience) to ensure that no case is adjourned out.

7.5 The CLCJC aims to achieve continuous listing so that cases should not have to be adjourned part heard. The Chancery Section pursues this objective. **Solicitors and counsel should note, therefore, that if a case overruns its trial estimate the Judge is likely to continue the hearing notwithstanding this, and they should arrange their diary commitments accordingly**. A case in the Chancery List will never be adjourned part heard for any significant length of time simply because it has overrun its trial estimate. However, a case which overruns from a Thursday may possibly be adjourned to the following week, to accommodate Friday case management business.

7.6 The parties' time estimates are critical to the objective of providing flexibility and continuous listing for the benefit of all litigants. Time estimates should always be practical and realistic. The parties should note the following:

7.6.1 Time estimates for Chancery cases should, if at all possible, be given in a form which indicates whether or not pre-reading time is included in the estimate (and in any event what pre-reading time requirement is expected) and also whether or not the estimate includes any time for the delivery of an immediate judgment.

7.6.2 In order to accommodate pre-reading, and to minimise waiting by the parties, the Chancery List will operate the following general rule regarding the parties' attendance on the first day, according to the estimated length of the hearing, and, where possible, this will be noted on case management directions:

| | |
|---|---|
| 1 or 2 day case: | 10.30 am |
| 3 day case | 11.30 am |
| 4 day or more case | 2 pm. |

If in doubt, the parties can contact the Chancery Section after 4 pm on the day before the hearing, to ascertain when their attendance is required.

7.6.3 Time estimates should assume that witness statements will be taken as read and that consequently no significant time will normally be required for oral evidence in chief. Pre-reading time should be calculated to allow for the reading of witness statements.

7.6.4 The trial judge will not normally expect to pre-read bundles of documents, apart from any key documents indicated as being required for a basic understanding of the case, unless arrangements are specifically made for this. If extensive reading of bundles is required, then the parties' advocates should decide whether this is best done before or during the hearing itself, and should make their time estimates and/or inform the court just before trial, accordingly.

7.6.5 Allowance should be made for any witnesses using interpreters. Experience indicates that the use of an interpreter trebles the length of time for a witness's oral evidence. The evidence of witnesses using a foreign language must carry the appropriate certification as to the witness's understanding, pursuant to the CPR.

7.7 Apart from the above, as a general rule, the parties should assume that, before the hearing, the judge will have been able to read the skeleton arguments, any key documents, and the witness statements, but not bundles of documentary evidence.

7.8 It is the duty of the parties to inform the Chancery Section Manager **immediately** of any changes in the time estimate of the case.

7.9 Advocates may assume that in Chancery cases, robes will be worn for trials and appeals, and that robes will not be worn for applications, except committal proceedings for contempt of court.

**8. Bundles and skeleton arguments**

**1A–249** 8.1 The practice set out in the Chancery Guide and in CPR part 39 should be followed in respect of bundles and skeleton arguments.

8.2 Bundles and skeleton arguments should be lodged in accordance with case management directions in the case, but at the very latest they **must** be lodged 24 hours prior to the time fixed for any hearing. They should be marked for the attention of the Chancery Section Manager **and delivered to the fourth floor office at 26 Park Crescent**.

8.3 Skeleton arguments should now be filed in accordance with the court's Skeleton Argument Protocol by email to CentralLondonCJSKEL@hmcourts-service.gsi.gov.uk (unless email is not available to the party). **The subject line MUST commence with the CHY No (without spaces) followed by case name**. If a party has no access to email then skeleton arguments can be filed in person or be sent by fax to "Reception" at 26 Park Crescent on 020 7917 7940. It is always advisable for a hard copy skeleton argument to be available at the hearing.

**9. Authorities**

**1A–250** 9.1 Bringing photocopies of authorities to court is helpful to the judges and is encouraged. It is also helpful if any bundle of authorities is provided with an index and appropriate tabs, and if bulky, is placed in a ring binder or lever arch file.

9.2 The court has a text book library including most of the usual Chancery, landlord and tenant and mercantile books. It maintains a set of Law Reports, the All England Law Reports, the Weekly Law Reports and an up-to-date set of Halsbury's Statutes and Halsbury's Laws. However, the provision of photocopied extracts from textbooks, especially specialist books, is of great assistance to the court.

**10. Orders**

**1A–251** 10.1 Orders made after a hearing, whether a trial or an application, will be drawn up and dispatched on the same day wherever possible. In some circumstances however, dispatch may not take place until the following day.

10.2 In order to assist the court, parties should draw up, in advance of the hearing, a minute of any order that they expect to ask the court to make.

***Paragraph numbers marked with a "+" can be found online and on CD.***

10.3 Where the terms of an order can only be finally decided at the hearing itself, solicitors and counsel should be prepared to draft a minute of the order after the hearing, to be handed in to the court clerk in order to assist the preparation of the sealed order. Alternatively, they may be asked to send in a minute to the court clerk by email, on returning to their office.

10.4 Where a party is granted relief at a hearing in the absence of the other party, the representative of the party obtaining the order should ensure either that the court confirms that it will be able to dispatch the sealed order within 24 hours, or that the judge gives any necessary direction for informing the absent party of the terms of the order in the interim.

10.5 Orders made after consideration of a case on paper will be drawn up and dispatched as soon as possible. However, as orders on hearings take priority, this may take up to a week. Counsel and solicitors should bear in mind the time constraints mentioned here and above at Paragraph 6.1–6.3 when making any application for an order without a hearing. This is especially important if the order sought is time-sensitive; an application for determination at a hearing may be more appropriate.

### 11. Transcripts

11.1 The court has a digital recording system in every courtroom. In the event of an appeal, therefore, a request should be made for a transcript of the evidence (if needed) and the judgment, if not handed down in writing. **1A–252**

11.2 Parties seeking to obtain a transcript should place an order with an approved member of the transcription panel and submit form EX107 to the court. Any enquiries related to transcripts should be directed in the first place as follows:

For hearings at 26 Park Crescent, to

CJ Support Section 020 7917 7938

For hearings at 13–14 Park Crescent to

Ms June Dodds 020 7917 5107

### 12. Central London Chancery Court User Group

12.1 The CLCJC Chancery Court User Group has been re-established, to meet periodically to monitor the operation of the Chancery List. **1A–253**

12.2 The Group comprises representatives from the Chancery and Property Bar Associations, the Property Litigation Association, the Association of Contentious Trust and Probate Solicitors, the Society of Trust and Estate Practitioners, the West London Law Society, the Westminster and Holborn Law Society, and representative local solicitors' firms. Meetings are held every four months and attended by the court's Chancery Judiciary and Chancery Section management.

12.3 The group is anxious to be kept informed of how the Chancery List is working in order to ensure that the best possible service can be delivered to meet the needs of users. Complaints, comments, suggestions and ideas for improvement may be communicated through any member of the group. However in the first place it will be useful if suggestions could be sent to either the Trial Centre Office Manager (Miss Michelle Bayley) or the Senior Chancery Judge (HH Judge Hazel Marshall QC) at 26 Park Crescent, London W1B1HT.

Nov 2009

## ANNEX A

## CASES SUITABLE FOR THE CHANCERY LIST AT CENTRAL LONDON CIVIL JUSTICE CENTRE

Any case in the following list which is either expressly transferred from the High **1A–254**

Court or is within the statutory jurisdiction of the County Court, which can be extended by agreement (see s 23 of the County Courts Act 1984)..

**Note**: Where a subject is noted * as being potentially suitable for either the Chancery or the General List, it is for the Claimant's solicitor to choose which is regarded as more appropriate in the first instance. Thereafter, the case will continue in that list unless transferred by the Court on case management, either of its own initiative, or upon application: see Paragraph 1.4 of the Guide

**Wills**

— Probate disputes
— Interpretation
— Inheritance Act.

**Administration of Estates**

**Trusts**

All matters relating to the validity of trusts and their administration but including especially

— Resulting and constructive trusts.
— Home sharing cases, ie *Stack v Dowden* cases: see s.14 of the Trusts of Land Act 1996.

(However two party cases with no complicating aspect may also be suitable for the General List*).

**Land**

— Sale of land (including specific performance claims)
— Contracts affecting land
— Disputes as to title
— Boundary disputes
— Land registration
— Right of way and other easements and rights over land
— Adverse possession
— Proprietary estoppel

**Landlord & Tenant**

Many landlord and tenant matters, and in particular business tenancy disputes under the 1954 Act, are suitable either for the Chancery or the General List.*

The Chancery List is particularly suitable for

— Substantial breach of covenant/forfeiture claims
— Rent review and other valuation matters
— Service charges and management (if not within the exclusive jurisdiction of the LVT.)
— Leasehold enfranchisement.
— Agricultural tenancies

It is less suitable, or necessary, for

— Residential tenancies
— Housing cases.

**Partnership Actions**

— Disputes as to the existence, terms, or termination of any partnership
— Administration or winding up of any partnership business.

**Company Law**

— Shareholders' agreements
— Disputes regarding the running or management of a company
— Breach of directors' duties (fiduciary and contractual)

But **NOT** cases within the exclusive statutory jurisdiction of the Companies Court.

It should also be noted that CLCJC has no jurisdiction in personal insolvency, and therefore has no original company winding up jurisdiction nor in matters depending on that jurisdiction, eg claims to set aside transactions in fraud of creditors under s 423 of the Companies Act 1986. However, such claims can be dealt with at CLCJC as High Court cases by specific authority being conferred on the specialist Chancery Judges, under s 9 of the Senior Courts Act 1981.

**Torts**

Torts in the property and commercial fields especially trespass, nuisance, and negligence in relation to assets and business or financial matters. (Many such matters will also be suitable for the General List.*)

— Fraud including constructive trusts and tracing

**Mortgages, banking and financial matters**

Mortgages, charges and securities including banking securities (other than simple mortgage possession cases where no defence is raised other than on the figure), but especially

— *O'Brien* defences.
— Disputes regarding priority of mortgages or charges
— Guarantees and indemnities
— Assignments of choses in action
— Subrogation

**Business litigation***

Business disputes may be suitable for either the General List or the Chancery List. The Chancery List may be an appropriate list for business litigation as an alternative to a mercantile list where, in particular, a complex point of legal principle or interpretation of contract may arise.

**Injunctions and equitable remedies**

All forms of equitable relief, including

— injunction,
— specific performance,
— declarations as to interests,
— tracing, and
— equitable accounting
— Claims in restitution

**Professional negligence related to any of the above topics**

— including solicitors, surveyors, valuers, architects, accountants, financial advisers.

## ANNEX B

## MODEL STANDARD CASE MANAGEMENT DIRECTIONS FOR CHANCERY LIST CASES AT CENTRAL LONDON CIVIL JUSTICE CENTRE—FORM MT3 (CHY)

Form MT 3 (CHY) **1A–255**

**Case Number:**

**Parties:**

**GENERAL**

1. Claim allocated to the Multi Track, to proceed as Chancery Business.

2. The parties do give serious consideration to using mediation with a view to reaching an early settlement. (Further particulars of the National Mediation Helpline can be accessed by phoning **0845 603 0809** (local rate) between 8.30am and 6.00pm. The parties may be assisted by reference to the National Mediation Helpline at *www.nationalmediationhelpline.com* and to HM Courts Service National Mediation website at *www.hmcourts-service.gov.uk/cms/14160.htm*. The parties will be expected to provide an explanation if mediation has not been attempted. Costs consequences may follow.

**DISCLOSURE**

3. Each party shall give to the other parties standard disclosure of documents on Form N265 by 4.00pm on [ ]

4. All requests for inspection of or a copy of a document must be made by 4.00pm on [*normally 7 days later*]. Copies of requested documents to be supplied by 4 pm on [*normally a further 7 days later*].

**WITNESS STATEMENTS**

5. The parties shall [serve][exchange] statements of witnesses of fact by 4.00pm on [ ].

**EXPERT EVIDENCE** *[Use (1) (2) or (3)]*

(1) *No expert evidence*

6. [It being agreed] [The court being of the view] that no expert evidence

is required, neither party has permission to rely on expert evidence without further order.

(2) *Single joint expert*

6. Expert evidence [on the issue of ] shall be limited to the written report of a single expert [name if available] to be jointly instructed by the parties. Unless the parties agree in writing or the court otherwise orders, the fees and expenses of the single expert shall be paid by the parties equally.
7. Parties are to agree a letter of instruction to the single joint expert by 4 pm on [ ]. Expert to provide a copy of his report to the parties and file his report with the court by 4 pm on [ ].
8. Each party to serve any questions to the single joint expert on the other parties and the single joint expert by 4 pm on [ ]. Expert to respond to such questions by 4 pm on [ ] by serving a copy of his answers on the parties and filing the answers with the court.
9. If the parties cannot agree by 4.00pm on [ ] [who the expert is to be] [the form of the letter of instruction] [the payment of the expert's fees] either party may apply to the court for further directions.

(3) *Parties' experts*

5. Each party has permission to rely on expert evidence of a [state discipline(s)].
6. Experts' written reports to be served by 4 pm on [ ].
7. Expert reports to be agreed if possible. If not, the experts shall hold without prejudice discussions and prepare and serve a statement of issues agreed and issues not agreed with a summary of the reasons for any disagreement by 4.00pm on [ ].
8. Experts to attend for cross examination at the trial unless agreed by the parties or otherwise ordered by the Court.

**VIEW** *(in appropriate cases)*

[ ]. Parties to co-operate in making arrangements for an early site inspection (aided by the provision of an agreed case summary and core bundle of key documents) by a Circuit Judge (to whom the case will then be reserved)[1].

**LISTING**

[ ]. The case is to be listed for trial before a Circuit Judge in the period from [ ] to [ ] with a time estimate of [ ] day/s, [including hours] [excluding any] pre-reading time for the court. [*For hearing of 3 days or more:* Parties not to attend until ................................on the first day][2]

[ ]. There will be a telephone listing appointment on [the first available date after namely] at ..... Each party must have dates to avoid for parties, witnesses and advocates. The listing appointment will be conducted as a telephone conference pursuant to PD 26.3; relevant information is attached. The parties are encouraged to agree a list of such dates, in which case one party may phone (without setting up a formal telephone conference) on behalf of all, provided he certifies that all others have agreed.

[ ]. On receipt of the required information the Court will arrange the date over the phone at the time of the call. If the telephone appointment is not set up and the required information is not received by the time stated, the court will proceed to list,. In either case a formal notice of hearing will also be sent by post or DX. Thereafter, the hearing date will not be altered except on application on notice to a Circuit Judge.

---

[1] This direction is for consideration in appropriate cases, namely where the dispute turns wholly or mainly on the interpretation of title deeds and/or plans. It may be employed at any stage of case management if and t appears likely to promote early narrowing of the issues and/or assistance with settlement.

[2] *(1) Trial window will in principle to be one month for each day of estimated length of trial, and will commence about 4 weeks after the projected time of the last step in pre-trial preparation, which will usually be either exchange of witness statements or finalisation of expert evidence. (2) Attendance on the first day will normally be 11.30 am for a case of 3 days and 2 pm for a hearing of 4 or more days, but the parties may vary this*

[ ]. No telephone call after the appointment date and time will be considered or otherwise dealt with unless directed by the Court.

**PREPARATION FOR TRIAL**

[ ]. *If considered necessary, direction for a Pre-Trial Review on an appropriate date, approximately 3–4 weeks before trial date. Provision can be made to vacate the PTR upon receipt of a joint certificate from the parties' solicitors, not less than three days before the PTR that the case is ready for trial and no further directions are required.*]

[ ]. Not less than [3] nor more than [7] days before the date fixed for trial, the Claimant is to prepare and file a trial bundle in accordance with the Practice Direction to Part 39 CPR. [Such trial bundle is to include [a chronology] [a case summary not exceeding .............................................................words] [a list of issues].]

[ ]. Skeleton arguments are to be exchanged. Skeleton arguments shall be filed at least [one] clear day before the hearing, and should be filed by email to CentralLondonCJSKEL@hmcourts-service.gsi.gov.uk in accordance with the court's CJ Skeleton Argument Protocol, unless email is not available to the party.

[ ]. Parties to inform the court immediately if the case should settle.

**COSTS**

[ ]. Costs of this [application] [case management conference] [hearing] be [*as appropriate*].

Dated:

HH Judge
Mr/Ms Recorder
District Judge
Deputy District Judge

# 1B QUEEN'S BENCH GUIDE

**Editorial note**

The coming into force of the Civil Procedure Rules 1998 highlighted the need for a Guide which would clarify the complexities of proceedings in the High Court in accordance with the new Rules. Here then is the first Queen's Bench Guide. **1B–1**

The Guide is intended to assist a litigant who wishes to bring a claim in the Queen's Bench Division at the Royal Courts of Justice by drawing his attention to the relevant Rules and Practice Directions, together with the procedures of the various offices within the Central office and of other related areas such as Listing.

The Guide will be updated at regular intervals as the need arises.

January 2007

## SECTION 1

### INTRODUCTION

#### 1.1 The Guide

1.1.1 This Guide has been prepared by the Senior Master, acting under the authority of the President of the Queen's Bench Division and provides a general explanation of the work and practice of the Queen's Bench Division with particular regard to proceedings started in the Central Office, and is designed to make it easier for parties to use and proceed in the Queen's Bench Division. **1B–2**

1.1.2 The Guide must be read with the Civil Procedure Rules ("CPR") and the supporting Practice Directions. Litigants and their advisers are responsible for acquainting themselves with the CPR; it is not the task of this Guide to summarise the CPR, nor should anyone regard it as a substitute for the CPR. It is intended to bring the Guide up to date at regular intervals as necessary.

1.1.3 The Guide does not have the force of law, but parties using the Queen's Bench Division will be expected to act in accordance with this Guide. Further guidance as to the practice of the Queen's Bench Division may be obtained from the Practice Master (see paragraph 6.1 below).

1.1.4 It is assumed throughout the Guide that the litigant intends to proceed in the Royal Courts of Justice. For all essential purposes, though, the Guide is equally applicable to the work of the District Registries, which deal with the work of the Queen's Bench Division outside London, but it should be borne in mind that there are some differences.

1.1.5 The telephone numbers and room numbers quoted in the Guide are correct at the time of going to press. However, the room numbers quoted for the Clerk of the Lists and the Listing Office are effective as from 2nd October 2000.

#### 1.2 The Civil Procedure Rules

1.2.1 The Overriding Objective set out in Part 1 of CPR is central to civil proceedings and enables the court to deal with cases justly. To further this aim the work is allocated to one of three tracks—the small claims track, the fast track and the multi-track—so as to dispose of the work in the most appropriate and effective way combined with active case management by the court. **1B–3**

1.2.2 The CPR are divided into Parts. A particular Part is referred to in the Guide as Part 7, etc., as the case may be. Any particular rule within a Part is referred to as Rule 6.4(2), and so on.

#### 1.3 The Practice Directions

1.3.1 Each Part—or almost each Part—has an accompanying Practice Direction or **1B–4**

Directions, and other Practice Directions deal with matters such as the Pre-Action Protocols and some former Rules of the Supreme Court and the County Court Rules, which are still applicable, and scheduled to Part 50.

1.3.2 The Practice Directions are made pursuant to statute, and have the same authority as do the CPR themselves. However, in case of any conflict between a Rule and a Practice Direction, the Rule will prevail. Each Practice Direction is referred to in the Guide with the number of any Part that it supplements preceding it; for example, the Practice Direction supplementing Part 6 is referred to as the Part 6 Practice Direction. But where there is more than one Practice Direction supplementing a Part it will also be described either by topic, for example, Part 25 Practice Direction—Interim Payments, or where appropriate, the Part 40B Practice Direction.

### 1.4 The Forms

**1B–5** 1.4.1 The Practice Direction supplementing Part 4 (Forms) lists the practice forms that are generally required to be used by or referred to in the CPR, and also those referred to in such of the Rules of the Supreme Court and the County Court Rules as are still in force (see Part 50 of the CPR; Schedules 1 and 2).

1.4.2 Those listed in Table 1 with a number prefixed by the letter N are forms that are referred to in and generally required to be used by Rules or Practice Directions. Those listed in Table 2 are Practice Forms that may be used as precedents. The Civil Procedure Forms Volume contains a comprehensive set of forms for use in the High Court and the county courts; these are listed under the same numbers that previously identified them.

1.4.3 The forms may be modified as circumstances in individual cases require, but it is essential that a modified form contains at least as full information or guidance as would have been given if the original form had been used.

1.4.4 Where the Royal Arms appears on any listed form it must appear on any modification of that form. The same format for the Royal Arms as is used on the listed forms need not be used. All that is necessary is that there is a complete Royal Arms.

1.4.5 Forms are available from the Court Service website at www.hmcourts-service.gov.uk

### 1.5 The Queen's Bench Division

**1B–6** 1.5.1 The Queen's Bench Division is one of the three divisions of the High Court, together with the Chancery Division and Family Division. A Lord Justice of Appeal, currently Lord Justice Judge has been appointed by the Lord Chief Justice to be the President of the Queen's Bench Division and Lord Justice May has been appointed as Vice-President; a High Court Judge is appointed as Judge in charge of the Lists and is currently Mr Justice Eady.

1.5.2 Outside London, the work of the Queen's Bench Division is administered in provincial offices known as District Registries. In London, the work is administered in the Central Office at the Royal Courts of Justice. The work in the Central Office of the Queen's Bench Division is the responsibility of the Senior Master, acting under the authority of the President of the Queen's Bench Division.

1.5.3 The work of the Queen's Bench Division is (with certain exceptions) governed by the CPR. The Administrative Court, the Admiralty Court, the Commercial Court and the Technology and Construction Court are all part of the Queen's Bench Division. However, each does specialised work requiring a distinct procedure that to some extent modifies the CPR. For that reason each has an individual Part of the CPR, its own Practice Direction and (except for the Administrative Court) its own Guide, to which reference should be made by parties wishing to proceed in the specialist courts.

1.5.4 The work of the Queen's Bench Division consists mainly of claims for;

(1) damages in respect of

(a) personal injury,

(b) negligence,

(c) breach of contract, and

(d) libel and slander (defamation),

(e) other tortious acts

(f) breach of statutory duty

(2) non-payment of a debt, and

(3) possession of land or property.

Proceedings retained to be dealt with in the Central Office of the Queen's Bench Division will almost invariably be multi-track claims.

1.5.5 In many types of claim—for example claims in respect of negligence by solicitors, accountants, etc. or claims for possession of land—the claimant has a choice whether to bring the claim in the Queen's Bench Division or in the Chancery Division. However, there are certain matters that may be brought only in the Queen's Bench Division, namely:

(1) High Court Enforcement Officer's interpleader proceedings,
(2) applications for the enrolment of deeds,
(3) registration of foreign judgments under the Civil Jurisdictions and Judgments Act 1982or the European Regulation,
(4) applications for bail in criminal proceedings,
(5) applications under the Administration of Justice Act 1920 and the Foreign Judgments (Reciprocal Enforcement) Act 1933 and European Regulations,
(6) registration and satisfaction of Bills of Sale,
(7) Election Petitions,
(8) applications for orders to obtain evidence for foreign courts.

**1.6 The Central Office**

1.6.1 The information in this and the following paragraph is to be found in the Part 2 Practice Direction at paragraph 2; it is reproduced here for the convenience of litigants. The Central Office is open for business from 10 a.m. to 4.30 p.m. (except during August when it is open from 10 a.m. to 2.30 p.m.) on every day of the year except; **1B–7**

(1) Saturdays and Sundays,
(2) Good Friday and the day after Easter Monday,
(3) Christmas Day and Boxing Day and, if these days are a Friday or Saturday, the Bank Holidays allotted in their place, then 28th December,
(4) Bank Holidays in England and Wales (under the Banking and Financial Dealings Act 1971), and
(5) such other days as the Lord Chancellor, with the concurrence or the Lord Chief Justice, the Master of the Rolls, the President of the Family Division and the Vice-Chancellor, may direct.

1.6.2 One of the Masters of the Queen's Bench Division is present on every day on which the Central Office is open for the purpose of superintending the business administered there and giving any directions that may be required on questions of practice and procedure. S/he is normally referred to as the "Practice Master". (See paragraph 6.1 below for information about the Practice Master and Masters in general.)

1.6.3 The Central Office consists of the Action Department, the Masters' Support Unit, the Foreign Process Section, the Masters' Secretary's Department, the Queen's Bench Associates' Department, the Clerk of the Lists, the Registry of the Technology and Construction Court and the Admiralty and Commercial Registry.

1.6.4 The Action Department deals with the issue of claims, responses to claims,

*Paragraph numbers marked with a "+" can be found online and on CD.*

admissions, undefended and summary judgments, enforcement, drawing up certain orders, public searches, provision of copies of court documents, enrolment of deeds, submission of references to the Court of Justice of the European Communities and registration of foreign judgments.

1.6.5 The Masters' Secretary's Department covers three discrete areas of work;

(1) the Masters' Support Unit which provides support (a) to the Masters, including assisting with case-management, and (b) to the Senior Master,
(2) Foreign Process, and
(3) Investment of Children's Funds.

Also one of the staff acts as the Chief Clerk to the Prescribed Officer for Election Petitions (the Senior Master).

1.6.6 The Queen's Bench Associates sit in court with the Judges during trials and certain interim hearings. The Chief Associate manages the Queen's Bench Associates and also provides support to the Senior Master as the Queen's Remembrancer. The Associates draw up the orders made in court at trial and those interim orders that the parties do not wish to draw up themselves, or directed by a Master to be drawn by the Court.

1.6.7 The Clerk of the Lists lists all trials and matters before the Judges (see Section 8 below).

1.6.8 The Technology and Construction Court deals with claims which involve issues or questions which are technically complex or for which a trial by a Judge of that court is for any other reason desirable (see the Part 49C Practice Direction—Technology and Construction Court).

1.6.9 The Admiralty and Commercial Court deals mainly with shipping collision claims and claims concerning charters and insurance, and commercial arbitrations. See the Commercial Court Guide and the Part 49D Practice Direction—Commercial Court, the Part 49F Practice Direction—Admiralty and the Part 49G Practice Direction—Arbitrations.

### 1.7 The Judiciary

**1B–8** 1.7.1 The judiciary in the Queen's Bench Division consist of the High Court Judges (The Honourable Mr/Mrs Justice ... and addressed in court as my Lord/my Lady) and in the Royal Courts of Justice the Masters (Master ...); in the District Registries the work of the Masters is conducted by District Judges.

1.7.2 Trials normally takes place before a High Court Judge (or Deputy High Court Judge)who may also hear pre-trial reviews and other interim applications. Wherever possible the judge before whom a trial has been fixed will hear any pre-trial review. A High Court Judge will hear applications to commit for contempt of court, applications for injunctions and most appeals from Masters' orders. (See the Practice Direction to Part 2B Allocation of cases to levels of Judiciary, and see paragraphs 7.11 and 7.12 below for more information on hearings and applications.)

1.7.3 The Masters deal with interim and some pre-action applications, and manage the claims so that they proceed without delay. The Masters' rooms are situated in the East Block of the Royal Courts of Justice. Hearings take place in these rooms or (short hearings only) in the Bear Garden.

1.7.4 Cases are assigned on issue by a court officer in the Action Department to Masters on a rota basis, and that Master is then known as the assigned Master in relation to that case. (See paragraphs 6.2 and 6.3 below for more information about assignment and the Masters' lists.)

1.7.5 General enquiries about the business dealt with by the Masters should initially be made in writing to the Masters' Support Unit in Room E16.

***Paragraph numbers marked with a "+" can be found online and on CD.***

## SECTION 2
## GENERAL

### 2.1 Essential matters

2.1.1 Before bringing any proceedings, the intending claimant should think carefully about the implications of so doing. (See Section 3 below about steps to be taken before issuing a claim form.) 1B–9

2.1.2 **A litigant who is acting in person faces a heavier burden in terms of time and effort than does a litigant who is legally represented, but all litigation calls for a high level of commitment from the parties. No intending claimant should underestimate this.**

2.1.3 The Overriding Objective of the CPR is to deal with cases justly, which means dealing with the claim in a way which is proportionate (amongst other things) to the amount of money involved. However, in all proceedings there are winners and losers; the loser is generally ordered to pay the costs of the winner and the costs of litigation can still be large. The risk of large costs is particularly acute in cases involving expert witnesses, barristers and solicitors. Also, the costs of an interim hearing are almost always summarily assessed and made payable by the unsuccessful party within 14 days after the order for costs is made. There may be a number of interim hearings before the trial itself is reached, so the costs must be paid as the claim progresses. (See also paragraph 2.5 Costs below.)

2.1.4 The intending claimant should also keep in mind that every claim must be proved, unless of course the defendant admits the allegations. There is little point in incurring the risks and expense of litigating if the claim cannot be proved. An intending claimant should therefore be taking steps to obtain statements from his/her prospective witnesses before starting the claim; if s/he delays until later, it may turn out that s/he is in fact unable to obtain the evidence that s/he needs to prove his/her claim. A defendant faces a similar task.

2.1.5 If s/he is to succeed, need an opinion from one or more expert witnesses, such as medical practitioners, engineers, accountants, or as the case may be. However s/he must remember that no expert evidence may be given at trial without the permission of the court. The services of such experts are in great demand, especially as, in some fields of expertise, there are few of them. It may take many months to obtain an opinion, and the cost may be high. (See paragraph 7.9 below for information about experts' evidence.) **If the claim is for compensation for personal injuries, the claimant must produce a medical report with his/her particulars of claim.**

2.1.6 The claimant must remember also not to allow the time limit for starting his/her claim to pass (see paragraph 2.3 below for information about time limits).

2.1.7 Any intending claimant should also have in mind that s/he will usually be required to give standard disclosure of the documents on which s/he relies. Although Rule 31.3(2) makes provision for a party not to be required to disclose documents if disclosure would be disproportionate to the value of the claim, in complex cases it may still be necessary to disclose relatively large quantities of documents, and this invariably involves much time, effort and expense. (See paragraph 7.8 below for information about disclosure.)

2.1.8 In many cases the parties will need legal assistance, whether by way of advice, drafting, representation at hearings or otherwise. It is not the function of court staff to give legal advice; however, subject to that, they will do their best to assist any litigant. Litigants in person who need assistance or funding should contact the Community Legal Service through their Information Points. The CLS are developing local networks of people giving legal assistance such as law centres, local solicitors or the Citizens Advice Bureaux. CLS Information Points are being set up in libraries and other public places. Litigants can telephone the CLS to find their nearest CLS

Information Point on 0845 608 1122 or can log on to the CLS website at www.justask.org.uk for the CLS directory and for legal information.

2.1.9 The RCJ Advice Bureau off the Main Hall at the Royal Courts of Justice is open Monday to Friday from 10.00am to 1.00pm and from 2.00pm to 5.00pm. The Bureau is run by lawyers in conjunction with the Citizens Advice Bureau and is independent of the court. It is also a registered Charity No 1050358. The Bureau operates on a "first come first served" basis, or telephone advice is available on 0845 120 3715 Monday to Friday from 11.00am to 12.00pm and from 3.00pm to 4.00pm.

### 2.2 Inspection and Copies of Documents

**1B-10** 2.2.1 Intending claimants must not expect to be able to keep the details of a claim away from public scrutiny. In addition to the right of a party to obtain copies of documents in the proceedings to which s/he is a party from the court record (on payment of the prescribed fee), (see CPR 5.4B), any person may obtain from the court records a copy of a claim form when it has been served, and the particulars of claim but not documents attached to the particulars of claim. This applies to claims issued from 2 October 2006. For claims issued before that date particulars of claim may only be inspected or copied where they are included in or served with the claim form, on request and payment of the appropriate fee. Any judgment or order made in public (whether made at a hearing or without a hearing) may also be obtained from the records of the court on payment of the appropriate fee. Additionally, under CPR 5.4 other specified documents may be obtained with the permission of the court, upon making an application in accordance with Part 23.

2.2.2 Witness statements used at trial are open to inspection, at the time of the trial, unless the court directs otherwise. Considerations of publicity are often particularly important in deciding whether to commence proceedings in respect of an alleged libel or slander; such a claim may, by its attendant publicity, do more damage than was ever inflicted by the original publication. In such proceedings the claimant may decide to serve his/her particulars of claim separately from the claim form, in which case they are not open to inspection by non-parties, without the permission of the court.

2.2.3 CPR 5.4(7) gives details of where the court, on application by a party or person identified in the claim form, may restrict inspection and obtaining of copies.

### 2.3 Time Limits

**1B-11** 2.3.1 There are strict time limits that apply to every claim. First, there are time limits fixed by the Limitation Act 1980 [and some other Statutes, such as the Human Rights Act 1998 and the Defamation Act 1996] within which proceedings must be brought. There are circumstances in which the court may extend those time limits, but this should be regarded as exceptional. In all other cases, once the relevant time limit has expired, it is rarely possible to start a claim.

2.3.2 Secondly, in order to try and bring the proceedings to an early trial date, a timetable will be set with which all parties must comply. Unless the CPR or a Practice Direction provides otherwise, or the court orders otherwise, the timetable may be varied by the written agreement of the parties. However, there are certain "milestone" events in the timetable for which the parties may not vary the time limits. Examples of these are;

(1) return of the Allocation Questionnaire/Reply to Defence, which should be returned together with the Allocation Questionnaire
(2) date for the case management conference
(3) return of the Pre Trial Checklist
(4) date fixed for trial
(5) Defence when time has elapsed following the days from service of Particulars of Claim on the Defendant (CPR 15.5).

Where parties have extended a time limit by agreement, the party for whom the time has been extended must advise the Registry Section in writing of the appropriate

*Paragraph numbers marked with a "+" can be found online and on CD.*

event in the proceedings for which the time has been extended and the new date by which it must be done. For example, if an extension is agreed for the filing of the defence, it is for the defendant to inform the Registry Section.

2.3.3 The court has power to impose a sanction on any party who fails to comply with a time limit. If the court considers that a prior warning should be given before a sanction is imposed, it will make an 'unless' order; in other words, the court will order that, unless that party performs his/her obligation by the time specified, s/he will be penalised in the manner set out in the order. This may involve the party in default having his/her claim or statement of case struck out and judgment given against him. **An Order striking out a claim or statement of case must be applied for after the time specified has expired, as this is not automatic unless the Unless Order so provides.**

### 2.4 Legal Representation

2.4.1 A party may act in person or be represented by a lawyer. A party who is acting in person may be assisted at any hearing by another person (often referred to as a McKenzie friend) subject to the discretion of the Court. The McKenzie friend is allowed to help by taking notes, quietly prompting the litigant and offering advice and suggestions. The litigant however, must conduct his/her own case; the McKenzie friend may not represent him and may only in very exceptional circumstances be allowed to address the court on behalf of the litigant (see s.27(2)(c) of the Courts and Legal Services Act 1990). **1B–12**

2.4.2 A written statement should be provided to the court at any hearing concerning the representation of the parties in accordance with paragraph 5.1 of the Part 39 Practice Direction (the Court Record Form, found outside the Masters' Rooms or in the Bear Garden)..

2.4.3 At a trial, a company or corporation may be represented by an employee if the company or corporation authorises him to do so and the court gives permission. Where this is to be the case, the permission of the Judge who is to hear the case may be sought informally; paragraph 5 of the Part 39 Practice Direction describes what is needed to obtain permission from the court for this purpose and mentions some of the considerations relevant to the grant or refusal of permission. A further statement concerning representation should be provided in accordance with paragraph 5.2 of the Part 39 Practice Direction.

2.4.4 Experienced outdoor clerks from solicitors firms are permitted to appear before the Masters. Barristers' clerks may attend before a Master to fix a hearing date for Counsel.

*The Personal Support Unit (PSU) is an independent charity, which supports litigants-in-person, witnesses, victims, their family members and other supporters attending the Royal Courts. There are now nearly 100 fully trained and experienced volunteers. Requests vary from the very simple to the complex. Some people just require directions or advice about procedures. Others need to unburden themselves, while others request the moral and emotional support of being accompanied in court. The PSU can be particularly helpful for clients with special needs.*

*The PSU*

*Room M104*

*Royal Courts of Justice*

*Strand*

*WC2A 2LL   Tel: 020 7947 7701/3   Fax: 020 7947 7702   email:* ***rcj@thepsu.co.uk***
*or: www.thepsu.co.uk*

***Paragraph numbers marked with a "+" can be found online and on CD.***

### 2.5 Costs

1B–13 2.5.1 Costs are dealt with in Parts 43 to 48. There are important new provisions in the costs rules, particularly with respect to;

(1) informing the client of costs orders,
(2) providing the court with estimates of costs, and
(3) summary assessment of costs,
(4) interim orders for costs, and
(5) interest on costs.

2.5.2 Solicitors now have a duty under Rule 44.2 to notify their client within 7 days if an order for costs is made against him in his/her absence. Solicitors must also notify any other person who has instructed them to act in the proceedings or who is liable to pay their fees (such as an insurer, trade union or the Legal Services Commission (LSC)). They must also inform these persons how the order came to be made (paragraphs 7.1 and 7.2 of the Costs Practice Direction).

2.5.3 The court may at any stage order any party to file an estimate of base costs (substantially in the form of Precedent H in the Schedule of Costs Precedents annexed to the Costs Practice Direction) and serve copies on all the other parties (paragraph 6.3 of the Costs Practice Direction). This will both assist the court in deciding what case management directions to make and inform the other parties as to their potential liability for payment of costs.

2.5.4 If a party seeks an order for his/her costs, in order to assist the court in making a summary assessment, s/he must prepare a written statement of the costs s/he intends to claim in accordance with paragraph 13.5 of the Costs Practice Direction, following as closely as possible Form N260. In addition, when an Allocation Questionnaire or a Pre Trial Checklist is filed, the party filing it must file and serve an estimate of costs on all the other parties.

2.5.5 If the parties have agreed the amount of costs, they do not need to file a statement of the costs, and summary assessment is unnecessary. Or, where the parties agree a consent order without any party attending on the application, the parties should insert either an agreed figure for costs or that there should be no order for costs in the order (paragraph 13.4 of the Costs Practice Direction).

2.5.6 Unless the court decides not to order an assessment of costs where, for example, it orders costs to be "costs in the case", it may either make a summary assessment of costs or order a detailed assessment to take place. The court will generally make a summary assessment of costs at any hearing which lasts for less than one day;

(1) "summary assessment" is where the court, when making an order for costs, assesses those costs and orders payment of a sum of money in respect of them, and
(2) "detailed assessment" is the procedure by which the amount of costs is decided by a Costs Judge or Costs Officer at a later date in accordance with Part 47.

The provision of summary assessment means that the paying party is likely to be paying the costs at an earlier stage than s/he would have done under the previous rules (and see paragraph 2.5.15 below).

2.5.7 The court will not make a summary assessment of the costs of a receiving party (the party to whom the costs are to be paid) where s/he is;

(1) a child or patient within the meaning of Part 21 unless the solicitor acting for the child or patient has waived the right to further costs, or
(2) an assisted person or a person in receipt of funded services under sections 4-11 of the Access to Justice Act 1999.

The costs payable by a party who is an assisted person or a person in receipt of funded services may be summarily assessed as the assessment is not by itself a determination of the assisted person's ability to pay those costs.

2.5.8 Rule 44.3A prevents the court from assessing an additional liability in respect of a funding agreement before the conclusion of the proceedings. At an interim hearing therefore, the court will assess only the base costs. (See paragraph 14.9 of the Costs Practice Direction for assessing an additional liability and Section 19 for information about funding arrangements.)

2.5.9 Interim orders for costs; where the court decides immediately who is to pay particular costs, but does not assess the costs summarily, for example after a trial lasting more than a day, so that the final amount of costs payable has to be fixed at a detailed assessment, the court may order the paying party to pay a sum or sums on account of the ultimate liability for costs.

2.5.10 Interest on costs; the court has power to award interest on costs from a date before the date of the order, so compensating the receiving party for the delay between incurring costs and receiving a payment in respect of them.

2.5.11 Parties should note that where the court makes an order which does not mention costs, no party is entitled to costs in relation to that order.

2.5.12 Rule 44.3 describes the court's discretion as to costs and the circumstances to be taken into account when exercising its discretion. Rules 44.4 and 44.5 set out the basis of assessment and the factors to be taken into account in deciding the amount of costs.

2.5.13 The amount of costs to be paid by one party to another may be ordered to be assessed on the standard basis or on the indemnity basis. The basis to be used is decided when the court decides that a party should pay the costs of another. Costs that are unreasonably incurred or are unreasonable in amount are not allowed on either basis.

2.5.14 The standard basis is the usual basis for assessment where only costs which are proportionate to the matters in issue, are allowed, and any doubt as to whether the costs were reasonably incurred or reasonable and proportionate in amount is resolved in favour of the paying party. On the indemnity basis, any such doubts are resolved in favour of the receiving party.

2.5.15 A party must normally pay summarily assessed costs awarded against him within 14 days of the assessment, but the court can extend that time, direct payment by instalments, or defer the liability to pay the costs until the end of the proceedings so that they can then be set off against any costs or judgment to which the paying party becomes entitled.

2.5.16 Fixed costs relating to default judgments, certain judgments on admissions and summary judgments etc. are set out in Part 45. Part 46 relates to fast track costs.

2.5.17 Part 47 and Sections 28 to 49 of the Costs Practice Direction contain the procedure for detailed assessment together with the default provisions. Precedents A,B,C and D set out in the Schedule of Costs Precedents annexed to the Costs Practice Direction are model forms of bills of costs for detailed assessment. Section 43 deals with costs payable out of the Community Legal Service fund, Section 44 deals with costs payable out of a fund other than the CLS fund and Section 49 deals with costs payable by the LSC. Part 48 and Sections 50 to 56 of the Costs Practice Direction deal with Special Cases, in particular;

(1) costs payable by or to a child or patient,
(2) litigants in person, (see CPR 48.6 The costs allowed under this rule must not exceed, except in the case of a disbursement, two-thirds of the amount which would have been allowed if the litigant in person had been represented by a legal representative) and
(3) wasted costs orders– personal liability of the legal representative.

2.5.18 Costs only proceedings are dealt with in Rule 44.12A and Section 17 of the Costs Practice Direction. They may be brought in the High Court only where the dispute was of such a value or type that had proceedings been brought they would have been commenced in the High Court. Proceedings are brought under Part 8 by the issue of a Claim Form in the Supreme Court Costs Office at Clifford's Inn, Fetter Lane, London EC4A 1DQ. (See also paragraphs 4.1.16 and 6.8.13 below.)

**2.6 Court Fees**

**1B–14** 2.6.1 The fees payable in the High Court as from 1 May 2008are set out in Schedule 1 to the Civil Proceedings Fees Order 2008 SI 2008/1053.

2.6.2 In the Royal Courts of Justice fees are paid in the Fees Room E01 and by way of receipt for the fee, it is usually stamped on the document to which they relate.

**2.7 Information Technology**

**1B–15** 2.7.1 To support the work of the Central Office in operating the provisions of the CPR, and to facilitate effective case management there is a limited computerised system to provide a record of proceedings and to produce some court forms and orders.

2.7.2 A number of specific applications of information technology have been well developed in recent years; the use of fax, the provision of skeleton arguments on disk and daily transcripts on disk have become commonplace. Short applications may be dealt with more economically by a conference telephone call, and taking evidence by video link has become more common and the available technology has improved considerably. The CPR contains certain provisions about the use of information technology, for example, Part 6 and the Part 6 Practice Direction deal with service of documents by Fax or other electronic means, the Part 23 Practice Direction refers to telephone hearings and video conferencing, Rule 32.3 allows the use of evidence given by video link and the Part 5 Practice Direction refers to the filing of documents at court by Fax.

2.7.3 Parties may agree to use information technology in the preparation, management and presentation of a case; however the agreement of the Judge or Master should be sought before providing the court with material in electronic form. Where permission has been given by a specific Master, the material for use at a hearing or in support of an application can be provided on a CD-Rom or in some cases by e-mail. The parties should check with the court which word-processing format should be used. This will normally be Word 6 or in some cases in PDF format.

2.7.4 A protocol has been prepared as a guide to all persons who are involved in the use of video conferencing equipment in civil proceedings in the High Court. It covers its use in courtrooms where the equipment may be installed, and also the situation where the court assembles in a commercial studio or conference room containing video conferencing equipment. Copies of the Video- conferencing Protocol may be obtained from the Bar Council at a charge of £2.50 to cover expenses. A room has now been made available as an audio/video conferencing courtroom for applications to Masters, as a pilot measure. More information may be obtained from the Senior Master through the Masters' Secretary's Department.

## SECTION 3

## STEPS BEFORE ISSUE OF A CLAIM FORM

**3.1 Settlement**

**1B–16** 3.1.1 So far as reasonably possible, a claimant should try to resolve his/her claim without litigation. The court is increasingly taking the view that litigation should be a last resort and parties may wish to consider the use of Alternative Dispute Resolution ("ADR"). (See paragraph 6.6 below.)

3.1.2 There are codes of practice for preliminary negotiations in certain types of claim. These codes of practice are called "Protocols" and are set out in a schedule to the Protocols Practice Direction to the CPR. Even if there is no protocol that applies to the claim, the parties will nonetheless be expected to comply with the spirit of the Overriding Objective (see paragraph 4 of the Protocols Practice Direction).

3.1.3 An offer to settle a claim may be made by either party whether before or after a claim is brought. The court will take account of any offer to settle made before proceedings are started when making any order as to costs after proceedings have started.

### 3.2 Disclosure Before Proceedings Are Started

3.2.1 An intending claimant may need documents to which s/he does not yet have access. If the documents are not disclosed voluntarily, in accordance with the Pre Action Protocols, then Rule 31.16 sets out the provisions for making an application for disclosure of documents before proceedings have started. An Application Notice under Part 23 is required together with the appropriate fee. This may be issued in the Registry Section, Room E07 and will be assigned to a Master for hearing. **1B–17**



3.2.2 Essentially, the court must be satisfied that the applicant and respondent to the application are likely to be parties when proceedings are brought, that the required documents are those that the respondent would be required to disclose under Rule 31.6 when proceedings are brought and that their early disclosure might dispose of or assist the disposal of anticipated proceedings or save costs.

### 3.3 Defamation proceedings: Offer of Amends

3.3.1 Application may be made to the court before a claim is brought for the court's assistance in accepting an offer of amends under section 3 of the Defamation Act 1996. The application is made by Part 8 Claim Form. For more information see paragraph 4.1.15 Part 8 procedure and paragraph 8.1 defamation below. **1B–18**

## SECTION 4

## STARTING PROCEEDINGS IN THE CENTRAL OFFICE

### 4.1 Issuing The Claim Form

4.1.1 All claims must be started by issuing a Claim Form. The great majority of claims involve a dispute of fact, and the Claim Form should be issued in accordance with Part 7 of the CPR. The Part 8 procedure may be followed in the types of claim described in paragraphs 4.1.14 to 4.1.16 below. **1B–19**

4.1.2 The requirements for issuing a Claim Form are set out in Part 7 and the Part 7 Practice Direction, the main points of which are summarised in the following paragraphs.

4.1.3 The Practice Direction at paragraphs 2, 3 and 4 provides information as to;

(1) where a claim should be started,
(2) certain matters that must be included in the Claim Form, and
(3) how the heading of the claim should be set out on the Claim Form.

In defamation cases, Part 53 and the Part 53 Practice Direction sets out matters that should be included in the Claim Form and particulars of claim. See also paragraph 12.7 below.

4.1.4 Proceedings are started when the court issues a Claim Form, and a Claim Form is issued on the date entered on the Claim Form by the court. However, where a Claim Form is received in the court office on an earlier date than the date of issue, then, for the purposes of the Limitation Act 1980, the claim is brought on the earlier date (see paragraphs 5.1 to 5.4 of the Part 7 Practice Direction).

4.1.5 To start proceedings in the Action Department, a claimant must use form N1 (or form N208 for a Part 8 claim) (or a form suitably modified as permitted by Part

*Paragraph numbers marked with a "+" can be found online and on CD.*

4), and should take or send the Claim Form to Room E07, Registry Section, Action Department, Central Office, Royal Courts of Justice, Strand, London WC2A 2LL. If the court is to serve the Claim Form, the claimant must provide sufficient copies for each defendant. The Claimant will be required to provide a Court copy, a Claimant's copy and one copy for each named Defendant. Copies of practice forms relevant to the work of the Action Department (including the Claim Form and Response Pack) are available from that office. Alternatively, claimants may produce their own forms, which may be modified as the circumstances require, provided that all essential information, especially any information or guidance that the form gives to the recipient, is included. (See Part 4 Forms.)

4.1.6 On issuing the Claim Form, the court will give or send the claimant a notice of issue endorsed with the date of issue of the Claim Form. If the claimant requires the court to serve the Claim Form, the date of posting and deemed date of service will also be endorsed on the notice of issue. Claimants and especially their solicitors who use the Action Department, are encouraged to serve their own documents but must inform the court when service has been effected (see paragraph 4.2.4 in relation to service by the claimant and the certificate of service). For certain types of claims, the notice of issue contains a request for judgment. (See paragraph 5 below for information about default judgments.)

4.1.7 A Claim Form must be served within 4 months after the date of issue (Rule 7.5) unless it is to be served out of the jurisdiction, when the period is 6 months; and Rule 7.6 and paragraph 7 of the Practice Direction set out how and on what grounds an extension of time for service of the Claim Form may be sought. (See Section 4.2 below about service.)

### 4.2 Particulars of Claim

**1B–20** 4.2.1 The particulars of claim may be;

(1) included in the Claim Form, (if served as part of the Claim Form they are available to be copied for any person under CPR 5.4—see para. 2.2 above)
(2) in a separate document served with the Claim Form, or
(3) in a separate document served within 14 days of service of the Claim Form provided that the particulars of claim are served within the latest time for serving the Claim Form.

4.2.2 A Claim Form that does not include particulars of claim must nonetheless contain a concise statement of the nature of the claim. Any Claim Form and/or Particulars of Claim that

(1) does not comply with the requirements of rule 16.2, or 16.4 or
(2) is garbled or abusive,

will be referred to a Master and is likely to be struck out by the court.

4.2.3 Where the particulars of claim are neither included in or served with the Claim Form;

(1) the Claim Form must contain a statement that particulars of claim will follow, and
(2) the particulars of claim must be served by the claimant and a copy then filed at the court together with a Certificate of Service (CPR 7.4(3))

However, where a Claim Form is to be served out of the jurisdiction, the particulars of claim, if not included in the claim form, must accompany it. (See paragraph 4.2.13 below.)

4.2.4 Certain forms must accompany the particulars of claim when they are served on the defendant. These forms are listed in Rule 7.8 and are included in a Response Pack, which is available from the Action Department.

4.2.5 A party who has entered into a funding arrangement and who wishes to claim

***Paragraph numbers marked with a "+" can be found online and on CD.***

an additional liability must give the Court and any other party information about that claim if s/he is to recover the additional liability. Where the funding arrangement has been entered into before proceedings are commenced, the claimant should file a notice of funding in form N251 when the Claim Form is issued.

4.2.6 Part 22 requires the Claim Form and particulars of claim to be verified by a statement of truth, and where the particulars of claim are not included in the Claim Form itself, these are to be separately verified by a statement of truth; see paragraph 6 of the Part 7 Practice Direction, and the Part 22 Practice Direction.

4.2.7 Part 16 and the Part 16 Practice Direction deal with statements of case, and in particular the contents of the Claim Form and the particulars of claim. Part 16 does not apply to claims in respect of which the Part 8 alternative procedure for claims is being used. See paragraph 5.6 below for more about statements of case. Note the requirements in relation to personal injury claims, fatal accident claims, hire purchase claims and recovery of land or goods.



**4.3 Part 8 Procedure**

4.3.1 A claimant may use the Part 8 procedure where; **1B–21**

(1) s/he seeks the court's decision on a question that is unlikely to involve a substantial dispute of fact, or
(2) a Rule or Practice Direction requires or permits the use of the Part 8 procedure,

however, the court may at any stage order the claim to continue as if the claimant had not used the Part 8 procedure.

4.3.2 Certain matters that must be included on the Claim Form when the Part 8 procedure is being used are set out in Rule 8.2. The types of claim for which the Part 8 procedure may be used include;

(1) a claim by or against a child or patient that has been settled before the commencement of proceedings, the sole purpose of the claim being to obtain the approval of the court to the settlement,
(2) provided there is unlikely to be a substantial dispute of fact, a claim for a summary order for possession against named or unnamed defendants occupying land or premises without the licence or consent of the person claiming possession (Schedule 1- RSC O.113),
(3) a claim for provisional damages that has been settled before the commencement of proceedings, the sole purpose of the claim being to obtain a judgment by consent,
(4) a claim under s.3 of the Defamation Act 1996 (made other than in existing proceedings) and
(5) a claim under Rule 44.12A where the parties have agreed all issues before the commencement of proceedings except the amount of costs and an order for costs is required.

4.3.3 In addition to the provisions of Rule 8.1, attention is drawn also to the Part 8(B) Practice Direction which deals with proceedings brought under "the Schedule Rules".

See Paragraph 6.7 below for more information regarding the Part 8 procedure.

**4.4 Service**

4.4.1 Service of documents is dealt with in Part 6; Section I (Rules 6.1 to 6.11) contains provisions relating to service generally and Section II (Rules 6.12 to 6.16) contains special provisions relating to service of the Claim Form. Section III (Rules 6.17 to 6.31) deals with service out of the jurisdiction. Some of the more important provisions are described below. **1B–22**

*Within the Jurisdiction*

4.4.2 The methods by which a document may be served are to be found in Rule 6.2. The court will serve a document that it has issued or prepared unless;

***Paragraph numbers marked with a "+" can be found online and on CD.***

(1) the party on whose behalf it is to be served notifies the court that s/he wishes to serve it himself,

(2) the court orders otherwise, or

(3) a Rule or Practice Direction provides otherwise.

It is anticipated that practitioners familiar with Central Office procedures will wish to continue to serve their own documents.

4.4.3 Where a party has entered into a funding agreement the notice of funding (form N251) must be served on all the other parties. If a claimant files his/her notice of funding when his/her Claim Form is issued, the Court will serve it on the other parties provided sufficient copies are provided. Otherwise the claimant must serve the notice of funding with the Claim Form. A defendant should file his/her notice of funding with his/her first document, i.e. his/her defence or acknowledgement of service etc. Sufficient copies of the notice should be provided for the Court to serve.

4.4.4 In all other circumstances a party must serve a notice of funding within 7 days of entering into the funding agreement.

4.4.5 Where the court has tried to serve a document but has been unable to serve it, the court will send a notice of non-service to the party on whose behalf it was to be served stating the method attempted. On receipt of this notice, the party should take steps to serve the document himself, as the court is under no further duty to effect service. The method of service used by the court will normally be first-class post.

4.4.6 Where a claimant has served a Claim Form, s/he must file a certificate of service that complies with the provisions of Rule 6.10. The certificate of service must be filed within 7 days of service of the Claim Form, and the claimant may not obtain judgment in default if it has not been filed.

4.4.7 Information as to how personal service is to be effected and as to service by electronic means is to be found in the Part 6 Practice Direction. Rule 6.6 deals with service on a child or patient.

4.4.8 A party must give an address for service within the jurisdiction. Rule 6.5 contains information as to the address for service.

4.2.9 A party may make an application for permission to serve a document by an alternative method to those set out in Rule 6.2. The application may be made without notice, and paragraph 9.1 of the Practice Direction sets out the evidence that will be required in support of the application. (Paragraph 7.12 below contains information in relation to applications.)

*Out of the Jurisdiction*

4.4.10 The provisions for service out of the jurisdiction are contained in Rules 6.17 to 6.31. Rule 6.19 sets out the provisions whereby a Claim Form may be served out of the jurisdiction without the permission of the court, and Rule 6.20 sets out the circumstances where the court's permission is required. Parties should also see the Practice Direction on service out of the jurisdiction.

4.4.11 A claimant may issue a Claim Form against defendants, one or some of whom appear to be out of the jurisdiction, without first having obtained permission for service out of the jurisdiction, provided that where the Claim Form is not one which may be served without the permission of the court under Rule 6.19, the Claim Form is endorsed by the court that it is "not for service out of jurisdiction".

4.4.12 Where a Claim Form is to be served in accordance with Rule 6.19 it must contain a statement of the grounds on which the claimant is entitled to serve it out of the jurisdiction. (See 6BPD.2). The statement should be as follows;

(1) "*I, (name) state that the High Court of England and Wales has power under the Civil Jurisdiction and Judgments Act 1982 to hear this claim and that no proceedings are*

*pending between the parties in Scotland, Northern Ireland or another Convention territory of any contracting state as defined by section 1(3) of the Act.",* or

(2) where the proceedings are those to which Article 16 of Schedule 1, 3C or 4 to the Act refers,

*"I, (name) state that the High Court of England and Wales has power under the Civil Jurisdiction and Judgments Act 1982, the claim having as its object rights in rem in immovable property or tenancies in immovable property (or otherwise in accordance with the provisions of Article 16 of Schedule 1, 3C or 4 to that Act) to which Article 16 of Schedule 1, 3C or 4 to that Act applies, to hear the claim and that no proceedings are pending between the parties in Scotland, Northern Ireland or another Convention territory of any contracting state as defined by section 1(3) of the Act.",* or

(3) where the defendant is party to an agreement conferring jurisdiction to which Article 17 of Schedule 1, 3C or 4 to that Act applies,

*"I, (name) state that the High Court of England and Wales has power under the Civil Jurisdiction and Judgments Act 1982, the defendant being a party to an agreement conferring jurisdiction to which Article 17 of Schedule 1, 3C or 4 to that Act applies, to hear the claim and that no proceedings are pending between the parties in Scotland, Northern Ireland or another Convention territory of any contracting state as defined by section 1(3) of the Act.".*

(4) where the Judgments Regulation applies (except where Articles 22 or 23 of the Regulation, or Rule 6.19(2) applies),

*"I, (name) state that the High Court of England and Wales has power under Council Regulation (EC) No 44/2001 of 22nd December 2000 (on jurisdiction and the recognition and enforcement of judgments in civil and commercial matters) to hear this claim and that no proceedings are pending between the parties in Scotland, Northern Ireland or any other Regulation state as defined by section 1(3) of the Civil Jurisdiction and Judgments Act 1982"*

(5) where Article 22 of the Judgments Regulation applies,

*"I, (name) state that the High Court of England and Wales has power under Council Regulation (EC) No 44/2001 of 22nd December 2000 (on jurisdiction and the recognition and enforcement of judgments in civil and commercial matters), the claim having as its object rights in rem in immovable property or tenancies in immovable property (or otherwise in accordance with the provisions of Article 22 of that Regulation) to which Article 22 of that Regulation applies, to hear this claim and that no proceedings are pending between the parties in Scotland, Northern Ireland or any other Regulation state as defined by section 1(3) of the Civil Jurisdiction and Judgments Act 1982"*

(6) where Article 23 of the Judgments Regulation applies,

*"I, (name) state that the High Court of England and Wales has power under Council Regulation (EC) No 44/2001 of 22nd December 2000 (on jurisdiction and the recognition and enforcement of judgments in civil and commercial matters), the defendant being party to an agreement conferring jurisdiction to which Article 23 of that Regulation applies, to hear this claim and that no proceedings are pending between the parties in Scotland, Northern Ireland or any other Regulation state as defined by section 1(3) of the Civil Jurisdiction and Judgments Act 1982"*

(7) where Rule 6.19(2) applies,

*"I, (name) state that the High Court of England and Wales has power to hear this claim under [state the provisions of the relevant enactment] which satisfies the requirements of rule 6.19(2), and that no proceedings are pending between the parties in Scotland, Northern Ireland, or in another Contracting State or Regulation State as defined by section 1(3) of the Civil Jurisdiction and Judgments Act 1982"*

4.4.13 The statement should be signed and have set out the full name of the signatory. If a Claim Form as specified in paragraph 4.2.10 above does not bear the appropriate above statement, the Claim Form will be endorsed "not for service out of the jurisdiction".

4.4.14 An application for an order for permission to issue a Claim Form for service out of the jurisdiction or to serve the Claim Form out of the jurisdiction should be made in accordance with Part 23 (form PF 6(A) may be used). The application must be supported by written evidence, and may be made without notice. The written evidence should state the requirements set out in Rule 6.21(1) and (2).

***Paragraph numbers marked with a "+" can be found online and on CD.***

4.4.15 An order giving permission for service out of the jurisdiction should be in form PF 6(B) and will;

(1) specify the country in which, or place at which, service is to be effected, and
(2) specify the number of days within which the defendant may either
    (a) file an acknowledgement of service,
    (b) file or serve an admission, or
    (c) file a defence to
    the claim, and where an acknowledgement of service is filed, specify a further 14 days within which the defendant may file a defence. (This information can be found in the Table in the Practice Direction to Part 6 (6BPD.13))

4.4.16 Where service is to be effected in a country which requires a translation of the documents to be served, it is the claimant's responsibility to provide the translation of all the documents for each defendant. In every case, it is the claimant's duty to ensure that the Response Pack clearly states the appropriate period for responding to the Claim Form, and form N9, form N1C and other relevant forms must be modified accordingly. Every translation must be accompanied by a statement by the person making it;

(1) that it is a correct translation, and
(2) including the person's name, address and qualifications for making the translation.

4.4.17 The periods for acknowledging service of a Claim Form served out of the jurisdiction are set out in Rule 6.22 and in the Table contained in the Part 6 Section III Practice Direction, and the periods for serving a defence to a Claim Form served out of the jurisdiction are set out in Rule 6.23 and in the Table in the Practice Direction. Rule 6.24 describes the methods of service.

4.4.18 Where the Claim Form is to be served through;

(1) the judicial authorities of the country where the Claim Form is to be served,
(2) a British Consular authority in that country,
(3) the authority designated under the Hague Convention in respect of that country, or
(4) the Government of that country, or
(5) where the court permits service on a State, the Foreign and Commonwealth Office,
(6) the Receiving Agency designated under Regulation (EC) 1348/2000

the claimant should provide the Senior Master with the following documents by forwarding them to the Foreign Process section, Room E 10;

(a) a request for service by the chosen method (in form **PF 7**),
(b) a sealed copy and a duplicate copy of the Claim Form,
(c) the Response Pack as referred to in paragraph 4.2.14,
(d) a translation in duplicate, and the statement referred to in paragraph 4.2.13, and
(e) any other relevant documents.

4.4.19 Where service has been requested in accordance with paragraph 4.2.16, the particulars of claim, if not included in the Claim Form, must accompany the Claim Form (in duplicate). Where the claimant is effecting service of the Claim Form direct (and not as in paragraph 4.2.16) and the Claim Form states that particulars of claim are to follow, the permission of the court is not required to serve the particulars of claim out of the jurisdiction.

4.2.20 Where an official certificate of service is received in a foreign language, it is the responsibility of the claimant to obtain a translation of the certificate. Where a defendant served out of the jurisdiction fails to attend a hearing, the official certificate of service is evidence of service. Otherwise the claimant may take no further steps

***Paragraph numbers marked with a "+" can be found online and on CD.***

against the defendant until written evidence showing that the Claim Form has been duly served is filed.

4.2.21 Further advice on service out of the jurisdiction may be obtained from the Foreign Process Section, Room E10.

## SECTION 5

## RESPONSE TO A PART 7 CLAIM

### 5.1 General

5.1.1 Responding to particulars of claim is dealt with in Part 9. A defendant may respond to the service of particulars of claim by; **1B–23**

(1) filing or serving an admission in accordance with Part 14,
(2) filing a defence in accordance with Part 15,
(3) doing both if part only of the claim is admitted, or
(4) filing an acknowledgement of service in accordance with Part 10.

5.1.2 Where a defendant receives a Claim Form that states that particulars of claim are to follow, s/he need not respond to the claim until the particulars of claim have been served on him.

5.1.3 If a defendant fails to;

(1) file an acknowledgement of service within the time specified in rule 10.3, and
(2) file a defence within the time specified in Rule 15.4, or
(3) file or serve an admission in accordance with Part 14

the claimant may obtain default judgment if Part 12 allows it. (See paragraph 5.5 below for information about default judgments.)

### 5.2 Acknowledgement of Service

5.2.1 Acknowledgements of service are dealt with in Part 10. A defendant may file an acknowledgement of service if; **1B–24**

(1) s/he is unable to file a defence within the period specified in Rule 15.4, or
(2) s/he wishes to dispute the court's jurisdiction. (CPR 11.7).

Filing an acknowledgement of service extends the time for filing the defence by 14 days.

5.2.2 A defendant who wishes to acknowledge service of a Claim Form should do so by using form **N9**. Rule 10.5 states that the acknowledgement of service must;

(1) be signed by the defendant or his/her legal representative, and
(2) include the defendant's address for service which must be within the jurisdiction of the court (CPR 6.5).

The Part 10 Practice Direction contains information relating to the acknowledgement of service and how it may be signed.

### 5.3 Admissions

5.3.1 The manner in which a defendant may make an admission of a claim or part of a claim is set out in Rules 14.1 and 14.2, and Rules 14.3 to 14.7 set out how judgment may be obtained on a written admission. **1B–25**

5.3.2 Included in the Response Pack that will accompany the Claim Form when it is served on the defendant, is an admission form (form N9A for a specified amount and form N9C for an unspecified amount). If the defendant makes an admission and requests time to pay, s/he should complete as fully as possible the statement of means contained in the admission form, or otherwise give in writing the same details of his/her means as could have been given in the admission form.

***Paragraph numbers marked with a "+" can be found online and on CD.***

5.3.3 Where the defendant has;

(1) made an admission in respect of a specified sum and requested time to pay, or

(2) made an admission in respect of an unspecified sum, offered a sum in satisfaction (which is accepted) and requested time to pay,

and the claimant has not accepted the request for time to pay, on receipt of the claimant's notice the court will enter judgment for the amount admitted or offered (less any payments made) to be paid at the time and rate of payment determined by the court.

5.3.4 Where the defendant has;

(1) made an admission for an unspecified amount, or

(2) made an admission for an unspecified amount and offered in satisfaction a sum that the claimant has not accepted,

on receipt of the claimant's request for judgment the court will enter judgment for an amount to be decided by the court and costs.

5.3.5 The matters that the court will take into account when determining the time and rate of payment are set out in paragraph 5.1 of the Part 14 Practice Direction.

5.3.6 The court may determine the time and rate of payment with or without a hearing, but, where a hearing is to take place, the proceedings must, where the provisions of Rule 14.12(2) apply, be transferred to the defendant's home court. Where the Claim Form was issued in the Royal Courts of Justice the defendant's home court will be the district registry for the district in which the defendant's address given in the admission form is situated. If there is no such district registry the proceedings will remain in the Royal Courts of Justice.

5.3.7 The procedure for an application for re-determination of a decision determining the time and rate of payment is to be found in Rule 14.13 and paragraphs 5.3 to 5.6 of the Practice Direction.

5.3.8 Where judgment has been entered for an amount to be decided by the court and costs, the court will give any directions that it considers appropriate, which may include allocating the case to a track. (See paragraph 6.5 below about allocation.)

5.3.9 Judgment will not be entered on an admission where;

(1) the defendant is a child or patient, or

(2) the claimant is a child or patient and the admission is made in respect of

(a) a specified amount of money, or

(b) a sum offered in satisfaction of a claim for an unspecified amount of money.

See Part 21 and the Part 21 Practice Direction, and in particular Rule 21.10 which provides that, where a claim is made by or on behalf of a child or patient or against a child or patient, no settlement, compromise or payment shall be valid, so far as it relates to that person's claim, without the approval of the court.

**5.4 Defence**

**1B–26** 5.4.1 A defendant who wishes to defend all or part of a claim must file a defence, and if s/he fails to do so, the claimant may obtain default judgment if Part 12 allows it.The time for filing a defence is set out in Rule 15.4.

5.4.2 A form for defending the claim is included in the Response Pack. The form for defending the claim also contains provision for making a counterclaim. Part 22 requires a defence to be verified by a statement of truth (see the Part 15 Practice Direction, paragraph 2; and see also Part 22 and the Part 22 Practice Direction).

5.4.3 The parties may, by agreement, extend the period specified in Rule 15.4 for filing a defence by up to 28 days. If the parties do so, the defendant must notify the court in writing of the date by which the defence must be filed. If the Claimant will not agree to extend time for filing of the Defence, or if a Defendant seeks further time beyond 28 days for filing a defence, the Defendant must issue an application (see Part 23) to obtain a court order for further time. A Claimant may consent to such an application.

**5.5 Default judgment**

5.5.1 A party may obtain default judgment under Part 12 except in the circumstances set out in Rules 12.2 and 12.3(3) and paragraphs 1.2 and 1.3 of the Part 12 Practice Direction, which list the circumstances where default judgment may not be obtained. **1B–27**



5.5.2 To obtain default judgment under the circumstances set out in Rules 12.4(1) and 12.9(1), a party may do so by filing a request. A court officer deals with a request and provided s/he is satisfied that the provisions of paragraph 4.1 of the Part 12 Practice Direction have been complied with, s/he will enter the default judgment.

5.5.3 Default judgment in respect of claims specified in Rules 12.4(2)(a), 12.9 and 12.10 must be obtained by making an application to a Master. The following are some of the types of claim that require an application for default judgment;

(1) against children and patients,
(2) for costs (other than fixed costs) only,
(3) for declaratory relief,
(4) by one spouse against the other on a claim in tort,
(5) for delivery up of goods where the defendant is not allowed the alternative of paying their value,
(6) against the Crown, and
(7) against a foreign State, diplomatic agents or persons or organisations who enjoy immunity from civil jurisdiction under the provisions of the International Organisations Acts 1968 and 1981.

Paragraph 4 of the Practice Direction provides information about the evidence required in support of an application for default judgment.

5.5.4 Where default judgment has been obtained for an amount to be decided by the court, the matter will be referred to a Master for directions to be given concerning the management of the case and any date to be fixed for a hearing.

**5.6 Statements of case**

5.6.1 Statements of case are defined in Rule 2.3(1) and comprise the particulars of claim and defence in the main proceedings and any further information given under Part 18 and also in any Part 20 proceedings, and any reply (which is optional); they are dealt with in Part 16. (Part 16 does not apply to claims proceeding under Part 8.) **1B–28**

5.6.2 The particulars of claim, whether contained in the Claim Form or served separately, should set out the claimant's claim clearly and fully. The same principle applies to the defence.

5.6.3 Part 16 sets out certain matters which must be included in a statement of case. Paragraphs 8 and 9 of the Part 16 Practice Direction contain matters which should be included in the particulars of claim in specific types of claim, and paragraph 10 lists matters which must be set out in the particulars of claim if relied on. In addition to the matters listed in paragraph 10, full particulars of any allegation of dishonesty or malice and, where any inference of fraud or dishonesty is alleged, the basis on which the inference is alleged should also be included. Points of law may be set out in any statement of case. For information in respect of statements of case in defamation claims see the Part 53 Practice Direction.

5.6.4 In addition to the information contained in Part 16 and the Part 16 Practice

Direction, the following guidelines on preparing a statement of case should be followed;

(1) a statement of case must be as brief and concise as possible and confined to setting out the bald facts and not the evidence of them,

(2) a statement of case should be set out in separate consecutively numbered paragraphs and sub-paragraphs,

(3) so far as possible each paragraph or sub-paragraph should contain no more than one allegation,

(4) the facts and other matters alleged should be set out as far as reasonably possible in chronological order,

(5) the statement of case should deal with the claim on a point-by-point basis, to allow a point-by-point response,

(6) where a party is required to give reasons, the allegation should be stated first and then the reasons listed one by one in separate numbered sub-paragraphs,

(7) a party wishing to advance a positive claim must identify that claim in the statement of case,

(8) any matter which, if not stated, might take another party by surprise, should be stated,

(9) where they will assist, headings, abbreviations and definitions should be used and a glossary annexed; contentious headings, abbreviations, paraphrasing and definitions should not be used and every effort should be made to ensure that they are in a form acceptable to the other parties,

(10) particulars of primary allegations should be stated as particulars and not as primary allegations,

(11) schedules or appendices should be used if this would be helpful, for example where lengthy particulars are necessary, and any response should also be stated in a schedule or appendix,

(12) any lengthy extracts from documents should be placed in a schedule.

5.6.5 A statement of case should be verified by a statement of truth. If a party fails to verify his/her statement of case, it will remain effective unless struck out, but that party may not rely on the statement of case as evidence of any of the matters contained in it; a statement of case verified by a statement of truth is advisable as evidence only at hearings other than the trial (see Rule 32.6(2)). Any party may apply to the court for an order to strike out a statement of case, which has not been verified.

## SECTION 6

## PRELIMINARY CASE MANAGEMENT

### 6.1 The Practice Master

1B–29 6.1.1 On every working day, the Practice Master is available from 10.30a.m. to 1.00p.m. and from 2.00p.m. to 4.30p.m. to answer questions about the practice of the Queen's Bench Division. Usually, one Master takes the Morning Practice, and another Master takes the Afternoon Practice. This will be shown on the Daily Cause List and is also on the notice boards in the Masters' corridors, and on the Listing Notice board outside The Masters Support Unit, Room E16. Also, a board is placed on the door of the Master who is sitting as Practice Master.(NOTE: the Practice Master will finish at 12 noon on those days where the High Court Enforcement Officers Interpleader list is listed- this usually takes place on the first Monday in each month).

6.1.2 The Practice Master cannot give advice, whether about a given case or about the law generally, s/he is there simply to answer general questions about the CPR and practice governing the work of the Queen's Bench Division, and can deal with any consent order, notwithstanding that the claim in which it is to be made has been assigned to another Master. The Practice Master may grant stays of execution and deal with urgent applications, which do not require notice to be given to the respondent. It is unnecessary to make an appointment to see the Practice Master and litigants are generally seen in order of arrival.

**6.2 Assignment to Masters**

6.2.1 A claim issued in the Central Office will normally be assigned upon issue to a particular Master as the procedural judge responsible for managing the claim. The Registry Section of the Action Department will endorse the name of the Assigned Master on the Claim Form. However, assignment may be triggered at an earlier stage, for example, by one of the following events; **1B-30**

(1) an application for pre-action disclosure under Rule 31.16,

(2) an application for an interim remedy before the commencement of a claim or where there is no relevant claim (Part 25).

It occasionally happens that a claim is assigned to a Master who may have an "interest" in the claim. In such cases the Senior Master will re-assign the claim to another Master.

6.2.2 Where either an application notice or Part 8 Claim Form is issued which requires a hearing date to be given immediately, the Registry will assign a Master and the Masters' Support Unit will give a hearing date.

6.2.3 The Senior Master may assign a particular Master to a class/group of claims or may re-assign work generally. At present Clinical negligence claims are assigned to Master Ungley and Master Yoxall. Claims for Mesothelioma are assigned to Master Whitaker. In the event of an assigned Master being on leave or for any other reason temporarily absent from the Royal Courts of Justice then the Masters' Support Unit may endorse on the appropriate document the name of another Master.

6.2.4 A court file will be opened when a Claim Form is issued. The name of the assigned Master will be endorsed on the Court File and entered on the Claim Forms. Any application notice in an assigned claim for hearing before a Master should have the name of the assigned Master entered on it by the solicitors/litigants making the application.

**6.3 Listing before Masters**

6.3.1 The Masters' lists consist of; **1B-31**

(1) the Chambers List - short applications in Rooms E102 and E110 ("the Bear Garden lists"),

(2) Private Room Appointments, (**using the prescribed PRA form**) and

(3) the High Court Enforcement Officer's Interpleader applications (formerly Sheriffs' applications).

6.3.2 2 Parties attending on all applications before the Masters are requested to complete the Court Record Sheet (form PF 48), which will be used to record details of the claim, representation and the nature of the application. Copies of this form may be found in the writing desks in the Masters' corridors and the Bear Garden. The form will be placed on the file when the hearing is concluded.

6.3.3 Masters will sit each day at 10.30am in the Bear Garden, Rooms E102 and E110 to hear applications in the Chambers Lists (Bear Garden lists). Applications of up to 30 minutes duration are listed at 10.30am, 11.00am and 11.30am. Solicitors and Counsel may attend any application in these lists although the costs of being represented by Counsel may be disallowed if not fully justified. **If the Master considers that the application is likely to take longer than 30 minutes s/he may adjourn it to a private room appointment.** The applicant must then complete the PRA form giving details of the parties' availability as fully as possible. Failure to do so may result in the request form being returned for further information thereby delaying the hearing date. The PRA form is available in the Masters Support Unit, Room E16 and available from the Court Service Website.

6.3.4 **Hearing dates** for the Chambers Lists (Bear Garden lists) are given by the Masters' Support Unit. The assigned Master gives hearing dates for private room

***Paragraph numbers marked with a "+" can be found online and on CD.***

appointments personally. The parties or their legal representatives must inform the Masters' Support Unit of any settlements as soon as possible. All time estimates must be updated as necessary. Any Order made which as a consequence results in a hearing being not required must be notified to the Master by using the Notice of Cancellation form available from the Judgments & Orders Section Room E15 – E17. This should be completed by the parties, and will be sent to the Assigned Master to note in the Diary accordingly.

6.3.5 Applications in the Chambers Lists (Bear Garden list) may, by agreement or where the application notice has not been served, be transferred for a private room appointment on a date to be specified by the Master, or may be re-listed for another date in the Chambers List. In all other cases an application for a postponement of the hearing date must be made to the Master to whom the claim has been assigned. An application may be re-listed in the Chambers List (Bear Garden list) without permission of a Master if for any reason the application has not been heard or has not been fully disposed of.

6.3.6 When an application in the Bear Garden list is adjourned by a Master s/he will specify the date to which it is adjourned.

*Adjournments*

6.3.7 An application for the adjournment of a private room appointment must be made to the Master who gave the appointment unless the application is by agreement of all parties and the Master approves. The Master will usually require details of parties' availability. Any adjournment will normally be to a new hearing date.

6.3.8 If the application for an adjournment is opposed by any other party, the party seeking the adjournment must issue an application for an adjournment, if time permits, and must give the court, and all other parties as much notice as possible of such application. Where possible, it is preferable that such application is heard before the date for the hearing. **The Master will not grant an adjournment readily where it is opposed by any other party. Good reason will need to be shown, and if the reason is illness of a party, an original (not a photocopy) medical certificate signed and dated by a medical practitioner, setting out the reasons why attendance at court is not possible, will be required.**

6.3.9 If an adjournment of a hearing is granted, the Master will usually require details of parties' availability. Any adjournment will normally be to a new hearing date.

6.3.10 **Where an application for which a Master has given a private room appointment has been settled, it is the duty of the parties or their legal representatives, particularly those who obtained that appointment, to notify the Master immediately.**

6.3.11 If the Master hearing an application considers that the result might affect the date fixed for a trial, s/he may refer the application to the Judge in Charge of the List. This possibility should be considered when making an application and a request should be included in the application notice asking the Master to refer the application to the Judge.

6.3.12 If the Master considers that an application should more properly be heard by a Judge, s/he may either during the hearing or before it takes place refer the application to the Interim Applications Judge. Among the circumstances that may make this appropriate are;

(1) that the time required for the hearing is longer than a Master could ordinarily make available,
(2) that the application raises issues of unusual difficulty or importance, etc. or
(3) that the outcome is likely to affect the trial date or window (in which case the referral will be to the Judge in Charge of the Lists).

***Paragraph numbers marked with a "+" can be found online and on CD.***

However, it is emphasised that no single factor or combination of factors is necessarily decisive, and the Master has a complete discretion.

6.3.13 The Sheriff's first return applications are interpleader applications (under RSC O.17 as set out in Schedule 1 to the CPR) and are listed at monthly intervals.

**6.4 Automatic transfer**

6.4.1 Part 26 requires certain claims to be transferred automatically. Where; **1B–32**

(1) the claim is for a specified amount of money,
(2) the claim has not been issued in a specialist list,
(3) the defendant, or one of the defendants is an individual,
(4) the claim has not been issued in the individual defendant's home court, and
(5) the claim has not already been transferred to another individual defendant's home court,

the claim will, on receipt of the defence, be transferred to the individual defendant's home court.



6.4.2 Where the Claim Form was issued in the Royal Courts of Justice the defendant's home court will be the district registry or county court for the district in which the defendant's address for service as shown on the defence is situated. If there is no such district registry or county court the proceedings will remain in the Royal Courts of Justice. If the claim is against more than one individual defendant, the claim will be transferred to the home court of the defendant who first files his/her defence. (See Section 6.9 below about transfer following an order.)

**6.5 Allocation**

6.5.1 When a defence to a claim is received in the Action Department from all the defendants, or from one or more of the defendants and the time for filing a defence has expired, the Action Department Registry will send an Allocation Questionnaire to all parties to an action, unless it has been dispensed with. If an Allocation Questionnaire is dispensed with the appropriate fee is still payable (CPR 26.3.3). **1B–33**

6.5.2 The Allocation Questionnaire to be used in accordance with Part 26 is form N150. The Allocation Questionnaire will state the time within which it must be filed, which will normally be at least 14 days after the day on which it is deemed served. Where proceedings are automatically transferred to a defendant's home court, notwithstanding that the issuing court will send out the Allocation Questionnaire before transfer, the Allocation Questionnaire should nevertheless be returned to the receiving court, the address for which will be on the covering letter.

6.5.3 Each party should state in his/her Allocation Questionnaire if there is any reason why the claim should be managed and tried at a court other than the Royal Courts of Justice or the trial centre for a particular district registry. Paragraph 2.6 of the Part 29 Practice Direction sets out certain types of claim that are suitable for trial in the Royal Courts of Justice. Form PF 52will be sent out to parties with the Allocation Questionnaire. Parties are encouraged to agree directions for the management of the claim, in the form of PF 52 or similar as prescribed by the Master.

6.5.4 Where a party fails to file his/her Allocation Questionnaire within the specified time the court officer will refer the proceedings to the Master for his/her directions. The Master's directions may include "the standard unless order", that is that unless the defaulting party files his/her Allocation Questionnaire within 7 days, his/her statement of case will be struck out.

6.5.5 Where one but not all of the parties has filed an Allocation Questionnaire the Master may allocate the claim to the multi-track where s/he considers that s/he has sufficient information to do so. Alternatively, the Master may order that an allocation hearing take place and that all or any particular parties must attend. The court officer will then send out a Notice of Allocation Hearing (form N153) giving reasons for the hearing and any other directions.

6.5.6 Parties requesting a stay to settle the proceedings should do so in their Allocation Questionnaire or otherwise in writing. The court encourages parties to consider the use of ADR (see paragraph 6.6 below). The Master will normally direct the proceedings to be stayed for one month, but parties may by agreement seek an extension of the stay. Paragraph 3 of the Part 26 Practice Direction sets out the procedure for seeking an extension.

6.5.7 Parties are reminded that an estimate of costs should be filed and served when the Allocation Questionnaire is filed (see paragraph 6.4 of the Costs Practice Direction).

6.5.8 On receipt of the Allocation Questionnaires or on an allocation hearing the Master will allocate the claim to the multi-track or transfer the claim to the appropriate county court. Rule 26.6 sets out the scope of each track. By operation of para 2.1 of Part 7A Practice Direction and Rule 26.6(4), claims proceeding in the Royal Courts of Justice must be allocated to the multi-track.

**6.6 Alternative Dispute Resolution ("ADR"):**

**1B–34** 6.6.1 Parties are encouraged to use ADR (such as, but not confined to, mediation and conciliation) to try to resolve their disputes or particular issues. Legal representatives should consider with their clients and the other parties the possibility of attempting to resolve the dispute or particular issues by ADR and they should ensure that their clients are fully informed as to the most cost effective means of resolving their dispute.

6.6.2 The settlement of disputes by ADR can;

(1) significantly reduce parties' costs,
(2) save parties the delay of litigation in resolving their disputes,
(3) assist parties to preserve their existing commercial relationships while resolving their disputes, and
(4) provide a wider range of remedies than those available through litigation.

The Master will in an appropriate case invite the parties to consider whether their dispute, or particular issues in it, could be resolved by ADR. The Master may also either stay proceedings for a specified period of time or extend the time for compliance with an order, a Rule or Practice Direction to encourage and enable the parties to use ADR. Parties may apply for directions seeking a stay for ADR at any time.

6.6.3 Information concerning ADR may be obtained from the Admiralty and Commercial Court Registry.

**6.7 Part 8—Alternative procedure for claims:**

**1B–35** 6.7.1 Paragraphs 4.3.14 to 4.3.16 above deal with issuing a Part 8 Claim Form. The alternative procedure set out in Part 8 ("the Part 8 procedure") may not be used if a Practice Direction provides that it does not apply in respect of a particular type of claim. A Rule or Practice Direction may require or permit the use of the Pt 8 procedure and may disapply or modify any of the Pt 8 rules in respect of specified types of proceedings. The Part 8B Practice Direction deals with commencement of proceedings under the Rules of the Supreme Court and the County Court Rules the provisions of which remain in force in Schedules 1 and 2 to the CPR ("the Schedule rules"). The Schedule rules and the Practice Directions supporting them may require certain proceedings to be commenced by the issue of a Part 8 Claim Form with appropriate modifications to the Part 8 procedure.

6.7.2 The main features of the Part 8 procedure are;

(1) Part 16 (statements of case) does not apply, but the claimant may be required to file Details of Claim when issuing,
(2) Part 15 (defence and reply) does not apply,
(3) judgment in default may not be obtained (Rule 12.2),
(4) Rules 14.4 to 14.7 (judgment by request on an admission) do not apply,
(5) a Part 8 claim shall be treated as being allocated to the multi-track.

6.7.3 All Part 8 Claim Forms will be referred to a Master for directions as soon as the Part 8 Claim Form is issued. These may include fixing a hearing date. Where a hearing date is fixed, notice of the hearing date must be served with the Claim Form. Where the Master does not fix a hearing date when the Claim Form is issued s/he will give directions for the disposal of the claim as soon as practicable after the receipt of the acknowledgement of service or as the case may be, the expiry of the period for acknowledging service.

6.7.4 Where a Part 8 Claim Form has been issued for the purpose of giving effect to a consent order for an award of damages to a child or patient or an award of provisional damages as in paragraph 4.1.15 (1) and (2) above, a draft of the order sought should be attached to the claim form. For more information see paragraphs 6.8.1 to 6.8.8 and 9.3.8 to 9.3.10 below about children and patients, and paragraphs 6.8.12, 9.3.11 and 9.3.12 below about provisional damages.

6.7.5 A defendant who wishes to respond to a Part 8 Claim Form should acknowledge service of it and may do so either by using form N210 or otherwise in writing giving the following information;
(1) whether s/he contests the claim, and
(2) where s/he is seeking a different remedy from that set out in the Claim Form, what that remedy is.

If a defendant does not acknowledge service of the Claim Form within the specified time, s/he may attend the hearing of the claim but may not take part in the hearing unless the court gives permission.

6.7.6 Rules 8.5 and 8.6 and paragraph 5 of the Part 8 Practice Direction (alternative procedure) deal with evidence to be relied on in Part 8 proceedings; **the claimant's evidence must be filed and served with the Claim Form, and the defendant's evidence (if any) must be filed with his/her acknowledgement of service.** If the defendant files written evidence s/he must at the same time serve it on the other parties. It is helpful to the court if, where the defendant does not intend to rely on written evidence, s/he notifies the court in writing to that effect.

6.7.7 Where a defendant contends that the Part 8 procedure should not be used, s/he should state the reasons for his/her contention on his/her acknowledgement of service. On receipt of the acknowledgement of service, the Master will give appropriate directions for the future management of the claim.

### 6.8 Specific matters which may be dealt with under the Part 8 procedure

*Settlements on behalf of children and patients*

6.8.1 Part 21 and the Part 21 Practice Direction set out the requirements for litigation by or against children and patients. References in Part 21, the Part 21 Practice Direction and in this guide to; **1B–36**
(1) "child" means a person under 18, and
(2) "patient" means a person who by reason of mental disorder within the meaning of the Mental Health Act 1983 is incapable of managing and administering his/her own property and affairs.

No settlement or compromise of a claim by or against a child or patient will be binding unless and until the court has approved it. In addition, a party may not obtain a default judgment against a child or patient without the permission of the court, and may not enter judgment on an admission against a child or patient.

***Paragraph numbers marked with a "+" can be found online and on CD.***

6.8.2 A patient must have a litigation friend to conduct proceedings on his/her behalf, and so must a child unless the court makes an order permitting the child to act on his/her own behalf. A litigation friend is someone who can fairly and competently conduct proceedings on behalf of the child or patient. S/he must have no interest in the proceedings adverse to that of the child or patient, and all steps s/he takes in the proceedings must be taken for the benefit of the child or patient. Rules 21.5 to 21.8 and paragraphs 2 and 3 of the Practice Direction set out how a person may become a litigation friend.

6.8.3 Applications for the approval of settlements or compromises of claims by or against a child or patient proceeding in the Central Office are heard by a Master. If the purpose of starting the claim is for the approval of a settlement, a Part 8 Claim Form should be issued in accordance with form PF 170(A) which must contain a request for approval of the settlement (or compromise) and, in addition to the details of the claim, must set out the terms of the settlement (or compromise) or must have attached to it a draft consent order. The draft consent order should be in form N292, and should include the child's National Insurance Number, so that the child can be subsequently traced. See paragraph 6 of the Practice Direction for further information which the Master will require.

6.8.4 Where parties reach a settlement (or compromise) in proceedings started by the issue of a Part 7 Claim Form (where the trial has not started) an application must be made to the Master, or if the amount of the proposed settlement exceeds £750,000, to the Judge, in accordance with Part 23 for the approval of the settlement. The application notice should be in form PF170(B) and should have attached to it a draft consent order in form N292. (See CPR 21.10 PD 21 paras 6 & 7.) The application notice should be lodged in Room E16. (See Section 7.12 below for information about applications.) If the trial has started, oral application may be made to the trial judge. Applications for approval of a settlement on behalf of a child or patient will normally be heard in public unless the Judge or Master orders otherwise. If a settlement is approved in private, the terms of settlement will be announced in public.

6.8.5 Paragraph 8 of the Practice Direction gives information about control of money recovered by or on behalf of a child or patient. Paragraph 10 deals with investment of money on behalf of a child and paragraph 11 deals with investment on behalf of a patient. Enquiries concerning investment for a child are dealt with in Room E105.

6.8.6 In respect of investment on behalf of a child, the litigation friend or his/her legal representative should provide the Master or a Judge with a completed form PF 172 (request for investment) for completion by the Master. The child's birth certificate should also be provided. When investment directions have been given, the PF 172 will then be forwarded to the Court Funds Office for their investment managers to make the appropriate investment. The Court of Protection is responsible for the administration of patients' funds (unless they are small). Paragraph 11 of the Practice Direction gives full information about procedure for investment by the Court of Protection. These procedures may also be used for investment of money on behalf of a child or patient following an award of damages at trial.

6.8.7 Damages may also be paid to a child or patient by way of a structured settlement. A Judge or Master must approve a structured settlement on behalf of a child or patient. The Court of Protection must also approve a structured settlement on behalf of a patient. (For more information about structured settlements see the Part 40C Practice Direction—Structured Settlements.)

6.8.8 Control of a child's fund, provided s/he is not also a patient, passes to him when s/he reaches the age of 18 (see paragraph 12.2 of the Practice Direction).

*Summary order for possession*

6.8.9 In practice such claims are usually dealt with in the appropriate County Court. Paragraph 1 of Part 55 Practice direction gives details of the limited circumstances where a claim may be brought in the High Court. High Court claims for the possession of land subject to a mortgage will be assigned to the Chancery Division.

*Settlement of a provisional damages claim*

6.8.12 A claim for provisional damages may proceed under Part 8 where the Claim Form is issued solely for the purpose of obtaining a consent judgment. The claimant must state in his/her Claim Form in addition to the matters set out in paragraph 4.4 of the Part 16 Practice Direction that the parties have reached agreement and request a consent judgment. A draft order in accordance with paragraph 4.2 of the Part 41 Practice Direction should be attached to the Claim Form. The claimant or his/her legal representative must lodge the case file documents (set out in the draft order) in Room E16. Once the Provisional damages claim has been approved the documents lodged will be compiled into a file and preserved by the Court. For more information about provisional damages claims and orders see Part 41 and the Part 41 Practice Direction, and section 9.3 below.

*Costs only proceedings*

6.8.13 Proceedings may be brought under Part 8 where the parties to a dispute have reached a written agreement before proceedings have been started but have been unable to agree an amount of costs. The costs only proceedings may be started by the issue of a Claim Form in the Supreme Court Costs Office at Clifford's Inn, Fetter Lane, London EC4A 1DQ. The Costs Practice Direction at Section 17 sets out in detail the provisions for issue and proceeding with the claim.

QB GUIDE

**6.9 Transfer**

6.9.1 Part 30 and the Part 30 Practice Direction deal with transfer of proceedings, within the High Court, from the High Court to the County Court and between County Courts. The jurisdiction of the High Court to transfer proceedings to the county courts is contained in s.40 of the County Courts Act 1984 as substituted by s.2(1) of the Courts and Legal Services Act 1990. Under that section the court has jurisdiction in certain circumstances to strike out claims that should have been started in a county court. **1B–37**

6.9.2 Rule 30.2 sets out the provisions for the transfer of proceedings between;
(1) county courts,
(2) the Royal Courts of Justice and a district registry of the High Court, and
(3) between district registries.

Rule 30.3 sets out the criteria to which the court will have regard when making an order for transfer. (See paragraph 6.4 above about automatic transfer.)

6.9.3 The High Court may order proceedings in any Division of the High Court to be transferred to another Division or to or from a specialist list. **An application for the transfer of proceedings to or from a specialist list must be made to a Judge dealing with claims in that list.**

6.9.4 A claim with an estimated value of less than £50,000 may generally be transferred to a county court, if the county court has jurisdiction, unless it is to proceed in the High Court under an enactment or in a specialist list

6.9.5 An order for transfer takes effect from the date it is made. When an order for transfer is sealed the court officer will immediately transfer the matter to the receiving court. At the same time, the court officer will also notify all parties of the transfer. An order for transfer to the High Court at the Royal Courts of Justice should state: "Transfer to the Central Office, Queen's Bench Division, [or as appropriate] at the Royal Courts of Justice."

6.9.6 Paragraph 5 of the Part 30 Practice Direction sets out the procedure for appealing an order for transfer. Where an order for transfer is made in the absence of notice given to a party, that party may apply to the court that made the order to have it set aside.

6.9.7 Where money has been paid into court before an order for transfer is made, the court may direct transfer of the money to the control of the receiving court.

***Paragraph numbers marked with a "+" can be found online and on CD.***

**6.10 Part 20 proceedings:**

**1B–38** 6.10.1 Part 20 deals with (a) counterclaims and (b) other additional claims, being claims for contribution or indemnity and what were formerly called "third party" claims. A Part 20 claim is treated as a claim for the purpose of the CPR with certain exceptions, for which see Rule 20.3.

6.10.2 A defendant may make a counterclaim by completing the defence and counterclaim form provided in the Response Pack. The fee for the Counterclaim will depend on the amount claimed, and will therefore be deemed the same as a fee for Issue of Claim (see Fees Annex 1). If the counterclaim is not filed with the defence, the permission of the court is required. Where a counterclaim brings in a new party, the defendant (Part 20 claimant) must apply to the court for an order in form PF 21A adding the new party as defendant.

6.10.3 A defendant claiming contribution or indemnity from another defendant may do so by filing a notice, in form PF 22, containing a statement of the nature and grounds of his/her claim and serving the notice on the other defendant.

6.10.4 Any other additional claim may be brought by the issue of a Part 20 Claim Form, N211. If the Part 20 Claim Form is issued at a time other than when the defence is filed, the permission of the court is required. Rule 20.8 deals with service of a Part 20 Claim Form and Rule 20.12 sets out the forms which must accompany the Part 20 Claim Form.

**6.11 Summary judgment**

**1B–39** 6.11.1 The court may give summary judgment under Part 24 against a claimant or defendant;

(1) if it considers that (a) the claimant has no real prospect of succeeding on the claim or issue, or (b) the defendant has no real prospect of successfully defending the claim, and

(2) there is no other reason why the claim or issue should be disposed of at a trial.

6.11.2 The court may give summary judgment against a claimant in any type of proceedings, and against a defendant in any type of proceedings except (a) proceedings for possession of residential premises against a mortgagor, or a tenant or person holding over after the end of his/her tenancy where occupancy is protected within the meaning of the Rent Act 1977 or the Housing Act 1988, (b) proceedings for an Admiralty claim in Rem, and (c) contentious probate proceedings. For information about summary disposal of defamation claims see Part 53, the Part 53 Practice Direction and paragraph 12 7 below.

6.11.3 An application for summary judgment should be made in accordance with Part 23 and the application notice should contain the information set out in paragraph 2 of the Part 24 Practice Direction (parties may use forms PF 11 and PF 12 as precedents). The application notice should be filed and served on the respondent giving at least 14 days notice of the date fixed for the hearing and the issues to be decided at the hearing. Unless the application notice contains all the evidence on which the applicant relies, the application notice should identify that evidence.

6.11.4 In claims which include a claim for;

(1) specific performance of an agreement,

(2) rescission of such an agreement, or

(3) forfeiture or return of a deposit made under such an agreement,

the application notice and any evidence in support must be served on the defendant not less than 4 days before the hearing. This replaces for such applications the 14 days notice usually required for summary judgment applications (Part 24 Practice Direction paragraph 7).

6.11.5 The application will normally be listed before a Master unless for example, an injunction is also sought. In that case the application notice should state that the application is intended to be made to a Judge.

***Paragraph numbers marked with a "+" can be found online and on CD.***

6.11.6 Where an order made on an application for summary judgment does not dispose of the claim or issue, the court will give case management directions in respect of the claim or issue.

### 6.12 Offers to settle and payments into and out of court:

6.12.1 A party may offer to settle a claim at any time. Part 36 deals with offers to settle and payments into court. An offer to settle made in accordance with Part 36 will have the costs and other consequences specified in that Part and may be made at any time after proceedings have started. Paragraph 1 of the Part 36 Practice Direction defines an offer made in accordance with Part 36. See also paragraph 5 of the Part 36 Practice Direction which contains general provisions concerning Part 36 offers and Part 36 payments. **1B–40**



6.12.2 A Part 36 offer may be made by any party, but to comply with Part 36 a defendant who makes an offer to settle for a specified sum must do so by way of a Part 36 payment into court. Paragraph 4.1(2) of the Part 36 Practice Direction sets out the requirements for making a Part 36 payment in respect of a claim proceeding in the Royal Courts of Justice. If a defendant has made a pre-action offer to settle and proceedings are then started, in order for the court to take account of his/her offers/he must make a Part 36 payment of not less than the amount offered within 14 days of service of the Claim Form. See also paragraph 10 of the Part 36 Practice Direction which deals with compensation recovery in respect of Part 36 payments.

6.12.3 The times for accepting a Part 36 offer or Part 36 payment are set out in Rules 36.11 and 36.12; the general rule is that a Part 36 offer or Part 36 payment made more than 21 days before the start of the trial may be accepted without the permission of the court, within 21 days after it was made. Otherwise, the permission of the court must be obtained. A Part 36 offer is made when received by the offeree. A Part 36 payment is made when the Part 36 payment notice (form N242A) is served on the claimant.

6.12.4 A party may accept a Part 36 offer or Part 36 payment by serving on the offeror a notice of acceptance (form N243 may be used to accept a Part 36 payment) within the times set out in Rules 36.11 and 36.12. When a Part 36 offer or Part 36 payment is accepted within those times, the general rule is that the claimant will be entitled to his/her costs up to the date of service of the notice of acceptance.

6.12.5 To obtain money out of court on acceptance of a Part 36 payment, the claimant should file a request for payment (form N243/N201) in the Action Department of the Central Office, and file a copy in the Court Funds Office. See paragraph 8 of the Part 36 Practice Direction for full details of the procedure for obtaining payment out of court.

6.12.6 The court's permission is required for acceptance of a Part 36 offer or Part 36 payment;

(1) which is not made or accepted within the times set out in Rules 36.11 and 36.12, or
(2) where acceptance is by or on behalf of a child or patient, or
(3) where a defence of tender has been put forward, or
(4) otherwise as mentioned in Rule 36.17.

6.12.7 Where a Part 36 offer or Part 36 payment is not accepted and a trial of the claim takes place, Rule 36.20 sets out the costs consequences where a claimant fails to do better than the Part 36 offer or Part 36 payment, and Rule 36.21 sets out the costs and other consequences where a claimant does better than s/he proposed in his/her Part 36 offer.

6.12.8 In the Action Department a Part 36 offer or payment, if not accepted, will be kept in a separate file held by the Manager of the Registry Section and not made available to the trial judge until after determination.

*Paragraph numbers marked with a "+" can be found online and on CD.*

6.12.9 **It should be noted that there will be extensive changes to the Part 36 procedure, and to the provisions about payments into court, which will come into force on 6th April 2007. The above notes reflect the position before that date. For details of the changes please see the revised Parts 36 and 37 (Schedules 1 and 2 to The Civil Procedure (Amendment No. 3) Rules 2006).**

## SECTION 7

## CASE MANAGEMENT AND INTERIM REMEDIES

### 7.1 Case management—general:

1B–41 7.1.1 CPR requires the court to provide a high degree of case management. Case management includes; identifying disputed issues at an early stage; fixing timetables; dealing with as many aspects of the claim as possible on the same occasion; controlling costs; disposing of proceedings summarily where appropriate; dealing with the applications without a hearing where appropriate; and giving directions to ensure that the trial of a claim proceeds quickly and efficiently. The court will expect the parties to co-operate with each other, and where appropriate, will encourage the parties to use ADR or otherwise help them settle the case.

7.1.2 Parties and their legal representatives will be expected to do all that they can to agree proposals for the management of the claim in accordance with Rule 29.4 and paragraphs 4.6 to 4.8 of the Part 29 Practice Direction. There is provision in the Allocation Questionnaire for proposing certain directions to be made, otherwise parties may use form PF 50 for making the application (attaching to it the draft form of order in form PF 52) and file it for the Master's approval. If the Master approves the proposals s/he will give directions accordingly.

### 7.2 The Case Management Conference:

1B–42 7.2.1 Parties who are unable to agree proposals for the management of the case, should notify the Court of the matters which they are unable to agree.

7.2.2 Where;

(1) the parties proposed directions are not approved, or
(2) parties are unable to agree proposed directions, or
(3) the Master wishes to make further directions,

the Master will generally either consult the parties or direct that a case management conference be held.

7.2.3 In relatively straightforward claims, the Court may give directions without holding a case management conference.

7.2.4 Any party who considers that a case management conference should be held before any directions are given should so state in his/her Allocation Questionnaire, (or in a Part 8 claim should notify the Master in writing), giving his/her reasons and supplying a realistic time estimate for the case management conference, with a list of any dates or times convenient to all parties, or most of them, in form PF 49.

7.2.5 Where a case management conference has been fixed, parties should ensure that any other applications are listed or made at that hearing. A party applying for directions at the case management conference should use form PF 50 for making their application and attach to it the draft order for directions (form PF 52).

7.2.6 Parties should consider whether a case summary would assist the Master at the Case Management Conference in dealing with the issues before him or her. Paragraph 5.7 of the Part 29 Practice Direction sets out the provisions for preparation of a case summary.

7.2.7 It may be appropriate for the advocates instructed or expected to be instructed to appear at the trial to attend any hearing at which case management directions are likely to be given. In any event, the legal representatives who attend the case management conference must be familiar with the case and have sufficient authority to deal with any issues which may arise. Where necessary, the court may order the attendance of a party.

**7.3 Preliminary issues:**

7.3.1 Costs can sometimes be saved by identifying decisive issues, or potentially decisive issues, and by the Court ordering that they be tried first. The decision of one issue, although not necessarily itself decisive of the claim as a whole, may enable the parties to settle the remainder of the dispute. In such a case, the trial of a preliminary issue may be appropriate. **1B–43**

7.3.2 At the allocation stage, at any case management conference and again at any pre-trial review, the court will consider whether the trial of a preliminary issue may be helpful. Where such an order is made, the parties and the court should consider whether the costs of the issue should be in the issue or in the claim as a whole.

7.3.3 Where there is an application for summary judgment, and issues of law or construction may be determined in the respondent's favour, it will usually be in the interests of the parties for such issues to be determined conclusively, rather than that the application should simply be dismissed.

**7.4 Trial timetable:**

7.4.1 To assist the court to set a trial timetable, a draft timetable should be prepared by the claimant's advocate(s) after consulting the other parties advocates. If there are differing views, those differences should be clearly indicated in the timetable. The draft timetable should be filed with the trial bundle. **1B–44**

7.4.2 The trial timetable will normally include times for giving evidence (whether of fact or opinion) and for oral submissions during the trial.

7.4.3 The trial timetable may be fixed at the case management conference, at any pre-trial review or at the beginning of the trial itself.

**7.5 Listing Questionnaire (Pre Trial Check List):**

7.5.1 The court will send out a Pre Trial Checklist (N170) to all parties for completion, specifying the date by which it must be returned. **1B–45**

7.5.2 Paragraph 6.4 of the Costs Practice Direction requires an estimate of costs to be filed and served with the Pre Trial Checklist.

**7.6 Pre-trial review:**

7.6.1 Where the trial of a claim is estimated to last more than 10 days, or where the circumstances require it, the Master may direct that a pre-trial review ("PTR") should be held. The PTR may be heard by a Master, but more usually is heard by a Judge. **1B–46**

7.6.2 Application should normally be made to the Queen's Bench Listing Officer for the PTR to be heard by the trial judge (if known), and the applicant should do all that s/he can to ensure that it is heard between 4 and 8 weeks before the trial date, and in any event long enough before the trial date to allow a realistic time in which to complete any outstanding matters.

7.6.3 The PTR should be attended by the advocates who are to represent the parties at the trial.

7.6.4 At least 7 days before the date fixed for the PTR, the applicant must serve the other parties with a list of matters to be considered at the PTR, and those other parties must serve their responses at least 2 days before the PTR. Account must be taken of the answers in any listing questionnaires filed. Realistic proposals must be put forward and if possible agreed as to the time likely to be required for each stage of the trial and as to the order in which witnesses are to be called.

7.6.5 The applicant should lodge a properly indexed bundle containing the listing questionnaires (if directed to be filed) and the lists of matters and the proposals, together with the results of discussions between the parties, and any other relevant material, in the Queen's Bench Listing Office, Room WG8, by no later than 10.30am on the day before the day fixed for the hearing of the PTR. If the PTR is to take place before a Master and he asks for the bundle in advance, it should be lodged in the Masters' Support Unit, Room E14. Otherwise it should be lodged at the hearing.

7.6.6 At the PTR, the court will review the parties' state of preparation, deal with any outstanding matters, and give any directions or further directions that may be necessary.

**7.7 Requests for further information:**

**1B–47** 7.7.1 A party seeking further information or clarification under Part 18 should serve a written request on the party from whom the information is sought before making an application to the court. Paragraph 1 of the Part 18 Practice Direction deals with how the request should be made, and paragraph 2 deals with the response. A statement of truth should verify a response. Parties may use form PF 56 for a combined request and reply, if they so wish.

7.7.2 If a party who has been asked to provide further information or clarification objects or is unable to do so, s/he must notify the party making the request in writing.

7.7.3 Where it is necessary to apply for an order for further information or clarification the party making the application should set out in or have attached to his/her application notice;

(1) the text of the order sought specifying the matters on which further information or clarification is sought, and
(2) whether a request has been made and, if so, the result of that request.

Applicants may use form PF 57 for their application notice.

**7.8 Disclosure and Inspection of Documents:**

**1B–48** Disclosure and inspection of documents involves two stages. First, disclosure of the existence of documents and claiming privilege from inspection for such documents as may attract privilege (e.g. those to which 'legal advice' privilege applies); and secondly, offering facilities to the opposing party for inspection of certain of those documents.

7.8.1 Under Part 31, there is no longer any general duty to disclose documents. Instead, a party is prevented from relying on any document that s/he has not disclosed, and is required to give inspection of any document to which s/he refers in his/her statement of case or in any witness statement, etc.. The intention is that disclosure should be proportionate to the value of the claim.

7.8.2 If an order for disclosure is made, unless the contrary is stated, the Court will order standard disclosure, namely disclosure of only;

(1) the documents on which a party relies,
(2) the documents that adversely affect his/her own or another party's case,
(3) the documents that support another party's case, and
(4) the documents required to be disclosed by a relevant practice direction.

Parties should give standard disclosure by completing form N265 and may list the documents by category.

7.8.3 The court may either limit or dispense with disclosure (and the parties may agree to do likewise). The court may also order disclosure of specified documents or

*Paragraph numbers marked with a "+" can be found online and on CD.*

specified classes of documents. In deciding whether to make any such order for specific disclosure, the court will want to be satisfied that the disclosure is necessary, that the cost of disclosure will not outweigh the benefits of disclosure and that a party's ability to continue the litigation would not be impaired by any such order.

7.8.4 The court will therefore seek to ensure that any specific disclosure ordered is appropriate to the particular case, taking into account the financial position of the parties, the importance of the case and the complexity of the issues.

7.8.5 If specific disclosure is sought, a separate application for specific disclosure should be made in accordance with Part 23; it is not a matter that would be routinely dealt with at the CMC. The parties should give careful thought to ways of limiting the burdens of such disclosure, whether by giving disclosure in stages, by dispensing with the need to produce copies of the same document, by requiring disclosure of documents sufficient merely for a limited purpose, or otherwise. They should also consider whether the need for disclosure could be reduced or eliminated by a request for further information.



7.8.6 A party who has the right to inspect a document should give written notice of his/her wish to inspect to the party disclosing the document. That party must permit inspection not more than 7 days after receipt of the notice.

**7.9 Experts and Assessors:**

7.9.1 The parties in a claim must bear in mind that under Part 35 no party may call **1B–49**
an expert or put in evidence an expert's report without the court's express permission, and the court is under a duty to restrict such evidence to what is reasonably required.

7.9.2 The duty of an expert called to give evidence is to assist the court. This duty overrides any obligation to the party instructing him or by whom s/he is being paid (see the Part 35 Practice Direction). In fulfilment of this duty, an expert must for instance make it clear if a particular question or issue falls outside his/her expertise or if s/he considers that insufficient information is available on which to express an opinion.

7.9.3 Before the Master gives permission, s/he must be told the field of expertise of the expert on whose evidence a party wishes to rely and where practicable the identity of the expert. Even then, s/he may, before giving permission, impose a limit on the extent to which the cost of such evidence may be recovered from the other parties in the claim.

7.9.4 Parties should always consider whether a single expert could be appointed in a particular claim or to deal with a particular issue. Before giving permission for the parties to call separate experts, the Master will always consider whether a single joint expert ought to be used, whether in relation to the issues as a whole or to a particular issue.

7.9.5 In many cases it is possible for the question of expert evidence or one or more of the areas of expert evidence to be dealt with by a single expert. Single experts are, for example, often appropriate to deal with questions of quantum in cases where primary issues are as to liability. Likewise, where expert evidence is required in order to acquaint the court with matters of expert fact, as opposed to opinion, a single expert will usually be appropriate. There remain, however, a body of cases where liability will turn upon expert opinion evidence and where it will be appropriate for the parties to instruct their own experts. For example, in cases where the issue for determination is as to whether a party acted in accordance with proper professional standards, it will often be of value to the court to hear the opinions of more than one expert as to the proper standard in order that the court becomes acquainted with the range of views existing upon the question and in order that the evidence can be tested in cross-examination.

7.9.6 It will not be a sufficient ground for objecting to an order for a single joint expert that the parties have already chosen their own experts. An order for a single joint expert does not prevent a party from having his/her own expert to advise him, though that is likely to be at his/her own cost, regardless of the outcome.

7.9.7 When the use of a single joint expert is being considered, the Master will expect the parties to co-operate in agreeing terms of reference for and instructions to the expert. In most cases, such terms of reference/instructions will include a statement of what the expert is asked to do, will identify any documents that s/he will be asked to consider and will specify any assumptions that s/he is asked to make.

7.9.8 The court will generally also order that experts in the same field confer on a 'without prejudice' basis, and then report in writing to the parties and the court on the extent of any agreement, giving reasons at least in summary for any continuing disagreement. A direction to 'confer' gives the experts the choice of discussing the matter by telephone or in any other convenient way, as an alternative to attending an actual meeting. Any material change of view of an expert should be communicated in writing to the other parties through their legal representatives, and when appropriate, to the court.

7.9.9 Written questions may be put to an expert within 28 days after service of his/her report, but must only be for purposes of clarification of the expert's report e.g. when the other party does not understand it. Questions going beyond this can only be put with the agreement of the parties or the Master's permission. The procedure of putting written questions to experts is not intended to interfere with the procedure for an exchange of professional opinion in discussions between experts or to inhibit that exchange of professional opinion. If questions that are oppressive in number or content are put without permission for any purpose other than clarification of the expert's report, the court is likely to disallow the questions and make an appropriate order for costs against the party putting them. (See paragraph 4.3 of the Part 35 Practice Direction with respect to payment of an expert's fees for answering questions under Rule 35.6.)

7.9.10 An expert may file with the court a written request for directions to assist him in carrying out his/her function as an expert. The expert should guard against accidentally informing the court about, or about matters connected with, communications or potential communications between the parties that are without prejudice or privileged. The expert may properly be asked to be privy to the content of these communications because s/he has been asked to assist the party instructing him to evaluate them.

7.9.11 Under Rule 35.15 the court may appoint an assessor to assist it in relation to any matter in which the assessor has skill and experience. The report of the assessor is made available to the parties. The remuneration of the assessor is decided by the court and forms part of the costs of the proceedings.

**7.10 Evidence:**

**1B–50** 7.10.1 Evidence is dealt with in the CPR in Parts 32, 33 and 34.

7.10.2 The most common form of written evidence is a witness statement. The Part 32 Practice Direction at paragraphs 17, 18 and 19 contains information about the heading, body (what it must contain) and format of a witness statement. The witness must sign a statement of truth to verify the witness statement; the wording of the statement of truth is set out in paragraph 20.2 of the Practice Direction.

7.10.3 A witness statement may be used as evidence in support of an interim application and, where it has been served on any other party to a claim, it may be relied on as a statement of the oral evidence of the witness at the trial. Part 33 contains provisions relating to the use of hearsay evidence in a witness statement.

7.10.4 In addition to the information and provisions for making a witness statement mentioned in paragraph 7.10.2, the following matters should be borne in mind;

(1) a witness statement must contain the truth, the whole truth and nothing but the truth on the issues it covers,

(2) those issues should consist only of the issues on which the party serving the witness statement wishes that witness to give evidence in chief and should not include commentary on the trial bundle or other matters which [may arise during the trial or] may have arisen during the proceedings,

(3) a witness statement should be as concise as the circumstances allow, inadmissible or irrelevant material should not be included,

(4) the cost of preparation of an over-elaborate witness statement may not be allowed,

(5) Rule 32.14 states that proceedings for contempt of court may be brought against a person if s/he makes, or causes to be made, a false statement in a document verified by a statement of truth without an honest belief in its truth,

(6) if a party discovers that a witness statement, which they have served, is incorrect they must inform the other parties immediately.

7.10.5 Evidence may also be given by affidavit but unless an affidavit is specifically required either in compliance with a court order, a Rule or Practice Direction, or an enactment, the party putting forward the affidavit may not recover from another party the cost of making an affidavit unless the court so orders.

7.10.6 The Part 32 Practice Direction at paragraphs 3 to 6 contains information about the heading, body, jurat (the sworn statement which authenticates the affidavit) and the format of an affidavit. The court will normally give directions as to whether a witness statement or, where appropriate, an affidavit is to be filed.

7.10.7 A statement of case, which has been verified by a statement of truth, and an application notice containing facts which have been verified by a statement of truth may also stand as evidence other than at the trial.

7.10.8 Evidence by deposition is dealt with in Part 34. A party may apply to a Master for an order for a person to be examined before a hearing takes place (Rule 34.8). Evidence obtained on an examination under that Rule is referred to as a deposition. The Master may order the person to be examined before either a Judge, an examiner of the court or such other person as the court appoints. The Part 34 Practice Direction at paragraph 4 sets out in detail how the examination should take place.

7.10.9 Provisions relating to applications for evidence by deposition to be taken either;

(1) in this country for use in a foreign court, or

(2) abroad for use in proceedings within the jurisdiction

are set out in detail in the Part 34 Practice Direction at paragraphs 5 and 6.

7.10.10 The procedure for issuing a witness summons is also dealt with in Part 34 and the Practice Direction. A witness summons may require a witness to;

(1) attend court, or

(2) produce documents to the court, or

(3) both,

on either a date fixed for the hearing or another date as the court may direct (but see also Rule 31.17 which may be used when there are areas of contention).

7.10.11 The court may also issue a witness summons in aid of a court or tribunal which does not have the power to issue a witness summons in relation to the proceedings before it (and see the Part 34 Practice Direction at paragraphs 1, 2 and 3).

7.10.12 To issue a witness summons, two copies should be filed in the Action Department, Room E07 for sealing; one copy will be retained on the court file.

7.10.13 A witness summons must be served at least 7 days before the date upon which the witness is required to attend. If this is not possible for any reason, an order must be sought from a Master that a witness summons is binding although it will be served less than 7 days before the date when the witness is required to attend. A Master will usually be prepared to deal with this in Practice, without notice.

7.10.14 A witness summons will be served by the court unless the party on whose behalf it is issued indicates in writing that s/he wishes to serve it himself. If time is a critical factor, it may be preferable for the party to serve the witness summons. For the method of service see the notes to Part 34 at paragraph 34.6.1.

7.10.15 At the time of service of the witness summons the witness must be offered "Conduct money" to defray his or her expenses of coming to, staying at, and returning from the place of the trial. Thus, where the court is to serve, the party on whose behalf it is issued must deposit the amount of conduct money in the court office. For the relevant amounts see the note at Part 34 paragraph 34.7.1.

**7.11 Hearings:**

*Hearings generally*

1B–51 **7.11.1 Hearings in public/private**

All hearings are in principle open to the public, even though in practice most of the hearings until the trial itself will be attended only by the parties and their representatives. However, in an appropriate case the court may decide to hold a hearing in private. Rule 39.2 lists the circumstances where it may be appropriate to hold a hearing in private. In addition, paragraph 1.5 of the Part 39 Practice Direction sets out certain types of hearings which may be listed in private.

7.11.2 The court also has the power under section 11 of the Contempt of Court Act 1981 to make an order forbidding publication of any details that might identify one or more of the parties. Such orders are granted only in exceptional cases.

7.11.3 References in the CPR and Practice Directions to hearings being in public or private do not restrict any existing rights of audience or confer any new rights of audience in respect of applications or proceedings which under the rules previously in force would have been heard in court or chambers respectively. Advocates (and judges) do not wear robes at interim hearings before High Court Judges. Robes are worn for trials and certain other proceedings such as preliminary issues, committals etc. It is not intended that the new routes of appeal should restrict the advocate's right of audience, in that, a solicitor who appeared in a county court matter which is the subject of an appeal to a High Court Judge would normally be allowed to appear at the appeal hearing.

**7.11.4 Conduct of the parties**

Parties are reminded that they are expected to act with courtesy and respect for the other parties present and for the proceedings of the court. Punctuality is particularly important; being late for hearings is unfair to the other parties and other court users, as well as being discourteous to them and to the court.

*Preparation for hearings*

7.11.5 To ensure court time is used efficiently there must be adequate preparation prior to the hearing. This includes the preparation and exchange of skeleton arguments, the compilation of bundles of documents and the giving of realistic time estimates. Where estimates prove inaccurate, a hearing may have to be adjourned to a later date, and the party responsible for the adjournment is likely to be ordered to pay the costs thrown away.

7.11.6 The parties should use their best endeavours to agree beforehand the issues, or main issues between them, and must co-operate with the court and each other to enable the court to deal with claims justly; parties may expect to be penalised for failing to do so.

***Paragraph numbers marked with a "+" can be found online and on CD.***

7.11.7 A bundle of documents must be compiled for the court's use at the trial, and also for hearings before the Interim Applications Judge or a Master where the documents to be referred to total 25 pages or more. The party lodging a trial or hearing bundle should supply identical bundles to all parties and for the use of witnesses. The efficient preparation of bundles is very important. Where bundles have been properly prepared, the claim will be easier to understand and present, and time and costs are likely to be saved. Where documents are copied unnecessarily or bundled incompetently, the costs may be disallowed. Paragraph 3 of the Part 39 Practice Direction sets out in full the requirements for compiling bundles of documents for hearings or trial.

7.11.8 The trial bundle must be filed not more than 7 and not less than 3 days before the start of the trial. Bundles for a Master's hearing should be brought to the hearing unless it is likely to assist the Master to read the bundle in advance in which case it should be lodged with the Masters' Support Unit or the Master directly 1–3 days in advance. The contents of the trial bundle should be agreed where possible, and it should be made clear whether in addition, they are agreeing that the documents in the bundle are authentic even if not previously disclosed and are evidence of the facts stated in them even if a notice under the Civil Evidence Act 1995 has not been served. If the trial/hearing bundles are extensive and either party wishes the judge to read certain documents in advance of the hearing, a reading list should be provided.



7.11.9 Lists of authorities for use at trial or at substantial hearings before a Judge should be provided to the usher by 9.00am on the first day of the hearing. For other applications before a Judge, or applications before a Master, copies of the authorities should be included in the bundle or in a separate bundle.

7.11.10 For trial and most hearings before a Judge, and substantial hearings before a Master, a chronology, a list of the persons involved and a list of the issues should be prepared and filed with the skeleton argument. A chronology should be non-contentious and agreed with the other parties if possible. If there is a material dispute about any event stated in the chronology, that should be stated.

7.11.11 Skeleton arguments should be prepared, filed and served;

(1) for trials, not less than 2 days before the trial in the Listing Office, and
(2) for substantial applications or appeals, not later than 1 day before the hearing in the Listing Office and, where the Master has requested papers in advance of the hearing, in the Masters' Support Unit Room E16 or directly with the Master. Parties should avoid handing skeleton arguments to the other party at the door of the court even for less substantial hearings, so that each party has time to consider the other party's case.

7.11.12 A skeleton argument should;

(1) concisely summarise the party's submissions in relation to each of the issues,
(2) cite the main authorities relied on, which may be attached,
(3) contain a reading list and an estimate of the time it will take the Judge to read,
(4) be as brief as the issues allow and not normally be longer than 20 pages of double-spaced A4 paper,
(5) be divided into numbered paragraphs and paged consecutively,
(6) avoid formality and use understandable abbreviations, and
(7) identify any core documents which it would be helpful to read beforehand.

7.11.13 Where a party decides not to call a witness whose witness statement has been served, to give oral evidence at trial, prompt notice of this decision should be given to all other parties. The party should also indicate whether s/he proposes to put, or seek to put, the witness statement in as hearsay evidence. If s/he does not, any other party may do so.

*Recording of proceedings*

7.11.14 At any hearing, including the trial, any oral evidence, the judgment or decision (including reasons) and any summing up to a jury will be recorded. At hearings before Masters, it is not normally practicable to record anything other than oral evidence and any judgment, but these will be recorded. If a party wishes the whole proceedings to be recorded that party should inform the Master at the start of the hearing. A party to the proceedings may obtain a transcript of the proceedings on payment of the appropriate charge, from the Courts Recording and Transcription Unit, Room WB14. A person who is not a party to the proceedings may not obtain a transcript of a hearing which took place in private without the permission of the court.

7.11.15 No person or party may use unofficial recording equipment at a hearing without the permission of the court; to do so constitutes a contempt of court.

**7.12 Applications:**

**1B–52** 7.12.1 Applications for court orders are governed by Part 23 and the Part 23 Practice Direction. Rule 23.6 and paragraph 2 of the Part 23 Practice Direction set out the matters an application notice must include. The Part 23 Practice Direction states that form N244 may be used, however, parties may prefer to use form PF 244 which is available for use in the Royal Courts of Justice only. To make an application the applicant must file an application notice unless a Rule or Practice Direction permits otherwise or the court dispenses with the requirement for an application notice. Except in cases of extreme urgency, or where giving notice might frustrate the order (as with a search order), an application notice must be served on every party unless a Rule or Practice Direction or a court order dispenses with service (see paragraph 7.12.3 below).A Master will not normally make an order on the basis of correspondence alone.

7.12.2 Applications for remedies which a Master has jurisdiction to grant should ordinarily be made to a Master. The Part 2 Practice Direction (Allocation of cases to levels of Judiciary) contains information about the types of applications which may be dealt with by Masters and Judges. An application notice for hearing by;

(1) a Judge should be issued in the Listing Office, Room WG8, and
(2) a Master should be issued in the Masters' Support Unit, Room E16,

and wherever possible should be accompanied by a draft in double spacing of the order sought.

7.12.3 The following are examples of applications which may be heard by a Master where service of the application notice is not required;

(1) service by an alternative method (Rule 6.8),
(2) service of a claim form out of the jurisdiction (section III of Part 6),
(3) default judgment under Rule 12.11(4) or (5),
(4) substituting a party under Rule 19.1(4),
(5) permission to issue a witness summons under Rule 34.3(2),
(6) deposition for use in a foreign court (CPR Part 34 Section II),
(7) Interim Charging Order (CPR Part 73)), and
(8) Interim Third Party Debt Order (CPR Part 72).

7.12.4 Paragraph 3 of the Part 23 Practice Direction states in addition that an application may be made without serving an application notice;

(1) where there is exceptional urgency,
(2) where the overriding objective is best furthered by doing so,
(3) by consent of all parties, and
(4) where a date for a hearing has been fixed and a party wishes to make an application at that hearing but does not have sufficient time to serve an application notice.

With the court's permission an application may also be made without serving an application notice where secrecy is essential.

7.12.5 Where an application is heard in the absence of one or more of the parties, it is the duty of the party attending to disclose fully all matters relevant to the application, even those matters adverse to the applicant. Failure to do so may result in the order being set aside. In addition any party who has not had notice of a hearing may apply to have the order set aside within 7 days of service of the order made at the hearing.

7.12.6 Where notice of an application is to be given, the application notice should be served as soon as practicable after issue and, if there is to be a hearing, at least 3 clear days before the hearing date, unless the CPR provides a longer period or for permission for shorter service is obtained from a Master. Where there is insufficient time to serve an application notice, informal notice of the application should be given unless the circumstances of the application require secrecy.

7.12.7 The court may deal with an application without a hearing if;

(1) the parties agree the terms of the order sought,

(2) the parties agree that the application should be dealt with without a hearing, or

(3) the court does not consider that a hearing would be appropriate.

7.12.8 The court may deal with an application or part of an application by telephone where it is convenient to do so or in matters of extreme urgency. Applications where there are a number of contested issues or where the hearing is likely to take longer than 45 minutes are not usually suitable for telephone hearings. The hearings most appropriate for a telephone hearing are Case Management Conferences and short applications for, e.g. extensions of time. See paragraph 6 of the Part 23 Practice Direction for the procedure to be followed.

**7.12.9 Urgent applications**

Applications of extreme urgency may be made out of hours and will be dealt with by the duty judge. An explanation will be required as to why it was not made or could not be made during normal court hours.

7.12.10 Initial contact should be made through the Security Office on 020 7947 6260 who will require the applicant's phone number. The clerk to the duty judge will then contact the applicant and will require the following information;

(1) the name of the party on whose behalf the application is to be made,

(2) the name and status of the person making the application,

(3) the nature of the application,

(4) the degree of urgency, and

(5) the contact telephone number(s).

7.12.11 The duty judge will indicate to his/her clerk if s/he thinks it appropriate for the application to be dealt with by telephone or in court. The clerk will inform the applicant and make the necessary arrangements. Where the duty judge decides to deal with the application by telephone, and the facility is available, it is likely that the judge will require a draft order to be faxed to him. An application for an injunction will be dealt with by telephone only where counsel or solicitors represent the applicant.

7.12.12 It is not normally possible to seal an order out of hours. The judge is likely to order the applicant to file the application notice and evidence in support on the same or next working day, together with two copies of the order for sealing.

**7.13 Interim remedies:**

7.13.1 Interim remedies which the court may grant are listed in Rule 25.1. An order for an interim remedy may be made at any time including before proceedings are started and after judgment has been given. Some of the most commonly sought remedies are injunctions, many of which are heard by the Interim Applications Judge. **1B–53**

***Paragraph numbers marked with a "+" can be found online and on CD.***

7.13.2 Where a Claim has been started, an application on notice for an injunction should be filed in the Listing Office, Room WG8 for a hearing to be listed. If the application is to be made without giving notice to the other parties in the first instance, the Application Notice stamped with the appropriate fee should be brought to the Interim Applications Court, Court 37, together with the evidence in support, a skeleton argument (where appropriate) and two copies of the Order sought. Applications without notice are heard in Court 37 at 10.00am and 2.00pm, and at such other times as the urgency of the application dictates.

7.13.3 Where an injunction is granted without the other party being present it will normally be for a limited period; a return date 1 to 2 weeks ahead. If the injunction order contains an undertaking to issue a Claim Form, this should be issued before the Application Notice for the return date is filed in Room WG8 prior to service.

7.13.4 The Part 25 (Interim Injunctions) Practice Direction at paragraph 4 deals fully with making urgent applications and those without notice, and paragraphs 6, 7 and 8 deal specifically with search orders and freezing injunctions, examples of which are annexed to the Practice Direction.

7.13.5 Certain applications may be heard in private if the judge thinks it appropriate to do so (Rule 39.2(3)). An application to go into private should be made at the outset of the hearing. Certain applications for search orders and freezing injunctions might be appropriate for hearing in private.

7.13.6 Applications for interim payments are heard by a Master. The application notice should be filed in the Masters' Support Unit, Room E14. The requirements for obtaining an order for an interim payment are fully dealt with in the Part 25 (Interim Payments) Practice Direction.

### 7.14 Interlocutory Orders

1B–54 **7.14.1 Orders made by the Masters**

In the majority of cases Orders by Masters in the Queen's Bench Division are drawn up by one of the parties, who must then arrange to have this sealed by the Judgment & Orders Section (Room E17) and effect service on all other parties. In a limited number of circumstances, e.g. where an order is made of the court's own initiative, the court will draw up, seal and serve an order.

7.14.2 Where an application notice has been issued, and there has been a hearing, the Master will endorse the order in handwriting upon the original application notice. (If the original is not at the hearing, the party drawing up the order will have to ask the Master's permission to treat a photocopy as an original). If the parties have provided a draft order, will endorse this, with or without amendment. The application notice would then be endorsed "Order in the form initialled". If the hearing is one where there is no application notice, for example a Case Management Conference, then the Master will endorse the order on any Notice of the hearing sent by the court, or will use a draft order provided by one of the parties to endorse the order.

7.14.3 The Master will usually direct which party should be responsible for drawing up the Order. In the absence of such direction, this will be the party who issued the application to which the order relates, or the Claimant where the order was made in a case management conference. The Master will also direct a date by which the order should be drawn up, sealed and served. If no date is specified, the order must be served within 14 days of the date it was made.

7.14.4 The party responsible for drawing up the order should lodge with the Judgments & Orders Section:

(i) The application notice (or other document) endorsed by the Master;
(ii) Clean copies for sealing, one for each party and one for the court file;
(iii) Evidence of payment of the court fee

***Paragraph numbers marked with a "+" can be found online and on CD.***

7.14.5 That party should serve the sealed order upon each other party to the action by the date specified. If not sealed and served by that date, a party will have to obtain the court's permission to file the order out of time, which should be sought from the Practice Master.

7.14.6 If an order is made without a hearing, then the party making the application must also draw up, file and serve the order in accordance with the procedure set out below.

### 7.14.7 Orders made by a High Court Judge

Order made by a Judge on an interim application will, where the parties have legal representation, generally be drawn up in the same way as orders made by the Masters. However, the court will draw, seal and serve orders on behalf of litigants in person, and also orders made in appeal proceedings.

### 7.15 Civil Restraint Orders:

7.15.1 The power of the court to make civil restraint order ("CROs") is governed by CPR 3.11, however the practice direction to Part 3 (Civil Restraint Orders) sets out the procedure in detail. **1B–55**

7.15.2 There are 3 types of CRO—limited civil restraint order, extended civil restraint order and general civil restraint order.

7.15.3 For a limited CRO ("LCRO") to be made, 2 or more findings that a litigant's application is totally without merit must first have been made. An LCRO may by made by a Judge of any court which includes a Master and District Judge. An LCRO restrains the litigant from making any further application in the proceedings in which the LCRO is made and usually remains in effect for the duration of those proceedings.

7.15.4 An extended CRO ("ECRO") may be made where a litigant has persistently issued claims or made applications which are totally without merit. An ECRO may be made (i) in respect of any court when made by a Judge of the Court of Appeal, (ii) in the High Court or any county court when made by a Judge of the High Court and (iii) in any county court when made by a Designated Civil Judge or his appointed deputy.

7.15.5 An ECRO restrains the litigant from making any further applications involving or relating to or touching or leading to the proceedings in which the ECRO is made and will be made for a specified period not exceeding 2 years.

7.15.6 A general CRO ("GCRO") may be made where, despite the existence of an ECRO, a litigant persists in issuing claims and making applications which are totally without merit.

7.15.7 A GCRO restrains the litigant from issuing any claim or making any application (i) in any court when made by a Judge of the Court of Appeal, (ii) in the High Court or any county court when made by a Judge of the High Court and (iii) in any county court when made by a Designated Civil Judge or his appointed deputy.

7.15.7 The CRO's provide for the litigant to seek in writing the court's permission to issue any claim or make any application which is restrained by the CRO. Both the CRO's and the practice direction set out in detail how such application is to be made and the consequences of failing to do so.

7.15.7 An application for a CRO may be made by another party in accordance with the provisions of Part 23, or may be made by the court of its own volition.

## SECTION 8

## DEFAMATION CLAIMS

Defamation claims are governed by Part 53 and the Part 53 Practice Direction. Paragraph 2 of the Practice Direction sets out the information which should be included in a statement of case. **1B–56**

***Paragraph numbers marked with a "+" can be found online and on CD.***

**8.1 Offer to make amends**

8.1.1 Under section 2 of the Defamation Act 1996 a person who has published a statement alleged to be defamatory of another may offer to make amends ("a section 2 offer"). The section 2 offer must;

(1) be in writing,

(2) be expressed to be an offer to make amends under section 2 of the Act, and

(3) state whether it is a qualified offer, and if so, set out the defamatory meaning in relation to which it is made.

A section 2 offer is an offer;

(1) to make a suitable correction of the statement complained of and sufficient apology,

(2) to publish the correction and apology in a manner that is reasonable and practicable in the circumstances, and

(3) to pay to the aggrieved party compensation (if any) and costs as may be agreed or determined to be payable.

8.1.2 Where a section 2 offer is accepted by an aggrieved person s/he may not bring or continue defamation proceedings against the person making the offer, but s/he may apply to the court under section 3 of the Act for an order that the other party fulfil his/her offer by taking the agreed steps. If the parties are unable to agree the amount of compensation or costs, the aggrieved party may apply to the court for the amount to be decided. (See para. 3 of the Defamation Practice Direction (Part 53)).

8.1.3 In the event that the parties are unable to agree on the steps to be taken, the person making the offer may take such steps as s/he thinks appropriate, including making an application for the court's approval of the terms of a statement to be read in Court containing a correction and apology. s/he may also give an undertaking to the court as to the manner of their publication.

8.1.4 In existing proceedings the above applications may be made in accordance with Part 23, otherwise a Part 8 Claim Form should be issued. The application or claim must be supported by written evidence as set out in the Part 53 Practice Direction at paragraph 3.3, and should be made to a Master. If the application or claim involves the court's approval for a statement to be read in Court, it should be made to the Senior Master. The Claim Form or application notice should be issued or filed in the Masters' Support Unit, Room E16.

**8.2 Ruling on meaning**

**1B–57** 8.2.1 An application for an order determining whether or not a statement complained of is capable of;

(1) having any meaning or meanings attributed to it in a statement of case,

(2) being defamatory of the claimant, or

(3) bearing any other meaning defamatory of the claimant,

should be made in accordance with Part 23 and may be made at any time after service of the particulars of claim. Paragraphs 4.3 and 4.4 or the Practice Direction state the information which must be included in the application notice and evidence in support.

8.2.2 The application notice should be filed in the Listing Office, Room WG8, for hearing by the Judge in charge of the Jury list, or another designated Judge.

**8.3 Summary disposal**

**1B–58** 8.3.1 Section 8 of the Act gives the court power to dispose summarily of the claimant's claim. The court may;

(1) dismiss the claim if it appears that it has no realistic prospect of success and there is no reason why it should be tried, or

(2) give judgment for the claimant and grant him summary relief.

8.3.2 Summary relief includes the following;

(1) a declaration that the statement was false and defamatory of the claimant,
(2) an order that the defendant publish or cause to be published a suitable correction and apology,
(3) damages not exceeding £10,000,
(4) an order restraining the defendant from publishing or further publishing the matter complained of.

8.3.3 Applications for summary disposal are dealt with in Rule 53.2 and paragraphs 5.1 to 5.3 of the Part 53 Practice Direction. Substantial claims and those involving the Police authorities or the Media or those seeking an order restraining publication will be dealt with by the Judge in charge of the Jury list or another designated Judge, and the application notice should be filed in the Listing Office, Room WG8. Applications for summary disposal in other defamation claims may be made at first instance to a Master.

8.3.4 An application notice for summary disposal must state;

(1) that it is an application for summary disposal made in accordance with section 8 of the Act,
(2) the matters set out in paragraph 2(3) of the Part 24 Practice Direction, and
(3) whether or not the defendant has made an offer to make amends under section 2 of the Act, and whether or not it has been withdrawn.

The application may be made at any time after service of the particulars of claim and the provisions of Rule 24.4(1)(a) and (b) do not apply.

8.3.5 Where the court has made an order for summary relief as in 12.7.9(2) above (specifying the date by which the parties should agree the content, time, manner, form and place of publication of the correction and apology) and the parties are unable to comply within the specified time, the claimant must prepare a summary of the court's judgment and serve it on the other parties within 3 days following the date specified in the order for the content to be agreed by the parties.

8.3.6 If the parties are unable to agree the summary, they must within 3 days of its receipt, apply to the court by;

(1) filing an application notice, and
(2) and serving on all the other parties a copy of the summary showing the revisions they wish to make to it.

The court (normally the Judge who delivered the judgment) will then settle the summary.

**8.4 Statements read in Court**

8.4.1 Paragraph 6 of the Practice Direction only applies where a party wishes to accept a Part 36 offer, Part 36 payment or other offer of settlement. **1B–59**

8.4.2 An application for permission to make the statement before a Judge in Court may be made before or after acceptance of the Part 36 offer, Part 36 payment or other offer to settle, and should be made in accordance with Part 23 to the Senior Master, or if s/he is not available, to the Practice Master. The application notice, together with a copy of the statement, should be filed in the Masters' Support Unit, Room E16.

8.4.3 Where permission has been given, the parties may take a copy of the order to the Listing Office, Room WG8 for the matter to be listed before the Judge in charge of the Jury List for mention. Otherwise, the Action Department will send the court file to the Listing Office for the matter to be listed.

***Paragraph numbers marked with a "+" can be found online and on CD.***

## SECTION 9

## LISTING BEFORE JUDGES

**9.1 Responsibility for Listing:**

**1B–60** 9.1.1 At the Case Management Conference hearing the Master will give a period of between one and three months within which the Clerk of the Lists is to arrange the trial. This is known as the "trial window". It should normally start on a Monday. The parties (usually counsel's clerks) attend before the Queen's Bench Listing Officer to agree a "trial period", usually a 3 day period, within which the trial will commence. A Master will not generally order a trial fixture without first consulting the Listing Officer.

9.1.2 The Clerk of the Lists (Room WG3, Royal Courts of Justice) is in general responsible for listing. All applications relating to listing should in the first instance be made to him. Any party dissatisfied with any decision of the Clerk of the Lists may, on one day's notice to all other parties, apply to the Judge in charge of the List.

9.1.3 The application should be made within 7 days of the decision of the Clerk of the Lists and should be arranged through the Queen's Bench Listing Office, Room WG5.

**9.2 The Lists:**

**1B–61** 9.2 There are three Lists, namely;
(1) the Jury List
(2) the Trial List, and
(3) the Interim Hearings List.

The Lists are described below.

**9.3 The Jury List:**

**1B–62** 9.3.1 Claims for damages for libel and slander (defamation), fraud, malicious prosecution and false imprisonment will be tried by a Judge and jury unless the court orders trial by a Judge alone.

9.3.2 Where a claim is being tried by a Judge and jury it is vitally important that the jury should not suffer hardship and inconvenience by having been misled by an incorrect time estimate. It is therefore essential that time estimates given to the court are accurate and realistic.

9.3.3 Dates for the trial of substantial claims will be fixed by the Listing Office within the trial window after consideration of the parties' views. In such cases the Listing Office may, in addition, impose an alternative reserve date several weeks or months in advance of the trial date, in an endeavour to dispose of claims more quickly and to fill gaps in the List created by frequent settlements. When a reserve date is so allocated a "cut off" date will be stated by the Clerk of the Lists again, after consideration of any views expressed by the parties and having regard to the complexity of the claim and the commitments of counsel and expert witnesses. On the cut off date a decision will be made by the Clerk of the Lists to break or confirm the reserved date for trial.

9.3.4 If a party considers that s/he will suffer significant prejudice as the result of the decision of the Clerk of the Lists relating to either a reserved date or the cut off dates/he may apply to the Judge in charge of the Jury List for reversal or variation of the decision, as set out in paragraph 9.1.2 above.

9.3.5 Jury applications will enter the Interim Warned List not less than two weeks from the date the application notice is filed. Parties may "offer" a date for hearing the application within the week for which they are warned. Subject to court availability, the application will be listed on the offered date. Any application not reached on the offered date will return to the current Warned List and will be taken from that List as and when required.

9.3.6 Applications in defamation claims in respect of "meaning" (for an explanation of "meaning" see paragraph 4.1 of the Part 53 Practice Direction) may be listed in private on a specific day allocated for such matters.

***Paragraph numbers marked with a "+" can be found online and on CD.***

9.3.7 Jury applications of length and/or complexity may be fixed by the same manner as set out in paragraph 8.3.6 above. (See the section below on The Trial List for general information about fixing trials).

9.3.8 Applications for directions and other applications within the Master's jurisdiction should firstly be made to a Master unless;

(1) a direction has been given for the arranging of a trial date, or
(2) a date has been fixed or a window given for the trial.

Interim applications made after (1) or (2) above should be made to the Judge. The Master will use his/her discretion to refer a matter to the Judge if s/he thinks it right to do so.

9.3.9 If a party believes that the Master is very likely to refer the application to the Judge, for example where there is a substantial application to strike out, the matter should first be referred to the Master or Practice Master on notice to the other parties without waiting for a private room appointment. The Master will then decide whether the application should be referred to the Judge.

**9.4 The Trial List:**

9.4.1 This List consists of trials (other than Jury trials), preliminary questions or issues ordered to be tried and proceedings to commit for contempt of court. **1B-63**

9.4.2 The Royal Courts of Justice presents unique problems in terms of fixing trial dates. The number of Judges and Masters involved and their geographical location has caused, for the time being at least, a different approach to the fixing of trials in the Chancery and Queen's Bench Divisions.

9.4.3 The requirement of Judges to go on Circuit, sit in the Criminal Division of the Court of Appeal, deal with cases in the Administrative Court and other lists make it difficult to fix dates for trials before particular Judges. Accordingly the following will only apply to the Listing Offices in the Royal Courts of Justice.

9.4.4 At as early an interim stage as practicable, the court will give directions with a view to fixing the trial date or period within which the trial is to begin (the trial window).

9.4.5 For that purpose the court may;

(1) direct that the trial do not begin earlier than a specified date calculated to provide enough time for the parties to complete any necessary preparations for trial, and/or
(2) direct that the trial date be within a specified period, and/or
(3) specify the trial date or window.

9.4.6 If directions under 8.4.5(1) or (2) are given the court will direct the parties to attend upon the Clerk of the Lists in Room W11 at such time and place as may be specified in order to fix the trial date or trial window.

9.4.7 The claimant must, unless some other party agrees to do so, take out an appointment with the Clerk of the Lists within 7 days of obtaining the direction in paragraph 8.4.6 above and give notice of the appointment to all other parties. If an appointment is not taken out within the 7 days, the Listing Office will appoint a date for a listing hearing and give notice of the date to all parties.

9.4.8 At the listing hearing the Clerk of the Lists will take account, in so far as it is practical to do so, of any difficulties the parties may have as to availability of counsel, experts and witnesses. The Clerk of the Lists will, nevertheless, try to ensure the speedy disposal of the trial by arranging a firm trial date as soon as possible within the trial window or, as the case may be, after the "not before" date directed by the court under paragraph 8.4.5 above. If exceptionally it appears to the Clerk of the Lists at the listing hearing that a trial date cannot be provided within a trial window,

***Paragraph numbers marked with a "+" can be found online and on CD.***

s/he may fix the trial date outside the trial period at the first available date. (If a case summary has been prepared (see the Part 29 Practice Direction The Multi-track, paragraphs 5.6 and 5.7) the claimant must produce a copy at the listing hearing together with a copy of particulars of claim and any orders relevant to the fixing of the trial date.)

9.4.9 The Listing Office will notify the Masters' Support Unit of any trial date or trial window given. In accordance with Rule 29.2(3) notice will also be given to all the parties.

9.4.10 A party who wishes to appeal a date or window allocated by the Listing Officer must, within 7 days of the notification, make an application to the Judge nominated by each Division to hear such applications. The application notice should be filed in the Listing Office and served, giving one days notice, on the other parties.

**9.5 The Interim Hearings List:**

**1B–64** 9.5.1 This List consists of interim applications, appeals and applications for judgment.

9.5.2 On each Thursday of Term and on such other days as may be appropriate, the Clerk of the Lists will publish a Warned List showing the matters in the Interim Hearings List that are liable to be heard in the following week. Any matters for which no date has been arranged will be liable to appear in the List for hearing with no warning save that given by the Cause List for the following day, posted each afternoon outside Room WG5.

9.5.3 Fixtures will only be given in exceptional circumstances. The parties may by agreement "offer" preferred dates for their matter to be heard, to be taken from the List on designated days, within the week following entry into the Warned List in accordance with Listing Office practice. Matters lasting less than a day are usually offered for two preferred consecutive days and matters lasting more than a day are usually offered for three preferred consecutive days.

**9.6 General:**

**1B–65** 9.6.1 In addition to the matters listed to be heard by individual Judges, the Daily Cause List for each day may list "unassigned cases". These are matters from the two Lists to be heard that day but not assigned to a particular Judge. If on any day a matter assigned to a particular Judge proves to be ineffective, s/he will hear an unassigned case. It is hoped that the great majority of unassigned cases will be heard on the day that they are listed but this cannot be absolutely guaranteed. Parties engaged in matters listed as unassigned should attend outside the court where the matter is listed. The Clerk of the Lists will notify them as soon as possible, which Judge is to hear the matter. It is not the practice to list cases as unassigned unless the parties consent and there are no witnesses.

9.6.2 Appeals from Masters' decisions will appear in the Interim Hearings List. The notices of appeal (stamped with the appropriate fee) must be filed in Room WG7. On being notified that the appeal has been set down the solicitors should immediately inform the Clerk of the Lists whether they intend to instruct counsel and, if so, the names of counsel.

**9.7 Listing before the Interim Applications Judge:**

**1B–66** 9.7.1 All interim applications on notice to the Interim Applications Judge will initially be entered in a List for hearing. They will be listed for hearing in Room E101 or some other nominated venue on any day of the week. Any matter which cannot be disposed of with within one hour will not be taken on the date given for the listed hearing.

9.7.2 If the parties agree that a matter cannot be disposed of within one hour, the applicant/appellant;

(1) may, on filing the application notice/notice of appeal, seek to have the matter placed directly into the Interim Hearings Warned List, or
(2) must as soon as practicable and in any event not later than 24 hours before the hearing date transfer the matter into the Interim Hearings List.

If the parties do not so agree, or agree less than 24 hours before the hearing date, the parties must attend on that date.

9.7.3 Matters in the Interim Hearings List will be listed by the Clerk of the Lists in Room WG3, and the parties will be notified by the Listing Office (Room WG5) of the date on which the matter will enter the Warned List. Matters in the Warned List may be listed for hearing at any time on or after that date.

9.7.4 In order to ensure that a complete set of papers in proper order is available for the Judge to read before the hearing, the parties must in advance of the hearing lodge in room WG4 a bundle, properly paginated in date order, and indexed, containing copies of the following documents;

(1) the application notice or notice of appeal,
(2) any statements of case,
(3) copies of all written evidence (together with copy exhibits) on which any party intends to rely, and
(4) any relevant order made in the proceedings.

9.7.5 The bundle should be agreed if possible. In all but simple cases a skeleton argument and, where that would be helpful, a chronology should also be lodged. (See paragraph 8.9.1 and 8.9.2 below in respect of skeleton arguments.)

9.7.6 Where a date for the hearing has been arranged the bundle must be lodged not later than 3 clear days before the fixed date. For application or appeals where there is no fixed date for hearing, the bundle must be lodged not later than 48 hours after the parties have been notified that the matter is to appear in the Warned List. (For information concerning trial bundles see the Part 39 Practice Direction.)

9.7.7 Except with the permission of the Judge no document may be used in evidence or relied on unless a copy of it has been included in the bundle referred to in paragraph 8.7.6 above. If any party seeks to rely on written evidence which has not been included in the bundle, that party should lodge the original (with copy exhibits) in Room WG5 in advance of the hearing, or otherwise with the Court Associate before the hearing commences.

9.7.8 In appeals from District Judges the provisions of paragraphs 8.7.4, 8.7.5, 8.7.6 and 8.7.7 should be complied with. In addition, the notes (if any) of reasons given by the District Judge, prepared by the District Judge, counsel or solicitors should be lodged.

9.7.9 Subject to the discretion of the Judge, any application or appeal normally made to the Interim Applications Judge may be made in the month of September. In the month of August, except with the permission of a Judge, only appeals in respect of orders;

(1) to set aside a claim form, or service of a claim form,
(2) to set aside judgment,
(3) for stay of execution,
(4) for any order by consent,
(5) for permission to enter judgment,
(6) for approval of settlements or for interim payment,
(7) for relief from forfeiture,
(8) for a Third Party Debt Order,
(9) for a garnishee order,
(10) for relief by way of High Court Enforcement Officer's interpleader,
(11) for relief by way of sheriff's interpleader,

***Paragraph numbers marked with a "+" can be found online and on CD.***

(12) for transfer to a county court or for trial by Master, or

(13) for time where time is running in the month of August,

may be heard, and only applications of real urgency will be dealt with, for example, urgent applications in respect of injunctions, or for possession (under RSC O.113 in Schedule 1 to Part 50).

9.7.10 It is desirable, where this is practical, that application notices or notices of appeal are submitted to the Practice Master or a Judge prior to the hearing of the application or appeal so that they can be marked "fit for August" or "fit for vacation". If they are so marked, then normally the Judge will be prepared to hear the application or appeal in August, if marked "fit for August" or in September if marked "fit for vacation". The application to a Judge to have the papers so marked should normally be made in writing, the application shortly setting out the nature of the application or appeal and the reasons why it should be dealt with in August or in September, as the case may be.

**9.8 The Lists generally:**

**1B–67** 9.8.1 Where a fixed date has been given it is the duty of the parties to keep the Clerk of the Lists fully informed as to the current position of the matter with regard to negotiations for settlement, whether all aspects of the claim are being proceeded with, an estimate of the length of the hearing, and so on.

9.8.2 Applications for adjournments will not be granted except for the most cogent reasons. If an application is made because solicitors were unaware of the state of the List they may be ordered personally to pay the costs of the application.

9.8.3 A party who seeks to have a hearing before a Judge adjourned must inform the Clerk of the Lists of his/her application as soon as possible. Applications for an adjournment immediately before a hearing begins should be avoided as they take up valuable time which could be used for dealing with effective matters and, if successful, may result in court time being wasted.

9.8.4 If the application is made by agreement, the parties should, in writing, apply to the Clerk of the Lists who will consult the Judge nominated to deal with such matters. The Judge may grant the application on conditions that may include giving directions for a new hearing date.

9.8.5 If the application is opposed the applicant should apply to either the nominated Judge or the Judge to whom the matter has been allocated. A hearing should then be arranged through the Clerk of the Lists. A short summary of the reasons for the adjournment should be lodged with the Listing Office where possible by 10.30am on the day before the application is to be made. Formal written evidence is not normally required.

9.8.6 The applicant will be expected to show that s/he has conducted his/her own case diligently. Any party should take all reasonable steps;

(1) to ensure his/her case is adequately prepared in sufficient time to enable the hearing to proceed, and

(2) to prepare and serve any document (including any evidence) required to be served on any other party in sufficient time to enable that party also to be prepared.

9.8.7 If a party or his/her solicitor's failure to take reasonable steps necessitates an adjournment, the court may dismiss the application or make any other order including an order penalising the defaulting party in costs.

**9.9 Listing Office—general matters:**

**1B–68** 9.9.1 To facilitate the efficient listing of proceedings, parties are reminded that skeleton arguments concisely summarising each party's submissions must be prepared and filed with the Listing Office;

***Paragraph numbers marked with a "+" can be found online and on CD.***

(1) for trials, not less than 3 days before the trial, and
(2) for substantial applications or appeals, not later than 1 day before the hearing.

9.9.2 If it is anticipated that a Skeleton Argument will be filed late, a letter of explanation should accompany it which will be shown to the Judge before whom the trial or hearing is to take place.

9.9.3 For parties' information, the following targets for the disposal of matters in the Lists have been agreed as set out below:

Interim Hearings Warned List within 4 weeks

From date of fixing;

Trials under 5 days within 4 months

Trials over 5 but under 10 days within 6 months

Trials over 10 but under 20 days within 9 months

Trials over 20 days within 12 months.

## SECTION 10

## TRIAL, JUDGMENTS AND ORDERS

### 10.1 General:

10.1.1 The trial of a claim in the Royal Courts of Justice normally takes place before a High Court Judge or a Deputy sitting as a High Court Judge. A Master may assess the damages or sum due to a party under a judgment and, subject to any Practice Direction, may try a claim which is **1B–69**

(1) treated as being allocated to the multi-track because it is proceeding under Part 8, or
(2) with the consent of the parties, allocated to the multi-track under Part 26.

10.1.2 Claims for defamation, malicious prosecution or false imprisonment will be tried by a Judge sitting with a Jury unless the court orders otherwise.

### 10.2 The Trial:

10.2.1 See paragraph 2.4 above about representation at the trial, and paragraphs 7.11.14 and 7.11.15 above about recording of proceedings. **1B–70**

10.2.2 Rule 39.3 sets out the consequences of a party's failure to attend the trial and see also paragraph 2 of the Part 39 Practice Direction.

10.2.3 The Judge may fix a timetable for evidence and submissions if it has not already been fixed. The claimant's advocate will normally begin the trial with a short opening speech, and the Judge may then allow the other party to make a short speech. Each party should provide written summaries of their opening speeches if the points are not covered in their skeleton arguments.

10.2.4 It is normally convenient for any outstanding procedural matters or applications to be dealt with in the course of, or immediately after, the opening speech. In a jury trial such matters would normally be dealt with before the jury is sworn in.

10.2.5 Unless the court orders otherwise, a witness statement will stand as the evidence in chief of the witness, provided s/he is called to give oral evidence. With the court's permission, a witness may amplify his/her witness statement or give evidence in relation to new matters which have arisen since the witness statement was served on the other parties.

10.2.6 The Court Associate will be responsible for any exhibits produced as evidence during the trial. After the trial, the exhibits are the responsibility of the party who produced them. Where a number of physical exhibits are involved, it is desirable, if possible, for the parties to agree a system of labelling and the manner of display, beforehand. The Associate will normally draw the Judgment or order made at the trial.

10.2.7 At a jury trial, it is the parties' responsibility to provide sufficient bundles of documents for the use of the jury.

10.2.8 Facilities are available to assist parties or witnesses with special needs. The Listing Office should be notified of any needs or requirements prior to the trial.

**10.3 Judgments and orders:**

**1B–71** 10.3.1 Part 40 deals with judgments and orders. Rule 40.2 contains the standard requirements of a judgment or order and Rule 40.3 contains provisions about drawing them up, see also paragraph 1 of the Part 40B Practice Direction for more information.

10.3.2 Provisions concerning consent orders are contained in Rule 40.6 which sets out in paragraph (3) the types of consent judgments and orders that may be sealed and entered by a court officer, provided;

(1) that none of the parties is a litigant in person, and
(2) the approval of the court is not required by a Rule, a Practice Direction or an enactment.

Other types of consent order require an application to be made to a Master or Judge for approval. It is common for a respondent to a consent order not to attend the hearing but to provide a written consent. The consent may either be written on the document or contained in a letter, and must be signed by the respondent, or where there are solicitors on record as acting for him, by his/her solicitors. Paragraph 3 of the Part 40B Practice Direction contains further information about consent orders.

10.3.3 Rule 40.11 sets out the time for complying with a judgment or order, which is 14 days unless the judgment or order specifies otherwise (for example by instalments), or a Rule specifies a different time, or the judgment or proceedings have been stayed.

10.3.4 The Part 40B Practice Direction contains further information about the effect of non-compliance with a judgment or order (and sets out the penal notice), adjustment of the final judgment sum in respect of interim payments and compensation recovery, and refers to various precedents for types of judgments and orders. See also;

(1) the Part 40 Practice Direction- Accounts and Enquiries, and
(2) the Part 40C Practice Direction- Structured Settlements which sets out the procedure to be followed both on settlement and after trial. Precedents for structured settlement orders, Parts 1 and 2, are annexed to the Practice Direction.

10.3.5 Where judgment is reserved, the Judge may deliver his/her judgment by handing down the written text without reading it out in open court. Where this is the case, the advocates will be supplied with the full text of the judgment in advance of delivery. The advocates should then familiarise themselves with the contents and be ready to deal with any points which may arise when the judgment is delivered. Any direction or requirement as to confidentiality must be complied with.

10.3.6 The judgment does not take effect until formally delivered in court. If the judgment is to be handed down in writing copies will then be made available to the parties and, if requested and so far as practicable, to the law reporters and the press.

10.3.7 The Judge will usually direct that the written judgment may be used for all purposes as the text of the judgment, and that no transcript need be made. Where such a direction is made, a copy will be provided to the court's Recording and Transcription Unit, Room WB14, from where further copies may be obtained (and see paragraph 7.11.14 above).

*Judgment or order for payment of money on behalf of a child or patient*

10.3.8 The usual order made at trial will make provision for any immediate payment to the litigation friend or his/her legal representative and for the balance of the award to be placed to a special investment account pending application to a Master or District Judge (in the case of a child) or the Court of Protection (in the case of a patient) for investment directions. The order will specify the time within which the application should be made. It should also deal with any interest accrued to the date of Judgment, and or any interest which accrues in the future. An Order should also refer to Majority directions, and decisions on investment of the fund in Court.

10.3.9 The litigation friend or his/her legal representative should then write to or make an appointment with;

(1) in the case of a child, the Master or District Judge in accordance with paragraph 6.8.6 above and the Part 21 Practice Direction, or

(2) in the case of a patient, the Court of Protection in accordance with paragraph 11 of the Part 21 Practice Direction.

10.3.10 Where after trial the Judge has found in favour of a child or patient, instead of judgment being given, the proposed award of damages may be paid by way of a structured settlement. The structure must be approved by the Judge, and in the case of a patient must also be approved by the Court of Protection. (See also the Part 40C Practice Direction—Structured Settlements.)

*Provisional damages*

10.3.11 Rule 41.1 defines an award of provisional damages. Where there is a chance that a claimant may in the future develop a particular disease or deterioration as a result of the event giving rise to the claim, s/he can seek an award of damages for personal injury on the assumption that s/he will not develop the disease or deterioration, with provision for him to make a further application within the time specified in the order, ifs/he does so develop the disease or deterioration.

10.3.12 The Part 41 Practice Direction gives further information about provisional damages awards and, in particular, about the preservation of the case file for the time specified in the order for making a further application, and the documents to be included in the case file. A precedent for a provisional damages judgment is annexed to the Practice Direction.

## SECTION 11
## APPEALS

**11.1 General:**

11.1.1 Appeals are governed by Part 52 and the Part 52 Practice Direction. The contents of Part 52 are divided into three sections; I—General Rules about Appeals, II—Special Provisions applying to the Court of Appeal,and III—Provisions about reopening Appeals. **1B–72**

11.1.2 The Practice Direction is divided into four sections; I—General Provisions about Appeals, II—General Provisions about Statutory Appeals and Appeals by way of Case Stated, III—Provisions about Specific Appeals and IV—Provisions about Reopening Appeals.

11.1.3 The following paragraphs apply to orders made after 2nd May 2000 and are intended only to draw parties' attention to the basic provisions for bringing an appeal in or from the Queen's Bench Division. For further information about these procedures and about other specific types of appeal, parties should refer to Part 52, the Practice Direction and the Civil Appeals Guide.

For the purposes of Part 52 and the Part 52 Practice Direction, except where the meaning indicates otherwise, the term "Judge" includes a Master or District Judge.

11.1.4 Routes of Appeal—An appeal will lie from the decision of:

A District Judge of a county court; to a Circuit Judge
A Master or a District Judge of a District Registry of the High Court; to a High Court Judge
A Circuit Judge; to a High Court Judge
A High Court Judge; to the Court of Appeal,

unless the decision to be appealed is a final decision in a claim allocated to the multi-track or in specialist proceedings (under the Companies Acts 1985 or 1989 or to which Sections I, II or III of Part 57 or any of Parts 58 to 63 apply), in which case the appeal will lie to the Court of Appeal.

11.1.5 Unless the lower court or the appeal court orders otherwise, filing an Appellant's Notice does not operate as a stay of any order or decision of the lower court. A stay must be specifically sought either in the Appellant's Notice or separately in accordance with Part 23.

**11.2 Permission to appeal:**

**1B–73** 11.2.1 Permission to appeal is required to appeal from a decision of a Judge in a county court or the High Court, except where the appeal is in respect of;

(1) a committal order,
(2) a refusal to grant habeas corpus,
(3) a secure accommodation order made under s.25 of The Children Act 1989,
(4) certain statutory appeals, or
(5) where a Practice Direction so provides.

11.2.2 Applicants are encouraged to seek permission at the hearing at which the decision to be appealed against is made. If it is not, or if it is sought and refused, permission should be sought from the court appealed to ("the appeal court"). Where permission is sought from the appeal court it must be requested in the Appellant's Notice. Permission may be granted, or refused, or granted in part (whether as to a part of the order, a ground of appeal or an issue) and refused as to the rest. (See paragraphs 4.1 to 4.24 of the Practice Direction in respect of permission to appeal.)

11.2.3 Refusal of permission at a hearing is, effectively, the end of the road (s.54(4) of the Access to Justice Act 1999 and paragraph 4.8 of the Practice Direction), save in extremely rare cases where the Court of Appeal or the High Court may reopen a final appeal or refusal of permission (52.17).

11.2.4 Where the decision sought to be appealed to the Court of Appeal was itself made on appeal to a county court or the High Court, permission must be sought from the Court of Appeal (52.13(1)). The Court of Appeal will not grant permission unless an important point of principle or practice is involved, or there is some other compelling reason.

11.2.5 Court Appeals Listing Office, Room WG7. An application for permission to appeal to the Court of Appeal is made by filing an Appellant's Notice in the Civil Appeals Office Registry, Room E307.

11.2.6 Before an application for permission can be considered, whether on the papers or at a hearing, the documents in support of the appeal must be lodged. The documents listed at section 11 of the Appellant's Notice should be lodged when the Appellant's Notice is filed. If the appellant needs more time to lodge the documents he/she must complete section 11 to obtain an extension of up to 14 days. This extension may be granted by a court officer. If the appellant is still unable to obtain the documents he/she may apply in writing for a further extension. This may also be granted by a court officer but any subsequent application for an extension must be made to a Judge.

11.2.7 Where the documents are not lodged in accordance with the extended time period and no further application for an extension is made, the matter will be placed in a Dismissal list before the Judge in charge of the List on notice to the appellant.

11.2.8 Where permission to appeal is being sought from the Court of Appeal, the Appellant must file the documents set out in paragraph 5.6, 5.6A, 5.9 and 5.12 of the Part 52 practice direction.

11.2.9 An application for permission is normally first considered on the papers without a hearing, although the application may be listed for a hearing at the outset, if the appellant requests it (52.3.5). Where permission is refused on the papers, the applicant may request that it be reconsidered at a hearing. The request should be made within 7 days of service of the notice of refusal.

11.2.10 The court will give notice of the permission hearing to the parties. A respondent who volunteers written submissions or attends the permission hearing will not normally be allowed his/her costs. If the court requests submissions from or the attendance of a Respondent, he/she will normally be allowed his/her costs if permission is refused (paragraphs 4.22–4.24 of the Part 52 practice direction).

**11.3 Notices:**

11.3.1 Rule 52.4 and paragraph 5 of the Practice Direction deal with the Appellant's Notice. The appellant must file 3 copies of his/her notice at the appeal court either within a period specified by the court appealed from ("the lower court") or, if no such period is specified, within 21 days of the date of the decision appealed from. The notice must be served on each respondent as soon as practicable, and in any event not later than 7 days after it is filed. **1B–74**

11.3.2 A respondent must file a notice where;

(1) he/she also wishes to appeal the lower court's decision,
(2) he/she wishes to uphold the decision of the lower court for different or additional reasons to those given by the lower court, or
(3) he/she is seeking permission to appeal from the appeal court.

11.3.3 The Respondent's Notice must be filed either within a period specified by the lower court or, if no such period is specified, within 14 days of;

(1) the date the respondent is served with the appellant's notice where
    (a) permission to appeal was given by the lower court or
    (b) permission to appeal is not required,
(2) the date the respondent is served with notification that the appeal court has given the appellant permission to appeal, or
(3) the date the respondent is served with notification that the application for permission to appeal and the appeal itself are to be heard together.

(Paragraph 7 of the Part 52 practice direction deals with the Respondent's Notice.)

11.3.4 The notices to be used are as follows;

(1) the Appellant's Notice—form N161, and
(2) the Respondent's Notice—form N162.

There is a leaflet available from the Listing Office, Room WG7 entitled "I want to appeal", which provides information about High Court appeals.

**11.4 Procedure where permission is obtained:**

1B–75 11.4.1 Where permission to appeal has been granted by the appeal court, the appellant must serve the appeal bundle on each respondent within 7 days of receiving the order giving permission to appeal.

11.4.2 The Appellant must include in the appeal bundle the Respondent's Notice and a skeleton argument (if any), any relevant transcripts of evidence, any documents which the parties have agreed are relevant and the order granting permission. If the order granting permission was made at an oral hearing, a transcript or note of the judgment should also be lodged. Where permission was refused in respect of a particular issue, any papers relating solely to that issue should be removed from the bundle. See paragraph 15.4 for more information on preparing the appeal bundle.

11.4.3 The High Court Appeals Office will notify the parties of either the hearing date or of the "listing window" during which the appeal is likely to be heard. Where the appeal is in the Court of Appeal, the Civil Appeals Office Registry will notify the parties of the "hear by" date and will send the appellant an Appeal Questionnaire. Paragraph 15.7 contains more information about listing in the Court of Appeal.

11.4.4 The Appeal Questionnaire must be completed and returned within 14 days of the date of the notification letter. The Appeal Questionnaire must contain the matters set out in paragraphs 6.5 and 6.6 of the Part 52 practice direction.

11.4.5 In the Court of Appeal, all the papers required for the hearing must be filed at least 7 days before the hearing. For an appeal to the High Court, all papers should be lodged not later than [2 days] before the hearing

**11.5 Disposing of applications for permission and appeals where the Appellant does not wish to proceed:**

1B–76 11.5.1 The following does not apply where any party to the proceedings is a child or patient.

11.5.2 The appellant may request that his/her application or appeal be dismissed. The request must state that the appellant is not a child or patient. If the request includes a statement from the respondent that he/she is not a child or patient and consents to the dismissal order being made without costs, the order will be so made. Otherwise the dismissal order will be made on the basis that the appellant pays the costs of the application or appeal.

**11.6 Appeals in cases of contempt of court:**

1B–77 11.6.1 Appellant's Notices which by paragraph 21.4 of the Part 52 Practice Direction (appeals in cases of contempt of court (s.13 of the Administration of Justice Act 1960)) are required to be served on "the court from whose order or decision the appeal is brought". In the case of appeals from the Queen's Bench Division, the Senior Master of the Queen's Bench Division should be served but service may be effected by leaving a copy of the Appellant's Notice with the High Court Appeals Office in Room WG7, Royal Courts of Justice, Strand, London WC2A 2LL.

## SECTION 12

## ENFORCEMENT

**12.1 General:**

1B–78 12.1.1 Enforcement in the High Court is governed by CPR Parts 70 and 74 together with RSC Orders 17, 45 to 47 and 52 as in Schedule 1 to the CPR.

12.1.2 RSC O. 45 deals with enforcement generally. A judgment or order for payment of money (other than into court) may be enforced by a writ of Fieri Facias, Third Party Debt Order Third Party Debt Order, a Charging Order or the appointment of a receiver. A judgment or order to do or abstain from doing an act may be enforced by a writ of sequestration (with the permission of the court) or an order of committal. A judgment or order for possession of land may be enforced by a writ of possession, and a judgment or order for delivery of goods without the alternative of paying their value by a writ of specific delivery. In each case, where RSC O.45 r.5 applies enforcement may also be by a writ of sequestration or an order of committal.

### 12.2 Writs of execution:

12.2.1 RSC O.46 deals with writs of execution generally. Rules 2 and 3 set out the circumstances when permission to issue a writ is necessary. Rule 4 contains provisions for making an application for permission. Rule 5 deals with applications for permission to issue a writ of sequestration. RSC O. 47 contains provisions concerning writs of Fieri Facias. Forms of writs of execution may be used as follows: **1B–79**

(1) writs of fieri facias in form Nos. 53 to 63,
(2) writs of delivery in form Nos. 64 and 65,
(3) writs of possession in form Nos. 66 and 66A,
(4) writ of sequestration in form No 67,
(5) writ of restitution in form No 68,
(6) writ of assistance in form No 69.

12.2.2 With certain exceptions, writs of execution issued in the Royal Courts of Justice are executed by the High Court Enforcement Officer. RSC O.46 r.6 sets out the provisions for issue of writs of execution. In the Queen's Bench Division writs of execution are issued in the Central Office in Room E15–E17. Before the Writ can be sealed for issue, a signed praecipe for its issue must be filed in one of forms PF 86 to 90, as appropriate, stamped with the appropriate fee. A copy of the judgment or order requiring enforcement should also be provided.

12.2.3 On an application for permission to issue a writ of possession under RSC O.45 r.3(2), if the property consists of a house of which various parts are sublet to, or in the occupation of, different persons, the evidence in support should show the nature and length of the notice which has been given to the various occupiers. Where the defendant or any other persons are in actual possession of the premises of which possession is sought, the evidence must contain the following information:

(1) whether the premises or any part of it is residential,
(2) if so,
   (a) what is the rateable value of the residential premises, and
   (b) whether it is let furnished or unfurnished and, if furnished, the amount of furniture it contains, and
(3) any other matters that will assist the Master in deciding whether any occupier is protected by the Rent Acts.

12.2.4 Where a party wishes to enforce a judgment or order expressed in a foreign currency by the issue of a writ of fieri facias, the praecipe must be endorsed with the following certificate:

> "I/We certify that the rate current in London for the purchase of (state the unit of foreign currency in which the judgment is expressed) at the close of business on (state the nearest preceding date to the date of issue of the writ of fieri facias) was (    ) to the £ sterling and at this rate the sum of (state amount of the judgment debt in the foreign currency) amounts to £    ."

The schedule to the writ of fieri facias should be amended;

(1) showing the amount of the judgment or order in the foreign currency at paragraph 1.
(2) inserting a new paragraph 2. as follows: "2. Amount of the sterling equivalent as appears from the certificate endorsed on the praecipe for issue of the writ    £    "
(3) renumbering the remaining paragraphs accordingly.

The writ of fieri facias will then be issued for the sterling equivalent of the judgment expressed in foreign currency as appears from the certificate.

***Paragraph numbers marked with a "+" can be found online and on CD.***

12.2.5 County Court judgments or orders to which Article 8(1) of the High Court and County Courts Jurisdiction Order 1991 applies may be enforced in the High Court, and since 26th April 1999, any County Court judgment for over £600 may be transferred to the High Court for enforcement by a High Court Enforcement Officer (except where it is a judgment arising from a regulated agreement under the Consumer Credit Act).

12.2.6 The party seeking enforcement should obtain from the appropriate county court a certificate of the judgment of the county court in compliance with CCR O. 22 r.8(1A) (in Schedule 2 to the CPR), setting out details of the judgment or order to be enforced, sealed with the seal of that court and dated and signed by an officer of that court and stating on its face that it is granted for the purpose of enforcing the judgment or order by execution against goods in the High Court. Form N293A is a "Combined Certificate of Judgment and Request for Writ of Fieri Facias" and should be used.

12.2.7 A correctly completed form N293A together with a copy should be filed in Room E15–E17 where the court officer will;

(1) allocate a reference number,
(2) date seal the Certificate and copy, returning the original to the party and retaining the copy, and
(3) enter the proceedings in a register kept for that purpose.

The certificate shall be treated for enforcement purposes as a High Court judgment and interest at the appropriate rate shall run from the date of the Certificate.

12.2.8 The title of all subsequent documents shall be set out as follows:

" IN THE HIGH COURT OF JUSTICE
QUEEN'S BENCH DIVISION
High Court Claim No.
County Court Claim No.

(Sent from the [ ] County Court by Certificate dated (*date*))

Claimant

Defendant "

When the writ of fieri facias is issued, the Certificate of judgment retained by the party shall be date sealed by the court officer on the bottom left hand corner and endorsed with the designation of the Sheriff to whom the writ is directed.

12.2.9 The Sheriffs Lodgement Centre at 20–21 Tooks Court, London EC4A 1LB provides a service for arranging transfer up of county court judgments. (A helpline is provided on 020 7205 2555)

12.2.10 It is important to remember in these cases that although any application for a stay of execution may be made to a Master in the High Court by application notice filed in accordance with Part 23, all other applications for enforcement or other relief must be made to the issuing county court. This practice is followed in the district registries with such variations as circumstances require.

12.2.11 When a writ of execution has been issued in the Royal Courts of Justice it may then be delivered to the Sheriffs Lodgement Centre. Value Added Tax is payable in addition to the High Court Enforcement Officer's fee on the services for

***Paragraph numbers marked with a "+" can be found online and on CD.***

which the fee is payable, and must be paid at the time of delivery of the writ. If the goods, chattels and property to be seized in execution are not within Greater London, the High Court Enforcement Officer will direct the writ to a High Court Enforcement Officer who is authorised to act in the appropriate district. Goods, which may not be seized in execution of a writ, are set out in s.138(3A) of the Senior Courts Act 1981 as follows:

(1) such tools, books, vehicles and other items of equipment as are necessary to that person for use personally by him in his/her employment, business or vocation,
(2) such clothing, bedding, furniture, household equipment and provisions as are necessary for satisfying the basic domestic needs of that person and his/her family,
(3) any money, bank notes, bills of exchange, promissory notes, bonds, specialties or securities for money belonging to that person.



12.2.12 When first executing a writ of fieri facias the High Court Enforcement Officer will deliver to the debtor or leave at each place where execution is levied a notice of seizure in form No 55. This is commonly known as "walking possession" and the notice explains to the debtor the situation with regard to the goods seized and what s/he then has to do.

12.2.13 After execution of a writ of execution, the High Court Enforcement Officer will endorse on the writ a statement of the manner in which s/he has executed it and will send a copy of the statement to the party issuing the writ.

**12.3 Interpleader proceedings (RSC O.17):**

12.3.1 Where a person is under liability in respect of a debt or property and has **1B–80**
been, or expects to be claimed against by two or more persons claiming the same debt or property, if the person under liability does not dispute the debt or claim the property, s/he may apply to the court for relief by way of interpleader, i.e. for the entitlement of the persons claiming the same debt or property to be established in separate proceedings between them.

12.3.2 Where the High Court Enforcement Officer has seized goods in execution and a person other than the person against whom the writ of execution was issued wishes to claim the goods seized, s/he must give notice of his/her claim to the High Court Enforcement Officer, including in his/her notice a statement of his/her address which will be his/her address for service. The High Court Enforcement Officer will then give notice of that claim to the judgment creditor on whose behalf the goods were seized, in form PF 23. The notice requires the judgment creditor to state whether s/he admits or disputes the claim. The claimant must do so within 7 days of receipt of the High Court Enforcement Officer's notice and may use form PF 24 to do so.

12.3.3 Where the judgment creditor admits the claim, the High Court Enforcement Officer will withdraw from possession of the goods and may apply under RSC O.17 r.2(4) for an order to restrain a claim being brought against him for having taken possession of the goods. Where the claimant disputes the claim, the High Court Enforcement Officer may apply for interpleader relief. An application for interpleader relief if made in existing proceedings is made by an application in accordance with Part 23, otherwise it is made by the issue of a Part 8 claim form.

12.3.4 The Master may deal with the claims summarily, or may direct an issue to be tried between the parties in dispute (see RSC O.17 r.5) or make such other order as is appropriate.

**12.4 Examination of judgment debtor (Part 71):**

12.4.1 Where a person ("the judgment creditor") has obtained a judgment or order **1B–81**
for payment of a sum of money against a person ("the judgment debtor"), the judgment creditor may apply for an order requiring the judgment debtor to attend to be orally examined concerning his assets and means. If the judgment debtor is a

company or corporation, the court will order a named officer of the company or corporation to attend for examination. In the case of a judgment or order which is not for payment of a sum of money, the court may make an order for the attendance of the party liable for his examination on such questions as may be specified in the order.

12.4.2 An application for an order under Part 71 should be made in accordance with Part 23 without notice to any other party. The application must be supported by evidence giving details of the judgment or order, including the amount still owing, and showing that the judgment creditor is entitled to enforce the judgment or order. Where the judgment debtor is a company or corporation the evidence must give details of the officer to be examined. Form PF 98 may be used as a precedent for the evidence in support. Where a judgment creditor has obtained judgments in several different proceedings against the same judgment debtor, only one application need be made, setting out in the body of the application details of all the judgments on which examination is sought.

12.4.3 The examination will take place before a Master, Registrar, district judge or nominated officer, as may be ordered, and will normally be at the court where the least expense will be incurred, usually the county court for the area where the judgment debtor lives. If a different court is requested by the applicant the reason why should be given in the application notice.

12.4.4 The application notice/evidence should be filed in the Masters' Support Unit Room E16 for consideration by a Master who will, if satisfied, make the order sought. Where the examination is to take place in a county court, the judgment creditor should lodge a copy of the order with the county court and obtain an appointment for the examination. If the examination is to take place in the Royal Courts of Justice, the order should be taken to Room E17 where the appointment will be endorsed on the order. In the Central Office the officers are nominated at the discretion of the Senior Master and their names may be obtained from Room E17.

12.4.5 The order (endorsed with the penal notice as set out in paragraph 9.1 of the Part 40B Practice Direction) together with details of the appointment must be served personally on the judgment debtor or on the officer of the judgment debtor company or corporation to be examined. A judgment debtor should be offered his/her conduct money, *i.e.* expenses of travelling to and from the examination and of attending to give evidence.

12.4.6 The officer conducting the examination will take down, or arrange to have taken down in writing the judgment debtor's statement. The officer will read the statement to the judgment debtor and will ask him or her to sign it. If he or she refuses to do so the officer will sign the statement. If the judgment debtor refuses to answer any question or if any other difficulties arise, the matter will be referred to the Interim Applications Judge in Court 37.

**12.5 Third Party Debt Order proceedings (CPR Part 72):**

**1B–82** 12.5.1 Where a judgment creditor has obtained a judgment or order for payment of a sum of money against a judgment debtor, and another person ("the Third Party") is indebted to the judgment debtor, the judgment creditor may apply to the Master for an order that the Third Party pays to the judgment creditor the amount of the debt due to the judgment debtor, or sufficient of it to satisfy the judgment debt.

12.5.2 The application should be made by filing an application notice in Practice Form N349, verified by a statement of truth, but the application notice need not be served on the judgment debtor. The application will normally be dealt with without a hearing and must be supported by evidence as set out in CPR 72 Practice Direction 1.2. If the Master is satisfied that such an order is appropriate, s/he will make an interim order in form N84specifying the debt attached and appointing a time for the Third Party and the judgment debtor to attend and show cause why the order should not be made final.

12.5.3 The Third Party Debt Order to show cause must be served on the Third Party, and on the judgment debtor, in accordance with CPR 72.5. Where the Third Party or the judgment debtor fails to attend the hearing or attends but does not dispute the debt, the Master may make a final Third Party Debt Order against the Third Party under CPR 72.8 in form N85 The final order may be enforced in the same manner as any other order for the payment of money. Where the Third Party or the judgment debtor disputes the debt, the Master may dispose of the matter as set out in CPR 72.8.

12.5.4 Where the judgment creditor seeks to enforce a judgment expressed in a foreign currency by Third Party Debt Order proceedings, the evidence in support of the application must contain words to the following effect:

> "The rate current in London for the purchase of (state the unit of foreign currency in which the judgment is expressed) at the close of business on (state the nearest preceding date to the date of verifying the evidence) was ( ) to the £ sterling, and at this rate the sum of (state the amount of the judgment debt in the foreign currency) amounts to £ . I have obtained this information from (state source) and believe it to be true."

**12.6 Charging Orders (CPR Part 73):**

12.6.1 A judgment creditor may apply for a charging order on the property or assets of the judgment debtor, which will have the effect of providing him with security over the property of the judgment debtor. The High Court has jurisdiction to impose a charging order in the following cases: **1B–83**

(1) where the property is a fund lodged in the High Court,
(2) where the order to be enforced is a maintenance order of the High Court, and
(3) where the judgment or order is made in the High Court and exceeds £5000.

The property and assets of the judgment debtor on which a charge may be imposed by a charging order are specified by s.2 of the Charging Orders Act 1979.

12.6.2 An interim charging order imposing a charge on land will be drawn in respect of the judgment debtors interest in the land and not the land itself, unless the court orders otherwise. If an interim charging order is made on stocks or shares in more than one company, a separate order must be drawn in respect of each company. A judgment creditor may apply in a single application notice for charging orders over more than one asset, but if the court makes charging orders over more than one asset, there will be separate orders relating to each asset. If the judgment debt is expressed in a foreign currency, the evidence in support of any application for a charging order should contain a similar provision to that set out in paragraph 12.5.4 above.

12.6.3 The application for a charging order is made to a Master and should be made in Practice Form N379if the application relates to land, or N380if the application relates to securities. The application is made without being served and will normally be dealt with without a hearing. If the Master is satisfied that such an order is appropriate, s/he will make an order in form N86appointing a time for the judgment debtor to attend and show cause why the order should not be made absolute.

12.6.4 The interim order and the application notice should be served in accordance with CPR 73.5, or otherwise as directed by the Master. After further consideration at the hearing the Master will either make the order Final (with or without modifications) as in form N87, or discharge it. Where the order is discharged or varied, the order of discharge must be served in accordance with CPR 73.9(3).

12.6.5 CPR 73.7 deals with the effects of a charging order on funds in court, which includes securities held in court.

12.6.6 Although the court may make a charging order in a foreign currency, to facilitate enforcement it is usually preferable for it to be expressed in sterling. Thus if the foreign debt is in a foreign currency the evidence in support of the application should contain the sterling equivalent and request the charging order to be made in sterling. (See paragraph 12.6.2 above).

#### 12.6.6 Enforcement of Charging Order

Proceedings for the enforcement of a charging order by sale of the property charged must be begun by a Part 8 Claim Form issued out of the Chancery Division of the High Court or a Chancery district registry unless the High Court has no jurisdiction, in which case application should be made to the appropriate County Court. (RSC O.50 r.9A). The County Court's limit at present is when the amount owing does not exceed £30,000.

### 12.7 Receivers; equitable execution (CPR Part 69):

1B–84 12.7.1 Equitable execution is a process which enables a judgment creditor to obtain payment of the judgment debt where the interest of the judgment debtor in property cannot be seized or reached by ordinary execution.

12.7.2 An application for appointment of a receiver by way of equitable execution may be made to a Master, who also has jurisdiction to grant an injunction if, and only so far as, the injunction is ancillary or incidental to the order. The procedure follows that set out in RSC O.30 rr.1 to 6, and the application should be made in accordance with Part 23 and the Part 23 Practice Direction as described in the following paragraphs.

12.7.3 If the judgment creditor seeks an injunction (as in 11.7.2 above) s/he should file his/her application notice based on form No 82 but setting out in addition the injunction sought, together with a witness statement or affidavit in support stating:

(1) the date and particulars of the judgment, and that it remains wholly unsatisfied, or to what extent it remains unsatisfied,

(2) the particulars and result of any execution which has been issued, and the nature of the High Court Enforcement Officer's return (if any),

(3) that the judgment debtor has no property which can be taken by the ordinary process of execution, (if s/he has, give reasons showing that legal execution would be futile),

(4) particulars of the property in respect of which it is proposed to appoint a receiver,

(5) the name and address of the receiver proposed to be appointed, and that in the deponent's judgments/he is a fit and proper person to be appointed receiver, and

(6) that the judgment debtor is in financial difficulties [that the immediate appointment of a receiver without the delay of giving security is of great importance] and that the deponent believes that the judgment debtor may assign or dispose of his/her estate or interest in (*give details of property*) unless restrained from doing so by the order and injunction of the court.

12.7.4 The judgment creditor need not give notice of this application which will normally be dealt with without a hearing. If the Master is satisfied with the evidence s/he will make an order in form No 83 for a hearing to take place in respect of the application for the appointment of the receiver and granting an injunction meanwhile.

12.7.5 If the judgment creditor does not seek an injunction, the application notice should be filed and served together with the evidence in support (as in paragraph 11.7.3 above but without paragraph (6)).

12.7.6 At the hearing of the application to appoint the receiver, the Master will, if s/he thinks fit, make an order in form No 84. A copy of the order appointing the receiver shall be served by the judgment creditor on the receiver and all other parties to the proceedings.

12.7.7 Where a receiver has been ordered to give security under RSC O.30 r.2, the judgment creditor should obtain an appointment before the Master who made the

***Paragraph numbers marked with a "+" can be found online and on CD.***

order appointing the receiver, to settle the form and amount of the security. Unless otherwise ordered, the security will be in the form of a guarantee. The judgment creditor should have prepared a draft form of guarantee for the Master to approve at the appointment. Form PF 30CH may be used as a precedent for the guarantee.

12.7.8 RSC O.30 r.3 deals with the remuneration of the receiver which may either be assessed by the Master or referred to a costs judge. RSC O.30 r.5 contains the provisions for submitting the receiver's accounts.

**12.8 Committals, etc. (RSC O.52):**

12.8.1 The court has power to punish contempt of court by an order of committal to prison or by other means. These may be by ordering the payment of a fine, by the issue of a writ of sequestration, or by making a hospital or guardianship order under certain provisions of the Mental Health Act 1983. Committal applications under RSC O.52 r.4 are always dealt with by a High Court Judge. The following provisions apply to applications made under RSC O.52 r.4. **1B–85**



12.8.2 The application should be made in existing proceedings by filing an application notice. If not in existing proceedings, a Part 8 Claim Form should be issued (see paragraphs 2.1 and 2.2 of the practice direction - Committal Applications). The Claim Form or application notice must contain a prominent notice stating the possible consequences of the court making a committal order. The notice is annexed at the end of the practice direction.

12.8.3 Evidence in support of a committal application must be by affidavit and, together with the Part 8 Claim Form or application notice, must be served personally on the person sought to be committed giving 14 days notice unless otherwise directed by the court (paragraph 4.2 of the practice direction). A date for the hearing must be obtained from the Listing Office, Room WG8 and endorsed on or served with the Claim Form or application notice.

12.8.4 Committal proceedings will normally be heard in public, but see RSC O.52 r.6 which sets out certain types of cases which may be heard in private, and see paragraph 9 of the Practice Direction.

12.8.5 Committal proceedings will normally be heard in public, but see RSC O.52 r.6 which sets out certain types of cases which may be heard in private (although brief details of the case must be read out in public) and see paragraph 9 of the Practice Direction.

12.8.6 Where the court makes a finding of contempt, details of the contempt and of the order or undertaking breached (where appropriate) must be set out in the order. The term of any period of committal must be stated in the order and must not exceed two years. A fine must be expressed as payable to Her Majesty the Queen and the order must state the amount of the fine and the date and time within which it must be paid. A contemnor and his solicitors will be notified separately as to how the fine should be paid. A precedent of the order is in form No. 85 and will normally be drawn by the court.

12.8.7 When an order for committal to prison is made, the court will issue a warrant to the Tipstaff authorising him to convey the contemnor to the appropriate prison. A copy of the order should be served on the prison governor and the Official Solicitor. RSC O.52 r.8 deals with the discharge of a person committed.

**12.9 Execution against property of Foreign or Commonwealth States:**

12.9.1 In cases where judgment has been obtained against a foreign or Commonwealth State and it is sought to execute the judgment by a writ of fieri facias, a charging order or a Third Party Debt Order, the following provisions apply: **1B–86**

(1) Before the writ of fieri facias is issued, the Master must be informed in writing and his/her direction sought. In cases where an application is to be made for a

***Paragraph numbers marked with a "+" can be found online and on CD.***

charging order to show cause or a Third Party to show cause, the evidence in support of the application must include a statement that the execution sought is against a foreign or Commonwealth State.

(2) The Master, having been so informed will, as soon as practicable, inform the Foreign and Commonwealth Office ("FCO") of the application and will not permit the issue of a writ of fieri facias, nor grant an order to show cause until the FCO has been so informed. The Protocol Division of the Head of Diplomatic Missions and International Organisations Unit of the FCO may be contacted by telephone on 020 7008 0991 or by Fax on 020 7008 0978.

(3) Having regard to all the circumstances of the case, the Master may postpone the decision whether to issue the writ or grant the order to show cause for so long as s/he considers reasonable for the purpose of enabling the FCO to furnish further information relevant to his/her decision, but not for longer than 3 days from the time of his/her contacting the FCO. In the event that no further information is received from the FCO within 24 hours of its being informed, then the writ of fieri facias may be issued or the order to show cause may be sealed without further delay.

**12.10 Recovery of enforcement costs:**

**1B–87** 12.10.1 Subsection (3) of section 15 of the Courts and Legal Services Act 1990 enables a person taking steps to enforce a money judgment in the High Court to recover the costs of any previous attempt to enforce that judgment. Subsection (4) of section 15 excludes costs that the court considers to have been unreasonably incurred.

12.10.2 The application for an enforcement costs order is made to a Master and should be made in accordance with Part 23 but the application notice need not be served on the judgment debtor. The application will normally be dealt with without a hearing and must be supported by evidence substantially as set out in form PF 205. The deponent should exhibit sufficient vouchers, receipts or other documents as are reasonably necessary to verify the amount of the costs of previous attempts to enforce the judgment.

12.10.3 If the Master is satisfied that such an order is appropriate, s/he will make an order for payment of the amount of such costs as s/he considers may be recoverable under subsection (3) of section 15. If the amount of such costs is less than that claimed by the judgment creditor, the Master may either disallow the balance or give directions for a detailed assessment or other determination of the balance. If after assessment or other determination it appears that the judgment creditor is entitled to further costs beyond those originally allowed, s/he may issue a further writ of fieri facias or take other lawful steps to enforce those costs. Interest on the costs runs either from the date the Master made the enforcement costs order or from the date of the costs certificate.

**12.11 Enforcement of Magistrates' Courts' orders:**

**1B–88** 12.11.1 The Magistrates' Courts Act 1980, s.87 provides that payment of a sum ordered to be paid on a conviction of a magistrates' court may be enforced by the High Court or a county court (otherwise than by the issue of a writ of fieri facias or other process against goods or by imprisonment or attachment of earnings) as if the sum were due to the clerk of the magistrates' court under a judgment of the High Court or county court, as the case may be.

12.11.2 In the Central Office, the application is made to a Master and should be made in accordance with Part 23. Where enforcement is sought by a Third Party Debt Order or charging order to show cause, the application will normally be dealt with without a hearing. Otherwise the application notice and evidence in support should be served on the defendant.

12.11.3 The application must be supported by a witness statement or affidavit in a form appropriate to the type of execution sought and must have exhibited to it the authority of the magistrates' court to take the proceedings which will recite the

*Paragraph numbers marked with a "+" can be found online and on CD.*

conviction, the amount outstanding and the nature of the proceedings authorised to be taken (Magistrates Courts Forms Rules 1981, Form 63).

12.11.4 The application notice and evidence in support together with an additional copy of the exhibit should be filed in Room E15 where it will be assigned a reference number from the register kept for that purpose. The Master according to the type of enforcement sought will then deal with the matter.

12.11.5 This practice will also be followed in the District Registries with such variations as circumstances may render necessary.

**12.12 Enforcement of Foreign Judgments and Enforcement of High Court Judgments Abroad**

12.12.1 CPR 74 deals with enforcement of judgments in different jurisdictions. Section 1 covers enforcement in England & Wales of judgments of foreign courts. **1B–89**

12.12.2 If a foreign court is not a party to an agreement with this country on mutual recognition and enforcement of judgments, then a fresh action will need to be brought based on that foreign judgment. Such an action can usually be made by a Part 8 claim.

12.12.3 Section 1 of the rule covers enforcement of judgments of foreign courts covered by the Administration of Justice Act 1933 ("the 1933 Act"), the Foreign Judgments (Reciprocal Enforcement) Act 1933 ("the 1933 Act"), the Civil Jurisdiction and Judgments Act 1982 ("the 1982 Act") and the Council Regulation (EC) No. 44/2001 of 22nd December 2000 ("the Judgments Regulation").

12.12.4 A list of the countries that are covered by each of the various Acts and the Judgments Regulation is set out in Her Majesty's Court Service 'Notes for Guidance' on the above Acts and Regulation, which can be obtained from the Judgments & Orders Section of the Action Department of the Central Office (Room E17). This also contains the standard forms used and sets out the procedure for applications for registration.

*Reciprocal enforcement; the Administration of Justice Act 1920 the Foreign Judgments (Reciprocal Enforcement) Act 1933, the Civil Jurisdiction and Judgments Act 1982 and the Judgments Regulation.*

12.12.5 CPR 74.4 sets out how an application for registration of a foreign judgment in the High Court under the 1920, 1933 or 1982 Acts under the Judgments Regulation may be made. The application should be made without notice being served on any other party, but the Master may direct that a Part 8 Claim Form should be issued and served.

12.12.6 CPR 74.4 (2)–(6) sets out what the evidence in support of the application should contain or have exhibited to it. The foreign judgment will be registered in the foreign currency in which it is expressed and must not be converted into Sterling in the evidence in support. When it comes to enforcing the foreign judgment, the amount should then be converted in accordance with the instructions set out above in paragraph 11 in respect of the type of enforcement sought.

12.12.7 The order giving permission to register the judgment must be drawn up by, or on behalf of the judgment creditor and will be entered in the Register of Judgments kept in the Action Department Room E17 of the Central Office for that purpose. The order will usually contain a direction that the costs of and caused by the application and the registration be assessed and added to the judgment as registered. The Order for registration of the judgment must state the matters set out in CPR 74.6 (3) including the right of the judgment debtor to apply, and the time within which s/he may do so, to have the registration set aside. The notice must be served on the judgment debtor in accordance with CPR 74.6 (1).

12.12.8 An application to set aside the registration of a judgment under CPR 74.7 (1) must be made in accordance with Part 23 and be supported by a witness statement or affidavit.



QB GUIDE

12.12.9 Section 2 of CPR 74 covers enforcement in foreign countries of judgments of the High Court and County Court of England & Wales. A judgment creditor who wishes to enforce such a judgment abroad must apply for a certified copy of the judgment.

12.12.10 Section 3 of CPR 74 deals with enforcement of UK Judgments in other parts of the UK. A person who wishes to enforce a judgment of the High Court or County Court of England & Wales in another part of the UK may apply for a certified copy of the judgment.

12.12.11 An application for a certified copy of a judgment entered in the High Court may be made without notice and must be supported by evidence, in accordance with CPR 74.13 for enforcement of High Court and County judgments in foreign countries, and in accordance with CPR 74.17 or 18 for enforcement of High Court and County judgments in other parts of the UK. The certified copy will be endorsed with a certificate signed by the Master. The forms of certificate are included in the 'Notes for Guidance' referred to in paragraph 11.12.4 above. Where the application was made under s. 10 of the Foreign Judgments (Reciprocal Enforcement) Act 1933, an additional certificate will be issued and signed by the Master [as in form PF 155.] Judgment creditors who intend to seek enforcement abroad should ensure that their judgment is endorsed as follows:

"This judgment carries interest from (date) at the rate of 8% per annum in accordance with the provisions of the Judgments Act 1838".

12.12.12 An application may also be made for registration in the High Court of a judgment given by a court in another part of the UK.

12.12.13 The certificate must be filed for registration in Room E15–E17 in the Action Department within 6 months from the date of its issue. Under paragraph 9 of schedule 6 to the Act of 1982 an application may be made to stay the enforcement of the certificate. The application may be made without notice being served on any other party supported by a witness statement or affidavit stating that the applicant is entitled and intends to apply to the judgment court to set aside or stay the judgment.

Applications under s.18 of the Act of 1982; judgment containing non-money provisions: The procedure is set out in CPR 74.16(3).

12.12.14 The certificates will be entered in the register of certificates in respect of judgments ordered to be registered under CPR 74 PD 3 kept in the Central Office for that purpose.

*Enforcement of European Community judgments*

12.12.15 Section 4 of CPR deals with enforcement of European Community judgments in England and Wales, that is, judgments not of the national courts of Member States but rather the judgments of the courts and institutes of the community itself.

12.12.16 CPR 74.19 An application for registration may be made without notice being served on any other party and must be supported by written evidence containing or having exhibited to it the matters referred to in CPR 74.21 (1).

12.12.17 The order for registration must contain the information and exhibit the documents required by CPR 74.22. The order for registration will be entered in the register of the Judgments and Orders kept in the Action Department Room E17, Central Office for that purpose. The registration order must be served on every person against whom judgment was given.

12.12.18 An application to vary or cancel a registration under the provisions of CPR 74.23 shall be made by application notice in accordance with Part 23, supported by written evidence, and must be made within 28 days of service of the registration order.

*Enforcement of recommendations etc. under the Merchant Shipping (Liner Conferences) Act 1982*

12.12.19 Applications under s. 9 of the Act of 1982 for registration of a recommendation, determination or award, are dealt with by a Commercial Judge and shall be made by the issue of a Part 8 Claim Form. The application should be supported by evidence in accordance with CPR 74 PD 12.

12.12.20 The order giving permission to register the recommendation, determination or award must be drawn up by or on behalf of the party making the application, and entered in the register of the recommendations, determinations and awards ordered to be registered under s. 9 of the Act of 1982, directed by the Senior Master to be kept in the Admiralty and Commercial Registry.

*Regulation (EC) No. 805/2004 of the European Parliament and of the Council of 21 April 2004 ("the European Enforcement Order")*

12.12.21 The European Enforcement Order (EEO) creates a simplified method of enforcement for uncontested claims throughout the EU member states (except Denmark). Details of the procedure are contained in Section V of Part 74.

12.12.22 An application for an EEO certificate must be made by Form N219or N219A depending upon whether the Judgment was by agreement/admission/settlement or in default of defence or objection. The application may be made without notice and will be dealt with without a hearing, unless the Master orders a hearing.

12.12.23 An application under Article 6(2) of the EEO Regulation for a certificate indicating the lack or limitation of enforceability of an EEO certificate must be made to the court of origin by application in accordance with Part 23.

12.12.24 An application under Article 10 of the EEO Regulation for rectification or withdrawal of an EEO certificate must be made to the court of origin and may be made by application in accordance with Part 23.

12.12.25 A person seeking to enforce an EEO in England and Wales must lodge at the court in which enforcement proceedings are to be brought the documents required by Article 20 of the EEO Regulation.

12.12.26 Where an EEO certificate has been lodged and the judgment debtor applies to stay or limit the enforcement proceedings under Article 23 of the EEO Regulation, such application must be made by application in accordance with Part 23 to the court in which the EEO is being enforced.

12.12.27 An application under Article 21 of the EEO Regulation that the court should refuse to enforce an EEO must be made by application in accordance with Part 23 to the court in which the EEO is being enforced.

## SECTION 13

## MISCELLANEOUS

### 13.1 Service of foreign process (RSC O.69):

13.1.1 RSC O.69 applies to the service on a person in England or Wales of any process in connection with civil or commercial proceedings in a foreign court or tribunal. A request for service is made to the Senior Master from either Her Majesty's Principal Secretary of State for Foreign and Commonwealth Affairs, or where the foreign court or tribunal is in a convention country, from a consular or other authority of that country. **1B–90**

13.1.2 Where the foreign court or tribunal certifies that the person to be served understands the language of the process, it is not necessary to provide a translation.

***Paragraph numbers marked with a "+" can be found online and on CD.***

RSC O.69 r.3 deals with the manner of service; the process may be served through the machinery of the county court and the usual practice is for the Senior Master to provide a certificate for the bailiff or county court officer to use. The Senior Master may make an order for service by an alternative method based on the bailiff's certificate.

13.1.3 When service has been effected, the Senior Master will send a certificate, together with a copy of the process served, to the authority who requested service, stating how service was effected, or why service could not be effected. There is a discretion to charge for the costs of service or attempted service, but recovery is usually sought only where the country requesting service does not provide a reciprocal free service.

13.1.4 Council Regulation (EC) No 1348/2000 ('the Service Regulation') applies to service on a person in England & Wales of proceedings in from courts in other European Union Member States, and provides a complete code for service of proceedings between member states. The Senior Master is the central body designated under Article 3 of the Regulation. The Regulation can be found at CPR Practice Direction 6.36.

**13.2 Rectification of register of deeds of arrangement (RSC O.94 r.4)**

**1B–91** 13.2.1 Deeds of arrangement must be registered. The registration office is at the Department of Trade.

13.2.2 An application for an order as set out in RSC O.94 r.4(1)(a) or (b) must be made to a Master of the Queen's Bench Division. Notice need not be served on any other party and a witness statement must support the application or affidavit as described in rule 4(2).

**13.3 Exercise of jurisdiction under the Representation of the People Acts (RSC O.94 r.5):**

**1B–92** 13.3.1 RSC O.94 r.5 describes the jurisdiction of the High Court under the above Acts. The practice is governed by the Election Petition Rules 1960 (as amended). The Senior Master is the Prescribed Officer.

13.3.2 Under Part III of the Representation of the People Act 1983, the result of a parliamentary or local government election may be questioned on the grounds of some irregularity either before or during the election. The provisions of Part III have also been applied to European Parliamentary elections.

13.3.3 The challenge is made by the issue of an Election Petition
(1) in respect of a Parliamentary election by one or more electors or
(2) in respect of a local government election by four or more electors,

or by an unsuccessful or alleged candidate.

The member/councillor whose election is complained of is a Respondent to the petition as is the Returning Officer if his/her conduct is complained of. The petition is issued in the Election Petitions Office, Room E08, normally within 21 days of the election (although this may be extended in certain circumstances).

13.3.4 The petition is tried by two High Court Judges of the Queen's Bench Division in respect of Parliamentary elections or by a Commissioner in respect of Local Government elections. The Commissioner must be a lawyer of not less than 10 years standing who neither resides nor practices in the area concerned. The trial usually takes place in the constituency/local government area for which the Election Petition has been issued, although preliminary matters are usually dealt with at the Royal Courts of Justice.

13.3.5 The election court may confirm the result of the election, or substitute another candidate as the member/councillor, or may order the election to be re-run.

13.3.6 Applications for remedies under various sections of the Representation of the People Act 1983 are also issued in the Election Petitions Office, and are usually heard by an Election Rota Judge.

13.3.7 Outside the court offices' opening times, but while the building is still open to the public, election petitions and applications may be left in the letterbox located outside Room E08. When the building is closed, Election Petitions and applications may be left with Security at the Main Entrance, up until midnight on the last day for service.

**13.4 Bills of Sale Acts 1878 and 1882 and the Industrial and Provident Societies Act 1967 (RSC O.95):**

13.4.1 Every bill of sale and absolute bill of sale to which the Act of 1878 applies must be registered under s.8 of that Act, within 7 clear days of its making, and, under s.11 of the Act of 1878, the registration of a bill of sale must be renewed at least once every 5 years. The register for the purpose of the Bills of Sale Acts contains the particulars of registered bills of sale and an alphabetical index of the names of the grantors, and is kept in the Action Department in Room E15–E17. **1B–93**



13.4.2 An application to register a bill of sale which is made within the prescribed time should be made by filing in Room E15–E17 the original bill of sale and any document annexed to it together with a witness statement or affidavit in form PF 179 or PF 180. An application to re-register a bill of sale which is made within the prescribed time should be made by filing in Room E15–E17 a witness statement or affidavit in form PF 181.

13.4.3 An application to rectify;

(1) an omission to register, by extending the time for registration, or

(2) an omission or mis-statement of the name, residence or occupation of a person in the register, by correcting the registration,

must be made by witness statement or affidavit to a Master of the Queen's Bench Division. In addition to the matters set out in forms PF 179 or PF 180, the evidence in support must also set out the particulars of the omission and state the grounds on which the application is made.

13.4.4 Where the residence of the grantor of the bill of sale or the person against whom the process is issued is outside the London bankruptcy district, or where the bill of sale describes the goods as being in a place outside that district, the Central Office will send copies of the bill of sale to the appropriate county court district judge.

13.4.5 The Master, on being satisfied that the omission or mis-statement of name, residence or occupation of a person in the register was accidental or due to inadvertence, may order the omission or mis-statement to be rectified by the insertion in the register of the correct name, residence or occupation of the person.

13.4.6 Where the Master is satisfied that the omission to register a bill of sale or a witness statement or affidavit of renewal within the prescribed time was accidental or due to inadvertence, s/he may extend the time for registration on such terms as s/he thinks fit. In order to protect any creditors who have accrued rights of property in the assets in respect of which the bill of sale was granted between the date of the bill and its actual registration, any order to extend the time for registration will normally be made "without prejudice" to those creditors. The order will be drawn up in form PF 182.

13.4.7 An application for an order that a memorandum of satisfaction be written on a registered copy of a bill of sale, made without the consent of the person entitled to the benefit of the bill of sale, must be made by the issue of a Part 8 Claim Form. Where the consent of the person entitled to the benefit of the bill of sale has been obtained, the application may be made by a witness statement or affidavit containing that consent and verifying the signature on it. Form PF 183 contains precedents for the evidence and forms of consent. Where the application is made with consent, the evidence need not be served on any other person. If the Master is satisfied on the evidence, s/he will endorse his/her approval on the witness statement or affidavit (an order is not normally drawn up) and send it to Room E17 for a memorandum of satisfaction to be entered on the copy of the Bill in the Registry. If a copy of the bill of sale has been sent to a county court district judge, a notice of satisfaction will be sent to that district judge.

13.4.8 Where the consent has not been obtained, the Claim Form must be served on the person entitled to the benefit of the bill of sale and must be supported by evidence that the debt (if any) for which the bill of sale was made has been satisfied or discharged.

13.4.9 An application to restrain removal on sale of goods seized in accordance with RSC O.95 r.3 and under the proviso to s.7 of the Bills of Sale Act (1878) Amendment Act 1882 must be made by the issue of a Part 8 Claim Form for hearing before the Interim Applications Judge.

13.4.10 Under the Industrial and Provident Societies Act 1967 an application to record an instrument creating a fixed or floating charge on the assets of a registered society or to rectify any omission or mis-statement in it must be made within 14 days beginning with the date of its execution.

13.4.11 Under RSC O.95 r.5 and in accordance with s.1(5) of the Act of 1967 the court may order;

(1) that the period for making an application for recording a charge be extended, or

(2) an omission or mis-statement in such an application be rectified.

The procedure for obtaining an order as in (1) or (2) above is similar to that under s.14 of the Bills of Sale Act 1878 and must be made by witness statement or affidavit to a Master of the Queen's Bench Division as in paragraph 12.4.3 above and must exhibit a copy of the instrument duly authenticated in the prescribed manner together with any other particulars relating to the charge.

13.4.12 RSC O.95 r.3 refers to the assignment of book debts; the register of assignments of book debts is kept in Room E15–E17 in the Central Office. An application for registration under s.344 of the Insolvency Act 1986 should be made in accordance with RSC O.95 r.6(2). Parties may use form PF 186 for their evidence in support. It is helpful if the original assignment is also produced.

**13.5 Enrolment of deeds and other documents:**

**1B–94** 13.5.1 Any deed or document which by virtue of any enactment is required or authorised to be enrolled in the Supreme Court may be enrolled in the Central Office. See the Part 5 Practice Direction at paragraph 6 which fully sets out the procedure for enrolment and contains in an appendix the Enrolment of Deeds (Change of Name) Regulations 1994.

**13.6 Bail (RSC O.79 r.9):**

**1B–95** 13.6.1 With the coming into force on 5th April 2004 of section 17of the Criminal Justice Act 2003, the Queen's Bench Division of the High Court no longer has the power to grant bail in criminal proceedings to a defendant in custody who has been refused bail, or to vary the arrangements for bail of an inferior court.

13.6.2 The limited remaining right of the High Court to grant bail in specific circumstances is exercised by the Administrative Court.

**13.7 References to the Court of Justice of the European Communities:**

**1B–96** 13.7.1 A party wishing to apply for an order under CPR 68 may do so by application before or at the trial or hearing. An application made before the trial or hearing should be made in accordance with Part 23.

13.7.2 Before making an order for reference, the Court will pay close attention to the terms of Part 68 of the CPR, to form PF 109 and to the "Guidance of the Court of Justice of the European Communities on References by National Courts for Preliminary Rulings" which may be found in the *Practice Direction (ECJ References: Procedure)* (1999) 1 WLR 260.

13.7.3 It is the responsibility of the Court, rather than the parties, to settle the terms of the reference. This should identify as clearly, succinctly and simply as the nature of the case permits the question to which the Court of England & Wales seeks an answer and it is very desirable that language should be used which lends itself readily to translation.

13.7.4 The referring court should, in a single document scheduled to the order (in form PF 109);

(1) identify the parties and summarise the nature and history of the proceedings,
(2) summarise the salient facts, indicating whether these are proved or admitted or assumed,
(3) make reference to the rules of national law (substantive and procedural) relevant to the dispute,
(4) summarise the contentions of the parties as far as relevant,
(5) explain why a ruling of the European Court is sought, identifying the EC provisions whose effect is in issue, and
(6) formulate, without avoidable complexity, the question(s) to which an answer is requested.

13.7.5 Where the document is in the form of a judgment, passages, which are not relevant to the reference, should be omitted from the text scheduled to the order. Incorporation of appendices, annexes or enclosures as part of the document should be avoided, unless the relevant passages lend themselves readily to translation and are clearly identified.

13.7.6 When the order of reference has been approved by the Judge and sealed by the court, the order, together with any other necessary documents should be promptly passed to Room E.209 where the Clerk will process the reference for the attention of the Senior Master of the Queen's Bench Division, for transmission to Luxembourg without avoidable delay.

**13.8 Group Litigation Orders "GLOs":**

13.8.1 Section III of Part 19 and the Practice Direction - Group Litigation deal with claims where multiple parties are claimants. **1B–97**

13.8.2 When considering applying for a GLO, the applicant should contact the Law Society at 113 Chancery Lane, London WC2A 1PL, who may be able to assist in putting the applicant in contact with other parties who may also be interested in applying for a GLO in the same matter.

13.8.3 The consent of either the Lord Chief Justice or the Vice-Chancellor to the GLO is required. In the Queen's Bench Division the application should be made to the Senior Master in accordance with Part 23. If the Senior Master is minded to make the GLO s/he will forward a copy of the application notice and any written evidence to the Lord Chief Justice. The application notice should include the information set out in paragraph 3.2 of the Practice Direction.

13.8.4 A group register will be set up and maintained by a party to the GLO of all the parties to the group of claims to be managed under the GLO. In order to publicise the GLO when it has been made, a copy should be supplied to the Law Society and to the Senior Master. A record of each GLO made will be maintained in the Central Office in a Nationwide Register of all GLO's notified to the Senior Master.

13.8.5 The Practice Direction sets out how the group litigation will be managed. In particular, a managing judge will be appointed. The case management directions are likely to direct;

(1) that a "Group Particulars of Claim" containing the various claims of the claimants on the group register are served,
(2) that one claim proceed as a "test" claim, and
(3) a cut-off date after which no additions may be made to the group register.
(4) that all documents in the GLO be headed in the name of the Group Litigation name

## Guide to Civil Proceedings Fees from 6 April 2006

1B–98 **Annex 1**

*Editorial note* —Annex 1 to the Guide contains the text of the Civil Proceedings Fees Order 2004 (SI 2004/3121),as amended to April 6, 2006. That Order has been replaced entirely (with effect from May 1, 2008) by the Civil Proceedings Fees Order 2008 (SI 2008/1053). For the complete text of that order, see Section 10 below.

1B–99 **Annex 2**

The following is a list of abbreviations commonly used by Masters on endorsements of orders, though there may be some variation as between individual Masters

| | |
|---|---|
| A.D.R | Alternative Dispute Resolution |
| Aff. | Affidavit |
| A.M-T | Allocate to Multi Track |
| A.N. | Appointment Notice |
| App. | Application |
| A.Q. | Allocation Questionnaire |
| A.S. | Assessed summarily |
| B.N.L.T. | By no later than |
| C.C. | County Court |
| C.I.A. | Costs in the application |
| C.I.A.E. | Costs in any event |
| C.I.C. | Costs in the case |
| Cl. | Claimant |
| Col. | Certificate for Counsel |
| C.M.C. | Case Management Conference |
| C.O.A. | Charging order absolute |
| C.O.C.B. | Costs of and caused by |
| C.O.S.C. | Charging order to show cause |
| C.R. | Costs reserved |
| C.T.R. | Costs of today reserved |
| D./Def. | Defendant/Defence |
| D.A.I/N.A. | Detailed assessment if not agreed |
| Disc. | Disclosure |
| Dism. | Dismissed |
| Disp. C/S. | Dispense with requirement of certificate of service |
| F.C. | Fixed costs |
| F.C.O. | Final Charging Order |
| F.I. | Further information |
| F.O. | Further order |
| F.O.D. | First open date |

| | |
|---|---|
| I.A.E. | In any event |
| I.B. | Indemnity basis |
| Insp. | Inspection |
| I.T.P.D.O. | Interim Third Party Debt Order |
| J. | Judgment |
| L.A. | Legal Aid |
| L.A.A. | Legal Aid assessment |
| L.Q. | Listing Questionnaire |
| O. | Order |
| On C.Serv. | On producing Certificate of Service |
| O. Exam. | Oral examination |
| P/C. | Particulars of claim |
| P.D. | Practice direction |
| Pm. | Permission |
| Pm. A. | Permission to apply/appeal |
| Pm. R. | Permission to restore |
| Pm. R.F.D. | Permission to restore for further directions |
| Pt. | Part |
| P.R.A. | Private Room Appointment |
| R. | Rule |
| S.A. | Set aside/Special allowance |
| S.O.J. | Service out of the jurisdiction |
| S/C | Statement of Case |
| S.B. | Standard basis |
| S/T | Statement of truth |
| Tfr. | Transfer |
| T.P.D.O | Third Party Debt Order |
| W.N. | Without notice |
| W.C.O. | Wasted Costs Order |
| W.N. | Without notice |
| W.S. | Witness Statement |

# 1C THE SUPREME COURT COSTS OFFICE GUIDE 2006

TABLE OF CONTENTS



***Paragraph numbers marked with a "+" can be found online and on CD.***



SCCO GUIDE

***Paragraph numbers marked with a "+" can be found online and on CD.***

***Paragraph numbers marked with a "+" can be found online and on CD.***

SCCO GUIDE

***Paragraph numbers marked with a "+" can be found online and on CD.***

***Paragraph numbers marked with a "+" can be found online and on CD.***



SCCO GUIDE

***Paragraph numbers marked with a "+" can be found online and on CD.***

***Paragraph numbers marked with a "+" can be found online and on CD.***

**APPENDIX—SOME STANDARD FORMS AND PRECEDENTS**



***Paragraph numbers marked with a "+" can be found online and on CD.***

LIST OF COSTS JUDGES AND COSTS OFFICERS 1C–2

| Costs Judge | Room |
|---|---|
| Chief Master Hurst (*Senior Costs Judge*) | 2.08 |
| Master Wright | 2.12 |
| Master Rogers | 2.24 |
| Master Rogers | 2.24 |
| Master O'Hare | 2.17 |
| Master Campbell | 2.23 |
| Master Simons | 2.22 |
| Master Gordon-Saker | 2.03 |
| Master Haworth | 2.02 |

| Costs Officer | Room |
|---|---|
| Mr D P O'Riordan (*Senior Costs Officer*) | 2.07 |
| Mr J Lambert (*Principal Costs Officer*) | 1.05 |
| Mr C J Baker | 1.09 |
| Mr J Martin | 1.17 |
| Mr F Edwards | 1.12 |
| Ms H Newman (*Acting Court Manager*) | 2.18 |
| Mr P Emery | 1.07 |
| Miss M Myers | 1.19 |
| Mrs I Sainthouse | 2.25 |
| Mrs A Alese | 1.13 |
| Mrs V Campbell | 1.15 |

**SCCO postal address**

Clifford's Inn
Fetter Lane
London EC4A 1DQ
(DX 44454 Strand)

**Telephone numbers**

| | |
|---|---|
| PA to Senior Costs Judge | 020 7947 6618 |
| Costs Judges Section | 020 7947 7124 |
| Costs Officers Section | 020 7947 7121 |
| Court of Protection | 020 7947 6469 |
| Issue Section | 020 7947 6163 |

**Certificates**

| | |
|---|---|
| Costs Judges' | 020 7947 7124 |
| Costs Officers' | 020 7947 7121 |

**Fax Numbers**

| | |
|---|---|
| Costs Judges Section | 020 7947 6247 |
| Costs Officers Section | 020 7947 6344 |
| General Office | 020 7947 6344 |

LIST OF REGIONAL COSTS JUDGES 1C–3

**Northern Circuit** — Bury
District Judge Duerden
Bury County Court
Tenterden Street
Bury, Lancs BL9 0HJ
DX 702615 BURY 2
Tel Number: 0161 7641344
Fax Number: 0161 7634995

**Wales and Chester Circuit** — Carmarthen
District Judge Davies
Carmarthen County Court
The Old Vicarage
Picton Terrace
Carmarthen
Wales SA31 1BJ
DX 99570 CARMARTHEN 2
Tel Number: 01267 228010
Fax Number: 01267 221844

***Paragraph numbers marked with a "+" can be found online and on CD.***

| | | | |
|---|---|---|---|
| District Judge Heyworth<br>Liverpool County Court<br>35 Vernon Street<br>Liverpool L2 1BX<br>DX 702600<br>LIVERPOOL 5<br>Tel Number: 0151 296 2200<br>Fax Number: 0151 296 2201 | Liverpool | District Judge Evans<br>Newport County Court<br>Olympia House, 3rd Floor<br>Upper Dock Street<br>Newport<br>Gwent NP20 1PQ<br>DX 99480<br>NEWPORT (SOUTH WALES) 4<br>Tel Number: 01633 227150<br>Fax Number: 01633 263820 | Newport |
| District Judge Park<br>Carlisle County Court<br>Courts of Justice<br>Earl Street<br>Carlisle, Cumbria CA1 1DJ<br>DX 65331 CARLISLE 2<br>Tel Number: 01228 520619<br>Fax Number: 590588 | Carlisle | District Judge Wallace<br>Macclesfield County Court<br>2nd Floor, Silk House<br>Park Green<br>Macclesfield<br>Cheshire SK11 7NA<br>DX 702498<br>MACCLESFIELD 3<br>Tel Number: 01625 412800<br>Fax Number: 01625 501262 | Macclesfield |
| District Judge Smedley<br>Liverpool County Court<br>Queen Elizabeth II Law Courts<br>Derby Square<br>Liverpool L2 1XA<br>DX 702600<br>LIVERPOOL 5<br>Tel Number: 0151 4737373<br>Fax Number: 0151 2581587 | Liverpool | **Western Circuit**<br>District Judge Dancey<br>Bournemouth County Court<br>The Courts of Justice<br>Deansleigh Road<br>Bournemouth BH7 7DS<br>DX 98420<br>BOURNEMOUTH 4<br>Tel Number: 01202 502800<br>Fax Number: 01202 502801 | Bournemouth |
| District Judge Turner<br>Blackpool County Court<br>The Law Courts<br>Chapel Street<br>Blackpool<br>Lancs FY1 5RJ<br>DX 724900<br>BLACKPOOL 10<br>Tel Number: 01253 754020<br>Fax Number: 01253 295255 | Blackpool | District Judge James<br>Aldershot & Farnham County Court<br>78/82 Victoria Road<br>Aldershot<br>Hants GU11 1SS<br>DX 98530 ALDERSHOT 2<br>Tel Number: 01252 796800<br>Fax Number: 01252 345705 | Aldershot & Farnham |

***Paragraph numbers marked with a "+" can be found online and on CD.***

| | | | |
|---|---|---|---|
| **North-Eastern Circuit**<br>District Judge Besford<br>Kingston-upon-Hull County Court<br>Lowgate<br>Kingston-upon-Hull<br>Hull HU1 2EZ<br>DX 703010 HULL 5<br>Tel Number: 01482 586161<br>Fax Number: 01482 588527 | Hull | District Judge Wainwright<br>Exeter County Court<br>The Castle<br>Exeter<br>Devon EX4 3PS<br>DX 98440 EXETER 2<br>Tel Number: 01392 210655<br>Fax Number: 01392 433546 | Exeter |
| District Judge Hill<br>Scarborough County Court<br>Pavilion House<br>Valley Bridge Road<br>Scarborough<br>North Yorkshire YO11 2JS<br>DX 65140 SCARBOROUGH 2<br>Tel Number: 01723 366361<br>Fax Number: 01723 501992 | Scarborough | **South-Eastern (North) Circuit**<br>District Judge Bazley-White<br>Ipswich County Court<br>8 Arcade Street<br>Ipswich, Suffolk IP1 1EJ<br>DX 97730 IPSWICH 3<br>Tel Number: 01473 214256<br>Fax Number: 01473 251797 | Ipswich |
| District Judge Spencer<br>Leeds County Court<br>The Courthouse<br>1 Oxford Row<br>Leeds LS1 3BG<br>DX 703016 LEEDS 6<br>Tel Number: 0113 2830040<br>Fax Number: 0113 2452305 | Leeds | District Judge Sparrow<br>Norwich County Court<br>The Law Courts<br>Bishopgate<br>Norwich NR3 1UR<br>DX 97385 NORWICH 5<br>Tel Number: 01603 728200<br>Fax Number: 01603 760863 | Norwich |
| **Midland Circuit**<br>District Judge Mackenzie<br>Worcester County Court<br>The Shirehall<br>Foregate Street<br>Worcester WR1 1EQ<br>DX 721120 WORCESTER 11<br>Tel Number: 01905 730800<br>Fax Number: 01905 730801 | Worcester | **South-East (South) Circuit**<br>District Judge Lethem<br>Tunbridge Wells County Court<br>Merevale House<br>42/46 London Road<br>Tunbridge Wells<br>Kent TN1 1DP<br>DX 98220 TUNBRIDGE WELLS 3<br>Tel Number: 01892 515515<br>Fax Number: 01892 513676 | Tunbridge Wells |
| District Judge Middleton<br>Birmingham County Court<br>The Priory Courts<br>33 Bull Street<br>Birmingham B4 6DS<br>DX 701987<br>Tel Number: 0121 6814441<br>Fax Number: 0121 681 3001/2 | Birmingham | District Judge Matthews<br>Oxford County Court<br>St Aldates<br>Oxford OX1 1TL<br>DX 964500 OXFORD 4<br>Tel Number: 01865 264200<br>Fax Number: 01865 790773 | Oxford |

SCCO GUIDE

*Paragraph numbers marked with a "+" can be found online and on CD.*

| | |
|---|---|
| District Judge Millard<br>Nottingham County Court<br>60 Canal Street<br>Nottingham NG1 7EJ<br>DX 702381<br>NOTTINGHAM 7<br>Tel Number: 0115 9103500<br>Fax Number: 0115 9103510 | Nottingham |

## FOREWORD

1C-4 Dealing with the costs of a case can often be just as complicated as the substantive issues themselves. This, the third (and largest) edition of the Senior Courts Costs Office Guide has been written by the Masters and Officers of the Senior Courts Costs Office who deal with the many complexities of costs issues on a daily basis. It does not seek to replace the rules set out in the Civil Procedure Rules and Practice Directions, but gives practical information and guidance for dealing with this area of law. As ever, like its predecessors, it will be an invaluable friend to anyone who uses it – whether they are lawyers or litigants.

**THE RIGHT HONOURABLE SIR ANTHONY CLARKE, MASTER OF THE ROLLS, HEAD OF CIVIL JUSTICE**

July 2006

GLOSSARY

1C-5

| | |
|---|---|
| **Additional liability** | Items of costs which are recoverable in certain circumstances: that part of a success fee (defined below) under a conditional fee agreement (also defined below) which is recoverable from a paying party (defined below) and/or a reasonable sum in respect of a relevant insurance premium (also defined below) and/or an additional amount which is sometimes recoverable in respect of "self insurance" notionally incurred by a litigant whose case is funded by a trade union or similar body. These three forms of additional liability are the items about which the paying party should have received a notice of funding (defined below). |
| **Applications clerk** | The clerk to whom all papers and enquiries should be directed concerning the issue of claim forms and application notices: the applications clerk's office is currently located in Room 2.13. |
| **Appropriate office** | The office in which a request for a detailed assessment hearing should be filed: it is the County Court Office or District Registry for the court in which the order for costs was made or, in all other cases, the Senior Courts Costs Office (SCCO). Where the SCCO is the appropriate office for the request, it is also the appropriate office for any request or application made earlier in the detailed assessment proceedings, eg, a request for a default costs certificate, a request or application to set aside such a certificate and applications for extension of time and sanctions for delay. |
| **Central Funds** | Money provided by Parliament out of which may be paid the costs of defendants in criminal cases in respect of which a "defendants costs order" has been made. |

| | |
|---|---|
| **Clerk of Appeals** | The clerk to whom all papers and enquiries should be directed which relate to SCCO work concerning criminal fee appeals. The Clerk of Appeal's office is currently located in Room 2.13. |
| **Conditional fee agreement** | An agreement with a legal representative which provides for the payment of fees or part of them only in specified circumstances. A party who wishes to recover a success fee payable under the agreement from his opponent should serve a notice of funding on the opponent at the outset of the claim. |
| **Costs between the parties** | Costs payable by one litigant to another litigant under the terms of an order made by the court. The expression is used in order to distinguish these costs from "solicitor and client costs" (costs payable by a client to a solicitor under the terms of a contract made between them) and "LSC only costs" (costs payable by the Legal Services Commission to a solicitor or barrister). |
| **Costs Judges** | Judges sitting in the SCCO (also known as Taxing Masters and as Masters of the SCCO). Costs Judges also act as District Judges of the Principal Registry of the Family Division, and as District Judges of the County Court when assessing costs from those courts. When assessing costs under an order of the Adjudicator to HM Land Registry they sit as his Deputy Adjudicators. |
| **Costs Officers** | Authorised court officers who assess most bills for sums not exceeding certain amounts specified from time to time. From their decisions, appeals lie as of right to the Costs Judges. |
| **Costs-only proceedings** | The procedure to be followed where, before court proceedings are commenced, the parties to a dispute reach an agreement on all issues, including which party is to pay costs, but are unable to agree the amount of those costs. |
| **Counsel** | One or more advocates acting for a litigant. Very senior advocates are awarded the title "Queen's Counsel". |
| **CPD** | The Costs Practice Direction, supplementing the CPR (defined below). |
| **CPR** | The Civil Procedure Rules which, supplemented by the CPD (defined above) govern the procedure to be followed in most civil cases brought in the SCCO. The text of the CPR and the CPD are set out in practitioner's books such as the White Book Service and the Civil Court Practice. Most of the relevant texts are also included on the SCCO page of the Court Service website (as to which, see para. 1.10, below). |
| **Detailed assessment** | The judicial process under which bills of costs are checked as to their reasonableness; the court may allow or disallow any items claimed in a bill or may vary any figures claimed in respect of them. |
| **Determining officer** | The court officer in criminal cases (only) who first assesses the costs payable to a defendant out of Central Funds (defined above) or payable by the LSC to solicitors and counsel under criminal legal aid orders. Costs Judges have jurisdiction to hear appeals from the decisions of Determining Officers. |

***Paragraph numbers marked with a "+" can be found online and on CD.***

| | |
|---|---|
| **Disbursements** | Sums of money, e.g., court fees, counsel's fees and witness expenses which are paid or payable by a "receiving party" (defined below) which cannot and do not include any element of profit for that party or for the solicitor acting for him. A special meaning is given to this term in the case of litigants in person (see para. 22.2, below). |
| **Form N252 and other N forms** | Court forms which are referred to in the CPD (defined above). Copies of the forms for use in the SCCO can be obtained from the SCCO itself or from the SCCO page of the Court Service Website (as to which, see para. 1.10, below). |
| **Funding arrangement** | An arrangement made by a litigant which gives rise to an additional liability (defined above). |
| **Insurance premium** | The sum paid or payable by a litigant who has taken out an "after the event" insurance policy taken out in respect of particular litigation and covering against the risk of losing that litigation. |
| **Litigant in person** | A party to any proceedings who does not have a solicitor or other legal representative duly authorised to represent him or her in those proceedings. |
| **LSC** | The Legal Services Commission, which is the body set up by Parliament to provide financial help as to the costs of legal services provided to litigants in civil claims and defendants in criminal cases who come within certain eligibility criteria. |
| **LSC funded client** | A litigant who has been granted financial help by the Legal Services Commission. |
| **Notice of Funding** | A notice (usually in Form **N251**) by which one party warns another of any additional liability (defined above) which may later be recoverable. |
| **Offer to settle** | An offer in writing made by one party to another in detailed assessment proceedings proposing the payment of a specific sum of money thereby avoiding the need for any further delay or expense. If the offer is not accepted and the costs in question are later subject to detailed assessment, neither party is allowed to reveal the existence of the offer to the Costs Judge or Costs Officer until the detailed assessment has been completed. The letter containing the offer should include the words "without prejudice save as to the costs of the detailed assessment" or words to that effect. |
| **Part 23 application** | Applications made by any party which relate to existing or intended detailed assessment proceedings. The notice of application should be in Form **N244** (as to which, see above). |
| **Part 36 offer or payment** | An offer in writing made by one litigant to another during the proceedings preceding the detailed assessment proceedings, proposing to settle those proceedings on specified terms. After proceedings have started an offer by a defendant to settle a money claim should be supported by a payment into court of the specific sum offered. |
| **Paying party** | The party to detailed assessment proceedings who is liable to pay the costs which are the subject of the assessment. The opposing party is referred to as the "receiving party" which is defined below. |

| | |
|---|---|
| **Points of dispute** | A written statement made by the paying party identifying the areas of disagreement as to the costs to be assessed. In respect of each item of costs which is disputed the statement should outline the reason for disputing it and, where a reduction is sought, should suggest the reduced figure. |
| **Profit costs** | Costs paid or payable in respect of work done by a solicitor which are not "disbursements" (defined above). |
| **Provisional assessment** | An assessment of costs made without a hearing. Subsequently the court notifies the receiving party of the sum proposed to be allowed and requires the receiving party to so inform the court office within 14 days if he wishes a hearing to be convened. |
| **RCJ** | The Royal Courts of Justice the postal address of which is Strand, London, WC2A 2LL. |
| **Receiving party** | A party to detailed assessment proceedings who is entitled to recover from another party the costs which are the subject of the assessment. In the case of "costs between the parties" (defined above) the receiving party is the person in whose favour the court's order for costs was made or the solicitor or other legal representative acting for such a person. In the case of "solicitor and client costs" (which is defined below) the receiving party is the solicitor. |
| **SCCO** | The Senior Courts Costs Office the postal address of which is Clifford's Inn, Fetter Lane, London, EC4A 1DQ. |
| **Sitting Master** | Each day the Master so nominated for that day deals with any applications in matters not yet assigned to other Masters and is also available to give guidance on points of practice to the Judges of the Senior Courts and other courts throughout the country and (via his clerk) to any litigants or lawyers seeking his help. |
| **Solicitor and client costs** | See "costs between the parties" above. |
| **Statement of truth** | A statement to be included in any claim form, application notice or witness statement which confirms that the facts stated therein are true. The statement of truth must be signed by the litigant, or his litigation friend or legal representative or witness as the case may be. |
| **Success fees** | An additional fee which is payable in certain circumstances under the terms of a conditional fee agreement. The success fee must be expressed as a percentage of the other profit costs payable under the agreement. |
| **Summary assessment** | The procedure by which the court, when making an award of costs, immediately calculates and specifies the sum of costs it allows. |
| **Wasted costs order** | An order against a legal representative which disallows, or, as the case may be, orders the legal representative to meet, the whole or any part of costs found to have been incurred as a result of improper, unreasonable or negligent acts or omissions on the part of the legal representative or any consequential costs. |

SCCO GUIDE

## SECTION 1

## INTRODUCTION

1C-6 **1.1 The work of the SCCO**

(a) The Senior Courts Costs Office (SCCO) is a distinct part of the High Court, separate from the Queens Bench Division, Chancery Division and Family Division. It has two ranks of judicial officer: Costs Judges (also known as Taxing Masters and as Masters of the SCCO) and costs officers (senior civil servants from whose decisions appeals lie as of right to a Costs Judge).

(b) The primary function of the SCCO is the assessment of costs which are recoverable from a litigant by another litigant or by a lawyer. In the past, assessments (then called "taxations") were conducted by specialist Judges appointed to each court. In 1842 the office of Taxing Master was created and Taxing Masters were appointed to each Division of the High Court. The Supreme Court Taxing Office was originally one of the Departments which made up the Central Office. At the start of the 20th century it took over the work of the Chancery Taxing Masters. In 1999 the Civil Procedure Rules ("CPR") adopted the term "detailed assessment" in place of "taxation" at which time the SCCO was created. It now has jurisdiction to assess costs awarded by any Judge of the Court of Appeal, High Court or County Court. Since 2000 it has had the jurisdiction to assess orders for costs made in the Family Division of the High Court and in the Principal Registry.

(c) Regional Costs Judges

Regional Costs Judges have been appointed on all circuits outside London. They are District Judges who have been appointed to hear detailed assessment of bills of costs that fall within the criteria of the scheme at a venue which is convenient to the parties and their legal representatives.

The criteria for a detailed assessment to be referred to a Regional Costs Judge, rather than the local District Judge, are as follows: the time estimate for the detailed assessment exceeds one day; and/or the sum claimed exceeds £50,000; and/or complex arguments on points of law, or an issue affecting a group of similar cases, are identified in the points of dispute or the reply or are referred to in argument at a detailed assessment hearing.

Once a request for detailed assessment in Form **N258** has been filed at court the bill will be referred to a District Judge who will consider whether it falls within the criteria for reference to a Regional Costs Judge. If it does, the bill will be referred to the appropriate Regional Costs Judge who will then decide whether to accept it and will give any directions required, including directions as to listing.

If a party wishes to make submissions as to whether any particular detailed assessment fulfils the criteria for reference to a Regional Costs Judge, or as to the most convenient court for any hearing before a Regional Costs Judge, they should first consult the other parties or their legal representatives before making submissions to the court. It is helpful if such submissions are filed with the court when the request for detailed assessment is lodged. If possible the parties should attempt to agree the reference to the Regional Costs Judge, any directions and the most convenient venue.

A list of the names and court addresses of the District Judges who were appointed Regional Costs Judges in 2005 is set out on pages 12 and 13 [para.1C-3], above.

**1.2 Representation**

1C-7 (a) Solicitors

In most cases parties will be represented by the solicitors who have acted for them in the litigation in which the order for costs has been made. The name, address, telephone and fax numbers and reference of each such solicitor is set out on the Statement of Parties which is lodged when a request for a detailed assessment hearing is made (see further, Section 8, below).

Where proceedings are brought by claim form under Part III of the Solicitors Act 1974, the name and other details of each party's solicitor are set out in the claim form or in the acknowledgment of service, as the case may be.

Solicitors remain on the record of the court until they obtain an order for their removal, or until another firm or the litigant in person files and serves a notice of acting. Notices of acting should be filed in the SCCO and also in the court office of the court in which the relevant order for costs was made if proceedings are still continuing in that court.

The firm on the record may be represented by a fee earner, for example, a partner, an assistant solicitor, a legal executive, a trainee solicitor or a paralegal or other clerk employed by the firm. Alternatively, firms outside London sometimes instruct a firm of solicitors in London to act on their behalf as an agent at any hearing.

(b) Bankrupt Party

A bankrupt has no right to be heard unless an order under Section 303 of the Insolvency Act 1986 has been made. It is normally for the trustee in bankruptcy to decide what steps to take on behalf of the bankrupt's estate in relation to any proceedings in the SCCO.

(c) Company

Under the CPR, companies are not required to act by a solicitor when starting proceedings or defending them. Thus, they may act by any duly authorised agent. Where a document is to be verified on behalf of a company a statement of truth as to that document may be signed by any person holding a senior position in the company. However, once a matter proceeds to a hearing, the company, by its officers or employees or otherwise, has no personal right of audience. CPR 39.6 permits the representation of a company "at trial" by an employee but this is not as of right; the rule states that the person wishing to speak for the company must obtain the court's permission. The Practice Direction to that rule sets out the information to be given to the court in such circumstances, states that such permission should be sought in advance and states that such permission may be obtained informally and without notice to the other parties. Although CPR 39.6 concerns representation at trial, the Practice Direction provisions concern representations at any hearing.

(d) Costs draftsmen

At present independent costs draftsmen have no rights of audience as such but, by concession, are treated as if they are in the employ of the firm of solicitors instructing them. They have no rights of audience on behalf of a litigant in person (but see McKenzie Friend below). In the near future the Association of Law Costs Draftsmen will be authorised to grant rights of audience and rights to conduct litigation to certain of its members when participating in detailed assessments.

(e) Patents agents, trademark agents and claims consultants

In any patent action conducted by a patent agent, the patent agent may have a right to appear. Similar rights have now been granted to trademark agents in respect of trademark cases. In certain cases (such as arbitrations and planning matters) surveyors and other persons acting as claims consultants who have conducted the proceedings may be permitted to appear.

(f) Counsel and counsel's clerks

Counsel properly briefed by solicitors or by the litigant have full rights of audience. However, if they appear on their own behalf without a brief they are not entitled to a fee. Counsel's clerks attending as such do not have any right of audience. However, in an exceptional case, counsel's clerk may be allowed a hearing on behalf of counsel if counsel so requests in writing and if the Costs Judge or costs officer so allows.

(g) McKenzie Friend

As a general rule, a litigant in person will be allowed to receive the assistance of a friend at the hearing to give advice and to take notes (but not to act as advocate).However, in a particular case, the court may refuse to allow such assistance to be given, or to be continued, if there are strong and compelling reasons for believing that such assistance will impede the efficient administration of justice.

### 1.3 Sitting Master 1C–8

Costs Judges act from time to time on a rota basis as Sitting Master to hear applications, in detailed assessment proceedings which have not been assigned to a particular Costs Judge or costs officer, to hear applications under the Solicitors Act 1974 and to deal with enquiries relating to practice and law arising out of assessments. Such enquiries may be made indirectly, via his clerk, or, in the case of Judges of the Senior Courts or other courts throughout the country, directly.

1C-9 **1.4 Office hours**

In common with other civil courts the SCCO is open from 10 am until 4.30 pm from Mondays to Fridays. It is closed on public holidays and on the Tuesday after Easter Monday.

1C-10 **1.5 SCCO Support Sections**

Once proceedings have been commenced in the SCCO further work done in preparation for hearings is dealt with by the clerks of the Costs Judges Section for hearings before a Master and by clerks of the Costs Officers Section for hearings before a costs officer. When an assessment has been completed and the appropriate fees paid these Sections will also deal with the issue of the final costs certificates. The clerks in these Sections deal with appointments, correspondence and telephone enquiries. They do not give legal advice to parties. However, assistance and guidance will be given in appropriate circumstances as to general office practice.

Assistance and guidance on technical matters which are complex and difficult may be referred to the Principal Costs Officer or to a designated senior clerk who will endeavour to help, possibly after consultation with the Costs Judge or costs officer to whom the case has been allocated.

1C-11 **1.6 The SCCO file**

On receiving the appropriate documents and court fees in respect of each application or request the court clerks will open a file and allocate to it a distinct file number. Subsequently further documents may be added to that file, eg, correspondence, witness statements, notes of hearings and the orders made thereon. Unless the court otherwise orders, any party to the proceedings is entitled, without permission, to obtain a copy of any document filed in the SCCO in respect of those proceedings if he pays any prescribed fee and files a written request for the document. Persons other than parties have much more limited rights of obtaining documents from the court file (CPR 5.4).

1C-12 **1.7 Referrals to the RCJ Citizens Advice Bureau**

(a) The Citizens Advice Bureau is able to give general legal advice to litigants in person and, for this purpose, maintains an office in the Royal Courts of Justice near the Main Hall.

(b) The Bureau operates on a "first come first served" basis. Clients will be seen first by a receptionist who will assess their eligibility for assistance by the Bureau. If they are eligible and the advice and assistance sought falls within the Bureau's remit they will be referred to a lawyer who will endeavour to provide the advice or assistance sought. Problems which can be resolved quickly will normally be dealt with there and then. If matters need more time, for example those involving a difficult point of law or procedure, or those requiring more information, research or the drafting of documents, the client will be asked to come back and an appointment made.

(c) Further information about the RCJ Citizens Advice Bureau and its referral scheme can be obtained from the SCCO Support Sections.

1C-13 **1.8 Contacting the SCCO by letter or fax**

(a) Although, during office hours, applications and other documents may be delivered by hand to the Costs Office, in practice most are delivered by letter or by fax. All such documentation should be sent with a covering letter stating any SCCO references relevant to the documentation. If a fee is payable the documentation should include a cheque or bankers draft made in favour of HM Paymaster General or HMPG. Parties who wish to pay court fees in cash must hand deliver the payment to Room E01 in the Royal Courts of Justice.

(b) Letters and documentation may be sent by post to:

The Court Manager
Senior Courts Costs Office

Cliffords Inn
Fetter Lane
London EC4A 1DQ

Or by document exchange (DX) to DX 44454 Strand.

(c) In an emergency urgent documents may be sent to the Costs Office by fax on number 020 7947 6247 or 020 7947 6344. If the fax relates to a hearing, the date and time of the hearing should be prominently displayed as well as the relevant SCCO reference number. Examples of urgent documents it is appropriate to send by fax are: documents required by the court at short notice before the hearing and letters informing the court of a settlement which obviates the need for some or all parties to attend a hearing. A fax should not be used to send letters or documents of a routine or non urgent nature, bills of costs, papers supporting bills or skeleton arguments.

(d) Where a document is filed by fax, the party filing it is not required in addition to send to the SCCO any further copy of that document, eg by post or document exchange. Documents sent by fax are not to be regarded as filed at court unless and until they are delivered by the court's fax machine. If a fax is delivered after 4 pm, or at any time on a day when the court office is closed, it will be treated as filed on the next day the court office is open.

**1.9 Contacting the SCCO by telephone** **1C–14**

(a) The SCCO can be contacted via the telephone numbers set out in the List of Costs Judges and Costs Officers (see page 11, [para.1C–2] above) or via the switchboard at the Royal Courts of Justice, the number of which is 020 7947 6000. Also once a file has been opened and the SCCO has entered into correspondence thereon the SCCO notepaper and compliments slips will show the telephone number of the relevant clerk. Parties should use this number when contact by letter or fax is not possible or not appropriate.

(b) In some cases the hearing of a detailed assessment may be conducted by telephone. If it is a hearing at which more than one party may be represented, the court will give directions as to who must arrange the conference call and the Costs Office number which should be used on that call. Most telephone hearings concern cases in which only one party wishes to attend. In those cases the court will give directions stating the Costs Office telephone number to be used, the date and time of the appointment and stating whether it should be by way of a conference call or an ordinary telephone call.

**1.10 SCCO page on the Court Service Website** **1C–15**

The SCCO page on the Court Service Website comprises a miscellany of information including the text of various guides and guideline figures published by the SCCO and the text of the Civil Procedure Rules and Practice Directions on Costs and summaries of recent costs appeals which contain important points of principle. The address of the SCCO page is www.hmcourts-service.gov.uk/infoabout/scco/index.htm.

## SECTION 2

## ENTITLEMENT TO COSTS

**2.1 The meaning of "Costs"** **1C–16**

(a) The word "costs" is defined in CPR 43.2. Costs normally fall into two categories:

(i) expenses of a type which solicitors frequently incur when acting on behalf of clients (such as counsel's fees, court fees, witness expenses etc). These are known as "disbursements".

(ii) The fees which a solicitor charges to his client. These are known as "solicitors' charges" or "profit costs".

(b) Costs payable by one party to another can, in appropriate circumstances, include costs incurred before the issue of proceedings (*In re Gibson's Settlement Trusts* [1981] Ch 179).

**2.2 Liability to pay costs** **1C–17**

(a) In litigation, no party has a right to costs. Costs are in the discretion of the court. If, however, the court sees fit to make an order as to the costs of the litigation,

***Paragraph numbers marked with a "+" can be found online and on CD.***

the general rule is that the unsuccessful party will be ordered to pay the costs of the successful party (CPR 44.3(2)(a)). The court may make an order for costs which reflects the extent to which each party has been successful in relation to different issues.

(b) Costs as between solicitor and client are payable to the solicitor according to the terms of any contract he has made with the client or, alternatively, in the case of an LSC funded client, according to the Regulations made under the Legal Aid Act 1988 and the Access to Justice Act 1999.

1C–18 **2.3 Orders which the Court may make**

(a) In deciding what order to make about costs the court is required to have regard to all the circumstances including the conduct of all the parties; whether a party has succeeded on part of his case, even if not wholly successful; and whether or not there has been a payment into court or an offer of settlement: (CPR 44.3(4)).

(b) The court has complete discretion as to what order for costs to make but those orders may include an order that a party must pay:

(i) a proportion of another party's costs;
(ii) a stated amount in respect of another party's costs;
(iii) costs from or until a certain date;
(iv) costs incurred before proceedings have begun;
(v) costs relating to particular steps in the proceedings;
(vi) costs relating only to a distinct part of the proceedings; and
(vii) interest on costs from or until a certain date.

(c) The court has, in addition, the power to order a party to pay an amount on account of costs before the costs are assessed (CPR 44.3(8)).

(d) Paragraph 8.5 of the Costs Practice Direction ("CPD") lists the more common costs orders which the court may make in proceedings before trial and explains their effect.

1C–19 **2.4 Bases of assessment**

(a) The court may order costs between the parties to be assessed on either the *standard basis* or the *indemnity basis*. The court will not allow costs which have been unreasonably incurred or which are unreasonable in amount.

(b) On the *standard basis*, the court will only allow costs which are proportionate to the matters in issue and will resolve any doubt which it may have as to whether costs were reasonably incurred or reasonable and proportionate in amount in favour of the paying party: (CPR 44.4(2)).

(c) Where the court assesses costs on the *indemnity basis* it will resolve any doubt which it may have as to whether costs were reasonably incurred or were reasonable in amount in favour of the receiving party (CPR 44.4(3)).

(d) In LSC funded cases, costs are payable to solicitors and counsel on the *standard basis* subject to Regulations which prescribe the amounts to be allowed in certain cases.

(e) In respect of costs payable to a solicitor by his client, the basis of assessment is the indemnity basis to which certain presumptions and limitations apply (see CPR 48.8 and CPD Section 54).

1C–20 **2.5 Methods of assessment of costs**

(a) When the court makes an order about costs, it may carry out a summary assessment then and there and order the payment of a sum of money in respect of costs, or it may order a detailed assessment of the costs. If a detailed assessment is ordered the receiving party must, amongst other things, prepare a bill setting out the work done and, ultimately, the court will go through that bill, hearing argument from both sides as to what items and amounts should and should not be allowed.

(b) The general rule is that the court will make a summary assessment of the costs at the conclusion of the trial of a case which has been dealt with on the fast track and at the conclusion of any other hearing which has lasted for not more than one day. In certain cases the Court of Appeal will also carry out a summary assessment. Summary assessment will be carried out unless there is good reason for not doing so, for example where the paying party shows substantial grounds for disputing the sum claimed for costs that cannot be dealt with summarily, or there is insufficient time to carry out a summary assessment (CPR 44.7; CPD Sections 12, 13 and 14).

### 2.6 The Indemnity Principle 1C–21

The principle is that a successful party cannot recover from an unsuccessful party more by way of costs than the successful party is liable to pay his or her legal representatives. There are several exceptions to the principle including the statutory exceptions concerning legal aid and conditional fee agreements. There have been calls for the total abolition of the principle. Unless and until that occurs the following three propositions continue to apply:

(i) A party in whose favour an order for costs has been made may not recover more than he is liable to pay his own solicitors: *Harold v Smith* [1860] 5 Hurl. &N. 381 at 385 and *Gundry v Sainsbury* [1910] 1KB 645 CA.

(ii) Where a party puts a statement of costs before the court for summary assessment that statement must be signed by the party or a legal representative. The form states: "The costs estimated above do not exceed the costs which the [*party*] is liable to pay in respect of the work which this estimate covers."

(iii) The signature of a statement of costs or a bill for detailed assessment by a solicitor is in normal circumstances sufficient to enable the court to be satisfied that the indemnity principle has not been breached: *Bailey v IBC Vehicles Ltd* [1998] 3 All ER 570 CA.

### 2.7 Duty to notify clients of adverse costs orders 1C–22

Where the court makes an order for costs against a person who is legally represented but is not present when the order is made, that party's solicitor must notify the client in writing of the costs order no later than seven days after the solicitor receives notice of the order (CPR 44.2).

### 2.8 Some special cases 1C–23

(a) In certain cases a right to costs on the *standard basis* arises even though the court does not make a specific order for costs. The occasions when this happens are under:

- (i) CPR 3.7(4) (defendant's right to costs where claim struck out for non payment of fees);
- (ii) CPR 36.13(1) (claimant's right to costs where he accepts defendants' Part 36 offer or Part 36 payment);
- (iii) CPR 36.14 (claimant's right to costs where defendant accepts the claimant's Part 36 offer); or
- (iv) CPR 38.6 (defendant's right to costs where claimant discontinues).

(b) In any other case, where the court makes an order but does not mention costs, no party is entitled to costs in relation to that order (CPR 44.13(1)).

(c) An appeal court may, unless it dismisses the appeal, make orders about costs of the proceedings in the lower court as well as the costs of the appeal (CPR 44.13(2)).

(d) Where proceedings are transferred from one court to another, the court to which they are transferred may (subject to any order made by the transferring court) deal with all the costs, including the costs before the transfer (CPR 44.13(3)).

(e) In a probate claim where a defendant has in his defence given notice that he requires the will to be proved in solemn form (as to which see CPR 57.7(5)), the court will not make an order for costs against the defendant unless it appears that there was no reasonable ground for opposing the will. The term "probate claim" is defined in CPR 57.1.

### 2.9 Costs where money is payable by or to a child or patient 1C–24

(a) Where a child or patient is ordered to pay money to another party the court may make a summary assessment of those costs or may order a detailed assessment.

(b) Where a child or patient is liable to pay money to his or her solicitor the court must order a detailed assessment of those costs (CPR 48.5) unless the case falls within one of those circumstances described in CPD Section 51 (eg another party has agreed to pay a specified sum in respect of costs and the solicitor acting for the child or patient has waived the right to claim further costs).

### 2.10 Costs of trustees and personal representatives 1C–25

Trustees and personal representatives who are parties to litigation are generally entitled to their costs, so far as not recovered from any other party, out of any fund

***Paragraph numbers marked with a "+" can be found online and on CD.***

which they hold as trustee or personal representative. The costs are assessed on the indemnity basis. If a trustee or personal representative has acted for a benefit other than that of the fund the court may make a different order (CPR 48.4).

1C–26 **2.11 Mortgagees' costs**

Depending on the terms of the mortgage, a mortgage lender is likely to be able to recover any costs incurred in litigation (except for costs which are unreasonably incurred or which are unreasonable in amount) as a matter of contract between the lender and the borrower. CPD Section 50 sets out the principles which apply to litigation costs relating to a mortgage (CPR 48.3).

1C–27 **2.12 Group Litigation Orders**

CPR Part 19 deals with Group Litigation Orders. CPR 48.6A provides that unless the court otherwise orders group litigants are severally (not jointly) liable for an equal proportion of the "common costs". ("Common costs" are defined in CPR 48.6A(2).) In addition, a group litigant is liable for the individual costs of his or her own claim. A group litigant coming late to the group register may be ordered to be liable for a proportion of the costs incurred before that litigant's name is entered on the register (CPR 48.6A(6)). Paragraph 16 of the Practice Direction Supplementing Part 19 provides that the Costs Judge will apportion the amounts of common costs and individual costs, if the court has not already done so.

1C–28 **2.13 Costs in the Companies Court**

In the Companies Court "the usual compulsory order" made on a winding-up petition includes provision for the payment of the petitioner's costs and one set of costs for the supporting creditors out of the assets of the company. Thus in a simple case if the usual compulsory order is made it will not generally be necessary to ask for a separate order for costs. If however there are opposing creditors and the petition succeeds, the costs of the opposing creditors are not paid out of the company's assets unless they are expressly allowed by the court.

1C–29 **2.14 Costs in family proceedings**

In family proceedings CPR Parts 43, 44 (except CPR 44.9 to 44.12), 47 and 48 apply to the assessment of costs; CPR 44.3(2) (costs follow the event) does not apply (Family Proceedings (Miscellaneous Amendments) Rules 1999 SI 1999 No.1012). The Costs Practice Direction applies to the extent that the CPR apply and references in the Direction to "claimant" and "defendant" should be read as references to the equivalent terms used in family proceedings.

1C–30 **2.15 Success fees and insurance premiums**

In certain cases the Access to Justice Act 1999 permits the recovery of costs under a conditional fee agreement which provides for a success fee and permits the recovery of sums paid or payable in respect of after the event insurance. Further information about these items of costs is given in Section 19 (below) and the procedures to be followed to deal with possible success fee disputes between legal representatives and clients are given in Section 20, below. It should be noted that, although family proceedings cannot be the subject of an enforceable conditional fee agreement (with or without a success fee) the reasonable cost of after the event insurance premiums in such proceedings may be recoverable.

1C–31 **2.16 Costs in relation to pre commencement disclosure and orders for disclosure against a non party**

Sections 33 and 34 of the Senior Courts Act 1981 and Sections 52 and 53 of the County Courts Act 1984 give the court powers, exercisable before commencement of proceedings, in relation to disclosure, and the power to make an order against a non party for disclosure of documents and inspection of property. The general rule is that the court will award the person against whom the order is sought, his costs of the application and of complying with any order which is made. If however that party has unreasonably opposed the application or failed to comply with any relevant pre-action protocol the court may well make a different order (CPR 48.1).

**2.17 Costs orders in favour of or against non parties** **1C–32**

(a) The court may order costs to be paid to or by a person who is not a party to the proceedings in which those costs have been incurred. Such an order is likely to be made only in exceptional circumstances. Where the court is considering making such an order, that person must be added as a party to the proceedings and must be given a reasonable opportunity to attend the hearing at which the court will consider the matter further (CPR 48.2 and see CPR Part 19 as to adding a person as a party). When the court makes such an order, the costs awarded can only be those incurred in the proceedings before it.

(b) The Court of Appeal has recently given guidance about the liabilities of professional funders, who have financed part of a Claimant's costs of litigation, to pay a contribution towards the costs of a successful defendant (see *Arkin v Borchard Lines Ltd* [2005] 1 WLR 3055; [2005] 3 All ER 613).

**2.18 Costs following acceptance of an offer to settle** **1C–33**

(a) CPR Part 36 deals with offers to settle and payments into court. Where a defendant's Part 36 offer or Part 36 payment is accepted without needing the permission of the court, the claimant is entitled to the costs of the proceedings up to the date of serving notice of acceptance (CPR 36.13(1)). Where a claimant's Part 36 offer is accepted without needing the permission of the court, the claimant is entitled to the costs of the proceedings up to the date upon which the defendant serves notice of acceptance (CPR 36.14). In these cases an order for costs is deemed to be made (see para 2.8 above).

(b) Where a claimant fails to do better than the defendant's Part 36 offer or Part 36 payment, the court will, unless it considers it unjust to do so, order the claimant to pay any costs incurred by the defendant after the latest date on which the payment or offer could have been accepted without needing the permission of the court (CPR 36.20).

(c) Where a claimant does better than was proposed in the claimant's Part 36 offer, the court may order interest at a rate not exceeding 10% above base rate, on the whole or part of the sum of money awarded to the claimant, for some or all of the periods starting with the latest date on which the defendant could have accepted the offer without needing the permission of the court. The court also has the power to order that the claimant is entitled to costs on the indemnity basis (as to which, see para 2.4, above) and to award interest on those costs at a rate not exceeding 10% above base rate (as to which, see Section 15, below). The court will make an order in such terms unless it considers it unjust to do so (CPR 36.21(4)).

(d) In deciding whether or not it would be unjust to make such an order, the court will take into account all the circumstances including the terms of the Part 36 offer, the stage in the proceedings when the offer was made, the information available to the parties at the time when the offer was made and the conduct of the parties with regard to the giving or refusing to give information for the purpose of enabling the offer to be made or evaluated (CPR 36.21(5)).

**2.19 Costs in small claims** **1C–34**

(a) In a case which has been allocated to the small claims track, the court may not order a party to pay costs to another party except in the limited circumstances set out in CPR 27.14(2). These include the fixed costs attributable to issuing the claim payable under CPR Part 45, and any costs which the court summarily assesses and orders to be paid by a party who has behaved unreasonably.

(b) The court also has the power to order a party to pay court fees paid by another party and expenses which a party or a witness has reasonably incurred in attending court. Paragraphs 7.2 and 7.3 of the Practice Direction Supplementing CPR Part 27 set out the maximum amount which the court may allow.

(c) The limits on costs also apply to any fee or reward for acting on behalf of a party to the proceedings, charged by a lay representative exercising a right of audience (CPR 27.14(4)).

(d) Where the parties consent to a claim being allocated to the small claims track, even though the amount of the claim exceeds the financial limit for small claims, the

*Paragraph numbers marked with a "+" can be found online and on CD.*

claim is treated for the purpose of costs as if it were proceeding on the fast track. In those circumstances the trial costs are in the discretion of the court but will not exceed the appropriate amount (having regard to the size of the claim) of fast track trial costs (CPR 27.14(5)).

(e) The effect on costs on allocation and reallocation to the small claims track is described in para 2.21, below.

1C-35 **2.20 Costs in fast track cases**

(a) In fast track cases the court's power to award trial costs is limited in accordance with CPR Part 46. Where the value of the claim does not exceed £3,000 the trial costs which the court may award will be £350. Where the value of the claim is more than £3,000 but not more than £10,000 the trial costs are £500 and where the value of the claim is more than £10,000 the trial costs are £750. The court may not award more or less than those amounts unless it decides not to award any trial costs or the circumstances set out in CPR 46.3 apply. The court has the power to apportion the amount awarded between the parties to reflect their respective degrees of success on the issues at trial (CPR 46.2(2)).

(b) The exceptional cases in which higher costs may be ordered are set out in CPR 46.3. These cover additional legal representatives, an additional liability in respect of a funding arrangement (see Section 19 below), separate trials, litigants in person, counterclaims and unreasonable and improper behaviour.

(c) Where a fast track case settles before the start of the trial and the court is assessing the amount of costs to be allowed in respect of a party's advocate for preparing for trial, it may not allow an amount exceeding the amount of fast track trial costs which would have been payable had the trial taken place (CPR 44.10).

1C-36 **2.21 Costs following allocation and reallocation**

The special rules which apply to small claims and fast track trial costs do not apply until the claim is allocated to a particular track. Once the claim is allocated to a particular track those special rules apply to the period before as well as after allocation except where the court or a Practice Direction provides otherwise (CPR 44.9). Any costs orders made before a claim is allocated to the small claims or fast track will not be affected by the allocation (CPR 44.11(1)). Where a claim is allocated to one track and subsequently re-allocated to a different track then, unless the court orders otherwise, any special rules about costs applying to the first track will apply to the claim up to the date of reallocation, and the rules applying to the second track will apply from the date of reallocation (CPR 44.11(2)).

1C-37 **2.22 Time for complying with orders for costs**

When the court makes an order for the payment of costs the paying party must make the payment within 14 days of the date of the order specifying the amount payable (CPR 44.8). The court may extend the time for payment, but if it does not do so and the costs are not paid within the 14 day period, the receiving party may take steps to enforce the order.

1C-38 **2.23 VAT**

(a) On an assessment of costs between the parties the receiving party must ensure that no claim for VAT is made in the bill if that party is able to recover it as input tax. Disputes as to the recoverability of VAT in bills between the parties are usually resolved by the making of a certificate as to the VAT position by the solicitors or auditors of the party receiving costs or by H M Revenue & Customs.

(b) Cases in which the receiving party cannot recover VAT on the costs payable by the paying party include the following:

- (i) the receiving party is a VAT registered taxable person and the supply of legal services was obtained for the purpose of his business;
- (ii) the receiving party is domiciled outside the European Union;
- (iii) the receiving party is domiciled outside the UK but is domiciled in the European Union and received the supply of legal services for the purposes of his business; or
- (iv) the receiving party is a legal representative representing himself (the "self supply" exception to VAT).

(c) CPD Section 5 sets out some special provisions relating to VAT.

***Paragraph numbers marked with a "+" can be found online and on CD.***

## SECTION 3

## FORM AND LAYOUT OF BILLS

### 3.1 Essential ingredients 1C–39

(a) Each bill should start with the full title of the proceedings, the name of the party whose bill it is and a description of the order for costs or other document giving the right to detailed assessment (as to which, see CPD 40.4).

(b) The bill should then give some background information about the case including a brief description of the proceedings, a statement of the status of the fee earners in respect of whom costs are claimed, the rates claimed for each such person and a brief explanation of any agreement or arrangement between the receiving party and his legal representatives which affects the costs claimed in the bill. There may also be a further matter to deal with if the party whose bill it is previously filed an estimate of costs in these proceedings. If there is a difference of 20% or more between the costs in the estimate and the costs (excluding the amount of any additional liability) claimed in the bill, the background information should state the reasons for that difference. See further as to differences between estimates and bills in paragraph 9.3 below.

(c) After the title and background information, it is convenient to divide the paper into several columns headed as follows: item number, date and description of work done, VAT, disbursements, profit costs.

(d) The bill should conclude with a summary showing the total costs claimed and with such of the certificates made by the receiving party or his legal representatives which are relevant (see further, paragraph 3.5 below).

### 3.2 Dividing bills of costs into separate parts 1C–40

Sometimes it is necessary or convenient to divide the section of the bill containing the actual items of costs into separate parts, numbered consecutively. For example, division into parts is necessary where there has been a change of solicitor, or where there has been some other change in the funding arrangements (eg to show costs incurred before, during and after the currency of LSC funding) to show costs claimed under different orders against different paying parties and to show costs before and after a change in the rate of VAT.

### 3.3 Dividing each part into separate items 1C–41

(a) In each part of a bill all the items claimed must be consecutively numbered and must be divided under such of the following heads as may be appropriate:

(1) Attendances on the court and counsel, in chronological order, up to the date of the notice of commencement.
(2) Attendances on and communications with the receiving party.
(3) Attendances on and communications with witnesses, including any expert witness.
(4) Attendances to inspect any property or place for the purposes of the proceedings.
(5) Attendances on and communications with other persons including officers of public records.
(6) Communications with the court and with counsel.
(7) Work done on documents: preparing and considering documentation, including documentation relating to pre action protocols where appropriate, work done in connection with arithmetical calculations of compensation and/or interest and time spent collating documents.
(8) Work done in connection with negotiations with a view to settlement if not already covered in the heads listed above.
(9) Attendances on and communications with London and other agents and work done by them.
(10) Other work done which was of or incidental to the proceedings which is not already covered in any of the heads listed above.

(b) In the list of items just given, the word "attendances" includes interviews and

***Paragraph numbers marked with a "+" can be found online and on CD.***

meetings and the word "communications" covers letters and e-mails sent and telephone calls.

(c) In each part of a bill which claims items under head 1 (attendances on court and counsel) a note should be made setting out, in chronological order with dates, all the relevant events in the proceedings including events which do not constitute chargeable items and including all orders for costs which the court has made (whether or not a claim is made in respect of those costs in this bill). Note that head 1 covers only attendances on the court and counsel. Communications with the court and counsel fall within head 6.

(d) Under heads 2 to 10, claims in respect of routine communications should be claimed as a single amount at the end of each head (*e.g.* "29 routine letters out at £x each and 8 routine telephone calls at £y each...£z"). If the number of attendances and non routine communications under a head is less than 20, each of them should be set out, in chronological order with dates. However, if under any head the number of attendances and non routine communications amount to 20 or more, the claim for the cost of those items in that part of the bill should be for the total only and should refer to a schedule in which the full record of dates and details is set out. Where bills contain more than one schedule each schedule should be numbered consecutively.

**1C-42** **3.4 Model forms of bills of costs**

The CPD contains several model forms of bill of costs. The use of these model forms is not compulsory but is recommended and, when a different form is used, a short explanation of why it has been adopted should appear in the narrative towards the beginning. Precedent A is the one which is most frequently used in practice: it is illustrated in the Appendix, below, para A-1.

**1C-43** **3.5 Certificates in bills of costs**

The final part of the bill of costs should contain such one or more of the prescribed certificates as are appropriate to the case and then the signature of the receiving party or his legal representative. These certificates give information on matters such as any rulings made as to entitlement to interest on costs, any payments made by the paying party on account of costs included in the bill and as to the receiving party's entitlement to recover from the paying party the VAT he is or has been liable to pay on the costs claimed. The text of the certificates is set out in the Appendix, below, para A-2.

**1C-44** **3.6 Disk copies of bills**

If the bill of costs is capable of being copied onto a computer disk, the paying party is entitled to demand a disk copy free of charge (CPD para 32.11).

## SECTION 4

## COMMENCEMENT OF DETAILED ASSESSMENT PROCEEDINGS

**1C-45** **4.1 Earliest time for commencement**

(a) Except where a summary assessment is carried out by the court, costs payable between the parties are not assessed until the conclusion of the proceedings out of which the order for costs arises, unless the court expressly orders an earlier detailed assessment (CPR 47.1). A Costs Judge or District Judge may make an order allowing detailed assessment proceedings to be commenced where there is no realistic prospect of the claim continuing (CPD para 28.1).

(b) Similarly where costs are payable out of the Community Legal Services Fund, detailed assessment should not be sought until the conclusion of the proceedings or until the discharge of the LSC certificate.

(c) Costs payable to a solicitor by his client are assessed if and when an order for detailed assessment is made (see further section 26 below).

(d) An appeal against an order for costs or an order for detailed assessment does not by itself operate as a stay of those proceedings unless the court so orders (CPR 47.2). An application for such a stay may be made either to the court whose order is being appealed or to the appeal court.

***Paragraph numbers marked with a "+" can be found online and on CD.***

**4.2 Latest time for commencement** 1C–46

(a) Detailed assessment proceedings must be commenced within three months after the judgment, order or event giving rise to the right to costs (CPR 47.7); in civil recovery proceedings under the Proceeds of Crime Act 2002 the time limit is reduced to two months, see further Section 32, below. The parties may agree between themselves to extend or shorten the time specified by the rule for commencing detailed assessment proceedings. A party may apply to the appropriate office (as to which, see para 8.1, below) for an order to extend or shorten the period of three months, but permission is not required to commence detailed assessment proceedings out of time.

(b) If the receiving party fails to commence detailed assessment proceedings within the period specified by the rule, or by order of the court, the paying party may apply for an order under CPR 47.8(1) requiring the receiving party to commence the proceedings within a specified time. The court may direct that unless the receiving party does commence the detailed assessment proceedings within the time specified by the court, all or part of the costs will be disallowed.

(c) Where the receiving party commences proceedings for detailed assessment out of time but the paying party has not made an application under CPR 47.8(1), the court may disallow all or part of the interest otherwise payable to the receiving party but the court will not impose any other sanction unless there has been misconduct (CPR 47.8(3)).

**4.3 Serving a notice of commencement** 1C–47

(a) Detailed assessment proceedings in respect of an order for costs between the parties are commenced by the receiving party serving on the paying party a notice of commencement in Form **N252** and a copy of the bill of costs. The notice of commencement must be completed to show the total amount of costs claimed in the bill and the extra sum which will be payable by way of fixed costs and court fees if a default costs certificate is obtained (CPR 47.6).

(b) The notice of commencement must be served on the paying party and on any other relevant persons, ie,

(i) any person who has taken part in the proceedings which gave rise to the assessment and who is directly liable under an order for costs made against him;

(ii) any person who has given to the receiving party notice in writing that he has a financial interest in the outcome of the assessment and wishes to be a party accordingly;

(iii) any other person whom the court orders to be treated as a relevant person (CPD para. 32.8).

**4.4 Documents to accompany the notice of commencement** 1C–48

(a) The list of documents to be served together with a notice of commencement depends upon whether or not the receiving party is seeking to recover an "additional liability", as to which see Section 19, below.

(b) If the detailed assessment is in respect of costs without any additional liability, the receiving party must serve, in addition to the notice of commencement and the bill of costs, copies of the fee notes of counsel and of any expert, in respect of fees claimed in the bill and written evidence as to any other disbursement claimed which exceeds £250, and a statement of parties giving the name and address for service of any person upon whom the receiving party intends to serve the notice of commencement (CPD para 32.3).

(c) If the detailed assessment is in respect of an additional liability only, the receiving party must serve, in addition to the notice of commencement and bill of costs, the relevant details of the additional liability and a statement of parties (CPD para 32.4). (Paragraph 19.6 below sets out the relevant details of additional liability which must be given.)

(d) If the detailed assessment is in respect of both costs and an additional liability, the receiving party must serve all the documents set out in (b) and (c) above.

**4.5 Procedure where costs are agreed** 1C–49

If the paying party and the receiving party agree the amount of costs, either may apply for a costs certificate (either interim or final) in the amount agreed (CPR 47.10 and, see further, para 17.9, below).

***Paragraph numbers marked with a "+" can be found online and on CD.***



SCCO GUIDE

1C–50 **4.6 Cases in which notices of commencement are unnecessary**

(a) In the following cases detailed assessment proceedings are commenced by the filing in court of a request for a detailed assessment hearing:

(i) costs of a LSC funded client which are payable only out of the Community Legal Service Fund (CPR 47.17 and see Form **N258A**).

(ii) Costs payable out of a fund other than the Community Legal Service Fund (CPR 47.17A and see Form **N258B**).

(iii) Costs to be assessed pursuant to an order under Part III of the Solicitors Act 1974 (CPR 48.8 and see Form **N258C**).

(b) In these cases there is no requirement to serve a notice of commencement on any party and there is no entitlement to the issue of a default costs certificate in respect of the assessment.

## SECTION 5

## POINTS OF DISPUTE AND REPLY

1C–51 **5.1 Time for Points of Dispute and consequences of not serving**

(a) Any party served with notice of commencement and the bill of costs may dispute any item in the bill by serving points of dispute on the receiving party and every other party to the detailed assessment proceedings. This must be done within 21 days after the date of service of the notice of commencement (CPR 47.9(2)), unless the parties agree to extend or shorten the time specified by the rule. A party may apply to the court for the time to be extended or shortened.

(b) Where a notice of commencement is served on a party outside England and Wales the period within which that party should serve points of dispute is to be calculated by reference to CPR Part 6 Section III (special provisions about service out of the jurisdiction) as if the notice of commencement was a claim form and as if the period for serving points of dispute were the period for filing a defence.

(c) If the receiving party is not served with any points of dispute and the period for doing so has expired, he may apply for a default costs certificate, as to which, see Section 6, below: (CPR 47.9(4)).

1C–52 **5.2 Form and contents of Points of Dispute**

(a) Points of dispute should be short and to the point and should follow as closely as possible Precedent G of the Schedule of Costs Precedents (see Appendix, para. A-3).

(b) The points of dispute should identify each item in the bill of costs which is disputed; state concisely the nature and grounds of the dispute and, where practicable, suggest a figure to be allowed instead of the figure which has been claimed. As a general rule, where details of an item are given in a schedule to the bill (eg, the Documents Item) it is not necessary for the Points of Dispute to deal separately with each individual entry in that schedule.

(c) A paying party may dispute a bill on the basis that the costs claimed therein exceed the amount of costs shown in an estimate of costs which the receiving party previously filed in the proceedings. In order to raise this dispute the paying party should include in his Points of Dispute a statement setting out his case if he:

(i) claims that he reasonably relied on the estimate of costs filed by the receiving party; or

(ii) wishes to rely upon the costs shown in the estimate in order to dispute the reasonable or proportionality of the costs claimed in the bill.

(N.B. the consequences of raising such a point of dispute are considered further in paragraph 9.3, below.)

(d) Where the receiving party claims an additional liability, a party serving points of dispute may include a request for information about other methods of financing costs which were available to the receiving party (CPD para 35.7(1)).

(e) The points of dispute should be signed by the party or his solicitor. If the points of dispute are capable of being copied onto a computer disk, the receiving party is entitled to demand a disk copy free of charge (CPD para 35.6).

1C–53 **5.3 Time limit for replies and their format**

(a) Where points of dispute are served the receiving party may serve a reply on the other parties to the assessment proceedings. The time limit for a reply is 21 days after service on him of the points of dispute (CPR 47.13).

(b) There is no obligation upon a receiving party to serve a reply. Before doing so the receiving party should consider whether the expense of a reply can be justified: it probably cannot if the reply will merely deny the points in dispute.

(c) The reply may take the form of an annotation to the points of dispute (see para 5.2(d) above) or may be set out on a separate document. Serving a reply on a separate document does not avoid the obligation to file points of dispute annotated as necessary in order to show which items have been agreed and their value and which items remain in dispute and their value (see further para 8.2, below).

**5.4 Where points of dispute challenge success fees** 1C–54

If a paying party challenges the amount of a success fee claimed on behalf of counsel or a solicitor, it may become necessary for the court to rule not only upon that point of dispute, but also upon the liability of the receiving party to pay to his legal representatives any disallowed amount. The procedure to be followed in such cases is set out in Section 20, below.

## SECTION 6

## OBTAINING A DEFAULT COSTS CERTIFICATE

**6.1 When and how to apply** 1C–55

(a) The deadline for serving points of dispute is 21 days after the date of service of notice of commencement (see para 5.1, above). A receiving party who is not served with points of dispute on or before that deadline can request the issue of a default costs certificate (CPR 47.9(4)) unless the case is one of those described in para 6.2, below.

(b) A request for a default costs certificate must be made in Form **N254** and must be accompanied by a copy of the order for costs or other document giving the right to detailed assessment (as to which, see CPD para 40.4). The form must be signed by the receiving party or his solicitor. A court fee is payable (see further, Section 27, below).

(c) The request in Form **N254** must be filed in the District Registry or County Court in which the case was being dealt with when the judgment or order for costs was made or when the event occurred which gave rise to the right to assessment, or to which it has subsequently been transferred; in all other cases the request must be filed in the SCCO.

**6.2 Cases in which the default costs certificate procedure does not apply** 1C–56

(a) If there is more than one paying party, the receiving party has no right to a default costs certificate if one or more of the paying parties serves points of dispute. However, paying parties who serve points of dispute late or who fail to serve them at all have no right to be heard at the subsequent detailed assessment unless the court gives permission (CPR 47.9 and 47.14).

(b) The default costs certificate procedure does not apply to costs of a LSC funded client which are payable out of the Community Legal Service Fund, costs payable out of a fund other than the Community Legal Service Fund, or costs to be assessed pursuant to an order under Part III of the Solicitors Act 1974. Further information concerning these cases is given in paras 4.6 and 8.1 of this Guide.

**6.3 Form of default costs certificate** 1C–57

(a) A default costs certificate will be in Form **N255**. It will include an order to pay the costs to which it relates, the fixed costs payable in respect of solicitor's charges on the issue of a default costs certificate and the fee paid on the request for the issue of a default costs certificate.

(b) The receiving party may either draw up a default costs certificate and deliver it to the court together with the request, or may leave it to the court to draw it up.

**6.4 Effect of a default costs certificate** 1C–58

(a) The amount certified in the default costs certificate must be paid within 14 days of the date of the certificate unless, upon an application made by either party, whether before or after the issue of the certificate, the court has specified some other date (CPR 44.8).

***Paragraph numbers marked with a "+" can be found online and on CD.***

(b) An application to stay enforcement of a default costs certificate issued by the SCCO may be made to a Costs Judge or to a court which has jurisdiction to enforce the certificate (see further Section 17, below). Proceedings for enforcement of a default costs certificate may not be issued in the SCCO (CPD para 37.7).

(c) Default costs certificates are addressed to the paying party. Where the receiving party is funded by the LSC, the issue of a default costs certificate does not prohibit, govern, or affect any detailed assessment of the same costs which may have to be made to determine the sum payable out of the Community Legal Service Fund (CPD para 37.5, and see further Section 24, below).

## SECTION 7

## APPLYING TO SET ASIDE A DEFAULT COSTS CERTIFICATE

1C-59 **7.1 Application by receiving party**

(a) Where (i) the receiving party has purported to serve the notice of commencement on the paying party; (ii) a default costs certificate has been issued; and (iii) the receiving party subsequently discovers that the notice of commencement did not reach the paying party at least 21 days before the default costs certificate was issued, the receiving party must file a request for the default costs certificate to be set aside (which can be done by a court clerk without any hearing) or apply to the court for directions. The receiving party may take no further steps in the detailed assessment proceedings or the enforcement of the default costs certificate until the certificate has been set aside or the court has given directions (CPR 47.12(4)).

(b) A receiving party who has obtained a default costs certificate for the wrong amount (whether for too much or for too little) may apply to the court for an order varying the certificate (as to applications generally, see Section 17, below).

1C-60 **7.2 Application by paying party**

(a) To obtain an order setting aside a default costs certificate a paying party should apply on notice in Form **N244** together with a copy of the bill of costs, a copy of the default costs certificate and a draft of the points of dispute he proposes to serve if his application is granted, and any other evidence supporting his application.

(b) In deciding whether to grant the application the court will consider, amongst other things, whether the application was made promptly and whether the applicant has shown some good reason why the order should be made. Where appropriate the court may make an order subject to conditions (such as a condition requiring the applicant to make a payment on account of the costs in question), or may instead of setting aside the certificate vary it (eg, to specify some other sum payable or some other date for payment).

1C-61 **7.3 Orders and directions on set aside applications**

(a) If a default costs certificate is set aside the court will give directions for the management of the detailed assessment proceedings.

(b) The Appendix, below, contains standard forms of order commonly made on set aside applications in the SCCO; a conditional order, an unconditional order, an order adjourning the application and an order dismissing the application (see para A-4).

## SECTION 8

## REQUESTS FOR A DETAILED ASSESSMENT HEARING

1C-62 **8.1 Forms of request**

(a) There are four forms of request:

(i) **N258**: request for detailed assessment hearing (general form).

(ii) **N258A**: request for detailed assessment (legal aid/LSC only).

(iii) **N258B**: request for detailed assessment (costs payable out of a fund other than the Community Legal Service Fund).

(iv) **N258C**: request for detailed assessment hearing pursuant to an order under Part 3 of the Solicitors Act 1974.

(b) The request should be filed in the District Registry or County Court in which the case was being dealt with when the judgment or order for costs was made or when

*Paragraph numbers marked with a "+" can be found online and on CD.*

the event occurred which gave rise to the right to assessment, or to which it has subsequently been transferred; in all other cases the request must be filed in the SCCO (CPR 47.4). Special provisions apply to cases proceeding in the London County Courts: see para 8.2, below.

(c) In cases in which Form **N258** is appropriate, the request should be filed within six months after the judgment, order or event giving rise to the right to costs. In cases in which any of the other three forms of request is appropriate, the request should be filed within three months after the judgment, order or event giving rise to the right to costs. As to the making of agreements or applications for an extension of this time limit, see para 17.5, below.

**8.2 Detailed assessment by the SCCO of costs of civil proceedings in London County Courts** **1C–63**

Where there is an order or judgment for costs in civil proceedings in the courts listed below, the receiving party must file the request for detailed assessment in the SCCO. All applications and requests must be made there. The relevant courts: Barnet, Bow, Brentford, Bromley, Central London, Clerkenwell, Croydon, Edmonton, Ilford, Lambeth, Mayors and City of London, Romford, Shoreditch, Uxbridge, Wandsworth, West London, Willesden and Woolwich.

**8.3 Documents to accompany the request** **1C–64**

(a) Each form of request contains a series of tick boxes which give guidance as to the documents which should accompany the request. In cases of difficulty or uncertainty litigants and their representatives should also refer to the full list of documents which is set out in the Costs Practice Direction at para. 40.2.

(b) As to the fee which may be payable when filing a request, further details are given in Section 27, below.

**8.4 Allocation to a Costs Officer or Costs Judge** **1C–65**

(a) As a general rule bills not exceeding £35,000, excluding VAT, will be allocated to a costs officer and larger bills will be allocated to a Costs Judge. Costs Judges also assess bills with a value below £35,000, excluding VAT, where they are linked to other bills which exceed that sum, or involve an assessment under the Solicitors Act 1974.

(b) On receipt of a form of request for a detailed assessment hearing, duly completed, the court clerk will enter the case on the computer, give it a reference number and then allocate the case by ballot to a particular costs officer or Costs Judge. The court clerk will then prepare an acknowledgement of the request which gives details of the reference number and the initials of the costs officer or Costs Judge to whom it has been assigned.

(c) Where the parties are agreed that the detailed assessment should not be made by a costs officer the receiving party should so inform the court clerk when filing the request. The court clerk will then allocate the case to a Costs Judge.

(d) If, after a case has been allocated to a costs officer, a party who objects to the detailed assessment being made by a costs officer must apply to a Costs Judge setting out the reasons for the objection. If sufficient reason is shown the court will direct that the bill should be assessed by a Costs Judge.

**8.5 Obtaining the date for the hearing** **1C–66**

(a) On receipt of the request for a detailed assessment hearing the court will fix a date for the hearing, or, if the costs officer or Costs Judge so decides, will give directions or fix a date for a preliminary appointment.

(b) The court will give at least 14 days notice of the time and place of the detailed assessment hearing to every person whose name and address appears on the statement of persons to who notice should be given which accompanies the request. When giving such notice the court will also distribute the annotated points of dispute lodged by the receiving party together with the request.

(c) Cases assigned to a costs officer are usually given a date for hearing not more than 12 weeks later than the date the request for a hearing was filed. Cases assigned to a Costs Judge are usually given a date for hearing not more than six months later than the date upon which the request for a hearing was filed. When filing the request the receiving party should also file a note of any dates upon which, to his knowledge, a detailed assessment hearing would be inconvenient for any party likely to attend.

(d) One or two cases every day will be listed before the Principal Costs Officer in Room 2.07 each day. The cases will be allocated on the day to a Costs Judge or costs officer who becomes available.

(e) As to the making of an application to change the date for hearing once fixed, see para. 17.6.

1C–67 **8.6 Application for an interim costs certificate**

(a) At any time after the receiving party has filed the request for a detailed assessment hearing, the receiving party may apply for the issue of an interim costs certificate. Further details about making applications are given in Section 17, below. The application should be listed before the costs officer or Costs Judge to whom the case has been allocated. If the detailed assessment has been allocated to a Deputy Costs Judge the application will be heard by the Sitting Master (see para 1.3).

(b) In determining what, if any, interim certificate to make, the court will consider, amongst other things, the bill of costs, points of dispute thereon and any reply thereto and the certificate in the bill as to any payments on account which have already been made.

(c) The form of interim costs certificate, **N257**, specifies the amount which must be paid, the time within which payment must be made and specifies whether the payment should be made to the receiving party or into court to await the issue of a final costs certificate. Payment into court is made at The Court Office, Kingsway, WC2B 6LE (DX 44455 Strand). Cheques must be made payable to the "Accountant General of the Senior Courts". The general form is the Form 100 Requests for Lodgment which must be accompanied by the relevant request for lodgment and proof that court proceedings exist.

(d) An application to amend, cancel or stay enforcement of an interim costs certificate may be made to a Costs Judge (but not to a costs officer) and applications to stay enforcement may also be made to any court which has jurisdiction to enforce the certificate. Proceedings for enforcement of an interim costs certificate may not be issued in the SCCO.

1C–68 **8.7 Lodging papers in support of the bill**

(a) Unless the court otherwise directs the receiving party must file with the court the papers in support of the bill not less than seven days before the date for the detailed assessment hearing and not more than 14 days before that date.

(b) Save as mentioned below the papers to be filed and the order in which they are to be arranged is as follows:

- (i) instructions and briefs to counsel arranged in chronological order together with all advices, opinions and drafts received and response to such instructions. Instructions are now frequently given by letter or email. These instructions should be separated or copied from the file if the original instructions sent to counsel are not available;
- (ii) reports and opinions of medical and other experts;
- (iii) any other relevant papers;
- (iv) a full set of any relevant pleadings to the extent that they have not already been filed in court;
- (v) correspondence, files and attendance notes;
- (vi) where the claim also includes a claim in respect of an additional liability (as to which, see Section 19, below) any paper relevant to the issues raised by the claim for additional liability.

(c) Where a claim is in respect of an additional liability only, the papers to be filed are such of those papers listed at (b) above as are relevant to the issues raised by the claim for additional liability.

(d) Further information about lodging documents and about orders for the production of documents is given in Section 10, below.

1C–69 **8.8 Obtaining files from other courts**

Where a District Registry or a County Court has directed that the detailed assessment hearing shall be at the SCCO, the District Registry or County Court will send their

*Paragraph numbers marked with a "+" can be found online and on CD.*

court file to the SCCO. The receiving party is responsible for filing all other papers at the SCCO. If, in cases in which the order for costs was made in the Royal Courts of Justice, the parties consider that the court file is required for the assessment proceedings, they should so notify the SCCO in sufficient time to enable the SCCO to obtain it.

## SECTION 9

## THE DETAILED ASSESSMENT HEARING

### 9.1 The conduct of the hearing 1C-70

(a) The general rule is that all hearings are in public (CPR 39.2). However, the court is not required to make special arrangements for accommodating members of the public who wish to attend and, therefore, members of the public have no right to admission if their admission is impracticable. The court may, if appropriate, adjourn the proceedings to a larger room or court in order to make their admission practicable.

(b) A hearing or any part of it may be private, for example if it involves confidential information (including information relating to personal financial matters) and publicity would damage that confidentiality. Other examples are set out in the Practice Direction to CPR 39. At the start of a public hearing, or during it, either party may request the court to rule that, thereafter, the hearing should be conducted in private. Any judgment or order given or made in private must, when drawn up, be clearly marked that the court was "sitting in private" (CPR 39 Practice Direction para 1.13).

(c) No person other than the receiving party, the paying party and any party who has served points of dispute may be heard at the detailed assessment hearing unless the court gives permission (CPR 47.14). As to the rights of audience of persons claiming to represent such parties, see para 1.2, above.

(d) No person other than the receiving party, the paying party and any party who has served points of dispute may be heard at the detailed assessment hearing unless the court gives permission (CPR 47.14). As to the rights of audience of persons claiming to represent such parties, see para 1.2, above.

### 9.2 The decisions made at the hearing 1C-71

(a) A hearing that takes place at a court will usually be tape recorded by the court. A party may obtain a transcript of such a recording on payment of the proper transcribing charges (Practice Direction para 5 to CPD 27). It is still important that the parties and/or their representatives keep a careful note of the submissions and the decisions which are given as the hearing proceeds.

(b) Having considered the evidence, both oral and written, and having heard argument, the court will normally give a decision orally in respect of each item as and when it deals with it. On any complicated matter that may arise, the costs officer or Costs Judge may reserve his decision and, if he does so, his decision on that matter may be delivered either at a subsequent hearing or in writing.

(c) The adverse rulings that may be made if a receiving party fails to abide by any estimate of costs he previously gave in the proceedings is considered in paragraph 9.3, below.

(d) Often, the final matter dealt with at the hearing is the award of the costs of the detailed assessment proceedings. As to this see further, Section 11, below.

(e) Some information about the possibility of bringing an appeal against any decision made, and the time limit in which to do so, is given in Section 13, below.

### 9.3 Relevance of estimates of costs previously given 1C-72

(a) On an assessment of the costs of a party, the court may have regard to any estimate previously filed by that party, or by any other party in the same proceedings. Such an estimate may be taken into account as a factor, among others, when assessing the reasonableness and proportionality of any costs claimed.

(b) If there is a difference of 20% or more between the costs claimed by a receiving party (excluding the amount of any additional liability claimed) and the costs shown in an estimate of costs filed by that party, the court may regard the difference as evidence that the costs claimed are unreasonable or disproportionate if—

(i) the receiving party has not provided a satisfactory explanation for that difference; or

*Paragraph numbers marked with a "+" can be found online and on CD.*



SCCO GUIDE

(ii) the court is satisfied that the paying party reasonably relied on the estimate of costs.

**1C-73** **9.4 Removing the papers in support**

Once the detailed assessment hearing has ended it is the responsibility of the receiving party and of any legal representative appearing for him to remove the papers filed in support of the bill. If it is not possible to remove the papers immediately after the hearing they may, by permission of the court be left with a court clerk for collection at a later date, within the next seven days.

**1C-74** **9.5 Hearing outside London**

If it is appropriate to do so, arrangements can be made for a Costs Judge to hear a detailed assessment in a court room outside London.

## SECTION 10

## PRODUCTION OF CONFIDENTIAL DOCUMENTS IN DETAILED ASSESSMENT HEARINGS

**1C-75** **10.1 Receiving party's duty to lodge documents**

(a) Unless the court directs otherwise, the receiving party must file with the court the papers in support of the bill not less than seven days before the date of a detailed assessment hearing and not more than 14 days before that date.

(b) The CPD gives further details about "the papers in support of the bill" (see para. 8.6, above). In respect of each item of costs claimed in the bill the papers in support include all of the papers relevant to that item, whether they are favourable to the receiving party's case or unfavourable, or whether or not they are confidential or privileged. The lodging of documents as required by the CPD does not amount to a waiver of any privilege in those documents.

**1C-76** **10.2 Court's power to order production of documents**

(a) The court may direct the receiving party to produce any document which, in the opinion of the court, is necessary to enable it to reach its decision. These documents will in the first instance be produced to the court, but the court may ask the receiving party to elect whether to disclose the particular document to the paying party in order to rely on the contents of that document, or whether to decline disclosure and instead rely on other evidence (CPD 40.14).

(b) The court's power to order production to the court of documents which the receiving party does not wish to produce will not be used to require production of those documents to the paying party. Because many of the documents in support of a bill are confidential and/or privileged there is no disclosure stage in detailed assessment hearings as there is in other civil proceedings.

**1C-77** **10.3 Deciding points of dispute in favour of the paying party**

If, having examined papers lodged with or produced to the court, the court makes a decision based on those documents wholly in favour of the paying party, the court will so inform the parties and give brief reasons therefor if necessary. The paying party has no right to see the documents relied on by the court in reaching a decision which is wholly favourable to the paying party.

**1C-78** **10.4 Deciding points of dispute in favour of the receiving party**

(a) If, having examined documents lodged with or produced to the court, the court is minded to determine a point of dispute wholly or partly in favour of the receiving party it does not automatically follow that the paying party will have a right to see all the documents relied on by the court in reaching that decision. The court should enquire of the paying party whether the paying party is content to accept that ruling (subject to appeal) or whether the paying party wishes to see the documents relied on by the court in making the ruling. In many cases the paying party will be content to agree that the court alone should see those documents. The alternatives (see below) may lead to additional delay and an increase in costs.

(b) If the paying party declines to accept the court's ruling without inspecting documents, then, save as explained in paras (f) to (h) below, the court will put the receiving party to his election between showing the documents in question to the paying party or not relying upon them and offering to prove the fact of which the document is evidence by some other means. Alternatively the receiving party may decide to withdraw the claim for the costs of it. The court may give directions enabling the receiving party to have a fair opportunity to provide other evidence. In reaching its final decision on the issue the court will not take account of documents which the receiving party has elected not to show to the paying party.

(c) If the receiving party elects to show the documents in question to the paying party, the court may give directions to ensure that this is done fairly and that the paying party is given a reasonable opportunity to consider the documents and to make observations thereon. When showing documents to the paying party it is permissible to blank out parts of the disclosed documents on the ground that they are irrelevant to the issue of costs.

(d) It is standard practice for the client care letter (redacted where appropriate) to be shown to the paying party. The Court of Appeal has held that it should become usual practice for a conditional fee agreement (redacted where appropriate) to be disclosed for the purpose of costs proceedings in which a success fee is claimed. If a conditional fee agreement with a success fee relates to court proceedings the Conditional Fee Agreements Regulations 2000 state that the agreement must provide for disclosure of the reasons for setting the percentage increase at the level stated in the agreement.

(e) No production of documents is appropriate where the court determines that the point of dispute raised is spurious or vexatious only.

(f) No production is appropriate in respect of documents which the court did not rely upon in reaching its decision and which the receiving party did not deploy.

(g) The court will not compel production of any documents where it is unnecessary or disproportionate to do so.

(h) The court will exercise its discretion to put the receiving party to his election having regard to the requirements of fairness and justice. In particular it may consider whether the production could be made to the paying party's legal representatives only, and whether any confidential matter which is irrelevant can be excluded from the production.

(i) If, in respect of any privileged documents, the receiving party elects to waive its privilege by showing them to the paying party, that waiver is for the purposes of the detailed assessment only and the privilege can be re-asserted in any subsequent context.

### 10.5 Avoiding or minimising the expense and delay of production 1C–79

The production of documents at a detailed assessment hearing may well cause substantial delay to that hearing and may prejudice or embarrass any appeal made in the proceedings in which the costs were awarded or in any similar proceedings between the same parties. Receiving parties should therefore consider in advance what voluntary disclosure to their opponents they are willing to make and, how such disclosure can be achieved before the detailed assessment hearing without substantially damaging any privilege they wish to retain. If necessary, directions can be made by consent. Directions can also be made providing split hearing dates or times so as to facilitate the orderly disposal of the points in dispute. If production of documents may substantially prejudice or embarrass any appeal or linked proceedings, orders can be made adjourning the detailed assessment proceedings pending the determination of the other proceedings and directing the payment of interim costs certificates in the meantime.

## SECTION 11

## COSTS OF DETAILED ASSESSMENT PROCEEDINGS

### 11.1 Entitlement 1C–80

(a) As a general rule the receiving party is entitled to the costs of the detailed assessment proceedings (CPR 47.18). For exceptions concerning non acceptance of offers to

***Paragraph numbers marked with a "+" can be found online and on CD.***

settle, findings of delay or misconduct and the special rules applicable to assessments under the Solicitors Act 1974, see below, para. 11.4 and Sections 16 and 26 respectively.

(b) In deciding whether to depart from the general rule, where it applies, the court must have regard to all the circumstances including the conduct of the parties, the amounts, if any by which the bill of costs has been reduced and whether it was reasonable for a party to claim or dispute any item.

(c) The costs of the detailed assessment proceedings are usually assessed at the end of the hearing, but, in an exceptional case, may be assessed at a subsequent hearing. It is not necessary to provide details of those costs in advance unless the court makes an order to that effect.

**1C–81** **11.2 Offers to settle: general provisions**

(a) Either party may make an offer to settle the claim for costs which is expressed to be "without prejudice, save as to the costs of the detailed assessment proceedings." Such an offer may relate to any issue in dispute between the parties. Its main purpose is to enable the parties to explore the possibility of negotiating a compromise which will not damage the subsequent presentation of their case if no compromise is reached.

(b) Paying parties should usually make their offers within 14 days after service of the notice of commencement. Receiving parties should usually make their offers within 14 days after service of the points of dispute. Offers made after these periods are likely to be given less weight unless there is good reason for the offer not having been made until the later time.

(c) The terms of the offer must be clear. There is no obligation to give details or a breakdown showing how the sum specified was arrived at, but unless the offer states otherwise, it will be treated as including the costs of the preparation of the bill, interest and VAT. A subsequent increased offer may be made.

**1C–82** **11.3 Where an offer to settle is accepted**

If an offer to settle is accepted an application may be made for an agreed costs certificate (as to which, see para 17.9, below). If, because of acceptance, the whole of the detailed assessment proceedings are now settled, the receiving party must give notice of that fact to the court immediately, preferably by fax. The current fax numbers are: 020 7947 6247 (Room 2.13) or 6344 (General Office).

**1C–83** **11.4 Where an offer to settle is not accepted**

(a) The existence of an offer to settle must not be communicated to the costs officer or Costs Judge conducting the hearing until the question of costs of the detailed assessment proceedings falls to be decided (CPR 47.19).

(b) When an offer to settle is properly brought to the attention of the court, the court may take it into account when deciding what, if any, order for costs to make. For example, if the court decides that an offer to settle made by the paying party ought reasonably to have been accepted by the receiving party, the court may:

(i) disallow the receiving party, wholly or in part, any costs of the detailed assessment, and/or

(ii) award costs in the detailed assessment to the paying party who made the offer.

## SECTION 12

## FINAL COSTS CERTIFICATES

**1C–84** **12.1 Completing the bill of costs**

(a) At the detailed assessment hearing, the court will note on the bill of costs all items allowed, disallowed or reduced. The receiving party must, after the hearing, make clear the correct figures agreed or allowed in respect of each item and recalculate the summary of the bill.

(b) The receiving party must file the completed bill of costs at the SCCO no later than 14 days after the detailed assessment hearing. When filing the bill of costs, the receiving party must lodge receipted fee notes and accounts in respect of all disbursements. However, there is no obligation to produce receipted fee notes or accounts in respect of disbursements (other than those relating to counsel's fees) which individually do not exceed £500 if the bill includes a certificate that such disbursements have been duly discharged (see Precedent F(5) which is illustrated in the Appendix, below, para A-2). Also, the court may have given a direction at the detailed assessment hearing which dispenses with the need for the production of some or all the fee notes and accounts in question. For example, the bill may be marked "vouching of [all disbursements] [expert's fees] is dispensed with.

**12.2 Failure to file completed bill of costs** **1C–85**

If the receiving party fails to file the completed bill of costs within 14 days of the detailed assessment hearing, the paying party may make an application for such directions as may be appropriate under the court's general powers of management. As to applications generally, see Section 17, below.

**12.3 Effect of final costs certificate** **1C–86**

(a) A final costs certificate will include an order to pay the costs to which it relates, unless the court orders otherwise (CPR 47.16)

(b) If the receiving party has failed to comply with the obligation to produce receipted fee notes and receipted accounts in respect of disbursements which have been allowed, the final costs certificate will be for an amount not exceeding the amount (if any) allowed in respect of profit costs and the amount of allowed disbursements in respect of which receipted fee notes or receipted accounts have been produced to the court but only to the extent indicated by those receipts.

(c) As a general rule the amount shown as payable in a final costs certificate will be the amount payable after taking into account the amount payable under any interim certificate already given and/or the amount payable under any order to pay costs on account. However, if the court is satisfied that no payments have been made in respect of previous certificates or orders, the certificate may include an order to pay the gross amount of costs payable. The text of such a certificate should, after stating the amount of the total costs, contain an endorsement such as:

*"and, no sums having been paid under the order of Mr Justice X dated...,or under the interim certificate issued herein dated...*

(d) The paying party must comply with the order for the payment of costs within 14 days of the date of the certificate or within such later date as the court may specify (CPR 44.8).

**12.4 Order to stay enforcement** **1C–87**

Any application to stay enforcement of an interim or final costs certificate issued by the SCCO must be made to a Costs Judge or to a court which has jurisdiction to enforce the certificate.

**12.5 Enforcement of certificate** **1C–88**

Proceedings for enforcement of an interim or final costs certificate may not be issued in the SCCO.

## SECTION 13

## APPEALS AGAINST DECISIONS IN DETAILED ASSESSMENT PROCEEDINGS

**13.1 Routes of appeal** **1C–89**

(a) From a decision of a costs officer in a High Court case there is a right of appeal (in other words, no permission to appeal is needed) to a Costs Judge with a further appeal (for which permission is required) to a High Court Judge.

(b) From a decision of a Costs Judge in a High Court matter parties may, if permission is granted, bring an appeal to a High Court Judge with a further appeal to the Court of Appeal.

(c) The route of an appeal from a decision of a Costs Judge in a County Court matter depends upon whether the Costs Judge heard the matter whilst sitting as a Deputy District Judge of the County Court. If he did so the parties may, if permission is granted, bring an appeal to a Circuit Judge in the County Court with a further appeal to the Court of Appeal.

***Paragraph numbers marked with a "+" can be found online and on CD.***

(d) In London County Court cases which are not transferred to the SCCO so as to become High Court cases, the appeal from a Costs Judge lies, if permission is granted, to the London Designated Civil Judge, sitting at the Central London County Court.

1C-90 **13.2 Seeking permission to appeal**

(a) No permission to appeal is required from any decision made by a costs officer.

(b) From any decision of a Costs Judge (including decisions made on an appeal from a costs officer) permission to appeal is required. The general test for permission is whether the appeal has any real prospect of success. The permission should normally be sought orally at the time of the hearing. If refused, or if not sought then, the intending appellant must include an application for permission in his appellant's notice (as to which, see para. 13.4, below).

(c) In order to bring a further appeal to the Court of Appeal from the decision of a High Court Judge permission is required from the Court of Appeal (CPR 52.13). The general test for permission in such a case is whether the appeal would raise an important point of principle or practice or whether there is some other compelling reason for the Court of Appeal to hear it.

(d) A permission to appeal may limit the issues which may be raised on the appeal and may be made subject to conditions.

1C-91 **13.3 Time limits for appeals**

(a) An intending appellant must file an appeal notice within 14 days after the date of the decision he wishes to appeal against (CPR 47.22 and 52.4). If a party has good reason for seeking a longer period in which to appeal he should apply for an extension of time, either on the occasion when the decision is made, or by including such an application in his appeal notice.

(b) The time for appeal runs from the date of the decision to be appealed against, not from the end of the detailed assessment. However, a costs officer or Costs Judge may make a direction that the time for appeal will not begin to run until the detailed assessment has been concluded.

1C-92 **13.4 Documentation on appeals**

(a) Form **N161** is the prescribed form of notice for all costs appeals. On an appeal from a costs officer the notice, once filed, will be served on other parties by the court office. On an appeal from a Costs Judge the appellant must arrange service of a copy of the notice on each respondent as soon as practicable and, in any event, within seven days after filing.

(b) Form **N161** summarises the documents which should be prepared in support of the appeal. In particular, the appellant must supply a suitable record of the judgment being appealed, ie, an approved transcript, alternatively a written judgment signed by the costs officer or Costs Judge, or alternatively in the case of a costs officer, the officer's comments written on the bill, or, in the case of a Costs Judge, a note of the judgment which is agreed by the respondent and/or approved by the Costs Judge.

(c) Form **N162** is the prescribed form of respondent's notice for all costs appeals. However, a respondent is not required to serve a respondent's notice if he intends to rely solely upon the judgment of the court below for the reasons given by that court.

1C-93 **13.5 Conduct of the appeal**

(a) On an appeal from a costs officer, the Costs Judge will rehear the proceedings which gave rise to the decision appealed against and may make any order and give any directions which he considers appropriate.

(b) An appeal from the decision of a Costs Judge is limited to a review of that decision, unless the court considers that it would be in the interests of justice to hold a rehearing.

(c) On an appeal from a decision of a Costs Judge it is customary for the court to sit with two assessors, one of whom will be a Costs Judge and the other will be a practising barrister or solicitor.

## SECTION 14

## CORRECTING ACCIDENTAL SLIPS OR OMISSIONS IN FINAL COSTS CERTIFICATES

1C-94 **14.1 The Slip Rule**

The court may at any time correct an accidental slip or omission in any certificate issued by the court and may vary any certificate in order to make the meaning and intention of the court clear: see CPR 40.12 (often known as the "slip rule") and the Practice Direction supplementing it. Although it is mainly used to correct typographical or arithmetical mistakes, the slip rule can also be used to correct other more substantial errors and omissions in expressing the manifest intention of the court.

**14.2 Applications for amendment** **1C–95**

An application under the slip rule may be made informally (eg, by letter) or formally, by application under Part 23 (as to which see Section 17, below). The application may be dealt with without a hearing if the applicant so requests, or with the consent of all parties, or where the court does not consider that a hearing would be appropriate. However, if the application is, or is likely to be, opposed, it should be listed for hearing before a Costs Judge.

## SECTION 15

## INTEREST ON COSTS

**15.1 Entitlement to interest on costs** **1C–96**

(a) In respect of costs payable by order and included in a bill of costs for detailed assessment the receiving party may be entitled to interest under Section 17 of the Judgments Act 1838 or Section 74 of the County Courts Act 1984. If so the entitlement to interest begins on the date upon which the order for costs was made (not the date upon which the costs were assessed) unless the court otherwise orders (CPR 40.8 and 44.3(6)(g)). However,

(i) In respect of the costs of the detailed assessment proceedings, the interest begins to run from the date of the default, interim or final costs certificate, as the case may be; and

(ii) Under CPR 44.3(6)g the court has power to order interest on costs to run from a date other than the date of judgment.

(b) In respect of costs payable by contract (eg, costs payable to a solicitor by his client or former client) the entitlement to interest normally depends upon the terms of that contract. However a statutory right to interest may arise under the Solicitors (Non Contentious Business) Remuneration Order 1994 or the Late Payment of Commercial Debts (Interest) Act 1998.

**15.2 Effect on final costs certificates** **1C–97**

(a) If the amount of costs payable under an order for costs proceeds to a detailed assessment, the final costs certificate issued will record the date of entitlement to interest and the effect of any rulings which the court has made as to interest. Where a bill of costs covers costs payable under an order or orders in respect of which the receiving party wishes to claim interest from different dates, the bill should be divided into separate parts so as to enable such interest to be calculated. If not so divided the date of entitlement to interest recorded in the certificate will be the latest of the relevant dates.

(b) Only in an exceptional case (eg where enforcement proceedings on a final costs certificate are to be taken abroad) will a final costs certificate record the amount of interest accrued up to the date of the certificate and/or the daily rate of interest accruing thereafter. In order to obtain such a certificate the receiving party should apply, on notice to the paying party, justifying the rate of interest claimed and, where payments on account have been made, explaining the effect which such payments have had on the calculation of interest.

(c) In respect of costs payable to a solicitor by his client or former client the final costs certificate will record neither the date of entitlement to any interest nor the amount of any interest accrued or accruing.

## SECTION 16

## APPLICATIONS CONCERNING DELAY, MISCONDUCT OR WASTED COSTS

**16.1 Sanction for delay in commencing detailed assessment proceedings** **1C–98**

(a) Under CPR 47.7 detailed assessment proceedings must be commenced within three months of the date of the order for costs or other event under which the right to



SCCO GUIDE

costs arose by the receiving party serving on the paying party the documents referred to in CPR 47.6(1) (see Section 4 above).

(b) Permission to commence detailed assessment proceedings out of time is not required (CPD 33.4) but if the receiving party has failed to commence detailed assessment proceedings within the deadline the paying party may apply for an order under CPR 47.8(1) disallowing all the costs to which the receiving party would otherwise be entitled unless the detailed assessment proceedings are commenced within such further time as the court may specify.

(c) An application for an order under Rule 47.8(1) must be made in writing, issued in the appropriate court office and served at least seven days before the hearing.

(d) If the receiving party commences proceedings for detailed assessment late but before the paying party makes an application under CPR 47.8(1) the court may disallow all or part of the interest on costs that would otherwise be payable but must not impose any other sanction except in accordance with CPR 44.14 (powers in relation to misconduct, see below).

1C-99 **16.2 Misconduct by litigants or legal representatives**

(a) The court may make an order under CPR 44.14 where—

(i) a litigant or his legal representative, in connection with a summary or detailed assessment, fails to comply with a rule, practice direction or court order; or

(ii) it appears to the court that the conduct of a party or his legal representative, before or during the proceedings which gave rise to the assessment proceedings, was unreasonable or improper.

(b) Examples of conduct which is unreasonable or improper includes steps which are calculated to prevent or inhibit the court from furthering its overriding objective which is to deal with cases justly.

(c) The sanctions which the Court can impose are:

(i) disallowance of all or part of the costs which are beng assessed; or

(ii) ordering the party at fault or his legal representative to pay the costs which the misconduct has caused any other party to incur.

(d) Before making such an order the Court must give the party or the legal representative in question a reasonable opportunity to attend a hearing to give reasons why such an order should not be made.

(e) Where the court makes an order under CPR 44.14 against a legally represented party and that party is not present when the order is made, that party's solicitor must notify his client in writing of the order no later than seven days after the solicitor receives notice of the order.

1C-100 **16.3 Personal liability of legal representatives for costs—wasted costs orders**

(a) In addition to the court's powers under CPR 44.14 the court can also order a *legal representative* to pay a specified sum of costs to a party or disallow a specific sum where costs have been wasted (CPR 48.7).

(b) The court may make a wasted costs order only if:—

(i) The legal representative has acted improperly, unreasonably or negligently;

(ii) his conduct has caused a party to incur unnecessary costs; and

(iii) it is just in all the circumstances to order him to compensate that party for the whole or part of those costs.

(c) Before making a wasted costs order a Court may direct a Costs Judge to inquire into the matter and report back to the Court. It may also refer the matter to a Costs Judge to deal with outright.

1C-101 **16.4 Principles on which wasted costs orders are made**

(a) The Court of Appeal laid down guidelines in *Ridehalgh v Horsefield* [1994] Ch 205, CA to assist the court in deciding whether a legal representative has acted improperly, unreasonably or negligently:

(i) acting "improperly" covers but is not confined to conduct which would ordinarily be held to justify disbarrment of barristers, striking off from the roll of solicitors, suspension from practice or other serious professional penalty;

(ii) acting "unreasonably" describes conduct which is vexatious, designed to harass the other side rather than advance the resolution of the case;

***Paragraph numbers marked with a "+" can be found online and on CD.***

(iii) acting "negligently" denotes, in an untechnical way, failure to act with the competence reasonably expected of ordinary members of the legal profession.

(b) In general, wasted costs applications should be left until after the end of the trial. It is usual for the aggrieved party rather than the Court to raise the issue of wasted costs, but the Court can make a wasted costs order against a legal representative of its own initiative.

**16.5 Procedural steps on applications for a wasted costs order** **1C-102**

(a) A party may apply for a wasted costs order by filing an application notice in accordance with Part 23 (as to which, see Section 17, below) or by making an application orally in the course of any hearing (CPD 53.3).

(b) A Part 23 application must be supported by evidence (CPD 53.8) which:

(i) sets out what the legal representative has done or failed to do; and,

(ii) identifies the costs that he may be ordered to pay or which are sought against him.

(c) The court will then give directions about the procedure to be followed in order to ensure that the issues are dealt with in a way which is as fair, simple and summary as the circumstances permit.

**16.6 Deciding whether to make a wasted costs order** **1C-103**

(a) As a general rule the court will consider whether to make a wasted costs order in two stages (CPD paragraph 53.6):

> *Stage One*—The Court must be satisfied that it has before it evidence or material, which, if unanswered, would be likely to lead to a wasted costs order being made, and that the wasted costs proceedings are justified notwithstanding the likely costs involved. If not so satisfied the Court will decide that further proceedings are not justified.
>
> *Stage Two*—The Court will give the legal representative an opportunity to give reasons why a wasted costs order should not be made before deciding whether to do so.

(b) If an application is made under Part 23 the Court can proceed direct to Stage Two if it is satisfied that the legal representative has already had a reasonable opportunity to give his reasons.

## SECTION 17

## OTHER APPLICATIONS IN DETAILED ASSESSMENT PROCEEDINGS

**17.1 Applications generally** **1C-104**

(a) Detailed assessment proceedings are commenced by the receiving party serving on the paying party a notice of commencement, a copy of the bill of costs and certain other documents. After that date, and sometimes even before that date, applications relating to the proceedings or intended proceedings can be made by any party.

(b) An application can be made in the SCCO if that is the "appropriate office" for the purposes of CPR 47.4 (and see para. 8.1, above). In order to make an application, the party must file in court a notice of application, copies of any documents relied on in support and the appropriate court fee, or a fee exemption certificate (see Section 27, below).

(c) The notice of application should be in Form **N244**. Note that the use of such a form and the requirement to pay a court fee may be avoided in some cases; if the SCCO has previously made an order or given directions in the detailed assessment proceedings, that order may include a "liberty to apply" which entitles the parties seeking a further order or directions to write to the court requesting it to restore the previous application rather than issuing a new one.

**17.2 Evidence in support of applications** **1C-105**

(a) All evidence relied on in support of an application must be filed in court, ideally at the same time the application notice is filed.

(b) Part C of Form **N244** enables the applicant to identify the evidence relied on in support of his application. The applicant can rely upon written evidence set out in the notice or in a separate witness statement. In either case such evidence must contain a statement of truth, ie, a statement in the following form:

***Paragraph numbers marked with a "+" can be found online and on CD.***

*[I believe] [the (claimant or as may be) believes] that the facts stated in this application notice (or witness statement as may be)] are true.*

The statement of truth must be signed by the litigant, or his litigation friend, or legal representative or witness, as may be.

(c) Other documents, not especially prepared for the purpose of the application, may also be relied on as evidence, eg, copies of letters received and letters sent.

1C–106 **17.3 Extension of time for commencing detailed assessment proceedings**

The time limit for commencing detailed assessment proceedings is summarised in para 4.2, above. The parties may agree to extend this time. Alternatively, the receiving party can make an application for an order extending the time limit. Note that permission to commence detailed assessment proceedings out of time is not required.

1C–107 **17.4 Extensions of time for service of points of dispute**

The time limit for service of points of dispute is summarised in para 5.1, above. Failure to serve points of dispute in time may lead to the receiving party obtaining a default costs certificate (as to which see Section 6, above). The parties may agree to extend the time for service of points of dispute, alternatively the paying party may apply to the appropriate office for an order extending the time limit.

1C–108 **17.5 Extension of other time limits**

The time limit for serving a reply to points of dispute is summarised in para 5.1 above and the time limit for filing a request for a detailed assessment hearing is summarised in para 8.1, above. In any case directions of the court may impose further time limits for the taking of certain steps, eg the service of witness statements. All these time limits may be extended by the agreement of the parties or, alternatively, by an order made upon an application.

1C–109 **17.6 Changing the date fixed for a detailed assessment hearing**

A date fixed for the hearing of a detailed assessment cannot be changed or cancelled merely by the agreement of the parties unless the parties agree a compromise and the detailed assessment proceedings are settled. If detailed assessment proceedings are settled the receiving party must give notice of that fact to the court immediately, preferably by fax. The current fax numbers are: 020 7947 6247 or 6344. In other cases, if one or all parties wishes to vary a date fixed, he or they must make an application in N244 or request the court to restore a previous application for hearing, if a "liberty to apply" has previously been given.

1C–110 **17.7 Amending bills of costs, points of dispute or replies**

If a party wishes to vary his bill of costs, points of dispute or reply, an amended or supplementary document must be filed with the court and copies of it must be served on all other relevant parties. Note that permission is not required but the court may later disallow the variation or permit it only upon conditions, including conditions as to the payment of any costs caused or wasted by the variation.

1C–111 **17.8 Case management directions**

Where appropriate any party can apply for case management directions, such as timetable directions for the exchange of witness statements and facilitating cross examination, or timetable directions concerning the detailed assessment of "linked bills", ie other bills of costs made in the same proceedings. Especially in the case of larger bills of costs, ie, bills exceeding £200,000, timetable directions may be given fixing a series of dates for the detailed assessment hearing. For example, if the estimated hearing time is five days, a one day appointment may be given for particular points of dispute (perhaps relating to VAT entitlement, solicitor's hourly rates, and all fees claimed in respect of the trial) with a four day appointment for the remaining points of dispute to take place some four weeks later. Splitting the hearing into two appointments usually enables the court to give an earlier appointment than it otherwise could. Also, by determining selected issues at the first appointment, the

***Paragraph numbers marked with a "+" can be found online and on CD.***

parties may be able to agree the remaining points so obviating the need for the later appointment.

**17.9 Agreed costs certificates** 1C–112

(a) Parties may agree all or part of the costs before or after the court has become involved in the detailed assessment proceedings. An interim or a final certificate can be issued.

(b) In the course of proceedings a receiving party may claim that the paying party has agreed to pay costs but will neither pay those costs nor join in a consent application. The receiving party may apply under Part 23 for an interim or final certificate to be issued. The application must be supported by evidence and will be heard by a Costs Judge.

**17.10 Change of solicitor** 1C–113

(a) Where a solicitor's business address has been properly given as the address for service of a party that solicitor is said to be "on the record" as acting for that party and, as such, will continue to be served with documents and will be expected to attend court hearings until such time as he is "off the record". That will not occur until a notice of change of solicitor is filed by or on behalf of the party, or, in a LSC funded case, until the solicitor files a notice of discharge of revocation of the funding certificate, or until the solicitor obtains an order for the removal of his name from the record.

(b) In practice, when a solicitor and client fall out and the client is not intending to instruct another solicitor, the former solicitor will often prepare a notice of change and either obtain the client's signature to it and then file it or will send it to the former client for him to sign and file. The former solicitor will no doubt warn the client that, if he refuses or unreasonably fails to serve and/or file the notice the solicitor may apply for an order that the solicitor has ceased to act together with an order for the costs of the application.

(c) An application for an order declaring that a solicitor has ceased to be the solicitor acting for a party should be made under Part 23 and should be supported by evidence. The notice of application and evidence should not be served on other parties to the proceedings but should be served on the former client unless the court directs otherwise.

(d) An applicant for an order declaring that he has ceased to be the solicitor acting for a party should consider whether he wishes the application to be dealt with without a hearing. As a general rule the court will make an order without a hearing (adding liberty to apply to stay, set aside or vary the order) if satisfied that the application is made by consent, is unopposed or appears overwhelmingly strong.

**17.11 Stay of detailed assessment proceedings** 1C–114

The bringing of an appeal against an order for costs does not stay the detailed assessment of those costs unless the court so orders (CPR 47.2). An application to stay the detailed assessment pending an appeal may be made either to the court whose order is being appealed or to the court who will hear the appeal. The application should not normally be made to the SCCO.

**17.11 Stay of enforcement of costs certificates** 1C–115

(a) Applications for an order staying enforcement of a default costs certificate, an interim costs certificate or a final costs certificate issued by the SCCO may be made either to the SCCO or to a court which has general jurisdiction to enforce the certificate. In the SCCO the application will be heard by the Costs Judge who assessed the costs in question or, if the costs were assessed by a costs officer, by the Sitting Master. The application should usually be accompanied by evidence of the paying party's income, assets, other liabilities and proposals for payment. The usual form of order granting a stay is on terms requiring the paying party to pay off the certified costs by specified instalments.

(b) If the certificate relates to the costs of a County Court case sent to the SCCO for assessment which nevertheless remains a County Court case, the paying party may, as an alternative to applying for a stay of enforcement, apply to the SCCO or the County Court for an order varying the certificate into an order for payment by instalments.

**17.13 Other applications** 1C–116

The paragraphs mentioned below contain notes on the following applications in detailed assessment proceedings:



SCCO Guide

- for assessment before conclusion of main proceedings (para. 4.1),
- for an order setting aside a default costs certificate (paras 7.1 and 7.2),
- for assignment from a costs officer to a Costs Judge (para. 8.3),
- for an interim costs certificate (para. 8.5),
- for permission to appeal (para. 13.2),
- for correcting accidental slips or omissions in certificates (para. 14.2),
- for sanctions for failure to commence in time (para. 16.1), and
- for a wasted costs order (para. 16.3).

## SECTION 18

## CASES TRANSFERRED FROM OTHER COURTS

1C–117 **18.1 Assessment of costs awarded in the High Court and the County Courts**

(a) Bills of costs in proceedings in the District Registries of the High Court and County Courts are frequently transferred to the SCCO either at the request of the parties or of the Court's own initiative. This is likely to occur when the District Judge considers the size and complexity of the bill warrants such a transfer.

(b) When bills are transferred from a District Registry or a County Court by an order of that Court, the parties will be served with a copy of that order. Sometimes such an order is made immediately prior to the date fixed for detailed assessment at that Court, which itself may be some time after the parties first requested a hearing date. Every effort is made by the SCCO to list the transferred case at the earliest opportunity. When, however, the parties have already waited for a significant time for their bill to be assessed by the local Court, they should notify the SCCO of this fact immediately after the order transferring the case is made, so that as early a hearing date as possible can be given. If this is not done, the parties may find themselves at the end of the queue of cases awaiting a hearing date at the SCCO.

(c) If it is appropriate to do so, arrangements can be made for a Costs Judge to hear a detailed assessment in a court room outside London. Receiving parties seeking such arrangements should request them by letter lodged with the Judge's clerk when the request for detailed assessment is lodged or when the matter has been transferred to the SCCO.

1C–118 **18.2 Assessment of costs awarded by other tribunals and bodies**

Various statutes give the SCCO jurisdiction to assess costs in litigation including the following:

(i) Election petitions

(ii) Proceedings under the Arbitration Acts

(iii) Proceedings before National Health Service Committees, Tribunals and other similar bodies

(iv) Proceedings before the Employment Appeal Tribunal

(v) Proceedings before VAT tribunals

(vi) Determinations by the Secretary of State for Environment or his appointed local planning inspectors as a result of local planning inquiries

(vii) Proceedings before the Solicitor's disciplinary tribunal

(viii) Proceedings before the Copyright Tribunal.

(ix) Competition appeals.

(x) Proceedings before the Financial Services and Markets Tribunal.

(xi) Proceedings under the Justices and Justices' Clerks (Costs) Regulations 2001

(xii) Proceedings under the General Commissioners of Income Tax (Costs) Regulations 2001.

## SECTION 19

## FUNDING ARRANGEMENTS

1C–119 **19.1 Introduction**

(a) The Access to Justice Act 1999 permits the recovery of costs under a conditional fee agreement which provides for a success fee. The Act also provides for recovery of after the event insurance premiums by way of costs, and recovery of an additional amount where a membership organisation undertakes to meet liabilities which members of the organisation, or other persons who are party to the proceedings may incur, to pay the costs of other parties to the proceedings (see Sections 27, 29 and 30 Access to Justice Act 1999). These arrangements are known as "funding arrangements" (CPR 43.2) and the percentage increase, insurance premium or additional amount in respect of provision made by a membership organisation is known as an "additional liability". Premiums in respect of before the event insurance polices (such as household and motor insurance policies) are not recoverable.

(b) The court will not assess any additional liability until the conclusion of the proceedings, or that part of the proceedings to which the funding arrangement relates. At the conclusion of the proceedings the court may make a summary assessment of all the costs, including any additional liability; make an order for detailed assessment of the additional liability but make a summary assessment of the other costs; or make an order for detailed assessment of all the costs (CPR 44.3A).

**19.2 Providing information about funding arrangements** **1C–120**

(a) A party who wishes to claim an additional liability from a paying party must give any other party information about the funding arrangement and must also provide similar information when the funding arrangement changes. Information is given on Form **N251**. The party must state whether he has entered into a conditional fee agreement which provides for a success fee; taken out an insurance policy to which Section 29 of the Access to Justice Act 1999 applies; or made an arrangement with a membership organisation for the purpose of Section 30 of the Access to Justice Act 1999 (CPR 44.15). CPD Section 19 gives further details about the information to be given.

(b) When giving notice of funding in respect of a conditional fee agreement with a success fee, the party must state the date of the agreement and identify the claim or claims to which it relates.

(c) Where the funding arrangement is an after the event insurance policy, the party must state, when giving notice of funding, the name of the insurer, the date of the policy and must identify the claim or claims to which it relates.

(d) To be recoverable the insurance premium must have been paid or must be payable for insurance against the risk of incurring a costs liability in the proceedings, which was taken out *after* the event that is the subject matter of the claim (CPR 43.2(1)(m)).

(e) Where the funding arrangement is with a membership organisation, the party must state when giving notice of funding, the name of the body and must set out the date and terms of the undertaking it has given and must identify the claim or claims to which it relates.

(f) Where a party has entered into more than one funding arrangement in respect of a claim, for example a conditional fee agreement and an insurance policy, a single notice containing the information set out in Form **N251** may contain the required information about both or all of them.

## SECTION 20

## ASSESSMENT OF SUCCESS FEES AND AFTER THE EVENT INSURANCE PREMIUMS

**20.1 Compliance with Conditional Fee Agreement and Collective Conditional Fee Agreement Regulations** **1C–121**

(a) The indemnity principle provides that a successful party cannot recover from an unsuccessful party more by way of costs than the successful party is liable to pay to his or her legal representatives (see Section 2.6). However the Access to Justice Act 1999 provides that a conditional fee agreement can now be made whereby the fees and expenses of the successful party's legal representatives will be payable even though the indemnity principle would otherwise prevent it.

(b) Until their revocation (see below) the Regulations which governed conditional fee agreements were the Conditional Fee Agreements Regulations 2000, the Access to Justice (Membership Organisations) Regulations 2000 and the Collective Conditional Fee Agreements Regulations 2000. With effect from 1 November 2005 the Access to

Justice (Membership Organisations) Regulations 2000 are replaced by new Regulations and the Conditional Fee Agreements Regulations 2000 and the Collective Conditional Fee Agreements Regulations 2000 have been replaced by the Solicitors Practice (Client Care) Amendment Rules 2005 and a new Law Society's Model CFA Agreement (for use in personal injury and clinical negligence cases).

(c) A conditional fee agreement is unenforceable unless it satisfies all the conditions imposed by Section 58 of the Courts and Legal Services Act 1990 (as amended by the Access to Justice Act 1999) and the Regulations made under it (where the CFA or CCFA was entered into before 1 November 2005).

(d) However the court will not declare a conditional fee agreement unenforceable unless the failure to satisfy those conditions has a materially adverse effect on the protection of the interests of the client or the proper administration of justice.

(e) If the court rules that a conditional fee agreement is unenforceable, the client under that agreement will not be liable to pay any fees or disbursements under it. Similarly, because of the indemnity principle, he will not be able to recover any of those fees and disbursements from any other litigant. However, the client may be able to recover any disbursements which he has already paid.

**1C–122** **20.2 Documents to accompany the bill**

Where a party seeks the detailed assessment of an additional liability the details which he must give together with the bill and notice of commencement are as follows:

(a) In the case of a conditional fee agreement with a success fee:

(i) a statement showing the amount of costs which have been summarily assessed or agreed and the percentage increase which has been claimed in respect of those costs; and

(ii) a statement of the reasons for the percentage increase (where the CFA or CCFA was entered into before 1 November 2005).

(b) If the additional liability is an after the event insurance premium a copy of the insurance certificate showing whether the policy covers:

(i) the receiving party's own costs;

(ii) his opponent's costs; or

(iii) his own costs and his opponent's costs; and

(iv) the maximum extent of that cover and the amount of the premium paid or payable.

(c) If the receiving party claims an additional amount under Section 30 of the Access to Justice Act 1999 (Membership Organisations) a statement setting out the basis upon which the receiving party's liability for the additional amount is calculated.

**1C–123** **20.3 Factors to be taken into account during assessment**

(a) A party may not recover as an additional liability—

(i) any proportion of a success fee which is to compensate the legal representative for the fact that he will have to wait to be paid his fees and expenses; or

(ii) any amount (when the agreement is made with a membership organisation) which exceeds the likely cost of taking out after the event insurance to cover another party's costs; or

(iii) any additional liability during a period in which he (or she) failed to provide to the other party the information required by the court or by the Rules and Practice Directions about the funding arrangements or the reasons for setting the level of a success fee.

(b) Where a success fee is irrecoverable for the reasons given in (a)(iii) above, the court may consider granting relief from the sanctions. CPR 3.9 sets out the circumstances in which the court may grant relief.

(c) The court will consider the amount of any additional liability separately from the base costs and a success fee will not be reduced simply because, when added to the base costs, it appears to be disproportionate.

(d) In deciding whether the base costs are reasonable the court will consider the factors set out in CPR 44.5.

(e) When considering the amount of an additional liability the court will have regard to the facts and circumstances as they reasonably appeared when the agreement was made (or varied).

(f) Factors to be taken into account in deciding whether a success fee is reasonable include:

(i) the risk that fees or expenses might not become payable;
(ii) the legal representative's liability to fund disbursements;
(iii) what other methods of funding the costs were available.

(g) In costs only proceedings (see Section 21) the court will have regard to the time when and the extent to which the claim had been settled without the need to commence proceedings.

(h) Factors to be taken into account in deciding whether an after the event insurance premium is reasonable include:

(i) how its cost compares with the likely cost of funding the case with a conditional fee agreement with a success fee and supporting insurance (if it is not already so funded);
(ii) the level and extent of the insurance cover provided;
(iii) the availability of pre-existing insurance cover;
(iv) whether any part of the premium would be rebated in the event of early settlement;
(v) the amount of commission payable to the receiving party or his legal representatives or agents.

(i) The additional amount recoverable in respect of the membership organisation must not exceed the likely cost of the premium of an insurance policy against the risk of incurring a liability to pay the costs of other parties to the proceedings.

**20.4 Fixed success fees** **1C–124**

CPR Part 45 provides for fixed success fees in certain road traffic accident disputes and certain Employers Liability claims.

**20.5 Disputes between legal representatives and their clients** **1C–125**

(a) The following notes in this section apply only to cases in which the relevant CFA or CCFA was entered into before 1 November 2005. The Regulations which continue to govern such agreements (see above) provide that, in certain circumstances, if a success fee allowed on assessment is lower than the contractual success fee, the disallowed amount ceases to be payable under the agreement unless the court is satisfied that it should continue to be so payable. CPR 44.16 and CPD Section 20 set out the procedure, summarised below, by which a ruling can be obtained as to whether the disallowed amount should continue to be payable by the client.

(b) If the points of dispute served by the paying party challenge a success fee claimed in respect of counsel's fees, the solicitor must so inform counsel within three days and counsel must reply within ten days or be taken to accept the reduction (unless the court otherwise orders).

(c) If points of dispute served by the paying party challenge the success fee of the solicitor or counsel, the solicitor must write to the client within three days giving a clear written explanation of the dispute and the effect it will have if it is upheld in whole or in part. The letter must also explain the client's right to attend any subsequent hearing at court when the matter is raised and should invite the client to inform the solicitors whether or not the client wishes to attend any subsequent hearings.

(d) When requesting a hearing date (see Section 8.1) the solicitor must certify:

(i) the existence of any dispute as to the success fee,
(ii) the intention (if it be the case) to apply for any disallowed amount to continue to be payable by the client,
(iii) that he has given a written explanation to the client, and
(iv) whether the client wishes to attend any subsequent hearing.

(e) On receipt of notice from the court of the date for an assessment hearing, the solicitor must, within the next seven days, give written notice to the client and, if appropriate, to counsel, stating the date, time and place of the hearing.

***Paragraph numbers marked with a "+" can be found online and on CD.***

(f) At the hearing attended by the paying party the receiving party, the solicitor and counsel may attend or may be separately represented and may make oral or written submissions.

(g) If a success fee payable by the paying party is assessed at a figure lower than the contractually agreed figure and the legal representative still wishes to recover the contractually agreed figure he may apply for an order that the disallowed amount should continue to be payable by his client and the court may adjourn the hearing to enable the client to be notified of the order sought and, if necessary to be separately represented (CPR 44.16). The order sought does not affect the paying party and, therefore, the paying party need not attend the adjourned hearing.

(h) The court may decide the issue, whether the disallowed amount should continue to be payable, without an adjournment if the receiving party and all relevant legal representatives consent to the court doing so, and if the receiving party (or if corporate, an officer thereof) is present in court and if the court is satisfied that the issue can be fairly decided without an adjournment. In any other case the court will give directions and fix the date for the hearing of the application.

## SECTION 21

## COSTS ONLY PROCEEDINGS

1C–126 **21.1 Introduction**

(a) CPR 44.12A sets out the procedure to be followed where, before court proceedings are commenced, the parties to a dispute reach agreement on all issues, including which party is to pay costs, but are unable to agree the amount of those costs.

(b) Two distinct steps are required: firstly an application under CPR Part 8 seeking an order for costs; and secondly detailed assessment of those costs.

(c) It is not appropriate for either party to take the first step unless:

(i) the parties must have reached an agreement on all the issues, including which party is to pay the costs;

(ii) that agreement has been made or confirmed in writing; and

(iii) no proceedings must have been started and the parties (*after a proper attempt at agreement*) must have failed to agree the amount of the costs.

1C–127 **21.2 The application under CPR Part 8**

(a) Either party may start costs only proceedings. The claim should be issued in the court in which the main proceedings would have been heard if that had been necessary.

(b) The Part 8 claim form (form **N208**) must: (i) identify the claim or dispute to which the agreement to pay costs relates; (ii) state the date and terms of the agreement on which the claimant relies; (iii) set out a draft of the order sought; (iv) state the amount of the costs claimed; and (v) state whether costs are claimed on the standard or the indemnity basis.

(c) The evidence filed in support of the claim must include copies of the documents relied upon to prove the agreement to pay costs.

1C–128 **21.3 Obtaining the order for costs**

(a) The court may make an order in the terms of the claim without the necessity of a hearing if:

(i) the defendant fails to file an acknowledgment of service within the time allowed to do so and the claimant has written to the court requesting an order; or

(ii) if the defendant files an acknowledgment of service stating that he does not contest the making of an order in the terms of the claim; or

(iii) if a consent order under CPR 40.6 is filed which is signed by or on behalf of all parties and none of them is a litigant in person and the approval of the court is not required by any other rule.

(b) In costs only proceedings to which CPR 45 Section II applies (ie certain road traffic accident claims where the total amount of agreed damages does not exceed £10,000) the court must assess the costs in the manner set out in that section (ie it should allow certain fixed recoverable costs plus success fee and disbursements: applications for greater amounts will be entertained only if the court considers that exceptional circumstances make it appropriate to do so).

(c) In cases in which CPR 45 Section II does not apply, the court will dismiss the claim without a hearing if it is opposed, ie, if the defendant files an acknowledgment of service stating that he intends to contest the proceedings or to seek a different remedy. A claim will not be treated as opposed and therefore dismissed merely because the defendant states in an acknowledgment of service that he disputes the amount of the claim for costs.

(d) Standard forms of order commonly made in the SCCO under CPR 44.12A are illustrated in the Appendix, below, para A-5.

(e) Unless all parties consent the order for costs will not include an order for a payment of costs on account. In costs only proceedings, the only issue to be decided by the court when making the order is whether or not there should be an assessment.

**21.4 Conducting the detailed assessment proceedings** **1C–129**

(a) An order for costs made under CPR 44.12A will be treated as an order for the amount of costs to be decided by a detailed assessment to which Part 47 applies, as to which, see Sections 3 to 17, above.

(b) As to the receiving party's entitlement to apply for an interim costs certificate once a request for a detailed assessment hearing has been made, see para. 8.5 above.

(c) In cases in which an additional liability is claimed (as to which, see Section 19, above) the court will have regard to the time when and the extent to which the claim has been settled and to the fact that the claim has been settled without the need to commence proceedings.

(d) CPR 45.13 and 45.14 provides that a costs penalty will be imposed upon any claimant in proceedings governed by CPR 45 Section II who claims costs greater than the fixed recoverable costs plus success fee and disbursements but fails to achieve an increase greater than 20% of the amount in respect of fixed recoverable costs: the claimant will be awarded only the fixed recoverable costs (unless in fact a lower sum has been assessed), plus success fee, plus disbursements and will be ordered to pay the defendant's costs of the proceedings.

## SECTION 22

## LITIGANTS IN PERSON

**22.1 Introduction** **1C–130**

(a) A person is a "litigant in person" during any stage of proceedings in court in which he or she is not represented by a solicitor or firm of solicitors. For this purpose the term "litigant in person" may include a company or other corporation, a barrister, a solicitor, a solicitor's employee or other authorised litigator who is acting for himself. However, the term does not include a solicitor who, instead of acting for himself, is represented in proceedings by his firm or by himself in his firm's name (CPD 52.5).

(b) Litigants in person have rights of audience in all detailed assessment proceedings. As to their entitlement to have a MacKenzie Friend present, see Section 1 para 1.2, above.

(c) The costs recoverable by parties in respect of periods when they are or were litigants in person are governed by the Litigants in Person (Costs and Expenses) Act 1975 and by CPR 48.6. This section of the Guide is intend to help parties understand the position. Reference must be made to the Act and the CPR if there is any doubt.

(d) The staff of the SCCO are not permitted to give rulings or legal advice on the Act or on the CPR nor to enter into any lengthy or technical advice as to the meaning of this Guide nor to recommend any individual solicitors or costs draftsmen who may be willing to give advice or assistance.

(e) Advice and assistance may be available from the Citizen's Advice Bureau in the Royal Courts of Justice. Further information as to this is given in Section 1 para 1.7, above.

(f) A litigant in person who is unable to obtain copies of any prescribed form needed may ask the Costs Office for help (see Section 1 paras 1.5, 1.8 and 1.9). Most of the "N" forms mentioned in this Guide can be supplied free of charge.

*Paragraph numbers marked with a "+" can be found online and on CD.*



SCCO GUIDE

1C–131 **22.2 Costs recoverable by litigants in person**

(a) The costs of litigants in person can be divided into four categories:

(i) out of pocket expenses (such as court fees, fares travelling to court, witness fees, etc) if they relate to work or disbursements which would have been done or made by a solicitor had a solicitor acted for the litigant in person.

(ii) Payments made to obtain expert assistance in connection with assessing the claim for costs. For this purpose a person is an expert if he is a barrister, solicitor, Fellow of the Institute of Legal Executives, Fellow of the Association of Law Costs Draftsmen, or a law costs draftsman who is a member of the Academy of Experts or the Expert Witness Institute. However, a litigant in person cannot recover any costs in respect of a person or entity whose services he retains to provide general assistance in litigation unless that person or entity has a right to conduct litigation within the meaning of s 28 Courts and Legal Services Act 1990 (see *Agassi v HM Inspector of Taxes*) [2005] EWCA Civ 1507. (Such a right is conferred by the Law Society, the Bar Council, the Institute of Legal Executives or an appropriate professional body.)

(iii) Costs for work done by the litigant in person which caused him or her pecuniary loss (for example, a litigant in person who is employed losing a day's pay through attending a court hearing or through going on a long journey to interview an essential witness).

(iv) Costs for work done by a litigant in person which did not cause him or her any pecuniary loss (eg, the examples just given if the work was done during leisure time).

1C–132 **22.3 Procedure on detailed assessment**

(a) The procedure by which a litigant in person seeks to obtain costs from another party is as set out in Sections 3 to 17 of this Guide (briefly, service of a bill plus notice of commencement and certain other documents, obtaining a default costs certificate or, if points of dispute are served, serving a reply and/or filing a request for a detailed assessment hearing).

(b) Where a litigant in person wishes to prove that he has suffered financial loss he should produce to the court any written evidence he relies on to support that claim and must serve a copy of that evidence on the paying party at the same time as serving the notice of commencement.

1C–133 **22.4 Calculation of charges for time spent by a litigant in person preparing the case**

(a) In order to determine charges for time spent, the costs officer or Costs Judge must decide four questions:

(i) What items of work were done and what time was actually spent on those items?

(ii) In respect of each item, how long was it reasonable for the litigant in person to spend? The time allowed may be less than the time actually spent by the litigant in person and more than the time that would have been spent by a solicitor, had a solicitor been employed to undertake that item.

(iii) What hourly rate or other rate is it reasonable to apply in respect of time reasonably spent by the litigant in person? Unless financial loss can be shown the rate allowed is £9.25 per hour under CPD Section 52.4 (£25 per hour in the Employment Appeal Tribunal).

(iv) If all the items of work for which costs are recoverable had been undertaken by a solicitor, what would a solicitor's reasonable charges have been for doing such work?

(b) The evidence to be served in support of a claim to prove financial loss should include what work a litigant carried out during the case, what employment the litigant may have taken up but for the case and what job offers were received and/or refused on account of the case (see *Mainwaring v Goldtech Investments Ltd*) [1997] 1 Costs LR 143 at page 156).

(c) There is an overall limit on charges for time spent preparing the case which can never be exceeded. The cost officer or Costs Judge cannot allow more than two thirds of the sum which a solicitor could reasonably have charged for doing the work (CPR Section 46(2)).

***Paragraph numbers marked with a "+" can be found online and on CD.***

**22.5 Calculation of disbursements** 1C–134

(a) The litigant in person will be allowed all his reasonable disbursements (such as court fees, out of pocket expenses) in full if the costs officer or Costs Judge decides all of the following questions in his or her favour:

(i) were these disbursements actually incurred?

(ii) If so, at the time they were incurred, did it then appear necessary or at least reasonable to incur them?

(iii) Are the sums claimed for each disbursement reasonable in amount?

(b) If, in respect of any disbursement the answers to questions (i) or (ii) is no, the amount claimed for that disbursement will be wholly disallowed.

(c) If, in respect of any disbursement, the answers to questions (i) and (ii) are yes but the answer to question (iii) is no, the costs officer or Costs Judge may allow a reduced amount for that disbursement.

(d) There is an overall limit on charges for time spent which can never be exceeded. The cost officer or Costs Judge cannot allow more than two thirds of the sum determined in answer to question (iv) above.

## SECTION 23

## COURT OF PROTECTION CASES

**23.1 Introduction** 1C–135

(a) The Court of Protection is an office of the Senior Courts and exercises jurisdiction in respect of the protection and management of the property and affairs of persons of who, by reason of mental disorder, are incapable of managing their own affairs ("patients").

(b) The relevant statutes and rules include the Mental Health Act 1983, the Enduring Powers of Attorney Act 1985 and the Court of Protection Rules 2001, relevant passages of all of which are set out and annotated in Volume 2 of Civil Procedure (the White Book)

(c) The Judges of the Court of Protection include the Master and his Deputies, from whom an appeal lies to the Judges of the Chancery and Family Divisions. A judge, the Master, or any nominated officer authorised under section 94 of the Mental Health Act 1983, may exercise the functions of the court.

(d) This Section of the Guide is published with the assistance and approval of the Master of the Court of Protection.

**23.2 Orders and directions as to costs** 1C–136

(a) All orders as to costs are at the discretion of the court and nothing in this guidance should be interpreted as removing or restricting the Court's discretion in any way.

(b) There are three methods of quantifying costs:

- Agreed costs,
- Fixed costs,
- Detailed assessment of costs.

**23.3 Agreed costs** 1C–137

(a) Agreed costs are not generally available. The procedure is now governed by the Practice Note of 11 October 2004. As a general principle, all bills of costs must be assessed, except where fixed costs are available. The procedure to assess bills below £3,000 should be used for all bills where professionals used to seek agreement.

(b) The Court of Protection recognises that in certain circumstances it would not be in the client's best interests to request an assessment, for example where the cost of assessment is disproportionate to the amount of the bill. The court may agree costs in such circumstances, as long as the fixed costs provisions do not cover the work. If solicitors consider that a costs assessment would not be appropriate, they should apply to the court setting out the reasons and requesting the court to agree the bill. Any request must be accompanied by a narrative bill setting out the hours spent and the level and status of the fee earner concerned, together with fee notes and vouchers for any disbursements. The court may also exercise its discretion to agree costs at any time whether or not it is in the context of a formal application.

1C-138 **23.4 Fixed costs**

(a) The Master of the Court of Protection specifies the amounts allowed under the categories of fixed costs in consultation with the Law Society. The rates are published annually in practice notes issued by the Master. The amounts allowed under each category are maximum amounts. Where there are reasonable grounds for thinking that costs will not exceed the maximum amount allowed, solicitors may take a lower figure without further reference to the Court or the PGO. For example if the professional reasonably believes the general management costs for the year will not exceed £400, then they may take that figure without drawing a bill.

(b) Solicitors may also take fixed costs for general management pro-rata if the period covered by the bill is less than one year, for example where the patient dies or the receiver retires before the anniversary date.

(c) Although fixed costs are set in consultation with the Law Society and apply mainly to the work of solicitors, accountants may elect to take an amount not exceeding fixed costs for any work covered in categories II III and VII below. The court may also apply the fixed costs procedure to any other non-solicitor if it is appropriate to do so, and it is open to any other professional to apply to the court for authority to receive fixed costs at any time.

(d) The categories of fixed costs are:

| | |
|---|---|
| Category I | Work up to and including the date upon which the First General Order or Short Order is entered |
| Category II | (a) Preparation and lodgment of a receivership account<br>(b) Preparation and lodgment of a receivership account which has been certified by a solicitor under the provisions of the Practice Notes dated 13 September 1984 and 5 March 1985 reported at [1984] 3 All ER 320 and [1985] 1 All ER 884 respectively |
| Category III | General management costs in the first year<br>(a) where there are lay receivers and the court has authorised the receiver to employ solicitors to carry out work not usually requiring professional assistance under rule 87 of the Court of Protection Rules 2001<br>(b) where there are professional receivers<br>General management work in the second and subsequent years<br>(c) where there are lay receivers and the court has authorised the receiver to employ solicitors to carry out work not usually requiring professional assistance under rule 87 of the Court of Protection Rules 2001<br>(d) where there are professional receivers<br>(e) Where a professional is dealing with the affairs of an individual under an order of the court, and the assets of the individual are less than £16,000, then the professional may take a general management fee of 2.5% of the patient's assets on the anniversary of the order appointing the professional to act (plus VAT). |
| Category IV | Applications under s.36 (9) or 54 of the Trustee Act 1925 or section 20 of the Trusts of Land and Appointment of Trustees Act 1996 for the appointment of a new trustee in the place of the patient and applications under section 96(1)(k) of the Mental Health Act 1983 for the authority to exercise any power vested in the patient whether beneficially, or as guardian or trustee, or otherwise. |
| Category V | Conveyancing costs, except where the sale or purchase is made by trustees. |

| | |
|---|---|
| Category VI | Work up to and including the date upon which an order appointing a replacement receiver is entered. |
| Category VII | Preparation of an Inland Revenue income tax return on behalf of a patient. |

(e) In most straightforward or routine receivership cases, solicitors will usually opt to take fixed costs because they can be paid quickly and easily. However, the court recognises that in some cases this will not be appropriate, therefore, in all categories of work, solicitors may, if they prefer, apply for an assessment of their costs.

### 23.5 Commencing detailed assessment 1C–139

(a) The detailed assessment of costs under orders or directions of the Court of Protection is dealt with in accordance with the CPR. Solicitors should lodge a request for a detailed assessment at the SCCO (not the Court of Protection or the PGO), using Form **N258B** if payable out of a fund, or Form **N258** if payable by one party to another, together with the authority for assessment, the bill of costs, all supporting papers and a lodgment fee (currently £200, or £100 for bills below £3,000 fee 4 COP Rules as amended).

(b) The authority for assessing a Court of Protection bill of costs must derive from an order or direction of the Court of Protection. The general rule is "one order-one bill" so the request should not consolidate two or more orders in one bill. The exception is a bill for the preparation of a receivership account, which may be included in a bill for general management.

### 23.6 Bill format 1C–140

(a) The bill of costs should be prepared in accordance with the model forms set out in the CPD (see para 3.4, above) except where the short form bill (described below) is appropriate. The bill should state correct title of the matter, the name and address, telephone number and reference of the solicitor. The bill should list each chargeable item of work in chronological order with dates. It should also show any relevant events even if it does not constitute a chargeable item. If the bill is for general management it should state the year covered (e.g. from 21 December 2004 to 20 December 2005).

(b) Where the amount of the bill does not exceed £3,000, excluding VAT and disbursements the solicitor may request the Costs Office to assess the costs using the short form bill. The procedure is the same as that for an application for detailed assessment, except that solicitors may use a simplified form of bill, which will not require the services of a costs draftsman. The cost of drawing a long form of bill will not usually be recoverable in cases where a short form bill is appropriate. A copy of the model short form bill is set out in the Appendix, below, para A-10.

### 23.7 Authorities to assess costs 1C–141

(a) The First General Order is the authority to assess the costs of the application to appoint the receiver. The Costs Office will treat costs of the application as ending on the issue date of the First General Order (which may be some time after the actual date of the order). The costs officer will treat any costs incurred after the issue of the order as general management costs.

(b) If the order provides for fixed costs, but solicitors elect for assessment, it is not necessary to apply to the Court of Protection for an amended direction. Instead, under a general direction issued by the Court of Protection and dated the 25 July 1990, solicitors may elect for assessment simply by lodging a bill with the Costs Office. The bill should contain a certificate stating that fixed costs have not been taken.

(c) If the application is for the assessment of general management costs, the costs officer will need to know that the court has agreed that the professional receiver is to be paid general management costs. When lodging the first year's general management bill, the receiver should send a copy of the First General Order authorising him or her to be paid professional costs. The Costs Office will keep a record so it is not necessary to send a copy of the First General Order in subsequent years. Unless there are any special circumstances, general management costs should be claimed annually, usually after passing the annual account.

(d) Any other solicitor in the matter will need to send the direction of the court, usually a letter, authorising the receiver to employ a solicitor to do work not usually requiring professional assistance (see para 23.9, below). They should also lodge a copy



SCCO GUIDE

of the First General Order so that the Costs Office can record who is receiver and note any specific directions.

(e) Costs for preparing the receiver's annual account are assessed after passing the receiver's account. Solicitors should enclose with their bill a copy of the letter from the PGO sent out when the account has been passed.

(f) In all cases, where fixed costs are available, solicitors should confirm, when lodging their bill for assessment, that they have not taken fixed costs for the work. The simplest way of doing this is to add an endorsement to the bill.

1C–142 **23.8 The detailed assessment**

(a) The Costs Office will deal with most assessments on a provisional basis by post. If the solicitor is not satisfied with the assessment he must inform the costs officer within 14 days of receipt of the provisional assessment. The Costs Office will then fix a date for hearing. In practice the costs officer will deal with any enquiries by telephone or letter.

(b) If the order provides for costs to be paid other than from the patient's estate, the solicitor must provide a statement of parties and Notice of Commencement. The Costs Office will send an appointment for the hearing to all parties. Rule 47.17A of the Civil Procedure Rules 1998 provides that a trustee, receiver or any other party managing the patient's fund or litigation, is a person who will be treated as having a financial interest in the outcome of a detailed assessment, therefore solicitors must provide their name, address and reference, in case the costs officer decides they should be sent the bill of costs or notice of assessment. As a matter of good practice, solicitors must serve a copy of the bill on the receiver prior to lodgement, as this will help to allay disputes where the receiver is unaware that costs have been claimed from the patient's estate until receipt of the final costs certificate.

(c) After completion of the assessment, the solicitor must complete the summary on the bill certifying the castings as correct, and return the original bill to the Costs Office for the issue of the costs certificate. There is no fee for sealing the certificate.

1C–143 **23.9 Solicitors and other professional persons carrying out receiver's work**

(a) Rule 87(1) of the Court of Protection Rules 2001 states that no receiver for a patient, other than the Official Solicitor, shall, unless authorised by the Court of Protection, be entitled at the expense of the patient's estate to employ a solicitor or other professional person to do any work not usually requiring professional assistance.

(b) The court may authorise professionals to be paid costs formally by way of an order or informally for example by letter. Although this guide describes the procedure in relation to solicitors' costs, the Court of Protection and the Costs Office will treat other professionals in a similar way.

(c) The Court of Protection has discretion to order assessment on either the standard or indemnity basis (rule 43 (remuneration) and rules 84 – 89 (costs) COP Rules). Definitions of standard and indemnity bases of costs are set out in para 2.4, above.

(d) As a general principle, the court will require assessment of costs on the standard basis. This is because the legal definition of the standard basis will only allow costs that are proportionate to the matters in issue. There is no test of proportionality in the definition of the indemnity basis, which precludes the costs officer from taking into account the amount of money involved, the financial position of the client and the complexity of the case.

(e) Following the Practice Direction issued by the Master of the Court of Protection on 2 March 2005, all orders providing for costs made on or after 1 April 2005 will, unless the court specifically directs otherwise, provide for assessment on the standard basis. This includes orders issued on or after that date providing for fixed costs, where the professional elects to seek an assessment pursuant to the general direction dated the 25 July 1990.

(f) The Court of Protection retains the discretion to order costs on the indemnity basis. Solicitors may apply to the court for an order for costs on the indemnity basis, if they feel the circumstances of the case justify it. However, solicitors undertaking work in expectation of receiving costs on the indemnity basis do so at their own risk that such an order may not be made.

(g) It is not possible to define exactly what circumstances might persuade the court to agree to assessment on the indemnity rather than standard basis. There are an infinite variety of situations that might justify the making of such an order and the judge has wide discretion in relation to the ordering of costs. The onus is therefore on the solicitors to persuade the court that costs should be paid on the indemnity basis.

### 23.10 Non-professional receivers 1C–144

(a) In cases where the receiver is not a professional person, he or she is required to carry out the full range of receivership duties. These duties are set out in the Receiver's Handbook published by the Public Guardianship Office and the Receiver's Declaration that applicants submit on applying for appointment as receiver.

(b) On occasions, the receiver may wish to employ at the client's expense a solicitor or other professional person to do work not usually requiring professional assistance. If a receiver engages a solicitor to assist in this way, the receiver or solicitor must apply to the court for authorisation under rule 87 of the COP Rules.

(c) Where an authorisation under rule 87 has been granted the solicitor must provide a copy of it to the Costs Office when submitting a bill for assessment. If no such authority has been obtained, the costs officer will disallow the claim, although they may still apply 'out of time' to the Court of Protection, for directions under rule 87. The court will usually provide retrospective authorisation where the professional has acted in good faith, for example in cases of emergency or where urgent action is required to protect the client's property. In most cases the court would expect the professional to seek advance authorisation.

(e) The court considers the completion of annual accounts to be work that sometimes requires professional assistance and therefore solicitors do not need to apply for directions under rule 87 if they are instructed by a receiver to prepare annual accounts.

### 23.11 General management work 1C–145

(a) The Court of Protection's jurisdiction extends only to the management and administration of the client's financial affairs. The court cannot give directions concerning aspects of clients' affairs that are not financial. It follows that solicitors will only be allowed costs for work relating to the client's financial affairs.

(b) If the costs officer disallows an item in a bill that the solicitor feels is properly chargeable as work relating to financial affairs, they should raise this upon review of the provisional assessment and if that is unsuccessful, take the question to appeal. Neither the court nor the PGO can intervene in the assessment process since this function is reserved to the SCCO by reason of rule 86 COP Rules.

(c) If the receiver is a solicitor or other professional person then, subject to the terms of the order appointing them as receiver, they may be paid costs for the whole of the receivership duties, as long as those duties relate to the management of the client's financial affairs. The interpretation of those duties may cause difficulties for professional receivers, as some of the duties listed in the Receiver's Handbook (published by the PGO) and the Receiver's Declaration do not relate directly to financial affairs. As a general rule the court would not expect professional receivers to undertake the non-financial duties of a receiver, but would expect the receiver to take reasonable steps to ensure that, wherever possible those duties were undertaken by someone else.

(d) On occasions some non-financial activities, such as visits to clients or attendance at case conferences, may be necessary in order to safeguard a client's financial affairs. In such cases, the costs officer may accept well-founded arguments that such general management costs should be allowed on assessment. If the circumstances of the case are unusual and require the receiver to be actively involved in the management of the client's day-to-day affairs, then the receiver should draw this to the costs officer's attention in a covering letter submitted with the bill. The costs officer would also expect that any receivership work, be it legal or non-legal, be undertaken by an appropriate fee earner in the firm, which may not necessarily be the appointed receiver.

### 23.12 Cost of sale or purchase of property 1C–146

(a) The assessment of costs of sale or purchase of a property will normally take place at the conclusion of the transaction unless the court has made other directions. The estate agent's charges should appear in the completion statement and not as a disbursement on the bill.

(b) If the sale was by trustees of a jointly owned property, the Costs Office will assess the costs of the application to appoint new trustees; but the conveyancing costs can only be approved by the trustees.

1C–147 **23.13 Deceased patients**

If the patient dies when the assessment of costs are pending, the solicitor should inform the Costs Office, who will suspend the assessment until after the court gives final directions. The solicitor must serve a copy of his bill upon the patient's personal representative upon resumption of the assessment process.

## SECTION 24

## LEGAL AID/LSC CASES

1C–148 **24.1 Introduction**

(a) Because of changes made by the Administration of Justice Act 1999 the old legal aid scheme, the Legal Aid Board and the Legal Aid Fund have all been replaced by a new funding scheme, the Legal Services Commission ("LSC") and the Community Legal Service Fund. Cases started under the old scheme continue largely as before but, on conclusion, will be paid for out of the Community Legal Service Fund.

(b) Under the old scheme legal aid paid for legal services supplied to "assisted persons". Under the new scheme legal aid provides legal services for "clients". In this Guide the term "LSC funded client" is used to cover both assisted persons and "clients".

(c) The modern form of order for what used to be called "legal aid taxation" is now "detailed assessment of the costs of the [party] which are payable out of the Community Legal Service Fund".

1C–149 **24.2 Costs payable by another person as well as out of the Fund**

(a) Where the costs are payable by another person as well as out of the Community Legal Service Fund, the rules governing commencement of detailed assessment proceedings, points of dispute and replies are the same as those which apply to between the parties cases generally (see Sections 3 and 17 above). The Schedule of Costs Precedents includes model forms of bills for use in such cases (Precedents C and D).

(b) The request for detailed assessment hearing must (in addition to the items set out in Section 8 above) be accompanied by:

(i) the legal aid certificate, the LSC certificate and relevant amendment certificate, any authorities and any certificates of discharge or revocation;

(ii) a certificate in Precedent F(3) and where appropriate a certificate in Precedent F(4) of the Schedule of Costs Precedents (as to which, see Appendix para A-2);

(iii) if the LSC funded client has a financial interest in the detailed assessment hearing and wishes to attend, the postal address of that person to which the court will send notice of any hearing;

(iv) if the rates payable out of the Community Legal Service Fund are prescribed rates (ie if the Civil Legal Aid (Remuneration) Regulations 1994 apply), a schedule (the "Legal Aid /LSC Schedule") setting out all the items in the bill which are claimed against other parties calculated at the legal aid prescribed rates. Precedent E of the Schedule of Costs Precedents should be followed as closely as possible;

(v) a copy of any default costs certificate in respect of the costs claimed in the bill.

(c) The LSC funded client should not be served with a copy of the notice of commencement and should only be served with a copy of the bill if he or she has a financial interest in the detailed assessment.

1C–150 **24.3 Procedure where costs are payable by another person as well as out of the Fund**

(a) Unless the legal aid/LSC only sections of the bill are comparatively small or otherwise easy to deal with, the detailed assessment will be conducted in two stages.

(i) In the first stage the court will consider only the between the parties sections of the bill, the points of dispute thereon and any replies made.

***Paragraph numbers marked with a "+" can be found online and on CD.***

(ii) In the second stage the court will consider the legal aid/LSC only sections of the bill and the Legal Aid/LSC Schedule.

(b) The Legal Aid/LSC Schedule is of no concern to the party against whom costs have been awarded between the parties and indeed that person should not normally attend the second stage of the detailed assessment.

(c) The LSC funded client's solicitor will have prepared the Legal Aid/LSC Schedule in advance of the detailed assessment. It may therefore be necessary to begin the second stage of the detailed assessment by altering the Schedule so as to update it, taking account of the decisions made during the first stage of the detailed assessment.

(d) In respect of any item appearing in the Legal Aid/LSC only sections of the bill, the court will consider what sum, if any, it is reasonable to allow in respect of that item.

(e) In respect of any item deleted or reduced in the Legal Aid/LSC Schedule so as to take into account decisions made during the first stage of the detailed assessment, the court may be requested to consider whether any part of that item can be restored via an appropriate alteration to the Legal Aid/LSC only sections of the bill.

**24.4 Costs of detailed assessment proceedings** **1C–151**

(a) Costs incurred on behalf of a LSC funded client in respect of a detailed assessment between the parties are treated in the same way as other costs incurred on his behalf, and whether or not they are payable by the other party, may also be claimed against the Community Legal Service Fund. In general the party whose bill is the subject of detailed assessment is entitled to the costs of the detailed assessment proceedings. However the court may make some other order in relation to all or part of the costs of the detailed assessment proceedings. (See Section 11 above.)

(b) The LSC funded client will not be required to make any contribution to the Community Legal Service Fund on account of the costs of the detailed assessment proceedings and the statutory charge does not apply in relation to any resulting increase in the net liability of the Fund arising from the costs of the detailed assessment proceedings. The cost of drawing up a bill of costs is however not included as part of the costs of the detailed assessment proceedings (Civil Legal Aid (General) Regulations 1989, Regulation 119 as amended).

**24.5 Costs payable only out of the Community Legal Service Fund** **1C–152**

(a) Where costs are payable only out of the Community Legal Service Fund, the solicitor representing the LSC funded client may request a detailed assessment of costs within 3 months after the date upon which the right to detailed assessment arose. The request must be in Form **N258A** and must be accompanied by a copy of the bill of costs and the other documents listed in paragraph 43.3 of the Costs Practice Direction.

(b) Where the solicitor has certified that the LSC funded client has a financial interest and wishes to attend, the court will, on receipt of the request for detailed assessment, fix a date for the detailed assessment hearing.

(c) Where the solicitor has certified that the LSC funded client has no financial interest or does not wish to attend the detailed assessment, the court will provisionally assess the costs without the attendance of the solicitor, unless it considers that a hearing is necessary. After the court has provisionally assessed the bill, it will return it to the solicitor. If the solicitor informs the court within 14 days after he receives the provisionally assessed bill that he wants the court to hold a detailed assessment hearing, the court will fix a date for such hearing.

**24.6 Duty to inform counsel** **1C–153**

It is the duty of the LSC funded client's solicitor to notify counsel in writing within 7 days after the detailed or provisional assessment where the fees claimed on his behalf have been reduced or disallowed on assessment and the solicitor must endorse the bill with the date on which such notice was given or that no such notice is necessary. If the bill is endorsed with the date upon which notice was given to counsel the court may not issue the certificate until 14 days have elapsed from the date so endorsed (see Civil Legal Aid (General) Regulations 1989, Regulation 112 and Precedent F(4) of the Schedule of Costs Precedents in Appendix 1, below, para A-2).

**24.7 Completing the bill and the legal aid assessment certificate** **1C–154**

It is the responsibility of the legal representative to complete the bill by entering in the bill the correct figures allowed in respect of each item, recalculating the summary of the bill appropriately and completing the Legal Aid Assessment certificate in Form **EX 80A**.

1C-155 **24.8 Agreement of between the parties costs**

(a) Where the Civil Legal Aid (Remuneration) Regulations 1994 do not apply to the detailed assessment (which is generally the case where the legal aid certificate was issued before 25 February 1994) the Civil Legal Aid (General) Regulations 1989, Regulation 106 remains applicable and an agreement of between the parties costs is not possible unless the agreement is accepted in full and final settlement of the costs ie with no further claim against the Fund. Therefore where in such cases the receiving party wishes to make a claim against the Fund, the parties will be informed that there will have to be a detailed assessment of the whole bill. However, because of the measure of agreement which has been reached, the detailed assessment of the between the parties sections of the bill may not take very long to complete.

(b) In cases where the Civil Legal Aid (Remuneration) Regulations do apply the Civil Legal Aid (General) Regulations 1989, Regulation 106A permits the LSC funded client's solicitor to apply for an assessment limited to legal aid/LSC only costs provided the between the parties costs have been both agreed and paid.

1C-156 **24.9 Costs appeals**

The solicitor for a LSC funded client may appeal against a decision of a Costs Judge or District Judge in detailed assessment proceedings in accordance with Rules of Court (ie CPR Part 52) and if counsel acting for the LSC funded client notifies the solicitor that he is dissatisfied with the decision the solicitor must appeal on counsel's behalf. The costs of any such appeal will only be payable out of the Community Legal Services Fund to the extent that the court hearing the appeal so orders. For the detailed Regulations relating to appeals involving LSC funded clients see Civil Legal Aid (General) Regulations 1989, Regulation 113 as amended and CPR 47.20(2).

## SECTION 25

## COSTS ORDERS AGAINST LSC FUNDED CLIENTS AND/OR THE LSC

1C-157 **25.1 The Access to Justice Act 1999 and the Regulations**

(a) Any costs ordered to be paid by a LSC funded client must not exceed the amount which is a reasonable one for him to pay having regard to all the circumstances including the financial resources of all the parties to the proceedings and their conduct in connection with the dispute to which the proceedings relate (Access to Justice Act 1999, Section 11).

(b) The Community Legal Service (Costs) Regulations 2000 ("the Costs Regulations") and the Community Legal Service (Costs Protection) Regulations 2000 ("the Costs Protection Regulations") are Regulations made under the Access to Justice Act 1999 and provide a code governing orders for costs against assisted persons/ LSC funded clients and against the LSC.

(c) The ordinary rules governing the assessment of costs (Parts 44 to 48 of the CPR) do not apply to the assessment of such costs. The procedure to be followed in such cases is set out in Sections 21–23 of the Costs Practice Direction.

1C-158 **25.2 Orders which the court awarding costs may make**

(a) If the court decides to make an order for costs against a LSC funded client it may either make an order that the amount of the costs payable by the LSC funded client is to be determined by a Costs Judge or District Judge or make an order which specifies the amount which the LSC funded client is to pay.

(b) If the court decides to make an order that the amount payable by the LSC funded client is to be determined by a Costs Judge or District Judge it may also state the amount which that person would, had costs protection not applied, have been ordered to pay ie the full costs which would be determined by summary assessment. Alternatively the court may make findings of facts eg about the conduct of all the parties which must be taken into account by the Costs Judge or District Judge in the subsequent determination proceedings.

(c) The court will not make an order which specifies the amount which the LSC funded client is to pay unless it considers that it has sufficient information before it to decide what amount is reasonable and either the order also states the amount of the full costs (ie the amount which that person would, had costs protection not applied, have been ordered to pay) or the court is satisfied that the full costs would exceed the amount which it has specified that the LSC funded client must pay.

(d) If the LSC funded client does not have costs protection in respect of all of the costs (eg the certificate was not in force during the whole of the proceeding) the order must also identify the sum payable in respect of which the LSC funded client had costs protection and the sum payable in respect of which he did not have costs protection. (See Section 22 of the Costs Practice Direction.)

(e) A specimen order for costs against a claimant who is a LSC funded client is set out in the Appendix, below, para. A-6.

**25.3 Costs against the LSC** **1C–159**

(a) If an application for an order for costs against the LSC is made the criteria set out in Regulation 5 of the Costs Protection Regulations will apply. Before the LSC can be ordered to pay the whole or any part of the costs incurred by a non-funded party all of several conditions must be satisfied:

(i) the costs ordered to be paid by the LSC funded client must be less than the full costs (ie the amount which that person would, had costs protection not applied, have been ordered to pay);

(ii) the proceedings must have been finally decided in favour of the non-funded party;

(iii) the non funded party must provide written notice of intention to seek an order against the LSC within 3 months of the making of the order for costs against the LSC funded client;

(iv) the court must be satisfied that it is just and equitable in the circumstances that provision for the costs should be made out of public funds; and,

(v) where the costs are incurred in a court of first instance, the proceedings must have been instituted by the LSC funded client and, the court must be satisfied that the non-funded party will suffer severe financial hardship unless the order is made.

(b) Where the application for funded services was made on or after 3 December 2001 the three months time limit referred to in (iii) above may be extended if there is a good reason for the delay; and in (v) above only a non funded party who is an individual may apply but the court will not have to be satisfied that the financial hardship he or she will suffer will be severe.

**25.4 Orders which a Costs Judge or District Judge may subsequently make** **1C–160**

(a) An order for costs to which Section 11(1) of the Access to Justice Act 1999 applies may specify the amount of full costs and may specify the amount payable by the LSC funded client. Where appropriate an application may be made to the District Judge or Costs Judge of the relevant court to determine:

(i) the amount of full costs;

(ii) the amount payable by the LSC funded client;

(iii) the amount payable by the LSC itself.

(b) The procedure for determination is set out in Section 23 of the Costs Practice Direction which is summarised below.

**25.5 Form of application** **1C–161**

Applications for such orders must be made in the appropriate court office on an application in Form **N244** accompanied by:

(i) the receiving party's bill of costs (unless the full costs have already been determined);

(ii) the receiving party's statement of resources (defined below); and

(iii) if the receiving party intends to seek costs against the LSC, written notice to that effect.

**25.6 The response by the LSC funded client** **1C–162**

(a) Within 21 days of being served with the application, the LSC funded client must respond by filing a statement of resources (defined below) and serving a copy of it on



SCCO GUIDE

the receiving party and, where relevant, on the Regional Director. The LSC funded client may also, within the same time limit, file and serve written points disputing the bill of costs.

(b) The 21 day time limit mentioned above may be extended by agreement between the parties or by order of the court.

1C-163 **25.7 Effect of non compliance by the LSC funded client**

If the LSC funded client fails to file a statement of resources without good reason, the court will determine his liability (and the amount of full costs if relevant) and need not hold an oral hearing for any such determination.

1C-164 **25.8 Further procedure where a statement of resources by the LSC funded client is filed or is not required**

(a) When the LSC funded client files a statement of resources the court will fix a hearing date and give the relevant parties at least 14 days notice. If the application is made only against the LSC the court may fix a hearing date at the time of issue of the application.

(b) Applications which proceed to a hearing to determine the liability of the LSC funded client will, in the first instance, be listed as a hearing to be held in private. At the start of the hearing, or during it, any party may request the court to rule that, thereafter, the hearing should be conducted in public.

1C-165 **25.9 Response by the Regional Director of the LSC**

The Regional Director of the LSC may appear at any hearing at which a costs order may be made against the LSC or may file a written statement as described in para. 23.10 of the Costs Practice Direction.

1C-166 **25.10 Costs of application**

When dealing with the application the court has a discretion as to whether the costs of the application are payable by one party to another, the amount of those costs, and (if relevant) when they are to be paid.

1C-167 **25.11 Statements of resources**

(a) A "statement of resources" should set out details of the financial resources and expectations of the maker of the statement and of his "partner" (a person with whom he or she lives as a couple). The resources of a partner are not treated as the LSC client's resources if the partner has a contrary interest in the proceedings.

(b) A full definition of "statement of resources" is given in para. 22.1 of the Costs Practice Direction. In order to comply with that paragraph the party making a statement of resources may be able to adapt the text of Form **N9A** a copy of which is obtainable from the court office or from a Citizens Advice Bureau.

(c) The Costs Regulations provide for the filing of statements of resources not only by the LSC funded client but also by the receiving party. As regards costs incurred in appeal proceedings, applications are often made by large commercial companies or litigants who are insured or who are publicly funded. In such cases a statement of resources stating merely that the applicant is "able to pay its costs out of its own resources" or "is insured" or "is a publicly funded body" will suffice. In such cases the court will assume that the applicant will not suffer any severe financial hardship if the application fails.

(d) Where the court is determining an application for a costs order against the LSC and the costs were not incurred in a court of first instance, a statement of resources does not have to filed by the receiving party.

1C-168 **25.12 Specimen forms of order**

Para A-6 of the Appendix, below, sets out a specimen order for costs against a claimant who is an LSC funded client and also a specimen order for use by a Costs Judge or District Judge when determining the amount of costs payable by an LSC funded client.

## SECTION 26

## APPLICATIONS UNDER THE SOLICITORS ACT 1974

1C-169 **26.1 Introduction**

(a) Application may be made under Section 70 of the Solicitors Act 1974 for an order for the detailed assessment of a solicitor's bill of costs. The application can relate to the whole bill, or can be limited to the profit costs only or to the disbursements only. Most such applications are made by the client or former client of the solicitor who delivered the bill. In practice solicitors make the application against their client or former client only where they wish to escape the consequences of a remuneration certificate issued by the Law Society. Although, in other cases, the solicitors may have a right to apply under Section 70 they almost invariably bring simple debt proceedings instead and, if prevented from obtaining a default judgment, seek summary judgment for an amount "to be assessed" (see High Court Practice Form 15).

(b) Application may also be made under Section 71 of the 1974 Act where a bill of costs is payable by a party who is not the client of the solicitors. For example beneficiaries under a will or a borrower whose mortgage or charge obliges him to pay the legal costs of the lender (usually a bank or a building society).

(c) The application is heard by a Costs Judge. If an order for detailed assessment is made, that detailed assessment will also be heard by a Costs Judge.

**26.2 Detailed assessment as of right or on terms** **1C–170**

(a) If the application is made within one calendar month of receipt of the bill, the Costs Judge must order detailed assessment.

(b) If the application is made more than one calendar month, but less than a year from receipt of the bill, the Costs Judge may impose conditions, for example, that the amount of the bill should be paid into court to abide the event.

(c) No order will be made, except in special circumstances, if:

(i) 12 months have elapsed from the delivery of the bill or

(ii) Judgment has been obtained for the recovery of the costs covered by the bill or

(iii) The bill has been paid less than 12 months before the date upon which the application was issued.

(d) If the bill has been paid more than 12 months before the date upon which the application was issued the Costs Judge has no power to order that bill be assessed.

**26.3 The forms to use** **1C–171**

(a) Application for the detailed assessment of a solicitor's bill of costs is made by a claim form to which CPR Part 8 applies. The specimen form is set out in the Appendix, below, para. A-7. This form is also used for other applications under the Act.

(b) If an order for detailed assessment is made there are two standard forms of order: precedents L and M in the Schedule of Costs Precedents included in the Costs Practice Direction (see further, para. 26.5, below)

**26.4 Commencing the application** **1C–172**

(a) Applicants must send or bring to the SCCO

(i) Three copies of the claim form with draft order sought.

(ii) A cheque for the fee made payable to H M Paymaster General (as to which, see para. 27.1, below).

(iii) The original bill(s) or copies of the original(s) which are certified by or on behalf of the applicants as being true and complete copies.

(b) Once the payment of the fee has been processed, the application will be passed to the application clerk in Room 2.13, who will list it for hearing before a Costs Judge. The court will serve the application unless there are particular reasons why the applicant should serve it. The application will usually be listed for a short appointment (15 minutes). If the hearing is likely to exceed the allotted time it may be necessary to adjourn it to a new date with a realistic time estimate. This step may become due, for example, when evidence is filed in reply to the application.

(c) In most cases, witness statement evidence is not required unless the application becomes contested, a certificate of special circumstances under Section 70(3) of the Act is sought or the Costs Judge so directs.

**26.5 The hearing of the application** **1C–173**

(a) Where an application is made by a litigant in person, an order will not be made in the absence of the parties. The litigant in person must attend in order that the Costs Judge may explain the effect of Section 70(9) of the Act ("the one-fifth rule", as to which, see para. 26.6 below).

(b) If no-one attends on behalf of the respondent, the Costs Judge may make the order sought, conditional upon adequate proof of service of the application.

(c) It is now common practice for a time-table to be incorporated into the order, based upon Rule 48.10 dealing with service of a breakdown of the bill, service of points of dispute, any reply and the request for a hearing date. A specimen order is included in the Appendix, below, para. A-8.

(d) The costs of the application will usually be treated as part of the costs of the detailed assessment and dealt with at the conclusion of the detailed assessment hearing.

(e) The order is usually drawn up by the court, and a copy served on all parties. The Costs Judge may direct that the order be drawn up by the successful party. In that event, three copies of the order must be lodged with the clerk to the Costs Judge. Copies will then be served on the parties.

1C-174 **26.6 The costs of the assessment**

(a) Statutory provisions apply where costs are assessed under Sections 70 or 71 of the Solicitors Act 1974. If the bill or bills are reduced by more than one fifth (excluding VAT) the solicitors will be ordered to pay the costs of the detailed assessment. If the bill or bills are reduced by less than one fifth the other party will be ordered to pay the costs of the detailed assessment. The Costs Judge may order otherwise if there are special circumstances.

(b) If on a detailed assessment of non-contentious costs, the costs allowed are less than one half of the costs claimed, the Costs Judge will report those facts to the Council of the Law Society. The report will be addressed to The Law Society Consumer Complaints Service, Victoria Court, 8 Dormer Place, Royal Leamington Spa, Warwickshire CV32 5AE.

## SECTION 27

## COURT FEES PAYABLE IN THE SCCO

1C-175 **27.1 Introductory**

(a) The fees payable for proceedings within the SCCO are set out in the Supreme Court(Review of Taxation in Criminal Cases) Fees Order 1984 (1994 No.340) as amended, the Civil Proceedings Fees Order 2004 and the Family Proceedings Fees Order 2004. Certain fees are prescribed by the Court of Protection Rules 2001 as amended. All of these orders and rules, except the first mentioned, are set out in practitioners' books such as the White Book and the Green Book. In cases of difficulty enquiry may be made at the Costs Office (see paras 1.5, 1.8 and 1.9, above).

(b) The following list, while not exhaustive, includes the fees most commonly encountered in matters before the SCCO, and are valid at the time of publication. The County Court fees and fees in Family Proceedings appear in brackets:

| | High Court | County Court | Family Proceedings |
|---|---|---|---|
| (i) Request for a default costs certificate: | £50 | (£45) | (£60) |
| (ii) Request or application to set aside a default costs certificate: | £100 | (£65) | (£65) |
| (iii) On filing request for a detailed assessment where the applicant is legally aided or publicly funded and no other party is ordered to pay the costs of the proceedings: | £120 | (£105) | (£140) |
| (iv) On filing request for a detailed assessment other than (iii) above (including assessment of costs payable to a solicitor by his client): | £600 | (£300) | (£250) |

***Paragraph numbers marked with a "+" can be found online and on CD.***

| | | | |
|---|---|---|---|
| (v) On applying for the court's approval of a certificate of costs payable from the Community Service Fund: | £50 | (£35) | (£35) |
| (vi) On any appeal against decisions in detailed assessment proceedings: | £200 | (£105) | (£105) |
| (vii) On an application for an order under Part III of the Solicitors Act 1974 for the assessment of costs payable to a solicitor by his client or on the commencement of costs only proceedings: | £50 | (£35) | (£35) |

The above fees apply to all cases where the order or authority for assessment of costs was made on or after 10 January 2006.

### 27.2 Time for payment 1C–176

Normally a request, an application or an appeal will not be accepted by the court office unless the appropriate fee is first paid. This should be in the form of a cheque payable to HM Paymaster General. In exceptional circumstances a costs officer may allow an application to be issued on an undertaking by the applicant or his solicitors that the appropriate fee will be paid within a limited period thereafter.

### 27.3 Exemptions 1C–177

(a) No fee is payable by a party who, at the time when the fee would otherwise be payable, is in receipt of a qualifying benefit and is not in receipt of legal aid or LSC funding for the purposes of the proceedings.

(b) "Qualifying benefits" referred to above are as follows:

(i) income support;

(ii) working tax credit provided that:

(a) child tax credit is being paid to the party or otherwise following a claim for child tax credit made jointly by members of a married couple or an unmarried couple as defined in Sections 3(5) and (6) of the Tax Credits Act 2002, which includes the party; or

(b) there is a disability element or severe disability element (or both) to the tax credit received by the party—

AND that the gross annual income taken into account for the calculations of the working tax credit is £14,600 or less;

(c) income based job seeker's allowance

(d) guarantee credit under the State Pension Credit Act, 2002.

(c) The Lord Chancellor may, where it appears that the payment of any fee would, owing to the exceptional circumstances of the particular case, involve undue financial hardship, reduce or remit the fee in the particular case.

(d) Where a fee has been paid which was not payable under the above provisions, or which has been reduced because of undue financial hardship, the fee will be refunded provided the party who paid the fee applies within six months of payment. The six month time limit may be extended if there is good reason for the application being made after the end of the six month period.

(e) In family proceedings no fee is payable by a person under 18 or in respect of whom an order for financial relief (under paragraph 2 of Schedule 1 to the Children Act 1989) is in force or is being applied for, provided that that person is not a beneficiary of a trust fund in court of a value of more than £50,000.

### 27.4 Appeal fee 1C–178

An appeal, whether from a Costs Judge to a High Court Judge, or from a costs officer to a Costs Judge, attracts a fee (currently £200). It is to be noted that informal appeals from costs officers to Costs Judges by letter are not permissible. The appropriate appeal notice must be used and the fee paid.

1C–179 **27.5 Fee for transcripts**

Although proceedings in the SCCO are recorded no transcripts of the recordings are made unless and until a party applies for a transcript and pays the fee. Application must be made by letter or telephone call to the Mechanical Recording Department at the RCJ, who will release the tapes only to one of the official tape transcribers (a list of whom is available from the Mechanical Recording Department). The amount of the fee payable for transcription will depend on the nature and length of the hearing.

1C–180 **27.6 Fee for providing copies**

In certain circumstances parties and other persons can inspect the SCCO file of a case and obtain copies of any document thereon (see para 1.6, above). The court fee charged is £1 for the first page and 20p for each subsequent page. For electronic copies the charge is £3 per disk.

## SECTION 28

## REMUNERATION OF COURT APPOINTED OFFICE HOLDERS

1C–181 **28.1 Introduction**

(a) Trustees in Bankruptcy, Joint Provisional Receivers and Liquidators are frequently appointed by Judges of the Companies Court to manage or wind up bankrupt estates or insolvent companies. The remuneration of such Court appointed Office Holders is generally met out of the assets of the insolvent estate in question. The amount which they are entitled to charge is fixed by the Court taking into account factors set out in the Insolvency Rules 1986 (see rule 4.30 and 6.138). These include the complexity of the case and the value and nature of the property the Trustee, the Receiver or Liquidator has to deal with.

(b) Guidance about the evidence required to support claims by Office Holders for remuneration is given in *Mirror Group Newspapers v Maxwell* [1998] BCC 324, Ferris J. Assistance can also be found in the report of Mr Justice Ferris' Working Party on the Remuneration of Office Holders dated July 1998 (in particular paragraph 4.3, and Section 8). The Statement of Insolvency Practice 9 (SIP9) issued by the Society of Insolvency Practitioners (now called 3R) gives additional guidance, in particular paragraph 3. Costs are now likely to be assessed on the indemnity if requested following BAI (Run Off) Ltd (Neuberger LJ, July 5, 2004, unrep.). Attention is also drawn to the Insolvency Practice Statement – "The fixing and approval of the remuneration of appointees" (2004).

1C–182 **28.2 Reference to a Costs Judge for report**

(a) The costs involved in receiverships and liquidations can be large, sometimes exceeding £1,000,000. In cases where substantial sums are involved, Judges and Registrars of the Companies Court may refer any request for remuneration made by a Court Appointed Office Holder to a Costs Judge for a report.

(b) The Companies Court order will direct the Court Appointed Office Holder to lodge a duplicate bundle of the documents presented to the Judge or Registrar at the Costs Office. It will also require him to apply to the Costs Judge assigned to the matter for a directions hearing. At that hearing the Costs Judge will give directions for the filing of any further evidence or documents.

(c) When all relevant material has been lodged, the Costs Judge will prepare a report for the use of the Companies Court Judge or Registrar. This report contains recommendations about the level of remuneration to allow. These are not binding and the ultimate decision as to the amount of the Office Holders' remuneration is taken by the Judge or Registrar.

1C–183 **28.3 Applications for interim payments**

In long running liquidations and receiverships, Office Holders frequently apply for interim payments of remuneration. Such applications can be made informally to the Costs Judge to whom the matter has been assigned. He will then make a recommendation to the Companies Court about the level of interim remuneration to allow.

## SECTION 29

## JUSTICES OF THE PEACE, JUSTICES' CLERKS AND GENERAL COMMISSIONERS OF INCOME TAX

### 29.1 Introduction 1C–184

(a) This Section of the Guide deals with the determination of costs where the court has made an order that the Lord Chancellor pay the costs of proceedings under Section 53A of the Justices of the Peace Act 1997 ("Section 53A") or under Section 2A of the Taxes Management Act 1970 ("Section 2A"). The amount of costs payable by the Lord Chancellor will be determined in accordance with the Justices and Justices Clerks (Costs) Regulations 2001 (SI 2001 No.1296) or the General Commissioners of Income Tax (Costs) Regulations 2001 (SI 2001 No.1304), and not in accordance with the CPR 47.

(b) The costs payable by the Lord Chancellor under an order under Section 53A are the costs of proceedings in respect of any act or omission of a Justice of the Peace or a Justices' Clerk in the execution (or purported execution) of his duty—

(i) as a single Justice; or

(ii) as a Justices' Clerk exercising, by virtue of any statutory provision, any of the functions of a single Justice.

(c) The costs payable by the Lord Chancellor under an order made under Section 2A are the costs of proceedings in respect of any act or omission of a General Commissioner in the execution (or purported execution) of his duty as a General Commissioner.

(d) The court will normally, when making the order for costs, determine the amount it considers sufficient reasonably to compensate the receiving party for any costs properly incurred by him in the proceedings and specify that amount in the order.

(e) The court may direct that the amount of costs be determined by a Costs Judge, where the hearing has lasted more than one day, or there is insufficient time for the court to determine the costs on the day of the hearing, or the court considers that there is other good reason for the Costs Judge to determine the amount of the costs.

(f) A court which makes an order under Section 53A or Section 2A which determines the amount payable by the Lord Chancellor or which directs that the amount be determined by a Costs Judge, must serve that order on the receiving party and on the Lord Chancellor.

### 29.2 Time limit for proceedings in the SCCO 1C–185

(a) Where the court orders the costs to be determined by a Costs Judge the receiving party is required by the Regulations to file a claim for costs and a copy of the order in the SCCO and to serve a copy of the claim on the Lord Chancellor.

(b) The time for filing and serving such a claim is no later than three months from (but excluding) the date on which the order was made. The Costs Judge may on the application of the receiving party, in exceptional circumstances, extend the period of three months.

### 29.3 Form of application 1C–186

(a) A claim for costs to be determined by a Costs Judge following an order under Section 53A or Section 2A is made by a claim form to which CPR Part 8 applies (Form **N208**) accompanied by copies of:

(i) the order of the court giving the right to costs;

(ii) a statement signed by the receiving party or his solicitor giving the name, address for service, reference and telephone number and fax number, if any, of (a) the receiving party and (b) the Lord Chancellor;

(iii) copies of any orders made by the court relating to the costs of the proceedings which are to be determined;

(iv) any fee notes of counsel;

(v) receipts or accounts for other disbursements relating to items claimed; and,

(vi) the relevant papers in support of the costs claimed.

***Paragraph numbers marked with a "+" can be found online and on CD.***

(b) In respect of the costs claimed, the receiving party may either:

(i) file with the claim form a bill of costs, the form and layout of which is similar to the bills referred to in Section 3 above; or

(ii) set out in the claim form a summary of the items of work done by a legal representative, or the receiving party as a litigant in person, as appropriate; the dates on which items of work were done; the time taken; and the sums claimed. The claims form must specify any disbursements claimed, including counsel's fees; the circumstances in which they were incurred and the amounts claimed in respect of them.

(c) If the receiving party wishes to draw any special circumstances to the attention of the Costs Judge those circumstances must be specified in the bill or in the claim form.

(d) The current court fee payable in respect of determinations under these Regulations is £120.

**1C–187** **29.4 Service on the Lord Chancellor**

(a) Within three months from the date on which the order under Section 53A or Section 2A was made, the receiving party must serve a sealed copy of the claim form together with copies of:

(i) the order of the court giving the right to costs;

(ii) any bill of costs filed;

(iii) any fee notes of counsel;

(iv) receipts or accounts for other disbursements relating to items claimed.

(b) The procedure for service of the claim form is governed by RSC Order 77 rule 4 which is scheduled to the CPR.

**1C–188** **29.5 Written representations and replies**

(a) The Lord Chancellor may, if so advised, no later than one month from (but excluding) the date on which he received the claim from the receiving party, file written representations in respect of the claim, at the SCCO and at the same time serve a copy of them on the receiving party.

(b) Where the Lord Chancellor makes written representations the receiving party may, if so advised, file a reply at the SCCO within 21 days after service of the written representations on the receiving party. A copy of the reply must be served on the Lord Chancellor at the same time.

**1C–189** **29.6 Case management directions**

The Costs Judge may give directions in respect of:

(i) the claim;

(ii) any written representations or reply;

(iii) the filing and serving of any further particulars or documents; and,

(iv) to ensure that the determination of costs is dealt with justly.

**1C–190** **29.7 The determination**

(a) After receiving points of dispute and/or a reply, or after the time for filing such documents has expired, if earlier, the Costs Judge will provisionally determine the amount of costs without the attendance of either party unless—

(i) either party has required the court to fix a date for a hearing; or

(ii) the court considers that a hearing is necessary.

(b) After a provisional determination, the court will give both parties notice of the amount which the court proposes to allow.

(c) The court will fix a date for hearing if either party informs the court, within 14 days after receipt of notice of provisional determination, that he wants the court to hold a hearing.

(d) Where the court fixes a date for a determination hearing, it will give at least 14 days notice to each party of the place, date and time of the hearing.

**1C–191** **29.8 Costs of proceedings in the SCCO**

In respect of costs incurred in the SCCO CPR 44.3 gives the court a discretion as to whether the costs of the application are payable by one party to another, the amount of those costs and when they are to be paid.

**29.9 Result of the determination** **1C–192**

(a) On a provisional determination, or at a determination hearing, the court will note on the bill of costs or claim form all items allowed, disallowed or reduced.

(b) Once the determination has been concluded—

(i) if the receiving party is legally represented, the legal representative should within the next 14 days make clear to the court the correct figures agreed or allowed in respect of each item and should recalculate the amount to be allowed; or

(ii) if the receiving party is not legally represented, the Lord Chancellor should, within the next 14 days make clear to the court the correct figures agreed or allowed in respect of each item and should recalculate the amount to be allowed.

(c) On the completion of the determination the court will draw up an order specifying the amount payable by the Lord Chancellor under the order made under Section 53A or Section 2A and specify what if any order for the costs of the proceedings in the SCCO was made and (if appropriate) the amount of those costs.

**29.10 Appeals** **1C–193**

CPR Part 52 applies to any appeal brought in respect of proceedings to which this section applies. Information about appeals and the time limits which apply is given in Section 13, above.

## SECTION 30

## THE FINANCIAL SERVICES AND MARKETS ACT 2000

**30.1 Orders for costs between the parties** **1C–194**

(a) The Financial Services and Markets Act 2000, Section 132 provides for the establishment of the Financial Services and Markets Tribunal as part of the scheme for the regulation of financial services and markets. Schedule 13 to the Act empowers the Tribunal to order payment of costs in certain circumstances by one party to another in proceedings before the Tribunal.

(b) The Financial Services and Markets Tribunal Rules 2001 (S.I. 2001 No.2476) provide that where the Tribunal makes a costs order it may order that an amount fixed by the Tribunal shall be paid by one party to another, or that the costs shall be assessed on such basis as it may specify "by a costs official" (Rule 21(3)).

(c) Where an order for costs to be assessed is made by the Tribunal the costs will be assessed in the SCCO in accordance with the procedure set out in Sections 3 to 17 of this Guide (briefly, service of a bill plus notice of commencement and certain other documents, obtaining a default costs certificate, or, if points of dispute are served, serving a reply and/or filing a request for a detailed assessment hearing).

**30.2 Costs under the Financial Services and Markets Tribunal Legal Assistance Scheme** **1C–195**

(a) The Financial Services and Markets Tribunal (Legal Assistance) Regulations 2001 (S.I. 2001 No. 3632) and the Financial Services and Markets Tribunal (Legal Assistance) Scheme (Costs) Regulations 2001 (S.I. 2001 No. 3633) are long and detailed. The provisions are similar to but not the same as those governing the assessment of costs in criminal proceedings. This Guide contains the barest outline and should not be relied upon as a comprehensive version of the Regulations. Reference should therefore be made to the Regulations themselves.

(b) The Legal Assistance Regulations govern the provision of legal assistance in respect of matters which are referred to the Tribunal by individuals against whom the Financial Services Authority has decided to take action in respect of alleged market abuse. The Costs Regulations make provision for the remuneration of work done under a legal assistance order in respect of cases before the Tribunal. They make provision for interim and staged payments in long cases and also for hardship payments. The two Schedules to the Costs Regulations set out details of the fees in respect of solicitors and advocates which are payable.

**30.3 Claims for costs by solicitors** **1C–196**

(a) Solicitors are required to submit their claims for costs within three months of the conclusion of the proceedings to which the claim relates. The costs will be determined by a costs officer of the SCCO. The claim should be documented in the same way, as far as possible, as a claim to a Crown Court determining officer would be, in respect of costs payable under a criminal legal aid order.

(b) The classes of work in respect of which a claim for costs may be made are:

(i) preparation, including taking instructions, advising, interviewing witnesses, ascertaining the Authority's case, preparing and perusing documents, dealing with letters and telephone calls which are not routine, preparing the advocacy, instructing an advocate and expert witnesses, conferences and consultations;

(ii) advocacy;

(iii) attending at court where an advocate is assigned, including conferences with the advocate at court;

(iv) travelling and waiting; and

(v) dealing with routine letters written and routine telephone calls (Regulation 13(1)).

(c) Fees will be allowed, as appropriate, to the following grades of fee earner:

(i) senior solicitor;

(ii) solicitor, legal executive or fee earner of equivalent experience;

(iii) trainee or fee earner of equivalent experience (Regulation 13(6)).

1C–197 **30.4 Claims for fees by an advocate**

(a) An advocate wishing to claim fees in respect of work done under a legal assistance order must submit the claim within three months of the conclusion of the proceedings to which it relates. The costs claimed will be detemined by a costs officer of the SCCO. The claim should be documented in the same way, as far as possible, as a claim to a Crown Court determining officer would be, in respect of costs payable under a criminal legal aid order.

(b) The classes of fee which may be allowed are as follows:

(i) a basic fee for preparation, including preparation for any hearing before the main hearing, and, where appropriate, the first day of the main hearing including where they took place on that day, short conferences, consultations, applications and appearances and any other preparation;

(ii) a refresher fee for any day or part of a day during which a hearing continued, including, where it took place on that day, short conferences, consultations, applications and appearances, and any other preparation;

(iii) subsidiary fees for:

(a) attendance at conferences and consultations not covered by (a) or (b) above;

(b) written advices or other written work; and

(c) attendance at hearings before the main hearing, applications and appearances not covered by (a) or (b) above (Regulation 16(2)).

1C–198 **30.5 Interim payments, staged payments and hardship payments**

(a) The Financial Services and Markets Tribunal (Legal Assistance) Scheme (Costs) Regulations 2001, Regs 6, 8, 9 and 10 permit the making of applications to a costs officer in respect of the interim payment of disbursements already made, staged payments in long cases, interim payments in respect of attendances already made before the Tribunal and hardship payments in certain other circumstances. The application should be made in writing addressed to the principal costs officer and should be in a form similar to that used in similar applications to Crown Court determining officers.

(b) The procedures for redetermination, appeal and further appeal (see below) do not apply to decisions made by a costs officer concerning interim payments or staged payments.

(c) At the conclusion of a case in which an interim payment, staged payment or hardship payment has been allowed:

(i) the representative must submit a claim for the determination of his overall remuneration whether or not such a claim will result in any payment additional to those already made; and

(ii) the costs officer will take into account any payments already made when determining what, if any, further sum is payable to the representative, or, as the case may be, what, if any, sum should be repaid by him.

***Paragraph numbers marked with a "+" can be found online and on CD.***

**30.6 Redetermination of costs** **1C-199**

(a) Where a representative is dissatisfied with the costs which have been determined, application may be made for redetermination of the costs. The application must be made within 21 days of the receipt of notification of the costs payable. The application should be made in writing to the costs officer specifying the matters in respect of which the application is made and the grounds of objection.

(b) The form of application should be similar to the form of application for redetermination used in the Crown Courts and should be accompanied by the particulars, information and documents supplied in connection with the original claim and must also state whether the applicant wishes to appear or be represented. If the applicant does wish to appear or be represented the costs officer will notify the applicant of the time and date of hearing.

(c) Having considered the applicant's submissions the costs officer will redetermine the costs, whether by way of increase or decrease, and will notify the applicant of the decision. The applicant may then request in writing that the appropriate officer give reasons for his decision. Such a request must be made within 21 days of the receipt of the notification of the decision on redetermination (Regulation 19).

**30.7 Appeals to a Costs Judge** **1C-200**

(a) Where a costs officer has given reasons for the decision on determination and redetermination a representative who is dissatisfied with the decision may appeal to a Costs Judge. The appeal must be brought within 21 days of the receipt of the costs officer's reasons. The appeal is by notice in writing to the Senior Costs Judge in a similar form to that used in criminal fee appeals (see Appendix, para. A-9).

(b) The notice of appeal must specify separately:

(i) each item appealed against, showing, where appropriate, the amount claimed for the item;

(ii) the amount determined and the grounds of the objection to the determination; and

(iii) state whether the appellant wishes to appear or to be represented, or whether he will accept a decision given in his absence.

(c) The notice of appeal must be accompanied by:

(i) a copy of the written representations made to the costs officer on the application for redetermination;

(ii) the costs officer's reasons for his decision on redetermination; and

(iii) the particulars, information and documents supplied to the costs officer on redetermination.

(d) If so directed by the Lord Chancellor, or in any other case where it appears appropriate to do so, the Senior Costs Judge will send to the Lord Chancellor a copy of the notice of appeal together with the supporting documents. The Lord Chancellor may arrange for written or oral representations to be made on his behalf and if he intends to do so he will inform the Senior Costs Judge and the appellant. The appellant will be permitted a reasonable opportunity to make representations in reply.

**30.8 Conduct of the appeal** **1C-201**

(a) The Costs Judge will inform the interested parties of the date of any hearing and may give directions as to the conduct of the appeal.

(b) The Costs Judge may consult the Tribunal or the costs officer and may require the appellant to provide any further information which is required for the purpose of the appeal.

(c) Unless the Costs Judge otherwise directs no further evidence will be received on the hearing of the appeal and no ground of objection will be valid which was not raised on the application for redetermination.

(d) The Costs Judge has the same powers as the costs officer and may alter the redetermination of the costs officer in respect of any sum allowed, whether by increase or decrease as he thinks fit.

(e) The decision of the Costs Judge will be given to the interested parties and the costs officer in writing. Except where he confirms or decreases sums redetermined, the Costs Judge may allow the appellant a sum in respect of part or all of any reasonable costs incurred in connection with the appeal.

1C–202 **30.9 Further appeals to a High Court Judge**

(a) The decision of the Costs Judge on appeal is final unless the Costs Judge certifies a point of principle of general importance. A representative who is dissatisfied with the decision of the Costs Judge on appeal may apply for such a certificate. That application must be made within 21 days of the notification of the Costs Judge's decision on appeal. Where the Costs Judge certifies a point of principle of general importance the representative may appeal to the High Court against the decision of the Costs Judge and the Lord Chancellor must be made a respondent to such an appeal. The appeal must be brought within 21 days of receipt of the Costs Judges certificate.

(b) If the Lord Chancellor is dissatisfied with the decision of the Costs Judge on appeal he may, if no appeal has been made by the representative, appeal to the High Court against that decision.

(c) An appeal to the High Court must be brought in the Queen's Bench Division and follow the procedure set out in CPR Part 8. The appeal will be heard and determined by a Single Judge whose decision is final. The Judge has the same powers as the costs officer and the Costs Judge and may reverse, affirm or amend the decision appealed against or make such other order as he thinks fit.

1C–203 **30.10 Extension of time limits**

(a) All the time limits referred to may for good reason be extended by the costs officer, the Costs Judge or the High Court as appropriate.

(b) Where a representative, without good reason has failed to comply with the time limit, time may be extended in exceptional circumstances and in such circumstances the costs officer, Costs Judge or High Court Judge will consider whether it is reasonable in the circumstances to reduce the costs. The representative will be allowed a reasonable opportunity to show cause orally or in writing why the costs should not be reduced. A representative may appeal to a Costs Judge against a decision under these provisions made by a costs officer under the procedure described in para. 30.8, above.

## SECTION 31

## CRIMINAL FEE APPEALS

1C–204 **31.1 Introductory**

(a) Costs Judges have jurisdiction to hear appeals from the decisions of Determining Officers of the Crown Court, the Divisional Court of the Queen's Bench Division and the Court of Appeal (Criminal Division) in each of the following cases:

(i) Appeals by parties awarded costs out of Central Funds (as to which see the Costs in Criminal Cases (General) Regulations 1986.

(ii) Appeals by solicitors and counsel entitled to remuneration under the Legal Aid Act 1988 (as to which see the Legal Aid in Criminal and Care Proceedings (Costs) Regulations 1989).

(iii) Appeals by solicitors and counsel entitled to remuneration under the Access to Justice Act, 1999 and the Criminal Defence Service (Funding) Order 2001.

(iv) Appeals by solicitors and advocates entitled to remuneration under the Criminal Procedure Rules 2005 (formerly the Crown Court Rules 1982 Part IV).

(v) Appeals by litigants in person having the benefit of costs orders under any of the above enactments.

(b) All Costs Judges have been appointed Deputy Adjudicators to HM Land Registry for the purpose of assessing such costs.

1C–205 **31.2 The Criminal Costs Practice Direction**

Detailed guidance as to the SCCO practice on criminal fee appeals and the procedure on further appeals to a High Court Judge is set out in the *Practice Direction (Criminal Proceedings: Costs)* [2004] 1 WLR 2657; [2004] 2 All ER 1070; [2004] 2 Cr App R395 (the "Criminal Costs Practice Direction).

1C–206 **31.3 Nominated Masters**

At present there are five Costs Judges who deal with criminal fee appeals, namely Chief Master Hurst (Senior Costs Judge), Master Rogers, Master Campbell, Master Simons and Master Gordon-Saker.

***Paragraph numbers marked with a "+" can be found online and on CD.***

**31.4 The Notice of Appeal** 1C-207

(a) The Notice of Appeal must be in writing and must be lodged with the Clerk of Appeals, together with the fee (currently £100) and the additional material referred to in the Criminal Costs Practice Direction within 21 days of receipt of the reasons given for the decision or within such longer time as the Costs Judge may direct; (under the Criminal Procedure Rules 2005 the period is 14 days). Papers are lodged with the Clerk of Appeals in Room 2.14.

(b) The Notice of Appeal should follow the Form A in Schedule 3 to the Criminal Costs Practice Direction and illustrated in the Appendix (para A-9, below). It is important that the Notice of Appeal should clearly identify (i) the matters which are being appealed to the Costs Judge and (ii) the amount in dispute in relation to each item.

(c) Notices of Appeal must be signed by advocates personally or by a partner in the appellant firm of Solicitors.

(d) It occasionally happens that appellants fail to serve the Determining Officer with a copy of the Notice of Appeal. The Regulations are mandatory in this respect and failure to do so may result in the appeal being dismissed without the merits being considered.

**31.5 The Grounds of Appeal** 1C-208

(a) The Grounds of Appeal should correspond with the Notice of Appeal. Points raised in the Notice of Appeal which are not supported by grounds may be dismissed and conversely matters included in the Grounds of Appeal which are not mentioned in the Notice of Appeal may not be separately decided.

(b) The Grounds of Appeal are an integral part of the Notice of Appeal and should be submitted at the same time. If for some reason the Grounds of Appeal cannot be prepared within the time allowed for lodging Notice of Appeal an application for an extension of time should be made.

(c) It is important to be both concise and specific in the Grounds of Appeal. Particular attention should be paid to the provisions of the Criminal Costs Practice Direction.

(d) Uncertified decisions of Costs Judges are not binding on Costs Judges or Determining Officers and will rarely if ever be of any assistance.

(e) Only in exceptional cases will a Costs Judge consider material not before the Determining Officer (leave is required in Schedule 1 to the 2001 Funding Order para 21(11) of Reg. 15(11) of the 1989 Regs; Reg. 9(11) of the 1986 Regs) or Reg 78.5(5) of the Criminal Procedure Rules 2005. Requests to consider such material should always be included in the Notice of Appeal.

**31.6 Supplementary Grounds of Appeal** 1C-209

Occasionally the Determining Officer does not give written Reasons in respect of all matters upon which the appellant wishes to bring before the Costs Judge. In that situation, provided the appellant has raised them at the re-determination stage, and in his/her request for written Reasons, the appellant should ask the Determining Officer for supplementary written Reasons and may then lodge supplementary Grounds of Appeal.

**31.7 Lodging of documents in support of appeal** 1C-210

(a) It frequently happens that far more material is lodged in support of the appeal than is either necessary or desirable. For instance in a case of a multi-handed appeal by a number of Counsel it is not normally necessary to lodge more than one set of depositions etc. Liaison between appellants is important.

(b) Before lodging substantial volumes of papers it is advisable to contact the Clerk of Appeals who will if necessary liaise with the Costs Judge as to what documents are required.

(c) The relevant documents should be lodged no more than 10 days prior to an oral hearing. In the case of appeals to be dealt with on paper only and without an attendance, all relevant papers should be lodged with the Notice and Grounds of Appeal.

**31.8 Appeals on paper only** 1C-211

(a) Appeals made on paper only and without an attendance may be dealt with more quickly than appeals dealt with by way of a hearing. All appellants should give careful

*Paragraph numbers marked with a "+" can be found online and on CD.*

consideration, at the stage of lodging their appeals, to the question of whether or not they consider it necessary to attend.

(b) An appellant seeking the costs of an appeal to be dealt with on paper only, should specify the particular sum claimed in a document accompanying the Grounds of Appeal or in a covering letter. If no sum is claimed, the Master will normally only order refund of the appeal fee paid.

**1C-212** **31.9 The hearing of an appeal**

All hearings may be attended by the counsel or representatives of the solicitors concerned in the matter or a duly authorised agent on their behalf, who may include another solicitor, another counsel or a costs draftsperson. Such oral hearings are informal and conducted in private. They are seldom of lengthy duration but where an appellant considers that an unusually lengthy hearing is necessary this should be indicated in a covering letter with the Notice and Grounds of Appeal.

**1C-213** **31.10 Multi-handed appeals**

Wherever possible appeals in relation to the same case by all or many of the advocates and/or solicitors concerned are listed together or at short consecutive intervals on the same day. Where this presents problems to individual appellants, representations should be made to the Clerk of Appeals who will consult the Costs Judge as to whether an exception can be made to this general rule. It may however be possible to hear all the appeals of advocates in one particular case on the same day and all the appeals of solicitors in relation to the same case on another day.

**1C-214** **31.11 Appeals by same advocate**

Where counsel, particularly from out of London, have a number of separate appeals every effort will be made to list these together to avoid unnecessary journeys.

**1C-215** **31.12 Appeals by telephone or video link**

All Costs Judges are prepared to hear criminal appeals by telephone or video link, especially where the sums involved are small or disproportionate to the costs of travel to London. Requests for any such hearing should be made to the Clerk of Appeals when lodging the appeal. Telephone appeals can usually be listed quite quickly but video appeals take longer because of pressure on the limited video facilities in the RCJ.

**1C-216** **31.13 Procedure subsequent to the appeal**

(a) In every case the Regulations require that the Master should give his reasons in writing. There is inevitably a time lag between the oral hearing and the despatch of the written Reasons. Only rarely will the Costs Judge consider material submitted after the hearing.

(b) A successful appellant is entitled to ask for his costs which are normally assessed by the Costs Judge at the end of the hearing. It is important that any appellant should submit details to the Costs Judge at the hearing of travelling expenses or any unusual expenditure in relation to the appeal.

(c) In all cases where an appeal is successful the court fee paid (currently £100) is added to the sums allowed, unless the Costs Judge otherwise directs.

**1C-217** **31.14 Further appeal**

(a) The Department of Constitutional Affairs has an independent right of appeal against any decisions adverse to the LSC Fund or Central Funds and in those cases no leave from the Costs Judge is required.

(b) In other cases, whether Central Funds or LSC funded cases, a further, and final, appeal is possible where the Costs Judge has certified that a point of principle of general importance is involved. It is necessary to apply within 21 days of receipt of the Master's written Reasons (14 days in the case of proposed appeals under the Criminal Procedure Rules 2005) for a certificate to be granted by the Costs Judge and, in accordance with the Criminal Costs Practice Direction, the form of certificate sought should wherever possible be submitted with the application.

(c) If the Costs Judge grants a certificate, the appeal lies to a Judge of the High Court, Queen's Bench Division who will normally sit with two assessors one of whom will be another Costs Judge.

(d) If the Costs Judge refuses a certificate no further appeal is possible.

(e) The decision of the High Court Judge is final, and no further appeal is permitted.

**31.15 Time limits** **1C–218**

(a) The time limits laid down by the Regulations and the Practice Direction should always be complied with. It is not a sufficient reason for granting an extension of time that the Determining Officer has taken many months to produce his or her Written Reasons which are being appealed to the Costs Judge. Further it is not sufficient to justify an extension of time that all the papers needed to support the appeal are not immediately available.

(b) It not infrequently happens particularly at Christmas, Easter and holiday times that it is difficult to comply with the strict 21 day time limit (14 days in the case of Criminal Procedure Rules 2005 appeals) laid down in the Regulations. In those situations, an appellant should always apply before the relevant time limit expires seeking a short extension and giving grounds in support of that application.

(c) Where the 21/14 day time limit has expired an application for leave to appeal out of time should be mounted at the first possible opportunity thereafter and should initially be submitted in writing. The letter should always be signed by the appellant, not by his clerk, or another solicitor within his office. It should give a full explanation for the delay and justification advanced for granting leave out of time.

(d) Such applications are in the first instance dealt with by one of the Costs Judges on the papers. Where such an application is refused the appellant may renew his application by asking for an oral hearing before the Costs Judge. Permission is sometimes granted subject to a percentage penalty reducing the amount of any increase in costs which would otherwise have been obtained on the appeal.

(e) Where such oral hearings take place the Costs Judge will try to dispose of the substantive appeal immediately after the leave application. Those attending such applications should come prepared to address the merits of the substantive appeal, having lodged all the relevant papers. An additional fee of £100 is payable, where such leave is granted.



**31.16 Divisional Court/Administrative Court central funds assessments** **1C–219**

All such determinations are currently dealt with by Costs Judge Rogers. He is treated as the Determining Officer in accordance with the 1986 Regulations. A dissatisfied party may ask him to redetermine those costs and thereafter to give his written reasons. Any party still dissatisfied may then appeal to the Senior Costs Judge who will follow the same procedure as in an appeal from a Determining Officer in the Crown Court or Court of Appeal.

## SECTION 32

## CIVIL RECOVERY PROCEEDINGS UNDER THE PROCEEDS OF CRIME ACT 2002

**32.1 Introductory** **1C–220**

(a) The Proceeds of Crime Act 2002 makes provision for the confiscation of the assets of persons convicted of criminal offences and, in certain circumstances, of those "tainted" by criminality. Where the Director of the Assets Recovery Agency is empowered to bring proceedings for a recovery order under the Act he may also apply to the High Court for a property freezing order or an interim receiving order which prohibits any person, to whose property the order applies, from dealing with that property. The court may make exclusions from that prohibition for certain purposes including the meeting of reasonable legal expenses.

(b) The Proceeds of Crime Act 2002 and the Regulations made thereunder make special provision for two types of proceedings in the SCCO:—

(i) during civil recovery proceedings, referrals to determine the amount which exclusions should allow for reasonable legal costs: and

***Paragraph numbers marked with a "+" can be found online and on CD.***

(ii) at the conclusion of civil recovery proceedings, the assessment of any person's reasonable legal expenses in those proceedings where the court has made a recovery order which provides for the payment of those expenses.

(c) The Proceeds of Crime Act 2002 (Legal Expenses in Civil Recovery Proceedings) Regulations 2005 (SI 2005/3382) specify the hourly rates of remuneration which may be allowed in respect of work done by legal representatives. Higher rates may be allowed for cases involving substantial, novel or complex issues of law or fact and the rates are increase for legal representatives whose offices are situated in certain London post code areas and districts.

**1C–221** **32.2 Exclusions to meet reasonable legal expenses**

(a) Where the court makes a property freezing order, or an interim receiving order, on an application without notice it will normally make an exclusion from the order to enable the respondent to meet his reasonable legal costs of taking advice in relation to the order, preparing a statement of assets and, if so advised, apply for the order to be set aside or varied. The initial exclusion will not normally exceed £3,000.

(b) When the court makes a property freezing order or an interim receiving order before a claim for a recovery order has been commenced, the court may also make an exclusion to enable the respondent to meet his reasonable legal costs, so that, when the claim is commenced, he may file an acknowledgment of service and any written evidence on which he intends to rely, or may apply for a further exclusion for the purpose of enabling him to meet his reasonable costs of the proceedings.

(c) Save as mentioned below, when the court makes an order or gives directions in civil recovery proceedings it will at the same time consider whether it is appropriate to make or vary an exclusion for the purpose of enabling any person affected by the order or directions to meet his reasonable legal costs. However, in order to obtain an exclusion going beyond the preliminary steps mentioned in sub paragraphs (a) and (b) above the person whose costs are to be provided for must make and file a statement of assets.

(d) The court will normally refer to a Costs Judge any question relating to the amount which an exclusion should allow for reasonable legal costs in respect of proceedings or a stage in the proceedings.

(e) An exclusion made for the purpose of enabling a person to meet his reasonable legal costs will specify:

(i) the stage or stages of civil recovery proceedings to which it relates;

(ii) the maximum amount which may be released in respect of legal costs for each specified stage; and

(iii) the total amount which may be released in respect of legal costs pursuant to the exclusion.

(f) Once expenses provided for by an exclusion have been incurred a person may seek the Director's agreement to the release of an interim payment in respect of those expenses. The amount which may be released is the amount which the Director agrees, or 65% of the amount claimed, whichever is the greater.

(g) If a person becomes aware that his legal costs have exceeded or will exceed the maximum amount allowed for a specified stage, or the total amount allowed for all stages, he should apply for a further exclusion or for a variation in the existing exclusion as soon as reasonably practicable.

**1C–222** **32.3 Procedure on referrals relating to exclusions**

(a) Where a matter has been referred to a Costs Judge, either party may make an application to the SCCO on Form N244 accompanied by a copy of the relevant order, copies of any evidence relied on in support and a statement of parties.

(b) If the application is made by the person whose reasonable legal costs are to be provided for:

(i) the evidence in support should include an estimate of costs substantially in the form illustrated in Precedent H in the Schedule of Costs Precedents annexed to the Costs Practice Direction; and

(ii) when fixing the date for hearing the Costs Judge will also give a direction as to the filing and service of any points of dispute on the estimated costs.

(c) A specimen form of order for directions on applications made by a person whose costs are to be provided for is included in the Appendix, below, para A-11.

(d) On receipt of an application the SCCO will endeavour to list it for a date for hearing not less than 14 days after nor more than 42 days after the date of issue. The party making the application should specify his preferred dates for hearing in that period. Ideally, he should specify at least one day in each week of that period.

**32.4 Assessment of costs following a recovery order** **1C–223**

(a) The Regulations set out the procedure for determining the amount payable in respect of legal expenses once the High Court has made a recovery order which vests property in the trustee for civil recovery and provides for the payment of those expenses out of that property. The Regulations also specify the hourly rates of remuneration which may be allowed in respect of work done by legal representatives.

(b) The amount of costs provided for by a recovery order may be agreed with the Director of the Assets Recovery Agency. In such a case the Director will give notice of the agreed sum to the person seeking costs and to the trustee for civil recovery.

(c) If the legal expenses are not agreed with the Director, the person seeking them must commence detailed assessment proceedings in accordance with CPR Part 47. Generally speaking the procedure is as set out in Sections 3 to 17 of this Guide (briefly, service of a bill plus notice of commencement and certain other documents, obtaining a default costs certificate or, if points of dispute are served, serving a reply and/or filing a request for a detailed assessment hearing).

(d) The notice of commencement plus other documents must be served not later than two months after the date of the recovery order.

(e) Unless the costs are subsequently agreed or unless a default costs certificate is obtained, a request for a detailed assessment hearing must be filed in the SCCO not later than two months after the expiration of the period for commencing the detailed assessment proceedings.

(f) Further details of the procedure to be followed are set out in Section 49A of the Costs Practice Direction. Notice in particular:

(i) the paying party is the trustee for civil recovery;

(ii) the notice of commencement must also be served on the Director of the Assets Recovery Agency;

(iii) in addition to the documents usually served with a notice of commencement (as to which, see para 4.4(b) of this Guide) the receiving party must also serve a statement giving the date, amount and source of all interim payments which have been released in respect of the costs in question;

(iv) in addition to the documents usually filed with a request for a detailed assessment hearing (as to which, see para 8.2(a) of this Guide) the receiving party must also file copies of all exclusions from property freezing orders or interim receiving orders which relate to the costs to be assessed and copies of every estimate of costs filed by the receiving party in support of an application for such an exclusion; and

(v) the costs will be assessed on the standard basis, subject to the Regulations specifying the hourly rates which may be allowed.

(g) If the sum payable in respect of a person's legal expenses exceeds the total amount which has been released in respect of those expenses, the trustee for civil recovery must pay the balance out of the assets recovered.

(h) The trustee for civil recovery may only make a payment in respect of a person's legal expenses to the solicitor who is instructed to act for that person or, where appropriate, to the solicitor who was so instructed when the legal expenses to which the sum relates were incurred.

(i) If the sum payable in respect of a person's legal expenses is less than the total amount which has been released in respect of those expenses, the person to whose expenses the sum relates must repay the balance to the trustee.

## SECTION 33

## COSTS ORDERS MADE BY THE ADJUDICATOR TO HM LAND REGISTRY

**33.1 Introductory** **1C–224**

(a) The Adjudicator to HM Land Registry (Practice and Procedure Rules) 2003 SI No.2003/2171 contains provisions about the making of orders for costs and the basis of

***Paragraph numbers marked with a "+" can be found online and on CD.***

assessment (standard or indemnity) and provides that the order may specify the amount of costs or, alternatively, may award "costs to be assessed".

(b) All Costs Judges have been appointed Deputy Adjudicators to HM Land Registry.

1C–225 **33.2 Assessments referred to the SCCO**

(a) The remaining paragraphs of this section set out the procedure to be followed where a party is awarded costs by an order of the Adjudicator to HM Land Registry and the order directs that that party may apply to the SCCO for assessment.

(b) On receiving the file from HM Land Registry the Costs Judge will issue standard directions with regard to the service and filing of Points of Dispute and the consequences of failing to do so.

(c) Either party may apply to the Costs Judge for further direction. If points of dispute have already been served (whether by order or voluntarily) the receiving party may file a *request for a detailed assessment hearing*. Such applications or requests are not governed by the CPR and, at present, no court fees are payable.

1C–226 **33.3 Applications for directions**

(a) The form of application should be similar to the form used in applications governed by the CPR, ie, Form **N244**, and should be accompanied by:

(i) a copy of the order for costs made by the Adjudicator,

(ii) a copy of the bill served pursuant to that order, and

(iii) a statement of parties.

(b) The application will normally be dealt with without a hearing.

(c) Two standards forms of order are illustrated in the appendix below, para A-12:—

(i) an order giving the defendant notice to show cause why the bill of costs should not be assessed as drawn because of his failure to comply with a direction by the Adjudicator to serve points of dispute;

(ii) directions for the service of points of dispute and (if the claimant so wishes) for the service of a reply. This form will also state the provisional date for a hearing if points of dispute are served and, if they are not, states that the claimant will be entitled to obtain an assessment of his bill as drawn.

1C–227 **33.4 Request for a detailed assessment hearing**

(a) The form of request should be similar to the form used in most cases governed by the CPR, ie, Form **N258**. This form contains a series of tick boxes which give guidance as to the documents which should accompany the request.

(b) On receipt of the request the court will fix a date for the hearing or, if the Costs Judge so decides, will give directions or fix a date a date for a preliminary appointment.

(c) The court will give at least 14 days notice of the time and place of the detailed assessment hearing to every person whose name and address appears on the statement of parties.

(d) On completion of the detailed assessment, the form of Order made is shown on A-13.

## SECTION 34

## SCCO CONSULTATION GROUPS

1C–228 **34.1 Costs Practitioners Group**

(a) This advisory group (formerly known as the Taxation Users Group) is run under the auspices of the SCCO. Two Costs Judges are members, one of whom acts as Chairman. The current Chairman is Master O'Hare. The Senior Costs Judge sometimes attends as does the Principal Costs Officer. The Council of Circuit Judges, The District Judges Association, the Bar Council, The Law Society, The London Solicitors Litigation Association, The Association of Personal Injury Lawyers (APIL), The Forum of Insurance Lawyers (FOIL) and the Association of Law Costs Draftsmen are all represented.

(b) The group generally meets twice a year in the SCCO, its function being to comment upon and make recommendations for the improvement of the current and evolving practice of assessment of costs. Although it is an advisory group, as it consists of representatives of all the principal "users" it is intended to be influential and to afford a regular opportunity for informal exchanges of views on existing practice and how the same can be improved. Minutes are taken and circulated.

(c) Organisations and bodies wishing to apply for membership of the Costs Practitioners Group should write to its Chairman, c/o the SCCO.

**34.2 SCCO Users Group** **1C–229**

(a) This Group, which is organised by the SCCO Court Manager, is open to any court user who wishes to attend. Meetings are held about three times each year, the dates of meetings being shown on the Customer Services Notice Board in Room 1.02. Persons stating their intention to attend the next meeting will later receive an invitation to contribute agenda items for that meeting.

(b) The main objective of the Group is to enable the SCCO to explain the services it provides and the standards of service it seeks to achieve. Commonly arising issues include statistics about waiting lists for hearings and turn around times for the issue of certificates.

(c) Meetings are usually attended by the Principal Costs Officer, the Court Manager, the Customer Services Manager and representatives from the Association of Law Costs Draftsmen, the Citizens Advice Bureau, the Law Society and the Legal Services Commission plus several members of the public. Minutes are taken and circulated.

## APPENDIX

## SOME STANDARD FORMS AND PRECEDENTS

**1C–230**

SCHEDULE OF COSTS PRECEDENTS
PRECEDENT A

IN THE HIGH COURT OF JUSTICE 2000 - B - 9999

QUEEN'S BENCH DIVISION

BRIGHTON DISTRICT REGISTRY

BETWEEN

AB Claimant

- and -

CD Defendant

**CLAIMANT'S BILL OF COSTS TO BE ASSESSED PURSUANT TO THE ORDER DATED 26th JULY 2000**

V.A.T. No. 33 4404 90

In these proceedings the claimant sought compensation for personal injuries and other losses suffered in a road accident which occurred on Friday 1st January 1999 near the junction between Bolingbroke Lane and Regency Road, Brighton, East Sussex. The claimant had been travelling as a front seat passenger in a car driven by the defendant. The claimant suffered severe injuries when, because of the defendant's negligence, the car left the road and collided with a brick wall.

The defendant was later convicted of various offences arising out of the accident including careless driving and driving under the influence of drink or drugs.

In the civil action the defendant alleged that immediately before the car journey began the claimant had known that the defendant was under the influence of alcohol and therefore consented to the risk of injury or was contributorily negligent as to it. It was also alleged that, immediately before the accident occurred, the claimant wrongfully took control of the steering wheel so causing the accident to occur.

The claimant first instructed solicitors, E F & Co, in this matter in July 2000. The claim form was issued in October 2000 and in February 2001 the proceedings were listed for a two day trial commencing 25th July 2001. At the trial the defendant was found liable but the compensation was reduced by 25% to take account of contributory negligence by the claimant. The claimant was awarded a total of £78,256.83 plus £1,207.16 interest plus costs.

The claimant instructed E F & Co under a conditional fee agreement dated 8th July 2000 which specifies the following base fees and success fees.

Partner - £180 per hour plus VAT
Assistant Solicitor - £140 per hour plus VAT
Other fee earners - £85 per hour plus VAT
Success fees exclusive of disbursement funding costs: 40%
Success fee in respect of disbursement funding costs: 7.5% (not claimed in this bill)

Except where the contrary is stated the proceedings were conducted on behalf of the claimant by an assistant solicitor, admitted November 1999.

E F & Co instructed Counsel (Miss GH, called 1992) under a conditional fee agreement dated 5th June 2001 which specifies a success fee of 75% and base fees, payable in various circumstances, of which the following are relevant

Fees for interim hearing whose estimated duration is up to 2 hours: £600
Brief for trial whose estimated duration is 2 days: £2,000
Fee for second and subsequent days: £650 per day

SCCO GUIDE

| Item No. | Description of work done | V.A.T. | Disburse -ments | Profit Costs |
|---|---|---|---|---|
| | 8th July 2000 - EF & Co instructed | | | |
| | 22nd July 2000 - AEI with Eastbird Legal Protection Ltd | | | |
| 1 | Premium for policy | - | £ 120.00 | |
| | 7th October 2000 - Claim issued | | | |
| 2 | Issue fee | - | £ 400.00 | |
| | 21st October 2000 - Particulars of claim served | | | |
| | 25th November 2000 - Time for service of defence extended by agreement to 14th January 2001 | | | |
| 3 | Fee on allocation | - | £ 80.00 | |
| | 20th January 2001 - case allocated to multi-track | | | |
| | 9th February 2001 - Case management conference at which costs were awarded to the claimant and the base costs were summarily assessed at £400 (paid on 24th February 2001) | | | |
| | 23rd February 2001 - Claimant's list of documents | | | |
| | 12th April 2001 - Payment into court of £25,126.33 | | | |
| | 13th April 2001 - Filing pre-trial checklist | | | |
| 4 | Fee on listing | - | £ 400.00 | |
| | 28th June 2001 - Pre trial review: costs in case<br>Engaged 1.5 hours £210.00<br>Travel and waiting 2.00 hours £280.00 | | | |
| 5 | Total solicitor's base fee for attending | | | £ 490.00 |
| 6 | Counsel's base fee for pre trial review (Miss GH) | | £ 600.00 | |
| | 25th July 2001 - Attending first day of trial: adjourned part heard<br>Engaged in Court 5.00 hours £700.00<br>Engaged in conference 0.75 hours £105.00<br>Travel and waiting 1.5 hours £210.00 | | | |
| 7 | Total solicitor's base fee for attending | | | £1,015.00 |
| 8 | Counsel's base fee for trial (Miss GH) | | £2,000.00 | |
| 9 | Fee of expert witness (Dr. IJ) | - | £ 850.00 | |
| 10 | Expenses of witnesses of fact | - | £ 84.00 | |
| | 26th July 2001 - Attending second day of trial when judgment was given for the claimant in the sum of £78,256.53 plus £1207.16 interest plus costs<br>Engaged in Court 3.00 hours £420.00<br>Engaged in conference 1.5 hours £210.00<br>Travel and waiting 1.5 hours £210.00 | | | |
| 11 | Total solicitor's base fee for attending | | | £ 840.00 |
| 12 | Counsel's base fee for second day (Miss GH) | | £ 650.00 | |
| | To Summary | £ - | £5,184.00 | £2,345.00 |

*Paragraph numbers marked with a "+" can be found online and on CD.*

| Item No. | Description of work done | V.A.T. | Disburse -ments | Profit Costs |
|---|---|---|---|---|
| | **Claimant** | | | |
| 13 | 8th July 2000 - First instructions: 0.75 hours by Partner: base fee | | | £ 135.00 |
| | Other timed attendances in person and by telephone - See Schedule 1 | | | |
| 14 | Total base fee for Schedule 1 - 7.5 hours | | | £1,050.00 |
| 15 | Routine letters out and telephone calls - 29 (17 + 12) total base fee | | | £ 406.00 |
| | **Witnesses of Fact** | | | |
| | Timed attendances in person, by letter out and by telephone - See Schedule 2 | | | |
| 16 | Total base fee for Schedule 2 - 5.2 hours | | | £ 728.00 |
| 17 | Routine letters out, e mails and telephone calls - 8 (4 + 2 + 2 )total base fee | | | £ 112.00 |
| 18 | Paid travelling on 9th October 2000 | £ 4.02 | £ 22.96 | |
| | **Medical expert (Dr. IJ)** | | | |
| 19 | 11th September 2000 - long letter out 0.33 hours: base fee | | | £ 46.20 |
| 20 | 30th January 2001 - long letter out 0.25 hours base fee | | | £ 35.00 |
| 21 | 23rd May 2001 - telephone call 0.2 hours base fee | | | £ 28.00 |
| 22 | Routine letters out and telephone calls - 10 (6 + 4) total base fee | | | £ 140.00 |
| 23 | Dr. IJ's fee for report | - | £ 350.00 | |
| | **Defendant and his solicitor** | | | |
| 24 | 8th July 2000 - timed letter sent 0.5 hours: base fee | | | £ 70.00 |
| 25 | 19th February 2001 - telephone call 0.25 hours: base fee | | | £ 35.00 |
| 26 | Routine letters out and telephone calls - 24 (18 + 6) total base fee | | | £ 336.00 |
| | **Communications with the court** | | | |
| 27 | Routine letters out and telephone calls - 9 (8 + 1) total base fee | | | £ 126.00 |
| | **Communications with Counsel** | | | |
| 28 | Routine letters out, e mails and telephone calls - 19 (4 + 7 + 8) total base fee | | | £ 266.00 |
| | **Work done on documents** | | | |
| | Timed attendances - See Schedule 3 | | | |
| 29 | Total base fees for Schedule 3 - 0.75 hours at £180, 44.5 hours at £140, 12 hours at £85 | | | £7,385.00 |
| | **Work done on negotiations** | | | |
| | 23rd March 2001 - meeting at offices of Solicitors for the Defendant | | | |
| | Engaged - 1.5 hours £210.00 | | | |
| | Travel and waiting - 1.25 hours £175.00 | | | |
| 30 | Total base fee for meeting | | | £ 385.00 |
| | **Other work done** | | | |
| | Preparing and checking bill | | | |
| | Engaged: Solicitor - 1 hour £140.00 | | | |
| | Engaged: Costs Draftsman - 4 hours £340.00 | | | |
| 31 | Total base fee on other work done | | | £ 480.00 |
| | To Summary | £ 4.02 | £ 372.96 | £11,763.20 |

SCCO GUIDE

*Paragraph numbers marked with a "+" can be found online and on CD.*

| Item No. | Description of work done | V.A.T. | Disburse -ments | Profit Costs |
|---|---|---|---|---|
| 32 | Success fee on solicitor's base fee on interim orders which were summarily assessed (40% of £400) plus VAT at 17.5% | £ 28.00 | | £ 160.00 |
| 33 | VAT on solicitor's other base fees (17.5% of £14,108.20) | £ 2,468.94 | | |
| 34 | Success fee on solicitor's other base fees (40% of £14,108.20) plus VAT at 17.5% | £ 987.58 | | £5,643.28 |
| 35 | VAT on Counsel's base fees (17.5% of £3,250)' | £ 568.75 | | |
| 36 | Success fee on Counsel's base fee (75% of £3,250) plus VAT at 17.5%' | £ 426.57 | £ 2,437.50 | |
| | To Summary | £ 4,479.84 | £ 2,437.50 | £ 5,803.28 |
| | **SUMMARY** | | | |
| | Page 3 £ | - | £ 5,184.00 | £ 2,345.00 |
| | Page 4 £ | 4.02 | £ 372.96 | £ 11,763.20 |
| | Page 5 £ | 4,479.84 | £2,437.50 | £ 5,803.28 |
| | Totals: | £ 4,483.86 | £ 7,994.46 | £ 19,911.48 |
| | Grand total: | | | £ 32,389.80 |

## A-2 Certificates in bills : Schedule of Costs Precedents, Precedent F

- Appropriate certificates under headings (1) and (2) are required in all cases. The appropriate certificate under (3) is required in all cases in which the receiving party is an assisted person or a LSC funded client. Certificates (4), (5) and (6) are optional. Certificate (6) may be included in the bill, or, if the dispute as to VAT recoverability arises after service of the bill, may be filed and served as a supplementary document amending the bill under paragraph 39.10 of this Practice Direction.

- All certificates must be signed by the receiving party or by his solicitor. Where the bill claims costs in respect of work done by more than one firm of solicitors, certificate (1), appropriately completed, should be signed on behalf of each firm.

**(1) CERTIFICATE AS TO ACCURACY**

I certify that this bill is both accurate and complete [ and ]

*(where the receiving party was funded by legal aid/LSC)*
☐ [in respect of Part(s) ..... of the bill] all the work claimed was done pursuant to a certificate issued by the Legal Aid Board/ Legal Services Commission granted to [the assisted person] [the LSC funded client].

*(where costs are claimed for work done by an employed solicitor)*
☐ [in respect of Part(s) .... of the bill] the case was conducted by a solicitor who is an employee of the receiving party.

*(other cases where costs are claimed for work done by a solicitor)*
☐ [in respect of Part(s) ..... of the bill] the costs claimed herein do not exceed the costs which the receiving party is required to pay me/my firm.

SCCO GUIDE

*Paragraph numbers marked with a "+" can be found online and on CD.*

**(2) CERTIFICATE AS TO INTEREST AND PAYMENTS**

I certify that:

☐ No rulings have been made in this case which affects my/the receiving party's entitlement (if any) to interest on costs.

or

☐ The only rulings made in this case as to interest are as follows:
*[give brief details as to the date of each ruling, the name of the Judge who made it and the text of the ruling]*

and

☐ No payments have been made by any paying party on account of costs included in this bill of costs.

or

☐ The following payments have been made on account of costs included in this bill of costs:
*[give brief details of the amounts, the dates of payment and the name of the person by or on whose behalf they were paid]*

**(3) CERTIFICATE AS TO INTEREST OF ASSISTED PERSON/ LSC FUNDED CLIENT PURSUANT TO REGULATION 119 OF THE CIVIL LEGAL AID (GENERAL) REGULATIONS 1989**

I certify that the assisted person/ LSC funded client has no financial interest in the detailed assessment.

or

I certify that a copy of this bill has been sent to the assisted person/ LSC funded client pursuant to Regulation 119 of the Civil Legal Aid General Regulations 1989 with an explanation of his/her interest in the detailed assessment and the steps which can be taken to safeguard that interest in the assessment. He/she has/has not requested that the costs officer be informed of his/her interest and has/has not requested that notice of the detailed assessment hearing be sent to him/her.

**(4) CONSENT TO THE SIGNING OF THE CERTIFICATE WITHIN 21 DAYS OF DETAILED ASSESSMENT PURSUANT TO REGULATION 112 AND 121 OF THE CIVIL LEGAL AID (GENERAL) REGULATIONS 1989**

I certify that notice of the fees reduced or disallowed on detailed assessment has been given in writing to counsel on [ date ].

or

I certify that: there having been no reduction or disallowance of counsel's fees it is not necessary to give notice to counsel.

I/we consent to the final costs certificate being issued immediately.

**(5) CERTIFICATE IN RESPECT OF DISBURSEMENTS NOT EXCEEDING £500**

I hereby certify that all disbursements listed in this bill which individually do not exceed £500 (other than those relating to counsel's fees) have been duly discharged.

**(6) CERTIFICATE AS TO RECOVERY OF VAT**

With reference to the pending assessment of the [claimant's/defendant's] costs and disbursements herein which are payable by the [claimant/defendant] we the undersigned [solicitors to] [auditors of] the [claimant/defendant] hereby certify that the [claimant/defendant] on the basis of its last completed VAT return [would/would not be entitled to recover would/be entitled to recover only percent of the] Value Added Tax on such costs and disbursements, as input tax pursuant to Section 14 of the Value Added Tax Act 1983.

**A-3 Points of dispute :** Schedule of Costs Precedents, Precedent G

IN THE HIGH COURT OF JUSTICE 2000 B 9999

QUEEN'S BENCH DIVISION

BRIGHTON DISTRICT REGISTRY

B E T W E E N

AB

Claimant

- and -

CD

Defendant

**POINTS OF DISPUTE SERVED BY THE DEFENDANT**

| Item | Dispute | Claimant's Comments |
|---|---|---|
| General point | Base rates claimed for the assistant solicitor and other fee earners are excessive. Reduce to £100 and £70 respectively plus VAT. Each item in which these rates are claimed should be recalculated at the reduced rates. | |
| (1) | The premium claimed is excessive. Reduce to £95. | |

| Item | Dispute | Claimant's Comments |
|---|---|---|
| (14) | The claim for timed attendances on claimant (schedule 1) is excessive. Reduce to 4 hours ie. £400 at reduced rates. | |

| | |
|---|---|
| (32) | The total claim for work done on documents by the assistant solicitor is excessive. A reasonable allowance in respect of documents concerning court and counsel is 8 hours, for documents concerning witnesses and the expert witness, 6.5 hours, for other documents, 5.5 hours. Reduce to 20 hours ie. £2,000 at reduced rates (£3,155 in total). |
| (34) | The time claimed is excessive. Reduce solicitors time to 0.5 hours ie. to £50 at reduced rates and reduce the costs draftsman's time to three hours ie. £210 (£260 in total). |
| (35) | The success fee claimed is excessive. Reduce to 25% ie. £100 plus VAT of £17.50. |
| (36) | The total base fees when recalculated on the basis of the above points amount to £7,788, upon which VAT is £1,362.90. |
| (37) | The success fee claimed is excessive. Reduce to 25% of £7,788 ie £1,947.50 plus VAT of £340.73. |
| (39) | The success fee claimed is excessive. Reduce to 50% ie £1,625 plus VAT of £284.38. |

Served on ................[date] by ............................ [name][solicitors for] the Defendant.

## A-4 Standard orders made on applications to set aside default costs certificates

### (a) Conditional order

**ORDER**

| | | |
|---|---|---|
| To Claimant's Solicitor | **In the High Court of Justice<br>Supreme Court Costs Office** | |
| [ ] | SCCO Ref: | |
| To Defendant's Solicitor | Claimant<br>(include Ref) | |
| [ ] | Defendants<br>(include Ref) | |
| | Date | |

**MASTER [ ] Costs Judge**

UPON THE APPLICATION of the [ ]

AND UPON HEARING the

AND UPON READING the documents on the court file.

IT IS ORDERED as follows:

(1) On or before 4 pm on [ ] the [ ] must pay to the [ ] [into court] the sum of [£ ] on account of the costs claimed by the [ ] herein and must forthwith give notice of any payment into court to the [ ].

(2) If and when the [ ] complies with paragraph (1) the default costs certificate issued herein will be automatically set aside and, on receiving notice of the payment, the [ ] must forthwith return the original certificate to the Supreme Court Costs Office to be so marked.

(3) If the default costs certificate issued herein is automatically set aside the following directions shall apply:

(a) Within [14 days] of the payment referred to in paragraph (1) the [ ] must serve Points of Dispute on the [ ] [and on the other parties hereto]. Points of Dispute should not be filed in court at that stage.

(b) Within [28] days of receipt of the Points of Dispute the [ ] must file a request for a detailed assessment hearing in Form N258.

(a) The [ ] having already served Points of Dispute, the [ ] must on or before 4 pm on [ ] file a request for a detailed assessment hearing in Form N258.

( ) The Form N258 to be filed by the [ ] must be duly completed and must specify the SCCO reference for this application.

( ) The [ ] has permission to serve a reply to the Points of Dispute if he does so before filing the request in Form N258.

(4) Enforcement of the default costs certificate is stayed until [ ] upon which date if it has not by then been automatically set aside, the [ ] can proceed to enforce it.

(5) The costs of and thrown away by this application are awarded to the [ ] and are summarily assessed at £ [including VAT] [VAT not recoverable] which sum is payable on or before [ ]

(6) There shall be a detailed assessment of the costs of the [ ] which are payable out of the Community Service Fund.

( ) Any party hereto may request a further hearing of this application in order to obtain further or other directions.

## (b) Unconditional order

[Heading and opening words as in A-4(a) above]

IT IS ORDERED as follows:

(1) The default costs certificate issued herein dated [ ] is hereby set aside and the [ ] must forthwith return the original certificate to the Supreme Court Costs Office to be so marked.

(2) On or before 4 pm on [ ] the [ ] must serve Points of Dispute on the [ ] [and on the other parties hereto]. Points of Dispute should not be filed in court at that stage.

(3) Within [28] days of receipt of the Points of Dispute the [ ] must file a request for a detailed assessment hearing in Form N258.

( ) The [ ] having already served Points of Dispute, the [ ] must on or before 4 pm on [ ] file a request for a detailed assessment hearing in Form N258.

( ) The Form N258 to be filed by the [ ] must be duly completed and must specify the SCCO reference for this application.

( ) The [ ] has permission to serve a reply to the Points of Dispute if he does so before filing the request in Form N258.

( ) The costs of and thrown away by this application are awarded to the [ ] and are summarily assessed at £ (including VAT) (VAT not recoverable) which sum [may be set off against any costs payable by the [ ] to the [ ]] [is payable on or before [ ]].

( ) There shall be a detailed assessment of the costs of the [ ] which are payable out of the Community Service Fund.

( ) Any party hereto may request a further hearing of this application in order to obtain further or other directions.

(c) Dismissal of application

[Heading and opening words as in A-4(a) above]

IT IS ORDERED as follows:

(1) The application to set aside the default costs certificate herein is dismissed
(2) Enforcement of the default costs certificate issued herein is stayed

(3) The costs of this application are awarded to the [ ] and are summarily assessed at £ (including VAT) (VAT not recoverable) which sum is payable on or before [ ].
(4) The costs of the application are awarded to [ ] to be assessed if not agreed.

(5) There shall be a detailed assessment of the costs of the [ ] which are payable out of the Community Service Fund.

(d) Adjournment of application

[Heading and opening words as in A-4(a) above]

IT IS ORDERED as follows:

(1) This application is adjourned to [ ] [ a date to be fixed].

(2) Enforcement of the default costs certificate issued herein is stayed until the conclusion of this application or further order.

*Paragraph numbers marked with a "+" can be found online and on CD.*

## A-5 Standard orders made in costs-only proceedings

### (a) Order for detailed assessment

[Heading as in A-4(a) above]

UPON THE APPLICATION of the Claimant.

AND UPON READING the documents on the Court file.

IT IS ORDERED:

(1) The Defendant must pay the Claimants costs of the claim relating to [the accident on ] in respect of which terms of settlement have been agreed.

(2) The Claimant must commence detailed assessment proceedings in accordance with CPR, Rule 47.6 for assessment on the Standard basis. (Rule 47.6 provides for the service of a Notice of Commencement and other documents).

(3) The costs of this application are costs in the assessment.

### (b) Dismissal of application

[Heading and opening words as in A-5(a) above]

IT IS ORDERED:

(1) Application dismissed.

(2) Liberty to both parties to apply to stay, set aside or vary this order.

(3) Liberty to both parties to apply for their costs of this application if such application is made within 28 days of any determination of the Claimant's entitlement to the costs of the claim relating to [the accident on ] which costs are the subject matter of this application.

### A-6 Standard orders made against Legal Services Commission funded clients

#### (a) Award of costs against a Claimant who is a Legal Services Commission funded client

[Heading and opening words as in A-4(a) above]

IT IS ORDERED THAT:

1. The claim is dismissed.

2. The full costs of this claim which have been incurred by the defendant are [summarily assessed at £ ] [to be determined by a Costs Judge or District Judge].

3. The claimant (a party who was in receipt of services funded by the Legal Services Commission) do pay to the Defendant [nil] [£ ] [an amount to be determined by a Costs Judge or District Judge]. [When determining such costs the Costs Judge or District Judge should take into account the following facts:

> [Here list any findings as to the party's conduct in the proceedings or otherwise which are relevant to the determination of the costs payable by the LSC funded client]

4. On or before (date) the claimant must pay into court £ on account of the costs payable under paragraph 2, above.

5. There be a detailed assessment of the costs of the claimant which are payable out of the Community Legal Service Fund.

#### (b) Order specifying the amounts payable, for use by a costs judge

[Heading and opening words as in A-4(a) above with (if relevant) the addition of the words "sitting in private"]

IT IS ORDERED THAT:

1. The full costs of the [defendant] herein, [including the costs of this application] are assessed at £

2. The amount of costs which it is reasonable for the [claimant] to pay to the [defendant] is [nil] [£ which sum is payable to the [defendant] on or before (date)].

3. The sum of £ paid into court on account of the costs specified in paragraph 2 above and any interest accruing thereon shall be paid out to the [defendant in part satisfaction] [claimant] as specified in the payment schedule to this Order.

4. The amount of costs payable by the Legal Services Commission to the [defendant] [including the costs of this application] is £ which sum is payable to the [defendant] on or before (date).

[Schedule in Form 200 (see Court Funds Rules 1987)]

**A-7 Claim form for remedies under Solicitors Act 1974:**
Schedule of Costs Precedents, Precedent J
**ROYAL ARMS**

IN THE HIGH COURT OF JUSTICE Claim No.

SUPREME COURT COSTS OFFICE

IN THE MATTER OF [name of solicitor or solicitors' firm]

Claimant

SEAL

Defendant(s)

**CLAIM FORM (CPR Part 8)**

Details of claim (see also overleaf)

The following orders are applied for:

( ) An order in standard form for the delivery of a bill of costs in [all causes and matters] [the following causes and matters
..............................................................................................
..............................................................................................................................
] in which the Defendant has acted for the Claimant(s).

( ) An order in standard form for the detailed assessment of the bill(s) dated .................. ..............................[and] [bearing the invoice numbers .................................................. delivered by the [claimant/Defendant] to the [Defendant/Claimant/person named ......................]

( ) An order dealing with the costs of this application

Defendant's name and address £

Court fee
Solicitor's costs
Issue date

The court office at the Supreme Court Costs Office, Cliffords Inn, Fetter Lane, London EC4A 1DQ is open between 10.00 am and 4.30 pm, Monday to Friday. When corresponding with the court, please address forms or letters to the Court Manager and quote the claim number.

Claim No.

Details of claim (continued)

Statement of Truth
*(I believe) (The Claimant believes) that the facts stated in these particulars of claim are true.
*I am duly authorised by the Claimant to sign this statement.

Full name ..........................................................................................................
Name of Claimant's solicitor's firm

Signed ........................................................ position or office held ...................................
*(Claimant) (Litigation friend) (Claimant's solicitor) (if signing on behalf of firm or company)

*delete as appropriate

Claimant's or claimant's solicitor's address to which documents should be sent if different from overleaf. If you are prepared to accept service by DX, fax or e-mail, please add details.

## A-8 Standard order in claim under Solicitors Act 1974: order on client's application

[Heading and opening words as in A-4(a) above]

IT IS ORDERED that:

(1) A detailed assessment must be made of the bill dated [ ] delivered to the Claimant by the Defendants.

(2) On making the detailed assessment, the court must also assess the costs of these proceedings and certify what is due to or from either party in respect of the bill and the costs of these proceedings.

(3) Until these proceedings are concluded the Defendants must not commence or continue any proceedings against the Claimant in respect of the bill mentioned above.

(4) Upon payment by the Claimant of any sum certified as due to the Defendants in these proceedings the Defendants must deliver to the Claimant all the documentation in the Defendant's possession or control which belong to the Claimant.

(5) CPR 48.9 applies, varied as follows:

(a) on or before the Defendants must serve a breakdown of costs (including a cash account);
(b) within 28 days of service of the breakdown of costs the Claimant must serve Points of Dispute thereon (ie, a brief statement identifying each item in the breakdown which is disputed, summarising the nature and grounds of dispute in respect of that item and, where practicable, suggesting a figure to be allowed for each item in respect of which a reduction is sought);
(c) if the Defendants wish to serve a reply, they must do so within 14 days of service on them of the Points of Dispute;
(d) either party may file a request for a hearing date upon payment of the appropriate fee and the filing of a time estimate –
(i) after Points of Dispute have been served, but;
(ii) no later than ;
(e) if a request for a hearing date is filed the matter is reserved to Master [ ] who has provisionally appointed it for hearing on .

(6) The costs of this application shall be treated as costs of the detailed assessment.

SCCO GUIDE

## A-9 Notice of appeal prescribed for criminal costs appeals

**FORM "A"**

**Form of Notice of Appeal**

Appeal Pursuant to the Costs in Criminal Cases (General) Regulations 1986/ The Legal Aid in Criminal and Care Proceedings (Costs) Regulations 1989/ The Crown Court Rules, 1982, the Criminal Defence Service (Funding) Order 2001

Crown Court/ Divisional
Court/ Court of Appeal Criminal Division
Regina v ...............................................................................................

Appeal of ...............................................................................................

Case No ....................................

To: A Costs Judge and to the appropriate authority of the
...............................................................................................

Crown Court/ Divisional Court/ Court of Appeal Criminal Division.

The Appellant ........................................... appeals to a Costs Judge against the redetermination of the costs in the above matter.

The following are the items in respect of which the Applicant appeals:

| Item | Description | Amount Claimed | Amount Allowed | Total Amount in Dispute After Redetermination |
|---|---|---|---|---|
| 1. | | | | |
| 2. | | | | |
| 3. etc | | | | £ ....................... |

Grounds of Objection (To Be Set Out in Full)
We confirm that a copy of this notice has been served upon the appropriate authority.

The Appellant should attach to this Notice of Appeal his/her Grounds of Objection and in so doing provide the Costs Judge with a detailed response to the written reasons provided by the Determining Officer.

Do you wish to attend the hearing of your Appeal: Yes/ No

Dated the day of

(Signed ...............................................................

...............................................................

Appellant

Address ...............................................................

...............................................................

...............................................................

Tel No. ...............................................................

Ref: ...............................................................

Fax No. ...............................................................

DX No. ...............................................................

E-Mail ...............................................................

**Form A-10**

**IN THE COURT OF PROTECTION**

Case No:- ..........................
SCCO reference ..........................
*(to be completed by the court)*

IN THE MATTER OF

........................................... (A patient)

Short form bill of costs of the Receiver of *(e.g.) General Management for the period............ to be assessed pursuant to the First General Order dated ............... and General Direction dated 19/11/82*

| **One paragraph summary of work carried out** |
|---|
| |

Fee earner category ........... Rate claimed .....................

| **Work done:-** | | **Charge:-** |
|---|---|---|
| Time spent in personal attendances | | |
| *22/9/02 45mins Upon patient* | | ........... |
| Time spent in travel ............ | | ........... |
| Letters Sent ............ | | ........... |
| Telephone Calls ............ | | ........... |
| Time spent on documents ............ | | ........... |
| Other work *(give details)* | | |
| ........................................................................................ | | ........... |
| ........................................................................................ | | ........... |
| | Sub Total | ........... |
| | V.A.T. | ........... |
| Disbursements (list below) | | |
| .............................................. | | |
| .............................................. | Disbursements | ........... |
| | V.A.T. | ........... |
| | Grand Total | ........... |

I certify that this bill is both accurate and complete.

.............................................

Partner

*Name, address and reference of solicitor filing bill*

**Short form bill of costs for use in Court of Protection assessments where the total costs claimed, excluding vat, do not exceed £3000.**

SCCO GUIDE

*Paragraph numbers marked with a "+" can be found online and on CD.*

1C–240

## A-11 Standard order for directions on a referral made in Civil Recovery Proceedings

[Heading as in A-4(a) above]

UPON THE APPLICATION of the Defendant AND UPON READING the documents on the court file IT IS ORDERED as follows:

1 This matter now stands adjourned to a hearing before Master [ ] in Room [ ] in the Supreme Court Costs Office on [*date to be fixed*] (2 hours allowed) for the Claimant to show cause why the exclusion in respect of the Defendant's reasonable legal costs should not specify;-

(1) the stage or stages in the civil recovery proceedings;
(2) the maximum amount which may be released in respect of legal costs for each specified stage; and
(3) the total amount which may be released in respect of legal costs pursuant to the exclusion

in the manner, and in the amounts, set out in the Defendant's estimate of costs which is referred to in the application notice herein.

2 On or before [*date to be fixed*] the Claimant must file in court and serve on the Defendant Points of Dispute on the estimate (i.e., a brief statement identifying each item in the estimate which is disputed, summarising the nature and grounds of dispute in respect of that item and, where practicable, suggesting a figure to be allowed for each item in respect of which a reduction is sought).

3 Liberty to [both] [all] parties to apply by letter to the Court requesting the Court to stay, set aside or vary this Order.

## A-12 Standard orders and directions in respect of costs awarded by the Adjudicator of HM Land Registry

***(a) Order for paying party to show cause following a failure to comply with an order to serve Points of Dispute***

[Heading as in A-4(a) above]

UPON THE APPLICATION of the Claimant AND UPON READING the documents on the court file IT IS ORDERED as follows:

1. This application now stands listed for hearing on [*date to be fixed*] in Room [ ] in the Supreme Court Costs Office (30 minutes allowed) for the Defendant to show cause why the Claimant's bill of costs served pursuant to the Order of the Adjudicator to HM Land Registry dated [ ] should not be assessed as drawn because of the Defendant's failure to serve Points of Dispute in compliance with that Order.

2. The costs of and incidental to this Order are reserved.

3. Liberty to all parties to apply by letter to the Court requesting the Court to stay, set aside or vary this Order.

***(b) Timetable directions for Points of Dispute and detailed assessment hearing***

[Heading and opening words as in A-12(a) above]

1. Within 21 days of service of this Order the Defendant must serve Points of Dispute on the Claimant's bill of costs served upon the Defendant pursuant to the Order of the Adjudicator to HM Land Registry dated [ ].

2. If the Defendant fails to serve Points of Dispute in compliance with this Order the Claimant may by letter, and without further notice to the Defendant, request Master [ ] to assess the Claimant's bill of costs as drawn.

3. The Claimant may file a request for a hearing date after Points of Dispute have been served, but no later than [*date to be fixed*].

4. If a request for a hearing date is filed the matter is reserved to Master [ ] who has provisionally appointed it for hearing on [*date to be fixed*].

5. If the Claimant wishes to serve a reply, he must do so before filing a request for a hearing date.

6. The costs of and incidental to this Order are reserved.

Liberty to all parties to apply by letter to the Court requesting the Court to stay, set aside or vary this Order.

**A-13 Costs certificate in respect of costs assessed on behalf of the Adjudicator of HM Land Registry**

**ORDER**

**ADJUDICATOR TO HER MAJESTY'S LAND REGISTRY**
**LAND REGISTRATION ACT 2002**

**IN THE MATTER OF A REFERENCE FROM H.M.LAND REGISTRY**

To Applicant's Solicitor

To Respondent's Solicitor

| SUPREME COURT COSTS OFFICE | |
|---|---|
| SCCO Ref. | |
| Case No. | |
| Applicant | |
| Respondent | |
| Date | 2006 |

**MASTER COSTS JUDGE**
**SITTING AS A DEPUTY ADJUDICATOR**

**PURSUANT TO THE ORDER** of the Adjudicator dated

I have assessed the costs of the in the sum of £ inclusive of the costs of assessment

The must pay the sum of £ to the by the day of 2006

The court office at Clifford's Inn, Fetter Lane, London, EC4A 1DQ is open between 10 am and 4.30 pm Monday to Friday. Address all communications to the Court Manager quoting the SCCO reference number.

# SECTION 2

## SPECIALIST PROCEEDINGS

# 2A COMMERCIAL COURT

## Part 58—Commercial Court

**Contents** 2A–1



**Editorial introduction**

Part 58 was added to the CPR by Civil Procedure (Amendment No.5) Rules 2001 (SI 2001/4015), and came into force on March 25, 2002. 2A–2

**Related sources** 2A–3

- Part 62—Arbitration Claims (see para.2E–7 *et seq.*)
- The Admiralty and Commercial Courts Guide (see para.2A–39 *et seq*).
- Practice Direction—Arbitrations (see para.2E–46 *et seq.*)
- Arbitration Act 1950 Pt II (see para.2E–57 *et seq.*)
- Arbitration Act 1996 (see para.2E–83 *et seq.*)
- Civil Procedure Rules including CPR 1, 2, 6, 7, 8, 9, 10, 11, 12, 14, 15, 16, 17, 18, 20, 22, 23, 24, 25, 32, 34, 35, 43, 48, 70, 71, 72, 73 and 74
- Heavy and Complex Cases—Checklist (see para. 2A–18.1)
- Practice Direction (Electronic Working Pilot Scheme)

**Forms** 2A–4

- **N1(CC)** Claim form
- **N1C(CC)** Notes for defendant
- **N9(CC)** Acknowledgment of service
- **N208(CC)** Claim form (Part 8)
- **N208C(CC)** Notes for defendant
- **N210(CC)** Acknowledgment of service (Part 8)
- **N211(CC)** Claim form (Part 20)
- **N211C(CC)** Notes for Part 20 defendant
- **N213(CC)** Acknowledgment of service (Part 20)
- **N244(CC)** Application Notice
- **N265(CC)** List of documents: standard disclosure

***Paragraph numbers marked with a "+" can be found online and on CD.***

### Scope of this Part and interpretation[1]

2A-5 **58.1—(1) This Part applies to claims in the Commercial Court of the Queen's Bench Division.**

**(2) In this Part and Practice Direction 58, "commercial claim" means any claim arising out of the transaction of trade and commerce and includes any claim relating to—**

**(a) a business document or contract;**
**(b) the export or import of goods;**
**(c) the carriage of goods by land, sea, air or pipeline;**
**(d) the exploitation of oil and gas reserves or other natural resources;**
**(e) insurance and re-insurance;**
**(f) banking and financial services;**
**(g) the operation of markets and exchanges;**
**(h) the purchase and sale of commodities;**
**(i) the construction of ships;**
**(j) business agency; and**
**(k) arbitration.**

2A-6 *Note*—The Commercial Court may continue to hear a banking case notwithstanding that the debt is secured by a mortgage and that High Court claims for possession of land subject to mortgage are assigned to the Chancery Division by Practice Direction—Possession Claims, supplementing CPR Pt 55 (*Midland Bank Ltd v Stamps* [1978] 1 W.L.R. 627; [1978] 3 All E.R. 1, a case under the pre-October 1, 2001 law). However *Midland Bank Ltd v Stamps* was not followed by the Court of Appeal in *National Westminster Bank Plc v Kitch* [1996] 1 W.L.R. 1316; [1996] 4 All E.R. 495.

### Specialist list[2]

2A-7 **58.2—(1) The commercial list is a specialist list for claims proceeding in the Commercial Court.**

**(2) One of the judges of the Commercial Court shall be in charge of the commercial list.**

### Application of the Civil Procedure Rules[3]

2A-8 **58.3 These Rules and their practice directions apply to claims in the commercial list unless this Part or a practice direction provides otherwise.**

### Proceedings in the commercial list[4]

2A-9 **58.4—(1) A commercial claim may be started in the commercial list.**

**(2) Rule 30.5 applies to claims in the commercial list, except**

---

[1] Introduced by the Civil Procedure (Amendment No.5) Rules 2001 (SI 2001/4015) and amended by the Civil Procedure (Amendment No.2) Rules 2009 (SI 2009/3390).
[2] Introduced by the Civil Procedure (Amendment No.5) Rules 2001 (SI 2001/4015).
[3] Introduced by the Civil Procedure (Amendment No.5) Rules 2001 (SI 2001/4015).
[4] Introduced by the Civil Procedure (Amendment No.5) Rules 2001 (SI 2001/4015) and amended by the Civil Procedure (Amendment No.4) Rules 2005 (SI 2005/3515).

**that a Commercial Court judge may order a claim to be transferred to any other specialist list.**

**(Rule 30.5(3) provides that an application for the transfer of proceedings to or from a specialist list must be made to a judge dealing with claims in that list).**

### Electronic working

2A–9.1

Practice Direction (Electronic Working Pilot Scheme), made by the Master of the Rolls, came into effect on April 1, 2009. It supplements CPR r.5.5 (Filing and sending documents) and provides for a pilot scheme, starting on April 1, 2009, and running (initially) until March 31, 2010, by which, in the circumstances set out in the practice direction, parties may avail themselves of arrangements for starting proceedings in the Commercial Court at the Royal Courts of Justice (and some other courts) electronically, and also for taking all subsequent steps in the proceedings electronically (so-called "Electronic Working"). In certain respects the practice direction modifies CPR provisions that would otherwise apply. Paragraph 1.3 states that, where proceedings to which CPR Pt 58 (Commercial Court) apply are issued, then the Electronic Working pilot scheme will apply subject to the provisions of that Part unless specifically excluded or revised by this practice direction.

The full text of this practice direction is published at para.5CPD.1 above.

Reference should be made to the Admiralty and Commercial Courts Guide, 8th edn (2009), section B, in particular to paragraph B2.4, which provides for the request for the issue of a Pt 7 or Pt 8 claim form being made when the Registry is closed and the circumstances when a party may request that a claim form be issued electronically; para.B3 which provides that the general directions with regard to the applicability of Protocols must be observed and that this may generally be done by a letter of claim which should be concise and not over elaborate.

Attention is also drawn to para.B13 of the Admiralty and Commercial Courts Guide which considers transfers to or from the Commercial Court and the appropriateness of commencing proceedings in the Mercantile Court before transfer into the Commercial List. See paras B13.2 and B13.5.

### Claim form and particulars of claim[1]

**58.5—(1) If, in a Part 7 claim, particulars of claim are not contained in or served with the claim form—** 2A–10

**(a) the claim form must state that, if an acknowledgment of service is filed which indicates an intention to defend the claim, particulars of claim will follow;**

**(b) when the claim form is served, it must be accompanied by the documents specified in rule 7.8(1);**

**(c) the claimant must serve particulars of claim within 28 days of the filing of an acknowledgment of service which indicates an intention to defend; and**

**(d) rule 7.4(2) does not apply.**

**(2) A statement of value is not required to be included in the claim form.**

**(3) If the claimant is claiming interest, he must—**

**(a) include a statement to that effect; and**

**(b) give the details set out in rule 16.4(2),**

**in both the claim form and the particulars of claim.**

*Note*—As to the claim form in a Pt 7 claim, see also the Admiralty and Commercial 2A–10.1

[1] Introduced by the Civil Procedure (Amendment No.5) Rules 2001 (SI 2001/4015).

***Paragraph numbers marked with a "+" can be found online and on CD.***

Courts Guide, 8th edn (2009), section B4, paras B4.1 to B4.10. Methods of service, applications for extensions of time, certificates of service and service of the claim form are considered in paras B7 to B8 of the Guide.

Further detail as to the form, content, serving and filing of the Particulars of Claim is to be found in section C of the Admiralty and Commercial Courts Guide, 8th edn (2009). As to form and content the following may be noted:

(a) statements of case should be brief and not set out evidence;
(b) they are limited to 25 pages unless permission for a longer statement of case has been obtained;
(c) they should not include lengthy portions of documents (if necessary such documents should be included in a schedule);
(d) the statement of case should be signed by the individual who drafted it and not, where the drafter is a solicitor in the name of the solicitor's firm.

As to service it is to be noted that all statements of case are to be served by the parties and not by the court (see PD58, para.9 and para.C1.8 of the Admiralty and Commercial Courts Guide, 8th edn (2009)). When filed, statements of case form part of the court record (see para C1.9 of the Admiralty and Commercial Courts Guide, 8th edn (2009)). Extensions of time for service may be agreed but the court must be notified (see PD 58 para.7.1 and para.C2.1 of the Admiralty and Commercial Courts Guide, 8th edn (2009)).

### Acknowledgment of service[1]

2A-11 **58.6—(1) A defendant must file an acknowledgment of service in every case.**

**(2) Unless paragraph (3) applies, the period for filing an acknowledgment of service is 14 days after service of the claim form.**

**(3) Where the claim form is served out of the jurisdiction, or on the agent of a defendant who is overseas, the time periods provided by rules 6.12(3), 6.35 and 6.37(5) apply after service of the claim form.**

2A-11.1 *Note*—As to acknowledgment of service in a Pt 7 claim see also the Admiralty and Commercial Courts Guide, 8th edn (2009) section B9, paras B9.1, B9.3 and B9.4.

### Disputing the court's jurisdiction[2]

2A-12 **58.7—(1) Part 11 applies to claims in the commercial list with the modifications set out in this rule.**

**(2) An application under rule 11(1) must be made within 28 days after filing an acknowledgment of service.**

**(3) If the defendant files an acknowledgment of service indicating an intention to dispute the court's jurisdiction, the claimant need not serve particulars of claim before the hearing of the application.**

2A-12.1 *Note*—As to disputing the court's jurisdiction in a Pt 7 claim see also the Admiralty and Commercial Courts Guide, 8th edn (2009) section B10, paras B10.1 and B10.3 of the Guide.

As to the appropriate time for serving a defence where the defendant has withdrawn

[1] Introduced by the Civil Procedure (Amendment No.5) Rules 2001 (SI 2001/4015) and amended by the Civil Procedure (Amendment) Rules 2008 (SI 2008/2178).
[2] Introduced by the Civil Procedure (Amendment No.5) Rules 2001 (SI 2001/4015).

its intention to dispute the court's jurisdiction, see *Flame SA v Primera Maritime (Hellas) Ltd* [2009] EWHC 1973 (Comm).

## Default judgment[1]

**58.8—(1) If, in a Part 7 claim in the commercial list, a defendant fails to file an acknowledgment of service, the claimant need not serve particulars of claim before he may obtain or apply for default judgment in accordance with Part 12.** 2A–13

**(2) Rule 12.6(1) applies with the modification that paragraph (a) shall be read as if it referred to the claim form instead of the particulars of claim.**

*Note* —As to default judgment see para.B11 of the Admiralty and Commercial Courts Guide, 8th edn (2009) which explains that the reason for the modification in r.58.8(2) is that in the Commercial Court the period for filing an acknowledgment of service is calculated from the service of the claim form. 2A–13.1

## Admissions[2]

**58.9—(1) Rule 14.5 does not apply to claims in the commercial list.** 2A–14

**(2) If the defendant admits part of a claim for a specified amount of money, the claimant may apply under rule 14.3 for judgment on the admission.**

**(3) Rule 14.14(1) applies with the modification that paragraph (a) shall be read as if it referred to the claim form instead of the particulars of claim.**

## Defence and Reply[3]

**58.10—(1) Part 15 (defence and reply) applies to claims in the commercial list with the modification to rule 15.8 that the claimant must—** 2A–15

**(a) file any reply to a defence; and**

**(b) serve it on all other parties,**

**within 21 days after service of the defence.**

**(2) Rule 6.35 (in relation to the period for filing a defence where the claim form is served out of the jurisdiction) applies to claims in the commercial list, except that if the particulars of claim are served after the defendant has filed an acknowledgment of service the period for filing a defence is 28 days from service of the particulars of claim.**

*Note* —With respect to the form, contents, serving and filing of a defence or reply see para.2A–10.1 above and see paras C.1.2, C3 and C4 of the Admiralty and Commercial Courts Guide, 8th edn (2009). It should be noted that a defendant (or Pt 20 defendant) who wishes to advance a positive case on mitigation (or on causation, or quantification of damages) must provide proper details of the case, see para.C1.2(g) of 2A–15.1

[1] Introduced by the Civil Procedure (Amendment No.5) Rules 2001 (SI 2001/4015).
[2] Introduced by the Civil Procedure (Amendment No.5) Rules 2001 (SI 2001/4015).
[3] Introduced by the Civil Procedure (Amendment No.5) Rules 2001 (SI 2001/4015) and amended by the Civil Procedure (Amendment) Rules 2008 (SI 2008/2178).

the Guide. As to extensions of time for serving and filing see para.C.3.1(b) of the Guide. With respect to the necessity to file a reply, see para.C4.2 of the Guide.

### Statements of case[1]

2A-16 **58.11 The court may at any time before or after the issue of the claim form order a claim in the commercial list to proceed without the filing or service of statements of case.**

2A-16.1 *Note* —Guidance as to amendments to a statement of case is provided at para.C5 of the Admiralty and Commercial Courts Guide, 8th edn (2009). It is to be noted that amendments must show the original text and may be shown by using footnotes or marginal notes provided that they identify where and when an amendment has been made (see also PD58, para.8). This procedure is to be contrasted with the practice contained in PD17 para.2.2 of the CPR.

### Part 8 claims[2]

2A-17 **58.12 Part 8 applies to claims in the commercial list, with the modification that a defendant to a Part 8 claim who wishes to rely on written evidence must file and serve it within 28 days after filing an acknowledgment of service.**

2A-17.1 *Note* —The Admiralty and Commercial Courts Guide, 8th edn (2009) provides specific information with respect to Pt 8 claims in the following paragraphs: para.B5 (commencement, statement of truth and time for filing evidence in opposition to a Part 8 claim), para.B9.2 filing an acknowledgment of service, and paras 10.2 and 10.3 disputing the court's jurisdiction.

### Case management[3]

2A-18 **58.13—(1) All proceedings in the commercial list are treated as being allocated to the multi-track and Part 26 does not apply.**

**(2) The following parts only of Part 29 apply—**

**(a) rule 29.3(2) (legal representative to attend case management conferences and pre-trial reviews);**

**(b) rule 29.5 (variation of case management timetable) with the exception of rule 29.5(1)(c).**

**(3) As soon as practicable the court will hold a case management conference which must be fixed in accordance with Practice Direction 58.**

**(4) At the case management conference or at any hearing at which the parties are represented the court may give such directions for the management of the case as it considers appropriate.**

#### Heavy and Complex Cases

2A-18.1 Reference should be made to paras 10 to 12 of the Practice Direction to Pt 58 and to section D of the Admiralty and Commercial Courts Guide, 8th edn (2009) which set out the procedure to be followed in detail. The Guide particularly emphasises the key features of case management in the Commercial Court (see para D2), how and when such management conferences are to be fixed (see para.D3); how cases which are

[1] Introduced by the Civil Procedure (Amendment No.5) Rules 2001 (SI 2001/4015).
[2] Introduced by the Civil Procedure (Amendment No.5) Rules 2001 (SI 2001/4015).
[3] Introduced by the Civil Procedure (Amendment No.5) Rules 2001 (SI 2001/4015) and amended by the Civil Procedure (Amendment No.2) Rules 2009 (SI 2009/3390).

exceptional in size or complexity may be allocated to a designated judge by order of the judge in charge of the List in which case ordinarily all applications will be made to the judge so designated who will also be the trial judge (see para.D4); the use of case memoranda (see para.D5); the use of the list of issues (see para.D6); the case management bundle and its preparation (see para.D7). Detailed consideration as to the procedure to be adopted with regard to the Case Management Conference itself, including applications, attendance and the conduct of the hearing itself are set out in para.D8 of the Guide. Paragraph D10 deals with case management of Pt 20 claims, para.D12 deals with progress monitoring and paras D16, D17 and D18 are concerned with fixing trial dates, the estimates of the length of trial and pre-trial review and trial timetable.

### Disclosure—ships papers[1]

**58.14—(1) If, in proceedings relating to a marine insurance policy, the underwriters apply for specific disclosure under rule 31.12, the court may—** 2A–19

- **(a) order a party to produce all the ships papers; and**
- **(b) require that party to use his best endeavours to obtain and disclose documents which are not or have not been in his control.**

**(2) An order under this rule may be made at any stage of the proceedings and on such terms, if any, as to staying the proceedings or otherwise, as the court thinks fit.**

#### The Order

(a) Although the insurer applying for an order is usually the defendant, the procedure is available to an insurer who is suing as claimant, e.g. to recover overpayments inducted by deception or mistake (*Boulton v Houlder Bros.* [1904] 1 K.B. 784, CA). 2A–20

(b) *Persons to whom the order is directed.* The order is usually directed to the claimant himself and to all persons interested in the proceeding and in the insurance (*China Steamship Co v Commercial Union Assurance Co* (1881) 8 QBD 142); "persons interested" means those interested on the claimant's side, not the underwriters themselves (*ibid.*). See also, as to the person to whom the order is to be directed, *China Traders Co v Royal Exchange Assurance* [1898] 2 Q.B. 187 at 189; *London Insurance Co v Chambers* (1900) 5 Com.Cas. 241. The affidavit or witness statement in answer must show the interest of the deponent or may be rejected as defective (*Avon v Miall*, November 27, 1925, unrep., Branson J. in Chambers) and must account for all documents in the possession and control of those to whom the order is addressed (*Graham etc. Co v Motor Union Co* [1922] 1 K.B. 563); if a particular "interested person" is thought to have relevant documents the order may expressly require an affidavit from him (*ibid.*).

(c) *Documents to be disclosed.* All material documents may be ordered to be disclosed and it is not a reason for refusing to make disclosure that they are not in the possession of the person to whom the order is directed: he must, in such a case, use all reasonable endeavors to obtain the documents and will only be excused on showing that these have been unavailing; thus a mortgagee must, if he can, obtain disclosure of the documents in possession of the mortgagor who operated the ship (*West of England Bank v Canton Insurance Co* (1877) 2 Ex.D. 472) and cargo owners suing as claimants must, if they can, obtain disclosure of the papers in possession of the shipowners or their servants (*Teneria Moderna Franco Espanola v New Zealand Insurance Co* [1924] 1 K.B. 79, CA).

(d) *Order staying proceedings.* The purpose of a stay may be to postpone the time for delivery of a defence or to ensure compliance with the order. It is a matter of discretion whether, and at what stage, a stay will be granted (*Probatina Shipping Co v Sun Insurance Office* [1974] Q.B. 635; [1974] 2 All E.R. 478, CA). It will be removed on

[1] Introduced by the Civil Procedure (Amendment No.5) Rules 2001 (SI 2001/4015).

compliance with the order or on showing to the Court that all reasonable endeavours have been made to comply (see cases cited in sub-paragraphs (b) and (c)).

A stay does not preclude the defendant from applying for a further and better information (*Abdela v Mutual Property Investment Ltd* [1921] W.N. 23, CA) nor prevent a party from recovering costs for the reasonable preparation of his case while the stay is in force (*Pecheries Ostendaises v Merchants' Marine Insurance Co* [1928] 1 K.B. 750, CA).

### Judgments and orders[1]

2A–21 **58.15—(1) Except for orders made by the court on its own initiative and unless the court orders otherwise, every judgment or order will be drawn up by the parties, and rule 40.3 is modified accordingly.**

**(2) An application for a consent order must include a draft of the proposed order signed on behalf of all the parties to whom it relates.**

**(3) Rule 40.6 (consent judgments and orders) does not apply.**

[1] Introduced by the Civil Procedure (Amendment No.5) Rules 2001 (SI 2001/4015).

*Paragraph numbers marked with a "+" can be found online and on CD.*

## PRACTICE DIRECTION 58—COMMERCIAL COURT

*This Practice Direction supplements CPR Part 58*

### General

**1.1** This practice direction applies to commercial claims proceeding in the commercial list of the Queen's Bench Division. It supersedes all previous practice directions and practice statements in the Commercial Court. **2A–22**

**1.2** All proceedings in the commercial list, including any appeal from a judgment, order or decision of a master or district judge before the proceedings were transferred to the Commercial Court, will be heard or determined by a Commercial Court judge, except that—

(1) another judge of the Queen's Bench Division or Chancery Division may hear urgent applications if no Commercial Court judge is available; and

(2) unless the court otherwise orders, any application relating to the enforcement of a Commercial Court judgment or order for the payment of money will be dealt with by a master of the Queen's Bench Division or a district judge.

**1.3** Provisions in other practice directions which refer to a master or district judge are to be read, in relation to claims in the commercial list, as if they referred to a Commercial Court judge.

**1.4** The Admiralty and Commercial Registry in the Royal Courts of Justice is the administrative office of the court for all proceedings in the commercial list.

### Starting proceedings in the Commercial Court

**2.1** Claims in the Commercial Court must be issued in the Admiralty and Commercial Registry. **2A–23**

**2.2** When the Registry is closed, a request to issue a claim form may be made by fax, using the procedure set out in Appendix A to this practice direction. If a request is made which complies with that procedure, the claim form is issued when the fax is received by the Registry.

**2.3** The claim form must be marked in the top right hand comer "Queen's Bench Division, Commercial Court".

**2.4** A claimant starting proceedings in the commercial list, other than an arbitration claim, must use practice form **N1(CC)** for Part 7 claims or practice form **N208(CC)** for Part 8 claims.

### Applications before proceedings are issued

**3.1** A party who intends to bring a claim in the commercial list must make any application before the claim form is issued to a Commercial Court judge. **2A–24**

**3.2** The written evidence in support of such an application must state that the claimant intends to bring proceedings in the commercial list.

**3.3** If the Commercial Court judge hearing the application considers that the proceedings should not be brought in the commercial list, he may adjourn the application to be heard by a master or by a judge who is not a Commercial Court judge.

**Transferring proceedings to or from the Commercial Court**

2A-25 **4.1** If an application is made to a court other than the Commercial Court to transfer proceedings to the commercial list, the other court may—

(1) adjourn the application to be heard by a Commercial Court judge; or

(2) dismiss the application.

**4.2** If the Commercial Court orders proceedings to be transferred to the commercial list—

(1) it will order them to be transferred to the Royal Courts of Justice; and

(2) it may give case management directions.

**4.3** An application by a defendant, including a Part 20 defendant, for an order transferring proceedings from the commercial list should be made promptly and normally not later than the first case management conference.

**4.4** A party applying to the Commercial Court to transfer a claim to the commercial list must give notice of the application to the court in which the claim is proceeding, and the Commercial Court will not make an order for transfer until it is satisfied that such notice has been given.

**Acknowledgment of service**

2A-26 **5.1** For Part 7 claims, a defendant must file an acknowledgment of service using practice form **N9(CC)**.

**5.2** For Part 8 claims, a defendant must file an acknowledgment of service using practice form **N210(CC)**.

**Default judgment and admissions**

2A-27 **6.** The practice directions supplementing Parts 12 and 14 apply with the following modifications—

(1) paragraph 4.1(1) of Practice Direction 12 is to be read as referring to the service of the claim form; and

(2) the references to "particulars of claim" in paragraphs 2.1, 3.1 and 3.2 of Practice Direction 14 are to be read as referring to the claim form.

**Variation of time limits**

2A-28 **7.1** If the parties, in accordance with rule 2.11, agree in writing to vary a time limit, the claimant must notify the court in writing, giving brief written reasons for the agreed variation.

**7.2** The court may make an order overriding an agreement by the parties varying a time limit.

**Amendments**

2A-29 **8.** Paragraph 2.2 of Practice Direction 17 is modified so that amendments to a statement of case must show the original text, unless the court orders otherwise.

*Paragraph numbers marked with a "+" can be found online and on CD.*

**Service of documents**

**9.** Unless the court orders otherwise, the Commercial Court will not serve documents or orders and service must be effected by the parties. **2A–30**

**Case management**

**10.1** The following parts only of Practice Direction 29 apply— **2A–31**

(1) paragraph 5 (case management conferences), excluding paragraph 5.9 and modified so far as is made necessary by other specific provisions of this practice direction; and

(2) paragraph 7 (failure to comply with case management directions).

**10.2** If the proceedings are started in the commercial list, the claimant must apply for a case management conference—

(a) for a Part 7 claim, within 14 days of the date when all defendants who intend to file and serve a defence have done so; and

(b) for a Part 8 claim, within 14 days of the date when all defendants who intend to serve evidence have done so.

**10.3** If the proceedings are transferred to the commercial list, the claimant must apply for a case management conference within 14 days of the date of the order transferring them, unless the judge held, or gave directions for, a case management conference when he made the order transferring the proceedings.

**10.4** Any party may, at a time earlier than that provided in paragraphs 10.2 or 10.3, apply in writing to the court to fix a case management conference.

**10.5** If the claimant does not make an application in accordance with paragraphs 10.2 or 10.3, any other party may apply for a case management conference.

**10.6** The court may fix a case management conference at any time on its own initiative. If it does so, the court will give at least 7 days notice to the parties, unless there are compelling reasons for a shorter period of notice.

**10.7** Not less than 7 days before a case management conference, each party must file and serve—

(1) a completed case management information sheet; and

(2) an application notice for any order which that party intends to seek at the case management conference, other than directions referred to in the case management information sheet.

**10.8** Unless the court orders otherwise, the claimant, in consultation with the other parties, must prepare—

(1) a case memorandum, containing a short and uncontroversial summary of what the case is about and of its material case history;

(2) a list of issues, with a section listing important matters which are not in dispute; and

(3) a case management bundle containing—

(a) the claim form;
(b) all statements of case (excluding schedules), except that, if a summary of a statement of case has been filed, the bundle should contain the summary, and not the full statement of case;
(c) the case memorandum;
(d) the list of issues;
(e) the case management information sheets and, if a pre-trial timetable has been agreed or ordered, that timetable;
(f) the principal orders of the court; and
(g) any agreement in writing made by the parties as to disclosure,

and provide copies of the case management bundle for the court and the other parties at least 7 days before the first case management conference or any earlier hearing at which the court may give case management directions.

**10.9** The claimant, in consultation with the other parties, must revise and update the documents referred to in paragraph 10.8 appropriately as the case proceeds. This must include making all necessary revisions and additions at least 7 days before any subsequent hearing at which the court may give case management directions.

**Pre-trial review**

2A-32 **11.1** At any pre-trial review or case management hearing, the court will ensure that case management directions have been complied with and give any further directions for the trial that are necessary.

**11.2** Advocates who are to represent the parties at the trial should represent them at the pre-trial review and any case management hearing at which arrangements for the trial are to be discussed.

**11.3** Before the pre-trial review, the parties must discuss and, if possible, agree a draft written timetable for the trial.

**11.4** The claimant must file a copy of the draft timetable for the trial at least two days before the hearing of the pre-trial review. Any parts of the timetable which are not agreed must be identified and short explanations of the disagreement must be given.

**11.5** At the pre-trial review, the court will set a timetable for the trial, unless a timetable has already been fixed or the court considers that it would be inappropriate to do so or appropriate to do so at a later time.

2A-32.1 *Editorial note*—See Heavy and Complex Cases at para. 2A-18.1 above.

**Case management where there is a Part 20 claim**

2A-33 **12.** Paragraph 5 of Practice Direction 20 applies, except that, unless the court otherwise orders, the court will give case management directions for Part 20 claims at the same case management conferences as it gives directions for the main claim.

**Evidence for applications**

2A-34 **13.1** The general requirement is that, unless the court orders otherwise—

***Paragraph numbers marked with a "+" can be found online and on CD.***

(1) evidence in support of an application must be filed and served with the application (see rule 23.7(3));
(2) evidence in answer must be filed and served within 14 days after the application is served; and
(3) evidence in reply must be filed and served within 7 days of the service of evidence in answer.

**13.2** In any case in which the application is likely to require an oral hearing of more than half a day the periods set out in paragraphs 13.1(2) and (3) will be 28 days and 14 days respectively.

**13.3** If the date fixed for the hearing of an application means that the times in paragraphs 13.1(2) and (3) cannot both be achieved, the evidence must be filed and served—
(1) as soon as possible; and
(2) in sufficient time to ensure that the application may fairly proceed on the date fixed.

**13.4** The parties may, in accordance with rule 2.11, agree different periods from those in paragraphs 13.1(2) and (3) provided that the agreement does not affect the date fixed for the hearing of the application.

### Judgments and orders

**14.1** An application for a consent order must include a draft of the proposed order signed on behalf of all parties to whom it relates (see paragraph 10.4 of Practice Direction 23). **2A–35**

**14.2** Judgments and orders are generally drawn up by the parties (see rule 58.15). The parties are not therefore required to supply draft orders on disk (see paragraph 12.1 of Practice Direction 23).

*APPENDIX A*

### Procedure for issue of claim form when Registry is closed—paragraph 2.2

**1.** A request to issue a claim form may be made by fax when the Registry is closed, provided that— **2A–36**
(a) the claim form is signed by a solicitor acting on behalf of the claimant; and
(b) it does not require the permission of the court for its issue (unless such permission has already been given).

**2.** The solicitor requesting the issue of the claim form ("the issuing solicitor") must—
(a) endorse on the claim form and sign the endorsement set out below;
(b) send a copy of the claim form so endorsed to the Registry by fax for issue under paragraph 2.2 of this practice direction; and
(c) complete and sign a certificate in the form set out below, certifying that he has received a transmission report confirming that the fax has been transmitted in full, and stating the time and date of transmission.

*Paragraph numbers marked with a "+" can be found online and on CD.*

**3.** When the Registry is next open to the public after the issue of a claim form in accordance with this procedure, the issuing solicitor or his agent must attend and deliver to the Registry—

(a) the original of the claim form which was sent by fax (including the endorsement and the certificate) or, if the claim form has been served, a true and certified copy of it;

(b) as many copies of the claim form as the Registry requires; and

(c) the transmission report.

**4.** When a court officer at the Registry has checked that—

(a) the claim form delivered under paragraph 3 matches the claim form received by fax; and

(b) the correct issue fee has been paid,

he will allocate a number to the case, and seal, mark as "original" and date the claim form with the date of issue (being the date when the fax is recorded at the Registry as having been received).

**5.** If the issuing solicitor has served the unsealed claim form on any person, that solicitor must as soon as practicable—

(a) inform that person of the case number; and

(b) if requested, serve him with a copy of the sealed and dated claim form at any address in the United Kingdom, unless the court orders otherwise.

**6.** Any person served with a claim form issued under this procedure may, without paying a fee, inspect and take copies of the documents lodged at the Registry under paragraphs 2 and 3 above.

**7.** The issue of a claim form in accordance with this procedure takes place when the fax is recorded at the Registry as having been received, and the claim form has the same effect for all purposes as a claim form issued under Part 7 or 8. Unless the court otherwise orders, the sealed version of the claim form retained by the Registry is conclusive proof that the claim form was issued at the time and on the date stated.

**8.** If the procedure set out in this Appendix is not complied with, the court may declare that a claim form shall be treated as not having been issued.

### Endorsement

**2A–37** A claim form issued pursuant to a request by fax must be endorsed as follows:

"1. This claim form is issued under paragraph 2.2 of Practice Direction 58 and may be served notwithstanding that it does not bear the seal of the Court.

2. A true copy of this claim form and endorsement has been sent to the Admiralty and Commercial Registry, Royal Courts of Justice, Strand, London WC2A 2LL, at the time and date certified below by the solicitor whose name appears below ("the issuing solicitor").

3. It is the duty of the issuing solicitor or his agent to attend at the Registry when it is next open to the public for the claim form to be sealed.

4. Any person served with this unsealed claim form—
   (a) will be notified by the issuing solicitor of the case number;
   (b) may require the issuing solicitor to serve that person with a copy of the sealed claim form at an address in the United Kingdom, unless the court orders otherwise.
   (c) may inspect without charge the documents lodged at the Registry by the issuing solicitor.
5. I, the issuing solicitor, undertake [to the Court, to the defendants named in this claim form, and to any other person served with this claim form]—
   (a) that the statement in paragraph 2 above is correct;
   (b) that the time and date given in the certificate with this endorsement are correct;
   (c) that this claim form is a claim form which may be issued under paragraph 2.2 and Appendix A of Practice Direction 58;
   (d) that I will comply in all respects with the requirements of Appendix A of Practice Direction 58; and
   (e) that I will indemnify any person served with the claim form before it is sealed against any loss suffered as a result of the claim form being or becoming invalid as a result of any failure to comply with Appendix A of Practice Direction 58.

   *(Signed)*

   Solicitor for the claimant"

   [**Note**: the endorsement may be signed in the name of the firm of solicitors rather than an individual solicitor, or by solicitors' agents in their capacity as agents acting on behalf of their professional clients.]

**Certificate**

The issuing solicitor must sign a certificate in the following form— **2A-38**

"I certify that I have received a transmission report confirming that the transmission of a copy of this claim form to the Registry by fax was fully completed and that the time and date of transmission to the Registry were *[enter the time and date shown on the transmission report]*.

Dated

*(Signed)*

Solicitor for the claimant"

[**Note**: the certificate must be signed in the name of the firm of solicitors rather than an individual solicitor, or by solicitors' agents in their capacity as agents acting on behalf of their professional clients.]

***Paragraph numbers marked with a "+" can be found online and on CD.***

# THE ADMIRALTY AND COMMERCIAL COURTS GUIDE



***Paragraph numbers marked with a "+" can be found online and on CD.***

*Paragraph numbers marked with a "+" can be found online and on CD.*

***Paragraph numbers marked with a "+" can be found online and on CD.***

8th Edition: 2009 **2A–39**

## INTRODUCTION

This edition of the Admiralty & Commercial Court Guide introduces changes designed to implement recommendations made by the Long Trials Working Party that were published in December 2007, following a pilot period in 2008 during which the Courts adopted the recommended procedures and subsequent consultations with practitioners. It also makes amendments in light of new procedures for issuing claims and applications and for communicating with the court electronically and other amendments suggested by practitioners or required by other developments. We are grateful to our colleagues for their assistance in revising the Guide, and in particular to Mr. Justice Flaux, who drew together the comments of practitioners on the proposals of the Working Party.

The Guide is intended to promote the efficient conduct of litigation in the Admiralty and Commercial Courts. It does not provide a complete blueprint for litigation and should be seen as providing guidance to be adopted flexibly and adapted to the exigencies of the particular case. It should not be understood to override in any way the Civil Procedure Rules or Practice Directions made under them, or as fettering the discretion of the judges.

We try to keep the Guide up to date, and suggestions for its improvement are always welcome.

The Hon Mr. Justice David Steel,
The Admiralty Judge

***Paragraph numbers marked with a "+" can be found online and on CD.***

The Hon Mr. Justice Andrew Smith,
Judge in charge of the Commercial Court
30 April 2009

## A.

## PRELIMINARY

### A1 The procedural framework

2A–40 A1.1 Proceedings in the Commercial Court are governed by the Civil Procedure Rules ("CPR") and Practice Directions. CPR Part 58 and its associated practice direction deal specifically with the Commercial Court. Part 61 deals with the Admiralty Court and Part 62 deals with arbitration applications. Parts 58 and 61 and their associated practice directions are set out in Appendix 1; Rule 62 and its associated practice direction is set out in Appendix 2.

A1.2 The Admiralty & Commercial Courts Guide is published with the approval of the Lord Chief Justice and the Head of Civil Justice in consultation with the Judges of the Admiralty and Commercial Courts and with the advice and support of the Admiralty Court and Commercial Court Users Committees. It is intended to provide guidance about the conduct of proceedings in the Admiralty and Commercial Courts and, within the framework of the Civil Procedure Rules and Practice Directions, to establish the practice to be followed in those courts.

A1.3 It is important to understand what the Guide is and what it is not. It provides guidance without prejudice to the provisions of the CPR and the Practice Directions. It is not itself a Practice Direction and does not constrain in any way how the judges might exercise their discretion under the Rules and Practice Directions in accordance with the overriding objective.

A1.4 Thus, the requirements of the Guide are designed to ensure effective management of proceedings in the Admiralty and Commercial Courts. On matters for which specific provision is not made by the Guide, the parties, their solicitors and counsel will be expected to act reasonably and in accordance with the spirit of the Guide.

A1.5 Pre-trial matters in the Admiralty and Commercial Courts are dealt with by the judges of those Courts: 58PD § 1.2.

A1.6 The Court expects a high level of co-operation and realism from the legal representatives of the parties. This applies to dealings (including correspondence) between legal representatives as well as to dealings with the Court.

A1.7 In order to avoid excessive repetition, the Guide has been written by reference to proceedings in the Commercial Court. Practitioners should treat the guidance as applicable to proceedings in the Admiralty Court unless the content of Part 61 or Section N of this Guide ("Admiralty") specifically requires otherwise.

A1.8 Parties may communicate with by e-mail with the Commercial and Admiralty Courts on certain matters: see Appendix 17.

A1.9 On 1 April 2009 the Commerical Court started an electronic working pilot scheme under PD Electronic Working Pilot Scheme. It is intended to develop the scheme incrementally in the Commerial and Admiralty Courts and in other courts, and up-to-date information about the scheme will be available on the Commerical Court website, www.hmcourts-service.gov.uk/infoabout/admiralcomm. See Appendix 18.

### A2 The Admiralty & Commercial Registry; the Commercial Court Listing Office

2A–41 A2.1 The administrative office for the Admiralty Court and the Commercial Court is the Admiralty & Commercial Registry ("the Registry") which is located at Room EB13 in the Royal Courts of Justice, Strand, London WC2A 2LL. The Commercial Court Listing Office ("the Listing Office") is located at Room EB09 in the Royal Courts of Justice, Strand, London WC2A 2LL.

A2.2 It is important that there is close liaison between legal representatives of the parties and both the Registry and the Listing Office.

### A3 The Commercial Court Users Committee

A3.1 The success of the Court's ability to meet the special problems and continually changing needs of the commercial community depends in part upon a steady flow of information and constructive suggestions between the Court, litigants and professional advisers. **2A–42**

A3.2 The Commercial Court Committee has assisted in this process for many years, and it is expected to continue to do so. It is expected to play an important part in helping to ensure that the procedures of the Court enable the achievement of the "overriding objective". All concerned with the Court are encouraged to make the fullest use of this important channel of communication. Correspondence raising matters for the consideration of the Committee should be addressed to the Clerk to the Commercial Court, Royal Courts of Justice, Strand, London WC2A 2LL.

### A4 Specialist associations

A4.1 There are a number of associations of legal representatives which liaise closely with the Commercial Court. These will also play an important part in helping to ensure that the Court remains responsive to the "overriding objective". **2A–43**

A4.2 The associations include the Commercial Bar Association ("COMBAR"), the London Common Law and Commercial Bar Association ("LCLCBA"), the City of London Law Society, the London Solicitors Litigation Association, the Commercial Litigators' Forum and the Admiralty Solicitors Group.

## B.

## COMMENCEMENT, TRANSFER AND REMOVAL

### B1 Commercial cases

B1.1 Rule 58.1(2) describes a "commercial claim" as follows: **2A–44**

"any claim arising out of the transaction of trade and commerce and includes any claim relating to—

(a) a business document or contract;
(b) the export or import of goods;
(c) the carriage of goods by land, sea, air or pipeline;
(d) the exploitation of oil and gas reserves or other natural resources;
(e) insurance and re-insurance;
(f) banking and financial services;
(g) the operation of markets and exchanges;
(h) the purchase and sale of commodities;
(i) the construction of ships;
(j) business agency; and
(k) arbitration."

### B2 Starting a case in the Commercial Court

B2.1 Except for arbitration applications which are governed by the provisions of CPR Part 62 and section O of the Guide, the case will be begun by a claim form under Part 7 or Part 8. **2A–45**

B2.2 Save where otherwise specified, references in this Guide to a claim form are to a Part 7 claim form.

B2.3 The Commercial Court may give a fixed date for trial (see section D16), but it does not give a fixed date for a hearing when it issues a claim. Rules 7.9 and 7.10 and their associated practice directions do not apply to the Commercial Court.

B2.4 A request for the issue of a Part 7 or a Part 8 claim form may be made by fax at certain times when the Registry is closed to the public: PD58 2.2. The procedure is set out in Appendix 3. Further details may be obtained from the Commercial Court website (www.hmcourts-service.gov.uk/infoabout/admiralcomm) or from the Registry. The fax number is 020 7947 6667.

B2.5 The Commercial Court may give a fixed date for trial (see section D16), but it does not give a fixed date for a hearing when it issues a claim. Rules 7.9 and 7.10 and their associated practice directions do not apply to the Commercial Court.

### B3 Pre-Action Protocols

**2A–45.1** B3.1 The Practice Direction – Protocols applies to actions in the Commercial Court and usually it should be observed, although it is sometimes necessary or proper to start proceedings without following the procedures there contemplated: for example, where delays in starting proceedings might prompt forum-shopping in other jurisdictions. There is no approved protocol for actions in the Commercial Court generally, but cases in the Commercial Court are sometimes covered by an approved protocol, such as the Professional Negligence Pre-Action Protocol.

B3.2 Subject to complying with the Practice Direction and any applicable approved protocol, the parties to proceedings in the Commercial Court are not required, or generally expected, to engage in elaborate or expensive pre-action procedures, and restraint is encouraged.

B3.3 Thus, the letter of claim should be concise and it is usually sufficient to explain the proposed claim(s), identifying key dates, so as to enable the potential defendant to understand and to investigate the allegations. Only essential documents need be supplied, and the period specified for a response should not be longer than one month without good reason.

B3.4 A potential defendant should respond to a letter of claim concisely and only essential documents need by supplied. It should often be possible to respond sufficiently within the 21 days referred to in para 4.4 of the Practice Direction for acknowledgment of the letter of claim. The Practice Direction (para 4.3(c)) requires a potential defendant to give reasons if he requires longer to respond than the period specified in the letter of claim, and even if the period specified is longer than one month, a potential defendant who needs longer should explain the reasons when acknowledging the letter of claim.

### B4 Part 7 claims

*The form*

**2A–46** B4.1 A claimant starting proceedings in the Commercial Court must use practice form **N1(CC)** for Part 7 claims: PD58 § 2.4.

*Marking*

B3.2 In accordance with PD58 § 2.3 the claim form should be marked in the top right hand corner with the words "Queen's Bench Division, Commercial Court", and on the issue of the claim form out of the Registry the case will be entered in the Commercial List. Marking the claim form in this way complies sufficiently with PD7 § 3.6(3).

*Statement of value*

B4.3 Rule 16.3, which provides for a statement of value to be included in the claim form, does not apply in the Commercial Court: rule 58.5(2).

*Particulars of claim and the claim form*

B4.4 Although particulars of claim may be served with the claim form, this is not a requirement in the Commercial Court. However, if the particulars of claim are not contained in or served with the claim form, the claim form must contain a statement that if an acknowledgment of service is filed indicating an intention to defend the claim, particulars of claim will follow: rule 58.5(1)(a).

B4.5 If particulars of claim do not accompany the claim form they must be served within 28 days after the defendant has filed an acknowledgment of service indicating an intention to defend the claim: rule 58.5(1)(c).

B4.6 The three forms specified in rule 7.8(1) must be served with the claim form. One of these is a form for acknowledging service: rule 58.5(1)(b).

*Statement of truth*

B4.7

(a) A claim form must be verified by a statement of truth: rule 22.1. Unless the court otherwise orders, any amendment to a claim form must also be verified: rule 22.1(2).
(b) The required form of statement of truth is set out at PD7 § 7.2.
(c) A claim form will remain effective even where not verified by a statement of truth, unless it is struck out: PD22 § 4.1.
(d) In certain cases the statement of truth may be signed by a person other than the party on whose behalf it is served or its legal representative: section C1.8–1.9.

*Trial without service of particulars of claim or a defence*

B4.8 The attention of the parties and their legal representatives is drawn to rule 58.11 which allows the court to order (before or after the issue of a claim form) that the case shall proceed without the filing or service of particulars of claim or defence or of any other statement of case. This facility is to be used with caution. It is unlikely to be appropriate unless all the issues have already been clearly defined in previous exchanges between the parties either in the course of a pre-claim form application or in previous correspondence and then only when the issues are of law or construction.

*Interest*

B4.9 The claim form (and not only the particulars of claim) must comply with the requirements of rules 16.4(1)(b) and 16.4(2) concerning interest: rule 58.5(3).

B4.10 References to particulars of claim in rule 12.6(1)(a) (referring to claims for interest where there is a default judgment) and rule 14.14(1)(a) (referring to claims for interest where there is a judgment on admissions) may be treated as references to the claim form: rules 58.8(2) and 58.9(3).

**B5 Part 8 claims**

*Form*

B5.1 A claimant who wishes to commence a claim under CPR Part 8 must use practice form **N208(CC)**: PD58 § 2.4. **2A–47**

B5.2 Attention is drawn to the requirement in rule 8.2(a) that where a claimant uses the Part 8 procedure his claim form must state that Part 8 applies. Similarly, PD7 § 3.3 requires that the claim form state (if it be the case) that the claimant wishes his claim to proceed under Part 8 or that the claim is required to proceed under Part 8.

*Marking and statement of truth*

B5.3 Sections B3.2 (marking) and B3.7 (statement of truth) also apply to a claim form issued under Part 8.

*Time for filing evidence in opposition to a Part 8 claim*

B5.4 A defendant to a Part 8 claim who wishes to rely on written evidence must file and serve it within 28 days after filing an acknowledgment of service: rule 58.12.

**B6 Part 20 claims**

*Form*

2A–48 B6.1 Adapted versions of the Part 20 claim form and acknowledgment of service (Practice Forms no. **N211** and **N213**) and of the related Notes to Part 20 claimant and Part 20 defendant have been approved for use in the Commercial Court.

**B7 Service of the claim form**

*Service by the parties*

2A–49 B7.1 Claim forms issued in the Commercial List are to be served by the parties, not by the Registry: PD58 § 9.

*Methods of service*

B7.2 Methods of service are set out in CPR Part 6, which is supplemented by a Practice Direction.

B7.3 PD6 § § 2.1 and 3.1 concern service by document exchange and other means, including fax and other electronic means. There are specific provisions about when a solicitor acting for a party may be served.

*Applications for extension of time*

B7.4 Applications for an extension of time in which to serve a claim form are governed by rule 7.6. Rule 7.6(3)(a), which refers to service of the claim form by the court, does not apply in the Commercial Court.

B7.5 The evidence required on an application for an extension of time is set out in PD7 § 8.2. In an appropriate case it may be presented by an application notice verified by a statement of truth and without a separate witness statement: rule 32.6(2).

*Certificate of service*

B7.6 When the claimant has served the claim form he must file a certificate of service: rule 6.14(2). Satisfaction of this requirement is relevant, in particular, to the claimant's ability to obtain judgment in default (see Part 12) and to the right of a non-party to search for, inspect and take a copy of the claim form under rule 5.4(2)(a).

**B8 Service of the claim form out of the jurisdiction**

2A–50 B8.1 Service of claim forms outside the jurisdiction without permission is governed by rules 6.32 – 6.35, and where rule 6.35(5) applies by PD6B.

B8.2 Applications for permission to serve a claim form out of the jurisdiction are governed by rules 6.36 and 6.37 and PD6B. A guide to the appropriate practice is set out in Appendix 15.

B8.3 Service of process in some foreign countries may take a long time to complete; it is therefore important that solicitors take prompt steps to effect service.

## B9 Acknowledgment of service

*Part 7 claims* 2A–51

B9.1

(a) A defendant must file an acknowledgment of service in every case: rule 58.6(1). An adapted version of practice form **N9** (which includes the acknowledgment of service) has been approved for use in the Commercial Court.

(b) The period for filing an acknowledgment of service is calculated from the service of the claim form, whether or not particulars of claim are contained in or accompany the claim form or are to follow service of the claim form. Rule 9.1(2), which provides that in certain circumstances the defendant need not respond to the claim until particulars of claim have been served on him, does not apply: rule 58.6(1).

*Part 8 claims*

B9.2

(a) A defendant must file an acknowledgment of service in every case: rule 58.6(1). An adapted version of practice form **N210** (acknowledgment of service of a Part 8 claim form) has been approved for use in the Commercial Court. A copy of this practice form (Form **N210(CC)**) is included at the end of the Guide, together with adapted versions of the notes for claimants and defendants on completing and replying to a Part 8 claim form.

(b) The time for filing an acknowledgment of service is calculated from the service of the claim form.

*Acknowledgment of service in a claim against a firm*

B9.3

(a) PD10 § 4.4 allows an acknowledgment of service to be signed on behalf of a partnership by any of the partners or a person having the control or management of the partnership business, whether he be a partner or not.

(b) However, attention is drawn to Schedule 1 to the CPR which includes, with modifications, provisions previously contained in RSC Order 81 concerning acknowledgment of service by a person served as a partner who denies his liability as such. (see also the note at the end of CPR Part 10).

*Time for filing acknowledgment of service*

B9.4

(a) Except in the circumstances described in section B8.4(b) and B8.4(c), or is otherwise ordered by the court, the period for filing an acknowledgment of service is 14 days after service of the claim form.

(b) If the claim form has been served out of the jurisdiction without the permission of the court under rules 6.32 and 33, the time for filing an acknowledgment of service is governed by rule 6.35, save that in all cases time runs from the service of the claim form: rule 58.6(3).

(c) If the claim form has been served out of the jurisdiction with the permission of the court under rule 6.36 the time for filing an acknowledgment of service is governed by rule 6.37.5, see Practice Direction B supplementing rule 6 and the table to which it refers, save that in all cases time runs from the service of the claim form: rule 58.6(3).

## B10 Disputing the court's jurisdiction

*Part 7 claims* 2A–52

B10.1

(a) If the defendant intends to dispute the court's jurisdiction or contend that the court should not exercise its jurisdiction he must:

(i) file an acknowledgment of service— rule 11(2); and

(ii) issue an application notice seeking the appropriate relief.

(b) An application to dispute the court's jurisdiction must be made within 28 days after filing an acknowledgment of service: rule 58.7(2).

***Paragraph numbers marked with a "+" can be found online and on CD.***

(c) If the defendant wishes to rely on written evidence in support of that application, he must file and serve that evidence when he issues the application. In an appropriate case it may be presented by an application notice verified by a statement of truth and without a separate witness statement: CPR 32.6(2).
(d) The parties to that application should consider at the time of the application or as soon as possible thereafter whether the application is a 'heavy application' within Section F6.1 likely to last more than half a day but for which the automatic timetable provisions in PD 58 para 13.2 and F6.3–F6.5 will not for any reason be appropriate. If any party considers that special timetabling is required otherwise than in accordance with those automatic provisions it should at once so inform all other parties and the Listing Office. Unless a timetable covering those matters covered by Section F6.3 to F6.5 can be agreed forthwith, the applicant must without delay inform the Listing Office that a directions hearing will be required. For the purposes of such a hearing all parties must by 1pm on the day before that hearing lodge with the Listing Office a brief summary of the issues of fact and law likely to arise on the application, a list of witnesses of fact whose witness statements or affidavits are likely to be adduced by that party, a list of expert witnesses on whose report that party intends to reply, an estimate of how long the hearing will take and how much pre-hearing reading will be required by the judge and a proposed pre-hearing timetable.
(e) If the defendant makes an application under rule 11(1), the claimant is not bound to serve particulars of claim until that application has been disposed of: rule 58.7(3).

*Part 8 claims*

B10.2

(a) The provisions of section B10.1(a)–(c) also apply in the case of Part 8 claims.
(b) If the defendant makes an application under rule 11(1), he is not bound to serve any written evidence on which he wishes to rely in opposition to the substantive claim until that application has been disposed of: rule 11.9.

*Effect of an application challenging the jurisdiction*

B10.3 An acknowledgment of service of a Part 7 or Part 8 claim form which is followed by an application challenging the jurisdiction under Part 11 does not constitute a submission by the defendant to the jurisdiction: rules 11(3) and 11(7).

B10.4 If an application under Part 11 is unsuccessful, and the court then considers giving directions for filing and serving statements of case (in the case of a Part 7 claim) or evidence (in the case of a Part 8 claim), a defendant does not submit to the jurisdiction merely by asking for time to serve and file his statement of case or evidence, as the case may be.

**B11 Default judgment**

2A–53 B11 Default judgment is governed by Part 12 and PD12. However, because in the Commercial Court the period for filing the acknowledgment of service is calculated from service of the claim form, the reference to "particulars of claim" in PD12 § 4.1(1) should be read as referring to the claim form: PD58 § 6(1).

2A–54 **B12 Admissions**

B12

(a) Admissions are governed by CPR Part 14, and PD14, except that the references to "particulars of claim" in PD14 § § 2.1, 3.1 and 3.2 should be read as referring to the claim form: PD58 § 6(2).
(b) Adapted versions of the practice forms of admission (practice forms no. **N9A** and no. **N9C**) have been approved for use in the Commercial Court.

***Paragraph numbers marked with a "+" can be found online and on CD.***

### B13 Transfer of cases into and out of the Commercial List

B13.1 The procedure for transfer and removal is set out in PD58 § 4. All such applications must be made to the Commercial Court: rule 30.5(3). **2A–55**

B13.2 Although an order to transfer a case to the Commercial List may be made at any stage, any application for such an order should normally be made at an early stage in the proceedings. It might be appropriate for some cases to be brought in a Mercantile Court and managed in its early stages in a Mercantile Court before being transferred to the Commercial List.

B13.3 Transfer to the Commercial List may be ordered for limited purposes only, but a transferred case will normally remain in the Commercial List until its conclusion.

B13.4 An order transferring a case out of the Commercial List may be made at any stage, but will not usually be made after a pre-trial timetable has been fixed at the case management conference (see section D8).

B13.5 Some commercial cases may more suitably, or as suitably, be dealt with in one of the Mercantile Courts or the London Mercantile Court. Parties should consider whether it would be more appropriate to begin proceedings in one of those courts and the Commercial Judge may on his own initiative order the case to be transferred there. Guidance on practical steps for transferring cases to the London Mercantile Court and to the Mercantile Courts is contained in a Guidance Note at Appendix 19.

## C.

## PARTICULARS OF CLAIM, DEFENCE AND REPLY

### C1 Form, content, serving and filing **2A–56**

C1.1

(a) Particulars of claim, the defence and any reply must be set out in separate consecutively numbered paragraphs and be as brief and concise as possible. They should not set out evidence.

(b) Statements of case should be limited to 25 pages in length. The court will give permission for a longer statement of case to be served where a party shows good reasons for doing so, and if it does the court might require that a summary of the statement of case is also served. Any application to serve a statement of case longer than 25 pages should be made on paper to the court briefly stating the reasons for exceeding the 25 page limit.

(c) It is seldom necessary for the proper understanding of the statement of case to include substantial parts of a lengthy document, but if this is necessary the passages in question should be set out in a schedule rather than in the body of the case.

(d) The document must be signed by the individual person or persons who drafted it, not, in the case of a solicitor, in the name of the firm alone.

(e) Documents should be in the form stipulated in the Practice Direction to CPR part 5, including that there should be numbered paragraphs and numbered pages.

C1.2

(a) Particulars of claim, the defence and also any reply must comply with the provisions of rules 16.4 and 16.5, save that rules 16.5(6) and 16.5(8) do not apply.

(b) The requirements of PD16 § 7.4–8.1 (which relate to claims based upon oral agreements, agreements by conduct and Consumer Credit Agreements and to reliance upon evidence of certain matters under the Civil Evidence Act 1968) should be treated as applying to the defence and reply as well as to the particulars of claim.

(i) full and specific details should be given of any allegation of fraud, dishonesty, malice or illegality; and

(ii) where an inference of fraud or dishonesty is alleged, the facts on the basis of which the inference is alleged must be fully set out.

(d) Any legislative provision upon which an allegation is based must be clearly identified and the basis of its application explained.

***Paragraph numbers marked with a "+" can be found online and on CD.***



COMMERCIAL COURTS

(e) Any provision of The Human Rights Act 1998 (including the Convention) on which a party relies in support of its case must be clearly identified and the basis of its application explained.

(f) Any principle of foreign law or foreign legislative provision upon which a party's case is based must be clearly identified and the basis of its application explained.

(g) It is important that if a defendant or Part 20 defendant wishes to advance by way of defence or defence to counterclaim a positive case on causation, mitigation or quantification of damages, proper details of that case should be included in the defence or Part 20 defence at the outset or, if not then available, as early as possible thereafter.

C1.3

(a) PD16 § 7.3 relating to a claim based upon a written agreement should be treated as also applying to the defence, unless the claim and the defence are based on the same agreement.

(b) In most cases attaching documents to or serving documents with a statement of case does not promote the efficient conduct of the proceedings and should be avoided.

(c) If documents are to be served at the same time as a statement of case they should normally be served separately from rather than attached to the statement of case.

(d) Only those documents which are obviously of critical importance and necessary for a proper understanding of the statement of case should be attached to or served with it. The statement of case must itself refer to the fact that documents are attached to or served with it.

(e) An expert's report should not be attached to the statement of case and should not be filed with the statement of case at the Registry. A party must obtain permission from the court in order to adduce expert evidence at trial and therefore any party which serves an expert's report without obtaining such permission does so at his own risk as to costs.

(f) Notwithstanding PD16 § 7.3(1), a true copy of the complete written agreement may be made available at any hearing unless the court orders otherwise.

Adapted versions of the practice forms of defence and counterclaim have been approved for use in the Commercial Court.

*Statement of truth*

C1.4 Particulars of claim, a defence and any reply must be verified by a statement of truth: rule 22.1. So too must any amendment, unless the court otherwise orders: rule 22.1(2); see also section C5.4.

C1.5 The required form of statement of truth is as follows:

(i) for particulars of claim, as set out in PD7 § 7.2 or PD16 § 3.4;

(ii) for a defence, as set out in PD15 § 2.2 or PD16 § 12.2;

(iii) for a reply the statement of truth should follow the form for the particulars of claim, but substituting the word "reply" for the words "particulars of claim" (see PD22 § 2.1).

C1.6 Rule 22.1(5), (6) and (8) and PD22 § 3 state who may sign a statement of truth. For example, if insurers are conducting proceedings on behalf of many claimants or defendants a statement of truth may be signed by a senior person responsible for the case at a lead insurer, but

(i) the person signing must specify the capacity in which he signs;

(ii) the statement of truth must be a statement that the lead insurer believes that the facts stated in the document are true; and

(iii) the court may order that a statement of truth also be signed by one or more of the parties.

See PD22 § 3.6B.

C1.7 A statement of case remains effective (although it may not be relied on as evidence) even where it is not verified by a statement of truth, unless it is struck out: PD22 § § 4.1–4.3.

*Service*

C1.8 All statements of case are served by the parties, not by the court: PD58 § 9.

*Filing*

C1.9 The statements of case filed with the court form part of the permanent record of the court.

### C2 Serving and filing particulars of claim

C2.1 Subject to any contrary order of the court and unless particulars of claim are contained in or accompany the claim form: **2A–57**

(i) the period for serving particulars of claim is 28 days after filing an acknowledgment of service: rule 58.5(1)(c);

(ii) the parties may agree extensions of the period for serving the particulars of claim. However, any such agreement and brief reasons must be evidenced in writing and notified to the court, addressed to the Listing Office: PD58 § 7.1;

C2.2 The court may make an order overriding any agreement by the parties varying a time limit: PD58 § 7.2.

C2.3 The claimant must serve the particulars of claim on all other parties. A copy of the claim form will be filed at the Registry on issue. If the claimant serves particulars of claim separately from the claim form he must file a copy within 7 days of service together with a certificate of service: rule 7.4(3).

### C3 Serving and filing a defence

C3.1 The defendant must serve the defence on all other parties and must at the same time file a copy with the court. **2A–58**

C3.2

(a) If the defendant files an acknowledgment of service which indicates an intention to defend the period for serving and filing a defence is 28 days after service of the particulars of claim, subject to the provisions of rule 15.4(2). (See also Appendix 15 for cases where the claim form has been served out of the jurisdiction).

(b) The defendant and the claimant may agree that the period for serving and filing a defence shall be extended by up to 28 days: rule 15.5(1). However, any such agreement and brief reasons must be evidenced in writing and notified to the court, addressed to the Case Management Unit: PD58 § 7.1.

(c) An application to the court is required for any further extension. If the parties are able to agree that a further extension should be granted, a draft consent order should be provided together with a brief explanation of the reasons for the extension.

C3.3 The general power to agree variations to time limits contained in rule 2.11 and PD58 § 7.1 enables parties to agree extensions of the period for serving and filing a defence that exceed 28 days. The length of extension must in all cases be specified, and any such agreement must be evidenced in writing and comply with the requirements of section C2.1.

C3.4 The claimant must notify the Listing Office by letter when all defendants who intend to serve a defence have done so. This information is material to the fixing of the case management conference (see section D3.1).

**C4 Serving and filing a reply**

2A–59 C4.1 Subject to section C4.3, the period for serving and filing a reply is 21 days after service of the defence: rule 58.10(1).

C4.2 A claimant who does not file a reply does not admit what is pleaded in the defence and a claimant who files a reply that does not deal with something pleaded in the defence is not taken to admit it. A reply should be served only when necessary and then only plead what is necessary: it should not repeat what is pleaded in the particulars of claim.

C4.3

(a) A reply must be filed at the same time as it is served: rule 15.8(b); rule 15.8(a) does not apply in proceedings in the Commercial List.

(b) The reply should be served before case management information sheets are provided to the court (see section D8.5). In the normal case, this will allow the parties to consider any reply before completing the case management information sheet, and allow time for the preparation of the case memorandum and the list of issues each of which is required for the case management conference (see sections D5–D7).

C4.3 In some cases, more than 21 days may be needed for the preparation, service and filing of a reply. In such cases an application should be made on paper for an extension of time and for a postponement of the case management conference. The procedure to be followed when making an application on paper is set out in section F4.

C4.4 Any reply must be served by the claimant on all other parties: rule 58.10(1).

2A–60 **C5 Amendment**

C5.1

(a) Amendments to a statement of case must show the original text, unless the court orders otherwise: PD58 § 8.

(b) Amendments may be shown by using footnotes or marginal notes, provided they identify precisely where and when an amendment has been made.

(c) Unless the court so orders, there is no need to show amendments by colour-coding.

(d) If there have been extensive amendments it may be desirable to prepare a fresh copy of the statement of case. However, a copy of the statement of case showing where and when amendments have been made must also be made available.

C5.2 All amendments to any statement of case must be verified by a statement of truth unless the court orders otherwise: rule 22.1(2).

C5.3 Questions of amendment, and consequential amendment, should wherever possible be dealt with by consent. A party should consent to a proposed amendment unless he has substantial grounds for objecting to it.

C5.4 Late amendments should be avoided and may be disallowed.

## D.

## CASE MANAGEMENT IN THE COMMERCIAL COURT

**D1 Generally**

2A–61 D1.1 All proceedings in the Commercial List will be subject to management by the court.

D1.2 All proceedings in the Commercial List are automatically allocated to the multi-track and consequently Part 26 and the rules relating to allocation do not apply: rule 58.13(1).

***Paragraph numbers marked with a "+" can be found online and on CD.***

D1.3 Except for rule 29.3(2) (legal representatives to attend case management conferences and pre-trial reviews) and rule 29.5 (variation of case management timetable), Part 29 does not apply to proceedings in the Commercial List: rule 58.13(2).

D1.4 If a party has a legal representative, all case management conferences must be attended by such a representative who is familiar with the case and has sufficient authority to deal with any issues that are likely to arise: rule 29.3(2).

**Editorial note**

See Heavy and Complex Cases at para.2A–18.1, above. **2A–61.1**

**D2 Key features of case management in the Commercial Court**

D2 Case management is governed by rule 58.13 and PD58 § 10. In a normal commercial case commenced by a Part 7 claim form, case management will include the following 12 key features: **2A–62**

(1) statements of case will be exchanged within fixed or monitored time periods;

(2) a case memorandum, a list of issues and a case management bundle will be produced at an early point in the case;

(3) the case memorandum, list of issues and case management bundle will be amended and updated or revised on a running basis throughout the life of the case and will be used by the court at every stage of the case. In particular the list of issues will be used as a tool to define what factual and expert evidence is necessary and the scope of disclosure;

(4) the court itself will approve or settle the list of issues and may require the further assistance of the parties and their legal representatives in order to do so;

(5) a mandatory case management conference will be held shortly after statements of case have been served, if not before (and preceded by the parties lodging case management information sheets identifying their views on the requirements of the case);

(6) at the case management conference the court will (as necessary) discuss the issues in the case and the requirements of the case with the advocates retained in the case. The court will set a pre-trial timetable and give any other directions as may be appropriate;

(7) after statements of case have been served, the parties will serve a disclosure schedule or schedules. At the first case management conference, the court will discuss with the advocates retained in the case by reference to the list of issues the strategy for disclosure set out in the disclosure schedules with a view to ensuring that disclosure and searches for documents are proportionate to the importance of the issues in the case to which the disclosure relates and avoiding subsequent applications for specific disclosure;

(8) before the progress monitoring date the parties will report to the court, using a progress monitoring information sheet, the extent of their compliance with the pre-trial timetable;

(9) on or shortly after the progress monitoring date a judge will (without a hearing) consider progress and give such further directions as he thinks appropriate;

(10) if at the progress monitoring date all parties have indicated that they will be ready for trial, all parties will complete a pre-trial checklist;

(11) in many cases there will be a pre-trial review; in such cases the parties will be required to prepare a trial timetable for consideration by the court;

(12) throughout the case there will be regular reviews of the estimated length of trial, including how much pre-trial reading should be undertaken by the judge.

**D3 Fixing a case management conference**

D3.1 A mandatory case management conference will normally take place on the first available date 6 weeks after all defendants who intend to serve a defence have done so. This will normally allow time for the preparation and service of any reply (see section C4). **2A–63**

*Paragraph numbers marked with a "+" can be found online and on CD.*

D3.2

(a) If proceedings have been started by service of a Part 7 claim form, the claimant must take steps to fix the date for the case management conference with the Listing Office in co-operation with the other parties within 14 days of the date when all defendants who intend to file and serve a defence have done so: PD58 § 10.2(a). The parties should bear in mind the need to allow time for the preparation and service of any reply.

(b) If proceedings have been begun by service of a Part 8 claim form, the claimant must take steps to fix a date for the case management conference with the Listing Office in co-operation with the other parties within 14 days of the date when all defendants who wish to serve evidence have done so: PD58 § 10.2(b).

D3.3

(a) In accordance with section C3 the Registry will expect a defence to be served and filed by the latest of:

(i) 28 days after service of particulars of claim (as certified by the certificate of service); or

(ii) any extended date for serving and filing a defence as notified to the court in writing following agreement between the parties; or

(iii) any extended date for serving and filing a defence as ordered by the court on an application.

(b) If within 28 days after the latest of these dates has passed for each defendant, the parties have not taken steps to fix the date for the case management conference, the Listing Office will inform the Judge in Charge of the List, and at his direction will take steps to fix a date for the case management conference without further reference to the parties.

D3.4 If the proceedings have been transferred to the Commercial List, the claimant must apply for a case management conference within 14 days of the date of the order transferring them, unless the judge held, or gave directions for, a case management conference when he made the order transferring the proceedings: PD58 § 10.3.

D3.5 If the claimant fails to make an application as required by the rules, any other party may apply for a case management conference: PD58 § 10.5.

D3.6

(a) In some cases it may be appropriate for a case management conference to take place at an earlier date.

(b) Any party may apply to the court in writing at an earlier time for a case management conference: PD58 § 10.4. A request by any party for an early case management conference should be made in writing to the Judge in Charge of the List, on notice to all other parties, at the earliest possible opportunity.

D3.7 If before the date on which the case management conference would be held in accordance with section D3 there is a hearing in the case at which the parties are represented, the business of the case management conference will normally be transacted at that hearing and there will be no separate case management conference.

D3.8 The court may fix a case management conference at any time on its own initiative. If it does so, the court will normally give at least 7 days notice to the parties: PD58 § 10.6.

D3.9 A case management conference may not be postponed or adjourned without an order of the court.

**D4 Designated judge**

**2A–64** D4.1 Cases which are exceptional in size or complexity or in having a propensity to give rise to numerous pre-trial applications may be allocated to a designated judge.

***Paragraph numbers marked with a "+" can be found online and on CD.***

D4.2 An application for the appointment of a designated judge should be made in writing to the Judge in Charge of the List at the time of fixing the case management conference.

D4.3 If an order is made for allocation to a designated judge, the designated judge will preside at all subsequent pre-trial case management conferences and other hearings. Normally all applications in the case, other than applications for an interim payment, will be determined by the designated judge and he will be the trial judge.

### D5 Case memorandum

D5.1 In order that the judge conducting the case management conference may be informed of the general nature of the case and the issues which are expected to arise, after service of the defence and any reply the solicitors and counsel for each party shall draft an agreed case memorandum. **2A–65**

D5.2 The case memorandum should contain:

(i) a short and uncontroversial description of what the case is about; and

(ii) a very short and uncontroversial summary of the material procedural history of the case.

D5.3 Unless otherwise ordered, the solicitors for the claimant are to be responsible for producing and filing the case memorandum, and where appropriate for revising it.

D5.4 The case memorandum should not refer to any application for an interim payment, to any order for an interim payment, to any voluntary interim payment, or to any payment or offer under CPR Part 36 or Part 37.

D5.5

(a) It should be clearly understood that the only purpose of the case memorandum is to help the judge understand broadly what the case is about. The case memorandum does not play any part in the trial. It is unnecessary, therefore, for parties to be unduly concerned about the precise terms in which it is drafted, provided it contains a reasonably fair and balanced description of the case. Above all the parties must do their best to spend as little time as practicable in drafting and negotiating the wording of the memorandum and keep clearly in mind the need to limit costs.

(b) Accordingly, in all but the most exceptional cases it should be possible for the parties to draft an agreed case memorandum. However, if it proves impossible to do so, the claimant must draft the case memorandum and send a copy to the defendant. The defendant may provide its comments to the court (with a copy to the claimant) separately.

(c) The failure of the parties to agree a case memorandum is a matter which the court may wish to take into account when dealing with the costs of the case management conference.

### D6 List of issues

D6.1 After service of the defence (and any reply), the solicitors and counsel for each party shall produce an agreed list of the important issues in the case. The list should include both issues of fact and issue of law. A separate section of the document should list what is common ground between the parties (or any of them, specifying which). **2A–66**

D6.2

(a) The list of issues is intended to be a neutral document for use as a case management tool at all stages of the case by the parties and the court. Neither party should attempt to draft the list in terms which advance one party's case over that of another.

(b) It is unnecessary, therefore, for parties to be unduly concerned about the precise terms in which the list of issues is drafted, provided it presents the structure of the case in a reasonably fair and balanced way. Above all the parties must do their best to spend as little time as practicable in drafting and negotiating the wording of the list of issues and keep clearly in mind the need to limit costs.

(c) Accordingly, in most cases it should be possible for the parties to draft an agreed list of issues. However, if it proves impossible to do so, the claimant must draft the list and send a copy to the defendant. The defendant may provide its comments or alternative suggested list to the court (with a copy to the claimant) separately.

D6.3

(a) A draft (or drafts) of the list of issues is to be available to the court prior to the first case management conference. It is intended that at that stage the draft list should be in a general form, identifying the key issues and the structure of the parties' contentions, rather than setting out all detailed sub-issues.

(b) At the first case management conference and any subsequent case management conferences which take place, the court will review and settle the draft list of issues with a view to refining it and identifying important sub-issues as appropriate and as required in order to manage the case. Accordingly the list of issues may be developed, by expansion or reduction as the case progresses.

D6.4 The list of issues will be used by the court and the parties as a case management tool as the case progresses to determine such matters as the scope of disclosure and of factual and expert evidence and to consider whether issues should be determined summarily or preliminary issues should be determined.

D6.5 The list of issues is a tool for case management purposes and is not intended to supersede the pleadings which remain the primary source for each party's case. If at any stage of the proceedings, any question arises as to the accuracy of the list of issues, it will be necessary to consult the pleadings, in order to determine what issues arise.

### D7 Case management bundle

*Preparation*

2A–67 D7.1 Before the case management conference (see sections D3 and D8), a case management bundle should be prepared by the solicitors for the claimant: PD58 § 10.8.

*Contents*

D7.2 The case management bundle should contain the documents listed below (where the documents have been created by the relevant time):

(i) the claim form;

(ii) all statements of case (excluding schedules), except that, if a summary has been prepared, the bundle should contain the summary, not the full statement of case;

(iii) the case memorandum (see section D5);

(iv) the list of issues (see section D6);

(v) the case management information sheets and the pre-trial timetable if one has already been established (see sections D8.5 and D8.9);

(vi) the principal orders in the case;

(vii) any agreement in writing made by the parties to disclose documents without making a list or any agreement in writing that disclosure (or inspection or both) shall take place in stages.

See generally PD58 § 10.8.

D7.3 It is also useful for the case management bundle to include all disclosure schedules stating what search each party intends to make pursuant to Rule 31.7 when giving standard disclosure of electronic and other documents and what search he expects of the other party (or parties).

D7.4 The case management bundle should not include a copy of any order for an interim payment.

*Lodging the case management bundle*

D7.5 The case management bundle should be lodged with the Listing Office at least 7 days before the (first) case management conference (or earlier hearing at which the parties are represented and at which the business of the case management conference may be transacted: see section D3.7).

*Preparation and upkeep*

D7.6 The claimant (or other party responsible for the preparation and upkeep of the case management bundle), in consultation with the other parties, must revise and update the case management bundle as the case proceeds: PD58 § 10.9. The claimant should attend at the Listing Office for this purpose at the following stages:

(i) within 10 days of the case management conference, in order to add the pre-trial timetable (or any other order made at the case management conference) and an updated case memorandum;

(ii) within 10 days of an order being made on an application, if in the light of the order or the application it is necessary to add a copy of the order made (as a principal order in the case) or an updated case memorandum;

(iii) within 14 days of the service of any amended statement of case (or summary), in order to substitute a copy of the amended statement of case (or summary) for that which it replaces and to incorporate an updated case memorandum and (if appropriate) a revised list of issues;

(iv) within 10 days of any other revision to the case memorandum or list of issues, in order to incorporate the revised document.

**D8 Case Management Conference**

*Application to postpone the case management conference* **2A–68**

D8.1

(a) An application to postpone the case management conference must be made within 21 days after all defendants who intend to serve a defence have done so.

(b) The application will be dealt with on paper unless the court considers it appropriate to direct an oral hearing.

*Attendance at the case management conference*

D8.2 Clients need not attend a case management conference unless the court otherwise orders. A representative who has conduct of the case must attend from each firm of solicitors instructed in the case. At least one of the advocates retained in the case on behalf of each party should also attend.

D8.3

(a) The case management conference is a very significant stage in the case. Although parties are encouraged to agree proposals for directions for the consideration of the court, directions will not normally be made by consent without the need for attendance.

(b) The general rule in the Commercial Court, as the Commercial and Admiralty Courts Guide makes clear, is that there must be an oral Case Management Conference (CMC) at court.

(c) However, there are cases which are out of the ordinary where it may be possible to dispense with an oral hearing if the issues are straightforward and the costs of an oral hearing cannot be justified.

***Paragraph numbers marked with a "+" can be found online and on CD.***

(d) In such a case, if the parties wish to ask the Court to consider holding the CMC on paper, they must lodge all the appropriate documents (see D8.3(e)) by no later than 12 noon on the Tuesday of the week in which the CMC is fixed for the Friday. That timing will be strictly enforced. If all the papers are not provided by that time, the CMC must be expected to go forward to an oral hearing. If the failure to lodge the papers is due to the fault of one party and it is for that reason an oral CMC takes place, that party will be at risk as to costs.

(e) With the papers (which will include the Case Management bundle with the information sheets fully completed by each party), the parties must lodge a draft Order and draft list of issues (both agreed by the parties) for consideration by the Judge and a statement signed by each advocate:

- (i) confirming that the parties have considered and discussed all the relevant issues and brought to the Court's attention anything that was unusual; and
- (ii) setting out information about any steps that had been taken to resolve the dispute by ADR, any future plans for ADR or an explanation as to why ADR would not be appropriate.
- (iii) giving a time estimate for the trial, specifically stating how much pre-trial reading by the judge will be required.

(f) In the ordinary course of things it would be unlikely that any case involving expert evidence or preliminary issues would be suitable for a CMC on paper. In cases involving expert evidence, the Court is anxious to give particular scrutiny to that evidence, given the cost such evidence usually involves and the need to focus that evidence. In cases where preliminary issues are sought, the Court will need to examine the formulation of those issues and discuss whether they are really appropriate.

*Applications*

D8.4

(a) If by the time of the case management conference a party wishes to apply for an order in respect of a matter not covered by Questions (1)–(16) in the case management information sheet, the application should be made at the case management conference.

(b) In some cases notice of such an application may be given in the case management information sheet itself: see section D8.5(c).

(c) In all other cases the applicant should ensure that an application notice and any supporting evidence is filed and served in time to enable the application to be heard at the case management conference.

*Materials: case management information sheet and case management bundle*

D8.5

(a) All parties attending a case management conference must complete a case management information sheet: PD58 § 10.7. A standard form of case management information sheet is set out in Appendix 6. The information sheet is intended to include reference to all applications which the parties would wish to make at a case management conference.

(b) A completed case management information sheet must be provided by each party to the court (and copied to all other parties) at least 7 days before the case management conference.

(c) Applications not covered by the standard questions raised in the case management information sheet should be entered under Question (17). No other application notice is necessary if written evidence will not be involved and the 7 day notice given by entering the application on the information sheet will in all the circumstances be sufficient to enable all other parties to deal with the application.

D8.6 The case management bundle must be provided to the court at least 7 days before the case management conference: PD58 § 10.8.

*The hearing*

D8.7 The court's power to give directions at the case management conference is to be found in rules 3.1 and 58.13(4). At the case management conference the judge will:

***Paragraph numbers marked with a "+" can be found online and on CD.***

(i) discuss the issues in the case by reference to the draft list of issues, and settle a list of issues;

(ii) discuss the requirements of the case (including issues of disclosure by reference to the disclosure schedule or schedules), with the advocates retained in the case;

(iii) fix the entire pre-trial timetable, or, if that is not practicable, fix as much of the pre-trial timetable as possible; and

(iv) in appropriate cases make an ADR order.

D8.8 At the Case Management Conference, and again at the Pre-Trial Review, active consideration will be given, by reference to the list of issues, to the possibility of the trial or summary determination of a preliminary issue or issues the resolution of which is likely to shorten the proceedings. An example is a relatively short question of law which can be tried without significant delay (though the implications of a possible appeal for the remainder of the case cannot be lost sight of). The court may suggest the trial of a preliminary issue, but it will rarely make an order without the concurrence of at least one of the parties. Active consideration will also be given to whether any issues are suitable for summary determination pursuant to CPR Part 24.

D8.9

(a) Rules 3.1(2) and 58.13(4) enable the court at the case management conference to stay the proceedings while the parties try to settle the case by alternative means. The case management information sheet requires the parties to indicate whether a stay for such purposes is sought.

(b) In an appropriate case an ADR order may be made without a stay of proceedings. The parties should consider carefully whether it may be possible to provide for ADR in the pre-trial timetable without affecting the date of trial.

(c) Where a stay has been granted for a fixed period for the purposes of ADR the court has power to extend it. If an extension of the stay is desired by all parties, a judge will normally be prepared to deal with an application for such an extension if it is made before the expiry of the stay by letter from the legal representatives of one of the parties. The letter should confirm that all parties consent to the application.

(d) An extension will not normally be granted for more than four weeks unless clear reasons are given to justify a longer period, but more than one extension may be granted.

*The pre-trial timetable*

D8.10 The pre-trial timetable will normally include:

(i) a progress monitoring date (see section D12 below); and

(ii) a direction that the parties attend upon the Clerk to the Commercial Court to obtain a fixed date for trial.

*Variations to the pre-trial timetable*

D8.11

(a) The parties may agree minor variations to the time periods set out in the pre-trial timetable without the case needing to be brought back to the court provided that the variation

(i) will not jeopardise the date fixed for trial;

(ii) does not relate to the progress monitoring date; and

(iii) does not provide for the completion after the progress monitoring date of any step which was previously scheduled to have been completed by that date.

(b) The court should be informed in writing of any such agreement.

D8.12 If in any case it becomes apparent that variations to the pre-trial timetable are required which do not fall within section D8.11 above, the parties should apply to have the case management conference reconvened immediately. The parties should not wait until the progress monitoring date.

**D9 Case management conference: Part 8 claims**

**2A–69** D9 In a case commenced by the issue of a Part 8 claim form, a case management conference will normally take place on the first available date 6 weeks after service and filing of the defendant's evidence. At that case management conference the Court will make such pre-trial directions as are necessary, adapting (where useful in the context of the particular claim) those of the case management procedures used for a claim commenced by the issue of a Part 7 claim form.

**D10 Case management conference: Part 20 claims**

**2A–70** D10.1 Wherever possible, any party who intends to make a Part 20 claim should do so before the hearing of the case management conference dealing with the main claim.

D10.2 Where permission to make a Part 20 claim is required it should be sought at the case management conference in the main claim.

D10.3 If the Part 20 claim is confined to a counterclaim by a defendant against a claimant alone, the court will give directions in the Part 20 claim at the case management conference in the main claim.

D10.4 If the Part 20 claim is not confined to a counterclaim by a defendant against a claimant alone, the case management conference in the main claim will be reconvened on the first available date 6 weeks after service by the defendant of the new party of parties to the proceedings.

D10.5 All parties to the proceedings (i.e. the parties to the main claim and the parties to the Part 20 claim) must attend the reconvened case management conference. There will not be a separate case management conference for the Part 20 claim alone.

D10.6 In any case involving a Part 20 claim the court will give case management directions at the same case management conferences as it gives directions for the main claim: PD58 § 12. The court will therefore normally only give case management directions at hearings attended by all parties to the proceedings.

D10.7 The provisions of D10.4, D10.5 and D10.6 apply equally to Part 20 claims brought by parties who are not also parties to the main claim.

**D11 Management throughout the case**

**2A–71** D11 The court will continue to take an active role in the management of the case throughout its progress to trial. Parties should be ready at all times to provide the court with such information and assistance as it may require for that purpose.

**D12 Progress monitoring**

*Fixing the progress monitoring date*

**2A–72** D12.1 The progress monitoring date will be fixed at the case management conference and will normally be after the date in the pre-trial timetable for exchange of witness statements and expert reports.

*Progress monitoring information sheet*

D12.2 At least 3 days (i.e. three clear days) before the progress monitoring date the parties must each send to the Case Management Unit (with a copy to all other parties) a progress monitoring information sheet to inform the court:

(i) whether they have complied with the pre-trial timetable, and if they have not, the respects in which they have not; and

(ii) whether they will be ready for a trial commencing on the fixed date specified in the pre-trial timetable, and if they will not be ready, why they will not be ready.

D12.3 A standard form of progress monitoring information sheet is set out in Appendix 12.

D12.4 The progress monitoring information sheets are referred to the judge in charge of the list.

D12.5 Upon considering progress monitoring information sheet, the court may, particularly if there has been significant non-compliance with the pre-trial timetable, direct a date by which further information sheet are to be sent to the court.

**D13 Reconvening the case management conference**

D13.1 If in the view of the court the information given in the progress monitoring sheets justifies this course, the court may direct that the case management conference be reconvened. **2A–73**

D13.2 At a reconvened hearing of the case management conference the court may make such orders and give such directions as it considers appropriate. If the court is of the view that due to the failure of the parties or any of them to comply with the case management timetable the trial cannot be fairly and efficiently conducted on the date fixed, it may vacate the trial date and make such order for costs as is appropriate.

**D14 Pre-trial checklist**

D14 Not later than three weeks before the date fixed for trial each party must send to the Listing Office (with a copy to all other parties) a completed checklist confirming final details for trial (a "pre-trial checklist") in the form set out in Appendix 13. **2A–74**

**D15 Further information** **2A–75**

D15.1

(a) If a party declines to provide further information requested under Part 18, the solicitors or counsel who are to appear at the application for the parties concerned must communicate directly with each other in an attempt to reach agreement before any application is made to the court.

(b) No application for an order that a party provide further information will normally be listed for hearing without prior written confirmation from the applicant that the requirements of this section D15.1(a) have been complied with.

(c) The court will only order further information to be provided if satisfied that the information requested is strictly necessary to understand another party's case.

D15.2 Because it falls within the definition of a statement of case (see rule 2.3(1))a response providing further information under CPR Part 18 must be verified by a statement of truth.

**D16 Fixed trial dates**

D16.1 Most cases will be given fixed trial dates immediately after the pre-trial timetable has been set at the case management conference. **2A–76**

D16.2 A fixed date for trial is given on the understanding that if previous fixtures have been substantially underestimated or other urgent matters need to be heard, the trial may be delayed. Where such delay might cause particular inconvenience to witnesses or others involved in the trial, the Clerk to the Commercial Court should be informed well in advance of the fixed date.

**D17 Estimates of length of trial**

D17.1 At the case management conference an estimate will be made of the minimum and maximum lengths of the trial. The estimate should include time for pre-trial **2A–77** reading by the judge and specify what time has been allowed for that purpose. The estimate will appear in the pre-trial timetable and will be the basis on which a date for trial will be fixed.

D17.2 The court examines with particular care longer estimates, and will wish to consider with the assistance of advocates whether in the case of particularly long trials all the issues in the trial should be heard at the same hearing: see section J2.

D17.3 If a party subsequently instructs new advocate(s) to appear on its behalf at the trial, the Listing Office should be notified of that fact within 14 days. Advocates newly instructed should review the estimate of the minimum and maximum lengths of the trial, and submit to the Listing Office a signed note revising or confirming the estimate as appropriate.

D17.4 A confirmed estimate of the minimum and maximum lengths of the trial, signed by the advocates who are to appear at the trial, should be attached to the pre-trial checklist.

D17.5 It is the duty of all advocates who are to appear at the trial to seek agreement, if possible, on the estimated minimum and maximum lengths of trial.

D17.6 The provisional estimate and (after it is given) the confirmed estimate must be kept under review by the advocates who are to appear at the trial. If at any stage an estimate needs to be revised, a signed revised estimate (whether agreed or not) should be submitted by the advocates to the Clerk to the Commercial Court.

D17.7 Accurate estimation of trial length is of great importance to the efficient functioning of the court. The court will be guided by, but will not necessarily accept, the estimates given by the parties.

### D18 Pre-Trial Review and trial timetable

2A-78 D18.1 The court will order a pre-trial review in any case in which it considers it appropriate to do so.

D18.2 A pre-trial review will normally take place between 8 and 4 weeks before the date fixed for trial, but might be earlier in particularly long or complex cases.

D18.3 Whenever possible the pre-trial review will be conducted by the trial judge. It should be attended by the advocates who are to appear at the trial: PD58 § 11.2.

D18.4 Before the pre-trial review or, if there is not to be one, not later than 7 days before the trial is due to commence, the parties must attempt to agree a timetable for the trial providing for oral submissions, examinations in chief (if any) and cross-examination of witnesses of fact and expert witnesses: PD58 § 11.3. The claimant must file a copy of the draft timetable at least two days before the date fixed for the pre-trial review; any differences of view should be clearly identified and briefly explained: PD58 § 11.4. At the pre-trial review the judge may set a timetable for the trial and give such other directions for the conduct of the trial as he considers appropriate.

### 2A-79 D19 Orders

D19.1

(a) Except for orders made by the court on its own initiative under rule 3.3, and unless the court otherwise orders, every judgment or order will be drawn up by the parties and rule 40.3 is modified accordingly: rule 58.15(1).

(b) Consent orders are to be drawn up in accordance with the procedure described in section F9.

(c) All other orders are to be drawn up in draft by the parties and dated in the draft with the date of the judge's decision. The claimant is to have responsibility for drafting the order, unless it was made on the application of another party in which case that other party is to have the responsibility.

(d) Two copies of the draft, signed by the parties themselves, or by their solicitors or counsel, must be lodged with the Registry **within five days** of the decision of the court reflected in the draft.

D19.2 If the court orders that an act be done by a certain date without specifying a time for compliance, the latest time for compliance is 4.30 p.m. on the day in question.

D19.3 Orders that are required to be served must be served by the parties, unless the court otherwise directs.

## E.
## DISCLOSURE

### E1 Generally

E1.1 The court will seek to ensure that disclosure is no wider than appropriate. Anything wider than standard disclosure will need to be justified. **2A–80**

E1.2 The obligations imposed by an order for disclosure continue until the proceedings come to an end. If, after a list of documents has been prepared and served, the existence (present or past) of further documents to which the order applies comes to the attention of the disclosing party, that party must prepare and serve a supplemental list.

E1.3 When making standard disclosure, a party is required to make a reasonable search for documents and state in his disclosure statement any limits that he has placed upon his search on the grounds that it would be unreasonable: rule 31.7.

### E2 Procedure in advance of disclosure

E2.1 At the first case management conference the court will normally wish to consider one or more of the following: **2A–81**

(i) ordering standard disclosure: rule 31.5(1);

(ii) dispensing with or limiting standard disclosure: rule 31.5(2);

(iii) ordering sample disclosure;

(iv) ordering disclosure in stages;

(v) ordering disclosure otherwise than by service of a list of documents, for example, by service of copy documents; and

(vi) ordering specific disclosure: rule 31.12.

E2.2 Among other things the court will normally wish to consider, by reference to the list of issues, the scope of standard disclosure. This is standard disclosure as defined by rule 31.6. Where standard disclosure is ordered a party is required to disclose only:

(i) the documents on which he relies; and

(ii) documents which—

— adversely affect his own case;

— adversely affect another party's case; or

— support another party's case; and

(iii) documents which he is required to disclose by any relevant practice direction.

E2.3 When considering disclosure at the first case management conference the court will normally be assisted by a disclosure schedule produced by each party, indicating (by reference to categories of documents, the location of documents and the period of time covered by the documentation and otherwise) what documentation the party recognises should be covered by standard disclosure, and whether he intends to place any, and if so what, limits upon his search on the basis that it would be unreasonable.

The court will normally invite the observations of other parties upon the proposals in a disclosure schedule with a view to determining the proper extent of disclosure and any proper limits upon the search for documents before the parties make disclosure.

E2.4 A party who contends that to search for a category or class of document would be unreasonable (see rule 31.7) should also indicate this in his case management information sheet (see Appendix 6).

E2.5 All parties should have regard to issues which may specifically arise concerning electronic data and documents in accordance with 31PD.2A:

(a) Rule 31.4 contains a broad definition of a document. This extends to electronic documents, including e-mail and other electronic communications, word processed documents and databases. In addition to documents that are readily accessible from computer systems and other electronic devices and media, the definition covers those documents that are stored on servers and back-up systems and electronic documents that have been "deleted". It also extends to additional information stored and associated with electronic documents known as metadata. In most cases metadata is unlikely to be relevant.

(b) The parties should, prior to the first Case Management Conference, discuss any issues that may arise regarding searches for and the preservation of electronic documents. This may involve the parties providing information about the categories of electronic documents within their control, the computer systems, electronic devices and media on which any relevant documents may be held, the storage systems maintained by the parties and their document retention policies. In the case of difficulty or disagreement, the matter should be referred to a judge for directions at the earliest practical date, if possible at the first Case Management Conference. For this purpose the parties should before any such hearing co-operate to provide the court with an explicit account of the issues as to retrieval and disclosure of electronic documents which have arisen and where proportionality is in issue each party should provide the court with an informed estimate of the volume of documents involved and the cost of their retrieval and disclosure.

(c) The parties should co-operate at an early stage as to the format in which electronic copy documents are to be provided on inspection. In the case of difficulty or disagreement, the matter should be referred to a Judge for directions at the earliest practical date, if possible at the first Case Management Conference.

(d) The existence of electronic documents impacts upon the extent of the reasonable search required by Rule 31.7 for the purposes of standard disclosure. The factors that may be relevant in deciding the reasonableness of a search for electronic documents include (but are not limited to) the following:

(i) The number of documents involved.

(ii) The nature and complexity of the proceedings.

(iii) The ease and expense of retrieval of any particular document. This includes:

(1) The accessibility of electronic documents or data including e-mail communications on computer systems, servers, back-up systems and other electronic devices or media that may contain such documents taking into account alterations or developments in hardware or software systems used by the disclosing party and/or available to enable access to such documents.

(2) The location of relevant electronic documents, data, computer systems, servers, back-up systems and other electronic devices or media that may contain such documents.

(3) The likelihood of locating relevant data.

(4) The cost of recovering any electronic documents.

(5) The cost of disclosing and providing inspection of any relevant electronic documents.

(6) The likelihood that electronic documents will be materially altered in the course of recovery, disclosure or inspection.

(iv) The significance of any document which is likely to be located during the search.

***Paragraph numbers marked with a "+" can be found online and on CD.***

(e) It may be reasonable to search some or all of the parties' electronic storage systems. In some circumstances, it may be reasonable to search for electronic documents by means of keyword searches (agreed as far as possible between the parties) even where a full review of each and every document would be unreasonable. There may be other forms of electronic search that may be appropriate in particular circumstances.

(f) Whether or not the parties draw to the court's attention particular areas of difference or disagreement, the court will normally at the first case management conference wish to consider whether the burden of dislcosure, in terms of time, cost and business disruption, can properly be reduced (for example by use of electronic search tools and deduplication software).

### E3 Disclosure procedure

E3.1 In order to comply with rule 31.10(3) (which requires the list to identify the documents in a convenient order and manner and as concisely as possible) it will normally be necessary to list the documents in date order, to number them consecutively and to give each a concise description. In some cases, it will be useful to give each document a "Bates number" identifying the party disclosing it (such as C101 or D(1) 202). However, where there is a large number of documents all falling within a particular category the disclosing party may (unless otherwise ordered) list those documents as a category rather than individually. **2A–82**

E3.2 Each party to the proceedings must serve a separate list of documents. This applies even if two or more parties are represented by the same firm of solicitors.

E3.3 If the physical structure of a file may be of evidential value (e.g. a placing or chartering file) solicitors should make one complete copy of the file in the form in which they received it before any documents are removed for the purpose of giving disclosure or inspection.

E3.4 Unless the Court directs otherwise, the disclosure statement must comply with the requirements of rules 31.7(3) and 31.10(6). In particular, it should

(i) expressly state that the disclosing party believes the extent of the search to have been reasonable in all the circumstances; and

(ii) draw attention to any particular limitations on the extent of the search adopted for reasons of proportionality and give the reasons why they were adopted.

E3.5 The disclosure statement for standard disclosure should begin with the following words:

"[I/we], [name(s)] state that [I/we] have carried out a reasonable and proportionate search to locate all the documents which [I am/here name the party is] required to disclose under [the order made by the Court or the agreement in writing made between the parties] on the [] day of [] 20[]."

E3.6 The disclosure statement for standard disclosure should end with the following certificate:

"[I/we] certify that [I/we] understand the duty of disclosure and to the best of [my/our] knowledge [I have/here name the party has] carried out that duty. [I/we] certify that the list above is a complete list of all documents which are or have been in [my/here name the party's] control and which [I am/here name the party is] obliged under [the said order or the said agreement in writing] to disclose."

E3.7 An adapted version of practice form N265 (list of documents: standard disclosure) has been approved for use in the Commercial Court. The court may at any stage order that a disclosure statement be verified by affidavit.

E3.8

(a) For the purposes of PD31 § 4.3 the court will normally regard as an appropriate person any person who is in a position responsibly and authoritatively to search for the documents required to be disclosed by that party and to make the statements contained in the disclosure statement concerning the documents which must be disclosed by that party.

(b) A legal representative may in certain cases be an appropriate person.

(c) An explanation why the person is considered an appropriate person must still be given in the disclosure statement.

(d) A person holding an office or position in the disclosing party but who is not in a position responsibly and authoritatively to make the statements contained in the disclosure statement will not be regarded as an appropriate person to make the disclosure statement of the party.

(e) The court may of its own initiative or on application require that a disclosure statement also be signed by another appropriate person.

### E4 Specific disclosure

**2A–83** E4.1 Specific disclosure is defined by rule 31.12(2).

E4.2 An order for specific disclosure under rule 31.12 may in an appropriate case direct a party to carry out a thorough search for any documents which it is reasonable to suppose may adversely affect his own case or support the case of the party applying for disclosure or which may lead to a train of enquiry which has either of these consequences and to disclose any documents located as a result of that search: PD31 § 5.5.

E4.3 Where an application is made for specific disclosure the party from whom disclosure is sought should provide to the applicant and to the Court information as to the factors listed in E2.5(d) above and its documents retention policy, to the extent such information is relevant to the application. At the hearing of the application, the Court may take into account the factors listed in E2.5(d) as well as the width of the request and the conduct of the parties.

E4.4 The court may at any stage order that specific disclosure be verified by affidavit or witness statement.

E4.5 Applications for ship's papers are provided for in rule 58.14.

### **2A–84** E5 Authenticity

E5.1

(a) Where the authenticity of any document disclosed to a party is not admitted, that party must serve notice that the document must be proved at trial in accordance with CPR 32.19. Such notice must be served by the latest date for serving witness statements or within 7 days of disclosure of the document, whichever is later.

(b) Where, apart from the authenticity of the document itself, the date upon which a document or an entry in it is stated to have been made or the person by whom the document states that it or any entry in it was made or any other feature of the document is to be challenged at the trial on grounds which may require a witness to be called at the trial to support the contents of the document, such challenge

(i) must be raised in good time in advance of the trial to enable such witness or witnesses to be called;

(ii) the grounds of challenge must be explicitly identified in the skeleton argument or outline submissions in advance of the trial.

(c) Where, due to the late disclosure of a document it or its contents or character cannot practicably be challenged within the time limits prescribed in (a) or (b), the challenge may only be raised with the permission of the court and having regard to the Overriding Objective (CPR 1.1).

## F.
## APPLICATIONS

### F1 Generally 2A–85

F1.1

(a) Applications are governed by CPR Part 23 and PD23 as modified by rule 58 and PD58. As a result

(i) PD23 § § 1 and 2.3–2.6 do not apply;

(ii) PD23 § § 2.8 and 2.10 apply only if the proposed (additional) application will not increase the time estimate (including the estimate for the judge's pre-hearing reading time) already given for the hearing for which a date has been fixed; and

(iii) PD23 § 3 is subject in all cases to the judge's agreeing that the application may proceed without an application notice being served.

(b) An adapted version of practice form **N244** (application notice) has been approved for use in the Commercial Court.

F1.2 An application for a consent order must include a draft of the proposed order signed on behalf of all parties to whom it relates: PD58 § 14.1.

F1.3 The requirement in PD23 § 12.1 that a draft order be supplied on disk does not apply in the Commercial Court since orders are generally drawn up by the parties: PD58 § 14.2.

*Service*

F1.4 Application notices are served by the parties, not by the court: PD58 § 9.

*Evidence*

F1.5

(a) Particular attention is drawn to PD23 § 9.1 which points out that even where no specific requirement for evidence is set out in the Rules or Practice Directions the court will in practice often need to be satisfied by evidence of the facts that are relied on in support of, or in opposition to, the application.

(b) Where convenient the written evidence relied on in support of an application may be included in the application notice, which may be lengthened for this purpose: see rule 32.6(2).

*Time for service of evidence*

F1.6 The time allowed for the service of evidence in relation to applications is governed by PD58 § 13.

*Hearings*

F1.7

(a) Applications (other than arbitration applications) will be heard in public in accordance with rule 39.2, save where otherwise ordered.

(b) With certain exceptions, arbitration applications will normally be heard in private: rule 62.10(3). See section O.

(c) An application without notice for a freezing injunction or a search order will often need to be heard in private in the interests of justice and therefore be heard in private: see rule 39.2(3).

F1.8 Parties should pay particular attention to PD23 § 2.9 which warns of the need to anticipate the court's wish to review the conduct of the case and give further management directions. The parties should be ready to give the court their assistance and should be able to answer any questions that the court may ask for this purpose.

F1.9 PD23 § § 6.1–6.5 and § 7 deal with the hearing of applications by telephone (other than an urgent applications out of court hours) and the hearing of applications

***Paragraph numbers marked with a "+" can be found online and on CD.***

COMMERCIAL COURTS

using video-conferencing facilities. These methods may be considered when an application needs to be made before a particular Commercial Judge who is currently on circuit. In most other cases applications are more conveniently dealt with in person.

**F2 Applications without notice**

**2A–86** F2.1 All applications should be made on notice, even if that notice has to be short, unless

(i) any rule or Practice Direction provides that the application may be made without notice; or

(ii) there are good reasons for making the application without notice, for example, because notice would or might defeat the object of the application.

F2.2 Where an application without notice does not involve the giving of undertakings to the court, it will normally be made and dealt with on paper, as, for example, applications for permission to serve a claim form out of the jurisdiction, and applications for an extension of time in which to serve a claim form.

F2.3 Any application for an interim injunction or similar remedy will require an oral hearing.

F2.4

(a) A party wishing to make an application without notice which requires an oral hearing before a judge should contact the Clerk to the Commercial Court at the earliest opportunity.

(b) If a party wishes to make an application without notice at a time when no commercial judge is available he should apply to the Queen's Bench Judge in Chambers (see section P1.1).

F2.5 On all applications without notice it is the duty of the applicant and those representing him to make full and frank disclosure of all matters relevant to the application.

F2.6 The papers lodged for the application should include two copies of a draft of the order sought. Save in exceptional circumstances where time does not permit, all the evidence relied upon in support of the application and any other relevant documents must be lodged in advance with the Clerk to the Commercial Court. If the application is urgent, the Clerk to the Commercial Court should be informed of the fact and of the reasons for the urgency. Counsel's estimate of reading time likely to be required by the court should also be provided.

**F3 Expedited applications**

**2A–87** F3.1 The Court will expedite the hearing of an application on notice in cases of sufficient urgency and importance.

F3.2 Where a party wishes to make an expedited application a request should be made to the Clerk to the Commercial Court on notice to all other parties.

**2A–88** **F4 Paper applications**

F4.1

(a) Although contested applications are usually best determined at an oral hearing, some applications may be suitable for determination on paper.

(b) Attention is drawn to the provisions of rule 23.8 and PD23 § 11. If the applicant considers that the application is suitable for determination on paper, he should ensure before lodging the papers with the court

(i) that the application notice together with any supporting evidence has been served on the respondent;

***Paragraph numbers marked with a "+" can be found online and on CD.***

(ii) that the respondent has been allowed the appropriate period of time in which to serve evidence in opposition;

(iii) that any evidence in reply has been served on the respondent; and

(iv) that there is included in the papers

(A) the written consent of the respondent to the disposal of the application without a hearing; or

(B) a statement by the applicant of the grounds on which he seeks to have the application disposed of without a hearing, together with confirmation that the application and a copy of the grounds for disposing of without a hearing have been served on the respondent and a statement of when they were served.

(c) Where a previous application in the case has been determined by a judge of the Commercial Court whether at a hearing or on paper, it is helpful for the application to indicate clearly when lodging the papers, the identity of the judge who last considered the matter, so that so far as reasonably practicable, the papers can be placed before that judge.

(d) Only in exceptional cases will the court dispose of an application without a hearing in the absence of the respondent's consent.

F4.2

(a) Certain applications relating to the management of proceedings may conveniently be made in correspondence without issuing an application notice.

(b) It must be clearly understood that such applications are not applications without notice and the applicant must therefore ensure that a copy of the letter making the application is sent to all other parties to the proceedings.

(c) Accordingly, the following procedure should be followed when making an application of this kind:

(i) the applicant should first ascertain whether the application is opposed by the other parties;

(ii) if it is, the applicant should apply to the court by letter stating the nature of the order which it seeks and the grounds on which the application is made;

(iii) a copy the letter should be sent (by email or fax, where possible) to all other parties at the same time as it is sent to the court;

(iv) any other party wishing to make representations should do so by letter within two days (i.e. two clear days) of the date of the applicant's letter of application. The representations should be sent (by email or fax, where possible) to the applicant and all other parties at the same time as they are sent to the court;

(v) the court will advise its decision by letter to the applicant. The applicant must forthwith copy the court's letter to all other parties, by email or fax where possible.

COMMERCIAL COURTS

### F5 Ordinary applications

F5.1 Applications likely to require an oral hearing lasting half a day or less are regarded as "ordinary" applications. **2A–89**

F5.2 Ordinary applications will generally be heard on Fridays, but may be heard on other days. Where possible, the Listing Office will have regard to the availability of advocates when fixing hearing dates.

F5.3

(a) The timetable for ordinary applications is set out in PD58 § 13.1 and is as follows:

(i) evidence in support must be filed and served with the application;

(ii) evidence in answer must be filed and served within 14 days thereafter;

(iii) evidence in reply (if any) must be filed and served within 7 days thereafter.

***Paragraph numbers marked with a "+" can be found online and on CD.***

(b) This timetable may be abridged or extended by agreement between the parties provided that any date fixed for the hearing of the application is not affected: PD58 § 13.4. In appropriate cases, this timetable may be abridged by the Court.

F5.4 An application bundle (see section F11) must be lodged with the Listing Office by 1 p.m. one clear day before the date fixed for the hearing. The case management bundle will also be required on the hearing; this file will be passed by the Listing Office to the judge.

F5.5 Save in very short and simple cases, skeleton arguments must be provided by all parties. These must be lodged with the Listing Office and served on the advocates for all other parties to the application by 1 p.m. on the day before the date fixed for the hearing (i.e. the immediately preceding day) together with an estimate of the reading time likely to be required by the court. Guidelines on the preparation of skeleton arguments are set out in Part 1 of Appendix 9.

**[EDITORIAL NOTE: The next paragraph is F5.7]**

F5.7 Thus, for an application estimated for a half day or less and due to be heard on a Friday:

(i) the application bundle must be lodged by 1 p.m. on Wednesday; and

(ii) skeleton arguments must be lodged by 1 p.m. on Thursday.

If, for reasons outside the reasonable control of the advocate a skeleton argument cannot be delivered to the Listing Office by 1pm, the clerk of the judge hearing the application should be informed before 1pm and the skeleton argument should be delivered direct to the clerk of the judge listed to hear the application and in any event not later than 4pm the day before the hearing.

F5.8 The applicant should, as a matter of course, provide all other parties to the application with a copy of the application bundle at the cost of the receiving party. Further copies should be supplied on request, again at the cost of the receiving party.

F5.9 Problems with the lodging of bundles or skeleton arguments should be notified to the Clerk to the Commercial Court as far in advance as possible. **If the application bundle or skeleton argument is not lodged by the time specified, the application may be stood out of the list without further warning.**

### F6 Heavy applications

2A–90 F6.1 Applications likely to require an oral hearing lasting more than half a day are regarded as "heavy" applications.

F6.2 Heavy applications normally involve a greater volume of evidence and other documents and more extensive issues. They accordingly require a longer lead-time for preparation and exchange of evidence. Where possible the Listing Office will have regard to the availability of advocates when fixing hearing dates.

F6.3 The timetable for heavy applications is set out in PD58 § 13.2 and is as follows:

(i) evidence in support must be filed and served with the application;

(ii) evidence in answer must be filed and served within 28 days thereafter;

(iii) evidence in reply (if any) must be filed and served as soon as possible, and in any event within 14 days of service of the evidence in answer.

F6.4 An application bundle (see section F11) must be lodged with the Listing Office by 4 p.m. two days (i.e. two clear days) before the date fixed for the hearing together with a reading list and an estimate for the reading time likely to be required by the court as agreed between the counsel or other advocates to appear on the application. The case management bundle will also be required on the hearing; this file will be passed by the Listing Office to the judge.

F6.5 Skeleton arguments must be lodged with the Listing Office and served on the advocates for all other parties to the application as follows:

***Paragraph numbers marked with a "+" can be found online and on CD.***

(i) applicant's skeleton argument (with chronology unless one is unnecessary, and with a dramatis personae if one is warranted), by 4 p.m. two days (i.e. two clear days) before the hearing;

(ii) respondent's skeleton argument, by 4 p.m. one day (i.e. one clear day) before the hearing.

Guidelines on the preparation of skeleton arguments are set out in Part 1 of Appendix 9.

F6.6 Thus, for an application estimated for more than half a day and due to be heard on a Thursday:

(i) the application bundle and the applicant's skeleton argument must be lodged by 4 p.m. on Monday;

(ii) the respondent's skeleton argument must be lodged by 4 p.m. on Tuesday.

F6.7 The applicant must, as a matter of course, provide all other parties to the application with a copy of the application bundle at the cost of the receiving party. Further copies must be supplied on request, again at the cost of the receiving party.

F6.8 Problems with the lodging of bundles or skeleton arguments should be notified to the Clerk to the Commercial Court as far in advance as possible. **If the application bundle or skeleton argument is not lodged by the time specified, the application may be stood out of the list without further warning.**

### F7 Evidence

F7.1 Although evidence may be given by affidavit, it should generally be given by witness statement, except where it can conveniently be given in the application notice (see rule 32.6(2) and except where PD32 requires evidence to be given on affidavit (as, for example, in the case of an application for a freezing injunction or a search order: PD32 § 1.4). In other cases the Court may order that evidence be given by affidavit: PD32 § 1.4(1) and 1.6. **2A–91**

F7.2 Witness statements and affidavits must comply with the requirements of PD32, save that photocopy documents should be used unless the court orders otherwise.

F7.3

(a) Witness statements must be verified by a statement of truth signed by the maker of the statement: rule 22.1.

(b) At hearings other than trial an applicant may rely on the application notice itself, and a party may rely on his statement of case, if the application notice or statement of case (as the case may be) is verified by a statement of truth: rule 32.6(2).

(c) A statement of truth in an application notice may also be signed as indicated in sections C1.8 and C1.9 above.

F7.4 Proceedings for contempt of court may be brought against a person who makes, or causes to be made, a false statement in a witness statement (or any other document verified by a statement of truth) without an honest belief in its truth: rule 32.14(1).

### F8 Reading time **2A–92**

F8

(a) It is essential for the efficient conduct of the court's business that the parties inform the court of the reading required in order to enable the judge to dispose of the application within the time allowed for the hearing and of the time likely to be required for that purpose. Accordingly

(i) in the case of all heavy applications and in the case of other applications if any advocate considers that the time required for reading is likely to exceed one hour, each party must lodge with the Listing Office not later than 1pm two clear days before the hearing of the application a reading list with an estimate of the time likely to be required by the court for reading;

(ii) in the case of all other applications each party must lodge with the Listing Office by 1pm on the day before the date fixed for the hearing of an application (ie the immediately preceding day) a reading list with an estimate of the time required to complete the reading;

(iii) each reading list should identify the material on both sides which the court needs to read.

(iv) if possible, the parties should provide the reading list in an agreed document, but if necessary each party should provide its own list.

(b) Failure to comply with these requirements may result in the adjournment of the hearing.

2A–93 **F9 Applications disposed of by consent**

F9.1

(a) Consent orders may be submitted to the court in draft for approval and initialling without the need for attendance.

(b) Two copies of the draft, one of which (or a counterpart) must be signed on behalf of all parties to whom it relates, should be lodged at the Registry. The copies should be undated. The order will be dated with the date on which the judge initials it, but that does not prevent the parties acting on their agreement immediately if they wish.

(c) The parties should act promptly in lodging the copies at the Registry. If it is important that the orders are made by a particular date, that fact (and the reasons for it) should be notified in writing to the Registry.

F9.2 For the avoidance of doubt, this procedure is not normally available in relation to a case management conference or a pre-trial review. Whether or not the parties are agreed as between themselves on the directions that the court should be asked to consider giving at a case management conference or a pre-trial review, attendance will normally be required. See section D8.3.

F9.3 Where an order provides a time by which something is to be done the order should wherever possible state the particular date by which the thing is to be done rather than specify a period of time from a particular date or event: rule 2.9.

**F10 Hearing dates, time estimates and time limits**

2A–94 F10.1 Dates for the hearing of applications to be attended by advocates are normally fixed after discussion with the counsel's clerks or with the solicitor concerned.

F10.2 The efficient working of the court depends on accurate estimates of the time needed for the oral hearing of an application including a considered estimate of the judge's pre-hearing reading. Over-estimating can be as wasteful as under-estimating.

F10.3 Subject to section F10.4, the Clerk to the Commercial Court will not accept or act on time estimates for the oral hearing of applications where those estimates exceed the following maxima:

| | |
|---|---|
| Application to set aside service: | 4 hours |
| Application for summary judgment: | 4 hours |
| Application to set aside or vary interim remedy: | 4 hours |
| Application to set aside or vary default judgment: | 2 hours |
| Application to amend statement of case: | 1 hour |
| Application for specific disclosure: | 1 hour |
| Application for security for costs: | 1 hour |

F10.4 A longer listing time will only be granted upon application in writing specifying the additional time required and giving reasons why it is required. A copy of the written application should be sent to the advocates for all other parties in the case at the same time as it is sent to the Listing Office.

F10.5

(a) Not later than five days before the date fixed for the hearing the applicant must provide the Listing Office with his current estimate of the time required to dispose of the application.

(b) If at any time either party considers that there is a material risk that the hearing of the application will exceed the time currently allowed it must inform the Listing Office immediately.

F10.6

(a) All time estimates should be given on the assumption that the judge will have read in advance the skeleton arguments and the documents identified in the reading list. In this connection attention is drawn to section F8.

(b) A time estimate for an ordinary application should allow time for judgment and consequential matters; a time estimate for a heavy application should not.

F10.7 Save in the situation referred to at section F10.8, a separate estimate must be given for each application, including any application issued after, but to be heard at the same time as, another application.

F10.8 A separate estimate need not be given for any application issued after, but to be heard at the same time as, another application where the advocate in the case certifies in writing that

(i) the determination of the application first issued will necessarily determine the application issued subsequently; or

(ii) the matters raised in the application issued subsequently are not contested.

F10.9 If it is found at the hearing that the time required for the hearing has been significantly underestimated, the judge hearing the application may adjourn the matter and may make any special costs orders (including orders for the immediate payment of costs and wasted costs orders) as may be appropriate.

F10.10 Failure to comply with the requirements for lodging bundles for the application will normally result in the application not being heard on the date fixed at the expense of the party in default (see further sections F5.9 and F6.8 above). An order for immediate payment of costs may be made.

### F11 Application bundles 2A–95

F11.1

(a) Attention is drawn to appendix 10, which deals with the preparation of bundles.

(b) Bundles for use on applications may be compiled in any convenient manner but must contain the following documents (preferably in separate sections in the following order)

(i) a copy of the application notice;

(ii) a draft of the order which the applicant seeks;

(iii) a copy of the statements of case;

(iv) copies of any previous orders which are relevant to the application;

(v) copies of the witness statements and affidavits filed in support of, or in opposition to, the application, together with any exhibits.

(c) Copies of the statements of case and of previous orders in the action should be provided in a separate section of the bundle. They should not be exhibited to witness statements.

(d) Witness statements and affidavits previously filed in the same proceedings should be included in the bundle at a convenient location. They should not be exhibited to witness statements.

(e) Where for the purpose of the application it is likely to be necessary for the court to read in chronological order correspondence or other documents located as exhibits to different affidavits or witness statements, copies of such documents should be filed and paged in chronological order in a separate composite bundle or bundles which should be agreed between the parties. If time does not permit agreement on the contents of the composite bundle, it is the responsibility of the applicant to prepare the composite bundle and to lodge it with the Listing Office by 4pm two clear days before the hearing in the case of heavy applications and one clear day before the hearing in the case of all other applications.

**F12 Chronologies, indices and dramatis personae**

**2A–96** F12.1 For most applications it is of assistance for the applicant to provide a chronology which should be cross-referenced to the documents. Dramatis personae are often useful as well.

F12.2 Guidelines on the preparation of chronologies and indices are set out in Part 2 of Appendix 9.

**F13 Authorities**

**2A–97** F13.1 On some applications there will be key authorities that it would be useful for the judge to read before the oral hearing of the application. Copies of these authorities should be provided with the skeleton arguments.

F13.2 It is also desirable for bundles of the authorities on which the parties wish to rely to be provided to the judge hearing the application as soon as possible after skeleton arguments have been exchanged.

F13.3 Authorities should only be cited when they contain some principle of law relevant to an issue arising on the application and where their substance is not to be found in the decision of a court of higher authority.

**F14 Costs**

**2A–98** F14.1 Costs are dealt with generally at section J13.

F14.2 Reference should be also be made to the rules governng the summary assessment of costs for shorter hearings contained in Parts 43 and 44. Active consideration will generally be given by the court to adopting the summary assessment procedure in all cases where the schedule of costs of the successful party is no more than £100,000, but the parties should always be prepared for the court to assess costs summarily even where the costs exceed this amount.

F14.3 In carrying out a summary assessment of costs, the court may have regard amongst other matters to

(i) advice from a Commercial Costs Judge or from the Chief Costs Judge on costs of specialist solicitors and counsel;

(ii) any survey published by the London Solicitors Litigation Association showing the average hourly expense rate for solicitors in London;

(iii) any information provided to the court at its request by one or more of the specialist associations (referred to at section A4.2) on average charges by specialist solicitors and counsel.

F14.4 Reference should also be made to CPR 44.3(8). Active consideration will generally be given by the court to making an order for a payment on account of costs if they are not assessed summarily.

## F15 Interim injunctions

*Generally*

2A-99

F15.1

(a) Applications for interim injunctions are governed by CPR Part 25.
(b) Applications must be made on notice in accordance with the procedure set out in CPR Part 23 unless there are good reasons for proceeding without notice.

F15.2 A party who wishes to make an application for an interim injunction must give the Clerk to the Commercial Court as much notice as possible.

F15.3

(a) Except when the application is so urgent that there has not been any opportunity to do so, the applicant must issue his claim form and obtain the evidence on which he wishes to rely in support of the application before making the application.
(b) On applications of any weight, and unless the urgency means that this is not possible, the applicant should provide the court at the earliest opportunity with a skeleton argument.
(c) An affidavit, and not a witness statement, is required on an application for a freezing order or a search order: PD25 § 3.1.

*Fortification of undertakings*

F15.4

(a) Where the applicant for an interim remedy is not able to show sufficient assets within the jurisdiction of the Court to provide substance to the undertakings given, particularly the undertaking in damages, he may be required to reinforce his undertakings by providing security.
(b) Security will be ordered in such form as the judge decides is appropriate but may, for example, take the form of a payment into court, a bond issued by an insurance company or a first demand guarantee or standby credit issued by a first-class bank.
(c) In an appropriate case the judge may order a payment to be made to the applicant's solicitors to be held by them as officers of the court pending further order. Sometimes the undertaking of a parent company may be acceptable.

*Form of order*

F15.5 Standard forms of wording for freezing injunctions and search orders are set out in Appendix 5. The forms have been adapted for use in the Commercial Court and should be followed unless the judge hearing a particular application orders otherwise.

F15.6 A phrase indicating that an interim remedy is to remain in force until judgment or further order means that it remains in force until the delivery of a final judgment. If an interim remedy continuing after judgment is required, say until judgment has been satisfied, an application to that effect must be made (see further section K1).

F15.7 It is good practice to draft an order for an interim remedy so that it includes a proviso which permits acts which would otherwise be a breach of the order to be done with the written consent of the solicitor of the other party or parties. This enables the parties to agree in effect to variations (or the discharge) of the order without the necessity of coming back to the court.

*Freezing injunctions*

F15.8

(a) Freezing injunctions made on an application without notice will provide for a return date, unless the judge otherwise orders: PD25 § 5.1(3). In the usual course,

***Paragraph numbers marked with a "+" can be found online and on CD.***

the return date given will be a Friday (unless a date for a case management conference has already been fixed, in which event the return date given will in the usual course be that date).

(b) If, after service or notification of the injunction, one or more of the parties considers that more than 15 minutes will be required to deal with the matter on the return date the Listing Office should be informed forthwith and in any event no later than 4 p.m. on the Wednesday before the Friday fixed as the return date.

(c) If the parties agree, the return date may be postponed to a later date on which all parties will be ready to deal with any substantive issues. In this event, an agreed form of order continuing the injunction to the postponed return date should be submitted for consideration by a judge and if the order is made in the terms submitted there will be no need for the parties to attend on the day originally fixed as the return date.

(d) In such a case the defendant and any other interested party will continue to have liberty to apply to vary or set aside the order.

F15.9 A provision for the defendant to give notice of any application to discharge or vary the order is usually included as a matter of convenience but it is not proper to attempt to fetter the right of the defendant to apply without notice or on short notice if need be.

F15.10 As regards freezing orders in respect of assets outside the jurisdiction, the standard wording in relation to effects on third parties should normally incorporate wording to enable overseas branches of banks or similar institutions which have offices within the jurisdiction to comply with what they reasonably believe to be their obligations under the laws of the country where the assets are located or under the proper law of the relevant banking or other contract relating to such assets.

F15.11 Any bank or third party served with, notified of or affected by a freezing injunction may apply to the court without notice to any party for directions, or notify the court in writing without notice to any party, in the event that the order affects or may affect the position of the bank or third party under legislation, regulations or procedures aimed to prevent money laundering.

*Search orders*

F15.12 Attention is drawn to the detailed requirements in respect of search orders set out in PD25 § § 7.1–8.3. The applicant for the search order will normally be required to undertake not to inform any third party of the search order or of the case until after a specified date.

*Applications to discharge or vary freezing injunctions and search orders*

F15.13 Applications to discharge or vary freezing injunctions and search orders are treated as matters of urgency for listing purposes. Those representing applicants for discharge or variation should ascertain before a date is fixed for the hearing whether, having regard to the evidence which they wish to adduce, the claimant would wish to adduce further evidence in opposition. If so, all reasonable steps must be taken by all parties to agree upon the earliest practicable date at which they can be ready for the hearing, so as to avoid the last minute need to vacate a fixed date. In cases of difficulty the matter should be referred to a judge who may be able to suggest temporary solutions pending the hearing.

F15.14 If a freezing injunction or a search order is discharged on an application to discharge or vary, or on the return date, the judge will consider whether it is appropriate that he should assess damages at once and direct immediate payment by the applicant. Where the judge considers that the hearing for the assessment of damages should be postponed to a future date he will give such case management directions as may be appropriate for the assessment hearing, including, if necessary, disclosure of documents and exchange of witness statements and experts' reports.

*Applications under section 25 of the Civil Jurisdiction and Judgments Act 1982*

F15.15 A Part 8 claim form (rather than an application notice: cf. rule 25.4(2)) must be used for an application under section 25 of the Civil Jurisdiction and Judgments

Act 1982 ("Interim relief in England and Wales and Northern Ireland in the absence of substantive proceedings"). The modified Part 8 procedure used in the Commercial Court is referred to at section B4 above.

### F16 Security for costs

F16.1 Applications for security for costs are governed by rules 25.12–14. **2A–100**

F16.2 The applicable practice is set out in Appendix 16.

## G.

## ALTERNATIVE DISPUTE RESOLUTION ("ADR")

### G1 Generally

G1.1 While emphasising its primary role as a forum for deciding commercial cases, the Commercial Court encourages parties to consider the use of ADR (such as, but not confined to, mediation and conciliation) as an alternative means of resolving disputes or particular issues. **2A–101**

G1.2 Whilst the Commercial Court remains an entirely appropriate forum for resolving most of the disputes which are entered in the Commercial List, the view of the Commercial Court is that the settlement of disputes by means of ADR

(i) significantly helps parties to save costs;

(ii) saves parties the delay of litigation in reaching finality in their disputes;

(iii) enables parties to achieve settlement of their disputes while preserving their existing commercial relationships and market reputation;

(iv) provides parties with a wider range of solutions than those offered by litigation; and

(v) is likely to make a substantial contribution to the more efficient use of judicial resources.

G1.3 The Commercial Judges will in appropriate cases invite the parties to consider whether their dispute, or particular issues in it, could be resolved through ADR.

G1.4 Legal representatives in all cases should consider with their clients and the other parties concerned the possibility of attempting to resolve the dispute or particular issues by ADR and should ensure that their clients are fully informed as to the most cost effective means of resolving their dispute.

G1.5 Parties who consider that ADR might be an appropriate means of resolving the dispute or particular issues in the dispute may apply for directions at any stage, including before service of the defence and before the case management conference.

G1.6 At the case management conference if it should appear to the judge that the case before him or any of the issues arising in it are particularly appropriate for an attempt at settlement by means of ADR but that the parties have not previously attempted settlement by such means, he may invite the parties to use ADR.

G1.7 The judge may, if he considers it appropriate, adjourn the case for a specified period of time to encourage and enable the parties to use ADR. He may for this purpose extend the time for compliance by the parties or any of them with any requirement under the rules, the Guide or any order of the Court. The judge in making an order providing for ADR will normally take into account, when considering at what point in the pre-trial timetable there should be compliance with such an order, such matters as the costs likely to be incurred at each stage in the pre-trial timetable if the claim is not settled, the costs of a mediation or other means of dispute resolution, how far the prospects of a successful mediation or other means of dispute resolution are likely to be enhanced by completion of pleadings, disclosure of documents, provision of further information under CPR 18, exchange of factual witness statements or exchange of experts' reports.

G1.8 The Judge may further consider in an appropriate case making an ADR Order in the terms set out in Appendix 7.

G1.9

(a) The Clerk to the Commercial Court keeps some published information on individuals and bodies that offer ADR and arbitration services. If the parties are unable to agree upon a neutral individual or panel of individuals to act as a mediator or give an early neutral evaluation, the normal form of ADR order set out in Appendix 7 contains at paragraph 3 a mandatory requirement that the case management conference should be restored to enable the court to facilitate agreement on a neutral or panel of neutrals. In order to avoid the cost of a restored case management hearing, the parties may agree to send to the court their respective list of available neutrals, so as to enable the judge to suggest a name from those lists. In any other case the parties may by consent refer to the judge for assistance in reaching such agreement.

(b) The court will not recommend any individual or body to act as a mediator or arbitrator.

G1.10 At the case management conference or at any other hearing in the course of which the judge makes an order providing for ADR he may make such order as to the costs that the parties may incur by reason of their using or attempting to use ADR as may in all the circumstances seem appropriate. The orders for costs are normally costs in the case, meaning that if the claim is not settled, the costs of the ADR procedures, will follow the ultimate event, or that each side shall bear its own costs of those procedures if the case is not settled.

G1.11 In some cases it may be appropriate that an ADR order should be made following judgment if application is made for permission to appeal. In such cases the court may adjourn the application for permission to appeal while making an ADR order providing for ADR procedures to be completed within a specified time and, failing settlement with that period, for the application for permission to appeal to be restored.

G1.12 At the case management conference the court may consider that an order directed to encouraging bilateral negotiations between the parties' respective legal representatives is likely to be a more cost-effective and productive route to settlement then can be offered by a formal ADR or ENE Order. In such a case the court will set a date by which there is to be a meeting between respective solicitors and their respective clients' officials responsible for decision-taking in relation to the case in question.

**G2 Early neutral evaluation**

2A–102 G2.1 In appropriate cases and with the agreement of all parties the court will provide a without-prejudice, non-binding, early neutral evaluation ("ENE") of a dispute or of particular issues.

G2.2 The approval of the Judge in Charge of the List must be obtained before any ENE is undertaken.

G2.3 If, after discussion with the advocates representing the parties, it appears to a judge that an ENE is likely to assist in the resolution of the dispute or of particular issues, he will, with the agreement of the parties, refer the matter to the Judge in Charge of the List.

G2.4

(a) The Judge in Charge of the List will nominate a judge to conduct the ENE.

(b) The judge who is to conduct the ENE will give such directions for its preparation and conduct as he considers appropriate.

***Paragraph numbers marked with a "+" can be found online and on CD.***

G2.5 The judge who conducts the ENE will take no further part in the case, either for the purpose of the hearing of applications or as the judge at trial, unless the parties agree otherwise.

## H.

## EVIDENCE FOR TRIAL

### H1 Witnesses of fact

*Preparation and form of witness statements*

H1.1 Witness statements must comply with the requirements of PD32. The following points are also emphasised **2A–103**

(i) the function of a witness statement is to set out in writing the evidence in chief of the witness; as far as possible, therefore, the statement should be in the witness's own words;

(ii) it should be as concise as the circumstances of the case allow without omitting any significant matters;

(iii) it should not contain lengthy quotations from documents;

(iv) it is seldom necessary to exhibit documents to a witness statement;

(v) it should not engage in (legal or other) argument;

(vi) it must indicate which of the statements made in it are made from the witness's own knowledge and which are made on information or belief, giving the source for any statement made on information or belief;

(vii) it must contain a statement by the witness that he believes the matters stated in it are true; proceedings for contempt of court may be brought against a person if he makes, or causes to be made, a false statement in a witness statement without an honest belief in its truth: rule 32.14(1).

(viii) it must comply with any direction of the court about its length.

H1.2 It is usually convenient for a witness statement to follow the chronological sequence of events or matters dealt with (32PD19.2). It is helpful for it to indicate to which issue in the list of issues the particular passage in the witness statement relates, either by a heading in the statement or in a marginal notation or by some other convenient method.

H1.3 It is improper to put pressure of any kind on a witness to give anything other than his own account of the matters with which his statement deals. It is also improper to serve a witness statement which is known to be false or which it is known the maker does not in all respects actually believe to be true.

*Fluency of witnesses*

H1.4 If a witness is not sufficiently fluent in English to give his evidence in English, the witness statement should be in the witness's own language and a translation provided.

H1.5 If a witness is not fluent in English but can make himself understood in broken English and can understand written English, the statement need not be in his own words provided that these matters are indicated in the statement itself. It must however be written so as to express as accurately as possible the substance of his evidence.

*Witness statement as evidence in chief*

H1.6

(a) Where a witness is called to give oral evidence, his witness statement is to stand as his evidence in chief unless the Court orders otherwise: rule 32.5(2).

***Paragraph numbers marked with a "+" can be found online and on CD.***

(b) In an appropriate case the trial judge may direct that the whole or any part of a witness's evidence in chief is to be given orally. Notice of any such application for such an order should be given as early as is reasonably convenient. It is usually reasonable for any such application to be made at a pre-trial review if one is held.

*Additional evidence from a witness*

H1.7

(a) A witness giving oral evidence at trial may with the permission of the court amplify his witness statement and give evidence in relation to new matters which have arisen since the witness statement was served: rule 32.5(3). Permission will be given only if the Court considers that there is good reason not to confine the evidence of the witness to the contents of his witness statement: rule 32.5(4).
(b) A supplemental witness statement should normally be served where the witness proposes materially to add to, alter, correct or retract from what is in his original statement. Permission will be required for the service of a supplemental statement. Such application should be made at the pre-trial review or, if there is no pre-trial review, as early as possible before the start of the trial. If application is made at any later stage, the applicant must provide compelling evidence explaining its delay in adducing such evidence.
(c) It is the duty of all parties to ensure that the statements of all factual witnesses intended to be called or whose statements are to be tendered as hearsay statements should be exchanged simultaneously unless the court has otherwise ordered. Witnesses additional to those whose statements have been initially exchanged may only be called with the permission of the court which will not normally be given unless prompt application is made supported by compelling evidence explaining the late introduction of that witness's evidence.

*Notice of decision not to call a witness*

H1.8

(a) If a party decides not to call to give oral evidence at trial a witness whose statement has been served but wishes to rely upon the evidence, he must put in the statement as hearsay evidence unless the court otherwise orders: rule 32.5. If he proposes to put the evidence in as hearsay evidence, reference should be made to rule 33.2.
(b) If the party who has served the statement does not put it in as hearsay evidence, any other party may do so: rule 32.5(5).

*Witness summonses*

H1.9

(a) Rules 34.2–34.8 deal with witness summonses, including a summons for a witness to attend court or to produce documents in advance of the date fixed for trial.
(b) Witness summonses are served by the parties, not the court.

**H2 Expert witnesses**

*Application for permission to call an expert witness*

2A–104 H2.1 Any application for permission to call an expert witness or serve an expert's report should normally be made at the case management conference. The party applying for such permission will normally be expected to identify to which issue or issues in the list of issues the proposed expert evidence relates, and to propose any amendments to the list of issues that might be required for this purpose. The court may limit the length of an expert report.

H2.2 Parties should bear in mind that expert evidence can lead to unnecessary expense and they should be prepared to consider the use of single joint experts in appropriate cases. In many cases the use of single joint experts is not appropriate and each party will generally be given permission to call one expert in each field requiring expert evidence. These are referred to in the Guide as "separate experts".

H2.3 When the use of a single joint expert is contemplated, the court will expect the parties to co-operate in developing, and agreeing to the greatest possible extent, terms of reference for that expert. In most cases the terms of reference will (in particular) identify in detail what the expert is asked to do, identify any documentary materials he is asked to consider and specify any assumptions he is asked to make.

*Provisions of general application in relation to expert evidence*

H2.4 The provisions set out in Appendix 11 to the Guide apply to all aspects of expert evidence (including expert reports, meetings of experts and expert evidence given orally) unless the court orders otherwise. Parties should ensure that they are drawn to the attention of any experts they instruct at the earliest opportunity.

*Form and content of expert's reports*

H2.5 Expert's reports must comply with the requirements of PD35 § § 1 and 2.

H2.6

(a) In stating the substance of all material instructions on the basis of which his report is written as required by rule 35.10(3) and PD35 § 1.2(8) an expert witness should state the facts or assumptions upon which his opinion is based.

(b) The expert must make it clear which, if any, of the facts stated are within his own direct knowledge.

(c) If a stated assumption is, in the opinion of the expert witness, unreasonable or unlikely he should state that clearly.

(d) The expert's report must be limited to matters relevant to the issue or issues in the list of issues to which the relevant expert evidence relates and for which permission to call such expert evidence has been given.

H2.7 It is useful if a report contains a glossary of significant technical terms.

H2.8 Where the evidence of an expert, such as a surveyor, assessor, adjuster, or other investigator is to be relied upon for the purpose of establishing primary facts, such as the condition of a ship or other property as found by him at a particular time, as well as for the purpose of deploying his expertise to express an opinion on any matter related to or in connection with the primary facts, that part of his evidence which is to be relied upon to establish the primary facts, is to be treated as factual evidence to be incorporated into a factual witness statement to be exchanged in accordance with the order for the exchange of factual witness statements. The purpose of this practice is to avoid postponing disclosure of a party's factual evidence until service of expert reports.

*Statement of truth*

H2.9

(a) The report must be signed by the expert and must contain a statement of truth in accordance with Part 35.

(b) Proceedings for contempt of court may be brought against a person if he makes, or causes to be made, without an honest belief in its truth, a false statement in an expert's report verified in the manner set out in this section.

*Request by an expert to the court for directions*

H2.10 An expert may file with the court a written request for directions to assist him in carrying out his function as expert, but

***Paragraph numbers marked with a "+" can be found online and on CD.***

(i) at least 7 days before he does so (or such shorter period as the court may direct) he should provide a copy of his proposed request to the party instructing him; and

(ii) at least 4 days before he does so (or such shorter period as the court may direct) he should provide a copy of his proposed request to all other parties.

*Exchange of reports*

H2.11 In appropriate cases the court will direct that the reports of expert witnesses be exchanged sequentially rather than simultaneously. The sequential exchange of expert reports may in many cases save time and costs by helping to focus the contents of responsive reports upon true rather than assumed issues of expert evidence and by avoiding repetition of detailed factual material as to which there is no real issue. Sequential exchange is likely to be particularly effective where experts are giving evidence of foreign law or are forensic accountants.This is an issue that the court will normally wish to consider at the case management conference.

*Meetings of expert witnesses*

H2.12 The court will normally direct a meeting or meetings of expert witnesses before trial. Sometimes it may be useful for there to be further meetings during the trial itself.

H2.13 The purposes of a meeting of experts are to give the experts the opportunity

(i) to discuss the expert issues;

(ii) to decide, with the benefit of that discussion, on which expert issues they share or can come to share the same expert opinion and on which expert issues there remains a difference of expert opinion between them (and what that difference is).

H2.14 Subject to section H2.16 below, the content of the discussion between the experts at or in connection with a meeting is without prejudice and shall not be referred to at the trial unless the parties so agree: rule 35.12(4).

H2.15 Subject to any directions of the court, the procedure to be adopted at a meeting of experts is a matter for the experts themselves, not the parties or their legal representatives.

H2.16 Neither the parties nor their legal representatives should seek to restrict the freedom of experts to identify and acknowledge the expert issues on which they agree at, or following further consideration after, meetings of experts.

H2.17 Unless the court orders otherwise, at or following any meeting the experts should prepare a joint memorandum for the court recording

(i) the fact that they have met and discussed the expert issues;

(ii) the issues on which they agree;

(iii) the issues on which they disagree; and

(iv) a brief summary of the reasons for their disagreement.

H2.18 If experts reach agreement on an issue that agreement shall not bind the parties unless they expressly agree to be bound by it.

*Written questions to experts*

H2.19

(a) Under rule 35.6 a party may, without the permission of the court, put written questions to an expert instructed by another party (or to a single joint expert) about his report. Unless the court gives permission or the other party agrees, such questions must be for the purpose only of clarifying the report.

(b) The court will pay close attention to the use of this procedure (especially where separate experts are instructed) to ensure that it remains an instrument for the helpful exchange of information. The court will not allow it to interfere with the procedure for an exchange of professional opinion at a meeting of experts, or to inhibit that exchange of professional opinion. In cases where (for example) questions that are oppressive in number or content are put, or questions are put for any purpose other than clarification of the report, the court will not hesitate to disallow the questions and to make an appropriate order for costs against the party putting them.

*Documents referred to in experts' reports*

H2.20 Unless they have already been provided on inspection of documents at the stage of disclosure, copies of any photographs, plans, analyses, measurements, survey reports or other similar documents relied on by an expert witness as well as copies of any unpublished sources must be provided to all parties at the same time as his report.

H2.21

(a) Rule 31.14(e) provides that (subject to rule 35.10(4)) a party may inspect a document mentioned in an expert's report. In a commercial case an expert's report will frequently, and helpfully, list all or many of the relevant previous papers (published or unpublished) or books written by the expert or to which the expert has contributed. Requiring inspection of this material may often be unrealistic, and the collating and copying burden could be huge.
(b) Accordingly, a party wishing to inspect a document in an expert report should (failing agreement) make an application to the court. The court will not permit inspection unless it is satisfied that it is necessary for the just disposal of the case and that the document is not reasonably available to the party making the application from an alternative source.

*Trial*

H2.22 At trial the evidence of expert witnesses is usually taken as a block, after the evidence of witnesses of fact has been given. The introduction of additional expert evidence after the commencement of the trial can have a severely disruptive effect. Not only is it likely to make necessary additional expert evidence in response, but it may also lead to applications for further disclosure of documents and also to applications to call further factual evidence from witnesses whose statements have not previously been exchanged. Accordingly, experts' supplementary reports must be completed and exchanged not later than the progress monitoring date and the introduction of additional expert evidence after that date will only be permitted upon application to the trial judge and if there are very strong grounds for admitting it.

**H3 Evidence by video link**

H3.1 In an appropriate case permission may be given for the evidence of a witness to be given by video link. If permission is given the court will give directions for the conduct of this part of the trial. **2A–105**



H3.2 The party seeking permission to call evidence by video link should prepare and serve on all parties and lodge with the Court a memorandum dealing with the matters outlined in the Video Conferencing Guidance contained in Annex 3 to PD32 (see Appendix 14) and setting out precisely what arrangements are proposed. Where the proposal involves transmission from a location with no existing video-link facility, experience shows that questions of feasibility, timing and cost will require particularly close investigation.

H3.3 An application for permission to call evidence by video link should be made, if possible, at the case management conference or, at the latest, at any pre-trial review. However, an application may be made at an even later stage if necessary. Particular attention should be given to the taking of evidence by video link whenever a proposed witness will have to travel from a substantial distance abroad and his evidence is likely to last no more than half a day.

H3.4 In considering whether to give permission for evidence to be given in this way the court will be concerned in particular to balance any potential savings of costs against the inability to observe the witness at first hand when giving evidence.

**H4 Taking evidence abroad**

**2A-106** H4.1 In an appropriate case permission may be given for the evidence of a witness to be taken abroad. CPR Part 34 contains provisions for the taking of evidence by deposition, and the issue of letters of request.

H4.2 In a very exceptional case, and subject in particular to all necessary approvals being obtained and diplomatic requirements being satisfied, the court may be willing to conduct part of the proceedings abroad. However, if there is any reasonable opportunity for the witness to give evidence by video link, the court is unlikely to take that course.

## J.

## TRIAL

**J1 Expedited trial**

**2A-107** J1.1 The Commercial Court is able to provide an expedited trial in cases of sufficient urgency and importance.

J1.2 A party seeking an expedited trial should apply to the Judge in Charge of the Commercial List on notice to all parties at the earliest possible opportunity. The application should normally be made after issue and service of the claim form but before service of particulars of claim.

**J2 Trials of issues**

**2A-108** J2.1 The court may direct a separate trial of any issue under rule 3.1(2)(i). It will sometimes be advantageous to have a separate trial of particular issues with other issues being heard either by the same judge or by another judge of the Commercial Court or in another court or tribunal. For example, where liability is tried first in the Commercial Court, the assessment of damages can be referred to a judge of the Technology and Construction Court or to a Master, or the parties may choose to ask an arbitrator to decide them. The same approach can be applied to other factual questions.

J2.2 Under rule 3.1(2)(j), (k) and (l) the court may decide the order in which issues are to be tried, may exclude an issue from consideration and may dismiss or give judgment on a claim after a decision on a preliminary issue. The court is likely to consider this by reference to the list of issues. Particularly in long trials, it will sometimes be advantageous to exercise these powers, and accordingly hear the evidence relevant to some issues before moving on to the evidence relevant to others; and the judge will sometimes decide some issues before moving on to hear the evidence relevant to other issues.

**J3 Documents for trial**

**2A-109** J3.1 Bundles of documents for the trial must be prepared in accordance with Appendix 10.

J3.2 The number, content and organisation of the trial bundles must be approved by the advocates with the conduct of the trial.

J3.3 Apart from certain specified documents, trial bundles should include only necessary documents: 39APD3.2(11). Consideration must always be given to what documents are and are not relevant and necessary. Where the court is of the opinion that costs have been wasted by the copying of unnecessary documents it will have no hesitation in making a special order for costs against the person responsible.

***Paragraph numbers marked with a "+" can be found online and on CD.***

J3.4 The number content and organisation of the trial bundles should be agreed in accordance with the following procedure

(i) the claimant must submit proposals to all other parties at least 6 weeks before the date fixed for trial; and

(ii) the other parties must submit details of additions they require and any suggestions for revision of the claimant's proposals to the claimant at least 4 weeks before the date fixed for trial.

This information must be supplied in a form that will be most convenient for the recipient to understand and respond to. The form to be used should be discussed between the parties before the details are supplied.

J3.5

(a) It is the responsibility of the claimant's legal representative to prepare and lodge the agreed trial bundles: see 39APD34.

(b) If another party wishes to put before the court a bundle that the claimant regards as unnecessary he must prepare and lodge it himself.

J3.6

(a) Preparation of the trial bundles must be completed not later than 2 weeks before the date fixed for trial unless the court orders otherwise.

(b) Any party preparing a trial bundle should, as a matter of course, provide all other parties who are to take part in the trial with a copy, at the cost of the receiving party: 39APD3.10. Further copies should be supplied on request, again at the cost of the receiving party.

J3.7 Unless the court orders otherwise, a full set of the trial bundles must be lodged with the Listing Office at least 7 days before the date fixed for trial.

J3.8 If bundles are lodged late, this may result in the trial not commencing on the date fixed, at the expense of the party in default. An order for immediate payment of costs may be made.

J3.9 If oral evidence is to be given at trial, the claimant should provide a clean unmarked set of all relevant trial bundles for use in the witness box: 39APD3.10. The claimant is responsible for ensuring that these bundles are kept up to date throughout the trial.

### J4 Information technology at trial

J4.1 The use of information technology at trial is encouraged where it is likely substantially to save time and cost or to increase accuracy. **2A–110**

J4.2 If any party considers that it might be advantageous to make use of information technology in preparation for, or at, trial, the matter should be raised at the first case management conference. This is particularly important if it is considered that document handling systems would assist disclosure and inspection of documents or the use of documents at trial. In any event, at the first case management conference, even if neither party itself raises the use of information technology, the parties must expect the court to consider its use, including its use in relation to trial bundles.

J4.3 Where information technology is to be used for the purposes of presenting the case at trial the same system must be used by all parties and must be made available to the court. In deciding whether and to what extent information technology should be used at the trial the court will have regard to the financial resources of the parties and will consider whether it is appropriate that, having regard to the parties' unequal financial resources, it is appropriate that the party applying for the use of such information technology should initially bear the cost subject to the court's ultimate order as to the overall costs following judgment.

### J5 Reading lists, authorities and trial timetable

2A–111 J5.1 Unless the court orders otherwise, a single reading list approved by all advocates must be lodged with the Listing Office not later than 1 p.m. two days (i.e. two clear days) before the date fixed for trial together with an estimate of the time required for reading.

J5.2

(a) If any party objects to the judge reading any document in advance of the trial, the objection and its grounds should be clearly stated in a letter accompanying the trial bundles and in the skeleton argument of that party.

(b) Parties should consider in particular whether they have any objection to the judge's reading the witness statements before the trial.

(c) In the absence of objection, the judge will be free to read the witness statements and documents in advance.

J5.3

(a) A composite bundle of the authorities referred to in the skeleton arguments should be lodged with the Listing Office as soon as possible after skeleton arguments have been exchanged.

(b) Unless otherwise agreed, the preparation of the bundle of authorities is the responsibility of the claimant, who should provide copies to all other parties. Advocates should liaise in relation to the production of bundles of authorities to ensure that the same authority does not appear in more than one bundle.

J5.4 Cases which are unreported and which are also not included in the index of Judgments of the Commercial Court and Admiralty Court of England and Wales should normally only be cited where the advocate is ready to give an assurance that the transcript contains a statement of some relevant principle of law of which the substance, as distinct from some mere choice of phraseology, is not to be found in any judgment that has appeared in one of the general or specialised series of law reports. The index of Judgments of the Commercial Court and Admiralty Court of England and Wales can be found www.hmcourt-service.gov.uk/infoabout/admiralcomm/index.htm via the link to "Searchable index of court cases" (at bottom of the box on right hand side of Commercial Court and Admiralty Court).

J5.5

(a) When lodging the reading list the claimant should also lodge a trial timetable.

(b) A trial timetable may have been fixed by the judge at the pre-trial review (section D18.4 above). If it has not, a trial timetable should be prepared by the advocate(s) for the claimant after consultation with the advocate(s) for all other parties.

(c) If there are differences of view between the advocate(s) for the claimant and the advocate(s) for other parties, these should be shown.

(d) The trial timetable will provide for oral submissions, witness evidence and expert evidence over the course of the trial. On the first day of the trial the judge may fix the trial timetable, subject to any further order.

(e) The court may restrict evidence or submissions to ensure compliance with the trial timetable.

### J6 Skeleton arguments etc. at trial

2A–112 J6.1 Written skeleton arguments should be prepared by each party. Guidelines on the preparation of skeleton arguments are set out in Part 1 of Appendix 9.

J6.2 Unless otherwise ordered, the skeleton arguments should be served on all other parties and lodged with the court as follows

***Paragraph numbers marked with a "+" can be found online and on CD.***

(i) by the claimant, not later than 1 p.m. two days (i.e. two clear days) before the start of the trial;

(ii) by each of the defendants, not later than 1 p.m. one day (i.e. one clear day) before the start of the trial.

J6.3 In heavier cases it will often be appropriate for skeleton arguments to be served and lodged at earlier times than indicated at section J6.2. The timetable should be discussed between the advocates and may be the subject of a direction in the pre-trial timetable or at any pre-trial review.

J6.4 The claimant should provide a chronology with his skeleton argument. Indices (i.e. documents that collate key references on particular points, or a substantive list of the contents of a particular bundle or bundles) and dramatis personae should also be provided where these are likely to be useful. Guidelines on the preparation of chronologies and indices are set out in Part 2 of Appendix 9.

J6.5 So far as possible skeleton arguments should be limited in length to 50 pages. Where the advocate or advocates for trial consider that it is not possible to comply with that limit, the matter should be discussed with the trial judge at the pre-trial review or in correspondence.

### J7 Trial sitting days and hearing trials in public

J7.1 Trial sitting days will not normally include Fridays. **2A–113**

J7.2 Where it is necessary in order to accommodate hearing evidence from certain witnesses or types of witness, the court may agree to sit outside normal hours.

J7.3 The general rule is that a hearing is to be in public: rule 39.2(1).

### J8 Oral opening statements at trial

J8.1 Oral opening statements should as far as possible be uncontroversial and in any **2A–114**
event no longer than the circumstances require. Even in a very heavy case, oral opening statements may be very short. There remains some confusion amongst advocates as to what is necessary to adduce a document other than a witness statement or expert report in evidence. Whereas there can be no doubt that any disclosed document can be relied on as evidence of the facts contained in it or as evidence of its existence or the use to which it was put, see Civil Evidence Act 1995 S.2(4) and CPR 32.19 the mere inclusion of a document in the agreed trial bundles does not in itself mean that it is being adduced in evidence by either party: see Appendix 10. For this to happen either the parties must agree that the document in question is to be treated as put in evidence by one or other of them and the judge so informed or they must actively adduce the document in evidence by some other means. This might be done by counsel inviting the judge to read the document relied upon before the calling of oral evidence. The appropriate procedure will be a matter for the judgment of the advocates in each case. However, whichever course is adopted, it will not normally be appropriate for reliance to be placed in final speeches on any document, not already specifically adduced in evidence by one of the means described.

J8.2 At the conclusion of the opening statement for the claimant the advocates for each of the other parties will usually each be invited to make a short opening statement.

### J9 Applications in the course of trial

J9.1 It will not normally be necessary for an application notice to be issued for an **2A–115**
application which is to be made during the course of the trial, but all other parties should be given adequate notice of the intention to apply.

J9.2 Unless the judge directs otherwise the parties should prepare skeleton arguments for the hearing of the application.

*Paragraph numbers marked with a "+" can be found online and on CD.*

**J10 Oral closing submissions at trial**

2A–116 J10.1 All parties will be expected to make oral closing submissions, whether or not closing submissions have been made in writing. It is a matter for the advocate to consider how in all the circumstances these oral submissions should be presented.

J10.2 Unless the trial judge directs otherwise, the claimant will make his oral closing submissions first, followed by the defendant(s) in the order in which they appear on the claim form with the claimant having a right of reply.

2A–117 **J11 Written closing submissions at trial**

J11.1

(a) In a more substantial trial, the court will normally also require closing submissions in writing before oral closing submissions.
(b) In such a case the court will normally allow an appropriate period of time after the conclusion of the evidence to allow the preparation of these submissions.
(c) Even in a less substantial trial the court will normally require a skeleton argument on matters of law.

2A–118 **J12 Judgment**

J12.1

(a) When judgment is reserved the judge may deliver judgment orally or by handing down a written judgment.
(b) If the judge intends to hand down a written judgment a copy of the draft text marked

*"Draft Judgment"*

and bearing the rubric:

*" This is a judgment to which the Practice Direction supplementing CPR Part 40 applies. It will be handed down on at in Court No . This Judgment is confidential to the parties and their legal representatives and accordingly neither the draft itself nor its substance may be disclosed to any other person or used in the public domain. The parties must take all reasonable steps to ensure that its confidentiality is preserved. No action is to be taken (other than internally) in response to the draft, before judgment has been formally pronounced. A breach of any of these obligations may be treated as a contempt of court. The official version of the judgment will be available from the Mechanical Recording Department of the Royal Courts of Justice once it has been approved by the judge.*

*The court is likely to wish to hand down its judgment in an approved final form. Counsel should therefore submit any list of typing corrections and other obvious errors in writing (Nil returns are required) to the clerk to , by fax to 020 7947 or via email at , by on , so that changes can be incorporated, if the judge accepts them, in the handed down judgment."*

will normally be supplied to the advocates one clear day before the judgment is to be delivered.
(c) Advocates should inform the judge's clerk not later than noon on the day before judgment is to be handed down of any typographical or other errors of a similar nature which the judge might wish to correct. This facility is confined to the correction of textual mistakes and is not to be used as the occasion for attempting to persuade the judge to change the decision on matters of substance.
(d) The requirement to treat the text as confidential must be strictly observed. Failure to do so amounts to a contempt of court.

J12.2

(a) Judgment is not delivered until it is formally pronounced in open court.
(b) Copies of the approved judgment will be made available to the parties, to law reporters and to any other person wanting a copy.

(c) The judge may direct that the written judgment stand as the definitive record and that no transcript need be made. Any editorial corrections made at the time of handing down will be incorporated in an approved official text as soon as possible, and the approved official text, so marked, will be available from the Mechanical Recording Department.

J12.3 If at the time of pronouncement of the judgment any party wishes to apply for permission to appeal to the Court of Appeal, that application should be supported by written draft grounds of appeal.

### J13 Costs

J13.1 The rules governing the award and assessment of costs are contained in CPR Parts 43 to 48. **2A–119**

J13.2 The summary assessment procedure provided for in Parts 43 and 44 also applies to trials lasting one day or less.

## K.

## AFTER TRIAL

### K1 Continuation, variation and discharge of interim remedies and undertakings **2A–120**

K1.1

(a) Applications to continue, vary or discharge interim remedies or undertakings should be made to a Commercial Judge, even after trial.
(b) If a party wishes to continue a freezing injunction after trial or judgment, care should be taken to ensure that the application is made before the existing freezing injunction has expired.

### K2 Accounts and enquiries

K2.1 The court may order that accounts and inquiries be referred to a judge of the Technology and Construction Court or to a Master. Alternatively, the parties may choose to refer the matter to arbitration. **2A–121**

### K3 Enforcement

K3.1 Unless the court orders otherwise, all proceedings for the enforcement of any judgment or order for the payment of money given or made in the Commercial Court will be referred automatically to a master of the Queen's Bench Division or a district judge: PD58 § 1.2(2). **2A–122**

K3.2 Applications in connection with the enforcement of a judgment or order for the payment of money should accordingly be directed to the Registry which will allocate them to the Admiralty Registrar or to one of the Queen's Bench masters as appropriate.

### K4 Assessment of damages or interest after a default judgment

K4.1 Unless the court orders otherwise, the assessment of damages or interest following the entry of a default judgment for damages or interest to be assessed will be carried out by the Admiralty Registrar or one of the Queen's Bench masters to whom the case is allocated by the Registry. **2A–123**

## L.

## MULTI-PARTY DISPUTES

### L1 Early consideration

2A–124 L1.1 Cases which involve, or are expected to involve, a large number of claimants or defendants require close case management from the earliest point. The same is true where there are, or are likely to be, a large number of separate cases involving the same or similar issues. Both classes of case are referred to as "multi-party" disputes.

L1.2

(a) The Judge in Charge of the List should be informed as soon as it becomes apparent that a multi-party dispute exists or is likely to exist and an early application for directions should be made.

(b) In an appropriate case an application for directions may be made before issue of a claim form. In some cases it may be appropriate for an application to be made without notice in the first instance.

### L2 Available procedures

2A–125 L2.1 In some cases it may be appropriate for the court to make a Group Litigation Order under Part 19 of the Rules. In other cases it may be more convenient for the court to exercise its general powers of management. These include powers

(i) to dispense with statements of case;

(ii) to direct parties to serve outline statements of case;

(iii) to direct that cases be consolidated or managed and tried together;

(iv) to direct that certain cases or issues be determined before others and to stay other proceedings in the meantime;

(v) to advance or put back the usual time for pre-trial steps to be taken (for example the disclosure of documents by one or more parties or a payment into court).

L2.2 Attention is drawn to the provisions of Section III of Part 19, rules 19.10–19.15 and the practice direction supplementing Section III of Part 19. Practitioners should note that the provisions of Section III of Part 19 give the court additional powers to manage disputes involving multiple claimants or defendants. They should also note that a Group Litigation Order may not be made without the consent of the Lord Chief Justice: PD19B § 3.3(1).

L2.3 An application for a Group Litigation Order should be made in the first instance to the Judge in Charge of the List: PD19B § 3.5.

## M.

## LITIGANTS IN PERSON

### M1 The litigant in person

2A–126 M1.1 Litigants in person appear less often in the Commercial Court than in some other courts. Their position requires special consideration.

### M2 Represented parties

2A–127 M2.1 Where a litigant in person is involved in a case the court will expect solicitors and counsel for other parties to do what they reasonably can to ensure that he has a fair opportunity to prepare and put his case.

M2.2 The duty of an advocate to ensure that the court is informed of all relevant decisions and legislative provisions of which he is aware (whether favourable to his case or not) and to bring any procedural irregularity to the attention of the court during the hearing is of particular importance in a case where a litigant in person is involved.

M2.3 Further, the court will expect solicitors and counsel appearing for other parties to ensure that the case memorandum, the list of issues and all necessary bundles are prepared and provided to the court in accordance with the Guide, even where the litigant in person is unwilling or unable to participate.

***Paragraph numbers marked with a "+" can be found online and on CD.***

M2.4 If the claimant is a litigant in person the judge at the case management conference will normally direct which of the parties is to have responsibility for the preparation and upkeep of the case management bundle.

M2.5 At the case management conference the court may give directions relating to the costs of providing application bundles, trial bundles and, if applicable, transcripts of hearings to the litigant in person.

**M3 Companies without representation**

M3.1 Although rule 39.6 allows a company or other corporation with the permission of the court to be represented at trial by an employee, the complexity of most cases in the Commercial Court makes that unsuitable. Accordingly, permission is likely to be given only in unusual circumstances. **2A–128**

## N.

## ADMIRALTY

**N1 General**

N1.1 Proceedings in the Admiralty Court are dealt with in Part 61 and its associated practice direction. **2A–129**

N1.2 The Admiralty & Commercial Courts Guide has been prepared in consultation with the Admiralty Judge. It has been adopted to provide guidance about the conduct of proceedings in the Admiralty Court. The Guide must be followed in the Admiralty Court unless the content of Part 61, its associated practice direction or the terms of this section N require otherwise.

N1.3 One significant area of difference between practice in the Commercial Court and practice in the Admiralty Court is that many interlocutory applications are heard by the Admiralty Registrar who has all the powers of the Admiralty judge save as provided otherwise: rule 61.1(4).

**N2 The Admiralty Court Committee**

N2.1 The Admiralty Court Committee provides a specific forum for contact and consultation between the Admiralty Court and its users. Its meetings are usually held in conjunction with the Commercial Court Users Committee. Any correspondence should be addressed to the Deputy Admiralty Marshal, Royal Courts of Justice, Strand, WC2A 2LL. **2A–130**

**N3 Commencement of proceedings, service of Statements of Case and associated matters**

N3.1 Sections B and C of this guide apply to all Admiralty claims except: **2A–131**

(i) a claim in rem;
(ii) a collision claim; and
(iii) a limitation claim.

**N4 Commencement and early stages of a claim in rem**

N4.1 The early stages of an in rem claim differ from those of other claims. **2A–132**

The procedure is governed generally by rule 61.3 and PD61 § § 3.1–3.11.

N4.2 In addition, the following sections of the Guide apply to claims in rem: B4.3, B4.7–B4.11, B7.4–B7.6, C1.1–C1.6, C1.8 and C2.1(ii)–C5.4.

N4.3 Subject to PD61 § 3.7, section C1.7 of the Guide also applies to claims in rem.

N4.4 After an acknowledgement of service has been filed a claim in rem follows the

*Paragraph numbers marked with a "+" can be found online and on CD.*

procedure applicable to a claim proceeding in the Commercial List, save that the Claimant is allowed 75 days in which to serve his particulars of claim: PD61 § 3.10.

### N5 The early stages of a Collision Claim

2A–133 N5.1 Where a collision claim is commenced in rem, the general procedure applicable to claims in rem applies subject to rule 61.4 and PD61 § § 4.1–4.5.

N5.2 Where a collision claim is not commenced in rem the general procedure applicable to claims proceeding in the Commercial List applies subject to rule 61.4 and PD61 § § 4.1–4.5.

N5.3 Service of a claim form out of the jurisdiction in a collision claim (other than a claim in rem) is permitted in the circumstances identified in rule 61.4(7) only and the procedure set out in Appendix 15 of the Guide should be adapted accordingly.

N5.4 One particular feature of a collision action is that the parties must prepare and file a Collision Statement of Case. Prior to the coming into force of Part 61, a Collision Statement of Case was known as a Preliminary Act and the law relating to Preliminary Acts continues to apply to Collision Statements of Case: PD61 § 4.5.

N5.5 The provisions of Appendix 4 apply to part 2 of a Collision Statement of Case (but not to part 1).

N5.6 Every party is required, so far as it is able, to provide full and complete answers to the questions contained in part 1 of the Collision Statement of Case. The answers should descend to a reasonable level of particularity.

N5.7 The answers to the questions contained in part 1 are treated as admissions made by the party answering the questions and leave to amend such answers will be granted only in exceptional circumstances. As to the principles applicable to the amendment of particulars of claim in a collision claim reference should be made to the judgment of Gross J. in *The Topaz* [2003] 2 Lloyd's Rep 19.

### N6 The early stages of a Limitation Claim

2A–134 N6.1 The procedure governing the early stages of a limitation claim differs significantly from the procedure relating to other claims and is contained in rule 61.11 and PD61 § 10.1.

N6.2 Service of a limitation claim form out of the jurisdiction is permitted in the circumstances identified in rule 61.11 (5) only and the procedure set out in Appendix 15 of the Guide should be adapted accordingly.

### N7 Issue of documents when the Registry is closed

2A–135 N7.1 When the Registry is closed (and only when it is closed) an Admiralty claim form may be issued on the following designated fax machine: 020 7947 6245 and only on that machine.

N7.2 The procedure to be followed is set out in Appendix 3 of the Guide.

N7.3 The issue of an Admiralty claim form in accordance with the procedure set out in Appendix 3 shall have the same effect for all purposes as a claim form issued in accordance with the relevant provisions of rule 61 and PD61.

N7.4 When the Registry is closed (and only when it is closed) a notice requesting a caution against release may be filed on the following designated fax machine: 020 7947 6245 and only on that machine. This machine is manned 24 hours a day by court security staff (telephone 020 7947 6260).

N7.5 The notice requesting the caution should be transmitted with a note in the following form for ease of identification by security staff:

"CAUTION AGAINST RELEASE
Please find notice requesting caution against release of the ... (*name ship/identify cargo*) ... for filing in the Admiralty & Commercial Registry."

N7.6 The notice must be in Admiralty Form No. **ADM11** and signed by a solicitor acting on behalf of the applicant.

N7.7 Subject to the provisions of sections N7.9 and N7.10 below, the filing of the notice takes place when the fax is recorded as having been received.

N7.8 When the Registry is next open to the public, the filing solicitor or his agent shall attend and deliver to the Registry the document which was transmitted by fax together with the transmission report. Upon satisfying himself that the document delivered fully accords with the document received by the Registry, the court officer shall stamp the document delivered with the time and date on which the notice was received, enter the same in the caution register and retain the same with the faxed copy.

N7.9 Unless otherwise ordered by the court, the stamped notice shall be conclusive proof that the notice was filed at the time and on the date stated.

N7.10 If the filing solicitor does not comply with the foregoing procedure, or if the notice is not stamped, the notice shall be deemed never to have been filed.

### N8 Case Management

N8.1 The case management provisions of the Guide apply to Admiralty claims save that **2A–136**

(i) In Admiralty claims the case management provisions of the Guide are supplemented by PD61 § § 2.1–2.3 which make provision for the early classification and streaming of cases;

(ii) In a collision case the claimant should apply for a case management conference within 7 days after the last Collision Statement of Case is filed;

(iii) In a limitation claim where the right to limit is not admitted and the claimant seeks a general limitation decree, the claimant must, within 7 days after the date of the filing of the defence of the defendant last served or the expiry of the time for doing so, apply to the Admiralty Registrar for a case management conference: PD61 § 10.7;

(iv) In a collision claim or a limitation claim a mandatory case management conference will normally take place on the first available date 5 weeks after the date when the claimant is required to take steps to fix a date for the case management conference;

(v) In a limitation claim, case management directions are initially given by the Registrar: PD61 § 10.8;

(vi) In the Admiralty Court, the Case Management Information Sheet should be in the form in Appendix 6 of this Guide but should also include the following questions

1. Do any of the issues contained in the List of Issues involve questions of navigation or other particular matters of an essentially Admiralty nature which require the trial to be before the Admiralty Judge?
2. Is the case suitable to be tried before a Deputy Judge nominated by the Admiralty Judge?
3. Do you consider that the court should sit with nautical or other assessors? If you intend to ask that the court sit with one or more assessors who is not a Trinity Master, please state the reasons for such an application.

### N9 Evidence

N9.1 In collision claims, section H1.5 and Appendix 8 are subject to the proviso that experience has shown that it is usually desirable for the main elements of a witness' evidence in chief to be adduced orally. **2A–137**

*Paragraph numbers marked with a "+" can be found online and on CD.*

*Authenticity*

N9.2

(a) Where the authenticity of any document disclosed to a party is not admitted, that party must serve notice that the document must be proved at trial in accordance with CPR 32.19. Such notice must be served by the latest date for serving witness statements or within 7 days of disclosure of the document, whichever is later.

(b) Where, apart from the authenticity of the document itself, the date upon which a document or an entry in it is stated to have been made or the person by whom the document states that it or any entry in it was made or any other feature of the document is to be challenged at the trial on grounds which may require a witness to be called at the trial to support the contents of the document, such challenge

(i) must be raised in good time in advance of the trial to enable such witness or witnesses to be called;

(ii) the grounds of challenge must be explicitly identified in the skeleton argument or outline submissions in advance of the trial.

(c) Where, due to the late disclosure of a document it or its contents or character cannot practicably be challenged within the time limits prescribed in (a) or (b), the challenge may only be raised with the permission of the court and having regard to the Overriding Objective (CPR 1.1).

*Skeleton arguments in Collision Claims*

N9.3 In collision claims the skeleton argument of each party must be accompanied by a plot or plots of that party's case or alternative cases as to the navigation of vessels during and leading to the collision. All plots must contain a sufficient indication of the assumptions used in the preparation of the plot.

**N10 Split trials, accounts, enquiries and enforcement**

**2A–138** N10.1 In collision claims it is usual for liability to be tried first and for the assessment of damages and interest to be referred to the Admiralty Registrar.

N10.2 Where the Admiralty Court refers an account, enquiry or enforcement, it will usually refer the matter to the Admiralty Registrar.

**N11 Release of vessels out of hours**

**2A–139** N11.1 This section makes provision for release from arrest when the Registry is closed.

N11.2 An application for release under rule 61.8(4)(c) or (d) may, when the Registry is closed, be made in, and only in, the following manner

(i) The solicitor for the arrestor or the other party applying must telephone the security staff at the Royal Courts of Justice (020 7947 6260) and ask to be contacted by the Admiralty Marshal, who will then respond as soon as practicably possible;

(ii) Upon being contacted by the Admiralty Marshal the solicitor must give oral instructions for the release and an oral undertaking to pay the fees and expenses of the Admiralty Marshal as required in Form No. **ADM12**;

(iii) The arrestor or other party applying must then send a written request and undertaking on Form No. **ADM12** by fax to a number given by the Admiralty Marshal;

(iv) The solicitor must provide written consent to the release from all persons who have entered cautions against release (and from the arrestor if the arrestor is not the party applying) by sending such consents by fax to the number supplied by the Admiralty Marshal;

(v) Upon the Admiralty Marshal being satisfied that no cautions against release are in force, or that all persons who have entered cautions against release, and if necessary the arrestor, have given their written consent to the release, the Admiralty Marshal shall effect the release as soon as practicable.

N11.3 Practitioners should note that the Admiralty Marshal is not formally on call and therefore at times may not be available to assist. Similarly the practicalities of releasing a ship in some localities may involve the services of others who may not be available outside court hours.

***Paragraph numbers marked with a "+" can be found online and on CD.***

N11.4 This service is offered to practitioners for use during reasonable hours and on the basis that if the Admiralty Marshal is available and can be contacted he will use his best endeavours to effect instructions to release but without guarantee as to their success.

**N12 Use of postal facilities in the Registry**

N12.1 Applications together with the requisite documents may be posted to: **2A-140**

The Admiralty and Commercial Registry,

Room EB15,

Royal Courts of Justice,

Strand,

London WC2A 2LL.

N12.2 In addition to the classes of business for which the use of postal facilities is permitted by the CPR or the Commercial Court Guide, the filing of the following classes of documents is also permitted in Admiralty matters

(i) Requests for cautions;

(ii) Collision Statements of Case.

N12.3

(a) Documents sent by post for filing must be accompanied by two copies of a list of the documents sent and an envelope properly addressed to the sender.

(b) On receipt of the documents in the Registry, the court officer will, if the circumstances are such that had the documents been presented personally they would have been filed, cause them to be filed and will, by post, notify the sender that this has been done. If the documents would not have been accepted if presented personally the court officer will not file them but will retain them in the Registry for collection by the sender and will, by post, so inform the sender.

(c) When documents received through the post are filed by the court officer they will be sealed and entered as filed on the date on which they were received in the Registry.

**N13 Insurance of arrested property**

N13.1 The Marshal will not insure any arrested property for the benefit of parties at any time during the period of arrest (whether before or after the lodging of an application for sale, if any). **2A-141**

N13.2 The Marshal will use his best endeavours (but without any legal liability for failure to do so) to advise all parties known to him as being on the record in actions in rem against the arrested property, including those who have filed cautions against release of that property, before any such property moves or is moved beyond the area covered by the usual port risks policy.

N13.3 In these circumstances, practitioners' attention is drawn to the necessity of considering the questions of insuring against port risks for the amount of their clients' interest in any property arrested in an Admiralty action and the inclusion in any policy of a "Held Covered" clause in case the ship moves or is moved outside the area covered by the usual port risks policy. The usual port risks policy provides, among other things, for a ship to be moved or towed from one berth to another up to a distance of five miles within the port where she is lying.

**N14 Assessors**

14.1 In collision claims and other cases involving issues of navigation and seamanship, the Admiralty Court usually sits with assessors. The parties are not **2A-142**

*Paragraph numbers marked with a "+" can be found online and on CD.*

COMMERCIAL COURTS

permitted to call expert evidence on such matters without the leave of the court: rule 61.13.

14.2 Parties are reminded of the practice with regard to the disclosure of any answers to the court's questions and the opportunity for comment on them as set out in the Judgment of Gross J. in *The Global Mariner* [2005] 1 Lloyd's Rep 699 at p702.

14.3 Provision is made in rule 35.15 for assessors' remuneration. Provisions for assessors' remuneration are set out in QB *Practice Direction* [2007] 1 WLR 2508. The usual practice is for the court to seek an undertaking from the claimant to pay the remuneration on demand after the case has concluded.

## O.

## ARBITRATION

**2A–143** **O1 Arbitration claims**

O1.1

(a) Applications to the court under the Arbitration Acts 1950 – 1996 and other applications relating to arbitrations are known as "arbitration claims".

(b) The procedure applicable to arbitration claims is to be found in Part 62 and its associated practice direction. Separate provision is made

(i) by Section I for claims relating to arbitrations to which the Arbitration Act 1996 applies;

(ii) by Section II for claims relating to arbitrations to which the Arbitration Acts 1950 – 1979 ("the old law") apply; and

(iii) by Section III for enforcement proceedings.

(c) For a full definition of the expression "arbitration claim" see rule 62.2(1) (claims under the 1996 Act) and rule 62.11(2) (claims under the old law).

(d) Part 58 applies to arbitration claims in the Commercial Court insofar as no specific provision is made by Part 62: rule 62.1(3).

**Claims under the Arbitration Act 1996**

*O2 Starting an arbitration claim*

**2A–144** O2.1 Subject to section O2.3 an arbitration claim must be started by the issue of an arbitration claim form in accordance with the Part 8 procedure: rule 62.3(1).

O2.2 The claim form must be substantially in the form set out in Appendix A to practice direction 62: PD62 § 2.2.

O2.3 An application to stay proceedings under section 9 of the Arbitration Act 1996 must be made by application notice in the proceedings: rule 62.3(2).

O2.4 Where a question arises as to whether an arbitration agreement is null and void, inoperative or incapable of being performed the court may deal with it in the same way as provided by rule 62.8(3) which applies where a question arises as to whether an arbitration agreement has been concluded or the dispute which is the subject matter of the proceedings falls within the terms of such an agreement.

*O3 The arbitration claim form*

O3.1 The arbitration claim form must contain, among other things, a concise statement of the remedy claimed and, if an award is challenged, the grounds for that challenge: rule 62.4(1).

O3.2 Reference in the arbitration claim form to a witness statement or affidavit filed in support of the claim is not sufficient to comply with the requirements of rule 62.4(1).

***Paragraph numbers marked with a "+" can be found online and on CD.***

*O4 Service of the arbitration claim form*

O4.1 An arbitration claim form issued in the Admiralty & Commercial Registry must be served by the claimant.

O4.2

(a) The rules governing service of the claim form are set out in Part 6 of the Civil Procedure Rules.
(b) Unless the court orders otherwise an arbitration claim form must be served on the defendant within 1 month from the date of issue: rule 62.4(2).

O4.3

(a) An arbitration claim form may be served out of the jurisdiction with the permission of the court: rule 62.5(1).
(b) Rules 6.40– 6.46 apply to the service of an arbitration claim form out of the jurisdiction: rule 62.5(3).

O4.4 The court may exercise its powers under rules 6.15 and/or 6.37(5)(b) to permit service of an arbitration claim form on a party at the address of the solicitor or other representative acting for him in the arbitration: PD62 § 3.1.

O4.5 The claimant must file a certificate of service within 7 days of serving the arbitration claim form: PD62 § 3.2.

*O5 Acknowledgment of service*

O5.1

(a) A defendant must file an acknowledgment of service of the arbitration claim form in every case: rule 58.6(1).
(b) An adapted version of practice form **N210** (acknowledgment of service of a Part 8 claim form) has been approved for use in the Commercial Court.

O5.2 The time for filing an acknowledgment of service is calculated from the service of the arbitration claim form.

*O6 Standard directions*

O6.1 The directions set out in PD62 § 6.2–6.7 apply unless the court orders otherwise.

O6.2 The claimant should apply for a hearing date as soon as possible after issuing an arbitration claim form or (in the case of an appeal) obtaining permission to appeal.

O6.3 A defendant who wishes to rely on evidence in opposition to the claim must file and serve his evidence within 21 days after the date by which he was required to acknowledge service: PD62 § 6.2.

O6.4 A claimant who wishes to rely on evidence in response to evidence served by the defendant must file and serve his evidence within 7 days after the service of the defendant's evidence: PD62 § 6.3.

O6.5 An application for directions in a pending arbitration claim should be made by application notice under Part 23. Where an arbitration application involves recognition and/or enforcement of an agreement to arbitrate and that application is challenged on the grounds that the parties to the application were not bound by an agreement to arbitrate, it will usually be necessary for the court to resolve that issue in order to determine the application. For this purpose it may be necessary for there to be disclosure of documents and/or factual and/or expert evidence. In that event, it

***Paragraph numbers marked with a "+" can be found online and on CD.***

is the responsibility of those advising the applicant to liaise with the other party and to arrange with the Listing Office for a case management conference to be listed as early as possible to enable the court to give directions as to the steps to be taken before the hearing of the application.

*O7 Interim remedies*

O7.1 An application for an interim remedy under section 44 of the Arbitration Act 1996 must be made in an arbitration claim form: PD62 § 8.1.

**O8 Challenging the award**

*Challenge by way of appeal*

**2A–145** O8.1 A party wishing to appeal against the award of an arbitrator or umpire must set out in the arbitration claim form

(i) the question of law on which the appeal is based; and

(ii) a succinct statement of the grounds of appeal,

identifying the relevant part(s) of the award and reasons.

O8.2 If the appeal is brought with the agreement of the other parties to the proceedings, a copy of their agreement in writing must be filed with the arbitration claim form.

O8.3 A party seeking permission to appeal must

(i) state in his arbitration claim form the grounds on which he contends that permission to appeal should be given PD62 § 12.1; and

(ii) file and serve with the arbitration claim form any written evidence on which he wishes to rely for the purposes of satisfying the court of the matters referred to in section 69(3) of the 1996 Act: PD62 § 12.2.

O8.4

(a) If the defendant wishes to oppose the claimant's application for permission to appeal he must file a witness statement setting out

(i) the grounds on which he opposes the grant of permission; and

(ii) any evidence on which he relies in relation to the matters mentioned in section 69(3) of the 1996 Act: PD62 § § 12.3(1) and (2).

(b) If the defendant wishes to contend that the award should be upheld for reasons other than those expressed in the award, he must set out those reasons in his witness statement: PD62 § 12.3(3).

O8.5 The court will normally determine applications for permission to appeal without an oral hearing. If the court considers that an oral hearing is required, it will give further directions as appropriate.

*Challenging an award for serious irregularity*

O8.6

(a) An arbitration claim challenging an award on the ground of serious irregularity under section 68 of the 1996 Act is appropriate only in cases where there are grounds for thinking

(i) that an irregularity has occurred which

(ii) has caused or will cause substantial injustice to the party making the challenge.

(b) An application challenging an award on the ground of serious irregularity should therefore not be regarded as an alternative to, or a means of supporting, an application for permission to appeal.

***Paragraph numbers marked with a "+" can be found online and on CD.***

O8.7 The challenge to the award must be supported by evidence of the circumstances on which the claimant relies as giving rise to the irregularity complained of and the nature of the injustice which has been or will be caused to him.

O8.8 If the nature of the challenge itself or the evidence filed in support of it leads the court to consider that the claim has no real prospect of success, the court may exercise its powers under rule 3.3(4) to dismiss the application summarily. In such cases the applicant will have the right to apply to the court to set aside the order and to seek directions for the hearing of the application.

*Multiple claims*

O8.9 If the arbitration claim form includes both a challenge to an award by way of appeal and a challenge on the ground of serious irregularity, the applications should be set out in separate sections of the arbitration claim form and the grounds on which they are made separately identified.

O8.10 In such cases the papers will be placed before a judge to consider how the applications may most appropriately be disposed of. It is usually more appropriate to dispose of the application to set aside or remit the award before considering the application for permission to appeal.

**O9 Time limits**

O9.1 An application to challenge an award under sections 67 or 68 of the 1996 Act or to appeal under section 69 of the Act must be brought within 28 days of the date of the award: **see** section 70(3). **2A–146**

O9.2 The court has power to vary the period of 28 days fixed by section 70(3) of the 1996 Act: rule 62.9(1). However, it is important that any challenge to an award be pursued without delay and the court will require cogent reasons for extending time.

O9.3 An application to extend time made **before** the expiry of the period of 28 days must be made in a Part 23 application notice, but the application notice need not be served on any other party: rule 62.9(2) and PD62 § 11.1(1).

O9.4 An application to extend time made **after** the expiry of the period of 28 days must be made in the arbitration claim form in which the applicant is seeking substantive relief: rule 62.9(3)(a).

O9.5 An application to vary the period of 28 days will normally be determined without a hearing and prior to the consideration of the substantive application: PD62 § 10.2.

**Claims under the Arbitration Acts 1950–1979**

*O10 Starting an arbitration claim*

O10.1 Subject to section O10.2 an arbitration claim must be started by the issue of an arbitration claim form in accordance with the Part 8 procedure: rule 62.13(1). **2A–147**

O10.2 The claim form must be substantially in the form set out in Appendix A to PD62 § 2.2.

O10.3 An application to stay proceedings on the grounds of an arbitration agreement must be made by application notice in the proceedings: rule 62.13(2).

*O11 The arbitration claim form*

O11.1 An arbitration claim form must state the grounds of the claim or appeal: rule 62.15(5)(a).

O11.2 Reference in the arbitration claim form to the witness statement or affidavit

*Paragraph numbers marked with a "+" can be found online and on CD.*



COMMERCIAL COURTS

filed in support of the claim is not sufficient to comply with the requirements of rule 62.15(5)(a).

*O12 Service of the arbitration claim form*

O12.1 An arbitration claim form issued in the Admiralty & Commercial Registry must be served by the claimant.

O12.2 The rules governing service of the claim form are set out in Part 6 of the Civil Procedure Rules.

O12.3

(a) An arbitration claim form may be served out of the jurisdiction with the permission of the court: rule 62.16(1).
(b) Rules 6.40– 6.46 apply to the service of an arbitration claim form out of the jurisdiction: rule 62.16(4).

O12.4 Although not expressly covered by PD62, the court may in an appropriate case exercise its powers under rule 6.15 and/or 6.37(5) to permit service of an arbitration claim form on a party at the address of the solicitor or other representative acting for him in the arbitration.

O12.5 The claimant must file a certificate of service within 7 days of serving the claim form.

2A-148 **O13 Acknowledgment of service**

O13.1

(a) A defendant must file an acknowledgment of service in every case: rule 58.6(1).
(b) An adapted version of practice form **N210** (acknowledgment of service of a Part 8 claim form) has been approved for use in the Commercial Court.

O13.2 The time for filing an acknowledgment of service is calculated from the service of the arbitration claim form.

*O14 Standard directions*

O14.1 Where the claim or appeal is based on written evidence, a copy of that evidence must be served with the arbitration claim form: rule 62.15(5)(b).

O14.2 Where the claim or appeal is made with the consent of the arbitrator or umpire or other parties, a copy of every written consent must be served with the arbitration claim form: rule 62.15(5)(c).

O14.3 An application for directions in a pending arbitration claim should be made by application notice under Part 23.

*O15 Interim remedies*

O15.1 An application for an interim remedy under section 12(6) of the 1950 Act must be made in accordance with Part 25.

O15.2 The application must be made by arbitration claim form.

O15.3 A claim under section 12(4) of the 1950 Act for an order for the issue of a witness summons to compel the attendance of a witness before an arbitrator or umpire where the attendance of the witness is required within the district of a District Registry may be started in that Registry: rule 62.14.

**O16 Challenging the award**

*Challenge by way of appeal*

O16.1 A party wishing to appeal against the award of an arbitrator or umpire must file and serve with the arbitration claim form a statement of the grounds for the appeal, specifying the relevant part(s) of the award and reasons: rule 62.15(6). **2A–149**

O16.2 A party seeking permission to appeal must also file and serve with the arbitration claim form any written evidence in support of the contention that the question of law concerns a term of the contract or an event which is not "one off": rule 62.15(6).

O16.3 Any written evidence in reply must be filed and served not less than 2 days before the hearing of the application for permission to appeal: rule 62.15(7).

O16.4 A party who wishes to contend that the award should be upheld for reasons other than those set out in the award and reasons must file and serve on the claimant a notice specifying the grounds of his contention not less than 2 days before the hearing of the application for permission to appeal: rule 62.15(8).

O16.5 Applications for permission to appeal will be heard orally, but will not normally be listed for longer than half an hour. Skeleton arguments should be lodged.

*Claims to set aside or remit the award*

O16.6 A claim to set aside or remit an award on the grounds of misconduct should not be regarded as an alternative to, or a means of supporting, an application for permission to appeal.

O16.7 The directions set out in PD62 § § 6.2–6.7 should be followed unless the court orders otherwise.

*Multiple claims*

O16.8 If the arbitration claim form includes both an appeal and an application to set aside or remit the award, the applications should be set out in separate sections of the arbitration claim form and the grounds on which they are made separately identified.

O16.9 The court may direct that one application be heard before the other or may direct that they be heard together, as may be appropriate. It is usually more appropriate to dispose of the application to set aside or remit the award before considering the application for permission to appeal.

**O17 Time limits** **2A–150**

O17.1

(a) Time limits governing claims under the 1950 and 1979 Acts are set out in rule 62.15.

(b) Different time limits apply to different claims. It is important to consult rule 62.15 to ensure that applications are made within the time prescribed.

(c) The court has power under rule 3.1(2) to vary the time limits prescribed by rule 62.15, but will require cogent reasons for doing so.

**O18 Provisions applicable to all arbitrations**

*Enforcement of awards*

O18.1 All applications for permission to enforce awards are governed by Section III of Part 62, rule 62.17. **2A–151**

O18.2 An application for permission to enforce an award in the same manner as a judgment may be made without notice, but the court may direct that the arbitration

***Paragraph numbers marked with a "+" can be found online and on CD.***

claim form be served, in which case the application will continue as an arbitration claim in accordance with the procedure set out in Section I: rule 62.18(1)–(3).

O18.3 An application for permission to enforce an award in the same manner as a judgment must be supported written evidence in accordance with rule 62.18(6).

O18.4

(a) Two copies of the draft order must accompany the application.

(b) If the claimant wishes to enter judgment, the form of the judgment must correspond to the terms of the award.

(c) The defendant has the right to apply to the court to set aside an order made without notice giving permission to enforce the award and the order itself must state in terms

(i) that the defendant may apply to set it aside within 14 days after service of the order or, if the order is to be served out of the jurisdiction, within such other period as the court may set; and

(ii) that it may not be enforced until after the end of that period or any application by the defendant to set it aside has been finally disposed of: rule 62.18(9) and (10).

**Matters of general application**

*O19 Transfer of arbitration claims*

2A–152 O19.1 An arbitration claim which raises no significant point of arbitration law or practice will normally be transferred

(i) if a rent-review arbitration, to the Chancery Division;

(ii) if a construction or engineering arbitration, to the Technology and Construction Court;

(iii) if an employment arbitration, to the Central London County Court Mercantile List.

O19.2 Salvage arbitrations will normally be transferred to the Admiralty Court.

*O20 Appointment of a Commercial Judge as sole arbitrator or umpire*

O20.1 Section 93 of the Arbitration Act 1996 provides for the appointment of a Commercial Judge as sole arbitrator or umpire. The Act limits the circumstances in which a Judge may accept such an appointment.

O20.2 Enquiries should be directed to the Judge in charge of the Commercial List or the Clerk to the Commercial Court.

## P.

## MISCELLANEOUS

2A–153 **P1 Out of hours emergency arrangements**

P1.1

(a) When the Listing Office is closed, solicitors or counsel's clerks should in an emergency contact the Clerk to the Queen's Bench Judge in Chambers by telephone through the security desk at the Royal Courts of Justice: PD58 § 2.2.

(b) The telephone number of the security desk is included in the list of addresses and contact details at the end of the Guide.

P1.2 When the Listing Office is closed an urgent hearing will initially be dealt with by the Queen's Bench Judge in Chambers who may dispose of the application himself or make orders allowing the matter to come before a Commercial Judge at the first available opportunity.

### P2 Index of decisions of the Commercial and Admiralty Courts

P2.1 An Index has been prepared on a subject-matter basis of unreported Commercial Court and Admiralty Court judgments from 1995 onwards. The Index is updated regularly. **2A–154**

P2.2 The Index is provided as a service to litigants and to the legal profession, and to assist the Commercial Court and the Admiralty Court to maintain reasonable consistency of approach in those areas of law and procedure most frequently before them.

P2.3 The index of Judgments of Commercial Court and Admiralty Court of England and Wales is available to all Internet users and can be found at: www.hmcourts-service.gov.uk/infoabout/admiralcomm/index.htm via the link to "Searchable index of court cases" (at bottom of the box on right hand side of Commercial Court and Admiralty Court).

P2.4 The judgments referred to in the Index are kept in the Registry. They may be consulted there.

P2.5 Copies of the judgments referred to in the Index may be obtained from the Registry (or where there is difficulty, from the clerk to the judge) unless the judgment is in the form of a transcript, in which case copies should be obtained from the shorthand writers or other transcript agency.

## APPENDIX 1

### Editorial note

**2A–155**

Part 58 (Commercial Court)—reproduced at paras 2A–1 *et seq.*
Part 61 (Admiralty Court)—reproduced at paras 2D–1 *et seq.*
Practice Direction to Part 58—reproduced at paras 2A–22 *et seq.*
Practice Direction to Part 61—reproduced at paras 2D–85 *et seq.*

## APPENDIX 2

### Editorial note

**2A–156**

Part 62 (Arbitration)—reproduced at paras 2E–1 *et seq.*
Practice Direction to Part 62—reproduced at paras 2E–46 *et seq.*

## APPENDIX 3

## PROCEDURE FOR ISSUE OF CLAIM FORM WHEN REGISTRY CLOSED

(See section B2.4 of the Guide.) **2A–157**

### Procedure

The procedure is as follows:

1. The claim form must be signed by a solicitor acting on behalf of the claimant, and must not require the permission of the Court for its issue (unless such permission has already been given).

2. The solicitor causing the claim form to be issued ("the issuing solicitor") must

(i) endorse on the claim form the endorsement shown below and sign that endorsement;

(ii) send a copy of the claim form so endorsed to the Registry by fax for issue under this section; and

(iii) when he has received a transmission report stating that the transmission of the claim form to the Registry was completed in full and the time and the date of the transmission, complete and sign the certificate shown below.

***Paragraph numbers marked with a "+" can be found online and on CD.***



COMMERCIAL COURTS

3. When the Registry is next open to the public after the issue of a claim form in accordance with this procedure the issuing solicitor or his agent shall attend and deliver to the Registry the document which was transmitted by fax (including the endorsement and the certificate), or if that document has been served, a true and certified copy of it, together with as many copies as the Registry shall require and the transmission report.

4. When the proper officer at the Registry has checked and is satisfied that the document delivered under paragraph 3 fully accords with the document received under paragraph 2, and that all proper fees for issue have been paid, he shall allocate a number to the case, and seal, mark as "original" and date the claim form with the date on which it was issued (being, as indicated below, the date when the fax is recorded at the Registry as having been received).

5. As soon as practicable thereafter the issuing solicitor shall inform any person served with the unsealed claim form of the case number, and (on request) shall serve any such person with a copy of the claim form sealed and dated under paragraph 4 above (at such address in England and Wales as the person may request) and the person may, without paying a fee, inspect and take copies of the documents lodged at the Registry under paragraphs 2 and 3 above.

### Effect of issue following request by fax

2A–158 The issue of a claim form in accordance with this procedure takes place when the fax is recorded at the Registry as having been received, and the claim form bearing the endorsement shall have the same effect for all purposes as a claim form issued under CPR Part 7 [or 8, as the case may be]. Unless otherwise ordered the sealed version of the claim form retained by the Registry shall be conclusive proof that the claim form was issued at the time and on the date stated. If the procedure set out in this Appendix is not complied with, the court may declare (on its own initiative or on application) that the claim form shall be treated as not having been issued.

### Endorsement

2A–159 A claim form issued pursuant to a request by fax must be endorsed as follows:

1. This claim form is issued under paragraph 2.2 of Practice Direction 58 and may be served notwithstanding that it does not bear the seal of the Court.

2. A true copy of this claim form and endorsement has been transmitted to the Admiralty and Commercial Registry, Royal Courts of Justice, Strand, London WC2A 2LL, at the time and date certified below by the solicitor whose name appears below ("the issuing solicitor").

3. It is the duty of the issuing solicitor or his agent to attend at the Registry when it is next open to the public for the claim form to be sealed.

4. Any person upon whom this unsealed claim form is served

(a) will be notified by the issuing solicitor of the number of the case;

(b) may require the issuing solicitor to serve a copy of the sealed claim form at an address in England and Wales; and

(c) may inspect without charge the documents which have been lodged at the Registry by the undersigned solicitor.

5. I, the issuing solicitor, undertake to the Court, to the defendants named in this claim form, and to any other person upon whom this claim form may be served:

(a) that the statement in paragraph 2 above is correct;

(b) that the time and date given in the certificate with this endorsement are correct;

(c) that this claim form is a claim form which may be issued under section 2.2 and Appendix A of Practice Direction 58;

(d) that I will comply in all respects with the requirements of Appendix A of Practice Direction 58;

(e) that I will indemnify any person served with the claim form before it is sealed against any loss suffered as a result of the claim form being or becoming invalid in accordance with Appendix A of Practice Direction 58.

*(Signed)*

Solicitor for the claimant"

[**Note**: the endorsement may be signed in the name of the firm of solicitors rather than an individual solicitor, or by solicitors' agents in their capacity as agents acting on behalf of their professional clients.]

**Certificate**

An issuing solicitor must sign a certificate in the following form: 2A–160

"I certify that I have received a transmission report confirming that the transmission of a copy of this claim form to the Registry by fax was fully completed and that the time and date of transmission to the Registry were *[enter the time and date shown on the transmission report]*.

Dated

*(Signed)*

Solicitor for the claimant."

[**Note**: the certificate may be signed in the name of the firm of solicitors rather than an individual solicitor, or by solicitors' agents in their capacity as agents acting on behalf of their professional clients.]

## APPENDIX 4

## STATEMENTS OF CASE

The following principles apply to all statements of case and should, as far as possible, also be observed when drafting a Part 8 claim form, which will not contain, or be followed by, particulars of claim: 2A–161

1. The document must be as brief and concise as possible.

2. The document must be set out in separate consecutively numbered paragraphs and sub-paragraphs.

3. So far as possible each paragraph or sub-paragraph should contain no more than one allegation.

4. The document must deal with the case on a point by point basis to allow a point by point response.

5. Where particulars are given of any allegation or reasons given for a denial, the allegation or denial should be stated first and the particulars or reasons for it listed one by one in separate numbered sub-paragraphs.

6. A party wishing to advance a positive case should set that case out in the document; a simple denial is not sufficient.

7. Any matter which, if not stated, might take another party by surprise should be stated.

8. Where they will assist:

(i) headings should be used; and

(ii) abbreviations and definitions should be established and used, and a glossary annexed.

9. Contentious headings, abbreviations and definitions should not be used. Every effort should be made to ensure that headings, abbreviations and definitions are in a form that will enable them to be adopted without issue by the other parties.

10. Particulars of primary allegations should be stated as particulars and not as primary allegations.

11. If it is necessary to rely upon a substantial amount of detailed factual information

or lengthy particulars in support of an allegation, these should be set out in schedules or appendices.

12. Particular care should be taken to set out only those factual allegations which are necessary to support the case. Evidence should not be included.

13. A response to particulars set out in a schedule should be set out in a corresponding schedule.

14. If it is necessary for the proper understanding of the statement of case to include substantial parts of a lengthy document the passages in question should be set out in a schedule rather than in the body of the case.

15. Contentious paraphrasing should be avoided.

16. The document must be signed by the individual person or persons who drafted it, not, in the case of a solicitor, in the name of the firm alone.

17. The document must not be longer than 25 pages unless the court has given permission for a longer document.

## APPENDIX 5

### FORMS OF FREEZING INJUNCTION AND SEARCH ORDER

2A–162 adapted for use in the Commercial Court

** FREEZING INJUNCTION **

**IN THE HIGH COURT OF JUSTICE**
**QUEEN'S BENCH DIVISION**
**COMMERCIAL COURT**

**Before The Honourable Mr Justice [ ]**

**Claim No.**

**BETWEEN**

**Claimant(s)/Applicant(s)**

– and –

**Defendant(s)/Respondent(s)**

---

**PENAL NOTICE**

**If you [ ] [1] disobey this order you may be held to be in contempt of court and may be imprisoned, fined or have your assets seized.**

**Any other person who knows of this order and does anything which helps or permits the Respondent to breach the terms of this order may also be held to be in contempt of court and may be imprisoned, fined or have their assets seized.**

**THIS ORDER**

1. This is a Freezing Injunction made against [ ] ("the Respondent") on [ ] by Mr Justice [ ] on the application of [ ] ("the Applicant").

---

[1] Insert name of Respondent(s).

2. This order was made at a hearing without notice to the Respondent. The Respondent has a right to apply to the court to vary or discharge the order—see paragraph 13 below.
3. There will be a further hearing in respect of this order on [ ] ("the return date" [1]).

[4. If there is more than one Respondent

(a) unless otherwise stated, references in this order to "the Respondent" mean both or all of them; and

(b) this order is effective against any Respondent on whom it is served or who is given notice of it.]

**FREEZING INJUNCTION**

*[For injunction limited to assets in England and Wales]*

5. Until after the return date or further order of the court, the Respondent must not remove from England and Wales or in any way dispose of, deal with or diminish the value of any of his assets which are in England and Wales up to the value of £

*[For worldwide injunction]*

5. Until the return date or further order of the court, the Respondent must not—

(1) remove from England and Wales any of his assets which are in England and Wales up to the value of £ ; or

(2) in any way dispose of, deal with or diminish the value of any of his assets whether they are in or outside England and Wales up to the same value.

*[For either form of injunction]*

6. Paragraph 5 applies to all the Respondent's assets whether or not they are in his own name, whether they are solely or jointly owned and whether the Respondent is interested in them legally, beneficially or otherwise. For the purpose of this order the Respondent's assets include any asset which he has the power, directly or indirectly, to dispose of or deal with as if it were his own. The Respondent is to be regarded as having such power if a third party holds or controls the asset in accordance with his direct or indirect instructions.
7. This prohibition includes the following assets in particular—

(a) the property known as [*title/address*] or the net sale money after payment of any mortgages if it has been sold;

(b) the property and assets of the Respondent's business [known as [*name*]] [carried on at [*address*]] or the sale money if any of them have been sold; and

(c) any money in the account numbered [*account number*] at [*title/address*].

(d) any interest under any trust or similar entity including any interest which can arise by virtue of the exercise of any power of appointment, discretion or otherwise howsoever.

*[For injunction limited to assets in England and Wales]*

8. If the total value free of charges or other securities ("unencumbered value") of the Respondent's assets in England and Wales exceeds £ , the Respondent may remove any of those assets from England and Wales or may dispose of or deal with them so long as the total unencumbered value of his assets still in England and Wales remains above £ .

*[For worldwide injunction]*

8.

(1) If the total value free of charges or other securities ("unencumbered value") of the Respondent's assets in England and Wales exceeds £ , the Respondent may remove any of those assets from England and

[1] In the Commercial Court, usually 14 days after the injunction was granted, particularly where parties are outside the jurisdiction.

Wales or may dispose of or deal with them so long as the total unencumbered value of the Respondent's assets still in England and Wales remains above £ .

(2) If the total unencumbered value of the Respondent's assets in England and Wales does not exceed £ , the Respondent must not remove any of those assets from England and Wales and must not dispose of or deal with any of them. If the Respondent has other assets outside England and Wales, he may dispose of or deal with those assets outside England and Wales so long as the total unencumbered value of all his assets whether in or outside England and Wales remains above £ .

**PROVISION OF INFORMATION**

9.

(1) Unless paragraph (2) applies, the Respondent must [within hours of service of this order] and to the best of his ability inform the Applicant's solicitors of all his assets [in England and Wales] [worldwide] [exceeding £ in value [1] ] whether in his own name or not and whether solely or jointly owned, giving the value, location and details of all such assets.

(2) If the provision of any of this information is likely to incriminate the Respondent, he may be entitled to refuse to provide it, but is recommended to take legal advice before refusing to provide the information. Wrongful refusal to provide the information is contempt of court and may render the Respondent liable to be imprisoned, fined or have his assets seized.

10. Within [] working days after being served with this order, the Respondent must swear and serve on the Applicant's solicitors an affidavit setting out the above information [2].]

**PROVISION OF INFORMATION**

11.

(1) This order does not prohibit the Respondent from spending £ a week towards his ordinary living expenses and also £ [*or* a reasonable sum] on legal advice and representation. [But before spending any money the Respondent must tell the Applicant's legal representatives where the money is to come from.]

[(2) This order does not prohibit the Respondent from dealing with or disposing of any of his assets in the ordinary and proper course of business, but before doing so the Respondent must tell the Applicant's legal representatives.]

(3) The Respondent may agree with the Applicant's legal representatives that the above spending limits should be increased or that this order should be varied in any other respect, but any agreement must be in writing.

(4) The order will cease to have effect if the Respondent—

(a) provides security by paying the sum of £ into court, to be held to the order of the court; or

(b) makes provision for security in that sum by another method agreed with the Applicant's legal representatives.

**COSTS**

12. The costs of this application are reserved to the judge hearing the application on the return date.

**VARIATION OR DISCHARGE OF THIS ORDER**

13. Anyone served with or notified of this order may apply to the court at any time to vary or discharge this order (or so much of it as affects that person), but they must first inform the Applicant's solicitors. If any evidence is to be

[1] In most cases, careful consideration will need to be given to inserting a lower limit of say £10,000 or equivalent below which value assets need not be disclosed.

[2] Consideration should also be given to amalgamating paragraphs 9 and 10 of the draft Order, so as to require only one disclosure exercise, verified by Affidavit.

relied upon in support of the application, the substance of it must be communicated in writing to the Applicant's solicitors in advance.

**INTERPRETATION OF THIS ORDER**

14. A Respondent who is an individual who is ordered not to do something must not do it himself or in any other way. He must not do it through others acting on his behalf or on his instructions or with his encouragement.

15. A Respondent which is not an individual which is ordered not to do something must not do it itself or by its directors, officers, partners, employees or agents or in any other way.

**PARTIES OTHER THAN THE APPLICANT AND RESPONDENT**

16. **Effect of this order**

It is a contempt of court for any person notified of this order knowingly to assist in or permit a breach of this order. Any person doing so may be imprisoned, fined or have their assets seized.

17. **Set off by banks**

This injunction does not prevent any bank from exercising any right of set off it may have in respect of any facility which it gave to the respondent before it was notified of this order.

18. **Withdrawals by the Respondent**

No bank need enquire as to the application or proposed application of any money withdrawn by the Respondent if the withdrawal appears to be permitted by this order.

*[For worldwide injunction]*

19. **Persons outside England and Wales**

(1) Except as provided in paragraph (2) below, the terms of this order do not affect or concern anyone outside the jurisdiction of this court.

(2) The terms of this order will affect the following persons in a country or state outside the jurisdiction of this court-

a. the Respondent or his officer or agent appointed by power of attorney;

b. any person who–

i. is subject to the jurisdiction of this court;

ii. has been given written notice of this order at his residence or place of business within the jurisdiction of this court; and

iii. is able to prevent acts or omissions outside the jurisdiction of this court which constitute or assist in a breach of the terms of this order; and

c. any other person, only to the extent that this order is declared enforceable by or is enforced by a court in that country or state.

*[For worldwide injunction]*

20. **Assets located outside England and Wales**

Nothing in this order shall, in respect of assets located outside England and Wales, prevent any third party from complying with—

(1) what it reasonably believes to be its obligations, contractual or otherwise, under the laws and obligations of the country or state in which those assets are situated or under the proper law of any contract between itself and the Respondent; and

(2) any orders of the courts of that country or state, provided that reasonable notice of any application for such an order is given to the Applicant's solicitors.

**COMMUNICATIONS WITH THE COURT**

All communications to the court about this order should be sent to Room EB09, Royal Courts of Justice, Strand, London WC2A 2LL quoting the case number. The telephone number is 020 7947 6826.

The offices are open between 10 a.m. and 4.30 p.m. Monday to Friday.

## SCHEDULE A—AFFIDAVITS

The Applicant relied on the following affidavits—

| | [name] | [number of affidavit] | [date sworn] | [filed on behalf of] |
|---|---|---|---|---|
| (1) | | | | |
| (2) | | | | |

## SCHEDULE B—UNDERTAKINGS GIVEN TO THE COURT BY THE APPLICANT

(1) If the court later finds that this order has caused loss to the Respondent, and decides that the Respondent should be compensated for that loss, the Applicant will comply with any order the court may make. (3) (4) (5)(i) copies of the affidavits and exhibits containing the evidence relied upon by the Applicant, and any other documents provided to the court on the making of the application; (ii) the claim form; and (iii) an application notice for continuation of the order.

[(2) The Applicant will—

(a) on or before [*date*] cause a written guarantee in the sum of £ to be issued from a bank with a place of business within England or Wales, in respect of any order the court may make pursuant to paragraph (1) above; and

(b) immediately upon issue of the guarantee, cause a copy of it to be served on the Respondent.]

(3) As soon as practicable the Applicant will issue and serve a claim form [in the form of the draft produced to the court] [claiming the appropriate relief].

(4) The Applicant will [swear and file an affidavit] [cause an affidavit to be sworn and filed] [substantially in the terms of the draft affidavit produced to the court] [confirming the substance of what was said to the court by the Applicant's counsel/solicitors].

(5) The Applicant will serve upon the Respondent [together with this order] [as soon as practicable]—

(i) copies of the affidavits and exhibits containing the evidence relied upon by the Applicant, and any other documents provided to the court on the making of the application;

(ii) the claim form; and

(ii) an application notice for continuation of the order.

[(6) Anyone notified of this order will be given a copy of it by the Applicant's legal representatives.]

(7) The Applicant will pay the reasonable costs of anyone other than the Respondent which have been incurred as a result of this order including the costs of finding out whether that person holds any of the Respondent's assets and if the court later finds that this order has caused such person loss, and decides that such person should be compensated for that loss, the Applicant will comply with any order the court may make.

(8) If this order ceases to have effect (for example, if the Respondent provides security or the Applicant does not provide a bank guarantee as provided for above) the Applicant will immediately take all reasonable steps to inform in writing anyone to whom he has given notice of this order, or who he has reasonable grounds for supposing may act upon this order, that it has ceased to have effect.

[(9) The Applicant will not without the permission of the court use any information obtained as a result of this order for the purpose of any civil or criminal proceedings, either in England and Wales or in any other jurisdiction, other than this claim.]

[(10) The Applicant will not without the permission of the court seek to enforce this order in any country outside England and Wales [or seek an order of a similar nature including orders conferring a charge or other security against the Respondent or the Respondent's assets].]

***Paragraph numbers marked with a "+" can be found online and on CD.***

**NAME AND ADDRESS OF APPLICANT'S LEGAL REPRESENTATIVES**

The Applicant's legal representatives are—

[Name, address, reference, fax and telephone numbers both in and out of office hours and e-mail]

****SEARCH ORDER**** **2A–162.1**

**IN THE HIGH COURT OF JUSTICE**
**QUEEN'S BENCH DIVISION**
**COMMERCIAL COURT**

**Before The Honourable Mr Justice [ ]**

**Claim No.**

**BETWEEN**

**Claimant(s)/Applicant(s)**

– and –

**Defendant(s)/Respondent(s)**

---

**PENAL NOTICE**

**If you [ ] [1] disobey this order you may be held to be in contempt of court and may be imprisoned, fined or have your assets seized.**

**Any other person who knows of this order and does anything which helps or permits the Respondent to breach the terms of this order may also be held to be in contempt of court and may be imprisoned, fined or have their assets seized.**

**THIS ORDER**

1. This is a Search Order made against [ ] ("the Respondent") on [ ] by Mr Justice [ ] on the application of [ ] ("the Applicant"). The Judge read the Affidavits listed in Schedule F and accepted the undertakings set out in Schedules C, D and E at the end of this order.
2. This order was made at a hearing without notice to the Respondent. The Respondent has a right to apply to the court to vary or discharge the order—see paragraph 27 below.
3. There will be a further hearing in respect of this order on [ ] ("the return date").
4. If there is more than one Respondent—
   (a) unless otherwise stated, references in this order to "the Respondent" mean both or all of them; and
   (b) this order is effective against any Respondent on whom it is served or who is given notice of it.
5. This order must be complied with by—
   (a) the Respondent;
   (b) any director, officer, partner or responsible employee of the Respondent; and
   (c) if the Respondent is an individual, any other person having responsible control of the premises to be searched.

---

[1] Insert name of Respondent(s).

**THE SEARCH**

6. The Respondent must permit the following persons [1]—
   (a) [ ] ("the Supervising Solicitor);
   (b) [ ], a solicitor in the firm of [ ], the Applicant's solicitors; and
   (c) up to [ ] other persons [2] being [their identity or capacity] accompanying them,

   (together "the search party"), to enter the premises mentioned in Schedule A to this order and any other premises of the Respondent disclosed under paragraph 18 below and any vehicles under the Respondent's control on or around the premises ("the premises") so that they can search for, inspect, photograph or photocopy, and deliver into the safekeeping of the Applicant's solicitors all the documents and articles which are listed in Schedule B to this order ("the listed items").
7. Having permitted the search party to enter the premises, the Respondent must allow the search party to remain on the premises until the search is complete. In the event that it becomes necessary for any of those persons to leave the premises before the search is complete, the Respondent must allow them to re-enter the premises immediately upon their seeking re-entry on the same or the following day in order to complete the search.

**RESTRICTIONS ON SEARCH**

8. This order may not be carried out at the same time as a police search warrant.
9. Before the Respondent allows anybody onto the premises to carry out this order, he is entitled to have the Supervising Solicitor explain to him what it means in everyday language.
10. The Respondent is entitled to seek legal advice and to ask the court to vary or discharge this order. Whilst doing so, he may ask the Supervising Solicitor to delay starting the search for up to 2 hours or such other longer period as the Supervising Solicitor may permit. However, the Respondent must—
    (a) comply with the terms of paragraph 27 below;
    (b) not disturb or remove any listed items; and
    (c) permit the Supervising Solicitor to enter, but not start to search.

**PROVISION OF INFORMATION**

11. Before permitting entry to the premises by any person other than the Supervising Solicitor, the Respondent may, for a short time (not to exceed two hours, unless the Supervising Solicitor agrees to a longer period), gather together any documents he believes may be [incriminating or] [3] privileged and hand them to the Supervising Solicitor for him to assess whether they are [incriminating or] privileged as claimed. If the Supervising Solicitor decides that any of the documents may be [incriminating or] privileged or is in any doubt as to their status, he will exclude them from the search and retain them in his possession pending further order of the court.
12. If the Respondent wishes to take legal advice and gather documents as permitted, he must first inform the Supervising Solicitor and keep him informed of the steps being taken.

**PROVISION OF INFORMATION**

13. No item may be removed from the premises until a list of the items to be removed has been prepared, and a copy of the list has been supplied to the Respondent, and he has been given a reasonable opportunity to check the list.

---

[1] Where the premises are likely to be occupied by an unaccompanied woman and the Supervising Solicitor is a man, at least one of the persons accompanying him should be a woman.

[2] None of these persons should be people who could gain personally or commercially from anything they might read or see on the premises, unless their presence is essential.

[3] References to incriminating documents should be omitted from orders made in intellectual property proceedings, where the privilege against self-incrimination does not apply – see paragraph 8.4 of the practice direction.

14. The premises must not be searched, and items must not be removed from them, except in the presence of the Respondent.
15. If the Supervising Solicitor is satisfied that full compliance with paragraphs 13 or 14 is not practicable, he may permit the search to proceed and items to be removed without fully complying with them.

**DELIVERY UP OF ARTICLES/DOCUMENTS**

16. The Respondent must immediately hand over to the Applicant's solicitors any of the listed items, which are in his possession or under his control, save for any computer or hard disk integral to any computer. Any items the subject of a dispute as to whether they are listed items must immediately be handed over to the Supervising Solicitor for safe keeping pending resolution of the dispute or further order of the court.
17. The Respondent must immediately give the search party effective access to the computers on the premises, with all necessary passwords, to enable the computers to be searched. If they contain any listed items the Respondent must cause the listed items to be displayed so that they can be read and copied.[1] The Respondent must provide the Applicant's Solicitors with copies of all listed items contained in the computers. All reasonable steps shall be taken by the Applicant and the Applicant's solicitors to ensure that no damage is done to any computer or data. The Applicant and his representatives may not themselves search the Respondent's computers unless they have sufficient expertise to do so without damaging the Respondent's system.

**PROVISION OF INFORMATION**

18. The Respondent must immediately inform the Applicant's Solicitors (in the presence of the Supervising Solicitor) so far as he is aware—
    (a) where all the listed items are;
    (b) the name and address of everyone who has supplied him, or offered to supply him, with listed items;
    (c) the name and address of everyone to whom he has supplied, or offered to supply, listed items; and
    (d) full details of the dates and quantities of every such supply and offer.
19. Within [ ] working days after being served with this order the Respondent must swear and serve an affidavit setting out the above information.[2]

**PROHIBITED ACTS**

20. Except for the purpose of obtaining legal advice, the Respondent must not directly or indirectly inform anyone of these proceedings or of the contents of this order, or warn anyone that proceedings have been or may be brought against him by the Applicant until 4.30 p.m. on the return date or further order of the court.
21. Until 4.30 p.m. on the return date the Respondent must not destroy, tamper with, cancel or part with possession, power, custody or control of the listed items otherwise than in accordance with the terms of this order.
22. [Insert any negative injunctions.]
23. [Insert any further order]

**COSTS**

24. The costs of this application are reserved to the judge hearing the application on the return date.

[1] If it is envisaged that the Respondent's computers are to be imaged (i.e. the hard drives are to be copied wholesale, thereby reproducing listed items and other items indiscriminately), special provision needs to be made and independent computer specialists need to be appointed, who should be required to give undertakings to the court.

[2] The period should ordinarily be longer than the period in paragraph (2) of Schedule D, if any of the information is likely to be included in listed items taken away of which the Respondent does not have copies.

**RESTRICTIONS ON SERVICE**

25. This order may only be served between [ ] a.m./p.m. and [ ] a.m./p.m. [and on a weekday].[1]
26. This order must be served by the Supervising Solicitor, and paragraph 6 of the order must be carried out in his presence and under his supervision.

**VARIATION AND DISCHARGE OF THIS ORDER**

27. Anyone served with or notified of this order may apply to the court at any time to vary or discharge this order (or so much of it as affects that person), but they must first inform the Applicant's solicitors. If any evidence is to be relied upon in support of the application, the substance of it must be communicated in writing to the Applicant's solicitors in advance.

**INTERPRETATION OF THIS ORDER**

28. Any requirement that something shall be done to or in the presence of the Respondent means—
    (a) if there is more than one Respondent, to or in the presence of any one of them; and
    (b) if a Respondent is not an individual, to or in the presence of a director, officer, partner or responsible employee.
29. A Respondent who is an individual who is ordered not to do something must not do it himself or in any other way. He must not do it through others acting on his behalf or on his instructions or with his encouragement.
30. A Respondent which is not an individual which is ordered not to do something must not do it itself or by its directors, officers, partners, employees or agents or in any other way.

**COMMUNICATIONS WITH THE COURT**

All communications to the court about this order should be sent to Room EB09, Royal Courts of Justice, Strand, London WC2A 2LL quoting the case number. The telephone number is 020 7947 6826.

The offices are open between 10 a.m. and 4.30 p.m. Monday to Friday.

**SCHEDULE A**
**THE PREMISES**

**SCHEDULE B**
**THE LISTED ITEMS**

**SCHEDULE C**
**UNDERTAKINGS GIVE TO THE COURT BY THE APPLICANT**

(1) If the court later finds that this order or carrying it out has caused loss to the Respondent, and decides that the Respondent should be compensated for that loss, the Applicant will comply with any order the court may make. Further if the carrying out of this order has been in breach of the terms of this order or otherwise in a manner inconsistent with the Applicant's solicitors' duties as officers of the court, the Applicant will comply with any order for damages the court may make.

[(2) As soon as practicable the Applicant will issue a claim form [in the form of the draft produced to the court] [claiming the appropriate relief].]

(3) The Applicant will [swear and file an affidavit] [cause an affidavit to be sworn and filed] [substantially in the terms of the draft affidavit produced to the court] [confirming the substance of what was said to the court by the Applicant's counsel/solicitors].

(4) The Applicant will not, without the permission of the court use any information or documents obtained as a result of carrying out this order nor inform

[1] Normally, the order should be served in the morning (not before 9.30 a.m.) and on a weekday to enable the Respondent more readily to obtain legal advice.

anyone else of these proceedings except for the purposes of these proceedings (including adding further Respondents) or commencing civil proceedings in relation to the same or related subject matter to these proceedings until after the return date.

(5) The Applicant will maintain pending further order the sum of £ [[0]11 ] in an account controlled by the Applicant's solicitors.]

[(6) The Applicant will insure the items removed from the premises.]

## SCHEDULE D
## UNDERTAKINGS GIVEN BY THE APPLICANT'S SOLICITORS

(1) The Applicant's solicitors will provide to the Supervising Solicitor for service on the Respondent—
   (i) a service copy of this order;
   (ii) the claim form (with defendant's response pack) or, if not issued, the draft produced to the court;
   (iii) an application for hearing on the return date;
   (iv) copies of the affidavits [or draft affidavits] and exhibits capable of being copied containing the evidence relied upon by the applicant;
   (v) a note of any allegation of fact made orally to the court where such allegation is not contained in the affidavits or draft affidavits read by the judge; and
   (vi) a copy of the skeleton argument produced to the court by the Applicant's [counsel/solicitors].

(2) The Applicants' solicitors will answer at once to the best of their ability any question whether a particular item is a listed item.

(3) Subject as provided below the Applicant's solicitors will retain in their own safe keeping all items obtained as a result of this order until the court directs otherwise.

(4) The Applicant's solicitors will return the originals of all documents obtained as a result of this order (except original documents which belong to the Applicant) as soon as possible and in any event within [two] working days of their removal.

## SCHEDULE E
## UNDERTAKINGS GIVEN BY THE SUPERVISING SOLICITOR

(1) The Supervising Solicitor will use his best endeavours to serve this order upon the Respondent and at the same time to serve upon the Respondent the other documents required to be served and referred to in paragraph (1) of Schedule D.

(2) The Supervising Solicitor will offer to explain to the person served with the order its meaning and effect fairly and in everyday language, and to inform him of his right to take legal advice (such advice to include an explanation that the Respondent may be entitled to avail himself of [the privilege against self-incrimination or] [legal professional privilege]) and to apply to vary or discharge this order as mentioned in paragraph 27 above.

(3) The Supervising Solicitor will retain in the safe keeping of his firm all items retained by him as a result of this order until the court directs otherwise.

(4) Within [48] hours of completion of the search the Supervising Solicitor will make and provide to the Applicant's solicitors, the Respondent or his solicitors and to the judge who made this order (for the purposes of the court file) a written report on the carrying out of the order.

**SCHEDULE F**
**AFFIDAVITS**

The Applicant relied on the following affidavits—

[name] [number of affidavit] [date sworn] [filed on behalf of]

(1)
(2)

**NAME AND ADDRESS OF APPLICANT'S SOLICITORS**

The Applicant's solicitors are—

[Name, address, reference, fax and telephone numbers both in and out of office hours.]

## APPENDIX 6

## CASE MANAGEMENT INFORMATION SHEET

2A-163 **The information supplied should be printed in bold characters**

Case Management Information Sheet

Party lodging information sheet:

Name of solicitors:

Name(s) of advocates for trial:

[Note: This Sheet should normally be completed with the involvement of the advocate(s) instructed for trial. If the claimant is a litigant in person this fact should be noted at the foot of the sheet and proposals made as to which party is to have responsibility for the preparation and upkeep of the case management bundle.]

(1) By what date can you give standard disclosure?

(2) In relation to standard disclosure, do you contend in relation to any category or class of document under rule 31.6(b) that to search for that category or class would be unreasonable? If so, what is the category or class and on what grounds do you so contend?

(3) Is specific disclosure required on any issue? If so, please specify.

(4) By what dates can you (a) give specific disclosure or (b) comply with a special disclosure order?

(5) May the time periods for inspection at rule 31.15 require adjustment, and if so by how much?

(6) Are amendments to or is information about any statement of case required? If yes, please give brief details of what is required.

(7) Can you make any additional admissions? If yes, please give brief details of the additional admissions.

(8) Are any of the issues in the case suitable for trial as preliminary issues?

(9) (a) On the evidence of how many witnesses of fact do you intend to rely at trial (subject to the directions of the Court)? Please give their names, or explain why this is not being done.

(b) By what date can you serve signed witness statements?

(c) How many of these witnesses of fact do you intend to call to give oral evidence at trial (subject to the directions of the Court)? Please give their names, or explain why this is not being done.

(d) Will interpreters be required for any witness?

(e) Do you wish any witness to give oral evidence by video link? Please give his or her name, or explain why this is not being done. Please state the country and city from which the witness will be asked to give evidence by video link.

(10) (a) On what issues may expert evidence be required?

(b) Is this a case in which the use of a single joint expert might be suitable (see rule 35.7)?

(c) On the evidence of how many expert witnesses do you intend to rely at trial (subject to the directions of the Court)? Please give their names, or explain why this is not being done. Please identify each expert's field of expertise.

(d) By what date can you serve signed expert reports?

(e) When will the experts be available for a meeting or meetings of experts?

(f) How many of these expert witnesses do you intend to call to give oral evidence at trial (subject to the directions of the Court)? Please give their names, or explain why this is not being done.

(g) Will interpreters be required for any expert witness?

(h) Do you wish any expert witness to give oral evidence by video link? Please give his or her name, or explain why this is not being done. Please state the country and city from which the witness will be asked to give evidence by video link.

(11) What are the advocates' present provisional estimates of the minimum and maximum lengths of the trial?

(12) What is the earliest date by which you believe you can be ready for trial?

(13) Is this a case in which a pre-trial review is likely to be useful?

(14) Is there any way in which the Court can assist the parties to resolve their dispute or particular issues in it without the need for a trial or a full trial?

(15) (a) Might some form of Alternative Dispute Resolution procedure assist to resolve or narrow the dispute or particular issues in it?

(b) Has the question at (a) been considered between the client and legal representatives (including the advocate(s) retained)?

(c) Has the question at (a) been explored with the other parties in the case?

(d) Do you request that the case is adjourned while the parties try to settle the case by Alternative Dispute Resolution or other means?

(e) Would an ADR order in the form of Appendix 7 to the Commercial Court Guide be appropriate?

(f) Are any other special directions needed to allow for Alternative Dispute Resolution?

(16) What other applications will you wish to make at the Case Management Conference?

(17) Does provision need to be made in the pre-trial timetable for any application or procedural step not otherwise dealt with above? If yes, please specify the application or procedural step.

(18) Are there, or are there likely in due course to be, any related proceedings (e.g. a Part 20 claim)? Please give brief details.

[Signature of solicitors]

Note: This information sheet must be lodged with the Clerk to the Commercial Court at least 7 days before the Case Management Conference (with a copy to all other parties): see section D8.5 of the Commercial Court Guide.

## APPENDIX 7

## DRAFT ADR ORDER

**2A–164** 1. On or before [*] the parties shall exchange lists of 3 neutral individuals who are available to conduct ADR procedures in this case prior to [*]. Each party may [in addition] [in the alternative] provide a list identifying the constitution of one or more panels of neutral individuals who are available to conduct ADR procedures in this case prior to [*].

2. On or before [*] the parties shall in good faith endeavour to agree a neutral individual or panel from the lists so exchanged and provided.

3. Failing such agreement by [*] the Case Management Conference will be restored to enable the Court to facilitate agreement on a neutral individual or panel.

4. The parties shall take such serious steps as they may be advised to resolve their disputes by ADR procedures before the neutral individual or panel so chosen by no later than [*].

5. If the case is not finally settled, the parties shall inform the Court by letter prior to [disclosure of documents/exchange of witness statements/exchange of experts' reports] what steps towards ADR have been taken and (without prejudice to matters of privilege) why such steps have failed. If the parties have failed to initiate ADR procedures the Case Management Conference is to be restored for further consideration of the case.

6. [Costs].

Note: The term "ADR procedures" is deliberately used in the draft ADR order. This is in order to emphasise that (save where otherwise provided) the parties are free to use the ADR procedure that they regard as most suitable, be it mediation, early neutral evaluation, non-binding arbitration etc.

## APPENDIX 8

## STANDARD PRE-TRIAL TIMETABLE

**2A–165** 1. [Standard disclosure is to be made by [*], with inspection [*] days after notice.]

2. Signed statements of witnesses of fact, and hearsay notices where required by rule 33.2, are to be exchanged not later than [*].

3. Unless otherwise ordered, witness statements are to stand as the evidence in chief of the witness at trial.

4. Signed reports of experts

(i) are to be confined to one expert for each party from each of the following fields of expertise: [*];

(ii) are to be confined to the following issues: [*];

(iii) are to be exchanged [sequentially/simultaneously];

(iv) are to be exchanged not later than [date or dates for each report in each field of expertise].

5. Meeting of experts

(i) The meeting of experts is to be by [*];

***Paragraph numbers marked with a "+" can be found online and on CD.***

(ii) The joint memorandum of the experts is to be completed by [*];

(iii) Any short supplemental expert reports are to be exchanged [sequentially/ simultaneously] by not later than [date or dates for each supplemental report].

6. [If the experts' reports cannot be agreed, the parties are to be at liberty to call expert witnesses at the trial, limited to those experts whose reports have been exchanged pursuant to 4. above.]

[Or: The parties are to be at liberty to apply to call as expert witnesses at the trial those experts whose reports they have exchanged pursuant to 4. above, such application to be made not earlier than [*] and not later than [*].]

7. Preparation of trial bundles to be completed in accordance with Appendix 10 to the Commercial Court Guide by not later than [*].

8. The provisional estimated length of the trial is [*]. This includes [*] pre-trial reading time.

9. Within [*] days the parties are to attend on the Clerk to the Commercial Court to fix the date for trial which shall be not before [*].

10. The progress monitoring date is [*]. Each party is to lodge a completed progress monitoring information sheet with the Clerk to the Commercial Court at least 3 days before the progress monitoring date (with a copy to all other parties).

11. Each party is to lodge a completed pre-trial checklist not later than 3 weeks before the date fixed for trial.

12. [There is to be a pre-trial review not earlier than [*] and not later than [*]].

13. Save as varied by this order or further order, the practice and procedures set out in the Admiralty & Commercial Courts Guide are to be followed.

14. Costs in the case.

15. Liberty to restore the Case Management Conference.

## APPENDIX 9

## SKELETON ARGUMENTS, CHRONOLOGIES AND INDICES

### Part 1 Skeleton arguments

1. A skeleton argument is intended to identify both for the parties and the court those points which are, and are not, in issue and the nature of the argument in relation to those points that are in issue. It is not a substitute for oral argument. **2A–166**

2. Skeleton arguments must therefore

(a) identify concisely:

(i) the nature of the case generally and the background facts insofar as they are relevant to the matter before the court;

(ii) the propositions of law relied on with references to the relevant authorities;

(iii) the submissions of fact to be made with references to the evidence;

(b) be in numbered paragraphs and state the name of the advocate(s) who prepared them; and

(c) should avoid arguing the case at length.

### Part 2 Chronologies and indices

3. As far as possible chronologies and indices should not be prepared in a tendentious form. The ideal is that the court and the parties should have a single point of reference that all find useful and are happy to work with. **2A–167**

***Paragraph numbers marked with a "+" can be found online and on CD.***

4. Where there is disagreement about a particular event or description, it is useful if that fact is indicated in neutral terms and the competing versions shortly stated.

5. If time and circumstances allow its preparation, a chronology or index to which all parties have contributed and agreed can be invaluable.

6. Chronologies and indices once prepared can be easily updated and are of continuing usefulness throughout the life of the case.

## APPENDIX 10

## PREPARATION OF BUNDLES

**2A–168** 1. The preparation of bundles requires a high level of co-operation between legal representatives for all parties. It is the duty of all legal representatives to co-operate to this high level.

2. Bundles should be prepared as follows:

(i) No more than one copy of any one document should be included, unless there is good reason for doing otherwise;

(ii) Contemporaneous documents, and correspondence, should be included in chronological order;

(iii) Where a contract or similar document is central to the case it may be included in a separate place provided that a page is inserted in the chronological run of documents to indicate

(A) the place the contract or similar document would have appeared had it appeared chronologically and

(B) where it may be found instead;

(iv) Documents in manuscript, or not fully legible, should be transcribed; the transcription should be marked and placed adjacent to the document transcribed;

(v) Documents in a foreign language should be translated; the translation should be marked and placed adjacent to the document transcribed; the translation should be agreed, or, if it cannot be agreed, each party's proposed translation should be included;

(vi) If a document has to be read across rather than down the page, it should be so placed in the bundle as to ensure that the top of the text is nearest the spine;

(vii) No bundle should contain more than 300 pages;

(viii) Bundles should not be overfilled, and should allow sufficient room for later insertions. Subject to this, the size of file used should not be a size that is larger than necessary for the present and anticipated contents;

(ix) Bundles should be paginated, in the bottom right hand corner and in a form that can clearly be distinguished from any existing pagination on the document;

(x) Bundles should be indexed, save that a chronological bundle of contemporaneous documents need not be indexed if an index is unlikely to be useful;

(xi) Bundles should be numbered and named on the outside and on the inside front cover, the label to include the short title of the case, and a description of the bundle (including its number, where relevant).

3. Documents within bundles should be marked as follows:

(i) When copy documents from exhibits have been included in the bundle(s), then unless clearly unnecessary, the copy of the affidavit or witness statement to which the documents were exhibited should be marked in the right hand margin (in manuscript if need be) to show where the document referred to may be found in the bundle(s).

(ii) Unless clearly unnecessary, where copy documents in a bundle are taken from the disclosure of more than one party the documents should be marked in the top right hand corner (in manuscript if need be) to show from which party's disclosure the copy document has been taken;

(iii) Where there is a reference in a statement of case or witness statement to a document which is contained in the trial bundles a note should be made in the margin (if necessary in manuscript) identifying the place where that document is to be found.

Unless otherwise agreed this is the responsibility of the party tendering the statement of case or witness statement.

4. For the trial a handy-sized core bundle should normally be provided containing the really important documents in the case. The documents in this bundle should be paginated, but each page should also bear its bundle and page number reference in the main bundles. It is particularly important to allow sufficient room for later insertions (see paragraph 2(viii) above).

5. Large documents, such as plans, should be placed in an easily accessible file.

6.

(a) When agreeing bundles for trial, legal representatives should bear in mind the effect of the Civil Evidence Act 1995 and of rules 33.2(3) (notice requiring proof of authenticity) and 32.19 (hearsay notices).

(b) Pursuant to those provisions, documents which have not been the subject of a notice served in accordance with rule 32.19(2) (requiring proof of authenticity) will be admissible as evidence of the truth of their contents even if there has been non-compliance with the notice requirements of s. 2(1) of the 1995 Act and rule 33.2 (see s. 2(4) of the Act). Accordingly, save for documents in respect of which there has been a timely notice to prove authenticity, all documents in the trial bundle will be admissible in evidence without more.

(c) The fact that documents in the trial bundle are admissible in evidence does not mean that all such documents form part of the evidence in the trial. It is the trial advocate's responsibility to indicate clearly to the court before closing his or her case the written evidence which forms part of that case. This should be done in the written opening statement or in the oral opening statement if the document is then available. Documents which have not previously been put in evidence before the closure of the parties' cases should not normally be referred to as evidence in the course of final speeches.

## APPENDIX 11

## EXPERT EVIDENCE—REQUIREMENTS OF GENERAL APPLICATION

1. It is the duty of an expert to help the court on the matters within his expertise: rule 35.3(1). This duty is paramount and overrides any obligation to the person from whom the expert has received instructions or by whom he is paid: rule 35.3(2). **2A–169**

2. Expert evidence presented to the court should be, and should be seen to be, the independent product of the expert uninfluenced by the pressures of litigation.

3. An expert witness should provide independent assistance to the court by way of objective unbiased opinion in relation to matters within his expertise. An expert witness should never assume the role of an advocate.

4. An expert witness should not omit to consider material facts which could detract from his concluded opinion.

5. An expert witness should make it clear when a particular question or issue falls outside his expertise.

6. If an expert's opinion is not properly researched because he considers that insufficient data is available, this must be stated in his report with an indication that the opinion is no more than a provisional one.

7. In a case where an expert witness who has prepared a report is unable to confirm that the report contains the truth, the whole truth and nothing but the truth without some qualification, that qualification must be stated in the report.

8. If, after exchange of reports, an expert witness changes his view on a material

matter having read another expert's report or for any other reason, such change of view should be communicated in writing (through the party's legal representatives) to the other side without delay, and when appropriate to the court.

## APPENDIX 12

### PROGRESS MONITORING INFORMATION SHEET

2A-170 **The information supplied should be printed in bold characters**

[SHORT TITLE OF CASE and FOLIO NUMBER]

Fixed trial date/provisional range of dates for trial specified in the pre-trial timetable:

Party lodging information sheet:

Name of solicitors:

Name(s) of advocates for trial:

[Note: this information sheet should normally be completed with the involvement of the advocate(s) instructed for trial]

(1) Have you complied with the pre-trial timetable in all respects?

(2) If you have not complied, in what respects have you not complied?

(3) Will you be ready for a trial commencing on the fixed date (or, where applicable, within the provisional range of dates) specified in the pre-trial timetable?

(4) If you will not be ready, why will you not be ready?

[*Signature of solicitors*]

**Note**: This information sheet must be lodged with the Listing Office at least 3 days before the progress monitoring date (with a copy to all other parties): see section D12.2 of the Guide.

## APPENDIX 13

### PRE-TRIAL CHECKLIST

2A-171 **The information supplied should be printed in bold characters**

[SHORT TITLE OF CASE and FOLIO NUMBER]

a. Trial date:

b. Party lodging checklist:

c. Name of solicitors:

d. Name(s) of advocates for trial:

[**Note**: this checklist should normally be completed with the involvement of the advocate(s) instructed for trial.]

1. Have you completed preparation of trial bundles in accordance with Appendix 10 to the Commercial Court Guide?
2. If not, when will the preparation of the trial bundles be completed?
3. Which witnesses of fact do you intend to call?
4. Which expert witness(es) do you intend to call (if directions for expert evidence have been given)?
5. Will an interpreter be required for any witness and if so, have any necessary directions already been given?
6. Have directions been given for any witness to give evidence by video link? If so, have all necessary arrangements been made?
7. What are the advocates' confirmed estimates of the minimum and maximum lengths of the trial? (A confirmed estimate of length signed by the advocates should be attached).
8. What is your estimate of costs already incurred and to be incurred at trial for the purposes of section 46 of the Practice Direction supplementing CPR Part 43 ? (If the trial is not expected to last more than **one day** the estimate should be substantially in the form of a statement of costs as illustrated in Form H of the Schedule of Costs Forms annexed to the Practice Direction).

[Signature of solicitors]

## VIDEO CONFERENCING GUIDANCE (ANNEX 3 TO PD32)

**Editorial note**

The Video Conferencing Guidance contained in this Appendix reproduces the Guidance in Annex 3 of Practice Direction—Evidence; see Vol.1 para. 32PD.33. **2A–172**

**[THE NEXT PARAGRAPH IS 2A–175.]**

## APPENDIX 15

## SERVICE OUT OF THE JURISDICTION: RELATED PRACTICE

**Service out of the jurisdiction without permission** **2A–175**

1.

(a) Before issuing a claim form or seeking permission to serve out of the jurisdiction, it is necessary to consider whether the jurisdiction of the English courts is affected by the Civil Jurisdiction and Judgments Act 1982. Where each claim in the claim form is a claim which the Court has by virtue of the Civil Jurisdiction and Judgments Act 1982 power to hear and determine, service of the claim form out of the jurisdiction may be effected without permission provided that, in the case of service in Scotland or Northern Ireland, the relevant requirements of rules 6.32 and 6.34 are satisfied; and, in the case of service out of the United Kingdom, the relevant requirements of rules 6.33 and 6.34 are satisfied.

These requirements include the requirement to file with the claim form a notice containing a statement of the grounds on which the claimant is entitled to serve the claim form out of the jurisdiction and to serve a copy of that notice with the claim form. In the case of service out of the jurisdiction of the United Kingdom, paragraph 2.1 of PD6B requires the notice to be in the form of practice form N510 in order to comply with rule 6.34. Rule 6.34(2) provides that, if the claimant fails to file such a notice, the consequence is that the claim form may only be served once the claimant has filed the requisite notice or if the court gives permission.

(b) Because of the significance of (amongst other things) the concept of "first seisure" in the context of Council Regulation (EC) No 44/2001 of 22 December 2001 on jurisdiction and the recognition and enforcement of judgments in civil and commercial matters ("the Judgment Regulation"), it is very important that the statement as to the grounds upon which the claimant is entitled to serve the claim form out of the jurisdiction is accurate and made with care. If entitlement to serve out of the jurisdiction without leave is wrongly asserted, a claimant may be ordered to pay the costs of a defendant's application to strike out the claim or set aside serve of the claim form on an indemnity basis.

(c) Rule 6.35 sets out the time periods during which a defendant must respond to a claim form where permission was not required for service, depending on whether the defendant is:

(i) in Scotland or Northern Ireland;
(ii) in a Member State or a Convention Territory; or
(iii) elsewhere.

Paragraph 6 of PDB sets out the periods for responding in the case of defendants served elsewhere.

These provisions are subject to the modifications set out in rule 58 in relation to Commercial Court Cases, including, but not limited to

(i) that a defendant must file an acknowledgement of service in every case; and
(ii) that the time periods provided by rule 6.35 apply after service of the claim form.

**Application for permission: statement in support** **2A–176**

2.

(a) The grounds upon which a claimant may apply for the court's permission to serve

*Paragraph numbers marked with a "+" can be found online and on CD.*



COMMERCIAL COURTS

a claim form out of the jurisdiction pursuant to rule 6.36 (in circumstances where neither rule 6.32 nor rule 6.33 applies) are set out in paragraph 3.1 of PDB.

(b) An application for permission under rule 6.36 must set out:

(i) the ground in PD6B relied on as giving the court jurisdiction to order service out, together with a summary of the facts relied on as bringing the case within each such paragraph;

(ii) where the application is made in respect of a claim referred to in paragraph 3.1(3) of PD6B, the grounds on which the claimant believes that there is between the claimant and the defendant a real issue which it is reasonable for the court to try;

(iii) the belief of the claimant that the claim has a reasonable prospect of success; and

(iv) the defendant's address or, if not known, in what place or country the defendant is or is likely to be found.

(c) The claimant should also present evidence of the considerations relied upon as showing that the case is a proper one in which to subject a party outside the jurisdiction to proceedings within it (stating the grounds of belief and sources of information); exhibit copies of the documents referred to and any other significant documents; and draw attention to any features which might reasonably be thought to weigh against the making of the order sought. Where convenient the written evidence should be included in the form of application notice, rather than in a separate witness statement. The form of application notice may be extended for this purpose.

**2A–177** **Application for permission: copies of draft order**

3.

(a) specify the periods within which the defendant must:

(i) file an acknowledgement of service;

(ii) serve or file an admission;

(iii) file a defence; and

(b) set out any other directions sought by the claimant as to:

(i) the method of service;

(ii) the terms of any order sought giving permission to serve other documents out of the jurisdiction;

The relevant periods referred to in sub-paragraphs (a)(i)–(iii) above are specified in paragraphs 6.1–6.6 of PDB, and in the Table at the end of that Practice Direction.

**Application for permission: copy or draft of claim form**

**2A–178** 4. A copy or draft of the claim form which the applicant intends to issue and serve must be provided to the judge who will usually initial it. If the endorsement to the claim form includes causes of action or claims not covered by the grounds on which permission to serve out of the jurisdiction can properly be granted, permission will be refused unless the draft is amended to restrict it to proper claims. Where the application is for the issue of a concurrent claim form, the documents submitted must also include a copy of the original claim form.

**Arbitration matters**

**2A–179** 5. Service out of the jurisdiction in arbitration matters is governed by Part 62. As to the 1968 Convention on Jurisdiction in the context of arbitration, see Article 1(4), which applies rules 6.40 – 6.46. The Judgment Regulation does not apply to "arbitration" (see Article 1.(2)(d)), but what proceedings fall within the category of arbitration and what do not, may be a difficult question: see The Front Comor, 10 February 2009, Case C-185/07.

**Practice under rules 6.32 and 6.33** **2A–180**

6.

(a) Although a Part 7 claim form may contain or be accompanied by particulars of claim, there is no need for it to do so and in many cases particulars of claim will be served after the claim form: rule 58.5.

(b) A defendant should acknowledge service in every case: rule 58.6(1).

(c) The period for filing an acknowledgment of service will be calculated from the service of the claim form, whether or not particulars of claim are to follow: rule 58.6.

(d) The periods for filing an acknowledgement of service and a defence are set out respectively in rule 6.35(2) (in relation to claim forms served in Scotland and Northern Ireland); in rule 6.35(3) (in relation to claim forms served pursuant to rule 6.33 on a defendant in a Convention Territory within Europe or a Member State); in rule 6.35(4) (in relation to claim forms served pursuant to rule 6.33 on a defendant in a Convention Territory outside Europe); and in paragraphs 6.1, 6.3, 6.4 and the Table in PDB in relation to claim forms served pursuant to rule 6.33 on a defendant in a country elsewhere: rule 6.35(5).

**Practice under rule 6.36** **2A–180.1**

7.

(a) Although a Part 7 claim form may contain or be accompanied by particulars of claim, there is no need for it to do so and in many cases particulars of claim will be served after the claim form: rule 58.5. If the claim form states that particulars of claim are to follow, there is no need to obtain further permission to serve out of the jurisdiction: rule 6.38(2).

However, permission must be obtained to serve any other document out of the jurisdiction: rule 6.38(2); other than in cases where the defendant has given an address for service in Scotland and Northern Ireland: rule 6.38(3).

(b) A defendant should acknowledge service in every case: rule 58.6(1).

(c) The periods for filing an acknowledgment of service will be calculated from the service of the claim form, whether or not particulars of claim are to follow: rule 58.6.

(d) The period for serving, and filing, particulars of claim (where they were not contained in the claim form and did not accompany the claim form) will be calculated from acknowledgment of service: rule 58.5(1)(c).

(e) The period for serving and filing the defence will be calculated from service of the particulars of claim: rule 58.10(2).

8. Time for serving and filing a defence is calculated:

(a) by reference to the number of days listed in the Table in PDB after service of the particulars of claim; or

(b) where the defendant has filed an acknowledgement of service, the number of days listed in the Table plus an additional 14 days after service of the particulars of claim: paragraph 6.4 of PDB.

9. There is some uncertainty whether the court's powers under rule 6.37 and rule 6.40 to give directions about the "method" of service include a specific power to make an order for service of documents to which Section IV of Part 6 applies by an alternative method (e.g. service on solicitors within the jurisdiction or service on a party by email); see the Notes in the 2009 Edition of Civil Procedure Rules Part 6 at paras 6.15.1 and 6.15.7. To date, the Commercial and Admiralty Court judges have taken the view that they do have such power and, in appropriate cases, have made orders providing for alternative methods of service, in cases where the criteria for serving the claim form out of the jurisdiction are satisfied. However, in circumstances where such alternative service is not permitted by the law of the country in which the defendant is to be served, rule 6.40(3) and (4) would appear to prevent such orders being made.

**Practice under rule 6.41—service in accordance with the Service Regulation**

10. If a party wishes to effect service of the claim form or other document in accordance with the Service Regulation, then the procedure to be adopted differs **2A–180.2**



COMMERCIAL COURTS

depending upon whether service is being made pursuant to rule 6.33 (service of the claim form, and other documents, out of the jurisdiction where the permission of the court is not required), or whether it is being made pursuant to rules 6.36 and 6.37 (service of the claim form, and other documents, out of the jurisdiction where the permission of the court is required).

11. In the former case (service without permission), the claimant must file the relevant documents referred to in rule 6.41(2) with the Registry. If the documents are in order, the relevant court officer will seal the claim form and forward the documents to the Senior Master of the Queen's Bench Division in accordance with rule 6.41(3).

12. In the latter case (service with permission), the claimant must first obtain permission from a judge to serve the relevant documents out of the jurisdiction, together with a direction pursuant to rule 6.37 that one, or the, method of service is to be in accordance with the Service Regulation. Once such an order has been made, the relevant court officer will seal the claim form and forward the documents to the Senior Master in accordance with rule 6.41(3).

13. In either case, once the documents have been forwarded by the Registry to the Senior Master, any queries thereafter about the progress of such service should be directed to the Senior Master.

## APPENDIX 16

## SECURITY FOR COSTS: RELATED PRACTICE

### First applications

**2A–181** 1. First applications for security for costs should not be made later than at the Case Management Conference and in any event any application should not be left until close to the trial date. Delay to the prejudice of the other party or the administration of justice might well cause the application to fail, as will any use of the application to harass the other party. Where it is intended to make an application for security at the Case Management Conference the procedure, and timetable for evidence, for an ordinary application must be followed (see section F5 of the Guide).

### Successive applications

**2A–182** 2. Successive applications for security can be granted where the circumstances warrant. If a claimant wishes to seek to preclude any further application it is incumbent on him to make that clear.

### Evidence

**2A–183** 3. An affidavit or witness statement in support of an application for security for costs should deal not only with the residence of the claimant (or other respondent to the application) and the location of his assets but also with the practical difficulties (if any) of enforcing an order for costs against him.

### Investigation of the merits of the case

**2A–184** 4. Investigation of the merits of the case on an application for security is strongly discouraged. It is usually only in those cases where it can be shown without detailed investigation of evidence or law that the claim is certain or almost certain to succeed or fail will the merits be taken into consideration.

### Undertaking by the applicant

**2A–185** 5. In appropriate cases an order for security for costs may only be made on terms that the applicant gives an undertaking to comply with any order that the court may make if the court later finds that the order for security for costs has caused loss to the

*Paragraph numbers marked with a "+" can be found online and on CD.*

claimant and that the claimant should be compensated for such loss. Such undertakings are intended to compensate claimants in cases where no order for costs is ultimately made in favour of the applicant.

**Stay of proceedings**

6. It is not usually convenient or appropriate to order an automatic stay of the proceedings pending the provision of the security. It leads to delay and may disrupt the preparation of the case for trial, or other hearing. Experience has shown that it is usually better to give the claimant (or other relevant party) a reasonable time within which to provide the security and the other party liberty to apply to the court in the event of default. This enables the court to put the claimant to his election and then, if appropriate, to dismiss the case. **2A–186**

**Amount of security**

7. Where the dispute on an application for security for costs relates to the correct evaluation of the amount of costs likely to be allowed to a successful defendant on an assessment of costs, parties should consider whether it would be advantageous for the judge hearing the application to sit with a Costs Judge as an informal assessor. The judge himself may take such an initiative. **2A–187**

## APPENDIX 17

## COMMERCIAL COURT USER E-MAIL GUIDANCE

**Introduction**

1. This guidance sets out how parties may communicate by e-mail with the Commercial and Admiralty Courts on certain matters. **2A–188**

**Restrictions**

2. A party should not use e-mail to take any step in a claim which requires a fee to be paid for that step. If a party sends by e-mail a document for which a fee is payable upon filing, the document will be treated as not having been filed. **2A–189**

3. Where a party sends or lodges a document by e-mail he should still comply with any rule or practice direction requiring the document to be served on any other person.

4. Nothing in this guidance requires any person to accept service of a document by e-mail.

**The subject line**

5. The subject line of the e-mail should contain only the following information which should be in the following order: **2A–190**

a. First, the proper title of the claim (abbreviated as necessary) with the claimant named first and the defendant named second; unless the action is an Admiralty action, the name of the ship should not be used:
b. Second, the claim number.

**Form and content of the e-mail**

6. Correspondence and documents may be sent either as text or attachments, except that documents required to be in a practice form should be sent in that form as attachments using one of the formats specified in paragraph 17. **2A–191**

7. Parties must not use e-mail to send any document which exceeds 40 pages in the aggregate of normal typescript in length or 2 MB whichever is the smaller. Documents may not be subdivided to comply with this requirement.

***Paragraph numbers marked with a "+" can be found online and on CD.***

8. Where a party files a document by e-mail, he should not send a hard copy in addition, unless there are good reasons for so doing or the Court requires.

9. Parties are advised to bear in mind when sending correspondence or documents of a confidential or sensitive nature that the security of e-mails cannot be guaranteed.

10. Where a time limit applies, it remains the responsibility of the party to ensure that the document is filed in time. Parties are advised to allow for delays or downtime on their server or the servers used by the Court.

### Attachments

2A–192 11. Attachments should be in one of the following formats:

a. Microsoft Word viewer/reader (.doc) in Word 1997 or later format
b. Rich Text Format as (.rtf) files
c. Plain/Formatted Text as (.txt) files
d. Hypertext documents as (.htm) files
e. Adobe Acrobat as (.pdf) files minimum viewer version 4

### Receipt of e-mail by the Court

2A–193 12. A document is not filed until the e-mail is received by the court at the addressee's computer terminal, whatever time it is shown to have been sent.

13. The time of receipt of an e-mail at the addressee's computer terminal will be recorded.

14. If an e-mail is received after 4 p.m. it will be treated as having been received on the next day the court office is open.

15. If a response to the subject matter of the e-mail is not received within a reasonable period, the sender should assume that the court has not received it and should send the e-mail again, or file the document by another means.

16. Parties should not telephone to enquire as to the receipt of an e-mail. They should observe the procedure set out in paragraph 15.

### Replies to e-mails sent to the court

2A–194 17. The court will normally send any reply by e-mail to documents or correspondence sent by e-mail.

a. All replies will be sent to the e-mail address from which the e-mail has been sent. If the sender wishes the reply to be copied to other parties or to another e-mail address used by the sender of the message, such e-mail addresses must be specified in the copy line.
b. The Court will not send copies to clients or others not on the record; the copy line must therefore not contain the addresses of such persons.
c. The e-mail should also contain in the body of the e-mail the name and telephone number of the sender.

**Note:** It is important that each firm or set of chambers considers putting in place a system to deal with the absence of the individual who has sent the e-mail and to whom the Court will ordinarily reply. Two possible solutions are:

a. A central mail box within each firm, either from which the e-mail is sent to the Court (and which will therefore receive the reply) or to which it is copied by the individual sender who sends it direct to the Court (and who will receive a copy of the reply);
b. a second individual e-mail address within the firm to which the reply will be copied so that any reply can be monitored.

It must be for each firm and set of chambers to devise its own system.

***Paragraph numbers marked with a "+" can be found online and on CD.***

**Communication with the Clerk to a Commercial Judge**

18. No documents or correspondence should be sent by e-mail to the Clerk to a Commercial Judge dealing with a case, unless: **2A–195**

a. an arrangement is made with the Clerk in each specific instance in which e-mail is to be used;

b. if such an arrangement is made, the e-mail must be copied to the appropriate Listing Office Address, The Registry Address, or the Admiralty Marshal Address, as the case may be.

## APPENDIX 18

## COMMERCIAL COURT ELECTRONIC WORKING PILOT SCHEME

**1. Introduction** **2A–196**

On 1 April 2009 the Commercial Court began a electronic working pilot scheme. It allows claims to be brought by issuing a claim form electronically, other documents to be filed electronically in those cases and an electronic court file to be used and inspected.

2. The intention is for the pilot scheme to be developed incrementally. Initially it covers only Part 7 claims in the Commercial Court and shortly such claims in the Admiralty Court issued by registered users. It is intended that it should soon be developed to include Part 8 claims and arbitration claims. Up-to-date information about the scheme can be found on the Commercial Court website (www.hmcourts-service.gov.uk/infoabout/admiralcomm).

3. The pilot scheme is taking place under Practice Direction (Electronic Working Pilot Scheme): see CPR Part 51. The practice direction is set out at the end of this appendix.

**4. Operation of the scheme**

The electronic scheme operated 24 hours every day and so claim forms can be issued and documents can be filed in cases to which the scheme applies outside normal court office opening hours. However, the scheme is not operated (i) during planned "down-time" and (ii) during "unplanned down-time". See PD (EWPS) 1.2(2). If the scheme is not operating, claim forms can be issued outside normal court hours by fax: see PD 58 2.2, and para B2.4 and Appendix 3 of the Guide.

**5. Fees**

Under the scheme fees may be paid by credit or debit card. If fees are not paid in accordance with the court's specifications, the court may make an order under CPR 3.3, including, in an appropriate case, an order striking out a claim or an application. See PD (EWPS) 3.1, 3.3, 8.1.

**6. Forms**

All forms filed at court under the scheme must be in PDF formal, and where they are available, the PDF forms created for the scheme must be used. If necessary forms must be converted into PDF format before they are filed. See PD (EWPS) para 4.1, 4.2, 4.3.

**7. Starting claims**

The procedure for starting a claim under the scheme is set out in PD (EWPS) para 6. The court will enter on the claim form as the issue date the date when the claim form was received by the court electronically: PD (EWPS) para 6.5. A claim form is issued on the date entered on the form by the court: CPR 7.2(2).

**8. Defendants**

Where a claim is started electronically, a defendant may file documents electronically. Any fees (for example, payable by a defendant making a counterclaim or an

*Paragraph numbers marked with a "+" can be found online and on CD.*

application) must be paid when and in the manner stipulated by the court. See para 5 above, and PD (EWPS) paras 7 and 8.

**9. Statements of truth and signatures**

Attention is drawn to paras 9 and 10 of the PD (EWPS), which deal with statements of truth and signatures.

**10. Hard copies of documents**

All trial bundles must be filed in hard copy format; PD (EWPS) para 14.

11. The court may require any other bundle to be provided in hard copy: PD (EWPS) para 13.

Note: During the course of this pilot scheme the court and Judges, with the assistance of court users, will be learning from experience what bundles (other than trial bundles) need be filed in hard copy. Please consult the Commercial Court website or telephone the court for up-to-date guidance.

## PRACTICE DIRECTION—ELECTRONIC WORKING PILOT

2A–197 *Note*—For text of practice direction, see para.5CPD.0 above.

**[THE NEXT PARAGRAPH IS 2A–214.]**

### APPENDIX 19

### GUIDANCE ON PRACTICAL STEPS FOR TRANSFERRING CASES TO THE MERCANTILE COURTS

2A–214 1. If a case is suitable for transfer to a Mercantile Court, either party can apply to the Commercial Judge prior to the CMC for transfer or, if no such application is made, the Commercial Judge will normally consider this with the parties at the CMC. He will expect the parties to have considered this issue prior to the CMC. Among the factors that the parties should consider are the size and complexity of the claim, the location of the parties and their legal advisers and the convenience of the witnesses. If transfer is contemplated, the parties should also contact the appropriate listing officer (at the telephone numbers set out at paragraph 9) to ascertain likely trial dates.

2. If the case is one that is suitable for transfer and a decision is made to transfer prior to the CMC, the Commercial Judge will order that the case be transferred to a Mercantile Court and the CMC will take place at the Mercantile Court.

3. If the case is one that is suitable for transfer and a decision is made to transfer at the CMC, the Commercial Judge will, in order to save the costs of a further hearing in the Mercantile Court, usually make all the directions with the appropriate timetable down to trial in the same way as if the case were to remain in the Commercial Court, including a direction to fix the trial date through the appropriate listing officer (see paragraph 9 below) within a specified period of time. If, as is usually the case, it is thought desirable to give the parties time to try and settle the case through direct negotiation or ADR, this will be built into the timetable.

4. The Commercial Judge will consider the time at which transfer is to take place and this must be specified in the Order. The Commercial Judge will decide whether he considers a PTR or further CMC appears necessary at that stage.

5. The Order must be drawn up in the usual way and lodged with the Commercial Registry Room EB13 in the RCJ.

- If the draft Order was not initialled in court by the Judge, the Order will then be sent to the Judge who made the Order to be approved. That normally takes 3–4 days.

- If the draft Order was initialled in court by the Judge at the hearing, the Order can be brought straight up to the Registry to be sealed.

6. Once the Order comes back, the Registry will put the Order in the various out trays for the solicitors clerks to collect. If the Order was sent in via the post, then the Registry will return it via the post or, if the firm of solicitors are not one of the regular users, the Registry will inform them of the procedure as to how to collect the Order.

7. Once the Order is sealed, the transfer from the Commercial Court is during normal circumstances effected by the Registry within one week; the transfer is effected by the Registry sending the court file and the Order to the Mercantile Court as the case may be. The Registry will also inform all parties on record once the case has been transferred.

8. The Mercantile Court will then receive all the papers which were on the Commercial Court file and they will give the case one of their own numbers and inform the parties.

9. The case will then continue in exactly the same way as if at the Commercial Court save that the hearing date must be fixed with the listing office at the Mercantile Court within the time limit specified in the Order. The parties must contact the specialist listing officer at the Court to which the case has been transferred. The telephone and fax numbers of the listing officers for the specialist list are:

London Mercantile Court

020 7947 6826

Fax 020 7947 7670

E-mail: comct.listing@hmcourts-service.gsi.gov.uk

Birmingham:

0121 681 3035

Fax 0121 250 6730

E-mail: birmingham.mercantile@hmcourts-service.gsi.gov.uk

Bristol:

0117 910 6706

Fax 0117 910 6727

E-mail: bristolmercantilelisting@hmcourts-service.gsi.gov.uk

Leeds:

0113 306 2461

Fax 0113 306 2392

E-mail: e-filing@leeds.countycourt.gsi.gov.uk

Newcastle:

0191 201 2047

Fax 0191 201 2000

E-mail: hearings@newcastle.countycourt.gsi.gov.uk

Liverpool/Manchester:

0161 240 5307

Fax 0161 240 5398

E-mail: highcourtspecialisthearings@manchester.countycourt.gsi.gov.uk

Wales and Chester:

02920 376483

Fax 02920 376475

E-mail: hearings@cardiff.countycourt.gsi.gov.uk

Parties are asked to speak to the specialist listing officers who will tell them of the facilities available at other Courts.

11. The Commercial Court monitors compliance with its Orders through the provision of progress monitoring information sheets which have to be provided by the Progress Monitoring Date specified in the Order. The standard directions for the Mercantile Courts provide for a Progress Monitoring Date; such a date should therefore be provided for in any Order. The Mercantile Courts monitor progress in accordance with paragraph 8 of the Mercantile Courts Practice Direction supplemental to Part 59. A PTR (either in court or by telephone conference) may be held in the Mercantile Courts if the parties make a request or the Mercantile Judge so directs.

12. The parties are expected to keep the listing officer of the Court to which the case is transferred apprised of any settlement of the case. Where the Commercial Judge has not made all the directions or the parties need to make an application either orally or in writing, then the appropriate directions will be considered and made by the Mercantile Judge.

## Addresses and Contact Details

2A–215 **The Admiralty Marshal:**

Room EB12
Royal Courts of Justice
Strand
London WC2A 2LL
Tel: 020 7947 6111

***Paragraph numbers marked with a "+" can be found online and on CD.***

Fax: 020 7947 7671

**The Admiralty & Commercial Registry:**

Room EB13
Royal Courts of Justice
Strand,
London WC2A 2LL
Tel: 020 7947 6112
Fax: 020 7947 6245
DX 44450 STRAND

**The Admiralty & Commercial Court Listing Office:**

Room EB09
Royal Courts of Justice
Strand,
London WC2A 2LL
Tel: 020 7947 6826
Fax: 020 7947 7670
DX 44450 STRAND

**The Secretary to the Commercial Court Committee:**

Mrs Angela Hodgson
Room EB09
Royal Courts of Justice
Strand
London WC2A 2LL
Tel: 020 7947 6826
Fax: 020 7947 7670
DX 44450 STRAND

**Out of hours emergency number:** (Security Office at Royal Courts of Justice): 020 7947 6260.

Fax number for the procedure under sections B3.11 and B4.4 of the Guide for the issue of claim forms when the Registry is closed: 020 7947 6667.

# 2B MERCANTILE COURTS

## PART 59—MERCANTILE COURTS

**Contents** 2B–1



**Editorial introduction**

Part 59 is added to the CPR by the Civil Procedure (Amendment No.5) Rules 2001 (SI 2001/4015) and came into force on March 25, 2002. 2B–2

**Related sources**

- The Mercantile Court website *http://www.hmcourts-service.gov.uk/cms/mercantile.htm* 2B–2.1
- The Mercantile Courts Directions Template (see para.2B–14.1 below)
- The Admiralty and Commercial Court Guide (see para.2A–39 and following, above)
- Practice Direction (Electronic Working Pilot Scheme)

### Scope of this Part and interpretation[1]

**59.1—(1) This Part applies to claims in Mercantile Courts.** 2B–3

**(2) A claim may only be started in a Mercantile Court if it—**

**(a) relates to a commercial or business matter in a broad sense; and**

**(b) is not required to proceed in the Chancery Division or in another specialist list.**

**(3) In this Part and Practice Direction 59—**

**(a) "Mercantile Court" means a specialist list established within the courts listed in Practice Direction 59;**

**(b) "mercantile claim" means a claim proceeding in a Mercantile Court; and**

**(c) "Mercantile judge" means a judge authorised to sit in a Mercantile Court.**

**Electronic working**

Practice Direction (Electronic Working Pilot Scheme), made by the Master of the 2B–4

[1] Introduced by the Civil Procedure (Amendment No.5) Rules 2001 (SI 2001/4015) and amended by the Civil Procedure (Amendment) Rules 2006 (SI 2006/1689) and the Civil Procedure (Amendment No.2) Rules 2009 (SI 2009/3390).

*Paragraph numbers marked with a "+" can be found online and on CD.*

Rolls, came into effect on April 1, 2009. It supplements CPR r.5.5 (Filing and sending documents) and provides for a pilot scheme, starting on April 1, 2009, and running (initially) until March 31, 2010, by which, in the circumstances set out in the practice direction, parties may avail themselves of arrangements for starting proceedings in The London Mercantile Court at the Royal Courts of Justice (and some other courts) electronically, and also for taking all subsequent steps in the proceedings electronically (so-called "Electronic Working"). In certain respects the practice direction modifies CPR provisions that would otherwise apply. Paragraph 1.3 states that, where proceedings to which CPR Pt 59 (Mercantile Courts) apply are issued, then the Electronic Working pilot scheme will apply subject to the provisions of that Part unless specifically excluded or revised by this practice direction.

The full text of this practice direction is published at para. 5CPD.1 above.

### Application of the Civil Procedure Rules[1]

2B–5 **59.2 These Rules and their practice directions apply to mercantile claims unless this Part or a practice direction provides otherwise.**

### Transfer of proceedings[2]

2B–6 **59.3 Rule 30.5 applies with the modifications that—**

**(a) a Mercantile judge may transfer a mercantile claim to another Mercantile Court; and**

**(b) a Commercial Court judge may transfer a claim from the Commercial Court to a Mercantile Court.**

**(Rule 30.5(3) provides that an application for the transfer of proceedings to or from a specialist list must be made to a judge dealing with claims in that list).**

### Claim form and particulars of claim[3]

2B–7 **59.4—(1) If particulars of claim are not contained in or served with the claim form—**

**(a) the claim form must state that, if an acknowledgment of service is filed which indicates an intention to defend the claim, particulars of claim will follow;**

**(b) when the claim form is served, it must be accompanied by the documents specified in rule 7.8(1);**

**(c) the claimant must serve particulars of claim within 28 days of the filing of an acknowledgment of service which indicates an intention to defend; and**

**(d) rule 7.4(2) does not apply.**

**(2) If the claimant is claiming interest, he must—**

**(a) include a statement to that effect; and**

**(b) give the details set out in rule 16.4(2),**

**in both the claim form and the particulars of claim.**

**(3) Rules 12.6(1)(a) and 14.14(1)(a) apply with the modification**

[1] Introduced by the Civil Procedure (Amendment No.5) Rules 2001 (SI 2001/4015).

[2] Introduced by the Civil Procedure (Amendment No.5) Rules 2001 (SI 2001/4015) and amended by the Civil Procedure (Amendment No.4) Rules 2005 (SI 2005/3515).

[3] Introduced by the Civil Procedure (Amendment No.5) Rules 2001 (SI 2001/4015).

**that references to the particulars of claim shall be read as if they referred to the claim form.**

### Acknowledgment of service[1]

**59.5—(1) A defendant must file an acknowledgment of service in every case.** 2B–8

**(2) Unless paragraph (3) applies, the period for filing an acknowledgment of service is 14 days after service of the claim form.**

**(3) Where the claim form is served out of the jurisdiction, or on the agent of a defendant who is overseas, the time periods provided by rules 6.12(3), 6.35 and 6.37(5)apply after service of the claim form.**

### Disputing the court's jurisdiction[2]

**59.6—(1) Part 11 applies to mercantile claims with the modifications set out in this rule.** 2B–9

**(2) An application under rule 11(1) must be made within 28 days after filing an acknowledgment of service.**

**(3) If the defendant files an acknowledgment of service indicating an intention to dispute the court's jurisdiction, the claimant need not serve particulars of claim before the hearing of the application.**

### Default judgment[3]

**59.7—(1) Part 12 applies to mercantile claims, except that rules 12.10 and 12.11 apply as modified by paragraphs (2) and (3) of this rule.** 2B–10

**(2) If, in any Part 7 claim—**

- **(a) the claim form has been served but no particulars of claim have been served; and**
- **(b) the defendant has failed to file an acknowledgment of service,**

**the claimant must make an application if he wishes to obtain a default judgment.**

**(3) The application may be made without notice, but the court may direct it to be served on the defendant.**

### Admissions[4]

**59.8—(1) Rule 14.5 does not apply to mercantile claims.** 2B–11

**(2) If the defendant admits part of a claim for a specified amount of money, the claimant may apply under rule 14.3 for judgment on the admission.**

---

[1] Introduced by the Civil Procedure (Amendment No.5) Rules 2001 (SI 2001/4015) and amended by the Civil Procedure (Amendment) Rules 2008 (SI 2008/2178).
[2] Introduced by the Civil Procedure (Amendment No.5) Rules 2001 (SI 2001/4015).
[3] Introduced by the Civil Procedure (Amendment No.5) Rules 2001 (SI 2001/4015).
[4] Introduced by the Civil Procedure (Amendment No.5) Rules 2001 (SI 2001/4015).

### Defence and Reply[1]

2B-12 **59.9—(1) Part 15 (Defence and Reply) applies to mercantile claims with the modification to rule 15.8 that the claimant must—**

**(a) file any reply to a defence; and**

**(b) serve it on all other parties,**

**within 21 days after service of the defence.**

**(2) Rule 6.35 (in relation to theperiod for filing a defence where the claim form is served out of the jurisdiction) applies to mercantile claims, except that if the particulars of claim are served after the defendant has filed an acknowledgment of service the period for filing a defence is 28 days from service of the particulars of claim.**

### Statements of case[2]

2B-13 **59.10 The court may at any time before or after issue of the claim form order a mercantile claim to proceed without the filing or service of statements of case.**

### Case management[3]

2B-14 **59.11—(1) All mercantile claims are treated as being allocated to the multi-track, and Part 26 does not apply.**

**(2) The following parts only of Part 29 apply—**

**(a) rule 29.3(2) (appropriate legal representative to attend case management conferences and pre-trial reviews); and**

**(b) rule 29.5 (variation of case management timetable) with the exception of rule 29.5(1)(c).**

**(3) As soon as practicable the court will hold a case management conference which must be fixed in accordance with Practice Direction 59.**

**(4) At the case management conference or at any hearing at which the parties are represented the court may give such directions for the management of the case as it considers appropriate.**

#### Directions

2B-14.1 A Mercantile Courts Directions template has been produced and approved for use by all Mercantile Courts in the country though it is the responsibility of each court to determine the appropriate directions for each case. Specimen directions for each Mercantile Court can be found in the template in the Forms section of the website: *http://www.hmcourts-service.gov.uk/cms/mercantile.htm*.

### Judgments and orders[4]

2B-15 **59.12—(1) Except for orders made by the court of its own initia-**

[1] Introduced by the Civil Procedure (Amendment No.5) Rules 2001 (SI 2001/4015) and amended by the Civil Procedure (Amendment) Rules 2008 (SI 2008/2178).

[2] Introduced by the Civil Procedure (Amendment No.5) Rules 2001 (SI 2001/4015).

[3] Introduced by the Civil Procedure (Amendment No.5) Rules 2001 (SI 2001/4015) and amended by the Civil Procedure (Amendment No.2) Rules 2009 (SI 2009/3390).

[4] Introduced by the Civil Procedure (Amendment No.5) Rules 2001 (SI 2001/4015).

**tive and unless the court otherwise orders every judgment or order will be drawn up by the parties, and rule 40.3 is modified accordingly.**

**(2) An application for a consent order must include a draft of the proposed order signed on behalf of all the parties to whom it relates.**

**(3) Rule 40.6 (consent judgments and orders) does not apply.**



*Paragraph numbers marked with a "+" can be found online and on CD.*

## PRACTICE DIRECTION 59—MERCANTILE COURTS

*This Practice Direction supplements Part 59*

### General

2B–16 **1.1** This practice direction applies to mercantile claims.

**1.2** Mercantile Courts are established in—

(1) the following district registries of the High Court—Birmingham, Bristol, Cardiff, Chester, Leeds, Liverpool, Manchester, Mold and Newcastle upon Tyne; and

(2) the Commercial Court of the Queen's Bench Division at the Royal Courts of Justice (called 'The London Mercantile Court').

**1.3** All mercantile claims will be heard or determined by a Mercantile judge, except that—

(1) an application may be heard and determined by any other judge who, if the claim were not a mercantile claim, would have jurisdiction to determine it, if—

(a) the application is urgent and no Mercantile judge is available to hear it; or

(b) a Mercantile judge directs it to be heard by another judge; and

(2) unless the court otherwise orders, all proceedings for the enforcement of a Mercantile Court judgment or order for the payment of money will be dealt with by a district judge.

**1.4** Provisions in other practice directions which refer to a master or district judge are to be read, in relation to mercantile claims, as if they referred to a Mercantile judge.

### Starting proceedings in a Mercantile Court

**2.1** A claim should only be started in a Mercantile Court if it will benefit from the expertise of a Mercantile judge.

**2.2** The claim form must be marked in the top right hand corner 'Queen's Bench Division, ..... District Registry, Mercantile Court' or 'Queen's Bench Division, the London Mercantile Court' as appropriate.

### Applications before proceedings are issued

**3.1** A party who intends to bring a claim in a Mercantile Court must make any application before the claim form is issued to a judge of that court.

**3.2** The written evidence in support of such an application should show why the claim is suitable to proceed as a mercantile claim.

### Transfer of proceedings to or from a Mercantile Court

**4.1** If a claim which has not been issued in a Mercantile Court is suitable to continue as a mercantile claim—

(1) any party wishing the claim to be transferred to a Mercantile Court may make an application for transfer to the court to which transfer is sought;

(2) if all parties consent to the transfer, the application may be

made by letter to the mercantile listing officer of the court to which transfer is sought, stating why the case is suitable to be transferred to that court and enclosing the written consents of the parties, the claim form and statements of case.

**4.2** If an application for transfer is made to a court which does not have power to make the order, that court may—

(1) adjourn the application to be heard by a Mercantile judge; or

(2) dismiss the application.

**4.3** A Mercantile judge may make an order under rule 59.3 of his own initiative.

### Default judgment and admissions

**5.** The practice directions supplementing Parts 12 and 14 apply with the following modifications—

(1) paragraph 4.1(1) of Practice Direction 12 is to be read as referring to the service of the claim form; and

(2) the references to "particulars of claim" in paragraphs 2.1, 3.1 and 3.2 of Practice Direction 14 are to be read as referring to the claim form.

### Variation of time limits by agreement

**6.1** If the parties, in accordance with rule 2.11, agree in writing to vary a time limit, the claimant must notify the court in writing, giving brief written reasons for the agreed variation.

**6.2** The court may make an order overriding an agreement by the parties varying a time limit.

### Case management

**7.1** The following parts only of Practice Direction 29 apply—

(1) paragraph 5 (case management conferences), excluding paragraph 5.9 and modified so far as is made necessary by other specific provisions of this practice direction; and

(2) paragraph 7 (failure to comply with case management directions).

**7.2** If proceedings are started in a Mercantile Court, the claimant must apply for a case management conference—

(1) for a Part 7 claim, within 14 days of the date when all defendants who intend to file and serve a defence have done so; and

(2) for a Part 8 claim, within 14 days of the date when all defendants who intend to serve evidence have done so.

**7.3** If proceedings are transferred to a Mercantile Court, the claimant must apply for a case management conference within 14 days of receiving an acknowledgment of the transfer from the receiving court, unless the judge held, or gave directions for, a case management conference when he made the order transferring the proceedings.

**7.4** Any party may, at a time earlier than that provided in paragraphs 7.2 or 7.3, apply in writing to the court to fix a case management conference.

**7.5** If the claimant does not make an application in accordance with paragraphs 7.2 or 7.3, any other party may apply for a case management conference.

**7.6** The court may fix a case management conference at any time on its own initiative. If it does so, the court will give at least seven days' notice to the parties, unless there are compelling reasons for a shorter period of notice.

**7.7** Not less than seven days before a case management conference—

(1) each party shall file and serve—
  (a) a case management information sheet substantially in the form set out at Appendix A to this practice direction; and
  (b) an application notice for any order which that party intends to seek at the case management conference, other than directions referred to in the case management information sheet; and

(2) the claimant (or other party applying for the conference) shall in addition file and serve—
  (a) a case management file containing—
  — the claim form;
  — the statements of case (excluding schedules of more than 15 pages);
  — any orders already made;
  — the case management information sheets; and
  — a short list of the principal issues to be prepared by the claimant; and
  (b) a draft order substantially in the form set out at Appendix B to this practice direction, setting out the directions which that party thinks appropriate.

**7.8** In appropriate cases—

(1) the parties may, not less than 7 days before the date fixed for the case management conference, submit agreed directions for the approval of the judge;

(2) the judge will then either—
  (a) make the directions proposed; or
  (b) make them with alterations; or
  (c) require the case management conference to proceed; but

(3) the parties must assume that the conference will proceed until informed to the contrary.

**7.9** If the parties submit agreed directions and the judge makes them with alterations, any party objecting to the alterations may, within 7 days of receiving the order containing the directions, apply to the court for the directions to be varied.

**7.10** The directions given at the case management conference—

(1) will normally cover all steps in the case through to trial, including the fixing of a trial date or window, or directions for the taking of steps to fix the trial date or window; and

(2) may include the fixing of a progress monitoring date or dates, and make provision for the court to be informed as to the progress of the case at the date or dates fixed.

**7.11** If the court fixes a progress monitoring date, it may after that date fix a further case management conference or a pre-trial review on its own initiative if—

(1) no or insufficient information is provided by the parties; or

(2) it is appropriate in view of the information provided.

### Pre-trial review and questionnaire

**8.1** The court may order a pre-trial review at any time.

**8.2** Each party must file and serve a completed pre-trial check list substantially in the form set out in Appendix C to this practice direction—

(1) if a pre-trial review has been ordered, not less than 7 days before the date of the review; or

(2) if no pre-trial review has been ordered, not less than 6 weeks before the trial date.

**8.3** When pre-trial check lists are filed under paragraph 8.2(2)–

(1) the judge will consider them and decide whether to order a pre-trial review; and

(2) if he does not order a pre-trial review, he may on his own initiative give directions for the further preparation of the case or as to the conduct of the trial.

**8.4** At a pre-trial review—

(1) the parties should if possible be represented by the advocates who will be appearing at the trial;

(2) any representatives appearing must be fully informed and authorised for the purposes of the review; and

(3) the court will give such directions for the conduct of the trial as it sees fit.

### Evidence for applications

**9.1** The general requirement is that, unless the court orders otherwise—

(1) evidence in support of an application must be filed and served with the application: see rule 23.7(3);

(2) evidence in answer must be filed and served within 14 days after the application is served;

(3) evidence in reply must be filed and served within 7 days of the service of the evidence in answer.

**9.2** In any case in which the application is likely to require an oral hearing of more than half a day the periods set out in paragraphs 9.1(2) and (3) will be 28 days and 14 days respectively.

**9.3** If the date fixed for the hearing of the application means that the times in paragraphs 9.1(2) and (3) cannot both be achieved, the evidence must be filed and served—

(1) as soon as possible; and

(2) in sufficient time to ensure that the application may fairly proceed on the date fixed.

**9.4** The parties may, in accordance with rule 2.11, agree different periods from those provided above, provided that the agreement does not affect the ability to proceed on the date fixed for the hearing of the application.

### Files for applications

**10.** Before the hearing of any application, the applicant must—

(1) provide to the court and each other party an appropriate indexed file for the application with consecutively numbered pages; and

(2) attach to the file an estimate of the reading time required by the judge.

### Judgments and orders

**11.1** After any hearing the claimant must draw up a draft order, unless the decision was made on the application of another party in which case that party must do so.

**11.2** A draft order must be submitted by the party responsible for drawing it up within 3 clear days of the decision, with sufficient copies for each party and for one to be retained by the court.

**11.3** The sealed orders will be returned to the party submitting them, who will be responsible for serving the order on the other parties.

**11.4** Orders must be dated with the date of the decision, except for consent orders submitted for approval, which must be left undated.

#### Editorial note

2B–16.1 See para.2B–14.1 Directions, above. In most cases the Mercantile Courts Directions template will be a more useful starting point than Annex B.

## Annex A

2B–17

### Case Management Information Sheet - Mercantile Courts

[Title of Case]

**This information sheet must be filed with Mercantile Listing at least 7 days before the Case Management Conference, and copies served on all other parties: see paragraph 7.7 of the Mercantile Courts Practice Direction.**

Party filing:
Solicitors:
Advocate(s) for trial:
Date:

**Substance of case**
1. What in about 20 words maximum is the case about?
   Please provide a separate concise list of issues in a complex case.

**Parties**
2. Are all parties still effective?
3. Do you intend to add any further party?

**Statements of case**
4. Do you intend to amend your statement of case?
5. Do you require any "further information" - see CPR 18?

**Disclosure**
6. By what date can you give standard disclosure?
7. Do you contend that to search for any type of document falling within CPR 31.6(b) would be unreasonable within CPR 31.7(2); if so, what type and on what grounds?
8. Is any specific disclosure required - CPR 31.12?
9. Is a full disclosure order appropriate?
10. By what dates could you give:
    (i) any specific disclosure referred to at 8; and
    (ii) full disclosure?

**Admissions**
11. Can you make any additional admissions?

**Preliminary issues**
12. Are any issues suitable for trial as preliminary issues? If yes, which?

**Witnesses of fact**
13. On how many witnesses of fact do you intend to rely at the trial (subject to the court's direction)?
14. Please name them, or explain why you do not.
15. Which of them will be called to give oral evidence?
16. When can you serve their witness statements?
17. Will any require an interpreter?

**Expert evidence**
18. Are there issues requiring expert evidence?
19. If yes, what issues?
20. Might a single joint expert be suitable on any issues (see CPR 35.7)?
21. What experts do you intend (subject to the court's direction) to call? Please give the number, their names and expertise.
22. By what date can you serve signed expert reports?
23. Should there be meetings of experts of like disciplines, of all disciplines? By when?
24. Which experts, if any, do you intend not to call at the trial?

MERCANTILE COURTS

25. Will any require an interpreter?

**Trial**

26. What are the advocates' present estimates of the length of the trial?
27. What is the earliest date that you think the case can be ready for trial?
28. Where should the trial be held?
29. Is a Pre-Trial Review advisable?

**A.D.R.**

30. Might some form of Alternative Dispute Resolution assist to resolve the dispute or some part of it?
31. Has this been considered with the client?
32. Has this been considered with the other parties?
33. Do you want the case to be stayed pending A.D.R. or other means of settlement - CPR 26.4; or any other directions relating to A.D.R.?

**Other applications**

34. What applications, if any, not covered above, will you be making at the conference?

**Costs**

35. What, do you estimate, are your costs to date?
36. What, do you estimate, will be your costs to end of trial?

[Signature of party/solicitor]

## Annex B

2B–18

**Standard Directions in Mercantile Courts**

[Title of case with Judge's name]

**Order for Directions**
made on [ ]

1. Standard disclosure is to be made by [ ].
Inspection on 48 hours notice to be completed by [ ].

2. Signed statements of witnesses of fact, and hearsay notices when required by CPR 33.2, are to be exchanged not later than [ ].

Unless otherwise ordered, the witness statements are to stand as the evidence in chief of the witnesses at trial.

3. Each party has permission to call at the trial expert witnesses as follows:

Number Expertise Issue(s) to be covered

whose reports are to be exchanged by [ ].

4. Experts of like disciplines are to:

(i) meet without prejudice by [ ] to identify the issues between them and to attempt to reach agreement on such issues, and

(ii) prepare a joint statement pursuant to CPR 35.12(3), by [ ].

*or*

3. Expert evidence in the following field(s) of expertise is limited to a written report by a single expert jointly instructed by the parties:

Expertise Issue(s) to be covered

4. (i) The report of the single joint expert is to be produced by [ ].

(ii) Any questions to the expert are to be presented to him by [ ] and answered by [ ].

(iii) Any party may apply not later than [ ] for an order that the expert witness shall give oral evidence at the trial.

5. The case will be tried in [ ] by judge alone, estimated length of trial [ ] days, [commencing on ] [not before ].
[The claimant is to apply to the mercantile listing officer to fix a date for the trial, not later than [ ], specifying dates which any party wishes to avoid.]

[6 . The progress monitoring date is [ ]. Each party is to notify the court in writing by that date (with a copy to all other parties) of the progress of the case, including -

(i) whether the directions have been complied with in all respects;

(ii) if any directions are outstanding, which of them and why; and

(iii) whether a further case management conference or a pre-trial review is required.]

7. There will be a pre-trial review on [ ].
[In the event of both parties notifying the court in writing not less than [ ] days before the pre-trial review that it is not required, then it will be vacated.]

8. Signed pre-trial check lists are to be filed and served by [ ] [not less than 7 days before the pre-trial review] [not less than 6 weeks before the trial date].

9. Trial bundles must be agreed, prepared and delivered to counsel not less than [ ] days before the trial date, and to the court not less than [ ] days before the trial date.

10. Costs in the case.

DATED

**Editorial note**

2B–18.1 See para.2B–14.1 above.

## Annex C

2B–19

### Pre-trial Check List - Mercantile Courts

[Title of Case]

**Where a Pre-trial Review has been ordered, this check list must be filed with Mercantile Listing not less than 7 days before the Pre-trial Review, and copies served on all other parties.**
**Where a Pre-trial Review has not been ordered, it must be filed and served not less than 6 weeks before the trial date .**
**See paragraph 8.2 of the Mercantile Courts Practice Direction.**

a. Trial Date:
b. Whether Pre-trial Review ordered:
c. Date of Review:
d. Party lodging:
e. Solicitors:
f. Advocate(s) for trial:
g. Date lodged:

[Note: this checklist should normally be completed with the involvement of the advocate(s) instructed for trial.]

1. Have all the directions made to date been carried out?
2. If not, what remains to be carried out? When will it be carried out?
3. Do you intend to take any further steps regarding:
   (i) statements of case?
   (ii) disclosure?
   (iii) witnesses and witness statements?
   (iv) experts and expert reports?
   If yes in any case, what and by when?
4. Will the preparation of trial bundles be completed not later than 3 weeks before the date fixed for trial? If not, what is the position?
5. What witnesses of fact do you intend to call?
6. (Where directions for expert evidence have been given) what experts do you intend to call?
7. Is any interpreter needed: for whom?
8. If a Pre-trial Review has not been ordered, do you think one would be useful?
9. What are the advocate(s)' confirmed estimates of the minimum and maximum lengths of the trial? A confirmed estimate signed by the advocate(s) and dated must be attached.
10 (i) Might some form of alternative dispute resolution now assist?
   (ii) Has the question been considered with the client?
   (iii) Has the question been explored with the other parties to the case?

[Signature of party/solicitor]

# 2C PROCEEDINGS IN THE TECHNOLOGY AND CONSTRUCTION COURT

## PART 60—TECHNOLOGY AND CONSTRUCTION COURT CLAIMS

**Contents** 2C–1



**Editorial introduction**

Part 60 is added to the CPR by Civil Procedure (Amendment No.5) Rules 2001 (SI 2001/4015) and came into force on March 25, 2002. 2C–2

**The Technology and Construction Court**

This court is the successor in title to the Official Referees Courts. The first Official Referees of the Supreme Court of Justice were appointed in 1876 under the Judicature Act s.1873– 1875. Any question could be referred for trial with or without consent of the parties if it involved the prolonged investigation of documents or accounts or of any scientific or local investigation. The report of an Official Referee on a trial had to be accepted as if it were the verdict of a jury but he could not give judgment or make any order as to costs. By the Judicature Act 1884 power was given for an Official Referee to give a judgment, make orders for costs and exercise the powers of a High Court judge in a case referred to him. The Arbitration Act of 1889 enabled parties to an arbitration agreement to require an Official Referee to sit as an arbitrator. From the outset much of the Official Referee's work was concerned with the construction industry in all its aspects. The Courts Act 1971 provided that in future "Official Referees business" should be dealt with by such Circuit Judges as the Lord Chancellor should determine. Although the title "Official Referee" was not legally preserved it continued to be used universally. By 1998 references were a rarity and most of the work tried in the court was commenced in the Official Referees Registry or transferred from the Chancery Division or the Queen's Bench Division. The description of the court was considered to be inaccurate and anachronistic and in October of 1998 the Lord Chancellor with the concurrence of the Lord Chief Justice directed that the court should be renamed the Technology and Construction Court of the High Court of Justice. The Technology and Construction Court (TCC) was opened by the Lord Chancellor on October 9, 1998. From that time the mode of address of all judges has been "my Lord". On April 26, 1999 the Civil Procedure Rules came into force incorporating many of the case management practices pioneered by the Official Referees during the 1980s and 1990s and reflecting the interventionist ethos of the court. 2C–3

*The Technology and Construction Courts in London* —There are eight courts situated on the second to sixth floors of St Dunstans House, 133–137 Fetter Lane, London EC4A 1HD. The Registry is on the third floor.

The constitution of the courts in London and elsewhere and assignment of cases is described in the Technology and Construction Court Guide (2nd edn) (see para.2C–37), and the Technology and Construction Court: Statement by the Lord Chief Justice of England and Wales, June 7, 2005 (LCJ Statement), (see para.2C–35) which deals with the interim arrangements pending a final determination as to the

***Paragraph numbers marked with a "+" can be found online and on CD.***

future of the TCC (para.5 of the LCJ Statement). The current position in London is that the judge in charge of the TCC, Ramsey J., sits as a full-time TCC judge. There are two further High Court judges (Akenhead and Coulson JJ.) who each sit in the TCC for at least half of each term, depending on the caseload and their other commitments. In addition, there are three Senior Circuit judges who are full-time TCC judges in London.

### General[1]

2C–4 **60.1—(1) This Part applies to Technology and Construction Court claims ("TCC claims").**

**(2) In this Part and Practice Direction 60—**

**(a) "TCC claim" means a claim which—**

**(i) satisfies the requirements of paragraph (3); and**

**(ii) has been issued in or transferred into the specialist list for such claims;**

**(b) "Technology and Construction Court" means any court in which TCC claims are dealt with in accordance with this Part or Practice Direction 60; and**

**(c) "TCC judge" means any judge authorised to hear TCC claims.**

**(3) A claim may be brought as a TCC claim if—**

**(a) it involves issues or questions which are technically complex; or**

**(b) a trial by a TCC judge is desirable.**

**(Practice Direction 60 gives examples of types of claims which it may be appropriate to bring as TCC claims).**

**(4) TCC claims include all official referees' business referred to in section 68(1)(a) of the Senior Courts Act 1981[2].**

**(5) TCC claims will be dealt with—**

**(a) in a Technology and Construction Court; and**

**(b) by a TCC judge, unless—**

**(i) this Part or Practice Direction 60 permits otherwise; or**

**(ii) a TCC judge directs otherwise.**

#### Comment

2C–5 A non-exhaustive list of the types of claim which are commonly dealt with in the TCC is set out at para.2.1 of the Pt 60 Practice Direction (para.2C–16 below). There is also a discussion of the wide variety of claims appropriate for the TCC at s.1.3.1 of the TCC Guide (2nd edn) at para.2C–41 below.

### Specialist list[3]

2C–6 **60.2—(1) TCC claims form a specialist list.**

**(2) A judge will be appointed to be the judge in charge of the TCC specialist list.**

---

[1] Introduced by the Civil Procedure (Amendment No.5) Rules 2001 (SI 2001/4015) and amended by the Civil Procedure (Amendment No.2) Rules 2009 (SI 2009/3390).

[2] 1981 c.54. Renamed by the Constitutional Reform Act 2005 s.59 and Sch.11, para.1 with effect from October 1, 2009 (SI 2009/1604).

[3] Introduced by the Civil Procedure (Amendment No.5) Rules 2001 (SI 2001/4015).

### Application of the Civil Procedure Rules[1]

**60.3 These Rules and their practice directions apply to TCC claims unless this Part or a practice direction provides otherwise.** 2C–7

### Issuing a TCC claim[2]

**60.4 A TCC claim must be issued in—** 2C–8

**(a) the High Court in London;**

**(b) a district registry of the High Court; or**

**(c) a county court specified in Practice Direction 60.**

#### Comment

Paragraph 3.1 of the Pt 60 Practice Direction sets out the correct way of starting a TCC claim (see para.2C–18 below). Detailed guidance as to the correct procedure on commencement in the TCC is set out in ss.3.1 to 3.4 of the TCC Guide (2nd edn), at paras 2C–51 to 2C–54 below. Guidance on the procedure for transferring a case started elsewhere into the TCC is set out in s.3.6 of the TCC Guide (para.2C–56 below). 2C–9

### Reply[3]

**60.5 Part 15 (Defence and Reply) applies to TCC claims with the modification to rule 15.8 that the claimant must—** 2C–10

**(a) file any reply to a defence; and**

**(b) serve it on all other parties,**

**within 21 days after service of the defence.**

### Case management[4]

**60.6—(1) All TCC claims are treated as being allocated to the multi-track and Part 26 does not apply.** 2C–11

**(2) Part 29 and Practice Direction 29 apply to the case management of TCC claims, except where they are varied by or inconsistent with Practice Direction 60.**

#### Comment

Case management is an extremely important part of the work of the TCC. In a complex case, the parties can expect to attend at least one case management conference at the outset of proceedings, one review case management conference, which will usually be heard after disclosure of documents and before the exchange of evidence, and a pre-trial review (PTR), listed to be heard about 4–6 weeks before the trial itself. Once a TCC claim has been issued or a claim has been transferred into the TCC specialist list, then the claim will be assigned to a named TCC judge who will have the primary responsibility for the case management of the claim (see para.6 of the Pt 60 Practice Direction at para.2C–23 below, and s.3.7 of the TCC Guide, at para.2C–57 below). The first case management conference will take place early, often before defences have been served (see para.8.1 of the Practice Direction at para.2C–27 below and s.5 of the TCC Guide at para.2C–66 below). Thereafter, in addition to any review CMCs and the PTR, noted above, the assigned TCC judge will also deal with any 2C–12

[1] Introduced by the Civil Procedure (Amendment No.5) Rules 2001 (SI 2001/4015).

[2] Introduced by the Civil Procedure (Amendment No.5) Rules 2001 (SI 2001/4015) and amended by the Civil Procedure (Amendment No.2) Rules 2009 (SI 2009/3390).

[3] Introduced by the Civil Procedure (Amendment No.5) Rules 2001 (SI 2001/4015).

[4] Introduced by the Civil Procedure (Amendment No.5) Rules 2001 (SI 2001/4015) and amended by the Civil Procedure (Amendment No.2) Rules 2009 (SI 2009/3390).

specific applications made by any party to the proceedings (see para.7 of the Pt 60 Practice Direction at para.2C–25 below, and s.6 of the TCC Guide at para.2C–76 below).

### Judgments and Orders[1]

2C–13 **60.7—(1) Except for orders made by the court of its own initiative and unless the court otherwise orders, every judgment or order made in claims proceeding in the Technology and Construction Court will be drawn up by the parties, and rule 40.3 is modified accordingly.**

**(2) An application for a consent order must include a draft of the proposed order signed on behalf of all the parties to whom it relates.**

**(3) Rule 40.6 (consent judgments and orders) does not apply.**

#### Comment

2C–14 At the first CMC, the court will almost always direct the claimant to draw up the relevant order within a specified time so that it can be approved by the court: see s.5.8.1 of the TCC Guide at para.2C–73 below. Similarly, at the conclusion of any application hearing, the court will usually require the applicant to draw up the necessary order: see s.6.6.4 of the TCC Guide at para.2C–81 below. Where the parties indicate to the court that they have agreed the terms of an order, the TCC judge will endeavour to endorse the terms which have been agreed, unless he or she considers that the agreed terms fail to take into account important features of the case as a whole, or the principles of the CPR. At the very least, the agreed terms will form the starting-point of the judge's consideration of the orders to be made: see s.5.7.1 of the TCC Guide at para.2C–72 below.

[1] Introduced by the Civil Procedure (Amendment No.3) Rules 2005 (SI 2005/2292).

# PRACTICE DIRECTION 60—TECHNOLOGY AND CONSTRUCTION COURT CLAIMS

*This Practice Direction supplements CPR Part 60*

## General

**1.** This practice direction applies to Technology and Construction Court claims ('TCC claims'). **2C–15**

## TCC claims

**2.1** The following are examples of the types of claim which it may be appropriate to bring as TCC claims— **2C–16**

(a) building or other construction disputes, including claims for the enforcement of the decisions of adjudicators under the Housing Grants, Construction and Regeneration Act 1996;

(b) engineering disputes;

(c) claims by and against engineers, architects, surveyors, accountants and other specialised advisers relating to the services they provide;

(d) claims by and against local authorities relating to their statutory duties concerning the development of land or the construction of buildings;

(e) claims relating to the design, supply and installation of computers, computer software and related network systems;

(f) claims relating to the quality of goods sold or hired, and work done, materials supplied or services rendered;

(g) claims between landlord and tenant for breach of a repairing covenant;

(h) claims between neighbours, owners and occupiers of land in trespass, nuisance etc.;

(i) claims relating to the environment (for example, pollution cases);

(j) claims arising out of fires;

(k) claims involving taking of accounts where these are complicated; and

(l) challenges to decisions of arbitrators in construction and engineering disputes including applications for permission to appeal and appeals.

**2.2** A claim given as an example in paragraph 2.1 will not be suitable for this specialist list unless it demonstrates the characteristics in rule 60.1(3). Similarly, the examples are not exhaustive and other types of claim may be appropriate to this specialist list.

### Comment

A TCC claim in rule 60.1(3) is one which involves issues or questions which are technically complex or for which a trial by a judge of a TCC is for any other reason desirable. The effect of the rule is that a TCC judge may try any case within the business of the Chancery and Queen's Bench divisions. The new rule is widely framed because the court has historically adapted itself to deal with new problems arising out of technical advances and customarily deals with cases involving multi-parties and cases which may occupy a great deal of time. See also section 1.3.1 of the TCC Guide, 2nd edition (see para.2C–41 below). **2C–17**

2C–17.1 A particular type of claim which is becoming much more common in the TCC concerns procurement. The Public Contracts Regulations 2006 set out detailed provisions concerning the appropriate method by which tenders for public contracts are to be obtained and evaluated. Claims by dissatisfied and unsuccessful tenderers in the TCC, to the effect that the Regulations have not been properly followed, have increased in both volume and size: see, by way of recent example, *Amaryllis Ltd v HM Treasury* [2009] EWHC 962 (TCC).

2C–17.2 Most TCC claims are commenced under CPR Pt 7. However, where the point at issue is a matter of construction of the contract, or some other clearly identifiable point of law, then the claimant may choose to start proceedings under CPR Pt 8. The advantage of this procedure in the TCC is that a hearing for the final disposition of the Pt 8 claim can usually be arranged within a matter of weeks. In such circumstances, it is necessary for the court to ensure that the claim is properly brought under Pt 8. It is anticipated that current economic difficulties will lead to an increase in the use of Pt 8 in the TCC: see *Walter Lilly and Co Ltd v DMW Developments Ltd* [2008] EWHC 3139 (TCC).

### How to start a TCC claim

2C–18 **3.1** TCC claims must be issued in the High Court or in a county court specified in this practice direction.

**3.2** The claim form must be marked in the top right-hand corner 'Technology and Construction Court' below the words 'The High Court, Queen's Bench Division' or 'The ______ County Court'.

**3.3** TCC claims brought in the High Court outside London may be issued in any District Registry, but it is preferable that wherever possible they should be issued in one of the following District Registries, in which a TCC judge will usually be available—Birmingham, Bristol, Cardiff, Chester, Exeter, Leeds, Liverpool, Manchester, Mold, Newcastle upon Tyne and Nottingham.

**3.4** The county courts in which a TCC claim may be issued are the following—Birmingham, Bristol, Cardiff, Central London, Chester, Exeter, Leeds, Liverpool, Manchester, Mold, Newcastle upon Tyne and Nottingham.

#### Comment

2C–19 TCC claims may be dealt with in the High Court or County Court. Hitherto TCC business (formerly O.R. business) fell only within the jurisdiction of the High Court. A claim with a value under the County Court limit can be issued in any of the County Courts named in 3.4.

A case of complexity or involving matters of public importance may be considered appropriate for transfer to the London Technology and Construction Court by way of example where a point on a contract is involved which may affect similar contracts commonly used in the construction industry. Otherwise such a case would proceed to trial in the appropriate County Court.

2C–19.1 Larger TCC claims may be appropriate for trial by a High Court Judge, but it may also be convenient for the parties for the litigation to be managed, and the trial to take place, in one of the TCC's regional centres. This potential problem was addressed by Ramsey J. in *Neath Port Talbot County BC v Currie and Brown Project Management Ltd* [2008] EWHC 1508 (TCC). He concluded that the case in question was suitable for trial by a High Court Judge but he refused to transfer the case from Bristol to London because Bristol formed a convenient location for the trial. He ruled that the case management would continue to be undertaken by the principal TCC judge in Bristol, and that the trial would be conducted by a High Court Judge, also in Bristol.

### Applications before proceedings are issued

2C–20 **4.1** A party who intends to issue a TCC claim must make any application before the claim form is issued to a TCC judge.

**4.2** The written evidence in support of such an application must state that the proposed claim is a TCC claim.

**Comment**

It is important to note that a party who intends to issue a TCC claim must comply with the Pre-Action Protocol for Construction and Engineering Disputes, which is set out at Section C5 of Vol.1 of Civil Procedure. The principal ingredients of this process are set out in s.2 of the TCC Guide, starting at para.2C–44 below. Unlike any other pre-action protocol, the Protocol for Construction and Engineering Disputes requires a pre-action meeting between the parties, which can often lead to an early resolution of the dispute. Failure to comply with the Pre-Action Protocol may well result in the TCC proceedings being stayed until such compliance has been achieved (see *Cundall Johnson & Partners LLP v Whipps Cross University Hospital NHS Trust* [2007] EWHC 2178 (TCC)). **2C–21**

**Comment**

Recent decisions have demonstrated that the TCC will adopt a pragmatic approach in circumstances where a party has failed to comply with the precise procedure set out in the Pre-action Protocol. What matters is compliance with the substance of the Protocol and, in particular, ensuring that each side has a clear understanding of the position of the other: see *Orange Personal Communications Services Ltd v Hoare Lea (A firm)* [2008] EWHC 223 (TCC). Depending on the circumstances, it will be unusual for seperate proceedings commenced subsequently against another defendant, or Pt 20 proceedings, to be made the subject of the Protocol; see *Alfred McAlpine Capital Projects Ltd v Siac Construction (UK) Ltd* [2006] B.L.R. 139. **2C–21.1**

The importance of considering the claimant's pre-action conduct in the round was stressed by Akenhead J. in *TJ Brent Ltd v Black and Veatch Consulting Ltd* [2008] EWHC 1497 (TCC) when he said that: **2C–21.2**

> "what the court should do in considering the Pre-action Protocol is to look at the matters in substance, not as a matter of semantics ... it is the court's job in reviewing this matter to look at matters in substance and not for technical non-compliances with the ... requirements in the Pre-action Protocol."

In that case he concluded that there had been substantial compliance with the Protocol.

One frequent complaint arising out of the Pre-Action Protocol process is that too often the process is allowed to take much longer than is prescribed, thereby increasing the costs, which might already be regarded as "front-loaded", to a significant degree. In *Roundstone Nurseries Ltd v Stephenson Holdings Ltd* [2009] EWHC 1431 (TCC) the judge was highly critical of a pre-action process which lasted a year and achieved almost nothing. In *Bovis Homes Ltd v Kendrick Construction Ltd* [2009] EWHC 1359 (TCC) the process took even longer and also achieved little, particularly given that, when the claimant eventually commenced proceedings in the TCC, the defendant raised, for the first time, the existence of an arbitration agreement and sought a stay pursuant to s.9 of the Arbitration Act 1996. The stay was allowed but the defendant was ordered to pay the costs thrown away as a result of its failure to raise the point during the protocol process. **2C–21.3**

**Pre-Action Mediation**

There will be cases in which, prior to the commencement of proceedings, the parties will engage in a mediation, either as part of the Protocol process or as a separate attempt at dispute resolution. The costs of such mediations can be significant. In *Lobster Group Ltd v Heidelberg Graphic Equipment* [2008] EWHC 413 (TCC) Coulson J. found that, as a general rule, the costs of a pre-action mediation were not recoverable in subsequent proceedings. He therefore concluded that such costs should be left out of account in any consideration of a subsequent application for security for costs under CPR Pt 23. **2C–21.4**

Sometimes, as a result of delays and concerns about limitation, a claimant may be obliged to commence proceedings in the TCC, which are then stayed whilst the Pre-Action Protocol process (and any mediation or ADR that the parties may have agreed to as part of that process) is completed. In such circumstances, the parties need to **2C–21.5** keep the court informed and to ensure that the proceedings remain stayed until after the mediation. In *Roundstone Nurseries* (above) the stay of the TCC proceedings had been allowed to expire by the parties. At the last minute, the defendant unreasonably cancelled the agreed mediation and, in retaliation, the claimant entered judgment in default. The judge found that the claimant was technically entitled so to do, but set that judgment aside on the grounds that there was an arguable defence. However the defendant was ordered to pay the costs thrown away by the late cancellation of the mediation.

#### Pre-Action Disclosure

2C–21.6 Given the volume of documents involved in many TCC disputes, it is common for prospective claimants to seek pre-action disclosure against prospective defendants pursuant to CPR 31.16. The relevant principles to be applied on such applications are set out by the Court of Appeal in *Black v Sumitomo Corporation* [2002] 1 W.L.R. 1562. One of the matters to be considered on such an application is the nature of the prospective claim and its prospects of success. In *Gwelhayl Ltd v Midas Construction Ltd* [2008] EWHC 2316, the application for pre-action disclosure failed because, on the facts, the judge was unable to conclude there would be any claim at all, let alone a claim with a real prospect of success.

### Transfer of proceedings

2C–22 **5.1** Where no TCC judge is available to deal with a claim which has been issued in a High Court District Registry or one of the county courts listed in paragraph 3.4 above, the claim may be transferred—

(1) if it has been issued in a District Registry, to another District Registry or to the High Court in London; or

(2) if it has been issued in a county court, to another county court where a TCC judge would be available.

**5.2** Paragraph 5.1 is without prejudice to the court's general powers to transfer proceedings under Part 30.

(Rule 30.5(3) provides that an application for the transfer of proceedings to or from a special list must be made to a judge dealing with claims in that list).

**5.3** A party applying to a TCC judge to transfer a claim to the TCC specialist list must give notice of the application to the court in which the claim is proceeding, and a TCC judge will not make an order for transfer until he is satisfied that such notice has been given.

#### Comment

2C–22.1 There have been three recent cases in which proceedings have been transferred into the TCC from other divisions of the High Court or courts outside London. They are *Fosse Me Ltd v Conde Nast* [2007] EWHC 2614 (TCC), a fire case; *Corby Group Litigation v Corby BC* [2007] EWHC 3174 (TCC), a personal injury case arising from reclamation and decontamination work at a former steel works complex; and *Brynley Collins v Raymond J Drumgold* [2008] EWHC 584 (TCC) a claim for some £300,000 arising out of allegedly defective foundations, transferred from the county court. In the last case the judge said that on applications to transfer in, the TCC would first consider whether the dispute in question was one of the types of claim which para.2.1 of the Pt 60 Practice Direction identified as being a claim suitable for the TCC. If so, the court would go on to ask whether the financial value of the claim and/or its complexity meant that, in accordance with the overriding objective, the case should be transferred to the TCC. He noted that what will often be critical is the view that the court takes of the complexity of the issues in the action itself. In addition, the court would consider broader questions of convenience to the parties.

As set out in App.D of the Technology and Construction Court Guide (para. 2C–151 below onwards) there are a number of district registries, civil justice centres, and county courts where there is at least one TCC judge. Accordingly, any application to transfer a case to the TCC in London from a provincial county court or district registry may depend, at least in part, upon the availability in that county court or district registry of a TCC judge. In *Brynley Collins v Raymond J Drumgold*, the absence of a TCC judge at the county court in question was a factor in the judge's decision to transfer the case to London.

Applications to transfer proceedings into the TCC from the Chancery Division are not uncommon. The correct approach was set out by Akenhead J. in *Natl Amusements (UK) Ltd v White City (Shepherd's Bush) Ltd Partnership* [2009] EWHC 2524 (TCC). At para.33 of his judgment, the judge said that the court considering the application for transfer was entitled to have regard to the relative appropriateness of the different Divisions, and the specialist courts within them, and needed to ascertain, if possible, where and in what areas of judicial expertise and experience the bulk or preponderance of the issues lay. If there was little or no significant difference between the appropriateness of the two venues, the court's discretion will generally be exercised in favour of the status quo, to reflect the fact that a claimant is entitled to issue proceedings in whatever Division it thinks fit. Akenhead J. also said that, where it was clear that significantly greater expedition would be achieved by one Division rather than another, or where there was a demonstrable difference in the costs, these too would be relevant factors for the court to take into account on an application to transfer. **2C–22.2**

The importance of the claimant's choice of venue was also emphasised in *Tai Ping Carpets UK Ltd v Arora Heathrow T5 Ltd* [2009] EWHC 2305 (TCC). In that case, the claimant commenced its claim in the District Registry in Birmingham. Both parties agreed that the matter should be transferred to the TCC, but whereas the claimant wanted it transferred to the TCC in Birmingham, the defendant wanted it transferred to the London TCC. There was little to choose between the perceived advantages and disadvantages of the two potential venues and Coulson J. found that, in the absence of any significant factors favouring the transfer to London, the case should be kept in Birmingham, because that is what the claimant had requested: **2C–22.3**

> "After all, it is the claimant who has gone to the trouble and expense of starting these proceedings and it is the claimant who runs the costs risk, to the extent that its claim may ultimately be unsuccessful. These are the claimant's proceedings and the responsibility for them rests with the claimant. If therefore the various other competing factors broadly cancel each other out, then it seems to me that I ought to give particular weight to the claimant's choice of location for case management and trial."

## Assignment of claim to a TCC judge

**6.1** When a TCC claim is issued or an order is made transferring a claim to the TCC specialist list, the court will assign the claim to a named TCC judge ('the assigned TCC judge') who will have the primary responsibility for the case management of that claim. **2C–23**

**6.2** All documents relating to the claim must be marked in similar manner to the claim form with the words 'Technology and Construction Court' and the name of the assigned TCC judge.

### Comment

As to assignment see section 3.7 of the TCC Guide, 2nd edition (see para.2C–57 below), and LCJ Statement (para.2C–35). **2C–24**

## Applications

**7.1** An application should normally be made to the assigned TCC judge. If the assigned TCC judge is not available, or the court gives permission, the application may be made to another TCC judge. **2C–25**

**7.2** If an application is urgent and there is no TCC judge available to deal with it, the application may be made to any judge who, if the claim were not a TCC claim, would be authorised to deal with the application.

**General**

2C-26 Applications to the assigned judge will cover a wide variety of topics. They will include applications for summary judgment or an interim payment; an interlocutory or permanent injunction; specific disclosure; or particular orders relating to delays in the provision of (or defects within) another party's pleadings and evidence. In addition, a party who has complied with the timetable or order of the court must make a specific application to the assigned judge if another party has failed to comply with that same timetable or order. It is important that, if one party is in significant delay, such default is brought to the attention of the assigned judge at the earliest opportunity, particularly if the delay threatens the feasibility of the trial date. The procedure to be followed in making and responding to applications is set out in s.6 of the TCC Guide (starting at para.2C-76 below).

**Preliminary issues**

2C-26.0 Given the complexity of many TCC cases, it is not uncommon for parties to seek the trial of preliminary issues. The principles which the assigned judge will apply when considering an application for the hearing of preliminary issues are set out in some detail in s.8 of the TCC Guide (starting at para.2C-90 below). Whilst preliminary issues can often be a superficially attractive method of saving time, and therefore costs, it is important to note that, all too often, the hearing of preliminary issues does not lead to any such saving. For a recent warning as to the dangers of ordering preliminary issues in a TCC case, see para.61 of the judgment of Sir John Chadwick in *Perrin v Northampton BC* [2007] EWCA Civ 1353. For a TCC case in which, on the facts, the judge concluded that the ordering of preliminary issues would not substantially save time or money and would not significantly improve the possibility of a settlement, see *Leading Rule v Phoenix Interiors Ltd* [2007] EWHC 2293 (TCC).

**Disclosure**

2C-26.1 One of the most common kind of applications in the TCC relates to specific disclosure and/or redacted documents. It is not uncommon for parties in TCC litigation to withhold numerous documents or to disclose them with parts redacted, and for the other side then to seek disclosure of the documents or to have the redactions removed. In *Atos Consultant Ltd v Avis PLC* [2007] EWHC 323 (TCC) the court had to consider whether the material being redacted was either privileged or relevant. The judge said that the right approach was, firstly, to consider the evidence produced on the application; secondly, if the court was satisfied that the right to withhold inspection (of all or part of the document) was established by the evidence and there were no sufficient grounds for challenging the correctness of that asserted right, the court would uphold the right; thirdly, if court was not satisfied that the right to withhold inspection was established (because, for instance, the evidence did not establish a legal right to withhold inspection), then the court would order inspection of the documents; fourthly, if sufficient grounds were shown for challenging the correctness of the asserted right then the court might order further evidence to be produced on oath or, if there was no other appropriate method of properly deciding whether the right to withhold inspection should be upheld, it might decide to inspect the documents; fifthly, if the court decided to inspect the documents then, having undertaken such an inspection, it might invite further representations from the parties.

**Without prejudice material**

2C-26.2 Another difficulty can arise out of the parties' attempts to compromise their disputes at the time, or shortly after, they first arose. During such attempts, one party may say something which, subsequently, the other party wishes to rely on. This can lead to arguments as to whether such statements were made as part of "without prejudice" negotiations (in which case the material will generally be inadmissible) or whether one of the exceptions to that general rule might apply (if, say, the communication did not unequivocally indicate the maker's intention to negotiate). The various authorities were summarised in *Galliford Try Construction Ltd v Mott MacDonald Ltd* [2008] EWHC 6030 (TCC) in which, on the facts, the judge concluded that the evidence in question arose out of genuine negotiations and was therefore the subject of the general "without prejudice" exclusion. He also found that the relevant privilege or admissibility had not been waived. The question of waiver also arose in *Farm Assist Ltd v The Secretary of State for Environment, Food and Rural Affairs* [2008] EWHC 3079 (TCC) in which Ramsey J. held that the documents in question were subject to legal advice privilege which had not been waived, notwithstanding the fact that the state of mind of the recipient of that legal advice was very much in issue in the case.

#### Applications under CPR Parts 24 and 25

A claimant with a large claim will often seek summary judgment pursuant to CPR Pt 24, or an interim payment pursuant to CPR Pt 25, in an attempt to recover a significant sum promptly. Such applications can lead the responding party to flood the court with paper in the hope that the judge will conclude that the matter is inappropriate for summary judgment. In *Jacobs UK Ltd v Skidmore Owings and Merrill LLP* [2008] EWHC 2847 (TCC) Coulson J. said: **2C-26.3**

> "In commercial cases, it is all too easy for a party who wishes to avoid summary judgment under CPR Part 24 to put in lengthy statements, and exhibit numerous documents, in the hope that the court will conclude that the issues will have to be dealt with at a trial, and that summary judgment is inappropriate. That risk is particularly acute in the TCC, where the parties often need no invitation to swamp the court with extraneous documentation. It is therefore incumbent on the court to consider the parties' submissions on the material provided and to see whether, no matter how detailed the documentation, the necessary tests have been made out."

He emphasised that, without undertaking this task, whatever the level of detail provided, it was not possible for the court to say whether there was a defence at all or, if there was, whether it had a "real prospect of success" and, even if it did, whether the defence raised could only be described as "possible", with the result that a conditional order might be appropriate under r.24.6.

#### Unless Orders

Where one party persistently fails to comply with court orders, it may be appropriate for the court to make an unless order, which will spell out in detail the consequences of any further non-compliance. In *E Group Ltd v Baker [t/a 'Hello']* [2008] EWHC 2349 (TCC) the defendant failed to comply with the number of orders of the court. An unless order was made against her with which she also failed to comply. The court was satisfied that the unless order was entirely justified, and that the automatic and draconian consequences of the defendant's non-compliance were therefore triggered. The defendant's defence was thus struck out. **2C-26.4**

#### Vacation

There is always a TCC judge on vacation duty. During quieter holiday periods, such as Christmas and New Year, any urgent hearings will usually be dealt with on a given day of the vacation week in question, often the Wednesday. In busier vacation periods, such as August and September, there will almost always be a TCC duty judge in London every working day. **2C-26.5**

## Case management conference

**8.1** The court will fix a case management conference within 14 days of the earliest of these events— **2C-27**

(1) the filing of an acknowledgment of service;

(2) the filing of a defence; or

(3) the date of an order transferring the claim to a TCC.

**8.2** When the court notifies the parties of the date and time of the case management conference, it will at the same time send each party a case management information sheet and a case management directions form.

(The case management information sheet and the case management directions form are in the form set out in Appendixes A and B to this practice direction).

**8.3** Not less than two days before the case management conference, each party must file and serve on all other parties—

(1) completed copies of the case management information sheet and case management directions form; and

(2) an application notice for any order which that party intends to seek at the case management conference, other than directions referred to in the case management directions form.

**8.4** The parties are encouraged to agree directions to propose to the court by reference to the case management directions form.

**8.5** If any party fails to file or serve the case management information sheet and the case management directions form by the date specified, the court may—

(1) impose such sanction as it sees fit; and

(2) either proceed with or adjourn the case management conference.

**8.6** The directions given at the case management conference will normally include the fixing of dates for—

(1) any further case management conferences;

(2) a pre-trial review;

(3) the trial of any preliminary issues that it orders to be tried; and

(4) the trial.

**General**

2C–28 Note that 8.3 gives a minimum time for exchange and return of the case management questionnaire and case management directions form. In substantial and complex cases it is desirable to exchange and serve at least four clear days before the hearing to assist the judge. An early exchange and return also gives the parties further opportunity to consider each other's proposals and agree matters before the hearing. 8.5 provides for sanctions and underlines the philosophy behind the rules and reflected in 4.3 (above) there should be no slippage and the time and resource of the court should not be wasted.

Paragraph 8.6—the Agenda for the first case conference will be based upon the form at Appendix B of the Practice Direction. Each case coming before the TCC varies as to its length, complexity and parties, and tailor made directions may be given or agreed to suit the case. For example, where a view is appropriate the timing of the view having regard to the changing state of the matter in dispute as when remedial work is being carried out. Directions may be given that a building or structure must not be altered before experts have had the proper opportunity to examine it fully; for the joint making of trial pits, bore holes, laboratory tests, or analyses; where a Scott schedule has been ordered, that the parties should select representative items for trial; arrangements for video displays, demonstrations and the like. It is at this stage that the court may consider whether an ADR direction may be given (see Pt 1.4(2)(E)) and whether it is necessary to extend time compliance requirements of the CPR to enable the parties to investigate ADR. Consideration may also be given at this stage as to whether an early neutral evaluation (ENE) would be appropriate by a judge of the court. It is open for the parties, should they so wish, in an appropriate case, to make an application that a judge of the court can be appointed to act as mediator. Note, that a judge acting as mediator thereafter ceases to take any part in the trial in, of the action. In the event of it proceeding it would be tried before another judge. In relation to resolution by trial, consideration will be given to the trial of an issue, or split trials of liability/damages.

Paragraph 8.6 contains provision that at the first case management conference, the court will usually fix the date for the trial of the case. This is so, but the direction will normally be in the following form:

| | |
|---|---|
| Trial: Week beginning ... | *For fees' purposes only this is not notice by the court of the trial date.* |
| Estimated length ... days | (see Supreme Court Fees Order 1999, para.2.2, Schedule 1, column 2). |

See also the guidance given in s.5 of the TCC Guide (2nd edn) (see para.2C–66 below). Paragraph 8.6(3) preliminary issues, see s.8 of the TCC Guide (2nd edn) (see para.2C–90 below).

It may be that, in the lead-up to or at the commencement of the first case management conference, the parties will be able to agree the orders to be made by the court. The assigned judge will take the agreed terms as the starting-point for his consideration of the orders to be made and, if appropriate, may often make the order in the precise terms that have been agreed: see s.5.7.1 of the TCC Guide at para.2C–72 below. If the terms have been agreed by the parties and approved by the judge well in advance of the case management conference, then it may be that there will be no need for a hearing at all. However, the assigned judge will usually want to see the parties at this early stage to identify any matters of potential concern; to explore the possibility of ADR; and to emphasise any particular aspects of the trial preparation which he or she considers to be of importance.

### Extending time for service

Often the CMC will be the first time that a defendant can seek to challenge any earlier court order, made ex-parte, extending the claimant's time for service of the original claim form. Parties need to be aware that any decision to extend time made ex-parte is capable of being modified, or even rescinded, when both parties are before the court. Of course, if the claims are statute-barred by the time of the CMC, and the order to extend time is discharged following a contested hearing, the claimant can be left without a remedy. The dangers of leaving it "until beyond the 11th hour" are highlighted in the decision of Christopher Clarke J. in *City and General (Holborn) Ltd v Structure Tone Ltd* [2009] EWHC 2139 (TCC). A more benevolent approach to the same problem can be seen in the decision of Ramsey J. in *Imperial Cancer Research Fund v Ove Arap and Partners Ltd* [2009] EWHC 1453 (TCC). **2C–28.1**

### Pleadings

At the CMC, orders will be made so as to achieve the prompt and cost-effective finalisation of the pleadings (if that has not already happened). In *Seele Austria GmbH and Co KG v Tokio Marine Europe Insurance Ltd* [2009] EWHC 2066 (TCC) the claimant's true claim, which had been through a wide variety of pleaded permutations, was not set out in the re-amended existing particulars of claim, and a belated attempt was made to set it out in the reply, which was served much later and at a time when the claim was statute barred. The reply was struck out and the claim therefore failed. **2C–28.2**

### Experts

The recent changes to CPR r.35 and the accompanying Practice Direction reflect what has been the practice in the TCC for some time. In particular, 35 PD.9 now makes it plain that the purpose of the without prejudice discussions between experts is to agree and narrow issues, and in particular to identify in a joint statement the matters agreed, the matters not agreed (with a short statement of the reasons for the disagreement) and the action, if any, which may be taken to resolve any matters of disagreement. The parties are obliged to discuss, and if possible agree, an agenda for the experts' meetings, to allow the experts to focus on the important issues which need to be discussed. Furthermore, the joint statement must be signed by the experts at the conclusion of their discussions, or as soon thereafter as practical, and no later than seven days thereafter. Importantly, experts are obliged to give their own opinions to assist the court and do not require the authority of the parties to sign the joint statement. **2C–28.3**

In defects cases, it is not uncommon for an employer to seek to blame both the contractor (workmanship) and the architect (design), although this can sometimes be logically difficult. In *Carillion JM Ltd v Bath and Northeast Somerset Council* [2009] EWHC

166 (TCC) the employer sought permission to call two different expert architects, one to give evidence in support of the employer's primary case, that the problems were all matters of workmanship, and one to give evidence of an alternative case that the problems were matters of architectural design and specification. The judge concluded that the employer was only entitled to call one expert architect, since the potential contradiction was inherent in the case that they were running. Further, the judge noted that the involvement of a second expert architect to deal with design would not spare the first expert architect from being cross-examined on that same issue, since the first expert architect would have had to have ruled out design deficiencies in order to conclude that all the problems were matters of workmanship.

### Costs

**2C–28.4** Costs remain a major problem in proceedings in the TCC. There are two ways in which the court will endeavour to limit the parties' costs early on and throughout the proceedings. One is by reference to costs capping orders; the other is by reference to costs estimates.

### Costs capping

**2C–28.5** CPR r.44.18 provides for costs capping orders. The new provisions reflect closely the words of Gage J. in *Smart v East Cheshire NHS Trust* [2004] 80 B.M.L.R. 175. It has been said that such orders will only be made in exceptional cases: see *Peacock v MGN Ltd* [2009] EWHC 769 (QB). That restrictive approach was followed in *Barr v Biffa Waste Services Ltd (No.2)* [2009] EWHC 2444 (TCC). In that case, it was noted that, since costs capping orders will not be made in circumstances where case management directions or post-trial cost assessments would control any risk that the claimant's costs would be disproportionately incurred, costs capping orders will be a rarity.

Costs capping orders will, however, be more common in cases where there has been a group litigation order: see *Willis v Nicholson* [2007] EWCA Civ 199 and *Corby Claimants v Corby BC* [2008] EWHC 619 (TCC). In the latter case, Akenhead J. had to consider how the costs should be assessed for the purposes of the order. He concluded that he should fix an overall cost cap but, in so doing, he had to have regard to the constituent elements of each parties' submitted costs estimates. He reiterated that an overall costs cap had to allow an element of flexibility, because in practice some of the costs would go down as well as up. Of course there is no guarantee that the cap would be the same for each party.

### Costs estimates

**2C–28.6** The parties are required at the first CMC to identify to the assigned judge the amount of costs incurred thus far, and the projected estimate of costs up to the conclusion of the trial. It is very important that this information is provided to the court at this early stage, because effective case management of the proceedings may not be possible without it. Furthermore, whilst it is illegitimate to use such an estimate as a straight replacement for a cost capping order (see *Leigh v Michelin Tyre* [2003] EWCA Civ 1766), it is permissible for the court to make an order that, subject to certain built-in safeguards and saving provisions, the costs of a party will not exceed the amount of the estimate. That was the approach adopted by Field J. in *Willis* (above), and by Coulson J. in *Barr v Biffa* (above).

Furthermore, the parties in TCC proceedings need to be aware that it is in their interests to get their costs estimates right, and that adverse consequences may flow from estimates that turn out to be significantly too low. For example, in *Fitzpatrick Contractors Ltd v Tyco Fire and Integrated Solutions (UK) Ltd* [2009] EWHC 274 (TCC), the claimant's costs estimate, provided some months before trial, was "£2m plus" through to the conclusion of the case. A few months later, the claimant alleged that, on settlement, it had actually incurred £3.7 million by way of costs, at a date that was before expert's reports had been exchanged, before counsels' briefs had been delivered, and long before there was a trial. The judge concluded that this was a startling discrepancy and that, following the settlement of the case, the assessment of an interim payment on costs otherwise due to the claimant had to reflect the possibility that the £3.7 million figure—being so much in excess of the estimate—may be neither reasonable nor recoverable.

### Assessors

**2C–28.7** Given the technical nature of most TCC work, it might be thought surprising that

TCC judges do not sit more often with assessors appointed pursuant to CPR 35.15. The principles applicable to the appointment of assessors were recently set out in *Balcombe Group PLC v London Development Agency* [2008] EWHC 1392 (TCC). On the facts of that case, the judge refused one party's application for the appointment of assessors, concluding that it would not be proportionate to make such an order on the facts of that case. He also said that:

"the evaluation of a lengthy list of individual items of claim, and the consideration of their reasonableness or (otherwise), is one of the principal functions of the TCC and there is no reason to distinguish this case from the ordinary run of quantum disputes arising out of property development and building work."

He concluded that, generally, such disputes were not suitable for assessors.

## Pre-trial review

**9.1** When the court fixes the date for a pre-trial review it will send each party a pre-trial review questionnaire. 2C-29

(The pre-trial review questionnaire is in the form set out in Appendix C to this practice direction).

**9.2** Each party must file and serve on all other parties completed copies of the questionnaire not less than two days before the date fixed for the pre-trial review.

**9.3** The parties are encouraged to agree directions to propose to the court.

**9.4** If any party fails to return or exchange the questionnaire by the date specified the court may—

(1) impose such sanction as it sees fit; and

(2) either proceed with or adjourn the pre-trial review.

**9.5** At the pre-trial review, the court will give such directions for the conduct of the trial as it sees fit.

### Comment

The parties will be reminded by a letter from the court of the date and time of the pre-trial review. That letter will contain the following text. 2C-30

"For the purposes of the fees order notice is now given that the trial has been fixed for (date) accordingly a fee of £600 must be paid within 14 days of the date of this notice, i.e. by (date 14 days from the date of dispatch of the letter) by the claimant or claimants, if the action is proceeding on the counter claim alone by the defendant. Payment is to be made (preferably by cheque) at the Registry of this Court or to the Fees Room in the Main Building (i.e. at the Royal Courts of Justice). The PTR questionnaire (see below) must be presented when payment is made as the receipt of payment of the fee is stamped on it.

If the fee is not paid by the date specified rule 3.7(4) states that the claim (or counterclaim) will be struck out automatically and that the claimant (or the defendant, as the case may be) will be liable for the costs incurred by the other party(ies) unless the Court orders otherwise.

You are reminded that as well as the completed Pre-Trial Reviews Questionnaires all proposed directions (which should be agreed wherever possible) be lodged by all parties with me not later than two clear days before the date of the PTR. Copies of the Questionnaire and the PTR Direction Form are obtainable from the Registry. Any questions relating to the fee should be addressed to the Registry but all other questions about the PTR must be addressed to me. Signed Clerk to the Judge."

Paragraph 9.2—see note to 8.3 above.

Paragraph 9.5—the court will take stock and ensure that there has been no unjustifiable slippage of the timetable. Where there has, directions will be given to ensure timely compliance. Since witness statements and experts may well have been exchanged this may be an appropriate time for parties to further consider ADR. In relation to conduct of the trial, further directions may be given to ensure that the proper issues are tried. The parties in the light of the pleadings, expert reports exchanged and witness statements served, may well have been required to provide a list of issues for trial to be considered at the PTR. If not already given, leave to call expert witnesses may be considered in the light of the exchange of expert reports and the identification of issues on which they are or are not agreed (see Pt 35.12(3)). Consideration will be given as to the necessity of supplemental witness/expert reports, and leave may be given. A trial timetable should be agreed by the parties and, failing such agreement, will be determined by the trial judge. Consideration will be given to such matters as the order of witnesses, e.g. the hearing of all witnesses' fact on both sides followed by the expert evidence, and to the organisation of trial bundles, i.e. indexing, time and service of index and proposed bundles, and the preparation of a core bundle(s) with cross references to the full trial bundles, where appropriate. Directions may be given at this as to whether the pleadings the claimant or defendant will open the trial and as to the service of written openings for the court/opposing party(ies) and written responses, if appropriate, and the provision of a chronology and cast list. A direction may be given as to the filing of disks (if obtainable) of the statements of case, witness statements, experts' reports, trial bundles and opening notes.

See also s.14 of the TCC Guid (2nd edn) (see para.2C–122).

Experience shows that the listing and hearing of a pre-trial review some weeks before the commencement date of the trial has two specific benefits. First, it provides a mechanism by which any minor slippage in the original timetable can be made good without endangering the trial date. In cases of significant default, however, it is critically important that the parties do not allow the fact that there is a forthcoming PTR to absolve them from making an earlier application to the court seeking compliance by the defaulting party. One party's failure to take a significant step (such as the service of witness statements or expert's reports) cannot be left to be resolved at the pre-trial review because, by that late stage, the delay in taking such a step, and the failure of any other party to bring that delay to the attention of the court, will leave the judge with the unpalatable choice between either adjourning the trial, or allowing the trial to go ahead with at least one party at a significant disadvantage.

Secondly, the PTR allows the assigned judge and the parties to resolve in some detail precisely how the trial will be conducted. This might even extend to resolving any questions of the admissibility of the evidence contained within the witness statements or expert's reports. Thus, because of the work that has been done at the PTR, the first day of a trial in the TCC will usually involve short oral openings and then, by mid-morning, the commencement of oral evidence. The PTR should ensure that valuable trial time is not lost in dealing with interlocutory and preliminary matters which should have been resolved weeks before.

### Listing

2C–31 **10** The provisions about listing questionnaires and listing in Part 29 and Practice Direction 29 do not apply to TCC claims.

### Trial

2C–32 **11.1** Whenever possible the trial of a claim will be heard by the assigned TCC judge.

**11.2** A TCC claim may be tried at any place where there is a TCC judge available to try the claim.

#### Comment

2C–33 The procedure to be followed where judgment is reserved is set out in sections 15.9.2 and 15.9.3 of the TCC Guide (see para.2C–135 below). In more complex cases, the judge will normally reserve judgment and hand down a written judgment as soon as possible thereafter. A draft copy of this judgment may be circulated in advance of the formal handing down, in order that the parties can notify the judge of any clerical errors or slips which they note in the judgment. The circulation of such a draft is not to be taken as an opportunity to re-argue the issues in the case. If the assigned judge wants further assistance on a particular point he will either request that assistance before circulating the draft, or will identify the particular paragraph or paragraphs in the draft which he requires the parties to check and/or comment upon, together with an explanation of the specific point on which their further assistance is being sought. Often in multi-party litigation, some of the claims and cross-claims will have been compromised immediately prior to the trial. This can give rise to an issue as to whether one party can utilise the expert's reports served by another party who, by then, is no longer part of the trial. In *Gurney Consulting Engineers v Gleeds Health and Safety Ltd* [2006] EWHC 43 (TCC) the court concluded that, where one party has disclosed an expert's report, any other party in the litigation may use that report as evidence at the trial, whether or not the party who originally commissioned the report was still a party to the proceedings. Precisely the same conclusion was reached in *Shepherd & Neame v EDF Energy Networks [SPN] Plc* [2008] EWHC 123 (TCC).

## *Appendices*

### Editorial note

The following forms which are annexed to this PD as Appendices A, B and C can be found in the *Civil Procedure Forms Volume*: **2C–34**

- **TCC/CM1**
- **TCC/CMCDIR**
- **TCC/PTR1**

## TECHNOLOGY AND CONSTRUCTION COURT: STATEMENT BY THE LORD CHIEF JUSTICE OF ENGLAND & WALES

2C–35 **1.** This announcement is made on behalf of myself and the Lord Chancellor. It reflects the importance which both the Lord Chancellor and I attach to the work of the Technology and Construction Court ("TCC").

**2.** The TCC is a specialist court, which operates at eleven court centres across the country. It comprises one High Court judge (who devotes about half of his working time to the business of the TCC) and 41 senior circuit and circuit judges. Of these circuit judges eight are full time TCC judges and the remainder spend only part of their time hearing TCC cases. Of the eight full time TCC judges, five are based at St Dunstan's House in London ("the London TCC"), one in Birmingham, one in Manchester and one in Liverpool. There are also 23 recorders who, because of their experience of the relevant classes of work, are specifically authorised to hear TCC cases when required. Most of the full time TCC judges (and all of those at the London TCC) are senior circuit judges.

**3.** The construction sector accounts for about 10% of the UK's GDP. The IT sector also accounts for a significant and growing proportion of GDP. Disputes within these industries or between providers and end users are often of considerable complexity. The sums at issue are huge. Some of the disputes arise from construction projects overseas or involve international parties. These disputes are of comparable size and importance to general commercial litigation. TCC judges try some of the most arduous and complex cases which come before the civil courts.

**4.** The existing TCC judges have a high degree of expertise in the management and trial of complex construction and IT cases. I pay tribute to the excellent work, which those judges are doing and have done for many years. Nevertheless the lack of involvement of High Court judges in the work of the TCC has been a source of concern within the IT and construction industries and within the profession. Hitherto the TCC has only had the services of one High Court judge for approximately half of his working time. It is now desirable for High Court judges to play a larger role in the management and trial of IT and construction litigation.

**5.** Arrangements for the longer term future of the TCC are currently under consideration by the Lord Chancellor, the Lord Chief Justice and the Master of the Rolls. In the meantime, however, we have decided that interim arrangements must be put in place, in order to ensure that all TCC cases are tried by appropriate judges. The interim arrangements, which will come into effect today, are as follows:

(i) The High Court judge in charge of the TCC (currently Jackson J) will no longer be required to spend half of each term away from the TCC. Instead he will be principally based at the TCC and will only sit in other courts when there is no TCC work requiring the immediate involvement of a High Court judge.

(ii) The judge in charge of the TCC will (with the assistance of the registry manager) consider every new case which is started in or transferred into the London TCC. He will classify each new case as "HCJ" or "SCJ". The most complex and heavy cases will be classified "HCJ". These will be managed and tried either by the judge in charge of the TCC or by another suitable High Court judge. The majority of cases, however, will be classified as "SCJ". These cases may be allocated to a named senior circuit judge by the judge in charge of the TCC; alternatively, they will be so allocated by operation of the rota.

(iii) It is neither practicable nor necessary for the judge in charge of the TCC to consider TCC cases which are commenced in, or transferred to, court centres outside London. Nevertheless, if any TCC case started outside London appears to require management and trial by a High Court judge, then the full time or principal TCC judge at that court centre should refer the case to the judge in charge of the TCC for a decision as to its future management and trial.

(iv) When proceedings are commenced in, or transferred to, the London TCC, any party to those proceedings may make brief representations by letter as to the appropriate classification.

**6.** Work is currently in progress on the preparation of a new edition of the TCC Guide. There has been widespread consultation with judges, court users and the profession about the contents of the Guide. The new edition of the Guide will set out the criteria which the judge in charge of the TCC will apply, when allocating cases to the appropriate level of judge. It will also provide that the judge in charge may change the classification of cases from "HCJ" to "SCJ", or vice versa, as appropriate.

**7.** I am confident that the TCC will continue, as it has done in the past, constantly seeking to improve the service which it provides to court users.

**The Right Honourable The Lord Woolf**
**Lord Chief Justice of England and Wales**
7th June 2005

**Comment**

The 2nd edition of the Technology and Construction Court Guide is set out below. As to allocation of cases in the London TCC, see Guide at ss.3.7.1–3.7.4 inclusive (see para.2C–57). **2C–36**

# Technology and Construction Court Guide

## Second Edition

*(issued 3 October 2005, revised with effect from 1 October 2007)*

2C–37 **INDEX**



**APPENDICES**



2C–38 *EXPLANATORY NOTE: This First Revision of the Second Edition of the TCC Guide makes the following changes:*

- *The contact details in Appendix D have been updated.*
- *Some minor inconsistencies in the provisions re time limits have been corrected.*
- *Paragraphs 2.1.3 and 2.4.2 have been revised to reflect amendments to the Pre-Action Protocol.*
- *Paragraphs 3.7.3 and 5.7.1 have been amended in the light of comments made by court users.*
- *Reference to the new Protocol re Provisional Bookings has been added to paragraph 3.7.4.*
- *Paragraph 4.5.5 has been deleted and paragraph 4.8.1 has been added in relation to lodging of documents.*
- *A sentence has been added to paragraph 5.2.1 to deal with the problem of fixing the first case management conference in multi-party cases.*
- *Paragraph 10.4.1 has been amended to reflect a recent decision.*

## SECTION 1.

## INTRODUCTION

### 1.1 Purpose of Guide

1.1.1 This new edition of the Technology and Construction Court ("TCC") Guide is intended to provide straightforward, practical guidance to the conduct of litigation in the TCC. Whilst it is intended to be comprehensive, it naturally concentrates on the most important aspects of such litigation. It therefore cannot cover all the procedural points that may arise. It does, however, describe the main elements of the practice that is likely to be followed in most TCC cases. **2C-39**

1.1.2 The Guide reflects the flexible framework within which litigation in the TCC is habitually conducted. The requirements set out in the Guide are designed to ensure effective management of proceedings in the TCC. It must always be remembered that, if parties fail to comply with these requirements, the court may impose sanctions including orders for costs.

1.1.3 In respect of those procedural areas for which specific provision is not made in this Guide, the parties, together with their advisors, will be expected to act reasonably and in accordance with both the spirit of the Guide and the overriding objective at CPR Rule 1.1

1.1.4 It is not the function of the Guide to summarise the Civil Procedure Rules ("the CPR"), and it should not be regarded as a substitute for the CPR. The parties and their advisors are expected to familiarise themselves with the CPR and, in particular, to understand the importance of the "overriding objective" of the CPR. The TCC endeavours to ensure that all its cases are dealt with justly and with proper proportionality. This includes ensuring that the parties are on an equal footing; taking all practicable steps to save expenditure; dealing with the dispute in ways which are proportionate to the size of the claim and cross-claim and the importance of the case to the parties; and managing the case throughout in a way that takes proper account of its complexity and the different financial positions of the parties. The court will also endeavour to ensure expedition, and to allot to each case an appropriate share of the court's resources.

1.1.5 This new edition of the TCC Guide has been prepared in consultation with the judges of the TCC in London, Cardiff, Birmingham, Manchester and Leeds, and with the advice and support of TECBAR, TeCSA, the Society for Computers and Law and the TCC Users' Committees in London, Cardiff, Birmingham, Manchester, Liverpool and Leeds. The TCC Guide is published with the approval of the Head of Civil Justice and the deputy Head of Civil Justice.

### 1.2 The CPR

1.2.1 Proceedings in the TCC are governed by the CPR and the supplementary Practice Directions. CPR Part 60 and its associated Practice Direction deal specifically with the practice and procedure of the TCC. **2C-40**

1.2.2 Other parts of the CPR that frequently arise in TCC cases include Part 8 (Alternative Procedure for Claims); Parts 12 and 13 (Default Judgment and Setting Aside); Part 17 (Amendments); Part 20 (Counterclaims and Other Additional Claims); Part 24 (Summary Judgment); Part 25 (Interim Remedies and Security for Costs); Part 26 (Case Management); Part 32 (Evidence); Part 35 (Experts and Assessors) and Part 62 (Arbitration Claims).

### 1.3 The TCC

1.3.1 What are TCC Claims? CPR Rules 60.1 (2) and (3) provide that a TCC claim is a claim which (i) involves technically complex issues or questions (or for which trial by a TCC judge is desirable) and (ii) has been issued in or transferred into the TCC **2C-41**

*Paragraph numbers marked with a "+" can be found online and on CD.*

specialist list. Paragraph 2.1 of the TCC Practice Direction identifies the following as examples of the types of claim which it may be appropriate to bring as TCC claims—

(a) building or other construction disputes, including claims for the enforcement of the decisions of adjudicators under the Housing Grants, Construction and Regeneration Act 1996;
(b) engineering disputes;
(c) claims by and against engineers, architects, surveyors, accountants and other specialised advisors relating to the services they provide;
(d) claims by and against local authorities relating to their statutory duties concerning the development of land or the construction of buildings;
(e) claims relating to the design, supply and installation of computers, computer software and related network systems;
(f) claims relating to the quality of goods sold or hired, and work done, materials supplied or services rendered;
(g) claims between landlord and tenant for breach of a repairing covenant;
(h) claims between neighbours, owners and occupiers of land in trespass, nuisance, etc.
(i) claims relating to the environment (for example, pollution cases);
(j) claims arising out of fires;
(k) claims involving taking of accounts where these are complicated; and
(l) challenges to decisions of arbitrators in construction and engineering disputes including applications for permission to appeal and appeals.

It should be noted that this list is not exhaustive and other types of claim may well be appropriate for the TCC.

1.3.2 <u>The Court.</u> Both the High Court and the county courts deal with TCC business. Circuit judges and recorders only have jurisdiction to manage and try TCC cases if they have been nominated by the Lord Chancellor pursuant to section 68 (1) (a) of the Senior Courts Act 1981. It should be noted that those circuit judges who have been nominated pursuant to section 68(1) of the Senior Courts Act 1981 fall into two categories: "full time" TCC judges and "part time" TCC judges. "Full time" TCC judges spend most of their time dealing with TCC business, although they will do other work when there is no TCC business requiring their immediate attention. "Part time" TCC judges are circuit judges who are only available to sit in the TCC for part of their time. They have substantial responsibilities outside the TCC.

In respect of a court centre where there is no full time TCC judge, the term "principal TCC judge" is used in this Guide to denote the circuit judge who has principal responsibility for TCC work.

The phrase "Technology and Construction Court" or "TCC" or "the court" is used in this Guide to denote any court which deals with TCC claims. All of the courts which deal with TCC claims form a composite group of courts. When those courts are dealing with TCC business, CPR Part 60, its accompanying Practice Direction and this Guide govern the procedures of those courts. The High Court judge in charge of the TCC ("the Judge in Charge"), although based principally in London, has overall responsibility for the judicial supervision of TCC business in those courts.

1.3.3 <u>The TCC in London.</u> The principal centre for TCC work is the High Court in London at St Dunstan's House, 133-137 Fetter Lane, London, EC4A 1HD. The Judge in Charge of the TCC sits principally at St Dunstan's House together with five full time TCC judges. Subject to paragraph 3.7.1 below, any communication or enquiry concerning a TCC case, which is proceeding at St Dunstan's House, should be directed to the clerk of the judge who is assigned to that case. The various contact details for the judges' clerks are set out in Appendix D.

The TCC judges who are based at St Dunstan's House will, when appropriate, sit at court centres outside London.

TCC county court cases in London are brought in (or transferred to) the Central London Civil Justice Centre, 13-14 Park Crescent, London W1N 4HT.

1.3.4 District Registries. TCC claims can be brought in the High Court outside London in any District Registry, although the Practice Direction states that it is preferable that, wherever possible, such claims should be issued in one of the following District Registries: Birmingham, Bristol, Cardiff, Chester, Exeter, Leeds, Liverpool, Newcastle, Nottingham and Salford (Manchester). There are full-time TCC Judges in Birmingham, Liverpool and Salford (Manchester). Contact details are again set out in Appendix D. There are part time TCC judges and/or recorders nominated to deal with TCC business available at most court centres throughout England and Wales.

In a number of regions a "TCC liaison district judge" has been appointed. It is the function of the TCC liaison district judge:

(a) To keep other district judges in that region well informed about the role and remit of the TCC (in order that appropriate cases may be transferred to the TCC at an early, rather than late, stage).
(b) To deal with any queries from colleagues concerning the TCC or cases which might merit transfer to the TCC.
(c) To deal with any subsidiary matter which a TCC judge directs should be determined by a district judge pursuant to rule 60.1(5)(b)(ii).
(d) To deal with urgent applications in TCC cases pursuant to paragraph 7.2 of the Practice Direction (i.e. no TCC judge is available and the matter is of a kind that falls within the district judge's jurisdiction).

1.3.5 County Courts outside London. TCC claims may also be brought in those county courts which are specified in the Part 60 Practice Direction. The specified county courts are: Birmingham, Bristol, Cardiff, Chester, Exeter, Leeds, Liverpool, Newcastle, Nottingham and Salford (Manchester). Contact details are again set out in Appendix D.

Where TCC proceedings are brought in a county court, statements of case and applications should be headed:

"In the ... County Court
Technology and Construction Court"

This heading is important because in TCC cases (subject to the limited exceptions mentioned in paragraph 1.3.4 above) district judges do not have jurisdiction to hear applications or make orders.

1.3.6 The division between High Court and county court TCC cases. As a general rule TCC claims for more than £50,000 are brought in the High Court, whilst claims for lower sums are brought in the county court. However, this is not a rigid dividing line. The monetary threshold for High Court TCC claims tends to be higher in London than in the regions. Regard must also be had to the complexity of the case and all other circumstances. Arbitration claims and claims to enforce or challenge adjudicators' awards are generally (but not invariably) brought in the High Court. The scale of fees differs in the High Court and the county court. This is a factor which should be borne in mind in borderline cases.

### 1.4 The TCC Users' Committees

1.4.1 The continuing ability of the TCC to meet the changing needs of all those involved in TCC litigation depends in large part upon a close working relationship between the TCC and its users. **2C–42**

1.4.2 London. The Judge in Charge chairs two meetings a year of the London TCC Users' Committee. The judge's clerk acts as secretary to the Committee and takes the minutes of meetings. That Committee is made up of representatives of the London TCC judges, the barristers and solicitors who regularly use the Court, the professional bodies, such as architects, engineers and arbitrators, whose members are affected by the decisions of the Court, and representatives of both employers and contractors' groups.

1.4.3 Outside London. There are similar meetings of TCC Users' Committees in Birmingham, Salford (Manchester), Liverpool, Cardiff and Leeds. Each Users' Committee is chaired by the full time TCC judge or the principal TCC judge in that location.

1.4.4 The TCC regards these channels of communication as extremely important and all those who are concerned with the work of the Court are encouraged to make full use of these meetings. Any suggestions or other correspondence raising matters for consideration by the Users' Committee should, in the first instance, be addressed to the clerk to the Judge in Charge at St. Dunstan's House or to the clerk to the appropriate TCC judge outside London.

### 1.5 Specialist Associations

2C–43 1.5.1 There are a number of associations of legal representatives which are represented on the Users' Committees and which also liaise closely with the Court. These contacts ensure that the Court remains responsive to the opinions and requirements of the professional users of the Court.

1.5.2 The relevant professional organisations are the TCC Bar Association ("TECBAR") and the TCC Solicitors Association ("TeCSA"). Details of the relevant contacts at these organisations are set out on their respective websites, namely www.tecbar.org and www.tecsa.org.

## SECTION 2.

## PRE-ACTION PROTOCOL

### 2.1 Introduction

2C–44 2.1.1 There is a Pre-Action Protocol for Construction and Engineering Disputes. Where the dispute involves a claim against architects, engineers or quantity surveyors, this Protocol prevails over the Professional Negligence Pre-Action Protocol: see paragraph 1.1 of the Protocol for Construction and Engineering Disputes and paragraph A.1 of the Professional Negligence Pre-Action Protocol. The current version of the Construction and Engineering Pre-Action Protocol ("the Protocol") is set out in volume 1 of the White Book at section C.

2.1.2 The purpose of the Protocol is to encourage the frank and early exchange of information about the prospective claim and any defence to it; to enable parties to avoid litigation by agreeing a settlement of the claim before the commencement of proceedings; and to support the efficient management of proceedings where litigation cannot be avoided.

2.1.3 Proportionality. The overriding objective (CPR rule 1.1) applies to the pre-action period. The Protocol must not be used as a tactical device to secure advantage for one party or to generate unnecessary costs. In lower value TCC claims (such as those likely to proceed in the county court), the letter of claim and the response should be simple and the costs of both sides should be kept to a modest level. In all cases the costs incurred at the Protocol stage should be proportionate to the complexity of the case and the amount of money which is at stake. The Protocol does not impose a requirement on the parties to marshal and disclose all the supporting details and evidence that may ultimately be required if the case proceeds to litigation.

### 2.2 To Which Claims Does The Protocol Apply?

2C–45 2.2.1 The court will expect all parties to have complied in substance with the provisions of the Protocol in all construction and engineering disputes. The only exceptions to this are identified in paragraph 2.3 below.

2.2.2 The court regards the Protocol as setting out normal and reasonable pre-action conduct. Accordingly, whilst the Protocol is not mandatory for a number of the claims noted by way of example in paragraph 1.3.1 above, such as computer cases or dilapidations claims, the court would, in the absence of a specific reason to the contrary, expect the Protocol generally to be followed in such cases prior to the commencement of proceedings in the TCC.

**2.3 What Are The Exceptions?**

2.3.1 A claimant does not have to comply with the Protocol if his claim: **2C–46**

(a) is to enforce the decision of an adjudicator;
(b) includes a claim for interim injunctive relief;
(c) will be the subject of a claim for summary judgment pursuant to Part 24 of the CPR; or
(d) relates to the same or substantially the same issues as have been the subject of a recent adjudication or some other formal alternative dispute resolution procedure.

2.3.2 In addition, a claimant need not comply with any part of the Protocol if, by so doing, his claim may become time-barred under the Limitation Act 1980. In those circumstances, a claimant should commence proceedings without complying with the Protocol and must, at the same time, apply for specific directions as to the timetable and form of procedure to be adopted. The court may order a stay of those proceedings pending completion of the steps set out in the Protocol.

**2.4 What Are The Essential Ingredients Of The Protocol?**

2.4.1 The Letter of Claim. The letter of claim must comply with Section 3 of the Protocol. Amongst other things, it must contain a clear summary of the facts on which each claim is based; the basis on which each claim is made; and details of the relief claimed, including a breakdown showing how any damages have been quantified. The claimant must also provide the names of experts already instructed and on whom he intends to rely. **2C–47**

2.4.2 The Defendant's Response. The defendant has 14 days to acknowledge the letter of claim and 28 days (from receipt of the letter of claim) either to take any jurisdiction objection or to respond in substance to the letter of claim. Paragraph 4.3.1 of the Protocol enables the parties to agree an extension of the 28 day period up to a maximum of 3 months. In any case of substance it is quite usual for an extension of time to be agreed for the defendant's response. The letter of response must comply with section 4 of the Protocol. Amongst other things, it must state which claims are accepted, which claims are rejected and on what basis. It must set out any counterclaim to be advanced by the defendant. The defendant should also provide the names of experts who have been instructed and on whom he intends to rely. If the defendant fails either to acknowledge or to respond to the letter of claim in time, the claimant is entitled to commence proceedings.

2.4.3 Pre-action Meeting. The Construction and Engineering Protocol is the only Protocol under the CPR that generally requires the parties to meet, without prejudice, at least once, in order to identify the main issues and the root causes of their disagreement on those issues. The purpose of the meeting is to see whether, and if so how, those issues might be resolved without recourse to litigation or, if litigation is unavoidable, what steps should be taken to ensure that it is conducted in accordance with the overriding objective. At or as a result of the meeting, the parties should consider whether some form of alternative dispute resolution ("ADR") would be more suitable than litigation and if so, they should endeavour to agree which form of ADR to adopt. Although the meeting is "without prejudice", any party who attended the meeting is at liberty to disclose to the Court at a later stage that the meeting took place; who attended and who refused to attend, together with the grounds for their refusal; and any agreements concluded between the parties.

**2.5 What Happens To The Material Generated By The Protocol?**

2.5.1 The letter of claim, the defendant's response, and the information relating to attendance (or otherwise) at the meeting are not confidential or 'without prejudice' **2C–48** and can therefore be referred to by the parties in any subsequent litigation. The detail of any discussion at the meeting(s) and/or any note of the meeting cannot be referred to the court unless all parties agree.

2.5.2 Normally the parties should include in the bundle for the first case management conference: (a) the letter of claim, (b) the response, and (c) any agreed note of the pre-action meeting: see Section 5 below. The documents attached to or enclosed with the letter and the response should not be included in the bundle.

**2.6 What If One Party Has Not Complied With The Protocol?**

**2C–49** 2.6.1 There can often be a complaint that one or other party has not complied with the Protocol. The court will consider any such complaints once proceedings have been commenced. If the court finds that the claimant has not complied with one part of the Protocol, then the court may stay the proceedings until the steps set out in the Protocol have been taken.

2.6.2 Paragraph 2.3 of the Practice Direction in respect of Protocols (section C of volume 1 of the White Book) makes plain that the court may make adverse costs orders against a party who has failed to comply with the Protocol. The court will exercise any sanctions available with the object of placing the innocent party in no worse a position than he would have been if the Protocol had been complied with.

2.6.3 The court is unlikely to be concerned with minor infringements of the Protocol or to engage in lengthy debates as to the precise quality of the information provided by one party to the other during the Protocol stages. The court will principally be concerned to ensure that, as a result of the Protocol stage, each party to any subsequent litigation has a clear understanding of the nature of the case that it has to meet at the commencement of those proceedings.

**2.7 Costs of compliance with the Protocol**

**2C–50** 2.7.1 If compliance with the Protocol results in settlement, the costs incurred will not be recoverable from the paying party, unless this is specifically agreed.

2.7.2 If compliance with the Protocol does not result in settlement, then the costs of the exercise cannot be recovered as costs, unless:

- those costs fall within the principles stated by Sir Robert Megarry V-C in *Re Gibson's Settlement Trusts* [1981] Ch 179; or
- the steps taken in compliance with the Protocol can properly be attributable to the conduct of the action.

## SECTION 3.

## COMMENCEMENT AND TRANSFER

**3.1 Claim Forms**

**2C–51** 3.1.1 All proceedings must be started using a claim form under CPR Part 7 or CPR Part 8. All claims allocated to the TCC are assigned to the Multi-Track: see CPR Rule 60.6(1).

**3.2 Part 7 Claims**

**2C–52** 3.2.1 The Part 7 claim form must be marked "Technology and Construction Court" in the appropriate place on the form.

3.2.2. Particulars of Claim may be served with the claim form, but this is not a mandatory requirement. If the Particulars of Claim are not contained in or served with the claim form, they must be served within **14 days** after service of the claim form.

***Paragraph numbers marked with a "+" can be found online and on CD.***

3.2.3 A claim form must be verified by a statement of truth, and this includes any amendment to a claim form, unless the court otherwise orders.

### 3.3 Part 8 Claims

3.3.1 The Part 8 claim form must be marked "Technology and Construction Court" in the appropriate place on the form. **2C–53**

3.3.2 A Part 8 claim form will normally be used where there is no substantial dispute of fact, such as the situation where the dispute turns on the construction of the contract or the interpretation of statute. For example, claims challenging the jurisdiction of an adjudicator or the validity of his decision are sometimes brought under Part 8. In those cases the relevant primary facts are often not in dispute. Part 8 claims will generally be disposed of on written evidence and oral submissions.

3.3.3 It is important that, where a claimant uses the Part 8 procedure, his claim form states that Part 8 applies and that the claimant wishes the claim to proceed under Part 8.

3.3.4 A statement of truth is again required on a Part 8 claim form.

### 3.4 Service

3.4.1 Claim forms issued in the TCC at St Dunstan's House in London are to be served by the claimant, not by the Registry. In some other court centres claim forms are served by the court, unless the claimant specifically requests otherwise. **2C–54**

3.4.2 The different methods of service are set out in CPR Part 6 and the accompanying Practice Direction.

3.4.3 Applications for an extension of time in which to serve a claim form are governed by CPR Rule 7.6. The evidence required on an application for an extension of time is set out in paragraph 8.2 of Practice Direction A supplementing CPR Part 7.

3.4.4 When the claimant has served the claim form, he must file a certificate of service: Rule 6.14(2). This is necessary if, for instance, the claimant wishes to obtain judgment in default (CPR Part 12).

3.4.5 Applications for permission to serve a claim form out of the jurisdiction are subject to Rules 6.19–6.31 inclusive.

### 3.5 Acknowledgement of Service

3.5.1 A defendant must file an acknowledgment of service in response to both Part 7 and Part 8 claims. Save in the special circumstances that arise when the claim form has been served out of the jurisdiction, the period for filing an acknowledgment of service is 14 days after service of the claim form. **2C–55**

### 3.6 Transfer

3.6.1 Proceedings may be transferred from any Division of the High Court or from any specialist list to the TCC pursuant to CPR rule 30.5. The order made by the transferring court should be expressed as being subject to the approval of a TCC judge. The decision whether to accept such a transfer must be made by a TCC judge: see rule 30.5(3). Many of these applications are uncontested, and may conveniently be dealt with on paper. Transfers from the TCC to other Divisions of the High Court or other specialist lists are also governed by CPR rule 30.5. In London there are quite often transfers between the Commercial Court and the TCC, in order to ensure that cases are dealt with by the most appropriate judge. Outside London there are quite often transfers between the TCC and the mercantile courts. **2C–56**

3.6.2 A TCC claim may be transferred from the High Court to one of the county courts noted above, and from any county court to the High Court, if the criteria stated in CPR Rule 30.3 are satisfied. In ordinary circumstances, proceedings will be transferred from the TCC in the High Court to the TCC in an appropriate county court if the amount of the claim does not exceed £50,000.

3.6.3 Where no TCC judge is available to deal with a TCC claim which has been issued in a district registry or one of the county courts noted above, the claim may be transferred to another district registry or county court or to the High Court TCC in London (depending upon which court is appropriate).

**3.7 Assignment**

**2C–57** 3.7.1 Where a claim has been issued at or transferred to the TCC at St Dunstan's House in London, the Judge in Charge of the TCC ("the Judge in Charge") shall with the assistance of court staff classify the case either "HCJ" or "SCJ".

- (i) If the case is classified "HCJ", it shall be managed and tried either by the Judge in Charge or by another High Court judge, who will be identified after consultation between the Judge in Charge and the Vice-President of the Queen's Bench Division. The clerical administration of "HCJ" cases will be carried out by the Case Administration Unit ("CAU") of the TCC at St Dunstan's House. The CAU will also deal with the listing of all applications and trials in such cases.
- (ii) If the case is classified "SCJ", it shall be managed and tried by one of the senior circuit judges, who is a full time TCC judge in London. Cases in the latter category will either (a) be assigned by the Judge in Charge to a specific senior circuit judge or (b) be assigned to a senior circuit judge by operation of the rota. The assigned judge will have primary responsibility for the management of that case.
- (iii) Although continuity of judge is regarded as important, it will sometimes be necessary for there to be a change of assigned judge. If no judge is available during the period fixed for trial, then the case may be tried by one of the deputy judges or recorders who has been nominated by the Lord Chancellor under section 68(1)(a) of the Senior Courts Act 1981.

3.7.2 When classifying a case "HCJ" or "SCJ", the Judge in Charge will take into account the following matters, as well as all the circumstances of the case:

1. The size and complexity of the case.
2. The nature and importance of any points of law arising.
3. The amount of money which is at stake.
4. Whether the case is one of public importance.
5. Whether the case has an international element or involves overseas parties.
6. The limited number of High Court judges and the needs of other court users, both civil and criminal.

Most TCC cases in London will be classified "SCJ". The Judge in Charge may change the classification of any case from "HCJ" to "SCJ" or from "SCJ" to "HCJ", if it becomes appropriate to do so. There will be a band of cases near the borderline between "HCJ" and "SCJ", where the classification will be liable to change depending upon the settlement rate of other cases and the availability of judges.

3.7.3 When proceedings are commenced in, or transferred to, the TCC at St Dunstan's House in London, any party to those proceedings may write to the court setting out matters relevant to classification. Any such letter should be clear and concise and should be copied to all other parties. A defendant who wishes to send such a letter should do so as soon as he becomes aware of the proceedings. Any party who believes that a case has been wrongly classified (whether "HCJ" or "SCJ") should write to the court promptly setting out his grounds for that belief. All letters referred to in this paragraph are referred to the judge in charge of the TCC or (in his absence) to the other TCC High Court judge for consideration.

3.7.4 When a case has been assigned to a named senior circuit judge in the TCC at St Dunstan's House, all communications to the court about the case (save for communications in respect of fees) shall be made to that judge's clerk. When a TCC case has been assigned to a named High Court judge, all such communications shall be made to the CAU or to the judge's clerk as appropriate. A Protocol on HMCS website sets out the procedure which will be followed when the CAU accepts a "provisional booking" for a High Court judge. All communications in respect of fees, however, should be sent to the Registry. All statements of case and applications should be marked with the name of the assigned judge.

3.7.5 There are full time TCC judges at Birmingham, Liverpool and Salford (Manchester). There are principal TCC judges at other court centres outside London. TCC cases at these court centres are assigned to judges either (a) by direction of the full time or principal TCC judge or (b) by operation of a rota. It will not generally be appropriate for the Judge in Charge (who is based in London) to consider TCC cases which are commenced in, or transferred to, court centres outside London. Nevertheless, if any TCC case brought in a court centre outside London appears to require management and trial by a High Court judge, then the full time or principal TCC judge at that court centre should refer the case to the Judge in Charge for a decision as to its future management and trial.

3.7.6 When a TCC case has been assigned to a named circuit judge at a court centre other than St Dunstan's House, all communications to the court about the case (save for communications in respect of fees) shall be made to that judge's clerk. All communications in respect of fees should be sent to the relevant registry. All statements of case and applications should be marked with the name of the assigned judge.

## SECTION 4.

## ACCESS TO THE COURT

### 4.1 General Approach

4.1.1 There may be a number of stages during the case management phase when the parties will make applications to the court for particular orders: see Section 6 below. There will also be the need for the court to give or vary directions, so as to enable the case to progress to trial. **2C-58**

4.1.2 The court is acutely aware of the costs that may be incurred when both parties prepare for an oral hearing in respect of such interlocutory matters and is always prepared to consider alternative, and less expensive, ways in which the parties may seek the court's assistance.

4.1.3 There are certain stages in the case management phase when it will generally be better for the parties to appear before the assigned judge. Those are identified at Section 4.2 below. But there are other stages, and/or particular applications which a party may wish to make, which could conveniently be dealt with by way of a telephone hearing (Section 4.3 below) or by way of a paper application (Section 4.4 below).

### 4.2 Hearings in Court

4.2.1 First Case Management Conference. The court will normally require the parties to attend an oral hearing for the purposes of the first Case Management Conference. This is because there may be matters which the judge would wish to raise with the parties arising out of the answers to the case management information sheets and the parties' proposed directions: see section 5.4 below. Even in circumstances where the directions and the case management timetable may be capable of being agreed by the parties and the court, the assigned judge may still wish to consider a range of case management matters face-to-face with the parties, including the possibility of ADR. See paragraphs 7.2.3, 7.3.2, 8.1.3, 11.1, 13.3, 13.4 and 16.3.2 below. **2C-59**

4.2.2 Whilst the previous paragraph sets out the ideal position, it is recognised that in low value cases the benefits of personal attendance might be outweighed by the costs involved. This is particularly so at court centres outside London, where the parties may have to travel substantial distances to court. Ultimately, the question whether personal attendance should be dispensed with at any particular case management conference must be decided by the judge, after considering any representations made and the circumstances of that particular case.

4.2.3 Pre-trial Review. It will normally be helpful for the parties to attend before the judge on a Pre-trial Review ("PTR"). It is always preferable for Counsel or other advocates who will be appearing at the trial to attend the PTR. Again, even if the parties can agree beforehand any outstanding directions and the detailed requirements for the management of the trial, it is still of assistance for the judge to raise matters of detailed trial management with the parties at an oral hearing. In appropriate cases, e.g. where the amount in issue is disproportionate to the costs of a full trial, the judge may wish to consider with the parties whether there are other ways in which the dispute might be resolved.

4.2.4 Whether or not other interlocutory applications require to be determined at an oral hearing will depend on the nature and effect of the application being made. Disputed applications for interim payments, summary judgment and security for costs will almost always require an oral hearing. Likewise, the resolution of a contested application to enforce an adjudicator's decision will normally be heard orally. At the other end of the scale, applications for extensions of time for the service of pleadings or to comply with other orders of the court can almost always be dealt with by way of a telephone hearing or in writing.

#### 4.3 Telephone Hearings

**2C–60** 4.3.1 Depending on the nature of the application and the extent of any dispute between the parties, the Court is content to deal with many case management matters and other interlocutory applications by way of a telephone conference.

4.3.2 Whilst it is not possible to lay down mandatory rules as to what applications should be dealt with in this way (rather than by way of an oral hearing in court), it may be helpful to identify certain situations which commonly arise and which can conveniently be dealt with by way of a telephone conference.

(a) If the location of the court is inconvenient for one or more of the parties, or the value of the claim is low, then the CMC and the PTR could, in the alternative to the procedure set out in Section 4.2 above, take place by way of a telephone conference. The judge's permission for such a procedure would have to be sought in advance.

(b) If the parties are broadly agreed on the orders to be made by the court, but they are in dispute in respect of one or two particular matters, then a telephone hearing is a convenient way in which those outstanding matters can be dealt with by the parties and the assigned judge.

(c) Similarly, specific arguments about costs, once a substantive application has been disposed of, or arguments consequential on a particular judgment or order having been handed down, may also conveniently be dealt with by way of telephone hearing.

(d) Other applications which, depending on their size and importance, may conveniently be dealt with by way of a telephone hearing include limited applications in respect of disclosure and specific applications as to the scope and content of factual or expert evidence exchanged by the parties.

4.3.3 Telephone hearings are not generally suitable for matters which are likely to last for more than an hour, although the judge may be prepared, in an appropriate case, to list a longer application for a telephone hearing.

4.3.4 Practical matters. Telephone hearings can be listed at any time between 8.30 a.m.and 5.30 p.m., subject to the convenience of the parties and the availability of the judge. Any party, who wishes to have an application dealt with by telephone, should make such request by letter or e-mail to the judge's clerk, sending copies to all other parties. Except in cases of urgency, the judge will allow a period of three days for the other parties to comment upon that request before deciding whether to deal with the application by telephone.

4.3.5 If permission is given for a telephone hearing, the court will normally indicate which party is to make all the necessary arrangements. In most cases, it will be the applicant. The procedure to be followed in setting up and holding a telephone hearing is that set out in section 6 of the Practice Direction supplementing CPR Part 23. The party making arrangements for the telephone hearing must ensure that all parties and the judge have a bundle for that hearing with identical pagination.

It is vital that the judge has all the necessary papers, in good time before the telephone conference, in order that it can be conducted efficiently and effectively.

### 4.4 Paper Applications

4.4.1 CPR rule 23.8 and section 11 of the accompanying Practice Direction enable certain applications to be dealt with in writing. Parties in a TCC case are encouraged to deal with applications in writing, whenever practicable. Applications for both abridgments of time and extensions of time can generally be dealt with in writing, as well as all other variations to existing directions which are wholly or largely agreed. Disputes over particular aspects of disclosure and evidence may also be capable of being resolved in this way. **2C–61**

4.4.2 If a party wishes to make an application to the court, it should ask itself the question: "Can this application be conveniently dealt with in writing?" If it can, then the party should issue the application and make its (short) written submissions both in support of its application and why it should be dealt with on paper. The application, any supporting evidence and the written submissions should be provided to all parties, as well as the court. These must include a draft of the precise order sought.

4.4.3 The party against whom the application is made, and any other interested party, should respond within 3 days dealing both with the substantive application and the request for it to be dealt with in writing.

4.4.4 The court can then decide whether or not to deal with the application in writing. If the parties are agreed that the court should deal with it in writing, it will be rare for the court to take a different view. If the parties disagree as to whether or not the application should be dealt with in writing, the court can decide that issue and, if it decides to deal with it in writing can go on to resolve the substantive point on the basis of the parties' written submissions.

4.4.5 Further guidance in respect of paper applications is set out in Section 6.7 below.

4.4.6 It is important for the parties to ensure that all documents provided to the court are also provided to all the other parties, so as to ensure that both the court and the parties are working on the basis of the same documentation. The pagination of any bundle which is provided to the court and the parties must be identical.

### 4.5 E-mail Communications

4.5.1 The general rules relating to communication and filing of documents by e-mail are set out in CPR Part 5, Practice Direction B. **2C–62**

4.5.2 The judges' clerks all have e-mail addresses identified in Appendix D. They welcome communication from the parties electronically. By agreement with the judge's clerk, it may also be possible to provide documents to the Court in this way. However, it should be noted that HM Court Service has imposed a blanket restriction of 2MB on the length of any e-mail, including its attachments. This equates to approximately 40 pages of normal typescript.

4.5.3 Depending on the particular circumstances of an individual trial, the assigned judge may ask for an e-mail contact address for each of the parties and may send e-mail communications to that address. In addition, the judge may provide a direct contact email address so that the parties can communicate directly with him out of court hours. In such circumstances, the judge and the parties should agree the times at which the respective e-mail addresses can be used.

4.5.4 Every e-mail communication to and from the judge must be simultaneously copied to all the other parties.

#### 4.6 Video Conferencing

**2C–63** 4.6.1 In appropriate cases, particularly where there are important matters in dispute and the parties' representatives are a long distance from one another and/or the court, the hearing may be conducted by way of a Video Conference ("VC"). Prior arrangements will be necessary for any such hearing.

4.6.2 In London, a VC can be arranged through the VC suite at the Royal Courts of Justice. However, this facility is popular and will need to be booked well in advance of the hearing. Alternatively, there are a number of other VC suites in the Strand/Fleet Street area which would be suitable. Details of these facilities are available from the judges' clerks.

4.6.3 Outside London, a VC can be arranged at the following TCC courts with the requisite facilities: Birmingham, Bristol, Cardiff, Central London, Chester, Exeter, Leeds, Liverpool, Newcastle-upon-Tyne, Nottingham, Salford (Manchester) and Winchester.

#### 4.7 Contacting the court out of hours

**2C–64** 4.7.1 Occasionally it is necessary to contact a TCC judge out of hours. For example, it may be necessary to apply for an injunction to prevent the commencement of building works which will damage adjoining property; or for an order to preserve evidence. A case may have settled and it may be necessary to inform the judge, before he/she spends an evening or a weekend reading the papers.

4.7.2 At St Dunstan's House. RCJ Security has been provided with the telephone numbers and other contact information of all the TCC judges based at St Dunstan's House and of the court manager. If contact is required with a judge out of hours, the initial approach should be to RCJ Security on 0207-947-6000. Security will then contact the judge and/or the court manager and pass on the message or other information. If direct contact with the judge or court manager is required, RCJ Security must be provided with an appropriate contact number. This number will then be passed to the judge and/or the court manager, who will decide whether it is appropriate for him or her to speak directly to the contacting party.

4.7.3 At other court centres. At the Central London Civil Justice Centre and at all court centres outside London there is a court officer who deals with out of hours applications.

#### 4.8 Lodging documents

**2C–65** 4.8.1 In general documents should be lodged in hard copy and not sent by email or fax. This causes unnecessary duplication as well as additional work for hard-pressed court staff. Only if matters are urgent may documents be sent by either email or fax, with a hard copy sent by way of confirmation and marked as such. In certain cases, the court may ask for documents to be submitted in electronic form by email or otherwise, where that is appropriate.

## SECTION 5.

## CASE MANAGEMENT AND THE FIRST CMC

### 5.1 General

5.1.1 The general approach of the TCC to case management is to give directions at the outset and then throughout the proceedings to serve the overriding objective of dealing with cases justly. The judge to whom the case has been assigned has wide case management powers, which will be exercised to ensure that: **2C–66**

- the real issues are identified early on and remain the focus of the ongoing proceedings;
- a realistic timetable is ordered which will allow for the fair and prompt resolution of the action;
- costs are properly controlled and reflect the value of the issues to the parties and their respective financial positions.

5.1.2 In order to assist the judge in the exercise of his case management functions, the parties will be expected to co-operate with one another at all times. See CPR rule 1.3. Costs sanctions may be applied, if the judge concludes that one party is not reasonably co-operating with the other parties.

5.1.3 A hearing at which the judge gives general procedural directions is a case management conference ("CMC"). CMCs are relatively informal and business-like occasions. Counsel are not robed. Representatives sit when addressing the judge.

5.1.4 The following procedures apply in order to facilitate effective case management:

- Upon commencement of a case in the TCC, it is allocated automatically to the multitrack. The provisions of CPR Part 29 apply to all TCC cases.
- The TCC encourages a structured exchange of proposals and submissions for CMCs in advance of the hearing, so as to enable the parties to respond on an informed basis to proposals made.
- The judges of the TCC operate pro-active case management. In order to avoid the parties being taken by surprise by any judicial initiative, the judge will consider giving prior notification of specific or unusual case management proposals to be raised at a case management conference.

5.1.5 The TCC's aim is to ensure that the trial of each case takes place before the judge who has managed the case since the first CMC. Whilst continuity of judge is not always possible, because of the need to double- or triple-book judges, or because cases can sometimes overrun their estimated length through no fault of the parties, this remains an aspiration of case management within the TCC.

### 5.2 The Fixing of the First CMC

5.2.1 Where a claim has been started in the TCC, or where it has been transferred into the TCC, paragraph 8.1 of the Part 60 Practice Direction requires the court to fix the first CMC within 14 days of the earliest of **2C–67**

- the filing by the defendant of an acknowledgement of service or
- the filing by the defendant of the defence or
- the date of the order transferring the case to the TCC.

If some defendants but not others are served with proceedings, the claimant's solicitors should so inform the court and liaise about the fixing of the first CMC.

5.2.2 This means that the first CMC takes place relatively early, sometimes before the defendant has filed a defence. However, if, as will usually be the case, the parties have complied with the protocol (Section 2 above) they will have a good idea of each other's respective positions, and an effective CMC can take place. If, on the other hand, there has been a failure to comply with the protocol, or there are other reasons why the issues are not clearly defined at the outset, then it may be important for the judge to be involved at an early stage.

***Paragraph numbers marked with a "+" can be found online and on CD.***

5.2.3 Despite the foregoing considerations, it is sometimes apparent to the parties that it will be more cost effective to postpone the first CMC until after service of the defence or the defences. If any of the parties wishes to delay the first CMC until then, they can write to the judge's clerk explaining why a delayed CMC is appropriate. If such a request is agreed by the other party or parties, it is likely that the judge will grant the request.

### 5.3 The Case Management Information Sheet and Other Documents

2C–68 5.3.1 All parties are expected to complete a detailed response to the case management information sheet sent out by the Registry when the case is commenced/transferred. A copy of a blank case management information sheet is attached as Appendix A. It is important that all parts of the form are completed, particularly those sections (e.g. concerned with estimated costs) that enable the judge to give directions in accordance with the overriding objective.

5.3.2 The Registry will also send out a blank standard directions form to each party. A copy is attached at Appendix B. This sets out the usual directions made on the first CMC. The parties should fill them in, indicating the directions and timetable sought. The parties should return both the questionnaire and the directions form to the court, so that the areas (if any) of potential debate at the CMC can be identified. The parties are encouraged to exchange proposals for directions and the timetable sought, with a view to agreeing the same before the CMC for consideration by the court.

5.3.3 If the case is large or complex, it is helpful for the advocates to prepare a Note to be provided to the judge the day before the CMC which can address the issues in the case, the suggested directions, and the principal areas of dispute between the parties. If such a Note is provided, it is unnecessary for the claimant also to prepare a Case Summary as well.

5.3.4 In smaller cases, a Case Summary for the CMC, explaining briefly the likely issues, can be helpful. Such Case Summaries should be non-contentious and should (if this is possible without incurring disproportionate cost) be agreed between the parties in advance of the hearing.

### 5.4 Checklist of Matters likely to be considered at the first CMC

2C–69 5.4.1 The following checklist identifies the matters which the judge is likely to want to consider at the first CMC, although it is not exhaustive:

- The need for, and content of, any further pleadings. This is dealt with in Section 5.5 below.
- The outcome of the Protocol process, and the possible further need for ADR. ADR is dealt with in Section 7 below.
- The desirability of dealing with particular disputes by way of a Preliminary Issue hearing. This is dealt with in Section 8 below.
- Whether the trial should be in stages (e.g. stage 1 liability and causation, stage 2 quantum). In very heavy cases this may be necessary in order to make the trial manageable. In more modest cases, where the quantum evidence will be extensive, a staged trial may be in the interest of all parties.
- The appropriate orders in respect of the disclosure of documents. This is dealt with in Section 11 below.
- The appropriate orders as to the exchange of written witness statements. This is dealt with in Section 12 below. It should be noted that, although it is normal for evidence-in-chief to be given by way of the written statements in the TCC, the judge may direct that evidence about particular disputes (such as what was said at an important meeting) should be given orally without reference to such statements.
- Whether it is appropriate for the parties to rely on expert evidence and, if so, what disciplines of experts should give evidence, and on what issues. This may be coupled with an order relating to the carrying out of inspections, the obtaining of samples, the conducting of experiments, or the performance of calculations. Considerations relating to expert evidence are dealt with in Section 13 below. The parties must be aware that, in accordance with the overriding objective, the judge will only give the parties permission to rely on expert evidence if it is both necessary and appropriate, and, even then, will wish to ensure that the scope of any such evidence is limited as far as possible.

- In certain cases the possibility of making a costs cap order. See section 16.3 below.
- The appropriate timetable for the taking of the various interlocutory steps noted above, and the fixing of dates for both the PTR and the trial itself (subject to paragraph 5.4.2 below). The parties will therefore need to provide the judge with an estimate for the length of the trial, assuming all issues remain in dispute. Unless there is good reason not to, the trial date will generally be fixed at the first CMC (although this may be more difficult at court centres with only one TCC judge). Therefore, to the extent that there are any relevant concerns as to availability of either witnesses or legal representatives, they need to be brought to the attention of the court on that occasion. The length of time fixed for the trial will depend on the parties' estimates, and also the judge's own view.

If the parties' estimate of trial length subsequently changes, they should inform the clerk of the assigned judge immediately.

5.4.2 The fixing of the trial date at the CMC is usually as a provisional fixture. Therefore no trial fee is payable at this stage. The court should at the same time specify a date upon which the fixture will cease to be "provisional" and, therefore, the trial fee will become payable. This should ordinarily be two months before the trial date. It should be noted that:

- if the trial fee is not paid within 14 days of the due date, then the whole claim will be struck out: see CPR rule 3.7(1)(a) and (4);
- if the court is notified at least 14 days before the trial date that the case is settled or discontinued, then the trial fee, which has been paid, shall be refunded: see fee 2.2 in Schedule 1 to the Civil Proceedings Fees Order 2004.

For all other purposes other than payment of the trial fee, the provisional date fixed at the CMC shall be regarded as a firm date.

5.4.3 Essentially, the judge's aim at the first CMC is to set down a detailed timetable which, in the majority of cases, will ensure that the parties need not return to court until the PTR.

### 5.5 Further Pleadings

5.5.1 Defence. If no defence has been served prior to the first CMC, then (except in cases where judgment in default is appropriate) the court will usually make an order for service of the defence within a specified period. The defendant must plead its positive case. Bare denials and non-admissions are, save in exceptional circumstances, unacceptable. 2C–70

5.5.2 Further Information. If the defendant wants to request further information of the Particulars of Claim, the request should, if possible, be formulated prior to the first CMC, so that it can be considered on that occasion. All requests for further information should be kept within reasonable limits, and concentrate on the important parts of the case.

5.5.3 Reply. A reply to the defence is not always necessary. However, where the defendant has raised a positive defence on a particular issue, it may be appropriate for the claimant to set out in a reply how it answers such a defence. If the defendant makes a counterclaim, the claimant's defence to counterclaim and its reply (if any) should be in the same document.

5.5.4 Part 20 Claims. The defendant should, at the first CMC, indicate (so far as possible) any Part 20 claims that it is proposing to make, whether against the claimant or any other party. Part 20 claims are required to be pleaded in the same detail as the original claim. They are a very common feature of TCC cases, because the widespread use of sub-contractors in the UK construction industry often makes it necessary to pass claims down a contractual chain. Defendants are encouraged to start any necessary Part 20 proceedings as soon as possible. It is undesirable for applications to join Part 20 defendants, to be made late in the proceedings.

***Paragraph numbers marked with a "+" can be found online and on CD.***

### 5.6 Scott Schedules

**2C–71** 5.6.1 It can sometimes be appropriate for elements of the claim, or any Part 20 claim, to be set out by way of a Scott Schedule. For example, claims involving a final account or numerous alleged defects or items of disrepair, may be best formulated in this way, which then allows for a detailed response from the defendant. Sometimes, even where all the damage has been caused by one event, such as a fire, it can be helpful for the individual items of loss and damage to be set out in a Scott Schedule. The secret of an effective Scott Schedule lies in the information that is to be provided. This is defined by the column headings. The judge may give directions for the relevant column headings for any Schedule ordered by the court. It is important that the defendant's responses to any such Schedule are as detailed as possible. Each party's entries on a Scott Schedule should be supported by a statement of truth.

5.6.2 Nevertheless, before any order is made or agreement is reached for the preparation of a Scott Schedule, both the parties and the court should consider whether this course (a) will genuinely lead to a saving of cost and time or (b) will lead to a wastage of costs and effort (because the Scott Schedule will simply duplicating earlier schedules, pleadings or expert reports). A Scott Schedule should only be ordered by the court, or agreed by the parties, in those cases where it is appropriate and proportionate.

5.6.3 When a Scott Schedule is ordered by the court or agreed by the parties, the format must always be specified. The parties must co-operate in the physical task of preparation. Electronic transfer between the parties of their respective entries in the columns will enable a clear and user-friendly Scott Schedule to be prepared, for the benefit of all involved in the trial.

### 5.7 Agreement Between the Parties

**2C–72** 5.7.1 Many, perhaps most, of the required directions at the first CMC may be agreed by the parties. If so, the judge will endeavour to make orders in the terms which have been agreed, unless he considers that the agreed terms fail to take into account important features of the case as a whole, or the principles of the CPR. The agreed terms will always, at the very least, form the starting-point of the judge's consideration of the orders to be made at the CMC. If the agreed terms are submitted to the judge 3 days in advance of the hearing date, it may be possible to avoid the need for a hearing altogether.

5.7.2 The approach outlined in paragraph 5.7.1 above is equally applicable to all other occasions when the parties come before the court with a draft order that is wholly or partly agreed.

### 5.8 Drawing Up of Orders

**2C–73** 5.8.1 Unless the court itself draws up the order, it will direct one party (usually the claimant or applicant) to do so within a specified time. That party must draw up the order and lodge it with the court for approval. Once approved, the order will be stamped by the court and returned to that party for service upon all other parties.

### 5.9 Further CMC

**2C–74** 5.9.1 In an appropriate case, the judge will fix a review CMC, to take place part way through the timetable that has been set down, in order to allow the court to review progress, and to allow the parties to raise any matters arising out of the steps that have been taken up to that point. This will not, however, be ordered automatically.

5.9.2 Each party will be required to give notice in writing to the other parties and the court of any order which it will be seeking at the review CMC, two days in advance of the hearing.

***Paragraph numbers marked with a "+" can be found online and on CD.***

### 5.10 The Permanent Case Management Bundle

5.10.1 In conjunction with the judge's clerk, the claimant's solicitor is responsible for ensuring that, for the first CMC and at all times thereafter, there is a permanent bundle of copy documents available to the judge, which contains: **2C–75**

- any relevant documents resulting from the Pre-Action Protocol;
- the claim form and all statements of case;
- all orders;
- all completed case management information sheets.

5.10.2 The permanent case management bundle can then be supplemented by the specific documents relevant to any particular application that may be made. Whether these supplementary documents should (a) become a permanent addition to the case management bundle or (b) be set on one side, will depend upon their nature. The permanent case management bundle may remain at court and be marked up by the judge; alternatively, the judge may direct that the permanent case management bundle be maintained at the offices of the claimant's solicitors and provided to the court when required.

## SECTION 6.

## APPLICATIONS AFTER THE FIRST CMC

### 6.1 Relevant parts of the CPR

6.1.1 The basic rules relating to all applications that any party may wish to make are set out in CPR Part 23 and its accompanying Practice Directions. **2C–76**

6.1.2 Part 7 of the Practice Direction accompanying CPR Part 60 is also of particular relevance.

### 6.2 Application Notice

6.2.1 As a general rule, any party to proceedings in the TCC wishing to make an application of any sort must file an application notice (rule 23.3) and serve that application notice on all relevant parties as soon as practicable after it has been filed (rule 23.4). Application notices should be served by the parties, unless (as happens in some court centres outside London) service is undertaken by the court. **2C–77**

6.2.2 The application notice must set out in clear terms what order is sought and, more briefly, the reasons for seeking that order: see rule 23.6.

6.2.3 The application notice must be served at least 3 days before the hearing at which the Court deals with the application: rule 23.7 (1). Such a short notice period is only appropriate for the most straight-forward type of application.

6.2.4 Most applications, in particular applications for summary judgment under CPR Part 24 or to strike out a statement of case under CPR rule 3.4, will necessitate a much longer notice period than 3 days. In such cases, it is imperative that the applicant obtain a suitable date and time for the hearing of the application from the assigned judge's clerk before the application notice is issued. The applicant must then serve his application notice and evidence in support sufficiently far ahead of the date fixed for the hearing of the application for there to be time to enable the respondent to serve evidence in response. Save in exceptional circumstances, there should be a minimum period of 10 working days between the service of the notice (and supporting evidence) and the hearing date. If any party considers that there is insufficient time before the hearing of the application or if the time estimate for the application itself is too short, that party must notify the Judge's clerk and the hearing may then be refixed by agreement.

6.2.5 When considering the application notice, the judge may give directions in writing as to the dates for the provision or exchange of evidence and any written submissions or skeleton arguments for the hearing.

***Paragraph numbers marked with a "+" can be found online and on CD.***

### 6.3 Evidence in Support

2C–78 6.3.1 The application notice when it is served must be accompanied by all evidence in support: rule 23.7 (2).

6.3.2 Unless the CPR expressly requires otherwise, evidence will be given by way of witness statements. Such statements must be verified by a statement of truth signed by the maker of the statement: rule 22.1.

### 6.4 Evidence in opposition and Evidence in reply

2C–79 6.4.1 Likewise, any evidence in opposition to the application should, unless the rules expressly provide otherwise, be given by way of witness statement verified by a statement of truth.

6.4.2 It is important to ensure that the evidence in opposition to the application is served in good time before the hearing so as to enable:

- the court to read and note up the evidence;
- the applicant to put in any further evidence in reply that may be considered necessary.

Such evidence should be served at least 5 working days before the hearing.

6.4.3 Any evidence in reply should be served not less than 3 working days before the hearing. Again, if there are disputes as to the time taken or to be taken for the preparation of evidence prior to a hearing, or any other matters in respect of a suitable timetable for that hearing, the court will consider the written positions of both parties and decide such disputes on paper. It will not normally be necessary for either a separate application to be issued or a hearing to be held for such a purpose.

6.4.4 If the hearing of an application has to be adjourned because of delays by one or other of the parties in serving evidence, the court is likely to order that party to pay the costs straight away, and to make a summary assessment of those costs.

### 6.5 Application Bundle

2C–80 6.5.1 The bundle for the hearing of anything other than the most simple and straightforward application should consist of:

- the permanent case management bundle (see Section 5.8 above);
- the witness statements provided in support of the application, together with any exhibits;
- the witness statements provided in opposition to the application together with exhibits;
- any witness statements in reply, together with exhibits.

6.5.2 The permanent case management bundle will either be with the court or with the claimant's solicitors, depending on the order made at the first CMC: see paragraph 5.9 above. If it is with the claimant's solicitors, it should be provided to the court not less than **2 working days** before the hearing. In any event, a paginated bundle (see paragraph 6.5.4 below) containing any material specific to the application should also be provided to the court not less than 2 working days before the hearing, unless otherwise directed by the judge. A failure to comply with this deadline may result in the adjournment of the hearing, and the costs thrown away being paid by the defaulting party.

6.5.3 In all but the simplest applications, the court will expect the parties to provide skeleton arguments and copies of any authorities to be relied on. The form and content of the skeleton argument is principally a matter for the author, although the judge will expect it to identify the issues that arise on the application, the important parts of the evidence relied on, and the applicable legal principles. For detailed guidance as to the form, content and length of skeleton arguments, please see paragraph 7.11.12 of the Queen's Bench Guide; Appendix 3 of the Chancery Guide; and Appendix 9 of the Commercial Court Guide.

6.5.4 For an application that is estimated to last ½ day or less, the skeleton should be provided no later than 1 pm on the last working day before the hearing. It should be accompanied by photocopies of the authorities relied on.

6.5.5 For an application that is estimated to last more than ½ day, the skeleton should be provided no later than 4 pm one clear working day before the hearing. It should be accompanied by photocopies of the authorities relied on.

6.5.6 The time limits at paragraphs 6.5.4 and 6.5.5 above will be regarded as the latest times by which such skeletons should be provided to the court. Save in exceptional circumstances, no extension to these periods will be permitted.

6.5.7 Pagination. It is generally necessary for there to be a paginated bundle for the hearing. Where the parties have produced skeleton arguments, these should be crossreferred to the bundle page numbers.

**6.6 Hearings**

6.6.1 Arbitration applications may be heard in private: see CPR rule 62.10. All other applications will be heard in public in accordance with CPR rule 39.2, save where otherwise ordered. **2C–81**

6.6.2 Provided that the application bundle and the skeletons have been lodged in accordance with the time limits set out above, the parties can assume that the court will have a good understanding of the points in issue. However, the court will expect to be taken to particular documents relied on by the parties and will also expect to be addressed on any important legal principles that arise.

6.6.3 It is important that the parties ensure that every application is dealt with in the estimated time period. Since many applications are dealt with on Fridays, it causes major disruption if application hearings are not disposed of within the estimated period. If the parties take too long in making their submissions, the application may be adjourned, part heard, and the Court may impose appropriate costs sanctions.

6.6.4 At the conclusion of the hearing, unless the court itself draws up the order, it will direct the applicant's solicitor to do so within a specified period.

**6.7 Paper Applications**

6.7.1 Contested applications are usually best disposed of at an oral hearing (either in court or by telephone). However, as noted in Section 4 above, some applications may be suitable for determination on paper. The procedure for dealing with paper applications is outlined in paragraph 4.4 above. **2C–82**

6.7.2 In addition, certain simple applications (particularly in lower value cases) arising out of the management of the proceedings may be capable of being dealt with by correspondence without the need for any formal application or order of the court. This is particularly true of applications to vary procedural orders, which variations are wholly or largely agreed, or proposals to vary the estimated length of the trial. In such cases, the applicant should write to the other parties indicating the nature of its application and to seek their agreement to it. If, however, it emerges that there is an issue to be resolved by the court, then a formal application must be issued and dealt with in the normal manner.

**6.8 Consent Orders**

6.8.1 Consent Orders may be submitted to the Court in draft for approval and initialling without the need for attendance. **2C–83**

6.8.2 Two copies of the draft order should be lodged, at least one of which should be signed. The copies should be undated.

*Paragraph numbers marked with a "+" can be found online and on CD.*

6.8.3 As noted above, whilst the parties can agree between themselves the orders to be made either at the Case Management Conference or the Pre-Trial Review, it is normally necessary for the Court to consider the case with the parties (either at an oral hearing or by way of a telephone conference) on those occasions in any event.

6.8.4 Generally, when giving directions, the court will endeavour to identify the date by which the relevant step must be taken, and will not simply provide a period during which that task should be performed. The parties should therefore ensure that any proposed consent order also identifies particular dates, rather then periods, by which the relevant steps must be taken.

#### 6.9 Costs

2C-84 6.9.1 Costs are dealt with generally at Section 16 below.

6.9.2 The costs of any application which took a day or less to be heard and disposed of will be dealt with summarily, unless there is a good reason for the court not to exercise its powers as to the summary assessment of costs.

6.9.3 Accordingly, it is necessary for parties to provide to the court and to one another their draft statements of costs no later than 24 hours before the start of the application hearing. Any costs which are incurred after these draft statements have been prepared, but which have not been allowed for (e.g. because the hearing has exceeded its anticipated length), can be mentioned at the hearing.

## SECTION 7.

## ADR

#### 7.1 General

2C-85 7.1.1 The court will provide encouragement to the parties to use alternative dispute resolution ("ADR") and will, whenever appropriate, facilitate the use of such a procedure. In this Guide, ADR is taken to mean any process through which the parties attempt to resolve their dispute, which is voluntary. In most cases, ADR takes the form of mediation conducted by a neutral mediator. Alternative forms of ADR include formal inter-party negotiations or (occasionally) early neutral evaluations. In an early neutral evaluation either a judge or some other neutral person receives a concise presentation from each party and then states his own evaluation of the case.

7.1.2 Although the TCC is an appropriate forum for the resolution of all IT and construction/engineering disputes, the use of ADR can lead to a significant saving of costs and may result in a settlement which is satisfactory to all parties.

7.1.3 Legal representatives in all TCC cases should ensure that their clients are fully aware of the benefits of ADR and that the use of ADR has been carefully considered prior to the first CMC.

#### 7.2 Timing

2C-86 7.2.1 ADR may be appropriate before the proceedings have begun or at any subsequent stage.

7.2.2 The TCC Pre-Action Protocol (Section 2 above) itself provides for a type of ADR, because it requires there to be at least one face-to-face meeting between the parties before the commencement of proceedings. At this meeting, there should be sufficient time to discuss and resolve the dispute. As a result of this procedure having taken place, the court will not necessarily grant a stay of proceedings upon demand and it will always need to be satisfied that an adjournment is actually necessary to enable ADR to take place.

7.2.3 However, at the first CMC, the court will want to be addressed on the parties' views as to the likely efficacy of ADR, the appropriate timing of ADR, and the advantages and disadvantages of a short stay of proceedings to allow ADR to take place. Having considered the representations of the parties, the court may order a short stay to facilitate ADR at that stage. Alternatively, the court may simply encourage the parties to seek ADR and allow for it to occur within the timetable for the resolution of the proceedings set down by the court.

7.2.4 At any stage after the first CMC and prior to the commencement of the trial, the court, will, either on its own initiative or if requested to do so by one or both of the parties, consider afresh the likely efficacy of ADR and whether or not a short stay of the proceedings should be granted, in order to facilitate ADR.

**7.3 Procedure**

7.3.1 In an appropriate case, the court may indicate the type of ADR that it considers suitable, but the decision in this regard must be made by the parties. In most cases, the appropriate ADR procedure will be mediation. **2C–87**

7.3.2 If at any stage in the proceedings the court considers it appropriate, an ADR order in the terms of Appendix E may be made. If such an order is made at the first CMC, the court may go on to give directions for the conduct of the action up to trial (in the event that the ADR fails). Such directions may include provision for a review CMC.

7.3.3 The court will not ordinarily recommend any individual or body to act as mediator or to perform any other ADR procedure. In the event that the parties fail to agree the identity of a mediator or other neutral person pursuant to an order in the terms of Appendix E, the court may select such a person from the lists provided by the parties. To facilitate this process, the court would also need to be furnished with the C.V's of each of the individuals on the lists.

7.3.4 Information as to the types of ADR procedures available and the individuals able to undertake such procedures is available from TeCSA, TECBAR, the Civil Mediation Council, and from some TCC court centres outside London.

**7.4 Non-Cooperation**

7.4.1 Generally. At the end of the trial, there may be costs arguments on the basis that one or more parties unreasonably refused to take part in ADR. The court will determine such issues having regard to all the circumstances of the particular case. In *Halsey v Milton Keynes General NHS Trust* [2004] EWCA Civ 576; [2004] 1 WLR 3002, the Court of Appeal identified six factors that may be relevant to any such consideration; **2C–88**

a) the nature of the dispute;
b) the merits of the case;
c) the extent to which other settlement methods have been attempted;
d) whether the costs of the ADR would be disproportionately high;
e) whether any delay in setting up and attending the ADR would have been prejudicial;
f) whether the ADR had a reasonable prospect of success.

7.4.2 If an ADR Order Has Been Made. The court will expect each party to co-operate fully with anyADR which takes place following an order of the court. If any other party considers that there has not been proper co-operation in relation to arrangements for the mediation, the complaint will be considered by the court and cost orders and/or other sanctions may be ordered against the defaulting party in consequence. However, nothing in this paragraph should be understood as modifying the rights of all parties to a mediation to keep confidential all that is said or done in the course of that mediation.

**7.5 Early Neutral Evaluation**

7.5.1 An early neutral evaluation ("ENE") may be carried out by any appropriately qualified person, whose opinion is likely to be respected by the parties. In an **2C–89** appropriate case, and with the consent of all parties, a TCC judge may provide an early neutral evaluation either in respect of the full case or of particular issues arising within it. Such an ENE will not, save with the agreement of the parties, be binding on the parties.

7.5.2 If the parties would like an ENE to be carried out by the court, then they can seek an appropriate order from the assigned judge either at the first CMC or at any time prior to the commencement of the trial.

7.5.3 The assigned judge may choose to do the ENE himself. In such instance, the judge will take no further part in the proceedings once he has produced the ENE, unless the parties expressly agree otherwise. Alternatively, the assigned judge will select another available TCC judge to undertake the ENE.

7.5.4 The judge undertaking the ENE will give appropriate directions for the preparation and conduct of the ENE. This may include a stay of the substantive proceedings whilst the ENE is carried out. The ENE may be carried out entirely on paper. Alternatively, there may be an oral hearing (either with or without evidence). The parties should agree whether the entire ENE procedure is to be without prejudice, or whether it can be referred to at any subsequent trial or hearing.

## SECTION 8.

## PRELIMINARY ISSUES

### 8.1 General

2C–90 8.1.1 The hearing of Preliminary Issues ("PI"), at which the court considers and delivers a binding judgment on particular issues in advance of the main trial, can be an extremely cost-effective and efficient way of narrowing the issues between the parties and, in certain cases, of resolving disputes altogether.

8.1.2 Some cases listed in the TCC lend themselves particularly well to this procedure. A PI hearing can address particular points which may be decisive of the whole proceedings; even if that is not the position, it is often possible for a PI hearing to cut down significantly on the scope (and therefore the costs) of the main trial.

8.1.3 At the first CMC the court will expect to be addressed on whether or not there are matters which should be taken by way of Preliminary Issues in advance of the main trial. Subject to paragraph 8.5 below, it is not generally appropriate for the court to make an order for the trial of preliminary issues until after the defence has been served. After the first CMC, and at any time during the litigation, any party is at liberty to raise with any other party the possibility of a PI hearing and the court will consider any application for the hearing of such Preliminary Issues. In many cases, although not invariably, a PI order will be made with the support of all parties.

8.1.4 Whilst, for obvious reasons, it is not possible to set out hard and fast rules for what is and what is not suitable for a PI hearing, the criteria set out in Section 8.2 below should assist the parties in deciding whether or not some or all of the disputes between them will be suitable for a PI hearing.

8.1.5 Drawbacks of preliminary issues in inappropriate cases. If preliminary issues are ordered inappropriately, they can have adverse effect. Evidence may be duplicated. The same witnesses may give evidence before different judges, in the event that there is a switch of assigned judge. Findings may be made at the PI hearing, which are affected by evidence called at the main hearing. The prospect of a PI hearing may delay the commencement of ADR or settlement negotiations. Also two trials are more expensive than one. For all these reasons, any proposal for preliminary issues needs to be examined carefully, so that the benefits and drawbacks can be evaluated. Also the court should give due weight to the views of the parties when deciding whether a PI hearing would be beneficial.

*Paragraph numbers marked with a "+" can be found online and on CD.*

8.1.6 Staged trials. The breaking down of a long trial into stages should be differentiated from the trial of preliminary issues. Sometimes it is sensible for liability (including causation) to be tried before quantum of damages. Occasionally the subject matter of the litigation is so extensive that for reasons of case management the trial needs to be broken down into separate stages.

**8.2 Guidelines**

8.2.1 The Significance of the Preliminary Issues. The court would expect that any issue proposed as a suitable PI would, if decided in a particular way, be capable of: **2C–91**

- resolving the whole proceedings or a significant element of the proceedings; or
- significantly reducing the scope, and therefore the costs, of the main trial; or
- significantly improving the possibility of a settlement of the whole proceedings.

8.2.2 Oral Evidence. The court would ordinarily expect that, if issues are to be dealt with by way of a PI hearing, there would be either no or relatively limited oral evidence. If extensive oral evidence was required on any proposed PI, then it may not be suitable for a PI hearing. Although it is difficult to give specific guidance on this point, it is generally considered that a PI hearing in a smaller case should not take more than about 2 days, and in a larger and more complex case, should not take more than about 4 days.

**8.3 Common Types of Preliminary Issue**

The following are commonly resolved by way of a PI hearing: **2C–92**

(a) Disputes as to whether or not there was a binding contract between the parties.
(b) Disputes as to what documents make up or are incorporated within the contract between the parties and disputes as to the contents or relevance of any conversations relied on as having contractual status or effect.
(c) Disputes as to the proper construction of the contract documents or the effect of an exclusion or similar clause.
(d) Disputes as to the correct application of a statute or binding authority to a situation where there is little or no factual dispute.
(e) Disputes as to the existence and/or scope of a statutory duty.
(f) Disputes as to the existence and/or scope of a duty of care at common law in circumstances where there is no or little dispute about the relevant facts.

**8.4 Other Possible Preliminary Issues**

The following can sometimes be resolved by way of a preliminary issue hearing, although a decision as to whether or not to have such a hearing will always depend on the facts of the individual case: **2C–93**

8.4.1 A Limitation Defence. It is often tempting to have limitation issues resolved in advance of the main trial. This can be a good idea because, if a complex claim is statutebarred, a decision to that effect will lead to a significant saving of costs. However, there is also a risk that extensive evidence relevant to the limitation defence (relating to matters such as when the damage occurred or whether or not there has been deliberate concealment) may also be relevant to the liability issues within the main trial. In such a case, a preliminary issue hearing may lead to a) extensive duplication of evidence and therefore costs and b) give rise to difficulty if the main trial is heard by a different judge.

8.4.2 Causation and 'No Loss' Points. Causation and 'No Loss' points may be suitable for a PI hearing, but again their suitability will diminish if it is necessary for the court to resolve numerous factual disputes as part of the proposed PI hearing. The most appropriate disputes of this type for a PI hearing are those where the defendant contends that, even accepting all the facts alleged by the claimant, the claim must fail by reason of causation or the absence of recoverable loss.

8.4.3 'One-Off' Issues. Issues which do not fall into any obvious category, like economic duress, or misrepresentation, may be suitable for resolution by way of a PI hearing, particularly if the whole case can be shown to turn on them.

### 8.5 Use of PI as an adjunct to ADR

2C-94 8.5.1 Sometimes parties wish to resolve their dispute by ADR, but there is one major issue which is a sticking point in any negotiation or mediation. The parties may wish to obtain the court's decision on that single issue, in the expectation that after that they can resolve their differences without further litigation.

8.5.2 In such a situation the parties may wish to bring proceedings under CPR Part 8, in order to obtain the court's decision on that issue. Such proceedings can be rapidly progressed. Alternatively, if the issue is not suitable for Part 8 proceedings, the parties may bring proceedings under Part 7 and then seek determination of the critical question as a preliminary issue. At the first CMC the position can be explained and the judge can be asked to order early trial of the proposed preliminary issue, possibly without the need for a defence or any further pleadings.

### 8.6 Precise Wording of PI

2C-95 8.6.1 If a party wishes to seek a PI hearing, either at the first CMC or thereafter, that party must circulate a precise draft of the proposed preliminary issues to the other parties and to the court well in advance of the relevant hearing.

8.6.2 If the court orders a PI hearing, it is likely to make such an order only by reference to specific and formulated issues, in order to avoid later debate as to the precise scope of the issues that have been ordered. Of course, the parties are at liberty to propose amendments to the issues before the PI hearing itself, but if such later amendments are not agreed by all parties, they are unlikely to be ordered.

### 8.7 Appeals

2C-96 8.7.1 When considering whether or not to order a PI hearing, the court will take into account the effect of any possible appeal against the PI judgment, and the concomitant delay caused.

8.7.2 At the time of ordering preliminary issues, both the parties and the court should specifically consider whether, in the event of an appeal against the PI judgment, it is desirable that the trial of the main action should (a) precede or (b) follow such appeal. It should be noted, however, that the first instance court has no power to control the timetable for an appeal. A first instance court's power to extend time under CPR rule 52.4(2)(a) for filing an appellant's notice is effectively limited to 14 days (see paragraph 5.19 of the Practice direction supplementing Part 52). The question whether an appeal should be (a) expedited or (b) stayed is entirely a matter for the Court of Appeal. Nevertheless, the Court of Appeal will take notice of any "indication" given by the lower court in this regard.

## SECTION 9.

## ADJUDICATION BUSINESS

### 9.1 Introduction

2C-97 9.1.1 The TCC is ordinarily the court in which the enforcement of an adjudicator's decision and any other business connected with adjudication is undertaken. Adjudicators' decisions predominantly arise out of adjudications which are governed by the mandatory provisions of the Housing Grants, Construction and Regeneration Act 1996 ("HGCRA"). These provisions apply automatically to any construction contract as defined in the legislation. Some Adjudicators' decisions arise out of standard form contracts which contain adjudication provisions, and others arise from ad-hoc agreements to adjudicate. The TCC enforcement procedure is the same for all three kinds of adjudication.

9.1.2 In addition to enforcement applications, declaratory relief is sometimes sought in the TCC at the outset of an adjudication in respect of matters such as the jurisdiction of the adjudicator or the validity of the adjudication. This kind of application is dealt with in Paragraph 9.4 below.

9.1.3 The HGCRA provides for a mandatory 28-day period within which the entire adjudication process must be completed, unless a) the referring party agrees to an additional 14 days, or b) both parties agree to a longer period. In consequence, the TCC has moulded a rapid procedure for enforcing an adjudication decision that has not been honoured. Other adjudication proceedings are ordinarily subject to similar rapidity.

### 9.2 Procedure In Enforcement Proceedings

9.2.1 Unlike arbitration business, there is neither a practice direction nor a claim form concerned with adjudication business. The enforcement proceedings normally seek a monetary judgment so that CPR Part 7 proceedings are usually appropriate. However, if the enforcement proceedings are known to raise a question which is unlikely to involve a substantial dispute of fact and no monetary judgment is sought, CPR Part 8 proceedings may be used instead. **2C–98**

9.2.2 The TCC has fashioned a procedure whereby enforcement applications are dealt with promptly. The details of this procedure are set out below.

9.2.3 The claim form should identify the construction contract, the jurisdiction of the adjudicator, the procedural rules under which the adjudication was conducted, the adjudicator's decision, the relief sought and the grounds for seeking that relief.

9.2.4 The claim form should be accompanied by an application notice that sets out the procedural directions that are sought. Commonly, the claimant's application will seek an abridgement of time for the various procedural steps, and summary judgment under CPR Part 24. The claim form and the application should be accompanied by a witness statement or statements setting out the evidence relied on in support of both the adjudication enforcement claim and the associated procedural application. This evidence should ordinarily include a copy of the adjudicator's decision.

9.2.5 The claim form, application notice and accompanying documents should be lodged in the appropriate registry or court centre clearly marked as being a "paper without notice adjudication enforcement claim and application for the urgent attention of a TCC judge". The parties will be informed that the enforcement proceedings will be assigned to a named judge. That judge will then manage the proceedings up to and including any hearing. He will ordinarily provide his directions made in connection with the procedural application within 3 working days of the receipt of the application notice at the courts.

9.2.6 The procedural application is dealt with by a TCC judge on paper, without notice. The paper application and the consequent directions should deal with:

(a) the abridged period of time in which the defendant is to file an acknowledgement of service;
(b) the time for service by the defendant of any witness statement in opposition to the relief being sought;
(c) an early return date for the hearing of the summary judgment application and a note of the time required or allowed for that hearing; and
(d) identification of the judgment, order or other relief being sought at the hearing of the adjudication claim.

The order made at this stage will always give the defendant liberty to apply.

9.2.7 A direction providing for a date by which the claim form, supporting evidence and court order providing for the hearing are to be served on the defendant should ordinarily also be given when the judge deals with the paper procedural application.

***Paragraph numbers marked with a "+" can be found online and on CD.***

9.2.8 The directions will ordinarily provide for an enforcement hearing within 28 days of the directions being made and for the defendant to be given at least 14 days from the date of service for the serving of any evidence in opposition to the adjudication application. In more straightforward cases, the abridged periods may be less.

9.2.9 Draft standard directions of the kind commonly made by the court on a procedural application by the claimant in an action to enforce the decision of an adjudicator are attached as Appendix F.

9.2.10 The claimant should, with the application, provide an estimate of the time needed for the hearing of the application. This estimate will be taken into account by the judge when fixing the date and length of the hearing. The parties should, if possible jointly, communicate any revised time estimate to the court promptly and the judge to whom the case has been allocated will consider whether to refix the hearing date or alter the time period that has been allocated for the hearing.

9.2.11 If the parties cannot agree on the date or time fixed for the hearing, a paper application must be made to the judge to whom the hearing has been allocated for directions.

**9.3 The Enforcement Hearing**

**2C–99** 9.3.1 Where there is any dispute to be resolved at the hearing, the judge should be provided with copies of the relevant sections of the HGCRA, the adjudication procedural rules under which the adjudication was conducted, the adjudicator's decision and copies of any adjudication provisions in the contract underlying the adjudication.

9.3.2 Subject to any more specific directions given by the court, the parties should lodge, by 4.00 p.m. one clear working day before the hearing, a bundle containing the documents that will be required at the hearing and copies of any authorities which are to be relied on. The parties should also file and serve short skeleton arguments, summarising their respective contentions as to why the adjudicator's decision is or is not enforceable or as to any other relief being sought. For a hearing that is expected to last half a day or less, the skeletons should be provided no later than 1 p.m. on the last working day before the hearing. For a hearing that is estimated to last more than half a day, the skeletons should be provided no later than 4 p.m. one clear working day before the hearing.

9.3.3 The parties should be ready to address the court on the limited grounds on which a defendant may resist an application seeking to enforce an adjudicator's decision or on which a court may provide any other relief to any party in relation to an adjudication or an adjudicator's decision.

**9.4 Other Proceedings Arising Out Of Adjudication**

**2C–100** 9.4.1 As noted above, the TCC will also hear any applications for declaratory relief arising out of the commencement of a disputed adjudication. Commonly, these will concern:

a) Disputes over the jurisdiction of an adjudicator. It can sometimes be appropriate to seek a declaration as to jurisdiction at the outset of an adjudication, rather than both parties incurring considerable costs in the adjudication itself, only for the jurisdiction point to emerge again at the enforcement hearing.
b) Disputes over whether there is a written contract between the parties or, in appropriate cases, whether there is a construction contract within the meaning of the Act.
c) Disputes over the permissible scope of the adjudication, and, in particular, whether the matters which the claimant seeks to raise in the adjudication are the subject of a pre-existing dispute between the parties.

9.4.2 Any such application will be immediately assigned to a named judge. In such circumstances, given the probable urgency of the application, the judge will usually require the parties to attend a CMC within 2 working days of the assignment of the case to him, and he will then give the necessary directions to ensure the speedy resolution of the dispute.

9.4.3 It sometimes happens that one party to an adjudication commences enforcement proceedings, whilst the other commences proceedings under Part 8, in order to challenge the validity of the adjudicator's award. This duplication of effort is unnecessary and it involves the parties in extra costs, especially if the two actions are commenced at different court centres. Accordingly there should be sensible discussions between the parties or their lawyers, in order to agree the appropriate venue and also to agree who shall be claimant and who defendant. All the issues raised by each party can and should be raised in a single action.

## SECTION 10.

## ARBITRATION

### 10.1 Arbitration Claims in the TCC

10.1.1 "Arbitration claims" are any application to the court under the Arbitration Act 1996 and any other claim concerned with an arbitration that is referred to in CPR 62.2(1). Common examples of arbitration claims are challenges to an award on grounds of jurisdiction under section 67, challenges to an award for serious irregularity under section 68 or appeals on points of law under section 69 of the Arbitration Act 1996. Arbitration claims may be started in the TCC, as is provided for in paragraph 2.3 of the Practice Direction—Arbitration which supplements CPR Part 62. **2C–101**

10.1.2 In practice, arbitration claims arising out of or connected with a construction or engineering arbitration (or any other arbitration where the subject matter involved one or more of the categories of work set out in paragraph 1.3.1 above) should be started in the TCC. The only arbitration claims that must be started in the Commercial Court are those (increasingly rare) claims to which the old law (i.e. the pre-1996 Act provisions) apply: see CPR rule 62.12.

10.1.3 The TCC follows the practice and procedure for arbitration claims established by CPR Part 62 and (broadly) the practice of the Commercial Court as summarised by Section O of the *Admiralty and Commercial Courts Guide*. In the absence of any specific directions given by the court, the automatic directions set out in section 6 of the Practice Direction supplementing CPR Part 62 govern the procedures to be followed in any arbitration claim from the date of service up to the substantive hearing.

### 10.2 Leave to appeal

10.2.1 Where a party is seeking to appeal a question of law arising out of an award pursuant to section 69 of the Arbitration Act 1996 and the parties have not in their underlying contract agreed that such an appeal may be brought, the party seeking to appeal must apply for leave to appeal pursuant to sections 69(2), 69(3) and 69(4) of that Act. That application must be included in the arbitration claim form as explained in paragraph 12 of the Practice Direction. **2C–102**

10.2.2 In conformity with the practice of the Commercial Court, the TCC will normally consider any application for permission to appeal on paper after the defendant has had an appropriate opportunity to answer in writing the application being raised.

10.2.3 The claimant must include within the claim form an application for permission to appeal. No separate application notice is required.

10.2.4 The claim form and supporting documents must be served on the defendant. The judge will not consider the application for permission to appeal until (a) a

***Paragraph numbers marked with a "+" can be found online and on CD.***

certificate of service has been filed at the appropriate TCC registry or court centre and (b) a further 28 days have elapsed, so as to enable the defendant to file written evidence in opposition. Save in exceptional circumstances, the only material admissible on an application for permission to appeal is (a) the award itself and any documents annexed to the award and (b) evidence relevant to the issue whether any identified question of law is of general public importance.

10.2.5 If necessary, the judge dealing with the application will direct an oral hearing with a date for the hearing. That hearing will, ordinarily, consist of brief submissions by each party. The judge dealing with the application will announce his decision in writing or, if a hearing has been directed, at the conclusion of the hearing with brief reasons if the application is refused.

10.2.6 Where the permission has been allowed in part and refused in part:

(a) Only those questions for which permission has been granted may be raised at the hearing of the appeal.

(b) Brief reasons will be given for refusing permission in respect of the other questions.

10.2.7 If the application is granted, the judge will fix the date for the appeal, and direct whether the same judge or a different judge shall hear the appeal.

**10.3 Appeals where leave to appeal is not required**

**2C-103** 10.3.1 Parties to a construction contract should check whether they have agreed in the underlying contract that an appeal may be brought without leave, since some construction and engineering standard forms of contract so provide. If that is the case, the appeal may be set down for a substantive hearing without leave being sought. The arbitration claim form should set out the clause or provision which it is contended provides for such agreement and the claim form should be marked "Arbitration Appeal—Leave not required".

10.3.2 Where leave is not required, the claimant should identify each question of law that it is contended arises out of the award and which it seeks to raise in an appeal under section 69. If the defendant does not accept that the questions thus identified are questions of law or maintains that they do not arise out of the award or that the appeal on those questions may not be brought for any other reason, then the defendant should notify the claimant and the court of its contentions and apply for a directions hearing before the judge nominated to hear the appeal on a date prior to the date fixed for the hearing of the appeal. Unless the judge hearing the appeal otherwise directs, the appeal will be confined to the questions of law identified in the arbitration claim form.

10.3.3 In an appropriate case, the judge may direct that the question of law to be raised and decided on the appeal should be reworded, so as to identify more accurately the real legal issue between the parties.

**10.4 The hearing of the appeal**

**2C-104** 10.4.1 Parties should ensure that the court is provided only with material that is relevant and admissible to the point of law. This will usually be limited to the award and any documents annexed to the award: see *Hok Sport Ltd v Aintree Racecourse Ltd* [2003] BLR 155 at 160. However, the court should also receive any document referred to in the award, which the court needs to read in order to determine a question of law arising out of the award: see *Kershaw Mechanical Services Ltd v Kendrick Construction Ltd* [2006] EWHC 727 (TCC).

10.4.2 On receiving notice of permission being granted, or on issuing an arbitration claim form in a case where leave to appeal is not required, the parties should notify the court of their joint estimate or differing estimates of the time needed for the hearing of the appeal.

10.4.3 The hearing of the appeal is to be in open court unless an application (with notice) has previously been made that the hearing should be wholly or in part held in private and the court has directed that this course should be followed.

**10.5 Section 68 applications—Serious Irregularity**

10.5.1 In some arbitration claims arising out of construction and engineering arbitrations, a party will seek to appeal a question of law and, at the same time, seek to challenge the award under section 68 of the Arbitration Act 1996 on the grounds of serious irregularity. This raises questions of procedure, since material may be admissible in a section 68 application which is inadmissible on an application or appeal under section 69. Similarly, it may not be appropriate for all applications to be heard together. A decision is needed as to the order in which the applications should be heard, whether there should be one or more separate hearings to deal with them and whether or not the same judge should deal with all applications. Where a party intends to raise applications under both sections of the Arbitration Act 1996, they should be issued in the same arbitration claim form or in separate claim forms issued together. The court should be informed that separate applications are intended and asked for directions as to how to proceed. **2C–105**

10.5.2 The court will give directions as to how the section 68 and section 69 applications will be dealt with before hearing or determining any application. These directions will normally be given in writing but, where necessary or if such is applied for by a party, the court will hold a directions hearing at which directions will be given. The directions will be given following the service of any documentation by the defendant in answer to all applications raised by the claimant.

**10.6 Successive awards and successive applications**

10.6.1 Some construction and engineering arbitrations give rise to two or more separate awards issued at different times. Where arbitration applications arise under more than one of these awards, any second or subsequent application, whether arising from the same or a different award, should be referred to the same judge who has heard previous applications. Where more than one judge has heard previous applications, the court should be asked to direct to which judge any subsequent application is to be referred. **2C–106**

**10.7 Other applications and Enforcement**

10.7.1 All other arbitration claims, and any other matter arising in an appeal or an application concerning alleged serious irregularity, will be dealt with by the TCC in the same manner as is provided for in CPR Part 62, Practice Direction—Arbitration and Section O of *The Admiralty and Commercial Courts Guide*. **2C–107**

10.7.2 All applications for permission to enforce arbitration awards are governed by Section III of Part 62 (rules 62.17–62.19).

10.7.3 An application for permission to enforce an award in the same manner as a judgment or order of the court may be made in an arbitration claim form without notice and must be supported by written evidence in accordance with rule 62.18(6). Two copies of the draft order must accompany the application, and the form of the order sought must correspond to the terms of the award.

10.7.4 An order made without notice giving permission to enforce the award:

(a) must give the defendant 14 days after service of the order (or longer, if the order is to be served outside the jurisdiction) to apply to set it aside;

(b) must state that it may not be enforced until after the expiry of the 14 days (or any longer period specified) or until any application to set aside the order has been finally disposed of: rule 62.18(9) and (10).

10.7.5 On considering an application to enforce without notice, the judge may direct that, instead, the arbitration claim form must be served on specified parties, with the result that the application will then continue as an arbitration claim in accordance with the procedure set out in Section I of Part 62: see rule 62.18(1)–(3).

***Paragraph numbers marked with a "+" can be found online and on CD.***

## SECTION 11.
## DISCLOSURE

### 11.1 Standard Disclosure

2C–108 11.1.1 The appropriate disclosure and inspection orders to be made will normally be considered and made at the first case management conference. This is governed by CPR Part 31 and the Practice Direction supplementing it. This procedure provides for standard disclosure, being disclosure and inspection in accordance with CPR Part 31 of:

(a) the documents upon which a party relies;
(b) the documents which adversely affect his or another party's case or support another party's case; and
(c) the documents which a party is required to disclose by any relevant practice direction.

### 11.2 Limiting disclosure and the cost of disclosure

2C–109 11.2.1 In many cases being conducted in the TCC, standard disclosure will not be appropriate. This may for any one or more of the following reasons:

(a) The amount of documentation may be considerable, given the complexity of the dispute and the underlying contract or contracts, and the process of giving standard disclosure may consequently be disproportionate to the issues and sums in dispute.
(b) The parties may have many of the documents in common from their previous dealings so that disclosure is not necessary or desirable.
(c) The parties may have provided informal disclosure and inspection of the majority of these documents, for example when complying with the pre-action Protocol.
(d) The cost of providing standard disclosure may be disproportionate.

In such cases, the parties should seek to agree upon a more limited form of disclosure or to dispense with formal disclosure altogether. Such an agreement could limit disclosure to specified categories of documents or to such documents as may be specifically applied for.

11.2.2 Where disclosure is to be provided, the parties should consider whether it is necessary for lists of documents to be prepared or whether special arrangements should be agreed as to the form of listing and identifying disclosable documents, the method, timing and location of inspection and the manner of copying or providing copies of documents. Where documents are scattered over several locations, or are located overseas or are in a foreign language, special arrangements will also need to be considered. Thought should also be given to providing disclosure in stages or to reducing the scope of disclosure by providing the relevant material in other forms.

11.2.3 Electronic data and documents give rise to particular problems as to searching, preserving, listing, inspecting and other aspects of discovery and inspection. These problems should be considered and, if necessary made the subject of special directions. Furthermore, in appropriate cases, disclosure, inspection and the provision of copies of hard copies may be undertaken using information technology. Attention is drawn to the relevant provisions in CPR Part 31, to *the Admiralty and Commercial Courts Guide* concerned with Electronic Disclosure, and to the TeCSA IT Protocol which provide guidance in relation to these matters. In appropriate cases the TCC will order that the provisions concerning electronic disclosure contained in section E of *the Admiralty and Commercial Courts Guide* shall apply.

11.2.4 All these matters should be agreed between the parties. If it is necessary to raise any of these matters with the court they should be raised, if possible, at the first

CMC. If points arise on disclosure after the first CMC, they may well be capable of being dealt with by the court on paper.

### 11.3 Service using information technology

11.3.1 The parties should consult with each other before the first CMC with a view to arranging the service and (where required) filing of pleadings, schedules, witness statements, experts' reports, disclosure lists and other documents in computer readable form as well as in hard copy. The parties should also consider whether to maintain a common running index, so that every document which has been exchanged between the parties has a unique reference number. Any agreement reached on these matters should be recorded and made the subject of an order for directions. Where agreement is not possible, the parties should raise these matters for decision at a CMC. **2C–110**

## SECTION 12.

## WITNESS STATEMENTS AND FACTUAL EVIDENCE FOR USE AT TRIAL

### 12.1 Witness statements

12.1.1 Witness statements should be prepared generally in accordance with CPR Part 22.1 (documents verified by a statement of truth) and CPR Part 32 (provisions governing the evidence of witnesses) and their practice directions, particularly paragraphs 17 to 22 of the Practice Direction supplementing CPR Part 32. **2C–111**

12.1.2 Unless otherwise directed by the court, witness statements should not have annexed to them copies of other documents and should not reproduce or paraphrase at length passages from other documents. The only exception arises where a specific document needs to be annexed to the statement in order to make that statement reasonably intelligible.

12.1.3 When preparing witness statements, attention should be paid to the following matters:

(a) Even when prepared by a legal representative or other professional, the witness statement should be, so far as practicable, in the witness's own words.
(b) The witness statement should indicate which matters are within the witness's own knowledge and which are matters of information and belief. Where the witness is stating matters of hearsay or of either information or belief, the source of that evidence should also be stated.
(c) The witness statement must include a statement by the witness that he believes the facts stated to be true.
(d) A witness statement should be no longer than necessary and should not be argumentative.

### 12.2 Other matters concerned with witness statements

12.2.1 Foreign language. If a witness is not sufficiently fluent in English to give his evidence in English, the witness statement should be in his or her own language and an authenticated translation provided. Where the witness has a broken command of English, the statement may be drafted by others so as to express the witness's evidence as accurately as possible. In that situation, however, the witness statement should indicate that this process of interpolation has occurred and also should explain the extent of the witness's command of English and how and to what parts of the witness statement the process of interpolation has occurred. **2C–112**

12.2.2 Reluctant witness. Sometimes a witness is unwilling or not permitted or is unavailable to provide a witness statement before the trial. The party seeking to adduce this evidence should comply with the provisions of CPR rule 32.9 concerned with the provision of witness summaries.

12.2.3 Hearsay. Parties should keep in mind the need to give appropriate notice of their intention to rely on hearsay evidence or the contents of documents without serving a witness statement from their maker or from the originator of the evidence contained in those documents. The appropriate procedure is contained in CPR rules 33.1–33.5.

#### 12.3 Cross-referencing

2C-113 12.3.1 Where a substantial number of documents will be adduced in evidence or contained in the trial bundles, it is of considerable assistance to the court and to all concerned if the relevant page references are annotated in the margins of the copy witness statements. It is accepted that this is a time-consuming exercise, the need for which will be considered at the PTR, and it will only be ordered where it is both appropriate and proportionate to do so. See further paragraphs 14.5.1 and 15.2.3 below.

#### 12.4 Video link

2C-114 12.4.1 If any witness (whose witness statement has been served and who is required to give oral evidence) is located outside England and Wales or would find a journey to court inconvenient or impracticable, his evidence might be given via a video link. Thought should be given before the PTR to the question whether this course would be appropriate and proportionate. Such evidence is regularly received by the TCC and facilities for its reception, whether in appropriate court premises or at a convenient venue outside the court building, are now readily available.

12.4.2 Any application for a video link direction and any question relating to the manner in which such evidence is to be given should be dealt with at the PTR. Attention is drawn to the Video-conferencing Protocol set out at Annex 3 to the Practice Direction—Witness Evidence. The procedure described in Annex 3 is followed by the TCC.

## SECTION 13.

## EXPERT EVIDENCE

#### 13.1 Nature of expert evidence

2C-115 13.1.1 Expert evidence is evidence as to matters of a technical or scientific nature and will generally include the opinions of the expert. The quality and reliability of expert evidence will depend upon (a) the experience and the technical or scientific qualifications of the expert and (b) the accuracy of the factual material that is used by the expert for his assessment. Expert evidence is dealt with in detail in CPR Part 35 ("Experts and Assessors") and in the Practice Direction supplementing Part 35. Particular attention should be paid to all these provisions, given the detailed reliance on expert evidence in most TCC actions. Particular attention should also be paid to the "Protocol for the instruction of experts to give evidence in civil claims" published by the Civil Justice Council in June 2005. This protocol has been approved by the Master of the Rolls.

13.1.2 The provisions in CPR Part 35 are concerned with the terms upon which the court may receive expert evidence. These provisions are principally applicable to independently instructed expert witnesses. In cases where a party is a professional or a professional has played a significant part in the subject matter of the action, opinion evidence will almost inevitably be included in the witness statements. Any points arising from such evidence (if they cannot be resolved by agreement) can be dealt with by the judge on an application or at the PTR.

#### 13.2 Control of expert evidence

2C-116 13.2.1 Expert evidence is frequently needed and used in TCC cases. Experts are often appointed at an early stage. Most types of case heard in the TCC involve more than one expertise and some, even when the dispute is concerned with relatively

*Paragraph numbers marked with a "+" can be found online and on CD.*

small sums, involve several different experts. Such disputes include those concerned with building failures and defects, delay and disruption, dilapidations, subsidence caused by tree roots and the supply of software systems. However, given the cost of preparing such evidence, the parties and the court must, from the earliest pre-action phase of a dispute until the conclusion of the trial, seek to make effective and proportionate use of experts. The scope of any expert evidence must be limited to what is necessary for the requirements of the particular case.

13.2.2 At the first CMC, or thereafter, the court may be asked to determine whether the cost of instructing experts is proportionate to the amount at issue in the proceedings, and the importance of the case to the parties. In dealing with any issues of proportionality, the court should be provided with estimates of the experts' costs.

13.2.3 The parties should also be aware that the court has the power to limit the amount of the expert's fees that a party may recover pursuant to CPR 35.4(4).

### 13.3 Prior to and at the first CMC

13.3.1 There is an unresolved tension arising from the need for parties to instruct and rely on expert opinions from an early pre-action stage and the need for the court to seek, wherever possible, to reduce the cost of expert evidence by dispensing with it altogether or by encouraging the appointment of jointly instructed experts. This tension arises because the court can only consider directing joint appointments or limiting expert evidence long after a party may have incurred the cost of obtaining expert evidence and have already relied on it. Parties should be aware of this tension. So far as possible, the parties should avoid incurring the costs of expert evidence on uncontroversial matters or matters of the kind referred to in paragraph 13.4.3 below, before the first CMC has been held. **2C–117**

13.3.2 In cases where it is not appropriate for the court to order a single joint expert, it is imperative that, wherever possible, the parties' experts co-operate fully with one another. This is particularly important where tests, surveys, investigations, sample gathering or other technical methods of obtaining primary factual evidence are needed. It is often critical to ensure that any laboratory testing or experiments are carried out by the experts together, pursuant to an agreed procedure. Alternatively, the respective experts may agree that a particular firm or laboratory shall carry out specified tests or analyses on behalf of all parties.

13.3.3 Parties should, where possible, disclose initial or preliminary reports to opposing parties prior to any pre-action protocol meeting, if only on a without prejudice basis. Such early disclosure will assist in early settlement or mediation discussions and in helping the parties to define and confine the issues in dispute with a corresponding saving in costs.

13.3.4 Before and at the first CMC and at each subsequent pre-trial stage of the action, the parties should give careful thought to the following matters:

(a) The number, disciplines and identity of the expert witnesses they are considering instructing as their own experts or as single joint experts.
(b) The precise issues which each expert is to address in his/her reports, to discuss without prejudice with opposing parties' experts and give evidence about at the trial.
(c) The timing of any meeting, agreed statement or report.
(d) Any appropriate or necessary tests, inspections, sampling or investigations that could be undertaken jointly or in collaboration with other experts. Any such measures should be preceded by a meeting of relevant experts at which an appropriate testing or other protocol is devised. This would cover (i) all matters connected with the process in question and its recording and (ii) the sharing and agreement of any resulting data or evidence.
(e) Any common method of analysis, investigation or reporting where it is appropriate or proportionate that such should be adopted by all relevant experts. An example of this would be an agreement as to the method to be used to ana-

lyse the cause and extent of any relevant period of delay in a construction project, where such is in issue in the case.

(f) The availability and length of time that experts will realistically require to complete the tasks assigned to them.

13.3.5 In so far as the matters set out in the previous paragraph cannot be agreed, the court will give appropriate directions. In giving permission for the reception of any expert evidence, the court will ordinarily order the exchange of such evidence, with a definition of the expert's area of expertise and a clear description of the issues about which that expert is permitted to give evidence. It is preferable that, at the first CMC or as soon as possible thereafter, the parties should provide the court with the name(s) of their expert(s).

**13.4 Single joint experts**

**2C–118** 13.4.1 An order may be made, at the first CMC or thereafter, that a single joint expert should address particular issues between the parties. Such an order would be made pursuant to CPR Parts 35.7 and 35.8.

13.4.2 Single joint experts are not usually appropriate for the principal liability disputes in a large case, or in a case where considerable sums have been spent on an expert in the pre-action stage. They are generally inappropriate where the issue involves questions of risk assessment or professional competence.

13.4.3 On the other hand, single joint experts can often be appropriate:

(a) in low value cases, where technical evidence is required but the cost of adversarial expert evidence may be prohibitive;

(b) where the topic with which the single joint expert's report deals is a separate and self-contained part of the case, such as the valuation of particular heads of claim;

(c) where there is a subsidiary issue, which requires particular expertise of a relatively uncontroversial nature to resolve;

(d) where testing or analysis is required, and this can conveniently be done by one laboratory or firm on behalf of all parties.

13.4.4 Where a single joint expert is to be appointed or is to be directed by the court, the parties should attempt to devise a protocol covering all relevant aspects of the appointment (save for those matters specifically provided for by CPR rules 35.6, 35.7 and 35.8).

13.4.5 The matters to be considered should include: any ceiling on fees and disbursements that are to be charged and payable by the parties; how, when and by whom fees will be paid to the expert on an interim basis pending any costs order in the proceedings; how the expert's fees will be secured; how the terms of reference are to be agreed; what is to happen if terms of reference cannot be agreed; how and to whom the jointly appointed expert may address further enquiries and from whom he should seek further information and documents; the timetable for preparing any report or for undertaking any other preparatory step; the possible effect on such timetable of any supplementary or further instructions. Where these matters cannot be agreed, an application to the court, which may often be capable of being dealt with as a paper application, will be necessary.

13.4.6 The usual procedure for a single joint expert will involve:

(a) The preparation of the expert's instructions. These instructions should clearly identify those issues or matters where the parties are in conflict, whether on the facts or on matters of opinion. If the parties can agree joint instructions, then a single set of instructions should be delivered to the expert. However, rule 35.8 expressly permits separate instructions and these are necessary where joint instructions cannot be agreed

(b) The preparation of the agreed bundle, which is to be provided to the expert. This bundle must include CPR Part 35, the Practice Direction supplementing Part 35 and the section 13 of the TCC Guide.

(c) The preparation and production of the expert's report.
(d) The provision to the expert of any written questions from the parties, which the expert must answer in writing.

13.4.7 In most cases the single joint expert's report, supplemented by any written answers to questions from the parties, will be sufficient for the purposes of the trial. Sometimes, however, it is necessary for a single joint expert to be called to give oral evidence. In those circumstances, the usual practice is for the judge to call the expert and then allow each party the opportunity to cross-examine. Such cross-examination should be conducted with appropriate restraint, since the witness has been instructed by the parties. Where the expert's report is strongly in favour of one party's position, it may be appropriate to allow only the other party to cross-examine.

**13.5 Meetings of experts**

13.5.1 The desirability of holding without prejudice meetings between experts at all stages of the pre-trial preparation should be kept in mind. The desired outcome of such meetings is to produce a document whose contents are agreed and which defines common positions or each expert's differing position. The purpose of such meetings includes the following: **2C–119**
(a) to define a party's technical case and to inform opposing parties of the details of that case;
(b) to clear up confusion and to remedy any lack of information or understanding of a party's technical case in the minds of opposing experts;
(c) to identify the issues about which any expert is to give evidence;
(d) to narrow differences and to reach agreement on as many "expert" issues as possible; and
(e) to assist in providing an agenda for the trial and for cross examination of expert witnesses, and to limit the scope and length of the trial as much as possible.

13.5.2 In many cases it will be helpful for the parties' respective legal advisors to provide assistance as to the agenda and topics to be discussed at an experts' meeting. However, (save in exceptional circumstances and with the permission of the judge) the legal advisors must not attend the meeting. They must not attempt to dictate what the experts say at the meeting.

13.5.3 Experts' meetings can sometimes usefully take place at the site of the dispute. Thought is needed as to who is to make the necessary arrangements for access, particularly where the site is occupied or in the control of a non-party. Expert meetings are often more productive, if (a) the expert of one party (usually the claimant) is appointed as chairman and (b) the experts exchange in advance agendas listing the topics each wishes to raise and identifying any relevant material which they intend to introduce or rely on during the meeting.

13.5.4 It is generally sensible for the experts to meet at least once before they exchange their reports.

**13.6 Experts' Joint Statements**

13.6.1 Following the experts' meetings, and pursuant to CPR 35.12 (3), the judge will almost always require the experts to produce a signed statement setting out the issues which have been agreed, and those issues which have not been agreed, together with a short summary of the reasons for their disagreement. In any TCC case in which expert evidence has an important role to play, this statement is a critical document and it must be as clear as possible. **2C–120**

13.6.2 It should be noted that, even where experts have been unable to agree very much, it is of considerable importance that the statement sets out their disagreements and the reasons for them. Such disagreements as formulated in the joint statement are likely to form an important element of the agenda for the trial of the action.

***Paragraph numbers marked with a "+" can be found online and on CD.***

13.6.3 Whilst the parties' legal advisors may assist in identifying issues which the statement should address, those legal advisors must not be involved in either negotiating or drafting the experts' joint statement.

### 13.7 Experts' Reports

**2C–121** 13.7.1 It is the duty of an expert to help the court on matters within his expertise. This duty overrides any duty to his client: CPR rule 35.3. Each expert's report must be independent and unbiased.

13.7.2 The parties must identify the issues with which each expert should deal in his report. Thereafter, it is for the expert to draft and decide upon the detailed contents and format of his report, so as to conform with section 2 of the Part 35 Practice Direction. It is appropriate, however, for the party instructing an expert to indicate that the report (a) should be as short as is reasonably possible; (b) should not set out copious extracts from other documents; (c) should identify the source of any opinion or data relied upon; and (d) should not annex or exhibit more than is reasonably necessary to support the opinions expressed in the report.

## SECTION 14.

## THE PRE-TRIAL REVIEW

### 14.1 Timing and Attendance

**2C–122** 14.1.1 The Pre-Trial Review ("PTR") will usually be fixed for a date that is 4–6 weeks in advance of the commencement of the trial itself. It is vital that the advocates, who are going to conduct the trial, should attend the PTR and every effort should be made to achieve this. It is usually appropriate for the PTR to be conducted by way of an oral hearing or, at the very least, a telephone conference.

### 14.2 Documents

**2C–123** 14.2.1 The parties must complete the PTR Questionnaire (a copy of which is at Appendix C attached) and return it in good time to the court. In addition, the judge may order the parties to provide other documents for the particular purposes of the PTR.

14.2.2 In an appropriate case, the advocates for each party should prepare a Note for the PTR, which addresses:

- any outstanding directions or interlocutory steps still to be taken;
- the issues for determination at the trial;
- the most efficient way in which those issues might be dealt with at the trial, including all questions of timetabling of witnesses.

These Notes should be provided to the court by 4 p.m. one clear day before the PTR.

14.2.3 The parties should also ensure that, for the PTR, the court has an up-to-date permanent case management bundle, together with a bundle of the evidence (factual and expert) that has been exchanged. This Bundle should also be made available to the court by 4 p.m. one clear day before the PTR.

### 14.3 Outstanding Directions

**2C–124** 14.3.1 It can sometimes be the case that there are still outstanding interlocutory steps to be taken at the time of the PTR. That will usually mean that one, or more, of the parties has not complied with an earlier direction of the court. In that event, the court is likely to require prompt compliance, and may make costs orders to reflect the delays.

14.3.2 Sometimes a party will wish to make an application to be heard at the same time as the PTR. Such a practice is unsatisfactory, because it uses up time allocated for the PTR, and it gives rise to potential uncertainty close to the trial date. It is always better for a party, if it possibly can, to make all necessary applications well in advance of the PTR. If that is not practicable, the court should be asked to allocate additional time for the PTR, in order to accommodate specific applications. If additional time is not available, such applications will not generally be entertained.

### 14.4 Issues

14.4.1 The parties should, if possible, provide the judge at the PTR with an agreed list of the Issues for the forthcoming trial (including, where appropriate, a separate list of technical issues to be covered by the experts). **2C–125**

14.4.2 If the parties are unable to agree the precise formulation of the issues, they should provide to the court their respective contentions as to what the issues are, and why.

14.4.3 In order to determine the best way to deal with the trial, it is necessary for the issues to be identified. If the precise formulation of the issues is a matter of dispute between the parties, the judge will note the parties' respective contentions, but is unlikely to give a ruling on this matter at the PTR.

### 14.5 Timetabling and Trial Logistics

14.5.1 Much of the PTR will be devoted to a consideration of the appropriate timetable for the trial, and other logistical matters. These will commonly include: **2C–126**

- Directions in respect of oral and written openings.
- Sequence of oral evidence; for example, whether all the factual evidence should be called before the expert evidence.
- Timetabling of oral evidence. (To facilitate this exercise, the advocates should tell the judge which witnesses need to be cross-examined and which evidence can be agreed.)
- Whether any form of time limits should be imposed. (Since the purpose of time limits is to ensure that that the costs incurred and the resources devoted to the trial are proportionate, this is for the benefit of the parties. The judge will endeavour to secure agreement to any time limits imposed.)
- Directions in respect of the trial bundle: when it should be agreed and lodged; the contents and structure of the bundle; avoidance of duplication; whether witness statements and/or expert reports should be annotated with cross references to page numbers in the main bundle (see paragraph 12.3 above); and similar matters.
- Whether there should be a core bundle; if so how it should be prepared and what it should contain. (The court will order a core bundle in any case where (a) there is substantial documentation and (b) having regard to the issues it is appropriate and proportionate to put the parties to cost of preparing a core bundle).
- Rules governing any email communication during trial between the parties and the court.
- Any directions relating to the use of simultaneous transcription at trial (this subject to agreement between the parties).

14.5.2 The topics identified in paragraph 14.5.1 are discussed in greater detail in section 15 below.

## SECTION 15.
## THE TRIAL

### 15.1 Arrangements prior to the trial—witnesses

15.1.1 Prior to the trial the parties' legal representatives should seek to agree on the following matters, in so far as they have not been resolved at the PTR: the order in **2C–127**

*Paragraph numbers marked with a "+" can be found online and on CD.*

which witnesses are to be called to give evidence; which witnesses are not required for cross examination and whose evidence in consequence may be adduced entirely from their witness statements; the timetable for the trial and the length of time each advocate is to be allowed for a brief opening speech. When planning the timetable, it should be noted that trials normally take place on Mondays to Thursdays, since Fridays are reserved for applications.

15.1.2 The witnesses should be notified in advance of the trial as to: (a) when each is required to attend court and (b) the approximate period of time for which he or she will be required to attend.

15.1.3 It is the parties' responsibility to ensure that their respective witnesses are ready to attend court at the appropriate time. It is never satisfactory for witnesses to be interposed, out of their proper place. It would require exceptional circumstances for the trial to be adjourned for any period of time because of the unavailability of a witness.

**15.2 Opening notes, trial bundle and oral openings**

**2C–128** 15.2.1 Opening notes. Unless the court has ordered otherwise, each party's advocate should provide an opening note, which outlines that party's case in relation to each of the issues identified at the PTR. Each opening note should indicate which documents (giving their page numbers in the trial bundle) that party considers that the judge should pre-read. The claimant's opening note should include a neutral summary of the background facts, as well as a chronology and cast list. The other parties' opening notes should be shorter and should assume familiarity with the factual background. In general terms, all opening notes should be of modest length and proportionate to the size and complexity of the case. Subject to any specific directions at the PTR, the claimant's opening note should be served two clear working days before the start of the trial; the other parties opening notes should be served by 1 p.m. on the last working day before the trial.

15.2.2 Trial bundles. Subject to any specific directions at the PTR, the trial bundles should be delivered to court at least three working days before the hearing. It is helpful for the party delivering the trial bundles to liaise in advance with the judge's clerk, in order to discuss practical arrangements, particularly when a large number of bundles are to be delivered. The parties should provide for the court an agreed index of all trial bundles. There should also be an index at the front of each bundle. This should be a helpful guide to the contents of that bundle. (An interminable list, itemising every letter or sheet of paper is not a helpful guide. Nor are bland descriptions, such as "exhibit "JT3", of much help to the bundle user.) The spines of bundles should be clearly labelled.

15.2.3 As a general rule the trial bundles should be clearly divided between statements of case, orders, contracts, witness statements, expert reports and correspondence/ minutes of meetings. The correspondence/ minutes of meetings should be in a separate bundle or bundles and in chronological order. Documents should only be included, if they are relevant to the issues in the case or helpful as background material. Documents should not be duplicated. Exhibits to witness statements should generally be omitted, since the documents to which the witnesses are referring will be found elsewhere in the bundles. The bundles of contract documents and correspondence/ minutes of meetings should be paginated, so that every page has a discrete number. The other bundles could be dealt with in one of two ways:

- The statements of case, witness statements and expert reports could be placed in bundles and continuously paginated.
- Alternatively, the statements of case, witness statements and expert reports could be placed behind tabbed divider cards, and then the internal numbering of each such document can be used at trial. If the latter course is adopted, it is vital that the internal page numbering of each expert report continues sequentially through the appendices to that report.

The ultimate objective is to create trial bundles, which are user friendly and in which any page can be identified with clarity and brevity (e.g. "bundle G page 273" or "defence page 3" or "Dr Smith page 12"). The core bundle, if there is one (as to which see paragraph 14.5.1 above), will be a separate bundle with its own pagination

15.2.4 Opening speeches. Subject to any directions made at the PTR, each party will be permitted to make an opening speech. These speeches should be prepared and presented on the basis that the judge will have pre-read the opening notes and the documents identified by the parties for pre-reading. The claimant's advocate may wish to highlight the main features of the claimant's case and/or to deal with matters raised in the other parties' opening notes. The other parties' advocates will then make shorter opening speeches, emphasising the main features of their own cases and/or responding to matters raised in the claimant's opening speech.

15.2.5 It is not usually necessary or desirable to embark upon legal argument during opening speeches. It is, however, helpful to foreshadow those legal arguments which (a) explain the relevance of particular parts of the evidence or (b) will assist the judge in following a party's case that is to be presented during the trial.

15.2.6 Narrowing of issues. Experience shows that often that the issues between the parties progressively narrow as the trial advances. Sometimes this process begins during the course of opening speeches. Weaker contentions may be abandoned and responses to those contentions may become irrelevant. The advocates will co-operate in focussing their submissions and the evidence on the true issues between the parties, as those issues are thrown into sharper relief by the adversarial process.

**15.3 Simultaneous transcription**

15.3.1 Many trials in the TCC, including the great majority of the longer trials, are conducted with simultaneous transcripts of the evidence being provided. There are a number of transcribing systems available. It is now common for a system to be used involving simultaneous transcription onto screens situated in court. However, systems involving the production of the transcript in hard or electronic form at the end of the day or even after a longer period of time are also used. The parties must make the necessary arrangements with one of the companies who provide this service. The court can provide a list, on request, of all companies who offer such a service. **2C-129**

15.3.2 In long trials or those which involve any significant amount of detailed or technical evidence, simultaneous transcripts are helpful. Furthermore, they enable all but the shortest trials to be conducted so as to reduce the overall length of the trial appreciably, since the judge does not have to note the evidence or submissions in longhand as the trial proceeds. Finally, a simultaneous transcript makes the task of summarising a case in closing submissions and preparing the judgment somewhat easier. It reduces both the risk of error or omission and the amount of time needed to prepare a reserved judgment.

15.3.3 If possible, the parties should have agreed at or before the PTR whether a simultaneous transcript is to be employed. It is usual for parties to agree to share the cost of a simultaneous transcript as an interim measure pending the assessment or agreement of costs, when this cost is assessable and payable as part of the costs in the case. Sometimes, a party cannot or will not agree to an interim cost sharing arrangement. If so, it is permissible for one party to bear the cost, but the court cannot be provided with a transcript unless all parties have equal access to the transcript. Unlike transcripts for use during an appeal, there is no available means of obtaining from public funds the cost of a transcript for use at the trial.

**15.4 Time limits**

15.4.1 Generally trials in the TCC are conducted under some form of time limit arrangement. Several variants of time limit arrangements are available, but the TCC has developed the practice of imposing flexible guidelines in the form of directions as to the sharing of the time allotted for the trial. These are not mandatory but an advocate should ordinarily be expected to comply with them. **2C-130**

15.4.2 The practice is, in the usual case, for the court to fix, or for the parties to agree, at the PTR or before trial an overall length of time for the trial and overall lengths of time within that period for the evidence and submissions. The part of those overall lengths of time that will be allocated to each party must then be agreed or directed.

15.4.3 The amount of time to be allotted to each party will not usually be the same. The guide is that each party should have as much time as is reasonably needed for it to present its case and to test and cross examine any opposing case, but no longer.

15.4.4 Before the trial, the parties should agree a running order of the witnesses and the approximate length of time required for each witness. A trial timetable should be provided to the court when the trial starts and, in long trials, regularly updated.

15.4.5 The practice of imposing a strict guillotine on the examination or cross examination of witnesses, is not normally appropriate. Flexibility is encouraged, but the agreed or directed time limits should not ordinarily be exceeded without good reason. It is unfair on a party, if that party's advocate has confined cross-examination to the agreed time limits, but an opposing party then greatly exceeds the corresponding time limits that it has been allocated.

15.4.6 An alternative form of time limit, which is sometimes agreed between the parties and approved by the court, is the "chess clock arrangement". The available time is divided equally between the parties, to be used by the parties as they see fit. Thus each side has X hours. One representative on each side operates the chess clock. The judge has discretion "to stop the clock" in exceptional circumstances. A chess clock arrangement is only practicable in a two-party case.

**15.5 Oral evidence**

**2C–131** 15.5.1 Evidence in chief is ordinarily adduced by the witness confirming on oath the truth and accuracy of the previously served witness statement or statements. A limited number of supplementary oral questions will usually be allowed (a) to give the witness an opportunity to become familiar with the procedure and (b) to cover points omitted by mistake from the witness statement or which have arisen subsequent to its preparation.

15.5.2 In some cases, particularly those involving allegations of dishonest, disreputable or culpable conduct or where significant disputes of fact are not documented or evidenced in writing, it is desirable that the core elements of a witness's evidence-in-chief are given orally. The giving of such evidence orally will often assist the court in assessing the credibility or reliability of a witness.

15.5.3 If any party wishes such evidence to be given orally, a direction should be sought either at the PTR or during the openings to that effect. Where evidence in chief is given orally, the rules relating to the use of witness statements in cross-examination and to the adducing of the statement in evidence at any subsequent stage of the trial remain in force and may be relied on by any party.

15.5.4 It is usual for all evidence of fact from all parties to be adduced before expert evidence and for the experts to give evidence in groups with all experts in a particular discipline giving their evidence in sequence. Usually, but not invariably, the order of witnesses will be such that the claimant's witnesses give their evidence first, followed by all the witnesses for each of the other parties in turn. If a party wishes a different order of witnesses to that normally followed, the agreement of the parties or a direction from the judge must be obtained in advance.

15.5.5 In a multi-party case, attention should be given (when the timetable is being discussed) to the order of cross-examination and to the extent to which particular topics will be covered by particular cross-examiners. Where these matters cannot be agreed, the order of cross-examination will (subject to any direction of the judge) follow the order in which the parties are set out in the pleadings. The judge will seek to limit cross examination on a topic which has been covered in detail by a preceding cross examination.

15.5.6 The coaching of witnesses or the suggestion of answers that may be given, before that witness starts to give evidence, is not permitted. Any prior discussion between the lawyers and the witness about the giving of evidence should be confined to factual information about the evidence-giving process. In short, witness familiarisation is permissible, but witness coaching is not. The boundary between witness familiarisation and witness coaching is discussed by the Court of Appeal in *R v Momodou* [2005] EWCA Crim 177 at [61]–[62]. Once a witness has started giving evidence, he cannot discuss the case or his evidence either with the lawyers or with anyone else until he has finally left the witness box. Occasionally a dispensation is needed (for example, an expert may need to participate in an experts' meeting about some new development). In those circumstances the necessary dispensation will either be agreed between the advocates or ordered by the judge.

### 15.6 Submissions during the trial

15.6.1 Submissions and legal argument should be kept to a minimum during the course of the trial. Where these are necessary, (a) they should, where possible, take place when a witness is not giving evidence and (b) the judge should be given forewarning of the need for submissions or legal argument. Where possible, the judge will fix a time for these submissions outside the agreed timetable for the evidence. **2C–132**

### 15.7 Closing submissions

15.7.1 The appropriate form of closing submissions can be determined during the course of the trial. Those submissions may take the form of (a) oral closing speeches or (b) written submission alone or (c) written submissions supplemented by oral closing speeches. In shorter or lower value cases, oral closing speeches immediately after the evidence may be the most cost effective way to proceed. Alternatively, if the evidence finishes in the late afternoon, a direction for written closing submissions to be delivered by specified (early) dates may avoid the cost of a further day's court hearing. In longer and heavier cases the judge may (in consultation with the advocates) set a timetable for the delivery of sequential written submissions (alternatively, an exchange of written submissions) followed by an oral hearing. In giving directions for oral and/or written closing submissions, the judge will have regard to the circumstances of the case and the overriding objective. **2C–133**

15.7.2 It is helpful if, in advance of preparing closing submissions, the parties can agree on the principal topics or issues that are to be covered. It is also helpful for the written and oral submissions of each party to be structured so as to cover those topics in the same order.

15.7.3 It is both customary and helpful for the judge to be provided with a photocopy of each authority and statutory provision that is to be cited in closing submissions.

### 15.8 Views

15.8.1 It is sometimes necessary or desirable for the judge to be taken to view the subjectmatter of the case. In normal circumstances, such a view is best arranged to take place immediately after the openings and before the evidence is called. However, if the subject matter of the case is going to be covered up or altered prior to the trial, the view must be arranged earlier. In that event, it becomes particularly important to avoid a change of judge. Accordingly, the court staff will note on the trial diary the fact that the assigned judge has attended a view. In all subsequent communications between the parties and court concerning trial date, the need to avoid a change of judge must be borne firmly in mind. **2C–134**

15.8.2 The matters viewed by the judge form part of the evidence that is received

*Paragraph numbers marked with a "+" can be found online and on CD.*

and may be relied on in deciding the case. However, nothing said during the view to (or in the earshot of) the judge, has any evidential status, unless there has been an agreement or order to that effect.

15.8.3 The parties should agree the arrangements for the view and then make those arrangements themselves. The judge will ordinarily travel to the view unaccompanied and, save in exceptional circumstances when the cost will be shared by all parties, will not require any travelling costs to be met by the parties.

**15.9 Judgments**

**2C–135** 15.9.1 Depending on the length and complexity of the trial, the judge may (a) give judgment orally immediately after closing speeches; (b) give judgment orally on the following day or soon afterwards; or (c) deliver a reserved judgment in writing at a later date.

15.9.2 Where judgment is reserved. The judge will normally indicate at the conclusion of the trial what arrangements will be followed in relation to (a) the making available of any draft reserved judgment and (b) the handing down of the reserved judgment in open court. If a judgment is reserved, it will be handed down as soon as possible. Save in exceptional circumstances, any reserved judgment will be handed down within 3 months of the conclusion of the trial. Any enquiries as to the progress of a reserved judgment should be addressed in the first instance to the judge's clerk, with notice of that enquiry being given to other parties. If concerns remain following the judge's response to the parties, further enquiries or communication should be addressed to the judge in charge of the TCC.

15.9.3 If the judge decides to release a draft judgment in advance of the formal hand down, this draft judgment will be confidential to the parties and their legal advisers. Solicitors and counsel on each side should send to the judge a note (if possible, agreed) of any clerical errors or slips which they note in the judgment. However, this is not to be taken as an opportunity to re-argue the issues in the case.

**15.10 Disposal of judge's bundle after conclusion of the case**

**2C–136** 15.10.1 The judge will have made notes and annotations on the bundle during the course of the trial. Accordingly, the normal practice is that the entire contents of the judge's bundle are disposed of as confidential waste. The empty ring files can be recovered by arrangement with the judge's clerk.

15.10.2 If any party wishes to retrieve from the judge's bundle any particular items of value which it has supplied (e.g. plans or photographs), a request for these items should be made to the judge's clerk promptly at the conclusion of the case. If the judge has not made annotations on those particular items, they will be released to the requesting party.

## SECTION 16.

## COSTS

**16.1 General**

**2C–137** 16.1.1 All disputes as to costs will be resolved in accordance with CPR Part 44, and in particular CPR rule 44.3.

16.1.2 The judge's usual approach will be to determine which party can be properly described as 'the successful party', and then to investigate whether there are any good reasons why that party should be deprived of some or all of their costs.

16.1.3 It should be noted that, in view of the complex nature of TCC cases, a consideration of the outcome on particular issues or areas of dispute can sometimes be an appropriate starting point for any decision on costs.

***Paragraph numbers marked with a "+" can be found online and on CD.***

**16.2 Summary Assessment of Costs**

16.2.1 Interlocutory hearings that last one day or less will usually be the subject of a summary assessment of costs in accordance with CPR 44.7 and section 13 of the Costs Practice Direction. The parties must ensure that their statements of costs, on which the summary assessment will be based, are provided to each other party, and the Court, no later than 24 hours before the hearing in question: see paragraph 6.9.3 above. **2C-138**

16.2.2 The *Supreme Court Costs Office Guide to the Summary Assessment of Costs* sets out clear advice and guidance as to the principles to be followed in any summary assessment. Generally summary assessment proceeds on the standard basis. In making an assessment on the standard basis, the court will only allow a reasonable amount in respect of costs reasonably incurred and any doubts must be resolved in favour of the paying party.

16.2.3 In arguments about the hourly rates claimed, the judge will have regard to the principles set out by the Court of Appeal in *Wraith v Sheffield Forgemasters Ltd* [1998] 1 WLR 132: i.e. the judge will consider whether the successful party acted reasonably in employing the solicitors who had been instructed and whether the costs they charged were reasonable compared with the broad average of charges made by similar firms practising in the same area.

16.2.4 In addition, when considering hourly rates, the judge in the TCC may have regard to the guideline rates published from time to time by TecSA.

16.2.5 The court will also consider whether unnecessary work was done or an unnecessary amount of time was spent on the work.

16.2.6 It may be that, because of pressures of time, and/or the nature and extent of the disputes about the level of costs incurred, the court is unable to carry out a satisfactory summary assessment of the costs. In those circumstances, the court will direct that costs be assessed on the standard (or indemnity) basis and will order an amount to be paid on account of costs under CPR Rule 44.3(8).

**16.3 Costs Cap Orders**

16.3.1 In exercising case management powers, the judge may make costs cap orders which, in normal circumstances, will be prospective only. He should only do so, however, where there is a real and substantial risk that without such an order: **2C-139**

(a) costs will be disproportionately or unreasonably incurred and
(b) such costs cannot be controlled by conventional case management and a detailed assessment of costs after a trial, and
(c) it is just to make such an order.

See CPR rule 3.1 and the notes to that rule in the White Book headed "Prospective costs cap orders".

16.3.2 The possibility of a costs cap order should be considered at the first CMC. The later such an order is sought, the more difficult it may be to impose an effective costs cap.

**16.4 Costs: Miscellaneous**

16.4.1 The court may at any stage order any party to file and serve on the other parties an estimate of costs: see CPR rule 3.1(2)(ii) and section 6 of the Costs Practice Direction. The case management information sheet for the first CMC requires such costs information. This information allows the court properly to exercise its case management functions. In appropriate cases (and where it is proportionate to do so) the judge will exercise his power under paragraph 3 of the Costs Practice Direction to direct the parties to file estimates of costs prepared in such a way as to demonstrate the likely effects of giving or not giving or not giving a particular case management direction. **2C-140**

*Paragraph numbers marked with a "+" can be found online and on CD.*

16.4.2 Pursuant to CPR Rule 44.2 and Section 7 of the Costs Practice Direction, solicitors have a duty to tell their clients within 7 days if an order for costs was made against the clients and they were not present at the hearing, explaining how the order came to be made. They must also give the same information to anyone else who has instructed them to act on the case or who is liable to pay their fees.

## SECTION 17.

## ENFORCEMENT

### 17.1 General

**2C-141** 17.1.1 The TCC is concerned with the enforcement of judgments and orders given by the TCC and with the enforcement of adjudicators' decisions and arbitrators' awards. Adjudication and arbitration enforcement have been dealt with in, respectively, sections 9 and 10 above.

### 17.2 High Court

**2C-142** 17.2.1 London. A party wishing to make use of any provision of the CPR concerned with the enforcement of judgments and orders made in the TCC in London can use the TCC Registry in London or any other convenient TCC District Registry listed in Appendix A.

17.2.2 Outside London. Where the judgment or order in respect of which enforcement is sought was made by a judge of the TCC out of London, the party seeking enforcement should use the Registry of the court in which the judgment or order was made.

17.2.3 Where orders are required or sought to support enforcement of a TCC judgment or order, a judge of the TCC is the appropriate judge for that purpose. If available, the judge who gave the relevant judgment or made the relevant order is the appropriate judge to whom all applications should be addressed.

### 17.3 County Court

**2C-143** 17.3.1 A TCC county court judgment (like any other county court judgment):

(a) if for less than £600, must be enforced in the county court;

(b) if for between £600 and £4999, can be enforced in either the county court or the High Court, at the option of the judgment creditor;

(c) if for £5,000 or more, must be enforced in the High Court.

17.3.2 If a judgment creditor in a TCC county court wishes to transfer any enforcement proceedings to any other county court (whether a TCC county court or not), he must make a written request to do so pursuant to section 2 of the Practice Direction supplementing Part 70. Alternatively, at the end of the trial the successful party may make an oral application to the trial judge to transfer the proceedings to some other specified county court for the purposes of enforcement.

### 17.4 Enforcement on paper

**2C-144** 17.4.1 Where the application or order is unopposed or does not involve any substantial dispute, the necessary order should be sought by way of a paper application.

## Section 18.

## The TCC Judge as Arbitrator

### 18.1 General

18.1.1 Section 93(1) of the Arbitration Act 1996 provides that a judge of the TCC (previously an Official Referee) may "if in all the circumstances he thinks fit, accept appointment as a sole arbitrator or as an umpire by or by virtue of an arbitration agreement." Judges of the TCC may accept appointments as arbitrators or umpires pursuant to these statutory provisions. A judge of the TCC may also accept an appointment as a member of a three-member panel of arbitrators pursuant to these provisions. **2C–145**

18.1.2 A TCC judge cannot accept such an appointment unless the Lord Chief Justice "has informed him that, having regard to the state of (TCC) business, he can be made available": see section 93(3) of the 1996 Act.

18.1.3 Application should be made in the first instance to the judge whose acceptance of the appointment is sought. If the judge is willing to accept the appointment, he will make application on behalf of the appointing party or parties, through the judge in charge of the TCC, to the Lord Chief Justice for his necessary approval. He will inform the party or parties applying for his appointment once the consent or refusal of consent has been obtained.

18.1.4 Subject to the workload of the court, such requests for judge arbitrators will generally be accepted. Particular advantages have been noted by both TECBAR and TeCSA in the appointment of a TCC judge to act as arbitrator where the dispute centres on the proper interpretation of a clause or clauses within one of the standard forms of building and engineering contracts.

### 18.2 Arbitration Management and Fees

18.2.1 Following the appointment of the judge arbitrator, the rules governing the arbitration will be decided upon, or directed, at the First Preliminary Meeting, when other appropriate directions will be given. The judge arbitrator will manage the reference to arbitration in a similar way to a TCC case. **2C–146**

18.2.2 The judge sitting as an arbitrator will sit in a TCC court room (suitably rearranged) unless the parties and the judge arbitrator agree to some other arrangement.

18.2.3 Fees are payable to the Court Service for the judge arbitrator's services and for any accommodation provided. The appropriate fee for the judge arbitrator, being a daily rate, is published in the Fees Order and should be paid through the TCC Registry.

### 18.3 Appeals

18.3.1 Section 2 of Schedule 2 to the Arbitration Act 1996 provides that any appeal from a judge arbitrator is to be heard, in the first instance, by the Court of Appeal. **2C–147**

## Appendix A

## Case Management Information Sheet

Appendix A to Part 60 Practice Direction—Form **TCC/CM1**—can be found in the *Civil Procedure Forms Volume.* **2C–148**

## Appendix B

## Case Management Directions Form

Appendix B—Form **TCC/CMD**—can be found in the *Civil Procedure Forms Volume.* **2C–149**

## Appendix C

## Pre-Trial Review Questionnaire

Appendix C to the Part 60 Practice Direction—Form **TCC/PTR1**—can be found in the *Civil Procedure Forms Volume.* **2C–150**

***Paragraph numbers marked with a "+" can be found online and on CD.***

## APPENDIX D

## CONTACT DETAILS FOR TECHNOLOGY AND CONSTRUCTION COURT

2C–151 **The High Court of Justice, Queen's Bench Division**
**Technology and Construction Court**
St Dunstan's House
133-137 Fetter Lane
London EC4A 1HD

### Comment

2C–152 Since Appendix D contains contact details, the information within it requires regular updating. The version of Appendix D above has been modified to bring it up to date.

### (a) Management

2C–153 Court Manager: Mr Wilf Lusty
Case Administration Unit Manager/Registry Manager: Mr Steven Gibbon (steven.gibbon@hmcourts-service.gsi.gov.uk)

Registry: Tel: 020 7947 6022
Fax: 020 7947 7428

Case Administration Unit: Tel: 020 7947 7156
Fax: 020 7947 6465

### (b) TCC Judges

2C–154 Mr Justice Ramsey
Clerk: Mr David Hamilton (david.hamilton5@hmcourts-service.gsi.gov.uk)
Tel: 0207 947 6331
Fax: 0207 073 4701

Mr Justice Akenhead
Clerk: Mr Sam Taylor (Sam.Taylor1@hmcourts-service.gsi.gov.uk)
Tel: 0207 947 7445

Mr Justice Coulson
TBA
Tel: 0207 947 6547

His Honour Judge Anthony Thornton QC
Clerk: Ms Anne Farrelly (anne.farrelly@hmcourts-service.gsi.gov.uk)
Tel: 020 7947 6457

His Honour Judge David Wilcox
Clerk: Ms Pam Gilham (pamela.gilham@hmcourts-service.gsi.gov.uk)
Tel: 020 7947 6450

His Honour Judge John Toulmin CMG QC
Clerk: Steven Gibbon (steven.gibbon@hmcourts-service.gsi.gov.uk)
Tel: 020 7947 6498

- The following seven High Court Judges will be available, when necessary and by arrangement with the Vice-President of the Queen's Bench Division, to sit in the TCC:

  Mr Justice Burton
  Mr Justice Elias
  Mr Justice Field

***Paragraph numbers marked with a "+" can be found online and on CD.***

Mr Justice Ouseley
Mr Justice Simon
Mr Justice Christopher Clarke
Mr Justice Teare

- The Case Administration Unit, headed by Steven Gibbon, administers cases classified as "HCJ" (see section 3.7 of guide).

**Birmingham District Registry: Birmingham County Court**
33 Bull Street
Birmingham B4 6DS
TCC listing and clerk to HH Judge Kirkham: Peter Duke (Peter.Duke@hmcourts-service.gsi.gov.uk)
Tel: 0121 681 3181
Fax: 0121 681 3121

**TCC Judges**
Her Honour Judge Frances Kirkham (full time TCC Judge)
Her Honour Judge Simon Brown QC (Mercantile Judge)
Her Honour Judge Caroline Alton (Mercantile Judge)
His Honour Judge Charles Purle QC (Chancery Judge)

Other judges in Birmingham who have been nominated to deal with TCC business are: His Honour Judge MacDuff Q.C.

**Bristol District Registry: Bristol County Court**
TCC Listing Office
The Law Courts
Small Street
Bristol BS1 1DA
**TCC Listing officers:** Dan Cuthbertson and Priya Patel
Email: bristolcclisting@hmcourts-service.gsi.gov.uk
Tel: 0117 910 6700
Fax: 0117 910 6727

**TCC Judges**
His Honour Judge Mark Havelock-Allan QC (principal TCC judge)
His Honour Judge Patrick McCahill QC

**Cardiff District Registry: Cardiff County Court**
Cardiff Civil Justice Centre
2 Park Street
Cardiff CF10 1 ET
Main switchboard: 02920 376 400
Fax: 02920 376 475
Listing office: 02920 376 412
**Circuit Judges Listing Manager**: Graham Driver
Tel: 02920 376483, graham.driver@hmcourts-service.gsi.gov.uk
**Specialist Listing Officer:** Tracey Davies
Tel: 02920 376412, tracey.davies@hmcourts-service.gsi.gov.uk

**TCC Judges**
His Honour Judge Gary Hickinbottom (principal TCC judge)
His Honour Judge Nicholas Chambers QC

**Central London Civil Justice Centre**
26 Park Crescent,

***Paragraph numbers marked with a "+" can be found online and on CD.***

London WIN 4HT
Listing office for TCC, Chancery and Mercantile Courts
Tel: 0207 917 7932 / 7933
Chancery and Specialist Section Manager: Ms Kathlyn Antoine
Tel: 0207 917 7889/ 7821
Fax: 0207 917 7935

**TCC Judges**
His Honour Judge Brian Knight QC (principal TCC judge)
His Honour Judge Paul Collins CBE
His Honour Judge Edward Bailey

**Chester District Registry: Chester County Court**
The Chester Civil Justice Centre
Trident House
Little St John Street
Chester CH1 1SN
Diary Manager: Julie Burgess
Email: Julie.burgess@hmcourts-service.gsi.gov.uk
Tel: 01244 404200
Fax: 01244 404300

**TCC Judge**
His Honour Judge Derek Halbert

**Exeter District Registry: Exeter County Court**
Southernhay Gardens
Exeter
Devon
EX1 1UH
Tel: 01392 415350
Fax: 01392 415645

**TCC Judge**
His Honour Judge Jeremy Griggs

**Leeds Combined Court Centre**
The Courthouse
1 Oxford Row
Leeds LS1 3BG

High Court Civil Listing Officers: David Eaton and Terence Pendlebury
Tel: 0113 306 2440/2441
Fax: 0113 242 6380
Email: david.eaton@hmcourts-service.gsi.gov.uk

**TCC Judges**
His Honour Judge John Cockroft (principal TCC judge)
His Honour Judge John Behrens
His Honour Judge Peter Langan QC
His Honour Judge Simon Grenfell
His Honour Judge Simon Hawkesworth QC
His Honour Judge Kaye QC

**Leicester District Registry: Leicester County Court**
90 Wellington Street

***Paragraph numbers marked with a "+" can be found online and on CD.***

Leicester LE1 6ZZ
Tel: 0116 222 5700
Fax: 0116 222 5763

**TCC Judge**
His Honour Judge David Brunning

**Liverpool District Registry: Liverpool Combined Court Centre**
Liverpool Civil & Family Courts
35 Vernon Street
Liverpool L2 2BX
**TCC listing officer:** Jackie Jones
Tel: 0151 296 2444
Fax: 0151 295 2201

**TCC Judges**
His Honour Judge David Mackay (full time TCC judge)
His Honour Judge Stephen Stewart QC
His Honour Judge Graham Platt

**Mold County Court**
Law Courts
Civic Centre
Mold Flintshire
Wales CH7 1AE
TCC listing officer: Selina Wilkes
Tel: 01352 707405
Fax: 01352 753874

**TCC Judges**
Will attend from Cardiff when required

**Newcastle upon Tyne Combined Court Centre**
The Law Courts
Quayside
Newcastle upon Tyne NE1 3LA
Tel: 0191 201 2029
Listing Officer: Mrs Carol Gallagher—carol.gallagher@hmcourts-service.gsi.gov.uk
Tel: 0191 201 2047
Fax: 0191 201 2001

**TCC Judge**
His Honour Judge Christopher Walton
District Judge Atherton

**Nottingham District Registry: Nottingham County Court**
60 Canal Street
Nottingham NG1 7EJ
Tel 0115 910 3500
Fax: 0115 910 3510

**TCC Judge**
His Honour Judge Richard Inglis

**Salford District Registry: Salford County Court**
Prince William House

Peel Cross Road
Salford M5 4RR
TCC clerks: Isobel Rich and David Fernandez
Tel: 0161 745 7511
Fax: 0161 745 7202
Email: Hearings@salford.countycourt.gsi.gov.uk

**TCC Judges**
His Honour Judge Phillip Raynor QC (full time TCC judge)
His Honour Judge Stephen Davies (full time TCC judge)

The following judges at Manchester are nominated to deal with TCC business: His Honour Judge Brendan Hegarty QC, His Honour Judge David Hodge QC, His Honour Judge Mark Pelling QC and His Honour Judge David Waksman QC.

**Sheffield Combined Court Centre**
The Law Courts
50 West Bar
Sheffield S3 8PH
Tel: 0114 281 2419
Fax: 0114 281 2585

**TCC Judge**
His Honour Judge John Bullimore

**Winchester Combined Court Centre**
The Law Courts
Winchester
Hampshire
SO23 9EL
Diary Manager: Mr Wayne Hacking—email wayne.hacking@hmcourts-service.gsi.gov.uk
Tel: 023 8021 3254
Civil Listing Officer: Mrs Karen Hart—email karen.hart@hmcourts-serviec.gsi.gov.uk
Tel: 01962 814 113
Switchboard: 01962 814100
Fax: 01962 814260

**TCC Judge**
His Honour Judge Iain Hughes QC

## APPENDIX E

## DRAFT ADR ORDER

2C–155 1. By [ ] the parties shall exchange lists of three neutral individuals who have indicated their availability to conduct a mediation/ENE in this case prior to [ ].

2. By [ ] the parties shall agree an individual from the exchanged lists to conduct the mediation/ENE by [ ]. If the parties are unable to agree on the neutral individual, they will apply to the Court in writing by [ ] and the Court will choose one of the listed individuals to conduct the mediation/ENE.

3. There will be a stay of the proceedings until [ ] to allow the mediation/ENE to take place. On or before that date, the Court shall be informed as to whether or not the case has been finally settled. If it has not been finally settled, the parties will:

a) comply with all outstanding directions made by the Court;
b) attend for a review CMC on [ ].

## APPENDIX F

### DRAFT DIRECTIONS IN ADJUDICATION ENFORCEMENT PROCEEDINGS

Upon reading the Claim Form, Particulars of Claim, the Claimant's without notice application dated the day of 200 and the evidence in support thereof **2C–156**

IT IS ORDERED THAT:

1. The Claimant's solicitor shall [as soon as practicable after receipt of this Order/ by 4pm on day of ] serve upon the Defendant
   a. The Claim Form and Response Pack
   b. This Order
   c. The Claimant's Application Pursuant to Part 24 and the Claimant's evidence in support.

2. The time for the Defendant to file its acknowledgement of service is abridged to [ ] days.

3. The Claimant hereby has permission to issue an application pursuant to CPR Part 24 without an acknowledgement of service or Defence having been filed.

4. The Part 24 application will be heard on the day of at am/pm at . Estimated Length of Hearing hours]

5. Any further evidence in relation to the Part 24 Application shall be served and filed
   a. By the Defendant, [14 days after the service of the documents in Paragraph 1 above/ at least 5 working days before the date fixed for the hearing of the Application] [on the day of ]
   b. By the Claimant, in response to that of the Defendant, [at least 3 working days before the date fixed for the hearing of the Application] [on the day of 200 ]

and in either case no later than 4.00pm upon that day.

6. The Claimant's solicitor shall file a paginated bundle comprising
   a. The witness statements provided in support of the application, together with any exhibits;
   b. The witness statements provided in opposition to the application together with exhibits;
   c. Any witness statements in reply, together with exhibits;
   d. Photocopies of relevant authorities.

This bundle is to be provided no later than [2 working days before the hearing of the Application] [on day of ].

7. The parties shall file and serve skeleton arguments by no later than [4.00pm one clear working day before the hearing/ 1pm the last working day before the hearing]* [on the day of ]

8. The costs of and incidental to these directions are reserved to the Part 24 hearing. Permission to apply in respect of such costs in the absence of such hearing.

9. The parties have permission to apply to the court on 48 hours written notice to the other to seek to set aside or vary these directions.

* Depending whether the hearing is estimated to last in excess of 1/2 day or not

# 2D ADMIRALTY JURISDICTION AND PROCEEDINGS

## PART 61—ADMIRALTY CLAIMS

**Contents** **2D–1**



**Editorial introduction**

This Part and its supplementing Practice Direction do not provide a complete code for these proceedings but have to be read in conjunction with the other CPR. The application of the CPR and the Practice Directions which supplement them is in Admiralty proceedings subject to the provisions of this Practice Direction. Part 61 also assigns certain claims to the QBD and provides that they are to be taken by the Admiralty court. **2D–2**

The following points are of importance:

- There is no jurisdiction in the County Court in Admiralty matters (see Civil Courts (Amendment) (No.2) Order 1999 (SI 1999/1011).
- All Admiralty claims *in rem* or *in personam* should be commenced in the Admiralty and Commercial Registry at the RCJ. In cases of urgency out of London reference should be made to the Admiralty and Commercial Registry at the RCJ.
- All arrests will be dealt with by the Admiralty Marshal at the Admiralty and Commercial Registry in London.
- As a general rule in cases where there is an arrest, the file and matter will be retained in the Admiralty and Commercial Registry for all purposes save as may be otherwise specifically ordered.
- All arrests are to be supported by a Solicitor's undertaking to pay the Marshal's arrest expenses or disbursements or by a payment in in respect thereof.
- The caveat system is preserved, but caveats are now termed cautions.
- An acknowledgment of service must be filed in every Admiralty claim *in rem* and in every other Admiralty claim formerly called claims *in personam* unless liability is admitted on **ADM16** in a limitation claim. Such acknowledgment must be filed within 14 days of service of the claim form irrespective of whether or not particulars of claim are served with it.
- An Admiralty other claim (see the Practice Direction—Admiralty Claims, para.12.1) is subject to the same rules as an ordinary claim where service is to be effected out of the jurisdiction save for the special rules set out in CPR r.6.20(17A) and as regards a limitation claim form only in r.61.11(5) and a collision claim form in r.61.4.

***Paragraph numbers marked with a "+" can be found online and on CD.***

— There are special rules as to times for service of a claim *in rem*.

(a) The validity for service of an *in rem* claim form is 12 months, see r.61.3(5)(b).

(b) The time for service of particulars of claim in an *in rem* claim if not served with the *in rem* claim form is 75 days after service of the *in rem* claim form, see r.61.3(3)(b).

Collision and limitation claims have their own special procedures see rr.61.4 and 6.11 respectively. The Preliminary Act procedure still applies in collision claims but Preliminary Acts are now termed Collision Statements of Case.

**Related sources**

2D-3
- Senior Courts Act 1981 ss.20–24, s.27 and s.150 (see paras 2D-145 *et seq.*)
- Hovercraft Act 1968 ss.2–4 (see paras 2D-203+ *et seq.*)
- Merchant Shipping Act 1995 ss.92–93, ss.185–189, ss.190, 192, 224 and 229–230 (see paras 2D-208 *et seq.*)
- The Admiralty and Commercial Courts Guide (see paras 2A-39 *et seq.*).
- Practice Direction (Electronic Working Pilot Scheme)

**Forms**

2D-4
- **ADM1** Claim form (Admiralty claim form *in rem*)
- **ADM1A** Claim form (Admiralty claim form for other claims)
- **ADM1C** Notes for defendant on replying to an *in rem* claim form
- **ADM2** Acknowledgment of service/response pack (Admiralty claim *in rem*)
- **ADM3** Collision Statement of Case
- **ADM4** Application and undertaking for arrest and custody
- **ADM5** Outline form of declaration in support of application for warrant of arrest
- **ADM6** Notice to consular officer of intention to apply for warrant of arrest
- **ADM7** Request for caution against arrest
- **ADM9** Warrant of arrest
- **ADM10** Standard directions to the admiralty marshal
- **ADM11** Request for caution against release
- **ADM12** Application and undertaking for release
- **ADM12A** Request for withdrawal of caution against release
- **ADM13** Application for judgment in default of filing an acknowledgment of service and/or defence or collision statement of case
- **ADM14** Order for sale of a ship
- **ADM15** Claim form (Admiralty limitation claim)
- **ADM15B** Notes for defendant (Admiralty limitation claim)
- **ADM16** Notice of admission of right of claimant to limit liability
- **ADM16A** Defence to admiralty limitation claim
- **ADM16B** Acknowledgment of service/response pack (Admiralty limitation claim)
- **ADM17** Application for restricted decree of limitation
- **ADM17A** Application for general limitation decree
- **ADM18** Restricted decree of limitation
- **ADM19** Decree of limitation
- **ADM20** Defendant's claim in a limitation claim
- **ADM21** Outline form of declaration as to inability of a defendant to file and serve statement of case under a decree of limitation

2D-5 *Note* —**ADM1A**—An Admiralty Claim *in personam* shall be commenced on a Pt 7 claim form as adapted for a Commercial Court claim, save for taking into consideration any logical or textual modifications made to the "Notes for Claimant on completing a claim form" in the Commercial Court, in order to accord with the practice of the Admiralty Court.

The formats for Pt 7 and Pt 8 claim forms for Commercial Court claims, the notes

***Paragraph numbers marked with a "+" can be found online and on CD.***

and response packs thereto together with certain other forms as adapted shall apply to an Admiralty action *in personam* (or *in rem*, if applicable) with the appropriate alterations.

**Electronic working**

Practice Direction (Electronic Working Pilot Scheme), made by the Master of the Rolls, came into effect on April 1, 2009. It supplements CPR r.5.5 (Filing and sending documents) and provides for a pilot scheme, starting on April 1, 2009, and running (initially) until March 31, 2010, by which, in the circumstances set out in the practice direction, parties may avail themselves of arrangements for starting proceedings in the Admiralty Court at the Royal Courts of Justice (and some other courts) electronically, and also for taking all subsequent steps in the proceedings electronically (so-called "Electronic Working"). In certain respects the practice direction modifies CPR provisions that would otherwise apply. Paragraph 1.3 states that, where proceedings to which CPR Pt 61 (Admiralty Claims) apply are issued, then the Electronic Working pilot scheme will apply subject to the provisions of that Part unless specifically excluded or revised by this practice direction. **2D–5.1**

## Scope and interpretation[1]

**61.1—(1) This Part applies to admiralty claims.** **2D–6**

**(2) In this Part—**

**(a) "admiralty claim" means a claim within the Admiralty jurisdiction of the High Court as set out in section 20 of the Senior Courts Act 1981[2];**

**(b) "the Admiralty Court" means the Admiralty Court of the Queen's Bench Division of the High Court of Justice;**

**(c) "claim in rem" means a claim in an admiralty action in rem;**

**(d) "collision claim" means a claim within section 20(3)(b) of the Senior Courts Act 1981;**

**(e) "limitation claim" means a claim under the Merchant Shipping Act 1995[3] for the limitation of liability in connection with a ship or other property;**

**(f) "salvage claim" means a claim—**

**(i) for or in the nature of salvage;**

**(ii) for special compensation under; Article 14 of Schedule 11 to the Merchant Shipping Act 1995**

**(iii) for the apportionment of salvage; and**

**(iv) arising out of or connected with any contract for salvage services;**

**(g) "caution against arrest" means a caution entered in the Register under rule 61.7;**

**(h) "caution against release" means a caution entered in the Register under rule 61.8;**

---

[1] Amended by the Civil Procedure (Amendment No.5) Rules 2001 (SI 2001/4015) and the Civil Procedure (Amendment No.2) Rules 2009 (SI 2009/3390).

[2] 1981 c.54; s.20 was amended by the Merchant Shipping (Salvage and Pollution) Act 1994 (c.28) s.1(6) and Sch. 2, para.6; the Merchant Shipping Act 1995 (c.21) s.314(2) and Sch.13, para.59 and by the Merchant Shipping and Maritime Security Act 1997 (c.28) s.29(1) and Sch. 6, para.2. Renamed by the Constitutional Reform Act 2005 s.59 and Sch.11, para.1 with effect from October 1, 2009 (SI 2009/1604).

[3] 1995 c.21.

*Paragraph numbers marked with a "+" can be found online and on CD.*

**(i) "the Register" means the Register of cautions against arrest and release which is open to inspection as provided by Practice Direction 61;**

**(j) "the Marshal" means the Admiralty Marshal;**

**(k) "ship" includes any vessel used in navigation; and**

**(l) "the Registrar" means the Queen's Bench Master with responsibility for Admiralty claims.**

**(3) Part 58 (Commercial Court) applies to claims in the Admiralty Court except where this Part provides otherwise.**

**(4) The Registrar has all the powers of the Admiralty judge except where a rule or practice direction provides otherwise.**

### Admiralty jurisdiction

**2D–7** As to the Admiralty jurisdiction of the High Court see SCA 1981 ss.20 to 24 (paras 2D–145 *et seq.* below), the Hovercraft Act 1968 as amended by SCA 1981 (paras 2D–203+ *et seq.*), the Merchant Shipping Act 1995 s.166.

The court is seised of a claim *in rem* from the moment of service of the claim form or of arrest of a ship (whichever is the earlier). Where, however, proceedings are brought against a ship already under arrest in High Court proceedings, the court will be seised of jurisdiction from the moment the claim form is issued. The court cannot have jurisdiction over a ship which does not come within the jurisdiction (*The Freccia del Nord* [1989] 1 Lloyd's Rep. 388). The court is seised of a claim *in personam* (see Practice Direction—Admiralty Claims, para.12, Other Claims) when the defendant is served with the claim form (*Neste Chemicals SA v D.K. Line SA The Sargasso* [1993] 1 Lloyd's Rep. 424, affirmed [1994] 3 All E.R. 180; [1994] 2 Lloyd's Rep. 6, CA). This is so whether service is to be effected within or without the jurisdiction and in the latter case may have first involved an application for permission to serve out of the jurisdiction. This is a matter of importance when considering Arts 21 and 22 of the Convention on Jurisdiction and the Enforcement of Judgments in Civil and Commercial Matters 1968.

Further, for cases subject to EC law, Council Regulation 44/2001 on jurisdiction and the recognition and enforcement of judgments in civil and commercial matters, effective from March 1, 2002, Section 9, *Lis pendens*—related actions, art.30 provides:

For the purposes of this Section, a court shall be deemed to be seised:

1. at the time when the document instituting the proceedings or an equivalent document is lodged with the court, provided that the plaintiff has not subsequently failed to take the steps he was required to take to have service effected on the defendant, or
2. if the document has to be served before being lodged with the court, at the time when it is received by the authority responsible for service, provided that the plaintiff has not subsequently failed to take the steps he was required to take to have the document lodged with the court.

Article 2 of the 1968 Brussels Convention on Jurisdiction and the Enforcement of Judgments in Civil and Commercial Matters covers all forms of proceedings in civil and commercial matters whether *in rem* or *in personam* and the word "sued" in Arts 2 and 3 of the Convention should be construed accordingly (*The Deichland* [1989] 2 Lloyd's Rep. 113, CA). Where an arrest within art.1(2) of the 1952 Arrest Convention is effected, the claimant is entitled to rely upon art.57 of the 1968 Convention as excluding the exclusive jurisdiction of another convention country which would otherwise apply under art.2 of the 1968 Convention in the absence of some exempting factor under art.5 of the 1968 Convention, see *The Anna H* [1994] 1 Lloyd's Rep. 287, affirmed [1995] 1 Lloyd's Rep. 11, CA. The Court of Appeal further held that the Arrest Convention required only that the legal consequences of judicial detention of the ship should be that it became security for a maritime claim not that the claimant's commercial motive must be to obtain security.

In *Canada Trust Co v Stolzenberg* [2000] 4 All E.R. 481, the House of Lords held that on the true construction of Articles 2 and 6 of the Lugano Convention on Jurisdiction and the Enforcement of Judgments in Civil and Commercial Matters 1988 (identical

*Paragraph numbers marked with a "+" can be found online and on CD.*

for present purposes to the terms of the 1968 Brussels Convention referred to above), the word "sued" referred to the initiation of proceedings, and accordingly the English court took jurisdiction over a defendant, for the purposes of those provisions, on the date that the writ [claim form] was issued. Such a conclusion was supported by the language of the convention which used the concepts "sued", "bring proceedings" and "instituted proceedings" interchangeably. Applied by Christopher Clarke J. in *Cherney v Deripsaka* [2008] EWHC 1530 (Comm); [2009] 1 All E.R. (Comm) 333.

**Admiralty Court**

This is part of the QBD. It has jurisdiction in all causes and matters assigned by SCA 1981 to that division which involve the exercise of the High Court's Admiralty jurisdiction or its jurisdiction as a prize court. See SCA 1981 ss.5, 6, 61 and 62 and Sch.1. **2D–8**

**Claim in rem**

Admiralty claims may be either *in rem* or *in personam*. (now known as other Admiralty Claims). **2D–9**

An Admiralty claim *in rem* is in effect a claim against a *res*. (*The Longford* (1888) 14 P.D. 34, *per* Lord Esher M.R. at 37; *The City of Mecca* (1879) 5 P.D. 28 at 33; 6 P.D. 106; *The Burns* [1907] P. 137; SCA 1981 s.21 (para.2D–178 below). A *res* is usually a ship but may in some cases be cargo or freight, an aircraft or hovercraft. In such a claim the claimant may cause the *res* to be arrested if it is within the jurisdiction (see rules 61.5 *et seq.*). If the *res* is arrested and the claimant's claim is successful then unless the *res* has been released (as to which see rr.61.8 *et seq.*) judgment may be given against the *res* and an order made for its appraisement and sale. The proceeds of sale will be paid into court and will, after deduction of the fees and expenses of the Admiralty Marshal in connection with the arrest, custody, appraisement and the sale of the *res*, be available in or towards satisfaction of the claimant's judgment. If, as is frequently the case, there is more than one claim against the *res*, payment out of the proceeds of sale will be ordered in accordance with the Admiralty rules as to the priorities of claims, claims of the same priority ranking *pari passu*. As to proceedings for the determination of priority of claims (see r.61.10).

A claim *in rem* may also be instituted against the proceeds of sale by the court of a *res*.

If in a claim *in rem* issue or service of the claim form has been acknowledged and the claim form is not set aside, the personal liability of the defendant who has appeared is added and judgment may be given against him as well as against the *res*. See *The Gemma* [1899] P.285, CA and *The August 8* [1983] 2 A.C. 450; [1983] 1 Lloyd's Rep. 351, PC.

In *Republic of India v India Steamship Co Ltd* [1997] 3 W.L.R. 818; [1998] 1 Lloyd's Rep. 1 HL(E) it was held that for the purposes of s.34 of the Civil Jurisdiction and Judgments Act 1982:

> "a [claim] *in rem* is an action against the owners from the moment that the Admiralty Court is seised with jurisdiction. The jurisdiction of the Admiralty Court is invoked by the service of a [claim form], or, where a [claim form] is deemed to be served, as a result of the acknowledgment of the issue of the [claim form] by the defendant before service (*The Banco* [1971] P.137). From that moment the owners are parties *in rem*".

Dicta of Lord Brandon in *The August 8* [1983] 2 A.C. 450; [1983] 2 W.L.R. 419 at 456, PC, and *The Deichland* [1990] 1 Q.B. 361, CA, applied and *The Nordglimt* [1988] Q.B. 183 overruled. The case reviews claims *in rem* generally and states that the idea that a ship can be a defendant in legal proceedings was always a legal fiction which can now be discarded holding that in reality a claim *in rem* is an action against the owners. *Quaere* the extent and effect of the reasoning in this case in claims *in rem* generally. The position in respect of cases involving a maritime lien was expressly reserved as requiring separate consideration. See too *The Irina Zharkikh* [2001] 2 Lloyd's Rep. 319 (N.Z. Ct.).

A defendant who has acknowledged issue or service of the claim form may provide security in order to avoid the arrest of the *res* or to obtain its release if it has been arrested.

Sale by the court in a claim *in rem* is a sale of the whole property and it is sold free of all claims, encumbrances, liens, etc., with a clean title (see, e.g. *The Acrux* [1962] 1 Lloyd's Rep. 405) all existing claims, etc., being transferred to the proceeds of sale, against which claims begun after the sale must be brought. See also *The Blitz* [1992] 2 Lloyd's Rep. 441—sale of vessel by a local authority pursuant to its powers under s.44 of the Harbours, Docks and Piers Clauses Act 1847 is a sale free from mortgages. The position regarding maritime liens is unclear.

In *The Cerro Colorado* [1993] 1 Lloyd's Rep. 58, the court declared that any conduct which impedes or is likely to impede the ability of the Admiralty Marshal to achieve a fair market value upon the sale of the vessel (including but not limited to published statements that the vessel will, after sale by the Admiralty Marshal, remain encumbered with existing claims) is an interference with the administration of justice. Such conduct may expose anyone responsible to proceedings for contempt of court.

The following are the main matters of procedure peculiar to a claim *in rem*:

(a) a special form of claim form is used. See PD 61 para.3.1;

(b) service of the claim form must be in a manner prescribed by PD 61 para.3.6;

(c) judgment in default of acknowledgment of service, defence, defence to counterclaim or the filing of a collision statement of case must be applied for by application under rule 61.9;

(d) a claim form *in rem* cannot be served outside the jurisdiction.

**Claims against two or more "sister" ships**

**2D–10** When the AJA 1956 came into force it became possible in many cases for a claimant to proceed *in rem* against any one of a number of ships in the same beneficial ownership, see s.3(4). The practice soon became established in such cases of issuing one claim form against some or all of the ships against which the claimant was entitled to proceed and later amending the claim form by striking out the names of all ships save the one in respect of which the claim form had been served or against which a warrant of arrest had been issued. The claim form should be amended immediately after service by deleting all but one of the ship's names upon it (*The Freccia del Nord* [1989] 1 Lloyd's Rep. 388 at 391).

In *The Banco* [1971] P. 137; [1971] 1 Lloyd's Rep. 49, CA, in which it was held that only one ship could be served with a claim form *in rem* or arrested in respect of one cause of action, the practice described above was, by a majority, approved. See now SCA 1981 s.21(8) (paras 2D–178 and 2D–190 below). *The Banco* was distinguished by the Singapore Court of Appeal in *Permina Samudra* [1978] 1 Lloyds Rep. 315 but subsequently applied in *The Berny* [1979] Q.B. 80; [1978 1 All E.R. 1065; [1977] 2 Lloyds Rep 533 and followed in Scotland by the Court of Sessions: *The Afala* [1995] 2 Lloyd's Rep 286 .

**Claims in rem and other claims**

**2D–11** If it is desired to commence proceedings both *in rem* and *in personam* separate claim forms must be issued. See para.2D–143.

**Cautions**

**2D–12** See rr.61.7 and 61.8.

**Limitation Claim**

**2D–13** See para.1.4, *British Shipping Laws*, Vols 1 and 11 (but note the change of onus of proof introduced since last publication of Vols 1 and 11). Limitation actions must be assigned to the Queen's Bench Division and taken by the Admiralty Court (r.61.2(i)(c)). For special rules relating to limitation actions see r.61.11 below.

**Ship**

**2D–14** Compare the definition of ship in SCA 1981 s.24 and see note "Ship" at para.2D–153 below.

A ship is equipment within the meaning of s.1 of the Employers'Liability (Defective Equipment) Act 1969 (*The Derbyshire* [1988] A.C. 276; [1988] 1 Lloyd's Rep. 109, HL).

**Limitation of claims**

**2D–15** There are special periods, subject to the court's discretion, in collision and salvage: Merchant Shipping Act 1995 ss.190 and 195.

***Paragraph numbers marked with a "+" can be found online and on CD.***

## Admiralty claims[1]

**61.2—(1) The following claims must be started in the Admiralty Court—** 2D–16

**(a) a claim—**

**(i) in rem;**

**(ii) for damage done by a ship;**

**(iii) concerning the ownership of a ship;**

**(iv) under the Merchant Shipping Act 1995;**

**(v) for loss of life or personal injury specified in section 20(2)(f) of the Senior Courts Act 1981[2];**

**(vi) by a master or member of a crew for wages;**

**(vii) in the nature of towage; or**

**(viii) in the nature of pilotage;**

**(b) a collision claim;**

**(c) a limitation claim; or**

**(d) a salvage claim.**

**(2) Any other admiralty claim may be started in the Admiralty Court.**

**(3) Rule 30.5 applies to claims in the Admiralty Court except that the Admiralty Court may order the transfer of a claim to—**

**(a) the Commercial list;**

**(b) a Mercantile Court;**

**(c) the Mercantile list at the Central London County Court; or**

**(d) any other appropriate court.**

### Restrictions on Admiralty jurisdiction

*(1) Collision and similar actions if in personam* —See SCA 1981 s.22 (para.2D–191). 2D–17

*(2) Wages actions* —Section 4 of the Consular Relations Act 1968, provides that Orders in Council may be made to exclude or limit the jurisdiction to entertain proceedings relating to the pay or conditions of service of the master or crew of any ship or aircraft belonging to a state specified in the Order unless the Consul has first been notifed of the intention to invoke the jurisdiction of the court and has not objected. Orders have been made in respect of Austria, Belgium, Bulgaria, Denmark, Federal Republic of Germany, Greece, Hungary, Italy, Japan, Mexico, Norway, Poland, Romania, Spain, Sweden, Yugoslavia, Czechoslovakia and Egypt. (See Statutory Instruments 1970 Nos. 1903–1905, 1907–1914, 1917, 1918 and 1920, 1971 No. 1846 1978 No. 275 1976/768 and 1986/217.) Each of these orders provides for a period of two weeks for objection. Following the dissolution of Yugoslavia and Czechoslovakia the position in respect of the individual former constituent member states is uncertain. It is suggested that the Consul of the individual state concerned is notified. 2D–18

The above-mentioned Orders in Council additionally require a statement to the effect that the consular officer of the state concerned has been notified of the intention to invoke the jurisdiction of the court and has not objected within a period of two weeks from the date of such notification to be included among the details on which the claim is based at the time when the proceedings are commenced.

---

[1] Amended by the Civil Procedure (Amendment No.5) Rules 2001 (SI 2001/4015) and the Civil Procedure (Amendment No.4) Rules 2005 (SI 2005/3515).

[2] 1981 c.54. Renamed by the Constitutional Reform Act 2005 s.59 and Sch.11, para.1 with effect from October 1, 2009 (SI 2009/1604)

***Paragraph numbers marked with a "+" can be found online and on CD.***

Further Orders in Council may be issued from time to time.

In *The Andrea Ursula* [1971] Fo. 61 and 81, it was held that proceedings were a nullity for non-compliance with the above mentioned statutory requirements.

**2D–19** *(3) Crown* —No claim *in rem* lies against the Crown, but in certain circumstances such a claim may be allowed to continue as if *in personam*: Crown Proceedings Act 1947 s.29 (Vol.2, Section 21L).

**2D–20** *(4) Foreign sovereign states, etc.* —As to claims against foreign sovereigns, foreign sovereign states, ambassadors and diplomatic agents, members of their suites and certain international organisations generally, see CPR r.12.10. As to claims *in rem* against state owned ships and cargoes see also the State Immunity Act 1978 ss.10, 12 and 13.

A ship, belonging to private owners, requisitioned by the Crown, cannot be arrested while in Government service though if a maritime lien attaches it may be enforced after derequisitioning (*The Broadmayne* [1916] P. 64) and though a claim lies against the owners of the ship if the crew remain their servants (*The Messicano* (1916) 32 T.L.R. 519; *The Crindon* (1918) 35 T.L.R. 81; *The Eolo* [1918] 2 Ir.R. 78).

**2D–21** *(5) Rhine Navigation Convention 1868* —No court in England or Wales has jurisdiction in cases falling to be determined in accordance with the provisions of this convention. See SCA 1981 s.23 (para.2D–194).

**2D–22** *(6) Nuclear Installations Act 1965* —This Act consolidates and repeals the Nuclear Installations (Licensing and Insurance) Act 1959, and (with one exception relating to the Electricity (Amendment) Act 1961) the Nuclear Installations (Amendment) Act 1965. In the event of an occurrence involving nuclear matter, reference should be made to the Act; in particular, s.14 (protection for ships and aircraft) makes claims *in rem* against ships or aircraft and limitation of liability under the Merchant Shipping Act 1995 unavailable: the Act substitutes a new approach. This Act was amended by the Nuclear Installations Act 1969.

**2D–23** *(7) Liquidation and bankruptcy* —As to liquidation see the Insolvency Act 1986 s.130. See also *The Constellation* [1966] 1 W.L.R. 272; [1965] 2 Lloyd's Rep. 538; *Re Aro Co Ltd* [1980] Ch. 196; [1980] 1 All E.R. 1067, CA.

### Claims in rem[1]

**2D–24** **61.3—(1) This rule applies to claims in rem.**

**(2) A claim in rem is started by the issue of an in rem claim form as set out in Practice Direction 61.**

**(3) Subject to rule 61.4, the particulars of claim must—**

**(a) be contained in or served with the claim form; or**

**(b) be served on the defendant by the claimant within 75 days after service of the claim form.**

**(4) An acknowledgment of service must be filed within 14 days after service of the claim form.**

**(5) The claim form must be served—**

**(a) in accordance with Practice Direction 61; and**

**(b) within 12 months after the date of issue and rules 7.5 and 7.6 are modified accordingly.**

**(6) If a claim form has been issued (whether served or not), any person who wishes to defend the claim may file an acknowledgment of service.**

[1] Amended by the Civil Procedure (Amendment No.5) Rules 2001 (SI 2001/4015) and the Civil Procedure (Amendment No.2) Rules 2009 (SI 2009/3390).

*Paragraph numbers marked with a "+" can be found online and on CD.*

### Claim in rem

A claim *in rem* may properly be issued only when the jurisdiction can be invoked by proceedings *in rem* under ss.21(2), (3), (4) or (5) of SCA 1981 (paras 2D–178 and 2D–179 to 2D–189). See too note "Claim in rem" under r.61.1.3 above. **2D–25**

### Renewal of a claim form

As to renewal of a claim form *in rem* on grounds of impossibility of service on the ship see *The Berny* [1979] Q.B. 80; [1978] 1 All E.R. 1065; [1977] 2 Lloyd's Rep. 533. As to renewal of a claim form generally see CPR r.7.6 and notes thereto. See also *The Helen Roth* [1980] Q.B. 273; [1980] 2 W.L.R. 549; [1980] 1 All E.R. 1078; [1980] 1 Lloyd's Rep. 477 as to the effect of a sale before the claim form was renewed. **2D–26**

### Acknowledgment of service before actual service

In a claim *in rem* or limitation claim *issue* of the claim form may be acknowledged, see r.61.3(6) above. **2D–27**

### Methods of service

For methods of service of a claim form *in rem* see PD 61 para.3.6 which includes service by an alternative method under CPR r.6.8 so long as *res* is within the jurisdiction. **2D–28**

## Special provisions relating to collision claims[1]

**61.4—(1) This rule applies to collision claims.** **2D–29**

**(2) A claim form need not contain or be followed by particulars of claim and rule 7.4 does not apply.**

**(3) An acknowledgment of service must be filed.**

**(4) A party who wishes to dispute the court's jurisdiction must make an application under Part 11 within 2 months after filing his acknowledgment of service.**

**(5) Every party must—**

**(a) within 2 months after the defendant files the acknowledgment of service; or**

**(b) where the defendant applies under Part 11 within 2 months after the defendant files the further acknowledgment of service,**

**file at the court a completed collision statement of case in the form specified in Practice Direction 61.**

**(6) A collision statement of case must be—**

**(a) in the form set out in Practice Direction 61; and**

**(b) verified by a statement of truth.**

**(7) A claim form in a collision claim may not be served out of the jurisdiction unless—**

**(a) the case falls within section 22(2)(a), (b) or (c) of the Senior Courts Act 1981 [2]; or**

**(b) the defendant has submitted to or agreed to submit to the jurisdiction; and**

---

[1] Amended by the Civil Procedure (Amendment No.5) Rules 2001 (SI 2001/4015), the Civil Procedure (Amendment) Rules 2008 (SI 2008/2178) and the Civil Procedure (Amendment No.2) Rules 2009 (SI 2009/3390).

[2] 1981 c.54. Renamed by the Constitutional Reform Act 2005 s.59 and Sch.11, para.1 with effect from October 1, 2009 (SI 2009/1604).

**the court gives permission in accordance with Section IV of Part 6.**

**(8) Where permission to serve a claim form out of the jurisdiction is given, the court will specify the period within which the defendant may file an acknowledgment of service and, where appropriate, a collision statement of case.**

**(9) Where, in a collision claim in rem ("the original claim")—**

**(a) (i) a Part 20 claim; or**

**(ii) a cross-claim in rem**

**arising out of the same collision or occurrence is made; and**

**(b) (i) the party bringing the original claim has caused the arrest of a ship or has obtained security in order to prevent such arrest; and**

**(ii) the party bringing the Part 20 claim or cross-claim is unable to arrest a ship or otherwise obtain security,**

**the party bringing the Part 20 claim or cross claim may apply to the court to stay the original claim until sufficient security is given to satisfy any judgment that may be given in favour of that party.**

**(10) The consequences set out in paragraph (11) apply where a party to a claim to establish liability for a collision claim (other than a claim for loss of life or personal injury)—**

**(a) makes an offer to settle in the form set out in paragraph (12) not less than 21 days before the start of the trial;**

**(b) that offer is not accepted; and**

**(c) the maker of the offer obtains at trial an apportionment equal to or more favourable than his offer.**

**(11) Where paragraph (10) applies the parties will, unless the court considers it unjust, be entitled to the following costs—**

**(a) the maker of the offer will be entitled to—**

**(i) all his costs from 21 days after the offer was made; and**

**(ii) his costs before then in the percentage to which he would have been entitled had the offer been accepted; and**

**(b) all other parties to whom the offer was made—**

**(i) will be entitled to their costs up to 21 days after the offer was made in the percentage to which they would have been entitled had the offer been accepted; but**

**(ii) will not be entitled to their costs thereafter.**

**(12) An offer under paragraph (10) must be in writing and must contain—**

**(a) an offer to settle liability at stated percentages;**

**(b) an offer to pay costs in accordance with the same percentages;**

*Paragraph numbers marked with a "+" can be found online and on CD.*

**(c) a term that the offer remain open for 21 days after the date it is made; and**

**(d) a term that, unless the court orders otherwise, on expiry of that period the offer remains open on the same terms except that the offeree should pay all the costs from that date until acceptance.**

**Collision statement of case, formerly called preliminary act**

"The object of the collision statement of case is to obtain from the parties statements of the facts at a time when they are fresh in their recollection" (per Sir Robert Phillimore, in *The Frankland* (1872) L.R. 3 A. & E. 511). The other main purpose is to force the parties to "plead blind" (*The Vortigern* (1859) Sw. 518). A statement of fact in a collision statement of case is a formal admission, binding the party making it, and can only be departed from by special permission (per Fletcher Moulton L.J. in *The Seacombe, The Devonshire* [1912] P.21, 59, *The Devonshire* [1912] P. 21, 59; see *The Ladybell* (1933) 49 T.L.R. 595; 46 Ll.L.Rep. 342). As a rule, therefore, the court will not allow either party subsequently to alter anything in his collision statement of case, not even to correct a clerical error (*The Miranda* (1882) 7 P.D. 185). But in *The Esso Brussels* (1968) Fo. 373, unrep., on this point, permission was given during the trial to amend Articles xii and xiv. Permission, however, is sometimes asked for and given to lead evidence not in accordance with the party's collision statement of case; if witnesses give evidence not in accordance with the collision statement of case and no leave is asked for, the court may hold the party to what is in the collision statement of case (see *The Semiramis* [1952] 2 Lloyd's Rep. 86 at 93). The court is not bound by the admissions in any collision statement of case (see, e.g. *The Vanessa* [1960] 1 Lloyd's Rep. 82; *The Geo. W. McKnight* (1947) 80 Ll.L.R. 419, HL). A party who has filed a defective collision statement of case, which does not give the information required by the rule, may be ordered on application by the other party to amend it (*The Godiva* (1886) 11 P.D. 20) or to give particulars. **2D–30**

Note that the present and previous rules are wider than the rule which they replaced. The old rule referred to "actions for damage by collision between vessels. ."; *The El Oso* (1925) 21 Ll.L.Rep. 340; *Armstrong v Gaselee* (1889) L.R. 22 QBD 250; *Secretary of State for India v Hewitt & Co* (1888) 6 Asp. 384; *The John Boyne* (1877) 36 L.T. 29; 3 Asp. M.L.C. 346, are cases decided under that rule. Each party is required in his collision statement of case to state the material facts upon which he founds his case and the court may order the costs of a collision statement of case which differs widely from the facts proved at the trial to be disallowed on taxation (*The Pelican I* (1926) 25 Ll.L.Rep. 150). The information must be given fully; any concealment will be viewed by the court with suspicion and, as stated, on the application of the other party, the court may order amendment (*The Godiva*, above) or particulars so that all the questions are answered properly. When a ship in a river is on a fixed course as opposed to a course which is constantly changed, either the magnetic or the true course should be stated (*The Rievaulx Abbey* (1910) 11 Asp. 437). In a collision case in which one ship is, or both ships are, at anchor, the collision statement of case or collision statements of case filed on behalf of the owners of the anchored ship or both anchored ships should state in art.vii the heading of the ship at anchor (*The Macroom* (1927) 17 Asp. 288 (one ship at anchor, the other under way); *The Erna* (1927) 27 Ll.L.Rep. 170 (a dragging case; both ships at anchor)). In *The Judith M.* (1968) 112 S.J. 859, a statement in the claimant's collision statement of case (art.(ix)(b)) and elsewhere that the defendants' ship was heading "across the bows" of the claimant's ship "from port to starboard" was criticised by Brandon J.; it was desirable to state such heading with greater particularity. A defendant is not entitled to demand of another defendant whom he blames in his defence that he shall file a collision statement of case, unless he issues a claim form against him (*The Carlston and the Balcombe* [1926] P. 82).

**Section 20(3)(b)(i) SCA 1981 "... collision between ships ..."**

A floating landing stage is not a ship, therefore no collision statements of case are required in an action arising from a collision between a steamship and it (*The Craighall* [1910] P. 207). On the other hand, where claimants whose ship, A, was in collision with another, B, blamed the owners of B and also the dock authority which had some **2D–31** measure of control over B it was held that all three parties must file collision statements of case; the dock authority were obliged to do the best they could to answer the questions in the collision statement of case (*The Beaverford* [1961] 1 W.L.R. 793; [1960] 3 All E.R. 612; [1960] 2 Lloyd's Rep. 216). This case was followed in *British Oil & Cake Mills Ltd v John H. Whitaker (Tankers) Ltd (The Grainger's No.4)* [1964] 1 W.L.R. 1474; [1964] 3 All E.R. 705; [1964] 2 Lloyd's Rep. 415. A collision statement of case is required of a widow whose husband has been killed in a collision (see *Webster v M. S. & L. Ry.* [1884] W.N. 1). This is so even where the ship has been sunk in the collision with the loss of all hands. See as to further information concerning information contained in collision statements of case: (*The Isle of Cyprus* (1890) 15 P.D. 134; *The Bernard* [1905] W.N. 73; *The Biola* (1876) 34 L.T. 185; *The Radnorshire* (1880) 5 P.D. 172).

#### Dispensing with or limiting collision statement of case

**2D-32** It is considered that the court retains power to order dispensing with or limiting the requirement under this paragraph of collision statements of case under its general CPR powers or inherent jurisdiction in appropriate though rare cases. An order to dispense with or limit the filing of collision statements of case will not be made on a consent application; the court will always require the parties to attend and explain the reasons for the application. Application is made by application notice before the Registrar.

#### Expert Witnesses etc

**2D-33** For guidance in use of expert witnesses, illustrative plotting and computer stimulation, see *Owners of the Pelopidas v Owners of the TRSL Concord* [1999] 2 All E.R. (Comm) 737.

#### Damages

**2D-33.1** In *Owners of the Front Ace v Owners of the Vicky 1 ("The Front Ace")* [2008] EWCA Civ 101; [2008] 2 All E.R. (Comm) 42; [2008] 2 Lloyd's Rep. 45; [2008] 1 C.L.C. 229, the Court of Appeal held that the ballast/laden or loss of use/loss of profit basis was not the appropriate methodology to be adopted in all cases where a shipowner lost a fixture as a result of a collision. On the question of whether a percentage deduction for loss of a chance was appropriate in the assessment of the quantum of damages in respect of a collision at sea, it held that where the expert witnesses had agreed the appropriate market rate for use of the vessel, in assessing the damages the Admiralty Registrar had been wrong to make a deduction of 20 per cent for "loss of a chance" from that agreed figure. The following cases, cited in *The Front Ace* , are also of importance in assessing damages: *The Oropesa* [1943] P. 32; [1943] 1 All E.R. 211; (1942) 74 Ll. L. Rep. 86 ; (CA) which provides that a claimant is entitled to damages unless there has been a break in the chain of causation; *Owners of the Steamship Gracie v Owners of the Steamship Argentino (The Argentino)* (1889) L.R. 14 App. Cas. 519 ; (HL) on the methodology to be adopted in cases where a claimant has lost a fixture as a result of the collision and *Allied Maples Group Ltd v Simmons & Simmons* [1995] 1 W.L.R. 1602; [1995] 4 All E.R. 907; [1996] C.L.C. 153 on the question of whether a deduction should be made for the chance of obtaining a replacement contract.

#### Costs

**2D-33.2** In *"KRYSIA" Maritime Inc v Intership Ltd* [2008] EWHC 1880 (Admlty) Aikens J. held that the general rule in CPR 44.3(2)(a) applies to claims where liability is apportioned, unless there was a good reason why it should not do so. He held that no rule or principle had been established in the Admiralty Court, where there is no counterclaim, that a claimant who is found at fault under s.87(1) and (2) of the Merchant Shipping Act 1995 should recover its costs in proportion to the percentage of liability of the defendant.

### Arrest[1]

**2D-34** **61.5—(1) In a claim in rem—**

[1] Amended by the Civil Procedure (Amendment No.5) Rules 2001 (SI 2001/4015) and the Civil Procedure (Amendment No.2) Rules 2009 (SI 2009/3390).

(a) a claimant; and

(b) a judgment creditor

may apply to have the property proceeded against arrested.

(2) Practice Direction 61 sets out the procedure for applying for arrest.

(3) A party making an application for arrest must—

(a) request a search to be made in the Register before the warrant is issued to determine whether there is a caution against arrest in force with respect to that property; and

(b) file a declaration in the form set out in Practice Direction 61.

(4) A warrant of arrest may not be issued as of right in the case of property in respect of which the beneficial ownership, as a result of a sale or disposal by any court in any jurisdiction exercising admiralty jurisdiction in rem, has changed since the claim form was issued.

(5) A warrant of arrest may not be issued against a ship owned by a State where by any convention or treaty, the United Kingdom has undertaken to minimise the possibility of arrest of ships of that State until—

(a) notice in the form set out in Practice Direction 61 has been served on a consular officer at the consular office of that State in London or the port at which it is intended to arrest the ship; and

(b) a copy of that notice is attached to any declaration under paragraph (3)(b).

(6) Except—

(a) with the permission of the court; or

(b) where notice has been given under paragraph (5),

a warrant of arrest may not be issued in a claim in rem against a foreign ship belonging to a port of a State in respect of which an order in council has been made under section 4 of the Consular Relations Act 1968,[1] until the expiration of 2 weeks from appropriate notice to the consul.

(7) A warrant of arrest is valid for 12 months but may only be executed if the claim form—

(a) has been served; or

(b) remains valid for service at the date of execution.

(8) Property may only be arrested by the Marshal or his substitute.

(9) Property under arrest—

(a) may not be moved unless the court orders otherwise; and

(b) may be immobilised or prevented from sailing in such manner as the Marshal may consider appropriate.

[1] 1968 c.18.

**(10) Where an in rem claim form has been issued and security sought, any person who has filed an acknowledgment of service may apply for an order specifying the amount and form of security to be provided.**

**General note**

2D–35 Where the Admiralty jurisdiction of the High Court may be and is invoked by a claim *in rem* the *res* proceeded against may be arrested if it is within the territorial jurisdiction of the court. For the circumstances in which the jurisdiction *in rem* may be invoked see SCA 1981 s.21 (para.2D–178). It will be observed that in some cases only the property concerned may be proceeded against *in rem* (s.21(2) *ibid.*) and that if a maritime lien has attached, a claim *in rem* may be brought against the ship or property in question regardless of any change of ownership since the cause of action arose other than by a judicial sale. In all other cases it is necessary to look at the person, if any, who was liable *in personam* at the time the cause of action arose; a claim *in rem* may be brought against ships of which he is the beneficial owner or demise charterer at the time of the issue of the claim provided he was the owner or charterer or in possession or control of the ship in connection with which the claim arose at the time when the claim arose. The expression "claim is brought" means "when the claim form is issued" (*The Carmania II* [1963] 2 Lloyd's Rep. 152). Once a claim is brought against a ship by issue of a claim form a sale of the ship by her owner will not deprive the claimant of any rights he may have (*The Monica S* [1968] P. 741; [1967] 3 All E.R. 740; [1967] 2 Lloyd's Rep. 113). But *quaere* the effect of *The Blitz* [1992] 2 Lloyd's Rep. 441. As to the requirements regarding personal liability in actions *in rem* generally and where there is a maritime lien in particular, see *The Father Thames* [1979] 2 Lloyd's Rep. 364.

Until the Civil Jurisdiction and Judgments Act 1982 the sole purpose of an action *in rem* was to obtain security in respect of a judgment of the court (or a sum due under a settlement) in that claim, the court had no jurisdiction to arrest ships or to keep ships under arrest for other purposes, see *The Cap Bon* [1967] 1 Lloyd's Rep. 543. Now s.26 of the 1982 Act enables the Admiralty Court to retain the security of the *res* or the security for the purpose of arbitration or other proceedings in a United Kingdom or overseas court. See also *The Jalamatsyr* [1987] 2 Lloyd's Rep. 164.

The issue of a warrant of arrest is not a discretionary remedy. If the statutory requirements set out in PD 61, para.61.5.3 are complied with the claimant is entitled to issue the warrant of arrest and if there is such compliance there is no further scope for the application of any duty of full and frank disclosure, *The Varna* [1993] 2 Lloyd's Rep. 253.

A vessel cannot remain in the custody of the Admiralty Marshal and yet be allowed to trade outside the jurisdiction (*The Bazias 3, The Bazias 4* [1993] Q.B. 673; [1993] 2 W.L.R. 854; [1993] 2 All E.R. 964; [1993] 1 Lloyd's Rep. 101, CA).

The Admiralty Marshal may pursuant to the undertaking in **ADM4** call for money on account of the expenses of an arrest as occasion demands.

**Merchant Shipping Act 1995**

2D–36 Where a state has enacted legislation giving effect to the provisions of the International Convention Relating to the Limitation of the Liability of Owners of Sea-Going Ships 1957, but not the International Convention on Limitation of Liability for Maritime Claims 1976, the setting up of a limitation fund in such a state will not prevent the arrest of a ship in another state which has enacted legislation giving effect to the 1976 Convention.

**Crown: foreign sovereign states, etc.**

2D–37 See notes under paras 2D–19 and 2D–20 above. Since the termination of the 1968 Treaty and Protocols between the UK and the USSR there is no longer any treaty or convention within 61.5(5) in force.

**Delay in prosecution of claim**

2D–38 The Marshal is not a shipkeeper and parties should not delay in prosecuting an action in which a vessel is under arrest (*The Italy II* [1987] 2 Lloyd's Rep. 162).

**Wrongful arrest**

2D–39 Whether a caution has been entered or not, if property is arrested by reason of *mala fides* or *crassa negligentia*, damages may be recovered in Admiralty or, indeed, at common law (*The Walter D. Wallett* [1893] P. 202; *The Evangelismos* (1858) 12 Moo. P.C. 352; Swa. 378; *The Strathnaver* (1875) 1 App. Cas. 58; *The Cathcart* (1867) L.R. 1 A. & E. 314; *The Eudora* (1879) 4 P.D. 208). Damages may also be recovered where an arrest has been unduly continued (*The Cheshire Witch* (1858) Br. & Lush. 362; *The Margaret and Jane* (1869) L.R. 2 A. & E. 345). As to claims for damages where release has been delayed owing to a caution against release and payment having been entered without good and sufficient reason, see r.61.8(5). See also r.61.7(5)(b).

**Rule 61.5(8)**

The warrant may only be executed by being served by the Marshal or his substitute upon the ship or property concerned in accordance with PD 61, para.61.5.5. The Marshal's officer acts as his substitute in London; elsewhere Customs officers and County Court bailiffs do so. See too *The Berny* [1977] 2 Lloyd's Rep. 533 at 548. **2D–40**

> "The court has to bear in mind that the duty of arresting a ship, and often at the time of serving a [claim form] on her, falls on the Admiralty Marshal or his deputies, and it should not adopt an approach to the matter which would or might expose these persons to unreasonable difficulties or dangers."

The claim form and warrant are frequently served at approximately the same time, but either may be served first. As to effect of failure to comply with the requirements as to service, see *The Prins Bernhard* [1964] P. 117; [1963] 3 All E.R. 735; [1963] 2 Lloyd's Rep. 236. As to the non-fatal character of a minor failure, see *The Sullivar* [1965] 2 Lloyd's Rep. 350.

Freight, being incorporeal, cannot be arrested nor can a claim form be served upon it, but where a claim is brought against freight, or cargo and freight, or ship, cargo and freight, the claim form can as against freight, be served on the cargo concerned or the ship in which it was carried, see PD 61 para.3.6(1) and a warrant can be executed against the cargo or ship or both (PD 61 para.5.5) in the manner prescribed.

**Contempt of court**

To move a ship from where she is lying with knowledge of the fact that a warrant has been issued, is contempt of court (*The Seraglio* (1885) 10 P.D. 120) and *a fortiori* after the warrant has been served. As to various acts amounting to contempt see *The Petrel* (1836) 3 Hagg. 299; *The Bure* (1850) 14 Jur. Pt 1, 1123; *The Armenian* (Sh.Gaz. March 1874); *The Rhenania* (Sh.Gaz. November 1909); *The Selina Stanford Times*, November 17, 1908. For modern examples see *The Jarlinn* [1965] 1 W.L.R. 1098; [1965] 2 All E.R. 886; [1965] 2 Lloyd's Rep. 191; *The Jarvis Brake* [1976] 2 All E.R. 886; [1976] 2 Lloyd's Rep. 320; *The Merdeka* [1982] 1 Lloyd's Rep. 401. **2D–41**

It is contempt to attempt to sell a ship in respect of which an order for sale by the court is in force (*The Jarvis Brake* [1976] 2 All E.R. 886. See also *Cerro Colorado* [1993] 1 Lloyd's Rep. 58).

## Security in claim in rem[1]

**61.6—(1) This rule applies if, in a claim in rem, security has been given to—** **2D–42**

**(a) obtain the release of property under arrest; or**

**(b) prevent the arrest of property.**

**(2) The court may order that the—**

**(a) amount of security be reduced and may stay the claim until the order is complied with; or**

**(b) claimant may arrest or re-arrest the property proceeded against to obtain further security.**

**(3) The court may not make an order under paragraph (2)(b) if the total security to be provided would exceed the value of the property at the time—**

[1] Amended by the Civil Procedure (Amendment No.5) Rules 2001 (SI 2001/4015).

*Paragraph numbers marked with a "+" can be found online and on CD.*

**(a) of the original arrest; or**

**(b) security was first given (if the property was not arrested).**

Rule 61.6.2(b)

2D–43 In *The Prinsengracht* [1993] 1 Lloyd's Rep. 41, applying *The Arctic Star*, *The Times*, February 5, 1985; it was held that arrest or re-arrest after security is given and before judgment is to be viewed in the light of whether the arrest or re-arrest is oppressive and vexatious in the circumstances of the particular case.

### Cautions against arrest[1]

2D–44 **61.7—(1) Any person may file a request for a caution against arrest.**

**(2) When a request under paragraph (1) is filed the court will enter the caution in the Register if the request is in the form set out in Practice Direction 61 and—**

**(a) the person filing the request undertakes—**

**(i) to file an acknowledgment of service; and**

**(ii) to give sufficient security to satisfy the claim with interest and costs; or**

**(b) where the person filing the request has constituted a limitation fund in accordance with Article 11 of the Convention on Limitation of Liability for Maritime Claims 1976[2] he—**

**(i) states that such a fund has been constituted; and**

**(ii) undertakes that the claimant will acknowledge service of the claim form by which any claim may be begun against the property described in the request.**

**(3) A caution against arrest—**

**(a) is valid for 12 months after the date it is entered in the Register; but**

**(b) may be renewed for a further 12 months by filing a further request.**

**(4) Paragraphs (1) and (2) apply to a further request under paragraph (3)(b).**

**(5) Property may be arrested if a caution against arrest has been entered in the Register but the court may order that—**

**(a) the arrest be discharged; and**

**(b) the party procuring the arrest pays compensation to the owner of or other persons interested in the arrested property.**

Rule 61.7(2)(b)

2D–45 The 1976 Convention is now to be found in Sch.7 to the Merchant Shipping Act 1995.

[1] Amended by the Civil Procedure (Amendment No.5) Rules 2001 (SI 2001/4015) and the Civil Procedure (Amendment No.2) Rules 2009 (SI 2009/3390).

[2] The text of the Convention is set out in Sch.7 to the Merchant Shipping Act 1995 (c.21).

**Entry of a caution against arrest**

The entry of a caution does not in fact prevent the issue or execution of a warrant of arrest but a person who causes property to be arrested despite the existence of a caution and without good and sufficient reason may be ordered to pay damages. See r.61.7(5). **2D–46**

**Withdrawal of a caution against arrest**

If a cautioner wishes to withdraw a current caution against arrest, application for such withdrawal must be made to the court, *The Iberian Ocean*, October 25, 2002, Admiralty Court. **2D–47**

## Release and cautions against release[1]

**61.8—(1) Where property is under arrest—** **2D–48**

**(a) an in rem claim form may be served upon it; and**

**(b) it may be arrested by any other person claiming to have an in rem claim against it.**

**(2) Any person who—**

**(a) claims to have an in rem right against any property under arrest; and**

**(b) wishes to be given notice of any application in respect of that property or its proceeds of sale,**

**may file a request for a caution against release in the form set out in Practice Direction 61.**

**(3) When a request under paragraph (2) is filed, a caution against release will be entered in the Register.**

**(4) Property will be released from arrest if—**

**(a) it is sold by the court;**

**(b) the court orders release on an application made by any party;**

**(c) (i) the arresting party; and**

**(ii) all persons who have entered cautions against release**

**file a request for release in the form set out in Practice Direction 61; or**

**(d) any party files—**

**(i) a request for release in the form set out in Practice Direction 61 (containing an undertaking); and**

**(ii) consents to the release of the arresting party and all persons who have entered cautions against release.**

**(5) Where the release of any property is delayed by the entry of a caution against release under this rule any person who has an interest in the property may apply for an order that the person who entered the caution pay damages for losses suffered by the applicant because of the delay.**

[1] Amended by the Civil Procedure (Amendment No.5) Rules 2001 (SI 2001/4015) and the Civil Procedure (Amendment No.2) Rules 2009 (SI 2009/3390).

*Paragraph numbers marked with a "+" can be found online and on CD.*

**(6) the court may not make an order under paragraph (5) if satisfied that there was good reason to—**

**(a) request the entry of; and**

**(b) maintain**

**the caution.**

**(7) Any person—**

**(a) interested in property under arrest or in the proceeds of sale of such property; or**

**(b) whose interests are affected by any order sought or made,**

**may be made a party to any claim in rem against the property or proceeds of sale.**

**(8) Where—**

**(a) (i) a ship is not under arrest but cargo on board her is; or**

**(ii) a ship is under arrest but cargo on board her is not; and**

**(b) persons interested in the ship or cargo wish to discharge the cargo,**

**they may, without being made parties, request the Marshal to authorise steps to discharge the cargo.**

**(9) If—**

**(a) the Marshal considers a request under paragraph (8) reasonable; and**

**(b) the applicant gives an undertaking in writing acceptable to the Marshal to pay—**

**(i) his fees; and**

**(ii) all expenses to be incurred by him or on his behalf**

**on demand,**

**the Marshall will apply to the court for an order to permit the discharge of the cargo.**

**(10) Where persons interested in the ship or cargo are unable or unwilling to give an undertaking as referred to in paragraph (9)(b), they may—**

**(a) be made parties to the claim; and**

**(b) apply to the court for an order for—**

**(i) discharge of the cargo; and**

**(ii) directions as to the fees and expenses of the Marshal with regard to the discharge and storage of the cargo.**

**Caution against release—general note**

2D–49 A caution under this paragraph may be entered by any person, whether he has begun a claim against the property under arrest (or the proceeds of sale) or not. A person entering a caution whose claim carries no maritime lien should consider the desirability of issuing a claim *in rem* in addition, to entering a caution because, if the *res* is sold by the owner while under arrest, the claimant's remedy against that *res* will be lost, though he may in some circumstances be able to proceed in a claim against a "sister ship". See SCA 1981 s.21(4). The effect of entering a caution is to prevent the release of the property or payment out of the proceeds of sale without the consent of the person entering a caution or order of the court. See rr.61.8(2) and 61.8(4). A party applying for an order for release or payment out notwithstanding the existence of a caution, should serve the application notice on any persons entering a caution. The principle is "no caution, no notice". All arrestors should consider advisability of entering caution.

Use of the caution procedure normally makes it unnecessary for a claimant in a claim *in rem* against property which is under arrest in another claim to issue a warrant for the arrest of that property. A claimant who has issued a claim *in rem* against a ship which is under arrest and has entered a caution under this paragraph will be considered as a secured creditor for the purpose of deciding whether or not the discretion of the court should be exercised in his favour under s.231 of the Companies Act 1948 (now Insolvency Act 1986 s.130) (*Re Aro Co Ltd* [1980] Ch. 196; [1980] 1 All E.R. 1067, CA).

### Release of property in a usual case

The owner may obtain the consent of the arresting party to the release by giving security to his satisfaction. There are many forms of security accepted but in almost all cases the arresting party is satisfied with a guarantee or undertaking given out of court, e.g. by the Defendant's P & I Club or by a bank or insurance company. Payment into court is sometimes used. Bail by bond is now a rarity. **2D–50**

The arresting party is "entitled to sufficient security to cover the amount of his claim with interest and costs on the basis of his reasonably arguable best case". (*The Moscanthy* [1971] 1 Lloyd's Rep. 37 at 44). Where the right to limit liability under the Merchant Shipping Acts is not disputed it seems that the proper amount is the limitation figure with interest and costs. It seems also that in no case can the amount exceed the value of the *res*. See *The Charlotte* [1920] P. 78. Where there is a dispute as to the amount of security to be provided, an application can be made to the court to determine the amount. See, for example, *The Moscanthy* [1971] 1 Lloyd's Rep. 37. The application should normally be made to the Admiralty Registrar by application notice in the claim asking for the release of the property upon provision of security for a stated amount. Where security has been provided in an excessive amount e.g., in order to obtain the prompt release of the property, an application may be made to the court for reduction of the amount of security.

It is, of course, always open to a party not to provide security and to allow his property to remain under arrest.

A party demanding excessive security may have to pay (1) the costs of a successful application to reduce the amount of that security and (2) the expense of providing the excess. Further as to security and release see British Shipping Laws, Vol. 1. The power to exact security must not be used oppressively; where there is a genuine dispute or discussion about the appropriate amount, the party seeking security ought to put his cards on the table and explain to the other party or his solicitors the grounds on which he claims to exercise this strong power: (*The Moscanthy* [1971] 1 Lloyd's Rep. 37 at 46–47).

### Letters of undertaking

See *C Itoh & Co Ltd v Campanhia De Navegaçao Lloyd Brasileiro and Steamship Mutual Underwriting Association (Bermuda) Ltd* [1999] 1 Lloyd's Rep. 115; *Same v Republic Federativa Do Brasil (The Rio Assu) (No.2)* [1999] 1 Lloyd's Rep. 115, CA held *inter alia* that on the true construction of the letter of undertaking the liability of the demise charterers' P & I Club under the letter of undertaking survived the demise of the demise charterer of the vessel. **2D–51**

See too *Galaxy Energy International Ltd v Assuranceforeningen Skuld (The Oakwell)* [1999] 1 Lloyd's Rep. 249 held *inter alia* that on a true construction of the letter of undertaking the obligation to instruct solicitors to accept service of the claim was unaffected by the fact that the vessel had been sold post provision of the letter and before proceedings issued.

### Release when claim stayed

In *The Bazias 3, The Bazias 4* [1993] Q.B. 673; [1993] 2 W.L.R. 854; [1993] 1 Lloyd's **2D–52**

Rep. 101, the Court of Appeal held that the effect of s.26 of the Civil Jurisdiction and Judgments Act 1982 was to assimilate *in rem* proceedings in the Admiralty Court with arbitration claims so that the discretion to release an arrested vessel was the same in both cases. Accordingly on an application to release a vessel held as security for a claim in arbitration the court would, in accordance with the usual practice, only exercise its discretion to release on provision of sufficient security to cover the claim, plus interest and costs on the basis of the claimant's reasonably arguable best case. Inconvenience and difficulty in finding sufficient liquid financial resources were not sufficient grounds for departing from the usual practice. There would be no cross-undertaking as to damages under s.26(2). The court granted a stay of action under s.1 of the Arbitration Act 1975 and ordered both vessels to remain under arrest pending further order.

**Release by setting aside warrant of arrest**

**2D–53** E.g. where the declaration leading to a warrant of arrest contains material inaccuracies relating to the statutory requirements set out in PD 61 para.5.3 and arrest cannot be validly maintained: in *The Varna* [1993] 2 Lloyd's Rep. 253, CA, the court held that beyond the establishment of the facts then required by O.75, r.5(9) and now by PD 61 para.61.5.3 there was no further scope for an attack upon the issue not being a discretionary remedy. The Court of Appeal, however, stated that a warrant might be set aside as a result of the claim *in rem* being struck out or the proceedings stayed and that there might be a general discretionary power on a with notice application to set aside the warrant on the basis that its continuance was in all the circumstances unjust.

**Release pursuant to Merchant Shipping Act 1995**

**2D–54** Section 185 and Sch.7 provide that the court may, and in certain circumstances must, order the release of a ship or other property which has been arrested, or the security given to prevent, or obtain release from, arrest. See also *The Putbus* [1969] P. 136; [1969] 2 All E.R. 676; [1969] 1 Lloyd's Rep. 253, CA). See also *The Wladyslaw Lokotiek* [1978] 2 Lloyd's Rep. 520 .

**Rule 61.8(5)**

**2D–55** For cases see *The Cormer* (1863) Br. & L. 161; *The Don Ricardo* (1880) 5 P.D. 121; 4 Asp. M.L.C. 225.

**Rule 61.8(7)**

**2D–56** The object of this provision is to enable a person who has a substantial interest in the *res* to intervene, if this interest may be injuriously affected by the claim against the *res* and to protect his interests (*The Dowthorpe* (1843) 2 W.Rob. 73, 77). The rights of an intervener are limited to the protection of his interest in the *res*, and he has no *locus standi* to raise issues which are not material to his purpose (*The Lord Strathcona* [1925] P. 143; see also *The Byzantion* (1922) 127 L.T. 756; 16 Asp. M.L.C. 19, as to defences which an intervener may and those which he may not set up). Application is to the Admiralty Registrar.

**Inherent jurisdiction**

**2D–57** The court has inherent jurisdiction to allow a person who has no interest in the property under arrest to intervene, if the effect of the arrest is to cause him serious hardship, difficulty or danger (*The Mardina Merchant* [1975] 1 W.L.R. 147; [1974] 3 All E.R. 749; [1974] 2 Lloyd's Rep. 424, in which the interests of a harbour authority were adversely affected by the presence of the arrested ship at one of their quays).

As to intervention for the purpose of applying to be added as a defendant or for other purposes see CPR r.19.

## Judgment in default[1]

**2D–58** **61.9—(1) In a claim in rem (other than a collision claim) the claimant may obtain judgment in default of—**

[1] Amended by the Civil Procedure (Amendment No.5) Rules 2001 (SI 2001/4015) and the Civil Procedure (Amendment No.2) Rules 2009 (SI 2009/3390).

**(a) an acknowledgment of service only if—**

**(i) the defendant has not filed an acknowledgment of service; and**

**(ii) the time for doing so set out in rule 61.3(4) has expired; and**

**(b) defence only if—**

**(i) a defence has not been filed; and**

**(ii) the relevant time limit for doing so has expired.**

**(2) In a collision claim, a party who has filed a collision statement of case within the time specified by rule 61.4(5) may obtain judgment in default of a collision statement of case only if—**

**(a) the party against whom judgment is sought has not filed a collision statement of case; and**

**(b) the time for doing so set out in rule 61.4(5) has expired.**

**(3) An application for judgment in default—**

**(a) under paragraph (1) or paragraph (2) in an in rem claim must be made by filing—**

**(i) an application notice as set out in Practice Direction 61;**

**(ii) a certificate proving service of the claim form; and**

**(iii) evidence proving the claim to the satisfaction of the court; and**

**(b) under paragraph (2) in any other claim must be made in accordance with Part 12 with any necessary modifications.**

**(4) An application notice seeking judgment in default and, unless the court orders otherwise, all evidence in support, must be served on all persons who have entered cautions against release on the Register.**

**(5) The court may set aside or vary any judgment in default entered under this rule.**

**(6) The claimant may apply to the court for judgment against a party at whose instance a notice against arrest was entered where—**

**(a) the claim form has been served on that party;**

**(b) the sum claimed in the claim form does not exceed the amount specified in the undertaking given by that party in accordance with rule 61.7(2)(a)(ii); and**

**(c) that party has not fulfilled that undertaking within 14 days after service on him of the claim form.**

#### Arrest of the res

The rule does not require the arrest of the *res* as a condition precedent to judgment in default (*The Nautik* [1895] P. 121). **2D–59**

#### Practice

It should be noted that before judgment in default can be obtained under this provision there must be adduced "evidence proving the claim to the satisfaction of the Admiralty Court". See r.61.9(3). It is therefore necessary for the claimant's case to be properly proved. **2D–60**

The usual practice is for evidence to be given by affidavit or certified statements and the court usually refuses to allow oral evidence to be adduced. See *The Nettuno*, Lloyd's List and Shipping Gazette, January 30, 1969.

The application notice and any evidence should be filed in the registry in good time in order that figures, etc. may be checked there before the hearing. If this is done it may be possible to obtain judgment for a specified sum and so avoid the expense of a reference. Any document in a foreign language must be accompanied by a translation which must itself be proved. If an order for appraisement and sale (r.61.10 below) is desired this should be stated in the application notice.

### Priorities

2D–61 If cautions have been entered under r.61.8(2) any decree made on the hearing of the application for judgment will usually reserve all questions of priorities. As to the determination of priorities and orders that may be made in connection therewith on an application for a judgment under this rule, see r.61.10.

### Payment out of proceeds of sale

2D–62 See r.61.10(5) below.

### Setting aside judgment

2D–63 It is not necessary for the defendant to have acknowledged service of the claim form when applying to set aside a judgment given in default (*The Ruben Martinez Villena* [1987] 1 Lloyd's Rep. 621).

## Sale by the court, priorities and payment out[1]

2D–64 **61.10—(1) An application for an order for the survey, appraisement or sale of a ship may be made in a claim in rem at any stage by any party.**

**(2) If the court makes an order for sale, it may—**

**(a) set a time within which notice of claims against the proceeds of sale must be filed; and**

**(b) the time and manner in which such notice must be advertised.**

**(3) Any party with a judgment against the property or proceeds of sale may at any time after the time referred to in paragraph (2) apply to the court for the determination of priorities.**

**(4) An application notice under paragraph (3) must be served on all persons who have filed a claim against the property.**

**(5) Payment out of the proceeds of sale will be made only to judgment creditors and—**

**(a) in accordance with the determination of priorities; or**

**(b) as the court orders.**

### Res must be under arrest

2D–65 The *res* must be in the hands of the court before an order for sale will be made (*The Wexford* (1888) 13 P.D. 10) but in special circumstances an order for arrest, appraisement and sale may be made where it is not (*The Berriz* 1905 Fo. 497). In *The Ricuna* 1974 Fo. 380 unrep., the practice of requiring that the *res* be under arrest in the claim in which an order for appraisement and sale is sought was approved. The power of the court in an Admiralty claim to order a court sale cannot be invoked in a claim *in personam* (*The Lady Tahilla* [1967] 1 Lloyd's Rep. 591 at 601). Appraisement and sale may be ordered *pendente lite*. As to the circumstances in which such an order will be

[1] Amended by the Civil Procedure (Amendment No. 5) Rules 2001 (SI 2001/4015).

made see *The Myrto* [1977] 2 Lloyd's Rep. 243 at 259. Such a sale was ordered on the *defendant's* application in *The Westport (No.1)* [1965] 1 W.L.R. 796.

The court may order a sale by the Admiralty Marshal without Appraisement to a specific buyer for a specific price.

An order for appraisement and sale however can only be made in claim in which the property is under arrest. Therefore, if the arresting claimant is dilatory or does not proceed with his claim it will become necessary for the claimant in a second or subsequent claim to issue a warrant and procure its execution so as to be in a position when he moves for judgment to apply for an order for appraisement and sale. The costs of a second or subsequent arrest are not normally allowed except in such circumstances.

**Property not under arrest**

If a ship under arrest is being adversely affected by property on board (e.g. perishables) which is not under arrest, an order, if granted, may include an order for sale of that property. **2D–66**

**Sale in foreign currency**

The Admiralty Marshal may if he thinks fit in order to obtain the best price in any particular case, invite offers and sell the property for a price in a foreign currency (*The Halcyon the Great* [1975] 1 W.L.R. 515; [1975] 1 All E.R. 882; [1975] 1 Lloyd's Rep. 518). **2D–67**

**Rule 61.10(3)**

An application under this paragraph should be made in the claim brought by the applicant. Notice of application must be served on all persons who have obtained judgment against the ship and on all cautioners. The names and addresses for service of these persons can be obtained from the Admiralty and Commercial Registry. **2D–68**

**Note**

As to priorities, see *British Shipping Laws, McGuffie: Admiralty Practice* and Halsbury's *Laws of England*; and Meeson, *Admiralty Jurisdiction and Practice*. See also as to variation of order determining priorities, *The Fairport (No.4)* [1967] 1 W.L.R. 964; [1967] 2 All E.R. 914n; [1967] 1 Lloyd's Rep. 602. For examples of subrogation of mortgagees to the rights and priorities of master and crew upon payment, *with permission of the court*, by the mortgagees of the master's and crew's wages, see *The Berostar* [1970] 2 Lloyd's Rep. 403 and *The Vasilia* [1972] 1 Lloyd's Rep. 51. **2D–69**

In *The Ruta* [2000] 1 W.L.R. 2068; [2001] 1 All E.R. 450, it was held that questions of priority were not capable of being compartmentalised in the form of strict rules of ranking, since the courts had adopted a broad discretionary approach, rival claims being ranked by reference to considerations of equity, public policy and commercial expediency, with the ultimate aim of doing that which was just in the circumstances of each case; and that, since the wage claimants had no alternative form of redress against the vessel owners and the only remedy open to them was to recover their unpaid wages from the proceeds of sale of the vessel, considerations of public policy justified according them a very high level of priority, giving them precedence over the damage claims and the contractual claim of the caveator.

**Payment out from proceeds of sale under rule 61.10(3) and (4)**

The court has no jurisdiction to order payment out from the proceeds of a sale by order of the court, to persons other than judgment holders or, in the case of the residue after all claims have been satisfied, the defendant (*The Saxon King* 1975 Fo. 253 unrep.). Exceptionally, payment out may be ordered to any person where the defendants and all other parties interested in the proceeds of sale (judgment holders, interveners and caveators) consent (*The Valiant* 1977 Fo. 446 unrep.). A payment out on account may be ordered where all parties consent, or where the priorities are such that it is clear the claimant will ultimately be entitled to at least the amount ordered. See *The Reina (No.2)* [1963] 2 Lloyd's Rep. 513. **2D–70**

**Charging and stop orders**

Payment out from proceeds of sale may be affected by a charging order or stop order pursuant to CPR Pt 74 or an application or order under CPR r.72.10. **2D–71**

***Paragraph numbers marked with a "+" can be found online and on CD.***

**Note**

2D–72 As to apportionment of a payment in a salvage action, see *The Talamba and the Troll* [1965] P. 433; [1965] 2 All E.R. 775; [1965] 2 Lloyd's Rep. 128.

In particular, note the observations of Sheen J. in *The Vasili Shelgunov* [1988] 2 Lloyd's Rep. 34, at 38 in relation to Admiralty claims *in personam*. Approved by Court of Appeal [1989] 1 Lloyd's Rep. 542, CA.

## Limitation claims[1]

2D–73 **61.11—(1) This rule applies to limitation claims.**

**(2) A claim is started by the issue of a limitation claim form as set out in Practice Direction 61.**

**(3) The—**

- **(a) claimant; and**
- **(b) at least one defendant**

**must be named in the claim form, but all other defendants may be described.**

**(4) The claim form—**

- **(a) must be served on all named defendants and any other defendant who requests service upon him; and**
- **(b) may be served on any other defendant.**

**(5) The claim form may not be served out of the jurisdiction unless—**

- **(a) the claim falls within section 22(2)(a), (b) or (c) of the Senior Courts Act 1981** [2] **;**
- **(b) the defendant has submitted to or agreed to submit to the jurisdiction of the court; or**
- **(c) the Admiralty Court has jurisdiction over the claim under any applicable Convention; and**

**the court grants permission in accordance with Section IV of Part 6.**

**(6) An acknowledgment of service is not required.**

**(7) Every defendant upon whom a claim form is served must—**

- **(a) within 28 days of service file—**
  - **(i) a defence; or**
  - **(ii) a notice that the defendant admits the right of the claimant to limit liability; or**
- **(b) if the defendant wishes to—**
  - **(i) dispute the jurisdiction of the court; or**
  - **(ii) argue that the court should not exercise its jurisdiction,**

**file within 14 days of service (or where the claim form is served out of the jurisdiction, within the time specified in rule 6.35) an acknowledgment of service as set out in Practice Direction 61.**

---

[1] Amended by the Civil Procedure (Amendment No.5) Rules 2001 (SI 2001/4015), the Civil Procedure (Amendment) Rules 2008 (SI 2008/2178) and the Civil Procedure (Amendment No.2) Rules 2009 (SI 2009/3390).

[2] 1981 c.54. Renamed by the Constitutional Reform Act 2005 s.59 and Sch.11, para.1 with effect from October 1, 2009 (SI 2009/1604).

(8) If a defendant files an acknowledgment of service under paragraph (7)(b) he will be treated as having accepted that the court has jurisdiction to hear the claim unless he applies under Part 11 within 14 days after filing the acknowledgment of service.

(9) Where one or more named defendants admits the right to limit—

(a) the claimant may apply for a restricted limitation decree in the form set out in Practice Direction 61; and

(b) the court will issue a decree in the form set out in Practice Direction 61 limiting liability only against those named defendants who have admitted the claimant's right to limit liability.

(10) A restricted limitation decree—

(a) may be obtained against any named defendant who fails to file a defence within the time specified for doing so; and

(b) need not be advertised, but a copy must be served on the defendants to whom it applies.

(11) Where all the defendants upon whom the claim form has been served admit the claimant's right to limit liability—

(a) the claimant may apply to the Admiralty Registrar for a general limitation decree in the form set out in Practice Direction 61; and

(b) the court will issue a limitation decree.

(12) Where one or more of the defendants upon whom the claim form has been served do not admit the claimant's right to limit, the claimant may apply for a general limitation decree in the form set out in Practice Direction 61.

(13) When a limitation decree is granted the court—

(a) may—

(i) order that any proceedings relating to any claim arising out of the occurrence be stayed;

(ii) order the claimant to establish a limitation fund if one has not been established or make such other arrangements for payment of claims against which liability is limited; or

(iii) if the decree is a restricted limitation decree, distribute the limitation fund; and

(b) will, if the decree is a general limitation decree, give directions as to advertisement of the decree and set a time within which notice of claims against the fund must be filed or an application made to set aside the decree.

(14) When the court grants a general limitation decree the claimant must—

(a) advertise it in such manner and within such time as the court directs; and

(b) file—

*Paragraph numbers marked with a "+" can be found online and on CD.*

**(i) a declaration that the decree has been advertised in accordance with paragraph (a); and**

**(ii) copies of the advertisements.**

**(15) No later than the time set in the decree for filing claims, each of the defendants who wishes to assert a claim must file and serve his statement of case on—**

**(a) the limiting party; and**

**(b) all other defendants except where the court orders otherwise.**

**(16) Any person other than a defendant upon whom the claim form has been served may apply to the court within the time fixed in the decree to have a general limitation decree set aside.**

**(17) An application under paragraph (16) must be supported by a declaration—**

**(a) stating that the applicant has a claim against the claimant arising out of the occurrence; and**

**(b) setting out grounds for contending that the claimant is not entitled to the decree, either in the amount of limitation or at all.**

**(18) The claimant may constitute a limitation fund by making a payment into court.**

**(19) A limitation fund may be established before or after a limitation claim has been started.**

**(20) If a limitation claim is not commenced within 75 days after the date the fund was established—**

**(a) the fund will lapse; and**

**(b) all money in court (including interest) will be repaid to the person who made the payment into court.**

**(21) Money paid into court under paragraph (18) will not be paid out except under an order of the court.**

**(22) A limitation claim for—**

**(a) a restricted decree may be brought by counterclaim; and**

**(b) a general decree may only be brought by counterclaim with the permission of the court.**

**Limitation claim**

**2D–74** For definition see r.61.1(2)(e). These claims are assigned to the Queen's Bench Division and taken by the Admiralty Court, see r.61.2(1)(c). See also SCA 1981 s.20(1)(b) and (3)(c). Limitation of liability may be relied on by way of defence to a claim or counterclaim.

A limitation decree or declaration can be granted before liability is established. The establishment of liability either by trial or agreement is not a precondition to the seeking and granting of a limitation decree or declaration, see *Bouygues Offshore SA. v Caspian Shipping Co* [1998] 2 Lloyd's Rep. 461. See further *The "Western Regent"* [2005] EWHC 240 (Admlty); [2005] 2 Lloyd's Rep 54 at para.20:

> "...an ability to constitute a limitation fund under Article 11.1 of the 1976 Convention is neither a pre-condition of the jurisdiction to hear and determine a limitation claim nor of the power given to the Court in an appropriate case to grant a limitation decree." (Affirmed [2005] EWCA Civ 985; [2005] 2 Lloyd's Rep 359, CA)

***Paragraph numbers marked with a "+" can be found online and on CD.***

In *Herceg Novi (Owners) v Ming Galaxy (Owners)* [1998] 4 All E.R. 238; [1998] 2 Lloyd's Rep. 454, CA, the court held that the 1976 Convention was not an internationally sanctioned and objective view of where substantial justice was viewed as lying, but was simply the view of some 30 states. Moreover, the preference for the 1976 Convention had no greater justification than for the 1957 regime and, in terms of abstract justice, neither convention was objectively more just than the other. Accordingly, since substantial justice would be done in Singapore, the appeal would be allowed and an unconditional stay of the English action would be granted.

In *MSC Mediterranean Shipping Co SA v Delmur BVBA (The Rosa M)* [2000] 2 All E.R. (Comm) 458, the court held that for it to be established that the claimant's liability was not limited under art.4 of the Convention, it was necessary for the defendant to prove that the casualty was caused by the personal act or omission of the charterers, that those personal acts or omissions were committed recklessly and at the time of those acts or omissions the *alter ego* of the charterers actually knew that the casualty would probably result. In the absence of any allegation of intent, the authorities made it clear that a person challenging the right to limit had to establish both reckless conduct and knowledge that the relevant loss would probably result, and "shut-eye" knowledge did not constitute "knowledge" for the purposes of art.4, which required actual knowledge. This approach has been affirmed by the Court of Appeal in *The Leerort* [2001] 2 Lloyd's Rep. 291, the court holding that it is only the personal act or omission of a shipowner which defeats the right to limit. A shipowner is defined in art 1 as the owner, charterer, manager or operator of a seagoing ship. Thus, to defeat the right to limit, it is necessary to identify the causative act or omission on the part of such a person that caused the loss. Furthermore, it is only conduct committed with intent to cause such loss, or recklessly with knowledge that such loss would probably result, that defeats the right to limit. It seems that person challenging the right to limit must establish both reckless conduct *and* knowledge that the relevant loss would probably result. In considering the relevant loss the court continued that it seems that where the loss in respect of which a claim is made resulted from a collision between ship A and ship B, the owners of ship A, or cargo in ship A, will only defeat the right to limit liability on the owner of ship B if they can prove that the owner of ship B intended that it should collide with ship A, or acted recklessly with the knowledge that it was likely to do so (para.13).

The alternative, which is perhaps arguable, is that the claimant merely has to prove that the owner of ship B intended that his ship should collide with another ship, or acted recklessly with the knowledge that it was likely to do so (*ibid.*, para.17).

On the facts of this case it is not necessary to decide which alternative is correct. In either event the reality is that when damage results from a collision the shipowner will only lose his right to limit if it can be proved that he deliberately or recklessly acted in way which he knew was likely to result in the loss of or damage to the property of another in circumstances where, inevitably, the same consequences would be likely to flow to his own vessel (*ibid.*, para.18).

Article 2.1(a) of the 1976 Convention does not extend the right to limit to a claim for damage to the vessel by reference to the tonnage of which limitation is to be calculated, see *CMA CGM SA v Classica Shipping Co Ltd (The CMA Djakarta)* [2004] EWCA Civ 114; [2004] 1 Lloyd's Rep. 460, CA. Nor does the Convention provide for a limitation on liablity for the costs of litigation, see *Thompson v Masterton* [2004] 1 Lloyd's Rep 304 [Roy. Ct. Guernsey]. See too *Newcastle Port Corp v Pevitt (The Robert Whitmore)* [2004] 2 Lloyd's Rep. 47 (NSWSC), fund is exclusive of costs.

**Claim form**

Special Admiralty Forms, Admiralty Limitation claim form, see the *Civil Procedure Forms Volume*. **2D–75**

**Service**

The claim form must be served on all named defendants in the claim form and not merely described. As to service out of the jurisdiction see r.61.11(5). **2D–76**

In the *ICL Shipping Ltd v Chin Tai Steel Enterprise Co Ltd (The ICL Vikraman)* [2003] EWHC 2320; [2004] 1 W.L.R. 2254; [2004] 1 Lloyd's Rep. 21 the court held that in CPR r.61.11(5)(c) the "claim" referred to is the claim to limit rather than any underlying claim and the words "any applicable convention" should be construed as covering the 1976 Convention. This case also concerns the construction and scope of Arts 11 and 13 of the 1976 Convention.

**Restricted decree**

2D–77 When a claimant in a limitation claim is satisfied that there will be no claims upon the fund other than the claims of the defendants who have acknowledged issue or service of the claim form the claimant may not want a decree which is good against the world. The claimant may apply to the Admiralty Registrar to amend the claim form by deleting reference to any defendants other than those named. The application should be accompanied by a letter signed by all consenting parties stating that in their view it is not anticipated that any further claims will emerge. The Registrar may then order payment out of the limitation fund in court.

If further claimants do emerge after payment out the claimant will be obliged to constitute a new fund should they wish to limit their liability against the new claimants. This practice arises from a decision of Sheen J. in an unreported case (*The Rena* [1979] Fo. 138).

**Owner-master**

2D–78 As to the right of an owner-master to limit his liability, see *The Annie Hay* [1968] P. 341; [1968] 1 All E.R. 657; [1968] 1 Lloyd's Rep. 141.

**Charterers**

2D–79 Charterers cannot limit their liability under the 1976 Convention in respect of claims brought by owners against them: see *Aegean Sea Traders Corp v Repsol Petroleo SA* [1998] 2 Lloyd's Rep. 39. See further *CMA CGM SA v Classica Shipping Co Ltd (The CMA Djakarta)* [2004] EWCA Civ 114; [2004] 1 Lloyd's Rep. 460, CA. The term charterers is to be given its ordinary meaning. Accordingly, the charterer's ability to limit will depend on the type of claim brought against him and not the capacity (e.g. qua owner) in which he was acting when his liability was incurred.

In *Metvale Ltd v Monsanto International SARL* [2008] EWHC 3002 (Admiralty Court), on the hearing of a preliminary issue, it was held that a slot charterer is within the definition of "shipowner" for the purposes of Art 1 of the 1976 Convention and were entitled to limit their liability under the Convention and under the Merchant Shipping Act 1995.

**Costs of application**

2D–80 The costs of an application for a decree of limitation under the former s.17 of the Merchant Shipping Act 1979, now s.185 of the Merchant Shipping Act 1995, should normally follow the event, see *The Capitan San Luis* [1994] Q.B. 465; [1994] 2 W.L.R. 465; [1994] 2 W.L.R. 299; [1994] 1 All E.R. 1016; [1993] 2 Lloyd's Rep. 573. In this case it was held that the shipowners should pay the costs of proving the matters which he had to establish in order to obtain the decree and that the claimant should pay the costs of investigating and determining the facts which the Convention provided he must prove, if at the end of the day he failed to establish those facts.

**Rule 61.11.13(a)(iii)**

2D–81 It seems that in a distribution pursuant to this paragraph, the court would order interest accrued on the limitation fund in court to be apportioned *pro rata* to the distribution.

## Stay of proceedings[1]

2D–82 **61.12 Where the court orders a stay of any claim in rem—**

**(a) any property under arrest in the claim remains under arrest; and**

**(b) any security representing the property remains in force,**

**unless the court orders otherwise.**

[1] Amended by the Civil Procedure (Amendment No.5) Rules 2001 (SI 2001/4015).

***Paragraph numbers marked with a "+" can be found online and on CD.***

## Assessors[1]

**61.13 The court may sit with assessors when hearing—** **2D–83**

**(a) collision claims; or**

**(b) other claims involving issues of navigation or seamanship, and**

**the parties will not be permitted to call expert witnesses unless the court orders otherwise.**

### Assessors

In the specified cases, nautical assessors usually advise the Court of Appeal and the Judge of the Admiralty Court upon questions of navigation and seamanship if such questions arise. In some cases only one nautical assessor is called in and occasionally their attendance is dispensed with altogether. In the Admiralty Court, the assessors are usually two of the Elder Brethren of Trinity House neither of whom should have been in the service of any party to the claim (*The Bremen* (1931) 47 T.L.R. 505) save where an Elder Brother is a retired officer of the Royal Navy and one of H.M. ships is involved. If Trinity House is a party, one or two of such Court of Appeal assessors as are not Elder Brethren may be called on. Where nautical assessors are present, evidence in the nature of expert opinion on matters of nautical skill and practice, and as to the deductions to be drawn from nautical facts, is usually inadmissible (*The Gazelle* (1842) 1 W.Rob. 471). In *The St Chad* [1965] 2 Lloyd's Rep. 1, affirming; [1965] 1 Lloyd's Rep. 107, however, an order made provided for a fishery assessor to assist the court and also for each side to be at liberty to call an experienced trawler skipper to give general evidence on the system of work in trawlers of the relevant type, as the system was said to have changed so recently that the new developments might be outside the practical experience of a fishery assessor. A comparable order was made in *The Bedford Earl* 1954 Fo. 218 unrep., but this case never came to trial. As to the Court of Appeal, see para.9A–213 below. **2D–84**

See generally CPR r.35.15 and Practice Direction—Experts and Assessors para.6.1 at 35–006 and the Admiralty and Commercial Courts Guide, Section N.14 and para. 2D–142 below.

Assessors may be called in to assist the Registrar at a reference, see PD 61 para.13.3. The function of nautical assessors is to advise the court upon nautical matters (*The City of Berlin* [1908] P. 110; see *The New Pelton* [1891] P. 258; *The River Derwent* (1891) 7 Asp. 467). There is no right of cross-examination. The decision of the case rests entirely with the judge (*The Gannet* [1900] A.C. 234; *Owners of SS. Australia v Owners of SS. Nautilus* [1927] A.C. 145; *San Onofre, The v Melanie, The (No.1)* [1925] A.C. 246; *Owners of the Artemisia v Owners of the Douglas* [1927] A.C. 164); this equally applies in the Court of Appeal (*The Llanelly* (1926) 25 Ll.L.Rep. 37, p.39, HL) and the Supreme Court, formerly the House of Lords, (*The Marinegra* [1960] 2 Lloyd's Rep. 1). Even in purely nautical matters the judge is not bound to follow the advice of his assessors, if it does not agree with his own opinion (see *The Magna Charta* (1872) 1 Asp. 153; *Aid, The* (1881) L.R. 6 P.D. 84; *Beryl, The* (1884) L.R. 9 P.D. 137, 141; *Swanland, The* (1855) 2 Sp. 107; *Fred, The* (1895) 7 Asp. 550; *Owners of SS. Melanie v Owners of SS. San Onofre (No.1)* [1925] A.C. 246; *Owners of SS. Australia v Owners of Cargo of SS. Nautilus*, above; *Spero, The* (1947-48) 81 Ll. L. Rep. 350 at 354 see *The British Resource* (1941) 70 Ll.L.Rep. 93 at 102, per du Parcq L.J., and *Carrick Coast, The* (1947-48) 81 Ll. L. Rep. 447 at 451, per Willmer J.) as to judging ordinary navigating officers by the exceptionally high standard of knowledge and experience of the Elder Brethren. The assessors should not be asked any question that is tantamount to asking them whether they would find for the claimant or the defendant (see *The Ausomia* (1920) 2 L.L.Rep. 123 at 124, HL). The assessors in an appeal court are not substituted for those previously consulted. They are additional but not to be preferred to them unless the advice given is such as in itself is more acceptable to the appellate court (*Sobieski, The* [1949] P. 313 at 379). There is no question of appeal from one set of assessors to another set (*Owners of SS. Australia v Owners of Cargo of SS. Nautilus*. See also *The Fina Canada* [1962] 2

[1] Amended by the Civil Procedure (Amendment No. 5) Rules 2001 (SI 2001/4015).

Lloyd's Rep. 445). In *The St Chad* [1965] 2 Lloyd's Rep. 1, CA, Willmer L.J. pointed out that nautical assessors in the Court of Appeal and the court below were of equal standing. He also said that it was their function to advise on nautical questions put to them by the court whether or not such question had been canvassed by counsel. If there is a difference of opinion between assessors and a judge cannot decide which advice is sound he must regard the point as not proven (see *The Dageld* (1947) 80 Ll.L.Rep. 517, reversing (1947) 80 Ll.L.Rep. 225 at 230; *Owners of S.S. Australiav Owners of Cargo of SS. Nautilus*) but he may reach a decision by rejecting the advice of one assessor and accepting that of the other (see *The Taiwan* (1947) 80 Ll.L.Rep. 580 at 586).

In order to comply with art.6(1) of the European Convention for the Protection of Human Rights and Fundamental Freedoms when a court has received evidence from an assessor it is appropriate, except in cases where such discussion is unnecessary in the light of submissions made earlier, that the preferable modern practice of putting questions to the assessors after discussion with counsel should be complemented by a practice of disclosing their answers to counsel, either orally or in writing—in order that any inappropriate submission can be made as to whether the judge should accept this advice, *Owners of the Bow Spring v Owners of the Manzanillo* [2004] EWCA Civ 1007; [2005] 1 W.L.R. 144; [2004] 4 All E.R. 899; [2005] 1 Lloyd's Rep 1, CA.

The Court of Appeal has been known to adopt the advice of Elder Brethren in the lower court, rejecting that of their own assessors (*The Sobieski*, above; see also *The Miraflores and The Abadesa* [1966] P. 18; [1966] 1 All E.R. 553; [1966] 1 Lloyd's Rep. 97 at 108, per Willmer L.J. A judge will not infrequently state in his judgment that he has sought advice on certain points, giving the results of having done so without detail, and saying whether he accepts or rejects the advice tendered (contrast *The Aurelian* [1957] 2 Lloyd's Rep. 417 at 422, where Willmer J. set out verbatim in his judgment the questions put to the Elder Brother). Questions and answers are in writing in the Court of Appeal.

As to assessors' fees, see para.2D–142 below; *mutatis mutandis* the fees in the High Court and Court of Appeal are the same.

***Paragraph numbers marked with a "+" can be found online and on CD.***

# PRACTICE DIRECTION 61—ADMIRALTY CLAIMS

*This Practice Direction supplements CPR Part 61*

## Scope

**1.1** Practice Direction 58 also applies to Admiralty claims except where it is inconsistent with Part 61 or this practice direction. **2D-85**

### Admiralty and Commercial Registry

RCJ Room EB13 (Tel. 020 7947 6112). Hours: 10.00–16.30. See PD to CPR Pt 2, at 2PD.2. **2D-86**

Inquiries as to practice may be made in person or by telephone. The Admiralty and Commercial Registry was initially established by *Practice Direction* [1987] 3 All E.R. 616 issued by the Lord Chief Justice with the concurrence of the Admiralty judge and the judge in charge of the Commercial List. In relation to Admiralty and Commercial matters it replaces and carries out all the functions of the Central Office including the issuing of processes. Fees are paid to the Supreme Court Accounts Office, but the Registry may accept payment of a fee for a single item by way of a Solicitor's cheque.

### Issue of claim form by fax

See Practice Direction—Commercial Court, para.2.2 and Appendix A thereto. **2D-87**

### Use of postal facilities in the Registry

Section N12 of the Admiralty and Commercial Courts Guide provides as follows: **2D-88**

N12.1 Applications together with the requisite documents may be posted to:

The Admiralty and Commercial Registry,
Room EB13,
Royal Courts of Justice,
Strand,
London WC2 2LL.

N12.2 In addition to the classes of business for which the use of postal facilities is permitted by the CPR or the Commercial Court Guide, the filing of the following classes of documents is also permitted in Admiralty matters:

(i) Requests for cautions;

(ii) Collision Statements of Case

N12.3 (a) Documents sent by post for filing must be accompanied by two copies of a list of the documents sent and an envelope properly addressed to the sender.

(b) On receipt of the documents in the Registry, the court officer will, if the circumstances are such that had the documents been presented personally they would have been filed, cause them to be filed and will, by post, notify the sender that this has been done. If the documents would not have been accepted if presented personally the court officer will not file them but will retain them in the Registry for collection by the sender and will, by post, so inform the sender.

(c) When documents received through the post are filed by the court officer they will be sealed and entered as filed on the date on which they were received in the Registry.

### Issuance of Admiralty Claim Forms and Warrants of Arrest out of High Court District Registries post March 25, 2002

It is not intended that the facility to issue Admiralty Claim Forms and Warrants of Arrest from District Registries of the High Court be removed under the new Part 61 and its associated Practice Direction. This facility should be continued. There must however be prior consultation with the Admiralty Marshal before any Warrant of Arrest is issued as has happened hitherto and the court file must be sent immediately upon the issue of the Claim Form and any Warrant of Arrest to the Admiralty and Commercial Registry at the Royal Courts of Justice as before in order that the **2D-89**

Admiralty Registrar may issue case management directions as required by the new Admiralty Practice Direction.

In so far as the new rule and Practice Direction read in conjunction with Part 58 and its Practice Direction provide that such facilities are to be provided out of the Admiralty and Commercial Registry the issuing District Registry will be deemed as providing the same on behalf of the Admiralty and Commercial Registry so long as the procedure outlined above is followed. District Registry numbering will continue to be used in the first place on issue. (Admiralty Registrar, March 18, 2002).

### Case management

2D–90 **2.1** After a claim form is issued the Registrar will issue a direction in writing stating—

(1) whether the claim will remain in the Admiralty Court or be transferred to another court; and

(2) if the claim remains in the Admiralty Court–

(a) whether it will be dealt with by–

(i) the Admiralty judge; or

(ii) the Registrar; and

(b) whether the trial will be in London or elsewhere.

**2.2** In making these directions the Registrar will have regard to–

(1) the nature of the issues and the sums in dispute; and

(2) the criteria set in rule 26.8 so far as they are applicable.

**2.3** Where the Registrar directs that the claim will be dealt with by the Admiralty judge, case management directions will be given and any case management conference or pre-trial review will be heard by the Admiralty judge.

#### Application to Judge and to Admiralty Registrar

2D–91 Any party wishing to make an application to an Admiralty Judge should apply to the Admiralty and Commercial Registry (Listing Office) where all necessary arrangements will be made. Applications to the Admiralty Registrar should be applied for in the Admiralty and Commercial Registry (General Office).

### Claims in rem

2D–92 **3.1** A claim form in rem must be in Form **ADM1**.

**3.2** The claimant in a claim in rem may be named or may be described, but if not named in the claim form must identify himself by name if requested to do so by any other party.

**3.3** The defendant must be described in the claim form.

**3.4** The acknowledgment of service must be in Form **ADM2**. The person who acknowledges service must identify himself by name.

**3.5** The period for acknowledging service under rule 61.3(4) applies irrespective of whether the claim form contains particulars of claim.

**3.6** A claim form in rem may be served in the following ways:

(1) on the property against which the claim is brought by fixing a copy of the claim form–

(a) on the outside of the property in a position which may reasonably be expected to be seen; or

(b) where the property is freight, either–

(i) on the cargo in respect of which the freight was earned; or

*Paragraph numbers marked with a "+" can be found online and on CD.*

(ii) on the ship on which the cargo was carried;

(2) if the property to be served is in the custody of a person who will not permit access to it, by leaving a copy of the claim form with that person;

(3) where the property has been sold by the Marshal, by filing the claim form at the court;

(4) where there is a notice against arrest, on the person named in the notice as being authorised to accept service;

(5) on any solicitor authorised to accept service;

(6) in accordance with any agreement providing for service of proceedings; or

(7) in any other manner as the court may direct under rule 6.15 provided that the property against which the claim is brought or part of it is within the jurisdiction of the court.

**3.7** In claims where the property—

(1) is to be arrested; or

(2) is already under arrest in current proceedings,

the Marshal will serve the in rem claim form if the claimant requests the court to do so.

**3.8** In all other cases in rem claim forms must be served by the claimant.

**3.9** Where the defendants are described and not named on the claim form (for example as "the Owners of the Ship X"), any acknowledgment of service in addition to stating that description must also state the full names of the persons acknowledging service and the nature of their ownership.

**3.10** After the acknowledgment of service has been filed, the claim will follow the procedure applicable to a claim proceeding in the Commercial list except that the claimant is allowed 75 days to serve the particulars of claim.

**3.11** A defendant who files an acknowledgment of service to an in rem claim does not lose any right he may have to dispute the jurisdiction of the court (see rule 10.1(3)(b) and Part 11).

**3.12** Any person who pays the prescribed fee may, during office hours, search for, inspect and take a copy of any claim form in rem whether or not it has been served.

#### Amendment of claim form

Where after the issue of a claim in an action *in rem* the defendants' vessel is sold, the title of the defendants should be amended to read "The Owners of the ship X, now named Y" (*The Mawan* [1988] 2 Lloyd's Rep. 459 at 460.) **2D–93**

#### Paragraph 61.3.6(3)

The property must have been sold by the court and part of the proceeds of sale must still be in court. Where property has been sold by an agent who retains the proceeds, a claim form cannot be served on those proceeds (*The Optima* (1905) 74 L.T.P. 94; *The Fornjot* (1907) 24 T.L.R. 26). In *The Eva* (1950) 84 Ll.L.R. 20 wartime compensation money was held not to be a *res* or represent a *res*. **2D–94**

### Collision claims

**4.1** A collision statement of case must be in Form **ADM3**. **2D–95**

***Paragraph numbers marked with a "+" can be found online and on CD.***

**4.2** A collision statement of case must contain—

(1) in Part 1 of the form, answers to the questions set out in that Part; and

(2) in Part 2 of the form, a statement—

(a) of any other facts and matters on which the party filing the collision statement of case relies;

(b) of all allegations of negligence or other fault which the party filing the collision statement of case makes; and

(c) of the remedy which the party filing the collision statement of case claims.

**4.3** When he files his collision statement of case each party must give notice to every other party that he has done so.

**4.4** Within 14 days after the last collision statement of case is filed each party must serve a copy of his collision statement of case on every other party.

**4.5** Before the coming into force of Part 61, a collision statement of case was known as a Preliminary Act and the law relating to Preliminary Acts will continue to apply to collision statements of case.

### Arrest

2D–96 **5.1** An application for arrest must be—

(1) in Form **ADM4** (which must also contain an undertaking); and

(2) accompanied by a declaration in Form **ADM5**.

**5.2** When it receives an application for arrest that complies with the rules and the practice direction the court will issue an arrest warrant.

**5.3** The declaration required by rule 61.5(3)(b) must be verified by a statement of truth and must state—

(1) in every claim–

(a) the nature of the claim or counterclaim and that it has not been satisfied and if it arises in connection with a ship, the name of that ship;

(b) the nature of the property to be arrested and, if the property is a ship, the name of the ship and her port of registry; and

(c) the amount of the security sought, if any.

(2) in a claim against a ship by virtue of section 21(4) of the Senior Courts Act 1981 —

(a) the name of the person who would be liable on the claim if it were not commenced in rem;

(b) that the person referred to in sub-paragraph (a) was, when the right to bring the claim arose

(i) the owner or charterer of; or

(ii) in possession or in control of,

the ship in connection with which the claim arose; and

(c) that at the time the claim form was issued the person referred to in sub-paragraph (a) was either—

(i) the beneficial owner of all the shares in the ship in respect of which the warrant is required; or

*Paragraph numbers marked with a "+" can be found online and on CD.*

(ii) the charterer of it under a charter by demise;

(3) in the cases set out in rules 61.5(5) and (6) that the relevant notice has been sent or served, as appropriate; and

(4) in the case of a claim in respect of liability incurred under section 153 of the Merchant Shipping Act 1995, the facts relied on as establishing that the court is not prevented from considering the claim by reason of section 166(2) of that Act.

**5.4** The notice required by rule 61.5(5)(a) must be in Form **ADM6**.

**5.5** Property is arrested—

(1) by service on it of an arrest warrant in Form **ADM9** in the manner set out at paragraph 3.6(1); or

(2) where it is not reasonably practicable to serve the warrant, by service of a notice of the issue of the warrant—

(a) in the manner set out in paragraph 3.6(1) on the property; or

(b) by giving notice to those in charge of the property.

**5.6** When property is arrested the Registrar will issue standard directions in Form **ADM10**.

**5.7** The Marshal does not insure property under arrest.

*Note* —Amended by the Constitutional Reform Act 2005 s.59 and Sch.11, para.1 with effect from October 1, 2009 (SI 2009/1604). **2D-96.1**

**Specific Applications**

An application to move a vessel under arrest (see r.61.5(9)) or to sell the same below the appraised value are made to the Admiralty Registrar or as he may direct. **2D-97**

As to the practice to be followed by the Marshal when a ship is under arrest and a harbour or dock authority claims or purports to exercise a statutory power of detention or sale in respect of unpaid dock dues, see *The Queen of the South* [1968] P. 449; [1968] 1 All E.R. 1163; [1968] 1 Lloyd's Rep. 182 and *The Freightline One* [1986] 1 Lloyd's Rep. 266. In *The Girl Irene* [1991] Fo. 774, the court directed that the Marshal was to follow the same practice in respect of a claim by Trinity House for unpaid light dues. Where some doubt arises as to the right of a harbour or dock authority to detain a ship, that authority should seek a declaration from the court (*The Baltico* (1982) H. No. 140. Hartlepool District Registry).

Mooring charges do not constitute "ship dues" within the meaning of s.26(3) of the Harbours Act 1964 and as defined by s.57(1) of the 1964 Act. Accordingly there is no power to distrain for non-payment of mooring charges under s.44 of the Harbours, Docks and Piers Clauses Act 1847: see *R. v Carrick DC Ex p. Prankerd (The Winnie Rigg)* [1998] 2 Lloyd's Rep. 675; [1999] Q.B. 1119.

As to applications to discharge cargo where ship or cargo is under arrest, see r.61.8(8) and (9).

Applications under r.61.5(4) and (6) are made without notice to the Admiralty Registrar.

**Insurance premiums**

Premiums paid by claimants to insure their interest in arrested property were held in *The Fairport* [1965] 2 Lloyd's Rep. 183 at 186, to be recoverable as costs but not to constitute a head of claim under AJA 1956 s.1 (see now SCA 1981 s.20). **2D-98**

**Insurance of arrested property**

Section N13 of the Admiralty and Commercial Courts Guide provides as follows: **2D-99**

N13.1 The Marshal will not insure any arrested property for the benefit of parties at any time during the period of arrest (whether before or after the lodging of an application for sale, if any).

N13.2 The Marshal will use his best endeavours (but without any legal liability for failure to do so) to advise all parties known to him as being on the record in actions in rem against the arrested property, including those who have filed cautions against release of that property, before any such property moves or is moved beyond the area covered by the usual port risks policy.

N13.3 In these circumstances, practitioners' attention is drawn to the necessity of considering the questions of insuring against port risks for the amount of their clients' interest in any property arrested in an Admiralty action and the inclusion in any policy of a "Held Covered "clause in case the ship moves or is moved outside the area covered by the usual port risks policy. The usual port risks policy provides, among other things, for a ship to be moved or towed from one berth to another up to a distance of five miles within the port where she is lying.

### Declarations

**2D–100** As to the contents of these declarations see PD 61 para.61.5.3 above.

### Paragraph 61.5.3 "... her port of registry ..."

**2D–101** The object of this requirement is to minimise the risk of the arrest of a different ship bearing the same name as the ship intended to be arrested. If the port of registry is not known this should be stated in the declaration.

### Practice

**2D–102** The declaration, warrant and a copy of it are taken to or transmitted to the Admiralty and Commercial Registry and a search of the Register requested. A clerk in the Registry will search the Register and inform the applicant whether a caution against arrest of the property is in force. If there is no caution against arrest in force or if it is desired to issue a warrant despite the existence of a caution, the declaration is filed and the warrant and copy lodged. The proper officer, if he is satisfied that the declaration complies with the requirements of this rule (or if permission to issue despite non-compliance has been given) will issue the warrant. The warrant and copy are retained in the Registry.

### False or inaccurate statement in declaration to lead warrant of arrest

**2D–103** If the statutory requirements set out in para.61.5.3 are complied with then there is no further scope for the application of any duty of full and frank disclosure see *The Varna* [1993] 2 Lloyd's Rep. 253 but as to such statutory requirements it is the duty of a declarant to correct promptly and frankly any false or inaccurate statement that he finds he has made in his declaration (*The Nordglimt* [1988] Q.B. 183; [1987] 2 Lloyd's Rep. 470).

## Cautions against arrest

**2D–104** **6.1** The entry of a caution against arrest is not treated as a submission to the jurisdiction of the court.

**6.2** The request for a caution against arrest must be in form **ADM7**.

**6.3** On the filing of such a request, a caution against arrest will be entered in the Register.

**6.4** The Register is open for inspection when the Admiralty and Commercial Registry is open.

### Para.61.6.2 and 3 "... the Register..."

**2D–105** There is only one book in which all cautions in Admiralty are entered; it is kept in the Admiralty and Commercial Registry at the Royal Courts of Justice in London where all cautions must be entered. As to cautions against arrest see r.61.7 and against release see r.61.8. As to searches see r.61.5 and PD 61 para.6.4.

## Release and cautions against release

**2D–106** **7.1** The request for a caution against release must be in Form **ADM11**.

***Paragraph numbers marked with a "+" can be found online and on CD.***

**7.2** On the filing of such a request, a caution against release will be entered in the Register.

**7.3** The Register is open for inspection when the Admiralty and Commercial Registry is open.

**7.4** A request for release under rule 61.8(4)(c) and (d) must be in Form **ADM12**.

**7.5** A withdrawal of a caution against release must be in form **ADM12A**.

### Application to secure release

In cases where an applicant wishes to secure release of his property whether held at the instance of the arrestor or any person who has entered a caution, the procedure in the Admiralty and Commercial Registry will be as set out below. The purpose of this procedure is to arrange that such an application is dealt with by the tribunal likely to be able to dispose of it most expeditiously and cheaply. **2D–107**

(1) The application notice should be issued normally before the Registrar with the date left blank.

(2) The applicant should attend at the Admiralty and Commercial Registry upon the issue of the application notice for the purpose of obtaining a direction by the Registrar as to whether the application will be heard before the Registrar or before the judge. Unless there is attendance at the Registry the application will be issued before the Registrar.

(3) The applicant attending upon the issue of the application notice should, if it is desired that the application be heard initially by the judge, be prepared to indicate orally why the application is more suitable for the judge than the Registrar (e.g. substantial savings in costs or time would normally be reasons militating in favour of initial hearing by the judge).

(4) A direction as to the hearing will normally be given forthwith and date and time set for the hearing.

### Release of vessels out of hours

Section N11 of the Admiralty and Commercial Courts Guide provides as follows: **2D–108**

N11.1 This section makes provision for release from arrest when the Registry is closed.

N11.2 An application for release under rule 61.8(4)(c) or (d) may, when the Registry is closed, be made in, and only in, the following manner:

(i) The solicitor for the arrestor or the other party applying must telephone the security staff at the Royal Courts of Justice (020 7947 6260) and ask to be contacted by the Admiralty Marshal, who will then respond as soon as practicably possible;

(ii) Upon being contacted by the Admiralty Marshal the solicitor must give oral instructions for the release and an oral undertaking to pay the fees and expenses of the Admiralty Marshal as required in Form **ADM12**;

(iii) The arrestor or other party applying must then send a written request and undertaking on Form **ADM12** by fax to a number given by the Admiralty Marshal;

(iv) The solicitor must provide written consent to the release from all persons who have entered cautions against release (and from the arrestor if the arrestor is not the party applying) by sending such consents by fax to the number supplied by the Admiralty Marshal;

(v) Upon the Admiralty Marshal being satisfied that no cautions against release are in force, or that all persons who have entered cautions against release, and if necessary the arrestor, have given their written consent to the release, the Admiralty Marshal shall effect the release as soon as practicable.

N11.3 Practitioners should note that the Admiralty Marshal is not formally on call and therefore at times may not be available to assist. Similarly the practicalities of releasing a ship in some localities may involve the services of others who may not be available outside court hours.

N11.4 This service is offered to practitioners for use during reasonable hours and on the basis that if the Admiralty Marshal is available and can be contacted he will use his best endeavours to effect instructions to release but without guarantee as to their success.

**Withdrawal of cautions**

2D–109 A caution against release may be withdrawn by lodging a written request in Form **ADM12A** (see para.7.5 above). Where a solicitor acts for more than one cautioner and wishes to withdraw some or all of their cautions, this may be done by a single request, adapted as necessary.

**"... the Register..."**

2D–110 See under para. 2D–105above.

## Judgment in default

2D–111 **8.1** An application notice for judgment in default must be in form **ADM13**.

## Sale by the court and priorities

2D–112 **9.1** Any application to the court concerning–

(1) the sale of the property under arrest; or

(2) the proceeds of sale of property sold by the court

will be heard in public and the application notice served on–

(a) all parties to the claim;

(b) all persons who have requested cautions against release with regard to the property or the proceeds of sale; and

(c) the Marshal.

**9.2** Unless the court orders otherwise an order for sale will be in form **ADM14**.

**9.3** An order for sale before judgment may only be made by the Admiralty judge.

**9.4** Unless the Admiralty judge orders otherwise, a determination of priorities may only be made by the Admiralty judge.

**9.5** When—

(1) proceeds of sale are paid into court by the Marshal; and

(2) such proceeds are in a foreign currency,

the funds will be placed on one day call interest bearing account unless the court orders otherwise.

**9.6** Unless made at the same time as an application for sale, or other prior application, an application to place foreign currency on longer term deposit may be made to the Registrar.

**9.7** Notice of the placement of foreign currency in an interest bearing account must be given to all parties interested in the fund by the party who made the application under paragraph 9.6.

**9.8** Any interested party who wishes to object to the mode of investment of foreign currency paid into court may apply to the Registrar for directions.

**Court Fees on Sale**

2D–113 On the sale of a ship or goods —

Subject to a minimum fee of £200,

*Paragraph numbers marked with a "+" can be found online and on CD.*

(a) for every £100 or fraction of £100 of the price up to £100,000 .......... £1

(b) for every £100 or fraction of £100 of the price exceeding £100,000 .......... 50p

Where there is sufficient proceeds of sale in court, fee 5.2 shall be taken by transfer from the proceeds of sale in court.

(See item 5.2 of Supreme Court Fees Order 1999, as amended). For other related charges see paras 2D–140 and 2D–141 below.

## Limitation claims

**10.1** The claim form in a limitation claim must be— **2D–114**

(1) in form **ADM15**; and

(2) accompanied by a declaration—

(a) setting out the facts upon which the claimant relies; and

(b) stating the names and addresses (if known) of all persons who, to the knowledge of the claimant, have claims against him in respect of the occurrence to which the claim relates (other than named defendants),

verified by a statement of truth.

**10.2** A defence to a limitation claim must be in form **ADM16A**.

**10.3** A notice admitting the right of the claimant to limit liability in a limitation claim must be in form **ADM16**.

**10.4** An acknowledgment of service in a limitation claim must be in form **ADM16B**.

**10.5** An application for a restricted limitation decree must be in form **ADM17** and the decree issued by the court on such an application must be in form **ADM18**.

**10.6** An application for a general limitation decree must be in form **ADM17A**.

**10.7** Where—

(1) the right to limit is not admitted; and

(2) the claimant seeks a general limitation decree in form **ADM17A**,

the claimant must, within 7 days after the date of the filing of the defence of the defendant last served or the expiry of the time for doing so, apply for an appointment before the Registrar for a case management conference.

**10.8** On an application under rule 61.11(12) the Registrar may—

(1) grant a general limitation decree; or

(2) if he does not grant a decree—

(a) order service of a defence;

(b) order disclosure by the claimant; or

(c) make such other case management directions as may be appropriate.

**10.9** The fact that a limitation fund has lapsed under rule 61.11(20)(a) does not prevent the establishment of a new fund.

**10.10** Where a limitation fund is established, it must be—

(1) the sterling equivalent of the number of special drawing rights to which [the claimant] claims to be entitled to limit his liability under the Merchant Shipping Act 1995; together with

*Paragraph numbers marked with a "+" can be found online and on CD.*

(2) interest from the date of the occurrence giving rise to his liability to the date of payment into court.

**10.11** Where the claimant does not know the sterling equivalent referred to in paragraph 10.10(1) on the date of payment into court he may—

(1) calculate it on the basis of the latest available published sterling equivalent of a special drawing right as fixed by the International Monetary Fund; and

(2) in the event of the sterling equivalent of a special drawing right on the date of payment into court being different from that used for calculating the amount of that payment into court the claimant may—

(a) make up any deficiency by making a further payment into court which, if made within 14 days after the payment into court, will be treated, except for the purpose of the rules relating to the accrual of interest on money paid into court, as if made on the date of that payment into court; or

(b) apply to the court for payment out of any excess amount (together with any interest accrued) paid into court.

**10.12** An application under paragraph 10.11(2)(b)—

(1) may be made without notice to any party; and

(2) must be supported by evidence proving, to the satisfaction of the court, the sterling equivalent of the appropriate number of special drawing rights on the date of payment into court.

**10.13** The claimant must give notice in writing to every named defendant of—

(1) any payment into court specifying—

(a) the date of the payment in;

(b) the amount paid in;

(c) the amount and rate of interest included; and

(d) the period to which it relates; and

(2) any excess amount (and interest) paid out to him under paragraph 10.11(2)(b).

**10.14** A claim against the fund must be in form **ADM20**.

**10.15** A defendant's statement of case filed and served in accordance with rule 61.11(15) must contain particulars of the defendant's claim.

**10.16** Any defendant who is unable to file and serve a statement of case in accordance with rule 61.11(15) and paragraph 10.15 must file a declaration, verified by a statement of truth, in form **ADM21** stating the reason for his inability.

**10.17** No later than 7 days after the time for filing claims [or declarations], the Registrar will fix a date for a case management conference at which directions will be given for the further conduct of the proceedings.

**10.18** Nothing in rule 61.11 prevents limitation being relied on by way of defence.

***Paragraph numbers marked with a "+" can be found online and on CD.***

**Limitation fund and interest**

Any person wishing to constitute a limitation fund must pay into court a fund constituted in accordance with s.185 and Sch.7 to the Merchant Shipping Act 1995, together with interest thereon from the date of the occurrence giving rise to his liability until the date of the constitution of the limitation fund pursuant to para.8(1) of Pt II of Sch.7 to the Act. The rate of interest is now fixed by the Merchant Shipping (Liability of Shipowners and Others) (Rate of Interest) Order 1999 (SI 1999/1922), effective September 1, 1999; by the Merchant Shipping (Liability of Shipowners and Others) (Rate of Interest) (Amendment) Order 2003 (SI 2003/3136) effective December 31, 2003 and the Merchant Shipping (Liability of Shipowners and Others) (New Rate of Interest) Order 2004 (SI 2004/931) effective April 28, 2004. **2D–115**

The rate of interest is:

(a) where the occurrence takes place before September 1, 1999 but the fund is constituted on or after that date:

(i) 12 per cent from the date of the occurrence until December 31, 1994;

(ii) 6.75 per cent on and after January 1, 1995 until August 31, 1998;

(iii) 8.5 per cent on and after September 1, 1998 until August 31, 1999, and

(iv) the prescribed rate on and after September 1, 1999, until December 30, 2003; or

(b) where the occurrence takes place on or after September 1, 1999, but before December 31, 2003 the prescribed rate.

Further, art.2 of SI 2003/3136 provides as follows:

"2. The rate of interest for the purposes of article 11(1) of the Convention on Limitation of Liability for Maritime Claims 1976 (b) shall be the prescribed rate—

(a) where the occurrence takes place before 31st December 2003, but the fund is constituted on or after that date; and

(b) where the occurrence takes place on or after 31st December 2003".

The prescribed rate is defined as one per cent more than the base rate quoted from time to time by the Bank of England or the rate of interest set by any body which may supersede it and, where there is for the time being more than one such rate, the lowest of them (art.2 of the SI 2004/931).

**Tonnage**

The limitation tonnage is usually proved in the case of a British registered ship by a certified copy of the Tonnage Certificate. As to the tonnage of ships of a foreign country which has adopted the British tonnage regulations, see Merchant Shipping Act 1995 s.12. For a list of these countries see *British Shipping Laws*, Vol.11, under s.84 of the Merchant Shipping Act 1894, now s.12 of the 1995 Act. See too the Merchant Shipping (Liability of Shipowners and Others) (Calculation of Tonnage) Order 1986 (SI 1986/1040); the Merchant Shipping (Tonnage) Regulations 1997 (SI 1997/1510) and the Merchant Shipping (Tonnage) (Fishing Vessels) Amendment Regulations 1998 (SI 1998/1916). **2D–116**

**Sterling equivalents**

For ascertainment of sterling equivalents, see Sch.7, Pt II, para.7 to the Merchant Shipping Act 1995. **2D–117**

**Paras 10.8 and 10.17 "... directions ..."**

An order will usually be made providing for statements of case, disclosure, and any other directions deemed necessary and the imposition of a set timetable for expeditious disposal of the matter. **2D–118**

## Proceeding against or concerning the International Oil Pollution Compensation Fund 1992 and the International Oil Pollution Supplementary Fund

**11.1** For the purposes of section 177 of the Merchant Shipping Act 1995 ('the Act'), the Fund may be given notice of proceedings by any **2D–119**

*Paragraph numbers marked with a "+" can be found online and on CD.*

party to a claim against an owner or guarantor in respect of liability under section 153 of the Act by that person serving a notice in writing on the Fund together with copies of the claim form and any statements of case served in the claim.

**11.2** Notice given to the Fund under paragraph 11.1 shall be deemed to have been given to the Supplementary Fund.

**11.3** The Fund or the Supplementary Fund may intervene in any claim to which paragraph 11.1 applies, (whether or not served with the notice), by serving notice of intervention on the—

(1) owner;

(2) guarantor; and

(3) court.

**11.4** Where a judgment is given against—

(1) the Fund in any claim under section 175 of the Act;

(2) the Supplementary Fund in any claim under section 176A of the Act,

the Registrar will arrange for a stamped copy of the judgment to be sent by post to—

(a) the Fund (where paragraph (1) applies);

(b) the Supplementary Fund (where paragraph (2) applies).

**11.5** Notice to the Registrar of the matters set out in—

(1) section 176(3)(b) of the Act in proceedings under section 175; or

(2) section 176B(2)(b) of the Act in proceedings under section 176A, must be given in writing and sent to the court by—

(a) the Fund (where paragraph (1) applies);

(b) the Supplementary Fund (where paragraph (2) applies).

### Pollution damage

2D–120 A claim by fish processors for the loss of profitable sales of processed whelks held to be secondary, derivative, relational and/or indirect, lacking in proximity and thus too remote. The "Sea Empress", [2002] EWHC 1095 (Admiralty); [2002] 2 All E.R. (Comm) 416; [2003] 1 Lloyd's Rep. 123, applying *Landcatch Ltd v The International Oil Pollution Compensation Fund* [1999] 2 Lloyd's Rep. 316; affirmed [2003] EWCA Civ 65 [2003] 2 All E.R. (Comm.) 1; [2003] 1 Lloyd's Rep 327, CA.

### Other claims

2D–121 **12.1** This section applies to admiralty claims which, before the coming into force of Part 61, would have been called claims in personam. Subject to the provisions of Part 61 and this practice direction relating to limitation claims and to collision claims, the following provisions apply to such claims.

**12.2** All such claims will proceed in accordance with Part 58 (Commercial Court).

**12.3** The claim form must be in Form **ADM1A** and must be served by the claimant.

**12.4** The claimant may be named or may be described, but if not named in the claim form must identify himself by name if requested to do so by any other party.

**12.5** The defendant must be named in the claim form.

**12.6** Any person who files a defence must identify himself by name in the defence.

**Claims in personam (now called other claims)**

An Admiralty action *in personam* is like an action in tort or contract in the QBD. It differs from such an action however in that it is subject to the rules of this order which modify those applicable to an ordinary QB action, e.g. collision cases, r.61.4 and the application of Pt 58 thereto unless inconsistent with Pt 61 and this practice direction. **2D–122**

**Duration of Admiralty Claim in personam (other claims) for service out of the jurisdiction**

The period of validity of a claim form *in personam* in admiralty proceedings for service out of the jurisdiction is six months. **2D–123**

## References to the Registrar

**13.1** The court may at any stage in the claim refer any question or issue for determination by the Registrar (a "reference"). **2D–124**

**13.2** Unless the court orders otherwise, where a reference has been ordered—

(1) if particulars of claim have not already been served, the claimant must file and serve particulars of claim on all other parties within 14 days after the date of the order; and

(2) any party opposing the claim must file a defence to the claim within 14 days after service of the particulars of claim on him.

**13.3** Within 7 days after the defence is filed, the claimant must apply for an appointment before the Registrar for a case management conference.

**General note**

It is the long-established practice of the Admiralty Court after liability has been determined, to refer to the Admiralty Registrar the matter of the assessment of the amount of the claimant's claim and of the counterclaim if there be one. There is, however, no rule that the assessment of damages must be referred (*The Fremantle* [1954] 2 Lloyd's Rep. 20) and in personal injury and Fatal Accidents Acts cases it is not unusual for the judge to assess damages. See, e.g. *Connell v Hellyer Brothers Ltd* [1963] 2 Lloyd's Rep. 249; *The St Chad (No.2)* [1965] 2 Lloyd's Rep. 347. **2D–125**

Questions of amount have occasionally been referred before trial. See, e.g. *The Happy Return* (1828) 2 Hagg. 198 at 207 but this has not been done for many years. In *The Lathara* (1930) 37 Ll.L.Rep. 160, it seems that all issues in the claim were referred to the Registrar.

Where the assessment of damages involves a question of causation this is in some cases decided by the judge at the trial or thereafter. See, e.g. *The Maid of Kent* (1881) 6 P.D. 178, *The Guildford* [1956] 2 Lloyd's Rep. 74; *The Lucile Bloomfield* [1967] 2 Lloyd's Rep. 308. If it is desired to have such questions decided by the judge at the trial this matter should be raised on the case management conference. In exercising its discretion the court will be guided by the consideration whether the matter is one which can better be dealt with by the court at the trial, or later at the reference (*The Maid of Kent* (1881) 6 P.D. 178, *ibid.*).

**Assessors**

In modern practice the Registrar decides questions without the assistance of merchants. Nautical and other assessors, however, are sometimes appointed. If the parties agree in desiring the Registrar to sit with a merchant (the full title is "merchant assessor") or other assessor, they should apply by letter to the Admiralty and Commercial Registry. In the event of disagreement between the parties an application should be made on notice. **2D–126**

**How references may rise**

A reference may arise out of the judgment or decree made on the trial or the hear- **2D–127**

*Paragraph numbers marked with a "+" can be found online and on CD.*

ing of an application; out of the decree in a limitation claim made on the hearing of an application under r.61.11, or an order on a consent application.

Where in an action *in personam* (other claim) judgment in default is entered "for an amount of money to be decided by the court" there can be no reference and the assessment is governed by CPR r.12.7.

**Claim in reference. See para.13.2 above**

**2D-128** The claim referred to in this provision should in the first place state in a few words how the claim arises; thus in a collision claim it would begin with a short statement giving the date of the collision, the voyage on which the vessel was engaged, and, if she was repaired, the place and date and duration of such repair. In every case the several heads of claim should then be set out and numbered consecutively. It is not correct and is confusing, to call the claim a statement of case. It is a claim in a reference. For content and format of forms of claim see *Atkin's Encyclopaedia of Court Forms in Civil Proceedings*, Vol.3, Form 185 (2008 Issue).

**Limitation references**

**2D-129** In references in limitation claim a claimant need not serve a copy of his claim on any other party. Any claimant may, however, on the payment of the proper fee, inspect and obtain a copy of the claim and any other documents filed by any other claimant against the fund. See CPR r.5.4(1). In practice copies of these documents are supplied on request by the solicitors concerned on payment of the usual copying charges.

If any claimant wishes to dispute the claim of another he should so inform the Admiralty and Commercial Registry by letter in order that he can be given notice of the appointment fixed for the hearing of that other's claim.

In a claim arising out of a collision between ships A and B if there are cross claims and both ships have been held to blame (or the matter has been settled on a both to blame basis) and the owners of A obtain a limitation decree it may be necessary to assess their claim in order to arrive at the amount which the owners of B are entitled to claim against the fund. It will be necessary to do this if there are other claimants against the fund. See *The Stoomvaart Maatschappij Nederland v The Peninsular and Oriental Steam Navigation Co* (1882) 7 App. Cas. 795. In this event the practice is for the owners of B to put forward in their claim a deduction in respect of the appropriate proportion of the damages of the owners of A as agreed or, failing agreement, estimated. This figure may be disputed by any other claimant.

**Filing amended claims**

**2D-130** A claimant should not amend his filed claim but should file another claim in amended form. No leave is required. If, however, the alterations are of such a character and are made at such a late stage as to embarrass the paying party at the reference, the Registrar may, in his discretion, adjourn the reference or take some other course as he thinks fit.

**Evidence**

**2D-131** The ordinary rules of evidence apply on the hearing of a reference but are, by agreement between the parties, frequently relaxed in order to save time and expense.

**Proved recoverable amount**

**2D-132** The convention of awarding one per cent of proved recoverable amount to compensate for disruption to business and expenditure of management available to shipowners does not extend to cargo owners (*Owners of the Ship Kumanovo v Owners of the Ship Massira* [1998] 2 Lloyd's Rep. 301). The convention itself was re-affirmed in *"The Charlotte C"* [2005] 2 Lloyd's Rep. 626.

**Hearing; general note**

**2D-133** A party to a reference may be represented by counsel, solicitor, legal executive or solicitor's clerk.

If a sum has been paid into court and the award is less than the amount paid in, the party who made the payment in is entitled to an order enabling him to take the balance out of court (*The Mona* [1894] P. 265).

***Paragraph numbers marked with a "+" can be found online and on CD.***

Inquiry regarding a shorthand record at references may be made of the Registry.

**Delay; interest**

See *The Nassau* [1965] 1 Lloyd's Rep. 236 and cases cited. 2D–134

**Interest: date for addition**

On compromising an Admiralty claim for collision damages interest should be 2D–135
added to each claim before striking the balance, such balance to be struck on the date of assessment or of agreement of claims; see *The Lu Shan* [1993] 2 Lloyd's Rep. 259.

**Interest in personal injury and fatal accident cases**

See SCA 1981 s.35A (see para.9A–122 below). 2D–136

**Costs of reference**

The costs of the reference are in the Registrar's discretion. Where two vessels are 2D–137
held to blame in a collision claim the costs in the reference of each claimant are dealt with on the basis of the reference being a separate proceeding from the claim (*The Consett* (1880) 5 P.D. 77). As to the effect of failure to give notice of survey, see *The Solace (No.2)* (1936) 55 Ll.L.Rep. 201. Usually where the claimant recovers a substantial proportion of the sum claimed he is given the costs of the reference, and where an offer has been made and the amount awarded in the reference is less, the offeror will usually be entitled to the costs after the offer was made (see *The Norseman* [1957] 1 Lloyd's Rep. 503; *The Reading* [1908] P. 162). If one claimant in a reference in a limitation claim puts forward a claim which is contested successfully by another, the former may be condemned to pay the costs of the successful claimant in contesting the claim, i.e. the costs over and above those of proving his own claim (*The Clan Canning* [1906] Fo. 206).

## Undertakings

**14.1** Where, in [Part 61] or this practice direction, any undertak- 2D–138
ing to the Marshal is required it must be given—

(1) in writing and to his satisfaction; or

(2) in accordance with such other arrangements as he may require.

**14.2** Where any party is dissatisfied with a direction given by the Marshal in this respect he may apply to the Registrar for a ruling.

**Note**

The personal undertaking of the party's solicitor is normally given. Where the ex- 2D–139
penses of effecting or maintaining the arrest are more than minimal, successive demands are likely to be made by the Marshal beginning soon after the arrest.

As to recovery from the proceeds of sale of sums paid to the Marshal by an arresting party, see *The Falcon* [1981] 1 Lloyd's Rep. 13. The Marshal's expenses of maintaining the arrest from the time of the order for appraisement and sale and the expenses of the sale are payable in the first instance by the party applying therefor. *The Falcon* [1981] 1 Lloyd's Rep. 13, above at 17. As to liability for the expenses of a second and subsequent arrests see *ibid.* As to recovery from the proceeds of sale of sums paid to the Marshal, insurance premiums, solicitors' costs of arrest, etc., crew's wages, interveners' costs and interest, see *The World Star* [1987] 1 Lloyd's Rep. 452.

For priorities and the method of determining the same see *British Shipping Laws*, Vol.1, para.1574, *The Falcon* [1981] 1 Lloyd's Rep. 13, above. *The World Star* [1987] 1 Lloyd's Rep. 452, above, and *The Rubi Sea* [1992] 1 Lloyd's Rep. 634.

The fees and commission paid by the Marshal to Brokers in addition to their reasonable expenses for carrying out a Judicial sale of a vessel are as follows:

**Scale of valuation fees as from May 25, 1998**

Not exceeding £20,000: £200 2D–140

Exceeding £20,000: £400

Where the condition of the ship and/or the state of the market make it advisable that there should be a dual valuation for both trading and demolition purposes the full fee will apply in respect of the valuation for trading and in addition a fee at half the above rates will apply in respect of the valuation for demolition.

**Scale of Commission as from May 25, 1998**

**2D–141** 6 per cent on the first £5,000
5 per cent on the next £10,000 up to £15,000
3 per cent on the next £15,000 up to £30,000
1 per cent on the balance over £30,000.

## OTHER ADMIRALTY PRACTICE DIRECTIONS AND STATEMENTS

### REMUNERATION OF NAUTICAL AND OTHER ASSESSORS PRACTICE DIRECTION [1994] 1 W.L.R. 599

**2D–142** See now CPR, r.35.13. The *Remuneration of Nautical and Other Assessors Practice Direction* [1994] 1 W.L.R. 599 has been revoked by Practice Direction (Admiralty: Assessors' Renumeration) QBD, [2007] 1 W.L.R. 2508. The following guidance has been given as to the level of renumeration which should normally be paid:

(1) Full day's attendance at hearing: £600
(2) Half-day's attendance at hearing: £300
(3) Attendance at court when case is not heard: £80 per hour
(4) Consultation with the court on a day when there is no hearing: £300
(5) Attendance to hear reserved judgment (including any consultation with the court on the same day): £150
(6) If notice of attendance is countermanded less than 2 days before the hearing: £300

and as before:

(1) Assessors should receive reasonable sums for their travelling expenses and subsistence.
(2) Where there is a cross appeal, or where appeals are heard together, or where actions are consolidated or tried together, the proceedings should be treated as one appeal or action as the case may be.
(3) In the absence of special directions given in a particular case, the remuneration and expenses should be paid by the appellant or the party setting down the action as the case may be without prejudice to any right to recover from any other party the amount so paid on taxation.

### USE OF CLAIM FORMS IN REM AND IN PERSONAM/OTHER CLAIMS

**2D–143** If it is desired to commence proceedings both *in rem* and *in personam* separate claim forms must be issued.

*See Practice Direction (Admiralty: [Claim Form])* [1979] 1 W.L.R. 426; [1979] 2 All E.R. 155.

## TAXATION OF COSTS

At the request of the Admiralty Registrar, all costs [other than those summarily assessed] in Admiralty matters will be taxed in the Supreme Court Taxing Office. **2D–144**

*Practice Direction (Admiralty Taxation of Costs)* [1986] 1 W.L.R. 1310.

# Senior Courts Act 1981

(1981 c.54) **2D–145**

Arrangement of Sections

Part II

Jurisdiction

*Admiralty jurisdiction*



### Introductory note

Sections 20–24 of this Act replace with amendments AJA 1956 ss.1 and 3–8 as amended. These sections were repealed by s.152 of and Sch.7 to this Act. Section 2 had been repealed by the Courts Act 1971 Sch.11. Amendments to ss.20–24 have been made from time to time and latterly by and consequent upon the Merchant Shipping Act 1995 which came into force on January 1, 1996. **2D–146**

The 1956 Act had replaced s.22 of the Judicature Act 1925 and extended the Admiralty jurisdiction to give effect to much of the International Convention Relating to the Arrest of Seagoing Ships and the International Convention on Certain Rules concerning Civil Jurisdiction in Matters of Collision both of which were signed at Brussels on May 10, 1952. See British Shipping Laws (Singh, International Maritime Law Conventions (1983)) for the texts of these conventions.

## Part II

## Jurisdiction

### *Admiralty Jurisdiction*

### Admiralty jurisdiction of High Court

**20.**—(1) The Admiralty jurisdiction of the High Court shall be as follows, that is to say— **2D–147**

***Paragraph numbers marked with a "+" can be found online and on CD.***

(a) jurisdiction to hear and determine any of the questions and claims mentioned in subsection (2);

(b) jurisdiction in relation to any of the proceedings mentioned in subsection (3);

(c) any other Admiralty jurisdiction which it had immediately before the commencement of this Act; and

(d) any jurisdiction connected with ships or aircraft which is vested in the High Court apart from this section and is for the time being by rules of court made or coming into force after the commencement of this Act assigned to the Queen's Bench Division and directed by the rules to be exercised by the Admiralty Court.

(2) The questions and claims referred to in subsection (1)(a) are—

(a) any claim to the possession or ownership of a ship or to the ownership of any share therein;

(b) any question arising between the co-owners of a ship as to possession, employment or earnings of that ship;

(c) any claim in respect of a mortgage of or charge on a ship or any share therein;

(d) any claim for damage received by a ship;

(e) any claim for damage done by a ship;

(f) any claim for loss of life or personal injury sustained in consequence of any defect in a ship or in her apparel or equipment, or in consequence of the wrongful act, neglect or default of—

(i) the owners, charterers or persons in possession or control of a ship; or

(ii) the master or crew of a ship, or any other person for whose wrongful acts, neglects or defaults the owners, charterers or persons in possession or control of a ship are responsible.

being an act, neglect or default in the navigation or management of a ship, in the loading, carriage or discharge of goods on, in or from the ship, or in the embarkation, carriage or disembarkation of persons on, in or from the ship;

(g) any claim for loss of or damage to goods carried in a ship;

(h) any claim arising out of any agreement relating to the carriage of goods in a ship or to the use or hire of a ship;

(j) any claim—

(i) under the Salvage Convention 1989;

(ii) under any contract for or in relation to salvage services; or

(iii) in the nature of salvage not falling within (i) or (ii) above;

or any corresponding claim in connection with an aircraft.

(k) any claim in the nature of towage in respect of a ship or an aircraft;

*Paragraph numbers marked with a "+" can be found online and on CD.*

(l) any claim in the nature of pilotage in respect of a ship or an aircraft;

(m) any claim in respect of goods or materials supplied to a ship for her operation or maintenance;

(n) any claim in respect of the construction, repair or equipment of a ship or dock charges or dues;

(o) any claim by a master or member of the crew of a ship for wages (including any sum allotted out of wages or adjudged by a superintendent to be due by way of wages);

(p) any claim by a master, shipper, charterer or agent in respect of disbursements made on account of a ship;

(q) any claim arising out of an act which is or is claimed to be a general average act;

(r) any claim arising out of bottomry;

(s) any claim for the forfeiture or condemnation of a ship or of goods which are being or have been carried, or have been attempted to be carried, in a ship, or for the restoration of a ship or any such goods after seizure, or for droits of Admiralty.

(3) The proceedings referred to in subsection (1)(b) are—

(a) any application to the High Court under the Merchant Shipping Act 1995.

(b) any action to enforce a claim for damage, loss of life or personal injury arising out of—

(i) a collision between ships; or

(ii) the carrying out of or omission to carry out a manoeuvre in the case of one or more of two or more ships; or

(iii) non-compliance, on the part of one or more of two or more ships, with the collision regulations;

(c) any action by shipowners or other persons under the Merchant Shipping Act 1995 for the limitation of the amount of their liability in connection with a ship or other property.

(4) The jurisdiction of the High Court under subsection (2)(b) includes power to settle any account outstanding and unsettled between the parties in relation to the ship, and to direct that the ship, or any share thereof, shall be sold, and to make such other order as the court thinks fit.

(5) Subsection (2)(e) extends to—

(a) any claim in respect of a liability incurred under Chapter III of Part VI of the Merchant Shipping Act 1995; and

(b) any claim in respect of a liability falling on the International Oil Pollution Compensation Fund, or on the International Oil Pollution Compensation Fund 1992 or on the International Oil Pollution Compensation Supplementary Fund 2003, under Chapter IV of Part VI of the Merchant Shipping Act 1995.

(6) In subsection 2(j)—

(a) the "Salvage Convention 1989" means the International Convention on Salvage, 1989 as it has effect under section 224 of the Merchant Shipping Act 1995;

(b) the reference to salvage services includes services rendered in saving life from a ship and the reference to any claim under any contract for or in relation to salvage services includes any claim arising out of such a contract whether or not arising during the provision of the services;

(c) the reference to a corresponding claim in connection with an aircraft is a reference to any claim corresponding to any claim mentioned in sub-paragraph (i) or (ii) of paragraph (j) which is available under section 87 of the Civil Aviation Act 1982.

(7) The preceding provisions of this section apply—

(a) in relation to all ships or aircraft, whether British or not and whether registered or not and wherever the residence or domicile of their owners may be;

(b) in relation to all claims, wherever arising (including, in the case of cargo or wreck salvage, claims in respect of cargo or wreck found on land); and

(c) so far as they relate to mortgages and charges, to all mortgages or charges, whether registered or not and whether legal or equitable, including mortgages and charges created under foreign law;

Provided that nothing in this subsection shall be construed as extending the cases in which money or property is recoverable under any of the provisions of the Merchant Shipping Act 1995.

**2D–148** *Note*.—Amended by SI 2006/1265, art.13, with effect from September 8, 2006, being the date on which the Supplementary Fund Protocol comes into force (London, Edinburgh and Belfast Gazettes, July 21, 2006).

**Admiralty jurisdiction generally**

**2D–149** The Admiralty Court can entertain a claim transferred to it, though it could not have been properly instituted in that court (*The Montrosa* [1917] P. 1).

The jurisdiction *in personam* is, in collision and similar cases, restricted (see s.22 and r.61.4(7) and r.61.11(5) and see r.6.20(17A). For other restrictions on the jurisdiction see paras 2D–17 *et seq.*.

As to the jurisdiction to restrain by injunction an act on the high seas, see *The Tubantia* [1924] P. 78.

Specific performance may be ordered in an Admiralty claim *in rem* (or *in personam*) (*The Conoco Britannia* [1972] 2 Q.B. 543; [1972] 2 All E.R. 283; [1972] 1 Lloyd's Rep. 342).

It is now possible for a judgment creditor in a claim *in rem* to arrest both in respect of a national judgment *in rem* as well as a foreign judgment *in rem*. See r.61.5(1) above at para.2D–34. Formerly it was only possible to arrest to enforce a foreign judgment *in rem*, see *The Despina G.K.* [1982] 3 W.L.R. 950; [1982] 2 Lloyd's Rep. 555.

The existence of an unsatisfied judgment *in personam* or arbitration award does not prevent the bringing of a claim *in rem* on the same cause of action. See *The Rena K* [1978] 1 Lloyd's Rep. 545 at 560 and cases there cited. See also *The Saint Anna* [1983] 1 Lloyd's Rep. 637. But see *The Bumbesti* noted at para.2D–164 below.

Admiralty claims *in personam* are now termed "other claims". See Practice Direction—Admiralty Claims, para.61.12.

**s.20(1)(c)**

Paragraph (c) of this subsection replaces the "sweeping up" provisions at the end of s.1(1) of the AJA 1956. In *The Queen of the South* [1968] P. 449; [1968] 1 All E.R. 1163; [1968] 1 Lloyd's Rep. 182, Brandon J., while expressing no concluded opinion, said that it appeared that the effect of this "sweeping up" provision in the AJA s.1(1) was to preserve to the court the jurisdiction over, *inter alia*, claims for what were known, before the coming into force of that Act, as "necessaries," a term not reproduced in it. **2D–150**

**Construction of paras (a)–(s)**

Where any provision of this Act which appears to be intended to give effect to the Arrest Convention of 1952 is capable of more than one meaning the court may look at the Convention in order to gain assistance in deciding which meaning is to be preferred. See *The Eschersheim* [1975] 1 W.L.R. 83 at 89; [1974] 3 All E.R. 307 at 314; [1974] 2 Lloyd's Rep. 188 at 192 and cases there cited. See also [1976] 1 W.L.R. 430 at 434; [1976] 1 All E.R. 920 at 924; [1976] 2 Lloyd's Rep. 1 at 6, HL(E). **2D–151**

As to resort to the *travaux préparatoires* of the Convention as an aid to interpretation, see *Gatoil International Inc v Arkwright-Boston Manufacturers Mutual Insurance Co* [1985] A.C. 255; [1985] 1 All E.R. 129, HL(Sc).

**Paragraph "(2)(a) any claim to the possession or ownership of a ship or to the ownership of any share therein ..."—Jurisdiction**

Jurisdiction to hear a claim for a declaration that the plaintiff is entitled to be registered as the owner of a British ship is given by this paragraph (*The Bineta* [1966] 2 Lloyd's Rep. 419). **2D–152**

**"Ship"**

See s.24(1), para.2D–195. See too s.313 of the Merchant Shipping Act 1995 which replaces s.742 of the Merchant Shipping Act 1894 and the cases cited in British Shipping Laws, (Temperley, *Merchant Shipping Acts*, 7th edn (1976)) under s.742 of the Merchant Shipping Act 1894. A sailing dinghy used on a reservoir for pleasure was held not to be a "vessel in navigation" within s.742 aforesaid, see *Curtis v Wild* [1991] 4 All E.R. 172; and a jet-ski was held not to be "a ship", see *Steedman v Scofield* [1992] 2 Lloyd's Rep. 163. See too *R. v Goodwin* [2005] EWCA Crim 3184; [2006] 1 W.L.R. 546; [2006] 2 All E.R. 519; [2006] 1 Lloyd's Rep. 432, CA, (a s.58(2)(b) and s.313(1) of the Merchant Shipping Act 1995 case) in which the Court of Appeal held that though it was not possible to conclude on the basis of its construction that the particular jet-ski involved was not a "vessel", the words "used in navigation" excluded craft such as a jet-ski which were used simply for having fun on the water without the object of going somewhere. See also the Hovercraft Act 1968 s.2(1), para.2D–203+. **2D–153**

**Foreigners**

The court has jurisdiction to entertain a claim between foreigners as to possession of a ship within the jurisdiction, see subs.(7)(a). But it seems it may refuse to adjudicate (*The Jupiter (No.2)* [1925] P. 69, CA). **2D–154**

**Paragraph "(2)(b) any question arising between the co-owners of a ship as to possession, employment or earnings of that ship"**

*Note*—This paragraph must be read with subs.(4) of this section. **2D–155**

**Paragraph "(2)(c) any claim in respect of a mortgage of or charge on a ship or any share therein"**

*Note*—See also subs.(7)(c), which provides that this paragraph shall apply to all mortgages and charges on ships. As to the meaning of "charge" see the note to s.21, paras 2D–179 to 2D–190. **2D–156**

As to the circumstances in which a mortgagee can recover payments made by him for insurance of the mortgaged ship, see *The Basildon* [1967] 2 Lloyd's Rep. 134.

***Paragraph numbers marked with a "+" can be found online and on CD.***

**Paragraph "(2)(d) any claim for damage received by a ship"**

**2D–157** *Note*—This includes damage done by something other than a ship; see *Mersey Docks and Harbour Board v Turner, The Zeta* [1893] A.C. 469 (collision with pierhead); *The Upcerne* [1912] P. 160 (collision with gas buoy).

Section 21, which provides for the mode of exercise of Admiralty jurisdiction, makes no provision for proceedings *in rem* in respect of claims falling within this paragraph. In practice, many such claims will fall within para.(2)(e) also.

**Paragraph "(2)(e) any claim for damage done by a ship"**

**2D–158** *Note*—This paragraph must be read with subs.(5), which extends it to certain claims in connection with oil pollution.

Damage done by a ship carries a maritime lien in the usual case; this is subject, however, to exceptions, e.g. no lien attaches under present law to a government ship.

**"Done by a ship"**

**2D–159**

> "The figurative phrase 'damage done by a ship' is a term of art in maritime law whose meaning is well settled by authority (*The Vera Cruz (No. 2)* (1884) 9 P. D. 96; *Currie v M'Knight* [1897] A.C. 97). To fall within the phrase not only must the damage be the direct result or natural consequence of something done by those engaged in the navigation of the ship but the ship itself must be the actual instrument by which the damage was done. The commonest case is that of collision, which is specifically mentioned in the Convention: but physical contact between the ship and whatever object sustains the damage is not essential—a ship may negligently cause a wash by which some other vessel or some property on shore is damaged"

per Lord Diplock, *The Eschersheim* [1976] 1 W.L.R. 430 at 438; [1976] 1 All E.R. 920 at 926; [1976] 2 Lloyd's Rep. 1 at 8. See also the judgments in the Court of Appeal [1976] 1 W.L.R. 339; [1976] 1 All E.R. 441; [1976] 1 Lloyd's Rep. 81. See also *The Minerva* [1933] P. 224; 46 Ll.L.Rep. 212 (part of a ship's derrick fell damaging a barge alongside); *The Chr. Knudsen* [1932] P. 153; 43 Ll.L.Rep. 423 (damage to dock by barge being sunk in it) and *The Dagmara and Ama Antxine* [1988] 1 Lloyd's Rep. 431(claimant's vessel forced to leave fishing grounds due to alleged dangerous navigation of defendant's vessel).

See too *The Rama* [1996] 2 Lloyd's Rep. 281; damages for deceit and/or for negligent misrepresentation in relation to a charterparty where the ship was not the active cause of the damage or the noxious instrument or the instrument in the physical sense of the loss was not damage done by a ship within s.20(2)(e) so as to give rise to a maritime lien.

**Paragraph "(2)(f) any claim for loss of life or personal injury"**

**2D–160** *Note*—This paragraph should be read together with subs.(1)(b) and subs.(3)(b).

**Paragraph "(2)(g) any claim for loss of or damage to goods carried in a ship"—"Loss"**

**2D–161** It is arguable that "loss" is wide enough to include a claim for conversion against a carrier (*The Wildgans*, 1976, Fo. 947).

**"Goods"**

**2D–162** "Goods" includes baggage, see s.24(1), para.2D–195. The term "baggage," however, covers the baggage of passengers or travellers only. The belongings of those on board a ship as employees of the shipowners in order to man and operate her are not baggage nor are they goods under this paragraph. (*The Eschersheim* [1975] 1 W.L.R. 83; [1974] 3 All E.R. 307; [1974] 2 Lloyd's Rep. 188).

The claims of crew members for lost or damaged belongings will in many cases come within para.(2)(e).

**Paragraph "(2)(h) any claim arising out of any agreement relating to the carriage of goods in a ship or to the use or hire of a ship"**

**2D–163** *Note*—Although this paragraph is in different terms from s.22(1)(a) (xii) of the JA

1925, which it replaces, it is wide enough to cover claims, whether in contract or in tort, arising out of any agreement relating to the carriage of goods in a ship (*The St Elefterio* [1957] P. 179; [1957] 2 All E.R. 374; [1957] 1 Lloyd's Rep. 283). This case was followed in *The Moscanthy* [1971] 1 Lloyd's Rep. 37.

An agreement for the payment of premiums on an insurance policy over goods to be carried by sea is not connected with the carriage of goods in a ship in a sufficiently direct sense to be capable of coming within this paragraph. See *Gatoil International Inc v Arkwright-Boston Manufacturers Mutual Insurance Co* [1985] A.C. 255; [1985] 1 All E.R. 129, HL(Sc.). See also *The Sea Friends* [1991] 2 Lloyd's Rep. 322.

An agreement for the hire by shipowners of containers to be carried in a ship is not within this paragraph (*ibid.*, at pp.263, 271 and 131, 137 of the respective reports). (See also the note to para.(m)). Nor is a claim on a salvage agreement for damages for breach of an undertaking to obtain security from cargo owners. (*The Tesaba* [1982] 1 Lloyd's Rep. 397, which is referred to in *Gatoil* above at pp.263, 268 and 131, 135 of the respective reports).

**"Arising out of"**

These words are to be given the wider meaning of "connected with" and not the narrower meaning of "arising under" (*The Antonis P. Lemos* [1985] A.C. 711; [1985] 1 All E.R. 695; [1985] 1 Lloyd's Rep. 283, HL). In *The Hamburg Star* [1994] 1 Lloyd's Rep. 399 claims for indemnity and contribution under the Civil Liability (Contribution) Act 1978 were held to be claims arising out of an agreement for carriage of containers and their contents. **2D–164**

In *The Bumbesti* [2000] Q.B. 559; [1999] 2 Lloyd's Rep. 481, the court held (inter alia) that the claim was an action on an arbitration award and arose out of an agreement to refer disputes which had arisen under a bare-boat charterparty and that such agreement to refer was not "an agreement in relation to the use and hire of a ship" but one distinct from the principal contract, i.e. the bare-boat charterparty. Accordingly the claim did not fall within subs.(h).

**"Goods"**

See note to para.(2)(g). **2D–165**

**"Use or hire"**

In deciding whether a particular agreement is an agreement relating to the use of a ship or not the court will look at the substances of the matter. See *The Eschersheim*, para.2D–151 in which it was held that a salvage agreement on Lloyd's form was, on the facts of that case, an agreement for the use of a ship. **2D–166**

In *The Stella Nora*, 1981, Com.L.R. 200 it was held that a management agreement, which provided that the managers would be solely entitled to enter into charterparties for the owners of the ship they were to manage, was an agreement relating to the use or hire of that ship.

To come within this paragraph the claim need not have its origin in an agreement between the claimant and the defendant (*The Antonis P. Lemos* [1985] A.C. 711; [1985] 1 All E.R. 695; [1985] 1 Lloyd's Rep. 283, HL).

**Paragraph "(2)(j) any claim ... Salvage Convention 1989 ..."**

*Note* —Derivation—s.1(6) and Sch.2 of the Merchant Shipping (Salvage and Pollution) Act 1994. The 1994 Act was repealed by the Merchant Shipping Act 1995 with saving and amendment of this provision and providing by s.224 the enactment of the Salvage Convention 1989 with a commencement date of January 1, 1995. **2D–167**

This paragraph must be read together with subss.(6) and (7)(b).

See, generally, British Shipping Laws (Kennedy, *Law of Salvage* , 7th edn (2002)); *Halsbury's Laws of England*, 4th edn (2001 Reissue).

This paragraph does not cover a claim by the owners of property salved against salvors for negligence in the salvage operations. *The Eschersheim* [1976] 1 W.L.R. 339 at 346, 353 and 359; [1976] 1 All E.R. 441 at 446, 452 and 458; [1976] 1 Lloyd's Rep. 81 at 89, 90 and 95.

The court has power to award interest on a salvage award (*The Aldora* [1975] Q.B. 748; [1975] 2 All E.R. 69; [1975] 1 Lloyd's Rep. 617).

Salvage services rendered in non-tidal waters do not give rise to a claim for salvage reward (*The Goring* [1988] 1 Lloyd's Rep. 397, HL).

In *The Sava Star* [1995] 2 Lloyd's Rep. 134; the court held that there was no reason in principle why cargo owners could not issue a salvage claim against an owner where services of a salvage nature were rendered voluntarily in the sense that they were not rendered pursuant to a duty owed to the ship owners and were not part of what might ordinarily be expected of a cargo owner such as providing advice about the characteristics of the cargo.

**Paragraph "(2)(k) any claim in the nature of towage in respect of a ship or an aircraft"**

**2D–168** *Note*—A "claim in the nature of towage" may include escorting without actually making fast: *The Leoborg* [1962] 2 Lloyd's Rep. 146. "Towage" in relation to an aircraft means towage when it is waterborne. See s.24(1), para.2D–195.

**Paragraph "(2)(l) any claim in the nature of pilotage in respect of a ship or an aircraft"**

**2D–169** *Note* — "Pilotage" in relation to an aircraft means pilotage when it is waterborne. See s.24(1), para.2D–195.

**Paragraph "(2)(m) any claim in respect of goods or materials supplied to a ship for her operation or maintenance"**

**2D–170** *Note*—In *The Fairport (No.5)* [1967] 2 Lloyd's Rep. 162 it was held that claims under this paragraph are certainly no narrower than claims which were formerly described as claims for necessaries in the Supreme Court of Judicature (Consolidation) Act 1925, and since there is authority that the word "necessaries" covers payment by way of advances to enable necessaries to be purchased then a similar construction should be given to this paragraph.

The words "in respect of" are wide words which should not be unduly restricted. They cover a claim for repayment of sums paid to sub-agents who had supplied goods to ships. *Centro Latino Americano de Commercio Exterior SA v Owners of the Ship Kommunar (No.1)* [1997] 1 Lloyd's Rep. 1.

Containers (in the sense in which that word is used in a commercial context) supplied whether by sale or lease to a shipowner to contain cargo loaded on board his ship or any sister ship available to him, are not supplied to that ship for her operation or maintenance within the meaning of this paragraph (*The River Rima* [1987] 2 Lloyd's Rep. 106, CA. Approved by HL [1988] 2 Lloyd's Rep. 193).

In *The Edinburgh Castle* [1999] 2 Lloyd's Rep. 362 the following were held to fall within s.20(2)(m) namely food, drink and other consumables supplied for use of the officers and crew; food, drink and other consumables supplied for the use or consumption of the passengers on the vessel; the provision of services, in particular, the provision of officers and crew of suitable calibre for the operation and manning of the vessel and a wide range of equipment supplied to the vessel. See too "*Nore Challenger*" and "*Nore Commander*" [2001] 2 Lloyd's Rep. 103.

**Paragraph "(2)(n) any claim in respect of the construction, repair or equipment of a ship or dock charges or dues"**

**2D–171** *Note*—In the *Stinne Peter* 1986 Fo. 171, Sheen J., on an ex parte motion, held that a classification certificate was part of the equipment of a ship and the classification society's claim for issuing it fell within this paragraph.

**Paragraph "(2)(o) any claim by a master or member of the crew of a ship for wages"**

**2D–172** *Note*—The jurisdiction in respect of wages is in relation to the ships of some foreign countries restricted by Orders in Council made under s.4 of the Consular Relations Act 1968, see para.2D–18. Furthermore, the court may refuse to entertain a claim for

***Paragraph numbers marked with a "+" can be found online and on CD.***

wages by the master or a member of the crew of a ship which is not a British ship, see s.24(2).

As to the recovery as wages of or other emoluments and sums payable but not paid by an employer in respect of, e.g. taxes, insurance and pension contributions, see *The Halcyon Skies* [1977] Q.B. 14; [1976] 1 All E.R. 856; [1976] 1 Lloyd's Rep. 461 and cases cited therein.

In *The Fairport* [1967] P. 167; [1966] 2 Lloyd's Rep. 7, it was held that *The Carolina* (1875) 3 Asp.M.C. 141 was wrongly decided and that accordingly the institution of a wages claim did not terminate a contract of service; wages thereafter accruing might be recovered as such in the action.

It is well settled that there is a maritime lien for wages. See *The Halcyon Skies* [1977] Q.B. 14; [1976] 1 All E.R. 856; [1976] 1 Lloyd's Rep. 461 at 26, 864 and 467 of the respective reports. See too *The Ever Success* [1999] 1 Lloyd's Rep. 824. This maritime lien applies only to the ship aboard which the wages were earned (*The El Hussein* 1982 Fo. 693). There is a right *in rem* in respect of wages earned aboard a sister ship. Thus, where a claim is brought against ship A for wages earned aboard her and aboard a sister ship B, on payment out of proceeds of sale, wages earned in A will rank before, and wages earned in B after, any mortgage. This should be considered together with s.21(8), at para.2D–178, before joining a claim for wages earned aboard a sister ship to a claim for wages earned aboard the ship proceeded against.

A master's claim for wages ranks *pari passu* with the claims of seamen (*The Royal Wells* [1984] 2 Lloyd's Rep. 255, not following earlier cases).

Severence pay is not wages within this sub-section and as opposed to wages does not give rise to a maritime lien (*The Tacoma City* [1991] 1 Lloyd's Rep. 330).

In *The Turiddu* [1999] 2 Lloyd's Rep. 401, CA, it was held that foreign members of a ship's crew requesting an allotted part of their wages to be paid through an agency to an identified person in their home country retained the benefit of a maritime lien over the vessel for unpaid wages in relation to that alloted part.

**Paragraph "(2)(p) any claim by a master, shipper, charterer or agent in respect of disbursements made on account of a ship"**

*Note* —A master has a maritime lien for his wages and for all disbursements or liabilities properly made or incurred by him on account of the ship. See the Merchant Shipping Act 1995 s.41 replacing the Merchant Shipping Act 1970 s.18 and the notes to that section in *British Shipping Laws* (Temperley, *Merchant Shipping Acts*, 7th edn (1976)). See also *The Fairport (No.3)* [1966] 2 Lloyd's Rep. 253. **2D–173**

**"Agent"**

It is arguable that the term agent in this paragraph is not restricted to a person carrying on a business as a ship's agent in the usually accepted sense but is wide enough to include a manager of a ship (*The Corona Energy* 1977 Fo. 174). However, the term agent does not extend to an insurance broker seeking to recover premiums paid out on behalf of ship's owners (*The Sea Friends* [1991] 2 Lloyd's Rep. 322). **2D–174**

Fees charged by agents for their services may be "disbursements" (*The Westport (No.3)* [1966] 1 Lloyd's Rep. 342).

**Paragraph "(2)(q) ... general average act ..." Paragraph "(2)(r) ... bottomry ..." Paragraph "(2)(s) ... forfeiture or condemnation of a ship or of goods"**

*Note* —In *The Skylark* [1965] P. 474; [1965] 2 Lloyd's Rep. 250, it was held that the Commissioners of Customs and Excise had a right to proceed *in rem* under the equivalent paragraph of the AJA 1956 for forfeiture of a ship under the Temporary Importation (Private Vehicles, Vessels and Aircraft) Regulations 1961. **2D–175**

**"Arising out of"**

See the first note at para.2D–164 above. **2D–176**

**Subsection (7)**

This paragraph applies only to aircraft referred to in s.20(2)(j), (k) and (l). The **2D–177**

Admiralty jurisdiction does not extend, therefore, to a claim in respect of a mortgage of an aircraft (*The Glider Standard Austria S.H.* [1965] P. 463; [1965] 2 All E.R. 1022; [1965] 2 Lloyd's Rep. 189).

## Mode of exercise of Admiralty jurisdiction

2D-178 **21.**—(1) Subject to section 22, an action in personam may be brought in the High Court in all cases within the Admiralty jurisdiction of that court.

(2) In the case of any such claim as is mentioned in section 20(2)(a), (c) or (s) or any such question as is mentioned in section 20(2)(b), an action in rem may be brought in the High Court against the ship or property in connection with which the claim or question arises.

(3) In any case in which there is a maritime lien or other charge on any ship, aircraft or other property for the amount claimed, an action in rem may be brought in the High Court against that ship, aircraft or property.

(4) In the case of any such claim as is mentioned in section 20(2)(e) to (r), where—

(a) the claim arises in connection with a ship; and

(b) the person who would be liable on the claim in an action in personam ("the relevant person") was, when the cause of action arose, the owner or charterer of, or in possession or in control of, the ship,

an action in rem may (whether or not the claim gives rise to a maritime lien on that ship) be brought in the High Court against—

(i) that ship, if at the time when the action is brought the relevant person is either the beneficial owner of that ship as respects all the shares in it or the charterer of it under a charter by demise; or

(ii) any other ship of which, at the time when the action is brought, the relevant person is the beneficial owner as respects all the shares in it.

(5) In the case of a claim in the nature of towage or pilotage in respect of an aircraft, an action in rem may be brought in the High Court against that aircraft if, at the time when the action is brought, it is beneficially owned by the person who would be liable on the claim in an action *in personam*.

(6) Where, in the exercise of its Admiralty jurisdiction, the High Court orders any ship, aircraft or other property to be sold, the court shall have jurisdiction to hear and determine any question arising as to the title to the proceeds of sale.

(7) In determining for the purposes of subsections (4) and (5)whether a person would be liable on a claim in an action in personam it shall be assumed that he has his habitual residence or a place of business within England or Wales.

(8) Where, as regards any such claim as is mentioned in section 20(2)(e) to (r), a ship has been served with a writ or arrested in an action in rem brought to enforce that claim, no other ship may be served with a writ or arrested in that or any other action in rem

brought to enforce that claim: but this subsection does not prevent the issue, in respect of any one such claim, of a writ naming more than one ship or of two or more writs each naming a different ship.

*Note*—Generally as to claims *in rem*, see CPR r.61.3 and notes thereunder and *British Shipping Laws*, Vol.1, *Admiralty Practice*. **2D–179**

**subs.(3) "... maritime lien ..."**

It is well settled that there is a maritime lien in respect of the following claims: damage done by a ship, salvage, wages, master's disbursements and bottomry. It is doubtful whether there is a maritime lien for pilotage. This question was left open in *The Ambatielos; The Cephalonia* [1923] P. 68. As to maritime liens generally see *The Tolten* [1946] P. 135 at 144 and 145 and cases there cited by Scott L.J. See also *The Father Thames* [1979] 2 Lloyd's Rep. 364. **2D–180**

**subs.(3) "... other charge ..."**

See *The St. Merriel* [1963] P. 247; [1963] 1 Lloyd's Rep. 63; *The Acrux* [1965] P. 391 at 403; [1965] 1 Lloyd's Rep. 565 at 572. **2D–181**

**subs.(4) "... in connection with a ship ..."**

As to the effect of these words in s.3(4) of the 1956 Act, see the passage in the speech of Lord Diplock in *The Eschersheim* [1976] 1 W.L.R. 430 at 436H; [1976] 1 All E.R. 920 at 925d; [1976] 2 Lloyd's Rep. 1, HL(E), in the respective reports. In *The Span Terza* [1982] 1 Lloyd's Rep. 225, the Court of Appeal held that this passage was *obiter* and by a majority allowed the arrest of the ship "X" where the claimant (owner of the ship "Y") was claiming for charter hire in a claim *in rem* against the ship "X" which was owned by the person to whom the "Y" had been chartered by the claimant. **2D–182**

**subs.(4) "... liable ... in personam ..."**

The purpose of the words "the person who would be liable on the claim in an action *in personam*" is to identify the person or persons whose ship or ships may be arrested (*The St Elefterio* [1957] P. 179 at 186; [1957] 2 All E.R. 374 at 377; [1957] 1 Lloyd's Rep. 283 at 287). But only one ship may be arrested, see subs.(8). **2D–183**

**subs.(4) "... beneficial owner ..."**

For the meaning of beneficial owner in this subsection see *The Andrea Ursula* [1973] Q.B. 265; [1971] 1 All E.R. 821; [1971] 1 Lloyd's Rep. 145 and *The I Congreso del Partido* [1981] 1 Lloyd's Rep. 536 at 560 *et seq.* in which *The Andrea Ursula* was not followed. See also *The Father Thames* [1979] 2 Lloyd's Rep. 364 at 366 and 367. **2D–184**

**subs.(4)(b)(i) "... charterer ..."**

The effect of these words in sub-para.(i) is to enable a claim *in rem* to be brought against a ship on demise charter if the demise charterer of it when the claim form is issued is the person who would be liable *in personam*, and was when the cause of action arose the owner, charterer or in possession or in control of the ship in connection with which the claim arose. **2D–185**

The "relevant person" can be a demise charterer within this subsection even in the absence of a consensual agreement between the parties in the nature of a demise charter if the legal relationship between the parties invests the "relevant person" with the right of a demise character against the owner of the vessel. See *Bridge Oil Ltd v Owners and/or Demise Charterers of the Ship Giuseppe di Vittorio* [1998] 1 Lloyd's Rep. 136, CA.

A slot charterer of spaces on a container ship for the carriage of goods is capable of coming within the definition of a charterer in s.21(4)(b) of the Senior Courts Act 1981 despite the fact that a slot charter gave control of only part of the vessel to the charterer, *MSC Mediterranean Shipping Company SA v Polish Ocean Lines (The Tychy)* [1999] 2 Lloyd's Rep. 11, CA.

**subs.(4) "... when the action is brought ..."**

This means when the claim form is issued (*The Carmania 11* [1963] 2 Lloyd's Rep. 152). **2D–186**

***Paragraph numbers marked with a "+" can be found online and on CD.***

**subs.(4) "... owner ..."**

2D–187 Section 21 does not confer a right to arrest a ship owned by a sister company of the owners of the ship giving rise to the cause of action (*The Evpo Agnic* [1988] 2 Lloyd's Rep. 411, CA). See too *The Nazym Khikmet and Other Ships* [1996] 2 Lloyd's Rep. 362, CA.

**subs.(4)(b)**

2D–188 It is not sufficient that the cause of action, being one falling within s.20(2)(e) to (r), should arise probably, but not necessarily, in connection with a ship owned by or demise chartered to or in the possession or control of the relevant person as defined by s.21(4)(b) (*The River Rima* [1987] 2 Lloyd's Rep. 106, CA. Approved by HL [1988] 2 Lloyd's Rep. 193). See too *The Lloyd Pacifico* [1995] 1 Lloyd's Rep. 54.

**Change of ownership after issue of claim form**

2D–189 This does not affect the claimant's right of claim *in rem* against the ship or prevent her arrest in the claim (*The Monica S* [1968] P. 741; [1967] 3 All E.R. 740; [1967] 2 Lloyd's Rep. 113 and see *The Andria*, renamed *The Vasso* (1984) 81 L.S.Gaz. 592).

**subs.(8)**

2D–190 Subsection (8) gives statutory effect to the decision of the Court of Appeal in *The Banco* [1971] P. 137; [1971] 1 All E.R. 524; [1971] 1 Lloyd's Rep. 49.

Where the claim form includes claims in respect of more than one ship, e.g. claims in respect of repairs to two or more ships in the same ownership, service of the claim form on or the arrest of any of the ships named in it will normally prevent valid service of that claim form on or the arrest of, any other ship named in it. Furthermore, after such service or arrest no other claim form *in rem* may be served or ship arrested in respect of any of the claims specified in the first claim form.

It seems however that in a case such as this if the claim form clearly shows what claims are made against each ship and there is no overlapping, all the ships against which claims are made in the claim form may be arrested and/or served with the claim form.

This subsection does not prevent the arrest of a ship where another has previously been arrested in the mistaken belief that she was a sister ship. The affidavit in support of the application for the second arrest should refer to the previous mistaken arrest and the reasons for it (*The Stephan J.* [1985] 2 Lloyd's Rep. 344).

## Restrictions on entertainment of actions in personam in collision and other similar cases

2D–191 **22.**—(1) This section applies to any claim for damage, loss of life or personal injury arising out of—

(a) a collision between ships; or

(b) the carrying out of, or omission to carry out, a manoeuvre in the case of one or more of two or more ships; or

(c) non-compliance, on the part of one or more of two or more ships, with the collision regulations.

(2) The High Court shall not entertain any action in personam to enforce a claim to which this section applies unless—

(a) the defendant has his habitual residence or a place of business within England or Wales; or

(b) the cause of action arose within inland waters of England or Wales or within the limits of a port of England or Wales; or

(c) an action arising out of the same incident or series of incidents is proceeding in the court or has been heard and determined in the court.

In this subsection—

"inland waters" includes any part of the sea adjacent to the coast of the United Kingdom certified by the Secretary of State to be waters falling by international law to be treated as within the territorial sovereignty of Her Majesty apart from the operation of that law in relation to territorial waters;

"port" means any port, harbour, river, estuary, haven, dock, canal or other place so long as a person or body of persons is empowered by or under an Act to make charges in respect of ships entering it or using the facilities therein, and "limits of a port" means the limits thereof as fixed by or under the Act in question or, as the case may be, by the relevant charter or custom;

"charges" means any charges with the exception of light dues, local light dues and any other charges in respect of lighthouses, buoys or beacons and of charges in respect of pilotage.

(3) The High Court shall not entertain any action in personam to enforce a claim to which this section applies until any proceedings previously brought by the plaintiff in any court outside England and Wales against the same defendant in respect of the same incident or series of incidents have been discontinued or otherwise come to an end.

(4) Subsections (2) and (3) shall apply to counterclaims (except counterclaims in proceedings arising out of the same incident or series of incidents) as they apply to actions, the references to the plaintiff and the defendant being for this purpose read as references to the plaintiff on the counterclaim and the defendant to the counterclaim respectively.

(5) Subsections (2) and (3) shall not apply to any action or counterclaim if the defendant thereto submits or has agreed to submit to the jurisdiction of the court.

(6) Subject to the provisions of subsection (3), the High Court shall have jurisdiction to entertain an action in personam to enforce a claim to which this section applies whenever any of the conditions specified in subsections (2)(a) to (c) is satisfied, and the rules of court relating to the service of process outside the jurisdiction shall make such provision as may appear to the rule-making authority to be appropriate having regard to the provisions of this subsection.

(7) Nothing in this section shall prevent an action which is brought in accordance with the provisions of this section in the High Court being transferred, in accordance with the enactments in that behalf, to some other court.

(8) For the avoidance of doubt it is hereby declared that this section applies in relation to the jurisdiction of the High Court not being Admiralty jurisdiction, as well as in relation to its Admiralty jurisdiction.

**subs.(2)(c)**

In *The World Harmony* [1967] P. 341; [1965] 2 All E.R. 139; [1965] 1 Lloyd's Rep. 244, it was held that the critical date under the equivalent provision in the AJA 1956(s.4(1)(c)), was the date when the claim form was issued and that when two claims are begun in two places on the same day, neither is previous or subsequent to the other. **2D–192**

**subs.(6) "... rules of court ..."**

2D–193 See CPR r.61.4(7) and r.6.20(17A).

## High Court not to have jurisdiction in cases within Rhine Convention

2D–194 **23.** The High Court shall not have jurisdiction to determine any claim or question certified by the Secretary of State to be a claim or question which, under the Rhine Navigation Convention, falls to be determined in accordance with the provisions of that Convention; and any proceedings to enforce such a claim which are commenced in the High Court shall be set aside.

## Supplementary provisions as to Admiralty jurisdiction

2D–195 **24.**—(1) In sections 20 to 23 and this section, unless the context otherwise requires—

"collision regulations" means safety regulations under section 85 of the Merchant Shipping Act 1995;

"goods" includes baggage;

"master" has the same meaning as in the Merchant Shipping Act 1995, and accordingly includes every person (except a pilot) having command or charge of a ship;

"the Rhine Navigation Convention" means the Convention of the 7th October 1868 as revised by any subsequent Convention;

"ship" includes any description of vessel used in navigation and (except in the definition of "port" in section 22(2)and in subsection (2)(c) of this section) includes, subject to section 2(3)of the Hovercraft Act 1968, a hovercraft;

"towage" and "pilotage", in relation to an aircraft, mean towage and pilotage while the aircraft is waterborne.

(2) Nothing in sections 20 to 23 shall—

(a) be construed as limiting the jurisdiction of the High Court to refuse to entertain an action for wages by the master or a member of the crew of a ship, not being a British ship;

(b) affect the provisions of section 226 of the Merchant Shipping Act 1995 (power of a receiver of wreck to detain a ship in respect of a salvage claim); or

(c) authorise proceedings in rem in respect of any claim against the Crown, or the arrest, detention or sale of any of Her Majesty's ships or Her Majesty's aircraft, or, subject to section 2(3)of the Hovercraft Act 1968, Her Majesty's hovercraft, or of any cargo or other property belonging to the Crown.

(3) In this section—

"Her Majesty's ships" and "Her Majesty's aircraft" have the meanings given by section 38(2) of the Crown Proceedings Act 1947;

"Her Majesty's hovercraft" means hovercraft belonging to the Crown in right of Her Majesty's Government in the United Kingdom or Her Majesty's Government in Northern Ireland.

*Paragraph numbers marked with a "+" can be found online and on CD.*

*Note*—Amended by the Merchant Shipping Act 1995 Sch.13. 2D–196

**Ship**

See further as to the meaning of ship, para.2D–153. 2D–197



*OTHER PARTICULAR FIELDS OF JURISDICTION*

* * * *

## Prize jurisdiction of High Court

**27.** The High Court shall, in accordance with section19(2), have as a prize court— 2D–198

(a) all such jurisdiction as is conferred on it by the Prize Acts 1864 to 1944 (in which references to the High Court of Admiralty are by virtue of paragraph 1 of Schedule 4 to this Act to be construed as references to the High Court); and

(b) all such other jurisdiction on the high seas and elsewhere as it has as a prize court immediately before the commencement of this Act.

*Note*—Derived from the JA 1925 s.23. 2D–199

# PART VI

## MISCELLANEOUS AND SUPPLEMENTARY

### *SUPPLEMENTARY*

* * * *

## Admiralty jurisdiction: provisions as to Channel Islands, Isle of Man, colonies, etc.

**150.**—(1) Her Majesty may by Order in Council— 2D–200

(a) direct that any of the provisions of sections 20 to 24 specified in the Order shall extend, with such exceptions, adaptations and modifications as may be so specified, to any of the Channel Islands or the Isle of Man; or

(b) make, for any of the Channel Islands or the Isle of Man, provision for any purposes corresponding to the purposes of any of the provisions of those sections.

(2) Her Majesty may by Order in Council direct, either generally or in relation to particular courts or territories, that the Colonial Courts of Admiralty Act 1890 shall have effect as if for the reference in section 2(2) of that Act to the Admiralty jurisdiction of the High Court in England there were substituted a reference to the Admiralty jurisdiction of that court as defined by section 20 of this Act, subject, however, to such adaptations and modifications of section 20 as may be specified in the Order.

(3) Her Majesty may by Order in Council direct that any of the provisions of sections 21 to 24 shall extend, with such exceptions,

adaptations and modifications as may be specified in the Order, to any colony or to any country outside Her Majesty's dominions in which Her Majesty has jurisdiction in right of the government of the United Kingdom.

(4) Subsections (1) and (3) shall each have effect as if the provisions there mentioned included section 2(2) of the Hovercraft Act 1968 (application of the law relating to maritime liens in relation to hovercraft and property connected with them).

**2D-201** *Note*—Derived from the AJA 1956 s.56.

## Hovercraft Act 1968

**2D-202** (1968 c.59)

ARRANGEMENT OF SECTIONS



**Paragraph numbers marked with a "+"denote content that is available on White Book on Westlaw UK or the Civil Procedure CD.**

## Merchant Shipping Act 1995

**2D-208** (1995 c.21)

ARRANGEMENT OF SECTIONS

PART IV

SAFETY

*ASSISTANCE AT SEA*



PART VII

LIABILITY OF SHIPOWNERS AND OTHERS

*LIMITATION OF LIABILITY OF SHIPOWNERS, ETC., AND SALVORS FOR MARITIME CLAIMS*



*MULTIPLE FAULT, APPORTIONMENT, LIABILITY AND CONTRIBUTION*



*TIME LIMIT FOR PROCEEDINGS AGAINST OWNERS OR SHIP*



*APPLICATION TO CROWN AND ITS SHIPS*



PART IX

SALVAGE AND WRECK

CHAPTER I

SALVAGE



***Paragraph numbers marked with a "+" can be found online and on CD.***

## PART IV

## SAFETY

### *ASSISTANCE AT SEA*

### Duty of ship to assist the other in case of collision

**92.**—(1) In every case of collision between two ships, it shall be the duty of the master of each ship, if and so far as he can do so without danger to his own ship, crew and passengers (if any)— **2D–209**

(a) to render to the other ship, its master, crew and passengers (if any) such assistance as may be practicable, and may be necessary to save them from any danger caused by the collision, and to stay by the other ship until he has ascertained that it has no need of further assistance; and

(b) to give to the master of the other ship the name of his own ship and also the names of the ports from which it comes and to which it is bound.

(2) The duties imposed on the master of a ship by subsection (1) above apply to the masters of United Kingdom ships and to the masters of foreign ships when in United Kingdom waters.

(3) The failure of the master of a ship to comply with the provisions of this section shall not raise any presumption of law that the collision was caused by his wrongful act, neglect, or default.

(4) [*Penalties for non compliance*].

*Note* —Derivation—Merchant Shipping Act 1894 s.422(1); the Merchant Shipping (Registration) Act 1993 Sch.4, para.6(2); and the Maritime Conventions Act 1911 s.4(2). **2D–210**

### Duty to assist aircraft in distress

**93.**—(1) The master of a ship, on receiving at sea a signal of distress from an aircraft or information from any source that an aircraft is in distress, shall proceed with all speed to the assistance of the persons in distress (informing them if possible that he is doing so) unless he is unable, or in the special circumstances of the case considers it unreasonable or unnecessary, to do so, or unless he is released from this duty under subsection (4) or (5) below. **2D–211**

(2) [...]

(3) The duties imposed on the master of a ship by subsection (1) above apply to the masters of United Kingdom ships and to the masters of foreign ships when in United Kingdom waters.

(4) [...]

(5) A master shall be released from the duty imposed by subsection (1) above, if he is informed by the persons in distress, or by the

master of any ship that has reached the persons in distress, that assistance is no longer required.

(6) [*Penalties for non compliance*].

(7) Compliance by the master of a ship with the provisions of this section shall not affect his right, or the right of any other person, to salvage.

2D–212 *Note* —Derivation—Merchant Shipping (Safety Convention) Act 1949 s.22(1) and (2); the Merchant Shipping (Registration, etc.) Act 1993 Sch.4, para.6(2); and the Merchant Shipping (Safety Convention) Act 1949 s.22(3), (4), (5) and (8) and s.37(3).

Section 93 has been amended by The Merchant Shipping (Distress Messages) Regulation 1998 (SI 1998/1691) reg.2.

**subs.(1)**

2D–213 A vessel which puts herself into unusual peril by reason of rendering assistance under this section is not to be regarded as negligent on that account. The principles of the common law as laid down in *Haynes v Harwood* [1935] 1 K.B. 146, apply (*The Gusty and the Daniel M.* [1940] P. 159, a case on the former s.6 of the Maritime Conventions Act 1911, see para.2D–221, below).

**subs.(7)**

2D–214 *The Tower Bridge* [1936] P. 30 is a case in which salvage is awarded in such circumstances.

## PART VII

## LIABILITY OF SHIPOWNERS AND OTHERS

* * * *

### *LIMITATION OF LIABILITY OF SHIPOWNERS, ETC., AND SALVORS FOR MARITIME CLAIMS*

### Limitation of liability for maritime claims

2D–215 **185.**—(1) The provisions of the Convention on Limitation of Liability for Maritime Claims 1976 as set out in Part I of Schedule 7 (in this section and Part II of that Schedule referred to as "the Convention") shall have the force of law in the United Kingdom.

(2) The provisions of Part II of that Schedule shall have effect in connection with the Convention, and subsection (1) above shall have effect subject to the provisions of that Part.

(2A) Her Majesty may by Order in Council make such modifications of Parts I and II of Schedule 7 as She considers appropriate in consequence of the revision of the Convention by the Protocol of 1996 amending the Convention (in this section referred to as "the 1996 Protocol").

(2B) If it appears to Her Majesty in Council that the Government of the United Kingdom has agreed to any further revision of the Convention or to any revision of article 8 of the 1996 Protocol, She may by Order in Council make such modifications of Parts I and II of Schedule 7 and subsections (2C) and (2D) below as She considers appropriate in consequence of the revision.

(2C) The Secretary of State may by order make such amendments of Parts I and II of Schedule 7 as appear to him to be appropriate for the purpose of giving effect to any amendment of a relevant limit which is adopted in accordance with article 8 of the 1996 Protocol.

(2D) In subsection (2C) above "a relevant limit" means any of the limits for the time being specified in either of the following provisions of the Convention—

(a) article 6, paragraph 1, and
(b) article 7, paragraph 1.

(2E) No modification made by virtue of subsection (2A), (2B) or (2C) above shall affect any rights or liabilities arising out of an occurrence which took place before the day on which the modification comes into force.

(3) The provisions having the force of law under this section shall apply in relation to Her Majesty's ships as they apply in relation to other ships.

(4) The provisions having the force of law under this section shall not apply to any liability in respect of loss of life or personal injury caused to, or loss of or damage to any property of, a person who is on board the ship in question or employed in connection with that ship or with the salvage operations in question if—

(a) he is so on board or employed under a contract of service governed by the law of any part of the United Kingdom; and
(b) the liability arises from an occurrence which took place after the commencement of this Act.

In this subsection, "ship"and "salvage operations" have the same meaning as in the Convention.

(5) A draft of an Order in Council proposed to be made by virtue of subsection (2A) or (2B) above shall not be submitted to Her Majesty in Council unless it has been approved by a resolution of each House of Parliament.

*Note*—Derivation—Merchant Shipping Act 1979 s.17, s.35(2) and Sch.5, para.3. Subsections (2A) to (2E) inserted by the Merchant Shipping and Maritime Security Act 1997 s.15. These subsections are now in force. As at December 2002 see only under s.185(2A), the Merchant Shipping (Convention on Limitation of Liability for Maritime Claims) (Amendment) Order 1998 (SI 1998/1258)—not in force until the 1996 Protocol amending the 1976 Convention on Liability for Maritime Claims comes into force internationally. **2D–216**

## Exclusion of liability

**186.**—(1) Subject to subsection (3) below, the owner of a United Kingdom ship shall not be liable for any loss or damage in the following cases, namely— **2D–217**

(a) where any property on board the ship is lost or damaged by reason of fire on board the ship; or
(b) where any gold, silver, watches, jewels or precious stones on board the ship are lost or damaged by reason of theft, robbery or other dishonest conduct and their nature and value were not at the time of shipment declared by

*Paragraph numbers marked with a "+" can be found online and on CD.*

their owner or shipper to the owner or master of the ship in the bill of lading or otherwise in writing.

(2) Subject to subsection (3) below, where the loss or damage arises from anything done or omitted by any person in his capacity of master or member of the crew or (otherwise than in that capacity) in the course of his employment as a servant of the owner of the ship, subsection (1) above shall also exclude the liability of—

(a) the master, member of the crew or servant; and

(b) in a case where the master or member of the crew is the servant of a person whose liability would not be excluded by that subsection apart from this paragraph, the person whose servant he is.

(3) This section does not exclude the liability of any person for any loss or damage resulting from any such personal act or omission of his as is mentioned in Article 4 of the Convention set out in Part I of Schedule 7.

(4) This section shall apply in relation to Her Majesty's ships as it applies in relation to other ships.

(5) In this section "owner", in relation to a ship, includes any part owner and any charterer, manager or operator of the ship.

**2D-218** *Note* —Derivation—Merchant Shipping Act 1979 s.18; and the Merchant Shipping (Registration, etc.) Act 1993 Sch.4, para.6(1).

### *MULTIPLE FAULT, APPORTIONMENT, LIABILITY AND CONTRIBUTION*

## Damage or loss: apportionment of liability

**2D-219** **187.**—(1) Where, by the fault of two or more ships, damage or loss is caused to one or more of those ships, to their cargoes or freight, or to any property on board, the liability to make good the damage or loss shall be in proportion to the degree in which each ship was in fault.

(2) If, in any such case, having regard to all the circumstances, it is not possible to establish different degrees of fault, the liability shall be apportioned equally.

(3) This section applies to persons other than the owners of a ship who are responsible for the fault of the ships, as well as to the owners of a ship and where, by virtue of any charter or demise, or for any other reason, the owners are not responsible for the navigation and management of the ship, this section applies to the charterers or other persons for the time being so responsible instead of the owners.

(4) Nothing in this section shall operate so as to render any ship liable for any loss or damage to which the fault of the ship has not contributed.

(5) Nothing in this section shall affect the liability of any person under a contract of carriage or any contract, or shall be construed as imposing any liability upon any person from which he is exempted by any contract or by any provision of law, or as affecting the right of any person to limit his liability in the manner provided by law.

(6) In this section "freight" includes passage money and hire.

(7) In this section references to damage or loss caused by the fault of a ship include references to any salvage or other expenses, consequent upon that fault, recoverable at law by way of damages.

*Note*—Derivation—Maritime Conventions Act 1911 s.1(1), s.1(1) proviso (a), (b) and (c), s.1(2) and s.9(4). **2D–220**

**General note**

The Merchant Shipping Act 1995 came into force on January 1, 1996, see s.315 of the 1995 Act. The 1995 Act is described as an act to consolidate the Merchant Shipping Acts 1894 to 1994 and other enactments relating to merchant shipping. Among those other enactments was the Maritime Conventions Act 1911 the text of which is to be found in the 1995 edition and earlier editions of this publication. In relation to s.1 of the 1911 Act (now s.187 of the 1995 Act set out above), s.3(1) of the Law Reform (Contributory Negligence) Act 1945 provided that the 1945 Act should not apply to any claim to which s.1 of the 1911 Act applied and that the 1911 Act should have effect as if the 1945 had not been passed. The intention of the 1911 Act and now of the provisions of the 1995 Act derived therefrom and of the 1945 Act is the same so that similar principles should be applied by the common law courts and the admiralty courts in the same way. See *Davies v Swan Motor Co (Swansea Corp Ltd and James, Third Parties)* [1949] 2 K.B. 291 at 319, per Evershed L.J. See also *The Miraflores and the Abadesa* [1966] P. 18 at 33; [1966] 1 Lloyd's Rep. 97 at 110, per Willmer L.J. Section 185 now applies in the case of ships belonging to Her Majesty as it applies in the case of other ships, see s.192(1) and (2) of the Merchant Shipping Act 1995. On the basis that the 1995 Act is a consolidating act case law previously appearing in the notes to the provisions of the 1911 Act has been retained. **2D–221**

**"Fault of two or more ships"**

For definition of "ship", see the Merchant Shipping Act 1995 s.313. See too the definitions of "vessel" and "ship" in the Merchant Shipping Act 1894 s.742 and the cases cited in the notes to that section in *British Shipping Laws* (Temperley, *Merchant Shipping Acts* 7th edn (1976)). A sailing dinghy used on a reservoir for pleasure has been held not to be a "vessel in navigation" within s.742 aforesaid, see *Curtis v Wild* [1991] 4 All E.R. 172; and a jet-ski not to be a "ship", see *Steedman v Scofield* [1992] 2 Lloyd's Rep. 163. See too *R. v Goodwin* noted at para.2D–153. **2D–222**

Of the Maritime Conventions Act 1911 (see under General Note above) it was said: "The ... Act personifies the vessel, treating it at one time as the actor, at another as suffering damage or loss, and at another as liable to make good such damage or loss. The truth is, of course, that for the purpose of ascertaining the legal effect, the word in one context connotes those responsible for the navigation of the vessel; in another, those who are interested in her, her cargo or freight; and in another, those who are in law answerable for the conduct of those in charge.", *per* Warrington J. in *The Cairnbahn* [1914] P. 25 at 34, CA.

The words "by the fault of two or more ships", and the words of s.190 "by the fault of that ship", are entirely general, and are wide enough to include not only faults of navigation but other faults as well. See *The Norwhale* [1975] Q.B. 589; [1975] 2 All E.R. 501; [1975] 1 Lloyd's Rep. 610, a case decided under ss.1(1) and 8 of the Maritime Conventions Act 1911.

As to the proof of "fault," the rule is the same as in common law cases, namely, that the onus is on the party setting up a case of negligence to prove both the breach of duty and the consequent damage (*SS. Heranger (Owners) v SS. Diamond (Owners)* [1939] A.C. 94). However, in *The Minosa* (1944) 77 L.R. 218 at 219, the judge said: "The fact that one ship does not allege any fault against the other seems to me to be quite immaterial if the court after inquiring into all the facts finds that such fault exists. I think, therefore, that this is a case in which liability should be apportioned." See also *The Shelbrit IV* (1945) 78 Ll.L.Rep. 50.

It should be noted, however, that the negligence of an officer on board a ship is not always to be treated as "the fault of the ship"; see *The Sobieski* [1949] P. 313, and *The Glaucus and the City of Florence* [1948] P. 95. In the former case a collision occurred between two ships, the S and the E, as the result of the negligence of each of them and as the result, also, of the negligence of a senior escort officer, L, on board a naval ship, the L A, which was escorting the S. L's negligence consisted of his failure to transmit information of the approach, detected by radar, of the E. It was held that L's negligence was not the negligence of his ship, the L A. Therefore, the court held, the Maritime Conventions Act (see under General Note above) had no application to the claim of the S against L, and that claim failed also at common law because of the contributory negligence of the S, the collision having occurred before the coming into force of the Law Reform (Contributory Negligence) Act 1945.

### "Damage or loss"

**2D–223** As to what may be recovered under the head of damages in a collision action, see *British Shipping Laws* (Marsden, Collisions at Sea).

"The word 'loss' is wide enough to include that form of pecuniary prejudice which consists in compensating third parties for wrong done to them by the fault of persons for whose conduct the party prejudiced must answer," *per* Lord Sumner in *The Cairnbahn* [1914] P. 25 at 33, CA. In *The Abadesa* [1966] 1 Lloyd's Rep. 118, a case under the Maritime Conventions Act 1911, however, it was decided that " Sect.1 deals with material claims, claims for material damage; Sects. 2 and 3 with personal injuries and loss of life." The corresponding sections are now ss.187, 188 and 189.

### "One or more of those ships"

**2D–224** An innocent third ship, not being one of "those ships" who were "at fault," can, it seems, still recover the whole of her damages from either of the vessels by the fault of which damage to her has been caused, leaving the ship which has paid to recover a proportionate share from the other ship at fault; see *The Cairnbahn* [1914] P. 25, where a collision occurred between a steamship and a barge in tow of and controlled by a tug. The tug-owners had no interest in the barge. The steamship and tug were found equally to blame for the collision. The owners of the innocent barge recovered the full amount of their damage from the steamship. In a subsequent claim against the tug the steamship was held entitled to include in her claim for damages half the amount of damages which she had paid to the barge. To bring the case within the section it is not necessary that the two ships on whom lies the liability to make good the damage should themselves have been in collision.

With this should be contrasted the decision in *The Umona* [1914] P. 141, where a collision occurred between a steamship and a dumb-barge in tow of and controlled by a tug whose owners also owned the barge. The fault was apportioned as to three-fourths to the steamship and one-fourth to the tug. The owners of cargo laden on the barge were held only entitled to recover from the steamship three-quarters of their damage in accordance with the doctrine enunciated in *The Milan* (1860) Lush. 388; 31 L.J.Ad. 105; followed in *The Drumlanrig* [1911] A.C. 16.

Only damage or loss to ships is within the section; so that, in *Manchester Ship Canal Co (Alpha) v Helgoy* (1924) 18 Ll.L.Rep. 191, a jetty belonging to the owners of ship A was damaged in collision between ships A and B, for which both A and B were equally to blame. Though a moiety of the damage to A and B was recoverable from the owners of B and A respectively, no part of the damage to the jetty was recoverable from the owners of B for the claim in respect of the damage to the jetty is a common law claim and, as the collision causing the damage occurred before the coming into force of the Law Reform (Contributory Negligence) Act 1945, was defeated by the defence based on the contributory negligence of the servants of the owners of A. *Quaere*, however, whether this decision is consistent with certain passages in the judgment in *The Cairnbahn* [1914] P. 25, which suggests that all forms of pecuniary loss suffered by owners of ships involved in a collision are within the section. See, too, as to collision with wreck, *The Manorbier Castle* (1922) 129 L.T. 31; 16 Asp.M.L.C. 151.

### "Cargoes"

**2D–225** The innocent owner of cargo on board either of the colliding ships could, prior to the JA 1873, recover in a common law action in tort the whole of his damages from either of the wrong-doing ships unless defeated as regards the carrying ship by the terms of the contract of carriage. In Admiralty, he could only recover half his damages against the other ship if both were found to blame for the collision (*The Milan* (1860)

Lush. 388; 31 L.J.Adm. 105). From 1873 until 1911 this Admiralty rule prevailed in all courts. Since the Maritime Conventions Act 1911 and now, under this Act, he can recover from the other ship a share of his damages proportionate to the degree in which such ship was in fault (*The Umona* [1914] P. 141). Nothing in this rule or the Act prevents the cargo owner from recovering his damages in full from the carrying ship should the terms of the contract of carriage permit (*The Bushire* (1886) 5 Asp.M.L.C. 416; 52 L.T. 740).

**"Liability to make good the damage or loss"**

These words are equivalent to "the burden of the damage or loss"; per Warrington J. in *The Cairnbahn* [1914] P. 25 at 37. Further as to liability, see para.2D–227. **2D–226**

Of s.1 of the Maritime Conventions Act 1911 (see under General Note above) it was said: Section 1 "is mandatory. It does not say that the liability shall be apportioned equally unless different degrees of fault are shown. It is the other way round. It says that the court must apportion the liability in proportion to the degree in which each vessel was at fault unless it is impossible to do so" (per Davies L.J., *The Anneliese* [1970] 1 Lloyd's Rep. 355 at 362, CA; see cases cited therein).

**Application of rule of division of loss when liability is limited**

In *Stoomvaart Maatschappij Nederland v Peninsular and Oriental S N Co (The Voorwaarts; The Khedive)* (1882) 7 App. Cas. 795, the House of Lords, following the rule laid down in *The Woodrop-Sims* (1815) 2 Dods. Ad. 83; *The Lord Melville* (1815) 5 Shaws Sc. App. Cas. 395; *The Petersfield and the Judith Randolph* (1789) Marsd. Ad. Cas. 332, decided that upon a finding of both to blame only one liability arose, namely, a liability upon the part of the owners of the ship that had done the greater damage to pay to the owners of the other ship the difference between the moieties of the losses suffered by the two ships, and that where the former limited their liability under the Merchant Shipping Acts (now the Merchant Shipping Act) the latter were only entitled to prove against the fund in court for this difference. **2D–227**

It is submitted that there is nothing in the present section to affect this rule as to unity of liability; but its application where both ships are held to blame with unequal degrees of fault may give rise to anomalous results even more striking than those which occurred under the old rule. It may happen that the ship which has been found to be at fault in the greater degree will, nevertheless, if she has also received the greater damage be entitled to some payment. Thus, for example, where the damage done to A amounts to £10,000 and to B £30,000, and the degree of fault in A is found to be $^1/_3$ and in B $^2/_3$, A, though only $^1/_3$ to blame, will have to pay B £3,333, i.e. the difference between £10,000 ($^1/_3$ of B's damage) and £6,666 ($^2/_3$ of A's damage). If A limits her liability, B can prove against the fund for £3,333.

**Three ships involved**

Where A, being towed by B, collides with C, and the court finds A and B one-half to blame and C one-half to blame, there is no obligation on the court to apportion the blame as between A and B. There is a joint and several liability in A and B to reimburse C in respect of a moiety of C's damage and a single liability in C to reimburse A and B in respect of a moiety of the damage, if any, sustained by them respectively (*The Socrates and the Champion* [1923] P. 76). **2D–228**

Where A collides with B while B is towing C, and the court finds that B and C are separately and distinctly at fault, the court will apportion blame as between B and C; see *The M.S.C. Panther and the Ericbank* [1957] P. 143 (distinguishing *The Socrates and the Champion* [1923] P. 76).

Where A goes aground negligently in avoiding B and C which have negligently collided, "the liability of each ship involved shall be assessed by comparison of her fault with the fault of each of the other ships involved individually, separately and in no way conjunctively." See *Miraflores v Owners of the George Livanos (The Miraflores, The Abadesa and The Livanos)* [1966] P. 18, per Winn L.J., affirmed by the House of Lords [1967] 1 A.C. 826; [1967] 1 All E.R. 672; [1967] 1 Lloyd's Rep. 191.

**No collision**

The section is not confined to cases where two ships have actually been in collision. **2D–229**
For example, where A, by her wash due to her excessive speed caused B, which was

improperly moored, to break adrift and suffer damage, the loss was found to be due to the fault of both A and B, and was accordingly apportioned. *The Batavier III* (1925) 134 L.T. 155; 42 T.L.R. 8. See too, *The Cairnbahn* [1914] P. 25.

**"Fault"**

2D–230 No definition of "fault" is given in the Act or the Convention (see Sch.7, Parts I & II). The basis of liability in a claim of damage by collision under the old Admiralty rule, and also, it seems, under the present section, is negligence causing or contributing to the *loss*. See, for example, *The Margaret* (1881) 6 P.D. 76, where, in a collision between a schooner at anchor and a dumb barge, the schooner, whose only fault consisted in having an anchor improperly suspended in such a position that it holed and sank the barge was held liable to pay for half the loss suffered by the barge, whose sole negligence caused the collision. See, too, *The Monte Rosa* [1893] P. 23, and presumably the same principle would be applied to cases under the present section. It is true that in *The Peter Benoit* (1915) 84 L.J.P. 197; 31 T.L.R. 227, CA; 85 L.J.P. 12; 32 T.L.R. 124, H.L.R. the Court of Appeal and the House of Lords held that the fault for which the liability is to be apportioned under this section must be "fault causing or contributing to the collision." But this decision must be read *secundum subjectam materiam*. The court was considering the effect of a breach of a local by-law (which, in fact, contributed neither to the collision nor to the loss) and must not be taken to have questioned the proposition of law illustrated above by *The Margaret* (1881) 6 P.D. 76, namely, that liability attaches to acts of negligence causing or contributing to the loss; see *The Kaiser Wilhelm II* (1916) 85. L.J.P. 34; 31 T.L.R. 615.

It is now well established that in assessing degrees of fault and apportioning blame, regard must be had both to the blameworthiness or culpability of the conduct and also its causative potency as a factor contributing to the collision and damage. See *Stapley v Gypsum Mines Ltd* [1953] A.C. 663 and *The British Aviator* [1965] 1 Lloyd's Rep. 271 at 277.

**Costs**

2D–231 Until the case of *The Modica* [1926] P. 72, the regular practice from the commencement of the Maritime Conventions Act in 1911 was that, where in a collision action it was found that each ship had been to blame, although in different degrees, the court would apply in cases under this Act the old rule of making each ship pay her own costs. This practice was based upon the rulings of Bargrave Deane J. in *The Rosalia* [1912] P. 109, and of Sir Samuel Evans P. in *The Bravo* (1912) 29 T.L.R. 122. In *The Modica*, however, Hill J., after reviewing the authorities, laid down the principle that the court, being guided by the particular circumstances in each case, was at liberty in a proper case to give to the party least in fault such proportion of that party's costs as on the particular facts appeared just, and in modern practice an order apportioning the costs is frequently made. It is, however, in each case, both in the court of first instance and in the appellate tribunals, a matter of pure discretion and not of legal right, and, unless the judge can be shown to have taken into consideration matters which are immaterial to the issue, his decision as to costs in unappealable: *The Young Sid* [1929] P. 190.

In *The Osprey* [1967] 1 Lloyd's Rep. 76 at 94, in which the plaintiffs' ship was held three-fifths and the defendants' ship two-fifths to blame, Brandon J. said, after hearing argument on costs and referring to *The Modica*, and to the then in force RSC O.62, rr.2(4) and 3(2): "It seems to me that if costs are to follow the event in a case where one party has done better than the other then the fact that party has done better than the other ought to be reflected in some way in the order for costs." The judge discussed three ways in which this might be done and finally ordered that the plaintiffs pay one-fifth of the defendants' costs. *The Osprey* has been followed in a number of cases.

**Appeal as to apportionment**

2D–232 See *The Peter Benoit* (1915) 84 L.J.P. 197; 31 T.L.R. 227, CA; 85 L.J.P. 12; 32 T.L.R. 124, HL. "I do not think this court ought lightly to interfere with the decision of the court below on the question of apportionment, unless it sees quite clearly that there has been some mistake of fact or some mistake of law which has led the learned judge to the conclusion to which he came": per Bankes L.J. at 91. See, too, *The Karamea* [1921] P. 76, CA; [1992] 1 A.C. 68; *The Clara Camus* (1926) 134 L.T. 50, CA; 136 L.T.

291, HL. In *The Testbank* [1942] P. 75 the Court of Appeal indicated that they regarded the principles laid down in *The Karamea* as placing too strict a limitation on the discretion of the Court of Appeal. But in *The MacGregor* [1943] A.C. 197, the House of Lords expressly approved *The Karamea* and disapproved the statement of principle in *The Testbank*.

The Court of Appeal will set aside the apportionment of the trial judge if persuaded that he has taken a wrong view of the material facts; see *The British Aviator* [1965] 1 Lloyd's Rep. 271 at 278.

**"(3) ... persons other than the owners of a ship who are responsible ..."**

Similar words under the former s.9(4) of the 1911 Act were held to include the commanding officer of a ship of the Royal Navy. *H.M.S. Archer* [1919] P. 1. See also *The Norwhale* [1975] Q.B. 589; [1975] 2 All E.R. 501; [1975] 1 Lloyd's Rep. 610. **2D–233**

**"Liability ... a contract"**

See, for example, *Chartered Mercantile Bank of India v Netherlands India Steam Navigation Co* (1883) 10 Q.B.D. 521, where the owner of cargo damaged in collision between two ships both belonging to the same shipowner and equally to blame, was held only to be entitled to recover from the shipowner half the amount of the damage, i.e. the half attaching to the non-carrying ship, the claim for the other half being defeated by the negligence clause in the bill of lading under which the goods were carried. **2D–234**

**"Limit his liability"**

For the provisions as to limitation of liability, see s.185 and Sch.7 replacing s.17 and Pts I and II of Sch.4 to the Merchant Shipping Act 1979, which itself came into force on December 1, 1986. **2D–235**

## Loss of life or personal injuries: joint and several liability

**188.**—(1) Where loss of life or personal injuries are suffered by any person on board a ship owing to the fault of that ship and of any other ship or ships, the liability of the owners of the ships shall be joint and several. **2D–236**

(2) Subsection (3) of section 187 applies also to this section.

(3) Nothing in this section shall be construed as depriving any person of any right of defence on which, apart from this section, he might have relied in an action brought against him by the person injured, or any person or persons entitled to sue in respect of such loss of life, or shall affect the right of any person to limit his liability in the manner provided by law.

(4) Subsection (7) of section 187 applies also for the interpretation of this section.

*Note* —Derivation—Maritime Conventions Act 1911 s.2, s.9(4), s.2 proviso and s.1(2). **2D–237**

**Crown ships**

This section now applies to ships belonging to Her Majesty as it applies in the case of other ships; see s.192(1) and (2) of the Merchant Shipping Act 1995. **2D–238**

**Loss of life and personal injuries**

Proceedings in respect of such damages may now be brought *in rem* or *in personam* (see the SCA 1981 s.20(1)(f), para.2D–147). **2D–239**

**"Fault"**

As to the personification of the ship, see s.187, at paras 2D–219 and 2D–222. **2D–240**

**"Owners"**

For meaning of this expression, see s.187(3) and para.2D–233. **2D–241**

**"Provided that ..."**

2D–242 Examples of defences preserved by this proviso are contributory negligence and an exempting term in a contract for the carriage of a passenger.

**"Limit his liability"**

2D–243 For the provisions as to limitation of liability, see s.185 of and Sch.7 to the 1995 Act.

## Loss of life or personal injuries: right of contribution

2D–244 **189.**—(1) Where loss of life or personal injuries are suffered by any person on board a ship owing to the fault of that ship and any other ship or ships, and a proportion of the damages is recovered against the owners of one of the ships which exceeds the proportion in which the ship was in fault, they may recover by way of contribution the amount of the excess from the owners of the other ship or ships to the extent to which those ships were respectively in fault.

(2) Subsection (3) of section 187 applies also to this section.

(3) Nothing in this section authorises the recovery of any amount which could not, by reason of any statutory or contractual limitation of, or exemption from, liability, or which could not for any other reason, have been recovered in the first instance as damages by the persons entitled to sue therefore.

(4) In addition to any other remedy provided by law, the persons entitled to any contribution recoverable under this section shall, for the purposes of recovering it, have the same rights and powers as the persons entitled to sue for damages in the first instance.

2D–245 *Note* —Derivation—Maritime Conventions Act 1911 s.3(1), s.9(4), s.3(1) proviso and s.3(2).

**Crown ships**

2D–246 This section now applies in the case of ships belonging to Her Majesty as it applied in the case of other vessels; see the Merchant Shipping Act 1995 s.192(1) and (2).

**General Note**

2D–247 If an innocent passenger on board ship A receives personal injuries in a collision between A and B, for which both ships are equally to blame, and recovers damages against A, A can recover a moiety from B subject to B's right to limit his liability in appropriate cases, for the passenger could have recovered against B in the first place.

An illustration of the working of subs.(3) formerly the proviso to s.3 of the Maritime Conventions Act 1911 is afforded by *The Cedric* [1920] P. 193. The representatives of the crew of a French sailing ship lost in collision with a British ship, for which both were equally to blame, had recovered in full the amount of the claims from the British ship. The owners of the latter were unable to recover a moiety of their damages in respect of these life claims in contribution from the French owners, on proof that by French law the representatives of the crew would have had no valid claim against the French ship.

**"Fault"**

2D–248 As to the personification of the ship, see s.187 at paras 2D–219, 2D–222. See too para.2D–230.

**Costs**

2D–249 Costs incurred in unreasonably disputing liability cannot be made the subject of contribution (*The Cairnbahn (No.2)* (1914) 30 T.L.R. 309, CA).

**"Recover by way of contribution"**

2D–250 It seems that this right of contribution can be enforced by the third party procedure provided for by CPR Pt 20.

Proceedings to endorce contribution must be commenced within one year of the date of payment (see s.190, below).

**"Statutory ... limitation"**

As to limitation of liability see s.185 of and Sch.7 to the Merchant Shipping Act 1995 which came into force on January 1, 1996 replacing s.17 and Pts I and IIof Sch.4 to the Merchant Shipping Act 1979. **2D–251**

**"The same rights and powers"**

i.e. a person claiming contribution can proceed *in rem* or *in personam*. See the SCA 1981 s.20(1)(f), para.2D–147. **2D–252**

*TIME LIMIT FOR PROCEEDINGS AGAINST OWNERS OR SHIP*

## Time limit for proceedings against owners or ship

**190.**—(1) This section applies to any proceedings to enforce any claim or lien against a ship or her owners— **2D–253**

(a) in respect of damage or loss caused by the fault of that ship to another ship, its cargo or freight or any property on board it; or

(b) for damages for loss of life or personal injury caused by the fault of that ship to any person on board another ship.

(2) The extent of the fault is immaterial for the purposes of this section.

(3) Subject to subsections (5) and (6) below, no proceedings to which this section applies shall be brought after the period of two years from the date when—

(a) the damage or loss was caused; or

(b) the loss of life or injury was suffered.

(4) Subject to subsections (5) and (6) below, no proceedings under any of sections 187 to 189 to enforce any contribution in respect of any overpaid proportion of any damages for loss of life or personal injury shall be brought after the period of one year from the date of payment.

(5) Any court having jurisdiction in such proceedings may, in accordance with rules of court, extend the period allowed for bringing proceedings to such extent and on such conditions as it thinks fit.

(6) Any such court, if satisfied that there has not been during any period allowed for bringing proceedings any reasonable opportunity of arresting the defendant ship within—

(a) the jurisdiction of the court, or

(b) the territorial sea of the country to which the plaintiff's ship belongs or in which the plaintiff resides or has his principal place of business,

shall extend the period allowed for bringing proceedings to an extent sufficient to give a reasonable opportunity of so arresting the ship.

*Note* —Derivation—Maritime Conventions Act 1911 s.8 and s.8 proviso. **2D–254**

**General note**

This section applies to claims against a ship or her owners for (1) damage sustained by a ship (2) damage sustained by cargo or goods aboard a ship (3) loss of life or **2D–255** personal injury of persons aboard a ship (4) contribution under s.189 of the Act. Further, in relation to the second and third types of claim it applies only to claims made against a ship (or the owners of a ship) other than the ship in which the cargo or goods or persons killed or injured were carried. See *The Niceto de Larrinaga* [1966] P. 80; [1965] 2 All E.R. 930; [1965] 2 Lloyd's Rep. 134.

**H.M. Ships**

**2D–256** With the exception of subs.(6) this section applies to H.M. ships, see the Merchant Shipping Act 1995 s.192(1).

**"...shall be brought"**

**2D–257** The effect of this section, like that of most of statutes of limitation, is not to extinguish the cause of action, but merely to bar the right to maintain the claim. See *The P.L.M. 8* [1920] P. 236; *The Dorie S.S. Co v Kamanetz Podolsk* (1923) 14 Ll.L.Rep. 512(Sc.).

The defence must be specifically pleaded; see CPR Pt 16 and Practice Direction—Statements of Case. As to the effect of omitting to plead, see *Re Robinson's Settlement* [1912] 1 Ch. 717 at 728, per Buckley L.J.

An entry of an acknowledgment of service to a claim form does not prevent the defendant from raising this defence (*The Llandovery Castle* [1920] P. 119).

If the defendant desires to raise any defence based on this section, he should raise it as a preliminary objection by way of application whether the claim is *in personam* or *in rem*. See *The Niceto de Larrinaga* [1965] 2 Lloyd's Rep. 134. On the hearing of such application the claimant may apply to the court for the exercise of its discretion in extending the time. If the objection is upheld the proper order is not that the claim form should be set aside, but that the claim is not maintainable; see *The P.L.M. 8* [1920] P. 236.

Section 190(3)(b) envisaged that there might be cases where time did not run from the date of collision and provided for cases where the date of loss of life or injury was not the same as the date of collision, see *Sweet v Owners of Blyth Lifeboat, The Times*, February 22, 2002 where time began to run from the date on which the claimant first developed a recognised psychiatric injury rather than from the date of collision between the vessels.

**"Owners"**

**2D–258** For the meaning of "owners," see s.187(3) and para.2D–233.

**"Damages for loss of life"**

**2D–259** In *The Alnwick sub nom. Robinson v Owners of the Motor Tug Alnwick* [1965] P. 357, CA, it was held that s.8 the precursor of this section was not affected by s.3 of the Law Reform (Limitation of Actions, etc.) Act 1954 and that the relevant period of limitation for an action in respect of loss of life which fell within s.8 was therefore two years. See the Limitation Act 1980 ss.31 *et seq.*

**"... caused by the fault of that ship ..."**

**2D–260** See para.2D–230.

**"... No proceedings ... shall be brought after the period of two years [or as appropriate, one year] ... "**

**2D–261** In *The Espanoleto* [1920] P. 223; 36 T.L.R. 554, it was held that inasmuch as the period of limitation provided by the precursor (s.8 of the Maritime Conventions Act) of this section was not absolute, the court should consider an application to renew on its merits and inquire whether the circumstances were such that the court would have given permission to *issue* the claim form notwithstanding that the time had expired, on the ground that the claimant had exercised due diligence in prosecuting his claim. If permission to issue the claim form would have been given, *a fortiori* a renewal of a claim form taken out within the prescribed time should be granted. See also *The World Harmony* [1965] 1 Lloyd's Rep. 244; [1967] P. 341; [1965] 2 All E.R. 139.

Where liability for damage has been proved or admitted, and the party liable has obtained a decree entitling him to limit his liability, claimants against the limitation fund may challenge the right of proof of other claimants who have not commenced

***Paragraph numbers marked with a "+" can be found online and on CD.***

proceedings within the periods prescribed by this section, for they are entitled to raise any defence which would have been open to the limiting person. But in such a case the court will generally consider the fact that limitation proceedings have been instituted as a sufficient ground for extending the time for commencing proceedings: *The Dispenser* [1920] P. 228. *Secus*, if the non-issue of the claim form resulted from the deliberate election of the claimant not to sue in this country (*The Nedenes* (1925) 23 Lloyd's Rep. 57).

**"May ... extend"**

Substantial grounds must be shown before the court will exercise its discretion to deprive the defendant of the limitation which he prima facie enjoys; and the Court of Appeal will not interfere with the exercise of this discretion unless it is shown that a wrong principle has been applied (*The Kashmir* [1923] P. 85, CA); *The James Westoll* [1923] P. 94n., CA, or, *semble*, unless the Court of Appeal considers that there were special circumstances or substantial reasons calling for an extension of the limitation period: *Robinson v Alnwick (Owners), The Alnwick* [1965] P. 357; [1965] 3 W.L.R. 118, CA; *sub nom. The Alnwick* [1965] 1 Lloyd's Rep. 69, reversed *ibid.*, 320, CA. See also *The Hesselmoor and the Sergeant* [1951] 1 Lloyd's Rep. 146 (where Willmer J. reviewed some of the earlier authorities) *The Sauria and the Trent* [1957] 1 Lloyd's Rep. 396, CA (where it was successfully contended that an informal admission of liability amounted to a contractual undertaking not to plead the defence of limitation of action) and three later decisions illustrating the application of the proviso to the Maritime Conventions Act 1911 s.8 from which this section is derived, *Bartlett v Admiralty (The Vadne)* [1959] 2 Lloyd's Rep. 480 (discretion exercised) and *The Vadne* [1960] 1 Lloyd's Rep. 260; and *The Sunpak* [1960] 2 Lloyd's Rep. 213 (exercise of discretion refused)). For a case in which the court exercised its discretion in favour of a counterclaiming defendant, see *The Fairplay XIV* [1939] P. 57. See also *The World Harmony* (exercise of discretion refused). In *The Al Tahith* [1995] 2 Lloyd's Rep. 336 a case under the former s.8, M.C.A. 1911, it was said that the test to be applied is the same as under the former RSC O.6, r.8 but note that CPR r.7.6 which replaces O.6, r.8 introduces a new approach. **2D–262**

There is no antithesis between subs.(5) and subs.(6). Thus, even in cases where there has been reasonable opportunity of arresting, the court may extend the period if satisfied that there were reasonable grounds for not issuing the claim form earlier, *The Arraiz* (1924) 19 Lloyd's Rep. 382; 132 L.T. 715, a case on the proviso to the former s.8 from which both present subss.(5)and (6)are derived.

**"And shall ... extend"**

Subsection (6) does not extend to Her Majesty's ships, see s.192(1) below. **2D–263**

**"Reasonable opportunity"**

The fact that the vessel has been within the jurisdiction for a few days within the period does not necessarily disprove lack of reasonable opportunity to arrest (*The Largo Law* (1920) 123 L.T. 560; 15 Asp.M.L.C. 104). See also *The Berny* [1977] 2 Lloyd's Rep. 533 at 547–549, where the question of reasonable opportunity to serve the claim form arose in connection with renewal of a claim form *in rem*. **2D–264**

* * * *

## *APPLICATION TO CROWN AND ITS SHIPS*

## Application to Crown and its ships

**192.**—(1) Sections 185, 186, 187, 188, 189 and 190 (except subsection (6)) apply in the case of Her Majesty's ships as they apply in relation to other ships and section 191 applies to the Crown in its capacity as an authority or person specified in subsection (1). **2D–265**

(2) In this section "Her Majesty's ships" means—

(a) ships of which the beneficial interest is vested in Her Majesty;

***Paragraph numbers marked with a "+" can be found online and on CD.***

(b) ships which are registered as Government ships;

(c) ships which are for the time being demised or sub-demised to or in the exclusive possession of the Crown;

except that it does not include any ship in which Her Majesty is interested otherwise than in right of Her Government in the United Kingdom unless that ship is for the time being demised or sub-demised to Her Majesty in right of Her Government in the United Kingdom or in the exclusive possession of Her Majesty in that right.

(3) In the application of subsection (2) above to Northern Ireland, any reference to Her Majesty's Government in the United Kingdom includes a reference to Her Government in Northern Ireland.

**2D–266** *Note*—Derivation—The Crown Proceedings Act 1947 ss.5, 6 , 7, 30(1) and 38(2); the Merchant Shipping Act 1979 Sch.5, para.3; and the Crown Proceedings Order 1981 (SI 1981/233) art.30(1).

## Compulsory insurance or security

**2D–267** **192A.**—(1) Subject to subsections (2) and (3) below, the Secretary of State may make regulations requiring that, in such cases as may be prescribed by the regulations, while a ship is in United Kingdom waters, there must be in force in respect of the ship—

(a) a contract of insurance insuring such person or persons as may be specified by the regulations against such liabilities as may be so specified and satisfying such other requirements as may be so specified, or

(b) such other security relating to those liabilities as satisfies requirements specified by or under the regulations.

(2) Regulations under this section shall not apply in relation to—

(a) a qualifying foreign ship while it is exercising—

(i) the right of innocent passage, or

(ii) the right of transit passage through straits used for international navigation,

(b) any warship, or

(c) any ship for the time being used by the government of any State for other than commercial purposes.

(3) Regulations under this section may not require insurance or security to be maintained in respect of a ship in relation to any liability in any case where an obligation to maintain insurance or security in respect of that ship in relation to that liability is imposed by section 163 or by or under an Order in Council under section 182B.

(4) Regulations under this section may require that, where a person is obliged to have in force in respect of a ship a contract of insurance or other security, such documentary evidence as may be specified by or under the regulations of the existence of the contract of insurance or other security must be carried in the ship and produced on demand, by such persons as may be specified in the regulations, to such persons as may be so specified.

(5) Regulations under this section may provide—

(a) that in such cases as are prescribed a ship which contravenes the regulations shall be liable to be detained and that section 284 shall have effect, with such modifications (if any) as are prescribed by the regulations, in relation to the ship,

(b) that a contravention of the regulations shall be an offence punishable on summary conviction by a fine of an amount not exceeding £50,000, or such less amount as is prescribed by the regulations, and on conviction on indictment by a fine, and

(c) that any such contravention shall be an offence punishable only on summary conviction by a fine of an amount not exceeding £50,000, or such less amount as is prescribed by the regulations.

(6) Regulations under this section may—

(a) make different provision for different cases,

(b) make provision in terms of any document which the Secretary of State or any person considers relevant from time to time, and

(c) include such incidental, supplemental and transitional provision as appears to the Secretary of State to be expedient for the purposes of the regulations.

*Note* —Inserted by the Merchant Shipping and Maritime Security Act 1997 s.16. This provision is now in force. As at December 2002 see hereunder the Merchant Shipping (Ship Receiving Transhipped Fish) Regulations 1998 (SI 1998/209), effective April 1998. **2D–268**

* * * *

## Part IX

## Salvage and Wreck

### Chapter I

### Salvage

### Salvage Convention 1989 to have force of law

**224.**—(1) The provisions of the International Convention on Salvage, 1989 as set out in Part I of Schedule 11 (in this Chapter referred to as "the Salvage Convention") shall have the force of law in the United Kingdom. **2D–269**

(2) The provisions of Part II of that Schedule shall have effect in connection with the Salvage Convention, and subsection (1) above shall have effect subject to the provisions of that Part.

(3) If it appears to Her Majesty in Council that the Government of the United Kingdom has agreed to any revision of the Salvage Convention She may by Order in Council make such modifications of Parts I and II of Schedule 11 as She considers appropriate in consequence of the revision.

*Paragraph numbers marked with a "+" can be found online and on CD.*

(4) Nothing in subsection (1) or (2) above shall affect any rights or liabilities arising out of any salvage operations started or other acts done before 1st January 1995.

(5) Nothing in any modification made by virtue of subsection (3) above shall affect any rights or liabilities arising out of any salvage operations started or other acts done before the day on which the modification comes into force.

(6) As respects any period before the entry into force of the Salvage Convention any reference in the Salvage Convention to a State Party to the Convention shall be read as a reference to the United Kingdom.

(7) A draft of an Order in Council proposed to be made by virtue of subsection (3) above shall not be submitted to Her Majesty in Council unless the draft has been approved by a resolution of each House of Parliament.

2D–270 *Note* —Derivation—Merchant Shipping (Salvage and Pollution) Act 1994. The derivation of Sch.7 (*q.v.*) is as to Pt I, Merchant Shipping Act 1979 Sch.4, Pt I and as to Pt II, Merchant Shipping Act 1979 s.49(5), Sch.4, Pt II; Merchant Shipping (Survey and Certification) Regulations 1995 (SI 1995/1210) reg.1(8).

* * * *

## Apportionment of salvage by the court

2D–271 **229.**—(1) Where—

(a) the aggregate amount of salvage payable in respect of salvage services rendered in United Kingdom waters has been finally determined and exceeds £5,000; or

(b) the aggregate amount of salvage payable in respect of salvage services rendered outside United Kingdom waters (of whatever amount) has been finally determined; but

(c) in either case, any delay or dispute arises as to the apportionment of the amount,

the court may cause the amount of salvage to be apportioned among the persons entitled to it in such manner as it thinks just.

(2) Any decision of the court under this section shall be made on the basis of the criteria contained in Article 13 of the Salvage Convention.

(3) For the purpose of making that apportionment, the court may—

(a) appoint any person to carry that apportionment into effect;

(b) compel any person in whose hands or under whose control the amount may be to distribute it or to pay it into court to be dealt with as the court directs; and

(c) issue such process as it thinks fit.

(4) In this section "the court" means the High Court or, in Scotland, the Court of Session or a sheriff.

2D–272 *Note* —Derivation—Merchant Shipping Act 1894 s.556; the Merchant Shipping

*Paragraph numbers marked with a "+" can be found online and on CD.*

(Registration, etc.) Act 1993 Sch.4, para.30; and the Merchant Shipping (Salvage and Pollution) Act 1994 Sch.2, para.1(5).



## Salvage claims against the Crown and Crown rights of salvage and regulation thereof

**230.**—(1) Subject to section 29 of the Crown Proceedings Act 1947 (exclusion of proceedings in rem against the Crown) (so far as consistent with the Salvage Convention) the law relating to civil salvage, whether of life or property, except sections 225, 226 and 227, shall apply in relation to salvage services in assisting any of Her Majesty's ships, or in saving life therefrom, or in saving any cargo or equipment belonging to Her Majesty in right of Her Government in the United Kingdom, in the same manner as if the ship, cargo or equipment belonged to a private person. **2D–273**

(2) Where salvage services are rendered by or on behalf of Her Majesty, whether in right of Her Government in the United Kingdom or otherwise, Her Majesty shall be entitled to claim salvage in respect of those services to the same extent as any other salvor, and shall have the same rights and remedies in respect of those services as any other salvor.

(3) No claim for salvage services by the commander or crew, or part of the crew, of any of Her Majesty's ships shall be finally adjudicated upon without the consent of the Secretary of State to the prosecution of the claim.

(4) Any document purporting to give the consent of the Secretary of State for the purposes of subsection (3)above and to be signed by an officer of the Ministry of Defence shall be evidence of that consent.

(5) If a claim is prosecuted without the consent required by subsection (3) above the claim shall be dismissed with costs.

(6) The reference in subsection (5) above to dismissal with costs shall in Scotland be construed as a reference to dismissal with the defender being found entitled to expenses.

(7) "Her Majesty's ships" has the same meaning in this section as in section 192.

(8) In the application of this section to Northern Ireland, any reference to Her Majesty's Government in the United Kingdom includes a reference to Her Government in Northern Ireland.

*Note* —Derivation—The Crown Proceedings Act 1947 s.8 and s.38(2); the Merchant Shipping Act 1894 s.557; the Merchant Shipping (Salvage and Pollution) Act 1994 Sch.2, para.3; the Defence (Transfer of Functions) Act 1964 ss.1(2) and 3(2); and the Crown Proceedings (Northern Ireland) Order 1981 (SI 1981/233) art.30(1). **2D–274**

# 2E ARBITRATION PROCEEDINGS

## Part 62—Arbitration Claims

**Contents**



**Editorial introduction**

Part I of Pt 62 is concerned with applications to which the Arbitration Act 1996 applies, Pt II is concerned with matters to which the old law applies, and Pt III with common enforcement procedures. 2E–2

"The old law" means the enactments specified in s.107 of the Arbitration Act 1996 as they stood before their amendment or repeal by the 1996 Act, namely the Arbitration Act 1950 (see SCP 1999, Vol.2, Section 21A, paras 21A–1 *et seq.*); the Arbitration Act 1975 (see SCP 1999, Vol.2, Section 21B, paras 21B–1 *et seq.*) and the Arbitration Act 1979 (see SCP 1999, Vol.2, Section 21C, paras 21C–1 *et seq.*).

The old law is preserved as a result of the provisions of s.109(2) of the Arbitration Act 1996 which provided that any order bringing the Act into force might contain any

***Paragraph numbers marked with a "+" can be found online and on CD.***

transitional provisions as might appear necessary and the provisions of the Arbitration Act 1996 (Commencement No.1) Order 1996, made on December 16, 1996, by way of transitional provision, provide that:

2. The old law shall continue to apply to:

(a) arbitral proceedings commenced before the appointed day [January 31, 1997];

(b) arbitration applications commenced or made before the appointed day;

(c) arbitration applications commenced or made on or after the appointed day relating to arbitral proceedings commenced before the appointed day;

and the provisions of the Act which would otherwise be applicable shall not apply.

### Note

2E–3 With the passage of time since the coming into force of the 1996 Act (January 31, 1997) the transitional concept of the "old law" is now (July 2005 onwards) considered to be for all practical purposes in a state of desuetude if not without any effect. See further at 2E–22.

Part II of the 1950 Act together with the First Schedule thereto were not repealed by the 1996 Act and survive in their own right independently of the transitional concept of "the old law" but are now rarely relied upon.

### The Application

2E–4 Arbitration applications under the 1996 Act (see Sect.I of Part 62) save for application under s.9, are made by use of an arbitration claim form (see rule 62.3, the Practice Direction—Arbitration and the reference to the form set out at Appendix A to the practice direction). Applications under s.9 are made by ordinary application process in the existing proceedings. The courts where the arbitration claim form may be issued are set out in the Practice Direction—Arbitration, para.62.2.3.

Applications under "the old law" see (Sect.II of Part 62) save for s.4 of the 1950 Act applications are made by the use of an arbitration claim form and must be stated in the Commercial Court and issued out of the Admiralty and Commercial Registry at the RCJ London and where required to be heard by a judge must be heard by a judge of that court unless he otherwise directs, see rule 62.12 and Practice Direction—Arbitration, para.62.14.1. Claims for the attendance of witnesses within the area of a district registry may be started within the relevant district registry, see r.62.14 and see the Practice Direction, para.7.2.

Applications for enforcement should be made using an arbitration claim form and may be considered by a Judge, Master, Admiralty Registrar or District Judge.

### Related sources

2E–5
- Arbitration Act 1950 Pt II (see paras 2E–57 *et seq.*).
- Arbitration Act 1996 (see paras 2E–83 *et seq.*).
- The preserved "old law"
  - — Arbitration Act 1950 Pt I (see SCP 1999, Vol.2, Section 21A).
  - — Arbitration Acts 1975 and 1979 (see SCP 1999, Vol.2, Sections 21B and 21C).
- High Court and County Court (Allocation of Arbitration Proceedings) Order 1996 (SI 1996/3215), as amended.
- CPR Pt 6.
- CPR Pt 8.
- CPR Pt 11
- CPR Pt 25.
- CPR Pt 34.
- CPR Pts 58 and 59.
- CPR Pt 74.
- The Admiralty and Commercial Courts Guide, Section O.
- The Technology and Construction Court Guide, Section 10.

### Forms

2E–6
- **N8** Claim form (arbitration)
- **N8A** Notes for claimant

***Paragraph numbers marked with a "+" can be found online and on CD.***

- **N8B** Notes for defendant
- **N15** Acknowledgment of service (arbitration claims)

## Scope of this Part and interpretation[1]

**62.1—(1) This Part contains rules about arbitration claims.** 2E–7

**(2) In this Part—**

**(a) "the 1950 Act" means the Arbitration Act 1950;**

**(b) "the 1975 Act" means the Arbitration Act 1975;**

**(c) "the 1979 Act" means the Arbitration Act 1979;**

**(d) "the 1996 Act" means the Arbitration Act 1996;**

**(e) references to—**

**(i) the 1996 Act; or**

**(ii) any particular section of that Act**

**include references to that Act or to the particular section of that Act as applied with modifications by the ACAS Arbitration Scheme (England and Wales) Order 2001; and**

**(f) "arbitration claim form" means a claim form in the form set out in Practice Direction 62.**

**(3) Part 58 (Commercial Court) applies to arbitration claims in the Commercial Court, Part 59 (Mercantile Court) applies to arbitration claims in the Mercantile Court and Part 60 (Technology and Construction Court claims) applies to arbitration claims in the Technology and Construction Court, except where this Part provides otherwise.**

### *I. Claims under the 1996 Act*

## Interpretation[2]

**62.2—(1) In this Section of this Part "arbitration claim" means—** 2E–8

**(a) any application to the court under the 1996 Act;**

**(b) a claim to determine—**

**(i) whether there is a valid arbitration agreement;**

**(ii) whether an arbitration tribunal is properly constituted; or what matters have been submitted to arbitration in accordance with an arbitration agreement;**

**(c) a claim to declare that an award by an arbitral tribunal is not binding on a party; and**

**(d) any other application affecting—**

**(i) arbitration proceedings (whether started or not); or**

**(ii) an arbitration agreement.**

**(2) This Section of this Part does not apply to an arbitration claim to which Sections II or III of this Part apply.**

[1] Amended by the Civil Procedure (Amendment No.5) Rules 2001 (SI 2001/4015) and the Civil Procedure (Amendment No.2) Rules 2009 (SI 2009/3390).

[2] Amended by the Civil Procedure (Amendment No.5) Rules 2001 (SI 2001/4015).

### Starting the claim[1]

2E–9 **62.3—(1) Except where paragraph (2) applies an arbitration claim must be started by the issue of an arbitration claim form in accordance with the Part 8 procedure.**

**(2) An application under section 9 of the 1996 Act to stay legal proceedings must be made by application notice to the court dealing with those proceedings.**

**(3) The courts in which an arbitration claim may be started are set out in Practice Direction 62.**

**(4) Rule 30.5 applies with the modification that a judge of the Technology and Construction Court may transfer the claim to any other court or specialist list.**

#### Note

2E–10 This rule is supplemented by Practice Direction—Arbitration para.2 (see para.2E–46 below). See too the High Court and County Courts (Allocation of Arbitration Proceedings) Order 1996 at paras 2E–375 *et seq*.

### Arbitration claim form[2]

2E–11 **62.4—(1) An arbitration claim form must—**

**(a) include a concise statement of—**

**(i) the remedy claimed; and**

**(ii) any questions on which the claimant seeks the decision of the court;**

**(b) give details of any arbitration award challenged by the claimant, identifying which part or parts of the award are challenged and specifying the grounds for the challenge;**

**(c) show that any statutory requirements have been met;**

**(d) specify under which section of the 1996 Act the claim is made;**

**(e) identify against which (if any) defendants a costs order is sought; and**

**(f) specify either—**

**(i) the persons on whom the arbitration claim form is to be served, stating their role in the arbitration and whether they are defendants; or**

**(ii) that the claim is made without notice under section 44(3) of the 1996 Act and the grounds relied on.**

**(2) Unless the court orders otherwise an arbitration claim form must be served on the defendant within 1 month from the date of issue and rules 7.5 and 7.6 are modified accordingly.**

**(3) Where the claimant applies for an order under section 12 of**

---

[1] Amended by the Civil Procedure (Amendment No.5) Rules 2001 (SI 2001/4015), the Civil Procedure (Amendment No.4) Rules 2005 (SI 2005/3515) and the Civil Procedure (Amendment No.2) Rules 2009 (SI 2009/3390).

[2] Amended by the Civil Procedure (Amendment No.5) Rules 2001 (SI 2001/4015).

**the 1996 Act (extension of time for beginning arbitral proceedings or other dispute resolution procedures), he may include in his arbitration claim form an alternative application for a declaration that such an order is not needed.**

### Service out of the jurisdiction[1]

**62.5—(1) The court may give permission to serve an arbitration claim form out of the jurisdiction if—** 2E–12

**(a) the claimant seeks to—**

**(i) challenge; or**

**(ii) appeal on a question of law arising out of,**

**an arbitration award made within the jurisdiction;**

**(The place where an award is treated as made is determined by section 53 of the 1996 Act).**

**(b) the claim is for an order under section 44 of the 1996 Act; or**

**(c) the claimant—**

**(i) seeks some other remedy or requires a question to be decided by the court affecting an arbitration (whether started or not), an arbitration agreement or an arbitration award; and**

**(ii) the seat of the arbitration is or will be within the jurisdiction or the conditions in section 2(4) of the 1996 Act are satisfied.**

**(2) An application for permission under paragraph (1) must be supported by written evidence—**

**(a) stating the grounds on which the application is made; and**

**(b) showing in what place or country the person to be served is, or probably may be found.**

(3) **Rules 6.40 to 6.46 apply to the service of an arbitration claim form under paragraph (1).**

**(4) An order giving permission to serve an arbitration claim form out of the jurisdiction must specify the period within which the defendant may file an acknowledgment of service.**

#### Note

Rule 62.5 applies only to applications by and against parties to an arbitration and does not allow service out of the jurisdiction on a non-party, *Vale Do Doce Navegacao SA v Shanghai Bao Steel Ocean Shipping Co Ltd* [2000] 2 Lloyd's Rep. 1 (attempt to serve brokers) a case under the forerunner to this rule. 2E–13

### Notice[2]

**62.6—(1) Where an arbitration claim is made under section 24, 28 or 56 of the 1996 Act, each arbitrator must be a defendant.** 2E–14

[1] Amended by the Civil Procedure (Amendment No.5) Rules 2001 (SI 2001/4015) and the Civil Procedure (Amendment) Rules 2008 (SI 2008/2178).

[2] Amended by the Civil Procedure (Amendment No.5) Rules 2001 (SI 2001/4015).

**(2) Where notice must be given to an arbitrator or any other person it may be given by sending him a copy of—**

**(a) the arbitration claim form; and**

**(b) any written evidence in support.**

**(3) Where the 1996 Act requires an application to the court to be made on notice to any other party to the arbitration, that notice must be given by making that party a defendant.**

### Case management[1]

2E–15 **62.7—(1) Part 26 and any other rule that requires a party to file an allocation questionnaire does not apply.**

**(2) Arbitration claims are allocated to the multi-track.**

**(3) Part 29 does not apply.**

**(4) The automatic directions set out in Practice Direction 62 apply unless the court orders otherwise.**

### Stay of legal proceedings[2]

2E–16 **62.8—(1) An application notice seeking a stay of legal proceedings under section 9 of the 1996 Act[3] must be served on all parties to those proceedings who have given an address for service.**

**(2) A copy of an application notice under paragraph (1) must be served on any other party to the legal proceedings (whether or not he is within the jurisdiction) who has not given an address for service, at—**

**(a) his last known address; or**

**(b) a place where it is likely to come to his attention.**

**(3) Where a question arises as to whether—**

**(a) an arbitration agreement has been concluded; or**

**(b) the dispute which is the subject-matter of the proceedings falls within the terms of such an agreement,**

**the court may decide that question or give directions to enable it to be decided and may order the proceedings to be stayed pending its decision.**

### Variation of time[4]

2E–17 **62.9—(1) The court may vary the period of 28 days fixed by section 70(3) of the 1996 Act for—**

**(a) challenging the award under section 67 or 68 of the Act; and**

**(b) appealing against an award under section 69 of the Act.**

**(2) An application for an order under paragraph (1) may be**

[1] Amended by the Civil Procedure (Amendment No.5) Rules 2001 (SI 2001/4015) and the Civil Procedure (Amendment No.2) Rules 2009 (SI 2009/3390).

[2] Amended by the Civil Procedure (Amendment No.5) Rules 2001 (SI 2001/4015).

[3] 1996 c.23.

[4] Amended by the Civil Procedure (Amendment No.5) Rules 2001 (SI 2001/4015).

*Paragraph numbers marked with a "+" can be found online and on CD.*

**made without notice being served on any other party before the period of 28 days expires.**

**(3) After the period of 28 days has expired—**

**(a) an application for an order extending time under paragraph (1) must—**

**(i) be made in the arbitration claim form; and**

**(ii) state the grounds on which the application is made;**

**(b) any defendant may file written evidence opposing the extension of time within 7 days after service of the arbitration claim form; and**

**(c) if the court extends the period of 28 days, each defendant's time for acknowledging service and serving evidence shall start to run as if the arbitration claim form had been served on the date when the court's order is served on that defendant.**



### Hearings[1]

**62.10—(1) The court may order that an arbitration claim be heard either in public or in private.** 2E–18

**(2) Rule 39.2 does not apply.**

**(3) Subject to any order made under paragraph (1)—**

**(a) the determination of—**

**(i) a preliminary point of law under section 45 of the 1996 Act; or**

**(ii) an appeal under section 69 of the 1996 Act on a question of law arising out of an award,**

**will be heard in public; and**

**(b) all other arbitration claims will be heard in private.**

**(4) Paragraph (3)(a) does not apply to—**

**(a) the preliminary question of whether the court is satisfied of the matters set out in section 45(2)(b); or**

**(b) an application for permission to appeal under section 69(2)(b).**

#### Application for variation of time

This rule is supplemented by Practice Direction—Arbitration para.11.1 (see para.2E–50 below). 2E–18.1

#### Note

In *Moscow City Council v Bankers Trust Co* [2004] EWCA Civ 314; [2005] Q.B. 207; [2004] 3 W.L.R. 533; [2004] 4 All E.R. 746; [2004] 2 Lloyd's Rep. 179, the Court of Appeal reviewed the several considerations material to deciding whether the hearing of an arbitration claim should be in public or in private and whether publication of any judgment given or order made should be restricted or not. At para.34, Mance L.J. said: 2E–19

> "The consideration that parties have elected to arbitrate confidentially and privately cannot dictate the position is respect of arbitration claims brought to

[1] Amended by the Civil Procedure (Amendment No.5) Rules 2001 (SI 2001/4015).

*Paragraph numbers marked with a "+" can be found online and on CD.*

court under CPR 62.10. CPR 62.10 therefore only represents a starting point. Such proceedings are no longer consensual. The possibility of pursuing them exists in the public interest. The courts, when called upon to exercise the supervisory role assigned to them under the Arbitration Act 1996, are acting as a branch of the state, not as a mere extension of the consensual arbitral process. Nevertheless, they are acting in the public interest to facilitate the fairness and well-being of a consensual method of dispute resolution, and both the Rule Committee and the courts can still take into account the parties' expectations regarding privacy and confidentiality when agreeing to arbitrate."

And at paras 38 and 39:

"...In arbitration claims relating to such arbitrations, the starting point may easily give way to a public hearing. In every case, while it will be appropriate to start the hearing in private as contemplated by CPR 62.10, the court should be ready to hear representations from one or other party that the hearing should be continued in public, and should anyway if appropriate raise this possibility with the parties, as Lord Woolf stressed in *Ex p. Kaim Todner*.

Further, even though the hearing may have been in private, the court should, when preparing and giving judgment, bear in mind that any judgment should be given in public, where this can be done without disclosing significant confidential information."

And at para.42:

"...It is, I think, better to describe CPR 62.10 and indeed 39.2 as establishing starting points, rather than as presumptions. If neither the parties nor the judge of his or her own motion raises any question about the appropriateness of private hearing, where that is the starting position, then the hearing will remain private. But, once the question of publication is raised, the judge's task is to weigh all relevant circumstances; and even where it is not raised by the parties, he or she may if appropriate raise it of his own motion."

See too *Emmott v Michael Wilson & Partners* [2008] EWCA Civ 184, [2008] 1 Lloyd's Rep. 616, CA,where the paramountcy of privacy in arbitration and the associated obligation of confidentiality and the exceptions thereto are reviewed. See also para. 31.22.1, above.

### *II. Other Arbitration Claims*

### Scope of this Section[1]

2E–20 **62.11—(1) This Section of this Part contains rules about arbitration claims to which the old law applies.**

**(2) In this Section—**

**(a) "the old law" means the enactments specified in Schedules 3 and 4 of the 1996 Act as they were in force before their amendment or repeal by that Act; and**

**(b) "arbitration claim" means any application to the court under the old law and includes an appeal (or application for permission to appeal) to the High Court under section 1(2) of the 1979 Act[2].**

**(3) This Section does not apply to—**

**(a) a claim to which Section III of this Part applies; or**

**(b) a claim on the award.**

[1] Amended by the Civil Procedure (Amendment No.5) Rules 2001 (SI 2001/4015).

[2] 1979 c.42; repealed by the Arbitration Act 1996 (c.23), s.107(2) and Sch.4 but continues to apply to claims commenced before January 31, 1997 by virtue of the Arbitration Act 1996 (Commencement No.1) Order 1996 (SI 1996/3146) art.4 and Sch.2.

*Paragraph numbers marked with a "+" can be found online and on CD.*

**Note**

"The old law" namely the Arbitration Act 1950; the Arbitration Act 1975; and the Arbitration Act 1979, the texts of which are set out in SCP 1999, Vol.2, Section 21 at paras 21A-1 *et seq.*, 21B–1 *et seq.*, and 21C–1 *et seq.* respectively. See too under Note at 2E–3 above. **2E–21**

**Other Arbitration Claims—Section II**

It is important to note that the provisions of Sect.II of Part 62 and Sect.II of its associated Practice Direction apply only to arbitration claims under "the old law". Such provisions should not be applied by analogy or otherwise to claims under the 1996 Act for which a more flexible regime consistent with the modern approach to arbitration is provided. In particular for 1996 Act claims a more flexible point of entry and jurisdiction is provided (see PD 62.2.3) allowing an arbitration claim to be issued and considered as appropriate to its subject matter in the Chancery Division, the Technology and Construction Court, the Mercantile lists (where established) and TCC lists of the High Court District Registries as well as the Commercial Court as hitherto. Applications for a stay under s.4 of the 1950 Act or under s.9 of the 1996 Act were and are in any event made in whatever court is dealing with the proceedings concerned. **2E–22**



## Applications to Judge[1]

**62.12 A claim—** **2E–23**

**(a) seeking permission to appeal under section 1(2) of the 1979 Act;**

**(b) under section 1(5) of that Act (including any claim seeking permission); or**

**(c) under section 5 of that Act,**

**must be made in the High Court and will be heard by a judge of the Commercial Court unless any such judge directs otherwise.**

**Effect of rule**

In connection with the following commentary it is suggested that reference be made first to the Note at 2E–3 and the Note at 2E–22 above. **2E–24**

Applications under s.1(5) of the 1979 Act must be made to a judge. These are applications to order the arbitrator or umpire concerned to state the reasons for his award in sufficient detail to enable the court, should an appeal be brought under s.1 of the 1979 Act, to consider any questions of law arising out of the award. The reason for this requirement is because of the likely complexity and importance of the questions which will probably arise in considering whether the award does or does not sufficiently set out the reasons for the award. An application under s.1(5) of the 1979 Act, including any application for permission is made by an arbitration form in accordance with Pt 8, which must be served on the arbitrator or umpire, as the case may be, and on all the parties to the reference (see r.62.13(3)).

Applications under s.5 of the 1979 Act must be made to a judge. These are applications to empower the arbitrator or umpire to continue with the reference in default of acknowledgment of service by any party or of non-compliance by a party with an order made by the arbitrator or umpire in the same manner as a Judge of the High Court might continue with proceedings where a party fails to comply with an order of the court or a requirement of the rules of court.

Applications for permission to appeal to the court under s.1(2) of the 1979 Act must be made to a judge. Section 1(2) provides that an appeal shall lie to the court on any question of law arising out of an award made on an arbitration agreement and in s.1(3) it is stated that an appeal may be brought by any of the parties to the reference (a) with the consent of all the other parties or (b) with the permission of the court.

Applications under this rule must be made, where a claim is pending by application

[1] Amended by the Civil Procedure (Amendment No.5) Rules 2001 (SI 2001/4015).

notice in the claim, and in any other case by a Pt 8 arbitration claim form (see r.62.13(1) and (2).

It should further be noted that applications under this rule which are required to be heard by a Judge must be heard by a Commercial judge, unless he directs otherwise (see r.62.12, and Practice Direction—Arbitration para.14.1).

Apart from the matters specified in this rule, all other applications arising under the Arbitration Act 1950, may be made in chambers and heard by the judge, Master or Admiralty Registrar. They include applications to stay proceedings under s.4, to appoint an arbitrator or umpire under s.10, for the issue of a witness summons, and all other matters included in s.12(6) of the Arbitration Act 1950. The effect of this rule is to negative the decisions in *Raymond and Reid v Granger* [1952] 2 All E.R. 1952, and *Kruger Townwear Ltd v Northern Assurance Co* [1953] 1 W.L.R. 1049; [1953] 2 All E.R. 727n.

#### Without notice applications for injunctions

2E–25 CPR r.25.2, which permits applications for injunctive relief in cases in urgency, before the issue of a Pt 7 claim form or a Pt 8 claim form. Where injunctive relief is granted in such circumstances, however, the claim form should be issued promptly thereafter. It is unacceptable that a *Mareva* injunction, for example, granted in aid of an arbitration, should remain in force for two months after its grant without any originating process to sustain it; accordingly such an injunction will be discharged (*Siporex Trade SA v Comdel Commodities Ltd* [1986] 2 Lloyd's Rep. 428; (1986) 136 N.L.J. 538).

#### Starting the claim[1]

2E–26 **62.13—(1) Except where paragraph (2) applies an arbitration claim must be started by the issue of an arbitration claim form in accordance with the Part 8 procedure.**

**(2) Where an arbitration claim is to be made in existing proceedings—**

**(a) it must be made by way of application notice; and**

**(b) any reference in this Section of this Part to an arbitration claim form includes a reference to an application notice.**

**(3) The arbitration claim form in an arbitration claim under section 1(5) of the 1979 Act (including any claim seeking permission) must be served on—**

**(a) the arbitrator or umpire; and**

**(b) any other party to the reference.**

#### Claims in District Registries[2]

2E–27 **62.14 If—**

**(a) a claim is to be made under section 12(4) of the 1950 Act[3] for an order for the issue of a witness summons to compel the attendance of the witness before an arbitrator or umpire; and**

[1] Amended by the Civil Procedure (Amendment No.5) Rules 2001 (SI 2001/4015).

[2] Amended by the Civil Procedure (Amendment No.5) Rules 2001 (SI 2001/4015).

[3] 1950 c.27; s.12(4) was repealed by the Arbitration Act 1996 (c.23), s.107(2) and Sch. 4 but continues to apply to claims commenced before January 31, 1997 by virtue of the Arbitration Act 1996 (Commencement No.1) Order 1996 (SI 1996/3146) art.4 and Sch.2.

(b) the attendance of the witness is required within the district of a District Registry,

the claim may be started in that Registry.

### Time limits and other special provisions about arbitration claims[1]

62.15—(1) An arbitration claim to— 2E–28

(a) remit an award under section 22 of the 1950 Act[2];

(b) set aside an award under section 23(2) of that Act[3] or otherwise; or

(c) direct an arbitrator or umpire to state the reasons for an award under section 1(5) of the 1979 Act,

must be made, and the arbitration claim form served, within 21 days after the award has been made and published to the parties.

(2) An arbitration claim to determine any question of law arising in the course of a reference under section 2(1) of the Arbitration Act 1979 must be made, and the arbitration claim form served, within 14 days after—

(a) the arbitrator or umpire gave his consent in writing to the claim being made; or

(b) the other parties so consented.

(3) An appeal under section 1(2) of the 1979 Act must be filed, and the arbitration claim form served, within 21 days after the award has been made and published to the parties.

(4) Where reasons material to an appeal under section 1(2) of the 1979 Act are given on a date subsequent to the publication of the award, the period of 21 days referred to in paragraph (3) will run from the date on which reasons are given.

(5) In every arbitration claim to which this rule applies—

(a) the arbitration claim form must state the grounds of the claim or appeal;

(b) where the claim or appeal is based on written evidence, a copy of that evidence must be served with the arbitration claim form; and

(c) where the claim or appeal is made with the consent of the arbitrator, the umpire or the other parties, a copy of every written consent must be served with the arbitration claim form.

(6) In an appeal under section 1(2) of the 1979 Act—

(a) a statement of the grounds for the appeal specifying the relevant parts of the award and reasons; and

---

1 Amended by the Civil Procedure (Amendment No.5) Rules 2001 (SI 2001/4015).

2 1950 c.27; s.22 was repealed by the Arbitration Act 1996 (c.23), s.107(2) and Sch.4 but continues to apply to claims commenced before January 31, 1997 by virtue of the Arbitration Act 1996 (Commencement No.1) Order 1996 (SI 1996/3146) art.4 and Sch.2.

3 1950 c.27; s.23(2) was repealed by the Arbitration Act 1996 (c.23), s.107(2) and Sch. 4 but continues to apply to claims commenced before January 31, 1997 by virtue of the Arbitration Act 1996 (Commencement No.1) Order 1996 (SI 1996/3146) art.4 and Sch.2.

**(b) where permission is required, any written evidence in support of the contention that the question of law concerns—**

**(i) a term of a contract; or**

**(ii) an event,**

**which is not a "one-off" term or event,**

**must be filed and served with the arbitration claim form.**

**(7) Any written evidence in reply to written evidence under paragraph (6)(b) must be filed and served on the claimant not less than 2 days before the hearing.**

**(8) A party to a claim seeking permission to appeal under section 1(2) of the 1979 Act who wishes to contend that the award should be upheld for reasons not expressed or fully expressed in the award and reasons must file and serve on the claimant, a notice specifying the grounds of his contention not less than 2 days before the hearing.**

#### General Note to 2E–30 and 2E–32 to 2E–36

2E–29 In connection with the above mentioned commentaries reference should be made first to the Note at 2E–3 and the Note at 2E–22.

#### Time for applying

2E–30 The 21–day time limit imposed by r.62.15(1) applies both to an application to set aside an award under s.23(2) of the Arbitration Act 1950 and to an application at common law for a declaration that an award is void on the grounds of the arbitrator's conduct. The time–limit cannot be circumvented simply by avoiding the use of the term "misconduct" in the application (*Cook International Inc v BV Handelsmaatschappij Jean Delvaux* [1985] 2 Lloyd's Rep. 225 at 233). The 21 day–time limit is not mandatory. The court has jurisdiction to extend time, see *Nagusina Naviera v Allied Maritime Inc* [2002] C.L.C. 385 (a case under s.1(2) of the Arbitration Act 1979 and concerning the relevance of CPR r.7.6).

#### "Made and published"

2E–31 An award is made and published when the arbitrator gives notice to the parties that it is ready. Delay in taking up the award does not extend the time for appealing or applying (*The Archipelagos* [1979] Lloyd's Rep. 289; *Selous Street Properties Ltd v Oronel Fabrics Ltd* (1984) 270 E.G. 643).

#### Appeal under s.1(2) of the Arbitration Act 1979—practice

2E–32 The practice is regulated by the provisions of r.62.15, and, in particular, by subrules (3) to (8) thereof inclusive. See too Section O of the Admiralty and Commercial Courts Guide and in particular paras O.16.1 *et seq.* at paras 2A–149 *et seq.* above.

### Service out of the jurisdiction[1]

2E–33 **62.16—(1) Subject to paragraph (2)—**

**(a) any arbitration claim form in an arbitration claim under the 1950 Act or the 1979 Act; or**

**(b) any order made in such a claim,**

**may be served out of the jurisdiction with the permission of the court if the arbitration to which the claim relates—**

**(i) is governed by the law of England and Wales; or**

[1] Amended by the Civil Procedure (Amendment No.5) Rules 2001 (SI 2001/4015) and the Civil Procedure (Amendment) Rules 2008 (SI 2008/2178).

**(ii) has been, is being, or will be, held within the jurisdiction.**

**(2) An arbitration claim form seeking permission to enforce an award may be served out of the jurisdiction with the permission of the court whether or not the arbitration is governed by the law of England and Wales.**

**(3) An application for permission to serve an arbitration claim form out of the jurisdiction must be supported by written evidence—**

**(a) stating the grounds on which the application is made; and**

**(b) showing in what place or country the person to be served is, or probably may be found.**

**(4) Rules 6.40 to 6.46 apply to the service of an arbitration claim form under paragraph (1).**

**(5) An order giving permission to serve an arbitration claim form out of the jursidiction must specify the period within which the defendant may file an acknowledgment of service.**

### Note

This rule is really an extension of CPR r.6.36, and an additional case in which service out of the jurisdiction is permissible with the permission of the court. For observations on the differences between service out of jurisdiction under the former RSC O.11 the forerunner of this rule and under this rule, see *Mayer Newman Co Ltd v Al Ferro Commodities Corp SA* [1990] 2 Lloyd's Rep. 290 at 293, CA, *per* Bingham L.J. The basis of the jurisdiction under this rule is that the "arbitration is to be or has been held within the jurisdiction". The practice under this rule is the same in all respects as under CPR r.6.36, including the requirement under CPR r.6.45 that translations be provided of documents for service on a foreign state in arbitration proceedings unless the official language or an official language of that State is English. **2E–34**

### Civil Jurisdiction and Judgments Acts 1982

Article 1 of the Brussels Convention, which forms the first Schedule to the Act, provides that the convention shall not apply to arbitration. The word "arbitration" in art.1 covers all matters connected with arbitration, including the question whether there is a valid arbitration agreement (*Marc Rich & Co AG v Societa Italiana Impianti pA (The Atlantic Emperor) (No.1)*, [1989] 1 Lloyd's Rep. 548). Thus where a claimant issues a Pt 8 arbitration claim form seeking the appointment of an arbitrator under s.10(3) of the Arbitration Act 1950, the Italian defendant having denied the existence of the alleged arbitration agreement, the claimant may properly seek permission to serve the Pt 8 arbitration claim form out of the jurisdiction under this rule, and should not attempt to serve without leave in Italy under the convention (*ibid.*). **2E–35**

### Application

This rule is concerned only with applications by and against parties to an arbitration which relate to the arbitration to which they are parties. Thus the natural meaning of the para.is that the application must be against the other party to the reference and not a non-party (as case under the pre-1997 RSC O.73, r.7 being *The Cienvik* [1996] 2 Lloyd's Rep. 395). The reasoning of the court in *The Cienvik* was adopted by the Court of Appeal in *Tate and Lyle Industries Ltd v CIA Usina Bulhoes and Cargill Inc* [1997] 1 Lloyd's Rep. 355, when holding that there is no jurisdiction to issue a without notice injunction against a proposed defendant not a party to the arbitration under s.12 of the 1950 Act. **2E–36**

***Paragraph numbers marked with a "+" can be found online and on CD.***

### III. Enforcement

**Scope of this Section**[1]

2E–37 **62.17 This Section of this Part applies to all arbitration enforcement proceedings other than by a claim on the award.**

**Enforcement of awards**[2]

2E–38 **62.18—(1) An application for permission under—**

**(a) section 66 of the 1996 Act**[3]**;**

**(b) section 101 of the 1996 Act;**

**(c) section 26 of the 1950 Act**[4]**; or**

**(d) section 3(1)(a) of the 1975 Act,**[5]

**to enforce an award in the same manner as a judgment or order may be made without notice in an arbitration claim form.**

**(2) The court may specify parties to the arbitration on whom the arbitration claim form must be served.**

**(3) The parties on whom the arbitration claim form is served must acknowledge service and the enforcement proceedings will continue as if they were an arbitration claim under Section I of this Part.**

**(4) With the permission of the court the arbitration claim form may be served out of the jurisdiction irrespective of where the award is, or is treated as, made.**

**(5) Where the applicant applies to enforce an agreed award within the meaning of section 51(2) of the 1996 Act—**

**(a) the arbitration claim form must state that the award is an agreed award; and**

**(b) any order made by the court must also contain such a statement.**

**(6) An application for permission must be supported by written evidence—**

**(a) exhibiting—**

**(i) where the application is made under section 66 of the 1996 Act or under section 26 of the 1950 Act, the arbitration agreement and the original award (or copies);**

**(ii) where the application is under section 101 of the**

[1] Amended by the Civil Procedure (Amendment No.5) Rules 2001 (SI 2001/4015).

[2] Amended by the Civil Procedure (Amendment No.5) Rules 2001 (SI 2001/4015) and the Civil Procedure (Amendment) Rules 2008 (SI 2008/2178).

[3] 1996 c.23.

[4] 1950 c.27; s.26 was repealed by the Arbitration Act 1996 (c. 23), s.107(2) and Sch. 4 but continues to apply to claims commenced before January 31, 1997 by virtue of the Arbitration Act 1996 (Commencement No.1) Order 1996 (SI 1996/3146) art.4 and Sch.2.

[5] 1975 c.3; repealed by the Arbitration Act 1996 (c.23), s.107(2) and Sch.4 but continues to apply to claims commenced before January 31, 1997 by virtue of the Arbitration Act 1996 (Commencement No.1) Order 1996 (SI 1996/3146) art.4 and Sch.2.

1996 Act, the documents required to be produced by section 102 of that Act; or

(iii) where the application is under section 3(1)(a) of the 1975 Act, the documents required to be produced by section 4 of that Act;

(b) stating the name and the usual or last known place of residence or business of the claimant and of the person against whom it is sought to enforce the award; and

(c) stating either—

(i) that the award has not been complied with; or

(ii) the extent to which it has not been complied with at the date of the application.

**(7) An order giving permission must—**

(a) be drawn up by the claimant; and

(b) be served on the defendant by—

(i) delivering a copy to him personally; or

(ii) sending a copy to him at his usual or last known place of residence or business.

(8) An order giving permission may be served out of the jurisdiction—

(a) without permission; and

(b) in accordance with rules 6.40 to 6.46 as if the order were an arbitration claim form.

(9) Within 14 days after service of the order or, if the order is to be served out of the jurisdiction, within such other period as the court may set—

(a) the defendant may apply to set aside the order; and

(b) the award must not be enforced until after—

(i) the end of that period; or

(ii) any application made by the defendant within that period has been finally disposed of.

(10) The order must contain a statement of—

(a) the right to make an application to set the order aside; and

(b) the restrictions on enforcement under rule 62.18(9)(b).

(11) Where a body corporate is a party any reference in this rule to place of residence or business shall have effect as if the reference were to the registered or principal address of the body corporate.

**Written evidence in support of application**

As to the importance of full and frank disclosure in any affidavit and by like token in any witness statement in support of application which in the first instance is made without notice, and the relevant considerations where non-disclosure is established (see *Curacao Trading Co BV v Harkisandas & Co* [1992] 21 Lloyd's Rep. 186). **2E-39**

**Copies of draft order/Contents of affidavit/Witness statement in support**

In addition to any written evidence Section O of the the Admiralty and Commercial Courts Guide, para.O18.4(a) requires two copies of a draft order to be provided and **2E-40** requires that care be taken to see that the affidavit or witness statement and the draft order meet the requirements of this provision.

### Interest on awards[1]

2E–41 **62.19—(1) Where an applicant seeks to enforce an award of interest the whole or any part of which relates to a period after the date of the award, he must file a statement giving the following particulars—**

**(a) whether simple or compound interest was awarded;**

**(b) the date from which interest was awarded;**

**(c) where rests were provided for, specifying them;**

**(d) the rate of interest awarded; and**

**(e) a calculation showing—**

**(i) the total amount claimed up to the date of the statement; and**

**(ii) any sum which will become due on a daily basis.**

**(2) A statement under paragraph (1) must be filed whenever the amount of interest has to be quantified for the purpose of—**

**(a) obtaining a judgment or order under section 66 of the 1996 Act (enforcement of the award); or**

**(b) enforcing such a judgment or order.**

### Registration in High Court of foreign awards[2]

2E–42 **62.20—(1) Where—**

**(a) an award is made in proceedings on an arbitration in any part of a British overseas territory or other territory to which Part I of the Foreign Judgments (Reciprocal Enforcement) Act 1933[3] ("the 1933 Act") extends;**

**(b) Part II of the Administration of Justice Act 1920[4] extended to that part immediately before Part I of the 1933 Act was extended to that part; and**

**(c) an award has, under the law in force in the place where it was made, become enforceable in the same manner as a judgment given by a court in that place,**

**rules 74.1 to 74.7 and 74.9 apply in relation to the award as they apply in relation to a judgment given by the court subject to the modifications in paragraph (2).**

**(2) The modifications referred to in paragraph (1) are as follows—**

**(a) for references to the State of origin are substituted references to the place where the award was made; and**

[1] Amended by the Civil Procedure (Amendment No.5) Rules 2001 (SI 2001/4015).

[2] Amended by the Civil Procedure (Amendment No.5) Rules 2001 (SI 2001/4015), the Civil Procedure (Amendment) Rules 2002 (SI 2002/2058) and the Civil Procedure (Amendment) Rules 2008 (SI 2008/2178).

[3] 1933 c.13 (23 & 24 Geo. 5).

[4] 1920 c.81 (10 & 11 Geo. 5); s.10 of Pt II was substituted by the Civil Jurisdiction and Judgments Act 1982 (c.27), s.35(2) and s.14 of Pt II was amended by the Civil Jurisdiction and Judgments Act 1982 (c.27), s.35(3).

(b) the written evidence required by rule 74.4 must state (in addition to the matters required by that rule) that to the best of the information or belief of the maker of the statement the award has, under the law in force in the place where it was made, become enforceable in the same manner as a judgment given by a court in that place.

**Note**

A foreign award expressed in a foreign currency must not be converted into sterling for the purposes of registration, see Rate of Exchange, para.74.11.9 in Vol.1 of *The White Book*. **2E–43**



## Registration of awards under the Arbitration (International Investment Disputes) Act 1966[1]

**62.21—(1) In this rule—** **2E–44**

**(a) "the 1966 Act" means the Arbitration (International Investment Disputes) Act 1966[2];**

**(b) "award" means an award under the Convention;**

**(c) "the Convention" means the Convention on the settlement of investment disputes between States and nationals of other States which was opened for signature in Washington on 18th March 1965[3];**

**(d) "judgment creditor" means the person seeking recognition or enforcement of an award; and**

**(e) "judgment debtor" means the other party to the award.**

**(2) Subject to the provisions of this rule, the following provisions of Part 74 apply with such modifications as may be necessary in relation to an award as they apply in relation to a judgment to which Part I of the Foreign Judgments (Reciprocal Enforcement) Act 1933 applies—**

**(a) rule 74.1;**

**(b) rule 74.3;**

**(c) rule 74.4(1), (2)(a) to (d), and (4);**

**(d) rule 74.6 (except paragraph (3)(c) to (e)); and**

**(e) rule 74.9(2).**

**(3) An application to have an award registered in the High Court under section 1 of the 1966 Act[4] must be made in accordance with the Part 8 procedure.**

**(4) The written evidence required by rule 74.4 in support of an application for registration must—**

[1] Amended by the Civil Procedure (AmendmentNo.5) Rules 2001 (SI 2001/4015) and the Civil Procedure (Amendment) Rules 2002 (SI 2002/2058).

[2] 1966 c.41.

[3] The text of the Convention is set out in the Schedule to the Arbitration (International Investment Disputes) Act 1966 (c.41).

[4] 1966 c.41; s.1 was amended by the Administration of Justice Act 1977 (c.38), ss.4 and 32(4) and Sch. 5, Pt I and by the Senior Courts Act 1981 (c.54), s.152(1) and Sch.5.

**(a) exhibit the award certified under the Convention instead of the judgment (or a copy of it); and**

**(b) in addition to stating the matters referred to in rule 74.4(2)(a) to (d), state whether—**

**(i) at the date of the application the enforcement of the award has been stayed (provisionally or otherwise) under the Convention; and**

**(ii) any, and if so what, application has been made under the Convention, which, if granted, might result in a stay of the enforcement of the award.**

**(5) Where, on granting permission to register an award or an application made by the judgment debtor after an award has been registered, the court considers—**

**(a) that the enforcement of the award has been stayed (whether provisionally or otherwise) under the Convention; or**

**(b) that an application has been made under the Convention which, if granted, might result in a stay of the enforcement of the award,**

**the court may stay the enforcement of the award for such time as it considers appropriate.**

### Scope of rule

2E–45 This rule provides the machinery for the registration of an award rendered pursuant to the Convention set out in the Schedule to the Arbitration (International Investment Disputes) Act 1966. The procedure follows, in large measure, but with the necessary modifications, the provisions of CPR r.74, since this Act is in many respects similar to the Foreign Judgments (Reciproal Enforcement) Act 1933.

Rule 62.21(2) makes it unecessary to convert an award under this Act expressed in foreign currency into sterling for the purposes of its registration.

## PRACTICE DIRECTION 62—ARBITRATION

*This Practice Direction supplements CPR Part 62*

### Section I

**1.1** This Section of this Practice Direction applies to arbitration claims to which Section I of Part 62 applies. **2E–46**

**1.2** In this Section "the 1996 Act" means the Arbitration Act 1996.

**1.3** Where a rule provides for a document to be sent, it may be sent—

(1) by first class post—

(2) through a document exchange; or

(3) fax, electronic mail or other means of electronic communication.

### 62.3 Starting the claim

**2.1** An arbitration claim under the 1996 Act (other than under section 9) must be started in accordance with the High Court and County Courts (Allocation of Arbitration Proceedings) Order 1996 by the issue of an arbitration claim form.

**2.2** An arbitration claim form must be substantially in the form set out in Appendix A to this practice direction.

**2.3** Subject to paragraph 2.1, an arbitration claim form—

(1) may be issued at the courts set out in column 1 of the table below and will be entered in the list set out against that court in column 2;

(2) relating to a landlord and tenant or partnership dispute must be issued in the Chancery Division of the High Court.

| Court | List |
|---|---|
| Admiralty and Commercial Registry at the Royal Courts of Justice, London | Commercial list |
| Technology and Construction Court Registry, St. Dunstan's House, London | TCC list |
| District Registry of the High Court (where mercantile court established) | Mercantile list |
| District Registry of the High Court (where arbitration claim form marked 'Technology and Construction Court' in top right hand corner) | TCC list |

**2.3A** An arbitration claim form must, in the case of an appeal, or application for permission to appeal, from a judge-adjudicator, be issued in the Civil Division of the Court of Appeal. The judge hearing the application may adjourn the matter for oral argument before two judges of that court.

***Paragraph numbers marked with a "+" can be found online and on CD.***

**Note**

2E–47 The High Court and County Courts (Allocation of Arbitration Proceedings) Order 1996 is SI 1996/3215 and came into force on January 31, 1997. It has been amended by SI 1999/1010.

**Appendix A**

2E–48 The Forms **N8,N8A**, **N8B** and **N15** can be found in the *Civil Procedure Forms Volume*.

**Fees**

2E–49 See the Supreme Court Fees Order 1999 (SI 1999/687) and, in particular, items 1.2, 2.4 and 2.5, and 4.4 and 4.5.

### 62.4 Arbitration claim form

#### 3.1 Service

2E–50 The court may exercise its powers under rule 6.15 to permit service of an arbitration claim form at an address of a party's solicitor or representative acting for that party in the arbitration.

**3.2** Where the arbitration claim form is served by the claimant he must file a certificate of service within 7 days of service of the arbitration claim form.

(Rule 6.17 specifies what a certificate of service must show).

#### 4.1 Acknowledgment of service or making representations by arbitrator or ACAS

Where—

(1) an arbitrator; or

(2) ACAS (in a claim under the 1996 Act as applied with modifications by the ACAS Arbitration Scheme (England and Wales) Order 2001)

is sent a copy of an arbitration claim form (including an arbitration claim form sent under rule 62.6(2)), that arbitrator or ACAS (as the case may be) may—

(a) apply to be made a defendant; or

(b) make representations to the court under paragraph 4.3.

**4.2** An application under paragraph 4.1(2)(a) to be made a defendant—

(1) must be served on the claimant; but

(2) need not be served on any other party.

**4.3** An arbitrator or ACAS may make representations by filing written evidence or in writing to the court.

#### 5.1 Supply of documents from court records

An arbitration claim form may only be inspected with the permission of the court.

### 62.7 Case management

**6.1** The following directions apply unless the court orders otherwise.

**6.2** A defendant who wishes to rely on evidence before the court must file and serve his written evidence—

(1) within 21 days after the date by which he was required to acknowledge service; or,

(2) where a defendant is not required to file an acknowledgement of service, within 21 days after service of the arbitration claim form.

**6.3** A claimant who wishes to rely on evidence in reply to written evidence filed under paragraph 6.2 must file and serve his written evidence within 7 days after service of the defendant's evidence.

**6.4** Agreed indexed and paginated bundles of all the evidence and other documents to be used at the hearing must be prepared by the claimant.

**6.5** Not later than 5 days before the hearing date estimates for the length of the hearing must be filed together with a complete set of the documents to be used.

**6.6** Not later than 2 days before the hearing date the claimant must file and serve—

(1) a chronology of the relevant events cross-referenced to the bundle of documents;

(2) (where necessary) a list of the persons involved; and

(3) a skeleton argument which lists succinctly—

(a) the issues which arise for decision;

(b) the grounds of relief (or opposing relief) to be relied upon;

(c) the submissions of fact to be made with the references to the evidence; and

(d) the submissions of law with references to the relevant authorities.

**6.7** Not later than the day before the hearing date the defendant must file and serve a skeleton argument which lists succinctly—

(1) the issues which arise for decision;

(2) the grounds of relief (or opposing relief) to be relied upon;

(3) the submissions of fact to be made with the references to the evidence; and

(4) the submissions of law with references to the relevant authorities.

### 7.1 Securing the attendance of witnesses

A party to arbitral proceedings being conducted in England or Wales who wishes to rely on section 43 of the 1996 Act to secure the attendance of a witness must apply for a witness summons in accordance with Part 34.

**7.2** If the attendance of the witness is required within the district of a district registry, the application may be made at that registry.

**7.3** A witness summons will not be issued until the applicant files written evidence showing that the application is made with—

(1) the permission of the tribunal; or

(2) the agreement of the other parties.

**8.1 Interim remedies**

An application for an interim remedy under section 44 of the 1996 Act must be made in an arbitration claim form.

**9.1 Applications under sections 32 and 45 of the 1996 Act**

This paragraph applies to arbitration claims for the determination of—

(1) a question as to the substantive jurisdiction of the arbitral tribunal under section 32 of the 1996 Act; and

(2) a preliminary point of law under section 45 of the 1996 Act.

**9.2** Where an arbitration claim is made without the agreement in writing of all the other parties to the arbitral proceedings but with the permission of the arbitral tribunal, the written evidence or witness statements filed by the parties must set out any evidence relied on by the parties in support of their contention that the court should, or should not, consider the claim.

**9.3** As soon as practicable after the written evidence is filed, the court will decide whether or not it should consider the claim and, unless the court otherwise directs, will so decide without a hearing.

**10.1 Decisions without a hearing**

Having regard to the overriding objective the court may decide particular issues without a hearing. For example, as set out in paragraph 9.3, the question whether the court is satisfied as to the matters set out in section 32(2)(b) or section 45(2)(b) of the 1996 Act.

**10.2** The court will generally decide whether to extend the time limit under section 70(3) of the 1996 Act without a hearing. Where the court makes an order extending the time limit, the defendant must file his written evidence within 21 days from service of the order.

**62.9 Variation of time**

**11.1** An application for an order under rule 62.9(1)—

(1) before the period of 28 days has expired, must be made in a Part 23 application notice; and

(2) after the period of 28 days has expired, must be set out in a separately identified part in the arbitration claim form.

**12.1 Applications for permission to appeal**

Where a party seeks permission to appeal to the court on a question of law arising out of an arbitration award, the arbitration claim form must—

(1) identify the question of law; and

(2) state the grounds

on which the party alleges that permission should be given.

**12.2** The written evidence in support of the application must set out any evidence relied on by the party for the purpose of satisfying the court—

(1) of the matters referred to in section 69(3) of the 1996 Act; and

*Paragraph numbers marked with a "+" can be found online and on CD.*

(2) that permission should be given.

**12.3** The written evidence filed by the respondent to the application must—

(1) state the grounds on which the respondent opposes the grant of permission;

(2) set out any evidence relied on by him relating to the matters mentioned in section 69(3) of the 1996 Act; and

(3) specify whether the respondent wishes to contend that the award should be upheld for reasons not expressed (or not fully expressed) in the award and, if so, state those reasons.

**12.4** The court will normally determine applications for permission to appeal without an oral hearing.

**12.5** Where the court refuses an application for permission to appeal without an oral hearing, it must provide brief reasons.

**12.6** Where the court considers that an oral hearing is required, it may give such further directions as are necessary.

*Section II*

**13.1** This Section of this Practice Direction applies to arbitration claims to which Section II of Part 62 applies.

## 62.13 Starting the claim

**14.1** An arbitration claim must be started in the Commercial Court and, where required to be heard by a judge, be heard by a judge of that court unless he otherwise directs.

### Effect of rule

The commentary which follows together with that at 2E–52 and 2E–53 should be read subject to the Note at 2E–3 and the Note at 2E–22 to which reference should be made. It is important to note that the requirement to channel arbitration applications through the Commercial Court as is necessary for Sect.II claims has been replaced in the case of 1996 Act claims by a more flexible regime. See further at 2E–22 and PD 62.2.3. **2E–51**

This rule has the effect of channelling all applications under Sect.II of Pt 62 in the first instance to the Commercial Court. The rule thus recognises that in practice the subject of arbitration is substantially a commercial matter and should be dealt with by a Commercial Judge both as a matter of convenience and the proper distribution of business in the High Court and also to enable uniformity of practice and procedure to be fostered and encouraged.

On the other hand, of course, there is a great volume of important arbitrations which may be described as "non-commercial" in the sense that the subject matter does not fall within the definition of a "commercial claim" and applications relating to such arbitrations which require to be heard by a judge under r.62.12, will no doubt be directed by a Commercial Judge to be heard by another judge of the High Court.

The normal practice should be that all applications for permission to appeal to the High Court are to be heard by a Commercial Judge unless any such judge otherwise directs, and if permission is granted, consideration could then be given to whether there should be a direction that the appeal itself should be heard by a judge who is not a Commercial Judge (*per* Donaldson L.J. in *F. G. Whitley & Sons Co Ltd v Clwyd CC*, *The Times*, August 6, 1982).

In *Ashbank Property Co Ltd v Department of Transport*, *The Times*, July 25, 1994; *Independent*, October 3, 1994; held that where a notice of application to set aside an arbitration award had been incorrectly issued in the Chancery Division it was inappropriate to transfer the same to the Commercial Court as that would be to grant an inappropriate extension of time for an appeal.

***Paragraph numbers marked with a "+" can be found online and on CD.***

It is the practice in the Commercial Court for one Judge to hear the application for permission to appeal under s.1(2) of the 1979 Act and for another judge to hear the appeal itself but there are exceptional cases where it would be quite right that the same judge should hear the appeal; ultimately, it must be a matter for the judge's discretion (*Hiscox v Outhwaite (No.2)* [1991] 1 W.L.R. 545, CA).

**Application**

2E–52 By arbitration claim form in accordance with Pt 8 procedure, unless claim made in existing proceedings by way of application notice. Matters referred to in r.62.12 and application in respect of matters referred to in r.62.15(1) and (2) are to be made by issuing an arbitration claim form and will be heard by a judge of the Commercial Court unless such judge otherwise directs.

Where permission to appeal is required, it should be applied for to a judge in private by an application in existing proceedings or by a Pt 8 claim if no existing proceedings issued in the Admiralty and Commercial Registry. Such permission is required under s.1(3) of the Act of 1979, unless all parties to the reference consent.

2E–53 For ss.22 and 23 of the Arbitration Act 1950 and ss.1 and 2 of the Arbitration Act 1979, see SCP 1999, Vol.2, Section 21.

### *Section III*

2E–54 **15.1** This Section of this Practice Direction applies to enforcement proceedings to which Section III of Part 62 applies.

### 62.21 Registration of awards under the Arbitration (International Investment Disputes) Act 1966

**16.1** Awards ordered to be registered under the 1966 Act and particulars will be entered in the Register kept for that purpose at the Admiralty and Commercial Registry.

**Editorial note**

2E–55 With the exception of ss.35 to 42 and the First and Second Schedule to the Arbitration Act 1950, the texts of the Arbitration Act 1950, of the Arbitration Act 1975 and of the Arbitration Act 1979 (the "old law") are not printed in this publication. Such texts and related annotations are to be found in SCP 1999, Vol.2 at Section 21A, paras 21A–1 *et seq.*, (the 1950 Act), paras 21B–1 *et seq.* (the 1975 Act) and paras 21C–1 *et seq.* (the 1979 Act) to which reference should be made as necessary.

**Appendix A**

2E–56 The following form which is contained in Appendix A to this PD can be found in the Civil Procedure Forms Volume:

- **N8**

## Arbitration Act 1950

2E–57 (14 Geo. 6 c.27)

Arrangement of Sections

Part II



***Paragraph numbers marked with a "+" can be found online and on CD.***

**Paragraph numbers marked with a "+" denote content that is available on White Book on Westlaw UK or the Civil Procedure CD.**

# Arbitration Act 1996

(1996 c.23)

2E–83

Arrangement of Sections

PART I

ARBITRATION PURSUANT TO AN ARBITRATION AGREEMENT

*Introductory*



***Paragraph numbers marked with a "+" can be found online and on CD.***



ARBITRATION

***Paragraph numbers marked with a "+" can be found online and on CD.***

**Paragraph numbers marked with a "+" denote content that is available on White Book on Westlaw UK or the Civil Procedure CD.**

### Introductory note

The provisions of the Arbitration Act 1996 save for a few exceptions were brought into force on January 31, 1997 by the Arbitration Act 1996 (Commencement No.1) Order 1996, made December 16, 1996. That Order also provides that "the old law" shall continue to apply to: 2E–84

(a) arbitral proceedings commenced before the appointed day (i.e. January 31, 1997);

(b) arbitration applications commenced or made before the appointed day;

(c) arbitration applications commenced or made on or after the appointed day relating to arbitral proceedings commenced before the appointed day;

and that the provisions of the Act which would otherwise be applicable shall not apply.

The Order also provides that the provisions of the Act which it brings into force shall apply to any other legal proceedings even though arbitral proceedings have not been commenced.

***Paragraph numbers marked with a "+" can be found online and on CD.***

Accordingly as from January 31, 1997 there are two alternative regimes though the enforcement provisions of Pt II of the Arbitration Act 1950 are common to both. It will be necessary therefore to determine according to the above application provisions which regime is appropriate. These application provisions are reflected in CPR Pt 62—Arbitration Claims and the Practice Direction—Arbitration supplementing CPR Pt 62.

The "old law" is defined in the said Order as the enactments mentioned in s.107 of the Act (the Consequential amendments and repeals provision). Included and now preserved in respect of the arbitral and legal proceedings referred to under (a), (b) and (c) above are the Arbitration Act 1950, the Arbitration Act 1975, and the Arbitration Act 1979.

**General note**

2E–85 The preamble to the 1996 Act states that it is "An act to restate and improve the law relating to arbitration pursuant to an arbitration agreement; to make other provision relating to arbitration and arbitration awards; and for connected purposes".

The 1996 Act applies to all arbitrations commenced after January 31, 1997 and to all applications made to the court on or after January 31, 1997, in respect of arbitrations yet to be commenced at the time of the application.

The Act enlarges the extent to which the principles of arbitration law are expressed in statutory form. It uses language that is "user friendly". It increases the authority of the parties to arbitral proceedings to regulate the proceedings themselves and restricts the role of the court to supporting the arbitral process save where court intervention is required to achieve justice between the parties.

Thus, for example access to the court to intervene is denied where the agreement provides a mechanism for resolving the question unless that mechanism has been tried and failed. The circumstances in which an award can be challenged are now more precisely defined as are the circumstances in which leave can be given for appealing against an award. There is statutory expression of an arbitral tribunal's powers to rule on matters affecting its own jurisdiction and of the guidelines developed by the court since 1979 on the circumstances in which leave to appeal against an award may be granted. The Act further specifies the grounds on which an award may be set aside or remitted or an arbitration removed thus removing the general discretion available under "the old law".

**The court**

2E–86 This is defined by s.105 of the Arbitration Act 1996 as meaning the High Court or a county court subject to powers vested in the Lord Chancellor by order to allocate and to impose restrictions in terms of specified proceedings and court.

By the High Court and County Courts (Allocation of Arbitration Proceedings) Order 1996 (SI 1996/3215) set out in full at paras 2E–375 *et seq.*, which came into force on January 31, 1997, it was inter alia provided:

"2. Subject to articles 3 to 5, proceedings under the Act shall be commenced and taken in the High Court.
3. Proceedings under section 9 of the Act (stay of legal proceedings) shall be commenced in the court in which the legal proceedings are pending.
4. Proceedings under sections 66 and 101(2) (enforcement of awards) of the Act may be commenced in any county court.
5. Proceedings under the Act may be commenced and taken in the Central London County Court Mercantile List." [Now without effect.]

**The Application**

2E–87 Arbitration applications under the 1996 Act (see Sect.I of Pt 62) save for application under s.9, are made by use of an arbitration claim form (see r.62.3, the Practice Direction—Arbitration and the reference to the form set out at Appendix A to the practice direction). Applications under s.9 are made by ordinary application process in the existing proceedings. The courts where the arbitration claim form may be issued are set ou in the Practice Direction—Arbitration.

Applications under "the old law" see (Sect.II of Pt 62) save for s.4 of the 1950 Act applications are made by the use of an arbitration claim form and must be started in the Commercial Court and issued out of the Admiralty and Commercial Registry at the R.C.J. London and where required to be heard by a judge must be heard by a judge of that court unless he otherwise directs, see r.62.12 and Practice Direction—Arbitration, para.14.1. Claims for the attendance of witnesses within the aread of a district registry may be started within the relevant district registry, see r.62.14.

Applications for enforcement should be made using an arbitration claim form and may be considered by a Judge, Master, Admiralty Registrar or District Judge.

**Definitions**

The following expressions are defined or otherwise explained by the provisions indicated: **2E–88**

| | |
|---|---|
| "agree" | section 5(1) |
| "agreement in writing" | section 5(2)–(6) |
| "arbitration agreement" | section 5(1) and 6 |
| "arbitrator" | section 82(1) |
| "available arbitral process" | section 82(1) |
| "claimant" | section 82(1) |
| "commencement of arbitral proceedings" | section 14 |
| "costs of arbitration" | section 82(1) |
| "court (the)" | section 105 |
| "dispute" | section 82(1) |
| "enactment" | section 82(1) |
| "legal proceedings" | section 82(1) |
| "limitation Acts" | section 13(4) |
| "notice" | section 76(6) |
| "notice (upon)" | section 80 |
| "party" | sections 82(2) and 106(4) |
| "peremptory order" | section 82(1) |
| "question of law" | section 82(1) |
| "recoverable costs" | sections 63 and 64 |
| "seat of arbitration" | section 3 |
| "serve and service" | section 76(6) |
| "statutory arbitration" | section 94(1) |
| "substantive jurisdiction" | sections 82(1) and 30(1)(a) to (c) |
| "time and periods" | section 78 |

ARBITRATION

# PART I

# ARBITRATION PURSUANT TO AN ARBITRATION AGREEMENT

## INTRODUCTORY

### General principles

**1.** The provisions of this Part are founded on the following principles, and shall be construed accordingly— **2E–89**

(a) the object of arbitration is to obtain the fair resolution of disputes by an impartial tribunal without unnecessary delay or expense;

*Paragraph numbers marked with a "+" can be found online and on CD.*

(b) the parties should be free to agree how their disputes are resolved, subject only to such safeguards as are necessary in the public interest;

(c) in matters governed by this Part the court should not intervene except as provided by this Part.

### Scope of application of provisions

2E–90 **2.**—(1) The provisions of this Part apply where the seat of the arbitration is in England and Wales or Northern Ireland.

(2) The following sections apply even if the seat of the arbitration is outside England and Wales or Northern Ireland or no seat has been designated or determined—

(a) sections 9 to 11 (stay of legal proceedings, etc.), and

(b) section 66 (enforcement of arbitral awards).

(3) The powers conferred by the following sections apply even if the seat of the arbitration is outside England and Wales or Northern Ireland or no seat has been designated or determined—

(a) section 43 (securing the attendance of witnesses), and

(b) section 44 (court powers exercisable in support of arbitral proceedings);

but the court may refuse to exercise any such power if, in the opinion of the court, the fact that the seat of the arbitration is outside England and Wales or Northern Ireland, or that when designated or determined the seat is likely to be outside England and Wales or Northern Ireland, makes it inappropriate to do so.

(4) The court may exercise a power conferred by any provision of this Part not mentioned in subsection (2) or (3) for the purpose of supporting the arbitral process where—

(a) no seat of the arbitration has been designated or determined, and

(b) by reason of a connection with England and Wales or Northern Ireland the court is satisfied that it is appropriate to do so.

(5) Section 7 separability of arbitration agreement and section 8 (death of a party) apply where the law applicable to the arbitration agreement is the law of England and Wales or Northern Ireland even if the seat of the arbitration is outside England and Wales or Northern Ireland or has not been designated or determined.

#### "...makes it inappropriate to do so"

2E–91 In *Commerce & Industry Co of Canada v Certain Underwriters at Lloyd's of London* [2002] 1 W.L.R. 1323; [2002] 2 All E.R. (Comm) 204; [2002] 1 Lloyd's Rep 219, the court held it inappropriate to order the examination of two witnesses in connection with New York arbitration proceedings pursuant to provisons of s.44 of the 1996 Act on basis that the procedure adopted under the curial law of New York differed from that of England and Wales and of Northern Ireland, in particular with regard to discovery of information by witness testimony.

### The seat of the arbitration

2E–92 **3.** In this Part "the seat of the arbitration" means the juridical seat of the arbitration designated—

(a) by the parties to the arbitration agreement, or

(b) by any arbitral or other institution or person vested by the parties with powers in that regard, or

(c) by the arbitral tribunal if so authorised by the parties, or determined, in the absence of any such designation, having regard to the parties' agreement and all the relevant circumstances.

**"the juridical seat of the arbitration"**

For factors relevant to the determination of the juridical seat of the arbitration, see *Dubai Islamic Bank PJSC v Paymentech Merchant Services Inc* [2001] 1 Lloyd's Rep. 65. **2E–93**

Choice of the seat of the arbitration will invariably (that is subject to agreement otherwise) coincide with the choice of procedural law; further agreement as to the seat of arbitration was akin to an exclusive jurisdiction clause and subject to an agreement otherwise determined the court having supervisory jurisdiction to the exclusion of the court of some other jurisdiction; *C v D* [2007] EWHC 1541(Comm); [2007] 2 Lloyd's Rep. 367 , affirmed on appeal [2007] EWCA Civ 1282; [2008] 1 Lloyd's Rep 239, CA . See for an instance of agreement to the contrary *Braes of Doune Wind Farm (Scotland) Ltd v Alfred McAlpine Business Services Ltd* [2008] EWHC 426 (TCC); [2008] 1 Lloyd's Rep. 608 (seat of arbitration Scotland, governing law English).

## Mandatory and non-mandatory provisions

**4.**—(1) The mandatory provisions of this Part are listed in Schedule 1 and have effect notwithstanding any agreement to the contrary. **2E–94**

(2) The other provisions of this Part (the "non-mandatory provisions") allow the parties to make their own arrangements by agreement but provide rules which apply in the absence of such agreement.

(3) The parties may make such arrangements by agreeing to the application of institutional rules or providing any other means by which a matter may be decided.

(4) It is immaterial whether or not the law applicable to the parties' agreement is the law of England and Wales or, as the case may be, Northern Ireland.

(5) The choice of a law other than the law of England and Wales or Northern Ireland as the applicable law in respect of a matter provided for by a non-mandatory provision of this Part is equivalent to an agreement making provision about that matter.

For this purpose an applicable law determined in accordance with the parties' agreement, or which is objectively determined in the absence of any express or implied choice, shall be treated as chosen by the parties.

## Agreements to be in writing

**5.**—(1) The provisions of this Part apply only where the arbitration agreement is in writing, and any other agreement between the parties as to any matter is effective for the purposes of this Part only if in writing. The expressions "agreement", "agree" and "agreed" shall be construed accordingly. **2E–95**

(2) There is an agreement in writing—

(a) if the agreement is made in writing (whether or not it is signed by the parties),

(b) if the agreement is made by exchange of communications in writing, or

(c) if the agreement is evidenced in writing.

(3) Where parties agree otherwise than in writing by reference to terms which are in writing, they make an agreement in writing.

(4) An agreement is evidenced in writing if an agreement made otherwise than in writing is recorded by one of the parties, or by a third party, with the authority of the parties to the agreement.

(5) An exchange of written submissions in arbitral or legal proceedings in which the existence of an agreement otherwise than in writing is alleged by one party against another party and not denied by the other party in his response constitutes as between those parties an agreement in writing to the effect alleged.

(6) References in this Part to anything being written or in writing include its being recorded by any means.

2E-96 *Note*—Compare s.32 of the 1950 Act and s.7(1) of the 1975 Act.

*THE ARBITRATION AGREEMENT*

## Definition of arbitration agreement

2E-97 **6.**—(1) In this Part an "arbitration agreement" means an agreement to submit to arbitration present or future disputes (whether they are contractual or not).

(2) The reference in an agreement to a written form of arbitration clause or to a document containing an arbitration clause constitutes an arbitration agreement if the reference is such as to make that clause part of the agreement.

2E-98 *Note*—Compare s.32 of the 1950 Act and s.7(1) of the 1975 Act.

### Agreement to submit to arbitration

2E-99 An agreement which gives one party alone the right to refer a dispute to arbitration was held to be a valid agreement to refer future disputes to arbitration within s.32 of the 1950 Act (*Pittalis v Sherefettin* [1986] 2 W.L.R. 1003; [1986] 2 All E.R. 227, CA). See too *Three Shipping Ltd v Harebell Shipping Ltd* [2004] EWHC 2001 (Comm); [2005] 1 Lloyd's Rep. 509 (a 1996 Act case).

The fact that a contractual agreement to refer disputes to arbitration depended upon the exercise of an option, even by the party claiming arbitration, does not prevent it from being "an agreement to refer future disputes" within s.27 of the 1950 Act (*Navigazione Alta Italia SpA v Concordia Maritime Chartering AB* [1990] 2 Lloyd's Rep. 234).

Where a bill of lading directs the reader to the charterparty which contains a clause providing for arbitration of disputes "arising ... out of this contract" the bill of lading incorporates the arbitration clause and the parties are bound by its terms (*Astro Valiente Compania Naviera SA v Pakistan Ministry of Food and Agriculture (No.2), The Emanuel Colocotronis* [1982] 1 W.L.R. 1096; [1982] 1 All E.R. 823).

A clause in a charterparty providing that "either party may elect to have the dispute referred to arbitration" is merely an agreement to agree to arbitrate, but once a valid election is made no further agreement is needed or contemplated for the arbitration to take place, and therefore once the election is duly made and the option to arbitrate exercised, and both the agreement and the option are expressed in writing, a binding written arbitration agreement comes into existence and there is no want of mutuality since either party could make election (*Westfal-Larsen & Co A/S v Ikerigi Compania Naviera SA, The Messiaki Bergen* [1983] 1 All E.R. 382; [1983] 1 Lloyd's Rep. 424).

***Paragraph numbers marked with a "+" can be found online and on CD.***

The words in sub-clause (2) "if the reference is such as to make that clause part of the agreement" were held in *Trygg Hansa Insurance Co v Equitas Ltd* [1998] 2 Lloyd's Rep. 439, to preserve the pre-existing law that general words of incorporation in an agreement were not appropriate to incorporate an arbitration clause. See too *Cigna Life Insurance v Intercaser SA* [2001] Lloyd's Rep. I.R. 821.

## Separability of arbitration agreement

**7.** Unless otherwise agreed by the parties, an arbitration agreement which forms or was intended to form part of another agreement (whether or not in writing) shall not be regarded as invalid, non-existent or ineffective because that other agreement is invalid, or did not come into existence or has become ineffective, and it shall for that purpose be treated as a distinct agreement. **2E-100**

*Note*—In *Fiona Trust and Holdings Corp v Privalov* [2007] UKHL 40; [2007] Bus L.R. 1719, HL the House of Lords held that s.7 of the 1996 Act was to be interpreted so that the main agreement and the arbitration agreement had to be treated as having been separately concluded and the arbitration agreement could be invalidated only on a ground which related to the arbitration agreement and was not merely a consequence of the invalidity of the main agreement. The doctrine of separability required direct impeachment of the arbitration agreement before it could be set aside. Further in construing the relevant clause the presumption should, in the absence of clear language to the contrary, that all disputes, including as to the validity of the contract, were to be decided by the same arbitral tribunal. **2E-101**

**For s.8 of the Arbitration Act 1996 (see Arrangement) plus any related commentary see paragraphs 2E-102+ to 2E-103+ on White Book on Westlaw UK or the Civil Procedure CD.**

*STAY OF LEGAL PROCEEDINGS*

## Stay of legal proceedings

**9.**—(1) A party to an arbitration agreement against whom legal proceedings are brought (whether by way of claim or counterclaim) in respect of a matter which under the agreement is to be referred to arbitration may (upon notice to the other parties to the proceedings) apply to the court in which the proceedings have been brought to stay the proceedings so far as they concern that matter. **2E-104**

(2) An application may be made notwithstanding that the matter is to be referred to arbitration only after the exhaustion of other dispute resolution procedures.

(3) An application may not be made by a person before taking the appropriate procedural step (if any) to acknowledge the legal proceedings against him or after he has taken any step in those proceedings to answer the substantive claim.

(4) On an application under this section the court shall grant a stay unless satisfied that the arbitration agreement is null and void, inoperative, or incapable of being performed.

(5) If the court refuses to stay the legal proceedings, any provision that an award is a condition precedent to the bringing of legal proceedings in respect of any matter is of no effect in relation to those proceedings.

*Note*—Compare s.4(1) of the 1950 Act and s.1 of the 1975 Act. This is a mandatory provision (see s.4) and applies even though the seat of arbitration is outside England **2E-105** and Wales or where no seat of arbitration has been designated (see s.2). Section 9(5) does not apply to statutory arbitrations. See further, para.9A–178.1 below.

### Appeal

2E–106 There is a right of appeal to the Court of Appeal, see *INCO Europe Ltd v First Choice Distribution* [1999] 1 W.L.R. 270; [1999] 1 All E.R. 820; [1999] C.L.C. 165, CA. The court held that the general terms of s.107 and Sch.3 of the 1996 Act (*q.v.*) were not to be construed as removing the right of appeal which had existed under earlier legislation (affirmed by HL(E) [2000] 1 W.L.R. 586; [2000] 2 All E.R. 109; [2000] 1 Lloyd's Rep 467.

### A Party to an arbitration agreement

2E–107 It is "a party" to an arbitration agreement against whom "legal proceedings are brought ...... in respect of a matter which under the agreement is to be referred to arbitration" who may apply under s.9(1) for a stay of such legal proceedings. In this context, "a party" includes "any person claiming under or through a party to the agreement" (s.82(2)). Section 9 cannot apply if the parties to the court proceedings are not the parties (or persons claiming through or under a party) to the abitration agreement, as it would be wholly inconsistent with the purpose and structure of the 1996 Act, and of s.9 in particular, if a stay could be obtained against a claimant who was not a party to the agreement (*City of London v Sancheti* [2008] EWCA Civ 1283; *The Times* December 1, 2008, CA (where held that a mere legal or commercial relationship between the applicant for a stay and the claimant was not sufficient)).

### Who may apply

2E–108 It is not necessary that all parties to the submission, other than the claimant in the claim, should join in application to stay (see *Willesford v Watson* (1872–73) L.R. 8 Ch.App. 473).

### The Application

2E–109 This is in by ordinary application notice and is made to the court in which the legal proceedings are pending (see r.62.3(2)).

### Form of Order

2E–110 See Queen's Bench Masters' Practice Forms, Form **PF 167** (see *Civil Procedure Forms Volume*).

### "... or after he has taken any step in those proceedings to answer the substantive claim"

2E–111 Though the application cannot precede the taking of the appropriate step if any to acknowledge the legal proceedings, the application must be made before taking any step to answer the substantive claim. So an application for security for costs was held to bar the defendant from obtaining a stay hereunder (*Adams v Cattley* (1892) 66 L.T. 687); so also the issue of an application for disclosure, see *Chappell v North* [1891] 2 Q.B. 252, cited above; so also attending an application for directions issued by the claimant and agreeing to or obtaining an order thereon (*County Theatres, etc. Ltd v Knowles* [1902] 1 K.B. 480; *Richardson v Le Maitre* [1903] 2 Ch. 222; *Stein v Buncle* [1902] W.N. 44; *Cohen v Arthur* (1912) 56 S.J. 344); or without an order being made, but an undertaking given to furnish an account (*Ochs v Ochs Bros.* [1909] 2 Ch. 121). After defence it is too late (*West London, etc. Co v Abbott* (1881) 29 W.R. 584). Also after defendant has obtained time to plead and agreed to take short notice of trial (*Smith v British Marine* [1883] W.N. 176). Opposition to an application for final judgment may constitute a step in the action; but no "step" is taken by a defendant opposing an application who not merely raises the matter of the arbitration clause in his affidavit (or witness statement), but also at the same time takes out an application to stay the claim (*Pitchers Ltd v Plaza (Queensbury) Ltd* [1940] 1 All E.R. 151, CA). *Cf.* also *Parker, Gaines & Co Ltd v Turpin* [1918] 1 K.B. 358.

The defendant must, however, act timeously. Thus if a defendant resists summary judgment proceedings by serving an affidavit or witness statement in opposition, but omits to issue an application to stay the claim until after a first hearing of the claimant's application which is merely adjourned for a further and fuller hearing, he will be deemed to have taken a step in the claim (*Turner & Goudy v McConnell* [1985] 1 W.L.R. 898; [1985] 2 All E.R. 34, CA; *Rumput (Panama) SA v Islamic Republic of Iran Shipping Lines, The League* [1984] 2 Lloyd's Rep. 259). A party who initiates an application for a stay pending an arbitration does not take a "step" in the proceedings within the meaning of s.9(3) of the 1996 Act if he, either simultaneously or subsquently, invokes or accepts the court's jurisdiction provided he does so only conditionally on his stay application failing (*Capital Trust Investments Ltd v Radio Design TJ AB* [2001] 3 All E.R. 756, affirmed [2002] 2 All E.R. 159, CA).

Similarly, if a defendant issues an application for an extension of time for defence, but omits to issue an application to stay until after the application for has been dealt with, he will be held to have taken a step in the proceedings (*Ford's Hotel Co Ltd v Bartlett* [1896] A.C. 1, HL). If, on the other hand, a defendant issues an application to stay, and, at the same time, issues an application for an extension of time for defence until after the hearing of the application to stay, he is unlikely to be held to have taken a step in the proceedings by the issue of the further time application (*London Sack & Bag Co Ltd v Dixon & Lugton Ltd* [1943] 2 All E.R. 763, CA).

Where defendant gave notice demanding particulars of case, that was held to be no step in the claim (*Ives v Willans* [1894] 1 Ch. 68; affirmed [1894] 2 Ch. 478; and *cf. Patteson v Northern Accident Ins. Soc.* [1901] 2 Ir.R. 262) and the same where the defendant before defence wrote to claimant under the former O.3, r.5 for further time to plead and obtained it (*Brighton Marine, etc. Co v Woodhouse* [1893] 2 Ch. 486); and where the defendant filed affidavits in the claim in answer to the claimant's affidavits in support of an application for a receiver, that was held to be no step in the claim (*Zalinoff v Hammond* [1898] 2 Ch. 92). The distinction seems to be that negotiation or correspondence between parties or their solicitors does not constitute a step in the claim, but an application, or the service of a pleading does. An application to strike out may be a step in the proceedings (*Leigh v English Property* [1976] 2 Lloyd's Rep. 298; *Eagle Star Insurance Co Ltd v Yuval Insurance Ltd* [1978] 1 Lloyd's Rep. 357).

A defendant did not take any step to answer the substantive claim so as to lose his right to apply for a stay by applying for relief which was otiose to the relief he needed in addition to the relief he did need; see *Patel v Patel* [2000] Q.B. 551, CA. In this case the defendant asked for the default judgment to be set aside (the relief he needed) but in addition and unnecessarily for leave to defend and counterclaim which he was entitled to do once default judgment was set aside.

The institution of an action within the time limit in a competent court in the United States between the same parties, which was subsequently stayed because it was brought in breach of a London arbitration clause, would not be regarded as steps having been taken under s.9 of the Arbitration Act 1996 when considering an application subsequently made out of time to appoint an arbitrator (*Thyssen Inc v Calypso Shipping Corp SA* [2000] 2 Lloyd's Rep. 243).

Whether additional matters sought to be raised by way of amendment to existing proceedings attract the stay provisions of s.9 of the 1996 Act depends on whether such additional matters "were part and parcel of the dispute of which the court was already seised or whether they were discrete matters in respect of which s.9 entitled the defendant to insist that they be arbitrated" (*Ahad v S Uddin* [2005] EWCA Civ 883).

#### Onus of showing that claim should proceed

It rests on the claimant to show that the dispute ought not to be referred to arbitration (*Hodgson v Ry. Passengers Assn. Co* (1882) 9 QBD 188; and see *Vawdrey v Simpson* [1896] 1 Ch. 166). The rule is now mandatory if the matters within subs.(4) are established. It is to be noted that the words "or that there was not in fact any dispute between the parties with regard to the matter agreed to be referred" (see s.1(1) of the 1975 Act) have not been re-enacted in s.9. Accordingly, where an amount due under an agreement was either disputed or simply not paid there was a dispute as to the amount due even though no answer to the claim existed in law or in fact. Such dispute was within the arbitration clause and proceedings at law brought to recover it had to be stayed (see *Halki Shipping Corp v Sopex Oils Ltd* [1997] 1 W.L.R. 1268; [1997] 3 All E.R. 833; [1998] 1 Lloyd's Rep. 49; affirmed by CA by a majority of 2:1, [1998] 1 W.L.R. 726; [1998] 2 All E.R. 23; [1998] 1 Lloyd's Rep. 465). 2E–112

In *Wealands v C.L.C. Contractors Ltd* [1998] C.L.C. 808, the court held on an application by a sub-contractor for third party proceedings against it by the contractor to be

***Paragraph numbers marked with a "+" can be found online and on CD.***

stayed under s.9 of the Arbitration Act 1996 that despite the disadvantages of the claim against the third party going to arbitration (if the plaintiff did not join the third party as a defendant) the 1996 Act gave priority to party autonomy and entitled the third party as of right to the stay which is sought (affirmed [1999] 2 Lloyd's Rep. 739, CA).

In *Prekons Insaat Sanayi AS v Rowlands Castle Contracting Group Ltd* [2006] EWHC 1367 (Comm); [2007] 1 Lloyd's Rep. 98 the court held that the only relevant ground upon which a stay under s.9 of the Arbitration Act 1996 can in these circumstances be resisted is if the claim under the agreement containing an arbitration clause, if made out, operates in partial or total extinction or defeasance of the claim under the contract/s not containing an arbitration agreement, relying on *Aectra Refining and Marketing Inc v Exmar NV* [1995] 1 Lloyd's Rep. 191 at 199–202 *per* Hoffmann L.J.

Where a party objected under s.9 of the 1996 Act to a matter being considered other than by arbitrators then a dispute as to whether or not an arbitration agreement was time barred by limitation should be considered by the arbitrators even though the claimant might, if he failed on such issue, need to seek the exercise of the court's discretion under s.12 of the 1996 Act; *Grimaldi Compagnia di Navigazione SpA v Sekihyo Line Ltd* [1999] 1 W.L.R. 708; [1998] 3 All E.R. 943.

In *Ahmad Al-Naimi (T/A Buildmaster Construction Services) v Islamic Press Agency Inc* [2000] 1 Lloyd's Rep. 522, CA the court held that—

(1) If the court decided that it was the court which should determine whether the matters the subject of the action were the subject of an arbitration clause, unless the parties were agreed that the matter should be resolved on affidavit then, if there was a triable issue, directions should be given for trying that issue: under the CPR the court had a wider discretion to rule what evidence it needed to decide any particular point; and

(2) On a proper construction of s.9 it could be said with force that a court should be satisfied (a) that that there was an arbitration clause and (b) that the subject of the action was within that clause before the court could grant a stay under that section; but a stay under the inherent jurisdiction might in fact be sensible in a situation where the court could not be sure of these matters but could see that good sense and litigation management made it desirable for an arbitrator to consider the whole matter first.

See too note at para. 2E–101.

In *Sonatrach Petroleum Corp (BVI) v Ferrell International Ltd* [2002] 1 All E.R. (Comm) 627 (head-charter provided for arbitration in Japan but sub-charter gave jurisdiction to English courts) held that the unenforceability of method of proper law selection in sub-charter did not mean the choice of forum was also void as the latter was free-standing and a stay was granted in respect of a claim brought under the sub-charter.

Section 9 does not apply to petitions under s.459 of the Companies Act 1985 as the shareholders statutory right to petition is inalienable and cannot be diminished by a contact for arbitration, *Exeter City AFC Ltd v Football Conference Ltd* [2004] EWHC 831(Ch); [2004] 1 W.L.R. 2910; [2004] 4 All E.R. 1179.

An agreement to arbitrate pursuant to the Football Association Rules did not infringe a party's right to a fair trial guaranteed by art.6 of the ECHR: *Stretford v Football Association Ltd* [2007] EWCA Civ 238; [2007] 2 All E.R. (Comm) 1; [2007] 2 Lloyd's Rep. 31, CA.

The court has no jurisdiction to order a stay under s.9(1) of the 1996 Act (as opposed to under its inherent jurisdiction if appropriate) unless it is satisfied: (a) that there was a concluded arbitration agreement; and (b) the issue was a matter which under the arbitration clause was to be referred to arbitration: see *Albon v Naza Motor Trading Sdn Bhd (No.3)* [2007] EWHC 665 (Ch); [2007] 2 All E.R. 1075; [2007] 2 Lloyd's Rep. 1 . The court also held that s.9(4) assumed that there was a concluded agreement but that the same was devoid of legal effect, e.g. for duress, mistake, fraud or waiver and that s.30 of the 1996 Act did not preclude the court itself from determining whether the arbitration agreement had been concluded. See too CPR r.62.8(3).

**Inoperative**

2E–113 An arbitration agreement is inoperative where a defendant had shown an intention not to be bound by the agreement to refer and the other party (the claimant) had accepted such repudiation, *Downing v Al Tameer Establishment* [2002] EWCA Civ 721; [2002] 2 All E.R. (Comm) 545, CA.

**"Incapable of being performed"**

The words in s.1(1) of the 1979 Act "incapable of being performed" were held to refer only to the question whether an arbitration agreement is capable of being performed up to the point when it results in an award and should not be construed as extending to the question whether, once an award has been made, the party against whom it is made will be incapable of satisfying it, for the impecuniosity of the loser rendering him unable to pay the amount of the award does not make the arbitration incapable of being performed (*The Rena K* [1979] Q.B. 377; [1979] 1 All E.R. 397; [1978] 1 Lloyd's Rep. 545). Nor was an arbitration agreement incapable of being performed within the meaning of s.1(1) of the Act merely because one party cannot afford the arbitration (*Paczy v Haendler & Natermann GmbH* [1981] F.S.R. 250). **2E–114**

## Reference of interpleader issue to arbitration

**10.**—(1) Where in legal proceedings relief by way of interpleader is granted and any issue between the claimants is one in respect of which there is an arbitration agreement between them, the court granting the relief shall direct that the issue be determined in accordance with the agreement unless the circumstances are such that proceedings brought by a claimant in respect of the matter would not be stayed. **2E–115**

(2) Where subsection (1) applies but the court does not direct that the issue be determined in accordance with the arbitration agreement, any provision that an award is a condition precedent to the bringing of legal proceedings in respect of any matter shall not affect the determination of that issue by the court.

*Note*—Compare s.5 of the 1950 Act. This is a mandatory provision (see s.4) and applies even though the seat of arbitration is outside England and Wales or where no seat of arbitration has been designated. Subsection (2) does not apply to statutory arbitrations. **2E–116**

## Retention of security where Admiralty proceedings stayed

**11.**—(1) Where Admiralty proceedings are stayed on the ground that the dispute in question should be submitted to arbitration, the court granting the stay may, if in those proceedings property has been arrested or bail or other security has been given to prevent or obtain release from arrest— **2E–117**

(a) order that the property arrested be retained as security for the satisfaction of any award given in the arbitration in respect of that dispute, or

(b) order that the stay of those proceedings be conditional on the provision of equivalent security for the satisfaction of any such award.

(2) Subject to any provision made by rules of court and to any necessary modifications, the same law and practice shall apply in relation to property retained in pursuance of an order as would apply if it were held for the purposes of proceedings in the court making the order.

*Note*—See s.26 of the Civil Jurisdiction and Judgments Act 1982. This is a mandatory provision (see s.4). **2E–118**



ARBITRATION

*COMMENCEMENT OF ARBITRAL PROCEEDINGS*

## Power of court to extend time for beginning arbitral proceedings, etc.

2E-119 **12.**—(1) Where an arbitration agreement to refer future disputes to arbitration provides that a claim shall be barred, or the claimant's right extinguished, unless the claimant takes within a time fixed by the agreement some step—

(a) to begin arbitral proceedings, or

(b) to begin other dispute resolution procedures which must be exhausted before arbitral proceedings can be begun,

the court may by order extend the time for taking that step.

(2) Any party to the arbitration agreement may apply for such an order (upon notice to the other parties), but only after a claim has arisen and after exhausting any available arbitral process for obtaining an extension of time.

(3) The court shall make an order only if satisfied—

(a) that the circumstances are such as were outside the reasonable contemplation of the parties when they agreed the provision in question, and that it would be just to extend the time, or

(b) that the conduct of one party makes it unjust to hold the other party to the strict terms of the provision in question.

(4) The court may extend the time for such period and on such terms as it thinks fit, and may do so whether or not the time previously fixed (by agreement or by a previous order) has expired.

(5) An order under this section does not affect the operation of the Limitation Acts (see section 13).

(6) The leave of the court is required for any appeal from a decision of the court under this section.

2E-120 *Note*—Compare s.27 of the 1950 Act. This is a mandatory provision (see s.4). This section does not apply to statutory arbitrations.

### "Claim"

2E-121 Under s.27 of the 1950 Act, it was held that the word claims therein was not to be construed as meaning "causes of action", but should be given a wide and liberal interpretation and it will thus extend to any claim to have determined by arbitration a matter in issue between the parties, e.g. a claim for arbitration so as to assess the proper amount of a salvage award (*Sioux Inc v China Salvage Co Kwangchow Branch* [1980] 1 W.L.R. 996; [1980] 3 All E.R. 154, CA).

### "... the Court may by order extend the time for taking that step"

2E-122 The court's powers hereunder are only in respect of provisions laying down time limits for commencing proceedings. Thus in *Crown Estate Commissioners v John Mowlem & Co Ltd* 70 B.L.R. 1 the Court of Appeal, disapproving *McLaughlin & Harvey Plc v P&O Developments Ltd* 55 B.L.R. 101, held that the court does not have power under this section to extend the time for commencing arbitration proceedings under clause 30.9.3. of the JCT Standard Form of Building Contract (1980 PwQ) since on its true construction that clause does not lay down any time limit for commencing proceedings but is concerned solely with the evidential effect of a final certificate in any proceedings which may be *commenced* and accordingly there was nothing for the court to extend (a case under s.27 of the 1950 Act).

Section 12 of the 1996 Act is markedly more restricted than its predecessor, s.27 of the 1950 Act. See in particular subs.3. It is now not possible to extend time because the court concludes in general terms that it would be just to do so (*Cathiship SA v Allanasons Ltd, The Catherine Helen* [1998] 3 All E.R. 714).

A party's failure properly to read a contractual provision relating to the time limit for commencing an arbitration was not a circumstance which triggered the court's power under s.12(3)(a) of the Arbitration Act 1996, to permit an extension of time for bringing arbitral proceedings. The aim of s.12(3) was to allow the court to consider an extension in relation to circumstances where the parties would not reasonably have contemplated them as being ones where the time-bar would apply (*Harbour and General Works Ltd v Environment Agency* [2000] 1 W.L.R. 950; [1999] 2 All E.R. (Comm) 686; [2000] 1 All E.R. 50; [2001] 1 Lloyd's Rep. 65, CA).

**For ss.13 to 23 of the Arbitration Act 1996 (see Arrangement) plus any related commentary see paragraphs 2E–123+ to 2E–145+ on White Book on Westlaw UK or the Civil Procedure CD.**

ARBITRATION

## Power of court to remove arbitrator

**24.**—(1) A party to arbitral proceedings may (upon notice to the other parties, to the arbitrator concerned and to any other arbitrator) apply to the court to remove an arbitrator on any of the following grounds— **2E–146**

(a) that circumstances exist that give rise to justifiable doubts as to his impartiality;

(b) that he does not possess the qualifications required by the arbitration agreement;

(c) that he is physically or mentally incapable of conducting the proceedings or there are justifiable doubts as to his capacity to do so;

(d) that he has refused or failed—

(i) properly to conduct the proceedings, or

(ii) to use all reasonable despatch in conducting the proceedings or making an award,

and that substantial injustice has been or will be caused to the applicant.

(2) If there is an arbitral or other institution or person vested by the parties with power to remove an arbitrator, the court shall not exercise its power of removal unless satisfied that the applicant has first exhausted any available recourse to that institution or person.

(3) The arbitral tribunal may continue the arbitral proceedings and make an award while an application to the court under this section is pending.

(4) Where the court removes an arbitrator, it may make such order as it thinks fit with respect to his entitlement (if any) to fees or expenses, or the repayment of any fees or expenses already paid.

(5) The arbitrator concerned is entitled to appear and be heard by the court before it makes any order under this section.

(6) The leave of the court is required for any appeal from a decision of the court under this section.

*Note*—Compare ss.13(3), 23 and 24(1) of the 1950 Act. This is a mandatory provision (see s.4). **2E–147**

***Paragraph numbers marked with a "+" can be found online and on CD.***

**"(a) circumstances exist that give rise to justifiable doubts as to his impartiality", etc.**

2E–148 In *Petroships Pte Ltd of Singapore v Petec Trading & Investment Corp of Vietnam (The Petro Ranger)* [2001] 2 Lloyd's Rep. 348 the court stated that careful regard should be had to paras 105 and 106 of the report on the Arbitration Bill by the Departmental Advisory Commitee on Arbitration Law, which provide as follows:

"105. We have included, as grounds for removal, the refusal or failure of an arbitrator properly to conduct the proceedings, as well as failing to use all reasonable despatch in conducting the proceedings or making an award, where the result has caused or will cause substantial injustices to the applicant. We trust that the courts will not allow the first of these matters to be abused by those intent on disrupting the arbitral process. To this end we have included a provision allowing the tribunal to continue while an application is made. There is also Clause 73 which effectively requires a party to 'put up or shut up' if a challenge is to be made.

106. We have every confidence that the courts will carry through the intent of this part of the Bill, which is that it should only be available where the conduct of the arbitrator is such as to go so beyond anything that could reasonably be defended that substantial injustice has resulted or will result. The provision is not intended to allow the Court to substitute its own view as to how the arbitral proceedings should be conducted. Thus the choice by an arbitrator of a particular proceedure, unless it breaches the duty laid on arbitrators by Clause 33, should on no view justify the removal of an arbitrator, even if the court would not itself have adopted that procedure. In short, this ground only exists to cover what we hope will be the very rare case where an arbitrator so conducts the proceedings that it can fairly be said that instead of carrying through the object of arbitration as stated in the Bill, he is in effect frustrating that object. Only if the Court confines itself in this way can this power of removal be justified as a measure supporting rather than subverting the arbitral process."

Where circumstances have made the arbitrator an interested party (e.g. litigation between the arbitrator and one of the parties) leave to revoke will be given (*Re Baring Bros. & Co and Doulton & Co* (1892) 61 L.J.Q. 704). But the mere fact that one of the parties has issued a claim form against the arbitrator is not sufficient to disqualify the latter from acting where he has taken no positive step in retaliation (*Belcher v Roedean School Site, etc. Ltd* (1901) 85 L.T. 468). The test is the same as that which applied to all who made judicial decisions, namely whether there was any real danger that the arbitrator was biased.

"...when deciding whether bias has been established, the Court personifies the reasonable man. The Court considers on all the material which is placed before it whether there is any real danger of unconscious bias on the part of the decision maker. This is the case irrespective of whether it is a Judge or an arbitrator who is the subject of the allegation of bias".

See *AT&T Construction v Saudi Cable Co* [2000] CLC 220; [2000] 2 Lloyd's Rep 127, CA at 136.

In *Laker Airways Inc v FLS Aerospace Ltd* [1999] 2 Lloyd's Rep. 45 (Barristers from the same Chambers appointed applicants' and respondents' arbitrators) the court stated at p.48:

"The test is an objective one—whether circumstances exist that give rise to justifiable doubts as to an arbitrator's impartiality. The test is thus objective in at least two respects: the Court must find that circumstances exist, and are not merely believed to exist (although I suppose that a belief may itself be a circumstance); and secondly, those cicumstances must justifiable or perhaps unreasonable doubt is not sufficient: it is not enough honestly to say that one has lost confidence in the arbitrator's impartiality. On the other hand, doubts, if justifiable, are sufficient: it is not necessary to prove actual bias."

The test for bias under s.24(1) is the same as that irregularity under s.68 where the application is made on the grounds of bias, see *Rustal Trading Ltd v Gill & Duffus SA* [2000] 1 Lloyd's Rep. 14.

In *ASM v HARRIS* [2007] EWHC 1513; [2008] 1 Lloyd's Rep. 61 it was held that bias of one arbitrator is not bias of all.

**Abortive arbitration**

2E–149 "When an arbitration for any reason becomes abortive it is the duty of a court of

***Paragraph numbers marked with a "+" can be found online and on CD.***

law, in working out a contract of which such arbitration is part of the practical machinery, to supply the defect which has occurred. It is the duty of a court in such circumstances to come to the assistance of parties by removal of the impasse and the extrication of their rights" (*Cameron v Caddy* [1914] A.C. 651 at 656).

So in *Neal v Richardson* [1938] 1 All E.R. 753, CA, where an architect being appointed to act as arbitrator, refused to grant certificates or to arbitrate, the court refused to stay a claim in which the builder sought relief *aliunde*. On the other hand apart from the specific agreement the architect does not act as an arbitrator between the parties in issuing interim certificates (*Sutcliffe v Thackrah* [1974] A.C. 727; [1974] 1 All E.R. 859, overruling *Chambers v Goldthorpe* [1901] 1 K.B. 624, CA).

**For ss.25 to 29 of the Arbitration Act 1996 (see Arrangement) plus any related commentary see paragraphs 2E-150+ to 2E-159+ on White Book on Westlaw UK or the Civil Procedure CD.**

*JURISDICTION OF THE ARBITRAL TRIBUNAL*

## Competence of tribunal to rule on its own jurisdiction

**30.**—(1) Unless otherwise agreed by the parties, the arbitral tribunal may rule on its own substantive jurisdiction, that is, as to— **2E-160**

(a) whether there is a valid arbitration agreement,

(b) whether the tribunal is properly constituted, and

(c) what matters have been submitted to arbitration in accordance with the arbitration agreement.

(2) Any such ruling may be challenged by any available arbitral process of appeal or review or in accordance with the provisions of this Part.

*Note*—This is a mandatory provision (see s.4). For adaptation of s.30(1)(a) in case of statutory arbitration see s.96 below. **2E-161**

### Counterclaims

Factors determining whether arbitrators may entertain a counterclaim are the true construction of the agreement to refer and whether the counterclaim is a transaction set-off or other true defence as opposed to a completely independent set-off, see *Metal Distributors (UK) Ltd v ZCCM Investment Holdings PLC* [2005] EWHC 156 (Comm); [2005] 2 Lloyd's Rep.37. However an arbitral tribunal's jurisdiction to determine and give effect to a transaction set-off depends upon the true construction of the arbitration agreement, see *Econet Satellite Services Ltd v Vee Networks Ltd* [2006] EWHC 1664 (Comm); [2006] 2 All E.R. (Comm) 989; [2006] 2 Lloyd's Rep. 423. **2E-162**

## Objection to substantive jurisdiction of tribunal

**31.**—(1) An objection that the arbitral tribunal lacks substantive jurisdiction at the outset of the proceedings must be raised by a party not later than the time he takes the first step in the proceedings to contest the merits of any matter in relation to which he challenges the tribunal's jurisdiction. A party is not precluded from raising such an objection by the fact that he has appointed or participated in the appointment of an arbitrator. **2E-163**

(2) Any objection during the course of the arbitral proceedings that the arbitral tribunal is exceeding its substantive jurisdiction must be made as soon as possible after the matter alleged to be beyond its jurisdiction is raised.

(3) The arbitral tribunal may admit an objection later than the time specified in subsection (1) or (2) if it considers the delay justified.

(4) Where an objection is duly taken to the tribunal's substantive jurisdiction and the tribunal has power to rule on its own jurisdiction, it may—

(a) rule on the matter in an award as to jurisdiction, or

(b) deal with the objection in its award on the merits.

If the parties agree which of these courses the tribunal should take, the tribunal shall proceed accordingly.

(5) The tribunal may in any case, and shall if the parties so agree, stay proceedings whilst an application is made to the court under section 32 (determination of preliminary point of jurisdiction).

**2E–164** *Note*—This is a mandatory provision (see s.4). The prescribed circumstances without which the application will not be considered are to be noted.

## Determination of preliminary point of jurisdiction

**2E–165** **32.**—(1) The court may, on the application of a party to arbitral proceedings (upon notice to the other parties), determine any question as to the substantive jurisdiction of the tribunal. A party may lose the right to object (see section 73).

(2) An application under this section shall not be considered unless—

(a) it is made with the agreement in writing of all the other parties to the proceedings, or

(b) it is made with the permission of the tribunal and the court is satisfied—

(i) that the determination of the question is likely to produce substantial savings in costs,

(ii) that the application was made without delay, and

(iii) that there is good reason why the matter should be decided by the court.

(3) An application under this section, unless made with the agreement of all the other parties to the proceedings, shall state the grounds on which it is said that the matter should be decided by the court.

(4) Unless otherwise agreed by the parties, the arbitral tribunal may continue the arbitral proceedings and make an award while an application to the court under this section is pending.

(5) Unless the court gives leave, no appeal lies from a decision of the court whether the conditions specified in subsection (2) are met.

(6) The decision of the court on the question of jurisdiction shall be treated as a judgment of the court for the purposes of an appeal.

But no appeal lies without the leave of the court which shall not be given unless the court considers that the question involves a point of law which is one of general importance or is one which for some other special reason should be considered by the Court of Appeal.

**2E–166** *Note*—This is a mandatory provision (see s.4).

#### Application of section

**2E–167** Guidance on the circumstances in which the court can entertain an application under s.32 by a party to arbitral proceedings is contained in *Vale do Rio doce Navegacao*

***Paragraph numbers marked with a "+" can be found online and on CD.***

*SA v Shanghai Bao Steel Ocean Shipping Co Ltd* [2000] 2 Lloyd's Rep. 1. The court should not intervene except in the limited circumstances specified. Where the other alleged party to an arbitration agreement denies he is a party thereto the court stated at para.54:

"The Act sets out in very clear terms the steps that a party who contends that there is another party to an arbitration agreement should take. First he should appoint an arbitrator. If the other party appoints an arbitrator, then s.31(1) makes it clear that his appointment of an arbitrator does not prevent him challenging the substantive jurisdiction of the tribunal. If the other party does not appoint an arbitrator, then the default provisions (s.17) or failure to appoint procedures (s.18) apply. Once the arbitral tribunal is constituted, then in accordance with the policy of the Act it is for that tribunal to rule on its own jurisdiction, save in the circumstances specified in s.32. Any award made can then be changed under s.67. The rights of the party who challenges the existence of the arbitration agreement and takes no part are protected by s.72; he is given the right to recourse to the Courts in the circumstances set out."

There is no jurisdiction under s.32 as regards non-parties to the arbitration (e.g. brokers). See further para.2E–13 above.

ARBITRATION

### *THE ARBITRAL PROCEEDINGS*

## General duty of the tribunal

**33.**—(1) The tribunal shall— **2E–168**

(a) act fairly and impartially as between the parties, giving each party a reasonable opportunity of putting his case and dealing with that of his opponent, and

(b) adopt procedures suitable to the circumstances of the particular case, avoiding unnecessary delay or expense, so as to provide a fair means for the resolution of the matters falling to be determined.

(2) The tribunal shall comply with that general duty in conducting the arbitral proceedings, in its decisions on matters of procedure and evidence and in the exercise of all other powers conferred on it.

*Note* —This is a mandatory provision (see s.4). **2E–169**

## Procedural and evidential matters

**34.**—(1) It shall be for the tribunal to decide all procedural and evidential matters, subject to the right of the parties to agree any matter. **2E–170**

(2) Procedural and evidential matters include—

(a) when and where any part of the proceedings is to be held;

(b) the language or languages to be used in the proceedings and whether translations of any relevant documents are to be supplied;

(c) whether any and if so what form of written statements of claim and defence are to be used, when these should be supplied and the extent to which such statements can be later amended;

(d) whether any and if so which documents or classes of documents should be disclosed between and produced by the parties and at what stage;

***Paragraph numbers marked with a "+" can be found online and on CD.***

(e) whether any and if so what questions should be put to and answered by the respective parties and when and in what form this should be done;

(f) whether to apply strict rules of evidence (or any other rules) as to the admissibility, relevance or weight of any material (oral, written or other) sought to be tendered on any matters of fact or opinion, and the time, manner and form in which such material should be exchanged and presented;

(g) whether and to what extent the tribunal should itself take the initiative in ascertaining the facts and the law;

(h) whether and to what extent there should be oral or written evidence or submissions.

(3) The tribunal may fix the time within which any directions given by it are to be complied with, and may if it thinks fit extend the time so fixed (whether or not it has expired).

## Consolidation of proceedings and concurrent hearings

2E–171 **35.**—(1) The parties are free to agree—

(a) that the arbitral proceedings shall be consolidated with other arbitral proceedings, or

(b) that concurrent hearings shall be held,

on such terms as may be agreed.

(2) Unless the parties agree to confer such power on the tribunal, the tribunal has no power to order consolidation of proceedings or concurrent hearings.

2E–172 *Note*—For adaptation where a statutory arbitration is involved, see s.96(3) below.

## Legal or other representation

2E–173 **36.** Unless otherwise agreed by the parties, a party to arbitral proceedings may be represented in the proceedings by a lawyer or other person chosen by him.

## Power to appoint experts, legal advisers or assessors

2E–174 **37.**—(1) Unless otherwise agreed by the parties—

(a) the tribunal may—

(i) appoint experts or legal advisers to report to it and the parties, or

(ii) appoint assessors to assist it on technical matters,

and may allow any such expert, legal adviser or assessor to attend the proceedings; and

(b) the parties shall be given a reasonable opportunity to comment on any information, opinion or advice offered by any such person.

(2) The fees and expenses of an expert, legal adviser or assessor appointed by the tribunal for which the arbitrators are liable are expenses of the arbitrators for the purposes of this Part.

2E–175 *Note*—Section 37(2) is a mandatory provision (see s.4).

***Paragraph numbers marked with a "+" can be found online and on CD.***

## General powers exercisable by the tribunal

**38.**—(1) The parties are free to agree on the powers exercisable by the arbitral tribunal for the purposes of and in relation to the proceedings. **2E–176**

(2) Unless otherwise agreed by the parties the tribunal has the following powers.

(3) The tribunal may order a claimant to provide security for the costs of the arbitration.

This power shall not be exercised on the ground that the claimant is—

(a) an individual ordinarily resident outside the United Kingdom, or

(b) a corporation or association incorporated or formed under the law of a country outside the United Kingdom, or whose central management and control is exercised outside the United Kingdom.

(4) The tribunal may give directions in relation to any property which is the subject of the proceedings or as to which any question arises in the proceedings, and which is owned by or is in the possession of a party to the proceedings—

(a) for the inspection, photographing, preservation, custody or detention of the property by the tribunal, an expert or a party, or

(b) ordering that samples be taken from, or any observation be made of or experiment conducted upon, the property.

(5) The tribunal may direct that a party or witness shall be examined on oath or affirmation, and may for that purpose administer any necessary oath or take any necessary affirmation.

(6) The tribunal may give directions to a party for the preservation for the purposes of the proceedings of any evidence in his custody or control.

*Note*—Compare s.12(1)–(3) and s.6(a) of the 1950 Act. The power to order security was new. **2E–177**

## Power to make provisional awards

**39.**—(1) The parties are free to agree that the tribunal shall have power to order on a provisional basis any relief which it would have power to grant in a final award. **2E–178**

(2) This includes, for instance, making—

(a) a provisional order for the payment of money or the disposition of property as between the parties, or

(b) an order to make an interim payment on account of the costs of the arbitration.

(3) Any such order shall be subject to the tribunal's final adjudication; and the tribunal's final award, on the merits or as to costs, shall take account of any such order.

(4) Unless the parties agree to confer such power on the tribunal, the tribunal has no such power.

This does not affect its powers under section 47 (awards on different issues, etc.).

2E–179 *Note*—Under this provision an arbitrator has power to make a freezing order on a provisional basis if the parties have so agreed, see *Kastner v Jason* [2004] EWHC 592 (Ch); [2004] 2 Lloyd's Rep. 233(Ch). Further reviewed and analysed on appeal [2004] EWCA Civ 1599; [2005] 1 Lloyd's Rep. 397.

### General duty of parties

2E–180 **40.**—(1) The parties shall do all things necessary for the proper and expeditious conduct of the arbitral proceedings.

(2) This includes—

(a) complying without delay with any determination of the tribunal as to procedural or evidential matters, or with any order or directions of the tribunal, and

(b) where appropriate, taking without delay any necessary steps to obtain a decision of the court on a preliminary question of jurisdiction or law (see sections 32 and 45).

2E–181 *Note*—This is a mandatory provision (see s.4).

### Powers of tribunal in case of party's default

2E–182 **41.**—(1) The parties are free to agree on the powers of the tribunal in case of a party's failure to do something necessary for the proper and expeditious conduct of the arbitration.

(2) Unless otherwise agreed by the parties, the following provisions apply.

(3) If the tribunal is satisfied that there has been inordinate and inexcusable delay on the part of the claimant in pursuing his claim and that the delay—

(a) gives rise, or is likely to give rise, to a substantial risk that it is not possible to have a fair resolution of the issues in that claim, or

(b) has caused, or is likely to cause, serious prejudice to the respondent,

the tribunal may make an award dismissing the claim.

(4) If without showing sufficient cause a party—

(a) fails to attend or be represented at an oral hearing of which due notice was given, or

(b) where matters are to be dealt with in writing, fails after due notice to submit written evidence or make written submissions,

the tribunal may continue the proceedings in the absence of that party or, as the case may be, without any written evidence or submissions on his behalf, and may make an award on the basis of the evidence before it.

(5) If without showing sufficient cause a party fails to comply with any order or directions of the tribunal, the tribunal may make a peremptory order to the same effect, prescribing such time for compliance with it as the tribunal considers appropriate.

(6) If a claimant fails to comply with a peremptory order of the tribunal to provide security for costs, the tribunal may make an award dismissing his claim.

(7) If a party fails to comply with any other kind of peremptory order, then, without prejudice to section 42 (enforcement by court of tribunal's peremptory orders), the tribunal may do any of the following—

(a) direct that the party in default shall not be entitled to rely upon any allegation or material which was the subject matter of the order;
(b) draw such adverse inferences from the act of non-compliance as the circumstances justify;
(c) proceed to an award on the basis of such materials as have been properly provided to it;
(d) make such order as it thinks fit as to the payment of costs of the arbitration incurred in consequence of the non-compliance.

*Note*—Compare s.13A of the 1950 Act. **2E–183**

**Unless otherwise agreed ... the following provisions apply**

The provisions reflect the principles laid down in *Birkett v James* [1978] A.C. 297, HL, and *Department of Transport v Smaller (Chris) Transport Ltd* [1989] A.C. 1197, HL. Thus in *James Lazenby & Co v McNicholas Construction Co Ltd* [1995] 1 W.L.R. 615; [1995] 2 Lloyd's Rep. 30, it was held that it was an error of law for an arbitrator to dismiss a claim within its limitation period in the absence of exceptional circumstances. **2E–184**

**Application**

Under the old law (s.13A) an arbitrator had power to dismiss a claim on the basis of inordinate and inexcusable delay occurring before (as well as after) the section came into force on January 1, 1992 and to such extent the provision has retrospective effect (*L'Office Cherifien des Phosphates and Unitramp SA v Yamashita-Shinnihom Steamship Co Ltd* [1994] 1 A.C. 486; [1994] 2 W.L.R. 39; [1994] 1 All E.R. 20; [1994] 1 Lloyd's Rep. 251, HL). **2E–185**

### *POWERS OF COURT IN RELATION TO ARBITRAL PROCEEDINGS*

## Enforcement of peremptory orders of tribunal

**42.**—(1) Unless otherwise agreed by the parties, the court may make an order requiring a party to comply with a peremptory order made by the tribunal. **2E–186**

(2) An application for an order under this section may be made—

(a) by the tribunal (upon notice to the parties),
(b) by a party to the arbitral proceedings with the permission of the tribunal (and upon notice to the other parties), or
(c) where the parties have agreed that the powers of the court under this section shall be available.

(3) The court shall not act unless it is satisfied that the applicant has exhausted any available arbitral process in respect of failure to comply with the tribunal's order.

(4) No order shall be made under this section unless the court is satisfied that the person to whom the tribunal's order was directed

***Paragraph numbers marked with a "+" can be found online and on CD.***

has failed to comply with it within the time prescribed in the order or, if no time was prescribed, within a reasonable time.

(5) The leave of the court is required for any appeal from a decision of the court under this section.

2E-187 *Note* —Compare s.5 of the 1979 Act. This section was amended by Scheme for Construction Contracts (England and Wales) Regulations 1998 (SI 1998/649) so far as construction contracts are concerned in that art.24 thereof provides as follows:

"**24.** Section 42 of the Arbitration Act 1996 shall apply to this Scheme subject to the following modifications—

(a) in subsection (2) for the word "tribunal" wherever it appears there shall be substituted the word "adjudicator",

(b) in subparagraph (b) of subsection (2) for the words "arbitral proceedings" there shall be substituted the word "adjudication",

(c) subparagraph (c) of subsection (2) shall be deleted, and

(d) subsection (3) shall be deleted."

## Securing the attendance of witnesses

2E-188 **43.**—(1) A party to arbitral proceedings may use the same court procedures as are available in relation to legal proceedings to secure the attendance before the tribunal of a witness in order to give oral testimony or to produce documents or other material evidence.

(2) This may only be done with the permission of the tribunal or the agreement of the other parties.

(3) The court procedures may only be used if—

(a) the witness is in the United Kingdom, and

(b) the arbitral proceedings are being conducted in England and Wales or, as the case may be, Northern Ireland.

(4) A person shall not be compelled by virtue of this section to produce any document or other material evidence which he could not be compelled to produce in legal proceedings.

2E-189 *Note* —Compare s.12(4) and (5) of the 1950 Act. This is a mandatory provision (see s.4).

### "A witness summons"

2E-190 Normally issues at the Admiralty and Commercial Registry at the Royal Courts of Justice, Strand, London WC2A 2LL, or a district registry where attendance of witness required within the district of the district registry (see Practice Direction—Arbitration, paras 7.1 to 7.3).

### Perjury

2E-191 It was held that perjury committed in an arbitration under the Workmen's Compensation Act was perjury at Common Law and punishable as such (*R. v Crossley* (1909) 100 L.T. 463, CA). See the Perjury Act 1911.

2E-192 *Note* —There is no power under s.43 for a court to order disclosure against a third party as opposed to issuing a witness summons for the production in evidence of specific documents. Nor are the court's powers under CPR r.31.17 to be translated into the context of arbitration, see *BNP Paribas v Deloitte & Touche LLP* [2003] EWHC 2874 (Comm).

## Court powers exercisable in support of arbitral proceedings

2E-193 **44.**—(1) Unless otherwise agreed by the parties, the court has for the purposes of and in relation to arbitral proceedings the same power of making orders about the matters listed below as it has for the purposes of and in relation to legal proceedings.

(2) Those matters are—

(a) the taking of the evidence of witnesses;

(b) the preservation of evidence;

(c) making orders relating to property which is the subject of the proceedings or as to which any question arises in the proceedings—

(i) for the inspection, photographing, preservation, custody or detention of the property, or

(ii) ordering that samples be taken from, or any observation be made of or experiment conducted upon, the property;

and for that purpose authorising any person to enter any premises in the possession or control of a party to the arbitration;

(d) the sale of any goods the subject of the proceedings;

(e) the granting of an interim injunction or the appointment of a receiver.

(3) If the case is one of urgency, the court may, on the application of a party or proposed party to the arbitral proceedings, make such orders as it thinks necessary for the purpose of preserving evidence or assets.

(4) If the case is not one of urgency, the court shall act only on the application of a party to the arbitral proceedings (upon notice to the other parties and to the tribunal) made with the permission of the tribunal or the agreement in writing of the other parties.

(5) In any case the court shall act only if or to the extent that the arbitral tribunal, and any arbitral or other institution or person vested by the parties with power in that regard, has no power or is unable for the time being to act effectively.

(6) If the court so orders, an order made by it under this section shall cease to have effect in whole or in part on the order of the tribunal or of any such arbitral or other institution or person having power to act in relation to the subject-matter of the order.

(7) The leave of the court is required for any appeal from a decision of the court under this section.

*Note*—Compare s.12(6) of the 1950 Act. **2E–194**

**Examination of Witness Order**

In *Commerce & Industry Co of Canada v Certain Underwriters at Lloyd's of London* [2002] 1 W.L.R. 1323; [2002] 2 All E.R. (Comm) 204; [2002] 1 Lloyd's Rep. 219, the court (a) declined a letter of request from New York arbitrators on the basis the reference in s.1 of the Evidence (Proceedings in Other Jurisdictions) Act 1975 to a "tribunal" did not include a private arbitral tribunal and (b) declined to exercise its power under s.44 in respect of ordering the taking of the evidence of witnesses which may be exercised even where the seat arbitration is outside England and Wales or Northern Ireland on the basis that it was inappropriate to do (see s.2(3) of the 1996 Act above) because of differences in procedure, namely the discovery of information by witness testimony under the curial law of New York which had never been part of English procedure. **2E–195**

**Preservation of Evidence etc**

Whilst s.44(2) did not provide for an order for disclosure by a non-party it permit- **2E–196**



ARBITRATION

ted an order for the inspection, photocopying and preservation of documents in the hands of third parties for the purpose of resolving an issue in the arbitration, (a feasibility study for deepening harbour in a breach of safe berth warranty claim) *Assimina Maritime Ltd v Pakistan National Shipping; The Tasmin Spirit* [2004] EWHC 3005 (Comm); [2005] 1 All E.R. (Comm) 460; [2005] 1 Lloyd's Rep. 525.

#### Interim Injunctions

2E–197 In *Channel Tunnel Group Ltd v Balfour Beatty Construction Ltd* [1993] A.C. 334; [1993] 2 W.L.R. 262; [1993] 1 All E.R. 664; [1993] 1 Lloyd's Rep. 291, the House of Lords held that on the true construction of s.12(6)(h) of the Arbitration Act 1950 there was no power to grant an interim injunction in respect of a foreign arbitration but that an interim injunction pursuant to s.37(1) of the Senior Courts Act 1981 could be granted to assist or reinforce a foreign arbitration if circumstances so required even though a stay of English proceedings was ordered. In the cited case an interim injunction was refused as to grant the same would have pre-empted the very decision the support of which formed the raison d'être of the injunction. The House of Lords also held that the court had an inherent power to stay proceedings brought before it in breach of agreement to decide disputes by an alternative method whether or not the procedure agreed amounted to an arbitration agreement within s.1 of the Arbitration Act 1975.

In *Cetelem SA v Roust Holdings Ltd* [2005] EWCA Civ 618; [2005] 1 W.L.R. 3555; [2005] 4 All E.R. 52; [2005] 2 Lloyd's Rep. 494 (an interim injunction case) the Court of Appeal held that:

> "on the true construction of s.44(3) of the 1996 Act if the case is one of urgency the court only has jurisdiction to make such orders as it thinks necessary for the purpose of preserving evidence or assets"

not following the wider approach of *Hiscox Underwriting Ltd v Dickson* [2004] EWHC 479; [2004] 1 All E.R. (Comm) 753; [2004] 2 Lloyd's Rep. 438 that s.44(3) was permissive and not restrictive of the powers conferred by s.44(1) and (2) and further holding that a contractual right could be an asset for the purposes of s.44(3).

#### Time when powers exercisable

2E–198 It is doubtful that there is jurisdiction under this provision to order pre-delivery tests and inspection of a vessel before a cause of action had arisen for defective condition upon delivery or circumstances giving rise to an injunction under (formerly) RSC O.29, r.1; see *Tsakos Shipping & Trading SA v Orizon Tanker Co Ltd (The Centaurus Mar)* [1998] C.L.C. 1003.

#### Sub-section (7)

2E–199 For the purposes of s.44(7) "the court" means the court of first instance but "...a decision of a judge which the court had no jurisdiction to make is not a decision 'under the section' within the meaning of s.44(7) of the 1996 Act", see *Cetelem SA* at para.2E–197, above.

## Determination of preliminary point of law

2E–200 **45.**—(1) Unless otherwise agreed by the parties, the court may on the application of a party to arbitral proceedings (upon notice to the other parties) determine any question of law arising in the course of the proceedings which the court is satisfied substantially affects the rights of one or more of the parties. An agreement to dispense with reasons for the tribunal's award shall be considered an agreement to exclude the court's jurisdiction under this section.

(2) An application under this section shall not be considered unless—

(a) it is made with the agreement of all the other parties to the proceedings, or

(b) it is made with the permission of the tribunal and the court is satisfied—

(i) that the determination of the question is likely to produce substantial savings in costs, and

(ii) that the application was made without delay.

(3) The application shall identify the question of law to be determined and, unless made with the agreement of all the other parties to the proceedings, shall state the grounds on which it is said that the question should be decided by the court.

(4) Unless otherwise agreed by the parties, the arbitral tribunal may continue the arbitral proceedings and make an award while an application to the court under this section is pending.

(5) Unless the court gives leave, no appeal lies from a decision of the court whether the conditions specified in subsection (2) are met.

(6) The decision of the court on the question of law shall be treated as a judgment of the court for the purposes of an appeal.

But no appeal lies without the leave of the court which shall not be given unless the court considers that the question is one of general importance, or is one which for some other special reason should be considered by the Court of Appeal.

*Note*—Compare s.2 of the 1979 Act. **2E-201**

**Determination of preliminary point of law**

The Act has a procedure under which an application may be made to the court to determine any question of law arising in the course of the reference, but restrictions are imposed on the making of such applications and the right to make an application may in specified circumstances also be excluded by agreement between the parties. **2E-202**

It should, however, be emphasised that s.45 provides for an essentially speedy procedure designed to interrupt the arbitration to the minimum possible extent and it is an exception to the general rule that the courts do not intervene in the course of an arbitration, and therefore, save in wholly exceptional cases, e.g. where the preliminary question of law would determine the whole dispute between the parties it is not to be used to obtain definitive decisions from the Court of Appeal or the House of Lords (*per* Donaldson L.J. in *Babanaft International Co SA v Avant Petroleum Inc* [1982] 1 W.L.R. 871 at 882; [1982] 3 All E.R. 244 at 252) a case on s.2 of the 1979 Act.

**For ss.46 to 64 of the Arbitration Act 1996 (see Arrangement) plus any related commentary see paragraphs 2E-203+ to 2E-239+ on White Book on Westlaw UK or the Civil Procedure CD.**

## Power to limit recoverable costs

**65.**—(1) Unless otherwise agreed by the parties, the tribunal may direct that the recoverable costs of the arbitration, or of any part of the arbitral proceedings, shall be limited to a specified amount. **2E-240**

(2) Any direction may be made or varied at any stage, but this must be done sufficiently in advance of the incurring of costs to which it relates, or the taking of any steps in the proceedings which may be affected by it, for the limit to be taken into account.

### *POWERS OF THE COURT IN RELATION TO AWARD*

## Enforcement of the award

**66.**—(1) An award made by the tribunal pursuant to an arbitration agreement may, by leave of the court, be enforced in the same manner as a judgment or order of the court to the same effect. **2E-241**



ARBITRATION

(2) Where leave is so given, judgment may be entered in terms of the award.

(3) Leave to enforce an award shall not be given where, or to the extent that, the person against whom it is sought to be enforced shows that the tribunal lacked substantive jurisdiction to make the award.

The right to raise such an objection may have been lost (see section 73).

(4) Nothing in this section affects the recognition or enforcement of an award under any other enactment or rule of law, in particular under Part II of the [1950 c. 27.] Arbitration Act 1950 (enforcement of awards under Geneva Convention) or the provisions of Part III of this Act relating to the recognition and enforcement of awards under the New York Convention or by an action on the award.

**2E–242** *Note* —Compare s.26(1) of the 1950 Act. This is a mandatory provision (see s.4).

**"By leave of the Court"**

**2E–243** Where the court is of opinion that the award is legally invalid, it may refuse permission to enforce it. *Cf. Re Stone and Hastie Arb.* [1903] 2 K.B. 463, CA. Permission should be given in nearly all cases to enforce an award as a judgment unless there is real ground for doubting the validity of the award, and the ambit of this section should not be circumscribed (*Middlemiss & Gould v Hartlepool Corp* [1972] 1 W.L.R. 1643; [1973] 1 All E.R. 172, CA, and see *Curacac Trading Co BV v Harkisandas & Co* [1992] 2 Lloyd's Rep. 186 at 192 approving statement in Mustill and Boyd, *Commercial Arbitration*, 2nd edn, p.419 to the effect that the court would probably now only refuse the application where the objection cannot properly be disposed of without trial.

**"Be enforced"**

**2E–244** This may be done by permission at any time, though the time for setting the award aside has not expired.

A person who obtains permission under this section to enforce an award is not thereby prevented from bringing a claim on the award (*China Steam Navigation Co v Van Laun* (1905) 22 T.L.R. 26). It is an implied term of an arbitration agreement that an award for the payment of money should be in a form which is capable of being enforced in the same manner as a judgment, and the court has power to remit such an award so that it may be amended to put it in such a form (*Margulies Ltd v Dafnis Thomaides Ltd* [1958] 1 W.L.R. 398; [1958] 1 All E.R. 777).

A confidentiality or non-disclosure agreement in respect of an arbitration should not be construed so as to prevent in terms of enforcement a party relying on an award in respect of rights declared in his favour by the award, *Associated Electric and Gas Insurance Services Ltd v European Reinsurance Co of Zurich* [2003] UKPC 11; [2003] 1 W.L.R. 1041.

In *Michael Carter v Harold Simpson Associates (Architects) Ltd*; [2004] UKPC 29; [2005] 1 W.L.R. 919; [2004] 2 Lloyd's Rep. 512, PC, (a case concerning Jamaican law) the Privy Council held that the unremitted parts of an award remain valid and can properly form the subject matter of enforcement. Effect of *Johnson v Latham* (1851) 20 L.J. Q.B. 236 considered.

**Claim on the award**

**2E–245** "It is well settled that procedure by [claim] upon an award is one that ought to be pursued where the objections raised are such as to render the validity of the award a matter of doubt. Where there are matters which may gravely affect the validity of the award, no order should be made giving [permission] to proceed summarily under the award." *Per* Swinfen Eady, M.R., *Re Boks & Co and Peters, Rushton & Co Arbn.* [1919] 1 K.B. 491. In this case Lush J. in Chambers refused permission to enforce the award as the contract between the parties was an illegal one. In *May v Mills* (1914) 30 T.L.R. 287, there was a doubt on the face of the proceedings whether there had been a valid

***Paragraph numbers marked with a "+" can be found online and on CD.***

arbitration. The Master refused leave to enforce the award. The Judge in Chambers reversed this decision, which was restored by the CA, who left the claimant to bring a claim on the award. The defendant had refused throughout to take any part in the arbitration. In the claim judgment was given for the defendant with costs of all the proceedings.

An application under s.66 is not a suitable procedure in a case where an objection is taken to the award which cannot properly be disposed of without a trial (*Allied Vision Ltd v VPS Film Entertainment GmbH* [1991] 1 Lloyd's Rep. 392), a case under s.26 of the 1950 Act.

When confronted with a clause which purports to provide that the rights of the parties shall be governed by a system of law which is neither English law nor the law of any other state, or which is a serious modification of such law, the court has to decide (a) whether the parties intend to create legally enforceable rights and obligations (b) whether the resulting agreement is sufficiently certain to constitute a legally enforceable contract, and (c) whether it will be contrary to public policy to enforce the award because there is some illegality present, or because enforcement will clearly be injurious to the public good (*Deutsche Schachtbau- und Tiefbohr GmbH v Ras Al Khaimah National Oil Co* [1987] 3 W.L.R. 1023; [1987] 2 All E.R. 796, CA reversed on another point *sub nom. Deutsche Schachtbau- und Tiefbohr GmbH v Shell International Petroleum Co Ltd* [1988] 3 W.L.R. 230; [1988] 2 All E.R. 833, HL). An award made by I.C.C. arbitrators in Geneva, applying a system of law which represented a common denominator of the principles underlying the laws of contract of various nations was held to be enforceable on application of these tests (*ibid.*).

**Counterclaim**

In a claim on an award the defendant is not estopped from counterclaiming for rectification of the agreement to refer (*Crane v Hegeman-Harris Co Inc* [1939] 1 All E.R. 662). **2E–246**

**Appeal from order to enforce award**

The principles applicable to obtaining permission to appeal out of time (see *C.M. Van Stillevoldt BV v E.L. Carviers Inc* [1983] 1 W.L.R. 207; and *Norwich and Peterborough Building Society v Steed* [1991] 1 W.L.R. 449) provided an appropriate guide to the court in exercising its discretion whether to extend time for permission to appeal where permission had been granted to enforce an award as a judgment and judgment had been entered (*Soinco Savi v Novokuznetsk Aluminium Plant* [1998] 2 Lloyd's Rep. 337, CA). **2E–247**

**Limitation**

On a claim to enforce or an application for permission to enforce an arbitration award in the same way as a judgment, the cause of action accrues when the party against whom the award has been made fails to honour the award, not when the breach of contract to which the award relates occurs (*Agromet Motoimport v Maulden Engineering Co (Beds) Ltd* [1985] 1 W.L.R. 762; [1985] 2 All E.R. 436). **2E–248**

**Practice—Methods of enforcement**

There are two methods of enforcement of an award which are open to the applicant namely: **2E–249**

1. By application directly to enforce the award (see para.2E–250 below) and if permission is granted.
2. By entering judgment in terms of the award and so to enforce the judgment by one or more of the usual forms of execution award.

These methods are not alternative, but successive. The applicant may apply for permission to enforce the award in the same manner as a judgment or order to the same effect, and if such permission is given, he may then proceed to enter judgment in the terms of the award. There is no need for a further application for permission to enter such a judgment, but it should be noted that there may be advantages in proceeding to the second stage of entering judgment instead of being content with an order granting leave to permission the award as a judgment, e.g. by suing upon the judgment or otherwise proceeding by execution or registration or other method of enforcement in a foreign court or by obtaining the recognition of the judgment in a foreign court or by relying on the judgment as *res judicata*.



ARBITRATION

### Application

**2E–250** (See generally CPR Pt 62—Arbitration Claims, r.62.18) In the light of the wider point of entry for enforcement matters application for permission to enforce an award under this section should be made in the first instance without notice to a Master, Admiralty Registrar or district judge of the district registry. The application should be made upon an arbitration claim form supported by written evidence such as an affidavit or witness statement which, in the QBD in London, should be left with the Admiralty and Commercial Registry in Room EB 13. The affidavit or witness statement should exhibit the arbitration agreement and the original award or copies thereof, and should state the name and the usual or last known place of abode or business of the applicant and the person against whom it is sought to enforce the award, and either that the award has not been complied with or the extent to which it has not been complied with at the date of the application (see Pt 62, r.62.18(6)). Where the application is under s.101 of the 1996 Act or s.3(1)(a) of the 1975 Act, different documents must be exhibited as specified in subss.6(a)(ii) and (iii). The Master may either grant the application on a without notice basis or direct the application to be issued. It should ask for "permission to enforce the award dated—in the above arbitration in the same manner as a judgment or order to the same effect"; and "that the respondent do pay the costs of this application to be taxed". The applicant must produce before the Master the original award (or a duplicate) and a copy thereof, together with an affidavit or witness statement intituled as above, verifying both the original, the copy award, and the arbitration agreement. On issuing execution without entering judgment, the copy award must be filed (no fee) at the Admiralty and Commercial Registry, together with the order for permission to enforce it. But if a judgment is to be signed, the award should first be filed and an office copy produced on signing judgment. In the QBD a reference number will be given on signing judgment or issuing execution as on the commencement of a claim. The award will be marked with a seal to indicate that execution has issued on it. All subsequent proceedings should bear the reference number. In the Chancery Division the papers are lodged in Chancery Chambers and a similar practice followed.

### Costs

**2E–251** The costs of the application for permission to enforce the award should be included in the order, no matter how small the amount awarded and the certificate for such costs produced on issuing execution.

Taxation of costs under the award may be obtained on production of the award either before or after permission to enforce it has been obtained. And this applies to taxation of the charges of the arbitrator, provided he has not himself taxed and fixed the amount of the costs of the reference and award by, and as part of, his award.

### Costs where judgment may be entered

**2E–252** If it is desired to enter judgment for the amount awarded, the application should be so framed as to provide for "the costs of any judgment which may be entered hereunder". If this precaution is not taken, it may be impossible to secure an order for the costs incurred in signing judgment.

### Service out of the jurisdiction

**2E–253** The application may, with permission, be served out of the jurisdiction, see r.62.18(4). Service out of the jurisdiction of an order giving permission to enforce does not require permission, see r.62.18(8).

### "Judgment ... in terms of the award"

**2E–254** A judgment so entered may be enforced in the usual way. But it is important to notice that no provision is made for the costs which may be incurred in making the necessary application under this section. The incidence of such costs will no doubt be settled, in the ordinary course, by the Master who hears that application, and his order can be enforced as if it were a judgment; but if it is proposed to enforce the award as a judgment—e.g. by suing upon it in a foreign court—no terms other than those to be found in the award can be included in the judgment. See for instance *Walker v Rowe* [2000] 1 Lloyd's Rep. 116—there is no power to add s.35 Senior Courts Act 1981 interest to an award which made no provision for post award interest because to do so would be to alter the terms of the award rather than entering judgment in terms of the award.

However by analogy with the decision in *Gater Assets Ltd v NAK Naftogaz Ukrainiy* [2008] EWHC 1108 (Comm); [2008] 1 Lloyd's Rep. 295 (Beatson J.), a New York Convention case, interest under the Judgments Act 1838 as amended is payable from the date of entry of the judgment even where no interest was awarded by the arbitrators.

## Challenging the award: substantive jurisdiction

**67.**—(1) A party to arbitral proceedings may (upon notice to the other parties and to the tribunal) apply to the court— **2E–255**

(a) challenging any award of the arbitral tribunal as to its substantive jurisdiction; or

(b) for an order declaring an award made by the tribunal on the merits to be of no effect, in whole or in part, because the tribunal did not have substantive jurisdiction.

A party may lose the right to object (see section 73) and the right to apply is subject to the restrictions in section 70(2) and (3).

(2) The arbitral tribunal may continue the arbitral proceedings and make a further award while an application to the court under this section is pending in relation to an award as to jurisdiction.

(3) On an application under this section challenging an award of the arbitral tribunal as to its substantive jurisdiction, the court may by order—

(a) confirm the award,

(b) vary the award, or

(c) set aside the award in whole or in part.

(4) The leave of the court is required for any appeal from a decision of the court under this section.

*Note*—Compare ss.22 and 23 of the 1950 Act. This is a mandatory provision (see s.4). A challenge under this section involves a re-hearing rather than a review, see *Azov Shipping Co v Baltic Shipping Co (No.1)* [1999] 1 All E.R. 476; [1999] 1 Lloyd's Rep. 68; *Peterson Farms Inc v C&M Farming Ltd* [2004] EWHC 121 (Comm); [2004] 1 Lloyd's Rep. 603. **2E–256**

The identification of parties to an aribitration agreement is a matter of substantive not procedural law, see *Peterson Farms Inc v C&M Farming Ltd* above in which award in favour of non-parties which were within the same group of companies as the company named in the arbitration agreement held to have been made without jurisdiction.

Arbitrators have to be appointed in compliance with any applicable procedure for appointment. Any irregularity in appointment invalidates the arbitration. There is no room in arbitration for the common law doctrine which can sometimes validate the acts of an apparent or reputed judge. See *Sumukan Ltd v Commonwealth Secretariat* [2007] EWCA Civ 1148; [2008] Bus L.R. 858; [2008] 1 Lloyd's Rep. 40, CA.

#### Section 67(1)(b)

See *Mohsin v Commonwealth Secretariat* [2002] EWHC 377 (Comm); March 1, 2002 for interplay of this section and s.73 of the 1996 Act (loss of right to object). **2E–257**

#### The leave of the court is required

Only the trial judge can grant permission to appeal against a decision under s.67. There is no jurisdiction in the Court of Appeal to do so: *Athletic Union of Constantinople v National Basketball Association* [2002] 1 W.L.R. 2863; [2002] 3 All E.R. 897, CA (see similarly *Henry Boot Construction v Malmaison Hotel* at para.2E–268 below). **2E–258**

#### Effect of an order pursuant to s.67(3)(c)

Upon an order setting aside the award or a declaration that the award was of no ef- **2E–259**

***Paragraph numbers marked with a "+" can be found online and on CD.***

fect, the arbitration reverted to the position it was in before the arbitrator published his award so that the arbitrator was not *functus officio, Hussman (Europe) Ltd v Pharaon* [2003] EWCA Civ 266; [2003] 1 All E.R. (Comm) 879, CA.

**Section 67(4)**

2E–259.1 It is not incompatible with the European Convention on Human Rights for Parliament to seek to further restrict second appeals as provided in subs.4, *Republic of Kazakhstan v Istil Group Ltd* [2007] EWCA Civ 471; [2007] 2 Lloyd's Rep. 548.

## Challenging the award: serious irregularity

2E–260 **68.**—(1) A party to arbitral proceedings may (upon notice to the other parties and to the tribunal) apply to the court challenging an award in the proceedings on the ground of serious irregularity affecting the tribunal, the proceedings or the award. A party may lose the right to object (see section 73) and the right to apply is subject to the restrictions in section 70(2) and (3).

(2) Serious irregularity means an irregularity of one or more of the following kinds which the court considers has caused or will cause substantial injustice to the applicant—

(a) failure by the tribunal to comply with section 33 (general duty of tribunal);

(b) the tribunal exceeding its powers (otherwise than by exceeding its substantive jurisdiction: see section 67);

(c) failure by the tribunal to conduct the proceedings in accordance with the procedure agreed by the parties;

(d) failure by the tribunal to deal with all the issues that were put to it;

(e) any arbitral or other institution or person vested by the parties with powers in relation to the proceedings or the award exceeding its powers;

(f) uncertainty or ambiguity as to the effect of the award;

(g) the award being obtained by fraud or the award or the way in which it was procured being contrary to public policy;

(h) failure to comply with the requirements as to the form of the award; or

(i) any irregularity in the conduct of the proceedings or in the award which is admitted by the tribunal or by any arbitral or other institution or person vested by the parties with powers in relation to the proceedings or the award.

(3) If there is shown to be serious irregularity affecting the tribunal, the proceedings or the award, the court may—

(a) remit the award to the tribunal, in whole or in part, for reconsideration,

(b) set the award aside in whole or in part, or

(c) declare the award to be of no effect, in whole or in part.

The court shall not exercise its power to set aside or to declare an award to be of no effect, in whole or in part, unless it is satisfied that it would be inappropriate to remit the matters in question to the tribunal for reconsideration.

(4) The leave of the court is required for any appeal from a decision of the court under this section.

*Note* —Compare ss.22 and 23 of the 1950 Act. This is a mandatory provision (see s.4). **2E-261**

**"On the ground of serious irregularity"**

This means irregularity of one or more of the kinds set out in sub-para.(2) which the court considers has or will cause substantial injustice to the applicant. In *Petroships Pte Ltd v Petec Trading and Investment Corp (The "Petro Ranger")* [2001] 2 Lloyd's Rep. 348, the following commentary on this section appears at p.351: **2E-262**

1. Section 68 sets out a closed list of irregularities (which it is not open to the court to extent).
2. Section 68 reflects the internationally accepted view that the court should be able to correct serious failure to comply with the "due process" of arbitral proceedings: *cf*. art.34 of the Model Law.
3. A serious irregularity has to pass the test of causing "substantial injustice" before the court can act (s.68(2)).
4. The test of "substantial injustice" is intended to be applied by way of support for the arbitral process, not by way of interference with that process. Thus it is only in those cases where it can be said that what has happened is so far removed from what could reasonably be expected of the arbitral process, that the court will take action.
5. The test is not what would have happened had the matter been litigated. To apply such a test would be to ignore the fact that the parties have agreed to arbitrate not litigate.
6. Having chosen arbitration, the parties cannot complain of substantial injustice, unless what has happened cannot on any view be defended as an acceptable consequence of that choice.
7. Section 68 is designed as a longstop, only available in extreme cases, where the tribunal has gone so wrong in its conduct of the arbitration in one of the respects listed in s.68, that justice calls out for it to be corrected.
8. Section 68 must not be used as a means of circumventing the restrictions upon the court's power to intervene in arbitral proceedings. Further, the distinction between s.68 and s.69 must be maintained. In addition, the court's powers under s.70(4) should be borne in mind (see below).
9. Section 68(2)(d) ("failure by the tribunal to deal with all issues which were put to it") does not require a tribunal to set out each step by which they reached their conclusion or to deal with each point made by a party. There is a distinction between criticism of the reasoning and a failure to deal with an issue (Mr Justice Thomas in *Hussmann (Europe) Ltd v Al Ameen Development & Trade Co* [2000] 2 Lloyd's Rep. 83, at p.97, col. 1).

In *Lesotho Highlands Development Authority v Impregilo SpA* [2005] UKHL 43 a case where "the issue was whether the tribunal had exceeded its powers within the meaning of s.68(2)(b)" and concerned ss.48(4) and 49(3) of the 1996 Act, Lord Steyn said:

> "**28** ... This is a mandatory provision. The policy in favour of party autonomy does not permit derogation from the provisions of section 68. A number of preliminary observations about section 68 are pertinent. First, unlike the position under the old law, intervention under section 68 is only permissible *after* an award has been made. Secondly, the requirement is a serious irregularity. It is a new concept in English arbitration law. Plainly a high threshold must be satisfied. Thirdly, it must be established that the irregularity caused or will cause substantial injustice to the applicant. This is designed to eliminate technical and unmeritorious challenges. It is also a new requirement in English arbitration law. Fourthly, the irregularity must fall within the closed list of categories set out in paragraphs (a) to (i).
>
> **29** It will be observed that the list of irregularities under section 68 may be divided into those which affect the arbitral procedure, and those which affect the award. But nowhere in section 68 is there any hint that a failure by the tribunal to arrive at the "correct decision" could afford a ground for challenge under section 68. On the other hand, section 68 has a meaningful role to play...

***Paragraph numbers marked with a "+" can be found online and on CD.***

**31** By its very terms section 68(2)(b) assumes that the tribunal acted within its substantive jurisdiction. It is aimed at the tribunal *exceeding its powers* under the arbitration agreement, terms of reference or the 1996 Act. Section 68(2)(b) does not permit a challenge on the ground that the tribunal arrived at a wrong conclusion as a matter of law or fact. It is not apt to cover a mere error of law. The view is reinforced if one takes into account that a mistake in interpreting the contract is the paradigm of a "question of law" which may in the circumstances specified in section 69 be appealed unless the parties have excluded that right by agreement. In cases where the right of appeal has by agreement, sanctioned by the Act, has been excluded, it would be curious to allow a challenge under section 68(2)(b) to be based on a mistaken interpretation of the underlying contract. Moreover, it would be strange where there is no exclusion agreement, to allow parallel challenges under section 68(2)(b) and section 69.

**32** In order to decide whether section 68(2)(b) is engaged it will be necessary to focus intensely on the particular power under an arbitration agreement, the terms of reference, or the 1996 Act which is involved, judged in all the circumstances of the case. In making this general observation it must always be borne in mind that the erroneous exercise of an available power cannot by itself amount to an excess of power. A mere error of law will not amount to an excess of power under section 68(2)(b)."

See also *Profilati Italia SRL v Painewebber Inc* [2001] 1 Lloyd's Rep. 715 (a case of innocent failure to disclosure) the court held that even where a successful party was said to have procured the award in a way which was contrary to public policy it would normally be necessary to satisfy the court that some form of reprehensible or unconscionable conduct on his part had contributed in a substantial way to obtaining an award in his favour; and the court should not be quick to interfere under s.68. Applied in *The Mariana* [2005] EWHC 219 (Comm); [2005] 1 Lloyd's Rep. 640.

See also *Cuflet Chartering v Carousel Shipping Co Ltd (The "Marie H")* [2001] 1 Lloyd's Rep. 707 (conduct alleged to have induced other party into believing that steps to obtaining an award would not be taken while negotiations were current), held that nothing short of unconscionable conduct (of which there had to be cogent evidence) would justify setting aside the award. Inadvertent conduct, however careless, would would not suffice.

In *Hussmann (Europe) Ltd v Al Ameen Development & Trade Co* (see above) it was also held that a meeting between the tribunal and an expert witness in the absence of the parties and without their knowledge, which was subsequently brought to the attention of the parties during oral examination of the expert with opportunity to cross-examine him, did not constitute a serious irregularity within the section.

The removal of one of three arbitrators for apparent bias did not, without more, result in a requirement that the remaining two should recuse themselves. *ASM Shipping Ltd v Harris* [2007] EWHC 1513 (Comm); *The Times* August 6, 2007.

A failure to address central issue by GAFA constituted a serious irregularity within s.68(2)(d), see *Ascot Commodities NV v Olam International Ltd* [2002] C.L.C 277.

For the interplay of s.73 (loss of right to object) of the 1996 Act upon s.68 see *Moshin v The Commonwealth Secretariat* [2002] EWHC 377 (Comm), March 1, 2002.

The court has a discretion to allow an arbitrator's confidential reasons to be adduced in evidence despite any agreement to treat the same as confidential. Indeed in the light of the issues raised by s.68 the court would allow confidential reasons to be adduced unless it was unnecessary to do so, or the allegations made were clearly groundless or there was some other exceptional reason not to do so, *Tame Shipping Ltd v Easy Navigation Ltd* [2004] EWHC 1862 (Comm); [2004] 2 All E.R. (Comm) 521; [2004] 2 Lloyd's Rep. 626, para.27.

For the extent to which and the circumstances in which an arbitrator may rely upon his own experience/knowledge without breaching his obligation under s.33 or so as to commit a serious irregularity under s.68 of the 1996 Act, see *Checkpoint Ltd v Strathclyde Pension Fund* [2003] EWCA Civ 84; [2003] UKPC D1, citing *Fox v P.G. Wellfair Ltd* [1981] 2 Lloyd's Rep 514, CA.

The following pre-1996 Act cases may still provide examples of irregularity:

(1) If the arbitrator, without proper notice to both parties, gave audience to one of the parties in the absence of the other, that is a good reason for setting aside the award (*Re Gregson and Armstrong Arbn.* (1894) 70 L.T. 106; and see *The Warwick* (1890)

***Paragraph numbers marked with a "+" can be found online and on CD.***

15 PD 189). Where the arbitrator heard the evidence of each party in the absence of the other, the award was set aside, although the party moving to set the award aside had made no objection at the time (*Ramsden & Co Ltd v Jacobs* [1922] 1 K.B. 640) but where a charterparty contained a clause that in the event of a dispute arising it should be referred to arbitration, each party to nominate an arbitrator who was to be a commercial man, and that if the arbitrators differed they should appoint an umpire, and where the umpire so appointed made his award after hearing the arbitrators, but without giving notice to or hearing the parties, it was held that, in view of the practice in commercial arbitrations, the award must stand (*French Government v Owners of S.S. Tsurushima Maru* (1921) 37 T.L.R. 961, CA).

(2) If the arbitrator wrongly rejects relevant evidence, his award will be set aside (*Trayfoot v Lock* [1957] 1 All E.R. 423). It is a settled principle that arbitrators must not take evidence in secret and therefore where an arbitrator who is an expert having special knowledge of the particular subject-matter is minded to use his special knowledge to form a different view of the facts from that given in evidence by expert witnesses called by the parties he should not do so without giving them an opportunity of dealing with it, and especially so where one party only appears before him (*Fisher v P.G. Wellfair Ltd* [1981] Com.L.R. 140; [1981] 2 Lloyd's Rep. 514, CA).

An arbitrator should use his special expertise to evaluate evidence, not to supply it. Furthermore he should not receive evidence in the absence of one of the parties or use any particular factual knowledge acquired by him in other proceedings (*Top Shop Estates Ltd v Danino* (1985) 273 E.G. 197).



**Jurisdiction of arbitrator on remission**

Where an award was remitted under s.22 of the Arbitration Act 1950 the arbitrator's jurisdiction was held to be limited to consideration of matters previously raised, together with any additional matters specified by the court in its order; he was not empowered to consider other issues (*Interbulk Ltd v Aiden Shipping Co Ltd*; *The Vimiera (No.3)* [1986] 2 Lloyd's Rep. 75). **2E–263**

## Appeal on point of law

**69.**—(1) Unless otherwise agreed by the parties, a party to arbitral proceedings may (upon notice to the other parties and to the tribunal) appeal to the court on a question of law arising out of an award made in the proceedings. An agreement to dispense with reasons for the tribunal's award shall be considered an agreement to exclude the court's jurisdiction under this section. **2E–264**

(2) An appeal shall not be brought under this section except—

(a) with the agreement of all the other parties to the proceedings, or

(b) with the leave of the court.

The right to appeal is also subject to the restrictions in section 70(2) and (3).

(3) Leave to appeal shall be given only if the court is satisfied—

(a) that the determination of the question will substantially affect the rights of one or more of the parties,

(b) that the question is one which the tribunal was asked to determine,

(c) that, on the basis of the findings of fact in the award—

(i) the decision of the tribunal on the question is obviously wrong, or

(ii) the question is one of general public importance and the decision of the tribunal is at least open to serious doubt, and

*Paragraph numbers marked with a "+" can be found online and on CD.*

(d) that, despite the agreement of the parties to resolve the matter by arbitration, it is just and proper in all the circumstances for the court to determine the question.

(4) An application for leave to appeal under this section shall identify the question of law to be determined and state the grounds on which it is alleged that leave to appeal should be granted.

(5) The court shall determine an application for leave to appeal under this section without a hearing unless it appears to the court that a hearing is required.

(6) The leave of the court is required for any appeal from a decision of the court under this section to grant or refuse leave to appeal.

(7) On an appeal under this section the court may by order—

(a) confirm the award,

(b) vary the award,

(c) remit the award to the tribunal, in whole or in part, for reconsideration in the light of the court's determination, or

(d) set aside the award in whole or in part.

The court shall not exercise its power to set aside an award, in whole or in part, unless it is satisfied that it would be inappropriate to remit the matters in question to the tribunal for reconsideration.

(8) The decision of the court on an appeal under this section shall be treated as a judgment of the court for the purposes of a further appeal.

But no such appeal lies without the leave of the court which shall not be given unless the court considers that the question is one of general importance or is one which for some other special reason should be considered by the Court of Appeal.

2E–265 *Note* —Compare ss.1 and 3 of the 1979 Act.

**Appeal to the High Court**

2E–266 The rules in Pt 62, s.II apply to appeals to the court under this section. Express provisions relating to applications for permission to appeal are found in Practice Direction—Arbitration para.12 (see para.2E–50 above).

The purpose and function of the restrictions on appeals on points of law imposed by s.69 and related provisions were examined in *Royal and Sun Alliance Insurance Plc v BAE Systems (Operations) Ltd* [2008] EWHC 743 (Comm); [2008] 1 Lloyd's Rep. 712 (Walker J.). In that case it was noted (at para.11) that, in relation to appeals under s.69, by s.4(2) of the 1996 Act parties are permitted to make their own arrangements by agreement with particular provisions of that section (including that requiring leave to appeal) and s.70 applying only in the absence of such agreement.

If no question of English law arises, there is no power in the English court to grant leave to appeal under s.69(1) interpolating the wording of s.82 of the Act, see *Reliance Industries Ltd v Enron Oil & Gas India Ltd* [2002] 1 Lloyd's Rep. 645 (arbitrators applying Indian law in construing the contract). Case also emphasised importance under s.69 to establish that, despite the agreement of the parties to resolve the matter by arbitration, it is just and proper in all the circumstances for the court to determine the question.

A judge should give sufficient reason for his decision so as to enable a party to understand why he had won or lost. What is sufficient will depend upon the issues involved in a particular case. The *Antaios* [1985] A.C. 191 guidance no longer holds good, see *North Range Shipping Ltd v Seatrans Shipping Corp (The Western Triumph)* [2002] EWCA Civ 405; [2002] 1 W.L.R. 2397; [2002] 4 All E.R. 390; [2002] 2 Lloyd's Rep. 1. The court said:

"Section 69(3) contains a variety of threshold tests. At the very least we think an unsuccessful applicant for leave should be told which of those tests he has failed ... But does the judge need to go further and explain in every case why the relevant threshold test has been failed? We think the answer to this question is "No". If the question is not one of law, does not substantially affect the rights of one or more of the parties or is not one which the tribunal was asked to determine, an adequate reason for the judge's decision will in almost all cases have been given simply by identifying the test or tests which the applicant has failed without the need to say more. The same applies we think to the question of general public importance. However, when one gets to whether the tribunal's decision was obviously wrong or not open to serious doubt, we do not think that it is possible to give an unqualified answer to the question we have posed. It may be enough simply to refer to the statutory test, but we do not think it is possible to say that this will always be so. It would be enough to say "For the reasons given by the arbitrators" if that was the judge's reason. Otherwise it may be necessary to go further. But any further reasons need only be brief so as to show the losing party why he has lost. Such reasons will of course be given against a background of a full hearing, a reasoned award and detailed submissions as to why leave to appeal should be granted. In other words, the judge's brief reasons are directed to a fully informed applicant."

See too the penumltimate and last paragraph of 2E–268 below.

In *The Agios Dimitrios* [2004] EWHC 2232 (Comm); [2005] 1 Lloyd's Rep. 23 the court at paras 5, 6 and 7 stated:

"5. The philosophy and purpose underlying the s.69 procedure requires the achievement of finality of awards consistently with the on-going judicial development of English commercial law. The s.69(3) tests are designed to reflect this philosophy and purpose. Section 69(3)(c) therefore distinguishes between cases where the material question of law is one of general public interest and cases where it is not. A different threshold test is to be applied in the former case (the serious doubt test) from the latter (the obviously wrong test), but in both cases the test is to be applied to the question of law strictly 'on the basis of the findings of facts in the award'. In other words the Court takes the findings of fact as an immutable basis for testing the correctness of the arbitrators' decision on the question of law unless the Court takes the view that the award does not contain reasons or 'does not set out the tribunal's reasons in sufficient detail to enable the Court properly to consider the application or appeal', in which case it can order the arbitrators to give reasons in sufficient detail under s.70(3).

6. The Court's function under s.69 is thus to look exclusively at the award for the purpose of ascertaining whether the threshold tests under s.69(3) have been satisfied. Above all, it does not go behind what appears on the face of the award and it is not concerned with the circumstances in which the award came to be made and in particular with whether those circumstances were such as to amount to serious irregularity which has caused or will cause substantial injustice to either of the parties. The Act provides, by s.68, an entirely self-contained procedural regime for dealing with such circumstances.

7. Consequently, the combination in one hearing of applications under both sections involves two quite distinct processes of judicial analysis. In many cases determination of the s.69 application for leave to appeal before that of the s.68 application may be logically preferable. This is because the determination by the Court of the question whether there has obviously been an error of law on such facts as have been found or whether there is serious doubt as to that, will often have a direct bearing on the question whether if there has been the serious irregularity complained of for the purposes of the s.68 application such irregularity has given rise to substantial injustice. In each case, however, it is a matter for the Court whether the application for leave to appeal should be tried first. There may be cases where the procedural irregularity complained of is of such a kind that it would be logically preferable for the s.68 application to be determined first so that, if it succeeds, the award can be set aside or remitted to the arbitrators before leave to appeal is considered. After all, following remission, the issue of law in question might not eventually arise."

It is not contrary to art.6 of the European Convention on Human Rights by agreement to restrict or exclude the supervisory regime of s.69; see *Sukuman Ltd v Commonwealth Secretariat* [2006] EWHC 304 (Comm); [2006] Lloyd's Rep. 53.

The words "final and binding" did not of themselves amount to an exclusion of the right to appeal but may together with other factors amount thereto; *Essex CC v Premier Recycling Ltd* [2007] B.L.R. 233, QBD (TCC).

Amongst other things, para.12 of Practice Direction—Arbitration (see para.2E–50 above) provides that the written evidence filed by a respondent to an application for permission to appeal under s.69 must specify whether that party wishes to contend that the award should be upheld for reasons not expressed in the award. In these circumstances, the grounds upon which the respondent relies (and as to which, inevitably, the court must come to its own conclusions) must be based on a point of law or points of law (*CTI Group Inc v Transclear SA (The "Mary Nour") (No.2)* [2008] EWHC 2340 (Comm); [2008] 1 Lloyd's Rep. 250 (Field J.)).

**Question of general public importance**

**2E–267** The requirement that the decision of the arbitrators is at least open to serious doubt is broader than that propounded by Lord Diplock in *"The Nema"* [1982] A.C. 724 (at p.743D) that there was a strong prima facie case that the arbitrator's decision was wrong, see *CMA CGM SA v Beteiligungs-Kommanditgesellscaft MS "Northern Pioneer" Schiffahrtgesellschaft MBH* [2002] EWCA Civ 1878; [2003] 1 W.L.R. 1015; [2003] 1 Lloyd's Rep 212; [2003] 3 All E.R. 330; [2003] 1 All E.R. (Comm) 204, CA.

**Appeals to the Court of Appeal**

**2E–268** In furtherance of the policy of injecting speed and finality in relation to arbitration awards, the Act re-enacts the far-reaching limitations on the right of appeal from decisions or orders of the High Court to the Court of Appeal.

Thus, it is provided that no appeal shall be to the Court of Appeal from a decision of the High Court on an appeal against an arbitration award under s.69 of the Act or from a decision determining a preliminary question of law (s.45) unless two conditions are satisfied, namely,

(a) the High Court or the Court of Appeal gives permission, and

(b) it is considered by the High Court that the question of law to which its decision relates, is either one of general public importance or is one which for some other special reason should be considered by the Court of Appeal under ss.69(8) and 45(6) of the Act,

Restrictions on the right of appeal to the Court of Appeal are contained in the Senior Courts Act 1981 s.18.

The mere fact that a High Court judge reaches a different conclusion from that of arbitrators he considers very experienced does not constitute a "special reason" justifying the granting of permission to appeal to the Court of Appeal (*Pera Shipping Corp v Petroship SA*, [1985] 2 Lloyd's Rep. 103, CA).

In *Henry Boot Construction (UK) Ltd v Malmaison Hotel (Manchester) Ltd* [2000] 2 Lloyd's Rep. 625 [2001] Q.B. 388; [2001] 1 All E.R. 257 CA, the court held (1) that on the true construction of s.69(8) of the Arbitration Act 1996 a party who wished to appeal from a decision of the High Court or a county court on appeal from an arbitration award required the permission of the High Court or the county court, as the case might be; and that the Court of Appeal had no jurisdiction either to grant permission itself or to review a refusal of the High Court or a county court to grant permission and (2) that s.55 of the Access to Justice Act 1999, which limited the right of appeal where there had already been one appeal, did not impliedly repeal s.69(8) of the Arbitration Act 1996; and that, accordingly (by a 2:1 majority), since s.55 of the Act of 1999 had no effect on s.69(8) of the Act of 1996, where the court which heard an appeal from an arbitrator gave permission to the Court of Appeal, there was no additional requirement to obtain the permission of the Court of Appeal.

In *CGU International Insurance plc v Astra Zeneca Insurance Co Ltd* [2006] EWCA Civ 1340; [2007] 1 Lloyd's Rep. 142, the court held that there was a residual discretion to permit an appeal despite the judge's refusal of leave where the refusal could be challenged on the ground of unfairness under art.6 of the European Convention on Human Rights. Courts would however not allow such power which existed to ensure that injustice was avoided to become itself an unfair instrument for subverting statute and undermining the process of arbitration. See too *ASM Shipping Ltd of India v TTMI Ltd of England* [2006] EWCA Civ 1341; [2007] 1 Lloyd's Rep. 136 (residual discretion not involved; no overarching principle in Human Rights Convention that an award tainted by apparent bias must be set aside: application of margin of appreciation in domestic court).

The exclusion of a right of appeal was not a matter of domestic law to be regarded as an onerous or unusual provision which had to be specifically drawn to the attention of the other party in order to be incorporated into the arbitration agreement nor did such exclusion infringe the other party's rights under art.6 of the ECHR: *Sumukan Ltd v The Commonwealth Secretariat* [2007] EWCA Civ 243; [2007] 3 All E.R. 342; [2007] 2 Lloyd's Rep. 87, CA.

## Challenge or appeal: supplementary provisions

**70.**—(1) The following provisions apply to an application or appeal under section 67, 68 or 69. **2E-269**

(2) An application or appeal may not be brought if the applicant or appellant has not first exhausted—

(a) any available arbitral process of appeal or review, and

(b) any available recourse under section 57 (correction of award or additional award).

(3) Any application or appeal must be brought within 28 days of the date of the award or, if there has been any arbitral process of appeal or review, of the date when the applicant or appellant was notified of the result of that process.

(4) If on an application or appeal it appears to the court that the award—

(a) does not contain the tribunal's reasons, or

(b) does not set out the tribunal's reasons in sufficient detail to enable the court properly to consider the application or appeal,

the court may order the tribunal to state the reasons for its award in sufficient detail for that purpose.

(5) Where the court makes an order under subsection (4), it may make such further order as it thinks fit with respect to any additional costs of the arbitration resulting from its order.

(6) The court may order the applicant or appellant to provide security for the costs of the application or appeal, and may direct that the application or appeal be dismissed if the order is not complied with.

The power to order security for costs shall not be exercised on the ground that the applicant or appellant is—

(a) an individual ordinarily resident outside the United Kingdom, or

(b) a corporation or association incorporated or formed under the law of a country outside the United Kingdom, or whose central management and control is exercised outside the United Kingdom.

(7) The court may order that any money payable under the award shall be brought into court or otherwise secured pending the determination of the application or appeal, and may direct that the application or appeal be dismissed if the order is not complied with.

(8) The court may grant leave to appeal subject to conditions to the same or similar effect as an order under subsection (6) or (7).

*Paragraph numbers marked with a "+" can be found online and on CD.*

This does not affect the general discretion of the court to grant leave subject to conditions.

2E–270 *Note*—Compare s.23(3) of the 1950 Act, and s.1(5) and (6) of the 1979 Act. This is a mandatory provision (see s.4).

**Time for appeal/Exhaustion of Specified Remedies s.70(2)**

2E–271 There is a 28 day time limit and the appellant must first have exhausted any available arbitral process of appeal or review or any available recourse under s.57.

This time limit may be extended, see s.80(5) below. For factors relevant to an application to extend time, see *Aoot Kalmneft v Glencore International AG* [2001] 2 All E.R. (Comm) 577.

For a case on exhaustion of any available recourse under s.57 see *Torch Offshore LLC v Cable Shipping Inc* [2004] EWHC 787 (Comm); [2004] 2 All E.R. (Comm) 365.

**Reasons for awards**

2E–272 By s.52(4) of the 1996 Act an award must contain reasons for the award unless it is an agreed award or the parties have agreed to dispense with reasons. Section 70(4) extends the power of the court to order reasons to applications under ss.67 and 68 as well as to applications under s.69. For an example of the existence of this power see *Petroships Pte Ltd v Petec Trading & Investment Corp* [2001] 2 Lloyd's Rep. 348.

**Terms**

2E–273 In granting permission to appeal, the High Court may impose such conditions as it considers reasonable (*ibid.*) as for example, that the minimum sum due to the successful party should be paid over to him or that the sum in dispute should be in some way secured, e.g. by payment into court or otherwise.

**Section 70(7)**

2E–274 In *Peterson Farms Inc v C&M Farming Ltd* [2003] EWHC 2298; [2004] 1 Lloyd's Rep. 614 the court considered factors material to the exercise of its discretion under s.70(7) holding inter alia that in most cases, it is likely that demonstration by the party against whom the jurisdictional challenge is made that the challenge is flimsy or otherwise lacks substance is likely to be regarded as a threshold requirement for the court's consideration whether in all the circumstances it is appropriate to require, as a condition of proceeding under s.67,that money payable under the award shall be brought into court or otherwise secured pending the determination of the application.

## Challenge or appeal: effect of order of court

2E–275 **71.**—(1) The following provisions have effect where the court makes an order under section 67, 68 or 69 with respect to an award.

(2) Where the award is varied, the variation has effect as part of the tribunal's award.

(3) Where the award is remitted to the tribunal, in whole or in part, for reconsideration, the tribunal shall make a fresh award in respect of the matters remitted within three months of the date of the order for remission or such longer or shorter period as the court may direct.

(4) Where the award is set aside or declared to be of no effect, in whole or in part, the court may also order that any provision that an award is a condition precedent to the bringing of legal proceedings in respect of a matter to which the arbitration agreement applies, is of no effect as regards the subject matter of the award or, as the case may be, the relevant part of the award.

2E–276 *Note*—Compare s.22(2) of the 1950 Act, and s.1(8) of the 1979 Act. This is a mandatory provision (see s.4). Section 71(4) does not apply to statutory arbitrations.

**For s.72 of the Arbitration Act 1996 (see Arrangement) plus any related commentary see paragraphs 2E–277+ to 2E–278+ on White Book on Westlaw UK or the Civil Procedure CD.**

## Loss of right to object

**73.**—(1) If a party to arbitral proceedings takes part, or continues to take part, in the proceedings without making, either forthwith or within such time as is allowed by the arbitration agreement or the tribunal or by any provision of this Part, any objection— 2E–279

(a) that the tribunal lacks substantive jurisdiction,

(b) that the proceedings have been improperly conducted,

(c) that there has been a failure to comply with the arbitration agreement or with any provision of this Part, or

(d) that there has been any other irregularity affecting the tribunal or the proceedings,

he may not raise that objection later, before the tribunal or the court, unless he shows that, at the time he took part or continued to take part in the proceedings, he did not know and could not with reasonable diligence have discovered the grounds for the objection.

(2) Where the arbitral tribunal rules that it has substantive jurisdiction and a party to arbitral proceedings who could have questioned that ruling—

(a) by any available arbitral process of appeal or review, or

(b) by challenging the award,

does not do so, or does not do so within the time allowed by the arbitration agreement or any provision of this Part, he may not object later to the tribunal's substantive jurisdiction on any ground which was the subject of that ruling.

*Note*—This is a mandatory provison (see s.4). See too *Rustal Trading Ltd v Gill & Duffus SA* [2002] 1 Lloyd's Rep. 14. 2E–280

**Examples:**

See *Rustal Trading Ltd v Gill & Duffus SA* [2000] 1 Lloyd's Rep. 14 and *Moshin v The Commonwealth Secretariat* [2002] EWHC 377 (Comm), March 1, 2002 (both cases of continuing to participate in the arbitral proceedings without objection with full knowledge and/a means of knowledge). See too *VEE Networks Ltd v Econet Wireless International Ltd* [2004] EWHC 2909; [2005] 1 All E.R. (Comm) 303; [2005] 1 Lloyd's Rep. 192. 2E–281

The words "any objection" and "that objection" mean any ground of objection and that ground of objection, see *Primetrade AG v Ythan Ltd* [2005] EWHC 2399 (Comm); [2006] 1 All E.R. 367; [2006] 1 Lloyd's Rep. 457. The ground should be looked at broadly. Case also considered the extent to which new evidence should be admitted in support of a new or different argument within an existing ground of objection. 2E–282

**For ss.74 to 78 of the Arbitration Act 1996 (see Arrangement) plus any related commentary see paragraphs 2E–283+ to 2E–289+ on White Book on Westlaw UK or the Civil Procedure CD.**

## Power of court to extend time limits relating to arbitral proceedings

**79.**—(1) Unless the parties otherwise agree, the court may by order extend any time limit agreed by them in relation to any matter relating to the arbitral proceedings or specified in any provision of 2E–290 this Part having effect in default of such agreement. This section does not apply to a time limit to which section 12 applies (power of court to extend time for beginning arbitral proceedings, etc.).

(2) An application for an order may be made—

(a) by any party to the arbitral proceedings (upon notice to the other parties and to the tribunal), or

(b) by the arbitral tribunal (upon notice to the parties).

(3) The court shall not exercise its power to extend a time limit unless it is satisfied—

(a) that any available recourse to the tribunal, or to any arbitral or other institution or person vested by the parties with power in that regard, has first been exhausted, and

(b) that a substantial injustice would otherwise be done.

(4) The court's power under this section may be exercised whether or not the time has already expired.

(5) An order under this section may be made on such terms as the court thinks fit.

(6) The leave of the court is required for any appeal from a decision of the court under this section.

**For ss.80 to 81 of the Arbitration Act 1996 (see Arrangement) plus any related commentary see paragraphs 2E–291+ to 2E–293+ on White Book on Westlaw UK or the Civil Procedure CD.**

## Minor definitions

2E–294 82.—(1) In this Part—

"arbitrator", unless the context otherwise requires, includes an umpire;

"available arbitral process", in relation to any matter, includes any process of appeal to or review by an arbitral or other institution or person vested by the parties with powers in relation to that matter;

"claimant", unless the context otherwise requires, includes a counterclaimant, and related expressions shall be construed accordingly;

"dispute" includes any difference;

"enactment" includes an enactment contained in Northern Ireland legislation;

"legal proceedings" means civil proceedings in the High Court or a county court;

"peremptory order" means an order made under section 41(5) or made in exercise of any corresponding power conferred by the parties;

"premises" includes land, buildings, moveable structures, vehicles, vessels, aircraft and hovercraft;

"question of law" means—

(a) for a court in England and Wales, a question of the law of England and Wales, and

*Paragraph numbers marked with a "+" can be found online and on CD.*

(b) for a court in Northern Ireland, a question of the law of Northern Ireland;

"substantive jurisdiction", in relation to an arbitral tribunal, refers to the matters specified in section 30(1)(a) to (c), and references to the tribunal exceeding its substantive jurisdiction shall be construed accordingly.

(2) References in this Part to a party to an arbitration agreement include any person claiming under or through a party to the agreement.

**For ss.83 to 98 of the Arbitration Act 1996 (see Arrangement) plus any related commentary see paragraphs 2E–295+ to 2E–343+ on White Book on Westlaw UK or the Civil Procedure CD.**



# PART III

# RECOGNITION AND ENFORCEMENT OF CERTAIN FOREIGN AWARDS

## *ENFORCEMENT OF GENEVA CONVENTION AWARDS*

### Continuation of Part II of the Arbitration Act 1950

**99.** Part II of the [1950 c. 27.] Arbitration Act 1950 (enforcement of certain foreign awards) continues to apply in relation to foreign awards within the meaning of that Part which are not also New York Convention awards. **2E–344**

*Note*—Compare ss.35 to 42 of the 1950 Act, and s.2 of the 1975 Act. **2E–345**

**Geneva Convention Countries**

Section 99 does not apply to countries which are also New York Convention States and the list below should be checked against the list at para.2E–350, below. **2E–346**

*List of Territories to which the Geneva Convention applies:*

The United Kingdom of Great Britain and Northern Ireland

| | |
|---|---|
| Anguilla | India |
| British Virgin Islands | Republic of Ireland |
| Cayman Islands | Israel |
| Falkland Islands | Italy |
| Falkland Islands Dependencies | Japan |
| Gibraltar | Kenya |
| Montserrat | Luxembourg |
| Turks and Caicos Islands | Malta |
| Antigua and Barbuda | Mauritius |
| Austria | Netherlands (including Curacao) |
| Bahamas | New Zealand |
| Bangladesh | Pakistan |
| Belgium | Portugal |
| Belize | Romania |
| †Czechoslovakia | Saint Christopher and Nevis |

| | |
|---|---|
| Denmark | St. Lucia |
| Dominica | Spain |
| Finland | Sweden |
| Federal Republic of Germany | Switzerland |
| France | Tanzania |
| *German Democratic Republic | Thailand |
| Greece | Western Samoa |
| Grenada | †Yugoslavia |
| Guyana | Zambia |

*The German Democratic Republic is now part of the Federal Republic of Germany.

† For the position of the former constituent states of Yugoslavia and of Czechoslovakia under this convention see *http://untreaty.un.org* but in any event such position is overshadowed where a state has acceded to the New York Convention (see below).

### *RECOGNITION AND ENFORCEMENT OF NEW YORK CONVENTION AWARDS*

## New York Convention awards

2E–347 **100.**—(1) In this Part a "New York Convention award" means an award made, in pursuance of an arbitration agreement, in the territory of a state (other than the United Kingdom) which is a party to the New York Convention.

(2) For the purposes of subsection (1) and of the provisions of this Part relating to such awards—

(a) "arbitration agreement" means an arbitration agreement in writing, and

(b) an award shall be treated as made at the seat of the arbitration, regardless of where it was signed, despatched or delivered to any of the parties.

In this subsection "agreement in writing" and "seat of the arbitration" have the same meaning as in Part I.

(3) If Her Majesty by Order in Council declares that a state specified in the Order is a party to the New York Convention, or is a party in respect of any territory so specified, the Order shall, while in force, be conclusive evidence of that fact.

(4) In this section "the New York Convention" means the Convention on the Recognition and Enforcement of Foreign Arbitral Awards adopted by the United Nations Conference on International Commercial Arbitration on 10th June 1958.

2E–348 *Note* —Compare s.7 of the 1975 Act.

#### New York Convention States

2E–349 The following states have been specified by Order in Council (as amended from time to time by the Arbitration (Foreign Awards) (Orders) as being parties to the New York Convention, namely:

| | |
|---|---|
| Algeria | Indonesia |
| Antigua and Barbuda | Republic of Ireland |
| Argentina | Israel |

***Paragraph numbers marked with a "+" can be found online and on CD.***

Australia (including all the external territories for the international relations of which Australia is responsible)
Austria
Bahrain
Belgium
Belize
Benin
Botswana
Bulgaria
Burkina Faso
Byelorussian Soviet Socialist Republic
Cambodia
Cameroon
Canada
Central African Republic
Chile
China
Colombia
Costa Rica
Cuba
Cyprus
Czechoslovakia‡
Denmark (including Greenland and the Faroe Islands)
Djibouti
Dominica
Ecuador
Egypt
Finland
France (including all the territories of the French Republic)
Federal Republic of Germany
German Democratic Republic*
Ghana
Greece
Guatemala
Haiti
Holy See
Hungary
India

Italy
Japan
Jordan
Kenya
Korea
Kuwait
Luxembourg
Madagascar
Malaysia
Mexico
Monaco
Morocco
Netherlands (including the Netherlands Antilles)
New Zealand
Niger
Nigeria
Norway
Panama
Peru
Philippines
Poland
Romania
San Marino
Singapore
South Africa
Spain
Sri Lanka
Sweden
Switzerland
Syria
Tanzania
Thailand
Trinidad and Tobago
Tunisia
Ukrainian Soviet Socialist Republic**
Uruguay

† The Union of Soviet Socialist Republics is now dissolved. In many respects the Russian Federation has succeeded to its international obligations but the precise position is uncertain. For the position of the countries which previously formed part of the Union of Soviet Socialist Republics but are not within the Russian Federation see the websites referred to under 2E–346 above.

United States of America (including all the territories for the international relations of which the United States of America is responsible)

***Paragraph numbers marked with a "+" can be found online and on CD.***

‡ For the signatory position of the former constituent states of Yugoslavia and Czechoslovakia consult the websites referred to under 2E–346 above.

*The German Democratic Republic is now part of the Federal Republic of Germany.

** The Ukrainian Soviet Socialist Republic is now the Ukraine.

2E–350 *Note* —The list at para.2E–349, above, identifies those signatories to the New York Convention in respect of whom an Order in Council envisaged under subs.(3) has been made. Not all signatories to the Convention are the subject of such an Order in Council. For a complete list of signatories recourse should be had to the website of the International Chamber of Commerce—Arbitration, or the website of the United Nations Commission on International Trade Law.

## Recognition and enforcement of awards

2E–351 **101.**—(1) A New York Convention award shall be recognised as binding on the persons as between whom it was made, and may accordingly be relied on by those persons by way of defence, set-off or otherwise in any legal proceedings in England and Wales or Northern Ireland.

(2) A New York Convention award may, by leave of the court, be enforced in the same manner as a judgment or order of the court to the same effect.

As to the meaning of "the court" see section 105.

(3) Where leave is so given, judgment may be entered in terms of the award.

2E–352 *Note* —Compare s.3 of the 1975 Act.

#### "... be enforced ...as a judgment" s.101(2)

2E–353 A foreign state which has agreed in writing to submit a dispute to arbitration cannot claim state immunity in respect of English proceedings to enforce the award: *Svenska Petroleum Exploration AB v Government of the Republic of Lithuania (No.2)* [2006] EWCA Civ 1529; [2007] Q.B. 886; [2007] 1 Lloyd's Rep. 193 applying s.9(1) of the State Immunity Act 1978.

Interest under the Judgments Act 1838 as amended is payable from the date of entry of the judgment even where interest was not ordered in the arbitral award. See *Gater Assets Ltd v NAK Naftogaz Ukrainiy* [2008] EWHC 1108 (Comm); [2008] 2 Lloyd's Rep. 295 (Beatson J.).

There is no objection in principle to enforcement of part only of an award, provided the part to be enforced could be ascertained from the face of the award and judgment could be given in the same terms as those in the award (*IPCO (Nigeria) Ltd v Nigerian National Petroleum Corp* [2008] EWCA Civ 1157; *The Times* November 11, 2008, CA.

#### Security for costs

2E–354 For opposing views as to whether there is or there is not jurisdiction to order security for costs in respect of an application to enforce the New York Convention award under this section, see *Gater Assets Ltd v NAK Naftogaz Ukrainiy* [2007] EWCA Civ 988; [2007] 2 Lloyd's Rep. 588, CA.

## Evidence to be produced by party seeking recognition or enforcement

2E–355 **102.**—(1) A party seeking the recognition or enforcement of a New York Convention award must produce—

(a) the duly authenticated original award or a duly certified copy of it, and

***Paragraph numbers marked with a "+" can be found online and on CD.***

(b) the original arbitration agreement or a duly certified copy of it.

(2) If the award or agreement is in a foreign language, the party must also produce a translation of it certified by an official or sworn translator or by a diplomatic or consular agent.

*Note* —Compare s.4 of the 1975 Act. 2E–356

## Refusal of recognition or enforcement

**103.**—(1) Recognition or enforcement of a New York Convention award shall not be refused except in the following cases. 2E–357

(2) Recognition or enforcement of the award may be refused if the person against whom it is invoked proves—

(a) that a party to the arbitration agreement was (under the law applicable to him) under some incapacity;

(b) that the arbitration agreement was not valid under the law to which the parties subjected it or, failing any indication thereon, under the law of the country where the award was made;

(c) that he was not given proper notice of the appointment of the arbitrator or of the arbitration proceedings or was otherwise unable to present his case;

(d) that the award deals with a difference not contemplated by or not falling within the terms of the submission to arbitration or contains decisions on matters beyond the scope of the submission to arbitration (but see subsection (4);

(e) that the composition of the arbitral tribunal or the arbitral procedure was not in accordance with the agreement of the parties or, failing such agreement, with the law of the country in which the arbitration took place;

(f) that the award has not yet become binding on the parties, or has been set aside or suspended by a competent authority of the country in which, or under the law of which, it was made.

(3) Recognition or enforcement of the award may also be refused if the award is in respect of a matter which is not capable of settlement by arbitration, or if it would be contrary to public policy to recognise or enforce the award.

(4) An award which contains decisions on matters not submitted to arbitration may be recognised or enforced to the extent that it contains decisions on matters submitted to arbitration which can be separated from those on matters not so submitted.

(5) Where an application for the setting aside or suspension of the award has been made to such a competent authority as is mentioned in subsection (2)(f), the court before which the award is sought to be relied upon may, if it considers it proper, adjourn the decision on the recognition or enforcement of the award.

It may also on the application of the party claiming recognition or enforcement of the award order the other party to give suitable security.

2E–358 *Note*—Compare s.5 of the 1975 Act.

**Enforcing court and curial court the same**

2E–359 Where the enforcing court and the court of the country whose law governs the award (the curial court) are the same, and application is made to that court to set aside or suspend a Convention award, that court may exercise both the curial court's power to set aside or suspend the award and, at the same time, the enforcing court's discretion to permit the pending supervisory process to continue and to refuse enforcement of the award if that process will result in the award being set aside or suspended by itself as the curial court, since, where the application is made to itself, as the curial court, to set aside or suspend the award it has as the enforcing court power under s.5(2) (now s.103(2)) to refuse enforcement of or reliance on the award and power under s.5(5) (now s.103(5)) to adjourn the proceedings, notwithstanding that the only proceedings consist of the application to itself as the curial court to set aside the award in which necessarily the award upon by the party seeking to have it set aside (*Hiscox v Outhwaite (No.1)* [1991] 3 All E.R. 641, HL).

In *Minmetals Germany GmbH v Ferco Steel Ltd* [1999] 1 All E.R. (Comm) 315; *The Times*, March 1, 1999 it was held that by agreeing the place of a foreign arbitration, a party not only agreed to submit all contractual disputes to arbitration but also agreed that the conduct of the arbitration should be subject to the supervisory jurisdiction of the courts of that place. Further the court stated that in a case where a party against whom enforcement was sought alleged that a New York Convention award should not be enforced on the ground that such enforcement would lead to substantial injustice and therefore be contrary to English public policy the following must normally be included among the relevant considerations:

1. The nature of the procedural injustice.
2. Whether that party had invoked the supervisory jurisdiction of the seat of the arbitration.
3. Whether a remedy was available under that jurisdiction.
4. Whether the courts of that jurisdiction had conclusively determined the enforcee's complaint in favour of upholding the award.
5. If that party had failed to invoke that remedial jurisdiction, what reason had he and, in particular, whether he was acting unreasonably in failing to do so.

**Grounds of refusal**

2E–360 In *Roseel NV v Oriental Commercial & Shipping Co (UK) Ltd* [1991] 2 Lloyd's Rep. 625, held that an agreement in parallel New York legal proceedings prior to award that any proceedings to confirm or vacate arbitration will be brought in New York did not constitute a ground within s.5(2)(f) of the Arbitration Act 1975 (now s.103(2)(f)) to refuse enforcement nor was it a precondition to enforcement that there should be assets within the jurisdiction.

In *Omnium de Traitement et de Valorisation SA v Hilmarton Ltd* [1999] 2 Lloyd's Rep. 222 (ICC arbitration where proper law of contract was Swiss law and curial seat of arbitration was the Canton of Geneva in a matter involving a business practice unlawful under Algerian law but involving no bribery or corruption and lawful under Swiss law) the court said that it was not adjudicating upon the underlying contract but deciding whether or not an arbitration award should be enforced in England and that in such context it seemed:

> "that (absent a finding of fact of corrupt practices which would give rise to obvious public policy considerations) the fact that English law would or might have arrived at a different result is nothing to the point. Indeed the reason for the different result is that Swiss law is different from English law, and the parties chose Swiss law and Swiss arbitration. If anything, this consideration dictates (as a matter of policy of the upholding of international arbitral awards) that the award should be enforced."

In *Kanoria v Guinness* [2006] EWCA Civ 222; [2006] 1 Lloyd's Rep. 701 the Court of Appeal upheld the refusal of enforcement where the enforcee had been unable to

***Paragraph numbers marked with a "+" can be found online and on CD.***

present his case because he had never been notified of the case made against him, approving the statement of Colman J. in the Minmetals case referred to at 2E–359 above at p.326 thereof that

> "the inability to present a case to arbitrators within s.103(2)(c) contemplates at least that the enforcee has been prevented from presenting his case by matters outside his control. This will normally cover the case where the procedure adopted has been operated in a manner contrary to the rules of natural justice."

**Subsection (5)**

On an application to adjourn an application for leave to enforce a foreign arbitration award because of a legal challenge to the validity of the award in a foreign jurisdiction, the court should consider the strength or otherwise of the argument for setting aside the award and the ease or difficulty of enforcing the award if an order for security was not made, together with any other relevant considerations (*Soleh Boneh International Ltd v Government of the Republic of Uganda* [1993] 2 Lloyd's Rep. 208). **2E–361**

## Saving for other bases of recognition or enforcement

**104.** Nothing in the preceding provisions of this Part affects any right to rely upon or enforce a New York Convention award at common law or under section 66. **2E–362**

*Note*—Compare s.6 of the 1975 Act. **2E–363**

# PART IV

# GENERAL PROVISIONS

## Meaning of "the court": jurisdiction of High Court and county court

**105.**—(1) In this Act "the court" means the High Court or a county court, subject to the following provisions. **2E–364**

(2) The Lord Chancellor may by order make provision—

(a) allocating proceedings under this Act to the High Court or to county courts; or

(b) specifying proceedings under this Act which may be commenced or taken only in the High Court or in a county court.

(3) The Lord Chancellor may by order make provision requiring proceedings of any specified description under this Act in relation to which a county court has jurisdiction to be commenced or taken in one or more specified county courts.

Any jurisdiction so exercisable by a specified county court is exercisable throughout England and Wales or, as the case may be, Northern Ireland.

[(3A) The Lord Chancellor must consult the Lord Chief Justice of England and Wales or the Lord Chief Justice of Northern Ireland (as the case may be) before making an order under this section.

(3B) The Lord Chief Justice of England and Wales may nominate a judicial office holder (as defined in section 109(4) of the Constitutional Reform Act 2005) to exercise his functions under this section.

(3C) The Lord Chief Justice of Northern Ireland may nominate any of the following to exercise his functions under this section–

***Paragraph numbers marked with a "+" can be found online and on CD.***

(a) the holder of one of the offices listed in Schedule 1 to the Justice (Northern Ireland) Act 2002;

(b) a Lord Justice of Appeal (as defined in section 88 of that Act).]

(4) An order under this section—

(a) may differentiate between categories of proceedings by reference to such criteria as the Lord Chancellor sees fit to specify, and

(b) may make such incidental or transitional provision as the Lord Chancellor considers necessary or expedient.

(5) An order under this section for England and Wales shall be made by statutory instrument which shall be subject to annulment in pursuance of a resolution of either House of Parliament.

(6) An order under this section for Northern Ireland shall be a statutory rule for the purposes of the [S.I. 1979/1573 (N.I. 12).] Statutory Rules (Northern Ireland) Order 1979 which shall be subject to annulment in pursuance of a resolution of either House of Parliament in like manner as a statutory instrument and section 5 of the [1946 c. 36.] Statutory Instruments Act 1946 shall apply accordingly.

**2E–365** *Note*—Subsections (3A)–(3C) inserted by the Constitutional Reform Act 2005 s.15(1), Sch.4, Pt 1, para.250, with effect from April 3, 2006 (SI 2006/1014).

**2E–366** *Note*—The proceedings under the Act have been allocated by the High Court and County Courts (Allocation of Arbitration Proceedings) Order 1996 (SI 1996/3215) at para.2E–375. Subsections (3A)–(3C) inserted by the Constitutional Reform Act 2005 , s.15(1), Sch.4, para.250.

## Crown application

**2E–367** **106.**—(1) Part I of this Act applies to any arbitration agreement to which Her Majesty, either in right of the Crown or of the Duchy of Lancaster or otherwise, or the Duke of Cornwall, is a party.

(2) Where Her Majesty is party to an arbitration agreement otherwise than in right of the Crown, Her Majesty shall be represented for the purposes of any arbitral proceedings—

(a) where the agreement was entered into by Her Majesty in right of the Duchy of Lancaster, by the Chancellor of the Duchy or such person as he may appoint, and

(b) in any other case, by such person as Her Majesty may appoint in writing under the Royal Sign Manual.

(3) Where the Duke of Cornwall is party to an arbitration agreement, he shall be represented for the purposes of any arbitral proceedings by such person as he may appoint.

(4) References in Part I to a party or the parties to the arbitration agreement or to arbitral proceedings shall be construed, where subsection (2) or (3) applies, as references to the person representing Her Majesty or the Duke of Cornwall.

**2E–368** *Note*—Compare s.30 of the 1950 Act.

**For ss.107 to 110 of the Arbitration Act 1996 (see Arrangement) plus any related commentary see paragraphs 2E–369+ to 2E–373+ on White Book on Westlaw UK or the Civil Procedure CD.**

***Paragraph numbers marked with a "+" can be found online and on CD.***

SECTION 4(1).

## SCHEDULE 1

MANDATORY PROVISIONS OF PART I

sections 9 to 11 (stay of legal proceedings); **2E–374**
section 12 (power of court to extend agreed time limits);
section 13 (application of Limitation Acts);
section 24 (power of court to remove arbitrator);
section 26(1) (effect of death of arbitrator);
section 28 (liability of parties for fees and expenses of arbitrators);
section 29 (immunity of arbitrator);
section 31 (objection to substantive jurisdiction of tribunal);
section 32 (determination of preliminary point of jurisdiction);
section 33 (general duty of tribunal);
section 37(2) (items to be treated as expenses of arbitrators);
section 40 (general duty of parties);
section 43 (securing the attendance of witnesses);
section 56 (power to withhold award in case of non-payment);
section 60 (effectiveness of agreement for payment of costs in any event);
section 66 (enforcement of award);
sections 67 and 68 (challenging the award; substantive jurisdiction and serious irregularity), and sections 70 and 71 (supplementary provisions; effect of order of court) so far as relating to those sections;
section 72 (saving for rights of person who takes no part in proceedings);
section 73 (loss of right to object);
section 74 (immunity of arbitral institutions, etc.);
section 75 (charge to secure payment of solicitors' costs).

## High Court and County Courts (Allocation of Arbitration Proceedings) Order 1996

(S.I. 1996 No. 3215)

**1.**—(1) This Order may be cited as the High Court and County Courts (Allocation of Arbitration Proceedings) Order 1996 and shall come into force on 31st January 1997. **2E–375**

(2) In this Order, "the Act" means the Arbitration Act 1996.

**2.** Subject to articles 3 to 5, proceedings under the Act shall be commenced and taken in the High Court. **2E–376**

**3.** Proceedings under section 9 of the Act (stay of legal proceedings) shall be commenced in the court in which the legal proceedings are pending. **2E–377**

**4.** Proceedings under sections 66 and 101(2) (enforcement of awards) of the Act may be commenced in any county court. **2E–378**

**5.**—(1) Proceedings under the Act may be commenced and taken in the Central London County Court Mercantile List. **2E–379**

(2) Where, in exercise of the powers conferred by sections 41 and 42 of the County Courts Act 1984(b) the High Court or the judge in charge of the Central London County Court Mercantile List orders the transfer of proceedings under the Act which were commenced in the Central London County Court Mercantile List to the High Court, those proceedings shall be taken in the High Court.

(3) Where, in exercise of its powers under section 40(2) of the County Courts Act 1984(c) the High Court orders the transfer of



ARBITRATION

proceedings under the Act which were commenced in the High Court to the Central London County Court Mercantile List, those proceedings shall be taken in the Central London County Court Mercantile List.

(4) In exercising the powers referred to in paragraphs (2) and (3) regard shall be had to the following criteria—

(a) the financial substance of the dispute referred to arbitration, including the value of any claim or counterclaim;

(b) the nature of the dispute referred to arbitration (for example, whether it arises out of a commercial or business transaction or relates to engineering, building or other construction work);

(c) whether the proceedings are otherwise important and, in particular, whether they raise questions of importance to persons who are not parties and

(d) the balance of convenience points to having the proceedings taken in the Central London County Court Mercantile List,

and, where the financial substance of the dispute exceeds £200,000, the proceedings shall be taken in the High Court unless the proceedings do not raise questions of general importance to persons who are not parties.

(5) The value of any claim or counterclaim shall be calculated in accordance with rule 16.3(6) of the Civil Procedure Rules 1998.

(6) In this article "the Central London County Court Mercantile List" means the Mercantile Court established at the Central London County Court pursuant to Part 59 of the Civil Procedure Rules 1998.

**2E-380** **6.** Nothing in this Order shall prevent the judge in charge of the commercial list (within the meaning of section 62(3) of the Senior Courts Act 1981) from transferring proceedings under the Act to another list, court or Division of the High Court to which he has power to transfer proceedings and, where such an order is made, the proceedings may be taken in that list, court or Division as the case may be.

**2E-381** *Note*—As amended by the High Court and County Courts (Allocation of Arbitration Proceedings) (Amendment) Order 1999 (SI 1999/1010) , the Civil Procedure (Modification of Enactments) Order 2002 and the Constitutional Reform Act 2005 s.59 and Sch.11, para.1 with effect from October 1, 2009 ( SI 2009/1604 ).

Throughout the Arbitration Act 1996, references to "the court" mean the High Court or a county court, but the jurisdiction of the two levels of court is not concurrent. By this Order, by exercise of powers under s.105, "proceedings under the Act" are allocated to the High Court and the county courts and proceedings which may be commenced or taken only in the High Court or in a county court are specified. The general rule stated in art.5 is that proceedings under the Act shall be commenced and taken in the High Court. This general rule is qualified by arts 3 and 4. It should also be noted that the High Court and County Courts Jurisdiction Order 1991 art.2(1)(c) provides that the county courts (as well as the High Court) shall have jurisdiction under s.26 of the Arbitration Act 1950. See also Pt 62 Arbitration Claims, r.62.1(3) and the Practice Direction—Arbitration, para.2, which is to be read in conjunction with this Order.

Article 5 provided a further qualification to the general rule in respect of the Central London County Court Mercantile List which no longer exists, such jurisdiction now being the province of the London Mercantile Court which operates as a separate list within the Commercial Court of the Queen's Bench Division. Article 5 is best regarded as defunct save as indicating the type of criteria determining which level of court will hear the application.

# 2F INTELLECTUAL PROPERTY PROCEEDINGS

## Part 63—Intellectual Property Claims

**Contents** 2F–1



*Note* —This part was substituted by the Civil Procedure (Amendment) Rules 2009 (SI 2009/2092) with effect from October 1, 2009. **2F–1.1**

**Editorial introduction**

These rules govern the procedure for registered and unregistered intellectual property rights. This part and its supplementing Practice Direction do not provide a complete guide for intellectual property proceedings and should be read in conjunction with other Civil Procedure Rules. The application of the other Civil Procedure Rules and their practice directions is subject to the provisions of these rules and the accompanying practice direction. **2F–1.2**

Part 63 and the Practice Direction thereto have been updated. They came into effect on October 1, 2009.

***Paragraph numbers marked with a "+" can be found online and on CD.***

**Related sources**

2F–1.3 • The Patents Court Guide, available on the Court Service website along with the Patents Court Diary

**Scope of this Part and interpretation**[1]

2F–2 **63.1—(1) This Part applies to all intellectual property claims including—**

**(a) registered intellectual property rights such as—**

**(i) patents;**

**(ii) registered designs; and**

**(iii) registered trade marks; and**

**(b) unregistered intellectual property rights such as—**

**(i) copyright;**

**(ii) design right;**

**(iii) the right to prevent passing off; and**

**(iv) the other rights set out in Practice Direction 63.**

**(2) In this Part—**

**(a) "the 1977 Act" means the Patents Act 1977;**

**(b) "the 1988 Act" means the Copyright, Designs and Patents Act 1988;**

**(c) "the 1994 Act" means the Trade Marks Act 1994;**

**(d) "the Comptroller" means the Comptroller General of Patents, Designs and Trade Marks;**

**(e) "patent" means a patent under the 1977 Actor a supplementary protection certificate granted by the Patent Office under Article 10(1) of Council Regulation (EEC) No. 1768/92 or of Regulation (EC) No. 1610/96 of the European Parliament and the Council and includes any application for a patent or supplementary protection certificate;**

**(f) "Patents Court" means the Patents Court of the High Court constituted as part of the Chancery Division by section 6(1) of the Senior Courts Act 1981;**

**(g) "patents county court" means a county court designated as a patents county court under section 287(1) of the 1988 Act;**

**(h) "patents judge" means a person nominated under section 291(1) of the 1988 Act as the patents judge of a patents county court;**

**(i) [omitted]**

**(j) "the register" means whichever of the following registers is appropriate—**

**(i) patents maintained by the Comptroller under section 32 of the 1977 Act;**

**(ii) designs maintained by the registrar under section 17 of the Registered Designs Act 1949;**

---

[1] Amended by the Civil Procedure (Amendment No.2) Rules 2009 (SI 2009/3390).

*Paragraph numbers marked with a "+" can be found online and on CD.*

**(iii) trade marks maintained by the registrar under section 63 of the 1994 Act;**

**(iv) Community trade marks maintained by the Office for Harmonisation in the Internal Market under Article 83 of Council Regulation (EC) 40/94;**

**(v) Community designs maintained by the Office for Harmonisation in the Internal Market under Article 72 of Council Regulation (EC) 6/2002; and**

**(vi) plant varieties maintained by the Controller under regulation 12 of the Plant Breeders' Rights Regulations 1998; and**

**(k) "the registrar" means—**

**(i) the registrar of trade marks; or**

**(ii) the registrar of registered designs,**

**whichever is appropriate.**

**(3) Claims to which this Part applies are allocated to the multi-track.**

*Note*—Substituted by the Civil Procedure (Amendment) Rules 2009 (SI 2009/2092) with effect from October 1, 2009. **2F–2.1**

**Note**

The old r.3.2 provided that the CPR and their practice directions apply to intellectual property claims unless Pt 63 or a practice direction provides otherwise (see *SmithKline Beecham Plc v Apotex Europe Ltd (Costs) (No.2)* [2004] EWCA Civ 1703). This rule is absent from the new Pt 63, presumably because it was and is self-evidently the case. **2F–2.2**

### *I. Patents and Registered Designs*

**Scope of Section I and allocation**

**63.2—(1) This Section applies to—** **2F–3**

**(a) any claim under—**

**(i) the 1977 Act;**

**(ii) the Registered Designs Act 1949;**

**(iii) the Defence Contracts Act 1958; and**

**(b) any claim relating to—**

**(i) Community registered designs;**

**(ii) semiconductor topography rights; or**

**(iii) plant varieties.**

**(2) Claims to which this Section applies must be started in—**

**(a) the Patents Court; or**

**(b) a patents county court.**

*Note*—Substituted by the Civil Procedure (Amendment) Rules 2009 (SI 2009/2092) with effect from October 1, 2009. **2F–3.1**

**Note**

The scope of the first section of Pt 63 which previously related to claims under the Patents Act 1977, the Registered Designs Act 1949 and the Defence Contracts Act 1958 has been extended to cover claims relating to Community registered designs, **2F–3.2** semiconductor topography rights and plant varieties cases. Whilst the practice direction and the rules (and hence the notes below) tend to refer only to patents and registered designs, the principles set out are appropriate for other cases falling under the auspices of this section (for example Community registered designs).

### Specialist list

2F-4 **63.3 Claims in the Patents Court and a patents county court form specialist lists for the purpose of rule 30.5.**

2F-4.1 *Note* —Substituted by the Civil Procedure (Amendment) Rules 2009 (SI 2009/2092) with effect from October 1, 2009.

### Patents judge

2F-5 **63.4—(1) Subject to paragraph (2), proceedings in a patents county court will be dealt with by the patents judge of that court.**

**(2) When a matter needs to be dealt with urgently and it is not practicable or appropriate for the patents judge to deal with such a matter, the matter may be dealt with by another judge with appropriate specialist experience nominated by the Chancellor of the High Court.**

2F-5.1 *Note* —Substituted by the Civil Procedure (Amendment) Rules 2009 (SI 2009/2092) with effect from October 1, 2009.

#### Transfer between Divisions and to and from a specialist list

2F-5.2 Rule 30.5 provides that the High Court may order proceedings in any Division of the High Court to be transferred to another Division and order proceedings to be transferred to or from a specialist list. Applications for the transfer of proceedings must be made to a judge dealing with claims in that list. In order to ensure access to justice for parties with limited financial resources, s.289 of the Copyright, Designs and Patents Act 1988 contains special provisions concerning transfer of proceedings between the High Court and a patents county court. Actions within the special jurisdiction of a patents county court may be ordered to be transferred to such a court by the High Court either of its own motion or on the application of any party to the proceedings. In considering whether to make such an order, the High Court shall have regard to the financial position of the parties and may order transfer notwithstanding that the proceedings are likely to raise an important question of law or fact. Such actions may also be ordered to be transferred from a patents county court to the High Court by the county court either of its own motion or on the application of any party to the proceedings. The county court is required to have regard to the financial position of the parties and may refrain from ordering transfer notwithstanding that the proceedings are likely to raise an important question of law or fact.

The High Court does not have the power to order proceedings within the special jurisdiction of a patents county court to be transferred from the Patents County Court. When an action is transferred to the Patents County Court, the court will, after consultation with the parties, give any directions deemed appropriate for the purpose of bringing the pleadings and any other documents in the case and outstanding procedural steps into conformity with its own procedures.

#### Role of a Patent County Court

2F-5.3 It is the role of a Patent County Court to make litigation cheaper and more accessible in the more straightforward disputes. In *Warheit v Olympia Tools Ltd (Costs)* [2002] EWCA Civ 1516, there was further argument on costs following an appeal from a two day trial in Patents County Court in which the costs claimed were in excess of £250,000. It was held that the costs should be subject to detailed assessment, and it was made clear that these costs were far in excess of what Lord Chancellor envisaged when setting up the Patents County Court. In future, it was said, efforts should be made to keep costs in proportion with the complexity of the proceedings. See e.g. *Unilin Beheer BV v Berry Floor NV* [2004] F.S.R. 14 on the wisdom of conducting experiments in the Patents County Court. It was not appropriate to start proceedings in the Patents County Court where the subject matter of the patents was complex and the ultimate time estimate of 15 days for the trial was amply justified—*Halliburton Energy Services Inc v Smith International (North Sea) Ltd* [2005] EWHC 1623 (Pat).

In the context of recent discussions relating to the effectiveness of the Patents County Court as a more low cost forum than the Patents Court, the above guidance is of particular relevance. It is for the parties as well as the Court to try and minimise the costs of proceedings in the Patents County Court.

#### Jurisdiction of Masters and District Judges

For provisions restricting the jurisdiction of Masters or district judges to make orders in proceedings in the Patents Court, see Practice Direction 2B (Allocation of Cases to Levels of Judiciary) para.5.1(k) (Vol.1para.2BPD.5). **2F–5.4**

## Starting the claim

**63.5 Claims to which this Section applies must be started—** **2F–6**

**(a) by a Part 7 claim form; or**

**(b) in existing proceedings under Part 20.**

*Note* —Substituted by the Civil Procedure (Amendment) Rules 2009 (SI 2009/2092) with effect from October 1, 2009. **2F–6.1**

#### Note

As regards the formalities of starting the claim, see the Practice Direction para.3.1—the claim form must be marked "Chancery Division Patents Court" or "Patents County Court" as appropriate in the top right hand corner below the title of the Court and must state the number of any patent or registered design to which the claim relates. **2F–6.2**

## Claim for infringement or challenge to validity of a patent or registered design[1]

**63.6 A statement of case in a claim for infringement or a claim in which the validity of a patent or registered design is challenged must contain particulars as set out in Practice Direction 63.** **2F–7**

*Note* —Substituted by the Civil Procedure (Amendment) Rules 2009 (SI 2009/2092) with effect from October 1, 2009. **2F–7.1**

#### Statements of case—Claims for infringement

Part 63.6 provides that a statement of case in a claim for infringement must contain particulars as set out in the practice direction. The relevant paragraph of the Practice Direction is para.4.1, which stipulates that the statement of case must show which of the claims of the patent are alleged to be infringed and must give at least one example of each type of infringement alleged, and a copy of each document referred to in the claim form (with translation if necessary). **2F–7.2**

The statement of case should be full but concise. It must set out all facts, matters and arguments relied on as establishing the allegations made and justifying the relief sought. It is the duty of the claimant to plead case on liability and relief (e.g. springboard relief) in advance (*Kirin-Amgen Inc v Transkaryotic Therapies Inc (No.2)* [2002] R.P.C. 3). That case sets out the factors that should be taken into account in considering whether it is just to permit the claimant to subsequently broaden relief.

Note that where a failure to address the question of the independent validity of

[1] Amended by the Civil Procedure (Amendment No.2) Rules 2009 (SI 2009/3390).

***Paragraph numbers marked with a "+" can be found online and on CD.***

subsidiary claims purposefully at an early stage caused an unnecessary increase in the defendant's costs then that is likely to be reflected in the costs order made in due course (see *Edwards Lifesciences AG v Cook Biotech Inc (Costs)* [2009] EWHC 1443 (Pat)).

**Particulars of infringements**

2F–7.3 The onus always rests on the claimant to prove infringement (*Whatmough v Morris Motors* (1940) 57 R.P.C. 177).

The patentee need not give his construction of his patent, the function of particulars of infringements being merely to point out to the defendant what specific act on his part is complained of so as to prevent surprise at the trial (*Wenham Co Ltd v Champion Gas Lamp Co* (1891) 8 R.P.C. 22; *Marsden v Albrecht* (1910) 27 R.P.C. 785). See also *Lux Traffic Controls Ltd v Staffordshire Public Works Company Ltd* [1991] R.P.C. 73.

The particulars may rely on inference. A case in which the basis of a claim for infringement was described as "somewhat thin" was nevertheless not struck out as an abuse of process where infringement was inferred from the suggestion that use of an infringing process would be the only economically viable method of manufacture: *Crystal Fibres A/S v Fianium Ltd* [2009] EWHC 2149 (Pat).

If the particulars allege as an instance a sale to A., and the defendants admit the sale of an exactly similar article to B., this will be admissible (*Sykes v Howarth* (1879) 12 Ch D 826 at 829).

Each type of infringement alleged constitutes a separate cause of action and must be separately particularised; see *Sorata Ltd v Gardex Ltd* [1984] R.P.C. 317, CA. However, see also *Building Product Design Ltd v Sandtoft Roof Tiles Ltd* [2004] F.S.R. 40 where the order was amended by the slip rule to include concrete as well as clay tiles. Note also *Building Product Design Ltd v Sandtoft Roof Tiles Ltd (No.2)* [2004] F.S.R. 41—having failed to also include angled tiles by the slip rule, the claimant sought to bring a second action in respect of angled tiles. CPR r.63.9 requires that the statement of case in a patent action must contain particulars as set out in the PD 63 para.11, which provides that the statement of case has to show both which of the claims in the specification of the patent had been infringed and at least one example of each type of alleged infringement. A claimant should therefore plead specific facts in relation to each potential way in which a patent is alleged to have been infringed and provide examples. See *Cranway Ltd v Playtech Ltd* [2007] EWHC 182 (Pat) — the requirement that each type of infringement had to be specifically pleaded in a patent infringement action recognised the importance of economy with regard to costs as well as in relation to the court's resources, the implementation of public policy regarding the finality of litigation and practical good sense.

It is of course preferable that all relevant infringements are considered at trial—see *Vax Appliances Ltd v Hoover PLC* [1990] R.P.C. 656 at 661 (line 45) to 662 (line 12), per Mummery J. It should be noted that this applies to defendants as well as claimants. In *MMI Research Ltd v CellXion Ltd* [2009] EWHC 1938 (Pat), after the trial CellXion invited the court to consider variants of the device considered at trial. The court held that parties who wish the court to consider such variants should do at the trial of the action, particularly where they were on the market and being sold at the material time (the position is likely to be different if a new variant is developed as a result of a judgment in a particular case). It is in the interests of the efficient management of litigation that, so far as reasonably practical, all the issues between the parties are determined at a single hearing: see CPR Pt 2 para.1.2(i). If parties do not reveal alternative embodiments until after the trial, this objective is frustrated.

Nevertheless, if such variants are raised after the trial, it may be appropriate (if it is still possible) to deal with them before a final order is made. (See also *Building Product Design Ltd v Sandtoft Roof Tiles Ltd* [2004] F.S.R. 40 whereby the order was formulated to include a variant on the products considered at trial by the slip rule.) The usual form of order is an order not to infringe the patent in suit. However whether or not a variant falls within the scope of the claims is not a matter which is suitable for determination on a contempt application—see *Multiform Displays v Whitmarley Displays (formerly Reay & Davis) (No.2)* [1957] R.P.C. 260 (HL). The alternative is to consider the variants on an account of profits or enquiry as to damages. The patentee is allowed on an inquiry as to damages or account of profits to claim relief for types of alleged infringement not ruled on by the trial court. This saves the formal issuance of fresh proceedings in respect of these and is permitted as a matter of convenience: see *General Tire &*

*Rubber Co v Firestone Tyre & Rubber Co Ltd* [1975] R.P.C. 203 at 207. If, in the inquiry or account, the patentee alleges a type of infringement not considered by the trial court, the court conducting the inquiry or account will have to rule on whether it falls within the scope of the patent (see *Unilin Beheer BV v Berry Floor NV* [2007] EWCA Civ 364; [2007] Bus. L.R. 1140).

**Statements of Case—Claims for invalidity**

The notes below are of course equally apposite for claims of invalidity and for counterclaims in which invalidity is raised. **2F–7.4**

See PD paras 4.2–4.6. Where the claim is for invalidity of a patent or registered design, the statement of case must contain particulars of the remedy sought and any issues which do not relate to the validity of the patent or registered design (PD para.4.2(1)). A separate document attached to the statement of case "and forming part of it" headed "Grounds of Invalidity" (i.e. the statement of case and the Grounds are physically separate but formally considered part of the same document) must specify the grounds of challenge, and include particulars "that will clearly define every issue (including any challenge to priority) (PD para.4.2(2)). The Grounds must include a copy of each document referred to with translations if necessary.

The Grounds of Invalidity must include the matters set out in the Practice Direction para.4.3. PD para.4.4 sets out the details which must be pleaded in relation to cases of prior publication and prior use.

The separate grounds of invalidity must be stated, for, apart from granting leave to amend, the court will not consider objections not pleaded, even if they appear on the evidence. See judgment of Lord Loreburn L.C. in *Alsop Flour Process Co v Flour Oxidising Co* (1908) 25 R.P.C. 490, and CA in *British United Shoe Machinery Co* v Fussell & Co (1908) 25 R.P.C. 631. Also, upon objection, the court may refuse to allow the admission of evidence or cross-examination relating to an insufficiently particularised plea of invalidity (*British Thomson-Houston Co Ltd v Tungstalite Ltd* (1940) 57 R.P.C. 271 at 275).

If party claiming invalidity also decides to rely upon common general knowledge he should plead it distinctly (*Phillips v Ivel Cycle Co Ltd* (1890) 7 R.P.C. 77). Ordinarily such a party need not give particulars of common general knowledge. However, particulars may be ordered of those portions of the specification relied upon by the defendant alleged to be common general knowledge (*Solaflex Signs Amalgamated Ltd v Allen Manufacturing Co Ltd* (1931) 48 R.P.C. 577). They were refused in *McCreath v Mayor, etc., of South Shields* (1932) 49 R.P.C. 349, but see *British Thomson-Houston Ltd v Tungstalite Ltd* (1940) 57 R.P.C. 271, where the defendants failed to give particulars ordered.

A party claiming insufficiency must set out in the Grounds of Invalidity which examples of the invention cannot be made to work or work in the manner described and in what respects (PD para.4.3(2). In response to a plea of insufficiency a patentee cannot be made to plead a positive case as against the whole world that his specification does sufficiently and fairly describe his invention and the manner of performing it. But in appropriate cases he can be made to give, in relation to each pleaded particular of insufficiency, particulars of the passage or passages in his complete specification alleged to contain a sufficient and fair description of that part of the invention and of the method by which it is to be performed, specifying in each case what it is alleged that a man skilled in the art would do in respect of that invention (*Polaroid Corp's Patent-Insufficiency Appeal* [1977] F.S.R. 233). However in most cases it seems that it will not be appropriate to order such particulars before experiments have been carried out (*Halcon International Inc v Shell Transport & Trading Co* [1977] F.S.R. 458).

Parties bringing counterclaims for invalidity of registered Community Designs must inform OHIM as set out in the Practice Direction at para.15.

**Commercial Success**

A party wishing to meet an attack on validity by relying on commercial success must state in the statement of case the grounds on which that party relies: PD para.4.6. **2F–7.5**

A case of commercial success inherently involves a number of substantial questions, e.g. is the success due to what is claimed, or to other matters such as advertising, or good manufacture, or the later development of the details (whether further inventions or not) which make for commercial success? Whether there was a long-felt want met by the alleged invention is likewise often a question of significance. In *Raychem Corp's*

INTELLECTUAL PROPERTY

*Patents* [1998] R.P.C. 31, Laddie J. went so far as to say that a plea of commercial success normally only added time and expense to the proceedings and served no useful purpose.

The essential elements of a commercial success argument, as well as some of the difficulties of such an argument, were set out by Kitchin J. in *Generics (UK) Ltd v H. Lundbeck A/S* [2007] EWHC 1040; (Pat); [2007] R.P.C. 32:

> "The essential elements of the argument are that there has been a "long felt want", that is to say a known problem in need of a solution, that the invention has achieved striking commercial success and that the monopoly is limited to embodiments which have the qualities giving rise to the success. Then, so the argument goes, the invention cannot be obvious or it would have been made before. Although these are the essential elements of the argument they must be approached with some caution. The commercial success may be attributable to factors other than the invention, for example effective advertising, better workmanship or more attractive presentation. Or it may be that those in the field were not aware of the prior art said to render the invention obvious or were unable to exploit any developments of it. Careful consideration must be given to all the circumstances, many of which were identified by Laddie J. in *Haberman v Jackel International Ltd* [1999] F.S.R. 683."

For disclosure in relation to commercial success, see para.XXX below. The Practice Direction provides for a schedule setting out various matters as further discussed below.

Foreign commercial success may be relevant (*Unilever v Gillette (UK) Ltd* [1989] R.P.C. 417).

**Declarations of non-infringement**

**2F–7.6** A patentee is required to particularise its positive case even though the burden of proof is on the claimant seeking a declaration of non-infringement. See *Baxter Healthcare Corporation v Abbott Laboratories* [2005] EWHC 2878 (Pat).

**Action by exclusive licensee under patent**

**2F–7.7** By s.67 of the 1977 Act an exclusive licensee may take proceedings in respect of infringements committed after the date of his licence. The patentee must be either joined as claimant or added as defendant (subs.(2)), although this is a formal procedure only, and it does not follow that that party must play a full or indeed any role in the proceedings. An interim injunction may be refused if the defendants did not know of the fact that the claimants were exclusive licensees (*Christian Salvesen (Oil Services) Ltd v Odfjell Drilling and Consulting Co (UK) Ltd* [1985] R.P.C. 569).

**Parties**

**2F–7.8** For proper parties and amendments to add parties see *PLG Research Ltd v Ardon International Ltd* [1992] F.S.R. 59. An equitable owner of a patent is entitled to commence proceedings without joining the assignor provided that at a later date the legal owner is made a party to proceedings; see *Baxter International Inc v Nederlands Produktielaboratorium voor Bloedtransusiapparatuur BV* [1998] R.P.C. 250. Exclusive licensees may sue for damages, but their licence must be registered; whilst a mere record of an older licence will justify damages from the date of the older licence, registration of a modification will not (*M.M.M. v Rennicks (UK) Ltd* [1992] F.S.R. 118).

As to particulars of acts alleged to have been performed by directors of a company personally joined as defendants in an action against the company, see *British Thomson Houston Co Ltd v Irradiant LampWorks Ltd* (1924) 41 R.P.C. 338. A director who merely facilitates infringement does not necessarily procure it: he will not be liable unless his involvement would be such as to render him liable as a joint tortfeasor if the company had not existed (*PLG Research Ltd v Ardon International Ltd* [1993] F.S.R. 197).

**Service out of the jurisdiction**

**2F–7.9** A foreign parent company and its UK subsidiary may have as good a common design to infringe a UK patent as any other joint tortfeasors, and if so, service outside the jurisdiction is proper (*Intel Corp v General Instrument Corp* [1991] R.P.C. 235). See also *Lubrizol v Esso (No.1)* [1992] R.P.C. 467, CA, where the parent company had not by taking procedural steps submitted to the jurisdiction, but was held to have admitted common design and the claimants had shown a good arguable case on infringement; but the joinder of the parent involved a new claim and relief against it would only run from six years previous to service upon it: *Molins v G.D SpA* [2000] F.S.R. 893—service of proceedings.

**Estoppel**

In *Chiron Corp v Organon Teknika Ltd (No.6)* [1994] F.S.R. 448, a defendant sued for a second time on the same patent, having unsuccessfully counterclaimed for its revocation in the first action, may not put the validity of the patent in issue in the second action (except possibly in exceptional circumstances). The matter was res judicata between the parties. *Chiron Corp v Organon Teknika Ltd (No.6)* has been reported in the Court of Appeal, where leave to appeal was obtained and then set aside (*Chiron Corp v Organon Teknika Ltd (No.14)* [1996] F.S.R. 701. Whether and to what extent estoppel may arise from the findings of foreign courts in parallel patent proceedings was considered in *Kirin Amgen Inc v Boehringer Mannheim GmbH* [1997] F.S.R. 289 and (regarding an unsuccessful opposition in the European Patent Office) *Buehler AG v Chronos Richardson Ltd* [1998] R.P.C. 609. **2F–7.10**

**Amendment to particulars of claim**

Patent actions are subject to the general provisions of CPR Pt 17 and the overriding objective that cases should be dealt with fairly. In general therefore amendments ought to be allowed so that the real dispute between the parties can be adjudicated upon provided that any prejudice to the other party caused by the amendment can be compensated for in costs, and the public administration of justice is not significantly harmed (see Gibson L.J. in *Cobbold v Greenwich LBC* August 9, 1999, unrep. (see notes to Pt 17)). Although the requirements of the Civil Procedure Rules are mandatory there is an element of discretion as to when the mandatory conditions need to be satisfied—see *Dendron GmbH v University of California (Amendment of Claim)* [2003] EWHC 2771. There is no special rule in patent cases that permits a patentee to amend its pleaded claim after judgment—see *Nikken Kosakusho Works v Pioneer Trading Co* [2005] EWCA Civ 906. However the court does have the power to permit an amendment which is sought after judgment has been given but before an order recording that judgment has been drawn up and sealed if there are exceptional circumstances or strong reasons for taking such a course (see *Stewart v Ebngel (permission to Amend)* [2000] 1 W.L.R. 2268 CA). **2F–7.11**

**Amendment to particulars of infringements**

If the claimant wants to recover relief for infringement of a claim of a patent, it must amend the pleadings to plead infringement of that claim. The request for further and other relief is not wide enough to encompass such an allegation. Moreover, a claimant seeking to so amend cannot require that the defendant shows it would have run its case differently in the light of such an amendment. A serious possibility that it would have done so was enough. See *Kirin-Amgen Inc v Transkaryotic Therapies Inc (No.2)* [2002] EWCA Civ 1096. **2F–7.12**

*Sandvik Aktiebolag v K. R. Pfiffner (UK) Limited* [2000] F.S.R. 17—"holding pleadings"; there is no automatic right to amend even if the other side could be compensated by costs; although the jurisdiction to strike out pleadings should be sparingly used.

In *Godfrey L. Cabot Inc v Philblack Ltd* [1961] R.P.C. 19, leave was given in a summons of the claimant to amend its own particulars of breaches to delete therefrom one instance of infringement and replace it with two others, even though the defendant objected that the two remaining instances of infringement were not sufficiently particularised. It was stated that the defendant's right to apply for fuller particulars of these two instances was not prejudiced by the amendment allowed. Abandonment of specific particulars was held not to be a discontinuance, in relation to subject-matter thereof, in *Anxionnaz v Rolls-Royce Ltd* [1963] R.P.C. 81. In *General Tire and Rubber Co v International Synthetic Rubber Co* [1968] R.P.C. 161, re-amendment of the statement of claim to allege a joint infringement was allowed. In *Dow Chemical AG v Spence Bryson and Co Ltd* [1982] F.S.R. 397, where the original particulars clearly complained of an infringement by manufacture, and all parties knew that manufacture had only taken place in Northern Ireland by the first defendant who operated there, an amendment to extend the particulars so as to more securely found an application for disclosure relating to Northern Ireland was allowable as involving no new cause of action.

***Paragraph numbers marked with a "+" can be found online and on CD.***

Whilst the practice in patent actions is that if one act of infringement is proved, a claimant will generally be granted an injunction in general terms to restrain infringement, and an inquiry as to damages suffered from infringing acts is not limited to the particular infringing act which has been pleaded and proved, it does not follow in the least that the particulars of infringement are no part of the cause of action, and that a claim in respect of a different manufactured product is necessarily part of the same cause of action as the original claim. The form of order for the inquiry as to damages, and the form of injunction, are matters of relief only, rather than indicating the cause of action for which relief is granted; *Sorata Ltd v Gardex Ltd* [1984] R.P.C. 317.

A proposed amendment to make a conditional allegation of infringement, on the basis that the claimant would only allege infringement of a second patent if unsuccessful in relation to an earlier, different patent is not a proper alternative plea and should not be allowed (*Beloit Technologies Inc v Valmet Paper Machinery Inc* [1994] R.P.C. 664).

The court has a complete discretion to impose terms where a claimant seeks to withdraw an allegation of infringement, and it is the practice of the Patents Court to require some kind of undertaking from the claimant in relation to future claims (Albright & Wilson Ltd v *SB Chemicals* [1994] R.P.C. 608). The imposition of terms is in the discretion of the court, and save in the strongest case the Court of Appeal will not interfere (*Wilson v Wilson* (1899) 16 R.P.C. 315).

### Amendment of Grounds of Invalidity

**2F-7.13** The general rules governing amendment set out by Pt 17 apply equally to amendment of Grounds of Invalidity. The general principle is to allow amendment of pleadings so as to determine the disputes between the parties however late they may be sought, provided that no injustice is caused thereby. In patent actions however there is also the public interest to take into account. See *Helitune Ltd v Stewart Hughes Ltd* [1991] R.P.C. 78:

> "Patents give to the patentee monopolies, and when validity is challenged in a patent action it is most unusual for any other parties who are subsequently sued under a patent to re-challenge the validity of the patent. Thus, in most cases, a decision that a patent is valid in effect decides the matter for all purposes. Thus, there is an important public interest that there is a full and proper inquiry when the validity of a patent becomes in question."

It follows that amendment to the Grounds of Invalidity ought to be more readily allowed in patent actions (and indeed in registered design cases for example). Where a point is foreshadowed in witness statements, amendments of pleadings will be allowed if necessary (see *Glaverbel SA v British Coal Corp (No.3)* [1993] F.S.R. 478).

Whilst the court has a discretion to make any appropriate order in the light of an amendment, particular costs consequences flowing from the introduction of further grounds of invalidity have been historically considered in relation to patents, in particular the ordering of *Earth Closet* and *See v Scott-Paine* orders (see *Baird v Moule's Patent Earth Closet Co Ltd* (1881) L.R. 17 Ch. D. 139 (Note)) and *See v Scott-Paine* (1933) 50 R.P.C. 56).

A *See v Scott-Paine* order is, in effect, an order that a patentee had a limited period within which to elect whether or not to abandon the patent in the light of a new ground of invalidity, and, if it did, it would have to pay the costs of the party attacking the patent only up to the date of the original grounds of invalidity (then "particulars of objection"), while the attacking party would bear the costs from that date to the date of the election. *Earth Closet* orders are to similar effect. The purpose of the *See v Scott-Paine* type of order was to impose on a party attacking the validity of a patent the obligation to take reasonable efforts to ensure that the full attack was put before the patentee at the earliest time. It was designed to impose a discipline on the proceedings which would help to reduce the costs involved. The rationale was explained by Slade L.J. in *Williamson v Moldline Ltd* [1986] R.P.C. 556. As set out in *GEC Alsthom Limited's Patent* [1996] F.S.R. 415 however, *See v Scott Paine* orders may result in serious injustice. It follows from *GEC Alsthom* and also from the judgment of Aldous J. (as he then was) in *CQR Security Systems' Patent* [1992] F.S.R. 303, that the imposition of a *See v Scott-Paine* order must be considered against the background of all the circumstances of the case (see *Cil International Ltd v Vitrashop Ltd* [2002] F.S.R. 4). A *See v Scott-Paine* order is discretionary and the court must consider the merits in each case; its aim is not to penalise a defendant but to encourage the pleading of all the objections known to him.

They are not to put the patentee in a "preferential" position (*Aumac Ltd's Patent* [1996] F.S.R. 843). See also *Robert Hewitt v P. McCann Ltd* [1998] F.S.R. 688 where a See v Scott-Paine order was refused where no serious criticism could be levelled at the defendant. The party seeking to amend the Grounds of Invalidity cannot have the best of both worlds however. In Instance v Denny Bros. Printing Ltd [1994] F.S.R. 396 the defendant sought a qualification on the usual *See v Scott-Paine* order that it be entitled to withdraw the amendments proposed at its election if the claimant chose to discontinue. The qualification was rejected on the basis that amendment is an indulgence. A defendant must decide whether to amend.

Where the claimant in a patent infringement action opted following the making of a *See v Scott-Paine* order to discontinue, and then sought to designate the United Kingdom in relation to a similar European divisional patent, the court would not re-open the *See v Scott Paine* order so as to prevent the claimant from suing on the European patent (*Aumac's Patent* [1995] F.S.R. 501).

The implication of *Helitune Ltd v Stewart Hughes Ltd* [1991] R.P.C. 78 is that if knowledge of a ground of invalidity (typically prior use by the patentee) comes to light only during cross examination, an amendment of the particulars of objections ought not to be subject to an *Earth Closet* or a *See v Scott-Paine* order. Further a distinction may be drawn between prior documents and prior uses. In the case of the latter, the defendant may only be able to discover them by chance, and in such circumstances it may not be appropriate to grant order (*La Baigne Magiglo v Multiglow Fires* [1994] R.P.C. 295).

Whilst the requirements of para.4 (then para.11) of the Practice Direction that particulars must be given in relation to an attack on novelty are mandatory, nonetheless the court has a discretion whether to allow amendments before they have been properly particularised (*Dendron GmbH v University of California (Amendment of Claim)* [2003] EWHC 2771 (Ch), unrep., Ch D). The court should however exercise that discretion to prevent amendments being made with a view to obtaining documents to discover a cause of action or defence. The court must judge whether the amendment is tantamount to a fishing expedition or not (see *Visx Inc v Nidek Co Ltd (No.2)* [1999] F.S.R. 91).



### Requests for further information

The usual rules in relation to requests (Pt 18) apply. In relation to patents in particular, if the defendant is unable to ascertain from the particulars with sufficient precision what type of machine or process is complained of, the onus will lie on him to make a request for further information, and to give some evidence to show that the information given is insufficient (*Haslam & Co v Hall* (1887) 4 R.P.C. 203); he should not wait until the trial to complain, but in appropriate cases further particulars will not be ordered until after disclosure and inspection (*Mullard Radio Valve Co Ltd v Tungsram Electric Lamp Works (Great Britain) Ltd* (1932) 49 R.P.C. 279). The exchange of witness statements may make the ordering of burdensome particulars undesirable however (*Lux Traffic Controls Ltd v Staffordshire Public Works Company Ltd* [1991] R.P.C. 73). **2F–7.14**

### Threats in patent proceedings

Section 70 of the 1977 Act provides a remedy for groundless threats of patent infringement proceedings. Section 70 permits threats to bring proceedings for an infringement alleged to consist of making or importing a product for disposal or of using a process. Section 70(4) allows threats to be made against primary infringers only in respect of acts of primary infringement, and does not allow threats against a primary infringer in relation to secondary acts of infringement, which remain actionable (*Cavity Trays Ltd v RMC Panel Products Ltd* [1996] R.P.C. 361). Mere notification of the existence of a patent does not constitute a threat. The threats may be direct or indirect, and the action may be brought by any person aggrieved thereby. Threats in respect of acts done while a patent application is pending are actionable within s.70(1) of the Patents Act 1977, as are threats to sue once the patent is granted. **2F–7.15**

In *Zeno Corp v BSM-Bionic Solutions Management GmbH* [2009] EWHC 1829 (Pat) it was held that an apparent request to stores stocking material as to whether that material infringed a patent was a veiled threat designed to discourage those stores from stocking the material, as evidenced by the sending of the letters to the stores rather than e.g. the head office. Lewison J applied the analogy of the interpretation of the proper construction of a notice of termination of a lease. See also *Grimme Landmaschinenfabrik GmbH & Co. KG v Derek Scott (t/a Scotts Potato Machinery)* [2009] EWHC 2691 (Pat):

> "It is well established that a threat can be implied as opposed to expressed. What needs to be considered is the effect that the letter would have on an ordinary recipient: see *Luna Advertising v Burnham* (1928) 45 R.P.C. 258".

An individual intimately connected with the management of a company against which threats are directed is a person aggrieved and able to sue for threats. See *Brain v Ingledew Brown Bennison and Garret* [1995] F.S.R. 552 (partially reversed on appeal, but not as to the legal findings). The threats must have been made within the jurisdiction (*Egg Fillers and Containers (Aust.) Proprietary Ltd v Holed-Tite Packing Corp and Packing Products Corp* (1934) 51 R.P.C. 9). The remedies are a declaration, injunction and damages unless the defendant proves that the act the subject of the threats would constitute an infringement of a patent or of rights arising from publication of a complete specification, in respect of a claim not shown by the claimant to be invalid. A defendant who pleads that any threat was justifiable must give particulars identifying the acts relied on as being infringing acts of the claimant in respect of which proceedings were threatened (*Reymes-Cole v Elite Hosiery Co Ltd* [1961] R.P.C. 277). The claimant is not entitled to relief even though some of the patents to which the threats related are invalid or uninfringed, if other such patents are valid and infringed. The defendant may counterclaim in respect of infringement, under the ordinary rules relating to counterclaims. Where the threats are admitted, the onus of proof shifts to the defendant who alleges infringement, and the defendant should then open the case (*Lewis Faulk v Jacobwitz* [1944] Ch. 64). A claim for threats may be made by way of counterclaim in an action for infringement (see, e.g. *Norton & Gregory Ltd v Jacobs* (1937) 54 R.P.C. 271). The fact that threats are malicious does not entitle the claimant to increased damages (*Berkeley & Young Ltd v Stillwell* (1940) 57 R.P.C. 291). An interlocutory injunction to restrain threats may be granted, even where threats are made only in solicitors' letters before action (*H.V.E. (Electric) Ltd v Cuffin Holdings Ltd* [1964] 1 W.L.R. 378; [1964] 1 All E.R. 674; [1964] R.P.C. 149, CA).

**Threats in registered design right proceedings**

2F–7.16 Section 26 of the 1949 Act provides a remedy for groundless threats of registered design right infringement proceedings. Section 26 permits threats to bring proceedings for an infringement alleged to consist of the making or importing of anything. A mere notification that a design is registered does not constitute a threat.

**Discontinuance**

2F–7.17 The normal rule in the event of a claimant discontinuing a claim is that the claimant has to pay the defendant's costs. The CPR gives the court a discretion however—see *Coca-Cola Company v Mabe* [2002] F.S.R. 47.

## Defence and reply

2F–8 **63.7 Part 15 applies with the modification—**

**(a) to rule 15.4(1)(b) that in a claim for infringement under rule 63.6, the period for filing a defence where the defendant files an acknowledgment of service under Part 10 is 42 days after service of the particulars of claim;**

**(b) that where rule 15.4(2) provides for a longer period to file a defence than in rule 63.7(a), then the period of time in rule 15.4(2) will apply; and**

**(c) to rule 15.8 that the claimant must—**

**(i) file any reply to a defence; and**

**(i) serve it on all other parties,**

**within 21 days of service of the defence.**

2F–8.1 *Note*—Substituted by the Civil Procedure (Amendment) Rules 2009 (SI 2009/2092) with effect from October 1, 2009.

***Paragraph numbers marked with a "+" can be found online and on CD***

**Time for defence**

The rules are self-explanatory. In a claim for infringement the defendant has 42 days from the service of the particulars of claim to serve a defence where he files an acknowledgment of service under Pt 10, unless a longer period applies in accordance with Pt 15.4(2) (for example if he has been served out of the jurisdiction). **2F–8.2**

The extended time for serving a defence applies to all claims for infringement, and not just those where the validity is challenged.

**Defences challenging validity**

For defences challenging the validity of a patent or registered design, see notes in relation to claims for invalidity above. **2F–8.3**

**Stay against one of several defendants who does not challenge validity**

Where one of two defendants does not raise the issue of invalidity, the action may be stayed against that defendant until after the action against the other defendant has been determined (*McCreath v Mayor, etc., of South Shields* (1932) 49 R.P.C. 349). As to addition of defendant, see *Anxionnaz v Rolls-Royce Ltd* [1963] R.P.C. 81. **2F–8.4**

**Defence that the patentee has granted licences with prohibited conditions**

This defence, given by the Patents Act 1977 s.44 exists where the patentee has imposed on licensees or purchasers or hirers certain conditions in restraint of trade attaching to the sale or use of the invention. If the prohibited contract has effect in the United Kingdom it is irrelevant that it is governed by a foreign law which does not have a provision similar to that in the United Kingdom (*Chiron Corp v Organon Teknika Ltd (No.2)* [1992] 3 C.M.L.R. 813; [1993] F.S.R. 324). Where a defendant succeeds on a s.44 defence there is jurisdiction to allow the claimant to alter the offending agreement after judgment and amend his pleadings after which the successful defence disappears; but leave to amend was refused in *Chiron Corp v Organon Teknika Ltd (No.4)* [1994] F.S.R. 252. A s.44 defence which is good against a claim by the patentee may fail against an exclusive licensee who was not a party to, and did not consent to, the offending agreement (*Chiron Corp v Organon Tekuka Ltd (No.12)* [1995] F.S.R. 153). **2F–8.5**

**Defence that use is for service of the Crown**

The question of whether there was a crown use defence is a matter which can and should be raised in the defence, not after the action in relation to the form of order (see *MMI Research Ltd v CellXion Ltd* [2009] EWHC 1533 (Pat)). **2F–8.6**

An action against the Crown for infringement of patent will be struck out: *Dory v Sheffield Health Authority* [1991] F.S.R. 221.

Before any act which would otherwise be an infringement ceased to be so by virtue of s.55, it had to be established that the person doing the act was a government department or person authorised in writing by a government department. In *MMI Research Ltd v CellXion Ltd* [2009] EWHC 1533 (Pat), there was no evidence as to what steps had been taken by CellXion to obtain an authorisation, whether the authorisation was intended to be of CellXion or the police forces who were using the device in question, nor was there evidence as to whether prospective or retrospective authorisation was being sought. The question in relation to police forces' use had was therefore hypothetical, the court did not entertain hypothetical questions and it would be wrong for the court to attempt to deal with points which might in future arise if C or the police obtained an authorisation to use the device from a government department.

**Striking out defences**

For an example of striking out Euro defences judged incapable of success, see *Chiron Corp v Organon Teknika Ltd (No.2)* [1992] 3 C.M.L.R. 813; [1993] F.S.R. 324, upheld on appeal: [1994] F.S.R. 187. **2F–8.7**

Where the defendants had been guilty of a number of significant breaches of court orders such that a fair trial was no longer possible it was appropriate to make a finding of contumacious default and strike out the defence see *Nutrinova Nutrition Specialties & Food Ingredients* [2002] EWHC 1729; (2002) 25(9) I.P.D. 25065. It was not appropriate to strike out aspects of a defence detailing the claimant's tactical motives in bringing a claim for declaratory relief in a patent action because the conduct and motives of a claimant could be taken into account. See *Interdigital Technology Corporation v Nokia*

*Corporation and Nokia Siemens Network Oy* [2008] EWHC 504 (Pat). The judge held in that case that it was concerned with a developing area of jurisprudence and so the court needed to exercise special caution when striking out claims. See also *Football Association Premier League Ltd v LCD Publishing Ltd* [2007] EWHC 3171, in which it was also inappropriate to strike out a competition defence raised by a defendant in response to claims for breach of copyright, infringement of trade mark and various economic torts, but it was appropriate to make an unless order requiring the company to provide particulars of its competition defence.

### Separate representation

**2F–8.8** *Bristol Myers Squibb Co v Baker Norton Pharmaceuticals Inc* [2001] R.P.C. 1—separately defended defendants will only fail to recover costs if it was unreasonable to have sought separate representation.

### Reply

**2F–8.9** *Time for reply* —Rule 15.8 stipulates that a claimant must file any reply to the defence at the same time as serving his allocation questionnaire and serve his reply on the other parties at the same time as he files it. Since r.26.3(6) (which sets out the period for filing the allocation questionnaire) is deemed not to apply by r.63.8(1) below, the period for filing any reply is set at within 21 days of service of the defence. This rule applies regardless of whether the case is a claim for infringement.

## Case management[1]

**2F–9** **63.8—(1) Parties do not need to file an allocation questionnaire.**

**(2) The following provisions only of Part 29 apply—**

**(a) rule 29.3(2) (legal representatives to attend case management conferences);**

**(b) rule 29.4 (the court's approval of agreed proposals for the management of proceedings); and**

**(c) rule 29.5 (variation of case management timetable) with the exception of paragraph (1)(b) and (c).**

**(3) As soon as practicable the court will hold a case management conference which must be fixed in accordance with Practice Direction 63.**

**2F–9.1** *Note* —Substituted by the Civil Procedure (Amendment) Rules 2009 (SI 2009/2092) with effect from October 1, 2009.

### Case management

**2F–9.2** The usual provisions relating to case management at the preliminary stage, i.e. those set out in r.26, do not apply to proceedings falling under this section. The court will hold a case management conference as soon as practicable. Paragraphs 5.1–5.12 of the Practice Direction supplementing Pt 63 deal generally with the procedure to be adopted in relation to case management. Paragraph 5 (except sub-para.5.9) and para.7 of the Practice Direction supplementing Pt 29 still apply, but only insofar as the provisions in that Practice Direction are consistent with the provisions of the Practice Direction supplementing Pt 63.

### Jurisdiction of Masters

**2F–9.3** Masters' jurisdiction is set out in the Practice Direction 63.8 (5.2). However parties should note the Direction, dated July 16, 2008, from Mr Justice Kitchin, the Senior Judge of the Patents Court, that a Master or a Deputy Master may deal with an application by a non-party under r.5.4C for a copy of the Grounds of Invalidity annexed

[1] Amended by the Civil Procedure (Amendment No.2) Rules 2009 (SI 2009/3390).

to a Statement of Case in which challenge is made to the validity of a patent or registered design.

**Legal representation at case management conferences**

One provision that still applies is r.29.3(2), which stipulates that parties' legal representatives at a case management conference should be familiar with the case and should have sufficient authority to deal with any issues that are likely to arise. As with r.29.3(2), if non-compliance with this rule leads to an adjournment the court will expect to make a wasted costs order (for which see r.48.7). **2F–9.4**

**Conduct of case management hearings**

See Practice Direction para.5.9 for the documents which should be included in the bundle for a case management conference—it should be provided at least four days before the first case management conference or earlier hearing for directions. The claimant is responsible for maintaining and updating those documents, and must make any necessary revisions at least seven days before any subsequent hearing (see Practice Direction para.5.12). As set out in the Practice Direction para.5.8, each party must file and serve an application notice for any order which that party intends to seek at the CMC. **2F–9.5**

If the parties can agree proposals for the management of the case they should notify the court and inform the court what the agreed proposals are. If the court thinks the agreed proposals suitable, a hearing may be unnecessary. Even if not all the proposals are suitable, those which are will be taken into account by the court when setting down directions. This is obviously beneficial in terms of time and cost. The parties should therefore attempt to come to some agreement about directions wherever possible in order to help the court to further the overriding objective (r.1.3). Parties who do so will be rewarded in costs. Parties who are combative are liable to be penalised in costs whether or not their case succeeds at trial. The court was entitled to expect that parties and their representatives acted in a professional and sensible manner and did not bring disputes which were unnecessary before the court. See *Dr Reddy's Laboratories (UK) Ltd v Eli Lilly* [2007] EWHC 1872 (Pat).

**Primers and Scientific Advisors**

In cases involving technical complexities, it has become the practice for the parties to prepare, where possible, an agreed statement of background technical facts (see, e.g. the "Phenothiazine Primer" used in *Olin Mathieson Chemical Corp v Biorex Laboratories Ltd* [1970] R.P.C. 157 at 197). In such cases the parties may also prepare written summaries of their submissions upon disputed matters. This was done, for example, in *Valensi v British Radio Corp Ltd* [1972] R.P.C. 373. In this case in the Court of Appeal, the defendants prepared a greatly extended explanatory document called a "Primer", and, although not an agreed document, it was greatly relied on by the court: [1973] R.P.C. 337 at 351, in *American Cyanamid Co's Patent* [1970] R.P.C. 306, the whole case was decided on agreed facts. **2F–9.6**

See also *Evans Medical Ltd's Patent* [1998] R.P.C. 517 and *Hoechst Celanese Corp v BP Chemicals Ltd* [1998] F.S.R. 586 for duties of parties in relation to primers. This is reflected in the practice direction at para.5.10(2), which states that at the case management conference the court may direct that a document setting out basic undisputed technology should be prepared. It should be emphasised that the purpose of a primer is to provide an undisputed summary of the technology. If there are matters that are contentious, then the dispute should be addressed in expert evidence. Nevertheless, the parties have a duty to try and agree the contents as far as they are able.

At the case management conference the court may direct that a scientific adviser under s.70(3) of the Senior Courts Act 1981 be appointed (it should be noted that r.35.15 applies to scientific advisers)—see Practice Direction 5.10(1).

See also *Kirin Amgen Inc v Hoechst Marion Roussel Ltd* [2004] UKHL 46, in which the appointment of a court expert to give the court a series of seminars in the material technology was approved of. It was suggested that such a course might usefully be adopted in future if the technology was "complex and undisputed" and the parties consented.

**Expert evidence**

*The Ikarian Reefer* [1993] F.S.R. 563 contains a discussion of the duties and responsibilities of expert witnesses. **2F–9.7**

***Paragraph numbers marked with a "+" can be found online and on CD.***

See *Cantor Fitzgerald International v Tradition (UK) Ltd* [2000] R.P.C. 95 for the dangers of an expert acting as advocate or holding back relevant information. Expert witnesses are relied upon by the court to express a disinterested view. Any pressure, and any act which may have the effect of placing pressure, on a witness may be a contempt of court and dealt with accordingly. See *Glaxo Group Ltd's Patent* [2004] EWHC 477 (Ch).

In a patent case the role of an expert is principally to educate the court in the technology so that it can establish what the skilled man would have thought. However the court must be careful not to weigh an expert's ability to teach or give evidence over the reasons for his views. What ultimately matters is what the skilled man would have thought—see *Apotex Europe Ltd v SmithKline Beecham Plc* [2004] EWCA Civ 1568.

A party should not have more than one independent expert witness on each topic (*Gerber Garment Technology Inc v Lectra Systems Ltd* [1994] F.S.R. 471). Parties are not entitled to repetitious expert evidence—courts did not decide cases by counting how many experts a party could get to say the same thing (see *Hoechst Celanese Corp v BP Chemicals Ltd* [1998] F.S.R. 586).

It is possible for an expert witness who lacks contemporaneous expertise to read himself into the state of the art. See *Inpro Licensing Sarl's Patent* [2006] EWHC 70 (Pat); [2006] R.P.C. 20.

**Expert evidence in registered design cases**

**2F–9.8** *Thermos Ltd v Aladdin Sales and Marketing Ltd* [2000] F.S.R. 402—the calling of expert evidence served little purpose in registered design actions concerned with ordinary consumer articles. In accordance with the CPR the court would need to be informed precisely at what areas the expert evidence would be directed, and it would exercise caution before admitting expert evidence. See also *Oren (Isaac) v Red Box Toy Factory Ltd* [1999] F.S.R. 785.

**Split trials**

**2F–9.9** For a discussion of the merits of splitting a trial between two different sets of patents ("system patents" and "device patents"), see *Research in Motion UK Limited v Motorola Inc* [2009] EWHC 42 (Pat).

**Time estimates and provisions for trial**

**2F–9.10** The Practice Direction at para.9 makes provisions for time estimates, trial bundles, reading guide etc. Attention is drawn to para.13 of the Patents Court Guide as to the need for realistic time estimates particularly in technologically difficult cases, as well as the duty to inform Chancery Listing of any unrealistic time estimates as soon as possible.

**Stays**

**2F–9.11** Where the likelihood was that validity proceedings in the Patents Court would more quickly resolve commercial uncertainty than proceedings in the EPO, it would normally be a proper exercise of discretion to decline to stay the Patents Court proceedings. See *Glaxo Group Ltd v Genentech Inc and Biogen Idec Inc* [2008] EWCA Civ 23. See also *Glaxosmithkline Biologicals SA v Novartis AG* [2009] EWHC 931 (Pat) and *InterDigital Technology Corp v Nokia Corp* [2008] EWHC 749 (Pat); (2008) 31(7) I.P.D. 31042 in which stays were refused.

**Experiments (see Practice Direction para.7)**

**2F–9.12** Where a party seeks to establish any fact by experimental proof conducted for the purpose of litigation he must, at least 21 days before service of the application notice for directions under para.7.1 of the practice direction, or within such other time as the court may direct, serve on all parties a notice stating the facts which he seeks to establish and giving full particulars of the experiments proposed to establish them. A party served with notice under para.7.1 of the practice direction must within 21 days after such service, serve on the other party a notice stating whether or not he admits each fact and may request the opportunity to inspect a repetition of all or a number of the experiments identified in the notice served under para.7.1. Where any fact which a party seeks to establish by experimental proof is not admitted, he must apply to the court for permission and directions by application notice (see practice direction paras

7.1 to 7.3). However, no automatic provisions for experiments should be made during the course of case management, and no permission at all should be granted for experiments that are directed at the issue of construction—see *Merck & Co Inc v Generics (UK) Ltd* [2003] EWHC 2842 (Pat).

Although experiments were not necessarily inappropriate in Patents County Court litigation, their appropriateness should be considered at the case management stage and adverse cost consequences may flow from any failure to take account of the realities of the case—see *Unilin Beheer BV v Berry Floor NV* [2004] F.S.R. 14 (overturned on appeal though no adverse comment made in relation to the above).

Where a party fails to permit the other party to see a repetition of an experiment, it is possible for that other party to apply to have the notice of experiments struck out. Whether this will be done depends on the circumstances (*American Cyanamid Co v Ethicon Ltd* [1978] R.P.C. 667, experiment not repeated because trial would be delayed and party wanting inspection partly to blame). Late applications to introduce experiments or like matter which may result in further delay and expense are likely to be refused (*H. & R. Johnson Tiles Ltd v Candy Tiles Ltd* [1985] F.S.R. 253 (late photographs relating to infringement refused)).

The regime for managing experimental evidence provided by the CPR should not be undermined. Poorly documented, unrepeated experiments coming into proceedings at a late stage should be strenuously avoided. Experimental evidence should be kept to a minimum, and that minimum should consist of inspected experiments. See *Monsanto Technology LLC v Cargill International SA* [2008] F.S.R. 7, where late experiments sought to be introduced by way of witness statements were excluded.

To prove that a skilled man carrying out a recipe would be able to do so using his ordinary skills, the recipe should ideally be given to a scientist of ordinary skills to try. There is a benefit if the experiment is carried out by a single court appointed expert, which the parties ought to consider when they apply for leave to adduce such evidence. See *Apotex Europe Ltd v SmithKline Beecham Plc* [2004] EWCA Civ 1568. A party was entitled to disclosure of documents relating to "work up experiments" that had been carried out for the purpose of litigation in which revocation of patents had been sought—*Mayne Pharma Pty Ltd v Debiopharm SA* [2006] EWHC 164. As to disclosure in relation to work-up experiments see para.XXX above.

**Use of models (see Practice Direction para.8)**

Where a party intends to rely on any model or apparatus, he must apply to the court for directions at the first case management conference (see practice direction 8.1). **2F–9.13**

**Relief**

For the appropriate scope of patent injunctions, see *Coflexip SA v Stolt Comex Seaway MS Ltd* [2001] R.P.C. 9, CA (general form of wording is appropriate). **2F–9.14**

There is no right to a stay of an injunction pending an appeal, far less to a stay pending an application for permission to appeal to the Court of Appeal which has yet to be determined. In order to determine whether a stay should be granted the court needs to be put properly into possession of the relevant facts, in order to answer the relevant questions which are: (a) what effect would the grant of an injunction, which later turned out ought not to have been granted, have on the defendants; (b) what effect would the refusal of the injunction have on the claimant who has at this stage established his right; and (c) what steps should the court take in order to place the appeal court in the best position to do justice between the parties? See *MMI Research Ltd v CellXion Ltd* [2009] EWHC 1533 (Pat).

As to the position regarding stay pending the outcome of EPO proceedings (and the effect of a final order in the UK courts prior to the outcome of EPO proceedings, see *Unilin Beheer BV v Berry Floor NV* [2007] EWCA Civ 364; [2007] Bus. L.R. 1140). The primary position is that the successful party is entitled to an injunction and an order for costs. Furthermore a party against whom an order for costs has been made is estopped from challenging the other party's entitlement to an account of profits or enquiry for damages even if the patent is later revoked by the EPO.

***Paragraph numbers marked with a "+" can be found online and on CD.***

## Disclosure and inspection[1]

2F-10 **63.9 Part 31 is modified to the extent set out in Practice Direction 63.**

2F-10.1 *Note*—Substituted by the Civil Procedure (Amendment) Rules 2009 (SI 2009/2092) with effect from October 1, 2009.

### Disclosure and inspection (see also Practice Direction para.6)

2F-10.2 *Product and Process descriptions*—Standard disclosure does not require the disclosure of documents relating to the infringement of a patent by a product or process if, before serving a list of documents, the defendant has served on the claimant and any other parties full particulars of the product or process alleged to infringe and any drawings or other illustrations explaining the product and process should they be necessary (See Practice Direction para.6.1(1)).

As for the duties incumbent on those serving product and process descriptions, see *Alfred Taylor v Ishida (Europe) Ltd* [2000] F.S.R. 224:

> "...the function of a product description is in all respects equivalent to that of disclosure. The duties of all parties, both the professionals and of the parties themselves, in relation to a product description, are the same as they would be in relation to disclosure...".

See also *Consafe Engineering (UK) Ltd v Emtunga UK Ltd* [1999] R.P.C. 154—a description of the product in general terms or including tendentious assertions is not acceptable. It was appropriate to grant an application by the claimants for disclosure, subject to appropriate safeguards, of the defendant's product description to technically qualified American attorneys in circumstances where, in the absence of such disclosure, it was impossible for the claimant's UK advisers to formulate any sensible request for further information—Intel Corp v VIA Technologies Inc (Application; Disclosure) [2002] EWHC 1434. Rockwater Ltd v Coflexip SA [2004] EWCA Civ 381 provided that where an alleged infringer provides a description of a product or process under PD 63 para.6.1 (then para.5.1), it should be formally proved by a witness at trial if required by the other party. That principle has now been enshrined in the new Practice Direction para.6.2, which provides that the Product and Process Description ("PPD") must be accompanied by a signed witness statement from a person acquainted with the facts to which the particulars relate. That person must verify the truth and completeness of the PPD and indicate his or her understanding that attendance for cross examination on the contents may be required. In some cases it is possible that it may be necessary for more than one person to attest to different aspects of a PPD.

### Disclosure in relation to validity

2F-10.3 Standard disclosure does not require the disclosure of documents relating to any ground on which the validity of a patent is put in issue, except documents which fall in the period starting two years before the earliest claimed priority date and two years following that date (See practice direction supplementing Pt 63, para.6.1(2)). See *Nokia Corp v Interdigital Technology Corp* [2004] EWHC 2920.

The question of disclosure in relation to validity was considered by the Court of Appeal in *Nichia Corp v Argos* [2007] EWCA Civ 741; [2007] F.S.R. 38. Whilst it was arguable that where obviousness was being considered what the inventor actually did was irrelevant, nevertheless the evidence of the inventor was admissible. That evidence was secondary evidence, and thus no more than an aid to assessing the primary evidence. Prima facie, Pt 63 required disclosure of primary documents required by standard disclosure, i.e. those that adversely affected a party's own case or supported another party's case, limited to a period of two years on either side of the earliest priority date. A reasonable search for such documents was required. The parties could agree to dispense with such disclosure, as could the court. The extent to which searches for such documents was reasonable in a given case would depend on factors such as the difficulties and expense of such a search, and the likelihood that the exercise would

[1] Amended by the Civil Procedure (Amendment No.2) Rules 2009 (SI 2009/3390).

result in documents of value or significance being disclosed. There is no blanket prima facie rule that disclosure would be dispensed with. In relation to potential limitations on disclosure in appropriate circumstances and the court's discretion as to disclosure, see *Novartis AG v Johnson & Johnson Medical Ltd* [2008] EWHC 295 (Pat); *MMI Research Ltd v Cellxion Ltd* [2007] EWHC 2611 (Pat); [2008] F.S.R. 23 and *Monsanto Technology LLC v Cargill International Plc* [2007] EWHC 1298 (Pat).

In *Edwards Lifesciences AG v Cook Biotech Inc (Costs)* [2009] EWHC 1443 (Pat) Kitchin described the disclosure exercise that had been undertaken as "a monumental waste of time and money" and said that it "provided a salutary reminder that disclosure in patent actions cost a great deal and was rarely of any use". He was of the view that "the court and the parties should be more robust in ensuring that disclosure exercises were not futile and that any disclosure was necessary and proportionate."

Discussion of disclosure in relation to issues of validity in older cases must be approached in the light of the above. Nonetheless the principles addressed in those cases may be of relevance in approaching a particular disclosure issue. Documents relating to the patentee's research leading to and concerned with the invention may be disclosable when obviousness, insufficiency or inutility are pleaded; see *Halcon International Inc v Shell Transport, etc. (Discovery No.2)* [1979] R.P.C. 459; *Wellcome Foundation v V.R. Laboratories (Australia) Pty Ltd* [1981] R.P.C. 35 and [1982] R.P.C. 343 (although see above regarding the likely utility of such disclosure). Since the reasons for alleged invalidity have to be specified in the grounds of invalidity it is not possible to get disclosure of the pleadings in earlier actions against different parties which were settled, on the suspicion—howsoever justified—that they disclosed much more relevant prior art (*Intalite Internationals NV v Cellular Ceilings Ltd (No.1)* [1987] R.P.C. 185).

In *Vickers Plc v Horsell Graphic Industries Ltd* [1988] R.P.C. 421, it emerged on disclosure that the patentee had expressed opinions in US proceedings that carrying out the process of a particular piece of prior art did not disclose his invention. Disclosure was ordered of documents relating to the like opinions expressed in yet other jurisdictions as disclosing the patentee's counter to attacks on validity and his approach to infringement. This case was not followed in *Glaverbel SA v British Coal Corp (No.2)* [1993] R.P.C. 90; [1992] F.S.R. 642, where documents relating to the patentees' opinion on obviousness were held not relevant; the effect on the need for disclosure of the modern practice of disclosing witness statements and the preferability of dealing with some matters by affidavit rather than disclosure were discussed; no disclosure of documents will be ordered unless it is certain they exist.

In *Intel Corp v General Instrument Corp* [1989] 1 F.S.R. 640, the authorities being conflicting, the court left open whether disclosure of documents showing grounds of invalidity not specifically pleaded could be ordered. (One case that does not appear to have been cited in that case was *Avery Ltd v Ashworth, Son & Co Ltd* (1915) 32 R.P.C. 561, in which it was said that disclosure can be obtained from the claimant only of such matters as are relevant to the plea of invalidity as made out in the particulars of objections, and he cannot be compelled to disclose any documents affecting the validity otherwise than as such documents are specifically pleaded).

### Disclosure in relation to commercial success

Standard disclosure does not require the disclosure of documents relating to commercial success except as set out in the practice direction (see practice direction supplementing Pt 63, para.6.1(3)). This reflects the fact that virtually every commercial document produced relating to a product or process may be relevant to the success of that product or process. In order to rationalise the disclosure relating to the commercial success of a product therefore, the patentee must serve a schedule: identifying the article or product (for example by product code number) made in accordance with the claims of the patent; a summary by convenient periods of sales of any such articles; a summary by convenient periods of any equivalent prior article or product marketed before the article in question (if any); and a summary by convenient periods of any advertising or promotional expenditure on the article. In relation to a process, the patentee must serve a schedule: identifying the process made in accordance with the claims of the patent; a summary by convenient periods of revenue received by the use of the process; a summary by convenient periods of any equivalent prior art process; and a summary by convenient periods of any expenditure supporting the use of the process. **2F–10.4**

**Disclosure generally**

2F–10.5 A defendant's obligation to give disclosure is confined to the issues raised in the particulars of infringements. He need not normally give disclosure of all his sales (*Belegging, etc. v Witten* [1979] F.S.R. 59, CA). Late applications for disclosure are very undesirable, but should not necessarily be refused on this ground alone (*Poseidon Industri A/B v Cerosa Ltd* [1975] F.S.R. 122). In *Kahn (David) Inc v Conway Stewart* [1972] R.P.C. 572 very late notice for inspection of the claimant's documents was permitted where no delay was likely to be caused. Correspondence between the patentee and the patent office relating to the application which matured into a patent in suit is not discoverable because it is not relevant (*Poseidon Industri A/B v Cerosa Ltd* [1975] F.S.R. 122).

Disclosure of documents relating to why foreign patents have more restricted claims will not be ordered as the question of fair basis is entirely a matter of construction for the court (*Schering Agrochemicals Ltd v A. B. M. Chemicals Ltd* [1987] R.P.C. 185). A patentee's equivalent foreign specifications cannot assist with construction of a UK patent and disclosure of the same will not be ordered (*Glaverbel SA v British Coal Corp (No.2)* [1993] R.P.C. 90; [1992] F.S.R. 642).

Where an alleged infringer is a licensee who imports without knowledge of the manufacturing process, and his licence entitles him to have information made available to him for the purposes of the licence, these purposes do not include litigation, and he will not be ordered to procure documents relating to manufacture (*Unilever Plc v Gillette UK Ltd* [1988] R.P.C. 416). Documents relating to a defendant's reaction to the claimant's patent and the indemnities he gives to his customers will not normally be relevant to the issue of obviousness and will not be ordered to be discovered (*Fuji Photo Film Co Ltd v Carr's Paper* [1989] R.P.C. 713). In a case involving benefit to an employer from a patent from an invention made by an employee, disclosure of documents relating to profit on patented articles is only relevant if the patent plays a major part in securing sales (*Memco-Med Ltd's Patent* [1992] R.P.C. 403).

**Disclosure in relation to common general knowledge**

2F–10.6 It is not normal for disclosure to be made in relation to common general knowledge (in relation to the question of commonplace designs which may be considered analogous it is only in exceptional circumstances that disclosure will be ordered in relation to the issue of whether or not a design was commonplace at the material time: see *Ultraframe Ltd v Eurocell Building Plastics Ltd (Disclosure)* [2003] EWHC 3258 (Ch); [2005] F.S.R. 2).

Evidence may be called generally on the issue of common general knowledge, but if it is apparent that the defendant is going to rely on particular documents, they should be disclosed as and when they come to hand (*Aluma Systems Inc v Hunnebeck GmbH* [1982] F.S.R. 239).

**Disclosure of work-up experiments**

2F–10.7 See *Mayne Pharma Pty Ltd v Debiopharm SA* [2006] EWHC 164 (Pat); [2006] F.S.R. 37, in which it was held that any legal professional privilege attaching to documents relating to workup experiments is waived by the service of a notice of experiments.

**Use of disclosed documents**

2F–10.8 In *Bourns Inc v Raychem Corp (No.2)* [2000] F.S.R. 841, it was held that there was an implied undertaking to use the documents disclosed only for purposes of taxation. See also *Smithkline Beecham Plc v Generics (UK) Ltd* [2003] EWCA Civ 1109 in which permission had been granted to the claimant to use disclosed documents in a co-pending revocation action brought by a third party, and the claimant had sought permission to use disclosed documents in a further action, and also *Dendron GmbH v University of California (No.2)* [2004] EWHC 589 (Pat).

**Disclosure as against non-parties**

2F–10.9 See *American Home Products Corp v Novartis Pharmaceuticals UK Ltd (No.2)* [2001] F.S.R. 41, in which the Court of Appeal held that s.34 of the Senior Courts Act 1981 provided jurisdiction to order disclosure of documents relevant to an issue, and the discretion to order such disclosure should be exercised when it would aid the administration of justice. See also *Coca-Cola Company v British Telecommunications Plc* [1999] F.S.R. 518 for appropriate considerations and factors to be taken into account.

***Paragraph numbers marked with a "+" can be found online and on CD.***

Where a claim is made against an innocent defendant for disclosure only (or also under the protective jurisdiction for any injunction) the claimant will normally bear the costs as against him, but will be able to recover these from the true infringer, either in the same or subsequent action (Smith, Kline & French Laboratories Ltd v *R. D. Harbottle (Mercantile) Ltd* [1980] R.P.C. 363; *Morton-Norwich Inc v Intercen* [1981] F.S.R. 337). See *Totalise Plc v The Motley Fool Ltd* [2002] F.S.R. 50 for the appropriate cost order to be made in Norwich Pharmacal Orders as against an innocent third party.

**Disclosure of infringing parties**

An action solely for an order compelling a defendant to give disclosure of the names and addresses of persons who are infringing the claimant's patent will lie against a defendant against whom the claimant has another cause of action (e.g. for infringement or breach of an equitable duty not to part with goods knowing that they infringe) and will also lie against an innocent defendant who, through no fault of his own and whether voluntarily or not, facilitated the infringement (*Norwich Pharmacal Co v Commrs. of Customs and Excise* [1974] A.C. 133; [1973] 2 All E.R. 943; [1974] R.P.C. 101, HL). **2F–10.10**

The question of whether, and in what circumstances, information relating to the infringement of other parties' rights discovered in the execution of an Anton Piller order can be passed to those other parties was considered in *Cobra Golf Inc v Rata* [1996] F.S.R. 819.

**Disclosure and inspection of secret processes and commercial secrets**

Where a defendant claims that the allegedly infringing process is a trade secret, he can claim limited disclosure. As to the principles upon which this is granted, see *Warner-Lambert & Co v Glaxo Laboratories Ltd* [1975] R.P.C. 354, CA. In that case, disclosure was ordered to one controlling intelligence in the company while the Court of Appeal accepted that there might be circumstances justifying no disclosure at all. See also *Roussel Uclaf v Imperial Chemical Industries Plc* [1989] R.P.C. 59, CA (disclosure to expert in France refused because of danger of leak). For further developments see *Roussel Uclaf v Imperial Chemical Industries Plc (No.2)* [1990] R.P.C. 45; [1990] F.S.R. 25; *British Thomson-Houston Co v Duram Ltd* (1915) 37 R.P.C. 121; *Coloured Asphalte Co Ltd v British Asphalt and Bitumen Ltd* (1936) 53 R.P.C. 89; *British Celanese Ltd v Courtaulds Ltd* (1932) 49 R.P.C. 345; *Helitune Ltd v Stewart Hughes Ltd* [1994] F.S.R. 422. Even non-confidential documents discovered in English proceedings may not be authorised to be proffered in foreign proceedings in which it is impossible to protect confidence, lest confidential documents have to be produced to explain them (*Halcon International v Shell Transport and Trading Co* [1979] R.P.C. 97). **2F–10.11**

Extensive guidance was given by Whitford J. as to the circumstances in which documents filed in the Patent Office and subsequently in the Patents Court should be treated as confidential. (1) The fact that a document is said to contain "sensitive commercial information" does not necessarily mean that this material, which would otherwise become public property is to be excluded from public inspection; apart from generalities there must be some real indication as to why disclosure would be harmful. (2) Those requesting confidentiality should put in evidence. (3) Material which is going to form no part of the decision can remain confidential. (4) Material supplied by a third party on the basis of confidence which involves minimal excisions from a decision should be maintained as confidential unless there is some overwhelming public interest which makes it desirable that the public should have sight of it. (5) The appropriate procedure is for the matter to be dealt with before hearing so that if ruled against the person proffering the document can make up his mind whether he will go forward publicly, or have the material withdrawn (*Diamond Shamrock Technologies SA's Patent* [1987] R.P.C. 91). (See also *Lilly Icos Ltd v Pfizer Ltd (No.2)* [2002]1 All E.R. 842 in which it was said that the court will only depart from normal rule of publicity of trials if very good reasons are given). See also *Smithkline Beecham Plc v Generics (UK) Ltd* [2003] EWCA Civ 1109 for discussion of the protection available to a party who discloses commercially sensitive documents in an action. See *Interdigital Technology Corporation v (1) Nokia Corporation (2) Nokia Siemens Networks Oy* [2008] EWHC 969 (Pat), in which the court considered the circumstances in which a party should be required to give disclosure of confidential business documents to representatives of the other party.

***Paragraph numbers marked with a "+" can be found online and on CD.***

The position is somewhat different when a claimant wins a case and is then forced to disclose potentially confidential documents before the account of profits or assessment of damages can take place. Just such a situation arose in *Dyson Limited v Hoover Limited (No.3)* [2002] R.P.C. 42. In that case it was said that it is only in exceptional cases that a party can be prevented from having access to information which would play a substantial part in the case. The burden is on the party seeking to restrict disclosure to show that the case was sufficiently exceptional that significant restrictions on disclosure had to be maintained. It is for the party trying to restrict disclosure to justify it and to show why, in all the circumstances, notwithstanding onerous undertakings as to confidentiality and the like, documents should not be shown to the other party.

**Privilege**

**2F–10.12** Apart from the usual legal professional privilege, privilege for communications with patent agents has been established by the Copyright Designs and Patents Act 1988 s.280. For a case involving both heads see *Soc. Francaise Hoechst v Allied Colloids Ltd* [1992] F.S.R. 66. Privilege at common law may extend to foreign lawyers giving advice on English law (*IBM v Phoenix International Computers Ltd* [1995] F.S.R. 184).

See *David Instance v Denny Bros. Printing Ltd* [2000] F.S.R. 869 for discussion of privilege in documents created for the purposes of negotiating settlements and mediation and their use in subsequent litigation. A defendant cannot rely on privilege against self-incrimination when he has accidentally handed over evidence of his own dishonesty; see *Bell Cablemedia Plc v Simmons* [2002] F.S.R. 34.

## Application to amend a patent specification in existing proceedings

**2F–11** **63.10—(1) An application under section 75 of the 1977 Act for permission to amend the specification of a patent by the proprietor of the patent must be made by application notice.**

**(2) The application notice must—**

**(a) give particulars of—**

**(i) the proposed amendment sought; and**

**(ii) the grounds upon which the amendment is sought;**

**(b) state whether the applicant will contend that the claims prior to the amendment are valid; and**

**(c) be served by the applicant on all parties and the Comptroller within 7 days of it being filed.**

**(3) The application notice must, if it is reasonably possible, be served on the Comptroller electronically.**

**(4) Unless the court otherwise orders, the Comptroller will, as soon as practicable, advertise the application to amend in the journal.**

**(5) The advertisement will state that any person may apply to the Comptroller for a copy of the application notice.**

**(6) Within 14 days of the first appearance of the advertisement any person who wishes to oppose the application must file and serve on all parties and the Comptroller a notice opposing the application which must include the grounds relied on.**

**(7) Within 28 days of the first appearance of the advertisement the applicant must apply to the court for directions.**

**(8) Unless the court otherwise orders, the applicant must within 7 days serve on the Comptroller any order of the court on the application.**

**(9) In this rule "the journal" means the journal published pursuant to rules under section 123(6) of the 1977 Act.**

*Note*—Substituted by the Civil Procedure (Amendment) Rules 2009 (SI 2009/2092) with effect from October 1, 2009. **2F–11.1**

Rule 63.10 provides for the procedure to be adopted in an application for amendment of a patent specification in existing proceedings under s.75 of the Patents Act 1977. It sets out the appropriate contents of the application notice as well as the steps to be taken as regards service on the Comptroller and the parties and advertisement etc. In appropriate circumstances those provisions may be short-circuited to an extent as set out below.

It does not follow from the fact that a party seeking to amend accepts that all of the unamended claims of the patent as granted are invalid that he has no cause of action and the claim should be struck out. See *Zipher Ltd v Markem Systems Ltd* [2007] EWHC 154 (Pat).

### Discretion to allow applications to amend

There are various instances in which applications to amend may arise. They are dealt with by Jacob L.J. in *Nikken Kosakusho Works v Pioneer Trading Co* [2005] EWCA Civ 906; [2006] F.S.R. 4. The discretion arises under s.75 of the Patents Act 1977 thus: **2F–11.2**

> "In any proceedings before the Court or the Comptroller in which the validity of the patent is put in issue, the court or, as the case may be, the Comptroller, may, subject to section 76 below, allow the proprietor of the patent to amend the specification of the patent in such a manner and subject to such terms as to advertising the proposed amendment and to costs, expenses or otherwise as the Court or Comptroller thinks fit."

As Jacob L.J. explained, there are different situations in which the exercise of the discretion may be sought:

> "(a) before a trial; (b) after trial, at which certain claims have been held valid but other claims held invalid, the patentee simply wishing to delete the invalid claims (I would include here also the case where the patentee wishes to re-write the claims so as to exclude various dependencies as in *Hallen Co v Brabantia (UK) Ltd* [1990] F.S.R. 134. There the patentee is in effect continuing to claim which he had claimed before but in a much smaller way); and (c) after a trial in which all claims have been held invalid but the patentee wishes to insert what he hopes are validating amendments."

### Prior to trial (position (a))

There is no difficulty with situation (a). As Jacob L.J. set out in *Nikken*: **2F–11.3**

> "Clearly, if the amendment is proposed in sufficient time before trial the defendant has a full opportunity to attack the proposed amended claims, not only on their allowability or in the exercise of discretion, but on their ultimate validity. The existing procedure for an application to amend the patent specification is governed by CPR Part 63.10. The procedure is by way of an application notice, service on the Comptroller, subsequent advertisement and so on. The procedures can, in appropriate circumstances, be gone through quickly or gone through provisionally on the basis that probably no third party will ever come in to oppose. It may be noted that the rules specifically require by Part 63.10 that the patentee must state whether he will contend that the claims prior to amendment are valid. That means that in advance of trial everyone knows where they stand. The patentee is either saying that the original claims are all right or not, and he is plainly also saying that the proposed amendment claims are all right."

Note that in appropriate circumstances the provisions set out in r.63.10 may be dealt with more quickly or on a provisional basis.

### After a trial (positions (b) and (c))

Position (b) is where effectively no more than claim dependency is being dealt with. Again there is no real difficulty with that situation. Following a conclusion that some claims are valid and others are not, the patentee is normally entitled to relief pursuant to s.63 of the Act. Normally the court will impose as a condition of relief that the invalid claims be amended by deletion. **2F–11.4**

***Paragraph numbers marked with a "+" can be found online and on CD.***



INTELLECTUAL PROPERTY

Note that where a patentee applied to amend after judgment to delete claims found invalid, the defendants in the action were not entitled to plead in opposition to the amendments sought that the valid claims were not supported by the description in the specification. There was no nexus between the support for those claims and the amendments sought and the reasons for seeking them (*Chiron Corp v Organon Teknika (No.11)* [1995] F.S.R. 589, CA).

Position (c) involves something different, a proposed claim which was not under attack and could not have been under attack prior to trial. As Jacob L.J. explained, if the court is to allow such a claim to be propounded after trial, there is almost bound to be a further battle which would arise in the proposed amendment proceedings. There were three reasons why such a course should not be allowed. The first was the straightforward application of the principles of *Henderson v Henderson* (1843) 3 Hare 100. The second was the practice of the Patents Courts of refusing this type of amendment if it would involve a second trial on validity (*Windsurfing International Inc v Tabur Marine (Great Britain) Ltd* [1985] R.P.C. 59 and *Lubrizol Corp v Esso Petroleum Co Ltd* [1998] R.P.C. 727). And the third was the provisions of the CPR requiring that cases are dealt with cheaply, expeditiously and fairly, all of which would be contravened by a second trial on validity.

For cases in which applications to amend post trial were refused, see *Aloys Wobben v Vestas-Celtic Wind Technology Limited* [2008] EWHC 235 (Pat) and *Qualcomm Inc v Nokia Corp* [2008] EWHC 776 (Ch); (2008) 31(5) I.P.D. 31034.

**Terms on which amendment allowed**

**2F–11.5** The form of the order will depend on the circumstances, and there is no form which is invariably to be followed in all cases (per Lindley L.J., in *Bray v Gardner* (1887) L.R. 34 Ch. D. 668 at 44). In general however it requires a special case before the court imposes conditions when permitting amendment (*Wilkinson Sword Ltd v Gillette Industries Ltd* [1975] R.P.C. 101; *General Tire & Rubber Co (Frost's) Patent* [1974] F.S.R. 433).

For terms on which liberty to apply to amend under the Act of 1883 was granted, see *Ludington Cigarette Machine Co v Baron Cigarette Machine Co* [1900] 1 Ch. 508; *Deeley v Perkes* [1896] A.C. 496; *Re Geipel's Patent* [1903] 2 Ch. 715; [1904] 1 Ch. 239; 20 R.P.C. 545; 21 R.P.C. 279. The form in the last-mentioned case was substantially followed in similar circumstances in *Gillette Safety Razor Co v Luna Safety Razor Co* [1910] 2 Ch. 373, followed in *Rheinische Gummi and Celluloid Fabrik v British Xylonite Co Ltd* (1912) 29 R.P.C. 672, where the order is set out in full. This form of order was slightly varied in *NV Hollandsche Glas-en Metaalbank v Rockware Glass Syndicate Ltd* (1931) 48 R.P.C. 181; see also *Lilley v Artistic Novelties Ltd* (1913) 30 R.P.C. 18, Rowland Edwards & C Ltd v *Three Star Accumulators Ltd* (1934) 51 R.P.C. 370, and *White's Application* [1958] R.P.C. 287. The application may be ordered to come on for hearing with the trial of the action (*British Celanese Ltd v Courtaulds Ltd* (1932) 49 R.P.C. 345; *Re Nier's Patent* (1938) 55 R.P.C. 1; *Astra A/B v Pharmaceutical Mfg Co* (1952) 69 R.P.C. 312) but this course may sometimes be inconvenient (*British Acoustic Films Ltd v Nettleford Productions* (1935) 52 R.P.C. 296; (1935) 53 R.P.C. 221, at 241; *Drysdale v Davey, Paxman & Co (Colchester) Ltd* (1938) 55 R.P.C. 95, at 108). The application may be allowed on the terms that consequential amendments may be made in the pleadings, in which case the defendant (or petitioner) will usually be given the costs occasioned thereby. See *Haslam Foundry and Engineering Co v Goodfellow* (1888) 5 R.P.C. 28; *Re Chatwood's Patent* (1899) 16 R.P.C. 370; *NV Hollandsche Glas-en Metaalbank v Rockware Glass Syndicate Ltd* (1931) 48 R.P.C. 425; *Chrome-Alloying Co Ltd v Metal Diffusions Ltd* [1962] R.P.C. 33. Leave to amend was given in Electrical & Musical Industries Ltd's Patent [1963] R.P.C. 241, but the question of terms was deferred to the full hearing. Where a perpetual injunction had been granted several years before the application to amend, the court as a term of the permission to amend dissolved the injunction (*Re Kenrick and Jefferson's Patent* (1912) 29 R.P.C. 25).

After amendment, a patentee must start a fresh action rather than seek to enforce any relief he has obtained in a previous action. That practice is based upon the fact that there has been no judgment on infringement and validity in relation to the amended patent and upon the statutory provisions that an amendment dates back to the grant (*PLG Research Ltd v Ardon International Ltd (No.2)* [1993] F.S.R. 698). Notwithstanding that, costs may be awarded to a successful patentee even though he later amends his specification and throws away all other relief obtained prior to amendment.

### Court's discretion to refuse amendment

As regards the court's discretion to refuse an amendment (as opposed to the discretion to allow an application for an amendment as discussed above), the position appears to have been brought into line with the EPC by the Patents Act 2004. Floyd J in *Zipher Ltd v Markem Systems Ltd* [2008] EWHC 1379 (Pat); [2009] F.S.R. 1 held as follows: **2F–11.6**

> "If a proper amendment is now brought forward in opposition proceedings in good time and which is necessary and appropriate to meeting the opposition, it seems inescapable that it will be allowed. It would, it seems to me, be an odd result if an amendment which would be available as of right under the central amendment procedure was refused simply because the patent was under opposition. Such a result would only be justified if either (a) the amendments would have no effect on the opposition and could accordingly be made after its conclusion if the patent survives or (b) procedural fairness to the opponents meant that it could not be considered. I appreciate that (b) might result in a patent being revoked before it could be amended: but if it were not so, the patentee could derail the proceedings by claiming the right to amend at the last moment. I think what I have derived so far can fairly be described as the principles on which in future, if not in the past, the power to allow amendment will be exercised in the EPO under the EPC. It follows that if I am to have regard to the principles applicable under the EPC, the discretion which I have to refuse amendments which comply with the Act has been limited. Considerations such as those formerly considered relevant to the discretion, such as the conduct of the patentee, are no longer relevant."

Only in exceptional circumstances will the Patents Court on appeal from the Patent Office consider amendments to the specification which make the specification substantially different to that considered in the decision of the patent office; here the exceptional circumstances were that there was a relevant decision of the CA intervening (*Schering Biotech Corp's Application* [1993] R.P.C. 249).

## Court's determination of question or application

**63.11—(1) This rule applies where the Comptroller—** **2F–12**

**(a) declines to deal with a question under section 8(7), 12(2), 37(8) or 61(5) of the 1977 Act;**

**(b) declines to deal with an application under section 40(5) of the 1977 Act; or**

**(c) certifies under section 72(7)(b) of the 1977 Act that the court should determine the question whether a patent should be revoked.**

**(2) Any person seeking the court's determination of that question or application must start a claim for that purpose within 14 days of receiving notification of the Comptroller's decision.**

**(3) A person who fails to start a claim within the time prescribed by rule 63.11(2) will be deemed to have abandoned the reference or application.**

**(4) A party may apply to the Comptroller or the court to extend the period for starting a claim prescribed by rule 63.11(2) even where the application is made after expiration of that period.**

*Note* —Substituted by the Civil Procedure (Amendment) Rules 2009 (SI 2009/2092) with effect from October 1, 2009. **2F–12.1**

## Application by employee for compensation

**63.12—(1) An application by an employee for compensation under section 40(1) or (2) of the 1977 Act must be made—** **2F–13**

*Paragraph numbers marked with a "+" can be found online and on CD.*

**(a) in a claim form; and**

**(b) within the period prescribed by paragraphs (2), (3) and (4).**

**(2) The prescribed period begins on the date of the grant of the patent and ends 1 year after the patent has ceased to have effect.**

**(3) Where the patent has ceased to have effect as a result of failure to pay renewal fees, the prescribed period continues as if the patent has remained continuously in effect provided that—**

**(a) the renewal fee and any additional fee are paid in accordance with section 25(4) of the 1977 Act; or**

**(b) restoration is ordered by the Comptroller following an application under section 28 of the 1977 Act.**

**(4) Where restoration is refused by the Comptroller following an application under section 28 of the 1977 Act, the prescribed period will end 1 year after the patent has ceased to have effect or 6 months after the date of refusal, whichever is the later.**

2F–13.1 *Note*—Substituted by the Civil Procedure (Amendment) Rules 2009 (SI 2009/2092) with effect from October 1, 2009.

For a discussion as to the appropriate principles concerning applications by employees for compensation, see *Kelly v GE Healthcare Limited* [2009] EWHC 181 (Pat). The procedure to be adopted is set out in r.63.12, and is self-explanatory.

### Case management of employee compensation claims

2F–13.2 Provision for the case management of employee compensation claims is made in para.12 of the Practice Direction.

In addition, disclosure will often be of considerable value to the applicant in s.40 proceedings, particularly when he or she is no longer employed by the proprietor. However it is up to an applicant to decide what is needed to support the application, and if at any stage it becomes apparent that discovery is needed, it should be requested promptly, not at the last minute, and in terms which are as specific as possible (see *Memco-Med Ltd's Patent* [1992] R.P.C. 403).

## *II. Registered Trade Marks and Other Intellectual Property Rights*

### Allocation[1]

2F–14 **63.13—(1) Claims relating to matters arising out of the 1994 Act and other intellectual property rights set out in Practice Direction 63 must be started in—**

**(a) the Chancery Division;**

**(b) a patents county court; or**

**(c) save as set out in Practice Direction 63, a county court where there is also a Chancery District Registry.**

2F–14.1 *Note*—Substituted by the Civil Procedure (Amendment) Rules 2009 (SI 2009/2092) with effect from October 1, 2009.

In the main the usual rules of the CPR apply to intellectual property cases in the specialist lists which do not fall under Section I above.

As regards the formalities of starting the claim, see the Practice Direction para.17—the claim form must be marked "Intellectual Property" in the top right hand corner

[1] Amended by the Civil Procedure (Amendment No.2) Rules 2009 (SI 2009/3390).

*Paragraph numbers marked with a "+" can be found online and on CD.*

below the title of the court in which it is issued, and must state the registration number of any trade mark to which the claim relates.

Where an application is made for delivery up, the claim form or application notice must be served on interested parties as set out in Practice Direction para.19.1, 23.1, and 24.1.

Parties bringing counterclaims for invalidity of Community Trade Marks must inform OHIM as set out in the Practice Direction para.21.

**Statements of case**

*Julian Higgins' Trade Mark Application* [2000] R.P.C. 321 and *Club Europe Trade Mark* [2000] R.P.C. 329—trade mark notice of oppositions and statements of grounds are in effect pleadings — it is the function of pleadings to define the issues between the parties. **2F–14.2**

Where fraud is pleaded it must be clearly set out (see *Claudius Ash v Invicta* (1912) 29 R.P.C., and where deception is alleged the party so alleging may be ordered to give details of the person or persons who was deceived (see *Humphries v Taylor* (1888) L.R. 39 Ch D 693.

The provision of material facts upon which an allegation was based is particularly important where an applicant for a declaration of invalidity relies upon s.5(4) of the 1994 Act (see *Geobank Trade Mark* [1999] R.P.C. 682).

Where a party seeks to revoke a trade mark from a date earlier than the date of the application for revocation, it should set out in the statement of grounds the date it contended for and explicitly allege that the grounds for revocation existed at an appropriate earlier date. See *Omega SA v Omega Engineering Inc* [2003] EWHC 1334.

There is no legislative bar to a party, having failed in opposition proceedings, launching proceedings for a declaration of invalidity. See *Special Effects Ltd v L'Oreal SA* [2007] EWCA Civ 1; [2007] E.T.M.R. 51. It would only be in unusual circumstances that a court would be justified in holding that a party who did take advantage of the second opportunity provided by the legislation was abusing the process of the court.

Particular considerations apply to the pleading of confidential information cases. The importance of, and need for, precision in setting out any information said to be confidential was dealt with at length by Laddie J. in *Ocular Sciences Ltd v Aspect Vision Care Ltd* [1997] R.P.C. 289.

A claimant who seeks additional damages for copyright or unregistered design right must set out that claim and its basis in the statement of case—see Practice Direction para.22.1.

**Case management**

Case management of intellectual property proceedings other than those referred to in Section I above will ordinarily take place before a Master. **2F–14.3**

**Survey evidence**

Survey evidence is often of little real value to the resolution of the issues, often because the wrong questions had been put. It was in the interests of saving costs and of shortening trials that any survey evidence which was called should be of value to the court. The prior leave of the court is usually required. An application with regard to adducing expert evidence in relation to that survey is also usually required. See *UK Channel Management Ltd v E! Entertainment Television Inc* [2007] EWHC 2339 (Ch); [2008] F.S.R. 5; and *O2 Ltd and O2 (UK) Ltd v Hutchison 3G Ltd* [2005] E.T.M.R. 61, Ch D. **2F–14.4**

The modern recommended approach is therefore that set out in *Esure Insurance v Direct Line Insurance plc* [2008] EWCA Civ 842; [2008] E.T.M.R 77, at para.63—64, in which Arden L.J. held that, since consumer surveys were costly to produce, can be based on the wrong questions and can thus produce irrelevant or unhelpful responses or for some other reason be of no evidential value, there was:

> "much to be said for the practice initiated by the late Pumfrey J. (as he then was) in *O2 Holdings Ltd v Hutchison 3G UK Ltd (Application for Interim Injunction)* [2005] E.T.M.R. 61, and subsequently followed by Rimer J. in *UK Channel Management Ltd v E! Entertainment Television Inc* [2008] F.S.R. 5".

Under that practice, case management directions are given at an interim stage which require the parties to seek the directions of the court as to the scope or methodology of any proposed consumer survey that the parties want to put in evidence at trial. Those directions can then be given in advance of the trial (see, for example, the further proceedings in the *UK Channel Management Ltd v E! Entertainment Television Inc* [2007] EWHC 2339 (Ch) case given by Lewison J.).

**Disclosure**

2F-14.5 Disclosure is governed by the usual rules of the CPR. Nevertheless many of the principles discussed in Section I above (such as the disclosure of commercial secrets) may be applicable to disclosure in relation to other intellectual property cases.

**Expert Evidence in trade mark cases**

2F-14.6 Confusion between trade marks was to be determined from the viewpoint of the average consumer in the light of all the relevant factors. Evidence of an expert as to his own opinion therefore added little when the tribunal could form its own view. There might, however, be a role for an expert witness where the markets in question were ones with which judges were unfamiliar. See *Esure Insurance Ltd v Direct Line Insurance Plc* [2008] EWCA Civ 842.

**Expert evidence in design right cases and copyright cases**

2F-14.7 Whilst sometimes it is of value for experts to tutor the court as to the differences between works of the parties, evidence as to whether or not there has been copying in a copyright case is unlikely to be useful. See *IPC Media Ltd v Highbury Leisure Publishing Ltd* [2004] EWHC 2985 (Ch).

Likewise the experts' views as to whether an article is commonplace are not helpful since this is a question for the court (even though such evidence is admissible under the Civil Evidence Act 1972). What matters are the reasons for any such opinion—see *Lambretta Clothing Co Ltd v Teddy Smith (UK) Ltd* [2004] EWCA Civ 886.Whilst sometimes it is of value for experts to tutor the court as to the differences between works of the parties, evidence as to whether or not there has been copying in a copyright case is unlikely to be useful. See *IPC Media Ltd v Highbury Leisure Publishing Ltd* [2004] EWHC 2985 (Ch).

**Similar fact evidence**

2F-14.9 See *Mattel Inc v Woolbro (Distributors) Ltd* [2003] EWHC 2412 (Ch) in which it was held that there was no automatic admission of "similar fact" evidence in cases involving copying—it would depend on the probative value of the evidence. The court should be careful not to allow the introduction of evidence which was unfair or oppressive.

**Discontinuance**

2F-14.10 The normal rule in the event of a claimant discontinuing a claim is that the claimant has to pay the defendant's costs. The CPR gives the court a discretion however—see *Coca-Cola Company v Mabe* [2002] F.S.R. 47.

**Stays**

2F-14.11 In trade mark cases the situation is not analogous to that outlined in relation to patents in the previous section. Where proceedings relating to a trade mark were pending both in the English courts and in the Office for Harmonisation in the Internal Market, there was no presumption that the English proceedings would be stayed. See *Kitfix Swallow Group Ltd v Great Gizmos Ltd* [2007] EWHC 2668 (Ch); [2008] Bus. L.R. 465; [2008] E.T.M.R. 11; [2008] F.S.R. 9.

A stay, or injunction preventing the pursuit of, proceedings in a lower tribunal may also be granted of where the issues therein are being pursued in the High Court (see *Sears v Sears Roebuck* [1993] R.P.C. 385).

### *III. Service of Documents and Participation by the Comptroller*

## Service of documents

2F-15 **63.14—(1) Subject to paragraph (2), Part 6 applies to service of a claim form and any document in any proceedings under this Part.**

***Paragraph numbers marked with a "+" can be found online and on CD.***

(2) A claim form relating to a registered right may be served—

(a) on a party who has registered the right at the address for service given for that right in the United Kingdom Patent Office register, provided the address is within the United Kingdom; or

(b) in accordance with rule 6.32(1), 6.33(1) or 6.33(2) on a party who has registered the right at the address for service given for that right in the appropriate register at—

(i) the United Kingdom Patent Office; or

(ii) the Office for Harmonisation in the Internal Market.

(3) Where a party seeks any remedy (whether by claim form, counterclaim or application notice), which would if granted affect an entry in any United Kingdom Patent Office register, that party must serve on the Comptroller or registrar—

(a) the claim form, counterclaim or application notice;

(b) any other statement of case where relevant (including any amended statement of case); and

(c) any accompanying documents.

*Note* —Substituted by the Civil Procedure (Amendment) Rules 2009 (SI 2009/2092) with effect from October 1, 2009. **2F–15.1**

Rule 63.14 relates to the service of documents in relation to registered rights. It is self-explanatory, though note should be taken of the requirement for service on the Comptroller or registrar of documents in circumstances where a claim or counterclaim would impact on the UKIPO register if the remedy sought were to be granted.



### Participation by the Comptroller

**63.15** Where the documents set out in rule 63.14(3) are served, the Comptroller or registrar— **2F–16**

(a) may take part in proceedings; and

(b) need not serve a defence or other statement of case unless the court orders otherwise.

*Note* —Substituted by the Civil Procedure (Amendment) Rules 2009 (SI 2009/2092) with effect from October 1, 2009. **2F–16.1**

## *IV. Appeals*

### Appeals from decisions of the Comptroller of the registrar

**63.16—(1)** Part 52 applies to appeals from decisions of the Comptroller and the registrar. **2F–17**

(2) Appeals about patents must be made to the Patents Court, and other appeals to the Chancery Division.

(3) Where Part 52 requires a document to be served, it must also be served on the Comptroller or registrar, as appropriate.

*Note* —Substituted by the Civil Procedure (Amendment) Rules 2009 (SI 2009/2092) with effect from October 1, 2009. **2F–17.1**

The new rule makes clear that Pt 52 applies not only to decisions from the Comptroller, but also the registrar.

**Nature of Appeal from the Comptroller and registrar**

2F–17.2 In general, in accordance with r.52.11, the appeal will be limited to a review of the comptroller or registrar's decision. See *Blacklight Power Inc v Comptroller General of Patents, Designs and Trade Marks* [2008] EWHC 2763 (Pat); [2009] Bus. L.R. 748—the appeal is limited to a review of the decision below unless the court considers in an individual case that it would be in the interests of justice to hold a rehearing.

See also *Ladney and Hendry's International Application* [1998] R.P.C. 319. Section 97(3) of the Patents Act 1977 has not been impliedly repealed or amended by s.55 of the Access to Justice Act 1999, nor had it been limited in its scope. The appropriate test for second appeals under s.97(3) of the Patents Act 1977 is thus whether the proposed appeal has a real prospect of success. See *Smith International Inc's Patent* [2005] EWCA Civ 1357; [2006] F.S.R. 25.

For the role of the appellate court in trade mark appeals, see also Harrison's Trade Mark Application ("Chinawhite") [2002] EWHC 3009; *REEF Trade Mark* [2003] R.P.C. 5, CA, *POLICE Trade Mark* [2004] R.P.C. 35 and *Du Pont Trade Mark* [2003] EWCA Civ 1368.

For the principles on which new evidence should be allowed in an appeal from the Trade Marks Registry, see *Ministere de l'Agriculture de la Foret v Bernard Matthews Plc, sub nom. LABEL ROUGE Trade Mark* [2002] EWHC 190 and also *Joop v Canadelle Ltd Partnership of Canada sub nom. WUNDERKIND Trade Mark* [2002] R.P.C. 45; *Du Pont Trade Mark* [2003] EWCA Civ 1368, and *Omega Engineering Inc v Omega SA* [2004] EWHC 2315.

The court will not refuse to entertain an appeal against a hearing officer's decision on an opinion given under the Patents Act 1977 s.74A on the basis that the procedure could only result in the production of non-binding opinions or decisions. The provision of non-binding opinions was potentially of great value to persons concerned with the validity or infringement of a patent, and as such did not involve a purely academic question but a living issue. The court should only decide that such an opinion was wrong if the hearing officer had failed to recognise that an examiner had made an error of principle or reached a conclusion that was clearly wrong. It was not the function of the court to express an opinion on the question that was the subject of the original request. See *In the matter of DLP Ltd* [2007] EWHC 2669 (Pat).

**Period for appeal: Practice Direction 52 para.17.3**

2F–17.3 Since an appeal from the comptroller constitutes a statutory appeal within the meaning of para.17.1 of Practice Direction 52, then in accordance with para.17.3 notice of appeal must be filed at the court within 28 days after the date of the comptroller's decision. There is no discretion for the comptroller to direct a different period. For trade mark appeals a period of 28 days also applies.

In accordance with r.52.4(3) and para.17.5 of Practice Direction 52, the appeal notice must be served on each respondent and on the comptroller as soon as practicable and in any event not later than seven days after it is filed.

**Extension of the appeal period: CPR r.52.6**

2F–17.4 In accordance with r.52.6(1) and paras 5.2 and 5.3 of Practice Direction 52, any application to extend the period for appeal must be made to the court. The parties cannot extend the period by agreement (r.52.6(2)).

An appellant who applies for an extension from the court must state the reasons for the delay and the steps taken prior to the application being made. The respondent has a right to be heard on the application.

**Appeals to the Appointed Person and the Registered Designs Appeal Tribunal Appointed Person**

2F–17.5 The period for appeal to the Appointed Person is 28 days under the Trade Marks Rules and the comptroller has sole jurisdiction to extend this period. In relation to the nature of the appeal, the Appointed Person is not bound by the CPR but is generally guided by the court's approach to the distinction between review and rehearing.

**Registered Designs Appeal Tribunal**

2F–17.6 The Registered Designs Appeal Tribunal Rules 1950 (as amended 1970) govern appeals to the Tribunal under s.28 of the Registered Designs Act 1949 (as amended by

*Paragraph numbers marked with a "+" can be found online and on CD.*

the Copyright, Designs and Patents Act 1988) and s.249 of the 1988 Act. Under these Rules the period for appeal is 14 days for a decision on a matter of procedure and six weeks for other decisions, and the comptroller may extend the period upon request made prior to its expiry.

### Costs on appeal

The normal rule in relation to appeals concerning matters arising under the 1977 Act is that the successful party is awarded his costs (*Extrude Hone Corp's Patent* [1982] R.P.C. 361, Whitford J.; *Omron's Patent* [1981] R.P.C. 125). This rule also applies to appeals to which the Comptroller is a party. If there is any further appeal the Court of Appeal apply the usual rule of assessed costs (*Associated British Combustion Ltd's Patent* [1978] R.P.C. 581). Costs may be awarded on an application to the Court of Appeal for leave to appeal (*International Paint Co's Appn* [1982] R.P.C. 247). **2F–17.7**

### Costs on appeal

The normal rule in relation to appeals concerning matters arising under the 1977 Act is that the successful party is awarded his costs (*Extrude Hone Corp's Patent* [1982] R.P.C. 361, Whitford J.; *Omron's Patent* [1981] R.P.C. 125). This rule also applies to appeals to which the Comptroller is a party. If there is any further appeal the Court of Appeal apply the usual rule of assessed costs (*Associated British Combustion Ltd's Patent* [1978] R.P.C. 581). Costs may be awarded on an application to the Court of Appeal for leave to appeal (*International Paint Co's Appn* [1982] R.P.C. 247). **2F–17.8**

### Notices regulating European Patent Appeals

**Notice from the Vice-President Directorate-General 3 dated 17 March 2008 concerning accelerated processing before the boards of appeal** **2F–17.9**

Parties with a legitimate interest may ask the boards of appeal to deal with their appeals rapidly. The boards can speed up an appeal as far as the procedural regulations allow. Requests for accelerated processing must be submitted to the competent board either at the beginning of or during proceedings. They should contain reasons for the urgency together with relevant documents; no particular form is required. This option is also available to the courts and competent authorities of the contracting states. By way of example, the following circumstances could justify an appeal being dealt with particularly rapidly:

— where infringement proceedings have been brought or are envisaged

— where the decision of potential licensees of the patent in suit, that is the patent which is the subject of an appeal, hinges upon the outcome of the appeal proceedings

— where an opposition which is to be given accelerated processing (see Notice of the EPO dated 17 March 2008, OJ EPO 2008, 221) has been made the subject of an appeal.

By way of exception, the board may accelerate the procedure ex officio, for example in view of the disadvantages which could ensue from the suspensive effect of the appeal in the case in question.

Whether or not a particular case is regarded as urgent will depend on the nature of the case and not merely on whether accelerated processing is requested by the parties. If, in view of the circumstances, the reasons given and the documents provided, the board decides to grant accelerated processing, this will involve in particular giving the appeal priority, and/or—with due respect for the parties' right to be heard and the fair administration of justice—adopting a strict framework for the procedure, for example concerning the time limits available before the final decision.

**Article 99—OJ 1998, 361 Notice from the President of the European Patent Office dated 19 May 1998 concerning accelerated processing of oppositions where infringement proceedings have been instituted**

1. In cases where an infringement action in respect of a European patent is pending before a national court of a contracting state a party to the opposition proceedings may request accelerated processing. The request may be filed at any time. It must be filed in written reasoned form. The Office will then make every effort to issue the next procedural action (e.g. communication, summons to oral proceedings) within three months of receipt of the request or where the request is already filed within the opposition period, within three months after receipt of the patent proprietor's response to the notice of opposition (whichever is the later).



INTELLECTUAL PROPERTY

2. In addition, the EPO will also accelerate the processing of the opposition if it is informed by the national court or competent authority of a contracting state that infringement actions are pending.

3. However, the EPO has to rely on the co-operation of the parties to the proceedings who are expected in particular to make their submissions promptly and in full and in any case strictly to adhere to the time limits set by the EPO for replying to communications or commenting on written submissions from the other parties. Requests to extend time limits over and above the normal four-month period can only be granted in exceptional, duly substantiated cases.

# PRACTICE DIRECTION 63—INTELLECTUAL PROPERTY CLAIMS

*This Practice Direction supplements CPR Part 63*

## Contents of this Practice Direction

**1.1** This practice direction is divided into four sections— 2F-18

- Section I—Provisions about patents and those other rights within the scope of Section I of Part 63
- Section II—Provisions about registered trade marks and other intellectual property rights
- Section III—Provisions about appeals.
- Section IV—Provisions about final orders

### *I. Provisions about Patents and those other Rights within the Scope of Section I of Part 63*

## Scope of Section I

**2.1** This Section applies to claims within the scope of Section 1 of Part 63. 2F-19

## Starting the claim (rule 63.5)

**3.1** A claim form to which this Section applies must— 2F-20

(a) be marked "Chancery Division Patents Court" or "Patents County Court" as the case may be, in the top right hand corner below the title of the court, and

(b) state the number of any patent or registered design to which the claim relates.

## Claim for infringement or challenge to validity (rule 63.6)

**4.1** In a claim for infringement of a patent— 2F-21

(1) the statement of case must—

(a) show which of the claims in the specification of the patent are alleged to be infringed; and

(b) give at least one example of each type of infringement alleged; and

(2) a copy of each document referred to in the statement of case, and where necessary a translation of the document, must be served with the statement of case.

**4.2** Where the validity of a patent or registered design is challenged—

(1) the statement of case must contain particulars of—

(a) the remedy sought; and

(b) the issues except those relating to validity of the patent or registered design;

(2) the statement of case must have a separate document attached to and forming part of it headed "Grounds of Invalidity" which must—

(a) specify the grounds on which validity of the patent or registered design is challenged; and

(b) include particulars that will clearly define every issue

***Paragraph numbers marked with a "+" can be found online and on CD.***



Intellectual Property

(including any challenge to any claimed priority date) which it is intended to raise; and

(3) a copy of each document referred to in the Grounds of Invalidity, and where necessary a translation of the document, must be served with the Grounds of Invalidity.

**4.3** Where in an application in which the validity of a patent or a registered design is challenged, the Grounds of Invalidity include an allegation—

(1) that the invention is not a patentable invention because it is not new or does not include an inventive step, the particulars must specify details of the matter in the state of the art relied on, as set out in paragraph 4.4;

(2) that the specification of the patent does not disclose the invention clearly enough and completely enough for it to be performed by a person skilled in the art, the particulars must state, if appropriate, which examples of the invention cannot be made to work and in which respects they do not work or do not work as described in the specification; or

(3) that the registered design is not new or lacks individual character, the particulars must specify details of any prior design relied on, as set out in paragraph 4.4.

**4.4** The details required under paragraphs 4.3(1) and 4.3(3) are—

(1) in the case of matter or a design made available to the public by written description, the date on which and the means by which it was so made available, unless this is clear from the fact of the matter; and

(2) in the case of matter or a design made available to the public by use—

(a) the date or dates of such use;
(b) the name of all persons making such use;
(c) the place of such use;
(d) any written material which identifies such use;
(e) the existence and location of any apparatus employed in such use; and
(f) all facts and matters relied on to establish that such matter was made available to the public.

**4.5** In any proceedings in which the validity of a patent is challenged, where a party alleges that machinery or apparatus was used before the priority date of the claim the court may order inspection of that machinery or apparatus.

**4.6** If the validity of a patent is challenged on the ground that the invention did not involve an inventive step, a party who wishes to rely on the commercial success of the patent must state in the statement of case the grounds on which that party so relies.

**Case management (rule 63.8)**

2F–22 **5.1** The following paragraphs only of Practice Direction 29 apply—

(1) paragraph 5 (case management conferences)—

(a) excluding paragraph 5.9; and

*Paragraph numbers marked with a "+" can be found online and on CD.*

(b) modified so far as is made necessary by other specific provisions of this practice direction; and

(2) paragraph 7 (failure to comply with case management directions).

**5.2** Case management will be dealt with by—

(1) a judge of the Patents Court, a patents judge or a Master, but

(2) a Master may only deal with the following matters—

(a) orders by way of settlement, except settlement of procedural disputes;

(b) applications for extension of time;

(c) applications for permission to serve out of the jurisdiction;

(d) applications for security for costs;

(e) other matters as directed by a judge of the court; and

(f) enforcement of money judgments.

**5.3** The claimant must apply for a case management conference within 14 days of the date when all defendants who intend to file and serve a defence have done so.

**5.4** Where the claim has been transferred, the claimant must apply for a case management conference within 14 days of the date of the order transferring the claim, unless the court held or gave directions for a case management conference when it made the order transferring the claim.

**5.5** Any party may, at a time earlier than that provided in paragraphs 5.3 and 5.4, apply in writing to the court to fix a case management conference.

**5.6** If the claimant does not make an application in accordance with paragraphs 5.3 and 5.4, any other party may apply for a case management conference.

**5.7** The court may fix a case management conference at any time on its own initiative.

**5.8** Not less than 4 days before a case management conference, each party must file and serve an application notice for any order which that party intends to seek at the case management conference.

**5.9** Unless the court orders otherwise, the claimant, or the party who makes an application under paragraph 5.6, in consultation with the other parties, must prepare a case management bundle containing—

(1) the claim form;

(2) all other statements of case (excluding schedules), except that, if a summary of a statement of case has been filed, the bundle must contain the summary, and not the full statement of case;

(3) a pre-trial timetable, if one has been agreed or ordered;

(4) the principal orders of the court; and

(5) any agreement in writing made by the parties as to disclosure,

*Paragraph numbers marked with a "+" can be found online and on CD.*



INTELLECTUAL PROPERTY

and provide copies of the case management bundle for the court and the other parties at least 4 days before the first case management conference or any earlier hearing at which the court may give case management directions.

**5.10** At the case management conference the court may direct that—

(1) a scientific adviser under section 70(3) of the Senior Courts Act 1981 or under section 63(1) of the County Courts Act 1984 be appointed; and

(2) a document setting out basic undisputed technology should be prepared.

(Rule 35.15 applies to scientific advisers.)

**5.11** Where a trial date has not been fixed by the court, a party may apply for a trial date by filing a certificate which must—

(1) state the estimated length of the trial, agreed if possible by all parties;

(2) detail the time required for the judge to consider the documents;

(3) identify the area of technology; and

(4) assess the complexity of the technical issues involved by indicating the complexity on a scale of 1 to 5 (with 1 being the least and 5 the most complex).

**5.12** The claimant, in consultation with the other parties, must revise and update the documents, referred to in paragraph 5.9 appropriately as the case proceeds. This must include making all necessary revisions and additions at least 7 days before any subsequent hearing at which the court may give case management directions.

### Disclosure and inspection (rule 63.9)

2F–23 **6.1** Standard disclosure does not require the disclosure of documents that relate to—

(1) the infringement of a patent by a product or process where—

(a) not less than 21 days before the date for service of a list of documents the defendant notifies the claimant and any other party of the defendant's intention to serve—

(i) full particulars of the product or process alleged to infringe; and

(ii) any necessary drawings or other illustrations; and

(b) on or before the date for service the defendant serves on the claimant and any other party the documents referred to in paragraph 6.1(1)(a);

(2) any ground on which the validity of a patent is put in issue, except documents which came into existence within the period—

(a) beginning two years before the earliest claimed priority date; and

(b) ending two years after that date; and

(3) the issue of commercial success.

**6.2** The particulars served under paragraph 6.1(1)(b) must be accompanied by a signed written statement which must state that the person making the statement—

(1) is personally acquainted with the facts to which the particulars relate;

(2) verifies that the particulars are a true and complete description of the product or process alleged to infringe; and

(3) understands that he or she may be required to attend court in order to be cross-examined on the contents of the particulars.

**6.3** Where the issue of commercial success arises, the patentee must, within such time limit as the court may direct, serve a schedule containing—

(1) where the commercial success relates to an article or product—
- (a) an identification of the article or product (for example by product code number) which the patentee asserts has been made in accordance with the claims of the patent;
- (b) a summary by convenient periods of sales of any such article or product;
- (c) a summary for the equivalent periods of sales, if any, of any equivalent prior article or product marketed before the article or product in sub-paragraph (a); and
- (d) a summary by convenient periods of any expenditure on advertising and promotion which supported the marketing of the articles or products in sub-paragraphs (a) and (c); or

(2) where the commercial success relates to the use of a process—
- (a) an identification of the process which the patentee asserts has been used in accordance with the claims of the patent;
- (b) a summary by convenient periods of the revenue received from the use of such process;
- (c) a summary for the equivalent periods of the revenues, if any, received from the use of any equivalent prior art process; and
- (d) a summary by convenient periods of any expenditure which supported the use of the process in sub-paragraphs (a) and (c).

### Experiments

**7.1** A party seeking to establish any fact by experimental proof conducted for the purpose of litigation must, at least 21 days before service of the application notice for directions under paragraph 7.3, or within such other time as the court may direct, serve on all parties a notice— **2F-24**

(1) stating the facts which the party seeks to establish; and

(2) giving full particulars of the experiments proposed to establish them.

*Paragraph numbers marked with a "+" can be found online and on CD.*

**7.2** A party served with a notice under paragraph 7.1—

(1) must within 21 days after such service, serve on the other party a notice stating whether or not each fact is admitted; and

(2) may request the opportunity to inspect a repetition of all or a number of the experiments identified in the notice served under paragraph 7.1.

**7.3** Where any fact which a party seeks to establish by experimental proof is not admitted, that party must apply to the court for permission and directions by application notice.

### Use of models or apparatus

2F–25 **8.1** A party that intends to rely on any model or apparatus must apply to the court for directions at the first case management conference.

### Time estimates for trial, trial bundle, reading guide and detailed trial timetable

2F–26 **9.1** Not less than one week before the beginning of the trial, each party must inform the court in writing of the estimated length of its—

(1) oral submissions;

(2) examination in chief, if any, of its own witnesses; and

(3) cross-examination of witnesses of any other party.

**9.2** At least four days before the date fixed for the trial, the claimant must file—

(1) the trial bundle;

(2) a reading guide for the judge; and

(3) a detailed trial timetable which should be agreed, if possible.

**9.3** The reading guide filed under paragraph 9.2 must—

(1) be short and, if possible, agreed;

(2) set out the issues, the parts of the documents that need to be read on each issue and the most convenient order in which they should be read;

(3) identify the relevant passages in text books and cases, if appropriate; and

(4) not contain argument.

### Application to amend a patent specification in existing proceedings (rule 63.10)

2F–27 **10.1** Where the application notice is served on the Comptroller electronically under rule 63.10(3), the applicant must comply with any requirements for the sending of electronic communications to the Comptroller.

**10.2** Not later than two days before the first hearing date the applicant, the Comptroller if wishing to be heard, the parties to the proceedings and any other opponent, must file and serve a document stating the directions sought.

### Request to limit a European patent (UK) under the European Patent Convention

2F–28 **11.1** Paragraphs 11.2 to 11.4 apply where there are proceedings before the court in which the validity of a European patent (UK) may be put in issue.

**11.2** Where the proprietor of the European patent (UK) intends to file a request under Article 105a of the European Patent Convention to limit the European patent (UK) by amendment of the claims, the proprietor must serve on all the parties to the proceedings a copy of the intended request (including a copy of the intended complete version of the amended claims and, as the case may be, of the amended description and drawings) at least 28 days prior to filing the request with the European Patent Office.

**11.3** Where a copy of an intended request is served on the party in accordance with paragraph 11.2, any party may apply to the court for such directions or other order as may be appropriate.

**11.4** Reference to "European Patent Convention" means the Convention on the Grant of European Patents of 5th October 1973 as amended from time to time.

### Application by employee for compensation (rule 63.12)

**12.1** Where an employee applies for compensation under section 40(1) or (2) of the 1977 Act, the court will at the case management conference give directions as to— **2F–29**

(1) the manner in which the evidence, including any accounts of expenditure and receipts relating to the claim, is to be given at the hearing of the claim and if written evidence is to be given, specify the period within which witness statements must be filed; and

(2) the provision to the claimant by the defendant or a person deputed by the defendant, of reasonable facilities for inspecting and taking extracts from the accounts by which the defendant proposes to verify the accounts in sub-paragraph (1) or from which those accounts have been derived.

### Communication of information to the European Patent Office

**13.1** The court may authorise the communication of any such information in the court files as the court thinks fit to— **2F–30**

(1) the European Patent Office; or

(2) the competent authority of any country which is a party to the European Patent Convention.

**13.2** Before authorising the communication of information under paragraph 13.1, the court will permit any party who may be affected by the disclosure to make representations, in writing or otherwise, on the question of whether the information should be disclosed.

### Order affecting entry in the register of patents or designs

**14.1** Where any order of the court affects the validity of an entry in the register, the party in whose favour the order is made, must serve a copy of such order on the Comptroller within 14 days. **2F–31**

**14.2** Where the order is in favour of more than one party, a copy of the order must be served by such party as the court directs.

### European Community designs

**15.1** The Patents Court and the patents county court at the Central **2F–32**

*Paragraph numbers marked with a "+" can be found online and on CD.*

London County Court are the designated Community design courts under Article 80(5) of Council Regulation (EC) 6/2002.

**15.2** Where a counterclaim is filed at the Community design court, for a declaration of invalidity of a registered Community design, the Community design court will inform the Office for Harmonisation in the Internal Market of the date on which the counterclaim was filed, in accordance with Article 86(2) of Council Regulation (EC) 6/2002.

**15.3** On filing a counterclaim under paragraph 15.2, the party filing it must inform the Community design court in writing that it is a counterclaim to which paragraph 15.2 applies and that the Office for Harmonisation in the Internal Market needs to be informed of the date on which the counterclaim was filed.

**15.4** Where a Community design court has given a judgment which has become final on a counterclaim for a declaration of invalidity of a registered Community design, the Community design court will send a copy of the judgment to the Office for Harmonisation in the Internal Market, in accordance with Article 86(4) of Council Regulation (EC) 6/2002.

**15.5** The party in whose favour judgment is given under paragraph 15.4 must inform the Community design court at the time of judgment that paragraph 15.4 applies and that the Office for Harmonisation in the Internal Market needs to be sent a copy of the judgment.

### *II. Provisions about Registered Trade Marks and Other Intellectual Property Rights*

**Allocation (rule 63.13)**

2F–33 **16.1** The other intellectual property rights referred to in rule 63.13 are—

(1) copyright;
(2) rights in performances;
(3) rights conferred under Part VII of the 1988 Act ;
(4) design right;
(5) Community design right;
(6) association rights;
(7) moral rights;
(8) database rights
(9) unauthorised decryption rights;
(10) hallmarks;
(11) technical trade secrets litigation;
(12) passing off;
(13) protected designations of origin, protected geographical indications and traditional speciality guarantees;
(14) registered trade marks; and
(15) Community trade marks.

**16.2** There are Chancery district registries at Birmingham, Bristol, Caernarfon, Cardiff, Leeds, Liverpool, Manchester, Mold, Newcastle upon Tyne and Preston.

**16.3** The county courts at Caernarfon, Mold and Preston do not have jurisdiction in relation to registered trade marks and Community trade marks.

**Starting the claim**

**17.1** A claim form to which Section II of Part 63 applies must be marked in the top right hand corner "Intellectual Property" below the title of the court in which it is issued. **2F–34**

**17.2** In the case of claims concerning registered trade marks and Community trade marks, the claim form must state the registration number of any trade mark to which the claim relates.

**Reference to the court by the registrar or the Comptroller**

**18.1** This paragraph applies where— **2F–35**

(1) an application is made to the registrar under the 1994 Act and the registrar refers the application to the court; or

(2) a reference is made to the Comptroller under section 246 of the 1988 Act and the Comptroller refers the whole proceedings or a particular question or issue to the court under section 251(1) of that Act.

**18.2** Where paragraph 18.1 applies, the applicant under the 1994 Act or the person making the reference under section 246 of the 1988 Act, as the case may be, must start a claim seeking the court's determination of the reference within 14 days of receiving notification of the decision to refer.

**18.3** If the person referred to in paragraph 18.2 does not start a claim within the period prescribed by that paragraph, that person will be deemed to have abandoned the reference.

**18.4** The period prescribed under paragraph 18.2 may be extended by—

(1) the registrar or the Comptroller as the case may be; or

(2) the court

where a party so applies, even if the application is not made until after the expiration of that period.

**Application to the court under section 19 of the 1994 Act**

**19.1** Where an application is made under section 19 of the 1994 Act, the applicant must serve the claim form or application notice on all identifiable persons having an interest in the goods, materials or articles within the meaning of section 19 of the 1994 Act. **2F–36**

**Order affecting entry in the register of trade marks**

**20.1** Where any order of the court affects the validity of an entry in the register, the provisions of paragraphs 14.1 and 14.2 apply. **2F–37**

**European Community trade marks**

**21.1** The Chancery Division, the patents county court at the Central London County Court and the county courts where there is also a Chancery district registry, except Caernarfon, Mold and Preston, are designated Community trade mark courts for the purposes of Article 91(1) of Council Regulation (EC) 40/94. **2F–38**

*Paragraph numbers marked with a "+" can be found online and on CD.*

**21.2** Where a counterclaim is filed at the Community trade mark court, for revocation or for a declaration of invalidity of a Community trade mark, the Community trade mark court will inform the Office of Harmonisation in the Internal Market of the date on which the counterclaim was filed, in accordance with Article 96(4) of Council Regulation (EC) 40/94.

**21.3** On filing a counterclaim under paragraph 21.2, the party filing it must inform the Community trade mark court in writing that it is a counterclaim to which paragraph 21.2 applies and that the Office for Harmonisation in the Internal Market needs to be informed of the date on which the counterclaim was filed.

**21.4** Where the Community trade mark court has given a judgment which has become final on a counterclaim for revocation or for a declaration of invalidity of a Community trade mark, the Community trade mark court will send a copy of the judgment to the Office for Harmonisation in the Internal Market, in accordance with Article 96(6) of Council Regulation (EC) 40/94.

**21.5** The party in whose favour judgment is given under paragraph 21.4 must inform the Community trade mark court at the time of judgment that paragraph 21.4 applies and that the Office for Harmonisation in the Internal Market needs to be sent a copy of the judgment.

### Claim for additional damages under section 97(2), section 191J(2) or section 229(3) of the 1988 Act

2F-39 **22.1** Where a claimant seeks to recover additional damages under section 97(2), section 191J(2) or section 229(3) of the 1988 Act, the particulars of claim must include—

(1) a statement to that effect; and
(2) the grounds for claiming them.

### Application for delivery up or forfeiture under the 1988 Act

2F-40 **23.1** An applicant who applies under section 99, 114, 195, 204, 230 or 231 of the 1988 Act for delivery up or forfeiture must serve—

(1) the claim form; or
(2) application notice, where appropriate,

on all identifiable persons who have an interest in the goods, material or articles within the meaning of section 114, 204 or 231 of the 1988 Act.

### Association rights

2F-41 **24.1** Where an application is made under regulations made under section 7 of the Olympic Symbol etc (Protection) Act 1995, the applicant must serve the claim form or application notice on all identifiable persons having an interest in the goods, materials or articles within the meaning of the regulations.

## *III. Provisions about Appeals*

### Reference to the court by an appointed person

2F-42 **25.1** This paragraph applies where a person appointed by the

*Paragraph numbers marked with a "+" can be found online and on CD.*

Lord Chancellor to hear and decide appeals under section 77 of the 1994 Act, refers an appeal to the Chancery Division under section 76(3) of the 1994 Act.

**25.2** The appellant must file a claim form seeking the court's determination of the appeal within 14 days of receiving notification of the decision to refer.

**25.3** The appeal will be deemed to have been abandoned if the appellant does not file a claim form within the period prescribed by paragraph 25.2.

**25.4** The period prescribed under paragraph 25.2 may be extended by—

(1) the person appointed by the Lord Chancellor; or

(2) the court

where the appellant so applies, even if such application is not made until after the expiration of that period.

*IV. Provisions about Final Orders*

**Costs**

**26.1** Where the court makes an order for delivery up or destruction of infringing goods, or articles designed or adapted to make such goods, the person against whom the order is made must pay the costs of complying with that order unless the court orders otherwise. **2F–43**

**26.2** Where the court finds that an intellectual property right has been infringed, the court may, at the request of the applicant, order appropriate measures for the dissemination and publication of the judgment to be taken at the expense of the infringer.

**[THE NEXT PARAGRAPH IS 2F–127.]**

# The Patents Court and Patents County Court Guide

Issued 7 July 2008 **2F–127**

By authority of the Chancellor of the High Court

**1. Introduction**

This guide applies to both the Patents Court and the Patents County Court.

The general guidance applicable to matters in the Chancery Division, as set out in the Chancery Guide also applies to patent actions unless specifically mentioned below. "63PD" refers to the Practice Direction–Patents and Other Intellectual Property Claims which supplements CPR Part 63. Thus practitioners should consult this guide together with the Chancery Guide.

**2. Allocation**

Actions proceeding in the Patents Court and the Patents County Court are allocated to the multi-track (Part 63.1(3)). Attention is drawn to Part 63.7 and 63PD.4 (case management). **2F–128**

**3. The judges of the Patents Court**

The judges of the Patents Court and their clerks are set out below. **2F–129**

Kitchin J (Clerk: Gillian Tarleton–tel 020 7947 6518, fax 020 7947 6439, (*Gillian.Tarleton@hmcourts-service.gsi.gov.uk*)–Senior Patents judge

Patten J (Clerk: Anne Bateman–tel 020 7947 7617, fax 020 7947 6650, (*Anne.Bateman@hmcourts-service.gsi.gov.uk*)

Lewison J (Clerk: Donald Bennett–tel 020 7947 6039, fax 020 7947 6894, (*Donald.Bennett@hmcourts-service.gsi.gov.uk*)

Mann J (Clerk: Patricia Swales–tel 020 7947 7964, fax 020 7947 6739, (*Patricia.Swales@hmcourts-service.gsi.gov.uk*)

Warren J (Clerk: Elizabeth Collum–tel 020 7947 7260, fax 020 7947 7740, (*Elizabeth.Collum2@hmcourts-service.gsi.gov.uk*)

Floyd J (Clerk: Alison Hall–tel 020 70731740, fax 020 7947 6593, (*Alison.Hall@hmcourts-service.gsi.gov.uk*)

Trials of cases with a technical difficulty rating of 4 or 5 will normally be heard by Kitchin J. or Floyd J.

**4. Patents County Court**

2F–130 4.1 The Patents County Court judge is His Honour Judge Fysh QC (Clerk: Kav Rekhi—tel 020 7073 4251, fax 020 7073 4253 (*kav.rekhi@hmcourts-service.gsi.gov.uk*). The Patents County Court is situated at:

Field House
15-25 Breams Buildings
London
EC4A 1DZ

4.2 The issue of claim forms for the Patents County Court and general inquiries relating to procedure, may be addressed to:

The Specialist Section
Central London Civil Justice Centre ("CLCC")
26 Park Crescent
London
W1N 4HT
DX 97325 REGENTS PARK 2
Tel: 020 7917 7821
Fax: 020 7917 7935

Enquiries relating to listing and existing patent cases should be addressed to the Chancery Listing Office (see para.12 below)

4.3 The issue of all interlocutory processes will continue to be dealt with as at present by the clerk of HHJ Fysh QC at Field House either by post or personal attendance. The payment of the fee will continue to be made at the Fees Office Room E01 in the Royal Courts of Justice.

4.4 All proceedings when issued are sent by CLCC to the Clerk of HH Judge Fysh QC. Enquiries relating to an existing case in the Patents County Court after the claim form has been issued (except for enforcement) may be addressed to

The Clerk to His Honour Judge Fysh QC
Field House
15-25 Breams Buildings
London
EC4A 1DZ
Tel: 020 7073 4251
Fax: 020 7073 4253

4.5 Any document (other than a claim form or one relating to enforcement) on which a fee is payable should be sent to:

Room E01
Royal Courts of Justice
Strand
London
WC2A 2LL
DX 44450 STRAND

**5. Judges able and willing to sit out of London**

If the parties so desire, for the purpose of saving time or costs, the Patents Court and Patents County Court will sit out of London. Before any approach is made to the Chancery Listing Officer, the parties should discuss between themselves the desirability of such a course. If there is a dispute as to venue, the court will resolve the matter on an application. Where there is no dispute, the Chancery Listing Officer should be contacted as soon as possible so that arrangements can be put in place well before the date of the proposed hearing. **2F–131**

**6. Intellectual Property Court Users' Committee**

This committee (the "IPCUC") considers the problems and concerns of intellectual property litigators. Membership of the committee includes the judges of the Patents Court and the Patents County Court, a representative of each of the Intellectual Property Bar Association, the Intellectual Property Lawyers Association, the Chartered Institute of Patent Attorneys, the Institute of Trade Mark Attorneys and the Trade Marks Patents and Designs Federation. Anyone having views concerning the improvement of intellectual property litigation is invited to make his or her views known to the committee, preferably through the relevant professional representative on the committee. They may also be communicated to the secretary (Philip Westmacott, Bristows, 100 Victoria Embankment, London EC4Y ODH Tel: 020 7400 8000 Fax: 020 7400 8050). **2F–132**

The Patents County Court also has a Users' Committee which has a membership and general remit similar to the IPCUC. Matters of specific interest to the Patents County Court do arise and are considered by this committee. Its secretary is Alan Johnson, Bristows (100 Victoria Embankment, London EC4Y ODH Tel: 020 7400 8000 Fax: 020 7400 8050).

## *Procedure in the Patents Court and Patents County Court*

**7. Statements of Case**

***Time Limits*** **2F–133**

7.1 In general, the time limits set out in Part 15 apply to litigation of patents and registered designs. However, Part 63.6 and 63.9 modify Part 15 in respect of the time limits for filing defences and replies.

***Content of statements of case***

7.2 In general, statements of case (i.e. the pleadings of all parties) must comply with the requirements of Part 16. Furthermore, they should comply with Part 63.9 and 63PD.11. Copies of important documents referred to in a statement of case (e.g. an advertisement referred to in a claim of infringement form or documents cited in Grounds of Invalidity) should be served with the statement of case. Where any such document requires translation, a translation should be served at the same time.

***Independent validity of claims***

7.3 Where one party raises the issue of validity of a patent, the patentee (or other relevant party) should identify which of the claims of the patent are alleged to have independent validity as early as possible.

**8. Active case management and streamlined procedure**

8.1 The claimants should apply for a case management conference ("CMC") within 14 days of the date when all defendants who intend to file and serve a defence have done so (63PD.4.3). If the claimants fail to do so, then any other party may apply for a CMC (63PD.4.6). Any party may apply in writing for a CMC prior to the above periods. Where a case has been transferred from another division or from another court, the claimants must file for a CMC within 14 days of the transfer (63PD.4.4). **2F–134**

8.2 Almost invariably CMCs in the Patents Court will be conducted by a judge. However, in the limited circumstances set out in 63PD.8.1 (see also para.16 below), a Master may conduct a CMC. Bundles in accordance with 63PD.4.9 should be filed with the court. In the Patents County Court, all CMCs are conducted by the judge of the Patents County Court and not by a district judge.

***Paragraph numbers marked with a "+" can be found online and on CD.***



INTELLECTUAL PROPERTY

8.3 In general, parties should endeavour to agree directions prior to the date fixed for the CMC. Although the court has the right to amend directions which have been agreed, this will only happen where there is manifest reason for doing so.

8.4 In accordance with the overriding objective, the court will actively manage the case. In making any order for directions, the court will consider all relevant matters and have regard to the overriding objective with particular emphasis on proportionality, the financial position of the parties, the degree of complexity of the case, the importance of the case and the amount of money at stake.

8.5 The parties are reminded of their continuing obligation to assist the court to further the overriding objective. Moreover, it is the duty of the parties' advisors to remind litigants of the existence of mediation or other forms of alternative dispute resolution as a possible means to resolve disputes. In particular, the parties should consider:

(a) The need for and/or scope of any oral testimony from factual or expert witnesses. The court may confine cross-examination to particular issues and to time limits. The parties should consider whether oral testimony of witnesses should be given by video facility.

(b) The need for, and scope of, any disclosure of documents.

(c) The need for any experiments, process or product descriptions.

(d) The need for an oral hearing or whether a decision can be made on the papers. If an oral hearing is considered to be appropriate, the court may order that the hearing be of a fixed duration.

(e) Whether there is a need for a document setting out the basic undisputed technology ("technical primer"), and if so, its scope and the steps to be taken to achieve agreement of it.

(f) Whether a scientific adviser should be appointed.

(g) Whether a costs-capping order should be made.

(h) Whether there should be a stay of proceedings for mediation or other form of alternative dispute resolution.

8.6 ***Streamlined procedure***

Any party may at any time apply to the court for a streamlined procedure in which:

(a) all factual and expert evidence is in writing;

(b) there is no requirement to give disclosure of documents;

(c) there are no experiments;

(d) cross-examination is only permitted on any topic or topics where it is necessary and is confined to those topics;

or for any variant on the above.

8.7 Prior to applying for a streamlined procedure, the party seeking it should put its proposal to other parties in the proceedings and should endeavour to agree a form of order.

8.8 If the parties agree to a streamlined procedure, the proposed form of order should be put to the judge for approval as a paper application.

### 9. Admissions

**2F–135** 9.1 With a view to early elimination of non-issues, practitioners are reminded of the necessity of making admissions as soon as possible. This should be done as early as possible, for instance, in a defence or reply. Thus, in a defence, a party may admit the acts complained of or that his article/process has certain of the features of a claim. In a reply a patentee may be able to admit prior publication of cited documents. For the effect of admissions, see Part 14.

9.2 Parties should also consider serving a notice to admit facts in accordance with Part 32.18 for the purpose of identification of points not in dispute. By asking whether or not the defendant disputes that his article/process has certain features of the claim the real dispute can be narrowed. Thus the ambit of disclosure and of witness and expert statements will be narrowed.

9.3 Parties are reminded that when deciding the issue of costs, a court can take into account the conduct of the parties, including whether it was reasonable for a party to contest a particular issue – Part 44.3(5)(b).

9.4 The position should be kept under constant review. If there is any alteration in the admissions that can be made, the identity of the claims said to have independent validity, or the claims alleged to be infringed, that information should be communicated forthwith to the other parties.

### 10. Alternative Dispute Resolution ("ADR")

10.1 While emphasising its primary role as a forum for deciding patent and registered design cases, the Patents Court and Patents County Court encourage parties to consider the use of ADR (such as, but not confined to, mediation and conciliation) as an alternative means of resolving disputes or particular issues within disputes. **2F–136**

10.2 Settlement of dispute by ADR has many advantages including significant saving of costs and providing parties with a wider range of solutions than can be offered by litigation. Legal representatives should consider and advise their clients as to the possibility of attempting to resolve the dispute via ADR. In an appropriate case, the Patents Court and Patents County Court may adjourn a case for a specified period of time to encourage and enable the parties to use ADR.

10.3 The clerk to the Patents County Court judge has a list of mediation service providers which is available on request.

### 11. Disclosure

11.1 Parties are obliged to provide disclosure in accordance with Part 31 as modified by Part 63.8 and 63PD.5 **2F–137**

***Process and Product Descriptions***

11.2 Where appropriate, parties are encouraged to provide a Process and/or Product Description ("PPD") instead of standard disclosure relating to processes or products which are alleged to infringe or are otherwise relevant to proceedings.

11.3 PPDs must be adequate to deal with the nature of the allegation that has been advanced by the other party or parties. The parties have joint responsibility at an early stage to determine the nature of the case advanced so that the PPD is adequate to deal with that case.

11.4 Parties should bear in mind when preparing a PPD that they may be called on to prove it at trial. Any material omission or inaccuracy could result in a costly adjournment with consequential adverse orders, including as to costs.

***Descriptions and drawings of processes or products***

11.5 Parties are encouraged to agree descriptions and drawings of processes and/or products which are the subject of infringement proceedings or are alleged to constitute relevant prior art.

***Models or apparatus of processes or products***

11.6 If a party wishes to adduce a model or apparatus at trial, it should, if practicable, ensure that directions for such are given at the first CMC (63PD.10). Parties should endeavour to view and agree the accuracy of such models or apparatus where possible well in advance of the date of trial.

## *General matters relating to hearings of applications and Trials*

### 12. Arrangements for listing

12.1 The Chancery Listing Officer is responsible for the listing of all work of the Patents Court and the Patents County Court. **2F–138**

12.2 The Chancery Listing Officer and his staff are located in Room WG04 in the Royal Courts of Justice. The office is open to the public from 10.00 am to 4.30 pm each day. The telephone numbers are 020 7947 6778/6690 and the fax number is 020 7947 7345.

12.3 Appointments to fix trials and interim applications are dealt with on Tuesdays and Thursdays between 11.00 am and 12.00 noon. The applicant should first obtain an appointment from the Chancery Listing Officer and give 3 clear days' notice to all interested parties of the date and time fixed.

***Paragraph numbers marked with a "+" can be found online and on CD.***

12.4 A party should not seek to list an application or cause the opposing advocate or counsel's clerk to "pencil in" a date for hearing prior to raising with the proposed respondent the subject-matter of the application so that, where possible, agreement may be reached on the subject-matter of the application. Applicants who fail properly to consult with the respondents prior to listing an application may be met with an adverse costs order.

***Short applications***

12.5 Short applications (i.e. those estimated to last no more than 1 hour) will usually be heard before the normal court day starts at 10.30 am e.g. 9.30 or 10 am. These can be issued and the hearing date arranged at any time by attendance at the Chancery Listing Office. Attention is drawn to 63PD.6 about the filing of documents and skeleton arguments.

***Urgent applications and Without Notice applications***

12.6 A party wishing to apply without notice to the respondent(s) should contact the Chancery Listing Office. In cases of emergency in vacation or out of normal court hours, the application should be made to the duty Chancery judge.

***September sittings***

12.7 The Patents Court and Patents County Court will endeavour, if the parties so desire and the case is urgent, to sit in September.

***Interim injunction hearings and expedited trials***

12.8 Applicants for interim remedies (in particular, interim injunctions) and respondents are encouraged to consider whether an expedited (speedy) trial would better meet the interests of justice. Applications for expedited trials may be made at any time but should be made as soon as possible and notice given to all parties.

12.9 When an application for an interim injunction is made the applicant should, where practicable, make prior investigations with the Chancery Listing Officer about trial dates on an unexpedited and expedited basis having regard to the estimated length of trial.

#### 13. Time estimates

2F-139 13.1 In providing appropriate time estimates, parties must appreciate the need to give realistic and accurate time estimates and ensure that the time estimate includes a discrete reading time for the court to read the papers prior to the hearing of the application or trial. In general, the court will wish to read the skeleton arguments, the patent (where relevant), the prior art (where relevant), expert reports and other key documents (e.g. important witness statements). Advisors should bear in mind the technical difficulty of the case when considering the reading time estimate. The court will consider the imposition of guillotines where time estimates are exceeded.

***Revised time estimates***

13.2 Where parties and their legal advisors consider that a time estimate that has been provided (e.g. at the CMC) is unrealistic, they have a duty to notify the new time estimate to the Chancery Listing Office or, where appropriate, the judge's clerk as soon as possible.

#### 14. Documents and timetable

2F-140 14.1 Bundling for the hearing of applications and trials is of considerable importance and should be approached intelligently. The general guidance given in Appendix 6 of the Chancery Guide should be followed. Solicitors or patent attorneys who fail to do so may be required to explain why and may be penalised personally in costs.

14.2 If it is known which judge will be taking the hearing, papers for the hearing should be lodged directly with that judge's clerk. If there is insufficient time to lodge hard copies before the deadline, faxed documents of significance (and particularly skeleton arguments) should be supplied, followed up by clean hard copies. Alternatively to faxing documents, by agreement, documents may be sent by e-mail to the clerk of the judge concerned.

14.3 It is the responsibility of both parties to ensure that all relevant documents are lodged with the clerk of the judge who will be taking the hearing by noon two days before the date fixed for hearing unless some longer or shorter period has been ordered by the judge or is prescribed by this guide.

14.4 The judges request that all important documents also be supplied to them on disk or via e-mail in a format convenient for the judge's use (normally the current or a recent version of Microsoft Word 2003 for Windows or as a text searchable pdf). These will usually include skeleton arguments, important patents and drawings, the witness statements and expert reports.

14.5 Prior to trial, parties should ensure that they comply with the requirements of 63PD.7 concerning the provision of a trial timetable, trial bundle and reading guide for the judge. The trial timetable should be detailed and set out the times and dates that witnesses will be required to give evidence.

14.6 Where a technical primer has been produced, the parties should identify those parts which are agreed to form part of the common general knowledge. Usually, this should be done shortly after exchange of expert reports but a reasonable time prior to trial.

14.7 [0]11Skeleton arguments should be lodged in time for the judge to read them before an application or trial.

(a) In the case of applications, this should normally be 10:30am the previous working day (or, in the case of short applications, 3pm)

(b) In the case of trials, this should normally be at least two working days before commencement of the trial. In substantial cases, a longer period (to be discussed with the clerk to the judge concerned) may be needed.

14.8 14.8[0]11Following the evidence in a substantial trial, a short adjournment may be granted to enable the parties to summarise their arguments in writing before oral argument.

***Transcripts***

14.9 In trials where a transcript of evidence is being made and supplied to the judge, the transcript should be supplied by e-mail and in hard copy.

### 15. Telephone applications

15.1 For short (20 minutes or less) matters, the judges of the Patents Court and Patents County Court are willing to hear applications by telephone conference in accordance with the Practice Direction under Part 23. The party making the application is responsible for setting up the telephone application and informing the parties, Counsels' clerks and Chancery Listing of the time of the conference call. **2F–141**

15.2 It is possible for the application to be recorded, and if recording by the court rather than by British Telecom (or other service provider) is requested, arrangements should be made with the Chancery Listing Officer. The recording will not be transcribed. The tape will be kept by the clerk to the judge hearing the application for a period of six months. Arrangements for transcription, if needed, must be made by the parties.

15.3 This procedure should be used where it will save costs.

## *Miscellaneous*

### 16. Jurisdiction of Masters

16.1 Masters have only a limited jurisdiction in patent matters (see 63PD.8). Generally it is more convenient for consent orders (on paper or in court) to be made by a judge even where a Master has jurisdiction to do so. **2F–142**

16.2 Where a Master makes a consent order disposing of an action which has been fixed, it is the duty of all the parties' representatives to inform the Chancery Listing Officer that the case has settled. Where the validity of the patent was in issue, the United Kingdom Intellectual Property Office ("UKIPO") should also be informed.

16.3 In the Patents County Court, all matters go to the appointed judge and not to a district judge. In many cases, such matters may be dealt with on paper.

NB Direction, dated 16th July 2008, from Mr Justice Kitchin, the Senior Judge of the Patents Court:

"Pursuant to paragraph 8.1(5) of the Practice Direction to CPR Part 63, I hereby

***Paragraph numbers marked with a "+" can be found online and on CD.***

direct that a Master or a Deputy Master may deal with an application by a non-party under CPR rule 5.4C for a copy of the Grounds of Invalidity annexed to a Statement of Case in which challenge is made to the validity of a patent or registered design."

**17. Consent orders**

2F-143 17.1 The court is normally willing to make consent orders without the need for the attendance of any parties. A draft of the agreed order and the written consent of all the parties' respective solicitors or counsel should be supplied to the Chancery Listing Office. Unless the judge considers a hearing is needed, he will make the order in the agreed terms by initialling it. It will be drawn up accordingly and sent to the parties.

17.2 In the Patents County Court, consent orders should be sent to the judge's clerk or to the Chancery Listing Office.

**18. Draft judgments**

2F-144 18.1 Many judgments, particularly after a full trial, will be reserved and handed down at a later date, as advised by the Chancery Listing Office. Prior to that, the practice has arisen to provide the parties' legal representatives (or litigants in person) with a copy of the draft judgment for advocates to notify the court of typographical and obvious errors (if any). The text may be shown, in confidence, to the parties, but only for the purpose of obtaining instructions and on the strict understanding that the judgment, or its effect, is not to be disclosed to any other person, or used in the public domain, and that no action is taken (other than internally) in response to the judgment. Reference is invited to 40EPD.1.

**19. Orders following judgment**

2F-145 19.1 Where a judgment is made available in draft before being given in open court the parties should, in advance of that occasion, exchange drafts of the desired consequential order. It is highly undesirable that one party should spring a proposal on the other for the first time when judgment is handed down. Where the parties are agreed as to the consequential order and have supplied to the judge a copy of the same signed by all parties or their representatives, attendance at the handing down of the judgment is not necessary.

**20. Appeals from the Comptroller-General of Patents, Designs and Trade Marks ("the Comptroller")**

2F-146 *Patents*

20.1 By virtue of statute, these lie only to the High Court and not the Patents County Court. They are now governed by Part 52 (see Part 63.17). Permission to appeal is not required. Note that the Comptroller must be served with a Notice of Appeal (Part 63.17(3)). The appellant has the conduct of the appeal and he or his representative should, within 2 weeks of lodging the appeal, contact the Chancery Listing Officer with a view to arranging a hearing date. The appellant must ensure that the appeal is set down as soon as is reasonably practicable after service of the notice of appeal. Parties are reminded that the provisions about the service of skeleton arguments apply to appeals from the Comptroller.

*Registered Designs*

20.2 Appeals in registered designs cases go to the Registered Designs Appeal Tribunal. This consists of one of the patent judges sitting as a tribunal. The CPR and PD do not apply to such appeals. Where such an appeal is desired, contact should be made direct with the Chancery Listing Officer.

*Trade Marks*

20.3 These are assigned to the Chancery Division as a whole, not the Patents Court (Part 63.17(2)). Permission to appeal is not required.

*Appeals on paper only*

20.4 The court will hear appeals on paper only if that is what the parties desire. If the appellant is willing for the appeal to be heard on paper only, he should contact the respondent and UKIPO at the earliest opportunity to discover

***Paragraph numbers marked with a "+" can be found online and on CD.***

whether such a way of proceeding is agreed. If it is, the Chancery Listing Office should be informed as soon as possible. The parties (and the Chancery Listing Officer if he/she desires) should liaise amongst themselves for early preparation of written submissions and bundles and provide the court with all necessary materials.

### *Specimen minute of order for directions*

A draft order is annexed below covering most normal eventualities. The directions are intended only as a guide and are not "standard directions". Not all paragraphs will be applicable in every case. **2F–147**

#### Form of order for directions

AND UPON the parties' legal advisors having advised the litigants of the existence of mediation as a possible means of resolving this claim and counterclaim **2F–148**

#### Transfer

1. [This claim and counterclaim be transferred to the Patents County Court.] (If this order is made, no other order will generally be necessary, though it will generally be desirable for procedural orders to be made at this time to save the costs of a further conference in the Patents County Court.)

#### Amendments to statements of case

2. The claimants have permission to amend their claim form shown in red on the copy [annexed to the application notice/as signed by the solicitors for the parties/annexed hereto] and [to re-serve the same on or before [date]/and that re-service be dispensed with] and that the defendants have permission to serve a consequentially amended defence within [number] days [thereafter/hereafter] and that the claimants have permission to serve a consequentially amended reply (if so advised) within [number] days thereafter.

3. (a) The defendants have permission to amend their defence and counterclaim [and grounds of invalidity] as shown in red on the copy [annexed to the application notice/as signed by the solicitors for the parties/annexed hereto] and [to re-serve the same within [number] days/on or before[date]] [and that re-service be dispensed with] and that the claimants have permission to serve a consequentially amended reply (if so advised) within [number] days thereafter.

[(b) The claimants do on or before [date] elect whether they will discontinue this claim and withdraw their defence to the amended counterclaim and consent to an order for the revocation of Patent No. ... ("the Patent") AND IF the claimants shall so elect and give notice thereof in the time aforesaid:

(i) the Patent be revoked;

(ii) the claimants shall pay the defendant's costs of the claim and counterclaim incurred up to and including [..............] (date of service of original defence and counterclaim) which shall include the costs of obtaining and giving effect to the order for revocation; and

(iii) the defendants shall pay the claimants' costs of the claim and counterclaim incurred thereafter.]

(c) The defendants' [claimants'] costs of and caused by the amendments to the claim form [particulars of claim] [defence and counterclaim] [reply] be the defendants [claimants] in any event.

#### Further Information and Clarification

5. (a) The [claimants/defendants] do on or before [date] serve on the [defendants/claimants] the further information or clarification of the [specify statement of case] as requested by the [claimants/defendants] by their request served on the [defendants/claimants] on [date] [and/or]

(b) The [claimants/defendants] do on or before [date] serve on the [defendants/claimants] [a response to their request for further information] [do answer the requests in their request for further information] or clarification of the [identify statement of case] served on the [defendants/claimants] on [date].

**Admissions**

6. The [claimants/defendants] do on or before [date] state in writing whether or not they admit the facts specified in the [defendants'/claimants'] notice to admit facts dated [date].

**Security**

7. The claimants/defendants do provide security for the defendants'/claimants' costs for its claim/counterclaim in the sum of £[state sum] by [paying such sums into court] [specify manner in which security to be given] and that:

(i) in the meantime the claim [counterclaim] be stayed [and/or];

(ii) unless security is given as ordered by the above date, the claim [counterclaim] be struck out without further order with the defendants'/claimants' costs of the claim [counterclaim] to be the subject of detailed assessment if not agreed.

**Lists of Documents**

8. (a) The claimants and the defendants respectively do on or before [state date] make and serve on the other of them a list in accordance with form N265 of the documents in their possession custody or control which they are required to disclose in accordance with the obligation of standard disclosure in accordance with Part 31 as modified by paragraph 5 of the Practice Direction - Patents etc. supplementing Part 63.

(b) In respect of those issues identified in Schedule [number] hereto disclosure shall be limited to those [documents/categories of documents] listed in Schedule [number].

**Inspection**

9. If any party wishes to inspect or have copies of such documents as are in another party's control, it shall give notice in writing that it wishes to do so and such inspection shall be allowed at all reasonable times upon reasonable notice and any copies shall be provided within [number] working days of the request upon the undertaking of the party requesting the copies to pay the reasonable copying charges.

**Experiments**

10. (a) Where a party desires to establish any fact by experimental proof, including an experiment conducted for the purposes of litigation or otherwise not being an experiment conducted in the normal course of research, that party shall on or before [date] serve on all the other parties a notice stating the facts which it desires to establish and giving full particulars of the experiments proposed to establish them.

(b) A party upon whom a notice is served under the preceding sub-paragraph shall within [number] days, serve on the party serving the notice a notice stating in respect of each fact whether or not that party admits it.

(c) Where any fact which a party wishes to establish by experimental proof is not admitted that party shall apply to the court for further directions in respect of such experiments.

[Or where paragraph 9 of the Practice Direction - Patents etc. supplementing CPR Part 63 has been complied with.]

11. (a) The claimants/defendants are to afford to the other parties an opportunity, if so requested, of inspecting a repetition of the experiments identified in paragraphs [specify them] of the notice[s] of experiments served on [date]. Any such inspection must be requested within [number] days of the date of this order and shall take place within [number] days of the date of the request.

(b) If any party shall wish to establish any fact in reply to experimental proof that party shall on or before [date] serve on all the other parties a notice stating the facts which it desires to establish and giving full particulars of the experiments proposed to establish them.

(c) A party upon whom a notice is served under the preceding sub-paragraph shall within [number] days serve on the party serving the notice a notice stating in respect of each fact whether or not that party admits it.

(d) Where any fact which a party wishes to establish by experimental proof in reply is not admitted the party may apply to the court for further directions in respect of such experiments.

**Notice of Models, etc.**

12. (a) If any party wishes to rely at the trial of this claim and counterclaim upon any model or apparatus, that party shall on or before [date] give notice thereof to all the other parties; shall afford the other parties an opportunity within [number] days of the service of such notice of inspecting the same and shall, if so requested, furnish the other party with copies or illustrations of such model or apparatus.

(b) No further or other model or apparatus shall be relied upon in evidence by either party save with consent or by permission of the court.

**Product or Process Description**

13. (a) The defendants/claimants do provide a written description together with relevant drawings of the following [product(s)] [process(es)] to the claimants/defendants by [...].

i. [description of product or process];

ii. [description of product or process]; etc.

(b) The description served under paragraph (a) shall be accompanied by a signed written statement which shall:

(i) state that the person making the statement is personally acquainted with the facts to which the description relates;

(ii) verify that the description is a true and complete description of the product or process; and

(iii) contain an acknowledgement by the person making the statement that he may be required to attend court in order to be cross-examined on the contents of the description.

**Technical Primer**

14. The parties shall use their best endeavours to agree on or before [date] a single technical primer setting out the basic undisputed technology and shall on or before [date] indicate which parts of the technical primer are agreed to form part of the common general knowledge.

**Scientific Adviser**

15. A.B is appointed a scientific adviser to assist the court in this claim and counterclaim, his/her costs to be met in the first instance in equal shares by the parties and to be costs in the claim and counterclaim, subject to any other order of the trial judge.

**Written Evidence**

16.(a) Each party shall on or before [date] serve on the other parties [signed] written statements of the oral evidence which the party intends to lead on any issues of fact to be decided at the trial, such statements to stand as the evidence in chief of the witness unless the court otherwise directs;

(b) Each party shall on or before [date] serve on the other parties [signed] written statements of the oral evidence which it intends to lead at trial in answer to facts and matters raised in the witness statements served on it under paragraph (a) and (b) above;

(c) Each party may call up to [number] expert witnesses in this claim and counterclaim provided that the said party:

(i) supplies the name of such expert to the other parties and to the court on or before [date]; and

(ii) no later than [date/[number days] before the date set for the hearing of this claim and counterclaim] serve upon the other parties a report of each such expert comprising the evidence which that expert intends to give at trial.

[(d) The claimant shall, with the cooperation of the other parties, arrange for the

***Paragraph numbers marked with a "+" can be found online and on CD.***



INTELLECTUAL PROPERTY

experts to meet on or before [date] to determine on what issues they agree and on what they disagree and the experts shall before [date] file a report stating where they agree and where they disagree and in the latter case, their reasons for disagreeing].

**Admissibility of Evidence**

17. A party who objects to any statements of any witness being read by the judge prior to the hearing of the trial, shall serve upon each other party a notice in writing to that effect setting out the grounds of the objection.

**Non-Compliance**

18. Where either party fails to comply with the directions relating to experiments and written evidence it shall not be entitled to adduce evidence to which such directions relate without the permission of the court.

**Trial Bundles**

19. Each party shall no later than [28] days before the date fixed for the trial of this claim and counterclaim serve upon the other parties a list of all the documents to be included in the trial bundles. The claimants shall no later than [21] days before the date fixed for trial serve upon the defendants ... sets of the bundles for use at trial.

20. The claimants must file with the court no later than [4] days before the date fixed for the trial:
(i) the trial bundle; and
(ii) a reading guide for the judge.

**Trial**

21. The trial of these proceedings shall be before an assigned judge alone in [London], estimated length [number] days which shall include a pre-trial reading estimate for the judge of [number] days. The technical difficulty rating is [].

**Liberty to Apply**

22. The parties are to be at liberty on two days' notice to apply for further directions and generally.

**Costs**

23. The costs of this application are to be costs in the claim and counterclaim.

*Paragraph numbers marked with a "+" can be found online and on CD.*

# 2G COMPANIES ACT PROCEEDINGS

## Companies Act 2006

(2006 c.46) 2G–1

ARRANGEMENT OF SECTIONS



### Derivative claims

**260.**—(1) This Chapter applies to proceedings in England and Wales or Northern Ireland by a member of a company— 2G–2

(a) in respect of a cause of action vested in the company, and

(b) seeking relief on behalf of the company. This is referred to in this Chapter as a "derivative claim".

(2) A derivative claim may only be brought—

(a) under this Chapter, or

(b) in pursuance of an order of the court in proceedings under section 994 (proceedings for protection of members against unfair prejudice).

(3) A derivative claim under this Chapter may be brought only in respect of a cause of action arising from an actual or proposed act or omission involving negligence, default, breach of duty or breach of trust by a director of the company.

The cause of action may be against the director or another person (or both).

(4) It is immaterial whether the cause of action arose before or after the person seeking to bring or continue the derivative claim became a member of the company.

(5) For the purposes of this Chapter—

(a) "director" includes a former director;

(b) a shadow director is treated as a director; and

(c) references to a member of a company include a person who is not a member but to whom shares in the company have been transferred or transmitted by operation of law.

### Application for permission to continue derivative claim

**261.**—(1) A member of a company who brings a derivative claim under this Chapter must apply to the court for permission (in Northern Ireland, leave) to continue it. 2G–3

(2) If it appears to the court that the application and the evidence filed by the applicant in support of it do not disclose a prima facie case for giving permission (or leave), the court—

*Paragraph numbers marked with a "+" can be found online and on CD.*

(a) must dismiss the application, and
(b) may make any consequential order it considers appropriate.

(3) If the application is not dismissed under subsection (2), the court—

(a) may give directions as to the evidence to be provided by the company, and
(b) may adjourn the proceedings to enable the evidence to be obtained.

(4) On hearing the application, the court may—

(a) give permission (or leave) to continue the claim on such terms as it thinks fit,
(b) refuse permission (or leave) and dismiss the claim, or
(c) adjourn the proceedings on the application and give such directions as it thinks fit.

## Application for permission to continue claim as a derivative claim

2G-4 **262.**—(1) This section applies where—

(a) a company has brought a claim, and
(b) the cause of action on which the claim is based could be pursued as a derivative claim under this Chapter.

(2) A member of the company may apply to the court for permission (in Northern Ireland, leave) to continue the claim as a derivative claim on the ground that—

(a) the manner in which the company commenced or continued the claim amounts to an abuse of the process of the court,
(b) the company has failed to prosecute the claim diligently, and
(c) it is appropriate for the member to continue the claim as a derivative claim.

(3) If it appears to the court that the application and the evidence filed by the applicant in support of it do not disclose a prima facie case for giving permission (or leave), the court—

(a) must dismiss the application, and
(b) may make any consequential order it considers appropriate.

(4) If the application is not dismissed under subsection (3), the court—

(a) may give directions as to the evidence to be provided by the company, and
(b) may adjourn the proceedings to enable the evidence to be obtained.

(5) On hearing the application, the court may—

(a) give permission (or leave) to continue the claim as a derivative claim on such terms as it thinks fit,
(b) refuse permission (or leave) and dismiss the application, or

(c) adjourn the proceedings on the application and give such directions as it thinks fit.

**Whether permission to be given**

**263.**—(1) The following provisions have effect where a member of a company applies for permission (in Northern Ireland, leave) under section 261 or 262. **2G–5**

(2) Permission (or leave) must be refused if the court is satisfied—

(a) that a person acting in accordance with section 172 (duty to promote the success of the company) would not seek to continue the claim, or

(b) where the cause of action arises from an act or omission that is yet to occur, that the act or omission has been authorised by the company, or

(c) where the cause of action arises from an act or omission that has already occurred, that the act or omission—

(i) was authorised by the company before it occurred, or

(ii) has been ratified by the company since it occurred.

(3) In considering whether to give permission (or leave) the court must take into account, in particular—

(a) whether the member is acting in good faith in seeking to continue the claim;

(b) the importance that a person acting in accordance with section 172 (duty to promote the success of the company) would attach to continuing it;

(c) where the cause of action results from an act or omission that is yet to occur, whether the act or omission could be, and in the circumstances would be likely to be—

(i) authorised by the company before it occurs, or

(ii) ratified by the company after it occurs;

(d) where the cause of action arises from an act or omission that has already occurred, whether the act or omission could be, and in the circumstances would be likely to be, ratified by the company;

(e) whether the company has decided not to pursue the claim;

(f) whether the act or omission in respect of which the claim is brought gives rise to a cause of action that the member could pursue in his own right rather than on behalf of the company.

(4) In considering whether to give permission (or leave) the court shall have particular regard to any evidence before it as to the views of members of the company who have no personal interest, direct or indirect, in the matter.

(5) The Secretary of State may by regulations—

(a) amend subsection (2) so as to alter or add to the circumstances in which permission (or leave) is to be refused;

(b) amend subsection (3) so as to alter or add to the matters that the court is required to take into account in considering whether to give permission (or leave).

(6) Before making any such regulations the Secretary of State shall consult such persons as he considers appropriate.

(7) Regulations under this section are subject to affirmative resolution procedure.

### Application for permission to continue derivative claim brought by another member

2G-6 **264.**—(1) This section applies where a member of a company ("the claimant")—

(a) has brought a derivative claim,

(b) has continued as a derivative claim a claim brought by the company, or

(c) has continued a derivative claim under this section.

(2) Another member of the company ("the applicant") may apply to the court for permission (in Northern Ireland, leave) to continue the claim on the ground that—

(a) the manner in which the proceedings have been commenced or continued by the claimant amounts to an abuse of the process of the court,

(b) the claimant has failed to prosecute the claim diligently, and

(c) it is appropriate for the applicant to continue the claim as a derivative claim.

(3) If it appears to the court that the application and the evidence filed by the applicant in support of it do not disclose a prima facie case for giving permission (or leave), the court—

(a) must dismiss the application, and

(b) may make any consequential order it considers appropriate.

(4) If the application is not dismissed under subsection (3), the court—

(a) may give directions as to the evidence to be provided by the company, and

(b) may adjourn the proceedings to enable the evidence to be obtained.

(5) On hearing the application, the court may—

(a) give permission (or leave) to continue the claim on such terms as it thinks fit,

(b) refuse permission (or leave) and dismiss the application, or

(c) adjourn the proceedings on the application and give such directions as it thinks fit.

2G-6.1 *Note*—The court procedure relating to the conduct of derivative claims is set out in Pt 19.9 of the Civil Procedure Rules. A full commentary can be found in Vol.1 under that rule.

## PRACTICE DIRECTION 49A—APPLICATIONS UNDER THE COMPANIES ACTS AND RELATED LEGISLATION

*This Practice Direction supplements CPR Part 49*

### *Section I.*

### *General*

**Definitions**

**1.** In this practice direction— **2G–7**

"the 1985 Act" means the Companies Act 1985;

"the 2006 Act" means the Companies Act 2006;

"the CJPA" means the Criminal Justice and Police Act 2001;

"the EC Regulation" means Council Regulation (EC) No. 2157/2001 of 8 October 2001 on the Statute for a European Company (SE);

"Part VII FSMA" means Part VII of the Financial Services and Markets Act 2000;

"the Cross-Border Mergers Regulations" means the Companies (Cross-Border Mergers) Regulations 2007.

**Application of this practice direction**

**2.** This practice direction applies to proceedings under— **2G–8**

(a) the 1985 Act;

(b) the 2006 Act (except proceedings under Chapter 1 of Part 11 or Part 30 of that Act);

(c) section 59 of the CJPA;

(d) Articles 22, 25 and 26 of the EC Regulation;

(e) Part VII FSMA; and

(f) the Cross-Border Mergers Regulations.

(Part 19 and Practice Direction 19C contain provisions about proceedings under Chapter 1 of Part 11 of the 2006 Act (derivative claims)).

**Application of this practice direction to certain proceedings in relation to limited liability partnerships**

**3.** This practice direction applies to proceedings under the 1985 Act and 2006 Act as applied to limited liability partnerships by regulations made under the Limited Liability Partnerships Act 2000. **2G–9**

**Title of documents**

**4.**(1) The claim form in proceedings under the 1985 Act, the 2006 Act, Part VII FSMA, the EC Regulation or the Cross-Border Mergers Regulations, and any application, affidavit, witness statement, notice or other document in such proceedings, must be entitled "In the matter of [the name of the company in question] and in the matter of [the relevant law]", where "[the relevant law]" means "the Companies Act 1985", "the Companies Act 2006", "Part VII of the Financial Services and Markets Act 2000", "Council Regulation (EC) **2G–10**

***Paragraph numbers marked with a "+" can be found online and on CD.***

No 2157/2001 of 8 October 2001 on the Statute for a European Company (SE)" or "the Companies (Cross-Border Merger) Regulations 2007", as the case may be.

(2) Where a company changes its name in the course of proceedings, the title must be altered by—
(a) substituting the new name for the old; and
(b) inserting the old name in brackets at the end of the title.

**Starting proceedings and notification of application made**

2G–11 **5.**(1) Proceedings to which this practice direction applies must be started by a Part 8 claim form—
(a) unless a provision of this or another practice direction provides otherwise, but
(b) subject to any modification of that procedure by this or any other practice direction.

(2) The claim form—
(a) will, where issued in the High Court, be issued out of the Companies Court or a Chancery district registry; or
(b) will, where issued in a county court, be issued out of a county court office.

(3) Where this practice direction requires a party to proceedings to notify another person of an application, such notification must, unless the court orders otherwise, be given by sending to that other person a copy of the claim form as soon as reasonably practicable after the claim form has been issued.

*Section II.*

*Particular applications under the 2006 Act*

**References to provisions of the 2006 Act in this Section**

2G–12 **6.** In this Section, a reference to a section by number, not otherwise identified, is to the section so numbered in the 2006 Act.

**Company generally to be made a party to a claim under the 2006 Act**

2G–13 **7.**(1) Where in a claim under the 2006 Act the company concerned is not the claimant, the company is to be made a defendant to the claim unless—
(a) any other enactment, the CPR or this or another practice direction makes a different provision; or
(b) the court orders otherwise.

(2) Where an application is made in the course of proceedings to which the company is or is required to be a defendant, the company must be made a respondent to the application unless—
(a) any other enactment, the CPR or this or another practice direction makes a different provision; or
(b) the court orders otherwise.

**Applications under section 169 (Director's right to protest against removal)**

**8.**(1) This paragraph applies to an application for an order under section 169(5). **2G–14**

(2) The claimant must notify the director concerned of the application.

**Applications under section 244 (Disclosure under court order of protected information)**

**9.**(1) This paragraph applies to an application for an order under section 244. **2G–15**

(2) The claimant must notify the director concerned of the application.

**Applications under section 295 (Application not to circulate members' statement) or section 317 (Application not to circulate members' statement)**

**10.**(1) This paragraph applies to an application for an order under section 295 or 317. **2G–16**

(2) The claimant must notify each member who requested the circulation of the relevant statement of the application.

**Proceedings under section 370 (Unauthorised donations – enforcement of directors' liabilities by shareholder action)**

**11.** Proceedings to enforce a director's liability under section 370 must be started by a Part 7 claim form. **2G–17**

**Proceedings under section 456 (Application in respect of defective accounts or directors' report)**

**12.**(1) This paragraph applies to an application for a declaration under section 456(1). **2G–18**

(2) The claimant must notify any former director who was a director at the time of the approval of the annual accounts or directors' report of the application.

**Proceedings under section 511, 514, 515 or 518 (Representations or statements made by the auditor)**

**13.**(1) This paragraph applies to an application for an order under section 511(6), 514(7), 515(7) or 518(9). **2G–19**

(2) The claimant must notify the auditor of the application.

**Proceedings under section 527 (Members' powers to require website publication of audit concerns)**

**14.**(1) This paragraph applies to an application for an order under section 527(5). **2G–20**

(2) The claimant must, unless the court orders otherwise, notify each member who requested a statement to be placed on the website of the application.

**Proceedings under Parts 26 and 27 of the 2006 Act (Applications to sanction a compromise or arrangement)**

**15.**(1) This paragraph applies to an application for an order under **2G–21**

*Paragraph numbers marked with a "+" can be found online and on CD.*

Parts 26 and 27 of the 2006 Act to sanction a compromise or arrangement.

(2) Where the application is made by the company concerned, or by a liquidator or administrator of the company, there need be no defendant to the claim unless the court so orders.

(3) The claim form must be supported by written evidence, including—

(a) statutory information about the company; and

(b) the terms of the proposed compromise or arrangement.

(4) The claim form must seek—

(a) directions for convening a meeting of creditors or members or both, as the case requires;

(b) the sanction of the court to the compromise or arrangement, if it is approved at the meeting or meetings, and a direction for a further hearing for that purpose; and

(c) a direction that the claimant files a copy of a report to the court by the chairman of the meeting or of each meeting.

**Proceedings under section 955 (Takeovers – enforcement by the court)**

2G–22 **16.** Proceedings for an order under section 955 must be started by a Part 7 claim form.

**Proceedings under section 968 (Takeovers – effect on contractual restrictions)**

2G–23 **17.** Proceedings to recover compensation under section 968(6) must be started by a Part 7 claim form.

**Applications under section 1132 (Production and inspection of documents where offence suspected)**

2G–24 **18.**(1) This paragraph applies to an application for an order under section 1132.

(2) No notice need be given to any person against whom the order is sought.

*Section III.*

*Other applications*

**Applications under the EC Regulation—Article 25**

2G–25 **19.**(1) In this paragraph and paragraphs 20 and 21—

(a) a reference to an Article by number is a reference to the Article so numbered in the EC Regulation; and

(b) 'SE' means a European public limited-liability company (Societas Europaea) within the meaning of the EC Regulation.

(1A) Any document that is filed with the court must, if not in English, be accompanied by a translation of that document into English—

***Paragraph numbers marked with a "+" can be found online and on CD.***

(a) certified by a notary public or other qualified person; or
(b) accompanied by written evidence confirming that the translation is accurate.

(2) An application for a certificate under Article 25(2)—
(a) must set out the pre-merger acts and formalities applicable to the applicant company;
(b) must be accompanied by evidence that those acts and formalities have been completed; and
(c) must be accompanied by copies of—
(i) the draft terms of merger, as provided for in Article 20;
(ii) the entry in the London Gazette containing the particulars specified in Article 21;
(iii) a directors' report;
(iv) an expert's report; and
(v) the resolution of the applicant company approving the draft terms of merger in accordance with Article 23.

(3) In paragraph (2)(c)—
'directors' report' in relation to a company means a report by the directors of the company containing the information required by section 908 of the 2006 Act;
'expert's report' in relation to a company means a report to the members of the company drawn up in accordance with—
(a) section 909 of the 2006 Act; or
(b) Article 22.

(4) There need be no defendant to the application.

### Applications under the EC Regulation—Article 22 (Appointment of an independent expert)

**20.**(1) An application under Article 22 for the appointment of an independent expert must be made— **2G–26**
(a) where the application is made at the same time as or after the application under Article 25(2) for the approval of the pre-merger acts and formalities has been filed with the court, by application notice pursuant to Part 23; or
(b) where no application under Article 25(2) has been made, by a Part 8 claim form.

(2) The application (whether by a claim form or application notice, as the case may be) must be accompanied by evidence in support of the application.

### Applications under the EC Regulation—Article 26

**21.**(1) Where under Article 26(2) a merging company is required to submit a certificate to the High Court, that company must, if no other merging company has begun proceedings under Article 26, start such proceedings by way of a Part 8 claim form. **2G–27**

(2) There need be no defendant to the claim.

(3) The claim form—

(a) must name the SE and all of the merging companies;

(b) must be accompanied by the documents referred to in sub-paragraph (5); and

(c) must be served on each of the other merging companies.

(4) Where under Article 26(2) a merging company is required to submit a certificate to the High Court, and proceedings under Article 26 have already been begun, the company—

(a) must, not more than 14 days after service on it of the claim form, file an acknowledgment of service and serve it on each of the other merging companies; and

(b) must file the documents, in relation to each merging company, referred to in sub-paragraph (5) within the time limit specified in Article 26(2), and serve copies of them on each of the other merging companies.

(5) The documents in relation to each merging company are—

(a) the certificate issued under Article 25(2) in respect of the company;

(b) a copy of the draft terms of merger approved by the company;

(c) evidence that arrangements for employee involvement have been determined by the company pursuant to Council Directive 2001/86/EC of 8 October 2001 supplementing the Statute for a European company with regard to the involvement of employees; and

(d) evidence that the SE has been formed in accordance with Article 26(4).

**Applications under the Cross-Border Mergers Regulations**

**2G–28** **22.**(1) In this paragraph and paragraphs 23 to 25 a reference to a regulation by number is a reference to the regulation so numbered in the Cross-Border Mergers Regulations.

(2) Any document that is filed with the court must, if not in English, be accompanied by a translation of that document into English—

(a) certified by a notary public or other qualified person; or

(b) accompanied by written evidence confirming that the translation is accurate.

**Application for approval of pre-merger requirements**

**2G–29** **23.**(1) This paragraph applies to an application under regulation 6.

(2) There need be no defendant to the application.

(3) The application must—.

(a) set out the pre-merger acts and formalities required by regulations 7 to 10 and 12 to 15 applicable to the applicant company; and

(b) be accompanied by evidence that those acts and formalities have been completed properly.

*Paragraph numbers marked with a "+" can be found online and on CD.*

(4) Where an application under regulation 11 to summon a meeting of creditors has been made, the court will not determine the application under regulation 6 to approve the pre-merger requirements until the result of the meeting is known.

(5) Where the court makes an order certifying that all pre-merger acts and formalities have been completed properly, the applicant must draw up the order and file it no later than 7 days after the date on which the order was made so that it can be sealed[GL] by the court. The court will seal[GL] and return the order to the applicant within 15 days of receipt.

**Application for appointment of independent expert or to summon a meeting of members or creditors**

**24.**(1) This paragraph applies to— **2G-30**

(a) an application for the appointment of an independent expert under regulation 9;

(b) an application under regulation 11 for an order to summon a meeting of members or creditors or both.

(2) The application must be made—

(a) where the application is made at the same time as or after the application for approval of the pre-merger acts and formalities under regulation 6 has been filed with the court, by application notice pursuant to Part 23; or

(b) where no application under regulation 6 has been made, by a Part 8 claim form.

(3) The application (whether by claim form or application notice, as the case may be) must be accompanied by evidence in support of the application.

**Application for the approval of the completion of the merger**

**25.**(1) This paragraph applies to an application under regulation 16. **2G-31**

(2) The application must be made by a Part 8 claim form.

(3) There need be no defendant to the application.

(4) The claim form must be accompanied by—

(a) the documents referred to in regulation 16(1)(b), (c) and (e);

(b) where appropriate, evidence that regulation 16(1)(f) has been complied with; and

(c) such other evidence as may be required to enable the court to decide the application.

(5) Where the court makes an order under regulation 16 approving the merger, it will fix a date on which the consequences of the merger are to take effect.

**Applications under section 59 of the CJPA**

**26.**(1) In sub-paragraphs (2) to (8)— **2G-32**

(a) a reference to a section by number, not otherwise identified, is a reference to the section so numbered in the CJPA; and

(b) references to a relevant interest in property have the same meaning as in section 59 of the CJPA.

(2) This paragraph applies to applications under section 59 in respect of property seized in exercise of the power conferred by section 448(3) of the 1985 Act (including any additional powers of seizure conferred by section 50 that are exercisable by reference to that power).

(3) The application must be supported by evidence—

(a) that the claimant has a relevant interest in the property to which the application relates; and

(b) in the case of an application under section 59(2), that one or more of the grounds set out in section 59(3) is satisfied in relation to the property.

(4) Where the claimant has a relevant interest in the property, the defendants to the claim are to be—

(a) the person in possession of the property; and

(b) any other person who appears to have a relevant interest in the property.

(5) Where the claimant is in possession of the property, the defendants are to be—

(a) the person from whom the property was seized; and

(b) any other person who appears to have a relevant interest in the property.

(6) In the case of an application for the return of seized property, the claimant must serve a copy of the claim form and the claimant's evidence in support of it on the person specified, by the notice given under section 52 when the property was seized, as the person to whom notice of such an application should be given.

(7) If the claimant knows the identity of the person who seized the property, the claimant must also notify that person of the application.

(8) When the court issues the claim form it will fix a date for the hearing.

## *Section IV.*

### *Conduct of proceedings*

### Reduction of capital—evidence

**2G–33** **27.**(1) In the case of an application to confirm a reduction in capital, if any shares were issued otherwise than for cash—

(a) for any shares so issued on or after 1st January 1901, it is sufficient to set out in the application the extent to which the shares are, or are treated as being, paid up; and

(b) for any shares so issued between 1st September 1867

and 31st December 1900, the application must also show that the requirement as to the filing of the relevant contract with the Registrar of Joint Stock Companies in section 25 of the Companies Act 1867 was complied with.

*Section V.*

*Miscellaneous*

### Service of documents

**28.** The parties are responsible for service of documents in proceedings to which this practice direction applies. **2G–34**

### Transitional provisions

**29.** A claim started, or an application made, before 1st October 2007 may be continued in accordance with the practice direction in force on 30th September 2007 as if it had not been revoked. **2G–35**

**[THE NEXT PARAGRAPH IS 2G–37.]**

#### Introduction

Although not expressly stated to be the case (see para.2) it would appear that the Practice Direction supersedes all previous directions relating to applications under the Companies Acts and related legislation, the related legislation being that referred to in paras 1 and 2. Note, however, that para.5 explicitly refers to other practice directions and the transitional provisions made by para.29. **2G–37**

#### Companies Act 2006

The Practice Direction appears to have been prompted by the Companies Act 2006 which received the royal assent on November 8, 2006. **2G–38**

#### Companies Court

Applications under the legislation covered by the Practice Direction should be made to the Companies Court. **2G–39**

Companies Court is not a separate and distinct part of the High Court but is a descriptive term given to the part of the Chancery Division of the High Court which deals with cases which are generally commenced before the bankruptcy registrar sitting in Companies Court from time to time, or in the case of a District registry the district judge sitting in the equivalent capacity (*Re Shilena Hosiery Co Ltd* [1980] Ch. 219).

#### Commencing proceedings

Proceedings should be commenced by Pt.8 claim form unless provision is made to the contrary (para.5). However, the use of petitions is still envisaged, e.g. in the case of proceedings under s.994 Companies Act 2006. **2G–40**

#### Issuing proceedings

All applications and proceedings under the legislation covered by the Practice Direction are listed for directions or determination before the registrar (or district judge in a District Registry) save for applications for injunctions. The majority of cases are heard and finally determined by the registrar. The following are always heard and tried by the judge: final hearings of applications to sanction a scheme of arrangement under the Companies Act 2006 or the Financial Services and Markets Act 2000; petitions under s.994 Companies Act 2006; applications for injunctions. **2G–41**

#### Urgent applications

Urgent applications estimated to last no more than 15 minutes may be listed by ar- **2G–42** rangement with the Companies Court clerks to be heard by the registrar at 10.15am. In addition, a registrar (covering both bankruptcy and companies work) is available at 2pm each Wednesday during term to hear urgent applications or other applications of a time critical nature (e.g. applications for a debarring order where there is urgency). Parties asking for an application to be dealt with in the urgent list must complete the certificate below:

No: ....................

IN THE HIGH COURT OF JUSTICE

CHANCERY DIVISION

COMPANIES COURT/IN BANKRUPTCY

IN THE MATTER OF/RE:

&

I estimate that this matter is likely to occupy the court for .................... mins/ hours.

I certify that it is urgent and fit for a without notice hearing for the following reasons:

..........................
[name of representative]

..........................
[telephone number]

Counsel/Solicitor for the ..........................

**WARNING. If, in the opinion of the Registrar, the application is not urgent then such sanction will be applied as is thought appropriate in all the circumstances.**

### Schemes, reductions and similar proceedings

2G–43 Arrangements for hearings of schemes and reductions (as well as those under the Financial Services and Markets Act 2000 and the Cross-Border Mergers Regulations

2007) in the Royal Courts of Justice should be made with the Companies Court case manager, Room TM 205 of the Thomas More Building, to whom inquiries may also be made by telephone (020 7947 6727). Papers should be lodged in TM 205 *at least* five working days before the hearing.

A claim form must now be used in place of a petition. It should contain the information which would previously have been set out in a petition including the date of incorporation of the company, the company number, the name of the company and any change, the situation of the registered office, the objects, capital history, relevant provisions in the articles of association, relevant share rights, details of the necessary special resolution, the purpose of the reduction and the form of the minute. The relief sought should include an order dealing with any enquiry as to creditors and directions for the first advertisement (which is most conveniently put in the first paragraph of the relief sought).

On issue of the claim form the court will endorse it with the time and date of the first hearing before the registrar. At the first hearing the court will deal with any enquiry as to creditors and advertisement and adjourn the matter to be heard by the registrar in open court at a subsequent date which should have been agreed in advance with the court case manager.

No application notice is now required. The claim will be adjourned after each hearing until the final order is made.

#### Schemes of arrangement

A claim form must now be used in place of a petition. As not all the information required by the court for the final hearing will be available at the time of issue of the claim form a short form of claim will be accepted seeking an order convening the necessary meeting(s), directions in relation thereto, an order requiring the chairman to report the result of the meeting(s) to the court and sanction of the scheme at the final hearing before the judge. The claim form should also set out the directions sought as regards creditors where the scheme involves a reduction. A copy of the latest print of the scheme should be annexed to the claim form. The directions hearing is listed before the registrar. **2G–44**

As the claim form will no longer contain all the matters which would otherwise have been contained in a petition (details of the company and its capital history and so on), those matters should be set out in the evidence. The evidence filed for the final hearing before the judge should explain any differences between the scheme annexed to the claim form and that in respect of which the final order is sought. The evidence must also include the chairman's report of the result of the meeting(s).

As in the case of reductions no application notice is now required. The claim will be adjourned after each hearing until the final order is made.

#### Applications to extend time for registering a charge or to rectify an omission or mis-statement

The relevant provisions are to be found in s.873 of the Companies Act 2006. **2G–45**

Section 873 enables a party to apply for relief from the consequences of failing to register on time and omissions or misstatements of any particular with respect to a charge or in a memorandum of satisfaction to be rectified.

The claim form should identify the charge in relation to which relief is sought. The company will generally be the claimant in which case no other party need be joined in the proceedings or given notice. If the claimant is a party other than the company the company should be made a defendant and served with the proceedings.

The claim should be supported by evidence as to the circumstances under which the documents in question were not registered, setting out in detail the sequence of events surrounding the default. It must show that the omission to register (or misstatement of any particulars) was (a) accidental or (b) due to inadvertence (the nature of the inadvertence being set out) or (c) some other sufficient cause or (d) is not of a nature to prejudice the position of creditors or shareholders or (e) that there are other grounds on which it is just and equitable to grant relief. It should exhibit a copy of the document to be registered. Up-to-date evidence of solvency should be filed confirming that no winding-up order has been made or resolution for winding-up passed, and that no winding up petition is pending, that no notice of a resolution to wind up has been given, that the company is continuing to carry on business, and that no judgment has been given against the company which remains unsatisfied (*Bootle Cold Storage, Re* [1901] WN 54; *Telomatic, Re* [1993] B.C.C. 404). Such evidence must be given by an officer of the company.

The original charge to be registered should be produced at the hearing.

In extending time the court will generally add to the order a provision that it is made without prejudice to the rights of any person acquired between the date of the creation of the charge and the date of its actual registration (*Re Joplin Brewery* [1902] 1 Ch 79; *Watson v Duff Morgan & Vermont (Holdings) Ltd* [1974] 1 All E.R. 794; *Re I. C. Johnson & Co* [1902] 2 Ch 101). For an exceptional case where the rights of intervening mortgagees were not preserved, see *Re Fablehill Ltd* [1991] B.C.L.C. 830.

The words in the order referred to above have been held not to put an unsecured creditor on the same footing as a debenture holder applying for an extension unless he has taken steps to enforce his debt or unless a winding up has intervened (*Re Ehrmann Bros.* [1906] 2 Ch 697) before actual registration (*Re Anglo Oriental Co* [1903] 1 Ch 914); but the court will not insert further words to protect unsecured creditors (*Re M. I. G. Trust Ltd* [1933] Ch 542, CA, affirmed in *Peat v Gresham Trust Ltd* [1934] A.C. 252).

As to the limits of the court's jurisdiction (e.g. to order the removal of unnecessary information) see *Re Calmex Ltd* [1989] 1 All E.R. 485; [1989] B.C.L.C. 299 ; *Igroup Ltd v Ocwen* [2003] EWHC 2431 (Ch); [2003] 4 All E.R. 1063 and in *Re Company (No.7466 of 2003)* [2004] EWHC 60. The court may, however, grant declaratory relief.

Where an order is sought for a declaration that a document wrongly filed on the register is of no effect the registrar of companies should be joined to and given notice of the proceedings.

**2G–46** *Re Charles orders* —Where at the date of the making of the order a winding up is likely the order may reserve the right of the liquidator to apply to discharge the order within 21 days of commencement of the winding up if it occurred within a month of the making of the order (*Re L. H. Charles & Co* [1935] WN 15; *Exeter Trust Ltd v Screenways Ltd* [1991] B.C.L.C. 888). The order, if made, will extend time for registration (or rectification) but subject to a proviso "that the company, acting by any liquidator or administrator, or any unsecured creditor of the company shall be at liberty to apply to discharge or vary this order within [a period of time] after the commencement of any voluntary winding up of the company or any order for the winding up of the company" (or as the case may be). Such an order may be made where, exceptionally, there is no evidence of solvency (*Re Kris Cruisers Ltd* [1949] Ch 138). However, *Kris Cruisers Ltd* was not followed in *Re Ashpurton Estates Ltd* [1983] Ch 110; [1982] 3 All E.R. 665 in which it was held that imminent liquidation was a factor to be taken into account and that an order extending time should not be made after a company has gone into liquidation (see *Re Resinoid and Mica Products Ltd (Note)* [1983] Ch 132; [1982] 3 All ER 677, but *cf. R. M. Arnold & Co Ltd* [1984] B.C.L.C. 505 where the circumstances were exceptional; see also *Re Braemar Investments Ltd* [1988] 3 W.L.R. 596; [1988] B.C.L.C. 556, where the court ordered a motion by the liquidator to discharge the registrar's order extending time). In *Re Chantry House Developments plc* [1990] B.C.L.C. 813 the court made an order extending time, notwithstanding the company being in administrative receivership, but on an undertaking that the mortgagee would notify substantial unsecured creditors of the company within seven days of the making of the order and on terms that they could apply within 14 days to discharge the order and that the mortgagee would abide by any order made in such circumstances. Generally, however, where insolvent liquidation seems inevitable the court should decline to extend time (*Re Barrow Borough Transport Ltd* [1989] 3 W.L.R. 858 and *Re Telomatic Ltd* [1993] B.C.C. 404).

The court will only extend time; it will not decide whether or not documents require registration (*Re Cunard Steamship Co* [1908] WN 160).

In *Exeter Trust Ltd v Screenways Ltd* [1991] B.C.L.C. 888 it was held that even if an order extending time was set aside the registrar of companies' certificate as to registration was conclusive evidence of the valid registration of the charge.

Following the decision in *Re Top Marques Car Rental Ltd* [2006] EWHC 109 (Ch), when making a *Re Charles* order the court will generally include the following provision:

"AND IT IS DIRECTED THAT the Registrar of Companies shall not issue a conclusive certificate of registration in respect of the [charge] until such time as the Registrar of Companies is satisfied that (1) no winding up or administration has commenced at the expiry of [28] days from the date of this order or (2) if a winding up or administration has commenced within [28] days from the date of this order no application has been made to vary or discharge this order by a liquidator or administrator within [56] days from the date of this order."

*COMPANIES ACT*

***Paragraph numbers marked with a "+" can be found online and on CD.***

## PRACTICE DIRECTION 49B—ORDER UNDER SECTION 127 INSOLVENCY ACT 1986

*This Practice Direction supplements CPR Part 49*

2G–47 **1.** Attention is drawn to the undesirability of asking as a matter of course for a winding up order as an alternative to an order under s.459 Companies Act 1985. The petition should not ask for a winding up order unless that is the remedy which the petitioner prefers or it is thought that it may be the only remedy to which the petitioner is entitled.

2G–48 **2.** Whenever a winding up order is asked for in a contributory's petition, the petition must state whether the petitioner consents or objects to an order under s.127 of the Insolvency Act 1986 ('a s.127 order') in the standard form. If he objects, the written evidence in support must contain a short statement of his reasons.

2G–49 **3.** If the petitioner objects to a s.127 order in the standard form but consents to such an order in a modified form, the petition must set out in the form of order to which he consents, and the written evidence in support must contain a short statement of his reasons for seeking the modification.

2G–50 **4.** If the petition contains a statement that the petitioner consents to a s.127 order, whether in the standard or a modified form, but the petitioner changes his mind before the first hearing of the petition, he must notify the respondents and may apply on notice to a Judge for an order directing that no s.127 order or a modified order only (as the case may be) shall be made by the Registrar, but validating dispositions made without notice of the order made by the Judge.

2G–51 **5.** If the petition contains a statement that the petitioner consents to a s.127 order, whether in the standard or a modified form, the Registrar shall without further enquiry make an order in such form at the first hearing unless an order to the contrary has been made by the Judge in the meantime.

2G–52 **6.** If the petition contains a statement that the petitioner objects to a s.127 order in the standard form, the company may apply (in the case of urgency, without notice) to the Judge for an order.

2G–53 **7.** Section 127 Order – Standard Form:

(Title etc.)

ORDER that notwithstanding the presentation of the said Petition

(1) payments made into or out of the bank accounts of the Company in the ordinary course of business of the Company and

(2) dispositions of the property of the Company made in the ordinary course of its business for proper value between the date of presentation of the Petition and the date of judgment on the Petition or further order in the meantime

shall not be void by virtue of the provisions of section 127 of the Insolvency Act 1986 in the event of an Order for the winding up of the Company being made on the said Petition provided that (the relevant bank) shall be under no obligation to verify for itself whether any transaction through the company's bank accounts is in the ordinary course of business, or that it represents full market value for the relevant transaction.

This form of Order may be departed from where the circumstances of the case require.

*Companies Court—Practice Note 1 of 2003*

**Claims for an order restoring the name of a company to the Register or declaring the dissolution of a company void**

With effect from April 29, 2003 claims for order of this type issued in the High Court in London will be given a return date three months in advance of the date of issue. This is designed to enable the applicant(s) to have sufficient opportunity to complete the requirements of the Registrar of Companies. In this way it is intended to prevent repeated adjournments pending completion of those requirements and to save the expense of unnecessary and repeated attendance at court by the parties. **2G–54**

When the requirements of the Registrar of Companies have been met and the Treasury Solicitor is able to approve the application, a consent order may be filed for approval by the court without attendance. If an undertaking is required to be given to the court it must be given by the solicitor (partner) for the claimant(s) in Form **U1** (attached) or by the claimant in person in Form **U2** (attached).

In such circumstances the papers which must be filed at court by the claimant(s) with the consent order are:

1. A copy of the claim
2. A copy of the witness statement in support
3. Original evidence of service of the application on the company (where appropriate)
4. Original evidence of service of the application on the Registrar of Companies
5. Original evidence of service of the application on the Treasury Solicitor dealing with bona vacantia assets on behalf of the Crown, or on the solicitor for the Duchy of Lancaster or the Duke of Cornwall dealing with bona vacantia assets in those areas, exhibiting in either case the bona vacantia waiver letter received in reply
6. The original signed copy of any undertaking required to be given to the court
7. Four copies of the agreed consent order, one of which should be signed by or on behalf of each party by way of consent to the form of order

In the normal course the above documents will be seen by the Registrar within three working days of delivery to the court. If the papers are in order, the Registrar will make the agreed order and the court will send two sealed copies of the order to the applicant and one to the Treasury Solicitor. If the papers are not in order (or the court for some reason requires), the matter will be listed for the parties to attend at the earliest convenient date and notice of this appointment will be given by the court to the parties.

Chief Bankruptcy Registrar
Royal Courts of Justice, Strand, London, WC2A 2LL
April 2003

**Editorial note**

2G–55 The following forms can be found in the *Civil Procedure Forms Volume*:

- **U1**
- **U2**

**Companies Act 2006**

2G–56 The Practice Note came into force in relation to the provisions of the Companies Act 1985. New provisions are made by ss.1003ff. and 1029ff. of the Companies Act 2006.

# SECTION 3

## OTHER PROCEEDINGS

# 3A HOUSING

## Common Law Procedure Act 1852

(15 & 16 Vict. c.76) 3A–0

Arrangement of Sections



**Paragraph numbers marked with a "+" denote content that is available on White Book on Westlaw UK or the Civil Procedure CD.**

## Law of Property Act 1925

(15 & 16 Geo. 5 c.20) 3A–7.1

Arrangement of Sections

Part III

Mortgages, Rent Charges, and Powers of Attorney

*Mortgages*



Part V

*Leases and Tenancies*



*Notices*



Part XII



**Paragraph numbers marked with a "+" denote content that is available on White Book on Westlaw UK or the Civil Procedure CD.**

## Part III

## Mortgages, Rent Charges, and Powers of Attorney

### *Mortgages*

### Sale of mortgaged property in action for redemption or foreclosure

**91.**—(1) Any person entitled to redeem mortgaged property may 3A–8
have a judgment or order for sale instead of for redemption in an ac-

***Paragraph numbers marked with a "+" can be found online and on CD.***

tion brought by him either for redemption alone, or for sale alone, or for sale or redemption in the alternative.

(2) In any action, whether for foreclosure, or for redemption, or for sale, or for the raising and payment in any manner of mortgage money, the court, on the request of the mortgagee, or of any person interested either in the mortgage money or in the right of redemption, and, notwithstanding that—

(a) any other person dissents; or

(b) the mortgagee or any person so interested does not appear in the action;

and without allowing any time for redemption or for payment of any mortgage money, may direct a sale of the mortgaged property, on such terms as it thinks fit, including the deposit in court of a reasonable sum fixed by the court to meet the expenses of sale and to secure performance of the terms.

(3) But, in an action brought by a person interested in the right of redemption and seeking a sale, the court may, in the application of any defendant, direct the plaintiff to give such security for costs as the court thinks fit, and may give the conduct of the sale to any defendant, and may give such directions as it thinks fit respecting the costs of the defendants or any of them.

(4) In any case within this section the court may, if it thinks fit, direct a sale without previously determining the priorities of incumbrancers.

(5) This section applies to actions brought either before or after the commencement of this Act.

(6) In this section "mortgaged property" includes the estate or interest which a mortgagee would have had power to convey if the statutory power of sale were applicable.

(7) For the purposes of this section the court may, in favour of a purchaser, make a vesting order conveying the mortgaged property, or appoint a person to do so, subject or not to any incumbrance, as the court may think fit; or, in the case of an equitable mortgage, may create and vest a mortgage term in the mortgagee to enable him to carry out the sale as if the mortgage had been made by deed by way of legal mortgage.

[(8) The county court has jurisdiction under this section where the amount owing in respect of the mortgage or charge at the commencement of the proceedings does not exceed £30,000].

**3A–9** *Note*—Amended by the County Courts Act 1984 s.148(1), Sch.2, Pt II, para.3(1); and the High Court and County Courts Jurisdiction Order 1991 (SI 1991/724) art.2(4) and (8).

**"mortgage"**

**3A–10** See s.205(xvi).

**"property"**

**3A–11** See s.205(xx).

**"sale"**

**3A–12** See s.205(xxiv).

***Paragraph numbers marked with a "+" can be found online and on CD.***

**"Sale of mortgaged property ..."**

Under this section the court (which includes the county court if the amount owing in respect of the mortgage at the commencement of proceedings does not exceed £30,000) on the application of any person entitled to redeem the mortgaged property may direct the sale of the premises on such terms as it thinks fit. The court has a wide discretion and may order a sale of mortgaged property against the wishes of the lender where it would be unfair to the borrower to postpone sale, even if the mortgage would not be redeemed. In exercising that discretion, the court should have regard to the interests of all concerned and to what is just and equitable (see *Palk v Mortgage Funding Services* [1993] Ch. 330; [1993] 2 W.L.R. 415; [1993] 2 All E.R. 481, CA; and *Polonski v Lloyds Bank* (1999) 31 H.L.R. 721; *The Times*, May 6, 1997, Ch D). **3A–13**

In *Cheltenham and Gloucester Building Society v Krausz* [1997] 1 W.L.R. 1558; [1997] 1 All E.R. 21, CA, Phillips L.J. stated that he did not consider:

> "that the County Court, as part of its inherent jurisdiction, can properly suspend an order or warrant for possession in order to enable a mortgagor to apply to the High Court for an order under s.91. It [is] incumbent on the mortgagor to seek from the High Court any relief which the court is empowered to give before the warrant takes effect."

He noted that Administration of Justice Act 1970 s.36 (see below) makes it clear that parliament did not intend that the court should have power to curtail mortgagees' rights to possession unless the proceeds of sale were likely to discharge the mortgage debt. Millett L.J. expressed serious doubts as to whether *Barrett v Halifax Building Society* (1995) 28 H.L.R. 634, Ch D, where an order allowing the borrowers to sell even though the proceeds of sale would not discharge the mortgage debt, was correctly decided.

If the proceeds of sale are likely to be sufficient to redeem the mortgage, it is normal for the court to give conduct of the sale to the borrower since he or she has a greater incentive to achieve the best price. In *Cheltenham and Gloucester plc v Booker* [1997] 19 E.G. 155; (1997) 73 P. & C.R. 412; (1997) 29 H.L.R. 634, CA, where the proceeds of sale were not likely to be sufficient to redeem the mortgage and where the court was unable to exercise its discretion under Administration of Justice Act 1970 s.36 (see below) it was held that the court may give conduct of the sale of premises to the lender while postponing execution of a warrant for possession until completion of the sale, thus allowing the borrower to remain in occupation. There is no reason in principle for the court to accede to a lender's insistence upon immediate possession if:

(a) possession will only be required on completion;
(b) the presence of the borrowers pending completion will enhance, or at least not depress, the sale price;
(c) the borrowers will co-operate in the sale; and
(d) they will give possession to the purchasers on completion.

However, Millett L.J. stated these conditions are seldom likely to be satisfied and the circumstances in which such a course would be appropriate are hard to imagine. Such an order would "certainly be a rarity".

* * * *

# PART V

## *LEASES AND TENANCIES*

### Restrictions on and relief against forfeiture of leases and underleases

**146.**—(1) A right of re-entry or forfeiture under any proviso or stipulation in a lease for a breach of any covenant or condition in the lease shall not be enforceable, by action or otherwise, unless and until the lessor serves on the lessee a notice— **3A–14**

***Paragraph numbers marked with a "+" can be found online and on CD.***

HOUSING

(a) specifying the particular breach complained of; and
(b) if the breach is capable of remedy, requiring the lessee to remedy the breach; and
(c) in any case, requiring the lessee to make compensation in money for the breach;

and the lessee fails, within a reasonable time thereafter, to remedy the breach, if it is capable of remedy, and to make reasonable compensation in money, to the satisfaction of the lessor, for the breach.

(2) Where a lessor is proceeding, by action by otherwise, to enforce such a right of re-entry or forfeiture, the lessee may, in the lessor's action, if any, or in any action brought by himself, apply to the court for relief; and the court may grant or refuse relief, as the court, having regard to the proceedings and conduct of the parties under the foregoing provisions of this section, and to all the other circumstances, thinks fit; and in case of relief may grant it on such terms, if any, as to costs, expenses, damages, compensation, penalty, or otherwise, including the granting of an injunction to restrain any like breach in the future, as the court, in the circumstances of each case, thinks fit.

(3) A lessor shall be entitled to recover as a debt due to him from a lessee, and in addition to damages (if any), all reasonable costs and expenses properly incurred by the lessor in the employment of a solicitor and surveyor or valuer, or otherwise, in reference to any breach giving rise to a right of re-entry or forfeiture which, at the request of the lessee, is waived by the lessor, or from which the lessee is relieved, under the provisions of this Act.

(4) Where a lessor is proceeding by action or otherwise to enforce a right of re-entry or forfeiture under any covenant, proviso, or stipulation in a lease, or for non-payment of rent, the court may, on application by any person claiming as under-lessee any estate or interest in the property comprised in the lease or any part thereof, either in the lessor's action (if any) or in any action brought by such person for that purpose, make an order vesting, for the whole term of the lease or any less term, the property comprised in the lease or any part thereof in any person entitled as under-lessee to any estate or interest in such property upon such conditions as to execution of any deed or other document, payment of rent, costs, expenses, damages, compensation, giving security, or otherwise, as the court in the circumstances of each case may think fit, but in no case shall any such under-lessee be entitled to require a lease to be granted to him for any longer term than he had under this original sub-lease.

(5) For the purposes of this section—

(a) "Lease" includes an original or derivative under-lease; also an agreement for a lease where the lessee has become entitled to have his lease granted; also a grant at a fee farm rent, or securing a rent by condition;
(b) "Lessee" includes an original or derivative under-lessee, and the persons deriving title under a lessee; also a grantee under any such grant as aforesaid and the persons deriving title under him;

*Paragraph numbers marked with a "+" can be found online and on CD.*

(c) "Lessor" includes an original or derivative under-lessor, and the persons deriving title under a lessor; also a person making such grant as aforesaid and the persons deriving title under him;

(d) "Under-lease" includes an agreement for an underlease where the underlessee has become entitled to have his underlease granted;

(e) "Underlessee" includes any person deriving title under an underlessee.

(6) This section applies although the proviso or stipulation under which the right of re-entry or forfeiture accrues is inserted in the lease in pursuance of the directions of any Act of Parliament.

(7) For the purposes of this section a lease limited to continue as long only as the lessee abstains from committing a breach of covenant shall be and take effect as a lease to continue for any longer term for which it could subsist, but determinable by a proviso for re-entry on such a breach.

(8) This section does not extend—

(i) To a covenant or condition against assigning, underletting, parting with the possession, or disposing of the land leased where the breach occurred before the commencement of this Act; or

(ii) In the case of a mining lease, to a covenant or condition for allowing the lessor to have access to or inspect books, accounts, records, weighing machines or other things, or to enter or inspect the mine or the working thereof.

(9) This section does not apply to a condition for forfeiture on the bankruptcy of the lessee or on taking in execution of the lessee's interest if contained in a lease of—

(a) Agricultural or pastoral land;

(b) Mines or minerals;

(c) A house used or intended to be used as a public-house or beershop;

(d) A house let as a dwelling-house, with the use of any furniture, books, works of art, or other chattels not being in the nature of fixtures;

(e) Any property with respect to which the personal qualifications of the tenant are of importance for the preservation of the value or character of the property, or on the ground of neighbourhood to the lessor, or to any person holding under him.

(10) Where a condition of forfeiture on the bankruptcy of the lessee or on taking in execution of the lessee's interest is contained in any lease, other than a lease of any of the classes mentioned in the last subsection, then—

(a) if the lessee's interest is sold within one year from the bankruptcy or taking in execution, this section applies to the forfeiture condition aforesaid;

(b) if the lessee's interest is not sold before the expiration of that year, this section only applies to the forfeiture condi-

*Paragraph numbers marked with a "+" can be found online and on CD.*

tion aforesaid during the first year from the date of the bankruptcy or taking in execution.

(11) This section does not, save as otherwise mentioned, affect the law relating to re-entry or forfeiture or relief in case of non-payment of rent.

(12) This section has affect notwithstanding any stipulation to the contrary.

(13) The county court has jurisdiction under this section.

**3A-15** *Note* —Amended by the High Court and County Courts Jurisdiction Order (SI 1991/724) art.2(1)(a) and (8). Subsection (13) was added by the County Courts Act 1984 s.148(1), Sch.2 and then amended by High Court and County Courts Jurisdiction Order 1991 (SI 1991/724) art.2(1)(a) and (8). County courts now have unlimited jurisdiction.

**No forfeiture notice before determination of breach.**

**3A-16** Commonhold and Leasehold Reform Act 2002 s.168 provides that a landlord under a long lease of a dwelling may not serve a notice under Law of Property Act 1925 s.146(1) unless it has been finally determined on an application under s.168(4) that the breach has occurred; or the tenant has admitted the breach; or a court in any proceedings, or an arbitral tribunal in proceedings pursuant to a post-dispute arbitration agreement, has finally determined that the breach has occurred. Section 168 is printed at para.3A-1593 below. Comonhold and Leasehold Reform Act 2002 s.76 provides that a lease is a long lease if it (a) is granted for a term of years certain exceeding 21 years; (b) is for a term fixed by law under a grant with a covenant or obligation for perpetual renewal (c) takes effect under Law of Property Act 1925 s.149(6) (leases terminable after a death or marriage); (d) was granted under the right to buy provisions of Housing Act 1985 Pt 5; (e) is a shared ownership lease; or (f) under Housing Act 1996 s.17 (the right to acquire). Section 77 contains certain exceptions.

**"rent"**

**3A-17** See s.205(xxiii).

**"lease", "lessee", "lessor", "under-lease" and "under-lessor"**

**3A-18** See s.146(5).

**"Restrictions on and relief against forfeiture ..."**

**3A-19** Note that this section does not, save as is otherwise mentioned, affect the law relating to re-entry or forfeiture or relief in the case of non-payment of rent (s.146(11)). See the Common Law Procedure Act 1852 ss.210–212, above, the Senior Courts Act 1981 s.38, below, and the County Courts Act 1984 ss.138–140, below.

For the restriction on forfeiture or re-entry for arrears of service charges see the Housing Act 1996 s.81, below.

For a statement of the circumstances in which a tenant may apply for relief, see *Billson v Residential Apartments Ltd* [1992] 1 A.C. 494; [1992] 2 W.L.R. 15; [1992] 1 All E.R. 141, HL, where Lord Templeman said:

> "A tenant may apply for ... relief from forfeiture under section 146(2) after the issue of a section 146 notice but he is not prejudiced if he does not do so. A tenant cannot apply for relief after a landlord has forfeited a lease by issuing and serving a writ, has recovered judgment and has entered into possession pursuant to that judgment. If the judgment is set aside or succesfully appealed, the tenant will be able to apply for relief in the landlord's action but the court in deciding whether to grant relief will take into account any consequences of the original order and repossession and the delay of the tenant. A tenant may apply for relief after a landlord has forfeited by re-entry without first obtaining a court order for that purpose, but the court in deciding whether to grant relief will take into account all the circumstances including delay on the part of the tenant."

Lord Templeman also indicated that he considered the practice of awarding indemnity costs as a condition of granting relief was ripe for reconsideration (but *cf.*

***Paragraph numbers marked with a "+" can be found online and on CD.***

*Church Commissioners v Ibrahim* [1997] 1 E.G.L.R. 13, CA and CPR r.48.3). See too *Fairview Investments Ltd v Sharma*, October 14, 1999, unrep. and *Gomba Holdings (UK) Ltd v Minories Finance Ltd (No.2)* [1993] Ch. 171 at p.194B, CA where the Court of Appeal stated that although costs are in the court's discretion, where there is a contractual right to costs, the discretion should ordinarily be exercised so as to reflect that contractual right. If a lessee is to be relieved from forfeiture, it should be on terms that reflect the lessee's breach of covenant and the lessor should not be left out of pocket by taking proper steps to protect his interests. Where a lessor has bargained for the protection afforded by a clause providing for payment of costs, a court should be slow to deprive him or her of that protection and should not do so without good reason.

## Relief against notice to effect decorative repairs

**147.**—(1) After a notice is served on a lessee relating to the internal decorative repairs to a house or other building, he may apply to the court for relief, and if, having regard to all the circumstances of the case (including in particular the length of the lessee's term or interest remaining unexpired), the court is satisfied that the notice is unreasonable, it may, by order, wholly or partially relieve the lessee from liability for such repairs. **3A-20**

(2) This section does not apply—

(i) where the liability arises under an express covenant or agreement to put the property in a decorative state of repair and the covenant or agreement has never been performed;

(ii) to any matter necessary or proper—

(a) for putting or keeping the property in a sanitary condition, or

(b) for the maintenance or preservation of the structure;

(iii) to any statutory liability to keep a house in all respects reasonably fit for human habitation;

(iv) to any covenant or stipulation to yield up the house or other building in a specified state of repair at the end of the term.

(3) In this section "lease" includes an underlease and an agreement for a lease, and "lessee" has a corresponding meaning and includes any person liable to effect the repairs.

(4) This section applies whether the notice is served before or after the commencement of this Act, and has effect notwithstanding any stipulation to the contrary.

(5) The county court has jurisdiction under this section.

*Note* —Subsection (5) added by the County Courts Act 1984 s.148(1), Sch.2; repealed in part by the High Court and County Courts Jurisdiction Order 1991 (SI 1991/724) art.2(8), Sch. County courts now have unlimited jurisdiction. **3A-21**

* * * *

### *NOTICES*

## Regulations respecting notices

**196.**—(1) Any notice required or authorised to be served or given by this Act shall be in writing. **3A-22**

***Paragraph numbers marked with a "+" can be found online and on CD.***

(2) Any notice required or authorised by this Act to be served on a lessee or mortgagor shall be sufficient, although only addressed to the lessee or mortgagor by that designation, without his name, or generally to the persons interested, without any name, and notwithstanding that any person to be affected by the notice is absent, under disability, unborn, or unascertained.

(3) Any notice required or authorised by this Act to be served shall be sufficiently served if it is left at the last-known place of abode or business in the United Kingdom of the lessee, lessor, mortgagee, mortgagor, or other person to be served, in case of a notice required or authorised to be served on a lessee or mortgagor, is affixed or left for him on the land or any house or building comprised in the lease or mortgage, or, in case of a mining lease, is left for the lessee at the office or counting-house of the mine.

(4) Any notice required or authorised by this Act to be served shall also be sufficiently served, if it is sent by post in a registered letter addressed to the lessee, lessor, mortgagee, mortgagor, or other person to be served, by name, at the aforesaid place of abode or business, office, or counting-house, and if that letter is not returned by the postal operator (within the meaning of the Postal Services Act 2000) concerned undelivered; and that service shall be deemed to be made at the time at which the registered letter would in the ordinary course be delivered.

(5) The provisions of this section shall extend to notices required to be served by any instrument affecting property executed or coming into operation after the commencement of this Act unless a contrary intention appears.

(6) This section does not apply to notices served in proceedings in the court.

**3A–23** *Note*—Amended by the Leasehold Property (Repairs) Act 1938 s.72; the Reserve and Auxiliary Forces (Protection of Civil Interests) Act 1951 s.29(b); the Recorded Delivery Service Act 1962 s.1, Sch.; and the Postal Services Act 2000 (Consequential Modifications No.1) Order (SI 2001/1149) Sch.1, para.7.

**"notices"**

**3A–24** It is good practice for landlords by an express provision to incorporate this section into tenancy agreements. If they do not do so, it cannot be implied. In the absence of express incorporation, landlords must prove that notices to quit or notices of intention to seek possession have come to the attention of the tenant (see *Wandsworth LBC v Attwell* (1995) 27 H.L.R. 536; (1996) 01 E.G. 100; (1996) 94 L.G.R. 419, CA; and *Enfield LBC v Devonish* (1997) 29 H.L.R. 691; *The Times*, December 12, 1996, CA.

**For s.205 of the Law of Property Act 1925 (see Arrangement) plus any related commentary see paragraphs 3A–25+ to 3A–26+ on White Book on Westlaw UK or the Civil Procedure CD.**

## National Assistance Act 1948

**3A–26.1** (11 & 12 GEO. 6 c.29)

ARRANGEMENT OF SECTIONS

PART III

LOCAL AUTHORITY SERVICES

*PROVISION OF ACCOMMODATION*



***Paragraph numbers marked with a "+" can be found online and on CD.***

*LOCAL AND CENTRAL AUTHORITIES*



# PART III

## LOCAL AUTHORITY SERVICES

### *PROVISION OF ACCOMMODATION*

**Duty of local authorities to provide accommodation**

**21.**—(1) Subject to and in accordance with the provisions of this Part of this Act, a local authority may with the approval of the Secretary of State, and to such extent as he may direct shall, make arrangements for providing— **3A–27**

(a) residential accommodation for persons aged eighteen or over who by reason of age, illness, disability or any other circumstances are in need of care and attention which is not otherwise available to them; and

(aa) residential accommodation for expectant and nursing mothers who are in need of care and attention which is not otherwise available to them.

(b) [...]

(1A) A person to whom section 115 of the Immigration and Asylum Act 1999 (exclusion from benefits) applies may not be provided with residential accommodation under subsection (1)(a) if his need for care and attention has arisen solely—

(a) because he is destitute; or

(b) because of the physical effects, or anticipated physical effects, of his being destitute.

(1B) Subsections (3) and (5) to (8) of section 95, of the Immigration and Asylum Act 1999 and paragraph 2 of Schedule 8 to that Act, apply for the purposes of subsection (1A) as they apply for the purposes of that section, but for the references in subsections (5) and (7) of that section and in that paragraph to the Secretary of State substitute references to a local authoity.

(2) In [making any such arrangements] a local authority shall have regard to the welfare of all persons for whom accommodation is provided, and in particular to the need for providing accommodation of different descriptions suited to different descriptions of such persons as are mentioned in the last foregoing subsection.

(2A) In determining for the purposes of paragraph (a) or (aa) of subsection (1) of this section whether care and attention are otherwise available to a person, a local authority shall disregard so much of the person's resources as may be specified in, or determined in accordance with, regulations made by the Secretary of State for the purposes of this subsection.

(2B) In subsection (2A) of this section the reference to a person's resources is a reference to his resources within the meaning of regulations made for the purposes of that subsection.

***Paragraph numbers marked with a "+" can be found online and on CD.***

(3) [...]

(4) Subject to the provisions of section 26 of this Act. Accommodation provided by a local authority in the exercise of their functions under this section shall be provided in premises managed by the authority or, to such extent as may be determined in accordance with the arrangements under this section, in such premises managed by another local authority as may be agreed between the two authorities and on such terms, including terms as to the reimbursement of expenditure incurred by the said other authority, as may be so agreed.

(5) References in this Act to accommodation provided under this Part thereof shall be construed as references to accommodation provided in accordance with this and the five next following sections, and as including references to board and other services, amenities and requisites provided in connection with the accommodation except where in the opinion of the authority managing the premises their provision is unnecessary.

(6) References in this Act to a local authority providing accommodation shall be construed, in any case where a local authority agree with another local authority for the provision of accommodation in premises managed by the said other authority, as references to the first-mentioned local authority.

(7) Without prejudice to the generality of the foregoing provisions of this section, a local authority may—

(a) provide, in such cases as they may consider appropriate, for the conveyance of persons to and from premises in which accommodation is provided for them under this Part of the Act;

(b) make arrangements for the provision on the premises in which accommodation is being provided for such other services as appear to the authority to be required.

(8) [...] nothing in this section shall authorise or require a local authority to make any provision authorised or required to be made (whether by that or by any other authority) by or under any enactment not contained in this Part of this Act [or for authorised or required to be provided under the National Health Service Act 2006 or the National Health Service (Wales) Act 2006.]

**3A–28** *Note* —Amended by the Local Government Act 1972 ss.195(6), 272(1), Sch.23, para.2(1), Sch.30; the National Health Service Reorganisation Act 1973 s.57(1), (2), Sch.4, para.44, Sch.5; the Housing (Homeless Persons) Act 1977 s.20(4), Sch.; the Children Act 1989 s.108(5), Sch.13, para.11(1); the National Health Service and Community Care Act 1990 s.42(1), 66, Sch.9, para.5(1)–(3), Sch.10; the Immigration and Asylum Act 1999 s.116; the Health and Social Care Act 2001 s.53; and by the National Health Service (Consequential Provisions) Act 2006 s.2 and Sch.1, para.2.

**Editorial introduction**

**3A–29** The National Assistance Act 1948 s.21(1)(a) gives social services authorities power to make arrangements for the accommodation of adults who are in need of care and attention not otherwise available to them as a result of age, illness, disability or any other circumstances. The Secretary of State has directed that authorities shall make arrangements under s.21(1)(a) to provide accommodation for adults who are ordinarily resident in their areas or are in urgent need thereof and who, by reason of age, illness, disability or any other circumstance, are in need of care and attention not otherwise available to them. Note that s.21 was amended by Immigration and Asylum Act 1999 s.116 to exclude the provision of accommodation under s.21 to destitute asylum seekers.

Section 21 is not a safety net on which any person short of money can rely. The proper test is whether a person is "in need of care and attention" (*R. v Newham LBC Ex p. Plastin* (1998) 30 H.L.R. 261, QBD). In *R (M) v Slough BC* [2008] UKHL 52, [2008] 1 W.L.R. 1808; [2008] 4 All E.R. 831, the House of Lords held that a person who only needed provision of normal housing (with a fridge) was not necessarily in need of "care and attention". In order to be so, a person had to need "looking after".In *R. v Southwark Ex p. Hong Cui* (1999) 31 H.L.R. 639, QBD David Pannick QC sitting as a deputy judge held that: (1) an applicant must show that s/he is in desperate need of care and attention and that otherwise there is a risk that there would be damage to his/her health or for some other reason assistance is urgently required. It is not enough to be destitute; and (2) authorities must consider the circumstances of each individual case. A local authority's duty is to assess and meet applicants' needs, not to satisfy their preferences. (*R (Khana and Karim) v Southwark LBC* [2001] EWCA Civ 999; [2002] H.L.R. 31).

**Children**

There is no express provision that obliges a local authority to meet the needs of an individual child after assessment. National Assistance Act 1948 s.21 involves the notion of a target duty that becomes crystallised and enforceable after a needs assessment (see *R. v Kensington & Chelsea RLBC Ex p. Kujtim* [1999] 4 All E.R. 161). However, the language and structure of Children Act 1989 s.17 are entirely different from s.21. A child previously accommodated by s.21 is catered for by s.20 of the 1989 Act. Where a child requires accommodation of a particular kind and is in a family unit so that s.20 is not invoked, provision would generally be made through the housing legislation. Section 17 of the 1989 Act creates a general duty to safeguard and promote the welfare of children in need. However in *A and W v Lambeth LBC*; *G v Barnet LBC* (also reported as *R.(G) v Barnet LBC)* [2003] UKHL 57; [2004] 2 A.C. 208; [2003] 3 W.L.R. 1194; [2004] 1 All E.R. 97, the House of Lords rejected claims that Children Act 1989 s.17 gives rise to an enforceable duty to accommodate the children with their families. Social services departments are not statutorily required to arrange or provide accommodation for families with children who are not entitled to be housed through the usual channels, although they can do so. Section 17(1) is an overriding duty, a statement of general principle. It provides the broad aims which local authorities are to bear in mind when performing other duties set out in the Children Act and the specific duties for facilitating the discharge of those general duties which were set out in Pt I of Sch.2. A child in need within the meaning of s.17(10) is eligible for the provision of those services, but has no absolute right to them. Section 17(1) sets out duties of a general character which are intended to be for the benefit of children in need in the local social services authority's area in general. The other duties and the specific duties which follow have to be performed in each individual case by reference to the general duties which s.17(1) sets out. Section 17 refers to a range and level of services appropriate to the children's needs. It is broadly expressed, with a view to giving the greatest possible scope to the local social services authority as to what it chooses to do in the provision of those services. Although the services which the authority provide may include the provision of accommodation (see s.17(6)), the provision of residential accommodation to house a child in need so that he or she can live with the family is not the principal or primary purpose of the legislation. Housing is the function of the local housing authority. Detailed provisions for the acquisition and management of housing stock are contained in the Housing Acts. Provisions of that kind are entirely absent from the Children Act. The expenditure of limited resources on the provision of residential accommodation for housing children with their families would be bound to mean that there was less available for expenditure on other services designed for the performance of the general duty which s.17(1) identified. It would also sit uneasily with the legislation in the Housing Acts. 3A–29.1

**"local authority"**

See s.33 below. 3A–30

**"destitute"**

See the Immigration and Asylum Act 1999 s.95(3). 3A–31

*Paragraph numbers marked with a "+" can be found online and on CD.*

### "resources"

3A-32 Where a local authority is satisfied that a person is in need of care and attention which is not otherwise available, lack of funds does not excuse it from performing its duty to make appropriate arrangements (*R. v Sefton MBC Ex p. Help the Aged* (1997-98) 1 C.C.L. Rep. 57, CA).

### "accommodation"

3A-33 In *R. v Newham LBC Ex p. Medical Foundation of the Care of Victims of Torture* (1998) 30 H.L.R. 955, QBD, Moses J. held that the phrase "residential accommodation" means no more than where a person lives. It does not mean "accommodation with an institutional quality". See too *R. v Newham LBC Ex p. C* (1999) 31 H.L.R. 567, QBD.

### Termination of duty

3A-34 See Immigration and Asylum Act 1999 Pt VI. The duty of central government to provide support to asylum seekers under Immigration and Asylum Act 1999 s.95 applies only where need arises solely from destitution rather than sickness, age or disability. Otherwise local authorities are obliged to provide accommodation under s.21. Regulation 6(4)of the Asylum Support Regulations 2000 (SI 2000/704) requires the secretary of state to take into account any other support available to an asylum seeker when determining whether that asylum seeker is destitute for the purposes of s.95(1). That regulation includes accomodation that the local authority is obliged to provide by s.21. See *R. (Westminster CC) v National Asylum Support Service* [2002] UKHL 38; [2002] 1 W.L.R. 2956.

Where a person's needs satisfy the criteria contained in the National Assistance Act 1948 s.21(1)(a), the authority has a continuing duty to provide accommodation while the person's needs remain the same. However an authority is entitled to treat its duty as discharged and to refuse to provide further accommodation if the person refuses accommodation offered or, following its provision manifests by his or her conduct a persistent and unequivocal refusal to observe the authority's reasonable requirements in relation to occupation of such accommodation. Before concluding that there has been such a refusal it is desirable that the authority write a final warning letter. Any decision by the authority to treat its duty as discharged by conduct requires a reassessment both of current need and careful consideration of the nature of that conduct, including any medical condition or infirmity known to the authority (*R. v Kensington and Chelsea RBC Ex p. Kutjim* [1999] 4 All E.R. 161, CA).

### Asylum Seekers

3A-35 Asylum seekers are to be supported under the Immigration and Asylum Act 1999 Pt VI until the conclusion of any appeal. Thereafter, if they have a need for care and attention that does not arise solely because of destitution, they qualify under s.21. See *R v Wandsworth LBC Ex p. O*; *R v Leicester CC Ex p. Bhika* [2000] 1 W.L.R. 2539; [2000] 4 All E.R. 590 where Simon Brown L.J. accepted submissions that:

> "if an applicant's need for care and attention is to any material extent made more acute by some circumstances other than the mere lack of accommodation and funds, then, despite being subject to immigration control, he qualifies for assistance. Other relevant circumstances include, of course, age, illness and disability, all of which are expressly mentioned in section 21(1) itself. If, for example, an immigrant, as well as being destitute, is old, ill or disabled, he is likely to be yet more vulnerable and less well able to survive than if he were merely destitute."

All other categories or persons from abroad, whether or not they have any pending immigration appeal qualify for assistance under s.21 if their need does not arise solely because of destitution. Where a destitute 'asylum-seeker' within the terms of Immigration and Asylum Act 1999 s.94(1) with children requires accommodation, a local authority's duty does not extend to accommodating the children. Responsibility for them falls on NASS rather than on the local authority and they are to be treated as "destitute" even though actually sheltered with their parent. In such circumstances, the appropriate practical solution is for the council to accommodate the whole family with NASS meeting the cost of accommodating the children (*R.(O) v Haringey LBC* [2004] EWCA Civ 535; [2004] H.L.R.44).

The fact that someone is unlawfully present in the United Kingdom does not preclude them from seeking accommodation under s.21 (*R. v Wandsworth LBC Ex p. O; R v Leicester CC Ex p. Bhika* [2000] 1 W.L.R. 2539; [2000] 4 All E.R. 590 where Simon Brown L.J. said:

> "section 21(1) affords the very last possibility of relief, the final hope of keeping the needy off the streets. Not even illegality should to my mind bar an applicant who otherwise qualifies for support. For my part I would hold that the local authority has no business with the applicant's immigration status save only for the purpose of learning why the care and attention 'is not otherwise available to them' as section 21(1) requires—and indeed . . for reporting such applications to the immigration authorities if they conclude that the Home Office is unaware of their presence here.")

Under National Assistance Act 1948 s.21(1A) the responsibility for meeting the care and accommodation needs of disabled asylum-seekers falls upon the local authorities, not the NASS. For the purposes of National Assistance Act 1948 s.21(1A), local authorities have to decide whether applicants are in need of care and attention not otherwise available to them. They cannot take into account the provision of asylum support under the Immigration and Asylum Act 1999 because the Asylum Support Regulations 2000 required them to disregard the provision of asylum support when deciding whether a person was destitute (*Murua v Croydon LBC* (2002) 5 C.C.L. Rep. 51).

A local authority is not relieved of its duty to provide residential accomodation under s.21 even if the asylum seeker has applied to NASS and has been accepted for provision of support by them. (Asylum Support Regulations 2000 (SI 2000/704), reg.23 and *R. (on the application of Mani) v Lambeth LBC* [2003] EWCA Civ 836.

**"discharge of duty"**

See *Anufrijeva v Southwark LBC* [2003] EWCA Civ 1406; [2004] Q.B. 1124; [2004] 2 W.L.R. 603; [2004] 1 All E.R. 833 where the claimants unsuccessfully brought proceedings for damages under the Human Rights Act 1998 for breach of ECHR, art.8 claiming that the defendant council had failed to discharge its duty under s.21 because a property in which they had been housed was unsuitable. The Court of Appeal held that there is a stage at which the dictates of humanity require the state to intervene to prevent any person within its territory suffering dire consequences as a result of deprivation of sustenance. If support is necessary to prevent a person in this country reaching the point of art.3 degradation, then that support should be provided. If such a basic standard exists, it must require intervention by the state, whether the claimant is an asylum seeker who has not sought asylum promptly on entry or is a citizen entitled to all the benefits of our system. Article 8 is capable of imposing on a state a positive obligation to provide support (*R. (Bernard) v Enfield LBC* [2002] EWHC 2282 (Admin); [2003] U.K.H.R.R. 148). Those obligations are not however absolute. There must be some ground for criticising the failure to act—an element of culpability and knowledge that the claimant's private and family life are at risk. If there is delay, there is no infringement of art.8 unless substantial prejudice has been caused to the applicant. Maladministration does not infringe art.8 unless the consequences are serious. Isolated acts of even significant carelessness are unlikely to suffice. At first instance courts dealing with claims for maladministration should adopt a broad-brush approach, without a close examination of authorities or a prolonged examination of the facts. Remedies have to be just and appropriate and necessary to afford just satisfaction. Levels of damages awarded in tort, by the CICB and local government ombudsmen might all provide some rough guidance. Courts should look critically at any attempt to recover damages for maladministration under the Human Rights Act 1998 other than in the Administrative Court. Before giving permission to apply for judicial review, the Administrative Court should require the claimant to explain why it is not more appropriate to use any internal complaints procedure. **3A–36**

* * * *

*LOCAL AND CENTRAL AUTHORITIES*

## Local Authorities for purposes of Part III

**33.**—(1) In this Part of this Act the expression "local authority" **3A–37**

***Paragraph numbers marked with a "+" can be found online and on CD.***

means a council which is a local authority for the purposes of the Local Authority Social Services Act 1970 in England or Wales, and a council constituted under section 2 of the Local Government, etc. (Scotland) Act 1994 in Scotland:

(2) [...]

## Administration of Justice Act 1970

3A–38 (1970 c.31)

ARRANGEMENT OF SECTIONS

PART IV

ACTIONS BY MORTGAGEES FOR POSSESSION

SECT.



## PART IV

## ACTIONS BY MORTGAGEES FOR POSSESSION

### Additional powers of court in action by mortgagee for possession of dwelling-house

3A–39 **36.**—(1) Where the mortgagee under a mortgage of land which consists of or includes a dwelling-house brings an action in which he claims possession of the mortgaged property, not being an action for foreclosure in which a claim for possession of the mortgaged property is also made, the court may exercise any of the powers conferred on it by subsection (2)below if it appears to the court that in the event of its exercising the power the mortgagor is likely to be able within a reasonable period to pay any sums due under the mortgage or to remedy a default consisting of a breach of any other obligation arising under or by virtue of the mortgage.

(2) The court—

(a) may adjourn the proceedings, or

(b) on giving judgment, or making an order, for delivery of possession of the mortgaged property, or at any time before the execution of such judgment or order, may—

(i) stay or suspend execution of the judgment or order, or

(ii) postpone the date for delivery of possession,

for such period or periods as the court thinks reasonable.

(3) Any such adjournment, stay, suspension or postponement as is referred to in subsection (2) above may be made subject to such conditions with regard to payment by the mortgagor of any sum secured by the mortgage or the remedying of any default as the court thinks fit.

(4) The court may from time to time vary or revoke any condition imposed by virtue of this section.

(5) [...]

(6) In the application of this section to Northern Ireland, "the court" means a judge of the High Court in Northern Ireland, and in subsection (1) the words from "not being" to "made" shall be omitted.

*Note*—Subsection (5) was repealed by the Statute Law (Repeals) Act 2004 s.1(1) and Sch.1, Pt 1. **3A-39.1**

**"Additional powers of court ..."**

For definitions of "dwelling-house", "mortgage", "mortgagee" and "mortgagor" see s.39 below. **3A-40**

See too the Administration of Justice Act 1973 s.8 (below).

At common law, where, under an instalment mortgage, by reason of default by the borrower, the whole money advanced has become payable, the lender is entitled to possession and the court has no jurisdiction to decline to make an order for possession or to adjourn the hearing, whether on terms of keeping up payments or paying arrears, if the mortgagee cannot be persuaded to agree to this course. To this the *sole exception* is that the application may be adjourned for a short time to afford the mortgagor a chance of paying off the mortgagee in full or otherwise satisfying him; but this should not be done if there is no reasonable prospect of this occurring (*Birmingham Citizens Permanent Building Society v Caunt* [1962] Ch. 883 at 912, Ch D). However, the Administration of Justice Act 1970 s.36 and the Administration of Justice Act 1973 s.8 (see below) give courts in mortgage possession proceedings power to adjourn, stay, suspend or postpone the date for the giving up of possession if it is likely that the arrears of instalments and interest can be repaid during a reasonable period. A bankrupt may make an application to the court for relief under Administration of Justice Acts 1970 and 1973 (*Nationwide BS v Purvis* [1998] B.P.I.R. 625, CA).

In *Royal Bank of Scotland v Miller* [2001] EWCA Civ 344; [2002] Q.B. 255; [2001] 3 W.L.R. 523, CA, it was held that (1) the relevant time for determining whether land consists of or includes a dwelling-house within the meaning of s.36 is the time when the mortgagee claims possession, not the date when the legal charge is entered into; and (2) breach of a term of the mortgage (e.g. occupation by a third party without consent) does not prevent s.36 from applying.

Section 8 does not apply to "all moneys" charges, since:

(a) the principal does not become due and cannot be sued upon until a written demand is made; and

(b) the charge does not provide for deferment after a written demand is made (*Habib Bank v Tailor* [1982] 1 W.L.R. 1218; [1982] 3 All E.R. 561, CA).

Accordingly a mortgagor with an all moneys charge against whom possession is sought can only rely upon s.36 if it is likely that all sums due (i.e. principal, interest and any other sums due under the mortgage) can be paid within a reasonable period.

An agreement to pay off outstanding sums drawn down from an overdraft facility secured by a charge by monthly instalments does not come within s.36 or s.8 either (*Rees Investments Ltd v Groves*, June 27, 2001, unrep., Ch D).

Administration of Justice Act 1970 s.36 has not abrogated the mortgagee's common law right to take possession of property where court proceedings are not needed, e.g. where premises are unoccupied or where premises are sold by receivers in accordance with Law of Property Act 1925 s.101 (see *Western Bank Ltd v Schindler* [1977] Ch. 1, CA; *Ropaigealach v Barclays Bank Plc* [2000] 1 Q.B. 263; [1999] 3 W.L.R. 17; [1999] 4 All E.R. 235, CA and *Horsham Properties Group Ltd v Clark* [2008] EWHC 2327 (Ch); October 8, 2008, where it was held that LPA 1925 s.101 is not incompatible with ECHR Article 1, Protocol 1). Parliament did not intend s.36 to give mortgagors protection from mortgagees who took possession without the assistance of the court (*cf*. Criminal Law Act 1977 s.6 and Consumer Credit Act 1974 s.126 where specific protection has been given to mortgagors from forcible re-entry).

Where the court exercises its power under s.36 to stay or suspend execution for such period as the court thinks reasonable, that period must be defined or rendered ascertainable. It is wrong to suspend in general terms without fixing any period for the length of the suspension (*Royal Trust Co of Canada v Markham* [1975] 3 All E.R. 433, CA).

The court cannot suspend an order for possession under s.36, however hard the circumstances, if there is no prospect of the borrower reducing the arrears (*Abbey National Mortgages v Bernard* (1995) 71 P. & C.R. 257, CA; see too *Abbey National Building Society v Mewton* [1995] 9 C.L. 346, CA).

Note also *Hyde Park Funding Ltd v Ioannou* [1999] 3 C.L.D. 428 (Barnet County Court) where mortgagees brought possession proceedings and a possession order was granted. Later they obtained a warrant. On the morning of the proposed eviction the borrower applied to a district judge to suspend the warrant. That application was dismissed and the borrower was evicted. The borrower appealed to a circuit judge. The lender contended that as the warrant had been executed, the court no longer had jurisdiction to suspend under Administration of Justice Act 1970 s.36. HHJ Connor allowed the appeal. On appeal from a district judge, a circuit judge can exercise all of the jurisdiction that the district judge had and can make any order that the district judge could have made. In view of new evidence adduced on the appeal, the correct order was to suspend on terms. The district judge's order was set aside and possession restored.

**"a reasonable period"**

3A-41 What is a reasonable period depends on the individual circumstances of each case, particularly the extent to which the mortgage and arrears are secured by the value of the property (*Bristol and West Building Society v Ellis* (1996) 73 P. & C.R. 158; (1996) 29 H.L.R. 282, CA). "The court should take as its starting point the full term of the mortgage and pose at the outset the question: would it be possible for the mortgagor to maintain payment-off of the arrears by instalments over that period?" (*Cheltenham and Gloucester Building Society v Norgan* [1996] 1 All E.R. 449 at 458; (1995) 28 H.L.R. 443; (1996) 72 P. & C.R. 46, CA, see too *First Middlesbrough Trading and Mortgage Co Ltd v Cunningham* (1974) 28 P. & C.R. 69, CA; and *Western Bank v Schindler* [1977] Ch. 1; [1976] 2 All E.R. 393, CA).

The court may exercise its discretion under s.36 without hearing formal sworn evidence on the basis of information given by defendants. "It must be possible for [judges] to act without evidence, especially where, as here, the mortgagor was present in court and available to be questioned and no objection to the reception of informal material is made by the mortgagee" (*Cheltenham and Gloucester Building Society v Grant* (1994) 26 H.L.R. 703 at 707, CA).

The court's powers under s.36 cease after a warrant has been executed (*Cheltenham and Gloucester Building Society v Obi* (1996) 28 H.L.R. 22, CA; and *National and Provincial Building Society v Ahmed* [1995] 38 E.G. 138, CA) unless the original order itself can be set aside, the warrant is obtained by fraud or there has been abuse of the process or oppression in its execution (*Hammersmith and Fulham LBC v Hill* [1994] 35 E.G. 124; (1995) 27 H.L.R. 368; [1994] 2 E.G.L.R. 51, CA).

See also *Mortgage Agency Services v Bal* (1998) 95(28) L.S.G. 31, CA (s.36 ceases to apply after execution of warrant).

**Mortgage Pre-Action Protocol**

3A-41.1 A new pre-action protocol for possession claims based on residential mortgage arrears came into force on November 19, 2008. See C12–001, the annotations thereto, CPR 55.10 and the commentary at 55.10.2.

**Forms of order**

3A-42 See County Court Forms **N29** (Order for possession (mortgaged property)) and **N31** (Order for possession of mortgaged land suspended under the Administration of Justice Act 1970 s.36 and the Administration of Justice Act 1973 s.8) as specified in the Practice Direction to CPR Pt 4, Table 3.

**European Convention of Human Rights**

3A-43 There is no inconsistency between Administration of Justice Act 1970 s.36 and Convention rights under art.8 or art.1 of the First Protocol (*Barclays Bank v Alcorn* [2002] EWCA Civ 817; June 17, 2002).

* * * *

**38A.** This Part of this Act shall not apply to a mortgage securing an agreement which is a regulated agreement within the meaning of the Consumer Credit Act 1974. **3A–44**

*Note*—Inserted by the Consumer Credit Act 1974 s.192(3)(a), Sch.4, Pt 1, para.30. **3A–45**

**Statutory protection**

For the statutory protection given to borrowers under the Consumer Credit Act 1974, see below. **3A–46**

* * * *

## Interpretation of Part IV

**39.**—(1) In this Part of this Act— **3A–47**

"dwelling-house" includes any building or part thereof which is used as a dwelling;

"mortgage" includes a charge and "mortgagor" and "mortgagee" shall be construed accordingly;

"mortgagor" and "mortgagee" includes any person deriving title under the original mortgagor or mortgagee.

(2) The fact that part of the premises comprised in a dwelling-house is used as a shop or office or for business, trade or professional purposes shall not prevent the dwelling-house from being a dwelling-house for the purposes of this Part of this Act.

## Defective Premises Act 1972

(1972 c.35) **3A–48**

ARRANGEMENT OF SECTIONS



## Duty to build dwellings properly

**1.**—(1) A person taking on work for or in connection with the provision of a dwelling (whether the dwelling is provided by the erection or by the conversion or enlargement of a building) owes a duty— **3A–49**

(a) if the dwelling is provided to the order of any person, to that person; and

(b) without prejudice to paragraph (a) above, to every person who acquires an interest (whether legal or equitable) in the dwelling;

to see that the work which he takes on is done in a workman-like



HOUSING

or, as the case may be, professional manner, with proper materials and so that as regards that work the dwelling will be fit for habitation when completed.

(2) A person who takes on any such work for another on terms that he is to do it in accordance with instructions given by or on behalf of that other shall, to the extent to which he does it properly in accordance with those instructions, be treated for the purposes of this section as discharging the duty imposed on him by subsection (1) above except where he owes a duty to that other to warn him of any defects in the instructions and fails to discharge that duty.

(3) A person shall not be treated for the purposes of subsection (2)above as having given instructions for the doing of work merely because he has agreed to the work being done in a specified manner, with specified materials or to a specified design.

(4) A person who—

(a) in the course of a business which consists of or includes providing or arranging for the provision of dwellings or installations in dwellings; or

(b) in the exercise of a power of making such provision or arrangements conferred by or by virtue of any enactment;

arranges for another to take on work for or in connection with the provision of a dwelling shall be treated for the purposes of this section as included among the persons who have taken on the work.

(5) Any cause of action in respect of a breach of the duty imposed by this section shall be deemed, for the purposes of the Limitation Act 1939, the Law Reform (Limitation of Actions, &c.) Act 1954 and the Limitation Act 1963, to have accrued at the time when the dwelling was completed, but if after that time a person who has done work for or in connection with the provision of the dwelling does further work to rectify the work he has already done, any such cause of action in respect of that further work shall be deemed for those purposes to have accrued at the time when the further work was finished.

**Duty to build dwellings properly**

**3A–50** This section imposes a duty to carry out work (whether by new building or conversion) for or in connection with the provision of a dwelling in a professional or workmanlike manner so that the premises are fit for habitation. It applies both to damage caused by the actual work and damage caused by failure to undertake necessary works (*Andrews v Schooling* [1991] 3 All E.R. 723; (1991) 23 H.L.R. 316, CA and *Mirza v Bhandal* August 1999, Legal Action 24, QBD).

For cases excluded from s.1, see s.2, below.

The duty only applies to work carried out after January 1, 1974.

As to limitation, see s.1(5) and *Alderson v Beetham Organisation Ltd* [2003] EWCA Civ 408; [2003] H.L.R. 60.

## Cases excluded from the remedy under section 1

**3A–51** **2.**—(1) Where—

(a) in connection with the provision of a dwelling or its first sale or letting for habitation any rights in respect of defects in the state of the dwelling are conferred by an approved scheme to which this section applies on a person having or acquiring an interest in the dwelling; and

(b) it is stated in a document of a type approved for the purposes of this section that the requirements as to design or construction imposed by or under the scheme have, or appear to have, been substantially complied with in relation to the dwelling;

no action shall be brought by any person having or acquiring an interest in the dwelling for breach of the duty imposed by section 1 above in relation to the dwelling.

(2) A scheme to which this section applies—

(a) may consist of any number of documents and any number of agreements or other transactions between any number of persons; but

(b) must confer, by virtue of agreements entered into with persons having or acquiring an interest in the dwellings to which the scheme applies, rights on such persons in respect of defects in the state of the dwellings.

(3) In this section "approved" means approved by the Secretary of State, and the power of the Secretary of State to approve a scheme or document for the purposes of this section shall be exercisable by order, except that any requirements as to construction or design imposed under a scheme to which this section applies may be approved by him without making any order or, if he thinks fit, by order.

(4) The Secretary of State—

(a) may approve a scheme or document for the purposes of this section with or without limiting the duration of his approval; and

(b) may by order revoke or vary a previous order under this section or, without such an order, revoke or vary a previous approval under this section given otherwise than by order.

(5) The production of a document purporting to be a copy of an approval given by the Secretary of State otherwise than by order and certified by an officer of the Secretary of State to be a true copy of the approval shall be conclusive evidence of the approval, and without proof of the handwriting or official position of the person purporting to sign the certificate.

(6) The power to make an order under this section shall be exercisable by statutory instrument which shall be subject to annulment in pursuance of a resolution by either House of Parliament.

(7) Where an interest in a dwelling is compulsorily acquired—

(a) no action shall be brought by the acquiring authority for breach of the duty imposed by section 1 above in respect of the dwelling; and

(b) if any work for or in connection with the provision of the dwelling was done otherwise than in the course of a business by the person in occupation of the dwelling at the time of the compulsory acquisition, the acquiring authority and not that person shall be treated as the person who took on the work and accordingly as owing that duty.

### Duty of care with respect to work done on premises not abated by disposal of premises

3A–52 **3.**—(1) Where work of construction, repair, maintenance or demolition or any other work is done on or in relation to premises, any duty of care owed, because of the doing of the work, to persons who might reasonably be expected to be affected by the defects in the state of the premises created by the doing of the work shall not be abated by the subsequent disposal of the premises by the persons who owed the duty.

(2) This section does not apply—

(a) in the case of premises which are let, where the relevant tenancy of the premises commenced, or the relevant tenancy agreement of the premises was entered into, before the commencement of this Act;

(b) in the case of premises disposed of in any other way, when the disposal of the premises was completed, or a contract for their disposal was entered into, before the commencement of this Act; or

(c) in either case, where the relevant transaction disposing of the premises is entered into in pursuance of an enforceable option by which the consideration for the disposal was fixed before the commencement of this Act.

#### "disposal"

3A–53 For the definition of "disposal", see s.6 below.

### Landlord's duty of care in virtue of obligation or right to repair premises demised

3A–54 **4.**—(1) Where premises are let under a tenancy which puts on the landlord an obligation to the tenant for the maintenance or repair of the premises, the landlord owes to all persons who might reasonably be expected to be affected by defects in the state of the premises a duty to take such care as is reasonable in all the circumstances to see that they are reasonably safe from personal injury or from damage to their property caused by a relevant defect.

(2) The said duty is owed if the landlord knows (whether as the result of being notified by the tenant or otherwise) or if he ought in all the circumstances to have known of the relevant defect.

(3) In this section "relevant defect" means a defect in the state of the premises existing at or after the material time and arising from, or continuing because of, an act or omission by the landlord which constitutes or would if he had had notice of the defect, have constituted a failure by him to carry out his obligation to the tenant for the maintenance or repair of the premises; and for the purposes of the foregoing provision "the material time" means—

*Paragraph numbers marked with a "+" can be found online and on CD.*

(a) where the tenancy commenced before this Act, the commencement of this Act; and

(b) in all other cases, the earliest of the following times, that is to say—

(i) the time when the tenancy commences;

(ii) the time when the tenancy agreement is entered into;

(iii) the time when possession is taken of the premises in contemplation of the letting.

(4) Where premises are let under a tenancy which expressly or impliedly gives the landlord the right to enter the premises to carry out any description of maintenance or repair of the premises, then, as from the time when he first is, or by notice or otherwise can put himself, in a position to exercise the right and so long as he is or can put himself in that position, he shall be treated for the purposes of subsections (1) to (3) above (but for no other purpose) as if he were under an obligation to the tenant for that description of maintenance or repair of the premises; but the landlord shall not owe the tenant any duty by virtue of this subsection in respect of any defect in the state of the premises arising from, or continuing because of, a failure to carry out an obligation expressly imposed on the tenant by the tenancy.

(5) For the purposes of this section obligations imposed or rights given by any enactment in virtue of a tenancy shall be treated as imposed or given by the tenancy.

(6) This section applies to a right of occupation given by contract or any enactment and not amounting to a tenancy as if the right were a tenancy, and "tenancy" and cognate expressions shall be construed accordingly.

**"Landlord's duty of care ..."**

Section 4 imposes on landlords a duty of care to all persons who might reasonably be affected by defects in the premises. The duty is to take such care as is reasonable in all the circumstances to see that they are reasonably safe from pesonal injury or from damage to their property (see, e.g. *Clarke v Taff Ely BC* (1983) 10 H.L.R. 44, QBD). The duty is owed if the landlord has the express or implied right under the agreement to enter the premises to carry out any description of maintenance or repair of the premises (e.g. *McAuley v Bristol City Council* [1992] 1 All E.R. 749; (1991) 23 H.L.R. 586; [1991] 46 E.G. 155, CA). See too the Rent Act 1977 ss.3(2) and 148 (below); and the Housing Act 1988 s.16 (below). **3A–55**

A tenant relying upon s.4 merely has to show a failure on the part of the landlord to take such care as is reasonable in the circumstances to see that the tenant is reasonably safe from personal injury. That duty is owed if the landlord "ought in all circumstances" to have known of the relevant defect. That is a general test of negligence. There is no express or implied exclusion of the tenant from the category of persons who might be affected. The burden of a tenant in establishing a breach of duty under s.4 should not be equated with the need under Landlord and Tenant Act 1987 s.11 to demonstrate notice (actual or constructive) of the actual defect giving rise to injury (*Sykes v Harry* [2001] EWCA Civ 167; [2001] Q.B. 1014).

The word "premises" may include a paved area built by a previous tenant outside a house (*Smith v Bradford MDC* (1982) 4 H.L.R. 86; (1982) P. & C.R. 171, CA).

As to liability at common law, see *Targett v Torfaen BC* [1992] 3 All E.R. 27; (1992) 24 H.L.R. 164, CA.

Works required to remedy a defect in design are not works of "repair", giving that word the meaning that it has to bear in this context. In such circumstances s.4 is not engaged (*Lee v Leeds City Council* [2002] All E.R. 124; [2002] 1 W.L.R. 1488, CA).

***Paragraph numbers marked with a "+" can be found online and on CD.***

## Application to Crown

3A–56 **5.** This Act shall bind the Crown, but as regards the Crown's liability in tort shall not bind the Crown further than the Crown is made liable in tort by the Crown Proceedings Act 1947.

## Supplemental

3A–57 **6.**—(1) In this Act—

"disposal", in relation to premises, includes a letting, and an assignment or surrender of a tenancy, of the premises and the creation by contract of any other right to occupy the premises, and "dispose" shall be construed accordingly;

"personal injury" includes any disease and any impairment of a person's physical or mental condition;

"tenancy" means—

(a) a tenancy created either immediately or derivatively out of the freehold, whether by a lease or underlease, by an agreement for a lease or underlease or by a tenancy agreement, but not including a mortgage term or any interest arising in favour of a mortgagor by his attorning tenant to his mortgagee; or

(b) a tenancy at will or a tenancy on sufferance; or

(c) a tenancy, whether or not constituting a tenancy at common law, created by or in pursuance of any enactment;

and cognate expressions shall be construed accordingly.

(2) Any duty imposed by or enforceable by virtue of any provision of this Act is in addition to any duty a person may owe apart from that provision.

(3) Any term of an agreement which purports to exclude or restrict, or has the effect of excluding or restricting, the operation of any of the provisions of this Act, or any liability arising by virtue of any such provision, shall be void.

(4) Section 4 of the Occupiers' Liability Act 1957 (repairing landlord's duty to visitors to premises) is hereby repealed.

## Local Government Act 1972

3A–57.1 (1972 c.70)

ARRANGEMENT OF SECTIONS

PART XI

LEGAL PROCEEDINGS



*Paragraph numbers marked with a "+" can be found online and on CD.*

## PART XI

## LEGAL PROCEEDINGS

### Power of local authorities to prosecute or defend legal proceedings

**222.**—(1) Where a local authority consider it expedient for the promotion or protection of the interests of the inhabitants of their area— **3A–57.2**

(a) they may prosecute or defend or appear in any legal proceedings and, in the case of civil proceedings, may institute them in their own name, and

(b) they may, in their own name, make representations in the interests of the inhabitants at any public inquiry held by or on behalf of any Minister or public body under any enactment.

(2) In this section "local authority" includes the Common Council and the London Fire and Emergency Planning Authority.

**Amendment**

Subsection (2): the words "and the London Fire and Emergency Planning Authority" in square brackets were inserted by the Greater London Authority Act 1999 s.328 and Sch.29, Pt I, para.20. **3A–57.3**

This section has effect as if a National Park authority were a principal council for the purposes of this Act and as if the relevant Park were the authority's area, by virtue of the Environment Act 1995 s.65, Sch.8, para.3(1).

See further the Local Government Reorganisation (Miscellaneous Provisions) Order 1990 (SI 1990/1765) art.4(3).

**Editorial introduction**

The purpose of s.222 is to enable local authorities to bring and defend proceedings in their own names without the involvement of the Attorney General. It does not give councils substantive powers. It is simply a procedural section which gives them powers formerly vested only in the Attorney General. The courts have considered the correct approach to the exercise of this power in the public interest in two principal contexts: the restraint of breaches of the criminal law and the suppression of public nuisances. Courts should be reluctant to grant injunctions in aid of the criminal law which, if disobeyed, may involve the infringer in sanctions far more onerous than the penalty imposed for the offence. See e.g. *Birmingham CC v Shafi* [2008] EWCA Civ 1186; [2009] 1 W.L.R. 1961; [2009] 3 All E.R. 127; October 30, 2008 where the terms of the injunction sought to restrain criminal behaviour were identical or almost identical to the terms of an ASBO. Sir Anthony Clarke M.R. and Rix L.J. stated that in such circumstances, **3A–57.4**

> "where Parliament has legislated in detail to deal with a particular problem, the courts should in general leave the matter to be dealt with as Parliament intended and, save perhaps in exceptional circumstances, refuse to grant injunctive relief of the kind which can be obtained by an ASBO [44]. ... [the courts] should not now develop a separate but parallel jurisprudence in respect of identical orders." [61]

Where an injunction is sought under s.222 to restrain a public nuisance, the principles which the court should apply should be less restrictive than in the case where it is sought to restrain the commission of a crime. See e.g. *Nottingham CC v Zain (a minor)* [2001] EWCA Civ 1248; [2002] 1 W.L.R. 607 where the Court of Appeal held that a local authority had the power to institute proceedings in its own name for injunctive relief to restrain a public nuisance provided that it considered it expedient for the promotion and protection of the interests of the inhabitants of its area.

***Paragraph numbers marked with a "+" can be found online and on CD.***

## Administration of Justice Act 1973

3A–57.5 (1973 c.15)

ARRANGEMENT OF SECTIONS

PART II

MISCELLANEOUS



## PART II

## MISCELLANEOUS

### Extension of powers of court in action by mortgagee of dwelling-house

3A–58 **8.**—(1) Where by a mortgage of land which consists of or includes a dwelling-house, or by any agreement between the mortgagee under such a mortgage and the mortgagor, the mortgagor is entitled or is to be permitted to pay the principal sum secured by instalments or otherwise to defer payment of it in whole or in part, but provision is also made for earlier payment in the event of any default by the mortgagor or of a demand by the mortgagee or otherwise, then for purposes of section 36 of the Administration of Justice Act 1970 (under which a court has power to delay giving a mortgagee possession of the mortgaged property so as to allow the mortgagor a reasonable time to pay any sums due under the mortgage) a court may treat as due under the mortgage on account of the principal sum secured and of interest on it only such amounts as the mortgagor would have expected to be required to pay if there had been no such provision for earlier payment.

(2) A court shall not exercise by virtue of subsection (1) above the powers conferred by section 36 of the Administration of Justice Act 1970 unless it appears to the court not only that the mortgagor is likely to be able within a reasonable period to pay any amounts regarded (in accordance with subsection (1) above) as due on account of the principal sum secured, together with the interest on those amounts, but also that he is likely to be able by the end of that period to pay any further amounts that he would have expected to be required to pay by then on account of that sum and of interest on it if there had been no such provision as is referred to in subsection (1)above for earlier payment.

(3) Where subsection (1) above would apply to an action in which a mortgagee only claimed possession of the mortgaged property, and the mortgagee brings an action for foreclosure (with or without also claiming possession of the property), then section 36 of the Administration of Justice Act 1970 together with subsections (1) and (2) above shall apply as they would apply if it were an action in which the mortgagee only claimed possession of the mortgaged property, except that—

(a) section 36(2)(b) shall apply only in relation to any claim for possession; and

(b) section 36(5) shall not apply.

(4) For purposes of this section the expressions "dwelling-house", "mortgage", "mortgagee" and "mortgagor" shall be construed in the same way as for the purposes of Part IV of the Administration of Justice Act 1970.

(5) [...]

(6) In the application of this section to Northern Ireland, subsection (3) shall be omitted.

*Note*—Repealed by the Statute Law (Repeals) Act 2004 s.1(1), Sch.1, Pt 1. **3A-59**

**"Extension of powers of court ..."**

See the Administration of Justice Act 1970 s.36, above and the commentary thereto. **3A-60**

The purpose of s.8 is to allow courts to exercise their powers to adjourn, stay, suspend or postpone the date for the giving up of possession in mortgage possession proceedings if it is likely that the arrears of instalments and interest can be repaid during a reasonable period, *cf. Halifax Building Society v Clark* [1973] Ch. 307; [1973] 2 All E.R. 33, where, prior to the passing of the 1973 Act, it was held that s.36 only applied where it was likely that all sums due (including the whole of the capital) could be paid during a reasonable period. Section 8 extends the possibility of relief under s.36 to mortgagors with endowment mortgages (*Bank of Scotland v Grimes* [1985] 2 All E.R. 254 and *Royal Bank of Scotland v Miller* [2001] EWCA Civ 344; [2002] Q.B. 255; [2001] 3 W.L.R. 523; see too *Habib Bank v Tailor* [1982] 1 W.L.R. 1218; [1982] 3 All E.R. 561).

## Welsh Development Agency Act 1975

(1975 c.70)

**For Sch.4 to the Welsh Development Agency Act 1975 plus any related commentary see paragraphs 3A-61+ to 3A-64+ on White Book on Westlaw UK or the Civil Procedure CD.** **3A-60.1**

## Protection from Eviction Act 1977

(1977 c.43) **3A-65**

Arrangement of Sections

Part I

Unlawful Eviction and Harassment



***Paragraph numbers marked with a "+" can be found online and on CD.***

## PART I

## UNLAWFUL EVICTION AND HARASSMENT

### Restriction on re-entry without due process of law

3A–66 **2.** Where any premises are let as a dwelling on a lease which is subject to a right of re-entry or forfeiture it shall not be lawful to enforce that right otherwise than by proceedings in the court while any person is lawfully residing in the premises or part of them.

**"court"**

3A–67 See s.9.

**"let"**

3A–68 See s.8(2).

The purpose of this section is to prevent peaceable re-entry of premises "let as a dwelling" while there is "any person lawfully residing" in them or any part of them. In such circumstances possession proceedings must be brought in court. The phrase "let as a dwelling" in s.2 means "let wholly or partly as a dwelling". It therefore applies to premises which are let for mixed residential and business purposes (*Pirabakaran v Patel* [2006] EWCA Civ 685; [2006] 1 W.L.R. 3112).

For the restriction on forfeiture or re-entry for arrears of service charges see the Housing Act 1996 s.81, and, generally, Commonhold and Leasehold Reform Act 2002 ss.167–171, below.

### Prohibition of eviction without due process of law

3A–69 **3.**—(1) Where any premises have been let as a dwelling under a tenancy which is neither a statutorily protected tenancy nor an excluded tenancy and—

(a) the tenancy (in this section referred to as the former tenancy) has come to an end, but

(b) the occupier continues to reside in the premises or part of them,

it shall not be lawful for the owner to enforce against the occupier, otherwise than by proceedings in the court, his right to recover possession of the premises.

(2) In this section "the occupier", in relation to any premises, means any person lawfully residing in the premises or part of them at the termination of the former tenancy.

(2A) Subsections (1) and (2) above apply in relation to any restricted contract (within the meaning of the Rent Act 1977) which—

(a) creates a licence; and

(b) is entered into after the commencement of section 69 of the Housing Act 1980;

as they apply in relation to a restricted contract which creates a tenancy.

(2B) Subsections (1) and (2) above apply in relation to any premises occupied as a dwelling under a licence, other than an excluded licence, as they apply in relation to premises let as a dwelling under a tenancy, and in those subsections the expressions "let" and "tenancy" shall be construed accordingly.

*Paragraph numbers marked with a "+" can be found online and on CD.*

(2C) References in the preceding provisions of this section and section 4(2A) below to an excluded tenancy do not apply to—

(a) a tenancy entered into before the date on which the Housing Act 1988 came into force, or

(b) a tenancy entered into on or after that date but pursuant to a contract made before that date,

but, subject to that, "excluded tenancy" and "excluded licence" shall be construed in accordance with section 3A below.

(3) This section shall, with the necessary modifications, apply where the owner's right to recover possession arises on the death of the tenant under a statutory tenancy within the meaning of the Rent Act 1977 or the Rent (Agriculture) Act 1976.

*Note* —Amended by the Housing Act 1980 s.69(1); and the Housing Act 1988 ss.30 and 40. **3A–70**

**"tenancy" and "statutorily protected tenancy"**

See s.8(1). **3A–71**

**"excluded tenancy"**

See s.3A. **3A–72**

**"owner"**

See s.8(3). **3A–73**

**"court"**

See s.9. **3A–74**

**"let"**

See s.8(2). **3A–75**

**Prohibition of eviction without due process of law**

This section prevents eviction without a court order. It applies to occupiers who are not statutorily protected (i.e. those who lack full security of tenure as defined in s.8(1), i.e. under Rent Act 1977, Rent (Agriculture) Act 1976, Landlord and Tenant Act 1954 Pt II, Agricultural Holdings Act 1986, Housing Act 1988 and Agricultural Tenancies Act 1995). Eviction of such tenants without a court order is unlawful. **3A–76**

It does not however apply to excluded tenants (see s.3A below). Excluded occupiers can be evicted without court orders.

Breach of s.3 is an actionable tort.

In *Mohamed v Manek and Kensington and Chelsea RLBC* (1995) 94 L.G.R. 211; (1995) 27 H.L.R. 439, CA, it was held that:

(a) the 1977 Act was not intended to apply to temporary housing provided by local authorities under the Housing Act 1985 s.63 (now Housing Act 1996 s.188; see too *Desnousse v Newham LBC* [2006] EWCA Civ 547; [2006] Q.B. 831—homeless person accommodated in self-contained accommodation owned by a private company, but managed by a housing association); and

(b) temporary accommodation in a hotel or hostel cannot be "premises occupied as a dwelling under a licence" for the purposes of s.3(2B).

## Excluded tenancies and licences

**3A.**—(1) Any reference in this Act to an excluded tenancy or an excluded licence is a reference to a tenancy or licence which is excluded by virtue of any of the following provisions of this section. **3A–77**

(2) A tenancy or licence is excluded if—

(a) under its terms the occupier shares any accommodation with the landlord or licensor; and

***Paragraph numbers marked with a "+" can be found online and on CD.***



HOUSING

(b) immediately before the tenancy or licence was granted and also at the time it comes to an end, the landlord or licensor occupied as his only or principal home premises of which the whole or part of the shared accommodation formed part.

(3) A tenancy or licence is also excluded if—

(a) under its terms the occupier shares any accommodation with a member of the family of the landlord or licensor;

(b) immediately before the tenancy or licence was granted and also at the time it comes to an end, the member of the family of the landlord or licensor occupied as his only or principal home premises of which the whole or part of the shared accommodation formed part; and

(c) immediately before the tenancy or licence was granted and also at the time it comes to an end, the landlord or licensor occupied as his only or principal home premises in the same building as the shared accommodation and that building is not a purpose-built block of flats.

(4) For the purposes of subsections (2) and (3) above, an occupier shares accommodation with another person if he has the use of it in common with that person (whether or not also in common with others) and any reference in those subsections to shared accommodation shall be construed accordingly, and if, in relation to any tenancy or licence, there is at any time more than one person who is the landlord of licensor, any reference in those subsections to the landlord or licensor shall be construed as a reference to any one of those persons.

(5) In subsections (2) to (4) above—

(a) "accommodation" includes neither an area used for storage nor a staircase, passage, corridor or other means of access;

(b) "occupier" means, in relation to a tenancy, the tenant and, in relation to a licence, the licensee; and

(c) "purpose-built block of flats" has the same meaning as in Part III of Schedule 1 to the Housing Act 1988;

and section 113 of the Housing Act 1985 shall apply to determine whether a person is for the purposes of subsection (3) above a member of another's family as it applies for the purposes of Part IV of that Act.

(6) A tenancy or licence is excluded if it was granted as a temporary expedient to a person who entered the premises in question or any other premises as a trespasser (whether or not, before the beginning of that tenancy or licence, another tenancy or licence to occupy the premises or any other premises had been granted to him).

(7) A tenancy or licence is excluded if—

(a) it confers on the tenant or licensee the right to occupy the premises for a holiday only; or

(b) it is granted otherwise than for money or money's worth.

(7A) A tenancy or licence is excluded if it is granted in order to provide accommodation under section 4 or Part VI of the Immigration and Asylum Act 1999.

(7B) Section 32 of the Nationality, Immigration and Asylum Act 2002 (accommodation centre: tenure) provides for a resident's licence to occupy an accommodation centre to be an excluded licence.

(7C) A tenancy or licence is excluded if it is granted in order to provide accommodation under the Displaced Persons (Temporary Protection) Regulations 2005.

(8) A licence is excluded if it confers rights of occupation in a hostel, within the meaning of the Housing Act 1985, which is provided by—

(a) the council of a county, county borough, district or London Borough, the Common Council of the City of London, the Council of the Isles of Scilly, the Inner London Education Authority, the London Fire and Emergency Planning Authority, a joint authority within the meaning of the Local Government Act 1985 or a residuary body within the meaning of that Act;

(b) a development corporation within the meaning of the New Towns Act 1981;

(c) the new towns residuary body;

(d) an urban development corporation established by an order under section 135 of the Local Government, Planning and Land Act 1980;

(e) a housing action trust established under Part III of the Housing Act 1988;

(f) [...]

(g) the Housing Corporation;

(ga) the Secretary of State under section 89 of the Housing Associations Act 1985;

(h) a housing trust (within the meaning of the Housing Associations Act 1985) which is a charity or a registered social landlord (within the meaning of the Housing Act 1985); or

(i) any other person who is, or who belongs to a class of person which is, specified in an order made by the Secretary of State.

(8A) In subsection (8)(c) above "new towns residuary body" means—

(a) in relation to England, the Homes and Communities Agency so far as exercising functions in relation to anything transferred (or to be transferred) to it as mentioned in section 52(1)(a) to (d) of the Housing and Regeneration Act 2008; and

(b) in relation to Wales, means the Welsh Ministers so far as exercising functions in relation to anything transferred (or to be transferred) to them as mentioned in section 36(1)(a)(i) to (iii) of the New Towns Act 1981.

(9) The power to make an order under subsection (8)(i) above shall be exercisable by statutory instrument which shall be subject to

annulment in pursuance of a resolution of either House of Parliament.

3A-78 *Note* —Added by the Housing Act 1988 s.31. Amended by the Local Government (Wales) Act 1994 Sch.8, para.4(1); the Housing Act 1996 (Consequential Provisions) Order 1996 (SI 1996/2325) art.5, Sch.2, para.7; the Government of Wales Act 1998 s.140 and Sch.16, para.2 and Sch.18, Pt IV the Immigration and Asylum Act 1996 Sch.14, para.73; Greater London Authority Act 1999 Sch.29, para.27; by the Nationality, Immigration and Asylum Act 2002 s.32(5); SI 2005/1379; and by the Immigration, Asylum and Nationality Act 2006 s.43(4)(a); by the Immigration, Asylum and Nationality Act 2006 s.43(4)(a); and by the Housing and Regeneration Act 2008 Sch.8 para.24.

**Excluded tenancies**

3A-79 For a case in which the Court of Appeal considered s.3A(2) see *Sumeghova v McMahon* [2002] EWCA Civ 1581; [2003] H.L.R. 26, and for a case where Elias J. considered whether premises were "a hostel" (s.3A(8)), see *Rogerson v Wigan MBC* [2004] EWHC 1677 (QB); [2005] H.L.R. 10 (residents allocated bedrooms with their own locks in flat but shared the facilities with other residents, warden with master key and terms of occupation including a nightly curfew, a prohibition on alcohol and drugs. The premises met the statutory definition of a "hostel" in Housing Act 1985 s.622 in that they provided residential accommodation with facilities for preparation of food "otherwise than in separate or self contained accommodation"). See too *Mohamed v Manek and Kensington and Chelsea RLBC* (1995) 27 H.L.R. 439, CA and *Desnousse v Newham LBC* [2006] EWCA Civ 547; [2006] Q.B. 831.

For an example of a licence granted for money's worth (s.3A(7)), see *Polarpark Enterprises Inc v Allason* [2007] EWHC (Ch) 1088; [2008] L. & T.R. 6.

* * * *

## PART II

## NOTICE TO QUIT

* * * *

### Validity of notices to quit

3A-80 **5.**—(1) Subject to subsection (1B) below no notice by a landlord or a tenant to quit any premises let (whether before or after the commencement of this Act) as a dwelling shall be valid unless—

(a) it is in writing and contains such information as may be prescribed, and

(b) it is given not less than 4 weeks before the date on which it is to take effect.

(1A) Subject to subsection (1B) below, no notice by a licensor or a licensee to determine a periodic licence to occupy premises as a dwelling (whether the licence was granted before or after the passing of this Act) shall be valid unless—

(a) it is in writing and contains such information as may be prescribed, and

(b) it is given not less than 4 weeks before the date on which it is to take effect.

(1B) Nothing in subsection (1) or subsection (1A) above applies to—

*Paragraph numbers marked with a "+" can be found online and on CD.*

(a) premises let on an excluded tenancy which is entered into on or after the date on which the Housing Act 1988 came into force unless it is entered into pursuant to a contract made before that date; or

(b) premises occupied under an excluded licence.

(2) In this section "prescribed" means prescribed by regulations made by the Secretary of State by statutory instrument, and a statutory instrument containing any such regulations shall be subject to annulment in pursuance of a resolution of either House of Parliament.

(3) Regulations under this section may make different provision in relation to different descriptions of lettings and different circumstances.

*Note* —Amended by the Housing Act 1988 s.32. **3A–81**

**Excluded tenancies**

Note that this section does not apply to excluded tenancies (see s.3A above, *Mohamed v Manek and Kensingson and Chelsea RLBC* (1995) 94 L.G.R. 211; (1995) 27 H.L.R. 439, CA and *Desnousse v Newham LBC* [2006] EWCA Civ 547; [2006] Q.B. 831). **3A–82**

**"let ... as a dwelling"**

Premises let as an agricultural holding, even if there is a dwelling upon the holding, do not constitute "premises let as a dwelling" for the purposes of this section (see *National Trust for Places of Historic Interest v Knipe* [1997] 40 E.G. 151; *The Times*, June 21, 1997, CA). **3A–83**

**"not less than 4 weeks"**

The statutory four-week period should be reckoned as a period which includes the first day of the notice but excludes the last day. The requirement for a minimum of four weeks' notice does not mean "28 clear days" (*Schnabel v Allard* [1967] 1 Q.B. 627; [1966] 3 All E.R. 816, CA). Note that the test generally applicable when interpreting a notice to quit is "Is the notice quite clear to a reasonable tenant reading it? Is it plain that he cannot be misled by it?" (*Carradine Properties Ltd v Aslam* [1976] 1 W.L.R. 442; [1976] 1 All E.R. 573, Ch D, where on September 6, 1974 landlords served a notice stating that they intended to terminate the lease on September 27, 1973. Their intention had been to determine it on September 27, 1975, but the reference to 1973 was a clerical error. The notice was held to be valid because the tenant reading the notice must have seen the mistake and realised that it was "obvious" that the landlord meant 1975. The decision in *Carradine Properties Ltd v Aslam* was approved by the House of Lords in *Mannai Investment Co Ltd v Eagle Star Life Assurance Co Ltd* [1997] A.C. 749; [1997] 2 W.L.R. 945; [1997] 3 All E.R. 352, HL. **3A–84**

It has been held that it is possible for a landlord and the tenant to waive the requirements of Protection from Eviction Act 1977 s.5 (*Hackney LBC v Snowden* (2001) 33 H.L.R. 49, CA; *Lewisham LBC v Lasisi-Agiri* [2003] EWHC 2392 (Ch); [2003] 45 E.G.C.S. 175).

**"such information as may be prescribed"**

See the Notices to Quit (Prescribed Information) Regulations 1988 (SI 1988/2201) which apply to notices to quit served by landlords. It is as follows: **3A–85**

(1) If the tenant or licensee does not leave the dwelling, the landlord or licensor must get an order for possession from the court before the tenant or licensee can lawfully be evicted. The landlord or licensor cannot apply for such an order before the notice to quit or notice to determine has run out.

(2) A tenant or licensee who does not know if he has any right to remain in possession after a notice to quit or notice to determine runs out can obtain advice from a solicitor. Help with all or part of the cost of legal advice and assistance

***Paragraph numbers marked with a "+" can be found online and on CD.***



HOUSING

may be available under the Legal Aid Scheme. He should also be able to obtain information from a Citizens' Advice Bureau, a Housing Aid Centre or a Rent Officer.

There is no prescribed information for notices to quit served by tenants.

It is not necessary that the precise form of wording of the current regulations should be set out (see *Beckerman v Durling* (1983) 6 H.L.R. 87, CA; *Swansea CC v Hearn* (1991) 23 H.L.R. 284, CA, and *Tadema Holdings v Ferguson* (2000)32 H.L.R. 866, cases where landlords used forms of notice to quit which complied with earlier regulations which had been superseded and where in substance all the information required by the then current regulations was contained in the notice served).

As to service of notices to quit, see *Wandsworth LBC v Attwell* (1995) 27 H.L.R. 536; [1996] 01 E.G. 100; (1996) 94 L.G.R. 419, CA; and *Enfield LBC v Devonish* (1997) 29 H.L.R. 691, CA.

## PART III

## SUPPLEMENTAL PROVISIONS

* * * *

### Interpretation

3A–86 **8.**—(1) In this Act "statutorily protected tenancy" means—

(a) a protected tenancy within the meaning of the Rent Act 1977 or a tenancy to which Part I of the Landlord and Tenant Act 1954 applies;

(b) a protected occupancy or statutory tenancy as defined in the Rent (Agriculture) Act 1976;

(c) a tenancy to which Part II of the Landlord and Tenant Act 1954 applies;

(d) a tenancy of an agricultural holding within the meaning of the Agricultural Holdings Act 1986 which is a tenancy in relation to which that Act applies.

(e) an assured tenancy or assured agricultural occupancy under Part I of the Housing Act 1988;

(f) a tenancy to which Schedule 10 to the Local Government and Housing Act 1989 applies;

(g) a farm business tenancy within the meaning of the Agricultural Tenancies Act 1995.

(2) For the purposes of Part I of this Act a person who, under the terms of his employment, had exclusive possession of any premises other than as a tenant shall be deemed to have been a tenant and the expressions "let" and "tenancy" shall be construed accordingly.

(3) In Part I of this Act "the owner", in relation to any premises, means the person who, as against the occupier, is entitled to possession thereof.

(4) In this Act "excluded tenancy" and "excluded licence" have the meaning assigned by section 3A of this Act.

(5) If, on or after the date on which the Housing Act 1988 came into force, the terms of an excluded tenancy or excluded licence entered into before that date are varied, then—

(a) if the variation affects the amount of the rent which is payable under the tenancy or licence, the tenancy or licence shall be treated for the purposes of sections 3(2C) and 5(1B) above as a new tenancy or licence entered into at the time of the variation; and

(b) if the variation does not affect the amount of the rent which is so payable, nothing in this Act shall affect the determination of the question whether the variation is such as to give rise to a new tenancy or licence.

(6) Any reference in subsection (5) above to a variation affecting the amount of the rent which is payable under a tenancy or licence does not include a reference to—

(a) a reduction or increase effected under Part III or Part VI of the Rent Act 1977 (rents under regulated tenancies and housing association tenancies), section 78 of that Act (power of rent tribunal in relation to restricted contracts) or sections 11 to 14 of the Rent (Agriculture) Act 1976; or

(b) a variation which is made by the parties and has the effect of making the rent expressed to be payable under the tenancy or licence the same as a rent for the dwelling which is entered in the register under Part IV or section 79 of the Rent Act 1977.

*Note* —Amended by the Agricultural Holdings Act 1986 Sch.14, para.61; the Housing Act 1988 s.33; the Local Government and Housing Act 1989 Sch.11, para.54; and the Agricultural Tenancies Act 1995 Sch., para.29. **3A–87**

## The court for purposes of Part I

**9.**—(1) The court for the purposes of Part I of this Act shall, subject to this section, be— **3A–88**

(a) the county court, in relation to premises with respect to which the county court has for the time being jurisdiction in actions for the recovery of land; and

(b) the High Court, in relation to other premises.

(2) Any powers of a county court in proceedings for the recovery of possession of any premises in the circumstances mentioned in section 3(1) of this Act may be exercised with the leave of the judge by any registrar of the court, except in so far as rules of court otherwise provide.

(3) Nothing in this Act shall affect the jurisdiction of the High Court in proceedings to enforce a lessor's right of re-entry or forfeiture or to enforce a mortgagee's right of possession in a case where the former tenancy was not binding on the mortgagee.

(4) Nothing in this Act shall affect the operation of—

(a) section 59 of the Pluralities Act 1838;

(b) section 19 of the Defence Act 1842;

(c) section 6 of the Lecturers and Parish Clerks Act 1844;

(d) paragraph 3 of Schedule 1 to the Sexual Offences Act 1956; or

***Paragraph numbers marked with a "+" can be found online and on CD.***

(e) section 13 of the Compulsory Purchase Act 1965.

## Rent Act 1977

3A–89 (1977 c.42)

Arrangement of Sections

Part I

Preliminary

*Protected and statutory tenancies*



Part VII

Security of Tenure

*Limitations on recovery of possession of dwelling-houses let on protected tenancies or subject to statutory tenancies*



***Paragraph numbers marked with a "+" can be found online and on CD.***

# PART I

# PRELIMINARY

## *PROTECTED AND STATUTORY TENANCIES*

### Protected tenants and tenancies

**1.** Subject to this Part of this Act, a tenancy under which a dwelling-house (which may be a house or part of a house) is let as a separate dwelling is a protected tenancy for the purposes of this Act. Any reference in this Act to a protected tenant shall be construed accordingly. **3A–90**

#### "let", "protected tenancy", "protected tenant" and "tenancy"

See s.152, below. **3A–91**

#### Protected tenants and tenancies

The Rent Act 1977 provided security of tenure and rent regulation for many tenancies created before January 15, 1989. The Housing Act 1988 s.34 (see below) lists three circumstances in which tenancies created on or after January 15, 1989 may also be **3A–92**

***Paragraph numbers marked with a "+" can be found online and on CD.***

within Rent Act protection. Otherwise private sector tenancies created after the implementation of the Housing Act 1988 are either assured tenancies, assured shorthold tenancies or tenancies with no security of tenure.

There can be no Rent Act protection if the occupant has a licence, as opposed to a tenancy (but see, e.g. *Street v Mountford* [1985] A.C. 809; [1985] 2 W.L.R. 877; [1985] 2 All E.R. 289, HL; *AG Securities v Vaughan* and *Antoniades v Villiers and Bridger* [1990] 1 A.C. 417; [1988] 3 W.L.R. 1205; [1988] 3 All E.R. 1058, HL; *Duke v Wynne* [1989] 3 All E.R. 130, CA; *Hadjiloucas v Crean* [1988] 1 W.L.R. 1006; [1987] 3 All E.R. 1008, CA; *Nicolau v Pitt* (1989) 21 H.L.R. 487; [1989] 21 E.G. 71, CA; *Aslan v Murphy* [1989] 3 All E.R. 130, CA; and *Crancour Ltd v Da Silvaesa* (1986) 18 H.L.R. 265; (1986) 278 E.G. 618, CA) or if any of the exceptions listed in Pt I of the Rent Act apply. Rent Act security of tenure operates by preventing landlords from recovering possession after termination of contractual tenancies unless they can prove a ground for possession and, when relying on certain grounds for possession, prove that it is reasonable to make a possession order (see the Rent Act 1977 s.98 and Sch.15, below).

See too *Gray v Taylor* [1998] 4 All E.R. 17, CA; and *Meynell Family Properties Ltd v Meynell*, June 1998, Legal Action 12, CA.

**"as a separate dwelling"**

3A–93 See *Goodrich v Paisner* [1957] A.C. 65; [1956] 2 All E.R. 176, HL; *Central London YMCA Housing Association Ltd v Goodman* (1992) 24 H.L.R. 109, CA; *Central London YMCA Housing Association Ltd v Saunders* (1991) 23 H.L.R. 212, CA; *Horford Investments v Lambert* [1976] Ch. 39; [1974] 1 All E.R. 131, CA; *Kavanagh v Lyroudias* [1985] 1 All E.R. 560, CA; *Mortgage Corp v Ubah* (1997) 73 P. & C.R. 500; (1997) 29 H.L.R. 48, CA; and *St Catherine's College v Dorling* [1980] 1 W.L.R. 66; [1979] 3 All E.R. 250, CA and *Mansfield DC v Langridge* [2008] EWCA Civ 264; [2008] H.L.R. 34

The word "dwelling" is not a term of art with a specialised legal meaning. It is "the place where [an occupier] lives and to which he returns and which forms the centre of his existence ... No doubt he will sleep there and usually eat there; he will often prepare at least some of his meals there." However there is no legislative requirement that cooking facilities must be available for premises to qualify as a dwelling. In deciding whether an occupant has security of tenure:

> "The first step is to identify the subject-matter of the tenancy agreement. If this is a house or part of a house of which the tenant has exclusive possession with no element of sharing, the only question is whether, at the date when proceedings were brought, it was the tenant's home. If so, it was his dwelling ... The presence or absence of cooking facilities in the part of the premises of which the tenant has exclusive occupation is not relevant."

(See *Uratemp Ventures Ltd v Collins and Carrell* [2001] UKHL 43; [2002] 1 A.C. 301; [2001] 3 W.L.R. 806; [2002] 1 All E.R. 46.)

## Statutory tenants and tenancies

3A–94 **2.**—(1) Subject to this Part of this Act—

(a) after the termination of a protected tenancy of a dwelling-house the person who, immediately before that termination, was the protected tenant of the dwelling-house shall, if and so long as he occupies the dwelling-house as his residence, be the statutory tenant of it; and

(b) Part I of Schedule 1to this Act shall have effect for determining what person (if any) is the statutory tenant of a dwelling-house or, as the case may be, is entitled to an assured tenancy of a dwelling-house by succession at any time after the death of a person who, immediately before his death, was either a protected tenant of the dwelling-house or the statutory tenant of it by virtue of paragraph (a) above.

(2) In this Act a dwelling-house is referred to as subject to a statutory tenancy when there is a statutory tenant of it.

***Paragraph numbers marked with a "+" can be found online and on CD.***

(3) In subsection (1)(a) above and in Part I of Schedule 1, the phrase "if and so long as he occupies the dwelling-house as his residence" shall be construed as it was immediately before the commencement of this Act (that is to say, in accordance with section 3(2) of the Rent Act 1968).

(4) A person who becomes a statutory tenant of a dwelling-house as mentioned in subsection (1)(a) above is, in this Act, referred to as a statutory tenant by virtue of his previous protected tenancy.

(5) A person who becomes a statutory tenant as mentioned in subsection (1)(b) above is, in this Act, referred to as a statutory tenant by succession.

*Note*—Amended by the Housing Act 1988 s.39(1). **3A-95**

**"dwelling-house"**

See ss.1 and 26. **3A-96**

**"let", "protected tenancy", "protected tenant" and "tenancy"**

See s.152 below. **3A-97**

**Statutory tenants and tenancies**

Section 2 provides that after termination of a contractual tenancy a statutory tenancy **3A-98** comes into existence if the tenant is still occupying the premises as a residence.

If two people are joint tenants under a protected tenancy, but one ceases to occupy the premises as a residence, the remaining tenant will become the statutory tenant on termination of the tenancy if s/he is still occupying them as a residence (*Lloyd v Sadler* [1978] Q.B. 774; [1978] 2 W.L.R. 721; [1978] 2 All E.R. 529, CA).

If tenants cease to occupy as a residence, there can be no statutory tenancy, and, if the contractual tenancy has been determined, tenants who cease to reside lose security of tenure (Rent Act 1977 s.2(1)(a)). Tenants who are temporarily absent may nevertheless still be occupying as a residence if they can show a de facto intention to return and some formal outward and visible sign of that intention—an *animus possidendi* and a *corpus possessionis*. A considerable body of case-law on this subject has built up over the years. See, e.g. *Hampstead Way Investments Ltd v Lewis-Weare* [1985] 1 W.L.R. 164; [1985] 1 All E.R. 564, HL; *Bevington v Crawford* (1974) 232 E.G. 191, CA; *Blanway Investments Ltd v Lynch* (1993) 25 H.L.R. 378, CA; *Brickfield Properties Ltd v Hughes* (1988) 20 H.L.R. 108; [1988] 24 E.G. 95, CA; *Brown v Brash* [1948] 2 K.B. 247; [1948] 1 All E.R. 922, CA; *DF Crocker Securities (Portsmouth) Ltd v Johal* (1989) 42 E.G. 103, CA; *Duke v Porter* (1986) 280 E.G. 633; (1987) 19 H.L.R. 1, CA; *Gofor Investments v Roberts* (1975) 29 P. & C.R. 366, CA; *Hall v King* (1987) 19 H.L.R. 440, CA; *Regalian Securities Ltd v Scheuer* (1981–82) 5 H.L.R. 48; (1982) 263 E.G. 973; (1984) 47 P. & C.R. 362, CA; *Richards v Green* (1984) 11 H.L.R. 1; (1983) 268 E.G. 443, CA; *Robert Thackray's Estate Ltd v Kaye* (1989) 21 H.L.R. 160, CA; *Tickner v Hearn* [1961] 1 All E.R. 65, CA; *Wigley v Leigh* [1950] 1 All E.R. 73, CA and *Prince v Robinson* (1999) 31 H.L.R. 89.

## Terms and conditions of statutory tenancies

**3.**—(1) So long as he retains possession, a statutory tenant shall **3A-99** observe and be entitled to the benefit of all the terms and conditions of the original contract of tenancy, so far as they are consistent with the provisions of this Act.

(2) It shall be a condition of a statutory tenancy of a dwelling-house that the statutory tenant shall afford to the landlord access to the dwelling-house and all reasonable facilities for executing therein any repairs which the landlord is entitled to execute.

(3) Subject to section 5 of the Protection from Eviction Act 1977 (under which at least 4 weeks' notice to quit is required), a statutory

tenant of a dwelling-house shall be entitled to give up possession of the dwelling-house if, and only if, he gives such notice as would have been required under the provisions of the original contract of tenancy, or, if no notice would have been so required, on giving not less than 3 months' notice.

(4) Notwithstanding anything in the contract of tenancy, a landlord who obtains an order for possession of a dwelling-house as against a statutory tenant shall not be required to give to the statutory tenant any notice to quit.

(5) Part II of Schedule 1 to this Act shall have effect in relation to the giving up of possession of statutory tenancies and the changing of statutory tenants by agreement.

**"dwelling-house"**

3A–100 See ss.1 and 26.

**"statutory tenant"**

3A–101 See ss.2 and 152.

**"let", "protected tenancy", "protected tenant", and "tenancy"**

3A–102 See ss.1 and 152.

## *EXCEPTIONS*

### Dwelling-houses above certain rateable values

3A–103 **4.**—(1) A tenancy which is entered into before April 1, 1990 or (where the dwelling-house had a rateable value on March 31, 1990) is entered into on or after April 1, 1990 in pursuance of a contract made before that date is not a protected tenancy if the dwelling-house falls within one of the Classes set out in subsection (2) below.

(2) Where alternative rateable values are mentioned in this subsection, the higher applies if the dwelling-house is in Greater London and the lower applies if it is elsewhere.

*Class A*

The appropriate day in relation to the dwelling-house falls or fell on or after April 1, 1973 and the dwelling-house on the appropriate day has or had a rateable value exceeding £1,500 or £750.

*Class B*

The appropriate day in relation to the dwelling-house fell on or after March 22, 1973, but before April 1, 1973, and the dwelling-house—

(a) on the appropriate day had a rateable value exceeding £600 or £800, and

(b) on April 1, 1973 had a rateable value exceeding £1,500 or £750.

*Class C*

The appropriate day in relation to the dwelling-house fell before March 22, 1973 and the dwelling-house—

(a) on the appropriate day had a rateable value exceeding £400 or £200, and

(b) on March 22, 1973 had a rateable value exceeding £600 or £300, and

(c) on April 1, 1973 had a rateable value exceeding £1,500 or £750.

(3) If any question arises in any proceedings whether a dwelling-house falls within a Class in subsection (2) above, by virtue of its rateable value at any time, it shall be deemed not to fall within that Class unless the contrary is shown.

(4) A tenancy is not a protected tenancy if—

(a) it is entered into on or after April 1, 1990 (otherwise than, where the dwelling-house had a rateable value on March 31, 1990, in pursuance of a contract made before April 1, 1990), and

(b) under it the rent payable for the time being is payable at a rate exceeding £25,000 a year.

(5) In subsection (4) above "rent" does not include any sum payable by the tenant as is expressed (in whatever terms) to be payable in respect of rates, council tax, services, repairs, maintenance or insurance, unless it could not have been regarded by the parties as a sum so payable.

(6) If any question arises in any proceedings whether a tenancy is precluded from being a protected tenancy by subsection (4) above, the tenancy shall be deemed to be a protected tenancy unless the contrary is shown.

(7) The Secretary of State may by order replace the amount referred to in subsection (4) above by an amount specified in the order; and such an order shall be made by statutory instrument which shall be subject to annulment in pursuance of a resolution of either House of Parliament.

*Note*—Amended by the References to Rating (Housing) Regulations 1990 (SI 1990/434) reg.2, Sch., paras 15 and 16; and (SI 1993/651), Sch.1, para.3. **3A–104**

**Dwelling-houses above certain rateable values**

The retrospective alteration of the rateable value does not bring a tenancy within protection (*Guest Heath plc v Mirza* (1990) 22 H.L.R. 399, QBD). **3A–105**

## Tenancies at low rents

**5.**—(1) A tenancy which was entered into before April 1, 1990 or (where the dwelling-house under the tenancy had a rateable value on March 31, 1990) is entered into on or after April 1, 1990 in pursuance of a contract made before that date is not a protected tenancy if under the tenancy either no rent is payable or, the rent payable is less than two-thirds of the rateable value which is or was the rateable value of the dwelling-house on the appropriate day. **3A–106**

(2) Where—

(a) the appropriate day in relation to a dwelling-house fell before March 22, 1973, and

(b) the dwelling-house had on the appropriate day a rateable value exceeding, if it is in Greater London, £400 or, if it is elsewhere, £200.



***Paragraph numbers marked with a "+" can be found online and on CD.***

subsection (1) above shall apply in relation to the dwelling-house as if the reference to the appropriate day were a reference to March 22, 1973.

(2A) A tenancy is not a protected tenancy if—

(a) it is entered into on or after April 1, 1990 (otherwise than, where the dwelling-house had a rateable value on March 31, 1990, in pursuance of a contract made before April 1, 1990), and

(b) under the tenancy for the time being either no rent is payable or the rent is payable at a rate of, if the dwelling-house is in Greater London, £1,000 or less a year, and, if the dwelling-house is elsewhere, £250 or less a year.

(2B) Subsection (7) of section 4 above shall apply to any amount referred to in subsection (2A) above as it applies to the amount referred to in subsection (4) of that section.

(3) In this Act a tenancy falling within subsection (1) above is referred to as a "tenancy at a low rent".

(4) In determining whether a long tenancy is a tenancy at a low rent, there shall be disregarded such part (if any) of the sums payable by the tenant as is expressed (in whatever terms) to be payable in respect of rates, council tax, services, repairs, maintenance, or insurance, unless it could not have been regarded by the parties as a part so payable.

(5) In subsection (4) above "long tenancy" means a tenancy granted for a term certain exceeding 21 years, other than a tenancy which is, or may become, terminable before the end of that term by notice given to the tenant.

3A–107 *Note* —Amended by the Housing Act 1980 s.152 and Sch.26; the References to Rating (Housing) Regulations 1990 (SI 1990/434) paras 17 and 18; and the Local Government Finance (Housing) (Consequential Amendments) Order 1993 (SI 1993/651) Sch.1, para.4.

**Tenancies at low rents**

3A–108 The Court of Appeal in *Bostock v Bryant* (1990) 22 H.L.R. 449; [1990] 39 E.G. 64, CA, stated that "if parties to an agreement describe a payment ... as rent, the court will normally accept that it is properly so described", but in that case "the more natural inference to be drawn from the payments by the tenants of the gas and electricity bills was that it was simply a payment of their part of the expenses incurred and a sharing of the expenses of the house" ((1990) 22 H.L.R. at 452). In those circumstances the inference should not be drawn that the payments were rent.

## Certain shared ownership leases

3A–109 **5A.**—(1) A tenancy is not a protected tenancy if it is a qualifying shared ownership lease, that is—

(a) a lease granted in pursuance of the right to be granted a shared ownership lease under Part V of the Housing Act 1985, or

(b) a lease granted by a housing association and which complies with the conditions set out in subsection (2) below.

(2) The conditions referred to in subsection (1)(b) above are that the lease—

*Paragraph numbers marked with a "+" can be found online and on CD.*

(a) was granted for a term of 99 years or more and is not (and cannot become) terminable except in pursuance of a provision for re-entry or forfeiture;

(b) was granted at a premium, calculated by reference to the value of the dwelling-house or the cost of providing it, of not less than 25 per cent, or such other percentage as may be prescribed, of the figure by reference to which it was calculated;

(c) provides for the tenant to acquire additional shares in the dwelling-house on terms specified in the lease and complying with such requirements as may be prescribed;

(d) does not restrict the tenant's powers to assign, mortgage or charge his interest in the dwelling-house;

(e) if it enables the landlord to require payment for outstanding shares in the dwelling-house, does so only in such circumstances as may be prescribed;

(f) provides, in the case of a house, for the tenant to acquire the landlord's interest on terms specified in the lease and complying with such requirements as may be prescribed; and

(g) states that the landlord's opinion that by virtue of this section the lease is excluded from the operation of this Act.

(3) The Secretary of State may by regulations prescribe anything requiring to be prescribed for the purposes of subsection (2) above.

(4) The regulations may—

(a) make different provision for different cases or descriptions of case, including different provision for different areas, and

(b) contain such incidental, supplementary or transitional provisions as the Secretary of State considers appropriate,

and shall be made by statutory instrument which shall be subject to annulment in pursuance of a resolution of either House of Parliament.

(5) In any proceedings the court may, if of opinion that it is just and equitable to do so, treat a lease as a qualifying shared ownership lease notwithstanding that the condition specified in subsection (2)(g) above is not satisfied.

(6) In this section—

"house" has the same meaning as in Part I of the Leasehold Reform Act 1967;

"housing association" has the same meaning as in the Housing Associations Act 1985; and

"lease" includes an agreement for a lease, and references to the grant of a lease shall be construed accordingly.

*Note*—Inserted by the Housing and Planning Act 1986 s.18 and Sch.4. 3A-110

## Dwelling-houses let with other land

**6.** Subject to section 26 of this Act, a tenancy is not a protected 3A-111

*Paragraph numbers marked with a "+" can be found online and on CD.*

tenancy if the dwelling-house which is subject to the tenancy is let together with land other than the site of the dwelling-house.

**"dwelling-house"**

3A–112 See ss.1 and 26.

**"let", "protected tenancy", "protected tenant" and "tenancy"**

3A–113 See ss.1 and 152.

## Payments for board or attendance

3A–114 7.—(1) A tenancy is not a protected tenancy if under the tenancy the dwelling-house is bona fide let at a rent which includes payments in respect of board or attendance.

(2) For the purposes of subsection (1) above, a dwelling-house shall not be taken to be bona fide let at a rent which includes payments in respect of attendance unless the amount of rent which is fairly attributable to attendance, having regard to the value of the attendance to the tenant, forms a substantial part of the whole rent.

**"dwelling-house"**

3A–115 See ss.1 and 26.

**"let", "protected tenancy", "protected tenant" and "tenancy"**

3A–116 See ss.1 and 152.

**Payments for board of attendance**

3A–117 A tenancy cannot be a Rent Act protected tenancy if the rent includes "payment in respect of board or attendance ... [and] the value of the attendance to the tenant forms a substantial part of the whole rent".

In *Otter v Norman* [1989] A.C. 129; [1988] 3 W.L.R. 321; [1988] 2 All E.R. 897, HL, Lord Bridge approved *dicta* in *Wilkes v Goodwin* [1923] 2 K.B. 86 that any amount of board suffices, provided it is not *de minimis*, but stressed the need for the tenant's rent to include "not only the cost of the food and drink provided but also all the housekeeping chores which must be undertaken in shopping for provisions, preparation and service of meals on the premises and cleaning and washing up after meals" ([1988] 2 All E.R. at 901). It is clear that the provision of a box of uncooked and unprepared groceries once a week is not sufficient to constitute board, although this might amount to an "attendance". Lord Bridge also pointed out that the "courts have consistently set their face against artificial and contrived devices whereby landlords have sought to deny to tenants the protection intended to be conferred by the Rent Acts" (at 901). "Attendance" means "services personal to the tenant" and the question of "proportionality" is a question of fact for the trial judge (*Nelson Developments Ltd v Taboada* [1992] 34 E.G. 72; (1992) 24 H.L.R. 462, CA).

## Lettings to students

3A–118 8.—(1) A tenancy is not a protected tenancy if it is granted to a person who is pursuing, or intends to pursue, a course of study provided by a specified educational institution and is so granted either by that institution or by another specified institution or body of persons.

(2) In subsection (1) above "specified" means specified, or of a class specified, for the purposes of this section by regulations made by the Secretary of State by statutory instrument.

(3) A statutory instrument containing any such regulations shall be subject to annulment in pursuance of a resolution of either House of Parliament.

***Paragraph numbers marked with a "+" can be found online and on CD.***

**"protected tenancy", and "tenancy"**

See ss.1 and 152. 3A–119

**"specified educational institution"**

See the Assured and Protected Tenancies (Lettings to Students) Regulations 1998 (SI 1998/1967) which define SEIs—basically any institution which provides higher or further education which is publicly funded and various other named institutions. 3A–120

## Holiday lettings

**9.** A tenancy is not a protected tenancy if the purpose of the tenancy is to confer on the tenant the right to occupy the dwelling-house for a holiday. 3A–121

**"dwelling-house"**

See ss.1 and 26. 3A–122

**"let", "protected tenancy", "protected tenant" and "tenancy"**

See ss.1 and 152. 3A–123

**Holiday lettings**

In *Buchmann v May* [1978] 2 All E.R. 993, CA, the Court of Appeal held that the labels put on a transaction are not conclusive, but that where a tenancy agreement expressly states the purpose for which it is made, that statement is evidence of that purpose unless the tenant can establish that it does not correspond with the true purpose, either because the express label is a sham or because it is a false label. Although a court will be "astute to detect a sham where it appears that a provision has been inserted for the purpose of depriving the tenant of statutory protection under the Rent Acts" ([1978] 2 All E.R. 993 at 999), the burden of proof lies on the tenant. In that case there was no evidence which displaced the express purpose and accordingly there was no Rent Act protection. The court accepted the dictionary definition of a holiday as "a period of cessation of work, or period of recreation". 3A–124

See too *R. v Rent Officer for Camden LBC Ex p. Plant* (1980) 257 E.G. 713; (1983) 7 H.L.R. 15, QBD, where there was "clear evidence that all the parties knew that [the applicants] were going to occupy it for the purpose of their work as students" and that that was "conclusive of the matter", and *McHale v Daneham* (1979) 249 E.G. 969, where H.H.J. Edwards, sitting at Bloomsbury and Marylebone County Court, held that there was "no reason why a working holiday should not fall within the provisions of s.9 of the Rent Act".

## Agricultural holdings

**10.**—(1) A tenancy is not a protected tenancy if— 3A–125

(a) the dwelling-house is comprised in an agricultural holding and is occupied by the person responsible for the control (whether as tenant or as servant or agent of the tenant) of the farming of the holding, or

(b) the dwelling-house is comprised in the holding held under a farm business tenancy and is occupied by the person responsible for the control (whether as tenant or as servant or agent of the tenant) of the management of the holding.

(2) In subsection (1) above—

"agricultural holding" means any agricultural holding within the meaning of the Agricultural Holdings Act 1986 held under a tenancy in relation to which that Act applies, and

"farm business tenancy" and "holding" in relation to such a

*Paragraph numbers marked with a "+" can be found online and on CD.*



HOUSING

tenancy, have the same meaning as in the Agricultural Tenancies Act 1995.

3A–126 *Note*—Substituted by the Agricultural Tenancies Act 1995 Sch., para.27.

## Licensed premises

3A–127 **11.** A tenancy of a dwelling-house which consists of or comprises premises which, by virtue of a premises licence under the Licensing Act 2003 may be used for the supply of alcohol (within the meaning of section 14 of that Act) for consumption on the premises shall not be a protected tenancy, nor shall such a dwelling-house be the subject of a statutory tenancy.

3A–128 *Note*—Amended by the Licensing Act 2003 s.198(1), Sch.6, para.67.

## Resident landlords

3A–129 **12.**—(1) Subject to subsection (2) below, a tenancy of a dwelling-house granted on or after August 14, 1974 shall not be a protected tenancy at any time if—

(a) the dwelling-house forms part only of a building and, except in a case where the dwelling-house also forms part of a flat, the building is not a purpose-built block of flats; and

(b) the tenancy was granted by a person who, at the time when he granted it, occupied as his residence another dwelling-house which—

(i) in the case mentioned in paragraph (a) above, also forms part of the flat; or

(ii) in any other case, also forms part of the building; and

(c) subject to paragraph 1 of Schedule 2 to this Act, at all times since the tenancy was granted the interest of the landlord under the tenancy has belonged to a person who, at the time he owned that interest, occupied as his residence another dwelling-house which—

(i) in the case mentioned in paragraph (a) above, also formed part of the flat; or

(ii) in any other case, also formed part of the building.

(2) This section does not apply to a tenancy of a dwelling-house which forms part of a building if the tenancy is granted to a person who, immediately before it was granted, was a protected or statutory tenant of that dwelling-house or of any other dwelling-house in that building.

(3) [...]

(4) Schedule 2 to this Act shall have effect for the purpose of supplementing this section.

3A–130 *Note*—Amended by the Housing Act 1980 ss.65(1) and 69(4).

**"dwelling-house"**

3A–131 See ss.1 and 26.

***Paragraph numbers marked with a "+" can be found online and on CD.***

**"statutory tenant"**

See ss.2 and 152. 3A–132

**"let", "protected tenancy", "protected tenant" and "tenancy"**

See ss.1 and 152. 3A–133

**"purpose-built block of flats"**

See Sch.2, para.4. 3A–134

**Resident landlords**

In *Cooper v Tait* (1984) 15 H.L.R. 98; (1984) 271 E.G. 105, CA, the Court of Appeal held that the residence requirements may be fulfilled by just one out of several joint landlords. 3A–135

When courts are considering whether a landlord is a resident landlord within the meaning of s.12 they should use the same test as when deciding whether a statutory tenant continues to occupy premises as a residence for the purposes of the Rent Act 1977 s.2 (see above). Landlords who are temporarily absent must leave in the premises some personal and visible sign of their intention to return (*Jackson v Pekic* [1989] 47 E.G. 141, CA).

Questions as to whether or not premises are part of the same building are essentially a question of fact for the county court judge. In *Griffiths v English* (1981) 2 H.L.R. 134; (1982) 261 E.G. 257, CA; *Barnes v Gorsuch* (1982) 43 P. & C.R. 294; (1982) 263 E.G. 253, CA; *Bardrick v Haycock* (1976) 1 P. & C.R. 420; (1981) 2 H.L.R. 118, CA; *Lewis-Graham v Conacher* [1992] 02 E.G. 171, CA, and *Wolff v Waddington* [1989] 47 E.G. 148, CA, the Court of Appeal declined to interfere with such findings.

## Landlord's interest belonging to Crown

**13.**—(1) Except as provided by subsection (2) below— 3A–136

(a) a tenancy shall not be a protected tenancy at any time when the interest of the landlord under the tenancy belongs to Her Majesty in right of the Crown or to a government department or is held in trust for Her Majesty for the purposes of a government department; and

(b) a person shall not at any time be a statutory tenant of a dwelling-house if the interest of his immediate landlord would at that time belong or be held as mentioned in paragraph (a) above.

(2) An interest belonging to Her Majesty in right of the Crown shall not prevent a tenancy from being a protected tenancy or a person from being a statutory tenant if the interest is under the management of the Crown Estate Commissioners.

*Note*—Substituted by the Housing Act 1980 s.73. See also the National Health Service and Community Care Act 1990 Sch.8, para.19. 3A–137

**"dwelling-house"**

See ss.1 and 26. 3A–138

**"statutory tenant"**

See ss.2 and 152. 3A–139

**"protected tenancy" and "tenancy"**

See ss.1 and 152. 3A–140

**"landlord"**

See s.152(1). 3A–141

*Paragraph numbers marked with a "+" can be found online and on CD.*

## Landlord's interest belonging to local authority, etc.

3A–142 **14.**—(1) A tenancy shall not be a protected tenancy at any time when the interest of the landlord under that tenancy belongs to—

(a) the council of a county or county borough;

(b) the council of a district or, in the application of this Act to the Isles of Scilly, the Council of the Isles of Scilly;

(bb) the Broads Authority;

(bc) a National Park Authority;

(c) the council of a London borough or the Common Council of the City of London;

(ca) [...]

(caa) a police authority established under section 3 of the Police Act 1996;

(caaa) [...];

(cba) an authority established for an area in England by an order under section 207 of the Local Government and Public Involvement in Health Act 2007 (joint waste authorities);

(cb) a joint authority established by Part IV of the Local Government Act 1985;

(d) the English new towns residuary body;

(e) a development corporation established by an order made, or having effect as if made, under the New Towns Act 1981; or

(f) [...]

(g) an urban development corporation within the meaning of Part XVI of the Local Government, Planning and Land Act 1980;

(h) a housing action trust established under Part III of the Housing Act 1988;

(i) the Residuary Body of Wales (Corff Gweddilliol Cymru);

nor shall a person at any time be a statutory tenant of a dwelling-house if the interest of his immediate landlord would belong at that time to any of those bodies.

(2) In subsection (1)(d) "English new towns residuary body" means the Homes and Communities Agency so far as exercising functions in relation to anything transferred (or to be transferred) to it as mentioned in section 52(1)(a) to (d) of the Housing and Regeneration Act 2008.

3A–143 *Note*—Amended by Local Government (Wales) Act 1994 Schs 8 and 13; the Police and Magistrates' Courts Act 1994 Sch.4; the Environment Act 1995 Sch.10; SI 1985/1884; the Local Government, Planning and Land Act 1980 s.155; the New Towns Act 1981 Sch.12; the Local Government Act 1985 Schs 14 and 17; the Norfolk and Suffolk Broads Act 1988 ss.21, 23, 27, Sch.6; the Housing Act 1988 s.62; the Education Reform Act 1988 s.237, Sch.13; the Police Act 1997 Sch.9, para.39; the Government of Wales Act 1998 Sch.18, Pt IV; the Criminal Justice and Police Act 2001 Sch.7, Pt 5; the Local Government and Public Involvement in Health Act 2007, s.209, Sch.13, para.35; and the Housing and Regeneration Act 2008 Sch.8 para.23.

### "dwelling-house"

3A–144 See ss.1 and 26.

***Paragraph numbers marked with a "+" can be found online and on CD.***

**"statutory tenant"**

See ss.2 and 152. 3A–145

**"protected tenancy", "protected tenant" and "tenancy"**

See ss.1 and 152. 3A–146

**"landlord"**

See s.152(1). 3A–147

**Welsh Development Agency**

Note that some tenants of the Welsh Development Agency do not enjoy security of tenure. See para.3A–60.1, The Welsh Development Agency Act 1975 Sch.4 as inserted by Government of Wales Act 1998 Sch.13. 3A–148

## Landlord's interest belonging to housing association, etc.

**15.**—(1) A tenancy shall not be a protected tenancy at any time when the interest of the landlord under that tenancy belongs to a housing association falling within subsection (3) below; nor shall a person at any time be a statutory tenant of a dwelling-house if the interest of his immediate landlord would belong at that time to such a housing asociation. 3A–149

(2) A tenancy shall not be a protected tenancy at any time when the interest of the landlord under that tenancy belongs to—

(a) the Housing Corporation; or

(aa) [...]

(b) a housing trust which is a charity within the meaning of the Charities Act 1993; nor shall a person at any time be a statutory tenant of a dwelling-house if the interest of his immediate landlord would belong at that time to any of those bodies.

(3) A housing association falls within this subsection if—

(a) it is a registered social landlord within the meaning of the Housing Act 1985(see section 5(4) and (5) of that Act); or

(b) it is a co-operative housing association within the meaning of the Housing Associations Act 1985; or

(c) [...]

(d) [...]

(4) [...]

(5) In subsection (2) above "housing trust" means a corporation or body of persons which—

(a) is required by the terms of its constituent instrument to use the whole of its funds, including any surplus which may arise from its operations, for the purpose of providing housing accommodation; or

(b) is required by the terms of its constituent instrument to devote the whole, or substantially the whole, of its funds to charitable purposes and in fact uses the whole, or substantially the whole, of its funds for the purpose of providing housing accommodation.

(6) [...]

*Note* —Amended by the Housing Act 1980 ss.74 and 152 and Sch.26; the Housing (Consequential Provisions) Act 1985 s.4, Sch.2; the Housing Act 1988 s.140, Sch.17, 3A–150 para.99; the Charities Act 1993 s.98(1), Sch.6; and Order 1996 art.5, Sch.2, para.66 and the Government of Wales Act 1998 Sch.18, Pt IV.

**"dwelling-house"**

3A–151 See ss.1 and 26.

**"statutory tenant"**

3A–152 See ss.2 and 152.

**"protected tenancy", "protected tenant" and "tenancy"**

3A–153 See ss.1 and 152.

**"landlord"**

3A–154 See ss.152(1).

**"registered social landlord"**

3A–155 See the Housing Act 1996 ss.1–7.

**"co-operative housing association"**

3A–156 See the Housing Associations Act 1985 s.1, which defines a housing association as a "society, body of trustees or company (a) which is established for the purpose of, or amongst whose objects or powers are included those of, providing, constructing, improving or managing, or facilitating or encouraging the construction or improvement of, housing accommodation, and (b) which does not trade for profit or whose constitution or rules prohibit the issue of capital with interest or dividend exceeding such rate as may be prescribed by the treasury, whether with or without differentiation between share and loan capital" and a co-operative housing association as "a fully mutual housing association which is a friendly society registered under the Industrial and Provident Societies Act 1965 ..."

## Landlord's interest belonging to housing co-operative

3A–157 **16.** A tenancy shall not be a protected tenancy at any time when the interest of the landlord under that tenancy belongs to a housing co-operative, within the meaning of section 27B of the Housing Act 1985 (agreements with housing co-operatives under certain superseded provisions) and the dwelling-house is comprised in a housing co-operative agreement within the meaning of that section.

3A–158 *Note*—Amended by the Housing and Planning Act 1986 s.24(1), (2), Sch.5, para.15.

**"dwelling-house"**

3A–159 See ss.1 and 26.

**"protected tenancy" and "tenancy"**

3A–160 See ss.1 and 152.

**"housing co-operative"**

3A–161 See the Housing Act 1985 s.5.

### *CONTROLLED AND REGULATED TENANCIES*

* * * *

## Regulated tenancies

3A–162 **18.**—(1) Subject to sections 24(3) and 143 of this Act, a "regulated tenancy" is, for the purposes of this Act, a protected or statutory tenancy.

***Paragraph numbers marked with a "+" can be found online and on CD.***

(2) Where a regulated tenancy is followed by a statutory tenancy of the same dwelling-house, the two shall be treated for the purposes of this Act as together constituting one regulated tenancy.

(3) [...]

(4) [...]

*Note*—Amended by the Housing Act 1980 Schs 25, and 26. **3A-163**

**"dwelling-house"**

See ss.1 and 26. **3A-164**

**"statutory tenant"**

See ss.2 and 152. **3A-165**

**"protected tenancy" and "tenancy"**

See ss.1 and 152. **3A-166**

## Modification of Act for controlled tenancies converted into regulated tenancies

**18A.** Schedule 17 to this Act applies for the purpose of modifying the provisions of this Act in relation to a tenancy which, by virtue of any of the following enactments, was converted from a controlled tenancy into a regulated tenancy, that is to say— **3A-167**

(a) section 18(3) of this Act;

(b) paragraph 5 of Schedule 2 to the Rent Act 1968 (which was superseded by section 18(3));

(c) Part VIII of this Act;

(d) Part III of the Housing Finance Act 1972 (which was superseded by Part VIII);

(e) Part IV of the Act of 1972 (conversion by reference to rateable values);

(f) section 64 of the Housing Act 1980 (conversion of remaining controlled tenancies into regulated tenancies).

*Note*—Added by the Housing Act 1980 Sch.25. **3A-168**

* * * *

### *SHARED ACCOMMODATION*

## Tenant sharing accommodation with persons other than landlord

**22.**—(1) Where a tenant has the exclusive occupation of any accommodation ("the separate accommodation") and— **3A-169**

(a) the terms as between the tenant and his landlord on which he holds the separate accommodation include the use of other accommodation ("the shared accommodation") in common with another person or other persons, not being or including the landlord, and

(b) by reason only of the circumstances mentioned in paragraph (a) above, the separate accommodation would

***Paragraph numbers marked with a "+" can be found online and on CD.***

not, apart from this section, be a dwelling-house let on or subject to a protected or statutory tenancy,

the separate accommodation shall be deemed to be a dwelling-house let on a protected tenancy or, as the case may be, subject to a statutory tenancy and the following provisions of this section shall have effect.

(2) For the avoidance of doubt it is hereby declared that where, for the purpose of determining the rateable value of the separate accommodation, it is necessary to make an apportionment under this Act, regard is to be had to the circumstances mentioned in subsection (1)(a) above.

(3) While the tenant is in possession of the separate accommodation (whether as a protected or statutory tenant), any term or condition of the contract of tenancy terminating or modifying, or providing for the termination or modification of, his right to use any of the shared accommodation which is living accommodation shall be of no effect.

(4) Where the terms and conditions of the contract of tenancy are such that at any time during the tenancy the persons in common with whom the tenant is entitled to the use of the shared accommodation could be varied, or their number could be increased, nothing in subsection (3) above shall prevent those terms and conditions from having effect so far as they relate to any such variation or increase.

(5) Without prejudice to the enforcement of any order made under subsection (6) below, while the tenant is in possession of the separate accommodation, no order shall be made for possession of any of the shared accommodation, whether on the application of the immediate landlord of the tenant or on the application of any person under whom that landlord derives title, unless a like order has been made, or is made at the same time, in respect of the separate accommodation; and the provisions of section 98(1) of this Act shall apply accordingly.

(6) On the application of the landlord, the county court may make such order either—

(a) terminating the right of the tenant to use the whole or any part of the shared accommodation other than living accommodation, or

(b) modifying his right to use the whole or any part of the shared accommodation, whether by varying the persons or increasing the number of persons entitled to the use of that accommodation, or otherwise,

as the court thinks just.

(7) No order shall be made under subsection (6) above so as to effect any termination or modification of the rights of the tenant which, apart from subsection (3) above, could not be effected by or under the terms of the contract of tenancy.

(8) In this section "living accommodation" means accommodation of such a nature that the fact that it constitutes or is included in the shared accommodation is (or, if the tenancy has ended, was) sufficient, apart from this section, to prevent the tenancy from constituting a protected tenancy of a dwelling-house.

**"dwelling-house"**

See ss.1 and 26. 3A–170

**"statutory tenant"**

See ss.2 and 152. 3A–171

**"landlord", "protected tenancy" and "tenant"**

See ss.1 and 152. 3A–172

*SUBLETTINGS*

## Certain sublettings not to exclude any part of sub-lessor's premises from protection

**23.**—(1) Where the tenant of any premises, consisting of a house or part of a house, has sublet a part but not the whole of the premises, then, as against his landlord or any superior landlord, no part of the premises shall be treated as not being a dwelling-house let on or subject to a protected or statutory tenancy by reason only that— 3A–173

(a) the terms on which any person claiming under the tenant holds any part of the premises include the use of accommodation in common with other persons; or

(b) part of the premises is let to any such person at a rent which includes payments in respect of board or attendance.

(2) Nothing in this section shall affect the rights against, and liabilities to, each other of the tenant and any person claiming under him, or of any two such persons.

**"dwelling-house"**

See ss.1 and 26. 3A–174

**"statutory tenant"**

See ss.2 and 152. 3A–175

**"landlord" and "protected tenancy"**

See ss.1 and 152. 3A–176

*BUSINESS PREMISES*

## Premises with a business use

**24.**—(1) [...] 3A–177

(2) [...]

(3) A tenancy shall not be a regulated tenancy if it is a tenancy to which Part II of the Landlord and Tenant Act 1954 applies (but this provision is without prejudice to the application of any other provision of this Act to a sub-tenancy of any part of the premises comprised in such a tenancy).

*Note*—Amended by the Housing Act 1980 s.152 and Sch.26. 3A–178

**Premises with business use**

Section 24 provides that a tenancy cannot be a regulated tenancy if it is a business tenancy to which the Landlord and Tenant Act 1954 Pt II applies. The Landlord and 3A–179

Tenant Act 1954 s.23(2) provides that "'business' includes trade, profession or employment".

Premises are only occupied "for the purposes of a business" where the business activity on the premises is a significant purpose of the occupation or part of the reason for the occupation. Where, however, the business use is merely incidental to residential occupation, there is Rent Act protection (*Cheryl Investments Ltd v Saldanha* [1979] 1 All E.R. 5; [1978] 1 W.L.R. 1329, CA). This is essentially a question of fact for the trial judge—*Gurton v Parrott* (1991) 23 H.L.R. 418; [1991] 18 E.G. 161, CA; *Pulleng v Curran* (1982) 44 P. & C.R. 58, CA; and *Wright v Mortimer* (1996) 28 H.L.R. 719; [1996] E.G.C.S. 51, CA, where the Court of Appeal held that whether or not business user is a significant element of occupation is a question of fact and degree which is particularly within the trial judge's ability to decide. It is permissible for the judge to take into account the tenant's attachment to the flat and the fact that an informed or reasonable person would conclude that the tenant is not carrying on a business at the premises.

See too *Florent v Horez* (1983) 268 E.G. 807; (1984) 12 H.L.R. 1; (1984) 48 P. & C.R. 166, CA, where the Court of Appeal stated that the phrase "business user" has a broad meaning and approved a statement by Lindley L.J. in *Rolls v Miller* (1884) 27 Ch D 71 at 88, that business "means almost anything which is an occupation, as distinguished from a pleasure—anything which is an occupation or duty which requires attention is a business". These authorities were reviewed in *Tan v Sitkowski* [2007] EWCA Civ 30; [2007] 1 W.L.R. 1628 where it was held that the mere fact that business use of premises had ceased, and that landlords continued to accept rent, could not amount to positive consent to the change of use.

## *MISCELLANEOUS*

### Rateable value and meaning of "appropriate day"

3A–180 **25.**—(1) Except where this Act otherwise provides, the rateable value on any day of a dwelling-house shall be ascertained for the purposes of this Act as follows—

(a) if the dwelling-house is a hereditament for which a rateable value is then shown in the valuation list, it shall be that rateable value;

(b) if the dwelling-house forms part only of such a hereditament or consists of or forms part of more than one such hereditament, its rateable value shall be taken to be such value as is found by a proper apportionment or aggregation of the rateable value or values so shown.

(2) Any question arising under this section as to the proper apportionment or aggregation of any value or values shall be determined by the county court, and the decision of the county court shall be final.

(3) In this Act "the appropriate day"—

(a) in relation to any dwelling-house which, on March 23, 1965, was or formed part of a hereditament for which a rateable value was shown in the valuation list then in force, or consisted or formed part of more than one such hereditament, means that date, and

(b) in relation to any other dwelling-house, means the date on which such a value is or was first shown in the valuation list.

(4) Where, after the date which is the appropriate day in relation to any dwelling-house, the valuation list is altered so as to vary the

rateable value of the hereditament of which the dwelling-house consists or forms part and the alteration has effect from a date not later than the appropriate day, the rateable value of the dwelling-house on the appropriate day shall be ascertained as if the value shown in the valuation list on the appropriate day had been the value shown in the list as altered.

(5) This section applies in relation to any other land as it applies in relation to a dwelling-house.

### Land and premises let with dwelling-house

**26.**—(1) For the purposes of this Act, any land or premises let together with a dwelling-house shall, unless it consists of agricultural land exceeding two acres in extent, be treated as part of the dwelling-house. **3A–181**

(2) For the purposes of subsection (1) above "agricultural land" has the meaning set out in section 26(3)(a) of the General Rate Act 1967(exclusion of agricultural land and premises from liability for rating).

* * * *

## PART VII

## SECURITY OF TENURE

### *LIMITATIONS ON RECOVERY OF POSSESSION OF DWELLING-HOUSES LET ON PROTECTED TENANCIES OR SUBJECT TO STATUTORY TENANCIES*

### Grounds for possession of certain dwelling-houses

**98.**—(1) Subject to this Part of this Act, a court shall not make an order for possession of a dwelling-house which is for the time being let on a protected tenancy or subject to a statutory tenancy unless the court considers it reasonable to make such an order and either— **3A–182**

(a) the court is satisfied that suitable alternative accommodation is available for the tenant or will be available for him when the order in question takes effect, or

(b) the circumstances are as specified in any of the Cases in Part I of Schedule 15 to this Act.

(2) If, apart from subsection (1) above, the landlord would be entitled to recover possession of a dwelling-house which is for the time being let on or subject to a regulated tenancy, the court shall make an order for possession if the circumstances of the case are as specified in any of the Cases in Part II of Schedule 15.

(3) Part III of Schedule 15 shall have effect in relation to Case 9 in that Schedule and for determining the relevant date for the purposes of the Cases in Part II of that Schedule.

(4) Part IV of Schedule 15 shall have effect for determining whether, for the purposes of subsection (1)(a) above, suitable alternative accommodation is or will be available for a tenant.

*Paragraph numbers marked with a "+" can be found online and on CD.*

(5) Part V of Schedule 15 shall have effect for the purpose of setting out conditions which are relevant to Cases 11 and 12 of that Schedule.

3A-183 *Note*—Amended by the Housing Act 1980 s.66.

**Grounds for possession of certain dwelling-houses**

3A-184 Section 98 contains the kernal of Rent Act security of tenure. In order to obtain possession a landlord must satisfy the court that a ground for possession (i.e. the availability of suitable alternative accommodation or one of the grounds in Sch.15) is made out, and, if the ground is a discretionary one, that it is reasonable to make an order for possession.

> "[I] f there is before the court a claim that the defendant is entitled to the benefit of the Rent Acts, the court may not make an order for possession unless it is satisfied, either by evidence or by admission by or on behalf of the defendant, that he is not entitled to that protection". (per Glidewell J. in *R. v Bloomsbury and Marylebone County Court, Ex p. Blackburne* (1984) 14 H.L.R. 56 at 67, QBD, approved by the Court of Appeal (1985) 275 E.G. 1273 at 1274). See also *Hounslow LBC v McBride* (1999) 31 H.L.R. 143, CA and *R. v Birmingham CC, Ex p. Foley*, March 2001, Legal Action 29, Queen's Bench Division.

Although not stated in s.98, landlords also have to ensure that any contractual tenancy has been determined.

**"dwelling-house"**

3A-185 See ss.1 and 26.

**"statuory tenant"**

3A-186 See ss.2 and 152.

**"landlord" and "protected tenancy"**

3A-187 See ss.1 and 152.

**"regulated tenancy"**

3A-188 See ss.18 and 152.

**Suitable alternative accommodation**

3A-189 See too Sch.15, Pt IV, below. Paragraph 5 provides that alternative accommodation must be reasonably suitable to the needs of the tenant and his family. In that context "needs" means "the needs for housing" or "need for accommodation for the purpose of habitation"—see *Hill v Rochard* [1983] 1 W.L.R. 478, CA and *Montross Associated Investments v Stone* March 2000, Legal Action 29, CA.

The court can properly take into account environmental matters (e.g. where the alternative accommodation offered had no garden, was on a busy thoroughfare, was next door to a fried-fish shop, near to a hospital, cinema and public house and with an open space to the rear which the local authority proposed to use as a transport depot), both when considering suitability to the tenant's needs and reasonableness (*Redspring v Francis* [1973] 1 W.L.R. 134; [1973] 1 All E.R. 640, CA), but only in so far as they relate to the property itself (not, e.g. matters such as the location of the tenant's friends, his mosque or cultural interests (*Siddiqui v Rashid* [1980] 1 W.L.R. 1018; [1980] 3 All E.R. 184, CA).

Part of a tenant's existing accommodation can amount to suitable alternative accommodation (see *Mykolyshyn v Noah* [1970] 1 W.L.R. 1271; [1971] 1 All E.R. 48, CA; *Thompson v Rolls* [1926] 2 K.B. 426; *Parmee v Mitchell* [1950] 1 All E.R. 872, CA; *McIntyre v Hardcastle* [1948] 1 All E.R. 696, CA; and *Scrace v Windust* [1955] 2 All E.R. 104, CA).

**Reasonable**

3A-190 See also commentary to the Housing Act 1985 s.84.

The question of reasonableness is an "overriding requirement" (*Smith v McGoldrick* (1976) 242 E.G. 1047) and gives the court a very wide discretion (*Bell London and*

*Provincial Properties Ltd v Reuben* [1946] 2 All E.R. 547; and *Plaschkes v Jones* (1983) 9 H.L.R. 110). In *Cumming v Danson* [1942] 2 All E.R. 653 at 655, Lord Greene M.R. said:

> "in considering reasonableness ... it is, in my opinion, perfectly clear that the duty of the judge is to take into account all relevant circumstances as they exist at the date of the hearing. That he must do in what I venture to call a broad common-sense way as a man of the world, and come to his conclusion giving such weight as he thinks right to the various factors in the situation. Some factors may have little or no weight, others may be decisive, but it is quite wrong for him to exclude from his consideration matters which he ought to take into account."

In *Shrimpton v Rabbits*, 131 L.T. 478, KBD, Swift J. said that in considering the question of reasonableness the court "must consider all the circumstances affecting the holding of the premises by the person who holds them and as they relate to the landlord who wants to hold them". Acton J. said, "Because a [landlord's] wish is reasonable, it does not follow that it is reasonable in a court to gratify it."

In *Lee v Whitehouse* [2009] EWCA Civ 375, May 14, 2009, Rimer L.J. said that:

> "the question is not whether it is reasonable for the landlord to claim possession, but whether it is reasonable to make the order" (para.29) ... It required [the trial judge] to look at the question from all the angles, in particular by considering the effect on the parties not just if an order was made, but also if it was not (para.30)".

In relation to rent arrears cases Denning L.J. (as he then was) has stated:

> "It would be very unusual indeed for the tenant to be ordered out on the ground of non-payment of rent when the full amount was already paid into court. If the tenant is in arrear, in these cases under the Rent Restriction Acts the everyday practice is to make an order for possession, but to suspend it so long as the current weekly rent and a payment on account of the rent in arrear are paid." (*Hayman v Rowlands* [1957] 1 W.L.R. 317; [1957] 1 All E.R. 321, CA; but *cf. Dellenty v Pellow* [1951] 2 All E.R. 716, CA; and *Lee-Steere v Jennings* (1987) 20 H.L.R. 1, CA).

The first requirement for a judge who has found a ground for possession to be proved is to ask whether it is reasonable to make a possession order at all and then to ask whether the order should be stayed or suspended under s.100(2). The correct approach is to determine the extent of the rent arrears and how quickly those are likely to be paid. It is wrong to take into account matters which have not been pleaded.

> "In considering whether it is reasonable to make an order ... the judge should consider all the relevant circumstances: but that is not a consideration at large. It is, or should be, a consideration in accordance with the pleadings. In my judgment, the matters proposed to be relied upon by the landlord in support of the contention that it would be reasonable to make an order for possession ... must be pleaded by the landlord." (per Sir Richard Scott V.-C. in *Raeuchle v Laimond Properties Ltd (Suspension of Possession Order)* (2001) 33 H.L.R. 10, CA); *cf. Taj v Ali* 97/17 L.S. Gaz., April 28, 2000, p.36, [2000] 43 E.G. 183; (2001) 33 H.L.R. 37, CA where it was said that a suspended possession order should not extend "into the mists of time" or where there were "no sensible terms on which the order could be suspended" (suspended possession order providing for payment of arrears over 55 years replaced with 28 day possession order).

Courts must consider whether it is reasonable to make an order for possession at the date of the hearing and not at an earlier stage (*Smith v McGoldrick* (1977) 242 E.G. 1047, CA). A judge's failure to consider reasonableness makes an order for possession a nullity (*Minchbourn Estates Ltd v Fernandez (No.2)* (1987) 19 H.L.R. 29; (1986) 280 E.G. 770, CA; and *Hounslow LBC v McBride* (1999) 31 H.L.R. 143, CA and *R. v Birmingham CC Ex p. Foley*, March 2001, Legal Action 29, QBD), even where an order is made "by consent"and money is paid to the tenant in return for the giving of vacant possession (*R. v Bloomsbury and Marylebone County Court Ex p. Blackburne* (1985) 275 E.G. 1273, CA). However, the Court of Appeal will "assume that the county court judge has taken all the relevant matters into account unless the contrary is clearly shown" and will only overrule a county court judge on the question of reasonableness "on very strong grounds" (*Dame Margaret Hungerford Charity Trustees v Beazeley* [1993] 29 E.G. 100, CA). See too *Battlespring Ltd v Gates* (1983) 268 E.G. 355, CA; *Dawncar Investments Ltd v Plews* [1993] 13 E.G. 110; (1993) 25 H.L.R. 639, CA; *Empson v Forde*

***Paragraph numbers marked with a "+" can be found online and on CD.***

[1990] 18 E.G. 99, CA and *Holloway v Povey* (1984) 15 H.L.R. 104; (1984) 271 E.G. 195, CA.

### Appeals on questions of reasonableness

3A–191 Although County Courts Act 1984 s.77(6) excludes appeals against judges' findings of fact, it does not exclude, in a proper case, the possibility of an appeal against a finding of reasonableness (*Castle Vale Housing Action Trust v Gallagher* [2001] EWCA Civ 944; (2001) 33 H.L.R. 810).

### ECHR Art 8 and reasonableness

3A–192 The Court of Appeal has doubted whether art.8 makes any difference to the way in which courts have approached questions of the reasonableness of making possessions order. Article 8 does, however, reinforce the importance of only making an order depriving someone of his or her home in circumstances where a clear case is made out (*Castle Vale Housing Action Trust v Gallagher* [2001] EWCA Civ 944; (2001) 33 H.L.R. 810, CA. See too *Newham LBC v Neal* [2003] EWCA Civ 541 February 25, 2003.). There is a need to find a fair balance and to protect the rights of the neighbours and other members of the public (*Lambeth LBC v Howard* [2001] EWCA Civ 468; (2001) 33 H.L.R. 636).

* * * *

## Extended discretion of court in claims for possession of certain dwelling-houses

3A–193 **100.**—(1) Subject to subsection (5) below, a court may adjourn, for such period or periods as it thinks fit, proceedings for possession of a dwelling-house which is let on a protected tenancy or subject to a statutory tenancy.

(2) On the making of an order for possession of such a dwelling-house, or at any time before the execution of such an order (whether made before or after the commencement of this Act), the court, subject to subsection (5) below, may—

(a) stay or suspend execution of the order, or

(b) postpone the date of possession.

for such period or periods as the court thinks fit.

(3) On any such adjournment as is referred to in subsection (1) above or any such stay, suspension or postponement as is referred to in subsection (2) above, the court shall, unless it considers that to do so would cause exceptional hardship to the tenant or would otherwise be unreasonable, impose conditions with regard to payment by the tenant of arrears of rent (if any) and rent or payments in respect of occupation after termination of the tenancy (mesne profits) and may impose such other conditions as it thinks fit.

(4) If any such conditions as are referred to in subsection (3) above are complied with, the court may, if it thinks fit, discharge or rescind any such order as is referred to in subsection (2) above.

(4A) Subsection (4B) below applies in any case where—

(a) proceedings are brought for possession of a dwelling-house which is let on a protected tenancy or subject to a statutory tenancy;

(b) the tenant's spouse or former spouse, having rights of occupation under the Matrimonial Homes Act 1967, is then in occupation of the dwelling-house; and

*Paragraph numbers marked with a "+" can be found online and on CD.*

(c) the tenancy is terminated as a result of those proceedings.

(4B) In any case to which this subsection applies, the spouse or former spouse shall, so long as he or she remains in occupation, have the same rights in relation to, or in connection with, any such adjournment as is referred to in subsection (1) above or any such stay, suspension or postponement as is referred to in subsection (2) above, as he or she would have if those rights of occupation were not affected by the termination of the tenancy.

(5) This section shall not apply if the circumstances are as specified in any of the Cases in Part II of Schedule 15.

*Note* —Amended by the Housing Act 1980 s.75. **3A–194**

**"dwelling-house"**

See ss.1 and 26. **3A–195**

**"statutory tenant"**

See ss.2 and 152. **3A–196**

**"protected tenancy"**

See ss.1 and 152. **3A–197**

**"tenant"**

See s.152. **3A–198**

**Extended discretion of court in claims for possession of certain dwelling-houses**

See commentary to the Housing Act 1985 s.85 and the Housing Act 1988 s.9. **3A–199**

## Overcrowded dwelling-houses

**101.** At any time when a dwelling-house is overcrowded, within the meaning of Part X of the Housing Act 1985, in such circumstances as to render the occupier guilty of an offence, nothing in this Part of this Act shall prevent the immediate landlord of the occupier from obtaining possession of the dwelling-house. **3A–200**

*Note* —Substituted by the Housing (Consequential Provisions) Act 1985 Sch.2, para.35. **3A–201**

**"overcrowding"**

See the Housing Act 1985 ss.324–328. **3A–202**

**Overcrowded dwelling-houses**

The Court of Appeal has held that where there is statutory overcrowding there is no jurisdiction to make a suspended possession order (*Henry Smith's Charity v Bartosiak-Jentys* (1992) 24 H.L.R. 627, CA). **3A–203**

## Compensation for misrepresentation or concealment in Cases 8 and 9

**102.** Where, in such circumstances as are specified in Case 8 or Case 9 in Schedule 15 to this Act, a landlord obtains an order for possession of a dwelling-house let on a protected tenancy or subject to a statutory tenancy and it is subsequently made to appear to the court that the order was obtained by misrepresentation or concealment of material facts, the court may order the landlord to pay to the former tenant such sum as appears sufficient as compensation for damage or loss sustained by that tenant as a result of the order. **3A–204**

**"dwelling-house"**

3A–205 See ss.1 and 26.

**"statutory tenant"**

3A–206 See ss.2 and 152.

**"protected tenancy"**

3A–207 See ss.1 and 152.

**"landlord" and "tenant"**

3A–208 See s.152.

**Compensation for misrepresentation or concealment in Cases 8 and 9**

3A–209 See, e.g. *Thorne v Smith* [1947] K.B. 307, CA and *Clements v Simmonds* [2002] EWHC 1652 (QB); [2002] 41 E.G. 178. Note that the power of the court to award compensation under s.102 where possession has been obtained as a result of misrepresentation or concealment is limited to Case 8 (former employee) and Case 9 (dwelling reasonably required for occupation by landlord or landlord's family) (*cf.* Housing Act 1988 s.12). There is, however, no reason why a tenant should not bring proceedings based upon the common law tort of deceit (see, e.g. *Mafo v Adams* [1970] 1 Q.B. 548, CA).

* * * *

### MISCELLANEOUS

## Interpretation of Part VII

3A–210 **107.**—(1) In this Part of this Act, except where the context otherwise requires—

"dwelling" means a house or part of a house;

"lessee" means the person to whom is granted, under a restricted contract, the right to occupy the dwelling in question as a residence and any person directly or indirectly deriving title from the grantee; and

"lessor" means the person who, under a restricted contract, grants to another the right to occupy the dwelling in question as a residence and any person directly or indirectly deriving title from the grantor.

(2) References in this Part of this Act to a party to a contract include references to any person directly or indirectly deriving title from such a party.

* * * *

### PART XI

### GENERAL

### SUBLETTINGS

## Effect on sub-tenancy of determination of superior tenancy

3A–211 **137.**—(1) If a court makes an order for possession of a dwelling-house from—

(a) a protected or statutory tenant, or

(b) a protected occupier or statutory tenant as defined in the Rent (Agriculture) Act 1976,

and the order is made by virtue of section 98(1) or 99(2) of this Act or, as the case may be, under Part I of Schedule 4 to that Act, nothing in the order shall affect the right of any sub-tenant to whom the dwelling-house or any part of it has been lawfully sublet before the commencement of the proceedings to retain possession by virtue of this Act, nor shall the order operate to give a right to possession against any such sub-tenant.

(2) Where a statutorily protected tenancy of a dwelling-house is determined, either as a result of an order for possession or for any other reason, any sub-tenant to whom the dwelling-house or any part of it has been lawfully sublet shall, subject to this Act, be deemed to become the tenant of the landlord on the same terms as if the tenant's statutorily protected tenancy had continued.

(3) Where a dwelling-house—

(a) forms part of premises which have been let as a whole on a superior tenancy but do not constitute a dwelling-house let on a statutorily protected tenancy; and

(b) is itself subject to a protected or statutory tenancy,

then, from the coming to an end of the superior tenancy, this Act shall apply in relation to the dwelling-house as if, in lieu of the superior tenancy, there had been separate tenancies of the dwelling-house and of the remainder of the premises, for the like purposes as under the superior tenancy, and at rents equal to the just proportion of the rent under the superior tenancy.

In this subsection "premises" includes, if the sub-tenancy in question is a protected or statutory tenancy to which section 99 of this Act applies, an agricultural holding within the meaning of the Agricultural Holdings Act 1986 held under a tenancy to which that Act applies, and land comprised in a farm business tenancy within the meaning of the Agricultural Tenancies Act 1995.

(4) In subsections (2) and (3) above "statutorily protected tenancy" means—

(a) a protected or statutory tenancy;

(b) a protected occupancy or statutory tenancy as defined in the Rent (Agricultural) Act 1976; or

(c) if the sub-tenancy in question is a protected or statutory tenancy to which section 99 of this Act applies,

(i) a tenancy of an agricultural holding within the meaning of the Agricultural Holdings Act 1986 which is a tenancy in relation to which that Act applies, or

(ii) a farm business tenancy within the meaning of the Agricultural Tenancies Act 1995.

(5) Subject to subsection (6) below, a long tenancy of a dwelling-house which is also a tenancy at a low rent but which, had it not been a tenancy at a low rent, would have been a protected tenancy or an assured tenancy within the meaning of Part I of the Housing Act

1988, shall be treated for the purposes of subsection (2) above as a statutorily protected tenancy.

(6) Notwithstanding anything in subsection (5) above, subsection (2) above shall not have effect where the sub-tenancy in question was created (whether immediately or derivatively) out of a long tenancy falling within subsection (5) above and, at the time of the creation of the sub-tenancy—

(a) a notice to terminate the long tenancy had been given under section 4(1) of the Landlord and Tenant Act 1954 or, as the case may be, served under paragraph 4(1) of Schedule 10 to the Local Government and Housing Act 1989; or

(b) the long tenancy was being continued by section 3(1) of the said Act of 1954 or, as the case may be, paragraph 3 of the said Schedule 10;

unless the sub-tenancy was created with the consent in writing of the person who at the time when it was created was the landlord, within the meaning of Part I of the said Act of 1954 or, as the case may be, the said Schedule 10.

(7) This section shall apply equally where a protected occupier of a dwelling-house, or part of a dwelling-house, has a relevant licence as defined in the Rent (Agriculture) Act 1976, and in this section "tenancy" and all cognate expressions shall be construed accordingly.

**3A–212** *Note*—Amended by the Agricultural Holdings Act 1986 Sch.14; the Housing Act 1988 s.140, Schs 17 and 18; the Local Government and Housing Act 1989 s.195, Sch.11, para.53; and the Agricultural Tenancies Act 1995 s.40, Sch.

**Effect on sub-tenancy of determination of superior tenancy**

**3A–213** Section 137 provides that in some cases, on termination of a head tenancy, the sub-tenant of any dwelling house which has been lawfully sublet is deemed to become the tenant of the landlord and so gives some protection to sub-tenants when head tenancies come to an end.

In three appeals heard together, reported as *Wellcome Trust v Hamad* [1998] Q.B. 638; [1998] 2 W.L.R. 156, CA, the Court of Appeal considered the construction of s.137(3) and the protection which it affords to sub-tenants. In each case buildings which comprised business premises (such as shops) on the ground floor and flats upstairs were let on long leases. These leases came within the provisions of the Landlord and Tenant Act 1954 Pt II. Subsequently Rent Act protected sub-tenancies of the residential parts of the buildings were granted. In all three cases county court judges relying on *Pittalis v Grant* [1989] Q.B. 605, CA, found that, after the termination of the head leases, the sub-tenants fell outside Rent Act protection. The sub-tenants appealed, contending that *Pittalis v Grant* had been decided per incuriam. After giving detailed consideration to the Rent Acts from a historical perspective the Court of Appeal granted the tenants' appeals and in two cases set aside possession orders made against them. Rent Act 1977 s.137(3) "appears to contemplate that where there is a flat over a shop, and the flat is lawfully sublet for residential use, so as to afford the sub-tenant protection under the Rent Act as against the tenant, the sub-tenant should continue to enjoy the same protection against the head landlord when the superior letting comes to an end". *Pittalis v Grant* had been decided *per incuriam* because:

(1) the argument relied upon that if a tenancy is not regulated, the premises cannot be treated as a dwelling house, was fallacious. Premises may amount to a dwelling house without being let on a regulated tenancy; and

(2) the Court of Appeal had overlooked all of the authorities in which the accepted principles referred to by Lord Wilberforce in *Maunsell v Olins* [1975]

***Paragraph numbers marked with a "+" can be found online and on CD.***

A.C. 373, HL, were contained. In each of the three cases the premises concerned constituted a dwelling-house and accordingly s.137(3) did afford protection to the sub-tenants.

A statutory tenant cannot grant an effective sub-tenancy, at least so far as the landlord is concerned. If a statutory tenant moves out and purports to sub-let, the premises cannot be lawfully sub-let under s.137 (*Moreland Properties (UK) Ltd v Dhokia* [2003] EWCA Civ 1639; October 21, 2003).

## Effect on furnished sub-tenancy of determination of superior unfurnished tenancy

**138.**—(1) If, in a case where section 137(2) of this Act applies, the conditions mentioned in subsection (2) below are fulfilled, the terms on which the sub-tenant is, by virtue of section 137(2), deemed to become the tenant of the landlord shall not include any terms as to the provision by the landlord of furniture or services. **3A–214**

(2) The conditions are—

(a) that the statutorily protected tenancy which is determined as mentioned in section 137(2) was neither a protected furnished tenancy nor a statutory furnished tenancy; and

(b) that, immediately before the determination of that statutorily protected tenancy, the sub-tenant referred to in section 137(2) was the tenant under a protected furnished tenancy or a statutory furnished tenancy; and

(c) that the landlord, within the period of six weeks beginning with the day on which the statutorily protected tenancy referred to in section 137(2) is determined, serves notice on the sub-tenant that this section is to apply to his tenancy or statutory tenancy.

(3) In this section "statutorily protected tenancy" has the same meaning as it has for the purposes of section 137(2) of this Act.

*Note* —Amended by the Housing Act 1980 s.152, Sch.25, para.51. **3A–215**

**"statutory furnished tenancy"**

See ss.2 and 152. **3A–216**

**"protected tenancy"**

See ss.1 and 152. **3A–217**

**"statutorily protected tenancy"**

See s.138(3). **3A–218**

**"landlord" and "tenant"**

See s.152. **3A–219**

* * * *

*JURISDICTION AND PROCEDURE*

## County court jurisdiction

**141.**—(1) A county court shall have jurisdiction, either in the course of any proceedings relating to a dwelling or on an application made **3A–220**

*Paragraph numbers marked with a "+" can be found online and on CD.*

HOUSING

for the purpose by the landlord or the tenant, to determine any question—

(a) as to whether a tenancy is a protected tenancy or whether any person is a statutory tenant of a dwelling-house; or

(b) as to the rent limit; or

(c) [...]

(d) as to the application of Part V and sections 103 to 106 of this Act to a contract; or

(e) as to whether a protected, statutory or regulated tenancy is a protected, statutory or regulated furnished tenancy;

or as to any matter which is or may become material for determining any such question.

(2) [...]

(3) A county court shall have jurisdiction to deal with any claim or other proceedings arising out of any of the provisions of this Act specified in subsection (5) below, notwithstanding that by reason of the amount of the claim or otherwise the case would not, apart from this subsection, be within the jurisdiction of a county court.

(4) If, under any of the provisions of this Act specified in subsection (5) below, a person takes proceedings in the High Court which he could have taken in the county court, he shall not be entitled to recover any costs.

(5) The provisions referred to in subsections (3) and (4) above are—

(a) [...]

(b) in Part III, section 57;

(c) Part VII, except sections 98(2) and 101;

(d) in Part IX, sections 125 and 126;

(e) in Part X, sections 133(1), 134 and 135; and

(f) in this Part of this Act, sections 145 and 147.

3A–221 *Note* —Amended by the Housing Act 1980 s.152, Sch.26.

**"dwelling-house"**

3A–222 See ss.1 and 26.

**"statutory furnished tenancy"**

3A–223 See ss.1 and 152.

**"protected tenancy" and "protected furnished tenancy"**

3A–224 See ss.1 and 152.

**"statutorily protected tenancy"**

3A–225 See s.138(3).

**"landlord"and "tenant"**

3A–226 See s.152.

**"regulated tenancy"**

3A–227 See ss.18 and 152.

## Rules as to procedure

3A–228 **142.** [...]

*Note*—Repealed by the Constitutional Reform Act 2005 ss.15(1), 146, Sch.4, para.94, Sch.18. 3A–229

* * * *

## MISCELLANEOUS

### Implied term in all protected tenancies

**148.** It shall be a condition of a protected tenancy of a dwelling-house that the tenant shall afford to the landlord access to the dwelling-house and all reasonable facilities for executing therein any repairs which the landlord is entitled to execute. 3A–230

**"protected tenancy"**

See ss.1 and 152. 3A–231

**"landlord" and "tenant"**

See s.152. 3A–232

**"dwelling-house"**

See ss.1 and 26. 3A–233

* * * *

## SUPPLEMENTAL

### Interpretation

**152.**—(1) In this Act, except where the context otherwise requires— 3A–234

"the appropriate day" has the meaning assigned to it by section 25(3) of this Act;

"landlord" includes any person from time to time deriving title under the original landlord and also includes, in relation to any dwelling-house, any person other than the tenant who is, or but for Part VII of this Act would be, entitled to possession of the dwelling-house;

"let" includes "sublet";

"long tenancy" means a tenancy granted for a term of years certain exceeding 21 years, whether or not subsequently extended by act of the parties or by any enactment;

"protected furnished tenancy", "regulated furnished tenancy" and "statutory furnished tenancy" means a protected or, as the case may be, regulated or statutory tenancy—

(a) under which the dwelling-house concerned is bona fide let at a rent which includes payments in respect of furniture, and

(b) in respect of which the amount of rent which is fairly attributable to the use of furniture, having regard to the value of that use to the tenant, forms a substantial part of the whole rent;

"protected tenant" and "protected tenancy" shall be construed in accordance with section 1 of this Act;

***Paragraph numbers marked with a "+" can be found online and on CD.***

"rates" includes water rates and charges but does not include an owner's drainage rate as defined in section 63(2)(a) of the Land Drainage Act 1976;

"rateable value" shall be construed in accordance with section 25 of this Act;

"regulated tenancy" shall be construed in accordance with section 18 of this Act;

"rent tribunal" has the meaning given by section 76(1) of this Act;

"rental period" means a period in respect of which a payment of rent falls to be made;

"restricted contract" shall be construed in accordance with section 19 of this Act;

"statutory tenant" and "statutory tenancy" shall be construed in accordance with section 2 of this Act;

"tenant" includes statutory tenant and also includes a sub-tenant and any person deriving title under the original tenant or sub-tenant;

"tenancy" includes "sub-tenancy";

"tenancy at a low rent" has the meaning assigned to it by section 5 of this Act.

(2) Except in so far as the context otherwise requires, any reference in this Act to any other enactment shall be taken as referring to that enactment as amended by or under any other enactment, including this Act.

**3A–235** *Note*—Amended by the Housing Act 1980 s.152, Sch.26.

# SCHEDULES

**SECTIONS 2 AND 3**

## SCHEDULE 1

### STATUTORY TENANCIES

### PART I

### STATUTORY TENANTS BY SUCCESSION

**3A–236** 1. Paragraph 2 below shall have effect, subject to section 2(3) of this Act, for the purpose of determining who is the statutory tenant of a dwelling-house by succession after the death of the person (in this Part of this Schedule referred to as "the original tenant") who, immediately before his death, was a protected tenant of the dwelling-house or the statutory tenant of it by virtue of his previous protected tenancy.

2.—(1) The surviving spouse, or civil partner, (if any) of the original tenant, if residing in the dwelling-house immediately before the death of the original tenant, shall after the death be the statutory tenant if and so long as he or she occupies the dwelling-house as his or her residence.

(2) For the purposes of this paragraph—

(a) a person who was living with the original tenant as his or her wife or husband shall be treated as the spouse of the original tenant, and

(b) a person who was living with the original tenant as if they were civil partners shall be treated as the civil partner of the original tenant.

(3) If, immediately after the death of the original tenant, there is, by virtue of

***Paragraph numbers marked with a "+" can be found online and on CD.***

sub-paragraph (2) above, more than one person who fulfils the conditions in sub-paragraph (1) above, such one of them as may be decided by agreement or, in default of agreement, by the county court shall for the purposes of this paragraph be treated (according to whether that one of them is of the opposite sex to, or of the same sex as, the original tenant) as the surviving spouse or the surviving civil partner.

3.—(1) Where paragraph 2 above does not apply, but a person was a member of the original tenant's family was residing with him in the dwelling-house at the time of and for the period of 2 years immediately before his death then, after his death, that person or if there is more than one such person such one of them as may be decided by agreement, or in default of agreement by the county court, shall be entitled to an assured tenancy of the dwelling-house by succession.

(2) If the original tenant died within the period of 18 months beginning on the operative date, then, for the purposes of this paragraph, a person who was residing in the dwelling-house with the original tenant at the time of his death and for the period which began 6 months before the operative date and ended at the time of his death shall be taken to have been residing with the original tenant for the period of 2 years immediately before his death.

4. A person who becomes the statutory tenant of a dwelling-house by virtue of paragraph 2 above is in this Part of this Schedule referred to as "the first successor".

5. If, immediately before his death, the first successor was still a statutory tenant, paragraph 6 below shall have effect for the purpose of determining who is entitled to an assured tenancy of the dwelling-house by succession after the death of the first successor.

6.—(1) Where a person who—

(a) was a member of the original tenant's family immediately before that tenant's death, and

(b) was a member of the first successor's family immediately before the first successor's death,

was residing in the dwelling-house with the first successor at the time of, and for the period of two years immediately before, the first successor's death, that person or, if there is more than one such person, such one of them as may be decided by agreement or, in default of agremeent, by the county court shall be entitled to an assured tenancy of the dwelling-house by succession.

(2) If the first successor died within the period of 18 months beginning on the operative date, then, for the purposes of this paragraph, a person who was residing in the dwelling-house with the first successor at the time of his death and for the period which began six months before the operative date and ended at the time of his death shall be taken to have been residing with the first successor for the period of two years immediately before his death.

7. [...]

8. [...]

9. Paragraphs 5 to 8 above do not apply where the statutory tenancy of the original tenant arose by virtue of section 4 of the Requisitioned Houses and Housing (Amendment) Act 1955 or section 20 of the Rent Act 1965.

10.—(1) Where after a succession the successor becomes the tenant of the dwelling-house by the grant to him of another tenancy, "the original tenant" and "the first successor" in this Part of this Schedule shall, in relation to that other tenancy, mean the persons who were respectively the original tenant and the first successor at the time of the succession, and accordingly—

(a) if the successor was the first successor, and, immediately before his death he was still the tenant (whether protected or statutory), paragraphs 6 and 7 above shall apply on his death,

(b) if the successor was not the first successor; no person shall become a statutory tenant on his death by virtue of this Part of this Schedule.

(2) Sub-paragraph (1) above applies—

(a) even if a successor enters into more than one other tenancy of the dwelling-house, and

***Paragraph numbers marked with a "+" can be found online and on CD.***

(b) even if both the first successor and the successor on his death enter into other tenancies of the dwelling-house.

(3) In this paragraph "succession" means the occasion on which a person becomes the statutory tenant of a dwelling-house by virtue of this Part of this Schedule and "successor" shall be construed accordingly.

(4) This paragraph shall apply as respects a succession which took place before August 27, 1972 if, and only if, the tenancy granted after the succession, or the first of those tenancies, was granted on or after that date, and where it does not apply as respects a succession, no account should be taken of that succession in applying this paragrpah as respects any later succession.

11.—(1) Paragraphs 5 to 8 above do not apply where—

(a) the tenancy of the original tenant was granted on or after the operative date within the meaning of the Rent (Agriculture) Act 1976, and

(b) both that tenancy and the statutory tenancy of the first successor were tenancies to which section 99 of this Act applies.

(2) If the tenants under both of the tenancies falling within sub-paragraph (1)(b) above were persons to whom paragraph 7 of Schedule 9 to the Rent (Agriculture) Act 1976 applies, the reference in sub-paragraph (1)(a) above to the operative date shall be taken as a reference to the date of operation for forestry workers within the meaning of that Act.

11A. In this Part of this Schedule "the operative date" means the date on which Part I of the Housing Act 1988 came into force.

**3A–237** *Note*—Paragraph 2 amended by the Civil Partnership Act 2004 s.81, Sch.8, para.13.

## PART II

## RELINQUISHING TENANCIES AND CHANGING TENANTS

*Payments demanded by statutory tenants as a condition of giving up possession*

**3A–238** 12.—(1) A statutory tenant of a dwelling-house who, as a condition of giving up possession of the dwelling-house, asks for or receives the payment of any sum, or the giving of any other consideration, by any person other than the landlord, shall be guilty of an offence.

(2) Where a statutory tenant of a dwelling-house requires that furniture or other articles shall be purchased as a condition of his giving up possession of the dwelling-house, the price demanded shall, at the request of the person on whom the demand is made, by stated in writing, and if the price exceeds the reasonable price of the articles the excess shall be treated, for the purposes of sub-paragraph (1) above, as a sum asked to be paid as a condition of giving up possession.

(3) A person guilty of an offence under this paragraph shall be liable to a fine not exceeding level 3 on the standard scale.

(4) The court by which a person is convicted of an offence under this paragraph may order the payment—

(a) to the person who made any such payment, or gave any such consideration, as is referred to in sub-paragraph (1) above, of the amount of that payment or the value of that consideration, or

(b) to the person who paid any such price as is referred to in sub-paragraph (2) above, of the amount by which the price paid exceeds the reasonable price.

*Change of statutory tenant by agreement*

**3A–239** 13.—(1) Where it is so agreed in writing between a statutory tenant ("the outgoing tenant") and a person proposing to occupy the dwelling ("the incoming tenant"), the incoming tenant shall be deemed to be the statutory tenant of the dwelling as from such date as may be specified in the agreement ("the transfer date").

(2) Such an agreement shall not have effect unless the landlord is a party thereto, and, if the consent of any superior landlord would have been required to an assignment of the previous contractual tenancy, the agreement shall not have effect unless the superior landlord is a party thereto.

***Paragraph numbers marked with a "+" can be found online and on CD.***

(3) If the outgoing tenant is the statutory tenant by virtue of his previous protected tenancy, then, subject to sub-paragraph (6) below, this Act shall have effect, on and after the transfer date, as if the incoming tenant had been a protected tenant and had become the statutory tenant by virtue of his previous protected tenancy.

(4) Subject to sub-paragraphs (5) and (6) below, if the outgoing tenant is a statutory tenant by succession, then, on and after the transfer date—

(a) this Act shall have effect as if the incoming tenant were a statutory tenant by succession, and

(b) the incoming tenant shall be deemed to have become a statutory tenant by virtue of that paragraph of Part I of this Schedule by virtue of which the outgoing tenant became (or is deemed to have become) a statutory tenant.

(5) If the outgoing tenant is a statutory tenant by succession, the agreement may provide that, notwithstanding anything in sub-paragraph (4) above, on and after the transfer date, this Act shall have effect, subject to sub-paragraph (6) below, as if the incoming tenant had been a protected tenant and had become the statutory tenant by virtue of his previous protected tenancy.

(6) Unless the incoming tenant is deemed, by virtue of sub-paragraph (4)(b) above, to have become a statutory tenant by virtue of paragraph 6 or 7 of Part I of this Schedule, paragraphs 5 to 7 of that Part shall not apply where a person has become a statutory tenant by virtue of this paragraph.

(7) In this paragraph "the dwelling" means the aggregate of the premises comprised in the statutory tenancy of the outgoing tenant.

*No pecuniary consideration to be required on change of tenant under paragraph 13*

14.—(1) Any person who requires the payment of any pecuniary consideration for entering into such an agreement as is referred to in paragraph 13(1) above shall be liable to a fine not exceeding level 3 on the standard scale. **3A–240**

(2) The court by which a person is convicted of an offence under sub-paragraph (1) above may order the amount of the payment to be repaid by the person to whom it was paid.

(3) Without prejudice to sub-paragraph (2) above, the amount of any such payment as is referred to in sub-paragraph (1) above shall be recoverable by the person by whom it was made either by proceedings for its recovery or, if it was made to the landlord by a person liable to pay rent to the landlord, by deduction from any rent so payable.

(4) Notwithstanding anything in sub-paragraph (1) above, if part from this paragraph he would be entitled to do so, the outgoing tenant may require the payment by the incoming tenant—

(a) of so much of any outgoings discharged by the outgoing tenant as is referable to any period after the transfer date;

(b) of a sum not exceeding the amount of any expenditure reasonably incurred by the outgoing tenant in carrying out any structural alteration of the dwelling or in providing or improving fixtures therein, being fixtures which, as against the landlord, the outgoing tenant is not entitled to remove;

(c) where the outgoing tenant became a tenant of the dwelling by virtue of an assignment of the previous protected tenancy, of a sum not exceeding any reasonable amount paid by him to his assignor in respect of expenditure incurred by the assignor, or by any previous assignor of the tenancy, in carrying out any such alteration or in providing or improving any such fixtures as are mentioned in paragraph (b) above; or

(d) where part of the dwelling is used as a shop or office, or for business, trade or professional purposes, of a reasonable amount in respect of any goodwill of the business, trade or profession, being goodwill transferred to the incoming tenant in connection with his becoming a statutory tenant of the dwelling or accruing to him in consequence thereof.

(5) In this paragraph "outgoing tenant", "incoming tenant", "the transfer date" and "the dwelling" have the same meanings as in paragraph 13 above.

*Note*—Amended by the Housing Act 1980 s.152, Sch.26; the Criminal Justice Act **3A–241**

***Paragraph numbers marked with a "+" can be found online and on CD.***

1982 ss.38 and 46; the Housing Act 1988 Schs 4 and 18; and the Civil Partnership Act 2004 s.81 and Sch.8, para.13.

Schedule 1 should be read in conjunction with ss.2 and 3 (see paras 3A–94 to 3A–102).

**Member of the original tenant's family**

**3A–242** A person of the same sex who has lived with the tenant for many years in a stable homosexual relationship may be a member of the tenant's family for the purposes of succession to a Rent Act tenancy (*Fitzpatrick v Sterling HA* [2001] 1 A.C. 27; [1999] 3 W.L.R. 1113; [1999] 4 All E.R. 705, HL). Further, same sex couples may be treated in the same way as a husband and wife. The House of Lords has held that the words "as his or her wife or husband" in para.2(2) must be read to mean "as if they were his or her wife or husband" in order to comply with the ECHR. Accordingly the survivor of a same sex couple who has been living in a loving and monogamous relationship with a tenant may acquire a statutory tenancy (*Ghaidan v Godin-Mendoza* [2004] UKHL 30; [2004] 2 A.C. 557).

SECTION 12(3)

## SCHEDULE 2

### RESIDENT LANDLORDS

### PART I

### PROVISIONS FOR DETERMINING APPLICATION OF SECTION 12

**3A–243** 1. In determining whether the condition in section 12(1)(c) of this Act is at any time fulfilled with respect to a tenancy, there shall be disregarded—

(a) any period of not more than 28 days beginning with the date on which the interest of the landlord under the tenancy becomes vested at law and in equity in an individual who, during that period, does not occupy as his residence another dwelling-house which forms part of the building or, as the case may be, flat concerned;

(b) if, within a period falling within paragraph (a) above, the individual concerned notifies the tenant in writing of his intention to occupy as his residence another dwelling-house in the building or, as the case may be, flat concerned, the period beginning with the date on which the interest of the landlord under the tenancy becomes vested in that individual as mentioned in that paragraph and ending—

(i) at the expiry of the period of six months beginning on that date, or

(ii) on the date on which that interest ceases to be so vested, or

(iii) on the date on which the condition in section 12(1)(c) again applies,whichever is the earlier; and

(c) any period of not more than two years beginning with the date on which the interest of the landlord under the tenancy becomes, and during which it remains, vested—

(i) […]

(ii) in trustees as such; or

(iii) by virtue of section 9 of the Administration of Estates Act 1925, in the Probate Judge or the Public Trustee.

2. During any period when—

(a) the interest of the landlord under the tenancy referred to in section 12(1) is vested in trustees as such, and

(b) that interest is held on trust for any person who occupies as his residence a dwelling-house which forms part of the building or, as the case may be, flat referred to in section 12(1)(a),the condition in section 12(1)(c) shall be deemed to be fulfilled and, accordingly, no part of that period shall be disregarded by virtue of paragraph 1 above.

2A.—(1) The tenancy referred to in section 12(1) falls within this paragraph if the interest of the landlord under the tenancy becomes vested in the personal representatives of a deceased person acting in that capacity.

***Paragraph numbers marked with a "+" can be found online and on CD.***

(2) If the tenancy falls within this paragraph, the condition in section 12(1)(c) shall be deemed to be fulfilled for any period, beginning with the date on which the interest becomes vested in the personal representatives and not exceeding two years, during which the interest of the landlord remains so vested.

3. Throughout any period which, by virtue of paragraph 1 above, falls to be disregarded for the purpose of determining whether the condition in section 12(1)(c) is fulfilled with respect to a tenancy, no order shall be made for possession of the dwelling-house subject to that tenancy, other than an order which might be made if that tenancy were or, as the case may be, had been a regulated tenancy.

4. For the purposes of section 12, a building is a purpose-built block of flats if as constructed it contained, and it contains, two or more flats; and for this purpose "flat" means a dwelling-house which—

(a) forms part only of a building; and

(b) is separated horizontally from another dwelling-house which forms part of the same building.

5. For the purposes of section 12, a person shall be treated as occupying a dwelling-house as his residence if, so far as the nature of the case allows, he fulfils the same conditions as, by virtue of section 2(3) of this Act, are required to be fulfilled by a statutory tenant of a dwelling-house.

## PART II

### TENANCIES CEASING TO FALL WITHIN SECTION 12

6.—(1) In any case where— **3A–244**

(a) a tenancy which, by virtue only of section 12, was precluded from being a protected tenancy ceases to be so precluded and accordingly becomes a protected tenancy, and

(b) before it became a protected tenancy a rent was registered for the dwelling concerned under Part V of this Act,

the amount which is so registered shall be deemed to be registered under Part IV of this Act as the rent for the dwelling-house which is let on that tenancy, and that registration shall be deemed to take effect on the day the tenancy becomes a protected tenancy.

(2) Section 67(3) of this Act shall not apply to an application for the registration under Part IV of a rent different from that which is deemed to be registered as mentioned in sub-paragraph (1) above.

(3) [...]

(4) If, immediately before a tenancy became a protected tenancy as mentioned in sub-paragraph (1)(a) above, the rates in respect of the dwelling-house concerned were borne as mentioned in sub-section (3) of section 79 of this Act and the fact that they were so borne was noted as required by that sub-section then, in the application of Part IV in relation to the protected tenancy, section 71(2) of this Act shall be deemed to apply.

7. If, in a case where a tenancy becomes a protected tenancy as mentioned in sub-paragraph (1)(a) above—

(a) a notice to quit had been served in respect of the dwelling concerned before the date on which the tenancy became a protected tenancy, and

(b) the period at the end of which that notice to quit takes effect had, before that date, been extended under Part VII of this Act, and

(c) that period has not expired before that date,

the notice to quit shall take effect on the day following that date (whenever it would otherwise take effect) and, accordingly, on that day the protected tenancy shall become a statutory tenancy.

*Note* —Amended by the Housing Act 1980 s.65, Sch.26; the Housing Act 1988 Sch.18; the Trusts of Land and Appointment of Trustees Act 1996 Sch.4; and the Law of Property (Miscellaneous Provisions) Act 1994 s.21(1), Sch.1. **3A–245**

Sch.2 should be read in conjunction with s.12 (see para.3A–129).

***Paragraph numbers marked with a "+" can be found online and on CD.***

* * * *

SECTION 98

# SCHEDULE 15

## GROUNDS FOR POSSESSION OF DWELLING-HOUSES LET ON OR SUBJECT TO PROTECTED OR STATUTORY TENANCIES

## PART I

## CASES IN WHICH COURT MAY ORDER POSSESSION

*Case 1*

**3A–246** Where any rent lawfully due from the tenant has not been paid, or any obligation of the protected or statutory tenancy which arises under this Act, or—

(a) in the case of a protected tenancy, any other obligation of the tenancy, in so far as is consistent with the provisions of Part VII of this Act, or

(b) in the case of a statutory tenancy, any other obligation of the previous protected tenancy which is applicable to the statutory tenancy,

has been broken or not performed.

*Case 2*

**3A–247** Where the tenant or any person residing or lodging with him or any sub-tenant of his has been guilty of conduct which is a nuisance or annoyance to adjoining occupiers, or has been convicted of using the dwelling-house or allowing the dwelling-house to be used for immoral or illegal purposes.

*Case 3*

**3A–248** Where the condition of the dwelling-house has, in the opinion of the court, deteriorated owing to acts of waste by, or the neglect or default of, the tenant or any person residing or lodging with him or any sub-tenant of his and, in the case of any act of waste by, or the neglect or default of, a person lodging with the tenant or sub-tenant of his, where the court is satisfied that the tenant has not, before the making of the order in question, taken such steps as he ought reasonably to have taken for the removal of the lodger or sub-tenant, as the case may be.

*Case 4*

**3A–249** Where the condition of any furniture provided for use under the tenancy has, in the opinion of the court, deteriorated owing to ill-treatment by the tenant or any person residing or lodging with him or any sub-tenant of his and, in the case of any ill-treatment by a person lodging with the tenant or a sub-tenant of his, where the court is satisfied that the tenant has not, before the making of the order in question, taken such steps as he ought reasonably to have taken for the removal of the lodger or sub-tenant, as the case may be.

*Case 5*

**3A–250** Where the tenant has given notice to quit and, in consequence of that notice, the landlord has contracted to sell or let the dwelling-house or has taken any other steps as the result of which he would, in the opinion of the court, be seriously prejudiced if he could not obtain possession.

*Case 6*

**3A–251** Where, without the consent of the landlord, the tenant has, at any time after—

(a) [...]

(b) 22nd March, 1973, in the case of a tenancy which became a regulated tenancy by virtue of section 14 of the Counter-Inflation Act 1973;

(bb) the commencement of section 73 of the Housing Act 1980, in the case of a tenancy which became a regulated tenancy by virtue of that section;

(c) 14th August, 1974, in the case of a regulated furnished tenancy; or

(d) 8th December, 1965, in the case of any other tenancy,

assigned or sublet the whole of the dwelling-house or sublet part of the dwelling-house, the remainder being already sublet.

*Case 7*

[...] 3A–252

*Case 8*

Where the dwelling-house is reasonably required by the landlord for occupation as a residence for some person engaged in his whole-time employment, or in the whole-time employment of some tenant from him or with whom, conditional on housing being provided, a contract for such employment has been entered into, and the tenant was in the employment of the landlord or a former landlord, and the dwelling-house was let to him in consequence of that employment and he has ceased to be in that employment. 3A–253

*Case 9*

Where the dwelling-house is reasonably required by the landlord for occupation as a residence for— 3A–254

(a) himself, or

(b) any son or daughter of his over 18 years of age, or

(c) his father or mother, or

(d) if the dwelling-house is let on or subject to a regulated tenancy, the father or mother of his spouse or civil partner,

and the landlord did not become landlord by purchasing the dwelling-house or any interest therein after—

(i) 7th November, 1956, in the case of a tenancy which was then a controlled tenancy;

(ii) 8th March, 1973, in the case of a tenancy which became a regulated tenancy by virtue of section 14 of the Counter-Inflation Act 1973;

(iii) 24th May, 1974, in the case of a regulated furnished tenancy; or

(iv) 23rd March, 1965, in the case of any other tenancy.

*Case 10*

Where the court is satisfied that the rent charged by the tenant— 3A–255

(a) for any sublet part of the dwelling-house which is a dwelling-house let on a protected tenancy or subject to a statutory tenancy is or was in excess of the maximum rent for the time being recoverable for that part, having regard to Part III of this Act, or

(b) for any sublet part of the dwelling-house which is subject to a restricted contract is or was in excess of the maximum (if any) which it is lawful for the lessor, within the meaning of Part V of this Act to require or receive having regard to the provisions of that Part.

*Note* —Case 9 amended by the Civil Partnership Act 2004 s.81, Sch.8, para.14. 3A–256

## PART II

## CASES IN WHICH COURT MUST ORDER POSSESSION WHERE DWELLIING-HOUSE SUBJECT TO REGULATED TENANCY

*Case 11*

Where a person (in this case referred to as the "owner-occupier") who let the dwelling-house on a regulated tenancy had, at any time before the letting, occupied it as his residence and— 3A–257

(a) not later than the relevant date the landlord gave notice, in writing to the tenant that possession might be recovered under this Case, and

(b) the dwelling-house has not, since—

***Paragraph numbers marked with a "+" can be found online and on CD.***

(i) March 22, 1973, in the case of a tenancy which became a regulated tenancy by virtue of section 14 of the Counter-Inflation Act 1973;

(ii) August 14, 1974, in the case of a regulated furnished tenancy; or

(iii) December 8, 1965, in the case of any other tenancy,

been let by the owner-occupier on a protected tenancy with respect to which the condition mentioned in paragraph (a) above was not satisfied, and

(c) the court is of the opinion that of the conditions set out in Part V of this Schedule one of those in paragraphs (a) and (c) to (f) is satisfied.

If the court is of the opinion that, notwithstanding that the condition in paragraph (a) or (b) above is not complied with, it is just and equitable to make an order for possession of the dwelling-house, the court may dispense with the requirements of either or both of these paragraphs, as the case may require.

The giving of a notice before August 14, 1974 under section 79 of the Rent Act 1968 shall be treated, in the case of a regulated furnished tenancy, as compliance with paragraph (a) of this Case.

Where the dwelling-house has been let by the owner-occupier on a protected tenancy (in this paragraph referred to as "the earlier tenancy") granted on or after November 16, 1984 but not later than the end of he period of two months beginning with the commencement of the Rent (Amendment) Act 1985 and either—

(i) the earlier tenancy was granted for a term certain (whether or not to be followed by a further term or to continue thereafter from year to year or some other period) and was during that term a protected shorthold tenancy as defined in section 52 of the Housing Act 1980, or

(ii) the conditions mentioned in paragraphs (a) to (c) of Case 20 were satisfied with respect to the dwelling-house and the earlier tenancy,

then for the purposes of paragraph (b) above the condition in paragraph (a) above is to be treated as having been satisfied with respect to the earlier tenancy.

*Case 12*

**3A–258** Where the landlord (in this Case referred to as "the owner") intends to occupy the dwelling-house as his residence at such time as he might retire from regular employment and has let it on a regulated tenancy before he has so retired and—

(a) not later than the relevant date the landlord gave notice in writing to the tenant that possession might be recovered under this Case; and

(b) the dwelling-house has not, since August 14, 1974, been let by the owner paragraph (a) above was not satisfied; and

(c) the court is of the opinion that of the conditions set out in Part V of this Schedule one of those in paragraphs (b) to (e) is satisfied.

If the court is of the opinion that, notwithstanding that the condition in paragraph (a) or (b) above is not complied with, it is just and equitable to make an order for possession of the dwelling-house, the court may dispense with the requirements of either or both of those paragraphs, as the case may require.

*Case 13*

**3A–259** Where the dwelling-house is let under a tenancy for a term of years certain not exceeding eight months and—

(a) not later than the relevant date the landlord gave notice in writing to the tenant that possession might be recovered under this Case; and

(b) that dwelling-house was, at some time within the period of 12 months ending on the relevant date, occupied under a right to occupy it for a holiday.

For the purposes of this Case a tenancy shall be treated as being for a term of years certain notwithstanding that it is liable to determination by re-entry or on the happening of any event other than the giving of notice by the landlord to determine the term.

*Case 14*

**3A–260** Where the dwelling-house is let under a tenancy for a term of years certain not exceeding 12 months and—

(a) not later than the relevant date the landlord gave notice in writing to the tenant that possession might be recovered under this Case; and

***Paragraph numbers marked with a "+" can be found online and on CD.***

(b) at some time within the period of 12 months ending on the relevant date, the dwelling-house was subject to such a tenancy as is referred to in section 8(1) of this Act.

For the purposes of this Case a tenancy shall be treated as being for a term of years certain notwithstanding that it is liable to determination by re-entry or on the happening of any event other than the giving of notice by the landlord to determine the term.

*Case 15*

Where the dwelling-house is held for the purpose of being available for occupation by a minister of religion as a residence from which to perform the duties of his office and— **3A–261**

(a) not later than the relevant date the tenant was given notice in writing that possession might be recovered under this Case, and

(b) the court is satisfied that the dwelling-house is required for occupation by a minister of religion as such a residence.

*Case 16*

Where the dwelling-house was at any time occupied by a person under the terms of his employment as a person employed in agriculture, and **3A–262**

(a) the tenant neither is nor at any time was so employed by the landlord and is not the widow of a person who was so employed, and

(b) not later than the relevant date, the tenant was given notice in writing that possession might be recovered under this Case, and

(c) the court is satisfied that the dwelling-house is required for occupation by a person employed, or to be employed, by the landlord in agriculture.

For the purposes of this Case "employed", "employment" and "agriculture" have the same meanings as in the Agricultural Wages Act 1948.

*Case 17*

Where proposals for amalgamation, approved for the purposes of a scheme under section 26 of the Agriculture Act 1967, have been carried out and, at the time when the proposals were submitted, the dwelling-house was occupied by a person responsible (whether as owner, tenant, or servant or agent of another) for the control of the farming of any part of the land comprised in the amalgamation and **3A–263**

(a) after the carrying out of the proposals, the dwelling-house was let on a regulated tenancy otherwise than to, or to the widow of, either a person ceasing to be so responsible as part of the amalgamation or a person who is, or at any time was, employed by the landlord in agriculture, and

(b) not later than the relevant date the tenant was given notice in writing that possession might be recovered under this Case, and

(c) the court is satisfied that the dwelling-house is required for occupation by a person employed, or to be employed, by the landlord in agriculture, and

(d) the proceedings for possession are commenced by the landlord at any time during the period of five years beginning with the date on which the proposals for the amalgamation were approved or, if occupation of the dwelling-house after the amalgamation continued in, or was first taken by, a person ceasing to be responsible as mentioned in paragraph (a) above or his widow, during a period expiring three years after the date on which the dwelling-house next became unoccupied.

For the purposes of this Case "employed" and "agriculture" have the same meanings as in the Agricultural Wages Act 1948 and "amalgamation" has the same meaning as in Part II of the Agriculture Act 1967.

*Case 18*

Where— **3A–264**

(a) the last occupier of the dwelling-house before the relevant date was a person, or the widow of a person, who was at some time during his occupation responsible (whether as owner, tenant, or servant or agent of another) for the control of the farming of land which formed, together with the dwelling-house, an agricultural unit within the meaning of the Agriculture Act 1947, and

(b) the tenant is neither—

(i) a person, or the widow of a person, who is or has at any time been responsible for the control of the farming of any part of the said land, nor

(ii) a person, or the widow of a person, who is or at any time was employed by the landlord in agriculture, and

(c) the creation of the tenancy was not preceded by the carrying out in connection with any of the said land of an amalgamation approved for the purposes of a scheme under section 26 of the Agriculture Act 1967, and

(d) not later than the relevant date the tenant was given notice in writing that possession might be recovered under this Case, and

(e) the court is satisfied that the dwelling-house is required for occupation either by a person responsible or to be responsible (whether as owner, tenant, or servant or agent of another) for the control of the farming of any part of the said land or by a person employed or to be employed by the landlord in agriculture, and

(f) in a case where the relevant date was before August 9, 1972, the proceedings for possession are commenced by the landlord before the expiry of five years from the date on which the occupier referred to in paragraph (a) above went out of occupation.

For the purposes of this Case "employed" and "agriculture" have the same meanings as in the Agricultural Wages Act 1948 and "amalgamation" has the same meaning as in Part II of the Agriculture Act 1967.

*Case 19*

**3A–265** Where the dwelling-house was let under a protected shorthold tenancy (or is treated under section 55 of the Housing Act 1980 as having been so let) and—

(a) there either has been no grant of a further tenancy of the dwelling-house since the end of the protected shorthold tenancy or, if there was such a grant, it was to a person the dwelling-house as a protected or statutory tenant; and

(b) the proceedings for possession were commenced after appropriate notice by the landlord to the tenant and not later than three months after the expiry of the notice.

A notice is appropriate for this Case if—

(i) it is in writing and states that proceedings for possession under this Case may be brought after its expiry; and

(ii) it expires not earlier than three months after it is served nor, if, when it is served, the tenancy is a periodic tenancy, before that periodic tenancy could be brought to an end by a notice to quit served by the landlord on the same day;

(iii) it is served—

(a) in the period of three months immediately preceding the date on which the protected shorthold tenancy comes to an end; or

(b) if that date has passed, in the period of three months immediately preceding any anniversary of that date; and

(iv) in a case where a previous notice has been served by the landlord on the tenant in respect of the dwelling-house, and that notice was an appropriate notice, it is served not earlier than three months after the expiry of the previous notice.

*Case 20*

**3A–266** Where the dwelling-house was let by a person (in this Case referred to as "the owner") at any time after the commencement of section 67 of the Housing Act 1980 and—

(a) at the time when the owner acquired the dwelling-house he was a member of the regular armed forces of the Crown;

(b) at the relevant date the owner was a member of the regular armed forces of the Crown;

(c) not later than the relevant date the owner gave notice in writing to the tenant that possession might be recovered under this Case;

***Paragraph numbers marked with a "+" can be found online and on CD.***

(d) the dwelling-house has not, since the commencement of section 67 of the Act of 1980 been let by the owner on a protected tenancy with respect to which the condition mentioned in paragraph (c) above was not satisfied; and

(e) the court is of the opinion that—

(i) the dwelling-house is required as a residence for the owner; or

(ii) of the conditions set out in Part V of this Schedule one of those in paragraphs (c) to (f) is satisfied.

If the court is of the opinion that, notwithstanding that the condition in paragraph (c) or (d) above is not complied with, it is just and equitable to make an order for possession of the dwelling-house, the court may dispense with the requirements of either or both of these paragraphs, as the case may require.

For the purposes of this Case "regular armed forces of the Crown" has the same meaning as in section 1 of the House of Commons Disqualification Act 1975.

## PART III

## PROVISIONS APPLICABLE TO CASE 9 AND PART II OF THIS SCHEDULE

*Provision for Case 9*

1. A court shall not make an order for possession of a dwelling-house by reason only that the circumstances of the case fall within Case 9 in Part I of this Schedule if the court is satisfied that, having regard to all the circumstances of the case, including the question whether other accommodation is available for the landlord or the tenant, greater hardship would be caused by granting the order than by refusing to grant it. **3A–267**

*Provision for Part II*

2. Any reference in Part II of this Schedule to the relevant date shall be construed as follows— **3A–268**

(a) except in a case falling within paragraph (b) or (c) below, if the protected tenancy, or, in the case of a statutory tenancy, the previous contractual tenancy, was created before December 8, 1965, the relevant date means June 7, 1966; and

(b) except in a case falling within paragraph (c) below, if the tenancy became a regulated tenancy by virtue of section 14 of the Counter-Inflation Act 1973 and the tenancy or, in the case of a statutory tenancy, the previous contractual tenancy, was created before March 22, 1973, the relevant date means September 22, 1973; and

(c) in the case of a regulated furnished tenancy, if the tenancy, or, in the case of a statutory furnished tenancy, the previous contractual tenancy was created before August 14, 1974, the relevant date means February 13, 1975; and

(d) in any other case, the relevant date means the date of the commencement of the regulated tenancy in question.

## PART IV

## SUITABLE ALTERNATIVE ACCOMMODATION

3. For the purposes of section 98(1)(a) of this Act, a certificate of the local housing authority for the district in which the dwelling-house in question is situated, certifying that the authority will provide suitable alternative accommodation for the tenant by a date specified in the certificate, shall be conclusive evidence that suitable alternative accommodation will be available for him by that date. **3A–269**

4.—(1) Where no such certificate as is mentioned in paragraph 3 above is produced to the court, accommodation shall be deemed to be suitable for the purposes of section 98(1)(a) of this Act if it consists of either—

(a) premises which are to be let as a separate dwelling such that they will then be let on a protected tenancy (other than one under which the landlord might recover possession of the dwelling-house under one of the cases in Part II of this Schedule), or

***Paragraph numbers marked with a "+" can be found online and on CD.***

(b) premises to be let as a separate dwelling on terms which will, in the opinion of the court, afford to the tenant security of tenure reasonably equivalent to the security afforded by Part VII of this Act in the case of a protected tenancy of a kind mentioned in paragraph (a) above,

and, in the opinion of the court, the accommodation fulfils the relevant conditions as defined in paragraph 5 below.

(2) […]

5.—(1) For the purposes of paragraph 4 above, the relevant conditions are that the accommodation is reasonably suitable to the needs of the tenant and his family as regards proximity to place of work, and either—

(a) similar as regards rental and extent to the accommodation afforded by dwelling-houses provided in the neighbourhood by any local housing authority for persons whose needs as regards extent are, in the opinion of the court, similar to those of the tenant and of his family; or

(b) reasonably suitable to the means of the tenant and to the needs of the tenant and his family as regards extent and character; and

that if any furniture was provided for use under the protected or statutory tenancy in question, furniture is provided for use in the accommodation which is either similar to that so provided or is reasonably suitable to the needs of the tenant and his family.

(2) For the purposes of sub-paragraph (1)(a) above, a certificate of a housing authority stating—

(a) the extent of the accommodation afforded by dwelling-houses provided by the authority to meet the needs of tenants with families of such number as may be specified in the certificate, and

(b) the amount of the rent charged by the authority for dwelling-houses affording accommodation of that extent,

shall be conclusive evidence of the facts so stated.

6. Accommodation shall not be deemed to be suitable to the needs of the tenant and his family if the result of their occupation of the accommodation would be that it would be an overcrowded dwelling-house for the purposes of Part X of the Housing Act 1985.

7. Any document purporting to be a certificate of a local housing authority named therein issued for the purposes of this Schedule and to be signed by the proper officer of that authority shall be received in evidence and, unless the contrary is shown, shall be deemed to be such a certificate without further proof.

8. In this Part "local housing authority" and "district" in relation to such an authority have the same meaning as in the Housing Act 1985.

## PART V

## PROVISIONS APPLYING TO CASES 11, 12 AND 20

**3A–270** 1. In this Part of this Schedule—

"mortgage" includes a charge and "mortgagee" shall be construed accordingly;

"owner" means, in relation to Case 11, the owner-occupied; and

"successor in title" means any person deriving title from the owner, other than a purchaser for value or a person deriving title from a purchaser for value.

2. The conditions referred to in paragraph (c) in each of Cases 11 and 12 and in paragraph (e)(ii) of Case 20 are that—

(a) the dwelling-house is required as a residence for the owner or any member of his family who resided with the owner when he last occupied the dwelling-house as a residence;

(b) the owner has retired from regular employment and requires the dwelling-house as a residence;

(c) the owner has died and the dwelling-house is required as a residence for a member of his family who was residing with him at the time of his death;

(d) the owner has died and the dwelling-house is required by a successor in title as his residence or for the purpose of disposing of it with vacant possession;

(e) the dwelling-house is subject to a mortgage, made by deed and granted before the tenancy, and the mortgagee—

(i) is entitled to exercise a power of sale conferred on him by the mortgage or by section 101 of the Law of Property Act 1925; and

(ii) requires the dwelling-house for the purpose of disposing of it with vacant possession in exercise of that power; and

(f) the dwelling-house is not reasonably suitable to the needs of the owner, having regard to his place of work, and he requires it for the purpose of disposing of it with vacant possession and of using the proceeds of that disposal in acquiring, as his residence, a dwelling-house which is more suitable to those needs.

*Note* —Amended by the Housing Act 1980 ss.55, 66 and 67, Schs 7, 8 and 25; the Housing (Consequential Provisions) Act 1985 s.4, Sch.2, para.35; the Rent (Amendment) Act 1985 ss.1, 66; the Housing and Planning Act 1986 s.13; the Housing Act 1988 s.140, Sch.18; and the Civil Partnership Act 2004 s.81 and Sch.8, para.14. **3A–271**

Schedule 15 should be read in conjunction with s.98 (see para.3A–182).

**Cases 1 to 10 are discretionary grounds**

The court may only make a possession order if it considers it reasonable to do so and the court has discretion to suspend any order in accordance with s.100 (see above). Cases 11 to 19 are mandatory grounds—if the ground is proved, the court must make a possession order to take effect in 14 days, or if there is exceptional hardship, a maximum of 42 days (see the Housing Act 1980 s.89, below). **3A–272**

**Case 1**

A landlord must prove either that there are rent arrears or that there has been a breach of a term or other obligation of the tenancy. **3A–273**

*Rent arrears* —A landlord must prove two things, first that rent was lawfully due from the tenant and second that some rent remained unpaid, at the date of issue of the claim. This applies only to rent which is due from the actual tenant against whom possession is claimed and not to that due from a predecessor of the present tenant (*Tickner v Clifton* [1929] 1 K.B. 207). Rent becomes lawfully due at midnight on the day when it is payable (*Aspinall v Aspinall* [1961] Ch. 526). If rent is tendered after the due date, but before the commencement of proceedings, that prevents rent from being "lawfully due" unless time has been made the essence of the contract. The words "lawfully due" mean that the obligation to pay rent must have arisen and not been discharged (*Bird v Hildage* [1948] 1 K.B. 91; [1947] 2 All E.R. 7, CA). However, once a landlord shows that there were arrears of rent at the commencement of proceedings, the court has jurisdiction to make a possession order even if rent arrears are paid before the hearing (*Dellenty v Pellow* [1951] 2 K.B. 858; [1951] 2 All E.R. 716, CA). Prima facie it would not ordinarily be reasonable to make a possession order in such circumstances (see *Hayman v Rowlands* [1957] 1 W.L.R. 317; [1957] 1 All E.R. 321, CA) but where the tenant has frequently been in arrears and proceedings have been issued on a number of occasions, it may be reasonable to make a possession order (*Dellenty v Pellow*, above. See too *Lee-Steere v Jennings* (1987) 20 H.L.R. 1, CA). See also *Laimond Properties Ltd v Raeuchle*, also reported as *Raeuchle v Laimond Properties Ltd (Suspension of Possession Order)* (2001) 33 H.L.R. 10. **3A–274**

Failure to provide a rent book does not disentitle a landlord from recovering rent (*Shaw v Groom* [1970] 2 Q.B. 504; [1970] 2 W.L.R. 299; [1970] 1 All E.R. 702, CA).

*Breach of any other tenancy obligation* —This limb of Case 1 is similar to the Housing Act 1988 Sch.2, Ground 12 (see below). **3A–275**

It should be noted that the original terms of the contractual tenancy continue to bind a statutory tenant in so far as they are consistent with the provisions of the Rent Act 1977 (see s.3(1) above).

A proviso in a contractual tenancy giving the landlord a right of re-entry if the tenant becomes bankrupt is an obligation under the subsequent statutory tenancy within the meaning of Case 1 *Cadogan Estates Ltd v McMahon* [2001] A.C. 378; [2000] 3 W.L.R. 1555; [2000] 4 All E.R. 897, HL.

**Case 2**

*Nuisance or annoyance* —"Nuisance" and "annoyance" are both used in the natural **3A–276**

***Paragraph numbers marked with a "+" can be found online and on CD.***

sense of the words. This ground may be satisfied by drunkenness, abusive behaviour, noise, obstructive behaviour towards other occupiers or violence (per Wood J. in *Cobstone Investments Ltd v Maxim* [1984] 2 All E.R. 635). Unknown people coming to the premises at all hours of the day and night may amount to an annoyance (*Florent v Horez* (1984) 12 H.L.R. 1; (1983) 268 E.G. 807, CA).

It is not necessary for the premises of people complaining of nuisance or annoyance to be contiguous in the sense that they are physically joined to the dwelling-house rented by a defendant. The word "adjoining" is used in the wider sense of "neighbouring" (*Cobstone Investments Ltd v Maxim* [1985] Q.B. 140; [1983] 3 W.L.R. 563; [1984] 2 All E.R. 635, CA). See too *Northampton BC v Lovatt* (1998) 30 H.L.R. 875; (1998) 07 E.G. 142; *The Times*, January 3, 1998, CA.

**3A–277** *Immoral of illegal purposes* —Where a landlord relies upon a conviction for using the dwelling-house or allowing the dwelling-house to be used for immoral or illegal purposes it is necessary to show that the crime has actually been committed on the premises and that the premises have been used for the purpose of committing the offence (*Abrahams v Wilson* [1971] 2 Q.B. 88; [1971] 2 W.L.R. 923; [1971] 2 All E.R. 114, CA). For example, there is a difference between drugs being in a defendant's immediate possession, on the one hand, and on the other hand the tenant using the premises to store drugs.

In a claim for possession based on nuisance or annoyance to adjoining occupiers, a judge may infer that adjoining occupiers have been affected, even if none of them gives evidence of actual nuisance (*Frederick Platts Co Ltd v Grigor* [1950] 1 All E.R. 941, CA).

**Case 3**

**3A–278** This ground is similar to Ground 13 in the Housing Act 1988 Sch.2, see below.

There is no need for a landlord to give advance warning of an intention to issue proceedings relying on this ground (*Lowe v Lendrum* (1950) 159 E.G. 423, CA) although failure to do so may be relevant when the court considers reasonableness and costs. See too *Holloway v Povey* (1984) 15 H.L.R. 104; (1984) 271 E.G. 195, CA.

**Case 5**

**3A–279** There must be a valid notice to quit before a landlord can rely on this ground for possession (*De Vries v Sparks* (1927) 137 L.T. 441). The words "notice to quit" have their normal technical meaning and the disappearance of a tenant followed by the return by him of the keys does not amount to "notice to quit" (*Standingford v Bruce* [1926] 1 K.B. 466).

**Case 6**

**3A–280** The ground applies even if there is no prohibition against assigning or subletting in the tenancy agreement and covers a vesting assent made by executors of a deceased tenant which takes effect as an assignment (*Pazgate Ltd v McGrath* (1985) 17 H.L.R. 127). It does not however apply unless all of the premises rented have been disposed of by assigning or subletting. In practice the ground is normally only of significance where there is subletting or assignment by a contractual tenant. If a statutory tenant sublets the whole of premises, Rent Act protection is lost because the tenant can no longer occupy the premises as his or her residence (see s.2 above, and *Poland v Cadogan (Earl)* [1980] 3 All E.R. 544, CA, dealing with similar provisions in the Leasehold Reform Act 1967 where the comparable wording is slightly different).

**Case 8**

**3A–281** This ground for possession is far more restrictive than Ground 16 in Sch.2 to the Housing Act 1988 (see below) which applies to assured tenants.

In order to succeed under this ground a landlord must prove that—

(a) *the tenant was in the employment of the landlord or a former landlord at the time when the premises were let* (*Fuggle (RF) Ltd v Gadsden* [1948] 2 K.B. 236). "Tenant" refers to the original contractual tenant (*Bolsover Colliery Co Ltd v Abbott* [1946] K.B. 8);

(b) *premises were let in consequence of that employment*. This is a question of fact in each case (*Long Eaton Co-op. v Smith* [1949] 1 All E.R. 633). The questions to be asked are—

***Paragraph numbers marked with a "+" can be found online and on CD.***

(i) "What was the reason for the landlord letting the premises to the tenant?"

(ii) "What was in the mind of the person who let the premises?"

(iii) "Was it let because of the tenant's employment or was there another reason?"

(*Braithwaite & Co Ltd v Elliot* [1946] 2 All E.R. 537 at 539);

(c) *employment has ceased*; and

(d) *the premises are reasonably required by the landlord for occupation as a residence by someone engaged in the whole-time employment of the landlord or someone with whom a contract of employment has been entered into which is conditional on housing being provided*. When the court considers whether or not the proposed new occupant is employed or whether a contract of employment has been entered into, the relevant date is the date of the court hearing (*Benninga v Bijstra* [1945] 2 All E.R. 433). Note that the premises must be reasonably required.

A tenant may be entitled to compensation if a landlord obtains an order for possession under Case 8 by misrepresentation or concealment. See s.102 above.

**Case 9**

*"Reasonably required"*—Case 9 applies where the premises are reasonably required as a residence by the landlord or certain specified members of the landlord's family. The words "reasonably required" mean more than a "desire" on the landlord's part, but less than "absolute necessity" (*Aitken v Shaw* 1933 S.L.T. (SHCT) 21; *Kennealy v Dunne* [1977] Q.B. 837). The court should consider whether this requirement is reasonable on the landlord's part, and in doing so the tenant's interests are not relevant (*Funnell v Armstrong* [1962] E.G.D. 319). The relevant date for deciding whether the premises are required is the date of the hearing, not the date of commencement of proceedings (*Alexander v Mohamadzadeh* (1985) 276 E.G. 1258, CA). **3A–282**

Where there are two or more joint beneficial owners, possession can be claimed under Case 9 only if possession is required for occupation as a residence for all or both of them (*McIntyre v Hardcastle* [1948] 2 K.B. 82; [1948] 1 All E.R. 696, CA. The position is different under Case 11—see *Tilling v Whiteman* [1979] 1 All E.R. 737, HL).

**Landlord by purchase**

Landlords are not entitled to rely on Case 9 if they became landlords by purchasing the premises after specified dates. **3A–283**

**"Greater hardship"**

Tenants have a complete defence to possession proceedings brought under Case 9 if they can prove that greater hardship would be caused to them by a possession order than would be caused to the landlord by refusing to grant the possession order. The burden of proving this lies on the tenant (*Smith v Penny* [1947] K.B. 230; [1946] 2 All E.R. 672, CA; *Sims v Wilson* [1946] 2 All E.R. 261). The court should consider how the balance of hardship will operate at the time when a possession order would take effect (*Wheeler v Evans* [1948] 1 K.B. 459). The "greater hardship test" gives the court a very wide discretion to take into account all factors which may affect both landlord and tenant (*Robinson v Donovan* [1946] 2 All E.R. 731). **3A–284**

Questions of greater hardship are essentially matters for county court judges, and their findings will normally only be overturned if no reasonable county court judge could have reached the same conclusion or if the decision was perverse. (*Hodges v Blee* (1987) 283 E.G. 1215; (1988) 20 H.L.R. 32, CA; *cf.*, however, *Manaton v Edwards* (1985) 276 E.G. 1256, CA, where, unusually, a county court judge's finding on greater hardship was overturned on appeal).

A tenant may be entitled to compensation if a landlord obtains an order for possession under Case 9 by misrepresentation or concealment. See s.102 above.

**Case 11**

This ground should be read in conjunction with Sch.15, Pt III, and Pt V. **3A–285**

The purpose of Case 11 was to allow owner-occupiers who intended to go away for a limited period but then to return home, to let the premises while they were away (per Griffiths L.J. in *Bradshaw v Baldwin-Wiseman* (1985) 17 H.L.R. 260; (1985) 49 P.&C.R. 382 at 264).

To rely on Case 11 a landlord must prove that—

(a) *prior to the granting of the tenancy in question, the landlord had at some time in the past occupied the premises as his or her residence.* It is no longer necessary for landlords to prove that they occupied the premises immediately before the granting of the tenancy. Residence at any time in the past is sufficient. It is sufficient for such previous residence to have been temporary and intermittent, although visits to a house by a landlord to stay with a girlfriend who lives there do not count as "occupation as a residence"(*Naish v Curzon* (1984) 17 H.L.R. 220, CA; *Mistry v Isidore* (1990) 22 H.L.R. 281; [1990] 2 E.G.L.R. 97, CA; and *Ibie v Trubshaw* (1990) 22 H.L.R. 191, CA);

(b) *notice of his or her intention to rely on Case 11 was given before the commencement of the tenancy.* The schedule provides that such notice must be in writing, although no particular form is necessary. It has been said that it is "of the utmost importance to a tenant that he should appreciate when he takes rented property whether or not he is obtaining security of tenure" (*Bradshaw v Baldwin-Wiseman*, above). Alternatively, the landlord may satisfy the court that it is just and equitable to dispense with service of the notice. The criteria which apply are the same as under the Housing Act 1988 Sch.2, Pt I and the Housing Act 1985 s.83(1)(b) (as amended) (see below).

(c) *all tenants to whom the premises have previously been let since the dates specified in Case 11 have been given written notice.* Again there is a provision which entitles the court to dispense with this requirement if it is considered just and equitable; and

(d) *one of the requirements in* sub-paragraphs (a), (c), (d), (e) or (f) in Sch.15, Pt V *is satisfied.* The most important of these is that the premises are "required as a residence". All that is required is that the landlord "bona fide wants" or "genuinely has the immediate intention" of occupying the premises (*Kennealy v Dunne* [1977] Q.B. 837, CA). The landlord need not require the premises as a permanent residence and fairly intermittent residence will be sufficient (*Naish v Curzon* (1984) 17 H.L.R. 220, CA; and *Davies v Peterson* (1989) 21 H.L.R. 63; (1989) 06 E.G. 130, CA). This is a question of fact in each case. It is sufficient if only one of two joint landlords requires the premises as a residence (*Tilling v Whiteman* [1979] 1 All E.R. 737, HL).

**Case 13**

**3A–286** *"right to occupy it for a holiday"* —See s.9 and commentary thereto, above.

**Case 14**

**3A–287** See s.8 and annotations thereto, above.

**Case 16**

**3A–288** The court cannot dispense with the requirement that notice must be served prior to the commencement of the tenancy. A term in a tenancy agreement that the tenant will vacate on 28 days' notice if the premises are required for another farm worker is not sufficient (*Fowler v Minchin* (1987) 19 H.L.R. 224, CA), but a certificate of fair rent which was handed to the tenant before the commencement of the tenancy and which stated that the tenancy was to be subject to Case 16 has been held to be sufficient (*Springfield Investments v Bell* (1990) 22 H.L.R. 440, CA).

***Paragraph numbers marked with a "+" can be found online and on CD.***

# Housing Act 1980

(1980 c.51) 3A-289

ARRANGEMENT OF SECTIONS

PART IV

JURISDICTION AND PROCEDURE



## PART IV

## JURISDICTION AND PROCEDURE

### Discretion of court in certain proceedings for possession

**88.**—(1) Where, under the terms of a rental purchase agreement, a person has been let into possession of a dwelling-house and, on the termination of the agreement or of his right to possession under it, proceedings are brought for the possession of the dwelling-house, the court may— 3A-290

(a) adjourn the proceedings; or

(b) on making an order for the possession of the dwelling-house, stay or suspend execution of the order or postpone the date of possession;

for such period or periods as the court thinks fit.

(2) On any such adjournment, stay, suspension or postponement the court may impose such conditions with regard to payments by the person in possession in respect of his continued occupation of the dwelling-house and such other conditions as the court thinks fit.

(3) The court may revoke or from time to time vary any condition imposed by virtue of this section.

(4) In this section "rental purchase agreement" means an agreement for the purchase of a dwelling-house (whether freehold or leasehold property) under which the whole or part of the purchase price is to be paid in three or more instalments and the completion of the purchase is deferred until the whole or a specified part of the purchase price has been paid.

(5) This section extends to proceedings for the possession of a dwelling-house which were begun before the commencement of this section unless an order for the possession of the dwelling-house was made in the proceedings and executed before the commencement of this section.

**"rental purchase agreement"**

See s.88(4). 3A-291

### Restriction on discretion of court in making orders for possession of land

**89.**—(1) Where a court makes an order for the possession of any land in a case not falling within the exceptions mentioned in subsec- 3A-292 tion (2) below, the giving up of possession shall not be postponed (whether by the order or any variation, suspension or stay of execution) to a date later than fourteen days after the making of the order, unless it appears to the court that exceptional hardship would be caused by requiring possession to be given up by that date; and shall not in any event be postponed to a date later than six weeks after the making of the order.

(2) The restrictions in subsection (1) above do not apply if—

(a) the order is made in an action by a mortgagee for possession; or

(b) the order is made in an action for forfeiture of a lease; or

(c) the court had power to make the order only if it considered it reasonable to make it; or

(d) the order relates to a dwelling-house which is the subject of a restricted contract (within the meaning of section 19 of the 1977 Act); or

(e) the order is made in proceedings brought as mentioned in section 88(1) above.

**Restriction on discretion of court in making orders for possession of land**

**3A–293** At common law judges had a discretion to allow occupiers a reasonable time before a possession order took effect even if they had no security of tenure (*Air Ministry v Harris* [1951] 2 All E.R. 862 (six months too long for licensees); *Sheffield Corp v Luxford* [1929] 2 K.B. 180 (one year too long); *Jones v Savery* [1951] 1 All E.R. 820 (one month reasonable)). However, this discretion was largely taken away by the Housing Act 1980. Apart from the exceptions contained in the section, orders for possession must now take effect not later than 14 days after the making of the order unless it would cause exceptional hardship, in which case the order can be postponed to a date which is not more than six weeks after the making of the order.

There are no reported decisions on the meaning of "exceptional hardship".

In *Hackney LBC v Side by Side (Kids) Ltd* [2003] EWHC 1813 (QBD); [2004] 1 W.L.R. 363, Stanley Burnton J. held that Housing Act 1980 s.89 applies as much to orders made in the High Court as to those made in the county court. The decision of Harman J. in *Bain & Co v Church Commissioners for England* [1989] 1 W.L.R. 24, Ch D, that "a court" meant "a county court" was clearly wrong. Further, Stanley Burnton J. held that the general words of s.89 "did not permit him to find that it did not apply to consent orders".

Section 89 does not restrict the power of the court to grant a stay pending appeal. (*Admiral Taverns (Cygnet) Ltd v Daniel and Daly* [2008] EWCA Civ 1501;[2009] 4 All E.R. 71).

## Senior Courts Act 1981

**3A–293.1** (1981 c.54)

ARRANGEMENT OF SECTIONS



### Relief against forfeiture for non-payment of rent

**3A–294** **38.**—(1) In any action in the High Court for the forfeiture of a lease for non-payment rent, the court shall have power to grant relief against forfeiture in a summary manner, and may do so subject to

*Paragraph numbers marked with a "+" can be found online and on CD.*

the same terms and conditions as to the payment of rent, costs or otherwise as could have been imposed by it in such an action immediately before the commencement of this Act.

(2) Where the lessee or a person deriving title under him is granted relief under this section, he shall hold the demised premises in accordance with the terms of the lease without the necessity for a new lease.

**Relief against forfeiture for non-payment of rent**

Relief from forfeiture for non-payment of rent may be obtained under the Common Law Procedure Act 1852 ss.210 to 212, or in a summary way under s.38 of the 1981 Act. **3A–295**

> "The Court, in exercising its jurisdiction to grant relief in cases of non-payment of rent is, of course, proceeding on the old principles of the Court of Equity which always regarded the condition of re-entry as being merely security for the payment of the rent and gave relief if the landlord could get his rent" (*Chandless-Chandless v Nicholson* [1942] 2 K.B. 321, CA, at 323 per Lord Greene M.R.).

Save in exceptional circumstances, therefore, the court grants relief where all the rent and costs have been paid or tendered (*Gill v Lewis* [1956] 2 Q.B. 1, CA).

Where an order is made giving relief in terms to be performed within a specified time, the court has power to extend the time, even though the original order did not expressly reserve "liberty to apply" (see *Chandless-Chandless v Nicholson*, above). Since the court can grant relief under this section in the exercise of the same powers as it could "immediately before the commencement of this Act," if relief from forfeiture is granted, the lessee will hold the demised premises according to the terms of the lease and without the necessity of any new lease (see s.46 of the Supreme Court of Judicature (Consolidation) Act 1925).

A statutory tenant under the Rent Act cannot claim relief under this section or s.146 of the LPA 1925 (see *Brewer v Jacobs* [1923] 1 K.B. 528).

As to relief against breaches of other covenants, see the LPA 1925 s.146.

Note also the County Courts Act 1984 s.138 (Provisions as to forfeiture for non-payment of rent), para.3A–297, below, and notes thereto, and, in particular, the explanation there of the effect of, and the legislative response to, *Di Palma v Victoria Square Property Co Ltd* [1986] Ch. 150; [1985] 2 All E.R. 676, CA.

## County Courts Act 1984

(1984 c.28) **3A–296**

Arrangement of Sections

*Forfeiture for non-payment of rent*



*Forfeiture for non-payment of rent*

### Provisions as to forfeiture for non-payment of rent

**138.**—(1) This section has effect where a lessor is proceeding by action in a county court (being an action in which the county court has jurisdiction) to enforce against a lessee a right of re-entry or forfeiture in respect of any land for non-payment of rent. **3A–297**

(2) If the lessee pays into court or to the lessor not less than 5 clear days before the return day all the rent in arrear and the costs of

Housing

the action, the action shall cease, and the lessee shall hold the land according to the lease without any new lease.

(3) If—

(a) the action does not cease under subsection (2); and

(b) the court at the trial is satisfied that the lessor is entitled to enforce the right of re-entry or forfeiture,

the court shall order possession of the land to be given to the lessor at the expiration of such period, not being less than 4 weeks from the date of the order, as the court thinks fit, unless within that period the lessee pays into court or to the lessor all the rent in arrear and the costs of the action.

(4) The court may extend the period specified under subsection (3) at any time before possession of the land is recovered in pursuance of the order under that subsection.

(5) [...] if—

(a) within the period specified in the order; or

(b) within that period as extended under subsection (4),

the lessee pays into court or to the lessor—

(i) all the rent in arrear; and

(ii) the costs of the action,

he shall hold the land acording to the lease without any new lease.

(6) Subsection (2) shall not apply where the lessor is proceeding in the same action to enforce a right of re-entry or forfeiture on any other ground as well as for non-payment of rent, or to enforce any other claim as well as the right of re-entry or forfeiture and the claim for arrears of rent.

(7) If the lessee does not—

(a) within the period specified in the order; or

(b) with that period as extended under subsection (4), pay into court or to the lessor—

(i) all the rent in arrear; and

(ii) the costs of the action,

the order shall be enforceable in the prescribed manner and so long as the order remains unreversed the lessee shall, subject to subsections (8) and (9A), be barred from all relief.

(8) The extension under subsection (4) of a period fixed by a court shall not be treated as relief from which the lessee is barred by subsection (7) if he fails to pay into court or to the lessor all the rent in arrear and the costs of the action within that period.

(9) Where the court extends a period under subsection (4) at a time when—

(a) that period has expired; and

(b) a warrant has been issued for the possession of the land, the court shall suspend the warrant for the extended period; and, if before the expiration period, the lessee pays into court or to the lessor all the rent in arrear and all the costs of the action, the court shall cancel the warrant.

***Paragraph numbers marked with a "+" can be found online and on CD.***

(9A) Where the lessor recovers possession of the land at any time after the making of the order under subsection (3) (whether as a result of the enforcement of the order or otherwise) the lessee may, at any time within six months from the date on which the lessor recovers possession, apply to the court for relief; and on any such application the court may, if it thinks fit, grant to the lessee such relief, subject to such terms and conditions, as it thinks fit.

(9B) Where the lessee is granted relief on an application under subsection (9A) he shall hold the land according to the lease without any new lease.

(9C) An application under subsection (9A) may be made by a person with an interest under a lease of the land derived (whether immediately or otherwise) from the lessee's interest therein in like manner as if he were the lessee; and on any such application the court may make an order which (subject to such terms and conditions as the court thinks fit) vests the land in such a person, as lessee of the lessor, for the remainder of the term of the lease under which he has any such interest as aforesaid, or for any lesser term.

In this subsection any reference to the land includes a reference to a part of the land.

(10) Nothing in this section or section 139 shall be taken to affect—

(a) the power of the court to make any order which it would otherwise have power to make as respects a right of re-entry or forfeiture on any ground other than non-payment of rent; or

(b) section 146(4) of the Law of Property Act 1925 (relief against forfeiture).

*Note* —Amended by the Administration of Justice Act 1985 ss.55 and 67(2), and Sch.8; and the Courts and Legal Services Act 1990 s.125(2), Sch.17, para.17. **3A–298**

See Form **N27** (*Civil Procedure Forms Volume*).

**General note**

Forfeiture is a remedy which may be available to a lessor against a lessee prior to expiry of a fixed term lease; it has the effect of dispossessing the lessee. The remedy may be available, not only where the lessee fails to pay rent, but also in other circumstances (e.g. breach of any other covenant). This section has effect where a lessor is proceeding by action in a county court to enforce against a lessee a right of re-entry or forfeiture in respect of any land for non-payment of rent. Where proceedings to enforce a right of re-entry or forfeiture are brought for non-payment of rent and for some other reason, or for some other reason alone, the Law of Property Act 1925 s.146 is likely to apply. The 1925 Act may also apply where land has been forfeited, not by action, but by the lessor's re-entry without action; see also s.139(2), below. **3A–299**

Peaceable re-entry of premises "let as a dwelling" is unlawful while there is "any person lawfully residing in them or any part of them" (see the Protection from Eviction Act 1977 s.2, above). In such circumstances possession proceedings must be brought in court.

For the restriction on forfeiture or re-entry for arrears of service charges see the Housing Act 1996 s.81, below.

In relation to proceedings in the High Court, legislation dealing with forfeiture for non-payment of rent is found in the Common Law Procedure Act 1852 ss.210 to 212 (re-enacting provisions in the Landlord and Tenant Act 1730). But this legislation is not as elaborate as s.138; case law supplies the deficiencies. Note also the SCA 1981 s.38 (summary relief against forfeiture for non-payment of rent) (see para.3A–294 and commentary thereto).

***Paragraph numbers marked with a "+" can be found online and on CD.***

In the CCA 1959, provisions as to the enforcement by action of a right of re-entry or forfeiture for non-payment of rent were found in s.191 (as amended by the Administration of Justice Act 1965 s.23). This section created certain difficulties, not all of which were remedied by the re-enactment of s.191, with some modifications, as s.138 of the 1984 Act. Consequently, the Administration of Justice Act 1985 s.55 added subss.(9A) to (9C) and made some minor amendments to subss.(5) and (7). The principal difficulty which had arisen was that the extent of the powers of the High Court, on the one hand, and of the county courts, on the other, differed and the relationship between the respective powers was a matter for doubt (see *Di Palma v Victoria Square Property Co Ltd* [1986] Ch. 150; [1985] 2 All E.R. 676, CA).

As a result of the Courts and Legal Services Act 1990 s.1 and Orders made under that section certain financial limits on the jurisdiction of county courts in relation to actions of the type referred to in subs.(1) of this section were removed and the jurisdictions of the High Court and the county courts became, in effect, co-terminous. At the same time, for the purpose of removing unnecessary distinctions between the two levels of jurisdiction, the words "or to the lessor" were added to subss.(2), (3), (5), (7), (8) and (9) by Sch.17, para.17 of the 1990 Act.

In effect, s.138 codifies an old equitable jurisdiction. The policy of the law stated in the section is to give lessees, against whom a right of re-entry or forfeiture may be enforced by a lessor for non-payment of rent, protections he would not otherwise enjoy, and which have the potential for enabling him to continue in occupation as lessee; where the protections apply, the lessee is relieved against forfeiture.

The section has no application to a case where there are arrears of service charges not deemed by the terms of the lease to be additional rent (*Escalus Properties Ltd v Robinson* [1996] Q.B. 231; [1995] 3 W.L.R. 524, CA).

Service by the lessor on the lessee of a notice under the Law of Property Act 1925 s.146, forfeiting a lease on grounds other than non-payment of rent, does not prevent the lessor subsequently claiming from the lessee under s.138 forfeiture for non-payment of rent due before service of the notice (*Church Commissioners for England v Nodjoumi* (1986) 51 P. & C.R. 155).

The broad scheme of s.138 is as follows. Subsection (2) states that, where a lessor brings an action to enforce a right of re-entry of forfeiture for non-payment of rent (but not for some other reason) and the action is not a mixed claim (see subs.(6)), then if the lessee pays arrears and costs within the time stipulated in that subsection he is relieved from forfeiture automatically; the action shall "cease" and the lease shall continue. Subss.(3) to (5) state that if the tenant does not so pay up and the court at trial is satisfied that the lessor is entitled to his remedy the court shall suspend the order for possession giving the lessee further time to pay. The time limit may be extended (and any warrant for possession suspended accordingly, see subs.(9)). If the tenant pays during the period of suspension, again he is relieved from forfeiture automatically (and any warrant is cancelled, see subs.(9)). If the tenant fails to pay, subs.(7) comes into play. This provision states that in these circumstances the order shall be enforceable in the prescribed manner and so long as the order remains unreversed the lessee shall "be barred from all relief", not only relief in any county court but also in the High Court. The lessor may proceed with a warrant for possession for the purpose of recovering possession. However, even in this event, from the tenant's point of view, all is not lost. At this late stage, if the lessor has not recovered possession (in pursuance of an order under subs.(3)), the tenant may still apply under subs.(4) for an extension (or a further extension) of the period for suspension of the order for possession fixed under subs.(3). It has been held in a county court that the divorced wife of a lessee, although not herself a lessee within the meaning of s.138, was a beneficial co-owner and so entitled to apply for an extension of time under s.138(4) and to pay the arrears on behalf of the lessee (*Bassett Road HA v Gough* [1998] 5 C.L.Y. 3653, Central London County Court). Further, if the lessor has recovered possession (whether as a result of the enforcement of the order or otherwise) the lessee may at any time within six months from the date on which the lessor recovered possession, apply to the court for relief (subs.(9A)). On such application relief is not automatic but discretionary; the court may grant relief as it thinks fit. (An application under subs.(9A) may be made by a person with an interest under a lease of land derived from the lessee's interest, subs.(9C), see further below.) In these two respects the lessee is not, in the terms of subs.(7), "barred from all relief" for his failure to pay within the period specified in the order for possession or as extended (as the case may be).

**"lessor","lessee","lease"**

For definitions, see s.140(1). "Lessee" includes mortgagee (*United Dominions Trust Ltd v Shellpoint Trustees Ltd* [1993] 4 All E.R. 310, CA). **3A-300**

**Service of claim**

If (a) one-half-year's rent is in arrear at the time of the commencement of the action, and (b) the lessor has a right to re-enter for non-payment of that rent, and (c) no sufficient distress is to be found on the premises countervailing the arrears then due, the service of the claim in the action shall stand in lieu of a demand and re-entry (s.139(1)). As to proof of insufficient distress, see *Rickett v Green* [1910] 1 K.B. 253. **3A-301**

**"not less than 5 clear days before the return day" (subs.(2))**

Section 147(1) states that "return day" means the day appointed in any summons or proceeding for the appearance of the defendant or any other day fixed for the hearing of any proceedings. In subs.(2) "return day" means the day so fixed, and not any later date upon which the action would fall actually to be tried in the absence of a payment under the subsection (*Swordheath Properties Ltd v Bolt* [1992] 2 E.G.L.R. 68; [1992] 38 E.G. 152, CA, following *R. v Registrar of the County Court at Leeds* (1885–86) L.R. 16 Q.B.D. 691, DC). **3A-302**

**Lessee paying into court or to lessor (subss.(2), (3), (5), (7), (8) & (9))**

Where payment into court or (semble) to the lessor of arrears of rent and costs is made by a person other than the lessee and that person does not make the payment on behalf of the lessee (e.g. an underlessee or mortgagee), the action does not "cease" by operation of subs.(2) as "lessee" in that subsection means the lessee against whom the action is brought as referred to in subs.(1) (*Matthews v Dobbins* [1963] 1 W.L.R. 227; [1963] 1 All E.R. 417, CA). **3A-303**

**"the court shall order possession" (subs.(3))**

Subsection (3) states that, if (a) the action does not cease under subs.(2), and (b) the court at the trial is satisfied that the lessor is entitled to enforce the right of re-entry or forfeiture, "the court shall order possession of the land". Where without doubt a lessor has established his claim he should be given judgment and the trial should not be adjourned against the wishes of the lessor except for good reason (*R. v Circuit Judge (sitting at Norwich Court) Ex p. Wathen* (1977) 33 P. & C.R. 423; (1976) 238 E.G. 45—in that case to give the lessee the opportunity to pay off the arrears). **3A-304**

**Possession to be given at expiration of specified period**

An order for possession under subs.(3) must be suspended as provided by that subsection. Subsection (4) provides that the period may be extended at any time before possession of the land is recovered "in pursuance of the order" under subs.(3). There is some authority for the proposition that recovery of possession "in pursuance of the order" means recovery under a warrant for possession and not by other means (*Gadsby and Mitchell v Price and Harrison* [1985] C.L.Y. 1877). **3A-305**

**"lessee pays...all the rent in arrear" (subss.(2), (3), (5), (7) & (9))**

The lease comes to an end when the claim is served. Rent is payable to the date of service and mesne profits thereafter. To facilitate the calculation of rent payable to date of service where rent is paid in arrears, the particulars of claim should state the daily rate at which the rent in arrear is to be calculated (PD 55 para.2.3(3)). Where the rent is payable in advance the lessor is entitled to be paid any rent due on a rent day which falls between issue and service (*Canas Property Co v KL Television Services* [1970] 2 Q.B. 433; [1970] 2 All E.R. 795, CA, see also *Capital and City Holdings Ltd v Dean Warburg Ltd* (1989) 58 P. & C.R. 346, CA). **3A-306**

In *Maryland Estates v Joseph* [1999] 1 W.L.R. 83; [1998] 3 All E.R. 193, CA, the Court of Appeal, held that the words used in County Courts Act 1984 s.138(3) ("the lessee pays into court ... all the rent in arrear") are not to be construed to mean that the court can order payment only of the rent in arrear at the date of the claim. It is to be assumed that leases continue after service of claims and that tenants remain under an obligation to pay sums reserved in leases as rent and that "all the rent in arrear" means the rent payable up to the date stated in the order.

**Lessee's application for relief under subs.(9A)**

Where the lessor recovers possession at any time after the making of the order for possession under subs.(3), whether as a result of the enforcement of the order or **3A-307**

*Paragraph numbers marked with a "+" can be found online and on CD.*

otherwise (e.g. where the lessee left voluntarily) the lessee may at any time within six months from the date on which the lessor recovers possession apply to the court for relief. Upon such application, the court "may, if it thinks fit, grant to the lessee such relief, subject to such terms and conditions, as it thinks fit". Guidance on the exercise of the power to grant relief was given in *Chandless-Chandless v Nicholson* [1942] 2 K.B. 321; [1942] 2 All E.R. 315, CA, and *Gill v Lewis* [1956] 2 Q.B. 1; [1956] 2 W.L.R. 962, CA. See also *Silverman v AFCO (UK) Ltd* (1988) 56 P. & C.R. 185, CA (very late application made after a new lease to a third party had been executed properly refused); *Varndean Estates Ltd v Buckland and Buckland* (1967) 111 S.J. 684, CA (period of 18 months for the payment of the arrears of rent reasonable in the special circumstances, and arrears should include amount owing under earlier judgment in respect of arrears); *Brompton Securities Ltd (No.2), Re* [1988] 3 All E.R. 677 (save in exceptional circumstances, relief may be granted notwithstanding lessor has been bad payer in past); *Three Stars Property Holdings v Driscoll* [1986] CA Transcript 927; [1988] C.L.Y. 2795 (full payment of costs incurred by lessor may be imposed as a condition notwithstanding lessee legally aided with a nil contribution).

#### Application "by a person with an interest... derived... from the lessee's interest" (subs.(9C))

**3A–308** PD 55 para.2.4 states that where the lessor knows of any person entitled to claim relief against forfeiture as underlessee (including a mortgagee) under subs.(9C) he shall give the name and address of that person in his particulars of claim and file a copy of the particulars for service on him. The holder of a charging order who has registered his interest is "a person with an interest under a lease" and may apply for relief from forfeiture under s.138(9C) (*Croydon (Unique) Ltd v Wright* [2001] Ch. 318; [2000] 2 W.L.R. 683; [1999] 4 All E.R. 257, CA).

An underlessee or mortgagee who fails to avail himself of the procedure for automatic relief provided for by subss.(2) and (5) may, by virtue of subs.(7), be barred from all relief, subject only to his right to apply for discretionary relief under subss.(9A) and (9C) within the specified six month period (*United Dominions Trust Ltd v Shellpoint Trustees Ltd* [1993] 4 All E.R. 310, CA; see also *Escalus Properties Ltd v Robinson* [1996] Q.B. 231; [1995] 3 W.L.R. 524, CA).

#### Law of Property Act 1925 s.146(4)

**3A–309** Section 138 has effect only where proceedings are brought for non-payment of rent. Subsection (10) states that nothing in this section (or in s.139) shall be taken to affect the power of the court to make any order which it would otherwise have power to make as respects a right of re-entry or forfeiture "on any ground other than non-payment of rent". Consequently, for example, the section does not affect the power of the court to grant relief from forfeiture to a lessee under s.146(2) of the 1925 Act, or to under-lessees claiming relief under s.146(4) of that Act. Relief from forfeiture may not be granted to a lessee under s.146(2) in proceedings based only on non-payment of rent (see s.146(11)). However, relief in proceedings based only on non-payment of rent, as well as proceedings based on other grounds (either additionally or alternatively), may be granted to an under-lessee under s.146(4). Because of this distinction between subss.(2) and (4) of s.146 of the 1925 Act subs.(10) of this section further provides that nothing in s.138 (or in s.139) shall be taken to affect s.146(4).

## Service of summons and re-entry

**3A–310** **139.**—(1) In a case where section 138 has effect, if—

(a) one-half-year's rent is in arrear at the time of the commencement of the action; and

(b) the lessor has a right to re-enter for non-payment of that rent; and

(c) no sufficient distress is to be found on the premises countervailing the arrears then due,

the service of the summons in the action in the prescribed manner shall stand in lieu of a demand and re-entry.

***Paragraph numbers marked with a "+" can be found online and on CD.***

(2) Where a lessor has enforced against a lessee, by re-entry without action, a right of re-entry or forfeiture as respects any land for non-payment of rent, the lessee may ... at any time within six months from the date on which the lessor re-entered apply to the county court for relief, and on any such application the court may, if it thinks fit, grant to the lessee such relief as the High Court could have granted.

(3) Subsections (9B) and (C) of section 138 shall have effect in relation to an application under subsection (2) of this section as they have effect in relation to an application under subsection (9A) of that section.

*Note* —Amended by the Administration of Justice Act 1985 s.55; and the High Court and County Courts Jurisdiction Order 1991 (SI 1991/724) Sch., Pt I. **3A–311**

The county court has unlimited jurisdiction.

**"lease", "lessee", "lessor", "under-lease", "under-lessee"**

See s.140. **3A–312**

## Interpretation of sections 138 and 139

**140.** For the purposes of sections 138 and 139— **3A–313**

"lease" includes—

(a) an original or derivative under-lease;

(b) an agreement for a lease where the lessee has become entitled to have his lease granted; and

(c) a grant at a fee farm rent, or under a grant securing a rent by condition;

"lessee" includes—

(a) an original or derivative under-lessee;

(b) the persons deriving title under a lessee;

(c) a grantee under a grant at a fee farm rent, or under a grant securing a rent by condition; and

(d) the persons deriving title under such a grantee;

"lessor" includes—

(a) an original or derivative under-lessor;

(b) the persons deriving title under a lessor;

(c) a person making a grant at a fee farm rent, or a grant securing a rent by condition; and

(d) the persons deriving title under such a grantor;

"under-lease" includes an agreement for an under-lease where the under-lessee has become entitled to have his underlease granted; and

"under-lessee" includes any person deriving title under an under-lessee.

# Housing Act 1985

3A–314 (1985 c.68)

ARRANGEMENT OF SECTIONS

PART I

INTRODUCTORY PROVISIONS

*LOCAL HOUSING AUTHORITIES*



***Paragraph numbers marked with a "+" can be found online and on CD.***

## PART I

## INTRODUCTORY PROVISIONS

### *LOCAL HOUSING AUTHORITIES*

### Local housing authorities

**1.** In this Act "local housing authority" means a district council, a London borough council, the Common Council of the City of London, a Welsh county council or county borough council, or the Council of the Isles of Scilly. **3A–315**

*Note*—Amended by the Local Government (Wales) Act 1994 Sch.8, para.5(1). **3A–316**

* * * *

### *OTHER AUTHORITIES AND BODIES*

### Other descriptions of authority

**4.** In this Act— **3A–317**

(a) "housing authority" means a local housing authority, or a new town corporation;

(b) "new town corporation" means a development corporation or the new towns residuary body;

(c) "development corporation" means a development corporation established by an order made, or having effect as if made, under the New Towns Act 1981;

(d) "urban development corporation" means an urban development corporation established under Part XVI of the Local Government, Planning and Land Act 1980;

(e) "local authority" means a county, county borough, district or London borough council, the Common Council of the City of London or the Council of the Isles of Scilly, in sections 43, 44 and 232 includes the Broads Authority, in sections 438, 441, 442, 443, and 458 includes the Broads Authority and a joint authority

***Paragraph numbers marked with a "+" can be found online and on CD.***

established by Part IV of the Local Government Act 1985 and the London Fire and Emergency Planning Authority, and in sections 45(2)(b), 50(2), 51(6), 80(1), 157(1), 171(2), 573(1), paragraph 2(1) of Schedule 1, grounds 7 and 12 in Schedule 2, ground 5 in Schedule 3, paragraph 7(1) of Schedule 4, paragraph 5(1)(b) of Schedule 5 and Schedule 16 includes the Broads Authority, a police authority established under section 3 of the Police Act 1996, [...] a joint authority established by Part IV of the Local Government Act 1985 and the London Fire and Emergency Planning Authority.

(f) "housing action trust" means a housing action established under Part III of the Housing Act 1988.

(g) "new towns residuary body" means—

(i) in relation to England, the Homes and Communities Agency so far as exercising functions in relation to anything transferred (or to be transferred) to it as mentioned in section 52(1)(a) to (d) of the Housing and Regeneration Act 2008; and

(ii) in relation to Wales, the Welsh Ministers so far as exercising functions in relation to anything transferred (or to be transferred) to them as mentioned in section 36(1)(a) (i) to (iii) of the New Towns Act 1981.

**3A–318** *Note*—Amended by SI 1986/1; the Norfolk and Suffolk Broads Act 1988 s.21, Sch.6, para.25; the Education Reform Act 1988 s.237(2), Sch.13; the Housing Act 1988 s.62(7); the Local Government (Wales) Act 1994 s.22(2), Sch.8, para.5(3); the Police and Magistrates' Courts Act 1994 ss.43, 93, Schs 4 and 9; the Police Act 1996 s.103(1) Sch.7; the Police Act 1997 Sch.9, para.49; the Government of Wales Act 1998 Sch.15, para.7; the Greater London Authority Act 1999 Sch.29, para.42; the Criminal Justice and Police Act 2001 Sch.7, Pt 5; the Police Reform Act 2002 Sch.8, para.1 and the Housing and Regeneration Act 2008 (Consequential Provisions) Order 2008 (SI 2008/3002), para.3.

## Housing associations

**3A–319** **5.**—(1) In this Act "housing association" means a society, body of trustees or company—

(a) which is established for the purpose of, or amongst whose objects or powers are included those of, providing, constructing, improving or managing, or facilitating or encouraging the construction or improvement of, housing accommodation, and

(b) which does not trade for profit or whose constitution or rules prohibit the issue of capital with interest or dividend exceeding such rate as may be prescribed by the Treasury, whether with or without differentiation as between share and loan capital.

(2) In this Act "fully mutual", in relation to a housing association, means that the rules of the association—

(a) restrict membership to persons who are tenants or prospective tenants of the association, and

(b) preclude the granting or assignment of tenancies to persons other than members;

and "co-operative housing association" means a fully mutual housing association which is a society registered under the Industrial and Provident Societies Act 1965.

(3) In this Act "self-build society" means a housing association whose object is to provide, for sale to, or occupation by, its members, dwellings built or improved principally with the use of its members' own labour.

(4) In this Act "registered social landlord" means—

(a) a housing association registered in the register maintained by the Housing Corporation under section 1 of the Housing Act 1996, or

(b) a housing association registered in the register maintained by the Secretary of State under section 1 of the Housing Act 1996,

subject as follows.

(5) References to registered social landlords include, where the context so permits, references to housing associations registered in the register maintained by Scottish Homes under section 3 of the Housing Associations Act 1985 (Scottish registered housing associations).

*Note* —Amended by the Housing Act 1996 (Consequential Provisions) Order 1996 (SI 1996/2325) art.5, Sch.2, para.14(1), (2); and the Government of Wales Act 1998 s.140 and Sch.16, para.6. See too *Qazi v Harrow LBC* [2003] UKHL 43; [2004] 1 A.C. 983; [2003] 3 W.L.R. 792 [2003] 4 All E.R. 461, where Lord Hope and Lord Scott said that contractual and property rights cannot be defeated by a defence based on art.8; *Lambeth LBC v Kay; Leeds CC v Price* [2006] UKHL 10; [2006] 2 A.C. 465; [2006] 2 W.L.R. 570 and *Birmingham City Council v Doherty* [2008] UKHL 57, [2009] 1 A.C. 367, [2008] 3 W.L.R. 636; *cf. McCann v UK App. No.19009/04, May 13, 2008, The Times*, May 23, 2008. **3A–320**

**Housing associations and the Human Rights Act 1998**

Whilst the activities of a housing association need not involve the performance of public functions, in taking over the responsibilities of a local housing authority as landlord of a tenant who had been granted a non-secure tenancy pending the determination of her application as a homeless person and in deciding to bring possession proceedings, the functions of a housing association were so closely assimilated to the council that it was properly to be regarded as a functional public authority within the meaning of the Human Rights Act 1998 s.6(1) (*Poplar Housing & Regeneration Community Association Ltd v Donoghue* [2001] EWCA Civ 595, [2002] Q.B. 48; [2001] 3 W.L.R—although it should be noted that this decision was disapproved in *YL v Birmingham CC* [2007] UKHL 27; [2008] 1 A.C. 95 where Baroness Hale and Lord Mance both criticised the Court of Appeal's reasoning for relying too heavily upon the historical links between the local authority and the registered social landlord, rather than upon the nature of the function itself which was the provision of social housing. See too *R. (on the application of Weaver) v London & Quadrant Housing Trust* [2009] EWCA Civ 587; June 18, 2009; (2009) *Times* August 26 (in determining whether a body is a public authority, the courts should adopt a "factor based approach". This requires the court to have regard to all the features or factors which may cast light on whether the particular function under consideration is a public function or not, and weigh them in the round. If an authority is a core public authority, all its functions are public functions, as are all acts pursuant to those functions. An authority is a hybrid authority if only some of its functions are public functions. Even then, the particular act is not subject to convention principles if it is a private act (Human Rights Act 1998 s.6(5)). **3A–321**

The character of an act is likely to take its colour from the character of the function of which it forms part. In this case, the provision of social housing was a public function. Elias L.J. found that seeking the termination of a social housing tenancy was not a private act. He said that "... the act of termination is so bound up with the provision of social housing that once the latter is seen, in the context of this particular body, as the exercise of a public function, then acts which are necessarily involved in the regulation of the function must also be public acts. The grant of a tenancy and its subsequent termination are part and parcel of determining who should be allowed to take advantage of this public benefit. This is not an act which is purely incidental or supplementary to the principal function ..." (para.76)).

### Housing trusts

3A–322 **6.** In this Act "housing trust" means a corporation or body of persons which—

(a) is required by the terms of its constituent instrument to use the whole of its funds, including any surplus which may arise from its operations, for the purpose of providing housing accommodation, or

(b) is required by the terms of its constituent instrument to devote the whole, or substantially the whole, of its funds for charitable purposes and in fact uses the whole, or substantially the whole, of its funds for the purpose of providing housing accommodation.

### Relevant Authority

3A–323 **6A.**—(1) In this Act "the Relevant Authority" means the Housing Corporation, the Secretary of State or Scottish Homes, subject as follows.

(2) In relation to a housing association which is—

(a) a registered charity which has its address for the purposes of registration by the Charity Commission in Wales,

(b) a society registered under the Industrial and Provident Societies Act 1965 which has its registered office for the purposes of that Act in Wales, or

(c) a company registered under the Companies Act 2006 which has its registered office for the purposes of that Act in Wales,

"the Relevant Authority" means the Secretary of State.

(3) In relation to a housing association which is a society registered under the Industrial and Provident Societies Act 1965 which has its registered office for the purposes of that Act in Scotland, "the Relevant Authority" means Scottish Homes.

(4) In relation to any other housing association which is a registered charity, a society registered under the Industrial and Provident Societies Act 1965 or a company registered under the Companies Act 1985, "the Relevant Authority" means the Housing Corporation.

(4A) This section is subject to any provision made elsewhere in this Act.

(5) In this section "registered charity" means a charity which is

registered under section 3 of the Charities Act 1993 and is not an exempt charity within the meaning of that Act.

*Note* —Inserted by the Housing Act 1988 Sch.17; substituted by the Housing Act 1996 (Consequential Provisions) Order 1996 (SI 1996/2325) art.5, Sch.2, para.14(1), (3). Amended by the Government of Wales Act 1998 s.140 and Sch.16, paras 5 and 7; the Charities Act 2006 s.75(1), Sch.8 para.77; the Housing and Regeneration Act 2008 (Consequential Provisions) Order 2008 (SI 2008/3002); and theCompanies Act 2006 (Consequential Amendments, Transitional Provisions and Savings) Order 2009 (SI 2009/1941) Sch.1 para.62, with effect from October 1, 2009.. **3A–324**

* * * *

# PART IV

# SECURE TENANCIES AND RIGHTS OF SECURE TENANTS

## *SECURITY OF TENURE*

### Secure tenancies

**79.**—(1) A tenancy under which a dwelling-house is let as a separate dwelling is a secure tenancy at any time when the conditions described in sections 80 and 81 as the landlord condition and the tenant condition are satisfied. **3A–325**

(2) Subsection (1) has effect subject to—

(a) the exceptions in Schedule 1 (tenancies which are not secure tenancies),

(b) sections 89(3) and (4) and 90(3) and (4) (tenancies ceasing to be secure after death of tenant), and

(c) sections 91(2) and 93(2) (tenancies ceasing to be secure in consequence of assignment or subletting).

(3) The provisions of this Part apply in relation to a licence to occupy a dwelling-house (whether or not granted for a consideration) as they apply in relation to a tenancy.

(4) Subsection (3) does not apply to a licence granted as a temporary expedient to a person who entered the dwelling-house or any other land as a trespasser (whether or not, before the grant of that licence, another licence to occupy that or another dwelling-house had been granted to him).

**"separate dwelling"**

See annotations to Rent Act 1977 s.1 above. **3A–326**

**"dwelling-house"**

See s.112. **3A–327**

**"landlord condition"**

See s.80. **3A–328**

**"tenant condition"**

See s.81. **3A–329**

**Secure tenancies**

This section provides the basic definition of a "secure tenancy" (or, in most circumstances, licence—see s.79(3) and (4)). The exceptions to security of tenure are set out **3A–330**

***Paragraph numbers marked with a "+" can be found online and on CD.***

in Sch.1, ss.89(3) and (4), 90(3) and (4), and 91(2) and (3). It is doubtful whether Parliament intended that a tenancy at will could be a secure tenancy, even where the conditions in ss.80 and s.81 are satisfied (*Banjo v Brent LBC* [2005] EWCA Civ 292; [2005] 1 W.L.R. 2520).

**Sub-tenancies**

**3A–331** A secure tenancy for the purpose of s.79 is one in which there is a direct landlord and tenant relationship between a landlord, satisfying the landlord condition in s.80, and a tenant, satisfying the tenant condition in s.81. If a local housing authority grants a lease to a charitable housing trust which in turn grants a sub-tenancy to an individual who lives in the property, the occupier's secure sub-tenancy persists while the intermediate lease continues, so long as the parties continue to meet the landlord and tenant conditions. As soon as either of them ceases to do so or the sub-lease in respect of which s.79 provided security ceases to exist, so also does the secure sub-tenancy (*Lambeth LBC v Kay* [2004] EWCA Civ 926; [2004] H.L.R. 56 and *Bruton v London and Quadrant Housing Trust* [2000] 1 A.C. 406; [1999] 3 W.L.R. 150, HL).

**Tenancies which are not secure tenancies and ECHR article 8**

**3A–331.1** Schedule 1 lists tenancies which are not secure tenancies. In recent years, there have been numerous reported cases in which the courts have considered whether or not ECHR art.8 can provide a defence to possession claims against occupants who lack security of tenure. For a summary, see "Article 8: La Lutta Continua?" [2009] J.H.L. 43. In *Harrow LBC v Qazi* [2003] UKHL 43; [2004] 1 A.C. 983; [2003] 3 W.L.R. 792, Lord Hope and Lord Scott said that contractual and property rights cannot be defeated by a defence based on art.8. See too *Newham LBC v Kibata* [2003] EWCA Civ 1785; [2004] H.L.R. 28; *Bradney v Birmingham CC*; *Birmingham CC v McCann* [2003] EWCA Civ 1783; [2004] H.L.R. 27; *Lambeth LBC v Kay*; *Leeds CC v Price* [2006] UKHL 10; [2006] 2 A.C. 465; [2006] 2 W.L.R. 570 and *Birmingham City Council v Doherty* [2008] UKHL 57; [2009] 1 A.C. 367; [2008] 3 W.L.R. 636; but cf. *McCann v UK* App. No.19009/04, *The Times* May 13, 2008, where the ECHR stated:

> "The loss of one's home is a most extreme form of interference with the right to respect for the home. Any person at risk of an interference of this magnitude should in principle be able to have the proportionality of the measure determined by an independent tribunal...(para.50)."

The "procedural safeguards" required by art.8 for the assessment of the proportionality of the interference are not met by the possibility of defendants in possession claims applying for judicial review. However, it would be only in very exceptional cases that occupiers would succeed in raising an arguable case which would require a court to examine the issue. In the great majority of cases, orders for possession could continue to be made "in summary proceedings".

See too *Liverpool City Council v Doran* [2009] EWCA Civ 146, March 3, 2009, where Toulson L.J. said that *Doherty v Birmingham City Council* [2008] UKHL 57; [2009] 1 A.C. 367; [2008] 3 W.L.R. 636 had "created a new battleground area" (para.46). He described the effect of Doherty as being two-fold:

> "49. First, there is no formulaic or formalistic restriction of the factors which may be relied upon by the licensee in support of an argument that the council's decision to serve a notice to quit, and seek a possession order, was one which no reasonable council would have taken. Such factors are not automatically irrelevant simply because they may include the licensee's personal circumstances, such as length of time of occupation." ...
>
> 50. Secondly, the question whether the council's decision was one which no reasonable person would have made is to be decided by applying public law principles as they have been developed at common law, and not through the lens of the convention."

Whether or not a "council's decision was unreasonable has to be decided by applying public law principles as they have been developed at common law [and] it is to be remembered that those principles are not frozen" (para.52). He continued "it is likely to be a rare case indeed where a council decides to issue a notice to quit and seek a possession order without any ground on which a reasonable council might have done so" (para.55).

See too *Central Bedfordshire Council v Taylor* [2009] EWCA Civ 613, June 23, 2009 and *Defence Estates v JL* [2009] EWHC 1049 (Admin), May 5, 2009.

***Paragraph numbers marked with a "+" can be found online and on CD.***

## The landlord condition

**80.**—(1) The landlord condition is that the interest of the landlord belongs to one of the following authorities or bodies— **3A–332**

a local authority,
a development corporation,
a housing action trust,
an urban development corporation, in the case of a tenancy falling within subsections (2A) to (2E), the Homes and Communities Agency or the Welsh Ministers (as the case may be), or
housing co-operative to which this section applies.

(2) [...]

(2A) A tenancy falls within this subsection if the interest of the landlord is transferred to—

(a) the Homes and Communities Agency as mentioned in section 52(1)(a) to (d) of the Housing and Regeneration Act 2008, or

(b) the Welsh Ministers as mentioned in section 36(1)(a)(i) to (iii) of the New Towns Act 1981.

(2B) A tenancy falls within this subsection if it is entered into pursuant to a contract under which the rights and liabilities of the prospective landlord are transferred to the Homes and Communities Agency or the Welsh Ministers as mentioned in subsection (2A)(a) or (b) (as the case may be).

(2C) A tenancy falls within this subsection if it is granted by the Homes and Communities Agency or the Welsh Ministers to a person (alone or jointly with others) who, immediately before it was entered into, was a secure tenant of the Homes and Communities Agency or the Welsh Ministers (as the case may be).

(2D) A tenancy falls within this subsection if—

(a) it is granted by the Homes and Communities Agency or the Welsh Ministers to a person (alone or jointly with others),

(b) before the grant of the tenancy, an order for possession of a dwelling-house let under a secure tenancy was made against the person (alone or jointly with others) and in favour of the Homes and Communities Agency or the Welsh Ministers (as the case may be) on the court being satisfied as mentioned in section 84(2)(b) or (c), and

(c) the tenancy is of the premises which constitute the suitable accommodation as to which the court was so satisfied.

(2E) A tenancy falls within this subsection if it is granted by the Homes and Communities Agency or the Welsh Ministers pursuant to an obligation under section 554(2A).

(3) If a co-operative housing association ceases to be a registered social landlord, it shall, within the period of 21 days beginning with the date on which it ceases to be a registered social landlord, notify each of its tenants who thereby becomes a secure tenant, in writing, that he has become a secure tenant.

(4) This section applies to a housing co-operative within the meaning of section 27B (agreements under certain superseded provisions) where the dwelling-house is comprised in a housing co-operative agreement within the meaning of that section.

(5) In this Act and in any provision made under this Act, or made by or under any other enactment, a reference to—

(a) a person within section 80 or 80(1) of this Act, or

(b) a person who satisfies the landlord condition under this section,

includes a reference to the Homes and Communities Agency or to the Welsh Ministers so far as acting in their capacity as landlord (or, in the case of disposals, former landlord) in respect of a tenancy which falls within subsections (2A) to (2E) above but, subject to this, does not include the Homes and Communities Agency or the Welsh Ministers.

(6) Subsection (5)—

(a) applies whether the person is described as an authority, body or landlord or in any other way and whether the reference is otherwise expressed in a different way, and

(b) is subject to any provision to the contrary.

3A–333 *Note*—Amended by the Housing Act 1996 (Consequential Provisions) Order 1996 (SI 1996/2325) art.5, Sch.2; the Housing Act 1988 Sch.18; the Housing and Planning Act 1986 Sch.5; Government of Wales Act 1998 Sch.18, Pt IV and the Housing and Regeneration Act 2008 (Consequential Provisions) Order 2008 (SI 2008/3002) Sch.1 para.10.

**"local authority"**

3A–334 See s.4.

**"housing action trust"**

3A–335 See s.4.

**"an urban development corporation"**

3A–336 See s.4.

**"housing co-operative"**

3A–337 See s.4.

**"registered social landlord"**

3A–338 See the Housing Act 1996 ss.1–7.

**The landlord condition**

3A–339 Note that if a housing association granted a tenancy before January 15, 1989, and all the other requirements of a secure tenancy exist, that tenancy remains a secure tenancy (see s.80(1) prior to amendment by the Housing Act 1988 and the Housing Act 1988 s.35). Tenancies granted by housing associations on or after January 15, 1989 are likely to be assured tenancies within the meaning of the Housing Act 1988.

The Court of Appeal has held that the landlord condition is not satisfied if there are joint landlords and only one of the joint landlords comes within the list of bodies specified in s.80(1) (see *R. v Council of City of Plymouth and Cornwall CC Ex p. Freeman* (1987) 19 H.L.R. 328, CA). See too *Knowsley Housing Trust v Revell*; *Helena Housing Ltd v Curtis* [2003] EWCA Civ 496; [2003] H.L.R. 63; *The Times*, April 17, 2003.

## The tenant condition

3A–340 **81.** The tenant condition is that the tenant is an individual and occupies the dwelling-house as his only or principal home; or, where the tenancy is a joint tenancy, that each of the joint tenants is an individual and at least one of them occupies the dwelling-house as his only or principal home.

**"dwelling-house"**

See s.112. 3A-341

**The tenant condition**

In order to gain or retain public sector security of tenure tenants must occupy premises as their "only or principal home"(*cf.* the Housing Act 1988 s.1(1)(b) ("as his only or principal home") the Leasehold Reform Act 1967 s.1 ("as his residence"), and the Rent Act 1977 s.2 ("as his residence")). Security of tenure and associated rights, such as the right to buy, are lost if secure tenants cease to occupy premises as their only or principal home (*Sutton LBC v Swann* (1986) 18 H.L.R. 140, CA) or if they sublet or part with possession of the whole (the Housing Act 1985 s.93). However, it is possible for tenants or licensees to have two or more homes in the public rented sector, but only the one which is the "principal" home can be secure. 3A-342

In order to maintain a "home" a tenant need not be physically resident, so long as there is an intention to return after a temporary absence and some physical sign of continued occupation (e.g. furniture and possessions in the property). Two houses can be occupied as a home at the same time—*Crawley BC v Sawyer* (1988) 20 H.L.R. 98, CA, where a council tenant went to live with his "girlfriend" for a period of approximately one-and-a-half years during which time the gas and electricity supplies to the premises which he rented from the council were cut off. Held that the rented premises remained his principal home throughout the period.

Temporary absence may be lengthy. In *Amoah v Barking and Dagenham LBC* (2001) 81 P. & C.R. D12; March 2001 Legal Action 27, Ch D a secure tenant was sentenced to 12 years' imprisonment. He left items of furniture in the property and appointed a relative to act as "caretaker" in his absence and intended to return on his release. Etherton J. held that he had retained his secure status.

The court should consider whether the tenant has an intention to return at the date of expiry of the notice to quit. It should focus on "the enduring intention" of the tenant and not on "fleeting changes of mind". This is particularly true of an elderly tenant in poor health whose intentions "may well have fluctuated from time to time and even from day to day". *Hammersmith and Fulham LBC v Clarke* (2001) 33 H.L.R. 77, CA.

It is possible for a tenant to lose security of tenure by reason of non-occupation but to regain it by re-occupying the property before service or a notice to quit—see *Hussey v Camden LBC* (1995) 27 H.L.R. 5, CA, where, as the tenant was occupying the property as his only or principal home at the time of service of the notice to quit, the Court of Appeal held that the earlier loss of security was irrelevant.

Subletting of the whole of premises means that any tenancy ceases to be secure (see *Jennings v Epping Forrest DC* (1993) 25 H.L.R. 241, CA; *Poland v Cadogan* [1980] 3 All E.R. 544, CA (the Leasehold Reform Act s.93(2)); *Muir Group Housing Association Ltd v Thornley* (1993) 25 H.L.R. 89, CA; *Brent LBC v Cronin* (1997) 30 H.L.R. 43, CA and *Ujima Housing Association v Asnah* (1998) 30 H.L.R. 831, CA (assured tenancy) *cf. Merton LBC v Salama* (1989) CAT No 89/169; June 1989 Legal Action 25, CA (parting with possession of part of premises)). Parting with possession is not to be inferred simply from the fact that another person has been allowed to use and occupy a tenant's home during his temporary absence (*Lam Kee Ying v Lam Shes Tong* [1975] A.C. 247, PC).

The Court of Appeal has held that (1) there is nothing in the Housing Act 1985 which renders it impossible or unlawful to grant a tenancy to a person not lawfully in this country; and (2) there is no public policy requirement that the word "lawfully" should be inserted into s.81 to limit security of tenure to those lawfully in occupation of their homes, see *Akinbolu v Hackney LBC* (1997) 29 H.L.R. 259, CA, where the council's claims that a tenancy was void because the tenant was an illegal overstayer and the council accordingly had no power to provide housing for him were rejected.

## Security of tenure

**82.**—(1) A secure tenancy which is either— 3A-343

*Paragraph numbers marked with a "+" can be found online and on CD.*

(a) a weekly or other periodic tenancy, or
(b) a tenancy for a term certain but subject to termination by the landlord,

cannot be brought to an end by the landlord except as mentioned in subsection (1A);

(1A) The tenancy may be brought to an end by the landlord—
(a) obtaining—
(i) an order of the court for the possession of the dwelling-house, and
(ii) the execution of the order,
(b) obtaining an order under subsection (3), or
(c) obtaining a demotion order under section 82A.

(2) In the case mentioned in subsection (1A)(a), the tenancy ends when the order is executed.

(3) Where a secure tenancy is a tenancy for a term certain but with a provision for re-entry or forfeiture, the court shall not order possession of the dwelling-house in pursuance of that provision, but in a case where the court would have made such an order it shall instead make an order terminating the tenancy on a date specified in the order and section 86 (periodic tenancy arising on termination of fixed term) shall apply.

(4) Section 146 of the Law of Property Act 1925 (restriction on and relief against forfeiture), except subsection (4) (vesting in under-lessee), and any other enactment or rule of law relating to forfeiture, shall apply in relation to proceedings for an order under subsection (3) of this section as if they were proceedings to enforce a right of re-entry or forfeiture.

**3A–344** *Note* —Section 82 has been amended by Anti-Social Behaviour Act 2003 s.14(1). This amendment was brought into force in England on June 30, 2004 by the Anti-Social Behaviour Act 2003 (Commencement No.3 and Savings) Order 2004 (SI 2004/1502) (c.61). It does not have effect in relation to any proceedings for the possession of a dwelling-house begun before June 30, 2004. It was brought into force in Wales on April 30, 2005 by the Anti-Social Behaviour Act 2003 (Commencement No.4) (Wales) Order 2005 (SI 2005/1225) (w.83) (c.55). The amendment allows a secure tenancy to be brought to an end by a demotion order. This section has also been amended by the Housing and Regeneration Act 2008 Sch.11, Pt I, para.2 (for transitional provisions see para.14) with effect from May 20, 2009 (SI 2009/1261) (c.66).

**Demotion order**

**3A–345** See s.82A.

**"dwelling-house"**

**3A–346** See s.112.

**"secure tenancy"**

**3A–347** See s.79.

**Security of tenure**

**3A–348** This important section provides that a secure tenancy cannot be brought to an end by a *landlord* except by obtaining an order of the court. It does not apply where the tenancy has ceased to be secure (e.g. as a result of the tenant ceasing to occupy as his or her only or principal home—see s.81, but note the need for a court order under the Protection from Eviction Act 1977) or where the termination is brought about by the action of a tenant (see, e.g. *Hammersmith and Fulham LBC v Monk* [1992] 1 A.C. 478;

***Paragraph numbers marked with a "+" can be found online and on CD.***

[1991] 3 W.L.R. 1144; [1992] 1 All E.R. 1, HL; *Harrow LBC v Johnstone* [1997] 1 W.L.R. 459; [1997] 1 All E.R. 929, HL; and *Greenwich LBC v McGrady* (1982) 81 L.G.R. 288; (1982) 46 P. & C.R. 223; (1983) 6 H.L.R. 361; (1982) 267 E.G. 515, CA and *Notting Hill Housing Trust v Brackley* [2001] EWCA Civ 601; [2001] 35 E.G. 106; [2002] H.L.R. 212; [2001] L. & T.R. 467). The Court of Appeal has held that there was no breach of ECHR, art.8 where a local authority took possession proceedings against the wife of a sole tenant after the husband (the tenant) had served a valid notice to quit upon the council (*Kensington and Chelsea v O'Sullivan* [2003] EWCA Civ 371; *The Times*, March 27, 2003. See too *Harrow LBC v Qazi* [2003] UKHL 43; [2004] 1 A.C. 983; [2003] 3 W.L.R. 792).

For the prerequisites for a possession order, see s.83 (notice of intention to bring proceedings) s.84 and Sch.2 (grounds for possession).

The tenancy ends on the date specified by the court (see, e.g. *Thompson v Elmbridge BC* [1987] 1 W.L.R. 1425; (1987) 19 H.L.R. 526, CA; *Leicester City Council v Aldwinkle* (1992) 24 H.L.R. 40, CA; and *Brent LBC v Knightley* (1997) 29 H.L.R. 857; *The Times*, February 26, 1997)—but note Housing and Regeneration Act 2008 Sch.11 below which will provide that secure tenancies will continue until any warrant for possession is executed. This amendment was brought into force on May 20, 2009 by the Housing and Regeneration Act 2008 (Commencement No.5) Order 2009 SI 2009/1261 (c.66).

## Demotion because of anti-social behaviour

**82A.**—(1) This section applies to a secure tenancy if the landlord is— **3A–349**

(a) a local housing authority;

(b) a housing action trust;

(c) a registered social landlord.

(2) The landlord may apply to a county court for a demotion order.

(3) A demotion order has the following effect—

(a) the secure tenancy is terminated with effect from the date specified in the order;

(b) if the tenant remains in occupation of the dwelling-house after that date a demoted tenancy is created with effect from that date;

(c) it is a term of the demoted tenancy that any arrears of rent payable at the termination of the secure tenancy become payable under the demoted tenancy;

(d) it is also a term of the demoted tenancy that any rent paid in advance or overpaid at the termination of the secure tenancy is credited to the tenant's liability to pay rent under the demoted tenancy.

(4) The court must not make a demotion order unless it is satisfied—

(a) that the tenant or a person residing in or visiting the dwelling-house has engaged or has threatened to engage in—

(i) housing-related anti-social conduct, or

(ii) conduct to which section 153B of the Housing Act 1996 (use of premises for unlawful purposes) applies, and

(b) that it is reasonable to make the order.

(5) Each of the following has effect in respect of a demoted

tenancy at the time it is created by virtue of an order under this section as it has effect in relation to the secure tenancy at the time it is terminated by virtue of the order—

(a) the parties to the tenancy;
(b) the period of the tenancy;
(c) the amount of the rent;
(d) the dates on which the rent is payable.

(6) Subsection (5)(b) does not apply if the secure tenancy was for a fixed term and in such a case the demoted tenancy is a weekly periodic tenancy.

(7) If the landlord of the demoted tenancy serves on the tenant a statement of any other express terms of the secure tenancy which are to apply to the demoted tenancy such terms are also terms of the demoted tenancy.

(7A) In subsection (4)(a) 'housing-related anti-social conduct' has the same meaning as in section 153A of the Housing Act 1996.

(8) For the purposes of this section a demoted tenancy is—

(a) a tenancy to which section 143A of the Housing Act 1996 applies if the landlord of the secure tenancy is a local housing authority or a housing action trust;
(b) a tenancy to which section 20B of the Housing Act 1988 applies if the landlord of the secure tenancy is a registered social landlord.

3A–350 *Note* —Inserted by the Anti-Social Behaviour Act 2003 s.14(2) and brought into force in relation to England on June 30 (SI 2004/1502) and in relation to Wales on April 30, 2005 (SI 2005/1225); amended by the Police and Justice Act 2006 s.52, Sch.14, para.12.

**Editorial note**

3A–351 This section was inserted by Anti-Social Behaviour Act 2003 s.14(2). This amendment was brought into force in England on June 30, 2004 by the Anti-Social Behaviour Act 2003 (Commencement No.3 and Savings) Order 2004 (SI 2004/1502) (c.61). It was brought into force in Wales on April 30, 2005 by the Anti-Social Behaviour Act 2003 (Commencement No.4) (Wales) Order 2005 (SI 2005/1225) (w.83) (c.55).

Section 82A provides that a local authority, a housing action trust or a registered social landlord can apply for a demotion order. A demotion order ends the secure tenancy on a specified date. If the tenant remains in occupation, a new demoted tenancy begins on the same date. The court may only make the order if the tenant, another resident of or visitor to the tenant's home has behaved in a way which is capable of causing nuisance or annoyance or if such a person has used the premises for illegal purposes. In addition the court must be satisfied that it is reasonable to make the order. As to reasonableness in the context of anti-social behaviour by a tenant's children and the use of hearsay evidence, see *Washington Housing Company Ltd v Morson* [2005] EWHC 3407 (CHY); October 25, 2005.

Demoted tenancies lack security of tenure. If the landlord follows the procedure set out in Housing Act 1996 ss.143E and F, the court must make an order for possession (see Housing Act 1996 s.143D). See *Manchester City Council v Pinnock* [2009] EWCA Civ 852, July 31, 2009, noted at para.3A–1147. Under a demoted tenancy, the parties, the period of the tenancy (unless it was for a fixed term) and rental terms remain the same, but a landlord may, apparently unilaterally, serve a statement of any other express terms of the secure tenancy which are to apply to the demoted tenancy. It was amended by the Police and Justice Act 2006 Sch.14, para.12.

**Demoted tenancy**

3A–352 See s.82A(8), Housing Act 1996 s.143A and Housing Act 1988 s.20B. Section

***Paragraph numbers marked with a "+" can be found online and on CD.***

82A(3)(c) and (d) confirm that any rent owed or overpaid on the tenant's rent account under the secure tenancy should be transferred across to the demoted tenancy. Section 82A(5) sets out certain basic terms of the demoted tenancy at the point at which it is created.

**Secure tenancy**

See s.79. **3A–353**

**A local housing authority**

See Housing Act 1996 s.230 and Housing Act 1985 ss.1 and 2(2). **3A–354**

**A housing action trust**

See Housing Act 1996 s.230 and Housing Act 1988 Pt III. **3A–355**

**A registered social landlord**

See Housing Act 1996 Pt I, ss.1 to 3. **3A–356**

**Anti-social behaviour or use of premises for unlawful purposes**

See Housing Act 1996 ss.153A and 153B. **3A–357**

## Proceedings for possession or termination: notice requirements

**83.**—(1) The court shall not entertain proceedings for an order mentioned in section 82(1A) unless— **3A–358**

(a) the landlord has served a notice on the tenant complying with the provisions of this section, or

(b) the court considers it just and equitable to dispense with the requirement of such a notice.

(2) A notice under this section shall—

(a) be in a form prescribed by regulations made by the Secretary of State,

(b) specify the ground on which the court will be asked to make the order, and

(c) give particulars of that ground.

(3) Where the tenancy is a periodic tenancy and the ground or one of the grounds specified in the notice is Ground 2 in Schedule 2 (nuisance or other anti-social behaviour), the notice—

(a) shall also—

(i) state that proceedings for the possession of the dwelling-house may be begun immediately, and

(ii) specify the date sought by the landlord as the date on which the tenant is to give up possession of the dwelling-house, and

(b) ceases to be in force twelve months after the date so specified.

(4) Where the tenancy is a periodic tenancy and Ground 2 in Schedule 2 is not specified in the notice, the notice—

(a) shall also specify the date after which proceedings for the possession of the dwelling-house may be begun, and

(b) ceases to be in force twelve months after the date so specified.

*Paragraph numbers marked with a "+" can be found online and on CD.*

(4A) If the proceedings are for a demotion order under section 82A the notice—

(a) must specify the date after which the proceedings may be begun;

(b) ceases to be in force twelve months after the date so specified.

(5) The date specified in accordance with subsection (3), (4) or (4A) must not be earlier than the date on which the tenancy could, apart from this Part, be brought to an end by notice to quit given by the landlord on the same date as the notice under this section.

(6) Where a notice under this section is served with respect to a secure tenancy for a term certain, it has effect also with respect to any periodic tenancy arising on the termination of that tenancy by virtue of section 86; and subsections (3) to (5) of this section do not apply to the notice.

(7) Regulations under this section shall be made by statutory instrument and may make different provision with respect to different cases or descriptions of case, including different provision for different areas.

**3A–359** *Note* —Substituted by the Housing Act 1996 s.147.

Section 83 has been amended by Anti-Social Behaviour Act 2003 s.14(3) and Sch.1. The amendments were brought into force in England on June 30, 2004 by the Anti-Social Behaviour Act 2003 (Commencement No.3 and Savings) Order 2004 (SI 2004/1502) (c.61). It was brought into force in Wales on April 30, 2005 by the Anti-Social Behaviour Act 2003 (Commencement No.4) (Wales) Order 2005 (SI 2005/1225) (w.83) (c.55).

### Proceedings for possession or termination: notice requirements

**3A–360** The Housing Act 1996 s.147 introduced completely new ss.83 and 83A which apply to notices served on or after February 12, 1997 (Housing Act 1996 (Commencement No.6) Order 1997 (SI 1997/66)). They are in similar form to the old s.83, but with two significant modifications, viz. the court may dispense with the requirement for a notice if it considers it just and equitable to do, and the notice may state that proceedings under new Ground 2 (nuisance or anti-social behaviour—see below) may be begun immediately.

For the prescribed forms of notice, see the Secure Tenancies (Notices) Regulations 1987 (SI 1987/775) (as amended by the Secure Tenancies (Notices) (Amendment) Regulations 1997 (SI 1997/71), the Secure Tenancies (Notices) (Amendment No.2) Regulations 1997 (SI 1997/377); the Secure Tenancies (Notices) (Amendment) (England) Regulations 2004 (SI 2004/1627) and the Secure Tenancies (Notices) (Amendment) (Wales) Regulations 2005 (SI 2005/1226) (w.84)). Paragraph 2(1) of the Regulations states that the notice should be "substantially to the same effect" as that contained in the Regulations. For cases where landlords used old versions of prescribed forms, see: *Beckerman v Durling* (1983) 6 H.L.R. 87, CA; *Swansea CC v Hearn* (1991) 23 H.L.R. 284, CA; and *Tadema Holdings v Ferguson* (2000) 32 H.L.R. 866, CA.

If the court does not consider it just and equitable to dispense with the notice requirement, s.83 precludes the court from granting an order for possession of a secure tenancy unless satisfied that a notice of intention to seek possession complying with the requirements of that section has been served. Such a notice must state the ground for possession and give "particulars" of the ground (s.83(2)(c)).

As to service see *Wandsworth LBC v Attwell* (1995) 27 H.L.R. 536; [1996] 01 E.G. 100; (1996) 94 L.G.R. 419, CA; *Enfield LBC v Devonish* (1997) 29 H.L.R. 691, CA and *Tadema Holdings v Ferguson* (2000) 32 H.L.R. 866, CA. If there are joint tenants, it should be addressed to all of them (*Newham LBC v Okotoro*, March 1993, Legal Action 11, Bow County Court).

Notices must specify a date which must not be earlier than the date on which the tenancy could otherwise be brought to an end by a notice to quit served by the landlord. (See also the Protection from Eviction Act 1977 s.5). However, a notice may state that proceedings under Ground 2 (nuisance or anti-social behaviour) may be begun immediately. In that case, the notice should state this and specify the date sought by the landlord as the date on which the tenant is to give up possession (s.83(3)).

Notices cease to be in force 12 months after the date specified in the notice. If that date passes, a new notice must be served (s.83(3)(b) and s.83A).

**"particulars of the ground"**

In rent arrears cases the particulars given must at least show the amount claimed, **3A–361** and in all cases the notice must be sufficiently particularised to "tell the tenant what he had to do to put matters right before proceedings are commenced" (*Torridge DC v Jones* (1986) 18 H.L.R. 107 at 114; (1985) 276 E.G. 1253, CA). ("The reasons for taking this action are non-payment of rent" not sufficient—notice invalid). See too *East Devon DC v Williams and Mills*, December 1996, Legal Action 13, Exeter County Court (possession claimed under Sch.2, Ground 1 (breach of the terms of the tenancy). The notice set out the relevant terms but in the section marked "Particulars" merely repeated the terms in full, without indicating the conduct relied upon—possession claim struck out); *Slough BC v Robbins* [1996] 12 C.L. 353, Slough County Court (notice seeking possession giving as particulars: "Numerous complaints have been received over a period of time that annoyance and nuisance is being caused to your neighbours by noise and disruptive behaviour. This nuisance and annoyance has been investigated by my staff and I believe the complaints to be substantiated" held to be defective, proceedings struck out); and *South Buckinghamshire CC v Frances* [1985] 11 C.L. 152; [1985] C.L.Y. 1900, Slough County Court (where it was held that the Housing Act 1980 s.33(2) (now the Housing Act 1985 s.83(2)(c)) required detailed particulars which should be similar to those required under the Law of Property Act 1925 s.146. It must be obvious to tenants what they must do. Although there was discretion to allow amendment of the notice (now contained in the Housing Act 1985 s.84(3)), the council would not be permitted "at a late stage" in the proceedings to amend the notice to include a schedule of dilapidations and particulars of nuisance which ought to have been included in the original notice).

However, in *Dudley MBC v Bailey* [1991] 10 E.G. 140; (1990) 22 H.L.R. 424, CA, Ralph Gibson L.J. stated that:

> "The question is whether, at the date of the notice, the landlord has in good faith stated the ground and given the particulars of that ground. The requirement of particulars is satisfied, in my judgment, if the landlord has stated in summary form the facts which he then intends to prove in support of the stated ground for possession. Error in the particulars does not, in my judgment, invalidate the notice, although it may well affect the decision of the court on the merits". ((1990) 22 H.L.R. 424 at 431).

See too *Marath v MacGillivray* (1996) 28 H.L.R. 484, CA, noted under the Housing Act 1988 s.8.

Section 83 expressly enables a court to give leave for a landlord to add to or alter the "grounds" on which possession is claimed (s.83(4)), but is silent about the addition or alteration of the "particulars" required by the notice. In *Camden LBC v Oppong* (1996) 28 H.L.R. 701, CA, the Court of Appeal held the s.83(4) power *ipso facto* extended to a power to add to or alter the particulars. The court stated that such leave would be granted only in circumstances where it would be just to do so and that the nature and extent of the addition or alteration would always be a critical factor.

The form of notice is prescribed by the Secure Tenancies (Notices) Regulations 1987 (SI 1987/775) (as amended by the Secure Tenancies (Notices) (Amendment) Regulations 1997 (SI 1997/71); the Secure Tenancies (Notices)(Amendment No.2) Regulations 1997 (SI 1997/377); the Secure Tenancies (Notices) (Amendment) (England) Regulations 2004 (SI 2004/1627); and the Secure Tenancies (Notices) (Amendment) (Wales) Regulations 2005 (SI 2005/1226) (w.84)). Paragraph 2(1) of the Regulations states that the notice should be "substantially to the same effect" as that contained in the Regulations. Minor variations are unlikely to invalidate a notice—see *Dudley MBC v Bailey* [1991] 10 E.G. 140; (1990) 22 H.L.R. 424, CA, where Ralph Gibson L.J. held that a notice, although not precisely in the prescribed form, was "substantially to the same effect". In *City of London v Devlin* (1995) 29 H.L.R. 58, CA, the Court of Appeal held that a notice seeking possession which had not been signed by the Director of Housing above that description which appeared on the printed form was "substantially to the same effect" as that prescribed and accordingly valid. Simon Brown L.J. stated that:

> "The reality here is that a series of aridly technical points raised by the applicant at trial were defeated by a series of creative, largely procedural rulings which were not even arguably impermissible."

**"the court considers it just and equitable to do dispense with the requirement of such a notice" (s.83(1)(b))**

3A–362 This provision brings secure tenancies into line with assured tenancies (*cf.* the Housing Act 1988 s.8(1)(b)). It is "obviously only in relatively exceptional cases where the court should be prepared to dispense with a section 83 notice". (*Braintree DC v Vincent* [2004] EWCA Civ 415—a case where the Court of Appeal held that a judge was entitled to dispense with the notice on unusual facts. A s.83 notice would have been of no benefit to the tenant—indeed it would have been to her disadvantage because it would have postponed the date for possession and added to her liability for rent.) In *Kelsey HA v King* (1995) 28 H.L.R. 270, CA, it was held that it was just and equitable to dispense with the notice requirement where a notice served was found to be invalid because it had not given adequate particulars of the complaints of nuisance. The court had regard, inter alia, to:

(a) developments since the commencement of proceedings; and
(b) the late stage in the proceedings at which any point about the deficiency in the notice was taken.

See too *North British HA v Sheridan* [1999] 2 E.G.L.R. 138; [2000] L. & T.R. 115; (2000) 32 H.L.R. 346; (1999) 78 P. & C.R. D38.

Although the effect is different, the same wording is also used in the Rent Act 1977 Sch.15, Case 11, and the Housing Act 1988 Sch.2, Ground 1, where the court may dispense with the requirement that notice be served *before the grant* of certain tenancies. Those provisions have been considered by the Court of Appeal in *Fernandes v Parvardin* (1981–82) 5 H.L.R. 33; *Bradshaw v Baldwin-Wiseman* (1985) 17 H.L.R. 260; (1985) 49 P. & C.R. 382; and *Boyle v Verrall* (1996) 29 H.L.R. 436. The decisions in those cases indicate that although the power to dispense with notices is not limited to exceptional cases and may be exercised where oral notice has been given, it is unlikely to be exercised where no intimation of an intention to require possession has been given.

## Additional requirements in relation to certain proceedings for possession

3A–363 **83A.**—(1) Where a notice under section 83 has been served on a tenant containing the information mentioned in subsection (3)(a) of that section, the court shall not entertain proceedings for the possession of the dwelling-house unless they are begun at a time when the notice is still in force.

(2) Where—

(a) a notice under section 83 has been served on a tenant, and
(b) a date after which proceedings may be begun has been specified in the notice in accordance with subsection (4)(a) of that section,

the court shall not entertain proceedings for the possession of the dwelling-house unless they are begun after the date so specified and at a time when the notice is still in force.

(3) Where—

(a) the ground or one of the grounds specified in a notice under section 83 is Ground 2A in Schedule 2 (domestic violence), and

*Paragraph numbers marked with a "+" can be found online and on CD.*

(b) the partner who has left the dwelling-house as mentioned in that ground is not a tenant of the dwelling-house,

the court shall not entertain proceedings for the possession of the dwelling-house unless it is satisfied that the landlord has served a copy of the notice on the partner who has left or has taken all reasonable steps to serve a copy of the notice on that partner.

This subsection has effect subject to subsection (5).

(4) Where—

(a) Ground 2A in Schedule 2 is added to a notice under section 83 with the leave of the court after proceedings for possession are begun, and

(b) the partner who has left the dwelling-house as mentioned in that ground is not a party to the proceedings,

the court shall not continue to entertain the proceedings unless it is satisfied that the landlord has served a notice under subsection (6) on the partner who has left or has taken all reasonable steps to serve such a notice on that partner.

This subsection has effect subject to subsection (5).

(5) Where subsection (3) or (4) applies and Ground 2 in Schedule 2 (nuisance or other anti-social behaviour) is also specified in the notice under section 83, the court may dispense with the requirements as to service in relation to the partner who has left the dwelling-house if it considers it just and equitable to do so.

(6) A notice under this subsection shall—

(a) state that proceedings for the possession of the dwelling-house have begun,

(b) specify the ground or grounds on which possession is being sought, and

(c) give particulars of the ground or grounds.

*Note*—Added by the Housing Act 1996 s.147. **3A–364**

**Additional requirements in relation to certain proceedings for possession**

This section contains special provisions concerning Ground 2A (domestic violence) (see Sch.2 below). **3A–365**

## Grounds for orders for possession

**84.**—(1) The court shall not make an order for the possession of a dwelling-house let under a secure tenancy except on one or more of the grounds set out in Schedule 2. **3A–366**

(2) The court shall not make an order for possession—

(a) on the grounds set out in Part I of that Schedule (grounds 1 to 8), unless it considers it reasonable to make the order,

(b) on the grounds set out in Part II of that Schedule (grounds 9 to 11), unless it is satisfied that suitable accommodation will be available for the tenant when the order takes effect,

(c) on the grounds set out in Part III of that Schedule (grounds 12 to 16), unless it both considers it reasonable to make the order and is satisfied that suitable accom-

HOUSING

modation will be available for the tenant when the order takes effect;

and Part IV of that Schedule has effect for determining whether suitable accommodation will be available for a tenant.

(3) Where a notice under section 83 has been served on the tenant, the court shall not make such an order on any of those grounds above unless the ground is specified in the notice; but the grounds so specified may be altered or added to with the leave of the court.

(4) Where a date is specified in a notice under section 83 in accordance with subsection (3) of that section, the court shall not make an order which requires the tenant to give up possession of the dwelling-house in question before the date so specified.

3A–367 *Note* —Amended by the Housing Act 1996 s.147.

**"dwelling-house"**

3A–368 See s.112.

**"secure tenancy"**

3A–369 See s.79.

**"notice"**

3A–370 See s.83. As to the alteration of grounds in notices, see the commentary to s.83.

**"suitable accommodation will be available"**

3A–371 See Sch.2, Pt IV.

**Grounds for orders for possession**

3A–372 The court may not make an order for possession against a secure tenant unless satisfied that one of the grounds for possession listed in Sch.2 is proved and in addition that, depending upon the ground, it is reasonable to make an order for possession, or that suitable alternative accommodation will be available, or that it is both reasonable to make an order for possession and suitable alternative accommodation will be available.

The service of a notice exercising the right to buy (Housing Act 1985 Pt V) does not prevent a public sector landlord from seeking possession of the property on any of the grounds permitted by the Housing Act 1985 Sch.2. However, if the ground requires the court to consider "reasonableness", the fact that the tenant has exercised the right to buy is a circumstance to be taken into account (*Enfield LBC v McKeon* [1986] 1 W.L.R. 1007; [1986] 2 All E.R. 730, CA). See too *Bristol CC v Lovell* [1998] 1 W.L.R. 446; [1998] 1 All E.R. 775, HL and *Basildon DC v Wahlen* [2006] EWCA Civ 326; [2006] 1 W.L.R. 2744.

**"reasonable"**

3A–373 See too the commentary to the Rent Act 1977 s.98. It is for the landlord to satisfy the court that it is reasonable to make a possession order. Note too the Protocol for Possession Claims Based on Rent Arrears at C11–001 which aims to encourage more pre-action contact between landlords and tenants and to enable court time to be used more effectively. Courts should take into account whether this protocol has been followed when considering what orders to make. The first requirement for a judge who has found a ground for possession to be proved is to ask whether it is reasonable to make a possession order at all and then to ask whether the order should be stayed, suspended or postponed under s.100(2). The correct approach is to determine the extent of the rent arrears and how quickly those were likely to be paid. It is wrong to take into account matters which have not been pleaded.

> "In considering whether it is reasonable to make an order…the judge should consider all the relevant circumstances: but that is not a consideration at large. It is, or should be, a consideration in accordance with the pleadings. In my judg-

ment, the matters proposed to be relied upon by the landlord in support of the contention that it would be reasonable to make an order for possession…must be pleaded by the landlord." (per Sir Richard Scott V.-C. in *Raeuchle v Laimond Properties Ltd (Suspension of Possession Order)* (2001) 33 H.L.R. 10, CA.

In view of the requirement that the appropriate grounds and conditions must be made out (e.g. as to reasonableness) "consent orders" have no place in public-sector proceedings. The court can have jurisdiction only if the necessary matters are proved by evidence or if there is express admission of the relevant facts (*Wandsworth LBC v Fadayomi* [1987] 3 All E.R. 474; (1987) 19 H.L.R. 512, CA; and *Hounslow LBC v McBride* (1999) 31 H.L.R. 143, CA, where after agreement between the parties in possession proceedings based upon Housing Act 1985 Grounds 1 and 2 a District Judge made a suspended possession order by consent without hearing evidence). Later the council alleged that Ms McBride had broken the conditions of the suspended order and applied for a warrant of possession. The Court of Appeal confirmed that both the possession order and the warrant should be set aside). See too *R. v Birmingham CC Ex p. Foley*, March 2001, Legal Action 29, Queen's Bench Division. A distinction has to be drawn between a form of order which contains an admission as to those matters on which the jurisdiction to make the order rests (e.g. reasonableness) and an order such as this one which did not.

**"reasonable"—rent arrears**

In rent arrears cases, the importance of ascertaining the position in respect of welfare benefits was stressed by the Court of Appeal in *Second WRVS Housing Society v Blair* (1987) 19 H.L.R. 104, CA, where the tenant became affected by a psychiatric illness. His life "fell apart" and arrears mounted. He received supplementary benefit towards the housing costs but spent it on food. The county court judge, finding that there were arrears of £1,198 and that the tenant was still on supplementary benefit, ordered possession (suspended for two months in case the debt could be cleared in that time) and costs of £140. The Court of Appeal set aside the order, as the judge had failed to consider in detail the question of reasonableness and, in particular, the available welfare benefits. The case was sent back for reconsideration to ascertain "more fully the benefits which could be obtained from DHSS in relation to arrears and more generally in relation to [the tenant's] condition". Dillon L.J. stated "it is well known that arrangements can be made with the DHSS when housing benefit is payable to see that the rent is paid direct to the landlord and I feel that is a matter which should have been taken into account". **3A–374**

Also important are the tenant's past record and the reason for the arrears. See *Woodspring DC v Taylor* (1981–82) 4 H.L.R. 95, CA, where the defendants, who were in their mid-fifties, had been tenants of the council for 24 years. They had a good rent record. However, Mr Taylor was made redundant and received a large tax demand. His wife became ill. As a result rent arrears accrued. They owed £557 at the launch of possession proceedings and £700 at the date of the hearing. By this time they were receiving benefit and the DHSS was paying current rent plus £1 per week off the arrears. In the county court a registrar made an absolute possession order. The Court of Appeal set aside the order, finding that no reasonable registrar could have found that it was reasonable to make the order. Waller L.J. stated that it was "hard to understand a conclusion that it was reasonable to make an order turning them out of their house" (at 99).

See also *Brent LBC v Marks* (1999) 31 H.L.R. 343, CA: appeal by tenant against suspended possession on terms that the tenant pay current rent and £2.50 allowed. Following *Second WRVS Housing Society v Blair* (1987) 19 H.L.R. 104, the judge ought to have had more regard to the fact that current rent was being paid by deductions made by the DSS quarterly in arrears and that the benefit system was both causing and then dealing with the arrears. Looking at the overall position this was a responsible tenant whose position had stabilised. On a new exercise of the court's discretion, a possession order might not be made.

If a defendant counterclaims unsuccessfully for breach of repairing obligations, in ordinary circumstances, it is not reasonable to make a possession order, if the tenant has made arrangements, in the event of the failure of his counterclaim, for the early discharge of the arrears. However, in exceptional circumstances where there has been a bad history of persistent delay in paying rent, it may be reasonable to make an absolute order for possession (*Haringey LBC v Stewart* (1991) 23 H.L.R. 557; [1991] 2 E.G.L.R. 252, CA).

In *Drew-Morgan v Hamid-Zadeh* (2000) 32 H.L.R. 316, CA the Court of Appeal held that a judge was entitled to conclude that it was reasonable to make a possession order in the light of persistent non-payment which was inexcusable because the tenant had received housing benefit. The non-payment was plainly deliberate and avoidable. The fact that the tenant paid arrears during the hearing underlined the fact that she had been in a position to pay but had chosen not to do so until the last moment. The judge was also entitled to take into account false allegations made by the tenant.

**"reasonable"—nuisance and annoyance**

**3A–375** *General approach* —In *Brent LBC v Doughan* [2007] EWCA Civ 135, February 6, 2007, May L.J. stated:

> "Eviction is likely to be a draconian step because the spectre of intentional homelessness under Pt 7 of the Housing Act 1996 looms over it. On the other hand the legislative policy is to enforce good behaviour between neighbours by court orders and thereby to protect others who may well be vulnerable from socially unacceptable behaviour."

*Serious or continuing conduct* —However, the proper approach in a case of the commission of "a most serious breach" of the tenancy agreement is that it will be reasonable to order possession in the absence of some exceptional circumstance—*Bristol CC v Mousah* (1998) 30 H.L.R. 32, CA (serious drug dealing). See too *Sandwell MBC v Hensley* [2007] EWCA Civ 1425; [2008] H.L.R. 22, November 1, 2007 (outright possession order substituted on appeal for suspended possession order where tenant had pleaded guilty to a charge of being knowingly concerned with the cultivation of cannabis. It was said that where an individual commits a criminal offence, a possession order should only be suspended in exceptional circumstances where there is cogent evidence to demonstrate that the offender's particular conduct had ceased); but cf. *North Devon Homes Ltd v Batchelor* [2008] EWCA Civ 840, July 22, 2008.

Similarly, where there is an admitted breach of covenant and an intention to continue with the breach a landlord should only be refused possession in a "very special case" (*Sheffield CC v Green* (1994) 26 H.L.R. 349, CA; cf.; *Accent Peerless Ltd (formerly Surrey Heath Housing Association Ltd) v Kingsdon* [2007] EWCA Civ 1314; December 12, 2007; Bell London & Provincial Properties Ltd v *Rueben* [1947] K.B. 157, CA). It is in the public interest that necessary and reasonable conditions in tenancy agreements are enforced fairly and effectively: *Sheffield CC v Jepson* (1993) 25 H.L.R. 299, CA (tenant keeping a dog in breach of an express term of the tenancy agreement. Although there was little evidence about the defendant's dog in particular, reasonable to make suspended possession order). In a case involving the parking of a caravan in a front garden in breach of the terms of a tenancy agreement, the Court of Appeal held that the propriety of the council's policy was not a factor relevant to the exercise of discretion. The judge should not have been concerned with the propriety or impropriety of the policy rule. His concern should have been with the reasonableness in the particular case of ordering possession; *Barking and Dagenham LBC v Hyatt and Hyatt* (1992) 24 H.L.R. 406, CA. See too *Camden LBC v Gilsenan* (1999) 31 H.L.R. 81, CA: decision by circuit judge that it was reasonable to make a possession order upheld. The trial judge had differentiated between acts done by the defendant and acts done by her visitors; and see *Newcastle Upon Tyne CC v Morrison* (2000) 32 H.L.R. 891, CA (single parent unable to control her "rampaging, destructive, intimidating and sometimes dangerous sons" with "quite appalling behaviour over a period of more than six years" involving "plain, repeated and grave breaches of the tenancy agreement, numerous offences affecting the neighbourhood and a dreadful catalogue of incidents". The Court of Appeal substituted a 28-day possession order for a suspended possession order). For a case in which a first instance judge dismissed a claim for possession but the Court of Appeal decided that it was reasonable to make a suspended possession order, see *Norwich City Council v Famuyiwa* [2004] EWCA Civ 1770; *The Times*, January 24, 2005. See too *Manchester City Council v Higgins* [2005] EWCA Civ 1423; [2006] H.L.R. 14 (suspended possession order replaced on appeal with outright possession order—misconduct so serious and persistent that it justified the making of an ASBO. This was strong but not conclusive evidence that the tenant would have forfeited any entitlement to retain possession).

*Effect upon other tenants*—In nuisance cases, the authority's obligations towards other tenants should be borne in mind. See s.85A below (statutory obligation to consider particular effects of nuisance and annoyance) and *Woking BC v Bystram* (1995) 27 H.L.R. 1; [1993] E.G.C.S. 208, CA (nuisance continuing—appropriate course was to make a suspended order for possession on terms that any further nuisance would lead to repossession in 28 days). See too *Solon South West Housing Association Ltd v James* [2004] EWCA Civ 1847; [2005] H.L.R. 24 (outright order confirmed by Court of Appeal).

*Cases where not reasonable to make outright order*—For examples of cases where the Court of Appeal has not found it reasonable to make an outright order, see *Wandsworth LBC v Hargreaves* (1995) 27 H.L.R. 142, CA (in breach of a term of the tenancy a visitor brought petrol into the flat to make petrol bombs, which were thrown from the window. A fire started in the flat from spilt petrol, causing £14,000 worth of damage. The Court of Appeal dismissed the council's appeal against a refusal of the county court judge to order possession); and *Greenwich LBC v Grogan* (2001) 33 H.L.R. 12, CA (17-year-old tenant pleaded guilty to handling stolen goods on the premises, sentenced to six months' youth custody. The Court of Appeal suspended the possession order for 12 months. In exercising its discretion, the court could take into account the wider public interest. The tenant was a young man trying to live a life free of crime and there was a serious possibility that that attempt would fail if he lost his flat. The council had a duty to consider its other tenants and people on its waiting list, but the balance was in favour of suspending the order).

*Other members of tenant's family*—An outright possession order may not be appropriate where the anti-social behaviour was not caused by the tenant, but by a member of the tenant's family who has since left the premises, with the result that the chances of recurrence are reduced (*Castle Vale Housing Action Trust v Gallagher* [2001] EWCA Civ 944; (2001) 33 H.L.R. 810, CA and *Wandsworth LBC v Webb* [2008] EWCA Civ 1421 November 12, 2008; The Times, January 5, 2009, where Sedley L.J. observed that it was not permissible to use a possession order as a means to bring pressure to bear on a tenant to modify the behaviour of an individual over whom they had no control). See too *Moat Housing Group South Ltd v Harris and Hartless* [2005] EWCA Civ 287; [2006] Q.B. 606; [2005] 3 W.L.R. 691; [2005] 4 All E.R. 1051, where having regard to good school reports, the absence of any criminal records or any serious record of police involvement with the tenant's family, and favourable testimonies given about the tenant, the Court of Appeal concluded that it would be right to suspend a possession order on the terms that there were no further breaches of the tenancy agreement. Cf. *Kensington and Chelsea RLBC v Simmonds* (1997) 29 H.L.R. 507, CA; *Northampton BC v Lovatt* (1998) 30 H.L.R. 875, CA; *Knowsley Housing Trust v McMullen* [2006] EWCA Civ 539; [2006] H.L.R. 43, CA and *Portsmouth City Council v Bryant* (2000) 32 H.L.R. 906; [2000] E.G.L.R. 287, CA.

*Effect of likely homelessness*—A local authority's housing obligations towards the defendant if made homeless, and in particular the question of whether rehousing is likely to be refused as a result of intentional homelessness, may have greater or lesser weight when considering reasonableness, depending on the circumstances—cf. *Rushcliffe BC v Watson* (1992) 24 H.L.R. 124, CA (the prospect that, if evicted, the tenant would probably be found to be intentionally homeless a very real consideration); *Bristol CC v Mousah* (1998) 30 H.L.R. 32, CA (whether the tenant would be rehoused as homeless was a matter for the council and not for the court); *Darlington BC v Sterling* (1997) 29 H.L.R. 309, CA (a decision by a Circuit Judge that as a District Judge had formed the view that the tenant ought not to be roofless he should not have ordered possession unless the council could show it would provide suitable alternative accommodation overturned by the Court of Appeal); and *Shrewsbury and Atcham BC v Evans* (1998) 30 H.L.R. 123, CA (the judge had not needed to consider how a tenant who had "flagrantly and deliberately lied about her circumstances" in order to obtain council housing would be rehoused). See too *Lewisham LBC v Adeyemi* (2000) 32 H.L.R. 414, CA where the court dismissed a tenant's appeal against a possession order, where the tenant claimed that the judge, when considering reasonableness, had failed to take into account whether the local authority would have a duty to rehouse under the Housing Act 1996 Pt VII. It is not for the court to make a pre-emptive decision on the possible outcome of an application that might or might not be made to the local authority. Entitlement to Pt VII accommodation is confined to the judgment of the local authority. It is not for the court to anticipate the outcome of that decision. The judge was well aware of the self-evident consequence of a possession order. The legal and practical consequences of homelessness however were not before the court, nor need they have been as they were for the local authority to determine; but cf. *North Devon Homes Ltd v Batchelor* [2008] EWCA Civ 840, July 22, 2008.

**Appeals on questions of reasonableness**

**3A–376** Although County Courts Act 1984 s.77(6) excludes appeals against judges' findings of fact, it does not exclude, in a proper case, the possibility of an appeal against a finding of reasonableness (*Castle Vale Housing Action Trust v Gallagher* [2001] EWCA Civ 944; (2001) 33 H.L.R. 810). In *Brent LBC v Doughan* [2007] EWCA Civ 135; February 6, 2007, May L.J. stated:

> "The judgment as to reasonableness is intrinsically one of judicial balance akin to the exercise of a judicial discretion. It is the kind of judgment with which [the Court of Appeal] is likely to be slow to interfere for well trodden reasons."

See too *Ealing LBC v Jama* [2008] EWCA Civ 896, June 25, 2008.

In *Bracknell Forest BC v Green* [2009] EWCA Civ 238, March 20, 2009 Mummery L.J. said that it is for judges in the county court to "carry out the balancing exercise and assess the relative weight of all the circumstances relevant to the decision". By its very nature a decision on reasonableness is difficult to appeal. "The role of the Court of Appeal under Pt 52 CPR is, in general, limited to a review of the decision of the lower court. The appeal is not a re-hearing or re-trial of the case" [22, 23]. He referred to Lord Hoffmann's "valuable analysis of the appellate function" in cases such as *Biogen v Medeva Plc* [1997] R.P.C. 1, and his overall conclusion that appellate courts should be "very cautious in differing from the judge's evaluation" of the facts in cases where a reference to, or an application of, an imprecise legal standard to the facts of the case is a matter of degree rather than of principle." In Mummery L.J.'s words:

> "the appeal process is not there merely for having another go at the kind of fact-based issue that the lower court is often better placed to assess than a law oriented appellate court is. ... [The Court of Appeal] should be slow to upset [a county court judge's] evaluation of reasonableness on the possession order issue, unless it is clear that he acted under an error of principle or unless his decision was obviously wrong" [29, 30].

**ECHR Article 8 and reasonableness**

**3A–377** The Court of Appeal has doubted whether art.8 makes any difference to the way in which courts have always approached questions of the reasonableness of making possessions order. Article 8 does, however, reinforce the importance of only making an order depriving someone of his or her home in circumstances where a clear case is made out (*Castle Vale Housing Action Trust v Gallagher* [2001] EWCA Civ 944; (2001) 33 H.L.R. 810). See too *Newham LBC v Neal* [2003] EWCA Civ 541; February 25, 2003. There is a need to find a fair balance and to protect the rights of the neighbours and other members of the public (*Lambeth LBC v Howard* [2001] EWCA Civ 468; (2001) 33 H.L.R. 636).

**Disability Discrimination Act 1995**

**3A–378** The effect of Disability Discrimination Act 1995 s.22(3)(c) is that it is unlawful to discriminate "by evicting [a] disabled person or subjecting him to any other detriment". Although unlawfulness under the Disability Discrimination Act is not a bar to a landlord seeking a possession order under the Housing Act, the fact that the eviction is unlawful and not justified is a highly relevant consideration for the s.7 discretion of whether or not to make a possession order. The Disability Discrimination Act contains its own code which requires a higher threshold than the Housing Act to justify an eviction (*North Devon Homes Ltd v Brazier* [2003] EWHC 574, QB). In *Manchester CC v Romano* [2004] EWCA (Civ) 834; [2005]1 W.L.R. 2775, the Court of Appeal, in a very thorough review of the legislation, stated that when a court considers the Disability

Discrimination Act 1995 in the context of possession proceedings, the first matter which has to be determined is whether the person who complains about disability discrimination is a "disabled person" within the meaning of the Disability Discrimination (Meaning of Disability) Regulations 1996 (SI 1996/1455), Sch.1, ss.1–3, and the *Guidance on matters to be taking into account in determining questions relating to the definition of disability* issued by the Secretary of State. Secondly, the court should consider whether or not there has been discrimination—i.e. treating a disabled person less favourably for a reason which relates to the disabled person's disability. Thirdly, the court should consider whether the landlord's treatment of the tenant is justified. It is only justified if in the landlord's opinion the treatment (viz the decision to set in motion proceedings for possession) is necessary in order not to endanger the health or safety of any of the people living in neighbouring houses and it is reasonable, in all the circumstances, for the landlord to hold that opinion. The landlord must prove that if it does not take this action someone's health or safety would be endangered. It does not have to prove that that person's health or safety has actually been damaged. However, in view of the decision in *Lewisham LBC v Malcolm* [2008] UKHL 43; [2008] 4 All E.R. 525 it will now be rare for tenants to be able to rely successfully on the Disability Discrimination Act when defending possession claims. Lord Scott stated that if the physical or mental condition that constitutes the tenant's disability has played no motivating part in the decision of the alleged discriminator to inflict on the disabled person the treatment complained of (e.g. bringing a possession claim), the alleged discriminator's reason for that treatment cannot relate to the disability.

**Forms of order**

See Forms **N26** (Order for possession), **N28** (Order for Possession (rented premises)(suspended)) and **N28A** (Order for Possession (rented premises) (postponed)). Notwithstanding the abolition of the status of "tolerated trespasser" (see para.3A–385 below), there may still be advantages to both landlords and tenants in using Form **N28A**. **3A–379**

## Extended discretion of court in certain proceedings for possession

**85.**—(1) Where proceedings are brought for possession of a dwelling-house let under a secure tenancy on any of the grounds set out in Part I or Part III of Schedule 2 (grounds 1 to 8 and 12 to 16: cases in which the court must be satisfied that it is reasonable to make a possession order), the court may adjourn the proceedings for such period or periods as it thinks fit. **3A–380**

(2) On the making of an order for possession of such a dwelling-house on any of those grounds, or at any time before the execution of the order, the court may—

(a) stay or suspend the execution of the order, or

(b) postpone the date of possession,

for such period or periods as the court thinks fit.

(3) On such an adjournment, stay, suspension or postponement the court—

(a) shall impose conditions with respect to the payment by the tenant of arrears of rent (if any) and rent, unless it considers that to do so would cause exceptional hardship to the tenant or would otherwise be unreasonable, and

(b) may impose such other conditions as it thinks fit.

(4) If the conditions are complied with, the court may, if it thinks fit, discharge or rescind the order for possession.

3A-381 *Note* —Amended by the Family Law Act 1996 Sch.8, para.53, the Civil Partnership Act 2004 s.82 and Sch.9, para.18 and the Housing and Regeneration Act 2008 Sch.11, Pt I, para.3(2), (4) (for transitional provisions see para.14) with effect from May 20, 2009 (SI 2009/1261) (c.66). The amendment made by Sch.11, Pt I, para.3(3) is not yet in force and is printed as part of the Housing and Regeneration Act 2008 —see below.

**"dwelling-house"**

3A-382 See s.112.

**"secure tenancy"**

3A-383 See s.79. See too Housing Act 1988 s.9.

**Extended discretion of court in certain proceedings for possession**

3A-384 The court's power to stay or suspend execution or postpone the date of possession may be exercised when making an order for possession or "at any time before the execution of the order" (s.85(2)).

A tenant against whom an outright order has been made under a discretionary ground is entitled to make a fresh application to a district judge to stay or suspend execution. Such an application:

> "is not in any way affected or fettered by the reasons given by [the district judge who heard the possession claim]...on such an application the district judge can take all relevant circumstances into account as they appear at the time of the application. Those will include any medical evidence which is before the court, any evidence as to the defendant's behaviour since the original order and the effect of an immediate order for possession which is not suspended upon the likelihood of the applicant being rehoused under the Housing Act 1996".

There is a continuing remedy in the county court (*Plymouth CC v Hoskin* [2002] EWCA Civ 684; May 1, 2002). See too *Ujima Housing Association v Smith*, April 2001 Legal Action 21; October 16, 2000, Ch D.

The right to apply for a postponement of an order for possession under s.85 is not an interest in land which is capable of being inherited. It is only available to the tenant, the tenant's spouse or former spouse in occupation (s.85(5), *Brent LBC v Knightley* (1997) 29 H.L.R. 857 , CA; *Marshall v Bradford MBC* [2001] EWCA Civ 594; [2002] H.L.R. 22) and *Austin v Southwark LBC* [2009] EWCA Civ 66, February 16, 2009).

For the circumstances in which it is reasonable to suspend or postpone a possession order, see the commentary to s.84 above. Section 85(2) gives the court a wide discretion and expressly allows the court to suspend for such period as it thinks fit. The court practice is to be merciful to tenants and to give them a realistic opportunity to pay arrears. The question of whether it is appropriate for a tenant who owes substantial arrears to have the threat of losing her home hanging over her for years is a political question and does not go to the correctness of making an order (*Henry v Lambeth LBC* (2000) 32 H.L.R. 874, CA).

Where there is a substantial dispute about the amount claimed and the tenant's compliance with the order, the up-to-date position has to be clearly and accurately established before considering an application to suspend under s.85 (*Haringey LBC v Powell* (1996) 28 H.L.R. 798, CA).

When exercising its powers under s.85 the court shall impose conditions with respect to the repayment of arrears of rent and mesne profits unless it considers that to do so would cause exceptional hardship (s.85(3)). There have been no reported Court of Appeal decisions as to what might constitute "exceptional hardship".

**The court's power to order the discharge of suspended possession orders**

3A-384.1 In *Knowsley Housing Trust v White*; *Islington LBC v Honeygan-Green*; *Porter v Shepherds Bush Housing Association* [2008] UKHL 70; [2009] 1 A.C. 636; [2009] 2 WLR 78, the House of Lords posed and answered the following questions:

(i) *Can the court, when making a suspended possession order under the Housing Act 1985, proleptically direct that the order be discharged once the terms have been complied with?* Yes. Section 85 permits a proleptic (i.e. anticipatory) discharge provision, not least because the court can always revisit the provision, effectively at the suit of the landlord, if the terms of the suspension are not complied with. Section 85

***Paragraph numbers marked with a "+" can be found online and on CD.***

should be construed, as far as permissible, to confer as much flexibility as possible on the court, and in such a way as to minimise future uncertainty and the need for further applications (para.96). (See too *Merton LBC v Hashmi* CAT 94/1147; September 1995, Legal Action 13, CA in relation to a former type of Form **N28**, which stated "When you have paid the total amount mentioned, the plaintiff will not be able to take any steps to evict you as a result of this order"—cheque for arrears handed to council on morning of execution. The council's contention that the judgment had not been satisfied because the cheque for £300 had not cleared before execution was rejected, since the tenants had been told that the further payment would satisfy all that was owed.)

(ii) *If so, can the court proleptically direct that the order be discharged even if the terms of the suspension have not been strictly complied with?* Yes. The terms on which a possession order for non-payment of rent is suspended should, almost as a matter of course, include precise dates on which any payment should be made. However, it does not follow that proleptic discharge should only be available if payment is made strictly on those dates (para.105). Nevertheless, the terms of a suspended order are to be literally applied and precisely complied with. If a tenant fails to comply strictly with any of the terms of suspension, the landlord can apply for a warrant (para.110).

(iii) *In the case of a suspended order under the Housing Act 1985, without a proleptic discharge provision, can a tenant who has not complied with the terms of suspension, but has paid off the arrears and costs, seek a discharge or variation of the order?* Yes. There is nothing in s.85(2), or elsewhere in the Act, which expressly or impliedly prevents a tenant, who has paid off all the arrears and costs, making an application to the court to exercise its powers under s.85(2) (para.113).

### Effect of breach of a suspended or postponed possession order

Until the implementation of the Housing and Regeneration Act 2008 Sch.11 on May 19, 2009, the effect of suspended (Form **N28**) or postponed possession orders (Form **N28A**) (e.g. with conditions that tenants pay current rent and a specified sum each week or month towards the arrears) was complex and depended on the changing forms of **N28** and, more recently **N28A**. The position was analysed in detail in the *White Book* 2009 Vol.2 para.3A–385. Many secure tenants became tolerated trespassers—sometimes immediately on breach of a suspended possession order; sometimes simply because of the wording of what was intended to be a suspended possession order (see e.g. *Thompson v Elmbridge BC* (1987) 19 H.L.R. 526, CA; *Burrows v Brent LBC* [1996] 1 W.L.R. 1448; [1996] 4 All E.R. 577 HL and *Harlow DC v Hall* [2006] EWCA Civ 156; [2006] 1 W.L.R. 2116). As a result of these difficulties, in *Bristol CC v Hassan*; *Bristol CC v Glastonbury* [2006] EWCA Civ 656; [2006] 1W.L.R. 2582, the Court of Appeal sanctioned a form of postponed order—now adopted as Form **N28A**. **3A–385**

The law has since been amended by Housing and Regeneration Act 2008 Sch.11 which prevents the creation of tolerated trespassers (by providing that secure and assured tenancies continue until any warrant for possession is executed); and restores tenancy status to former tolerated trespassers (by providing that a new "replacement tenancy" is deemed to arise provided that the former tenant continues to occupy the dwelling as his or her home).

Part 1 of Sch.11 amends the Housing Act 1985 to provide that where a possession order is made against a secure tenant, the tenancy ends on the date the tenant is evicted (unless the tenant ends the tenancy before that date). Part 2 of Sch.11 (see para.3A–1704) deals with replacement tenancies.

### Procedure on breach

If a tenant breaches a suspended order in Form **N28** and the landlord wishes to evict, generally the landlord files a Request for Warrant for Possession of Land in Form **N325**. In most circumstances, the issue of a Warrant for Possession of Land in Form **N49** is an administrative act. No hearing is required. A hearing is required, however, if the words "No warrant to be issued without prior application on notice" (or similar) are added to the normal form of suspended possession order. **3A–386**

A postponed order in Form **N28A** does not give a date for possession. Accordingly, a landlord who claims that a tenant has breached the terms of a postponed possession order must apply to the court for the court to fix a date for possession. In *Wandsworth*

*LBC v Whibley* [2008] EWCA Civ 1259; [2009] H.L.R. 26, the Court of Appeal rejected the council's attempt to establish a general rule that applications to fix a date for possession following the making and breach of a postponed possession order should be dealt with summarily. Courts have an obligation to consider whether or not it is right to make an order and to examine the circumstances. Sedley L.J. said:

> "if, on being notified of the impending application [to fix a date for possession] and invited to respond, the defendant remains silent or puts in a plainly spurious or irrelevant response, an order may properly be made summarily. But if, as is more probable in nuisance cases, an issue is raised which is capable of affecting the court's decision, justice will require the defendant to be given an opportunity to put his or her case. The court will of course be astute not to let merely factitious [sic] or obstructive responses impede a summary disposal; but, inconvenient though it will be for the lessor and for a time nightmarish for the neighbours, it is not permissible for a tenant who has a possible tenable answer to lose his or her home unheard " [12].

He continued:

> "What will not suffice to procure a hearing is an unsupported assertion that the tenant has an answer. Nor will a bare denial amount to an answer: save in exceptional cases the court will expect details, since a tenant who has already, by definition, breached the terms of the agreement has to have a cogent answer once there is prima facie evidence of repetition." [18]

At hearings to determine whether or not terms of a postponed possession order have been breached, the law permits the use of hearsay and enables most hearings to be conducted expeditiously. "Everything depends . . on a judicial appraisal of how the issues can be fairly and economically determined."

### Relevance of other conduct after a possession order has been made

**3A–387** (a) *on a landlord's application*—After a suspended possession order has been made, liberty to apply to the court by the landlord is implicit, without the need to start new proceedings for possession. If a landlord wishes to put new allegations before the court, the court can make a new order, even if the old order has not expired. Such a new order may provide for possession to be given up forthwith. The court has, on such an application, to bear in mind the guidance given in cases such as *Sheffield City Council v Hopkins* [2001] EWCA Civ 1023; [2002] H.L.R. 12; [2001] 26 E.G. 163, as to the exercise of its discretion in such a situation, and should be astute to ensure that tenants are not taken by surprise. However, that does not necessarily extend to insisting that the proceedings be delayed by the equivalent of the extra time that would have been taken had the landlord had to begin new proceedings (*Manchester City Council v Finn* [2002] EWCA Civ 1998; [2003] H.L.R. 41).

(b) *on a tenant's application*—The court, exercising its discretion on an application to suspend a warrant under s.85, may take account of matters (e.g. breaches of the terms of the tenancy agreement or anti-social behaviour) other than those relied upon as grounds for making the original possession order—although it is not always right to do so (*Sheffield City Council v Hopkins* [2001] EWCA Civ 1023; [2002] H.L.R. 12; [2001] 26 E.G. 163). Whilst not attempting to fetter the discretion of District Judges, the Court of Appeal stated that the following points are relevant: (1) The discretion should be used so as to further the policy of Housing Act 1985, Pt IV, reinforced by ECHR, art.8. The policy is only to evict after a serious breach of an obligation, where it is reasonable to do so and where the tenant is proved to have breached any condition of suspension; (2) The overriding objective of the Civil Procedure Rules, especially the need for applications to be dealt with in a summary and proportionate way, means that wider issues may not be able to be dealt with on an application to suspend or vary. They may need to be dealt with in some other way; (3) The tenant should have clear evidence of what is alleged, especially where the allegations were not contained in the original claim; (4) The fact that the landlord had or had not included the allegations as part of the original proceedings is relevant; (5) The discretion to consider other allegations should generally be exercised more readily in respect of matters occurring after commencement of the proceedings; (6) The court should also consider the practicalities of dealing with matters on the execution of a warrant; (7) The fact that the tenant is at the mercy of the court and the responsibilities of a public landlord to its other tenants. The list is not exhaustive. District Judges have to exercise the discretion bearing in mind the importance of the issue to the tenant, at risk of losing his home, and the responsibilities of social landlords to their other tenants. However it would appear that the court cannot take into account allegations which have not been proved or admitted by the tenant.

### After execution of a warrant

The court's power to stay or suspend execution or postpone the date of possession only applies before the execution of the order (*Hammersmith and Fulham LBC v Hill* (1995) 27 H.L.R. 368; [2001] L. & T.R. 423; [1994] 2 E.G.L.R. 51, CA and *Leicester CC v Aldwinkle* (1992) 24 H.L.R. 40, CA). After execution an occupier can only be restored to possession if either the possession order is set aside (see, e.g. *Governors of Peabody Donation Fund v Hay* (1987) 19 H.L.R. 145, CA; *Hackney LBC v White* (1996) 28 H.L.R. 219, CA; and *Tower Hamlets LBC v Abadie* (1990) 22 H.L.R. 264, CA) or the warrant has been obtained by fraud, abuse of process or oppression (*Hammersmith and Fulham LBC v Hill* (1995) 27 H.L.R. 368; [2001] L. & T.R. 423; [1994] 2 E.G.L.R. 51, CA (arguable that the council had behaved "oppressively" where the tenant claimed that after issue of the warrant, but before execution, council officers had said that the defendant would have no chance of having the warrant suspended unless she was able to pay £1,000 within 24 hours); *Saint v Barking and Dagenham LBC* (1999) 31 H.L.R. 620, CA (oppression where warrant executed without prior notification to tenant who was in prison and without inviting him to renew his application for housing benefit); and *William Sutton HT v Breen*, February 2000, Legal Action. See too *Islington LBC v Harridge, The Times*, June 30, 1993, CA. **3A–388**

In *Southwark LBC v Sarfo* (2000) 32 H.L.R. 602, CA, Roch L.J. said:

> "Oppression may be very difficult if not impossible to define, but it is not difficult to recognise. It is the insistence by a public authority on its strict rights in circumstances which make that insistence manifestly unfair. The categories of oppression are not closed because no-one can envisage all the sets of circumstances which could make the execution of a warrant oppressive".

"Oppression" is not limited to acts by the landlord. Misleading information from a court office, depriving a tenant of taking steps to have execution of a warrant for possession stayed prior to execution, may amount to oppression (*Hammersmith and Fulham LBC v Lemeh* (2001) 33 H.L.R. 23; [2001] L & T R. 423, CA). See too *Lambeth LBC v Hughes* (2001) 33 H.L.R. 33, CA where the Court of Appeal held that:

(1) a council's letter that only payment in full could prevent eviction was misleading and oppressive;
(2) the failure of the court office to advise the defendant of the procedure when he sought assistance in person was oppressive and
(3) the failure to despatch the bailiff's letter in sufficient time for it to be received and acted upon again made the execution oppressive.

However it has also been held that (1) a possession warrant obtained and executed against a secure tenant without fault on anyone's part cannot properly be set aside as oppressive or an abuse of process; (2) oppression cannot exist without the unfair use of court procedures; and (3) something more than the mere use of the eviction process "some action on someone's part which was open to criticism" is required before the court's procedures can be said to have been unfairly used (*Jephson Homes HA v Moisejevs* [2001] 2 All E.R. 901, CA). See too *Circle 33 Housing Trust Ltd v Ellis* [2005] EWCA Civ 1233; [2006] H.L.R. 7.

There is no power under s.85(2) to stay or postpone the date for giving up possession under an existing possession order if tenants have already given up possession without the need for execution of the order. The words "at any time before the execution of the order" in s.85(2) have to be read subject to the qualification "and for so long as execution is required to give effect to that order" (*Dunn v Bradford MDC* [2002] EWCA Civ 1137; [2003] H.L.R. 15, *Marston v Leeds City Council* [2002] EWCA Civ 1137; [2003] H.L.R. 15).

### Warrants and the ECHR

The Court of Appeal has held that the procedure which allows the issue of a war- **3A–389** rant of possession and the arrangements for execution following breach of a suspended possession order do not infringe tenants' rights under ECHR, Arts 6, 8 or 14. Tenants' rights to possession of premises are determined, when suspended possession orders are made. The issue of the warrant of possession is simply a step authorised to be taken to enforce that order. It does not alter the legal status of the tenant or make any kind of decision in relation to his or her rights, and so is not required to be the subject of a separate hearing. Secondly, although possession proceedings may interfere with tenants' right of respect for their homes, they are clearly in accordance with the law and are a legitimate and proportionate response to non-payment of rent. (*Southwark LBC v St. Brice* [2001] EWCA Civ 1138; [2002] 1 W.L.R. 1537).

Nevertheless, the Lord Chancellor's Department (LCD) has improved the information available to occupiers when an eviction is due to take place. Bailiffs must deliver Form **N54** (Notice of Eviction) to all addresses where evictions are due to take place and hand it to the defendant personally or leave it at the property in an envelope addressed to the defendant(s) by name and "any other occupiers". The notice points out that in some circumstances the court can decide to suspend the warrant and explains the procedure to be followed. In *Southwark LBC v St. Brice*, Kennedy L.J. said: "It is important that so far as possible tenants should receive such notice in time to enable time to take advice and, if so advised, bring the matter back to the court before the date fixed for eviction."

## Proceedings for possession: anti-social behaviour

3A–390 **85A.**—(1) This section applies if the court is considering under section 84(2)(a) whether it is reasonable to make an order for possession on ground 2 set out in Part 1 of Schedule 2 (conduct of tenant or other person).

(2) The court must consider, in particular—

(a) the effect that the nuisance or annoyance has had on persons other than the person against whom the order is sought;

(b) any continuing effect the nuisance or annoyance is likely to have on such persons;

(c) the effect that the nuisance or annoyance would be likely to have on such persons if the conduct is repeated.

### Editorial note

3A–391 This section was inserted by Anti-Social Behaviour Act 2003 s.16. It was brought into force in England on June 30, 2004 by the Anti-Social Behaviour Act 2003 (Commencement No.3 and Savings) Order 2004 (SI 2004/1502) (c.61). It does not have effect in relation to any proceedings for the possession of a dwelling-house begun before June 30, 2004. It was brought into force in Wales on April 30, 2005 by the Anti-Social Behaviour Act 2003 (Commencement No.4) (Wales) Order 2005 (SI 2005/1225) (w.83) (c.55).

### Reasonable

3A–392 When considering whether or not to make a possession order and/or whether or not to make a suspended possession order under Sch.2, Ground 2, the court must consider whether it is reasonable to make such an order—see the commentary to s.84 at para.3A–373 *et seq*. Section 85A adds to that general consideration a requirement that the court must consider, in particular, the effect that the nuisance or annoyance has had and would be likely to have if continued on persons other than the defendant, e.g. neighbours.

## Periodic tenancy arising on termination of fixed term

3A–393 **86.**—(1) Where a secure tenancy ("the first tenancy") is a tenancy for a term certain and comes to an end—

*Paragraph numbers marked with a "+" can be found online and on CD.*

(a) by effluxion of time, or

(b) by an order of the court under section 82(3) (termination in pursuance of provision for re-entry or forfeiture),

a periodic tenancy of the same dwelling-house arises by virtue of this section, unless the tenant is granted another secure tenancy of the same dwelling-house (whether a tenancy for a term certain or a periodic tenancy) to begin on the coming to an end of the first tenancy.

(2) Where a periodic tenancy arises by virtue of this section—

(a) the periods of the tenancy are the same as those for which rent was last payable under the first tenancy, and

(b) the parties and the terms of the tenancy are the same as those of the first tenancy at the end of it;

except that the terms are confined to those which are compatible with a periodic tenancy and do not include any provision for re-entry or forfeiture.

**"dwelling-house"**
See s.112. **3A-394**

**"secure tenancy"**
See s.79. See *Banjo v Brent LBC* [2005] EWCA Civ 292; *The Times* March 29, 2005, where the Court of Appeal held that no periodic tenancy arose on the determination a long lease, either under s.86 (because the fixed term tenancy which the tenant had previously held was not itself a secure tenancy) or by implication from the demand, payment or acceptance of rent. Security of tenure is dependent on there being a tenancy that the landlord cannot bring to an end without obtaining an order for possession. **3A-395**

*SUCCESSION ON DEATH OF TENANT*

## Persons qualified to succeed tenant

**87.** A person is qualified to succeed the tenant under a secure tenancy if he occupies the dwelling-house as his only or principal home at the time of the tenant's death and either— **3A-396**

(a) he is the tenant's spouse or civil partner, or

(b) he is another member of the tenant's family and has resided with the tenant throughout the period of twelve months ending with the tenant's death;

unless, in either case, the tenant was himself a successor, as defined in section 88.

*Note*—Amended by the Civil Partnership Act 2004 s.81 and Sch.8, para.20. **3A-397**

**"dwelling-house"**
See s.112. **3A-398**

**"secure tenancy"**
See s.79. **3A-399**

**"member of the tenant's family"**
See s.113. **3A-400**

**"successor"**
See s.88. **3A-401**

*Paragraph numbers marked with a "+" can be found online and on CD.*

### Persons qualified to succeed tenant

3A–402 On the death of a secure tenant, another person living in the dwelling as his or her only or principal home may succeed to the tenancy if s/he is either the spouse of the tenant or a member of the tenant's family who has resided with the tenant throughout the 12 months ending with the death.

In "family member" succession cases, the burden of proof is on successors to show that they are family members, that they have lived with the tenant for the 12 months and that the dwelling is their only or principal home (*Peabody Donation Fund Governors v Grant* (1983) 6 H.L.R. 41; (1982) 264 E.G. 925, CA).

The term "member of the family" can only be satisfied by the relationships listed in Housing Act 1985 s.113. First cousins, even if thought of as brothers in African culture, cannot be within the section (*Brent LBC v Fofana* [2000] Ed. C.R. 425).

Co-habitees count as family members (s.113). The Court of Appeal has held that the Housing Act 1985 s.87, when read together with the words "living together as husband and wife" in s.113, means that in order to be entitled to succeed a cohabitee must not only have lived with the deceased for a year but have lived as "husband or wife" for the whole year. Succession cannot be established where the cohabitation "as husband and wife" has been for only part of the 12 months of co-residence (*Westminster CC v Peart* (1992) 24 H.L.R. 389, CA).

Same sex couples may be treated in the same way as a husband and wife. The House of Lords has held that the words "as his or her wife or husband" in Rent Act 1977 Sch.1 para.2(2) must be read to mean "as if they were his or her wife or husband" in order to comply with the ECHR. Accordingly the survivor of a same sex couple who has been living in a loving and monogamous relationship with a tenant may be able to succeed to a secure tenancy (see *Ghaidan v Godin-Mendoza* [2004] UKHL 30; [2004] 2 A.C. 557; cf. *Harrogate BC v Simpson* (1985) 17 H.L.R. 205, CA and *Fitzpatrick v Sterling Housing Association* [2001] 1 A.C. 27; [1999] 3 W.L.R. 1113; [1999] 4 All E.R. 705, HL).

It is not possible for there to be a joint succession to a secure tenancy (*Newham LBC v Phillips* (1998) 30 H.L.R. 859; (1998) 96 L.G.R. 788, CA).

A minor who satisfies the succession conditions may succeed to a secure tenancy. In that case, a secure tenancy in equity vests in the minor. The Trusts of Land and Appointment of Trustees Act 1996 Sch.1 operates in such a way that the legal tenancy to which the minor succeeded is held on trust until the age of majority is reached (*Kingston upon Thames RLBC v Prince* [1999] 1 F.L.R. 593 and *Newham LBC v R (A Child)* [2004] EWCA Civ 41).

The term "residence" is interpreted in much the same way as in the Rent Act 1977 s.2, the Housing Act 1985 s.81, and the Housing Act 1988 s.1. Periods of temporary absence (if there is an intention to return and a physical manifestation of that intention) or residence at other premises do not necessarily prevent "residence" continuing. See, e.g. *Peabody Donation Fund Governors v Grant* (1983) 6 H.L.R. 41; (1982) 264 E.G. 925, CA (daughter moved in to live with father who was ill for part of each week in order to look after him. She stayed in her father's flat four nights a week, kept her clothes and books there and regarded the flat as her home. She was entitled to succeed); *Camden LBC v Goldenberg* (1996) 28 H.L.R. 727; (1997) 73. P & C.R. 376, CA (grandson moved out after marriage, but he and his wife could not find alternative accommodation and as a result he moved back after ten weeks) and *Marsh v Lewisham LBC* December 1989, Legal Action 14, CA. However, mere physical presence is not enough to amount to "residing with" for the purposes of s.87. There must, to a significant degree, be an intention which can be characterised as making a home with the tenant. Just staying in the property is not enough (*Islington LBC v Freeman* [2009] EWCA Civ 536; June 11, 2009 and *Swanbrae Ltd v Elliott* (1987) 19 H.L.R. 86, CA).

The 12-month residence requirement may be satisfied by residence with the deceased council tenant in any premises or combination of premises (not necessarily subject to secure tenancies for the whole period) for the one year ending with the date of death (*Waltham Forest LBC v Thomas* [1992] 2 A.C. 198; [1992] 3 W.L.R. 131; [1992] 3 All E.R. 244, HL, overruling *South Northamptonshire DC v Power* [1987] 1 W.L.R. 1433, CA).

The right to succeed only applies where a secure tenancy is still in existence. The law used to be that such tenancies came to an end if the terms of a suspended possession order were breached (s.85(5) and *Brent LBC v Knightley* (1997) 29 H.L.R. 857 , CA)—but now the Housing and Regeneration Act 2008 Sch.11 provides that secure tenancies continue until any warrant for possession is executed.

Security of tenure is commonly lost when a tenant dies and there is no person qualified to succeed to the tenancy. In such circumstances the tenancy passes to the late tenant's executors or administrators. In the case of intestacy, the tenancy now passes to the Public Trustee (Law of Property (Miscellaneous Provisions) Act 1994 s.14). A Practice Direction (Probate: Notice to Quit [1995] 1 W.L.R. 1120) indicates how a notice to quit may be served on the Public Trustee to bring the continuing tenancy to an end.

See too Sch.2 Ground 16 (ground for possession where dwelling more extensive than reasonably required after succession).

Section 87 is also relevant to the question of assignment of secure tenancies, since one of the exceptions to the general prohibition against assignment of secure tenancies (s.91) applies where the assignee is "a person who would be qualified to succeed the tenant if the tenant died immediately before the assignment".

## Cases where the tenant is a successor

**88.**—(1) The tenant is himself a successor if— **3A–403**

(a) the tenancy vested in him by virtue of section 89 (succession to a periodic tenancy), or

(b) he was a joint tenant and has become the sole tenant, or

(c) the tenancy arose by virtue of section 86 (periodic tenancy arising on ending of term certain) and the first tenancy there mentioned was granted to another person or jointly to him and another person, or

(d) he became the tenant on the tenancy being assigned to him (but subject to subsections (2) to (3)), or

(e) he became the tenant on the tenancy being vested in him on the death of the previous tenant, or

(f) the tenancy was previously an introductory tenancy and he was a successor to the introductory tenancy.

(2) A tenant to whom the tenancy was assigned in pursuance of an order under section 23A or 24 of the Matrimonial Causes Act 1973 (property adjustment orders in connection with matrimonial proceedings) or section 17(1) of the Matrimonial and Family Proceedings Act 1984 (property adjustment orders after overseas divorce) is a successor only if the other party to the marriage was a successor.

(2A) A tenant to whom the tenancy was assigned in pursuance of an order under Part 2 of Schedule 5, or paragraph 9(2) or (3) of Schedule 7, to the Civil Partnership Act 2004 (property adjustment orders in connection with civil partnership proceedings or after overseas dissolution of civil partnership, etc.) is a successor only if the other civil partner was a successor.

(3) A tenant to whom the tenancy was assigned by virtue of section 92 (assignments by way of exchange) is a successor only if he was a successor in relation to the tenancy which he himself assigned by virtue of that section.

(4) Where within six months of the coming to an end of a secure tenancy which is a periodic tenancy ("the former tenancy") the tenant becomes a tenant under another secure tenancy which is a periodic tenancy, and—

(a) the tenant was a successor in relation to the former tenancy, and

(b) under the other tenancy either the dwelling-house or

the landlord, or both, are the same as under the former tenancy,

the tenant is also a successor in relation to the other tenancy unless the agreement creating that tenancy otherwise provides.

3A-404 *Note*—Amended by the Housing Act 1996 Sch.14, para.1, Sch.18, para.9; the Family Law Act 1996 Sch.8, para.34; and the Civil Partnership Act 2004 s.81 and Sch.8, para.21.

**"successor"**

3A-405 A person who was a joint tenant and became a sole tenant by right of survivorship before the implementation of the Housing Act 1980 is not "a successor" for the purposes of the Housing Act 1985 s.88 (*Birmingham City Council v Walker* [2007] UKHL 22; [2007] 2 A.C. 262; [2007] 2 W.L.R. 1057).

**"dwelling-house"**

3A-406 See s.112.

**"secure tenancy"**

3A-407 See s.79.

**"introductory tenancy"**

3A-408 See s.115A and the Housing Act 1996 s.124.

## Succession to periodic tenancy

3A-409 **89.**—(1) This section applies where a secure tenant dies and the tenancy is a periodic tenancy.

(2) Where there is a person qualified to succeed the tenant, the tenancy vests by virtue of this section in that person, or if there is more than one such person in the one to be preferred in accordance with the following rules—

(a) the tenant's spouse or civil partner is to be preferred to another member of the tenant's family;

(b) of two or more other members of the tenant's family such of them is to be preferred as may be agreed between them or as may, where there is no such agreement, be selected by the landlord.

(3) Where there is no person qualified to succeed the tenant, the tenancy ceases to be a secure tenancy—

(a) where it is vested or otherwise disposed of in the course of the administration of the tenants' estate, unless the vesting or other disposal is in pursuance of an order made under—

(i) section 23A or 24 of the Matrimonial Causes Act 1973 (property adjustment orders made in connection with matrimonial proceedings),

(ii) section 17(1) of the Matrimonial and Family Proceedings Act 1984 (property adjustment orders after overseas divorce), or

(iii) paragraph 1 of Schedule 1 to the Children Act 1989 (orders for financial relief against parents), or

(iv) Part 2 of Schedule 5, or paragraph 9(2) or (3) of Schedule 7, to the Civil Partnership Act 2004 (property adjustment orders in connection with civil partnership proceedings or after overseas dissolution of civil partnership, etc.)

(b) When it is known that when the tenancy is so vested or disposed of it will not be in pursuance of such an order.

(4) A tenancy which ceases to be a secure tenancy by virtue of this section cannot subsequently become a secure tenancy.

*Note* —Amended by the Housing Act 1996 Sch.18, para.10; the Family Law Act 1996 Sch.8, para.34; and the Civil Partnership Act 2004 ss.81, 261(4), Sch.8, para.22, Sch.30. **3A–410**

**"secure tenancy"**

See s.79. **3A–411**

**"member of the tenant's family"**

See s.113. Section 113 contains an exhaustive list of categories of family members eligible to succeed a secure tenant. Although that section is discriminatory in relation to a matter within the scope of ECHR, art.8 (the "home") and so art.14 is engaged, there is an objective justification for establishing a "closed" list in s.113, namely "certainty" in determining which members of a secure tenant's family are eligible to succeed and accordingly art.14 is not infringed. The fact that the Rent Acts contain no exhaustive definition of "member of the family" is not relevant to the construction of the section because the schemes of the Rent Act and the Housing Act tenancies are so different that a potential successor in one scheme has no "comparator" in the other scheme. On a claim for possession against a non-successor, the county court is not required to investigate the individual circumstances of the defendant in order to find the conditions of ECHR, art.8(2) made out. (*Michalak v Wandsworth LBC* [2002] EWCA Civ 271; [2003] 1 W.L.R. 617). See too *R. (Gangera) v Hounslow LBC* [2003] EWHC 794 Admin; [2003] H.L.R. 68 (where Moses J. held that the provisions prohibiting people in categories other than those listed in s.113 from succeeding to secure tenancies do not infringe ECHR, art.14 read with art.8) and *Harrow LBC v Qazi* [2003] UKHL 43; [2004] 1 A.C. 983; [2003] 3 W.L.R. 792; (where Lord Hope and Lord Scott approved these decisions and said that contractual and property rights cannot be defeated by a defence based on Article 8). **3A–412**

**"qualified to succeed"**

See s.87. **3A–413**

It has been held that if a minor would be entitled to succeed, by operation of the Trusts of Land and Appointment of Trustees Act 1996 Sch.1, the tenancy should be held on trust for him or her: *Kingston upon Thames RLBC v Prince* (1999) 31 H.L.R. 794; [1999] L.G.R. 333, CA.

## Devolution of term certain

**90.**—(1) This section applies where a secure tenant dies and the tenancy is a tenancy for a term certain. **3A–414**

(2) The tenancy remains a secure tenancy until—

(a) it vested or otherwise disposed of in the course of the administration of the tenant's estate, as mentioned in subsection (3), or

(b) it is known that when it is so vested or disposed of it will not be a secure tenancy.

(3) The tenancy ceases to be a secure tenancy on being vested or otherwise disposed of in the course of administration of the tenant's estate, unless—

(a) the vesting or other disposal is in pursuance of an order made under—

(i) section 23A or 24 of the Matrimonial Causes Act 1973 (property adjustment orders in connection with matrimonial proceedings),

(ii) section 17(1) of the Matrimonial and Family Proceedings Act 1984 (property adjustment orders after overseas divorce),

(iii) paragraph 1 of Schedule 1 to the Children Act 1989 (orders for financial relief against parents), or

(iv) Part 2 of Schedule 5, or paragraph 9(2) or (3) of Schedule 7, to the Civil Partnership Act 2004 (property adjustment orders in connection with civil partnership proceedings or after overseas dissolution of civil partnership, etc.), or

(b) the vesting or other disposal is to a person qualified to succeed the tenant.

(4) A tenancy which ceases to be a secure tenancy by virtue of this section cannot subsequently become a secure tenancy.

**3A–415** *Note* —Amended by the Housing Act 1996 Sch.18, para.11; the Family Law Act 1996; and the Civil Partnership Act 2004 ss.81, 261(4) and Sch.8, para.24, Sch.30.

**"secure tenancy"**

**3A–416** See s.79.

**"qualified to succeed"**

**3A–417** See s.87.

### *ASSIGNMENT, LODGERS AND SUBLETTING*

**3A–418** **91.**—(1) A secure tenancy which is—

(a) a periodic tenancy, or

(b) a tenancy for a term certain granted on or after 5th November 1982, is not capable of being assigned except in the cases mentioned in subsection (3).

(2) If a secure tenancy for a term certain granted before 5th November 1982 is assigned, then, except in the cases mentioned in subsection (3), it ceases to be a secure tenancy and cannot subsequently become a secure tenancy.

(3) The exceptions are—

(a) an assignment in accordance with section 92 (assignment by way of exchange);

(b) an assignment in pursuance of an order made under—

(i) section 23A or 24 of the Matrimonial Causes Act 1973 (property adjustment orders in connection with matrimonial proceedings),

(ii) section 17(1) of the Matrimonial and Family Proceedings Act 1984 (property adjustment orders after overseas divorce),

***Paragraph numbers marked with a "+" can be found online and on CD.***

(iii) paragraph 1 of Schedule 1 to the Children Act 1989 (orders for financial relief against parents), or

(iv) Part 2 of Schedule 5, or paragraph 9(2) or (3) of Schedule 7, to the Civil Partnership Act 2004 (property adjustment orders in connection with civil partnership proceedings or after overseas dissolution of civil partnership, etc.)

(c) an assignment to a person who would be qualified to succeed the tenant if the tenant died immediately before the assignment.

*Note* —Amended by the Housing Act 1996 Sch.18, para.12; the Family Law Act 1996 Sch.8, para.34; and the Civil Partnership Act 2004 ss.81, 261(4), Sch.8, para.24, Sch.30. **3A–419**

**"secure tenancy"**

See s.79. **3A–420**

**"qualified to succeed"**

See s.87. **3A–421**

**Deed of Release**

The prohibition on assignment in s.91(1) applies equally to deeds of assignment and deeds of release (*Burton v Camden LBC* [2000] 2 A.C. 399; [2000] 2 W.L.R. 427, [2000] 1 All E.R. 943, HL). **3A–422**

## Assignments by way of exchange

**92.**—(1) It is a term of every secure tenancy that the tenant may, with the written consent of the landlord, assign the tenancy to another secure tenant who satisfies the condition in subsection (2) or to an assured tenant who satisfies the conditions in subsection 2A. **3A–423**

(2) The condition is that the other secure tenant has the written consent of his landlord to an assignment of his tenancy either to the first-mentioned tenant or to another secure tenant who satisfies the condition in this subsection.

(2A) The conditions to be satisfied with respect to an assured tenant are—

(a) that the landlord under is assured tenancy is either the Housing Corporation, the Secretary of State, a registered housing association or a housing trust which is a charity; and

(b) that he intends to assign his assured tenancy to the secure tenant referred to in subsection (1) or to another secure tenant who satisfies the condition in subsection (2).

(3) The consent required by virtue of this section shall not be withheld except on one or more of the grounds set out in Schedule 3, and if withheld otherwise than on one of those grounds shall be treated as given.

(4) The landlord may not rely on any of the grounds set out in Schedule 3 unless he has, within 42 days of the tenant's application

for the consent, served on the tenant a notice specifying the ground and giving particulars of it.

(5) Where rent lawfully due from the tenant has not been paid or an obligation of the tenancy has been broken or not performed, the consent required by virtue of this section may be given subject to a condition requiring the tenant to pay the outstanding rent, remedy the breach or perform the obligation.

(6) Except as provided by subsection (5), a consent required by virtue of this section cannot be given subject to a condition, and a condition imposed otherwise than as so provided shall be disregarded.

3A–424 *Note*—Amended by the Local Government and Housing Act 1989 s.163; the Housing Act 1996 (Consequential Provisions) Order 1996 (SI 1996/2325) art.5, Sch.2, para.14 and the Government of Wales Act 1998 s.140 and Sch.16, para.10 and Sch.18, Pt VI.

**"secure tenancy"**

3A–425 See s.79.

**"term"**

3A–426 See s.116.

**"assured tenancy"**

3A–427 See ss. 117 and 622, and the Housing Act 1988 s.1. See too Sch.2, Ground 6 (ground for possession where premium charged on mutual exchange), and Sch.3 (grounds for withholding consent to assignment).

**Assignments by way of exchange**

3A–428 The right to "mutual exchange" may be exercised between secure and assured tenants provided that they have the written consent of their landlords. Consent may only be withheld on the grounds set out in Sch.3. If it is withheld other than on such grounds, it is to be treated as having been given (s.91(3)).

To be effective an assignment must be by deed (Law of Property Act 1925 s.52, and *Crago v Julian* [1992] 1 W.L.R. 372; (1991) 24 H.L.R. 306, CA).

See also *Sanctuary Housing Association v Baker* (1998) 30 H.L.R. 809, CA.

## Lodgers and subletting

3A–429 **93.**—(1) It is a term of every secure tenancy that the tenant—

(a) may allow any persons to reside as lodgers in the dwelling-house, but

(b) will not, without the written consent of the landlord, sublet or part with possession of part of the dwelling-house.

(2) If the tenant under a secure tenancy parts with the possession of the dwelling-house or sublets the whole of it (or sublets first part of it and then the remainder), the tenancy ceases to be a secure tenancy and cannot subsequently become a secure tenancy.

**"secure tenancy"**

3A–430 See s.79.

**"dwelling-house"**

3A–431 See s.112.

**"lodgers"**

3A–432 Not defined in the Housing Act 1985, but see *Street v Mountford* [1985] A.C. 809;

[1985] 2 W.L.R. 877; [1985] 2 All E.R. 289; (1985) 17 H.L.R. 402, HL; *Aslan v Murphy* [1989] 3 All E.R. 130; [1989] 38 E.G. 109; (1989) 21 H.L.R. 532, CA; *Crancour Ltd v Da Silvaesa* (1986) 18 H.L.R. 265; (1986) 278 E.G. 618, CA; *Huwyer v Ruddy* (1996) 28 H.L.R. 550, CA; and *Monmouth BC v Marlog* (1994) 27 H.L.R. 30, CA.

**"sub-letting or parting with possession"**

See *Muir Group Housing Association Ltd v Thornley* (1993) 25 H.L.R. 89, CA; and *Brent LBC v Cronin* (1997) 30 H.L.R. 43, CA, *cf. Merton LBC v Salama* (1989) CAT No.89/169; June 1989, Legal Action 25, CA (parting with possession of part of premises); and *Hussey v Camden LBC* (1994) 27 H.L.R. 5, CA. Parting with possession is not to be inferred simply from the fact that another person has been allowed to use and occupy a tenant's home during his temporary absence (*Lam Kee Ying v Lam Shes Tong* [1975] A.C. 247, PC). See too the commentary to s.81. Section 93(2) is not incompatible with ECHR art.8 or art.1 of the First Protocol (*Delson v Lambeth LBC* [2002] EWCA Civ 1894; November 19, 2002). **3A–433**

**"consent of the landlord"**

See s.94. **3A–434**

## Consent to subletting

**94.**—(1) This section applies to the consent required by virtue of section 93(1)(b)(landlord's consent to subletting of part of dwelling-house). **3A–435**

(2) Consent shall not be unreasonably withheld (and if unreasonably withheld shall be treated as given), and if a question arises whether the withholding of consent was unreasonable it is for the landlord to show that it was not.

(3) In determining that question the following matters, if shown by the landlord, are among those to be taken into account—

(a) that the consent would lead to overcrowding of the dwelling-house within the meaning of Part X (overcrowding);

(b) that the landlord proposes to carry out works on the dwelling-house, or on the building of which it forms part, and that the proposed works will affect the accommodation likely to be used by the sub-tenant who would reside in the dwelling-house as a result of the consent.

(4) Consent may be validly given notwithstanding that it follows, instead of preceding, the action requiring it.

(5) Consent cannot be given subject to a condition (and if purporting to be given subject to a condition shall be treated as given unconditionally).

(6) Where the tenant has applied in writing for consent, then—

(a) if the landlord refuses to give consent, it shall give the tenant a written statement of the reasons why consent was refused, and

(b) if the landlord neither gives nor refuses to give consent within a reasonable time, consent shall be taken to have been withheld.

**"dwelling-house"**

See s.112. **3A–436**

**"overcrowding"**

See s.324. **3A–437**

*Paragraph numbers marked with a "+" can be found online and on CD.*

### Assignment or subletting where tenant condition not satisfied

3A–438 **95.**—(1) This section applies to a tenancy which is not a secure tenancy but would be if the tenant condition referred to in section 81 (occupation by the tenant) were satisfied.

(2) Sections 91 and 93(2) (restrictions on assignment or subletting of whole dwelling-house) apply to such a tenancy as they apply to a secure tenancy, except that—

(a) section 91(3)(b) and (c) (assignments expected from restrictions) do not apply to such a tenancy for a term certain granted before 5th November 1982, and

(b) references to the tenancy ceasing to be secure shall be disregarded, without prejudice to the application of the remainder of the provisions in which those references occur.

**"secure tenancy"**

3A–439 See s.79.

**"tenant condition"**

3A–440 See s.81.

* * * *

### Acquisition of dwelling-house subject to statutory tenancy

3A–441 **109A.** Where an authority or body within section 80 (the landlord condition for secure tenancies) becomes the landlord of a dwelling-house subject to a statutory tenancy, the tenancy shall be treated for all purposes as if it were a contractual tenancy on the same terms, and the provisions of this Part apply accordingly.

3A–442 *Note*—Inserted by Housing and Planning Act 1986 s.24(1)(b), Sch.5, Pt 1, para.2.

## *SUPPLEMENTARY PROVISIONS*

### Jurisdiction of county court

3A–443 **110.**—(1) A county court has jurisdiction to determine questions arising under this Part and to entertain proceedings brought under this Part and claims, for whatever amount, in connection with a secure tenancy.

(2) That jurisdiction includes jurisdiction to entertain proceedings on the following questions—

(a) whether a consent required by section 92 (assignment by way of exchange) was withheld otherwise than on one or more of the grounds set out in Schedule 3,

(b) whether a consent required by section 93(1)(b) or 97(1) (landlord's consent to subletting of part of dwelling-house or to carrying out of improvements) was withheld or unreasonably withheld, or

(c) whether a statement supplied in pursuance of section

104(2)(b)(written statement of certain terms of tenancy) is accurate,

notwithstanding that no other relief is sought than a declaration.

(3) If a person takes proceedings in the High Court which, by virtue of this section, he could have taken in the county court, he is not entitled to recover any costs.

## County court rules and directions

**111.** [...] **3A–444**

*Note* —Repealed by the Constitutional Reform Act 2005 ss.15(1), 146, Sch.4, paras 180, 181, Sch.18. **3A–445**

## Introductory tenancies

**111A.** Sections 102(1), (2) and (3)(a), 103 and 108 apply in relation to introductory tenancies as they apply in relation to secure tenancies. **3A–446**

*Note* —Inserted by the Housing Act 1996 (Consequential Amendments) Order 1997 (SI 1997/74) art.2, Sch., para.3(a), (i). **3A–447**

See also s.115A and the Housing Act 1996 s.124.

## Meaning of "dwelling-house"

**112.**—(1) For the purposes of this Part a dwelling-house may be a house or a part of a house. **3A–448**

(2) Land let together with a dwelling-house shall be treated for the purposes of this Part as part of the dwelling-house unless the land is agricultural land (as defined in section 26(3)(a) of the General Rate Act 1967) exceeding two acres.

## Members of a person's family

**113.**—(1) A person is a member of another's family within the meaning of this Part if— **3A–449**

(a) he is the spouse or civil partner of that person, or he and that person live together as husband and wife or as if they were civil partners, or

(b) he is that person's parent, grandparent, child, grandchild, brother, sister, uncle, aunt, nephew or niece.

(2) For the purpose of subsection (1)(b)—

(a) a relationship by marriage or civil partnership shall be treated as a relationship by blood,

(b) a relationship of the half-blood shall be treated as a relationship of the whole blood,

(c) the stepchild of a person shall be treated as his child, and

(d) an illegitimate child shall be treated as the legitimate child of his mother and reputed father.

*Note* —Amended by the Civil Partnership Act 2004 s.81 and Sch.8, para.27. **3A–450**

### Members of a person's family

See commentary to s.87. **3A–451**

***Paragraph numbers marked with a "+" can be found online and on CD.***

## Meaning of "landlord authority"

3A–452 **114.**—(1) In this Part "landlord authority" means—

a local housing authority,

a registered social landlord other than a co-operative housing association,

a housing trust which is a charity,

a development corporation,

a housing action trust, or

an urban development corporation

other than an authority in respect of which an exemption certificate has been issued.

(2) The Secretary of State may, on an application duly made by the authority concerned, issue an exemption certificate to—

a development corporation,

a housing action trust, or

an urban development corporation,

if he is satisfied that it has transferred, or otherwise disposed of, at least three-quarters of the dwellings which have at any time before the making of the application been vested in it.

(3) The application shall be in such form and shall be accompanied by such information as the Secretary of State may, either generally or in relation to a particular case, direct.

3A–453 *Note*—Amended by the Housing Act 1988 s.83; the Housing Act 1996 (Consequential Provisions) Order 1996 (SI 1996/2325) art.5, Sch.2, para.14 and the Government of Wales Act 1998 Sch.15, para.10 and Sch.18, Pt IV.

**"local housing authority"**

3A–454 See ss.1 and 2.

**"housing action trust"**

3A–455 See s.4.

**"housing trust"**

3A–456 See s.6.

**"an urban development corporation"**

3A–457 See s.4.

**"development corporation"**

3A–458 See s.4.

**"registered social landlord"**

3A–459 See the Housing Act 1996 ss.1–7.

## Meaning of "long tenancy"

3A–460 **115.**—(1) The following are long tenancies for the purposes of this Part, subject to subsection (2)—

(a) a tenancy granted for a term certain exceeding 21 years, whether or not it is (or may become) terminable before the end of that term by notice given by the tenant or by re-entry or forfeiture;

(b) a tenancy for a term fixed by law under a grant with a covenant or obligation for perpetual renewal, other than a tenancy by sub-demise from one which is not a long tenancy;

(c) any tenancy granted in pursuance of Part V (the right to buy), including any tenancy granted in pursuance of that Part as it has effect by virtue of section 17 of the Housing Act 1996 (the right to acquire).

(2) A tenancy granted so as to become terminable by notice after a death is not a long tenancy for the purposes of this Part, unless—

(a) it is granted by a housing association which at the time of the grant is a registered social landlord

(b) it is granted at a premium calculated by reference to a percentage of the value of the dwelling-house or of the cost of providing it, and

(c) at the time it is granted it complies with the requirements of the regulations then in force under section 140(4)(b) of the Housing Act 1980 or paragraph 4(2)(b) of Schedule 4A to the Leasehold Reform Act 1967 (conditions for exclusion of shared ownership leases from Part I of the Leasehold Reform Act 1967) or, in the case of a tenancy granted before any such regulations were brought into force, with the first such regulations to be in force.

*Note* —Amended by the Housing Act 1988 s.140, Sch.17, para.40; and the Housing Act 1996 (Consequential Provisions) Order 1996 (SI 1996/2325) art.5, Sch.2, para.14; and the Housing Act 1996 (Consequential Amendments No.2) Order 1997 (SI 1997/627) Sch.2, para.3. **3A–461**

## Meaning of "introductory tenancy"

**115A.** In this Part "introductory tenancy" has the same meaning as in Chapter I of Part V of the Housing Act 1996. **3A–462**

*Note* —Inserted by the Housing Act 1996 s.141(1), Sch.14, para.3. See also the Housing Act 1996 s.124. **3A–463**

## Minor definitions

**116.** In this Part— **3A–464**

"common parts", in relation to a dwelling-house let under a tenancy, means any part of a building comprising the dwelling-house and any other premises which the tenant is entitled under the terms of the tenancy to use in common with the occupiers of other dwelling-houses let by the landlord;

"housing purposes" means the purposes for which dwelling-houses are held by local housing authorities under Part II (provision of housing) or purposes corresponding to those purposes;

"rental period" means a period in respect of which a payment of rent falls to be made;

"term", in relation to a secure tenancy, includes a condition of the tenancy.

## Index of defined expressions: Part IV

3A–465 **117.** The following Table shows provisions defining or otherwise explaining expressions used in this Part (other than provisions defining or explaining an expression in the same section or paragraph)—

| | |
|---|---|
| assured tenancy | section 622 |
| cemetery | section 622 |
| charity | section 622 |
| common parts (in relation to a dwelling-house let under a tenancy) | section 116 |
| consent | Schedule 3A, para.2(3) |
| co-operative housing association | section 5(2) |
| development corporation | section 4(c) |
| dwelling-house | section 112 |
| family (member of) | section 113 |
| housing association | section 5(1) |
| housing authority | section 4(a) |
| housing purposes | section 116 |
| housing trust | section 6 |
| improvement | section 97(2) |
| introductory tenancy | section 115A |
| landlord | Schedule 2 Part V, para.7 |
| landlord authority | section 114 |
| local authority | section 4(e) |
| local housing authority | section 1, 2(2) |
| long tenancy | section 115 |
| management agreement and manager | section 27(2) and 27B(4) |
| new town corporation | section 4(b) |
| qualified to succeed (on the death of a secure tenant) | section 87 |
| registered social landlord | section 5(4) and (5) |
| relevant Authority | section 6A |
| rental period | section 116 |
| secure tenancy | section 79 |
| term (in relation to a secure tenancy) | section 116 |

3A–466 *Note* —Amended by the Housing and Planning Act 1986 s.24(1), (2), Sch.5; the Housing Act 1988 s.140, Sch.17; the Housing Act 1996 s.141(1), Sch.14, para.4; the Housing Act 1996 (Consequential Provisions) Order 1996 (SI 1996/2325) art.5, Sch.2, para.14 and the Government of Wales Act 1998 Sch.16, para.11 and Sch.18, Pt VI.

***Paragraph numbers marked with a "+" can be found online and on CD.***

* * * *

*DEMOLITION ORDERS*

## Demolition orders: recovery of possession of building to be demolished

**270.**—(1) Where a demolition order has become operative with respect to any premises, the local housing authority shall serve on any occupier of the premises or any part of the premises a notice— **3A–467**

(a) stating the effect of the order,

(b) specifying the date by which the order requires the premises to be vacated, and

(c) requiring him to quit the premises before that date or before the expiration of 28 days from the service of the notice, whichever may be the later.

(2) If any person is in occupation of the premises, or any part of them, at any time after the date on which the notice requires the premises to be vacated, the local housing authority or an owner of the premises may apply to the county court which shall thereupon order vacant possession of the premises or part to be given to the applicant within such period, of not less than two or more than four weeks, as the court may determine.

(3) Nothing in the Rent Acts or Part I of the Housing Act 1988 affects the provisions of this section relating to the obtaining possession of any premises.

(4) Expenses incurred by the local housing authority under this section in obtaining possession of any premises, or part of any premises, may be recovered by them by action from the owner, or from any of the owners, of the premises.

(5) A person who, knowing that a demolition order has become operative and applies to any premises—

(a) enters into occupation of the premises, or a part of them, after the date by which the order requires them to be vacated, or

(b) permits another person to enter into such occupation after that date,

commits a summary offence and is liable on conviction to a fine not exceeding level 5 on the standard scale and to a further fine not exceeding £5 for every day or part of a day on which the occupation continues after conviction.

*Note*—Amended by the Local Government and Housing Act 1989 Sch.9; and the Housing Act 1988 Sch.17. **3A–468**

**"demolition order"**

Is defined by s.267 as "an order requiring that the premises—(a) be vacated within a specified period (of at least 28 days) from the date on which the order becomes operative, and (b) be demolished within six weeks after the end of that period, after the date on which it is vacated or, in either case, within such longer period as in the circumstances the local housing authority consider it reasonable to specify." **3A–469**

***Paragraph numbers marked with a "+" can be found online and on CD.***

**"local housing authority"**

3A–470 See ss.1 and 2.

**"owner"**

3A–471 Is defined by s.322:

"(a) ... a person (other than a mortgagee not in possession) who is for the time being entitled to dispose of the fee simple in premises, whether in possession or in the reversion, and

(b) includes also a person holding or entitled to the rents and profits of the premises under a lease of which the unexpired term exceeds three years."

**"premises"**

3A–472 Are defined by s.322 as "the dwelling-house, house in multiple occupation, building or part of building in respect of which the closing order or, as the case may be, demolition order is made." "Dwelling house" includes "any yard, garden outhouses and appurtenances belonging to it or usually enjoyed with it ..."

**"Rent Acts"**

3A–473 Are defined by s.622 as the Rent Act 1977 and the Rent (Agriculture) Act 1976.

**Demolition orders**

3A–474 A tenant is not entitled to rely upon the protection of the Rent Act 1977 or the Housing Act 1988 when a demolition order is in force in relation to the premises (see *Marela v Machorowski* [1953] 1 Q.B. 565; and *Beaney v Branchett* (1987) 19 H.L.R. 471, CA). The effect of a demolition order is to remove security of tenure (*Johnson v Felton*; (1995) 27 H.L.R. 265, CA). However, any tenancy must still be terminated in the normal way (e.g. by notice to quit) (see *Aslan v Murphy (No.2)* [1990] 1 W.L.R. 766; [1989] 3 All E.R. 130, CA).

**[THE NEXT PARAGRAPH IS 3A–482.]**

## SCHEDULES

**SECTION 79** SCHEDULE 1

### TENANCIES WHICH ARE NOT SECURE TENANCIES

*Long leases*

3A–482 1. A tenancy is not a secure tenancy if it is a long tenancy.

*Introductory tenancies*

3A–483 1A. A tenancy is not a secure tenancy if it is an introductory tenancy or a tenancy which has ceased to be an introductory tenancy—

(a) by virtue of section 133(3) of the Housing Act 1996 (disposal on death to non-qualifying person), or

(b) by virtue of the tenant, or in the case of a joint tenancy every tenant, ceasing to occupy the dwelling-house as his only or principal home.

*Demoted tenancies*

3A–484 1B. A tenancy is not a secure tenancy if it is a demoted tenancy within the meaning of section 143A of the Housing Act 1996.

*Premises occupied in connection with employment*

3A–485 2.—(1) Subject to sub-paragraph 4B, a tenancy is not a secure tenancy if the tenant is an employee of the landlord or of—

a local authority,
a development corporation,
a housing action trust,
an urban development corporation, or

*Paragraph numbers marked with a "+" can be found online and on CD.*

the governors of an aided school,

and his contract of employment requires him to occupy the dwelling-house for the better performance of his duties.

(2) Subject to sub-paragraph 4B, a tenancy is not a secure tenancy if the tenant is a member of a police force and the dwelling-house is provided for him free of rent and rates in pursuance of regulations made under section 50 of the Police Act 1996(general regulations as to government, administration and conditions of service of police forces).

(3) Subject to sub-paragraph 4B, a tenancy is not a secure tenancy if the tenant is an employee of a fire and rescue authority and—

(a) his contract of employment requires him to live in close proximity to a particular fire station, and

(b) the dwelling-house was let to him by the authority in consequence of that requirement;

(4) Subject to sub-paragraph (4A) and (4B), a tenancy is not a secure tenancy if—

(a) within the period of three years immediately preceding the grant the conditions mentioned in sub-paragraph (1), (2) or (3) have been satisfied with respect to a tenancy of the dwelling-house, and

(b) before the grant the landlord notified the tenant in writing of the circumstances in which this exception applies and that in its opinion the proposed tenancy would fall within this exception;

(4A) Except where the landlord is a local housing authority, a tenancy under sub-paragraph (4) shall become a secure tenancy when the periods during which the conditions mentioned in sub-paragraph (1), (2) or (3) are not satisfied with respect to the tenancy amount in aggregate to more than three years.

(4B) Where the landlord is a local housing authority, a tenancy under sub-paragraph (1), (2), (3) or (4) shall become a secure tenancy if the authority notify the tenant that the tenancy is to be regarded as a secure tenancy.

(5) In this paragraph "contract of employment" means a contract of service or apprenticeship, whether express or implied and (if express) whether oral or in writing.

*Land acquired for development*

3.—(1) A tenancy is not a secure tenancy if the dwelling-house is on land which has been acquired for development and the dwelling-house is used by the landlord, pending development of the land, as temporary housing accommodation. **3A–486**

(2) In this paragraph "development" has the meaning given by section 55 of the Town and Country Planning Act 1990 (general definition of development for purposes of that Act).

*Accommodation for homeless persons*

4. A tenancy granted in pursuance of any function under Part VII of the Housing Act 1996 (homelessness) is not a secure tenancy unless the local housing authority concerned have notified the tenant that the tenancy is to be regarded as a secure tenancy. **3A–487**

*Family intervention tenancies*

4ZA.—(1) A tenancy is not a secure tenancy if it is a family intervention tenancy. **3A–487.1**

(2) But a tenancy mentioned in sub-paragraph (1) becomes a secure tenancy if the landlord notifies the tenant that it is to be regarded as a secure tenancy.

(3) In this paragraph "a family intervention tenancy" means, subject to sub-paragraph (4), a tenancy granted by a local housing authority in respect of a dwelling-house—

(a) to a person ("the new tenant") against whom a possession order under section 84 in respect of another dwelling-house—

(i) has been made, in relation to a secure tenancy, on ground 2 or 2A of Part 1 of Schedule 2;

(ii) could, in the opinion of the authority, have been so made in relation to such a tenancy; or

(iii) could, in the opinion of the authority, have been so made if the person had had such a tenancy; and

(b) for the purposes of the provision of behaviour support services.

(4) A tenancy is not a family intervention tenancy for the purposes of this paragraph if the local housing authority has failed to serve a notice under sub-paragraph (5) on the new tenant before the new tenant entered into the tenancy.

(5) A notice under this sub-paragraph is a notice stating—

(a) the reasons for offering the tenancy to the new tenant;

(b) the dwelling-house in respect of which the tenancy is to be granted;

(c) the other main terms of the tenancy (including any requirements on the new tenant in respect of behaviour support services);

(d) the security of tenure available under the tenancy and any loss of security of tenure which is likely to result from the new tenant agreeing to enter into the tenancy;

(e) that the new tenant is not obliged to enter into the tenancy or (unless otherwise required to do so) to surrender any existing tenancy or possession of a dwelling-house;

(f) any likely action by the local housing authority if the new tenant does not enter into the tenancy or surrender any existing tenancy or possession of a dwelling-house.

(6) The appropriate national authority may by regulations made by statutory instrument amend sub-paragraph (5).

(7) A notice under sub-paragraph (5) must contain advice to the new tenant as to how the new tenant may be able to obtain assistance in relation to the notice.

(8) The appropriate national authority may by regulations made by statutory instrument make provision about the type of advice to be provided in such notices.

(9) Regulations under this paragraph may contain such transitional, transitory or saving provision as the appropriate national authority considers appropriate.

(10) A statutory instrument containing (whether alone or with other provision) regulations under this paragraph which amend or repeal any of paragraphs (a) to (f) of sub-paragraph (5) may not be made—

(a) by the Secretary of State unless a draft of the instrument has been laid before, and approved by a resolution of, each House of Parliament; and

(b) by the Welsh Ministers unless a draft of the instrument has been laid before, and approved by a resolution of, the National Assembly for Wales.

(11) Subject to this, a statutory instrument containing regulations made under this paragraph—

(a) by the Secretary of State is subject to annulment in pursuance of a resolution of either House of Parliament; and

(b) by the Welsh Ministers is subject to annulment in pursuance of a resolution of the National Assembly for Wales.

(12) In this paragraph— "appropriate national authority"—

(a) in relation to England, means the Secretary of State; and

(b) in relation to Wales, means the Welsh Ministers;

"behaviour support agreement" means an agreement in writing about behaviour and the provision of support services made between the new tenant and the local housing authority concerned (or between persons who include those persons);

"behaviour support services" means relevant support services to be provided by any person to—

(a) the new tenant; or

(b) any person who is to reside with the new tenant; for the purpose of addressing the kind of behaviour which led to the new tenant falling within sub-paragraph (3)(a);

***Paragraph numbers marked with a "+" can be found online and on CD.***

"family intervention tenancy" has the meaning given by sub-paragraph (3);

"family intervention tenancy" has the meaning given by sub-paragraph (3);

"the new tenant" has the meaning given by sub-paragraph (3)(a);

"relevant support services" means support services of a kind identified in a behaviour support agreement and designed to meet such needs of the recipient as are identified in the agreement.

*Accommodation for Asylum Seekers*

4A.—(1) A tenancy is not a secure tenancy if it is granted in order to provide accommodation under section 4 or Part VI of the Immigration and Asylum Act 1999. **3A–488**

(2) A tenancy mentioned in sub-paragraph (1) becomes a secure tenancy if the landlord notifies the tenant that it is to be regarded as a secure tenancy.

*Temporary accommodation for persons taking up employment*

5.—(1) Subject to sub-paragraphs (1A and 1B), a tenancy is not a secure tenancy if— **3A–489**

(a) the person to whom the tenancy was granted was not, immediately before the grant, resident in the district in which the dwelling-house is situated,

(b) before the grant of the tenancy, he obtained employment, or an offer of employment, in the district or its surrounding area,

(c) the tenancy was granted to him for the purpose of meeting his need for temporary accommodation in the district or its surrounding area in order to work there, and of enabling him to find permanent accommodation there, and

(d) the landlord notified him in writing of the circumstances in which this exception applies and that in its opinion the proposed tenancy would fall within this exception;

(1A) Except where the landlord is a local housing authority, a tenancy under sub-paragraph (1) shall become a secure tenancy on the expiry of one year from the grant or on earlier notification by the landlord to the tenant that the tenancy is to be regarded as a secure tenancy.

(1B) Where the landlord is a local housing authority, a tenancy under sub-paragraph (1) shall become a secure tenancy is at any time the authority notify the tenant that the tenancy is to be regarded as a secure tenancy.

(2) In this paragraph—

"district" means district of a local housing authority; and

"surrounding area", in relation to a district, means the area consisting of each district that adjoins it.

*Short-term arrangements*

6. A tenancy is not a secure tenancy if— **3A–490**

(a) the dwelling-house has been leased to the landlord with vacant possession for use as temporary housing accommodation,

(b) the terms on which it has been leased include provision for the lessor to obtain vacant possession from the landlord on the expiry of a specified period or when required by the lessor,

(c) the lessor is not a body which is capable of granting secure tenancies, and

(d) the landlord has no interest in the dwelling-house other than under the lease in question or as a mortgagee.

*Temporary accommodation during works*

7. A tenancy is not a secure tenancy if— **3A–491**

(a) the dwelling-house has been made available for occupation by the tenant (or a predecessor in title of his) while works are carried out on the dwelling-house which he previously occupied as his home, and

(b) the tenant or predecessor was not a secure tenant of that other dwelling-house at the time when he ceased to occupy it as his home.

*Agricultural holding etc.*

**3A-492** 8.—(1) A tenancy is not secure if—

(a) the dwelling-house is comprised in an agricultural holding and is occupied by the person responsible for the control (whether as tenant or as servant or agent of the tenant) of the farming of the holding, or

(b) the dwelling-house is comprised in the holding held under a farm business tenancy and is occupied by the person responsible for the control (whether a tenant or as servant or agent of the tenant) of the management of the holding.

(2) In sub-paragraph (1) above—

"agricultural holding" means any agricultural holding within the meaning of the Agricultural Holdings Act 1986 held under a tenancy in relation to which that Act applies, and

"farm business tenancy" and

"holding" in relation to such a tenancy, have the same meaning as in the Agricultural Tenancies Act 1995.

*Licensed premises*

**3A-493** 9. A tenancy is not a secure tenancy if the dwelling-house consists of or includes premises which, by virtue of a premises licence under the Licensing Act 2003, may be used for the supply of alcohol (within the meaning of section 14 of that Act) for consumption on the premises.

*Student lettings*

**3A-494** 10.—(1) Subject to sub-paragraphs (2A) and (2B), a tenancy of a dwelling-house is not a secure tenancy if—

(a) it is granted for the purpose of enabling the tenant to attend a designated course at an educational establishment, and

(b) before the grant of the tenancy the landlord notified him in writing of the circumstances in which this exception applies and that in its opinion the proposed tenancy would fall within this exception.

(2) A landlord's notice under sub-paragraph (1)(b) shall specify the educational establishment which the person concerned proposes to attend.

(2A) Except where the landlord is a local housing authority, a tenancy under sub-paragraph (1) shall become a secure tenancy on the expiry of the period specified in sub-paragraph (3) or on earlier notification by the landlord to the tenant that the tenancy is to be regarded as a secure tenancy.

(2B) Where the landlord is a local housing authority, a tenancy under sub-paragraph (1) shall become a secure tenancy if at any time the authority notify the tenant that the tenancy is to be regarded as a secure tenancy.

(3) The period referred to in sub-paragraph (2A) is—

(a) in a case where the tenant attends a designated course at the educational establishment specified in the landlord's notice, the period ending six months after the tenant ceases to attend that (or any other) designated course at that establishment;

(b) in any other case, the period ending six months after the grant of the tenancy.

(4) In this paragraph—

"designated course" means a course of any kind designated by regulations made by the Secretary of State for the purposes of this paragraph;

"educational establishment" means a university or institution which provides higher education or further education (or both); and for the purposes of this definition

"higher education" and "further education" have the same meaning as in the

Education Act 1996.

(5) Regulations under sub-paragraph (4) shall be made by statutory instrument and may make different provision with respect to different cases or descriptions of case, including different provision for different areas.

*1954 Act tenancies*

11. A tenancy is not a secure tenancy if it is one to which Part II of the Landlord and Tenant Act 1954 applies (tenancies of premises occupied for business purposes). **3A–495**

*Almshouses*

12. A licence to occupy a dwelling-house is not a secure tenancy of— **3A–496**

(a) the dwelling-house is an almshouse, and

(b) the licence was granted by or on behalf of a charity which—

(i) is authorised under its trusts to maintain the dwelling-house as an almshouse, and

(ii) has no power under its trusts to grant a tenancy of the dwelling-house;

and in this paragraph "almshouse" means any premises maintained as an almshouse, whether they are called an almshouse or not and "trusts" in relation to a charity, means the provisions establishing it as a charity and regulating its purposes and administration, whether those provisions take effect by way of trust or not.

*Note*—Amended by the Housing Act 1988 s.83; the Planning (Consequential Provisions) Act 1990, the Charities Act 1992; the Agricultural Holdings Act 1986 Sch.14; the Education Reform Act 1988 Sch.12; the Housing Act 1996 Schs 16 and 17; the Education Act 1996 Sch.7; the Agricultural Tenancies Act 1995 s.40, Sch.; the Police Act 1996 s.103, Sch.7, para.40 the Government of Wales Act 1998 Sch.18, Pt IV; the Immigration and Asylum Act 1999 Sch.14, para.81; the Anti-Social Behaviour Act 2003 s.14(5) and Sch.1; and by the Fire and Rescue Services Act 2004 s.53(1), Sch.1, para.62(1), (3); the Licensing Act 2003 Sch.6, paras 102, 104; the Fire and Rescue Services Act 2004 s.53(1), Sch.1, para.62(1), (3); theImmigration, Asylum and Nationality Act 2006 s.43(4), the Housing and Regeneration Act 2008 (Consequential Provisions) Order 2008 (SI 2008/3002) para.28, and the Housing and Regeneration Act 2008 s.297 with effect from January 1, 2009 (CO 2008/3068). **3A–497**

Schedule 1 lists those types of tenancies and licences (see s.79) which cannot be secure.

**Sch.1, para.1A—introductory tenancies**

See para.3A–1063. **3A–498**

**Sch.1, para.1B—Demoted Tenancies**

This paragraph was inserted by the Anti-Social Behaviour Act 2003. See 3A–1117. **3A–499**

## [THE NEXT PARAGRAPH IS 3A-501]

**Sch.1, para.3—temporary use pending development**

Schedule 1, para.3 provides that a tenancy of premises acquired for development and temporarily used as housing accommodation pending that or other development is not secure. **3A–501**

There are two distinct requirements, firstly, that the premises are on land acquired for development, and secondly, that they are used as temporary accommodation pending development. The immediate landlord need not be the body which acquired the land for development (*Hyde Housing Association Ltd v Harrison* (1991) 23 H.L.R. 57, CA.

In *Attley v Cherwell DC* (1989) 21 H.L.R. 613, CA, the Court of Appeal found development was intended and so the tenancy was not secure, even though the

***Paragraph numbers marked with a "+" can be found online and on CD.***

development might not be the same type of development as had originally been envisaged (*cf. Lillieshall Road Housing Co-operative Ltd v Brennan* (1992) 24 H.L.R. 195, CA).

**Sch.1, para.4—accommodation for homeless persons**

3A–502 Article 8 does not entitle non-secure local authority tenants to have a county court judge (or the judicial review court) decide on the particular facts whether eviction was disproportionate to the council's aim of managing its housing stock properly. The effect of this would be to convert non-secure tenancies enjoyed by homeless persons into a form of secure tenancy. The balance of interests arising under Article 8(2) has in all its essentials been struck by the legislature when enacting the current scheme for the housing of homeless persons and their eviction (*Sheffield CC v Smart* [2002] EWCA Civ 4; [2002] H.L.R. 34).

For the interrelationship between Sch.1, paras 4 and 6, see *City of Westminster v Boraliu* [2007] EWCA Civ 1339; [2008] 1 W.L.R. 2408.

**Sch.1, para.4ZA—family intervention tenancies**

3A–502.1 See para.3A–1664.

**Sch.1, para.6—private sector leasing**

3A–503 Schedule 1, para.6 excepts premises let under what are commonly called "private sector leasing" schemes. It applies when a private owner leases a property with vacant possession for use as temporary housing to a public landlord, which then sublets to an individual occupier. The sub-tenancy is excepted from secure status to ensure that vacant possession can be obtained at the expiry of the head lease.

See *Tower Hamlets LBC v Abdi* (1992) 91 L.G.R. 300; (1993) 25 H.L.R. 80, CA; *Hackney LBC v Lambourne* (1993) 25 H.L.R. 172, CA and *Haringey LBC v Hickey* [2006] EWCA 373; [2006] H.L.R. 36. For the interrelationship between Sch.1, paras 4 and 6, see *City of Westminster v Boraliu* [2007] EWCA Civ 1339; [2008] 1 W.L.R. 2408, November 2, 2007.

**SECTION 84**

## SCHEDULE 2

### GROUNDS FOR POSSESSION OF DWELLING-HOUSES LET UNDER SECURE TENANCIES

### PART I

### GROUNDS ON WHICH COURT MAY ORDER POSSESSION IF IT CONSIDERS IT REASONABLE

*Ground 1*

3A–504 Rent lawfully due from the tenant has not been paid or an obligation of the tenancy has been broken or not performed.

*Ground 2*

3A–505 The tenant or a person residing in or visiting the dwelling-house—

(a) has been guilty of conduct causing or likely to cause a nuisance or annoyance to a person residing, visiting or otherwise engaging in a lawful activity in the locality, or

(b) has been convicted of—

(i) using the dwelling-house of allowing it to be used for immoral or illegal purposes, or

(ii) an indictable offence committed in, or in the locality of, the dwelling-house.

*Ground 2A*

3A–506 The dwelling-house was occupied (whether alone or with others) by a married couple, a couple who are civil partners of each other, or a couple living together as husband and wife or a couple living together as if they were civil partners and—

(a) one or both of the partners is a tenant of the dwelling-house,

(b) one partner has left because of violence or threats of violence by the other towards—

***Paragraph numbers marked with a "+" can be found online and on CD.***

(i) that partner, or

(ii) a member of the family of that partner who was residing with that partner immediately before the partner left, and

(c) the court is satisfied that the partner who has left is unlikely to return.

*Ground 3*

The condition of the dwelling-house or of any of the common parts has deteriorated owing to acts of waste by, or the neglect or default of, the tenant or a person residing in the dwelling-house and, in the case of an act of waste by, or the neglect or default of, a person lodging with the tenant or a sub-tenant of his, the tenant has not taken such steps as he ought reasonably to have taken for the removal of the lodger or sub-tenant. **3A–507**

*Ground 4*

The condition of furniture provided by the landlord for use under the tenancy, or for use in the common parts, has deteriorated owing to ill-treatment by the tenant or a person residing in the dwelling-house and, in the case of ill-treatment by a person lodging with the tenant or a sub-tenant of his, the tenant has not taken such steps as he ought reasonably to have taken for the removal of the lodger or sub-tenant. **3A–508**

*Ground 5*

The tenant is the person, or one of the persons, to whom the tenancy was granted and the landlord was induced to grant the tenancy by a false statement made knowingly or recklessly by **3A–509**

(a) the tenant, or

(b) a person acting at the tenants instigation.

*Ground 6*

The tenancy was assigned to the tenant, or to a predecessor in title of his who is a member of his family and is residing in the dwelling-house, by an assignment made by virtue of section 92 (assignments by way of exchange) and a premium was paid either in connection with that assignment or the assignment which the tenant or predecessor himself made by virtue of that section. **3A–510**

In this paragraph "premium" means any fine or other like sum and any other pecuniary consideration in addition to rent.

*Ground 7*

The dwelling-house forms part of, or is within the curtilage of, a building which, or so much of it as is held by the landlord, is held mainly for purposes other than housing purposes and consists mainly of accommodation other than housing accommodation, and— **3A–511**

(a) the dwelling-house was let to the tenant or a predecessor in title of his in consequence of the tenant or predecessor being in the employment of the landlord, or of—

a local authority,
a development corporation,
a housing action trust,
an urban development corporation, or
the governors of an aided school,
and

(b) the tenant or a person residing in the dwelling-house has been guilty of conduct such that, having regard to the purpose for which the building is used, it would not be right for him to continue in occupation of the dwelling-house.

*Ground 8*

The dwelling-house was made available for occupation by the tenant (or a predecessor in title of his) while works were carried out on the dwelling-house which he previously occupied as his only or principal home and— **3A–512**

(a) the tenant (or predecessor) was a secure tenant of the other dwelling-house at the time when he ceased to occupy it as his home,

(b) the tenant (or predecessor) accepted the tenancy of the dwelling-house of which possession is sought on the understanding that he would give up occupation when, on completion of the works, the other dwelling-house was again available for occupation by him under a secure tenancy, and

(c) the works have been completed and the other dwelling-house is so available.

## PART II

## GROUNDS ON WHICH THE COURT MAY ORDER POSSESSION IF SUITABLE ALTERNATIVE ACCOMMODATION IS AVAILABLE

*Ground 9*

**3A–513** The dwelling-house is overcrowded, within the meaning of Part X, in such circumstances as to render the occupier guilty of an offence.

*Ground 10*

**3A–514** The landlord intends, within a reasonable time of obtaining possession of the dwelling-house—

(a) to demolish or reconstruct the building or part of the building comprising the dwelling-house, or

(b) to carry out work on that building or on land let together with, and thus treated as part of, the dwelling-house.

and cannot reasonably do so without obtaining possession of the dwelling-house.

*Ground 10A*

**3A–515** The dwelling-house is in an area which is the subject of a redevelopment scheme approved by the Secretary of State or the Housing Corporation or Scottish Homes in accordance with Part V of this Schedule and the landlord intends a reasonable time of obtaining possession to dispose of the dwelling-house in accordance with the scheme.

*or*

Part of the dwelling-house is in such an area and the landlord intends within a reasonable time of obtaining possession to dispose of that part in accordance with the scheme and for that purpose reasonably requires possession of the dwelling-house.

*Ground 11*

**3A–516** The landlord is a charity and the tenant's continued occupation of the dwelling-house would conflict with the objects of the charity.

## PART III

## GROUNDS ON WHICH THE COURT MAY ORDER POSSESSION IF IT CONSIDERS IT REASONABLE AND SUITABLE ALTERNATIVE ACCOMMODATION IS AVAILABLE

*Ground 12*

**3A–517** The dwelling-house forms part of, or is within the curtilage of, a building which, or so much of it as is held by the landlord, is held mainly for purposes other than housing purposes and consists mainly of accommodation other than housing accommodation, or is situated in a cemetery, and—

(a) the dwelling-house was let to the tenant or a predecessor in title of his in consequence of the tenant or predecessor being in the employment of the landlord or of—

a local authority,
a development corporation,
a housing action trust,
an urban development corporation, or
the governors of an aided school,
and that employment has ceased, and

(b) the landlord reasonably requires the dwelling-house for occupation as a residence for some person either engaged in the employment of the landlord, or of such a body, or with whom a contract for such employment has been entered into conditional on housing being provided.

*Ground 13*

The dwelling-house has features which are substantially different from those of ordinary dwelling-houses and which are designed to make it suitable for occupation by a physically disabled person who requires accommodation of a kind provided by the dwelling-house and— **3A–518**

(a) there is no longer such a person residing in the dwelling-house, and

(b) the landlord requires it for occupation (whether alone or with members of his family) by such a person.

*Ground 14*

The landlord is a housing association or housing trust which lets dwelling-houses only for occupation (whether alone or with others) by persons whose circumstances (other than merely financial circumstances) make it especially difficult for them to satisfy their need for housing, and— **3A–519**

(a) either there is no longer such a person residing in the dwelling-house or the tenant has received from a local housing authority an offer of accommodation in premises which are to be let as a separate dwelling under a secure tenancy, and

(b) the landlord requires the dwelling-house for occupation (whether alone or with members of his family) by such a person.

*Ground 15*

The dwelling-house is one of a group of dwelling-houses which it is the practice of the landlord to let for occupation by persons with special needs and— **3A–520**

(a) a social service or special facility is provided in close proximity to the group of dwelling-houses in order to assist persons with those special needs,

(b) there is no longer a person with those special needs residing in the dwelling-house, and

(c) the landlord requires the dwelling-house for occupation (whether alone or with members of his family) by a person who had those special needs.

*Ground 16*

The accommodation afforded by the dwelling-house is more extensive than is reasonably required by the tenant and— **3A–521**

(a) the tenancy vested in the tenant by virtue of section 89 (succession to periodic tenancy), the tenant being qualified to succeed by virtue of section 87(b)(members of family other than spouse), and

(b) notice of the proceedings for possession was served under section 83 or, where no such notice was served, the proceedings for possession were begun more than six months but less than twelve months after the date of the previous tenant's death.

The matters to be taken into account by the court in determining whether it is reasonable to make an order on this ground include—

(a) the age of the tenant,

(b) the period during which the tenant has occupied the dwelling-house as his only or principal home, and

(c) any financial or other support given by the tenant to the previous tenant.

## PART IV

### SUITABILITY OF ACCOMMODATION

1. For the purposes of section 84(2)(b) and (c) (case in which court is not to make an order for possession unless satisfied that suitable accommodation will be available) accommodation is suitable if it consists of premises— **3A–522**

(a) which are to be let as a separate dwelling under a secure tenancy, or

(b) which are to be let as a separate dwelling under a protected tenancy, not being a tenancy under which the landlord might recover possession under one of the

Cases in Part II of Schedule 15 to the Rent Act 1977 (cases where court must order possession),

(c) which are to be let as a separate dwelling under an assured tenancy which is neither an assured shorthold tenancy, within the meaning of Part I of the Housing Act 1988, nor a tenancy under which the landlord might recover possession under any of Grounds 1 to 5 in Schedule 2 to that Act,

and, in the opinion of the court, the accommodation is reasonably suitable to the needs of the tenant and his family.

2. In determining whether the accommodation is reasonably suitable to the needs of the tenant and his family, regard shall be had to—

(a) the nature of the accommodation which it is the practice of the landlord to allocate to persons with similar needs;

(b) the distance of the accommodation available from the place of work or education of the tenant and of any members of his family;

(c) its distance from the home of any member of the tenant's family if proximity to it is essential to that member's or the tenant's well-being;

(d) the needs (as regards extent of accommodation) and means of the tenant and his family;

(e) the terms on which the accommodation is available and the terms of the secure tenancy;

(f) if furniture was provided by the landlord for use under the secure tenancy, whether furniture is to be provided for use in the other accommodation, and if so the nature of the furniture to be provided.

3. Where possession of a dwelling-house is sought on ground 9 (overcrowding such as to render occupier guilty of offence), other accommodation may be reasonably suitable to the needs of the tenant and his family notwithstanding that the permitted number of persons for that accommodation, as defined in section 326(3) (overcrowding: the space standard), is less than the number of persons living in the dwelling-house of which possession is sought.

4.—(1) A certificate of the appropriate local housing authority that they will provide suitable accommodation for the tenant by a date specified in the certificate is conclusive evidence that suitable accommodation will be available for him by that date.

(2) The appropriate local housing authority is the authority for the district in which the dwelling-house of which possession is sought is situated.

(3) This paragraph does not apply where the landlord is a local housing authority.

## PART V

### APPROVAL OF REDEVELOPMENT SCHEMES FOR PURPOSES OF GROUND 10A

**3A-523** 1.—(1) The Secretary of State may, on the application of the landlord, approve for the purposes of ground 10A in Part II of this Schedule a scheme for the disposal and redevelopment of an area of land consisting of or including the whole or part of one or more dwelling-houses.

(2) For this purpose—

(a) "disposal" means a disposal of any interest in the land (including the grant of an option), and

(b) "redevelopment" means the demolition or reconstruction of buildings or the carrying out of other works to buildings or land;

and it is immaterial whether the disposal is to precede or follow the redevelopment.

(3) The Secretary of State may on the application of the landlord approve a variation of a scheme previously approved by him and may, in particular, approve a variation adding land to the area subject to the scheme.

2.—(1) Where a landlord proposes to apply to the Secretary of State for the approval of a scheme or variation it shall serve a notice in writing on any secure tenant of a dwelling-house affected by the proposal stating—

(a) the main features of the proposed scheme or, as the case may be, the scheme as proposed to be varied,

***Paragraph numbers marked with a "+" can be found online and on CD.***

(b) that the landlord proposes to apply to the Secretary of State for approval of the scheme or variation, and

(c) the effect of such approval, by virtue of section 84 and ground 10A in Part II of this Schedule, in relation to proceedings for possession of the dwelling-house,

and informing the tenant that he may, within such period as the landlord may allow (which shall be at least 28 days from service of the notice), make representations to the landlord about the proposal.

(2) The landlord shall not apply to the Secretary of State until it has considered any representations made to it within that period.

(3) In the case of a landlord to which section 105 applies (consultation on matters of housing management) the provisions of this paragraph apply in place of the provisions of that section in relation to the approval or variation of a redevelopment scheme.

3.—(1) In considering whether to give his approval to a scheme or variation the Secretary of State shall take into account, in particular—

(a) the effect of the scheme on the extent and character of housing accommodation in the neighbourhood,

(b) over what period of time it is proposed that the disposal and redevelopment will take place in accordance with the scheme, and

(c) to what extent the scheme includes provision for housing provided under the scheme to be sold or let to existing tenants or persons nominated by the landlord;

and he shall take into account any representations made to him and, so far as they are brought to his notice, any representations made to the landlord.

(2) The landlord shall give to the Secretary of State such information as to the representations made to it, and other relevant matters, as the Secretary of State may require.

4. The Secretary of State shall not approve a scheme or variation so as to include in the area subject to the scheme—

(a) part only of one or more dwelling-houses, or

(b) one or more dwelling-houses not themselves affected by the works involved in redevelopment but which are proposed to be disposed of along with other land which is so affected,

unless he is satisfied that the inclusion is justified in the circumstances.

5.—(1) Approval may be given subject to conditions and may be expressed to expire after a specified period.

(2) The Secretary of State, on the application of the landlord or otherwise, may vary an approval so as to—

(a) add, remove or vary conditions to which the approval is subject; or

(b) extend or restrict the period after which the approval is to expire.

(3) Where approval is given subject to conditions, the landlord may serve a notice under section 83 (notice of proceedings for possession) specifying ground 10A notwithstanding that the conditions are not yet fulfilled but the court shall not make an order for possession on that ground unless satisfied that they are or will be fulfilled.

6. Where the landlord is a social landlord registered in the register maintained by the Housing Corporation under section 1 of the Housing Act 1996 or a housing association registered in the register maintained by Scottish Homes under section 3 of the Housing Associations Act 1985, the Housing Corporation, or Scottish Homes (and not the Secretary of State), has the functions conferred by this Part of this Schedule.

7. In this Part of this Schedule references to the landlord of a dwelling-house include any authority or body within section 80 (the landlord condition for secure tenancies) having an interest of any description in the dwelling-house.

*Note*—Schedule 2 amended by the Housing and Planning Act 1986 s.9; the Housing Act 1988 s.83 and Sch.17, para.65; the Housing Act 1996 ss.144–146; the Housing Act 1996 (Consequential Provisions) Order 1996 (SI 1996/2325), the Government of Wales Act 1998 s.140 and Sch.16, para.21 and Sch.18, Pt IV; the Civil Partnership Act 2004 s.81 and Sch.8, para.33, the Serious Organised Crime and Police Act 2005 s.111, **3A–524**

Sch.7, para.45 and the Housing and Regeneration Act 2008 (Consequential Provisions) Order 2008 (SI 2008/3002) para.29.

**Sch.2, Ground 1—arrears or breach of obligation**

3A–525 See the commentary to the Rent Act 1977 Sch.15, Case 1.

As to reasonableness in claims for possession under "Ground 1", see commentary to s.84, above.

**Sch.2, Ground 2—nuisance or annoyance**

3A–526 As substituted by Housing Act 1996 s.144.

For the definition of "indictable offences", see the Interpretation Act 1978 Sch.1, which provides that "indictable offence" means an offence which, if committed by an adult, is triable on indictment, whether it is exclusively so triable or triable either way.

In *Kensington & Chelsea RLBC v Simmonds* (1997) 29 H.L.R. 507; *The Times*, July 15, 1996, CA, where conduct which was a nuisance or annoyance had persisted over a number of months, the Court of Appeal held that there was ample basis for the judge's findings that the tenant had allowed her son to abuse the neighbours. The Court also rejected the argument that it was necessary to show "fault" on the part of the tenant before a possession order could be made. The Court had to consider not only the interests of the tenant but also those of neighbours. It would be quite intolerable if neighbours were deprived of the possibility of relief because the tenant was incapable of controlling her son. See too *Portsmouth City Council v Bryant* (2000) 32 H.L.R. 906; [2000] E.H.L.R. 287, CA (claimant does not have to establish fault or even knowledge on part of tenant, but the extent of personal fault is relevant when considering reasonableness.) In *Northampton BC v Lovatt* (1998) 30 H.L.R. 875; [1998] 07 E.G. 142; *The Times*, January 3, 1998, CA, the Court of Appeal confirmed that a tenant can be held responsible for acts of a minor child.

In relation to subpara.(b), indictable offences do not have to have been committed during the currency of the tenancy if a tenant pleads guilty or is convicted after the grant of the tenancy. See *Raglan Housing Association Ltd v Fairclough* [2007] EWCA Civ 1087; [2008] H.L.R. 21, where the defendant was arrested before the grant of his assured tenancy, but pleaded guilty after its grant. The Court of Appeal stated that a tenant who is convicted of supplying illegal drugs or of burgling his neighbours' houses poses no less a continuing threat if the offences were committed before he became a tenant than he would if they had been committed afterwards. The Court of Appeal was not agreed as to whether the ground could only be satisfied if the conviction itself (though not the facts on which it was based) occurred during the currency of the tenancy, but did not have to decide that point.

As to reasonableness in claims for possession under Ground 2, see commentary to s.84, above and s.85A.

**Sch.2, Ground 2A—domestic violence**

3A–527 As inserted by the Housing Act 1996 s.145 and amended by the Civil Partnership Act 2004 s.81, Sch.8, para.33.

The Housing Act 1996 s.145 introduced this ground for possession where there has been domestic violence. Ground 2A applies where one or both partners is a tenant and:

(a) one partner has left because of violence or threats of violence by the other towards that partner or a member of that partner's family; and

(b) the court is satisfied that the partner who has left is unlikely to return.

Landlords seeking to rely upon this ground must satisfy the court that notice of proceedings for possession has been served on the partner who has left the home or that they have taken reasonable steps to effect service (Housing Act 1996 s.147).

Where possession is sought under Ground 2A, it is not sufficient that the alleged violence or threats of violence were merely one of a range of causes of equal efficacy in the victim's departure from the property. For the ground to be made out it has to be established that the alleged violence or threat of violence was the dominant, principal and real cause of the departure (*Camden LBC v Mallett* (2001) 33 H.L.R. 20, CA).

**Sched.2, Ground 5—tenancy obtained by false statement**

3A–528 The Housing Act 1996 s.146 amended Ground 5 by widening it to include a statement made by "a person acting at the tenant's instigation". The word "instigate" means "to bring about or initiate". The Latin source of the word is *instigare*, to urge or incite. The Ground refers to "instigation" and not merely to someone "acting on behalf of the tenant". To come within Ground 5, the instigation must be of the false statement and not merely instigation of action in general on behalf of the tenant (*Merton LBC v Richards* [2005] EWCA Civ 639; May 11, 2005).

Ground 5 is only available where the defendant is the person to whom the tenancy was granted. The language of Ground 5 is clear and unambiguous and only refers to the current tenant—the person against whom possession is sought. The first seventeen words of Ground 5 make it clear that, if there has been an assignment, the word "tenant" does not include any predecessor in title who made the misrepresentation relied upon (*Islington LBC v Uckac* [2006] EWCA Civ 340; [2006] 1 W.L.R. 1303).

In *Rushcliffe BC v Watson* (1992) 24 H.L.R. 124, CA, Nourse L.J. approved comments made by the judge at first instance that the burden of proof in cases brought under Ground 5 was akin to the criminal standard because of the seriousness of the allegation. See too *Waltham Forest LBC v Roberts* [2004] EWCA Civ 940; [2005] H.L.R. 2.

In *Shrewsbury and Atcham BC v Evans* (1997) 30 H.L.R. 123, CA, where the tenant had "flagrantly and deliberately lied about her circumstances" in order to obtain council housing, Beldam L.J. said that:

> "It would have been an affront to those who put forward their claims honestly, wait patiently and rely upon the local authority to deal fairly with their claims, if a judge had concluded that in the circumstances of this case it was not reasonable to make an order for possession."

As to reasonableness in claims for possession under Ground 5, see commentary to s.84, above and *Lewisham LBC v Adeyenni* (2000) 32 H.L.R. 414, CA.

**Sch.2, Ground 10—property required for demolition or redevelopment**

This ground for possession may arise if a public landlord requires possession in order to carry out demolition or redevelopment work and cannot reasonably carry out the work without obtaining possession. **3A–529**

In *Wansbeck DC v Marley* (1988) 20 H.L.R. 247, CA, the Court of Appeal held that it was for the landlord to prove:

(a) that it intended to carry out works; and

(b) that such work could not reasonably be done without obtaining possession.

In this case there was no evidence on which the judge could have reached such conclusions. The tenant's appeal against a possession order was allowed.

**Sch.2, Ground 10A—redevelopment**

As inserted by the Housing and Planning Act 1986 s.9. **3A–530**

**Sch.2, Ground 16—dwelling more extensive than reasonably required after succession**

As amended by the Housing Act 1996 s.147(3). When considering whether or not to make a possession order under Ground 16, the court should consider family members living with the tenant. The correct date for establishing whether family members are residing with a tenant who has succeeded to a secure tenancy is the date of the hearing before the court, not the date of succession: *Wandsworth LBC v Randall* [2007] EWCA Civ 1126; *Wandsworth LBC v Randall* [2007] EWCA Civ 1126; [2008] 1 W.L.R. 359. **3A–531**

[THE NEXT PARAGRAPH IS 3A–545.]

## Landlord and Tenant Act 1985

(1985 c.70) **3A–545**

Arrangement of Sections

*Repairing obligations*



***Paragraph numbers marked with a "+" can be found online and on CD.***

### *Repairing obligations*

## Repairing obligations in short leases

3A–546 **11.**—(1) In a lease to which this section applies (as to which, see sections 13 and 14) there is implied a covenant by the lessor—

(a) to keep in repair the structure and exterior of the dwelling-house (including drains, gutters and external pipes),

(b) to keep in repair and proper working order the installations in the dwelling-house for the supply of water, gas and electricity and for sanitation (including basins, sinks, baths and sanitary conveniences, but not other fixtures, fittings and appliances for making use of the supply of water, gas or electricity), and

(c) to keep in repair and proper working order the installations in the dwelling-house for space heating and heating water.

(1A) If a lease to which this section applies is a lease of a dwelling-house which forms part only of a building, then, subject to subsection (1B), the covenant implied by subsection (1) shall have effect as if—

(a) the reference in paragraph (a) of that subsection to the dwelling-house included a reference to any part of the building in which the lessor has an estate or interest; and

(b) any reference in paragraphs (b) and (c) of that subsection to an installation in the dwelling-house included a reference to an installation which, directly or indirectly, serves the dwelling-house and which either—

(i) forms part of any part of a building in which the lessor has an estate or interest; or

(ii) is owned by the lessor or under his control.

(1B) Nothing in subsection (1A) shall be construed as requiring the lessor to carry out any works or repairs unless the disrepair (or failure to maintain in working order) is such as to affect the lessee's enjoyment of the dwelling-house or of any common parts, as defined in section 60(1) of the Landlord and Tenant Act 1987, which the lessee, as such, is entitled to use.

(2) The covenant implied by subsection (1) ("the lessor's repairing covenant") shall not be construed as requiring the lessor—

(a) to carry out works or repairs for which the lessee is liable by virtue of his duty to use the premises in a tenant-like manner, or would be so liable but for an express covenant on his part,

(b) to rebuild or reinstate the premises in the case of destruction or damage by fire, or by tempest, flood or other inevitable accident, or

(c) to keep in repair or maintain anything which the lessee is entitled to remove from the dwelling-house.

(3) In determining the standard of repair required by the lessor's repairing covenant, regard shall be had to the age, character and prospective life of the dwelling-house and the locality in which it is situated.

(3A) In any case where—

(a) the lessor's repairing covenant has effect as mentioned in subsection (1A), and

(b) in order to comply with the covenant the lessor needs to carry out works or repairs otherwise than in, or to an installation in, the dwelling-house, and

(c) the lessor does not have a sufficient right in the part of the building or the installation concerned to enable him to carry out the required works or repairs,

then, in any proceedings relating to a failure to comply with the lessor's repairing covenant, so far as it requires the lessor to carry out the works or repairs in question, it shall be a defence for the lessor to prove that he used all reasonable endeavours to obtain, but was unable to obtain, such rights as would be adequate to enable him to carry out the works or repairs.

(4) A covenant by the lessee for the repair of the premises is of no effect so far as it relates to the matters mentioned in subsection (1)(a) to (c), except so far as it imposes on the lessee any of the requirements mentioned in subsection (2)(a) or (c).

(5) The reference in subsection (4) to a covenant by the lessee for the repair of the premises includes a covenant—

(a) to put in repair or deliver up in repair,

(b) to paint, point or render,

(c) to pay money in lieu of repairs by the lessee, or

(d) to pay money on account of repairs by the lessor.

(6) In a lease in which the lessor's repairing covenant is implied there is also implied a covenant by the lessee that the lessor, or any person authorised by him in writing, may at reasonable times of the day and on giving 24 hours' notice in writing to the occupier, enter the premises comprised in the lease for the purpose of viewing their condition and state of repair.

*Note*—Amended by the Housing Act 1988 s.116. **3A-547**

**"dwelling-house"**

See s.16. **3A-548**

**"lease"**

See s.16. **3A-549**

**"lessor"**

See s.16. **3A-550**

**Protocol**

There is a Pre-action Protocol for Housing Disrepair Cases. See Vol.1, C10–001. **3A-551**

**Repairing obligations in short leases**

The Landlord and Tenant Act 1985 s.11 (which re-enacts with some modifications the Housing Act 1961 s.32) implies into leases granted on or after October 24, 1961 **3A-552**

*Paragraph numbers marked with a "+" can be found online and on CD.*

(see s.13) for a term of less than seven years a covenant requiring landlords to keep in repair the structure and exterior of dwellings let to tenants. This includes drains, gutters and external pipes. Landlords are also obliged to keep in repair and proper working order installations in dwelling-houses for the supply of water, gas and electricity, for sanitation, for space heating and for heating hot water. To be in breach of this implied contractual duty landlords must:

(a) have knowledge of the defect; and

(b) then fail to carry out the repair within a reasonable period.

The repairing obligation cannot be transferred to tenants by express terms in the tenancy agreement (s.11(4), but see s.12 below). It does not apply to tenancies for a term of seven years or more.

Two important changes were made by the Housing Act 1988 s.116 to the landlord's obligations to repair found in s.11. First, the covenant to repair the "structure and exterior" was extended beyond the tenant's dwelling to cover "any part of the same building in which the lessor has an estate or interest". Secondly, the obligation to repair and maintain installations was extended from those in the dwelling to any installation which "directly or indirectly" serves the dwelling and is either part of the same building or owned by the landlord. Only tenancies granted after the commencement of the Housing Act 1988 (January 15, 1989) are affected by these changes. As to common parts, see though *Liverpool City Council v Irwin* [1977] A.C. 239; [1976] 2 All E.R. 39; (1984) 13 H.L.R. 38, HL.

Local authorities do not owe a higher repairing obligation under s.11 than other landlords (*Wainwright v Leeds City Council* (1984) 13 H.L.R. 117; (1984) 270 E.G. 1289, CA).

Section 11 does not apply where the Crown is the landlord (*Department of Transport v Egoroff* (1986) 278 E.G. 1361; (1986) 18 H.L.R. 326, CA) unless the lease is under the management of the Crown Estates Commissioners or a government department or a person holding in trust for Her Majesty for the purposes of a government department (s.14(5)).

**Notice**

3A–553 A landlord is not in breach of the implied covenant until a reasonable period has elapsed after the giving of notice of the defect (*O'Brien v Robinson* [1973] A.C. 912; [1973] 2 W.L.R. 393; [1973] 1 All E.R. 583, HL—collapse of bedroom ceiling due to a latent defect. Neither the tenant nor the landlord was aware of the defect until the collapse occurred. The House of Lords held that no liability under the Housing Act 1961 s.32 (now the Landlord and Tenant Act 1985 s.11) arose until the landlord had information about the existence of a defect in the premises which would put a reasonable person on enquiry as to whether works of repair were needed). See too *McGreal v Wake* (1984) 269 E.G. 1254; (1984) 13 H.L.R. 107, CA. The onus of proving that a reasonable period has passed is on the tenant (*Morris v Liverpool City Council* (1988) 14 E.G. 59; (1988) 20 H.L.R. 498, CA).

Notice of disrepair need not specify the precise nature or degree of want of repair. A letter from the solicitors which did not give details or enclose estimates or a report will normally be sufficient to put the landlord under an obligation to attend and inspect and thereafter carry out the repair (*Al Hassani v Merrigan* [1988] 03 E.G. 88; (1988) 20 H.L.R. 238, CA). The Court of Appeal has also held that a landlord local authority had notice of disrepair where an officer of the environmental health department had visited the property and seen the defects and the chief executive had received a report from the district valuer—prepared after a right to buy application—which drew attention to the defects, even though the tenancy agreement stated that notice of disrepair should be given direct to the architectural service of the council (*Dinefwr BC v Jones* (1987) 19 H.L.R. 445, CA). See too *Hall v Howard* (1988) 20 H.L.R. 566, CA (inspection report setting out items of disrepair taken into account in reaching a valuation of the property); and *Sheldon v West Bromwich Corp* (1984) 13 H.L.R. 23; (1984) 25 P. & C.R. 360, CA, where the Court of Appeal held that the state of discoloration of the water in a tank and the tank's age were sufficient to give the landlords actual knowledge of the need to repair. Information about the existence of such a defect which would put a reasonable person on inquiry as to whether works of repair are needed is sufficient for the landlord's repairing obligation to commence.

The requirement for notice to the landlord does not apply where reliance is placed upon the Defective Premises Act 1972 s.4 (see above) or where the disrepair is within part of a building retained by the landlord. See *British Telecommunications Plc v Sun Life Plc* [1995] 3 W.L.R. 622; [1995] 4 All E.R. 44; [1996] Ch. 69, CA, where Nourse L.J. stated:

> "The general rule is that a covenant to keep premises in repair obliges the covenantor to keep them in repair at all times, so that there is breach of the obligation immediately a defect occurs. There is an exception where the obligation is the landlord's and the defect occurs in the demised premises themselves, in which case he is in breach of his obligation only when he has information about the existence of a defect such as would put a reasonable landlord on enquiry as to whether works of repair are needed and he has failed to carry out the works with reasonable expedition thereafter" ([1995] 4 All E.R. at 52).

In *Loria v Hammer* E.G.L.R. 249, Ch D, the cause of dampness was a failure to keep in repair the water tanks in the roof space and gutters around the roof. As these were in the common parts of a building, the landlord was held to be liable to repair irrespective of any notice.

**"structure and exterior"**

Outside walls of premises are part of the structure and so covered by the implied covenant, even if the lease expressly excludes them from the demise (*Campden Hill Towers Ltd v Gardner* [1977] Q.B. 823; [1977] 1 All E.R. 739; (1984) 13 H.L.R. 64, CA). The roof above a flat is capable of being part of the structure and exterior' of the dwelling comprising the flat within the meaning of the Housing Act 1961 s.32 (now the Landlord and the Tenant Act 1985 s.11), whether or not the roof is part of the demised premises (*Douglas-Scott v Scorgie* [1984] 1 W.L.R. 716; [1984] 1 All E.R. 1086, CA). See too *Ravenseft Properties Ltd v Davstone (Holdings) Ltd* [1980] Q.B. 12; [1979] 2 W.L.R. 897; [1979] 1 All E.R. 929, QBD. **3A–554**

However, in *Brown v Liverpool Corporation* [1969] 3 All E.R. 1345; (1984) 13 H.L.R. 1, CA, the Court of Appeal held that four shallow steps and a path made of flagstones between the house and the street were not part of the structure of the house and so not within the implied covenant. Similarly, in *Hopwood v Cannock Chase DC (formerly Rugeley UDC)* [1975] 1 W.L.R. 373; [1975] 1 All E.R. 796, CA, where the widow of the tenant tripped and fell on the edge of a paving slab in the yard behind the house, the Court of Appeal held that the yard did not form part of the essential means of access to the property and so was not part of the structure or exterior of the dwelling house for the purposes of the Housing Act 1961 s.32 (now the Landlord and Tenant Act 1985 s.11). See too *King v South Northamptonshire DC* [1992] 06 E.G. 152; (1992) 24 H.L.R. 284, CA.

In *Irvine v Morgan* (1992) 24 H.L.R. 1; [1991] 1 E.G.L.R. 261, QBD, Recorder Thayne Forbes, Q.C. held that the words "structure and exterior" do not mean that landlords are liable to repair the whole of the house. On the other hand, "structure" is not limited to the load-bearing parts. It consists of those elements of the overall dwelling-house which give it its essential stability and shape. The expression does not extend to the many and various ways in which the dwelling-house will be fitted out, equipped, decorated and generally made habitable. Applying that test to the specific items, he held that:

- the separate garage and gates were not within the implied covenant;
- internal wall plaster and door furniture were decorative and therefore not part of the structure;
- external windows and doors and their constituent parts (including sashes) were either part of the structure or exterior;
- external painting was part of the obligation to repair the exterior;
- internal decorative painting of installations such as radiators was purely decorative and not part of the implied covenant.

See too *Quick v Taff Ely BC* [1986] 1 Q.B. 809; [1985] 3 W.L.R. 981; [1985] 3 All E.R. 321, CA (very severe condensation making house virtually unfit for human habitation not a breach of the s.11 covenant in the absence of evidence of disrepair to the structure or exterior) where Dillon L.J. stated:

> "In the present case the liability of the council was to keep the structure and exterior of the house in repair—not the decorations. Though there is ample evi-

HOUSING

dence of damage to the decorations and to bedding, clothing and other fabrics, evidence of damage to the subject-matter of the covenant, the structure and exterior of the house, is far too seek ... there is no evidence at all of physical damage to the walls—as opposed to the decorations—or the windows" ([1985] 3 All E.R. at 326).

Lawton L.J. stated:

"It follows that, on the evidence in this case, the trial judge should first have identified the parts of the exterior and structure of the house which were out of repair and then have gone on to decide whether, in order to remedy the defects, it was reasonably necessary to replace the concrete lintels over the windows, which caused 'cold bridging', and the single-glazed metal windows ..." (*ibid.*, at 328).

In *Lee v Leeds City Council* [2002] 1 W.L.R. 1488; [2002] All E.R. 124, CA the Court of Appeal held that: (1) *Quick* was not decided per incuriam because of a failure to consider the meaning given to "repair" in *Proudfoot v Hart* (1890) 25 QBD 42. Even if *Quick* was decided in ignorance of *Proudfoot*, both cases were before the court in *Post Office v Aquarius Properties Ltd* [1987] 1 All E.R. 1055 and the court did not regard them as inconsistent; and (2) In view of an express covenant to keep the structure in repair and the similar covenant which was otherwise implied under s.11, the court would not imply into local authority tenancies a term that the landlord was to keep the property "in good condition".

However, in *Staves v Leeds City Council* (1991) 23 H.L.R. 107; [1992] 29 E.G. 119, CA, where the condensation was so bad that the wall plaster had become saturated in places, the council conceded that the internal plasterwork was part of the structure. It argued, however, that, although the plaster was saturated, the patches concerned were minimal and the plaster was not in "disrepair". The Court of Appeal upheld H.H.J. Coles Q.C.'s finding that plaster when saturated is in disrepair and dismissed the *de minimis* argument. The plaster was in such poor condition that it required complete renewal. An award of £5,000 general damages (December 1990, Legal Action 17) was not disturbed. See too *Hussein v Mehman* [1992] 32 E.G. 59, Wood Green Trial Centre, where Assistant Recorder Sedley held that defective plaster on a bedroom ceiling was part of the "structure" for the purposes of s.11.

**"age, character and prospective life of the dwelling-house"—(s.11(3))**

**3A–555** In *Dame Margaret Hungerford Charity Trustees v Beazeley* [1993] 29 E.G. 100, CA, the main allegation was that the landlords had failed to keep in repair a stone tile and wooden peg roof, probably 150 to 180 years old. The trial judge was satisfied that by 1989 the roof was in need of complete repair but that since that date the landlords had simply undertaken "running repairs" by replacing individual rotten pegs and slipped tiles. Preferring the evidence of the landlords' expert, and having regard to the age, character and prospective life of the dwelling, he held that the landlords were not in breach of the repairing covenant. Although replacing the roof would be ideal, it was no breach simply to keep patching up the old roof. The Court of Appeal dismissed the tenant's appeal, declining to interfere with the judge's findings of fact. See too *Newham LBC v Patel* 13 H.L.R. 77, CA; and *Murray v Birmingham City Council* (1988) 20 H.L.R. 39, CA, where the roof of a rented property built in 1908 had repeatedly failed, causing six incidents of rainwater penetration in six years. Although each had "sooner or later" been repaired by retiling or other minor work, the tenant pressed for complete replacement. The Court of Appeal dismissed the tenant's appeal against a county court finding in favour of the landlord. Slade L.J. said:

"I accept that in any case where a landlord or a tenant for that matter is under an obligation to keep in repair an old roof, the stage may come where the only practicable way of performing that covenant is to replace the roof altogether." (p.43)

However, dismissing the appeal, the Court of Appeal found that by the end of the tenancy in 1982 that stage had not been reached. If a tenant wanted to make good the assertion that the whole roof should be replaced, it would require evidence as to its general condition, its construction, the condition of battens and joists, the fixing of slates and expert evidence as to why piecemeal repair was no longer practicable.

On the other hand, a landlord was not entitled to rely upon s.11(3) where the property which was not near the end of its life, had been in disrepair for three years and would cost only £1,200 to repair (*McLean v Liverpool City Council* (1988) 20 H.L.R. 25; (1987) 283 E.G. 1395, CA).

**"repair"**

Section 11 obliges landlords to repair. The distinction between what is a repair and an improvement is therefore important. In *McDougall v Easington DC* (1989) 21 H.L.R. 310, CA (where the works involved reducing each property to its original concrete framework and then fitting new roofs, new windows and new internal fittings and retiling the floors), Mustill L.J. stated that: **3A–556**

> "... three different tests may be discerned, which may be applied separately or concurrently as the circumstances of the individual case may demand, but all are to be approached in the light of the nature and age of the premises, their condition when the tenant went into occupation, and the other express terms of the tenancy—
>
> (i) whether the alterations went to the whole of the structure or only to a subsidiary part;
>
> (ii) whether the effect of the alterations was to produce a building of a wholly different character than that which had been let;
>
> (iii) what was the cost of the works in relation to the previous value of the building, and what was their effect on the value and lifespan of the building." (p.316)

See too *Wainwright v Leeds City Council* (1984) 13 H.L.R. 117; (1984) 270 E.G. 1289, CA, a case involving rising damp, where the Court of Appeal rejected the tenant's contention that the defendants were in breach of the Housing Act 1961 s.32 (now the Landlord and Tenant Act 1985 s.11) because they had failed to install a damp-proof course in a house which had originally been built without one. Landlords have no obligation to go beyond repairing the subject-matter of the demise (in that case a house with no damp-proof course); *cf. Elmcroft Developments Ltd v Tankersley-Sawyer* (1984) 15 H.L.R. 63; (1984) 270 E.G. 140, CA, where a landlord was obliged to repair a *defective* damp proof course.

In *Stent v Monmouth DC* (1987) 19 H.L.R. 269; (1987) 282 E.G. 705, CA, where the accumulation of water beneath the front door caused parts of the door to rot and required repeated replacement, the Court of Appeal held that the landlord was obliged to replace the existing door with a weatherproof door.

**Proper working order**

An installation for the supply of water is in proper working order if it is able to function under those conditions of supply that it is reasonable to anticipate will prevail. An unanticipated change in the nature of the supply of a utility may occur in a varierty of circumstances. If a change is imposed deliberately because of some scientific or technical advance, the change is likely to be introduced in a manner and subject to conditions under which it is reasonable to expect customers to modify their installations to accomodate the change and business efficacy would suggest that the landlord's duty to keep installations in proper working order would require him to make necessary modifications. In other circumstances, if the change is likely to be short-lived, the cost of modification might be disproportionate. Where the changed circumstances are likely to persist for a lengthy period it might seem wholly unreasonable for the landlord to leave his tenants deprived of a satisfactory supply of water for want of relatively modest expenditure on modifications. (*O'Connor v Old Etonians Housing Association Ltd* [2002] EWCA Civ 150; [2002] Ch. 295)—water pipes reduced from 1.25 inch diameter to 1 inch—unable to supply water during period when water pressure reduced). **3A–557**

The Court of Appeal has held that landlords were not obliged by the Housing Act 1961 s.32 (now the Landlord and Tenant Act 1985 s.11) to lag pipes which function satisfactorily in all but the most extreme weather conditions. Accordingly there was no liability on the part of landlords for damage caused by the bursting of an unlagged pipe in very severe cold (*Wycombe Health Authority v Barnett* (1982) 5 H.L.R. 84; (1982) 264 E.G. 619, CA).

The implied covenant to repair under s.11(1A)(b)(i) does not extend to installations located in parts of a building in which the lessor does not have an estate or interest, even if the lessor has an estate or interest in other parts of the same building (*Niazi Services Ltd v Van der Loo* [2004] EWCA Civ 53; [2004] 1 W.L.R. 1254—inadequate wa-

HOUSING

ter pressure in top floor flat caused by works in ground floor/basement restaurant in which the mesne lessor of the top floor had no interest).

**Specific performance**

3A–558 See s.17, below.

**Damages**

3A–559 "The object of awarding damages against a landlord for breach of his covenant to repair is not to punish the landlord but, so far as money can, to restore the tenant to the position he would have been in had there been no breach. This object will not be acheived by applying one set of rules to all cases regardless of particular circumstances of the case. The facts of each case must be looked at carefully to see what damage the tenant has suffered and how he may be fairly compensated by a monetary award."

per Griffiths L.J. in *Calabar Properties Ltd v Stitcher* [1984] 1 W.L.R. 287; [1983] 3 All E.R. 759 at 768, CA).

In *Wallace v Manchester City Council* (1998) 30 H.L.R. 1111; *The Times*, July 23, 1998; [1998] 41 E.G. 223, CA, Morritt L.J. said:

"First, the question in all cases of damages for breach of obligation to repair is what sum will, so far as money can, place the tenant in the position he would have been in if the obligation to repair had been duly performed by the landlord. Second, the answer to that question inevitably involves a comparison of the property as it was for the period when the landlord was in breach of his obligation with what it would have been if the obligation had been performed. Third, for the periods when the tenant remained in occupation of the property, notwithstanding the breach of the obligation to repair the loss to him requiring compensation is the loss of comfort and convenience which results from living in a property which was not in the state of repair it ought to have been if the landlord performed his obligation ... Fourth, if the tenant does not remain in occupation but, being entitled to do so, is forced by the landlord's failure to repair to sell or sublet the property he may diminution of the price or recoverable rent occasioned by the landlord's failure to perform his covenant to repair."

He continued:

"... the sum required to compensate the tenant for the distress and inconvenience ... may be ascertained in a number of different ways, including but not limited to a notional reduction in the rent. Some judges may prefer to use that method alone ... some may prefer a global award for discomfort and inconvenience ... and others may prefer a mixture of the two ... But, in my judgment, they are not bound to assess damages separately under heads of both diminution in value and discomfort because in cases within the third proposition those heads are alternative ways of expressing the same concept."

Morritt L.J. said that the source of the money with which to pay the rent (e.g. housing benefit) is irrelevant to the extent of the discomfort and inconvenience suffered by the tenant and what would be proper monetary compensation for it.

In *Shine v English Churches Housing Group* [2004] EWCA Civ 434; [2004] H.L.R. 42, the Court of Appeal stated that although the guidelines in *Wallace* "are not to be applied in a mechanistic or dogmatic way", and that there are cases "where the level of distress or inconvenience experienced by a tenant may require an award in excess of the level of rent payable" if an award is made in excess of the rent payable, "clear reasons need to be given". The Court referred to "a basic rule of thumb that—all other things being equal—the maximum award of damages should be the rental value of the premises." Where a global award of damages is made, it should be cross-checked against the annual rent to ensure that damages are neither too high nor too low.

On the other hand, in *Earle v Charalambous* [2006] EWCA Civ 1090; [2007] H.L.R. 8; it was said:

"A long-lease of a residential property is not only a home, but is also a valuable property asset. Distress and inconvenience caused by disrepair are not free-standing heads of claim, but are symptomatic of interference with the lessee's enjoyment of that asset. If the lessor's breach of covenant has the effect of depriving the lessee of that enjoyment, wholly or partially, for a significant period, a notional judgment of the resulting reduction in rental value is likely to be the most appropriate starting point for assessment of damages. Generally, this reduction will not be capable of precise estimation; ... it will be a matter for the judgment for the court, rather than for expert valuation evidence."

The fact that offers of alternative accommodation have been made but not taken up "cannot ... affect the question of damages" (per Parker L.J. in *Lubren v Lambeth LBC* (1988) 20 H.L.R. 165, CA).

Even if a landlord is not at fault in carrying out its repairing obligations, there is an obligation to reinstate the property after completion of works to a reasonable standard, and that includes putting right damage done to decorations (*Bradley v Chorley BC* (1985) 17 H.L.R. 305, CA). See too *McGreal v Wake* (1984) 269 E.G. 1254; (1984) 13 H.L.R. 107, CA.

Damages may include loss of rent where it was foreseeable that the tenant might sub-let (*Mira v Aylmer Square Investments Ltd* [1990] 22 E.G. 61; (1990) 22 H.L.R. 182, CA).

Registration of a fair rent does not preclude recovery of damages for breach of repairing covenants (*Sturolson and Co v Mauroux* (1988) 20 H.L.R. 332, CA).

As to *quantum* generally, see *Brent LBC v Murphy (Carmel)* (1996) 28 H.L.R. 203, CA; *Chiodi v De Marney* [1988] 41 E.G. 80; (1989) 21 H.L.R. 6, CA; *Davies v Peterson* (1989) 21 H.L.R. 63, CA; *Dean v Ainley* [1987] 3 All E.R. 748, CA; *Elmcroft Developments Ltd v Tankersley-Sawyer* (1984) 15 H.L.R. 63, CA; *Taylor v Knowsley BC* (1985) 17 H.L.R. 376, CA; and *Televantos v McCulloch* [1991] 19 E.G. 18; (1991) 23 H.L.R. 412, CA.

**Repairing obligations and the ECHR**

In *Lee v Leeds City Council* [2002] EWCA Civ 6; [2002] 1 W.L.R. 1488; [2002] All **3A–560**
E.R. 124, CA, the Court of Appeal held that Human Rights Act 1998 s.6 imposes an obligation on local authority landlords to take steps to ensure that the condition of dwelling houses which they let for social housing are such that the tenants' rights to respect for home and family life under art.8 are not infringed. However rights under art.8 are not unqualified (*Southwark LBC v Tanner* [2001] 1 A.C. 1) and there is nothing in the Strasbourg jurisprudence to support the proposition that s.6 and art.8 impose a general and unqualified obligation on local authorities in relation to the condition of their housing stock. There might though be cases where a local authority that had let a property that was unfit for human habitation or prejudicial to health would be in breach of the positive duty imposed by s.6 and art.8. In this case there was no such breach of duty. The conditions complained of did not seem to be sufficiently serious (*Lopez Ostra v Spain* (1994) 20 E.H.R.R. 277).

## Restriction on contracting out of s.11

**12.**—(1) A covenant or agreement, whether contained in a lease to **3A–561**
which section 11 applies or in an agreement collateral to such a lease, is void in so far as it purports—

(a) to exclude or limit the obligations of the lessor or the immunities of the lessee under that section, or

(b) to authorise any forfeiture or impose on the lessee any penalty, disability or obligation in the event of his enforcing or relying upon those obligations or immunities,

unless the inclusion of the provision was authorised by the county court.

(2) The county court may, by order made with the consent of the parties, authorise the inclusion in a lease, or in an agreement collateral to a lease, of provisions excluding or modifying in relation to the lease, the provisions of section 11 with respect to the repairing obligations of the parties if it appears to the court that it is reasonable to do so, having regard to all the circumstances of the case, including the other terms and conditions of the lease.

**"lease"**

See s.16. **3A–562**

***Paragraph numbers marked with a "+" can be found online and on CD.***

**"lessor"**

3A–563 See s.16.

**"lessee"**

3A–564 See s.16.

## Leases to which s.11 applies: general rule

3A–565 **13.**—(1) Section 11 (repairing obligations) applies to a lease of a dwelling-house granted on or after 24th October 1961 for a term of less than seven years.

(2) In determining whether a lease is one to which section 11 applies—

(a) any part of the term which falls before the grant shall be left out of account and the lease shall be treated as a lease for a term commencing with the grant,

(b) a lease which is determinable at the option of the lessor before the expiration of seven years from the commencement of the term shall be treated as a lease for a term of less than seven years, and

(c) a lease (other than a lease to which paragraph (b) applies) shall not be treated as a lease for a term of less than seven years if it confers on the lessee an option for renewal for a term which, together with the original term, amounts to seven years or more.

(3) This section has effect subject to—

section 14 (leases to which section 11 applies: exceptions), and

section 32(2) (provisions not applying to tenancies within Part II of the Landlord and Tenant Act 1954).

**"dwelling-house"**

3A–566 See s.16.

**"lease"**

3A–567 See s.16.

**"lessor"**

3A–568 See s.16.

**"lessee"**

3A–569 See s.16.

**"for a term of less than seven years"**

3A–570 In *Brikom Investments Ltd v Seaford* [1981] 1 W.L.R. 863; [1981] 2 All E.R. 783, CA, a tenant was allowed into possession in accordance with an agreement for a lease for a term of seven years on November 1. The lease was executed some days later but provided for a term of seven years commencing on November 1. The landlord contended that the Housing Act 1961 s.32 (now the Landlord and the Tenant Act 1985 s.11) did not apply because of the reference in s.32(1) to any lease "for a term of less than seven years". The Court of Appeal held that, in view of s.33(5) (now s.13(2)(a)), for the purposes of s.32 the commencement of the term was November 1 (*cf. Roberts v Church Commissioners* [1972] 1 Q.B. 278, CA). However, the landlord was estopped from denying that s.32 (now s.11) applied where the rent officer had registered a rent on the basis that the implied covenant applied, the rent registered had not been challenged or rectified and the landlord had been receiving the higher

***Paragraph numbers marked with a "+" can be found online and on CD.***

rent (*cf. Demetriou v Poolaction Ltd* [1991] 25 E.G. 113, CA). See too *Tomkins v Basildon DC* [2002] EWCA Civ 876; [2002] 43 E.G. 206.

## Leases to which s.11 applies: exceptions

**14.**—(1) Section 11 (repairing obligations) does not apply to a new lease granted to an existing tenant, or to a former tenant still in possession, if the previous lease was not a lease to which section 11 applied (and, in the case of a lease granted before 24th October 1961, would not have been if it had been granted on or after that date). **3A–571**

(2) In subsection (1)—

"existing tenant" means a person who is when, or immediately before, the new lease is granted, the lessee under another lease of the dwelling-house;

"former tenant still in possession" means a person who—

(a) was the lessee under another lease of the dwelling-house which terminated at some time before the new lease was granted, and

(b) between the termination of that other lease and the grant of the new lease was continuously in possession of the dwelling-house or of the rents and profits of the dwelling-house; and

"the previous lease" means the other lease referred to in the above definitions.

(3) Section 11 does not apply to a lease of a dwelling-house which is a tenancy of an agricultural holding within the meaning of the Agricultural Holdings Act 1986 and in relation to which that Act applies or to a farm business tenancy within the meaning of the Agricultural Tenancies Act 1995.

(4) Section 11 does not apply to a lease granted on or after 3rd October 1980 to—

a local authority,

a National Park authority

a new town corporation,

an urban development corporation,

the Development Board for Rural Wales,

a registered social landlord,

a co-operative housing association, or

an educational institution or other body specified, or of a class specified, by regulations under section 8 of the Rent Act 1977or paragraph 8 of Schedule I to the Housing Act 1988 (bodies making student lettings).

a housing action trust established under Part III of the Housing Act 1988.

(5) Section 11 does not apply to a lease granted on or after 3rd October 1980 to—

(a) Her Majesty in right of the Crown (unless the lease is under the management of the Crown Estate Commissioners), or

(b) a government department or a person holding in trust

***Paragraph numbers marked with a "+" can be found online and on CD.***

for Her Majesty for the purposes of a government department.

3A–572 *Note*—Amended by the Agricultural Holdings Act 1986 Sch.14, para.64; the Housing Act 1988 s.116; the Local Government and Housing Act 1989 Sch.11, para.89; the Housing Act 1996 (Consequential Provisions) Order 1996 (SI 1996/2325) Sch.2, para.16; and the Agricultural Tenancies Act 1995 Sch.

**"dwelling-house"**

3A–573 See s.16.

**"lease"**

3A–574 See s.16.

**"lessor"**

3A–575 See s.16.

**"lessee"**

3A–576 See s.16.

**"local authority"**

3A–577 See s.38.

**[THE NEXT PARAGRAPH IS 3A–707.1.]**

## Landlord and Tenant Act 1987

3A–707.1 (1987 c.31)

ARRANGEMENT OF SECTIONS

PART VI



**Paragraph numbers marked with a "+" denote content that is available on White Book on Westlaw UK or the Civil Procedure CD.**

## Housing Act 1988

3A–722 (1988 c.50)

ARRANGEMENT OF SECTIONS

PART I

RENTED ACCOMMODATION

CHAPTER I

ASSURED TENANCIES

*MEANING OF ASSURED TENANCY ETC.*



***Paragraph numbers marked with a "+" can be found online and on CD.***

***Paragraph numbers marked with a "+" can be found online and on CD.***

## PART I

## RENTED ACCOMMODATION

### CHAPTER I

### ASSURED TENANCIES

### *MEANING OF ASSURED TENANCY ETC.*

### Assured tenancies

**3A–723** **1.**—(1) A tenancy under which a dwelling-house is let as a separate dwelling is for the purposes of this Act an assured tenancy if and so long as—

(a) the tenant or, as the case may be, each of the joint tenants is an individual; and
(b) the tenant or, as the case may be, at least one of the joint tenants occupies the dwelling-house as his only or principal home; and
(c) the tenancy is not one which, by virtue of subsection (2) or subsection (6) below, cannot be an assured tenancy.

(2) Subject to subsection (3) below, if and so long as a tenancy falls within any paragraph in Part I of Schedule 1 to this Act, it cannot be an assured tenancy; and in that Schedule—

(a) "tenancy" means a tenancy under which a dwelling-house is let as a separate dwelling;
(b) Part II has effect for determining the rateable value of a dwelling-house for the purposes of Part I; and
(c) Part III has effect for supplementing paragraph 10 in Part I.

(2A) The Secretary of State may by order replace any amount referred to in paragraphs 2 and 3A of Schedule 1 to this Act by such amount as is specified in the order; and such an order shall be made by statutory instrument which shall be subject to annulment in pursuance of a resolution of either House of Parliament.

(3) Except as provided in Chapter V below, at the commencement of this Act, a tenancy—

(a) under which a dwelling-house was then let as a separate dwelling, and

***Paragraph numbers marked with a "+" can be found online and on CD.***

(b) which immediately before that commencement was an assured tenancy for the purposes of sections 56 to 58 of the Housing Act 1980 (tenancies granted by approved bodies),

shall become an assured tenancy for the purposes of this Act.

(4) In relation to an assured tenancy falling within subsection (3) above—

(a) Part I of Schedule 1 to this Act shall have effect, subject to subsection (5) below, as if it consisted only of paragraphs 11 and 12; and

(b) sections 56 to 58 of the Housing Act 1980 (and Schedule 5 to that Act) shall not apply after the commencement of this Act.

(5) In any case where—

(a) immediately before the commencement of this Act the landlord under a tenancy is a fully mutual housing association, and

(b) at the commencement of this Act the tenancy becomes an assured tenancy by virtue of subsection (3) above,

then, so long as that association remains the landlord under that tenancy (and under any statutory periodic tenancy which arises on the coming to an end of that tenancy), paragraph 12 of Schedule 1 to this Act shall have effect in relation to that tenancy with the omission of sub-paragraph (1)(h).

(6) [...]

(7) [...]

*Note* —Subsection (2A) added by the References to Rating (Housing) Regulations 1990 (SI 1990/434) para.27. Subsections (6) and (7) repealed by the Housing Act 1996 Sch.19, Pt VIII. **3A–724**

**"tenant"**

See s.45. **3A–725**

**"dwelling-house"**

See s.45. **3A–726**

**"let"**

See s.45. **3A–727**

**"fully mutual housing association"**

See the Housing Associations Act 1985 s.1, which defines a housing association as a "society, body of trustees or company (a) which is established for the purpose of, or amongst whose objects or powers are included those of, providing, constructing, improving or managing, or facilitating or encouraging the construction or improvement of, housing accommodation, and (b) which does not trade for profit or whose constitution or rules prohibit the issue of capital with interest or dividend exceeding such rate as may be prescribed by the treasury, whether with or without differentiation between share and loan capital". **3A–728**

HOUSING

**"A tenancy under which a dwelling-house is let"**

Section 1 refers to: "A tenancy under which a dwelling-house is let ..." Therefore, there can only be an assured tenancy if there is a tenancy. There can be no such thing as an "assured licence". For the distinction between tenancies and licences see, e.g. *Street v Mountford* [1985] A.C. 809; [1985] 2 W.L.R. 877; [1985] 2 All E.R. 289, HL; *AG* **3A–729**

*Securities v Vaughan* and *Antoniades v Villiers and Bridger* [1990] 1 A.C. 417; [1988] 3 W.L.R. 1205; [1988] 3 All E.R. 1058, HL; *Duke v Wynne* [1989] 3 All E.R. 130, CA; *Hadjiloucas v Crean* [1988] 1 W.L.R. 1006; [1987] 3 All E.R. 1008, CA; *Nicolau v Pitt* (1989) 21 H.L.R. 487; [1989] 21 E.G. 71, CA; *Aslan v Murphy* [1989] 3 All E.R. 130, CA; and *Crancour Ltd v Da Silvaesa* (1986) 18 H.L.R. 265; (1986) 78 E.G. 618, CA.

Section 1 contains four pre-requisites for the creation of an assured tenancy:

(a) The dwelling-house must be let as a separate dwelling. This is the well known phrase which appears in the Rent Act 1977 s.1. If a tenancy comprises two or more separate units of accommodation which are let together to a tenant, there can be no assured tenancy (*St Catherine's College v Dorling* [1980] 1 W.L.R. 66; and *Kavanaghv Lyroudias* [1985] 1 All E.R. 560). See also *Central YMCA Housing Association v Goodman* (1992) 24 H.L.R. 109, CA, where Dillon L.J. referring to a furnished twin-bedded room in a hostel with a private bathroom and lavatory en suite, said that "… this room was no more a dwelling-house than a hotel room is a dwelling-house"); *Central YMCA Housing Association v Saunders* (1990) 23 H.L.R. 212, CA; *Parkins v Westminister CC* (1998) 30 H.L.R. 894, CA; and *R. v Rent Officer for Nottingham Ex p. Allen* (1985) 17 H.L.R. 481.

The word "dwelling" is not a term of art with a specialised legal meaning. It is: "the place where [an occupier] lives and to which he returns and which forms the centre of his existence…No doubt he will sleep there and usually eat there; he will often prepare at least some of his meals there".

However there is no legislative requirement that cooking facilities must be available for premises to qualify as a dwelling. In deciding whether an occupant has security of tenure: "The first step is to identify the subject-matter of the tenancy agreement. If this is a house or part of a house of which the tenant has exclusive possession with no element of sharing, the only question is whether, at the date when proceedings were brought, it was the tenant's home. If so, it was his dwelling … The presence or absence of cooking facilities in the part of the premises of which the tenant has exclusive occupation is not relevant."

(See *Uratemp Ventures Ltd v Collins and Carrell* [2001] UKHL 43; [2002] 1 A.C. 301; [2001] 3 W.L.R. 806; [2002] 1 All E.R. 46, HL).

Section 3 provides that if a tenant enjoys exclusive occupation of some rented accommodation with a right to share other accommodation with other people, apart from the landlord, the mere fact that the other accommodation is shared, does not prevent the tenant from occupying the accommodation which is not shared as a separate dwelling (compare the Rent Act 1977 s.22 and the Housing Act 1985 s.79).

(b) The tenant, or if there are joint tenants, each of the joint tenants, must be individuals. A genuine letting to a company can never be an assured tenancy. See, e.g. *Hiller v United Dairies* [1934] 1 K.B. 57, CA; *Hilton v Plustitle Ltd* [1989] 1 W.L.R. 149; [1988] 3 All E.R. 1051, CA; *Kaye v Massbetter Ltd and Kanter* (1992) 24 H.L.R. 28, CA; and *Estavest Investments Ltd v Commercial Express Travel Ltd* (1989) 21 H.L.R. 106, CA and *Eaton Square Properties Ltd v O'Higgins* (2001) 33 H.L.R. 68, CA. In such cases, the tenancy is unprotected and may come to an end by effluxion of time or may be terminated by service of a notice to quit. If this occurs, a landlord who brings possession proceedings is automatically entitled to possession without having to prove any ground for possession.

(c) The tenant, or if there are joint tenants, at least one of them, must occupy the premises as his or her only or principal home (*cf.* the Housing Act 1985 s.81 ("as his only or principal home"), the Leasehold Reform Act 1967 s.1 ("as his residence") and the Rent Act 1977 s.2 ("as his residence"). It is not possible for assured tenants to maintain assured tenancies in more than one home at the same time, although there is no reason why an assured tenant should not be temporarily absent from the premises in question provided that they remain his or her only or main home. Tenancies cease to be assured if tenants cease to occupy premises as their only or principal home (*cf. Sutton LBC v Swann* (1986) 18 H.L.R. 140, CA).

In order to maintain a "home" a tenant need not be physically resident, so long as there is an intention to return after a temporary absence and some

***Paragraph numbers marked with a "+" can be found online and on CD.***

physical sign of continued occupation (e.g. furniture and possessions in the property). Two houses can be occupied as a home at the same time—*Crawley BC v Sawyer* (1988) 20 H.L.R. 98, CA, where a council tenant went to live with his "girlfriend" for a period of approximately one and a half years during which time the gas and electricity supplies to the premises which he rented from the council were cut off. Held that the rented premises remained his principal home throughout the period. However, if two houses are occupied, they cannot both be assured tenancies.

It is possible for a tenant to lose security of tenure by reason of non-occupation but to regain it by re-occupying the property before service of a notice to quit—see *Hussey v Camden LBC* (1995) 27 H.L.R. 5, CA, where, as the tenant was occupying the property as his only or principal home at the time of service of the notice to quit, the Court of Appeal held that the earlier loss of security was irrelevant.

Subletting of the whole of premises means that any tenancy cases to be assured—see *Ujima Housing v Ansah* (1998) 30 H.L.R. 831, CA; *Jennings v Epping Forest DC* (1993) 25 H.L.R. 241, CA; *Poland v Cadogan* [1980] 3 All E.R. 544, CA (Leasehold Reform Act 1993 s.93(2)); *Muir Group Housing Association Ltd v Thornley* (1993) 25 H.L.R. 89, CA; and *Brent LBC v Cronin* (1997) 30 H.L.R. 43, CA, *cf. Waltham Forest CBHA v Fanning* July 2001 Legal Action 33, (2001) March 12, QBD and *Merton LBC v Salama* (1989) CAT No.89/169; June 1989, *Legal Action 25*, CA (parting with possession of part of premises). Parting with possession is not to be inferred simply from the fact that another person has been allowed to use and occupy a tenant's home during his temporary absence (*Lam Kee Ying v Lam Shes Tong* [1975] A.C. 247, PC).

(d) A tenancy cannot be an assured tenancy if any of the exceptions listed in Sch.1 applies (see below). Many of these exceptions are similar to those set out in the Rent Act 1977 Pt I.

Note also that a tenancy granted by a private landlord under arrangements made by a local housing authority in accordance with their functions under Housing Act 1996 ss.188, 190, 200 or 204 (interim duties towards the homeless) cannot be an assured tenancy within twelve months of the date of notification of the local authority's decision or the determination of any Housing Act 1996 s.202 review or s.204 appeal, unless the landlord notifies the tenant that the tenancy is to be an assured shorthold tenancy—see Housing Act 1996 s.209 as substituted by Homelessness Act 2002 Sch.1, para.19.

## Letting of a dwelling-house together with other land

**2.**—(1) If, under a tenancy, a dwelling-house is let together with other land then, for the purposes of this Part of this Act— **3A–730**

(a) if and so long as the main purpose of the letting is the provision of a home for the tenant or, where there are joint tenants, at least one of them, the other land shall be treated as part of the dwelling-house; and

(b) if and so long as the main purpose of the letting is not as mentioned in paragraph (a) above, the tenancy shall be treated as not being one under which a dwelling-house is let as a separate dwelling.

(2) Nothing in subsection (1) above affects any question whether a tenancy is precluded from being an assured tenancy by virtue of any provision of Schedule 1 to this Act.

**"tenancy"**

See s.45. **3A–731**

**"tenant"**

See s.45. **3A–732**

***Paragraph numbers marked with a "+" can be found online and on CD.***

**"dwelling-house"**

3A–733 See s.45.

**"let"**

3A–734 See s.45.

## Tenant sharing accommodation with persons other than landlord

3A–735 **3.**—(1) Where a tenant has the exclusive occupation of any accommodation (in this section referred to as "the separate accommodation") and—

(a) the terms as between the tenant and his landlord on which he holds the separate accommodation include the use of other accommodation (in this section referred to as "the shared accommodation") in common with another person or other persons, not being or including the landlord, and

(b) by reason only of the circumstances mentioned in paragraph (a) above, the separate accommodation would not, apart from this section, be a dwelling-house let on an assured tenancy,

the separate accommodation shall be deemed to be a dwelling-house let on an assured tenancy and the following provisions of this section shall have effect.

(2) For the avoidance of doubt it is hereby declared that where, for the purpose of determining the rateable value of the separate accommodation, it is necessary to make an apportionment under Part II of Schedule 1 to this Act, regard is to be had to the circumstances mentioned in subsection (1)(a) above.

(3) While the tenant is in possession of the separate accommodation, any term of the tenancy terminating or modifying, or providing for the termination or modification of, his right to the use of any of the shared accommodation which is living accommodation shall be of no effect.

(4) Where the terms of the tenancy are such that, at any time during the tenancy, the persons in common with whom the tenant is entitled to the use of the shared accommodation could be varied or their number could be increased, nothing in subsection (3) above shall prevent those terms from having effect so far as they relate to any such variation or increase.

(5) In this section "living accommodation" means accommodation of such a nature that the fact that it constitutes or is included in the shared accommodation is sufficient, apart from this section, to prevent the tenancy from constituting an assured tenancy of a dwelling-house.

**"assured tenancy"**

3A–736 See s.1.

**"tenancy"**

3A–737 See s.45.

**"tenant"**

3A–738 See s.45.

*Paragraph numbers marked with a "+" can be found online and on CD.*

**"dwelling-house"**

See s.45. 3A–739

**"let"**

See s.45. 3A–740

**Sharing accommodation**

Note *Miller v Eyo* (1999) 31 H.L.R. 306, CA where the terms of the plaintiff's tenancy 3A–741
were that she had exclusive use of her bedroom with shared use of a living room, kitchen and bathroom/WC. Initially the only other bedroom in the flat was occupied by another tenant, but when she moved out the landlord and her family moved into the other bedroom and started to share the other parts of the flat with the plaintiff. Following *Gray v Brown* (1993) 25 H.L.R. 144, CA the Court of Appeal held that in the absence of an express term in the tenancy that the landlord had the right to re-enter and occupy, the tenancy came with s.3 and was assured. For a landlord to avoid this situation, a landlord's right to re-enter must be "clear and specific".

## Certain sublettings not to exclude any part of sub-lessor's premises from assured tenancy

**4.**—(1) Where the tenant of a dwelling-house has sub-let a part but 3A–742
not the whole of the dwelling-house, then, as against his landlord or any superior landlord, no part of the dwelling-house shall be treated as excluded from being a dwelling-house let on an assured tenancy by reason only that the terms on which any person claiming under the tenant holds any part of the dwelling-house include the use of accommodation in common with other persons.

(2) Nothing in this section affects the rights against, and liabilities to, each other of the tenant and any person claiming under him, or of any two such persons.

**"assured tenancy"**

See s.1. 3A–743

**"tenancy"**

See s.45. 3A–744

**"tenant"**

See s.45. 3A–745

**"dwelling-house"**

See s.45. 3A–746

**"let"**

See s.45. 3A–747

### *SECURITY OF TENURE*

## Security of tenure

**5.**—(1) An assured tenancy cannot be brought to an end by the 3A–748
landlord except by—

(a) obtaining—

(i) an order of the court for possession of the dwelling-house under section 7 or 21, and

(ii) the execution of the order,

***Paragraph numbers marked with a "+" can be found online and on CD.***

(b) obtaining an order of the court under section 6A (demotion order), or

(c) in the case of a fixed term tenancy which contains power for the landlord to determine the tenancy in certain circumstances, by the exercise of that power, and, accordingly, the service by the landlord of a notice to quit is of no effect in relation to a periodic assured tenancy.

(1A) Where an order of the court for possession of the dwelling-house is obtained, the tenancy ends when the order is executed.

(2) If an assured tenancy which is a fixed term tenancy comes to an end otherwise than by virtue of—

(a) an order of the court of the kind mentioned in subsection (1)(a) or (b) or any other order of the court, or

(b) a surrender or other action on the part of the tenant,

then, subject to section 7 and Chapter II below, the tenant shall be entitled to remain in possession of the dwelling-house let under that tenancy and, subject to subsection (4) below, his right to possession shall depend upon a periodic tenancy arising by virtue of this section.

(3) The periodic tenancy referred to in subsection (2) above is one—

(a) taking effect in possession immediately on the coming to an end of the fixed term tenancy;

(b) deemed to have been granted by the person who was the landlord under the fixed term tenancy immediately before it came to an end to the person who was then the tenant under that tenancy;

(c) under which the premises which are let are the same dwelling-house as was let under the fixed term tenancy;

(d) under which the periods of the tenancy are the same as those for which rent was last payable under the fixed term tenancy; and

(e) under which, subject to the following provisions of this Part of this Act, the other terms are the same as those of the fixed term tenancy immediately before it came to an end, except that any term which makes provision for determination by the landlord or the tenant shall not have effect while the tenancy remains an assured tenancy;

(4) The periodic tenancy referred to in subsection (2) above shall not arise if, on the coming to an end of the fixed term tenancy, the tenant is entitled, by virtue of the grant of another tenancy, to possession of the same or substantially the same dwelling-house as was let to him under the fixed term tenancy.

(5) If, on or before the date on which a tenancy is entered into or is deemed to have been granted as mentioned in subsection (3)(b) above, the person who is to be the tenant under that tenancy—

(a) enters into an obligation to do any act which (apart from this subsection) will cause the tenancy to come to an end at a time when it is an assured tenancy, or

(b) executes, signs or gives any surrender, notice to quit or other document which (apart from this subsection) has the effect of bringing the tenancy to an end at a time when it is an assured tenancy,

the obligation referred to in paragraph (a) above shall not be enforceable or, as the case may be, the surrender, notice to quit or other document referred to in paragraph (b) above shall be of no effect.

(5A) Nothing in subsection (5) affects any right of pre-emption—

(a) which is exercisable by the landlord under a tenancy in circumstances where the tenant indicates his intention to dispose of the whole of his interest under the tenancy, and

(b) in pursuance of which the landlord would be required to pay, in respect of the acquisition of that interest, an amount representing its market value.

"Dispose" means dispose by assignment or surrender, and "acquisition" has a corresponding meaning.

(6) If, by virtue of any provision of this Part of this Act, Part I of Schedule 1 to this Act has effect in relation to a fixed term tenancy as if it consisted only of paragraphs 11 and 12, that Part shall have the like effect in relation to any periodic tenancy which arises by virtue of this section on the coming to an end of the fixed term tenancy.

(7) Any reference in this Part of this Act to a statutory periodic tenancy is a reference to a periodic tenancy arising by virtue of this section.

*Note* —Amended by the Housing Act 2004 s.222(1) and (2). This section has also been amended by the Housing and Regeneration Act 2008 Sch.11, Pt I, para.6 (for transitional provisions see para.14) with effect from May 20, 2009 (SI 2009/1261) (c.66). **3A–749**

**"assured tenancy"**

See s.1. **3A–750**

**"tenancy"**

See s.45. **3A–751**

**"tenant"**

See s.45. **3A–752**

**"dwelling-house"**

See s.45. **3A–753**

**"let"**

See s.45. **3A–754**

**"fixed term tenancy"**

See s.45. **3A–755**

**Security of tenure**

Section 5 provides that a periodic assured tenancy can only be brought to an end by a landlord by obtaining an order of the court or by surrender. Section 5(1) makes it clear that notices to quit served by landlords have no effect upon periodic assured tenancies. Service of a notice to quit by a tenant does terminate an assured tenancy (see, e.g. *Hammersmith and Fulham LBC v Monk* [1992] 1 A.C. 478; [1991] 3 W.L.R. 1144; [1992] All E.R. 1, HL; *Harrow LBC v Johnstone* [1997] 1 W.L.R. 459; [1997] All E.R. 929, HL; and *Greenwich LBC v McGrady* (1982) 81 L.G.R. 288; (1982) 46 P. & C.R. **3A–756**

223; (1983) 6 H.L.R. 361; (1982) 267 E.G. 515, CA and *Notting Hill Housing Trust v Brackley* [2001] EWCA Civ 601; [2002] H.L.R. 212; [2001] L. & T.R. 467; [2001] 35 E.G. 106, CA).

If a contractual fixed term assured tenancy is brought to an end, other than by an order of a court or by surrender, a periodic assured tenancy (called a "statutory periodic tenancy") normally comes into existence immediately after the fixed term tenancy has come to an end. In some ways this is similar to a Rent Act statutory tenancy, but there are differences. The most important of these is the provision for fixing the terms of the statutory periodic tenancy. The basic rule is that the terms of the new statutory periodic tenancy are the same as for the former contractual assured tenancy (s.5(3)(e)). As to the period of a statutory periodic tenancy, see *Church Commissioners for England v Meya* [2006] EWCA Civ 821; [2007] H.L.R. 4.

## Fixing of terms of statutory periodic tenancy

**3A–757** **6.**—(1) In this section, in relation to a statutory periodic tenancy—

(a) "the former tenancy" means the fixed term tenancy on the coming to an end of which the statutory periodic tenancy arises, and

(b) "the implied terms" means the terms of the tenancy which have effect by virtue of section 5(3)(e) above, other than terms as to the amount of the rent;

but nothing in the following provisions of this section applies to a statutory periodic tenancy at a time when, by virtue of paragraph 11 or paragraph 12 in Part I of Schedule 1 to this Act, it cannot be an assured tenancy.

(2) Not later than the first anniversary of the day on which the former tenancy came to an end, the landlord may serve on the tenant, or the tenant may serve on the landlord, a notice in the prescribed form proposing terms of the statutory periodic tenancy different from the implied terms and, if the landlord or the tenant considers it appropriate, proposing an adjustment of the amount of the rent to take account of the proposed terms.

(3) Where a notice has been served under subsection (2) above—

(a) within the period of three months beginning on the date on which the notice was served on him, the landlord or the tenant, as the case may be, may, by an application in the prescribed form, refer the notice to a rent assessment committee under subsection (4) below; and

(b) if the notice is not so referred, then, with effect from such date, not falling within the period referred to in paragraph (a) above, as may be specified in the notice, the terms proposed in the notice shall become terms of the tenancy in substitution for any of the implied terms dealing with the same subject matter and the amount of the rent shall be varied in accordance with any adjustment so proposed.

(4) Where a notice under subsection (2) above is referred to a rent assessment committee, the committee shall consider the terms proposed in the notice and shall determine whether those terms, or some other terms (dealing with the same subject matter as the proposed terms), are such as, in the committee's opinion, might reasonably be expected to be found in an assured periodic tenancy of the dwelling-house concerned, being a tenancy—

(a) which begins on the coming to an end of the former tenancy; and

(b) which is granted by a willing landlord on terms which, except in so far as they relate to the subject matter of the proposed terms, are those of the statutory periodic tenancy at the time of the committee's consideration.

(5) Whether or not a notice under subsection (2) above proposes an adjustment of the amount of the rent under the statutory periodic tenancy, where a rent assessment committee determine any terms under subsection (4) above, they shall, if they consider it appropriate, specify such an adjustment to take account of the terms so determined.

(6) In making a determination under subsection (4) above, or specifying an adjustment of an amount of rent under subsection (5) above, there shall be disregarded any effect on the terms or the amount of the rent attributable to the granting of a tenancy to a sitting tenant.

(7) Where a notice under subsection (2) above is referred to a rent assessment committee, then, unless the landlord and the tenant otherwise agree, with effect from such date as the committee may direct—

(a) the terms determined by the committee shall become terms of the statutory periodic tenancy in substitution for any of the implied terms dealing with the same subject matter; and

(b) the amount of the rent under the statutory periodic tenancy shall be altered to accord with any adjustment specified by the committee;

but for the purposes of paragraph (b) above the committee shall not direct a date earlier than the date specified, in accordance with subsection (3)(b) above, in the notice referred to them.

(8) Nothing in this section requires a rent assessment committee to continue with a determination under subsection (4) above if the landlord and tenant give notice in writing that they no longer require such a determination or if the tenancy has come to an end.

**"tenancy"**

See s.45. **3A–758**

**"tenant"**

See s.45. **3A–759**

**"fixed term tenancy"**

See s.45. **3A–760**

**"landlord"**

See s.45. **3A–761**

**"statutory periodic tenancy"**

See s.5(7). **3A–762**

**"prescribed"**

See s.45 and the Assured Tenancies and Agricultural Occupancies (Forms) Regula- **3A–763**

HOUSING

tions 1997 (SI 1997/194). Note that a notice conforms with the regulations if it is "substantially to the same effect" as that prescribed (para.2).

**Fixing of terms of statutory periodic tenancy**

**3A–764** Section 6 provides a mechanism by which landlords and tenants may propose new terms for a statutory period tenancy which has come into existence by virtue of s.5. At any time up to one year after the former tenancy has come to an end, either party may serve a notice proposing new terms. The notice must be in "the prescribed form" (see Assured Tenancies and Agricultural Occupancies (Forms) Regulations 1997 (SI 1997/194). If either party wishes to object to the proposed new terms, he or she may apply to the Rent Assessment Committee to determine whether they are terms which "might reasonably be expected to be found in an assured periodic tenancy of the dwelling-house concerned" granted by a willing landlord. The RAC may specify an adjustment of rent, even if none is sought, to take into account any new terms, if they consider it appropriate.

An application to a RAC must be made within three months of service of the notice proposing new terms. If no application is made to the RAC within the three-month time limit, the proposed new terms automatically take effect.

## Demotion because of anti-social behaviour

**3A–765** **6A.**—(1) This section applies to an assured tenancy if the landlord is a registered social landlord.

(2) The landlord may apply to a county court for a demotion order.

(3) A demotion order has the following effect—

(a) the assured tenancy is terminated with effect from the date specified in the order;

(b) if the tenant remains in occupation of the dwelling-house after that date a demoted tenancy is created with effect from that date;

(c) it is a term of the demoted tenancy that any arrears of rent payable at the termination of the assured tenancy become payable under the demoted tenancy;

(d) it is also a term of the demoted tenancy that any rent paid in advance or overpaid at the termination of the assured tenancy is credited to the tenant's liability to pay rent under the demoted tenancy.

(4) The court must not make a demotion order unless it is satisfied—

(a) that the tenant or a person residing in or visiting the dwelling-house has engaged or has threatened to engage in—

(i) housing-related anti-social conduct, or

(ii) conduct to which section 153B of the Housing Act 1996 (use of premises for unlawful purposes) applies, and

(b) that it is reasonable to make the order.

(5) The court must not entertain proceedings for a demotion order unless—

(a) the landlord has served on the tenant a notice under subsection (6), or

(b) the court thinks it is just and equitable to dispense with the requirement of the notice.

(6) The notice must—

(a) give particulars of the conduct in respect of which the order is sought;

(b) state that the proceedings will not begin before the date specified in the notice;

(c) state that the proceedings will not begin after the end of the period of twelve months beginning with the date of service of the notice.

(7) The date specified for the purposes of subsection (6)(b) must not be before the end of the period of two weeks beginning with the date of service of the notice.

(8) Each of the following has effect in respect of a demoted tenancy at the time it is created by virtue of an order under this section as it has effect in relation to the assured tenancy at the time it is terminated by virtue of the order—

(a) the parties to the tenancy;

(b) the period of the tenancy;

(c) the amount of the rent;

(d) the dates on which the rent is payable.

(9) Subsection (8)(b) does not apply if the assured tenancy was for a fixed term and in such a case the demoted tenancy is a weekly periodic tenancy.

(10) If the landlord of the demoted tenancy serves on the tenant a statement of any other express terms of the assured tenancy which are to apply to the demoted tenancy such terms are also terms of the demoted tenancy.

(10A) In subsection (4)(a) 'housing-related anti-social conduct' has the same meaning as in section 153A of the Housing Act 1996.

(11) For the purposes of this section a demoted tenancy is a tenancy to which section 20B of the Housing Act 1988 applies.

**Editorial note**

This section was inserted by Anti-Social Behaviour Act 2003 s.14(4). It was amended by the Police and Justice Act 2006 Sch.14, para.15. It was brought into force in England on June 30, 2004 by the Anti-Social Behaviour Act 2003 (Commencement No.3 and Savings) Order 2004 (SI 2004/1502) (c.61). It was brought into force in Wales on 30 April 2005 by the Anti-Social Behaviour Act 2003 (Commencement No.4) (Wales) Order 2005 (SI 2005/1225) (w.83) (c.55). Section 6A provides that a demotion order ends an assured tenancy on a specified date. If the tenant remains in occupation, a new demoted assured shorthold tenancy begins on the same date. The court may only make the order if the tenant, another resident of or visitor to the tenant's home has behaved in a way which is capable of causing nuisance or annoyance or if such a person has used the premises for illegal purposes. In addition the court must be satisfied that it is reasonable to make the order. Sections 6A(3)(c) and (d) confirm that any rent owed or overpaid on the tenant's rent account under the secure tenancy should be transferred across to the new demoted tenancy. Section 6A(5) requires landlords to serve notice on assured tenants before issuing demotion proceedings, and specify the information which the notice should contain. However the court may dispense with the requirement for notice if it thinks it is just and equitable to do so. For consideration of the words "just and equitable" in other contexts, see the commentary at paras 3A–362 and 3A–795. **3A–766**

**Registered social landlord**

See Housing Act 1996 s.230, subss.1 to 3. **3A–767**

*Paragraph numbers marked with a "+" can be found online and on CD.*

**Housing Act 1988, s.20B**

3A–768 See para.3A–884.

## Orders for possession

3A–769 **7.**—(1) The court shall not make an order for possession of a dwelling-house let on an assured tenancy except on one or more of the grounds set out in Schedule 2 to this Act; but nothing in this Part of this Act relates to proceedings for possession of such a dwelling-house which are brought by a mortgagee, within the meaning of the Law of Property Act 1925, who has lent money on the security of the assured tenancy.

(2) The following provisions of this section have effect, subject to section 8 below, in relation to proceedings for the recovery of possession of a dwelling-house let on an assured tenancy.

(3) If the court is satisfied that any of the grounds in Part I of Schedule 2 to this Act is established then, subject to subsections (5A) and (6) below, the court shall make an order for possession.

(4) If the court is satisfied that any of the grounds in Part II of Schedule 2 to this Act is established, then, subject to subsections (5A) and (6) below, the court may make an order for possession if it considers it reasonable to do so.

(5) Part III of Schedule 2 to this Act shall have effect for supplementing Ground 9 in that Schedule and Part IV of that Schedule shall have effect in relation to notices given as mentioned in Grounds 1 to 5 of that Schedule.

(5A) The court shall not make an order for possession of a dwelling-house let on an assured periodic tenancy arising under Schedule 10 to the Local Government and Housing Act 1989 on any of the following grounds, that is to say,—

(a) Grounds 1, 2 and 5 in Part I of Schedule 2 to this Act;

(b) Ground 16 in Part II of that Schedule; and

(c) if the assured periodic tenancy arose on the termination of a former 1954 Act tenancy, within the meaning of the said Schedule 10, Ground 6 in Part I of Schedule 2 to this Act.

(6) The court shall not make an order for possession of a dwelling-house to take effect at a time when it is let on an assured fixed term tenancy unless—

(a) the ground for possession is Ground 2 or Ground 8 in Part I of Schedule 2 to this Act or any of the grounds in Part II of that Schedule, other than Ground 9 or Ground 16; and

(b) the terms of the tenancy make provision for it to be brought to an end on the ground in question (whether that provision takes the form of a provision for re-entry, for forfeiture, for determination by notice or otherwise).

(7) Subject to the preceding provisions of this section, the court may make an order for possession of a dwelling-house on grounds relating to a fixed term tenancy which has come to an end; and where an order is made in such circumstances, any statutory periodic

*Paragraph numbers marked with a "+" can be found online and on CD.*

tenancy which has arisen on the ending of the fixed term tenancy shall end (without any notice and regardless of the period) in accordance with section 5(1A).

*Note* —Amended by the Local Government and Housing Act 1989 Sch.11. This section has also been amended by the Housing and Regeneration Act 2008 Sch.11, Pt I, para.7 (for transitional provisions see para.14) with effect from May 20, 2009 (SI 2009/ 1261) (c.66). **3A–770**

**"assured tenancy"**

See s.1. **3A–771**

**"tenancy"**

See s.45. **3A–772**

**"dwelling-house"**

See s.45. **3A–773**

**"let"**

See s.45. **3A–774**

**"fixed term"**

See s.45. **3A–775**

**Orders for possession**

Like the Rent Act 1977 s.98 and the Housing Act 1985 s.84, this section provides that a court may only make an order for possession against an assured tenant if a ground for possession is made out. The grounds are specified in Sch.2 (see below). In addition, depending upon the ground relied upon, the landlord may have to satisfy the court that it is reasonable to make an order for possession. For reasonableness, see the commentary to the Housing Act 1985 s.84, above. As to reasonableness (s.7(4)) see *West Kent Housing Association v Davis* (1991) 31 H.L.R. 415, CA; *New Charter Housing (North) Ltd v Ashcroft* [2004] EWCA Civ 310; [2004] H.L.R. 36 , *Knowsley Housing Trust v McMullen* [2006] EWCA Civ 539; [2006] H.L.R. 43 and *Moat Housing Group South Ltd v Harris and Hartless* [2005] EWCA Civ 287; [2006] Q.B. 606; [2005] 3 W.L.R. 691; [2005] 4 All E.R. 1051. **3A–776**

In relation to claims for possession where registered social landlords rely upon arrears of rent, see the Protocol for Possession Claims Based on Rent Arrears at C11–001 which aims to encourage more pre-action contact between landlords and tenants and to enable court time to be used more effectively. Courts should take into account whether this protocol has been followed when considering what orders to make.

A fixed term assured or assured shorthold tenancy can be terminated during the fixed term if the landlord can prove that any of Grounds 2 (premises required by mortgagee), 8 (two months' rent arrears), 10 (rent arrears), 11 (persistent rent arrears), 12 (breach of obligation), 13 (deterioration), 14 (nuisance or annoyance) or 15 (deterioration of furniture) (see Sch.2) exist and provided that the tenancy contains a provision entitling the landlord to do so (see s.7(6)).

**Mandatory grounds for possession**

Where a landlord is seeking possession under one of the mandatory grounds for possession (e.g. Ground 8) during the fixed term of a tenancy, the court has no power to grant relief from forfeiture under the County Courts Act 1984 s.138. In *Artesian Residential Investments Ltd v Beck* [2000] Q.B. 541; [2000] 2 W.L.R. 357; [1999] 3 All E.R. 113, CA a fixed term assured tenancy agreement included a proviso for re-entry and determination if the rent was at any stage 14 days in arrears. The defendant fell into rent arrears before the expiry of the term and, the landlord brought possession proceedings relying on the Housing Act 1988 Sch.2, Grounds 8 and 10. A possession order was made, but the defendant later paid all the arrears and applied for suspension of the possession order, relying upon the relief from forfeiture provisions of the County Courts Act 1984 s.138. H.H.J. Mitchell granted relief but the Court of Appeal **3A–777**

*Paragraph numbers marked with a "+" can be found online and on CD.*

held that the Housing Act 1988 s.5(1) sets out the only routes for bringing an assured tenancy to an end. There is no need for a parallel claim for forfeiture to prevent the contractual tenancy continuing after the granting of an order for possession under the Act. By its express words, s.5(1) makes it abundantly clear that an order for possession brings a tenancy to an end. This construction is also borne out by s.7(7) which provides that, when the court makes an order for possession on grounds relating to a fixed term tenancy which has come to an end, any ensuing statutory periodic tenancy which arises on the ending of the fixed term tenancy ends (without any notice or regardless of the period) on the day on which the order takes effect.

Furthermore, s.7(3) is explicit, obliging the court mandatorily to make an order for possession if satisfied that any of the grounds in Sch.2 is established subject, inter alia, to s.6. Section 7(6)(b) does no more than require provision for, e.g., forfeiture to be included in the terms of the tenancy, and does not set up forfeiture as an independent ground for terminating the tenancy. As a matter of principle there is no room for applying s.138. As there is no exercise of a right of re-entry or forfeiture for non-payment of rent, its requirements are not met.

Difficulties may arise where arrears are due to housing benefit problems. In *North British Housing Association Limited v Matthews* [2004] EWCA Civ 1736; [2005] 1 W.L.R. 3133; [2005] 2 All E.R. 667, when dismissing appeals by tenants who had been refused adjournments in order to attempt to resolve housing benefit problems, the Court of Appeal held that:

- The court cannot be satisfied that the landlord is entitled to possession before the date of the hearing. The date of the hearing is the date when the claim is heard. It is not the date fixed for the hearing if, on that date, an adjournment is granted without a hearing taking place at all.
- There is no doubt that it is a perfectly proper exercise of the court's discretion to adjourn, if a case has to be taken out of the list because there is no judge available, or because there has been over-listing, or because the defendant is prevented by ill-health from attending court.
- The court retains jurisdiction to grant an adjournment before it is satisfied that the landlord is entitled to possession. It may be a proper exercise of discretion to adjourn the hearing before the court is satisfied that the landlord is entitled to possession—e.g. where there is an arguable claim for damages which can be set-off against arrears; where the tenant shows that there is an arguable defence based on accord and satisfaction or estoppel arising from an agreement whereby the landlord accepts an offer by the tenant to pay off the current rent and arrears at a certain rate in return for not pursuing the claim for possession; or where the court is satisfied that there is a real chance that the tenant would be given permission to apply for judicial review of the landlord's decision to claim possession because of abuse of power.
- However it is not legitimate to adjourn to enable the tenant to pay off arrears and so defeat the claim for possession, unless there are exceptional circumstances—e.g. if a tenant is robbed on the way to court, or if a computer failure prevents the housing benefit authority from being able to pay benefit due until the day after the hearing date. The fact that arrears are attributable to maladministration on the part of the housing benefit authority is not an exceptional circumstance.
- Once the court has expressed the conclusion that it is satisfied that the landlord is entitled to possession, there is no power to grant an adjournment in any circumstances (see ss.7(3) and 9(6)). The court cannot be "satisfied" within the meaning of s.9(6) until the judge has given a judgment and effect is given to that judgment in a perfected order of the court.
- The Housing Corporation may consider it wise to expand its advice in Regulatory Circular 07/04 (see November 2004 Legal Action 23) about the need for effective liaison between landlords and housing benefit departments right up to the time when a possession claim for rent arrears is heard.

In a case where an outright order for possession was made under Ground 8, but the landlord subsequently accepted the tenant's offer to pay rent and £100 per month off arrears, the Court of Appeal held that the landlord had done nothing to affect the legal relations between the parties. No new or different terms were come to. The landlord had no intention to create a new tenancy. The legal relations between the parties were governed by the terms of the order until the landlord took a position inconsistent with the order (*Stirling v Leadenhall Residential 2 Ltd* [2001] EWCA Civ 1011; [2001] 3 All E.R. 645; [2002] 1 W.L.R. 499, CA).

Where an order for possession is made under one of the mandatory grounds in the Housing Act 1988 Sch.2, then that ground should be stated on the face of the order. It is not proper to return to the judge at a later date to find out the grounds on which he made the order to find out if it was made in exercise of his discretion. Accordingly, where an order for possession under those grounds failed to state the ground on the face of the order, it could be regarded as having been granted on uncertain grounds, and in those circumstances, a court could revisit the exercise of discretion by the previous judge (*Diab v Countrywide Rentals 1 Plc Independent*, November 5, 2001 (c.S)).

**Disability Discrimination Act 1995**

The effect of Disability Discrimination Act 1995 s.22(3)(c) is that it is unlawful to discriminate "by evicting [a] disabled person or subjecting him to any other detriment". Although unlawfulness under the Disability Discrimination Act is not a bar to a landlord seeking a possession order under the Housing Act, the fact that the eviction is unlawful and not justified is a highly relevant consideration for the s.7 discretion of whether or not to make a possession order. The Disability Discrimination Act contains its own code which requires a higher threshold than the Housing Act to justify an eviction (*North Devon Homes Ltd v Brazier* [2003] EWHC 574 (QB); [2003] 22 EG 141). In *Manchester CC v Romano* [2004] EWCA Civ 834; [2005] 1 W.L.R. 2775, the Court of Appeal, in a very thorough review of the legislation, stated that when a court considers the Disability Discrimination Act 1995 in the context of possession proceedings, the first matter which has to be determined is whether the person who complains about disability discrimination is a "disabled person" within the meaning of the Disability Discrimination (Meaning of Disability) Regulations 1996 (SI 1996/1455), Sch.1, ss.1-3 and the *Guidance on matters to be taking into account in determining questions relating to the definition of disability* issued by the Secretary of State. Secondly, the court should consider whether or not there has been discrimination— i.e. treating a disabled person less favourably for a reason which relates to the disabled person's disability. Thirdly, the court should consider whether the landlord's treatment of the tenant is justified. It is only justified if in the landlord's opinion the treatment (viz. the decision to set in motion proceedings for possession) is necessary in order not to endanger the health or safety of any of the people living in neighbouring houses and it is reasonable, in all the circumstances, for the landlord to hold that opinion. The landlord must prove that if it does not take this action someone's health or safety would be endangered. It does not have to prove that that person's health or safety has actually been damaged. However, in view of the decision in *Lewisham LBC v Malcolm* [2008] UKHL 43; [2008] 4 All E.R. 525, it will now be rare for tenants to be able to rely successfully on the Disability Discrimination Act when defending possession claims. Lord Scott stated that if the physical or mental condition that constitutes the tenant's disability has played no motivating part in the decision of the alleged discriminator to inflict on the disabled person the treatment complained of (e.g. bringing a possession claim), the alleged discriminator's reason for that treatment cannot relate to the disability. **3A–778**

**"consent orders"**

The jurisdiction of the court to make an order for possession under s.7 is limited. If the court is not satisfied that a ground under Sch.2 has been established it does not have jurisdiction to make the order. A court is under a duty to determine whether the relevant ground has been established, whether or not it has been raised by the parties. Where a court lacks jurisdiction, it cannot be conferred merely by consent. To confer jurisdiction an admission that a ground is satisfied, either express or implied, has to be clearly shown. Any consent order should clearly spell out in express terms the admission made by the tenant, or the court should ask the tenant what admission was being made, so that there can be no room for confusion or doubt in the future (*Baygreen Properties Ltd v Gil* [2002] EWCA Civ 1340; [2003] H.L.R. 12; [2002] 49 EG 126—"possession order by consent" approved by circuit judge set aside). **3A–779**

**appeals on questions of reasonableness**

Although County Courts Act 1984 s.77(6) excludes appeals against judges' findings **3A–780**



HOUSING

of fact, it does not exclude, in a proper case, the possibility of an appeal against a finding of reasonableness *Castle Vale Housing Action Trust v Gallagher* [2001] EWCA Civ 944; (2001) 33 H.L.R. 810, CA.

#### ECHR art 8 and reasonableness

3A–781 The Court of Appeal has doubted whether art.8 makes any difference to the way in which courts have always approached questions of the reasonableness of making possessions order. Article 8 does, however, reinforce the importance of only making an order depriving someone of his or her home in circumstances where a clear case is made out (*Castle Vale Housing Action Trust v Gallagher* [2001] EWCA Civ 944; (2001) 33 H.L.R. 810. See too *Newham LBC v Neal* [2003] EWCA Civ 541, February 25, 2003.) There is a need to find a fair balance and to protect the rights of the neighbours and other members of the public. (*Lambeth LBC v Howard* [2001] EWCA Civ 468; (2001) 33 H.L.R. 636.

#### Forms of order

3A–782 See Forms **N26A** (Order that Claimant have possession (Assured tenancies)) and **N28** (Order for Possession (rented premises) (suspended)) and **N28A** (Order for possession (rented premises) (postponed)) as specified in the Practice Direction to CPR Pt 4, Table 3.

#### Breach of suspended possession orders

3A–783 Breach of a suspended order did not convert an assured tenant into a tolerated trespasser—see *Knowsley Housing Trust v White* [2008] UKHL 70; [2009] 1 AC 636; [2009] 2 W.L.R. 78—but, in any event, see now Housing and Regeneration Act 2008 Sch.11, noted at para.3A–385.

### Notice of proceedings for possession

3A–784 **8.**—(1) The court shall not entertain proceedings for possession of dwelling-house let on an assured tenancy unless—

(a) the landlord or, in the case of joint landlords, at least one of them has served on the tenant a notice in accordance with this section and the proceedings are begun within the time limits stated in the notice in accordance with subsections (3) to (4B) below, or

(b) the court considers it just and equitable to dispense with the requirement of such a notice.

(2) The court shall not make an order for possession on any of the grounds in Schedule 2 to this Act unless that ground and particulars of it are specified in the notice under this section; but the grounds specified in such a notice may be altered or added to with the leave of the court.

(3) A notice under this section is one in the prescribed form informing the tenant that—

(a) the landlord intends to begin proceedings for possession of the dwelling-house on one or more of the grounds specified in the notice; and

(b) those proceedings will not begin earlier than a date specified in the notice in accordance with subsections (4) to (4B) below; and

(c) those proceedings will not begin later than twelve months from the date of service of the notice.

(4) If a notice under this section specifies in accordance with subsection (3)(a) above Ground 14 in Schedule 2 to this Act (whether

with or without other grounds), the date specified in the notice as mentioned in subsection (3)(b) above shall not be earlier than the date of the service of the notice.

(4A) If a notice under this section specifies in accordance with subsection (3)(a) above, any of Grounds 1, 2, 5 to 7, 9 and 16 in Schedule 2 to this Act (whether without other grounds or with any ground other than Ground 14), the date specified in the notice as mentioned in subsection (3)(b) above shall not be earlier than—

(a) two months from the date of service of the notice; and

(b) if the tenancy is a periodic tenancy, the earliest date on which, apart from section 5(1) above, the tenancy could be brought to an end by a notice to quit given by the landlord on the same date as the date of service of the notice under this section.

(4B) In any other case, the date specified in the notice as mentioned in subsection (3)(b) above shall not be earlier than the expiry of the period of two weeks from the date of the service of the notice.

(5) The court may not exercise the power conferred by subsection (1)(b) above if the landlord seeks to recover possession on Ground 8 in Schedule 2 to this Act.

(6) Where a notice under this section—

(a) is served at a time when the dwelling-house is let on a fixed term tenancy, or

(b) is served after a fixed term tenancy has come to an end but relates (in whole or in part) to events occurring during that tenancy,

the notice shall have effect notwithstanding that the tenant becomes or has become tenant under a statutory periodic tenancy arising on the coming to an end of the fixed term tenancy.

*Note*—Amended by the Housing Act 1996 s.151. **3A–785**

**"assured tenancy"**

See s.1. **3A–786**

**"landlord", "tenancy" and "tenant"**

See s.45. **3A–787**

**"dwelling-house"**

See s.45. **3A–788**

**"fixed term"**

See s.45. **3A–789**

**"prescribed"**

See s.45 and the Assured Tenancies and Agricultural Occupancies (Forms) Regulations 1997 (SI 1997/194). For cases where landlords used old versions of prescribed forms, see: *Beckerman v Durling* (1983) 6 H.L.R. 87, CA; *Swansea CC v Hearn* (1991) 23 H.L.R. 284, CA; and *Tadema Holdings v Ferguson*, (2000) 32 H.L.R. 866; *The Times*, November 25, 1999, CA. **3A–790**

**Notice of proceedings for possession**

Before bringing possession proceedings against assured tenants, landlords must either serve a "notice of proceedings for possession" in accordance with the Housing Act **3A–791**

1988 s.8, or (in cases other than Ground 8) persuade the court that it is just and equitable to dispense with that requirement. The relevant form is contained in the Assured Tenancies and Agricultural Occupancies (Forms) Regulations 1997 (SI 1997/194). Note that a notice conforms with the regulations if it is "substantially to the same effect" as that prescribed (para.2). The relevant form (Form 3) states that the landlord must, inter alia, "give the full text ... of each ground which is being relied upon". It is similar to the form of notice used in connection with public sector secure tenancies (Housing Act 1985 s.83). Particulars of the grounds relied upon have to be included, as well as the ground itself.

Normally notices of intention to bring possession proceedings against assured tenants only have to give two weeks notice, but in the case of Grounds 1 (landlord's occupation), 2 (mortgagee seeking to exercise power of sale), 5 (ministers of religion), 6 (housing association wishing to demolish or reconstruct), 7 (death of tenant), 9 (suitable alternative accommodation) and 16 (letting in consequence of employment) (all set out below) at least two months notice or notice equivalent to the contractual period of the tenancy, whichever is longer, has to be given. If the landlord relies upon Ground 14 (nuisance or annoyance) proceedings may be begun immediately after service (s.8(4)).

Proceedings must be begun within 12 months of service of the notice, otherwise a new notice must be served. There is no need for a landlord of an assured tenant to serve a notice to quit as well as a notice of intention to bring proceedings (s.5(1)).

As to assured tenancy agreements that provide that (1) before bringing possession proceedings landlords will give four weeks notice and (2) that they will only rely upon certain grounds for possession, see *North British HA v Sheridan* (2000) 32 H.L.R. 346; [2000] L & T.R. 115, CA.

#### Service of section 8 notices

**3A–792** The word "service" in ss.8 and 13 is an ordinary English word connoting delivery of a document to a particular person. It carries no implication that the document has to be read, understood or indeed known by the recipient to have been delivered as long as delivery is to the correct address. Such meaning does not change according to the capacity of the intended recipient. See *Tadema Holdings v Ferguson* (2000) 32 H.L.R. 866, CA.

#### "ground"

**3A–793** Although the full text of the ground as set out in the Housing Act 1988 Sch.2 may not have to be repeated verbatim, "the words used [must] set out fully the substance of the ground so that the notice is adequate to achieve the legislative purpose of the provision. That purpose ... is to give ... information ... to enable the tenant to consider what she should do and, with or without advice, to do that which is in her power and which will best protect her against the loss of her home" (*Mountain v Hastings* [1993] 29 E.G. 96; (1993) 25 H.L.R. 427 at 433, CA, where the notice was held to be defective because it had omitted the words "both at the date of service of the Notice...and at the date of the hearing" and the explanation that "'rent' means rent lawfully due from the tenant"). In *Mountain v Hastings* the Court of Appeal also held that the words in s.8(2) which allow a court to alter or add to the grounds specified in a notice assume that there is a valid notice and are solely directed to the possibility of adding to or deleting grounds.

#### particulars of the ground (s.8(2))

**3A–794** See also the commentary to the Housing Act 1985 s.83.

The Court of Appeal has held that the particulars in a notice from a landlord to a tenant relying upon Ground 8 comply with the Housing Act 1988 s.8 provided that "it is made clear...that more than [two] months rent is at the date of that notice unpaid and due and provided also that in some way or other that notice makes it clear either how much, or how the tenant can ascertain how much, is alleged to be due". It is not necessary for the notice to contain a schedule of the arrears (*Marath v MacGillivray* (1996) 28 H.L.R. 484, CA, where the notice stated, as particulars of the arrears: "At a meeting between the landlord and tenant on July 24, 1994 the arrears were agreed at £103.29...Since that date no payments of rent have been made..." without giving a figure for the arrears as at the date of the notice was given). In *Marath* the Court of

Appeal also indicated that under s.8(2) a court may allow particulars to be added if they have not been given earlier.

**"the court considers it just and equitable to dispense with the requirement of such a notice" (s.8(1)(b))**

See the commentary to the Housing Act 1985 s.83(1)(b). Note that there is no power to dispense with service of a notice if Ground 8 (i.e. 8 weeks' arrears) is relied upon. **3A–795**

It is "obviously only in relatively exceptional cases where the court should be prepared to dispense with a...notice" (*Braintree DC v Vincent* [2004] EWCA Civ 415—a case where the Court of Appeal held that a judge was entitled to dispense with a statutory notice on unusual facts. A notice would have been of no benefit to the tenant—indeed it would have been to her disadvantage because it would have postponed the date for possession and added to her liability for rent). In *Kelsey HA v King* (1995) 28 H.L.R. 270, CA, it was held that in deciding whether it is just and equitable to dispense with service a court should "weigh all the factors before it" and "take all the circumstances into account, both from the view of the landlord and the tenant". In many cases, the fact that tenants have not been given "an opportunity to put right what it is alleged had gone wrong" would be significant, but in this case where full particulars were annexed to the Particulars of Claim the Defendant had had ample time.

See too the Rent Act cases such as *Fernandes v Parvardin* (1982) 264 E.G. 49; (1981–82) 5 H.L.R. 33, CA; and *Bradshaw v Baldwin-Wiseman* (1985) 17 H.L.R. 260; (1985) 49 P.&C.R. 382, CA.

Applications to strike out possession proceedings where there has been a failure to comply with s.8 should be made promptly.

Where local authority landlords transfer their housing stock to registered social landlords, and as a result, the landlords are no longer within the landlord condition (Housing Act 1985 s.80(1)), tenancies cease to be secure and, by virtue of Housing Act 1988 s.1(1), become assured tenancies. In such circumstances courts have no jurisdiction to entertain possession claims unless s.8 notices are served, or the court exercises the power to dispense with notice under s.8(1)(b). This applies even where local authorities serve notices seeking possession under Housing Act 1985 s.83 before the stock transfer. The court's discretion is wide enough to allow substitution of the new landlord as claimant and dispensation of a s.8 notice where the reality is that the new landlord relies upon the same breach of the same term and the relief sought is no different. However, it is not legitimate for a court to dispense with s.8 notices without some consideration of any objection which might be taken by tenants by reference to the facts of their cases (*Knowsley Housing Trust v Revell*; *Helena Housing Ltd v Curtis* [2003] EWCA Civ 496; [2003] H.L.R. 63). See too *North British HA v Sheridan*, (2000) 32 H.L.R. 346; [1999] 2 E.G.L.R. 138, CA.

In *McShane v William Sutton Trust* (1997) 1 L. & T. Rev D67; December 1997, Legal Action 13, Warrington County Court, H.H.J. Daley held that although there is nothing in the rules preventing a landlord from applying ex parte to dispense with service of a s.8 notice, following *Kelsey HA v King* (1995) 28 H.L.R. 270, CA, it is not possible for a judge deciding whether or not to dispense with service to weigh up all factors from both points of view without the tenant being in court and that a decision by a district judge ex parte to dispense with service was "plainly wrong".

See too *Hegab v Shamash*, June 1998, Legal Action 13, CA: appeal by tenant against decision to dispense with requirement for notice allowed because the judge had failed to take into account two matters, namely the fact that the tenant had paid a deposit of £4,000 in relation to a proposed purchase of the premises which had not been refunded and that the landlord had not paid the costs of the earlier proceedings concerning an illegal eviction.

## Additional notice requirements: ground of domestic violence

**8A.**—(1) Where the ground specified in a notice under section 8 (whether with or without other grounds) is Ground 14A in Schedule 2 to this Act and the partner who has left the dwelling-house as mentioned in that ground is not a tenant of the dwelling-house, the court shall not entertain proceedings for possession of the dwelling-house unless— **3A–796**

*Paragraph numbers marked with a "+" can be found online and on CD.*



HOUSING

(a) the landlord or, in the case of joint landlords, at least one of them has served on the partner who has left a copy of the notice or has taken all reasonable steps to serve a copy of the notice on that partner, or

(b) the court considers it just and equitable to dispense with such requirements as to service.

(2) Where Ground 14A in Schedule 2 to this Act is added to a notice under section 8 with the leave of the court after proceedings for possession are begun and the partner who has left the dwelling-house as mentioned in that ground is not a party to the proceedings, the court shall not continue to entertain the proceedings unless—

(a) the landlord or, in the case of joint landlords, at least one of them has served a notice under subsection (3) below on the partner who has left or has taken all reasonable steps to serve such a notice on that partner, or

(b) the court considers it just and equitable to dispense with the requirement of such a notice.

(3) A notice under this subsection shall—

(a) state that proceedings for the possession of the dwelling-house have begun,

(b) specify the ground or grounds on which possession is being sought, and

(c) give particulars of the ground or grounds.

3A–797 *Note*—Added by the Housing Act 1996 s.150.

**"landlord", "tenancy" and "tenant"**

3A–798 See s.45.

**"dwelling-house"**

3A–799 See s.45.

**"notice"**

3A–800 See s.8.

**"the court considers it just and equitable to dispense with the requirement of such a notice"**

3A–801 See s.8(1)(b). See also commentary to Ground 14A, below.

## Extended discretion of court in possession claims

3A–802 **9.**—(1) Subject to subsection (6) below, the court may adjourn for such period or periods as it thinks fit proceedings for possession of a dwelling-house let on an assured tenancy.

(2) On the making of an order for possession of a dwelling-house let on an assured tenancy or at any time before the execution of such an order, the court, subject to subsection (6) below, may—

(a) stay or suspend execution of the order, or

(b) postpone the date of possession,

for such period or periods as the court thinks just.

(3) On any such adjournment as is referred to in subsection (1) above or on any such stay, suspension or postponement as is referred to in subsection (2) above, the court, unless it considers that to do so

would cause exceptional hardship to the tenant or would otherwise be unreasonable, shall impose conditions with regard to payment by the tenant of arrears of rent (if any) and rent and may impose such other conditions as it thinks fit.

(4) If any such conditions as are referred to in subsection (3) above are complied with, the court may, if it thinks fit, discharge or rescind any such order as is referred to in subsection (2) above.

(5) […]

(5A) […]

(6) This section does not apply if the court is satisfied that the landlord is entitled to possession of the dwelling-house—

(a) on any of the grounds in Part I of Schedule 2 to this Act, or

(b) by virtue of subsection (1) or subsection (4) of section 21 below.

*Note*—Amended by the Family Law Act 1996 Sch.8, para.59 and the Civil Partnership Act 2004 s.82, Sch.9, para.23. This section has also been amended by the Housing and Regeneration Act 2008 Sch.11, Pt I, para.8(2), (4) (for transitional provisions see para.14) with effect from May 20, 2009 (SI 2009/1261) (c.66). The amendment made by Sch.11, Pt I, para.8(3) is not yet in force and is printed as part of the Housing and Regeneration Act 2008 —see below. **3A–803**

**"assured tenancy"**

See s.1. **3A–804**

**"landlord", "tenancy" and "tenant"**

See s.45. **3A–805**

**"dwelling-house"**

See s.45. **3A–806**

**Extended discretion of court in possession claims**

See also commentary to the Housing Act 1985 s.85. This section gives the court a wide discretion, firstly at trial when considering the form of possession order to make and secondly after the making of a possession order at "*any time before the execution of such an order.*" See, e.g. *R. v Ilkeston County Court Ex p. Kruza* (1985) 17 H.L.R. 539, QBD, s.9 "gives a wide power to stay or suspend an order for possession which is applicable to all cases except those where it is expressly excluded by statute." The power may be exercised where circumstances have changed since the original hearing, even where an outright order was made by a different judge, (*Ujima HA v Smith* Legal Action 22, October 16, 2000, Ch D, April 2001, where the defendant was by the time of the application to suspend accepting her legal responsibility for serious damage to a shared kitchen and offering to pay £150 in compensation). See too *Plymouth CC v Hoskin* [2002] EWCA Civ 684; May 1, 2002 where the Court of Appeal said "There is a continuing remedy in the county court." However, the power only applies where there is a discretionary ground for possession (as opposed to a mandatory ground where the court's discretion is limited by the Housing Act 1980 s.89 (see above). **3A–807**

When exercising its powers under s.9 the court should impose conditions with respect to the repayment of arrears of rent and mesne profits unless it considers that to do so would cause exceptional hardship (s.9(3)). There have been no reported Court of Appeal decisions as to what might constitute "exceptional hardship".

Where there is a substantial dispute about the amount claimed and the tenant's compliance with the order, the up-to-date position has to be clearly and accurately established before considering an application to suspend under s.9 (*Haringey LBC v Powell* (1996) 28 H.L.R. 798, CA).

The court, exercising its discretion on an application to suspend a warrant under s.9, may take account of matters (*e.g.* breaches of the terms of the tenancy agreement or anti-social behaviour) other than those relied upon as grounds for making the original possession order—although it is not always be right to do so. (See *Sheffield City Council v Hopkins* [2001] EWCA Civ 1023; [2002] H.L.R. 12, CA) and the more detailed commentary at para.3A–387).

After execution an occupier can only be restored to possession if either the whole proceedings are set aside (see the commentary at 3A–388; *Leicester City Council v Aldwinkle* (1992) 24 H.L.R. 40, CA; *cf. Governors of Peabody Donation Fund v Hay* (1987) 19 H.L.R. 145, CA; and *Tower Hamlets LBC v Abadie* (1990) 22 H.L.R. 264, CA) or the warrant had been obtained by fraud, abuse of process or oppression (see *Hammersmith and Fulham LBC v Hill* (1995) 27 H.L.R. 368; [1994] 2 E.G.L.R. 51, CA; *Hackney LBC v White* (1995) 28 H.L.R. 219, CA; and *Tower Hamlets LBC v Azad* (1998) 30 H.L.R. 241, CA; but *cf. Islington LBC v Harridge, The Times*, 30 June, 1993, CA).

See also *Saint v Barking and Dagenham LBC* (1999) 31 H.L.R. 620, CA (oppression where warrant executed without prior notification to tenant who was in prison and without inviting him to renew his application for housing benefit).

**On any of the grounds in Part I**

**3A–808** The extended discretion to stay or suspend does not apply where the landlord has satisfied one of the mandatory grounds for possession—s.9(6). See however *Capital Prime Plus Plc v Wills* (1999) 31 H.L.R. 926, CA where the landlord had consented to the suspension of the original possession order even though there were over two months' arrears. The Court of Appeal held that the order had not been made under Ground 8 and so, on subsequent default, the court did have power to suspend a warrant and *Diab v Countrywide Rentals 1 Plc, Independent*, November 5, 2001 (c.S) , noted at para.3A–777.

## Proceedings for possession: anti-social behaviour

**3A–809** **9A.**—(1) This section applies if the court is considering under section 7(4) whether it is reasonable to make an order for possession on ground 14 set out in Part 2 of Schedule 2 (conduct of tenant or other person).

(2) The court must consider, in particular—

(a) the effect that the nuisance or annoyance has had on persons other than the person against whom the order is sought;

(b) any continuing effect the nuisance or annoyance is likely to have on such persons;

(c) the effect that the nuisance or annoyance would be likely to have on such persons if the conduct is repeated.

**Editorial note**

**3A–810** This section was inserted by Anti-Social Behaviour Act 2003 s.14(6). It was brought into force in England on June 30, 2004 by the Anti-Social Behaviour Act 2003 (Commencement No.3 and Savings) Order 2004 (SI 2004/1502) (c.61). It was brought into force in Wales on April 30, 2005 by the Anti-Social Behaviour Act 2003 (Commencement No.4) (Wales) Order 2005SI No.1225 (w.83)(c.55).

**Reasonable**

**3A–811** When considering whether or not to make a possession order and/or whether or not to make a suspended possession order under Sch.2, Ground 14, the court must consider whether it is reasonable to make such an order—see the commentary to s.7 at paras 3A–190 and 3A–373. Section 9A adds to that general consideration a requirement that the court must consider, in particular, the effect that the nuisance or annoyance has had and would be likely to have if continued on persons other than the defendant, e.g. neighbours.

## Special provisions applicable to shared accommodation

**3A–812** **10.**—(1) This section applies in a case falling within subsection (1) of section 3 above and expressions used in this section have the same meaning as in that section.

(2) Without prejudice to the enforcement of any order made under subsection (3) below, while the tenant is in possession of the separate accommodation, no order shall be made for possession of any of the shared accommodation, whether on the application of the immediate landlord of the tenant or on the application of any person under whom that landlord derives title, unless a like order has been made, or is made at the same time, in respect of the separate accommodation; and the provisions of section 6 above shall have effect accordingly.

(3) On the application of the landlord, the court may make such order as it thinks just either—

(a) terminating the right of the tenant to use the whole or any part of the shared accommodation other than living accommodation; or

(b) modifying his right to use the whole or any part of the shared accommodation, whether by varying the persons or increasing the number of persons entitled to the use of that accommodation or otherwise.

(4) No order shall be made under subsection (3) above so as to effect any termination or modification of the rights of the tenant which, apart from section 3(3) above, could not be effected by or under the terms of the tenancy.

**"landlord", "tenancy" and "tenant"**

See s.45. **3A–813**

**"separate accommodation"**

See s.3. **3A–814**

**"shared accommodation"**

See s.3. **3A–815**

## Payment of removal expenses in certain cases

**11.**—(1) Where a court makes an order for possession of a dwelling-house let on an assured tenancy on Ground 6 or Ground 9 in Schedule 2 to this Act (but not on any other ground), the landlord shall pay to the tenant a sum equal to the reasonable expenses likely to be incurred by the tenant in removing from the dwelling-house. **3A–816**

(2) Any question as to the amount of the sum referred in subsection (1) above shall be determined by agreement between the landlord and the tenant or, in default of agreement, by the court.

(3) Any sum payable to a tenant by virtue of this section shall be recoverable as a civil debt due from the landlord.

**"assured tenancy"**

See s.1. **3A–817**

**"landlord", and "tenant"**

See s.45. **3A–818**

**"dwelling-house"**

See s.45. **3A–819**

*Paragraph numbers marked with a "+" can be found online and on CD.*

**Payment of removal expenses in certain cases**

3A–820 The court may only order a landlord to pay removal expenses if possession is claimed under Ground 6 (housing association wishing to demolish or reconstruct), or Ground 9 (suitable alternative accommodation).

## Compensation for misrepresentation or concealment

3A–821 **12.** Where a landlord obtains an order for possession of a dwelling-house let on an assured tenancy on one or more of the grounds in Schedule 2 to this Act and it is subsequently made to appear to the court that the order was obtained by misrepresentation or concealment of material facts, the court may order the landlord to pay to the former tenant such sum as appears sufficient as compensation for damage or loss sustained by that tenant as a result of the order.

**"assured tenancy"**

3A–822 See s.1.

**"landlord" and "tenant"**

3A–823 See s.45.

**"dwelling-house"**

3A–824 See s.45.

**Compensation for misrepresentation or concealment**

3A–825 *cf.* the Rent Act 1977 s.102. See also *Mafo v Adams* [1970] 1 Q.B. 548, CA (proceedings based upon the common law tort of deceit).

### *RENT AND OTHER TERMS*

## Increase of rent under assured periodic tenancies

3A–826 **13.**—(1) This section applies to—

(a) a statutory periodic tenancy other than one which, by virtue of paragraph 11 or paragraph 12 in Part I of Schedule 1 to this Act, cannot for the time being be an assured tenancy; and

(b) any other periodic tenancy which is an assured tenancy, other than one in relation to which there is a provision, for the time being binding on the tenant, under which the rent for a particular period of the tenancy will or may be greater than the rent for an earlier period.

(2) For the purpose of securing an increase in the rent under a tenancy to which this section applies, the landlord may serve on the tenant a notice in the prescribed form proposing a new rent to take effect at the beginning of a new period of the tenancy specified in the notice, being a period beginning not earlier than—

(a) the minimum period after the date of the service of the notice; and

(b) except in the case of a statutory tenancy—

(i) in the case of an assured agricultural occupancy, the first anniversary of the date on which the first period of the tenancy began;

(ii) in any other case, on the date that falls 52 weeks

after the date on which the first period of the tenancy began; and;

(c) if the rent under the tenancy has previously been increased by virtue of a notice under this subsection or a determination under section 14 below—

(i) in the case of an assured agricultural occupancy, the first anniversary of the date on which the increased rent took effect;

(ii) in any other case, the appropriate date.

(3) The minimum period referred to in subsection (2) above is—

(a) in the case of a yearly tenancy, six months;

(b) in the case of a tenancy where the period is less than a month, one month; and

(c) in any other case, a period equal to the period of the tenancy,

(3A) The appropriate date referred to in subsection (2)(c)(ii) above is—

(a) in a case to which subsection (3B) below applies, the date that falls 53 weeks after the date on which the increased rent took effect;

(b) in any other case, the date that falls 52 weeks after the date on which the increased rent took effect.

(3B) This subsection applies where—

(a) the rent under the tenancy has been increased by virtue of a notice under this section or a determination under section 14 below on at least one occasion after the coming into force of the Regulatory Reform (Assured Periodic Tenancies) (Rent Increases) Order 2003; and

(b) the fifty-third week after the date on which the last such increase took effect begins more than six days before the anniversary of the date on which the first such increase took effect.

(4) Where a notice is served under subsection (2) above, a new rent specified in the notice shall take effect as mentioned in the notice unless, before the beginning of the new period specified in the notice—

(a) the tenant by an application in the prescribed form refers the notice to a rent assessment committee; or

(b) the landlord and the tenant agree on a variation of the rent which is different from that proposed in the notice or agree that the rent should not be varied.

(5) Nothing in this section (or in section 14 below) affects the right of the landlord and the tenant under an assured tenancy to vary by agreement any term of the tenancy (including a term relating to rent).

*Note*—Amended by the Regulatory Reform (Assured Periodic Tenancies) (Rent Increases) Order 2003 (SI 2003/259). The amendment was designed to overcome the argument that a strict interpretation of former s.13(2)(c) rendered many rent increases made by registered social landlords invalid because, although increases may have oc- **3A–827**

HOUSING

curred annually, in some years they may have purported to take effect a few days earlier than "the first anniversary of the date" when the last increase took effect. The effect of the amendment is to enable landlords to set a fixed day (e.g. the first Monday in April) on which rent increases are to take effect. The first time that the rent is increased after the Order came into force on February 10, 2003, the increase may take effect not less than 52 weeks after the start of the tenancy or, if the rent has already been increased, not less than 52 weeks after the date of the last increase. On the second and subsequent occasions, the increase may take effect not less than 52 weeks after the last increase, unless that would result in the increase taking effect on a date falling a week or more before the anniversary of the first increase after the date on which the Order comes into force. In such a case the increase may not take effect until 53 weeks after the date of the last increase. As a result of this change the Assured Tenancies and Agricultural (Forms) (Amendment) (England) Regulations 2003 (SI 2003/260) prescribe new forms to be used by landlords when proposing new rents under s.13(2) from April 11, 2003. The Assured Tenancies and Agricultural Occupancies (Forms) (Amendment) (Wales) Regulations 2003 (SI 2003/307) (w.46) prescribe the new forms to be used in Wales.

**"assured tenancy"**

**3A–828** See s.1.

**"landlord", and "tenant"**

**3A–829** See s.45.

**"dwelling-house"**

**3A–830** See s.45.

**"statutory periodic tenancy"**

**3A–831** See s.5(7).

**"refers"**

**3A–832** The word "refers" in s.13(4)(b) bears the ordinary and obvious meaning "deliver to". A rent assessment committee has no jurisdiction unless the application is received before the beginning of the new period. An application cannot be referred until it has been received (*R. (Lester) v London Rent Assessment Committee* [2003] EWCA Civ 319; [2003] 1 W.L.R. 1449).

**"prescribed"**

**3A–833** See s.45 and the Assured Tenancies and Agricultural Occupancies (Forms) Regulations 1997 (SI 1997/194). Note that a notice conforms with the regulations if it is "substantially to the same effect" as that prescribed (para.2).

In *Tadema Holdings v Ferguson* (2000) 32 H.L.R. 866, CA, landlords, seeking to rely upon s.13, used an older version of the prescribed form since replaced by the Assured Tenancies and Agricultural Occupancies (Forms) Regulations 1997, Form 4. It gave the landlord's address as being "c/o the agent" and an annualised figure rather than a monthly figure for rent. It also stipulated the wrong date for the date on which each new period of tenancy started. Arrears accrued. The landlord served a s.8 notice and brought possession proceedings. The tenant defended claiming that the s.13 notice was invalid. The tenant appealed unsuccessfully against a possession order. There was no basis for confusion.

**Increase of rent under assured periodic tenancies**

**3A–834** Sections 13 and 14 give Rent Assessment Committees power to determine the rent payable by an assured tenant where there is a periodic tenancy which does not contain a contractual provision allowing for the variation of rent or a statutory periodic tenancy. On the expiry of a fixed term, a statutory periodic tenancy may come into being. In such circumstances, s.13 provides a statutory scheme governing the increase of rent. Section 13(1) draws a distinction between two different categories of assured periodic tenancy. Section 13(1)(a) is concerned with statutory periodic tenancies other than those which cannot be an assured tenancy due to Sch.1 paras 11 and 12. Section 13(1)(b) is concerned with any other assured periodic tenancies. In respect of the latter category, the statutory scheme expressly does not apply where there is a contractual rent review clause binding on the tenant. The natural reading of s.13, given the contrast between the subsections, is that a rent review clause in the original assured tenancy does not oust the mechanism for increasing rent found in s.13 once that assured tenancy has been superseded by a statutory periodic tenancy. (*London District Properties Management Ltd v Goolamy* [2009] EWHC 1367 (Admin), June 16, 2009).

The rent to be determined is the rent at which "the dwelling house concerned might reasonably be expected to be let in the open market by a willing landlord under an assured tenancy" (see s.14(1)).

**Service**

The word "service" in ss.8 and 13 is an ordinary English word connoting delivery of a document to a particular person. It carries no implication that the document has to be read, understood or indeed known by the recipient to have been delivered as long as delivery is to the correct address. Such meaning does not change according to the capacity of the intended recipient. See *Tadema Holdings v Ferguson* (2000) 32 H.L.R. 866, CA. **3A–835**

## Determination of rent by rent assessment committee

**14.**—(1) Where, under subsection (4)(a) of section 13 above, a tenant refers to a rent assessment committee a notice under subsection (2) of that section, the committee shall determine the rent at which, subject to subsections (2) and (4) below, the committee consider that the dwelling-house concerned might reasonably be expected to be let in the open market by a willing landlord under an assured tenancy— **3A–836**

(a) which is a periodic tenancy having the same periods as those of the tenancy to which the notice relates;

(b) which begins at the beginning of the new period specified in the notice;

(c) the terms of which (other than relating to the amount of the rent) are the same as those of the tenancy to which the notice relates; and

(d) in respect of which the same notices, if any, have been given under any of Grounds 1 to 5 of Schedule 2 to this Act, as have been given (or have effect as if given) in relation to the tenancy to which the notice relates.

(2) In making a determination under this section there shall be disregarded—

(a) any effect on the rent attributable to the granting of a tenancy to a sitting tenant;

(b) any increase in the value of the dwelling-house attributable to a relevant improvement carried out by a person who at the time it was carried out was the tenant, if the improvement—

(i) was carried out otherwise than in pursuance of an obligation to his immediate landlord, or

(ii) was carried out pursuant to an obligation to his immediate landlord being an obligation which did not relate to the specific improvement concerned but arose by reference to consent given to the carrying out of that improvement; and

(c) any reduction in the value of the dwelling-house attributable to a failure by the tenant to comply with any terms of the tenancy.

(3) For the purposes of subsection (2)(b) above, in relation to a notice which is referred by a tenant as mentioned in subsection (1) above, an improvement is a relevant improvement if either it was carried out during the tenancy to which the notice relates or the following conditions are satisfied, namely—

(a) that it was carried out not more than twenty-one years before the date of service of the notice; and

(b) that, at all times during the period beginning when the improvement was carried out and ending on the date of service of the notice, the dwelling-house has been let under an assured tenancy; and

(c) that, on the coming to an end of an assured tenancy at any time during that period, the tenant (or, in the case of joint tenants, at least one of them) did not quit.

(3A) In making a determination under this section in any case where under Part I of the Local Government Finance Act 1992 the landlord or a superior landlord is liable to pay council tax in respect of a hereditament ("the relevant hereditament") of which the dwelling-house forms part, the rent assessment committee shall have regard to the amount of council tax which, as at the date on which the notice under section 13(2) above was served, was set by the billing authority—

(a) for the financial year in which that notice was served, and

(b) for the category of dwellings within which the relevant hereditament fell on that date,

but any discount or other reduction affecting the amount of council tax payable shall be disregarded.

(3B) In subsection (3A) above—

(a) "hereditament" means a dwelling within the meaning of Part I of the Local Government Finance Act 1992,

(b) "billing authority" has the same meaning as in that Part of that Act, and

(c) "category of dwellings" has the same meaning as in section 30(1) and (2) of that Act.

(4) In this section "rent" does not include any service charge, within the meaning of section 18 of the Landlord and Tenant Act 1985, but, subject to that, includes any sums payable by the tenant to the landlord on account of the use of furniture, in respect of council tax, or for any of the matters referred to in subsection (1)(a) of that section, whether or not those sums are separate from the sums payable for the occupation of the dwelling-house concerned or are payable under separate agreements.

(5) Where any rates in respect of the dwelling-house concerned are borne by the landlord or a superior landlord, the rent assessment committee shall make their determination under this section as if the rates were not so borne.

(6) In any case where—

(a) a rent assessment committee have before them at the same time the reference of a notice under section 6(2) above relating to a tenancy (in this subsection referred to as "the section 6 reference") and the reference of a notice under section 13(2) above relating to the same tenancy (in this subsection referred to as "the section 13 reference"), and

(b) the date specified in the notice under section 6(2) above is not later than the first day of the new period specified in the notice under section 13(2) above, and

(c) the committee propose to hear the two references together,

the committee shall make a determination in relation to the section 6 reference before making their determination in relation to the section 13 reference and, accordingly, in such a case the reference in subsection (1)(c) above to the terms of the tenancy to which the notice relates shall be construed as a reference to those terms as varied by virtue of the determination made in relation to the section 6 reference.

(7) Where a notice under section 13(2) above has been referred to a rent assessment committee, then, unless the landlord and the tenant otherwise agree, the rent determined by the committee (subject, in a case where subsection (5) above applies, to the addition of the appropriate amount in respect of rates) shall be the rent under the tenancy with effect from the beginning of the new period specified in the notice or, if it appears to the rent assessment committee that that would cause undue hardship to the tenant, with effect from such later date (not being later than the date the rent is determined) as the committee may direct.

(8) Nothing in this section requires a rent assessment committee to continue with their determination of a rent for a dwelling-house if the landlord and tenant give notice in writing that they no longer require such a determination or if the tenancy has come to an end.

(9) This section shall apply in relation to an assured shorthold tenancy as if in subsection (1)the reference to an assured tenancy were a reference to an assured shorthold tenancy.

*Note* —Amended by the Local Government Finance (Housing) (Consequential Amendments) Order 1993 (SI 1993/651); and the Housing Act 1996 Sch.8, para.2(2). **3A–837**

**"assured tenancy"**

See s.1. **3A–838**

**"landlord", and "tenant"**

See s.45. **3A–839**

**"dwelling-house"**

See s.45. **3A–840**

**Determination of rent by rent assessment committee**

Section 14(1) requires RACs to assess the rent at which "the dwelling-house concerned might reasonably be expected to be let in the open market by a willing landlord under an assured tenancy" even if the rent assessed by the RAC is in excess of £25,000 and this means the tenancy ceases to be an assured tenancy. Parliament did **3A–841**

***Paragraph numbers marked with a "+" can be found online and on CD.***



HOUSING

not intend the References to Rating (Housing) Regulations 1990 (SI 1990/434) (para.29) (tenancies at a high rent cannot be assured tenancies) to introduce a rent cap (*R. v London RAP Ex p. Cadogan Estates* [1998] Q.B. 398; [1997] 3 W.L.R. 833, QBD).

In *N & D (London) Ltd v Gadson* (1992) 24 H.L.R. 64; [1992] 02 E.G. 176, QBD, Auld J. held that Housing Act 1988 s.14(2)(c), when stating that rent assessment committees should disregard "any reduction in the value of the dwelling-house attributable to a failure by the tenant to comply with any terms of the tenancy" only referred to default by the current tenant. They were obliged to take into account the current condition of the premises, even if that had been brought about by the default of the tenant's father before his death.

When applying the disregard for tenant's improvements (s.14(2)) the committee should not apply a de-capitalised discount based upon the cost of the works. They should simply take as the value of the property its current value less the improvements carried out (*Rowe v South West Rent Assessment Panel* [2001] EWHC 865 (Admin), October 23, 2001).

Note that ss.14A and 14B (inserted by the Local Government Finance (Housing) (Consequential Amendments) Order 1993 (SI 1993/651), provided for interim increases prior to April 1, 1994 where the landlord was liable for council tax.

Where a property is in disrepair, there is no requirement that the RAC should perform a two stage process of first calculating the open market rental of the property in good condition, and then indicating by a figure or percentage discount what allowance has been made for the actual condition of the property (*Ghani v London Rent Assessment Committee* [2002] EWHC 1167 (Admin); May 28, 2002).

## Interim increase before 1st April 1994 of rent under assured periodic tenancies in certain cases where landlord liable for council tax

3A–842 **14A.**—(1) In any case where—

(a) under Part I of the Local Government Finance Act 1992 the landlord of a dwelling-house let under an assured tenancy to which section 13 above applies or a superior landlord is liable to pay council tax in respect of a dwelling (within the meaning of that Part of that Act) which includes that dwelling-house,

(b) under the terms of the tenancy (or an agreement collateral to the tenancy) the tenant is liable to make payments to the landlord in respect of council tax,

(c) the case falls within subsection (2) or subsection (3) below, and

(d) no previous notice under this subsection has been served in relation to the dwelling-house,

the landlord may serve on the tenant a notice in the prescribed form proposing an increased rent to take account of the tenant's liability to make payments to the landlord in respect of council tax, such increased rent to take effect at the beginning of a new period of the tenancy specified in the notice being a period beginning not earlier than one month after the date on which the notice was served.

(2) The case falls within this subsection if—

(a) the rent under the tenancy has previously been increased by virtue of a notice under section 13(2) above or under a determination under section 14 above, and

(b) the first anniversary of the date on which the increased rent took effect has not yet occurred.

*Paragraph numbers marked with a "+" can be found online and on CD.*

(3) The case falls within this subsection if a notice has been served under section 13(2) above before 1st April 1993 but no increased rent has taken effect before that date.

(4) No notice may be served under subsection (1) above after 31st March 1994.

(5) Where a notice is served under subsection (1) above, the new rent specified in the notice shall take effect as mentioned in the notice unless, before the beginning of the new period specified in the notice—

(a) the tenant by an application in the prescribed form refers the notice to a rent assessment committee, or

(b) the landlord and the tenant agree on a variation of the rent which is different from that proposed in the notice or agree that the rent should not be varied.

(6) Nothing in this section (or in section 14B below) affects the right of the landlord and the tenant under an assured tenancy to vary by agreement any term of the tenancy (including a term relating to rent).

*Note*—Note that ss.14A and 14B (inserted by the Local Government Finance (Housing) (Consequential Amendments) Order 1993 (SI 1993/651), provided for interim increases prior to April 1, 1994 where the landlord was liable for council tax. **3A–843**

**Interim determination of rent by rent assessment committee**

**14B.**—(1) Where, under subsection (5)(a) of section 14A above, a tenant refers to a rent assessment committee a notice under subsection (1) of that section, the committee shall determine the amount by which, having regard to the provisions of section 14(3A) above, the existing rent might reasonably be increased to take account of the tenant's liability to make payments to the landlord in respect of council tax. **3A–844**

(2) Where a notice under section 14A(1) above has been referred to a rent assessment committee, then, unless the landlord and the tenant otherwise agree, the existing rent shall be increased by the amount determined by the committee with effect from the beginning of the new period specified in the notice or, if it appears to the committee that that would cause undue hardship to the tenant, with effect from such later date (not being later than the date the increase is determined) as the committee may direct.

(3) In any case where—

(a) a rent assessment committee have before them at the same time the reference of a notice under section 13(2) above relating to a tenancy (in this subsection referred to as "the section 13 reference") and the reference of a notice under section 14A(1) above relating to the same tenancy (in this subsection referred to as "the section 14A reference"); and

(b) the committee propose to hear the two references together,

the committee shall make a determination in relation to the section 13 reference before making their determination in relation to the section 14A reference, and if in such a case the date specified in the notice under section 13(2) above is later than the date specified in the notice under section 14A(1) above, the rent determined under the section 14A reference shall not take effect until the date specified in the notice under section 13(2).

(4) In this section "rent" has the same meaning as in section 14 above; and section 14(4) above applies to a determination under this section as it applies to a determination under that section.

3A-845 *Note* —Added by the Local Government Finance (Housing) (Consequential Amendments) Order 1993 (SI 1993/651) Sch.2.

### Limited prohibition on assignment etc. without consent

3A-846 **15.**—(1) Subject to subsection (3) below, it shall be an implied term of every assured tenancy which is a periodic tenancy that, except with the consent of the landlord, the tenant shall not—

(a) assign the tenancy (in whole or in part); or

(b) sub-let or part with possession of the whole or any part of the dwelling-house let on the tenancy.

(2) Section 19 of the Landlord and Tenant Act 1927 (consents to assign not to be unreasonably withheld etc.) shall not apply to a term which is implied into an assured tenancy by subsection (1) above.

(3) In the case of a periodic tenancy which is not a statutory periodic tenancy or an assured periodic tenancy arising under Schedule 10 to the Local Government and Housing Act 1989, subsection (1) above does not apply if—

(a) there is a provision (whether contained in the tenancy or not) under which the tenant is prohibited (whether absolutely or conditionally) from assigning or sub-letting or parting with possession or is permitted (whether absolutely or conditionally) to assign, sub-let or part with possession; or

(b) a premium is required to be paid on the grant or renewal of the tenancy.

(4) In subsection (3)(b) above "premium" includes—

(a) any fine or other like sum;

(b) any other pecuniary consideration in addition to rent; and

(c) any sum paid by way of deposit, other than one which does not exceed one-sixth of the annual rent payable under the tenancy immediately after the grant or renewal in question.

3A-847 *Note* —Amended by the Local Government and Housing Act 1989 Sch.11, para.102.

**"assured tenancy"**

3A-848 See s.1.

**"landlord", and "tenant"**

3A-849 See s.45.

**"dwelling-house"**

3A-850 See s.45

**"statutory periodic tenancy"**
See s.5(7). 3A–851

## Access for repairs

**16.** It shall be an implied term of every assured tenancy that the tenant shall afford to the landlord access to the dwelling-house let on the tenancy and all reasonable facilities for executing therein any repairs which the landlord is entitled to execute. 3A–852

**"assured tenancy"**
See s.1. 3A–853

**"landlord", "tenancy" and "tenant"**
See s.45. 3A–854

**"dwelling-house"**
See s.45. 3A–855

### *MISCELLANEOUS*

## Succession to assured periodic tenancy by spouse

**17.**—(1) In any case where— 3A–856

(a) the sole tenant under an assured periodic tenancy dies, and

(b) immediately before the death, the tenant's spouse or civil partner was occupying the dwelling-house as his or her only or principal home, and

(c) the tenant was not himself a successor, as defined in subsection (2) or subsection (3) below,

then, on the death, the tenancy vests by virtue of this section in the spouse or civil partner (and, accordingly, does not devolve under the tenant's will or intestacy).

(2) For the purposes of this section, a tenant is a successor in relation to a tenancy if—

(a) the tenancy became vested in him either by virtue of this section or under the will or intestacy of a previous tenant; or

(b) at some time before the tenant's death the tenancy was a joint tenancy held by himself and one or more other persons and, prior to his death, he became the sole tenant by survivorship; or

(c) he became entitled to the tenancy as mentioned in section 39(5) below.

(3) For the purposes of this section, a tenant is also a successor in relation to a tenancy (in this subsection referred to as "the new tenancy") which was granted to him (alone or jointly with others) if—

(a) at some time before the grant of the new tenancy, he was, by virtue of subsection (2) above, a successor in relation to an earlier tenancy of the same or substantially the same dwelling-house as is let under the new tenancy; and

***Paragraph numbers marked with a "+" can be found online and on CD.***

HOUSING

(b) at all times since he became such a successor he has been a tenant (alone or jointly with others) of the dwelling-house which is let under the new tenancy or of a dwelling-house which is substantially the same as that dwelling-house.

(4) For the purposes of this section—

(a) a person who was living with the tenant as his or her wife or husband shall be treated as the tenant's spouse, and

(b) a person who was living with the tenant as if they were civil partners shall be treated as the tenant's civil partner.

(5) If, on the death of the tenant, there is, by virtue of subsection (4) above, more than one person who fulfils the condition in subsection (1)(b) above, such one of them as may be decided by agreement or, in default of agreement, by the county court shall for the purposes of this section be treated (according to whether that one of them is of the opposite sex to, or of the same sex as, the tenant) as the tenant's spouse or the tenant's civil partner.

3A–857 *Note*—Amended by the Civil Partnership Act 2004 s.81 and Sch.8, para.41.

**"assured tenancy"**

3A–858 See s.1.

**"landlord", "tenancy" and "tenant"**

3A–859 See s.45.

**"dwelling-house"**

3A–860 See s.45.

**Succession to assured periodic tenancy by spouse**

3A–861 This section provides for succession to an assured tenancy by a spouse who was occupying the dwelling-house as his or her only or principal home. "Spouse" includes "a person who was living with the tenant as his or her wife or husband" even if they were not married. Same sex couples may be treated in the same way as a husband and wife. The House of Lords has held that the words "as his or her wife or husband" in Rent Act 1977 Sch.1, para.2(2) must be read to mean "as if they were his or her wife or husband" in order to comply with the ECHR. Accordingly the survivor of a same sex couple who has been living in a loving and monogamous relationship with a tenant may be able to succeed to an assured tenancy (see *Ghaidan v Godin-Mendoza* [2004] UKHL 30; [2004] 2 A.C. 557; *cf. Harrogate BC v Simpson* (1985) 17 H.L.R. 205, CA and *Fitzpatrick v Sterling Housing Association* [2001] 1 A.C. 27; [1999] 3 W.L.R. 1113; [1999] 4 All E.R. 705, HL). In *Nutting v Southern Housing Group Ltd* [2004] EWHC 2982 (Ch); [2005] H.L.R. 25 Evans-Lombe J. held that without a lifetime commitment at least at some point in a same sex relationship, there is no sufficient similarity to marriage. Such a relationship must be "openly and unequivocally displayed to the outside world".

Note that Ground 7 does not apply to a successor under this section since the tenancy has not "devolved under the will or intestacy".

## Provisions as to reversions on assured tenancies

3A–862 **18.**—(1) If at any time—

(a) a dwelling-house is for the time being lawfully let on an assured tenancy, and

(b) the landlord under the assured tenancy is himself a tenant under a superior tenancy, and

***Paragraph numbers marked with a "+" can be found online and on CD.***

(c) the superior tenancy comes to an end,

then, subject to subsection (2) below, the assured tenancy shall continue in existence as a tenancy held of the person whose interest would, apart from the continuance of the assured tenancy, entitle him to actual possession of the dwelling-house at that time.

(2) Subsection (1) above does not apply to an assured tenancy if the interest which, by virtue of that subsection, would become that of the landlord, is such that, by virtue of Schedule 1 to this Act, the tenancy could not be an assured tenancy.

(3) Where, by virtue of any provision of this Part of this Act, an assured tenancy which is a periodic tenancy (including a statutory periodic tenancy) continues beyond the beginning of a reversionary tenancy which was granted (whether before, on or after the commencement of this Act) so as to begin on or after—

(a) the date on which the previous contractual assured tenancy came to an end, or

(b) a date on which, apart from any provision of this Part, the periodic tenancy could have been brought to an end by the landlord by notice to quit,

the reversionary tenancy shall have effect as if it had been granted subject to the periodic tenancy.

(4) The reference in subsection (3) above to the previous contractual assured tenancy applies only where the periodic tenancy referred to in that subsection is a statutory periodic tenancy and is a reference to the fixed-term tenancy which immediately preceded the statutory periodic tenancy.

**"assured tenancy"**

See s.1. 3A-863

**"landlord", and "tenant"**

See s.45. 3A-864

**"dwelling-house"**

See s.45. 3A-865

**"statutory periodic tenancy"**

See s.5(7). 3A-866

## Restriction on levy of distress for rent.

**19.**—(1) Subject to subsection (2) below, no distress for the rent of any dwelling-house let on an assured tenancy shall be levied except with the leave of the county court; and, with respect to any application for such leave, the court shall have the same powers with respect to adjournment, stay, suspension, postponement and otherwise as are conferred by section 9 above in relation to proceedings for possession of such a dwelling-house. 3A-867

(2) Nothing in subsection (1) above applies to distress levied under section 102 of the County Courts Act 1984.

**"assured tenancy"**

See s.1. 3A-867.1

***Paragraph numbers marked with a "+" can be found online and on CD.***

**"dwelling-house"**

3A–867.2 See s.45.

* * * *

CHAPTER II

ASSURED SHORTHOLD TENANCIES

## Assured shorthold tenancies: post-Housing Act 1996 tenancies

3A–868 **19A.** An assured tenancy which—

(a) is entered into on or after the day on which section 96 of the Housing Act 1996 comes into force (otherwise than pursuant to a contract made before that day), or

(b) comes into being by virtue of section 5 above on the coming to an end of an assured tenancy within paragraph (a) above,

is an assured shorthold tenancy unless it falls within any paragraph in Schedule 2A to this Act.

3A–869 *Note* —Added by the Housing Act 1996 s.96(1).

**"assured tenancy"**

3A–870 See s.1.

**Assured shorthold tenancies: post-Housing Act 1996 tenancies**

3A–871 Housing Act 1996 s.96 and Sch.7 take effect as a new Housing Act 1988 s.19A and Sch.2A. They provide that all new tenancies entered into after this provision came into force on February 28, 1997 which would otherwise have been assured tenancies are automatically *assured shorthold* tenancies lacking long term security of tenure. This applies whether the tenancy is granted orally or by a written agreement. In other words, the requirement of a s.20 notice (see below) informing the tenant that the tenancy will be an assured shorthold tenancy has been abolished. There are though several exceptions. The new rule does not apply where:

- the new tenancy is made pursuant to a contract made before the new provisions come into force (Housing Act 1996 s.96); or
- the landlord serves a notice before entering into the tenancy stating that the tenancy is not to be an assured shorthold tenancy (Housing Act 1996 Sch.7, para.1); or
- the landlord serves a notice after the grant of the tenancy stating that the tenancy is no longer an assured shorthold tenancy (Housing Act 1996 Sch.7, para.2); or
- there is a provision in the tenancy agreement stating that the tenancy is not an assured shorthold tenancy (Housing Act 1996 Sch.7, para.3); or
- the tenancy is an assured tenancy by succession—i.e. a spouse or member of the family of a statutory tenant under the Rent Act 1977 or the Rent (Agriculture) Act 1976 became an assured tenant after the death of the original tenant (Rent Act 1977 s.2(1)(b) and Sch.1; Housing Act 1988 s.39; and Housing Act 1996 Sch.7, para.4); or
- the tenancy was formerly a secure tenancy and became an assured tenancy, e.g. on transfer of housing stock from a local housing authority to a housing association or other landlord (Housing Act 1985 Pt IV; Housing Act 1988 s.38; and Housing Act 1996 Sch.7, para.5); or
- an assured tenancy came into existence on the ending of a long residential tenancy (Landlord and Tenant Act 1954 Pt I; Local Government and Housing Act 1989 s.186 and Sch.10; and Housing Act 1996 Sch.7, para.6); or

- the tenancy is granted to someone who immediately before its grant was an assured tenant (as opposed to an assured *shorthold* tenant) and is granted by someone who was the landlord under the old tenancy (Housing Act 1996 Sch.7, para.7); or
- in some cases the tenancy or licence is an assured agricultural occupancy (Rent (Agriculture) Act 1976; Housing Act 1988 s.24 and Sch.3; and Housing Act 1996 Sch.7, para.9).

## Assured shorthold tenancies: pre-Housing Act 1996 tenancies

**20.**—(1) Subject to subsection (3) below, an assured tenancy which is not one to which section 19A above applies is an assured shorthold tenancy if— **3A–872**

(a) it is a fixed term tenancy granted for a term certain of not less than six months,

(b) there is no power for the landlord to determine the tenancy at any time earlier than six months from the beginning of the tenancy, and

(c) a notice in respect of it is served as mentioned in subsection (2) below.

(2) The notice referred to in subsection (1)(c) above is one which—

(a) is in such form as may be prescribed;

(b) is served before the assured tenancy is entered into;

(c) is served by the person who is to be the landlord under the assured tenancy on the person who is to be the tenant under that tenancy; and

(d) states that the assured tenancy to which it relates is to be a shorthold tenancy.

(3) Notwithstanding anything in subsection (1) above, where—

(a) immediately before a tenancy (in this subsection referred to as "the new tenancy") is granted, the person to whom it is granted or, as the case may be, at least one of the persons to whom it is granted was a tenant under an assured tenancy which was not a shorthold tenancy, and

(b) the new tenancy is granted by the person who, immediately before the beginning of the tenancy, was the landlord under the assured tenancy referred to in paragraph (a) above,

the new tenancy cannot be an assured shorthold tenancy.

(4) Subject to subsection (5) below, if, on the coming to an end of an assured shorthold tenancy (including a tenancy which was an assured shorthold but ceased to be assured before it came to an end), a new tenancy of the same or substantially the same premises comes into being under which the landlord and the tenant are the same as at the coming to an end of the earlier tenancy, then, if and so long as the new tenancy is an assured tenancy, it shall be an assured shorthold tenancy, whether or not it fulfils the conditions in paragraphs (a) to (c) of subsection (1) above.

(5) Subsection (4) above does not apply if, before the new tenancy is entered into (or, in the case of a statutory periodic tenancy, takes

effect in possession), the landlord serves notice on the tenant that the new tenancy is not to be a shorthold tenancy.

(5A) Subsections (3) and (4) above do not apply where the new tenancy is one to which section 19A above applies.

(6) In the case of joint landlords—

(a) the reference in subsection (2)(c) above to the person who is to be the landlord is a reference to at least one of the persons who are to be joint landlords; and

(b) the reference in subsection (5) above to the landlord is a reference to at least one of the joint landlords.

**3A-873** *Note* —Amended by the Housing Act 1996 Schs 8 and 19.

**"assured tenancy"**

**3A-874** See s.1.

**"landlord", and "tenant"**

**3A-875** See s.45.

**"statutory periodic tenancy"**

**3A-876** See s.5(7).

**"prescribed"**

**3A-877** See s.45 and the Assured Tenancies and Agricultural Occupancies (Forms) Regulations 1988 (SI 1988/2203). Note that a notice conforms with the regulations if it is "substantially to the same effect" as that prescribed (para.2).

**Assured shorthold tenancies: pre-Housing Act 1996 tenancies**

**3A-878** This section now only applies to tenancies granted prior to February 28, 1997 (but note the exceptions listed in s.19A). For tenancies granted after that date, see s.19A, above.

Section 20 provides that for a tenancy granted before February 28, 1997 to be an assured shorthold tenancy:

(a) there had to be a tenancy granted for a fixed term of not less than six months (A tenancy granted for "a term certain of one year ... and ... thereafter from month to month" is a tenancy granted for a term certain within the meaning of s.20(1)(a) which was capable of being an assured shorthold tenancy. (*Goodman v Evely* [2001] EWCA Civ 104; [2002] H.L.R. 53; [2001] L.& T.R. 436, CA)); and

(b) there could be no power enabling the landlord to determine the tenancy within the first six months;

Section 45(4) provides that a power of re-entry or forfeiture for breach of a condition does *not* count as a provision enabling the landlord to determine the tenancy for this purpose; and

(c) a notice in the prescribed form had to be served on the prospective tenant before the tenancy was entered into, stating that the tenancy was to be an assured shorthold tenancy.

This requirement was *mandatory*. There is no provision which allows the court to dispense with the service of a notice before the initial grant of a pre-February 28, 1997 assured shorthold tenancy.

Service earlier on the day when the tenancy commenced was sufficient (*Bedding v McCarthy* [1994] 41 E.G. 151, CA). This is a pure question of fact. It was good practice, although not a statutory requirement, for landlords to ensure that tenants endorsed a note confirming receipt on a copy of the notice. A s.20 notice may be served upon a prospective tenant's agent (*Yenula Properties Ltd v Naidu* [2002] EWCA Civ 719; [2003] H.L.R. 18; [2002] 42 E.G.162).

Section 20 notices have been held to be invalid where the landlord inserted an incorrect date (*Panayi v Roberts* (1993) 25 H.L.R. 421, CA), where the dates in the notice and the tenancy were "in complete conflict" *(Clickex Ltd v McCann* (2000) 32 H.L.R. 324; [1999] 30 EG 96, CA; where the four bullet points giving instructions and advice to the tenant were omitted (*Manel v Memon* [2000] 33 E.G. 74, CA), where no date for termination was inserted (*Mistry v Dave*, June 1995, Legal Action 20(cc)), where the landlord's name, address and telephone number were missing (*Stephens v Lamb*, March 1996, Legal Action 12(cc)), and where the landlord's name was spelt incorrectly and the notice was not signed (*Symons v Warren* [1995] C.L.W. 33/95(cc)).

However all these cases now have to be reconsidered in the light of cases such as *Ravenseft Proeprties Ltd v Hall* and *B. Osborn & Co Ltd v Dior* [2003] H.L.R. 45 where the Court of Appeal held that there is no statutory or common law doctrine of "obvious mistake" or any requirement to apply a two-stage test in which the court has first to consider whether the error in the notice is obvious or evident before proceeding to consider whether the notice read in context is sufficiently clear to leave a reasonable recipient in no reasonable doubt as to the terms of the notice. There is only one statutory question, which is whether, notwithstanding any errors or omissions, the notice is "substantially to the same effect" as a correct notice in accomplishing the purpose of telling the proposed tenant of the special nature of an assured shorthold tenancy (*Mannai Investment Co Ltd v Eagle Star Life Assurance Co Ltd* [1997] A.C. 749, HL). This is a matter of fact and degree in each case. The resolution of that question is not a decision on a point of law that is binding on later courts (*White v Chubb; Kasseer v Freeman* [2001] EWCA Civ 2034; *Ravenseft Properties Ltd v Hall* [2001] EWCA Civ 2034; [2002] H.L.R. 33; [2002] 11 E.G. 156).

See too *York and Ross v Casey* (1999) 31 H.L.R. 209; [1998] 30 E.G. 110, CA where, following *Mannai Investment Co Ltd v Eagle Star Life Assurance Co Ltd* [1997] A.C. 749; [1997] 2 W.L.R. 945; [1997] 3 All E.R. 352, HL, the Court of Appeal held that a notice is valid even if it contains a minor misdescription if, in its contextual setting, it informs a reasonably minded recipient how the notice is to operate. There is no material difference between contractual and statutory notices and accordingly the *Mannai* test is equally applicable to statutory notices. In this case where the section 20 notice gave a commencement date of September 28, 1996 but a date for termination of the tenancy of September 6, 1996, there was no doubt that the termination date was wrong. The real question was whether the correct termination date was sufficiently clear. In looking at a letter which accompanied the notice, there was no doubt that the termination date was understood to be March 27, 1997. See too *Garston v Scottish Widows* [1998] 1 W.L.R. 1583, CA.

See too *B. Osborn & Co Ltd v Dior* [2003] H.L.R. 45 where it was held that omission of landlords' particulars from a s.20 notice is not fatal. The question is whether the form is substantially to the same effect as the prescribed form.

#### Tenancy of same premises

Note though that if a new tenancy of substantially the same premises was granted **3A–879** and at least one of the tenants was previously an assured shorthold tenant of the same landlord, the new tenancy automatically became an assured shorthold tenancy even if conditions (a) to (c) were not complied with (s.20(4)).

## Post-Housing Act 1996 tenancies: duty of landlord to provide statement as to terms of tenancy

**20A.**—(1) Subject to subsection (3) below, a tenant under an assured shorthold tenancy to which section 19A above applies may, by notice in writing, require the landlord under that tenancy to provide him with a written statement of any term of the tenancy which— **3A–880**

(a) falls within subsection (2) below, and

(b) is not evidenced in writing.

(2) The following terms of a tenancy fall within this subsection, namely—

(a) the date on which the tenancy began or, if it is a statutory periodic tenancy or a tenancy to which section 39(7) below applies, the date on which the tenancy came into being,

(b) the rent payable under the tenancy and the dates on which that rent is payable,

(c) any term providing for a review of the rent payable under the tenancy, and

(d) in the case of a fixed term tenancy, the length of the fixed term.

(3) No notice may be given under subsection (1) above in relation to a term of the tenancy if—

(a) the landlord under the tenancy has provided a statement of that term in response to an earlier notice under that subsection given by the tenant under the tenancy, and

(b) the term has not been varied since the provision of the statement referred to in paragraph (a) above.

(4) A landlord who fails, without reasonable excuse, to comply with a notice under subsection (1) above within the period of 28 days beginning with the date on which he received the notice is liable on summary conviction to a fine not exceeding level 4 on the standard scale.

(5) A statement provided for the purposes of subsection (1) above shall not be regarded as conclusive evidence of what was agreed by the parties to the tenancy in question.

(6) Where—

(a) a term of a statutory periodic tenancy is one which has effect by virtue of section 5(3)(e) above, or

(b) a term of a tenancy to which subsection (7) of section 39 below applies is one which has effect by virtue of subsection (6)(e) of that section,

subsection (1) above shall have effect in relation to it as if paragraph (b) related to the term of the tenancy from which it derives.

(7) In subsections (1) and (3) above—

(a) references to the tenant under the tenancy shall, in the case of joint tenants, be taken to be references to any of the tenants, and

(b) references to the landlord under the tenancy shall, in the case of joint landlords, be taken to be references to any of the landlords.

3A–881 *Note*—Added by the Housing Act 1996 s.97.

**"assured shorthold tenancy"**

3A–882 See ss.19A and 20.

**"landlord", and "tenant"**

3A–883 See s.45.

### Demoted assured shorthold tenancies

3A–884 **20B.**—(1) An assured tenancy is an assured shorthold tenancy to which this section applies (a demoted assured shorthold tenancy) if—

***Paragraph numbers marked with a "+" can be found online and on CD.***

(a) the tenancy is created by virtue of an order of the court under section 82A of the Housing Act 1985 or section 6A of this Act (a demotion order), and

(b) the landlord is a registered social landlord.

(2) At the end of the period of one year starting with the day when the demotion order takes effect a demoted assured shorthold tenancy ceases to be an assured shorthold tenancy unless subsection (3) applies.

(3) This subsection applies if before the end of the period mentioned in subsection (2) the landlord gives notice of proceedings for possession of the dwelling house.

(4) If subsection (3) applies the tenancy continues to be a demoted assured shorthold tenancy until the end of the period mentioned in subsection (2) or (if later) until one of the following occurs—

(a) the notice of proceedings for possession is withdrawn;

(b) the proceedings are determined in favour of the tenant;

(c) the period of six months beginning with the date on which the notice is given ends and no proceedings for possession have been brought.

(5) Registered social landlord has the same meaning as in Part 1 of the Housing Act 1996.

**Editorial note**

This section was inserted by Anti-Social Behaviour Act 2003 s.15(1). It was brought into force in England on June 30, 2004 by the Anti-Social Behaviour Act 2003 (Commencement No.3 and Savings) Order 2004 (SI 2004/1502) (c.61). It was brought into force in Wales on April 30, 2005 by the Anti-Social Behaviour Act 2003 (Commencement No.4) (Wales) Order 2005 (SI 2005/1225) (w.83) (c.55). **3A–885**

Section 20B sets out the legal basis for the form of demoted tenancy that can be used by registered social landlords. A demoted assured shorthold tenancy is an assured shorthold tenancy during the demoted period but there is provision for the demoted assured shorthold tenancy automatically to turn into an assured tenancy after one year unless the landlord has issued a notice of proceedings for possession during that year. If a notice is issued, the tenancy remains a demoted assured shorthold tenancy beyond the first year until the notice is withdrawn or six months have passed and no proceedings have been issued; or, if proceedings have been issued, until they are determined in favour of the tenant. A demoted assured shorthold tenancy can be ended at any time during the demotion period. Unlike non-demoted assured shorthold tenancies a possession order granted on the basis that the landlord has given the required notice under s.21(4) of the Housing Act 1988 can take effect within the first six months of the tenancy.

**Assured tenancy**

See s.1. **3A–886**

**Assured shorthold tenancy**

See ss.19A and 20. **3A–887**

**Registered social landlord**

See Housing Act 1996 Part I, ss.1 to 3. **3A–888**

## Recovery of possession on expiry or termination of assured shorthold tenancy

**21.**—(1) Without prejudice to any right of the landlord under an assured shorthold tenancy to recover possession of the dwelling- **3A–889**

house let on the tenancy in accordance with Chapter I above, on or after the coming to an end of an assured shorthold tenancy which was a fixed term tenancy, a court shall make an order for possession of the dwelling-house if it is satisfied—

(a) that the assured shorthold tenancy has come to an end and no further assured tenancy (whether shorthold or not) is for the time being in existence, other than an assured shorthold periodic tenancy (whether statutory or not); and

(b) the landlord or, in the case of joint landlords, at least one of them has given to the tenant not less than two months' notice in writing stating that he requires possession of the dwelling-house.

(2) A notice under paragraph (b) of subsection (1) above may be given before or on the day on which the tenancy comes to an end; and that subsection shall have effect notwithstanding that on the coming to an end of the fixed term tenancy a statutory periodic tenancy arises.

(3) Where a court makes an order for possession of a dwelling-house by virtue of subsection (1) above, any statutory periodic tenancy which has arisen on the coming to an end of the assured shorthold tenancy shall end (without further notice and regardless of the period) in accordance with section 5(1A).

(4) Without prejudice to any such right as is referred to in subsection (1) above, a court shall make an order for possession of a dwelling-house let on an assured shorthold tenancy which is a periodic tenancy if the court is satisfied—

(a) that the landlord or, in the case of joint landlords, at least one of them has given to the tenant a notice in writing stating that, after a date specified in the notice, being the last day of a period of the tenancy and not earlier than two months after the date the notice was given, possession of the dwelling-house is required by virtue of this section; and

(b) that the date specified in the notice under paragraph (a) above is not earlier than the earliest day on which, apart from section 5(1) above, the tenancy could be brought to an end by a notice to quit given by the landlord on the same date as the notice under paragraph (a) above.

(4A) Where a court makes an order for possession of a dwelling-house by virtue of subsection (4) above, the assured shorthold tenancy shall end in accordance with section 5(1A).

(5) Where an order for possession under subsection (1) or (4) above is made in relation to a dwelling-house let on a tenancy to which section 19A above applies, the order may not be made so as to take effect earlier than—

(a) in the case of a tenancy which is not a replacement tenancy, six months after the beginning of the tenancy, and

(b) in the case of a replacement tenancy, six months after the beginning of the original tenancy.

***Paragraph numbers marked with a "+" can be found online and on CD.***

(5A) Subsection (5) above does not apply to an assured shorthold tenancy to which section 20B (demoted assured shorthold tenancies) applies.

(6) In subsection (5)(b) above, the reference to the original tenancy is—

(a) where the replacement tenancy came into being on the coming to an end of a tenancy which was not a replacement tenancy, to the immediately preceding tenancy, and

(b) where there have been successive replacement tenancies, to the tenancy immediately preceding the first in the succession of replacement tenancies.

(7) For the purposes of this section, a replacement tenancy is a tenancy—

(a) which comes into being on the coming to an end of an assured short-hold tenancy, and

(b) under which, on its coming into being—

(i) the landlord and tenant are the same as under the earlier tenancy as at its coming to an end, and

(ii) the premises let are the same or substantially the same as those let under the earlier tenancy as at that time.

*Note* —Amended by the Local Government and Housing Act 1989 Sch.11, the Housing Act 1996 ss.98 and 99 and the Anti-Social Behaviour Act 2003 s.15(2). **3A–890**

This section has also been amended by the Housing and Regeneration Act 2008 Sch.11, Pt I, para.9 (for transitional provisions see para.14) with effect from May 20, 2009 (SI 2009/1261) (c.66).

**"assured shorthold tenancy"**

See ss.19A and 20. **3A–891**

**"landlord", and "tenant"**

See s.45. **3A–892**

**"statutory periodic tenancy"**

See s.5(7). **3A–893**

**Tenancy deposits and s.21 notices**

Housing Act 2004 s.215(1) provides that if a tenancy deposit (see Housing Act s.212(8)) has been paid in connection with an assured shorthold tenancy, no s.21 notice may be given in relation to the tenancy at any time when (a) the deposit is not being held in accordance with an authorised scheme (see Housing Act 2004 s.213(4)), or (b) the initial requirements of such a scheme (see s.213(4)) have not been complied with in relation to the deposit. These provisions were brought into force on April 6, 2007 by the Housing Act 2004 (Commencement No.7) (England) Order 2007 (SI 2007/1068) and the Housing Act 2004 (Commencement No.4) (Wales) Order 2007 (SI 2007/305). They apply to deposits paid on or after that date. **3A–894**

**Houses in multiple occupation and s.21 notices**

Note that no s.21 notice may be given in relation to an assured shorthold tenancy in a house in multiple occupation if the house is not licensed in accordance with the provisions of the Housing Act 2004 Pt 2—see s.75. **3A–895**

**Recovery of possession on expiry or termination of assured shorthold tenancy**

Assured shorthold tenancies lack long-term security of tenure. If the initial tenancy **3A–896**

***Paragraph numbers marked with a "+" can be found online and on CD.***

was for a fixed term and the tenant continues to occupy premises as his or her only or principal home, a statutory periodic tenancy arises, but all that a landlord need do to recover possession is to:

(a) prove that any fixed term tenancy has come to an end and that no new fixed term tenancy has been granted; and

(b) give at least two months notice to the tenant that the landlord requires possession. Such notice may be given before the fixed term expires.

There are no requirements as to the form of the notice, although it should be in writing (s.21(1)(b) and s.21(4)(a), as amended by the Housing Act 1996 s.98).

Although s.21(4)(a) refers to "a date specified in the notice", the Court of Appeal has held that no date need be specified in a s.21 notice provided that "the tenant knows or can easily ascertain the date referred to ... The word 'specified' ... means no more than 'made clear'" (*Lower Street Properties v Jones* (1996) 28 H.L.R. 877; [1996] 2 E.G.L.R. 67). Accordingly a notice which does not contain a date, but which provides a formula for calculating a date which complies with s.21(4)(a) (e.g. "at the end of the period of your tenancy which will end next after the expiration of two months from the service upon you of this notice") is valid.

If landlords comply with these requirements, they are automatically entitled to possession. The court has no power to suspend possession orders, apart from the Housing Act 1980 s.89(1) (see above). It has been held in the county court that a s.21 notice served before the commencement of the tenancy is not valid because at that stage there was no relationship of landlord and tenant, as required by s.21(1)(b)—see *Turpitt v Elizabeth*, August 1998, Legal Action 21, Edmonton County Court—although the better view is that such a notice is valid.

Uncertainty has been caused by the dichotomy between the Housing Act 1988 s.21(1)(b) and s.21(4)(a). Section 21(1)(b) merely provides that the landlord must give "the tenant not less than two months' notice stating that he requires possession of the dwelling-house". However, s.21(4)(a) provides that the date specified in a notice where there is "a periodic tenancy" shall be "the last day of a period of the tenancy". Although it has been argued that s.21(1) and s.21(4) are simply alternatives that may be used as landlords choose, the better view is that there is no need for the two months notice to expire on "the last day of a period of the tenancy" if the notice is served during a fixed term assured shorthold but this requirement has to be satisfied if the notice is served after the expiry of a fixed term (i.e. during a statutory periodic assured shorthold tenancy). The use of the words "without prejudice ... to ... subsection (1)" in s.21(4) clearly shows that the two subsections are alternatives and that s.21(4) is not an additional requirement for all s.21(1) notices. The words in s.21(2) ("A notice under paragraph (b) of subsection (1) above may be given before or on the day on which the tenancy comes to an end") indicate that a s.21(1) notice is one which can be served during a fixed term. In contrast, the use of the words "let on an assured shorthold tenancy which is a periodic tenancy" in s.21(4) indicate that the s.21(4)(b) requirement applies whenever a notice is served during a periodic tenancy—and that includes a statutory periodic tenancy (*cf.* s.13(1)(a) and (b) and s.15(3)). This approach is also supported by the Housing Act 1996 s.98 which refers to s.21(1) notices as being given "under a fixed term" and s.21(4) as the "corresponding provision for periodic tenancies".

In *Gracechurch SA v Tribhovan and Abdul* (2001) 33 H.L.R. 28, CA, Simon Brown L.J., while hearing an appeal on another issue, described the dismissal of possession proceedings, because a notice requiring possession from a periodic tenant did not expire on the last day of a period of the tenancy, as "clearly correct". This was confirmed by the Court of Appeal in *McDonald v Fernandez* [2003] EWCA Civ 1219; [2004] 1 W.L.R. 1027, when rejecting a landlord's contention that s.21 should be construed in the same way as the common law rules relating to notices to quit. It might be possible to give a notice to quit that expired on either the first day or the last day of a period of the tenancy, but that was not because there were two last days. It was because the last day ended at midnight and the first day of the new period would begin thereafter. A s.21 notice is not a notice to quit. The niceties of contractual notices to quit should not be imported into the plain words of the statute. Section 21(4)(a) requires the notice to specify the last date of the period. It is not a situation where the legislation permits the form to be substantially to the same effect. The subsection is clear and precise. Accordingly, a notice served during a periodic assured shorthold tenancy which does not expire "on the last day of a period of the tenancy" is unlikely to be valid.

In order to be valid, a notice served upon a periodic assured shorthold tenant—

(1) must specify a date after which possession is required—either by inserting a particular date or by using a formula, as in *Lower Street Properties v Jones* (above);

(2) give a date which is the last day of a period of the tenancy, and not any other day. The fact that the notice is too long does not save it from being defective. (*McDonald v Fernandez* [2003] EWCA Civ 1219 (above));

(3) make it clear that possession is required after that date. In *Notting Hill Housing Trust v Roomus* [2006] EWCA Civ 407; [2006] 1 W.L.R. 1375, the Court of Appeal found that a s.21 notice which stated "Possession is required of the premises which you hold as tenant(s) at the end of the period of your tenancy which will end after expiry of two months from the service upon you of this notice" was valid because the phrase "at the end of the ... tenancy" in the notice meant "after the end of the tenancy".

The Housing Act 1996 s.99, by inserting subss.(5) to (7), provides that possession orders made against tenants occupying under the Housing Act 1988 s.19A assured shorthold tenancies cannot take effect earlier than six months after the beginning of the tenancy. There is, however, no reason why a s.21(4) notice should not be served and proceedings commenced within six months of the grant of the tenancy.

A landlord relying upon s.21 may in most circumstances use the Accelerated Possession Procedure, using Form **N5A**, which if not defended, may result in a possession order without a hearing—(see CPR rr.55.11 to 55.19). In *Manel v Memon* [2000] 33 E.G. 74, CA, Holman J. said "[The accelerated possession procedure] is a robust machinery. It depends upon district judges rigorously considering the documents which have been filed. Some replies may be little more than a plea, however genuine, for mercy. But if, on the face of the reply, a matter has been raised which, if true, might arguably raise a defence; or if the documents filed by the claimant might arguably disclose a defect in his claim, then the district judge must necessarily be "not satisfied" within the meaning of CCR O.49, r.6A(16) and a hearing on notice must be fixed."

The same applies to cases brought under CPR rr.55.11 to 55.19.

### Section 21 and ECHR art.8

Notwithstanding its mandatory terms, the right to possession contained in s.21(4) **3A–897**
does not conflict with tenants' rights under ECHR art.8. The section is clearly necessary in a democratic society insofar as there has to be a procedure for recovering possession of property at the end of a tenancy. The court would defer to Parliament as to whether the restricted power of the court under that section was legitimate and proportionate (*Donoghue v Poplar HARCA* [2001] 3 W.L.R. 183, CA); also reported as *Poplar Housing & Regeneration Community Association Ltd v Donoghue* [2001] EWCA Civ 595 *Poplar Housing & Regeneration Community Association Ltd v Donoghue* [2001] EWCA Civ 595; [2002] Q.B. 48. (Note that in *Qazi v Harrow LBC* [2003] UKHL 43; [2004] 1 A.C. 983, Lord Scott stated that this case was correctly decided, but for the wrong reason.

## Reference of excessive rents to rent assessment committee

**22.**—(1) Subject to section 23 and subsection (2) below, the tenant **3A–898**
under an assured shorthold tenancy may make an application in the prescribed form to a rent assessment committee for a determination of the rent which, in the committee's opinion, the landlord might reasonably be expected to obtain under the assured shorthold tenancy.

(2) No application may be made under this section if—

(a) the rent payable under the tenancy is a rent previously determined under this section;

(aa) the tenancy is one to which section 19A above applies

*Paragraph numbers marked with a "+" can be found online and on CD.*

and more than six months have elapsed since the beginning of the tenancy or, in the case of a replacement tenancy, since the beginning of the original tenancy; or

(b) the tenancy is an assured shorthold tenancy falling within subsection (4) of section 20 above (and, accordingly, is one in respect of which notice need not have been served as mentioned in subsection (2) of that section).

(3) Where an application is made to a rent assessment committee under subsection (1) above with respect to the rent under an assured shorthold tenancy, the committee shall not make such a determination as is referred to in that subsection unless they consider—

(a) that there is a sufficient number of similar dwelling-houses in the locality let on assured tenancies (whether shorthold or not); and

(b) that the rent payable under the assured shorthold tenancy in question is significantly higher than the rent which the landlord might reasonably be expected to be able to obtain under the tenancy, having regard to the level of rents payable under the tenancies referred to in paragraph (a) above.

(4) Where, on an application under this section, a rent assessment committee make a determination of a rent for an assured shorthold tenancy—

(a) the determination shall have effect from such date as the committee may direct, not being earlier than the date of the application;

(b) if, at any time on or after the determination takes effect, the rent which, apart from this paragraph, would be payable under the tenancy exceeds the rent so determined, the excess shall be irrecoverable from the tenant; and

(c) no notice may be served under section 13(2) above with respect to a tenancy of the dwelling-house in question until after the first anniversary of the date on which the determination takes effect.

(5) Subsections (4), (5) and (8) of section 14 above apply in relation to a determination of rent under this section as they apply in relation to a determination under that section and, accordingly, where subsection (5) of that section applies, any reference in subsection (4)(b) above to rent is a reference to rent exclusive of the amount attributable to rates.

(5A) Where—

(a) an assured tenancy ceases to be an assured shorthold tenancy by virtue of falling within paragraph 2 of Schedule 2A to this Act, and

(b) at the time when it so ceases to be an assured shorthold tenancy there is pending before a rent assessment committee an application in relation to it under this section,

the fact that it so ceases to be an assured shorthold tenancy shall, in relation to that application, be disregarded for the purposes of this section.

(6) In subsection (2)(aa) above, the references to the original tenancy and to a replacement tenancy shall be construed in accordance with subsections (6) and (7) respectively of section 21 above.

*Note*—Amended by the Housing Act 1996 s.10, Sch.8, para.2, Sch.19, Pt IV. **3A–899**

**"assured shorthold tenancy"**

See ss.19A and 20. **3A–900**

**"landlord", and "tenant"**

See s.45. **3A–901**

**"statutory periodic tenancy"**

See s.5(7). **3A–902**

**"dwelling-house"**

See s.45. **3A–903**

**Reference of excessive rents to rent assessment committee**

Assured shorthold tenants may apply to the rent assessment committee if they consider that the rent is excessive. This right cannot be exercised if more than six months have elapsed from the beginning of a s.19A tenancy. **3A–904**

## Termination of rent assessment committee's functions

**23.**—(1) If the Secretary of State by order made by statutory instrument so provides, section 22 above shall not apply in such cases or to tenancies of dwelling-houses in such areas or in such other circumstances as may be specified in the order. **3A–905**

(2) An order under this section may contain such transitional, incidental and supplementary provisions as appear to the Secretary of State to be desirable.

(3) No order shall be made under this section unless a draft of the order has been laid before, and approved by a resolution of, each House of Parliament.

**"dwelling-house"**

See s.45. **3A–906**

**"tenancy"**

See s.45. **3A–907**

* * * *

CHAPTER IV

PROTECTION FROM EVICTION

## Damages for unlawful eviction

**27.**—(1) This section applies if, at any time after 9th June 1988, a landlord (in this section referred to as "the landlord in default") or any person acting on behalf of the landlord in default unlawfully deprives the residential occupier of any premises of his occupation of the whole or part of the premises. **3A–908**

(2) This section also applies if, at any time after 9th June 1988, a landlord (in this section referred to as "the landlord in default") or any person acting on behalf of the landlord in default—

*Paragraph numbers marked with a "+" can be found online and on CD.*

(a) attempts unlawfully to deprive the residential occupier of any premises of his occupation of the whole or part of the premises, or

(b) knowing or having reasonable cause to believe that the conduct is likely to cause the residential occupier of any premises—

(i) to give up his occupation of the premises or any part thereof, or

(ii) to refrain from exercising any right or pursuing any remedy in respect of the premises or any part thereof,

does acts likely to interfere with the peace or comfort of the residential occupier or members of his household, or persistently withdraws or withholds services reasonably required for the occupation of the premises as a residence,

and, as a result, the residential occupier gives up his occupation of the premises as a residence.

(3) Subject to the following provisions of this section, where this section applies, the landlord in default shall, by virtue of this section, be liable to pay to the former residential occupier, in respect of his loss of the right to occupy the premises in question as his residence, damages assessed on the basis set out in section 28 below.

(4) Any liability arising by virtue of subsection (3) above—

(a) shall be in the nature of a liability in tort; and

(b) subject to subsection (5) below, shall be in addition to any liability arising apart from this section (whether in tort, contract or otherwise).

(5) Nothing in this section affects the right of a residential occupier to enforce any liability which arises apart from this section in respect of his loss of the right to occupy premises as his residence; but damages shall not be awarded both in respect of such a liability and in respect of a liability arising by virtue of this section on account of the same loss.

(6) No liability shall arise by virtue of subsection (3) above if—

(a) before the date on which proceedings to enforce the liability are finally disposed of, the former residential occupier is reinstated in the premises in question in such circumstances that he becomes again the residential occupier of them; or

(b) at the request of the former residential occupier, a court makes an order (whether in the nature of an injunction or otherwise) as a result of which he is reinstated as mentioned in paragraph (a) above;

and, for the purposes of paragraph (a) above, proceedings to enforce a liability are finally disposed of on the earliest date by which the proceedings (including any proceedings on or in consequence of an appeal) have been determined and any time for appealing or further appealing has expired, except that if any appeal is abandoned, the proceedings shall be taken to be disposed of on the date of the abandonment.

(7) If, in proceedings to enforce a liability arising by virtue of subsection (3) above, it appears to the court—

(a) that, prior to the event which gave rise to the liability, the conduct of the former residential occupier or any person living with him in the premises concerned was such that it is reasonable to mitigate the damages for which the landlord in default would otherwise be liable, or

(b) that, before the proceedings were begun, the landlord in default offered to reinstate the former residential occupier in the premises in question and either it was unreasonable of the former residential occupier to refuse that offer or, if he had obtained alternative accommodation before the offer was made, it would have been unreasonable of him to refuse that offer if he had not obtained that accommodation,

the court may reduce the amount of damages which would otherwise be payable by such amount as it thinks appropriate.

(8) In proceedings to enforce a liability arising by virtue of subsection (3) above, it shall be a defence for the defendant to prove that he believed, and had reasonable cause to believe—

(a) that the residential occupier had ceased to reside in the premises in question at the time when he was deprived of occupation as mentioned in subsection (1) above or, as the case may be, when the attempt was made or the acts were done as a result of which he gave up his occupation of those premises; or

(b) that, where the liability would otherwise arise by virtue only of the doing of acts or the withdrawal or withholding of services, he had reasonable grounds for doing the acts or withdrawing or withholding the services in question.

(9) In this section—

(a) "residential occupier", in relation to any premises, has the same meaning as in section 1 of the 1977 Act;

(b) "the right to occupy", in relation to a residential occupier, includes any restriction on the right of another person to recover possession of the premises in question;

(c) "landlord", in relation to a residential occupier, means the person who, but for the occupier's right to occupy, would be entitled to occupation of the premises and any superior landlord under whom that person derives title;

(d) "former residential occupier", in relation to any premises, means the person who was the residential occupier until he was deprived of or gave up his occupation as mentioned in subsection (1) or subsection (2) above (and, in relation to a former residential occupier, "the right to occupy" and "landlord" shall be construed accordingly).

**"landlord"**

See subs.(9). 3A–909

**"residential occupier"**

3A–910 See subs.(9) and the Protection from Eviction Act 1977 s.1 which defines "residential occupier" as "a person occupying the premises as a residence, whether under a contract or by virtue of any enactment or rule of law giving him the right to remain in occupation or restricting the right of any other person to recover possession of the premises."

**"the 1977 Act"**

3A–911 See s.33 which, for the purposes of this Chapter, states that this means the Protection from Eviction Act 1977.

**Damages for unlawful eviction**

3A–912 Section 27 provides a cause of action where a landlord or any person acting on behalf of the landlord:

(i) Unlawfully deprives a residential occupier of the whole or part of any premises which are occupied; or

(ii) Attempts unlawfully to deprive a residential occupier or the whole or part of any premises which are occupied; or

(iii) Causes a residential occupier to give up premises by either—

(a) Doing "acts likely to interfere with the peace or comfort of the residential occupier" or members of his or her household, or

(b) Persistently withdrawing or withholding services reasonably required for the occupation of premises as a residence, and

(c) the landlord or person acting on behalf of the landlord knows or has reasonable cause to believe that this conduct is likely to cause the residential occupier to give up occupation of the premises or to refrain from exercising any right or pursuing any remedy in respect of the premises.

Much of the wording of the section is derived from the Protection from Eviction Act 1977.

It has been held by the Court of Session in Scotland, that the expression "acting on his behalf" in Housing (Scotland) Act 1988 s.36 (the Scottish equivalent to Housing Act 1988 s.27) is clear and unambiguous and encompasses anyone who is acting either as direct agent of the landlord, or as someone employed to do a particular act, or to undertake the management of the property with no particular fetter. It should not be read as imposing liability only where a landlord instigated or at least connived at his agent's illegitimate activities (*Scott v Thomson* 2003 S.L.T. 99, Court of Session, Ex Div.)

The word "unlawfully" means that the section applies not only to acts or omissions which are a trespass or a breach of contract, but also to acts which amount to breaches of the Protection from Eviction Act 1977 s.2 (Re-entry without court order), and s.3 (Eviction of former unprotected tenant or licensee without taking court proceedings).

Purchasers who are let into occupation as licensees before completion of the sale of premises may come within the definition of "landlord" in s.27(9)(c) (*Jones v Miah* (1992) 24 H.L.R. 578; [1992] 33 E.G. 59, CA). However, ss.27 and 28 impose liability on landlords alone to pay damages and accordingly no claim under these sections can lie against a landlord's agent as a joint tortfeasor (*Sampson v Wilson* [1996] Ch. 39; [1995] 3 W.L.R. 455, CA).

Landlords have a defence to proceedings if they can show that they "believed, or had reasonable cause to believe" that the occupier had ceased to occupy the premises, or that there were "reasonable grounds" for withdrawing or withholding services. It should also be noted that no damages are recoverable under ss.27 and 28 if the residential occupier is reinstated in the premises by the time at which any civil proceedings are disposed of or if a landlord has offered to reinstate the tenant and it was unreasonable of the tenant to refuse the offer of reinstatement (s.27(6) and (7)). In *Tagro v Cafane and Patel* [1991] 2 All E.R. 235, CA, the Court of Appeal held that, even though the tenant had obtained an injunction and even though the landlords had offered a key to a room which had been "wrecked", there had not been a reinstatement satisfying the Housing Act 1988 s.27(6)(b). See too *Wandsworth LBC v Osei-Bonsu* [1999] 1 All E.R. 265, CA.

A landlord's contention that s.27 only applies where "the seriousness of the

***Paragraph numbers marked with a "+" can be found online and on CD.***

landlord's conduct is established to a high degree and where he makes the tenant's position so intolerable that he is driven out of the property" was rejected by the Court of Appeal in *Abbott v Bayley* (2000) 32 H.L.R. 72, CA.

The real significance of s.27 is not the scope of the cause of action, which is narrower than the covenant for quiet enjoyment, but the way in which damages are to be assessed (see commentary to s.28 below).

## The measure of damages

**28.**—(1) The basis for the assessment of damages referred to in section 27(3) above is the difference in value, determined as at the time immediately before the residential occupier ceased to occupy the premises in question as his residence, between— **3A–913**

(a) the value of the interest of the landlord in default determined on the assumption that the residential occupier continues to have the same right to occupy the premises as before that time; and

(b) the value of that interest determined on the assumption that the residential occupier has ceased to have that right.

(2) In relation to any premises, any reference in this section to the interest of the landlord in default is a reference to his interest in the building in which the premises in question are comprised (whether or not that building contains any other premises) together with its curtilage.

(3) For the purposes of the valuations referred to in subsection (1) above, it shall be assumed—

(a) that the landlord in default is selling his interest on the open market to a willing buyer;

(b) that neither the residential occupier nor any member of his family wishes to buy; and

(c) that it is unlawful to carry out any substantial development of any of the land in which the landlord's interest subsists or to demolish the whole or part of any building on that land.

(4) In this section "the landlord in default" has the same meaning as in section 27 above and subsection (9) of that section applies in relation to this section as it applies in relation to that.

(5) Section 113 of the Housing Act 1985 (meaning of "members of a person's family") applies for the purposes of subsection (3)(b) above.

(6) The reference in subsection (3)(c) above to substantial development of any of the land in which the landlord's interest subsists is a reference to any development other than—

(a) development for which planning permission is granted by a general development order for the time being in force and which is carried out so as to comply with any condition or limitation subject to which planning permission is so granted; or

(b) a change of use resulting in the building referred to in subsection (2) above or any part of it being used as, or as part of, one or more dwelling-houses;

and in this subsection "general development order" has the meaning given in section 56(6) of the Town and Country Planning Act 1990 and other expressions have the same meaning as in that Act.

3A–914 *Note* —Amended by the Planning (Consequential Provisions) Act 1990 Sch.2, para.79(1).

**"landlord"**

3A–915 See s.27(9).

**"residential occupier"**

3A–916 See s.27(9) and the Protection from Eviction Act 1977 s.1, which defines "residential occupier" as "a person occupying the premises as a residence, whether under a contract or by virtue of any enactment or rule of law giving him the right to remain in occupation or restricting the right of any other person to recover possession of the premises."

**"member of his family"**

3A–917 See the Housing Act 1985 s.113.

**The measure of damages**

3A–918 Section 28 provides that damages are to be determined by subtracting the value of the premises if the tenant had remained in occupation from the value of the premises with vacant possession. In making such valuations, it is assumed that:

(i) The landlord is selling on the open market to a willing buyer; and
(ii) Neither the tenant nor any member of the tenant's family wishes to buy; and
(iii) No substantial development on the premises can be carried out unless planning permission has been granted by general development order within the meaning of the Town & County Planning Act 1990 s.56(6)).

Where a tenant is wrongfully evicted, but the eviction makes no difference to the value of the landlord's interest in the property, no damages can be awarded under the Housing Act 1988 ss.27 and 28 (*Melville v Bruton* (1997) 29 H.L.R. 319, CA).

In *Regalgrand Ltd v Dickerson* (1997) 29 H.L.R. 620; (1997) 75 P. & C.R. 313, CA, the judge reduced the tenants' damages from £12,000 to £1,500 pursuant to s.27(7)(a) because their conduct "was such that it [was] reasonable to mitigate the damages". The relevant conduct which she took into acount were:

(a) the withholding of rent without giving prior notice and without justification;
(b) the tenants' failure to inform the landlord that his installation of a new boiler had failed to cure the heating problems; and
(c) their intention to vacate in any event.

The tenants appealed on the grounds that the landlord had failed to plead mitigation, that the judge had failed to specify how she had arrived at the figure of £1,500, that their omissions were not "conduct" and that the judge had been wrong to take into account the arrears of rent. The Court of Appeal dismissed the appeal. Failure to pay rent was conduct. Although a mere intention (e.g. to leave) cannot amount to conduct, here the intention to leave has been partly acted upon because the tenants had moved their belongings and only very occasionally resided in the flat.

In view of s.27(5), damages awarded at common law for the loss of the right to occupy premises should be set off against damages awarded under ss.27 and 28 (*Mason v Nwokorie* (1994) 26 H.L.R. 60; [1994] 05 E.G. 155, CA). However, *Mason v Nwokorie* was distinguished in *Kaur (Kashmir) v Gill*, *The Times*, June 15, 1995, CA, where an award of general damages in addition to ss.27-28 damages was upheld because the damages had not been awarded for any loss of right to occupy, but rather for breaches of the covenant for quite enjoyment. Note that:

> "... where damages have been awarded to the tenant against the landlord under sections 27 and 28, there is no place for a further award of exemplary damages against either the landlord or against the person who assisted her in the eviction", but that principle does not prevent the award of aggravated damages" (per Sir Iain Glidewell in *Francis v Brown* (1997) 30 H.L.R. 143, CA).

In relation to damages, see also *Murray v Aslam* (1995) 27 H.L.R. 284, CA; *Francis v*

***Paragraph numbers marked with a "+" can be found online and on CD.***

*Brown* (1997) 30 H.L.R. 143, CA; *King v Jackson* (1998) 30 H.L.R. 541; [1998] 03 E.G. 138, CA and *Wandsworth LBC v Osei-Bonsu* [1999] 1 All E.R. 265, CA.

* * * *

CHAPTER V

PHASING OUT OF RENT ACTS AND OTHER TRANSITIONAL PROVISIONS

## New protected tenancies and agricultural occupancies restricted to special cases

**34.**—(1) A tenancy which is entered into on or after the commencement of this Act cannot be a protected tenancy, unless— **3A–919**

(a) it is entered into in pursuance of a contract made before the commencement of this Act; or

(b) it is granted to a person (alone or jointly with others) who, immediately before the tenancy was granted, was a protected or statutory tenant and is so granted by the person who at that time was the landlord (or one of the joint landlords) under the protected or statutory tenancy; or

(c) it is granted to a person (alone or jointly with others) in the following circumstances—

(i) prior to the grant of the tenancy, an order for possession of a dwelling-house was made against him (alone or jointly with others) on the court being satisfied as mentioned in section 98(1)(a) of, or Case 1 in Schedule 16 to the Rent Act 1977 or Case 1 in Schedule 4 to the Rent (Agriculture) Act 1976 (suitable alternative accommodation available); and

(ii) the tenancy is of the premises which constitute the suitable alternative accommodation as to which the court was so satisfied; and

(iii) in the proceedings for possession the court considered that, in the circumstances, the grant of an assured tenancy would not afford the required security and, accordingly, directed that the tenancy would be a protected tenancy; or

(d) it is a tenancy under which the interest of the landlord was at the time the tenancy was granted held by a the Commission for the New Towns or a development corporation, within the meaning of section 80 of the Housing Act 1985, and, before the date which has effect by virtue of paragraph (a) or paragraph (b) of subsection (4) of section 38 below, ceased to be so held by virtue of a disposal by the commission for the New Towns made pursuant to a direction under section 37 of the New Towns Act 1981.

(2) In subsection (1)(b) above "protected tenant" and "statutory tenant" do not include—

***Paragraph numbers marked with a "+" can be found online and on CD.***

(a) a tenant under a protected shorthold tenancy;

(b) a protected or statutory tenant of a dwelling-house which was let under a protected shorthold tenancy which ended before the commencement of this Act and in respect of which at that commencement either there has been no grant of a further tenancy or any grant of a further tenancy has been to the person who, immediately before the grant, was in possession of the dwelling-house as a protected or statutory tenant;

and in this subsection "protected shorthold tenancy" includes a tenancy which, in proceedings for possession under Case 19 in Schedule 15 to the Rent Act 1977, is treated as a protected shorthold tenancy.

(3) In any case where—

(a) by virtue of subsections (1) and (2) above, a tenancy entered into on or after the commencement of this Act is an assured tenancy, but

(b) apart from subsection (2) above, the effect of subsection (1)(b) above would be that the tenancy would be a protected tenancy, and

(c) the landlord and the tenant under the tenancy are the same as at the coming to an end of the protected or statutory tenancy which, apart from subsection (2) above, would fall within subsection (1)(b) above,

the tenancy shall be an assured shorthold tenancy (whether or not in the case of a tenancy to which the provision applies it fulfils the conditions in section 20(1) above) unless, before the tenancy is entered into, the landlord serves notice on the tenant that it is not to be a shorthold tenancy.

(4) A licence or tenancy which is entered into on or after the commencement of this Act cannot be a relevant licence or relevant tenancy for the purposes of the Rent (Agriculture) Act 1976 (in this subsection referred to as "the 1976 Act") unless—

(a) it is entered into in pursuance of a contract made before the commencement of this Act, or

(b) it is granted to a person (alone or jointly with others) who, immediately before the licence or tenancy was granted, was a protected occupier or statutory tenant, within the meaning of the 1976 Act, and is so granted by the person who at that time was the landlord or licensor (or one of the joint landlords or licensors) under the protected occupancy or statutory tenancy in question.

(5) Except as provided in subsection (4) above, expressions used in this section have the same meaning as in the Rent Act 1977.

**3A–920** *Note* —Amended by the Local Government and Housing Act 1989 s.195, Sch.11; Housing Act 1996 s.104, Sch.8, para.2 and the Housing and Regeneration Act 2008 (Consequential Provisions) Order 2008 (SI 2008/3002) para.37.

**"commencement of this Act"**

**3A–921** See s.141(2), which provides that Pt I shall come into force "at the expiry of the period of two months beginning on the day it is passed"—i.e. January 15, 1989.

***Paragraph numbers marked with a "+" can be found online and on CD.***

**"assured shorthold tenancy"**

See ss.19A and 20. **3A-922**

**"protected shorthold tenancy"**

See the Housing Act 1980 s.52. **3A-923**

**"landlord", and "tenancy"**

See s.45. **3A-924**

**New protected tenancies and agricultural occupancies restricted to special cases**

Section 34 provides that no new Rent Act protected tenancies can be created after the Act came into force unless one of three exceptions applies. All new tenancies created on or after January 15, 1989 are assured or assured shorthold tenancies or totally unprotected tenancies unless: **3A-925**

(1) The tenancy was entered into in pursuance of a contract made before January 15, 1989, or

(2) The tenancy was granted to an existing 1977 Rent Act protected or statutory tenant by the same landlord. If there are joint tenants or joints landlords, it is sufficient for only one of the joint tenants to have been a protected tenant and for only one of the joint landlords to have been the landlord of the existing tenant or tenants. In *Secretarial Nominee Co Ltd v Thomas* [2005] EWCA Civ 1008; [2006] H.L.R. 5, the Court of Appeal held that s.34 "begins with the concept of a person who, after the commencement of the 1988 Act, is both a Rent Act tenant and has entered into a new tenancy. Such a person, moreover, has to have been a Rent Act tenant already before the new tenancy". The words "and prior to the commencement of this Act" in s.34 "have to be understood (in addition to the express requirement of "immediately before the tenancy was granted") as inherently qualifying the words "was a protected or statutory tenant". It is for the sake of such a tenant, and no other that the transitional protection of a protected tenancy is extended." The statutory language shows that the protection is for a particular person. Section 34 accordingly gave no rights to a person who had never been a joint tenant with a Rent Act tenant.

It is clear from *Hansard* (June 30, 1988, cols 75 and 87) that Parliament's intention was that this exception should apply even if the tenant was a protected tenant in other accommodation but has been granted a new post-January 15, 1989 tenancy in, say, a different building. This was confirmed by the Court of Appeal in *Laimond Properites Ltd v Al-Shakarchi* (1998) 30 H.L.R. 1099, CA, where the Court of Appeal held that s.34(1)(a), (b) and (c) deal with three separate situations. Section 34(1)(b) has no application in a case where the landlords have obtained an order for possession since the court "will have considered whether the new tenancy affords 'the required security' and whether the court should direct that the new tenancy be a protected tenancy". Roch L.J. also: (1) accepted submissions that s.34(1)(b) was mandatory, not permissive; and (2) approving *Gorringe v Twinsectra Ltd*, June 1994, Legal Action 11(cc), held that s.34(1)(b) protection applies both to new tenancies of the same premises and to tenancies of other premises granted by the same landlords. See too *Rajah v Arogol Co Ltd* [2001] EWCA Civ 454; [2002] H.L.R. 21, CA. It is the identity of the landlord and tenant that matters, not the identity of the premises. Further, the fact that the landlord has changed between the grant of the two tenancies does not affect the position. Section 34(1)(b) clearly refers to a grant at a later date by the person who was the landlord at the time of the later grant. Note too in *McAllister v Queens Cross Housing Association Ltd*, 2003 S.L.T. 971, a case involving a similar provision in Housing (Scotland) Act 1987 s.43(3)(c), where it was held that there is no requirement that the earlier tenancy should be of the same premises.

(3) Before the grant of the new tenancy an order for possession was made on the grounds of suitable alternative accommodation against a protected or statutory tenant (Rent Act 1977 s.98(1)(a) or Sched.16, Case 1) and in the possession proceedings relating to the earlier tenancy, the court directed that the tenancy of the suitable alternative accommodation shall be held on a protected tenancy. The court may make such a direction if an assured tenancy "would not afford the required security".

HOUSING

***Paragraph numbers marked with a "+" can be found online and on CD.***

**"restricted contracts"**

3A–926 For the effect of Housing Act 1988 ss.34(1) and 36(2)(a) on restricted contracts, see *Rowe v Matthews* (2001) 33 H.L.R. 81, QBD.

## Removal of special regimes for tenancies of housing associations etc.

3A–927 **35.**—(1) In this section "housing association tenancy" has the same meaning as in Part VI of the Rent Act 1977.

(2) A tenancy which is entered into on or after the commencement of this Act cannot be a housing association tenancy unless—

(a) it is entered into in pursuance of a contract made before the commencement of this Act, or

(b) it is granted to a person (alone or jointly with others) who, immediately before the tenancy was granted, was a tenant under a housing association tenancy and is so granted by the person who at that time was the landlord under that housing association tenancy; or

(c) it is granted to a person (alone or jointly with others) in the following circumstances—

(i) prior to the grant of the tenancy, an order for possession of a dwelling-house was made against him (alone or jointly with others) on the court being satisfied as mentioned in paragraph (b) or paragraph (c) of subsection (2) of section 84 of the Housing Act 1985; and

(ii) the tenancy is of the premises which constitute the suitable accommodation as to which the court was so satisfied; and

(iii) in the proceedings for possession the court directed that the tenancy would be a housing association tenancy; or

(d) it is a tenancy under which the interest of the landlord was at the time the tenancy was granted held by the Commission for the New Towns or a development corporation, within the meaning of section 80 of the Housing Act 1985, and, before the date which has effect by virtue of paragraph (a) or paragraph (b) of subsection (4) of section 38 below, ceased to be so held by virtue of a disposal by the Commission for the New Towns made pursuant to a direction under section 37 of the New Towns Act 1981.

(3) Where, on or after the commencement of this Act, a registered social landlord, within the meaning of the Housing Act 1985 (see section 5(4) and (5) of that Act), grants a secure tenancy pursuant to an obligation under section 554(2A) of the Housing Act 1985 (as set out in Schedule 17 to this Act) then, in determining whether that tenancy is a housing association tenancy, it shall be assumed for the purposes only of section 86(2)(b) of the Rent Act 1977 (tenancy would be a protected tenancy but for section 15 or 16 of that Act) that the tenancy was granted before the commencement of this Act.

(4) Subject to section 38(4A) below a tenancy or licence which is entered into on or after the commencement of this Act cannot be a secure tenancy unless—

(a) the interest of the landlord belongs to a local authority, a development corporation or an urban development corporation, all within the meaning of section 80 of the Housing Act 1985, or a housing action trust established under Part III of this Act; or

(b) the interest of the landlord belongs to a housing co-operative within the meaning of section 27B of the Housing Act 1985 (agreements between local housing authorities and housing co-operatives) and the tenancy or licence is of a dwelling-house comprised in a housing co-operative agreement falling within that section, or

(ba) the interest of the landlord belongs to the Homes and Communities Agency or the Welsh Ministers and the tenancy or licence falls within section 80(2A) to (2E) of the Housing Act 1985; or

(c) it is entered into in pursuance of a contract made before the commencement of this Act, or

(d) it is granted to a person (alone or jointly with others) who, immediately before it was entered into, was a secure tenant and is so granted by the body which at that time was the landlord or licensor under the secure tenancy, or

(e) it is granted to a person (alone or jointly with others) in the following circumstances—

(i) prior to the grant of the tenancy or licence, an order for possession of a dwelling-house was made against him (alone or jointly with others) on the court being satisfied as mentioned in paragraph (b) or paragraph (c) of subsection (2) of section 84 of the Housing Act 1985; and

(ii) the tenancy or licence is of the premises which constitute the suitable accommodation as to which the court was so satisfied; and

(iii) in the proceedings for possession the court considered that, in the circumstances, the grant of an assured tenancy would not afford the required security and, accordingly, directed that the tenancy or licence would be a secure tenancy; or

(f) it is granted pursuant to an obligation under section 554(2A) of the Housing Act 1985 (as set out in Schedule 17 to this Act).

(5) If, on or after the commencement of this Act, the interest of the landlord under a protected or statutory tenancy becomes held by a housing association, a housing trust or the Housing Corporation or, where that interest becomes held by him as a result of the exercise by him of the functions under Part III of the Housing Associations Act 1985, the Secretary of State, nothing in the preceding provisions

of this section shall prevent the tenancy from being a housing association tenancy or a secure tenancy and, accordingly, in such a case section 80 of the Housing Act 1985 (and any enactment which refers to that section) shall have effect without regard to the repeal of provisions of that section effected by this Act.

(6) In subsection (5) above "housing association" and "housing trust" have the same meaning as in the Housing Act 1985.

3A–928 *Note*—Amended by the Local Government and Housing Act 1989 s.195, Sch.11; the Housing Act 1996 (Consequential Provisions) Order 1996 (SI 1996/2325) art.5, Sch.2, para.18, Government of Wales Act 1998 Sch.15, para.15; Government of Wales Act 1998 (Housing) (Amendments) Order 1999 (SI 1999/61) and the Housing and Regeneration Act 2008 (Consequential Provisions) Order 2008 (SI 2008/3002) para.38.

**"commencement of this Act"**

3A–929 See s.141(2) which provides that Pt I shall come into force "at the expiry of the period of two months beginning on the day it is passed"—i.e. January 15, 1989.

**"housing association tenancy"**

3A–930 See the Rent Act 1977 s.86.

**"secure tenancy"**

3A–931 See s.45 and the Housing Act 1985 s.79 (above).

**"landlord" and "tenancy"**

3A–932 See s.45.

## New restricted contracts limited to transitional cases

3A–933 **36.**—(1) A tenancy or other contract entered into after the commencement of this Act cannot be a restricted contract for the purposes of the Rent Act 1977 unless it is entered into in pursuance of a contract made before the commencement of this Act.

(2) If the terms of a restricted contract are varied after this Act comes into force then, subject to subsection (3) below,—

(a) if the variation affects the amount of the rent which, under the contract, is payable for the dwelling in question, the contract shall be treated as a new contract entered into at the time of the variation (and subsection (1) above shall have effect accordingly); and

(b) if the variation does not affect the amount of the rent which, under the contract, is so payable, nothing in this section shall affect the determination of the question whether the variation is such as to give rise to a new contract.

(3) Any reference in subsection (2) above to a variation affecting the amount of the rent which, under a contract, is payable for a dwelling does not include a reference to—

(a) a reduction or increase effected under section 78 of the Rent Act 1977(power of rent tribunal); or

(b) a variation which is made by the parties and has the effect of making the rent expressed to be payable under the contract the same as the rent for the dwelling which is entered in the register under section 79 of the Rent Act 1977.

(4) In subsection (1) of section 81A of the Rent Act 1977 (cancellation of registration of rent relating to a restricted contract) paragraph (a) (no cancellation until two years have elapsed since the date of the entry) shall cease to have effect.

(5) In this section "rent" has the same meaning as in Part V of the Rent Act 1977.

**"restricted contract"**

See the Rent Act 1977 ss.19 and 20. For the effect of Housing Act 1988 ss.34(1) and 36(2)(a) on restricted contracts, see *Rowe v Matthews* (2001) 33 H.L.R. 81, QBD. **3A–934**

**"commencement of this Act"**

See s.141(2), which provides that Pt I shall come into force "at the expiry of the period of two months beginning on the day it is passed"—i.e. January 15, 1989. **3A–935**

**"landlord" and "tenancy"**

See s.45. **3A–936**

**"rent"**

See the Rent Act 1977 s.85(3). **3A–937**

* * * *

CHAPTER VI

GENERAL PROVISIONS

## Jurisdiction of county courts

**40.**—(1) A county court shall have jurisdiction to hear and determine any question arising under any provision of— **3A–938**

(a) Chapters I to III and V above, or

(b) sections 27 and 28 above,

other than a question falling within the jurisdiction of a rent assessment committee by virtue of any such provision.

(2) [...]

(3) Where any proceedings under any provision mentioned in subsection (1) above are being taken in a county court, the court shall have jurisdiction to hear and determine any other proceedings joined with those proceedings, notwithstanding that, apart from this subsection, those other proceedings would be outside the court's jurisdiction.

(4) If any person takes any proceedings under any provision mentioned in subsection (1) above in the High Court, he shall not be entitled to recover any more costs of those proceedings than those to which he would have been entitled if the proceedings had been taken in a county court: and in such a case the taxing master shall have the same power of directing on what county court scale costs are to be allowed, and of allowing any item of costs, as the judge would have had if the proceedings had been taken in a county court.

(5) Subsection (4) above shall not apply where the purpose of taking the proceedings in the High Court was to enable them to be joined with any proceedings already pending before that court (not being proceedings taken under any provision mentioned in subsection (1) above).

***Paragraph numbers marked with a "+" can be found online and on CD.***

3A–939 *Note*—Amended by the High Court and County Courts Jurisdiction Order 1991 (SI 1991/724).

* * * *

## Interpretation of Part I

3A–940 **45.**—(1) In this part of this Act, except where the context otherwise requires—

"dwelling-house" may be a house or part of a house;

"fixed term tenancy" means any tenancy other than a periodic tenancy;

"fully mutual housing association" has the same meaning as in Part I of the Housing Associations Act 1985;

"landlord" includes any person from time to time deriving title under the original landlord and also includes, in relation to a dwelling-house, any person other than a tenant who is, or but for the existence of an assured tenancy would be, entitled to possession of the dwelling-house;

"let" includes "sub-let";

"prescribed" means prescribed by regulations made by the Secretary of State by statutory instrument;

"rates" includes water rates and charges but does not include an owner's drainage rate, as defined in section 63(2)(a) of the Land Drainage Act 1976;

"secure tenancy" has the meaning assigned by section 79 of the Housing Act 1985;

"statutory periodic tenancy" has the meaning assigned by section 5(7) above;

"tenancy" includes a sub-tenancy and an agreement for a tenancy or sub-tenancy; and

"tenant" includes a sub-tenant and any person deriving title under the original tenant or sub-tenant.

(2) Subject to paragraph 11 of Schedule 2 to this Act, any reference in this Part of this Act to the beginning of a tenancy is a reference to the day on which the tenancy is entered into or, if it is later, the day on which, under the terms of any lease, agreement or other document, the tenant is entitled to possession under the tenancy.

(3) Where two or more persons jointly constitute either the landlord or the tenant in relation to a tenancy, then, except where this Part of this Act otherwise provides, any reference to the landlord or to the tenant is a reference to all the persons who jointly constitute the landlord or the tenant, as the case may require.

(4) For the avoidance of doubt, it hereby declared that any reference in this Part of this Act (however expressed) to a power for a landlord to determine a tenancy does not include a reference to a power of re-entry or forfeiture for breach of any term or condition of the tenancy.

(5) Regulations under subsection (1) above may make different provision with respect to different cases or descriptions of case, including different provisions for different areas.

**Prescribed**

See the Assured Tenancies and Agricultural Occupancies (Forms) Regulations (SI 1988/2203), amended by the Assured Tenancies and Agricultural Occupancies (Forms) (Amendment) Regulations (SI 1989/146); the Assured Tenancies and Agricultural Occupancies (Forms) (Amendment) Regulations 1990 (SI 1990/1532); the Assured Tenancies and Agricultural Occupancies (Forms) (Amendment) Regulations 1993 (SI 1993/654); the Assured Tenancies and Agricultural Occupancies (Forms) Regulations 1997 (SI 1997/194) and the Assured Tenancies and Agricultural (Forms) (Amendment) (England) Regulations 2003 (SI 2003/260). **3A–941**

* * * *

SECTION 1

# SCHEDULE 1

## TENANCIES WHICH CANNOT BE ASSURED TENANCIES

## PART I

## THE TENANCIES

*Tenancies entered into before commencement*

1. A tenancy which is entered into before, or pursuant to a contract made before, the commencement of this Act. **3A–942**

*Tenancies of dwelling-houses with high rateable values*

2.—(1) A tenancy— **3A–943**

(a) which is entered into on or after 1st April 1990 (otherwise than, where the dwelling-house had a rateable value on 31st March 1990, in pursuance of a contract made before 1st April 1990), and

(b) under which the rent payable for the time being is payable at a rate exceeding £25,000 a year.

(2) In sub-paragraph (1) "rent" does not include any sum payable by the tenant as is expressed (in whatever terms) to be payable in respect of rates, council tax, services, management, repairs, maintenance or insurance, unless it could not have been regarded by the parties to the tenancy as a sum so payable.

(2A.) A tenancy—

(a) which was entered into before the 1st April 1990, or on or after that date in pursuance of a contract made before that date, and

(b) under which the dwelling-house had a rateable value on 31st March 1990 which, if it is in Greater London, exceeded £1,500 and, if it is elsewhere, exceeded £750.

*Tenancies at a low rent*

3. A tenancy under which for the time being no rent is payable. **3A–944**

(3A.) A tenancy—

(a) which is entered into on or after 1st April 1990 (otherwise than, where the dwelling-house had a rateable value on 31st March 1990, in pursuance of a contract made before 1st April 1990), and

(b) under which the rent payable for the time being is payable at a rate of, if the dwelling-house is in Greater London, £1,000 or less a year and, if it is elsewhere, £250 or less a year.

(3B.) A tenancy—

(a) which was entered into before 1st April 1990 or, where the dwelling-house had a rateable value on the 31st March 1990, on or after 1st April 1990 in pursuance of a contract made before that date, and

(b) under which the rent for the time being payable is less than two-thirds of the rateable value of the dwelling-house on 31st March 1990.

(3C.) Paragraph 2(2) above applies for the purposes of paragraphs 3, 3A and 3B as it applies for the purposes of paragraph 2(1).

***Paragraph numbers marked with a "+" can be found online and on CD.***

*Business tenancies*

3A–945 4. A tenancy to which Part II of the Landlord and Tenant Act 1954 applies (business tenancies).

*Licensed premises*

3A–946 5. A tenancy under which the dwelling-house consists of or premises which, by virtue of a premises licence under the Licensing Act 2003 may be used for the supply of alcohol (within the meaning of section 14 of that Act) for consumption on the premises.

*Tenancies of agricultural land*

3A–947 6.—(1) A tenancy under which agricultural land, exceeding two acres, is let together with the dwelling-house.

(2) In this paragraph "agricultural land" has the meaning set out in section 26(3)(a) of the General Rate Act 1967(exclusion of agricultural land and premises from liability for rating).

*Tenancies of agricultural holdings etc*

3A–948 7.—(1) A tenancy under which the dwelling-house—

(a) is comprised in an agricultural holding, and

(b) is occupied by the person responsible for the control (whether as tenant or as servant or agent of the tenant) of the farming of the holding.

(2) A tenancy under which the dwelling-house—

(a) is comprised in the holding held under a farm business tenancy, and

(b) is occupied by the person responsible for the control (whether as tenant or as servant or agent of the tenant) of the management of the holding.

(3) In this paragraph—

"agricultural holding" means any agricultural holding within the meaning of the Agricultural Holdings Act 1986 held under a tenancy in relation to which that Act applies, and

"farm business tenancy" and "holding", in relation to such a tenancy, have the same meaning as in the Agricultural Tenancies Act 1995.

*Lettings to students*

3A–949 8.—(1) A tenancy which is granted to a person who is pursuing, or intends to pursue, a course of study provided by a specified educational institution and is so granted either by that institution or by another specified institution or body of persons.

(2) In sub-paragraph (1) above "specified" means specified, or of a class specified, for the purposes of this paragraph by regulations made by the Secretary of State by statutory instrument.

(3) A statutory instrument made in the exercise of the power conferred by sub-paragraph (2) above shall be subject to annulment in pursuance of a resolution of either House of Parliament.

*Holiday lettings*

3A–950 9. A tenancy the purpose of which is to confer on the tenant the right to occupy the dwelling-house for a holiday.

*Resident landlords*

3A–951 10.—(1) A tenancy in respect of which the following conditions are fulfilled—

(a) that the dwelling-house forms part only of a building and, except in a case where the dwelling-house also forms part of a flat, the building is not a purpose-built block of flats, and

(b) that, subject to Part III of this Schedule, the tenancy was granted by an individual who, at the time when the tenancy was granted, occupied as his only or principal home another dwelling-house which,—

(i) in the case mentioned in paragraph (a) above, also forms part of the flat; or

(ii) in any other case, also forms part of the building; and

***Paragraph numbers marked with a "+" can be found online and on CD.***

(c) that, subject to Part III of this Schedule, at all times since the tenancy was granted the interest of the landlord under the tenancy has belonged to an individual who, at the time he owned that interest, occupied as his only or principal home another dwelling-house which,—

(i) in the case mentioned in paragraph (a) above, also formed part of the flat, or

(ii) in any other case, also formed part of the building; and

(d) that the tenancy is not one which is excluded from this sub-paragraph by sub-paragraph (3) below.

(2) If a tenancy was granted by two or more persons jointly, the reference in sub-paragraph (1)(b) above to an individual is a reference to any one of those persons and if the interest of the landlord is for the time being held by two or more persons jointly, the reference in sub-paragraph (1)(c) above to an individual is a reference to any one of those persons.

(3) A tenancy (in this sub-paragraph referred to as "the new tenancy") is excluded from sub-paragraph (1) above if—

(a) it is granted to a person (alone, or jointly with others) who, immediately before it was granted, was a tenant under an assured tenancy (in this sub-paragraph referred to as "the former tenancy") of the same dwelling-house or of another dwelling-house which forms part of the building in question; and

(b) the landlord under the new tenancy and under the former tenancy is the same person or, if either of those tenancies is or was granted by two or more persons jointly, the same person is the landlord or one of the landlords under each tenancy.

*Crown tenancies*

11.—(1) A tenancy under which the interest of the landlord belongs to Her Majesty in right of the Crown or to a government department or is held in trust for Her Majesty for the purpose of a government department. **3A–952**

(2) The reference in sub-paragraph (1) above to the case where the interest of the landlord belongs to Her Majesty in right of the Crown does not include the case where that interest is under the management of the Crown Estate Commissioners or it is held by him as a result of the exercise by him of the functions under Part III 1985 of the Housing Associations Act 1985.

*Local authority tenancies etc.*

12.—(1) A tenancy under which the interest of the landlord belongs to— **3A–953**

(a) a local authority, as defined in sub-paragraph (2) below;

(b) the Homes and Communities Agency but only if the tenancy falls within subsections (2A) to (2E) of section 80 of the Housing Act 1985;

(ba) the Welsh Ministers but only if the tenancy falls within subsections (2A) to (2E) of section 80 of the Housing Act 1985;

(c) [...]

(d) an urban development corporation established by an order under section 135 of the Local Government, Planning and Land Act 1980;

(e) a development corporation, within the meaning of the New Towns Act 1981;

(f) an authority established under section 10 of the Local Government Act 1985 (waste disposal authorities);

(fa) an authority established for an area in England by an order under section 207 of the Local Government and Public Involvement in Health Act 2007 (joint waste authorities);

(g) a residuary body, within the meaning of the Local Government Act 1985; or

(gg) The Residuary Body for Wales (Corff Gweddilliol Cymru);

(h) a fully mutual housing association; or

(i) a housing action trust established under Part III of this Act.

(2) The following are local authorities for the purposes of sub-paragraph (1)(a) above—

(a) the council of a county, county borough, district or London borough;

***Paragraph numbers marked with a "+" can be found online and on CD.***

HOUSING

(b) the Common Council of the City of London;

(c) the Council of the Isles of Scilly;

(d) the Broads Authority;

(da) a National Park authority;

(e) the Inner London Education Authority; and

(f) a joint authority, within the meaning of the Local Government Act 1985.

(g) a police authority established under section 3 of the Police Act 1964.

*Family intervention tenancies*

**3A–953.1** 12ZA.—(1) A family intervention tenancy.

(2) But a family intervention tenancy becomes an assured tenancy if the landlord notifies the tenant that it is to be regarded as an assured tenancy.

(3) In this paragraph "a family intervention tenancy" means, subject to sub-paragraph (4), a tenancy granted by a registered provider of social housing or a registered social landlord ("the landlord") in respect of a dwelling-house—

(a) to a person ("the new tenant") against whom a possession order under section 7 in respect of another dwelling-house—

(i) has been made, in relation to an assured tenancy, on ground 14 or 14A of Part 2 of Schedule 2;

(ii) could, in the opinion of the landlord, have been so made in relation to such a tenancy; or

(iii) could, in the opinion of the landlord, have been so made if the person had had such a tenancy; and

(b) for the purposes of the provision of behaviour support services.

(4) A tenancy is not a family intervention tenancy for the purposes of this paragraph if the landlord has failed to serve a notice under sub-paragraph (5) on the new tenant before the new tenant entered into the tenancy.

(5) A notice under this sub-paragraph is a notice stating—

(a) the reasons for offering the tenancy to the new tenant;

(b) the dwelling-house in respect of which the tenancy is to be granted;

(c) the other main terms of the tenancy (including any requirements on the new tenant in respect of behaviour support services);

(d) the security of tenure available under the tenancy and any loss of security of tenure which is likely to result from the new tenant agreeing to enter into the tenancy;

(e) that the new tenant is not obliged to enter into the tenancy or (unless otherwise required to do so) to surrender any existing tenancy or possession of a dwelling-house;

(f) any likely action by the landlord if the new tenant does not enter into the tenancy or surrender any existing tenancy or possession of a dwelling-house.

(6) The appropriate national authority may by regulations made by statutory instrument amend sub-paragraph (5).

(7) A notice under sub-paragraph (5) must contain advice to the new tenant as to how the new tenant may be able to obtain assistance in relation to the notice.

(8) The appropriate national authority may by regulations made by statutory instrument make provision about the type of advice to be provided in such notices.

(9) Regulations under this paragraph may contain such transitional, transitory or saving provision as the appropriate national authority considers appropriate.

(10) A statutory instrument containing (whether alone or with other provision) regulations under this paragraph which amend or repeal any of paragraphs (a) to (f) of sub-paragraph (5) may not be made—

(a) by the Secretary of State unless a draft of the instrument has been laid before, and approved by a resolution of, each House of Parliament; and

(b) by the Welsh Ministers unless a draft of the instrument has been laid before, and approved by a resolution of, the National Assembly for Wales.

(11) Subject to this, a statutory instrument containing regulations made under this paragraph—

(a) by the Secretary of State is subject to annulment in pursuance of a resolution of either House of Parliament; and

(b) by the Welsh Ministers is subject to annulment in pursuance of a resolution of the National Assembly for Wales.

(12) In this paragraph—

"appropriate national authority"—

(a) in relation to England, means the Secretary of State; and

(b) in relation to Wales, means the Welsh Ministers;

"behaviour support agreement" means an agreement in writing about behaviour and the provision of support services made between the new tenant, the landlord and the local housing authority for the district in which the dwelling-house which is to be subject to the new tenancy is situated (or between persons who include those persons);

"behaviour support services" means relevant support services to be provided by any person to—

(a) the new tenant; or

(b) any person who is to reside with the new tenant; for the purpose of addressing the kind of behaviour which led to the new tenant falling within sub-paragraph (3)(a);

"family intervention tenancy" has the meaning given by sub-paragraph (3);

"family intervention tenancy" has the meaning given by sub-paragraph (3);

"landlord" has the meaning given by sub-paragraph (3);

"local housing authority" (and the reference to its district) has the same meaning as in the Housing Act 1985 (see sections 1 and 2(1) of that Act);

In this paragraph—

"the new tenant" has the meaning given by sub-paragraph (3)(a);

"registered social landlord" has the same meaning as in Part 1 of the Housing Act 1996;

"relevant support services" means support services of a kind identified in a behaviour support agreement and designed to meet such needs of the recipient as are identified in the agreement.

*Accommodation for asylum-seekers*

12A.—(1) A tenancy granted by a private landlord under arrangements for the provision of support for asylum-seekers or dependants or asylum-seekers made under section 4 or Part VI of the Immigration and Asylum Act 1999. **3A-954**

(2) Private landlord means a landlord who is not within section 80(1) of the Housing Act 1985.

12B.—(1) A tenancy granted by a private landlord under arrangements for the provision of accommodation for persons with temporary protection made under the Displaced Persons (Temporary Protection) Regulations 2005.

(2) "Private landlord" means a landlord who is not within section 80(1) of the Housing Act 1985.

*Transitional cases*

13.—(1) A protected tenancy, within the meaning of the Rent Act 1977. **3A-955**

(2) A housing association tenancy, within the meaning of Part VI of that Act.

(3) A secure tenancy.

(4) Where a person is a protected occupier of a dwelling-house, within the meaning of the Rent (Agriculture) Act 1976, the relevant tenancy, within the meaning of that Act, by virtue of which he occupies the dwelling-house.

## PART II

## RATEABLE VALUES

14.—(1) The rateable value of a dwelling-house at any time shall be ascertained for the purposes of Part I of this Schedule as follows— **3A-956**

(a) if the dwelling-house is a hereditament for which a rateable value is then shown in the valuation list, it shall be that rateable value;

***Paragraph numbers marked with a "+" can be found online and on CD.***

(b) if the dwelling-house forms part only of such a hereditament or consists of or forms part of more than one such hereditament, its rateable value shall be taken to be such value as is found by a proper apportionment or aggregation of the rateable value or values so shown.

(2) Any question arising under this Part of this Schedule as to the proper apportionment or aggregation of any value or values shall be determined by the county court and the decision of that court shall be final.

15. Where, after the time at which the rateable value of a dwelling-house is material for the purposes of any provision of Part I of this Schedule, the valuation list is altered so as to vary the rateable value of the hereditament of which the dwelling-house consists (in whole or in part) or forms part and the alteration has effect from that time or from an earlier time, the rateable value of the dwelling-house at the material time shall be ascertained as if the value shown in the valuation list at the material time had been the value shown in the list as altered.

16. Paragraphs 14 and 15 above apply in relation to any other land which, under section 2 of this Act, is treated as part of a dwelling-house as they apply in relation to the dwelling-house itself.

## PART III

## PROVISIONS FOR DETERMINING APPLICATION OF PARAGRAPH 10 (RESIDENT LANDLORDS)

3A–957 17.—(1) In determining whether the condition in paragraph 10(1)(c) above is at any time fulfilled with respect to a tenancy, there shall be disregarded—

(a) any period of not more than twenty-eight days, beginning with the date on which the interest of the landlord under the tenancy becomes vested at law and in equity in an individual who, during that period, does not occupy as his only or principal home another dwelling-house which forms part of the building or, as the case may be, flat concerned;

(b) if, within a period falling within paragraph (a) above, the individual concerned notifies the tenant in writing of his intention to occupy as his only or principal home another dwelling-house in the building or, as the case may be, flat concerned, the period beginning with the date on which the interest of the landlord under the tenancy becomes vested in that individual as mentioned in that paragraph and ending—

(i) at the expiry of the period of six months beginning on that date, or

(ii) on the date on which that interest ceases to be so vested, or

(iii) on the date on which that interest becomes again vested in such an individual as is mentioned in paragraph 10(1)(c) or the condition in that paragraph becomes deemed to be fulfilled by virtue of paragraph 18(1) or paragraph 20 below,

whichever is the earlier; and

(c) any period of not more than two years beginning with the date on which the interest of the landlord under the tenancy becomes, and during which it remains, vested—

(i) in trustees as such; or

(ii) by virtue of section 9 of the Administration of Estates Act 1925, in the Probate Judge or the Public Trustee, within the meaning of that Act.

(2) Where the interest of the landlord under a tenancy becomes vested at law and in equity in two or more persons jointly, of whom at least one was an individual, sub-paragraph (1) above shall have effect subject to the following modifications—

(a) in paragraph (a) for the words from "an individual" to "occupy" there shall be substituted "the joint landlords if, during that period none of them occupies"; and

(b) in paragraph (b) for the words "the individual concerned" there shall be substituted "any of the joint landlords who is an individual"and for the words "that individual" there shall be substituted "the joint landlords".

18.—(1) During any period when—

*Paragraph numbers marked with a "+" can be found online and on CD.*

(a) the interest of the landlord under the tenancy referred to in paragraph 10 above is vested in trustees as such, and
(b) that interest is held on trust for any person who or for two or more persons of whom at least one occupies as his only or principal home a dwelling-house which forms part of the building or, as the case may be, flat referred to in paragraph 10(1)(a),

the condition in paragraph 10(1)(c) shall be deemed to be fulfilled and accordingly, no part of that period shall be disregarded by virtue of paragraph 17 above.

(2) If a period during which the condition in paragraph 10(1)(c) is deemed to be fulfilled by virtue of sub-paragraph (1) above comes to an end on the death of a person who was in occupation of a dwelling-house as mentioned in paragraph (b) of that sub-paragraph, then, in determining whether that condition is at any time thereafter fulfilled, there shall be disregarded any period—

(a) which begins on the date of the death;
(b) during which the interest of the landlord remains vested as mentioned in sub-paragraph (1)(a) above; and
(c) which ends at the expiry of the period of two years beginning on the date of the death or on any earlier date on which the condition in paragraph 10(1)(c)becomes again deemed to be fulfilled by virtue of sub-paragraph (1) above.

19. In any case where—

(a) immediately before a tenancy comes to an end the condition in paragraph 10(1)(c) is deemed to be fulfilled by virtue of paragraph 18(1) above, and
(b) on the coming to an end of that tenancy the trustees in whom the interest of the landlord is vested grant a new tenancy of the same or substantially the same dwelling-house to a person (alone or jointly with others) who was the tenant or one of the tenants under the previous tenancy,

the condition in paragraph 10(1)(b) above shall be deemed to be fulfilled with respect to the new tenancy.

20.—(1) The tenancy referred to in paragraph 10 above falls within this paragraph if the interest of the landlord under the tenancy becomes vested in the personal representatives of a deceased person acting in that capacity.

(2) If the tenancy falls within this paragraph, the condition in paragraph 10(1)(c) shall be deemed to be fulfilled for any period, beginning with the date on which the interest becomes vested in the personal representatives and not exceeding two years, during which the interest of the landlord remains so vested.

21. Throughout any period which, by virtue of paragraph 17 or paragraph 18(2) above, falls to be disregarded for the purpose of determining whether the condition in paragraph 10(1)(c) is fulfilled with respect to a tenancy, no order shall be made for possession of the dwelling-house subject to that tenancy, other than an order which might be made if that tenancy were or, as the case may be, had been an assured tenancy.

22. For the purposes of paragraph 10 above, a building is a purpose-built block of flats if as constructed it contained, and it contains, two or more flats; and for this purpose "flat" means a dwelling-house which—

(a) forms part only of a building; and
(b) is separated horizontally from another dwelling-house which forms part of the same building.

*Note* —Amended by the Reference to Rating (Housing) Regulations 1990 (SI 1990/434); the Local Government (Wales) Act 1994 Sch.9, para.9, and Sch.13, para.31; the Law of Property (Miscellaneous Provisions) Act 1994 Sch.1, para.11; the Local Government Finance (Housing) (Consequential Amendments) Order 1993 (SI 1993/651); and the Police and Magistrates' Court Act 1994 Sch.4, para.62; the Environmental Act 1995 s.78, Sch.10, para.28; the Agricultural Tenancies 1995 Sch., para.34; the Trusts of Land and Appointment of Trustees Act 1996 s.25(2), Sch.4; the Government of Wales Act 1998 Sch.18, Pt IV; the Government of Wales Act 1998 (Housing) (Amendments) Order 1999 (SI 1999/61); the Immigration and Asylum Act 1999 Sch.14, **3A–958** para.88; the Licensing Act 2003 s.198(1), Sch.6, para.108; SI 2005/1379; the Immigration, Nationality and Asylum Act 2006 s.43(4); the Local Government and Public Involvement in Health Act 2007 s.209(2), Sch.13, Pt.II, para.44 with effect from April 1, 2008 (SI 2008/917), the Housing and Regeneration Act 2008 (Consequential Provisions) Order 2008 (SI 2008/3002) para.40, and the Housing and Regeneration Act 2008 s.297 with effect from January 1, 2009 (CO 2008/3068).

**Schedule 1**

3A-959 This Schedule lists types of tenancies which cannot be assured tenancies:

**Paragraph 1**

3A-960 A tenancy which is entered into before or pursuant to a contract made before January 15, 1989.

**"commencement of this Act"**

3A-961 See s.141(2) which provides that Pt I shall come into force "at the expiry of the period of two months beginning on the day it is passed"—i.e. January 15, 1989.

**Paragraph 2**

3A-962 Tenancies of dwelling-houses with high rateable values—i.e. over £1,500 in Greater London, over £750 elsewhere (compare the Rent Act 1977 s.4). Note that the References to Rating (Housing) Regulations 1990 (SI 1990/434) provide that where tenancies are granted after April 1, 1990, they cannot be assured if the rent is more than £25,000 per annum. "Rent" does not include sums paid in respect of services, repairs, maintenance or insurance.

In *Bankway Properties v Dunsford* [2001] EWCA Civ 528; [2001] 1 W.L.R. 1369, CA the Court of Appeal found that a clause permitting a landlord to increase the rent of a tenant in receipt of housing benefit to £25,000 per annum was a mere device, which enabled the landlord, effectively when it chose, to recover possession. In those circumstances it was unenforceable and the landlord's claim for possession based upon arrears was dismissed.

**Paragraph 3**

3A-963 Tenancies at a low rent—either where no rent is payable or where the rent is less than two thirds of the rateable value. The date for determining whether a tenancy is a tenancy at a low rent is the date when the relevant issue arises (*Woozley v Woodall Smith* [1950] 1 K.B. 325). In effect a tenancy may drift in and out of being an assured tenancy, subject to fluctuating costs (compare the Rent Act 1977 s.5). Note that The References to Rating (Housing) Regulations provide that tenancies granted after April 1, 1990 cannot be assured if the *rent* is less than £1,000 per annum in London or less than £250 per annum outside London.

**Paragraph 4**

3A-964 Business tenancies—see Pt II of the Landlord & Tenant Act 1954 (compare the Rent Act 1977 ss.2 and 24 and see commentary thereto) and *Broadway Investments Hackney Ltd v Grant* [2006] EWCA Civ 1709; [2007] H.L.R. 23; where, Lloyd L.J., after considering the Landlord and Tenant Act 1954 s.23, said that the question posed by that section:

> "is a factual one. Does the tenant occupy all or part of the premises comprised in the tenancy, and if so does he occupy them, or part of them, for the purposes of a business carried on by him, or for those and other purposes?"

**Paragraph 5**

3A-965 Tenancies under which dwelling-houses consists of or comprise premises licensed for the sale of intoxicating liquors for consumption on the premises (compare the Rent Act 1977 s.11).

**Paragraphs 6 and 7**

3A-966 Tenancies under which agricultural land, exceeding two acres is let together with the dwelling-house and agricultural holdings within the meaning of the Agricultural Holdings Act 1986 (compare the Rent Act 1977 s.10).

**Paragraph 8**

Lettings to students by a specified educational institution. See the Assured and Protected Tenancies (Lettings to Students) Regulations 1998 (SI 1998/1967), as amended, which define SEIs—basically any institution which provides higher or further education which is publicly funded and various other named institutions. Note also that lettings by registered housing associations to students cannot be assured tenancies (compare the Rent Act 1977 s.8). **3A-967**

**Paragraph 9**

Holiday lettings—where the purpose of the tenancy is to confer on the tenant the right to occupy the dwelling-house for a holiday (see commentary to the Rent Act 1977 s.9). In *Buchmann v May* [1978] 2 All E.R. 993; (1976) 240 E.G. 49, CA, the Court of Appeal held that the labels put on a transaction are not conclusive, but that where a tenancy agreement expressly states the purpose for which it is made, that statement is evidence of that purpose unless the tenant can establish that it does not correspond with the true purpose, either because the express label is a sham or because it is a false label. Although a court will be "astute to detect a sham where it appears that a provision has been inserted for the purpose of depriving the tenant of statutory protection under the Rent Acts" ([1978] 2 All E.R. at 999), the burden of proof lies on the tenant. In that case there was no evidence which displaced the express purpose and accordingly there was no Rent Act protection. The court accepted the dictionary definition of a holiday as "a period of cessation of work, or period of recreation". See also *R. v Rent Officer for Camden LBC Ex p. Plant* (1980) 257 E.G. 713; (1983) 7 H.L.R. 15, QBD, where there was "clear evidence that all the parties knew that [the applicants] were going to occupy it for the purpose of their work as students' and that that was "conclusive of the matter". **3A-968**

**Paragraph 10**

Compare the Rent Act 1977 s.12 and the commentary to that section. **3A-969**

The provision of "Board" is *not* an exception (compare the Rent Act 1977 s.7).

**Paragraph 12**

Welsh Development Agency—Note that some tenants of the Welsh Development Agency do not enjoy security of tenure. See para.3A-60.1,the Welsh Development Agency Act 1975 Sch.4 as inserted by the Government of Wales Act 1998 Sch.13. **3A-970**

If one of the exceptions in Sch.1 applies, the tenant has no security of tenure. Once a notice to quit has been served and has expired the tenant has no statutory protection, except, in some cases, for the Protection from Eviction Act 1977 s.3 which provides that it is unlawful for a landlord to evict such a tenant without taking court proceedings. The landlord need only prove that the contractual tenancy has been terminated.

**12ZA. Family intervention tenancies**

See para.3A-1664. **3A-970.1**

**SECTION 7**

## SCHEDULE 2

## GROUNDS FOR POSSESSION OF DWELLING-HOUSES LET ON ASSURED TENANCIES

### PART I

### GROUNDS ON WHICH COURT MUST ORDER POSSESSION

*Ground 1*

Not later than the beginning of the tenancy the landlord gave notice in writing to the tenant that possession might be recovered on this ground or the court is of the opinion that it is just and equitable to dispense with the requirement of notice and (in either case)— **3A-971**

***Paragraph numbers marked with a "+" can be found online and on CD.***

(a) at some time before the beginning of the tenancy, the landlord who is seeking possession or, in the case of joint landlords seeking possession, at least one of them occupied the dwelling-house as his only or principal home; or

(b) the landlord who is seeking possession or, in the case of joint landlords seeking possession, at least one of them requires the dwelling-house as his, his spouse's or his civil partner's only or principal home and neither the landlord (or, in the case of joint landlords, any one of them) nor any other person who, as landlord, derived title under the landlord who gave the notice mentioned above acquired the reversion on the tenancy for money or money's worth.

*Ground 2*

**3A-972** The dwelling-house is subject to a mortgage granted before the beginning of the tenancy and—

(a) the mortgagee is entitled to exercise a power of sale conferred on him by the mortgage or by section 101 of the Law of Property Act 1925; and

(b) the mortgagee requires possession of the dwelling-house for the purpose of disposing of it with vacant possession in exercise of that power; and

(c) either notice was given as mentioned in Ground 1 above or the court is satisfied that it is just and equitable to dispense with the requirement of notice;

and for the purposes of this ground "mortgage" includes a charge and "mortgagee" shall be construed accordingly.

*Ground 3*

**3A-973** The tenancy is a fixed term tenancy for a term not exceeding eight months and—

(a) not later than the beginning of the tenancy the landlord gave notice in writing to the tenant that possession might be recovered on this ground; and

(b) at some time within the period of twelve months ending with the beginning of the tenancy, the dwelling-house was occupied under a right to occupy it for a holiday.

*Ground 4*

**3A-974** The tenancy is a fixed term tenancy for a term not exceeding twelve months and—

(a) not later than the beginning of the tenancy the landlord gave notice in writing to the tenant that possession might be recovered on this ground, and

(b) at some time within the period of twelve months ending with the beginning of the tenancy, the dwelling-house was let on a tenancy falling within paragraph 8 of Schedule 1 to this Act.

*Ground 5*

**3A-975** The dwelling-house is held for the purpose of being available for occupation by a minister of religion as a residence from which to perform the duties of his office and—

(a) not later than the beginning of the tenancy the landlord gave notice in writing to the tenant that possession might be recovered on this ground; and

(b) the court is satisfied that the dwelling-house is required for occupation by a minister of religion as such a residence.

*Ground 6*

**3A-976** The landlord who is seeking possession or, if that landlord is a registered social landlord or charitable housing trust, a superior landlord intends to demolish or reconstruct the whole or a substantial part of the dwelling-house or to carry out substantial works on the dwelling-house or any part thereof or any building of which it forms part and the following conditions are fulfilled—

(a) the intended work cannot reasonably be carried out without the tenant giving up possession of the dwelling-house because—

(i) the tenant is not willing to agree to such a variation of the terms of the tenancy as would give such access and other facilities as would permit the intended work to be carried out, or

(ii) the nature of the intended work is such that no such variation is practicable, or

***Paragraph numbers marked with a "+" can be found online and on CD.***

(iii) the tenant is not willing to accept an assured tenancy of such part only of the dwelling-house (in this sub-paragraph referred to as "the reduced part") as would leave in the possession of his landlord so much of the dwelling-house as would be reasonable to enable the intended work to be carried out and, where appropriate, as would give such access and other facilities over the reduced part as would permit the intended work to be carried out, or

(iv) the nature of the intended work is such that such a tenancy is not practicable; and

(b) either the landlord seeking possession acquired his interest in the dwelling-house before the grant of the tenancy or that interest was in existence at the time of that grant and neither that landlord (or, in the case of joint landlords, any of them) nor any other person who, alone or jointly with others, has acquired that interest since that time acquired it for money or money's worth; and

(c) the assured tenancy on which the dwelling-house is let did not come into being by virtue of any provision of Schedule 1 to the Rent Act 1977, as amended by Part I of Schedule 4 to this Act or, as the case may be, section 4 of the Rent (Agriculture) Act 1976, as amended by Part II of that Schedule.

For the purposes of this ground, if, immediately before the grant of the tenancy, the tenant to whom it was granted or, if it was granted to joint tenants, any of them was the tenant or one of the joint tenants of the dwelling-house concerned under an earlier assured tenancy or, as the case may be, under a tenancy to which Schedule 10 to the Local Government and Housing Act 1989 applied, any reference in paragraph (b) above to the grant of the tenancy is a reference to the grant of that or, as the case may be, to the grant of the tenancy to which the said Schedule 10 applied.

For the purposes of this ground "registered social landlord" has the same meaning as in the Housing Act 1985 (see section 5(4) and (5) of that Act) and "charitable housing trust" means a housing trust, within the meaning of the Housing Associations Act 1985, which is a charity, within the meaning of the Charities Act 1993.

For the purposes of this ground, every acquisition under Part IV of this Act shall be taken to be an acquisition for money or money's worth; and in any case where—

(i) the tenancy (in this paragraph referred to as "the current tenancy") was granted to a person (alone or jointly with others) who, immediately before it was granted, was a tenant under a tenancy of a different dwelling-house (in this paragraph referred to as "the earlier tenancy"), and

(ii) the landlord under the current tenancy is the person who, immediately before that tenancy was granted, was the landlord under the earlier tenancy, and

(iii) the condition in paragraph (b) above could not have been fulfilled with respect to the earlier tenancy by virtue of an acquisition under Part IV of this Act (including one taken to be such an acquisition by virtue of the previous operation of this paragraph),

the acquisition of the landlord's interest under the current tenancy shall be taken to have been under that Part and the landlord shall be taken to have acquired that interest after the grant of the current tenancy.

*Ground 7*

The tenancy is a periodic tenancy (including a statutory periodic tenancy) which has devolved under the will or intestacy of the former tenant and the proceedings for the recovery of possession are begun not later than twelve months after the death of the former tenant or, if the court so directs, after the date on which, in the opinion of the court, the landlord or, in the case of joint landlords, any one of them became aware of the former tenant's death. **3A–977**

For the purposes of this ground, the acceptance by the landlord of rent from a new tenant after the death of the former tenant shall not be regarded as creating a new periodic tenancy, unless the landlord agrees in writing to a change (as compared with the tenancy before the death) in the amount of the rent, the period of the tenancy, the premises which are let or any other term of the tenancy.

*Ground 8*

Both at the date of the service of the notice under section 8 of this Act relating to the proceedings for possession and at the date of the hearing— **3A–978**

(a) if rent is payable weekly or fortnightly, at least eight weeks rent is unpaid;
(b) if rent is payable monthly, at least two months rent is unpaid;
(c) if rent is payable quarterly, at least one quarter's rent is more than three months in arrears; and
(d) if rent is payable yearly, at least three months' rent is more than three months in arrears;

and for the purpose of this ground "rent" means rent lawfully due from the tenant.

## PART II

## GROUNDS ON WHICH COURT MAY ORDER POSSESSION

### Ground 9

3A-979 Suitable alternative accommodation is available for the tenant or will be available for him when the order for possession takes effect.

### Ground 10

3A-980 Some rent lawfully due from the tenant—

(a) is unpaid on the date on which the proceedings for possession are begun; and
(b) except where subsection (1)(b) of section 8 of this Act applies, was in arrears at the date of the service of the notice under that section relating to those proceedings.

### Ground 11

3A-981 Whether or not any rent is in arrears on the date on which proceedings for possession are begun, the tenant has persistently delayed paying rent which has become lawfully due.

### Ground 12

3A-982 Any obligation of the tenancy (other than one related to the payment of rent) has been broken or not performed.

### Ground 13

3A-983 The condition of the dwelling-house or any of the common parts has deteriorated owing to acts of waste by, or the neglect or default of, the tenant or any other person residing in the dwelling-house and, in the case of an act of waste by, or the neglect or default of, a person lodging with the tenant or a sub-tenant of his, the tenant has not taken such steps as he ought reasonably to have taken for the removal of the lodger or sub-tenant.

For the purposes of this ground, "common parts" means any part of a building comprising the dwelling-house and any other premises which the tenant is entitled under the terms of the tenancy to use in common with the occupiers of other dwelling-houses in which the landlord has an estate or interest.

### Ground 14

3A-984 The tenant or a person residing in or visiting the dwelling-house—

(a) has been guilty of conduct causing or likely to cause a nuisance or annoyance to a person residing, visiting or otherwise engaging in a lawful activity in the locality, or
(b) has been convicted of—
  (i) using the dwelling-house or allowing it to be used immoral or illegal purposes, or
  (ii) an indictable offence committed in, or in the locality of, the dwelling-house.

### Ground 14A

3A-985 The dwelling-house was occupied (whether alone or with others) by a married couple, a couple who are civil partners of each other, or a couple living together as husband and wife or a couple living together as if they were civil partners and—

***Paragraph numbers marked with a "+" can be found online and on CD.***

(a) one or both of the partners is a tenant of the dwelling-house,

(b) the landlord who is seeking possession is a registered social landlord or a charitable housing trust,

(c) one partner has left the dwelling-house because of violence or threats of violence by the other towards—

(i) that partner, or

(ii) children of the partnership.

(d) the court is satisfied that the partner who has left is unlikely to return.

For the purposes of this ground "registered social landlord" and "member of the family" have the same meaning as in Part I of the Housing Act 1996 and "charitable housing trust" means a housing trust, within the meaning of the Housing Associations Act 1985, which is a charity within the meaning of the Charities Act 1993.

*Ground 15*

The condition of any furniture provided for use under the tenancy has, in the opinion of the court, deteriorated owing to ill-treatment by the tenant or any other person residing in the dwelling-house and, in the case of ill-treatment by a person lodging with the tenant or by a sub-tenant of his, the tenant has not taken such steps as he ought reasonably to have taken for the removal of the lodger or sub-tenant. **3A–986**

*Ground 16*

The dwelling-house was let to the tenant in consequence of his employment by the landlord seeking possession or a previous landlord under the tenancy and the tenant has ceased to be in that employment. **3A–987**

For the purposes of this ground, at a time when the landlord is or was the Secretary of State, employment by a health service body, as defined in section 60(7) of the National Health Service and Community Care Act 1990, shall be regarded as employment by the Secretary of State.

*Ground 17*

The tenant is the person, or one of the persons, to whom the tenancy was granted and the landlord was induced to grant the tenancy by a false statement made knowingly or recklessly by— **3A–988**

(a) the tenant or,

(b) a person acting at the tenant's instigation.

## PART III

## SUITABLE ALTERNATIVE ACCOMMODATION

1. For the purposes of Ground 9 above, a certificate of the local housing authority for the district in which the dwelling-house in question is situated, certifying that the authority will provide suitable alternative accommodation for the tenant by a date specified in the certificate, shall be conclusive evidence that suitable alternative accommodation will be available for him by that date. **3A–989**

2. Where no such certificate as is mentioned in paragraph 1 above is produced to the court, accommodation shall be deemed to be suitable for the purposes of Ground 9 above if it consists of either—

(a) premises which are to be let as a separate dwelling such that they will then be let on an assured tenancy, other than—

(i) a tenancy in respect of which notice is given not later than the beginning of the tenancy that possession might be recovered on any of Grounds 1 to 5 above, or

(ii) an assured shorthold tenancy, within the meaning of Chapter II of Part I of this Act, or

(b) premises to be let as a separate dwelling on terms which will, in the opinion of the court, afford to the tenant security of tenure reasonably equivalent to the security afforded by Chapter I of Part I of this Act in the case of an assured tenancy of a kind mentioned in sub-paragraph (a) above,

***Paragraph numbers marked with a "+" can be found online and on CD.***

and, in the opinion of the court, the accommodation fulfils the relevant conditions as defined in paragraph 3 below.

3.—(1) For the purposes of paragraph 2 above, the relevant conditions are that the accommodation is reasonably suitable to the needs of the tenant and his family as regards proximity to place of work, and either—

(a) similar as regards rental and extent to the accommodation afforded by dwelling-houses provided in the neighbourhood by any local housing authority for persons whose needs as regards extent are, in the opinion of the court, similar to those of the tenant and of his family; or

(b) reasonably suitable to the means of the tenant and to the needs of the tenant and his family as regards extent and character; and

that if any furniture was provided for use under the assured tenancy in question, furniture is provided for use in the accommodation which is either similar to that so provided or is reasonably suitable to the needs of the tenant and his family.

(2) For the purposes of sub-paragraph (1)(a) above, a certificate of a local housing authority stating—

(a) the extent of the accommodation afforded by dwelling-houses provided by the authority to meet the needs of tenants with families of such number as may be specified in the certificate, and

(b) the amount of the rent charged by the authority for dwelling-houses affording accommodation of that extent,

shall be conclusive evidence of the facts so stated.

4. Accommodation shall not be deemed to be suitable to the needs of the tenant and his family if the result of their occupation of the accommodation would be that it would be an overcrowded dwelling-house for the purposes of Part X of the Housing Act 1985.

5. Any document purporting to be a certificate of a local housing authority named therein issued for the purposes of this Part of this Schedule and to be signed by the proper officer of that authority shall be received in evidence and, unless the contrary is shown, shall be deemed to be such a certificate without further proof.

6. In this Part of this Schedule "local housing authority" and "district", in relation to such an authority, have the same meaning as in the Housing Act 1985.

## PART IV

## NOTICES RELATING TO RECOVERY OF POSSESSION

**3A–990** 7. Any reference in Grounds 1 to 5 in Part I of this Schedule or in the following provisions of this Part to the landlord giving a notice in writing to the tenant is, in the case of joint landlords, a reference to at least one of the joint landlords giving such a notice.

8.—(1) If, not later than the beginning of a tenancy (in this paragraph referred to as "the earlier tenancy"), the landlord gives such a notice in writing to the tenant as is mentioned in any of Grounds 1 to 5 in Part I of this Schedule, then, for the purposes of the ground in question and any further application of this paragraph, that notice shall also have effect as if it had been given immediately before the beginning of any later tenancy falling within sub-paragraph (2) below.

(2) Subject to sub-paragraph (3) below, sub-paragraph (1) above applies to a later tenancy—

(a) which takes effect immediately on the coming to an end of the earlier tenancy; and

(b) which is granted (or deemed to be granted) to the person who was the tenant under the earlier tenancy immediately before it came to an end; and

(c) which is of substantially the same dwelling-house as the earlier tenancy.

(3) Sub-paragraph (1) above does not apply in relation to a later tenancy if, not later than the beginning of the tenancy, the landlord gave notice in writing to the tenant that the tenancy is not one in respect of which possession can be recovered on the ground in question.

9. Where paragraph 8(1) above has effect in relation to a notice given as mentioned in Ground 1 in Part I of this Schedule, the reference in paragraph (b) of that ground to the reversion on the tenancy is a reference to the reversion on the earlier tenancy and on any later tenancy falling within paragraph 8(2) above.

10. Where paragraph 8(1) above has effect in relation to a notice given as mentioned in Ground 3 or Ground 4 in Part I of this Schedule, any second or subsequent tenancy in relation to which the notice has effect shall be treated for the purpose of that ground as beginning at the beginning of the tenancy in respect of which the notice was actually given.

11. Any reference in Grounds 1 to 5 in Part I of this Schedule to a notice being given not later than the beginning of the tenancy is a reference to its being given not later than the day on which the tenancy is entered into and, accordingly, section 45(2) of this Act shall not apply to any such reference.

*Note* —Amended by the Local Government and Housing Act 1989 s.195, Sch.11, paras 108 and 109; the NHS and Community Care Act 1990 Sch.8; the Charities Act 1993 s.98(1), Sch.6; the Housing Act 1996 ss.10, 101, 102, 148 and 149, Sch.19, Pt IX; the Housing Act 1996 (Consequential Provisions) Order 1996 (SI 1996/2325) art.5 and Sch.2, para.18; the Civil Partnership Act 2004 s.81 and Sch. 8, para.43 and the Serious Organised Crime and Police Act 2005 s.111, Sch.7, para.46. **3A-991**

**Mandatory Grounds**

*Ground 1*

*Returning Owner Occupier:* This ground is similar to Case 11 in the Rent Act 1977 Sch.15, but more widely drafted. A landlord must prove that: **3A-992**

(a) At, or before, the grant of the tenancy the landlord gave notice in writing that possession might be recovered on this ground. The notice need not be in any particular form and may be included as a recital in any tenancy agreement provided that the agreement does not operate retrospectively. The court has power to dispense with such a notice if it considers it just and equitable.

AND EITHER

(b) At some time before the grant of the tenancy the landlord, or if there are joint landlords, at least one of them, occupied the dwelling-house as his or her only or principal residence. A landlord's previous occupation may be temporary and intermittent in order to suffice (see *Naish v Curzon* (1984) 17 H.L.R. 220; and *Mistry v Isidore* (1990) 22 H.L.R. 281, *cf. Ibie v Trubshaw* (1990) 22 H.L.R. 191).

*OR*

(c) The landlord (or at least one of them) "requires the dwelling-house as his or his spouse's only or principal home". The landlord need not show that the premises are reasonably required, merely that the landlord "bona fide wants" or "genuinely has the immediate intention" of occupying the premises (*Kennealy v Dunne* [1977] Q.B. 837). Premises need not be required as a permanent residence and fairly intermittent residence will be sufficient (*Naish v Curzon* (1984) 17 H.L.R. 220).

This ground for possession is not available to a new landlord who has acquired the premises "for money or money's worth" from an original landlord who gave a notice that possession might be recovered under this ground (*Epps v Rothnie* [1945] K.B. 562).

HOUSING

*Ground 2*

*Mortgagees:* This ground applies if: **3A-993**

(a) a mortgagee is entitled to exercise a power of sale (e.g. if the mortgagor has defaulted on instalments of the mortgage), and

(b) the mortgagee requires vacant possession to exercise that power, and

(c) a Ground 1 notice was given before the commencement of the tenancy or the court considers it just and equitable to dispense with the notice.

Note the comments of Lord Denning M.R. in *Quennell v Maltby* [1979] 1 W.L.R. 318) that:

"A mortgagee will be restrained from getting possesion except when it is sought bona fide and reasonably for the purpose of enforcing the security and then only subject to such conditions as the court thinks fit to impose" (approved in *Albany Homes Ltd v Massey* [1997] 2 All E.R. 609, CA).

*Ground 3*

3A–994 *Tenancy preceded by "holiday let":* This ground is almost identical to the Rent Act 1977 Sch.15, Case 13. A landlord must prove that:

(a) not later than the grant of the tenancy, notice was given that possession might be recovered under this ground and;

(b) at some time during the twelve months prior to the grant of the tenancy, the dwelling-house was occupied for a holiday.

The court has no power to dispense with service of the notice required prior to the grant of the tenancy (*Fowler v Minchin* (1987) 19 H.L.R. 224, but *cf. Springfied Investments v Bell* (1990) 22 H.L.R. 440).

*Ground 4*

3A–995 *Educational Institutions:* This ground applies where, during the twelve months preceding the tenancy, premises were let by a specified educational institution. As with Ground 3, notice stating that this ground may be relied upon has to be served before the commencement of the tenancy. It is almost identical to the Rent Act 1977 Sch.15, Case 14.

**"specified educational institution"**

3A–996 See the Assured and Protected Tenancies (Lettings to Students) Regulations 1998 (SI 1998/1967) which also provide that lettings by registered housing associations to students cannot be assured tenancies.

*Ground 5*

3A–997 *Ministers of Religion:* This ground applies to premises which are "held for the purpose of being available for occupation by a minister of religion as a residence from which to perform duties of his office". Note that possession might be required must be served before the grant of the tenancy and the landlord must satisfy the court that the property is required for occupation by a minister of religion as a residence.

*Ground 6*

3A–998 *Demolition or Reconstruction:* This ground is available for a landlord who "intends to demolish or reconstruct the whole or a substantial part of the dwelling-house or to carry out substantial works". This ground is very similar to the Landlord and Tenant Act 1954 s.30(1)(f):

(a) It has been held that "reconstruction" means "a substantial interference with the structure of the premises and then a rebuilding, in probably a different form, of such part of the premises as has been demolished by reason of the interference with the structure (*Joel v Swaddle* [1957] 3 All E.R. 325 at 329; see too *Barth v Pritchard* [1990] 20 E.G. 65).

(b) The landlord must show that the intention will be fulfilled shortly after the date of the hearing (*Betty's Cafe v Phillips* [1958] 1 All E.R. 607, HL). There are two elements to the concept of intention—

  (i) a genuine desire that the result will come about, and

  (ii) a reasonable prospect of bringing about that result. See too *Edwards v Thompson* [1990] 29 E.G. 41, where the landlord failed to prevent the grant of a new tenancy because she had not found a developer at the time of the hearing and "there was a real possibility that [she] would not be in a position to carry out the entire development on the termination of the current tenancy. ... She had failed to show that she had the means and ability; she had not established the necessary intention." It is not essential that a landlord obtain planning permission in advance if it can be shown that there is a reasonable prospect of getting consent (*Gregson v Cyril Lord* [1962] 3 All E.R. 907).

(c) The landlord must show that, because of one of four specified reasons, the intended work cannot reasonably be carried out without the tenant giving up possession of the premises. "Possession" means "putting an end to legal rights of possession" and not merely access (*Heath v Drown* [1972] 2 All E.R. 561; and the Housing Act 1988 s.16).

(d) This ground is not available to a landlord who has acquired his or her interest in the property by purchasing it after the grant of the tenancy.

(e) When a possession order is made under this ground the landlord must pay a sum equal to the tenant's reasonable removal expenses (s.11(1)).

*Ground 7*

*Death of the Tenant:* Although an assured tenancy may pass by will or on intestacy after the death of a tenant, the landlord may obtain possession if proceedings are brought within twelve months of the death of the tenant or the date upon which the landlord became aware of the death. "Proceedings for possession" means court proceedings, not the service of a s.8 notice (*Shepping v Osada* (2001) 33 H.L.R. 13; [2000] L. & T.R. 489; [2000] 2 E.G.L.R. 38, CA). This ground does not apply if a spouse succeeds to the tenancy under s.17. The Act specifies that acceptance of rent after the death of the former tenant should not be regarded as creating a new tenancy unless the landlord has agreed in writing to a change in the terms of the tenancy, such as an increase in rent. **3A–999**

*Ground 8*

*Two months' rent arrears:* This is the first of three distinct grounds for possession based on rent arrears, although in practice landlords frequently plead all three in the alternative. Under Ground 8, two months' rent arrears (or eight weeks' arrears in the case of a weekly tenancy) give a landlord an automatic right to a possession order. However the landlord must prove that there are two months' arrears, both at the time when the notice of the landlord's intention to bring proceedings is served and at the date of the hearing. It should be borne in mind that delays on the part of a local authority or the Benefits Agency in making housing benefit payments do not provide a defence to proceedings brought under Ground 8 (*Marath v MacGillivray* (1996) 28 H.L.R. 484, CA). As to the restrictions on the court's power to adjourn in such circumstances, see ss.7(3) and 9(6) and the commentary at 3A–777. **3A–1000**

In *Day v Coltrane* [2003] EWCA Civ 342; [2003] 1 W.L.R. 1379 a tenant, facing a Ground 8 possession claim, handed the landlord a cheque for all the arrears on the day of the hearing. The landlord accepted the cheque and it was paid on first presentation. The Court of Appeal, allowing an appeal from a possession order, held that delivery of a cheque is a conditional payment. If the cheque is met, it is an actual payment from the date of delivery (*Homes v Smith* [2000] Lloyd's Rep. Bank. 139). That principle applies to Ground 8. If the cheque cleared, the debt was paid when the cheque was delivered. An uncleared cheque delivered to the landlord at or before the hearing and which was accepted by him, or which he was bound by an earlier agreement to accept, is to be treated as payment on the date of delivery provided it was subsequently paid on first presentation. At the date of the hearing there was jurisdiction to adjourn the claim to see whether the cheque would be paid.

Note that the court cannot dispense with the requirement for a s.8 notice when Ground 8 is relied upon (see s.8(5)).

## *Discretionary Grounds*

*Ground 9*

*Suitable Alternative Accommodation:* As with the Rent Act 1977 s.98(1)(a), the availability of suitable alternative accommodation, either at the time of the hearing or when the order is to take effect, is a ground for possession. (See commentary to the Rent Act 1977 s.98). Pt III of Sch.2 gives further clarification as to the matters to be taken into account when determining whether or not accommodation is suitable. They are similar to those set out in the Rent Act 1977 Sch.15, Pt IV. **3A–1001**

When a possession order is made under this ground, the landlord must pay a sum equal to the tenant's reasonable removal expenses (s.11(1)).

### Ground 10

3A-1002 *Rent Arrears:* A landlord must prove that there were rent arrears both at the date when proceedings were begun and, unless the court considers it "just and equitable" to dispense with the need for service of a notice prior to issue, that there were arrears when the notice was served. This is the ground for possession which is most similar to Case 1 in Sch.15 to the Rent Act (see commentary thereto). A possession order may be made even if the arrears are paid off before the hearing, although in most circumstances there would be strong grounds for arguing that it would not be reasonable to make an order. See *Dellenty v Pellow* [1951] 2 All E.R. 716, CA; and *Lee-Steere v Jennings* (1987) 20 H.L.R. 1, CA.

### Ground 11

3A-1003 *Persistent Delay in Paying Rent:* Even if there are no arrears on the date when possession proceedings are issued, persistent delay in paying rent which is due is a ground for possession. The phrase "persistent delay" is not defined, but is likely to have the same meaning as in the Landlord and Tenant Act 1954 s.30(1)(b)—i.e. one instalment of rent has been in arrears for a significant period of time or instalments have persistently been paid late, or both (see *Hopcutt v Carver* (1969) 209 E.G. 1069, CA; and *Horowitz v Ferand* [1956] C.L.Y. 4843). For an example of the court's exercise of its powers under Landlord and Tenant Act 1954 s.30(1)(b) (persistent delay in paying rent), see *Hazel v Akhtar* [2001] EWCA Civ 1883; [2002] 07 E.G. 124.

### Ground 12

3A-1004 *Breach of any obligtion:* This ground for possession is similar to the second limb of Case 1 in the Rent Act 1977 Sch.15 and applies if "any obligation of the tenancy (other than one related to the payment of rent) has been broken or not performed". See commentary to Case 1.

### Ground 13

3A-1005 *Waste or Neglect:* This ground is similar to Case 3 in the Rent Act 1977 Sch.15, but slightly wider in that it applies not only to the premises let, but also to common parts.

There is no need for a landlord to give advance warning of an intention to issue proceedings relying on this ground (*Lowe v Lendrum* (1950) 159 E.G. 423, CA) although failure to do so may be relevant when the court considers reasonableness and costs. See too *Holloway v Povey* (1984) 15 H.L.R. 104; (1984) 271 E.G. 195, CA.

### Ground 14

3A-1006 *Nuisance or annoyance or conviction for illegal or immoral user:* The Housing Act 1996 s.148 introduced new Ground 14 which replaces the former "nuisance or annoyance" ground. For detailed commentary on Housing Act 1985 Sched 2, Ground 2, the comparable ground relating to secure tenants, see para.3A–505.

There is no requirement that any person visiting the premises and causing a nuisance should be there lawfully. The ground is wide enough, for example, to encompass behaviour by a former partner of a tenant who has been excluded, but returns contrary to the tenant's wishes. The widening of the ground from conduct which *is* a nuisance or annoyance to neighbours to conduct which *is likely to cause nuisance or annoyance* is designed to meet two problems. Firstly the new ground avoids the apparent need for landlords to produce neighbours as witnesses to whom nuisance or annoyance has been caused (but *cf. Frederick Platts Co v Grigor* [1950] 1 All E.R. 941, CA, where it was held that the court can infer that nuisance or annoyance has been caused without hearing evidence from anyone affected.) Secondly, the amended ground covers nuisance or annoyance to people who are not neighbours—e.g. housing officers (but *cf.* the wide definition of "neighbour" adopted by the Court of Appeal in *Northampton BC v Lovatt* (1998) 30 H.L.R. 875; 91 L.G.R. 548; [1998] 07 E.G. 142, CA. As to the meaning of locality in the context of Housing Act 1996 s.152, see *Manchester CC v Lawler* (1999) 31 H.L.R. 119, CA where it was said that it is a matter of fact for the judge in each case to determine whether the conduct complained of has occurred in the locality (held that an incident in a shopping centre three streets away from the property was "in the locality").

For the definition of indictable offences, see the Interpretation Act 1978 Sch.1, which provides "indictable offence" means an offence which, if committed by an adult, is triable on indictment, whether it is exclusively so triable or triable either way. Ground 14 is not restricted to offences committed during the currency of the tenancy. (*Raglan Housing Association Ltd v Fairclough* [2007] EWCA Civ 1087; (2007) *The Times* November 28, 2007; November 1, 2007 where the defendant was arrested before the grant of his tenancy, but pleaded guilty after its grant. The Court of Appeal stated that a tenant who is convicted of supplying illegal drugs or of burgling his neighbours' houses poses no less a continuing threat if the offences were committed before he became a tenant than he would if they had been committed afterwards. The Court of Appeal was not agreed as to whether the ground could only be satisfied if the conviction itself (though not the facts on which it was based) occurred during the currency of the tenancy, but did not have to decide that point.

*Ground 14A*

*Domestic Violence:* **3A–1007**

*"registered social landlord"*

See the Housing Act 1996 ss.1– 7 and the Housing Act 1985 s.5.

The Housing Act 1996 s.149 introduced a new ground for possession against assured tenants of registered social landlords or charitable housing trusts where there has been domestic violence. Ground 14A applies where one partner is or both partners are tenants and:

(a) one partner has left because of violence or threats of violence by the other towards that partner or a member of that partner's family; and

(b) the court is satisfied that the partner who has left is unlikely to return.

Landlords seeking to rely upon this ground must satisfy the court that notice of proceedings for possession has been served on the partner who has left the home or that they have taken reasonable steps to effect service (Housing Act 1996 s.150, inserting new Housing Act 1988 s.8A).

Where possession is sought under Ground 14A, it is not sufficient that the alleged violence or threats of violence were merely one of a range of causes of equal efficacy in the victim's departure from the property. For the ground to be made out it has to be established that the alleged violence or threat of violence was the dominant, principal and real cause of the departure (*Camden LBC v Mallett* (2001) 33 H.L.R. 20, CA).

*Ground 15*

*Deterioration of furniture: cf.* the Rent Act 1977 Sch.15, Case 4. **3A–1008**

*Ground 16*

*Premises let to employees:* An employer who has let accommodation to an employee "in consequence" of employment may claim possession if the tenant has "ceased to be in that employment". This ground for possession is wider than Case 8, the comparable Rent Act ground. It applies whether or not the employer requires the premises for another employee. **3A–1009**

*Ground 17*

See commentary to the Housing Act 1985 Sch.2, Ground 5. **3A–1010**

## SCHEDULE 2A

### ASSURED TENANCIES: NON-SHORTHOLDS

*Tenancies excluded by notice*

1.—(1) An assured tenancy in respect of which a notice is served as mentioned in sub-paragraph (2) below. **3A–1011**

(2) The notice referred to in sub-paragraph (1) above is one which—

(a) is served before the assured tenancy is entered into,

(b) is served by the person who is to be the landlord under the assured tenancy on the person who is to be the tenant under that tenancy, and

(c) states that the assured tenancy to which it relates is not to be an assured shorthold tenancy.

2.—(1) An assured tenancy in respect of which a notice is served as mentioned in sub-paragraph (2) below.

(2) The notice referred to in sub-paragraph (1) above is one which—

(a) is served after the assured tenancy has been entered into,

***Paragraph numbers marked with a "+" can be found online and on CD.***

(b) is served by the landlord under the assured tenancy on the tenant under that tenancy, and

(c) states that the assured tenancy to which it relates is no longer an assured shorthold tenancy.

*Tenancies containing exclusionary provision*

3A–1012 3. An assured tenancy which contains a provision to the effect that the tenancy is not an assured shorthold tenancy.

*Tenancies under section 39*

3A–1013 4. An assured tenancy arising by virtue of section 39 above, other than one to which subsection (7) of that section applies.

*Former secure tenancies*

3A–1014 5. An assured tenancy which became an assured tenancy on ceasing to be a secure tenancy.

*Former demoted tenancies*

3A–1015 5A. An assured tenancy which ceases to be an assured shorthold tenancy by virtue of section 20B(2) or (4).

*Tenancies under Schedule 10 to the Local Government and Housing Act 1989*

3A–1016 6. An assured tenancy arising by virtue of Schedule 10 to the Local Government and Housing Act 1989 (security of tenure on ending of long residential tenancies).

*Tenancies replacing non-shortholds*

3A–1017 7.—(1) An assured tenancy which—

(a) is granted to a person (alone or jointly with others) who, immediately before the tenancy was granted, was the tenant (or, in the case of joint tenants, one of the tenants) under an assured tenancy other than a shorthold tenancy ("the old tenancy"),

(b) is granted (alone or jointly with others) by a person who was at that time the landlord (or one of the joint landlords) under the old tenancy, and

(c) is not one in respect of which a notice is served as mentioned in sub-paragraph (2) below.

(2) The notice referred to in sub-paragraph (1)(c) above is one which—

(a) is in such form as may be prescribed,

(b) is served before the assured tenancy is entered into,

(c) is served by the person who is to be the tenant under the assured tenancy on the person who is to be the landlord under that tenancy (or, in the case of joint landlords, on at least one of the persons who are to be joint landlords), and

(d) states that the assured tenancy to which it relates is to be a shorthold tenancy.

8. An assured tenancy which comes into being by virtue of section 5 above on the coming to an end of an assured tenancy which is not a shorthold tenancy.

*Assured agricultural occupancies*

3A–1018 9.—(1) An assured tenancy—

(a) in the case of which the agricultural worker condition is, by virtue of any provision of Schedule 3 to this Act, for the time being fulfilled with respect to the dwelling-house subject to the tenancy, and

(b) which does not fall within sub-paragraph (2) or (4) below.

(2) An assured tenancy falls within this sub-paragraph if—

(a) before it is entered into, a notice—

(i) in such form as may be prescribed, and

(ii) stating that the tenancy is to be a shorthold tenancy,

is served by the person who is to be the landlord under the tenancy on the person who is to be the tenant under it, and

(b) it is not an excepted tenancy.

***Paragraph numbers marked with a "+" can be found online and on CD.***

(3) For the purposes of sub-paragraph (2)(b) above, an assured tenancy is an excepted tenancy if—

(a) the person to whom it is granted or, as the case may be, at least one of the persons to whom it is granted was, immediately before it is granted, a tenant or licensee under an assured agricultural occupancy, and

(b) the person by whom it is granted or, as the case may be, at least one of the persons by whom it is granted was, immediately before it is granted, a landlord or licensor under the assured agricultural occupancy referred to in paragraph (a) above.

(4) An assured tenancy falls within this sub-paragraph if it comes into being by virtue of section 5 above on the coming to an end of a tenancy falling within sub-paragraph (2) above.

*Note*—Added by the Housing Act 1996 s.96, Sch.7. **3A–1019**

Section 21 has been amended by Anti-Social Behaviour Act 2003 s.15(2) and para.5A has been inserted by Anti-Social Behaviour Act 2003 s.15(3). The amendment was brought into force in England on June 30, 2004 by the Anti-Social Behaviour Act 2003 (Commencement No.3 and Savings) Order 2004 (SI 2004/1502) (c.61). It was brought into force in Wales on 30 April 2005 by the Anti-Social Behaviour Act 2003 (Commencement No.4) (Wales) Order 2005 (SI 2005/1225) (w.83) (c.55). It has been held that the words 'assured tenancy' on the cover of a rent book were not a statement "that the assured tenancy to which it relates is not to be an assured shorthold tenancy" (para.1(2)(c)), because an assured shorthold tenancy is itself a type of assured tenancy. Further, the reference in para.1 to "a notice" being "served" is a reference to the service of a written notice. The rent book was clearly intended and used simply to record the payment of rent (*Andrews v Cunningham* [2007] EWCA Civ 762; [2008] H.L.R. 13; [2008] L. & T.R. 1).).

**[THE NEXT PARAGRAPH IS 3A–1021.]**

## Criminal Justice and Public Order Act 1994

(1994 c.33) **3A–1021**

Arrangement of Sections



### Interim possession orders: false or misleading statements

**75.**—(1) A person commits an offence if, for the purpose of obtaining an interim possession order, he— **3A–1022**

(a) makes a statement which he knows to be false or misleading in a material particular; or

(b) recklessly makes a statement which is false or misleading in a material particular.

(2) A person commits an offence if, for the purpose of resisting the making of an interim possession order, he—

(a) makes a statement which he knows to be false or misleading in a material particular; or

(b) recklessly makes a statement which is false or misleading in a material particular.

(3) A person guilty of an offence under this section shall be liable—

(a) on conviction on indictment, to imprisonment for a term not exceeding two years or a fine or both;

(b) on summary conviction, to imprisonment for a term not exceeding six months or a fine not exceeding the statutory maximum or both.

(4) In this section—

"interim possession order" means an interim possession order (so entitled) made under rules of court for the bringing of summary proceedings for possession of premises which are occupied by trespassers;

"premises" has the same meaning as in Part II of the Criminal Law Act 1977 (offences relating to entering and remaining on property); and

"statement", in relation to an interim possession order, means any statement, in writing or oral and whether as to fact or belief, made in or for the purposes of the proceedings.

**Premises**

3A-1023 See Criminal Law Act 1977 s.12(1) which states:

"(a) 'premises' means any building, any part of a building under separate occupation, any land ancillary to a building, the site comprising any building or buildings together with any land ancillary thereto..."

3A-1024 Section 12(2) provides that references to a building shall apply also to any structure other than a movable one, and to any movable structure, vehicle or vessel designed or adapted for use for residential purposes. Part of a building is under separate occupation if anyone is in occupation or entitled to occupation of that part as distinct from the whole. Land is ancillary to a building if it is adjacent to it and used (or intended for use) in connection with the occupation of that building or any part of it.

**Interim possession order**

3A-1025 See s.75(4) and CPR rr.55.22 to 55.28.

**Editorial note**

3A-1026 Criminal Justice and Public Order Act 1994 ss.75 and 76 created interim possession orders (IPOs). They can only be granted against trespassers. Failure to comply with an IPO is a criminal offence. The IPO procedure can only be used if:

— the claimant is only seeking possession. A claimant cannot seek an IPO if there is a claim for another remedy (e.g. damages);
— the claimant has an immediate right to possession and has had such a right throughout the period of unlawful occupation;
— the defendants entered premises as trespassers. It cannot be used against former licensees, tenants or sub-tenants.

The procedure for obtaining an IPO is set out in CPR rr.55.22 to 55.28.

3A-1027 If an IPO has been made and served, any person who is present on the premises as a trespasser at any time during the currency of the order commits an offence unless he or she leaves the premises within 24 hours of service of the order (and does not return) or a copy of the order is not fixed to the premises. It is also an offence if a person who was on the premises when the order was served and who has left then re-enters or attempts to do so as a trespasser after the expiry of the order but within one year of the date of service of the order. Offences are triable summarily.

## Interim possession orders: trespassing during currency of order

3A-1028 **76.**—(1) This section applies where an interim possession order has been made in respect of any premises and served in accordance with rules of court; and references to "the order" and "the premises" shall be construed accordingly.

***Paragraph numbers marked with a "+" can be found online and on CD.***

(2) Subject to subsection (3), a person who is present on the premises as a trespasser at any time during the currency of the order commits an offence.

(3) No offence under subsection (2) is committed by a person if—

(a) he leaves the premises within 24 hours of the time of service of the order and does not return; or

(b) a copy of the order was not fixed to the premises in accordance with rules of court.

(4) A person who was in occupation of the premises at the time of service of the order but leaves them commits an offence if he re-enters the premises as a trespasser or attempts to do so after the expiry of the order but within the period of one year beginning with the day on which it was served.

(5) A person guilty of an offence under this section shall be liable on summary conviction to imprisonment for a term not exceeding six months or a fine not exceeding level 5 on the standard scale or both.

(6) A person who is in occupation of the premises at the time of service of the order shall be treated for the purposes of this section as being present as a trespasser.

(7) [...]

(8) In this section—

"interim possession order" has the same meaning as in section 75 above and "rules of court" is to be construed accordingly; and

"premises" has the same meaning as in that section that is to say the same meaning as in Part II of the Criminal Law Act 1977 (offences relating to entering and remaining on property).

*Note* —Amended by the Serious Organised Crime and Police Act 2005 s.111, Sch.7, para.31, Sch.17. **3A–1029**

**Interim possession order**

See s.75(4). **3A–1030**

**Rules of court**

See CPR rr.55.22 to 55.28. **3A–1031**

**Premises**

See commentary to s.75 and Criminal Law Act 1977 s.12. **3A–1032**

**[THE NEXT PARAGRAPH IS 3A–1045.]**

## Housing Act 1996

(2006 c.52) **3A–1045**

ARRANGEMENT OF SECTIONS

PART III

LANDLORD AND TENANT

CHAPTER I

TENANTS' RIGHTS

*FORFEITURE*



***Paragraph numbers marked with a "+" can be found online and on CD.***

***Paragraph numbers marked with a "+" can be found online and on CD.***

***Paragraph numbers marked with a "+" can be found online and on CD.***

# PART III

## LANDLORD AND TENANT

### CHAPTER I

### TENANTS' RIGHTS

### *FORFEITURE*

## Restriction on termination of tenancy for failure to pay service charge

**81.**—(1) A landlord may not, in relation to premises let as a dwelling, exercise a right of re-entry or forfeiture for failure by a tenant to pay a service charge or administartion charge unless—

(a) it is finally determined by (or on appeal from) a leasehold valuation tribunal or by a court, or by an arbitral tribunal in proceedings pursuant to a post-dispute arbitration agreement, that the amount of the service charge or administration charge is payable by him, or

(b) the tenant has admitted that it is so payable.

(2) The landlord may not exercise a right of re-entry or forfeiture

by virtue of subsection (1)(a) until after the end of the period of 14 days beginning with the day after that on which the final determination is made.

(3) For the purposes of this section it is finally determined that the amount of a service charge or administration charge is payable—

(a) if a decision that it is payable is not appealed against or otherwise challenged, at the end of the time for bringing an appeal or other challenge, or

(b) if such a decision is appealed against or otherwise challenged and not set aside in consequence of the appeal or other challenge, at the time specified in subsection (3A).

(3A) The time referred to in subsection (3)(b) is the time when the appeal or other challenge is disposed of—

(a) by the determination of the appeal or other challenge and the expiry of the time for bringing a subsequent appeal (if any), or

(b) by its being abandoned or otherwise ceasing to have effect.

(4) The reference in subsection (1) to premises let as a dwelling does not include premises let on—

(a) a tenancy to which Part II of the Landlord and Tenant Act 1954 applies (business tenancies),

(b) a tenancy of an agricultural holding within the meaning of the Agricultural Holdings Act 1986 in relation to which that Act applies, or

(c) a farm business tenancy within the meaning of the Agricultural Tenancies Act 1995.

(4A) References in this section to the exercise of a right of re-entry or forfeiture include the service of a notice under section 146(1) of the Law of Property Act 1925 (restriction on re-entry or forfeiture).

(5) In this section—

(a) "administration charge" has the meaning given by Part 1 of Schedule 11 to the Commonhold and Leasehold Reform Act 2002,

(b) "arbitration agreement" and "arbitral tribunal" have the same meaning as in Part 1 of the Arbitration Act 1996 (c.23) and "post-dispute arbitration agreement", in relation to any matter, means an arbitration agreement made after a dispute about the matter has arisen,

(c) "dwelling" has the same meaning as in the Landlord and Tenant Act 1985 (c.70), and (d).

(5A) Any order of a court to give effect to a determination of a leasehold valuation tribunal shall be treated as a determination by the court for the purposes of this section.

(6) Nothing in this section affects the exercise of a right of re-entry or forfeiture on other grounds.

*Note* —Amended by Commonhold and Leasehold Reform Act 2002 s.170. **3A–1046**

**"Crown land"**

Section 81 applies in relation to Crown land as in relation to other land (see the Commonhold and Leasehold Reform Act 2002 s.172, which also defines "Crown land". **3A–1047**

***Paragraph numbers marked with a "+" can be found online and on CD.***

**"service charge"**

3A–1048 See the Landlord and Tenant Act 1985 s.18, above.

**"arbitral tribunal"**

3A–1049 See the Arbitration Act 1996 Pt I.

**"dwelling"**

3A–1050 See Landlord and Tenant Act 1985 s.38.

**"landlord, tenant, lease, tenancy"**

3A–1051 See Landlord and Tenant Act 1985 s.36, para.3A–702+.

**"administration charge"**

3A–1052 See Sch.11, Pt 1.

**"post-dispute arbitration agreement"**

3A–1053 See s.169(5). It means an arbitration agreement made after a breach has occurred (or is alleged to have occurred).

**Restriction on termination of tenancy for failure to pay service charge**

3A–1054 Section 81 prevents landlords from exercising a right of re-entry or forfeiture of premises let as a dwelling for failure to pay service charges unless the amount claimed is either agreed or admitted by the lessee or has been determined by a court or an arbitral tribunal in accordance with the Arbitration Act 1996 Pt I. If the service charge has been determined by a court or tribunal, the landlord cannot commence forfeiture proceedings until 14 days after the determination. Section 82 provides that the Law of Property Act 1925 s.146 notices relating to arrears of service charges must refer to s.81 and state that s.81 has been complied with. "Service charge" has the same meaning as in the Landlord and Tenant Act 1985 s.18(1)—i.e. sums payable "directly or indirectly, for services, repairs, maintenance, improvements or insurance or the landlord's costs of management" and which vary according to the relevant costs. The aim of this provision was to prevent freeholders from pressurising lessees who have genuine disputes about service charges (or their mortgagees) into paying up rather than face forfeiture proceedings. It came into force on September 24, 1996 (Housing Act 1996 s.232(2)).

Courts are probably obliged to take s.81 into account even if it is not pleaded (*Mohammadi v Anston Investments Ltd* [2003] EWCA Civ 981; [2004] H.L.R. 8).

In *Southwark LBC v Tornaritis* [1999] CLY 3744, Lambeth County Court, H.H.J. Cox held that an earlier default judgment in respect of service charge arrears was a "determination" within the meaning of Housing Act 1996 s.81. He held that the phrase "determination by a court" did not require a judicial determination. However, in *Hillbrow (Richmond) Ltd v Alogaily Wandsworth County Court* [2006] CLY 2707, H.H.J. Rose held that the making of a default judgment did not amount to a determination of any issue other than those laid down in CPR Pt 12.3. An analysis of the issues was required before a "determination" could be said to have taken place. (It should be noted that the amendment to s.81 made by Commonhold and Leasehold Reform Act 2002 s.170 came into force before the *Hillbrow* case was decided and that may be a reason why the latter approach should be preferred.)

Section 81 has to be read in conjunction with the Landlord and Tenant Act 1985 s.19, as amended by the Housing Act 1996 s.83 which provides that lessors and lessees may apply to RACs sitting as Leasehold Valuation Tribunals (LVTs) to determine whether costs incurred for services, repairs, maintenance, etc. were reasonably incurred, whether such services or works were of a reasonable standard and whether sums payable by lessees before costs have been incurred are reasonable. There is a right of appeal to the Lands Tribunal, but only with the leave of the LVT or the Lands Tribunal (Housing Act 1996 s.83).

## Notice under s.146 of the Law of Property Act 1925

3A–1055 **82.** [...]

3A–1056 *Note*—Repealed by the Commonhold and Leasehold Reform Act 2002 s.180, Sch.14.

***Paragraph numbers marked with a "+" can be found online and on CD.***

* * * *

SERVICE CHARGES

## Right to appoint surveyor to advise on matters relating to service charges

**84.**—(1) A recognised tenants' association may appoint a surveyor for the purposes of this section to advise on any matters relating to, or which may give rise to, service charges payable to a landlord by one or more members of the association. The provisions of Schedule 4 have effect for conferring on a surveyor so appointed rights of access to documents and premises. **3A–1057**

(2) A person shall not be so appointed unless he is a qualified surveyor.

For this purpose "qualified surveyor" has the same meaning as in section 78(4)(a) of the Leasehold Reform, Housing and Urban Development Act 1993 (persons qualified for appointment to carry out management audit).

(3) The appointment shall take effect for the purposes of this section upon notice in writing being given to the landlord by the association stating the name and address of the surveyor, the duration of his appointment and the matters in respect of which he is appointed.

(4) An appointment shall cease to have effect for the purposes of this section if the association gives notice in writing to the landlord to that effect or if the association ceases to exist.

(5) A notice is duly given under this section to a landlord of any tenants if it is given to a person who receives on behalf of the landlord the rent payable by those tenants; and a person to whom such a notice is so given shall forward it as soon as may be to the landlord.

(6) In this section—

"recognised tenants' association" has the same meaning as in the provisions of the Landlord and Tenant Act 1985 relating to service charges (see section 29 of that Act); and

"service charge" means a service charge within the meaning of section 18(1) of that Act, other than one excluded from that section by section 27 of that Act (rent of dwelling registered and not entered as variable).

### Application

Commonhold and Leasehold Reform Act 2002 s.172 provides that Housing Act 1996 s.84 applies in relation to Crown land as in relation to other land. The phrase "Crown land" is defined by Commonhold and Leasehold Reform Act 2002 s.172. That section was brought into force on September 30, 2003 by the Commonhold and Leasehold Reform Act (Commencement No.2 and Savings) (England) Order 2003 (SI 2003/1986) (c.82). **3A–1058**

### "recognised tenants' association"

See the Landlord and Tenant Act 1985 s.29 which refers to an association of qualifying tenants being recognised "either—(a) by a notice in writing given by the landlord to the secretary of the association, or (b) by a certificate of a member of the local rent assessment committee panel." **3A–1059**

**"service charge"**

3A–1060 See commentary to s.81 and the Landlord and Tenant Act 1985 s.18.

**"qualified surveyor"**

3A–1061 See the Leasehold Reform, Housing and Urban Development Act 1993 s.78(4)(a) which states that a person is a "qualified surveyor" if "(a) ... he is a qualified surveyor; (b) he is not disqualified from acting within the meaning of the Landlord and Tenant Act 1985 s.28(1); and (c) he is not the tenant of any premises contained in the relevant premises." See also the Leasehold Reform, Housing and Urban Development Act 1993 s.78(5).

Schedule 4 gives such a surveyor the right to inspect documents and premises.

* * * *

*SUPPLEMENTARY*

## Jurisdiction of county courts

3A–1062 **95.**—(1) Any jurisdiction expressed by a provision to which this section applies to be conferred on the court shall be exercised by a county court.

(2) There shall also be brought in a county court any proceedings for determining any question arising under or by virtue of any provision to which this section applies.

(3) Where, however, other proceedings are properly brought in the High Court, that court has jurisdiction to hear and determine proceedings to which subsection (1) or (2) applies which are joined with those proceedings.

(4) Where proceedings are brought in a county court by virtue of subsection (1) or (2), that court has jurisdiction to hear and determine other proceedings joined with those proceedings despite the fact that they would otherwise be outside its jurisdiction.

(5) The provisions to which this section applies are—

(a) section 81 (restriction on termination of tenancy for failure to pay service charge), and

(b) section 84 (right to appoint surveyor to advise on matters relating to service charges) and Schedule 4 (rights exercisable by surveyor appointed by tenants' association).

* * * *

# PART V

## CONDUCT OF TENANTS

### CHAPTER I

### INTRODUCTORY TENANCIES

*GENERAL PROVISIONS*

## Introductory tenancies

3A–1063 **124.**—(1) A local housing authority or a housing action trust may elect to operate an introductory tenancy regime.

*Paragraph numbers marked with a "+" can be found online and on CD.*

(2) When such an election is in force, every periodic tenancy of a dwelling-house entered into or adopted by the authority or trust shall, if it would otherwise be a secure tenancy, be an introductory tenancy, unless immediately before the tenancy was entered into or adopted the tenant or, in the case of joint tenants, one or more of them was—

(a) a secure tenant of the same or another dwelling-house, or

(b) an assured tenant of a registered social landlord (otherwise than under an assured shorthold tenancy) in respect of the same or another dwelling-house.

(3) Subsection (2) does not apply to a tenancy entered into or adopted in pursuance of a contract made before the election was made.

(4) For the purposes of this Chapter a periodic tenancy is adopted by a person if that person becomes the landlord under the tenancy, whether on a disposal or surrender of the interest of the former landlord.

(5) An election under this section may be revoked at any time, without prejudice to the making of a further election.

**"local housing authority"**

See s.230 which refers to Housing Act 1985 (see the Housing Act 1985 ss.1 and 2 above). **3A–1064**

**"housing action trust"**

See s.230 which refers to the Housing Act 1988. See the Housing Act 1985 s.4 above. **3A–1065**

**"dwelling house"**

See s.139. **3A–1066**

**"secure tenant"**

See s.230 which refers to the Housing Act 1985 Pt IV. See the Housing Act 1985 s.79 above. **3A–1067**

**"assured tenant"**

See s.230 which refers to the Housing Act 1988 Pt I. See the Housing Act 1988 s.1 above. **3A–1068**

**"assured shorthold tenancy"**

See s.230 which refers to the Housing Act 1988 Pt I. See the Housing Act 1988 ss.19A and 20 above. **3A–1069**

**Introductory tenancies**

Introductory tenancies are a form of probationary tenancy granted by some local authorities lacking security of tenure within the first year of the tenancy. Housing Act 1985 Sch.1, para.1A provides that introductory tenancies cannot be secure tenancies (Housing Act 1996 Sch.14, para.5). **3A–1070**

Section 124 provides that "a local housing authority or housing action trust (HAT) may elect to operate an introductory tenancy regime". The Department of the Environment's Circular on Introductory Tenancies (2/97) suggests that local authorities should consult with existing tenants in accordance with the Housing Act 1985 s.105 before setting up an introductory tenancy regime (para.6). Where such an election is made, all new periodic tenancies and licences (Housing Act 1996 s.126) which would otherwise be secure tenancies will be introductory tenancies or licences unless immediately before the new tenancy, one or more of the tenants was either a secure tenant or an assured tenant of a registered social landlord. Tenancies remain introductory tenancies until the end of the "trial period" which lasts for one year after the date on which the tenancy was entered into, or the date on which the tenant was first entitled to possession, whichever is later. Note also that s.125A provides for the possible extension of the trial period by a further six months. Earlier periods when the tenant had another introductory tenancy or had an assured shorthold tenancy granted by a registered social landlord count towards the trial period provided that there is no gap between them.

Tenancies cease to be introductory tenancies if:

- the circumstances are such that the tenancy could not be secure; or
- a person or body other than a local housing authority or HAT becomes the landlord; or
- the election is revoked; or
- the tenant dies and there is no-one qualified to succeed (Housing Act 1996 ss.125 and 133(3)).

The Department of the Environment's Circular on Introductory Tenancies (2/97) suggests that landlords should ensure "that introductory tenancies can never be used as a weapon against vulnerable individuals and ensure that there are safeguards to protect such tenants...[They] must be vigilant to ensure that neighbours are not able to make a case for eviction against a vulnerable tenant whose behaviour may be different through no fault of their own (paras 9 and 11)". Where there are vulnerable tenants, they should liaise with social services and should have arrangements "for automatic notification to social services at an early stage once any problems arise (para.12)". The Circular also states that "eviction is not necessarily appropriate when problems arise between a vulnerable tenant and neighbours (para.14)" and that "landlords should have fair and rigorous procedures in place to investigate complaints against tenants (para.19)." The local authority associations have produced comprehensive good practice guidance on running an introductory regime which should be read in conjunction with the circular.

Landlords may only bring introductory tenancies to an end by obtaining a possession order in court (Housing Act 1996 s.127). Before bringing proceedings landlords must serve notices giving reasons for the decision to seek a possession order and specifying a date after which court proceedings may be begun. The notice given must be equivalent to that which would otherwise be needed to terminate the tenancy by notice to quit. It must also inform tenants of their right to "request a review of the landlord's decision" and that they may seek advice from a CAB, housing aid centre, law centre or solicitor (Housing Act 1996 s.128). The circular states:

> "As good practice landlords should include a full statement of the reasons for seeking possession which could include a case history of the sequence of events (para.16)."

Where a landlord serves a Housing Act 1996 s.128 notice based upon the arrears, but then also relies upon allegations of nuisance, the correct procedure is normally for the landlord to serve an additional notice. However in a case where the tenant had not suffered any prejudice, and the same decision would have been reached, even without the allegations of nuisance, a tenant's challenge to the review process was dismissed (*R.(Laporte) v Newham LBC* [2004] EWHC 227 (Admin); [2004] 2 All E.R. 874).

"The precise way in which a landlord chooses to conduct...a review is for each landlord to determine" (DoE Circular: 2/97 para.22)." However, the Introductory Tenants (Review) Regulations 1997 (SI 1997/72) set out certain basic requirements to be followed on reviews. Reviews are not to be by way of a hearing unless tenants inform their landlords that they wish to have an oral hearing (para.2). A request for an oral hearing must be made within 14 days after receipt of the notice seeking possession. Reviews must be carried out by a person who was not involved in the original decision to seek possession (para.3). If the review is not to be conducted by an oral hearing, the tenant may make written representations (para.4). If there is an oral hearing, the tenant has a right to:

(a) be heard and accompanied or represented by another person;
(b) call persons to give evidence;
(c) put questions to anyone who gives evidence; and

***Paragraph numbers marked with a "+" can be found online and on CD.***

(d) make representations in writing (para.5).

The tenant must be notified of the time, date and place of any hearing. It must take place not less than five days after the request for a hearing (para.6). The Regulations do not, however, specify a minimum period between notification of the date of the hearing and the hearing itself.

The review must be carried out and the tenant notified of the result before the date specified as the date after which proceedings may be begun.

If a landlord serves a notice which expires and then brings proceedings against an introductory tenant, the court must make a possession order. It is not necessary for the landlord to give evidence about the reason for seeking possession. All that is necessary is to prove that notice was served and that any review has been determined or that the period specified in the notice has expired (s.127). "Suspended possession orders ... are not appropriate for introductory tenancies. Applications to court for possession must lead to eviction" (DoE, para.20).

See too *Manchester City Council v Cochrane* [1999] 1 W.L.R. 809, CA where the Court of Appeal held that the word "shall" in s.127(2) means that once the requirements of s.128 have been complied with, the county court has no discretion but to make an order for possession.

In a case where a landlord served a s.128 notice, but then told the tenant that proceedings would not be issued if she cleared the arrears at a rate of £3 per week, the Court of Appeal held that there was no requirement to give a further or second notice when the arrears started to increase again. Housing Act 1996 s.127 imposes a mandatory duty on the court to grant possession if "a" notice has been served in compliance with s.128. A requirement to serve a further notice would introduce unnecessary formality and might deter an authority from taking a humane "wait and see" approach before issuing proceedings. *Cardiff City Council v Stone* [2002] EWCA Civ 298; [2003] H.L.R. 47, CA. However, for a case where there was in reality a decision to reverse or quash the original decision, albeit with a warning about future conduct, see *Forbes v Lambeth LBC* [2003] EWHC 222 (Admin); [2003] H.L.R. 49. Crane J. stated that where the reasons for a decision have changed, the tenant ought at least to be given an opportunity to seek a review, not only to question the alleged facts, but also, crucially, to argue that it was not reasonable to require possession. If that were not done, the scheme of the Act would not be ECHR compliant.

The Act is silent as to the methods by which tenants may challenge review decisions. This is not dealt with in the Introductory Tenancies (Review) Regulations either and so tenants' only redress if they are dissatisfied with a review decision is to apply for judicial review. In view of the decisions in *Manchester CC v Cochrane* [1999] 1 W.L.R. 809, CA, and *Avon CC v Buscott* [1988] Q.B. 656; [1988] 1 All E.R. 841, CA, the traditional view was that county courts hearing subsequent possession proceedings could not consider public law defences based upon tenants' complaints about the review procedure or decisions. It was thought that the private law rights of tenants under introductory tenancies were no more than a right to remain in possession until an order for possession was made. The remedy for tenants in such cases, was to apply for the possession proceedings to be adjourned pending determination of their applications for judicial review. Whether or not that view still represents the law is arguable in view of the recognition by the House of Lords (albeit in a different scenario) in *Birmingham City Council v Doherty* [2008] UKHL 57, [2009] 1 A.C. 367, [2008] 3 W.L.R. 636; that judicial review-type scrutiny of the fairness and legality of a council's decision to bring proceedings may be presented by way of a defence to the possession claim.

In determining whether proceedings are started before the end of the trial period, proceedings are started by the issue of the claim form by the court (CPR r.7.2 and PD7, para.5.1), not when the claim form is received by the court (*Salford City Council v Garner* [2004] EWCA Civ 364; [2004] H.L.R. 35). If the "trial period" ends before determination of the possession proceedings, the tenancy will remain an introductory tenancy until the determination of proceedings or the date on which possession is to be given up, whichever is later (s.130(2)).

Although introductory tenants lack security of tenure, the Act gives them some rights which are equivalent to those of secure tenants, e.g. succession (Housing Act 1996 ss.131– 133 and 140) and information and consultation (ss.136– 137). The right to repair scheme (Housing Act 1985 s.96) has been extended to introductory tenancies by the Secure Tenancies (Right to Repair) (Amendment) Regulations 1997 (SI 1997/

73). Assignment of introductory tenancies is in general prohibited although they may be transferred by orders made under the Matrimonial Causes Act 1973 s.24, the Matrimonial and Family Proceedings Act 1984, the Children Act 1989 Sch.1 and to a person who would be qualified to succeed the tenant if the tenant died immediately before the assignment (Housing Act 1996 s.134).

The provisions relating to introductory tenancies were brought into force on February 12, 1997 by the Housing Act 1996 (Commencement No.6 and Savings) Order 1997 (SI 1997/66).

**Introductory tenants and the Human Rights Act 1998**

3A–1071 In *R. (McLellan) v Bracknell Forest DC* [2001] EWCA Civ 1510; [2002] Q.B. 1129; [2002] 2 W.L.R. 1448; [2002] 1 All E.R. 899, the Court of Appeal held that:

(1) Eviction of an introductory tenant falls within ECHR art.8(1) (*Lambeth LBC v Howard* (2001) 33 HR 58, CA). Accordingly it is necessary to consider under art.8(2) whether an eviction is in accordance with the law and whether it is necessary for the protection of the rights of others. A tenant under an introductory tenancy has the right to raise the question whether it is reasonable in the particular case to insist on eviction, i.e. whether the eviction can be justified under art.8(2) (*Donoghue v Poplar HARCA* [2001] EWCA Civ 595 also reported as *Poplar HARCA v Donoghue* [2002] Q.B. 48, and Human Rights Act 1998 s.7(1)(b)). The review procedure taken together with the availability of judicial review provides adequate protection. Section 127 does not prevent tenants from relying on Convention rights if the procedure in *Manchester City Council v Cochrane* [1999] 1 W.L.R. 809 is followed. The fact that the tenant has failed to seek judicial review of the decision to seek possession does not deprive the county court of the power to consider whether there is arguably a breach of the Convention and to adjourn if necessary. Therefore the introductory tenancy scheme is not as such incompatible with Art 8 and there is no reason to think that individuals' rights will be infringed without remedy from the courts. If the pace of eviction is too fast the court may grant a limited extension of time under Housing Act 1980 s.89(1). Section 89 is not itself incompatible with art.8.

(2) The decision of the review panel involves the determination of an introductory tenant's civil rights and so ECHR art.6 is engaged. However the combination of the review panel plus judicial review is enough to meet the requirements of art.6. There is no requirement that a council must be satisfied that there has been a breach of the terms of the tenancy before serving notice—the question is whether, in the light of allegation and counter-allegation, it was reasonable for the council to take a decision to proceed with termination of the tenancy. There is no reason to believe that the review procedure will not be operated fairly, nor any reason to believe that judicial review will not provide an adequate safeguard to tenants enabling them to challenge any unfairness or infringement of their Convention rights, bearing in mind that the courts will "examine the decision maker's actions more rigorously" where a discretionary power is liable to interfere with fundamental human rights. Where a review has taken place it should be the norm for the council to set out in an affidavit before the county court how the review procedure was operated in each case so that the court has the necessary information to decide whether to adjourn pending an application for judicial review.

In *Merton LBC v Williams* [2002] EWCA Civ 980; [2003] H.L.R. 20, the Court of Appeal confirmed (following *McLellan*) that county courts hearing possession claims against introductory tenants have a general duty to consider the procedure that has been followed and to ensure that it complies both with the statutory procedure and the tenant's rights under the ECHR—although in the instant case a possession order should have been made because was no realistic prospect that any judicial review proceedings would succeed. See though *Harrow LBC v Qazi* [2003] UKHL 43; [2004] 1 A.C. 983; [2003] 3 W.L.R. 79 where Lord Hope and Lord Scott said that contractual and property rights cannot be defeated by a defence based on art.8; *Lambeth LBC v Kay; Leeds CC v Price* [2006] UKHL 10; [2006] 2 A.C. 465; [2006] 2 W.L.R. 570 and *Birmingham City Council v Doherty* [2008] UKHL 57, [2009] 1 A.C. 367, [2008] 3 W.L.R. 636. Note that in *Harrow LBC v Qazi* [2003] UKHL 43; [2004] 1 A.C. 983; [2003] 3 W.L.R. 79, Lord Scott also stated that *McLellan* was correctly decided, but for the wrong reason.

## Duration of introductory tenancy

3A–1072 **125.**—(1) A tenancy remains an introductory tenancy until the end

***Paragraph numbers marked with a "+" can be found online and on CD.***

of the trial period, unless one of the events mentioned in subsection (5) occurs before the end of that period.

(2) The "trial period" is the period of one year beginning with—

(a) in the case of a tenancy which was entered into by a local housing authority or housing action trust—

(i) the date on which the tenancy was entered into, or

(ii) if later, the date on which a tenant was first entitled to possession under the tenancy; or

(b) in the case of a tenancy which was adopted by a local housing authority or housing action trust, the date of adoption;

but this is subject to subsections (3) and (4) and to section 125A (extension of trial period by 6 months).

(3) Where the tenant under an introductory tenancy was formerly a tenant under another introductory tenancy, or held an assured shorthold tenancy from a registered social landlord, any period or periods during which he was such a tenant shall count towards the trial period, provided—

(a) if there was one such period, it ended immediately before the date specified in subsection (2), and

(b) if there was more than one such period, the most recent period ended immediately before that date and each period succeeded the other without interruption.

(4) Where there are joint tenants under an introductory tenancy, the reference in subsection (3) to the tenant shall be construed as referring to the joint tenant in whose case the application of that subsection produces the earliest starting date for the trial period.

(5) A tenancy ceases to be an introductory tenancy if, before the end of the trial period—

(a) the circumstances are such that the tenancy would not otherwise be a secure tenancy,

(b) a person or body other than a local housing authority or housing action trust becomes the landlord under the tenancy,

(c) the election in force when the tenancy was entered into or adopted is revoked, or

(d) the tenancy ceases to be an introductory tenancy by virtue of section 133(3)(succession).

(6) A tenancy does not come to an end merely because it ceases to be an introductory tenancy, but a tenancy which has once ceased to be an introductory tenancy cannot subsequently become an introductory tenancy.

(7) This section has effect subject to section 130 (effect of beginning proceedings for possession).

Amended by the Housing Act 2004 s.179. 3A–1073

**Duration of introductory tenancy**

See commentary to s.124. 3A–1074

**"introductory tenancy"**

See s.124. 3A–1075

**"local housing authority"**

3A–1076 See s.230 which refers to the Housing Act 1985 (see the Housing Act 1985 ss.1 and 2 above).

**"housing action trust"**

3A–1077 See s.230 which refers to the Housing Act 1988. See the Housing Act 1985 s.4 above.

**"dwelling house"**

3A–1078 See s.139.

**"secure tenant"**

3A–1079 See s.230 which refers to the Housing Act 1985 Pt IV. See the Housing Act 1985 s.79 above.

**"assured tenant"**

3A–1080 See s.230 which refers to the Housing Act 1988 Pt I. See the Housing Act 1988 s.1 above.

**"assured shorthold tenancy"**

3A–1081 See s.230 which refers to the Housing Act 1988 Pt I. See the Housing Act 1988 ss.19A and 20 above.

**"registered social landlord"**

3A–1082 See s.1.

## Extension of trial period by 6 months

3A–1083 **125A.**—(1) If both of the following conditions are met in relation to an introductory tenancy, the trial period is extended by 6 months.

(2) The first condition is that the landlord has served a notice of extension on the tenant at least 8 weeks before the original expiry date.

(3) The second condition is that either—

(a) the tenant has not requested a review under section 125B in accordance with subsection (1) of that section, or

(b) if he has, the decision on the review was to confirm the landlord's decision to extend the trial period.

(4) A notice of extension is a notice—

(a) stating that the landlord has decided that the period for which the tenancy is to be an introductory tenancy should be extended by 6 months, and

(b) complying with subsection (5).

(5) A notice of extension must—

(a) set out the reasons for the landlord's decision, and

(b) inform the tenant of his right to request a review of the landlord's decision and of the time within which such a request must be made.

(6) In this section and section 125B "the original expiry date" means the last day of the period of one year that would apply as the trial period apart from this section.

3A–1084 *Note*—Inserted by the Housing Act 2004 s.179.

**Trial period**

See s.125(2). 3A–1085

**Review**

See s.125B. 3A–1086

## Review of decision to extend trial period

**125B.**—(1) A request for review of the landlord's decision that the trial period for an introductory tenancy should be extended under section 125A must be made before the end of the period of 14 days beginning with the day on which the notice of extension is served. 3A–1087

(2) On a request being duly made to it, the landlord shall review its decision.

(3) The Secretary of State may make provision by regulations as to the procedure to be followed in connection with a review under this section.

Nothing in the following provisions affects the generality of this power.

(4) Provision may be made by regulations—

(a) requiring the decision on review to be made by a person of appropriate seniority who was not involved in the original decision, and

(b) as to the circumstances in which the person concerned is entitled to an oral hearing, and whether and by whom he may be represented at such a hearing.

(5) The landlord shall notify the tenant of the decision on the review.

If the decision is to confirm the original decision, the landlord shall also notify him of the reasons for the decision.

(6) The review shall be carried out and the tenant notified before the original expiry date.

*Note*—Inserted by the Housing Act 2004 s.179. 3A–1088

**Regulations**

See the Introductory Tenancies (Review of Decisions to Extend a Trial Period) (England) Regulations 2006 (SI 2006/1077) and the Introductory Tenancies (Review of Decisions to Extend a Trial Period) (Wales) Regulations 2006 (SI 2006/2983) (w.274). 3A–1089

**The original expiry date**

See s.125A(6). 3A–1090

## Licences

**126.**—(1) The provisions of this Chapter apply in relation to a licence to occupy a dwelling-house (whether or not granted for a consideration) as they apply in relation to a tenancy. 3A–1091

(2) Subsection (1) does not apply to a licence granted as a temporary expedient to a person who entered the dwelling-house or any other land as a trespasser (whether or not, before the grant of that licence, another licence to occupy that or another dwelling-house had been granted to him).

**Licences**

3A-1092 See commentary to s.124.

**"dwelling house"**

3A-1093 See s.139.

**"temporary expedient"**

3A-1094 *cf.* Housing Act 1985 s.79(4).

*PROCEEDINGS FOR POSSESSION*

## Proceedings for possession

3A-1095 **127.**—(1) The landlord may only bring an introductory tenancy to an end by obtaining—

(a) an order of the court for the possession of the dwelling-house, and

(b) the execution of the order.

(1A) In such a case, the tenancy ends when the order is executed.

(2) The court shall make an order of the kind mentioned in subsection (1)(a) unless the provisions of section 128 apply.

**Amendment**

3A-1095.1 Amended by the Housing and Regeneration Act 2008 Sch.11, Pt I, para.11 (for transitional provisions see para.14) with effect from May 20, 2009 (SI 2009/1261) (c.66).

**Proceedings for possession**

3A-1096 See commentary to s.124 and *Manchester City Council v Cochrane* [1999] 1 W.L.R. 809, CA.

**"dwelling house"**

3A-1097 See s.139.

## Notice of proceedings for possession

3A-1098 **128.**—(1) The court shall not entertain proceedings for the possession of a dwelling-house let under an introductory tenancy unless the landlord has served on the tenant a notice of proceedings complying with this section.

(2) The notice shall state that the court will be asked to make an order for the possession of the dwelling-house.

(3) The notice shall set out the reasons for the landlord's decision to apply for such an order.

(4) The notice shall specify a date after which proceedings for the possession of the dwelling-house may be begun.

The date so specified must not be earlier than the date on which the tenancy could, apart from this Chapter, be brought to an end by notice to quit given by the landlord on the same date as the notice of proceedings.

(5) The court shall not entertain any proceedings for possession of the dwelling-house unless they are begun after the date specified in the notice of proceedings.

(6) The notice shall inform the tenant of his right to request a

review of the landlord's decision to seek an order for possession and of the time within which such a request must be made.

(7) The notice shall also inform the tenant that if he needs help or advice about the notice, and what to do about it, he should take it immediately to a Citizens' Advice Bureau, a housing aid centre, a law centre or a solicitor.

**Notice of proceedings of possession**

See commentary to s.124. **3A–1099**

**"dwelling house"**

See s.139. **3A–1100**

**"introductory tenancy"**

See s.124. **3A–1101**

## Review of decision to seek possession

**129.**—(1) A request for review of the landlord's decision to seek an order for possession of a dwelling-house let under an introductory tenancy must be made before the end of the period of 14 days beginning with the day on which the notice of proceedings is served. **3A–1102**

(2) On a request being duly made to it, the landlord shall review its decision.

(3) The Secretary of State may make provision by regulations as to the procedure to be followed in connection with a review under this section.

Nothing in the following provisions affects the generality of this power.

(4) Provision may be made by regulations—

(a) requiring the decision on review to be made by a person of appropriate seniority who was not involved in the original decision, and

(b) as to the circumstances in which the person concerned is entitled to an oral hearing, and whether and by whom he may be represented at such a hearing.

(5) The landlord shall notify the person concerned of the decision on the review.

If the decision is to confirm the original decision, the landlord shall also notify him of the reasons for the decision.

(6) The review shall be carried out and the tenant notified before the date specified in the notice of proceedings as the date after which proceedings for the possession of the dwelling-house may be begun.

**Review of decision to seek possession**

See commentary to s.124. **3A–1103**

**"dwelling house"**

See s.139. **3A–1104**

**"introductory tenancy"**

See s.124. **3A–1105**

**"regulations"**

See the Introductory Tenants (Review) Regulations 1997 (SI 1997/72). **3A–1106**

### Effect of beginning proceedings for possession

3A–1107 **130.**—(1) This section applies where the landlord has begun proceedings for the possession of a dwelling-house let under an introductory tenancy and—

(a) the trial period ends, or

(b) any of the events specified in section 125(5) occurs (events on which a tenancy ceases to be an introductory tenancy).

(2) Subject to the following provisions, the tenancy remains an introductory tenancy until—

(a) the tenancy comes to an end in accordance with section 127(1A), or

(b) the proceedings are otherwise finally determined.

(3) If any of the events specified in section 125(5)(b) to (d) occurs, the tenancy shall thereupon cease to be an introductory tenancy but—

(a) the landlord (or, as the case may be, the new landlord) may continue the proceedings, and

(b) if he does so, section 127(1A) and (2) (termination by landlord) apply as if the tenancy had remained an introductory tenancy.

(4) Where in accordance with subsection (3) a tenancy ceases to be an introductory tenancy and becomes a secure tenancy, the tenant is not entitled to exercise the right to buy under Part V of the Housing Act 1985 unless and until the proceedings are finally determined on terms such that he is not required to give up possession of the dwelling-house.

(5) For the purposes of this section proceedings shall be treated as finally determined if they are withdrawn or any appeal is abandoned or the time for appealing expires without an appeal being brought.

#### Amendment

3A–1107.1 Amended by the Housing and Regeneration Act Sch.11, Pt I, para.12 (for transitional provisions see para.14) with effect from May 20, 2009 (SI 2009/1261) (c.66).

#### Effect of beginning proceedings for possession

3A–1108 See commentary to s.124.

#### "dwelling house"

3A–1109 See s.139.

#### "introductory tenancy"

3A–1110 See s.124.

#### "trial period"

3A–1111 See s.125(2).

* * * *

## SUPPLEMENTARY

### Jurisdiction of county court

3A–1112 **138.**—(1) A county court has jurisdiction to determine questions arising under this Chapter and to entertain proceedings brought under this Chapter and claims, for whatever amount, in connection with an introductory tenancy.

(2) That jurisdiction includes jurisdiction to entertain proceedings as to whether a statement supplied in pursuance of section 136(2)(b) (written statement of certain terms of tenancy) is accurate notwithstanding that no other relief is sought than a declaration.

(3) If a person takes proceedings in the High Court which, by virtue of this section, he could have taken in the county court, he is not entitled to recover any costs.

(4)—(6) [...]

*Note* —Amended by the Constitutional Reform Act 2005 ss.15(1), 146, Sch.4, para.256 and 257, Sch.18. **3A–1113**

### Meaning of "dwelling-house"

**139.**—(1) For the purposes of this Chapter a dwelling-house may be a house or a part of a house. **3A–1114**

(2) Land let together with a dwelling-house shall be treated for the purposes of this Chapter as part of the dwelling-house unless the land is agricultural land which would not be treated as part of a dwelling-house for the purposes of Part IV of the Housing Act 1985 (see section 112(2) of that Act).

### Members of a person's family: Chapter I

**140.**—(1) A person is a member of another's family within the meaning of this Chapter if— **3A–1115**

(a) he is the spouse or civil partner of that person, or he and that person live together as husband and wife or as if they were civil partners, or

(b) he is that person's parent, grandparent, child, grandchild, brother, sister, uncle, aunt, nephew or niece.

(2) For the purpose of subsection (1)(b)—

(a) a relationship by marriage or civil partnership shall be treated as a relationship by blood,

(b) a relationship of the half-blood shall be treated as a relationship of the whole blood, and

(c) the stepchild of a person shall be treated as his child.

*Note* —This section has been amended by the Civil Partnership Act 2004 s.81 and Sch.8, para.51. **3A–1116**

* * * *

Chapter 1A

## DEMOTED TENANCIES

*General provisions*

### Demoted tenancies

**143A.**—(1) This section applies to a periodic tenancy of a dwelling-house if each of the following conditions is satisfied. **3A–1117**

*Paragraph numbers marked with a "+" can be found online and on CD.*

(2) The first condition is that the landlord is either a local housing authority or a housing action trust.

(3) The second condition is that the tenant condition in section 81 of the Housing Act 1985 is satisfied.

(4) The third condition is that the tenancy is created by virtue of a demotion order under section 82A of that Act.

(5) In this Chapter—

(a) a tenancy to which this section applies is referred to as a demoted tenancy;

(b) references to demoted tenants must be construed accordingly.

3A–1118 *Note* —This section was inserted by Anti-Social Behaviour Act 2003 s.14(5) and Sch.1, para.1.

**Editorial note**

3A–1119 Demoted tenancies lack security of tenure. If the landlord follows the procedure set out in the Housing Act 1996 s.143E and F, the court must make an order for possession (see the Housing Act 1996 s.143D).

**"dwelling house"**

3A–1120 See s.143O which provides that a dwelling house may be a house or a part of a house and that land let together with a dwelling-house must be treated for as part of the dwelling-house unless the land is agricultural land which would not be treated as part of a dwelling-house for the purposes of the Housing Act 1985 Pt 4.

**Local housing authority**

3A–1121 See the Housing Act 1996 s.230 and the Housing Act 1985 ss.1 and 2(2).

**Housing action trust**

3A–1122 See the Housing Act 1996 s.230 and the Housing Act 1988 Pt III.

**Tenant condition**

3A–1123 See the Housing Act 1985 s.81.

## Duration of demoted tenancy

3A–1124 **143B.**—(1) A demoted tenancy becomes a secure tenancy at the end of the period of one year (the demotion period) starting with the day the demotion order takes effect; but this is subject to subsections (2) to (5).

(2) A tenancy ceases to be a demoted tenancy if any of the following paragraphs applies—

(a) either of the first or second conditions in section 143A ceases to be satisfied;

(b) the demotion order is quashed;

(c) the tenant dies and no one is entitled to succeed to the tenancy.

(3) If at any time before the end of the demotion period the landlord serves a notice of proceedings for possession of the dwelling-house subsection (4) applies.

(4) The tenancy continues as a demoted tenancy until the end of the demotion period or (if later) until any of the following occurs—

(a) the notice of proceedings is withdrawn by the landlord;

(b) the proceedings are determined in favour of the tenant;

*Paragraph numbers marked with a "+" can be found online and on CD.*

(c) the period of 6 months beginning with the date on which the notice is served ends and no proceedings for possession have been brought.

(5) A tenancy does not come to an end merely because it ceases to be a demoted tenancy.

*Note* —This section was inserted by Anti-Social Behaviour Act 2003 s.14(5), Sch.1, para.1. **3A–1125**

**Secure tenancy**

See Housing Act 1985 s.79. **3A–1126**

**Demoted tenancy**

See Housing Act 1985 s.82A and s.143A, above. This section only applies to former secure tenancies while the tenant condition (see Housing Act 1985 s.81) continues to apply. Demoted tenancies lack security of tenure. If the landlord follows the procedure set out in Housing Act 1996 ss.143E and F, the court must make an order for possession (see Housing Act 1996 s.143D). **3A–1127**

## Change of landlord

**143C.**—(1) A tenancy continues to be a demoted tenancy for the duration of the demotion period if— **3A–1128**

(a) at the time the demoted tenancy is created the interest of the landlord belongs to a local housing authority or a housing action trust, and

(b) during the demotion period the interest of the landlord transfers to another person who is a local housing authority or a housing action trust.

(2) Subsections (3) and (4) apply if—

(a) at the time the demoted tenancy is created the interest of the landlord belongs to a local housing authority or a housing action trust, and

(b) during the demotion period the interest of the landlord transfers to a person who is not such a body.

(3) If the new landlord is a registered social landlord or a person who does not satisfy the landlord condition the tenancy becomes an assured shorthold tenancy.

(4) If the new landlord is not a registered social landlord and does satisfy the landlord condition the tenancy becomes a secure tenancy.

(5) The landlord condition must be construed in accordance with section 80 of the Housing Act 1985.

*Note* —This section was inserted by Anti-Social Behaviour Act 2003 s.14(5), Sch.1, para.1. **3A–1129**

**Registered social landlord**

See Housing Act 1996 s.230 referring back to Pt I (ss.1 to 3). **3A–1130**

**Local housing authority**

See Housing Act 1996 s.230 and Housing Act 1985 ss.1 and 2(2). **3A–1131**

**Housing action trust**

See Housing Act 1996 s.230 and Housing Act 1988 Pt III. **3A–1132**

***Paragraph numbers marked with a "+" can be found online and on CD.***

**Demoted tenancy**

3A–1133 See Housing Act 1985 s.82A and s.143A, above. This section only applies to former secure tenancies while the tenant condition (see Housing Act 1985 s.81) continues to apply.

**Secure tenancy**

3A–1134 See Housing Act 1985 s.79.

**Landlord condition**

3A–1135 See Housing Act 1985 s.80 and the commentary at para.3A–332.

**Assured shorthold tenancy**

3A–1136 See Housing Act 1988 ss.19A and 20.

*PROCEEDINGS FOR POSSESSION*

## Proceedings for possession

3A–1137 **143D.**—(1) The landlord may only bring a demoted tenancy to an end by obtaining —

(a) an order of the court for the possession of the dwelling-house, and

(b) the execution of the order.

(1A) In such a case, the tenancy ends when the order is executed.

(2) The court must make an order for possession unless it thinks that the procedure under sections 143E and 143F has not been followed.

**Amendment**

3A–1137.1 Amended by the Housing and Regeneration Act Sch.11, Pt I, para.13 (for transitional provisions see para.14) with effect from May 20, 2009 (SI 2009/1261) (c.66).

3A–1138 *Note* —This section was inserted by Anti-Social Behaviour Act 2003 s.14(5), Sch.1 para.1. Amended by the Housing and Regeneration Act Sch.11 Pt I para.13 (for transitional provisions see para.14) with effect from May 20, 2009 (SI 2009/1261) (c.66).

**Demoted tenancy**

3A–1139 See Housing Act 1985 s.82A and s.143A, above. This section only applies to former secure tenancies while the tenant condition (see Housing Act 1985 s.81) continues to apply.

## Notice of proceedings for possession

3A–1140 **143E.**—(1) Proceedings for possession of a dwelling-house let under a demoted tenancy must not be brought unless the landlord has served on the tenant a notice of proceedings under this section.

(2) The notice must—

(a) state that the court will be asked to make an order for the possession of the dwelling-house;

(b) set out the reasons for the landlord's decision to apply for the order;

(c) specify the date after which proceedings for the possession of the dwelling-house may be begun;

(d) inform the tenant of his right to request a review of the landlord's decision and of the time within which the request must be made.

(3) The date specified under subsection (2)(c) must not be earlier than the date on which the tenancy could (apart from this Chapter) be brought to an end by notice to quit given by the landlord on the same date as the notice of proceedings.

(4) The court must not entertain proceedings begun on or before the date specified under subsection (2)(c).

(5) The notice must also inform the tenant that if he needs help or advice—

(a) about the notice, or

(b) about what to do about the notice,

he must take the notice immediately to a Citizen's Advice Bureau, a housing aid centre, a law centre or a solicitor.

*Note* —This section was inserted by Anti-Social Behaviour Act 2003 s.14(5), Sch.1, para.1. **3A–1141**

**Editorial note**

Demoted tenancies lack security of tenure. If a landlord follows the procedure set out in ss.143E and F, the court must make an order for possession (see Housing Act 1996 s.143D). **3A–1142**

**Demoted tenancy**

See Housing Act 1985 s.82A and s.143A, above. This section only applies to former secure tenancies while the tenant condition (see Housing Act 1985 s.81) continues to apply. **3A–1143**

**Notice**

A landlord must serve notice of proceedings on a demoted tenant before bringing possession proceedings. There is no prescribed form of notice. The notice must, among other things, set out the reasons for the landlord's decision to apply for a possession order and specify the date after which proceedings for possession may be begun. The date specified must not be earlier than the date on which the tenancy could be brought to an end by notice to quit—in most cases, in view of Protection from Eviction Act 1977 s.5, 28 days. Court proceedings should not be begun before that date. The notice must also inform the tenant of the right to request a review of the landlord's decision and of the time within which the request must be made—see s.143F. **3A–1144**

## Review of decision to seek possession

**143F.**—(1) Before the end of the period of 14 days beginning with the date of service of a notice for possession of a dwelling-house let under a demoted tenancy the tenant may request the landlord to review its decision to seek an order for possession. **3A–1145**

(2) If a request is made in accordance with subsection (1) the landlord must review the decision.

(3) The Secretary of State may by regulations make provision as to the procedure to be followed in connection with a review under this section.

(4) The regulations may include provision—

(a) requiring the decision on review to be made by a person of appropriate seniority who was not involved in the original decision;

(b) as to the circumstances in which the tenant is entitled to an oral hearing, and whether and by whom he may be represented at the hearing.

(5) The landlord must notify the tenant—

(a) of the decision on the review;

(b) of the reasons for the decision.

(6) The review must be carried out and notice given under subsection (5) before the date specified in the notice of proceedings as the date after which proceedings for possession of the dwelling-house may be begun.

3A–1146 *Note*—This section was inserted by Anti-Social Behaviour Act 2003 s.14(5), Sch.1, para.1.

**Regulations**

3A–1147 See the Demoted Tenancies (Review of Decisions) (England) Regulations 2004 (SI 2004/1679) and the Demoted Tenancies (Review of Decisions) (Wales) Regulations 2005 (SI 2005/1228) (w.86).

The provisions for an internal local authority review of the decision to seek possession conferred by the Demoted Tenancies (Review of Decisions) Regulations, when taken with the judicial review jurisdiction, satisfy the requirements of ECHR art.6 (*R (on the application of Gilboy) v Liverpool City Council* [2008] EWCA Civ 751; [2009] 3 W.L.R. 300; [2008] 4 All E.R. 127). In *Manchester City Council v Pinnock* [2009] EWCA Civ 852, July 31, 2009 Stanley Burnton L.J. said:

> "The obtaining of possession of a property subject to a demoted tenancy is the second part of a two-stage process, and the whole process must be considered if the landlord's decision is to be fairly and lawfully considered in its context. The first stage is the application under section 82A ... for a demotion order. That order is made in a procedure that clearly complies with article 6. ... [W]hen a demotion order has been made, the court has found the removal of security a necessary and proportionate response to the conduct of the tenant or those residing with or visiting him. ... When ... the conduct ... has been so serious as to justify a demotion order, very little is required to justify the landlord's decision to obtain possession. It would be wholly wrong, and inconsistent with the statutory scheme, to scrutinise the landlord's decision at the second stage with the rigour required of the county court at the first stage. ... Proportionality at the second stage is not a high test, and I see no real difference at the second stage between it and the domestic requirement ... that the landlord's decision must not be one that no reasonable person would consider justifiable. If on review the landlord considers for good reason ... that it is necessary or appropriate to obtain possession of a dwelling-house let on a demoted tenancy, and its decision is one that no reasonable person would consider unjustifiable, the requirement of proportionality will be satisfied (paras 27–30)."

Housing Act 1996 s s.143D, 143E and 143F are "quite clear": if the court concludes the procedure has not been followed, it will not make an order for possession. If it has been followed, it must make the order (*Pinnock* at [50]).

**Demoted tenancy**

3A–1148 See Housing Act 1985 s.82A and s.143A, above. This section only applies to former secure tenancies while the tenant condition (see Housing Act 1985 s.81) continues to apply.

**Request for review**

3A–1149 A tenant who seeks to challenge a decision to bring proceedings may request that the landlord review its decision. However a request for a review must be made before the end of the period of 14 days beginning with the date of service of the notice for possession. The court has no power to grant an extension of time. The statutory framework is similar to that for introductory tenancies—see Housing Act 1996 s.129

and the commentary at para.3A–1102. Decisions of review panels are susceptible to judicial review by the Administrative Court. However, failure to comply with s.143F(6) (completing the review in time) should not of itself invalidate a review (*Manchester City Council v Pinnock* [2009] EWCA Civ 852, July 31, 2009).

## Effect of proceedings for possession

**143G.**—(1) This section applies if the landlord has begun proceedings for the possession of a dwelling-house let under a demoted tenancy and— **3A–1150**

(a) the demotion period ends, or

(b) any of paragraphs (a) to (c) of section 143B(2) applies (circumstances in which a tenancy ceases to be a demoted tenancy).

(2) If any of paragraphs (a) to (c) of section 143B(2) applies the tenancy ceases to be a demoted tenancy but the landlord (or the new landlord as the case may be) may continue the proceedings.

(3) Subsection (4) applies if in accordance with subsection (2) a tenancy ceases to be a demoted tenancy and becomes a secure tenancy.

(4) The tenant is not entitled to exercise the right to buy unless—

(a) the proceedings are finally determined, and

(b) he is not required to give up possession of the dwelling-house.

(5) The proceedings must be treated as finally determined if—

(a) they are withdrawn;

(b) any appeal is abandoned;

(c) the time for appealing expires without an appeal being brought.

*Note*—This section was inserted by Anti-Social Behaviour Act 2003 s.14(5), Sch.1, para.1. **3A–1151**

#### Demoted tenancy

See Housing Act 1985 s.82A and s.143A, above. This section only applies to former secure tenancies while the tenant condition (see Housing Act 1985 s.81) continues to apply. **3A–1152**

#### Secure tenancy

See Housing Act 1985 s.79. **3A–1153**

#### Right to buy

See Housing Act 1985 Pt V. **3A–1154**

### *SUCCESSION TO DEMOTED TENANCY*

## Succession to demoted tenancy

**143H.**—(1) This section applies if the tenant under a demoted tenancy dies **3A–1155**

(2) If the tenant was a successor, the tenancy—

(a) ceases to be a demoted tenancy, but

(b) does not become a secure tenancy.

(3) In any other case a person is qualified to succeed the tenant if—

(a) he occupies the dwelling-house as his only or principal home at the time of the tenant's death,

(b) he is a member of the tenant's family, and

(c) he has resided with the tenant throughout the period of 12 months ending with the tenant's death.

(4) If only one person is qualified to succeed under subsection (3) the tenancy vests in him by virtue of this section.

(5) If there is more than one such person the tenancy vests by virtue of this section in the person preferred in accordance with the following rules—

(a) the tenant's spouse or civil partner (if the tenant has neither spouse or civil partner) the person mentioned in section 143P(1)(b) is to be preferred to another member of the tenant's family;

(b) if there are two or more other members of the tenant's family the person preferred may be agreed between them or (if there is no such agreement) selected by the landlord.

3A-1156 *Note*—This section was inserted by Anti-Social Behaviour Act 2003 s.14(5), Sch.1, para.1 and amended by the Civil Partnership Act 2004 s.81 Sch.8, para.55.

**Editorial note**

3A-1157 Section 143H provides for succession to demoted tenancies by members of a deceased tenant's family *cf*. Housing Act 1985 s.88 and the commentary at para.3A-402. There can only be one succession.

**Demoted tenancy**

3A-1158 See Housing Act 1985 s.82A and s.143A, above. This section only applies to former secure tenancies while the tenant condition (see Housing Act 1985 s.81) continues to apply.

**Secure tenancy**

3A-1159 See Housing Act 1985 s.79.

**Only or principal home**

3A-1160 This is the phrase which is used in the tenant condition for secure tenancies—see Housing Act 1985 s.81 and the commentary at para.3A-342.

**Member of the tenant's family**

3A-1161 See s.143P.

## No successor tenant: termination

3A-1162 **143I.**—(1) This section applies if the demoted tenant dies and no person is qualified to succeed to the tenancy as mentioned in section 143H(3).

(2) The tenancy ceases to be a demoted tenancy if either subsection (3) or (4) applies.

(3) This subsection applies if the tenancy is vested or otherwise disposed of in the course of the administration of the tenant's estate unless the vesting or other disposal is in pursuance of an order under—

(a) section 23A or 24 of the Matrimonial Causes Act 1973 (property adjustment orders in connection with matrimonial proceedings);
(b) section 17(1) of the Matrimonial and Family Proceedings Act 1984 (property adjustment orders after overseas divorce, etc);
(c) paragraph 1 of Schedule 1 to the Children Act 1989 (orders for financial relief against parents).
(d) Part 2 of Schedule 5, or paragraph 9(2) or (3) of Schedule 7, to the Civil Partnership Act 2004 (property adjustment orders in connection with civil partnership proceedings or after overseas dissolution of civil partnership, etc).

(4) This subsection applies if it is known that when the tenancy is vested or otherwise disposed of in the course of the administration of the tenant's estate it will not be in pursuance of an order mentioned in subsection (3).

(5) A tenancy which ceases to be a demoted tenancy by virtue of this section cannot subsequently become a secure tenancy.

*Note*—This section was inserted by Anti-Social Behaviour Act 2003 s.14(5), Sch.1, para.1; amended by the Civil Partnership Act 2004 s.81, Sch.8, para.56. **3A–1163**

**Demoted tenancy**

See Housing Act 1985 s.82A and s.143A, above. This section only applies to former secure tenancies while the tenant condition (see Housing Act 1985 s.81) continues to apply. **3A–1164**

**Secure tenancy**

See Housing Act 1985 s.79. **3A–1165**

**Person is qualified to succeed**

See ss.143H and 143P. **3A–1166**

## Successor tenants

**143J.**—(1) This section applies for the purpose of sections 143H and 143I. **3A–1167**

(2) A person is a successor to a secure tenancy which is terminated by a demotion order if any of subsections (3) to (6) applies to him.

(3) The tenancy vested in him—
(a) by virtue of section 89 of the Housing Act 1985 or section 133 of this Act;
(b) under the will or intestacy of the preceding tenant.

(4) The tenancy arose by virtue of section 86 of the Housing Act 1985 and the original fixed term was granted—
(a) to another person, or
(b) to him jointly with another person.

(5) He became the tenant on the tenancy being assigned to him unless—
(a) the tenancy was assigned—
(i) in proceedings under section 24 of the Matrimonial Causes Act 1973 (property adjustment orders

*Paragraph numbers marked with a "+" can be found online and on CD.*

in connection with matrimonial proceedings) or section 17(1) of the Matrimonial and Family Proceedings Act 1984 (property adjustment orders after overseas divorce, etc), or

(ii) in proceedings under Part 2 of Schedule 5, or paragraph 9(2) or (3) of Schedule 7, to the Civil Partnership Act 2004 (property adjustment orders in connection with civil partnership proceedings or after overseas dissolution of civil partnership, etc),

(b) where the tenancy was assigned as mentioned in paragraph (a)(i), neither he nor the other party to the marriage was a successor, and

(c) where the tenancy was assigned as mentioned in paragraph (a)(ii), neither he nor the other civil partner was a successor.

(6) He became the tenant on assignment under section 92 of the Housing Act 1985 if he himself was a successor to the tenancy which he assigned in exchange.

(7) A person is the successor to a demoted tenancy if the tenancy vested in him by virtue of section 143H(4) or (5).

(8) A person is the successor to a joint tenancy if he has become the sole tenant.

3A–1168 *Note*—This section was inserted by Anti-Social Behaviour Act 2003 s.14(5), Sch.1, para.1 and amended by the Civil Partnership Act 2004 s.81, Sch.8, para.57.

**Demoted tenancy**

3A–1169 See Housing Act 1985 s.82A and s.143A, above. This section only applies to former secure tenancies while the tenant condition (see Housing Act 1985 s.81) continues to apply.

**Secure tenancy**

3A–1170 See Housing Act 1985 s.79.

**Successor**

3A–1171 See ss.143H and 143P.

*ASSIGNMENT*

## Restriction on assignment

3A–1172 **143K.**—(1) A demoted tenancy is not capable of being assigned except as mentioned in subsection (2).

(2) The exceptions are assignment in pursuance of an order made under—

(a) section 24 of the Matrimonial Causes Act 1973 (property adjustment orders in connection with matrimonial proceedings);

(b) section 17(1) of the Matrimonial and Family Proceedings Act 1984 (property adjustment orders after overseas divorce, etc.);

(c) paragraph 1 of Schedule 1 to the Children Act 1989 (orders for financial relief against parents).

(d) Part 2 of Schedule 5, or paragraph 9(2) or (3) of Schedule 7, to the Civil Partnership Act 2004 (property adjustment orders in connection with civil partnership proceedings or after overseas dissolution of civil partnership, etc).

*Note* —This section was inserted by Anti-Social Behaviour Act 2003 s.14(5), Sch.1, para.1 and amended by the Civil Partnership Act 2004 s.81, Sch.8, para.58. **3A–1173**

**Editorial note**

Section 143K provides that a demoted tenancy cannot be assigned except in matrimonial proceedings or under Children Act 1989 *cf.* Housing Act 1985 s.91. There is no provision for mutual exchange *cf.* Housing Act 1985 s.92. **3A–1174**

**Demoted tenancy**

See Housing Act 1985 s.82A and s.143A, above. This section only applies to former secure tenancies while the tenant condition (see Housing Act 1985 s.81) continues to apply. **3A–1175**

### *REPAIRS*

## Right to carry out repairs

**143L.** The Secretary of State may by regulations under section 96 of the Housing Act 1985 (secure tenants: right to carry out repairs) apply to demoted tenants any provision made under that section in relation to secure tenants. **3A–1176**

*Note* —This section was inserted by Anti-Social Behaviour Act 2003 s.14(5), Sch.1, para.1. **3A–1177**

**Demoted tenancy**

See Housing Act 1985 s.82A and s.143A, above. This section only applies to former secure tenancies while the tenant condition (see Housing Act 1985 s.81) continues to apply. **3A–1178**

**Secure tenants: right to carry out repairs**

See Housing Act 1985 s.96. **3A–1179**

**Regulations**

There are not yet any regulations. **3A–1180**

### *PROVISION OF INFORMATION*

## Provision of information

**143M.**—(1) This section applies to a local housing authority or a housing action trust if it is the landlord of a demoted tenancy. **3A–1181**

(2) The landlord must from time to time publish information about the demoted tenancy in such form as it thinks best suited to explain in simple terms and so far as it considers appropriate the effect of—

(a) the express terms of the demoted tenancy;

(b) the provisions of this Chapter;

*Paragraph numbers marked with a "+" can be found online and on CD.*

(c) the provisions of sections 11 to 16 of the Landlord and Tenant Act 1985 (landlord's repairing obligations).

(3) The landlord must ensure that information published under subsection (2) is, so far as is reasonably practicable, kept up to date.

(4) The landlord must supply the tenant with—

(a) a copy of the information published under subsection (2);

(b) a written statement of the terms of the tenancy, so far as they are neither expressed in the lease or written tenancy agreement (if any) nor implied by law.

(5) The statement required by subsection (4)(b) must be supplied on the grant of the tenancy or as soon as practicable afterwards.

**3A–1182** *Note* —This section was inserted by Anti-Social Behaviour Act 2003 s.14(5), Sch.1, para.1.

**Demoted tenancy**

**3A–1183** See Housing Act 1985 s.82A and s.143A, above. This section only applies to former secure tenancies while the tenant condition (see Housing Act 1985 s.81) continues to apply.

**Sections 11 to 16 of the Landlord and Tenant Act 1985**

**3A–1184** See para.3A–546 *et seq.*

*SUPPLEMENTARY*

## Jurisdiction of county court

**3A–1185** **143N.**—(1) A county court has jurisdiction—

(a) to determine questions arising under this Chapter;

(b) to determine questions arising under this Chapter;

(c) to determine claims (for whatever amount) in connection with a demoted tenancy.

(2) The jurisdiction includes jurisdiction to entertain proceedings as to whether a statement supplied in pursuance of section 143M(4)(b) (written statement of certain terms of tenancy) is accurate.

(3) For the purposes of subsection (2) it is immaterial that no relief other than a declaration is sought.

(4) If a person takes proceedings in the High Court which, by virtue of this section, he could have taken in the county court he is not entitled to recover any costs.

(5) The Lord Chancellor may make such rules and give such directions as he thinks fit for the purposes of giving effect to this section.

(6) The rules and directions may provide—

(a) for the exercise by a district judge of a county court of any jurisdiction exercisable under this section;

(b) for the conduct of proceedings in private.

(7) The power to make rules must be exercised by statutory instrument subject to annulment in pursuance of a resolution of either House of Parliament.

*Note* —This section was inserted by Anti-Social Behaviour Act 2003 s.14(5), Sch.1, para.1. **3A–1186**

**Demoted tenancy**

See Housing Act 1985 s.82A and s.143A, above. This section only applies to former secure tenancies while the tenant condition (see Housing Act 1985 s.81) continues to apply. **3A–1187**

**Rules and directions**

See CPR Pt 65 and PD 65. **3A–1188**

## Meaning of dwelling house

**143O.**—(1) For the purposes of this Chapter a dwelling-house may be a house or a part of a house. **3A–1189**

(2) Land let together with a dwelling-house must be treated for the purposes of this Chapter as part of the dwelling-house unless the land is agricultural land which would not be treated as part of a dwelling-house for the purposes of Part 4 of the Housing Act 1985.

*Note* —This section was inserted by Anti-Social Behaviour Act 2003 s.14(5), Sch.1, para.1. **3A–1190**

## Members of a person's family

**143P.**—(1) For the purposes of this Chapter a person is a member of another's family if— **3A–1191**

(a) he is the spouse or civil partner of that person;

(b) he and that person live together as a couple in an enduring family relationship, but he does not fall within paragraph (c);

(c) he is that person's parent, grandparent, child, grandchild, brother, sister, uncle, aunt, nephew or niece.

(2) For the purposes of subsection (1)(b) it is immaterial that two persons living together in an enduring family relationship are of the same sex.

(3) For the purposes of subsection (1)(c)—

(a) a relationship by marriage or civil partnership must be treated as a relationship by blood;

(b) a relationship of the half-blood must be treated as a relationship of the whole blood;

(c) a stepchild of a person must be treated as his child.

*Note* —This section has been amended by the Anti-Social Behaviour Act 2003 s.14(5), Sch.1, para.1; amended by the Civil Partnership Act 2004 s.81, Sch.8, para.59. **3A–1192**

**Member of another's family**

*Cf.* Housing Act 1985 s.113 and the commentary at para.3A–412. Section 143P(2) gives effect to the decision in *Ghaidan v Godin-Mendoza* [2004] UKHL 30; [2004] 2 A.C. 557; [2004] 3 W.L.R. 113. **3A–1193**

**Editorial note**

This section was inserted by Anti-Social Behaviour Act 2003 s.14(5) and Sch.1. It was brought into force in England on June 30, 2004 by the Anti-Social Behaviour Act 2003 (Commencement No.3 and Savings) Order 2004 (SI 2004/1502) (c.61). It was **3A–1194** brought into force in Wales on 30 April 2005 by the Anti-Social Behaviour Act 2003 (Commencement No.4) (Wales) Order 2005 (SI 2005/1225) (w.83) (c.55).

* * * *

CHAPTER III

INJUNCTIONS AGAINST ANTI-SOCIAL BEHAVIOUR

### Power to grant injunctions against anti-social behaviour

3A–1195 **152.** [...]

### Power of arrest for breach of other injunctions against anti-social behaviour

3A–1196 **153.** [...]

3A–1197 *Note* — Sections 152 and 153 were repealed by the Anti-Social Behaviour Act 2003, s.13 and replaced by new ss.153A—E below.

### Anti-social behaviour injunction

3A–1198 **153A.**—(1) In this section— "anti-social behaviour injunction" means an injunction that prohibits the person in respect of whom it is granted from engaging in housing-related anti-social conduct of a kind specified in the injunction; "anti-social conduct" means conduct capable of causing nuisance or annoyance to some person (who need not be a particular identified person); "conduct" means conduct anywhere; "housing-related" means directly or indirectly relating to or affecting the housing management functions of a relevant landlord.

(2) The court on the application of a relevant landlord may grant an anti-social behaviour injunction if the condition in subsection (3) is satisfied.

(3) The condition is that the person against whom the injunction is sought is engaging, has engaged or threatens to engage in housing-related conduct capable of causing a nuisance or annoyance to—

(a) a person with a right (of whatever description) to reside in or occupy housing accommodation owned or managed by a relevant landlord,

(b) a person with a right (of whatever description) to reside in or occupy other housing accommodation in the neighbourhood of housing accommodation mentioned in paragraph (a),

(c) a person engaged in lawful activity in, or in the neighbourhood of, housing accommodation mentioned in paragraph (a), or

(d) a person employed (whether or not by a relevant landlord) in connection with the exercise of a relevant landlord's housing management functions.

(4) Without prejudice to the generality of the court's power under subsection (2), a kind of conduct may be described in an anti-social behaviour injunction by reference to a person or persons and, if it is, may (in particular) be described by reference—

(a) to persons generally,
(b) to persons of a description specified in the injunction, or
(c) to persons, or a person, specified in the injunction.

*Note* —Note: This section was inserted by the Police and Justice Act 2006 s.26. It was brought into force on April 6, 2007 by the Police and Justice Act 2006 (Commencement No.2, Transitional and Saving Provisions) Order 2007 (SI 2007/709) (c.30). It replaces an earlier version inserted by Anti-Social Behaviour Act 2003 s.13. **3A–1199**

**Editorial note**

Section 153A(1) allows relevant landlords to obtain anti-social behaviour injunctions. **3A–1200** It provides that the conduct to which that provision applies is conduct capable of causing nuisance or annoyance to some person (who need not be a particular identified person) even if no complaint has been made. The conduct must be "housing-related"—i.e. directly or indirectly relating to or affecting the housing management functions of a relevant landlord. The conduct may take place "anywhere"". Injunctions may be obtained against people who are engaging, have engaged or threaten to engage in housing-related conduct capable of causing a nuisance or annoyance to—

(a) a person with a right to reside in or occupy housing accommodation owned or managed by a relevant landlord,
(b) a person with a right to reside in or occupy other housing accommodation in the neighbourhood of housing accommodation mentioned in para.(a),
(c) a person engaged in lawful activity in, or in the neighbourhood of, housing accommodation mentioned in para.(a), or
(d) a person employed (whether or not by a relevant landlord) in connection with the exercise of a relevant landlord's housing management functions.

**Relevant landlord**

An application for an anti-social behaviour injunction may only be made by a relevant landlord. **3A–1201** Section 153E(7) specifies bodies which may be relevant landlords. Housing action trusts (see the Housing Act 1996 s.230 and the Housing Act 1988 Part III), local authorities (see the Housing Act 1985 s.4(e)) and registered social landlords (see the Housing Act 1996 s.230 referring back to Part I (ss.1 to 3)) are all relevant landlords for the purposes of s.153A. A charitable housing trust which is not a registered social landlord is not a relevant landlord for the purposes of s.153A.

**Court**

This means either the High Court or a county court (s.153E(6)). In practice applications for anti-social behaviour injunctions should always be made to a county court. **3A–1202**

**Housing accommodation**

See s.153E(9). Housing accommodation includes flats, lodging-houses and hostels **3A–1203** and any yard, garden, outhouses and appurtenances belonging to the accommodation or usually enjoyed with it. In relation to a neighbourhood, it includes the whole of the housing accommodation owned or managed by a relevant landlord in the neighbourhood and any common areas used in connection with the accommodation. Housing accommodation is owned (s.153A(4)) by a relevant landlord if either it is a person (other than a mortgagee not in possession) who is for the time being entitled to dispose of the fee simple in the premises, whether in possession or in reversion or holds or is entitled to the rents and profits of the premises under a lease which (when granted) was for a term of not less than three years.

**Housing management functions**

See s.153E(11). The housing management functions of a relevant landlord include **3A–1204** functions conferred by or under any enactment and the powers and duties of the landlord as the holder of an estate or interest in housing accommodation.

**Minors**

In *Enfield LBC v B (A Minor)* [2000] 1 W.L.R. 2259, CA, the Court of Appeal doubted **3A–1205** but left open the proposition that former s.152 could not apply to minors—but see *H*

***Paragraph numbers marked with a "+" can be found online and on CD.***

*v H (A Child) (Occupation Order: Power of Arrest)* [2001] 1 F.L.R. 641; [2001] 1 F.C.R. 370; [2001] Fam. Law 261, CA. (The court has the power to attach a power of arrest to an occupation order made under Family Law Act 1996 s.47(2) against a minor. By suggesting that such a power of arrest could not be made against a 17 year old, wording was implied upon the provisions of s.47(2) of the Act that just was not there) *Wookey v Wookey* [1991] Fam. 121; [1991] 3 W.L.R. 135, CA. But see *G v Harrow LBC* [2004] EWHC 17 (QB). (Complaints against 14 year old. The council obtained an injunction against him under Housing Act 1996 s.152 with a power of arrest. Roderick Evans J. granted the appeal. G was too young to be sent to prison for contempt. In the absence of evidence to the contrary, common sense and experience dictated that G would have no source of income or goods that could be sequestered. The injunction could not be properly or effectively enforced and so should not have been granted. Roderick Evans J. stated that if a council did seek an injunction against a minor, it should be in a position to place evidence before the judge of the minor's circumstances which would make enforcement by a way of a fine or sequestration of assets an effective sanction for breach).

**Procedure**

**3A–1206** The County Court (Amendment) Rules 1997 set out the procedure to be followed on applications for injunctions to restrain anti-social behaviour under Housing Act 1996 ss.152 and 153 by creating a new CCR O.49, r.6B, as amended by the Civil Procedure (Amendment No.4) Rules 2001. They have been replaced by a new CPR Pt 65 (Anti-social Behaviour and Harassment) and PD 65. CPR Pt 65 also contains provisions dealing with demoted tenancies, ASBOs and the Protection from Harassment Act 1997. The old procedure was also partly governed by a Practice Direction made by the Lord Chancellor on August 28, 1997. It has been revoked and not replaced.

(i) *Applications for anti-social behaviour injunctions.* Applications for injunctions under ss.153A, 153B or 153D must be made in Form **N16A** and follow the Pt 8 procedure. They must be made in the court for the district in which the defendant resides or the conduct complained of occurred. (CPR r.65.3; PD 65 para.1; *cf.* CCR O.49, r.6B(1)).

(ii) All applications must state the terms of the injunction applied for and be supported by written evidence. They must be made on two days notice unless the court otherwise directs. The defendant must be served personally. If the application is made without notice the affidavit should explain why notice has not been given. (CPR r.65.3; *cf.* CCR O.49, r.6B(2)–(4))

(iii) Unless otherwise directed applications made on notice should be heard in public. (CPR r.39.2; *cf.* PD to CCR O.49, r.6B(5)). In *Moat Housing Group South Ltd v Harris and Hartless* [2005] EWCA Civ 287; [2006] Q.B. 606; [2005] 3 W.L.R. 691; [2005] 4 All E.R. 1051, Brooke L.J., giving the judgment of the court, stressed that the grant of an injunction without notice is an exceptional remedy.

> "It is hard to envisage a more intrusive 'without notice' order than one which requires a mother and her four young children to vacate their home immediately. .... As a matter of principle no order should be made in civil or family proceedings without notice to the other side unless there is a very good reason for departing from the general rule that notice must be given. Needless to say, the more intrusive the order, the stronger must be the reasons for the departure. It is one thing to restrain a defendant from what would in any event be anti-social behaviour for a short time until a hearing can be arranged at which both sides can be heard. It is quite another thing to make a 'without notice' order directing defendants to leave their home immediately and banning them from re-entering a large part of the area where they live."

After reviewing family law authorities on ouster injunctions, Brooke L.J. said that when deciding whether to exercise their discretion to make ASBIs without notice, judges should follow the guidance given in Family Law Act 1996 s.45(2)(a). Further, it is:

> "inconceivable that a court would grant an ASBI without notice unless there was both violence (or a threat of violence) in the past and a risk of significant harm to one of the relevant persons during the short period between the time of service of the order and the time of the court hearing on notice."

(iv) Applications for injunctions must be made in Form **N16A** (PD65, para.1). Injunctions should be in Form **N16**. Wherever possible the claimant should file a draft of the order sought with the application and a disc with the draft order should be available to the court (PD 25 para.2.4). Injunctions must be "framed in terms appropriate and proportionate to the facts of the case". If there is a risk of significant harm to a particular person or persons it is usually appropriate for the injunction to identify that person or those persons. However, in order to justify granting a wider injunction, restraining someone from causing a nuisance or annoyance to, "a person of a similar description," it is normally necessary for the judge to make a finding that there has been use or threats of violence to persons of a similar description, and that there is a risk of significant harm to persons of a similar description if an injunction is not granted in respect of them. (*Manchester City Council v Lee* [2003] EWCA Civ 1256; [2004] 1 W.L.R. 349).

(v) If a power of arrest is sought, each provision which is to be subject to the power of arrest, must be set out in a separate clause of the injunction (CPR r.65.4). Powers of arrest may be sought in claim forms, acknowledgements of service or Pt 23 applications. They must be supported by written evidence. If made on notice, not less than two days notice must be given (CPR r.65.9) It is important to spell out in the injunction the specific activities which are forbidden and confine the power of arrest to those specific activities alone. Under ECHR law, citizens must be able, if necessary with appropriate advice, to foresee to a reasonable degree the consequences that a given action may produce (*Silver v United Kingdom* (1983) 5 E.H.R.R. 347, at paras 87–8). Summary arrest and detention are clearly an extremely serious interference with a person's private life, which can only be justified by an order which is "particularly precise" (*Kopp v Switzerland* (1999) 27 E.H.R.R. 91, at para.72). See too *Manchester City Council v Lee* [2003] EWCA Civ 1256; [2004] 1 W.L.R. 349 and, in a domestic violence context, *Hale v Tanner* [2000] 1 W.L.R. 2377, CA, which suggests a power of arrest be attached only to paragraphs prohibiting violence or physical proximity. This is confirmed by s.153C.

(vi) A without notice court order with a power of arrest attached deserves and demands early re-consideration, ideally within 14 days. There is nothing wrong in a without notice order being for a duration of six months, provided that it is of a non-intrusive type (such as a typical non-molestation or non-nuisance order) and the on notice hearing takes place timeously (*Moat Housing Group South Ltd v Harris and Hartless* [2005] EWCA Civ 287; [2006] Q.B. 606; [2005] 3 W.L.R. 691; [2005] 4 All E.R. 1051).

(vii) The claimant must deliver a copy of an injunction with a Power of Arrest to any police station for the area where the conduct occurred—but if it was granted without notice, only after service on the defendant (CPR r.65.4 and Form **N110A**; *cf.* CCR O.49, r.6B(6)). The claimant must immediately inform the police station if an injunction containing a power of arrest is varied or discharged.

(viii) The question of jurisdiction has been dealt with by an amendment to PD2B. The former position was that the jurisdiction of the court under ss.152 and 153 could be exercised by district judges as well as circuit judges. The amendment to PD2B makes it clear that district and deputy district judges have jurisdiction to grant anti-social behaviour injunctions and to commit for contempt. There is no longer any requirement that district judges and deputy district judges have to have had appropriate training before exercising the jurisdiction (*cf.* the Practice Direction made by the Lord Chancellor on August 28, 1997 which has been revoked and not replaced). Notwithstanding the suggestion in some quarters that the former rule giving district judges jurisdiction was ultra vires, it is now accepted that this is not the case—see County Courts Act 1984 s.75(3)(d), repealed by Civil Procedure Act 1997 Sch.2, but Sch.1 of that Act provides that the Civil Procedure Rules may deal with the subjects contained in the former rules.

(ix) An application for a warrant of arrest under s.155(3) must be made in accordance with CPR Pt 23 and may be made without notice. A claimant seeking a warrant must file an affidavit setting out grounds for the application or give oral evidence. A warrant shall not be issued unless the application is substantiated on oath and the judge has reasonable grounds for believing the defendant has failed to comply with the injunction (CPR r.65.5).

(x) The judge before whom an arrested person is brought may deal with the matter or adjourn proceedings (CPR r.65.6). In such circumstances the arrested person may be remanded or released. If the person is released, the matter shall be dealt with by the same or another judge within 28 days of the date the arrested person appears in court. At least two days notice of the adjourned hearing must be given. (CPR r.65.6; *cf.* CCR O.49, r.6B(8B)).

(xi) Applications for bail. An application for bail made by a person arrested under a power of arrest attached to an injunction or a warrant of arrest issued under s.155(3) may be made either orally or in an application notice. An application notice seeking bail must contain (1) the full name of the person making the application; (2) the address of the place where the person making the application is detained; (3) the address where s/he would reside if bail were granted; (4) the amount of any proposed recognizance; and (5) the grounds for the application and, where a previous application has been refused, full details of any change in circumstances which has occurred since that refusal. A copy of the application notice must be served on the person who obtained the injunction. (PD 65 para.2; *cf.* PD to CCR O.49, r.6B)

(xii) If a person is bailed, subject to a recognizance, the recognizance may subsequently be taken by a judge, a justice of the peace, a justice's clerk, a senior police officer or the governor of a prison (CPR r.65.7; *cf.* CCR O.49, r.6B(11)).

**Sentences for breach of s.153A injunctions**

**3A–1207** In *Tower Hamlets LBC v Long* (2000) 32 H.L.R. 219, CA, the Court of Appeal held that an immediate sentence of imprisonment was appropriate where a tenant had waged a personal vendetta against another tenant in breach of an injunction. However a prison sentence of three months was reduced to three weeks. In *Nottingham City Council v Cutts* (2001) 33 H.L.R. 7, CA, the Court of Appeal dismissed an appeal against an immediate sentence of twelve months imprisonment where there had been previous breaches and where the actual breaches consisted of attempts to punch, racist and other foul language, threats to kill and kicking and banging of doors. The judge "was undoubtedly right in the case to impose a substantial term of imprisonment". Although the sentence was "a stiff one" it was not "manifestly excessive". See too *Leicester City Council v Lewis* (2001) 33 H.L.R. 37, CA and *Leeds CC v MacDonald* , November 20, 2007, unrep.

In *Barnet LBC v Hurst* [2002] EWCA Civ 1009; [2003] 1 W.L.R. 722, the Court of Appeal held that a sentence of nine months imprisonment for a defendant who had breached an undertaking not to assault, threaten, harass or cause nuisance to anyone residing in or visiting a block of flats where his father lived by being loud and noisy and disturbing the neighbours' sleep was manifestly too long. The sentence was reduced to three months. The maximum sentence of two years imprisonment should be reserved for the worst cases (*Turnbull v Middlesbrough BC* [2003] EWCA Civ 1327).

In *Longhurst Homes Ltd v Killen* [2008] EWCA Civ 402; March 11, 2008, a case of repeated, unpleasant and intimidating behaviour, but where no actual violence had been used, the Court of Appeal dismissed an appeal against nine months' imprisonment, stating that the judge was entitled to reach the conclusion that an immediate sentence of imprisonment was called for in the face of breaches of the injunction which had been deliberate and repeated. Although the overall sentence was stiff, and one which would not necessarily have been imposed by every judge, the judge had not stepped outside the bracket legitimately available to her.

In *Birmingham City Council v Flatt* [2008] EWCA Civ 739, June 12, 2008, the Court of Appeal stated that it does not follow that imprisonment is to be regarded as the automatic consequence of breach of an order and it is common practice to take some other course on the first occasion when someone breaches an injunction. However, in this case, the defendant had a history of violent and threatening conduct towards others. He had denied the breaches and shown no remorse. A sentence of imprisonment was not wrong in principle. Although the length of the sentence (four months' imprisonment for driving a vehicle at a neighbour, causing him injury and making false accusations about other neighbours) was at the top end of the range of sentences available for such a breach, it was not manifestly excessive and the judge had been entitled to take the view that this was not a case for a suspended sentence order.

Time spent in custody on remand is not deducted from the sentence imposed on a committal for contempt of court (*Delaney v Delaney* [1996] Q.B. 387, CA; *Sevketoglu v Sevketoglu* [2003] EWCA Civ 1570)—but it is important to note that pursuant to Criminal Justice Act 2003 s.258, a defendant can expect to serve half of the period of imprisonment imposed (see *Wear Valley DC v Robson* [2008] EWCA Civ 1470; [2009]

***Paragraph numbers marked with a "+" can be found online and on CD.***

H.L.R. 27—six months' imprisonment for breaching an ASBI on five separate occasions by playing loud music, banging on residents' doors, using foul language, behaving in a drunken and abusive manner, allowing other alcoholics to visit his flat and threatening to smash up the flat evicted, described as a severe sentence, but wholly appropriate.).

## Injunction against unlawful use of premises

**153B.**—(1) This section applies to conduct which consists of or involves using or threatening to use housing accommodation owned or managed by a relevant landlord for an unlawful purpose. **3A-1208**

(2) The court on the application of the relevant landlord may grant an injunction prohibiting the person in respect of whom the injunction is granted from engaging in conduct to which this section applies.

*Note*—This section was inserted by Anti-Social Behaviour Act 2003 s.13. **3A-1209**

### Relevant landlord

An application for an anti-social behaviour injunction may only be made by a relevant landlord. Section 153E(7) specifies bodies which may be relevant landlords. Housing action trusts (see Housing Act 1996 s.230 and Housing Act 1988 Pt III), local authorities (see Housing Act 1985 s.4(e)) and registered social landlords (see Housing Act 1996 s.230 referring back to Part I (ss.1 to 3)) are all relevant landlords for the purposes of s.153A. A charitable housing trust which is not a registered social landlord is not a relevant landlord for the purposes of s.153B. **3A-1210**

### Court

This means either the High Court or a county court (s.153E(6)). In practice applications for anti-social behaviour injunctions should always be made to a county court. **3A-1211**

### Housing accommodation

See s.153E(9). Housing accommodation includes flats, lodging-houses and hostels and any yard, garden, outhouses and appurtenances belonging to the accommodation or usually enjoyed with it. In relation to a neighbourhood, it includes the whole of the housing accommodation owned or managed by a relevant landlord in the neighbourhood and any common areas used in connection with the accommodation. Housing accommodation is owned (s.153A(4)) by a relevant landlord if either it is a person (other than a mortgagee not in possession) who is for the time being entitled to dispose of the fee simple in the premises, whether in possession or in reversion or holds or is entitled to the rents and profits of the premises under a lease which (when granted) was for a term of not less than three years. **3A-1212**

### Unlawful purpose

This phrase is not defined. Clearly the section includes any conduct which amounts to a criminal offence. The most obvious examples are drug dealing or use of the premises as a brothel. In view of s.153D, it is unlikely that it includes conduct which is merely a breach of the terms of a tenancy agreement and not a criminal offence. **3A-1213**

## Injunctions: exclusion order and power of arrest

**153C.**—(1) This section applies if the court grants an injunction under subsection (2) of section 153A or 153B and it thinks that either of the following paragraphs applies— **3A-1214**

(a) the conduct consists of or includes the use or threatened use of violence;

(b) there is a significant risk of harm to a person mentioned in any of paragraphs (a) to (d) of section 153A(3).

*Paragraph numbers marked with a "+" can be found online and on CD.*

HOUSING

(2) The court may include in the injunction a provision prohibiting the person in respect of whom it is granted from entering or being in—

(a) any premises specified in the injunction;

(b) any area specified in the injunction.

(3) The court may attach a power of arrest to any provision of the injunction.

3A-1215 *Note* —This section was inserted by Anti-Social Behaviour Act 2003 s.13. It was amended by the Police and Justice Act 2006 Sch.14, para.32, with effect from April 6, 2007 (SI 2007/709).

**Editorial note**

3A-1216 Section 153C allows the court granting an injunction under ss.153A or 153B to attach a power of arrest or to exclude a person from specified premises or a specified area where there is the use or threat of violence or a significant risk of harm to any person mentioned in s.153A(4). Consequently a power of arrest is available in cases where there is a significant risk of harm even if there has been no actual or threatened violence.

**Power of arrest**

3A-1217 See s.154 and the commentary to that section.

**Exclusion orders**

3A-1218 Although courts have power to make ouster orders and/or exclusion orders without notice if the facts are sufficiently serious to warrant such a draconian order, very great care is needed. Further, judges making such orders should generally be scrupulous to prescribe that the order may only be served at a reasonable time of the day (for example, between 9 am and 4.30 pm on a weekday) (*Moat Housing Group South Ltd v Harris and Hartless* [2005] EWCA Civ 287; [2006] Q.B. 606; [2005] 3 W.L.R. 691; [2005] 4 All E.R. 1051).

**Court**

3A-1219 This means either the High Court or a county court (s.153E(6)). In practice applications for anti-social behaviour injunctions, exclusion orders and/or powers of arrest should always be made to a county court.

**Harm**

3A-1220 See s.153E(12). Harm includes serious ill-treatment or abuse (whether physical or not). The government's intention (see the explanatory notes to the Act) was that it should include emotional or psychological harm. This could apply, for example, in cases of racial or sexual harassment. The former repealed provisions only allowed a power of arrest when there was either violence or threatened violence together with a significant risk of harm.

## Injunction against breach of tenancy agreement

3A-1221 **153D.**—(1) This section applies if a relevant landlord applies for an injunction against a tenant in respect of the breach or anticipated breach of a tenancy agreement on the grounds that the tenant—

(a) is engaging or threatening to engage in conduct that is capable of causing nuisance or annoyance to any person, or

(b) is allowing, inciting or encouraging any other person to engage or threaten to engage in such conduct.

(2) The court may proceed under subsection (3) or (4) if it is satisfied—

***Paragraph numbers marked with a "+" can be found online and on CD.***

(a) that the conduct includes the use or threatened use of violence, or

(b) that there is a significant risk of harm to any person.

(3) The court may include in the injunction a provision prohibiting the person in respect of whom it is granted from entering or being in—

(a) any premises specified in the injunction;

(b) any area specified in the injunction.

(4) The court may attach a power of arrest to any provision of the injunction.

(5) Tenancy agreement includes any agreement for the occupation of residential accommodation owned or managed by a relevant landlord.

*Note* —This section was inserted by Anti-Social Behaviour Act 2003 s.13. **3A–1222**

**Editorial note**

Section 153D applies in relation to injunctions sought by a local authority, a housing action trust, a registered social landlord or a charitable housing trust on the grounds of a breach or anticipated breach of a tenancy agreement by a tenant. If the behaviour is prohibited by the terms of the tenancy agreement and satisfies the criteria ss.153D(1)(a) and (b), the court may exclude a person from specified premises or a specified area and attach a power of arrest to any provision of the injunction. The breach (or anticipated breach) of the tenancy agreement must relate to conduct which is capable of causing nuisance or annoyance to any person. The tenant may have engaged or threatened to engage in the conduct directly or have allowed, incited or encouraged another person to engage in such conduct. In addition the conduct must include violence or the threat of violence or a significant risk of harm to any person. **3A–1223**

**Relevant landlord**

An application for an anti-social behaviour injunction may only be made by a relevant landlord. Section 153E(7) specifies bodies which may be relevant landlords. Housing action trusts (see Housing Act 1996 s.230 and Housing Act 1988 Pt III), local authorities (see Housing Act 1985 s.4(e)) and registered social landlords (see Housing Act 1996 s.230 referring back to Pt I (ss.1 to 3)) are all relevant landlords for the purposes of s.153A. A charitable housing trust which is not a registered social landlord is not a relevant landlord for the purposes of s.153D (see s.153E(8)). **3A–1224**

**Court**

This means either the High Court or a county court (s.153E(6)). In practice applications for injunctions to prevent a breach of a tenancy agreement should always be made to a county court. **3A–1225**

**Power of arrest**

See s.154 and the commentary to that section. **3A–1226**

## Injunctions: supplementary

**153E.**—(1) This section applies for the purposes of sections 153A to 153D. **3A–1227**

(2) An injunction may—

(a) be made for a specified period or until varied or discharged;

(b) have the effect of excluding a person from his normal place of residence.

(3) An injunction may be varied or discharged by the court on an application by—

*Paragraph numbers marked with a "+" can be found online and on CD.*

(a) the person in respect of whom it is made;
(b) the relevant landlord.

(4) If the court thinks it just and convenient it may grant or vary an injunction without the respondent having been given such notice as is otherwise required by rules of court.

(5) If the court acts under subsection (4) it must give the person against whom the injunction is made an opportunity to make representations in relation to the injunction as soon as it is practicable for him to do so.

(6) The court is the High Court or a county court.

(7) Each of the following is a relevant landlord—
(a) a housing action trust;
(b) a local authority (within the meaning of the Housing Act 1985);
(c) a registered social landlord.

(8) A charitable housing trust which is not a registered social landlord is also a relevant landlord for the purposes of section 153D.

(9) Housing accommodation includes—
(a) flats, lodging-houses and hostels;
(b) any yard, garden, outhouses and appurtenances belonging to the accommodation or usually enjoyed with it;
(c) in relation to a neighbourhood, the whole of the housing accommodation owned or managed by a relevant landlord in the neighbourhood and any common areas used in connection with the accommodation.

(10) A landlord owns housing accommodation if either of the following paragraphs applies to him—
(a) he is a person (other than a mortgagee not in possession) who is for the time being entitled to dispose of the fee simple in the premises, whether in possession or in reversion;
(b) he is a person who holds or is entitled to the rents and profits of the premises under a lease which (when granted) was for a term of not less than three years.

(11) The housing management functions of a relevant landlord include—
(a) functions conferred by or under any enactment;
(b) the powers and duties of the landlord as the holder of an estate or interest in housing accommodation.

(12) Harm includes serious ill-treatment or abuse (whether physical or not).

**3A–1228** *Note*—This section was inserted by Anti-Social Behaviour Act 2003 s.13.

**Registered social landlord**

**3A–1229** See Housing Act 1996 s.230 referring back to Pt I, ss.1 to 3.

## Powers of arrest: ex-parte applications for injunctions

**3A–1230** **154.**—(1) In determining whether to exercise its power under section 153C(3) or 153D(4) to attach a power of arrest to an injunction which it intends to grant on an ex-parte application, the High Court or a county court shall have regard to all the circumstances including—

(a) whether it is likely that the applicant will be deterred or prevented from seeking the exercise of the power if the power is not exercised immediately, and

(b) whether there is reason to believe that the respondent is aware of the proceedings for the injunction but is deliberately evading service and that the applicant or any person of a description mentioned in any of paragraphs (a) to (d) of section 153A(3) (as the case may be) will be seriously prejudiced if the decision as to whether to exercise the power were delayed until substituted service is effected.

(2) Where the court exercises its power as mentioned in subsection (1), it shall afford the respondent an opportunity to make representations relating to the exercise of the power as soon as just and convenient at a hearing of which notice has been given to all the parties in accordance with rules of court.

*Note* —This section was amended by the Anti-Social Behaviour Act 2003 s.13(4). It was amended by the Police and Justice Act 2006 Sch.14, para.32, with effect from April 6, 2007 (SI 2007/709). **3A–1231**

**Powers of arrest: ex parte applications for injunctions**

See commentary to ss.153A–E. **3A–1232**

## Arrest and remand

**155.**—(1) If a power of arrest is attached to certain provisions of an injunction by virtue of section 153C(3) or 153D(4), a constable may arrest without warrant a person whom he has reasonable cause for suspecting to be in breach of any such provision or otherwise in contempt of court in relation to a breach of any such provision. A constable shall after making any such arrest forthwith inform the person on whose application the injunction was granted. **3A–1233**

(2) Where a person is arrested under subsection (1)—

(a) he shall be brought before the relevant judge within the period of 24 hours beginning at the time of his arrest, and

(b) if the matter is not then disposed of forthwith, the judge may remand him.

In reckoning for the purposes of this subsection any period of 24 hours no account shall be taken of Christmas Day, Good Friday or any Sunday.

(3) If the court has granted an injunction in circumstances such that a power of arrest could have been attached under section 153C(3) or 153D(4) but—

(a) has not attached a power of arrest under the section in question to any provisions of the injunction, or

(b) has attached that power only to certain provisions of the injunction, then, if at any time the applicant considers that the respondent has failed to comply with the injunction, he may apply to the relevant judge for the issue of a warrant for the arrest of the respondent.

(4) The relevant judge shall not issue a warrant on an application under subsection (3) unless—

(a) the application is substantiated on oath, and

(b) he has reasonable grounds for believing that the respondent has failed to comply with the injunction.

(5) If a person is brought before a court by virtue of a warrant issued under subsection (4) and the court does not dispose of the matter forthwith, the court may remand him.

(6) Schedule 15 (which makes provision corresponding to that applying in magistrates' courts in civil cases under sections 128 and 129 of the Magistrates' Courts Act 1980) applies in relation to the powers of the High Court and a county court to remand a person under this section.

(7) If a person remanded under this section is granted bail by virtue of subsection (6), he may be required by the relevant judge to comply, before release on bail or later, with such requirements as appear to the judge to be necessary to secure that he does not interfere with witnesses or otherwise obstruct the course of justice.

3A–1234 *Note*—This section was amended by Anti-Social Behaviour Act 2003 s.13(5).

**"relevant judge"**

3A–1235 See s.158 and the commentary at 3A–1206, para.(viii)

**Arrest and remand**

3A–1236 See commentary to ss.152 and 153 and Form **N148**.

Note that s.155(2)(b) and s.155(3)–(7) were implemented on October 15, 2001 by the Housing Act 1996 (Commencement No.13) Order 2001 (SI 2001/3164) (c.100). See too *Braintree DC v Clark* [1998] C.L.Y. 3724, CA. The county court has power to review a decision to grant bail or to remand in custody, especially when there has been a change in circumstance. Accordingly, the Court of Appeal's task on any appeal against a refusal to grant bail is one of review rather than rehearing. (*Newham LBC v Jones* [2002] EWCA Civ 1779 a case where an appeal was dismissed. Although the circuit judge did not specifically refer to the Bail Act 1976 when refusing bail, he did express concerns over the seriousness of the allegations and further breaches of the injunction).

## Remand for medical examination and report

3A–1237 **156.**—(1) If the relevant judge has reason to consider that a medical report will be required, any power to remand a person under section 155 may be exercised for the purpose of enabling a medical examination and report to be made.

(2) If such a power is so exercised the adjournment shall not be for more than 4 weeks at a time unless the judge remands the accused in custody.

(3) If the judge so remands the accused, the adjournment shall not be for more than 3 weeks at a time.

(4) If there is reason to suspect that a person who has been arrested—

(a) under section 155(1), or

(b) under a warrant issued under section 155(4),

is suffering from mental disorder within the meaning of the Mental Health Act 1983, the relevant judge shall have the same power to make an order under that section (remand for report on accused's mental condition) as the Crown Court has under section 35 of that Act in the case of an accused person within the meaning of that section.

*Note* —Amended (subject to savings) by the Mental Health Act 2007 s.1(4), Sch.1, Pt.2, para.21 with effect from November 3 2008 (SI 2008/1900). 3A–1237.1

**"relevant judge"**

See s.158 and the commentary at 3A–1206, para.(vii). 3A–1238

**Remand for medical examination and report**

See commentary to ss.152 and 153. 3A–1239

Note that ss.155(2)(b) (remands in custody) and 155(3)–(7) (warrants for arrest), 156 (remand for medical examination), and Sch.15 (provisions corresponding with civil procedure in magistrates' courts) were implemented on October 15, 2001 by the Housing Act 1996 (Commencement No.13) Order 2001 (SI 2001/3164) (c.100).

## Powers of arrest: supplementary provisions

**157.**—(1) If in exercise of its power under section 153C(3) or 153D(4) the High Court or a county court attaches a power of arrest to any provisions of an injunction, it may provide that the power of arrest is to have effect for a shorter period than the other provisions of the injunction. 3A–1240

(2) Any period specified for the purposes of subsection (1) may be extended by the court (on one or more occasions) on an application to vary or discharge the injunction.

(3) If a power of arrest has been attached to certain provisions of an injunction by virtue of section 153C(3) or 153D(4), the court may vary or discharge the injunction in so far as it confers a power of arrest (whether or not any application has been made to vary or discharge any other provision of the injunction).

(4) An injunction may be varied or discharged under subsection (3) on an application by the respondent or the person on whose application the injunction was made.

*Note* —This section was amended by the Anti-Social Behaviour Act 2003 s.13(6). 3A–1241

**Powers of arrest: supplementary provisions**

See commentary at 3A–1206. 3A–1242

## Interpretation: Chapter III

**158.**—(1) For the purposes of this Chapter— 3A–1243

"charitable housing trust" means a housing trust, within the meaning of the Housing Associations Act 1985, which is a charity within the meaning of the Charities Act 1993;

"child" means a person under the age of 18 years;

"harm"—

(a) in relation to a person who has reached the age of 18 years, means ill-treatment or the impairment of health, and

*Paragraph numbers marked with a "+" can be found online and on CD.*

(b) in relation to a child, means ill-treatment or the impairment of health or development;

"health" includes physical or mental health;

"ill-treatment", in relation to a child, includes sexual abuse and forms of ill-treatment which are not physical;

"relevant judge", in relation to an injunction, means—

(a) where the injunction was granted by the High Court, a judge of that court,

(b) where the injunction was granted by a county court, a judge or district judge of that or any other county court;

"tenancy" includes a licence, and "tenant" and "landlord" shall be construed accordingly.

(2) Where the question of whether harm suffered by a child is significant turns on the child's health or development, his health or development shall be compared with that which could reasonably be expected of a similar child.

3A–1244 *Note* —This section was amended by the Anti-Social Behaviour Act 2003 s.13(7).

**Interpretation: Chapter III**

3A–1245 See commentary to ss.152 and 153.

**"relevant judge"**

3A–1246 See the commentary at para.3A–1206.

* * * *

## PART VII

## HOMELESSNESS

**Housing Act 1996—Pt VII**

3A–1247 Pt VII completely replaced the homelessness provisions formerly found in the Housing Act 1985 Pt III (see the Housing Act 1996 Sch.19, Pt VIII) with a new statutory code contained in ss.175 to 218). Some of the old provisions were re-enacted without alteration (e.g. s.189 (priority need)) or with only minor amendments (e.g. ss.175–177 (definition of homelessness), s.188 (interim duty to accommodate), ss.198–199 (local connection), and ss.211–212 (protection of property)). However, other changes were far more significant. Significant amendments to the 1996 Act were also made by the Homelessness Act 2002.

When implementing the provisions of Pt VII authorities must have regard to the Guidance issued by the Department of the Environment (s.182). The current *Code of Guidance* was issued in July 2002 by the Office of the Deputy Prime Minister to reflect changes introduced by the Homelessness Act 2002. Copies are available from the Office of the Deputy Prime Minister, PO Box 236, Wetherby, West Yorkshire LS23 7NB. There is a separate Welsh Code of Guidance issued by the Welsh Assembly Government. Failure to consider the current edition of the *Code* may provide grounds for quashing a decision (*R. v Newham LBC Ex p. Bones* (1998) 30 H.L.R. 261, QBD). However the Code of Guidance is not a source of law. Although councils must take it into account and give reasons for departing from it, it is not binding on them (*Khatun v Newham LBC* [2004] EWCA Civ 55; [2005] Q.B. 37; [2004] 3 W.L.R. 417). Where the Code of Guidance is in conflict with the Act, the words of the Act prevail (*Griffin v Westminster City Council* [2004] EWCA Civ 108; [2004] H.L.R. 32).

***Paragraph numbers marked with a "+" can be found online and on CD.***

See too Homelessness Act 2002 Pt I.

## Homelessness and threatened homelessness

**175.**—(1) A person is homeless if he has no accommodation available for his occupation, in the United Kingdom or elsewhere, which he— **3A–1248**

(a) is entitled to occupy by virtue of an interest in it or by virtue of an order of a court,

(b) has an express or implied licence to occupy, or

(c) occupies as a residence by virtue of any enactment or rule of law giving him the right to remain in occupation or restricting the right of another person to recover possession.

(2) A person is also homeless if he has accommodation but—

(a) he cannot secure entry to it, or

(b) it consists of a moveable structure, vehicle or vessel designed or adapted for human habitation and there is no place where he is entitled or permitted both to place it and to reside in it.

(3) A person shall not be treated as having accommodation unless it is accommodation which it would be reasonable for him to continue to occupy.

(4) A person is threatened with homelessness if it is likely that he will become homeless within 28 days.

### "accommodation available for his occupation"

See s.176. Prison is not accommodation. It does not fall within s.175(a), (b) or (c). **3A–1249**
For accommodation to exist there has to be a right to occupy which is enforceable or defensible in law. A prisoner cannot be said to have such a right of occupation. Detention is the antithesis of any such right. (*Stewart v Lambeth LBC* [2002] EWCA Civ 753; [2002] H.L.R. 40 and *R. (B) v Southwark LBC* [2003] EWHC 1678 (Admin); [2004] H.L.R. 3).

### "any enactment or rule of law"

A person remaining in possession of premises after the date on which an order for **3A–1250**
possession has become effective but before the warrant for possession has been executed is occupying a residence by virtue of an enactment restricting the right of the landlord to recover possession within s.175(1)(c). Enactment in that section includes rules of court under which the warrant was obtained. That is the position under the Protection from Eviction Act 1977 (*Haniff v Robinson* [1993] Q.B. 419; [1992] 3 W.L.R. 875; [1993] 1 All E.R. 185). Therefore a person only becomes homeless when the warrant for possession is executed (*R. (Sacupima) v Newham LBC* [2001] 1 W.L.R. 563, QBD). See too *R. v Newham LBC Ex p. Khan* (2001) 33 H.L.R. 29, QBD.

### "reasonable to continue to occupy"

See s.177. In assessing whether it is "reasonable to continue to occupy" existing ac- **3A–1251**
commodation, councils are entitled to take account of the existence of many families even more severely overcrowded in their area (s.177(2)). It does not automatically follow that because a home is statutorily overcrowded, or that an offence is being committed by remaining in it, that it cannot be reasonable for a tenant to continue in occupation. Furthermore, and in parallel to ss.175(3) and 177(2), s.210 (dealing with suitability of accommodation) does not provide that overcrowded accommodation can never be suitable, simply that the overcrowding provisions needed to be taken into account by the housing authority in deciding what to offer (*Harouki v RBK&C* [2007] EWCA Civ 1000; [2008] 1 W.L.R. 797, although it should be noted that the judgment contains the pre-2006 version of s.210).

*Paragraph numbers marked with a "+" can be found online and on CD.*

**Homelessness and threatened homelessness**

3A–1252 Sections 175, 176 and 177 re-enact the provisions defining homelessness ("A person is homeless if he has no accommodation available for his occupation ...") and what is accommodation which it is reasonable to occupy, formerly found in the Housing Act 1985 ss.58 and 75 with minor amendments. Section 177(3)provides that the Secretary of State may specify other circumstances to be taken into account in determining whether or not it is reasonable to continue in occupation. This has been done by the Homelessness (Suitability of Accommodation) Order 1996 (SI 1996/3204) which states that in considering whether it would have been reasonable for a person to continue to occupy accommodation, authorities should take into account the applicant's financial resources, including various specified forms of income, various specified costs relating to accommodation and other reasonable living expenses. See *Odunsi v Brent LBC*, unreported, 1999, Willesden County Court, where it was held that Homelessness (Suitability of Accommodation) Order 1996 art.2 requires councils to consider whether property is affordable. This is a mandatory obligation. The procedure is inquisitorial, not adversarial.

**Cannot secure entry**

3A–1253 The condition in section 175(2)(a) requiring a person to be able to secure entry to accommodation refers to some kind of physical bar to gaining entry at the premises themselves (e.g. displacement by unlawful eviction, squatting and the like) and not to some difficulty, for whatever reason, of travelling to them (*Begum v Tower Hamlets LBC*; [2000] Q.B. 133; [2000] 1 W.L.R. 306, CA).

**reasonable to occupy**

3A–1254 In *R. v Westminster City Council Ex p.Alouat* (1989) 21 H.L.R. 477, QBD, Schiemann J. held that in the Housing Act 1985 s.58(2A)(now the Housing Act 1996 s.175(3)) "reasonableness" is not limited to statutory factors—non-statutory overcrowding, medical need and other matters should also be considered by local authorities. When determining whether it is reasonable to continue to occupy accommodation for the purposes of Pt 7, local authorities should have regard to the Housing Act 1985 Pt 10 (statutory overcrowding): *Elrify v Westminster City Council* [2007] EWCA Civ 332; [2007] H.L.R. 36. See too *Osei v Southwark LBC* [2007] EWCA Civ 787; [2008] H.L.R. 15 and *Waltham Forest LBC v Maloba* [2007] EWCA Civ 1281; [2008] H.L.R. 26.

**Domestic violence**

3A–1255 The provisions relating to homelessness as a result of domestic violence (Housing Act 1985 s.83(3)) have been re-enacted and broadened (Housing Act 1996 s.177(1)).

Even before the introduction of the specific reference to domestic violence in s.177(1), threats of violence were likely to be a relevant factor when considering whether or not it was reasonable for an applicant to continue to occupy premises. In *R. v Broxbourne BC Ex p. Willmoth* (1990) 22 H.L.R. 118, CA, the Court of Appeal (following and applying *R. v Kensington and Chelsea RBC Ex p. Hammell* [1989] 1 Q.B. 518; [1989] 2 W.L.R. 90; [1989] 1 All E.R. 1202, CA) held that s.58(2A) (now the Housing Act 1996 s.175(3)) required consideration of all matters related to continued occupation. Sir John Megaw said the reasonableness test is:

> "not necessarily or solely confined to looking at the actual quality of the accommodation within the four walls of the house or the room or flat which is the accommodation available. It may be the duty of the housing authority to consider also circumstances, matters and factors which may fall outside the limited consideration of the actual quality of physical accommodation itself ... Just as the difficulties created by a staircase or other approach to accommodation, to an applicant with physical infirmities, is relevant to reasonableness, so also are threats of violence, even though those threats come from one who is not resident in the accommodation (p.127)".

The Court of Appeal has held that the probability test in s.177(1), (namely whether it is probable that continued occupation would lead to domestic violence) is clear and unequivocal. It is a question of fact devoid of value judgments about what an applicant might or might not have done. Available measures that would probably prove effective in preventing actual or threatened violence might reduce the level of risk below one of probability. However, councils are not entitled to assume that such measures would be

***Paragraph numbers marked with a "+" can be found online and on CD.***

taken or would be effective if taken (*Bond v Leicester City Council* [2001] EWCA Civ 1544; [2002] H.L.R. 6).

A woman who flees domestic violence and is taken in by a women's refuge normally remains "homeless" while at the refuge because it is not accommodation that it would be reasonable for her to continue to occupy indefinitely (for the purposes of s.175(3)) (*Moran v Manchester City Council* [2009] UKHL 36, July 1, 2009; *The Times*, July 7, 2009. See too *R. v Ealing LBC ex p Sidhu* (1982) 2 H.L.R. 41, CA).

**Other Violence**

Homelessness Act 2002 s.10 amended s.177 so as to provide that violence other than domestic violence may mean that it is not reasonable to continue to occupy existing accommodation. Violence includes threats of violence which are likely to be carried out. In England, this amendment was brought into force on July 31, 2002 by the Homelessness Act 2002 (Commencement No.1) (England) Order 2002 (SI 2002/1799) (c.56). In Wales, this amendment was brought into force on September 30, 2002 by the Homelessness Act 2002 (Commencement) (Wales) Order 2002 (SI 2002/1736) (w.166) (c.53). **3A-1256**

**Temporary accommodation**

The amendment of the definition of homelessness in the Housing Act 1985 s.58 by the Housing and Planning Act 1986 s.14(2), which added a new s.58(2A)(now the Housing Act 1996 s.175(3)) which states that, "a person shall not be treated as having accommodation unless it is accommodation which it would be reasonable for him to continue to occupy", and a new s.58(2B)(now the Housing Act 1996 s.177(2)) which states that in determining whether it is reasonable to continue to occupy accommodation, regard may be had to the general circumstances prevailing in relation to housing in the district of the local housing authority to whom the applicant has applied for accommodation, have reversed the effect of the decision of the House of Lords in *R. v Hillingdon LBC Ex p. Puhlhofer* [1986] A.C. 484; [1986] 2 W.L.R. 259; [1986] 1 All E.R. 467, HL. **3A-1257**

The mere fact that accommodation is temporary does not mean that a person is homeless. In *R. v Brent LBC Ex p. Awua* [1996] A.C. 55; [1995] 3 W.L.R. 215; [1995] 3 All E.R. 493, HL, Lord Hoffmann, giving the leading speech, observed that nothing in the Housing Act 1985 s.58 (now the Housing Act 1996 s.175) caused a person to be homeless simply because their accommodation was temporary, short-term or precarious until they were within 28 days of losing it (s.58(4)—now s.175(4)). He found it hard to imagine a case in which it could be said that it was not reasonable to continue to occupy accommodation simply on the basis it was temporary but he observed that:

> "On the other hand, the extent to which the accommodation is physically suitable, so that it would be reasonable for a person to continue to occupy it, must be related to the time for which he has been there and is expected to stay. A housing authority could take the view that a family like the Puhlhofers, put into a cramped and squalid bedroom, can be expected to make do for a temporary period. On the other hand, there will come a time at which it is no longer reasonable to expect them to continue to occupy such accommodation. At this point they come back within the definition of homelessness in section 58(1)" (now s.175(1)) ([1995] 3 All E.R. 498).

A council does not have to be satisfied that accommodation has some degree of permanence before it can conclude that a person is not homeless by reason of the availability of accommodation which it would be reasonable for him to occupy under s.175(3) (*Begum v Tower Hamlets LBC* [2000] Q.B. 133, CA).

## Meaning of accommodation available for occupation

**176.** Accommodation shall be regarded as available for a person's occupation only if it is available for occupation by him together with— **3A-1258**

(a) any other person who normally resides with him as a member of his family, or

(b) any other person who might reasonably be expected to reside with him.

***Paragraph numbers marked with a "+" can be found online and on CD.***

References in this Part to securing that accommodation is available for a person's occupation shall be construed accordingly.

**Meaning of accommodation available for occupation**

3A–1259 See commentary to s.175.

## Whether it is reasonable to continue to occupy accommodation

3A–1260 **177.**—(1) It is not reasonable for a person to continue to occupy accommodation if it is probable that this will lead to domestic violence or other violenceagainst him, or against—

(a) a person who normally resides with him as a member of his family, or

(b) any other person who might reasonably be expected to reside with him.

(1A) For this purpose "violence" means—

(a) violence from another person; or

(b) threats of violence from another person which are likely to be carried out; and violence is "domestic violence" if it is from a person who is associated with the victim.

(2) In determining whether it would be, or would have been, reasonable for a person to continue to occupy accommodation, regard may be had to the general circumstances prevailing in relation to housing in the district of the local housing authority to whom he has applied for accommodation or for assistance in obtaining accommodation.

(3) The Secretary of State may by order specify—

(a) other circumstances in which it is to be regarded as reasonable or not reasonable for a person to continue to occupy accommodation, and

(b) other matters to be taken into account or disregarded in determining whether it would be, or would have been, reasonable for a person to continue to occupy accommodation.

3A–1261 *Note* — Amended by Homelessness Act 2002 s.10. In England, this amendment was brought into force on July 31, 2002 by the Homelessness Act 2002 (Commencement No.1) (England) Order 2002 (SI 2002/1799) (c.56). In Wales, this amendment was brought into force on September 30, 2002 by the Homelessness Act 2002 (Commencement) (Wales) Order 2002 (SI 2002/1736) (w.166) (c.53).

**Whether it is reasonable to continue to occupy accommodation**

3A–1262 See commentary to s.175.

## Meaning of associated person

3A–1263 **178.**—(1) For the purposes of this Part, a person is associated with another person if—

(a) they are or have been married to each other;

(aa) they are or have been civil partners of each other,

(b) they are cohabitants or former cohabitants;

(c) they live or have lived in the same household;

(d) they are relatives;

(e) they have agreed to marry one another (whether or not that agreement has been terminated);

(ea) they have entered into a civil partnership agreement between them (whether or not that agreement has been terminated);

(f) in relation to a child, each of them is a parent of the child or has, or has had, parental responsibility for the child.

(2) If a child has been adopted or falls within subsection (2A) two persons are also associated with each other for the purposes of this Part if—

(a) one is a natural parent of the child or a parent of such a natural parent, and

(b) the other is the child or a person—

(i) who has become a parent of the child by virtue of an adoption order or who has applied for an adoption order, or

(ii) with whom the child has at any time been placed for adoption.

(2A) A child falls within this subsection if—

(a) an adoption agency, within the meaning of section 2 of the Adoption and Children Act 2002, is authorised to place him for adoption under section 19 of that Act (placing children with parental consent) or he has become the subject of an order under section 21 of that Act (placement orders), or

(b) he is freed for adoption by virtue of an order made—

(i) in England and Wales, under section 18 of the Adoption Act 1976,

(ii) in Scotland, under section 18 of the Adoption (Scotland) Act 1978, or

(iii) in Northern Ireland, under Article 17(1) or 18(1) of the Adoption (Northern Ireland) Order 1987.

(3) In this section—

"adoption order" means an adoption order within the meaning of section 72(1) of the Adoption Act 1976 or section 46(1) of the Adoption and Children Act 2002;

"child" means a person under the age of 18 years;

"civil partnership agreement" has the meaning given by section 73 of the Civil Partnership Act 2004;

"cohabitants" means —

(a) a man and a woman who, although not married to each other, are living together as husband and wife, or

(b) two people of the same sex who, although not civil partners of each other, are living together as if they were civil partners;, and "former cohabitants" shall be construed accordingly;

*Paragraph numbers marked with a "+" can be found online and on CD.*

"parental responsibility" has the same meaning as in the Children Act 1989; and

"relative", in relation to a person, means—

(a) the father, mother, stepfather, stepmother, son, daughter, stepson, stepdaughter, grandmother, grandfather, grandson or granddaughter of that person or of that person's spouse, civil partner or former spouse or former civil partner, or

(b) the brother, sister, uncle, aunt, niece or nephew (whether of the full blood or of the half blood or by marriage or civil partnership) of that person or of that person's spouse, civil partner or former spouse or former civil partner,

and includes, in relation to a person who is living or has lived with another person as husband and wife, a person who would fall within paragraph (a) or (b) if the parties were married to each other.

3A–1264 *Note* —This section has been amended by the Adoption and Children Act 2002 s.139(1), Sch.3, paras 89, 90, 91 and 92; and the Civil Partnership Act 2004 s.81 and Sch.8, para.61.

**Meaning of associated person**

3A–1265 See commentary to s.175.

*GENERAL FUNCTIONS IN RELATION TO HOMELESSNESS OR THREATENED HOMELESSNESS*

## Duty of local housing authority to provide advisory services

3A–1266 **179.**—(1) Every local housing authority shall secure that advice and information about homelessness, and the prevention of homelessness, is available free of charge to any person in their district.

(2) The authority may give to any person by whom such advice and information is provided on behalf of the authority assistance by way of grant or loan.

(3) A local housing authority may also assist any such person—

(a) by permitting him to use premises belonging to the authority,

(b) by making available furniture or other goods, whether by way of gift, loan or otherwise, and

(c) by making available the services of staff employed by the authority.

**"local housing authority"**

3A–1267 See ss.217, 218, and 230 which refers to the Housing Act 1985—see the Housing Act 1985 ss.1 and 2 above.

## Assistance for voluntary organisations

3A–1268 **180.**—(1) The Secretary of State or a local housing authority may give assistance by way of grant or loan to voluntary organisations concerned with homelessness or matters relating to homelessness.

(2) A local housing authority may also assist any such organisation—

(a) by permitting them to use premises belonging to the authority,

(b) by making available furniture or other goods, whether by way of gift, loan or otherwise, and

(c) by making available the services of staff employed by the authority.

(3) A "voluntary organisation" means a body (other than a public or local authority) whose activities are not carried on for profit.

**"local housing authority"**

See ss.217, 218 and 230 which refers to the Housing Act 1985—see the Housing Act 1985 ss.1 and 2 above. **3A-1269**

## Terms and conditions of assistance

**181.**—(1) This section has effect as to the terms and conditions on which assistance is given under section 179 or 180. **3A-1270**

(2) Assistance shall be on such terms, and subject to such conditions, as the person giving the assistance may determine.

(3) No assistance shall be given unless the person to whom it is given undertakes—

(a) to use the money, furniture or other goods or premises for a specified purpose, and

(b) to provide such information as may reasonably be required as to the manner in which the assistance is being used.

The person giving the assistance may require such information by notice in writing, which shall be complied with within 21 days beginning with the date on which the notice is served.

(4) The conditions subject to which assistance is given shall in all cases include conditions requiring the person to whom the assistance is given—

(a) to keep proper books of account and have them audited in such manner as may be specified,

(b) to keep records indicating how he has used the money, furniture or other goods or premises, and

(c) to submit the books of account and records for inspection by the person giving the assistance.

(5) If it appears to the person giving the assistance that the person to whom it was given has failed to carry out his undertaking as to the purpose for which the assistance was to be used, he shall take all reasonable steps to recover from that person an amount equal to the amount of the assistance.

(6) He must first serve on the person to whom the assistance was given a notice specifying the amount which in his opinion is recoverable and the basis on which that amount has been calculated.

## Guidance by the Secretary of State

**182.**—(1) In the exercise of their functions relating to homeless- **3A-1271**

ness and the prevention of homelessness, a local housing authority or social services authority shall have regard to such guidance as may from time to time be given by the Secretary of State.

(2) The Secretary of State may give guidance either generally or to specified descriptions of authorities.

**"local housing authority"**

3A–1272 See ss.217, 218, and 230 which refers to the Housing Act 1985—see the Housing Act 1985 ss.1 and 2 above.

**"social services authority"**

3A–1273 See s.217.

**Guidance by the Secretary of State**

3A–1274 When implementing the provisions of Pt VII authorities must have regard to the issued by the Department of the Environment (s.182). The current *Code of Guidance* was issued in July 2002 by the Office of the Deputy Prime Minister to reflect changes introduced by the Homelessness Act 2002. Copies are available from the Office of the Deputy Prime Minister, PO Box 236, Wetherby, West Yorkshire LS23 7NB. There is a separate Welsh Code of Guidance issued by the Welsh Assembly Government. The Code of Guidance is not a source of law. Although councils must take it into account and give reasons for departing from it, it is not binding on them (*R. (on the application of Khatun) v Newham LBC* [2004] EWCA Civ 55; [2005] Q.B. 37; [2004] 3 W.L.R. 417). Where the Code of Guidance is in conflict with the Act, the words of the Act prevail (*Griffin v Westminster City Council* [2004] EWCA Civ 108; [2004] H.L.R. 12.

### *APPLICATION FOR ASSISTANCE IN CASE OF HOMELESSNESS OR THREATENED HOMELESSNESS*

## Application for assistance

3A–1275 **183.**—(1) The following provisions of this Part apply where a person applies to a local housing authority for accommodation, or for assistance in obtaining accommodation, and the authority have reason to believe that he is or may be homeless or threatened with homelessness.

(2) In this Part—

"applicant" means a person making such an application,

"assistance under this Part" means the benefit of any function under the following provisions of this Part relating to accommodation or assistance in obtaining accommodation, and

"eligible for assistance" means not excluded from such assistance by section 185 (persons from abroad not eligible for housing assistance).

(3) Nothing in this section or the following provisions of this Part affects a person's entitlement to advice and information under section 179 (duty to provide advisory services).

3A–1276 *Note*—Amended by Immigration and Asylum Act 1999 Sch.14, para.116.

**"homeless"**

3A–1277 See s.175.

**"threatened with homelessness"**

3A–1278 See s.175.

***Paragraph numbers marked with a "+" can be found online and on CD.***

**"local housing authority"**

See ss.217, 218, and 230 which refers to the Housing Act 1985—see the Housing Act 1985 ss.1 and 2, above. **3A–1279**

**"application"**

The House of Lords has held that a child dependent on an adult cannot make an application for accommodation capable of triggering the duties under the Housing Act 1985 Pt III (now the Housing Act 1996 Pt VII). The Housing Act 1985 s.59(1)(b) (now s.189(1)(b)) plainly indicates that parliament intended dependent children to be the subject of applications by their carer (*R. v Oldham MBC Ex p. G* [1993] A.C. 509; [1993] 2 W.L.R. 609; [1993] 2 All E.R. 65 (also reported as *Garlick v Oldham MBC*, HL). Similarly, an adult lacking mental capacity was not owed duties under the Housing Act 1985 Pt III (now the Housing Act 1996 Pt VII). It is for local authorities to determine whether an applicant has sufficient mental capacity (i.e. the capacity to understand and deal with the concept of being offered accommodation) and their decisions can only be challenged if they are manifestly perverse or otherwise wrong on *Wednesbury* grounds (*R. v Tower Hamlets LBC Ex p. Begum (Ferdous)* [1993] A.C. 509; [1993] 2 W.L.R. 609; [1993] 2 All E.R. 65, HL). **3A–1280**

## Inquiry into cases of homelessness or threatened homelessness

**184.**—(1) If the local housing authority have reason to believe that an applicant may be homeless or threatened with homelessness, they shall make such inquiries as are necessary to satisfy themselves— **3A–1281**

(a) whether he is eligible for assistance, and

(b) if so, whether any duty, and if so what duty, is owed to him under the following provisions of this Part.

(2) They may also make inquiries whether he has a local connection with the district of another local housing authority in England, Wales or Scotland.

(3) On completing their inquiries the authority shall notify the applicant of their decision and, so far as any issue is decided against his interests, inform him of the reasons for their decision.

(3A) If the authority decide that a duty is owed to the applicant under section 193(2) or 195(2) but would not have done so without having had regard to a restricted person, the notice under subsection (3) must also—

(a) inform the applicant that their decision was reached on that basis,

(b) include the name of the restricted person,

(c) explain why the person is a restricted person, and

(d) explain the effect of section 193(7AD) or (as the case may be) section 195(4A).

(4) If the authority have notified or intend to notify another local housing authority under section 198 (referral of cases), they shall at the same time notify the applicant of that decision and inform him of the reasons for it.

(5) A notice under subsection (3) or (4) shall also inform the applicant of his right to request a review of the decision and of the time within which such a request must be made (see section 202).

(6) Notice required to be given to a person under this section shall be given in writing and, if not received by him, shall be treated

as having been given to him if it is made available at the authority's office for a reasonable period for collection by him or on his behalf.

(7) In this Part "a restricted person" means a person—

(a) who is not eligible for assistance under this Part,

(b) who is subject to immigration control within the meaning of the Asylum and Immigration Act 1996, and

(c) either—

(i) who does not have leave to enter or remain in the United Kingdom, or

(ii) whose leave to enter or remain in the United Kingdom is subject to a condition to maintain and accommodate himself, and any dependants, without recourse to public funds.

**Amendment**

**3A-1281.1** Amended for certain purposes by the Housing and Regeneration Act 2008 Sch.15, Pt I, para.3, with effect from March 2, 2009 (SI 2009/415; for purposes see art.2).

**"homeless"**

**3A-1282** See s.175.

**"threatened with homelessness"**

**3A-1283** See s.175.

**"local housing authority"**

**3A-1284** See ss.217, 218, and 230 which refers to the Housing Act 1985—see the Housing Act 1985 ss.1 and 2 above.

**"applicant"**

**3A-1285** See s.183 and the commentary thereto.

**"eligible for assistance"**

**3A-1286** See s.185.

**"local connection"**

**3A-1287** See s.199.

**Inquiry into cases of homelessness or threatened homelessness**

**3A-1288** Section 184 sets out the matters into which a council must enquire on receiving an application from a potentially homeless applicant. These are such enquiries as are necessary to satisfy themselves as to:

(a) whether he or she is eligible for assistance; and

(b) if so, whether any duty, and if so, what duty is owed.

Inadequate inquiries will leave a council decision (irrespective of its merit) open to challenge for failure to have regard to all relevant considerations.

In *Cramp v Hastings LBC*; *Phillips v Camden LBC* [2005] EWCA Civ 1005; [2005] 4 All E.R. 1014, the Court of Appeal stated that Parliament imposed the duty to make the necessary inquiries upon housing officers, and, if there is a review, upon senior housing officers. It is for councils to judge what inquiries are necessary, and they are susceptible to successful challenges on a point of law if and only if a judge in the county court considers that no reasonable council could have failed to regard as necessary the further inquiries suggested by the appellant. As a matter of law a quashing order cannot be justified on the grounds "that it would have been helpful" if particular inquiries had been made, or that "there might well have been additional information" which further inquiries might have produced. Whether to make such inquiries is a matter for the reviewing officer. The Court of Appeal stated that

"these two cases evidence a worrying tendency in judges at [county court] level to overlook the fact that it will never be easy for a judge to say that an experienced senior housing officer on a homelessness review, who has considered all the reports readily available, and all the representations made by the applicant's solicitors, has made an error of law when she considered that it was unnecessary to put in train further detailed inquiries, not suggested by the applicant's solicitors, before she could properly make a decision on the review. The need to correct that tendency raises an important point of practice".

For other Court of Appeal decisions on the adequacy of inquiries under the 1985 Act, see *R. v Brent LBC Ex p. Grossett* (1996) 28 H.L.R. 9, CA; *R. v Exeter City Council Ex p. Tranckle* (1994) 26 H.L.R. 244, CA; *R. v Kensington and Chelsea RBC Ex p. Bayani* (1990) 22 H.L.R. 406, CA; *R. v Kensington and Chelsea RBC Ex p. Cunha* (1989) 21 H.L.R. 16, CA; *R. v Northavon DC Ex p. Palmer* (1995) 27 H.L.R. 576; (1995) 94 L.G.R. 568, CA; *R. v Sevenoaks DC Ex p. Reynolds* (1990) 22 H.L.R. 250, CA; *R. v Tower Hamlets LBC Ex p. Shafia Khatun* (1995) 27 H.L.R. 465, CA and *Kacar v Enfield LBC* (2001) 33 H.L.R. 64, CA. Faced with an application based upon threatened homelessness, a council has to take immediate steps under s.184 to determine whether the applicant is eligible for assistance and what duty is owed. Where satisfied that the applicant is threatened with homelessness, eligible for assistance and in priority need, the duty to take steps to secure accommodation arises under section 195. The council cannot remain inactive (*R. v Newham LBC Ex p. Khan* (2001) 33 H.L.R. 29, QBD).

## *Eligibility for Assistance*

### Persons from abroad not eligible for housing assistance

**185.**—(1) A person is not eligible for assistance under this Part if he is a person from abroad who is ineligible for housing assistance. **3A–1289**

(2) A person who is subject to immigration control within the meaning of the Asylum and Immigration Act 1996 is not eligible for housing assistance unless he is of a class prescribed by regulations made by the Secretary of State.

(2A) No person who is excluded from entitlement to housing benefit by section 115 of the Immigration and Asylum Act 1999 (exclusion from benefits) shall be included in any class prescribed under subsection (2).

(3) The Secretary of State may make provision by regulations as to other descriptions of persons who are to be treated for the purposes of this Part as persons from abroad who are ineligible for housing assistance.

(4) A person from abroad who is not eligible for housing assistance shall be disregarded in determining for the purposes of this Part whether a person falling within subsection (5) —

(a) is homeless or threatened with homelessness, or

(b) has a priority need for accommodation.

(5) A person falls within this subsection if the person—

(a) falls within a class prescribed by regulations made under subsection (2); but

(b) is not a national of an EEA State or Switzerland.

*Note*—This section is amended by the Immigration and Asylum Act 1999 s.117 and the Homelessness Act 2002 Sch.1, para.7. Amended for certain purposes by the Housing and Regeneration Act 2008 Sch.15, Pt I, para.4, with effect from March 2, 2009 (SI 2009/415; for purposes see art.2). **3A–1290**

**"assistance"**

See s.183. **3A–1291**

***Paragraph numbers marked with a "+" can be found online and on CD.***

**"regulations"**

3A-1292 See below.

**"homeless"**

3A-1293 See s.175.

**"threatened with homelessness"**

3A-1294 See s.175.

**"priority need"**

3A-1295 See s.189.

**Persons from abroad not eligible for housing assistance**

3A-1296 Section 185 provides that applicants *are not eligible* for assistance under Pt VII if—

(a) they are persons from abroad who are subject to immigration control under the Asylum and Immigration Act 1996. (Under the Immigration and Asylum Act 1999 Part VI, all people who applied for asylum after April 3, 2000 must rely upon the National Asylum Support Service, which, in some circumstances is obliged to provide accommodation); or

(b) they are persons who are not habitually resident in the Common Travel Area (s.185(2A) and Homelessness (England) Regulations 2000 No.701, para.4).

Both these provisions are subject to exceptions contained in the Allocation of Housing and Homelessness (Eligibility) (England) Regulations 2006 SI 2006/1294 and the Allocation of Housing and Homelessness (Miscellaneous Provisions) (England) Regulations 2006 SI 2006/2527, as amended by the Allocation of Housing and Homelessness (Eligibility) (England) (Amendment) (No.2) Regulations 2006 (SI 2006/3340) which apply to homelessness applications made on or after January 1, 2007 by Romanian and Bulgarian nationals. Note that an accession state national who is not working is prima facie not "eligible" under the Housing Act 1996 s.185. In such circumstances councils have no power to accommodate pending any appeal against that decision (save on human rights grounds) because of the prohibition in the Nationality, Immigration & Asylum Act 2002 Sch.3. (*Putans v Tower Hamlets LBC* [2006] EWHC 1634 (Ch); [2007] H.L.R. 10). (For Wales, see the Homelessness (Wales) Regulations 2006 SI 2006/2624 (w.227).)

First, the Allocation of Housing and Homelessness (Eligibility) (England) (Amendment) Regulations 2006 (SI 2006/1294), para.5 as amended by the Allocation of Housing and Homelessness (Miscellaneous Provisions) (England) Regulations 2006 SI 2006/2527 sets out five classes of persons who, although subject to immigration control, are eligible for housing assistance. (As indicated above, the intention of the government is that post-April 3, 2000 asylum seekers should seek accommodation through the National Asylum Support Service.) The classes eligible for housing assistance are:

- **Class A**—a person who is recorded by the Secretary of State as a refugee within the definition in Article 1 of the Refugee Convention and who has leave to enter or remain in the United Kingdom;
- **Class B**—a person—
  - (i) who has exceptional leave to enter or remain in the United Kingdom granted outside the provisions of the Immigration Rules; and
  - (ii) whose leave to enter or remain is not subject to a condition requiring him to maintain and accommodate himself, and any person who is dependent on him, without recourse to public funds;
- **Class C**—a person who is habitually resident in the United Kingdom, the Channel Islands, the Isle of Man or the Republic of Ireland and whose leave to enter or remain in the United Kingdom is not subject to any limitation or condition, other than a person—
  - (i) who has been given leave to enter or remain in the United Kingdom upon an undertaking given by his sponsor;
  - (ii) who has been resident in the United Kingdom, the Channel Islands, the Isle of Man or the Republic of Ireland for less than five years beginning on the date of entry or the date on which his sponsor gave the undertaking in respect of him, whichever date is the later; and

***Paragraph numbers marked with a "+" can be found online and on CD.***

(iii) whose sponsor or, where there is more than one sponsor, at least one of whose sponsors, is still alive;

- **Class D**—a person who has humanitarian protection granted under the Immigration Rules; and
- **Class E**—a person who is an asylum-seeker whose claim for asylum is recorded by the Secretary of State as having been made before April 3, 2000 and in the circumstances mentioned in one of the following paragraphs—

(i) on arrival (other than on his re-entry) in the United Kingdom from a country outside the United Kingdom, the Channel Islands, the Isle of Man or the Republic of Ireland;

(ii) within three months from the day on which the Secretary of State made a relevant declaration, and the applicant was in Great Britain on the day on which the declaration was made; or

(iii) on or before February 4, 1996 by an applicant who was on February 4, 1996 entitled to benefit under reg.7A of the Housing Benefit (General) Regulations 1987 (persons from abroad).

The Allocation of Housing and Homelessness (Eligibility) (England) (Amendment) Regulations 2009 (SI 2009/358) provide that certain British citizens who were living in Zimbabwe but who came or come to the UK between February 28, 2009 and March 18, 2011, pursuant to an offer from the government to assist their settlement in the UK, are to be treated as eligible, notwithstanding that they are not habitually resident in the United Kingdom.

The purpose of s.185(2A), an amendment brought about by the Homelessness Act 2002, (as of the subsection originally inserted by Immigration and Asylum Act 1999) is to limit the power of the Secretary of State to make regulations prescribing classes of persons subject to immigration control who may be eligible for assistance under Part VII. Section 185, as amended, excludes from the Housing Act 1996 Part VII people from abroad who are not entitled to housing benefit.

Local authorities may request information from the Secretary of State about a person's immigration status (Housing Act 1996 s.187). When considering an application for interim accommodation under s.188, local authorities have a duty to make enquiries, but where the Secretary of State has refused a non-EEA national's application for a resident's permit, a local authority is entitled to take such a refusal at face value. It is reasonable not to make further enquiries (*R. (on the application of Burns) v Southwark LBC* [2004] EWHC 1901 (Admin)).

### Persons from abroad and priority need

Housing and Regeneration Act 2008 Sch.15 amended s.185(4) to remedy the declaration of incompatibility with the European Convention of Human Rights made in *R. (Morris) v Westminster CC* [2005] EWCA Civ 1184; [2006] H.L.R. 8. Section 185(4) formerly required local housing authorities in England and Wales to disregard ineligible household members when deciding whether an applicant for housing assistance was homeless or had a priority need for accommodation. The effect of Sch.15 is that the disregards no longer apply in the case of an applicant for housing assistance who is a British citizen, a Commonwealth citizen with a right of abode in the United Kingdom, or an EEA or Swiss national exercising an EU Treaty right to reside in the United Kingdom. **3A-1297**

Schedule 15 also changed the way in which the duty owed to applicants who are found to be homeless and to have a priority need only by reliance on a household member who is a "restricted person" (a person who requires leave to enter or remain in the United Kingdom and does not have it, or a person who does have the required leave but that leave was granted on the condition that the person would have "no recourse to public funds") may be discharged. In such a case, local housing authorities are required, so far as possible, to bring their duty to secure accommodation to an end by ensuring that an offer of accommodation for a period of at least 12 months in the private rented sector is made to the applicant. If such an offer is made the duty is discharged whether or not the applicant accepts the offer.

## Asylum-seekers and their dependents

**186.** [...] **3A-1298**

***Paragraph numbers marked with a "+" can be found online and on CD.***

**Note**

3A-1299 This section was repealed by Immigration and Asylum Act 1999 s.117(5) and Sch.16. Any accommodation which is to be made available for asylum seekers and their dependents should now be provided by via the National Asylum Support Service. See the Immigration and Asylum Act 1999 ss.94–100.

## Provision of information by Secretary of State

3A-1300 **187.**—(1) The Secretary of State shall, at the request of a local housing authority, provide the authority with such information as they may require—

(a) as to whether a person is a person to whom section 115 of the Immigration and Asylum Act 1999 (exclusion from benefits) applies, and

(b) to enable them to determine whether such a person is eligible for assistance under this Part under section 185 (persons from abroad not eligible for housing assistance).

(2) Where that information is given otherwise than in writing, the Secretary of State shall confirm it in writing if a written request is made to him by the authority.

(3) If it appears to the Secretary of State that any application, decision or other change of circumstances has affected the status of a person about whom information was previously provided by him to a local housing authority under this section, he shall inform the authority in writing of that fact, the reason for it and the date on which the previous information became inaccurate.

3A-1301 *Note*—Amended by the Immigration and Asylum Act 1999 s.117(8).

**"asylum seeker"**

3A-1302 See s.186.

**"dependent of asylum seeker"**

3A-1303 See s.186.

**"local housing authority"**

3A-1304 See ss.217, 218, and 230 which refers to the Housing Act 1985—see the Housing Act 1985 ss.1 and 2, above.

**Provision of information by Secretary of State**

3A-1305 See commentary to s.185.

## Interim duty to accommodate in case of apparent priority need

3A-1306 **188.**—(1) If the local housing authority have reason to believe that an applicant may be homeless, eligible for assistance and have a priority need, they shall secure that accommodation is available for his occupation pending a decision as to the duty (if any) owed to him under the following provisions of this Part.

(2) The duty under this section arises irrespective of any possibility of the referral of the applicant's case to another local housing authority (see sections 198 to 200).

(3) The duty ceases when the authority's decision is notified to the applicant, even if the applicant requests a review of the decision (see section 202).

The authority may secure that accommodation is available for the applicant's occupation pending a decision on a review.

*Note* —Amended by the Homelessness Act 2002 Sch.1, para.8. **3A–1307**

**"eligible for assistance"**

See s.185. **3A–1308**

**"assistance"**

See s.183. **3A–1309**

**"local housing authority"**

See ss.217, 218, and 230 which refer to the Housing Act 1985—see the Housing Act 1985 ss.1 and 2, above. **3A–1310**

**"homeless"**

See s.175. **3A–1311**

**"threatened with homelessness"**

See s.175. **3A–1312**

**"applicant"**

See s.183 and the commentary thereto. **3A–1313**

**"priority need"**

See s.189. **3A–1314**

**"available for his occupation"**

See s.176. **3A–1315**

**Interim duty to accommodate**

See *R. v Camden LBC Ex p. Mohammed* (1998) 30 H.L.R. 315, QBD (summarised at para.3A–1426); *R. v Newham LBC Ex p. Idowu*, August 1998, Legal Action 21, QBD; and *R. v Haringey LBC Ex p. Erdogan*, August 1998, Legal Action 23, QBD. **3A–1316**

**Suitability of interim accommodation**

Accommodation provided under the interim duty to accommodate must be suitable. Lack of resources does not relieve councils from this mandatory duty. Section 188, when read with s.176, does not permit councils to split families in accommodation in separate dwellings (*Ealing LBC v Surdonja* (1999) 31 H.L.R. 686, QBD affirmed on appeal; [2001] Q.B. 97; [2000] 2 All E.R. 597, CA and [2001] UKHL 57; [2002] 1 A.C. 547; [2001] 3 W.L.R. 1339; [2001] 1 All E.R. 176, HL). When discharging their interim duties under s.188 local authorities should give individual consideration to the circumstances of particular applicants. The duty cannot be met by booking all applicants into bed and breakfast accommodation—*R. v Newham LBC Ex p. Ojuri (No.3)* (1999) 31 H.L.R. 452, CA, (Collins J.). **3A–1317**

The question whether or not the accommodation is suitable requires an assessment of all the qualities of the accommodation in the light of the needs and requirements of the homeless person and his or her family. That means that the location of the accommodation may be relevant to an assessment of suitability. A council may act unlawfully in failing to have regard to the particular educational, employment and medical requirements of the family (*R.(Sacupima) v Newham LBC* [2001] 1 W.L.R. 563, CA, where a decision to provide bed and breakfast accommodation outside its area was quashed).

## Priority need for accommodation

**189.**—(1) The following have a priority need for accommodation— **3A–1318**

(a) a pregnant woman or a person with whom she resides or might reasonably be expected to reside;

***Paragraph numbers marked with a "+" can be found online and on CD.***

(b) a person with whom dependent children reside or might reasonably be expected to reside;

(c) a person who is vulnerable as a result of old age, mental illness or handicap or physical disability or other special reason, or with whom such a person resides or might reasonably be expected to reside;

(d) a person who is homeless or threatened with homelessness as a result of an emergency such as flood, fire or other disaster.

(2) The Secretary of State may by order—

(a) specify further descriptions of persons as having a priority need for accommodation, and

(b) amend or repeal any part of subsection (1).

(3) Before making such an order the Secretary of State shall consult such associations representing relevant authorities, and such other persons, as he considers appropriate.

(4) No such order shall be made unless a draft of it has been approved by resolution of each House of Parliament.

**Priority need for accommodation**

**3A–1319** Categories of priority need are set out in Housing Act 1996 s.189, the Homelessness (Priority Need for Accommodation) (England) Order 2002 (SI 2002/2051) and the Homeless Persons (Priority Need) (Wales) Order 2001 (SI 2001/607 (w.3)). Section 189(1), lists four categories of priority need, namely:

(a) She is pregnant or the applicant is a person with whom a pregnant woman resides or might reasonably be expected to reside.

(b) S/he has dependent children. There are two routes to priority need through dependent children (s.189(1)(b)). One is if dependent children are residing with the applicant. The other is if, although the children do not at present reside with the applicant, it is reasonable to expect them to do so in the future. The second route may apply if a parent who does not have day-to-day care and control of children but intends to have prolonged staying contact. The Act contains no definition of "dependent child" but the Homelessness Code of Guidance suggests that it should include "all children under 16, and all children aged 16 to 18 who are in, or are about to begin, full-time education or training" (para.14.2).

(c) S/he is vulnerable as a result of old age, mental illness or handicap or physical disability or other special reason, or is someone with whom such a person resides or might reasonably be expected to reside (s.189(1)(c)).

(d) S/he is homeless or threatened with homelessness as a result of an emergency such as a flood, fire or other disaster (s.189(1)(d)). If such a person is not intentionally homeless, the local authority must ensure that permanent alternative accommodation is made available.

**The Homelessness (Priority Need for Accommodation) (England) Order 2002**

**3A–1320** In addition the Homelessness (Priority Need for Accommodation) (England) Order 2002 (SI 2002/2051) provides that the following categories of people have a priority need for accommodation for the purposes of Pt 7 of the Housing Act 1996:

**Children aged 16 or 17**

**3.**—(1) A person (other than a person to whom paragraph (2) below applies) aged sixteen or seventeen who is not a relevant child for the purposes of section 23A of the Children Act 1989.

(2) This paragraph applies to a person to whom a local authority owe a duty to provide accommodation under section 20 of that Act (provision of accommodation for children in need).

**Young people under 21**

**4.**—(1) A person (other than a relevant student) who—

(a) is under twenty-one; and

(b) at any time after reaching the age of sixteen, but while still under eighteen, was, but is no longer, looked after, accommodated or fostered.

**Vulnerability: institutional backgrounds**

**5.**—(1) A person (other than a relevant student) who has reached the age of twenty-one and who is vulnerable as a result of having been looked after, accommodated or fostered.

(2) A person who is vulnerable as a result of having been a member of Her Majesty's regular naval, military or air forces.

(3) A person who is vulnerable as a result of—

(a) having served a custodial sentence (within the meaning of section 76 of the Powers of Criminal Courts (Sentencing) Act 2000);

(b) having been committed for contempt of court or any other kindred offence;

(c) having been remanded in custody (within the meaning of paragraph (b), (c) or (d) of section 88(1) of that Act).

**Vulnerability: fleeing violence or threats of violence**

**6.**—A person who is vulnerable as a result of ceasing to occupy accommodation by reason of violence from another person or threats of violence from another person which are likely to be carried out.

### Priority need in Wales

The Homeless Persons (Priority Need) (Wales) Order 2001 (SI 2001/607 (w.3)) extended the priority need categories in s.189 to include anyone applying as a homeless person in Wales who is: **3A–1321**

- aged 16 or 17;
- aged 18, 19 or 20 (who had been in local authority care and is at particular risk of sexual or financial exploitation);
- fleeing domestic violence or in fear of such violence if s/he returns home;
- homeless since leaving the regular armed forces; or
- homeless since leaving custody as a prisoner (and who has a local connection with the authority applied to).

It came into force on March 1, 2001.

### Priority need and the ECHR

The provisions of s.189 do not breach ECHR art.8(1) in enacting a scheme of priorities whereby applications for accommodation by homeless persons are to be determined by local housing authorities. In assessing priorities, Parliament was entitled to take into account considerations such as vulnerability, which might or might not have an impact on family life, as well as those that inevitably did. Specifically art.8(1) does not require applicants with child spouses to be given priority over applicants with adult spouses or over other categories of applicant. (*Hackney LBC v Ekinci* [2001] EWCA Civ 776; [2002] H.L.R. 2). **3A–1322**

### Dependent children

The function of the priority need provisions relating to dependent children in Part VII is to keep families together. That brings them within the ambit of ECHR art.8 dealing with the right to respect for "family life" (*R. (Morris) v Westminster City Council* [2005] EWCA Civ 1184; [2006] H.L.R. 8). The term "dependent child" in s.189(1) does not include a wife under the age of 18 who is in full-time education and dependent upon her husband (*Ekinci v Hackney LBC* [2001] EWCA Civ 1776, CA; [2002] H.L.R. 2). **3A–1323**

A child in full-time employment cannot be dependent. However, there may be circumstances where 16 or 17-year-olds who are not financially dependent on their parents may be dependent on them in other ways, bringing them within s.189(1)(b). (*R. v Kensington and Chelsea RBC Ex p. Hammell* [1989] Q.B. 518, CA—son aged 16, who was on a two-year YTS course at a training workshop, not dependent).

See also *R. v Kingswood BC Ex p. Smith-Morse* [1995] 2 F.L.R. 137, QBD; *R. v Lambeth LBC Ex p. Bodunrin* (1992) 24 H.L.R. 647, QBD.

***Paragraph numbers marked with a "+" can be found online and on CD.***

It has been held that the test to be applied under Housing Act 1985 s.59(1)(b) (now Housing Act 1996 s.189(1)(b)) was whether dependent children resided with the applicant, not whether there was any "greater residency" with another adult (*R. v Leeds CC Ex p. Collier*, June 1998, Legal Action 14, QBD) —but see now *Holmes-Moorehouse v Richmond-upon-Thames RLBC* [2009] 1 W.L.R. 413; [2009] 3 All E.R. 277. If parents have separated, in considering whether a child might reasonably be expected to live with an applicant, a local authority is entitled to take account of the fact that the child may already have a home with the other parent and that the consequence of awarding priority need might be the provision of accommodation to the applicant which would be under-occupied for much of the time. As a result:

> "it will be only in exceptional circumstances that it would be reasonable to expect a child who has a home with one parent to be provided under Part VII with another so that he can reside with the other parent as well" (para.21).

Such "exceptional circumstances" might arise where there is a disabled child and care of both parents is imperative.

See too *Robinson v Hammersmith & Fulham LBC* [2006] EWCA Civ 1122; [2006] 1 W.L.R. 3295 where the applicant was about to turn 18 at the time of her application.

**Vulnerable**

**3A–1324** Vulnerable means vulnerable in housing terms (*R. v Bath City Council Ex p. Sangermano* (1985) 17 H.L.R. 94, QBD). See too *R. v Lambeth LBC Ex p. Carroll* (1988) 20 H.L.R. 142, QBD, where Webster J. confirmed that "vulnerable" means less able to fend for oneself when homeless or in finding and keeping accommodation.

Note that the Housing Act 1996 s.189(1)(c) draws a distinction between mental illness and mental handicap which is not concerned with illness but with either subnormality or severe subnormality (*R. v Bath City Council Ex p. Sangermano* (1985) 17 H.L.R. 94, QBD).

In *R. v Waveney DC Ex p. Bowers* [1983] Q.B. 238; [1982] 3 All E.R. 727, CA, the Court of Appeal held that although alcoholism does not normally give an applicant priority need, in this case Mr Bowers's brain injury, whether described as a mental handicap or other social reason, had increased his vulnerability to such an extent that he had priority need (*cf. R. v Westminster City Council Ex p. Ortiz* (1995) 27 H.L.R. 364, CA).

In relation to epilepsy, *cf. R. v Reigate and Banstead BC Ex p. Di Dominico* (1988) 20 H.L.R. 153, QBD; and *R. v Wandsworth BC Ex p. Banbury* (1987) 19 H.L.R. 76, QBD.

In *R. v Camden LBC Ex p. Pereira* (1999) 31 H.L.R. 317, CA, after reviewing recent authorities, the Court of Appeal stated that vulnerability involves not just the issue of whether applicants can find and keep accommodation, but also whether they are less able to fend for themselves in coping with the state of homelessness. The assessment required is a composite one and an individual is not homeless under the "coping with homelessness" approach unless s/he would suffer injury of detriment which an ordinary homeless person would not. See too *Thorne v Winchester CC*, April 2000, Legal Action 32, CA. Although the Code of Guidance (July 2002) para.8.13 states that the critical test in applying s.189(1)(c) is whether an applicant is less likely to be unable to fend for himself so that he is likely to suffer injury or detriment, the Court of Appeal has noted that the word "likelihood" does not appear in the relevant provisions of the Act. Although local authorities must have regard to the Code of Guidance when exercising their functions under the Act, where the Code of Guidance is in conflict with the Act, the words of the Act prevail. The correct test under s.189(1)(c) is whether homeless persons are less able to fend for themselves so that they will suffer injury or detriment, not whether they are likely to suffer injury or detriment. It is not necessary to put the gloss of likeliness into the statutory test (*Griffin v Westminster City Council* [2004] EWCA Civ 108; [2004] H.L.R. 32). See too *Chowdhoury v Islington LBC* [2004] EWCA Civ 08; *Osmani v Camden LBC* [2004] EWCA Civ 1706; [2005] H.L.R. 22; *Bellouti v Wandsworth LBC* [2005] EWCA Civ 602; *Aman v Camden LBC* [2006] EWCA Civ 750; May 11, 2006; *Tetteh v Kingston upon Thames RLBC* [2004] EWCA Civ 1775; [2005] H.L.R. 21 and *Allison v Wandsworth LBC* [2008] EWCA Civ 354, April 15, 2008.

As to the obligation of local authorities to make inquiries, see s.184 and (in relation to alleged vulnerability) *Cramp v Hastings LBC*; *Phillips v Camden LBC* [2005] EWCA Civ 1005; [2005] 4 All E.R. 1014.

Although it is proper for a local authority to consider medical opinion, the question of whether or not someone is vulnerable for "some other special reason" is to be answered by the authority itself, not by the medical adviser. Local authorities are therefore obliged to consider any other available evidence and make whatever appropriate enquiries are necessary beyond obtaining their own officers' opinions (*R. v Lambeth LBC Ex p. Carroll* (1988) 20 H.L.R. 142, QBD). In In *Shala v Birmingham CC* [2007] EWCA Civ 624; [2008] H.L.R. 8 the Court of Appeal gave extended guidance on the commissioning and use of medical advice by local housing authorities in deciding "priority need" cases. It stated that:

(i) Although it is acceptable for local authorities to take specialist advice about medical evidence, care has to be taken not to appear to be using professional medical advisors simply to provide or shore up reasons for not accepting that an appellant is vulnerable.

(ii) There is no harm and some good in medical advisers directly addressing those matters within their professional competence about which the local authority have to make a decision, so long as both they and the local authority recognise that it is for the latter to make their own appraisal of every opinion.

(iii) Where an authority's medical expert is not a qualified psychiatrist, a local authority weighing his comments against the report of a qualified psychiatrist must not fall into the trap of thinking that it is comparing like with like; the authority's expert has the function of enabling the authority to understand the medical issues and to evaluate for themselves the expert evidence.

(iv) Absent an examination of the patient, the authority's medical adviser's advice cannot itself constitute expert evidence of the applicant's condition.

(v) Where an authority's medical adviser has not examined an applicant, he may, with consent, speak to the applicant's medical advisor on an informal basis about matters which need discussion.

There is no duty on authorities to refer every medical report to their medical advisors. (*Simms v Islington LBC* [2008] EWCA Civ 1083; [2009] H.L.R. 20).

**"emergency"**

The phrase "emergency such as a flood, fire or other disaster" involves the sudden **3A–1325**
and wholly unexpected loss of a home in circumstances outside an applicant's control. It is not necessary to show that a home has been lost through some physical disaster. The disappearance of a caravan in unexplained circumstances may be an emergency under s.189(1)(d) (*Higgs v Brighton and Hove City Council* [2003] EWCA Civ 895; [2003] 1 W.L.R. 2241; [2003] 3 All E.R. 753). However a demolition order is not "an emergency such as a flood, fire or any other disaster" (*Noble v South Hertfordshire DC* (1985) 17 H.L.R. 80, CA). Similarly, the Court of Appeal has held that a person made homeless by an unlawful eviction is not homeless "as a result of an emergency" within the Housing Act 1985 s.59(1)(d)(now s.189(1)(d)) (*R. v Bristol City Council Ex p. Bradic* (1995) 94 L.G.R. 257; 27 H.L.R. 584, CA). The word "emergency" is qualified by the phrase "such as flood, fire or other disaster". However, emergencies giving rise to priority need are not limited to those with "natural" causes. Fires or floods caused by humans can give rise to priority need, but there must be physical damage which causes the accommodation to be uninhabitable.

### *DUTIES TO PERSONS FOUND TO BE HOMELESS OR THREATENED WITH HOMELESSNESS*

## Duties to persons becoming homeless intentionally

**190.**—(1) This section applies where the local housing authority **3A–1326**
are satisfied that an applicant is homeless and is eligible for assistance but are also satisfied that he became homeless intentionally.

(2) If the authority are satisfied that the applicant has a priority need, they shall—

(a) secure that accommodation is available for his occupa-

***Paragraph numbers marked with a "+" can be found online and on CD.***

tion for such period as they consider will give him a reasonable opportunity of securing accommodation for his occupation, and

(b) provide him with (or secure that he is provided with) advice and assistance in any attempts he may make to secure that accommodation becomes available for his occupation.

(3) If they are not satisfied that he has a priority need, they shall provide him with (or secure that he is provided with) advice and assistance in any attempts he may make to secure that accommodation becomes available for his occupation.

(4) The applicant's housing needs shall be assessed before advice and assistance is provided under subsection (2)(b) or (3).

(5) The advice and assistance provided under subsection (2)(b) or (3) must include information about the likely availability in the authority's district of types of accommodation appropriate to the applicant's housing needs (including, in particular, the location and sources of such types of accommodation).

**3A-1327** *Note*—Amended by Homelessness Act 2002 Sch.1, paras 9 and 10.

**"eligible for assistance"**

**3A-1328** See s.185.

**"assistance"**

**3A-1329** See s.183.

**"local housing authority"**

**3A-1330** See ss.217, 218, and 230 which refer to the Housing Act 1985—see the Housing Act 1985 ss.1 and 2 above.

**"homeless"**

**3A-1331** See s.175.

**"applicant"**

**3A-1332** See s.183 and the commentary thereto.

**"priority need"**

**3A-1333** See s.189.

**"available for his occupation"**

**3A-1334** See s.176.

**"homeless intentionally"**

**3A-1335** See s.191.

**"a reasonable opportunity"**

**3A-1336** See *R. (Conville) v Richmond Upon Thames RLBC* [2006] EWCA Civ 718; [2006] 1 W.L.R. 2808 and *R. (Nipyo) v Croydon LBC* [2008] EWHC 847 (Admin); [2008] H.L.R. 37.

**Duties to persons becoming homeless intentionally**

**3A-1337** Local authorities only have minimal obligations to applicants who are intentionally homeless. The definition of intentional homelessness in the Housing Act 1996 s.191(1) has five component parts. The homeless person must have:

(a) done a deliberate act,

***Paragraph numbers marked with a "+" can be found online and on CD.***

(b) which caused the loss of housing,
(c) which s/he ceased to occupy,
(d) which was available to him or her, and
(e) which it would have been reasonable to continue to occupy.

In addition a person is to be treated as becoming homeless intentionally if he or she enters "into an arrangement under which he is required to cease to occupy accommodation which it would be reasonable for him to continue to occupy, and ... the purpose of the arrangement is to enable him to become entitled to assistance" in accordance with Part VII of the Act "and there is no other good reason why he is homeless" (Housing Act 1996 s.191(3)).

A person is threatened with homelessness intentionally if homelessness is the "likely result" of his or her deliberate act or omission.

It is for each local authority to make its own enquiries and to form its own view as to whether homelessness is intentional or not (*R. v Slough BC Ex p. Ealing LBC* [1981] Q.B. 801; [1981] 1 All E.R. 601; [1981] 2 W.L.R. 399, CA; *Noh v Hammersmith and Fulham LBC* [2001] EWCA Civ 905; [2002] H.L.R. 54, and *R. v Basingstoke and Deane DC Ex p. Webb*; December 1989; Legal Action 15, QBD).

The material date for determining whether a person became homeless intentionally or unintentionally is the date on which s/he left the accommodation. What may have happened afterwards is irrelevant (*Din v Wandsworth LBC* [1983] 1 A.C. 657; [1981] 3 All E.R. 881, HL). See too *R. v Islington LBC Ex p. Hassan* (1995) 27 H.L.R. 485, QBD, where Deputy Judge Roger Toulson, QC quashed a finding of intentional homelessness because the council had erred in believing that it could take account of developments after the applicant became homeless but before his actual departure from the premises.

The burden is on local authorities to satisfy themselves that an applicant has become homeless intentionally. If there is doubt or uncertainty, the issue must be resolved in the applicant's favour (*R. v Gravesham BC Ex p. Winchester* (1986) 18 H.L.R. 207, QBD—finding upheld).

Note that a homeless person cannot be intentionally homeless for refusing an offer of permanent accommodation, as it has never been occupied (*R. v Brent LBC Ex p. Awua* [1996] A.C. 55; [1995] 3 W.L.R. 215; [1995] 3 All E.R. 493, HL, below). However, such a refusal may mean that a local authority has discharged its duty and owes no further obligations towards the homeless person.

There is no practical or policy reason why a woman who has been sent to prison for theft should not be regarded as having made herself intentionally homeless, even though she moved house between the commission of the offence and the start of her sentence (*Minchin v Sheffield City Council*, *The Times*, April 26, 2000, CA). See too *Stewart v Lambeth LBC* [2002] EWCA Civ 753; [2002] H.L.R. 40, noted above.

**"deliberately does or fails to do ..."**

In *Dyson v Kerrier DC* [1980] 1 W.L.R. 1205; [1980] 3 All E.R. 313, CA, the applicant **3A-1338**
had surrendered her tenancy of a council flat in Cambridgeshire and gone to Cornwall where she had relatives. She took an unprotected holiday let for about four-and-a-half months. Not long before the holiday let was due to expire she approached the council for accommodation. It decided that her impending homelessness had been caused "intentionally" by her giving up the flat in Cambridgeshire. The Court of Appeal held that the council was entitled to take into account the fact that if she had not surrendered the Cambridgeshire tenancy she would not have become homeless. See too *R. v Barking and Dagenham LBC Ex p. Okuneye* (1996) 28 H.L.R. 174, QBD and *R. v Tower Hamlets LBC Ex p. Abdul Jolil*, October 1998, Legal Action 22, QBD.

However, in *R. v Tower Hamlets LBC Ex p. Rouf* (1991) 23 H.L.R. 460, CA, the applicant who had been in Britain since 1963 returned to Bangladesh in 1985 for three years. During his absence, he allowed a friend to occupy his council flat. The friend did not pay the rent and the flat was repossessed. In 1988, after obtaining entry clearance for his family, the applicant returned to England with them. He found the flat boarded up and applied to the council as a homeless person. Following an interview during which the applicant gave details of the accommodation he had used in Bangladesh (two small rooms), the authority declared him intentionally homeless for leaving the family home in Bangladesh. The interviewing officer failed to raise with the applicant two of the crucial issues contained in the definition of intentional homelessness (Housing Act 1985 s.60(1)—now the Housing Act 1996 s.191(1))—first, was the accommodation available for his continued occupation, and secondly, was it reasonable for him to have continued in occupation? The interviewer "deduced" positive answers from the discussion with the applicant. The Court of Appeal quashed the decision. The applicant had returned to England unaware that his flat had been repossessed. He had accordingly acted in ignorance and his action could not be "deliberate" for the purposes of s.60(1), if he had acted in good faith (s.60(3)—now Housing Act 1996 s.191(2)). The council had not addressed the good faith point in either its enquiries or its decision letter. See too *Kacar v Enfield LBC* (2001) 33 H.L.R. 5, CA.

A family cannot become intentionally homeless simply because they choose to have additional children (*R. v Eastleigh BC Ex p. Beattie (No.1)* (1983) 10 H.L.R. 134, QBD).

**Eviction following arrears**

**3A–1339** The key issue if arrears result in eviction and subsequent homelessness is whether the accrual of arrears, or more commonly, the circumstances which led to the arrears, were "a deliberate act." Eviction as a result of rent arrears is not intentional if it is the result of spending assets on the necessities of life. The "necessities of life" may vary from family to family. It is for the authority to consider whether a failure to pay rent is deliberate or whether it is due to a tenant having insufficient money to pay for the necessities of life, not for the court. It is not for the authority to investigate every detail in an applicant's figures of income and expenditure and it is not necessary for them to put to applicants their opinion that certain items are not a necessity (*R. v Brent LBC Ex p. Baruwa* (1997) 29 H.L.R. 915, CA, where a finding of intentional homelessness was upheld). See too *R. v Brent LBC Ex p. Grossett* (1996) 28 H.L.R. 9, CA; *R. v Exeter City Council Ex p. Tranckle* (1994) 26 H.L.R. 244, CA; and *R. v Wandsworth LBC Ex p. Onwudiwe* (1994) 26 H.L.R. 302, CA. A finding of intentionality was also upheld in *Hobbs v Sutton LBC* (1994) 26 H.L.R. 132, CA (eviction following rent arrears but claims by the applicants that there had been confusion about the whereabouts of their landlord and their entitlement to housing benefit.) Similarly, in *R. v Barnet LBC Ex p. Rughooputh* (1993) 25 H.L.R. 607, CA, the applicant was made homeless following mortgage possession proceedings. The deliberate act which caused the loss of the home was the applicant's taking out a mortgage in 1987 beyond her means—she was unemployed, but had claimed to have an earned income of £18,000. The council's finding of intentional homelessness was upheld. The taking out of the mortgage was the act that caused the homelessness. It had been induced by fraudulent misrepresentation and so the Housing Act 1985 s.60(3) (now the Housing Act 1996 s.190(2)) could not apply to prevent the act from being "deliberate". See too *Watchman v Ipswich BC* [2007] EWCA Civ 348; [2007] H.L.R. 33 (council had been entitled to find that it was the taking out of a mortgage (and not the loss of a job) that had caused the homelessness).

On the other hand, in *R. v Wandsworth LBC Ex p. Hawthorne* [1995] 2 All E.R. 331; (1995) 27 H.L.R. 59, CA, a finding of intentional homelessness was quashed where the applicant had been evicted from her council home for rent arrears of over £3,000. She claimed that she had been unable to afford the rent, having had so low an income after her husband left her that she had been driven to choose between maintaining her children and paying the council. Nourse L.J. stated:

> "The purpose of Part III of the 1985 Act [now the Housing Act 1996 Part VII] is to house the homeless. Admittedly, it is no part of that purpose to house those whose homelessness has been brought upon them by their own fault. But equally it is no part of it to refuse housing to those whose homelessness has been brought upon them without fault on their part, for example by disability, sickness, poverty or even a simple inability to make ends meet."

The council had not considered the matters which had caused the applicant not to pay her rent. That was a fatal omission. It was no answer to assert that there had been a considered decision not to pay. The true question is: "What caused that decision?" See too *R. v Hillingdon LBC Ex p. Tinn* (1988) 20 H.L.R. 305, QBD, below; *R. v Shrewsbury and Atcham BC Ex p. Griffiths* (1993) 25 H.L.R. 613, QBD (decision of intentional homelessness after eviction for mortgage arrears quashed); *R. v Southwark LBC Ex p. Davies* (1994) 26 H.L.R. 677, QBD; and *R. v Camden LBC Ex p. Cosma* (1998) 30 H.L.R. 817, QBD (return to England following the failure of the applicant's restaurant enterprise in Cyprus. Finding of intentional homelessness quashed because of failure to make sufficient enquiries into the arrangements the applicant might (or might not) have been) able to make with lenders to stave off her eviction and accordingly whether it would have been reasonable for the applicant to have continued to occupy her home in Cyprus).

### Eviction after anti-social behaviour

It is not necessary for authorities to show that the applicants have deliberately done something with the intention of being evicted. See *Devenport v Salford City Council* (1983) 8 H.L.R. 54, CA, where a finding of intentional homelessness was upheld after failure by parents to take any steps to control their children and the children's conduct resulted in the making of a possession order. Findings of intentional homelessness were also upheld in *R. v Rochester-upon-Medway City Council Ex p. Williams* (1994) 26 H.L.R. 588, QBD (failure to control children); *R. v Hammersmith and Fulham LBC Ex p. P* (1990) 22 H.L.R. 21, QBD (anti-social and criminal behaviour leading to the loss of homes); and *Denton v Southwark LBC* [2007] EWCA Civ 623; [2008] H.L.R. 11 ("deliberate act" of breaking mother's house rules led to be applicant being thrown out). **3A–1340**

### Acquiescence in conduct of partner

A woman who lives with a man who becomes intentionally homeless is not necessarily barred from relief by his conduct or by the fact that he may benefit undeservingly. However, depending on the facts, an authority may be entitled to assume that, in the absence of evidence to the contrary, she had acquiesced in his conduct and that accordingly she herself had become intentionally homeless (*R. v North Devon DC Ex p. Lewis* [1981] 1 W.L.R. 328; [1981] 1 All E.R. 27, QBD). See too *R. v Nottingham CC Ex p. Caine* (1995) 28 H.L.R. 374, CA (the applicant's partner had decided to withhold rent, for which housing benefit was being paid, because of the landlord's failure to carry out repairs. As a result of the arrears, the couple were evicted. Finding of intentional homelessness upheld because the applicant had acquiesced in the decision not to pay the rent and to use the housing benefit in the family budget); *R. v Tower Hamlets LBC Ex p. Khatun* (1995) 27 H.L.R. 344, CA (wife content in the marriage to leave decisions to her husband. The Court of Appeal held that she might properly be treated as having "joined" in her husband's decision to move accommodation); *R. v Barnet LBC Ex p. O'Connor* (1990) 22 H.L.R. 486, QBD; *R. v Ealing LBC Ex p. Salmons* (1991) 23 H.L.R. 272, QBD; *R. v East Herts DC Ex p. Bannon* (1986) 18 H.L.R. 515, QBD (acquiescence in nuisance); *R. v Swansea City Council Ex p. John* (1983) 9 H.L.R. 56, QBD (council entitled to reach conclusion that wife has acquiesced in husband's drunkenness which had led to eviction). **3A–1341**

*Cf.* however, *R. v East Northamptonshire DC Ex p. Spruce* (1988) 20 H.L.R. 508, QBD (finding of intentional homelessness quashed because of insufficient inquiries into alleged acquiescence); *R. v Eastleigh BC Ex p. Beattie (No.2)* (1985) 17 H.L.R. 168, QBD (decision not to pay mortgage instalments based on legal advice; evidence that Mrs Beattie had protested about her husband not paying the mortgage. Finding of intentional homelessness quashed); *R. v Penwith DC Ex p. Trevena* (1985) 17 H.L.R. 526, QBD (no material on which the authority could conclude that Mr Trevena had been a party to the surrender of a tenancy by his wife or that it was a joint surrender or abandonment); *R.v Mole Valley DC Ex p. Burton* (1988) 20 H.L.R. 479, QBD; and *R. v Thanet DC Ex p. Groves* (1990) 22 H.L.R. 223, QBD (failure by council to have regard to wife's assertions that she did not know of, or participate in, the accumulation of arrears).

### "act or omission in good faith"

An act or omission in good faith on the part of a person who was unaware of any relevant fact shall not be treated as deliberate (s.191(2)). When considering this question "there is a distinction between honest blundering and carelessness on the one hand, where a person can still act in good faith, and dishonesty on the other, where there can be no question of the person acting in good faith" (per Roch J. in *R. v Hammersmith and Fulham LBC Ex p. Lusi* (1991) 23 H.L.R. 260, QBD). The use of the phrase "good faith" carries a connotation of some kind of impropriety, or some element of misuse or abuse of the legislation (*Ugiagbe v Southwark LBC* [2009] EWCA Civ 31, February 10, 2009; *The Times*, February 18, 2009, where the claimant had been in ignorance of a relevant fact and had acted in "good faith"—not intentionally homeless). See too *R. v Westminster CC Ex p. Obeid* (1997) 29 H.L.R. 389, QBD (ignorance about **3A–1342** housing benefit); and *R. v Wandsworth LBC Ex p. Rose* (1984) 11 H.L.R. 105, QBD (applicant came to stay with her father but asked to leave because his accommodation was not satisfactory. The council was not entitled to assume, without making proper enquiries, that simply because the applicant had failed to ask her father about accommodation, she had acted other than in good faith about a relevant fact).

In *R. v Westminster CC Ex p. N'Dormadingar, The Times*, November 20, 1997, QBD, Lightman J. enumerated the following principles which apply where someone gives up accommodation but claims not to be intentionally homeless because he or she is unaware of a material fact:

(1) An applicant must show that he or she is unaware of some relevant fact existing at the date that he or she gave up accommodation;
(2) Whether an applicant makes enquiries into the existence of the fact is relevant to his or her awareness of it;
(3) A fact is relevant where, had the applicant been aware of it, he or she would have taken it into account in deciding to give up accommodation;
(4) A fact must be sufficiently clear and definite for its existence to be objectively determined;
(5) Lack of, or deficiency in, foresight of the future does not constitute unawareness of an existing fact. To establish such unawareness it is necessary to show the existence at the relevant date of a factual state of affairs which falsifies the applicant's predictions.

In a case turning on whether ignorance was in good faith, the council should in interview tell an applicant if it believes that he or she is not acting in good faith (*R. v Westminster City Council Ex p. Moozary-Oraky* (1994) 26 H.L.R. 213, QBD).

**"reasonable for him to continue to occupy"**

**3A–1343** In considering whether or not it is reasonable to continue to occupy accommodation, local authorities are not limited to housing issues and can have regard to things like employment prospects and loss of benefits in that locality (per Woolf J. in *R. v Hammersmith and Fulham LBC Ex p. Duro-Rama* (1983) 9 H.L.R. 71, QBD). See too *R. v Hillingdon LBC Ex p. Tinn* (1988) 20 H.L.R. 305, QBD, where Kennedy J. said:

> "it cannot be reasonable [within the meaning of section 60 of the 1985 Act—(now Housing Act 1996 s.191)] for a person to continue to occupy accommodation when they can no longer discharge the fiscal obligations ... in relation to that accommodation without so straining their resources as to deprive themselves of the ordinary necessities of life, such as food, clothing, heat, transport and so forth" (p.308).

See too *R. v Camden LBC Ex p. Aranda* (1998) 30 H.L.R. 76, CA (surrender of London council flat under a scheme involving the receipt of a substantial sum to help them to buy privately followed by acquisition of a bungalow in Colombia. Applicant returned to London after failure to find work and being abandoned by her husband without financial support. Camden's finding of intentional homelessness was quashed. Any finding that the giving up of the Colombian home was intentional was impossible—no reasonable authority could have found, given the financial circumstances, that it would have been reasonable to continue in occupation); *R. v Basingstoke and Deane BC Ex p. Bassett* (1983) 10 H.L.R. 125, QBD (applicant not homeless as a result of leaving that accommodation, but rather as a result of the breakdown in the marriage and in particular her husband's conduct, which made it unreasonable for her to live with him); *R. v Islington LBC Ex p. Bibi* (1997) 29 H.L.R. 498, QBD (applicant left her home in Bangladesh because she had no access to sufficient monies to feed her family. Finding of intentional homelessness quashed); and *R. v Tower Hamlets LBC Ex p. Ojo* (1991) 23 H.L.R. 488, QBD (council gave "no proper consideration" to the question of whether, as a result of overcrowding of the applicant's home in Nigeria, it could be said that it was not reasonable to continue to occupy the accommodation).

See also *R. v Hillingdon LBC Ex p. Islam* [1983] 1 A.C. 688; [1981] 3 W.L.R. 109; [1981] 3 All E.R. 901, HL (husband, wife and several children evicted from shared room); *De Falco v Crawley BC* [1980] Q.B. 460; [1980] 2 W.L.R. 664; [1980] 1 All E.R. 913, CA (reasonable to have continued to occupy the accommodation in Italy); *cf. R. v Westminster City Council Ex p. Guilarte*, June 1994, Legal Action 13, QBD (applicant left accommodation in Venezuela because of the poor economy and high inflation in that country and because he thought he would find a better standard of living in Britain.

Decision quashed because the council had failed to make enquiries as to (a) whether he could have remained in the specific accommodation he occupied in Venezuela, and, if so (b) why he chose to leave it).

In *R. v Wandsworth LBC Ex p. Henderson* (1986) 18 H.L.R. 522, QBD, there was acute disrepair and, as a result, the council served statutory notices. The tenants withheld rent and arrears accrued. The landlord began possession proceedings based on rent arrears. Even though the tenants counterclaimed and were represented by counsel, a possession order was made. The council decided that they had consented to the possession order and had become homeless intentionally. McNeill J. dismissed an application for judicial review. Even though the necessary repairs were very extensive and being carried out slowly, the local authority was entitled to decide that the tenants had "deliberately" left available accommodation. See too *R. v Waltham Forest LBC Ex p. Green* December 1997, Legal Action 15, QBD.

As to living conditions in shared accommodation, contrast *R. v Brent LBC Ex p. Yusuf* (1997) 29 H.L.R. 48, QBD; and *R. v Brent LBC Ex p. Bariise* (1999) 31 H.L.R. 50, CA.

### Departure after violence

See *R. v Croydon LBC Ex p. Toth* (1988) 20 H.L.R. 576, CA (departure after threats **3A–1344** by associates of applicant's husband, who had disappeared and was being sought in relation to an armed robbery. Finding of intentional homelessness upheld); *R. v Newham LBC Ex p. McIlroy* (1991) 23 H.L.R. 570, QBD (council was entitled to conclude that the family could have continued in their home or temporary accommodation in Belfast pending an urgent transfer application notwithstanding sectarian violence which had led to one of the applicants being shot at); *cf. R. v Brent LBC Ex p. McManus* (1993) 25 H.L.R. 643, CA (sectarian violence); *R. v Hillingdon LBC Ex p. H* (1988) 20 H.L.R. 554, QBD (intimidation and violence in Northern Ireland); *R. v Westminster City Council Ex p. Bishop* (1993) 25 H.L.R. 459, CA (departure of applicant's daughter from flat after she had been harassed and molested by drug-dealers followed by the applicant leaving as a result of violence and harassment from a former partner. Finding of intentional homelessness quashed); *R. v Westminster City Council Ex p. Ermakov* [1996] 2 All E.R. 302, CA; *R. v Barnet LBC Ex p. Babalola* (1996) 28 H.L.R. 196, QBD; *R. v Hillingdon LBC Ex p. McDowell*, December 1992, Legal Action 22, QBD (harassment from neighbours, culminating in the systematic wrecking of her car and ransacking of her flat. Finding of intentional homelessness quashed); *R. v Tynedale DC Ex p. McCabe* (1992) 24 H.L.R. 384, QBD (domestic violence); *R. v Northampton BC Ex p. Clarkson* (1992) 24 H.L.R. 529, QBD (sexual abuse) and *R. (McAuley and Stewart) v Highland Council*, Court of Session (Outer House), July 22, 2003 (harassment, threats and violence).

### Affordability

The question of whether accommodation is affordable and accordingly whether it is **3A–1345** reasonable to continue to occupy is not to be "judged on a Micawber test as to whether one's income exceeds, or fails to measure up to, the rent one is required to pay" (per Sir Thomas Bingham M.R. in *R. v Croydon LBC Ex p. Graham* (1994) 26 H.L.R. 286, CA, where the applicant had not acted unreasonably in moving (without prospect of homelessness) to cheaper suitable accommodation. See too *R. v Tower Hamlets LBC Ex p. Ullah* (1992) 24 H.L.R. 680, QBD (applicant sold house to repay loans. Finding of intentional homelessness quashed because council had failed to enquire into the loans, their terms and all the surrounding circumstances to determine where on the scale of necessity this situation fell). But *cf. R. v Leeds City Council Ex p. Adamiec* (1992) 24 H.L.R. 138, QBD, where although a home-owner fell into financial difficulties and mortgage arrears developed, no action was taken by the lender to enforce the loan and there was no threat of repossession proceedings. The owner sold the home, repaid the debt and applied to the council as a homeless person. The council decided that he was intentionally homeless. Webster J. dismissed an application for judicial review, but said "if [the family] had been threatened with repossession, then it would have been unreasonable for the council not to rehouse them". See also *R. v Westminster City Council Ex p. Ali* (1997) 29 H.L.R. 580, QBD.

### Settled accommodation

Where someone applies to a local authority after leaving accommodation which is **3A–1346**

***Paragraph numbers marked with a "+" can be found online and on CD.***

not settled, the council must first identify the last "settled" accommodation, the loss of which caused the present homelessness. For someone to remain intentionally homeless, there must be a causal link between past intentionality and present homelessness. Such a link may be broken if the applicant secures further "settled accommodation" after the original intentional homelessness. See, e.g. *R. v Brent LBC, Ex p. Awua* [1996] A.C. 55; [1995] 3 W.L.R. 215; [1995] 3 All E.R. 493, HL, where the applicant when originally homeless applied to Tower Hamlets LBC for accommodation. She accepted temporary accommodation pending enquiries. Subsequently, in discharge of the full housing duty, she was offered a housing association tenancy (Housing Act 1985 ss.65(2) and 69(1)(b)) but rejected it. Tower Hamlets accordingly terminated her right to occupy the temporary accommodation. The applicant then applied to Brent LBC, with which she also had a local connection. Brent declared her intentionally homeless due to her eviction from the temporary accommodation granted by Tower Hamlets. The House of Lords upheld Brent's decision. What Ms Awua had lost was plainly "accommodation". It did not matter whether that accommodation was temporary or otherwise. What mattered was whether by her act or omission she had lost it. On the facts, her failure to take up an offer of suitable permanent accommodation made through Tower Hamlets had caused the loss of the temporary accommodation and she was intentionally homeless. See too *R. v East Herts DC Ex p. Hunt* (1986) 18 H.L.R. 51, QBD (accommodation provided pending full discharge of council's duty was settled accommodation); but *cf. R. v Rushcliffe DC Ex p. Summerson and Buckley* (1993) 25 H.L.R. 577, QBD (a single hostel room without facilities intended for only very short-term occupation could not be regarded as settled); *Mohamed v Westminster CC* [2005] EWCA Civ 796;15 June 2005 (assured shorthold tenancy where housing benefit was capped at less than the rent due, resultant arrears of rent and an order for possession. Council decision that applicant had not had "settled" accommodation since her last application because the private sector accommodation had been unaffordable and overcrowded from the outset and the loss of it had been inevitable, upheld by Court of Appeal); and *Stewart v Lambeth LBC* [2002] EWCA Civ 753; [2002] H.L.R. 40, (tenant sentenced to imprisonment and then evicted for rent arrears. Held (1) the applicant had had no "settled accommodation" since the loss of his flat as prison could not be treated as a settled home. He had been detained against his will and so it was "incarceration" rather than a "home"; and (2) the causal connection between the offending and the homelessness had not been broken by an arrangement with the applicant's sister that she would pay the rent and her failure to perform it).

In *Lambert v Ealing LBC* [1982] 1 W.L.R. 550; [1982] 2 All E.R. 394, CA, a French widower left accommodation in Grenoble and came to England with three teenage daughters to occupy premises in Ealing on a holiday let. When the holiday let was terminated, he sought accommodation from the local authority. The Court of Appeal held that the accommodation which a person left "intentionally" did not have to be the same as the accommodation inhabited immediately before his/her ultimate homelessness. As Mr Lambert had not acquired any settled accommodation in the UK, he had become homeless intentionally when he left the home in Grenoble. See too *R. v Croydon LBC Ex p. Easom* (1993) 25 H.L.R. 262, QBD (series of tenancies in Australia where applicants were illegal immigrants not settled accommodation); *cf. R. v Camden LBC Ex p. Aranda* (1998) 30 H.L.R. 76, CA.

An assured shorthold tenancy may be settled accommodation. In *Knight v Vale Royal BC* [2003] EWCA Civ 1258; [2004] H.L.R. 9,the Court of Appeal stated that occupation under an assured shorthold tenancy is "likely to be settled rather than temporary" and that it is not right to assume that occupation for a period of as little as six months "is likely to be temporary rather than settled". However, it does not follow that occupation under an assured shorthold tenancy always constitutes settled accommodation. That remains a question of fact and degree "although the existence of an assured shorthold tenancy will normally be a significant pointer to the accommodation being settled". The question of whether or not such a tenancy is settled accommodation is a question of degree and judgment for the local authority (*R. v Christchurch BC Ex p. Conway* (1987) 19 H.L.R. 238, QBD (finding of intentional homelessness upheld); and *R. v Rochester-upon-Medway City Council Ex p. Williams* (1994) 26 H.L.R. 588, QBD (application for judicial review dismissed). See too *R. v Harrow LBC Ex p. Fahia* [1998] 1 W.L.R. 1396; [1998] 4 All E.R. 137, HL; *R. v Hackney LBC Ex p. Ajayi* [1997] August C.L.D. 306; June 1997, Legal Action 23, CA; and *R. v Merton LBC Ex p. Ruffle* (1989) 21 H.L.R. 361, QBD.

## Becoming homeless intentionally

**191.**—(1) A person becomes homeless intentionally if he deliberately does or fails to do anything in consequence of which he ceases to occupy accommodation which is available for his occupation and which it would have been reasonable for him to continue to occupy. **3A–1347**

(2) For the purposes of subsection (1) an act or omission in good faith on the part of a person who was unaware of any relevant fact shall not be treated as deliberate.

(3) A person shall be treated as becoming homeless intentionally if—

(a) he enters into an arrangement under which he is required to cease to occupy accommodation which it would have been reasonable for him to continue to occupy, and

(b) the purpose of the arrangement is to enable him to become entitled to assistance under this Part,

and there is no other good reason why he is homeless.

(4) [...]

*Note*—Amended by the Homelessness Act 2002 Sch.1, para.1. **3A–1348**

**"available for his occupation"**

See s.176. **3A–1349**

**Becoming homeless intentionally**

See commentary to s.190. **3A–1350**

## Duty to persons not in priority need who are not homeless intentionally

**192.**—(1) This section applies where the local housing authority— **3A–1351**

(a) are satisfied that an applicant is homeless and eligible for assistance, and

(b) are not satisfied that he became homeless intentionally,

but are not satisfied that he has a priority need.

(2) The authority shall provide the applicant with (or secure that he is provided with) advice and assistance in any attempts he may make to secure that accommodation becomes available for his occupation.

(3) The authority may secure that accommodation is available for occupation by the applicant.

(4) The applicant's housing needs shall be assessed before advice and assistance is provided under subsection (2).

(5) The advice and assistance provided under subsection (2) must include information about the likely availability in the authority's district of types of accommodation appropriate to the applicant's housing needs (including, in particular, the location and sources of such types of accommodation).

*Note*—Amended by Homelessness Act 2002 Sch.1, paras 11 and 12. **3A–1352**

**"eligible for assistance"**

See s.185. **3A–1353**

***Paragraph numbers marked with a "+" can be found online and on CD.***

**"assistance"**

3A-1354 See s.183.

**"local housing authority"**

3A-1355 See ss.217, 218, and 230 which refer to the Housing Act 1985—see the Housing Act 1985 ss.1 and 2, above.

**"homeless"**

3A-1356 See s.175.

**"applicant"**

3A-1357 See s.183 and the commentary thereto.

**"priority need"**

3A-1358 See s.189.

**"homeless intentionally"**

3A-1359 See s.191.

**Duty and Power**

3A-1360 The only *duty* to persons not in priority need who are homeless unintentionally is to provide advice and assistance. However the amendment effected by Homelessness Act 2002 gives local housing authorities a *power* to secure that accommodation is made available.

## Duty to persons with priority need who are not homeless intentionally

3A-1361 **193.**—(1) This section applies where the local housing authority are satisfied that an applicant is homeless, eligible for assistance and has a priority need, and are not satisfied that he became homeless intentionally.

(2) Unless the authority refer the application to another local housing authority (see section 198), they shall secure that accommodation is available for occupation by the applicant.

(3) The authority are subject to the duty under this section until it ceases by virtue of any of the following provisions of this section.

(3A) The authority shall, on becoming subject to the duty under this section in a case which is not a restricted case, give the applicant a copy of the statement included in their allocation scheme by virtue of section 167(1A) (policy on offering choice to people allocated housing accommodation under Part 6).

(3B) In this section "a restricted case" means a case where the local housing authority would not be satisfied as mentioned in subsection (1) without having had regard to a restricted person.

(5) The local housing authority shall cease to be subject to the duty under this section if the applicant, having been informed by the authority of the possible consequence of refusal and of his right to request a review of the suitability of the accommodation, refuses an offer of accommodation which the authority are satisfied is suitable for him and the authority notify him that they regard themselves as having discharged their duty under this section.

(6) The local housing authority shall cease to be subject to the duty under this section if the applicant—

(a) ceases to be eligible for assistance,

(b) becomes homeless intentionally from the accommodation made available for his occupation,

(c) accepts an offer of accommodation under Part VI (allocation of housing), or

(cc) accepts an offer of an assured tenancy (other than an assured shorthold tenancy) from a private landlord,

(d) otherwise voluntarily ceases to occupy as his only or principal home the accommodation made available for his occupation.

(7) The local housing authority shall also cease to be subject to the duty under this section if the applicant, having been informed of the possible consequence of refusal and of his right to request a review of the suitability of the accommodation, refuses a final offer of accommodation under Part 6.

(7A) An offer of accommodation under Part 6 is a final offer for the purposes of subsection (7) if it is made in writing and states that it is a final offer for the purposes of subsection (7).

(7AA) In a restricted case the authority shall also cease to be subject to the duty under this section if the applicant, having been informed of the matters mentioned in subsection (7AB) —

(a) accepts a private accommodation offer, or

(b) refuses such an offer.

(7AB) The matters are—

(a) the possible consequence of refusal of the offer, and

(b) that the applicant has the right to request a review of the suitability of the accommodation.

(7AC) For the purposes of this section an offer is a private accommodation offer if—

(a) it is an offer of an assured shorthold tenancy made by a private landlord to the applicant in relation to any accommodation which is, or may become, available for the applicant's occupation,

(b) it is made, with the approval of the authority, in pursuance of arrangements made by the authority with the landlord with a view to bringing the authority's duty under this section to an end, and

(c) the tenancy being offered is a fixed term tenancy (within the meaning of Part 1 of the Housing Act 1988) for a period of at least 12 months.

(7AD) In a restricted case the authority shall, so far as reasonably practicable, bring their duty under this section to an end as mentioned in subsection (7AA).

(7B) In a case which is not a restricted case, the authority shall also cease to be subject to the duty under this section if the applicant accepts a qualifying offer of an assured shorthold tenancy which is made by a private landlord in relation to any accommodation which is, or may become, available for the applicant's occupation.

(7C) In a case which is not a restricted case, the applicant is free to reject a qualifying offer without affecting the duty owed to him under this section by the authority.

(7D) For the purposes of subsection (7B) an offer of an assured shorthold tenancy is a qualifying offer if—

(a) it is made, with the approval of the authority, in pursuance of arrangements made by the authority with the landlord with a view to bringing the authority's duty under this section to an end;

(b) the tenancy being offered is a fixed term tenancy (within the meaning of Part 1 of the Housing Act 1988 (c. 50)); and

(c) it is accompanied by a statement in writing which states the term of the tenancy being offered and explains in ordinary language that—

(i) there is no obligation to accept the offer, but

(ii) if the offer is accepted the local housing authority will cease to be subject to the duty under this section in relation to the applicant.

(7E) An acceptance of a qualifying offer is only effective for the purposes of subsection (7B) if the applicant signs a statement acknowledging that he has understood the statement mentioned in subsection (7D).

(7F) The local housing authority shall not—

(a) make a final offer of accommodation under Part 6 for the purposes of subsection (7); or

(ab) approve a private accommodation offer; or

(b) approve an offer of an assured shorthold tenancy for the purposes of subsection (7B), unless they are satisfied that the accommodation is suitable for the applicant and that it is reasonable for him to accept the offer.

(8) For the purposes of subsection (7F) an applicant may reasonably be expected to accept an offer even though he is under contractual or other obligations in respect of his existing accommodation, provided he is able to bring those obligations to an end before he is required to take up the offer.

(9) A person who ceases to be owed the duty under this section may make a fresh application to the authority for accommodation or assistance in obtaining accommodation.

**3A-1362** *Note* —Amended by Homelessness Act 2002 Sch.1, para.13. Amended for certain purposes by the Housing and Regeneration Act 2008 Sch.15, Pt I, para.5, with effect from March 2, 2009 (SI 2009/415; for purposes see art.2).

#### Restricted case and restricted person

**3A-1362.1** See Housing Act 1996 s.184(7). New s.193(7AA) provides that an authority may cease to be subject to the s.193 duty in a restricted case if an applicant who has been informed of the consequences of refusal and of his right to request a review on the grounds of suitability, accepts or refuses a private accommodation offer. A private accommodation offer is defined as an offer of a fixed-term assured shorthold tenancy for a period of at least 12 months, made by a private landlord with the approval of the authority, in pursuance of arrangements made by the authority with a view to bringing the s.193 duty to an end (new s.193(7AB), (7AC)). Local authorities are obliged, in a restricted case, as far as reasonably practicable, to bring their duty under this section to an end by such an offer: s.193(7AD).

**"assured tenancy"**

See Housing Act 1988 s.1. 3A-1363

**"assured shorthold tenancy"**

See Housing Act 1988 ss.19A and 20. 3A-1364

**"fixed term tenancy"**

See Housing Act 1988 s.45. 3A-1365

**"eligible for assistance"**

See s.185. 3A-1366

**"assistance"**

See s.183. 3A-1367

**"local housing authority"**

See ss.217, 218, and 230 which refer to the Housing Act 1985—see the Housing Act 1985 ss.1 and 2 above. 3A-1368

**"homeless"**

See s.175. 3A-1369

**"applicant"**

See s.183 and the commentary thereto. 3A-1370

**"priority need"**

See s.189. 3A-1371

**"homeless intentionally"**

See s.191. 3A-1372

**They are satisfied that the accommodation is suitable (s.193(7F))**

See s.210 below and commentary at para.3A-1376, sub-paragraph (b). 3A-1373

**Duty to persons with priority need who are not homeless intentionally**

If local housing authorities are satisfied that applicants are homeless, eligible for assistance, in priority need and not satisfied that they became homeless intentionally, they have two possible courses of action: 3A-1374

(a) to refer to another local authority. See Housing Act 1996 s.198 and the commentary at 3A-1402. Section 198 is almost exactly the same as the previous "local connection" provisions (Housing Act 1985 s.67), but it has been extended to include referral back to another authority where that other authority originally dealt with the applicant's homeless application and as a result placed the applicant in accommodation outside its boundaries; or

(b) secure that suitable accommodation is made available for occupation (Housing Act 1996 ss.193(2) and 206). Once the conditions in s.193(1) are met, the duty to accommodate is triggered and it is unlawful to impose "any further hurdle or proviso before accepting that the duty arises". (e.g. service of notice to quit in relation to joint tenancy). See *R. (Hammia) v Wandsworth LBC* [2005] EWHC 1127; [2005] H.L.R. 45.

Under s.193, it is only in exceptional circumstances, if at all, that councils are allowed to "earmark" properties in advance because when a property actually becomes available it has to be offered to the family highest placed in the council's allocation scheme at that date (*R. (Amirun Begum) v Tower Hamlets LBC* [2002] EWHC 633 (Admin); [2003] H.L.R. 8).

No claim lies for damages in tort for breach of the statutory duties owed to the homeless (*O'Rourke v Camden LBC* [1998] A.C. 188; [1997] 3 W.L.R. 86; [1997] 3 All E.R. 23, HL).

Although ECHR art.8 does not impose on the state a duty to provide a home and the simple fact of "homelessness" does not therefore breach art.8, there may though

***Paragraph numbers marked with a "+" can be found online and on CD.***



HOUSING

be cases where it assists if homelessness causes interference with the claimant's family life or private life (*R. (Morris) v Newham LBC* [2002] EWHC 1262 (Admin); May 24, 2002—on the facts, claim dismissed).

**"secure that accommodation is available for occupation"**

3A-1375 The Housing Act 1996 s.176 requires that accommodation be secured not only for occupation by an applicant, but also for "any other person who normally resides with him as a member of his family". In *R. v Newham LBC Ex p. Khan* (2001) 33 H.L.R. 29, QBD Collins J. held that the decision to "split" a family who had lived together prior to homelessness was unlawful. *cf. R. v Westminster CC Ex p. Abo-Ragheed*, April 2001, Legal Action 22, November 27, 2001, QBD Admin Ct.

In *Birmingham City Council v Ali and Aweys* [2009] UKHL 36; [2009] 1 W.L.R. 1506 , it was held that an authority can perform its main housing duty under the Housing Act 1996 Pt 7 by arranging for an applicant to stay in existing unsatisfactory accommodation for a short period, but is not performing its duty if it simply accepts the homelessness application and adds the applicant to its allocation scheme for long term housing;

Authorities must secure accommodation which is "suitable"—see the Housing Act 1996 s.206. See e.g. *R. v Newham LBC Ex p. Dada* [1996] Q.B. 507; [1995] 3 W.L.R. 540; [1995] 2 All E.R. 522. The requirement that accommodation is suitable means suitable for the persons to whom the duty is owed. It encompasses considerations of the range, nature and location of accommodation as well as its standard of condition, and likely duration of the applicant's occupancy (*Codona v Mid-Bedfordshire DC* [2004] EWCA Civ 925; [2005] H.L.R. 1). In considering whether accommodation is suitable authorities should have regard to the Housing Act 1985 Pts IX, X and XI (slum clearance, overcrowding and HMOs and the applicant's financial resources, including various specified forms of income, various specified costs relating to accommodation and other reasonable living expenses (Housing Act 1996 s.210 and the Homelessness (Suitability of Accommodation) Order 1996 (SI 1996/3204).

In addition, the Homelessness (Suitability of Accommodation) (England) Order 2003 (SI 2003/3326) prescribes the accommodation which is suitable for a person with family commitments—i.e. someone who is pregnant or with whom a pregnant woman or dependent children reside or might reasonably be expected to reside. Accommodation is not to be regarded as suitable if it is "B&B accommodation". B&B accommodation is accommodation which, whether or not breakfast is provided, is not self contained or which involves sharing certain amenities with another household. However there are exceptions. If there is no available accommodation, other than B&B accommodation, a local housing authority may house someone with family commitments in B&B accommodation, but only for a period or total of periods not exceeding six weeks.

An offer can only discharge the main housing duty under s.193(7F) if the authority is satisfied both that the accommodation is suitable and that it would be reasonable for the applicant to accept the offer. The particular needs of the applicant, for example to be protected from domestic violence and to be located near support networks, are relevant when considering suitability but that does not mean that those matters are material only to suitability. The submission that if premises were suitable it had to follow that it was reasonable to accept them was rejected in *Slater v Lewisham LBC* [2006] EWCA Civ 394; [2006] H.L.R. 37. There may be circumstances in which it is reasonable to refuse accommodation that is objectively suitable.

An offer of accommodation which is not suitable for occupation at the date it falls to be accepted can operate as a performance of the housing duty if accompanied with certain binding and enforceable assurances about what work will be carried out to it after acceptance (*Boreh v Ealing LBC* [2008] EWCA Civ 1176, [2009] H.L.R. 22).

In *R. (Yumsak) v Enfield LBC* [2002] EWHC 280; [2003] H.L.R. 1, Maurice Kay L.J. said that cases in which local authorities have been successfully challenged (in relation to suitability of accommodation offered) have been described as "exceptional" and that those who seek to challenge them have to surmount a high hurdle" (at [32]).

**"cease to be subject to the duty"**

3A-1376 Authorities cease to be under if a duty if the applicant:

- after being informed about the possible consequences of refusal, refuses an offer of accommodation which the authority are satisfied is suitable (Housing Act 1996 s.193(5)); or

- ceases to be eligible for assistance (Housing Act 1996 s.193(6)(a)); or
- becomes homeless intentionally from the accommodation made available for occupation (Housing Act 1996 s.193(6)(b)); or
- accepts an offer of housing under the Housing Act 1996 Pt VI or otherwise ceases to occupy as his or her only or principal home the accommodation made available (Housing Act 1996 s.193(6)(c) and (d)); or
- after being informed of the possible consequences refuses an offer of Pt VI accommodation which the authority are satisfied was suitable (Housing Act 1996 s.193(7)(a)).
- the applicant accepts an offer of an assured tenancy from a private landlord (s.193(7B)).

The offer of an assured shorthold tenancy from a private landlord only ends the local housing authority's duty if it is a qualifying offer of a fixed term tenancy. The authority must be satisfied that it is suitable for the applicant and that it is reasonable for him or her to accept it. The landlord's offer must be accompanied by a written statement setting out the terms of the tenancy being offered and explaining that there is no obligation to accept the offer.

Under the Housing Act 1996 s.193(6), unless there is fraud, a local authority does not cease to be under a duty to accommodate simply because an applicant ceases to have priority need. (*R. v Brent LBC Ex p. Sadiq* (2001) 33 H.L.R. 47, CA). After a determination has been made, if a council considers that it was wrong, it may conduct a further "extra-statutory review". Decisions under the Housing Act 1996 as to whether applicants are in priority need or whether they are intentionally homeless are questions of public law. Accordingly once a decision has been taken the authority is permitted to revisit its conclusion (*Crawley BC v B* (2000) 32 H.L.R. 636, CA). See too *Porteous v West Dorset DC* [2004] EWCA Civ 244).

**Refuses a final offer of accommodation (s.193(5) and (7))**

Provided that an offer letter actually conveys the point that it is a "final" offer of suitable accommodation and otherwise complies with s.193(7), the precise rubric need not be used (*Omar v Birmingham CC* [2007] EWCA Civ 610; [2007] H.L.R. 43). **3A–1377**

The Court of Appeal considered the situation where an offer is refused, but a homeless person then makes a further application in *Tower Hamlets LBC v Rikha Begum* [2005] EWCA Civ 340; [2005] 1 W.L.R. 2103. It held that there was no test of "material change of circumstances" and that (applying *R. v Harrow LBC Ex p. Fahia* [1998] 1 W.L.R. 1396):

- an authority has to accept and consider a second application if it is not factually "identical" to the earlier one;
- this test of "exactly the same facts" was harder for an authority to use to refuse an application than the "material change of circumstances" approach;
- any new facts raised in the second approach to a council (provided not trivial or fanciful) require that it be treated as a fresh application;
- the question is whether the facts as presented are "new" and comparison has to be made by contrasting the material put forward on the new approach with the facts as they had stood when the earlier application was "disposed of" by an initial or review decision (as opposed to the date that the earlier application had been made);
- that question does not involve any "inquiries" by an authority, nor any investigation as to whether the asserted new facts are accurate (per Neuberger and Keene L.JJ.). The issue is simply whether, in the purported new application, the applicant has put forward facts which are different and the differences are neither fanciful nor trivial. A safeguard against applicants "inventing" new facts is the possibility of criminal prosecution. Pill L.J., however, considered that "some inquiry" might be necessary to establish (a) what matters are now relied upon and (b) whether they are the same matters or new matters.

**Reviews**

A decision as to suitability of s.193 accommodation is amenable to review under **3A–1378**

***Paragraph numbers marked with a "+" can be found online and on CD.***

s.202(1)(f) and subsequent appeal to the county court under s.204. That is the appropriate route for any challenge. Would-be applicants should bear in mind that remedy and should not apply for judicial review (*R. v Merton LBC Ex p. Sembi* (2000) 32 H.L.R. 439, QBD). After a determination has been made, if a council considers that it was wrong, it may conduct a further "extra-statutory review". Decisions under Housing Act 1996 as to whether applicants are in priority need or whether they are intentionally homeless are questions of public law. Accordingly once a decision has been taken the authority is permitted to revisit its conclusion (*Crawley BC v B* (2000) 32 H.L.R. 636, CA. See too *Porteous v West Dorset DC* [2004] EWCA Civ 244; [2004] H.L.R. 30).

**3A-1379** *Note* — Section 194 has been repealed by Homelessness Act 2002 s.6(4) which provides that Housing Act 1996 s.194 (power to continue to secure accommodation after minimum period of two years, formerly contained in s.193) shall cease to have effect. The section is unnecessary in the light of the abolition of the former provisions of s.193 limiting the duty to two years. In England, this amendment was brought into force on July 31, 2002 by the Homelessness Act 2002 (Commencement No.1) (England) Order 2002 (SI 2002/1799) (c.56). In Wales, this amendment was brought into force on September 30, 2002 by the Homelessness Act 2002 (Commencement) (Wales) Order 2002 (SI 2002/1736) (w.166) (c.53). Any person for whom a local housing authority was exercising their power under s.194 to continue to secure accommodation, immediately before implementation, is to be treated as a person to whom the authority owe the main duty under s.193 (Homelessness Act 2002 s.6(4)).

* * *

## Duties in case of threatened homelessness

**3A-1380** **195.**—(1) This section applies where the local housing authority are satisfied that an applicant is threatened with homelessness and is eligible for assistance.

(2) If the authority—

(a) are satisfied that he has a priority need, and

(b) are not satisfied that he became threatened with homelessness intentionally,

they shall take reasonable steps to secure that accommodation does not cease to be available for his occupation.

(3) Subsection (2) does not affect any right of the authority, whether by virtue of a contract, enactment or rule of law, to secure vacant possession of any accommodation.

(3A) The authority shall, on becoming subject to the duty under this section in a case which is not a restricted threatened homelessness case, give the applicant a copy of the statement included in their allocation scheme by virtue of section 167(1A) (policy on offering choice to people allocated housing accommodation under Part 6).

(4) Where in a case which is not a restricted threatened homelessness case, in pursuance of the duty under subsection (2) the authority secure that accommodation other than that occupied by the applicant when he made his application is available for occupation by him, the provisions of section 193(3) to (9) (period for which duty owed) apply, with any necessary modifications, in relation to the duty under this section as they apply in relation to the duty under section 193 in a case which is not a restricted case (within the meaning of that section).

(4A) Where, in a restricted threatened homelessness case, in

*Paragraph numbers marked with a "+" can be found online and on CD.*

pursuance of the duty under subsection (2) the authority secure that accommodation other than that occupied by the applicant when he made his application is available for occupation by him, the provisions of section 193(3) to (9) (period for which duty owed) apply, with any necessary modifications, in relation to the duty under this section as they apply in relation to the duty under section 193 in a restricted case (within the meaning of that section).

(4B) In subsections (3A) to (4A) "a restricted threatened homelessness case" means a case where the local housing authority would not be satisfied as mentioned in subsection (1) without having had regard to a restricted person.

(5) If the authority—

(a) are not satisfied that the applicant has a priority need, or

(b) are satisfied that he has a priority need but are also satisfied that he became threatened with homelessness intentionally,

they shall provide him with (or secure that he is provided with) advice and assistance; in any attempts he may make to secure that accommodation does not cease to be available for his occupation.

(6) The applicant's housing needs shall be assessed before advice and assistance is provided under subsection (5).

(7) The advice and assistance provided under subsection (5) must include information about the likely availability in the authority's district of types of accommodation appropriate to the applicant's housing needs (including, in particular, the location and sources of such types of accommodation)."

(8) If the authority decide that they owe the applicant the duty under subsection (5) by virtue of paragraph (b) of that subsection, they may, pending a decision on a review of that decision—

(a) secure that accommodation does not cease to be available for his occupation; and

(b) if he becomes homeless, secure that accommodation is so available.

(9) If the authority—

(a) are not satisfied that the applicant has a priority need; and

(b) are not satisfied that he became threatened with homelessness intentionally,

the authority may take reasonable steps to secure that accommodation does not cease to be available for the applicant's occupation."

*Note*—Amended by the Homelessness Act 2002 Sch.1, para.14. Amended for certain purposes by the Housing and Regeneration Act 2008 Sch.15, Pt I, para.6, with effect from March 2, 2009 (SI 2009/415; for purposes see art.2). **3A–1381**

**Duties in case of threatened homelessness**

See commentary to s.193. **3A–1382**

**"local housing authority"**

See ss.217, 218, and 230 which refer to the Housing Act 1985—see the Housing Act 1985 ss.1 and 2 above. **3A–1383**

***Paragraph numbers marked with a "+" can be found online and on CD.***

**"available for his occupation"**

3A-1384 See s.176.

**"priority need"**

3A-1385 See s.189.

**"eligible for assistance"**

3A-1386 See s.185.

## Becoming threatened with homelessness intentionally

3A-1387 **196.**—(1) A person becomes threatened with homelessness intentionally if he deliberately does or fails to do anything the likely result of which is that he will be forced to leave accommodation which is available for his occupation and which it would have been reasonable for him to continue to occupy.

(2) For the purposes of subsection (1) an act or omission in good faith on the part of a person who was unaware of any relevant fact shall not be treated as deliberate.

(3) A person shall be treated as becoming threatened with homelessness intentionally if—

(a) he enters into an arrangement under which he is required to cease to occupy accommodation which it would have been reasonable for him to continue to occupy, and

(b) the purpose of the arrangement is to enable him to become entitled to assistance under this Part,

and there is no other good reason why he is threatened with homelessness.

(4) […]

3A-1388 *Note* —Amended by the Homelessness Act 2002 s.5(1), Sch.2.

**Becoming threatened with homelessness intentionally**

3A-1389 See commentary to ss.190 and 193.

**"available for his occupation"**

3A-1390 See s.176.

**"threatened with homelessness intentionally"**

3A-1391 See s.195.

**Duty where other suitable accommodation available**

3A-1392 Homelessness Act s.9 provides that Housing Act 1996 s.197 (duty where other suitable accomodation available in their district) shall cease to have effect. In England, this amendment was brought into force on July 31, 2002 by the Homelessness Act 2002 (Commencement No.1) (England) Order 2002 (SI 2002/1799) (c.56). In Wales, this amendment was brought into force on September 30, 2002 by the Homelessness Act 2002 (Commencement) (Wales) Order 2002 (SI 2002/1736) (w.166) (c.56)). Any person for whom a local housing authority was exercising their power under s.197, immediately before implementation, is to be treated as a person to whom the authority owe the duty under s.193 (the main homelessness duty) (Homelessness Act 2002 s.6(4)).

**"local housing authority"**

3A-1393 See ss.217, 218, and 230 which refer to the Housing Act 1985—see the Housing Act 1985, ss.1 and 2, above.

*Paragraph numbers marked with a "+" can be found online and on CD.*

**"available for his occupation"**

See s.176. **3A–1394**

*Note*—Section 197 was repealed by the Homelessness Act 2002 ss.9(1), 18(2), Sch.2. **3A–1395**

* * * *

*REFERRAL TO ANOTHER LOCAL HOUSING AUTHORITY*

## Referral of case to another local housing authority

**198.**—(1) If the local housing authority would be subject to the duty under section 193 (accommodation for those with priority need who are not homeless intentionally) but consider that the conditions are met for referral of the case to another local housing authority, they may notify that other authority of their opinion. **3A–1396**

(2) The conditions for referral of the case to another authority are met if—

- (a) neither the applicant nor any person who might reasonably be expected to reside with him has a local connection with the district of the authority to whom his application was made,
- (b) the applicant or a person who might reasonably be expected to reside with him has a local connection with the district of that other authority, and
- (c) neither the applicant nor any person who might reasonably be expected to reside with him will run the risk of domestic violence in that other district.

(2A) But the conditions for referral mentioned in subsection (2) are not met if—

- (a) the applicant or any person who might reasonably be expected to reside with him has suffered violence (other than domestic violence) in the district of the other authority; and
- (b) it is probable that the return to that district of the victim will lead to further violence of a similar kind against him.

(3) For the purposes of subsections (2) and (2A) "violence" means—

- (a) violence from another person; or
- (b) threats of violence from another person which are likely to be carried out; and violence is "domestic violence" if it is from a person who is associated with the victim.

(4) The conditions for referral of the case to another authority are also met if—

- (a) the applicant was on a previous application made to that other authority placed (in pursuance of their functions under this Part) in accommodation in the district of the authority to whom his application is now made, and
- (b) the previous application was within such period as may be prescribed of the present application.

(5) The question whether the conditions for referral of a case are satisfied shall be decided by agreement between the notifying authority and the notified authority or, in default of agreement, in accordance with such arrangements as the Secretary of State may direct by order.

(6) An order may direct that the arrangements shall be—

(a) those agreed by any relevant authorities or associations of relevant authorities, or

(b) in default of such agreement, such arrangements as appear to the Secretary of State to be suitable, after consultation with such associations representing relevant authorities, and such other persons, as he thinks appropriate.

(7) No such order shall be made unless a draft of the order has been approved by a resolution of each House of Parliament.

3A–1397 *Note* —Amended by Homelessness Act 2002 s.10.

**Editorial note**

3A–1398 The Allocation of Housing and Homelessness (Review Procedures) Regulations 1999 (SI 1999/71) include a specific provision for reviews of decisions made under s.198(5). See too the Homelessness (Decisions on Referrals) Order 1998 (SI 1998/1578).

**"local housing authority"**

3A–1399 See ss.217, 218, and 230 which refer to the Housing Act 1985—see the Housing Act 1985 ss.1 and 2 above.

**"within such period as may be prescribed"**

3A–1400 See the Allocation of Housing and Homelessness (Miscellaneous Provisions) (England) Regulations 2006 (SI 2006/2527).

**"district"**

3A–1401 See s.217(3).

**Referral of case to another local housing authority**

3A–1402 A local housing authority which finds itself subject to a duty under the Housing Act 1996 s.193 to an applicant who is unintentionally homeless and in priority need may, if the conditions in s.198 are fulfilled, refer the duty to another housing authority with which the applicant has a local connection. By s.199 an applicant can have a local connection with an area for one of four reasons:

(a) residence;
(b) employment;
(c) family; or
(d) special circumstances.

The onus of establishing a local connection rests on the applicant. Applicants must show that they have built up a real connection based on a period of residence, employment, family associations or other special circumstances. Where the claim is based on residence there is no reason why a local authority should not have guidelines that residence short of six months in the preceding year does not suffice (*R. v Eastleigh BC Ex p. Betts* [1983] 2 A.C. 613; [1983] 3 W.L.R. 397; [1983] 2 All E.R. 1111, HL).

The House of Lords has held that (1) on a statutory review of a decision to refer an application for accommodation to another authority on the basis that there is no local connection, any occupation by the applicant of interim accommodation within the first authority's district prior to the date of the review may constitute normal residence and so be taken into account as evidence of a local connection. So long as the place where someone eats and sleeps is voluntarily accepted by him, the reason why he is there rather than somewhere else does not prevent that place from being his normal residence; (2) the correct date to decide whether a person has a local connection is the date of the decision or, if there is a review, the date of the review—whether in the meantime the applicant has acquired or lost, by moving away, his local connection (*Mohamed v Hammersmith and Fulham LBC* [2001] UKHL 57; [2002] 1 A.C. 547; [2001] 3 W.L.R. 1339; [2002] 1 All E.R. 176.

For cases in the Court of Appeal on "local connection", see *R. v Greenwich LBC Ex p. Patterson* (1994) 26 H.L.R. 159, CA; *R. v Hammersmith & Fulham LBC Ex p.Duro-Rama* (1983) 9 H.L.R. 71, CA; *R. v Newham LBC Ex p. Tower Hamlets LBC* (1990) 23 H.L.R. 62, CA; *R. v Slough BC Ex p. Ealing LBC* [1981] Q.B. 801; [1981] 1 All E.R. 601; [1981] 2 W.L.R. 399, CA; *R. v Tower Hamlets LBC Ex p. Ali and Bibi* (1993) 25 H.L.R. 158, CA; *R. v Westminster CC Ex p. Benniche* (1996) 29 H.L.R. 230, *The Times*, April 15, 1996, CA. *R. v Ealing LBC Ex p. Fox*, (1998) 95(11) L.S.G. 35; *The Times*, March 9, 1998, QBD: voluntary work may be employment for the purposes of s.199(1)(b)) and *Ozbek v Ipswich BC* [2006] EWCA Civ 534; [2006] H.L.R. 41 (family associations too tenuous to amount to a "local connection").

The effect of the decision in *Al-Ameri v Kensington and Chelsea RLBC* [2004] UKHL 4; [2004] 2 A.C. 159; [2004] 2 W.L.R. 354 (that residence in a district in accommodation provided to a destitute asylum seeker under Immigration and Asylum Act 1999 was not capable of being regarded as residence in that district of the asylum seeker's own choice) has been reversed by Asylum and Immigration (Treatment of Claimants, etc) Act 2004 s.11 which added new ss.(6) and (7) to s.199. See 3A–1608+.

There is no statutory right to review of an authority's decision not to refer an application under s.198. Accordingly there is no right of appeal to a county court on that issue under s.204. The county court has no jurisdiction to consider on appeal whether local authorities have a duty to investigate the issue of local connection (*Sareen v Hackney LBC* [2003] EWCA Civ 351; [2003] H.L.R. 54).

### Violence

Note that a referral to another authority may not be made if the applicant or a person who might reasonably be expected to live with the applicant runs the risk of violence in the other district. Since the amendment of s.198 by Homelessness Act 2002 s.10, "violence" is not limited to "domestic violence". "Violence" includes actual threats of physical violence which are likely to be carried out but not general racially motivated aggression and gestures (*Kensington & Chelsea RLBC v Danesh* [2006] EWCA Civ 1404; [2007] H.L.R. 17). **3A–1403**

### Disputes

Homelessness (Decisions on Referrals) Order 1998 (SI 1998/1578) provides a mechanism for resolving disputes between housing authorities about whether or not the conditions of referral from one authority to another exist. Such questions are to be decided by a person to be appointed from a panel established by the Local Government Association. **3A–1404**

## Local connection

**199.**—(1) A person has a local connection with the district of a local housing authority if he has a connection with it— **3A–1405**

(a) because he is, or in the past was, normally resident there, and that residence is or was of his own choice,

(b) because he is employed there,

(c) because of family associations, or

(d) because of special circumstances.

(2) …

(3) Residence in a district is not of a person's own choice if—

(a) …

(b) he, or a person who might reasonably be expected to

***Paragraph numbers marked with a "+" can be found online and on CD.***

reside with him, becomes resident there because he is detained under the authority of an Act of Parliament.

(4) ...

(5) The Secretary of State may by order specify ...circumstances in which—

(a) a person is not to be treated as employed in a district, or

(b) residence in a district is not to be treated as of a person's own choice.

(6) A person has a local connection with the district of a local housing authority if he was (at any time) provided with accommodation in that district under section 95 of the Act 1999 (support for asylum seekers).

(7) But subsection (6) does not apply—

(a) to the provision of accommodation for a person in a district of a local housing authority if he was subsequently provided with accommodation in the district of another local housing authority under section 95 of that Act, or

(b) to the provision of accommodation in an accommodation centre by virtue of section 22 of the Nationality, Immigration and Asylum Act 2002 (c.41) (use of accommodation centres for section 95 support).

**3A-1406** *Note*—Amended by the Asylum and Immigration (Treatment of Claimants, etc) Act 2004, s.11. The effect of the amendment is to reverse the effect of *Al-Ameri v Kensington and Chelsea RLBC* [2004] UKHL 4; [2004] 2 A.C. 159; [2004] 2 W.L.R. 354; [2004] 1 W.L.R. 1104. This section has also been amended by Housing and Regeneration Act 2008 s.315 so as to allow members of the armed forces to acquire a local connection. The amendment was brought into force in England on December 1, 2008 by the Housing and Regeneration Act 2008 (Commencement No.2 and Transitional, Saving and Transitory Provisions) Order 2008 (SI 2008/3068) and in Wales on March 30, 2009 by the Housing and Regeneration Act 2008 (Commencement No.1) (Wales) Order 2009 (SI 2009/773) (w.65) (c.48).. The effect of the amendment is that a person in the armed forces is now able to establish a local connection with a district through residence or employment there, in the same way as a civilian.

#### Local connection

**3A-1407** See commentary to s.198.

#### "local housing authority"

**3A-1408** See ss.217, 218, and 230 which refer to the Housing Act 1985—see the Housing Act 1985 ss.1 and 2, above.

#### "district"

**3A-1409** See s.217(3).

### Duties to applicant whose case is considered for referral or referred

**3A-1410** **200.**—(1) Where a local housing authority notify an applicant that they intend to notify or have notified another local housing authority of their opinion that the conditions are met for the referral of his case to that other authority—

(a) they cease to be subject to any duty under section 188 (interim duty to accommodate in case of apparent priority need), and

*Paragraph numbers marked with a "+" can be found online and on CD.*

(b) they are not subject to any duty under section 193 (the main housing duty),

but they shall secure that accommodation is available for occupation by the applicant until he is notified of the decision whether the conditions for referral of his case are met.

(2) When it has been decided whether the conditions for referral are met, the notifying authority shall notify the applicant of the decision and inform him of the reasons for it.

The notice shall also inform the applicant of his right to request a review of the decision and of the time within which such a request must be made.

(3) If it is decided that the conditions for referral are not met, the notifying authority are subject to the duty under section 193 (the main housing duty).

(4) If it is decided that those conditions are met, the notified authority are subject to the duty under section 193 (the main housing duty).

(5) The duty under subsection (1) ceases as provided in that subsection even if the applicant requests a review of the authority's decision (see section 202).

The authority may secure that accommodation is available for the applicant's occupation pending the decision on a review.

(6) Notice required to be given to an applicant under this section shall be given in writing and, if not received by him, shall be treated as having been given to him if it is made available at the authority's office for a reasonable period for collection by him or on his behalf.

*Note*—Amended by Homelessness Act 2002 s.5(1), Sch.1, para.15. **3A-1411**

**Duties to applicant whose case is considered for referral or referred**

See commentary to ss.193 and 198. **3A-1412**

**"local housing authority"**

See ss.217, 218, and 230 which refers to the Housing Act 1985—see the Housing Act 1985 ss.1 and 2 above. **3A-1413**

**"district"**

See s.217(3). **3A-1414**

**"other suitable accommodation"**

See s.197. **3A-1415**

## Application of referral provisions to cases arising in Scotland

**201.** Sections 198 and 200 (referral of application to another local housing authority and duties to applicant whose case is considered for referral or referred) apply— **3A-1416**

(a) to applications referred by a local authority in Scotland in pursuance of sections 33 and 34 of the Housing (Scotland) Act 1987, and

(b) to persons whose applications are so transferred,

as they apply to cases arising under this Part (the reference in section 198 to this Part being construed as a reference to Part II of that Act).

**Right to request review of decision**

3A-1417 **202.**—(1) An applicant has the right to request a review of—

(a) any decision of a local housing authority as to his eligibility for assistance,

(b) any decision of a local housing authority as to what duty (if any) is owed to him under sections 190 to 193 and 195 to 196 (duties to persons found to be homeless or threatened with homelessness),

(c) any decision of a local housing authority to notify another authority under section 198(1) (referral of cases),

(d) any decision under section 198(5) whether the conditions are met for the referral of his case,

(e) any decision under section 200(3) or (4) (decision as to duty owed to applicant whose case is considered for referral or referred)

(f) any decision of a local housing authority as to the suitability of accommodation offered to him in discharge of their duty under any of the provisions mentioned in paragraph (b) or (e) or as to the suitability of accommodation offered to him as mentioned in section 193(7), or

(g) any decision of a local housing authority as to the suitability of accommodation offered to him by way of a private accommodation offer (within the meaning of section 193).

(1A) An applicant who is offered accommodation as mentioned in section 193(5), (7) or (7AA) may under subsection (1)(f) or (as the case may be) (g) request a review of the suitability of the accommodation offered to him whether or not he has accepted the offer.

(2) There is no right to request a review of the decision reached on an earlier review.

(3) A request for review must be made before the end of the period of 21 days beginning with the day on which he is notified of the authority's decision or such longer period as the authority may in writing allow.

(4) On a request being duly made to them, the authority or authorities concerned shall review their decision.

3A-1418 *Note*—Amended by the Homelessness Act 2002 s.5(1), Sch.1, para.16 and the Housing and Regeneration Act 2008 Sch.16 with effect from December 1, 2008 (SI 2008/3068), and Sch.15, Pt I, para.7 and Sch.16, for certain purposes with effect from March 2, 2009 (SI 2009/415; for purposes see art.2)..

**"available for his occupation"**

3A-1419 See s.176.

**"threatened with homelessness intentionally"**

3A-1420 See s.195.

*Paragraph numbers marked with a "+" can be found online and on CD.*

**"assistance"**

See s.183. 3A–1421

**"local housing authority"**

See ss.217, 218, and 230 which refer to the Housing Act 1985—see the Housing Act 1985 ss.1 and 2 above. 3A–1422

**"homeless"**

See s.175. 3A–1423

**"applicant"**

See s.183 and the commentary thereto. 3A–1424

**Reviews**

On concluding their enquiries authorities, when they notify applicants of their decisions and give their reasons, are also obliged to inform applicants of the right to request a review of the decision in accordance with the Housing Act 1996 s.202 (Housing Act 1996 s.184(5)). 3A–1425

The *Code of Guidance* states that it is good practice to notify applicants of decisions within three working days of the decision being made. Where possible decisions should not only be provided in writing but also explained in person to the applicant (para.17.3).

The Housing Act 1996 s.202 provides that applicants have a right to request a review of any decision within 21 days of notification. The 21 day period may be extended by the authority. The Allocation of Housing and Homelessness (Review Procedures) Regulations 1999 (SI 1999/71) provide that:

- if the decision is to be reviewed by an officer of the authority, the review shall be carried out by a person who was not involved in the original decision and who is senior to the officer who made the original decision (*cf. Saunders v Hammersmith and Fulham LBC* [1999] 6 C.L.D. 347, West London County Court, where the officer who had made the original decision participated in the review with a more senior officer, Appeal allowed);
- the applicant should be notified that written representations may be made and shall be informed of the procedure to be followed;
- if the reviewer considers that there is deficiency or irregularity in the original decision or in the manner in which it was made but is minded nevertheless to make a decision which is against the interests of the applicant on one or more issues the reviewer shall notify the applicant (a) that the reviewer is so minded, and the reasons why; and (b) that the applicant, or someone acting on his behalf, may make representations to the reviewer orally or in writing or both orally and in writing (reg 8(2). In *Hall v Wandsworth LBC*; *Carter v Wandsworth LBC* [2004] EWCA Civ 1740, Carnwath L.J. said (para.30): "To summarise, the reviewing officer should treat regulation 8(2) as applicable, not merely when he finds some significant legal or procedural error in the decision, but whenever (looking at the matter broadly and untechnically) he considers that an important aspect of the case was either not addressed, or not addressed adequately, by the original decision-maker. In such a case, if he intends to confirm the decision, he must give notice of the grounds on which he intends to do so, and provide an opportunity for written and (if requested) oral representations."

  See too *Johnston v Lambeth LBC* [2008] EWCA Civ 690; [2009] H.L.R. 10; *The Times* June 30, 2008, June 19, 2008; where Rimer L.J. said: "...regulation 8(2) is not a discretionary option that the review officer can apply or disapply according to whether or not he or she considers that the service of a 'minded to find' notice would be of material benefit to the applicant. Regulation 8(2) imposes a dual, mandatory obligation upon the review officer. First, to 'consider' whether there was a deficiency or irregularity in the original decision or in the manner in which it was made. Secondly, if there was—and if the review officer is nonetheless minded to make a decision adverse to the applicant on one or more issues—to serve a 'minded to find' notice on the ap-

***Paragraph numbers marked with a "+" can be found online and on CD.***



HOUSING

plicant explaining his reasons for his provisional views. In my judgment, there is no discretion on the review officer to give himself a dispensation from complying with either of those obligations."

Even if, on a literal construction of the words of Allocation of Housing and Homelessness (Review Procedures) Regulations (SI 1999/71) reg.8(2), there has been no "deficiency or irregularity" in the original decision, a broad reading of the regulation requires a reviewing officer to give an applicant an opportunity to address him or her (orally or in writing) before making an adverse decision on wholly different grounds (*Banks v Kingston-upon-Thames RLBC* [2008] EWCA Civ 1443, [2009] H.L.R. 29); cf. *Gilby v Westminster CC* [2007] EWCA Civ 604; [2008] H.L.R. 7 (no shift in reasoning which required the reviewing officer to comply with the "minded-to"provisions of reg.8(2).

- decisions on reviews shall be notified to applicants within eight weeks of the day on which the request is made or such longer period as may be agreed by the applicant in writing.

With regards the adequacy of reasons given, courts would be slow to intervene and would only interfere where it was clear that the process of review was capable of being described as unfair.

An officer conducting a review must consider all the facts afresh, including information relevant to the period before the first decision, but only obtained thereafter, and to matters occurring after the initial decision, (*Mohamed v Hammersmith and Fulham LBC* [2001] UKHL 57; [2002] 1 A.C. 547; [2001] 3 W.L.R. 1339; [2002] 1 All E.R. 176, HL and *Sarahid v Camden LBC* [2004] EWCA Civ 1485; October 26, 2004). Reviewing officers acting under the Housing Act 1996 s.202 should consider the facts as at the date of the refusal. Although reviewing officers are entitled to take account of facts as at that date—even if previously unknown to the council—material dealing with what has occurred since then is irrelevant (*Omar v City of Westminster* [2008] EWCA Civ 421; [2008] H.L.R. 36).Where issues have been put to an applicant in interview, there is no reason why a review panel should offer an oral hearing (*Lomotey v Enfield LBC* [2004] EWCA Civ 627; [2004] H.L.R. 45. See too *Connors v Northampton BC* [2004] EWCA Civ 427).

There is no statutory right to a review of an authority's decision not to refer an application under s.198 (referral of case to another local housing authority). Accordingly there is no right of appeal to a county court on that issue under s.204 (*Sareen v Hackney LBC* [2003] EWCA Civ 351; [2003] H.L.R. 54).

### Accommodation pending reviews and appeals

**3A–1426** In *R.v Camden LBC Ex p. Mohammed* (1998) 30 H.L.R. 315, QBD, Latham J. considered the circumstances in which authorities should provide accommodation pursuant to s.188(3) pending a review. Camden's policy was that no interim accommodation was to be made available to an applicant pending a review of a refusal of an application for housing assistance under the Housing Act 1996 Pt.VII unless there were exceptional circumstances. Latham J. dismissed an application for a declaration that the policy was ultra vires. He considered the Housing Act 1996 ss.188(3), 202 and 204 and found that the council had a wide discretion. Use of the phrase "exceptional reasons" was a rational way of describing the approach to be adopted provided that the council carried out a balancing act and considered:

(1) the merits of the case itself and the extent to which it could properly be said that the decision was contrary to the merits of the case or was one which was finely balanced which could go either way;
(2) whether there was any new material which could have a real effect upon the decision under review; and
(3) the personal circumstances of the applicant and the consequence of an adverse decision.

Neither the statutory scheme nor any general principle of fairness nor the need to avoid the appearance of bias requires that a decision as to whether or not accommodation should be provided pending review should be taken by a different officer who was not involved in the initial decision on the homelessness application (*R (Abdi) v Lambeth LBC* [2007] EWHC 1565 (Admin); [2008] H.L.R. 5).

Section 204A, as inserted by Homelessness Act 2002 s.11, allows an applicant to appeal to the county court against a refusal by a local housing authority to exercise its

***Paragraph numbers marked with a "+" can be found online and on CD.***

powers to provide accommodation pending the hearing of a county court appeal, or against their decision to exercise the power for a limited period, or to cease from exercising that power. The county court should determine any such appeal on judicial review principles. There is however no right to appeal to the county court against a refusal to provide accommodation pending a review—any such challenge must still be brought by judicial review, as in *R. v Camden LBC Ex p. Mohammed* (above).

The effect of s.202(1A) is to reverse the effect of *Alghile v Westminster City Council* [2001] EWCA Civ 363; (2001) 33 H.L.R. 57 where it was held that an applicant could not accept accommodation *and* seek a review as to its suitability.

**Failure to apply for review within 21 days**

Councils have a discretion under s.202(3) to extend time to request a review, but **3A–1427** that discretion has to be exercised in a principled way. This requires a consideration of the statutory scheme. Reasons for delay and the prospects of success are relevant but do not have to be balanced against each other. (*R. (C) v Lewisham LBC* [2003] EWCA Civ 927; [2003] 3 All E.R. 1277). See too *R.(Minhas) v Wandsworth LBC* [2004] EWHC 805).

**Reconsideration of review**

Councils are not precluded from reconsidering review decisions, but there is no **3A–1428** requirement that they should do so. If a council fails to reconsider a review, the remedy for the applicant is to appeal the original review decision in the county court in accordance with s.204. The High Court should not entertain an application for judicial review in such circumstances because another remedy (i.e. appeal in the county court) is available—*R. v Westminster CC Ex p. Ellioua* (1999) 31 H.L.R. 440, CA. In *Demetri v Westminster CC* [2000] 1 W.L.R. 772, CA, the Court of Appeal held that: (1) while an applicant has no right to seek a review of a review decision (see s.202(2)) a council can agree to re-open its earlier decision (*R. v Westminster CC Ex p. Ellioua* (1999) 31 H.L.R. 440). If it does so, the council should make clear whether it is treating the earlier review decision as withdrawn and is conducting a new review or is simply "reconsidering" its earlier decision; (2) where an applicant is legally represented, the onus is on the advisers either to lodge an appeal within 21 days of the original review decision or to obtain clear agreement from the council that the review is being re-run and the earlier decision treated as non-existent. In the instant case no appeal had been lodged in time, no clear agreement to withdraw the earlier decision had been reached, and the council's agreement to "reconsider" the review decision did not have the effect of extending the time for appealing against it. Any judicial review challenge to a decision made on an extra-statutory reconsideration is unlikely to succeed (*R. (C) v Lewisham LBC* [2003] EWCA Civ 927; [2003] 3 All E.R. 1277 applying the test in *R. v Brighton and Hove BC Ex p. Nacion* (1999) 31 H.L.R. 1095, CA).

The Court of Appeal has held that, in the absence of any exceptional circumstances, there is nothing objectionable in the same officer conducting a review and then (if it is agreed or ordered that there should be a further review) conducting a re-review or second review. This is because the reviewing officer does not review his or her own earlier decision but starts afresh to review a decision made by a more junior officer. There is nothing unfair about that. Further, as the Allocation of Housing and Homelessness (Review Procedures) Regulations 1999 (SI 1999/71) give no guidance as to who is to conduct a review the second time and there is nothing to suggest that it has to be someone who was not involved in the first decision, there is no breach of those regulations if the same officer conducts the further review (*Feld v Barnet LBC* [2004] EWCA Civ 1307; [2005] H.L.R. 9; *Pour v Westminster CC* [2004] EWCA Civ 1307; *The Times*, October 26, 2004).

**Reasons**

Section 203 requires local housing authorities to give reasons if the decision on **3A–1429** review is to confirm the original decision. In *R. v Westminster CC Ex p. Ermakov* [1996] 2 All E.R. 302, a case involving Housing Act 1985, s.64 (now Housing Act 1996 s.184(3)), Hutchison L.J. said that the Act:

> "requires a decision and at the same time reasons and if no reasons, which is the reality of the present case, or wholly deficient reasons are given, the applicant is prima facie entitled to have the decision quashed as unlawful".

He stated that the reasons given must be proper, adequate and intelligible and deal with the substantial points that have been raised. In *Hijazi v Kensington and Chelsea RLBC* [2003] EWCA Civ 692; [2003] H.L.R. 72, a case in which a circuit judge hearing a s.204 appeal had allowed further evidence from the reviewing officer that he had taken a doctor's report into account but had found that it did not take matters further, the Court of Appeal, dismissing a further appeal, held that while further evidence ought not to be considered where it added to, or supplemented, the reasons given in a review decision (see *R. v Westminster CC Ex p. Ermakov* [1996] 2 All E.R. 302), the statement in this case simply elucidated the reasons already given. For a case in which the Court of Appeal considered the adequacy of reasons given on review, see *Bernard v Enfield LBC* [2001] EWCA Civ 1831; [2002] H.L.R. 46.

### Appeals

**3A–1430** If the review results in confirmation of the original decision, reasons must be given. The Act does not specify that they must be in writing. There is a right of appeal from a review decision to the county court on a point of law. Prior to amendment by Homelessness Act 2002 Sch.1, appeals to the court had to be brought within 21 days of "the date on which [the applicant] should have been notified" of the review decision (Housing Act 1996 s.204).

For the procedure for appeals, see CPR 52 and the commentary at 3A–1440.

In *Begum v Tower Hamlets LBC* [2000] Q.B. 133; [2000] 1 W.L.R. 306, CA it was held that the judge at first instance was right in construing the words "point of law" which qualify the right of appeal to the county court in s.204 as being wide enough to embrace any ground of challenge that would have been available in proceedings for judicial review (including *Wednesbury* irrationality). See too *Chief Adjudication Officer v Foster* [1993] A.C. 754, HL.

Where there is an appeal to a county court, the question for the court is whether the whole of the circumstances justify any relief in public law. A new ground for refusing accommodation should only be ignored if it can be faulted on public law grounds (*Crawley BC v B* (2000) 32 H.L.R. 636, CA). Where a court identifies procedural flaws in a local authority's decision making process, the decision may only be upheld if a court is satisfied that a properly directed local authority would inevitably have reached the same decision. The test of inevitability is a strict test. (*Ali and Nessa v Newham LBC* [2001] EWCA Civ 73; [2002] H.L.R. 20).

### No duty owed

**3A–1431** In *Warsame v Hounslow LBC* (2000) 32 H.L.R. 335; [2000] 1 W.L.R. 696, CA the council decided that a duty which it had owed to the applicants under the Housing Act 1996 s.193 ended upon the refusal by the applicants of an offer of a secure council tenancy made under the Housing Act Part VI, s.193(7). Reversing a circuit judge's decision that he had no jurisdiction to consider an appeal, the Court of Appeal held that a decision that "no duty was owed" was a decision as to "what duty (if any)" was owed by the council and accordingly was brought by Housing Act 1996 s.202(1)(b) within the statutory mechanism for review and appeal. It followed that the applicants could challenge the findings by the council which had led to the "no duty" decision (e.g. on the "suitability" and "acceptability" issues in s.193(7) itself). It would seem from the court's approach that a decision that "no (further) duty is owed" must be given in writing with reasons and must notify the right to review: Housing Act 1996 s.184.

### Section 202 reviews, s.204 appeals and the ECHR

**3A–1432** The House of Lords considered whether this procedure is ECHR compliant in *Begum (Runa) v Tower Hamlets LBC* [2003] UKHL 5; [2003] 2 A.C. 430; [2003] 2 W.L.R. 388; [2003] 1 All E.R. 731. (1) The House of Lords assumed, without deciding, that decisions made under Housing Act 1996 Pt VII do give rise to "civil rights" for the purposes of ECHR, art.6, although Lord Bingham stated that:

> "to hold that the right enjoyed by [a homeless person] is a 'civil right' for the purposes of article 6 would ... be to go further than the Strasbourg court has yet gone...".

(2) The s.202 review process does not comply with article 6 because the reviewing officer is not an "independent and impartial tribunal"—an employee cannot be independent of the authority. (3) However an appeal to the county court on a point of law

(s.204) gives a right of access to a court of "full jurisdiction" for art.6 purposes. For reasons of good administration, the absence of a full fact finding jurisdiction in the court or tribunal to which an appeal lies from an administrative decision making body does not disqualify it for the purposes of art.6.

> "'Full jurisdiction' in this context does not necessarily mean full jurisdiction on fact or law, but ... 'jurisdiction to deal with the case as the nature of the decision requires'" (Lord Millett).

An authority's factual findings are "only staging posts on the way to much the broader judgments which the authority has to make." Lord Bingham stated that he:

> "would expect the county court judge to be alert to any indication that an applicant's case might not have been resolved by the authority in a fair, objective and even-handed way",

but could:

> "see no warrant for applying in this context notions of 'anxious scrutiny' ... or [an] enhanced approach to judicial review ... [or] 'a close and rigorous analysis' if by that is meant an analysis closer or more rigorous than would ordinarily be conducted by a careful and competent judge determining an application for judicial review."

Lord Hoffmann considered that the conventional principles of judicial review are sufficient.

The House of Lords declined to follow and apply dicta in *Adan v Newham LBC* [2001] EWCA Civ 1916; [2002] 1 All E.R. 931 that the limited right of appeal under s.204 means that the county court is not a court of full jurisdiction and that a local authority may use its contracting-out powers under the Local Authorities (Contracting Out of Allocation of Housing and Homelessness Functions) Order 1996 (SI 1996/3205) to appoint an independent and impartial tribunal to conduct the review in cases where a material dispute of primary fact has to be resolved. See too *Ali v Birmingham City Council* [2008] EWCA Civ 1228, November 7, 2008; [2009] 2 All E.R. 501.

## Procedure on a review

**203.**—(1) The Secretary of State may make provision by regulations as to the procedure to be followed in connection with a review under section 202. Nothing in the following provisions affects the generality of this power. **3A–1433**

(2) Provision may be made by regulations—

(a) requiring the decision on review to be made by a person of appropriate seniority who was not involved in the original decision, and

(b) as to the circumstances in which the applicant is entitled to an oral hearing, and whether and by whom he may be represented at such a hearing.

(3) The authority, or as the case may be either of the authorities, concerned shall notify the applicant of the decision on the review.

(4) If the decision is—

(a) to confirm the original decision on any issue against the interests of the applicant, or

(b) to confirm a previous decision—

(i) to notify another authority under section 198 (referral of cases), or

(ii) that the conditions are met for the referral of his case,

they shall also notify him of the reasons for the decision.

(5) In any case they shall inform the applicant of his right to ap-

***Paragraph numbers marked with a "+" can be found online and on CD.***

peal to a county court on a point of law, and of the period within which such an appeal must be made (see section 204).

(6) Notice of the decision shall not be treated as given unless and until subsection (5), and where applicable subsection (4), is complied with.

(7) Provision may be made by regulations as to the period within which the review must be carried out and notice given of the decision.

(8) Notice required to be given to a person under this section shall be given in writing and, if not received by him, shall be treated as having been given if it is made available at the authority's office for a reasonable period for collection by him or on his behalf.

**Procedure on a review**

**3A–1434** See the commentary to s.202.

**"regulations"**

**3A–1435** See the Allocation of Housing and Homelessness (Review Procedures) Regulations 1999 (SI 1999/71).

## Right of appeal to county court on point of law

**3A–1436** **204.**—(1) If an applicant who has requested a review under section 202—

(a) is dissatisfied with the decision on the review, or

(b) is not notified of the decision on the review within the time prescribed under section 203,

he may appeal to the county court on any point of law arising from the decision or, as the case may be, the original decision.

(2) An appeal must be brought within 21 days of his being notified of the decision or, as the case may be, of the date on which he should have been notified of a decision on review.

(2A) The court may give permission for an appeal to be brought after the end of the period allowed by subsection (2), but only if it is satisfied—

(a) where permission is sought before the end of that period, that there is a good reason for the applicant to be unable to bring the appeal in time; or

(b) where permission is sought after that time, that there was a good reason for the applicant's failure to bring the appeal in time and for any delay in applying for permission.

(3) On appeal the court may make such order confirming, quashing or varying the decision as it thinks fit.

(4) Where the authority were under a duty under section 188, 190 or 200 to secure that accommodation is available for the applicant's occupation, or had the power under section 195(8) to do so, they may secure that accommodation is so available—

(a) during the period for appealing under this section against the authority's decision, and

(b) if an appeal is brought, until the appeal (and any further appeal) is finally determined.

*Paragraph numbers marked with a "+" can be found online and on CD.*

*Note*—Amended by the Homelessness Act 2002 s.5(1), Sch.1, para.17. 3A–1437

**Right of appeal to county court on point of law**

See the commentary to s.202. 3A–1438

**"review"**

See ss.202 and 203. 3A–1439

**Procedure for appeal**

CPR Pt 52 (Appeals) applies to s.204 appeals. Appellants' notices in Form **N161** must be filed and served in all cases (PD 52 para.5.1). Appellants must also file bundles of documents with appellants' notices. Such bundles should include all documents which the appellant reasonably considers necessary to enable the court to reach its decision on the hearing of the appeal (para.5.6). If it is not possible to file all documents, the appellant must indicate which documents have not yet been filed and the reasons why they are not currently available (para.5.7). 3A–1440

Appeals to the county court provided by s.204 are appeals for the purposes of the Access to Justice Act 1999 (Destination of Appeals) Order 2000 (SI 2000/1071). Accordingly appeals from the county court lie to the Court of Appeal and the more restrictive test for permission to appeal, as prescribed by Access to Justice Act 1999 s.55, applies (*Azimi v Newham LBC* (2001) 33 H.L.R. 51, CA).

District judges may not hear appeals pursuant to s.204 (PD 2B para.9A and *Crawley BC v B* (2000) 32 H.L.R. 636, CA).

Under CPR Pt 2.3 an appeal is brought by filing the notice of appeal. Filing means delivering by post or otherwise. Delivery of the appeal notice to the appropriate court is sufficient to constitute filing within the CPR, even if the court offices are closed. There is no need for a person to have received or authenticated it (*Van Aken v Camden LBC* [2002] EWCA Civ 1724; [2003] 1 W.L.R. 684; [2003] 1 All E.R. 552). See to *Aadan v Brent LBC* (2000) 32 H.L.R. 848, CA. Appeals must be brought within 21 days of applicants being notified of the decision or, as the case may be, of the date on which he should have been notified of a decision on review. Time to appeal does not run from the date of the review decision letter, but from the earliest date on which, on the facts, the review decision letter could have come to the applicant's attention (*Barrett v Southwark LBC* [2008] EWHC 1568 (QB)).

**"extension of time for bringing appeal"**

Section 204(2A) was inserted by Homelessness Act 2002, Sch.1. An extension of time may only be granted if permission is sought before the end of the period allowed by s.204(2) or there is a good reason for the applicant's failure to bring the appeal in time and for any delay in applying for permission. The word "only" in s.204(2A) provides a threshold which has to be passed before the merits can be considered. It is not open to a judge to have regard to the criteria in CPR r.3.9, or any other criteria, other than those specified in s.204(2A). If a judge is not satisfied that there are good reasons for a failure to bring an appeal in time, it is not possible to go on to consider the merits (*Short v Birmingham CC* [2004] EWHC 2112 (QB); [2005] H.L.R. 6). The concept of good reason was analogous to "good cause" used in social security provisions and explained by the social security commissioner in R(S) 2/63 (T) (*Barrett v Southwark LBC* [2008] EWHC 1538(QB)). 3A–1441

**Judicial review**

An application for judicial review is an abuse of the process, and not available, where a homeless person does not exhaust the right to a statutory review and appeal to the county court under ss.202 and 204 (*R. (on the application of Campbell) v Enfield LBC* [2001] EWHC Admin 354), but *cf. R. (Van der Stolk) v Camden LBC* [2002] EWHC 1261 (Admin); July 2002 Legal Action 26 (although judicial review would not normally lie where the claimant had not availed himself of a county court appeal, judicial review allowed in "an unusual case" where the claimant's health was poor and deteriorating and the medical report did add materially to what had been known about its effects on the claimant. His homelessness application should be reconsidered in the light of it). 3A–1442

**New evidence on appeal**

In *Cramp v Hastings LBC*; [2005] EWCA Civ 1005; [2005] 4 All E.R. 1014, the Court of Appeal stated that: 3A–1443

***Paragraph numbers marked with a "+" can be found online and on CD.***

"...judges in the county court need to be astute to ensure that evidential material over and above the contents of the housing file and the reviewing officer's decision is limited to that which is necessary to illuminate the points of law that are to be relied on in the appeal, or the issue of what, if any, relief ought to be granted. An undisciplined approach to the admission of new evidence may lead to the danger that the reviewing officer is found guilty of an error of law for not taking into account evidence that was never before her, notwithstanding the applicant's opportunity to make representations about the original decision."

## Section 204(4): appeals

3A–1444 **204A.**—(1) This section applies where an applicant has the right to appeal to the county court against a local housing authority's decision on a review.

(2) If the applicant is dissatisfied with a decision by the authority—

(a) not to exercise their power under section 204(4) ("the section 204(4) power") in his case;

(b) to exercise that power for a limited period ending before the final determination by the county court of his appeal under section 204(1) ("the main appeal"); or

(c) to cease exercising that power before that time,

he may appeal to the county court against the decision.

(3) An appeal under this section may not be brought after the final determination by the county court of the main appeal.

(4) On an appeal under this section the court—

(a) may order the authority to secure that accommodation is available for the applicant's occupation until the determination of the appeal (or such earlier time as the court may specify); and

(b) shall confirm or quash the decision appealed against,

and in considering whether to confirm or quash the decision the court shall apply the principles applied by the High Court on an application for judicial review.

(5) If the court quashes the decision it may order the authority to exercise the section 204(4) power in the applicant's case for such period as may be specified in the order.

(6) An order under subsection (5)—

(a) may only be made if the court is satisfied that failure to exercise the section 204(4) power in accordance with the order would substantially prejudice the applicant's ability to pursue the main appeal;

(b) may not specify any period ending after the final determination by the county court of the main appeal.

3A–1445 *Note*—Inserted by Homelessness Act 2002 s.11. Note that PD 52 para.24.2 provides that

- an appeal under s.204A should be made in the same appellant's notice (Form **N161**) as a s.204 appeal or (if that is not possible) in separate appellant's notices;
- an application for an interim injunction in a s.204A appeal may be included in the appellant's notice; and

***Paragraph numbers marked with a "+" can be found online and on CD.***

- where such an interim injunction is made without notice to the housing authority, that order will normally require that accommodation is secured only until a hearing date on which the authority can make representations.

PD2B, para.9 provides that appeals under s.204A may be not be heard by district judges.

When hearing a s.204A appeal, the county court should apply the same approach as directed in *R. v Brighton & Hove BC Ex p. Nacion* (1999) 31 H.L.R. 1095, CA unless the court decides that the local authority did not direct itself in accordance with *R. v London Borough of Camden Ex p. Mohammed* (1998) 30 H.L.R. 315, QBD. In that case it should quash the decision and decide whether it should itself exercise the s.204A(5) power to order the authority to provide temporary accommodation. There is no question of the county court embarking on an assessment of the merits of the appeal. That would be to go beyond the scope of the appeal as set out in *Nacion*. A challenge to the exercise of powers under s.188 of the Act still has to be brought by way of judicial review (see *Francis v Kensington and Chelsea RLBC* [2003] EWCA Civ 443; [2003] 1 W.L.R. 2248; [2003] 2 All E.R. 1052).

### SUPPLEMENTARY PROVISIONS

## Discharge of functions: introductory

**205.**—(1) The following sections have effect in relation to the discharge by a local housing authority of their functions under this Part to secure that accommodation is available for the occupation of a person— **3A–1446**

section 206 (general provisions),
section 208 (out-of-area placements),
section 209 (arrangements with private landlord).

(2) In sections 206 and 208 those functions are referred to as the authority's "housing functions under this Part".

*Note*—Amended by the Homelessness Act 2002 s.5(1), Sch.1, para.18. **3A–1447**

## Discharge of functions by local housing authorities

**206.**—(1) A local housing authority may discharge their housing functions under this Part only in the following ways— **3A–1448**

(a) by securing that suitable accommodation provided by them is available,
(b) by securing that he obtains suitable accommodation from some other person, or
(c) by giving him such advice and assistance as will secure that suitable accommodation is available from some other person.

(2) A local housing authority may require a person in relation to whom they are discharging such functions—

(a) to pay such reasonable charges as they may determine in respect of accommodation which they secure for his occupation (either by making it available themselves or otherwise), or
(b) to pay such reasonable amount as they may determine in respect of sums payable by them for accommodation made available by another person.

**Discharge of functions by local housing authorities**

See the commentary to s.193. **3A–1449**

***Paragraph numbers marked with a "+" can be found online and on CD.***



HOUSING

**"local housing authority"**

3A–1450 See ss.217, 218, and 230 which refer to the Housing Act 1985—see the Housing Act 1985 ss.1 and 2, above.

## Discharge of functions: provision of accommodation by the authority

3A–1451 **207.** [...]

3A–1452 *Note* —This section was repealed by the Homelessness Act 2002, Sch.2.

## Discharge of functions: out-of-area placements

3A–1453 **208.**—(1) So far as reasonably practicable a local housing authority shall in discharging their housing functions under this Part secure that accommodation is available for the occupation of the applicant in their district.

(2) If they secure that accommodation is available for the occupation of the applicant outside their district, they shall give notice to the local housing authority in whose district the accommodation is situated.

(3) The notice shall state—

(a) the name of the applicant,

(b) the number and description of other persons who normally reside with him as a member of his family or might reasonably be expected to reside with him,

(c) the address of the accommodation,

(d) the date on which the accommodation was made available to him, and

(e) which function under this Part the authority was discharging in securing that the accommodation is available for his occupation.

(4) The notice must be in writing, and must be given before the end of the period of 14 days beginning with the day on which the accommodation was made available to the applicant.

**Discharge of functions: out-of-area placements**

3A–1454 See the commentary to s.193.

**"local housing authority"**

3A–1455 See ss.217, 218, and 230 which refer to the Housing Act 1985—see the Housing Act 1985 ss.1 and 2 above.

**"district"**

3A–1456 See s.217(3).

**"available for his occupation"**

3A–1457 See s.176.

## Discharge of interim duties: arrangements with private landlord

3A–1458 **209.**—(1) This section applies where in pursuance of any of their housing functions under section 188, 190, 200 or 204(4) (interim duties) a local housing authority make arrangements with a private landlord to provide accommodation.

(2) A tenancy granted to the applicant in pursuance of the arrangements cannot be an assured tenancy before the end of the period of twelve months beginning with—

(a) the date on which the applicant was notified of the authority's decision under section 184(3) or 198(5); or

(b) if there is a review of that decision under section 202 or an appeal to the court under section 204, the date on which he is notified of the decision on review or the appeal is finally determined,

unless, before or during that period, the tenant is notified by the landlord (or in the case of joint landlords, at least one of them) that the tenancy is to be regarded as an assured shorthold tenancy or an assured tenancy other than an assured shorthold tenancy.

*Note* —Amended by Homelessness Act 2002 s.5(1), Sch.1, para.19. **3A–1459**

**private landlord**

See s.217(1), as amended by Homelessness Act 2002 Sch.1, para.20. **3A–1460**

**assured shorthold tenancy**

See Housing Act 1988 ss.19A and 20. **3A–1461**

**Discharge of functions: arrangements with private landlord**

See the commentary to s.193. **3A–1462**

**"local housing authority"**

See ss.217, 218, and 230 which refer to the Housing Act 1985—see the Housing Act 1985 ss.1 and 2 above. **3A–1463**

**"available for his occupation"**

See s.176. **3A–1464**

**"assured tenancy"**

See s.230 which refers to the Housing Act 1988 Pt I. See the Housing Act 1988 s.1 above. **3A–1465**

**"registered social landlord"**

See s.1. **3A–1466**

## Suitability of accommodation

**210.**—(1) In determining for the purposes of this Part whether accommodation is suitable for a person, the local housing authority shall have regard to Parts 9 and 10 of the Housing Act 1985 (slum clearance and overcrowding) and Parts 1 to 4 of the Housing Act 2004). **3A–1467**

(2) The Secretary of State may by order specify—

(a) circumstances in which accommodation is or is not to be regarded as suitable for a person, and

(b) matters to be taken into account or disregarded in

determining whether accommodation is suitable for a person.

3A–1468 *Note* —Amended by the Housing Act 2004Sch.15, paras 40 and 43.

**Suitability of accommodation**

3A–1469 See the commentary to s.193, the Homelessness (Suitability of Accommodation (England) Order 2003 (SI 2003/3326) and the Homelessness (Suitability of Accommodation) (Wales) Order 2006 (SI 2006/650 (w.71)).

**"local housing authority"**

3A–1470 See ss.217, 218, and 230 which refer to the Housing Act 1985—see the Housing Act 1985 ss.1 and 2 above.

## Protection of property of homeless persons and persons threatened with homelessness

3A–1471 **211.**—(1) This section applies where a local housing authority have reason to believe that—

(a) there is danger of loss of, or damage to, any personal property of an applicant by reason of his inability to protect it or deal with it, and

(b) no other suitable arrangements have been or are being made.

(2) If the authority have become subject to a duty towards the applicant under—

section 188 (interim duty to accommodate),

section 190, 193 or 195 (duties to persons found to be homeless or threatened with homelessness), or

section 200 (duties to applicant whose case is considered for referral or referred),

then, whether or not they are still subject to such a duty, they shall take reasonable steps to prevent the loss of the property or prevent or mitigate damage to it.

(3) If they have not become subject to such a duty, they may take any steps they consider reasonable for that purpose.

(4) The authority may decline to take action under this section except upon such conditions as they consider appropriate in the particular case, which may include conditions as to—

(a) the making and recovery by the authority of reasonable charges for the action taken, or

(b) the disposal by the authority, in such circumstances as may be specified, of property in relation to which they have taken action.

(5) References in this section to personal property of the applicant include personal property of any person who might reasonably be expected to reside with him.

(6) Section 212 contains provisions supplementing this section.

**"local housing authority"**

3A–1472 See ss.217, 218, and 230 which refer to the Housing Act 1985—see the Housing Act 1985 ss.1 and 2 above.

*Paragraph numbers marked with a "+" can be found online and on CD.*

For there to be a cause of action for a claim under s.211 the local authority must have reason to believe that: (a) there is a danger of loss or damage to property as a result of the owner being unable to protect it; and (b) no other suitable arrangements can be made (see ss.211(1)(a) and (b)). In view of the use of the word "danger", there has to be a likelihood of harm and not just the possibility of injury (*Deadman v Southwark LBC* (2001) 33 H.L.R. 865, CA). 3A–1473

## Protection of property: supplementary provisions

**212.**—(1) The authority may for the purposes of section 211 (protection of property of homeless persons or persons threatened with homelessness)— 3A–1474

(a) enter, at all reasonable times, any premises which are the usual place of residence of the applicant or which were his last usual place of residence, and

(b) deal with any personal property of his in any way which is reasonably necessary, in particular by storing it or arranging for its storage.

(2) Where the applicant asks the authority to move his property to a particular location nominated by him, the authority—

(a) may, if it appears to them that his request is reasonable, discharge their responsibilities under section 211 by doing as he asks, and

(b) having done so, have no further duty or power to take action under that section in relation to that property.

If such a request is made, the authority shall before complying with it inform the applicant of the consequence of their doing so.

(3) If no such request is made (or, if made, is not acted upon) the authority cease to have any duty or power to take action under section 211 when, in their opinion, there is no longer any reason to believe that there is a danger of loss of or damage to a person's personal property by reason of his inability to protect it or deal with it.

But property stored by virtue of their having taken such action may be kept in store and any conditions upon which it was taken into store continue to have effect, with any necessary modifications.

(4) Where the authority—

(a) cease to be subject to a duty to take action under section 211 in respect of an applicant's property, or

(b) cease to have power to take such action, having previously taken such action,

they shall notify the applicant of that fact and of the reason for it.

(5) The notification shall be given to the applicant—

(a) by delivering it to him, or

(b) by leaving it, or sending it to him, at his last known address.

(6) References in this section to personal property of the applicant include personal property of any person who might reasonably be expected to reside with him.

## Co-operation between relevant housing authorities and bodies

**213.**—(1) Where a local housing authority— 3A–1475

*Paragraph numbers marked with a "+" can be found online and on CD.*

(a) request another relevant housing authority or body, in England, Wales or Scotland, to assist them in the discharge of their functions under this Part, or

(b) request a social services authority, in England, Wales or Scotland, to exercise any of their functions in relation to a case which the local housing authority are dealing with under this Part,

the authority or body to whom the request is made shall co-operate in rendering such assistance in the discharge of the functions to which the request relates as is reasonable in the circumstances.

(2) In subsection (1)(a) "relevant housing authority or body" means—

(a) in relation to England and Wales, a local housing authority, a new town corporation, a registered social landlord or a housing action trust;

(b) in relation to Scotland, a local authority, a development corporation, a registered housing association or Scottish Homes.

Expressions used in paragraph (a) have the same meaning as in the Housing Act 1985; and expressions used in paragraph (b) have the same meaning as in the Housing (Scotland) Act 1987.

(3) Subsection (1) above applies to a request by a local authority in Scotland under section 38 of the Housing (Scotland) Act 1987 as it applies to a request by a local housing authority in England and Wales (the references to this Part being construed, in relation to such a request, as references to Part II of that Act).

**"local housing authority"**

**3A–1476** See ss.217, 218, and 230 which refer to the Housing Act 1985—see the Housing Act 1985 ss.1 and 2, above.

**"social services authority"**

**3A–1477** See s.217.

## Co-operation in certain cases involving children

**3A–1478** **213A.**—(1) This section applies where a local housing authority have reason to believe that an applicant with whom a person under the age of 18 normally resides, or might reasonably be expected to reside—

(a) may be ineligible for assistance;

(b) may be homeless and may have become so intentionally; or

(c) may be threatened with homelessness intentionally.

(2) A local housing authority shall make arrangements for ensuring that, where this section applies—

(a) the applicant is invited to consent to the referral of the essential facts of his case to the social services authority for the district of the housing authority (where that is a different authority); and

(b) if the applicant has given that consent, the social services authority are made aware of those facts and of the subsequent decision of the housing authority in respect of his case.

(3) Where the local housing authority and the social services authority for a district are the same authority (a "unitary authority"), that authority shall make arrangements for ensuring that, where this section applies—

(a) the applicant is invited to consent to the referral to the social services department of the essential facts of his case; and

(b) if the applicant has given that consent, the social services department is made aware of those facts and of the subsequent decision of the authority in respect of his case.

(4) Nothing in subsection (2) or (3) affects any power apart from this section to disclose information relating to the applicant's case to the social services authority or to the social services department (as the case may be) without the consent of the applicant.

(5) Where a social services authority—

(a) are aware of a decision of a local housing authority that the applicant is ineligible for assistance, became homeless intentionally or became threatened with homelessness intentionally, and

(b) request the local housing authority to provide them with advice and assistance in the exercise of their social services functions under Part 3 of the Children Act 1989, the local housing authority shall provide them with such advice and assistance as is reasonable in the circumstances.

(6) A unitary authority shall make arrangements for ensuring that, where they make a decision of a kind mentioned in subsection (5)(a), the housing department provide the social services department with such advice and assistance as the social services department may reasonably request.

(7) In this section, in relation to a unitary authority

"the housing department" means those persons responsible for the exercise of their housing functions; and

"the social services department" means those persons responsible for the exercise of their social services functions under Part 3 of the Children Act 1989.

*Note* —Amended by the Homelessness Act 2002 s.12. **3A–1479**

**Local housing authority**—see Housing Act 1985 s.1.

**Ineligible for assistance**—see s.185.

**Homeless intentionally**—see s.191.

**Threatened with homelessness intentionally**—see s.191.

**Unitary authority**—see s.213A(3).

**Social services authority**—see s.213A(7) and the Children Act 1989 Pt III.

**Co-operation with social services authority**—If a local housing authority decide that an applicant, with whom a person under the age of 18 normally resides, may be ineligible for assistance, intentionally homeless, or threatened with homelessness intentionally, they must, subject to the consent of the applicant, make arrangements to ensure that the essential facts of the case are referred to the social services authority.

**Children Act 1989**—Local authorities have a power to provide assistance by way of accommodation under Children Act 1989 s.17. However s.17 does not impose an enforceable duty to provide assistance—see *A and W v Lambeth LBC; G v Barnet LBC* (also reported as *R.(on the application of G) v Barnet LBC*) [2003] UKHL 57; [2004] 2 A.C. 208; [2003] 3 W.L.R. 1194 and the commentary at 3A–29 above.

### *GENERAL PROVISIONS*

## False statements, withholding information and failure to disclose change of circumstances

3A–1480 **214.**—(1) It is an offence for a person, with intent to induce a local housing authority to believe in connection with the exercise of their functions under this Part that he or another person is entitled to accommodation or assistance in accordance with the provisions of this Part, or is entitled to accommodation or assistance of a particular description—

(a) knowingly or recklessly to make a statement which is false in a material particular, or

(b) knowingly to withhold information which the authority have reasonably required him to give in connection with the exercise of those functions.

(2) If before an applicant receives notification of the local housing authority's decision on his application there is any change of facts material to his case, he shall notify the authority as soon as possible.

The authority shall explain to every applicant, in ordinary language, the duty imposed on him by this subsection and the effect of subsection (3).

(3) A person who fails to comply with subsection (2) commits an offence unless he shows that he was not given the explanation required by that subsection or that he had some other reasonable excuse for non-compliance.

(4) A person guilty of an offence under this section is liable on summary conviction to a fine not exceeding level 5 on the standard scale.

**"local housing authority"**

3A–1481 See ss.217, 218 and 230 which refer to the Housing Act 1985—see the Housing Act 1985 ss.1 and 2 above.

See too the Housing Act 1985 Sch.2, Ground 5 above.

## Regulations and orders

3A–1482 **215.**—(1) In this Part "prescribed" means prescribed by regulations of the Secretary of State.

(2) Regulations or an order under this Part may make different provision for different purposes, including different provision for different areas.

(3) Regulations or an order under this Part shall be made by statutory instrument.

(4) Unless required to be approved in draft, regulations or an order under this Part shall be subject to annulment in pursuance of a resolution of either House of Parliament.

## Transitional and consequential matters

**216.**—(1) The provisions of this Part have effect in place of the provisions of Part III of the Housing Act 1985 (housing the homeless) and shall be construed as one with that Act. **3A–1483**

(2) Subject to any transitional provision contained in an order under section 232(4) (power to include transitional provision in commencement order), the provisions of this Part do not apply in relation to an applicant whose application for accommodation or assistance in obtaining accommodation was made before the commencement of this Part.

(3) The enactments mentioned in Schedule 17 have effect with the amendments specified there which are consequential on the provisions of this Part.

## Minor definitions: Part VII

**217.**—(1) In this Part, subject to subsection (2)— **3A–1484**

"private landlord" means a landlord who is not within section 80(1) of the Housing Act 1985 (c.68) (the landlord condition for secure tenancies); and

"relevant authority" means a local housing authority or a social services authority; and

"social services authority" means a local authority for the purposes of the Local Authority Social Services Act 1970, as defined in section 1 of that Act.

(2) In this Part, in relation to Scotland—

(a) "local housing authority" means a local authority within the meaning of the Housing (Scotland) Act 1988, and

(b) "social services authority" means a local authority for the purposes of the Social Work (Scotland) Act 1968.

(3) References in this Part to the district of a local housing authority—

(a) have the same meaning in relation to an authority in England or Wales as in the Housing Act 1985, and

(b) in relation to an authority in Scotland, mean the area of the local authority concerned.

*Note* —Amended by the Homelessness Act 2002 s.5(1) Sch.1, para.20. **3A–1485**

## Index of defined expressions: Part VII

**218.** The following Table shows provisions defining or otherwise explaining expressions used in this Part (other than provisions defining or explaining an expression used in the same section)— **3A–1486**

| | |
|---|---|
| accommodation available for occupation | section 176 |
| applicant | section 183(2) |

*Paragraph numbers marked with a "+" can be found online and on CD.*

| | |
|---|---|
| assistance under this Part | section 183(2) |
| associated (in relation to a person) | section 178 |
| assured tenancy and assured shorthold tenancy | section 230 |
| district (of local housing authority) | section 217(3) |
| eligible for assistance | section 183(2) |
| homeless | section 175(1) |
| housing functions under this Part (in sections 206 and 208) | section 205(2) |
| intentionally homeless | section 191 |
| intentionally threatened with homelessness | section 196 |
| local connection | section 199 |
| local housing authority— | |
| —in England and Wales | section 230 |
| —in Scotland | section 217(2)(a) |
| minimum period (for purposes of section 193) | section 193(3) and (4) |
| prescribed | section 215(1) |
| priority need | section 189 |
| private landlord | section 217(1) |
| reasonable to continue to occupy accommodation | section 177 |
| registered social landlord | section 230 |
| relevant authority | section 217(1) |
| restricted person | section 184(7) |
| social services authority | section 217(1) and (2)(b) |
| threatened with homelessness | section 175(4) |

**3A–1487** *Note* —Amended by Homelessness Act 2002 s.5(1), Sch.1, para.21 and the Housing and Regeneration Act 2008 Sch.15, para.8, for certain purposes with effect from March 2, 2009 (SI 2009/415; for purposes see art.2).

## Anti-social behaviour: landlords' policies and procedures

**3A–1488** **218A.**—(1) This section applies to the following landlords—

(a) a local housing authority;
(b) a housing action trust;
(c) a registered social landlord.

(2) The landlord must prepare—

(a) a policy in relation to anti-social behaviour;
(b) procedures for dealing with occurrences of anti-social behaviour.

(3) The landlord must not later than 6 months after the commencement of section 12 of the Anti-Social Behaviour Act 2003 publish a statement of the policy and procedures prepared under subsection (2).

(4) The landlord must from time to time keep the policy and

procedures under review and, when it thinks appropriate, publish a revised statement.

(5) A copy of a statement published under subsection (3) or (4)—

(a) must be available for inspection at all reasonable hours at the landlord's principal office;

(b) must be provided on payment of a reasonable fee to any person who requests it.

(6) The landlord must also—

(a) prepare a summary of its current policy and procedures;

(b) provide without charge a copy of the summary to any person who requests it.

(7) In preparing and reviewing the policy and procedures the landlord must have regard to guidance issued—

(a) by the Secretary of State in the case of a local housing authority or a housing action trust;

(b) by the Relevant Authority under section 36 in the case of a registered social landlord.

(8) Anti-social behaviour is—

(a) any housing-related anti-social conduct, or

(b) any conduct to which section 153B applies.

(8A) Housing-related anti-social conduct has the same meaning as in section 153A.

(9) Relevant Authority has the same meaning as in Part 1.

*Note*—This section was inserted by the Anti-Social Behaviour Act 2003 s.12. It was amended by the Police and Justice Act 2006 Sch.14, para.33, with effect from April 6, 2007 (SI 2007/709). **3A–1489**

**A local housing authority**

See the Housing Act 1996 s.230 and Housing Act 1985 ss.1 and 2(2). **3A–1490**

**A housing action trust**

See the Housing Act 1996 s.230 and Housing Act 1988 Pt III. **3A–1491**

**A registered social landlord**

See the Housing Act 1996 s.230 referring back to Pt I (ss.1 to 3). **3A–1492**

**Anti-social behaviour**

See the ss.153A and 153B above. **3A–1493**

**Relevant authority**

See Housing Act 1996 s.56—i.e. the Housing Corporation or Housing for Wales. **3A–1494**

**Guidance**

Guidance may be issued to local housing authorities or housing action trusts in England by the Secretary of State or, in Wales, by the National Assembly for Wales. Guidance to registered social landlords may be issued by the Housing Corporation in England or, in Wales, by the National Assembly for Wales. At present no guidance has been issued. **3A–1495**

* * * *

## PART VIII

## MISCELLANEOUS AND GENERAL PROVISIONS

### *GENERAL*

### Meaning of "lease" and "tenancy" and related expressions

3A–1496 **229.**—(1) In this Act "lease" and "tenancy" have the same meaning.

(2) Both expressions include—

(a) a sub-lease or a sub-tenancy, and

(b) an agreement for a lease or tenancy (or sub-lease or sub-tenancy).

(3) The expressions "lessor" and "lessee" and "landlord" and "tenant", and references to letting, to the grant of a lease or to covenants or terms, shall be construed accordingly.

* * * *

**SECTION 155(6)** SCHEDULE 15

ARREST FOR ANTI-SOCIAL BEHAVIOUR: POWERS OF HIGH COURT AND COUNTY COURT TO REMAND

*Introductory*

3A–1497 1.—(1) The provisions of this Schedule apply where the court has power to remand a person under section 155(2) or (5) (arrest for breach of injunction, &c.).

(2) In this Schedule "the court" means the High Court or a county court and includes—

(a) in relation to the High Court, a judge of that court, and

(b) in relation to a county court, a judge or district judge of that court.

*Remand in custody or on bail*

3A–1498 2.—(1) The court may—

(a) remand him in custody, that is, commit him to custody to be brought before the court at the end of the period of remand or at such earlier time as the court may require, or

(b) remand him on bail, in accordance with the following provisions.

(2) The court may remand him on bail—

(a) by taking from him a recognizance, with or without sureties, conditioned as provided in paragraph 3, or

(b) by fixing the amount of the recognizances with a view to their being taken subsequently, and in the meantime committing him to custody as mentioned in sub-paragraph (1)(a).

(3) Where a person is brought before the court after remand, the court may further remand him.

3.—(1) Where a person is remanded on bail, the court may direct that his recognizance be conditioned for his appearance—

(a) before that court at the end of the period of remand, or

***Paragraph numbers marked with a "+" can be found online and on CD.***

(b) at every time and place to which during the course of the proceedings the hearing may from time to time be adjourned.

(2) Where a recognizance is conditioned for a person's appearance as mentioned in sub-paragraph (1)(b), the fixing of any time for him next to appear shall be deemed to be a remand.

(3) Nothing in this paragraph affects the power of the court at any subsequent hearing to remand him afresh.

4.—(1) The court shall not remand a person for a period exceeding 8 clear days, except that—

(a) if the court remands him on bail, it may remand him for a longer period if he and the other party consent, and

(b) if the court adjourns a case under section 156(1) (remand for medical examination and report), the court may remand him for the period of the adjournment.

(2) Where the court has power to remand a person in custody it may, if the remand is for a period not exceeding 3 clear days, commit him to the custody of a constable.

*Further remand*

5.—(1) If the court is satisfied that a person who has been remanded is unable by reason of illness or accident to appear or be brought before the court at the expiration of the period for which he was remanded, the court may, in his absence, remand him for a further time. This power may, in the case of a person who was remanded on bail, be exercised by enlarging his recognizance and those of any sureties for him to a later time. **3A–1499**

(2) Where a person remanded on bail is bound to appear before the court at any time and the court has no power to remand him under sub-paragraph (1) the court may in his absence enlarge his recognizance and those of any sureties for him to a later time. The enlargement of his recognizance shall be deemed to be a further remand.

(3) Paragraph 4(1) (limit of period of remand) does not apply to the exercise of the powers conferred by this paragraph.

*Postponement of taking of recognizance*

6. Where under paragraph 2(2)(b) the court fixes the amount in which the principal and his sureties, if any, are to be bound, the recognizance may afterwards be taken by such person as may be prescribed by rules of court, with the same consequences as if it had been entered into before the court. **3A–1500**

**Schedule 15**

See the commentary to ss.153 to 155 above. **3A–1501**

Note that ss.155(2)(b) (remands in custody), 155(3)–(7) (warrants for arrest), 156 (remand for medical examination), and Sch.15 (provisions corresponding with civil procedure in magistrate's courts) were implemented on October 15, 2001 by the Housing Act 1996 (Commencement No.13) Order 2001 (SI 2001/3164).

## Crime and Disorder Act 1998

(1998 c.37) **3A–1502**

ARRANGEMENT OF SECTIONS

*CRIME AND DISORDER: GENERAL*

SECT.



*CRIME AND DISORDER: GENERAL*

## Anti-social behaviour orders

**1.**—(1) An application for an order under this section may be made **3A–1503**

***Paragraph numbers marked with a "+" can be found online and on CD.***

by a relevant authority if it appears to the authority that the following conditions are fulfilled with respect to any person aged 10 or over, namely—

(a) that the person has acted, since the commencement date, in an anti-social manner, that is to say, in a manner that caused or was likely to cause harassment, alarm or distress to one or more persons not of the same household as himself; and

(b) that such an order is necessary to protect relevant persons from further anti-social acts by him.

(1A) In this section and sections 1AA, 1B, 1CA, 1E and 1F 'relevant authority' means —

(a) the council for a local governmenjt area;

(aa) in relation to England, a county council;

(b) the chief officer of police of any police force maintained for a police area;

(c) the chief constable of the British Transport Police Force;

(d) any person registered under section 1 of the Housing Act 1996 (c.52) as a social landlord who provides or manages any houses or hostel in a local government area; or

(e) a housing action trust established by order in pursuance of section 62 of the Housing Act 1988.

(1B) In this section 'relevant persons' means—

(a) in relation to a relevant authority falling within paragraph (a) of subsection (1A), persons within the local government area of that council;

(aa) in relation to a relevant authority falling within paragraph (aa) of subsection (1A), persons within the county of the county council;

(b) in relation to a relevant authority falling within paragraph (b) of that subsection, persons within the police area;

(c) in relation to a relevant authority falling within paragraph (c) of that subsection—

(i) persons who are within or likely to be within a place specified in section 31(1)(a) to (f) of the Railways and Transport Safety Act 2003 in a local government area; or

(ii) persons who are within or likely to be within such a place;

(d) in relation to a relevant authority falling within paragraph (d) or (e) of that subsection—

(i) persons who are residing in or who are otherwise on or likely to be on premises provided or managed by that authority; or

(ii) persons who are in the vicinity of or likely to be in the vicinity of such premises.

[...]

(3) Such an application shall be made by complaint to a magistrates' court.

(4) If, on such an application, it is proved that the conditions mentioned in subsection (1) above are fulfilled, the magistrates' court may make an order under this section (an "anti-social behaviour order") which prohibits the defendant from doing anything described in the order.

(5) For the purpose of determining whether the condition mentioned in subsection (1)(a) above is fulfilled, the court shall disregard any act of the defendant which he shows was reasonable in the circumstances.

(5A) Nothing in this section affects the operation of section 127 of the Magistrates' Courts Act 1980 (limitation of time in respect of informations laid or complaints made in magistrates' court).

(6) The prohibitions that may be imposed by an anti-social behaviour order are those necessary for the purpose of protecting persons (whether relevant persons or persons elsewhere in England and Wales) from further anti-social acts by the defendant.

(7) An anti-social behaviour order shall have effect for a period (not less than two years) specified in the order or until further order.

(8) Subject to subsection (9) below, the applicant or the defendant may apply by complaint to the court which made an anti-social behaviour order for it to be varied or discharged by a further order.

(9) Except with the consent of both parties, no anti-social behaviour order shall be discharged before the end of the period of two years beginning with the date of service of the order.

(10) If without reasonable excuse a person does anything which he is prohibited from doing by an anti-social behaviour order, he is guilty of an offence and liable—

(a) on summary conviction, to imprisonment for a term not exceeding six months or to a fine not exceeding the statutory maximum, or to both; or

(b) on conviction on indictment, to imprisonment for a term not exceeding five years or to a fine, or to both.

(10A) The following may bring proceedings for an offence under subsection (10)—

(a) a council which is a relevant authority;

(b) the council for the local government area in which a person in respect of whom an anti-social behaviour order has been made resides or appears to reside.

(c) Transport for London, where the anti-social behaviour order was made on an application by Transport for London.

(10B) If proceedings for an offence under subsection (10) are brought in a youth court section 47(2) of the Children and Young Persons Act 1933 (c. 12) has effect as if the persons entitled to be present at a sitting for the purposes of those proceedings include one person authorised to be present by a relevant authority.

(10C) In proceedings for an offence under subsection (10), a copy of the original anti-social behaviour order, certified as such by the proper officer of the court which made it, is admissible as evidence of its having been made and of its contents to the same extent that oral evidence of those things is admissible in those proceedings.

(10D) In relation to proceedings brought against a child or a young person for an offence under subsection (10)—

(a) section 49 of the Children and Young Persons Act 1933 (restrictions on reports of proceedings in which children and young persons are concerned) does not apply in respect of the child or young person against whom the proceedings are brought;

(b) section 45 of the Youth Justice and Criminal Evidence Act 1999 (power to restrict reporting of criminal proceedings involving persons under 18) does so apply.

(10E) If, in relation to any such proceedings, the court does exercise its power to give a direction under section 45 of the Youth Justice and Criminal Evidence Act 1999, it shall give its reasons for doing so.

(11) Where a person is convicted of an offence under subsection (10) above, it shall not be open to the court by or before which he is so convicted to make an order under subsection (1)(b) (conditional discharge) of section 12 of the Powers of Criminal Courts (Sentencing) Act 2000 in respect of the offence.

(12) In this section—

"British Transport Police Force" means the force of constables appointed under section 53 of the British Transport Commission Act 1949 (c. xxix);

"child" and "young person" shall have the same meaning as in the Children and Young Persons Act 1933;

"the commencement date" means the date of the commencement of this section;

"local government area" means —

(a) in relation to England, a district or London borough, the City of London, the Isle of Wight and the Isles of Scilly;

(b) in relation to Wales, a county or county borough.

"policed premises" has the meaning given by section 53(3) of the British Transport Commission Act 1949.

**3A–1504** *Note* —Amended by the Powers of the Court (Sentencing) Act 2000 s.165(1), Sch.9, para.192; the Police Reform Act 2002 s.61; the Anti-Social Behaviour Act 2003 s.85; SI 2004/1573; SI 2005/886; the Serious Organised Crime and Police Act 2005 ss.139(2), 140(2), 141(2), 142(2); the Violent Crime Reduction Act 2006 s.59(1) with effect from April 6, 2008 (SI 2008/791); the Transport for London Act 2008 s.29(a) with effect from July 22, 2008; and the Criminal Justice and Immigration Act 2008 s.124(4) with effect from February 1, 2009 (SI 2009/140).

#### Anti-social behaviour order

**3A–1505** Such an order (an ASBO) may be granted if a person has acted in an anti-social manner, that is to say, in a manner that caused or was likely to cause harassment, alarm or distress to one or more persons not of the same household as himself and such an order is necessary to protect relevant persons from further anti-social acts (s.1(1)). When considering whether a person's conduct has caused or is likely to cause

*Paragraph numbers marked with a "+" can be found online and on CD.*

harassment, alarm or distress to others within the meaning of Crime and Disorder Act 1998 s.1(1)(a) "likely" means "more probable than not". The likelihood has to be proved to the criminal standard (see *Chief Constable of Lancashire v Potter* [2003] EWHC 2272 (Admin) and *R. (McCann) v Manchester Crown Court* [2002] UKHL 39; [2003] 1 A.C. 787; [2002] 3 W.L.R. 1313).. An ASBO may prohibit the defendant from doing anything described in the order. The prohibitions that may be imposed by an ASBO are "those necessary for the purpose of protecting persons (whether relevant persons or persons elsewhere in England and Wales) from further anti-social acts by the defendant" (s.1(4)and (6)). ASBOs have effect for the period (not less than two years) specified in the order or until further order (s.1(7)). Although ASBOs should be substantially and not just formally prohibitory, a restraint upon leaving or travelling between specified premises between particular times meets that test. Further there is nothing legally objectionable to a curfew provision in an ASBO if it is necessary for the protection of relevant people. Courts should however consider carefully the need for and duration of curfew provisions when making ASBOs. Just because ASBOs have to run for a minimum of two years, it does not follow that each and every prohibition within a particular ASBO has to endure for the life of the order (*R. (Lonergan) v Lewes Crown Court* [2005] EWHC 457 (Admin); [2005] 1 W.L.R. 2570).

Breach of an ASBO may be punished on summary conviction by imprisonment for a term not exceeding six months or a fine or both; or on conviction on indictment, by imprisonment for a term not exceeding five years or to a fine, or to both (s.1(10)).

In *Moat Housing Group South Ltd v Harris and Hartless* [2005] EWCA Civ 287; [2006] Q.B. 606; [2005] 3 W.L.R. 691; [2005] 4 All E.R. 1051, the Court of Appeal left open "the important question whether a failure to control one's children from being a nuisance, although it may constitute a breach of a tenancy agreement, is an 'act' of the type referred to in" Crime and Disorder Act 1998 s.1(1)(a).

As to the relationship between ASBOs and possession claims based upon anti-social behaviour, see e.g. *Knowsley Housing Trust v McMullen* [2006] EWCA Civ 539; [2006] H.L.R. 43.

**A relevant authority**

See s.1(1A), namely the council for a local government area, a county council, the chief officer of police of any police force maintained for a police area, the chief constable of the British Transport Police Force, a social landlord who provides or manages any houses or hostel which is registered under Housing Act 1996 s.1 or a housing action trust (see Housing Act 1988 s.62). The Crime and Disorder Act 1998 (Relevant Authorities and Relevant Persons) Order 2006 (SI 2006/2137) added the Environment Agency and Transport for London to the list of organisations which may apply for ASBOs. Any person (or employee of that person) who exercises a local housing authority's management functions pursuant to an agreement under the Housing Act 1985 s.27, (such as an Arms Length Management Organisation—ALMO) may discharge the authority's functions under the Crime and Disorder Act 1998 ss.1– 1E (the Local Authorities (Contracting Out of Anti-Social Behaviour Order Functions) (England) Order 2007 SI 2007/1441). **3A–1506**

**Relevant persons**

See s.1(1B). **3A–1507**

**An application**

Applications for ASBOs could originally only be made by complaint in the Magistrates Court, but see s.1B below (introduced by Police Reform Act 2002 s.63) which provides that ASBOs can be made in the county court if a relevant authority considers it is reasonable to make such an application. If the relevant authority or the person against whom the ASBO is sought is not already a party to the principal proceedings, an application can be made for him or her to be joined as a party. However a person may only be joined if his or her anti-social acts are material in relation to the principal proceedings (see s.1B(3C) below). **3A–1508**

## Power of Secretary of State to add to relevant authorities

**1A.**—(1) The Secretary of State may by order provide that the **3A–1509**

chief officer of a body of constables maintained otherwise than by a police authority is, in such cases and circumstances as may be prescribed by the order, to be a relevant authority for the purposes of section 1 above.

(2) The Secretary of State may by order—

(a) provide that a person or body of any other description specified in the order is, in such cases and circumstances as may be prescribed by the order, to be a relevant authority for the purposes of such of sections 1 above and 1B, 1CA, 1E and 1F below as are specified in the order; and

(b) prescribe the description of persons who are to be "relevant persons" in relation to that person or body.

**3A-1510** *Note*—Inserted by the Police Reform Act 2002 s.62(1); amended by the Serious Organised Crime and Police Act 2005 s.139(3) s.142(2).

**By order**

**3A-1511** See the Crime and Disorder Act 1998 (Relevant Authorities and Relevant Persons) Order 2006 (SI 2006/2137).

## Orders in county court proceedings

**3A-1512** **1B.**—(1) This section applies to any proceedings in a county court ('the principal proceedings').

(2) If a relevant authority—

(a) is a party to the principal proceedings, and

(b) considers that a party to those proceedings is a person in relation to whom it would be reasonable for it to make an application under section 1,

it may make an application in those proceedings for an order under subsection (4).

(3) If a relevant authority—

(a) is not a party to the principal proceedings, and

(b) considers that a party to those proceedings is a person in relation to whom it would be reasonable for it to make an application under section 1,

it may make an application to be joined to those proceedings to enable it to apply for an order under subsection (4) and, if it is so joined, may apply for such an order.

(3A) Subsection (3B) applies if a relevant authority is a party to the principal proceedings and considers—

(a) that a person who is not a party to the proceedings has acted in an anti-social manner, and

(b) that the person's anti-social acts are material in relation to the principal proceedings.

(3B) The relevant authority may—

(a) make an application for the person mentioned in subsection (3A)(a) to be joined to the principal proceedings to enable an order under subsection (4) to be made in relation to that person;

*Paragraph numbers marked with a "+" can be found online and on CD.*

(b) if that person is so joined, apply for an order under subsection (4).

(3C) But a person must not be joined to proceedings in pursuance of subsection (3B) unless his anti-social acts are material in relation to the principal proceedings.

(4) If, on an application for an order under this subsection, it is proved that the conditions mentioned in section 1(1) are fulfilled as respects that other party, the court may make an order which prohibits him from doing anything described in the order.

(5) Subject to subsection (6), the person against whom an order under this section has been made and the relevant authority on whose application that order was made may apply to the county court which made an order under this section for it to be varied or discharged by a further order.

(6) Except with the consent of the relevant authority and the person subject to the order, no order under this section shall be discharged before the end of the period of two years beginning with the date of service of the order.

(7) Subsections (5) to (7) and (10) to (12) of section 1 apply for the purposes of the making and effect of orders made under this section as they apply for the purposes of the making and effect of anti-social behaviour orders.

(8) Sections 1AA and 1AB apply in relation to orders under this section, with any necessary modifications, as they apply in relation to anti-social behaviour orders.

(9) In their application by virtue of subsection (8), sections 1AA(1A)(b) and 1AB(6) have effect as if the words "by complaint" were omitted.

*Note* —Section 1B was inserted by the Police Reform Act 2002 s.63 and has been amended by the Anti-Social Behaviour Act 2003 s.85(5), (6); and the Criminal Justice and Immigration Act 2008 s.124(4) with effect from February 1, 2009 (SI 2009/140). **3A–1513**

**A relevant authority**

See s.1(1A), namely the council for a local government area, a county council, the chief officer of police of any police force maintained for a police area, the chief constable of the British Transport Police Force, a social landlord who provides or manages any houses or hostel which is registered under Housing Act 1996 s.1 or a housing action trust (see Housing Act 1988 s.62). The Crime and Disorder Act 1998 (Relevant Authorities and Relevant Persons) Order 2006 (SI 2006/2137) added the Environment Agency and Transport for London to the list of organisations which may apply for ASBOs. Any person (or employee of that person) who exercises a local housing authority's management functions pursuant to an agreement under the Housing Act 1985 s.27, (such as an Arms Length Management Organisation—ALMO) may discharge the authority's functions under the Crime and Disorder Act 1998 ss.1– 1E (the Local Authorities (Contracting Out of Anti-social Behaviour Order Functions) (England) Order 2007 SI 2007/1441). **3A–1514**

**Anti-social acts**

See s.1(1)(a) which refers to behaviour that has caused or was likely to cause harassment, alarm or distress. **3A–1515**

**Principal proceedings**

See s.1B(1). **3A–1516**

**Procedure**

Applications for relevant authorities or persons against whom ASBOs are sought to **3A–1517** be joined to the principal proceedings are made in accordance with CPR Pt 65. See CPR r.65.23 and the commentary thereto. Note that a person may only be joined if his or her "anti-social acts are material in relation to the principal proceedings" (s.1B(3C)). As ASBOs are civil and not criminal orders (*R. (McCann) v Manchester Crown Court* [2002] UKHL 39; [2003] 1 A.C. 787) it follows that hearsay evidence is admissible under the Civil Evidence Act 1995. See too *R. (on the application of W) v Acton Youth Court* [2005] EWHC 954 (Admin); May 19, 2005. However "the willingness of a civil court to admit hearsay evidence carries with it inherent dangers". Claimants should state, by convincing direct evidence, why it is not reasonable and practicable to produce the original makers of statements as witnesses. If statements involve multiple hearsay, the route by which the original statement came to the attention of the person attesting to it should be identified as far as practicable. When hearing such applications, it is better for judges to start their judgments with an analysis of the direct oral evidence received, and then to move onto the evidence of the absent named witnesses and anonymous witnesses. (See *Moat Housing Group South Ltd v Harris and Hartless* [2005] EWCA Civ 287; [2006] Q.B. 606; [2005] 3 W.L.R. 691; [2005] 4 All E.R. 1051.)

**Children**

**3A–1518** County courts do not now have jurisdiction to make ASBOs against children. The pilot scheme provided for by Anti-Social Behaviour Act 2003 (Commencement No.4) Order 2004 (SI 2004/2168) has lapsed.

* * * *

## Interim orders

**3A–1519** **1D.**—(1) This section applies where—

(a) an application is made for an anti-social behaviour order;

(b) an application is made for an order under section 1B;

(c) a request is made by the prosecution for an order under section 1C; or

(d) the court is minded to make an order under section 1C of its own motion.

(2) If, before determining the application or request, or before deciding whether to make an order under section 1C of its own motion, the court considers that it is just to make an order under this section pending the determination of that application or request or before making that decision, it may make such an order.

(3) An order under this section is an order which prohibits the defendant from doing anything described in the order.

(4) An order under this section—

(a) shall be for a fixed period;

(b) may be varied, renewed or discharged;

(c) shall, if it has not previously ceased to have effect, cease to have effect on the determination of the application or request mentioned in subsection (1), or on the court's making a decision as to whether or not to make an order under section 1C of its own motion.

(5) In relation to cases to which this section applies by virtue of paragraph (a) or (b) of subsection (1), subsection (6), (8) and (10) to (12) of section 1 apply for the purposes of the making and effect of orders under this section as they apply for the purposes of the making and effect of anti-social behaviour orders.

***Paragraph numbers marked with a "+" can be found online and on CD.***

(6) In relation to cases to which this section applies by virtue of paragraph (c) or (d) of subsection (1)—

(a) subsections (6) and (10) to (12) of section 1 apply for the purposes of the making and effect of orders under this section as they apply for the purposes of the making and effect of anti-social behaviour orders; and

(b) section 1CA applies for the purposes of the variation or discharge of an order under this section as it applies for the purposes of the variation or discharge of an order under section 1C.

*Note* —Section 1D was inserted by Police Reform Act 2002 s.65; amended by the Serious Organised Crime and Police Act 2005 s.139(6)– (9). **3A–1520**

**Interim ASBOs**

The court may make an interim ASBO if it considers that it is just to make such an order pending the determination of the main application. Interim ASBOs should be made for a fixed period, but may be varied, renewed or discharged. An interim ASBO obtained without notice to the defendant does not breach the right to a fair trial under ECHR art.6 (*R.(M) v Secretary of State for Constitutional Affairs* [2004] EWCA Civ 312; [2004] 1 W.L.R. 2298). **3A–1521**

## Consultation requirements

**1E.**—(1) This section applies to— **3A–1522**

(a) applications for an anti-social behaviour order; and

(b) applications for an order under section 1B.

(2) Before making an application to which this section applies, the council for a local government area shall consult the chief officer of police of the police force maintained for the police area within which that local government area lies.

(3) Before making an application to which this section applies, a chief officer of police shall consult the council for the local government area in which the person in relation to whom the application is to be made resides or appears to reside.

(4) Before making an application to which this section applies, a relevant authority other than a council for a local government area or a chief officer of police shall consult—

(a) the council for the local government area in which the person in relation to whom the application is to be made resides or appears to reside; and

(b) the chief officer of police of the police force maintained for the police area within which that local government area lies.

(5) Subsection (4)(a) does not apply if the relevant authority is a county council for a county in which there are no districts.

*Note* —Section 1E was inserted by Police Reform Act 2002 s.66 and amended by the Anti-Social Behaviour Act 2003 s.85. **3A–1523**

**A relevant authority**

See s.1(1A), namely the council for a local government area, a county council, the chief officer of police of any police force maintained for a police area, the chief constable of the British Transport Police Force, a social landlord who provides or manages **3A–1524** any houses or hostel which is registered under Housing Act 1996 s.1 or a housing action trust (see Housing Act 1988 s.62). The Crime and Disorder Act 1998 (Relevant Authorities and Relevant Persons) Order 2006 (SI 2006/2137) added the Environment Agency and Transport for London to the list of organisations which may apply for ASBOs. Any person (or employee of that person) who exercises a local housing authority's management functions pursuant to an agreement under the Housing Act 1985 s.27, (such as an Arms Length Management Organisation—ALMO) may discharge the authority's functions under the Crime and Disorder Act 1998 ss.1– 1E (the Local Authorities (Contracting Out of Anti-social Behaviour Order Functions) (England) Order 2007 SI 2007/1441). The Order imposes conditions whereby an authority may only make arrangements permitting a person to apply for an ASBO if the arrangements also provide that the person exercises the authority's functions in relation to consultation under s.1E.

**Consultation**

**3A–1525** In considering whether to impose an interim ASBO, the county court not only has the jurisdiction to consider whether the local authority has complied with the consultation requirements of s.1E, but is obliged to do so (*Manchester CC v M* [2006] EWCA Civ 423; March 20, 2006). See too *McC v Wigan MBC*, October 30, 2003, unrep. where the lead role in seeking ASBOs was taken by a management company, which, although solely owned by the council, was a separate entity to the council. As such, in the absence of authorisation form the council, it was not authorised to consult. It was also apparent that there was a lack of knowledge on the part of the tenancy relations manager about the Home Office Guidance and an unstructured approach to the process. However these failings did not result in a substantial failure to comply with the consultation requirements. The requirement for consultation between the police and local authority in s.1E is fulfilled by substantial compliance, even though there may not have been full compliance. Information had been exchanged before making the application.

In *Wareham v Purbeck DC* [2005] EWHC 358 (Admin); March 14, 2005; (2005) *The Times* March 28, the Divisional Court, dismissing an appeal by way of case stated, held that a failure to invite the proposed defendant to put his view at an anti-social behaviour case conference convened prior to the decision to apply for an ASBO does not amount to an infringement of any right under ECHR. The defendant had a full opportunity to put his case before the magistrates' court.

**3A–1526** *Note* —Serious Organised Crime and Police Act 2005 ss.142 and s.143 introduce new s.1F (contracting out of local authority functions) and 11 (special measures for witnesses). Drugs Act 2005 s.20 inserts new ss.1G and 1H (intervention orders).

## Homelessness Act 2002

**3A–1526.1** (2002 c.7)

Arrangement of Sections



**Paragraph numbers marked with a "+" denote content that is available on White Book on Westlaw UK or the Civil Procedure CD.**

***Paragraph numbers marked with a "+" can be found online and on CD.***

# Land Registration Act 2002

(2002 c.9) 3A–1552.1

ARRANGEMENT OF SECTIONS

PART 9



**Paragraph numbers marked with a "+" denote content that is available on White Book on Westlaw UK or the Civil Procedure CD.**

# Commonhold and Leasehold Reform Act 2002

(2002 c.15) 3A–1580

ARRANGEMENT OF SECTIONS



**Editorial introduction**

Chapter 5 of the Commonhold and Leasehold Reform Act 2002 makes a number of changes to the leasehold management provisions of the Landlord and Tenant Act 1985. It 3A–1581

- extends the definition of 'service charge' for the purposes of the 1985 Act to include any charge which is required to be paid under the terms of the lease to cover the costs of improvements;
- extends the jurisdiction of Leasehold Valuation Tribunals so that they can determine whether or not leaseholders are liable to pay service charges as well as the reasonableness of such charges;
- makes a number of changes to the existing requirements in the Landlord and Tenant Acts.1985 and 1987 covering the accounting and safeguarding of service charge monies. Under the Act service charge funds have to be held in separate designated trust accounts for each property or group of service charge payers. Leaseholders have a new right to withhold payment of further service charges if key requirements are not met;
- introduces a new concept of 'administration charge' covering charges which are required to be paid under leases for approvals, for the provision of information, as a result of a failure to pay rent or other charges on time, or as a result of a breach of a covenant or condition of a lease. It sets out a require-

HOUSING

***Paragraph numbers marked with a "+" can be found online and on CD.***

ment that administration charges must be reasonable. Lessees may challenge the liability to pay such charges, or their reasonableness, in Leasehold Valuation Tribunals;

- replaces Landlord and Tenant Act 1985 s.20 (which provides that landlords must consult leaseholders before carrying out works costing more than a prescribed sum which are recoverable through service charges) with a revised section. This extends the consultation requirements to include contracts for works or other services of more than 12 months duration, but with a power to exempt, by regulations, specified types of contract or in specified circumstances. It enables the consultation procedures to be prescribed by regulations and provides that LVTs (rather than county courts) may grant dispensation from the procedures in particular cases where they consider it reasonable to do so; and
- introduces a new requirement that ground rent is not payable unless it has been demanded by giving the tenant a prescribed notice, and prevents the application of any provisions of a lease relating to late or non-payment (e.g. additional charges) if the rent is paid within 30 days of the demand being issued. It also introduces additional restrictions on the commencement of forfeiture proceedings for breaches of covenants or conditions of a lease. It modifies Housing Act 1996 s.81 to prohibit the commencement of forfeiture proceedings, including the issue of a notice under Law of Property Act 1925 s.146, in respect of non-payment of service charges or administration charges unless the charge has been agreed or admitted by the tenant, or a court or a Leasehold Valuation Tribunal has determined that it is reasonable and due. It also prohibits the commencement of forfeiture proceedings for other breaches unless a court or Leasehold Valuation Tribunal has determined that a breach has occurred.

The amendments to Landlord and Tenant Act 1985 have now been incorporated into the main text.

#### Implementation and Transitional Provisions

3A–1582 See the Commonhold and Leasehold Reform Act 2002 (Commencement No.1, Savings and Transitional Provisions) (England) Order 2002 (SI 2002/1912) (c.58),the Commonhold and Leasehold Reform Act 2002 (Commencement No.1, Savings and Transitional Provisions) (Wales) Order 2002 (SI 2002/3012) (w.284) (c.96), the Commonhold and Leasehold Reform Act 2002 (Commencement No.2 and Savings) (England) Order 2003 (SI 2003/1986) (c.82) and the Commonhold and Leasehold Reform Act 2002 (Commencement No.2 and Savings) (Wales) Order 2004 (SI 2004/669) (w.62) (c.25).

### Administration charges

3A–1583 **158.** Schedule 11 (which makes provision about administration charges payable by tenants of dwellings) has effect.

#### Implementation

3A–1584 Section 158 and Sch.11 were brought into force, subject to savings, on September 30, 2003 in England and on March 30, 2004 in Wales by the Commonhold and Leasehold Reform Act 2002 (Commencement No.2 and Savings) (England) Order 2003 (SI 2003/1986) (c.82) and the Commonhold and Leasehold Reform Act 2002 (Commencement No.2 and Savings) (Wales) Order 2004 (SI 2004/669) (w.62) (c.25).

* * * *

## *GROUND RENT*

### Requirement to notify long leaseholders that rent is due

3A–1585 **166.**—(1) A tenant under a long lease of a dwelling is not liable to make a payment of rent under the lease unless the landlord has

*Paragraph numbers marked with a "+" can be found online and on CD.*

given him a notice relating to the payment; and the date on which he is liable to make the payment is that specified in the notice.

(2) The notice must specify—

(a) the amount of the payment,

(b) the date on which the tenant is liable to make it, and

(c) if different from that date, the date on which he would have been liable to make it in accordance with the lease,

and shall contain any such further information as may be prescribed.

(3) The date on which the tenant is liable to make the payment must not be—

(a) either less than 30 days or more than 60 days after the day on which the notice is given, or

(b) before that on which he would have been liable to make it in accordance with the lease.

(4) If the date on which the tenant is liable to make the payment is after that on which he would have been liable to make it in accordance with the lease, any provisions of the lease relating to non-payment or late payment of rent have effect accordingly.

(5) The notice—

(a) must be in the prescribed form, and

(b) may be sent by post.

(6) If the notice is sent by post, it must be addressed to a tenant at the dwelling unless he has notified the landlord in writing of a different address in England and Wales at which he wishes to be given notices under this section (in which case it must be addressed to him there).

(7) In this section "rent" does not include—

(a) a service charge (within the meaning of section 18(1) of the 1985 Act), or

(b) an administration charge (within the meaning of Part 1 of Schedule 11 to this Act).

(8) In this section "long lease of a dwelling" does not include—

(a) a tenancy to which Part 2 of the Landlord and Tenant Act 1954 (c.56) (business tenancies) applies,

(b) a tenancy of an agricultural holding within the meaning of the Agricultural Holdings Act 1986 (c.5) in relation to which that Act applies, or

(c) a farm business tenancy within the meaning of the Agricultural Tenancies Act 1995 (c.8).

(9) In this section—

"dwelling" has the same meaning as in the 1985 Act,

"landlord" and "tenant" have the same meanings as in Chapter 1 of this Part,

"long lease" has the meaning given by sections 76 and 77 of this Act, and

"prescribed" means prescribed by regulations made by the appropriate national authority.

**Implementation**

3A–1586 Section 166 was brought into force in so far as it confers power to make regulations on July 26, 2002 in England and on January 1, 2003 in Wales by the Commonhold and Leasehold Reform Act 2002 (Commencement No.1, Savings and Transitional Provisions) (England) Order 2002 (SI 2002/1912) (c.58) and the Commonhold and Leasehold Reform Act 2002 (Commencement No.1, Savings and Transitional Provisions) (Wales) Order 2002 (SI 2002/3012) (w.284) (c.96). It was brought fully into force in England on February 28, 2005 by the Commonhold and Leasehold Reform Act 2002 (Commencement No.5 and Saving and Transitional Provision) Order 2004 (SI 2004/3056) (c.127) and in Wales on May 31, 2005 by the Commonhold and Leasehold Reform Act 2002 (Commencement No.3 and Saving and Transitional Provision) (Wales) Order 2005 (SI 2005/1353) (w.101) (c.59).

**Editorial introduction**

3A–1587 Section 166(1) provides that a long lessee is not liable to make a payment of rent unless notice has been served. Section 166(2) provides that such a notice must specify the amount due, the date on which the lessee is liable to make the payment and, if different, the date on which the lessee would have been liable to make the payment in accordance with the lease. Section 166(2) is supplemented by the Landlord and Tenant (Notice of Rent) (England) Regulations 2004 (SI 2004/3096) and the Landlord and Tenant (Notice of Rent) (Wales) Regulations 2005 (SI 2005/1355) (w.103) which contain additional requirements, namely notes for both lessees and lessors. The content of the notes is set out in the Schedule to the Regulations, as part of the prescribed form of notice under s.166(1).

**Dwelling**

3A–1588 See Landlord and Tenant Act 1985 s.38.

**landlord, tenant, lease, tenancy**—see Landlord and Tenant Act 1985 s.36, para.3A–702+.

**regulations**—see the Landlord and Tenant (Notice of Rent) (England) Regulations 2004 (SI 2004/3096) and the Landlord and Tenant (Notice of Rent) (Wales) Regulations 2005 (SI 2005/1355) (w.103).

**long lease**—see s.76 which provides that a lease is a long lease if it (a) is granted for a term of years certain exceeding 21 years; (b) is for a term fixed by law under a grant with a covenant or obligation for perpetual renewal (c) takes effect under Law of Property Act 1925 s.149(6) (leases terminable after a death or marriage); (d) was granted under the right to buy provisions of Housing Act 1985 Pt 5; (e) is a shared ownership lease; or (f) under Housing Act 1996 s.17 (the right to acquire). Section 77 contains certain exceptions.

**administration charge**—see Sch.11, Pt 1.

*FORFEITURE OF LEASES OF DWELLINGS*

## Failure to pay small amount for short period

3A–1589 **167.**—(1) A landlord under a long lease of a dwelling may not exercise a right of re-entry or forfeiture for failure by a tenant to pay an amount consisting of rent, service charges or administration charges (or a combination of them) ("the unpaid amount") unless the unpaid amount—

(a) exceeds the prescribed sum, or

(b) consists of or includes an amount which has been payable for more than a prescribed period.

(2) The sum prescribed under subsection (1)(a) must not exceed £500.

(3) If the unpaid amount includes a default charge, it is to be treated for the purposes of subsection (1)(a) as reduced by the

*Paragraph numbers marked with a "+" can be found online and on CD.*

amount of the charge; and for this purpose "default charge" means an administration charge payable in respect of the tenant's failure to pay any part of the unpaid amount.

(4) In this section "long lease of a dwelling" does not include—

(a) a tenancy to which Part 2 of the Landlord and Tenant Act 1954 (c.56) (business tenancies) applies,

(b) a tenancy of an agricultural holding within the meaning of the Agricultural Holdings Act 1986 (c.5) in relation to which that Act applies, or

(c) a farm business tenancy within the meaning of the Agricultural Tenancies Act 1995 (c.8).

(5) In this section—

"administration charge" has the same meaning as in Part 1 of Schedule 11,

"dwelling" has the same meaning as in the 1985 Act,

"landlord" and "tenant" have the same meaning as in Chapter 1 of this Part,

"long lease" has the meaning given by sections 76 and 77 of this Act, except that a shared ownership lease is a long lease whatever the tenant's total share,

"prescribed" means prescribed by regulations made by the appropriate national authority, and

"service charge" has the meaning given by section 18(1) of the 1985 Act.

**Implementation**

Section 167 was brought into force in so far as it confers power to make regulations on July 26, 2002 in England and on January 1, 2003 in Wales by the Commonhold and Leasehold Reform Act 2002 (Commencement No.1, Savings and Transitional Provisions) (England) Order 2002 (SI 2002/1912) (c.58) and the Commonhold and Leasehold Reform Act 2002 (Commencement No.1, Savings and Transitional Provisions) (Wales) Order 2002 (SI 2002/3012) (w.284) (c.96). It was brought fully into force in England on February 28, 2005 by the Commonhold and Leasehold Reform Act 2002 (Commencement No.5 and Saving and Transitional Provision) Order 2004 (SI 2004/3056) (c.127) and in Wales on May 31, 2005 by the Commonhold and Leasehold Reform Act 2002 (Commencement No.3 and Saving and Transitional Provision) (Wales) Order 2005 (SI 2005/1353) (w.101) (c.59). **3A–1590**

**Editorial introduction**

Section 167(1) prevents a landlord under a long lease of a dwelling from exercising a right of re-entry or forfeiture for failure by a tenant to pay an amount consisting of rent, service charges or administration charges (or a combination of them) unless the unpaid amount exceeds the prescribed sum or consists of, or includes, an amount which has been payable for more than a prescribed period. The Rights of Re-entry and Forfeiture (Prescribed Sum and Period) (England) Regulations 2004 (SI 2004/3086), and the Rights of Re-entry and Forfeiture (Prescribed Sum and Period) (Wales) Regulations 2005 (SI 2005/1352) (w.100), which prescribe the sum of £350 and a period of three years. **3A–1591**

**"service charges"**

See Landlord and Tenant Act 1985 s.18 as amended by Commonhold and Leasehold Reform Act 2002 Sch.9.. **3A–1592**

**administration charge**—see Sch.11, Pt 1.

**dwelling**—see Landlord and Tenant Act 1985 s.38.

**landlord, tenant, lease, tenancy**—see Landlord and Tenant Act 1985 s.36.

***Paragraph numbers marked with a "+" can be found online and on CD.***

**regulations**—See the Rights of Re-entry and Forfeiture (Prescribed Sum and Period) (England) Regulations 2004 (SI 2004/3086) and the Rights of Re-entry and Forfeiture (Prescribed Sum and Period) (Wales) Regulations 2005 (SI 2005/1352) (w.100).

**long lease**—see s.76 which provides that a lease is a long lease if it (a) is granted for a term of years certain exceeding 21 years; (b) is for a term fixed by law under a grant with a covenant or obligation for perpetual renewal (c) takes effect under Law of Property Act 1925 s.149(6) (leases terminable after a death or marriage); (d) was granted under the right to buy provisions of Housing Act 1985 Pt 5; (e) is a shared ownership lease; or (f) under Housing Act 1996 s.17 (the right to acquire). Section 77 contains certain exceptions.

## No forfeiture notice before determination of breach

3A–1593 **168.**—(1) A landlord under a long lease of a dwelling may not serve a notice under section 146(1) of the Law of Property Act 1925 (c.20) (restriction on forfeiture) in respect of a breach by a tenant of a covenant or condition in the lease unless subsection (2) is satisfied.

(2) This subsection is satisfied if—

(a) it has been finally determined on an application under subsection (4) that the breach has occurred,

(b) the tenant has admitted the breach, or

(c) a court in any proceedings, or an arbitral tribunal in proceedings pursuant to a post-dispute arbitration agreement, has finally determined that the breach has occurred.

(3) But a notice may not be served by virtue of subsection (2)(a) or (c) until after the end of the period of 14 days beginning with the day after that on which the final determination is made.

(4) A landlord under a long lease of a dwelling may make an application to a leasehold valuation tribunal for a determination that a breach of a covenant or condition in the lease has occurred.

(5) But a landlord may not make an application under subsection (4) in respect of a matter which—

(a) has been, or is to be, referred to arbitration pursuant to a post-dispute arbitration agreement to which the tenant is a party,

(b) has been the subject of determination by a court, or

(c) has been the subject of determination by an arbitral tribunal pursuant to a post-dispute arbitration agreement.

3A–1594 **implementation**—This section was brought into force in England on February 28, 2005 by the Commonhold and Leasehold Reform Act 2002 (Commencement No.5 and Saving and Transitional Provision) Order 2004 (SI 2004/3056) (c.127) and in Wales on May 31, 2005 by the Commonhold and Leasehold Reform Act 2002 (Commencement No.3 and Saving and Transitional Provision) (Wales) Order 2005 (SI 2005/1353) (w.101) (c.59).

**dwelling**—see Landlord and Tenant Act 1985 s.38.

**landlord, tenant, lease, tenancy**—see Landlord and Tenant Act 1985 s.36, para.3A–702+.

**long lease**—see s.169 and s.76 which provides that a lease is a long lease if it (a) is granted for a term of years certain exceeding 21 years; (b) is for a term fixed by law under a grant with a covenant or obligation for perpetual renewal (c) takes effect under Law of Property Act 1925 s.149(6) (leases terminable after a death or marriage); (d) was granted under the right to buy provisions of Housing Act 1985 Pt 5; (e) is a

*Paragraph numbers marked with a "+" can be found online and on CD.*

shared ownership lease; or (f) under Housing Act 1996 s.17 (the right to acquire). Section 77 contains certain exceptions.

**arbitration agreement, arbitral tribunal**—see s.169(5) and Arbitration Act 1996 Pt 1.

**post-dispute arbitration agreement**—see s.169(5). It means an arbitration agreement made after a breach has occurred (or is alleged to have occurred).

## Section 168: supplementary

**169.**—(1) An agreement by a tenant under a long lease of a dwelling (other than a post-dispute arbitration agreement) is void in so far as it purports to provide for a determination— **3A–1595**

(a) in a particular manner, or

(b) on particular evidence,

of any question which may be the subject of an application under section 168(4).

(2) For the purposes of section 168 it is finally determined that a breach of a covenant or condition in a lease has occurred—

(a) if a decision that it has occurred is not appealed against or otherwise challenged, at the end of the period for bringing an appeal or other challenge, or

(b) if such a decision is appealed against or otherwise challenged and not set aside in consequence of the appeal or other challenge, at the time specified in subsection (3).

(3) The time referred to in subsection (2)(b) is the time when the appeal or other challenge is disposed of—

(a) by the determination of the appeal or other challenge and the expiry of the time for bringing a subsequent appeal (if any), or

(b) by its being abandoned or otherwise ceasing to have effect.

(4) In section 168 and this section "long lease of a dwelling" does not include—

(a) a tenancy to which Part 2 of the Landlord and Tenant Act 1954 (c.56) (business tenancies) applies,

(b) a tenancy of an agricultural holding within the meaning of the Agricultural Holdings Act 1986 (c.5) in relation to which that Act applies, or

(c) a farm business tenancy within the meaning of the Agricultural Tenancies Act 1995 (c.8).

(5) In section 168 and this section—

"arbitration agreement" and "arbitral tribunal" have the same meaning as in Part 1 of the Arbitration Act 1996 (c.23) and "post-dispute arbitration agreement", in relation to any breach (or alleged breach), means an arbitration agreement made after the breach has occurred (or is alleged to have occurred),

"dwelling" has the same meaning as in the 1985 Act,

"landlord" and "tenant" have the same meaning as in Chapter 1 of this Part, and

"long lease" has the meaning given by sections 76 and 77 of this

Act, except that a shared ownership lease is a long lease whatever the tenant's total share.

(6) Section 146(7) of the Law of Property Act 1925 (c.20) applies for the purposes of section 168 and this section.

(7) Nothing in section 168 affects the service of a notice under section 146(1) of the Law of Property Act 1925 in respect of a failure to pay—

(a) a service charge (within the meaning of section 18(1) of the 1985 Act), or

(b) an administration charge (within the meaning of Part 1 of Schedule 11 to this Act).

3A–1596 **implementation**—This section was brought into force in England on February 28, 2005 by the Commonhold and Leasehold Reform Act 2002 (Commencement No.5 and Saving and Transitional Provision) Order 2004 (SI 2004/3056) (c.127) and in Wales on May 31, 2005 by the Commonhold and Leasehold Reform Act 2002 (Commencement No.3 and Saving and Transitional Provision) (Wales) Order 2005 (SI 2005/1353) (w.101) (c.59).

**dwelling**—see Landlord and Tenant Act 1985 s.38.

**service charges**—see Landlord and Tenant Act 1985 s.18 as amended by Commonhold and Leasehold Reform Act 2002 Sch.9.

**landlord, tenant, lease, tenancy**—see Landlord and Tenant Act 1985 s.36, para.3A–702+.

**administration charge**—see Sch.11, Pt 1.

* * * *

## Power to prescribe additional or different requirements

3A–1597 **171.**—(1) The appropriate national authority may by regulations prescribe requirements which must be met before a right of re-entry or forfeiture may be exercised in relation to a breach of a covenant or condition in a long lease of an unmortgaged dwelling.

(2) The regulations may specify that the requirements are to be in addition to, or instead of, requirements imposed otherwise than by the regulations.

(3) In this section "long lease of a dwelling" does not include—

(a) a tenancy to which Part 2 of the Landlord and Tenant Act 1954 (c.56) (business tenancies) applies,

(b) a tenancy of an agricultural holding within the meaning of the Agricultural Holdings Act 1986 (c.5) in relation to which that Act applies, or

(c) a farm business tenancy within the meaning of the Agricultural Tenancies Act 1995 (c.8).

(4) For the purposes of this section a dwelling is unmortgaged if it is not subject to a mortgage, charge or lien.

(5) In this section—

"dwelling" has the same meaning as in the 1985 Act, and

"long lease" has the meaning given by sections 76 and 77 of this Act, except that a shared ownership lease is a long lease whatever the tenant's total share.

### Implementation

3A–1598 Section 171 was brought into force in so far as it confers power to make regulations

*Paragraph numbers marked with a "+" can be found online and on CD.*

on July 26, 2002 in England and on January 1, 2003 in Wales by the Commonhold and Leasehold Reform Act 2002 (Commencement No.1, Savings and Transitional Provisions) (England) Order 2002 (SI 2002/1912) (c.58) and the Commonhold and Leasehold Reform Act 2002 (Commencement No.1, Savings and Transitional Provisions) (Wales) Order 2002 (SI 2002/3012) (w.284) (c.96). It was brought fully into force in England on February 28, 2005 by the Commonhold and Leasehold Reform Act 2002 (Commencement No.5 and Saving and Transitional Provision) Order 2004 (SI 2004/3056) (c.127).

**"regulations"**

At present, there are no regulations. **3A–1599**

**dwelling**—see Landlord and Tenant Act 1985 s.38.

**long lease**—see s.76 which provides that a lease is a long lease if it (a) is granted for a term of years certain exceeding 21 years; (b) is for a term fixed by law under a grant with a covenant or obligation for perpetual renewal (c) takes effect under Law of Property Act 1925 s.149(6) (leases terminable after a death or marriage); (d) was granted under the right to buy provisions of Housing Act 1985 Pt 5; (e) is a shared ownership lease; or (f) under Housing Act 1996 s.17 (the right to acquire). Section 77 contains certain exceptions.

## *CROWN APPLICATION*

## Application to Crown

**172.**—(1) The following provisions apply in relation to Crown land (as in relation to other land)— **3A–1600**

(a) sections 18 to 30B of (and the Schedule to) the 1985 Act (service charges, insurance and managing agents),

[...]

(d) sections 46 to 49 of the 1987 Act (information to be furnished to tenants),

[...]

(f) section 81 of the Housing Act 1996 (c.52) (restriction on termination of tenancy for failure to pay service charge etc.),

(g) section 84 of (and Schedule 4 to) that Act (right to appoint surveyor), and

(h) in this Chapter, the provisions relating to any of the provisions within paragraphs (a) to (g), Part 1 of Schedule 11 and sections 164 to 171.

(2) Land is Crown land if there is or has at any time been an interest or estate in the land—

(a) comprised in the Crown Estate,

(b) belonging to Her Majesty in right of the Duchy of Lancaster,

(c) belonging to the Duchy of Cornwall, or

(d) belonging to a government department or held on behalf of Her Majesty for the purposes of a government department.

(3) No failure by the Crown to perform a duty imposed by or by virtue of any of sections 21 to 23A of, or any of paragraphs 2 to 4A of the Schedule to, the 1985 Act makes the Crown criminally liable; but the High Court may declare any such failure without reasonable excuse to be unlawful.

*Paragraph numbers marked with a "+" can be found online and on CD.*

**Implementation**

3A-1601 Section 172 was partially brought into force, on 30 September 2003 in England and on March 30, 2004 in Wales by the Commonhold and Leasehold Reform Act 2002 (Commencement No.2 and Savings) (England) Order 2003 (SI 2003/1986) (c.82) and the Commonhold and Leasehold Reform Act 2002 (Commencement No.2 and Savings) (Wales) Order 2004 (SI 2004/669) (w.62) (c.25). See too the Commonhold and Leasehold Reform Act 2002 (Commencement No.5 and Saving and Transitional Provision) Order 2004 (SI 2004/3056) (c.127).

* * * *

## SCHEDULE 11

### ADMINISTRATION CHARGES

*Part 1 Reasonableness of Administration Charges*

*Meaning of "administration charge"*

3A-1602 1.—(1) In this Part of this Schedule "administration charge" means an amount payable by a tenant of a dwelling as part of or in addition to the rent which is payable, directly or indirectly—

(a) for or in connection with the grant of approvals under his lease, or applications for such approvals,

(b) for or in connection with the provision of information or documents by or on behalf of the landlord or a person who is party to his lease otherwise than as landlord or tenant,

(c) in respect of a failure by the tenant to make a payment by the due date to the landlord or a person who is party to his lease otherwise than as landlord or tenant, or

(d) in connection with a breach (or alleged breach) of a covenant or condition in his lease.

(2) But an amount payable by the tenant of a dwelling the rent of which is registered under Part 4 of the Rent Act 1977 (c.42) is not an administration charge, unless the amount registered is entered as a variable amount in pursuance of section 71(4) of that Act.

(3) In this Part of this Schedule "variable administration charge" means an administration charge payable by a tenant which is neither—

(a) specified in his lease, nor

(b) calculated in accordance with a formula specified in his lease.

(4) An order amending sub-paragraph (1) may be made by the appropriate national authority.

*Reasonableness of administration charges*

3A-1603 2. A variable administration charge is payable only to the extent that the amount of the charge is reasonable.

3A-1604 3.—(1) Any party to a lease of a dwelling may apply to a leasehold valuation tribunal for an order varying the lease in such manner as is specified in the application on the grounds that—

(a) any administration charge specified in the lease is unreasonable, or

(b) any formula specified in the lease in accordance with which any administration charge is calculated is unreasonable.

(2) If the grounds on which the application was made are established to the satisfaction of the tribunal, it may make an order varying the lease in such manner as is specified in the order.

(3) The variation specified in the order may be—

(a) the variation specified in the application, or

(b) such other variation as the tribunal thinks fit.

(4) The tribunal may, instead of making an order varying the lease in such manner

as is specified in the order, make an order directing the parties to the lease to vary it in such manner as is so specified.

(5) The tribunal may by order direct that a memorandum of any variation of a lease effected by virtue of this paragraph be endorsed on such documents as are specified in the order.

(6) Any such variation of a lease shall be binding not only on the parties to the lease for the time being but also on other persons (including any predecessors in title), whether or not they were parties to the proceedings in which the order was made.

*Notice in connection with demands for administration charges*

4.—(1) A demand for the payment of an administration charge must be accompanied by a summary of the rights and obligations of tenants of dwellings in relation to administration charges. **3A–1605**

(2) The appropriate national authority may make regulations prescribing requirements as to the form and content of such summaries of rights and obligations.

(3) A tenant may withhold payment of an administration charge which has been demanded from him if sub-paragraph (1) is not complied with in relation to the demand.

(4) Where a tenant withholds an administration charge under this paragraph, any provisions of the lease relating to non-payment or late payment of administration charges do not have effect in relation to the period for which he so withholds it.

*Liability to pay administration charges*

5.—(1) An application may be made to a leasehold valuation tribunal for a determination whether an administration charge is payable and, if it is, as to— **3A–1606**

(a) the person by whom it is payable,
(b) the person to whom it is payable,
(c) the amount which is payable,
(d) the date at or by which it is payable, and
(e) the manner in which it is payable.

(2) Sub-paragraph (1) applies whether or not any payment has been made.

(3) The jurisdiction conferred on a leasehold valuation tribunal in respect of any matter by virtue of sub-paragraph (1) is in addition to any jurisdiction of a court in respect of the matter.

(4) No application under sub-paragraph (1) may be made in respect of a matter which—

(a) has been agreed or admitted by the tenant,
(b) has been, or is to be, referred to arbitration pursuant to a post-dispute arbitration agreement to which the tenant is a party,
(c) has been the subject of determination by a court, or
(d) has been the subject of determination by an arbitral tribunal pursuant to a post-dispute arbitration agreement.

(5) But the tenant is not to be taken to have agreed or admitted any matter by reason only of having made any payment.

(6) An agreement by the tenant of a dwelling (other than a post-dispute arbitration agreement) is void in so far as it purports to provide for a determination—

(a) in a particular manner, or
(b) on particular evidence,

of any question which may be the subject matter of an application under sub-paragraph (1).

*Interpretation*

6.—(1) This paragraph applies for the purposes of this Part of this Schedule. **3A–1607**

(2) "Tenant" includes a statutory tenant.

(3) "Dwelling" and "statutory tenant" (and "landlord" in relation to a statutory tenant) have the same meanings as in the 1985 Act.

(4) "Post-dispute arbitration agreement", in relation to any matter, means an arbitration agreement made after a dispute about the matter has arisen.

***Paragraph numbers marked with a "+" can be found online and on CD.***

(5) "Arbitration agreement" and "arbitral tribunal" have the same meanings as in Part 1 of the Arbitration Act 1996 (c.23).

## Asylum and Immigration (Treatment of Claimants, etc.) Act 2004

3A–1607.1 (2004 c.19)

ARRANGEMENT OF SECTIONS



**Paragraph numbers marked with a "+" denote content that is available on White Book on Westlaw UK or the Civil Procedure CD.**

## Housing Act 2004

3A–1611 (2004 c.34)

ARRANGEMENT OF SECTIONS

CHAPTER 4

TENANCY DEPOSIT SCHEMES



### CHAPTER 4

### TENANCY DEPOSIT SCHEMES

## Tenancy deposit schemes

3A–1612 **212.**—(1) The appropriate national authority must make arrangements for securing that one or more tenancy deposit schemes are available for the purpose of safeguarding tenancy deposits paid in connection with shorthold tenancies.

(2) For the purposes of this Chapter a "tenancy deposit scheme" is a scheme which—

(a) is made for the purpose of safeguarding tenancy deposits paid in connection with shorthold tenancies and facilitating the resolution of disputes arising in connection with such deposits, and

(b) complies with the requirements of Schedule 10.

(3) Arrangements under subsection (1) must be arrangements made with any body or person under which the body or person ("the scheme administrator") undertakes to establish and maintain a tenancy deposit scheme of a description specified in the arrangements.

***Paragraph numbers marked with a "+" can be found online and on CD.***

(4) The appropriate national authority may—

(a) give financial assistance to the scheme administrator;

(b) make payments to the scheme administrator (otherwise than as financial assistance) in pursuance of arrangements under subsection (1).

(5) The appropriate national authority may, in such manner and on such terms as it thinks fit, guarantee the discharge of any financial obligation incurred by the scheme administrator in connection with arrangements under subsection (1).

(6) Arrangements under subsection (1) must require the scheme administrator to give the appropriate national authority, in such manner and at such times as it may specify, such information and facilities for obtaining information as it may specify.

(7) The appropriate national authority may make regulations conferring or imposing—

(a) on scheme administrators, or

(b) on scheme administrators of any description specified in the regulations,

such powers or duties in connection with arrangements under subsection (1) as are so specified.

(8) In this Chapter—

"authorised", in relation to a tenancy deposit scheme, means that the scheme is in force in accordance with arrangements under subsection (1);

"custodial scheme" and "insurance scheme" have the meaning given by paragraph 1(2) and (3) of Schedule 10);

"money" means money in the form of cash or otherwise;

"shorthold tenancy" means an assured shorthold tenancy within the meaning of Chapter 2 of Part 1 of the Housing Act 1988 (c. 50);

"tenancy deposit", in relation to a shorthold tenancy, means any money intended to be held (by the landlord or otherwise) as security for–

(a) the performance of any obligations of the tenant, or

(b) the discharge of any liability of his, arising under or in connection with the tenancy.

(9) In this Chapter—

(a) references to a landlord or landlords in relation to any shorthold tenancy or tenancies include references to a person or persons acting on his or their behalf in relation to the tenancy or tenancies, and

(b) references to a tenancy deposit being held in accordance with a scheme include, in the case of a custodial scheme, references to an amount representing the deposit being held in accordance with the scheme.

3A-1613 *Note*—Brought into force on April 6, 2007, in relation to England by SI 2007/1068 and in relation to Wales by SI 2007/305.

**Editorial introduction**

3A–1614 Tenancy deposit schemes have two main purposes. They aim to safeguard tenancy deposits paid in connection with assured shorthold tenancies and to facilitate the resolution of disputes arising in connection with such deposits. All authorised tenancy deposit schemes must comply with the requirements of Sch.10. Schemes are expected to be self-financing, but s.212(4) allows the appropriate national authority to give financial assistance. Tenancy deposit schemes must be either a custodial scheme or an insurance scheme (Sch.10, para.1(1)). Landlords may choose with which type of scheme to comply. A custodial scheme requires a landlord to pay any deposit money received to a scheme administrator, who is to keep the money in a separate account until the end of the tenancy when it will be returned to the landlord or the tenant, as appropriate. An insurance scheme allows a landlord to retain the deposit during the tenancy. At its end, if the tenant disputes any amount of the deposit that the landlord proposes to retain, the landlord must pay the disputed amount into an account held by the scheme administrator, who will hold it until the dispute is resolved. If the landlord has opted for this scheme, the scheme administrator is obliged to pay the tenant any sum that he is entitled to recover following the determination of the dispute, whether or not the landlord complies with his obligation to pay that amount into the scheme. Accordingly, the scheme administrator must maintain insurance to cover any failure by the landlord to do so, contributions towards the cost of which may be passed on to those landlords who opt for this approach as part of the administrators' costs (Sch.10, paras 5–8).

The primary sanction for non-compliance with the scheme is that landlords may not serve the Housing Act 1988 s.21 notices at any time where a deposit is not being safeguarded in accordance with an authorised scheme or where either the initial requirements of the scheme have not been met or the prescribed information regarding the safeguarding the deposit has not been given. See s.215 below. In addition tenants are entitled to claim a sum equivalent to three times the amount of the deposit from a defaulting landlord—see s.214 below.

**Tenancy deposit**

3A–1615 See s.212(8).

**Shorthold tenancy**

3A–1616 See s.212(8) and (9) and Housing Act 1988 s.19.

**"regulations"**

3A–1617 See Housing (Tenancy Deposit Schemes) Order 2007 (SI 2007/796), Housing (Tenancy Deposits) (Prescribed Information) Order 2007 (SI 2007/797) and Housing (Tenancy Deposits) (Specified Interest Rate) Order 2007 (SI 2007/798).

## Requirements relating to tenancy deposits

3A–1618 **213.**—(1) Any tenancy deposit paid to a person in connection with a shorthold tenancy must, as from the time when it is received, be dealt with in accordance with an authorised scheme.

(2) No person may require the payment of a tenancy deposit in connection with a shorthold tenancy which is not to be subject to the requirement in subsection (1).

(3) Where a landlord receives a tenancy deposit in connection with a shorthold tenancy, the initial requirements of an authorised scheme must be complied with by the landlord in relation to the deposit within the period of 14 days beginning with the date on which it is received.

(4) For the purposes of this section "the initial requirements" of an authorised scheme are such requirements imposed by the scheme as fall to be complied with by a landlord on receiving such a tenancy deposit.

(5) A landlord who has received such a tenancy deposit must give the tenant and any relevant person such information relating to—

(a) the authorised scheme applying to the deposit,

(b) compliance by the landlord with the initial requirements of the scheme in relation to the deposit, and

(c) the operation of provisions of this Chapter in relation to the deposit,

as may be prescribed.

(6) The information required by subsection (5) must be given to the tenant and any relevant person—

(a) in the prescribed form or in a form substantially to the same effect, and

(b) within the period of 14 days beginning with the date on which the deposit is received by the landlord.

(7) No person may, in connection with a shorthold tenancy, require a deposit which consists of property other than money.

(8) In subsection (7) "deposit" means a transfer of property intended to be held (by the landlord or otherwise) as security for—

(a) the performance of any obligations of the tenant, or

(b) the discharge of any liability of his, arising under or in connection with the tenancy.

(9) The provisions of this section apply despite any agreement to the contrary.

(10) In this section—

"prescribed" means prescribed by an order made by the appropriate national authority;

"property" means moveable property;

"relevant person" means any person who, in accordance with arrangements made with the tenant, paid the deposit on behalf of the tenant.

*Note* —Brought into force on April 6, 2007, in relation to England by SI 2007/1068 and in relation to Wales by SI 2007/305. **3A–1619**

**"tenancy deposit"**

See s.212(8). **3A–1620**

**"authorised"**

See s.212(8). **3A–1620.1**

**"prescribed"**

See s.213(10) and the Housing (Tenancy Deposits) (Prescribed Information) Order 2007 (SI 2007/797). **3A–1620.2**

**"shorthold tenancy"**

See s.212(8) and (9) and Housing Act 1988 s.19. **3A–1621**

## Proceedings relating to tenancy deposits

**214.**—(1) Where a tenancy deposit has been paid in connection with a shorthold tenancy, the tenant or any relevant person (as defined by section 213(10)) may make an application to a county court on the grounds— **3A–1622**

(a) that the initial requirements of an authorised scheme (see section 213(4)) have not, or section 213(6)(a) has not, been complied with in relation to the deposit; or

(b) that he has been notified by the landlord that a particular authorised scheme applies to the deposit but has been unable to obtain confirmation from the scheme administrator that the deposit is being held in accordance with the scheme.

(2) Subsections (3) and (4) apply if on such an application the court—

(a) is satisfied that those requirements have not, or section 213(6)(a) has not, been complied with in relation to the deposit, or

(b) is not satisfied that the deposit is being held in accordance with an authorised scheme,

as the case may be.

(3) The court must, as it thinks fit, either—

(a) order the person who appears to the court to be holding the deposit to repay it to the applicant, or

(b) order that person to pay the deposit into the designated account held by the scheme administrator under an authorised custodial scheme,

within the period of 14 days beginning with the date of the making of the order.

(4) The court must also order the landlord to pay to the applicant a sum of money equal to three times the amount of the deposit within the period of 14 days beginning with the date of the making of the order.

(5) Where any deposit given in connection with a shorthold tenancy could not be lawfully required as a result of section 213(7), the property in question is recoverable from the person holding it by the person by whom it was given as a deposit.

(6) In subsection (5) "deposit" has the meaning given by section 213(8).

3A–1623 *Note* —Brought into force on April 6, 2007, in relation to England bySI 2007/1068 and in relation to Wales by SI 2007/305.

**"tenancy deposit"**

3A–1624 See s.212(8).

**"relevant person"**

3A–1625 See s.213(10).

**"shorthold tenancy"**

3A–1626 See s.212(8) and (9) and Housing Act 1988 s.19.

**"authorised scheme"**

3A–1627 See s.213(4).

**Procedure**

3A–1627.1 Any application by a tenant for an order for repayment of the deposit, or an order for it to be paid into a designated account under a custodial scheme and for an order

*Paragraph numbers marked with a "+" can be found online and on CD.*

that the landlord pay a sum equivalent to three times the amount of the deposit should be started in the county court for the district in which the land is situated in accordance with CPR Pt 56. See s.214(1) and the commentary to CPR Pt 56.

**Proceedings relating to tenancy deposits**

See in general the editorial introduction above. It appears that if landlords fail to comply with the requirements of s.213, courts have no discretion and must make orders sought under s.214. However, it has been held in the county court that provision of prescribed information outside the fourteen days required by s.213(5) and (6) does not trigger the right to a sum equivalent to three times the deposit, if the information is supplied before any application is made. (*Harvey v Bamforth* Sheffield County Court, August 8, 2008, November 2008 *Legal Action* 18). **3A–1627.2**

## Sanctions for non-compliance

**215.**—(1) If a tenancy deposit has been paid in connection with a shorthold tenancy, no section 21 notice may be given in relation to the tenancy at a time when— **3A–1628**

(a) the deposit is not being held in accordance with an authorised scheme, or

(b) the initial requirements of such a scheme (see section 213(4)) have not been complied with in relation to the deposit.

(2) If section 213(6) is not complied with in relation to a deposit given in connection with a shorthold tenancy, no section 21 notice may be given in relation to the tenancy until such time as section 213(6)(a) is complied with.

(3) If any deposit given in connection with a shorthold tenancy could not be lawfully required as a result of section 213(7), no section 21 notice may be given in relation to the tenancy until such time as the property in question is returned to the person by whom it was given as a deposit.

(4) In subsection (3) "deposit" has the meaning given by section 213(8).

(5) In this section a "section 21 notice" means a notice under section 21(1)(b) or (4)(a) of the Housing Act 1988 (recovery of possession on termination of shorthold tenancy).

*Note* —Brought into force on April 6, 2007, in relation to England by SI 2007/1068 and in relation to Wales by SI 2007/305. **3A–1629**

Landlords may not serve notices under Housing Act 1988 s.21 at any time where a deposit is not being safeguarded in accordance with an authorised scheme or where either the initial requirements of the scheme have not been met or the prescribed information regarding the safeguarding the deposit has not been given. **3A–1630**

**"tenancy deposit"**

See s.212(8). **3A–1631**

**"shorthold tenancy"**

See s.212(8) and (9) and Housing Act 1988 s.19. **3A–1632**

**"section 21 notice"**

See Housing Act 1988 s.21 at 3A–889 and commentary at 3A–896. **3A–1632.1**

**"authorised scheme"**

See s.213(4). **3A–1633**

***Paragraph numbers marked with a "+" can be found online and on CD.***

* * * *

SECTION 212

## SCHEDULE 10

### PROVISIONS RELATING TO TENANCY DEPOSIT SCHEMES

*Schemes to be custodial schemes or insurance schemes*

3A-1634 1.—(1)A tenancy deposit scheme must be either—

(a) a custodial scheme, or

(b) an insurance scheme.

(2) A "custodial scheme" is a scheme under which—

(a) tenancy deposits in connection with shorthold tenancies are paid to the landlords under the tenancies,

(b) amounts representing the deposits are then paid by the landlords into a designated account held by the scheme administrator, and

(c) those amounts are kept by the scheme administrator in that account until such time as, in accordance with the scheme, they fall to be paid (wholly or in part) to the landlords or tenants under the tenancies.

(3) An "insurance scheme" is a scheme under which—

(a) tenancy deposits in connection with shorthold tenancies are paid to the landlords under the tenancies,

(b) such deposits are retained by the landlords on the basis that, at the end of the tenancies—

(i) such amounts in respect of the deposits as are agreed between the tenants and the landlords will be repaid to the tenants, and

(ii) such amounts as the tenants request to be repaid to them and which are not so repaid will, in accordance with directions given by the scheme administrator, be paid into a designated account held by the scheme administrator,

(c) amounts paid into that account are kept by the scheme administrator in the account until such time as, in accordance with the scheme, they fall to be paid (wholly or in part) to the landlords or tenants under the tenancies,

(d) landlords undertake to reimburse the scheme administrator, in accordance with directions given by him, in respect of any amounts in respect of the deposits paid to the tenants by the scheme administrator (other than amounts paid to the tenants as mentioned in paragraph (c)), and

(e) insurance is maintained by the scheme administrator in respect of failures by landlords to comply with such directions.

*Provisions applying to custodial and insurance schemes*

3A-1635 2.—(1)A custodial scheme must conform with the following provisions—

paragraphs 3 to 4C, and

paragraphs 9 to 10C.

(2) An insurance scheme must conform with the following provisions—

paragraphs 5 to 8, and

paragraphs 9 and 10.

*Custodial schemes: general*

3A-1636 3.—(1)This paragraph applies to a custodial scheme.

(2) The scheme must provide for any landlord who receives a tenancy deposit in connection with a shorthold tenancy to pay an amount equal to the deposit into a designated account held by the scheme administrator.

(3) The designated account must not contain anything other than amounts paid into it as mentioned in sub-paragraph (2) and any interest accruing on such amounts.

***Paragraph numbers marked with a "+" can be found online and on CD.***

(4) Subject to sub-paragraph (5), the scheme administrator may retain any interest accruing on such amounts.

(5) The relevant arrangements under section 212(1) may provide for any amount paid in accordance with paragraph 4 or 4C to be paid with interest—

(a) in respect of the period during which the relevant amount has remained in the designated account, and

(b) at such rate as the appropriate national authority may specify by order.

(6) With the exception of any interest retained in accordance with sub-paragraph (4), nothing contained in the designated account may be used to fund the administration of the scheme.

(7) In this paragraph "the relevant amount", in relation to a tenancy deposit, means the amount paid into the designated account in respect of the deposit.

*Custodial schemes: termination of tenancies*

4.—(1)A custodial scheme must make provision— **3A–1637**

(a) for enabling the tenant and the landlord under a shorthold tenancy in connection with which a tenancy deposit is held in accordance with the scheme to apply, at any time after the tenancy has ended, for the whole or part of the relevant amount to be paid to him, and

(b) for such an application to be dealt with by the scheme administrator in accordance with the following provisions of this paragraph.

(2) Sub-paragraph (3) applies where the tenant and the landlord notify the scheme administrator that they have agreed that the relevant amount should be paid—

(a) wholly to one of them, or

(b) partly to the one and partly to the other.

(3) If, having received such a notification, the scheme administrator is satisfied that the tenant and the landlord have so agreed, the scheme administrator must arrange for the relevant amount to be paid, in accordance with the agreement, within the period of 10 days beginning with the date on which the notification is received by the scheme administrator.

(4) Sub-paragraph (5) applies where the tenant or the landlord notifies the scheme administrator that—

(a) a court has decided that the relevant amount is payable either wholly to one of them or partly to the one and partly to the other, and

(b) that decision has become final.

(4A) Sub-paragraph (5) also applies where the tenant or the landlord notifies the scheme administrator that a person acting as an adjudicator under the provision made under paragraph 10 has made a binding decision that the relevant amount is payable either wholly to one of them or partly to one and partly to the other.

(5) If, having received a notification as mentioned in sub-paragraph (4) or (4A), the scheme administrator is satisfied as to the matters mentioned in that sub-paragraph, the scheme administrator must arrange for the relevant amount to be paid, in accordance with the decision, within the period of 10 days beginning with the date on which the notification is received by the scheme administrator.

(6) For the purposes of this Schedule a decision becomes final—

(a) if not appealed against, at the end of the period for bringing an appeal, or

(b) if appealed against, at the time when the appeal (or any further appeal) is disposed of.

(7) An appeal is disposed of—

(a) if it is determined and the period for bringing any further appeal has ended, or

(b) if it is abandoned or otherwise ceases to have effect.

(8) In this paragraph "the relevant amount" has the meaning given by paragraph 3(7).

*Custodial schemes: termination of tenancies—absent or un-cooperative landlord or tenant*

4A.—(1) The provision made by a custodial scheme for the purposes of paragraph 4(1) in relation to the treatment of the relevant amount at the end of a tenancy must include provision— **3A–1638**

(a) for enabling the landlord, if he considers that the conditions set out in sub-paragraph (2) are met, to apply to the scheme administrator for the whole or a specified part of the relevant amount ("the amount claimed") to be paid to him; and

(b) for such an application to be dealt with by the scheme administrator in accordance with the provisions of paragraph 4C.

(2) Such an application may be made if—

(a) at least 14 days have elapsed since the day on which the tenancy ended;

(b) the landlord and tenant have not reached an agreement under paragraph 4(2) with respect to the amount claimed;

(c) either sub-paragraph (3) or sub-paragraph (4) applies; and

(d) the landlord believes that he is entitled to be paid the amount claimed and that the amount claimed is referable to sums falling within sub-paragraph (5).

(3) This sub-paragraph applies if the landlord has no current address for, or other means of contacting, the tenant.

(4) This sub-paragraph applies if—

(a) the tenant has, since the tenancy ended, received from the landlord a written notice asking whether the tenant accepts that the landlord should be paid the whole or a specified part of the relevant amount; and

(b) the tenant has failed to respond to that notice within the period of 14 days beginning with the day on which he received the notice by indicating to the landlord whether he accepts that the landlord should be paid the relevant amount or the specified part of it (as the case may be).

(5) The amount claimed must be referable to—

(a) an amount of unpaid rent or any other sum due under the terms of the tenancy; or

(b) a liability of the tenant to the landlord arising under or in connection with the tenancy in respect of—

(i) damage to the premises subject to the tenancy, or

(ii) loss of or damage to property on those premises, other than damage caused by fair wear and tear.

(6) If sub-paragraph (4) applies and the notice specifies part of the relevant amount, the amount claimed in the application must not exceed the specified part.

(7) The application must be accompanied by a statutory declaration made by the landlord stating—

(a) the date on which the tenancy ended;

(b) that the landlord and the tenant have not reached any agreement under paragraph 4(2) with respect to the amount claimed, with details of any communications between them since that date (whether relating to the relevant amount or otherwise);

(c) the basis on which the amount claimed is calculated, with particulars of any facts relied on to justify claiming that amount;

(d) if the landlord relies on the condition in sub-paragraph (3), that he has no current address for, or other means of contacting, the tenant, giving particulars of any address (other than the premises subject to the tenancy) and other contact details (including telephone numbers or e mail addresses) which the landlord has had for the tenant;

(e) if the landlord relies on the condition in sub-paragraph (4), that the condition is met, with particulars of the facts relied on to demonstrate that it is met and attaching a copy of the notice given to the tenant;

(f) any information he has as to the whereabouts of the tenant;

(g) that he gives his consent, in the event of the tenant disputing that the landlord should be paid the amount claimed, for the dispute to be resolved through the use of the dispute resolution service;

(h) that he considers that he is entitled to be paid the amount claimed; and

(f) that he makes the statutory declaration knowing that if he knowingly and wilfully makes a false declaration he may be liable to prosecution under the Perjury Act 1911[2].

4B.—(1) The provision made by a custodial scheme for the purposes of paragraph 4(1) in relation to the treatment of the relevant amount at the end of a tenancy must include provision—

(a) for enabling the tenant, if he considers that the conditions set out in sub-paragraph (2) are met, to apply to the scheme administrator for the whole or a specified part of the relevant amount ("the amount claimed") to be paid to him; and

(b) for such an application to be dealt with by the scheme administrator in accordance with the provisions of paragraph 4C.

(2) Such an application may be made if—

(a) at least 14 days have elapsed since the day on which the tenancy ended;

(b) the landlord and tenant have not reached an agreement under paragraph 4(2) with respect to the amount claimed;

(c) either sub-paragraph (3) or sub-paragraph (4) applies; and

(d) the tenant believes that he is entitled to be paid the amount claimed.

(3) This sub-paragraph applies if the tenant has no current address for, or other means of contacting, the landlord.

(4) This sub-paragraph applies if—

(a) the landlord has, since the tenancy ended, received from the tenant a written notice asking whether the landlord accepts that the tenant should be paid the whole or a specified part of the relevant amount; and

(b) the landlord has failed to respond to that notice within the period of 14 days beginning with the day on which he received the notice by indicating to the tenant whether he accepts that the tenant should be paid the relevant amount or the specified part of it (as the case may be).

(5) If sub-paragraph (4) applies and the notice specifies part of the relevant amount, the amount claimed in the application must not exceed the specified part.

(6) The application must be accompanied by a statutory declaration made by the tenant stating—

(a) the date on which the tenancy ended;

(b) that the landlord and the tenant have not reached any agreement under paragraph 4(2) with respect to the amount claimed, with details of any communications between them since that date (whether relating to the relevant amount or otherwise);

(c) if the tenant relies on the condition in sub-paragraph (3), that he has no current address for, or other means of contacting, the landlord, giving particulars of any address and other contact details (including telephone numbers or e mail addresses) which the tenant has had for the landlord;

(d) if the tenant relies on the condition in sub-paragraph (4), that the condition is met, with particulars of the facts relied on to demonstrate that it is met and attaching a copy of the notice given to the landlord;

(e) any information he has as to the whereabouts of the landlord;

(f) that he gives his consent, in the event of the landlord disputing that the tenant should be paid the amount claimed, for the dispute to be resolved through the use of the dispute resolution service;

(g) that he considers that he is entitled to be paid the amount claimed; and

(h) that he makes the statutory declaration knowing that if he knowingly and wilfully makes a false declaration he may be liable to prosecution under the Perjury Act 1911[3].

4C.—(1) Immediately upon receipt of—

(a) a duly completed application from the landlord, accompanied by a statutory declaration which appears to meet the requirements of paragraph 4A(7), or

***Paragraph numbers marked with a "+" can be found online and on CD.***



HOUSING

(b) a duly completed application from the tenant, accompanied by a statutory declaration which appears to meet the requirements of paragraph 4B(6), the scheme administrator must give to the tenant or, as the case may be, the landlord ("the other party") a copy of the application and accompanying statutory declaration and a notice under sub-paragraph (2).

(2) A notice under this sub-paragraph is a notice—

(a) asking the other party to indicate—

(i) whether he accepts that the applicant should be paid the whole or part of the amount claimed;

(ii) if he accepts that part of the amount claimed should be paid, the amount he accepts should be paid; and

(iii) if he does not accept that the applicant should be paid the whole of the amount claimed, whether he consents to the dispute being resolved through the use of the dispute resolution service; and

(b) warning the other party that—

(i) the amount claimed will be paid to the applicant unless, within the relevant period, the other party informs the scheme administrator that he does not accept that the whole of the amount claimed should be paid to the applicant; and

(ii) if the other party responds to the scheme administrator informing him that he does not accept that the whole of the amount claimed should be paid to the applicant, but fails to respond within the relevant period to the question mentioned in paragraph (a)(iii), he will be treated as having given his consent for the dispute to be resolved through the use of the dispute resolution service.

(3) If within the relevant period the scheme administrator receives a response from the other party to the effect that he accepts that the amount claimed should be paid to the applicant—

(a) the application must be granted; and

(b) the scheme administrator must arrange for the amount claimed to be paid to the applicant within the period of 10 days beginning with the day on which the scheme administrator receives that response.

(4) If within the relevant period the scheme administrator receives a response from the other party to the effect that he does not accept that the applicant should be paid any of the amount claimed—

(a) the application must be refused;

(b) the scheme administrator must not pay the amount claimed to either party except in accordance with the relevant provisions of paragraph 4; and

(c) the scheme administrator must inform the applicant of the other party's response to the questions asked in the notice under sub-paragraph (2).

(5) If within the relevant period the scheme administrator receives a response from the other party to the effect that he accepts that part of the amount claimed should be paid to the applicant—

(a) sub-paragraph (3) applies in relation to that part of the amount claimed; and

(b) sub-paragraph (4) applies to so much of the application as relates to the rest of the amount claimed.

(6) If the scheme administrator does not, within the relevant period, receive a response from the other party indicating whether he accepts that the whole or part of the amount claimed should be paid to the applicant, the scheme administrator must arrange for the amount claimed to be paid to the applicant within the period of 10 days beginning with the day after the last day of the relevant period.

(7) If within the relevant period the scheme administrator receives a response from the other party to the effect that he does not accept that the applicant should be paid the whole of the amount claimed but the other party fails within that period to indicate whether he consents to the dispute being resolved through the use of the dispute resolution service—

(a) the other party is to be treated as having given his consent to the use of that service; and

(b) the scheme administrator must inform the applicant that such consent is treated as having been given.

(8) In this paragraph "the relevant period", in relation to the application, means the period of 14 days beginning with the day on which the notice mentioned in sub-paragraph (2) is received by the other party.

*Insurance schemes: general*

5.—(1)This paragraph applies to an insurance scheme. **3A–1639**

[(1A) The scheme must make provision as to the requirements that fall to be complied with by the landlord or by the scheme administrator where—

(a) a landlord wishes to retain a tenancy deposit under the scheme; or

(b) a landlord retaining a tenancy deposit under the scheme (in relation to a tenancy that has not terminated) gives notice to the scheme administrator that he no longer wishes to retain the deposit under that scheme.]

(2) The scheme must provide that any landlord by whom a tenancy deposit is retained under the scheme must give the scheme administrator an undertaking that, if the scheme administrator directs the landlord to pay him any amount in respect of the deposit in accordance with paragraph 6(3) or (7), the landlord will comply with such a direction.

(3) The scheme must require the scheme administrator to effect, and maintain in force, adequate insurance in respect of failures by landlords by whom tenancy deposits are retained under the scheme to comply with such directions as are mentioned in sub-paragraph (2).

(3A) The scheme may make provision enabling the scheme administrator to determine that, by virtue of the landlord's failure to comply with a relevant obligation, a tenancy deposit which has previously been retained by a landlord under the scheme (and which relates to a tenancy which has not ended) is to cease to be retained under the scheme.

(3B) Provision under sub-paragraph (3A) must require the scheme administrator, before making a determination, to give a notice to the landlord stating that the scheme administrator proposes to make such a determination and the reasons for the proposal.

(4) If the scheme provides for landlords participating in the scheme to be members of the scheme, the scheme may provide for a landlord's membership to be terminated by the scheme administrator in the event of any failure by the landlord to comply with a relevant obligation.

(4A) Provision made under sub-paragraph (4) must require the scheme administrator, before determining that the landlord's membership be terminated, to give a notice to the landlord stating that the scheme administrator proposes to make such a determination and the reasons for the proposal.

(4B) On the termination of a landlord's membership under sub-paragraph (4)—

(a) any tenancy deposits previously retained by the landlord under the scheme (in relation to tenancies which had not ended before the termination) cease to be retained under the scheme; but

(b) the scheme continues to apply to a tenancy deposit retained by the landlord under the scheme in relation to a tenancy which ended before the termination as if the landlord were still a member.

(5) The scheme may provide for landlords participating in the scheme to pay to the scheme administrator—

(a) fees in respect of the administration of the scheme, and

(b) contributions in respect of the cost of the insurance referred to in sub-paragraph (3).

(6) Paragraph 5A makes further provision in relation to the procedure to be followed after a notice of the kind mentioned in sub-paragraph (1A)(b), (3B) or (4A) has been given in accordance with the scheme.

(7) In this paragraph "relevant obligation" means—

(a) the duty to comply with a direction mentioned in sub-paragraph (2); or

(b) any obligation under the scheme which is specified in the scheme as a relevant obligation for the purposes of this paragraph.

Requirements where deposit is to cease to be retained under an insurance scheme

***Paragraph numbers marked with a "+" can be found online and on CD.***

5A.—(1) This paragraph applies in relation to—

(a) notice of the kind mentioned in paragraph 5(1A)(b) or (3B), or

(b) a notice from the scheme administrator stating that he proposes to terminate a landlord's membership of the scheme under paragraph 5(4), given in accordance with an insurance scheme.

given in accordance with an insurance scheme.

(2) The scheme must make provision for the scheme administrator, in the case of a notice of the kind mentioned in paragraph 5(1A)(b) which has not been not withdrawn—

(a) to determine the date on which the tenancy deposit is to cease to be retained under the scheme; and

(b) to give a notice under sub-paragraph (4) to the landlord and to the tenant.

(3) The scheme must make provision for the scheme administrator, in the case of a notice of the kind mentioned in paragraph 5(3B), to take the following steps after the end of the period of 14 days beginning with the day on which that notice is received—

(a) to determine whether the deposit should cease to be retained under the scheme and, if so, the date on which it is to cease to be so retained;

(b) if the determination is that the deposit should continue to be retained under the scheme, to give a notice of the determination to the landlord;

(c) if the determination is that the deposit should cease to be so retained, to give a notice under sub-paragraph (4) to the landlord and to the tenant.

(4) A notice under this sub-paragraph is a notice—

(a) identifying the tenancy deposit in question;

(b) informing the recipients of the notice of the determination made by the scheme administrator and stating the date when the deposit ceases to be retained under the scheme; and

(c) giving a general explanation of the continuing effect of sections 213 to 215 of this Act in relation to the deposit (including in particular the effect of section 213 as modified by sub-paragraph (9)).

(5) The scheme must make provision for the scheme administrator, in the case of a notice of the kind mentioned in sub-paragraph (1)(b), to take the following steps after the end of the period of 14 days beginning with the day on which that notice is received—

(a) to determine whether to terminate the landlord's membership and, if so, the date on which his membership is to terminate;

(b) if the determination is that the landlord should continue as a member, to give a notice of the determination to the landlord; and

(c) if the determination is that the membership should be terminated, to give a notice under sub-paragraph (6) to the landlord and to the tenant under any tenancy in relation to which a deposit affected by the determination is retained under the scheme.

(6) A notice under this sub-paragraph is a notice—

(a) informing the recipients of the notice of the determination by the scheme administrator that the landlord's membership of the scheme is to be terminated and stating the date on which his membership terminates;

(b) giving a general explanation of the effect of the termination on any tenancy deposits retained by the landlord under the scheme; and

(c) giving a general explanation of the continuing effect of sections 213 to 215 of this Act in relation to any tenancy deposits that cease to be retained under the scheme as a result of the termination of membership (including in particular the effect of section 213 as modified by sub-paragraph (9)).

(7) The date determined under sub-paragraph (2)(a), (3)(a) or (5)(a) must not be within the period of three months beginning with the day on which the original notice mentioned in sub-paragraph (1) was received.

(8) A notice under sub-paragraph (4) or (6) must be given at least two months before the date on which the deposit ceases to be retained under the scheme or the landlord's membership terminates (as the case may be).

***Paragraph numbers marked with a "+" can be found online and on CD.***

(9) In the application of section 213 to a tenancy deposit which ceases to be retained under an insurance scheme ("the old scheme") by virtue of a determination mentioned in this paragraph—

(a) references to receiving the deposit include a reference to ceasing to retain it under the terms of the old scheme;

(b) subsection (3) has effect as if for the words "within the period of 14 days beginning with the date on which it is received" there were substituted "before the deposit ceases to be retained under the old scheme"; and

(c) subsection (6)(b) has effect as if the reference to the date on which the landlord receives the deposit were a reference to the date on which the deposit ceases to be retained under the old scheme.

*Insurance schemes: termination of tenancies*

6.—(1)An insurance scheme must make provision in accordance with this paragraph and paragraphs 6A to 8 in relation to the respective obligations of the landlord and the scheme administrator where— **3A–1640**

(a) a tenancy deposit has been retained by the landlord under the scheme, and

(b) the tenancy has ended.

(2) Sub-paragraphs (3) to (9) apply where the tenant notifies the scheme administrator that—

(a) the tenant has requested the landlord to repay to him the whole or any part of the deposit, and

(b) the amount in question ("the outstanding amount") has not been repaid to him within the period of 10 days beginning with the date on which the request was made.

(2A) When a tenant gives notice under sub-paragraph (2) he must also indicate whether he consents to any dispute as to the amount to be repaid to him being resolved through the use of the dispute resolution service.

(3) On receiving a notification in accordance with sub-paragraph (2), the scheme administrator must direct the landlord—

(a) to pay an amount equal to the outstanding amount into a designated account held by the scheme administrator, and

(b) to do so within the period of 10 days beginning with the date on which the direction is received by the landlord.

(4) The following sub-paragraphs apply where the tenant or the landlord notifies the scheme administrator—

(a) that a court has decided that the outstanding amount is payable either wholly to one of them or partly to the one and partly to the other and the decision has become final (see paragraph 4(6) and (7)),

(b) that the tenant and landlord have agreed that such an amount is to be paid either wholly to one of them or partly to the one and partly to the other; or

(c) that a person acting as an adjudicator under the provision made under paragraph 10 has made a binding decision that the outstanding amount is payable either wholly to one of them or partly to one and partly to the other.

(5) If the scheme administrator is satisfied as to the matters mentioned in sub-paragraph (4)(a), (b) or (c) (as the case may be), he must—

(a) pay to the tenant any amount due to him in accordance with the decision or agreement (and, to the extent possible, pay that amount out of any amount held by him by virtue of sub-paragraph (3)), and

(b) comply with sub-paragraph (6) or (7), as the case may be.

(6) Where any amount held by the scheme administrator by virtue of sub-paragraph (3) is more than any amount due to the tenant in accordance with the decision or agreement, the scheme administrator must pay the balance to the landlord.

(7) Where any amount so held by the scheme administrator is less than any amount so due to the tenant, the scheme administrator must direct the landlord to pay him the difference within the period of 10 days beginning with the date on which the direction is received by the landlord.

***Paragraph numbers marked with a "+" can be found online and on CD.***

(8) The scheme administrator must pay any amounts required to be paid to the tenant or the landlord as mentioned in sub-paragraph (5)(a) or (6) within 10 days beginning with the date on which the notification is received by the scheme administrator.

(9) The landlord must comply with any direction given in accordance with sub-paragraph (3) or (7).

*Notice to be sent to landlord when a direction under paragraph 6(3) is given*

3A–1641 6A.—(1) This paragraph applies where the scheme administrator of an insurance scheme gives a direction under paragraph 6(3) to a landlord.

(2) The scheme administrator must also send to the landlord a notice—

(a) asking the landlord to indicate—

(i) whether he accepts that the tenant should be repaid the whole or part of the outstanding amount;

(ii) if he accepts that part of it should be repaid, the amount he accepts should be repaid; and

(iii) if he does not accept that the tenant should be repaid the whole of the outstanding amount, whether he consents to the dispute being resolved through the use of the dispute resolution service; and

(b) warning the landlord that if he does not accept that the tenant should be repaid the whole of the outstanding amount but fails to respond within the relevant period to the question mentioned in paragraph (a)(iii), he will be treated as having given his consent for the dispute to be resolved through the use of that service.

(3) If the scheme administrator does not, within the relevant period, receive a response from the landlord indicating whether he accepts that the whole or part of the outstanding amount should be paid to the tenant—

(a) the scheme administrator must treat the lack of a response as an indication that the landlord does not accept that the tenant should be repaid any of the outstanding amount;

(b) the scheme administrator must determine forthwith whether he is satisfied that the notice was received by the landlord;

(c) if the scheme administrator determines that he is satisfied that it was so received, the landlord is to be treated as having given his consent for the dispute to be resolved through the use of the dispute resolution service; and

(d) the scheme administrator must inform the tenant and the landlord whether or not such consent is to be treated as having been given.

(4) If within the relevant period the scheme administrator receives a response to the notice under sub-paragraph (2) to the effect that the landlord does not accept that the tenant should be repaid the whole of the outstanding amount but the landlord fails within that period to indicate whether he consents to the dispute being resolved through the dispute resolution service—

(a) the landlord is to be treated as having given his consent for the dispute to be resolved through the use of that service; and

(b) the scheme administrator must inform the tenant and the landlord that such consent is to be treated as given.

(5) In this paragraph—

"the outstanding amount" has the same meaning as in paragraph 6;

"the relevant period" means the period of 10 working days beginning with the day after that on which the notice referred to in sub-paragraph (2) is sent; and

"working days" shall be taken to exclude Saturdays, Sundays, Christmas Day, Good Friday and any day which, under the Banking and Financial Dealings Act 1971, is a bank holiday in England and Wales.

*Insurance schemes—supplementary provisions*

3A–1642 7.—(1)The designated account held by the scheme administrator must not contain anything other than amounts paid into it as mentioned in paragraph 6(3) and any interest accruing on such amounts.

***Paragraph numbers marked with a "+" can be found online and on CD.***

(2) Subject to sub-paragraph (3), the scheme administrator may retain any interest accruing on such amounts.

(3) The relevant arrangements under section 212(1) may provide for any amount paid in accordance with paragraph 6(5)(a) or (6) to be paid with interest—

(a) in respect of the period during which the relevant amount has remained in the designated account, and

(b) at such rate as the appropriate national authority may specify for the purposes of paragraph 3(5)(b).

(4) With the exception of any interest retained in accordance with sub-paragraph (2), nothing contained in the designated account may be used to fund the administration of the scheme.

(5) In this paragraph "the relevant amount", in relation to a tenancy deposit, means the amount, in respect of the deposit, paid into the designated account by virtue of a direction given in accordance with paragraph 6(3).

8.—(1)The scheme must make provision for preventing double recovery by a tenant in respect of the whole or part of the deposit, and may in that connection make provision— **3A–1643**

(a) for excluding or modifying any requirement imposed by the scheme in accordance with paragraph 6 or 7, and

(b) for requiring the repayment of amounts paid to the tenant by the scheme administrator.

(2) In this paragraph "double recovery", in relation to an amount of a tenancy deposit, means recovering that amount both from the scheme administrator and from the landlord.

*Notifications to tenants*

9.—(1)Every custodial scheme or insurance scheme must provide for the scheme administrator to respond as soon as is practicable to any request within sub-paragraph (2) made by the tenant under a shorthold tenancy. **3A–1644**

(2) A request is within this sub-paragraph if it is a request by the tenant to receive confirmation that a deposit paid in connection with the tenancy is being held in accordance with the scheme.

*Dispute resolution procedures*

10.—(1)Every custodial scheme or insurance scheme must provide for facilities to be available for enabling disputes relating to tenancy deposits subject to the scheme to be resolved without recourse to litigation. **3A–1645**

(2) The scheme must not, however, make the use of such facilities compulsory in the event of such a dispute.

(3) The provision made under this paragraph may confer power on a person acting as an adjudicator in relation to such a dispute to decline to proceed, or continue to proceed, with the case.

(4) In this Schedule, in relation to a custodial scheme or an insurance scheme, "the dispute resolution service"means the facilities provided by the scheme in accordance with this paragraph.

*Service of documents: general*

10A. A tenancy deposit scheme may make provision as to the methods which may be used for giving or sending any direction, notice or other document which falls to be given or sent under the scheme. **3A–1646**

*Service of documents by scheme administrator on landlords*

10.B—(1) The provision made by a tenancy deposit scheme under paragraph 10A may include provision for any direction, notice or other document mentioned in this Schedule which is to be given or sent to a landlord by the scheme administrator to be treated as having been received on the second day after the day on which it is sent by first class post to the landlord at the address last provided by him to the scheme administrator as the postal address to which correspondence may be sent. **3A–1647**

(2) Sub-paragraph (1) does not apply to the notice mentioned in paragraph 6A(2).

(3) Provision made under sub-paragraph (1) may require the scheme administrator—

(a) to send a document to an address other than that mentioned in that sub-paragraph; or

(b) to use or attempt to use any other available means of communication,

before sending a document which is to be treated as having been received as mentioned in that sub-paragraph.

3A-1648

*Service of documents by scheme administrator on tenants*

10C.—(1) The provision made by a tenancy deposit scheme under paragraph 10A may include provision for any notice or other document mentioned in this Schedule which is to be given or sent to a tenant by the scheme administrator to be treated as having been received on the second day after the day on which it is sent by first class post to the tenant at the proper address.

(2) In the case of a notice mentioned in paragraph 4C(2), the proper address is—

(a) the address (if any) last provided to the scheme administrator as the address to which correspondence may be sent; or

(b) if no such address has been provided, the address given in the landlord's statutory declaration as the tenant's last known address or, if the scheme administrator has a more recent address for the tenant, that address.

(3) In the case of a notice of the kind mentioned in paragraph 5A(4) or (6), the proper address is the address of the premises subject to the tenancy in question.

(4) Provision made under sub-paragraph (1) may require the scheme administrator—

3A-1649

(a) to send a document to an address other than the proper address, or

(b) to use or attempt to use any other available means of communication, before sending a document which is to be treated as having been received as mentioned in that sub-paragraph.

3A-1650

*Power to amend*

11. The appropriate national authority may by order make such amendments of

3A-1651 this Schedule as it considers appropriate.

*Interpretation*

12. In this Schedule references to tenants under shorthold tenancies include references to persons who, in accordance with arrangements made with such tenants, have paid tenancy deposits on behalf of the tenants.

*Note* —Amended by the Housing (Tenancy Deposit Schemes) Order 2007 (SI 2007/796).

# Housing and Regeneration Act 2008

(2008 c.17) 3A–1652

ARRANGEMENT OF SECTIONS

SECT.



## [THE NEXT PARAGRAPH IS 3A–1664.]

### Family intervention tenancies

Local housing authorities and registered providers of social housing (in England) and registered social landlords (in Wales) are able to offer family intervention tenancies, which are not secure or assured, to tenants who have lost or are potentially at risk of losing their secure or assured tenancies. These tenancies are offered to provide behavioural support services to tenants against whom a possession order for anti-social behaviour has been made or to tenants who could face possession proceedings on the grounds of anti-social behaviour. Family intervention tenancies were created by Housing and Regeneration Act 2008 s.297 by inserting new para.4ZA into Housing Act 1985 Sch.1 (tenancies which are not secure tenancies) and new para.12ZA into Housing Act 1988 Sch.1 to the (tenancies which cannot be assured tenancies). 3A–1664

Family intervention tenancies are voluntary. There is provision for the service of notices prior to the grant of family intervention tenancies. If no notice is served, the new tenancy cannot be a family intervention tenancy.

Family intervention tenants do not enjoy security of tenure, but can become secure or assured tenancies if the landlord so notifies the tenant.

Paragraphs 4ZA (3) and 12ZA(3) (see paras 3A–502.1 and 3A–970.1) define a family intervention tenancy "as a tenancy granted by a local authority to a person for the purposes of the provision of behaviour support services and against whom a possession order in respect of another dwelling-house:

- has been made in relation to a secure tenancy on the grounds of anti-social behaviour; or
- could have been so made in relation to a secure tenancy; or
- could have been so made if the tenant had had such a tenancy.

Paragraphs 4ZA (4) and 12ZA(4) provide that the new tenancy is not a family intervention tenancy unless the local housing authority has served a notice under sub-para.(5). Sub-paragraph (5) provides the information the notice must contain including that the tenant is under no obligation to enter into the tenancy or unless otherwise required to do so to surrender any existing tenancy or possession of a dwelling-house. Sub-paragraph (6) provides that the contents of the notice may be amended by regulations made by statutory instrument. In addition the notice must contain advice to the tenant as to how he or she may be able to obtain assistance in relation to the notice (sub-para.(7)). The type of advice to be included in notices may be provided for by regulations (sub-para.(8)) made by statutory instrument.

Paragraphs 4ZA (12) and 12ZA(12) provide definitions for the terms used in the new para.4ZA. In particular, "behaviour support services" are defined as those support services which are identified in a behaviour support agreement and are provided by any person to the new tenant or persons living with them for the purposes of addressing the anti-social behaviour which has led to the local authority taking possession action or of being of the opinion that such a possession claim could be made. A "behaviour support agreement" is an agreement between the tenant and the local housing authority about behaviour and the provision of support services.

***Paragraph numbers marked with a "+" can be found online and on CD.***

For the term "registered social landlord", see Housing Act 1996 Pt 1. Registered charities which are housing associations are eligible for registration as social landlords under Housing Act 1996 s.2. In addition s.2 provides that societies registered under the Industrial and Provident Societies Act 1965 and companies registered under the Companies Act 1985 are eligible for registration if they are non-profit-making and established for the purpose of, or have among their objects or powers, the provision, construction, improvement or management of:

(a) houses to be kept available for letting;

(b) houses for occupation by members of the body, where the rules of the body restrict membership to persons entitled or prospectively entitled (as tenants or otherwise) to occupy a house provided or managed by the body; or

(c) hostels.

Section 297(3) provides that the provisions in new para.4ZA of Sch.1 to the Housing Act 1985 and para.12ZA of Pt 1 of Sch.1 to the Housing Act 1988 do not apply to any tenancy granted before this section came into force—i.e. January 1, 2009.

## Certain family intervention tenancies: termination

3A–1665 **298**—(1) A local housing authority must not serve a notice to quit on the tenant of a family intervention tenancy unless—

(a) the authority has served a notice under subsection (2) on the tenant, and

(b) either—

(i) the tenant has not requested a review of the kind mentioned in subsection (2)(e) within the period of 14 days beginning with the service of the notice,

(ii) any such request has been withdrawn, or

(iii) the authority has served a notice on the tenant under subsection (4)(b).

(2) A notice under this subsection is a notice in writing stating—

(a) that the authority has decided to serve a notice to quit on the tenant,

(b) the effect of serving a notice to quit,

(c) the reasons for the authority's decision,

(d) when the authority is intending to serve the notice to quit, and

(e) that the tenant has the right to request, within the period of 14 days beginning with the service of the notice under this subsection, a review of the authority's decision.

(3) Subsection (4) applies if the tenant requests a review of the kind mentioned in subsection (2)(e) within the period of 14 days beginning with the service of the notice under subsection (2) and the request is not withdrawn.

(4) The local housing authority must—

(a) review its decision to serve a notice to quit on the tenant, and

(b) serve a notice on the tenant informing the tenant of the decision of the authority on the review and the reasons for it.

(5) The appropriate national authority may by regulations make

provision about the procedure to be followed in connection with such a review.

(6) Regulations under subsection (5) may, in particular—

(a) specify the description of person who is to make the decision on a review,

(b) specify the circumstances in which the tenant is entitled to an oral hearing on a review,

(c) specify whether, and by whom, the tenant is entitled to be represented at such a hearing.

(7) A notice under subsection (2), and a notice to quit, served by a local housing authority in respect of a family intervention tenancy must contain advice to the tenant as to how the tenant may be able to obtain assistance in relation to the notice.

(8) The appropriate national authority may by regulations make provision about the type of advice to be provided in such notices.

(9) In this section—

"appropriate national authority" means –

(a) in relation to England, the Secretary of State, and

(b) in relation to Wales, the Welsh Ministers,

"family intervention tenancy" has the same meaning as in paragraph 4ZA of Schedule 1 to the Housing Act 1985 (c. 68), and other expressions used in this section and in paragraph 4ZA of that Schedule have the same meaning as in that paragraph.

(10) This section does not apply to any tenancy granted before the coming into force of this section.

**Implementation**

Brought into force on January 1, 2009 by the Housing and Regeneration Act 2008 (Commencement No.2 and Transitional, Saving and Transitory Provisions) Order 2008 (SI 2008/3068) art.4(11). **3A–1666**

**Extent**

This section applies to England and Wales. **3A–1667**

**Local housing authority**

See Housing Act 1985 s.1 and 2(1)—i.e. a district council, a London borough council, the Common Council of the City of London, a Welsh county council or county borough council or the Council of the Isles of Scilly. **3A–1668**

**Family intervention tenancy**

See s.297. **3A–1669**

**Appropriate national authority**

See (9)—i.e. the Secretary of State in England and the Welsh Ministers in Wales. **3A–1670**

**Regulations**

See the Family Intervention Tenancies (Review of Local Authority Decisions) (England) Regulations 2008 SI No.3111. **3A–1671**

**Review**

In view of *R. (McLellan) v Bracknell Forest DC* [2001] EWCA 1510; [2002] QB 1129; and *R. (Gilboy) v Liverpool City Council* [2008] EWCA Civ 751; [2009] 3 W.L.R. 300; **3A–1672**



HOUSING

[2008] 4 All E.R. 127, the procedure for reviews does not appear to be incompatible with ECHR art.8 and there is no reason to think that individuals' rights will be infringed without remedy from the courts.

**Editorial introduction**

3A–1673 This section makes provision for the termination of local housing authority family intervention tenancies. Subsection (1) provides that local authorities should not serve notices to quit on tenants of family intervention tenancies unless notice under subs.(2) has been served on the tenant and either:

- the tenant has not requested a review of the kind specified in the notice (right to request, within 14 days of the service of the notice, a review of the authority's decision to evict);
- the tenant withdraws the request for a review; or
- a notice under subs.(4)(b) has been served on the tenant (notice of the reasoning and decision of the requested review).

Subsection (2) sets out the required contents of the notice. Subsections (3) and (4) explain what a local authority must do if a tenant requests a review of the local authority's decision within 14 days of the service of the notice under subs.(2). The local authority must carry out the review and serve notice of its decision and the reasons for it on the tenant. The procedure to be followed on review may be provided by regulations made by statutory instrument. The regulations may contain:

- a description of the person who makes the review decision;
- the circumstances under which the tenant would be entitled to an oral review;
- whether or not and by whom the tenant can be represented during the review hearing.

Subsection (7) provides that any notice to quit or notice under subs.(2) served in respect of a family intervention tenancy, must also contain advice to the tenant about obtaining assistance in relation to the notice. Subsection (8) provides that the type of advice the notice to quit or notice under subs.(2) must include may be provided by regulations subject to the negative resolution procedure. Subsection (10) effectively applies the provisions of this section only to tenancies granted on or after the coming into force of this section. The review provisions only apply to family intervention tenancies granted by local authorities. As family intervention tenancies lack security of tenure, and s.298 only applies to local authorities, registered social landlords who seek to terminate family intervention tenancies merely have to serve a notice to quit—but see *R. (on the application of Weaver) v London & Quadrant Housing Trust* [2009] EWCA Civ 587, June 18, 2009; (2009) *Times* August 26, noted at para.3A–331.

## Possession orders relating to certain tenancies

3A–1674 **299** Schedule 11 (which makes provision about possession orders and their effect on secure tenancies, assured tenancies, introductory tenancies and demoted tenancies including provision about the status of existing occupiers) has effect.

**Commencement**

3A–1674.1 Brought into force on December 1, 2008 for certain purposes, by the Housing and Regeneration Act 2008 (Commencement No.2 and Transitional, Saving and Transitory Provisions) Order 2008 (SI 2008/3068) art.4(4).

**Editorial introduction**

3A–1674.2 See para.3A–1681.

**Secure tenancies**

3A–1675 See Housing Act 1985 s.79 above.

**Assured tenancies**

3A–1676 See Housing Act 1988 s.1 above.

**Introductory tenancies**

3A–1677 See Housing Act 1996 ss.124 above.

**Demoted tenancies**

See Housing Act 1985 s.82A, Housing Act 1988 ss.6A and 20B and Housing Act 1996 s.143A, above. **3A–1678**

**[THE NEXT PARAGRAPH IS 3A–1680.]**

**Extent**

This section applies to England and Wales. **3A–1680**

**Section 299 and Sch.11—abolition of tolerated trespassers**

The purpose of these provisions is to abolish the status of "tolerated trespasser" (see para.3A–385). Part 1 achieved this by making amendments to Housing Act 1985 and Housing Act 1988. The key amendment in each Act is that tenancies continue until a warrant for possession is executed. In so far as these provisions have been implemented, they have been incorporated into the text of the relevant sections. (Housing and Regeneration Act 2008 (Commencement No.5) Order 2009 SI 1261 did not bring into force parts of paras 3, 8 or 14 of Pt 1 of Sch.1 – they are still not yet in force.) **3A–1681**

Part 2 of the Schedule provides new tenancies for tenants of "original tenancies" who had become tolerated trespassers. "An original tenancy" is one which ended as a result of a possession order (but not as a result of execution of the order—i.e. eviction). Paragraph 16(1) provides that a new tenancy of the dwelling-house let under the original tenancy is treated as arising on the commencement date (i.e. May 20, 2009), between the ex-landlord and the ex-tenant, if three conditions are satisfied. These conditions are, firstly, that the home condition is met; secondly, that the ex-landlord is entitled to let the dwelling-house; and thirdly, that the ex-landlord and ex-tenant have not in the meantime entered into a new tenancy. The second and third of those conditions have been amended by the Housing (Replacement of Terminated Tenancies) (Successor Landlords) (England) Order 2009 SI 1262 and the Housing (Replacement of Terminated Tenancies) (Successor Landlords) (Wales) Order 2009 SI 1260.

Paragraph 16(2) provides that the dwelling-house must have been the only or principal home of the ex-tenant throughout the termination period, and still be so on the commencement date.

In general, replacement tenancies are the same type as the original tenancy (para.17). In general, the terms and conditions of the original tenancy immediately before it ended apply to the new tenancy (para.18) Arrears of "rent" owed for the termination period are owed in respect of the new tenancy. Paragraph 19(1) provides that any statutory provisions relating to secure, assured, introductory or demoted tenancies apply to any replacement tenancy under Pt 2 of the Schedule.

Paragraph 20 deals with the effect which court orders made in the course of the possession proceedings in respect of the original tenancy have on the new tenancy. The possession order itself is to be treated, so far as practicable, as applying to the new tenancy, and para.20(2) provides that any other court orders relating to occupation of the dwelling-house and made in contemplation of, in consequence of, or otherwise in connection with the possession order, and which are in force on the commencement date, must also be treated (so far as practicable) as applying to the new tenancy.

## Service charges: provision of information and designated accounts

**303** Schedule 12 (which relates to the provision of information about service charges and to service charge funds) has effect. **3A–1682**

**Commencement**

Brought into force with effect from December 1, 2008 for certain purposes, by the Housing and Regeneration Act 2008 (Commencement No.2 and Transitional, Saving and Transitory Provisions) Order 2008 (SI 2008/3068) art.4(4). **3A–1683**

**Schedule 12: provision of information and designated accounts**

Schedule 12 makes changes to the requirements in the Landlord and Tenant Act **3A–1684**

1985 and the Landlord and Tenant Act 1987 regarding the information that landlords must supply to service charge payers and how service charge monies are to be held. The changes were originally proposed in set out in *Commonhold and Leasehold Reform Act 2002: A Consultation Paper on Regular Statements of Account and Designated Client Accounts*, published on July 25, 2007.

The main amendments are to Landlord and Tenant Act 1985 s.21 (as substituted by the Commonhold and Leasehold Reform Act 2002) and Landlord and Tenant Act 1987 s.42A (as inserted by the 2002 Act). Section 21 and s.42A, as amended or introduced by the 2002 Act, have not been brought into force.

Paragraph 2 broadly replicates the effect of s.21. Subsection (1) provides the appropriate national authority (the Secretary of State in England, and the Welsh Ministers in Wales) with power to make regulations about the provision by landlords of dwellings of service charge information. Subsection (2) sets out the types of information that should be dealt with in those regulations. In particular, the regulations must, subject to exceptions, require a landlord to provide information about the service charges of the tenant and any "associated charges" (defined in subs.(10)); and the relevant costs relating to the service charges. Subsection (3) provides that the regulations must (subject to exceptions) require that a report by a qualified person be supplied with the information provided. Subsection (4) sets out the additional matters about which provision may be made in the regulations. In particular the regulations may make provision about the information and reports that need to be provided, the periods in relation to which information or reports are to be provided, the times at or by which they need to be provided, and the form and manner in which they may be provided. The regulations may also describe the persons who are "qualified persons" for the purposes of preparing the report that must accompany the information supplied by the landlord. Subsection (5) provides that the power under subs.(1) to make regulations is not limited in any way by the provisions of subss.(2) to (4). Subsection (6) allows regulations made under s.21 to make different provision for different cases, descriptions of case or different purposes and to make supplementary, incidental, consequential, transitional or saving provision that is considered to be appropriate. Subsection (7) provides that, subject to subss.(8) and (9), the regulations will be subject to the negative procedure. Subsections (8) and (9) provides that the first use of the regulation making powers by the appropriate national authority will be subject to the affirmative resolution procedure. Subsection (10) contains definitions.

Paragraphs 3 to 8 of the Schedule make amendments to Landlord and Tenant Act 1985 ss.21A, 22, 23, 26 and 27, which are consequential on the new terminology used in s.21.

Paragraph 9 repeals Landlord and Tenant Act 1985 s.28, which defines the meaning of "qualified accountant" for the purposes of providing a certificate supporting information supplied under the existing s.21. This is being replaced with the power to specify in regulations made under the new s.21(4) the persons who are qualified to provide a report on such information.

**[THE NEXT PARAGRAPH IS 3A–1691.]**

## SCHEDULE 11

### POSSESSION ORDERS RELATING TO CERTAIN TENANCIES

### PART 1

### AMENDMENTS TO THE HOUSING ACTS OF 1985, 1988 AND 1996

*Housing Act 1985 (c. 68)*

**3A–1691** 1. The Housing Act 1985 is amended as follows.

* * * *

**[THE NEXT PARAGRAPH IS 3A–1693.]**

3.—(1)Section 85 (extended discretion of court in certain proceedings for possession) is amended as follows. 3A–1693

(3) For subsection (4) substitute—

"(4) The court may discharge or rescind the order for possession if it thinks it appropriate to do so having had regard to—

(a) any conditions imposed under subsection (3), and

(b) the conduct of the tenant in connection with those conditions."

* * * *

*Housing Act 1988 (c. 50)*

5. The Housing Act 1988 is amended as follows. 3A–1694

## [THE NEXT PARAGRAPH IS 3A–1697.]

8.—(1)Section 9 (extended discretion of court in possession claims) is amended as follows. 3A–1697

(3) For subsection (4) substitute—

"(4) The court may discharge or rescind any such order as is referred to in subsection (2) if it thinks it appropriate to do so having had regard to—

(a) any conditions imposed under subsection (3), and

(b) the conduct of the tenant in connection with those conditions."

* * * *

## [THE NEXT PARAGRAPH IS 3A–1703.]

*Transitional provisions*

14.—(1)Subject as follows, this Part of this Schedule does not apply to any possession order made before the commencement date. 3A–1703

(2) This Part of this Schedule does apply to a possession order made before the commencement date if the order applies to—

(a) a new tenancy by virtue of paragraph 20, or

(b) a tenancy which has not ended pursuant to the order before that date.

(3) Paragraphs 3(3) and 8(3) apply to any possession order regardless of when it was made.

(4) In determining for the purposes of sub-paragraph (2) whether a tenancy has ended, any ending which was temporary because the tenancy was restored in consequence of a court order is to be ignored.

(5) In this paragraph "the commencement date" means the day on which section 299 comes into force for purposes other than the purposes of the Secretary of State or the Welsh Ministers making orders under Part 2 of this Schedule.

*Note*—This Part was brought into force by SI 2009/1261, with effect from May, 20, 2009, except paras 3(3), 8(3), 14(3). The amendments to the Housing Acts 1985, 1988, 1996 now in force are shown in the text of those acts as set out earlier in this section. 3A–1703.1

## PART 2

## REPLACEMENT OF CERTAIN TERMINATED TENANCIES

*Circumstances in which replacement tenancies arise*

15. In this Part of this Schedule "an original tenancy" means any secure tenancy, assured tenancy, introductory tenancy or demoted tenancy— 3A–1704

(a) in respect of which a possession order was made before the commencement date, and

(b) which ended before that date pursuant to the order but not on the execution of the order.

3A–1705 16.—(1) A new tenancy of the dwelling-house which was let under the original tenancy is treated as arising on the commencement date between the [successor landlord] and the ex-tenant if—

(a) on that date—

(i) the home condition is met, and

(ii) the [successor landlord] is entitled to let the dwelling-house, and

[(b) the ex-tenant has not entered into another tenancy with—

(i) the successor landlord, or

(ii) the [successor landlord] is entitled to let the dwelling-house, andany initial transferee or subsequent transferee who is not the successor landlord,

after the date on which the original tenancy ended but before the commencement date.]

(2) The home condition is that the dwelling-house which was let under the original tenancy—

(a) is, on the commencement date, the only or principal home of the ex-tenant, and

(b) has been the only or principal home of the ex-tenant throughout the termination period.

(3) In this Part of this Schedule "the termination period" means the period—

(a) beginning with the end of the original tenancy, and

(b) ending with the commencement date.

(4) For the purposes of sub-paragraph (2)(a) the dwelling-house is the only or principal home of the ex-tenant on the commencement date even though the ex-tenant is then absent from the dwelling-house as a result of having been evicted in pursuance of a warrant if the warrant is subsequently set aside but the possession order under which it was granted remains in force.

(5) In that case, the new tenancy is treated as arising on the first day (if any) on which the ex-tenant resumes occupation of the dwelling-house as that person's only or principal home.

(6) For the purposes of sub-paragraph (2)(b) any period of time within the termination period is to be ignored if—

(a) it is a period in which the ex-tenant was absent from the dwelling-house as a result of having been evicted in pursuance of a warrant which was then set aside although the possession order under which it was granted remained in force, and

(b) the ex-tenant subsequently resumes occupation of the dwelling-house as the ex-tenant's only or principal home.

(7) The appropriate national authority may by order provide for particular cases or descriptions of case, or particular circumstances, where the home condition is met where it would not otherwise be met.

3A–1705.1 *Note*—Paragraph 16 was amended by the Housing (Replacement of Terminated Tenancies) (Successor Landlords) (England) Order 2009 SI No.1262 art.3.

*Nature of replacement tenancies*

3A–1706 [17. The new tenancy is to be—

(a) a secure tenancy if—

(i) the original tenancy was—

(aa) a secure tenancy,

(bb) an assured tenancy (whether or not an assured shorthold tenancy),

(cc) an introductory tenancy, or

***Paragraph numbers marked with a "+" can be found online and on CD.***

(dd) a demoted tenancy,

(ii) the new tenancy satisfies the conditions for a secure tenancy in accordance with Part IV of the Housing Act 1985,

(iii) the new tenancy is one which, by virtue of subsection (2) of section 1 of the Housing Act 1988, cannot be an assured tenancy,

(iv) where the original tenancy was an assured shorthold tenancy or an introductory tenancy, no election by the successor landlord under section 124 of the Housing Act 1996 is in force on the day on which the new tenancy arises, and

(v) where the original tenancy was a demoted tenancy, the successor landlord is not a person entitled to apply for an order of the court under section 82A of the Housing Act 1985 (a demotion order),

(b) an assured shorthold tenancy if—

(i) the original tenancy was—

(aa) an assured shorthold tenancy,

(bb) an introductory tenancy, or

(cc) a demoted tenancy

(ii) the new tenancy is not one which, by virtue of subsection (2) of section 1 of the Housing Act 1988, cannot be an assured tenancy,

(iii) the new tenancy is not one which falls within any paragraph of Schedule 2A to the Housing Act 1988,

(iv) the new tenancy does not satisfy the conditions for a secure tenancy in accordance with Part IV of the Housing Act 1985, and

(v) where the original tenancy was a demoted tenancy, the successor landlord is not a registered social landlord,

(c) an assured tenancy which is not an assured shorthold tenancy if—

(i) the original tenancy was—

(aa) an assured tenancy which was not an assured shorthold tenancy, or

(bb) a secure tenancy,

(ii) the new tenancy is not one which, by virtue of subsection (2) of section 1 of the Housing Act 1988, cannot be an assured tenancy, and

(iii) the new tenancy does not satisfy the conditions for a secure tenancy in accordance with Part IV of the Housing Act 1985,

(d) an introductory tenancy if—

(i) the original tenancy was—

(aa) an introductory tenancy, or

(bb) an assured shorthold tenancy,

(ii) the new tenancy is one which, by virtue of subsection (2) of section 1 of the Housing Act 1988, cannot be an assured tenancy,

(iii) an election by the successor landlord under section 124 of the Housing Act 1996 is in force on the day on which the new tenancy arises, and

(iv) but for that election, the new tenancy would be a secure tenancy because it satisfies the conditions for a secure tenancy in accordance with Part IV of the Housing Act 1985,

(e) a demoted tenancy to which section 20B of the Housing Act 1988 applies if—

(i) the original tenancy was a demoted tenancy, and

(ii) the successor landlord is a registered social landlord, or

(f) a demoted tenancy to which section 143A of the Housing Act 1996 applies if—

***Paragraph numbers marked with a "+" can be found online and on CD.***

(i) the original tenancy was a demoted tenancy, and

(ii) the new tenancy satisfies the first and second conditions in section 143A of the Housing Act 1996.]

3A–1706.1 *Note* —The current para.17 was substituted by the Housing (Replacement of Terminated Tenancies) (Successor Landlords) (England) Order 2009 SI No.1262 art.4.

3A–1707 18.—(1) The new tenancy is, subject as follows, to have effect on the same terms and conditions as those applicable to the original tenancy immediately before it ended.

(2) The terms and conditions of the new tenancy are to be treated as modified so as to reflect, so far as applicable, any changes made during the termination period to the level of payments for the ex-tenant's occupation of the dwelling-house or to the other terms and conditions of the occupation.

(3) The terms and conditions of the new tenancy are to be treated as modified so that any outstanding liabilities owed by the ex-tenant to the [successor landlord] in respect of payments for the ex-tenant's occupation of the dwelling-house during the termination period are liabilities in respect of rent under the new tenancy.

(4) The appropriate national authority may by order provide for other modifications of the terms and conditions of the new tenancy.

(5) Nothing in sub-paragraphs (2) to (4) is to be read as permitting modifications of the new tenancy which would not have been possible if the original tenancy had remained a tenancy throughout the termination period.

[(6) The terms and conditions of a new secure tenancy which arises by virtue of paragraph 17(a), where the original tenancy was—

(a) an assured tenancy,

(b) an introductory tenancy, or

(c) a demoted tenancy

are to be treated as modified so far as necessary to reflect the fact that the new tenancy is a secure tenancy and not an assured tenancy, an introductory tenancy or a demoted tenancy (as the case may be).

(7) The terms and conditions of a new assured shorthold tenancy which arises by virtue of paragraph 17(b), where the original tenancy was—

(a) an introductory tenancy, or

(b) a demoted tenancy,

are to be treated as modified so far as necessary to reflect the fact that the new tenancy is an assured shorthold tenancy and not an introductory tenancy or a demoted tenancy (as the case may be).

(8) The terms and conditions of a new assured tenancy which arises by virtue of paragraph 17(c), where the original tenancy was a secure tenancy, are to be treated as modified so far as necessary to reflect the fact that the new tenancy is an assured tenancy and not a secure tenancy.

(9) The terms and conditions of a new introductory tenancy which arises by virtue of paragraph 17(d), where the original tenancy was an assured shorthold tenancy, are to be treated as modified so far as necessary to reflect the fact that the new tenancy is an introductory tenancy and not an assured shorthold tenancy.

(10) The terms and conditions of a new demoted tenancy which arises by virtue of paragraph 17(e), where the original tenancy was a demoted tenancy to which section 143A of the Housing Act 1996 applied, are to be treated as modified so far as necessary to reflect the fact that the new tenancy is a demoted tenancy to which section 20B of the Housing Act 1988 applies and not a demoted tenancy to which section 143A of the Housing Act 1996 applies.

(11) The terms and conditions of a new demoted tenancy which arises by virtue of

paragraph 17(f), where the original tenancy was a demoted tenancy to which section 20B of the Housing Act 1988 applied, are to be treated as modified so far as necessary to reflect the fact that the new tenancy is a demoted tenancy to which section 143A of the Housing Act 1996 applies and not a demoted tenancy to which section 20B of the Housing Act 1988 applies.]

*Note* —Paragraph 18 was amended by the Housing (Replacement of Terminated Tenancies) (Successor Landlords) (England) Order 2009 SI No.1262 art.5. **3A–1707.1**

19.—(1) Any provision which is made by or under an enactment and relates to a secure tenancy, assured tenancy, introductory tenancy or demoted tenancy applies, subject as follows, to a new tenancy of a corresponding kind. **3A–1708**

(2) Any such provision which relates to an introductory tenancy applies to a new tenancy which is an introductory tenancy as if the trial period mentioned in section 125(2) of the Housing Act 1996 (c. 52) were the period of one year beginning with the day on which the new tenancy arises.

(3) Any such provision which relates to a demoted tenancy applies to a new tenancy which is a demoted tenancy as if the demotion period mentioned in section 20B(2) of the Housing Act 1988 (c. 50) or section 143B(1) of the Housing Act 1996 were the period of one year beginning with the day on which the new tenancy arises.

(4) The appropriate national authority may by order modify any provision made by or under an enactment in its application to a new tenancy.

*Status of possession order and other court orders*

20.—(1) The possession order in pursuance of which the original tenancy ended is to be treated, so far as practicable, as if it applies to the new tenancy. **3A–1709**

(2) Any court orders made before the commencement date which—

(a) are in force on that date,
(b) relate to the occupation of the dwelling-house, and
(c) were made in contemplation of, in consequence of or otherwise in connection with the possession order,

are to be treated, so far as practicable, as if they apply to the new tenancy.

*Continuity of tenancies*

21.—(1) The new tenancy and the original tenancy are to be treated for the relevant purposes as— **3A–1710**

(a) the same tenancy, and
(b) a tenancy which continued uninterrupted throughout the termination period.

(2) The relevant purposes are—

[...]

(b) calculating on or after the commencement date the period qualifying, or the aggregate of such periods, under Schedule 4 to the Housing Act 1985 (c. 68) (qualifying period for right to buy and discount),
(c) determining on or after the commencement date whether the condition set out in paragraph (b) of Ground 8 of Schedule 2 to that Act is met, and
(d) any other purposes specified by the appropriate national authority by order.

[(2A) Where the ex-tenant was a successor in relation to the original tenancy, the ex-tenant shall be treated as a successor in relation to the new tenancy.]

[(3) In proceedings on a claim of a description specified in sub-paragraph (7), the court concerned may order that, for the purposes of the claim, the original tenancy is to be treated as having continued during the termination period until the relevant interest was transferred to the initial transferee.

(4) In proceedings on a claim of a description specified in sub-paragraph (8), the court concerned may order that, for the purposes of the claim, the original tenancy is to be treated as having continued during the termination period until the relevant interest was transferred to the successor landlord.

(5) In proceedings on a claim of a description specified in sub-paragraph (9), the court concerned may order that, for the purposes of the claim, the new tenancy is to

***Paragraph numbers marked with a "+" can be found online and on CD.***

be treated as having commenced when the relevant interest was transferred to the successor landlord.

(6) In proceedings on a claim of a description specified in sub-paragraph (8) together with a claim of a description specified in sub-paragraph (9), where those claims relate to the same alleged breach, the court concerned may order that, for the purposes of the claims, the original tenancy and the new tenancy are to be treated as—

(a) the same tenancy, and

(b) a tenancy which continued uninterrupted throughout the termination period.

(7) The following are claims specified for the purposes of sub-paragraph (3)—

(a) a claim by the ex-tenant or the ex-landlord against the other for breach of a term or condition of the original tenancy—

(i) in respect of which proceedings are brought on or after the commencement date, or

(ii) in respect of which proceedings were brought, but were not finally determined, before that date, and

(b) a claim by the ex-tenant against the ex-landlord for breach of statutory duty—

(i) where the alleged breach occurred before the relevant interest was transferred to the initial transferee, and

(ii) in respect of which proceedings are or were brought as mentioned in paragraph (a)(i) or (ii).

(8) Where any rights or liabilities in relation to the original tenancy were transferred to the successor landlord, the following is a claim specified for the purposes of sub-paragraph (4): a claim by the ex-tenant or the successor landlord against the other for breach of a term or condition of the original tenancy in respect of which proceedings are or were brought as mentioned in sub-paragraph (7)(a)(i) or (ii).

(9) The following are claims specified for the purposes of sub-paragraph (5)—

(a) a claim by the ex-tenant or the successor landlord against the other for breach of a term or condition of the new tenancy, and

(b) a claim by the ex-tenant against the successor landlord for breach of statutory duty, where the alleged breach occurred after the relevant interest was transferred to the successor landlord,

in respect of which proceedings are brought as mentioned in sub-paragraph (7)(a)(i) or (ii).

(10) For the purposes of sub-paragraphs (7) to (9) proceedings must be treated as finally determined if—

(a) they are withdrawn,

(b) any appeal is abandoned, or

(c) the time for appealing has expired without an appeal being brought.]

**3A–1710.1** *Note* —Paragraph 21 was amended by the Housing (Replacement of Terminated Tenancies) (Successor Landlords) (England) Order 2009 SI No.1262 art.6.

*Compliance with consultation requirements*

**3A–1711** 22.—(1) The fact that—

(a) the views of the ex-tenant during the termination period were not sought or taken into account when they should have been sought or taken into account, or

(b) the views of the ex-tenant during that period were sought or taken into account when they should not have been sought or taken into account,

is not to be taken to mean that the consultation requirements were not complied with.

(2) The consultation requirements are—

(a) the requirements under—

(i) section 105(1) of the Housing Act 1985 (c. 68),

(ii) paragraphs 3 and 4 of Schedule 3A to that Act,

(iii) regulations made under section 27AB of that Act which relate to arranging for ballots or polls with respect to a proposal to enter into a management agreement, and

***Paragraph numbers marked with a "+" can be found online and on CD.***

(iv) section 137(2) of the Housing Act 1996 (c. 52), and

(b) any other requirements specified by the appropriate national authority by order.

*Joint tenancies*

23.—(1) In the application of this Part of this Schedule in relation to an original tenancy which was a joint tenancy, a reference to the dwelling-house being the only or principal home of the ex-tenant is to be treated as a reference to the dwelling-house being the only or principal home of at least one of the extenants of the joint tenancy. **3A-1712**

(2) The appropriate national authority may by order provide for this Part of this Schedule to apply in relation to an original tenancy which was a joint tenancy subject to such additional modifications as may be specified in the order.

*Successor landlords*

24.—(1) The appropriate national authority may by order provide for this Part of this Schedule to apply, subject to such modifications as may be specified in the order, to successor landlord cases. **3A-1713**

(2) For the purposes of sub-paragraph (1) a successor landlord case is a case, in relation to an original tenancy, where the interest of the ex-landlord in the dwelling-house—

(a) has been transferred to another person after the end of the original tenancy and before the commencement date, and

(b) on the commencement date, belongs to the person to whom it has been transferred or a subsequent transferee.

*Supplementary*

25. In determining for the purposes of this Part of this Schedule whether a tenancy has ended, any ending which was temporary because the tenancy was restored in consequence of a court order is to be ignored. **3A-1714**

26.—(1)In this Part of this Schedule— **3A-1715**

"appropriate national authority" means –

(a) in relation to a dwelling-house in England, the Secretary of State, and

(b) in relation to a dwelling-house in Wales, the Welsh Ministers,

"assured shorthold tenancy" and "assured tenancy" have the same meanings as in Part 1 of the Housing Act 1988 (c. 50) but do not include a demoted tenancy to which section 20B of that Act applies,

"the commencement date" means the day on which section 299 comes into force for purposes other than the purposes of the Secretary of State or the Welsh Ministers making orders under this Part of this Schedule,

"demoted tenancy" means a tenancy to which section 20B of the Act of 1988 or section 143A of the Housing Act 1996 (c. 52) applies,

"dwelling-house" –

(a) in relation to an assured tenancy, or a tenancy to which section 20B of the Act of 1988 applies, has the same meaning as in Part 1 of that Act,

(b) in relation to a tenancy to which section 143A of the Act of 1996 applies, has the same meaning as in Chapter 1A of Part 5 of that Act,

(c) in relation to an introductory tenancy, has the meaning given by section 139 of the Act of 1996, and

(d) in relation to a secure tenancy, has the meaning given by section 112 of the Housing Act 1985 (c. 68),

"ex-landlord" means the person who was the landlord under an original tenancy,

"ex-tenant" means the person who was the tenant under an original tenancy,

["initial transferee" means the person to whom the relevant interest was transferred by the ex-landlord after the end of the original tenancy and before the commencement date,]

"introductory tenancy" has the same meaning as in Chapter 1 of Part 5 of the Act of 1996,

"modification" includes omission,

"new tenancy" means a tenancy which is treated as arising by virtue of paragraph

HOUSING

16,

"original tenancy" has the meaning given by paragraph 15,

"possession order", in relation to a tenancy, means a court order for the possession of the dwelling-house,

["registered social landlord" has the same meaning as in Part 1 of the Housing Act 1996,

"relevant interest" means the interest of the ex-landlord in the dwelling-house which was let under an original tenancy,]

"secure tenancy" has the same meaning as in Part 4 of the Act of 1985,

["subsequent transferee" means any person to whom, before the commencement date, the relevant interest was transferred after the transfer from the ex-landlord to the initial transferee,]

"successor"[, except in the expression "successor landlord] –

(a) in relation to [an original tenancy which was, or a new tenancy which is] an assured tenancy[, or in relation to an original tenancy which was, or a new tenancy which is, a demoted tenancy] to which section 20B of the Act of 1988 applies, has the same meaning as in section 17 of that Act,

(b) in relation to [an original tenancy which was, or a new tenancy which is] a demoted tenancy to which section 143A of the Act of 1996 applies, has the meaning given by section 143J of that Act,

(c) in relation to [an original tenancy which was, or a new tenancy which is] an introductory tenancy, has the same meaning as in section 132 of the Act of 1996, and

(d) in relation to [an original tenancy which was, or a new tenancy which is] a secure tenancy, has the same meaning as in section 88 of the Act of 1985.

["successor landlord" means the initial transferee, or, as the case may be, a subsequent transferee, to whom the relevant interest belongs on the commencement date,]

"termination period" has the meaning given by paragraph 16(3).

(2) For the purposes of the definition of "appropriate national authority" in sub-paragraph (1) a dwelling-house which is partly in England and partly in Wales is to be treated—

(a) as being in England if it is treated as situated in the area of a billing authority in England by virtue of regulations under section 1(3) of the Local Government Finance Act 1992 (c. 14) (council tax in respect of dwellings), and

(b) as being in Wales if it is treated as situated in the area of a billing authority in Wales by virtue of regulations under that section.

**Commencement**

**3A–1716** Part 2 brought into force for the purpose of enabling the appropriate national authority to make orders under that Part, with effect from December 1, 2008 by the Housing and Regeneration Act 2008 (Commencement No.2 and Transitional, Saving and Transitory Provisions) Order 2008 (SI 2008/3068) art.4(4). Amended by the Housing (Replacement of Terminated Tenancies) (Successor Landlords) (England) Order 2009 SI No.1262 and the Housing (Replacement of Terminated Tenancies) (Successor Landlords) (Wales) Order 2009 (SI 2009/1260).

# 3B BUSINESS TENANCIES

## Landlord and Tenant Act 1927

(17 & 18 Geo. 5 c.36) 3B–1

Arrangement of Sections

Part I

*Compensation for Improvements and Goodwill on the Termination of Tenancies of Business Premises*



## PART I

## *COMPENSATION FOR IMPROVEMENTS AND GOODWILL ON THE TERMINATION OF TENANCIES OF BUSINESS PREMISES*

### Tenant's right to compensation for improvements

**1.**—(1) Subject to the provisions of this Part of this Act, a tenant of a holding to which this Part of this Act applies shall, if a claim for the purpose is made in the prescribed manner [and within the time limited by section forty-seven of the Landlord and Tenant Act, 1954] be entitled, at the termination of the tenancy, on quitting his holding, to be paid by his landlord compensation in respect of any 3B–2

***Paragraph numbers marked with a "+" can be found online and on CD.***

improvement (including the erection of any building) on his holding made by him or his predecessors in title, not being a trade or other fixture which the tenant is by law entitled to remove, which at the termination of the tenancy adds to the letting value of the holding: Provided that the sum to be paid as compensation for any improvement shall not exceed—

(a) the net addition to the value of the holding as a whole which may be determined to be the direct result of the improvement; or

(b) the reasonable cost of carrying out the improvement at the termination of the tenancy, subject to a deduction of an amount equal to the cost (if any) of putting the works constituting the improvement into a reasonable state of repair, except so far as such cost is covered by the liability of the tenant under any covenant or agreement as to the repair of the premises.

(2) In determining the amount of such net addition as aforesaid, regard shall be had to the purposes for which it is intended that the premises shall be used after the termination of the tenancy, and if it is shown that it is intended to demolish or to make structural alterations in the premises or any part thereof or to use the premises for a different purpose, regard shall be had to the effect of such demolition, alteration or change of user on the additional value attributable to the improvement, and to the length of time likely to elapse between the termination of the tenancy and the demolition, alteration or change of user.

(3) In the absence of agreement between the parties, all questions as to the right to compensation under this section, or as to the amount thereof, shall be determined by the tribunal hereinafter mentioned, and if the tribunal determines that, on account of the intention to demolish or alter or to change the user of the premises, no compensation or a reduced amount of compensation shall be paid, the tribunal may authorise a further application for compensation to be made by the tenant if effect is not given to the intention within such time as may be fixed by the tribunal.

**3B–3** *Note* —Section 1 was amended by Landlord and Tenant Act 1954 s.1(1)(a)(b) and s.47(5).

**Editorial Note**

**3B–4** The Landlord and Tenant Act 1927 allows certain business tenants who carry out improvements to their holdings to claim compensation on quitting. This does not apply to tenants of mining leases (see s.25(1)) or tenancies of agricultural holdings (s.17(1)) or tenants who hold any office, appointment or employment from the landlord (s.17(2)). Tenants have to follow the strict procedures laid down in Pt I of this Act and comply with the time limit provided by Landlord and Tenant Act 1954 s.47—i.e. within the period of three months beginning on the date on which notice is given.

Sections 4 to 7 were repealed by Landlord and Tenant Act 1954 s.45 and Sch.7, Pt I.

**Holding**

**3B–5** i.e. premises held under a lease. See s.17.

**Improvement**

**3B–6** There is no definition of improvement in the Act, but s.1(1) provides that it must be

*Paragraph numbers marked with a "+" can be found online and on CD.*

something which at the termination of the tenancy adds to the letting value of the holding. Erection of a new building on unoccupied land may be an improvement within the Act (s.1(1) and *National Electric Theatres v Hudgell* [1939] Ch 553; [1939] 1 All E.R. 567). Section 2 provides that a tenant is not entitled to claim compensation in respect of certain types of improvements.

**Tenant**

Any person entitled in possession to the holding under any contract of tenancy, whether the interest of such tenant was acquired by original contract, assignment, operation of law or otherwise (s.25). This includes sub-tenants. Note that the designation of landlord and tenant continues to apply to the parties until the conclusion of any proceedings taken under or in pursuance of this Act in respect of compensation (s.25(2)). **3B–7**

**Landlord**

Any person who under a lease is, as between himself and the tenant or other lessee, for the time being entitled to the rents and profits of the demised premises payable under the lease (s.25). **3B–8**

**Trade or business**

There is no definition of trade or business in the 1927 Act. It is generally accepted that the phrase is to be interpreted in a narrower sense than in the 1954 Act (see e.g. *Stuchbery v General Accident Fire and Life Assurance Corp* [1949] 2 K.B. 256; [1949] 1 All E.R. 1026, CA—solicitors carrying on profession, not trade or business, not entitled to compensation under the 1927 Act, but see s.17(3) and (4)). **3B–9**

**Procedural requirements**

A tenant must serve on the landlord notice of intention to make improvements before carrying them out. The notice must be accompanied by a plan (s.3(1)). There is no prescribed form. Notice may be given in the form of a letter. See *Deerfield Travel Services v Wardens and Society of the Mistery or Art of the Leather Sellers* (1983) 46 P& C.R. 132, CA. The tenant may carry out the works if the landlord raises no objection within three months, even if a covenant in the lease provides otherwise. If the landlord objects, the tenant may apply to the court for a certificate that the improvement is a proper one (s.3(1)). **3B–10**

**Tribunal**

i.e. a county court or the High Court. See s.21 and Landlord and Tenant Act 1954 s.63. For the procedure see Vol.1, PD 56 para.5. **3B–11**

**The amount of compensation**

See s.1(1). The landlord pays for the benefit received from the improvement. The sum to be paid shall not exceed the net addition to the value of the holding as a whole or the reasonable cost of carrying out the improvement at the termination of the tenancy. **3B–12**

## Limitation on tenant's right to compensation in certain cases

**2.**—(1) A tenant shall not be entitled to compensation under this Part of this Act— **3B–13**

(a) in respect of any improvement made before the commencement of this Act; or

(b) in respect of any improvement made in pursuance of a statutory obligation, or of any improvement which the tenant or his predecessors in title were under an obligation to make in pursuance of a contract entered into, whether before or after the passing of this Act, for valuable consideration, including a building lease; or

(c) in respect of any improvement made less than three years before the termination of the tenancy; or

***Paragraph numbers marked with a "+" can be found online and on CD.***

(d) if within two months after the making of the claim under section one, subsection (1), of this Act the landlord serves on the tenant notice that he is willing and able to grant to the tenant, or obtain the grant to him of, a renewal of the tenancy at such rent and for such term as, failing agreement, the tribunal may consider reasonable; and, where such a notice is so served and the tenant does not within one month from the service of the notice send to the landlord an acceptance in writing of the offer, the tenant shall be deemed to have declined the offer.

(2) Where an offer of the renewal of a tenancy by the landlord under this section is accepted by the tenant, the rent fixed by the tribunal shall be the rent which in the opinion of the tribunal a willing lessee other than the tenant would agree to give and a willing lessor would agree to accept for the premises, having regard to the terms of the lease, but irrespective of the value attributable to the improvement in respect of which compensation would have been payable.

(3) The tribunal in determining the compensation for an improvement shall in reduction of the tenant's claim take into consideration any benefits which the tenant or his predecessors in title may have received from the landlord or his predecessors in title in consideration expressly or impliedly of the improvement.

**3B–14** *Note*—The effect of s.2(1)(b) is restricted by Landlord and Tenant Act 1954 s.48(1).

**Tenant**

**3B–15** Any person entitled in possession to the holding under any contract of tenancy, whether the interest of such tenant was acquired by original contract, assignment, operation of law or otherwise (s.25). This includes sub-tenants. Note that the designation of landlord and tenant continues to apply to the parties until the conclusion of any proceedings taken under or in pursuance of this Act in respect of compensation (s.25(2)).

**Landlord**

**3B–16** Any person who under a lease is, as between himself and the tenant or other lessee, for the time being entitled to the rents and profits of the demised premises payable under the lease (s.25).

**Improvement**

**3B–17** See commentary to s.1.

**Tribunal**

**3B–18** i.e. a county court or the High Court. See s.21 and Landlord and Tenant Act 1954 s.63.

## Landlord's right to object

**3B–19** **3.**—(1) Where a tenant of a holding to which this Part of this Act applies proposes to make an improvement on his holding, he shall serve on his landlord notice of his intention to make such improvement, together with a specification and plan showing the proposed improvement and the part of the existing premises affected thereby, and if the landlord, within three months after the service of the notice, serves on the tenant notice of objection, the tenant may, in the prescribed manner, apply to the tribunal, and the tribunal may, after ascertaining that notice of such intention has been served upon any superior landlords interested and after giving such persons an opportunity of being heard, if satisfied that the improvement—

(a) is of such a nature as to be calculated to add to the letting value of the holding at the termination of the tenancy; and
(b) is reasonable and suitable to the character thereof; and
(c) will not diminish the value of any other property belonging to the same landlord, or to any superior landlord from whom the immediate landlord of the tenant directly or indirectly holds;

and after making such modifications (if any) in the specification or plan as the tribunal thinks fit, or imposing such other conditions as the tribunal may think reasonable, certify in the prescribed manner that the improvement is a proper improvement.

Provided that, if the landlord proves that he has offered to execute the improvement himself in consideration of a reasonable increase of rent, or of such increase of rent as the tribunal may determine, the tribunal shall not give a certificate under this section unless it is subsequently shown to the satisfaction of the tribunal that the landlord has failed to carry out his undertaking.

(2) In considering whether the improvement is reasonable and suitable to the character of the holding, the tribunal shall have regard to any evidence brought before it by the landlord or any superior landlord (but not any other person) that the improvement is calculated to injure the amenity or convenience of the neighbourhood.

(3) The tenant shall, at the request of any superior landlord or at the request of the tribunal, supply such copies of the plans and specifications of the proposed improvement as may be required.

(4) Where no such notice of objection as aforesaid to a proposed improvement has been served within the time allowed by this section, or where the tribunal has certified an improvement to be a proper improvement, it shall be lawful for the tenant as against the immediate and any superior landlord to execute the improvement according to the plan and specification served on the landlord, or according to such plan and specification as modified by the tribunal or by agreement between the tenant and the landlord or landlords affected, anything in any lease of the premises to the contrary notwithstanding:

Provided that nothing in this subsection shall authorise a tenant to execute an improvement in contravention of any restriction created or imposed—

(a) for naval, military or air force purposes;
(b) for civil aviation purposes under the powers of the Air Navigation Act, 1920;
(c) for securing any rights of the public over the foreshore or bed of the sea.

(5) A tenant shall not be entitled to claim compensation under

this Part of this Act in respect of any improvement unless he has, or his predecessors in title have, served notice of the proposal to make the improvement under this section, and (in case the landlord has served notice of objection thereto) the improvement has been certified by the tribunal to be a proper improvement and the tenant has complied with the conditions, if any, imposed by the tribunal, nor unless the improvement is completed within such time after the service on the landlord of the notice of the proposed improvement as may be agreed between the tenant and the landlord or may be fixed by the tribunal, and where proceedings have been taken before the tribunal, the tribunal may defer making any order as to costs until the expiration of the time so fixed for the completion of the improvement.

(6) Where a tenant has executed an improvement of which he has served notice in accordance with this section and with respect to which either no notice of objection has been served by the landlord or a certificate that it is a proper improvement has been obtained from the tribunal, the tenant may require the landlord to furnish to him a certificate that the improvement has been duly executed; and if the landlord refuses or fails within one month after the service of the requisition to do so, the tenant may apply to the tribunal who, if satisfied that the improvement has been duly executed, shall give a certificate to that effect.

Where the landlord furnishes such a certificate, the tenant shall be liable to pay any reasonable expenses incurred for the purpose by the landlord, and if any question arises as to the reasonableness of such expenses, it shall be determined by the tribunal.

**3B–20** *Note*—Section 3 is restricted by Landlord and Tenant Act 1954 s.48(1).

**Holding**

**3B–21** i.e. premises held under a lease. See s.17.

**Tenant**

**3B–22** Any person entitled in possession to the holding under any contract of tenancy, whether the interest of such tenant was acquired by original contract, assignment, operation of law or otherwise (s.25). This includes sub-tenants. Note that the designation of landlord and tenant continues to apply to the parties until the conclusion of any proceedings taken under or in pursuance of this Act in respect of compensation (s.25(2)).

**Landlord**

**3B–23** Any person who under a lease is, as between himself and the tenant or other lessee, for the time being entitled to the rents and profits of the demised premises payable under the lease (s.25).

**Change of mind**

**3B–24** See commentary to s.1, above. Where a tenant serves a notice under s.3 stating an intention to carry out improvements, but then withdraws the notice after the landlord has served a counter notice, the landlord is not entitled to carry out the improvements (*Norfolk Capital Group Ltd v Cadogan Estates Ltd* [2004] EWHC 384 (ChD); [2004] 32 E.G. 64; [2004] 1 W.L.R. 1458).

**Improvement**

**3B–25** There is no definition of improvement in the Act, but s.1(1) provides that it must be something which at the termination of the tenancy adds to the letting value of the holding. See commentary to s.1, above.

**Tribunal**

i.e. a county court or the High Court. See s.21 and Landlord and Tenant Act 1954 s.63. 3B–26

* * * *

## Rights of mesne landlords

**8.**—(1) Where, in the case of any holding, there are several persons standing in the relation to each other of lessor and lessee, the following provisions shall apply:— Any mesne landlord who has paid or is liable to pay compensation under this Part of this Act, shall, at the end of his term, be entitled to compensation from his immediate landlord in like manner and on the same conditions as if he had himself made the improvement [.] in question, except that it shall be sufficient if the claim for compensation is made at least two months before the expiration of his term: A mesne landlord shall not be entitled to make a claim under this section unless he has, within the time and in the manner prescribed, served on his immediate superior landlord copies of all documents relating to proposed improvements and claims which have been sent to him in pursuance of this Part of this Act: Where such copies are so served, the said superior landlord shall have, in addition to the mesne landlord, the powers conferred by or in pursuance of this Part of this Act in like manner as if he were the immediate landlord of the occupying tenant, and shall, in the manner and to the extent prescribed, be at liberty to appear before the tribunal and shall be bound by the proceedings: 3B–27

(2) In this section, references to a landlord shall include references to his predecessors in title.

*Note* —Section 8 was amended by Landlord and Tenant Act 1954, s.45 and Sch.7, Pts I and II. 3B–28

**Holding**

i.e. premises held under a lease. See s.17. 3B–29

**Tenant**

Any person entitled in possession to the holding under any contract of tenancy, whether the interest of such tenant was acquired by original contract, assignment, operation of law or otherwise (s.25). This includes sub-tenants. Note that the designation of landlord and tenant continues to apply to the parties until the conclusion of any proceedings taken under or in pursuance of this Act in respect of compensation (s.25(2)). 3B–30

**Landlord**

Any person who under a lease is, as between himself and the tenant or other lessee, for the time being entitled to the rents and profits of the demised premises payable under the lease (s.25). 3B–31

**Tribunal**

i.e. a county court or the High Court. See s.21 and Landlord and Tenant Act 1954 s.63. 3B–32

## Restriction on contracting out

**9.** This Part of this Act shall apply notwithstanding any contract to 3B–33 the contrary, being a contract made at any time after the eighth day of February, nineteen hundred and twenty-seven.

3B-34 *Note* —The former proviso to s.9 was repealed by Landlord and Tenant Act 1954 s.49.

## Right of entry

3B-35 **10.** The landlord of a holding to which this Part of this Act applies, or any person authorised by him may at all reasonable times enter on the holding or any part of it, for the purpose of executing any improvement he has undertaken to execute and of making any inspection of the premises which may reasonably be required for the purposes of this Part of this Act.

**Landlord**

3B-36 Any person who under a lease is, as between himself and the tenant or other lessee, for the time being entitled to the rents and profits of the demised premises payable under the lease (s.25).

**Holding**

3B-37 i.e. premises held under a lease. See s.17.

## Right to make deductions

3B-38 **11.**—(1) Out of any money payable to a tenant by way of compensation under this Part of this Act, the landlord shall be entitled to deduct any sum due to him from the tenant under or in respect of the tenancy.

(2) Out of any money due to the landlord from the tenant under or in respect of the tenancy, the tenant shall be entitled to deduct any sum payable to him by the landlord by way of compensation under this Part of this Act.

**Tenant**

3B-39 Any person entitled in possession to the holding under any contract of tenancy, whether the interest of such tenant was acquired by original contract, assignment, operation of law or otherwise (s.25). This includes sub-tenants. Note that the designation of landlord and tenant continues to apply to the parties until the conclusion of any proceedings taken under or in pursuance of this Act in respect of compensation (s.25(2)).

**Landlord**

3B-40 Any person who under a lease is, as between himself and the tenant or other lessee, for the time being entitled to the rents and profits of the demised premises payable under the lease (s.25).

## Application of 13 & 14 Geo. 5. c.9. s.20

3B-41 **12.** Section twenty of the Agricultural Holdings Act, 1923 (which relates to charges in respect of money paid for compensation), as set out and modified in the First Schedule to this Act, shall apply to the case of money paid for compensation under this Part of this Act, including any proper costs, charges, or expenses incurred by a landlord in opposing any proposal by a tenant to execute an improvement, or in contesting a claim for compensation, and to money expended by a landlord in executing an improvement the notice of a proposal to execute which has been served on him by a tenant under this Part of this Act.

**Tenant**

Any person entitled in possession to the holding under any contract of tenancy, whether the interest of such tenant was acquired by original contract, assignment, operation of law or otherwise (s.25). This includes sub-tenants. Note that the designation of landlord and tenant continues to apply to the parties until the conclusion of any proceedings taken under or in pursuance of this Act in respect of compensation (s.25(2)). **3B–42**

**Landlord**

Any person who under a lease is, as between himself and the tenant or other lessee, for the time being entitled to the rents and profits of the demised premises payable under the lease (s.25). **3B–43**

## Power to apply and raise capital money

**13.**—(1) Capital money arising under the Settled Land Act, 1925 […] section twenty-eight of the Law of Property Act, 1925, or under the University and College Estates Act, 1925, may be applied— **3B–44**

(a) in payment as for an improvement authorised by the Act of any money expended and costs incurred by a landlord under or in pursuance of this Part of this Act in or about the execution of any improvement;

(b) in payment of any sum due to a tenant under this Part of this Act in respect of compensation for an improvement […] and any costs, charges, and expenses incidental thereto;

(c) in payment of the costs, charges, and expenses of opposing any proposal by a tenant to execute an improvement.

(2) The satisfaction of a claim for such compensation as aforesaid shall be included amongst the purposes for which a tenant for life, statutory owner, trustee for sale, or personal representative may raise money under section seventy-one of the Settled Land Act, 1925.

(3) Where the landlord liable to pay compensation for an improvement […] is a tenant for life or in a fiduciary position, he may require the sum payable as compensation and any costs, charges, and expenses incidental thereto, to be paid out of any capital money held on the same trusts as the settled land.

In this subsection "capital money" includes any personal estate held on the same trusts as the land, and "settled land" includes land held on trust for sale or vested in a personal representative.

*Note*—Section 13 was amended by Trusts of Landand Appointment of Trustees Act 1925 Sch.4 and by Landlord and Tenant Act 1954 s.45, Sch.7, Pt I. **3B–45**

**Tenant**

Any person entitled in possession to the holding under any contract of tenancy, whether the interest of such tenant was acquired by original contract, assignment, operation of law or otherwise (s.25). This includes sub-tenants. Note that the designation of landlord and tenant continues to apply to the parties until the conclusion of any proceedings taken under or in pursuance of this Act in respect of compensation (s.25(2)). **3B–46**

**Landlord**

Any person who under a lease is, as between himself and the tenant or other lessee, **3B–47** for the time being entitled to the rents and profits of the demised premises payable under the lease (s.25).

## Power to sell or grant leases notwithstanding restrictions

3B–48 **14.** Where the powers of a landlord to sell or grant leases are subject to any statutory or other restrictions, he shall, notwithstanding any such restrictions or any rule of law to the contrary, be entitled to offer to sell or grant any such reversion or lease as would under this Part of this Act relieve him from liability to pay compensation thereunder, and to convey and grant the same, and to execute any lease which he may be ordered to grant under this Part of this Act.

### Landlord

3B–49 Any person who under a lease is, as between himself and the tenant or other lessee, for the time being entitled to the rents and profits of the demised premises payable under the lease (s.25).

## Provisions as to reversionary leases

3B–50 **15.**—(1) Where the amount which a landlord is liable to pay as compensation for an improvement under this Part of this Act has been determined by agreement or by an award of the tribunal, and the landlord had before the passing of this Act granted or agreed to grant a reversionary lease commencing on or after the termination of the then existing tenancy, the rent payable under the reversionary lease shall, if the tribunal so directs, be increased by such amount as, failing agreement, may be determined by the tribunal having regard to the addition to the letting value of the holding attributable to the improvement: Provided that no such increase shall be permissible unless the landlord has served or caused to be served on the reversionary lessee copies of all documents relating to the improvement when proposed which were sent to the landlord in pursuance of this Part of this Act.

(2) The reversionary lessee shall have the same right of objection to the proposed improvement and of appearing and being heard at any proceedings before the tribunal relative to the proposed improvement as if he were a superior landlord, and if the amount of compensation for the improvement is determined by the tribunal, any question as to the increase of rent under the reversionary lease shall, where practicable, be settled in the course of the same proceedings.

3B–51 *Note*—Section 15 was amended by Landlord and Tenant Act 1954 Sch.7, Pt II.

### Holding

3B–52 i.e. premises held under a lease. See s.17.

### Landlord

3B–53 Any person who under a lease is, as between himself and the tenant or other lessee, for the time being entitled to the rents and profits of the demised premises payable under the lease (s.25).

### Tribunal

3B–54 i.e. a county court or the High Court. See s.21 and Landlord and Tenant Act 1954 s.63.

***Paragraph numbers marked with a "+" can be found online and on CD.***

## Landlord's right to reimbursement of increased taxes, rates or insurance premiums

**16.** Where the landlord is liable to pay any […] rates (including water rate) in respect of any premises comprised in a holding, or has undertaken to pay the premiums on any fire insurance policy on any such premises, and in consequence of any improvement executed by the tenant on the premises under this Act the assessment of the premises or the rate of premium on the policy is increased, the tenant shall be liable to pay to the landlord sums equal to the amount by which— **3B–55**

(a) the […] rates payable by the landlord are increased by reason of the increase of such assessment;

(b) the fire premium payable by the landlord is increased by reason of the increase in the rate of premium;

and the sums so payable by the tenant shall be deemed to be in the nature of rent and shall be recoverable as such from the tenant, […].

*Note*—Section 16 was amended by Rent Act 1968 s.67(2); Finance Act 1963 Sch.13, Pt IV; and Housing Act 1980 s.152 and Sch.26. **3B–56**

**Tenant**

Any person entitled in possession to the holding under any contract of tenancy, whether the interest of such tenant was acquired by original contract, assignment, operation of law or otherwise (s.25). This includes sub-tenants. Note that the designation of landlord and tenant continues to apply to the parties until the conclusion of any proceedings taken under or in pursuance of this Act in respect of compensation (s.25(2)). **3B–57**

**Landlord**

Any person who under a lease is, as between himself and the tenant or other lessee, for the time being entitled to the rents and profits of the demised premises payable under the lease (s.25). **3B–58**

**Holding**

i.e. premises held under a lease. See s.17. **3B–59**

## Holdings to which Part I. applies

**17.**—(1) The holdings to which this Part of this Act applies are any premises held under a lease, other than a mining lease, made whether before or after the commencement of this Act, and used wholly or partly for carrying on thereat any trade or business, and [not being— **3B–60**

(a) agricultural holdings within the meaning of the Agricultural Holdings Act 1986 held under leases in relation to which that Act applies, or

(b) holdings held under farm business tenancies within the meaning of the Agricultural Tenancies Act 1995]

(2) This Part of this Act shall not apply to any holding let to a tenant as the holder of any office, appointment or employment, from the landlord, and continuing so long as the tenant holds such office, appointment or employment, but in the case of a tenancy created after the commencement of this Act, only if the contract is in writing and expresses the purpose for which the tenancy is created.

*Paragraph numbers marked with a "+" can be found online and on CD.*

(3) For the purposes of this section, premises shall not be deemed to be premises used for carrying on thereat a trade or business—

(a) by reason of their being used for the purpose of carrying on thereat any profession;

(b) by reason that the tenant thereof carries on the business of subletting the premises as residential flats, whether or not the provision of meals or any other service for the occupants of the flats is undertaken by the tenant.

Provided that, so far as this Part of this Act relates to improvements, premises regularly used for carrying on a profession shall be deemed to be premises used for carrying on a trade or business.

(4) In the case of premises used partly for purposes of a trade or business and partly for other purposes, this Part of this Act shall apply to improvements only if and so far as they are improvements in relation to the trade or business.

**3B–61** *Note*—Section 17 was amended by the Agricultural Tenancies Act 1995 Sch.1.

**Tenant**

**3B–62** Any person entitled in possession to the holding under any contract of tenancy, whether the interest of such tenant was acquired by original contract, assignment, operation of law or otherwise (s.25). This includes sub-tenants. Note that the designation of landlord and tenant continues to apply to the parties until the conclusion of any proceedings taken under or in pursuance of this Act in respect of compensation (s.25(2)).

**Landlord**

**3B–63** Any person who under a lease is, as between himself and the tenant or other lessee, for the time being entitled to the rents and profits of the demised premises payable under the lease (s.25).

**Mining lease**

**3B–64** A lease for any mining purpose or purposes connected therewith, and "mining purposes" include the sinking and searching for, winning, working, getting, making merchantable, smelting or otherwise converting or working for the purposes of any manufacture, carrying away, and disposing of mines and minerals, in or under land, and the erection of buildings, and the execution of engineering and other works suitable for those purposes (s.25)

**Trade or business**

**3B–65** There is no definition of trade or business in the 1927 Act. It is generally accepted that the phrase is to be interpreted in a narrower sense than in the 1954 Act (see e.g. *Stuchbery v General Accident Fire and Life Assurance Corp* [1949] 2 K.B. 256; [1949] 1 All E.R. 1026, CA—solicitors carrying on profession, not trade or business, not entitled to compensation under the 1927 Act, but see s.17(3) and (4)).

# PART II

## GENERAL AMENDMENTS OF THE LAW OF LANDLORD AND TENANT

### Provisions as to covenants to repair

**3B–66** **18.**—(1) Damages for a breach of a covenant or agreement to keep or put premises in repair during the currency of a lease, or to leave or put premises in repair at the termination of a lease, whether such covenant or agreement is expressed or implied, and whether general or specific, shall in no case exceed the amount (if any) by which the value of the reversion (whether immediate or not) in the premises is diminished owing to the breach of such covenant or agreement as aforesaid; and in particular no damage shall be recovered for a breach of any such covenant or agreement to leave or put premises in repair at the termination of a lease, if it is shown that the premises, in whatever state of repair they might be, would at or shortly after the termination of the tenancy have been or be pulled down, or such structural alterations made therein as would render valueless the repairs covered by the covenant or agreement.

(2) A right of re-entry or forfeiture for a breach of any such covenant or agreement as aforesaid shall not be enforceable, by action or otherwise, unless the lessor proves that the fact that such a notice as is required by section one hundred and forty-six of the Law of Property Act, 1925, had been served on the lessee was known either—

(a) to the lessee; or

(b) to an under-lessee holding under an under-lease which reserved a nominal reversion only to the lessee; or

(c) to the person who last paid the rent due under the lease either on his own behalf or as agent for the lessee or under-lessee;

and that a time reasonably sufficient to enable the repairs to be executed had elapsed since the time when the fact of the service of the notice came to the knowledge of any such person.

Where a notice has been sent by registered post addressed to a person at his last known place of abode in the United Kingdom, then, for the purposes of this subsection, that person shall be deemed, unless the contrary is proved, to have had knowledge of the fact that the notice had been served as from the time at which the letter would have been delivered in the ordinary course of post.

This subsection shall be construed as one with section one hundred and forty-six of the Law of Property Act, 1925.

(3) This section applies whether the lease was created before or after the commencement of this Act.

*Note*—Section 18 was amended by the Recorded Delivery Service Act 1962 s.1, Sch. **3B–67**

**Introduction**

Section 18(1) of the 1927 Act limits the amount of damages that a landlord may recover for breach of repairing covenants. There are two limbs to this subsection. Under the first limb the damages are limited to the amount by which the value of the landlord's interest in the property is damaged by the breach. The second limb precludes any recovery at all where that limb applies (the property will at or shortly after termination be pulled down, or structural alterations that would render the repairs valueless). **3B–67.1**

Where the court is considering whether or not there has been a diminution in value under the first limb, if the repairs have been carried out or are going to be carried out the cost of those repairs is likely to be a good guide to the amount of the diminution in value of the property (*Jones v Herxheimer* [1950] 2 K.B. 106; [1950] 1 All E.R. 323). Generally speaking if the repairs are not going to be carried out the cost of them is unlikely to be a good guide (*Smiley v Townshend* [1950] 2 K.B. 311; [1950] 1 All E.R. 530); and it will be necessary to obtain valuation evidence. In *Latimer v Carney* [2006] EWCA Civ 1417; [2007] 1 P. & C.R. 13; [2006] 3 E.G.L.R. 13) the Court of Appeal held that an estimated cost of repairs in a schedule of dilapidations could be used to establish diminution in value. The landlord did not carry out the works in the schedule but something rather different for an incoming tenant. The landlord was able to rely upon the estimated cost to establish that there was some diminution in value but the amount of its claim was substantially reduced to take account of the uncertainty. The lesson is that in all but the most simple cases there should be proper expert evidence as to diminution in value.

The second limb is difficult to establish and is not often relied upon. However, even where it is not possible to establish that the second limb applies the tenant may still be able to rely upon the first limb where the property is ripe for development. If any potential purchaser would develop the property and the development would render otiose the carrying out of most of the repairs claimed by the landlord there is unlikely to be much if any diminution in value (*Ravengate Estates Ltd v Horizon Housing Group Ltd* [2007] EWCA Civ 1368).

**Repair**

**3B–67.2** A covenant to decorate is a covenant to repair and so is subject to the limitations in s.18 (*Latimer v Carney* [2006] EWCA Civ 1417; [2006] 3 E.G.L.R. 13). Other covenants such as a covenant not to re-instate alterations, or to comply with statutory obligations, are not covenants to repair. Thus, s.18 will not afford the tenant any protection. However, since the House of Lords decision in *Ruxley v Forsyth* [1996] A.C. 344; [1995] 3 W.L.R. 268; [1995] 3 All E.R. 268 it is likely that the same principles apply at common law (see *Latimer v Carney* [2006] EWCA Civ 1417; [2007] 1 P. & C.R.13; [2006] 3 E.G.L.R. 13, per Arden L.J. at [24] and [60]).

**Re-entry or forfeiture**

**3B–68** See the commentary to Law of Property Act 1925 s.146 at para.3A–16.

**Deemed knowledge**

**3B–69** See the commentary to s.23 below.

## Provisions as to covenants not to assign, &c. without licence or consent

**3B–70** **19.**—(1) In all leases whether made before or after the commencement of this Act containing a covenant condition or agreement against assigning, underletting, charging or parting with the possession of demised premises or any part thereof without licence or consent, such covenant condition or agreement shall, notwithstanding any express provision to the contrary, be deemed to be subject—

(a) to a proviso to the effect that such licence or consent is not to be unreasonably withheld, but this proviso does not preclude the right of the landlord to require payment of a reasonable sum in respect of any legal or other expenses incurred in connection with such licence or, consent; and

(b) (if the lease is for more than forty years, and is made in consideration wholly or partially of the erection, or the substantial improvement, addition or alteration of buildings, and the lessor is not a Government department or local or public authority, or a statutory or public utility company) to a proviso to the effect that in the case of any assignment, under-letting, charging or parting with the possession (whether by the holders of the lease or any under-tenant whether immediate or not) effected more than seven years before the end of the term no

*Paragraph numbers marked with a "+" can be found online and on CD.*

consent or licence shall be required, if notice in writing of the transaction is given to the lessor within six months after the transaction is effected.

(1A) Where the landlord and the tenant under a qualifying lease have entered into an agreement specifying for the purposes of this subsection—

(a) any circumstances in which the landlord may withhold his licence or consent to an assignment of the demised premises or any part of them, or

(b) any conditions subject to which any such licence or consent may be granted,

then the landlord—

(i) shall not be regarded as unreasonably withholding his licence or consent to any such assignment if he withholds it on the ground (and it is the case) that any such circumstances exist, and

(ii) if he gives any such licence or consent subject to any such conditions, shall not be regarded as giving it subject to unreasonable conditions;

and section 1 of the Landlord and Tenant Act 1988 (qualified duty to consent to assignment etc.) shall have effect subject to the provisions of this subsection.

(1B) Subsection (1A) of this section applies to such an agreement as is mentioned in that subsection—

(a) whether it is contained in the lease or not, and

(b) whether it is made at the time when the lease is granted or at any other time falling before the application for the landlord's licence or consent is made.

(1C) Subsection (1A) shall not, however, apply to any such agreement to the extent that any circumstances or conditions specified in it are framed by reference to any matter falling to be determined by the landlord or by any other person for the purposes of the agreement, unless under the terms of the agreement—

(a) that person's power to determine that matter is required to be exercised reasonably, or

(b) the tenant is given an unrestricted right to have any such determination reviewed by a person independent of both landlord and tenant whose identity is ascertainable by reference to the agreement,

and in the latter case the agreement provides for the determination made by any such independent person on the review to be conclusive as to the matter in question.

(1D) In its application to a qualifying lease, subsection (1)(b) of this section shall not have effect in relation to any assignment of the lease.

(1E) In subsection (1A) and (1D) of this section—

(a) "qualifying lease" means any lease which is a new tenancy for the purposes of section 1 of the Landlord and Tenant (Covenants) Act 1995 other than a residential lease, namely a lease by which a building or part of a building is let wholly or mainly as a single private residence; and

(b) references to assignment include parting with possession on assignment.

(2) In all leases whether made before or after the commencement of this Act containing a covenant condition or agreement against the making of improvements without a licence or consent, such covenant condition or agreement shall be deemed, notwithstanding any express provision to the contrary, to be subject to a proviso that such licence or consent is not to be unreasonably withheld; but this proviso does not preclude the right to require as a condition of such licence or consent the payment of a reasonable sum in respect of any damage to or diminution in the value of the premises or any neighbouring premises belonging to the landlord, and of any legal or other expenses properly incurred in connection with such licence or consent nor, in the case of an improvement which does not add to the letting value of the holding, does it preclude the right to require as a condition of such licence or consent, where such a requirement would be reasonable, an undertaking on the part of the tenant to reinstate the premises in the condition in which they were before the improvement was executed.

(3) In all leases whether made before or after the commencement of this Act containing a covenant condition or agreement against the alteration of the user of the demised premises, without licence or consent, such covenant condition or agreement shall, if the alteration does not involve any structural alteration of the premises, be deemed, notwithstanding any express provision to the contrary, to be subject to a proviso that no fine or sum of money in the nature of a fine, whether by way of increase of rent or otherwise, shall be payable for or in respect of such licence or consent; but this proviso does not preclude the right of the landlord to require payment of a reasonable sum in respect of any damage to or diminution in the value of the premises or any neighbouring premises belonging to him and of any legal or other expenses incurred in connection with such licence or consent.

Where a dispute as to the reasonableness of any such sum has been determined by a court of competent jurisdiction, the landlord shall be bound to grant the licence or consent on payment of the sum so determined to be reasonable.

(4) This section shall not apply to leases of agricultural holdings within the meaning of the [Agricultural Holdings Act 1986], and paragraph (b) of subsection (1), subsection (2) and subsection (3) of this section shall not apply to mining leases.

**3B–71** *Note*—Section 19 has been superseded in relation to secure tenancies by Housing Act 1985 s.97, s.109. It was amended by Agricultural Holdings Act 1986 ss.99 and 100, Sch.13, para.3 and Sch.14, para.15. See too Landlord and Tenant Act 1988.

**Tenant**

**3B–72** Any person entitled in possession to the holding under any contract of tenancy, whether the interest of such tenant was acquired by original contract, assignment, operation of law or otherwise (s.25). This includes sub-tenants. Note that the designation of landlord and tenant continues to apply to the parties until the conclusion of any proceedings taken under or in pursuance of this Act in respect of compensation (s.25(2)).

### Landlord

Any person who under a lease is, as between himself and the tenant or other lessee, for the time being entitled to the rents and profits of the demised premises payable under the lease (s.25). **3B–73**

### Mining lease

A lease for any mining purpose or purposes connected therewith, and "mining purposes" include the sinking and searching for, winning, working, getting, making merchantable, smelting or otherwise converting or working for the purposes of any manufacture, carrying away, and disposing of mines and minerals, in or under land, and the erection of buildings, and the execution of engineering and other works suitable for those purposes (s.25). **3B–74**

### Reasonableness

Section 19(1)(a) implies a proviso into leases that the "licence or consent is not to be unreasonably withheld". The leading case for determining whether or not the landlord has acted reasonably is *International Drilling Fluids Ltd v Louisville Investments (Uxbridge) Ltd* [1986] Ch 513; [1986] 2 W.L.R. 581; [1986] 1 All E.R. 321. The main principles as stated in that case are as follows (Balcombe J. at 325): **3B–75**

- The purpose of a covenant against assignment without the consent of the landlord, such consent not to be unreasonably withheld is to protect the lessor from having his premises used or occupied in an undesirable way or by an undesirable tenant or assignee.
- As a corollary a landlord is not entitled to refuse his consent to an assignment on grounds which have nothing to do with the relationship of landlord and tenant in regard to the subject matter of the lease.
- It is not necessary for the landlord to prove that the conclusions which led him to refuse consent were justified, if they were conclusions which might be reached by a reasonable man in the circumstances.
- If may be reasonable for the landlord to refuse his consent for an assignment on the ground of the purpose for which the proposed assignee intends to use the premises, even though that purpose is not forbidden by the lease.
- There is a divergence of authority on the question, in considering whether the landlord's refusal of consent is reasonable, whether it is permissible to have regard to the consequences to the tenant if consent to the proposed assignment is withheld. A proper reconciliation of the authorities can be achieved by saying that while a landlord need usually only consider his own relevant interest, there may be cases where there is such a disproportion between the benefit to the landlord and the detriment to the tenant if the landlord withholds his consent to an assignment, that it is unreasonable for the landlord to refuse consent.
- Subject to the propositions set out above, it is, in each case a question of fact, depending on all the circumstances, whether consent is being unreasonably withheld.

At the time of *International Drilling* the onus of proof was on the tenant, who had to prove that the consent had been unreasonably withheld. However, the position was reversed by s.1(6)(c) of the 1988 Act so that the burden is now on the landlord to prove that his refusal was reasonable (*Norwich v Shopmoor* [1998] 3 All E.R. 32).

When a court is determining whether or not a landlord's consent was reasonable, the landlord cannot rely upon matters that did not influence him at the time he refused his consent. The time at which the landlord's refusal must be judged is the time at which he refuses consent (*CIN Properties v Gill* [1993] 2 E.G.L.R. 97; *Go West v Spigarolo* [2003] EWCA Civ 17; [2003] Q.B. 1140; [2003] 2 W.L.R. 986). However, he may elaborate a reason already given (*Ashworth Frazer v Gloucester City Council (No.2)* [2001] UKHL 59; [2001] 1 W.L.R. 2180; *The Royal Bank of Scotland v Victoria Street (No.3) Ltd* [2008] EWHC 3052 (Ch); [2009] L. & T.R. 17—Morgan J at [37]: "the essential distinction in this area is between something which is an elaboration of the reasons stated in the letter, which is permitted, and something which is a different reason to that stated in the letter, which is not permitted.").

A refusal to give consent to an assignment on the ground that the intended use by

***Paragraph numbers marked with a "+" can be found online and on CD.***

the assignee would be a breach of covenant is not automatically unreasonable. It is necessary to consider what the reasonable landlord would do in the particular circumstances of the case (*Ashworth Frazer Ltd v Gloucester City Council (No.2)* [2001] UKHL 59; [2001] 1 W.L.R. 2180).

## Apportionment of rents

3B–76 **20.**—(1) An order of apportionment of a rent reserved by a lease or any such other rent or payment as is mentioned in section ten of the Inclosure Act, 1854, may be made by the under sections ten to fourteen of that Act, on the application of any person interested in the rent or payment, or any part thereof, or in the land in respect of which such rent or payment is payable, without the concurrence of any other person: Provided that the Minister may in any such case, on the application of any person entitled to the rent or payment or any part thereof, require as a condition of making the order that any apportioned part of the rent or payment which does not exceed the yearly sum of [£5] shall be redeemed forthwith [in accordance with sections 8 to 10 of the Rentcharges Act 1977(which, for the purposes of this section, shall have effect with the necessary modifications)].

[(1A) An order of apportionment under sections 10 to 14 of the said Act of 1854 may provide for the amount apportioned to any part of the land in respect of which the rent or payment is payable to be nil.]

(2) Where the reason for the application was due to any action taken by a person other than the applicant, the Minister shall, notwithstanding anything in section fourteen of the Inclosure Act, 1854, have power to direct by whom and in what manner the expenses of the application or any part thereof are to be paid.

3B–77 *Note*—Section 20 was amended by Housing Act 1980, s.143(1), the Rentcharges Act 1977 s.17(1) and Sch. 1, para.3 and by Housing Act 1980 s.143(3). The functions of the Minister of Agriculture and Fisheries under s.20 are now exercisable by the Secretary of State: see Transfer of Functions (Ministry of Food) Order 1955 (SI 1995/554); Minister of Land and Natural Resources Order 1965 (SI 1965/143); Ministry of Land and Natural Resources (Dissolution) Order 1967 (SI 1967/156) and Secretary of State for the Environment Order 1970 (SI 1970/1681).

# PART III

## GENERAL

## The tribunal

3B–78 **21.** The tribunal for the purposes of Part I of this Act shall be the court exercising jurisdiction in accordance with the provisions of section sixty-three of the Landlord and Tenant Act, 1954.

3B–79 *Note*—The current s.21 was substituted by Landlord and Tenant Act 1954 s.63(10).

* * * *

## Service of notices

3B–80 **23.**—(1) Any notice, request, demand or other instrument under

*Paragraph numbers marked with a "+" can be found online and on CD.*

this Act shall be in writing and may be served on the person on whom it is to be served either personally, or by leaving it for him at his last known place of abode in England or Wales, or by sending it through the post in a registered letter addressed to him there, or, in the case of a local or public authority or a statutory or a public utility company, to the secretary or other proper officer at the principal office of such authority or company, and in the case of a notice to a landlord, the person on whom it is to be served shall include any agent of the landlord duly authorised in that behalf.

(1A) Occupation or the carrying on of a business—

(a) by a company in which the tenant has a controlling interest; or

(b) where the tenant is a company, by a person with a controlling interest in the company,

shall be treated for the purposes of this section as equivalent to occupation or, as the case may be, the carrying on of a business by the tenant.

(1B) Accordingly references (however expressed) in this Part of this Act to the business of, or to use, occupation or enjoyment by, the tenant shall be construed as including references to the business of, or to use, occupation or enjoyment by, a company falling within subsection (1A)(a) above or a person falling within subsection (1A)(b) above.

(2) Unless or until a tenant of a holding shall have received notice that the person theretofore entitled to the rents and profits of the holding (hereinafter referred to as "the original landlord") has ceased to be so entitled, and also notice of the name and address of the person who has become entitled to such rents and profits, any claim, notice, request, demand, or other instrument which the tenant shall serve upon or deliver to the original landlord shall be deemed to have been served upon or delivered to the landlord of such holding.

*Note* —Section 23 was amended by the Recorded Delivery Service Act 1962 s.1. **3B–81**

**Tenant**

Any person entitled in possession to the holding under any contract of tenancy, whether the interest of such tenant was acquired by original contract, assignment, operation of law or otherwise (s.25). This includes sub-tenants. Note that the designation of landlord and tenant continues to apply to the parties until the conclusion of any proceedings taken under or in pursuance of this Act in respect of compensation (s.25(2)). **3B–82**

**Landlord**

Any person who under a lease is, as between himself and the tenant or other lessee, for the time being entitled to the rents and profits of the demised premises payable under the lease (s.25). **3B–83**

**Service of notices**

Section 23 provides that any notice, request, demand or other instrument can be served personally or left at the last known place of abode (which includes place of business—*Price v West London Investment Building Society Ltd* [1964] 1 W.L.R. 616; [1964] 2 All E.R. 318, CA; *cf. Arundel Corp v Khokher* [2003] EWCA Civ 1784; [2004 148 S.J.L.B. 25) of the person to be served or posted by registered or recorded delivery (s.1 of the Recorded Delivery Service Act 1962). (As to change of landlords, see s.23(2)). **3B–84**

***Paragraph numbers marked with a "+" can be found online and on CD.***

If one of these methods of service is adopted, service is deemed to be effected even if the document is not received by the intended recipient, if, for example, it is returned by the Post Office (*Blunden v Frogmore Investments Ltd* [2002] EWCA Civ 573; [2003] 2 P. & C.R. 6; [2003] 29 E.G. 153). If a notice is sent by recorded delivery, it is irrefutably deemed to have been served on the date that the notice was put in the post and not on the date of actual receipt (*Beanby Estates Ltd v Egg Stores (Stamford Hill) Ltd* [2003] EWHC 1252 (Ch); [2003] 1 W.L.R. 2064) and *CA Webber (Transport) Ltd v Network Rail Infrastructure Ltd (formerly Railtrack Plc)* [2003] EWCA Civ 1167; [2004] 1 W.L.R. 320; [2004] 3 All E.R. 202).

## Application to Crown, Duchy, ecclesiastical and charity lands

**3B–85** **24.**—(1) This Act shall apply to land belonging to His Majesty in right of the Crown or the Duchy of Lancaster and to land belonging to the Duchy of Cornwall, and to land belonging to any Government department, and for that purpose the provisions of the Agricultural Holdings Act, 1923, relating to Crown and Duchy lands, as set out and adapted in Part I of the Second Schedule to this Act, shall have effect.

(2) The provisions of the Agricultural Holdings Act, 1923, with respect to the application of that Act to ecclesiastical and charity lands, as set out and adapted in Part II of the Second Schedule to this Act, shall apply for the purposes of this Act.

(3) [Repealed by Endowments and Glebe Measure 1976 (No. 4), s. 47(4), Sch. 8].

(4) Where any land is vested in the [official custodian for charities] in trust for any charity, the trustees of the charity and not the [custodian] shall be deemed to be the landlord for the purposes of this Act.

**3B–86** *Note* —Section 24 was amended by Charities Act 1960 Sch.6. The functions of the Ecclesiastical Commissioners are now exercisable by the Church Commissioners—see Church Commissioners Measure 1947 (No.2), s.2.

## Interpretation

**3B–87** **25.**—(1) For the purposes of this Act, unless the context otherwise requires—

The expression "tenant" means any person entitled in possession to the holding under any contract of tenancy, whether the interest of such tenant was acquired by original contract, assignment, operation of law or otherwise;

The expression "landlord" means any person who under a lease is, as between himself and the tenant or other lessee, for the time being entitled to the rents and profits of the demised premises payable under the lease;

The expression "predecessor in title" in relation to a tenant or landlord means any person through whom the tenant or landlord has derived title, whether by assignment, by will, by intestacy, or by operation of law;

The expression "lease" means a lease, under-lease or other tenancy, assignment operating as a lease or under-lease, or an agreement for such lease, under-lease tenancy, or assignment;

The expression "mining lease" means a lease for any mining purpose or purposes connected therewith, and

***Paragraph numbers marked with a "+" can be found online and on CD.***

"mining purposes" include the sinking and searching for, winning, working, getting, making merchantable, smelting or otherwise converting or working for the purposes of any manufacture, carrying away, and disposing of mines and minerals, in or under land, and the erection of buildings, and the execution of engineering and other works suitable for those purposes;

The expression "term of years absolute" has the same meaning as in the Law of Property Act, 1925;

The expression "statutory company" means any company constituted by or under an Act of Parliament to construct, work or carry on any [...], tramway, hydraulic power, dock, canal or railway undertaking;

and the expression "public utility company" means any company within the meaning of the Companies (Consolidation) Act, 1908, or a society registered under the Industrial and Provident Societies Acts, 1893 to 1913, carrying on any such undertaking;

The expression "prescribed" means [prescribed by rules of court or by a practice direction].

(2) The designation of landlord and tenant shall continue to apply to the parties until the conclusion of any proceedings taken under or in pursuance of this Act in respect of compensation.

*Note* —Section 25 was amended by the Gas Act 1986 s.67(3)(4), Sch.8, para.17, Sch.9, Pt 1, the Water Act 1989 s.190(3), Sch.27, Pt 1, the Electricity Act 1989 s.112(3)(4), Sch.17, para.35(1), Sch.18 and by SI 2001/2717, art.3. **3B–88**

## Short title, commencement and extent

**26.**—(1) This Act may be cited as the Landlord and Tenant Act 1927. **3B–89**

(2) [Repealed by Statute Law Revision Act 1950 (c. 6)]

(3) This Act shall extend to England and Wales only.

## Landlord and Tenant Act 1954

(2 & 3 Eliz. 2 c.56) **3B–90**

Arrangement of Sections

Part II

Security of Tenure for Business, Professional and Other Tenants



***Paragraph numbers marked with a "+" can be found online and on CD.***

# PART II

## SECURITY OF TENURE FOR BUSINESS, PROFESSIONAL AND OTHER TENANTS

**Editorial note**

3B–91 Part II of the Landlord and Tenant Act 1954 contains provisions regulating security of tenure as between landlords and tenants of business premises. Significant amendments were made by the Regulatory Reform (Business Tenancies) (England and Wales) Order 2003 (SI 2003/3096). These amendments apply to cases where the

***Paragraph numbers marked with a "+" can be found online and on CD.***

landlord gave a statutory notice of termination, or the tenant made a statutory request for a new tenancy on or after June 1, 2004—see the Regulatory Reform (Business Tenancies) (England and Wales) Order 2003 (SI 2003/3096) para.29(1). The full text of para.29 is as at 3B–93:

Part II of the Act is reproduced as amended by the 2003 Reform Order. It will be necessary to refer to the Act in its unamended form where the transitional provisions apply. 3B–92

The Order implemented most of the recommendations of the Law Commission contained in their 1992 paper Business Tenancies: A Periodic Review of the Landlord and Tenant Act Pt II (Law Com No.208).

In brief, the Order—

- changed the procedures to be followed to renew a tenancy or to terminate it without renewal. Both landlords and tenants are permitted to apply to the court for the terms of a new tenancy to be settled. Landlords are permitted to apply for an order that the tenancy be terminated without renewal if they can make out one of the statutory grounds for opposition. The requirement for a tenant to serve a counter-notice to a landlord's notice of termination is abolished.
- substituted new time limits for applications to the court to renew tenancies and enables the parties to agree to extend these.
- widened the circumstances in which landlord and tenant can operate the statutory procedures of Pt II. An individual and any company s/he controls should be treated as one and the same for the purposes of those procedures. Companies controlled by one individual should be treated as members of a group of companies.
- introduced several changes relating to interim rent. Tenants as well as landlords are allowed to apply to the court for interim rent. The date from which any interim rent determined by the court is payable becomes the earliest date for renewal of the tenancy which could have been specified in the statutory notice served by the landlord or tenant. A new method for the calculation of the amount of interim rent is introduced where the landlord does not oppose renewal. The interim rent is set at the same level as the rent for the new tenancy (i.e. usually, the open market rent), but subject to adjustment where market conditions or the occupational terms of the tenancy change significantly during the interim period. In other circumstances, the rules for calculation of interim rent formerly in s.24A(3), and now contained in s.24D(2), continue to apply although in a slightly modified form.
- amended the rules relating to the compensation that tenants may claim where their tenancies are not renewed. It changes the method of calculation of compensation where the tenant has occupied different parts of premises for different periods of time, and where different landlords control different parts. It also enables a tenant to claim compensation if induced not to apply to court, or to withdraw an application for renewal, because of a misrepresentation.
- replaced the requirement for both parties to apply to court for approval to an agreement to exclude security of tenure or to surrender a tenancy. The new procedure requires a landlord to serve a prescribed notice on the tenant at least 14 days before the parties enter into such an agreement. Tenants must sign a simple declaration that they have received and accepted the consequences of the notice. If the parties wish to waive the 14 day period, tenants have to sign a statutory declaration, rather than a simple declaration, that they have received and accepted the consequences of the notice. In the case of an agreement to exclude security of tenure, the declaration must be made before the tenant enters into the tenancy or becomes contractually bound to do so. In the case of an agreement to surrender, the declaration must be made before entering into the agreement. The forms of the notice, the simple declaration and the statutory declaration are set out in Scheds 1 to 4 to the Order.
- increased the categories of information which a landlord and tenant can require the other to provide towards the end of a tenancy term, in order to enable effective use of the statutory renewal or termination process. They also impose an obligation to keep such information up to date for six months, make provision for parties which transfer their interests and clarify the powers

of the court where a party fails to comply with obligations to provide or update information.

- clarified what a tenant must do to terminate a tenancy to which Pt II applies. If a tenant has ceased to occupy the business premises at the expiry of the contractual term, no continuation tenancy arises. Where a tenancy has continued beyond the end of the fixed contractual term, the tenant must give three months notice, ending on any day. Where necessary, rent is apportioned.
- increased the length of the term of a new tenancy that the court may order from 14 to 15 years.

### Transitional provisions

3B-93 Paragraph 29 of the 2003 Reform Order contains transitional provisions. The most important of these for the purposes of proceedings is contained in para. 29(1). The effect of this paragraph is that Pt II of the 1954 Act as amended only applies where the s.25 notice or s.26 request was served on or after June 1, 2004 (when the 2003 Reform Order came into force). Where the notice or request was served before that date Pt II in its unamended form continues to apply. The full text of para.29 of the 2003 Reform Order is as follows:

"**29.**—(1) Where, before this Order came into force—

(a) the landlord gave the tenant notice under section 25 of the Act; or

(b) the tenant made a request for a new tenancy in accordance with section 26 of the Act,

nothing in this Order has effect in relation to the notice or request or anything done in consequence of it.

(2) Nothing in this Order has effect in relation—

(a) to an agreement—

(i) for the surrender of a tenancy which was made before this Order came into force and which fell within section 24(2)(b) of the Act; or

(ii) which was authorised by the court under section 38(4) of the Act before this Order came into force; or

(b) to a notice under section 27(2) of the Act which was given by the tenant to the immediate landlord before this Order came into force.

(3) Any provision in a tenancy which requires an order under section 38(4) of the Act to be obtained in respect of any subtenancy shall, so far as is necessary after the coming into force of this Order, be construed as if it required the procedure mentioned in section 38A of the Act to be followed, and any related requirement shall be construed accordingly.

(4) If a person has, before the coming into force of this Order, entered into an agreement to take a tenancy, any provision in that agreement which requires an order under section 38(4) of the Act to be obtained in respect of the tenancy shall continue to be effective, notwithstanding the repeal of that provision by Article 21(2) of this Order, and the court shall retain jurisdiction to make such an order.

(5) Article 20 above does not have effect where the tenant quit the holding before this Order came into force.

(6) Nothing in Articles 23 and 24 above applies to a notice under section 40 of the Act served before this Order came into force."

## Tenancies to which Part II applies

3B-94 **23.**—(1) Subject to the provisions of this Act, this Part of this Act applies to any tenancy where the property comprised in the tenancy is or includes premises which are occupied by the tenant and are so occupied for the purposes of a business carried on by him or for those and other purposes.

(1A) Occupation or the carrying on of a business—

(a) by a company in which the tenant has a controlling interest; or

*Paragraph numbers marked with a "+" can be found online and on CD.*

(b) where the tenant is a company, by a person with a controlling interest in the company, shall be treated for the purposes of this section as equivalent to occupation or, as the case may be, the carrying on of a business by the tenant.

(1B) Accordingly references (however expressed) in this Part of this Act to the business of, or to use, occupation or enjoyment by, the tenant shall be construed as including references to the business of, or to use, occupation or enjoyment by, a company falling within subsection (1A)(a) above or a person falling within subsection (1A)(b) above.

(2) In this Part of this Act the expression "business" includes a trade, profession or employment and includes any activity carried on by a body of persons, whether corporate or unincorporate.

(3) In the following provisions of this Part of this Act the expression "the holding", in relation to a tenancy to which this Part of this Act applies, means the property comprised in the tenancy, there being excluded any part thereof which is occupied neither by the tenant nor by a person employed by the tenant and so employed for the purposes of a business by reason of which the tenancy is one to which this Part of this Act applies.

(4) Where the tenant is carrying on a business, in all or any part of the property comprised in a tenancy, in breach of a prohibition (however expressed) of use for business purposes which subsists under the terms of the tenancy and extends to the whole of that property, this Part of this Act shall not apply to the tenancy unless the immediate landlord or his predecessor in title has consented to the breach or the immediate landlord has acquiesced therein.

In this subsection the reference to a prohibition of use for business purposes does not include a prohibition of use for the purposes of a specified business, or of use for purposes of any but a specified business, but save as aforesaid includes a prohibition of use for the purposes of some one or more only of the classes of business specified in the definition of that expression in subsection (2) of this section.

*Note*—Paragraphs (1A) and (1B) were added by para.13 of the Regulatory Reform (Business Tenancies)(England and Wales) Order 2003 (SI 2003/3096). **3B–95**

**Tenancy**

See s.69(1). The definition includes an agreement for a lease or underlease, but does not include a mortgage. It also makes it clear that the Act applies to tenancies which have already been renewed under the provisions of the Act. Part II applies to sub tenancies. If a sub tenancy is granted in breach of a covenant, the superior landlord is not bound by the sub tenancy and may exercise rights of forfeiture, but the sub tenant, as against the mesne landlord may exercise the rights given by the Act (see s.69(1), *HL Bolton Engineering Co Ltd v TJ Graham & Sons Ltd* [1957] 1 Q.B. 159; [1956] 3 W.L.R. 804; [1956] 3 All E.R. 624, CA, and *D'Silva v Lister House Developments Ltd* [1971] Ch. 17; [1970] 2 W.L.R. 563; [1970] 1 All E.R. 858 (ChD)). **3B–96**

However, Landlord and Tenant Act 1954 Pt II does not apply to licences—see e.g. *Shell-Mex and BP v Manchester Garages* [1971] 1 W.L.R. 612; [1971] 1 All E.R. 841, CA (licence of petrol filling station) and *Dresden Estates v Collinson* (1988) 55 P. & C.R. 47, CA (licence of workshop and store) *National Car Parks Ltd v Trinity Development Co (Banbury) Ltd* [2001] L. & T.R. 33 (car park) and *Clear Channel UK Ltd v Manchester City Council* [2005] EWCA Civ 1304 ; [2006] L. & T.R. 7(advertising hoardings). *In Clear*

*Channel*, in deciding that the agreement was a licence, the Court of Appeal had regard to a term that stated as follows: "This Agreement shall constitute a licence in respect of each Site and confers no tenancy on [the company] and possession of each Site is retained by [the Council] subject however to the rights and obligations created by this Agreement". Parker L.J. made it clear that he did not intend to cast any doubt on the principles of *Street v Mountford* but nonetheless stated: "On the other hand the fact remains that this was a contract negotiated between two substantial parties of equal bargaining power and with the benefit of full legal advice. Where the contract so negotiated contains not merely a label but a clause which sets out in unequivocal terms the parties' intention as to its legal effect, I would in any event have taken some persuading that its true effect was directly contrary to that expressed intention."

Tenancies at will are also excluded from statutory protection, although courts will look carefully at any agreements which are alleged to be tenancies at will (*Hagee (London) Ltd v AB Erikson and Larson* [1976] Q.B. 209; [1975] 3 W.L.R. 272; [1975] 3 All E.R. 234; (1975) 29 P. & C.R. 512, CA and *Manfield & Sons v Botchin* [1970] 2 Q.B. 612; [1970] 3 W.L.R 120; [1970] 3 All E.R. 143, QBD).

**Tenant**

**3B–97** If there are joint tenants, for the purposes of the Act, "tenant" means all the joint tenants in whom the legal estate is vested (*Jacobs v Chaudhuri* [1968] 2 Q.B. 470; [1968] 2 W.L.R. 1098; [1968] 2 All E.R. 124, CA) As to partnerships, see s.41A below and for groups of companies, see s.42 below.

**Premises**

**3B–98** Parking spaces (and other incorporeal hereditaments) are "premises" that can be "occupied" for the purposes of s.23 (*Pointon York Group plc v Poulton* [2006] EWCA Civ 1001). Arden L.J.:

> "That conclusion may in some cases lead to the conclusion that a tenancy may qualify under section 23 even though only the incorporeal hereditament is occupied for business purposes. But I do not see why in such a case that should not be possible if the incorporeal hereditament is capable of being occupied. It is possible to have a business use of the incorporeal hereditament alone, such as where a house is let with right to use garages or stables which are occupied used for business purposes. It is difficult to see why this business use should not be protected even though the house is not used as part of the business. Section 23 expressly applies where only part of the premises is occupied for business use."

On the facts of this case, the judge had found that the tenant had occupied the parking spaces during business hours; and that was sufficient.

**Occupation by tenant for purposes of a business**

**3B–99** See ss.23(1) and (2). Landlord and Tenant Act 1954 Pt II only applies where the property comprised in the tenancy is occupied by the tenant for the purposes of a business carried on by him. As to "business", see s.46 and s.23(2) which provides that "business" includes a trade, profession or employment and includes any activity carried on by a body of persons, whether corporate or unincorporate. Residential premises may be occupied for the purpose of a business if the business activity is "a significant purpose" (see e.g. *Cheryl Investments v Saldanha* [1978] 1 W.L.R. 1329; [1979] 1 All E.R. 5, CA; *Gurton v Parrott* (1991) 23 H.L.R. 418; [1991] 18 E.G. 161, CA; *Florent v Horez* (1984) 12 H.L.R. 1; *Lewis v Weldcrest* [1978] 1 W.L.R. 1107; [1978] 3 All E.R. 1226, CA; and *Wright v Mortimer* (1996) 28 H.L.R. 719, CA).

Premises are occupied if the tenant physically uses them and is able to control the day to day use of them by other persons (*Commissioner of Valuation for Northern Ireland v Fermanagh Protestant Board of Education* [1969] 1 W.L.R. 1708; [1969] 3 All E.R. 352, HL (a rating case). See too *Hancock & Willis v G.M.S. Syndicate* [1983] 1 E.G.L.R. 70, CA; *Graysim Holdings Ltd v P&O Property Holdings Ltd* [1994] 1 W.L.R. 992; [1994] 3 All E.R. 897, CA; [1996] A.C. 329; [1995] 3 W.L.R. 854; [1995] 4 All E.R. 831, HL). There can be no continuation tenancy if the tenant has ceased to occupy the premises for business purposes before the expiry of the contractual tenancy (*Esselte AB v Pearl Assurance Plc* [1997] 1 W.L.R. 891; [1997] 2 All E.R. 41, CA and see now s.27(1A) below). Occupation for the purposes of a business is a question of fact and degree. The mere fact that premises are empty does not take them outside Pt II—e.g. if structural repairs are needed (*I&H Caplan Ltd v Caplan (No.2)* [1963] 1 W.L.R. 1247; [1963] 2 All E.R. 930, Ch D—where the tenant closed down a general clothing and footwear business, sold off stock, but remained in occupation prior to re-opening solely selling ladies' garments). Premises may be occupied through employees, agents or managers (*Linden v Department of Health and Social Security* [1986] 1 W.L.R. 164; [1986] 1 All E.R. 691, ChD.) Protection is not lost if premises are shared but if the whole of premises are sub-let, it is the sub-tenant who is likely to be in occupation, not the mesne tenant (*Graysim Holdings Ltd v P&O Property Holdings Ltd* [1994] 1 W.L.R. 992; [1994] 3 All E.R. 897, CA; [1996] A.C. 329; [1995] 3 W.L.R. 854; [1995] 4 All E.R. 831, HL; *Bagettes Ltd v GP Estates Co Ltd* [1956] Ch. 290; [1956] 2 W.L.R. 773; [1956] 1 All E.R. 729, CA).

The county court has considered the question of shared occupation and its effect on security under Part II of the Act. In *Smith v Titanate Ltd* [2005] 2 E.G.L.R. 63 (HH Judge Roger Cooke at Central London County Court) the property was divided into six flats. The tenant ran a business of letting out the flats. The longer term lettings were on standard assured shorthold tenancies. Other lettings were on terms that included the provision of services but the judge held that these were tenancies. The question for the court was whether the tenant was in occupation of the individual flats for the purpose of a business. Held: No. The 1954 Act did not therefore apply (*Graysim Holdings Ltd v P&O Property Holdings Ltd* [1996] A.C. 329 applied). The judge analysed three different types of situation that might arise:

- Cases where flats are let on conventional terms, with the landlord doing no more than receiving the rents and performing the landlord's covenants. In those cases there is no business occupation of the flats.
- At the other end of the spectrum cases such as common lodging houses, or hostel/student halls of residence, where there is a high degree of control and the services are performed in circumstances in which the landlord has an unfettered access to the rooms for that purpose.
- Cases in the middle where there is some degree of control and/or less restricted access and/or a greater degree of intrusive service provision. Depending on the facts these may fall on either side of the line.

If a tenant voluntarily moves out after issuing a claim for a new tenancy, the claim may be struck out. On the other hand if events over which the tenant has no control (e.g. a fire) lead to absence from the premises, the tenant may continue to claim occupancy (*Morrison Holdings Ltd v Manders Property (Wolverhampton) Ltd* [1976] 1 W.L.R. 533; [1976] 2 All E.R. 205, CA and *Flairline Properties v Hassan* [1999] 1 EGLR 138 Anthony Hacking Q.C., Deputy High Court Judge).

Premises occupied for the purpose of a business in breach of a covenant against business or trade use in general are outside Pt II, unless the immediate landlord or his predecessor in title has consented to the breach or the immediate landlord has acquiesced therein. However a business carried out in breach of a covenant stipulated or prohibiting a particular type of business may come within Pt II (see s.23(4)). For government departments, see s.56(3).

The issue of a short gap between the tenant's physical occupation and the end of the lease was considered in the context of compensation in the case of *Bacciocchi v Academic Agency Ltd* [1998] 3 E.G.L.R. 157. *Pointon York Group plc v Poulton* [2006] EWCA Civ 1001 has confirmed that the principles in that case apply to occupation under s.23 so that "...a tenant need not be physically present in the premises if he is using them in some other way as an incident in the ordinary course or conduct of business life, provided that the premises are occupied by no other business occupier and are not used for any non-business purpose." (para.31). Prior to the end of the sublease, the subtenants employed contractors to decorate the offices and put in new carpets. While this work was being carried out the tenant's staff went to the premises to check on the progress of the work. The tenant intended to use the premises for its own business after expiry of the sublease and wanted to plan how the offices could be used in the future. The decorating and re-carpeting was finished the day after the sublease expired. On that day a director of the tenant went to the premises and spoke to the carpet layers. He confirmed that the works were suitable for the company's business occupation. It was also necessary to put in new wiring and computer systems but this could not be done in the few days between the end of the sublease and the end of the lease and were left to be carried out shortly afterwards. This was sufficient to constitute occupation and the landlord's action in evicting T the day after the expiry date in the headlease was unlawful. The lease had continued under Pt II of the 1954 Act.

### Excluded tenancies

**3B–100** Part II does *not* apply to—

— agricultural holdings (see s.43(1)(a));
— farm business tenancies (see s.43(1)(aa));
— mining leases (see s.43(1)(b));
— most premises licensed for the sale of intoxicating liquor for consumption on the premises (see s.43(1)(d) below, but note the exceptions);
— most residential tenancies (see Rent Act 1977 s.24(3); Housing Act 1985 Sch.1, para.11 and Housing Act 1988 Sch.1, para.4)
— tenancies granted by reason of office, appointment or employment (see s.43(2));
— tenancies not exceeding six months (see s.43(3), but note the exceptions);
— where contracting out was authorised under the old s.38(4);

### Holding

**3B–101** See s.23(3) and s.32—i.e. prima facie the whole subject-matter of the tenancy (*Heath v Drown* [1973] A.C. 498; [1972] 2 W.L.R. 1306; [1976] 2 All E.R. 561, HL) except for those parts not occupied by the tenant or employees for business purposes.

### The landlord

**3B–102** See s.44(1) which provides that "the landlord" means the person (whether or not he is the immediate landlord) who is the owner of that interest in the property comprised in the relevant tenancy which for the time being fulfils the conditions contained in ss.44(1)(a) and (b).

### Procedure

**3B–103** See CPR Pt 56, PD 56 and the commentary thereto.

## Continuation of tenancies to which Part II applies and grant of new tenancies

**3B–104** **24.**—(1) A tenancy to which this Part of this Act applies shall not come to an end unless terminated in accordance with the provisions of this Part of this Act; and, subject to the following provisions of this Act either the tenant or the landlord under such a tenancy may apply to the court for an order for the grant of a new tenancy—

(a) if the landlord has given notice under section 25 of this Act to terminate the tenancy, or

(b) if the tenant has made a request for a new tenancy in accordance with section 26 of this Act.

(2) The last foregoing subsection shall not prevent the coming to an end of a tenancy by notice to quit given by the tenant, by surrender or forfeiture, or by the forfeiture of a superior tenancy, unless—

(a) in the case of a notice to quit, the notice was given before the tenant had been in occupation in right of the tenancy for one month; or

(b) [...]

(2A) Neither the tenant nor the landlord may make an application under subsection (1) above if the other has made such an application and the application has been served.

(2B) Neither the tenant nor the landlord may make such an application if the landlord has made an application under section 29(2) of this Act and the application has been served.

(2C) The landlord may not withdraw an application under subsection (1) above unless the tenant consents to its withdrawal.

(3) Notwithstanding anything in subsection (1) of this section—

(a) where a tenancy to which this Part of this Act applies ceases to be such a tenancy, it shall not come to an end by reason only of the cesser, but if it was granted for a term of years certain and has been continued by subsection (1) of this section then (without prejudice to the termination thereof in accordance with any terms of the tenancy) it may be terminated by not less than three nor more than six months' notice in writing given by the landlord to the tenant;

(b) where, at a time when a tenancy is not one to which this Part of this Act applies, the landlord gives notice to quit, the operation of the notice shall not be affected by reason that the tenancy becomes one to which this Part of this Act applies after the giving of the notice.

*Note*—The current s.24 was substituted by Law of Property Act 1969 s.15, Sch.1. It was amended by the Regulatory Reform (Business Tenancies) (England and Wales) Order 2003 (SI 2003/3096) art.3. Subsection (2)(b) was repealed by Sch.6. See too Landlord and Tenant (Licensed Premises) Act 1990 s.1(2); Leasehold Reform Act 1967 s.35(2); Rent Act 1977 s.108(3) and Opencast Coal Act 1958 s.37, Sch.7, para.22. **3B–105**

**Tenancy**

See s.69(1) and the commentary to s.23 above. The definition includes an agreement for a lease or underlease, but does not include a mortgage. **3B–106**

**Notice to quit**

Means a notice to quit given by the immediate landlord (see s.44(2)). **3B–107**

**The landlord**

See s.44(1) which provides that "the landlord" means the person (whether or not he is the immediate landlord) who is the owner of that interest in the property comprised in the relevant tenancy which for the time being fulfils the conditions contained in ss.44(1)(a) and (b). **3B–108**

**Continuation**

Business tenancies within the ambit of Pt II do not come to an end, notwithstanding effluxion of time, unless terminated in accordance with the provisions of the Act. On effluxion they are continued automatically by s.24(1) until terminated by notice in the prescribed form given either by the landlord (as defined in s.44) or tenant. All the terms and conditions of the contractual tenancy (apart from those relating to termination) continue to apply (see e.g. *Poster v Slough Estates Ltd* [1969] 1 Ch. 495; [1968] 1 W.L.R. 1515; [1968] 3 All E.R. 257, Ch D). The contractual rent continues to be payable, unless the landlord or the tenant applies to the court in accordance with s.24A for an interim rent. However, unless there is a clear and express provision in the contractual tenancy agreement, where the tenancy has been assigned, it is only the assignee who is liable for rent under the continuation tenancy (*City of London Corp v Fell* [1993] Q.B. 589; [1993] 3 W.L.R. 1164; [1993] 2 All E.R. 449, CA (affirmed in House of Lords, [1994] 1 A.C. 458; [1993] 2 W.L.R. 710; [1993] 4 All E.R. 968); *cf. GMS Syndicate Ltd v Gary Elliott Ltd* [1982] Ch. 1; [1981] 2 W.L.R. 478; [1981] 1 All E.R. 619, ChD). If the tenant vacates before the contractual expiry of the tenancy, he is not in occupation, and so no continuation tenancy can arise. In such circumstances there is no continuing liability for rent, even if an application has been made to the court for a new tenancy (*Surrey CC v Single Horse Properties Ltd* [2002] EWCA Civ 367; [2002] 1 W.L.R. 2106; [2002] 4 All E.R. 143). **3B–109**

***Paragraph numbers marked with a "+" can be found online and on CD.***

**Termination**

3B–110 Business tenancies may be terminated by—

- a section 25 notice given by the landlord as defined by s.44, although, if agreement for a new tenancy is not reached, the tenant or the landlord may apply to the court for a new tenancy;
- a section 26 request by the tenant for a new tenancy. Again, if agreement is not reached, the tenant or the landlord may apply to the court for a new tenancy;
- a notice to quit, or notice exercising a break clause, given by the tenant (s.24(2), but note the exceptions);
- surrender (s.24(2) but see s.38 below); or
- forfeiture (s.24(2)).

**Application to the court**

3B–111 See s.29, CPR Pt 56 and PD 56.

## Applications for determination of interim rent while tenancy continues

3B–112 **24A.**

(1) Subject to subsection (2) below, if—

(a) the landlord of a tenancy to which this Part of this Act applies has given notice under section 25 of this Act to terminate the tenancy; or

(b) the tenant of such a tenancy has made a request for a new tenancy in accordance with section 26 of this Act,

either of them may make an application to the court to determine a rent (an "interim rent") which the tenant is to pay while the tenancy ("the relevant tenancy") continues by virtue of section 24 of this Act and the court may order payment of an interim rent in accordance with section 24C or 24D of this Act.

(2) Neither the tenant nor the landlord may make an application under subsection (1) above if the other has made such an application and has not withdrawn it.

(3) No application shall be entertained under subsection (1) above if it is made more than six months after the termination of the relevant tenancy.

3B–113 *Note* —New s.24A was inserted by the Regulatory Reform (Business Tenancies) (England and Wales) Order 2003 (SI 2003/3096).

**Tenancy**

3B–114 See s.69(1) and the commentary to s.23 above. The definition includes an agreement for a lease or underlease, but does not include a mortgage.

**The landlord**

3B–115 See s.44(1) which provides that "the landlord" means the person (whether or not he is the immediate landlord) who is the owner of that interest in the property comprised in the relevant tenancy which for the time being fulfils the conditions contained in ss.44(1)(a) and (b).

## Date from which interim rent is payable

3B–116 **24B.**—(1) The interim rent determined on an application under section 24A(1) of this Act shall be payable from the appropriate date.

(2) If an application under section 24A(1) of this Act is made in a case where the landlord has given a notice under section 25 of this

Act, the appropriate date is the earliest date of termination that could have been specified in the landlord's notice.

(3) If an application under section 24A(1) of this Act is made in a case where the tenant has made a request for a new tenancy under section 26 of this Act, the appropriate date is the earliest date that could have been specified in the tenant's request as the date from which the new tenancy is to begin.

*Note* —New s.24B was inserted by the Regulatory Reform (Business Tenancies) (England and Wales) Order 2003 (SI 2003/3096), art.18. **3B–117**

## Amount of interim rent where new tenancy of whole premises granted and landlord not opposed

**24C.**—(1) This section applies where— **3B–118**

(a) the landlord gave a notice under section 25 of this Act at a time when the tenant was in occupation of the whole of the property comprised in the relevant tenancy for purposes such as are mentioned in section 23(1) of this Act and stated in the notice that he was not opposed to the grant of a new tenancy; or

(b) the tenant made a request for a new tenancy under section 26 of this Act at a time when he was in occupation of the whole of that property for such purposes and the landlord did not give notice under subsection (6) of that section, and the landlord grants a new tenancy of the whole of the property comprised in the relevant tenancy to the tenant (whether as a result of an order for the grant of a new tenancy or otherwise).

(2) Subject to the following provisions of this section, the rent payable under and at the commencement of the new tenancy shall also be the interim rent.

(3) Subsection (2) above does not apply where—

(a) the landlord or the tenant shows to the satisfaction of the court that the interim rent under that subsection differs substantially from the relevant rent; or

(b) the landlord or the tenant shows to the satisfaction of the court that the terms of the new tenancy differ from the terms of the relevant tenancy to such an extent that the interim rent under that subsection is substantially different from the rent which (in default of such agreement) the court would have determined under section 34 of this Act to be payable under a tenancy which commenced on the same day as the new tenancy and whose other terms were the same as the relevant tenancy.

(4) In this section "the relevant rent" means the rent which (in default of agreement between the landlord and the tenant) the court would have determined under section 34 of this Act to be payable under the new tenancy if the new tenancy had commenced on the appropriate date (within the meaning of section 24B of this Act).

(5) The interim rent in a case where subsection (2) above does

*Paragraph numbers marked with a "+" can be found online and on CD.*

not apply by virtue only of subsection (3)(a) above is the relevant rent.

(6) The interim rent in a case where subsection (2) above does not apply by virtue only of subsection (3)(b) above, or by virtue of subsection (3)(a) and (b) above, is the rent which it is reasonable for the tenant to pay while the relevant tenancy continues by virtue of section 24 of this Act.

(7) In determining the interim rent under subsection (6) above the court shall have regard—

(a) to the rent payable under the terms of the relevant tenancy; and

(b) to the rent payable under any sub-tenancy of part of the property comprised in the relevant tenancy,

but otherwise subsections (1) and (2) of section 34 of this Act shall apply to the determination as they would apply to the determination of a rent under that section if a new tenancy of the whole of the property comprised in the relevant tenancy were granted to the tenant by order of the court and the duration of that new tenancy were the same as the duration of the new tenancy which is actually granted to the tenant.

(8) In this section and section 24D of this Act "the relevant tenancy" has the same meaning as in section 24A of this Act.

3B–119 *Note* —New s.24C was inserted by the Regulatory Reform (Business Tenancies) (England and Wales) Order 2003 (SI 2003/3096), art.18.

## Amount of interim rent in any other case

3B–120 **24D.**—(1) The interim rent in a case where section 24C of this Act does not apply is the rent which it is reasonable for the tenant to pay while the relevant tenancy continues by virtue of section 24 of this Act.

(2) In determining the interim rent under subsection (1) above the court shall have regard—

(a) to the rent payable under the terms of the relevant tenancy; and

(b) to the rent payable under any sub-tenancy of part of the property comprised in the relevant tenancy,

but otherwise subsections (1) and (2) of section 34 of this Act shall apply to the determination as they would apply to the determination of a rent under that section if a new tenancy from year to year of the whole of the property comprised in the relevant tenancy were granted to the tenant by order of the court.

(3) If the court—

(a) has made an order for the grant of a new tenancy and has ordered payment of interim rent in accordance with section 24C of this Act, but

(b) either—

(i) it subsequently revokes under section 36(2) of this Act the order for the grant of a new tenancy; or

(ii) the landlord and tenant agree not to act on the order,

the court on the application of the landlord or the tenant shall determine a new interim rent in accordance with subsections (1) and (2) above without a further application under section 24A(1) of this Act.

*Note* —New s.24D was inserted by the Regulatory Reform (Business Tenancies) (England and Wales) Order 2003 (SI 2003/3096), art.18. **3B–121**

## Termination of tenancy by the landlord

**25.**—(1) The landlord may terminate a tenancy to which this Part of this Act applies by a notice given to the tenant in the prescribed form specifying the date at which the tenancy is to come to an end (hereinafter referred to as "the date of termination"): Provided that this subsection has effect subject to the provisions of section 29B(4) of this Act and the provisions of Part IV of this Act as to the interim continuation of tenancies pending the disposal of applications to the court. **3B–122**

(2) Subject to the provisions of the next following subsection, a notice under this section shall not have effect unless it is given not more than twelve nor less than six months before the date of termination specified therein.

(3) In the case of a tenancy which apart from this Act could have been brought to an end by notice to quit given by the landlord—

(a) the date of termination specified in a notice under this section shall not be earlier than the earliest date on which apart from this Part of this Act the tenancy could have been brought to an end by notice to quit given by the landlord on the date of the giving of the notice under this section; and

(b) where apart from this Part of this Act more than six months' notice to quit would have been required to bring the tenancy to an end, the last foregoing subsection shall have effect with the substitution for twelve months of a period six months longer than the length of notice to quit which would have been required as aforesaid.

(4) In the case of any other tenancy, a notice under this section shall not specify a date of termination earlier than the date on which apart from this Part of this Act the tenancy would have come to an end by effluxion of time.

(5) [...]

(6) A notice under this section shall not have effect unless it states whether the landlord is opposed to the grant of a new tenancy to the tenant.

(7) A notice under this section which states that the landlord is opposed to the grant of a new tenancy to the tenant shall not have effect unless it also specifies one or more of the grounds specified in section 30(1) of this Act as the ground or grounds for his opposition.

(8) A notice under this section which states that the landlord is not opposed to the grant of a new tenancy to the tenant shall not have effect unless it sets out the landlord's proposals as to—

*Paragraph numbers marked with a "+" can be found online and on CD.*

(a) the property to be comprised in the new tenancy (being either the whole or part of the property comprised in the current tenancy);

(b) the rent to be payable under the new tenancy; and

(c) the other terms of the new tenancy.

3B–123 *Note*—Subsection (5) was repealed by the Regulatory Reform (Business Tenancies) (England and Wales) Order 2003 (SI 2003/3096) which also inserted new subss. (6) to (8). Those amendments came into force June 1, 2004. They only apply where a landlord has given a tenant notice under s.25 or a tenant has made a request for a new tenancy in accordance with s.26 on or after that date.

**Tenancy**

3B–124 See s.69(1) and the commentary to s.23 above. The definition includes an agreement for a lease or underlease, but does not include a mortgage.

**Date of termination**

3B–125 See s.46 and s.25(1)—the date specified in the landlord's s.25 notice at which the tenancy is to come to an end.

**Termination**

3B–126 A s.25 notice is used to exercise a break clause, to terminate a tenancy which would have expired by effluxion of time at common law, to terminate a tenancy continuing under s.24 and to terminate a periodic tenancy.

**Notice to quit**

3B–127 Means a notice to quit given by the immediate landlord (see s.44(2)). A s.25 notice is not technically a notice to quit, although it has the effect of terminating the tenancy.

**Requirements of a s.25 notice**

3B–128 A s.25 notice must:

(a) **be given by the landlord**—see s.44(1) which provides that "the landlord" means the person (whether or not he is the immediate landlord) who is the owner of that interest in the property comprised in the relevant tenancy which for the time being fulfils the conditions contained in s.44(1)(a) and (b). Notice may be served by an agent with the landlord's authority (*Tennant v London CC* (1957) 121 J.P. 428, CA; *London CC v Farren* [1956] 1 W.L.R. 1297; [1956] 3 All E.R. 401, CA) but the correct landlord must be named (*Morrow v Nadeem* [1986] 1 W.L.R. 1381; [1987] 1 All E.R. 237, CA). If there are joint landlords, all must join in giving the notice (*Dodson Bull Carpet Co Ltd v City of London Corp* [1975] 1 W.L.R. 781; [1975] 2 All E.R. 497, CA).

(b) **be given to the tenant.** If there are joint tenants, notice must be given to all of them (*Jacobs v Chaudhuri* [1968] 2 Q.B. 470; [1968] 2 W.L.R. 1098; [1968] 2 All E.R. 124, CA), but in the case of partners, see s.41A(4).

(c) **relate to the whole of the property comprised in the tenancy.** A notice which purports to apply to only part of the premises is ineffective (*Dodson Bull Carpet Co Ltd v City of London Corp.* [1975] 1 W.L.R. 781; [1975] 2 All E.R. 497, CA; *Kaiser Engineers & Contractors v Suibb (E.R.) & Sons* [1971] E.G.D. 553, CA).

(d) **specify a date for termination which complies with tenancy and the Act**—see ss.25(1) and (3). The date of termination specified in the notice cannot be earlier than the earliest date on which, contractually, the tenancy could be brought to an end by a notice to quit or break clause, or the date on which a fixed term tenancy would have expired by effluxion of time (*Crowhurst Park, Re* [1974] 1 W.L.R. 583; [1974] 1 All E.R. 991, Ch D). The notice must also be given not more than twelve nor less than six-months before the date of termination unless more than six months notice would have been required at common law. In calculating that period, the date on which the notice is given must be disregarded, with the result that the relevant period is the specified number of months which end on the corresponding day of the appropriate

***Paragraph numbers marked with a "+" can be found online and on CD.***

subsequent month (*Dodds v Walker* [1981] 1 W.L.R. 1027; [1981] 2 All E.R. 609, HL, a case on s.29). An obvious error as to the date may be corrected where it is clear that the tenant cannot be misled (*Carradine Properties Ltd v Aslam* [1976] 1 W.L.R. 442; [1976] 1 All E.R. 573, CA).

(e) **be in the prescribed form or substantially to the like effect.** There have been a number of new prescribed forms since June 1, 2004 (when the 2003 Reform Order amending Pt II of the 1954 Act came into effect) dealing with various different situations (the Landlord and Tenant Act 1954, Part 2 (Notices) (England and Wales) Regulations 2004 (SI 2004/1005). A full list is set out in Sch.1 to those regulations; and the forms themselves are in Sch.2. The two main forms that will be used in most cases are: (i) Form 1—to be used where the landlord is not opposed to the grant of a new tenancy; and (ii) Form 2—to be used where the landlord is opposed to the grant of a new tenancy. Where the landlord is not opposed to a new tenancy he must, in his s.25 notice, set out his proposals as to (i) the property to be comprised in the new tenancy, being either the whole or part of the property comprised in the tenancy; (ii) the rent to be payable under the new tenancy and (iii) the other terms of the new tenancy. The landlord must use the appropriate form listed in the schedule or "a form substantially to the same effect" (reg. 2(2)). The notes on the back of each form are part of the prescribed form and must be used. If they are omitted they will not be regarded as being in "a form substantially to same effect". These are important parts of the form and must be included. The fact that the tenant is not misled by their omission is irrelevant (*Sabella Ltd v Montgomery* [1998] 1 E.G.L.R. 65, CA).

### Service of notice

See Landlord and Tenant Act 1927, s.23 which provides that any notice, request, demand or other instrument can be served personally or left at the last known place of abode (which includes place of business—*Price v West London Investment Building Society Ltd* [1964] 1 W.L.R. 616; [1964] 2 All E.R. 318, CA) of the person to be served or posted by registered or recorded delivery. (As to change of landlords, see Landlord and Tenant Act 1927 s.23(2)). If one of these methods of service is adopted, service is deemed to be effected even if the document is not received by the intended recipient, if, for example, it is returned by the Post Office (*Blunden v Frogmore Investments Ltd* [2002] EWCA Civ 573; [2003] 29 E.G. 153). If a notice is sent by recorded delivery it is irrefutably deemed to have been served on the date that the notice was put in the post and not on the date of actual receipt (*Beanby Estates Ltd v Egg Stores (Stamford Hill) Ltd* [2003] EWHC 1252 (Ch); [2003] 1 W.L.R. 2064 and *CA Webber (Transport) Ltd v Network Rail Infrastructure Ltd (formerly Railtrack Plc)* [2003] EWCA Civ 1167; [2004] 1 W.L.R. 320; [2004] 3All E.R. 202). **3B–129**

### Withdrawal of notice

For the limited circumstances in which a valid s.25 notice may be withdrawn, see Landlord and Tenant Act 1954 Sch.6, para.6. **3B–130**

### More than one notice

For the position where a party serves more than one notice and the notices are contradictory, see *Barclays Bank Plc v Bee* [2001] EWCA Civ 1126; [2001] 37 E.G. 153. **3B–131**

## Tenant's request for a new tenancy

**26.**—(1) A tenant's request for a new tenancy may be made where the current tenancy is a tenancy granted for a term of years certain exceeding one year, whether or not continued by section twenty-four of this Act, or granted for a term of years certain and thereafter from year to year. **3B–132**

(2) A tenant's request for a new tenancy shall be for a tenancy beginning with such date, not more than twelve nor less than six months after the making of the request, as may be specified therein:

Provided that the said date shall not be earlier than the date on

*Paragraph numbers marked with a "+" can be found online and on CD.*

which apart from this Act the current tenancy would come to an end by effluxion of time or could be brought to an end by notice to quit given by the tenant.

(3) A tenant's request for a new tenancy shall not have effect unless it is made by notice in the prescribed form given to the landlord and sets out the tenant's proposals as to the property to be comprised in the new tenancy (being either the whole or part of the property comprised in the current tenancy), as to the rent to be payable under the new tenancy and as to the other terms of the new tenancy.

(4) A tenant's request for a new tenancy shall not be made if the landlord has already given notice under the last foregoing section to terminate the current tenancy, or if the tenant has already given notice to quit or notice under the next following section; and no such notice shall be given by the landlord or the tenant after the making by the tenant of a request for a new tenancy.

(5) Where the tenant makes a request for a new tenancy in accordance with the foregoing provisions of this section, the current tenancy shall, subject to the provisions of sections 29B(4) and 36(2) of this Act and the provisions of Part IV of this Act as to the interim continuation of tenancies, terminate immediately before the date specified in the request for the beginning of the new tenancy.

(6) Within two months of the making of a tenant's request for a new tenancy the landlord may give notice to the tenant that he will oppose an application to the court for the grant of a new tenancy, and any such notice shall state on which of the grounds mentioned in section thirty of this Act the landlord will oppose the application.

**3B–133** *Note* —Section 26 is excluded by Leasehold Reform Act 1967 ss.17, 18, Sch.2, para.6(1). It was amended by the Regulatory Reform (Business Tenancies) (England and Wales) Order 2003 (SI 2003/3096). The amendment came into force June 1, 2004. It only applies where a landlord has given a tenant notice under s.25 or a tenant has made a request for a new tenancy in accordance with s.26 on or after that date.

**Tenancy**

**3B–134** See s.69(1) and the commentary to s.23 above. The definition includes an agreement for a lease or underlease, but does not include a mortgage. Note that that it is not possible for a tenant to serve a request for a new tenancy under s.26 unless the lease is for a "for a term of years certain exceeding one year" (e.g. see *Manton Securities Ltd v Nazam* [2008] EWCA Civ 805).

**Current tenancy**

**3B–135** See s.46 and s.26(1)—the tenancy under which the tenant holds for the time being.

**Notice to quit**

**3B–136** Means a notice to quit given by the immediate landlord (see s.44(2)).

**The landlord**

**3B–137** See s.44(1) which provides that "the landlord" means the person (whether or not he is the immediate landlord) who is the owner of that interest in the property comprised in the relevant tenancy which for the time being fulfils the conditions contained in ss.44(1)(a) and (b).

**Prescribed form**

**3B–138** See the Landlord and Tenant Act 1954, Part 2 (Notices) Regulations 2004 (SI 2004/1005). Regulation 2(2) allows a "form substantially to the like effect" of those contained in the regulations. See the commentary to s.25 above.

**Tenant's request**

Section 26 does not apply where (i) the landlord has already served a s.25 notice; (ii) the tenant has already given notice to quit; (iii) or the tenant has already given a s.27 notice to avoid continuance under the Act. If there are joint tenants, all must join in the request, unless they are partners (see s.41A). The request must be served upon the competent landlord or the landlord's authorised agent and set out the tenant's proposals as to the new tenancy. The request brings the existing tenancy to an end, but an interim continuation tenancy then comes into being (s.26(2)). Within two months of receipt the landlord may give a counter-notice stating that the grant of a new tenancy will be opposed on one of the s.30 grounds. Failure to give a counter-notice during the prescribed period prevents the landlord form opposing the grant of a new tenancy. There is no prescribed form for a landlord's counter-notice. As to contents, see *Marks (Morris) v British Waterways Board* [1963] 1 W.L.R. 1008; [1963] 3 All E.R. 28, CA. **3B–139**

A tenant's motive for requesting a new tenancy is irrelevant (*Sun Life Assurance Plc v Thales Tracs Ltd (formerly Racal Tracs Ltd)* [2001] EWCA Civ 704; [2001] 1 W.L.R. 1562; [2002] 1 All E.R. 64 notice served only to preserve compensation rights).

**Service**

See commentary to s.25. **3B–140**

## Termination by tenant of tenancy for fixed term

**27.**—(1) Where the tenant under a tenancy to which this Part of this Act applies, being a tenancy granted for a term of years certain, gives to the immediate landlord, not later than three months before the date on which apart from this Act the tenancy would come to an end by effluxion of time, a notice in writing that the tenant does not desire the tenancy to be continued, section 24 of this Act shall not have effect in relation to the tenancy, unless the notice is given before the tenant has been in occupation in right of the tenancy for one month. **3B–141**

(1A) Section 24 of this Act shall not have effect in relation to a tenancy for a term of years certain where the tenant is not in occupation of the property comprised in the tenancy at the time when, apart from this Act, the tenancy would come to an end by effluxion of time.

(2) A tenancy granted for a term of years certain which is continuing by virtue of section 24 of this Act shall not come to an end by reason only of the tenant ceasing to occupy the property comprised in the tenancy but may be brought to an end on any day by not less than three months' notice in writing given by the tenant to the immediate landlord, whether the notice is given after the date on which apart from this Act the tenancy would have come to an end or before that date, but not before the tenant has been in occupation in right of the tenancy for one month.

(3) Where a tenancy is terminated under subsection (2) above, any rent payable in respect of a period which begins before, and ends after, the tenancy is terminated shall be apportioned, and any rent paid by the tenant in excess of the amount apportioned to the period before termination shall be recoverable by him.

*Note*—The current s.27 was substituted by Law of Property Act 1969 s.15, Sch.1 and amended by the Regulatory Reform (Business Tenancies) (England and Wales) Order 2003 (SI 2003/3096). The amendment came into force June 1, 2004. It does not have effect in relation to a notice given under s.27(2) prior to that date. **3B–142**

**Tenancy**

3B–143 See s.69(1) and the commentary to s.23 above. The definition includes an agreement for a lease or underlease, but does not include a mortgage.

**The landlord**

3B–144 See s.44(1) which provides that "the landlord" means the person (whether or not he is the immediate landlord) who is the owner of that interest in the property comprised in the relevant tenancy which for the time being fulfils the conditions contained in ss.44(1)(a) and (b).

## Renewal of tenancies by agreement

3B–145 **28.** Where the landlord and tenant agree for the grant to the tenant of a future tenancy of the holding, or of the holding with other land, on terms and from a date specified in the agreement, the current tenancy shall continue until that date but no longer, and shall not be a tenancy to which this Part of this Act applies.

**Tenancy**

3B–146 See s.69(1) and the commentary to s.23 above. The definition includes an agreement for a lease or underlease, but does not include a mortgage.

**Current tenancy**

3B–147 See s.46 and s.26(1)—the tenancy under which the tenant holds for the time being.

**holding**

3B–148 See s.46, s.32 and s.23(3) which provides that the expression "the holding" means the property comprised in the tenancy, there being excluded any part thereof which is occupied neither by the tenant nor by a person employed by the tenant ... for the purposes of a business by reason of which the tenancy is one to which this Part of this Act applies.

**The landlord**

3B–149 See s.44(1) which provides that "the landlord" means the person (whether or not he is the immediate landlord) who is the owner of that interest in the property comprised in the relevant tenancy which for the time being fulfils the conditions contained in ss.44(1)(a) and (b).

**Aagree**

3B–150 Any agreement must be in writing (s.69(2)). Note too Law of Property (Miscellaneous Provisions) Act 1989 s.2.

## Order by court for grant of new tenancy or termination of current tenancy

3B–151 **29.**—(1) Subject to the provisions of this Act, on an application under section 24(1) of this Act, the court shall make an order for the grant of a new tenancy and accordingly for the termination of the current tenancy immediately before the commencement of the new tenancy.

(2) Subject to the following provisions of this Act, a landlord may apply to the court for an order for the termination of a tenancy to which this Part of this Act applies without the grant of a new tenancy—

(a) if he has given notice under section 25 of this Act that he is opposed to the grant of a new tenancy to the tenant; or

*Paragraph numbers marked with a "+" can be found online and on CD.*

(b) if the tenant has made a request for a new tenancy in accordance with section 26 of this Act and the landlord has given notice under subsection (6) of that section.

(3) The landlord may not make an application under subsection (2) above if either the tenant or the landlord has made an application under section 24(1) of this Act.

(4) Subject to the provisions of this Act, where the landlord makes an application under subsection (2) above—

(a) if he establishes, to the satisfaction of the court, any of the grounds on which he is entitled to make the application in accordance with section 30 of this Act, the court shall make an order for the termination of the current tenancy in accordance with section 64 of this Act without the grant of a new tenancy; and

(b) if not, it shall make an order for the grant of a new tenancy and accordingly for the termination of the current tenancy immediately before the commencement of the new tenancy.

(5) The court shall dismiss an application by the landlord under section 24(1) of this Act if the tenant informs the court that he does not want a new tenancy.

(6) The landlord may not withdraw an application under subsection (2) above unless the tenant consents to its withdrawal.

*Note* —A new s.29 was substituted by the Regulatory Reform (Business Tenancies) (England and Wales) Order 2003 (SI 2003/3096), art.5. The amendment came into force June 1, 2004 but only applies where the s.25 notice or s.26 request was served on or after that date. **3B–152**

**Such property**

See s.32. **3B–153**

**Such rent**

See s.34. **3B–154**

**Such other terms**

See s.35. **3B–155**

**Tenancy**

See section 69(1) and the commentary to s.23 above. The definition includes an agreement for a lease or underlease, but does not include a mortgage. **3B–156**

**Date of termination**

See s.46 and s.25(1)—the date specified in the landlord's s.25 notice at which the tenancy is to come to an end. **3B–157**

**The landlord**

See s.44(1) which provides that "the landlord" means the person (whether or not he is the immediate landlord) who is the owner of that interest in the property comprised in the relevant tenancy which for the time being fulfils the conditions contained in ss.44(1)(a) and (b). **3B–158**

**Procedure**

See CPR Pt 56, Vol.1, para.56.0.1. Section 29 applications may be made to the county court (the norm—CPR r.56.2) in which the land is situated or the High Court. They are Part 8 claims and Form **N208** should be used. **3B–159**

***Paragraph numbers marked with a "+" can be found online and on CD.***

### Landlord in administration

3B–159.1 An application by a tenant for a new lease under Pt II of the 1954 Act is a "legal process" within para.43 Sch.B1 Insolvency Act 1986. This means that if the landlord goes into administration the tenant cannot proceed with the claim without the consent of the administrator or the permission of the court (*Somerfield Stores Ltd v Spring (Sutton Coldfield) Ltd* [2009] EWHC 2384 (Ch)—tenant given permission to pursue the claim because the tenant's need for certainty in relation to the new lease outweighed the administrator's possible plans for development at some point in the future. If appropriate the court on the application for the new lease could grant a short term or a lease with a break clause).

### Dismissing application

3B–160 Since the changes to Pt II of the 1954 Act, the landlord as well as the tenant has been able to apply for an order that the court do grant the tenant a new lease. The purpose of the change was to limit delay and to allow the landlord to start things off if the tenant has not got on and applied for a new lease. This gives rise to the following difficulty: What if the landlord applies for a new lease when the tenant does not want one? To deal with this possibility a new s.29(5) states as follows:

> "The court shall dismiss an application by the landlord under s.24(1) of this Act if the tenant informs the court that he does not want a new tenancy".

However, neither the Act nor the rules provide for orders for costs if the tenant does so inform the court. One can easily see factual situations where this might be unfair to the landlord. *Trustees of the Portman Estate v Drexler* [2007] EWCA Civ 464 was one of them. After some negotiations the landlord made an application for renewal. Crucially, the tenant filed an acknowledgement of service agreeing to the grant of a new lease but disputing the terms. Subsequently, the tenant found another property and then informed the court, pursuant to s.29(5), that it did not want to take on the new lease.

The judge at first instance made no order for costs because he treated the proceedings as having been compromised and felt that he was therefore required by guidance given in *BCT Software Solutions Ltd v C Brewer & Sons Ltd* [2003] EWCA Civ 939 to make no order for costs.

On appeal, the CA pointed out that the proceedings were not compromised. Rather, the tenant had unilaterally decided not to proceed with the renewal. The CA considered that service a notice under s.29(5) was equivalent to a discontinuance. The tenant should therefore pay for the costs of the action. Evans-Lombe J. at paras 20 (ii) and (ii):

> "... by entering an acknowledgement of service assenting to such grant, the defendants were, in effect, themselves launching proceedings for the granting of a new tenancy but upon terms more favourable to them than the Claimants were prepared to offer ... It seems to me that the service on the court by the Defendants of notice under s.29(5) was the equivalent of a notice to discontinue proceedings in which they had been seeking an order from the court awarding them a new tenancy upon terms settled by the court. It follows that the judge should have placed the burden of proof on the Defendants to establish facts which would justify his departure from the normal order in these circumstances."

## Time limits for applications to court

3B–161 **29A.**—(1) Subject to section 29B of this Act, the court shall not entertain an application—

(a) by the tenant or the landlord under section 24(1) of this Act; or

(b) by the landlord under section 29(2) of this Act,

if it is made after the end of the statutory period.

(2) In this section and section 29B of this Act "the statutory period" means a period ending—

(a) where the landlord gave a notice under section 25 of this Act, on the date specified in his notice; and

***Paragraph numbers marked with a "+" can be found online and on CD.***

(b) where the tenant made a request for a new tenancy under section 26 of this Act, immediately before the date specified in his request.

(3) Where the tenant has made a request for a new tenancy under section 26 of this Act, the court shall not entertain an application under section 24(1) of this Act which is made before the end of the period of two months beginning with the date of the making of the request, unless the application is made after the landlord has given a notice under section 26(6) of this Act.

*Note* —New s.29A was substituted by the Regulatory Reform (Business Tenancies) (England and Wales) Order 2003 (SI 2003/3096). The amendment came into force June 1, 2004. **3B–162**

#### Time limits

Under the law prior to June 1, 2004 the tenant's application for a new tenancy had to be made "not less than two nor more than four months" after the giving of the landlord's s.25 or as the case may be the tenant's s.26 request. Many tenants missed this window of opportunity and lost their right to apply for a new tenancy. Since June 1, 2004 the deadline in respect of notices served on or after that date has been: **3B–163**

- the date specified in the s.25 notice; or
- the date immediately before the date specified in the s.26 request (s.29A(2)).

However, it should be noted (by tenants in particular) that where a s.26 request has been made by the tenant an application for a new tenancy cannot be made until the landlord has served a counter-notice or the time for so doing has passed (s.29A(3)). Thus, there still remains a potential trap that could invalidate applications.

#### No application shall be entertained

The court has no power to extend time (*Hodgson v Armstrong* [1967] 2 Q.B. 299; [1967] 2 W.L.R. 311; [1967] 1 All E.R. 307, CA). Strict compliance with the timetable may be waived by the parties (*Kammins Ballrooms Co Ltd v Zenith Investments (Torquay) Ltd (No.1)* [1971] A.C. 850; [1970] 2 All E.R. 871, HL), but the landlord cannot agree to confer jurisdiction which the court does not have (e.g. because the application was made after the tenant ceased to be a tenant—*Meah v Sector Properties Ltd* [1974] 1 W.L.R. 547; [1974] 1 All E.R. 1074, CA). However note that the parties can agree to extend time before issue—see s.29B below. **3B–164**

If the tenant ceases to occupy for purposes of a business, the protection of Pt II is lost and the landlord may apply to have the claim dismissed or struck out (*I&H Caplan Ltd v Caplan (No.2)* [1963] 1 W.L.R. 1247; [1963] 2 All E.R. 930, Ch D).

## Agreements extending time limits

**29B.**—(1) After the landlord has given a notice under section 25 of this Act, or the tenant has made a request under section 26 of this Act, but before the end of the statutory period, the landlord and tenant may agree that an application such as is mentioned in section 29A(1) of this Act, may be made before the end of a period specified in the agreement which will expire after the end of the statutory period. **3B–165**

(2) The landlord and tenant may from time to time by agreement further extend the period for making such an application, but any such agreement must be made before the end of the period specified in the current agreement.

(3) Where an agreement is made under this section, the court may entertain an application such as is mentioned in section 29A(1) of this Act if it is made before the end of the period specified in the agreement.

***Paragraph numbers marked with a "+" can be found online and on CD.***

(4) Where an agreement is made under this section, or two or more agreements are made under this section, the landlord's notice under section 25 of this Act or tenant's request under section 26 of this Act shall be treated as terminating the tenancy at the end of the period specified in the agreement or, as the case may be, at the end of the period specified in the last of those agreements.

**3B-166** *Note* —New s.29B was substituted by the Regulatory Reform (Business Tenancies) (England and Wales) Order 2003 (SI 2003/3096). The amendment came into force June 1, 2004 but only applies where the s.25 or s.26 notice was served on or after that date.

**Agreement in writing**

**3B-167** The agreement to extend the time limit must be in writing (s.69(2)). Is an agreement by email in writing? Almost certainly yes. Section 5 and Sch.1 of the Interpretation Act 1978 provides that "writing" includes "typing, printing, lithography, photography and other modes of representing or reproducing words in a visible form, and expressions referring to writing are construed accordingly". However, any practitioner who has any doubt about this should insist upon an agreement in old fashioned correspondence. If the agreement is not forthcoming the application should be made before the time limit expires.

**Time of expiry**

**3B-168** When agreeing a new deadline the parties should use whole days not specific moments in time (e.g. 3.30pm on ...). Although the statute does not expressly forbid times it does seem to follow from the definition of "the statutory period" in s.29A(2) that only whole days are allowed. Indeed, generally speaking, the law does not recognise parts of days when dealing with notices.

**Agreement before time expires**

**3B-169** If no application to the court is made before the expiry of the deadline or any agreed extension, the right to apply to the court will be lost and the tenancy will come to an end (s.29B(3)(4)).

## Opposition by landlord to application for new tenancy

**3B-170** **30.**—(1) The grounds on which a landlord may oppose an application under section 24(1) of this Act, or make an application under section 29(2) of this Act, are such of the following grounds as may be stated in the landlord's notice under section 25 of this Act or, as the case may be, under subsection (6) of section 26 thereof, that is to say:—

(a) where under the current tenancy the tenant has any obligations as respects the repair and maintenance of the holding, that the tenant ought not to be granted a new tenancy in view of the state of repair of the holding, being a state resulting from the tenant's failure to comply with the said obligations;

(b) that the tenant ought not to be granted a new tenancy in view of his persistent delay in paying rent which has become due;

(c) that the tenant ought not to be granted a new tenancy in view of other substantial breaches by him of his obligations under the current tenancy, or for any other reason connected with the tenant's use or management of the holding;

(d) that the landlord has offered and is willing to provide or secure the provision of alternative accommodation for the tenant, that the terms on which the alternative accommodation is available are reasonable having regard to the terms of the current tenancy and to all other relevant circumstances, and that the accommodation and the time at which it will be available are suitable for the tenant's requirements (including the requirement to preserve goodwill) having regard to the nature and class of his business and to the situation and extent of, and facilities afforded by, the holding;

(e) where the current tenancy was created by the sub-letting of part only of the property comprised in a superior tenancy and the landlord is the owner of an interest in reversion expectant on the termination of that superior tenancy, that the aggregate of the rents reasonably obtainable on separate lettings of the holding and the remainder of that property would be substantially less than the rent reasonably obtainable on a letting of that property as a whole, that on the termination of the current tenancy the landlord requires possession of the holding for the purpose of letting or otherwise disposing of the said property as a whole, and that in view thereof the tenant ought not to be granted a new tenancy;

(f) that on the termination of the current tenancy the landlord intends to demolish or reconstruct the premises comprised in the holding or a substantial part of those premises or to carry out substantial work of construction on the holding or part thereof and that he could not reasonably do so without obtaining possession of the holding;

(g) subject as hereinafter provided, that on the termination of the current tenancy the landlord intends to occupy the holding for the purposes, or partly for the purposes, of a business to be carried on by him therein, or as his residence.

(1A) Where the landlord has a controlling interest in a company, the reference in subsection (1)(g) above to the landlord shall be construed as a reference to the landlord or that company.

(1B) Subject to subsection (2A) below, where the landlord is a company and a person has a controlling interest in the company, the reference in subsection (1)(g) above to the landlord shall be construed as a reference to the landlord or that person.

(2) The landlord shall not be entitled to oppose an application under section 24(1) of this Act, or make an application under section 29(2) of this Act,on the ground specified in paragraph (g) of the last foregoing subsection if the interest of the landlord, or an interest which has merged in that interest and but for the merger would be the interest of the landlord, was purchased or created after the beginning of the period of five years which ends with the termination of

the current tenancy, and at all times since the purchase or creation thereof the holding has been comprised in a tenancy or successive tenancies of the description specified in subsection (1) of section 23 of this Act.

(2A) Subsection (1B) above shall not apply if the controlling interest was acquired after the beginning of the period of five years which ends with the termination of the current tenancy, and at all times since the acquisition of the controlling interest the holding has been comprised in a tenancy or successive tenancies of the description specified in section 23(1) of this Act.

(3) [...]

3B–171 *Note*—The current s.30 was substituted by the Law of Property Act 1969 s.15, Sch.1 and amended by the Regulatory Reform (Business Tenancies) (England and Wales) Order 2003 (SI 2003/3096) arts 6, 14 and subs.(3) was repealed by Sch.6, para.1. The amendments came into force June 1, 2004 but only apply where the s.25 notice or s.26 request was served after that date.

**Business**

3B–172 See s.46 and s.23(2) which provides that "business" includes a trade, profession or employment and includes any activity carried on by a body of persons, whether corporate or unincorporate. See too the commentary to s.23 above.

**Current tenancy**

3B–173 See s.46 and s.26(1)—the tenancy under which the tenant holds for the time being.

**Holding**

3B–174 See s.46, s.32 and s.23(3) which provides that the expression "the holding" means the property comprised in the tenancy, there being excluded any part thereof which is occupied neither by the tenant nor by a person employed by the tenant ... for the purposes of a business by reason of which the tenancy is one to which this Part of this Act applies.

**The landlord**

3B–175 See s.44(1) which provides that "the landlord" means the person (whether or not he is the immediate landlord) who is the owner of that interest in the property comprised in the relevant tenancy which for the time being fulfils the conditions contained in ss.44(1)(a) and (b).

**Grounds**

3B–176 Landlords may only rely upon grounds for opposing the grant of a new tenancy or termination under s.29(2) if they are specified in a s.25 notice or a counter-notice served in response to a tenant's s.26 notice.

**s.30(1)(a) state of repair**

3B–177 The state of repair of the holding is only a ground for opposing the grant of a new tenancy if it results form the tenant's failure to comply with obligations. To be relied upon, the neglect to repair must be "substantial" (*Lyons v Central Commercial Properties* [1958] 1 W.L.R. 869; [1958] 2 All E.R. 767, CA). Even then, the court has a discretion and should have regard to the overall conduct of the tenant in relation to his obligations and the reason for any breach. There is no entitlement to compensation if this ground is established.

**s.30(1)(b) persistent delay in paying rent**

3B–178 There may be "persistent delay" if one instalment of rent has been in arrears for a significant period of time or instalments have persistently been paid late, or both (*Hopcutt v Carver* (1969) 209 E.G. 1069, CA; *Horowitz v Ferrand* [1956] C.L.Y. 4843. In exercising its discretion, the court may take into account both the conduct of the tenant and the landlord in relation to the late payments (*Hazel v Akhtar* [2001] EWCA Civ

***Paragraph numbers marked with a "+" can be found online and on CD.***

1883; [2002] 07 E.G. 124—landlord who accepted late payment without complaint prevented form relying upon s.30(1)(b)). There is no entitlement to compensation if this ground is established.

**s.30(1)(c) other substantial breaches of obligations, or any other reason connected with the tenant's use or management of the holding**

The court has a discretion and should have regard to the overall conduct of the tenant in relation to his obligations and the reason for any breach (*Eichner v Midland Bank Executor and Trustee Co* [1970] 1 W.L.R. 1120; [1970] 2 All E.R. 597, CA). There is no entitlement to compensation if this ground is established. **3B–179**

In *Fowles v Heathrow Airport Ltd* [2008] EWCA Civ 1270 the trial judge found that the tenant had been in flagrant and persistent breaches of planning control some of which at least amounted to the commission of criminal offences and refused to order the grant of a new lease. On appeal the tenant submitted that it was "only if the renewal of the tenancy necessarily involves a criminal offence in the use of the land that such a prospect becomes a relevant consideration". The submission was rejected as "virtually unarguable". It was contrary to common sense and the broad language of para.(c). The judge was entitled to exercise the discretion in the way that he did. Indeed "it would have been perverse for the court to have ordered the respondent to grant the new tenancy to the appellant" (per Lawrence Collins L.J.).

**s.30(1)(d) offer of alternative accommodation for the tenant**

Alternative accommodation must be suitable for the tenant's requirements. For a case in which possession was refused because the alternative accommodation would have adversely affected the way in which the tenant's business was conducted, see *Singh v Malayan Theatres* [1953] A.C. 632; [1953] 3 W.L.R. 491, PC. The terms on which it is offered must be reasonable having regard to the terms of the current tenancy and all other circumstances. Accommodation must have been offered and still be available at the time of the court hearing. If this ground is established, the court has no discretion and must dismiss the application for a new tenancy. There is no entitlement to compensation if this ground is established. **3B–180**

**s30(1)(e) aggregate of the rents reasonably obtainable on separate lettings less than the rent reasonably obtainable on a letting of that property as a whole**

This ground is rarely used in practice. It is designed to prevent a landlord from suffering prejudice as a result of sub-lettings created by a tenant. Even if the ground is established, the court has a discretion. **3B–181**

**s.30(1)(f) intention of landlord to demolish or reconstruct**

See too s.31A. The landlord must show that the intention to demolish or reconstruct exists at the time of the hearing and will be fulfilled shortly after the date of the hearing. (*Betty's Cafes Ltd v Phillips Furnishing Stores Ltd (No.1)* [1959] A.C. 20; [1958] 2 W.L.R. 513; [1958] 1 All E.R. 607, HL). The intention must be genuine, firm, and settled, and unlikely to be changed (*Fleet Electrics v Jacey Investments* [1956] 1 W.L.R. 1027; [1956] 3 All E.R. 99, CA). There are two elements to the concept of intention: first, a genuine desire that the result will come about and, secondly, a reasonable prospect of bringing about that result. For example, in *Edwards v Thompson* (1990) 60 P. & C.R. 222, CA, a landlord failed to prevent the grant of a new tenancy because she had not found a developer at the time of the hearing and "there was a real possibility that [she] would not be in a position to carry out the entire development on the termination of the current tenancy ... She had failed to show that she had the means and ability; she had not established the necessary intention." (See too *Capocci v Goble* (1987) 284 E.G. 230, CA). A landlordís case is stronger if planning permission has been obtained in advance of the institution of court proceedings, but this is not essential if it can be shown that there is a reasonable prospect of getting consent (*Gregson v Cyril Lord Ltd* [1963] 1 W.L.R. 41; [1962] 3 All E.R. 907, CA). **3B–182**

It has been held that "reconstruction" means "a substantial interference with the structure of the premises and then a rebuilding, in probably a different form, of such part of the premises as has been demolished by reason of the interference with the structure" (*Joel v Swaddle* [1957] 1 W.L.R. 1094; [1957] 3 All E.R. 325 at p.329, CA—removal of internal walls and replacement with reinforced steel joists amounted to

***Paragraph numbers marked with a "+" can be found online and on CD.***

reconstruction of a substantial part). See too *Barth v Pritchard* [1990] 20 E.G. 65, CA and *Cook v Mott* (1961) 178 E.G. 637, CA). There is no requirement of demolition or construction of structural or load bearing features as a condition of applicability (*Ivorygrove Ltd v Global Grange Ltd* [2003] EWHC 1409 (Ch); [2003] 1 W.L.R. 2090).

The landlord must also show that the intended work cannot reasonably be carried out without the tenant giving up possession of the premises. "Possession" means "putting an end to legal rights of possession" and not merely access. For example, in *Heath v Drown* [1973] A.C. 498; [1972] 2 W.L.R. 1306; [1972] 2 All E.R. 561, HL a business tenant successfully defeated the landlordís claim even though the front wall of the premises had to be entirely rebuilt and it would not be possible to occupy the premises while such work was carried out. The landlord must show that the work cannot be carried out while the tenancy still exists.

If this ground is established, the court has no discretion and must dismiss the application for a new tenancy.

In *Wessex Reserve Forces and Cadets Association v White* [2005] EWCA Civ 1744(CA) the landlord relied upon s.30(1)(f) as a ground of opposition, stating that it intended to demolish some huts on the land. However, the huts were tenants' fixtures. These were the most substantial structures on the land and under the terms of the lease the tenant was required to remove them upon termination of its tenancy. The landlord could not therefore establish that it was going to demolish them.

In *Dogan v Semali Investments Ltd* [2005] EWCA Civ 1036 the issue was whether there was a reasonable prospect of obtaining planning permission for the landlord's proposals. The case reminds us that the burden on the landlord is not a high one and that (contrary to popular belief) it is not necessary (although as a matter of tactics highly desirable) to have planning permission at the date of the hearing. *Gatwick Parking Services Ltd v Sargent* [2000] 2 E.G.L.R. 45 applied.

**s.30(1)(g) intention of landlord to occupy the holding for the purposes of a business or as his residence**

**3B–183** For "intention" see the commentary to s.30(1)(f) above. The landlord need not intend to occupy personally. It is sufficient to intend to carry on the business through an agent or manager (*Hills (Patents) Ltd v University College Hospital Board of Governors* [1956] 1 Q.B. 90; [1955] 3 W.L.R. 523; [1955] 3 All E.R. 365, CA). An intention to sublet the whole is inconsistent with an intention to occupy (*Crowhurst Park, Re* [1974] 1 W.L.R. 583; [1974] 1 All E.R. 991, Ch D). As to trustees, see s.41(2) and groups of companies, s.42(3).

Note that this ground cannot be relied upon by a landlord who has purchased within the preceding five years if the premises have been let during the whole of that period (s.30(2)—see too *Northcote Laundry v Donnelly (Frederick)* [1968] 1 W.L.R. 562; [1968] 2 All E.R. 50, CA). The period of five years is calculated backwards from the date of determination of the current tenancy (see *Frederick Lawrence Ltd v Freeman Hardy & Willis Ltd (No.1)* [1959] Ch. 731; [1959] 3 W.L.R. 275; [1959] 3 All E.R. 77, CA). If this ground is established, the court has no discretion and must dismiss the application for a new tenancy.

**Application dismissed**

**3B–184** Any continuation tenancy terminates on the expiry of three months beginning with the date on which the application is finally disposed of (Sch.6, para.4(3)).

**Misrepresentation or concealment**

**3B–185** If the court refuses a new tenancy, and it later appears that the court was induced to refuse it by misrepresentation or concealment, the court may order compensation (s.37A).

## Dismissal of application for new tenancy where landlord successfully opposes

**3B–186** **31.**—(1) If the landlord opposes an application under subsection (1) of section twenty-four of this Act on grounds on which he is entitled to oppose it in accordance with the last foregoing section and

*Paragraph numbers marked with a "+" can be found online and on CD.*

establishes any of those grounds to the satisfaction of the court, the court shall not make an order for the grant of a new tenancy.

(2) Where the landlord opposes an application under section 24(1) of this Act, or makes an application under section 29(2) of this Act, on one or more of the grounds specified in section 30(1)(d) to (f) of this Act but establishes none of those grounds, and none of the other grounds specified in section 30(1) of this Act, to the satisfaction of the court, then if the court would have been satisfied on any of the grounds specified in section 30(1)(d) to (f) of this Act, if the date of termination specified in the landlord's notice or, as the case may be, the date specified in the tenant's request for a new tenancy as the date from which the new tenancy is to begin, had been such later date as the court may determine, being a date not more than one year later than the date so specified—

(a) the court shall make a declaration to that effect, stating of which of the said grounds the court would have been satisfied as aforesaid and specifying the date determined by the court as aforesaid, but shall not make an order for the grant of a new tenancy;

(b) if, within fourteen days after the making of the declaration, the tenant so requires the court shall make an order substituting the said date for the date specified in the said landlord's notice or tenant's request, and thereupon that notice or request shall have effect accordingly.

*Note* —Note s.31 was amended by the Regulatory Reform (Business Tenancies) (England and Wales) Order 2003 (SI 2003/3096), art.7. The amendments came into force June 1, 2004 but only applies where the s.25 notice or s.26 request was served on or after that date. **3B–187**

**Date of termination**

See s.46 and s.25(1)—the date specified in the landlord's s.25 notice at which the tenancy is to come to an end. **3B–188**

**The landlord**

See s.44(1) which provides that "the landlord" means the person (whether or not he is the immediate landlord) who is the owner of that interest in the property comprised in the relevant tenancy which for the time being fulfils the conditions contained in ss.44(1)(a) and (b). **3B–189**

## Grant of new tenancy in some cases where s. 30(1)(f) applies

**31A.**—(1) Where the landlord opposes an application under section 24(1) of this Act on the ground specified in paragraph (f) of section 30(1) of this Act, or makes an application under section 29(2) of this Act on that ground,the court shall not hold that the landlord could not reasonably carry out the demolition, reconstruction or work of construction intended without obtaining possession of the holding if— **3B–190**

(a) the tenant agrees to the inclusion in the terms of the new tenancy of terms giving the landlord access and other facilities for carrying out the work intended and,

*Paragraph numbers marked with a "+" can be found online and on CD.*

given that access and those facilities, the landlord could reasonably carry out the work without obtaining possession of the holding and without interfering to a substantial extent or for a substantial time with the use of the holding for the purposes of the business carried on by the tenant; or

(b) the tenant is willing to accept a tenancy of an economically separable part of the holding and either paragraph (a) of this section is satisfied with respect to that part or possession of the remainder of the holding would be reasonably sufficient to enable the landlord to carry out the intended work.

(2) For the purposes of subsection (1)(b) of this section a part of a holding shall be deemed to be an economically separate part if, and only if, the aggregate of the rents which, after the completion of the intended work, would be reasonably obtainable on separate lettings of that part and the remainder of the premises affected by or resulting from the work would not be substantially less than the rent which would then be reasonably obtainable on a letting of those premises as a whole.

**3B–191** *Note*—Section 31A was inserted by Law of Property Act 1969 s.7(1) and amended by the Regulatory Reform (Business Tenancies) (England and Wales) Order 2003 (SI 2003/3096), art.8. The amendment came into force June 1, 2004.

**Business**

**3B–192** See s.46 and s.23(2) which provides that "business" includes a trade, profession or employment and includes any activity carried on by a body of persons, whether corporate or unincorporate. See too the commentary to s.23 above.

**Holding**

**3B–193** See s.46, s.32 and s.23(3) which provides that the expression "the holding" means the property comprised in the tenancy, there being excluded any part thereof which is occupied neither by the tenant nor by a person employed by the tenant ... for the purposes of a business by reason of which the tenancy is one to which this Part of this Act applies.

**The landlord**

**3B–194** See s.44(1) which provides that "the landlord" means the person (whether or not he is the immediate landlord) who is the owner of that interest in the property comprised in the relevant tenancy which for the time being fulfils the conditions contained in ss.44(1)(a) and (b).

## Property to be comprised in new tenancy

**3B–195** **32.**—(1) Subject to the following provisions of this section, an order under section 29 of this Act for the grant of a new tenancy shall be an order for the grant of a new tenancy of the holding; and in the absence of agreement between the landlord and the tenant as to the property which constitutes the holding the court shall in the order designate that property by reference to the circumstances existing at the date of the order.

(1A) Where the court, by virtue of paragraph (b) of section 31A(1) of this Act, makes an order under section 29 of this Act for the grant of a new tenancy in a case where the tenant is willing to accept a

*Paragraph numbers marked with a "+" can be found online and on CD.*

tenancy of part of the holding, the order shall be an order for the grant of a new tenancy of that part only.

(2) The foregoing provisions of this section shall not apply in a case where the property comprised in the current tenancy includes other property besides the holding and the landlord requires any new tenancy ordered to be granted under section 29 of this Act to be a tenancy of the whole of the property comprised in the current tenancy; but in any such case—

(a) any order under the said section 29 for the grant of a new tenancy shall be an order for the grant of a new tenancy of the whole of the property comprised in the current tenancy, and

(b) references in the following provisions of this Part of this Act to the holding shall be construed as references to the whole of that property.

(3) Where the current tenancy includes rights enjoyed by the tenant in connection with the holding, those rights shall be included in a tenancy ordered to be granted under section 29 of this Act, except as otherwise agreed between the landlord and the tenant or, in default of such agreement, determined by the court.

*Note*—The current s.32 was substituted by the Law of Property Act 1969 s.15, Sch.1. **3B–196**

**Holding**

The tenant is only entitled to require the grant of a new tenancy of his or her holding. For holdings, see s.46, s.32 and s.23(3) which provides that the expression "the holding" means the property comprised in the tenancy, there being excluded any part thereof which is occupied neither by the tenant nor by a person employed by the tenant ... for the purposes of a business by reason of which the tenancy is one to which this Part of this Act applies. **3B–197**

**Current tenancy**

See s.46 and s.26(1)—the tenancy under which the tenant holds for the time being. **3B–198**

**The landlord**

See s.44(1) which provides that "the landlord" means the person (whether or not he is the immediate landlord) who is the owner of that interest in the property comprised in the relevant tenancy which for the time being fulfils the conditions contained in ss.44(1)(a) and (b). **3B–199**

**parking previously under permission**

Facilities enjoyed by licence under the original lease are outside s.32(3). Thus, in *The Picture Warehouse Ltd v Cornhill Investments Ltd* [2008] EWHC 45 (QB) the tenant had the benefit of a licence from the landlord for its customers and delivery men to park on the forecourt outside the demised premises. However, there was no right under the lease to that effect. On renewing the lease the tenant was unable to obtain a term of the new lease giving it parking rights. Further, there is no jurisdiction under s.35(1) of the 1954 Act to enlarge the holding by ordering the grant of a right over the landlord's land that the tenant had not previously enjoyed. **3B–199.1**

## Duration of new tenancy

**33.** Where on an application under this Part of this Act the court makes an order for the grant of a new tenancy, the new tenancy shall be such tenancy as may be agreed between the landlord and the tenant, or, in default of such an agreement, shall be such a tenancy as **3B–200**

may be determined by the court to be reasonable in all the circumstances, being, if it is a tenancy for a term of years certain, a tenancy for a term not exceeding fifteen years, and shall begin on the coming to an end of the current tenancy.

**3B–201** *Note* —Section 33 was amended by the Regulatory Reform (Business Tenancies) (England and Wales) Order 2003 (SI 2003/3096), art.26. The amendment came into force June 1, 2004 but only applies where the s.25 notice or s.26 request was served on or after that date.

**Duration**

**3B–202** The norm is for the term of any new tenancy to be agreed between the landlord and the tenant. In the absence of agreement, the court determines a term which is "reasonable in all the circumstances". The court cannot order a tenancy for a term of more than fifteen years, but the parties are free to agree a longer term. The starting point is the length of the current term, but the court must strike a reasonable balance between conflicting considerations (*Edwards (J.H.) & Sons v Central London Commercial Estates* [1984] 2 E.G.L.R. 103, CA; *Upsons v Robins (E)* [1956] 1 Q.B. 131; [1955] 3 W.L.R. 584; [1955] 3 All E.R. 348, CA). For a list of the considerations that the court might take into account when deciding what term is "reasonable in all the circumstances", see *Woodfall*, para.23.146.

**Current tenancy**

**3B–203** See s.46 and s.26(1)—the tenancy under which the tenant holds for the time being.

**The landlord**

**3B–204** See s.44(1) which provides that "the landlord" means the person (whether or not he is the immediate landlord) who is the owner of that interest in the property comprised in the relevant tenancy which for the time being fulfils the conditions contained in ss.44(1)(a) and (b).

## Rent under new tenancy

**3B–205** **34.**—(1) The rent payable under a tenancy granted by order of the court under this Part of this Act shall be such as may be agreed between the landlord and the tenant or as, in default of such agreement, may be determined by the court to be that at which, having regard to the terms of the tenancy (other than those relating to rent), the holding might reasonably be expected to be let in the open market by a willing lessor, there being disregarded—

(a) any effect on rent of the fact that the tenant has or his predecessors in title have been in occupation of the holding,

(b) any goodwill attached to the holding by reason of the carrying on thereat of the business of the tenant (whether by him or by a predecessor of his in that business),

(c) any effect on rent of an improvement to which this paragraph applies,

(d) in the case of a holding comprising licensed premises, any addition to its value attributable to the licence, if it appears to the court that having regard to the terms of the current tenancy and any other relevant circumstances the benefit of the licence belongs to the tenant.

(2) Paragraph (c) of the foregoing subsection applies to any improvement carried out by a person who at the time it was carried

*Paragraph numbers marked with a "+" can be found online and on CD.*

out was the tenant, but only if it was carried out otherwise than in pursuance of an obligation to his immediate landlord and either it was carried out during the current tenancy or the following conditions are satisfied, that is to say,—

(a) that it was completed not more than twenty-one years before the application to the court was made; and

(b) that the holding or any part of it affected by the improvement has at all times since the completion of the improvement been comprised in tenancies of the description specified in section 23(1) of this Act; and

(c) that at the termination of each of those tenancies the tenant did not quit.

(2A) If this Part of this Act applies by virtue of section 23(1A) of this Act, the reference in subsection (1)(d) above to the tenant shall be construed as including—

(a) a company in which the tenant has a controlling interest, or

(b) where the tenant is a company, a person with a controlling interest in the company.

(3) Where the rent is determined by the court the court may, if it thinks fit, further determine that the terms of the tenancy shall include such provision for varying the rent as may be specified in the determination.

(4) It is hereby declared that the matters which are to be taken into account by the court in determining the rent include any effect on rent of the operation of the provisions of the Landlord and Tenant (Covenants) Act 1995.

*Note*—The current s.34 was substituted by the Law of Property Act 1969, s.15, Sch.1; s.34(4) was added by the Landlord and Tenant (Covenants) Act 1995 Sch.1 para.3. Section 34(2)(a) was amended and s.34(2A) inserted by the Regulatory Reform (Business Tenancies) (England and Wales) Order 2003 (SI 2003/3096), art.15. **3B–206**

**Rent**

In the absence of agreement between the parties, the court determines the rent at which, having regard to the terms of the tenancy, the holding might reasonably be expected to be let in the open market by a willing lessor, subject to a number of disregards. In view of the requirement to have regard to the terms of the tenancy, the court should determine any other disputed terms, before deciding the rent. (*O'May v City of London Real Property Co Ltd* [1983] 2 A.C. 726; [1982] 2 W.L.R. 407; [1982] 1 All E.R. 660, HL; *Cardshops v Davies* [1971] 1 W.L.R. 591; [1971] 2 All E.R. 721, CA) The best evidence of a reasonable open market rent is normally that of valuers relying upon comparables. The disregards in s.34(1) are principally matters related to the particular tenant—e.g. the effect of the tenant's occupation, any goodwill derived from the tenant's business and the effect of any improvements to which the section applies. It is possible for the court to fix a rent which increases by instalments (s.34(3), *Fawke v Viscount Chelsea* [1980] Q.B. 441; [1979] 3 W.L.R. 508; [1979] 3 All E.R. 568, CA and *88 High Road, Kilburn, Re* [1959] 1 W.L.R. 279; [1959] 1 All E.R. 527, Ch D—upwards only rent review). **3B–207**

In *Trans-World Investments Ltd v Anita Dadarwalla* [2007] EWCA Civ 480 it was held that the trial judge was wrong to disregard the passing rent of the subject property under the lease. He was also wrong to disregard valuation evidence of a neighbouring property as a "rogue figure" on the basis that there was no evidence as to the circumstances in which the rent was calculated. Mummery L.J. at para.30:

"In my judgment, the judge was wrong to disregard the passing rent and the

***Paragraph numbers marked with a "+" can be found online and on CD.***

rent of No 106 on the basis stated by him. The rents under the current lease and of the adjoining property at No 106 are relevant valuation evidence of market rent of the Property without the need for the court to require the party relying on those rents to produce positive evidence of the circumstances in which they were determined. Rather it is for the party who challenges the relevance of the passing rent and/or the rent of the adjoining property to adduce evidence of circumstances relied on to show that the rents are not relevant factors in the valuation exercise of determining the open market rent."

**Business**

3B–208 See s.46 and s.23(2) which provides that "business" includes a trade, profession or employment and includes any activity carried on by a body of persons, whether corporate or unincorporate. See too the commentary to s.23 above.

**Current tenancy**

3B–209 See s.46 and s.26(1)—the tenancy under which the tenant holds for the time being.

**Holding**

3B–210 See s.46, s.32 and s.23(3) which provides that the expression "the holding" means the property comprised in the tenancy, there being excluded any part thereof which is occupied neither by the tenant nor by a person employed by the tenant ... for the purposes of a business by reason of which the tenancy is one to which this Part of this Act applies.

**The landlord**

3B–211 See s.44(1) which provides that "the landlord" means the person (whether or not he is the immediate landlord) who is the owner of that interest in the property comprised in the relevant tenancy which for the time being fulfils the conditions contained in ss.44(1)(a) and (b).

## Other terms of new tenancy

3B–212 **35.**—(1) The terms of a tenancy granted by order of the court under this Part of this Act (other than terms as to the duration thereof and as to the rent payable thereunder), including, where different persons own interests which fulfil the conditions specified in section 44(1) of this Act in different parts of it, terms as to the apportionment of the rent,shall be such as may be agreed between the landlord and the tenant or as, in default of such agreement, may be determined by the court; and in determining those terms the court shall have regard to the terms of the current tenancy and to all relevant circumstances.

(2) In subsection (1) of this section the reference to all relevant circumstances includes (without prejudice to the generality of that reference) a reference to the operation of the provisions of the Landlord and Tenant (Covenants) Act 1995.

3B–213 *Note* —Subsections (1) and (2) were inserted by the Landlord and Tenant (Covenants) Act 1995 Sch.1, paras 4(1) and (2) and amended by the Regulatory Reform (Business Tenancies) (England and Wales) Order 2003 (SI 2003/3096), art.27(3). The amendment came into force June 1, 2004 but only applies where the s.25 notice or s.26 request was served on or after that date.

**Other terms**

3B–214 In the absence of agreement between the parties, the court determines any other terms, having regard to the terms of the current tenancy, and all relevant circumstances. The court will normally follow the terms of the current tenancy—any party wishing to depart from them must give a reason (*O'May v City of London Real*

***Paragraph numbers marked with a "+" can be found online and on CD.***

*Property Co Ltd* [1983] 2 A.C. 726; [1982] 2 W.L.R. 407; [1982] 1 All E.R. 660, HL). Any change must be fair and reasonable and take into account the comparatively weak negotiating position of a sitting tenant seeking renewal (*Cardshops v Davies* [1971] 1 W.L.R. 591; [1971] 2 All E.R. 721, CA. See too *No.1 Albemarle Street, Re* [1959] Ch. 531; [1959] 1 All E.R. 250; Ch D). A facility enjoyed pursuant to a licence under the old lease cannot became a term of the new lease—see para. 3B–199A.

**Current tenancy**

See s.46 and s.26(1)—the tenancy under which the tenant holds for the time being. **3B–215**

**The landlord**

See s.44(1) which provides that "the landlord" means the person (whether or not he is the immediate landlord) who is the owner of that interest in the property comprised in the relevant tenancy which for the time being fulfils the conditions contained in ss.44(1)(a) and (b). **3B–216**

## Carrying out of order for new tenancy

**36.**—(1) Where under this Part of this Act the court makes an order for the grant of a new tenancy, then, unless the order is revoked under the next following subsection or the landlord and the tenant agree not to act upon the order, the landlord shall be bound to execute or make in favour of the tenant, and the tenant shall be bound to accept, a lease or agreement for a tenancy of the holding embodying the terms agreed between the landlord and the tenant or determined by the court in accordance with the foregoing provisions of this Part of this Act; and where the landlord executes or makes such a lease or agreement the tenant shall be bound, if so required by the landlord, to execute a counterpart or duplicate thereof. **3B–217**

(2) If the tenant, within fourteen days after the making of an order under this Part of this Act for the grant of a new tenancy, applies to the court for the revocation of the order the court shall revoke the order; and where the order is so revoked, then, if it is so agreed between the landlord and the tenant or determined by the court, the current tenancy shall continue, beyond the date at which it would have come to an end apart from this subsection, for such period as may be so agreed or determined to be necessary to afford to the landlord a reasonable opportunity for reletting or otherwise disposing of the premises which would have been comprised in the new tenancy; and while the current tenancy continues by virtue of this subsection it shall not be a tenancy to which this Part of this Act applies.

(3) Where an order is revoked under the last foregoing subsection any provision thereof as to payment of costs shall not cease to have effect by reason only of the revocation; but the court may, if it thinks fit, revoke or vary any such provision or, where no costs have been awarded in the proceedings for the revoked order, award such costs.

(4) A lease executed or agreement made under this section, in a case where the interest of the lessor is subject to a mortgage, shall be deemed to be one authorised by section ninety-nine of the Law of Property Act 1925 (which confers certain powers of leasing on mortgagors in possession), and subsection (13) of that section (which allows those powers to be restricted or excluded by agreement) shall not have effect in relation to such a lease or agreement.

**Carrying out of order for new tenancy**

3B-218 If the court orders the grant of a new tenancy, the landlord is bound to make and the tenant is bound to accept a new lease embodying the terms agreed or determined by the court, unless—

(a) the landlord and the tenant agree not to act on the order; or
(b) the tenant elects not to take the tenancy on the terms ordered. In such circumstances the tenant may apply to the court within 14 days of the making of the order for the revocation of the order. On such an application the court must revoke the order (s.36(2)).

See e.g. *88 High Road, Kilburn, Re* [1959] 1 W.L.R. 279; [1959] 1 All E.R. 527 where the order was revoked, but the tenant was ordered to pay the costs of the action and of the application to revoke.

**Current tenancy**

3B-219 See s.46 and s.26(1)—the tenancy under which the tenant holds for the time being.

**Holding**

3B-220 See s.46, s.32 and s.23(3) which provides that the expression "the holding" means the property comprised in the tenancy, there being excluded any part thereof which is occupied neither by the tenant nor by a person employed by the tenant ... for the purposes of a business by reason of which the tenancy is one to which this Part of this Act applies.

**The landlord**

3B-221 See s.44(1) which provides that "the landlord" means the person (whether or not he is the immediate landlord) who is the owner of that interest in the property comprised in the relevant tenancy which for the time being fulfils the conditions contained in ss.44(1)(a) and (b).

## Compensation where order for new tenancy precluded on certain grounds

3B-222 **37.**—(1) Subject to the provisions of this Act, in a case specified in subsection (1A), (1B) or (1C) below (a "compensation case") the tenant shall be entitled on quitting the holding to recover from the landlord by way of compensation an amount determined in accordance with this section.

(1A) The first compensation case is where on the making of an application by the tenant under section 24(1) of this Act the court is precluded (whether by subsection (1) or subsection (2) of section 31 of this Act) from making an order for the grant of a new tenancy by reason of any of the grounds specified in paragraphs (e), (f) and (g) of section 30(1) of this Act (the "compensation grounds") and not of any grounds specified in any other paragraph of section 30(1).

(1B) The second compensation case is where on the making of an application under section 29(2) of this Act the court is precluded (whether by section 29(4)(a) or section 31(2) of this Act) from making an order for the grant of a new tenancy by reason of any of the compensation grounds and not of any other grounds specified in section 30(1) of this Act.

(1C) The third compensation case is where—

(a) the landlord's notice under section 25 of this Act or, as the case may be, under section 26(6) of this Act, states his opposition to the grant of a new tenancy on any of the compensation grounds and not on any other grounds specified in section 30(1) of this Act; and

*Paragraph numbers marked with a "+" can be found online and on CD.*

(b) either—

(i) no application is made by the tenant under section 24(1) of this Act or by the landlord under section 29(2) of this Act; or

(ii) such an application is made but is subsequently withdrawn.

(2) Subject to the following provisions of this section, compensation under this section shall be as follows, that is to say—

(a) where the conditions specified in the next following subsection are satisfied in relation to the whole of the holding it shall be the product of the appropriate multiplier and twice the rateable value of the holding,

(b) in any other case it shall be [the product of the appropriate multiplier and] the rateable value of the holding.

(3) The said conditions are—

(a) that, during the whole of the fourteen years immediately preceding the termination of the current tenancy, premises being or comprised in the holding have been occupied for the purposes of a business carried on by the occupier or for those and other purposes;

(b) that, if during those fourteen years there was a change in the occupier of the premises, the person who was the occupier immediately after the change was the successor to the business carried on by the person who was the occupier immediately before the change.

(3A) If the conditions specified in subsection (3) above are satisfied in relation to part of the holding but not in relation to the other part, the amount of compensation shall be the aggregate of sums calculated separately as compensation in respect of each part, and accordingly, for the purpose of calculating compensation in respect of a part any reference in this section to the holding shall be construed as a reference to that part.

(3B) Where section 44(1A) of this Act applies, the compensation shall be determined separately for each part and compensation determined for any part shall be recoverable only from the person who is the owner of an interest in that part which fulfils the conditions specified in section 44(1) of this Act.

(4) Where the court is precluded from making an order for the grant of a new tenancy under this Part of this Act in a compensation case, the court shall on the application of the tenant certify that fact.

(5) For the purposes of subsection (2) of this section the rateable value of the holding shall be determined as follows:—

(a) where in the valuation list in force at the date on which the landlord's notice under section 25 or, as the case may be, subsection (6) of section 26 of this Act is given a value is then shown as the annual value (as hereinafter defined) of the holding, the rateable value of the holding shall be taken to be that value;

(b) where no such value is so shown with respect to the holding but such a value or such values is or are so shown

*Paragraph numbers marked with a "+" can be found online and on CD.*

with respect to premises comprised in or comprising the holding or part of it, the rateable value of the holding shall be taken to be such value as is found by a proper apportionment or aggregation of the value or values so shown;

(c) where the rateable value of the holding cannot be ascertained in accordance with the foregoing paragraphs of this subsection, it shall be taken to be the value which, apart from any exemption from assessment to rates, would on a proper assessment be the value to be entered in the said valuation list as the annual value of the holding;

and any dispute arising, whether in proceedings before the court or otherwise, as to the determination for those purposes of the rateable value of the holding shall be referred to the Commissioners of Inland Revenue for decision by a valuation officer.

An appeal shall lie to the Lands Tribunal from any decision of a valuation officer under this subsection, but subject thereto any such decision shall be final.

(5A) If part of the holding is domestic property, as defined in section 66 of the Local Government Finance Act 1988—

(a) the domestic property shall be disregarded in determining the rateable value of the holding under subsection (5) of this section; and

(b) if, on the date specified in subsection (5)(a) of this section, the tenant occupied the whole or any part of the domestic property, the amount of compensation to which he is entitled under subsection (1) of this section shall be increased by the addition of a sum equal to his reasonable expenses in removing from the domestic property.

(5B) Any question as to the amount of the sum referred to in paragraph (b) of subsection (5A) of this section shall be determined by agreement between the landlord and the tenant or, in default of agreement, by the court.

(5C) If the whole of the holding is domestic property, as defined in section 66 of the Local Government Finance Act 1988, for the purposes of subsection (2) of this section the rateable value of the holding shall be taken to be an amount equal to the rent at which it is estimated the holding might reasonably be expected to let from year to year if the tenant undertook to pay all usual tenant's rates and taxes and to bear the cost of the repairs and insurance and the other expenses (if any) necessary to maintain the holding in a state to command that rent.

(5D) The following provisions shall have effect as regards a determination of an amount mentioned in subsection (5C) of this section—

(a) the date by reference to which such a determination is to be made is the date on which the landlord's notice under section 25 or, as the case may be, subsection (6) of section 26 of this Act is given;

(b) any dispute arising, whether in proceedings before the court or otherwise, as to such a determination shall be referred to the Commissioners of Inland Revenue for decision by a valuation officer;

(c) an appeal shall lie to the Lands Tribunal from such a decision but, subject to that, such a decision shall be final.

(5E) Any deduction made under paragraph 2A of Schedule 6 to the Local Government Finance Act 1988 (deduction from valuation of hereditaments used for breeding horses etc.) shall be disregarded, to the extent that it relates to the holding, in determining the rateable value of the holding under subsection (5) of this section.

(6) The Commissioners of Inland Revenue may by statutory instrument make rules prescribing the procedure in connection with references under this section.

(7) In this section—

the reference to the termination of the current tenancy is a reference to the date of termination specified in the landlord's notice under section 25 of this Act or, as the case may be, the date specified in the tenant's request for a new tenancy as the date from which the new tenancy is to begin;

the expression "annual value" means rateable value except that where the rateable value differs from the net annual value the said expression means net annual value;

the expression "valuation officer" means any officer of the Commissioners of Inland Revenue for the time being authorised by a certificate of the Commissioners to act in relation to a valuation list.

(8) In subsection (2) of this section "the appropriate multiplier" means such multiplier as the Secretary of State may by order made by statutory instrument prescribe and different multipliers may be so prescribed in relation to different cases.

(9) A statutory instrument containing an order under subsection (8) of this section shall be subject to annulment in pursuance of a resolution of either House of Parliament.

*Note*—Section 37 was amended by the Local Government, Planning and Land Act 1980 Sch.33, paras 4(1) and 4(2); the Local Government and Housing Act 1989 s.149 and Sch.7, paras 2(2), 2(3), 2(4) and 4 and by the Local Government Finance (Miscellaneous Amendments and Repeal) Order 1990 (SI 1990/1285) art.2, Sch. Pt I, para.4(a) and by the Regulatory Reform (Business Tenancies) (England and Wales) Order 2003 (SI 2003/3096), art.19. The latter amendment came into force June 1, 2004 but only applies where the s.25 notice or s.26 request was served on or after that date. **3B–223**

**Business**

See s.46 and s.23(2) which provides that "business" includes a trade, profession or employment and includes any activity carried on by a body of persons, whether corporate or unincorporate. See too the commentary to s.23 above. **3B–224**

**Current tenancy**

See s.46 and s.26(1)—the tenancy under which the tenant holds for the time being. **3B–225**

**Date of termination**

See s.46 and s.25(1)—the date specified in the landlord's s.25 notice at which the tenancy is to come to an end. **3B–226**

**Holding**

3B–227 See s.46, s.32 and s.23(3) which provides that the expression "the holding" means the property comprised in the tenancy, there being excluded any part thereof which is occupied neither by the tenant nor by a person employed by the tenant ... for the purposes of a business by reason of which the tenancy is one to which this Part of this Act applies.

**The landlord**

3B–228 See s.44(1) which provides that "the landlord" means the person (whether or not he is the immediate landlord) who is the owner of that interest in the property comprised in the relevant tenancy which for the time being fulfils the conditions contained in ss.44(1)(a) and (b).

**Compensation**

3B–229 Put simply, a tenant is entitled to compensation if a landlord successfully relies upon s.30(1)(e) (aggregate of the rents reasonably obtainable on separate lettings less than the rent reasonably obtainable on a letting of that property as a whole), s.30(1)(f) (intention of landlord to demolish or reconstruct) or s.30(1)(g) (intention of landlord to occupy the holding for the purposes of a business or as his residence). If a court refuses the grant of a new tenancy on any these three grounds it must certify that fact (s.37(4)). The amount of compensation is either the product of the appropriate multiplier and the rateable value or the product of the appropriate multiplier and twice the rateable value. (See s.37 and the Landlord and Tenant Act 1954 (Appropriate Multiplier) Order 1990 (SI 1990/363)).

**Restriction on contracting out**

3B–230 See s.38(2).

## Compensation for possession obtained by misrepresentation

3B–231 **37A.**—(1) Where the court—

(a) makes an order for the termination of the current tenancy but does not make an order for the grant of a new tenancy, or

(b) refuses an order for the grant of a new tenancy,

and it subsequently made to appear to the court that the order was obtained, or the court was induced to refuse the grant, by misrepresentation or the concealment of material facts, the court may order the landlord to pay to the tenant such sum as appears sufficient as compensation for damage or loss sustained by the tenant as the result of the order or refusal.

(2) Where—

(a) the tenant has quit the holding—

(i) after making but withdrawing an application under section 24(1) of this Act; or

(ii) without making such an application; and

(b) it is made to appear to the court that he did so by reason of misrepresentation or the concealment of material facts,

the court may order the landlord to pay to the tenant such sum as appears sufficient as compensation for damage or loss sustained by the tenant as the result of quitting the holding.

3B–232 *Note* —New s.37A was inserted by the Regulatory Reform (Business Tenancies) (England and Wales) Order 2003 (SI 2003/3096), art.20. The amendment came into force June 1, 2004 but only where the tenant quit the holding before that date

***Paragraph numbers marked with a "+" can be found online and on CD.***

(reg.29(5) of 2003 Order) but only where the tenant quit the holding before that date (reg.29(5) of 2003 Order; para.3B–93).

A landlord who told a tenant in a letter accompanying a s.25 notice that he intended to redevelop but subsequently changed his mind, without telling the tenant, was held liable to the tenant for damages under s.37A. There was a continuing representation, in the letter, that had been made false by the change in circumstances (*Inclusive Technology v Williamson* [2009] EWCA Civ 718).

## Restriction on agreements excluding provisions of Part II

**38.**—(1) Any agreement relating to a tenancy to which this Part of this Act applies (whether contained in the instrument creating the tenancy or not) shall be void (except as provided by section 38A of this Act) in so far as it purports to preclude the tenant from making an application or request under this Part of this Act or provides for the termination or the surrender of the tenancy in the event of his making such an application or request or for the imposition of any penalty or disability on the tenant in that event. **3B–233**

(2) Where—

(a) during the whole of the five years immediately preceding the date on which the tenant under a tenancy to which this Part of this Act applies is to quit the holding, premises being or comprised in the holding have been occupied for the purposes of a business carried on by the occupier or for those and other purposes, and

(b) if during those five years there was a change in the occupier of the premises, the person who was the occupier immediately after the change was the successor to the business carried on by the person who was the occupier immediately before the change,

any agreement (whether contained in the instrument creating the tenancy or not and whether made before or after the termination of that tenancy) which purports to exclude or reduce compensation under section 37 of this Act shall to that extent be void, so however that this subsection shall not affect any agreement as to the amount of any such compensation which is made after the right to compensation has accrued.

(3) In a case not falling within the last foregoing subsection the right to compensation conferred by section 37 of this Act may be excluded or modified by agreement.

(4) [...]

*Note*—The current s.38 was substituted by Law of Property Act 1969 s.15, Sch.1 and was amended by the Regulatory Reform (Business Tenancies) (England and Wales) Order 2003 (SI 2003/3096), art.21 and Sch.5, para.4. Subsection (4) was repealed by Sch.6, para.1. The amendment came into force June 1, 2004. It does not apply to an agreement to contract out nor does it apply to an agreement for the surrender for a tenancy which was authorised by the court under s.38(4) before that date. (Regulation 29(2)(a)(ii) of the 2003 Order—for further transitional provisions see reg. 29(3) and (4); para.3B–93). **3B–234**

## Agreements to exclude provisions of Part 2

**38A.**—(1) The persons who will be the landlord and the tenant in **3B–235**

relation to a tenancy to be granted for a term of years certain which will be a tenancy to which this Part of this Act applies may agree that the provisions of sections 24 to 28 of this Act shall be excluded in relation to that tenancy.

(2) The persons who are the landlord and the tenant in relation to a tenancy to which this Part of this Act applies may agree that the tenancy shall be surrendered on such date or in such circumstances as may be specified in the agreement and on such terms (if any) as may be so specified.

(3) An agreement under subsection (1) above shall be void unless—

(a) the landlord has served on the tenant a notice in the form, or substantially in the form, set out in Schedule 1 to the Regulatory Reform (Business Tenancies) (England and Wales) Order 2003 ("the 2003 Order"); and

(b) the requirements specified in Schedule 2 to that Order are met.

(4) An agreement under subsection (2) above shall be void unless—

(a) the landlord has served on the tenant a notice in the form, or substantially in the form, set out in Schedule 3 to the 2003 Order; and

(b) the requirements specified in Schedule 4 to that Order are met.

**3B–236** *Note* —New s.38A was inserted by the Regulatory Reform (Business Tenancies) (England and Wales) Order 2003 (SI 2003/3096). The amendment came into force June 1, 2004. Section 38A sets out a completely new procedure for contracting out of the security provisions of Pt II of the 1954 Act and for agreements to surrender where Pt II of the Act applies. The procedure in each case is based upon three elements (i) notice in a prescribed form served upon the tenant by the landlord, (ii) a declaration from the tenant acknowledging receipt of the notice and (iii) a reference to the notice in the lease/agreement to surrender. The details are contained in Schs 1 to 4 of 2003 Reform Order—not set out in the *White Book*. Note that both under the old system of contracting out and the new it is necessary for the tenancy to be "for a term of years certain". In *London Borough of Newham v Thomas-Van Staden* [2008] EWCA Civ 1414 the term was not, on a proper construction of the lease, for a term of years certain. Thus, even though the court (under the old system) had a made court order approving the agreement to contract out the tenancy was in fact protected by the 1954 Act and the tenant was entitled to remain in possession.

Where a notice informing a prospective tenant that the lease is to be contracted out of Pt II of the 1954 Act is served more than 14 days before the lease is entered into, para.3 of Schedule 2 to the Regulatory Reform (Business Tenancies) (England and Wales) Order 2003 says that the tenant (or duly authorised person) "must" sign a simple declaration. However, if he in fact signs a statutory declaration that will still be effective (see *The Chiltern Railway Company Ltd v Patel* [2008] EWCA Civ 178:

> "It would ... be 'bordering on the absurd' if a statutory declaration was held to be ineffective on the grounds that it differed from the prescribed form because a) it was both expressly and in law in a more solemn form than that form; and b) although it stated that notice was served before the lease was entered into, it did not state that it was served more than fourteen days before the lease was entered into" (Lord Neuberger sitting in the Court of Appeal at para.11).

## Saving for compulsory acquisitions

**3B–237** **39.**—(1) [...]

*Paragraph numbers marked with a "+" can be found online and on CD.*

(2) If the amount of the compensation which would have been payable under section thirty-seven of this Act if the tenancy had come to an end in circumstances giving rise to compensation under that section and the date at which the acquiring authority obtained possession had been the termination of the current tenancy exceeds the amount of [the compensation payable under section 121 of the Lands Clauses Consolidation Act 1845 or section 20 of the Compulsory Purchase Act 1965in the case of a tenancy to which this Part of this Act applies], that compensation shall be increased by the amount of the excess.

(3) Nothing in section twenty-four of this Act shall affect the operation of the said section one hundred and twenty-one.

*Note* —Amended by Land Compensation Act 1973 s.47(3). Subsection (1) was repealed by Land Compensation Act 1973, Sch. 3. **3B–238**

**Current tenancy**

See s.46 and s.26(1)—the tenancy under which the tenant holds for the time being. **3B–239**

## Duty of tenants and landlords of business premises to give information to each other

**40.**—(1) Where a person who is an owner of an interest in reversion expectant (whether immediately or not) on a tenancy of any business premises has served on the tenant a notice in the prescribed form requiring him to do so, it shall be the duty of the tenant to give the appropriate person in writing the information specified in subsection (2) below. **3B–240**

(2) That information is—

(a) whether the tenant occupies the premises or any part of them wholly or partly for the purposes of a business carried on by him;

(b) whether his tenancy has effect subject to any sub-tenancy on which his tenancy is immediately expectant and, if so—

(i) what premises are comprised in the sub-tenancy;

(ii) for what term it has effect (or, if it is terminable by notice, by what notice it can be terminated);

(iii) what is the rent payable under it;

(iv) who is the sub-tenant;

(v) (to the best of his knowledge and belief) whether the sub-tenant is in occupation of the premises or of part of the premises comprised in the sub-tenancy and, if not, what is the sub-tenant's address;

(vi) whether an agreement is in force excluding in relation to the sub-tenancy the provisions of sections 24 to 28 of this Act; and

(vii) whether a notice has been given under section 25 or 26(6) of this Act, or a request has been made under section 26 of this Act, in relation to the sub-

*Paragraph numbers marked with a "+" can be found online and on CD.*

tenancy and, if so, details of the notice or request; and

(c) (to the best of his knowledge and belief) the name and address of any other person who owns an interest in reversion in any part of the premises.

(3) Where the tenant of any business premises who is a tenant under such a tenancy as is mentioned in section 26(1) of this Act has served on a reversioner or a reversioner's mortgagee in possession a notice in the prescribed form requiring him to do so, it shall be the duty of the person on whom the notice is served to give the appropriate person in writing the information specified in subsection (4) below.

(4) That information is—

(a) whether he is the owner of the fee simple in respect of the premises or any part of them or the mortgagee in possession of such an owner,

(b) if he is not, then (to the best of his knowledge and belief)—

(i) the name and address of the person who is his or, as the case may be, his mortgagor's immediate landlord in respect of those premises or of the part in respect of which he or his mortgagor is not the owner in fee simple;

(ii) for what term his or his mortgagor's tenancy has effect and what is the earliest date (if any) at which that tenancy is terminable by notice to quit given by the landlord; and

(iii) whether a notice has been given under section 25 or 26(6) of this Act, or a request has been made under section 26 of this Act, in relation to the tenancy and, if so, details of the notice or request;

(c) (to the best of his knowledge and belief) the name and address of any other person who owns an interest in reversion in any part of the premises; and

(d) if he is a reversioner, whether there is a mortgagee in possession of his interest in the premises and, if so, (to the best of his knowledge and belief) what is the name and address of the mortgagee.

(5) A duty imposed on a person by this section is a duty—

(a) to give the information concerned within the period of one month beginning with the date of service of the notice; and

(b) if within the period of six months beginning with the date of service of the notice that person becomes aware that any information which has been given in pursuance of the notice is not, or is no longer, correct, to give the appropriate person correct information within the period of one month beginning with the date on which he becomes aware.

(6) This section shall not apply to a notice served by or on the tenant more than two years before the date on which apart from this Act his tenancy would come to an end by effluxion of time or could be brought to an end by notice to quit given by the landlord.

(7) Except as provided by section 40A of this Act, the appropriate person for the purposes of this section and section 40A(1) of this Act is the person who served the notice under subsection (1) or (3) above.

(8) In this section—

"business premises" means premises used wholly or partly for the purposes of a business;

"mortgagee in possession" includes a receiver appointed by the mortgagee or by the court who is in receipt of the rents and profits, and "his mortgagor" shall be construed accordingly;

"reversioner" means any person having an interest in the premises, being an interest in reversion expectant (whether immediately or not) on the tenancy;

"reversioner's mortgagee in possession" means any person being a mortgagee in possession in respect of such an interest; and

"sub-tenant" includes a person retaining possession of any premises by virtue of the Rent (Agriculture) Act 1976 or the Rent Act 1977 after the coming to an end of a sub-tenancy, and "sub-tenancy" includes a right so to retain possession.

*Note* —New s.40 was inserted by the Regulatory Reform (Business Tenancies) (England and Wales) Order 2003 (SI 2003/3096). The amendment came into force June 1, 2004. It does not apply to a notice under s.40 served before that date (reg. 29(6) of the 2003 Reform Order—see para.3B–93). **3B–241**

#### Tenancy

See s.69(1) and the commentary to s.23 above. The definition includes an agreement for a lease or underlease, but does not include a mortgage. **3B–242**

#### Business

See s.46 and s.23(2) which provides that "business" includes a trade, profession or employment and includes any activity carried on by a body of persons, whether corporate or unincorporate. See too the commentary to s.23 above. **3B–243**

#### Prescribed form

See the Landlord and Tenant Act 1954, Pt 2 (Notices) Regulations 2004 (SI 2004/1005). Regulation 2(2) allows a "form substantially to the like effect" of those contained in the regulations. **3B–244**

#### Notice to quit

Means a notice to quit given by the immediate landlord (see s.44(2)). **3B–245**

#### The landlord

See s.44(1) which provides that "the landlord" means the person (whether or not he is the immediate landlord) who is the owner of that interest in the property comprised in the relevant tenancy which for the time being fulfils the conditions contained in ss.44(1)(a) and (b). **3B–246**

### Duties in transfer cases

**40A.**—(1) If a person on whom a notice under section 40(1) or (3) of this Act has been served has transferred his interest in the premises **3B–247**

*Paragraph numbers marked with a "+" can be found online and on CD.*

or any part of them to some other person and gives the appropriate person notice in writing—

(a) of the transfer of his interest; and

(b) of the name and address of the person to whom he transferred it,

on giving the notice he ceases in relation to the premises or (as the case may be) to that part to be under any duty imposed by section 40 of this Act.

(2) If—

(a) the person who served the notice under section 40(1) or (3) of this Act ("the transferor") has transferred his interest in the premises to some other person ("the transferee"); and

(b) the transferor or the transferee has given the person required to give the information notice in writing—

(i) of the transfer; and

(ii) of the transferee's name and address,

the appropriate person for the purposes of section 40 of this Act and subsection (1) above is the transferee.

(3) If—

(a) a transfer such as is mentioned in paragraph (a) of subsection (2) above has taken place; but

(b) neither the transferor nor the transferee has given a notice such as is mentioned in paragraph (b) of that subsection,

any duty imposed by section 40 of this Act may be performed by giving the information either to the transferor or to the transferee.

**3B–248** *Note* —New s.40A was inserted by the Regulatory Reform (Business Tenancies) (England and Wales) Order 2003 (SI 2003/3096). The amendment came into force June 1, 2004. It does not apply to a notice under s.40 served before that date.

## Proceedings for breach of duties to give information

**3B–249** **40B.** A claim that a person has broken any duty imposed by section 40 of this Act may be made the subject of civil proceedings for breach of statutory duty; and in any such proceedings a court may order that person to comply with that duty and may make an award of damages.

**3B–250** *Note* —New s.40B was inserted by the Regulatory Reform (Business Tenancies) (England and Wales) Order 2003 (SI 2003/3096). The amendment came into force June 1, 2004. It does not apply to a notice under s.40 served before that date.

## Trusts

**3B–251** **41.**—(1) Where a tenancy is held on trust, occupation by all or any of the beneficiaries under the trust, and the carrying on of a business by all or any of the beneficiaries, shall be treated for the purposes of section twenty-three of this Act as equivalent to occupation or the carrying on of a business by the tenant; and in relation to a tenancy to which this Part of this Act applies by virtue of the foregoing provisions of this subsection—

*Paragraph numbers marked with a "+" can be found online and on CD.*

(a) references (however expressed) in this Part of this Act and in the Ninth Schedule to this Act to the business of, or to carrying on of business, use, occupation or enjoyment by, the tenant shall be construed as including references to the business of, or to carrying on of business, use, occupation or enjoyment by, the beneficiaries or beneficiary;

(b) the reference in paragraph (d) of [subsection (1) of] section thirty-four of this Act to the tenant shall be construed as including the beneficiaries or beneficiary; and

(c) a change in the persons of the trustees shall not be treated as a change in the person of the tenant.

(2) Where the landlord's interest is held on trust the references in paragraph (g) of subsection (1) of section thirty of this Act to the landlord shall be construed as including references to the beneficiaries under the trust or any of them; but, except in the case of a trust arising under a will or on the intestacy of any person, the reference in subsection (2) of that section to the creation of the interest therein mentioned shall be construed as including the creation of the trust.

*Note*—Amended by the Law of Property Act 1969 s.1(2). **3B–252**

**Tenancy**

See s.69(1) and the commentary to s.23 above. The definition includes an agreement for a lease or underlease, but does not include a mortgage. **3B–253**

**Business**

See s.46 and s.23(2) which provides that "business" includes a trade, profession or employment and includes any activity carried on by a body of persons, whether corporate or unincorporate. See too the commentary to s.23 above. **3B–254**

**The landlord**

See s.44(1) which provides that "the landlord" means the person (whether or not he is the immediate landlord) who is the owner of that interest in the property comprised in the relevant tenancy which for the time being fulfils the conditions contained in ss.44(1)(a) and (b). **3B–255**

## Partnerships

**41A.**—(1) The following provisions of this section shall apply where— **3B–256**

(a) a tenancy is held jointly by two or more persons (in this section referred to as the joint tenants); and

(b) the property comprised in the tenancy is or includes premises occupied for the purposes of a business; and

(c) the business (or some other business) was at some time during the existence of the tenancy carried on in partnership by all the persons who were then the joint tenants or by those and other persons and the joint tenants' interest in the premises was then partnership property; and

(d) the business is carried on (whether alone or in partnership with other persons) by one or some only of the joint tenants and no part of the property comprised in the tenancy is occupied, in right of the tenancy, for the purposes of a business carried on (whether alone or in partnership with other persons) by the other or others.

(2) In the following provisions of this section those of the joint tenants who for the time being carry on the business are referred to as the business tenants and the others as the other joint tenants.

(3) Any notice given by the business tenants which, had it been given by all the joint tenants, would have been—

(a) a tenant's request for a new tenancy made in accordance with section 26 of this Act; or

(b) a notice under subsection (1) or subsection (2) of section 27 of this Act;

shall be treated as such if it states that it is given by virtue of this section and sets out the facts by virtue of which the persons giving it are the business tenants; and references in those sections and in section 24A of this Act to the tenant shall be construed accordingly.

(4) A notice given by the landlord to the business tenants which, had it been given to all the joint tenants, would have been a notice under section 25 of this Act shall be treated as such a notice, and references in that section to the tenant shall be construed accordingly.

(5) An application under section 24(1) of this Act for a new tenancy may, instead of being made by all the joint tenants, be made by the business tenants alone; and where it is so made—

(a) this Part of this Act shall have effect, in relation to it, as if the references therein to the tenant included references to the business tenants alone; and

(b) the business tenants shall be liable, to the exclusion of the other joint tenants, for the payment of rent and the discharge of any other obligation under the current tenancy for any rental period beginning after the date specified in the landlord's notice under section 25 of this Act or, as the case may be, beginning on or after the date specified in their request for a new tenancy.

(6) Where the court makes an order under section 29 of this Act for the grant of a new tenancy it may order the grant to be made to the business tenants or to them jointly with the persons carrying on the business in partnership with them, and may order the grant to be made subject to the satisfaction, within a time specified by the order, of such conditions as to guarantors, sureties or otherwise as appear to the court equitable, having regard to the omission of the other joint tenants from the persons who will be the tenants under the new tenancy.

(7) The business tenants shall be entitled to recover any amount payable by way of compensation under section 37 or section 59 of this Act.

**3B–257** *Note*—Section 41A was inserted by Law of Property Act 1969 s.9 and amended by the Regulatory Reform (Business Tenancies) (England and Wales) Order 2003 (SI 2003/3096), Sch.5, para.5.

**Business**

**3B–258** See s.46 and s.23(2) which provides that "business" includes a trade, profession or

***Paragraph numbers marked with a "+" can be found online and on CD.***

employment and includes any activity carried on by a body of persons, whether corporate or unincorporate. See too the commentary to s.23 above.

**Current tenancy**

See s.46 and s.26(1)—the tenancy under which the tenant holds for the time being. **3B–259**

**The landlord**

See s.44(1) which provides that "the landlord" means the person (whether or not he is the immediate landlord) who is the owner of that interest in the property comprised in the relevant tenancy which for the time being fulfils the conditions contained in ss.44(1)(a) and (b). **3B–260**

## Groups of companies

**42.**—(1) For the purposes of this section two bodies corporate shall be taken to be members of a group if and only if one is a subsidiary of the other or both are subsidiaries of a third body corporate or the same person has a controlling interest in both. **3B–261**

(2) Where a tenancy is held by a member of a group, occupation by another member of the group, and the carrying on of a business by another member of the group, shall be treated for the purposes of section 23 of this Act as equivalent to occupation or the carrying on of a business by the member of the group holding the tenancy; and in relation to a tenancy to which this Part of this Act applies by virtue of the foregoing provisions of this subsection—

(a) references (however expressed) in this Part of this Act and in the Ninth Schedule to this Act to the business of or to use occupation or enjoyment by the tenant shall be construed as including references to the business of or to use occupation or enjoyment by the said other member;

(b) the reference in paragraph (d) of subsection (1) of section 34 of this Act to the tenant shall be construed as including the said other member; and

(c) an assignment of the tenancy from one member of the group to another shall not be treated as a change in the person of the tenant.

(3) Where the landlord's interest is held by a member of a group—

(a) the reference in paragraph (g) of subsection (1) of section 30 of this Act to intended occupation by the landlord for the purposes of a business to be carried on by him shall be construed as including intended occupation by any member of the group for the purposes of a business to be carried on by that member; and

(b) the reference in subsection (2) of that section to the purchase or creation of any interest shall be construed as a reference to a purchase from or creation by a person other than a member of the group.

*Note*—The current s.42 was substituted by the Law of Property Act 1969 s.15, Sch.1 and amended by Companies Act 1989 s.144(4), s.213(2), s.215(2), Sch.18 para.3 and by the Regulatory Reform (Business Tenancies) (England and Wales) Order 2003 (SI 2003/3096) but only applies where the s.25 notice or s.26 request was served on or after that date. **3B–262**

***Paragraph numbers marked with a "+" can be found online and on CD.***

**Business**

3B–263 See s.46 and s.23(2) which provides that "business" includes a trade, profession or employment and includes any activity carried on by a body of persons, whether corporate or unincorporate.

**The landlord**

3B–264 See s.44(1) which provides that "the landlord" means the person (whether or not he is the immediate landlord) who is the owner of that interest in the property comprised in the relevant tenancy which for the time being fulfils the conditions contained in ss.44(1)(a) and (b).

## Tenancies excluded from Part II

3B–265 **43.**—(1) This Part of this Act does not apply—

(a) to a tenancy of an agricultural holding [[which is a tenancy in relation to which the Agricultural Holdings Act 1986 applies or a tenancy which would be a tenancy of an agricultural holding in relation to which that Act applied if subsection (3) of section 2 of that Act] did not have effect or, in a case where approval was given under subsection (1) of that section], if that approval had not been given;]

(aa) [to a farm business tenancy;]

(b) to a tenancy created by a mining lease;

(c) [...]

(d) [...]

(2) This Part of this Act does not apply to a tenancy granted by reason that the tenant was the holder of an office, appointment or employment from the grantor thereof and continuing only so long as the tenant holds the office, appointment or employment, or terminable by the grantor on the tenant's ceasing to hold it, or coming to an end at a time fixed by reference to the time at which the tenant ceases to hold it:

Provided that this subsection shall not have effect in relation to a tenancy granted after the commencement of this Act unless the tenancy was granted by an instrument in writing which expressed the purpose for which the tenancy was granted.

[(3) This Part of this Act does not apply to a tenancy granted for a term certain not exceeding six months unless—

(a) the tenancy contains provision for renewing the term or for extending it beyond six months from its beginning; or

(b) the tenant has been in occupation for a period which, together with any period during which any predecessor in the carrying on of the business carried on by the tenant was in occupation, exceeds twelve months.]

3B–266 *Note* —Amended by Agricultural Tenancies Act 1995 Sch.1, para.10; Agricultural Holdings Act 1986 s.99, s.100, Sch.13, para.3, Sch.14, para.21; Agriculture Act 1958 Sch.1, Pt I, para.29; Housing Act 1980 Sch.26; Finance Act 1959 Sch.2, para.5; Landlord and Tenant (Licensed Premises) Act 1990 s.1(1)(2), s.2(2)(a); and Law of Property Act 1969 s.15, Sch.1.

**Tenancy**

3B–267 See s.69(1) and the commentary to s.23 above. The definition includes an agreement for a lease or underlease, but does not include a mortgage.

***Paragraph numbers marked with a "+" can be found online and on CD.***

**Mining lease**

See s.46 and Landlord and Tenant Act 1927, s.25 which defines "mining lease" as a lease for any mining purpose or purposes connected therewith, and "mining purposes" include the sinking and searching for, winning, working, getting, making merchantable, smelting or otherwise converting or working for the purposes of any manufacture, carrying away, and disposing of mines and minerals, in or under land, and the erection of buildings, and the execution of engineering and other works suitable for those purposes. **3B–268**

## Jurisdiction of county court to make declaration

**43A.** Where the rateable value of the holding is such that the jurisdiction conferred on the court by any other provision of this Part of this Act is, by virtue of section 63 of this Act, exercisable by the county court, the county court shall have jurisdiction (but without prejudice to the jurisdiction of the High Court) to make any declaration as to any matter arising under this Part of this Act, whether or not any other relief is sought in the proceedings. **3B–269**

*Note* —Section 43A was inserted by the Law of Property Act 1969 s.13. Claims under Pt II should normally be brought in the county court. Only exceptional circumstances justify starting such a claim in the High Court (CPR r.56.2 and PD 56.2). **3B–270**

**Holding**

See s.46, s.32 and s.23(3) which provides that the expression "the holding" means the property comprised in the tenancy, there being excluded any part thereof which is occupied neither by the tenant nor by a person employed by the tenant ... for the purposes of a business by reason of which the tenancy is one to which this Part of this Act applies. **3B–271**

## Meaning of "the landlord" in Part II, and provisions as to mesne landlords, etc.

**44.**—(1) Subject to subsections (1A) and (2) below, in this Part of this Act the expression "the landlord", in relation to a tenancy (in this section referred to as "the relevant tenancy"), means the person (whether or not he is the immediate landlord) who is the owner of that interest in the property comprised in the relevant tenancy which for the time being fulfils the following conditions, that is to say— **3B–272**

(a) that it is an interest in reversion expectant (whether immediately or not) on the termination of the relevant tenancy, and

(b) that it is either the fee simple or a tenancy which will not come to an end within fourteen months by effluxion of time and, if it is such a tenancy, that no notice has been given by virtue of which it will come to an end within fourteen months or any further time by which it may be continued under section 36(2) or section 64 of this Act, and is not itself in reversion expectant (whether immediately or not) on an interest which fulfils those conditions.

(1A) The reference in subsection (1) above to a person who is the owner of an interest such as is mentioned in that subsection is to be construed, where different persons own such interests in different parts of the property, as a reference to all those persons collectively.

*Paragraph numbers marked with a "+" can be found online and on CD.*

(2) References in this Part of this Act to a notice to quit given by the landlord are references to a notice to quit given by the immediate landlord.

(3) The provisions of the Sixth Schedule to this Act shall have effect for the application of this Part of this Act to cases where the immediate landlord of the tenant is not the owner of the fee simple in respect of the holding.

**3B–273** *Note*—The current s.44 was substituted by the Law of Property Act 1969 s.15, Sch.1 and amended by the Regulatory Reform (Business Tenancies) (England and Wales) Order 2003 (SI 2003/3096), art.27(2). The latter amendment came into force June 1, 2004 but only applies where the s.25 notice or s.26 request was served on or after that date.

**Landlord**

**3B–274** Only the competent landlord may give a s.25 notice or receive a s.26 request for a new tenancy. There can only be one competent landlord at any given time. Effectively it is the first person in the chain of landlords who has more than a nominal reversion. A mesne landlord, whose own tenancy is continuing under s.24 may be the landlord in relation to a sub-tenant of part of the premises, despite the uncertain duration of his own tenancy (*Bowes Lyon v Green* [1963] A.C. 420; [1961] 3 W.L.R. 1044; [1961] 3 All E.R. 843, HL). The landlord means the person with legal title to the land and so it is trustees rather than beneficiaries who are the competent landlord (*Biles v Caesar* [1957] 1 W.L.R. 156; [1957] 1 All E.R. 151, CA; *Morar v Chauhan* [1985] 1 W.L.R. 1263; [1985] 3 All E.R. 493, CA). Note s.40 which provides a mechanism allowing tenants to serve notices to obtain information as to the identity of the competent landlord.

**Holding**

**3B–275** See s.46, s.32 and s.23(3) which provides that the expression "the holding" means the property comprised in the tenancy, there being excluded any part thereof which is occupied neither by the tenant nor by a person employed by the tenant ... for the purposes of a business by reason of which the tenancy is one to which this Part of this Act applies.

**3B–276** **45.** [...]

**3B–277** *Note*—Repealed by Statute Law (Repeals) Act 1974 (C.22), Pt XI.

## Interpretation of Part II

**3B–278** **46.**—(1) In this Part of this Act:—

"business" has the meaning assigned to it by subsection (2) of section twenty-three of this Act;

"current tenancy" means the tenancy under which the tenant holds for the time being;

"date of termination" has the meaning assigned to it by subsection (1) of section twenty-five of this Act;

subject to the provisions of section thirty-two of this Act, "the holding" has the meaning assigned to it by subsection (3) of section twenty-three of this Act;

"interim rent" has the meaning given by section 24A(1) of this Act;

"mining lease" has the same meaning as in the Landlord and Tenant Act 1927.

(2) For the purposes of this Part of this Act, a person has a controlling interest in a company, if, had he been a company, the other company would have been its subsidiary; and in this Part—

"company" has the meaning given by section 1(1) of the Companies Act 2006; and

"subsidiary" has the meaning given by section 1159 of that Act.

*Note* — Section 46 was amended by the Regulatory Reform (Business Tenancies) (England and Wales) Order 2003 (SI 2003/3096). The amendment came into force June 1, 2004 but only applies where the s.25 notice or s.26 request was served on or after that date. Further amended by the Companies Act 2006 (Consequential Amendments, Transitional Provisions and Savings) Order 2009 (SI 2009/1941) Sch.1 para.7 with effect from October 1, 2009. **3B–279**

* * * *

## PART IV

### *MISCELLANEOUS AND SUPPLEMENTARY*

### Jurisdiction of court for purposes of Parts I and II and of Part I of Landlord and Tenant Act 1927

**63.**—(1) Any jurisdiction conferred on the court by any provision of Part I of this Act shall be exercised by the county court. **3B–280**

(2) Any jurisdiction conferred on the court by any provision of Part II of this Act or conferred on the tribunal by Part I of the Landlord and Tenant Act 1927, shall, subject to the provisions of this section, be exercised [by the High Court or a county court]

(3) [...]

(4) The following provisions shall have effect as respects transfer of proceedings from or to the High Court or the county court, that is to say—

(a) where an application is made to the one but by virtue of [an Order under section 1 of the Courts and Legal Services Act 1990] cannot be entertained except by the other, the application shall not be treated as improperly made but any proceedings thereon shall be transferred to the other court;

(b) any proceedings under the provisions of Part II of this Act or of Part I of the Landlord and Tenant Act 1927, which are pending before one of those courts may by order of that court made on the application of any person interested be transferred to the other court, if it appears to the court making the order that it is desirable that the proceedings and any proceedings before the other court should both be entertained by the other court.

(5) In any proceedings where in accordance with the foregoing provisions of this section the county court exercises jurisdiction the powers of the judge of summoning one or more assessors under subsection (1) of section 91 of the County Courts Act 1959, may be exercised notwithstanding that no application is made in that behalf by any party to the proceedings.

(6) Where in any such proceedings an assessor is summoned by a judge under the said subsection (1),—

***Paragraph numbers marked with a "+" can be found online and on CD.***

(a) he may, if so directed by the judge, inspect the land to which the proceedings relate without the judge and report to the judge in writing thereon;

(b) the judge may on consideration of the report and any observations of the parties thereon give such judgment or make such order in the proceedings as may be just;

(c) the remuneration of the assessor shall be at such rate as may be determined by the Lord Chancellor with the approval of the Treasury and shall be defrayed out of moneys provided by Parliament.

(7) In this section the expression "the holding"—

(a) in relation to proceedings under Part II of this Act, has the meaning assigned to it by subsection (3) of section twenty-three of this Act,

(b) in relation to proceedings under Part I of the Landlord and Tenant Act 1927, has the same meaning as in the said Part I.

(8) […]

(9) Nothing in this section shall prejudice the operation of section 41 of the County Courts Act 1984 (which relates to the removal into the High Court of proceedings commenced in a county court).

(10) In accordance with the foregoing provisions of this section, for section 21 of the Landlord and Tenant Act 1927, there shall be substituted the following section—

The Tribunal

21. The tribunal for the purposes of Part I of this Act shall be the court exercising jurisdiction in accordance with the provisions of section sixty-three of the Landlord and Tenant Act 1954.

**3B–281** *Note*—See the reference to s.63(2) in the High Court and County Courts Jurisdiction Order 1991 (SI 1991/724).

## Interim continuation of tenancies pending determination by court

**3B–282** **64.**—(1) In any case where—

(a) a notice to terminate a tenancy has been given under Part I or Part II of this Act or a request for a new tenancy has been made under Part II thereof, and

(b) an application to the court has been made under the said Part I or under section 24(1) or 29(2) of this Act, as the case may be, and

(c) apart from this section the effect of the notice or request would be to terminate the tenancy before the expiration of the period of three months beginning with the date on which the application is finally disposed of,

the effect of the notice or request shall be to terminate the tenancy at the expiration of the said period of three months and not at any other time.

(2) The reference in paragraph (c) of subsection (1) of this section to the date on which an application is finally disposed of shall be

construed as a reference to the earliest date by which the proceedings on the application (including any proceedings on or in consequence of an appeal) have been determined and any time for appealing or further appealing has expired, except that if the application is withdrawn or any appeal is abandoned the reference shall be construed as a reference to the date of the withdrawal or abandonment.

## Provisions as to reversions

**65.**—(1) Where by virtue of any provision of this Act a tenancy (in this subsection referred to as "the inferior tenancy") is continued for a period such as to extend to or beyond the end of the term of a superior tenancy, the superior tenancy shall, for the purposes of this Act and of any other enactment and of any rule of law, be deemed so long as it subsists to be an interest in reversion expectant upon the termination of the inferior tenancy and, if there is no intermediate tenancy, to be the interest in reversion immediately expectant upon the termination thereof. **3B–283**

(2) In the case of a tenancy continuing by virtue of any provision of this Act after the coming to an end of the interest in reversion immediately expectant upon the termination thereof, subsection (1) of section one hundred and thirty-nine of the Law of Property Act 1925 (which relates to the effect of the extinguishment of a reversion) shall apply as if references in the said subsection (1) to the surrender or merger of the reversion included references to the coming to an end of the reversion for any reason other than surrender or merger.

(3) Where by virtue of any provision of this Act a tenancy (in this subsection referred to as "the continuing tenancy") is continued beyond the beginning of a reversionary tenancy which was granted (whether before or after the commencement of this Act) so as to begin on or after the date on which apart from this Act the continuing tenancy would have come to an end, the reversionary tenancy shall have effect as if it had been granted subject to the continuing tenancy.

(4) Where by virtue of any provision of this Act a tenancy (in this subsection referred to as "the new tenancy") is granted for a period beginning on the same date as a reversionary tenancy or for a period such as to extend beyond the beginning of the term of a reversionary tenancy, whether the reversionary tenancy in question was granted before or after the commencement of this Act, the reversionary tenancy shall have effect as if it had been granted subject to the new tenancy.

## Provisions as to notices

**66.**—(1) Any form of notice required by this Act to be prescribed shall be prescribed by regulations made by the Lord Chancellor by statutory instrument. **3B–284**

(2) Where the form of a notice to be served on persons of any description is to be prescribed for any of the purposes of this Act, the form to be prescribed shall include such an explanation of the rele-

vant provisions of this Act as appears to the Lord Chancellor requisite for informing persons of that description of their rights and obligations under those provisions.

(3) Different forms of notice may be prescribed for the purposes of the operation of any provision of this Act in relation to different cases.

(4) Section twenty-three of the Landlord and Tenant Act 1927 (which relates to the service of notices) shall apply for the purposes of this Act.

(5) Any statutory instrument under this section shall be subject to annulment in pursuance of a resolution of either House of Parliament.

**Wales**

3B–285 The functions of the Secretary of State, exercisable in relation to Wales, were transferred to the National Assembly for Wales, by the National Assembly for Wales (Transfer of Functions) Order 1999 (SI 1999/672).

**Prescribed ... by statutory instrument**

3B–286 See the Landlord and Tenant Act 1954, Part 2 (Notices) Regulations 2004 (SI 2004/1005). Regulation 2(2) of the 2004 Regulations allows a "form substantially to the like effect" of those contained in the regulations.

## Provisions as to mortgagees in possession

3B–287 **67.** Anything authorised or required by the provisions of this Act, other than subsection (3) of section forty, to be done at any time by, to or with the landlord, or a landlord of a specified description, shall, if at that time the interest of the landlord in question is subject to a mortgage and the mortgagee is in possession or a receiver appointed by the mortgagee or by the court is in receipt of the rents and profits, be deemed to be authorised or required to be done by, to or with the mortgagee instead of that landlord.

3B–288 *Note* — Section 67 was amended by the Regulatory Reform (Business Tenancies) (England and Wales) Order 2003 (SI 2003/3096). The amendment came into force June 1, 2004.

* * * *

## Interpretation

3B–289 **69.**—(1) In this Act the following expressions have the meanings hereby assigned to them respectively, that is to say:—

"agricultural holding" has the same meaning as in the [ Agricultural Holdings Act 1986];

"development corporation" has the same meaning as in the New Towns Act 1946;

'farm business tenancy' has the same meaning as in the Agricultural Tenancies Act 1995;

"local authority" [[means any local authority within the meaning of the Town and Country Planning Act 1990, any National Park authority, an authority established for an area in England by an order under section 207 of the Local Government and

*Paragraph numbers marked with a "+" can be found online and on CD.*

Public Involvement in Health Act 2007 (joint waste authorities), the Broads Authority[, the London Fire and Emergency Planning Authority] or] .. a joint authority established by Part IV of the Local Government Act 1985];

"mortgage" includes a charge or lien and "mortgagor" and "mortgagee" shall be construed accordingly;

"notice to quit" means a notice to terminate a tenancy (whether a periodical tenancy or a tenancy for a term of years certain) given in accordance with the provisions (whether express or implied) of that tenancy;

"repairs" includes any work of maintenance, decoration or restoration, and references to repairing, to keeping or yielding up in repair and to state of repair shall be construed accordingly;

"statutory undertakers" has the same meaning as in the Town and Country Planning Act 1971[...];

"tenancy" means a tenancy created either immediately or derivatively out of the freehold, whether by a lease or underlease, by an agreement for a lease or underlease or by a tenancy agreement or in pursuance of any enactment (including this Act), but does not include a mortgage term or any interest arising in favour of a mortgagor by his attorning tenant to his mortgagee, and references to the granting of a tenancy and to demised property shall be construed accordingly;

"terms", in relation to a tenancy, includes conditions.

(2) References in this Act to an agreement between the landlord and the tenant (except in section seventeen and subsections (1) and (2) of section thirty-eight thereof) shall be construed as references to an agreement in writing between them.

(3) References in this Act to an action for any relief shall be construed as including references to a claim for that relief by way of counterclaim in any proceedings.

*Note*—Section 69 was amended by the Agricultural Holdings Act 1986 s.100, Sch.14, para.22; the Agricultural Tenancies Act 1995 s.40, para.12; the Local Government Act 1985 s.84, Sch.14, para.36; the Environment Act 1995 s.78, Sch.10, para.3; the Greater London Authority Act 1999 s.328, Sch.29, Pt I, para.1; the Education Reform Act 1988 s.237, Sch.13, Pt I; the Coal Industry Act 1994 s.67, Sch.9, para.5, Sch.11, Pt II and the Local Government and Public Involvement in Health Act 2007 s.209(2), Sch.13, Pt.II, para.25 with effect from April 1 2008 (SI 2008/917). **3B–290**

* * * *

**SECTION 44**

## SCHEDULE 6

### Provisions for Purposes of Part II where Immediate Landlord is not the Freeholder **3B–291**

**Definitions**

1. In this Schedule the following expressions have the meanings hereby assigned to them in relation to a tenancy (in this Schedule referred to as "the relevant tenancy"), that is to say:— **3B–292**

"the competent landlord" means the person who in relation to the tenancy is for

*Paragraph numbers marked with a "+" can be found online and on CD.*

the time being the landlord (as defined by section 44) of this Act) for the purposes of Part II of this Act;

"mesne landlord" means a tenant whose interest is intermediate between the relevant tenancy and the interest of the competent landlord; and

"superior landlord" means a person (whether the owner of the fee simple or a tenant) whose interest is superior to the interest of the competent landlord.

**Power of court to order reversionary tenancies**

**3B-293** 2. Where the period for which in accordance with the provisions of Part II of this Act it is agreed or determined by the court that a new tenancy should be granted thereunder will extend beyond the date on which the interest of the immediate landlord will come to an end, the power of the court under Part II of this Act to order such a grant shall include power to order the grant of a new tenancy until the expiration of that interest and also to order the grant of such a reversionary tenancy or reversionary tenancies as may be required to secure that the combined effects of those grants will be equivalent to the grant of a tenancy for that period; and the provisions of Part II of this Act shall, subject to the necessary modifications, apply in relation to the grant of a tenancy together with one or more reversionary tenancies as they apply in relation to the grant of one new tenancy.

**Acts of competent landlord binding on other landlords**

**3B-294** 3.—(1) Any notice given by the competent landlord under Part II of this Act to terminate the relevant tenancy, and any agreement made between that landlord and the tenant as to the granting, duration, or terms of a future tenancy, being an agreement made for the purposes of the said Part II, shall bind the interest of any mesne landlord notwithstanding that he has not consented to the giving of the notice or was not a party to the agreement.

(2) The competent landlord shall have power for the purposes of Part II of this Act to give effect to any agreement with the tenant for the grant of a new tenancy beginning with the coming to an end of the relevant tenancy, notwithstanding that the competent landlord will not be the immediate landlord at the commencement of the new tenancy, and any instrument made in the exercise of the power conferred by this sub-paragraph shall have effect as if the mesne landlord had been a party thereto.

(3) Nothing in the foregoing provisions of this paragraph shall prejudice the provisions of the next following paragraph.

**3B-295** 4.—(1) If the competent landlord, not being the immediate landlord, gives any such notice or makes any such agreements as is mentioned in sub-paragraph (1) of the last foregoing paragraph without the consent of every mesne landlord, any mesne landlord whose consent has not been given thereto shall be entitled to compensation from the competent landlord for any loss arising in consequence of the giving of the notice or the making of the agreement.

(2) If the competent landlord applies to any mesne landlord for his consent to such a notice or agreement, that consent shall not be unreasonably withheld, but may be given subject to any conditions which may be reasonable (including conditions as to the modification of the proposed notice or agreement or as to the payment of compensation by the competent landlord).

(3) Any question arising under this paragraph whether consent has been unreasonably withheld or whether any conditions imposed on the giving of consent are unreasonable shall be determined by the court.

**3B-296** 5. An agreement between the competent landlord and the tenant made for the purposes of Part II of this Act in a case where—

(a) the competent landlord is himself a tenant, and

(b) the agreement would apart from this paragraph operate as respects any period after the coming to an end of the interest of the competent landlord,

shall not have effect unless every superior landlord who will be the immediate landlord of the tenant during any part of that period is a party to the agreement.

**3B-297** 6. Where the competent landlord has given a notice under section 25 of this Act to terminate the relevant tenancy and, within two months after the giving of the notice, a superior landlord—

(a) becomes the competent landlord; and

(b) gives to the tenant notice in the prescribed form that he withdraws the notice previously given;

the notice under section 25 of this Act shall cease to have effect, but without prejudice to the giving of a further notice under that section by the competent landlord.

7. If the competent landlord's interest in the property comprised in the relevant tenancy is a tenancy which will come or can be brought to an end within sixteen months (or any further time by which it may be continued under section 36(2) or section 64 of this Act) and he gives to the tenant under the relevant tenancy a notice under section 25 of this Act to terminate the tenancy or is given by him a notice under section 26(3) of this Act:— **3B–298**

(a) the competent landlord shall forthwith send a copy of the notice to his immediate landlord; and

(b) any superior landlord whose interest in the property is a tenancy shall forthwith send to his immediate landlord any copy which has been sent to him in pursuance of the preceding sub-paragraph or this sub-paragraph.

## Landlord and Tenant Act 1988

(1988 c.26) **3B–299**

ARRANGEMENT OF SECTIONS

SECT.



### Qualified duty to consent to assigning, underletting etc. of premises

**1.**—(1) This section applies in any case where— **3B–300**

(a) a tenancy includes a covenant on the part of the tenant not to enter into one or more of the following transactions, that is—

(i) assigning,

(ii) underletting,

(iii) charging, or

(iv) parting with the possession of,

the premises comprised in the tenancy or any part of the premises without the consent of the landlord or some other person, but

(b) the covenant is subject to the qualification that the consent is not to be unreasonably withheld (whether or not it is also subject to any other qualification).

(2) In this section and section 2 of this Act—

(a) references to a proposed transaction are to any assignment, underletting, charging or parting with possession to which the covenant relates, and

(b) references to the person who may consent to such a transaction are to the person who under the covenant may consent to the tenant entering into the proposed transaction.

*Paragraph numbers marked with a "+" can be found online and on CD.*

(3) Where there is served on the person who may consent to a proposed transaction a written application by the tenant for consent to the transaction, he owes a duty to the tenant within a reasonable time—

(a) to give consent, except in a case where it is reasonable not to give consent,

(b) to serve on the tenant written notice of his decision whether or not to give consent specifying in addition—

(i) if the consent is given subject to conditions, the conditions,

(ii) if the consent is withheld, the reasons for withholding it.

(4) Giving consent subject to any condition that is not a reasonable condition does not satisfy the duty under subsection (3)(a) above.

(5) For the purposes of this Act it is reasonable for a person not to give consent to a proposed transaction only in a case where, if he withheld consent and the tenant completed the transaction, the tenant would be in breach of a covenant.

(6) It is for the person who owed any duty under subsection (3) above—

(a) if he gave consent and the question arises whether he gave it within a reasonable time, to show that he did,

(b) if he gave consent subject to any condition and the question arises whether the condition was a reasonable condition, to show that it was,

(c) if he did not give consent and the question arises whether it was reasonable for him not to do so, to show that it was reasonable,

and, if the question arises whether he served notice under that subsection within a reasonable time, to show that he did.

#### Reasonable time

3B–301 See e.g. *Blockbuster Entertainment Ltd v Barnsdale Properties Ltd* [2003] EWHC 2912, (Ch D); November 11, 2003 (landlord breached its statutory duty under s.1(3) by failing to consent to a proposed sublease within a reasonable time. There was a delay of two months and as a result the proposed sub-lessee withdrew its offer, leaving the premises empty for over a year. Lloyd J. held that there was no basis for withholding consent and the landlord should have consented within a week. Damages of over £70,000 were awarded to compensate the tenant for rent, contributions to insurance costs and rates).

In *NCR Ltd v Riverland Portfolio No.1 Ltd (No.2)* [2005] EWCA Civ 312; [2005] 22 EG 134 there was a covenant not to sublet without consent not to be unreasonably withheld. The landlord refused to consent to the tenant's proposed subletting. The tenant made two complaints: (i) that there had been an unreasonable delay and (ii) that the refusal was unreasonable. The judge found in favour of T but his decision was overturned in the CA. The case essentially turns upon its own facts and the evidence, including expert evidence, before the court but it does contain a useful summary of the law (paragraph 11 of the judgment). On the question of the reasonableness of the time taken to give a decision the judge considered that a period of two weeks was sufficient time for a decision once all the relevant information was available. This was criticised by Carnwarth LJ in the Court of Appeal, at para 21:

"In my view, whatever earlier discussions there had been, Riverland was entitled to adequate time following receipt of the completed application to consider the serious financial and legal implications of a refusal with its advisers, and if necessary to report to the relevant Board. In the absence of special exceptional circumstances, a period of less than three weeks (particularly in the holiday period) cannot in my view be categorised as inherently unreasonable for that process.".

**Conditions**

A landlord imposing a condition can only rely upon written reasons given within a reasonable time of receiving the tenant's application and within a reasonable time of imposing the condition. The question of reasonableness is determined by the information available to the landlord at the time he imposed the condition (*London & Argyll Developments Ltd v Mount Cook Land Ltd* [2002] 50 E.G. 111 (C.S.).) **3B–302**

**"covenant", "consent", "tenancy" and "tenant"**

See s.5 and *Go West Ltd v Spigarolo* [2003] EWCA Civ 17; [2003] Q.B. 1140; [2003] 2 W.L.R. 986; [2003] 2 All E.R. 141; *The Times*, February 10, 2003, *Norwich Union Life Insurance Society v Shopmoor Ltd* [1999] 1 W.L.R. 531; *Footwear Corp Ltd v Amplight Properties Ltd* [1999] 1 W.L.R. 551 and *Mount Eden Land Ltd v Folia Ltd* [2003] EWHC 1815 (Ch); July 23, 2003 (minor breaches not a valid basis for refusing licence to under-let). **3B–303**

Once the landlord has given written notice with reasons refusing consent the period of reasonable time for giving consent has passed. The landlord cannot subsequently change his mind and say that the change has occurred within a reasonable time of the request. The fact that there were subsequent attempts to negotiate permission to assign did not deprive the tenant on the facts to its rights under the 1988 Act (*Go West Ltd v Spigarolo*, above).

## Duty to pass on applications

**2.**—(1) If, in a case where section 1 of this Act applies, any person receives a written application by the tenant for consent to a proposed transaction and that person— **3B–304**

(a) is a person who may consent to the transaction or (though not such a person) is the landlord, and

(b) believes that another person, other than a person who he believes has received that application or a copy of it, is a person who may consent to the transaction,

he owes a duty to the tenant (whether or not he owes him any duty under section 1 of this Act) to take such steps as are reasonable to secure the receipt within a reasonable time by the other person of a copy of the application.

(2) The reference in section 1(3) of this Act to the service of an application on a person who may consent to a proposed transaction includes a reference to the receipt by him of an application or a copy of an application (whether it is for his consent or that of another).

**"consent" and "tenancy"**

See s.5. **3B–305**

**"person who may consent"**

See s.1(2). **3B–306**

**"proposed transaction"**

See s.1(2). **3B–307**

## Qualified duty to approve consent by another

**3.**—(1) This section applies in any case where— **3B–308**

***Paragraph numbers marked with a "+" can be found online and on CD.***

(a) a tenancy includes a covenant on the part of the tenant not without the approval of the landlord to consent to the sub-tenant—
(i) assigning,
(ii) underletting,
(iii) charging, or
(iv) parting with the possession of, the premises comprised in the sub-tenancy or any part of the premises, but
(b) the covenant is subject to the qualification that the approval is not to be unreasonably withheld (whether or not it is also subject to any other qualification).

(2) Where there is served on the landlord a written application by the tenant for approval or a copy of a written application to the tenant by the sub-tenant for consent to a transaction to which the covenant relates the landlord owes a duty to the sub-tenant within a reasonable time—
(a) to give approval, except in a case where it is reasonable not to give approval,
(b) to serve on the tenant and the sub-tenant written notice of his decision whether or not to give approval specifying in addition—
(i) if approval is given subject to conditions, the conditions,
(ii) if approval is withheld, the reasons for withholding it.

(3) Giving approval subject to any condition that is not a reasonable condition does not satisfy the duty under subsection (2)(a) above.

(4) For the purposes of this section it is reasonable for the landlord not to give approval only in a case where, if he withheld approval and the tenant gave his consent, the tenant would be in breach of covenant.

(5) It is for a landlord who owed any duty under subsection (2) above—
(a) if he gave approval and the question arises whether he gave it within a reasonable time, to show that he did,
(b) if he gave approval subject to any condition and the question arises whether the condition was a reasonable condition, to show that it was,
(c) if he did not give approval and the question arises whether it was reasonable for him not to do so, to show that it was reasonable,

and if the question arises whether he served notice under that subsection within a reasonable time, to show that he did.

**"covenant", "consent", "landlord", "tenancy" and "tenant"**

**3B–309** See s.5.

**Not to be unreasonably withheld**

**3B–310** Unless it can be shown that a trial judge has misdirected himself by erring in principle or by reaching a conclusion that no reasonable judge could have reached, the Court of Appeal will be slow to differ from his measurements of reasonableness (*Arundel Corp v Khokher* [2003] EWCA Civ 1784; December 9, 2003).

**"served"**

See s.5(2). **3B–311**

## Breach of duty

**4.** A claim that a person has broken any duty under this Act may be made the subject of civil proceedings in like manner as any other claim in tort for breach of statutory duty. **3B–312**

**damages**

Where a landlord has all relevant information to enable it to make a decision under s.1(3) as to whether or not to give licence to assign, but fails to respond and operates in a cynical way designed to frustrate the assignment of premises, the court may mark its disapproval by awarding a sum of exemplary damages that would cause the landlord to consider seriously its future conduct (*Design Progression Ltd v ThurloeProperties Ltd* [2004] EWHC 324, (Ch); *The Times*, March 2, 2004—award of £25,000 exemplary damages plus £75,000 for loss of a premium and some other sums). **3B–313**

## Interpretation

**5.**—(1) In this Act— **3B–314**

"covenant" includes condition and agreement,

"consent" includes licence,

"landlord" includes any superior landlord from whom the tenant's immediate landlord directly or indirectly holds,

"tenancy", subject to subsection (3) below, means any lease or other tenancy (whether made before or after the coming into force of this Act) and includes—

(a) a sub-tenancy, and

(b) an agreement for a tenancy and references in this Act to the landlord and to the tenant are to be interpreted accordingly, and

"tenant", where the tenancy is affected by a mortgage (within the meaning of the Law of Property Act 1925) and the mortgagee proposes to exercise his statutory or express power of sale, includes the mortgagee.

(2) An application or notice is to be treated as served for the purposes of this Act if—

(a) served in any manner provided in the tenancy, and
(b) in respect of any matter for which the tenancy makes no provision, served in any manner provided by section 23 of the Landlord and Tenant Act 1927.

(3) This Act does not apply to a secure tenancy (defined in section 79 of the Housing Act 1985) or to an introductory tenancy (within the meaning of Chapter I of Part V of the Housing Act 1996).

(4) This Act applies only to applications for consent or approval served after its coming into force.

# 3C CONTEMPT OF COURT ACT 1981



## Contempt of Court Act 1981

(1981 c.49) 3C–1

ARRANGEMENT OF SECTIONS



## STRICT LIABILITY

### The strict liability rule

**1.** In this Act "the strict liability rule" means the rule of law whereby conduct may be treated as a contempt of court as tending to interfere with the course of justice in particular legal proceedings regardless of intent to do so. **3C–2**

### Limitation of scope of strict liability

**2.**—(1) The strict liability rule applies only in relation to publications, and for this purpose "publication" includes any speech, writing, programme included in a cable programme service or other communication in whatever form, which is addressed to the public at large or any section of the public. **3C–3**

(2) The strict liability rule applies only to a publication which creates a substantial risk that the course of justice in the proceedings in question will be seriously impeded or prejudiced.

(3) The strict liability rule applies to a publication only if the

proceedings in question are active within the meaning of this section at the time of publication.

(4) Schedule 1 applies for determining the times at which proceedings are to be treated as active within the meaning of this section.

(5) In this section "programme service" has the same meaning as in the Broadcasting Act 1990.

3C–4 *Note* —Amended by the Cable and Broadcasting Act 1984, Sch.5, para.39; and the Broadcasting Act 1990, s.203, Sch.20, para.31.

**Meaning of "substantial risk" and "seriously impeded or prejudiced"**

3C–5 "Substantial" describes the degree of risk; "seriously" describes the degree of impediment or prejudice to the course of justice; in combination the two words are intended to exclude a risk that is only remote (per Lord Diplock in *Attorney General v English* [1983] 1 A.C. 116; [1982] 2 All E.R. 903 at 919, HL). See also *Attorney General v Times Newspapers Ltd*; *The Times*, February 12, 1983, CA; and *Attorney General v BBC, Independent*, January 3, 1992.

"Substantial," as a qualification of "risk," does not have the meaning of "weighty," but rather "not insubstantial" or "not minimal"; the risk part of the test will usually be of importance in the context of the width of the publication, the court needing to consider whether there is an element of public interest in the publication which ought to be permitted and whether the proceedings sought to be protected are sufficiently proximate to the apprehended publication to require protection; proximity in time between the publication and the proceedings will probably have a greater bearing on the risk limb than on the seriousness limb, but may go to both (*Attorney General v News Group Newspapers Ltd* [1987] Q.B. 1, CA). Where the trial will not take place for at least ten months, the impact of the publication may be blunted (*ibid.*). Thus where nine months had elapsed between a single broadcast of an ephemeral nature and publication in a newspaper of limited circulation and the eventual trial, no contempt was held to have been committed (*Attorney General v Independent Television News Ltd* [1995] 2 All E.R. 370).

The publication of a statement that a defendant in criminal proceedings is awaiting trial on other charges does not, for the purposes of s.2(2) of the 1981 Act, necessarily create a substantial risk that the course of justice would be seriously impeded. The test is whether the statement created a substantial risk not whether it was the type of publication inherently liable to create such a risk. The risk has to be practical risk rather than a theoretical one (*Attorney General v Guardian Newspapers Ltd (No.3)* [1992] 1 W.L.R. 874.

Assessment of the risk will involve a consideration of the possible impact of the publication upon readers. Where an article appeared in an obscure weekly publication the possibility of any prospective juror having read the publication would be small and that small risk would be overwhelmed by a lengthy and complex trial. *Attorney General v Sunday Newspapers Ltd* [1999] C.O.D. 11.

On an application under s.2(2) it is not necessary to demonstrate the degree of prejudice which would justify an order by the trial judge for a stay of the criminal proceedings. It is a sufficient basis for a finding of contempt that the publication created a seriously arguable ground of appeal against conviction. *Attorney General v Birmingham Post and Mail Ltd* [1999] 1 W.L.R. 361 (Simon Brown L.J. and Thomas J.).

A distinction should be drawn between private pressure on a litigant, by an opposing litigant or a third party, and publication to a wide section of the public. As regards the latter, publication will not generally constitute contempt if it contains nothing more than fair and temperate criticism of a litigant; an article that goes beyond such criticism may create a substantial risk of prejudice (*Attorney General v Hislop* [1991] 2 W.L.R. 219; [1991] 1 Q.B. 514, CA).

Expressions of regret cannot excuse a breach of the strict liability rule although they might mitigate penalty. This is so even where the publishers did not intend such a consequence to ensue from the publication or foresee that it would or might have such an effect (*Attorney General v BBC, Independent*, January 3, 1992).

A publication referring to particular legal proceedings is less likely to be held to create a substantial risk that the course of justice in those proceedings will be seriously impeded or prejudiced if the proceedings are to be heard by a judge rather than tried by a jury. The possibility that an appellate court will be influenced is even more remote. Hence a publication which prejudges appeal proceedings pending before the House of Lords, and which is unlikely to deter the parties from contesting the appeal, does not constitute a contempt of court (*Re Lonrho plc* [1989] 2 All E.R. 1100, HL). A litigant who seeks a judicial remedy to compel a particular course of action is not guilty of contempt of court under s.2(2) of the Act if he resorts to self-help to obtain the remedy without the assistance of the courts, since the fact that the litigant thereby pre-empts the decision of the courts does not amount to impeding or prejudicing the course of justice (*ibid.*).

Documents in a court file do not become available for inspection unless access to a particular document is granted by operation of the rules or by leave of the court in a particular case. Where a person inspects documents in the court file by deception or subterfuge and then publishes that which he discovers he interferes with the administration of justice and commits a contempt of court *Dobson v Hastings* (1991) 141 New L.J. 1625.

A stay of proceedings, which stops the continuance of proceedings before a court or tribunal, is not an order enforceable by proceedings for contempt because it is not capable of being breached by a party to the proceedings (*Minister of Foreign Affairs, Trade and Industry v Vehicle and Supplies Ltd* [1991] 1 W.L.R. 550, PC; [1990] 4 All E.R. 65).

The fact that words were spoken in a humorous, irreverent and often rude television programme ("Have I Got News for You") some six months before the trial did not diminish the risk of serious prejudice to the course of justice (*Attorney General v BBC* [1997] E.M.L.R. 76).

In determining the degree of risk the court will look at each publication separately, but the mere fact that by reason of earlier publications there is already some risk of prejudice does not prevent a finding that the latest publication has created a further risk. The crucial matter will be the residual impact of the publication on a notional juror at the time of the trial. It may be proper for a trial judge to stay proceedings on the ground of prejudice albeit that no individual is subsequently found to be guilty of contempt (*Attorney General v MGN Ltd* [1997] 1 All E.R. 456).

A third party will not be held liable for contempt in acting inconsistently with a court order unless that order is clear and precise both in its effect and scope. Moreover where it is sought to impose indirect liability on a third party it is not necessary to show that the relevant proceedings had been wholly frustrated or rendered utterly futile but rather some significant and adverse effect upon the administration of justice. Conduct by a third party which is inconsistent with a court order only in a trivial or technical way should not expose him to conviction for contempt (*Attorney General v Newspaper Publishing Plc* [1997] 1 W.L.R. 926).

**"... If the proceedings in question are active"**

The rules for determining the times at which proceedings are to be treated as active **3C–6**
are set out in Sch.1 (see paras 3C–56 *et seq.* below). Proceedings in a Coroner's Court become active as soon as the inquest is opened, even where there has been an adjournment of all contentious matters after non-contentious matters have been dealt with (*Peacock v London Weekend Television Ltd*, *The Times*, November 27, 1985, CA).

Whether or not an action is in the High Court warned list, or is less than three months from the date fixed for trial, are not matters which can be substituted for the test of "activity" prescribed by paras 12 and 13 of Sch.1 (see para.3C–58, below) (*Attorney General v News Group Newspapers Ltd* [1987] Q.B. 1; [1986] 2 All E.R. 833, CA).

In cases where no active steps have been taken in any prosecution against a plaintiff (so that the strict liability rule under ss.1 and 2 of the Contempt of Court Act 1981 did not apply), but it is sought to restrain publication of material on the ground of contempt of court at common law, it is necessary for the court to be sure (a) that publication would create a risk of real prejudice if and when the prosecution proceeded, and (b) the material would be published with the specific intention of causing that risk (*Coe v Central Television, Cook and Thorne*, *Independent*, August 11, 1993).

## Defence of innocent publication or distribution

**3.**—(1) A person is not guilty of contempt of court under the strict **3C–7**

***Paragraph numbers marked with a "+" can be found online and on CD.***

liability rule as the publisher of any matter to which that rule applies if at the time of publication (having taken all reasonable care) he does not know and has no reason to suspect that relevant proceedings are active.

(2) A person is not guilty of contempt of court under the strict liability rule as the distributor of a publication containing any such matter if at the time of distribution (having taken all reasonable care) he does not know that it contains such matter and has no reason to suspect that it is likely to do so.

(3) The burden of proof of any fact tending to establish a defence afforded by this section to any person lies upon that person.

(4) [...]

3C-8 *Note* —Subsection (4) repealed by the Statute Law (Repeals) Act 2004, s.1(1), Sch.1, Pt 1.

## Contemporary reports of proceedings

3C-9 **4.**—(1) Subject to this section a person is not guilty of contempt of court under the strict liability rule in respect of a fair and accurate report of legal proceedings held in public, published contemporaneously and in good faith.

(2) In any such proceedings the court may, where it appears to be necessary for avoiding a substantial risk of prejudice to the administration of justice in those proceedings, or in any other proceedings pending or imminent, order that the publication of any report of the proceedings, or any part of the proceedings, be postponed for such period as the court thinks necessary for that purpose.

(2A) Where in proceedings for any offence which is an administration of justice offence for the purposes of section 54 of the Criminal Procedure and Investigations Act 1996 (acquittal tainted by an administration of justice offence) it appears to the court that there is a possibility that (by virtue of that section) proceedings may be taken against a person for an offence of which he has been acquitted, subsection (2) of this section shall apply as if those proceedings were pending or imminent.

(3) For the purposes of subsection (1) of this section a report of proceedings shall be treated as published contemporaneously—

(a) in the case of a report of which publication is postponed pursuant to an order under subsection (2) of this section, if published as soon as practicable after that order expires;

(b) in the case of a report of committal proceedings of which publication is permitted by virtue only of subsection (3) of section 8 of the Magistrates' Courts Act, if published as soon as practicable after publication is so permitted.

(4) [...]

3C-10 *Note* —Amended by the Criminal Justice and Public Order Act 1994, s.44, Sch.4, para.50; the Criminal Procedure and Investigations Act 1996, s.57; and the Defamation Act 1996, s.16, Sch.2; subs.(4) repealed by the Statute Law (Repeals) Act 2004, s.1(1), Sch.1, Pt 1.

***Paragraph numbers marked with a "+" can be found online and on CD.***

## Legal proceedings held in public

The expression "legal proceedings held in public" refers to court proceedings, and not to events preceding them. Thus an arrest of a defendant is not a legal proceeding held in public and a film of the arrest cannot be the subject of an order under s.4(2); if the showing of the film is likely to prejudice the trial, the proper remedy is for the person affected to apply for an injunction in the High Court (*R. v Rhuddlan Justices Ex p. HTV Ltd* [1986] Crim.L.R. 329, DC). **3C–11**

## Postponement of reports of proceedings

A magistrates' court in considering whether to make or continue a reporting restriction order under s.4(2) of the Contempt of Court Act 1981 has, like the Crown Court, a discretionary power to hear representations from the press and it was to be expected that the power would ordinarily be exercised when the media asked to be heard (*R. v Clerkenwell Stipendiary Magistrates Ex p. The Telegraph plc* (1992) 142 New L.J. 1541; *Independent*, October 16, 1992), indeed, members of the media should be asked whether they wish to make submissions, *Crawford v DPP The Times*, February 20, 2008 (Thomas L.J. and Dobbs J.).. **3C–12**

In relation to committal proceedings s.8 of the Magistrates' Courts Act 1980 already imposes restrictions on the reporting of such proceedings and, as a matter of general policy, justices should therefore be slow to make additional orders under s.4(2) of the 1981 Act (*R. v Beaconsfield Justices Ex p. Westminster Press Ltd, The Times*, June 28, 1994).

In considering whether to make an order under s.4(2) the court should seek to answer three questions: (i) was there a substantial risk of prejudice to the administration of justice? (ii) did it appear necessary for the avoidance of that prejudice that there should be some order made postponing publication of a report? (iii) if so, should the court, in its discretion, make an order and, if so, in what terms? *MGN Pensions Trustees Ltd v Bank of America National Trust and Savings Association* [1995] 2 All E.R. 355 (Lindsay J.). In determining whether publication of matter would cause a substantial risk of prejudice to a future trial, a court should credit the jury with the will and ability to abide by the judge's direction to decide the case only on the evidence before them. The court should also bear in mind that the staying power and detail of publicity, even in cases of notoriety, are limited and that the nature of a trial is to focus the jury's minds on the evidence put before them, rather than on matters outside the courtroom. The Court of Appeal's function on an appeal under s.159 of the Criminal Justice Act 1988 was to form its own view on the material before it. *Ex p. The Telegraph plc* [1993] 1 W.L.R. 980.

In considering whether it is "necessary" to make an order, both in the sense contemplated by s.4(2) and in the different sense contemplated by Art.10 of the European Convention on Human Rights, "restrictions ... as are prescribed by law and are necessary in a democratic society ..." the court should apply a three part test:

(1) Whether reporting would give rise to a "not unsubstantial" risk of prejudice to the administration of justice in the relevant proceedings. if not, that will be the end of the matter.

(2) If such a risk is perceived to exist, would a s.4(2) order eliminate it? If not there could be no necessity to impose such a ban and, again, that will be the end of the matter. If, however, an order would achieve the objective the judge must still consider whether the risk could be satisfactorily overcome by less restrictive means.

(3) If the judge concludes that there is indeed no other way of eliminating the risk of prejudice he must still ask whether the degree of risk contemplated should be regarded as tolerable in the sense of being "the lesser of two evils". At that stage value judgments may have to be made as to the priority between "competing public interests": *Ex p. The Telegraph Group PLC* [2001] 1 W.L.R. 1983 (Longmore L.J., Douglas Brown and Eady JJ.).

Since it is necessary to keep a permanent record of all orders made under s.4(2), all such orders must be formulated in precise terms, having regard to the decision in *R. v Horsham Justices Ex p. Farquharson* [1982] Q.B. 762; [1982] 2 All E.R. 269, and all orders under this section as well as under s.11 must be committed to writing either by the judge personally or by the clerk of the Court under the judges' direction. Such an order must state (a) its precise scope (b) the time at which it will cease to have effect if appropriate and (c) the specific purpose of making the order.

Courts will normally give notice to the press in some form that an order has been made under either section of the Act and court staff should be prepared to answer any inquiry about a specific case, but it is, and will remain, the responsibility of those reporting cases, and their editors, to ensure that no breach of any order occurs and the onus rests with them to make inquiry in any case of doubt (Practice Direction (Contempt: Reporting Restrictions) [1982] 1 W.L.R. 1475; [1983] 1 All E.R. 64).

When making an order the courts should be diligent in accommodating and understanding the legitimate interests of the press and such an order should be drafted and made public in a way which makes it clear what may or may not be published, both as regards the proceedings themselves and the terms of the order. It is desirable that it be made in advance of the trial and the judge is at liberty to adjourn consideration of reporting restrictions until the press have been heard (*Attorney General v Guardian Newspapers Ltd (No.3)* [1992] 1 W.L.R. 874; [1992] 3 All E.R. 38).

Care should be taken over the wording of any notice pinned to the door of the court or given in some other form which may be read by jurors. Where the complete text of an order made under s.4(2), making it clear that the defendant faces further trials, is pinned to the door of the court and is seen to be read by a juror trying the case, there is a real possibility of prejudice to the defendant and the jury should be discharged (*R. v Hutton* [1990] Crim.L.R. 875, CA (Crim. Div)).

Where a jury has retired to spend a night at an hotel it is not necessary to postpone reports of the proceedings on television or radio for fear that members of the jury may watch television or listen to the radio while at the hotel; if it is considered necessary to insulate the members of the jury from the media, they can be deprived of access to television or radio, just as they can be denied access to newspapers, while at the hotel (*Re Central Independent Television plc* [1991] 1 All E.R. 347, CA (Crim. Div)).

A Judge's decision whether or not to order reporting restrictions under s.4(2) involves an exercise of discretion based on fact, and does not involve any question of law such as to entitle the Court of Appeal to interfere with the decision, unless it can be demonstrated that such discretion has been exercised on a fundamentally flawed basis (*Re Saunders*, *The Times*, February 8, 1990; *Independent*, February 8, 1990, CA).

It is important that there should be freedom of information unless some necessity is shown to prevent it. Thus where the managers of a company are alleged to have removed assets in breach of their duties, and where a receiver is appointed to ensure that certain funds should be secured until the Court can decide who is the true owner, there is no reason to restrict reporting of the judgment whereby the receiver is appointed. Nothing in such a judgment is likely to prejudice a fair trial of the managers involved, and any report that does not make it clear that, as yet, there are only unsubstantiated allegations, will not be fair and accurate, and itself will be a contempt of court by virtue of s.4 (*Barlow Clowes Gilt Managers Ltd v Clowes*, *The Times*, February 2, 1990).

Section 4(2) is designed to enable the court to prevent the publication of a report of proceedings, where the publication would prejudice the conduct of those proceedings or specific pending proceedings. The need for postponement cannot subsist beyond the end of the proceedings in question. In *Re Times Newspapers Ltd* [2008] 1 W.L.R. 234 (Lord Phillips of Worth Matravers C.J., Elias and Griffith Williams JJ.).

## Discussion of public affairs

3C-13 **5.** A publication made as or as part of a discussion in good faith of public affairs or other matters of general public interest is not to be treated as a contempt of court under the strict liability rule if the risk of impediment or prejudice to particular legal proceedings is merely incidental to the discussion.

### Incidental to the discussion

3C-14 The protection afforded by s.5 is intended to prevent the suppression of bona fide discussion in the media of controversial matters of public interest, merely by reason that contemporaneous legal proceedings exist in which some particular instance of such matters may be in issue, and the burden is on the Attorney General to prove that the publication does not fall within s.5 and that the risk of prejudice to a fair trial is

*Paragraph numbers marked with a "+" can be found online and on CD.*

not "merely incidental" to the discussion. Where a newspaper article forms part of a wider campaign and controversy as to the justiciability of mercy killing, it does not prejudice the fair trial of the doctor accused of the murder of a severely disabled baby, since it is no more than an incidental consequence of a discussion of a matter of general public interest, and is not a contempt of court (*Attorney General v English* [1983] A.C. 116; [1982] 2 All E.R. 903, HL. See also *Attorney General v Times Newspapers Ltd*, *The Times*, February 12, 1983, CA).

In considering whether a publication is a contempt of court by reason of prejudice to particular legal proceedings, or is merely incidental to discussion of matters of general public interest, it is appropriate to look at the subject matter of the discussion in the publication and to see how closely it relates to the particular legal proceedings; where the theme of the discussion is narrowly directed to the activities of a small group of identifiable persons, and where such activities are the subject matter of indictments charging one or more of those persons, it is impossible to categorise the discussion as no more than incidental to discussion of matters of general public interest (*Attorney General v TVS Television Ltd*, *The Times*, July 7, 1989; *Independent*, July 7, 1989).

## Savings

**6.** Nothing in the foregoing provisions of this Act— **3C–15**

(a) prejudices any defence available at common law to a charge of contempt of court under the strict liability rule;

(b) implies that any publication is punishable as contempt of court under that rule which would not be so punishable apart from those provisions;

(c) restricts liability for contempt of court in respect of conduct intended to impede or prejudice the administration of justice.

### "Conduct intended to impede or prejudice the administration of justice"

A person not named in an interlocutory injunction may be in contempt of court by acting in a way contrary to the terms of that injunction. Such action may constitute "conduct intended to impede or prejudice the administration of justice", even though such intention is not the sole or principal intention of the contemnor (*Attorney General v Newspaper Publishing plc* [1987] 3 W.L.R. 942, CA. See also *Attorney General v Guardian Newspaper Publishing Ltd (No.2)*, *Independent*, October 17, 1987; *The Times*, October 20, 1987). **3C–16**

A person who is not a party to an action in which an injunction has been granted, commits a contempt of court if he knowingly does an act which is in breach of the injunction and which has the effect of destroying in whole or in part the subject matter of the action, so that the purpose of the trial of the action is wholly or partly nullified. (*Attorney General v Times Newspapers Ltd*, *The Times*, February 12, 1983, HL).

The purpose the Court seeks to achieve in granting an interlocutory injunction is to prevent the restrained acts from being done, pending a decision by the Court on the claims in the proceedings. Third parties will be in contempt if they wilfully interfere with the administration of justice by thwarting the achievement of *this* purpose in *those* proceedings. This is so, even if the injunction is drawn in seemingly over-wide terms. The remedy of the third party whose conduct is affected by the order is to apply to the court for the order to be varied. See *Attorney Generalv Punch Ltd* [2002] UKHL 50; [2003] 1 A.C. 1046; [2003] 2 W.L.R. 49, an appeal from [2001] EWCA Civ 403.

The Act makes extensive provision for what may be called statutory contempts, but the saving contained in s.6(c) indicates that something which falls short of contempt under the statute may still be contempt at common law. Hence a newspaper which publishes articles with specific intention of interfering with the course of justice in criminal proceedings which, though not pending, are virtually certain to be commenced in the near future may be guilty of contempt at a common law even if the articles do not come within the strict liability provisions of sections 1 and 2 (*Attorney General v News Group Newspapers Ltd* [1988] 3 W.L.R. 163; [1988] 2 All E.R. 907).

In *Attorney General v Sport Newspapers Ltd* [1991] 1 W.L.R. 1194; [1992] 1 All E.R.

503, Bingham L.J. followed *Attorney General v News Group Newspapers plc* [1989] Q.B. 110, holding that, if publication creates a real risk of prejudice to the due administration of justice, and if the alleged contemnor publishes with the specific intent of causing such risk, contempt may be committed even though proceedings are neither in existence nor imminent. In the same case, however, Hogson J., disapproving *Attorney General v News Group Newspapers plc* (above), took the view that the time when the summary jurisdiction of judges over intentional publications contempts begins is when the relevant proceedings become pending, and that the ambit of such summary procedure should not be widened.

## Consent required for institution of proceedings

3C–17 7. Proceedings for a contempt of court under the strict liability rule (other than Scottish proceedings) shall not be instituted except by or with the consent of the Attorney-General or on the motion of a court having jurisdiction to deal with it.

### Consent of the Attorney General

3C–18 An application to commit a person for an alleged contempt which falls within the strict liability rule will be dismissed where the consent of the Attorney General has not been obtained (*Roger Bullivant Ltd v Ellis, Financial Times*, April 16, 1986).

Although a circuit judge has jurisdiction to deal with a contempt in the face of the court, he has no jurisdiction to deal with a contempt alleged to have been committed by the publication of a book, shortly before the commencement of criminal proceedings against a defendant, in which reference is made to the defendant being involved in serious organised crime, and which thereby tends, contrary to "the strict liability rule" prescribed by s.1, to interfere with the course of justice in those proceedings; except in the narrow range of cases where proceedings for contempt can be instituted under s.7 on the motion of the Court having jurisdiction to deal with the matter, proceedings for contempt under "the strict liability rule" can be commenced only by or with the consent of the Attorney General (*Taylor v Topping*, *The Times*, February 15, 1990; *Independent*, February 20, 1990). The decision of the law officers not to institute proceedings under s.7 cannot be challenged by way of an application for judicial review. *R. v Solicitor General Ex p. Taylor and Taylor* [1996] C.O.D. 61).

*OTHER ASPECTS OF LAW AND PROCEDURE*

## Confidentiality of jury's deliberations

3C–19 8.—(1) Subject to subsection (2) below, it is a contempt of court to obtain, disclose or solicit any particulars of statements made, opinions expressed, arguments advanced or votes cast by members of a jury in the course of their deliberations in any legal proceedings.

(2) This section does not apply to any disclosure of any particulars—

(a) in the proceedings in question for the purpose of enabling the jury to arrive at their verdict, or in connection with the delivery of that verdict, or

(b) in evidence in any subsequent proceedings for an offence alleged to have been committed in relation to the jury in the first mentioned proceedings,

or to the publication of any particulars so disclosed.

(3) Proceedings for a contempt of court under this section (other than Scottish proceedings) shall not be instituted except by or with the consent of the Attorney-General or on the motion of a court having jurisdiction to deal with it.

*Paragraph numbers marked with a "+" can be found online and on CD.*

**Confidentiality of jury's deliberations**

Any approach or attempt to take statements from jurors which might have the effect of breaching s.8 is to run the risk of committing a contempt of court or even of an attempt to pervert the course of justice. In relation to enquiries concerning the jury the trial judge is *functus officio* after verdict and sentence and in such cases the proper course is to seek the consent of the Court of Appeal (*R. v Mickleburgh*, *The Times*, July 26, 1994). **3C-20**

The prohibitions contained in s.8 apply equally to the Court of Appeal as they do to others. It would therefore be a breach of s.8 for the court to enquire into the jury's deliberations in the retiring room. However, the section does not prevent the court from enquiring into what may have taken place at an hotel where the jury had stayed overnight before returning to court to resume its deliberations (*R. v Young (Stephen)*, [1995] Q.B. 324). In s.8(1) the word "disclose" is apt to include not only disclosure by a juror but also disclosure by some other, but not the republication of information already in the public domain (*Attorney General v Associated Newspapers* [1994] 2 W.L.R. 277; [1994] 1 All E.R. 556, HL). For a review of the authorities, see *HM Attorney General v Seckenson and The Times* Newspapers Ltd [2009] EWHC 1023 (Admin) (Pill L.J and Sweeney J.).

A request by a judge for the names of jurors to which a note related was a breach of section 8(1), which applies to the court as it does to others, and of the long established principle that there is no right in anyone to enquire as to what occurred in the jury room, a principle reaffirmed in *Andrew Brown* (1907) 7 N.S.W. St.Rep. 291 and *R. v Thompson* [1962] 1 All E.R. 65 CA *R. v Schot and Barclay*, *The Times*, May 14, 1997).

## Use of tape recorders

**9.**—(1) Subject to subsection (4) below, it is a contempt of court— **3C-21**

(a) to use in court, or bring into court for use, any tape recorder or other instrument for recording sound, except with the leave of the court;

(b) to publish a recording of legal proceedings made by means of any such instrument, or any recording derived directly or indirectly from it, by playing it in the hearing of the public or any section of the public, or to dispose of it or any recording so derived, with a view to such publication;

(c) to use any such recording in contravention of any conditions of leave granted under paragraph (a).

(2) Leave under paragraph (a) of subsection (1) may be granted or refused at the discretion of the court, and if granted may be granted subject to such conditions as the court thinks proper with respect to the use of any recording made pursuant to the leave; and where leave has been granted the court may at the like discretion withdraw or amend it either generally or in relation to any particular part of the proceedings.

(3) Without prejudice to any other power to deal with an act of contempt under paragraph (a) of subsection (1), the court may order the instrument, or any recording made with it, or both, to be forfeited; and any object so forfeited shall (unless the court otherwise determines on application by a person appearing to be the owner) be sold or otherwise disposed of in such manner as the court may direct.

(4) This section does not apply to the making or use of sound recordings for purposes of official transcripts of proceedings.

**Use of tape recorders in court**

The following Practice Direction was issued on November 19, 1981. See *Practice Direction (Tape Recorders)* [1981] 1 W.L.R. 1526; [1981] 3 All E.R. 848: **3C-22**

***Paragraph numbers marked with a "+" can be found online and on CD.***

1. Section 9 of the Contempt of Court Act 1981 contains provisions governing the unofficial use of tape recorders in court. Among other things it provides that it is a contempt of court to use in court, or bring into court for use, any tape recorder or other instrument for recording sound, except with the leave of the court; and it is also a contempt of court to publish a recording of legal proceedings or to use any such recording in contravention of any conditions which the court may have attached to the grant of permission to use the machine in court. These provisions do not apply to the making or use of sound recordings for purposes of official transcripts of proceedings, on which the Act imposes no restriction whatever.

2. The discretion given to the court to grant, withhold or withdraw leave to use tape recorders or to impose conditions as to the use of the recording is unlimited, but the following factors may be relevant to its exercise:

(a) the existence of any reasonable need on the part of the applicant for leave, whether a litigant or a person connected with the press or broadcasting, for the recording to be made;

(b) in a criminal case, or a civil case in which a direction has been given excluding one or more witnesses from the court, the risk that the recording could be used for the purpose of briefing witnesses out of court;

(c) any possibility that the use of a recorder would disturb the proceedings or distract or worry any witnesses or other participants.

3. Consideration should always be given whether conditions as to the use of a recording made pursuant to leave should be imposed. The identity and role of the applicant for leave and the nature of the subject matter of the proceedings may be relevant to this.

4. The particular restriction imposed by s.9(1)(b) of the 1981 Act applies in every case, but may not be present to the mind of every applicant to whom leave is given. It may, therefore, be desirable on occasion for this provision to be drawn to the attention of those to whom leave is given.

5. The transcript of a permitted recording is intended for the use of the person given leave to make it and is not intended to be used as, or to compete with, the official transcript mentioned in s.9(4) of the 1981 Act.

## Sources of information

3C–23 **10.** No court may require a person to disclose, nor is any person guilty of contempt of court for refusing to disclose, the source of information contained in a publication for which he is responsible, unless it be established to the satisfaction of the court that disclosure is necessary in the interests of justice or national security or for the prevention of disorder or crime.

### Application of section

3C–24 Section 10 is not directly applicable to a requirement made of a journalist by inspectors investigating possible offences under the Companies Acts, because such inspectors are not a court. The section, however, is indicative of the general policy prescribed by Parliament which should be applied by way of analogy on a reference arising out of such a requirement. If, therefore, the journalist is in a position to show that, if the inspectors were a court, he could rely on s.10 to support refusal to disclose his source of information, he has "reasonable excuse" for his refusal, within the meaning of s.178(2) of the Financial Services Act 1986, and will not be punishable as for a contempt of court under that section (*Re an Inquiry under the Company Securities (Insider Dealing) Act 1985* [1988] A.C. 660; [1988] 1 All E.R. 203, HL).

### Interests of national security

3C–25 The prohibition in s.10 against the court making an order to disclose a source of information is of wide and general application, subject only to the four exceptions specified in the section, namely that disclosure is necessary in the interests of justice or national security or for the prevention of disorder or crime. Accordingly it is sufficient to attract the protection of s.10 if the order for disclosure might, but not necessarily would have the effect of disclosing a source of information. Moreover a publisher is not precluded from relying on s.10 in the face of a proprietary claim by an owner for the delivery up of his property. The onus of proving that the case falls within one of the four exceptions specified in the section lies on the party seeking the order, and the standard of proof required to satisfy the court that disclosure is necessary is the balance of probabilities. The interests of national security require that the identity of a person who discloses to a newspaper a memorandum of the Secretary of State for Defence classified as "secret" should be disclosed, where the risk to national security lies not in the publication of the particular document but in the possibility that the person who discloses it may in future disclose other classified documents, the disclosure of which would have more serious consequences for national security (*Secretary of State for Defence v Guardian Newspapers Ltd* [1985] A.C. 339; [1984] 3 All E.R. 601, HL).

**Interests of justice**

"The interests of justice" refer to the administration of justice in the course of legal proceedings in a court of law, a tribunal or a body exercising judicial power of the state, and not to the concept of justice in the abstract (*Secretary of State for Defence v Guardian Newspapers Ltd* (above)). The words "in the interests of justice" are to be construed in the technical sense of the administration of legal proceedings in a court of law; s.10 requires it to be established that disclosure is necessary for the administration of justice in that sense, and not merely that disclosure is expedient (*Maxwell v Pressdram Ltd* [1987] 1 W.L.R. 298; [1987] 1 All E.R. 656, CA). The public interest in the non-disclosure of journalists' sources may in a particular case outweigh the requirement that the sources be named in the interest of justice (*ibid.*). **3C–26**

To construe "justice" as the antonym of "injustice" is too wide but to confine it to the technical sense of the administration of justice in court of legal proceedings in a court of law is too narrow. It is in the interests of justice, within the meaning of the section, that persons should be enabled to exercise important legal rights and to protect themselves from serious legal wrongs, whether or not resort to legal proceedings in a court of law will be necessary to attain such objectives. It will not be sufficient, by itself, to establish the necessity of disclosure, for a party seeking disclosure of a source to show merely that he will be unable, without disclosure, to exercise the legal right or avert the threatened legal wrong on which he bases his claim. If the party seeking disclosure shows that his livelihood depends on it, that will put the case near one end of the spectrum. The greater the legitimate public interest in the information, the greater will be the importance of protecting the source. If the information is obtained illegally, that will diminish the importance of protecting the source unless, for example, the source has acted for the purpose of exposing iniquity (*X Ltd v Morgan Grampian (Publishers) Ltd* [1990] 2 All E.R. 1, HL). Hence disclosure of a journalist's source of confidential information about a company is necessary in the interests of justice, where the importance of protecting the source, whose complicity in obtaining the information is not counterbalanced by any legitimate public interest in publication of the information, is outweighed by the threat of severe damage to the company's business which can be avoided only if the information is recovered (*ibid.*). But now see the decision of the European Court of Human Rights that the order requiring the journalist to reveal his source of information, and the fine imposed on him for having refused to do so, constituted a violation of Art.10 of the European Convention of Human Rights (*Goodwin v UK*, *The Times*, March 28, 1996).

The question whether a publisher is to be required to disclose the source of information or return documents which would necessarily identify that source is to be determined in accordance with English law, as set out in s.10 and interpreted by the English courts in *X Ltd v Morgan-Grampian (Publishers) Ltd* [1991] 1 A.C. 1 (it being clear and unambiguous) and not therefore by the application of the decision of the European Court of Human Rights in *Goodwin v United Kingdom* (1996) 22 E.C.H.R. 123 (based on the same facts) and the interpretation of Art.10 of the ECHR (*Camelot Group plc v Centaur Communications Ltd*, *The Times*, July 15, 1997, per Kay J.).

Before the court will require journalists to break the important professional obligation to protect a source, the minimum requirement is that other avenues of enquiry should be explored in an attempt to identify the source. A single leak of counsel's draft advice was not sufficient to warrant an order for disclosure under s.10 of the Act. *John v Express Newspapers* [2000] 1 W.L.R.1931 (Lord Woolf M.R., Pill and May L.JJ.).

***Paragraph numbers marked with a "+" can be found online and on CD.***

An order for disclosure may be made, even if the information is not required for the purpose of bringing an action. The important protection which both s.10 and Art.10 provide for freedom of expression required however that the Court should scrutinise diligently any request for relief which would result in the Court interfering with freedom of expression including ordering the disclosure of journalists services. Both s.10 and Art.10 of the European Convention on Human Rights are one in making clear that the Court has to be sure that a sufficiently strong positive case has been made out in favour of disclosure before it will be ordered, *Ashworth Hospital Authority v MGN Ltd* [2002] 4 All E.R. 193 (House of Lords).

For the court to order a journalist to disclose the name of his source it must be established that it is both necessary, in the sense of there being an overriding interest, amounting to a pressing social need, and proportionate: *Mersey Care NHS Trust v Ackroyd* [2007] EWCA Civ 101; *The Times*, February 26, 2007, CA.

#### "Necessary for the prevention of crime"

**3C–27** "Necessary" has a meaning that lies somewhere between "indispensable" on the one hand and "useful" or "convenient" on the other. It is a word which takes colour from its context. Whether a particular measure is necessary in a particular case involves an exercise of judgment on the established facts. "The prevention of crime" refers to the prevention of crime generally rather than to the prevention of a particular identifiable future crime. The court must be presented with sufficient material to enable it to exercise an independent judgment on the extent of the need for disclosure. It will pay proper regard to the views of those seeking disclosure, but must not act as a rubber stamp for those views (*Re an Inquiry under the Company Securities (Insider Dealing) Act 1985* [1988] A.C. 660; [1988] 1 All E.R. 203, HL). Disclosure by a defendant cannot be said to be necessary for the prevention of crime in circumstances where the prevention of crime is not the plaintiff's task, and where a criminal investigation would not be a likely consequence if the defendant's source were disclosed (*X (Health Authority) v Y.* [1988] 2 All E.R. 648). In considering whether it is "necessary" to require a journalist to reveal the source of a leaked document, the court will consider whether the applicant for the disclosure order has itself attempted to discover the source of the leak, otherwise than by applying to the Court (*Broadmoor Hospital v Hyde*, *The Times*, March 18, 1994; *Independent*, March 4, 1994).

## Publication of matters exempted from disclosure in court

**3C–28** **11.** In any case where a court (having power to do so) allows a name or other matter to be withheld from the public in proceedings before the court, the court may give such directions prohibiting the publication of that name or matter in connection with the proceedings as appear to the court to be necessary for the purpose for which it was so withheld.

#### Directions prohibiting publication

**3C–29** The jurisdiction to order disclosure of the identity of a wrongdoer is one of general application, exisiting in equity. The "interests of justice" in s.10 means interests which were justifiable, and was not confined to the technical sense of the administration of justice in the course of legal proceedings in a court of law, *Ashworth Hospital Authority v MGN Ltd* [2001] 1 W.L.R. 515, (Lord Phillips of Worth Matravers M.R., May and Laws L.JJ.).

The Q.B. Divisional Court has no jurisdiction to entertain an application for judicial review of an order made under s.11 by a Crown Court in relation to a trial on indictment. The Divisional Court has noted, however, an increasing tendency to make orders under s.11, even where the name of a witness which it was forbidden to publish outside court had been referred to in the proceedings. It is doubtful whether s.11 has any application in such circumstances. It is of vital constitutional importance that criminal trials are held in public and freely reported. This consideration must outweigh the individual interests of particular persons who may feel embarrassment as a result of allegations made in the course of a trial (*R. v Central Criminal Court Ex p. Crook* (1985) 82 L.S.Gaz. 1408, DC; *The Times*, November 8, 1984).

***Paragraph numbers marked with a "+" can be found online and on CD.***

A court has no power under s.11 to prohibit the press from publishing the name of a defendant if, earlier in the proceedings, that name has not been withheld from the public (*R. v Arundel JJ. Ex p. Westminster Press Ltd* [1985] 1 W.L.R. 708; [1985] 2 All E.R. 390).

The general principle of law is that all evidence communicated to a court should be communicated publicly (*Attorney General v Leveller Magazine Ltd* [1979] A.C. 440, [1979] 2 All E.R. 745, HL). The general rule should not be departed from save where the nature of circumstances of the proceedings are such that its application would frustrate or render impracticable the administration of justice. Such circumstances are rare. It is a misuse of s.11 for magistrates to prohibit the publication of a defendant's address in order to protect him from possible harassment by his former wife (*R. v Evesham Justices Ex p. McDonagh* [1988] Q.B. 553; [1988] 1 All E.R. 371). A magistrate making an order under s.37 of the Public Health (Control of Disease) Act 1984 directing the removal to hospital of a person with a "notifiable disease" is a court for the purposes of s.11 of the Contempt of Court Act 1981 and has power to allow a patient's name to be withheld from the public. It is however a constrained power and exercisable only in so far as reasonably necessary to serve the ends of justice. While it would be unfair to allow publication of a patient's identity when subject to an ex parte order, once all reasonable opportunity to challenge that order had passed, no interest of justice was any longer involved. Any wish to protect privacy or avoid embarrassment is not a ground for the continuance of such a prohibition. *Birmingham Post & Mail Ltd v Birmingham City Council*, *Independent*, November 25, 1993). The power to make an order under s.11 must be exercised carefully and cannot be used simply to protect privacy or avoid embarrassment. In proceedings for judicial review any application for anonymity should usually be made at the same time as the application for leave to move. However, where the applicant's name alone might itself give rise to publicity, enquiry should first be made of the Crown Office, so that the application for an order under s.11 can be made as soon as the papers are lodged (*R. v Westminster City Council Ex p. Castelli and Garcia*, *The Times*, August 14, 1995).

The fact that publication of the summonses giving rise to the proceedings may have dire economic consequences leading to the closure of the defendant's business does not constitute an exceptional circumstances justifying magistrates making an order restricting publication under s.11 (*R. v Dover Justices Ex p. Dover DC*, *The Times*, October 21, 1991; *Independent*, October 21, 1991). It would be very rare indeed to find circumstances justifying departure from the general rule to prevent publication of material relating to a defendant's acquittal (*ibid.*).

Where, however, application is made to a court to hear proceedings *in camera* and for a direction under s.11 prohibiting publication of the proceedings, the court should accede to a request to hear the reasons for the application *in camera*, so that a decision may be made whether there is substance in the application without prejudicing the applicant (*R. v Tower Bridge Justices Ex p. Osborne* [1988] Crim.L.R. 382).

In relation to an application for judicial review it may sometimes be appropriate to make an interim order under s.11 of the Act at the ex parte leave stage so as to enable the applicant to provide more substantial evidence at the substantive hearing as to the damage which might be caused by disclosure. This case also contains an examination of the more recent authorities on s.11 (*R. v Somerset Health Authority Ex p. S* [1996] C.O.D. 244, per Brooke J.).

## Offences of contempt of magistrates' courts

**12.**—(1) A magistrates' court has jurisdiction under this section to deal with any person who— **3C-30**

(a) wilfully insults the justice or justices, any witness before or officer of the court or any solicitor or counsel having business in the court, during his or their sitting or attendance in court or in going to or returning from the court; or

(b) wilfully interrupts the proceedings of the court or otherwise misbehaves in court.

***Paragraph numbers marked with a "+" can be found online and on CD.***

(2) In any such case the court may order any officer of the court, or any constable, to take the offender into custody and detain him until the rising of the court; and the court may, if it thinks fit, commit the offender to custody for a specified period not exceeding one month or impose on him a fine not exceeding £2,500, or both.

(2A) A fine imposed under subsection (2) above shall be deemed, for the purposes of any enactment, to be a sum adjudged to be paid by a conviction.

(3) [...]

(4) A magistrates' court may at any time revoke an order of committal made under subsection (2) and, if the offender is in custody, order his discharge.

(5) Section 135 of the Powers of Criminal Courts (Sentencing) Act 2000, Sched. 9, para. 83(a) and the following provisions of the Magistrates' Courts Act 1980 apply in relation to an order under this section as they apply in relation to a sentence on conviction or finding of guilty of an offence, namely: section 36 (restriction on fines in respect of young persons); sections 75 to 91 (enforcement); section 108 (appeal to Crown Court); section 136 (overnight detention in default of payment); and section 142(1) (power to rectify mistakes).

3C-31 *Note*—Amended by the Criminal Justice Act 1991, s.17(3), Sch.4; and the Criminal Justice Act 1993, s.65(3) (4) and Sch.3.

**Jurisdiction of magistrates' courts**

3C-32 A committal of a person to custody under s.12(2) for wilfully interrupting the proceedings of the Court does not amount to a summary conviction giving the person a right to legal representation before a sentence of imprisonment can be imposed. Nor does natural justice require the contemnor to be so represented (see *R. v Newbury Justices Ex p. du Pont* (1984) 148 J.P. 248; (1984) 78 Cr.App.R. 255).

By virtue of s.1(1) of the Criminal Justice Act 1982 a magistrates' court has no power to commit a person under the age of 17 for contempt; by virtue of s.9(1) of that Act and s.12 of this Act such a court does have power to commit for contempt a person between the ages of 17 and 21, but such power should be exercised only if the court is of opinion that no other method of dealing with the person is appropriate (*R. v Selby Justices Ex p. Frame* [1991] 2 All E.R. 344).

Where a defendant persisted in seeking to occupy that part of the court reserved for professional advocates, she was rightly held to be in contempt. The court should, however, never act in haste and should always give the alleged contemnor an opportunity to obtain legal advice and to apologise to the court (*R. v Pateley Bridge Justices Ex p. Percy* [1994] C.O.D. 453).

**"Wilfully insults"**

3C-33 "Insult" is to be given its ordinary meaning in the English language. Hence an alleged contemnor who threatens a witness does not thereby "wilfully insult" him as to confer jurisdiction on justices with the matter under s.12(1)(a) (*R. v Havant JJ. Ex p. Palmer* (1985) 149 J.P. 609; [1985] Crim.L.R. 658).

The provisions of s.12 of the Contempt of Court Act 1981 give a good indication of the type of behaviour which may amount to contempt in the face of the court at common law. Thus a wolf whistle directed at a juror returning into court was potentially insulting, offensive and a serious interference with the administration of justice and the courts. Jurors did not come to courts in order to have comments made about their personal appearance. The appropriate penalty was a moderate fine or detention until the end of the day or over the luncheon adjournment (*R. v Powell*, *The Times*, June 3, 1993).

Justices who peremptorily committed a solicitor to custody under s.12 of the Act for criticising the court's listing system had acted unreasonably. This was a classic case of a storm in a tea cup and like most storms so located no one had acted with entire good sense (*R. v Tamworth Justices Ex p. Walsh*, *The Times*, March 3, 1994; [1994] C.O.D. 277).

**"Wilfully interrupts"**

Magistrates have jurisdiction under s.12(1)(b) to deal with a person who "wilfully interrupts the proceedings of the court," whether the interruptions result from acts done inside or outside the court. In addition to the deliberate commission of the acts causing the interruptions, the mental element of intention that they should interrupt the proceedings must be established. Recklessness, in the sense that the interrupter knows that there is a risk that his acts will interrupt the proceedings but nevertheless goes on to do such acts, will be sufficient (*Bodden v Commissioner of Police for the Metropolis* [1990] 2 W.L.R. 76; [1989] 3 All E.R. 833, CA). **3C–34**

**Appeal to Crown Court**

An appeal from a conviction, or a sentence, for contempt of a Magistrates Court lies to the Crown Court under s.12(5) of the 1981 Act, but an appeal to the High Court by way of case stated or proceedings for judicial review may be brought where appropriate: *Haw v Westminster Magistrates Court* [2008] 3 W.L.R. 465 (Thomas L.J. and Gross J.). **3C–35**

## Legal aid

**13.** [...] **3C–36**

*Note*—Repealed by the Legal Aid Act 1988 s.45, Sch.6, and effectively replaced by s.29 of that Act. **3C–37**

*PENALTIES FOR CONTEMPT AND KINDRED OFFENCES*

## Proceedings in England and Wales

**14.**—(1) In any case where a court has power to commit a person to prison for contempt of court and (apart from this provision) no limitation applies to the period of committal, the committal shall (without prejudice to the power of the court to order his earlier discharge) be for a fixed term, and that term shall not on any occasion exceed two years in the case of committal by a superior court, or one month in the case of committal by an inferior court. **3C–38**

(2) In any case where an inferior court has power to fine a person for contempt of court and (apart from this provision) no limit applies to the amount of the fine, the fine shall not on any occasion exceed £2,500.

(2A) In the exercise of jurisdiction to commit for contempt of court or any kindred offence the court shall not deal with the offender by making an order under section 60 of the Powers of Criminal Courts (Sentencing) Act 2000 (an attendance centre order) if it appears to the court, after considering any available evidence, that he is under 17 years of age.

(3) [...]

(4) Each of the superior courts shall have the like power to make a hospital order or guardianship order under section 37 of the Mental Health Act 1983 or an interim hospital order under section 38 of that Act in the case of a person suffering from mental disorder within the meaning of that Act who could otherwise be committed to prison for contempt of court as the Crown Court has under that section in the case of a person convicted of an offence.

***Paragraph numbers marked with a "+" can be found online and on CD.***

(4A) Each of the superior courts shall have the like power to make an order under section 35 of the said Act of 1983 (remand for report on accused's mental condition) where there is reason to suspect that a person who could be committed to prison for contempt of court is suffering from mental disorder within the meaning of that Act as the Crown Court has under that section in the case of an accused person within the meaning of that section.

(4A) For the purposes of the preceding provisions of this section a county court shall be treated as a superior court and not as an inferior court.

(5) The enactments specified in Part II of Schedule 2 shall have effect subject to the amendments set out in that Part, being amendments relating to the penalties and procedure in respect of certain offences of contempt in coroners' courts, county courts and magistrates' courts.

**3C-39** *Note* —Amended by the Mental Health (Amendment) Act 1982 s.65(1), Sch.3; the Mental Health Act 1983 s.148, Sch.4; the County Courts (Penalties for Contempt) Act 1983 s.1; the Criminal Justice Act 1991 s.17(3), Sch.4; and the Criminal Justice Act 1993 s.65(3) (4), Sch.3. There are two subss.(2A) and (4A). The first subs.(2A) was inserted by the Criminal Justice Act 1982 s.77, Sch.14, para.60, Sch.16 and is amended by the Powers of Criminal Courts (Sentencing) Act 2000, Sch.9, para.84. Subsection (4) and the first subs.(4A) are amended by the Mental Health Act 2007 s.1(4), Sch.1, Pt.2, para.19 with effect from November 3, 2008 (SI 2008/1900).

**"In any case where a court has power to commit a person to prison for contempt of court**

**3C-40** Section 14 applies to civil contempts (*Linnett v Coles* [1987] Q.B. 555; [1986] 3 All E.R. 652, CA). For guidance on sentencing where the contempt is constituted by a witness's refusal to give evidence see *R. v Montgomery (James)* [1995] 2 All E.R. 28. For general guidance on sentencing see *Hale v Tanner* [2000] 1 W.L.R. 2377. However this guidance was modified by *Lomas v Parle* [2002] EWCA Civ 1804 which pointed out that, if there are parallel criminal proceedings arising out of the same incident it is not for the first court to sentence to anticipate or allow for a likely further sentence. Rather it is for the second court to reflect the prior sentence to ensure that the defendant is not punished twice for the same act.

**Mitigation**

**3C-41** Where an alleged contemnor is liable to imprisonment the court must afford him, whether or not he is legally represented, proper opportunity to mitigate, especially where the court has indicated that it was reluctant to consider any sentence other than one of immediate imprisonment (*Taylor v Persico*, *The Times*, February 12, 1992, CA).

A judge exercising the jurisdiction to punish for contempt will be well advised to invite, although he cannot require, the alleged contemnor to be legally represented. In this way he will obtain the assistance of counsel or solicitors in considering his powers and the circumstances of the case (*R. v Tyne Tees Television Ltd*, *The Times*, October 20, 1997, per Beldam L.J., Ognall and Buckley L.JJ.).

See further Practice Direction—Committal Applications at scpd52.1. This PD is distilled from a series of Court of Appeal decisions and should be treated as authoratitive.

**"A fixed term"**

**3C-42** The term, once imposed, may not be varied so as to increase its duration (*Westcott v Westcott* (1985) Fam.Law. 278, CA). An order committing a person to prison for contempt for an indefinite period, even if suspended for a fixed number of days, is not a committal for a fixed term and is ultra vires (*C (A Minor), Re*, *The Times*, July 22, 1985, CA).

Where, however, there has been no unfairness or material irregularity in the com-

***Paragraph numbers marked with a "+" can be found online and on CD.***

mittal proceedings, and where there has been nothing more than an irregularity in the drawing up of the committal order, the irregularity can be corrected on appeal by virtue of A.J.A. 1960, s.13(3), and the term varied so as to make the order lawful (*Linnett v Coles* [1987] Q.B. 555; [1986] 3 All E.R. 652, CA).

A Court dealing with a person for criminal contempt, whether at first instance or on appeal, has no power to make a probation order (*R. v Palmer* [1992] 1 W.L.R. 568).

S.14(1) does not enable the court on any one occasion to impose consecutive sentences which cumulatively exceed the two year maximum. Thus where a judge purported to give a contemnor credit for admitting breaches of an undertaking, but thereafter imposed consecutive sentences to a total of two years he could not be said to have made the reduction in sentence which he had promised (*Re R. (a Minor) (Contempt Sentence)* [1994] 1 W.L.R. 487; [1994] 2 All E.R. 144). The court cannot, moreover, on the same occasion both activate a suspended sentence and impose a new consecutive sentence which together exceed the two year maximum (*Villiers v Villiers* [1994] 2 All E.R. 149).

Where the contempt consists of a refusal to give evidence in a criminal trial the Court of Appeal, Criminal Division, has set out the principles to which a court should have regard in determining the appropriate sentence (*R. v Montgomery*, *The Times*, July 19, 1994).

A judge sitting in the county court who has found a party guilty of contempt, in breaching an order or undertaking, has no power to detain the contemnor in custody pending consideration of the sentence to be imposed (*Delaney v Delaney*, [1996] Q.B. 387). A High Court judge has only a very limited power (see *Wilkinson v S & anor* [2003] 1 W.L.R. 1254).

In considering what order to make against a local authority for its contempt in breaching its undertaking to perform its repairing obligations under a lease a judge was entitled to take judicial notice of numerous instances of past contempt in other claims against that authority by its tenants (*Hackney LBC v Mullen*, *Independent*, November 18, 1996).

#### Superior Court

For the meaning of superior court see s.19 below. The County Courts (Penalties for Contempt) Act 1983, which came into force on May 13, 1983, provides for county courts to be treated as superior courts for the purposes of this section (see subs.(4A) inserted by that Act), thus reversing the effect of the House of Lords' decision in *Peart v Stewart* [1983] 2 A.C. 109; [1983] 1 All E.R. 859. **3C–43**

#### Inferior court

A coroner's court is an inferior court of record which has power to punish a person for contempt of court committed in the face of the court, since it was necessary for the coroner to keep order in the proceedings which he has the duty of conducting (*R. v West Yorkshire Coroner Ex p. Smith* [1985] Q.B. 1096; [1985] 1 All E.R. 100). An industrial tribunal is also an inferior court and the Queen's Bench Divisional Court therefore has power to punish for contempt of that tribunal (*Peach Grey & Co (a firm) v Sommers* [1995] 2 All E.R. 513). **3C–44**

#### Suspension of order

A county court now has like power as the High Court to suspend a committal order for contempt of court upon stated conditions, and to impose consecutive sentences for separate contempts (*Lee v Walker* [1985] Q.B. 1191; [1985] 1 All E.R. 781, CA). **3C–45**

* * * *

## Enforcement of fines imposed by certain superior courts

**16.**—(1) Payment of a fine for contempt of court imposed by a superior court, other than the Crown Court or one of the courts specified in subsection (4) below, may be enforced upon the order of the court— **3C–46**

(a) in like manner as a judgment of the High Court for the payment of money; or

***Paragraph numbers marked with a "+" can be found online and on CD.***

(b) in like manner as a fine imposed by the Crown Court.

(2) Where payment of a fine imposed by any court falls to be enforced as mentioned in paragraph (a) of subsection (1)—

(a) the court shall, if the fine is not paid in full forthwith or within such time as the court may allow, certify to Her Majesty's Remembrancer the sum payable;

(b) Her Majesty's Remembrancer shall thereupon proceed to enforce payment of that sum as if it were due to him as a judgment debt;

(c) [...].

(3) Where payment of a fine imposed by any court falls to be enforced as mentioned in paragraph (b) of subsection (1), the provisions of sections 139 and 140 of the Powers of Criminal Courts (Sentencing) Act 2000 shall apply as they apply to a fine imposed by the Crown Court.

(4) Subsection (1) of this section does not apply to fines imposed by the criminal division of the Court of Appeal or by the Supreme Court on appeal from that division.

(5) The Fines Act 1833 shall not apply to a fine to which subsection (1) of this section applies.

(6) [...].

3C–47 *Note* —Amended by the Senior Courts Act 1981 s.152(4) and Sch.7; the Industrial Tribunals Act 1996 s.45 and Sch.3, the Powers of Criminal Courts (Sentencing) Act 2000 Sch.9, para.85 and the Constitutional Reform Act 2005 s.40 and Sch.9, para.35(2), with effect from October 1, 2009 (SI 2009/1604).

**Superior Court**

3C–48 See s.19, para.3C–50 and note under s.14, para.3C–38.

### Disobedience to certain orders of magistrates' courts

3C–49 **17.**—(1) The powers of a magistrates' court under subsection (3) of section 63 of the Magistrates' Court Act 1980 (punishment by fine or committal for disobeying an order to do anything other than the payment of money or to abstain from doing anything) may be exercised either of the court's own motion or by order on complaint.

(2) In relation to the exercise of those powers the provisions of the Magistrates'Court Act 1980 shall apply subject to the modifications set out in Schedule 3 to this Act.

* * * *

SUPPLEMENTAL

### Interpretation

3C–50 **19.** In this Act—

"court" includes any tribunal or body exercising the judicial power of the State, and "legal proceedings" shall be construed accordingly;

"publication" has the meaning assigned by subsection (1) of section 2, and "publish" (except in section 9) shall be construed accordingly;

*Paragraph numbers marked with a "+" can be found online and on CD.*

"Scottish proceedings" means proceedings before any court, including the Courts-Martial Appeal Court, the Restrictive Practices Court and Employment Appeal Tribunal, sitting in Scotland, and includes proceedings before the Supreme Court in the exercise of any appellate jurisdiction over proceedings in such a court;

"the strict liability rule" has the meaning assigned by section 1;

"superior court" means Supreme Court, the Court of Appeal, the High Court, the Crown Court, the Courts-Martial Appeal Court, the Restrictive Practices Court, the Employment Appeal Tribunal and any other court exercising in relation to its proceedings powers equivalent to those of the High Court..

*Note*—Amended by the Senior Courts Act 1981 s.152(4) and Sch.7; the Industrial Tribunals Act 1996 s.45 and Sch.3, the Powers of Criminal Courts (Sentencing) Act 2000, Sch.9, para.85 and the Constitutional Reform Act 2005 s.40 and Sch.9, para.35(2), with effect from October 1, 2009 (SI 2009/1604). **3C–51**

#### Court

A mental health review tribunal is a court for inter alia the purposes of s.19 (*Pickering v Liverpool Daily Post & Echo Newspapers plc* [1990] 2 W.L.R. 494; [1990] 1 All E.R. 335, CA; affd. on this ground (although reversed on others) [1991] 1 All E.R. 622, HL). The decision to the contrary in *Attorney General v Associated Newspapers Group plc* [1989] 1 W.L.R. 322; [1989] 1 All E.R. 604, is wrong (*ibid.*). See also generally the note at para.13A–45. **3C–52**

#### Superior Court

See n. "Superior court", para.3C–48. **3C–53**

### Tribunals of Inquiry

**20.**—(1) In relation to any tribunal to which the Tribunals of Inquiry (Evidence) Act 1921 applies, and the proceedings of such a tribunal, the provisions of this Act (except subsection (3) of section 9) apply as they apply in relation to courts and legal proceedings; and references to the course of justice or the administration of justice in legal proceedings shall be construed accordingly. **3C–54**

(2) The proceedings of a tribunal established under the said Act shall be treated as active within the meaning of section 2 from the time when the tribunal is appointed until its report is presented to Parliament.

### Short title, commencement and extent

**21.**—(1) This Act may be cited as the Contempt of Court Act 1981. **3C–55**

(2) The provisions of this Act relating to legal aid in England and Wales shall come into force on such day as the Lord Chancellor may appoint by order made by statutory instrument; and the provisions of this Act relating to legal aid in Scotland and Northern Ireland shall come into force on such day or days as the Secretary of State may so appoint.

Different days may be appointed under this subsection in relation to different courts.

(3) Subject to subsection (2), this Act shall come into force at the

expiration of the period of one month beginning with the day on which it is passed.

(4) Sections 7, 8(3), 12, 13(1) to (3), 14, 16, 17 and 18, Parts I and III of Schedule 2 and Schedules 3 and 4 of this Act do not extend to Scotland.

(5) This Act, except sections 15 and 17 and Schedules 2 and 3, extends to Northern Ireland.

## SCHEDULE 1

### TIMES WHEN PROCEEDINGS ARE ACTIVE FOR PURPOSES OF SECTION 2

*Preliminary*

**3C–56** 1. In this Schedule "criminal proceedings" means proceedings against a person in respect of an offence, not being appellate proceedings or proceedings commenced by motion for committal or attachment in England and Wales or Northern Ireland; and "appellate proceedings" means proceedings on appeal from or for the review of the decision of a court in any proceedings.

2. Criminal, appellate and other proceedings are active within the meaning of section 2 at the times respectively prescribed by the following paragraphs of this Schedule; and in relation to proceedings in which more than one of the steps described in any of those paragraphs is taken, the reference in that paragraph is a reference to the first of those steps.

*Criminal proceedings*

**3C–57** 3. Subject to the following provisions of this Schedule, criminal proceedings are active from the relevant initial step specified in paragraph 4 or 4A until concluded as described in paragraph 5.

4. The initial steps of criminal proceedings are—

(a) arrest without warrant;

(b) the issue, or in Scotland the grant, of a warrant for arrest;

(c) the issue of a summons to appear, or in Scotland the grant of a warrant to cite;

(d) the service of an indictment or other document specifying the charge;

(e) except in Scotland, oral charge.

4A. Where as a result of an order under section 54 of the Criminal Procedure and Investigations Act 1996 (acquittal tainted by an administration of justice offence) proceedings are brought against a person for an offence of which he has previously been acquitted, the initial step of the proceedings is a certification under subsection (2) of that section; and paragraph 4 has effect subject to this.

5. Criminal proceedings are concluded—

(a) by acquittal or, as the case may be, by sentence;

(b) by any other verdict, finding, order or decision which puts an end to the proceedings;

(c) by discontinuance or by operation of law.

6. The reference in paragraph 5(a) to sentence includes any order or decision consequent on conviction or finding of guilt which disposes of the case, either absolutely or subject to future events, and a deferment of sentence under section 1 of the Powers of Criminal Courts (Sentencing) Act 2000, s.219 or 432 of the Criminal Procedure (Scotland) Act 1975 or Article 14 of the Treatment of Offenders (Northern Ireland) Order 1976.

7. Proceedings are discontinued within the meaning of paragraph 5(c)—

(a) in England and Wales or Northern Ireland, if the charge or summons is withdrawn or a *nolle prosequi* entered;

(aa) in England and Wales, if they are discontinued by virtue of section 23 of the Prosecution of Offences Act 1985;

(b) in Scotland, if the proceedings are expressly abandoned by the prosecutor or are deserted *simpliciter*;

***Paragraph numbers marked with a "+" can be found online and on CD.***

(c) in the case of proceedings in England and Wales or Northern Ireland commenced by arrest without warrant, if the person arrested is released, otherwise than on bail, without having been charged.

8. Criminal proceedings before a court-martial or standing civilian court are not concluded until the completion of any review of finding or sentence.

9. Criminal proceedings in England and Wales or Northern Ireland cease to be active if an order is made for the charge to lie on the file, but become active again if leave is later given for the proceedings to continue.

9A. Where proceedings in England and Wales have been discontinued by virtue of section 23 of the Prosecution of Offences Act 1985, but notice is given by the accused under subsection (7) of that section to the effect that he wants the proceedings to continue, they become active again with the giving of that notice.

10. Without prejudice to paragraph 5(b) above, criminal proceedings against a person cease to be active—

(a) if the accused is found to be under a disability such as to render him unfit to be tried or unfit to plead or, in Scotland, is found to be insane in bar of trial; or

(b) if a hospital order is made in his case under section 51(5) of the Mental Health Act 1983 or Article 57(5) of the Mental Health (Northern Ireland) Order 1986 or, in Scotland, where an assessment order or a treatment order ceases to have effect by virtue of sections 52H or 52R respectively of the Criminal Procedure (Scotland) Act 1995

but become active again if they are later resumed.

11. Criminal proceedings against a person which become active on the issue or the grant of a warrant for his arrest cease to be active at the end of the period of twelve months beginning with the date of the warrant unless he has been arrested within that period, but become active again if he is subsequently arrested.

*Other proceedings at first instance*

12. Proceedings other than criminal proceedings and appellate proceedings are active from the time when arrangements for the hearing are made or, if no such arrangements are previously made, from the time the hearing begins, until the proceedings are disposed of or discontinued or withdrawn; and for the purposes of this paragraph any motion or application made in or for the purposes of any proceedings, and any pre-trial review in the county court, is to be treated as a distinct proceeding. **3C–58**

13. In England and Wales or Northern Ireland arrangements for the hearing of proceedings to which paragraph 12 applies are made within the meaning of that paragraph—

(a) in the case of proceedings in the High Court for which provision is made by rules of court for setting down for trial, when the case is set down;

(b) in the case of any proceedings, when a date for the trial or hearing is fixed.

14. [*Proceedings in Scotland.*]

*Appellate proceedings*

15. Appellate proceedings are active from the time when they are commenced— **3C–59**

(a) by application for leave to appeal or apply for review, or by notice of such an application;

(b) by notice of appeal or of application for review;

(c) by other originating process,

until disposed of or abandoned, discontinued or withdrawn.

16. Where, in appellate proceedings relating to criminal proceedings, the court—

(a) remits the case to the court below; or

(b) orders a new trial or a *venire de novo*, or in Scotland grants authority to bring a new prosecution,

any further or new proceedings which result shall be treated as active from the conclusion of the appellate proceedings.

*Note* —Amended by the Mental Health Act 1983, Sch.4, paras 57(c) and 59(c); the Prosecution of Offences Act 1985, s.31, Sch.1, paras 4 and 5; the Mental Health **3C–60**

(Scotland) Act 1984, s.17, s.127(1), Sch.3, para.48; the Criminal Procedure and Investigations Act 1996, s.57 and by the Powers of Criminal Courts (Sentencing) Act 2000, Sch.9, para.86; and by SI 2005/465.

**Power of a county court to commit for contempt**

3C–61 For the power of a county court to commit for contempt see s.118 of the County Courts Act 1984 (para.9A–654).

*Paragraph numbers marked with a "+" can be found online and on CD.*

# 3D PROCEEDINGS UNDER THE HUMAN RIGHTS ACT 1998

## Human Rights Act 1998

(1998 c.42) **3D–1**

ARRANGEMENT OF SECTIONS



*INTRODUCTION*

### The Convention rights

**1.**—(1) In this Act, "the convention rights" means the rights and fundamental freedoms set out in— **3D–2**

***Paragraph numbers marked with a "+" can be found online and on CD.***

(a) Articles 2 to 12 and 14 of the Convention,

(b) Articles 1 to 3 of the First Protocol, and

(c) Article 1 of the Thirteenth Protocol.

as read with Articles 16 to 18 of the Convention.

(2) Those Articles are to have effect for the purposes of this Act subject to any designated derogation or reservation (as to which see sections 14 and 15).

(3) The Articles are set out in Schedule 1.

(4) The Secretary of State may by order make such amendments to this Act as he considers appropriate to reflect the effect, in relation to the United Kingdom, of a protocol.

(5) In subsection (4) "protocol" means a protocol to the Convention—

(a) which the United Kingdom has ratified; or

(b) which the United Kingdom has signed with a view to ratification.

(6) No amendment may be made by an order under subsection (4) so as to come into force before the protocol concerned is in force in relation to the United Kingdom.

**Section 1(1)**

**3D–3** "The Convention" here means "the Convention ...as it has effect for the time being in relation to the United Kingdom", as defined in s.21(1). Thus if the effect of a provision of the Convention is limited or extinguished by some other, overriding provision of international law, such as a UN Security Council Resolution, that limitation affects the interpretation of the convention rights in the United Kingdom: *R (on the application of Al Jedda) v Secretary of State for Defence* [2007] UKHL 58; [2008] 1 A.C. 332; [2008] 2 W.L.R. 31. Also *R. (Quark Fishing Ltd) v Foreign Secretary* [2005] UKHL 57; [2005] 3 W.L.R. 837; [2005] 3 W.L.R. 837 at paras 25, 32, 56, 87 and 97 and *Al-Skeini v Secretary of State for Defence* [2007] UKHL 26; [2008] 1 A.C. 153; [2007] 3 W.L.R. 33; [2007] 3 All E.R. 685. The effect of the Convention is usually, but not always territorially limited. See all cases above and also *R. (Bancoult)* v Secretary of State for Foreign & Commonwealth Affairs [2008] UKHL 61; 2009 1 A.C. 453.

**Section 1(1)(c)**

**3D–4** Substituted by the Human Rights Act 1998 (Amendment) Order 2004 (SI 2004/1574), art.2(1) to reflect the coming into force of Protocol 13 of the ECHR, concerning abolition of the death penalty.

**Section 1(2)**

**3D–5** The United Kingdom entered a derogation to art.5 of the ECHR in order to enact Pt IV of the Anti-Terrorism Crime and Security Act 2001. This was contained in the Human Rights Act 1998 (Designated Derogation) Order 2001 (SI 2001/3644). However, that Order was quashed by the House of Lords in *A v Secretary of State for the Home Department* [2005] UKHL 71, [2006] 2 A.C. 221; [2005] 3 W.L.R. 1249; [2006] 1 All E.R. 575; [2006] H.R.L.R. 6; [2006] U.K.H.R.R. 225. Part IV of the Anti-Terrorism Crime and Security Act 2001 was repealed by the Prevention of Terrorism Act 2005, with effect from March 14, 2005, and the Human Rights Act 1998 (Amendment) Order 2005 (SI 2005/1071) of April 8, 2005, reflected the withdrawal of the derogation from art.5 in response to this.

**Section 1(4)**

**3D–6** For procedure for making of an order under this section, see s.20(4).

## Interpretation of Convention rights

**3D–7** **2.**—(1) A court or tribunal determining a question which has arisen under this Act in connection with a Convention right must take into account any—

(a) judgment, decision, declaration or advisory opinion of the European Court of Human Rights,

(b) opinion of the Commission given in a report adopted under Article 31 of the Convention,

(c) decision of the Commission in connection with Article 26 or 27(2) of the Convention, or

(d) decision of the Committee of Ministers taken under Article 46 of the Convention,

whenever made or given, so far as, in the opinion of the court or tribunal, it is relevant to the proceedings in which that question has arisen.

(2) Evidence of any judgment, decision, declaration or opinion of which account may have to be taken under this section is to be given in proceedings before any court or tribunal in such manner as may be provided by rules.

(3) In this section "rules" means rules of court or, in the case of proceedings before a tribunal, rules made for the purposes of this section—

(a) by the Lord Chancellor or the Secretary of State, in relation to any proceedings outside Scotland;

(b) by the Secretary of State, in relation to proceedings in Scotland; or

(c) by a Northern Ireland department, in relation to proceedings before a tribunal in Northern Ireland—

(i) which deals with transferred matters; and

(ii) for which no rules made under paragraph (a) are in force.

*Note*—Amended by SI 2003/1887 and SI 2005/3429. **3D–8**

**Section 2(1)**

This requires any court or tribunal determining a question which has arisen under any Act in connection with a Convention right to "take into account" the decisions of the Strasbourg organs, whenever made or given so far as, in the opinion of the court or tribunal, it is relevant to the proceedings in which that question has arisen. The courts will not without good reason depart from the principles laid down in a carefully considered judgment of the ECHR sitting as a Grand Chamber: *R. (Anderson) v Secretary of State for the Home Department* [2002] UKHL 46; [2003] 1 A.C. 837; [2002] 3 W.L.R. 1800; [2002] 4 All E.R. 1089 per Lord Bingham at para.18. In the absence of some special circumstance, a court should follow any clear and consistent jurisprudence of the ECHR: *R. (on the application of Holding and Barnes plc) v Secretary of State for the Environment* [2001] UKHL 23, [2003] 2 A.C. 295, [2001] 2 W.L.R. 1389 HL, per Lord Slynn. This principle was interpreted in a limited way by the majority of the Court of Appeal in *Copsey v WWB Devon Clays Ltd* [2005] EWCA Civ 932; [2005] I.C.R. 1789; [2005] I.R.L.R. 811; 2005 H.R.L.R. 32. It may, however, be appropriate for a court to decline to follow the reasoning of the ECHR if it is unpersuasive: see *R. v Spear* [2002] UKHL 31, [2003] 1 A.C. 734 HL paras 12–13 and 65–66 and *R. v Lyons* [2002] UKHL 44, [2003] 1 A.C. 976, para.46. **3D–9**

The purpose of s.2 is to ensure that the same Convention rights are enforced under the HRA by courts within the United Kingdom as would be enforced by the ECHR in Strasbourg. It is not intended to provide Convention rights with a domestically autonomous meaning: *N v Secretary of State for the Home Department* [2005] UKHL 31; [2005]

***Paragraph numbers marked with a "+" can be found online and on CD.***

2 A.C. 296; [2005] 2 W.L.R. 1124; [2005] 4 All E.R. 1017 per Lord Hope, para.25 and *R (on the application of Al Jedda) v Secretary of State for Defence* [2007] UKHL 58; [2008] 1 A.C. 332; [2008] 2 W.L.R. 31. See too *R. (Quark Fishing Ltd) v Foreign Secretary* [2005] UKHL 57; [2005] 3 W.L.R. 837, *Aston Cantlow PCC v Wallbank* [2003] UKHL 37; [2004] 1 A.C. 546 at para 6 and *R. (Greenfield) v Home Secretary* [2005] UKHL 14; [2005] 1 W.L.R. 673; [2005] 2 All E.R. 240; [2005] H.R.L.R. 13; [2005] U.K.H.R.R. 323 at para.19. A national court should not, without strong reason, dilute or weaken the effect of Strasbourg case-law. Nor should the provision of more generous rights be the product of interpretation of the Convention by the national courts, since the meaning of the Convention should be uniform throughout the states party to it: *R. v Special Adjudicator Ex p. Ullah*, sub nom. *Doh v Secretary of State for the Home Department* [2004] UKHL 26, [2004] 2 A.C. 323; [2004] 3 W.L.R. 23 per Lord Bingham. See too *R. (SB) v Denbigh High School* [2006] UKHL 15; [2007] 1 A.C. 100; [2006] 2 W.L.R. 719 at para.29.

However (per Moses J at first instance in *Al-Jedda* [2005] EWHC 1809 (Admin); [2005] H.R.L.R. 39 at para.41), the "less than imperative terms" of the drafting were necessary to allow a distinction to be drawn between the ECHR approach and that of a domestic court, in that, for example, domestic courts may have a narrower area of discretion. Note s.11 of the Act: reliance on Convention rights does not restrict other wider rights available otherwise.

The principle of *stare decisis* compels domestic courts to follow the earlier decisions of higher courts, even if they conflict with later Strasbourg authority. See *Kay v Lambeth LBC* [2006] UKHL 10; [2006] 2 A.C. 465; [2006] 2 W.L.R. 570; [2006] U.K.R.R. 640. See too *R. (Animal Defenders International) v Secretary of State for Culture, Media & Sport* [2008] UKHL 15; [2008] 2 W.L.R. 781, and *R. (RJM) v Secretary of State for Work & Pensions* [2008] UKHL 63 at 59–67; *A v Hoare* [2006] EWCA Civ 395, *R (on the application of Gilboy) v Liverpool City Council* [2007] EWHC 2335; [2007] B.L.G.R. 837 and *Doherty v Birmingham CC* [2008] UKHL 57; [2009] 1 A.C. 367 [2008] 3 W.L.R. 636; [2009] 1 All E.R. 653.

**Section 2(1)(b)**

**3D–10** This refers to opinions given under art.31 of the Convention as it existed before amendment by the 11th Protocol. Article 31 dealt with the duty of the European Commission of Human Rights to report in the event that it did not secure a friendly settlement of an application which it had declared admissible. art.31(1) provided:

> "If a solution is not reached, the Commission shall draw up a Report on the facts and state its opinion as to whether the facts found disclose a breach by the State concerned of its obligations under the Convention. The opinions of all the members of the Commission on this point may be stated in the Report."

**Section 2(1)(c)**

**3D–11** This refers to art.26 of the Convention before it was amended by the 11th Protocol, which provided:

> "The Commission may only deal with the matter [i.e. non-state applications] after all domestic remedies have been exhausted, according to the generally recognised rules of international law, and within a period of six months from the date on which the final decision was taken."

Article 27(2) of the unamended Convention provided:

> "3. The Commission shall declare inadmissible any individual application submitted under art.25 which it considers incompatible with the provisions of the present Convention, manifestly ill-founded, or an abuse of the right of petition".

See now art.35 of the Convention as amended.

**Section 2(1)(d)**

**3D–12**

> "Article 46—Binding force and execution of judgments
> 1. The High Contracting Parties undertake to abide by the final judgment of the Court in any case to which they are parties.
> 2. The final judgment of the Court shall be transmitted to the Committee of Ministers, which shall supervise its execution."

The reference to art.46 includes a reference to Arts 32 and 54 of the Convention

***Paragraph numbers marked with a "+" can be found online and on CD.***

before it was amended by the 11th Protocol: see s.21(3). Article 32(1) provided that if, after the Commission had adopted a Report under art.31, the case was not referred to the ECHR, "the Committee of Ministers [of the Council of Europe] shall decide by a majority of two-thirds of the members entitled to sit on the Committee whether there has been a violation of the Convention". Article 54 was virtually identical to the new art.46.

**Section 2(2)**

As to citation of Strasbourg authorities, see para.8 of the Practice Direction—Miscellaneous Provisions Relating to Hearings: 39 PD.8. Excessive citation of authority is to be avoided. Decisions of the ECHR tend to repeat the same principles in successive cases in order to apply them to different situations. Citation of a single case may therefore be all that is required: *A v B Plc* [2002] EWCA Civ 337; [2003] Q.B. 195; [2002] 3 W.L.R. 542 paras 8–9. **3D–13**

**Section 2(3)**

The power to make rules under this subsection for England and Wales is exercisable by statutory instrument: see s.20(2). It can be annulled by resolution of either House of Parliament: see ss.20(5) and 20(7). **3D–14**

For citation of authorities concerning human rights see CPR Practice Direction supplementing r.39, para.8.1.

### *LEGISLATION*

## Interpretation of legislation

**3.**—(1) So far as it is possible to do so, primary legislation and subordinate legislation must be read and given effect in a way which is compatible with the Convention rights. **3D–15**

(2) This section—

(a) applies to primary legislation and subordinate legislation whenever enacted;

(b) does not affect the validity, continuing operation or enforcement of any incompatible primary legislation; and

(c) does not affect the validity, continuing operation or enforcement of any incompatible subordinate legislation if (disregarding any possibility of revocation) primary legislation prevents removal of the incompatibility.

Like the court's general free-standing jurisdiction to declare the meaning of legislation, the interpretative obligation in s.3(1) is a general one. A claimant seeking a declaration as to the meaning of legislation under s.3(1) need not be a victim: it is sufficient that he or she has an interest and standing: see *R. (on the application of Rusbridger) v AG* [2003] UKHL 38; [2004] A.C. 357; [2003] 3 W.L.R. 232 para.21, per Lord Steyn. However, see para.3D–19 concerning declarations of incompatibility. **3D–16**

Section 3(1) introduced a new canon of construction, a "strong adjuration" to interpret legislation compatibly with the Convention, which may involve adopting a meaning other than the natural and ordinary meaning of the statutory words: see *R. v DPP Ex p. Kebilene* [2000] 2 A.C. 326; [1999] 3 W.L.R. 972; [1999] 4 All E.R. 801, per Lord Cooke of Thorndon. For a review of s.3 case-law, see the speech of Lord Steyn in *Ghaidan v Godin-Mendoza* [2004] UKHL 30; [2004] 2 A.C. 557; [2004] 3 W.L.R. 113. See also *R. v Holding* [2006] EWCA Crim 3185; [2006] 1 W.L.R. 1040; *Culnane v Morris* [2005] EWHC 2438 (Admin); [2006] 2 All E.R. 149 and *Secretary of State for the Home Department v MB* [2006] EWCA Civ 1140; [2008] 1 A.C. 440; [2006] 3 W.L.R. 831; [2006] H.R.L.R. 37, in which a declaration of incompatibility made by the High Court was reversed by the Court of Appeal, applying HRA s.3 so as to achieve an HRA-

***Paragraph numbers marked with a "+" can be found online and on CD.***

compatible construction of the Prevention of Terrorism Act 2005. See too the decision of the House of Lords: [2007] UKHL 46; [2008] 1 A.C. 440; [2007] 3 W.L.R. 681.

The particular statutory provision which is said to contravene Convention rights must be identified with precision by the claimant: see *R. v A (Complainant's Sexual History)* [2001] UKHL 25; [2001] 1 A.C. 45; [2001] 2 W.L.R. 1546, HL, per Lord Hope at 1582, 153 para.110; *R. v Lambert* [2001] 3 W.L.R. 206 at 234 para.8; *Re S (Care Order: Implementation of Care Plan)* [2002] UKHL 10; [2002] 2 A.C. 291; [2002] 2 W.L.R 720; [2002] 2 All E.R. 192 per Lord Nicholls at para.41.

The court must first ask whether, on ordinary construction, the statutory provision is compatible with Convention rights. If not, it must consider whether it is possible to read the provision in a manner which is compatible: *Brown v Stott* [2003] 1 A.C. 681; [2001] 2 All E.R. 97. These steps require the Court to identify the scope of the Convention right in question: *Brown*, per Lord Roger. As to what is "possible" see the case law on European Community law, e.g. *Marleasing SA v La Comercial Internacional de Alimentacion SA (C106/89)* [1990] E.C.R. I-4135 and *Litster v Forth Dry Dock & Engineering Company Limited* [1990] 1 A.C. 546. Techniques involved may be reading down of express language in a statute, or reading in. Section 3 may require a court to depart from the unambiguous meaning which the legislation would bear other than by reference to the purpose of compatibility with the Convention: see *Ghaidan v Godin-Mendoza* [2004] UKHL 30; [2004] 2 A.C. 557; [2004] 3 W.L.R. 113, per Lord Nicholls at para.30. This may involve departure from the intention of the Parliament which enacted the legislation. See also *R. v Holding* [2006] EWCA Crim 3185; [2006] 1 W.L.R. 1040, *Culnane v Morris* [2005] EWHC 2438; [2006] 2 All E.R. 149 and *R. (MB) v Secretary of State for the Home Department* [2006] EWHC (Admin), and [2006] EWCA Civ 1157, in which a declaration of incompatibility made by the High Court was reversed by the Court of Appeal, applying HRA s.3 so as to achieve an HRA-compatible construction of the Prevention of Terrorism Act 2005. See too the decision of the House of Lords in [2007] UKHL 46; [2008] 1 A.C. 440; [2007] 3 W.L.R. 681. Parliament's intention is normally to be deduced from the statutory language. It is seldom necessary to have regard to matters stated in Parliament by resort to Hansard: *Wilson v First County Trust Ltd (No.2)* [2003] UKHL 40; [2004] 1 A.C. 816; [2003] 3 W.L.R. 568; [2003] 4 All E.R. 97.

A compatible interpretation must be sought unless it is plainly impossible: the search is for a "possible" meaning, not one which is "reasonably possible": *R. v A (No 2)* [2001] UKHL 25; [2002] 1 A.C. 45; [2001] 2 W.L.R. 1546 HL; cf *R. (on the application of H) v Mental Health Review Tribunal for North and East London Region* [2001] EWCA Civ 415; [2002] Q.B. 1; [2001] 3 W.L.R. 512). See too *R (Hammond) v Secretary of State for the Home Department* [2005] UKHL 69; (2006) 1 A.C. 603 and *R. (MB) v Secretary of State for the Home Department* [2007] UKHL 46; [2007] 3 W.L.R. 681.

A s.3 interpretation is only invoked where it is necessary for it to be applied in order to arrive at a Convention compatible interpretation. Otherwise the court must afford the legislation its ordinary meaning. See *R. (Hurst) v Commissioner of Police for the Metropolis* [2007] UKHL 13; [2007] 2 A.C. 189; [2007] 2 W.L.R. 726; [2007] 2 All E.R. 1025.

The exercise is, however, one of interpretation not legislation. A Convention-compatible interpretation cannot be given to legislation if it is contrary to express statutory words or the necessary implication of the statute: *Poplar Housing & Regeneration Community Association Ltd v Donoghue* [2001] EWCA Civ 595; [2002] Q.B. 48; [2001] 3 W.L.R. 183, CA; *R (Anderson) v Secretary of State for the Home Department* [2002] UKHL 46; [2003] 1 A.C. 837; [2002] 3 W.L.R. 1800; [2002] 4 All E.R. 1089. See too *R. (Wright) v Secretary of State for Health* [2009] UKHL 3; [2009] 1 A.C. 739; [2009] 2 W.L.R. 267. There are two circumstances in which it would not be possible to use s.3 to achieve compatibility. First, a meaning which departs substantially from a fundamental feature of an Act of Parliament is likely to have crossed the boundary between interpretation and amendment: *Re S (Care Order: Implementation of Care Plan)* [2002] 2 A.C. 291; [2002] 2 W.L.R. 720; [2002] 2 All E.R. 192; [2002] 1 F.L.R. 815 per Lord Nicholls at para.40. Secondly, compatible interpretation would be impossible where the legislation in issue had wide ramifications, raising policy issues ill-suited for determination by the courts or court procedures, or would require the construction of a wide-ranging new extra-statutory scheme: *Re S (supra); Bellinger v Bellinger* [2003] UKHL 21; [2003] 2 A.C. 467; [2003] 2 W.L.R. 1174; [2003] 2 All E.R. 593 For the boundary between interpretation and amendment see too *AS (Somalia) v Secretary of State for the Home Department* [2009] UKHL 32; [2009] 1 W.L.R. 1385.

Where a court does rely on s.3 it should limit the extent of the modified meaning to that necessary to achieve compatibility: see *Poplar Housing & Regeneration Community Association Ltd v Donoghue* [2001] EWCA Civ 595; *R. (Middleton) v HM Coroner for Western Somerset* [2004] UKHL 10; [2004] 2 A.C. 182; [2004] 2 W.L.R. 800; [2004] 2 All E.R. 465 (para 34).

For the relationship between ss.3, 4 and 6, see *Nasseri v Secretary of State for the Home Department* [2009] UKHL 23; [2009] 2 W.L.R. 1190 per Lord Hoffmann at [19].

## Declaration of incompatibility

**4.**—(1) Subsection (2) applies in any proceedings in which a court determines whether a provision of primary legislation is compatible with a Convention right. **3D-17**

(2) If the court is satisfied that the provision is incompatible with a Convention right, it may make a declaration of that incompatibility.

(3) Subsection (4) applies in any proceedings in which a court determines whether a provision of subordinate legislation, made in the exercise of a power conferred by primary legislation, is compatible with a Convention right.

(4) If the court is satisfied—

(a) that the provision is incompatible with a Convention right, and

(b) that (disregarding any possibility of revocation) the primary legislation concerned prevents removal of the incompatibility,

it may make a declaration of that incompatibility.

(5) In this section "court" means—

(a) the Supreme Court;

(b) the Judicial Committee of the Privy Council;

(c) the Courts-Martial Appeal Court;

(d) in Scotland, the High Court of Justiciary sitting otherwise than as a trial court or the Court of Session;

(e) in England and Wales or Northern Ireland, the High Court or the Court of Appeal;

(f) the Court of Protection, in any matter being dealt with by the President of the Family Division, the Vice-Chancellor or a puisne judge of the High Court.

(6) A declaration under this section ("a declaration of incompatibility")—

(a) does not affect the validity, continuing operation or enforcement of the provision in respect of which it is given; and

(b) is not binding on the parties to the proceedings in which it is made.

*Note*—Amended by the Mental Capacity Act 2005 s.67 and Sch.6, para.43. Further amended by the Constitutional Reform Act 2005 s.40 Sch.9 para.66 with effect from October 1, 2009 (SI 2009/1604). **3D-18**

***Paragraph numbers marked with a "+" can be found online and on CD.***

3D–19 There is no strict requirement that a person who seeks a declaration of incompatibility is a "victim" within s.7, provided he or she has a sufficient interest and standing: *R. (on the application of Rusbridger) v Att-Gen* [2003] UKHL 38; [2004] 1 A.C. 357; [2003] 3 W.L.R. 232 para.21, per Lord Steyn. Ordinarily, however, the court will only grant a declaration of incompatibility to a person who is a victim of an actual or proposed breach of a Convention right: *Re S (Care Order: Implementation of Care Plan)* [2002] 2 A.C. 291; [2002] 2 W.L.R. 720; [2002] 2 All E.R. 192; [2002] 1 F.L.R. 815 per Lord Nicholls; *Bellinger v Bellinger* [2003] UKHL 21; [2003] 2 A.C. 467; [2003] 2 W.L.R. 1174; [2003] 2 All E.R. 593. In any event, a person cannot apply for a declaration of incompatibility on the basis of a hypothetical argument, nor unless they are adversely affected by the impugned measure: *Joseph Taylor v Lancashire CC and Secretary of State for the Environment, Food & Rural Affairs* [2005] EWCA Civ 284; [2005] 1 W.L.R. 2668; [2005] H.R.L.R. 17; [2005] U.K.H.R.R. 766, per Woolf, C.J.

Unlike a claim under s.7, which can be considered by any court, only superior courts of record can make declarations of incompatibility (s.4(5)). When considering whether to make an order transferring proceedings from the County Court to the High Court, the court must have regard to the question of whether the making of a declaration of incompatibility has arisen or may arise: CPR r.30.3(2)(g). It is not, however, necessary to transfer the proceedings to the High Court merely because a breach of a Convention right is alleged, nor where an application for a declaration of incompatibility has been made which stands no chance of success: *V (A Child) (Care Proceedings: Human Rights Claims, Re* [2004] EWCA Civ 54; [2004] 1 W.L.R. 1433; [2004] 1 All E.R. 997; [2004] 1 F.W.L.R. 944.

A statutory lacuna is not the same as an incompatibility: see *S (Children) (Care Order: Implementation of Care Plan), Re* [2002] UKHL 10; [2002] 2 A.C. 291; [2002] 2 W.L.R. 720, per Lord Nicholls. See also s.6(3)(b) and s.6(6): failure to legislate does not amount to a breach of s.6(1).

Whether to make a declaration of incompatibility is a matter for the court's discretion. Such a declaration should only be made if the primary remedies under ss.6 and 3 cannot be used. See *Nasseri v Secretary of State for the Home Department* [2009] UKHL 23; [2009] 2 W.L.R. 1190 per Lord Hoffmann at [19]. A declaration of incompatibility is a remedy of last resort: it must be avoided unless it is plainly impossible to do so: *R. v A (No 2)* [2001] UKHL 25; [2002] 1 A.C. 45; [2001] 2 W.L.R. 1546 (see also commentary on s.3, above). Even where it is not possible to interpret a provision compatibly with the ECHR, the Court retains a discretion as to whether to grant a declaration, to be exercised according to the normal principles governing the grant of declarations. As to circumstances in which a declaration might be made, see *Wilson v First County Trust Ltd (No.2)* [2001] EWCA 633; [2002] Q.B. 74; [2001] 3 W.L.R. 42 (CA) (overruled on other grounds in *Wilson v first County Trust Ltd (No.2)* [2003] UKHL 40; [2004] 1 A.C. 816; [2003] 3 W.L.R. 568; [2003] 4 All E.R. 97).

Extrinsic evidence of legislative policy is admissible only in relation to a declaration of incompatibility: see also *Wilson v First County Trust Ltd (No.2)* [2003] UKHL 40; [2004] 1 A.C. 816; [2003] 3 W.L.R. 568; [2003] 4 All E.R. 97 at paras 61–67, per Lord Nicholls; *Evans v Amicus Healthcare Ltd* [2004] EWCA Civ 727, CA; [2005] Fam. 1; [2004] 3 W.L.R. 681; [2004] 3 All E.R. 1025, CA and *R. (on the application of Morris) v Westminster City Council (No.3)* [2005] EWCA Civ 1184; [2006] 1 W.L.R. 505; [2005] H.R.L.R. 43; [2006] U.K.H.R.R. 165, para.39, per Sedley L.J.

The fact that another power may achieve the same result as that which is prohibited by the operation of s.6(2), and which results in a declaration of incompatibility, does not mean that a statement of incompatibility is unnecessary if the impugned measure is incompatible with a Convention right. Other forms of statutory protection are immaterial. See *R. (on the application of Morris) v Westminster City Council (No.3)* [2005] EWCA Civ 1184; [2006] 1 W.L.R. 505; [2005] H.R.L.R. 43; [2006] U.K.H.R.R. 165, paras 53–55 and 82.

As to the procedure for making declarations of incompatibility, see s.5 post, and CPR, r.19.4A inserted by reg.3 of the Civil Procedure (Amendment No 4) Rules 2000 (SI 2000/2092).

3D–20 A request for a declaration of incompatibility should not be made on the basis of a hypothetical argument because a person cannot apply for a declaration under s.4(2) unless they are adversely affected by the legislation in question: *Joseph Taylor (Appellant) v Lancashire County Council (Respondent) & Secretary of State for Environment, Food and Ru-*

*ral Affairs (Intervener)* [2005] EWCA Civ 284; [2005] 1 W.L.R. 2668; [2005] H.R.L.R. 17; [2005] U.K.H.R.R. 766, para.43, per Woolf, C.J.

## Right of Crown to intervene

**5.**—(1) Where a court is considering whether to make a declaration of incompatibility, the Crown is entitled to notice in accordance with rules of court. **3D–21**

(2) In any case to which subsection (1) applies—

(a) a Minister of the Crown (or a person nominated by him),

(b) a member of the Scottish Executive,

(c) a Northern Ireland Minister,

(d) a Northern Ireland department,

is entitled, on giving notice in accordance with rules of court, to be joined as a party to the proceedings.

(3) Notice under subsection (2) may be given at any time during the proceedings.

(4) A person who has been made a party to criminal proceedings (other than in Scotland) as the result of a notice under subsection (2) may, with leave, appeal to the House of Lords against any declaration of incompatibility made in the proceedings.

(5) In subsection (4)—

"criminal proceedings" includes all proceedings before the Courts-Martial Appeal Court; and

"leave" means leave granted by the court making the declaration of incompatibility or by the Supreme Court.

*Note*—Amended by the Constitutional Reform Act 2005 s.40 Sch.9 para.66 with effect from October 1, 2009 (SI 2009/1604). **3D–21.1**

As to the procedure for giving notice to the Crown, see CPR r.19.4A. **3D–22**

The parties should also give as much informal notice as possible to the Crown of the proceedings and the issues involved, and should copy this notice to the court: *Poplar Housing & Regeneration Community Association Ltd v Donoghue* [2001] EWCA Civ 595; [2002] Q.B. 48; [2001] 4 All E.R. 604; [2001] 3 W.L.R. 183, CA. "The Crown" means a person named in a list under the Crown Proceedings Act 1947 s.17, *ibid.* See e.g. *Wilkinson v Kitzinger & Attorney General (Lord Chancellor Intervening)* [2006] EWHC 2022 (Fam); [2007] 1 F.L.R. 295; [2007] 1 F.C.R. 183; [2006] H.R.L.R. 36.

### *PUBLIC AUTHORITIES*

## Acts of public authorities

**6.**—(1) It is unlawful for a public authority to act in a way which is incompatible with a Convention right. **3D–23**

(2) Subsection (1) does not apply to an act if—

(a) as the result of one or more provisions of primary legislation, the authority could not have acted differently; or

(b) in the case of one or more provisions of, or made under, primary legislation which cannot be read or given effect in a way which is compatible with the Convention rights, the authority was acting so as to give effect to or enforce those provisions.

***Paragraph numbers marked with a "+" can be found online and on CD.***

(3) In this section "public authority" includes—

(a) a court or tribunal, and

(b) any person certain of whose functions are functions of a public nature,

but does not include either House of Parliament or a person exercising functions in connection with proceedings in Parliament.

(4) [Omitted]

(5) In relation to a particular act, a person is not a public authority by virtue only of subsection (3)(b) if the nature of the act is private.

(6) "An act" includes a failure to act but does not include a failure to—

(a) introduce in, or lay before, Parliament a proposal for legislation; or

(b) make any primary legislation or remedial order.

**3D–23.1** *Note* —Amended by the Constitutional Reform Act 2005 s.40 Sch.11 para.1 with effect from October 1, 2009 (SI 2009/1604).

**Section 6(1)**

**3D–24** Section 6(1) only applies to territory to which relevant provisions of the law have been extended by the United Kingdom: *R (on the application of Quark Fishing Limited) v Secretary of State for Foreign & Commonwealth Affairs* [2005] UKHL 57; [2005] 3 W.L.R. 837.

As to whether the Court should declare that a Defendant has acted in breach of s.6, compare the approaches of Simon Brown and Carnwarth L.JJ. in *R. (on the application of Purja) v Ministry of Defence* [2003] EWCA Civ 1345; [2004] 1 W.L.R. 289; [2004] U.K.H.R.R. 309; *The Times*, October 16, 2003. See also the decision of the House of Lords in *MB v Secretary of State for the Home Department* [2007] UKHL 46; [2008] 2 A.C. 440; [2008] 3 W.L.R. 681.

**Section 6(1) and 6(3)**

**3D–25** As to the meaning of "public authority" see *YL v Birmingham City Council* [2007] UKHL 27; [2008] 1 A.C. 95; [2007] 3 W.L.R. 112; [2007] 3 All E.R. 957. See too *Poplar Housing & Regeneration Community Association Limited v Donoghue* [2001] EWCA Civ 395; [2002] Q.B. 48; [2001] 3 W.L.R. 183 CA; *Austin Hall Building Ltd v Buckland Securities* [2001] B.L.R. 272; *R (on the application of A) v Partnerships in Care Ltd* [2002] EWHC 529; [2002] 1 W.L.R. 2610; *R. (on the application of Heather) v Leonard Cheshire Foundation* [2002] EWCA Civ 366; [2002] 2 All E.R. 936; [2002] H.R.L.R. 30; [2002] U.K.H.R.R. 883, *Aston Cantlow & Wilmcote with Billesley Parochial Church Council v Wallbank* [2003] UKHL 37; [2004] 1 A.C. 546; *Hampshire CC v Beer (t/a Hammer Trout Farm) sub nom. R. (on the application of Beer (t/a Hammer Trout Farm)) v Hampshire Farmers Markets Ltd* [2003] EWCA Civ 1056; [2004] 1 W.L.R. 233; [2004] U.K.H.R.R. 727; *Re Malcolm; Malcolm v Benedict Mackenzie (A Firm)* [2004] EWCA Civ 1748; [2005] 1 W.L.R. 1238 at [30]; *R. (on the application of West) v Lloyds of London* [2004] EWCA Civ 506; [2004] 3 All E.R. 251; [2004] 2 All E.R. (Comm) 1; *Cameron v Network Rail Infrastructure Ltd (formerly Railtrack Plc)* [2006] EWHC 1133; [2007] 1 W.L.R. 163 at [29] and *London & Quadrant Housing Trust v Weaver* [2009] EWCA Civ 587; [2009] 4 All E.R. 865; [2009] H.R.L.R. 40; [2009] B.L.G.R. 962. For the meaning of "public authority" under the provisions of the Freedom of Information Act 2000 see *Sugar v British Broadcasting Corporation* [2009] UKHL 9; [2009] 1 W.L.R. 430.

**Section 6(2)**

**3D–26** As to the extent and effect of s.6(2), see *Ghaidan v Ghodin-Mendoza* [2004] UKHL 30; [2004] 2 A.C. 557; [2004] 3 W.L.R. 113 at para.18; *Hooper v Department for Work & Pensions* [2005] UKHL 29 at paras 49–51.

Section 6(2) disapplies s.6(1) only if the public authority is acting so as to give effect to one or more provisions of primary legislation which cannot be read or given effect in a way which is compatible with Convention rights, having read the legislation, under s.3(1), in a way which is, if possible, compatible with the Convention: see *Brown v Stott* [2001] 2 W.L.R. 817, [2001] 2 All E.R. 97, per Lord Roger.

As to the effect of a finding that s.6(2) applies on the exercise of another power, see *R. (on the application of Morris) v Westminster City Council (No.3)* [2005] EWCA Civ 1184; [2006] 1 W.L.R. 505; [2005] H.R.L.R. 43; [2006] U.K.H.R.R. 165, paras 53–55 and 82.

The fact that a statute provides a specific scheme of enforcement by reference to specified public authorities does not confine any s.6(1) action to those bodies: *Marcic v Thames Water Utilities* [2003] UKHL 66; [2004] 2 A.C. 42; [2004] 1 All E.R. 135; [2003] 3 W.L.R. 1603, HL.

**Section 6(3)**

The fact that courts are public authorities under s.6(1) may affect the approach they adopt in proceedings between two private bodies: for example, in the approach they take to determining whether to award an interim injunction to give effect to Arts 8 and 10 of the Convention: *A v B plc* [2002] EWCA Civ 337; [2003] Q.B. 195; [2002] 3 W.L.R. 542. **3D–27**

**Section 6(4)**

Subsection (4) provided that "Parliament" in subs.(3) did not include the House of Lords in its judicial capacity. Upon the establishment of the Supreme Court of the United Kingdom this subsection was omitted by the Constitutional Reform Act 2005 s.40 Sch.9 para.66. **3D–27.1**

## Proceedings

**7.**—(1) A person who claims that a public authority has acted (or proposes to act) in a way which is made unlawful by section 6(1) may— **3D–28**

(a) bring proceedings against the authority under this Act in the appropriate court or tribunal, or

(b) rely on the Convention right or rights concerned in any legal proceedings,

but only if he is (or would be) a victim of the unlawful act.

(2) In subsection (1)(a) "appropriate court or tribunal" means such court or tribunal as may be determined in accordance with rules; and proceedings against an authority include a counterclaim or similar proceeding.

(3) If the proceedings are brought on an application for judicial review, the applicant is to be taken to have a sufficient interest in relation to the unlawful act only if he is, or would be, a victim of that act.

(4) If the proceedings are made by way of a petition for judicial review in Scotland, the applicant shall be taken to have title and interest to sue in relation to the unlawful act only is he is, or would be, a victim of that act.

(5) Proceedings under subsection (1)(a) must be brought before the end of—

(a) the period of one year beginning with the date on which the act complained of took place; or

(b) such longer period as the court or tribunal considers equitable having regard to all the circumstances,

but that is subject to any rule imposing a stricter time limit in relation to the procedure in question.

(6) In subsection (1)(b) "legal proceedings" includes—

(a) proceedings brought by or at the instigation of a public authority; and

(b) an appeal against the decision of a court or tribunal.

(7) For the purposes of this section, a person is a victim of an unlawful act only if he would be a victim for the purposes of Article 34 of the Convention if proceedings were brought in the European Court of Human Rights in respect of that act.

(8) Nothing in this Act creates a criminal offence.

(9) In this section "rules" means—

(a) in relation to proceedings before a court or tribunal outside Scotland, rules made by the Lord Chancellor or the Secretary of State for the purposes of this section or rules of court,

(b) in relation to proceedings before a court or tribunal in Scotland, rules made by the Secretary of State for those purposes,

(c) in relation to proceedings before a tribunal in Northern Ireland—

(i) which deals with transferred matters; and

(ii) for which no rules made under paragraph (a) are in force, rules made by a Northern Ireland department for those purposes,

and includes provision made by order under section 1 of the Courts and Legal Services Act 1990.

(10) In making rules regard must be had to section 9.

(11) The Minister who has power to make rules in relation to a particular tribunal may, to the extent he considers it necessary to ensure that the tribunal can provide an appropriate remedy in relation to an act (or proposed act) of a public authority which is (or would be) unlawful as a result of section 6(1), by order add to—

(a) the relief or remedies which the tribunal may grant; or

(b) the grounds on which it may grant any of them.

(12) An order made under subsection (11) may contain such incidental, supplemental, consequential or transitional provision as the Minister making it considers appropriate.

(13) "The Minister" includes the Northern Ireland department concerned.

**3D–29** *Note* —Amended by SI 2003/1887 and SI 2005/3429.

**Sections 7(1) "public authority"**

**3D–30** As to meaning of public authority, see para.3D–25 above (*Birmingham City Council* [2007] UKHL 27; [2008] 1 A.C. 95; [2007] 3 W.L.R. 112; [2007] 3 All E.R. 957).

**Section 7(1), 7(3) and 7(7) "victim"**

**3D–31** As to the meaning of "victim" in art.34 (formerly art.25) of the Convention, see: Lester, Pannick and Herberg, *Human Rights Law & Practice, 3rd edn* (LexisNexis, 2009) para 2.7.2 and Wadham, Mountfield, Gallagher and Prochaska, *Blackstone's Guide to the Human Rights Act 1998, 5th edn* (OUP, 2009) paras 4.20–4.23. See too *Director General of Fair Trading v Proprietary Association of Great Britain* [2001] EWCA Civ 1217; [2002] 1

W.L.R. 269 (CA) (association could not be a "victim" where its rights were not affected and where it had not been formally declared to be the representative of its members' interests). A person may continue to claim to be a victim where there is a continuing violation of a positive procedural obligation, even if he has received compensation for feelings of frustration, distress and anxiety from the ECHR: *Re McKerr* [2004] UKHL 12; [2004] 1 W.L.R. 807; [2004] 2 All E.R. 409; [2004] N.I. 212.

**Section 7(1)(a) and 7(2) "appropriate court or tribunal"**

This is determined by the subject matter of the claim, and rules issued under the Act. See the Civil Procedure (Amendment No.4) Rules 2000 (SI 2000/2092) concerning procedure for treatment of human rights issues in the Administrative Court; the Family Proceedings (Amendment) Rules 2000 (SI 2000/2267) for family courts; Pt 33 CPR and Practice Direction 30 concerning transfer between courts; Criminal Appeals (Amendment) Rules 2000 (SI 2000/2036) concerning human rights issues in criminal courts; and the House of Lords: Practice Directions and Standing Orders Applicable to Civil Appeals and Practice Directions and Standing Orders Applicable to Criminal Appeals. **3D–32**

**Practice Directions and Standard Orders Applicable to Civil Appeals and Practice Directions and Standing Orders Applicable to Criminal Appeals**

It is not necessary to transfer proceedings to the High Court merely because a breach of a Convention right is alleged, or where there is a claim for a declaration of incompatibility if it has no chance of success: *V (A Child) (Care Proceedings: Human Rights Claims, Re* [2004] EWCA Civ 54; [2004] 1 W.L.R. 1433; [2004] 1 All E.R. 997; [2004] 1 F.W.L.R. 944. **3D–33**

For employment claims where a declaration of incompatibility may be sought see *Whittaker v Watson (t/a P & M Watson Haulage)* [2002] I.C.R. 1244; [2002] 67 B.M.L.R. 28.

The Proscribed Organisation Appeals Commission is the appropriate tribunal in relation to matters related to proscription of a terrorist organisation under the Terrorism Act 2000: *R (Kurdistan Workers' Party) v Secretary of State for the Home Department* [2002] EWHC 644 (Admin); [2002] A.C.D. 99. See the Proscribed Organisations Appeal Commission (Human Rights Act Proceedings) Rules 2006 (SI 2006/2298).

**Section 7(2)**

In *Anufrijeva v Southwark LBC* [2003] EWCA Civ 1406; [2004] Q.B. 1124; [2004] 2 W.L.R. 613; [2004] 1 All E.R. 833, the Court of Appeal gave guidance as to the approach in considering claims for damages for breaches of Convention rights involving maladministration. The Court also laid down the following procedural guidelines: **3D–34**

(i) Courts should look critically at any attempt to recover HRA damages for maladministration by any procedure other than judicial review.

(ii) A claim for damages alone cannot be brought by judicial review (r.54.3(2)) but it should still be brought in the Administrative Court by an ordinary claim. (see also para.53). Note, however, that this refers only to an ordinary claim before the Administrative Court, that is to say a claim asserting breach of a public law duty (i.e. maladministration) which requires permission to enable it to proceed: *Andrews v Reading BC* [2004] EWHC 970; [2005] Env. L.R. 2; [2004]; [2004] U.K.H.R.R. 599, para.9 (Collins J).

(iii) Before giving permission to apply for judicial review, the Administrative Court judge should require the claimant to explain why it would not be more appropriate to use any available internal complaint procedure or proceed by making a claim to the Parliamentary or Local Government Ombudsman at least in the first instance.

(iv) If there is a legitimate claim for other relief, permission should if appropriate be limited to that relief and consideration given to deferring permission for the damages claim, adjourning or staying that claim until use has been made of ADR, whether by a reference to a mediator or an ombudsman or otherwise, or remitting that claim to a district judge or master if it cannot be dismissed summarily on grounds that in any event an award of damages is not required to achieve just satisfaction.

(v) It is hoped that in future, claims that have to be determined by the courts can be determined by the appropriate level of judge in a summary manner by the judge reading the relevant evidence. The citing of more than three authorities should be justified and the hearing should be limited to half a day except in exceptional circumstances.

These guidelines may create certain practical difficulties and, it is suggested, may not be appropriate outside the area to which the cases related, namely allegations of breaches of positive obligations in the social welfare and immigration fields, arising out of delay caused by maladministration.

**Section 7(5)**

3D–34.1 See *Dunn v Parole Board* [2008] EWCA Civ 374; [2008] H.R.L.R. 32 and [2008] U.K.H.R.R. 711. The defence under s.7(5) is a limitation defence in the ordinary sense and does not limit the jurisdiction of the court: see *M(A Child) v Ministry of Justice* [2009] EWCA Civ 419.

**Section 7(6)(b)**

3D–35 Proceedings brought by or at the instigation of a public authority include not only the trial but also a victim's appeal in such proceedings: *R. v DPP Ex p. Kebilene* [2000] 2 A.C. 326; [1999] 3 W.L.R. 972; [1999] 4 All E.R. 801, per Lord Steyn.

As to the requirements of a statement of case relying on the Human Rights Act 1998 see PD 16, para.15.1 As to the requirements of an appellant's notice see PD 52, paras 5.1A and 5.1B.

Applications for judicial review are not brought by or at the instigation of a public authority: *R. v Haringey LBC Ex p. Ben-Abdelaziz* [2001] EWCA Civ 809; [2001] 1 W.L.R. 1485; [2001] A.C.D. 88.

**Section 7(9)**

3D–36 The power to make rules under this subsection for England and Wales is exercisable by statutory instrument: see s.20(2). It can be annulled by resolution of either House of Parliament: see ss.20(5) and 20(7).

**Section 7(11)**

3D–37 For the procedure for making orders under this sub-section, see s.20(4).

## Judicial remedies

3D–38 8.—(1) In relation to any act (or proposed act) of a public authority which the court finds is (or would be) unlawful, it may grant such relief or remedy, or make such order, within its powers as it considers just and appropriate.

(2) But damages may be awarded only by a court which has power to award damages, or to order the payment of compensation, in civil proceedings.

(3) No award of damages is to be made unless, taking account of all the circumstances of the case, including—

(a) any other relief or remedy granted, or order made, in relation to the act in question (by that or any other court), and

(b) the consequences of any decision (of that or any other court) in respect of that act,

the court is satisfied that the award is necessary to afford just satisfaction to the person in whose favour it is made.

(4) In determining—

(a) whether to award damages, or

(b) the amount of an award,

the court must take into account the principles applied by the

European Court of Human Rights in relation to the award of compensation under Article 41 of the Convention.

(5) A public authority against which damages are awarded is to be treated—

(a) in Scotland, for the purposes of section 3 of the Law Reform (Miscellaneous Provisions) (Scotland) Act 1940 as if the award were made in an action of damages in which the authority has been found liable in respect of loss or damage to the person to whom the award is made;

(b) for the purposes of the Civil Liability (Contribution) Act 1978 as liable in respect of damage suffered by the person to whom the award is made.

(6) In this section—

"court" includes a tribunal;

"damages" means damages for an unlawful act of a public authority; and

"unlawful" means unlawful under section 6(1).



Remedies available under s.8 of the Act are all those within the court's powers, unconstrained by any new principles except in relation to damages, where ss.8(2)–8(4) apply. **3D–39**

**Sections 8(3) and 8(4)**

As to the meaning of "just satisfaction", the principles applied by the ECHR must be taken into account (though they are not binding). **3D–40**

A domestic court should not award damages under s.8 unless it is satisfied it is necessary to do so. Damages under s.8 should only be awarded if, taking into account other awards which could be made under different heads, it is necessary to do so in order to afford just satisfaction: see *Dobson v Thames Water Utilities Ltd* [2009] EWCA Civ 28; [2009] 3 All ER 319; [2009] UKHRR 617. A causal connection is required between the violation and the loss for which compensation is claimed (see *R. (on the application of Greenfield) v Secretary of State for the Home Department* [2005] UKHL 14; [2005] 1 W.L.R. 637; [2005] 2 All E.R. 240; [2005] H.R.L.R. 13, per Lord Bingham, para.11). The Court of Appeal gave guidelines as to the award of damages in *Anufrijeva v Southwark LBC* [2003] EWCA Civ 1406; [2004] Q.B. 1124; [2004] 2 W.L.R. 613; [2004] 1 All E.R. 833. The Court made clear its view that damages are not available as of right like damages for tort, but only as a discretionary remedy of last resort. The guiding remedial principle is *restitutio in integrum*, so that the claimant should, so far as possible, be put in the position in which he would have found himself if his Convention rights had not been infringed. However, account must first be taken of the effect of any other remedies which the court has already been able to provide. Any remaining significant pecuniary loss caused by the breach should usually be assessed and awarded; but caution is to be exercised when deciding whether to award damages for non-pecuniary loss, and if so how much. The consequences of the breach must be serious, the damage must be more than distress and frustration, and the scale and manner of the violation can be taken into account. In cases of maladministration, awards by the Parliamentary or Local Government Ombudsman may be the only guide. The Court of Appeal also approved the approach of Sullivan J. in *R. (on the application of Bernard) v Enfield LBC* [2002] EWHC 2282; [2003] H.R.L.R. 4; [2003] U.K.H.R.R. 148, where damages were awarded a severely disabled woman and her husband-carer, who had been left in unsuitable accommodation for 20 months in breach of art.8. **3D–41**

In *R. (on the application of H) v Secretary of State for the Home Department* [2003] UKHL 1; [2003] H.R.L.R. 570; [2003] 1 W.L.R. 411; [2003] 1 All E.R. 497, the House of Lords declined to award damages to a mental health patient since the violation had been publicly acknowledged and his right had been vindicated, the law had been amended in a way which should prevent similar violations in future, and he had not been the victim of unlawful detention, which art.5 is intended to avoid. For analysis of the principles applied in cases involving loss of opportunity or distress see *Re Cf (A Child), Sub Nom Re P; P v South Gloucestershire Council; Re C (Breach of Human Rights: Damages); Re P* [2007] EWCA Civ 2; [2007] 1 F.L.R. 1957.

Reported cases in which HRA damages have been awarded include *R. (Bernard) v Enfield LBC* (above); *R. (KB) v Mental Health Review Tribunal* [2003] EWHC 193; [2004] Q.B. 936; [2003] 3 W.L.R. 185; [2003] 2 All E.R. 209 and *Van Colle v Chief Constable of Hertfordshire* [2006] EWHC 360; [2006] 3 All E.R. 963; [2006] 1 F.C.R. 755; [2006] H.R.L.R. 25 and [2007] EWCA Civ 325 though the *Van Colle* decision on liability was overturned by the House of Lords: see *Chief Constable of Hertfordshire v Van Colle* [2008] UKHL 50; [2009] 1 A.C. 225, [2008] 3 W.L.R. 598; [2008] 3 All E.R. 977.

For authority on obligation of the courts to ensure effective protection of fundamental rights and to fashion new remedies where necessary see *Gairy v Attorney General of Grenada*, [2001] UKPC 30; [2001] 3 W.L.R. 779, PC. The limitation in s.21(1) read with s.38(2) of the Crown Proceedings Act 1947 must now be reading accordance with the provisions of the Human Rights Act.

## Judicial acts

**3D–42** **9.**—(1) Proceedings under section 7(1)(a) in respect of a judicial act may be brought only—

(a) by exercising a right of appeal;

(b) on any application (in Scotland a petition) for judicial review; or

(c) in such other forum as may be prescribed by rules.

(2) That does not affect any rule of law which prevents a court from being the subject of judicial review.

(3) In proceedings under this Act in respect of a judicial act done in good faith, damages may not be awarded otherwise than to compensate a person to the extent required by Article 5(5) of the Convention.

(4) An award of damages permitted by subsection (3) is to be made against the Crown, but no award may be made unless the appropriate person, if not a party to the proceedings, is joined.

(5) In this section—

"appropriate person" means the Minister responsible for the court concerned, or a person or government department nominated by him;

"court" includes a tribunal;

"judge" includes a member of a tribunal, a justice of the peace and a clerk or other officer entitled to exercise the jurisdiction of a court;

"judicial act" means a judicial act of a court and includes an act done on the instructions, or on behalf, of a judge; and

"rules" has the same meaning as in section 7(9).

**3D–43** As to evidence in a claim in respect of a judicial act, see CPR r.33.9.

It is arguable that in *R. v Director General of Fair Trading v Proprietary Association of Great Britain* [2001] EWCA Civ. 1217; [2002] 1 W.L.R. 269, CA, the court should have found that there was a breach of ECHR art.6(1) arising out of the lack of independence of the first instance court, but refused the application for costs on the basis of s.9(3).

**Section 9(2)**

**3D–44** See s.29(3) of the Senior CourtsAct 1981. Considered in *R. v DPP Ex p. Kebilene*

***Paragraph numbers marked with a "+" can be found online and on CD.***

[2000] 2 A.C. 326; [1999] 3 W.L.R. 972; [1999] 4 All E.R. 801. See also *R. v Hertfordshire CC Ex p. Green Environmental Industries Ltd* [2000] 2 A.C. 412; [2000] 2 W.L.R. 373; [2000] 1 All E.R. 733, per Lord Cooke of Thorndon and Lord Hobhouse of Woodborough.

### *REMEDIAL ACTION*

## Power to take remedial action

**10.**—(1) This section applies if— 3D-45

(a) a provision of legislation has been declared under section 4 to be incompatible with a Convention right and, if an appeal lies—

(i) all persons who may appeal have stated in writing that they do not intended to do so;

(ii) the time for bringing an appeal has expired and no appeal has been brought within that time; or

(iii) an appeal brought within that time has been determined or abandoned; or

(b) it appears to a Minister of the Crown or Her Majesty in Council that, having regard to a finding of the European Court of Human Rights made after the coming into force of this section in proceedings against the United Kingdom, a provision of legislation is incompatible with an obligation of the United Kingdom arising from the Convention.

(2) If a Minister of the Crown considers that there are compelling reasons for proceeding under this section, he may by order make such amendments to the legislation as he considers necessary to remove the incompatibility.

(3) If, in the case of subordinate legislation, a Minister of the Crown considers—

(a) that it is necessary to amend the primary legislation under which the subordinate legislation in question was made, in order to enable the incompatibility to be removed; and

(b) that there are compelling reasons for proceeding under this section,

he may by order make such amendments to the primary legislation as he considers necessary.

(4) This section also applies where the provision in question is in subordinate legislation and has been quashed, or declared invalid, by reason of incompatibility with a Convention right and the Minister proposes to proceed under paragraph 2(b) of Schedule 2.

(5) If the legislation is an Order in Council, the power conferred by subsection (2) or (3) is exercisable by Her Majesty in Council.

(6) In this section "legislation" does not include a Measure of the Church Assembly or of the General Synod of the Church of England.

(7) Schedule 2 makes further provision about remedial orders.

3D–45.1 A declaration of incompatibility may serve a useful purpose even if the government has already indicated an intention to change the law. See *Bellinger v Bellinger* (2003) UKHL 21; [2003] 2 A.C. 467.

### *OTHER RIGHTS AND PROCEEDINGS*

## Safeguard for existing human rights

3D–46 **11.** A person's reliance on a Convention right does not restrict—

(a) any other right or freedom conferred on him by or under any law having effect in any part of the United Kingdom; or

(b) his right to make any claim or bring any proceedings which he could make or bring apart from sections 7 to 9.

3D–46.1 See *R. (Morgan Grenfell) v Special Commissioner of Income Tax* [2001] EWCA Civ 329; [2003] 1 A.C. 563; *R. (Wooder) v Feggetter* [2002] EWCA Civ 554; [2003] Q.B. 549, and *C plc v P* [2006] EWHC 1226 Ch; [2006] Ch. 549.

## Freedom of expression

3D–47 **12.**—(1) This section applies if a court is considering whether to grant any relief which, if granted might affect the exercise of the Convention right to freedom of expression.

(2) If the person against whom the application for relief is made ("the respondent") is neither present nor represented, no such relief is to be granted unless the court is satisfied—

(a) that the applicant has taken all practicable steps to notify the respondent; or

(b) that there are compelling reasons why the respondent should not be notified.

(3) No such relief is to be granted so as to restrain publication before trial unless the court is satisfied that the applicant is likely to establish that publication should not be allowed.

(4) The court must have particular regard to the importance of the Convention right to freedom of expression and, where the proceedings relate to material which the respondent claims, or which appears to the court, to be journalistic, literary or artistic material (or to conduct connected with such material), to—

(a) the extent to which—

(i) the material has, or is about to, become available to the public; or

(ii) it is, or would be, in the public interest for the material to be published;

(b) any relevant privacy code.

(5) In this section—

"court" includes a tribunal; and

"relief" includes any remedy or order (other than in criminal proceedings).

3D–48 The Court of Appeal gave guidance as to the application of s.12 in *A v B Plc* [2002] EWCA Civ 337; [2003] Q.B. 195; [2002] H.R.L.R. 25. See the approach of the Court of Appeal in *Clayton v Clayton* [2006] EWCA Civ 878. See too *Re Ward; BBC v CAFCASS Legal* [2007] EWHC 616 (Fam).

***Paragraph numbers marked with a "+" can be found online and on CD.***

For the procedure to be followed in seeking to exclude the media from family law proceedings, see *Re (X) (A Child)* [2009] EWCA 1728, Fam. **3D–48.1**

**Section 12(3)**

In *Cream Holdings Ltd v Bannerjee* [2004] UKHL 44; [2005] 1 A.C. 253 it was held that, at this interlocutory stage, the test of likelihood was higher than the normal threshold for the grant of an interlocutory injunction in *American Cyanamid v Ethicon Ltd* [1975] A.C. 396 (whether the claim had a "real prospect" of success) but not so high as being that the claim was "more likely than not" to succeed, which standard was unworkable in practice. The standard is a flexible one: the degree of likelihood of success at trial needed to satisfy s.12(3) must depend on the circumstances. There is no automatic priority, or presumption that art.10 ECHR has greater weight than art.8, and the court should evaluate whether it is necessary in any given case to qualify the one right in order to protect the other: *Campbell v MGN Limited* [2004] UKHL 22; [2004] 2 A.C. 457; [2004] 2 W.L.R. 1232, para.55 (Lord Hoffmann) and para.141 (Baroness Hale). See also *Douglas v Hello! Ltd* [2001] Q.B. 967, para.150 per Keene L.J. and *Mahmud v Galloway & McKay* [2006] EWHC 1286; [2006] E.M.L.R. 26.See also *Boehringer Ingelheim Ltd v Vetplus Ltd* [2007] EWCA Civ 583; [2007] Bus. L.R. 1456; [2007] H.R.L.R. 33. **3D–49**

**Section 12(4)**

The court cannot have "particular regard" to art.10 without having regard to the qualifications in art.10(2), such as the rights and freedoms of others: *Douglas v Hello! Ltd (No.1)* [2001] Q.B. 967, per Sedley L.J., para.133. Thus, the sub-section does not give either art.8 or 10 pre-eminence over the other: *S (A Child) (Identification: Restrictions on Publication), Re* [2004] UKHL 47; [2005] 1 A.C. 593; [2004] 3 W.L.R. 1129, Hale L.J. When the values of two rights are in conflict, it is necessary to focus intensely on their comparative importance. This includes consideration of the justifications for interfering with or restricting each right and the application of the proportionality test: *A Local Authority v PD* [2005] EWHC 1832; [2005] E.M.L.R. 35. See too *CC v AB* [2006] EWHC 3083. **3D–50**

The fact that an injunction will interfere with freedom of the press is of particular importance: *A v B Plc* [2002] EWCA Civ 337; [2003] Q.B. 195; [2002] 3 W.L.R. 542; [2002] All E.R. 545, para.11(iv). The reference to the "public interest" does not mean that the court is justified in interfering where there is no identifiable special public interest in any particular material to be published. Any interference with publication must be justified: *ibid.*, para.11(v). "Any relevant privacy code" includes the Press Complaints Commission Code of Practice, but this is only one factor. Courts should discourage advocates from seeking to rely on individual PCC decisions: *ibid.*, paras 11(xiv) and 11(xv). Where the balance does not clearly point in either direction, interim relief should be refused: *ibid.*, para.12. Note that although the lack of media challenge to an application does not in itself justify the grant of an order interfering with the rights of the press, it nevertheless demonstrates that the press does not believe that a significant inhibition of the exercise of its rights under art.10 exists: *Maxine Carr v News Group Newspapers Ltd* [2005] EWHC 971, QB. See also Paul Dougan "Anonymity Orders and Media Censorship in the 'New Era' of Human Rights", Ent. L.R. 2005, 16(6), 150–152.

## Freedom of thought, conscience and religion

**13.**—(1) If a court's determination of any question arising under this Act might affect the exercise by a religious organisation (itself or its members collectively) of the Convention right to freedom of thought, conscience and religion, it must have particular regard to the importance of that right. **3D–51**

(2) In this section, "court" includes a tribunal.

See *R. (Williamson) v Secretary of State for Education* [2002] EWCA Civ 1926, [2003] Q.B. 1300 (also discussed in HL, but discussion of s.13 in CA); *R. (Amicus) v Secretary of State for Trade & Industry* [2004] EWHC 860 Admin, [2004] E.L.R. 311; *R. (Playfoot) v Governing Body of Millais School* [2007] EWHC 1698 Admin; [2007] 3 F.C.R. 754, [2007] E.L.R. 489 and *Surayanda v Welsh Ministers* [2007] EWCA Civ 893. **3D–51.1**

***Paragraph numbers marked with a "+" can be found online and on CD.***



HUMAN RIGHTS

## Derogations

3D–52 **14.**—(1) In this Act "designated derogation" means any derogation by the United Kingdom from an Article of the Convention, or of any protocol to the Convention, which is designated for the purposes of this Act in an order made by the Secretary of State.

(2) The derogation referred to in subsection (1)(a) is set out in Part I of Schedule 3.

(3) If a designated derogation is amended or replaced it ceases to be a designated derogation.

(4) But subsection (3) does not prevent the Secretary of State from exercising his power under subsection (1) to make a fresh designation order in respect of the Article concerned.

(5) The Secretary of State must by order make such amendments to Schedule 3 as he considers appropriate to reflect—

(a) any designation order; or

(b) the effect of subsection (3).

(6) A designation order may be made in anticipation of the making by the United Kingdom of a proposed derogation.

3D–53 *Note*—The text of the UK's derogation is contained in Sch.3.

The power to make such an order is exercisable by statutory instrument: s.20(1). For procedure for making of an order under this section, see s.20(3).

Amended by the Secretary of State for Constitutional Affairs Order 2003 (SI 2003/1884) Sch.2, para.10.

The original derogation in Pt I of Sch.3 of the Act as enacted was deleted by the Human Rights Act (Amendment) Order 2001 (SI 2001/1216). A new derogation from ECHR art.5 was designated in order to enact Pt IV of the Anti-Terrorism Crime and Security Act 2001. This was contained in the Human Rights Act 1998 (Designated Derogation) Order 2001 (SI 2001/3644). However, that Order was quashed by the House of Lords in *A v Secretary of State for the Home Department* [2005] UKHL 71, [2006] 2 A.C. 221; [2005] 3 W.L.R. 1249; [2006] 1 All E.R. 575; [2006] H.R.L.R. 6; [2006] U.K.H.R.R. 225. Part IV of the Anti-Terrorism Crime and Security Act 2001 was repealed by the Prevention of Terrorism Act 2005, with effect from March 14, 2005, and the Human Rights Act 1998 (Amendment) Order 2005 (SI 2005/1071), of April 8, 2005, reflected the withdrawal of the derogation from art.5 in response to this.

## Reservations

3D–54 **15.**—(1) In this Act, "designated reservation" means—

(a) the United Kingdom's reservation to Article 2 of the First Protocol to the Convention; and

(b) any other reservation by the United Kingdom to an Article of the Convention, or of any protocol to the Convention, which is designated for the purposes of this Act in an order made by the Secretary of State.

(2) The text of the reservation referred to in subsection (1)(a) is set out in Part II of Schedule 3.

(3) If a designated reservation is withdrawn wholly or in part it ceases to be a designated reservation.

(4) But subsection (3) does not prevent the Secretary of State from exercising his power under subsection (1)(b) to make a fresh designation order in respect of the Article concerned.

(5) The Secretary of State must by order make such amendments to this Act as he considers appropriate to reflect—

(a) any designation order; or

(b) the effect of subsection (3).

*Note*—The text of the UK's reservation is contained in Sch.3.

The power to make such an order is exercisable by statutory instrument: s.20(1). For procedure for making of an order under this section, see s.20(3).



## Period for which designated derogations have effect

**16.**—(1) If it has not already been withdrawn by the United Kingdom, a designated derogation ceases to have effect for the purposes of this Act, at the end of the period of five years beginning with the date on which the order designating it was made. **3D–55**

(2) At any time before the period—

(a) fixed by subsection (1), or

(b) extended by an order under this subsection,

comes to an end, the Secretary of State may by order extend it by a further period of five years.

(3) An order under section 14(1) ceases to have effect at the end of the period for consideration, unless a resolution has been passed by each House approving the order.

(4) Subsection (3) does not affect—

(a) anything done in reliance on the order; or

(b) the power to make a fresh order under section 14(1).

(5) In subsection (3) "period for consideration" means the period of forty days beginning with the day on which the order was made.

(6) In calculating the period for consideration, no account is to be taken of any time during which—

(a) Parliament is dissolved or prorogued; or

(b) both Houses are adjourned for more than four days.

(7) If a designated derogation is withdrawn by the United Kingdom, the Secretary of State must by order make such amendments to this Act as he considers are required to reflect that withdrawal.

*Note*—Amended by the Secretary of State for Constitutional Affairs Order (SI 2003/1887), Sch.2, para.10. **3D–56**

### Section 16(2)

The power to make such an order is exercisable by statutory instrument: s.20(1). For procedure for making an order under this sub-section, see s.20(4). **3D–57**

### Section 16(7)

The power to make such an order is exercisable by statutory instrument: s.20(1). For procedure for making an order under this sub-section, see s.20(3). **3D–58**

## Periodic review of designated reservations

**17.**—(1) The appropriate Minister must review the designated reservation referred to in section 15(1)(a)— **3D–59**

(a) before the end of the period of five years beginning with the date on which section 1(2) came into force; and

(b) if that designation is still in force, before the end of the period of five years beginning with the date on which the last report relating to it was laid under subsection (3).

(2) The appropriate Minister must review each of the other designated reservations (if any)—

(a) before the end of the period of five years beginning with the date on which the order designating the reservation first came into force; and

(b) if the designation is still in force, before the end of the period of five years beginning with the date on which the last report relating to it was laid under subsection (3).

(3) The Minister conducting a review under this section must prepare a report on the result of the review and lay a copy of it before each House of Parliament.

*JUDGES OF THE EUROPEAN COURT OF HUMAN RIGHTS*

## Appointment to European Court of Human Rights

3D–60 **18.**—(1) In this section "judicial office" means the office of—

(a) Lord Justice of Appeal, Justice of the High Court or Circuit judge, in England and Wales;

(b) judge of the Court of Session or sheriff, in Scotland;

(c) Lord Justice of Appeal, judge of the High Court or county court judge, in Northern Ireland.

(2) The holder of a judicial office may become a judge of the European Court of Human Rights ("the Court") without being required to relinquish his office.

(3) But he is not required to perform the duties of his judicial office while he is a judge of the Court.

(4) In respect of any period during which he is a judge of the Court—

(a) a Lord Justice of Appeal or Justice of the High Court is not to count as a judge of the relevant court for the purposes of section 2(1) or 4(1) of the Senior Courts Act 1981 (maximum number of judges) nor as a judge of the Supreme Court for the purposes of section 12(1) to (6) of that Act (salaries etc.);

(b) a judge of the Court of Session is not to count as a judge of that court for the purposes of section 1(1) of the Court of Session Act 1988 (maximum number of judges) or of section 9(1)(c) of the Administration of Justice Act 1973 ("the 1973 Act") (salaries etc.);

(c) a Lord Justice of Appeal or judge of the High Court in Northern Ireland is not to count as a judge of the relevant court for the purposes of section 2(1) or 3(1) of the

Judicature (Northern Ireland) Act 1978 (maximum number of judges) nor as a judge of the Supreme Court of Northern Ireland for the purposes of section 9(1)(d) of the 1973 Act (salaries etc.);

(d) a Circuit judge is not to count as such for the purposes of section 18 of the Courts Act 1971 (salaries etc.);

(e) a sheriff is not to count as such for the purposes of section 14 of the Sheriff Courts (Scotland) Act 1907 (salaries etc.);

(f) a county court judge of Northern Ireland is not to count as such for the purposes of section 106 of the County Courts Act (Northern Ireland) 1959 (salaries etc.).

(5) If a sheriff principal is appointed a judge of the Court, section 11(1) of the Sheriff Courts (Scotland) Act 1971 (temporary appointment of sheriff principal) applies, while he holds that appointment, as if his office is vacant.

(6) Schedule 4 makes provision about judicial pensions in relation to the holder of a judicial office who serves as a judge of the Court.

(7) The Lord Chancellor or the Secretary of State may by order make such transitional provision (including, in particular, provision for a temporary increase in the maximum number of judges) as he considers appropriate in relation to any holder of a judicial office who has completed his service as a judge of the Court.

(7A) The following paragraphs apply to the making of an order under subsection (7) in relation to any holder of a judicial office listed in subsection (1)(a)—

(a) before deciding what transitional provision it is appropriate to make, the person making the order must consult the Lord Chief Justice of England and Wales;

(b) before making the order, that person must consult the Lord Chief Justice of England and Wales.

(7B) The following paragraphs apply to the making of an order under subsection (7) in relation to any holder of a judicial office listed in subsection (1)(c)—

(a) before deciding what transitional provision it is appropriate to make, the person making the order must consult the Lord Chief Justice of Northern Ireland;

(b) before making the order, that person must consult the Lord Chief Justice of Northern Ireland.

(7C) The Lord Chief Justice of England and Wales may nominate a judicial office holder (within the meaning of section 109(4) of the Constitutional Reform Act 2005) to exercise his functions under this section.

(7D) The Lord Chief Justice of Northern Ireland may nominate any of the following to exercise his functions under this section—

(a) the holder of one of the offices listed in Schedule 1 to the Justice (Northern Ireland) Act 2002;

(b) a Lord Justice of Appeal (as defined in section 88 of that Act).

3D–61 *Note* —Amended by the Constitutional Reform Act 2005 ss.15(1) and 59, Sch.4, para.278 and Sch.11, para.1.

## PARLIAMENTARY PROCEDURE

### Statements of compatibility

3D–62 **19.**—(1) A Minister of the Crown in charge of a Bill in either House of Parliament must, before Second Reading of the Bill—

(a) make a statement to the effect that in his view the provisions of the Bill are compatible with the Convention rights ("a statement of compatibility"); or

(b) make a statement to the effect that although he is unable to make a statement of compatibility the government nevertheless wishes the House to proceed with the Bill.

(2) The statement must be in writing and be published in such manner as the Minister making it considers appropriate.

3D–63 *Note* —This section came into force on November 24, 1998: The Human Rights Act 1998 (Commencement) Order 1998 (SI 1998/2882).

3D–64 "The Convention" has been held to mean "The Convention as given effect by the Act for the time being in relation to the United Kingdom": that is, the Convention and rights of the same scope as would be perceived in Strasbourg: see.*R (on the application of Al Jedda) v Secretary of State for Defence* [2007] UKHL 58; [2008] 2 W.L.R. 31. See also *R. (Quark Shipping Ltd) v Foreign Secretary* [2005] UKHL 57; [2005] 3 W.L.R. 837 at paras 25, 32, 56, 87 and 97, paras 59–63 and 112.

## SUPPLEMENTAL

### Orders, etc., under this Act

3D–65 **20.**—(1) Any power of a Minister of the Crown to make an order under this Act is exercisable by statutory instrument.

(2) The power of the Lord Chancellor or the Secretary of State to make rules (other than rules of court) under section 2(3) or 7(9) is exercisable by statutory instrument.

(3) Any statutory instrument made under section 14, 15 or 16(7) must be laid before Parliament.

(4) No order may be made by the Lord Chancellor or the Secretary of State under section 1(4), 7(11) or 16(2) unless a draft of the order has been laid before, and approved by, each House of Parliament.

(5) Any statutory instrument made under section 18(7) or Schedule 4, or to which subsection (2) applies, shall be subject to annulment in pursuance of a resolution of either House of Parliament.

(6) The power of a Northern Ireland department to make—

(a) rules under section 2(3)(c) or 7(9)(c), or

(b) an order under section 7(11),

is exercisable by statutory rule for the purposes of the Statutory Rules (Northern Ireland) Order 1979.

(7) Any rules made under section 2(3)(c) or 7(9)(c) shall be subject to negative resolution; and section 41(6) of the Interpretation Act (Northern Ireland) 1954 (meaning of "subject to negative resolu-

tion") shall apply as if the power to make the rules were conferred by an Act of the Northern Ireland Assembly.

(8) No order may be made by a Northern Ireland department under section 7(11) unless a draft of the order has been laid before, and approved by, the Northern Ireland Assembly.

*Note* —Amended by SI 2003/1887 and SI 2005/3429. **3D-66**

## Interpretation, etc.

**21.**—(1) In this Act— **3D-67**

"amend" includes repeal and apply (with or without modification);

"the appropriate Minister" means the Minister of the Crown having charge of the appropriate authorised government department (within the meaning of the Crown Proceedings Act 1947);

"the Commission" means the European Commission of Human Rights;

"the Convention" means the Convention for the Protection of Human Rights and Fundamental Freedoms, agreed by the Council of Europe at Rome on November 4, 1950 as it has effect for the time being in relation to the United Kingdom;

"declaration of incompatibility" means a declaration under section 4;

"Minister of the Crown" has the same meaning as in the Ministers of the Crown Act 1975;

"Northern Ireland Minister" includes the First Minister and the deputy First Minister in Northern Ireland;

"primary legislation" means any—

(a) public general Act;

(b) local and personal Act;

(c) private Act;

(d) Measure of the Church Assembly;

(e) Measure of the General Synod of the Church of England;

(f) Order in Council—

(i) made in exercise of Her Majesty's Royal Prerogative;

(ii) made under section 38(1)(a) of the Northern Ireland Constitution Act 1973 of the corresponding provision of the Northern Ireland Act 1998; or

(iii) amending an Act of a kind mentioned in paragraph (a), (b) or (c); and includes an order or other instrument made under primary legislation (otherwise than by the National Assembly for Wales, Welsh Ministers, the First Minister for Wales, the Counsel General to the Welsh Assembly Government, a member of the

*Paragraph numbers marked with a "+" can be found online and on CD.*

Scottish Executive, a Northern Ireland Minister or a Northern Ireland department) to the extent to which it operates to bring one or more provisions of that legislation into force or amends any primary legislation;

"the First Protocol" means the protocol to the Convention agreed at Paris on March 20, 1952;

"the Eleventh Protocol" means the protocol to the Convention (restructuring the control machinery established by the Convention) agreed at Strasbourg on May 11, 1994;

"the Thirteenth Protocol" means the protocol to the Convention (concerning the abolition of the death penalty in all circumstances) agreed at Vilnius on 3rd May 2002;

"remedial order" means an order under section 10;

"subordinate legislation" means any—

(a) Order in Council other than one—

(i) made in exercise of Her Majesty's Royal Prerogative;

(ii) made under section 38(1)(a) of the Northern Ireland Constitution Act 1973 or the corresponding provision of the Northern Ireland Act 1998; or;

(iii) amending an Act of a kind mentioned in the definition of primary legislation;

(b) Act of the Scottish Parliament;

(ba) Measure of the National Assembly for Wales;

(bb) Act of the National Assembly for Wales;

(c) Act of the Parliament of Northern Ireland;

(d) Measure of the Assembly established under section 1 of the Northern Ireland Assembly Act 1973;

(e) Act of the Northern Ireland Assembly;

(f) order, rules, regulations, scheme, warrant, byelaw or other instrument made under primary legislation (except to the extent to which it operates to bring one or more provisions of that legislation into force or amends any primary legislation);

(g) order, rules, regulations, scheme, warrant, byelaw or other instrument made under legislation mentioned in paragraph (b), (c), (d) or (e) or made under an Order in Council applying only to Northern Ireland;

(h) order, rules, regulations, scheme, warrant, byelaw or other instrument made by a member of the Scottish Executive, Welsh Ministers, the First Minister for Wales, the Counsel General to the Welsh Assembly Government, a Northern Ireland Minister or Northern Ireland department in exercise of prerogative or other executive functions of Her Majesty which are exercisable by such a person on behalf of Her Majesty;

"transferred matters" has the same meaning as in the Northern Ireland Act 1998; and "tribunal" means any tribunal in which legal proceedings may be brought.

(2) The references in paragraphs (b) and (c) of section 2(1) to Articles are to Articles of the Convention as they had effect immediately before the coming into force of the 11th Protocol.

(3) The reference in paragraph (d) of section 2(1) to Article 46 includes a reference to Articles 32 and 54 of the Convention as they had effect immediately before the coming into force of the Eleventh Protocol.

(4) The references in section 2(1) to a report or decision of the Commission or a decision of the Committee of Ministers include references to a report or decision made as provided by paragraphs 3, 4 and 6 of Article 5 of the 11th Protocol (transitional provisions).

(5) Any liability under the Army Act 1955, the Air Force Act 1955 or the Naval Discipline Act 1957 to suffer death for an offence is replaced by a liability to imprisonment for life or any less punishment authorised by those Acts; and those Acts shall accordingly have effect with the necessary modifications.

*Note* —Amended by SI 2004/1574; and by the Government of Wales Act 2006 s.160(1), Sch.10, para.56, with effect immediately after the date of the 2007 ordinary election (see ss.3 and 161 of the 2006 Act). **3D–68**

## Short title, commencement, application and extent

**22.**—(1) This Act may be cited as the Human Rights Act 1998. **3D–69**

(2) Sections 18, 20 and 21(5) and this section come into force on the passing of this Act.

(3) The other provisions of this Act come into force on such day as the Secretary of State may by order appoint; and different days may be appointed for different purposes.

(4) Paragraph (b) of subsection (1) of section 7 applies to proceedings brought by or at the instigation of a public authority whenever the act in question took place; but otherwise that subsection does not apply to an act taking place before the coming into force of that section.

(5) This Act binds the Crown.

(6) This Act extends to Northern Ireland.

(7) Section 21(5), so far as it relates to any provision contained in the Army Act 1955, the Air Force Act 1955 or the Naval Discipline Act 1957, extends to any place to which that provision extends.

### Section 22(2) & 22(3)

The date on which the Act received Royal Assent was November 9, 1998. Section 19 came into force on November 24, 1998: The Human Rights Act 1998 (Commencement) Order 1998 (SI 1998/2882). The remainder of the Act came into force on October 2, 2000: The Human Rights Act 1998 (Commencement No 2) Order 2000 (SI 2000/1851). **3D–70**

### Section 22(4)

As to what constitutes an act "brought by or at the instigation of a public authority", see commentary to s.7, and *R. v Haringey LBC, Ex p. Ben-Abdelaziz* [2001] EWCA Civ **3D–71**

***Paragraph numbers marked with a "+" can be found online and on CD.***

809; [2001] 1 W.L.R. 1485; [2001] A.C.D. 88, *Advocate General for Scotland v MacDonald; Pearce v Governing Body of Mayfield School* [2003] UKHL 34; [2004] 1 All E.R. 339; *Malcolm v Mackenzie* [2004] EWHC 339; [2004] EWCA Civ 1748; [2005] 1 W.L.R. 1238 (Ch).

The object of s.22(4) is to protect defendants to proceedings brought by or at the instigation of a public authority: see *Wilson v First County Trust Ltd (No.2)* [2001] EWCA Civ 633; [2002] Q.B. 74; [2001] 3 W.L.R. 42; [2001] 3 All E.R. 229, CA, para.90.

Limited retrospective effect of s.3 may be permitted if no unfairness would be caused to any individual: *Commissioner of Police for the Metropolis v Hurst* [2005] EWCA Civ 890; [2005] 1 W.L.R. 3892; [2005] H.R.L.R. 31; [2005] U.K.H.R.R. 1259.

Acts of courts or tribunals which took place before October 2, 2000, which were required by primary legislation and which were done according to the meaning of the legislation which applied at the time are not affected by the provisions of the Act: *R. v Kansal* [2001] UKHL 62, [2002] 2 A.C. 69; [2001] 3 W.L.R. 1562 and *R. v Lyons* [2002] UKHL 44; [2003] H.R.L.R. 6. (Though *cf R. v DPPEx p Kebilene* [2000] 2 A.C. 326; [1999] 3 W.L.R. 972; [1999] 4 All E.R. 801 HL and *R. v Lambert* [2001] 3 All E.R. 577 HL).

The Act cannot be relied upon to make conduct which was lawful at the time when it took place retrospectively unlawful: see *Wainwright v Home Office* [2001] EWCA Civ 2081; [2002] Q.B. 1334, CA. However, a continuing failure to act dating from before the entry into force of the Act may become unlawful from the entry into force of the Act, though damages may only be claimed from the date of the coming into force of the Act: *Marcic v Thames Water Utilities* [2002] EWCA Civ 64 (overruled on other grounds by *Marcic v Thames Water Utilities Ltd* [2003] UKHL 66; [2004] 2 A.C. 42; [2003] 3 W.L.R. 1603; [2004] 1 All E.R. 135).

For continuing violation of positive obligations to investigate under art.2 or art.3 see *Re McKerr* [2004] UKHL 12; [2004] 1 W.L.R. 807; [2004] 2 All E.R. 409; [2004] N.I. 212.

## SCHEDULE 1

### THE ARTICLES

### PART I

### THE CONVENTION

### RIGHTS AND FREEDOMS

#### *Article 2—Right to life*

3D–72 1. Everyone's right to life shall be protected by law. No one shall be deprived of his life intentionally save in the execution of a sentence of a court following his conviction of a crime for which this penalty is provided by law.

2. Deprivation of life shall not be regarded as inflicted in contravention of this Article when it results from the use of force which is no more than absolutely necessary:

(a) in defence of any person from unlawful violence;

(b) in order to effect a lawful arrest or to prevent the escape of a person lawfully detained;

(c) in action lawfully taken for the purpose of quelling a riot or insurrection.

#### *Article 3—Prohibition of torture*

3D–73 No one shall be subjected to torture or to inhuman or degrading treatment or punishment.

#### *Article 4—Prohibition of slavery and forced labour*

3D–74 1. No one shall be held in slavery or servitude.

2. No one shall be required to perform forced or compulsory labour.

***Paragraph numbers marked with a "+" can be found online and on CD.***

3. For the purpose of this Article the term "forced or compulsory labour" shall not include:

(a) any work required to be done in the ordinary course of detention imposed according to the provisions of Article 5 of this Convention or during conditional release from such detention;

(b) any service of a military character or, in case of conscientious objectors in countries where they are recognised, service exacted instead of compulsory military service;

(c) any service exacted in case of an emergency or calamity threatening the life or well-being of the community;

(d) any work or service which forms part of normal civic obligations.

*Article 5—Right to liberty and security*

1. Everyone has the right to liberty and security of person. No one shall be deprived of his liberty save in the following cases and in accordance with a procedure prescribed by law: **3D–75**

(a) the lawful detention of a person after conviction by a competent court;

(b) the lawful arrest or detention of a person for non-compliance with the lawful order of a court or in order to secure the fulfilment of any obligation prescribed by law;

(c) the lawful arrest or detention of a person effected for the purpose of bringing him before the competent legal authority on reasonable suspicion of having committed an offence or when it is reasonably considered necessary to prevent his committing an offence or fleeing after having done so;

(d) the detention of a minor by lawful order for the purpose of educational supervision or his lawful detention for the purpose of bringing him before the competent legal authority;

(e) the lawful detention of persons for the prevention of the spreading of infectious diseases, of persons of unsound mind, alcoholics or drug addicts or vagrants;

(f) the lawful arrest or detention of a person to prevent his effecting an unauthorised entry into the country or of a person against whom action is being taken with a view to deportation or extradition.

2. Everyone who is arrested shall be informed promptly, in a language which he understands, of the reasons for his arrest and of any charge against him.

3. Everyone arrested or detained in accordance with the provisions of paragraph 1(c) of this Article shall be brought promptly before a judge or other officer authorised by law to exercise judicial power and shall be entitled to trial within a reasonable time or to release pending trial. Release may be conditioned by guarantees to appear for trial.

4. Everyone who is deprived of his liberty by arrest or detention shall be entitled to take proceedings by which the lawfulness of his detention shall be decided speedily by a court and his release ordered if the detention is not lawful.

5. Everyone who has been the victim of arrest or detention in contravention of the provisions of this Article shall have an enforceable right to compensation.

*Article 6—Right to a fair trial*

1. In the determination of his civil rights and obligations or of any criminal charge against him, everyone is entitled to a fair and public hearing within a reasonable time by an independent and impartial tribunal established by law. Judgment shall be pronounced publicly but the press and public may be excluded from all or part of the trial in the interest of morals, public order or national security in a democratic society, where the interests of juveniles or the protection of the private life of the parties so require, or to the extent strictly necessary in the opinion of the court in special circumstances where publicity would prejudice the interests of justice. **3D–76**

2. Everyone charged with a criminal offence shall be presumed innocent until proved guilty according to law.

3. Everyone charged with a criminal offence has the following minimum rights:

(a) to be informed promptly, in a language which he understands and in detail, of the nature and cause of the accusation against him;

(b) to have adequate time and facilities for the preparation of his defence;

(c) to defend himself in person or through legal assistance of his own choosing or, if he has not sufficient means to pay for legal assistance, to be given it free when the interest of justice so require;

(d) to examine or have examined witnesses against him and to obtain the attendance and examination of witnesses on his behalf under the same conditions as witnesses against him;

(e) to have the free assistance of an interpreter if he cannot understand or speak the language used in court.

*Article 7—No punishment without law*

**3D–77** 1. No one shall be held guilty of any criminal offence on account of any act or omission which did not constitute a criminal offence under national or international law at the time when it was committed. Nor shall a heavier penalty be imposed than the one that was applicable at the time the criminal offence was committed.

2. The Article shall not prejudice the trial and punishment of any person for any act or omission which, at the time when it was committed, was criminal according to the general principles of law recognised by civilised nations.

*Article 8—Right to respect for private and family life*

**3D–78** 1. Everyone has the right to respect for his private and family life, his home and his correspondence.

2. There shall be no interference by a public authority with the exercise of this right except such as is in accordance with the law and is necessary in a democratic society in the interests of national security, public safety or the economic well-being of the country, for the prevention of disorder or crime, for the protection of health or morals, or for the protection of the rights and freedoms of others.

*Article 9—Freedom of thought, conscience and religion*

**3D–79** 1. Everyone has the right to freedom of thought, conscience and religion; this right includes freedom to change his religion or belief and freedom, either alone or in community with others and in public or private, to manifest his religion or belief, in worship, teaching, practice and observance.

2. Freedom to manifest one's religion or beliefs shall be subject only to such limitations as are prescribed by law and are necessary in a democratic society in the interests of public safety, for the protection of public order, health or morals, or for the protection of the rights and freedoms of others.

*Article 10—Freedom of expression*

**3D–80** 1. Everyone has the right to freedom of expression. This right shall include freedom to hold opinions and to receive and impart information and ideas without interference by public authority and regardless of frontiers. This Article shall not prevent States from requiring the licensing of broadcasting, television or cinema enterprises.

2. The exercise of these freedoms, since it carries with it duties and responsibilities, may be subject to such formalities, conditions, restrictions or penalties as are prescribed by law and are necessary in a democratic society, in the interests of national security, territorial integrity or public safety, for the prevention of disorder or crime, for the protection of health or morals, for the protection of the reputation or rights of others, for preventing the disclosure of information received in confidence, or for maintaining the authority and impartiality of the judiciary.

*Article 11—Freedom of assembly and association*

**3D–81** 1. Everyone has the right to freedom of peaceful assembly and to freedom of association with others, including the right to formand to join trade unions for the protection of his interests.

2. No restrictions shall be placed on the exercise of these rights other than such as are prescribed by law and are necessary in a democratic society in the interests of national security or public safety, for the prevention of disorder or crime, for the

protection of health or morals or for the protection of the rights and freedoms of others. This Article shall not prevent the imposition of lawful restrictions on the exercise of these rights by members of the armed forces, of the police or of the administration of the State.

*Article 12—Right to marry*

Men and women of marriageable age have the right to marry and to found a family, according to the national laws governing the exercise of this right. **3D–82**

*Article 14—Prohibition of discrimination*

The enjoyment of the rights and freedoms set forth in this Convention shall be secured without discrimination on any ground such as sex, race, colour, language, religion, political or other opinion, national or social origin, association with a national minority, property, birth or other status. **3D–83**

*Article 16—Restrictions on political activity of aliens*

Nothing in Articles 10, 11 and 14 shall be regarded as preventing the High Contracting Parties from imposing restrictions on the political activity of aliens. **3D–84**

*Article 17—Prohibition of abuse of rights*

Nothing in this Convention may be interpreted as implying for any State, group or person any right to engage in any activity or perform any act aimed at the destruction of any of the rights and freedoms set forth herein or at their limitation to a greater extent than is provided for in the Convention. **3D–85**

*Article 18—Limitation on use of restrictions on rights*

The restrictions permitted under this Convention to the said rights and freedoms shall not be applied for any purpose other than those for which they have been prescribed. **3D–86**

## PART II

## THE FIRST PROTOCOL

*Article 1—Protection of property*

Every natural or legal person is entitled to the peaceful enjoyment of his possessions. No one shall be deprived of his possessions except in the public interest and subject to the conditions provided for by law and by the general principles of international law. **3D–87**

The preceding provisions shall not, however, in any way impair the right of a State to enforce such laws as it deems necessary to control the use of property in accordance with the general interest or to secure the payment of taxes or other contributions or penalties.

*Article 2—Right to education*

No person shall be denied the right to education. In the exercise of any functions which it assumes in relation to education and to teaching, the State shall respect the right of parents to ensure such education and teaching in conformity with their own religious and philosophical convictions. **3D–88**

*Article 3—Right to free elections*

The High Contracting Parties undertake to hold free elections at reasonable intervals by secret ballot, under conditions which will ensure the free expression of the opinion of the people in the choice of the legislature. **3D–89**

## PART III

## THE THIRTEENTH PROTOCOL

*Article 1—Abolition of the death penalty*

The death penalty shall be abolished. No one shall be condemned to such penalty or executed. **3D–90**



HUMAN RIGHTS

3D–91 *Note* —Substituted by the Human Rights Act 1998 (Amendment) Order 2004 (SI 2004/1574), art.2(3).

*Article 2—Death penalty in time of war*

3D–92 A State may make provision in its law for the death penalty in respect of acts committed in time of war or of imminent threat of war; such penalty shall be applied only in the instances laid down in the law and in accordance with its provisions. The State shall communicate to the Secretary General of the Council of Europe the relevant provisions of that law.

# European Convention on Human Rights

## *Article 1*

### *Obligation to respect human rights*

3D–93 The High Contracting Parties shall secure to everyone within their jurisdiction the rights and freedoms defined in Section I of this Convention.

* * * *

## *Article 13*

### *Right to an effective remedy*

3D–94 Everyone whose rights and freedoms as set forth in this Convention are violated shall have an effective remedy before a national authority notwithstanding that the violation has been committed by persons acting in an official capacity.

3D–95 *Editorial note* —Although not among the Convention rights to which s.1(2) of the Human Rights Act 1998 gives effect, Arts 1 and 13 of the Convention are also of significance. Their text is set out above.

***Paragraph numbers marked with a "+" can be found online and on CD.***

# 3E INSOLVENCY PROCEEDINGS

## PRACTICE DIRECTION—INSOLVENCY PROCEEDINGS

*Part One*

### 1. General

**1.1** In this Practice Direction: 3E–1

(1) "The Act" means the Insolvency Act 1986 and includes the Act as applied to limited liability partnerships by the Limited Liability Partnerships Regulations 2001;

(2) "The Insolvency Rules" means the rules for the time being in force and made under s.411 and s.412 of the Act in relation to insolvency proceedings;

(3) "CPR" means the Civil Procedure Rules and "CPR" followed by a Part or rule by number means the Part or rule with that number in those Rules;

(4) "RSC" followed by an Order by number means the Order with that number set out in Schedule 1 to the CPR;

(5) "Insolvency proceedings" means any proceedings under the Act, the Insolvency Rules, the Administration of Insolvent Estates of Deceased Persons Order 1986 (SI 1986/1999), the Insolvent Partnership Order 1986 (SI 1986/2142), the Insolvent Partnerships Order 1994 (SI 1994/2421) or the Limited Liability Partnerships Regulations 2001.

(6) Referencesto a 'company' shall include a limited liability partnership and references to a 'contributory' shall include a member of a limited liability partnership.

**1.2** This Practice Direction shall come into effect on 26th April 1999 and shall replace all previous Practice Notes and Practice Directions relating to insolvency proceedings.

**1.3** Except where the Insolvency Rules otherwise provide, service of documents in insolvency proceedings in the High Court will be the responsibility of the parties and will not be undertaken by the court.

**1.4** Where CPR Part 2.4 provides for the court to perform any act, that act may be performed by a Registrar in Bankruptcy for the purpose of insolvency proceedings in the High Court.

**1.5** A writ of execution to enforce any order made in insolvency proceedings in the High Court may be issued on the authority of a Registrar.

**1.6**(1) This paragraph applies where an insolvency practitioner ("the outgoing office holder") holds office as a liquidator, administrator, trustee or supervisor in more than one case and dies, retires from practice as an insolvency practitioner or is otherwise unable or unwilling to continue in office.

(2) A single application may be made to a Judge of the Chancery Division of the High Court by way of ordinary application in Form 7.2 for the appointment of a substitute office



INSOLVENCY

holder or office holders in all cases in which the outgoing office holder holds office, and for the transfer of each such case to the High Court for the purpose only of making such an order.

(3) The application may be made by any of the following:
 (i) the outgoing office holder (if he is able and willing to do so);
 (ii) any person who holds office jointly with the outgoing office holder;
 (iii) any person who is proposed to be appointed as a substitute for the outgoing office holder; or
 (iv) any creditor in the cases where the substitution is proposed to be made.

(4) The outgoing office holder (if he is not the applicant) and every person who holds office jointly with the office holder must be made a respondent to the application, but it is not necessary to join any other person as a respondent or to serve the application upon any other person unless the Judge or Registrar in the High Court so directs.

(5) The application should contain schedules setting out the nature of the office held, the identity of the Court currently having jurisdiction over each case and its name and number.

(6) The application must be supported by evidence setting out the circumstances which have given rise to the need to make a substitution and exhibiting the written consent to act of each person who is proposed to be appointed in place of the outgoing office holder.

(7) The Judge will in the first instance consider the application on paper and make such order as he thinks fit. In particular he may do any of the following:
 (i) make an order directing the transfer to the High Court of those cases not already within its jurisdiction for the purpose only of the substantive application;
 (ii) if he considers that the papers are in order and that the matter is straightforward, make an order on the substantive application;
 (iii) give any directions which he considers to be necessary including (if appropriate) directions for the joinder of any additional respondents or requiring the service of the application on any person or requiring additional evidence to be provided;
 (iv) if he does not himself make an order on the substantive application when the matter is first before him, give directions for the further consideration of the substantive application by himself or another Judge of the Chancery Division or adjourn the substantive application to the Registrar for him to make such order upon it as is appropriate.

(8) An order of the kind referred to in sub-paragraph (6)(i)

***Paragraph numbers marked with a "+" can be found online and on CD.***

shall follow the draft order in **Form PDIP 3** set out in the Schedule hereto and an order granting the substantive application shall follow the draft order in **Form PDIP 4** set out in the schedule hereto (subject in each case to such modifications as may be necessary or appropriate).

(9) It is the duty of the applicant to ensure that a sealed copy of every order transferring any case to the High Court and of every order which is made on a substantive application is lodged with the court having jurisdiction over each case affected by such order for filing on the court file relating to that case.

(10) It will not be necessary for the file relating to any case which is transferred to the High Court in accordance with this paragraph to be sent to the High Court unless a Judge or Registrar so directs.

## *Part Two*

## *Companies*

### 2. Advertisement of winding up petition

**2.1** Insolvency Rule 4.11(2)(b) is mandatory, and designed to ensure that the class remedy of winding up by the court is made available to all creditors, and is not used as a means of putting pressure on the company to pay the petitioner's debt. Failure to comply with the rule, without good reason accepted by the court, may lead to the summary dismissal of the petition on the return date (Insolvency Rule 4.11(5)). If the court, in its discretion, grants an adjournment, this will be on condition that the petition is advertised in due time for the adjourned hearing. No further adjournment for the purpose of advertisement will normally be granted. **3E–2**

**2.2** Copies of every advertisement published in connection with a winding up petition must be lodged with the Court as soon as possible after publication and in any event not later than the day specified in Insolvency Rule 4.14 of the Insolvency Rules 1986. This direction applies even if the advertisement is defective in any way (*e.g.* is published at a date not in accordance with the Insolvency Rules, or omits or misprints some important words) or if the petitioner decides not to pursue the petition (e.g. on receiving payment).

### 3. Certificate of compliance—time for filing

**3.1** In the High Court in order to assist practitioners and the Court the time laid down by Insolvency Rule 4.14 of the Insolvency Rules 1986, for filing a certificate of compliance and a copy of the advertisement, is hereby extended to not later than 4.30 p.m. on the Friday preceding the day on which the petition is to be heard. Applications to file the certificate and the copy advertisement after 4.30 p.m. on the Friday will only be allowed if some good reason is shown for the delay. **3E–3**

### 4. Errors in petitions

3E–4 **4.1** Applications for leave to amend errors in petitions which are discovered subsequent to a winding up order being made should be made to the Court Manager in the High Court and to the District Judge in the county court.

**4.2** Where the error is an error in the name of the company, the Court Manager in the High Court and the District Judge in the county court may make any necessary amendments to ensure that the winding up order is drawn with the correct name of the company inserted. If there is any doubt, e.g. where there might be another company in existence which could be confused with the company to be wound up, the Court Manager will refer the application to the Registrar and the District Judge may refer it to the Judge.

**4.3** Where an error is an error in the registered office of the company and any director or member of the company claims that the company was unaware of the petition by reason of it having been served at the wrong registered office, it will be open to them to apply to rescind the winding up order in the usual way.

**4.4** Where it is discovered that the company had been struck off the Register of Companies prior to the winding up order being made, the matter must be restored to the list before the order is entered to enable an order for the restoration of the name to be made as well as the order to wind up.

### 5. Distribution of business

3E–5 **5.1** The following applications shall be made direct to the Judge and, unless otherwise ordered, shall be heard in public—

(1) Applications to commit any person to prison for contempt;

(2) Applications for urgent interim relief (*e.g.* applications pursuant to s.127 of the Act prior to any winding up order being made);

(3) Applications to restrain the presentation or advertisement of a petition to wind up; or

(4) Applications for the appointment of a provisional liquidator;

(5) Petitions for administration orders or an interim order upon such a Petition;

(6) Applications after an administration order has been made pursuant to s.14(3) of the Act (for directions) or s.18(3) of the Act (to vary or discharge the order);

(7) Petitions to discharge administration orders and to wind up;

(8) Applications pursuant to s.5(3) of the Act (to stay a winding up or discharge an administration order or for directions) where a voluntary arrangement has been approved;

(9) Appeals from a decision made by a County Court or by a Registrar of the High Court.

**5.2** Subject to paragraph 5.4 below all other applications shall be made to the Registrar or the District Judge in the first instance who may give any necessary directions and may, in the exercise of his discretion, either hear and determine it himself or refer it to the Judge.

*Paragraph numbers marked with a "+" can be found online and on CD.*

**5.3** The following matters will also be heard in public—

(1) Petitions to wind up;

(2) Public examinations;

(3) All matters and applications heard by the Judge, except those referred by the Registrar or the District Judge to be heard in private or so directed by the Judge to be heard.

**5.4** In accordance with directions given by the Lord Chancellor the Registrar has authorised certain applications in the High Court to be dealt with by the Court Manager of the Companies Court, pursuant to Insolvency Rule 13.2(2). The applications are:

(1) To extend or abridge time prescribed by the Insolvency Rules in connection with winding up (Insolvency Rule 4.3 and 12.9);

(2) For substituted service of winding up petitions (Insolvency Rule 4.8(6));

(3) To withdraw petitions (Insolvency Rule 4.15);

(4) For the substitution of a petitioner (Insolvency Rule 4.19);

(5) By the Official Receiver for limited disclosure of a statement of affairs (Insolvency Rule 4.35);

(6) By the Official Receiver for relief from duties imposed upon him by the rules (Insolvency Rule 4.47);

(7) By the Official Receiver for permission to give notice of a meeting by advertisement only (Insolvency Rule 4.59);

(8) To transfer proceedings from the High Court to a County Court (Insolvency Rule 7.11);

(9) For permission to amend any originating application.

[N.B. In District Registries all such applications must be made to the District Judge].

### 6. Drawing up of orders

**6.1** The Court will draw up all orders except orders on the application of the Official Receiver or for which the Treasury Solicitor is responsible under the existing practice. **3E–6**

### 7. Rescission of a winding up order

**7.1** Any application for the rescission of a winding up order shall be made within seven days after the date on which the order was made (Insolvency Rule 7.47(4)). Notice of any such application must be given to the Official Receiver. **3E–7**

**7.2** Applications will only be entertained if made (a) by a creditor, or (b) by a contributory, or (c) by the company jointly with a creditor or with a contributory. The application must be supported by written evidence of assets and liabilities.

**7.3** In the case of an unsuccessful application the costs of the petitioning creditor, the supporting creditors and of the Official Receiver will normally be ordered to be paid by the creditor or the contributory making or joining in the application. The reason for this is that if the costs of an unsuccessful application are made payable by the company, they fall unfairly on the general body of creditors.

*Paragraph numbers marked with a "+" can be found online and on CD.*

**7.4** Cases in which the making of the winding up order has not been opposed may, if the application is made promptly, be dealt with on a statement by the applicant's legal representative of the circumstances; but apart from such cases, the court will normally require any application to be supported by written evidence.

**7.5** There is no need to issue a form of application (Form 7.2) as the petition is restored before the Court.

### 8. Restraint of presentation of a winding-up petition

3E–8 **8.1** An application to restrain presentation of a Winding-up petition must be made to the Judge by the issue of an Originating Application (Form 7.1).

*Part Three*

*Personal Insolvency—Bankruptcy*

### 9. Distribution of business

3E–9 **9.1** The following applications shall be made direct to the Judge and unless otherwise ordered shall be heard in public:

(1) Applications for the committal of any person to prison for contempt;

(2) Application for injunctions or for the modification or discharge of injunctions;

(3) Applications for interlocutory relief or directions after the matter has been referred to the Judge.

**9.2** All other applications shall be made to the Registrar or the District Judge in the first instance. He shall give any necessary directions and may, if the application is within his jurisdiction to determine, in his discretion either hear and determine it himself or refer it to the Judge.

**9.3** The following matters shall be heard in public:

(1) The public examination of debtors;

(2) Opposed applications for discharge or for the suspension or lifting of the suspension of discharge;

(3) Opposed applications for permission to be a director;

(4) In any case where the petition was presented or the receiving order or order for adjudication was made before the appointed day, those matters and applications specified in Rule 8 of the Bankruptcy Rules 1952;

(5) All matters and applications heard by the Judge, except matters and applications referred by the Registrar or the District Judge to be heard by the Judge in private or directed by the Judge to be so heard.

**9.4** All petitions presented will be listed under the name of the debtor.

**9.5** In accordance with Directions given by the Lord Chancellor the Registrar has authorised certain applications in the High Court to be dealt with by the Court Manager of the Bankruptcy Court pursuant to Insolvency Rule 13.2(2). The applications are:

(1) by petitioning creditors: to extend time for hearing petitions (s.376 of the Act).

(2) by the Official Receiver:

(a) To transfer proceedings from the High Court to a County Court (Insolvency Rule 7.13);

(b) to amend the full title of the proceedings (Insolvency Rule 6.35 and 6.47).

[N.B. In District Registries all such applications must be made to the District Judge].

## 10. Service abroad of statutory demand

**10.1** A statutory demand is not a document issued by the Court. Leave to serve out of the jurisdiction is not, therefore, required. **3E–10**

**10.2** Insolvency Rule 6.3(2) ("Requirements as to service") applies to service of the statutory demand whether outside or within the jurisdiction.

**10.3** A creditor wishing to serve a statutory demand outside the jurisdiction in a foreign country with which a civil procedure convention has been made (including the Hague Convention) may and, if the assistance of a British Consul is desired, must adopt the procedure prescribed by CPR Part 6.25. In the case of any doubt whether the country is a "convention country", enquiries should be made of the Queen's Bench Masters' Secretary Department, Room E216, Royal Courts of Justice.

**10.4** In all other cases, service of the demand must be effected by private arrangement in accordance with Insolvency Rule 6.3(2) and local foreign law.

**10.5** When a statutory demand is to be served out of the jurisdiction, the time limits of 21 days and 18 days respectively referred to in the demand must be amended. For this purpose reference should be made to the table set out in Practice Direction 6B.

**10.6** A creditor should amend the statutory demand as follows:

(1) For any reference to 18 days there must be substituted the appropriate number of days set out in the table plus 4 days, and

(2) for any reference to 21 days there must be substituted the appropriate number of days in the table plus 7 days.

Attention is drawn to the fact that in all forms of the statutory demand the figure 18 and the figure 21 occurs in more than one place.

## 11. Substituted service

*Statutory demands*

**11.1** The creditor is under an obligation to do all that is reasonable to bring the statutory demand to the debtor's attention and, if practicable, to cause personal service to be effected. Where it is not possible to effect prompt personal service, service may be effected by other means such as first class post or by insertion through a letter box. **3E–11**

*Paragraph numbers marked with a "+" can be found online and on CD.*

**11.2** Advertisement can only be used as a means of substituted service where:

(1) The demand is based on a judgment or order of any Court;

(2) The debtor has absconded or is keeping out of the way with a view to avoiding service and,

(3) There is no real prospect of the sum due being recovered by execution or other process.

As there is no statutory form of advertisement, the Court will accept an advertisement in the following form:

STATUTORY DEMAND

(Debt for liquidated sum payable immediately following a judgment or order of the Court)

---

To (Block letters)

of

TAKE NOTICE that a statutory demand has been issued by:

Name of Creditor:

Address:

The creditor demands payment of £ the amount now due on a judgment or order of the (High Court of Justice Division) (.........County Court) dated the day of 199 .

The statutory demand is an important document and it is deemed to have been served on you on the date of the first appearance of this advertisement. You must deal with this demand within 21 days of the service upon you or you could be made bankrupt and your property and goods taken away from you. If you are in any doubt as to your position, you should seek advice immediately from a solicitor or your nearest Citizens' Advice Bureau. The statutory demand can be obtained or is available for inspection and collection from:

Name:

Address:

(Solicitor for) the Creditor

Tel. No. Reference:

You have only 21 days from the date of the first appearance of this advertisement before the creditor may present a Bankruptcy Petition. You have only 18 days within which to apply to the Court to set aside the demand.

**11.3** In all cases where substituted service is effected, the creditor must have taken all those steps which would justify the Court making an order for substituted service of a petition. The steps to be taken to obtain an order for substituted service of a petition are set out below. Failure to comply with these requirements may result in the Court declining to file the petition: Insolvency Rule 6.11(9).

*Petitions*

**11.4** In most cases, evidence of the following steps will suffice to justify an order for substituted service:

(1) One personal call at the residence and place of business of the debtor where both are known or at either of such places as is known. Where it is known that the debtor has more than one residential or business address, personal calls should be made at all the addresses.

(2) Should the creditor fail to effect service, a first class prepaid letter should be written to the debtor referring to the call(s), the purpose of the same and the failure to meet with the debtor, adding that a further call will be made for the same purpose on the day of 19 at hours at (place). At least two business days notice should be given of the appointment and copies of the letter sent to all known addresses of the debtor. The appointment letter should also state that

(a) in the event of the time and place not being convenient, the debtor is to name some other time and place reasonably convenient for the purpose;

(b) (Statutory Demands) if the debtor fails to keep the appointment the creditor proposes to serve the debtor by [advertisement] [post] [insertion through a letter box] or as the case may be, and that, in the event of a bankruptcy petition being presented, the Court will be asked to treat such service as service of the demand on the debtor;

(c) (Petitions) if the debtor fails to keep the appointment, application will be made to the Court for an order for substituted service either by advertisement, or in such other manner as the Court may think fit.

(3) In attending any appointment made by letter, inquiry should be made as to whether the debtor has received all letters left for him. If the debtor is away, inquiry should also be made as to whether or not letters are being forwarded to an address within the jurisdiction (England and Wales) or elsewhere.

(4) If the debtor is represented by a Solicitor, an attempt should be made to arrange an appointment for personal service through such Solicitor. The Insolvency Rules enable a Solicitor to accept service of a statutory demand on behalf of his client but there is no similar provision in respect of service of a bankruptcy petition.

(5) The written evidence filed pursuant to Insolvency Rule 6.11 should deal with all the above matters including all relevant facts as to the debtor's whereabouts and whether the appointment letter(s) have been returned.

**11.5** Where the Court makes an order for service by first class ordinary post, the order will normally provide that service be deemed to be effected on the seventh day after posting. The same method of calculating service may be applied to calculating the date of service of a statutory demand.

**12. Setting aside a statutory demand**

3E–12 **12.1** The application (Form 6.4) and written evidence in support (Form 6.5) exhibiting a copy of the statutory demand must be filed in Court within 18 days of service of the statutory demand on the debtor. Where service is effected by advertisement in a newspaper the period of 18 days is calculated from the date of the first appearance of the advertisement. Three copies of each document must be lodged with the application to enable the Court to serve notice of the hearing date on the applicant, the creditor and the person named in Part B of the statutory demand.

**12.2** Where, to avoid expense, copies of the documents are not lodged with the application in the High Court, any order of the Registrar fixing a venue is conditional upon copies of the documents being lodged on the next business day after the Registrar's order otherwise the application will be deemed to have been dismissed.

**12.3** Where the statutory demand is based on a judgment or order, the Court will not at this stage go behind the judgment or order and inquire into the validity of the debt nor, as a general rule, will it adjourn the application to await the result of an application to set aside the judgment or order.

**12.4** Where the debtor (a) claims to have a counterclaim, set off or cross demand (whether or not he could have raised it in the action in which the judgment or order was obtained) which equals or exceeds the amount of the debt or debts specified in the statutory demand or (b) disputes the debt (not being a debt subject to a judgment or order) the Court will normally set aside the statutory demand if, in its opinion, on the evidence there is a genuine triable issue.

**12.5** A debtor who wishes to apply to set aside a statutory demand after the expiration of 18 days from the date of service of the statutory demand must apply for an extension of time within which to apply. If the applicant wishes to apply for an injunction to restrain presentation of a petition the application must be made to the Judge. Paragraphs 1 and 2 of Form 6.5 (Affidavit in Support of Application to set Aside Statutory Demand) should be used in support of the application for an extension of time with the following additional paragraphs:

"3. That to the best of my knowledge and belief the creditor(s) named in the demand has/have not presented a petition against me.

4. That the reasons for my failure to apply to set aside the demand within 18 days after service are as follows: ..."

If application is made to restrain presentation of a bankruptcy petition the following additional paragraph should be added:

"5. Unless restrained by injunction the creditor(s) may present a bankruptcy petition against me."

### 13. Proof of service of a statutory demand

**13.1** Insolvency Rule 6.11(3) provides that, if the Statutory Demand has been served personally, the written evidence must be provided by the person who effected that service. Insolvency Rule 6.11(4) provides that, if service of the demand (however effected) has been acknowledged in writing, the evidence of service must be provided by the creditor or by a person acting on his behalf. Insolvency Rule 6.11(5) provides that, if neither paragraphs (3) or (4) apply, the written evidence must be provided by a person having direct knowledge of the means adopted for serving the demand. **3E-13**

**13.2** Form 6.11 (Evidence of personal service of the statutory demand): this form should only be used where the demand has been served personally and acknowledged in writing (see Insolvency Rule 6.11(4)). If the demand has not been acknowledged in writing, the written evidence should be provided by the Process Server and Paragraphs 2 and 3 (part of Form 6.11) should be omitted (See Insolvency Rule 6.11(3)).

**13.3** Form 6.12 (Evidence of Substituted Service of the Statutory Demand): this form can be used whether or not service of the demand has been acknowledged in writing. Paragraphs 4 and 5 (part) provide for the alternatives. Practitioners are reminded, however, that the appropriate person to provide the written evidence may not be the same in both cases. If the demand has been acknowledged in writing, the appropriate person is the creditor or a person acting on his behalf. If the demand has not been acknowledged, that person must be someone having direct knowledge of the means adopted for serving the demand.

Practitioners may find it more convenient to allow process servers to carry out the necessary investigation whilst reserving to themselves the service of the demand. In these circumstances Paragraph 1 should be deleted and the following paragraph substituted:

"1. Attempts have been made to serve the demand, full details of which are set out in the accompanying affidavit of ..."

**13.4** "Written evidence" means an affidavit or a witness statement.

### 14. Extension of hearing date of petition

**14.1** Late applications for extension of hearing dates under Insolvency Rule 6.28, and failure to attend on the listed hearing of a petition, will be dealt with as follows: **3E-14**

(1) If an application is submitted less than two clear working days before the hearing date (for example, later than Monday for Thursday, or Wednesday for Monday) the costs of the application will not be allowed under Insolvency Rule 6.28(3).

(2) If the petition has not been served and no extension has been granted by the time fixed for the hearing of the petition, and if no one attends for the hearing, the petition will be re-listed for hearing about 21 days later. The Court will notify the petitioning creditor's solicitors (or the petitioning creditor in person), and any known supporting or opposing

creditors or their solicitors, of the new date and times. Written evidence should then be filed on behalf of the petitioning creditor explaining fully the reasons for the failure to apply for an extension or to appear at the hearing, and (if appropriate) giving reasons why the petition should not be dismissed.

(3) On the re-listed hearing the Court may dismiss the petition if not satisfied it should be adjourned or a further extension granted.

**14.2** All applications for extension should include a statement of the date fixed for the hearing of the petition.

**14.3** The petitioning creditor should attend (by solicitors or in person) on or before the hearing date to ascertain whether the application has reached the file and been dealt with. It should not be assumed that an extension will be granted.

### 15. Bankruptcy petition

3E–15 **15.** To help in the completion of the form of a creditor's bankruptcy petition, attention is drawn to the following points:

**15.1** The petition does not require dating, signing or witnessing.

**15.2** In the title it is only necessary to recite the debtor's name, *e.g.* Re John William Smith or Re J W Smith (Male). Any alias or trading name will appear in the body of the petition. This also applies to all other statutory forms other than those which require the "full title".

**15.3** Where the petition is based on a statutory demand, only the debt claimed in the demand may be included in the petition.

**15.4** In completing Paragraph 2 of the petition, attention is drawn to Insolvency Rule 6.8(1)(a) to (c), particularly where the "aggregate sum" is made up of a number of debts.

**15.5** Date of service of the statutory demand (paragraph 4 of the petition):

(1) In the case of personal service, the date of service as set out in the affidavit of service should be recited and whether service is effected before/after 1700 hours on Monday to Friday or at any time on a Saturday or a Sunday: see CPR Part 6.7(2) and (3).

(2) In the case of substituted service (otherwise than by advertisement), the date alleged in the affidavit of service should be recited: see "11. Substituted Service" above.

(3) In the strictly limited case of service by advertisement under Insolvency Rule 6.3, the date to be alleged is the date of the advertisement's appearance or, as the case may be, its first appearance: see Insolvency Rules 6.3(3) and 6.11(8).

**15.6** There is no need to include in the petition details of the person authorised to present it.

**15.7** Certificates at the end of the petition:

(1) The period of search for prior petitions has been reduced to eighteen months.

(2) Where a statutory demand is based wholly or in part on a

County Court judgment, the following certificate is to be added:

"I/We certify that on the day of 19 I/We attended on the County Court and was/were informed by an officer of the Court that no money had been paid into Court in the action or matter v Claim No pursuant to the statutory demand."

This certificate will not be required when the demand also requires payment of a separate debt, not based on a County Court judgment, the amount of which exceeds the bankruptcy level (at present £750).

**15.8** Deposit on petition: the deposit will be taken by the Court and forwarded to the Official Receiver. In the High Court, the petition fee and deposit should be handed to the Senior Courts Accounts Office, Fee Stamping Room, who will record the receipt and will impress two entries on the original petition, one in respect of the Court fee and the other in respect of the deposit. In the County Court, the petition fee and deposit should be handed to the duly authorised officer of the Court's staff who will record its receipt.

In all cases cheque(s) for the whole amount should be made payable to "HM Paymaster General".

**15.9** On the hearing of a petition for a bankruptcy order, in order to satisfy the Court that the debt on which the petition is founded has not been paid or secured or compounded the Court will normally accept as sufficient a certificate signed by the person representing the petitioning creditor in the following form:

"I certify that I have/my firm has made enquiries of the petitioning creditor(s) within the last business day prior to the hearing/adjourned hearing and to the best of my knowledge and belief the debt on which the petition is founded is still due and owing and has not been paid or secured or compounded save as to

Signed Dated"

For convenience in the High Court this certificate will be incorporated in the attendance slip, which will be filed after the hearing. A fresh certificate will be required on each adjourned hearing.

**15.10** On the occasion of the adjourned hearing of a petition for a bankruptcy order, in order to satisfy the Court that the petitioner has complied with Insolvency Rule 6.29, the petitioner will be required to file written evidence of the manner in which notice of the making of the order of adjournment and of the venue for the adjourned hearing has been sent to:

(i) the debtor, and

(ii) any creditor who has given notice under Insolvency Rule 6.23 but was not present at the hearing when the order for adjournment was made.

**16. Orders without attendance**

**16.1** In suitable cases the Court will normally be prepared to make **3E–16**

*Paragraph numbers marked with a "+" can be found online and on CD.*



INSOLVENCY

orders under Part VIII of the Act (Individual Voluntary Arrangements), without the attendance of either party, provided there is no bankruptcy order in existence and (so far as is known) no pending petition. The orders are:

(1) A fourteen day interim order with the application adjourned 14 days for consideration of the nominee's report, where the papers are in order, and the nominee's signed consent to act includes a waiver of notice of the application or a consent by the nominee to the making of an interim order without attendance.

(2) A standard order on consideration of the nominee's report, extending the interim order to a date 7 weeks after the date of the proposed meeting, directing the meeting to be summoned and adjourning to a date about 3 weeks after the meeting. Such an Order may be made without attendance if the nominee's report has been delivered to the Court and complies with Section 256(1) of the Act and Insolvency Rule 5.10(2) and (3) and proposes a date for the meeting not less than 14 days from that on which the nominee's report is filed in Court under Insolvency Rule 5.10 nor more than 28 days from that on which that report is considered by the Court under Insolvency Rule 5.12.

(3) A "concertina" Order, combining orders as under (1) and (2) above. Such an order may be made without attendance if the initial application for an interim order is accompanied by a report of the nominee and the conditions set out in (1) and (2) above are satisfied.

(4) A final order on consideration of the Chairman's report. Such an order may be made without attendance if the Chairman's report has been filed and complies with Insolvency Rule 5.22(1). The order will record the effect of the Chairman's report and may discharge the interim order.

**16.2** Provided that the conditions as under 16.1(2) and (4) above are satisfied and that the appropriate report has been lodged with the Court in due time the parties need not attend or be represented on the adjourned hearing for consideration of the Nominee's report or of the Chairman's report (as the case may be) unless they are notified by the Court that attendance is required. Sealed copies of the order made (in all four cases as above) will be posted by the Court to the applicant or his Solicitor and to the Nominee.

**16.3** In suitable cases the Court may also make consent orders without attendance by the parties. The written consent of the parties will be required. Examples of such orders are as follows:

(1) <u>On applications to set aside a statutory demand</u>, orders:

(a) dismissing the application, with or without an order for costs as may be agreed (permission will be given to present a petition on or after the seventh day after the date of the order, unless a different date is agreed);

(b) setting aside the demand, with or without an order for costs as may be agreed; or

(c) giving permission to withdraw the application with or without an order for costs as may be agreed.

(2) On petitions: where there is a list of supporting or opposing creditors in Form 6.21, or a statement signed by or on behalf of the petitioning creditor that no notices have been received from supporting or opposing creditors, orders:

(a) dismissing the petition, with or without an order for costs as may be agreed, or

(b) if the petition has not been served, giving permission to withdraw the petition (with no order for costs).

(3) On other applications, orders:

(a) for sale of property, possession of property, disposal of proceeds of sale

(b) giving interim directions

(c) dismissing the application, with or without an order for costs as may be agreed

(d) giving permission to withdraw the application, with or without an order for costs as may be agreed.

If (as may often be the case with orders under subparagraphs (3)(a) or (b) above), an adjournment is required, whether generally with liberty to restore or to a fixed date, the order by consent may include an order for the adjournment. If adjournment to a date is requested, a time estimate should be given and the Court will fix the first available date and time on or after the date requested.

**16.4** The above lists should not be regarded as exhaustive, nor should it be assumed that an order will be made without attendance as requested.

**16.5** The procedure outlined above is designed to save time and costs but is not intended to discourage attendance.

**16.6** Applications for consent orders without attendance should be lodged at least two clear working days (and preferably longer) before any fixed hearing date.

**16.7** Whenever a document is lodged or a letter sent, the correct case number, code (if any) and year (for example 123/SD/99 or 234/99) should be quoted. A note should also be given of the date and time of the next hearing (if any).

**16.8** Attention is drawn to Paragraph 4.4(4) of the Costs Practice Direction.

## 16A. Bankruptcy Restrictions Orders

*Making the application*

**16A.1** An application for a bankruptcy restrictions order is made as an ordinary application in the bankruptcy. **3E–17**

**16A.2** The application must be made within one year beginning with the date of the bankruptcy order unless the court gives permission for the application to be made after that period. The one year period does not run while the bankrupt's discharge has been suspended under section 279(3) of the Insolvency Act 1986.

*Paragraph numbers marked with a "+" can be found online and on CD.*

**16A.3** An application for a bankruptcy restrictions order may be made by the Secretary of State or the Official Receiver ('the Applicant'). The application must be supported by a report which must include:

(a) a statement of the conduct by reference to which it is alleged that it is appropriate for a bankruptcy restrictions order to be made; and

(b) the evidence relied on in support of the application (r.6.241 Insolvency Rules 1986).

**16A.4** The report is treated as if it were an affidavit (r.7.9(2) Insolvency Rules 1986) and is prima facie evidence of any matter contained in it (r.7.9(3)).

**16A.5** The application may be supported by evidence from other witnesses which may be given by affidavit or (by reason of r.7.57(5) Insolvency Rules 1986) by witness statement verified by a statement of truth.

**16A.6** The court will fix a first hearing which must be not less than 8 weeks from the date when the hearing is fixed (r.6.241(4) Insolvency Rules 1986).

**16A.7** Notice of the application and the venue fixed by the court must be served by the Applicant on the bankrupt not more than 14 days after the application is made. Service of notice must be accompanied by a copy of the application together with the evidence in support and a form of acknowledgment of service.

**16A.8** The bankrupt must file in court an acknowledgment of service not more than 14 days after service of the application on him, indicating whether or not he contests the application. If he fails to do so he may attend the hearing of the application but may not take part in the hearing unless the court gives permission.

*Opposing the application*

**16A.9** If the bankrupt wishes to oppose the application, he must within 28 days of service on him of the application and the evidence in support (or such longer period as the court may allow) file in court and (within three days thereof) serve on the Applicant any evidence which he wishes the court to take into consideration. Such evidence should normally be in the form of an affidavit or a witness statement verified by a statement of truth.

**16A.10** The Applicant must file any evidence in reply within 14 days of receiving the evidence of the bankrupt (or such longer period as the court may allow) and must serve it on the bankrupt as soon as reasonably practicable.

*Hearings*

**16A.11** Any hearing of an application for a bankruptcy restrictions order must be in public (r.6.241(5) Insolvency Rules 1986). The hearing will generally be before the registrar or district judge in the first instance who may:

(1) adjourn the application and give directions;

(2) make a bankruptcy restrictions order; or

(3) adjourn the application to the judge.

*Making a bankruptcy restrictions order*

**16A.12** When the court is considering whether to make a bankruptcy restrictions order, it must not take into account any conduct of the bankrupt prior to 1 April 2004 (art. 7 Enterprise Act (Commencement No. 4 and Transitional Provisions and Savings) Order 2003).

**16A.13** The court may make a bankruptcy restrictions order in the absence of the bankrupt and whether or not he has filed evidence (r.6.244 Insolvency Rules 1986).

**16A.14** When a bankruptcy restrictions order is made the court must send two sealed copies of the order to the Applicant (r.6.244(2) Insolvency Rules 1986), and as soon as reasonably practicable after receipt, the Applicant must send one sealed copy to the bankrupt (r.6.244(3)).

**16A.15** A bankruptcy restrictions order comes into force when it is made and must specify the date on which it will cease to have effect, which must be between two and 15 years from the date on which it is made.

*Interim bankruptcy restriction orders*

**16A.16** An application for an interim bankruptcy restrictions order may be made any time between the institution of an application for a bankruptcy restrictions order and the determination of that application (Sch 4A para. 5 Insolvency Act 1986). The application is made as an ordinary application in the bankruptcy.

**16A.17** The application must be supported by a report as evidence in support of the application (r.6.246(1) Insolvency Rules 1986) which must include evidence of the bankrupt's conduct which is alleged to constitute the grounds for making an interim bankruptcy restrictions order and evidence of matters relating to the public interest in making the order.

**16A.18** Notice of the application must be given to the bankrupt at least two business days before the date fixed for the hearing unless the court directs otherwise (r.6.245).

**16A.19** Any hearing of the application must be in public (r.6.245).

**16A.20** The court may make an interim bankruptcy restrictions order in the absence of the bankrupt and whether or not he has filed evidence (r.6.247).

**16A.21** The bankrupt may apply to the court to set aside an interim bankruptcy restrictions order. The application is made by ordinary application in the bankruptcy and must be supported by an affidavit or witness statement verified by a statement of truth stating the grounds on which the application is made (r.6.248(2)).

**16A.22** The bankrupt must send the Secretary of State, not less than 7 days before the hearing, notice of his application, notice of the venue, a copy of his application and a copy of the supporting affidavit. The Secretary of State may attend the hearing and call the attention of the court to any matters which seem to him to be relevant, and may himself give evidence or call witnesses.

***Paragraph numbers marked with a "+" can be found online and on CD.***



INSOLVENCY

**16A.23** Where the court sets aside an interim bankruptcy restrictions order, two sealed copies of the order must be sent by the court, as soon as reasonably practicable, to the Secretary of State.

**16A.24** As soon as reasonably practicable after receipt of sealed copies of the order, the Secretary of State must send a sealed copy to the bankrupt.

*Bankruptcy restrictions undertakings*

**16A.25** Where a bankrupt has given a bankruptcy restrictions undertaking, the Secretary of State must file a copy in court and send a copy to the bankrupt as soon as reasonably practicable (r.6.250).

**16A.26** The bankrupt may apply to annul a bankruptcy restrictions undertaking. The application is made as an ordinary application in the bankruptcy and must be supported by an affidavit or witness statement verified by a statement of truth stating the grounds on which it is made.

**16A.27** The bankrupt must give notice of his application and the venue together with a copy of his affidavit in support to the Secretary of State at least 28 days before the date fixed for the hearing.

**16A.28** The Secretary of State may attend the hearing and call the attention of the court to any matters which seem to him to be relevant and may himself give evidence or call witnesses.

**16A.29** The court must send a sealed copy of any order annulling or varying the bankruptcy restrictions undertaking to the Secretary of State and the bankrupt.

*Part Four*

*Appeals*

### 17. Appeals in insolvency proceedings

3E–18 **17.1** This Part shall come into effect on 2nd May 2000 and shall replace and revoke Paragraph 17 of, and be read in conjunction with the Practice Direction—Insolvency Proceedings which came into effect on 26th April 1999 as amended.

**17.2**(1) An appeal from a decision of a County Court (whether made by a District Judge or a Circuit Judge) or of a Registrar of the High Court in insolvency proceedings ("a first appeal") lies to a Judge of the High Court pursuant to s.375(2) of the Act and Insolvency Rules 7.47(2) and 7.48(2) (as amended by s.55 of the Access to Justice Act 1999).

(2) The procedure and practice for a first appeal are governed by Insolvency Rule 7.49 which imports the procedure and practice of the Court of Appeal. The procedure and practice of the Court of Appeal is governed by CPR Part 52 and Practice Direction 52, which are subject to the provisions of the Act, the Insolvency Rules and this Practice Direction: see CPR Part 52 rule 1(4).

***Paragraph numbers marked with a "+" can be found online and on CD.***

(3) A first appeal (as defined above) does not include an appeal from a decision of a Judge of the High Court.

**17.3**(1) Section 55 of the Access to Justice Act 1999 has amended s.375(2) of the Act and Insolvency Rules 7.47(2) and 7.48(2) so that an appeal from a decision of a Judge of the High Court made on a first appeal lies, with the permission of the Court of Appeal, to the Court of Appeal.

(2) An appeal from a Judge of the High Court in insolvency proceedings which is not a decision on a first appeal lies, with the permission of the Judge or of the Court of Appeal, to the Court of Appeal (see CPR Part 52, rule 3);

(3) The procedure and practice for appeals from a decision of a Judge of the High Court in insolvency proceedings (whether made on a first appeal or not) are also governed by Insolvency Rule 7.49 which imports the procedure and practice of the Court of Appeal as stated at Paragraph 17.2(2) above.

**17.4** CPR Part 52 and Practice Direction 52 and the forms required by them apply to appeals from a decision of a Judge of the High Court in insolvency proceedings.

**17.5** An appeal from a decision of a judge of the High Court in insolvency proceedings requires permission set out in Paragraph 17.3(1) and (2) above.

**17.6** A first appeal is subject to the permission requirement in CPR Part 52, rule 3.

**17.7** Except as provided in this Part, CPR Part 52 and Practice Direction 52 and Forms do not apply to first appeals, but Paragraphs 17.8 to 17.23 inclusive of this Part apply only to first appeals.

**17.8** Interpretation:

(a) the expressions "appeal court", "lower court", "appellant", "respondent" and "appeal notice" have the meanings given in CPR Part 52.1(3);

(b) "Registrar of Appeals" means—
 (i) in relation to an appeal filed at the Royal Courts of Justice in London, a registrar in bankruptcy; and
 (ii) in relation to an appeal filed in a district registry, a district judge of that district registry.

(c) "appeal date" means the date fixed by the appeal court for the hearing of the appeal or the date fixed by the appeal court upon which the period within which the appeal will be heard commences.

**17.9** An appellant's notice and a respondent's notice shall be in Form **PDIP 1** and **PDIP 2** set out in the Schedule hereto.

**17.10**(1) An appeal from a decision of a registrar in bankruptcy must be filed at the Royal Courts of Justice in London.

(2) An appeal from a decision of a district judge sitting in a district registry may be filed—
 (a) at the Royal Courts of Justice in London; or
 (b) in that district registry.

*Paragraph numbers marked with a "+" can be found online and on CD.*

(3) An appeal from a decision made in a county court may be filed—
(a) at the Royal Courts of Justice in London; or
(b) in the Chancery district registry for the area within which the county court exercises jurisdiction.

(There are Chancery district registries of the High Court at Birmingham, Bristol, Caernarfon, Cardiff, Leeds, Liverpool, Manchester, Mold, Newcastle upon Tyne and Preston. The county court districts that each district registry covers are set out in Schedule 1 to the Civil Courts Order 1983.)

**17.11**(1) Where a party seeks an extension of time in which to file an appeal notice it must be requested in the appeal notice and the appeal notice should state the reason for the delay and the steps taken prior to the application being made; the court will fix a date for the hearing of the application and notify the parties of the date and place of hearing;

(2) The appellant must file the appellant's notice at the appeal court within—
(a) such period as may be directed by the lower court; or
(b) where the court makes no such direction, 21 days after the date of the decision of the lower court which the appellant wishes to appeal.

(3) Unless the appeal court orders otherwise, an appeal notice must be served by the appellant on each respondent—
(a) as soon as practicable; and
(b) in any event not later than 7 days, after it is filed.

**17.12**(1) A respondent may file and serve a respondent's notice.

(2) A respondent who wishes to ask the appeal court to uphold the order of the lower court for reasons different from or additional to those given by the lower court must file a respondent's notice.

(3) A respondent's notice must be filed within—
(a) such period as may be directed by the lower court; or
(b) where the court makes no such direction, 14 days after the date on which the respondent is served with the appellant's notice.

(4) Unless the appeal court orders otherwise a respondent's notice must be served by the respondent on the appellant and any other respondent—
(a) as soon as practicable; and
(b) in any event not later than 7 days, after it is filed.

**17.13**(1) An application to vary the time limit for filing an appeal notice must be made to the appeal court.

(2) The parties may not agree to extend any date or time limit set by—
(a) this Practice Direction; or
(b) an order of the appeal court or the lower court.

**17.14** Unless the appeal court or the lower court orders otherwise an appeal shall not operate as a stay of any order or decision of the lower court.

**17.15** An appeal notice may not be amended without the permission of the appeal court.

**17.16** A Judge of the appeal court may strike out the whole or part of an appeal notice where there is compelling reason for doing so.

**17.17**(1) In relation to an appeal the appeal court has all the powers of the lower court.

(2) The appeal court has power to—

(a) affirm, set aside or vary any order or judgment made or given by the lower court;

(b) refer any claim or issue for determination by the lower court;

(c) order a new trial or hearing;

(d) make a costs order.

(3) The appeal court may exercise its powers in relation to the whole or part of an order of the lower court.

**17.18**(1) Every appeal shall be limited to a review of the decision of the lower court.

(2) Unless it orders otherwise, the appeal court will not receive—

(a) oral evidence; or

(b) evidence which was not before the lower court.

(3) The appeal court will allow an appeal where the decision of the lower court was—

(a) wrong; or

(b) unjust because of a serious procedural or other irregularity in the proceedings in the lower court.

(4) The appeal court may draw any inference of fact which it considers justified on the evidence.

(5) At the hearing of the appeal a party may not rely on a matter not contained in his appeal notice unless the appeal court gives permission.

**17.19** The following applications shall be made to a Judge of the appeal court:

(1) for injunctions pending a substantive hearing of the appeal;

(2) for expedition or vacation of the hearing date of an appeal;

(3) for an order striking out the whole or part of an appeal notice pursuant to Paragraph 17.16 above;

(4) for a final order on paper pursuant to Paragraph 17.22(8) below.

**17.20**(1) All other interim applications shall be made to the Registrar of Appeals in the first instance who may in his discretion either hear and determine it himself or refer it to the Judge.

(2) An appeal from a decision of a Registrar of Appeals lies to

*Paragraph numbers marked with a "+" can be found online and on CD.*



INSOLVENCY

a Judge of the appeal court and does not require the permission of either the Registrar of Appeals or the Judge.

**17.21** The procedure for interim applications is by way of ordinary application (see Insolvency Rule 12.7 and Schedule 4, Form 7.2).

**17.22** The following practice applies to all first appeals to a Judge of the High Court whether filed at the Royal Courts of Justice in London, or filed at one of the other venues referred to in Paragraph 17.10 above:

(1) on filing an appellant's notice in accordance with Paragraph 17.11(2) above, the appellant must file:

(a) two copies of the appeal notice for the use of the court, one of which must be stamped with the appropriate fee, and a number of additional copies equal to the number of persons who are to be served with it pursuant to Paragraph 17.22(4) below;

(aa) an approved transcript of the judgment of the lower court or, where there is no official record of the judgment, a document referred to in paragraph 5.12 of the Practice Direction 52;

(b) a copy of the order under appeal; and

(c) an estimate of time for the hearing.

(2) the above documents may be lodged personally or by post and shall be lodged at the address of the appropriate venue listed below:

(a) if the appeal is to be heard at the Royal Courts of Justice in London the documents must be lodged at Room 110, Thomas More Building, The Royal Courts of Justice, Strand, London WC2A 2LL;

(b) if the appeal is to be heard in Birmingham, the documents must be lodged at the District Registry of the Chancery Division of the High Court, 33 Bull Street, Birmingham B4 6DS;

(c) if the appeal is to be heard in Bristol the documents must be lodged at the District Registry of the Chancery Division of the High Court, Third Floor, Greyfriars, Lewins Mead, Bristol, BS1 2NR;

(ca) if the appeal is to be heard in Caernarfon the documents must be lodged at the District Registry of the Chancery Division of the High Court, Llanberis Road, Caernarfon, LL55 2DF;

(d) if the appeal is to be heard in Cardiff the documents must be lodged at the District Registry in the Chancery Division of the High Court, First Floor, 2 Park Street, Cardiff, CF10 1ET;

(e) if the appeal is to be heard in Leeds the documents must be lodged at the District Registry of the Chancery Division of the High Court, The Court House, 1 Oxford Row, Leeds LS1 3BG;

(f) if the appeal is to be heard in Liverpool the documents

must be lodged at the District Registry of the Chancery Division of the High Court, Liverpool Combined Court Centre, Derby Square, Liverpool L2 1XA;

(g) if the appeal is to be heard in Manchester the documents must be lodged at the District Registry of the Chancery Division of the High Court, Courts of Justice, Crown Square, Manchester, M60 9DJ;

(ga) if the appeal is to be heard in Mold the documents must be lodged at the District Registry of the Chancery Division of the High Court, Law Courts, Civic Centre, Mold, CH7 1AE;

(h) if the appeal is to be heard at Newcastle upon Tyne the documents must be lodged at the District Registry of the Chancery Division of the High Court, The Law Courts, Quayside, Newcastle upon Tyne NE1 3LA;

(i) if the appeal is to be heard in Preston the documents must be lodged at the District Registry of the Chancery Division of the High Court, The Combined Court Centre, Ringway, Preston PR1 2LL.

(3) if the documents are correct and in order the court at which the documents are filed will fix the appeal date and will also fix the place of hearing. That court will send letters to all the parties to the appeal informing them of the appeal date and of the place of hearing and indicating the time estimate given by the appellant. The parties will be invited to notify the court of any alternative or revised time estimates. In the absence of any such notification the estimate of the appellant will be taken as agreed. The court will also send to the appellant a document setting out the court's requirement concerning the form and content of the bundle of documents for the use of the Judge. Not later than 7 days before the appeal date the bundle of documents must be filed by the appellant at the address of the relevant venue as set out in sub-paragraph 17.22(2) above and a copy of it must be served by the appellant on each respondent.

(4) the appeal notice must be served on all parties to the proceedings in the lower court who are directly affected by the appeal. This may include the Official Receiver, liquidator or trustee in bankruptcy.

(5) the appeal notice must be served by the appellant or by the legal representative of the appellant and may be effected by:

(a) any of the methods referred to in CPR Part 6 rule 2; or

(b) with permission of the court, an alternative method pursuant to CPR Part 6 rule 8.

(6) service of an appeal notice shall be proved by a Certificate of Service in accordance with CPR Part 6, rule 10 (CPR

***Paragraph numbers marked with a "+" can be found online and on CD.***

Form **N215**) which must be filed at the relevant venue referred to at Paragraph 17.22(2) above immediately after service.

(7) Subject to sub-paragraphs (7A) and (7B), the appellant's notice must be accompanied by a skeleton argument and a written chronology of events relevant to the appeal. Alternatively, the skeleton argument and chronology may be included in the appellant's notice. Where the skeleton argument and chronology are so included they do not form part of the notice for the purposes of rule 52.8.

(7A) Where it is impracticable for the appellant's skeleton argument and chronology to accompany the appellant's notice they must be filed and served on all respondents within 14 days of filing the notice.

(7B) An appellant who is not represented need not file a skeleton argument nor a written chronology but is encouraged to do so since these documents may be helpful to the court.

(8) where an appeal has been settled or where an apellant does not wish to continue with the appeal, the appeal may be disposed of on paper without a hearing. It may be dismissed by consent but the appeal court will not make an order allowing an appeal unless it is satisfied that the decision of the lower court was wrong. Any consent order signed by each party or letters of consent from each party must be lodged not later than 24 hours before the date fixed for the hearing of the appeal at the address of the appropriate venue as set out in sub-paragraph 17.22(2) above and will be dealt with by the Judge of the appeal court. Attention is drawn to paragraph 13.4 of the Costs Practice Direction regarding costs where an order is made by consent without attendance.

**17.23** Only the following paragraphs of Practice Direction 52, with any necessary modifications, shall apply to first appeals: 5.10 to 5.20 inclusive.

**17.24**(1) Where, under the procedure relating to appeals in insolvency proceedings prior to the coming into effect of this Part of this Practice Direction, an appeal has been set down in the High Court or permission to appeal to the Court of Appeal has been granted before 2nd May 2000, the procedure and practice set out in this Part of this Practice Direction shall apply to such an appeal after that date.

(2) Where, under the procedure relating to appeals in insolvency proceedings prior to the coming into effect of this Part of this Practice Direction, any person has failed before 2nd May 2000 either:

(a) in the case of a first appeal, to set down in the High Court an appeal which relates to an order made (County Court) or sealed (High Court) after March 27, 2000 and before May 2, 2000, or

***Paragraph numbers marked with a "+" can be found online and on CD.***

(b) in the case of an appeal from a decision of a Judge of the High Court, to obtain any requisite permission to appeal to the Court of Appeal which relates to an order sealed in the same period,

the time for filing an appeal notice is extended to May 16, 2000 and application for any such permission should be made in the appeal notice.

**17.25** This paragraph applies where a judge of the High Court has made a Bankruptcy order or a winding-up order or dismissed an appeal against such an order and an application is made for a stay of proceedings pending appeal.

(1) the judge will not normally grant a stay of all proceedings but will confine himself to a stay of advertisement of the proceedings.

(2) where the judge has granted permission to appeal any stay of advertisement will normally be until the hearing of the appeal but on terms that the stay will determine without further order if an appellant's notice is not filed within the period prescribed by the rules.

(3) where the judge has refused permission to appeal any stay of advertisement will normally be for a period not exceeding 28 days. Application for any further stay of advertisement should be made to the Court of Appeal.



### Insolvency proceedings

The law relating to insolvency is found primarily in the Insolvency Act 1986 (as amended) and the Insolvency Rules 1986 (as amended) (SI 1986/1925). The law governing the insolvency of partnerships is to be found in the Insolvent Partnerships Order 1994 (SI 1994/2421) as amended by the Insolvent Partnerships (Amendment) Order 2005 (SI 2005/1516) and that governing the insolvency of limited liability partnerships in the Limited Liability Partnerships Act 2000 and related secondary legislation. The administration of the estates of deceased insolvent individuals is governed by the Administration of Insolvent Estates of Deceased Persons Order 1986 (SI 1986/1999). **3E–19**

The Bankruptcy Act 1914 and the Bankruptcy Rules 1952 continue to govern bankruptcies commenced under that Act. The Companies Act 1948 and the Companies (Winding-Up) Rules 1949 (SI 1949/330) continue to apply to corporate insolvencies commenced under the 1948 Act.

Insolvency proceedings are defined as proceedings under the Insolvency Act 1986 and the Insolvency Rules 1986 (r.13.7, Insolvency Rules 1986).

### Procedure

Insolvency proceedings are governed primarily by the Insolvency Act 1986 and the Insolvency Rules 1986 and not by the CPR. However, where the Act and the Rules do not make provision for procedure, the CPR may be invoked (see para.2.1.4 and r.7.51(1) of the Insolvency Rules 1986). All insolvency proceedings are multi-track (r.7.51(2) of the Insolvency Rules 1986). **3E–20**

Chapters 19 and 20 of the Chancery Guide (paras 1A–152 *et seq.* above) give further guidance on the procedure in the Bankruptcy and Companies Courts.

### Applications in insolvency proceedings

Part 7 of the Insolvency Rules 1986 deals with particular matters applying to procedure in insolvency proceedings including rules as to the form and content of applications (r.7.3). **3E–21**

Applications in insolvency proceedings (other than those made by petition) may only be made by originating application or ordinary application. An originating application is an application made to the court which is not an application in pending proceedings before the court. An ordinary application is any other application to the court (r.7.2(1)). Every application must be in the appropriate form (r.7.2(2)). Rule 7.3 provides general rules as to the form and content of applications. Particular rules deal with the form and content of other documents such as statutory demands and petitions as well as prescribing forms for particular uses.

**Urgent applications**

3E–22 Urgent applications in Companies Court may be heard at 10.15am. In addition a duty registrar (covering both bankruptcy and companies work) will be available at 2pm each Wednesday during term to hear urgent applications or applications of a time critical nature (e.g. applications for a debarring order where there is urgency). Parties seeking to list an urgent companies application should attend room TM 405 and those seeking to list an urgent bankruptcy application TM110 with a certificate bearing the heading of the case and the following information:

> I estimate that this matter is likely to occupy the court for ..............mins/hours.
> I certify that it is urgent and fit for a without notice hearing for the following reasons: [*give brief reasons*]".

The certificate should be signed by the solicitor or counsel with conduct of the application and provide a telephone number. It should include the following warning: "WARNING. If, in the opinion of the Registrar, the application is not urgent then such sanction will be applied as is thought appropriate in all the circumstances".

Urgent applications which may be heard by a registrar should not be listed before the judge in the applications court.

**Evidence in insolvency proceedings**

3E–23 Evidence may be given by witness statement or affidavit following the coming into force of the CPR. As to evidence that must be given by affidavit see the Insolvency Rules 1986, r.7.57.

The official receiver or a deputy official receiver may file a report; an administrator, liquidator, trustee in bankruptcy, provisional liquidator or interim receiver, a special manager or an insolvency practitioner appointed under s.273(2) may also file a report unless the application to which it relates involves other parties or the court otherwise directs (r.7.9).

**Jurisdiction—Companies Court**

3E–24 Applications concerning companies and partnerships made under the Insolvency Act 1986, the Insolvency Act 2000 and the Insolvency Partnerships Order 1994 (SI 1994/ 2421) are dealt with by the Companies Court.

Although paragraph 5.1 of the Practice Direction has not been formally amended, on May 23, 2005 the Vice-Chancellor issued a Practice Note on the Hearing of Insolvency Proceedings which sets out a much simplified scheme for the distribution of work between the judges and registrars and district judges (see para. 3E–124).

**Jurisdiction—Bankruptcy**

3E–25 Section 265(1) of the Insolvency Act 1986 provides that certain jurisdictional conditions have to be satisfied in respect of a debtor. The debtor must be domiciled in England and Wales, or personally present in England and Wales on the day on which the petition is presented, or at any time in the three year period ending with that day, have been ordinarily resident or had a place of residence in England and Wales or carried on business in England and Wales. Section 265 is now subject to Art.3 of the EC Regulation on Insolvency Proceedings (see s.265(3) and para.3E–26).

Although para.9 of the Practice Direction had not been formally amended, on May 23, 2005 the Vice-Chancellor issued a Practice Note on the Hearing of Insolvency Proceedings which sets out a much simplified scheme for the distribution of work between the judges and registrars and district judges (see para. 3E–124).

**The EC Regulation on Insolvency Proceedings**

3E–26 The Council of the European Union Regulation on Insolvency Proceedings 1346/ 2000 (O.J. L160, 30.6.2000) came into force on May 31, 2002 and has direct application as domestic law. It applies to all the EU member states, except Denmark. It applies to "collective insolvency proceedings which entail the partial or total divestment of a debtor and the appointment of a liquidator" (Art.1(1)); see also *In re Eurofood IFSC Ltd* [2006] Ch. 508; [2007] 2 B.C.L.C. 151.Such proceedings are: winding up by the court, creditors' voluntary winding up with confirmation of the court (as to which see para.3E–88), administration, voluntary arrangements and bankruptcy (Art.2(a) and Annex A), and the term "liquidator" includes the relevant office holder in relation thereto (Art.2(b) and Annex C). The Regulation does not apply to insurance and certain other financial undertakings (Art.1(2)), nor does it apply to members' voluntary winding-up, schemes of arrangement, winding-up on the just and equitable ground or winding-up in the public interest (*Marann Brooks CSV Ltd, Re* [2003] B.P.I.R. 1159.

The Regulation provides for insolvency proceedings to be main proceedings or secondary (or territorial) proceedings (Art.3(1) and (2)). Jurisdiction is founded by reference to the debtor's centre of main interests, which in the case of a company is presumed (in the absence of proof to the contrary) to be its registered office (Art.3(1)) and in the case of an individual is likely to be the place of the debtor's business or his place of ordinary residence (in the absence of evidence to the contrary). Main proceedings are proceedings brought in the place of the debtor's centre of main interests and are universal in scope. Secondary or territorial proceedings may be brought in a country in which the debtor has an establishment, i.e. a "place of operations where the debtor carries out a non-transitory economic activity with human means and goods" (Arts.2(h) and 3(2)). Such proceedings are limited to assets within the territory. The court is thus obliged to consider whether it has jurisdiction before making an order, and when making an order, to state whether the Regulation applies and if so whether the proceedings are main, territorial or secondary. (For examples of the court's consideration of the jurisdictional issue see *A Company, Re (No.6394/2002)* [2002] All E.R. (D) 223 (Oct); *Marann Brooks CSV Ltd, Re* [2003] B.P.I.R. 1159; *BRAC Rent-A-Car Internaional Inc, Re* [2003] 2 All E.R. 201; [2003] 1 W.L.R. 1421; *Re Salvage Association* [2003] B.C.C. 504; *Skjevesland v Geveran Trading Co Ltd* [2003] B.P.I.R. 73; [2003] B.P.I.R. 924, *A Bankrupt, Re (No.136 of 2003)* [2003] All E.R. (D) 36 (Dec); *Shierson v Vlieland-Boddy* [2005] B.P.I.R. 1170; *Re Staubitz-Schreiber* (C-1/07) [2006] E.C.R. 1-701; [2006] B.P.I.R. 510, ECJ; *Stojevic v Official Receiver* [2007] B.P.I.R. 141.)

The place where proceedings are opened (usually by the making of an order (Art.2(f)) determines the law applicable to the insolvency (Art.4(1)), but subject to various exceptions set out in detail in the Regulation.

The Regulation provides for automatic recognition of insolvency proceedings in member states (Arts.17 and 25). A creditors' voluntary liquidation requires "confirmation of the court" for such purposes (Annex A) (see para.3E–88).

#### The UNCITRAL model law

The UNCITRAL model law on cross-border insolvency, implementing the model law and enabling representatives of foreign insolvency proceedings to seek recognition and other relief in Great Britain, came into force on April 4, 2006 (Insolvency Act 2000, s.14; the Cross-Border Insolvency Regulations 2006 (SI 2006/1030)). **3E–27**

#### Company

"Company" means a company formed and registered under the Companies Act 1985 or under the former Companies Acts (i.e. the Joint Stock Companies Act, the Companies Act 1862, the Companies (Consolidation) Act 1908, the Companies Act 1929 and the Companies Act 1948 to 1983) but excluding those in what was Ireland (s.735(1) of the Companies Act 1985). As to jurisdiction in relation to a company incorporated by royal charter, see *Re Salvage Association* [2003] B.C.C. 504. As to the meaning of a UK-registered company see s.1158 of the Companies Act 2006. **3E–28**

#### Partnerships

The insolvency of partnerships is dealt with largely by reference to the legislation on company insolvency (with appropriate modifications) Thus a partnership may propose a partnership voluntary arrangement under provisions set out in Sch.1 of the Insolvent Partnerships Order 1994 (as amended), seek an administration order or be wound up under Pt V of the Insolvency Act 1986. **3E–29**

**Limited liability partnerships**

3E–30 The Limited Liability Partnerships Act 2000 created a new legal entity, the limited liability partnership and provided for the recognition of oversea limited liability partnerships. Pursuant to s.14 of the Limited Liability Partnerships Act 2000 and the Limited Liability Partnership Regulations 2001 (SI 2001/1090) Pts I, II, III, IV, VI and VII of the Insolvency Act 1986 apply with modifications to limited liability partnerships.

## *Company voluntary arrangements (Part I Insolvency Act 1986)*

**Company voluntary arrangements without moratorium**

3E–31 The directors of a company, its administrator (where an administration order is in force) or its liquidator (where the company is being wound up) may propose to the creditors of the company a composition in satisfaction of its debts or a scheme of arrangement (a company voluntary arrangement) (s.1). The proposal must be made to all the company's creditors, and it must be for a composition of debts or a scheme of arrangement (as to which see *March Estates plc v Gunmark Ltd* [1996] 2 B.C.L.C. 1). Within 28 days (or any longer period the courts allow) the nominee must submit a report to the court stating whether a meeting of creditors and members of the company should be summoned to consider the proposal (s.2). The meetings must then be held at the time, date and place proposed (s.3(2)) The chairman of the meetings must report to the court the result of the meetings (s.4(6)). Members vote according to the rights attaching to their shares (r.1.18(1)) but are entitled to vote even where no voting rights attach to their shares (r.1.18(2)). A resolution to approve or modify the proposal must be passed by a majority in excess of three-quarters in value of creditors present in person or by proxy (r.1.19(1)).

**Company voluntary arrangements with moratorium**

3E–32 Under the provisions of the Insolvency Act 2000, which came into force on January 1, 2003, an "eligible company" (as defined by ss.2–4 of Sch.A1 of the Insolvency Act 1986), which must be a small company (as defined by s.247(3) of the Companies Act 1985), may obtain a moratorium without making an application for an administration order (s.1A). The moratorium commences when the directors file in court the company's proposal, a statement of affairs, a statement that the company is eligible for a moratorium and a statement from the nominee that he has consented to act and that in his opinion (a) the arrangement has a reasonable prospect of being approved and implemented, (b) the company is likely to have sufficient funds available during the moratorium to enable it to carry on its business, and (c) meetings of the company and its creditors should be summoned to consider the proposal. The moratorium lasts for 28 days but may be extended by resolution for up to two months after the date when the meetings were first held.

**Filing of company voluntary arrangements**

3E–33 In the High Court in London the proposal and accompanying documents should be filed in the issue room on the second floor, Thomas More Building, Royal Courts of Justice.

**Partnership voluntary arrangements**

3E–34 A partnership voluntary arrangement is made in much the same way as a company voluntary arrangement (Insolvent Partnerships Order 1994 (as amended by the Insolvent Partnerships (Amendment) Order 2005). The moratorium provisions also apply to a partnership voluntary arrangement (Insolvent Partnerships (Amendment) (No.2) Order 2002 (SI 2002/2708)). A limited liability partnership may also propose a voluntary arrangement.

**Challenges**

3E–35 Within 28 days of the day on which the chairman's reports have been filed (as to which see *Re Bournemouth and Boscombe v AFC Co Ltd* [1998] B.P.I.R. 153) a person entitled to vote at a meeting or who would have been so entitled if he had notice of it, the nominee or his replacement, or (if applicable) the liquidator or administrator, may apply to challenge the approval of the arrangement on the ground of unfair prejudice or material irregularity at or in relation to the meetings (s.6). The application should be made initially to the registrar and be supported by written evidence detailing the matters complained of.

## Administration orders (Part II Insolvency Act 1986)

Section 248 of the Enterprise Act 2002 created a new statutory regime for administrations the details of which are to be found in Insolvency Act 1986, Sch.B1. The Insolvency (Amendment) Rules 2003 (SI 2003/1730) substitute a new Pt 2 in the Insolvency Rules 1986 dealing with the rules governing the new forms of administration. **3E-36**

Paragraph 3(1) of Sch.B1 provides that the administrator must perform his functions with the objective of— **3E-37**

(a) rescuing the company as a going concern, or
(b) achieving a better result for the company's creditors as a whole than would be likely if the company were wound up (without first being in administration), or
(c) realising property in order to make a distribution to one or more secured or preferential creditors.

### Administration by court order

An administrator may be appointed by order of the court. The application may be made by the company, the directors of the company, one or more creditors of the company, the justices' chief executive for a magistrates' court (in relation to a fine) or any combination of the above (para.12(1)). It is made by a prescribed form of application (Form 2.1B) and must be supported by an affidavit containing details of the company's financial position (including assets and liabilities), details of any security held, details of any existing insolvency proceedings, (where more than one administrator is to be appointed) details of which functions are to be carried out by them jointly or separately (para.100(2), Sch.B1), any other relevant matters, (where the application is made by the holder of a qualifying floating charge) details to satisfy the court of the charge-holder's entitlement to appoint an administrator, a statement as to the application of the EC Regulation on Insolvency Proceedings and whether the proceedings are main or territorial (r.2.4, Insolvency Rules 1986). **3E-38**

Notice of the making of the application must be given to any person who has appointed an administrative receiver, any person who may be entitled to appoint one, the holder of any qualifying floating charge (para.12(2), Sch.B1); in addition the application must be served on any administrative receiver who has been appointed, any person who has presented a winding up petition, any liquidator appointed in main proceedings in a member state, the proposed administrator, the company (unless it is the applicant) and the supervisor of a voluntary arrangement under Pt I Insolvency Act 1986 (r.2.6, Insolvency Rules 1986). **3E-39**

Before making an administration order the court must be satisfied that the company is or is likely to become unable to pay its debts and that the administration order is reasonably likely to achieve the purpose of the administration (para.11, Sch. B1). **3E-40**

On the hearing of the application the court may make the administration order, dismiss the application, adjourn the hearing conditionally or unconditionally, make an interim order, treat the application as a winding up petition and make any order it could make under s.125 of the Insolvency Act 1986 or make any other order it thinks appropriate (para.13(1), Sch.B1). **3E-41**

Where a qualifying charge holder applies for an order (as opposed to appointing out of court) there is no obligation to satisfy the court that the company is or is likely to become unable to pay its debts, but the application must state that it is being made under para.35 of Sch.B1. **3E-42**

### Administration out of court

The holder of a qualifying floating charge may appoint an administrator out of court (paras 14 to 21 of Sch.B1, Insolvency Act 1986 and rr.2.15 to 2.19, Insolvency (Amendment) Rules 2003). A floating charge "qualifies" if it is created by an instrument which states that para.14, Sch.B1 applies to it, purports to empower the holder to appoint an administrator, purports to empower the holder to make an appointment of what would otherwise be an administrative receiver (para.14(2)). **3E-43**

3E–44 The appointment becomes effective when a notice of appointment in the prescribed form accompanied by the administrator's consent to act and a statement by him that in his opinion the purpose of the administration is likely to be achieved have been filed in court. Rule 2.19 makes special provision for filing notice of appointment by fax out of business hours (Form 2.7B). The fax number for filing notice in the Royal Courts of Justice is 020 7947 6607.

3E–45 Similar provisions (but excluding that relating to appointment out of hours) are made for the appointment of an administrator by the company or its directors (paras 22 to 34 and rr.2.20 to 2.26).

**Effects of administration**

3E–46 The effects of administration are set out in paras 40 to 45 of Sch.B1. On the making of an administration order any petition to wind up the company (except in the public interest or under the Financial Services and Markets Act 2000) must be dismissed or (in the case of an appointment by the holder of a qualifying charge) suspended and any administrative receiver must vacate office (paras 40 and 41).

3E–47 Both court and out of court administrations create a statutory moratorium during which no resolution to wind up the company may be passed, no winding up order may be made (save in the public interest or under the Financial Services and Markets Act 2000), no steps may be taken to enforce any security or repossess goods subject to hire purchase except with the consent of the administrator or the permission of the court, no landlord may forfeit except with such consent or permission and no legal process (including legal proceedings, execution and distress) may be instituted or continued against the company or its property except with such consent or permission (paras 42 and 43).

3E–48 An application for an administration order creates an interim moratorium which has the same effect as paras 42 and 43, save that the proviso relating to the consent of the administrator does not apply (para.44).

As to the ability to appoint an administrator while a winding up petition is pending see *Re Blights Builders Ltd* [2006] EWHC 3549(Ch); [2007] 3 All E.R. 776.

**Application for directions and extensions**

3E–49 As to the ability of an administrator to apply to court for directions see *Re Transbus International Ltd* [2004] 2 All E.R. 911.

Applications to extend administrations should be made promptly. Failure to apply promptly may result in the court depriving the administrator of his remuneration and his legal advisers of their costs. It would seem that the test the court should apply will be similar to that applicable to the making of an administration order and that the benefit of any extension will outweigh any potential prejudice (see *Re Trident Fashions plc*, unrep. and cf. generally *Re Cosslett (Contractors Ltd)* [2004] EWHC 658).

## *Receivership (Part III Insolvency Act 1986)*

3E–50 Applications to the court in relation to receiverships are relatively rare, since the conduct of the receivership is governed by the provisions of the Insolvency Act and the terms of the debenture under which the receiver has been appointed.

**Applications for directions**

3E–51 Section 35 enables a receiver to apply to the court for directions.The application should be made initially to the registrar who will give directions for its determination either before himself or the judge.

**Applications for extensions of time**

3E–52 The Act imposes on a receiver obligations to give various notices and to file returns, accounts and other documents in relation to the receivership. Application to extend the time limits for so doing are made to the registrar and should be supported by written evidence setting out the reasons why the extension is required. Application may also be made to extend time for the submission of a statement of affairs (s.47).

**The Enterprise Act 2002**

3E–53 Amendments effected by the Enterprise Act 2002 now permit the holders of floating

***Paragraph numbers marked with a "+" can be found online and on CD.***

charges to appoint an administrator as an alternative to an administrative receiver. This is intended as an alternative to administrative receivership, since s.250 of the Enterprise Act 2002 (inserting new Chap. IV in the Insolvency Act 1986) will in future prevent the appointment of administrative receivers except in relation to charges created before the new act came into force and certain charges in relation to capital market, public-private partnership and utilities charges and similar (ss.72A–72H).

## *Winding-up petitions (Parts IV and V Insolvency Act 1986)*

Part IV of the Insolvency Act 1986 deals with the winding up of registered companies and Pt V with the winding up of unregistered companies. **3E–54**

### Jurisdiction

Section 117(1) of the Insolvency Act 1986 provides that the High Court has jurisdiction to wind up any company registered in England and Wales, and s.117(2) gives concurrent jurisdiction to the county court of the district in which the company's registered office is situated where the amount of the company's share capital paid up or credited as paid up does not exceed £120,000. A company which has no share capital (e.g. a company limited by guarantee) may be wound up only in the High Court (*Re North of England Iron Steamship Insurance Association* [1900] 1 Ch. 481). A company's registered office for the purpose of s.117 of the Insolvency Act 1986 is the place which has longest been its registered office during the six months immediately preceding the presentation of a petition for winding up (s.117(6)). The relevant date for the purpose of determining jurisdiction is the date when proceedings are commenced, which need not be the date on which the company went into liquidation (*Re Lichfield Freight Terminal Ltd* [1997] B.C.C. 11). **3E–55**

Proceedings taken in the wrong court are not invalidated (s.118(1)).

### Grounds on which a company may be wound up

A company may be wound up by the court if: **3E–56**

(a) it has resolved by special resolution that it be wound up by the court;
(b) it is a public limited company and fails within one year of registration as such to obtain a certificate from the registrar of companies under s.117 of the Companies Act 1985;
(c) it is an old public company within the meaning of the Companies Consolidation (Consequential Provisions) Act 1985 (i.e. it has failed to comply with the requirements of re-registration following the re-definition of a public company in the Companies Act 1980);
(d) it has not commenced its business within a year from its incorporation or suspends its business for a whole year;
(e) except in the case of a private company limited by shares or by guarantee, the number of members is reduced below two;
(f) the company is unable to pay its debts;
(g) the court is of the opinion that it is just and equitable that the company should be wound up (s.122(1)).

### Inability to pay debts

A company is deemed unable to pay its debts: **3E–57**

(a) if a creditor (by assignment or otherwise) to whom the company is indebted in a sum exceeding £750 then due has served on the company, by leaving at the company's registered office, a written demand in the prescribed form (a statutory demand) requiring the company to pay the sum so due, and the company has for three weeks thereafter neglected to pay the sum or to secure or compound for it to the reasonable satisfaction of the creditor; or
(b) if execution or other process issued on a judgment, decree or order of any court in favour of a creditor of the company is returned unsatisfied in whole or in part; or
(c) if it is proved to the satisfaction of the court that the company is unable to pay its debts as they fall due (other than by reason of its failure to satisfy a statutory demand);
(d) if it is proved to the satisfaction of the court that the value of the company's as-

INSOLVENCY

sets is less than the amount of its liabilities, taking into account its contingent and prospective liabilities (s.123(1) and (2)).

As to the form of a statutory demand for the purpose of s.123(1)(a) see rr.4.4-4.6 of the Insolvency Rules 1986.

Note that the minimum level of indebtedness (£750) applies only to proof of inability to pay by service of a statutory demand. It is open to a creditor to petition for a lesser sum, relying on ground (d) above. The court may refuse to make the order (as it did in *Re Fancy Dress Balls Co* [1899] W.N. 109), but it may make the order where the company flagrantly refuses to pay (*Re World Industrial Bank Ltd* [1909] W.N. 148).

Service of a statutory demand is not an essential prerequisite to presentation of a petition. Inability to pay may be established without service of a demand, for example if the company fails to pay an undisputed debt (*Re Taylor's Industrial Flooring Ltd* [1990] BCC 44, *Taylor's Industrial Flooring Ltd v M & H Plant Hire (Manchester) Ltd* [1990] B.C.L.C. 216, CA).

A creditor with a debt which is not disputed is entitled to a winding-up order as a matter of right (*Bowes v Hope Life Insurance Co Ltd* [1895] All E.R. 1383). However, the court will not make a winding-up order where the petition has been issued improperly or simply as a debt collecting exercise, for some private purpose, or to put pressure on a solvent company to pay a debt (*Re Lympne Investments Ltd* [1972] 1 W.L.R. 523; *Re a Company* [1983] B.C.L.C. 492) nor will it make an order on the basis of a debt which is disputed on genuine grounds (see, for example, *Re London & Paris Banking Corp* (1874–75) L.R. 19 Eq. 444; *Re Richbell Strategic Holdings Ltd* [1997] 2 B.C.L.C. 429). The dispute must be genuine: a bare allegation that the debt is in dispute will not suffice to establish that the dispute is genuine (*Re a Company No.006685 of 1996* [1997] B.C.C. 830). A winding-up order will not be made on a debt which is time barred (*Re Karnos Property Co Ltd* (1989) 5 B.C.C. 14).

**The petition**

**3E–58** A petition to wind up a company may be presented by the following:

(a) the company itself;
(b) its directors
(c) one or more of its creditors (including an actual, contingent or prospective creditor);
(d) one or more of its contributories;
(e) a clerk to a magistrates' court to enforce a fine;
(f) any combination of the above (s.124(1));
(g) the official receiver (where the company is in voluntary liquidation) (s.124(5));
(h) the supervisor of the company's voluntary arrangement (s.7(4)(b));
(i) an administrator (s.14(1)(b); Sch.1, para.21);
(j) an administrative receiver (s.42(1); Sch.1, para.1);
(k) a voluntary liquidator (s.165(3); Sch.4, Pt II, para.4).

It should contain statutory information about the company and state the basis on which it is contended the company is unable to pay its debts.It should deal with jurisdiction under the EC Regulation on Insolvency proceedings (see para.3E–26). It should expressly state that "the company is insolvent and unable to pay its debts" and contend, "In the circumstances it is just and equitable that the company should be wound up". It should conclude with the prayers, "(1) that the company may be wound up by the court under the provisions of the Insolvency Act 1986; or (2) that such other order may be made as the court thinks fit".

**Evidence**

**3E–59** The petition must be verified by an affidavit or witness statement (r.4.7(1) and r.4.12) which should be sworn or made no more than 10 days before the date of issue of the petition.

**Service and advertisement**

**3E–60** The petition (unless it is the company's own petition) must be served (r.4.8; see also r.4.10), and service must be proved (r.4.9).

The petition must be advertised not less than seven business days after service on the company and not less than seven business days before the date appointed for the hearing of the petition (r.4.11). As to the contents of the advertisement see r.4.11(4).

**Applications to restrain presentation or advertisement of a petition**

A company which has been served with a statutory demand or is otherwise made aware that it is intended to present a petition may apply with or without notice for an order restraining presentation of a petition or advertisement of any petition which has already been presented. The application should be supported by full written evidence in support setting out in detail why the petition should not be presented or advertised (usually because the petition debt is disputed). Since the application is for an injunction it is made direct to the judge. There is no provision to apply for a statutory demand to be set aside. **3E-61**

The court will not restrain a creditor from prosecuting a petition where the company can demonstrate solvency but has failed to pay a debt that is due (*Cornhill Insurance plc v Improvement Services Ltd* [1986] 1 W.L.R. 114).

**Failure to advertise**

Winding up is a class remedy. Accordingly the court attaches importance to the advertisement of a winding up petition. The petition should be advertised in the London Gazette (r.4.11(1)), but may be advertised elsewhere if the court so orders (r.4.11(3)). If a petition has not been advertised in accordance with r.4.11 the court may dismiss it (r.4.11(5) and para.2 of the Practice Direction). The court will not, as a general rule, dismiss the petition by reason only of a failure to advertise, at the first hearing of the petition. It will, however, do so as a general rule if the petition has not been advertised by any adjourned hearing unless there are exceptional circumstances for not complying with the general rule. It will almost certainly dismiss any petition that has not been advertised with a view to holding the unadvertised petition over the company's head for the purpose of obtaining costs from the company without an order of the court. If the court does adjourn the petition as a result of a failure to advertise it may do so on terms that the petitioner should have no costs in respect of the ineffective hearing. **3E-62**

Premature advertisement of the petition may result in dismissal if the breach of the rule appears to have been culpable, but will generally be waived if the petition is unopposed and no prejudice has been suffered by the company. The court may waive up to two days lateness in advertisement but will generally adjourn if the advertisement is more than two days late. The court may also waive minor errors in the advertisement (e.g. misspelling of the company's address) so long as the name and identity of the company in the advertisement are clear.

**Certificate of compliance**

The Petitioner must, at least five days before the hearing of the petition, file in court a certificate of compliance relating to service and advertisement of the petition (r.4.14(1)). It must show the date of presentation of the petition, the date fixed for the hearing, the dates of service and advertisement, and it must be accompanied by a copy of the advertisement of the petition. Failure to file a certificate of compliance may also result in dismissal of the petition (r.4.14(3)). **3E-63**

**List of appearances**

Any person who intends to appear on the hearing of the petition must give notice to the petitioner of his intention to do so, state whether he intends to support or oppose the petition and give details of the amount and nature of his debt (r.4.16). The petitioner must prepare a list of the persons who have given notice under r.4.16 and hand a copy of the list to the court before the hearing (r.4.17). **3E-64**

**Hearing of the petition**

In the High Court in London winding up petitions are heard on Wednesdays by the registrar. **3E-65**

At the hearing of the petition the petitioner may appear as may the company and any supporting or opposing creditor who has given notice under r.4.16 or has failed to give such notice but has been permitted by the court to appear (r.4.16(5)). The company may appear by a director or employee as well as by solicitors or counsel. However, the court will not generally allow accountants right of audience.

At the hearing, the court may dismiss the petition, adjourn it conditionally or unconditionally, or make an interim order or any other order it thinks fit (s.125(1)). It may also make an order that the company be wound up.

***Paragraph numbers marked with a "+" can be found online and on CD.***



INSOLVENCY

3E–66 *Petition contested* —If the company opposes the making of a winding up order it should file in court and serve on the petitioner evidence in opposition not less than seven days before the date fixed for the hearing of the petition (r.4.18). In practice, if the company appears and indicates that it opposes the making of an order on grounds that appear to be substantial, the court will give directions for the filing and service of evidence in opposition and evidence in reply and order the petition to be heard at a later date, notwithstanding any failure to comply with the provisions of r.4.18.

3E–67 *Substitution of petitioner* —Where the petitioner is unable to proceed with his petition (e.g. because the petition debt is disputed) or is unable to seek a winding up order (e.g. because restrained by injunction from advertising, because he has failed to advertise or otherwise comply with the rules) or does not seek a winding up order for some other reason (e.g. because his debt has been paid), a creditor or contributory who would himself be entitled to present a petition may seek substitution. The application may be made informally at the hearing and without notice. If more than one creditor seeks substitution the court will generally substitute the creditor with the largest debt or the debt least likely to be disputed. The court will direct that the petition be amended and re-verified; it may order re-service but will generally dispense with re-advertisement if the petition has already been advertised. It will adjourn the petition so as to allow sufficient time for those steps to be taken.

3E–68 *Dismissal of the petition* —If the petitioner fails to appear, if the petitioner accepts that the petition debt is capable of dispute, or if the petition debt has been paid and no creditor or contributory seeks substitution, the court will generally dismiss the petition. It may also dismiss the petition for failure to advertise or for some other failure to comply with the Insolvency Rules 1986 (e.g. rr.4.11(5) and 4.14(3)).

The court must dismiss a petition for the winding up of a company in respect of which an administration order has been made (Sch.B1, para.40(1)(a)). It must suspend the petition where an administration has been appointed by the holder of a floating charge (Sch.B1, para.40(b). As to costs in such cases see para. 3E–72.

3E–69 *Usual compulsory order* —If the court is satisfied that the provisions of the Insolvency Act 1986 and the Insolvency Rules 1986 have been complied with and that the petition debt is not disputed on grounds which are substantial and that it is just and equitable to wind up the company it will make "the usual compulsory order", i.e. an order that the company be wound up by the court under the provisions of the Insolvency Act 1986. It will also make a declaration as to whether or not the EC Regulation on Insolvency Proceedings applies to the winding up and whether (if it does) the proceedings are main or secondary/territorial proceedings.

3E–70 *Double barrelled order* —Where a company has been struck off the register by the registrar of companies the court may order the company to be restored and wound up

3E–71 *After administration* —Where an administrator applies for the administration to cease and, with the approval of the creditors, petitions for the company to be wound up, the court will generally make the winding up order at the same time as the administrator seeks other relief, provided it is satisfied that all parties concerned, including the company, have had notice of his intention to do so. Where a petition has been suspended by virtue of para.40(1)(b) of Sch.B1 to the Act, the petition may be listed with the administrator's application for relief so that a winding up order may be made on the petition, provided that the petitioner appears and asks for the order to be made. The winding up order may be made whether or not the petition has been advertised and may be made at the first directions hearing without adjournment into the normal winding up list.

3E–72 *Costs and supervening insolvency* —Where after presentation of a petition a supervening insolvency event is initiated and then occurs (such as an administration order, voluntary arrangement or creditors' voluntary liquidation) the court will generally dismiss the petition and order that the costs be paid as an expense of the supervening insolvency (whether or not the petition has been advertised, but provided it has been served) and, where the insolvency practitioner in the supervening insolvency has not given consent to the payment of costs, give liberty to apply to vary or discharge

***Paragraph numbers marked with a "+" can be found online and on CD.***

the costs order provided it is exercised within 28 days of the making or service of the order. Where an administrator is appointed by the holder of a qualifying floating charge pursuant to para.14 of Sch.B1 after the presentation of the petition, the petition must be suspended by the court, but the court will usually order that the petitioner's costs be paid as an expense of the administration (whether or not it has been advertised, but provided it has been served) and give the administrator liberty to apply to vary or discharge the costs order provided it is exercised within 28 days of the making or service of the order.

*Appointment of liquidator*—Where a winding-up order is made immediately on the discharge of an administration order, the court may appoint the former administrator as liquidator (s.140(1)). The court may also appoint as liquidator a person who was the supervisor of a voluntary arrangement under Pt I of the Act (s.140(2)). **3E–73**

Where a petition presented by an administrator or supervisor contains a request for his appointment as liquidator the person whose appointment is sought must, not less than two days before the return day of the petition, file in court a report including particulars of the date on which he notified creditors of his intention to seek appointment and details of any response received to such notification (r.4.7(10)).

A winding-up petition should not be used as a mechanism to oust a liquidator appointed in a creditors' voluntary liquidation to whose appointment the petitioning creditor objects (*Re Inside Sport Ltd (In Liquidation)* [2000] B.C.C. 40; [2000] 1 B.C.L.C. 302). **3E–74**

*Costs*—The court has a discretion as to the making of any order for costs. **3E–75**

Where an order is made for the company to be wound up, unless otherwise stated, the petitioner will be entitled to his costs as a claim in the winding up of the company. The supporting creditors may also be awarded one set of costs to be shared among them provided they have given notice of intention to appear or been given permission to appear (r.4.16). Such costs are payable out of the assets of the company in accordance with the order of priority prescribed by r.4.218 of the Insolvency Rules 1986 (see r.4.218(1)(h) as to the costs of the petitioner and any other person appearing).

Where the petition is dismissed because the petition debt has been paid, the court will generally award the petitioner his costs provided that the petitioner has complied with the provisions of the Act and the Rules or if the company consents to pay the costs.Where the petition is dismissed because it has been successfully opposed by the company, the court will generally order the petitioner to pay the company's costs.

Where the petition is dismissed because the company has obtained approval for a voluntary arrangement under Pt I of the Act or because an administration order has been made, the court will generally order the company to pay the petitioner's costs and may order such costs to be in the voluntary arrangement or the administration. The court will not necessarily order the costs of a petition to be in the voluntary winding up of the company where the company goes into creditors' voluntary liquidation, even if the liquidator agrees that they should be paid on that basis.

Where the petition is adjourned, unless the contrary is said, the costs will generally be in the petition.

If there is argument as to costs the registrar will normally adjourn the question of costs to be dealt with at a later date and give directions for evidence to be filed.

**Withdrawal of petition**

The petitioner may apply to withdraw a winding up petition provided that the application is made at least five days before the date fixed for hearing the petition, the petition has not been advertised, no notices in support of or in opposition to the petition have been received and the company consents to an order being made (r.4.15). The order may also be made without the consent of the company if the company has not been served. The application may be made without notice by ordinary application and will generally be heard by the clerk to the companies court if made at least five days before the hearing. Otherwise the application should be made to the registrar. Permission to withdraw a petition will almost never be given after the petition has been heard in court or advertised. **3E–76**

**Rescinding a winding up order**

The court may review, rescind or vary any order made by it in the exercise of its ju- **3E–76.1** risdiction to wind up a company (r.7.47(1)). Any application for the rescission of a winding-up order should be made within seven days after the date on which the order was made (r.7.47(3)). It is possible to apply to extend time (r.4.3). The application may only be made by (a) a creditor, (b) a contributory or (c) by the company jointly with a creditor or contributory (Practice Direction para.7.2). As to evidence in support see para.7.4 of the Practice Direction. If an application is made to extend time the evidence will need to explain any delay.

Notice of making the application should be given to the official receiver (Practice Direction para.7.1), the petitioner and any supporting or opposing creditors (although oddly this is not mentioned in the Practice Direction).

As to rescission generally see *Papanicola v Humphreys* [2005] EWHC 335 (Ch); [2205] 2 All E.R. 418; *In re Baxter Ltd* WN June 25, 1898; *Re Intermain Properties Ltd* [1986] B.C.L.C. 265; [1983–85] 1 B.C.C. 99; *Re Calmex Ltd* [1989] 1 All E.R. 485; [1989] B.C.L.C. 299; *Re Virgo Systems Ltd* (1989) 5 B.C.C. 833; *Re Dollar Land (Feltham) Ltd* [1995] 2 B.C.L.C. 370. As to circumstances in which relief has been refused see *Re Piccadilly Property Management Ltd* [1999] 2 B.C.L.C. 145; *Re Thirty-Eight Building Ltd (in liquidation) (No 2)* [2000] 1 B.C.L.C. 201; *Leicester v Stevenson* [2002] EWHC 2831 (Ch); [2003] 2 B.C.L.C. 97; and *Re Turnstem Ltd* [2004] EWHC 1765(Ch); [2005] 1 B.C.L.C. 388.

**Winding up unregistered companies**

**3E–77** The court has power to wind up an unregistered company (as defined by s.220) (s.221). The provision is generally applied in the case of a company incorporated outside England and Wales which has established a place of business within the jurisdiction or has some other sufficient connection with the jurisdiction (see para.3E–78) or to wind up an insolvent partnership (which is treated as an unregistered company under the provisions of the Insolvent Partnerships Order 1994 (SI 1994/2421)).

**Winding up a foreign company**

**3E–78** The power of the court to wind up a foreign company as an unregistered company is now restricted by the terms of the EC Regulation on Insolvency Proceedings (see para.3E–26). However, the power still has effect in relation to foreign companies not covered by the Regulation. Furthermore, the courts have construed the power in relation to foreign companies narrowly, so that the court will not assume jurisdiction over matters which properly lie in the competence of the courts of other countries (*Banque des Marchands de Moscou (Koupetschesky) v Kindersley* [1951] Ch. 112; [1950] 2 All E.R. 549). The court will be reluctant to make an order where the foreign company is continuing to trade in its place of incorporation and elsewhere in the world save in exceptional circumstances (*Banco Nacional de Cuba v Cosmos Trading Corp* [2000] B.C.C. 910; [2000] 1 B.C.L.C. 812).

The court will generally have to be satisfied, before assuming jurisdiction and making an order in relation to a foreign company, that (a) there is a sufficient connection with the jurisdiction, (b) that there is a reasonable possibility of a benefit to the petitioner if an order is made to wind-up the company, and (c) that one or more persons interested in the distribution of assets is a person over whom the court can exercise jurisdiction (*Stocznia Gdanska v Latreefers Inc* [1999] 1 B.C.L.C. 271).

**Winding up in the public interest**

**3E–79** Where it appears to the Secretary of State for Trade and Industry that it is expedient in the public interest that a company should be wound up he may present a petition to the court for an order that the company be wound up (s.124A). A public interest petition is dealt with in the same way as any other petition under the Act, save that a contested public interest petition is always heard by the judge. Uncontested public interest petitions as well as any interim applications in connection with such petitions (save for an application to appoint a provisional liquidator) are heard by the registrar.

The court will not generally accept an undertaking as an alternative to making an order (*Re Supporting Link Alliance Ltd* [2004] EWHC 523; [2004] 1 W.L.R. 1549).

The Housing Corporation may petition for the winding up of a registered social landlord (Housing Act 1996, Sch. 1) and the Financial Services Authority may petition for the winding up of an authorised person or appointed representative (Financial Services and Markets Act 2000, s.367).

***Paragraph numbers marked with a "+" can be found online and on CD.***

**Contributory's petition**

A contributory's petition (unlike a creditor's petition) is not listed straight away for hearing but is given a first return date on which the petitioner and the company should attend before the registrar for directions to be given (r.4.22(2)). The petition must be served on the company at least 14 days before the hearing (r.4.22(4)). As to the range of directions which the court may give see r.4.23. **3E–80**

**Supervisor's petition**

A winding up petition presented by the supervisor of a voluntary arrangement under Part I of the Act must be presented to the court in which the nominee's report was filed (r.4.7(8)) and is treated as a petition presented by a contributory (r.4.7(9)). As to the appointment of the supervisor as liquidator see para.3E–73. **3E–81**

**Applications for relief from the effects of s.127**

Section 127 of the Insolvency Act 1986 renders certain transactions made after commencement of the winding up void. Thus, advertisement of a winding up petition will generally have the effect of freezing any bank accounts of the company. The company may apply for relief from the effects of the provisions of s.127 to the judge (if the application is urgent) or otherwise to the registrar. Any order made is commonly referred to as a validation order. For the form of the order see para. 7 of the Practice Direction Order under s.127 of the Insolvency Act 1986 (see para.2G–53). As to the principles governing such applications see *Re Gray's Inn Construction Co Ltd* [1980] 1 W.L.R. 711; [1980] 1 All E.R. 814; and *Re SA & D Wright Ltd, Denny v John Hudson & Co Ltd* [1992] B.C.C. 503 **3E–82**

The application should generally be made to the registrar (see para.3E–125).

**Applications for the appointment of a provisional liquidator**

The court may appoint a provisional liquidator of a company at any time after presentation of a winding up petition and before the making of a winding up order (s.135(1)). Such an appointment is generally made only where assets of the company are in jeopardy or in connection with a public interest petition. The application may be (and commonly is) made without notice to the company and is always made direct to the judge (see para. 3E–124.). It should be supported by full written evidence (as to the contents of which see r.4.25(2)). **3E–83**

INSOLVENCY

## *Applications in the liquidation of companies*

The winding up of a company (whether voluntary or by the court) does not bring the life of the company to an end. The company, acting by its liquidator, may bring proceedings in its own name even after it has been wound up. Thus, the company may by its liquidator and in its own name issue proceedings to collect a debt or to enforce any other right. Such proceedings should generally be issued in the court having the appropriate jurisdiction: the county court, for example, in the case of a debt action, the Chancery Division in the case of an action regarding intellectual property rights, and so on. However, the breadth of proceedings which the companies court may entertain is wide (*Re Shilena Hosiery Co Ltd* [1980] Ch. 219). **3E–84**

**Applications to recover assets or relating to prior transactions**

The Insolvency Act 1986 provides the administrator, administrative receiver or liquidator of a company with a wide range of remedies to enable him to recover assets of the company or undo the effects of prior transactions (see, for example in liquidations, s.127 (void transactions), ss.206–207 (fraud), s.212 (misfeasance etc.), ss.212–213 (fraudulent and wrongful trading), s.238 (transactions at an undervalue), s.239 (preferences), s.244 (extortionate credit transactions), s.245 (avoidance of floating charges) and s.246 (liens etc.)). Any application to enforce a right of the liquidator or to review or appeal against the conduct of a liquidator should be made to the court having jurisdiction in the winding up. The application should be made by originating or ordinary application (see para.3E–21) and be supported by written evidence. It will be listed for directions before the registrar and determined by him or the judge depending on the length and complexity of the case **3E–85**

**Applications for directions in the winding up of a company**

Section 112 of the Insolvency Act 1986 allows a liquidator, contributory or creditor **3E–86** to apply to the court to determine any question arising in the winding up of a company. The application should be made by originating or ordinary application (see para.3E–21) and supported by written evidence. It will be listed for directions before the registrar and determined by him or the judge depending on the length and complexity of the case.

### Applications for private examinations

**3E–87** Section 236 of the Insolvency Act 1986 enables an office holder to apply to the court for an order summoning to appear before it (a) any officer of the company, (b) any person known or suspected to have in his possession any property of the company or supposed to be indebted to the company, (c) any person whom the court thinks capable of giving information concerning the promotion, formation, business, dealings, affairs or property of the company (subs.2). Such person may be examined on oath (s.237(3) and (4)). Failure to attend may give rise to the issue of a warrant for the arrest of the person concerned (s.236(5)).

The case law relating to s.236 relief is voluminous and complex. The making of an order is a matter for the discretion of the court, but the discretion will generally be exercised in favour an office holder (*Joint Liquidators of Sasea Finance Ltd v KPMG* [1998] B.C.C. 216) provided the application is made to enable him to carry out his proper functions (*British & Commonwealth Holdings plc v Spicer & Oppenheim (Re British & Commonwealth Holdings plc (No.2))* [1993] A.C. 426; [1992] B.C.C. 977). The formation of the liquidator of an intention to bring proceedings against the proposed examinee may be a factor weighing against the exercise of the discretion to make an order (*Re Castle New Homes Ltd* [1979] 1 W.L.R. 1075; [1979] 2 All E.R. 775 and *Re Cloverbay Ltd* [1991] Ch 90; [1990] B.C.C. 414; [1990] B.C.L.C. 449); an order will not be made to give the office holder a litigation advantage (*Re Atlantic Computers plc* [1998] B.C.C. 200); however an order may be made for the purpose of obtaining information other than for the administration of the liquidation (e.g. for the purposes of disqualification proceedings, *Re Pantmaenog Timber Co Ltd* [2003] UKHL 49; [2003] 3 W.L.R. 767; [2003] B.C.C. 659, HL). As to the use of compelled evidence in subsequent criminal proceedings see s.219(2A) of the Insolvency Act 1986.

### Applications for confirmation by the court of a creditors' voluntary winding up

**3E–88** The EC Regulation on Insolvency Proceedings (see para.3E–26) applies to creditors' voluntary winding up with confirmation by the court (Annex A). Article 19 of the Regulation provides that the appointment of a liquidator must be evidenced by a copy of the decision appointing him or by some other certificate issued by the court with jurisdiction. The procedure for applying for an order confirming a creditors' voluntary winding up is provided for by rr.7.62 *et seq.* of the Insolvency Rules 1986.

The application is made pursuant to r.7.62(1) and must be made by prescribed form 7.20 which incorporates the application, the evidence in support and the order to be made. The evidence must state the name of the applicant and of the company and its registered number, the date of the resolution to wind up the company, that the application is accompanied by the required documents and that the copies submitted are true copies, that the Regulation applies to the company, and whether the proceedings are main, territorial or secondary proceedings (r.7.62(2)). The application must be filed together with a copy and be accompanied by a copy of the resolution to wind up the company, evidence of the applicant's appointment as liquidator and the statement of affairs (r.7.62(3)). Whilst provision is made for the order to be made by a member of the court staff (r.7.62(7)), in the High Court the application should be made to the registrar who will make the order without a hearing provided that the papers are in order. The application need not be served on any other party (r.7.62(4)).

The order is made by the court completing and sealing the order section of the prescribed form and returning a completed and sealed copy to the applicant.

### Applications to convert proceedings

**3E–89** The EC Regulation on Insolvency Proceedings provides that the liquidator in main proceedings may request that proceedings listed in Annex A previously opened in another member state be converted into winding up proceedings if this is in the interests of creditors in the main proceedings (Art.37). The court may, on such an application, order that any such proceedings be converted into one of the proceedings listed in

***Paragraph numbers marked with a "+" can be found online and on CD.***

Annex B (i.e. winding up by or subject to the supervision of the court, creditors' voluntary winding up with confirmation by the court (see para.3E–88) or bankruptcy).

### *Individual Voluntary Arrangements (Part VIII Insolvency Act 1986)*

Part VIII of the Insolvency Act 1986 allows a debtor to make a proposal to his creditors for what must be either a composition with his creditors or a scheme of arrangement of his affairs. A composition is effectively an agreement whereby creditors agree to accept a lesser sum in satisfaction of their debt; a scheme of arrangement may take any form which is acceptable to the parties but must provide for someone to act either as a trustee or otherwise for the purpose of supervising its implementation. As to compositions and schemes generally, see *Re Griffth* (1886) 3 Morr.111 and *Inland Revenue Commissioners v Adam & Partners Ltd* [2001] 1 B.C.L.C. 222. In practice the procedure to be followed in each case is the same and can be summarised as follows. A proposal is formulated, reviewed by the nominee who will then present it to the creditors at a meeting summoned for that purpose; if approved by a majority of in excess of three quarters of creditors in value it then becomes binding on the creditors. **3E–90**

The Insolvency Act 2000, ss.3 and 4 and Sch.3, and the Insolvency (Amendment) (No.2) Rules 2002 (SI 2712/2002) which came into force on January 1, 2003, enable the debtor to choose whether or not to apply for an interim order. If the debtor needs protection from his creditors, which now includes protection against peaceable re-entry by his landlord or distress (except with the permission of the court), then an interim order will be required and an application will need to be made to the court as before. The procedure has not changed and is set out in Pt 5 of the Insolvency Rules 1986. If protection is not required then the debtor may submit his proposal, which must comply with r.5.3 (as amended) and statement of affairs to the intended nominee who, if he is of the opinion that the debtor is an undischarged bankrupt or is able to petition for his own bankruptcy and is prepared to act, can call the meeting of creditors. The nominee must within 14 days (or such longer period as the court may allow) after receiving the proposal and statement of affairs submit a report to the court in which he must state whether in his opinion the voluntary arrangement has a reasonable prospect of being approved and implemented, whether a meeting of creditors should be summoned and if so the date, time and venue. This must be filed along with a copy of the proposal, the statement of affairs and form 5.5 (which contains the statement that it is not intended to apply for an interim order). The court will not read the report unless an application is made under the Act or Rules in relation to the proposal, for example to challenge the decision of the creditors' meeting under s.262 of the Insolvency Act 1986, (see r.5.14(1)). **3E–91**

The appropriate court in which to file is the court in which the debtor should file his own bankruptcy petition (r.6.40), or if an undischarged bankrupt the court with the conduct of the bankruptcy. Where the debtor is an undischarged bankrupt the nominee must send copies of his report, the proposal and the statement of affairs to the official receiver or trustee and to any petitioning creditor if a petition has been filed (r.5.5A(3)).

The nominee or supervisor appointed must either be a licensed insolvency practitioner or a member of a body recognised by the secretary of state for that purpose. To date no other body has been given such recognition. In either case he must have in force security for the proper performance of his functions. **3E–92**

In his report the nominee must state whether in his opinion the proposal has a reasonable prospect of being approved and implemented (ss.256 as amended by para.3 and para.5 of Sch.3 of the Insolvency Act 2000). An application may be made to the court for an order replacing a nominee where it is impractical or inappropriate for the nominee to continue to act. Section 260 of the Insolvency Act 1986 as amended by s.3 and para.10 of Sch.3 of the Insolvency Act 2000 provides that approval of a voluntary arrangement binds every person who in accordance with the rules was entitled to vote at the meeting (whether or not he was present or represented at it), or would have been so entitled had he had notice of it. The classes of person who may challenge the outcome of the meeting under s.262 of the Insolvency Act 1986 includes any person who was entitled, in accordance with the rules, to vote at the creditors' meeting or would have been so entitled had he had notice of it (r.5.3(2)). The content of the debtor's proposal must now state how it is proposed to deal with the claims of any person who is bound by the arrangement by virtue of this provision.



INSOLVENCY

Section 262A, Insolvency Act 1986, as enacted by s.3 and para.12 of Sch.3 of the Insolvency Act 2000, makes it an offence for a debtor to make any false representation or fraudulently to do, or omit to do, anything for the purpose of obtaining the approval of his creditors to a proposal, whether approved or not.

### The Proposal

3E–93 The debtor must ensure that his proposal complies with the requirements of r.5.3 of the Insolvency Rules 1986 as amended. In particular it must deal with the EC Regulation on Insolvency Proceedings (see para.3E–26) and give details of the debtor's centre of main interests and/or his establishment (r.5.3(2)(q)). It is also necessary to set out not only the fees to be charged by the intended nominee but also to list the disbursements (r.5.3 (2)(g)).

### Application for interim order

3E–94 If the debtor decides that he needs the protection of an interim order then the steps set out in Pt 5 of the Insolvency Rules must be followed. The debtor must give written notice of his proposal together with a copy of the proposal to the intended nominee (r.5.4(1)). If he is an undischarged bankrupt then he must also give notice to the or his trustee (r.5.4(5)). If the nominee is prepared to act he endorses his consent on the notice (r.5.4(3)) and returns it to the debtor. The debtor then has 7 days, or such longer period as the nominee may allow, to give the nominee his statement of affairs (r.5.8(2)).

The application may be made by the debtor where he is not bankrupt or by the debtor, the official receiver or his trustee where he is (s.253(3) of the Insolvency Act 1986). The application is by way of originating application accompanied by an affidavit or witness statement in support. The evidence must comply with r.5.1 of the Insolvency Rules 1986: it should give the reason for the application, details of any execution or other legal process, state whether the debtor is an undischarged bankrupt or able to file his own petition, confirm that there has been no other application within the last 12 months, name the nominee and confirm that he is qualified to act and is willing to act. A copy of the notice served upon the nominee endorsed with his consent to act must be exhibited to the written evidence (r.5.5(2)). If the nominee has completed his enquiries the application may be accompanied by his report.

### Interim order

3E–95 Where it is not necessary to give any other party notice the court will often deal with the application in the absence of the parties and will only require a hearing if the papers are not in order. In the absence of a nominee's report the court will make an interim order for 14 days commencing the day following the making of the order and will fix a hearing date within the 14 day period to consider the nominee's report (r.5.6(3)). At the adjourned hearing if the nominee's report has not been filed the court may extend the 14 day period in certain circumstances, if appropriate. Where it has been filed and a date, time and venue have been given for the meeting of creditors (which is not less than 14 days from the date on which it was filed and not more than 28 days from the date on which it is considered by the court) the court will extend the interim order to a date 7 weeks after the proposed date of the meeting and adjourn the application to a date about 3 weeks after the date of the meeting for consideration of the chairman's report. The time scale allows for possible adjournment of the meeting. If the nominee's report accompanies the application the court may make a "concertina order" which combines the two orders set out above. The nominee must state in his report whether the debtor's proposal has a reasonable prospect of being approved (s.256 as amended). As to the obligations of a nominee in reporting to the court see *Greystoke v Hamilton-Smith* [1996] 2 B.C.L.C. 429; [1997] B.P.I.R. 24).

Where it has been necessary to give notice to other parties a hearing date will be fixed for consideration of the application when the parties will have the opportunity to make representations to the court about the proposal.

The court has a discretion as to whether or not to make an interim order. It will not make an order if the proposal is not viable (*Cooper v Fearnley* [1997] B.P.I.R. 20; *Hook v Jewson Ltd* [1997] B.C.C. 752) or cannot achieve the requisite majority (*Re Cove* [1990] 1 All E.R. 949). As to the importance of adhering to the statutory regime applicable to interim orders and individual voluntary arrangements see, for example,

*Greystoke v Hamilton-Smith* [1996] 2 B.C.L.C. 429; [1997] B.P.I.R. 24; *Fletcher v Vooght* [2000] B.P.I.R. 435 and *Re N (a debtor)* [2002] B.P.I.R. 1024.

**Chairman's report**

The chairman's report must state whether the proposal was approved, with or without modifications, or rejected, set out the resolutions and the decision on each one, list the creditors who were present and how they voted, indicate whether it is governed by the E.C. Regulation on Insolvency Proceedings and if so whether the proceedings are main or territorial proceedings and include any other information he thinks should be made known to the court (r.5.22(2)). As to the chairman's obligations in conducting the meeting of creditors see *Re a Debtor (No.222 of 1990) Ex p. Bank of Ireland* [1992] B.C.L.C. 137; [1993] B.C.L.C. 233; as to his obligations in reporting to the court see *Re N (a debtor)* [2002] B.P.I.R. 1024. **3E–96**

**Challenges**

Within 28 days of the day on which the chairman's report was made to the court the debtor, a person entitled to vote at the creditors' meeting, the nominee, and, where the debtor is an undischarged bankrupt, the official receiver or trustee, may apply to challenge the approval of the arrangement on the ground of unfair prejudice or material irregularity at or in relation to the meeting (s.262 of the Insolvency Act 1986). The 28–day period may be extended (*Tager v Westpac Banking Corp* [1998] B.C.C. 73; [1997] 1 B.C.L.C. 313; [1997] B.P.I.R. 543.The application is made initially to the registrar and must be supported by written evidence detailing the matters complained of. As to creditors bound who did not receive notice, see para.3E–92, above. **3E–97**

## *Bankruptcy (Part IX Insolvency Act 1986)*

Part IX of the Act enables a petition for a bankruptcy order to be presented by a creditor or creditors, the debtor, a temporary administrator within the meaning of Art.38 of the EC Regulation, a liquidator within the meaning of Art.2(b) appointed in proceedings by virtue of art.3(1) of the EC Regulation and the supervisor of a voluntary arrangement (s.264(1) of the Insolvency Act 1986). **3E–98**

**Presentation of petition**

A creditor's petition is normally presented to the court in whose insolvency district the debtor has carried on business; this may be different from the insolvency district in which the debtor resides. Petitions presented by government departments are always presented in the High Court. If the debtor is resident or carries on business in the London insolvency district or is not resident in England and Wales or his place of business or residence is not known the petition may also be presented in the High Court. See generally r.6.9 of the Insolvency Rules 1986. **3E–99**

**Grounds of a creditor's petition**

The grounds for a creditor's petition are set out in s.267(2) of the Insolvency Act 1986. A creditor may present a petition where the amount of the debt or debts is equal to or greater than the bankruptcy level, currently £750, the debt or debts are for a liquidated sum payable either immediately or at some future time and are unsecured and the debtor appears either to be unable to pay or to have no reasonable prospect of paying the debt or debts. Also there must be no outstanding application to set aside a statutory demand. It is possible for creditors to join in the presentation of a creditor's petition: the debts do not need to be interrelated but can be entirely separate. The creditor has a duty to disclose whether he holds any security though he may undertake in the petition to give it up for the benefit of all the creditors (s.269(1)(a)). **3E–100**

*Inability to pay debts*—The debtor is deemed to be unable to pay his debts if 3 weeks have elapsed since service of a statutory demand and the demand has not been complied with or set aside, or if execution of a judgment or court order in favour of the petitioner has been returned unsatisfied (s.268). As to the requirements in relation to unsatisfied execution see *Re a debtor (No.340 of 1992)* [1996] 2 All E.R. 211. **3E–101**

**Statutory demand**

The form of the statutory demand and the information it must contain is prescribed by rr.6.1 and 6.2. The form to be used will vary depending on the nature of the debt. **3E–102**



INSOLVENCY

The creditor is under an obligation to do all that is reasonable to bring the demand to the debtor's attention and, if practicable, to cause personal service to be effected (r.6.3(2)). The Practice Direction sets out in detail the steps to be taken to effect service. Where substituted service is effected the court will need to be satisfied that the creditor has taken all steps which would justify the court making an order for substituted service of a petition

### Application to set aside statutory demand

3E-103 The debtor may apply to the court to set aside the statutory demand within 18 days of its service upon him. The court will consider the application and will dismiss it summarily if it considers that it has no real prospect of success (r.6.5(1)); for example where the demand is based on a judgment, the court will not go behind it at this stage. In all other cases a date will be fixed for a directions hearing. As to the grounds on which the court will set aside a demand see r.6.5(4) of the Insolvency Rules 1986.

Paragraph 12 of the Practice Direction refers to the need to show a genuine triable issue. It would appear that the decision in *BPR Graphic Engineers (Yorks) Ltd* [2002] B.P.I.R. 544 to the effect that the test is lower than that applicable on an application for summary judgement no longer applies. The Court of Appeal has now held that there is no practical difference between a "genuine triable issue" and a "real prospect of success" for the purpose of an application to set aside a demand (*Ashworth v Newnote Ltd* [2007] EWCA Civ 793; [2007] B.P.I.R. 1012).

A petition (other than an expedited petition) may not be presented until the application is dealt with.

### Expedited petition

3E-104 Although the prescribed period for compliance with a statutory demand is 3 weeks, if a creditor can establish that there is a serious possibility that before the end of the 3 week period the value of the debtor's property will be significantly diminished then the court may allow a petition to be presented before the expiry of the 3 weeks but no bankruptcy order can be made until 3 weeks have elapsed (s.270).

### Petition

3E-105 The content of the petition (as to which see rr.6.6 – 6.11) must be verified (r.6.12(1)) and if it relies upon an unsatisfied statutory demand written evidence must be filed establishing service of the demand. The requirements to satisfy the court that service has been properly affected are set out in para.13 of the Practice Direction. If the petition relies upon a demand served more than 4 months before the filing of the petition the reason for the delay must be explained in the affidavit of verification, r.6.12(7).

The petition must be served personally. If this proves to be impossible then an application for substituted service may be made (see para.11 of the Practice Direction). The court may order service by post or other appropriate means, advertisement in a national newspaper or (rarely) the London Gazette. Again the Practice Direction sets out the criteria for this. The petition must comply with the EC Regulation and state whether it will apply and if so whether the proceedings will be main, territorial or secondary proceedings and the debtor's centre of main interests. Once presented the court fixes a date, time and place for the hearing and seals sufficient copies for service.

### Service of the petition

3E-106 The petition must be served at least 14 days before the hearing date, but if service proves to be difficult an application may be made to the court on paper for an extension of the hearing date of the petition (r.6.28 of the Insolvency Rules 1986 and para.14 of the Practice Direction). The application should be made in advance of the hearing date; if made less than 2 days before the hearing costs will not be allowed.

A first extension will generally be granted without evidence, but where a further application is made by written evidence in support may be required.

### Hearing of the petition

3E-107 The court will not make a bankruptcy order unless it is satisfied that the debt on which the petition is based is either (a) a debt which has not been paid, secured or compounded for or (b) a debt which the debtor has no reasonable prospect of being able to pay when it falls due (s.271(1)). Thus, at the hearing of the petition the court will need to be satisfied that that the debt remains due and payable. The petitioner must complete a certificate of continuing debt so as to satisfy the court that the petition debt remains due (r.6.25). In the High Court in London this is incorporated in the attendance sheet. A fresh certificate is required for each adjourned hearing.

When a petition is adjourned the court will also need to be satisfied at the adjourned hearing that the petitioner has complied with r.6.29 and given written notice to the debtor of the adjourned hearing date and time, regardless of whether the debtor attended the previous hearing. The petitioner is also required to give notice to any creditor who has given notice under r.6.23 but was not present at the hearing when the adjournment was made.

At the hearing the petitioning creditor, the debtor, any supervisor under a voluntary arrangement and any other creditor who has given notice may be heard (r.6.18(3)). If the debtor intends to oppose the petition he must file with the court and serve the petitioning creditor with a notice setting out his grounds of opposition not less than 7 days before the hearing (r.6.21). The petitioning creditor must prepare a list of supporting/opposing creditors (r.6.24).

At the hearing the court, upon being satisfied that the papers are in order, may make a bankruptcy order noting in the record the time when the order was made. The court also has general power to dismiss stay or adjourn a petition for any reason and if stayed to impose conditions (s.266(3)). The court will not allow repeated adjournments to see if a debtor maintains payments by an instalment arrangement agreed with the petitioner.

#### Withdrawal, substitution and change of carriage of petition

Once issued a petition may not be withdrawn without the permission of the court (s.266(2)). Permission will only be given at a hearing. **3E–108**

At the hearing of the petition any creditor who has given notice and was in a position to issue his own petition at the date the petition was filed may apply to be substituted as petitioner (r.6.30). This will require amendment and possibly re-service of the petition.

Where a creditor who has given proper notice but was not in a position to file a petition at the time the petition was presented appears, and the petition debt remains unpaid, he may apply to the court for carriage of the petition (r.6.31). Amendment of the petition will not be necessary. As to change of carriage generally see *Re Purvis and another* [1997] 3 All E.R. 663.

#### Debtor's petition

The only ground upon which a debtor may present his own petition is that he is unable to pay his debts (s.272(1) and rr.6.37 to 6.50). The petition must contain sufficient information to establish that it is being brought in the right court and be accompanied by a statement of affairs detailing the debtor's assets and liabilities. The court will usually hear the petition immediately. Generally the High Court will make the order in the absence of the debtor. Where a bankruptcy order is made the court will notify the official receiver immediately. **3E–109**

#### Review, rescind or vary

Section 375(1) of the Insolvency Act gives the court power to review, rescind or vary any order made by it in the exercise of its jurisdiction. This provision is of very broad application but should not be used in place of an appeal. The fact that an appeal is pending does not prevent to court from rehearing a matter and reviewing any order made. The exercise of the power should be confined to cases in which there has been a change of circumstance since the making of the original order. The court may apply this provision to a bankruptcy order in circumstances where annulment is not possible (*Fitch v Official Receiver* [1996] 1 W.L.R. 242). For a detailed analysis of the jurisdiction see *Papanicola v Humphreys* [2005] EWHC 335 (Ch); [2005] 2 All E.R. 418. **3E–110**

#### Annulment

The jurisdiction to annul a bankruptcy order is found in ss.261 and 282 of the Insolvency Act. Section 261(1)(a) allows a bankrupt to apply for the annulment of the bankruptcy order if his creditors have at a meeting called for the purpose approved a proposal for a voluntary arrangement. The court cannot make the order before the **3E–111** end of the period of 28 days beginning with the day on which the chairman's report was made to the court (s.261(2)). The official receiver and trustee (if appointed) are necessary parties and must be given notice of the application but they are not required to file any report. If the court feels that a relevant obligation under the arrangement has yet to be fulfilled, for example if a third party is to make a single lump sum payment, then the court may adjourn the annulment application until the payment has been received.

Section 282(1) gives the court power to annul a bankruptcy order on the basis that either (a) on grounds existing at the time the order was made it should not have been made or (b) the bankrupt has paid or secured his debts in full. Rules 6.206(1)(a), (2)–(4) as amended relate to ground (a) above. A report is required from the trustee or official receiver. The courts will generally be sympathetic if the debtor can provide a reasonable explanation for non-attendance in circumstances where his attendance would in all probability have led to the adjournment or dismissal of the petition. In such cases the annulment will be on terms that he pays the official receiver's fees, costs charges and expenses and the creditor's costs of the annulment application. Further, unless the creditor agrees to the petition being dismissed, it will be restored to the list for hearing. There is no point in annulling if the debtor is hopelessly insolvent or if the trustee's inquiries reveal that there is a strong case that the bankrupt has entered into antecedent transactions.

Annulment under s.282(1)(b) can only be granted where the official receiver or trustee confirms that he is satisfied it is appropriate and files with the court a detailed report to this effect (r.6.207). In the absence of such report the annulment cannot be granted. Note that before the court makes the order it must generally be satisfied that the debts and costs of the bankruptcy have been paid: the provisions relating to security for bankruptcy costs and debts relate only to those which are disputed or are claimed by creditors who cannot be traced (r.6.211).

The annulment of a bankruptcy order is a matter of discretion, and the court will not make an order where the bankrupt has not, for example, complied with his obligations to the official receiver or where there has been misconduct.

Where after the annulment has been granted a trustee wants an order for his release he must make a separate fee paid application.

### Discharge

**3E–112** Section 279 of the Insolvency Act 1986 provides for automatic discharge for the majority of bankrupts after one year (s.279(1)) or earlier if the official receiver files notice (see r.6.214A) that the affairs of the bankrupt do not require investigation or that such investigation has been concluded (s.279(2)) in which case the bankrupt is discharged when the notice is filed. The trustee (where one has been appointed) or a creditor may, within 28 days of receiving notice from the official receiver of his intention to file a notice under s.279(2), inform the official receiver that he objects to the proposed course of action (r.6.214A(5)). Reasons for objection must be given. The official receiver may reject the objection, he must also give reasons and the trustee or creditor may appeal (r.6.214A(5)(b) and r.7.50, Insolvency Rules 1986). Any appeal must be made within 14 days of the notification by the official receiver of his decision (r.7.50(2)). The official receiver may still apply to suspend discharge if a bankrupt fails to comply with his obligations. Section 279(3) provides that the official receiver may apply to suspend discharge until the end of a specified period or until the fulfilment of a specified condition (see also r.6.215).

### The bankrupt's home

**3E–113** Section 283A of the Insolvency Act 1986 introduces restrictions on the right of a trustee to realise the home of the bankrupt. Under this provision, where the bankrupt had an interest in a dwelling-house which was the sole or principal residence of the bankrupt, the bankrupt's spouse or former spouse at the date of the bankruptcy order, that interest ceases to be comprised in the bankrupt's estate at the end of three years beginning with the date of the bankruptcy and revests automatically in the bankrupt unless the trustee makes an application within the three year period or takes any of the other steps set out in the section. The three year period may be extended (s.283A(6)).

### Bankruptcy Restrictions Order

**3E–114** Section 281A and Sch.4A of the Insolvency Act 1986 set out post-discharge restrictions, the bankruptcy restrictions order and undertaking.

***Paragraph numbers marked with a "+" can be found online and on CD.***

The Secretary of State for Trade and Industry or the official receiver may make the application for a bankruptcy restrictions order (para.1, Sch.4A, Insolvency Act 1986). It is made as an ordinary application in the bankruptcy and must be supported by a report setting out the conduct relied on (r.6.241). The timing of the application is crucial and it must be made before the end of one year, beginning with the commencement of the bankruptcy (i.e. the making of the bankruptcy order) unless the discharge period has been suspended (para.3, Sch.4A). The application and supporting evidence must be served not more than 14 days after making the application (r.6.242(1)) and the defendant must file an acknowledgment of service indicating whether or not he contests the application not more than 14 days after service upon him (r.6.242(3)). Evidence in opposition must be filed within 28 days of service of the application and served on the Secretary of State within 3 days of filing it at the court (r.6.243(1)). The Secretary of State must file any evidence in reply within 14 days of receipt of the evidence in opposition and serve this on the bankrupt as soon as is reasonably practicable (r.6.243(2)).

A number of grounds of conduct likely to lead to the making of an order are set out in para.2(2) of Sch.4A but these are not exhaustive. The making of an order is obligatory if the court reaches the conclusion that it is appropriate to make one having regard to the bankrupt's conduct (para.2(1), Sch.4A). The order comes into force when it is made and may be for a period of between two and fifteen years (para.3, Sch.4A). The Act and the Rules also allow the court to make an interim bankruptcy restrictions order (see rr.6.245 to 6.248, Insolvency Rules 1986).

See generally *Randhawa v Official Receiver* [2006] EWHC 2946 (Ch); [2007] 1 W.L.R. 1700.

A bankrupt may enter into an undertaking, which has the same effect as an order (paras 7 to 9, Sch.4A; see also r.6.249, Insolvency Rules 1986). As to the circumstances in which it is appropriate to make an interim bankruptcy restrictions order see *Official Receiver v Merchant* [2006] B.P.I.R. 1525.



#### Appeal

Section 375(2) provides that an appeal from a decision of a County Court or a registrar of the High Court lies to a single judge of the High Court, and an appeal from the decision of that judge is to the Court of Appeal. Paragraph 17 of the Practice Direction sets out the procedure for first and second appeals. The appeal is a true appeal limited to a review of the decision of the lower court (*Vadher v Wesigard* [1997] B.C.C. 219) and will only be allowed if the decision was wrong or unjust because of a serious procedural irregularity or other irregularity in the proceedings. Permission is required for a second appeal and will only be given where either the appeal raises an important point of principle or practice or there is some other compelling reason. Where the first decision has been given by a judge of the High Court then either his permission is required or, if he refuses, the permission of the Court of Appeal is required before the appeal can proceed. **3E–115**

With effect from October 2, 2006 a first appeal in insolvency proceedings is subject to the permission requirement in CPR, r.52.3. The time in which to appeal is extended from 14 to 21 days. See also para.3E–123 below.

### *Applications to fix an office holder's remuneration*

The Insolvency Act 1986 and the Insolvency Rules 1986 allow an office holder to apply to the court for his remuneration to be fixed. An administrator may apply (rr.2.47(6) and 2.49(1)), as may a liquidator in relation to the remuneration of a receiver (s.36(1)) or in relation to his own remuneration (rr.4.130(1)) and 4.148A(6)). The court will not generally interfere in relation to the remuneration of a receiver unless it is excessive (*Potters Oils, Re (No.2)* [1986] 1 W.L.R. 201; [1985] 1 B.C.C. 99). The remuneration of a provisional liquidator must be fixed by the court (r.4.30(1)). **3E–116**

Detailed guidance on office holders' remuneration is contained in the Report (July 1998), Statement of Insolvency Practice 9 (Recovery Professionals) and the Practice Statement—The Fixing and Approval of the Remuneration of Appointees (2004) the text of which can be found at para.3E–117 to 3E–123.

As to recent case law see *Barker v Bajjon* [2008] B.P.I.R. 771; *Cabletel Installations Ltd (In Liquidation), Re* [2005] B.P.I.R. 28, Ch D; *Independent Insurance Co Ltd (No.1), Re*

[2002] EWHC 1577 (Ch); [2003] B.P.I.R. 562; [2002] 2 B.C.L.C. 709, Ch D; *Independent Insurance Co Ltd (No.2)*; Re [2003] EWHC 51 (Ch); [2003] B.P.I.R. 577; [2003] 1 B.C.L.C. 640, Ch D; *Mirror Group Newspapers plc v Maxwell (No.2)* [1998] 1 B.C.L.C. 638; [1998] B.C.C. 324; Ch D; *Simion v Brown* [2007] EWHC 511 (Ch); [2007] B.P.I.R. 412, *UIC Insurance Company Ltd (In Provisional Liquidation) (No.1)*, Re [2006] EWHC 2717 (Ch); [2007] B.P.I.R. 494, Ch D; *UIC Insurance Company Ltd (In Provisional Liquidation) (No.2), Re* [2007] B.P.I.R. 589 Ch D.

### *Practice Statement—The Fixing and Approval of the Remuneration of Appointees (2004)*

**For "Practice Statement—The Fixing and Approval of the Remuneration of Appointees (2004)" see paragraphs 3E–118+ to 3E–123+ on White Book on Westlaw UK or the Civil Procedure CD.**

### *Practice Note on the Hearing of Insolvency Proceedings*

**3E–124** 1. The following statement was issued by the Vice-Chancellor.

2. This Practice Note supersedes all previous Practice Statements of the Bankruptcy Registrars dealing with jurisdiction and work distribution and the Guidelines issued by the Insolvency Court Users' Committee in November 1988.

3. As a general rule all petitions, claims and applications (except for those listed in paragraph 4 below) should be listed for initial hearing before a registrar or district judge in accordance with rule 7.6(2) Insolvency Rules 1986.

4. The following applications should always be listed before a judge:

**Proceedings relating to insolvent companies**

- applications for committal for contempt
- applications for an administration order
- applications for an injunction
- applications for the appointment of a provisional liquidator
- interim applications and applications for directions or case management after any proceedings have been referred or adjourned to the judge (except where liberty to apply to the registrar or district judge has been given);

**Proceedings relating to insolvent individuals**

- applications for committal for contempt
- applications for an injunction
- interim applications and applications for directions or case management after any proceedings have been referred or adjourned to the judge (except where liberty to apply to the registrar or district judge has been given).

5. When deciding whether to hear proceedings themselves or refer or adjourn them to the judge, the registrar or district judge should have regard to the following factors:

- the complexity of the proceedings
- whether the proceedings raise new or controversial points of law
- the likely date and length of the hearing

***Paragraph numbers marked with a "+" can be found online and on CD.***

- public interest in the proceedings
- the availability in the court which is likely to hear the proceedings of relevant specialist expertise.

6. Litigants and their advisors are reminded that paragraph 17 of the Practice Direction on Insolvency Proceedings applies to appeals and that an appeal from a registrar, district judge or County Court judge lies, in the first instance and without permission, to a single judge of the High Court.

23rd May 2005

### *Practice Note—Validation Orders (ss.127 and 284 Insolvency Act 1986)*

The following Practice Note was issued by the Chancellor of the High Court. **3E–125.0**

## Companies **3E–125**

1. Section 127(1) Insolvency Act 1986 provides,

> "In a winding up by the court, any disposition of the company's property, and any transfer of shares, or alteration in the status of the company's members, made after the commencement of the winding up is, unless the court otherwise orders, void".

Section 129(2) Insolvency Act 1986 provides that,

> "[T]he winding up of a company by the court is deemed to commence at the time of the presentation of the petition for winding up".

2. A company against which a winding up petition has been presented ("the company") may apply to the court after presentation of the petition for relief from the effects of the foregoing provisions by seeking an order that a disposition or dispositions of its property, including payments out of its bank account (whether such account is in credit or overdrawn), shall not be void in the event of a winding up order being made on the hearing of the petition (a "validation order").

3. In accordance with the *Practice Note on the Hearing of Insolvency Proceedings of 23 May 2005* [2005] BCC 456, [2005] B.P.I.R. 688 an application for a validation order should generally be made to the registrar or district judge. An application should be made to the judge only (a) where it is urgent and no registrar or district judge is available to hear it, or (b) where it is complex or raises new or controversial points of law, or (c) is estimated to last longer than 30 minutes.

4. Save in exceptional circumstances, notice of the making of the application should be given to (a) the petitioning creditor, (b) any person entitled to receive a copy of the petition pursuant to r. 4.10 Insolvency Rules 1986, (c) any creditor who has given notice to the petitioner of his intention to appear on the hearing of the petition pursuant to r. 4.16 Insolvency Rules 1986 and (d) any creditor who has been substituted as petitioner pursuant to r. 4.19 Insolvency Rules 1986.

5. The application should be supported by written evidence in the form of an affidavit or witness statement which, save in exceptional circumstances, should be made by a director or officer of the company who is intimately acquainted with the company's affairs and financial

circumstances. If appropriate, supporting evidence in the form of an affidavit or witness statement from the company's accountant should also be produced.

6. The extent and contents of the evidence will vary according to the circumstances and the nature of the relief sought, but in the majority of cases it should include, as a minimum, the following information:

(a) when and to whom notice has been given in accordance with paragraph 4 above;
(b) the company's registered office;
(c) company's nominal and paid up capital;
(d) details of the circumstances leading to presentation of the petition;
(e) how the company became aware of presentation of the petition;
(f) whether the petition debt is admitted or disputed and, if the latter, brief details of the basis on which the debt is disputed;
(g) full details of the company's financial position including details of its assets (including details of any security and the amount(s) secured) and liabilities, which should be supported, as far as possible, by documentary evidence, e.g. the latest filed accounts, any draft audited accounts, management accounts or estimated statement of affairs;
(h) a cash flow forecast and profit and loss projection for the period for which the order is sought;
(i) details of the dispositions or payments in respect of which an order is sought;
(j) the reasons relied on in support of the need for such dispositions or payments to be made;
(k) other information relevant to the exercise of the court's discretion;
(l) details of any consents obtained from the persons mentioned in paragraph 4 above (supported by documentary evidence where appropriate).

7. Where an application is made urgently to enable payments to be made which are essential to continued trading (e.g. wages) and it is not possible to assemble all the evidence listed above, the court may consider granting limited relief for a short period, but there should be sufficient evidence to satisfy the court that the interests of creditors are unlikely to be prejudiced.

8. Where the application involves a disposition of property the court will need details of the property (including its title number if the property is land) and to be satisfied that any proposed disposal will be at a proper value. Accordingly an independent valuation should be obtained and exhibited to the evidence.

9. The court will need to be satisfied by credible evidence that the company is solvent and able to pay its debts as they fall due or that a particular transaction or series of transactions in respect of which the order is sought will be beneficial to or will not prejudice the interests

of all the unsecured creditors as a class (*Denney v John Hudson & Co Ltd* [1992] B.C.L.C. 901, [1992] BCC 503, CA; *Re Fairway Graphics Ltd* [1991] B.C.L.C. 468).

10. A draft of the order sought should be attached to the application.

**Individuals**

11. Section 284 Insolvency Act 1986 provides, inter alia,

"(1) Where a person is adjudged bankrupt, any disposition of property made by that person in the period to which this section applies is void except to the extent that it is or was made with the consent of the court, or is or was subsequently ratified by the court.

"(2) Subsection (1) applies to a payment (whether in cash or otherwise) as it applies to a disposition of property and, accordingly, where any payment is void by virtue of that subsection, the person shall hold the sum paid for the bankrupt as part of his estate.

"(3) This section applies to the period beginning with the day of the presentation of the petition for the bankruptcy order and ending with the vesting, under Chapter IV of this Part [of the Act], of the bankrupt's estate in a trustee".

12. A person against whom a bankruptcy petition has been presented ("the debtor") may apply to the court after presentation of the petition for relief from the effects of the foregoing provisions by seeking an order that any disposition of his assets or payment made out of his funds, including any bank account (whether it is in credit or overdrawn), shall not be void in the event of a bankruptcy order being made on the petition (a "validation order").

13. In accordance with the *Practice Note on the Hearing of Insolvency Proceedings of 23 May 2005* [2005] BCC 456, [2005] BPIR 688 an application for a validation order should be made to the registrar or district judge.

14. Save in exceptional circumstances, notice of the making of the application should be given to (a) the petitioning creditor(s) or other petitioner, (b) any creditor who has given notice to the petitioner of his intention to appear on the hearing of the petition pursuant to r. 6.23 Insolvency Rules 1986, (c) any creditor who has been substituted as petitioner pursuant to r. 6.30 Insolvency Rules 1986 and (d) any creditor who has carriage of the petition pursuant to r. 6.3 1 Insolvency Rules 1986.

15. The application should be supported by written evidence in the form of an affidavit or witness statement which, save in exceptional circumstances, should be made by the debtor. If appropriate, supporting evidence in the form of an affidavit or witness statement from the debtor's accountant should also be produced.

16. The extent and contents of the evidence will vary according to the circumstances and the nature of the relief sought, but in a case where the debtor is trading or carrying on business it should include, as a minimum, the following information:

(a) when and to whom notice has been given in accordance with paragraph 14 above;

(b) brief details of the circumstances leading to presentation of the petition;
(c) how the debtor became aware of the presentation of the petition;
(d) whether the petition debt is admitted or disputed and, if the latter, brief details of the basis on which the debt is disputed;
(e) full details of the debtor's financial position including details of his assets (including details of any security and the amount(s) secured) and liabilities, which should be supported, as far as possible, by documentary evidence, e.g. accounts, draft accounts, management accounts or estimated statement of affairs;
(f) a cash flow forecast and profit and loss projection for the period for which the order is sought;
(g) details of the dispositions or payments in respect of which an order is sought;
(h) the reasons relied on in support of the need for such dispositions or payments to be made;
(i) any other information relevant to the exercise of the court's discretion;
(j) details of any consents obtained from the persons mentioned in paragraph 14 above (supported by documentary evidence where appropriate).

17. Where an application is made urgently to enable payments to be made which are essential to continued trading (e.g. wages) and it is not possible to assemble ali the evidence listed above, the court may consider granting limited relief for a short period, but there should be sufficient evidence to satisfy the court that the interests of creditors are unlikely to be prejudiced.

18. Where the debtor is not trading or carrying on business and the application relates only to a proposed sale, mortgage or re-mortgage of the debtor's home evidence of the following will generally suffice:
(a) when and to whom notice has been given in accordance with paragraph 14 above;
(b) whether the petition debt is admitted or disputed and, if the latter, brief details of the basis on which the debt is disputed;
(c) details of the property to be sold, mortgaged or re-mortgaged (including its title number);
(d) the value of the property and the proposed sale price, or details of the mortgage or re-mortgage;
(e) details of any existing mortgages or charges on the property and redemption figures;
(f) the costs of sale (e.g. solicitors' or agents' costs);
(g) how and by whom any net proceeds of sale (or sums coming into the debtor's hands as a result of any mortgage or re-mortgage) are to be held pending the final hearing of the petition;

(h) any other information relevant to the exercise of the court's discretion;

(i) details of any consents obtained from the persons mentioned in paragraph 14 above (supported by documentary evidence where appropriate).

19. Whether or not the debtor is trading or carrying on business, where the application involves a disposition of property the court will need to be satisfied that any proposed disposal will be at a proper value. Accordingly an independent valuation should be obtained and exhibited to the evidence.

20. The court will need to be satisfied by credible evidence that the debtor is solvent and able to pay his debts as they fall due or that a particular transaction or series of transactions in respect of which the order is sought will be beneficial to or will not prejudice the interests of all the unsecured creditors as a class (*Denney v John Hudson & Co Ltd* [1992] B.C.L.C. 901; [1992] BCC 503, CA; *Re Fairway Graphics Ltd* [1991] B.C.L.C. 468).

21. A draft of the order sought should be attached to the application.

**Ratification of transactions**

22. Similar considerations to those set out above are likely to apply to applications seeking ratification of a transaction or payment after the making of a winding up order or bankruptcy order.

11th January 2007

INSOLVENCY

## Insolvency Act 1986

1986 c. 45 **3E–126**

ARRANGEMENT OF SECTIONS

PART I



***Paragraph numbers marked with a "+" can be found online and on CD.***

***Paragraph numbers marked with a "+" can be found online and on CD.***

CHAPTER II



CHAPTER III



CHAPTER IV



CHAPTER V



CHAPTER VI



***Paragraph numbers marked with a "+" can be found online and on CD.***

CHAPTER VII



CHAPTER VIII



***Paragraph numbers marked with a "+" can be found online and on CD.***

***Paragraph numbers marked with a "+" can be found online and on CD.***



INSOLVENCY

PART VI



PART VII



PART VIIA



PART VIII



***Paragraph numbers marked with a "+" can be found online and on CD.***

***Paragraph numbers marked with a "+" can be found online and on CD.***

***Paragraph numbers marked with a "+" can be found online and on CD.***

***Paragraph numbers marked with a "+" can be found online and on CD.***



INSOLVENCY

***Paragraph numbers marked with a "+" can be found online and on CD.***

**Paragraph numbers marked with a "+" denote content that is available on White Book on Westlaw UK or the Civil Procedure CD.**

***Paragraph numbers marked with a "+" can be found online and on CD.***

# The Insolvency Rules 1986

3E–1365

## 1986/1925

ARRANGEMENT OF SECTIONS



***Paragraph numbers marked with a "+" can be found online and on CD.***

***Paragraph numbers marked with a "+" can be found online and on CD.***

***Paragraph numbers marked with a "+" can be found online and on CD.***

***Paragraph numbers marked with a "+" can be found online and on CD.***

***Paragraph numbers marked with a "+" can be found online and on CD.***

***Paragraph numbers marked with a "+" can be found online and on CD.***

INSOLVENCY

***Paragraph numbers marked with a "+" can be found online and on CD.***

***Paragraph numbers marked with a "+" can be found online and on CD.***

***Paragraph numbers marked with a "+" can be found online and on CD.***

***Paragraph numbers marked with a "+" can be found online and on CD.***

***Paragraph numbers marked with a "+" can be found online and on CD.***

***Paragraph numbers marked with a "+" can be found online and on CD.***

***Paragraph numbers marked with a "+" can be found online and on CD.***

***Paragraph numbers marked with a "+" can be found online and on CD.***



INSOLVENCY

***Paragraph numbers marked with a "+" can be found online and on CD.***

Schedule 2—Alternative Courts
Schedule 3—Shorthand Writers' Remuneration
Schedule 4—Forms
Schedule 5—Punishment of Offences Under The Rules
Schedule 6—Determination of Insolvency Office Holder's Remuneration
Paragraph numbers marked with a "+" denote content that is available on the White Book on Westlaw UK Service or the Civil Procedure CD.

### Debt Relief Orders

Section 251A in Pt 7A of the Insolvency Act 1986 (inserted by the Tribunals, Courts and Enforcement Act 2007) provides for "Debt Relief Orders" ("DRO"). Such orders are very limited in scope but where one is available is an alternative to a Bankruptcy Order, or possibly even a county court administration order. **3E–2859**

The Insolvency (Amendment) Rules 2009 (SI 2009/642) brought these orders into force as from April 1, 2009. They are a new form of personal insolvency procedure that entails the making administratively by the Official Receiver (not the court) of a DRO on the application of the individual debtor. The effect of the order is to stay enforcement by creditors and to discharge the debts after a period of one year. While the DRO is in force the debtor is subject to similar restrictions to bankruptcy.

The court plays no part in the making of a DRO. Application is direct to the Official Receiver through an approved intermediary (see *http://www.insolvency.gov.uk* [Accessed May 14, 2009] for more details and a list of approved intermediaries). The Official Receiver makes the order if satisfied that the criteria are met.

### Criteria for a Debt Relief Order

To apply for a DRO debtors must: **3E–2860**

(a) be unable to pay their debts;
(b) owe less than £15,000;
(c) not own their own home;
(d) have assets with a total value not exceeding £300 (additionally, a car not exceeding a value of £1,000 is permitted);
(e) after tax, national insurance and normal household expenses, have disposable income of no more than £50 a month;
(f) be domiciled in England and Wales;
(g) not have been subject of a DRO within the last six years;
(h) not be involved in another formal insolvency procedure.

### Limited role of the court

The DRO is made by the Official Receiver not the court. However, any debtor or creditor dissatisfied with the decision of the Official Receiver may apply to the court. Further, the Official Receiver can apply to the court for directions and either a debtor or creditor can apply for an extension of the moratorium period. Additionally, the court could refuse to make a bankruptcy order or an administration order if satisfied that a DRO would be more appropriate. **3E–2861**

Schedule 2—Alternative Courts
Schedule 3—Shorthand Writers' Remuneration
Schedule 4—Forms
Schedule 5—Punishment of Offences Under the Rules
Schedule 6—Determination of Insolvency Office Holder's Remuneration
Paragraph numbers marked with a + denote content that is available on the White Book on Westlaw UK Service or the Civil Procedure CD.

**Debt Relief Orders**

3E-2859 Section 251A in Pt 7A of the Insolvency Act 1986 (inserted by the Tribunals, Courts and Enforcement Act 2007) provides for "Debt Relief Orders" ("DROs"). Such orders are very limited in scope but where one is available is an alternative to a Bankruptcy Order, or possibly even a county court administration order.

The Insolvency (Amendment) Rules 2009 (SI 2009/642) brought these orders into force as from April 6, 2009. They are a new form of personal insolvency proceeding that involve the making administratively by the Official Receiver (not the court) of a DRO on the application of the individual debtor. The effect of the order is to stay enforcement by creditors and to discharge the debts after a period of one year. While the DRO is in force the debtor is subject to similar restrictions to bankruptcy.

The court plays no part in the making of a DRO. Application is direct to the Official Receiver through an approved intermediary (see *http://www.insolvency.gov.uk* [Accessed May 13, 2009] for more details and a list of approved intermediaries). The Official Receiver makes the order if satisfied that the criteria are met.

**Criteria for a Debt Relief Order**

3E-2860 To apply for a DRO debtors must:

(a) be unable to pay their debts;

(b) owe less than £15,000;

(c) not own their own homes;

(d) have assets with a total value not exceeding £300 (additionally a car not exceeding a value of £1000 is permitted);

(e) after tax, national insurance and normal household expenses, have disposable income of no more than £50 a month;

(f) be domiciled in England and Wales;

(g) not have been subject of a DRO within the last six years;

(h) not be involved in another formal insolvency procedure.

**Limited role of the court**

3E-2861 The DRO is made by the Official Receiver not the court. However, any debtor or creditor dissatisfied with the decision of the Official Receiver may apply to the court. Further, the Official Receiver can apply to the court for directions and either a debtor or creditor can apply for an extension of the moratorium period. Additionally, the court could refuse to make a bankruptcy order or an administration order if satisfied that a DRO would be more appropriate.

*Paragraph numbers marked with a + can be found online and on CD.*

# 3F PERSONAL INJURY

## Introduction

Personal injury litigation forms a significant percentage of the work of the civil courts. This section includes materials which will be of special use to practitioners in this important area. Of course, the CPR apply to all types of litigation and this Section therefore supplements the rules and commentary in Vol.1. The CPR heralded a major change of direction for the adversarial system. Litigation is not the first option but is to be resorted to because there is no alternative. Thus the Pre-Action Protocol for Personal Injury Claims (C2–001) and the Pre-Action Protocol for Resolution of Clinical Disputes (C3–001) are the most widely used of the pre-action protocols. **3F–1**

A number of rules in the CPR make special provision for personal injury cases. These include:

r.2.3(1)—definition of "claim for personal injuries"

r.14.1A—Pre-action admissions

r.16.3(3)—pleading requirement for "statement of value"

PD 16 para.4—pleading requirements for PI claims, including the requirement to attach a medical report to the Particulars of Claim where the claimant is relying on the evidence of a medical practitioner

PD 16 para.5—pleading requirements for Fatal Accident Act cases

r.26.6—different financial values in PI cases for purpose of allocation to track

Pt 41—Provisional Damages

In addition the following rules, though not confined to PI cases, are often encountered:

Pt 25.1—Interim Remedies

PD 25B—Interim Payments

PD 26 para.12.4—Disposal Hearings

Part 28—The Fast Track (most fast track cases are PI cases)

r.31.6—standard disclosure

r.31.16—pre-action disclosure

Pt 35—Expert Evidence

Pt 36—Offers to Settle and Payments into Court

Pt 41, Sect.II—the courts powers to order periodical payments in PI cases

There are relatively few rules that have no application at all to PI cases. Thus Parts not specifically mentioned here should be referred to as the need arises.

In addition to statutes thought to be of particular use to PI practitioners this section includes the Rehabilitation Code of Practice. Rehabilitation is a welcome development and is something to be considered in all cases. It is of particular importance where the claimant has suffered serious injury. Rehabilitation concentrates on assessing the claimant's needs (including medical treatment) and for the defendant's insurers to meet the cost of providing them at an early stage. This marks a departure from thinking of claims solely in terms of money. Successful rehabilitation provides both a quicker and better outcome for the claimant and a lower cost for insurers. The Code provides a framework supported by all the main associations for insurers and PI lawyers in the UK. Note that the Rehabilitation Protocol now formally forms part of the Personal Injury Pre-Action protocol.

## Material relevant to personal injury located elsewhere in this work

*Statutes and Regulations* **3F–2**



***Paragraph numbers marked with a "+" can be found online and on CD.***

## Access to Health Records Act 1990

3F–3 (1990 c.23)

ARRANGEMENT OF SECTIONS



**Paragraph numbers marked with a "+" denote content that is available on White Book on Westlaw UK or the Civil Procedure CD.**

### General note

3F–4 *The Access to Health Records Act 1990 came into force on 1st November 1991.*

The practical application of the parts of this Act included here, following the modifications introduced by the Data Protection Act 1998 is to enable the obtaining of the health records (as defined in s.1) of (in Scotland) persons who lack capacity, and more generally in relation to the medical records of deceased persons (where the application may be made by the Personal Representative of the Deceased or any person having a claim arising from the Deceased's death. The categories of persons entitled to apply under this Act were restricted in favour of the general personal data access regime contained in the Data Protection Act 1998, but use of the Access to Health Records Act 1990 may still be required for the two categories of application just referred to. Only the sections of direct relevance to personal injury claims are set out here.

### Obtaining medical records: the 1990 Act and the Data Protection Act 1998

3F–5 In general patients (in the non-CPR sense of that term) have a right to have copies of their medical records, but in exceptional circumstances the law allows for records to be withheld. The Data Protection Act 1998 (most cases) and the Access to Health Records Act 1990 (in the two situations referred to in the preceding note) set out the legal code which applies, but in practice what is required in the first instance is to contact the medical professional concerned or to the Medical Records section or department in the case of larger institutions such as hospitals. The Clinical Disputes protocol at C3–001 in this work contains further information and pro-forma documents to assist. See also Health Service Circular HSC 2000/009 on the topic of patient information. A strictly limited fee may be charged for providing copies, under the provisions of the Data Protection Act 1998. (For a note on fees see the notes to section 4 below).

Disclosure of medical records under the 1990 Act may be refused on the basis set out in s.5. (Similarly under the Data Protection Act 1998 a record holder may refuse to supply records if he/she believes that disclosure of the contents may have an adverse affect on the patient's health (Data Protection (Subject Access Modification) (Health) Order 2000 (SI 2000/413)), or may identify a third party (Data Protection Act 1998 s.7(4)). Under the 1998 Act refusal is permitted if copying requires "disproportionate effort" for which see the provisions of the Data Protection (Conditions under Paragraph 3 of Part II of Schedule 1) Order 2000 (SI 2000/185).)

***Paragraph numbers marked with a "+" can be found online and on CD.***

### Medical Reports prepared for insurers/employers—Access to Medical Records Act 1988

For the law relating to access to medical reports prepared on behalf of insurers or employers, see s.1 of the Access to Medical Reports Act 1988 which states: **3F–6**

"It shall be the right of an individual to have access, in accordance with the provisions of this Act, to any medical report relating to the individual which is to be, or has been, supplied by a medical practitioner for employment purposes or insurance purposes".

That Act thus allows patients to obtain access to reports for insurers or employers and provides for the patient to ask for amendments. The patient can require that his/her own comments are appended if the report is not corrected. The Act also requires the patient's consent before any information is released to a third party in the context of reports requested by insurers or employers. The patient must be provided with the report before it is sent if the patient so wishes and the patient also has a right to refuse consent for the provision of a report.

### Disclosure by doctor to own legal advisers

Note that there is some authority to the effect that a doctor who discloses a patient's medical records to his own solicitors, for the purpose of seeking legal advice as to whether the doctor is obliged to disclose the records in the course of litigation brought by the patient against him, does not thereby act in breach of the Data Protection legislation or the Access to Health Records Act 1990, or the general law of confidentiality (*Matthew Yeboah Mensah v Robert H Jones* [2004] EWHC 2699 (Ch D)). It was held that the disclosure was necessary to allow the doctor to obtain legal advice as to the extent of his obligation to make disclosure. **3F–7**

### Relevant Pre-action Protocols

See the Protocol for the Resolution of Clinical Disputes in Vol.1 of this work at C3–001 and the Protocol for Obtaining Hospital Records at C3–019. **3F–8**

### Definitions

"health record" "patient" "holder" see s.1 **3F–9**

"health professional" see s.2

"care" "general practitoner" "Health Authority" "Health Board" "health service body" "information" "make" "Primary Care Trust" "Special Health Authority" "Strategic Health Authority" see s.11

**For ss.1 to 6 of the Access to Health Records Act 1990 (see Arrangement) plus any related commentary see paragraphs 3F–10+ to 3F–29+ on White Book on Westlaw UK or the Civil Procedure CD.**

* * * *

## Applications to the court

**8.**—(1) Subject to subsection (2) below, where the court is satisfied, on an application made by the person concerned within such period as may be prescribed by rules of court, that the holder of a health record has failed to comply with any requirement of this Act, the court may order the holder to comply with that requirement. **3F–30**

(2) The court shall not entertain an application under subsection (1) above unless it is satisfied that the applicant has taken all such steps to secure compliance with the requirement as may be prescribed by regulations made by the Secretary of State.

(3) For the purposes of subsection (2) above, the Secretary of State may by regulations require the holders of health records to make such arrangements for dealing with complaints that they have

*Paragraph numbers marked with a "+" can be found online and on CD.*

PERSONAL INJURY

failed to comply with any requirements of this Act as may be prescribed by the regulations.

(4) For the purpose of determining any question whether an applicant is entitled to be given access under section 3(2) above to any health record, or any part of a health record, the court—

(a) may require the record or part to be made available for its own inspection; but

(b) shall not, pending determination of that question in the applicant's favour, require the record or part to be disclosed to him or his representatives whether by discovery (or, in Scotland, recovery) or otherwise.

**For s.11 of the Access to Health Records Act 1990 (see Arrangement) plus any related commentary see paragraphs 3F–31+ to 3F–32+on White Book on Westlaw UK or the Civil Procedure CD.**

## Damages Act 1996

3F–33 (1996 c.48)

ARRANGEMENT OF SECTIONS



**Paragraph numbers marked with a "+" denote content that is available on White Book on Westlaw UK or the Civil Procedure CD.**

### Note

3F–34 By s.8 (not reproduced in this work) this Act came into force two months after date of passage, i.e. in force from September 24, 1996.

### The Courts Act 2003

3F–35 By s.100 and s.101 of the Courts Act 2003, which received Royal Assent on November 20, 2003, and which came into force on April 1, 2005 (SI 2005/910); ss.2, 2A, 2B and 4 were extensively substituted, and the text is shown here as amended by that Act.

### Assumed rate of return on investment of damages

3F–36 **1.**—(1) In determining the return to be expected from the investment of a sum awarded as damages for future pecuniary loss in an action for personal injury the court shall, subject to and in accordance with rules of court made for the purposes of this section, take into account such rate of return (if any) as may from time to time be prescribed by an order made by the Lord Chancellor.

(2) Subsection (1) above shall not however prevent the court taking a different rate of return into account if any party to the proceedings shows that it is more appropriate in the case in question.

(3) An order under subsection (1) above may prescribe different rates of return for different classes of case.

(4) Before making an order under subsection (1) above the Lord Chancellor shall consult the Government Actuary and the Treasury; and any order under that subsection shall be made by statutory instrument subject to annulment in pursuance of a resolution of either House of Parliament.

[(5) In the application of this section to Scotland—

(a) for the reference to the Lord Chancellor in subsections (1) and (4) there is substituted a reference to the Scottish Ministers; and

(b) in subsection (4)—

(i) "and the Treasury" is omitted; and

(ii) for "either House of Parliament" there is substituted "the Scottish Parliament".]

*Note* —Subsection (5) substituted by (Scotland Act 1998 (Consequential Modifications) (No.2) Order (SI 1999/1820) Sch.2(I), para.126(2). **3F–37**

**"personal injury"**

By s.7 (not printed here), "personal injury" includes any disease and any impairment of a person's physical or mental condition and references to a claim or action for personal injury include references to such a claim or action brought by virtue of the Law Reform (Miscellaneous Provisions) Act 1934 and to a claim or action brought by virtue of the Fatal Accidents Act 1976. **3F–38**

**Orders and regulations under this section**

The Damages (Personal Injury) Order 2001 (SI 2002/2301). **3F–39**

**Note**

Section 10 of the Civil Evidence Act 1995 (see 9B–1080) provides that the H.M. Government Actuary's Department's tables known as the Ogden Tables are admissible in evidence when that section comes into force. In practice such tables are regularly used in court in any event: see *Wells v Wells* [1999] 1 A.C. 345 referred to more fully below, and *Longden v British Coal Corp* (1998) A.C. 653 at 671; [1997] 3 W.L.R. 1336 and in Scotland it has been held that the court can take judicial notice of the Ogden Tables at least for some purposes: *O'Brien's Curator Bonis v British Steel Plc* 1991 S.C. 315. In simple terms a claimant who receives a lump sum at trial representing future lost income is expected to be able to derive an investment income from that lump sum whilst also drawing down on the funds. An award of the full amount of the loss as a lump sum would overcompensate the claimant. **3F–40**

Section 1 of the Damages Act 1996 provides that the Lord Chancellor may by order specify a particular assumed rate of annual return for the calculation of lump sum awards for future pecuniary loss, representing what is in effect the presumed rate of investment return available on the money without undue risk to the capital, on the footing that the capital is gradually drawn down and should be precisely exhausted by the end of the period of anticipated loss. The courts are enjoined by subs.(1) to "take into account" such a specified rate of return in accordance with court rules.

**The Lord Chancellor's discount rate**

By the Damages (Personal Injury) Order 2001 which came into force on June 28, 2001 the Lord Chancellor specified a rate of 2.5 per cent for this purpose, frequently referred to as the "discount rate". **3F–41**

In practice the manner in which practitioners approach the calculation of future pecuniary loss in a straightforward case making use of the 2.5 per cent rate is to consult the 2.5 per cent discount rate column within the Ogden tables, at the row representing the period of time over which the loss will occur. That provides a multiplier for the loss which takes into account normal likelihood of death (other than where there is a particular raised chance of death over and above normal mortality levels) and takes into account the accelerated recovery due to an estimated 2.5 per cent investment income on the lump sum whilst drawing down on the capital over the number of years specified as the loss period.

For general principles of calculation of lump sum damages see the judgment of Stephen J. in the High Court of Australia in *Todorovic v Waller* [1981] 56 A.L.J.R. 59 at 498 (approved in *Wells v Wells*; *Thomas v Brighton Health Authority*; [1999] 1 A.C. 345.) See also *Kemp and Kemp Quantum of Damages* vol.1, para.7–010), Judgment of Lord Pearson in *Taylor v O'Connor* [1971] A.C. 115, 140, and Lord Oliver of Aylmerton in *Hodgson v Trapp* [1989] A.C. 807, 826.

Prior to the announcement of the 2.5 per cent rate by the Lord Chancellor the prevailing rate was set by common law in the absence of any order under s.1. In *Wells v Wells*; *Thomas v Brighton Health Authority*; *Page v Sheerness Steel Co Plc* [1999] 1 A.C. 345 the House of Lords set a guideline rate of 3 per cent based on the average rate of return of Index Linked Government Securities, the House stressing that it was not in their view appropriate to assume a higher rate based on a premise that injured parties will invest in more hazardous forms of investment, per Lord Steyn:

> "The premise that plaintiffs, who have perhaps been very seriously injured, are in the same position as ordinary investors is not one that I can accept. Such plaintiffs have not chosen to invest: the tort and its consequences compel them to do so. For plaintiffs an investment in equities is inherently risky, notably in regard to the timing of the investment…
>
> Typically, by investing in equities an ordinary investor takes a calculated risk which he can bear in order to improve his financial position. On the other hand, the typical plaintiff requires the return from an award of damages to provide the necessities of life. For such a plaintiff it is not possible to cut back on medical and nursing care as well as other essential services. His objective must be to ensure that the damages awarded do not run out. It is money that he cannot afford to lose … It is therefore unrealistic to treat such a plaintiff as an ordinary investor. It seems to me entirely reasonable for such a plaintiff to be cautious and conservative … it seems to me difficult to say that an investment in index-linked securities by plaintiffs would be unreasonable."

The analysis of the underlying principles is informative notwithstanding the later decision of the Lord Chancellor to set a 2.5 per cent rather than 3 per cent rate and many of the reported cases between 1999 and 2001 refer to a 3 per cent rate in accordance with the *Wells v Wells* judgment.

The Damages (Personal Injury) Order 2001 (SI 2001/2301) sets the "discount rate" which the courts must take into account when awarding damages for future pecuniary loss in personal injury cases, under s.1 of the Damages Act 1996. Prior to the making of this Order the rate in use was fixed by Common Law at 3 per cent following the case of *Wells v Wells*; *Thomas v Brighton Health Authority*; *Page v Sheerness Steel Co Plc* [1999] 1 A.C. 345; [1998] 3 All E.R. 481 HL. The 2001 Order sets the rate at 2.5 per cent with effect from June 28, 2001

### Basis for the Lord Chancellor's decision to set the rate

**3F–42** The Lord Chancellor has a wide discretion to decide upon the most appropriate rate. His reasons for setting the 2.5 per cent were set out in his Reasons dated July 27, 2001 (*http://www.dca.gov.uk/civil/discount.htm#part3* [Accessed March 30, 2007]) at length, inter alia basing his decision on then current average gross redemption yield figures for Index linked Government Stock:

> "it is highly desirable to exercise my powers under the Act so as to produce a situation in which claimants and defendants may have a reasonably clear idea about the impact of the discount rate upon their cases, so as to facilitate negotiation of settlements and the presentation of cases in court. In order to promote this objective, I have concluded that I should:
>
> a. set a single rate to cover all cases.
>
> b. set a rate which is easy for all parties and their lawyers to apply in practice and which reflects the fact that the rate is bound to be applied in a range of different circumstances over a period of time. For this reason, I consider it appropriate to set the discount rate to the nearest half per cent…
>
> c. set a rate which should obtain for the foreseeable future. I consider it would be very detrimental to the reasonable certainty which is necessary

to promote the just and efficient resolution of disputes (by settlement as well as by hearing in court) to make frequent changes to the discount rate. Therefore, whilst I will remain ready to review the discount rate whenever I find there is a significant and established change in the relevant real rates of return to be expected, I do not propose to tinker with the rate frequently to take account of every transient shift in market conditions."

**Court's discretion to depart from the 2.5 per cent rate**

Whilst the court must take the rate set under this section "into account" the court is not bound to apply it. By s.1(2) the court may take into account a different rate if any party shows that a different rate is more appropriate, though on the strict wording it appears that a court may not decide to take into account a different rate merely of its own motion in the absence of submissions by a party. The courts will be prepared to depart from the rate, it seems, only with great reluctance for example if the Lord Chancellor's reasons for setting a particular rate were demonstrably wrong or omitted to take into account a significant factor. For two failed attempts to vary the former 3 per cent rate (decisions of the Court of Appeal in the period between judgment of the House of Lords in *Wells v Wells* and the announcement of the Lord Chancellor's rate of 2.5 per cent) see *Warriner v Warriner* [2002] 1 W.L.R. 1703 and *Warren v Northern General Hospital NHS Trust* [2000] 1 W.L.R. 1404. **3F–43**

Similarly, attempts to depart from the 2.5 per cent rate by the "back door", based on evidence that future care costs for the claimant would increase at a significantly steeper rate than general inflation, failed in three conjoined appeals to the Court of Appeal handed down on October 16, 2003 (*Cooke v United Bristol Healthcare NHS Trust* [2003] EWCA Civ 1370; *Sheppard v Stibbe* and another; *Page v Lee* [2003] EWCA Civ 1370) in which it was held that such would constitute an illegitimate attempt to subvert the "discount rate" set by the Lord Chancellor to be applied when assessing the multiplier for future loss.

In *Page v Plymouth Hospitals NHS Trust* [2004] EWHC 1154 All E.R. 367 (QB), the courtrejected any argument that the Lord Chancellor when fixing the discount rate did so with the intention of abiding by the fudamental principle of full compensation, and had wished to achieve certainty and consistency. He was essentially prescribing the discount rate by reference to index-linked gilt-edged stock and not a mixed portfolio, and it was inherent in the Lord Chancellor's reasons for the 2001 Order that the costs of investment advice were taken into account in setting the discount rate. Accordingly predicted costs of investment advice and fund management charges incurred in the management of the claimant's award of damages could not be recovered as damages.

## Periodical payments

**2.**—(1) A court awarding damages for future pecuniary loss in respect of personal injury— **3F–44**

(a) may order that the damages are wholly or partly to take the form of periodical payments, and
(b) shall consider whether to make that order.

(2) A court awarding other damages in respect of personal injury may, if the parties consent, order that the damages are wholly or partly to take the form of periodical payments.

(3) A court may not make an order for periodical payments unless satisfied that the continuity of payment under the order is reasonably secure.

(4) For the purpose of subsection (3) the continuity of payment under an order is reasonably secure if—

(a) it is protected by a guarantee given under section 6 of or the Schedule to this Act,
(b) it is protected by a scheme under section 213 of the Fi-

***Paragraph numbers marked with a "+" can be found online and on CD.***

nancial Services and Markets Act 2000 (compensation) (whether or not as modified by section 4 of this Act), or

(c) the source of payment is a government or health service body.

(5) An order for periodical payments may include provision—

(a) requiring the party responsible for the payments to use a method (selected or to be selected by him) under which the continuity of payment is reasonably secure by virtue of subsection (4);

(b) about how the payments are to be made, if not by a method under which the continuity of payment is reasonably secure by virtue of subsection (4);

(c) requiring the party responsible for the payments to take specified action to secure continuity of payment, where continuity is not reasonably secure by virtue of subsection (4);

(d) enabling a party to apply for a variation of provision included under paragraph (a), (b) or (c).

(6) Where a person has a right to receive payments under an order for periodical payments, or where an arrangement is entered into in satisfaction of an order which gives a person a right to receive periodical payments, that person's right under the order or arrangement may not be assigned or charged without the approval of the court which made the order; and—

(a) a court shall not approve an assignment or charge unless satisfied that special circumstances make it necessary, and

(b) a purported assignment or charge, or agreement to assign or charge, is void unless approved by the court.

(7) Where an order is made for periodical payments, an alteration of the method by which the payments are made shall be treated as a breach of the order (whether or not the method was specified under subsection (5)(b)) unless—

(a) the court which made the order declares its satisfaction that the continuity of payment under the new method is reasonably secure,

(b) the new method is protected by a guarantee given under section 6 of or the Schedule to this Act,

(c) the new method is protected by a scheme under section 213 of the Financial Services and Markets Act 2000 (compensation) (whether or not as modified by section 4 of this Act), or

(d) the source of payment under the new method is a government or health service body.

(8) An order for periodical payments shall be treated as providing for the amount of payments to vary by reference to the retail prices index (within the meaning of section 833(2) of the Income and Corporation Taxes Act 1988) at such times, and in such a manner, as may be determined by or in accordance with Civil Procedure Rules.

(9) But an order for periodical payments may include provision—

(a) disapplying subsection (8), or

(b) modifying the effect of subsection (8).

*Note* —The above new text of s.2, and the text of ss.2A and 2B (below) were substituted for the old text of s.2 with effect from April 1, 2005 by SI 2005/901 by virtue of the Courts Act 2003 s.100. The Courts Act 2003 received Royal Assent on November 20, 2003. The 37th Update of the Civil Procedure Rules, published December 17, 2004, included provisions for periodical payments, and the amended rules appear in CPR, Pt 41, Sect.II. Those rules came into force on the date of entry into force of ss.100 and 101 of the Courts Act 2003 (namely April 1, 2005). **3F-45**

**Note**

For the court rules which relate to periodical payments, see CPR 41 Part II elsewhere in this work. The references to "government or health service body" in subs. (4)(c) and 7(d) are defined in section 2A below, and itemized in the Statutory Instrument which is referred to in the Note to that section below headed "Designated Government and Health Service Bodies". **3F-46**

The original text of s.2 did not provide the court with the power to impose a periodical payments order in a personal injury case, rather the court could make such an order only with the consent of the parties. The new sections 2, 2A and 2B reproduced here and below brought in a regime from April 1, 2005 where consent is not required for such an order where the damages are for future pecuniary loss for personal injury (and the court is now—under the new section 2(b)— required to consider whether such an order should be made. (Consent remains necessary for other forms of loss). This was in accordance with the recommendation of the Law Commission Report No.224 Cm. 2646 "Structured Settlements and Interim and Provisional Damages". The Law Commission recommended that in the absence of agreement there should be no judicial power to impose a structured settlement (paras 3.37–3.53 of the Report). Judicially however the power for the courts to order periodical payments was called for: See per Lord Steyn in *Wells v Wells*; *Thomas v Brighton Health Authority*; *Page v Sheerness Steel Co Plc* [1999] 1 A.C. 345 at 384B where s.2(1) was described as a "dead letter". **3F-47**

See also the Lord Chancellor's consultative document "Damages For Future Loss: Giving the Courts the Power to Order Periodical Payments for Future Loss and Care Costs in Personal Injury Cases", March 2002, which resulted in the Courts Act 2003 ss.100 and 101 to address the absence of a power to order periodical payments. The result was the scheme now set out in sections 2.2A and 2B reproduced below and which replaced this section from April 1, 2005 (SI 2005/910).

One of the potential problems with a periodical payment structured settlement, which can be over the course of the remainder of the claimant's life, is that the insurer or other source of funds for the payments may go into liquidation or otherwise cease to be able to pay at some date in the future, ss.4 to 6 provide a protective regime to deal with such eventualities.

**Case law**

For an example of s.2(1) in action, see *Peter Godbold v Rashid Mahmood* [2005] EWHC 1002 (QB). A periodical payments order under s.2(1)(a) was made for care and related costs which would recur over time. It was held that a periodical payments order eliminated uncertainty and risks of unfairness, and met the Claimant's needs having regard to factors in CPR PD41B. The order was also preferred because it facilitated budgeting by the Claimant because his income was secure. **3F-48**

As to the power provided under s.29(9), in *Lee Thompstone v Tameside and Glossop Acute Services NHS Trust* [2006] EWHC 2904 (QB) it was held the court was to determine the way to meet the claimant's needs and that in applying ss.2(8) and 2(9) the claimant bore an evidential burden to adduce evidence sufficient to establish that the Retail Prices Index was inappropriate and that some other measure was appropriate. It was held that there was a probability that the expense of carers which the claimant needed would increase significantly more than the RPI would suggest. Indexation would therefore be insufficient. The court decided that on the facts of the case an indexation in payments linked to the 75th percentile of the annual survey of hours and earnings (ASHE) 6115 (the survey relating to occupational earnings for care assistants and home carers) was appropriate and would provide a reasonably accurate indicator of the growth of the earnings of carers of the type to be employed by the claimant. See also *Flora v Wakom (Heathrow)* [2005] EWHC 2822 (QB) and *A (A Child) v B Hospitals NHS Trust* [2006] EWHC 2833 (Admin), for the ASHE survey, visit *http://www.statistics.gov.uk/StatBase/Product.asp?vlnk=13101* [Accessed March 30, 2007]

*Flora v Wakom (Heathrow) Ltd* was appealed unsuccessfully (at [2006] EWCA Civ 1103) where it was confirmed that there was nothing in the language of s.2(8) or (9) to suggest that the power to make provision disapplying or modifying the effect of s.2(8) could only be triggered in an exceptional case. A periodical payments order was not the same as a lump sum order and nothing in the Act suggested that Parliament had intended to provide compensation by periodical payments lower than would be awarded through the usual rule that that a victim of a tort was to be compensated as nearly as possible in full for pecuniary losses. It was noted that the courts should not consider questions of affordability when determining what order to make. Flora was applied, e.g. in *Sarwar v Kamran Ali* [2007] EWHC 1255 (QB). See also *RH v United Bristol Healthcare NHS Trust* [2007] EWHC 1441 (QB) where it was accepted on the facts that it was appropriate to index future periodic payments for the cost of care by reference to the earnings related index 6115 in the ASHE rather than the retail price index. *Thompstone v Tameside and Glossop Acute Services NHS Trust* was appealed, unsuccessfully, at [2008] EWCA Civ 5 and the Court of Appeal there rejected an argument that *Flora* was decided per incuriam.

**Model orders**

3F–48.1 In In *Thompstone v Tameside Hospital NHS Foundation Trust* [2008] EWHC 2948 (QB), December 2, 2008, unrep. the High Court extensively discussed the form of order under s.2 where the court makes provision as to the mechanics of indexation of periodical payments, and the judgment provides model forms of order. The model forms of order are available at para. 3F–48.60.2+.

**For ss.2A and 2B of the Damages Act 1996 (see Arrangement) plus any related commentary see paragraphs 3F–49+ to 3F–53+ on White Book on Westlaw UK or the Civil Procedure CD.**

## Provisional damages and fatal accident claims

3F–54 **3.**—(1) This section applies where a person—

(a) is awarded provisional damages; and

(b) subsequently dies as a result of the act or omission which gave rise to the cause of action for which the damages were awarded.

(2) The award of the provisional damages shall not operate as a bar to an action in respect of that person's death under the Fatal Accidents Act 1976

(3) Such part (if any) of—

(a) the provisional damages; and

(b) any further damages awarded to the person in question before his death,

as was intended to compensate him for pecuniary loss in a period which in the event falls after his death shall be taken into account in assessing the amount of any loss of support suffered by the person or persons for whose benefit the action under the Fatal Accidents Act 1976 is brought.

(4) No award of further damages made in respect of that person after his death shall include any amount for loss of income in respect of any period after his death.

*Paragraph numbers marked with a "+" can be found online and on CD.*

(5) In this section "provisional damages" means damages awarded by virtue of subsection (2)(a) of section 32A of the Senior Courts Act 1981 or section 51 of the County Courts Act 1984 and "further damages" means damages awarded by virtue of subsection (2)(b) of either of those sections.

(6) Subsection (2) above applies whether the award of provisional damages was before or after the coming into force of that subsection; and subsections (3) and (4) apply to any award of damages under the 1976 Act or, as the case may be, further damages after the coming into force of those subsections.

*Note* —Amended by the Constitutional Reform Act 2005 s.40 Sch.9 para.66 with effect from October 1, 2009 (SI 2009/1604). **3F–54.1**

**Note**

This section clarifies the linkage between provisional damages, the rights of the dependants of the deceased under the Inheritance (Provision for Family and Dependants) Act 1975, and damages under the Fatal Accidents Act 1976. The section applies where a person was awarded provisional damages—(damages awarded on the basis that there is a recognised specific risk of future development of a medical condition, or of further deterioration, which has not yet resulted in harm) but which will entitle the claimant to pursue a "further" damages claim in the event that the risk crystallises. For "provisional damages" see s.32A(2)(a) of the SCA 1981 and s.51 of the CCA 1984. **3F–55**

If the claimant in due course dies as a result of the tort which gave rise to the cause of action for which provisional damages were awarded, the fact that that award was made will not amount to a bar on the commencement of a claim by the deceased's dependants under the Fatal Accidents Act 1976 (see subs.(2)).

To extent that the award of damages was intended to be compensation for loss covering a period which in the event fell after the deceased died, then by subs.(3) the amount of the damages for that period must be taken into account by the court when it comes to assess damages for loss of support under the Fatal Accidents Act 1976. Relatedly subs.(4) provides that courts may not award amounts of "further damages" in respect loss of income under a provisional damages order after that persons' death. This avoids a risk of double recovery by relatives under both the Fatal Accidents Act 1976 and under the terms of the provisional order made within the deceased's original personal injury claim. For the meaning of "further damages" see s.32A(2)(b) of the SCA 1981 and s.51(2)(b) of the CCA 1984.

**For ss.4 and 6 of the Damages Act 1996 (see Arrangement) and Periodical Payments Order—Model Schedule plus any related commentary see paragraphs 3F–56+ to 3F–60.2+ on White Book on Westlaw UK or the Civil Procedure CD.**

## The Damages (Variation of Periodical Payments) Order 2005

(S.I. 2005 No. 841)

*Note* —Section 2B(6) allows the Lord Chancellor to specify the circumstances in which a court may vary a periodical payments order. The Damages (Variation of Periodical Payments) Order 2005 (SI 2005/841) provides for such circumstances and the text of the body of the Order appears below. **3F–61**

### Citation, commencement, interpretation and extent

**1.**—(1) This Order may be cited as the Damages (Variation of Periodical Payments) Order 2005 and shall come into force on the fourteenth day after the day on which it is made.

(2) In this Order—

(a) "the Act" means the Damages Act 1996;

(b) "agreement" means an agreement by parties to a claim or action for damages which settles the claim or action and which provides for periodical payments;

(c) "damages" means damages for future pecuniary loss in respect of personal injury;

(d) "defence society" means the Medical Defence Union or the Medical Protection Society;

(e) "variable agreement" means an agreement which contains a provision referred to in Article 9(1);

(f) "variable order" means an order for periodical payments which contains a provision referred to in Article 2.

(3) In the application of this Order to Northern Ireland—

(a) "claimant" means plaintiff;

(b) "permission" means leave;

(c) "statements of case" means, in the High Court, the writ and pleadings and, in the county court, the civil bill and any notice of intention to defend, defence, notice for particulars, replies and counterclaim.

(4) This Order extends to England and Wales and Northern Ireland.

(5) This Order applies to proceedings begun on or after the date on which it comes into force.

**Power to make variable orders**

**2.** If there is proved or admitted to be a chance that at some definite or indefinite time in the future the claimant will—

(a) as a result of the act or omission which gave rise to the cause of action, develop some serious disease or suffer some serious deterioration, or

(b) enjoy some significant improvement, in his physical or mental condition, where that condition had been adversely affected as a result of that act or omission,

the court may, on the application of a party, with the agreement of all the parties, or of its own initiative, provide in an order for periodical payments that it may be varied.

**Defendant's financial resources**

**3.** Unless—

(a) the defendant is insured in respect of the claim,

(b) the source of payment under the order for periodical payments is a government or health service body within the meaning of section 2A(2) of the Act,

(c) the payment is guaranteed under section 6 of or the Schedule to the Act, or

(d) the order is made by consent and the claimant is neither a child, nor a person who lacks capacity within the meaning of the Mental Capacity Act 2005 (c.9) to administer and manage his property and affairs nor a patient within the meaning of Part VII of the Mental Health (Northern Ireland) Order 1986,

the court will take into account the defendant's likely future financial resources in considering whether to make a variable order.

### Award of provisional damages

**4.** The court may make a variable order in addition to an order for an award of provisional damages made by virtue of section 32A of the Senior Courts Act 1981 or section 51 of the County Courts Act 1984 or, in relation to Northern Ireland, paragraph 10(2)(a) of Schedule 6 to the Administration of Justice Act 1982.

### Contents of variable order

**5.** Where the court makes a variable order—

(a) the damages must be assessed or agreed on the assumption that the disease, deterioration or improvement will not occur;

(b) the order must specify the disease or type of deterioration or improvement;

(c) the order may specify a period within which an application for it to be varied may be made;

(d) the order may specify more than one disease or type of deterioration or improvement and may, in respect of each, specify a different period within which an application for it to be varied may be made;

(e) the order must provide that a party must obtain the court's permission to apply for it to be varied, unless the court otherwise orders.

### Applications to extend period for applying for permission to vary

**6.** Where a period is specified under Article 5(c) or (d)—

(a) a party may make more than one application to extend the period, and such an application is not to be treated as an application to vary a variable order for the purposes of Article 7;

(b) a party may not make an application for the variable order to be varied after the end of the period specified or such period as extended by the court.

### Limit on number of applications to vary

**7.** A party may make only one application to vary a variable order in respect of each specified disease or type of deterioration or improvement.

### Case file

**8.**—(1) Where the court makes a variable order, the case file documents must be preserved by the court until the end of the period or periods specified under Article 5(c) or (d) or of any extension of them or, if no such period was specified, until the death of the claimant.

*Paragraph numbers marked with a "+" can be found online and on CD.*

(2) The case file documents are, unless the court otherwise orders—

(a) the judgment as entered;
(b) the statements of case;
(c) the schedule of expenses and losses;
(d) a transcript of the judge's oral judgment;
(e) all medical reports relied on;
(f) a transcript of any parts of the claimant's own evidence which the judge considers necessary;
(g) any subsequent orders.

(3) A court officer must ensure that the case file documents are provided by the parties where necessary and filed on the court file.

(4) Where a variable order has been made, the legal representatives of the parties and, if the parties are insured, their insurers, must also preserve their own case file until the end of the period or periods specified under Article 5(c) or (d) or of any extension of them or, if no such period was specified, until the death of the claimant.

**Variable agreements**

**9.**—(1) If there is agreed to be a chance that at some definite or indefinite time in the future the claimant will—

(a) as a result of the act or omission which gave rise to the cause of action, develop some serious disease or suffer some serious deterioration, or
(b) enjoy some significant improvement, in his physical or mental condition, where that condition had been adversely affected as a result of that act or omission,

the parties to an agreement may agree that a party to it may apply to the court subsequently for its terms to be varied.

(2) Where the parties agree to permit an application to vary the terms of an agreement, the agreement—

(a) must expressly state that a party to it may apply to the court for its terms to be varied;
(b) must specify the disease or type of deterioration or improvement;
(c) may specify a period within which an application for it to be varied may be made;
(d) may specify more than one disease or type of deterioration or improvement and may, in respect of each, specify a different period within which an application for it to be varied may be made.

(3) A party who is permitted by an agreement to apply for its terms to be varied must obtain the court's permission to apply for it to be varied.

**Application for permission**

**10.**—(1) An application for permission to apply for a variable order or a variable agreement to be varied must be accompanied by evidence—

(a) that the disease, deterioration or improvement specified in the order or agreement has occurred, and

(b) that it has caused or is likely to cause an increase or decrease in the pecuniary loss suffered by the claimant.

(2) Where the applicant is the claimant and he knows that the defendant is insured in respect of the claim and the identity of the defendant's insurers, he must serve the application notice on the insurers as well as on the defendant.

(3) Where the applicant is the claimant and he knows that the defendant is a member of a defence society and the identity of the defence society, he must serve the application notice on the defence society as well as on the defendant.

(4) The respondent to the application may, within 28 days after service of the application, serve written representations on the applicant and, if he does, must file them with the court.

(5) The court will deal with the application without a hearing.

## Refusal of permission

**11.**—(1) Where permission is refused, the applicant may, within 14 days after service of the order, request the decision to be reconsidered at a hearing.

(2) No appeal lies from an order refusing permission after reconsideration.

## Grant of permission

**12.**—(1) Where permission is granted, the court will also give directions as to the application for the variation of the variable order or the variable agreement.

(2) Directions must include directions as to—

(a) the date by which the application for variation must be served and filed;

(b) the service and filing of evidence.

(3) No appeal lies from an order granting permission.

## Order for variation

**13.**—(1) On an application for the variation of a variable order or a variable agreement, if the court is satisfied—

(a) that the disease, deterioration or improvement specified in the order or agreement has occurred, and

(b) that it has caused or is likely to cause an increase or decrease in the pecuniary loss suffered by the claimant,

it may order—

(i) the amount of annual payments to be varied, either from the date of the application for permission or from the date of the application to vary if the order did not require the permission of the court for an application to vary, or

*Paragraph numbers marked with a "+" can be found online and on CD.*

from such later date as it may specify in the order;

(ii) how each payment is to be made during the year and at what intervals;

(iii) a lump sum to be paid in addition to the existing periodical payments.

(2) Section 2(3) to (9) of the Act applies to orders under this Order as it applies to orders for periodical payments.

**Application of rules of court**

**14.** In England and Wales, the Civil Procedure Rules 1998 and in Northern Ireland, rules of court apply to applications under this Order, except where this Order makes provision inconsistent with Civil Procedure Rules or rules of court.

3F–62 *Note*—Articles 5, 3(b), 3(c) and (3)(d) are amended by the Mental Capacity Act 2005 (Transitional and Consequential Provisions) Order 2007 (SI 2007/1898). Paragraph 3(d) was substituted by SI 2007/1898, art.6, Sch.1, para.37. Article 4 amended by the Constitutional Reform Act 2005 s.59 and Sch.11, para.1 with effect from October 1, 2009 (SI 2009/1604).

**Fatal Accidents Act 1976**

3F–63 (1976 c.30)

ARRANGEMENT OF SECTIONS



3F–64 *Note*—The Act still retains its regnal year though it was virtually re-enacted by s.3 of the AJA 1982, subs.(1) substituting the following ss.1 to 4, and subs.(2) amending s.5.

**Right of action for wrongful act causing death**

3F–65 **1.**—(1) If death is caused by any wrongful act, neglect or default which is such as would (if death had not ensued) have entitled the person injured to maintain an action and recover damages in respect thereof, the person who would have been liable if death had not ensued shall be liable to an action for damages, notwithstanding the death of the person injured.

(2) Subject to section 1A(2) below, every such action shall be for the benefit of the dependants of the person ("the deceased") whose death has been so caused.

(3) In this Act "dependant" means—

(a) the wife or husband or former wife or husband of the deceased;

(aa) the civil partner or former civil partner of the deceased;

(b) any person who—

*Paragraph numbers marked with a "+" can be found online and on CD.*

(i) was living with the deceased in the same household immediately before the date of the death; and

(ii) had been living with the deceased in the same household for at least two years before that date; and

(iii) was living during the whole of that period as the husband or wife or civil partner of the deceased;

(c) any parent or other ascendant of the deceased;

(d) any person who was treated by the deceased as his parent;

(e) any child or other descendant of the deceased;

(f) any person (not being a child of the deceased) who, in the case of any marriage to which the deceased was at any time a party, was treated by the deceased as a child of the family in relation to that marriage;

(fa) any person (not being a child of the deceased) who, in the case of any civil partnership in which the deceased was at any time a civil partner, was treated by the deceased as a child of the family in relation to that civil partnership;

(g) any person who is, or is the issue of, a brother, sister, uncle or aunt of the deceased.

(4) The reference to the former wife or husband of the deceased in subsection (3)(a) above includes a reference to a person whose marriage to the deceased has been annulled or declared void as well as a person whose marriage to the deceased has been dissolved.

(4A) The reference to the former civil partner of the deceased in subsection (3)(aa) above includes a reference to a person whose civil partnership with the deceased has been annulled as well as a person whose civil partnership with the deceased has been dissolved.

(5) In deducing any relationship for the purposes of subsection (3) above—

(a) any relationship by marriage or civil partnership shall be treated as a relationship by consanguinity, any relationship of the half blood as a relationship of the whole blood, and the stepchild of any person as his child, and

(b) an illegitimate person shall be treated as the legitimate child of his mother and reputed father.

(6) Any reference in this Act to injury includes any disease and any impairment of a person's physical or mental condition.

*Note*—Amended by the Civil Partnership Act 2004 s.83. **3F-66**

Note that in *Kotke v Saffarini* [2005] EWCA Civ 221 it was held that for the purposes of the "living together as husband and wife" test of subs.(3)(b)(iii) (and presumably therefore the "living together as civil partners" test, the trial judge had been correct to approach the test by drawing a distinction between wanting and intending to live in the same household, planning to do so and actually living in the same household. On the facts the deceased had retained his own home, leaving his clothes and belongings and keeping overnight bag at his partner's house. That lasted until he was able to dispose of his own house in order to purchase a new home with the Claimant. The mere sharing of shopping expenses was not the establishment of a joint household.

## Bereavement

**1A.**—(1) An action under this Act may consist of or include a claim for damages for bereavement. **3F-67**

*Paragraph numbers marked with a "+" can be found online and on CD.*



PERSONAL INJURY

(2) A claim for damages for bereavement shall only be for the benefit—

(a) of the wife or husband or civil partner of the deceased; and

(b) where the deceased was a minor who was never married or a civil partner—

(i) of his parents, if he was legitimate; and

(ii) of his mother, if he was illegitimate.

(3) Subject to subsection (5) below, the sum to be awarded as damages under this section shall be £11,800.

(4) Where there is a claim for damages under this section for the benefit of both the parents of the deceased, the sum awarded shall be divided equally between them (subject to any deduction falling to be made in respect of costs not recovered from the defendant).

(5) The Lord Chancellor may by order made by statutory instrument, subject to annulment in pursuance of a resolution of either House of Parliament, amend this section by varying the sum of the time being specified in subsection (3) above.

**3F-68** *Note*—Amended (to insert the sum of £11,800 for causes of action which accrue on or after January 1, 2008) by the Damages for Bereavement (Variation of Sum) (England and Wales) Order 2007 (SI 2007/3489), art.2. Prior to January 1, 2008 the relevant sum was £10,000. The section was also amended by the Civil Partnership Act 2004 s.83.

## Persons entitled to bring the action

**3F-69** **2.**—(1) The action shall be brought by and in the name of the executor or administrator of the deceased.

(2) If—

(a) there is no executor or administrator of the deceased, or

(b) no action is brought within six months after the death by and in the name of an executor or administrator of the deceased,

the action may be brought by and in the name of all or any of the persons for whose benefit an executor or administrator could have brought it.

(3) Not more than one action shall lie for and in respect of the same subject matter of complaint.

(4) The plaintiff in the action shall be required to deliver to the defendant or his solicitor full particulars of the persons for whom and on whose behalf the action is brought and of the nature of the claim in respect of which damages are sought to be recovered.

### "more than one action"

**3F-70** Section 2(3) has to be construed compatibly with the ECHR (see Human Rights Act 1998 Sch.1), and "action" is to be interpreted as referring to "served process" (*Cachia v Faluyl* [2001] EWCA Civ 998; [2001] 1 W.L.R. 1966, CA).

In *Thompson v Arnold* [2007] EWHC 1875 (QB) it was held that statutory construction which prevented dependants from suing on the basis that the deceased had during her lifetime settled a claim in respect of the injuries, did not offend against Art.6 or Art.8 of the Convention. Not to permit a further claim where the defendant had already satisfied one claim during the deceased's lifetime did not show lack of respect for private or family life: *Reader v Molesworths Bright Clegg Solicitors* [2007] EWCA Civ 169 applied.

## Assessment of damages

**3.**—(1) In the action such damages, other than damages for bereavement, may be awarded as are proportioned to the injury resulting from the death to the dependants respectively. **3F-71**

(2) After deducting the costs not recovered from the defendant any amount recovered otherwise than as damages for bereavement shall be divided among the dependants in such shares as may be directed.

(3) In an action under this Act where there fall to be assessed damages payable to a widow in respect of the death of her husband there shall not be taken into account the re-marriage of the widow or her prospects of re-marriage.

(4) In an action under this Act where there fall to be assessed damages payable to a person who is a dependant by virtue of section 1(3)(b) above in respect of the death of the person with whom the dependant was living as husband or wife or civil partner there shall be taken into account (together with any other matter that appears to the court to be relevant to the action) the fact that the dependant had no enforceable right to financial support by the deceased as a result of their living together.

(5) If the dependants have incurred funeral expenses in respect of the deceased, damages may be awarded in respect of those expenses.

(6) Money paid into court in satisfaction of a cause of action under this Act may be in one sum without specifying any person's share.

*Note*—Amended by the Civil Partnership Act 2004 s.83. **3F-72**

### Assessment of damages

Where the husband was in receipt of a retirement pension from his former employers' pension fund which constituted the whole or part of his income, the widow on his death suffered a loss of dependency and thus an "injury" under s.3(1) of the Act for which she was entitled to damages, and the allowances paid to her after her husband's death could be disregarded, since these were benefits which accrued to her as a result of his death under s.4 (*Pidduck v Eastern Scottish Omnibuses Ltd* [1990] 1 W.L.R. 993; [1990] 2 All E.R. 69, CA). **3F-73**

See also *Welsh Ambulance Services NHS Trust v Williams* [2008] EWCA Civ 81 (financial benefit that two children brought to the family subsequent to their father's death was irrelevant to the assessment of the dependency under s.3 of the Act. A dependant could not by their conduct after the death affect the value of the dependency).

## Assessment of damages: disregard of benefits

**4.** In assessing damages in respect of a person's death in an action under this Act, benefits which have accrued or will or may accrue to any person from his estate or otherwise as a result of his death shall be disregarded. **3F-74**

### "Benefits"

A pension and a widow's allowance received from an employer's pension fund are benefits for the purposes of s.4 and are to be disregarded in assessing damages for the deceased's death: *Pidduck v Eastern Scottish Omnibuses Ltd* [1989] 1 W.L.R. 317; [1989] 2 **3F-75**

***Paragraph numbers marked with a "+" can be found online and on CD.***

All E.R. 261. Monies awarded by virtue of the Pneumoconiosis etc. (Workers' Compensation) Act 1979 are not a 'benefit' within s.4 and must be taken into account when assessing damages under the Act: *Cameron v Vinters Defence Systems Ltd* [2007] EWHC 2267 (QB).

In *Arnup v MW White Ltd* [2008] EWCA Civ 447 the Court of Appeal held that the expression "or otherwise as a result of his death" in s.4 was wide enough to cover benefits in kind which accrued as a result of the death, and any other kind of benefit which might not yet have been identified.

## Contributory negligence

3F-76 **5.** Where any person dies as the result partly of his own fault and partly by the fault of any other person or persons, and accordingly if an action were brought for the benefit of the estate under the Law Reform (Miscellaneous Provisions) Act 1934 the damages recoverable could be reduced under section 1(1) of the Law Reform (Contributory Negligence) Act 1945, any damages recoverable in an action under this Act shall be reduced by a proportionate extent.

### Note

3F-77 Amended by the AJA 1982 s.3(2).

### Premature action by dependants

3F-78 An action by the dependants of the deceased claiming damages as dependants under the Fatal Accidents Act commenced within six months of the death of deceased, although premature and perhaps irregular, is nevertheless valid and sustainable where it appears that no executor or administrator of the deceased started proceedings against the defendant within six months of the death of the deceased and that the defendant has not suffered any prejudice by the action by the dependants (*Austin v Hart* [1983] 2 A.C. 640; [1983] 2 All E.R. 341, PC (decided on the provision in an Ordinance in Trinidad and Tobago substantially similar to the Fatal Accidents Act 1976 s.2)).

### Premature claims for funeral expenses

3F-78.1 Note that claims for funeral expenses in personal injury cases can arise firstly, where expenses are incurred by the dependents of the deceased and the Fatal Accidents Act 1976 s.3(5) applies (supra.), and also where they are incurred by the deceased's estate and the Law Reform (Miscellaneous Provisions) Act 1934 s.1(2)(c) applies. A living claimant cannot claim for anticipated funeral expenses based on a reduced life expectancy. See *Watson v Cakebread Robey Ltd* [2009] EWHC 1695 (QB).

## Road Traffic Act 1988

3F-79 (1988 c.52)

Arrangement of Sections



**Paragraph numbers marked with a "+" denote content that is available on White Book on Westlaw UK or the Civil Procedure CD.**

***Paragraph numbers marked with a "+" can be found online and on CD.***

# Law Reform (Personal Injuries) Act 1948

(11 & 12 GEO. 6 c.41) 3F–99

ARRANGEMENT OF SECTIONS



*Paragraph 1—Common employment*

## Common employment

**1.**—(1) It shall not be a defence to an employer who is sued in respect of personal injuries caused by the negligence of a person employed by him, that that person was at the time the injuries were caused in common employment with the person injured. 3F–100

(2) Accordingly the Employers'Liability Act 1880, shall cease to have effect, and is hereby repealed.

(3) Any provision contained in a contract of service or apprenticeship, or in an agreement collateral thereto (including a contract or agreement entered into before the commencement of this Act) shall be void in so far as it would have the effect of excluding or limiting any liability of the employer in respect of personal injuries caused to the person employed or apprenticed by the negligence of persons in common employment with him.

## Measure of damages

**2.**— [...] 3F–101

(4) In an action for damages for personal injuries (including any such action arising out of a contract), there shall be disregarded, in determining the reasonableness of any expenses, the possibility of avoiding those expenses or part of them by taking advantage of facilities under the the National Health Service Act 2006 or the National Health Service (Wales) Act 2006 or the National Health Service (Scotland) Act 1978, or of any corresponding facilities in Northern Ireland.

[...]

*Note* —Amended by the Fatal Accidents Act 1959; the Social Security (Consequential Provisions) Act 1975 s.1(3) and Sch.2. Social Security Pensions Act 1975 s.65(1) and Sch.4; the National Health Service Act 1977 s.129 and Sch.15; the Health and Social Security Act 1984 Sch.4, para.1; the Social Security Act 1989 Schs 4 and 9; and the Social Security Act 1990 Sch.1; subs. (1), (1A), (3), and (6) omitted by the Social Security (Recovery of Benefits) Act 1997 (1997 c.27), Sch.3 para.1; and the National Health Service (Consequential Provisions) Act 2006 s.2, Sch.1, paras 10, 11. 3F–102

### "Rights"—"value of rights"

For the procedure in relation to Recoupment of Benefits from damages awards in personal injury cases see the Social Security (Recovery of Benefits) Act 1997 (1997 c.27) and regulations thereunder. 3F–103

## Definition of "personal injury"

**3.** In this Act the expression "personal injury" includes any disease 3F–104

***Paragraph numbers marked with a "+" can be found online and on CD.***

and any impairment of a person's physical or mental condition, and the expression "injured" shall be construed accordingly.

### Application to Crown

3F–105 **4.** This Act shall bind the Crown.

* * * *

### Short title and commencement

3F–106 **6.**—(1) This Act may be cited as the Law Reform (Personal Injuries) Act 1948.

(2) Section one and subsection (1) of section two of this Act shall apply only where the cause of action accrues on or after the day appointed for the National Insurance (Industrial Injuries) Act 1946, to take effect; but subsections (4) and (5) of the said section two shall apply whether the cause of action accrued or the action was commenced before or after the commencement of this Act.

## *Untraced Drivers' Agreement Department of Transport Motor Insurers' Bureau (Compensation of Victims of Untraced Drivers) and the Supplementary Untraced Drivers' Agreement England, Scotland and Wales 2008*

3F–107.0.0 **For the text of the "Untraced Drivers' Agreement Department of Transport Motor Insurers' Bureau (Compensation of Victims of Untraced Drivers)" and the "Supplementary Untraced Drivers' Agreement England, Scotland and Wales 2008" plus any related commentary see paragraphs 3F–107+ to 3F–143.0.2+ on White Book on Westlaw UK or the Civil Procedure CD.**

## *Motor Insurers' Bureau (Compensation of Victims of Uninsured Drivers) Text of an Agreement dated the 13th August 1999 between the Secretary of State for the Environment, Transport and the Regions and Motor Insurers' Bureau together with some notes on its scope and purpose*

3F–143.1 **For "The Motor Insurers' Bureau (Compensation of Victims of Uninsured Drivers) Text of an Agreement" plus any related commentary see paragraphs 3F–144+ to 3F–167+ on White Book on Westlaw UK or the Civil Procedure CD.**

## *Notes for the Guidance of Victims of Road Traffic Accidents*

3F–167.1 **For "Notes for the Guidance of Victims of Road Traffic Accidents" and the "Supplementary Uninsured Drivers Agreement 2008" plus any related commentary see paragraphs 3F–168+ to 3F–181.1+ on White Book on Westlaw UK or the Civil Procedure CD.**

***Paragraph numbers marked with a "+" can be found online and on CD.***

# Compensation Act 2006

(2006 c.29) **3F–182**

ARRANGEMENT OF SECTIONS

PART 1

STANDARD OF CARE



**Paragraph numbers marked with a "+" denote content that is available on White Book on Westlaw UK or the Civil Procedure CD.**

PERSONAL INJURY

### General note

Part 1 of the Compensation Act 2006 reproduced here came into force on the date of Royal Assent (June 25, 2006) but s.16 of the Act makes special provision for s.3 which is discussed there and which has the effect of modifying the date from which s.3 takes effect. The Compensation Act as a whole contains provisions in relation to the law on negligence and breach of statutory duty, damages for mesothelioma, and in relation to the regulation of claims management services. The part reproduced here is that relating to negligence and breach of statutory duty, and damages for mesothelioma. **3F–183**

## PART 1

## STANDARD OF CARE

### Deterrent effect of potential liability

**1.** A court considering a claim in negligence or breach of statutory duty may, in determining whether the defendant should have taken particular steps to meet a standard of care (whether by taking precautions against a risk or otherwise), have regard to whether a requirement to take those steps might— **3F–184**

(a) prevent a desirable activity from being undertaken at all, to a particular extent or in a particular way, or

(b) discourage persons from undertaking functions in connection with a desirable activity.

*Paragraph numbers marked with a "+" can be found online and on CD.*

### Note

3F-185 Section 1 deals arises from the report of the "Better Regulation Task Force" in May 2004 entitled "Better Routes to Redress". A widespread misapprehension of the law relating to standard of care was perceived to lead to fear of litigation and, in consequence, risk averse behaviour which could be undesirable. The section seeks to clarify the law relating to what constitutes a breach of duty of care and addresses the issue of what amounts to 'reasonable care' when a court is deciding whether that standard has been met. What amounts to 'reasonable care in any particular case varies according to the circumstances. In some cases, what would be required to prevent injury of the kind suffered may be such that to demand it would be to demand more than is reasonable. Section 1 of the Act makes explicit the principle that a court may in determining whether the defendant should have taken particular steps to meet a standard of care take into account whether a requirement to take those steps might prevent a desirable activity from being undertaken, or discourage persons from undertaking functions in connection with a desirable activity. The section appears to be aimed at making explicit the net effects of judgments such as *Tomlinson v Congleton BC* [2003] UKHL 47 (and see *Ratcliff v McConnell* [1999] 1 W.L.R. 670 and *Donoghue v Folkestone Properties Ltd* [2003] 2 W.L.R. 1138). In *Tomlinson* a young man dived into a pool which had been formed from a flooded sand quarry, on a hot day. He had dived there before safely for much of his life but on this occasion struck his head on the sandy bottom and suffered catastrophic injury rendering him tetraplegic. He accepted that he had been a trespasser and relied on the common duty of care owed to him under s.1 of the Occupiers Liability Act 1984 namely to "take such care as is reasonable in all the circumstances of the case to see that he [did] not suffer injury on the premises by reason of the danger concerned". The defendant local authority had for many years prohibited swimming there and Notices had been erected saying "Dangerous Water. No Swimming". As Lord Hoffman noted in judgment, the policy had not been altogether effective because many people ignored the notices. The Claimant argued that the notices had been ineffectual and therefore it was necessary to take more drastic measures to prevent people from going into the water. Various schemes had been considered in the past for rendering the site safe and more attractive but none had been carried out, albeit a scheme had recently been approved and was pending implementation, following a council report which observed "To provide a facility that is open to the public and which contains beach and water areas is, [...] an open invitation and temptation to swim and engage in other water's edge activities despite the cautionary note that is struck by deterrent notices etc., and in that type of situation accidents become inevitable. We must therefore do everything that is reasonably possible to deter, discourage and prevent people from swimming or paddling in the lake or diving into the lake." Their Lordships concuded that there had been no breach, giving speeches in notably strong terms about interference with public freedom to take risk. Per Lord Hoffman at paras 34 and 46 with added italic emphasis indicating the foreshadowing of s.1 of the Compensation Act 2006:

> "34. My Lords, the majority of the Court of Appeal appear to have proceeded on the basis that if there was a foreseeable risk of serious injury, the Council was under a duty to do what was necessary to prevent it. But this in my opinion is an oversimplification. Even in the case of the duty owed to a lawful visitor under section 2(2) of the 1957 Act and even if the risk had been attributable to the state of the premises rather than the acts of Mr Tomlinson, the question of what amounts to "such care as in all the circumstances of the case is reasonable" depends upon assessing, as in the case of common law negligence, not only the likelihood that someone may be injured and the seriousness of the injury which may occur, but also the social value of the activity which gives rise to the risk and the cost of preventative measures. These factors have to be balanced against each other."

> "46 ... I think that there is an important question of freedom at stake. It is unjust that the harmless recreation of responsible parents and children with buckets and spades on the beaches should be prohibited in order to comply with what is thought to be a legal duty to safeguard irresponsible visitors against dangers which are perfectly obvious. The fact that such people take no notice of warnings cannot create a duty to take other steps to protect them. I find it difficult to express with appropriate moderation my disagreement with the proposition of Sedley LJ (at para. 45) that it is "only where the risk is so obvious that the occupier can safely assume that nobody will take it that there will be no liability". A duty to protect against obvious risks or self-inflicted harm exists only in cases

***Paragraph numbers marked with a "+" can be found online and on CD.***

in which there is no genuine and informed choice, as in the case of employees, or some lack of capacity, such as the inability of children to recognise danger (*British Railways Board v Herrington* [1972] AC 877) or the despair of prisoners which may lead them to inflict injury on themselves (*Reeves v Commissioner of Police* [2000] 1 AC 360)."

See also per Lord Hobhouse of Woodborough at 81:

"81 ... it is not, and should never be, the policy of the law to require the protection of the foolhardy or reckless few to deprive, or interfere with, the enjoyment by the remainder of society of the liberties and amenities to which they are rightly entitled. Does the law require that all trees be cut down because some youths may climb them and fall? Does the law require the coast line and other beauty spots to be lined with warning notices? Does the law require that attractive water side picnic spots be destroyed because of a few foolhardy individuals who choose to ignore warning notices and indulge in activities dangerous only to themselves? The answer to all these questions is, of course, no. [...] In truth, the arguments for the claimant have involved an attack upon the liberties of the citizen which should not be countenanced. They attack the liberty of the individual to engage in dangerous, but otherwise harmless, pastimes at his own risk and the liberty of citizens as a whole fully to enjoy the variety and quality of the landscape of this country. The pursuit of an unrestrained culture of blame and compensation has many evil consequences and one is certainly the interference with the liberty of the citizen. The discussion of social utility in the Illinois Supreme Court is to the same effect: *Bucheleres v Chicago Park District* 171 Ill 2d 435, at 457–8."

The scope of s.1 of the Compensation Act especially where overseas theatres of war are concerned (but with relevance to other cases) was considered in *Graham Hopps v Mott Macdonald and MoD* [2009] EWHC 1881 (QB). The claimant claimed damages against his employer and the MOD for injuries suffered in a bombing in Iraq. Clarke J. held that: **3F–185.1**

"92 ... It was at one stage submitted on behalf of the claimant that this section was not retrospective and could not affect the outcome of this claim. I disagree for two reasons. Firstly, the section must, as it seems to me, be applicable to this claim since it is a claim which the court is "considering". Secondly thepurpose of the section is to draw attention to, and to some extent, to expound the principle of the common law expounded by the House of Lords in *Tomlinson v Congleton Borough Council* [2004] 1 AC 46.

93 It was suggested that the section can have no real application to a claim for personal injuries suffered in theatre; and is more applicable to desirable activities such as the provision of public amenities or the playing of sports and games or the pursuit of pastimes. I do not accept this. It seems to me that in determining whether particular steps (e.g. confinement to the airport until armoured vehicles were available for transport) should have been taken I am entitled to have regard to whether such steps would prevent the desirable activity of reconstruction of a shattered infrastructure after a war in a territory occupied by HM forces, particularly when failure to expedite that work would carry with it risks to the safety of coalition forces and civilian contractors in Iraq as a whole."

## Apologies, offers of treatment or other redress

**2.** An apology, an offer of treatment or other redress, shall not of itself amount to an admission of negligence or breach of statutory duty. **3F–186**

**Note**

The section is self-explanatory and codifies existing law. **3F–187**

## Mesothelioma: damages

**3.**—(1) This section applies where— **3F–188**

(a) a person ("the responsible person") has negligently or in breach of statutory duty caused or permitted another person ("the victim") to be exposed to asbestos,

*Paragraph numbers marked with a "+" can be found online and on CD.*

(b) the victim has contracted mesothelioma as a result of exposure to asbestos,

(c) because of the nature of mesothelioma and the state of medical science, it is not possible to determine with certainty whether it was the exposure mentioned in paragraph (a) or another exposure which caused the victim to become ill, and

(d) the responsible person is liable in tort, by virtue of the exposure mentioned in paragraph (a), in connection with damage caused to the victim by the disease (whether by reason of having materially increased a risk or for any other reason).

(2) The responsible person shall be liable—

(a) in respect of the whole of the damage caused to the victim by the disease (irrespective of whether the victim was also exposed to asbestos—

(i) other than by the responsible person, whether or not in circumstances in which another person has liability in tort, or

(ii) by the responsible person in circumstances in which he has no liability in tort), and

(b) jointly and severally with any other responsible person.

(3) Subsection (2) does not prevent—

(a) one responsible person from claiming a contribution from another, or

(b) a finding of contributory negligence.

(4) In determining the extent of contributions of different responsible persons in accordance with subsection (3)(a), a court shall have regard to the relative lengths of the periods of exposure for which each was responsible; but this subsection shall not apply—

(a) if or to the extent that responsible persons agree to apportion responsibility amongst themselves on some other basis, or

(b) if or to the extent that the court thinks that another basis for determining contributions is more appropriate in the circumstances of a particular case.

(5) In subsection (1) the reference to causing or permitting a person to be exposed to asbestos includes a reference to failing to protect a person from exposure to asbestos.

(6) In the application of this section to Scotland—

(a) a reference to tort shall be taken as a reference to delict, and

(b) a reference to a court shall be taken to include a reference to a jury.

(7) The Treasury may make regulations about the provision of compensation to a responsible person where—

(a) he claims, or would claim, a contribution from another responsible person in accordance with subsection (3)(a), but

(b) he is unable or likely to be unable to obtain the contribution, because an insurer of the other responsible person is unable or likely to be unable to satisfy the claim for a contribution.

*[Subsections (8)–(11) not reproduced]*

### Commencement

Section 16 of the Act makes special provision for the commencement of s.3 in terms of the effect which it has, or may have, on settlements of compensation cases in relation to mesothelioma inasmuch as it is partially retrospective. The relevant part of s.16 states as follows **3F–189**

"16.—[...]

(3) Section 16 shall be treated as having always had effect.

(4) But the section shall have no effect in relation to—

(a) a claim which is settled before 3rd May 2006 (whether or not legal proceedings in relation to the claim have been instituted), or

(b) legal proceedings which are determined before that date.

(5) Where a claim is settled on or after that date and before the date on which this Act is passed, a party to the settlement may apply to a relevant court to have the settlement varied; and—

(a) a court is a relevant court for that purpose if it had, or would have had, jurisdiction to determine the claim by way of legal proceedings,

(b) an application shall be brought as an application in, or by way of, proceedings on the claim, and

(c) a court to which an application is made shall vary the settlement to such extent (if any) as appears appropriate to reflect the effect of section 16.

(6) Where legal proceedings are determined on or after that date and before the date on which this Act is passed, a party to the proceedings may apply to the court to vary the determination; and—

(a) "the court" means the court which determined the proceedings,

(b) the application shall be treated as an application in the proceedings, and

(c) the court shall vary the determination to such extent (if any) as appears appropriate to reflect the effect of section 3."

### Note

*Regulations unders this section* —See the Compensation Act 2006 (Contribution for Mesothelioma Claims) Regulations 2006 (SI 2006/3259). **3F–189.1**

### Note to s.3

In *Fairchild v Glenhaven Funeral Services Ltd* [2002] UKHL 22, the House of Lords it was held that a claimant who contracted mesothelioma after exposure to asbestos at different times by several negligent defendants could sue any of them. Such applied even though he could not prove which exposure was the cause of the disease. Fairchild did not resolve whether liability should be joint and several. In the later case of *Barker v Corus UK Ltd* [2006] UKHL 20, the House of Lords decided that damages were to be apportioned according to the relative degree of contribution by the liable parties to the risk that the person would contract the disease. Section 3 of the Act endeavours to reverse *Barker* inasmuch as that decision meant that the risk of any of the defendants being insolvent and unable to pay the appropriate share would fall on the claimant such that the claimant would need to trace all defendants before liability could be apportioned, or commence multiple claims. Subsections (2) and (3) reverse the effects of the *Barker* judgment by allowing claimants to recover full compensation from any liable person, who in turn may seek a contribution from other liable persons. Subsection (3) also makes clear the existing law that if the victim is found to have negligently exposed himself to asbestos then damages may be reduced by way of contributory negligence. Subsection (4) provides guidance as to how the court should at- **3F–190** tribute liability, namely by having regard to the relative lengths of exposure to asbestos due to the negligence of each responsible person, though if the responsible persons agree otherwise or the court so decides then a different approach may be taken.

Subsections (7) onwards [not fully reproduced here] provide a power for HM Treasury to make provisions intended to accelerate the payment of damages to mesothelioma victims. Such provisions would enable responsible persons to claim money back from the Financial Services Compensation Scheme in circumstances in which previously only the claimant would have had such a right when another responsible person and their insurer are both insolvent.

**For ss.4 to 18 of and Sch.1 to the Compensation Act 2006 (see Arrangement) plus any related commentary see paragraphs 3F–191+ to 3F–220+ on White Book on Westlaw UK or the Civil Procedure CD.**

## NHS Redress Act 2006

3F–221 (2006 c.44)

ARRANGEMENT OF SECTIONS

SECT.



**Paragraph numbers marked with a "+" denote content that is available on White Book on Westlaw UK or the Civil Procedure CD.**

# 3G DATA PROTECTION ACT 1998

**Introduction**

The Data Protection Act ("the Act" or "DPA") was passed to implement Directive 95/46 of October 24, 1995 on the protection of individuals with regard to the processing of personal data and the free movement of such data ("Directive 95/46"). It repealed the Data Protection Act 1984 which had been passed to enable the UK to ratify the Convention for the Protection of Individuals with regard to automatic processing of Personal Data ("Treaty 108"). The courts have referred to the Directive, Treaty 108 and the Convention Rights under the ECHRFF, particularly art.8, in interpreting cases on the Act. In case law since the Act came into force the courts have tended to consider the law of confidence and the emerging privacy rights under art.8 in conjunction with the Act. Further specific rights in relation to telecommunications services and electronic marketing are contained in the Privacy and Electronic Communications (EC Directive) Regulations 2003 (see para.3G–17). Retention of personal data derived from public telecommunications services is mandated by Directive 2006/24. In cases ECJ C–317/04 and C–317/05 the European Court of Justice held that Commission Decision 2004/535 on the transfer of Passenger Name Record on air passengers to the United States was outside the powers of the European Commission under Directive 95/46. **3G–1**

## Data Protection Act 1998

(1998 c.29)

PART I **3G–2**

PRELIMINARY

### Basic interpretative provisions

**1.**—(1) In this Act, unless the context otherwise requires— **3G–3**

"data" means information which—

(a) is being processed by means of equipment operating automatically in response to instructions given for that purpose,

(b) is recorded with the intention that it should be processed by means of such equipment,

(c) is recorded as part of a relevant filing system or with the intention that it should form part of a relevant filing system,

(d) does not fall within paragraph (a), (b) or (c) but forms part of an accessible record as defined by section 68;

(e) is recorded information held by a public authority and does not fall within paragraphs (a) to (d).

"data controller" means, subject to subsection (4), a person who (either alone or jointly or in common with other persons) determines the purposes for which and the manner in which any personal data are, or are to be, processed;

"data processor", in relation to personal data, means any person (other than an employee of the data controller) who processes the data on behalf of the data controller;

"data subject" means an individual who is the subject of personal data;

*Paragraph numbers marked with a "+" can be found online and on CD.*

"personal data" means data which relate to a living individual who can be identified—

(a) from those data, or

(b) from those data and other information which is in the possession of, or is likely to come into the possession of, the data controller,

and includes any expression of opinion about the individual and any indication of the intentions of the data controller or any other person in respect of the individual;

"processing", in relation to information or data, means obtaining, recording or holding the information or data or carrying out any operation or set of operations on the information or data, including—

(a) organisation, adaptation or alteration of the information or data,

(b) retrieval, consultation or use of the information or data,

(c) disclosure of the information or data by transmission, dissemination or otherwise making available, or

(d) alignment, combination, blocking, erasure or destruction of the information or data;

"Public authority" has the same meaning as in the Freeedom of Information Act 2000;

"relevant filing system"means any set of information relating to individuals to the extent that, although the information is not processed by means of equipment operating automatically in response to instructions given for that purpose, the set is structured, either by reference to individuals or by reference to criteria relating to individuals, in such a way that specific information relating to a particular individual is readily accessible.

**Notes**

**3G–4** "Data"—although the definition limits the scope of the Act by reference to the form in which information is held, material which would fall outside this definition may also be covered because it is the product of the processing of data. In *Campbell v Mirror Group Newspapers* [2003] 2 W.L.R. 80 it was held that the Act covered text and photographs printed in newspapers which were the immediate result of data processing. See para.3G–8 in relation to "processing". Confirmed (para.230) in *Michael Douglas, Catherine Zeta-Jones and Northern Shell Plc v Hello* [2003] EWHC 786. Conversely information held in machine readable form which can no longer be accessed because the technology is no longer available should fall outside the definition. In *Smith v Lloyds Bank Plc* [2005] EWHC 246 (Ch) the court rejected a contention that hard copy should be regarded as "data" because it could be scanned and become data or because it was produced from data within 1(1)(a).

Some types of manual filing systems are caught by this provision. See the definition of "relevant filing system" and para.3G–9.

"Accessible records" are manual records to which access was available under the Access to Health Records Act 1990 (health records) and the Access to Personal Files Act 1987 (personal information held for social work purposes by specified authorities and in relation to public sector tenancies). Accessible records are defined in s.68 and Scheds 11 and 12 of the Act. The rights of access are slightly modified in respect of such records. Such records are covered only by the rights of access and correction under the Act until October 2007, after which the Act applies in full.

Where information falls within the definition because it is intended to process it as

***Paragraph numbers marked with a "+" can be found online and on CD.***

data or include it in a relevant filing system s.1(3) provides that it is immaterial that the processing or inclusion should occur outside the EEA.

Subsection (e) was added by s.68 of the Freedom of Information Act 2000. "Public authority" has the same meaning as in that Act. The effect of this, and further amendments made by ss.69–72 is to extend the right of subject access (see 3G–10), rectification etc. (see 3G–22) and compensation for inaccuracy (see 3G–20) to all types of information after January 1, 2005. The amendments impact only on public sector bodies (see also note 3G–9).

"Data controller"—this is a two part definition, the second part being in s.1(4). The terms "jointly" and "in common" are not defined. **3G–5**

The controller must determine both the manner and purpose of the processing. There may be two or more controllers sharing control in different ways. The Information Commissioner has suggested that:

"the determination of the purposes for which personal data are to be processed is paramount in deciding whether or not a person is a data controller"

Legal Guidance October 2001. The approach has not been tested by the courts and possibly should be treated with caution.

"Data processor"—a data controller who uses a data processor must ensure that the relationship is governed by a contract made or evidenced in writing covering security and control of the data. See Principle 7 Sch.1. **3G–6**

"Personal data" was considered in *Durant v Financial Services Authority* [2003] EWCA Civ 1746; [2004] F.S.R. 28; [2004] IP & T 814. Mr Durant had applied for access to information under s.7 of the Act. The court considered the meaning of the words "relate to" and the extent to which, if any, information must have the data subject as its focus, or main focus, before it is considered to relate to him. It held that the term has a narrow meaning: **3G–7**

> "...not all information retrieved from a computer search against an individual's name is personal data within the Act. Mere mention of the data subject in a document held by a data controller does not necessarily amount to his personal data. Whether it does so in any particular instance depends on where it falls in a continuum of relevance or proximity to the data subject as distinct, say, from transactions or matters in which he may have been involved in a greater or lesser degree. It seems to me that there are two notions which may be of assistance. The first is whether the information is biographical in a significant sense, that is going beyond the recording of the putative data subject's involvement in a matter or an event that has no personal connotations, a life event in respect of which his privacy could not be said to be compromised. The second is one of focus. The information should have the putative data subject as its focus rather than some other person with whom he may have been involved or some other transaction or event in which he may have figured or had an interest, for example as in this case an investigation into some other person's or body's conduct that he may have instigated. In short it is information that affects his privacy, whether in his personal or family life, business or professional capacity."

per Auld L.J. at para.28. It should be noted that he went on to refer to the judgment of the European Court in the case of *Criminal Proceedings against Lindqvist Aklagarkammgrei Jonkoping* Case C-101/01 in which the court held that the term "personal data" covered name and identifying data such as a telephone number. Thus the name, and information immediately associated with the name, such as a statement in a report of a meeting that Mr X was present, will fall within the definition but the remainder of the report will not be personal data about Mr X merely by virtue of that one reference.

It is arguable that the definition has been narrowed in transposition from the definition in art.2 of the Directive in which it covers identifiable natural persons that is:

> "one who can be identified, directly or indirectly, in particular by reference to an identification number or to one or more factors specific to his physical, physiological, mental, economic, cultural or social identity".

In *Lindqvist* the court held that the name of a person or identification of him by some other means, for instance by giving his telephone number, or information about his working conditions or hobbies, constituted personal data about the individual. *Durant* was applied in *Johnson v The Medical Defence Union Ltd* [2004] EWHC 2509.

In the Joined Cases C–465/00 *Rechnugshof and Osterreichischer Rundfunk* and

***Paragraph numbers marked with a "+" can be found online and on CD.***

C–139/01 *Joseph Lauermann and Osterreichischer Rundfunk*, an information request about the salaries paid to senior public servants was held to be information relating to identifiable natural persons and was therefore personal data. Activities of a professional nature should not be excluded from the ambit of personal data.

The EU Commission has reviewed the question of UK compliance with Directive 95/46 but no infrigement proceedings have yet been issued. The term has also been considered in a number of regulatory decisions under the FOIA and FOISA.

The House of Lords in *The Common Services Agency and The Scottish Information Commissioner* [2008] UKHL 47 held that the incidences of childhood leukaemia in Dumfries and Galloway were not personal data if the data was effectively anonymised because individual sufferers could not be identified.

In the consolidated appeals of *The Corporate Officer of the House of Commons v The Information Commissioner* EA/2006/0015 and 0016, the Information Tribunal held that the disclosure of the amount of expenses claimed by MPs did not contravene the DPA. Under Principle 1, fair processing notices were only required to be provided "so far as is practical" and failure to provide a notice should not prevent disclosure. Principle 2 was not contravened because the expenses of MPs are already published. The decision was upheld by the High Court on appeal, case [2008] EWHC 1084 (Admin). The expenses of Scottish MPs have also been disclosed, following *Paul Hutcheon, The Sunday Herald and the Scottish Parliamentary Corporate Body* (Decision 033/2005).

As the definition covers only living individuals, the Act affords no protection for records relating to deceased persons. However in a decision of the Information Tribunal it was held that a form of confidentiality could endure after death to protect such information. See *Pauline Bluck v Information Commission* Appeal EA/2006/0090.

"Sensitive personal data" is defined in s.2 as information about racial or ethnic origin, political opinions, religious beliefs and a number of other specific categories set out in the section. Particular care should be taken when processing such types of data. Before processing such data the controller must ensure that he can rely on one or more of the grounds set out in Sch.3 as well as the normal grounds set out in Sch.2, SI 2000/417, SI 2006/2068 or SI 2009/1811. Considered in *Lindqvist* where the court held that information that an individual had injured her foot and was working half-time on medical grounds was sensitive personal data.

**Notes**

**3G–8** "Processing"—was considered by the Court of Appeal in *Campbell v MGN* [2003] 2 W.L.R. 80 per Lord Phillips MR at para.122 who held that the publication in hard copy, where data had previously been automatically processed, formed part of the processing and falls within the Act. The point was not specifically considered in the House of Lords but appears to have been accepted, per Lord Nicholls of Birkenhead at para.32: "It is not necessary for me to pursue the claim based on the Data Protection Act 1998. The parties were agreed that this claim stands or falls with the outcome of the main claim." If the House did not accept that publication in these circumstances fell under the Data Protection Act, the claim under that Act would have failed irrespective of the failure or success of the main claim. It was further considered in *Paul Johnson v Medical Defence Union* [2007] EWCA Civ 262 where the Court of Appeal held that the act of reading material, some from computerised and some from manual files and summarising the files was not within the definition of processing.

Information, as well as data, may be processed, thus the collection of information orally before it is captured as data may fall within the scope of the Act. This is made explicit in s.1(2).

It is for the data controller to determine the purposes for which personal data are processed, as long as those are lawful and specified: *Chief Constable of Humberside Police v Information Commissioner* [2009] EWCA Civ 1079.

**Notes**

**3G–9** "Relevant filing system"—in *Durant* (see para.3G–7 above) the Court of Appeal considered three files and a sheaf of papers and agreed with the ruling in the High Court that in each case the material did not satisfy all the elements necessary to fall within the definition:

— one file was not structured by reference to individuals at all;

— one was referenced to the claimant but documents were filed in date order

***Paragraph numbers marked with a "+" can be found online and on CD.***

only; the other was referenced by issues and although it did contain a section on the claimant, there was no further internal structure of the material so that specific information could not be said to be readily accessible.

"I conclude....that a "relevant filing system" for the purpose of the Act is limited to a system:

(1) in which the files forming part of it are structured or referenced in such a way as clearly to indicate at the outset of the search whether specific information capable of amounting to personal data of an individual requesting it under section 7 is held within the system, and, if so, in which file or files it is held; and

(2) which has, as part of its own structure or referencing mechanism, a sufficiently sophisticated and detailed means of readily indicating whether and where in an individual files or files specific criteria or information about the applicant can be located"

per Auld L.J. at para.50.

The definition is the starting point for the exclusory definitions of "recorded" and "unstructured" manual information in s.68 and s.69 of the Freedom of Information Act 2000. Section 69 inserts a new s.9A in the DPA which applies to public authorities in England, Wales and Northern Ireland. Equivalent amendments have been made to impact in Scotland by the Freedom of Information (Scotland) Act 2002 (consequential modifications) Order 2004 (SI 2004/3089) made under the Scotland Act 2000 as the Freedom of Information (Scotland) Act 2002, being devolved legislation, could not be used to amend the Data Protection Act 1998. Thus the definition of a relevant filing system excludes material which would fall within these categories of information.

The term derives from "personal data filing system" in the Directive which provides that a data set may exist irrespective of whether the data set is: "centralised, decentralised or dispersed on a functional or geographic basis".

The Directive appears to allow Member States some margin of appreciation in how far they apply the Directive to manual files see art.4 and Recitals 15 and 27. The Government aimed at the narrowest possible coverage. Relevant material can be found in Hansard at Vol 587 No.95 col 467 Lords Rep March 16, 1998.

"Grounds for processing"—a data controller may only process personal data if he can rely on one or more of the six grounds set out in Sch.2. Where sensitive personal data (defined s.2) are to be processed the controller must rely on one or more of the further grounds set out in Sch.3, SI 2000/417, SI 2006/2068 or SI 2009/1811. Where the term "necessary" is used in the Schedules, the word bears the same meaning as in the ECHRFF para.60: *Michael Stone v SE Coast Strategic Health Authority* [2006] EWHC 1668. Where a party has it within its power to comply with the requirements of the Act it cannot use a possible breach of the Data Protection Act as a reason for failure to meet a contractual obligation: *Grow with us v Green Thumb* [2006] EWHC 379.

"Personal or domestic"—data processed only for the personal, domestic or recreational purposes by an individual are exempt from most of the Act including the Principles and the individual rights. It follows that no remedies will be available whatever the use where the controller processes for such purposes s.36.

In *Lindqvist* the European Court had regard to the relevant preamble to the Directive in interpreting the equivalent exemption in the Swedish law. The court held a narrow interpretation applied so material posted on the internet would not fall within the exemption.

* * * *

## Right of access to personal data

**7.**—(1) Subject to the following provisions of this section and to sections 8 and 9, an individual is entitled— **3G–10**

(a) to be informed by any data controller whether personal data of which that individual is the data subject are being processed by or on behalf of that data controller,

(b) if that is the case, to be given by the data controller a description of—

*Paragraph numbers marked with a "+" can be found online and on CD.*

(i) the personal data of which that individual is the data subject,

(ii) the purposes for which they are being or are to be processed, and

(iii) the recipients or classes of recipients to whom they are or may be disclosed,

(c) to have communicated to him in an intelligible form—

(i) the information constituting any personal data of which that individual is the data subject, and

(ii) any information available to the data controller as to the source of those data, and

(d) where the processing by automatic means of personal data of which that individual is the data subject for the purpose of evaluating matters relating to him such as, for example, his performance at work, his credit worthiness, his reliability or his conduct, has constituted or is likely to constitute the sole basis for any decision significantly affecting him, to be informed by the data controller of the logic involved in that decision-taking.

(2) A data controller is not obliged to supply any information under subsection (1) unless he has received—

(a) a request in writing, and

(b) except in prescribed cases, such fee (not exceeding the prescribed maximum) as he may require.

(3) Where a data controller—

(a) reasonably requires further information in order to satisfy himself as to the identity of the person making a request under this section and to locate the information which that person seeks, and

(b) has informed him of that requirement,

the data controller is not obliged to comply with the request unless he is supplied with that further information.

(4) Where a data controller cannot comply with the request without disclosing information relating to another individual who can be identified from that information, he is not obliged to comply with the request unless—

(a) the other individual has consented to the disclosure of the information to the person making the request, or

(b) it is reasonable in all the circumstances to comply with the request without the consent of the other individual.

(5) In subsection (4) the reference to information relating to another individual includes a reference to information identifying that individual as the source of the information sought by the request; and that subsection is not to be construed as excusing a data controller from communicating so much of the information sought by the request as can be communicated without disclosing the identity of the other individual concerned, whether by the omission of names or other identifying particulars or otherwise.

(6) In determining for the purposes of subsection (4)(b) whether

it is reasonable in all the circumstances to comply with the request without the consent of the other individual concerned, regard shall be had, in particular, to—

(a) any duty of confidentiality owed to the other individual,

(b) any steps taken by the data controller with a view to seeking the consent of the other individual,

(c) whether the other individual is capable of giving consent, and

(d) any express refusal of consent by the other individual.

(7) An individual making a request under this section may, in such cases as may be prescribed, specify that his request is limited to personal data of any prescribed description.

(8) Subject to subsection (4), a data controller shall comply with a request under this section promptly and in any event before the end of the prescribed period beginning with the relevant day.

(9) If a court is satisfied on the application of any person who has made a request under the foregoing provisions of this section that the data controller in question has failed to comply with the request in contravention of those provisions, the court may order him to comply with the request.

(10) In this section—

"prescribed" means prescribed by the Secretary of State by regulations:

"the prescribed maximum" means such amount as may be prescribed:

"the prescribed period" means forty days or such other period as may be prescribed:

"the relevant day", in relation to a request under this section, means the day on which the data controller receives the request or, if later, the first day on which the data controller has both the required fee and the information referred to in subsection (3).

(11) Different amounts or periods may be prescribed under this section in relation to different cases.

**Notes**

Subject access is one of the "rights of data subjects" under Principle 6 of Sch.1 (interpretation of the provision at para.8a of Pt II of Sch.1). Accordingly failure to comply with it may not only be the basis for an application to court by the data subject but also the subject of a request for assessment of processing by a data subject to the Information Commissioner under s.42. Failure to comply with a subject access request may give rise to the exercise of the Commissioner's supervisory jurisdiction. A data subject who has referred a failure to comply to the Commissioner is not bound to await the Commissioner's response before commencing action but may take independent action under s.7(9), *R. (Lord) v Secretary of State for the Home Department* [2003] EWHC 2073 (Admin). The appropriate procedure for handling an application to the court was considered in *Ezsias v Welsh Ministers* [2007] All E.R. (D) 65. **3G–11**

Since the Human Rights Act 1998 came into force a court must have regard to any relevant jurisprudence of the Court of Human Rights when interpreting legislation. Section 7(5) derives from the judgment of the ECtHR in *Gaskin v UK* [1990] 1 FLR 167; (1990) 12 E.H.R.R. 36 although the case was not referred to in *Lord* which considered (inter alia) this provision.

This section is one of the "subject information provisions" s.27(2). By virtue of s.27(5) the subject information provisions "shall have effect notwithstanding any enactment or rule of law prohibiting or restricting the disclosure or authorising the withholding of information" except as provided by Pt IV. Part IV sets out the exemptions. It follows that, if personal data are properly requested by a data subject from a data controller (see para.3G–5 above) in accordance with this section the data controller must supply them unless one of the exemptions listed in Pt IV applies. Part IV incorporates the exemptions in Sch.7.

In a second case brought by Mr Johnson (see para.3G–7 above) *Johnson v The Medical Defence Union Ltd* [2004] EWHC 2509 the court held that the fact that documents did not contain personal data, and were therefore not available to him under a subject access request, did not preclude a claimant from seeking disclosure under CPR, Pt 31.

Rights of Access may also be founded on Convention rights. The European Court of Human Rights has ordered access be provided to information under art.8 rights in *Roche v UK (App.3255/96)* 20 BHRC 99; [2005] All E.R. (D.) 212 (Oct).

**Exemptions**

Class exemptions apply to personal data processed only for domestic and recreational purposes (s.36) (see para.3G–9 above), information available to the public by or under any enactment (s.34), references provided in confidence when in the hands of the giver only (para.1 Sch.7), judicial appointments and honours (para.3 Sch.7), certain Crown Offices exempt under Data Protection (Crown Appointments) Order 2000 (SI 2000/416), examination scripts (para.9 Sch.7) and where legal professional privilege or the equivalent privilege in Scotland, would apply (para.10 Sch.7).

Other exemptions are limited in extent: national security if "required for the purpose of safeguarding national security", s.28. A claim for exemption under s.28 must be supported by a Ministerial certificate. The breadth of a certificate issued by the Home Secretary was successfully challenged under s.28(6) before the National Security Panel of the Information Tribunal in the case of *Norman Baker MP v Secretary of State for the Home Department* [2001] U.K.H.R.R. 1275. The Panel concluded that the Minister was not justified in issuing a certificate which permitted the Security Service to issue a "neither confirm nor deny" response to a request made under s.7(1)(a) regardless of whether national security would be harmed in the particular case. Where the service of a s.43 notice by the Commissioner is met by the production of a s.28 certificate the Commissioner may appeal it as a person "directly affected" under s.28(4). On the appeal the Tribunal may make appropriate determinations in those proceedings, including ordering that the Commissioner be given access to the material covered by the certificate. It followed that a certificate issued under s.28(2) which purported to wholly exclude the possible disclosure of information to which the certificate related to the Commissioner would be quashed: *R. (on the application of SSHD) v Information Tribunal*—Interested Party the Information Commissioner [2006] EWHC 2958.

Access to a number of classes of personal data is affected by modification orders which apply specific exemptions. These cover health information in accordance with the Data Protection (Subject Access Modification) (Health) Order 2000 (SI 2000/413), social work data in accordance with the Data Protection (Subject Access Modification) (Social Work) Order 2000 (SI 2000/415) and the Data Protection (Subject Access Modification) (Social Work) (Amendment) Order 2005, education information in accordance with the Data Protection (Subject Access Modification) (Education) Order 2000 (SI 2000/414) and a variety of additional special cases, such as material about embryos and adoption, covered by the Data Protection (Miscellaneous Subject Access Exemption) Order 2000 (SI 2000/419).

The remaining exemptions cover material held for the purposes of journalistic, literary or artistic work (s.32), information held for research purposes (s.33) (both exemptions only applicable where particular conditions apply), information which would be prejudicial to:

— the purposes of the detection of crime and related purposes (s.29);
— a range of regulatory activities (s.31);
— management forecasting or management planning (Sch.7 para.5);
— and negotiation (Sch.7 para.7).

In *R. (Alan Lord) v Secretary of State for the Home Department* [2003] EWHC 2073 the court held that s.29(1) requires the issue of whether disclosure is likely to prejudice

***Paragraph numbers marked with a "+" can be found online and on CD.***

the prevention or detection of crime to be determined in relation to each individual case (paras 122–127).

There are special provisions for access to examination marks to ensure that access rights cannot be used to obtain premature disclosure.

The remaining exemptions cover corporate finance under the Data Protection (Corporate Finance Exemption) Order 2000 (SI 2000/184) and preserve the privilege against self incrimination (Sch.7 para.11).

The Act imposes no obligation on a data controller to give reasons for a refusal of a subject access request or an explanation of an exemption relied upon. However, a court asked to renew the application of an exemption should apply an "anxious scrutiny" to determine whether a controller has complied with its obligations: *Clive Roberts v Nottinghamshire Healthcare NHS Trust* [2008] EWHC 1934 (QB).

Information which is disclosed under a subject access obligation is not admissible against the disclosing data controller in proceedings for an offence under the Act, (Sch.7 para.11). Note however that the Act itself does not restrict the use of material disclosed as evidence in a prosecution for any other offence. Material disclosed can be used in civil proceedings and a subject access request is often a precursor of proceedings.

Two new exemptions are inserted by the Freedom of Information Act 2000 covering material which would infringe the privileges of the Houses of Parliament (Sch.6 paras 2–5) and information relating to personnel matters (s.33A inserted by s.70). The latter only applies to manual data held in structured and unstructured files (see para.3G–9).

**Note**: the number and extent of exemptions has been criticised, as has the proliferation of class exemptions, as being open to challenge for being wider than those permissible under the Directive.

"Previous access rights"—access rights previously exercised by individuals under the Consumer Credit Act 1974, Access to Health Records Act 1990 and Access to Personal Files Act 1987 have been consolidated under the DPA although some of the detailed rules remain different.

For "data controller", "personal data" and "processed" see definitions above.

"Extent of obligations"—the controller must provide a description of the nature of the data and the purposes for which they are held as well as a copy of the information constituting the data. Note that the data subject has to be informed of the purposes for which the data are held and not the grounds for the processing relied on by the controller. Nevertheless the information provided may assist the data subject to determine whether he is entitled to exercise his right to object to processing under s.10 (see below). Where the information falls into the definition of unstructured personal data the data subject must describe the data requested and his request may be refused if it is estimated that the cost of compliance would exceed the appropriate limit (s.9A)

"Prescribed fee"—the fee is £10 for a subject access request, although different limits apply to applications for consumer credit files, medical data and unstructured personal data. Fees and time limits for response, which also differ with the type of application, are set out in the Data Protection (Subject Access) (Fees and Miscellaneous Provisions) Regulations 2000 (SI 2000/191). A request for information under one part of s.7 is taken to be a request for information under the first three sub-sections but is only to be taken as applying to s.7(1)(d) if the application shows an express intention to that effect.

In *R. v Chief Constable of B County Constabulary and the Director of the National Identification Service Ex p. R*, November 1997, unrep., a case under the equivalent provisions of the 1984 Act, it was held that the section establishes a simple duty to supply the data subject with all the information held upon him when he makes a request, with the implication that the data subject may not, as the claimant wished in that case, cherry pick particular material or omit some from the record. As a matter of practice it is common for data controllers to ask the data subject which material he wishes to receive and for data subjects to limit their request to particular files or types of data. It is submitted that this is not incompatible with the judgment in *Ex p. R* and the two issues can be distinguished. The mischief addressed by the decision in *R* was the desire of the data subject for the data controller to "doctor" the response to omit specific material for presentation to a third party.

***Paragraph numbers marked with a "+" can be found online and on CD.***

"Personal data"—only "personal data" of which the applicant is the subject is available to him in response to an access request; the mere fact that a document may be retrievable by reference to an individual's name does not entitle him to a copy of it. The court considered the purpose of the right in *Durant* as being:

"to enable him to check whether the data controller's processing of it unlawfully infringes his privacy and, if so, to take such steps as the Act provides, for example in section 10 to 14, to protect it"

per Auld L.J. at para.27 (see para.3G–7).

"Third party data"—material may be omitted or "redacted" where the disclosure of such material would encroach upon the legitimate privacy or confidentiality of a third party but the controller must apply an appropriate balancing test to ensure that the interests of both the data subject and the third party are protected. This follows the ruling of the ECtHR in *Gaskin v UK* [1990]1 F.L.R. 167. The issue only arises where the personal data about the individual includes such third party material in such a manner that it is impossible to separate the two. If the "personal data" about the applicant can be provided by omitting material about others that course should be followed i.e. there should be no unnecessary or gratuitous disclosure of information about third parties.

In *R. (on the application of Alan Lord) v Secretary of State for the Home Department* [2003] EWHC 2073 held information about individuals in an employment capacity is personal data in which privacy interests subsist (para.46). A blanket policy of non-disclosure does not meet the balancing test required by 7(4); a selective and targeted approach to redaction of third party information is required (para.148).

The "data controller" must determine whether it is "reasonable in all the circumstances" to make the disclosure. The court when considering this will not review the entire sets of material but will proceed by examining the approach of the data controller to the decisions to omit material. It will ask what, if any, legitimate interest the data subject has in the disclosure of the identity of another individual named in or identifiable from personal data to which he is otherwise entitled (*Durant* para.61) The court will generally not substitute its own view for the view of the data controller as long as the data controller is shown to have approached the decision in a balanced and fair way, taking account of the relevant considerations.

"Jurisdiction"—exercisable by the High Court or a county court or, in Scotland Court of Session or the sheriff: s.15(1).

"Powers of the court"—applications for remedial orders may be made to the High Court or a county court. Section 7(9) provides that, where a court is satisfied on the application of a data subject that the data controller has failed to comply with a valid request, the court may order the controller to comply with the request. The judgments in the cases of *P v Wozencroft* [2002] EWHC 1724, *Durant* and *Lord* appear to regard this as affording the court a wide discretion. In *Durant* the judge in the High Court commented on the applicant's motives for making the access request as relevant to the nature of the judgment which he would have been prepared to make. On appeal it was argued that such an approach diverges from the requirements of the Directive or even the Act itself. The Directive provides in art.22 for Member States to provide for:

> "the right of every person to a judicial remedy for any breach of the rights guaranteed him by the national law applicable to the processing in question,"

subject only to limited grounds of exemption. On appeal the court confirmed the breadth of judicial discretion. In the Act the considerations which are incorporated in s.8 are limited to whether the individual has made unreasonably frequent requests, whether the information would disclose a trade secret or whether the data relate to third parties, in addition the court may accept that the data should not be provided by means of a copy where to do so would involve disproportionate effort but the right may be satisfied by the adoption of another mechanism, for example inspection of the material. In *Lindqvist* the European Court addressed the issue of how prescriptive the terms of the Directive are where a private right may conflict with other rights or interests. It accepts that in some areas the State will have room to manoeuvre and must strike a balance between competing rights and interests (para.85). In *Lord*, the court commented that where the court has held that there are no grounds to withhold data, whether under an exemption, s.7(4) or8(2)(a) the Act:

> "points powerfully in favour of the Court exercising its discretion in favour of

the data subject ... at least where as here it is the data subjects' liberty interests that are at stake" (para.163).

A lower court does not appear to be able to order that an access request be complied with in part. In a case in which the court might be minded to seek to curtail the scope of an order it could deal with the problem by giving leave to amend the application for an order under its case management powers.

"Special purposes"—the special purposes are journalistic, literary and artistic purposes s.3. These are not further defined. Extensive exemptions are available to those who process personal data for the special purposes if publication would be in the public interest and compliance with the Act would be incompatible with the special purposes. In *Campbell v MGN (No.2)* the Court of Appeal overruled the High Court and held that the data controller has the benefit of s.32 **after** publication as well as before where the grounds are made out (para.130). It was suggested by the court that news media would usually be entitled to rely on the exemption.

Where personal data are processed for the special purposes with a view to the publication of material not previously published a court must stay proceedings brought under this section until a determination has been made by the Commissioner under s.45 or the claim is withdrawn s.32(4) and (5). The Information Commissioner may provide legal assistance to a claimant where a case involves the special purposes s.53 and Sch.10.

Where a controller has refused to respond to a repeated request he may be able to apply to strike out an action against him for failure to provide access under CPR, r.3.4 on the ground that the statement of claim discloses no reasonable ground for bringing a claim.

"Access to material to inspect"—a court considering an application under s.7(9) is entitled to inspect any relevant data or information as to the logic involved in any decision making in order to determine the case s.15(2). The court cannot permit disclosure to the claimant prior to the determination of the case or to representatives acting on behalf of the claimant (*Clive Roberts v Nottinghamshire*). In the event that the court rules against the data controller the court must order access be provided by the controller. It is not the role of the court itself to provide access.

"Position pending appeal"—under CPR, r.52.7 unless the Appeal Court or the lower Court orders otherwise an appeal does not operate as a stay of an order or decision. A "data controller" who intends to appeal against an order that he provide access to personal data should apply to the Information Tribunal for an appropriate order on the grounds of r.52.7.1.

"Compensation for breach"—if a failure to provide subject access has caused the data subject to suffer damage he may seek compensation under s.13. Where damage has been suffered the subject may also claim for any associated distress. There is a defence of due diligence against a compensation claim s.13(3).

## Provisions supplementary to section 7

**8.**—(1) The Secretary of State may by regulations provide that, in such cases as may be prescribed, a request for information under any provision of subsection (1) of section 7 is to be treated as extending also to information under other provisions of that subsection. **3G–12**

(2) The obligation imposed by section 7(1)(c)(i) must be complied with by supplying the data subject with a copy of the information in permanent form unless—

(a) the supply of such a copy is not possible or would involve disproportionate effort, or

(b) the data subject agrees otherwise;

and where any of the information referred to in section 7(1)(c)(i) is expressed in terms which are not intelligible without explanation the copy must be accompanied by an explanation of those terms.

(3) Where a data controller has previously complied with a

request made under section 7 by an individual, the data controller is not obliged to comply with a subsequent identical or similar request under that section by that individual unless a reasonable interval has elapsed between compliance with the previous request and the making of the current request.

(4) In determining for the purposes of subsection (3) whether requests under section 7 are made at reasonable intervals, regard shall be had to the nature of the data, the purposes for which the data are processed and the frequency with which the data are altered.

(5) Section 7(1)(d) is not to be regarded as requiring the provision of information as to the logic involved in any decision-taking if, and to the extent that, the information constitutes a trade secret.

(6) The information to be supplied pursuant to a request under section 7 must be supplied by reference to the data in question at the time when the request is received, except that it may take account of any amendment or deletion made between that time and the time when the information is supplied, being an amendment or deletion that would have been made regardless of the receipt of the request.

(7) For the purposes of section 7(4) and (5) another individual can be identified from the information being disclosed if he can be identified from that information, or from that and any other information which, in the reasonable belief of the data controller, is likely to be in, or to come into, the possession of the data subject making the request.

**Notes**

3G–13 "Disproportionate effort"—*R. (Lord) v SSHD* held s.8(2)(a) cannot justify withholding information in the form in which the data subject would otherwise be entitled to receive it para.155.

* * * *

## Right to prevent processing likely to cause damage or distress

3G–14 **10.**—(1) Subject to subsection (2), an individual is entitled at any time by notice in writing to a data controller to require the data controller at the end of such period as is reasonable in the circumstances to cease, or not to begin, processing, or processing for a specified purpose or in a specified manner, any personal data in respect of which he is the data subject, on the ground that, for specified reasons—

(a) the processing of those data or their processing for that purpose or in that manner is causing or is likely to cause substantial damage or substantial distress to him or to another, and

(b) that damage or distress is or would be unwarranted.

(2) Subsection (1) does not apply—

(a) in a case where any of the conditions in paragraphs 1 to 4 of Schedule 2 is met, or

(b) in such other cases as may be prescribed by the Secretary of State by order.

(3) The data controller must within twenty-one days of receiving a notice under subsection (1) ("the data subject notice") give the individual who gave it a written notice—

(a) stating that he has complied or intends to comply with the data subject notice, or

(b) stating his reasons for regarding the data subject notice as to any extent unjustified and the extent (if any) to which he has complied or intends to comply with it.

(4) If a court is satisfied, on the application of any person who has given a notice under subsection (1) which appears to the court to be justified (or to be justified to any extent), that the data controller in question has failed to comply with the notice, the court may order him to take such steps for complying with the notice (or for complying with it to that extent) as the court thinks fit.

(5) The failure by a data subject to exercise the right conferred by subsection (1) or section 11(1) does not affect any other right conferred on him by this Part.

**Notes**

This is one of the two rights to prevent processing; the other being an absolute right relating to use of personal data for direct marketing only in s.11. **3G–15**

The right to object to processing is limited to those cases in which the controller relies for his justification for processing on the general discretionary powers as set out in grounds 5 and 6 of Sch.2.

It appears that the burden of showing that the data controller was **not** relying on one of the other grounds falls on the claimant as the right to serve the notice does not apply where the relevant conditions in the Schedule are met.

Where sensitive personal data, as defined in s.2 (see para.3G–7 above), are processed it is more likely that damage or distress may be caused to the individual however s.10 includes no specific reference to the categories of sensitive personal data.

In *Michael Douglas, Catherine Zeta Jones and Northern Shell Plc v Hello!* [2003] EWHC 786 it was initially argued that the film stars had exercised their right of objection under the DPA when they had first heard of the proposal by *Hello!* magazine to publish unauthorised pictures of their wedding day but the point was not pursued at trial.

**Note**: the provision has been restrictively transposed from the Directive, art.14 of which provides that the data subject must be granted the right to:

> "object at any time on compelling legitimate grounds relating to his particular situation to the processing of personal data relating to him....Where there is a justified objection, the processing instigated by the controller may no longer involve those data".

"Powers of the court"—s.10(4) a court may order the controller to desist from processing to the same extent that the individual could where it is satisfied that the controller has failed to comply with a valid notice.

"Special purposes"—where personal data are processed for the special purposes with a view to the publication of material not previously published a court must stay proceedings brought under this section until a determination has been made by the Commissioner under s.45 or the claim is withdrawn s.32(4) and (5). The information Commissioner may fund legal advice or representation for a claimant where a case concerns the special purposes s.53 and Sch.10.

"Jurisdiction"—exercisable by the High Court or a county court or, in Scotland Court of Session or the sheriff s.15(1).

The court has a wide discretion as to the appropriate remedy when dealing with an application under this section (contrast s.7 see above) and may require partial compliance with the notice.

"Form of order"—as the order will be binding on the controller and failure to comply may involve penalties orders should be drawn with the care exercised in relation to mandatory injunctions. The order should specify the processing in question, the purpose of the processing the duration and any other relevant matters.

DATA PROTECTION

"Non-disclosure exemptions"—the obligations to respond to notices of objection under ss.10 and 11 are included in the non-disclosure provisions by s.27(4)(c) and are disapplied in a number of cases where the disclosure would be inconsistent with the protection of the interest protected by the exemption. Non-disclosure exemptions apply where disclosures are required for the purposes of the prevention or detection of crimes.29, national security s.28, the special purposes s.32, information available under an enactment s.34 or disclosures required by law or for legal purposes s.35. Thus a data subject could not use a notice of objection to processing under s.10 to restrict a disclosure made for one of those purposes in accordance with the terms of the individual exemption.

"Compensation for breach"—if a failure to deal with a proper objection has caused the data subject to suffer damage he may seek compensation under s.13. Where damage has been suffered the subject may also claim for any associated distress. There is a defence of due diligence against a compensation claim s.13(3).

## Right to prevent processing for purposes of direct marketing

3G-16 **11.**—(1) An individual is entitled at any time by notice in writing to a data controller to require the data controller at the end of such period as is reasonable in the circumstances to cease, or not to begin, processing for the purposes of direct marketing personal data in respect of which he is the data subject.

(2) If the court is satisfied, on the application of any person who has given a notice under subsection (1), that the data controller has failed to comply with the notice, the court may order him to take such steps for complying with the notice as the court thinks fit.

(3) In this section "direct marketing" means the communication (by whatever means) of any advertising or marketing material which is directed to particular individuals.

### Notes

3G-17 This is an absolute right.

The terms advertising or marketing materials are not defined. The court took a very broad view of what amounts to processing for the purposes of direct marketing in *R. (on the application of Robertson) v Wakefield MDC* [2001] EWHC Admin 915; [2002] Q.B. 1052; [2002] 2 W.L.R. 889 to include uses made of the data by third parties to whom the data are passed, as long as the controller is aware of those uses. Mr Robertson objected to the fact that the electoral roll was sold, pursuant to a statutory requirement in regulations, to any person who wished to purchase it. This resulted in the data derived from the roll being used in a wide range of commercial applications, including direct marketing. In a judicial review of the relevant provisions of the regulations the judge held that the Electoral Registration Officer (ERO) was acting in breach of s.11 and art.14 of the Directive, as well as the right to a free and fair election under art.3 of the First Protocol of the Convention Rights. The breach was the processing by the ERO to disclose the electoral roll without providing individuals with a right of objection in the knowledge that at least some of the purchasers would use the data for direct marketing. The judge found that the register was sold for marketing:

> "and for many years the data contained in the Register have been purchased by commercial interests and it has been obvious to EROs and to others that the data so purchased have been used, for among other things, direct marketing".

Additional provisions apply to marketing by telephone, facsimile and e-mail or short messaging services (SMS). From December 11, 2003 these are contained in the Privacy and Electronic Communication (EU Directive) Regulations 2003 (SI 2003/2426) which replace the Telecommunications (Data Protection and Privacy) Regulations 1999. These are based on Directive 2002/58. They apply in addition to the provisions of the DPA. In brief the use by any person of automated dialling machines for marketing requires prior consent of any subscriber; fax marketing to individual subscribers requires prior consent, other subscribers may opt-out of fax marketing; individual subscribers have a right to opt-out of telephone marketing both by registering on the Stop list and by notice to the person using the telephone line to carry out direct marketing, other subscribers can only opt-out by giving notice to the person using the telephone line to carry out direct marketing; any electronic marketing such as e-mail or SMS requires the consent of an individual subscriber except where the marketer is marketing similar goods and services to existing customers or prospects and the customer or prospect has been made aware, and continues to be made aware, of the opportunity to opt out of the use. The use of electronic mail for marketing to subscribers who are not individuals is subject to no restriction.

The provisions were extended by the Privacy and Electronic Communications (EC Directive) (Amendment) Regulations 2004 (SI 2004/1039). These regulations, which came into force on June 25, 2004, implement the corporate telephone preference service.

**Note**: Regulation 30 provides for a specific right to apply to the court for compensation for damage suffered as a result of breach of the special rules relating to electronic marketing. In *Microsoft Corp v McDonald* [2006] EWHC 3410 the court held this entitled Microsoft to apply for an injunction against a spammer whose activities had caused damage to their services. The general right under s.11 applies irrespective of how the marketing complained of is carried out. The Commissioner's powers of enforcement and individual rights for compensation for breach apply to electronic marketing under the Regulations (see para.3G–25 re appeals against enforcement notices and para.3G–20 re compensation).

"Powers of the court"—a court which is satisfied that a data subject has made an objection in accordance with the Act under s.11 which has not been complied with by the data controller may order the controller to take appropriate steps to comply.

"Compensation for breach"—if a failure to respond to a proper objection has caused the data subject to suffer damage he may seek compensation under s.13. Where damage has been suffered the subject may also claim for any associated distress. There is a defence of due diligence against a compensation claim: s.13(3).

"Jurisdiction"—exercisable by the High Court or a county court or, in Scotland Court of Session or the sheriff: s.15(1).

## Rights in relation to automated decision-taking

**12.**—(1) An individual is entitled at any time, by notice in writing to any data controller, to require the data controller to ensure that no decision taken by or on behalf of the data controller which significantly affects that individual is based solely on the processing by automatic means of personal data in respect of which that individual is the data subject for the purpose of evaluating matters relating to him such as, for example, his performance at work, his credit worthiness, his reliability or his conduct. **3G–18**

(2) Where, in a case where no notice under subsection (1) has effect, a decision which significantly affects an individual is based solely on such processing as is mentioned in subsection (1)—

(a) the data controller must as soon as reasonably practicable notify the individual that the decision was taken on that basis, and

(b) the individual is entitled, within twenty-one days of receiving that notification from the data controller, by notice in writing to require the data controller to reconsider the decision or to take a new decision otherwise than on that basis.

(3) The data controller must, within twenty-one days of receiving a notice under subsection (2)(b) ("the data subject notice") give the individual a written notice specifying the steps that he intends to take to comply with the data subject notice.

***Paragraph numbers marked with a "+" can be found online and on CD.***

(4) A notice under subsection (1) does not have effect in relation to an exempt decision; and nothing in subsection (2) applies to an exempt decision.

(5) In subsection (4) "exempt decision" means any decision—

(a) in respect of which the condition in subsection (6) and the condition in subsection (7) are met, or

(b) which is made in such other circumstances as may be prescribed by the Secretary of State by order.

(6) The condition in this subsection is that the decision—

(a) is taken in the course of steps taken—

(i) for the purpose of considering whether to enter into a contract with the data subject,

(ii) with a view to entering into such a contract, or

(iii) in the course of performing such a contract, or

(b) is authorised or required by or under any enactment.

(7) The condition in this subsection is that either—

(a) the effect of the decision is to grant a request of the data subject, or

(b) steps have been taken to safeguard the legitimate interests of the data subject (for example, by allowing him to make representations).

(8) If a court is satisfied on the application of a data subject that a person taking a decision in respect of him ("the responsible person") has failed to comply with subsection (1) or (2)(b), the court may order the responsible person to reconsider the decision, or to take a new decision which is not based solely on such processing as is mentioned in subsection (1).

(9) An order under subsection (8) shall not affect the rights of any person other than the data subject and the responsible person.

**Notes**

3G–19 There is no case law on this section. It is a complex provision. There are two aspects to the right:

(1) the right to stop a data controller from taking a relevant (non-exempt) decision by automated means; and

(2) the right to object to such a decision after the event and require it to be reviewed.

In order to ensure that individuals are aware of automated decisions data controllers must notify data subjects where such decisions are made, although there is no sanction if the controller fails to do so. **Note**: that the court may make an order against the "responsible person". It appears therefore that a person other than the relevant data controller for the personal data processed may be held responsible for the making of an automated decision.

"Exempt decisions"—may either be in relation to contractual situations or where the controller is processing on the basis of a statutory power. Either the effect of the decision must have been to grant the request of the individual or his interests must be protected in some other way e.g. by being entitled to make representations about the decision.

"Powers of the court"—a court which is satisfied that a data subject has served a notice in accordance with the Act under s.12 which has not been complied with by the data controller may order the controller to take appropriate steps to comply.

"Special purposes"—where personal data are processed for the special purposes with a view to the publication of material not previously published a court must stay

*Paragraph numbers marked with a "+" can be found online and on CD.*

proceedings brought under this section until a determination has been made by the Commissioner under s.45 or the claim is withdrawn s.32(4) and (5). The Information Commissioner may fund legal advice or assistance for a claimant where a case concerns the special purposes s.53 and Sch.10.

"Compensation for breach"—if a failure to respond to a proper objection has caused the data subject to suffer damage he may seek compensation under s.13. Where damage has been suffered the subject may also claim for any associated distress. There is a defence of due diligence against a compensation claim s.13(3).

"Jurisdiction"—exercisable by the High Court or a county court or, in Scotland Court of Session or the sheriff: s.15(1).

## Compensation for failure to comply with certain requirements

**13.**—(1) An individual who suffers damage by reason of any contravention by a data controller of any of the requirements of this Act is entitled to compensation from the data controller for that damage. 3G-20

(2) An individual who suffers distress by reason of any contravention by a data controller of any of the requirements of this Act is entitled to compensation from the data controller for that distress if—

(a) the individual also suffers damage by reason of the contravention, or

(b) the contravention relates to the processing of personal data for the special purposes.

(3) In proceedings brought against a person by virtue of this section it is a defence to prove that he had taken such care as in all the circumstances was reasonably required to comply with the requirement concerned.

### Notes

"Extent of right to compensation"—compensation is not only available for damage caused by failure to comply with the individual rights as noted above but for damage (and associated distress) caused by any contravention of the Act. The claimant need not be a data subject in order to bring proceedings, although it may be unlikely that damage will be caused to anyone who is not a data subject. The other provisions of the Act which might give rise to claims for damages are breach of the Principles, particularly Principle 7 which covers the requirements of adequate security for information. Under s.13(3) there is a defence of due diligence against a compensation claim. 3G-21

In *Lord Ashcroft v Attorney General* [2002] EWHC 1122; [2002] All E.R. (D) 521, QBD Lord Ashcroft, having been unsuccessful in his claim for damages for breach of Principle under the 1984 Act, claimed damages under s.13 for the continued holding of irrelevant and inaccurate data post March 2000, when the 1998 Act came into force. The judge agreed that it was an arguable claim however it did not proceed to hearing.

In *Paul Johnson v Medical Defence Union* [2006] EWHC 321 the court held that compensation for distress may only be awarded for distress arising from the occurrence giving rise to the right to damages. Unlike defamation the damages for distress are not at large.

In *Abayomi Sofola v Lloyds TSB Bank* [2005] EWHC 1335 Tugendhat J., in a hearing in which he gave permission for a claimant to re-open an appeal so that claims under the Act could be considered, considered it arguable that the retention of material alleging a fraud on file for nine years without evidence could breach Principles 4 and 5.

"Compensation"—November 2003 it was reported that the Chief Constable of Greater Manchester had paid compensation of £2000 for psychiatric harm to a lady whose details had been accessed by a police officer neighbour; in *A v London Borough of*

***Paragraph numbers marked with a "+" can be found online and on CD.***

*Newham* it was reported that the Borough paid £5,000 to the parents of a child who was wrongly stigmatised as being HIV positive, the picture of the child having used on the front of a Council publication on HIV and Children. The Borough had continued to use the picture in that way even after the parents had complained. In *Douglas v Hello! Ltd (No.1)* [2001] Q.B. 967 Michael Douglas and his wife, Catherine Zeta Jones, received modest damages of £3750 each plus expenses of £50 each by way of nominal damages for breach of the Act in the High Court. However they received damages for a breach of confidence, described by the court as "abuse of private information", and the court stated that the DPA should not be seen as adding a separate route to recovery for damage or distress beyond the nominal amount, (para.239). The failure of the lower courts to grant the Douglases a permanent injunction and then to compensate for abuse of their private information was regretted by the Court of Appeal on appeal, *Douglas v Hello! Ltd (No.6)* [2005] EWCA Civ 595,which confirmed the award of damages was an appropriate level.The Court of Appeal took same view in *Ogle v Chief Constable of Thames Valley* [2001] EWCA Civ 598; [2001] All E.R. (D) 231, a claim for compensation arising from inaccurate data. The Claimant could not recover additional damages to those recovered on same facts for wrongful arrest.

"Special purposes"—where the processing is for those purposes but outside the scope of the exemptions the claimant can seek compensation for distress alone, and need not show damage. In *Campbell v MGN* [2002] EWCA Civ 1373 the model who had been surreptitiously photographed by the Mirror newspaper attending a clinic was awarded £2,500 for damage and hurt feelings plus £1,000 for aggravated damages for a subsequent offensive article, although the judgment was overturned by Court of Appeal it was reinstated by the House of Lords which considered the case under the application of the law of confidence rather than as a Data Protection Act claim, see para.3G–8.

Where personal data are processed for the special purposes with a view to the publication of material not previously published a court must stay proceedings brought under this section until a determination has been made by the Commissioner under s.45 or the claim is withdrawn s.32(4) and (5). The Information Commissioner may fund legal advice or assistance for a claimant where a case concerns the special purposes s.53 and Sch.10.

"Injunction"—where the purpose of the claimant is to protect his privacy a claim may also lie in art.8 of the HRA 1998. There are difficulties for a claimant seeking to use the DPA in order to restrain the publication of material because of the provisions in ss.32 (4) which restrict the bringing of proceedings in relation to the special purposes until a determination has been made by the Commissioner under s.45.

"Jurisdiction"—exercisable by the High Court or a county court or, in Scotland Court of Session or the sheriff: s.15(1).

"Data Protection Principles"—s.4 and Sch.1. It is the duty of a data controller to comply with the data protection principles in relation to all personal data in respect of which he is the data controller. The eight principles require that personal data:

(1) are processed fairly and lawfully and in accordance with the fair processing rules set out in the Schedule;
(2) are processed for limited purposes and not in a manner incompatible with the notified purposes;
(3) are adequate relevant and not excessive in relation to those purposes;
(4) are accurate;
(5) are not kept for longer than is necessary;
(6) are processed in accordance with the rights of data subjects;
(7) are kept secure and
(8) are not transferred outside the EEA without adequate protection.

Information may be disclosed without breach of the principles in reliance on one or more of the non-disclosure exemptions s.27. In *Matthew Yeboah Mensah v Robert H Jones* [2004] EWHC 2699 (Ch) the data subject could not resist the disclosure of his medical records by his doctor for the purpose of seeking legal advice where the doctor had relied on the non-disclosure exemption in s.35(2).

Disclosure of information about non-payment of a debit to a credit reference agency was neither unfair nor unlawful despite the fact the debt was not enforceable due to a defect in the credit agreement: *McGuffick v RBS Plc* [2009] EWHC 2386.

***Paragraph numbers marked with a "+" can be found online and on CD.***

There is no breach of Principle 1 where information provided by a taxpayer via self-assessment tax return is used to cross-reference to assess liability for VAT: *Webster Shrowder v Revenue and Customs Commissioners* (VADT 20912).

In *Lindqvist* the European Court ruled that the posting of personal details on the internet where the site is hosted in the EEA does not amount to a transfer of the personal data.

Personal data may be transferred outside the EEA where one or more of the derogations in Sch.4 apply. Grounds 4(1) and 5(a) under the Schedule were relied on to sanction the transfer of personal data to the trustee in bankruptcy in the USA: *Re Madoff Securities International Ltd* ChD February 27, 2009.

In the Tribunal case of *S. Yorks v Information Commissioner Information Tribunal* (October 12, 2005) in 2005 the Tribunal held that the retention of records of criminal convictions did not breach Principle 5 as long as the records were retained for policing purposes. The tribunal reversed its decision via subsequent cases but was overruled by the Court of Appeal which held that where the police take a view information is reasonably necessary for policing, the information commissioner was not entitled to substitute his own judgment "unless that view is perversely or unreasonably held", per Lord Justice Hughes para.107. The court further held the proper purposes of policing include the retention of information for use by others with a legitimate need: *Chief Constable of Humberside v Information Commission* [2009] EWCA Civ 1079.

The Privacy and Electronic Communications (EC Directive) Regulations 2003 include a mirror provision in reg.30 which entitles any person who has suffered damage (but not distress) by reason of a contravention of the Regulations by any other person to claim compensation for the damage, subject to a defence of due diligence. The damage would have to be specific to the electronic marketing and additional to damage suffered by reason of breach of the Act itself. An Internet service provider which suffers damage by its goodwill may bring proceedings under this provision against senders of unsolicited marketing emails. In an appropriate case the court will grant injunctive relief: *Microsoft Corp v McDonald*, December 12, 2006, unrep.

## Rectification, blocking, erasure and destruction

**14.**—(1) If a court is satisfied on the application of a data subject that personal data of which the applicant is the subject are inaccurate, the court may order the data controller to rectify, block, erase or destroy those data and any other personal data in respect of which he is the data controller and which contain an expression of opinion which appears to the court to be based on the inaccurate data. **3G-22**

(2) Subsection (1) applies whether or not the data accurately record information received or obtained by the data controller from the data subject or a third party but where the data accurately record such information, then—

(a) if the requirements mentioned in paragraph 7 of Part II of Schedule 1 have been complied with, the court may, instead of making an order under subsection (1), make an order requiring the data to be supplemented by such statement of the true facts relating to the matters dealt with by the data as the court may approve, and

(b) if all or any of those requirements have not been complied with, the court may, instead of making an order under that subsection, make such order as it thinks fit for securing compliance with those requirements with or without a further order requiring the data to be supplemented by such a statement as is mentioned in paragraph (a).

(3) Where the court—

*Paragraph numbers marked with a "+" can be found online and on CD.*

(a) makes an order under subsection (1), or

(b) is satisfied on the application of a data subject that personal data of which he was the data subject and which have been rectified, blocked, erased or destroyed were inaccurate,

it may, where it considers it reasonably practicable, order the data controller to notify third parties to whom the data have been disclosed of the rectification, blocking, erasure or destruction.

(4) If a court is satisfied on the application of a data subject—

(a) that he has suffered damage by reason of any contravention by a data controller of any of the requirements of this Act in respect of any personal data, in circumstances entitling him to compensation under section 13, and

(b) that there is a substantial risk of further contravention in respect of those data in such circumstances,

the court may order the rectification, blocking, erasure or destruction of any of those data.

(5) Where the court makes an order under subsection (4) it may, where it considers it reasonably practicable, order the data controller to notify third parties to whom the data have been disclosed of the rectification, blocking, erasure or destruction.

(6) In determining whether it is reasonably practicable to require such notification as is mentioned in subsection (3) or (5) the court shall have regard, in particular, to the number of persons who would have to be notified.

**Notes**

**3G–23** "Accuracy"—personal data are inaccurate if they are "incorrect or misleading as to any matter of fact" s.70(2).

"Information received from a third party"—where data accurately reflect information received from the data subject or a third party and the controller has taken reasonable care to ensure accuracy, taking account of the purposes and, if the data subject notifies the controller that he regards the data as inaccurate, the controller marks the data to indicate that fact then there is no breach of the relevant Principle Sch.1, Pt II, para.7, nevertheless the data subject may ask the court to order deletion, blocking etc.

"Rectification, blocking, erasure and destruction"—are not defined terms. If rectification involves the alteration or removal of data it may conflict with requirements to maintain an audit trail for security purposes. Blocking appears to cover the case where the data remain on the record but access is forbidden either generally or to specific persons or for specific purposes. Erasure and destruction appear to import different meanings. It is suggested that erasure takes place where the media on which the data are held is not destroyed and destruction where the media are also destroyed.

In *P v Wozencroft* [2002] EWHC 1724, Fam the court considered an application under the DPA to amend an expert report which had been relied upon in family proceedings on the basis that the report was inaccurate. The judge ruled that it would be an abuse of process to seek to challenge an expert's report in satellite proceedings under the DPA and dismissed the case.

"Powers of the court"—a court which is satisfied that personal data are inaccurate may make any of the orders noted above as well as ordering enquiries to be made and data to be traced where it has been shown that inaccurate data have been disclosed to third parties.

"Special purposes"—where personal data are processed for the special purposes with a view to the publication of material not previously published a court must stay proceedings brought under this section until a determination has been made by the

Commissioner under s.45 or the claim is withdrawn s.32(4) and (5). The Information Commissioner may fund legal advice or assistance for a claimant where a case concerns the special purposes s.53 and Sch.10.

"Compensation for breach"—if a failure to maintain accurate data or the dissemination of inaccurate data has caused the data subject to suffer damage he may seek compensation under s.13. Where damage has been suffered the subject may also claim for any associated distress. There is a defence of due diligence under s.13(3).

"Jurisdiction"—exercisable by the High Court or a county court or, in Scotland Court of Session or the sheriff: s.15(1).

**Part V**

Appeals from that Tribunal may be made to the High Court. 3G–24

* * * *

## Rights of appeal

**48.**—(1) A person on whom an enforcement notice, an information notice or a special information notice has been served may appeal to the Tribunal against the notice. 3G–25

(2) A person on whom an enforcement notice has been served may appeal to the Tribunal against the refusal of an application under section 41(2) for cancellation or variation of the notice.

(3) Where an enforcement notice, an information notice or a special information notice contains a statement by the Commissioner in accordance with section 40(8), 43(5) or 44(6) then, whether or not the person appeals against the notice, he may appeal against—

(a) the Commissioner's decision to include the statement in the notice, or

(b) the effect of the inclusion of the statement as respects any part of the notice.

(4) A data controller in respect of whom a determination has been made under section 45 may appeal to the Tribunal against the determination.

(5) Schedule 6 has effect in relation to appeals under this section and the proceedings of the Tribunal in respect of any such appeal.

**Notes**

"Information Tribunal Rules"—the Act continued the Data Protection Tribunal which became the Information Tribunal following the implementation of s.18(2) of the Freedom of Information Act 2000. The Tribunal operates under the Data Protection Tribunal (Enforcement Appeals) Rules 2000 (SI 2000/189), as amended by the Information Tribunal (Enforcement Appeal) (Amendment) Rules 2002 (SI 2002/2722). The amending Regulations were necessary to provide for cases under the Freedom of Information Act 2000 before January 2005. Further amendments have been made in the Information Tribunal (Enforcement appeals) Rules 2005 (SI 2005/14), The Information Tribunal (Enforcement Appeals) (Amendment) Rules 2005 (SI 2005/450) and the Information Tribunal (National Security Appeals) Rules 2005 (SI 2005/13). Separate rules of procedure, the Data Protection Tribunal (National Security Appeals) Rules 2000 (SI 2000/206), apply to hearings in relation to national security certificates under s.28(4). From January 2010 the Tribunal will become part of the two-tier system under the Tribunals, Courts and Enforcemnet Act 2007. 3G–26

"Appeals"—the Tribunal hears appeals against a range of orders which can be made by the Information Commissioner. Under the Data Protection Act 1998 it hears appeals against enforcement notices, information notices and special information notices, against the inclusion of urgency provisions in any of the notices, a determination that personal data are not held for the special purposes or the refusal to vary or cancel an enforcement notice. Sitting in special panel the Tribunal also hears appeals against the extent of national security certificates. Under the Freedom of Information Act 2000 it hears appeals against enforcement information notices, and decision notices under the Freedom of Information Act 2000 and the extent of national security certificates issued under that Act. Under the Privacy and Electronic Communications (EC Directive) Regulations 2003 it hears appeals against enforcement notices, information notices, against the inclusion of urgency provisions in a notice or the refusal to vary or cancel an enforcement notice.

In *R. v Ewing (Terence Patrick)* [1983] Q.B. 1039 held that the Information Tribunal was, for the purpose of hearing appeals against the issue of certificates on the grounds of national security, a court within the meaning of Senior CourtsAct 1981 s.42 and a vexatious litigant requires leave to bring such proceedings.

## Determination of appeals

3G–27 **49.**—(1) If on an appeal under section 48(1) the Tribunal considers—

(a) that the notice against which the appeal is brought is not in accordance with the law, or

(b) to the extent that the notice involved an exercise of discretion by the Commissioner, that he ought to have exercised his discretion differently,

the Tribunal shall allow the appeal or substitute such other notice or decision as could have been served or made by the Commissioner; and in any other case the Tribunal shall dismiss the appeal.

(2) On such an appeal, the Tribunal may review any determination of fact on which the notice in question was based.

(3) If on an appeal under section 48(2) the Tribunal considers that the enforcement notice ought to be cancelled or varied by reason of a change in circumstances, the Tribunal shall cancel or vary the notice.

(4) On an appeal under subsection (3) of section 48 the Tribunal may direct—

(a) that the notice in question shall have effect as if it did not contain any such statement as is mentioned in that subsection, or

(b) that the inclusion of the statement shall not have effect in relation to any part of the notice,

and may make such modifications in the notice as may be required for giving effect to the direction.

(5) On an appeal under section 48(4), the Tribunal may cancel the determination of the Commissioner.

(6) Any party to an appeal to the Tribunal under section 48 may appeal from the decision of the Tribunal on a point of law to the appropriate court; and that court shall be—

(a) the High Court of Justice in England if the address of the person who was the appellant before the Tribunal is in England or Wales,

(b) the Court of Session if that address is in Scotland, and

(c) the High Court of Justice in Northern Ireland if that address is in Northern Ireland.

(7) For the purposes of subsection (6)—

(a) the address of a registered company is that of its registered office, and

(b) the address of a person (other than a registered company) carrying on a business is that of his principal place of business in the United Kingdom.

**Notes**

A significant number of appeals have been heard by the FOIA since January 2005, however few have raised procedural points. In *S. Yorks v Information Commissioner Information Tribunal* (October 12, 2005) the Tribunal appears to have reserved a power to vary its order on subsequent application. **3G–28**

The powers of the Tribunal in dealing with appeals apply also to appeals under the Privacy and Electronic Communications (EU Directive) Regulations 2003 and the Freedom of Information Act 2000.

## Powers of entry and inspection

**50.** Schedule 9 (powers of entry and inspection) has effect. **3G–29**

* * * *

**SECTION 50**

## SCHEDULE 9

### POWERS OF ENTRY AND INSPECTION

*Issue of warrants*

1.—(1) If a circuit judge is satisfied by information on oath supplied by the Commissioner that there are reasonable grounds for suspecting— **3G–30**

(a) that a data controller has contravened or is contravening any of the data protection principles, or

(b) that an offence under this Act has been or is being committed,

and that evidence of the contravention or of the commission of the offence is to be found on any premises specified in the information, he may, subject to sub-paragraph (2) and paragraph 2, grant a warrant to the Commissioner.

(2) A judge shall not issue a warrant under this Schedule in respect of any personal data processed for the special purposes unless a determination by the Commissioner under section 45 with respect to those data has taken effect.

(3) A warrant issued under sub-paragraph (1) shall authorise the Commissioner or any of his officers or staff at any time within seven days of the date of the warrant to enter the premises, to search them, to inspect, examine, operate and test any equipment found there which is used or intended to be used for the processing of personal data and to inspect and seize any documents or other material found there which may be such evidence as is mentioned in that sub-paragraph.

2.—(1) A judge shall not issue a warrant under this Schedule unless he is satisfied— **3G–31**

(a) that the Commissioner has given seven days' notice in writing to the occupier of the premises in question demanding access to the premises, and

(b) that either—

(i) access was demanded at a reasonable hour and was unreasonably refused, or

(ii) although entry to the premises was granted, the occupier unreasonably refused to comply with a request by the Commissioner or any of the Commissioner's officers or staff to permit the Commissioner or the officer or member of staff to do any of the things referred to in paragraph 1(3), and

(c) that the occupier, has, after the refusal, been notified by the Commissioner of the application for the warrant and has had an opportunity of being heard by the judge on the question whether or not it should be issued.

***Paragraph numbers marked with a "+" can be found online and on CD.***

(2) Sub-paragraph (1) shall not apply if the judge is satisfied that the case is one of urgency or that compliance with those provisions would defeat the object of the entry.

3G–32 3. A judge who issues a warrant under this Schedule shall also issue two copies of it and certify them clearly as copies.

*Execution of warrants*

3G–33 4. A person executing a warrant issued under this Schedule may use such reasonable force as may be necessary.

3G–34 5. A warrant issued under this Schedule shall be executed at a reasonable hour unless it appears to the person executing it that there are grounds for suspecting that the evidence in question would not be found if it were so executed.

3G–35 6. If the person who occupies the premises in respect of which a warrant is issued under this Schedule is present when the warrant is executed, he shall be shown the warrant and supplied with a copy of it; and if that person is not present a copy of the warrant shall be left in a prominent place on the premises.

3G–36 7.—(1) A person seizing anything in pursuance of a warrant under this Schedule shall give a receipt for it if asked to do so.

(2) Anything so seized may be retained for so long as is necessary in all the circumstances but the person in occupation of the premises in question shall be given a copy of anything that is seized if he so requests and the person executing the warrant considers that it can be done without undue delay.

*Matters exempt from inspection and seizure*

3G–37 8. The powers of inspection and seizure conferred by a warrant issued under this Schedule shall not be exercisable in respect of personal data which by virtue of section 28 are exempt from any of the provisions of this Act.

3G–38 9.—(1) Subject to the provisions of this paragraph, the powers of inspection and seizure conferred by a warrant issued under this Schedule shall not be exercisable in respect of—

(a) any communication between a professional legal adviser and his client in connection with the giving of legal advice to the client with respect to his obligations, liabilities or rights under this Act, or

(b) any communication between a professional legal adviser and his client, or between such an adviser or his client and any other person, made in connection with or in contemplation of proceedings under or arising out of this Act (including proceedings before the Tribunal) and for the purposes of such proceedings.

(2) Sub-paragraph (1) applies also to—

(a) any copy or other record of any such communication as is there mentioned, and

(b) any document or article enclosed with or referred to in any such communication if made in connection with the giving of any advice or, as the case may be, in connection with or in contemplation of and for the purposes of such proceedings as are there mentioned.

(3) This paragraph does not apply to anything in the possession of any person other than the professional legal adviser or his client or to anything held with the intention of furthering a criminal purpose.

(4) In this paragraph references to the client of a professional legal adviser include references to any person representing such a client.

3G–39 10. If the person in occupation of any premises in respect of which a warrant is issued under this Schedule objects to the inspection or seizure under the warrant of any material on the grounds that it consists partly of matters in respect of which those powers are not exercisable, he shall, if the person executing the warrant so requests, furnish that person with a copy of so much of the material as is not exempt from those powers.

*Return of warrants*

3G–40 11. A warrant issued under this Schedule shall be returned to the court from which it was issued—

***Paragraph numbers marked with a "+" can be found online and on CD.***

(a) after being executed, or

(b) if not executed within the time authorised for its execution;

and the person by whom any such warrant is executed shall make an endorsement on it stating what powers have been exercised by him under the warrant.

*Offences*

12. Any person who— **3G–41**

(a) intentionally obstructs a person in the execution of a warrant issued under this Schedule, or

(b) fails without reasonable excuse to give any person executing such a warrant such assistance as he may reasonably require for the execution of the warrant,

is guilty of an offence.

*Vessels, vehicles etc.*

13. In this Schedule "premises" includes any vessel, vehicle, aircraft or hovercraft, and references to the occupier of any premises include references to the person in charge of any vessel, vehicle, aircraft or hovercraft. **3G–42**

*Scotland and Northern Ireland*

14. In the application of this Schedule to Scotland— **3G–43**

(a) for any reference to a circuit judge there is substituted a reference to the sheriff,

(b) for any reference to information on oath there is substituted a reference to evidence on oath, and

(c) for the reference to the court from which the warrant was issued there is substituted a reference to the sheriff clerk.

15. In the application of this Schedule to Northern Ireland— **3G–44**

(a) for any reference to a circuit judge there is substituted a reference to a county court judge, and

(b) for any reference to information on oath there is substituted a reference to a complaint on oath.

**Notes**

Privacy and Electronic Communications (EC Directive) Regulations 2003 the power to apply for warrant of entry is extended to circumstances where a person has contravened or is contravening the requirements of those Regulations (para.10(a) Sch.1 PECR). **3G–45**

"Without notice"—warrant may be granted without notice having been given to the occupier in limited circumstances where the matter is one of urgency or compliance would defeat the object of the entry. The burden of establishing that notice would defeat the object of the entry falls upon the applicant for the warrant. The provisions are silent as to the standard of proof required. The issue and execution of a warrant will amount to a breach of the art.8 rights of the occupier and therefore the requirement of proportionality will apply.

The Codes of Practices made pursuant to the Police and Criminal Evidence Act 1984 do not apply to warrants issued under this provision but it is thought that those executing warrants should ensure that equivalent standards are met.

"Seizure of property"—difficult questions may arise where the material which the investigator wishes to inspect appears to be held on computer. The officer executing the warrant is entitled to inspect, examine and test material on the premises and only to seize material which is evidence of breach of the Act. Therefore if the officer wishes to take a computer in order to carry out tests off site the consent of the occupier will be required to remove the computer or to take a forensic copy of the disk unless the inspection shows that the computer contains evidence of a breach.

"Copies"—the occupier must be provided with copies of material seized if he so requests. The Commissioner's office has in the past refused to provide copies if they were not requested at the execution of the warrant so anyone subject to a warrant is advised to require copies during the execution of the warrant.

"Legal privilege"—the investigator is not entitled to seize material which is subject

***Paragraph numbers marked with a "+" can be found online and on CD.***

to legal professional privilege. Note that this is an absolute provision and does not depend on the reasonable belief of the investigator that the material is not privileged.

## Assistance by Commissioner in cases involving processing for the special purposes

3G-46 **53.**—(1) An individual who is an actual or prospective party to any proceedings under section 7(9), 10(4), 12(8), 12A(3) or 14 or by virtue of section 13 which relate to personal data processed for the special purposes may apply to the Commissioner for assistance in relation to those proceedings.

(2) The Commissioner shall, as soon as reasonably practicable after receiving an application under subsection (1), consider it and decide whether and to what extent to grant it, but he shall not grant the application unless, in his opinion, the case involves a matter of substantial public importance.

(3) If the Commissioner decides to provide assistance, he shall, as soon as reasonably practicable after making the decision, notify the applicant, stating the extent of the assistance to be provided.

(4) If the Commissioner decides not to provide assistance, he shall, as soon as reasonably practicable after making the decision, notify the applicant of his decision and, if he thinks fit, the reasons for it.

(5) In this section—

(a) references to "proceedings" include references to prospective proceedings, and

(b) "applicant", in relation to assistance under this section, means an individual who applies for assistance.

(6) Schedule 10 has effect for supplementing this section.

**SECTION 53(6)** SCHEDULE 10

FURTHER PROVISIONS RELATING TO ASSISTANCE UNDER SECTION 53

3G-47 1. In this Schedule "applicant" and "proceedings" have the same meaning as in section 53.

3G-48 2. The assistance provided under section 53 may include the making of arrangements for, or for the Commissioner to bear the costs of—

(a) the giving of advice or assistance by a solicitor or counsel, and

(b) the representation of the applicant, or the provision to him of such assistance as is usually given by a solicitor or counsel—

(i) in steps preliminary or incidental to the proceedings, or

(ii) in arriving at or giving effect to a compromise to avoid or bring an end to the proceedings.

3G-49 3. Where assistance is provided with respect to the conduct of proceedings—

(a) it shall include an agreement by the Commissioner to indemnify the applicant (subject only to any exceptions specified in the notification) in respect of any liability to pay costs or expenses arising by virtue of any judgment or order of the court in the proceedings,

(b) it may include an agreement by the Commissioner to indemnify the applicant in respect of any liability to pay costs or expenses arising by virtue of any compromise or settlement arrived at in order to avoid the proceedings or bring the proceedings to an end, and

(c) it may include an agreement by the Commissioner to indemnify the applicant in respect of any liability to pay damages pursuant to an undertaking given on the grant of interlocutory relief (in Scotland, an interim order) to the applicant.

4. Where the Commissioner provides assistance in relation to any proceedings, he shall do so on such terms, or make such other arrangements, as will secure that a person against whom the proceedings have been or are commenced is informed that assistance has been or is being provided by the Commissioner in relation to them. **3G–50**

5. In England and Wales or Northern Ireland, the recovery of expenses incurred by the Commissioner in providing an applicant with assistance (as taxed or assessed in such manner as may be prescribed by rules of court) shall constitute a first charge for the benefit of the Commissioner— **3G–51**

(a) on any costs which, by virtue of any judgment or order of the court, are payable to the applicant by any other person in respect of the matter in connection with which the assistance is provided, and

(b) on any sum payable to the applicant under a compromise or settlement arrived at in connection with that matter to avoid or bring to an end any proceedings.

6. In Scotland, the recovery of such expenses (as taxed or assessed in such manner as may be prescribed by rules of court) shall be paid to the Commissioner, in priority to other debts— **3G–52**

(a) out of any expenses which, by virtue of any judgment or order of the court, are payable to the applicant by any other person in respect of the matter in connection with which the assistance is provided, and

(b) out of any sum payable to the applicant under a compromise or settlement arrived at in connection with that matter to avoid or bring to an end any proceedings.

**Notes**

See para.3G–11 in relation to the actions in respect of which the data subject may wish to seek support from the Commissioner. **3G–53**

**Notes**

"Provision"—gives the Tribunal power to deal with behaviour that might result in punishment for contempt of court were it to be perpetrated before a court. **3G–54**

## Unlawful obtaining etc. of personal data

**55.**—(1) A person must not knowingly or recklessly, without the consent of the data controller— **3G–55**

(a) obtain or disclose personal data or the information contained in personal data, or

(b) procure the disclosure to another person of the information contained in personal data.

(2) Subsection (1) does not apply to a person who shows—

(a) that the obtaining, disclosing or procuring—

(i) was necessary for the purpose of preventing or detecting crime, or

(ii) was required or authorised by or under any enactment, by any rule of law or by the order of a court,

(b) that he acted in the reasonable belief that he had in law the right to obtain or disclose the data or information or, as the case may be, to procure the disclosure of the information to the other person,

(c) that he acted in the reasonable belief that he would have had the consent of the data controller if the data controller had known of the obtaining, disclosing or procuring and the circumstances of it, or

DATA PROTECTION

***Paragraph numbers marked with a "+" can be found online and on CD.***

(ca) that he acted—

(i) for the special purposes,

(ii) with a view to the publication by any person of any journalistic, literary or artistic material, and

(iii) in the reasonable belief that in the particular circumstances the obtaining, disclosing or procuring was justified as being in the public interest,

(d) that in the particular circumstances the obtaining, disclosing or procuring was justified as being in the public interest.

(3) A person who contravenes subsection (1) is guilty of an offence.

(4) A person who sells personal data is guilty of an offence if he has obtained the data in contravention of subsection (1).

(5) A person who offers to sell personal data is guilty of an offence if—

(a) he has obtained the data in contravention of subsection (1), or

(b) he subsequently obtains the data in contravention of that subsection.

(6) For the purposes of subsection (5), an advertisement indicating that personal data are or may be for sale is an offer to sell the data.

(7) Section 1(2) does not apply for the purposes of this section; and for the purposes of subsections (4) to (6), "personal data" includes information extracted from personal data.

(8) References in this section to personal data do not include references to personal data which by virtue of section 28 are exempt from this section.

**Notes**

3G–56 In *R. v Rooney* [2006] EWCA Crim 1841 the court held that the disclosure that a couple had moved to "a new address in Tunstall" was a disclosure of information contained in personal data within s.55(1)(a) even though the identity of the individuals was not disclosed.

Section (ca) was added by s.78 of the Criminal Justice and Immigration Act 2008 and is not in force as at November 2009.

Pre-action disclosure may be granted under CPR, r.31.16 against a party which has unlawfully obtained personal data in breach of s.55: *Hughes v Carratu International Plc* [2006] EWHC 1791.

*Monetary penalties*

### 3G–57 Power of Commissioner to impose monetary penalty

**55A.**—(1) The Commissioner may serve a data controller with a monetary penalty notice if the Commissioner is satisfied that—

(a) there has been a serious contravention of section 4(4) by the data controller,

(b) the contravention was of a kind likely to cause substantial damage or substantial distress, and

(c) subsection (2) or (3) applies.

(2) This subsection applies if the contravention was deliberate.

***Paragraph numbers marked with a "+" can be found online and on CD.***

(3) This subsection applies if the data controller—

(a) knew or ought to have known —

(i) that there was a risk that the contravention would occur, and

(ii) that such a contravention would be of a kind likely to cause substantial damage or substantial distress, but

(b) failed to take reasonable steps to prevent the contravention.

(4) A monetary penalty notice is a notice requiring the data controller to pay to the Commissioner a monetary penalty of an amount determined by the Commissioner and specified in the notice.

(5) The amount determined by the Commissioner must not exceed the prescribed amount.

(6) The monetary penalty must be paid to the Commissioner within the period specified in the notice.

(7) The notice must contain such information as may be prescribed.

(8) Any sum received by the Commissioner by virtue of this section must be paid into the Consolidated Fund.

(9) In this section—

"data controller" does not include the Crown Estate Commissioners or a person who is a data controller by virtue of section 63(3);

"prescribed" means prescribed by regulations made by the Secretary of State.

## Monetary penalty notices: procedural rights

**55B.**—(1) Before serving a monetary penalty notice, the Commissioner must serve the data controller with a notice of intent. **3G–58**

(2) A notice of intent is a notice that the Commissioner proposes to serve a monetary penalty notice.

(3) A notice of intent must—

(a) inform the data controller that he may make written representations in relation to the Commissioner's proposal within a period specified in the notice, and

(b) contain such other information as may be prescribed.

(4) The Commissioner may not serve a monetary penalty notice until the time within which the data controller may make representations has expired.

(5) A person on whom a monetary penalty notice is served may appeal to the Tribunal against—

(a) the issue of the monetary penalty notice;

(b) the amount of the penalty specified in the notice.

(6) In this section, "prescribed" means prescribed by regulations made by the Secretary of State.

## Guidance about monetary penalty notices

**55C.**—(1) The Commissioner must prepare and issue guidance on **3G–59**

*Paragraph numbers marked with a "+" can be found online and on CD.*

how he proposes to exercise his functions under sections 55A and 55B.

(2) The guidance must, in particular, deal with—

(a) the circumstances in which he would consider it appropriate to issue a monetary penalty notice, and

(b) how he will determine the amount of the penalty.

(3) The Commissioner may alter or replace the guidance.

(4) If the guidance is altered or replaced, the Commissioner must issue the altered or replacement guidance.

(5) The Commissioner may not issue guidance under this section without the approval of the Secretary of State.

(6) The Commissioner must lay any guidance issued under this section before each House of Parliament.

(7) The Commissioner must arrange for the publication of any guidance issued under this section in such form and manner as he considers appropriate.

(8) In subsections (5) to (7), "guidance" includes altered or replacement guidance.

### Monetary penalty notices: enforcement

3G-60 **55D.**—(1) This section applies in relation to any penalty payable to the Commissioner by virtue of section 55A.

(2) In England and Wales, the penalty is recoverable—

(a) if a county court so orders, as if it were payable under an order of that court;

(b) if the High Court so orders, as if it were payable under an order of that court.

(3) In Scotland, the penalty may be enforced in the same manner as an extract registered decree arbitral bearing a warrant for execution issued by the sheriff court of any sheriffdom in Scotland.

(4) In Northern Ireland, the penalty is recoverable—

(a) if a county court so orders, as if it were payable under an order of that court;

(b) if the High Court so orders, as if it were payable under an order of that court.

### Notices under sections 55A and 55B: supplemental

3G-61 **55E.**—(1) The Secretary of State may by order make further provision in connection with monetary penalty notices and notices of intent.

(2) An order under this section may in particular—

(a) provide that a monetary penalty notice may not be served on a data controller with respect to the processing of personal data for the special purposes except in circumstances specified in the order;

(b) make provision for the cancellation or variation of monetary penalty notices;

(c) confer rights of appeal to the Tribunal against decisions of the Commissioner in relation to the cancellation or variation of such notices;

(d) make provision for the proceedings of the Tribunal in respect of appeals under section 55B(5) or appeals made by virtue of paragraph (c);

(e) make provision for the determination of such appeals;

(f) confer rights of appeal against any decision of the Tribunal in relation to monetary penalty notices or their cancellation or variation.

(3) An order under this section may apply any provision of this Act with such modifications as may be specified in the order.

(4) An order under this section may amend this Act.

*Note* —These provisions were inserted by s.144 of the Criminal Justice and Immigration Act 2008 but are not yet in force (as at November 2009). Implementation is anticipated Spring 2010. **3G–62**

### Criminal Justice and Immigration Act 1998

(2008 c.4)

## Power to alter penalty for unlawfully obtaining etc. personal data

**77.** (1)The Secretary of State may by order provide for a person who is guilty of an offence under section 55 of the Data Protection Act 1998 (c. 29) (unlawful obtaining etc. of personal data) to be liable— **3G–63**

(a) on summary conviction, to imprisonment for a term not exceeding the specified period or to a fine not exceeding the statutory maximum or to both,

(b) on conviction on indictment, to imprisonment for a term not exceeding the specified period or to a fine or to both.

(2) In subsection (1)(a) and (b) "specified period" means a period provided for by the order but the period must not exceed—

(a) in the case of summary conviction, 12 months (or, in Northern Ireland, 6 months), and

(b) in the case of conviction on indictment, two years.

(3) The Secretary of State must ensure that any specified period for England and Wales which, in the case of summary conviction, exceeds 6 months is to be read as a reference to 6 months so far as it relates to an offence committed before the commencement of section 282(1) of the Criminal Justice Act 2003 (c. 44) (increase in sentencing powers of magistrates' courts from 6 to 12 months for certain offences triable either way).

(4) Before making an order under this section, the Secretary of State must consult—

(a) the Information Commissioner,

(b) such media organisations as the Secretary of State considers appropriate, and

(c) such other persons as the Secretary of State considers appropriate.

(5) An order under this section may, in particular, amend the Data Protection Act 1998.

3G–64 *Note* —This provision came into force on May 8, 2008 but no orders have been made to date. The Ministry of Justice published a consultation document CP 22/09 on October 15, 2009 on the introduction of orders under the section.

# 3H CONSUMER CREDIT AND CONSUMER LAW

### Introduction

The legislation in this section includes key provisions of the Consumer Credit Act 1974 and of other legislation relating to proceedings by and against consumers. 3H–1

### Jurisdiction

In relation to consumer contracts there is a special jurisdiction regime governing contracts made within EU Member States and other states which were members of the European Free Trade Association. Under that regime, the general position is that a claim against the consumer must be brought in the state of the consumer's domicile but that a claim by the consumer may be brought either in the state of his own domicile or in the state where the supplier is domiciled or has a branch, agency or establishment whose operation has given rise to the dispute. For the special jurisdiction regime, see para.6.19.23, paras 5–69 to 5–71, paras 5–150 to 5–152 and paras 5–229 to 5–231. Where the UK is the country where the consumer or the supplier is domiciled (or the latter has a branch, agency or establishment), the above rule applies in relation to that part of the UK where the consumer or supplier is domiciled (or the latter has the relevant branch, agency or establishment): Civil Jurisdiction and Judgments Act 1982 ss.10 and 44 (see paras 5–21 and 5–39). For connected lender liability claims relating to overseas transactions made using a UK credit card (or other UK credit), see the commentary to s.75 of the Consumer Credit Act 1974. 3H–2

### Case management

Consumer claims are generally suitable for the small claims track (see 26PD.8.1). See also CPR r.27.1 and commentary. 3H–3

### Introductory note about procedure in consumer credit cases

*Jurisdiction and parties* —The county court has exclusive jurisdiction to hear a claim to enforce a regulated agreement against a debtor or hirer, s.141. For requirements as to joinder of parties, see s.141(5). For procedural requirements where claim is brought by debtor or hirer or where the claim is to enforce an exempt agreement, see commentaries to ss.129, 139, 140B and 141. Where a claim relating to a consumer credit agreement is issued in the High Court, e.g. by a debtor, the particulars of claim must contain a statement that the action is not one to which s.141 of the Consumer Credit Act 1974 applies (16PD.7.6). 3H–4

*Land* —Claims for the possession of land, including mortgage possession actions, must be brought under the procedure set out in CPR Pt 55, as supplemented by the Practice Direction to that Part (see para.55APD.1). That Practice Direction includes special pleading requirements for regulated consumer credit agreements: see paras 2.5(2)(c), 2.5(4), 2.5(5) (all at para.55APD.4); see also para.55.4.4. 3H–5

*Goods* —Claims to enforce regulated consumer hire agreements and regulated consumer credit agreements relating to goods shall be made in accordance with the "Consumer Credit Act procedure" (at para.7BPD.1) in the Consumer Credit Practice Direction (which supplements CPR r.7.9). This procedure applies in addition to the rest of the CPR (which are modified only to the extent that they are inconsistent with it). This Consumer Credit Act procedure (para.7BPD.1) includes requirements for what must be included in the particulars of claim, including specific requirements when the claim is for delivery of goods let, other than to a corporate body, under a regulated hire-purchase or conditional sale agreement. (For the requirements where the hire-purchase or conditional sale agreement is *not* regulated by the Consumer Credit Act, see (at para.16PD.6) para.6.1 of the Statements of Case Practice Direction (which supplements CPR Pt 16)). 3H–6

*Money claims* —For money claims by the creditor or owner which do not relate to the recovery of land, the relevant procedure is as follows: 3H–7

***Paragraph numbers marked with a "+" can be found online and on CD.***

(a) Where the agreement relates to goods, the Consumer Credit Act procedure (para.7BPD.1) applies.

(b) Where the agreement does not relate to goods but the creditor or owner, in order to be able to enforce the agreement (or security) against the defendant, requires a court order under any of ss.65(1), 86(2), 90, 92(1), 105(7)(a) or (b), 111(2), 124(1) or (2), the Consumer Credit Act procedure (para.7BPD.1) applies.

(c) In other cases where the agreement relates only to money, the Consumer Credit Act procedure does not apply. Instead such a claim must be started by the issue of a Pt 7 claim form (see para.7BPD.1, para.3.3).

No doubt in many cases, the claimant will not know or believe, or will be unwilling to acknowledge, that he requires an order under one of the sections listed at (b), e.g. that the documentation requirements were not complied with when the agreement was made and that he consequently requires an order under s.65(1) in order to enforce the agreement. In that case if the agreement does not relate to goods or land, the claimant is likely to start proceedings by the issue of a Pt 7 claim form ignoring the Consumer Credit Act procedure. In that case, it is for the defendant to raise the issue by way of defence.

**3H-8** *The Consumer Credit Act Procedure* —Stated (at para.7BPD.1) in the Consumer Credit Act Practice Direction which supplements CPR r.7.9, this procedure

- is a fixed-date procedure
- in which the claimant must serve the particulars of claim with the claim form,
- where the defendant is not required to, but may, serve an acknowledgement of service or file a defence
- where default judgment is not available (see CPR r.12.2, commentary at paras 12.2.1 and 12.4.5 and also 12PD.1).

See "Goods" and "Money claims" above for when this procedure is to be used.

**3H-9** *Applications by debtor or hirer* —Except where the claim relates to the recovery of land, the Consumer Credit Act procedure is to be used for originating applications by the debtor or hirer for an order under s.129 (a time order), under s.140B (unfair debtor/creditor relationship) or under s.139(1) (extortionate credit bargain). Where a regulated agreement is secured by a land mortgage, the position is not clear. Arguably, in such a case, an *originating* application for a time order or for an order on the basis that the creditor/debtor relationship is unfair, does not "relate to the recovery of land", in which case the Consumer Credit Act procedure is to be used. If it does "relate to the recovery of land", then the CPR appear to have no special provision for such an application. Of course applications under ss.129 and 140B can be made by a defendant whatever procedure has been used by the claimant/creditor.

**3H-10** *Default judgment* —A judgment in default of acknowledgement of service or in default of defence is not obtainable on a claim for delivery of goods which are subject to a regulated agreement, CPR r.12.2(a). It is not available in any case where the claimant is using the Consumer Credit Act procedure (para.7BPD.5 at para.5.5).

**3H-11** *Interest on judgments* —The County Courts (Interest on Judgment Debts) Order 1991 (SI 1991/1184) as amended provides for interest to be carried on judgment debts that are unsatisfied. By way of exception, interest under the Order is not payable on a judgment in proceedings to recover money under an agreement regulated by the Consumer Credit Act 1974 (see paras 40.8.2 and 9B-72). A regulated agreement may, however, expressly provide for payment of interest on such a judgment. In *Director General of Fair Trading v First National Bank* [2002] 1 A.C. 48, the House of Lords held that such a contractual provision was not unfair within the Unfair Terms in Consumer Contracts Regulations 1994. Default interest under a regulated agreement must not be at a rate higher than that applicable to the agreement as a whole (see Consumer Credit Act 1974 s.93 below). There is also, from October 1, 2008, a notice giving requirement before the creditor or owner can become entitled to recover any post-judgment interest (see the Consumer Credit Act 1974 s.130A below). See also ss.86A to 86F of the 1974 Act, which are designed to prevent a debtor sleepwalking into ever increasing debt by requiring him to be given information as to sums in arrears and the attendant risks.

***Paragraph numbers marked with a "+" can be found online and on CD.***

*Hearings* —Proceedings brought under the Consumer Credit Act shall in the first instance be listed by the court as a hearing in private under CPR r.39.2(3)(c)—see para.39APD.1, para.1.5. **3H-12**

*Costs* —For claims for "fixed commencement costs" and for recovery of "fixed costs on entry of judgment" for delivery up of goods, see CPR Pt 45. In relation to such costs issues in the case of a summary judgment, see also para.24.6.7. **3H-13**

*Enforcement of judgments* —A County Court judgment which arose out of an agreement regulated by the Consumer Credit Act 1974 cannot be transferred to the High Court for enforcement: s.141 of the 1974 Act and art.8 of the High Court and County Courts Jurisdiction Order 1991 (para.9B–928). See also paras 70.3.2, sc.46.1.48, and cc25.13.1. **3H-14**

*Bills of Sale* —For registration of bills of sale, renewals of registration, entry of satisfaction, search of the register and related matters, see paras sc95.0.1 to sc95.4.1 and the Practice Direction supplementing RSC O.95 (at scpd95.1). **3H-15**

**Exempt agreements (ss.16, 16A, 16B and 16C)**

Section 16 of the Consumer Credit Act 1974 states that the Act does not regulate a consumer credit or consumer hire agreement if it falls into one of a series of categories. The matter is more finely regulated by an Order made under s.16, the Consumer Credit (Exempt Agreements) Order 1989 (as amended). Sections 16A, 16B and 16C provide for exemptions where the debtor or hirer is of high net worth (s.16A) or in business (s.16B) or takes buy-to-let credit (s.16C). For the terms of these four sections and detailed commentary, see para.3H–45+ *et seq.* available on the White Book on Westlaw UK Service or the Civil Procedure CD. Most exempt credit agreements are, however, subject to an order being made against the creditor under s.140B of the Act, if the court finds the relationship between the creditor and debtor to be unfair. **3H-16**

**Consumer Credit Act 2006**

The Consumer Credit Act 2006 has no substantive provisions but made significant amendments to the Consumer Credit Act 1974. The principal changes made by the 2006 Act (with the commencement dates shown in brackets) are the following: **3H-17**

- Removal of the financial limit in the definition of regulated agreement in ss.8 and 15 of the 1974 Act (as from April 6, 2008).
- Repeal of subss.(3) to (5) of s.127 of the 1974 Act, which in certain circumstances made improperly executed agreements irredeemably unenforceable against the debtor or hirer (as from April 6, 2007).
- Replacement of the court's power to re-open an extortionate credit bargain (under ss.137–140) with similar powers (under new ss.140A–140D) where the court finds the relationship between creditor and debtor arising out of the agreement to be "unfair", a wider concept than that of an "extortionate credit bargain" (as from April 6, 2007).
- Expansion of the definition of ancillary credit business (in s.145 of the 1974 Act) to include "debt administration" and "credit information services" (as from October 1, 2008).
- Extension of the ombudsman scheme established under the Financial Services and Markets Act 2000, to include consumer credit jurisdiction thereby enabling it to be used by an individual bringing a consumer credit complaint (as from April 6, 2007).
- Strengthening of the requirements to give notice and information to debtors and hirers in default/arrears (as from October 1, 2008).

The effect of transitional provisions is explained in commentary to the relevant sections of the 1974 Act (below).

***Paragraph numbers marked with a "+" can be found online and on CD.***

# Consumer Credit Act 1974

3H–18 (1974 c.39)

ARRANGEMENT OF SECTIONS

PART II

CREDIT AGREEMENTS, HIRE AGREEMENTS AND LINKED TRANSACTIONS



***Paragraph numbers marked with a "+" can be found online and on CD.***

***Paragraph numbers marked with a "+" can be found online and on CD.***

***Paragraph numbers marked with a "+" can be found online and on CD.***

**Paragraph numbers marked with a "+" denote content that is available on White Book on Westlaw UK or the Civil Procedure CD.**

**[THE NEXT PARAGRAPH IS 3H–20.]**

# PART II

# CREDIT AGREEMENTS, HIRE AGREEMENTS AND LINKED TRANSACTIONS

## Consumer credit agreements

**8.**—(1) A consumer credit agreement is an agreement between an individual ("the debtor") and any other person ("the creditor") by which the creditor provides the debtor with credit of any amount. **3H–20**

(2) [...]

(3) A consumer credit agreement is a regulated agreement within the meaning of this Act if it is not an agreement (an "exempt agreement") specified in or under section 16, 16A, 16B or 16C.

*Note* —Amended by the Consumer Credit (Increase of Monetary Limits) Order 1983 (SI 1983/1878); and the Consumer Credit (Increase of Monetary Limits) (Amendment) Order 1998 (SI 1998/996). Further amended and subs.(2) repealed by the Consumer Credit Act 2006 ss.2 and 70 and Sch.4 with effect from April 6, 2008 for certain purposes (SI 2007/3300 and SI 2008/831) and for remaining purposes October 31, 2008 (SI 2008/831 as amended by SI 2008/2444). Further amended by the Legislative Reform (Consumer Credit) Order 2008 (SI 2008/2826). **3H–21**

### Consumer credit agreements

As a general rule the Act and the regulations made under it apply only to "regulated" agreements. There are two kinds of regulated agreement: **3H–22**

(i) those defined in this section, i.e. regulated consumer credit agreements; and

(ii) those defined in s.15, i.e. regulated consumer hire agreements.

"Exempt agreements"—An "exempt agreement" is not a "regulated agreement". There are, nevertheless, certain provisions in the Act which apply to most exempt agreements, namely the unfair relationships provisions in ss.140A to 140C and (in re-

***Paragraph numbers marked with a "+" can be found online and on CD.***

lation to certain agreements made before April 6, 2007) the extortionate credit bargain provisions in ss.137–140. See, further, the commentary to s.140A below.

"Individual"—No agreement is a consumer credit agreement or a regulated agreement unless the debtor is an "individual". A corporate body is not an individual. A partnership of up to three people is an "individual". Prior to April 6, 2007 a partnership of any number of people was an "individual"— see the definition of "individual" in s.189(1) and commentary to that section.

"Credit"—For the meaning of "credit" see s.9. "Credit" can be provided under an agreement—and that agreement can thus be a consumer credit agreement and a regulated agreement—even though the credit is never actually used. Thus a bank may agree to a customer having authority to go overdrawn to, say, a maximum of £10,000. Credit is provided even though the customer may subsequently choose not to use the overdraft facility. "Credit" is provided when the customer is granted the facility. Similarly, credit is provided when a credit card agreement is made and a credit card issued to the customer. A credit card agreement will normally be a regulated consumer credit agreement, i.e. unless the debtor is a company or other corporate body. A charge card agreement, however, will normally be an exempt agreement under s.16.

**Financial limit**

**3H–23** Prior to amendments effected by the Consumer Credit Act 2006, the definition of "consumer credit agreement" included a financial limit. Thus any agreement which was made prior to April 6, 2008 and which provided an individual with credit exceeding a specified figure was not—and still is not—a consumer credit agreement. When the 1974 Act came into force, the specified figure was £5,000. From May 20, 1985 it became £15,000. In respect of any agreement made on or after May 1, 1998 the figure was £25,000. In relation to the specified figure there was an important distinction between fixed-sum credit and running-account credit, which terms are defined in s.10. When dealing with fixed-sum credit, the important question was whether the amount of the *credit* exceeded the specified figure. A loan of £25,000 was within the limit even though the repayments (i.e. including interest) would exceed £25,000. Similarly a hire-purchase or conditional sale agreement involving an initial down-payment of £2,000 and instalment payments totalling £27,000 was within the £25,000 figure provided that the instalment payments included a figure of at least £2,000 for interest (or credit charge). Neither the down payment nor the credit charges form part of the "credit". (For the rule that credit charges do not form part of the credit, see s.9(4).) As a rule of thumb, when dealing with a hire-purchase, conditional sale or credit sale agreement, one can ascertain the amount of the credit by deducting the down payment and any trade-in allowance from the cash price of the item being purchased; the resulting figure is the amount which, in common parlance, is being "borrowed", i.e. is the amount of "credit" (see also Sch.II, Pt II, Example 10). When dealing with running-account credit, e.g. a credit card agreement or an overdraft, the important question is whether the "credit-limit" (defined in s.10(2)) exceeded the figure specified, though there were anti-avoidance provisions in s.10(3).

**3H–24** *Removal of financial limit—transitional provisions* —Article 4 of the Consumer Credit Act 2006 (Commencement No.4 and Transitional Provisions) Order 2008 (SI 2008/831), sets out transitional provisions. Article 4 prevents s.82(2) of the Consumer Credit Act 1974 applying in certain cases, with the following effect. An agreement made before April 6, 2008 under which the creditor provided the debtor with credit exceeding £25,000 will remain unregulated even if (a) it is varied or supplemented by a later agreement which does not provide for a cash loan, or (b) it is varied or supplemented by a later agreement which is an exempt agreement.

Subsection (2) was repealed and the financial limit was removed (subject to one exception) in relation to agreements made on or after April 6, 2008. The exception was buy-to-let credit agreements (defined and termed "relevant agreements" in Sch.1 to the Consumer Credit Act 2006 (Commencement No.4 and Transitional Provisions) Order 2008). In relation to these buy-to-let agreements, the relevant commencement date was October 1, 2008. Also on October 1, 2008, the Legislative Reform (Consumer Credit) Order 2008 (SI 2008/2826) came into effect. It ensured that buy-to-let credit agreements remained exempt by inserting a new s.16C into the Consumer Credit Act 1974 making certain agreements exempt—those agreements being defined exactly the same as "relevant agreements" had been defined in Sch.1 to SI 2008/831.

## Meaning of credit

**9.**—(1) In this Act "credit" includes a cash loan, and any other form of financial accommodation. **3H–25**

(2) Where credit is provided otherwise than in sterling it shall be treated for the purposes of this Act as provided in sterling of an equivalent amount.

(3) Without prejudice to the generality of subsection (1), the person by whom goods are bailed or (in Scotland) hired to an individual under a hire-purchase agreement shall be taken to provide him with fixed-sum credit to finance the transaction of an amount equal to the total price of the goods less the aggregate of the deposit (if any) and the total charge for credit.

(4) For the purposes of this Act, an item entering into the total charge for credit shall not be treated as credit even though time is allowed for its payment.

### Meaning of credit

*Subsection (1)*—"Credit" appears intended to embrace the classic form of credit summed up in the phrase "Have now, pay later", or expressed as the deferment of an obligation to pay. An agreement for the provision of advertising services provided for payment to be made in full on the primary date (i.e. the signing of the agreement) or by instalments; this was held to be the provision of credit in that customers were permitted to defer payment beyond the primary date (*Stolink UK v Thomas* [1996] 1 C.L.Y. 1225). The term "credit hire agreement" is sometimes used to describe a hire agreement under which payment for the hire of goods is deferred for a period after the hire has come to an end. It involves the provision of credit because the duty to pay is contractually deferred for a significant period after payment has been earned: *Hatfield v Hiscock* [1998] C.C.L.R. 68 and *Dimond v Lovell* [2002] 1 A.C. 384, HL. (See further the notes to s.11.) **3H–26**

Whether a contract provides credit is to be determined as at the time the contract is made. Where at that time it is uncertain whether the arrangements between the parties will give rise to a debt at all, there is no "credit" merely because the contract postpones any obligation to pay until the possible indebtedness has crystallised: *Nejad v City Index Ltd* [2000] C.C.L.R. 7; *McMillan Williams (A Firm) v Range* [2004] C.C.L.R. 3; [2004] 1 W.L.R. 1858. A publishing contract, which provided for the author to be paid an advance on royalties coupled with a requirement for the author to repay after three years such amount of the advance as the sales in those three years had failed to earn, would not provide the author with credit. That conclusion might be different, however, if the amount of the advance was so great as to show that it was in reality a loan dressed up as an advance on royalties.

Professionally drafted contracts for the sale by J of a farm, for its lease-back to J and for J to have an option to re-purchase it later, were held not to amount to the provision of credit even though they were transactions made in order to enable J to cope with substantial financial problems: *Lavin v Johnson* [2002] EWCA Civ 1138.

Under a funding agreement the claimants were to provide funds of 50 millions of euros, to use the funds to purchase share warrants, to transfer these warrants to the borrower, a special purchase vehicle (an SPV) (to be set up by the defendants) and then to have the funds repaid one year later by the borrower (the SPV) together with an uplift of 25 per cent. Until the SPV (a corporate body) was set up, the defendants were to be jointly and severally liable for the borrower's liability under the agreement. This funding agreement was held not to amount to the provision of "credit" to the defendants: *Maple Leaf Macro Volatility Master Fund v Rouvroy and Trylinski* [2009] EWHC 257 (Comm); [2009] C.C.L.R. 9

*After the event (ATE) insurance*: a claimant in a personal injury claim action may well fund the proceedings by a conditional fee arrangement (CFA). If the claimant loses, the claimant will not have to pay legal fees but may well have costs awarded against

***Paragraph numbers marked with a "+" can be found online and on CD.***

her requiring her to pay the defendant's legal costs. The claimant therefore may, at the time of entering her CFA, take out an insurance policy to cover herself against that risk. Such a policy, known as "after the event" (ATE) insurance, may provide that the premium is not payable until the conclusion of the case. If so, does that amount to the provision of "credit", i.e. insurance cover now, pay later? In *Tilby v Perfect Pizza Ltd* [2003] C.C.L.R. 9 (also available on Court Service website), Senior Costs Judge Hurst held that there was no provision of "credit" unless payment of the premium was deferred for a significant period beyond the conclusion of the case. For the recoverability of an ATE insurance premium as part of a successful claimant's costs: see para.44.3A.3.

**3H–27** *Subsection(2)* —This is relevant to the various financial limits in the Act. Most of these are relevant at the time the agreement is made. For example an agreement made before April 6, 2008 and involving credit of more than £25,000 is not a regulated agreement (see s.8). Thus the relevant exchange rate to apply is that operative on the date of the making of the agreement. An agreement is either a regulated agreement or it is not; it cannot become one, or cease to be one, at some later date simply because the exchange rate has moved.

**3H–28** *Subsection(3)* —This makes it clear that hire-purchase agreements are treated by the Act as consumer credit agreements and not as consumer hire agreements. Where the Act uses the terms "creditor or owner" and "debtor or hirer", in each case it is the former which is relevant to hire-purchase agreements. A hire-purchase agreement may itself use the terms "owner" and "hirer"; nevertheless, in the terminology employed in the Act, the parties are "creditor"and "debtor". The terms "owner" and "hirer", when used in the Act, refer only to the parties to consumer hire agreements.

**3H–29** *Subsection(4)* —The "total charge for credit" is defined in the Consumer Credit (Total Charge for Credit) Regulations 1980, made under s.20. In determining whether a fixed-sum credit agreement (made before April 6, 2008) is within the financial limit to bring it within the definition of a regulated consumer credit agreement (see s.8(2)), any item which is part of the total charge for credit is to be ignored. In *Humberclyde Finance Ltd v Thompson* [1997] C.C.L.R. 23, CA, the debtor contracted to buy a car on conditional sale terms. The balance of the cash price (i.e. after deduction of the initial down payment which was paid by a part-exchange) was £14,497. However, the agreement contained also a payment waiver option which the debtor adopted and which provided that if the debtor (Mr Thompson) died within five years, Mrs Thompson would be relieved from having to pay any instalments which had not fallen due before his death. The fee for this option was £796. Despite the fact that, under the agreement, payment of this fee was a deferred obligation, it was held that the fee did not form part of the "credit", because it fell within the definition of the "total charge for credit". Thus the agreement involved "credit" of less than £15,000 (the then figure specified in s.8(2)) and was a regulated agreement. [*Query* whether the fee was *correctly* held to be within the definition of the total charge for credit—see Consumer Credit (Total Charge for Credit) Regulations 1980 below]. For further examples of the application of s.9(4), see *Huntpast Ltd v. Leadbeater* [1993] C.C.L.R. 15, CA and *Watchtower Investments Ltd v Payne* [2001] EWCA Civ 1159; [2003] C.C.L.R. 10 and *McGinn v Grangewood Securities Ltd* [2002] EWCA Civ 522; [2003] C.C.L.R. 11, *London North Securities Ltd v Meadows* [2005] EWCA Civ 956; [2005] C.C.L.R. 7 and *Blackhorse Ltd v Hanson* [2009] EWCA Civ 73; [2009] C.C.L.R. 6 —all explained at para.3H–432+. See also *Wilson v First County Trust (No.1)* [2001] Q.B. 407; [2003] C.C.L.R. 1—discussed in the commentary to s.127(3) below.

## Running-account credit and fixed-sum credit

**3H–30** **10.**—(1) For the purposes of this Act—

(a) running-account credit is a facility under a consumer credit agreement whereby the debtor is enabled to receive from time to time (whether in his own person, or by another person) from the creditor or a third party cash, goods and services (or any of them) to an amount or value such that, taking into account payments made by or to the credit of the debtor, the credit limit (if any) is not at any time exceeded; and

(b) fixed-sum credit is any other facility under a consumer credit agreement whereby the debtor is enabled to receive credit (whether in one amount or by instalments).

(2) In relation to running-account credit, "credit limit" means, as respects any period, the maximum debit balance which, under the credit agreement, is allowed to stand on the account during that period, disregarding any term of the agreement allowing that maximum to be exceeded merely temporarily.

(3) For the purposes of paragraph (a) of section 16B(1), running-account credit shall be taken not to exceed the amount specified in that paragraph ("the specified amount") if—

(a) the credit limit does not exceed the specified amount; or

(b) whether or not there is a credit limit, and if there is, notwithstanding that it exceeds the specified amount,—

(i) the debtor is not enabled to draw at any one time an amount which, so far as (having regard to section 9(4)) it represents credit, exceeds the specified amount, or

(ii) the agreement provides that, if the debit balance rises above a given amount (not exceeding the specified amount), the rate of the total charge for credit increases or any other condition favouring the creditor or his associate comes into operation, or

(iii) at the time the agreement is made it is probable, having regard to the terms of the agreement and any other relevant considerations, that the debit balance will not at any time rise above the specified amount.

*Note*—Amended by Consumer Credit Act 2006 s.5(2), with effect from April 6, 2008 (SI 2007/3300). **3H–31**

**Running-account credit and fixed-sum credit**

Typical examples of fixed-sum credits are: hire-purchase, conditional sale and credit sale agreements, bank loans (whether advanced as a lump sum or in instalments), pawnbrokers' loans, check trading credit (see also Sch.II, Pt II, Examples 9, 10, 17 and 23). A "credit hire" agreement has been held to be an example of fixed-sum credit (see notes to s.11). Typical examples of running-account credit are: credit card agreements, bank overdraft agreements, shop budget accounts (see also Sch.II, Pt II, Examples 15, 16, 18 and 23). Suppose a consumer applies to have a store credit card which is offered at the time the consumer decides to make a purchase and that both parties know and intend that the first debit to the account will be the price of the item being purchased. The fact that, when the credit agreement is made, the parties know that an exact sum is to be advanced under the credit agreement, is not enough to make the credit agreement one which is in part a fixed-sum credit agreement. That debit is merely the first drawing against a running-account facility: *Goshawk Dedicated (No.2) Ltd v The Governor and Company of the Bank of Scotland* [2005] EWHC 2906 (Ch); [2006] 2 All E.R. 610. The distinction between fixed-sum and running-account credit is important for the purposes of calculation of the "specified amount" in s.16B(1)(a). **3H–32**

***Paragraph numbers marked with a "+" can be found online and on CD.***

In relation to an agreement made before April 6, 2008, it is important for the purposes of the calculation of the specified figure which until that date was part of the definition (in s.8) of a consumer credit agreement. An agreement made prior to April 6, 2008 was not (and still is not) a consumer credit agreement if it provided credit exceeding £25,000—see commentary to s.8. As regards running-account agreements, the primary rule is that the credit limit is the determining factor. However, even if there is no credit limit or if the credit limit is higher than the specified amount (£25,000 prior to April 6, 2008), the agreement may nevertheless be taken, by virtue of s.10(3), to provide credit not exceeding that figure. Section 10(3) is an anti-avoidance provision to cope with the situation where an unrealistically high credit limit is agreed. A term that the interest rate increases if the debit balance rises above £25,000 (or any lower figure), would cause the application of s.10(3)(b)(ii)—(see also Sch.II, Pt II, Example 6). If the agreement contains a term signifying that in the opinion of the parties s.10(3)(b)(iii) does not apply to the agreement, it (i.e. s.10(3)(b)(iii)) shall be taken not to apply unless the contrary is proved, see s.171(1)(see also Sch.II, Pt II, Example 6). By s.10(2) a term of the agreement allowing the debtor to exceed the credit limit merely temporarily is to be ignored (see also s.18(5) and Sch.II, Pt II, Examples 22 and 23).

## Restricted-use credit and unrestricted-use credit

3H–33 **11.**—(1) A restricted-use credit agreement is a regulated consumer credit agreement—

(a) to finance a transaction between the debtor and the creditor, whether forming part of that agreement or not, or

(b) to finance a transaction between the debtor and a person (the "supplier") other than the creditor, or

(c) to refinance any existing indebtedness of the debtor's, whether to the creditor or another person,

and "restricted-use credit" shall be construed accordingly.

(2) An unrestricted-use credit agreement is a regulated consumer credit agreement not falling within subsection (1), and "unrestricted-use credit" shall be construed accordingly.

(3) An agreement does not fall within subsection (1) if the credit is in fact provided in such a way as to leave the debtor free to use it as he chooses, even though certain uses would contravene that or any other agreement.

(4) An agreement may fall within subsection (1)(b) although the identity of the supplier is unknown at the time the agreement is made.

### Restricted-use credit and unrestricted-use credit

3H–34 Credit is either restricted-use credit or unrestricted-use credit. These two definitions interrelate with those (in ss.12 and 13) of debtor-creditor agreement and debtor-creditor-supplier agreement. Also they are relevant to the definitions of some exempt agreements (see commentary to s.16). Where the credit is advanced in such a way that the debtor can spend it in any way he chooses (e.g. cash is put into the debtor's hands or into his current account), the credit is inevitably unrestricted-use credit (s.11(3)). That is so even if the debtor has agreed to use the credit only in a particular way. Where goods or services are supplied on credit, then the credit is tied to that particular purpose and the agreement will therefore fall within s.11(1)(a) or s.11(1)(b). It will be a s.11(1)(a) situation where the person providing the credit (the creditor) and the person contracting with the debtor to supply the goods or services (the supplier) are one and the same person, e.g. where a retailer supplies a fridge on terms that the debtor pays the retailer for it in instalments later. A s.11(1)(b) situation arises where the creditor and the supplier are two different persons, e.g. where the customer uses his regulated credit card to pay for goods or services. The credit card issuer (the creditor) provides credit to the customer to enable the customer to buy from the retailer. The customer's contract of purchase is with the retailer; his credit card agreement with the card issuer is a restricted-use credit agreement within s.11(1)(b). It is "restricted" use because, although the card can no doubt be used at many retail outlets, it is not available for use absolutely anywhere. If the card-holder (the debtor) is able to draw cash on his credit card account, he is, of course, free to use that cash as he chooses. In that case the credit card agreement is a "multiple agreement"(within s.18(1)(a)): when the debtor uses the card to pay for goods or services, the agreement is one for restricted-use credit within s.11(1)(b); when the debtor uses it to draw cash, it is an unrestricted-use credit agreement (see Sch.II, Pt II, Example 16).

*Hatfield v Hiscock* [1998] C.C.L.R. 68, involved a "credit hire" agreement for the hire of a motor vehicle for a period not exceeding three months and under which the payment for the hire was deferred for a period after the hire had come to an end. This agreement was held to involve fixed-sum credit, albeit the amount of the credit was incapable of being quantified until some weeks or months after the agreement was made. In *Dimond v Lovell* [2000] Q.B. 216; [1999] 3 W.L.R. 561, the Court of Appeal held a similar "credit hire" agreement to be: a personal credit agreement within s.8(1); a consumer credit agreement within s.8(2); an agreement for fixed-sum credit within s.10(1)(b), and; a debtor-credit-supplier agreement within s.12(a). This analysis was apparently approved when a further appeal in *Dimond v Lovell* [2002] 1 A.C. 384 was dismissed by the House of Lords.

A hire-purchase agreement (or a conditional sale or credit sale agreement) entered into between the customer and a finance company to whom the customer has been introduced by a dealer for the purpose of enabling the customer to buy goods of the dealer on credit terms, may appear at first sight to be a s.11(1)(b) agreement. In fact it is not. In this scenario, the finance company buys the goods from the dealer and in turn contracts to supply them to the customer/debtor. The finance company is both creditor and supplier. It is the latter because under the hire-purchase contract the finance company contracts to supply the goods. It is to the finance company that the debtor can look if the goods are not delivered or if, say, there is a breach of the statutory implied terms (as to description, satisfactory quality, etc.). The credit in these cases is provided by the finance company to finance a transaction (i.e. for the supply of the goods) between the finance company and the debtor. Thus every regulated hire-purchase agreement, every regulated conditional sale agreement and every regulated credit sale agreement is a s.11(1)(a) agreement.

An agreement can be "to finance ..." or "to refinance ..." within s.11 only where it contains an express or implied term that the credit shall be used for that purpose. It is not enough that the parties had a common purpose or intention that the credit be used for that purpose, *National Westminster Bank v Story and Pallister* [1999] C.C.L.R. 70, CA.

## Debtor-creditor-supplier agreements

**12.** A debtor-creditor-supplier agreement is a regulated consumer credit agreement being— **3H-35**

(a) a restricted-use credit agreement which falls within section 11(1)(a), or

(b) a restricted-use credit agreement which falls within section 11(1)(b)and is made by the creditor under pre-existing arrangements, or in contemplation of future arrangements, between himself and the supplier, or

(c) an unrestricted-use credit agreement which is made by the creditor under pre-existing arrangements between himself and a person (the "supplier") other than the debtor in the knowledge that the credit is to be used to finance a transaction between the debtor and the supplier.

### Debtor-creditor-supplier agreements

Every regulated agreement is either a debtor-creditor-supplier agreement (within **3H-36**

***Paragraph numbers marked with a "+" can be found online and on CD.***

s.12) or a debtor-creditor agreement (within s.13). The former identifies regulated consumer credit agreements: first where the creditor and the supplier are one and the same person (s.12(a)); and, secondly, where, though the creditor and supplier are separate persons, there is a business link between them such that the credit contract and the supply contract are linked in a business sense (s.12(b) and (c)). Later sections provide for the dealer to be deemed to be agent of the creditor in antecedent negotiations (s.56) and for the creditor to be jointly and severally liable for misrepresentations and breaches of contract committed by the supplier when the supplier is a different person from the creditor (s.75). These sections do not apply to debtor-creditor agreements.

Every regulated hire-purchase agreement, every regulated conditional sale agreement and every regulated credit sale agreement is a debtor-creditor-supplier agreement within s.12(a) (see commentary to s.11 above). A regulated credit card agreement will be a debtor-creditor-supplier agreement within s.12(b) when the credit card is used to pay for goods or services and will be a debtor-creditor agreement within s.13(c) when used to withdraw cash (see commentary to s.11 above). A "credit hire" agreement is a debtor-creditor-supplier agreement within s.12(a)—see notes to s.11.

"Arrangements" is a key word intended to identify the link between the credit agreement and the supply agreement. The Crowther Report, which the Act was passed to implement, referred to the situation where the creditor and supplier were in effect in a "joint venture for mutual profit". For "arrangements", see s.187. An agreement for an individual to have an overdraft (with a credit limit of £25,000 or less) is a regulated consumer credit agreement; it is a debtor-creditor agreement. That is so irrespective of whether payment (for goods or services) out of that account is by means of either a cheque (whether or not backed by a cheque guarantee card) or an electronic debit card (e.g. Delta or Switch), see s.187(3) and (3A). It would be a debtor-creditor-supplier agreement (within s.12(b) or (c)) in the very unlikely event that the bank agreed to the overdraft pursuant to arrangements between the bank and a supplier whereby the bank agreed to grant credit to customers to enable them to make purchases from the supplier. Such a scenario would be more likely to occur, however, in the case of a bank loan (i.e. rather than an overdraft agreement). If that scenario did exist, the loan would be a debtor-creditor-supplier agreement even if the loan were advanced by means of unrestricted-use credit (e.g. if the bank advanced the credit, albeit under a separate loan agreement, by simply crediting it to the debtor's current account). In that case, if the loan was made under the arrangements between the bank and the supplier, and if the bank knew that it was to be used to finance a transaction between the debtor and the supplier, it would be a debtor-creditor-supplier agreement within s.12(c).

In relation to debtor-creditor-supplier and debtor-creditor agreements, see Sch.II, Pt II, Examples 8, 16, 17, 18 and 21.

### Debtor-creditor agreements

3H–37 **13.** A debtor-creditor agreement is a regulated consumer credit agreement being—

(a) a restricted-use credit agreement which falls within section 11(1)(b) but is not made by the creditor under pre-existing arrangements, or in contemplation of future arrangements, between himself and the supplier, or

(b) a restricted-use credit agreement which falls within section 11(1)(c), or

(c) an unrestricted-use credit agreement which is not made by the creditor under pre-existing arrangements between himself and a person (the "supplier") other than the debtor in the knowledge that the credit is to be used to finance a transaction between the debtor and the supplier.

**Debtor-creditor agreements**

3H–38 See commentary to s.12.

***Paragraph numbers marked with a "+" can be found online and on CD.***

## Credit-token agreements

**14.**—(1) A credit-token is a card, check, voucher, coupon, stamp, form, booklet or other document or thing given to an individual by a person carrying on a consumer credit business, who undertakes— 3H–39

(a) that on the production of it (whether or not some other action is also required) he will supply cash, goods and services (or any of them) on credit, or

(b) that where, on the production of it to a third party (whether or not any other action is also required), the third party supplies cash, goods and services (or any of them), he will pay the third party for them (whether or not deducting any discount or commission), in return for payment to him by the individual.

(2) A credit-token agreement is a regulated agreement for the provision of credit in connection with the use of a credit-token.

(3) Without prejudice to the generality of section 9(1), the person who gives to an individual an undertaking falling within subsection (1)(b) shall be taken to provide him with credit drawn on whenever a third party supplies him with cash, goods or services.

(4) For the purposes of subsection (1), use of an object to operate a machine provided by the person giving the object or a third party shall be treated as the production of the object to him.

### Credit-token agreements

The basic concept of a credit-token is of an object on production of which cash, goods or services may be supplied on credit. The credit card is the typical case, but the term also covers trading vouchers, trading checks, and in some circumstances electronic debit (Delta or Swift) cards. 3H–40

This section contains two definitions: "credit-token"; and "credit-token agreement". Only a regulated agreement can be a credit-token agreement. A credit-token can exist, on the other hand in relation to an agreement which is not a regulated agreement—though it can only be a credit-token if it is given by someone carrying on a "consumer credit business". *Query* whether a token issued in relation to an exempt agreement (e.g. an exempt charge card) by someone who also carries on a "consumer credit business" (e.g. issues regulated credit cards) can be a "credit-token"? See the definition of "consumer credit business" in s.189(1). It seems that an electronic debit card which can be used only to withdraw cash from machines operated by the bank which issued the card will be a credit-token only if the bank has agreed to the card holder having a debit balance on his account, since if the card is to be used simply to withdraw money from an account with a credit balance, the card does not fall within s.14(1)(a), there being no "credit" involved. If, on the other hand, the card can be used to withdraw money from a machine operated by a third party (e.g. another bank) the card appears capable of falling within s.14(1)(b). In that case it appears to be irrelevant (if it is the case) that the card is able to be used only in relation to a credit balance, since by s.14(3) the issuing bank is "taken" to provide the card holder with credit. Or does the reference in s.14(1)to the object being given by a person carrying on a consumer credit business imply that it is confined to objects issued in relation to regulated consumer credit agreements?

It is an offence to give an unsolicited credit-token, s.51(1). In that context, it has been held that the word "undertakes" in s.14(1) does not imply a requirement of a contract or of a binding undertaking, *Elliott v Director General of Fair Trading* [1980] 1 W.L.R. 977; [1980] C.C.L.R. 23. In that case a card having the appearance of a credit card was on its face stated to be a credit card available for immediate use. It was held that this was a credit-token even though a customer first presenting the card would have been required to enter a formal agreement and complete other formalities before getting credit.

## Consumer hire agreements

3H-41 **15.**—(1) A consumer hire agreement is an agreement made by a person with an individual (the "hirer") for the bailment or (in Scotland) the hiring of goods to the hirer, being an agreement which—

(a) is not a hire-purchase agreement, and

(b) is capable of subsisting for more than three months.

(c) [...]

(2) A consumer hire agreement is a regulated agreement if it is not an exempt agreement.

3H-42 *Note* —Amended by the Consumer Credit (Increase of Monetary Limits) Order 1983 (SI 1983/1878); and the Consumer Credit (Increase of Monetary Limits) (Amendment) Order 1988 (SI 1998/996). Subsection (1)(c) was repealed with effect from April 6, 2008 by the Consumer Credit Act 2006 ss.2(2), 70, Sch.4 (SI 2007/ 3300 and SI 2008/ 831).

### Consumer hire agreements

3H-43 For "individual" see commentary to s.8. A hire-purchase agreement cannot be a consumer hire agreement. Hire-purchase agreements are credit agreements (see s.9(2)). The parties to a consumer hire agreement are referred to in the Act as "owner" and "hirer". An agreement is not a hire agreement if it does not provide for the bailee to pay (or provide some other reward) for the hire: *TRM Copy Centres (UK) Ltd v Lanwall Services Ltd* [2009] UKHL 35; [2009] 1 W.L.R. 1375, (not hire when retailer agreed to have a photocopier on retailer's premises with no obligation to make any payment to the photocopier owner other than to account, less a commission, for payments made by members of the public for use of the machine). A hire agreement which is stated to have a duration of two months and which contains an option to renew the agreement for a further two months (whether exercisable by the hirer or the owner) is capable of subsisting for more than three months. Until April 6, 2008, subs.(1) contained a third paragraph—paragraph (c)—setting out a financial limit. Thus any hire agreement made before that date was not (and still is not) a consumer hire agreement if it required the hirer to make payments exceeding a specified figure. When the Act came into force, the figure in s.15(1)(c) was £5,000. On May 20, 1985, it was raised to £15,000. For agreements made on or after May 1, 1998 the figure was £25,000. An agreement, made before April 6, 2008, which was stated to last for seven years, which contained no clause entitling either party to terminate it before the expiry of the seven years, and which provided for quarterly rentals each of £1,000, was not a consumer hire agreement. This is because it required the debtor to make payments amounting to £28,000, i.e. exceeding £25,000. If, on the other hand, the agreement had contained a clause entitling the hirer to terminate the agreement at the end of three and a half years, it would have been a consumer hire agreement because it would then require the hirer to make payments of only £14,000, i.e. not exceeding £25,000. See also Sch.II, Pt II, Examples 20 and 24. The financial limit is no part of the definition in relation to agreements made after April 6, 2008. For "exempt" agreements, see ss.16, 16A and 16B.

### Credit-hire agreements

3H-44 If the *bailment* is not capable of subsisting for more than three months, then the agreement is not a consumer hire agreement. That is so, even if the agreement is a "credit-hire" agreement and thus the period allowed for payment of the hire charges is much longer than three months: *Lagden v O'Connor* [2003] Q.B. 36; [2002] EWCA Civ 510. For whether a "credit-hire" agreement is a consumer credit agreement, see the commentaries to ss.8 and 11. For whether it is exempt, see commentary to s.16 (at the sixth bullet point).

**For ss.16 to 16C of the Consumer Credit Act 1974 (see Arrangement) plus any related commentary see paragraphs 3H–45+ to 3H–54.0.2+ on White Book on Westlaw UK or the Civil Procedure CD.**

***Paragraph numbers marked with a "+" can be found online and on CD.***

## Small agreements

**17.**—(1) A small agreement is— 3H–54

(a) a regulated consumer credit agreement for credit not exceeding £50, other than a hire-purchase or conditional sale agreement; or

(b) a regulated consumer hire agreement which does not require the hirer to make payments exceeding £50,

being an agreement which is either unsecured or secured by a guarantee or indemnity only (whether or not the guarantee or indemnity is itself secured).

(2) Section 10(3)(a) applies for the purposes of subsection (1) as it applies for the purposes of section 16B(1)(a).

(3) Where—

(a) two or more small agreements are made at or about the same time between the same parties, and

(b) it appears probable that they would instead have been made as a single agreement but for the desire to avoid the operation of provisions of this Act which would have applied to that single agreement but, apart from this subsection, are not applicable to the small agreements,

this Act applies to the small agreements as if they were regulated agreements other than small agreements.

(4) If, apart from this subsection, subsection (3) does not apply to any agreements but would apply if, for any party or parties to any of the agreements, there were substituted an associate of that party, or associates of each of those parties, as the case may be, then subsection (3) shall apply to the agreements.

*Note*—Amended by the Consumer Credit (Increase of Monetary Limits) Order 1983 (SI 1983/1878). Also amended by s.5(3) of the Consumer Credit Act 2006 with effect from April 6, 2008 (SI 2007/3300). 3H–55

### Small agreements

This definition identifies agreements of low value and enables later sections to except some of them from some of the requirements of the Act, e.g. from the documentation requirements (see s.74). From the coming into force of the Act until January 1, 1984 the figure in s.17(1)(a) was £30. Since that date the figure has been £50. See Sch.II, Pt II, Examples 16, 17 and 22. 3H–56

## Multiple agreements

**18.**—(1) This section applies to an agreement (a "multiple agreement") if its terms are such as— 3H–57

(a) to place a part of it within one category of agreement mentioned in this Act, and another part of it within a different category of agreement so mentioned, or within a category of agreement not so mentioned, or

(b) to place it, or a part of it, within two or more categories of agreement so mentioned.

(2) Where a part of an agreement falls within subsection (1), that part shall be treated for the purposes of this Act as a separate agreement.

*Paragraph numbers marked with a "+" can be found online and on CD.*

(3) Where an agreement falls within subsection (1)(b), it shall be treated as an agreement in each of the categories in question, and this Act shall apply to it accordingly.

(4) Where under subsection (2) a part of a multiple agreement is to be treated as a separate agreement, the multiple agreement shall (with any necessary modifications) be construed accordingly; and any sum payable under the multiple agreement, if not apportioned by the parties, shall for the purposes of proceedings in any court relating to the multiple agreement be apportioned by the court as may be requisite.

(5) In the case of an agreement for running-account credit, a term of the agreement allowing the credit limit to be exceeded merely temporarily shall not be treated as a separate agreement or as providing fixed-sum credit in respect of the excess.

(6) This Act does not apply to a multiple agreement so far as the agreement relates to goods if under the agreement payments are to be made in respect of the goods in the form of rent (other than a rentcharge) issuing out of land.

**Multiple agreements**

3H–58 In *Southern Pacific Mortgage Ltd v Heath* [2009] EWCA Civ 1135; [2010] C.C.L.R.4 the Court of Appeal held that paragraphs (a) and (b) of s.18(1) are mutually exclusive. They both cover cases where elements of the agreement fall within two or more disparate categories, "categories" having the same meaning in both paragraphs. Paragraph (a) deals with the case where the respective elements within the agreement can be seen as constituting separate parts of the agreement, whereas para.(b) deals with the situation where they cannot be seen as constituting separate parts. The court also held that the final sentence of the analysis to Example 16 in Sch.1 to the Act (see para.3H–407+) is wrong in that it implicitly states that a credit card agreement, the whole of which falls into two disparate categories of agreement (for unrestricted-use and restricted-use credit), is an agreement within s.18(1)(a). Such an agreement, unlike (possibly) the current account/informal overdraft agreement in Example 18, is not an agreement "in parts". The features of the informal overdraft example which (possibly) cause it to be an agreement "in parts" and thus to fall within s.18(1)(a) apparently are: (i) the two elements, the current account when in credit and the overdraft facility, can each be operated separately by the debtor; and (ii) different contract terms apply to those two elements ("parts") of the agreement. *Southern Pacific Mortgage Ltd v Heath* settled a controversy as to the proper interpretation of s.18 between Professor Goode (see his *Consumer Credit Legislation*) and the draftsman of the Act, Francis Bennion (see his articles at *http://www.francisbennion.com* [Accessed November 9, 2009]). For the earlier case law relating to the controversy, see commentary to s.18 in the *White Book* 2009.

## Linked transactions

3H–59 **19.**—(1) A transaction entered into by the debtor or hirer, or a relative of his, with any other person ("the other party"), except one for the provision of security, is a linked transaction in relation to an actual or prospective regulated agreement (the "principal agreement") of which it does not form part if—

(a) the transaction is entered into in compliance with a term of the principal agreement; or

(b) the principal agreement is a debtor-creditor-supplier agreement and the transaction is financed, or to be financed, by the principal agreement, or

(c) the other party is a person mentioned in subsection (2), and a person so mentioned initiated the transaction by suggesting it to the debtor or hirer, or his relative, who enters into it—

(i) to induce the creditor or owner to enter into the principal agreement, or

(ii) for another purpose related to the principal agreement, or

(iii) where the principal agreement is a restricted-use credit agreement, for a purpose related to a transaction financed, or to be financed, by the principal agreement.

(2) The persons referred to in subsection (1)(c) are—

(a) the creditor or owner, or his associate;

(b) a person who, in the negotiation of the transaction, is represented by a credit-broker who is also a negotiator in antecedent negotiations for the principal agreement;

(c) a person who, at the time the transaction is initiated, knows that the principal agreement has been made or contemplates that it might be made.

(3) A linked transaction entered into before the making of the principal agreement has no effect until such time (if any) as that agreement is made.

(4) Regulations may exclude linked transactions of the prescribed description from the operation of subsection (3).

#### Linked transactions

For the meaning of the many technical terms in this section, see s.189(1). Three provisions in particular have an impact upon linked transactions: ss.19(3), 69(1) and 96(1). If the debtor or hirer withdraws an offer to enter a regulated agreement or exercises his right to cancel a cancellable agreement, any linked transaction is automatically withdrawn from or cancelled (ss.19(3) and 69(1)). If for any reason the debtor's indebtedness is discharged early, the debtor is discharged from any further liability under any linked transaction (s.96(1)). However, by virtue of the Consumer Credit (Linked Transactions) (Exemptions) Regulations 1983 (SI 1983/1560), three types of linked transaction are exempted from the three provisions just mentioned which would otherwise have applied to them. Those three types of linked transaction are: **3H–60**

(i) contracts of insurance;

(ii) written guarantees of goods; and

(iii) any transaction which is (or is made under) an agreement for the operation of a savings, deposit or current account.

**For ss.20, 40 and 55 of the Consumer Credit Act 1974 (see Arrangement) plus any related commentary see paragraphs 3H–61+ to 3H–71+ on White Book on Westlaw UK or the Civil Procedure CD.**

## Antecedent negotiations

**56.**—(1) In this Act "antecedent negotiations" means any negotiations with the debtor or hirer— **3H–72**

(a) conducted by the creditor or owner in relation to the making of any regulated agreement, or

(b) conducted by a credit-broker in relation to goods sold or proposed to be sold by the credit-broker to the creditor before forming the subject-matter of a debtor-creditor-supplier agreement within section 12(a), or

(c) conducted by the supplier in relation to a transaction financed or proposed to be financed by a debtor-creditor-supplier agreement within section 12(b) or (c),

and "negotiator" means the person by whom negotiations are so conducted with the debtor or hirer.

(2) Negotiations with the debtor in a case falling within subsection (1)(b) or (c) shall be deemed to be conducted by the negotiator in the capacity of agent of the creditor as well as in his actual capacity.

(3) An agreement is void if, and to the extent that, it purports in relation to an actual or prospective regulated agreement—

(a) to provided that a person acting as, or on behalf of, a negotiator is to be treated as the agent of the debtor or hirer, or

(b) to relieve a person from liability for acts or omissions of any person acting as, or on behalf of, a negotiator.

(4) For the purposes of this Act, antecedent negotiations shall be taken to begin when the negotiator and the debtor or hirer first enter into communication (including communication by advertisement), and to include any representations made by the negotiator to the debtor or hirer and any other dealings between them.

*Antecedent negotiations*

**Subsection (1)**

3H–73 The definition of antecedent negotiations is significant for two reasons:

(i) the agency provision in s.56(2);

(ii) no agreement will be cancellable under s.67 unless oral representations were made during "antecedent negotiations".

Section 56(1)(b) covers the triangular situation where the dealer sells the goods to a finance company which in turn contracts with the debtor to supply the goods to the debtor on hire-purchase, conditional sale or credit sale agreement terms. In that situation the dealer who introduces the debtor to the finance company is a "credit-broker" (s.189(1)). Section 56(1)(b) does not, however, cover the situation where the contract made by the finance company with the customer is a regulated consumer hire agreement (*Moorgate Mercantile Leasing Ltd v Gell and Ugolini* [1988] C.C.L.R. 1). Section 56(1)(c) covers the situation where, pursuant to arrangements between the creditor and the supplier, the creditor provides credit for the debtor to pay for goods or services supplied by the supplier, e.g. the debtor pays for the goods using his (regulated) credit card.

**Deemed agency**

3H–74 Subsection (2) reverses the common law rule whereby the dealer (e.g. in the hire-purchase triangular situation) is not normally the agent of the finance company (*Branwhite v Worcester Works Finance* [1969] 1 A.C. 552). It means, inter alia, that statements, promises, etc., made to the debtor by the dealer are regarded as also made by the creditor who can accordingly be liable for misrepresentation or breach of a contractual promise. The deemed agency, in a s.56(1)(b) situation, relates only to statements and promises "in relation to" the goods being supplied to the debtor. This *does*, however, include, where the debtor has traded in a vehicle in part exchange for the new one (the "goods"), a promise by the dealer to use the part exchange allowance (or part of it) to discharge the debtor's indebtedness under the credit agreement by which the debtor acquired the traded in vehicle (*Forthright Finance Ltd v Ingate* [1997] 4 All E.R.

99; [1997] C.C.L.R. 95). Negotiations relating to the part-exchange and to the new vehicle were all part of the same transaction. *Forthright Finance Ltd v Ingate* was, however, distinguished in the situation where the dealer, having promised the debtor that he would pay off the debtor's indebtedness, used an intermediary credit broker to arrange the finance for the new vehicle: *Black Horse Ltd v Langford* [2007] EWHC 907; [2007] C.C.L.R. 5.

For a situation where at common law the dealer was held (contrary to the usual position) to have been expressly authorised by the finance company to accept the debtor's offer to enter a conditional sale agreement, thereby making the agreement by releasing the vehicle to the debtor upon the latter signing the finance company's proposal form, see *Carlyle Finance Ltd v Pallas Industrial Finance Ltd* [1999] C.C.L.R. 85, CA.

## Withdrawal from prospective agreement

**57.**—(1) The withdrawal of a party from a prospective regulated agreement shall operate to apply this Part to the agreement, any linked transaction and any other thing done in anticipation of the making of the agreement as it would apply if the agreement were made and then cancelled under section 69. **3H–75**

(2) The giving to a party of a written or oral notice which, however expressed, indicates the intention of the other party to withdraw from a prospective regulated agreement operates as a withdrawal from it.

(3) Each of the following shall be deemed to be the agent of the creditor or owner for the purpose of receiving a notice under subsection (2)—

(a) a credit-broker or supplier who is the negotiator in antecedent negotiations, and

(b) any person who, in the course of a business carried on by him, acts on behalf of the debtor or hirer in any negotiations for the agreement.

(4) Where the agreement, if made, would not be a cancellable agreement, subsection (1) shall nevertheless apply as if the contrary were the case.

*Withdrawal from prospective agreement*

### Deemed cancellation

By s.57(1) a prospective agreement which is withdrawn from, is deemed to have been made, to have been a cancellable one and to have been cancelled, with the result that ss.67–73 below apply. For those linked transactions to which this provision does not apply, see commentary to s.19. **3H–76**

### Deemed agency

A wider range of persons than negotiator in antecedent negotiations is deemed agent of the creditor or owner for the purpose of receiving notice of the withdrawal. It could, for example, include the debtor's solicitor if he helped the debtor arrange the prospective agreement. A person deemed to receive a notice as agent of the creditor or owner is under a duty to transmit the notice to the creditor or owner forthwith (s.175). **3H–77**

Section 57 does not apply to agreements listed in ss.74 and 82(4).

**For ss.58 and 59 of the Consumer Credit Act 1974 (see Arrangement) plus any related commentary see paragraphs 3H–78+ to 3H–81+ on White Book on Westlaw UK or the Civil Procedure CD.**

***Paragraph numbers marked with a "+" can be found online and on CD.***

## Form and content of agreements

3H–82 **60.**—(1) The Secretary of State shall make regulations as to the form and content of documents embodying regulated agreements, and the regulations shall contain such provisions as appear to him appropriate with a view to ensuring that the debtor or hirer is made aware of—

(a) the rights and duties conferred or imposed on him by the agreement,

(b) the amount and rate of the total charge for credit (in the case of a consumer credit agreement),

(c) the protection and remedies available to him under this Act, and

(d) any other matters which, in the opinion of the Secretary of State, it is desirable for him to know about in connection with the agreement.

(2) Regulations under subsection (1) may in particular—

(a) require specified information to be included in the prescribed manner in documents, and other specified material to be excluded;

(b) contain requirements to ensure that specified information is clearly brought to the attention of the debtor or hirer, and that one part of a document is not given insufficient or excessive prominence compared with another.

(3) If, on an application made to the OFT by a person carrying on a consumer credit business or a consumer hire business, it appears to the OFT impracticable for the applicant to comply with any requirement of regulations under subsection (1) in a particular case, it may, by notice to the applicant direct that the requirement be waived or varied in relation to such agreements, and subject to such conditions (if any), as it may specify, and this Act and the regulations shall have effect accordingly.

(4) The OFT shall give a notice under subsection (3) only if it is satisfied that to do so would not prejudice the interests of debtors or hirers.

3H–83 *Note*—Amended by the Enterprise Act 2002 s.278 and Sch.25.

### Form and content of agreements

3H–84 The Consumer Credit (Agreements) Regulations 1983 (SI 1983/1553), as amended with effect from May 31, 2005 by the Consumer Credit (Agreements)(Amendment) Regulations 2004 (SI 2004/1482), lay down detailed requirements as to form and content. Failure to comply with the regulations will result in the agreement being improperly executed (see ss.61(1) and 65). These sections—and the regulations—do not apply to agreements listed in ss.74 and 82(4).

3H–85 *Dispensations*—Granted under subss.(3) and (4) by the Office of Fair Trading are entered in the Consumer Credit Public Register.

**For ss.61 to 64 of the Consumer Credit Act 1974 (see Arrangement) plus any related commentary see paragraphs 3H–86+ to 3H–98+ on White Book on Westlaw UK or the Civil Procedure CD.**

***Paragraph numbers marked with a "+" can be found online and on CD.***

## Consequences of improper execution

**65.**—(1) An improperly-executed regulated agreement is enforceable against the debtor or hirer on an order of the court only. **3H–99**

(2) A retaking of goods or land to which a regulated agreement relates is an enforcement of the agreement.

### Consequences of improper execution

An agreement is "improperly-executed" if the documentation requirements in ss.57– 63 are not complied with. The effect of unenforceability under s.65 (apart from in the human rights context, see *Wilson v First County Trust Ltd (No.2)* [2003] UKHL 40; [2004] 1 A.C. 816) is that the rights of creditor or owner and the corresponding liabilities or obligations of the debtor or hirer exist but are not enforceable without a court order: *McGuffick v Royal Bank of Scotland Plc* [2009] EWHC 2386 (Comm); [2010] C.C.L.R. 2. The court's power to grant an order is restricted by s.127 (*q.v.*). For the effect of this on "security", see s.113. None of the following amounts to "enforcement" for the purposes of the Consumer Credit Act: (i) reporting information about the state of the debtor's account to credit reference agencies; (ii) reporting such information without also telling them that the agreement is currently unenforceable; (iii) disseminating or threatening to disseminate the debtor's personal data in respect of the agreement to third parties: *McGuffick* (above). Section 65(2) does not preclude the retaking of goods or land where it is done with the consent of the debtor or hirer given at the time of the re-possession (see s.173(3)). If the debtor or hirer has disposed of the goods wrongfully to a third party, then arguably recovery of them from that third party would not be prohibited since it would not be an enforcement of the agreement "against the debtor or hirer". See the case law on the rather different wording of s.90. Similarly, if say a hire purchase or consumer hire agreement has terminated leaving the creditor with ownership, the creditor has a right to recover the goods independently of the agreement, i.e. on the basis of his ownership, and, arguably, in recovering the goods would not be enforcing the agreement but relying on his ownership as the basis of the claim (see *Bowmaker v Barnet Instruments Ltd* [1945] K.B. 65). Section 65(2) appears to deny such an argument. **3H–100**

There is no sanction provided for breach of s.65 but such a breach may be taken into account by the Office of Fair Trading in determining if the creditor or owner is fit to have a licence (see s.170(1) and (2)).

Section 65 does not apply to agreements listed in ss.74 and 82(4).

### Procedure

For the relevant procedural rules see the notes to s.127 and the Introductory Note About Procedure in Consumer Credit Cases, immediately before the start of this Act, at para.3H–4 et seq. above. **3H–101**

**For s.66 of the Consumer Credit Act 1974 (see Arrangement) plus any related commentary see paragraphs 3H–102+ to 3H–103+ on White Book on Westlaw UK or the Civil Procedure CD.**

*CANCELLATION OF CERTAIN AGREEMENTS WITHIN COOLING-OFF PERIOD*

## Cancellable agreements

**67.** A regulated agreement may be cancelled by the debtor or hirer in accordance with this Part if the antecedent negotiations included oral representations made when in the presence of the debtor or hirer by an individual acting as, or on behalf of, the negotiator, unless— **3H–104**

(a) the agreement is secured on land, or is a restricted-use credit agreement to finance the purchase of land or is an agreement for a bridging loan in connection with the purchase of land, or

***Paragraph numbers marked with a "+" can be found online and on CD.***

(b) the unexecuted agreement is signed by the debtor or hirer at premises at which any of the following is carrying on any business (whether on a permanent or temporary basis)—

(i) the creditor or owner;

(ii) any party to a linked transaction (other than the debtor or hirer or a relative of his);

(iii) the negotiator in any antecedent negotiations.

#### Cancellable agreements

3H-105 A statement is not a "representation" unless it:

(a) is a statement of fact or opinion or an undertaking as to the future; and

(b) is capable of inducing the proposed debtor or hirer to enter the regulated agreement (*Moorgate Services Ltd v Kabir* [1995] C.C.L.R. 74, CA).

A regulated agreement is cancellable if four conditions are satisfied:

(i) antecedent negotiations included oral representations made in the presence of the debtor or hirer by or on behalf of the creditor or owner;

(ii) the unexecuted agreement was signed by the debtor or hirer away from business premises identified in s.67(b);

(iii) the agreement does not fall within s.67(a), s.74(1) or (2), or s.82(4) or (6);

(iv) the agreement is not cancellable under the provisions of the Timeshare Act 1992.

Where negotiations are conducted by a dealer leading up to the common tripartite arrangement whereby the dealer sells the goods to a finance company which in turn contracts with the debtor to supply them to the debtor on hire-purchase terms, the first of these conditions will be satisfied. Where, however, the resultant agreement between the finance company is a consumer hire agreement, the negotiations between the dealer and the customer are not antecedent negotiations (*Lloyds Bowmaker Leasing Ltd v MacDonald* [1993] C.C.L.R. 65). For antecedent negotiations, see s.56. Note that an agreement may be cancellable if signed at the debtor's or hirer's own business premises. In relation to agreements within s.67(a), see ss.58 and 61(2) and (3). An agreement which is not cancellable (i.e. within the meaning of the Consumer Credit Act) may nevertheless be cancellable by virtue of other legislation, e.g. the Cancellation of Contracts made in a Consumer's Home or Place of Work, etc. Regulations 2008; or the Timeshare Act 1992. When an agreement appears to be cancellable under both the Consumer Credit Act 1974 and the 2008 Regulations just mentioned, the latter do not apply and it is cancellable only under the Consumer Credit Act. On the other hand where an agreement prima facie appears to be cancellable under both the Consumer Credit Act 1974 and the Timeshare Act 1992, it is in fact cancellable only under the Timeshare Act 1992. When the Timeshare Act 1992 was first enacted, the opposite solution was adopted (i.e. an agreement prima facie falling within the cancellation provisions of both enactments would in fact be cancellable only under the Consumer Credit Act). That position was reversed by s.1(6A) of the Timeshare Act 1992 which was inserted by the Timeshare Regulations 1997 (SI 1997/1081).

An agreement which is not cancellable under the Consumer Credit Act may be cancellable under the Consumer Protection (Distance Selling) Regulations 2000, which are set out at para.3H–906 below. An agreement is unlikely to be cancellable under both, since for an agreement to be cancellable under the former there have to be representations made in the presence of the debtor or hirer, whereas the latter apply only to "distance contracts", namely where the contract is concluded entirely by distance communication. Where a distance contract is cancellable under the regulations and is cancelled, that cancellation operates (reg.15) also to cancel any "related credit agreement".

Related to the concept of cancellation is that of canvassing off trade premises (defined in s.48). A regulated agreement made following canvassing off trade premises by someone whose licence did not specifically cover that activity may be unenforceable by virtue of s.40 (*q.v.*).

#### Distance credit contracts

3H-106 A credit agreement made entirely by distance communication, though not cancellable under the Consumer Credit Act, may be cancellable under the Financial Services (Distance Marketing) Regulations 2004 (SI 2004/2095) which implemented the European Directive on the distance marketing of financial services (2002/65). Under these regulations a credit agreement concluded at a distance with a consumer (an individual acting outside any business of his) is cancellable by the consumer for a period of 14 days after the day on which the contract is made. This right of cancellation does not apply to: a "related credit agreement" cancelled under reg.15(1) of the Consumer Protection (Distance Selling) Regulations 2000; a credit agreement cancelled under reg.6A of the Timeshare Act 1992; a credit agreement where the consumer's obligation to repay is secured by a legal mortgage on land; a restricted-use credit agreement to finance the purchase of land or an existing building, or an agreement for a bridging loan in connection with the purchase of land or an existing building.

**For ss.68 to 73 of the Consumer Credit Act 1974 (see Arrangement) plus any related commentary see paragraphs 3H–107+ to 3H–121+ on White Book on Westlaw UK or the Civil Procedure CD.**

## *Exclusion of certain agreements from Part V*

### Exclusion of certain agreements from Part V

**74.**—(1) This part (except section 56) does not apply to— 3H–122

(a) a non-commercial agreement, or

(b) a debtor-creditor agreement enabling the debtor to overdraw on a current account, or

(c) a debtor-creditor agreement to finance the making of such payments arising on, or connected with, the death of a person as may be prescribed.

(2) This Part (except sections 55 and 56) does not apply to a small debtor-creditor-supplier agreement for restricted-use credit.

(2A) In the case of an agreement to which the Cancellation of Contracts made in a Consumer's Home or Place of Work etc. Regulations 2008 apply the reference in subsection (2) to a small agreement shall be construed as if in section 17(1)(a) and (b) "£35" were substituted for "£50".

(3) Subsection (1)(b) or (c) applies only where the OFT so determines, and such a determination—

(a) may be made subject to such conditions as the OFT thinks fit, and

(b) shall be made only if the OFT is of opinion that it is not against the interests of debtors.

(3A) Notwithstanding anything in subsection (3)(b) above, in relation to a debtor-creditor agreement under which the creditor is the Bank of England or a bank within the meaning of the Bankers' Books Evidence Act 1879, the OFT shall make a determination that subsection (1)(b) above applies unless it considers that it would be against the public interest to do so.

(4) If any term of an agreement falling within subsection (1)(c) or (2) is expressed in writing, regulations under section 60(1) shall apply to that term (subject to section 60(3)) as if the agreement were a regulated agreement not falling within subsection (1)(c) or (2).

*Note* —Amended by the Banking Act 1979 s.38 and SI 1987/2117 reg.9; the Enterprise Act 2002 s.278 and Sch.25 and by SI 2008/1816. 3H–123

***Paragraph numbers marked with a "+" can be found online and on CD.***

**Exclusion of certain agreements from Part V**

3H–124 For "non-commercial agreement" see s.189(1).

3H–125 *Subsection (1)(b)* —"current account" is not defined. The determination (dated December 21, 1989) of the Director General of Fair Trading (now the OFT) covers both formal and informal overdraft agreements where the creditor is a bank.

The determination contains conditions requiring the debtor to be given specified information as to the rate of interest and other credit charges incurred in relation to the overdraft. For interpretation of those conditions, see *Coutts & Co v Sebestyen* [2005] EWCA Civ 473, [2005] C.C.L.R. 4.

3H–126 *Subsection (1)(c)* —Covers only agreements financing payments prescribed by the Consumer Credit (Payments Arising on Death) Regulations 1983 (SI 1983/1554), namely: capital transfer tax; court fees for grant of probate or of letters of administration (or the resealing in the UK of a Commonwealth or colonial grant); payments to a surety in connection with a guarantee required as a condition of the grant of probate or of letters of administration. The determination (dated December 21, 1989) of the Director General of Fair Trading (now the OFT) limits the effect of subs.(1)(c) to credit granted by a bank to a debtor who is acting in the course of his trade or profession.

## PART VI

## MATTERS ARISING DURING CURRENCY OF CREDIT OR HIRE AGREEMENTS

### Liability of creditor for breaches by supplier

3H–127 **75.**—(1) If the debtor under a debtor-creditor-supplier agreement falling within section 12(b) or (c) has, in relation to a transaction financed by the agreement, any claim against the supplier in respect of a misrepresentation or breach of contract, he shall have a like claim against the creditor, who, with the supplier, shall accordingly be jointly and severally liable to the debtor.

(2) Subject to any agreement between them, the creditor shall be entitled to be indemnified by the supplier for loss suffered by the creditor in satisfying his liability under subsection (1), including costs reasonably incurred by him in defending proceedings instituted by the debtor.

(3) Subsection (1) does not apply to a claim—

(a) under a non-commercial agreement, or

(b) so far as the claim relates to any single item to which the supplier has attached a cash price not exceeding £100 or more than £30,000.

(4) This section applies notwithstanding that the debtor, in entering into the transaction, exceeded the credit limit or otherwise contravened any term of the agreement.

(5) In an action brought against the creditor under subsection (1) he shall be entitled, in accordance with rules of court, to have the supplier made a party to the proceedings.

3H–128 *Note* —Amended by the Consumer Credit (Increase of Monetary Limits) Order 1983 (SI 1983/1878).

**Liability of creditor for breaches by supplier**

3H–129 This section implements the recommendation of the Crowther Committee that there should be "connected lender liability" where the creditor and the supplier are

***Paragraph numbers marked with a "+" can be found online and on CD.***

two different persons and the creditor is, by arrangement with the supplier, providing credit to finance the debtor's purchase (of goods or services) from the supplier. The creditor is jointly and severally liable for the supplier's default but is entitled to an indemnity from the supplier. In the event of the supplier's insolvency the creditor will end up carrying the loss, unless the creditor can claim indemnity against anyone else, e.g. under the Civil Liability (Contribution) Act 1978. There is no doubt that s.75 applies where a (regulated) credit card is used by the debtor to pay for goods or services (within the limits in subs.(3)(b)). Credit card companies have variously maintained that s.75 does not apply:

(i) to cards (including replacement cards) issued under agreements made before July 1, 1997 (the commencement date of s.75);

(ii) where it is a second authorised card-holder on the debtor's account who used the card;

(iii) to "four party" credit card transactions i.e. where it was not the creditor (the card issuer) who was the "merchant acquirer" who signed up the particular retailer to the credit-card payment system (e.g. VISA);

(iv) where a British credit card is used to make a payment abroad.

The first two of these have not been determined in any reported decision. (i) is probably correct, but not in the case of an agreement which has been modified by agreement since July 1, 1977 (see s.82(2)); in any case the credit card companies have agreed "voluntarily" to accept s.75 liability (up to the amount of the credit used on the transaction in question) in relation to pre-July 1977 agreements. (ii) is arguable, but perhaps the second card holder *is* within the definition of "debtor" in s.189(1), see "credit" in s.9(1). (iii) and (iv) were considered in *Office of Fair Trading v Lloyds TSB Bank Plc* [2006] EWCA Civ 268; [2007] Q.B. 1, where it was held that s.75(1) does apply to "four party" credit card agreements and is not confined to applying only to transactions in the UK and hence does apply where a UK credit card is used in relation to transactions abroad. This decision was upheld in the House of Lords [2007] UKHL 48; [2007] 3 W.L.R.733. In *Bank of Scotland v Alfred Truman* [2005] EWHC 583, [2005] C.C.L.R.3, customers of a car dealer used their credit cards to pay deposits on cars to be supplied by the dealer. The dealer did not have credit card payment processing facilities. The defendant firm of solicitors had such facilities, having signed a merchant services agreement with the firm's bank. The defendant firm used its card processing facilities to process, on behalf of the dealer, the payments of deposits by the car dealer's customers. It was held that section 75 applied to these *five* party credit card transactions.

In *Jarrett v Barclays Bank and Royal Bank of Scotland* [1999] Q.B. 1; [1997] C.C.L.R. 32, CA, credit was advanced under a credit card agreement and under other regulated agreements to finance the purchase of timeshares in Portugal and Spain. Though in each case a claim by the debtor against the timeshare supplier was, by virtue of the Brussels Convention, subject to the exclusive jurisdiction of the Portuguese or Spanish court, it was held that that did not apply to actions under s.75 against the creditors, i.e. the British banks.

Where, relying on a breach of contract or misrepresentation, the debtor rescinds the supply agreement which was financed by a loan agreement within s.12(b) or (c), then a "like claim" under s.75 means a claim to rescind the loan agreement (*United Dominions Trust v Taylor* [1980] S.L.T. (Sh. Ct.) 28; [1980] C.C.L.R. 29, followed, despite academic criticism, in *Forward Trust Ltd v Hornsby* [1996] C.C.L.R. 18).

*Subsection (3)* —The original figures were increased to the current ones of £100 and £30,000 as from January 1, 1984 (SI 1983/1878). The limit refers to the cash price attached to the "item". This is arguably inconsistent with the Consumer Credit Directive (87/102) which allows a lower limit only where "the *transaction* in question is for an amount less than 200 ECU". **3H–130**

## Duty to give notice before taking certain action

**76.**—(1) The creditor or owner is not entitled to enforce a term of a regulated agreement by— **3H–131**

(a) demanding earlier payment of any sum, or

(b) recovering possession of any goods or land, or

***Paragraph numbers marked with a "+" can be found online and on CD.***



CONSUMER

(c) treating any right conferred on the debtor or hirer by the agreement as terminated, restricted or deferred,

except by or after giving the debtor or hirer not less than seven days' notice of his intention to do so.

(2) Subsection (1) applies only where—

(a) a period for the duration of the agreement is specified in the agreement, and

(b) that period has not ended when the creditor or owner does an act mentioned in subsection (1),

but so applies notwithstanding that, under the agreement, any party is entitled to terminate it before the end of the period so specified.

(3) A notice under subsection (1) is ineffective if not in the prescribed form.

(4) Subsection (1) does not prevent a creditor from treating the right to draw on any credit as restricted or deferred and taking such steps as may be necessary to make the restriction or deferment effective.

(5) Regulations may provide that subsection (1) is not to apply to agreements described by the regulations.

(6) Subsection (1) does not apply to a right of enforcement arising by reason of any breach by the debtor or hirer of the regulated agreement.

**Duty to give notice before taking certain action**

3H–132 See commentary to s.98.

**For ss.77 to 80 of the Consumer Credit Act 1974 (see Arrangement) plus any related commentary see paragraphs 3H–133+ to 3H–146+ on White Book on Westlaw UK or the Civil Procedure CD.**

## Appropriation of payments

3H–147 **81.**—(1) Where a debtor or hirer is liable to make to the same person payments in respect of two or more regulated agreements, he shall be entitled, on making any payment in respect of the agreements which is not sufficient to discharge the total amount then due under all the agreements, to appropriate the sum so paid by him—

(a) in or towards the satisfaction of the sum due under any one of the agreements, or

(b) in or towards the satisfaction of the sums due under any two or more of the agreements in such proportions as he thinks fit.

(2) If the debtor or hirer fails to make any such appropriation where one or more of the agreements is—

(a) a hire-purchase agreement or conditional sale agreement, or

(b) a consumer hire agreement, or

(c) an agreement in relation to which any security is provided,

the payment shall be appropriated towards the satisfaction of the

*Paragraph numbers marked with a "+" can be found online and on CD.*

sums due under the several agreements respectively in the proportions which those sums bear to one another.

**Appropriation of payments**

At common law, where the debtor owes two or more debts that have fallen due and they are payable by him to the same person (e.g. the debts are both owed to the same creditor, but under different contracts), then the debtor when he makes a payment can appropriate that payment as he chooses between the different debts. If when he pays he communicates no such appropriation to the payee (i.e. usually the creditor), the latter may appropriate the payments as the creditor chooses. No appropriation by the creditor is effective until it is communicated to the debtor. An unequivocal appropriation becomes both effective and irrevocable when communicated to the debtor (*Julian Hodge Bank Ltd v Hall* [1998] C.C.L.R. 14, CA). Where it applies, s.81(2) removes the creditor's common law right of appropriation and provides its own automatic appropriation. It appropriates the payment according to the sums that have fallen "due" under the different agreements. This then takes no account of instalments that have not fallen due at the time of the repayment. Where s.81(2) does not apply, e.g. when allocating a payment as between (a) instalments that have already fallen due, and (b) default interest that has accrued under the same agreement for failing to pay the instalments on time, the common law rules apply. In the case of a regulated hire purchase agreement this can have crucial significance in determining whether goods are "protected goods" within s.90 (*Julian Hodge Bank Ltd v Hall*, above). **3H–148**

## Variation of agreements

**82.**—(1) Where, under a power contained in a regulated agreement the creditor or owner varies the agreement, the variation shall not take effect before notice of it is given to the debtor or hirer in the prescribed manner. **3H–149**

(2) Where an agreement (a "modifying agreement") varies or supplements an earlier agreement, the modifying agreement shall for the purposes of this Act be treated as—

(a) revoking the earlier agreement, and

(b) containing provisions reproducing the combined effect of the two agreements,

and obligations outstanding in relation to the earlier agreement shall accordingly be treated as outstanding instead in relation to the modifying agreement.

(2A) Subsection (2) does not apply if the earlier agreement or the modifying agreement is an exempt agreement as a result of section 16(6C) or 16C.

(3) If the earlier agreement is a regulated agreement but (apart from this subsection) the modifying agreement is not then, unless the modifying agreement is—

(a) for running account credit; or

(b) an exempt agreement as a result of section 16(6C) or 16C,

it shall be treated as a regulated agreement.

(4) If the earlier agreement is a regulated agreement for running-account credit, and by the modifying agreement the creditor allows the credit limit to be exceeded but intends the excess to be merely temporary, Part V (except section 56) shall not apply to the modifying agreement.

(5) If—

***Paragraph numbers marked with a "+" can be found online and on CD.***

(a) the earlier agreement is a cancellable agreement, and

(b) the modifying agreement is made within the period applicable under section 68 to the earlier agreement,

then, whether or not the modifying agreement would, apart from this subsection, be a cancellable agreement, it shall be treated as a cancellable agreement in respect of which a notice may be served under section 68 not later than the end of the period applicable under that section to the earlier agreement.

(5A) Subsection (5) does not apply where the modifying agreement is an exempt agreement as a result of section 16(6C) or 16C.

(6) Except under subsection (5), a modifying agreement shall not be treated as a cancellable agreement.

(7) This section does not apply to a non-commercial agreement.

*Note*—Subsections (2A) and (5A) added and subs.(3) amended by the Financial Services and Markets Act 2000 (Consequential Amendments) Order 2005 (SI 2005/2967). Subsection (2A) amended by the Financial Services and Markets Act 2000 (Consequential Amendments) Order 2008 (SI 2008/733). References to s.16C added by the Legislative Reform (Consumer Credit) Order 2008 (SI 2008/2826).

**Variation of agreements**

**3H–150** Subsection (1) deals with a variation which can be made unilaterally by the creditor or owner; i.e. because he has that power under the agreement. Subsections (2)–(5) deal with a variation which comes about by a subsequent agreement between the parties.

**3H–151** *Unilateral variation*—The Consumer Credit (Notice of Variation of Agreements) Regulations 1977 (SI 1977/328), as amended, prescribe a general rule that the debtor or hirer must be given at least seven days' written notice of the change, but that changes in interest rate may normally be given by public notices placed in newspapers and in the creditor's business premises.

**3H–152** *Modifying agreements*—An agreement varying an earlier agreement is a modifying agreement. Section 82(2)(b) means that an agreed variation could turn an unregulated agreement into a regulated one. A fixed-sum credit agreement made in 2006 providing the debtor with credit of £30,000 would not be a regulated agreement, because, prior to April 6, 2008 an agreement providing credit of more than £25,000 was not a consumer credit agreement. If in February 2009, the parties agreed to vary that agreement (e.g. by adding a further advance), that is regarded as a termination of the old agreement and the making of a new agreement. Unless it is an exempt agreement, the new agreement is a regulated agreement, the amount of the credit being irrelevant after April 6, 2008 when the financial limit was removed from the definition of a consumer credit agreement. A regulated modifying agreement will normally be subject to the documentation requirements in s.55 and ss.57–65, though not normally (see s.82(6)) to the cancellation provisions. The Consumer Credit (Agreements) Regulations 1983 (SI 1983/1553) make provision for the form and contents of modifying agreements.

## Liability for misuse of credit facilities

**3H–153** **83.**—(1) The debtor under a regulated consumer credit agreement shall not be liable to the creditor for any loss arising from use of the credit facility by another person not acting, or to be treated as acting, as the debtor's agent.

(2) This section does not apply to a non-commercial agreement, or to any loss in so far as it arises from misuse of an instrument to which section 4 of the Cheques Act 1957 applies.

### Liability for misuse of credit facilities

Section 83(1) states a general rule which is subject to exceptions stated in s.84. The **3H–154** protection afforded does not, however, extend to the fraudulent use of payment cards (e.g. many charge cards) which are issued under exempt agreements (for "exempt agreements" see s.16 above). Similarly it does not apply to the unauthorised use of a cash withdrawal token to withdraw cash from an account, e.g. a current account, which has a credit balance—since the protection afforded by s.83 extends only to the unauthorised use of a "credit" facility. In the latter case the Banking Code of Practice (subscribed to by banks and building societies) offers a similar degree of protection to that afforded by ss.83 and 84 (taken together) in the case of misuse of a credit facility.

### Fraudulent use of payment card in connection with distance contract

In the case of a distance contract, the Consumer Protection (Distance Selling) **3H–155** Regulations 2000 (SI 2000/2334) give protection to a consumer against the fraudulent use of any "payment card". A "payment card" includes credit cards, charge cards, debit cards and store cards. By reg.21, a consumer is entitled to cancel a payment where fraudulent (unauthorised) use has been made of his payment card in connection with a distance contract. Upon cancelling a payment, the consumer is entitled to be re-credited, or to have all sums returned by the card issuer. The regulations are set out at para.3H–906 below.

**For ss.84 to 85 of the Consumer Credit Act 1974 (see Arrangement) plus any related commentary see paragraphs 3H–156+ to 3H–159.1+ on theWhite Book on Westlaw UK or the Civil Procedure CD.**

## Death of debtor or hirer

**86.**—(1) The creditor or owner under a regulated agreement is not **3H–160** entitled, by reason of the death of the debtor or hirer, to do an act specified in paragraphs (a) to (e) section 87(1) if at the death the agreement is fully secured.

(2) If at the death of the debtor or hirer a regulated agreement is only partly secured or is unsecured, the creditor or owner is entitled, by reason of the death of the debtor or hirer, to do an act specified in paragraphs (a) to (e) section 87(1) on an order of the court only.

(3) This section applies in relation to the termination of an agreement only where—

(a) a period for its duration is specified in the agreement, and

(b) that period has not ended when the creditor or owner purports to terminate the agreement,

but so applies notwithstanding that, under the agreement, any party is entitled to terminate it before the end of the period so specified.

(4) This section does not prevent the creditor from treating the right to draw on any credit as restricted or deferred, and taking such steps as may be necessary to make the restriction or deferment effective.

(5) This section does not affect the operation of any agreement providing for payment of sums—

(a) due under the regulated agreement, or

(b) becoming due under it on the death of the debtor or hirer,

out of the proceeds of a policy of assurance on his life.

(6) For the purposes of this section an act is done by reason of the

*Paragraph numbers marked with a "+" can be found online and on CD.*

death of the debtor or hirer if it is done under a power conferred by the agreement which is—

(a) exercisable on his death, or

(b) exercisable at will and exercised at any time after his death.

**Death of debtor or hirer**

3H–161 The object is to prevent the creditor or owner being entitled to terminate an agreement (other than in the sense of refusing to allow further drawings of credit, e.g. under a credit card agreement) simply because of the death of the debtor or hirer (or of any one of the debtors or hirers—s.185(4)). If the agreement is not "fully secured" then the creditor may be able to terminate the agreement by an order of the court, but only if he can satisfy the requirements in s.128. The same restrictions apply to prevent the creditor doing any of the other acts listed in s.87(1). Even though the debtor may have died, s.86 does not, however, prevent the creditor being entitled to do one of those things for some reason other than the death, e.g. by reason of a breach of the agreement (providing in that case that s.87 is complied with). "Fully secured" is not defined, but presumably means an agreement in relation to which there is security which if realised at the time of the debtor's or hirer's death would cover the whole of the outstanding debt under the agreement.

**Procedure**

3H–162 Where a court order is required under s.86(2) then the claim is governed by the Consumer Credit Act procedure in the Consumer Credit Practice Direction at para.7BPD.1, unless the claim relates to the recovery of land. If it is a mortgage repossession action, the procedure set out in CPR Pt 55 should be used. See further, the Note About Procedure in Consumer Credit Cases, immediately before the start of this Act, at para.3H–4 *et seq.* above.

## PART VII

## DEFAULT AND TERMINATION

### *INFORMATION SHEETS*

### OFT to prepare information sheets on arrears and default

3H–163 **86A.**—(1) The OFT shall prepare, and give general notice of, an arrears information sheet and a default information sheet.

(2) The arrears information sheet shall include information to help debtors and hirers who receive notices under section 86B or 86C.

(3) The default information sheet shall include information to help debtors and hirers who receive default notices.

(4) Regulations may make provision about the information to be included in an information sheet.

(5) An information sheet takes effect for the purposes of this Part at the end of the period of three months beginning with the day on which general notice of it is given.

(6) If the OFT revises an information sheet after general notice of it has been given, it shall give general notice of the information sheet as revised.

(7) A revised information sheet takes effect for the purposes of this Part at the end of the period of three months beginning with the day on which general notice of it is given.

*__Paragraph numbers marked with a "+" can be found online and on CD.__*

*Note* —Inserted subject to transitional provisions by the Consumer Credit Act 2006 s.8 (for transitional provisions see Sch.3, para.5), with effect from January 31, 2007 (SI 2007/123). Sections 86B to 86F are inserted by the Consumer Credit Act 2006 ss.9–13. Subsections 86B(8), 86C(6) and 86E(2) and (7) were brought into force with effect from June 16, 2006 (SI 2006/1508); remaining subsections of ss.86B to 86F are in force with effect from October 1, 2008 (SI 2007/3300). For transitional provisions relating to ss.86A to 86F, see Consumer Credit Act 2006 Sch.3, paras 5– 9. **3H–164**

**Arrears and default**

Sections 86A to 86F have been fully in force since October 1, 2008. They require the creditor to give notice of sums in arrears, including an arrears information sheet (prepared by the OFT), to the debtor. They require this to be done after the debtor has fallen into arrears by, broadly, more than two monthly (or four weekly) payments. The creditor is required to serve a notice (a notice of default sums) before becoming entitled to recover any "default sum" and is not entitled to any interest on a default sum in respect of the first 28 days after service of the notice. The creditor is not in any case entitled to recover any such interest at all unless it is simple interest. For "default sum", see s.187A. **3H–165**

### *SUMS IN ARREARS AND DEFAULT SUMS*

## Notice of sums in arrears under fixed-sum credit agreements etc

**86B.**—(1) This section applies where at any time the following conditions are satisfied— **3H–166**

(a) that the debtor or hirer under an applicable agreement is required to have made at least two payments under the agreement before that time;

(b) that the total sum paid under the agreement by him is less than the total sum which he is required to have paid before that time;

(c) that the amount of the shortfall is no less than the sum of the last two payments which he is required to have made before that time;

(d) that the creditor or owner is not already under a duty to give him notices under this section in relation to the agreement; and

(e) if a judgment has been given in relation to the agreement before that time, that there is no sum still to be paid under the judgment by the debtor or hirer.

(2) The creditor or owner—

(a) shall, within the period of 14 days beginning with the day on which the conditions mentioned in subsection (1) are satisfied, give the debtor or hirer a notice under this section; and

(b) after the giving of that notice, shall give him further notices under this section at intervals of not more than six months.

(3) The duty of the creditor or owner to give the debtor or hirer notices under this section shall cease when either of the conditions mentioned in subsection (4) is satisfied; but if either of those conditions is satisfied before the notice required by subsection (2)(a) is given, the duty shall not cease until that notice is given.

***Paragraph numbers marked with a "+" can be found online and on CD.***



CONSUMER

(4) The conditions referred to in subsection (3) are—

(a) that the debtor or hirer ceases to be in arrears;

(b) that a judgment is given in relation to the agreement under which a sum is required to be paid by the debtor or hirer.

(5) For the purposes of subsection (4)(a) the debtor or hirer ceases to be in arrears when—

(a) no payments, which he has ever failed to make under the agreement when required, are still owing;

(b) no default sum, which has ever become payable under the agreement in connection with his failure to pay any sum under the agreement when required, is still owing;

(c) no sum of interest, which has ever become payable under the agreement in connection with such a default sum, is still owing; and

(d) no other sum of interest, which has ever become payable under the agreement in connection with his failure to pay any sum under the agreement when required, is still owing.

(6) A notice under this section shall include a copy of the current arrears information sheet under section 86A.

(7) The debtor or hirer shall have no liability to pay any sum in connection with the preparation or the giving to him of a notice under this section.

(8) Regulations may make provision about the form and content of notices under this section.

(9) In the case of an applicable agreement under which the debtor or hirer must make all payments he is required to make at intervals of one week or less, this section shall have effect as if in subsection (1)(a) and (c) for 'two' there were substituted 'four'.

(10) If an agreement mentioned in subsection (9) was made before the beginning of the relevant period, only amounts resulting from failures by the debtor or hirer to make payments he is required to have made during that period shall be taken into account in determining any shortfall for the purposes of subsection (1)(c).

(11) In subsection (10) "relevant period" means the period of 20 weeks ending with the day on which the debtor or hirer is required to have made the most recent payment under the agreement.

(12) In this section "applicable agreement" means an agreement which

(a) is a regulated agreement for fixed-sum credit or a regulated consumer hire agreement; and

(b) is neither a non-commercial agreement nor a small agreement.

(13) In this section—

(a) "payments" in relation to an applicable agreement which is a regulated agreement for fixed-sum credit means payments to be made at predetermined intervals provided for under the terms of the agreement; and

*Paragraph numbers marked with a "+" can be found online and on CD.*

(b) "payments" in relation to an applicable agreement which is a regulated consumer hire agreement means any payments to be made by the hirer in relation to any period in consideration of the bailment or hiring to him of goods under the agreement.

*Note*—Inserted by the Consumer Credit Act 2006 s.9. Subsection (8) was brought into force with effect from June 16, 2006 (SI 2006/1508); remaining subsections are in force with effect from October 1, 2008 (SI 2007/3300). Subsection (5) amended and subs.(13) added by the Legislative Reform (Consumer Credit) Order 2008 (SI 2008/2826). **3H–167**

*Subsection (8)*—See the Consumer Credit (Information Requirements and Duration of Licences and Charges) Regulations 2007 (SI 2007/1167). **3H–168**

**Notice of sums in arrears under fixed-sum and consumer hire agreements**

See the note to s.86A above and the comments there about arrears and default. **3H–169**

## Notice of sums in arrears under running-account credit agreements

**86C.**—(1) This section applies where at any time the following conditions are satisfied— **3H–170**

(a) that the debtor under an applicable agreement is required to have made at least two payments under the agreement before that time;

(b) that the last two payments which he is required to have made before that time have not been made;

(c) that the creditor has not already been required to give a notice under this section in relation to either of those payments; and

(d) if a judgment has been given in relation to the agreement before that time, that there is no sum still to be paid under the judgment by the debtor.

(2) The creditor shall, no later than the end of the period within which he is next required to give a statement under section 78(4) in relation to the agreement, give the debtor a notice under this section.

(3) The notice shall include a copy of the current arrears information sheet under section 86A.

(4) The notice may be incorporated in a statement or other notice which the creditor gives the debtor in relation to the agreement by virtue of another provision of this Act.

(5) The debtor shall have no liability to pay any sum in connection with the preparation or the giving to him of the notice.

(6) Regulations may make provision about the form and content of notices under this section.

(7) In this section 'applicable agreement' means an agreement which—

(a) is a regulated agreement for running-account credit; and

(b) is neither a non-commercial agreement nor a small agreement.

*Paragraph numbers marked with a "+" can be found online and on CD.*

(8) In this section "payments" means payments to be made at predetermined intervals provided for under the terms of the agreement.

3H–171 *Note*—Inserted by the Consumer Credit Act 2006 s.10. Subsection (6) was brought into force with effect from June 16, 2006 (SI 2006/1508); remaining subsections are in force with effect from October 1, 2008 (SI 2007/3300). Subsection (8) added by the Legislative Reform (Consumer Credit) Order 2008 (SI 2008/2826).

3H–172 *Subsection (6)*—See the Consumer Credit (Information Requirements and Duration of Licences and Charges) Regulations 2007 (SI 2007/1167).

**Notice of sums in arrears under running-account credit agreements**

3H–173 See the note to s.86A above and the comments there about arrears and default.

## Failure to give notice of sums in arrears

3H–174 **86D.**—(1) This section applies where the creditor or owner under an agreement is under a duty to give the debtor or hirer notices under section 86B but fails to give him such a notice—

(a) within the period mentioned in subsection (2)(a) of that section; or

(b) within the period of six months beginning with the day after the day on which such a notice was last given to him.

(2) This section also applies where the creditor under an agreement is under a duty to give the debtor a notice under section 86C but fails to do so before the end of the period mentioned in subsection (2) of that section.

(3) The creditor or owner shall not be entitled to enforce the agreement during the period of non-compliance.

(4) The debtor or hirer shall have no liability to pay—

(a) any sum of interest to the extent calculated by reference to the period of non-compliance or to any part of it; or

(b) any default sum which (apart from this paragraph)—

(i) would have become payable during the period of non-compliance; or

(ii) would have become payable after the end of that period in connection with a breach of the agreement which occurs during that period (whether or not the breach continues after the end of that period).

(5) In this section 'the period of non-compliance' means, in relation to a failure to give a notice under section 86B or 86C to the debtor or hirer, the period which—

(a) begins immediately after the end of the period mentioned in (as the case may be) subsection (1)(a) or (b) or (2); and

(b) ends at the end of the day mentioned in subsection (6).

(6) That day is—

(a) in the case of a failure to give a notice under section 86B as mentioned in subsection (1)(a) of this section, the day on which the notice is given to the debtor or hirer;

(b) in the case of a failure to give a notice under that section as mentioned in subsection (1)(b) of this section, the earlier of the following—

(i) the day on which the notice is given to the debtor or hirer;

(ii) the day on which the condition mentioned in subsection (4)(a) of that section is satisfied;

(c) in the case of a failure to give a notice under section 86C, the day on which the notice is given to the debtor.

*Note* —Inserted by the Consumer Credit Act 2006 s.11, with effect from October 1, 2008 (SI 2007/3300). **3H–175**

**Failure to give notice of sums in arrears**

See the note to s.86A above and the comments there about arrears and default. **3H–176**

## Notice of default sums

**86E.**—(1) This section applies where a default sum becomes payable under a regulated agreement by the debtor or hirer. **3H–177**

(2) The creditor or owner shall, within the prescribed period after the default sum becomes payable, give the debtor or hirer a notice under this section.

(3) The notice under this section may be incorporated in a statement or other notice which the creditor or owner gives the debtor or hirer in relation to the agreement by virtue of another provision of this Act.

(4) The debtor or hirer shall have no liability to pay interest in connection with the default sum to the extent that the interest is calculated by reference to a period occurring before the 29th day after the day on which the debtor or hirer is given the notice under this section.

(5) If the creditor or owner fails to give the debtor or hirer the notice under this section within the period mentioned in subsection (2), he shall not be entitled to enforce the agreement until the notice is given to the debtor or hirer.

(6) The debtor or hirer shall have no liability to pay any sum in connection with the preparation or the giving to him of the notice under this section.

(7) Regulations may—

(a) provide that this section does not apply in relation to a default sum which is less than a prescribed amount;

(b) make provision about the form and content of notices under this section.

(8) This section does not apply in relation to a non-commercial agreement or to a small agreement.

*Note* —Inserted by the Consumer Credit Act 2006 s.12. Subss.(2), (7) were brought into force with effect from June 16, 2006 (SI 2006/1508); remaining subsections are in force with effect from October 1, 2008 (SI 2007/3300). **3H–178**

*Subsection (2) and (7)(b)* —For the prescribed period and the form and contents of notices, see the Consumer Credit (Information Requirements and Duration of Licences **3H–179** and Charges) Regulations 2007 (SI 2007/1167). The prescribed period is 35 days from a default sum becoming payable by the debtor or hirer.

#### Notice of default sums

3H-180 See the note to s.86A above and the comments there about arrears and default. For "default sum", see s.187A.

### Interest on default sums

3H-181 **86F.**—(1) This section applies where a default sum becomes payable under a regulated agreement by the debtor or hirer.

(2) The debtor or hirer shall only be liable to pay interest in connection with the default sum if the interest is simple interest.

3H-182 *Note*—Inserted by the Consumer Credit Act 2006 s.13, with effect from October 1, 2008 (SI 2007/3300).

#### Interest on default sums

3H-183 For "default sum", see s.187A. See the note to s.86A above and the comments there about arrears and default.

## DEFAULT NOTICES

### Need for default notice

3H-184 **87.**—(1) Service of a notice on the debtor or hirer in accordance with section 88 (a "default notice") is necessary before the creditor or owner can become entitled, by reason of any breach by the debtor or hirer of a regulated agreement—

(a) to terminate the agreement, or
(b) to demand earlier payment of any sum, or
(c) to recover possession of any goods or land, or
(d) to treat any right conferred on the debtor or hirer by the agreement as terminated, restricted or deferred, or
(e) to enforce any security.

(2) Subsection (1) does not prevent the creditor from treating the right to draw upon any credit as restricted or deferred, and taking such steps as may be necessary to make the restriction or deferment effective.

(3) The doing of an act by which a floating charge becomes fixed is not enforcement of a security.

(4) Regulations may provide that subsection (1) is not to apply to agreements described by the regulations.

#### Need for default notice

3H-185 Section 87 does not give the creditor or owner the right to take any of the actions listed in s.87(1). Its effect is that if he has that right, e.g. by virtue of a provision in the agreement or because of a repudiation by the debtor, he will not be entitled to exercise it until a default notice has been served (and has expired without the default having been rectified). This restriction applies only where the right to do one of those acts arises by reason of a breach of the agreement by the debtor or hirer. Where, however, it arises by some other reason (e.g. the agreement gives the creditor the right to terminate the agreement on the debtor becoming unemployed), then ss.76 and 98 may require prior service of a notice. The inclusion of s.87(1)(b) in the list means that an accelerated payments clause cannot be activated without service of a default notice (or a notice under s.76). Copies of any default notice must be served on each debtor or hirer (i.e. where there is more than one), s.185(1)(a) and on any surety (s.111). Notices served on the debtor or hirer under ss.76(1), 87(1) and 98(1) must be given in paper form: the Consumer Credit (Enforcement, Default and Termination Notices) Regulations 1983 (SI 1983/1561), as amended. The same regulations state that ss.76(1), 87(1) and 98(1) do not apply to non-commercial agreements in relation to which no security has been provided. For content and effect of default notice, see s.88. For default notice sent by post and never arriving, see s.176.

## Contents and effect of default notice

**88.**—(1) The default notice must be in the prescribed form and specify— **3H–186**

(a) the nature of the alleged breach;

(b) if the breach is capable of remedy, what action is required to remedy it and the date before which that action is to be taken;

(c) if the breach is not capable of remedy, the sum (if any) required to be paid as compensation for the breach, and the date before which it is to be paid.

(2) A date specified under subsection (1) must not be less than 14 days after the date of service of the default notice, and the creditor or owner shall not take action such as is mentioned in section 87(1) before the date so specified or (if no requirement is made under subsection (1)) before those 14 days have elapsed.

(3) The default notice must not treat as a breach failure to comply with a provision of the agreement which becomes operative only on breach of some other provision, but if the breach of that other provision is not duly remedied or compensation demanded under subsection (1) is not duly paid, or (where no requirement is made under subsection (1)) if the 14 days mentioned in subsection (2) have elapsed, the creditor or owner may treat the failure as a breach and section 87(1) shall not apply to it.

(4) The default notice must contain information in the prescribed terms about the consequences of failure to comply with it and any other prescribed matters relating to the agreement.

(4A) The default notice must also include a copy of the current default information sheet under section 86A.

(5) A default notice making a requirement under subsection (1) may include a provision for the taking of action such as is mentioned in section 87(1) at any time after the restriction imposed by subsection (2) will cease, together with a statement that the provision will be ineffective if the breach is duly remedied or the compensation duly paid.

*Note* —Amended by Consumer Credit Act 2006 s.14(1) and (2); subs.(4A) inserted by the Consumer Credit Act 2006 s.14(3), with effect from October 1, 2008 (SI 2007/3300). **3H–187**

### Contents and effects of default notice

For the prescribed form, see the Consumer Credit (Enforcement, Default and Termination Notices) Regulations 1983 (SI 1983/1561), as amended by the Consumer Credit (Information Requirements and Duration of Licences and Charges) Regulations 2007 (SI 2007/1167). The usual default is a failure to pay instalments. In that case, the action required to remedy the default, and which s.88(1)(b) requires the default notice to specify, is payment of the arrears together with any default interest **3H–188** owing on those arrears. If the default notice specifies a figure more than the giver of the notice is entitled to demand, then the default notice is invalid, *Woodchester Lease Management Services Ltd v Swain* [1999] 1 W.L.R. 263; [1999] C.C.L.R. 8, CA, although the court might overlook an error which was no more than de minimis. Besides complying with s.88 and with the regulations, the default notice must not put upon the debtor a repudiation when he has not committed one and must make clear when it expires (*Eshun v Moorgate Mercantile Co* [1971] 1 W.L.R. 722 (decided under the earlier provisions of the Hire Purchase Act 1965)). If the debtor or hirer rectifies the breach (i.e. by taking the action specified in s.88(1)(b) or (c)) the breach is taken not to have occurred (s.89). As soon as a default notice is served, the debtor or hirer is eligible to apply for a time order under s.129, under which the court could grant extra time for paying off arrears or remedying the breach. Even if the debtor does not apply for a time order and the breach is not rectified before the default notice expires, the creditor or owner may still face a restriction on enforcing the agreement. Thus he may not be entitled to recover goods or enter land without a court order (ss.90 and 92) and, if he brings proceedings to enforce the agreement, the debtor or hirer may in those proceedings apply for a time order.

**Consumer Credit Act 2006**

**3H–189** Section 14(1) of the 2006 Act, which came into force on October 1, 2006 and applies to default notices served after that date even though the default may have occurred before that date, increased from seven to 14 days the period of notice specified in s.88(2) and (3). Subsection (4A) comes into force on October 1, 2008. It requires that the default notice includes a copy of a default information sheet (prepared by the OFT).

## Compliance with default notice

**3H–190** **89.** If before the date specified for that purpose in the default notice the debtor or hirer takes the action specified under section 88(1)(b) or (c) the breach shall be treated as not having occurred.

*FURTHER RESTRICTION OF REMEDIES FOR DEFAULT*

## Retaking of protected hire-purchase, etc., goods

**3H–191** **90.**—(1) At any time when—

(a) the debtor is in breach of a regulated hire-purchase or a regulated conditional sale agreement relating to goods, and

(b) the debtor has paid to the creditor one-third or more of the total price of the goods, and

(c) the property in the goods remains in the creditor,

the creditor is not entitled to recover possession of the goods from the debtor except on an order of the court.

(2) Where under a hire-purchase or conditional sale agreement the creditor is required to carry out any installation and the agreement specifies, as part of the total price, the amount to be paid in respect of the installation (the "installation charge") the reference in subsection (1)(b) to one-third of the total price shall be construed as a reference to the aggregate of the installation charge and one-third of the remainder of the total price.

(3) In a case where—

(a) subsection (1)(a) is satisfied, but not subsection (1)(b), and

*Paragraph numbers marked with a "+" can be found online and on CD.*

(b) subsection (1)(b) was satisfied on a previous occasion in relation to an earlier agreement, being a regulated hire-purchase or regulated conditional sale agreement, between the same parties, and relating to any of the goods comprised in the later agreement (whether or not other goods were also included),

subsection (1) shall apply to the later agreement with the omission of paragraph (b).

(4) If the later agreement is a modifying agreement, subsection (3) shall apply with the substitution, for the second reference to the later agreement, of a reference to the modifying agreement.

(5) Subsection (1) shall not apply, or shall cease to apply, to an agreement if the debtor has terminated, or terminates, the agreement.

(6) Where subsection (1) applies to an agreement at the death of the debtor, it shall continue to apply (in relation to the possessor of the goods) until the grant of probate or administration, or (in Scotland) confirmation (on which the personal representative would fall to be treated as the debtor).

(7) Goods falling within this section are in this Act referred to as "protected goods".

**Retaking of protected hire-purchase, etc., goods**

Forcing the creditor to have to apply for a court order to recover possession of protected goods, makes it more likely that the debtor may apply for a time order (s.129), hoping thereby to prevent what would usually otherwise be for the debtor the rather disastrous financial consequences of termination of a hire-purchase or conditional sale agreement. Section 90 prevents the creditor being entitled, without a court order, to recover possession of protected goods "from the debtor". This does not prevent recovery of them from someone to whom the debtor has sold them or if the debtor has abandoned them but does prevent recovery from someone to whom the debtor has temporarily bailed them (e.g. lent them to a friend or left them at a garage for repair) (*Bentinck v Cromwell Engineering Ltd* [1971] 1 Q.B. 324). Nor does it prohibit recovery of the goods with the debtor's consent given at the time of the repossession (s.173(3)). For the consequences of recovering possession in contravention of s.90, see s.91. **3H–192**

*Subsection (1)(b)*—The term "payment" includes tender (s.189(1)). The "total price" (s.189(1)) does not include default interest that may accrue following lateness in paying off instalments. If after having fallen into arrears and after default interest has accrued, the debtor makes a further payment he can appropriate that payment as between applying it to paying off (a) instalments overdue, or (b) the accrued default interest. If he does not, the creditor has the right to make such appropriation. Applying it to (a) will, but applying it to (b) will not, increase the amount of the total price that has been paid and may make the crucial difference as to whether one third or more of the total price has been paid (*Julian Hodge Bank Ltd v Hall* [1998] C.C.L.R. 14, CA; and see s.81 as to appropriation of payments). **3H–193**

**Procedure**

For a claim for a court order under s.90(1), the relevant procedure is the Consumer Credit procedure, set out in the Consumer Credit Practice Direction at para.7BPD.1. In a claim to which s.90(1) applies, the defendant may admit the claim and offer terms on which a return order should be suspended under s.135(1)(b)—see para.7BPD.8 for the relevant procedure. See also the Introductory Note About Procedure in Consumer Credit Cases, immediately before the start of this Act, at para.3H–4 *et seq.* above. **3H–194**

## Consequences of breach of s.90

**91.** If goods are recovered by the creditor in contravention of section 90— **3H–195**

(a) the regulated agreement, if not previously terminated shall terminate, and

(b) the debtor shall be released from all liability under the agreement, and shall be entitled to recover from the creditor all sums paid by the debtor under the agreement.

### Recovery of possession of goods or land

3H–196 **92.**—(1) Except under an order of the court, the creditor or owner shall not be entitled to enter any premises to take possession of goods subject to a regulated hire-purchase agreement, regulated conditional sale agreement or regulated consumer hire agreement.

(2) At any time when the debtor is in breach of a regulated conditional sale agreement relating to land, the creditor is entitled to recover possession of the land from the debtor, or any person claiming under him, on an order of the court only.

(3) An entry in contravention of subsection (1) or (2) is actionable as a breach of statutory duty.

#### Recovery of possesion of goods or land

3H–197 Section 90 does not prevent recovery of the goods or land with consent of the relevant person(s) given at the time of the repossession (s.173(3)).

#### Procedure

3H–198 The relevant procedural rules are: (i) for a claim under subs.(1), the Consumer Credit Act procedure in the Consumer Credit Practice Direction at para.7BPD.1, and, (ii) for a claim under subs.(2), the procedure set out in CPR Pt 55. See further, the Introductory Note About Procedure at the start of this Act.

### Interest not to be increased on default

3H–199 **93.** The debtor under a regulated consumer credit agreement shall not be obliged to pay interest on sums which, in breach of the agreement, are unpaid by him at a rate—

(a) where the total charge for credit includes an item in respect of interest, exceeding the rate of that interest, or

(b) in any other case, exceeding what would be the rate of the total charge for credit if any items included in the total charge for credit by virtue of section 20(2) were disregarded.

#### Interest not to be increased on default

3H–200 Section 93 prevents the debtor being charged default interest at a rate in excess of the rate of the APR payable under the agreement. For the effect of a contract clause providing for interest (at the same APR as that payable under the agreement as whole) to be payable on arrears, including after judgment has been given for those arrears, see commentary to s.136 below and at 3H–891. With effect from October 1, 2008, only simple interest can be charged on a "default sum" (s.86F above). For "default sum", see s.187A.

**For ss.93A to 125 of the Consumer Credit Act 1974 (see Arrangement) plus any related commentary see paragraphs 3H–201+ to 3H–279+ on White Book on Westlaw UK or the Civil Procedure CD.**

*LAND MORTGAGES*

### Enforcement of land mortgages

3H–280 **126.** A land mortgage securing a regulated agreement is enforce-

*Paragraph numbers marked with a "+" can be found online and on CD.*

able (so far as provided in relation to the agreement) on an order of the court only.

**Enforcement of land mortgages**

This section also applies to a land mortgage which secures an agreement which is exempt by virtue of s.16(6C) and which would, but for s.16(6C), be a regulated agreement: see s.16(6D). Section 126 presumably prevents the creditor from retaking possession and from selling the property without a court order. It does not prevent anything, e.g. repossession, being done with the consent of the relevant person (the mortgagor?) given at the time of the repossession (s.173(3)). The relevant procedure for an application for an order under this section (being a claim for recovery of land) is the procedure set out in CPR Pt 55. **3H–281**

# Part IX

# Judicial Control

## *Enforcement of certain regulated agreements and securities*

### Enforcement orders in cases of infringement

**127.**—(1) In the case of an application for an enforcement order under— **3H–282**

(a) section 65(1) (improperly executed agreements), or
(b) section 105(7)(a) or (b) (improperly executed security instruments), or
(c) section 111(2) (failure to serve copy of notice on surety), or
(d) section 124(1) or (2) (taking of negotiable instruments in contravention of section 123),

the court shall dismiss the application if, but only if, it considers it just to do so having regard to—

(i) prejudice caused to any person by the contravention in question, and the degree of culpability for it; and
(ii) the powers conferred on the court by subsection (2) and sections 135 and 136.

(2) If it appears to the court just to do so, it may in an enforcement order reduce or discharge any sum payable by the debtor or hirer, or any surety, so as to compensate him for prejudice suffered as a result of the contravention in question.

*Note*—Subsections (3) to (5) were repealed with savings by the Consumer Credit Act 2006 ss.15 and 70, and Sch.4 (for savings see Sch.3, para.11), with effect from April 6, 2007 (SI 2007/123). **3H–283**

*Enforcement orders in cases of infringement*

**No enforcement order possible before April 2007**

By virtue of subss.(3) to (5), certain agreements which had been improperly executed (e.g. where no agreement was signed or where the signed agreement did not contain certain basic minimum terms) were "irredeemably unenforceable": *Dimond v Lovell* [2000] Q.B. 216, confirmed in the House of Lords [2002] 1 A.C. 384. Subsection (3) to (5) ceased to have effect on April 6, 2007, except in relation to agreements made **3H–284** before that date (see the "savings" referred to in the note above). For their wording and the considerable case law to which they gave rise, see the *White Book 2006*.

**Court's discretion**

3H-285 Except where in relation to an agreement made before April 6, 2007 the court is prevented from granting an enforcement order by subss.(3)–(5), the court has a discretion whether to do so. It has a discretion to refuse to grant an enforcement order taking into account the factors spelt out in s.127(1)(i) and (ii). It might grant an enforcement order without any qualification if, despite the infringement, the debtor or hirer has suffered no prejudice (*Nissan Finance v Lockhart* [1993] C.C.L.R. 39, CA). It might refuse to grant an enforcement order, e.g. where the debtor or hirer would not have entered the agreement if it had been properly executed (*P.B. Leasing Ltd v Patel and Patel* [1995] C.C.L.R. 82). It might grant an enforcement order but (under ss.127(2) and 136) reduce the rate of interest where a failure to give the debtor an advance copy of the agreement and leave the debtor a pre-contract consideration period (under ss.58 and 61) has deprived the debtor of the opportunity of securing a loan elsewhere at a lower rate of interest (*National Guardian Mortgage Corp v Wilkes* [1993] C.C.L.R. 1). It might considerably reduce (under ss.127(2) and 136) the amount of an accelerated payment due after termination of a consumer hire agreement, where the documentation failed to include that information (*Rank Xerox v Hepple* [1994] C.C.L.R. 1). The Court of Appeal will not normally interfere with the exercise of the judge's discretion under s.127 unless it has not been exercised on the right principles (*Nissan Finance UK v Lockhart*, above).

**Procedure**

3H-286 In the case of an application under any of the sections referred to in s.127(1) the relevant procedural rules are as follows: (i) for a claim relating to the recovery of land, the procedure set out in CPR Pt 55; (ii) for any other claim, the Consumer Credit Act procedure in the Consumer Credit Practice Direction at para.7BPD.1. See further the Introductory Note About Procedure in Consumer Credit Cases, immediately before the start of this Act, at para.3H-4 *et seq*. above.

## Enforcement orders on death of debtor or hirer

3H-287 **128.** The court shall make an order under section 86(2) if, but only if, the creditor or owner proves that he has been unable to satisfy himself that the present and future obligations of the debtor or hirer under the agreement are likely to be discharged.

*EXTENSION OF TIME*

## Time orders

3H-288 **129.**—(1) Subject to subsection (3) below, if it appears to the court just to do so—

(a) on an application for an enforcement order; or

(b) on an application made by a debtor or hirer under this paragraph after service on him of—

(i) a default notice, or

(ii) a notice under section 76(1) or 98(1); or

(ba) on an application made by a debtor or hirer under this paragraph after he has been given a notice under section 86B or 86C; or

(c) in an action brought by a creditor or owner to enforce a regulated agreement or any security, or recover possession of any goods or land to which a regulated agreement relates,

***Paragraph numbers marked with a "+" can be found online and on CD.***

the court may make an order under this section (a "time order").

(2) A time order shall provide for one or both of the following, as the court considers just—

(a) the payment by the debtor or hirer or any surety of any sum owed under a regulated agreement or a security by such instalments, payable at such times, as the court, having regard to the means of the debtor or hirer and any surety, considers reasonable;

(b) the remedying by the debtor or hirer of any breach of a regulated agreement (other than non-payment of money) within such period as the court may specify.

(3) Where in Scotland a time to pay direction or a time to pay order has been made in relation to a debt, it shall not thereafter be competent to make a time order in relation to the same debt.

*Note* —Amended by the Debtors (Scotland) Act 1987 Sch.6. Paragraph (ba) inserted in subs.(1) by s.16 of the Consumer Credit Act 2006, with effect from October 1, 2008 (SI 2007/3300). **3H–289**

### Time orders

The court's power under s.129(2)(a) to allow time for the payment is limited to "any sum owed". This must mean, and is confined to, sums that have actually fallen due, since otherwise there would be no need, in s.130(2), to extend the power, "in the case of a hire-purchase and conditional sale agreement only", to allow the court to grant the order in respect also of payments that have not yet fallen due. Where an accelerated payments clause has been activated (i.e. after expiry of a default notice under s.87), then the whole outstanding balance will have fallen due by virtue of the clause; in that case the court's power under s.129(2)(a) extends to the whole balance, irrespective of whether the agreement is a hire-purchase or conditional sale agreement. Where a land mortgage has been granted as security for a loan and, after the debtor's default, the creditor (no doubt after expiry of a default notice under s.87) commences repossession proceedings, that amounts to a "calling-in" of the loan entitling the creditor to the whole of the outstanding balance; in that case, the court's power under s.127(2)(a) extends to the whole debt including future instalments that would not otherwise have fallen due yet (*Southern District Finance plc v Barnes* [1995] C.C.L.R. 62, CA). According to this case, when a time order is made, it should normally be for a stipulated period on account of temporary financial difficulty; the correct judicial approach is first to consider whether it is just to make a time order, bearing in mind the positions of both parties. See also *First National Bank plc v Syed* [1991] 2 All E.R. 250; [1991] C.C.L.R. 37; there is no point making a time order involving payments that would be insufficient even to keep down the interest accruing on the account. If a time order is made, the court should suspend (see s.135) any possession order it also makes, for so long as the terms of the time order are complied with. **3H–290**

For supplementary matters see s.130 and for the court's power to vary the rate of interest or otherwise amend the agreement in consequence of a term of a time order, see s.136.

A time order is a final order (*Jenkins v Cedar Holdings Ltd* [1988] C.C.L.R. 34).

### Procedure

An application under s.129(1) will no doubt often be made by way of defence to an action begun by the creditor. In relation to mortgage possession claims, the Practice Direction supplementing CPR Pt 55 states at para.7.1 that the defendant may make an application for a time order under s.129 of the Consumer Credit Act 1974 either in his defence or by application notice in the proceedings (see 55APD.10). **3H–291**

An *originating* application for a time order (i.e. under s.129(1)(b) or (ba)), unless it "relates to the recovery of land", should be made using the Consumer Credit Act procedure, set out in the Consumer Credit Practice Direction at para.7BPD.1 and it

***Paragraph numbers marked with a "+" can be found online and on CD.***

should be made in the county court where the claimant resides or carries on business (para.4.3 of the Consumer Credit Act procedure). See further the Note About Procedure in Consumer Credit Cases, immediately before the start of this Act, at para.3H–4 *et seq.* above. An application under s.129(1)(ba) may be made only if the debtor or hirer has given notice of intent which complies with s.129A. An application under s.129(1)(ba) can be made regardless of when the agreement was made (Consumer Credit Act 2006 Sch.3, para.12).

For the evidentiary effect (for the purposes of s.129(2)(a)) of a defendant's admission and offer in a claim relating to "protected goods" under a regulated hire-purchase or conditional sale agreement, see 7BPD.8 and the commentary to s.90 above.

## Debtor or hirer to give notice of intent etc. to creditor or owner

3H–292 **129A.**—(1) A debtor or hirer may make an application under section 129(1)(ba) in relation to a regulated agreement only if—

(a) following his being given the notice under section 86B or 86C, he gave a notice within subsection (2) to the creditor or owner; and

(b) a period of at least 14 days has elapsed after the day on which he gave that notice to the creditor or owner.

(2) A notice is within this subsection if it—

(a) indicates that the debtor or hirer intends to make the application;

(b) indicates that he wants to make a proposal to the creditor or owner in relation to his making of payments under the agreement; and

(c) gives details of that proposal.

3H–293 *Note* —Section 129A inserted by s.16 of the Consumer Credit Act 2006 with effect from October 1, 2008 (SI 2007/3300).

### Notice of intent

3H–294 The purpose of s.129A is to encourage the parties to agree on a repayment arrangement without the need for the debtor to start proceedings for a time order.

## Supplemental provisions about time orders

3H–295 **130.**—(1) Where in accordance with rules of court an offer to pay any sum by instalments is made by the debtor or hirer and accepted by the creditor or owner, the court may in accordance with rules of court make a time order under section 129(2)(a) giving effect to the offer without hearing evidence of means.

(2) In the case of a hire-purchase or conditional sale agreement only, a time order under section 129(2)(a) may deal with sums which, although not payable by the debtor at the time the order is made, would if the agreement continued in force become payable under it subsequently.

(3) A time order under section 129(2)(a) shall not be made where the regulated agreement is secured by a pledge if, by virtue of regulations made under section 76(5), 87(4) or 98(5), service of a notice is not necessary for enforcement of the pledge.

(4) Where, following the making of a time order in relation to a regulated hire-purchase or conditional sale agreement or a regulated

*Paragraph numbers marked with a "+" can be found online and on CD.*

consumer hire agreement, the debtor or hirer is in possession of the goods, he shall be treated (except in the case of a debtor to whom the creditor's title has passed) as a bailee or (in Scotland) a custodier of the goods under the terms of the agreement, notwithstanding that the agreement has been terminated.

(5) Without prejudice to anything done by the creditor or owner before the commencement of the period specified in a time order made under section 129(2)(b)("the relevant period"),—

(a) he shall not while the relevant period subsists take in relation to the agreement any action such as is mentioned in section 87(1);

(b) where—

(i) a provision of the agreement ("the secondary provision") becomes operative only on breach of another provision of the agreement ("the primary provision"), and

(ii) the time order provides for the remedying of such a breach of the primary provision within the relevant period,

he shall not treat the secondary provision as operative before the end of that period;

(c) if while the relevant period subsists the breach to which the order relates is remedied it shall be treated as not having occurred.

(6) On the application of any person affected by a time order, the court may vary or revoke the order.

**Supplemental provisions about time orders**

See commentary to s.129. **3H–296**

## Interest payable on judgment debts etc.

**130A.**—(1) If the creditor or owner under a regulated agreement wants to be able to recover from the debtor or hirer post-judgment interest in connection with a sum that is required to be paid under a judgment given in relation to the agreement (the 'judgment sum'), he— **3H–297**

(a) after the giving of that judgment, shall give the debtor or hirer a notice under this section (the 'first required notice'); and

(b) after the giving of the first required notice, shall give the debtor or hirer further notices under this section at intervals of not more than six months.

(2) The debtor or hirer shall have no liability to pay post-judgment interest in connection with the judgment sum to the extent that the interest is calculated by reference to a period occurring before the day on which he is given the first required notice.

(3) If the creditor or owner fails to give the debtor or hirer a notice under this section within the period of six months beginning with the day after the day on which such a notice was last given to the debtor or hirer, the debtor or hirer shall have no liability to pay

post-judgment interest in connection with the judgment sum to the extent that the interest is calculated by reference to the whole or to a part of the period which—

(a) begins immediately after the end of that period of six months; and

(b) ends at the end of the day on which the notice is given to the debtor or hirer.

(4) The debtor or hirer shall have no liability to pay any sum in connection with the preparation or the giving to him of a notice under this section.

(5) A notice under this section may be incorporated in a statement or other notice which the creditor or owner gives the debtor or hirer in relation to the agreement by virtue of another provision of this Act.

(6) Regulations may make provision about the form and content of notices under this section.

(7) This section does not apply in relation to post-judgment interest which is required to be paid by virtue of any of the following—

(a) section 4 of the Administration of Justice (Scotland) Act 1972;

(b) Article 127 of the Judgments Enforcement (Northern Ireland) Order 1981;

(c) section 74 of the County Courts Act 1984.

(8) This section does not apply in relation to a non-commercial agreement or to a small agreement.

(9) In this section 'post-judgment interest' means interest to the extent calculated by reference to a period occurring after the giving of the judgment under which the judgment sum is required to be paid.

3H–298 *Note*—Section 17 of the Consumer Credit Act 2006 provides for s.130A to be added. Subsections (6) and (9) inserted with effect from June 16, 2006 (SI 2006/1508); remaining subsections inserted with effect from October 1, 2008 (SI 2007/3300).

3H–299 *Subsection (6)*—See the Consumer Credit (Information Requirements and Duration of Licences and Charges) Regulations 2007 (SI 2007/1167).

**Interest on judgment debts**

3H–300 As from October 1, 2008, s.130A requires the creditor or owner to give notice to the debtor or hirer before being allowed to recover any post-judgment interest on any debts. It further requires the notice to be given at least every six months thereafter. Section 130A applies in relation to agreements whenever made but does not apply to sums payable under judgments given before October 1, 2008 (Consumer Credit Act 2006 Sch.3, para.13). See further para.40.8.16.

### *PROTECTION OF PROPERTY PENDING PROCEEDINGS*

## Protection orders

3H–301 **131.** The court, on the application of the creditor or owner under a regulated agreement, may make such orders as it thinks just for protecting any property of the creditor or owner, or property subject to any security, from damage or depreciation pending the determination of any proceedings under this Act, including orders restricting or prohibiting use of the property or giving directions as to its custody.

**Protection orders**

For powers to impose conditions or suspend the operation of the order or to vary agreements in consequence of the order, see ss.135 and 136. The Consumer Credit Act Practice Direction (para.7BPD.1) makes no reference to claims under this section, which appear from the wording of the section to be necessarily interim applications. Presumably an application under s.131 must comply with the rules about Applications for Court Orders (CPR Pt 23) and Interim Remedies (CPR Pt 25). **3H–302**

### *HIRE AND HIRE-PURCHASE, ETC., AGREEMENTS*

## Financial relief for hirer

**132.**—(1) Where the owner under a regulated consumer hire agreement recovers possession of goods to which the agreement relates otherwise than by action, the hirer may apply to the court for an order that— **3H–303**

(a) the whole or part of any sum paid by the hirer to the owner in respect of the goods shall be repaid, and

(b) the obligation to pay the whole or part of any sum owed by the hirer to the owner in respect of the goods shall cease,

and if it appears to the court just to do so, having regard to the extent of the enjoyment of the goods by the hirer, the court shall grant the application in full or in part.

(2) Where in proceedings relating to a regulated consumer hire agreement the court makes an order for the delivery to the owner of goods to which the agreement relates the court may include in the order the like provision as may be made in an order under subsection (1).

**Financial relief for hirer**

In *Automotive Financial Services v Henderson* [1993] C.C.L.R. 55; [1992] S.L.T. Sh.Ct. 63, the defenders suggested two different formulae for determining whether relief should be granted—one based on the interest and the administrative costs of the owner, the other based on the value of the goods supplied and their subsequent depreciation. The Sheriff Principal held that it would be wrong to control the application of s.132 by any formula not in the Act. Presumably, as with s.127 (see the commentary thereto), the Court of Appeal will not normally interfere with the exercise of the judge's discretion unless it has not been exercised on the right principles—or is patently unreasonable. **3H–304**

Where the owner claims under a liquidated damages clause (e.g. after an early termination of the agreement), the hirer may have alternative ways to challenge the claim by: (i) applying for relief under s.132; (ii) seeking relief at common law; (iii) challenging the validity of the clause on the ground that it is a penalty. For relief at common law, see *Starside Properties Ltd v Mustapha* [1974] 1 W.L.R. 816. The principles relating to penalties applicable in hire-purchase cases (see *Bridge v Campbell Discount Co Ltd* [1962] A.C. 600; [1962] 2 W.L.R. 439)are applicable also to consumer hire agreements: *Volkswagen Financial Services (UK) Ltd v Ramage* [2008] C.C.L.R. 3 (Cambridge Cty Ct) and see also *Robophone Facilities Ltd v Blank* [1966] 1 W.L.R. 1428.

## Hire-purchase, etc., agreements: special powers of court

**133.**—(1) If, in relation to a regulated hire-purchase or conditional sale agreement, it appears to the court just to do so— **3H–305**

(a) on an application for an enforcement order or time order; or
(b) in an action brought by the creditor to recover possession of goods to which the agreement relates,

the court may—
(i) make an order (a "return order") for the return to the creditor of goods to which the agreement relates;
(ii) make an order (a "transfer order") for the transfer to the debtor of the creditor's title to certain goods to which the agreement relates ("the transferred goods"), and the return to the creditor of the remainder of the goods.

(2) In determining for the purposes of this section how much of the total price has been paid ("the paid-up sum"), the court may—
(a) treat any sum paid by the debtor, or owed by the creditor, in relation to the goods as part of the paid-up sum;
(b) deduct any sum owed by the debtor in relation to the goods (otherwise than as part of the total price) from the paid-up sum,

and make corresponding reductions in amounts so owed.

(3) Where a transfer order is made, the transferred goods shall be such of the goods to which the agreement relates as the court thinks just; but a transfer order shall be made only where the paid-up sum exceeds the part of the total price referable to the transferred goods by an amount equal to at least one-third of the unpaid balance of the total price.

(4) Notwithstanding the making of a return order or transfer order, the debtor may at any time before the goods enter the possession of the creditor, on payment of the balance of the total price and the fulfilment of any other necessary conditions, claim the goods ordered to be returned to the creditor.

(5) When, in pursuance of a time order or under this section, the total price of goods under a regulated hire-purchase agreement or regulated conditional sale agreement is paid and any other necessary conditions are fulfilled, the creditor's title to the goods vests in the debtor.

(6) If, in contravention of a return order or transfer order, any goods to which the order relates are not returned to the creditor, the court, on the application of the creditor, may—
(a) revoke so much of the order as relates to those goods, and
(b) order the debtor to pay the creditor the unpaid portion of so much of the total price as is referable to those goods.

(7) For the purposes of this section, the part of the total price referable to any goods is the part assigned to those goods by the agreement or (if no such assignment is made) the part determined by the court to be reasonable.

**Hire-purchase, etc., agreements: special powers of court**

**3H–306** Section 133 provides for two possible orders in the case of a regulated hire-purchase or conditional sale agreement. A transfer order will be possible only where the goods subject to the agreement are divisible. Another way of expressing the formula, is that a transfer order is not possible unless the debtor has paid both (a) that part of the total price referable to the "transferred goods" and also (b) one quarter of the rest of the total price. This formula may need adjusting, however, by virtue of subs.(2). In the usual case, the choice before the court will be whether to make a return order or whether to make, if one is applied for, a time order (under s.129). If it decides to make a time order, it could make a return order, suspended, e.g. for so long as the debtor observes the terms of the time order, see s.135.

## Evidence of adverse detention in hire purchase, etc., cases

**134.**—(1) Where goods are comprised in a regulated hire-purchase agreement, regulated conditional sale agreement or regulated consumer hire agreement, and the creditor or owner— **3H-307**

(a) brings an action or makes an application to enforce a right to recover possession of the goods from the debtor or hirer, and

(b) proves that a demand for the delivery of the goods was included in the default notice under section 88(5), or that, after the right to recover possession of the goods accrued but before the action was begun or the application was made, he made a request in writing to the debtor or hirer to surrender the goods,

then, for the purposes of the claim of the creditor or owner to recover possession of the goods, the possession of them by the debtor or hirer shall be deemed to be adverse to the creditor or owner.

(2) In subsection (1) "the debtor or hirer" includes a person in possession of the goods at any time between the debtor's or hirer's death and the grant of probate or administration, or (in Scotland) confirmation.

(3) Nothing in this section affects a claim for damages for conversion or (in Scotland) for delict.

### *SUPPLEMENTAL PROVISIONS AS TO ORDERS*

## Power to impose conditions, or suspend operation of order

**135.**—(1) If it considers it just to do so, the court may in an order made by it in relation to a regulated agreement include provisions— **3H-308**

(a) making the operation of any term of the order conditional on the doing of specified acts by any party to the proceedings;

(b) suspending the operation of any term of the order either—

(i) until such time as the court subsequently directs, or

(ii) until the occurrence of a specified act or omission.

(2) The court shall not suspend the operation of a term requiring the delivery up of goods by any person unless satisfied that the goods are in his possession or control.

(3) In the case of a consumer hire agreement, the court shall not

*Paragraph numbers marked with a "+" can be found online and on CD.*

so use its powers under subsection (1)(b) as to extend the period for which, under the terms of the agreement, the hirer is entitled to possession of the goods to which the agreement relates.

(4) On the application of any person affected by a provision included under subsection (1), the court may vary the provision.

**Power to impose conditions, or suspend operation of order**

3H–309 These powers are relevant to ss.127(1)(ii), 129, 131, 132 and 133 (see commentaries to ss.127, 129 and 133). In a claim to which s.90(1) applies (protected goods under a hire-purchase or conditional sale agreement), the defendant may admit the claim and offer terms on which a return order should be suspended under s.135(1)(b)—see 7BPD.8 for the relevant procedure and for the evidentiary effect of such an admission in relation to s.135(2).

## Power to vary agreements and securities

3H–310 **136.** The court may in an order made by it under this Act include such provision as it considers just for amending any agreement or security in consequence of a term of the order.

**Power to vary agreements and securities**

3H–311 When a time order is made, then unless the contemplated amendment under s.136 is truly a consequence of the time order, and the making of it is also just, there is no power to make it (*Southern & District Finance plc v Barnes* [1995] C.C.L.R. 62). When a time order is made in relation to future instalments that have not yet fallen due (i.e. in one of those limited types of case where that is possible), there will inevitably be consequences for the term of the loan or the rate of interest or both; in such a case the court has power to reduce the rate of interest in re-scheduling the debt (*ibid.*). The decision in *Southern & District Finance plc v Barnes* was, however, rather ambiguous since in that case the Court of Appeal having confirmed the above mentioned limitations on the court's power conferred by section 136, nevertheless then went on to confirm its use in an apparently very wide set of circumstances. In *Director General of Fair Trading v First National Bank* [2000] 1 W.L.R. 98; [2000] 1 All E.R. 240 Evans Lombe J. considered (obiter) that the court's powers under section 136 (as explained and applied in *Southern & District Finance v Barnes*) were ample to prevent the imposition on a borrower of post-judgment interest where it would not be just to impose such interest. [The case was brought under the Unfair Terms in Consumer Contracts Regulations 1994 and ultimately reached the House of Lords—see para.3H–891.] The court has wider powers to amend the agreement where it finds the parties' relationship to be unfair (ss.140A–140C). As regards interest on "default sums", see s.86F.

*EXTORTIONATE CREDIT BARGAINS*

## Extortionate credit bargains

3H–312 **137.**—(1) If the court finds a credit bargain extortionate it may reopen the credit agreement so as to do justice between the parties.

(2) In this section and sections 138 to 140,—

(a) "credit agreement" means any agreement (other than an agreement which is an exempt agreement as a result of section 16(6C)) between an individual (the "debtor") and any other person (the "creditor") by which the creditor provides the debtor with credit of any amount, and

(b) "credit bargain"—

(i) where no transaction other than the credit agreement is to be taken into account in computing the

*Paragraph numbers marked with a "+" can be found online and on CD.*

total charge for credit, means the credit agreement, or

(ii) where one or more other transactions are to be so taken into account, means the credit agreement and those other transactions, taken together.

*Note* —Repealed subject to savings and transitional provisions by the Consumer Credit Act 2006 ss.22(3) and 70, and Sch.4, (for savings and transitional provisions see Sch.3, para.15 and notes to s.140A below), with effect from April 6, 2007 (SI 2007/123). The original text was amended by the Financial Services and Markets Act 2000 (Regulated Activities) Order 2001 (SI 2001/544) (see notes to s.16). **3H–313**

**Extortionate credit bargains**

Sections 137–140 deal with extortionate credit bargains. They apply not just to regulated consumer credit agreements, but to any "personal credit agreement", e.g. an exempt agreement or an agreement to provide an individual with credit of £30,000. Section 137 enables the court to re-open a "credit agreement" where a "credit bargain" is found to be extortionate. The definition of "credit agreement" (identical to that of "personal credit agreement" in s.8(1)), is not as wide as that of "credit bargain". For the definition of extortionate, see s.138. For court's powers on re-opening a credit agreement, see s.139. For applications to re-open the credit agreement and for possible rules as to limitation, see s.139 and commentary thereon. **3H–314**

**Repeal of extortionate credit bargain provisions**

The extortionate credit bargain provisions (in ss.137–140) were replaced by the provisions on unfair creditor/debtor relationships (in ss.140A to 140D). In one respect, however, they remain relevant: a debtor can apply to the court to have an agreement re-opened under the extortionate credit bargain provisions, if the agreement was made before April 6, 2007 and was fully performed before April 6, 2008. Sections 140A to 140D do not apply, and ss.137–140 continue to apply, in relation to such agreements. **3H–314.1**

## When bargains are extortionate

**138.**—(1) A credit bargain is extortionate if it— **3H–315**

(a) requires the debtor or a relative of his to make payments (whether unconditionally, or on certain contingencies) which are grossly exorbitant, or

(b) otherwise grossly contravenes ordinary principles of fair dealing.

(2) In determining whether a credit bargain is extortionate, regard shall be had to such evidence as is adduced concerning—

(a) interest rates prevailing at the time it was made,

(b) the factors mentioned in subsections (3) to (5), and

(c) any other relevant considerations.

(3) Factors applicable under subsection (2) in relation to the debtor include—

(a) his age, experience, business capacity and state of health; and

(b) the degree to which, at the time of making the credit bargain, he was under financial pressure, and the nature of that pressure.

(4) Factors applicable under subsection (2) in relation to the creditor include—

(a) the degree of risk accepted by him, having regard to the value of any security provided;

(b) his relationship to the debtor; and

(c) whether or not a colourable cash price was quoted for any goods or services included in the credit bargain.

(5) Factors applicable under subsection (2) in relation to a linked transaction include the question how far the transaction was reasonably required for the protection of debtor or creditor, or was in the interest of the debtor.

3H-316 *Note* —Repealed subject to savings and transitional provisions by the Consumer Credit Act 2006 ss.22(3) and 70 and Sch.4 (for savings and transitional provisions see Sch.3, para.15 and notes to s.140A below), with effect from April 6, 2007 (SI 2007/123).

**When bargains are extortionate**

3H-317 *Burden of proof* —Rests upon the creditor (s.171(7)).

3H-318 *"Evidence ... adduced"* —The court will normally have regard to the "evidence adduced" about the factors listed. However, the court can take judicial notice, relying on its own general knowledge, e.g. of interest rates (*Castle Phillips Finance v Williams* [1986] C.C.L.R. 13).

3H-319 *Interest rates* —The court should consider rates for similar types of transaction prevailing at the time the agreement was made. It is essential to compare like with like. For example, a short term loan will not be exorbitant simply because the interest rate is higher than that obtainable for long term loans. A different approach might be possible if, say, an unworldly debtor has been talked into making an agreement in an expensive sector of the market when she could have equally well have obtained the credit via a less expensive type of agreement. In making comparison between the interest rate under the agreement and prevailing rates the APR should be used (*Davies v Direct Loans Ltd* [1986] 1 W.L.R. 823). Sometimes a credit agreement confers on the creditor a power to vary the rate of interest. In *Paragon Finance Plc v Nash* [2002] 1 W.L.R. 685; [2002] C.C.L.R. 2 the Court of Appeal declined to follow *Lombard Tricity Finance v Paton* [1989] 1 All E.R. 918, CA, and held: (i) post-contract variations to the rate of interest are irrelevant to whether the credit bargain is extortionate; (ii) the contractual power to vary the rate of interest is subject to an implied contractual term that the creditor will not exercise that power dishonestly, for an improper purpose, arbitrarily, capricously or unreasonably. A creditor which raised its interest rate in an attempt to alleviate serious financial difficulties by passing on its increased costs to its borrowers, was held not to be in breach of that implied term—even though the variation increased the gap between the rate charged by the creditor and that charged by other lenders. A commercial lender is free to conduct its business in what it genuinely believes to be its best commercial interests: *Paragon Finance Ltd v Pender and Pender* [2005] EWCA Civ 760; [2005] 1 W.L.R. 3412; [2005] C.C.L.R. 5. The implied terms which in *Paragon* the Court of Appeal was prepared to imply are all negative and *Paragon* does not open the door to an implied term that a lender may have a positive obligation to reduce a rate of interest: *Sterling Credit v Rahman (No.2)* [2002] EWHC 3008 (Ch); [2003] C.C.L.R. 13.

If a creditor has a policy of not exercising a contractual power to vary the interest rate (or the APR) even when market rates fall substantially, then failure to inform the debtor, at the time the agreement is made, about that policy is a relevant factor. If, however, the debtor would have entered the agreement even with that information, that factor is unlikely on its own to be sufficient to render the agreement extortionate: *Broadwick Financial Services Ltd v Spencer* [2002] EWCA Civ 35; [2002] 1 All E.R. (Comm) 446; [2002] C.C.L.R. 3. There were two further aspects of *Broadwick*. First, the debtor, a non-status borrower, was allowed to make payments based on a lower rate of interest than the contractual rate. This was by virtue of a "concession letter" given to the debtor at the time the agreement was made. The letter stated that it was "not intended to be legally binding" and that the lower rate was an "*ex gratia* concession". Secondly, the agreement provided for a rebate on early settlement calculated according to the "Rule of 78". Both these features of the case were irrelevant to the issue of whether the agreement was extortionate: the first because the concession was not intended to be legally binding and the concessionary rate was not substantially lower than the contractual interest rate; the second because calculating the rebate according to the "Rule of 78" was sanctioned by the Consumer Credit (Rebate on Early Settlement) Regulations 1983.

*Alternative challenges* —A debtor may be able to challenge terms of the agreement (other than "core" terms, such as those which set the rate of interest payable under a loan agreement) as being "unfair" within the meaning of the Unfair Terms in Consumer Contracts Regulations 1994 (if the agreement was made after June 30, 1995 and before October 1, 1999) or the Unfair Terms in Consumer Contracts Regulations 1999 (if the agreement was made on or after October 1, 1999). For the 1999 regulations see para.3H–886 below. In *Falco Finance Ltd v Gough* [1999] C.C.L.R. 16 (Macclesfield County Court), the court considerd three features of a long term mortgage loan, namely: (i) its "dual rate" clause by which a lower ("concessionary") rate of interest was charged unless and until the debtor fell into arrears at any point; (ii) a clause providing for a rebate on redemption calculated on the "rule of 78" coupled with six months' notional deferral; and (iii) the charging of interest on a "flat rate" basis. The first was held to be extortionate within the meaning of s.138 while all three features were held to be unfair within the 1994 regulations. For an analysis of the application of the 1994 Regulations to a clause in a loan agreement imposing default interest at the contractual rate on outstanding arrears, including after judgment, see *Director General of Fair Trading v First National Bank plc* at para.3H–891 below. **3H–320**

## Reopening of extortionate agreements

**139.**—(1) A credit agreement may, if the court thinks just, be reopened on the ground that the credit bargain is extortionate— **3H–321**

(a) on an application for the purpose made by the debtor or any surety to the High Court, county court or sheriff court; or

(b) at the instance of the debtor or a surety in any proceedings to which the debtor and creditor are parties, being proceedings to enforce the credit agreement, any security relating to it, or any linked transaction; or

(c) at the instance of the debtor or a surety in other proceedings in any court where the amount paid or payable under the credit agreement is relevant.

(2) In reopening the agreement, the court may, for the purpose of relieving the debtor or a surety from payment of any sum in excess of that fairly due and reasonable, by order—

(a) direct accounts to be taken, or (in Scotland) an accounting to be made, between any persons,

(b) set aside the whole or part of any obligation imposed on the debtor or a surety by the credit bargain or any related agreement,

(c) require the creditor to repay the whole or part of any sum paid under the credit bargain or any related agreement by the debtor or a surety, whether paid to the creditor or any other person,

(d) direct the return to the surety of any property provided for the purposes of the security, or

(e) alter the terms of the credit agreement or any security instrument.

(3) An order may be under subsection (2) notwithstanding that its effect is to place a burden on the creditor in respect of an advantage unfairly enjoyed by another person who is a party to a linked transaction.

(4) An order under subsection (2) shall not alter the effect of any judgment.

(5) In England and Wales an application under subsection (1)(a) shall be brought only in the county court in the case of—

(a) a regulated agreement, or

(b) an agreement (not being a regulated agreement) under which the creditor provides the debtor with fixed-sum credit or running-account credit.

(5A) [...]

(6) In Scotland an application under subsection (1)(a) may be brought in the sheriff court for the district in which the debtor or surety resides or carries on business.

(7) In Northern Ireland an application under subsection (1)(a) may be brought in the county court in the case of—

(a) a regulated agreement, or

(b) an agreement (not being a regulated agreement) under which the creditor provides the debtor with fixed-sum credit not exceeding £5,000 or running-account credit on which the credit limit does not exceed £5,000.

**3H–322** *Note*—Repealed subject to savings and transitional provisions by the Consumer Credit Act 2006 ss.22(3) and 70, and Sch.4, (for savings and transitional provisions see Sch.3, para.15 and notes to s.140A below), with effect from April 6, 2007 (SI 2007/123).

Amended by the Debtors (Scotland) Act 1987 Sch.6; the Administration of Justice (Northern Ireland) Order 1975 (SI 1975/816) art.9(1), Sch.1; the County Courts Jurisdiction Order 1977 (SI 1977/600); the County Courts Jurisdiction Order 1981 (SI 1981/1123); the Administration of Justice Act 1982 Sch.3; the County Courts (Amendment) Rules (Northern Ireland) 1982 (SI 1982/120); the County Courts Act Sch.2; and the High Court and County Courts Jurisdiction Order 1991 (SI 1991/724).

#### Reopening of extortionate agreements

**3H–323** *Restrictions on court's ability to re-open agreement*—An application under s.139(1) must be made within any relevant limitation period under the Limitation Act 1980. The proper approach, it is submitted, is that the Limitation Act has no application at all where the debtor makes the application to re-open the credit agreement (e.g. to be relieved of the obligation to pay a sum) as part of his *defence*, but that it may apply to a claim or counterclaim—see also *Extortionate Credit Bargain Claims and the Limitation Rules* (1998) 412 S.J. 274 and *Extortionate Loans: the Limitation Act revisited* (1999) 143 S.J. 646. Where an application under s.139 is for a remedy or remedies, other than for repayment of any sum, the claim is an action upon a specialty within s.8 of the Limitation Act 1980 and the relevant period limitation period expires 12 years after the agreement was made, *Rahman v Sterling Credit Ltd* [2001] 1 W.L.R. 496. The period is six years where the remedy claimed is repayment of any sum, Limitation Act 1980 s.9. The Court of Appeal in *Rahman* did not decide, but nevertheless appeared to imply, that the six year period under s.9 began when the agreement was made. This is surely wrong, because the period does not start until the cause of action accrues and the cause of action to recover a sum of money cannot accrue until that sum has first been

*Paragraph numbers marked with a "+" can be found online and on CD.*

paid—see the articles referred to above. *Rahman* did not deal with the situation where an extortionate credit bargain claim is made purely by way of defence. It involved a secure loan made in 1989 in respect of which a possession order had been made in 1990 but never executed. In 1998, the debtor wished to apply, by way of a counterclaim in the possession proceedings, to have the agreement re-opened as being extortionate. Holding that the 12 year limitation period had not expired, the Court of Appeal granted him permission under CPR 20.4 to file that counterclaim (which did not include a claim for repayment of any sum). The court declined to refuse permission on the grounds of issue stoppel, since the counterclaim was part of the same original action in which the possession order had been claimed. It was not a new action in which the defendant was seeking to raise an issue which should have been raised in an earlier action.

In *Nolan v Wright* [2009] EWHC 305; [2009] C.C.L.R. 8 Judge Hodge Q.C., held that a claim to re-open a credit bargain as being extortionate was statute barred after 12 years from the date of the agreement unless the claim extended to a claim for repayment of money previously paid in which case the relevant period was six years, the period in the latter case possibly not beginning until the date the money had been paid to the creditor. Considering himself bound to do so by the decision in *Rahman*, he rejected the suggestion (at the start of this paragraph) that "the Limitation Act has no application all where the debtor makes the application to re-open the credit agreement (e.g. to be relieved of the obligation to pay a sum) as part of his *defence*".

*Procedure* —An application under s.139(1) will no doubt often be made by the debtor (or surety) in an action begun by the creditor. Written notice of an intention to make such an application should be served on the court and all other parties within 14 days after the service of the claim form on the applicant: see para.7BPD.10. If such a notice is served, the applicant will be treated as having filed a defence. An originating application should be made using the Consumer Credit Act procedure, set out in the Consumer Credit Practice Direction at para.7BPD.1, unless it relates to the recovery of land. See further the Introductory Note About Procedure in Consumer Credit Cases, immediately before the start of this Act, at para.3H–4 *et seq.* above. **3H–324**

## Interpretation of sections 137 to 139

**140.** Where the credit agreement is not a regulated agreement, expressions used in sections 137 to 139 which, apart from this section, apply only to regulated agreements, shall be construed as nearly as may be as if the credit agreement were a regulated agreement. **3H–325**

*Note* —Repealed subject to savings and transitional provisions by the Consumer Credit Act 2006 ss.22(3) and 70, and Sch.4, (for savings and transitional provisions see Sch.3, para.15 and notes to s.140A below), with effect from April 6, 2007 (SI 2007/123). **3H–326**

## Unfair relationships between creditors and debtors

**140A.**—(1) The court may make an order under section 140B in connection with a credit agreement if it determines that the relationship between the creditor and the debtor arising out of the agreement (or the agreement taken with any related agreement) is unfair to the debtor because of one or more of the following— **3H–327**

(a) any of the terms of the agreement or of any related agreement;

(b) the way in which the creditor has exercised or enforced any of his rights under the agreement or any related agreement;

(c) any other thing done (or not done) by, or on behalf of, the creditor (either before or after the making of the agreement or any related agreement).

***Paragraph numbers marked with a "+" can be found online and on CD.***

(2) In deciding whether to make a determination under this section the court shall have regard to all matters it thinks relevant (including matters relating to the creditor and matters relating to the debtor).

(3) For the purposes of this section the court shall (except to the extent that it is not appropriate to do so) treat anything done (or not done) by, or on behalf of, or in relation to, an associate or a former associate of the creditor as if done (or not done) by, or on behalf of, or in relation to, the creditor.

(4) A determination may be made under this section in relation to a relationship notwithstanding that the relationship may have ended.

(5) An order under section 140B shall not be made in connection with a credit agreement which is an exempt agreement by virtue of section 16(6C).

**3H-328** *Note* —Inserted by the Consumer Credit Act 2006 s.19, with effect from April 6, 2007 (SI 2007/123).

**Unfair relationships**

**3H-329** The powers available to the court under ss.140A to 140C effectively enable the court to remove any unfairness where the court determines that the relationship between creditor and debtor is unfair to the debtor. For an unsuccessful claim that there was unfair relationship within s.140A(1), see *Tamimi v Khodari* [2009] EWCA Civ 1109; [2010] C.C.L.R. 3, confirming *Khodari v Tamimi* [2008] EWHC 3065; [2009] C.C.L.R. 5.

**Agreements to which unfair relationships provisions apply**

**3H-330** Sections 140A to 140C apply (see s.140C(1)) to agreements where credit is provided to an individual (which includes a partnership of up to three partners). Thus they apply not only to regulated credit agreements but also to exempt agreements. By way of exception, they do not apply (see s.140A(5)) to agreements which are exempt agreements by virtue of s.16(6C)(a). The latter are those subject to the regulatory regime under the Financial Services and Markets Act 2000 which are, broadly, any loan secured by a first legal mortgage on a dwelling in which the debtor or his family resides—see further the commentary to s.16 (at the third bullet point).

**Limitation rules**

**3H-331** For the application of the limitation rules under ss.137–140, see *Rahman v Sterling Credit Ltd* [2001] 1 W.L.R. 496 and the commentary to s.139 above. In s.140B there is a clear distinction between the words "on an application made by" in s.140B(2)(a) and the words "at the instance of" in s.140B(2)(b) and (c). Thus, whereas the limitation rules will apply to an application under s.140B(2)(a), it is submitted that they have no application at all to the situation where the debtor or surety raises the issue of unfair relationship by way of defence. In relation to an application under s.140B(2) for a remedy or remedies other than for the repayment of money, the limitation period expires 12 years after the credit agreement was made, since such a claim is an action upon a specialty: *Rahman*, above. Where the remedy claimed in an application under s.140B(2)(a) is the repayment to the debtor or surety of money which he has paid, the limitation period is six years beginning with when the cause of action accrued: Limitation Act 1980 s.9. That period does not, it is submitted, begin until the date when the debtor or surety paid the money which is now being reclaimed, since the cause of action of action entitling the debtor or surety to reclaim that money cannot have accrued until he had first paid it. The latter limitation period will thus not finally expire until six years after the date of the debtor's final payment under the agreement. See further the articles cited in the notes to s.139.

**Commencement and transitional provisions relating to unfair relationships**

**3H-332** Sections 140A to 140D were added by the Consumer Credit Act 2006, with effect

***Paragraph numbers marked with a "+" can be found online and on CD.***

from April 6, 2007: the Consumer Credit Act 2006 (Commencement No.2 and Transitional Provisions and Savings) Order 2007 (SI 2007/123). The transitional period, set out in paras 14 to 16 of Sch.3 to the Consumer Credit Act 2006 ended on April 5, 2008. After the transitional period (i.e. currently), ss.140A to 140C (and not ss.137–140) apply to agreements whenever made. There is one exception to that. The exception is that ss.137–140 (and not ss.140A to 140C) continue to apply to agreements which were made before April 6, 2007 and were fully performed before April 6, 2008. Thus, in the case of an agreement made before April 6, 2007 and fully performed before April 6, 2008, the debtor can seek to have the agreement re-opened under the extortionate credit bargain provisions but cannot challenge the agreement under the unfair relationship provisions.

#### Alternative challenges

For the possibility of a challenge that the terms of a credit agreement are "unfair" within the meaning of the Unfair Terms in Consumer Contracts Regulations 1999, see those Regulations at para.3H-886 below and also the commentary to s.138 above. **3H–333**

### Powers of court in relation to unfair relationships

**140B.**—(1) An order under this section in connection with a credit agreement may do one or more of the following— **3H–334**

- (a) require the creditor, or any associate or former associate of his, to repay (in whole or in part) any sum paid by the debtor or by a surety by virtue of the agreement or any related agreement (whether paid to the creditor, the associate or the former associate or to any other person);
- (b) require the creditor, or any associate or former associate of his, to do or not to do (or to cease doing) anything specified in the order in connection with the agreement or any related agreement;
- (c) reduce or discharge any sum payable by the debtor or by a surety by virtue of the agreement or any related agreement;
- (d) direct the return to a surety of any property provided by him for the purposes of a security;
- (e) otherwise set aside (in whole or in part) any duty imposed on the debtor or on a surety by virtue of the agreement or any related agreement;
- (f) alter the terms of the agreement or of any related agreement;
- (g) direct accounts to be taken, or (in Scotland) an accounting to be made, between any persons.

(2) An order under this section may be made in connection with a credit agreement only—

- (a) on an application made by the debtor or by a surety;
- (b) at the instance of the debtor or a surety in any proceedings in any court to which the debtor and the creditor are parties, being proceedings to enforce the agreement or any related agreement; or
- (c) at the instance of the debtor or a surety in any other proceedings in any court where the amount paid or payable under the agreement or any related agreement is relevant.

*Paragraph numbers marked with a "+" can be found online and on CD.*

(3) An order under this section may be made notwithstanding that its effect is to place on the creditor, or any associate or former associate of his, a burden in respect of an advantage enjoyed by another person.

(4) An application under subsection (2)(a) may only be made—

(a) in England and Wales, to the county court;

(b) in Scotland, to the sheriff court;

(c) in Northern Ireland, to the High Court (subject to subsection (6)).

(5) In Scotland such an application may be made in the sheriff court for the district in which the debtor or surety resides or carries on business.

(6) In Northern Ireland such an application may be made to the county court if the credit agreement is an agreement under which the creditor provides the debtor with—

(a) fixed-sum credit not exceeding £15,000; or

(b) running-account credit on which the credit limit does not exceed £15,000.

(7) Without prejudice to any provision which may be made by rules of court made in relation to county courts in Northern Ireland, such rules may provide that an application made by virtue of subsection (6) may be made in the county court for the division in which the debtor or surety resides or carries on business.

(8) A party to any proceedings mentioned in subsection (2) shall be entitled, in accordance with rules of court, to have any person who might be the subject of an order under this section made a party to the proceedings.

(9) If, in any such proceedings, the debtor or a surety alleges that the relationship between the creditor and the debtor is unfair to the debtor, it is for the creditor to prove to the contrary.

**3H–335** *Note*—Inserted subject to transitional provisions by the Consumer Credit Act 2006 s.20 (for transitional provisions see Sch.3, paras 14 and 16), with effect from April 6, 2007 (SI 2007/123).

**Powers of court in relation to unfair relationships**

**3H–336** See the commentary to s.140A.

**3H–337** *Procedure*—An application under s.140B(2)(b) or (c) will no doubt often be made by the debtor (or surety) in an action begun by the creditor. Written notice of an intention to make such an application should be served on the court and all other parties within 14 days after the service of the claim form on the applicant: see para.7BPD.10. If such a notice is served, the applicant will be treated as having filed a defence.

## Interpretation of ss.140A and 140B

**3H–338** **140C.**—(1) In this section and in sections 140A and 140B 'credit agreement' means any agreement between an individual (the 'debtor') and any other person (the 'creditor') by which the creditor provides the debtor with credit of any amount.

(2) References in this section and in sections 140A and 140B to the creditor or to the debtor under a credit agreement include—

(a) references to the person to whom his rights and duties under the agreement have passed by assignment or operation of law;

(b) where two or more persons are the creditor or the debtor, references to any one or more of those persons.

(3) The definition of 'court' in section 189(1) does not apply for the purposes of sections 140A and 140B.

(4) References in sections 140A and 140B to an agreement related to a credit agreement (the 'main agreement') are references to—

(a) a credit agreement consolidated by the main agreement;

(b) a linked transaction in relation to the main agreement or to a credit agreement within paragraph (a);

(c) a security provided in relation to the main agreement, to a credit agreement within paragraph (a) or to a linked transaction within paragraph (b).

(5) In the case of a credit agreement which is not a regulated consumer credit agreement, for the purposes of subsection (4) a transaction shall be treated as being a linked transaction in relation to that agreement if it would have been such a transaction had that agreement been a regulated consumer credit agreement.

(6) For the purposes of this section and section 140B the definitions of 'security' and 'surety' in section 189(1) apply (with any appropriate changes) in relation to—

(a) a credit agreement which is not a consumer credit agreement as if it were a consumer credit agreement; and

(b) a transaction which is a linked transaction by virtue of subsection (5).

(7) For the purposes of this section a credit agreement (the 'earlier agreement') is consolidated by another credit agreement (the 'later agreement') if—

(a) the later agreement is entered into by the debtor (in whole or in part) for purposes connected with debts owed by virtue of the earlier agreement; and

(b) at any time prior to the later agreement being entered into the parties to the earlier agreement included—

(i) the debtor under the later agreement; and

(ii) the creditor under the later agreement or an associate or a former associate of his.

(8) Further, if the later agreement is itself consolidated by another credit agreement (whether by virtue of this subsection or subsection (7)), then the earlier agreement is consolidated by that other agreement as well.

*Note* —Inserted subject to transitional provisions by the Consumer Credit Act 2006 s.21 (for transitional provisions see Sch.3, para.16), with effect from April 6, 2007 (SI 2007/123). **3H–339**

**Interpretation of ss. 140A and 140B**

See the commentary to s.140A. **3H–340**

*Paragraph numbers marked with a "+" can be found online and on CD.*

## Advice and information

3H–341 **140D.** The advice and information published by the OFT under section 229 of the Enterprise Act 2002 shall indicate how the OFT expects sections 140A to 140C of this Act to interact with Part 8 of that Act.

3H–342 *Note* —Inserted by the Consumer Credit Act 2006 s.22, with effect from April 6, 2007 (SI 2007/123).

### *MISCELLANEOUS*

## Jurisdiction and parties

3H–343 **141.**—(1) In England and Wales the county court shall have jurisdiction to hear and determine—

(a) any action by the creditor or owner to enforce a regulated agreement or any security relating to it;

(b) any action to enforce any linked transaction against the debtor or hirer or his relative,

and such an action shall not be brought in any other court.

(2) Where an action or application is brought in the High Court which, by virtue of this Act, ought to have been brought in the county court it shall not be treated as improperly brought, but shall be transferred to the county court.

(3) In Scotland the sheriff court shall have jurisdiction to hear and determine any action referred to in subsection (1) and such an action shall not be brought in any other court.

(3A) Subject to subsection (3B) an action which is brought in the sheriff court by virtue of subsection (3) shall be brought only in one of the following courts, namely—

(a) the court for the place where the debtor of hirer is domiciled (within the meaning of section 41 or 42 of the Civil Jurisdiction and Judgments Act 1982);

(b) the court for the place where the debtor of hirer carries on business; and

(c) where the purpose of the action is to assert, declare or determine proprietary or possessory rights, or rights of security, in or over moveable property, or to obtain authority to dispose of moveable property, the court for the place the property is situated.

(3B) Subsection (3A) shall not apply—

(a) where Rule 3 of Schedule 8 to the said Act of 1982 applies; or

(b) where the jurisdiction of another court has been prorogated by an agreement entered into after the dispute has arisen.

(4) In Northern Ireland the county court shall have jurisdiction to hear and determine any action or application falling within subsection (1).

(5) Except as may be provided by rules of court, all the parties to

a regulated agreement, and any surety, shall be made parties to any proceedings relating to the agreement.

*Note* —Amended by the Civil Jurisdiction and Judgments Act 1982 Sch.12. **3H–344**

**Jurisdiction and parties**

The Consumer Credit Practice direction (which supplements CPR r.7.9) indicates in which county court a claim to recover goods, or an originating application for a time order (under s.129(1)(b)), may be started—generally the court in the district where the debtor or hirer resides or carries on business (para.7BPD.1, para.4). For the appropriate forum where the claim is between parties in different European states, see para.6.19.23. **3H–345**

*Subsection (2)* —Despite the words "which shall not be treated as improperly brought", the court now has, by virtue of the County Courts Act 1984 s.40(1)(b) (as substituted by the Courts and Legal Services Act 1990), discretion to strike out the proceedings if satisfied that the claimant knew or ought to have known that they should have been brought in the County Court (*Barclays Bank Plc v Brooks* [1997] C.C.L.R. 60). In any claim issued in the High Court in relation to a consumer credit agreement (e.g. a claim by the debtor or in relation to an exempt agreement), the particulars of claim must contain a statement that the action is not one to which s.141 applies (see para.7.6 of the Practice Direction supplementing CPR Pt 16 at para.16PD.7). **3H–346**

*Subsection (5)* —For additional requirements as to parties and for the court's power to dispense with the requirements of this subsection, see para.9 of the Consumer Credit Practice Direction (para.7BPD.1). **3H–347**

**Procedure**

A claim by a creditor or owner to enforce a regulated agreement will be subject to one of the following three sets of procedure: **3H–348**

- The procedure set out in CPR Pt 55, if it is a claim relating to recovery of land;
- The Consumer Credit Act procedure, set out in the Consumer Credit Practice Direction at para.7BPD.1, if either
  - (i) the agreement relates to goods, or
  - (ii) the agreement relates only to money and the claim involves an application for an order under any of ss.65(1), 86(2), 90, 92(1), 105(7)(a) or (b), 111(2), 124(1) or (2);
- A Pt 7 claim form (but not using the Consumer Credit Act procedure), if the agreement relates only to money and the claim does not involve an application under one of the above mentioned sections.

See further, the Note About Procedure in Consumer Credit Cases, immediately before the start of this Act, at para.3H–4 *et seq.* above.

## Power to declare rights of parties

**142.**—(1) Where under any provision of this Act a thing can be done by a creditor or owner on an enforcement order only, and either— **3H–349**

(a) the court dismisses (except on technical grounds only) an application for an enforcement order, or

(b) where no such application has been made or such an application has been dismissed on technical grounds only, an interested party applies to the court for a declaration under this subsection,

the court may if it thinks just make a declaration that the creditor or owner is not entitled to do that thing, and thereafter no application for an enforcement order in respect of it shall be entertained.

***Paragraph numbers marked with a "+" can be found online and on CD.***

(2) Where—

(a) a regulated agreement or linked transaction is cancelled under section 69(1), or becomes subject to section 69(2), or

(b) a regulated agreement is terminated under section 91,

and an interested party applies to the court for a declaration under this subsection, the court may make a declaration to that effect.

**Power to declare rights of parties**

3H–350 For the effect on security of a declaration under subs.(1), see s.113(3)(d) and (4). A court has no power to grant a section 142 declaration where an agreement is closed, that is where the regulated agreement has been fully performed and it is therefore impossible for the creditor to apply for an enforcement order: *Watson v Progressive Financial Services Ltd, T/A Welcome Finance* [2009] C.C.L.R.10 (Liverpool Cty Ct).

**For ss.143 to 144 and ss.148 to 149 of the Consumer Credit Act 1974 (see Arrangement) plus any related commentary see paragraphs 3H–351+ to 3H–360+ on White Book on Westlaw UK or the Civil Procedure CD.**

## PART XI

## ENFORCEMENT OF ACT

* * * *

### No further sanctions for breach of Act

3H–361 **170.**—(1) A breach of any requirement made (otherwise than by any court) by or under this Act shall incur no civil or criminal sanction as being such a breach, except to the extent (if any) expressly provided by or under this Act.

(2) In exercising its functions under this Act the OFT may take account of any matter appearing to it to constitute a breach of a requirement made by or under this Act, whether or not any sanction for that breach is provided by or under this Act and, if it is so provided, whether or not proceedings have been brought in respect of the breach.

(3) Subsection (1) does not prevent the grant of an injunction, or the making of an order of certiorari, mandamus or prohibition or as respects Scotland the grant of an interdict or of an order under section 91 of the Court of Session Act 1868 (order for specific performance of statutory duty).

3H–362 *Note* —Amended by the Enterprise Act 2002 s.278 and Sch.25.

### Onus of proof in various proceedings

3H–363 **171.**—(1) If an agreement contains a term signifying that in the opinion of the parties section 10(3)(b)(iii) does not apply to the agreement, it shall be taken not to apply unless the contrary is proved.

(2) It shall be assumed in any proceedings, unless the contrary is proved that when a person initiated a transaction as mentioned in section 19(1)(c) he knew the principal agreement had been made, or contemplated that it might be made.

*Paragraph numbers marked with a "+" can be found online and on CD.*

(3) Regulations under section 44 or 52 may make provision as to the onus of proof in any proceedings to enforce the regulations.

(4) In proceedings brought by the creditor under a credit-token agreement—

(a) it is for the creditor to prove that the credit-token was lawfully supplied to the debtor, and was accepted by him, and

(b) if the debtor alleges that any use made of the credit-token was not authorised by him, it is for the creditor to prove either—

(i) that the use was so authorised, or

(ii) that the use occurred before the creditor had been given notice under section 84(3).

(5) In proceedings under section 50(1) in respect of a document received by a minor at any school or other educational establishment for minors, it is for the person sending it to him at that establishment to prove that he did not know or suspect it to be such an establishment.

(6) In proceedings under section 119(1) it is for the pawnee to prove that he had reasonable cause to refuse to allow the pawn to be redeemed.

(7) ...

*Note* —Amended by the Consumer Credit Act 2006 s.70 and Sch 4, with effect from April 6, 2007 (SI 2007/123). **3H–364**

## Statements by creditor or owner to be binding

**172.**—(1) A statement by a creditor or owner is binding on him if given under— **3H–365**

section 77(1),
section 78(1),
section 79(1),
section 97(1),
section 107(1)(c),
section 108(1)(c),
section 109(1)(c).

(2) Where a trader—

(a) gives a customer a notice in compliance with section 103(1)(b), or

(b) gives a customer a notice under section 103(1) asserting that the customer is not indebted to him under an agreement,

the notice is binding on the trader.

(3) Where in proceedings before any court—

(a) it is sought to rely on a statement or notice given as mentioned in subsection (1) or (2), and

(b) the statement or notice is shown to be incorrect,

the court may direct such relief (if any) to be given to the creditor or owner from the operation of subsection (1) or (2) as appears to the court to be just.

**Statements by creditor or owner to be binding**

3H–366 It would seem likely in exercising its discretion under subs.(3), the court will follow a very similar approach to that in estoppel cases. Indeed, a debtor may well seek to rely on s.172 and on estoppel as alternatives. For cases on estoppel see *United Overseas Bank v Jiwani* [1976] 1 W.L.R. 964 (bank, which had credited debtor's account erroneously, not estopped from reclaiming money from debtor as debtor had not altered his position on basis of the error), and *Lombard North Central v Stobart* [1990] C.C.L.R. 53, CA (creditor issuing settlement statement in relation to unregulated conditional sale agreement for purchase of car—statement understating amount required to pay off outstanding debt—debtor selling the car in consequence of error—creditor estopped from making claim in contract or conversion).

## Contracting-out forbidden

3H–367 **173.**—(1) A term contained in a regulated agreement or linked transaction, or in any other agreement relating to an actual or prospective regulated agreement or linked transaction, is void if, and to the extent that, it is inconsistent with a provision for the protection of the debtor or hirer or his relative or any surety contained in this Act or in any regulation made under this Act.

(2) Where a provision specified the duty or liability of the debtor or hirer or his relative or any surety in certain circumstances, a term is inconsistent with that provision if it purports to impose, directly or indirectly, an additional duty or liability on him in those circumstances.

(3) Notwithstanding subsection (1), a provision of this Act under which a thing may be done in relation to any person on an order of the court or the OFT only shall not be taken to prevent its being done at any time with that person's consent given at that time, but the refusal of such consent shall not give rise to any liability.

3H–368 *Note*—Amended by the Enterprise Act 2002 s.278 and Sch.25.

3H–369 *Consensual enforcement*—For apparently conflicting rulings on whether s.173(3) enables a debtor to give effective consent to enforcement of the agreement against himself where, without that consent, s.127(3) (now repealed) rendered the agreement unenforceable against him, see commentary to s.127 in the *White Book* 2006.

## PART XII

## SUPPLEMENTAL

### *GENERAL*

* * * *

## Service of documents

3H–370 **176.**—(1) A document to be served under this act by one person ("the server") on another person ("the subject") is to be treated as properly served on the subject if dealt with as mentioned in the following subsections.

(2) The document may be delivered or sent by an appropriate method to the subject, or addressed to him by name and left at his proper address.

***Paragraph numbers marked with a "+" can be found online and on CD.***

(3) For the purposes of this Act, a document sent by post to, or left at, the address last known to the server as the address of a person shall be treated as sent by post to, or left at, his proper address.

(4) Where the document is to be served on the subject as being the person having any interest in land, and it is not practicable after reasonable inquiry to ascertain the subject's name or address, the document may be served by—

(a) addressing it to the subject by the description of the person having that interest in the land (naming it), and

(b) delivering the document to some responsible person on the land or affixing it, or a copy of it, in a conspicuous position on the land.

(5) Where a document to be served on the subject as being a debtor, hirer or surety, or as having any other capacity relevant for the purposes of this Act, is served at any time on another person who—

(a) is the person last known to the server as having that capacity, but

(b) before that time had ceased to have it,

the document shall be treated as having been served at that time on the subject.

(6) Anything done to a document in relation to a person who (whether to the knowledge of the server or not) has died shall be treated for the purposes of subsection (5) as service of the document on that person if it would have been so treated had he not died.

(7) The following enactments shall not be construed as authorising service on the Public Trustee (in England and Wales) or the Probate Judge (in Northern Ireland) of any document which is to be served under this Act—

section 9 of the Administration of Estates Act 1925;

section 3 of the Administration of Estates Act (Northern Ireland) 1955.

(8) References in the preceding subsections to the serving of a document on a person include the giving of the document to that person.

*Note* —Amended by the Law of Property (Miscellaneous Provisions) Act 1994 Sch.1 and by the Consumer Credit Act 1974 (Electronic Communications) Order 2004 (SI 2004/3236). **3H–371**

**Service of documents**

In *Lombard North Central v Power-Hines* [1995] C.C.L.R. 24, the debtor claimed in vain, that a default notice (under s.87) had not been received by him either because the postman was unreliable or because the debtor's young son had intercepted it. It was held that the fact that it did not come to the debtor's attention did not mean that he did not receive it. Section 176(2) was designed to apply where through no fault of the creditor the document does not come to the attention of the debtor. The court was entitled to assume that where the letter was not returned, it had been delivered. **3H–372**

## Electronic transmission of documents

**176A.**—(1) A document is transmitted in accordance with this subsection if— **3H–373**

(a) the person to whom it is transmitted agrees that it may be delivered to him by being transmitted to a particular electronic address in a particular electronic form,

(b) it is transmitted to that address in that form, and

(c) the form in which the document is transmitted is such that any information in the document which is addressed to the person to whom the document is transmitted is capable of being stored for future reference for an appropriate period in a way which allows the information to be reproduced without change.

(2) A document transmitted in accordance with subsection (1) shall, unless the contrary is proved, be treated for the purposes of this Act, except section 69, as having been delivered on the working day immediately following the day on which it is transmitted.

(3) In this section, "electronic address" includes any number or address used for the purposes of receiving electronic communications.

3H–374 *Note*—Section 176A was added by the Consumer Credit Act 1974 (Electronic Communications) Order 2004 (SI 2004/3236).

*INTERPRETATION*

* * * *

## Arrangements between creditor and supplier

3H–375 **187.**—(1) A consumer credit agreement shall be treated as entered into under pre-existing arrangements between a creditor and a supplier if it is entered into in accordance with, or in furtherance of, arrangements previously made between persons mentioned in subsection (4)(a), (b) or (c).

(2) A consumer credit agreement shall be treated as entered into in contemplation of future arrangements between a creditor and a supplier if it is entered into in the expectation that arrangements will subsequently be made between persons mentioned in subsection (4)(a), (b) or (c) for the supply of cash, goods and services (or any of them) to be financed by the consumer credit agreement.

(3) Arrangements shall be disregarded for the purposes of subsection (1) or (2) if—

(a) they are arrangements for the making, in specified circumstances, of payments to the supplier by the creditor, and

(b) the creditor holds himself out as willing to make, in such circumstances, payments of the kind to suppliers generally.

(3A) Subsections (1) and (2) do not apply to any disclosure of information by the Director to the Bank of England for the purpose of enabling or assisting the Bank to discharge its functions under the Banking Act 1987or the Director to discharge his functions under this Act.

(4) The persons referred to in subsections (1) and (2) are—

(a) the creditor and the supplier;

(b) one of them and an associate of the other's;

(c) an associate of one and an associate of the other's.

(5) Where the creditor is an associate of the supplier's, the consumer credit agreement shall be treated, unless the contrary is proved, as entered into under pre-existing arrangements between the creditor and the supplier.

*Note* —Amended by the Banking Act 1987 s.89. 3H–376

**Arrangements between creditor and supplier**

See commentary to s.12. 3H–377

*Subsection (1)* —This does not define the only kind of arrangements that are capable of falling within s.12(b). The expression "treated as" was used to extend, rather than restrict, the scope of that section: *OFT v Lloyds Bank TSB* [2006] EWCA Civ 268; [2007] Q.B. 1, at para.65.

## Definition of 'default sum'

**187A.**—(1) In this Act 'default sum' means, in relation to the debtor or hirer under a regulated agreement, a sum (other than a sum of interest) which is payable by him under the agreement in connection with a breach of the agreement by him. 3H–378

(2) But a sum is not a default sum in relation to the debtor or hirer simply because, as a consequence of his breach of the agreement, he is required to pay it earlier than he would otherwise have had to.

*Note* —Inserted by the Consumer Credit Act 2006 s.18. 3H–379

**Default sum**

A repayment which the debtor has failed to pay under the agreement and in respect of which the debtor is thus in arrears is not a "default sum". A default sum is a sum which only becomes due because the debtor has defaulted, e.g. a fee payable by a debtor for late payment of an instalment or for exceeding his credit card limit. 3H–380

See ss.86E and 86F above regarding (a) the notice required to be given when a default sum has become due and (b) interest on default sums.

*Subsection (2)* —A payment falling due earlier than it otherwise would have done, e.g. under an accelerated payments clause is not a default sum. 3H–381

**For ss.188 to 191 of and Sch.2 to the Consumer Credit Act 1974 (see Arrangement) plus any related commentary see paragraphs 3H–382+ to 3H–415+ on White Book on Westlaw UK or the Civil Procedure CD.**

***Paragraph numbers marked with a "+" can be found online and on CD.***

## Consumer Credit (Total Charge for Credit) Regulations 1980

3H–416 (S.I. 1980 No. 51)

ARRANGEMENT OF REGULATIONS



**Paragraph numbers marked with a "+" denote content that is available on White Book on WestlawUK or the Civil Procedure CD.**

## Consumer Credit (Agreements) Regulations 1983

3H–462 (S.I. 1983 No. 1553)

ARRANGEMENT OF REGULATIONS



***Paragraph numbers marked with a "+" can be found online and on CD.***

**Paragraph numbers marked with a "+" denote content that is available on White Book on Westlaw UK or the Civil Procedure CD.**

# The Consumer Credit (Exempt Agreements) Order 1989

(S.I. 1989 No. 869)

**For The Consumer Credit (Exempt Agreements) Order 1989 see paragraphs 3H–499+ to 3H–516+ on White Book on Westlaw UK or the Civil Procedure CD.** **3H–498**

# Misrepresentation Act 1967

(1967 c.7) **3H–517**

ARRANGEMENT OF SECTIONS



**Paragraph numbers marked with a "+" denote content that is available on White Book on Westlaw UK or the Civil Procedure CD.**

# Supply of Goods (Implied Terms) Act 1973

(1973 c.13) **3H–526**

ARRANGEMENT OF SECTIONS



**Paragraph numbers marked with a "+" denote content that is available on White Book on Westlaw UK or the Civil Procedure CD.**

### General note

The only sections of this Act remaining unrepealed are s.14 and those sections relating to the terms as to title, description, satisfactory quality, fitness for purpose, and sample which are implied in hire-purchase contracts. The sections that imply these terms in hire-purchase agreements are s.8 (title), s.9 (description), s.10 (satisfactory quality and fitness for purpose) and s.11 (sample). These implied terms are word for word the same as the equivalent sections (12–15) of the Sale of Goods Act 1979 (*q.v.*) except for necessary changes of wording to adapt the provisions to apply to hire-purchase agreements. Thus, instead of "seller" and "buyer" the terms "creditor" and **3H–527** "debtor" are used to describe the parties. These are the same terms as used by the Consumer Credit Act 1974 to describe the parties to a hire-purchase agreement. The terms implied by the Supply of Goods (Implied Terms) Act 1973 are implied into all hire-purchase agreements, not just those which are regulated by the Consumer Credit Act 1974.

**Exclusion of liability**

**3H–528** The statutory restrictions on excluding liability for breach of these terms are exactly the same as they are in relation to the implied terms in ss.12–15 of the Sale of Goods Act 1979 (see, in particular, the Unfair Contract Terms Act 1977 s.6).

**Remedies**

**3H–529** The same terms are conditions as are the equivalent implied terms in ss.12–15 of the Sale of Goods Act 1979. As with a contract of sale of goods, a breach of one of these conditions entitles the debtor to reject the goods. In sale of goods a buyer who is not "dealing as a consumer" has no right to reject the goods for breach of the implied conditions if the breach is so slight that it would be unreasonable to reject the goods (Sale of Goods Act 1979 s.15A). The position is exactly the same under the Supply of Goods (Implied Terms) Act 1973 for a debtor who is not "dealing as a consumer" (s.11A). One small difference in the law, however, is that the sale of goods doctrine that the right of rejection is lost by "acceptance" (within the meaning of the Sale of Goods Act 1979 s.35) does not apply to hire-purchase agreements. The difference is small because the debtor under a hire-purchase agreement is subject to the doctrine of affirmation whereby he loses any right of rejection he may have when he affirms the contract (*U.C.B. Leasing Ltd v Holtom* [1987] C.C.L.R. 101; [1987] R.T.R. 82, CA). See also *Feldaroll Foundry Plc v Hermes Leasing (London) Ltd* [2004] EWCA Civ 747; [2004] C.C.L.R. 8.

In relation to remedies, the law relating to conditional sale agreements is exactly as just explained in relation to hire-purchase agreements. That is the effect of s.14, which, in relation to conditional sale agreements, disapplies s.11(4) of the Sale of Goods Act 1979.

**For ss.8 to 11A and 14 to 15 of Supply of Goods (Implied Terms) Act 1973 (see Arrangement) plus any related commentary see paragraph 3H–530+ to 3H–545+ on White Book on Westlaw UK or the Civil Procedure CD.**

## Unfair Contract Terms Act 1977

**3H–546** (1977 c.50)

ARRANGEMENT OF SECTIONS

PART I

*INTRODUCTORY*



***Paragraph numbers marked with a "+" can be found online and on CD.***

**Introductory note**

This Act implemented, with some modifications, the recommendations in the Second Report on Exemption Clauses of the Law Commissions (Law. Com. No.69; Scot. Law Com. No.39). The Act does not apply to all contract terms, but only to those which purport to exempt or limit the liability of one of the parties to the contract. It restricts the ability of the parties to exclude or limit liability for: breach of contract, negligence or misrepresentation. It also restricts the exclusion of tortious liability by non-contractual notices. For legislation which applies to other contractual terms which are unfair: see the Unfair Terms in Consumer Contracts Regulations 1999 (below) and (in relation to unfair creditor/debtor relationships) the Consumer Credit Act 1974 ss.140A to 140C. Hitherto the privity of contract rule meant that generally speaking, a third party (X) could not rely upon a contractual exclusion clause in a contract between A and B, *Scruttons v Midland Silicones* [1962] A.C. 446. In such a case the provisions of the Unfair Contract Terms Act 1977 were irrelevant. The Contracts (Rights of Third Parties) Act 1999 has (subject to some exceptions) removed the inability of a third party to rely upon an exclusion clause where the clause was intended by the parties to benefit the third party and the third party was identified by name, class or description. In that case, the Unfair Contract Terms Act 1977 may then operate to restrict the effectiveness of the clause. A clause which is not affected by this Act may be rendered ineffective by the Unfair Terms in Consumer Contracts Regulations 1999 (see para.3H–886 below). 3H–547

# PART I

## *INTRODUCTORY*

### Scope of Part I

**1.**—(1) For the purposes of this Part of this Act, "negligence" means the breach— 3H–548

(a) of any obligation, arising from the express or implied terms of a contract, to take reasonable care or exercise reasonable skill in the performance of the contract;

(b) of any common law duty to take reasonable care or exercise reasonable skill (but not any stricter duty);

(c) of the common duty of care imposed by the Occupiers' Liability Act 1957 or the Occupiers' Liability Act (Northern Ireland) 1957.

(2) This Part of this Act is subject to Part III; and in relation to contracts, the operation of sections 2 to 4 and 7 is subject to the exceptions made by Schedule 1.

(3) In the case of both contract and tort, sections 2 to 7 apply (except where the contrary is stated in section 6(4)) only to business liability, that is liability for breach of obligations or duties arising—

(a) from things done or to be done by a person in the course of a business (whether his own business or another's); or

(b) from the occupation of premises used for business purposes of the occupier;

*Paragraph numbers marked with a "+" can be found online and on CD.*

and references to liability are to be read accordingly, but liability of an occupier of premises for breach of an obligation or duty towards a person obtaining access to the premises for recreational or educational purposes, being liability for loss or damage suffered by reason of the dangerous state of the premises, is not a business liability of the occupier unless granting that person such access for the purposes concerned falls within the business purposes of the occupier.

(4) In relation to any breach of duty or obligation, it is immaterial for any purpose of this Part of this Act whether the breach was inadvertent or intentional, or whether liability for it arises directly or vicariously.

3H–549 *Note*—Amended by the Occupiers' Liability Act 1984 s.2.

*Scope of Part I*

3H–550 *Subsection (2)*—The effect of Pt III is that the Act does not apply to: international supply contracts where possession or ownership of goods is to pass (s.26); foreign contracts where the parties have chosen English Law as the applicable law (s.27); exemption clauses allowed by UK legislation implementing international conventions (ss.28 and 29); and, contracts within Sch.1, para.1 of the Act. The latter include: insurance contracts; land transactions; formation and dissolution of companies; securities transactions. A contract of employment, which excluded the employer's liability for the employee's loss of share option rights in the event that the employee was wrongfully dismissed, related to the creation or transfer of securities (share option rights) and to that extent was outside the scope of the Act, *Micklefield v S.A.C. Technology Ltd* [1990] 1 W.L.R. 1002. Except in favour of a person dealing as a consumer, the Act, apart from s.2(1), does not apply to charterparties, marine salvage, contracts of carriage by ship or hovercraft (Sch.1, para.2).

3H–551 *Subsection (3)*—the expression "in the course of a business" has been held to have a restricted meaning in s.12. Even if that is correct in relation to s.12, it seems more likely that the expression here includes any transaction made by a business, whether or not such a transaction was the regular trade of that business. See the commentary to s.12.

*AVOIDANCE OF LIABILITY FOR NEGLIGENCE, BREACH OF CONTRACTS, ETC.*

## Negligence liability

3H–552 **2.**—(1) A person cannot by reference to any contract term or to a notice given to persons generally or to particular persons exclude or restrict his liability for death or personal injury resulting from negligence.

(2) In the case of other loss or damage, a person cannot so exclude or restrict his liability for negligence except in so far as the term or notice satisfies the requirement of reasonableness.

(3) Where a contract term or notice purports to exclude or restrict liability for negligence a person's agreement to or awareness of it is not of itself to be taken as indicating his voluntary acceptance of any risk.

*Negligence liability*

3H–553 *Subsection (1)*—Two cases both concerned the same standard clause in a contract to hire a crane and driver. The clause provided that as between supplier and hirer, the driver would be regarded for all purposes as employee of the hirer. In *Phillips Products Ltd v Hyland* [1987] 1 W.L.R. 659 where the negligent driver drove the crane into a building belonging to the hirer, thereby damaging it, the hirer was the victim and claimed damages from the supplier for the negligence of the supplier's employee. The hirer succeeded in having the clause declared ineffective under subs.(2) as not satisfying the test of reasonableness. This case was distinguished in *Thomson v T. Lohan (Plant Hire) Ltd* [1987] 1 W.L.R. 649 where the driver brought a claim (successfully) against one employer (the hirer) for his injuries and the hirer sought to recover contribution from the supplier. The supplier was able to rely on the clause, since a clause which does not restrict the victim's ability to bring a claim but which merely apportions or allocates liability between potential defendants is not affected by s.2.

*Subsection (2)*—For the requirement of reasonableness, see s.11. Even if a term satisfied the requirement of reasonableness, it would still be ineffective to exclude liability for negligence if either (a) it was not incorporated into the contract or (b) as a matter of construction, it does not operate to exclude liability for negligence or the loss in question. The language may not be sufficiently plain to exclude liability for negligence, *Hollier v Rambler Motors* [1972] 2 Q.B. 71. A disclaimer by a professional valuer giving a valuation of a house to a prospective lender and foreseeably relied upon by the borrower/buyer has been held invalid under this provision, *Smith v Eric S. Bush* [1990] 1 A.C. 381. **3H–554**

## Liability arising in contract

**3.**—(1) This section applies as between contracting parties where one of them deals as consumer or on the other's written standard terms of business. **3H–555**

(2) As against that party, the other cannot by reference to any contract term—

(a) when himself in breach of contract, exclude or restrict any liability of his in respect of the breach; or

(b) claim to be entitled—

(i) to render a contractual performance substantially different from that which was reasonably expected of him, or

(ii) in respect of the whole or any part of his contractual obligation, to render no performance at all,

except in so far as (in any of the cases mentioned above in this subsection) the contract term satisfies the requirement of reasonableness.

### Liability arising in contract

For the requirement of reasonableness, see s.11. For "deals as a consumer" see s.12. There is no definition of "standard terms of business". It certainly includes both (i) clauses prepared by a trade association or similar body for use generally in the trade and (ii) those prepared just by an individual contractor with no particular contract in mind. **3H–556**

## Unreasonable indemnity clauses

**4.**—(1) A person dealing as consumer cannot by reference to any contract term be made to indemnify another person (whether a party to the contract or not) in respect of liability that may be incurred by the other for negligence or breach of contract, except in so far as the contract term satisfies the requirement of reasonableness. **3H–557**

(2) This section applies whether the liability in question—

***Paragraph numbers marked with a "+" can be found online and on CD.***

(a) is directly that of the person to be indemnified or is incurred by him vicariously:

(b) is to the person dealing as consumer or to someone else.

*LIABILITY ARISING FROM SALE OR SUPPLY OF GOODS*

### "Guarantee" of consumer goods

3H–558 **5.**—(1) In the case of goods of a type ordinarily supplied for private use or consumption, where loss or damage—

(a) arises from the goods proving defective while in consumer use; and

(b) results from the negligence of a person concerned the manufacture or distribution of the goods,

liability for the loss or damage cannot be excluded or restricted by reference to any contract term or notice contained in or operating by reference to a guarantee of the goods.

(2) For these purposes—

(a) goods are to be regarded as "in consumer use" when a person is using them, or has them in his possession for use, otherwise than exclusively for the purposes of a business; and

(b) anything in writing is a guarantee if it contains or purports to contain some promise or assurance (however worded or presented) that defects will be made good by complete or partial replacement, or by repair, monetary compensation or otherwise.

(3) This section does not apply as between the parties to a contract under or in pursuance of which possession or ownership of the goods passed.

### Sale and hire-purchase

3H–559 **6.**—(1) Liability for breach of the obligations arising from—

(a) section 12 of the Sale of Goods Act 1979 (seller's implied undertakings as to title, etc.);

(b) section 8 of the Supply of Goods (Implied Terms) Act 1973 (the corresponding thing in relation to hire-purchase),

cannot be excluded or restricted by reference to any contract term.

(2) As against *a* person dealing as consumer, liability for breach of the obligations arising from—

(a) section 13, 14 or 15 of the 1979 Act (seller's implied undertakings as to conformity of goods with description or sample, or as to their quality or fitness for a particular purpose);

(b) section 9, 10 or 11 of the 1973 Act (the corresponding things in relation to hire-purchase),

cannot be excluded or restricted by reference to any contract term.

(3) As against a person dealing otherwise than as consumer, the liability specified in subsection (2) above can be excluded or restricted by reference to a contract term, but only in so far as the term satisfies the requirement of reasonableness.

(4) The liabilities referred to in this section are not only the business liabilities defined by section 1(3), but include those arising under any contract of sale of goods or hire-purchase agreement.

*Note* —Amended by the Sale of Goods Act 1979 s.63(2) and Sch.2. **3H–560**

**Sale and hire-purchase**

This section restates provisions previously stated in the Sale of Goods Act 1893 s.55 as amended by the Supply of Goods (Implied Terms) Act 1973 and in the 1973 Act itself. For "dealing as a consumer", see s.12. For "requirement of reasonableness", see s.11 and Sch.2. **3H–561**

## Miscellaneous contracts under which goods pass

**7.**—(1) Where the possession or ownership of goods passes under or in pursuance of a contract not governed by the law of sale of goods or hire-purchase, subsections (2) to (4) below apply as regards the effect (if any) to be given to contract terms excluding or restricting liability for breach of obligation arising by implication of law from the nature of the contract. **3H–562**

(2) As against a person dealing as consumer, liability in respect of the goods' correspondence with description or sample, or their quality or fitness for any particular purpose, cannot be excluded or restricted by reference to any such term.

(3) As against a person dealing otherwise than as consumer, that liability can be excluded or restricted by reference to such a term, but only in so far as the term satisfies the requirement of reasonableness.

(3A) Liability for breach of the obligations arising under section 2 of the Supply of Goods and Services Act 1982 (implied terms about title etc. in certain contracts for the transfer of the property in goods) cannot be excluded or restricted by references to any such term.

(4) Liability in respect of—

(a) the right to transfer ownership of the goods, or give possession; or

(b) the assurance of quiet possession to a person taking goods in pursuance of the contract, cannot (in a case to which subsection (3A) above does not apply) be excluded or restricted by reference to any such term except in so far as the term satisfies the requirement of reasonableness.

*Note* —Amended, and subs.(3A) added, by the Supply of Goods and Services Act 1982 s.17; subs.(5) repealed by The Regulatory Reform (Trading Stamps) Order 2005 (SI 2005/871). **3H–563**

**Miscellaneous contracts**

The principal examples of contracts capable of falling within subs.(1) are: contracts of barter or exchange, contracts for services which involve the supply of goods; contracts of hire. See further, the commentary to the Sale of Goods Act 1979 s.2 (below). **3H–564**

***Paragraph numbers marked with a "+" can be found online and on CD.***

## Misrepresentation

3H–565 **8.**—(1) In the Misrepresentation Act 1967, the following is substituted for section 3— "Avoidance of provision excluding liability for misrepresentation

3. If a contract contains a term which would exclude or restrict—

(a) any liability to which a party to a contract may be subject by reason of any misrepresentation made by him before the contract was made; or

(b) any remedy available to another party to the contract by reason of such a misrepresentation,

the term shall be of no effect except in so far as it satisfies the requirement of reasonableness as stated in section 11(1) of the Unfair Contract Terms Act 1977; and it is for those claiming that the term satisfies that requirement to show that it does"

(2) The same section is substituted for section 3 of the Misrepresentation Act (Northern Ireland) 1967.

#### Misrepresentation

3H–566 This section does not in any way qualify the right of a principal to limit the authority (actual or ostensible) of his agent, *Overbrooke Estates v Glencombe Park Properties* [1974] 1 W.L.R. 1335.

## Effect of breach

3H–567 **9.**—(1) Where for reliance upon it a contract term has to satisfy the requirement of reasonableness, it may be found to do so and be given effect accordingly notwithstanding that the contract has been terminated either by breach or by a party electing to treat it as repudiated.

(2) Where on a breach the contract is nevertheless affirmed by a party entitled to treat it as repudiated, this does not of itself exclude the requirement of reasonableness in relation to any contract term.

#### Effect of breach

3H–568 If an exemption clause (a) is properly incorporated into the contract, (b), as a matter of construction, covers the breach in question and, (c) satisfies the requirement of reasonableness, then it may be relied upon notwithstanding the termination of the contract.

## Evasion by means of secondary contract

3H–569 **10.** A person is not bound by any contract term prejudicing or taking away rights of his which arise under, or in connection with the performance of, another contract, so far as those rights extend to the enforcement of another's liability which this Part of this Act prevents that other from excluding or restricting.

#### Evasion by secondary contract

3H–570 This section applies only to clauses in a contract which seek to modify or exempt future liability and does not affect retrospective waivers of existing claims, *Tudor Grange Holdings Ltd v Citibank NA* [1992] Ch 53.

## The "reasonableness" test

**11.**—(1) In relation to a contract term, the requirement of reasonableness for the purposes of this Part of this Act, section 3 of the Misrepresentation Act 1967 and section 3 of the Misrepresentation Act (Northern Ireland) 1967 is that the term shall have been a fair and reasonable one to be included having regard to the circumstances which were, or ought reasonably to have been, known to or in the contemplation of the parties when the contract was made. **3H–571**

(2) In determining for the purposes of section 6 or 7 above whether a contract term satisfies the requirement of reasonableness, regard shall be had in particular to the matters specified in Schedule 2 to this Act; but this subsection does not prevent the court or arbitrator from holding, in accordance with any rule of law, that a term which purports to exclude or restrict any relevant liability is not a term of the contract.

(3) In relation to a notice (not being a notice having contractual effect), the requirement of reasonableness under this Act is that it should be fair and reasonable to allow reliance on it, having regard to all the circumstances obtaining when the liability arose or (but for the notice) would have arisen.

(4) Where by reference to a contract term or notice a person seeks to restrict liability to a specified sum of money, and the question arises (under this or any other Act) whether the term or notice satisfies the requirement of reasonableness, regard shall be had in particular (but without prejudice to subsection (2) above in the case of contract terms) to—

(a) the resources which he could expect to be available to him for the purpose of meeting the liability should it arise; and

(b) how far it was open to him to cover himself by insurance.

(5) It is for those claiming that a contract term or notice satisfies the requirement of reasonableness to show that it does.

### The reasonableness test

In applying the test, the courts have to weigh relevant factors. When applying it for the purposes of ss.6 and 7 the court is given guidelines in Sch.2. These, however, are not exhaustive of the factors to be taken into account. The judge's task in weighing the various factors is akin to the exercise of a discretion and his decision on the issue of reasonableness will not be disturbed by an appellate court unless it proceeded on some erroneous principle or was plainly and obviously wrong, *Mitchell (George) v Finney Lock Seeds* [1983] 2 A.C. 803. In that case, a contract by which a farmer bought some seeds contained a clause limiting the liability of the sellers to no more than the purchase price of the seeds. The wrong seeds were supplied and the farmer's crop consequently failed. It was held in the House of Lords that the clause did not satisfy the test of reasonableness bearing in mind, inter alia, the following: (i) it had not been negotiated by any representative body; (ii) the buyers could not have discovered the error until after the crop had been sown; (iii) the buyers could not reasonably have been expected to cover the risk (of crop failure) by insurance whereas the sellers could easily, and at modest cost, have obtained liability insurance. An international computer firm's standard term limiting the firm's liability to a maximum of £100,000 has been held unreasonable, *St Albans DC v I.C.L. Ltd* [1996] 4 All E.R. 481, relevant factors including: (i) the parties were of unequal bargaining power; (ii) the limit of £100,000 was small in relation to the potential risk; (iii) the defendants held an aggregate of £50M of insurance cover world wide; (iv) the defendants were in a better position to insure. In as- **3H–572**

***Paragraph numbers marked with a "+" can be found online and on CD.***

sessing the reasonableness of a clause the court must consider the whole scope of the clause and not just that part upon which the defendant seeks to rely, *Stewart Gill Ltd v Horatio Myer & Co Ltd* [1992] Q.B. 600. In principle, a standard form clause which removes one party's right of set-off is subject to the requirement of reasonableness by virtue of s.3 as extended by s.13. Whether it will satisfy the requirement may depend upon whether the clause contains a further limitation of liability. In *Overland Shoes Ltd v Schenkers Ltd* [1998] 1 Lloyd's Rep. 498, a clause of the British International Freight Association which provided that customers must make prompt payment "without reduction or deferment on account of any claim, counterclaim or set-off" was held to satisfy the requirement. It had been drafted following wide consultation in the industry, was in common use, having been accepted by the trade as fair and reasonable and it merely defined the method of resolving competing claims, rather than seeking to limit liability. For more cases on the reasonableness test, see commentary to the Guidelines in Sch.2 below.

## "Dealing as consumer"

**3H-573** **12.**—(1) A party to a contract "deals as consumer" in relation to another party if—

(a) he neither makes the contract in the course of a business nor holds himself out as doing so; and

(b) the other party does make the contract in the course of a business; and

(c) in the case of a contract governed by the law of sale of goods or hire-purchase, or by section 7 of this Act, the goods passing under or in pursuance of the contract are of a type ordinarily supplied for private use or consumption.

(1A) But if the first party mentioned in subsection (1) is an individual paragraph (c) of that subsection must be ignored.

(2) But the buyer is not in any circumstances to be regarded as dealing as consumer—

(a) if he is an individual and the goods are second hand goods sold at public auction at which individuals have the opportunity of attending the sale in person;

(b) if he is not an individual and the goods are sold by auction or by competitive tender.

**3H-574** *Note*—Amended, and subs.(1A) added, by the Sale and Supply of Goods to Consumers Regulations 2002 (SI 2002/3045).

### In the course of a business

**3H-575** Where a business buys something in which it deals (e.g. a butcher buying meat) that is clearly a purchase in the course of a business. Where, however, a business buys something which is incidental to its business (e.g. the butcher buys a car for his business), then it has been held that the purchase is not "in the course of a business" unless the business makes such transactions regularly—two or three times in five years being insufficiently regular—*R & B Customs Brokers Co Ltd v United Dominions Trust* [1988] 1 W.L.R. 321. This decision seemed very doubtful in the light of the reasoning and the decision in *Stevenson v Rogers* [1999] Q.B. 1028, see commentary to Sale of Goods Act 1979 s.14. It was nevertheless followed and applied by the Court of Appeal in *Feldaroll Foundry Plc v Hermes Leasing (London) Ltd* [2004] EWCA Civ 747; [2004] C.C.L.R. 8. The amendments effected by the Sale and Supply of Goods to Consumers Regulations 2002 brought the definition of "dealing as a consumer" as it applies to non-corporate customers into line with the Directive on Certain Aspects of Sale of Goods and Consumer Guarantees (1999/3). See the Sale of Goods Act 1979 ss.14(2D) and 48A and commentaries, below.

## Varieties of exemption clause

**13.**—(1) To the extent that this Part of this Act prevents the exclusion or restriction of any liability it also prevents— **3H–576**

(a) making the liability or its enforcement subject to restrictive or onerous conditions;

(b) excluding or restricting any right or remedy in respect of the liability, or subjecting a person to any prejudice in consequence of his pursuing any such right or remedy;

(c) excluding or restricting rules of evidence or procedure;

and (to that extent) sections 2 and 5 to 7 also prevent excluding or restricting liability by reference to terms and notices which exclude or restrict the relevant obligation or duty.

(2) But an agreement in writing to submit present or future differences to arbitration is not to be treated under this Part of this Act as excluding or restricting any liability.

#### Varieties of exemption clause

A clause which removes one party's right of set-off is a clause which excludes or restricts a right or remedy, see commentary to s.11 above. **3H–577**

## Interpretation of Part I

**14.** In this Part of this Act— **3H–578**

"business" includes a profession and the activities of any government department or local or public authority;

"goods" has the same meaning as in the Sale of Goods Act 1979;

"hire-purchase agreement" has the same meaning as in the Consumer Credit Act 1974;

"negligence" had the meaning given by section 1(1);

"notice" includes an announcement, whether or not in writing, and any other communication or pretended communication; and

"personal injury" includes any disease and any impairment of physical or mental condition.

*Note* —Amended by the Sale of Goods Act 1979 s.63(2) and Sch.2. **3H–579**

* * * * *

## SCHEDULES
## SCHEDULE 2

"GUIDELINES" FOR APPLICATION OF REASONABLENESS TEST **3H–580**

The matters to which regard is to be had in particular for the purposes of sections 6(3), 7(3) and (4), 20 and 21 are any of the following which appear to be relevant—

(a) the strength of the bargaining positions of the parties relative to each other, taking into account (among other things) alternative means by which the customer's requirements could have been met;

(b) whether the customer received an inducement to agree to the term, or in accepting it had an opportunity of entering into a similar contract with other persons, but without having to accept a similar term;

(c) whether the customer knew or ought reasonably to have known of the existence and extent of the term (having regard, among other things, to any custom of the trade and any previous course of dealing between the parties);

***Paragraph numbers marked with a "+" can be found online and on CD.***

(d) where the term excludes or restricts any relevant liability if some condition is not complied with, whether it was reasonable at the time of the contract to expect that compliance with that condition would be practicable;

(e) whether the goods were manufactured, processed or adapted to the special order of the customer.

### Guidelines for Application of Reasonableness Test

3H–581 An exclusion clause may well be incorporated into the contract by virtue of being part of the small print on a standard form contract of one of the parties. The other party, typically a buyer, may not be aware of its existence or extent, e.g. may not have read the form or may not have understood it fully before signing it. Paragraph (c) of the Guidelines does not equate the position of a party who knows of the existence of an exclusion clause with a party who "ought to have known" of its existence: *Britvic Soft Drinks Ltd v Messer UK Ltd* [2002] 2 Lloyd's Rep. 368; [2002] EWCA Civ 548. A clause of which the buyer was unaware and which purported to exclude liability for lack of satisfactory quality or fitness for purpose in a contract to sell an ingredient for use in making soft drinks failed the test in *Britvic*. Where, on the other hand, the buyer was aware of and had succeeded in getting amended (albeit not substantially) a clause excluding liability for consequential loss in a contract to supply software (which is notoriously liable to present problems), the clause was held to pass the test: *Watford Electronics Ltd v Sanderson CFL Ltd* [2001] 1 All E.R. (Comm) 696 and see also *SAM Business Systems Ltd v Hedley & Co* [2002] EWHC 2733; [2003] 1 All E.R.(Comm) 465.

## Sale of Goods Act 1979

3H–582 (1979 c.54)

ARRANGEMENT OF SECTIONS

PART I



***Paragraph numbers marked with a "+" can be found online and on CD.***

***Paragraph numbers marked with a "+" can be found online and on CD.***

**Paragraph numbers marked with a "+" denote content that is available on White Book on Westlaw UK or the Civil Procedure CD.**

**For s.1 of the Sale of Goods Act 1979 (see Arrangement) plus any related commentary see paragraph 3H–583+ on White Book on Westlaw UK or the Civil Procedure CD.**

## Contract of sale

**3H–584** **2.**—(1) A contract of sale of goods is a contract by which the seller transfers or agrees to transfer the property in goods to the buyer for a money consideration, called the price.

(2) There may be a contract of sale between one part owner and another.

(3) A contract of sale may be absolute or conditional.

(4) Where under a contract of sale the property in the goods is transferred from the seller to the buyer the contract is called a sale.

(5) Where under a contract of sale the transfer of the property in the goods is to take place at a future time or subject to some condition later to be fulfilled the contract is called an agreement to sell.

(6) An agreement to sell becomes a sale when the time elapses or the conditions are fulfilled subject to which the property in the goods is to be transferred.

### Contracts of sale of goods

**3H–585** Into contracts which are not contracts of sale of goods but which are analogous, terms are implied relating to goods supplied under the contract which terms are very similar to those implied in sale of goods contracts by ss.12–15 of the Sale of Goods Act. Those analogous contracts and the related implied terms provisions are as follows: hire-purchase agreements (Supply of Goods (Implied Terms) Act 1973 ss.8– 11); contracts of barter and contracts for services which involve the passing of property in goods (Supply of Goods and Services Act 1982 ss.2– 5A); contracts of hire (Supply of Goods and Services Act 1982 ss.6– 10A). Where under a contract no property in goods transfers and no goods are hired, it is possible that nevertheless goods are consumed in the course of providing a service to the customer—e.g. shampoo used in washing hair. In that case the common law may imply terms as to quality similar to those implied by statute in the above mentioned contracts, *Ingham v Emes* [1955] 2 Q.B. 366. A contract to supply computer software on disk is a sale of goods contract, whereas a contract to supply computer software in purely intangible form is not; in the latter case the court will be prepared to imply a term at common law that the software will be reasonably fit for its intended purpose, *St Albans DC v ICL* [1996] 4 All E.R. 481, CA.

**For ss.3 to 10 of the Sale of Goods Act 1979 (see Arrangement) plus any related commentary see paragraphs 3H–586+ to 3H–596+ on White Book on Westlaw UK or the Civil Procedure CD.**

***Paragraph numbers marked with a "+" can be found online and on CD.***

## When condition to be treated as warranty

**11.**—(1) This section does not apply to Scotland. **3H–597**

(2)Where a contract of sale is subject to a condition to be fulfilled by the seller, the buyer may waive the condition, or may elect to treat the breach of the condition as a breach of warranty and not as a ground for treating the contract as repudiated.

(3)Whether a stipulation in a contract of sale is a condition, the breach of which may give rise to a right to treat the contract as repudiated, or a warranty, the breach of which may give rise to a claim for damages but not to a right to reject the goods and treat the contract as repudiated, depends in each case on the construction of the contract; and a stipulation may be a condition, though called a warranty in the contract.

(4)Subject to section 35A below where a contract of sale is not severable and the buyer has accepted the goods or part of them, the breach of a condition to be fulfilled by the seller can only be treated as a breach of warranty, and not as a ground for rejecting the goods and treating the contract as repudiated, unless there is an express or implied term of the contract to that effect.

(5)[...]

(6)Nothing in this section affects a condition or warranty whose fulfilment is excused by law by reason of impossibility or otherwise.

(7)Paragraph 2 of Schedule 1 below applies in relation to a contract made before 22 April 1967 or (in the application of this Act to Northern Ireland) 28 July 1967.

*Note* —Subsection (1) substituted, subs.(4) amended and subs.(5) repealed by the Sale and Supply of Goods Act 1994 ss.3(2), 7, Sch.2, para.5(2), Sch.3. **3H–598**

For "acceptance" and the loss of right of rejection see ss.35 and 35A and commentaries, below.

### Conditional sale agreements

Subsection (4) does not—and thus the doctrine of "acceptance" does not—apply to a conditional sale agreement where the buyer deals as a consumer within s.12 of the Unfair Contract Terms Act 1977 (i.e. irrespective of whether the conditional sale agreement is regulated by the Consumer Credit Act 1974). In such a case the buyer's right to reject goods for breach of a condition is not lost by his "acceptance" but may be lost, as in the case of a hire-purchase agreement, by his affirmation of the contract. That is the effect of s.14 of the Supply of Goods (Implied Terms) Act 1973. **3H–599**

## Implied terms about title, etc

**12.**—(1) In a contract of sale, other than one to which subsection (3) below applies, there is an implied term on the part of the seller that in the case of a sale he has a right to sell the goods, and in the case of an agreement to sell he will have such a right at the time when the property is to pass. **3H–600**

(2) In a contract of sale, other than one to which subsection (3) below applies, there is also an implied term that—

(a) the goods are free, and will remain free until the time when the property is to pass, from any charge or encumbrance not disclosed or known to the buyer before the contract is made, and

***Paragraph numbers marked with a "+" can be found online and on CD.***

(b) the buyer will enjoy quiet possession of the goods except so far as it may be disturbed by the owner or other person entitled to the benefit of any charge or encumbrance so disclosed or known.

(3) This subsection applies to a contract of sale in the case of which there appears from the contract or is to be inferred from its circumstances an intention that the seller should transfer only such title as he or a third person may have.

(4) In a contract to which subsection (3) above applies there is an implied term that all charges or encumbrances known to the seller and not known to the buyer have been disclosed to the buyer before the contract is made.

(5) In a contract to which subsection (3) above applies there is also an implied term that none of the following will disturb the buyer's quiet possession of the goods, namely—

(a) the seller;

(b) in a case where the parties to the contract intend that the seller should transfer only such title as a third person may have, that person;

(c) anyone claiming through or under the seller or that third person otherwise than under a charge or encumbrance disclosed or known to the buyer before the contract is made.

(5A) As regards England and Wales and Northern Ireland, the term implied by subsection (1) above is a condition and the terms implied by subsections (2), (4) and (5) above are warranties.

(6) Paragraph 3 of Schedule 1below applies in relation to a contract made before 18 May 1973.

**3H-601** *Note*—Subsections (1), (2), (4), (5) amended and subs.(5A) inserted by the Sale and Supply of Goods Act 1994 s.7, Sch.2, para.5(3).

**Title to goods**

**3H-602** The classic example of a breach of the condition in s.12(1) is where the seller is not the owner and does not have the owner's authority to sell the goods. It makes no difference whether the seller knows that he is not the owner. He may honestly believe himself to be the owner (e.g. having in all innocence "bought" the goods from someone who had stolen them from the true owner). He is still in breach of this condition. It may be that the buyer does not discover until some months later that the seller was not the owner of the goods. If he then rejects the goods for breach of this condition, he is entitled to recover the whole of the purchase price as being money had and received on a total failure of consideration, *Rowland v Divall* [1923] 2 K.B. 500. This is so notwithstanding that the buyer has had the enjoyment of the goods for several months. The position is exactly the same where the contract is not a contract of sale of goods but one of hire-purchase, *Warman v Southern Counties Finance* [1949] 2 K.B. 576 (approved in *Barber v N.W.S. Bank* [1996] 1 W.L.R. 641, CA). For the corresponding condition as to title in contracts of hire-purchase, see Supply of Goods (Implied Terms) Act 1973 s.8.

The buyer's right to reject the goods for breach of the condition in s.12(1) is, apparently, not lost by his "acceptance" of the goods within the meaning of s.35. It will be lost, however, if the title is "fed" to him, *Butterworth v Kingsway Motors* [1954] 1 W.L.R. 1286. This typically occurs where the buyer buys goods from someone who acquired them on hire-purchase or conditional sale terms and who at the time of the sale has not become the owner (i.e. because he has not completed his instalment payments under the hire-purchase or conditional sale agreement). Here the seller is in breach of

***Paragraph numbers marked with a "+" can be found online and on CD.***

the implied condition as to title. If, however, at some later stage he completes his instalment payments, then the seller will at that moment acquire title which automatically and immediately will be fed to his buyer. If at that moment the buyer has not already rejected the goods, then he loses that right. He does, however, have a claim for damages (see s.53(1)) and the prima facie measure of damages will be the difference between the value of the goods at the time when the buyer should have acquired good title and their (lower) value at the time he did acquire good title, *Butterworth v Kingsway Motors* (above).

Normally, someone who sells goods which he does not own (and who does not have the owner's authority to sell) cannot transfer title to the buyer. *Nemo dat quod non habet*—a seller cannot give a good title which he does not himself have (Sale of Goods Act 1979 s.21(1)). There are, however, some exceptions to this principle, the main ones being: (i) where the true owner is estopped from asserting that the sale was unauthorised; (ii) where the seller is a mercantile agent in possession of the goods with the consent of the owner, is acting in the ordinary course of business of a mercantile agent and sells the goods to someone who takes in good faith and is unaware that the seller has no authority to make the sale (Factors Act 1889 s.2(1)); (iii) where the seller has a voidable title to the goods and that title has not been avoided at the time of the sale and the seller sells to someone buying in good faith without notice of the seller's defect of title (Sale of Goods Act 1979 s.23); (iv) where the seller is someone who has already sold the goods to someone else but who has retained the goods (or documents of title) and who then sells and delivers them to the buyer who receives them in good faith without notice of the earlier sale (Sale of Goods Act 1979 s.24); (v) where the seller is someone who had agreed to buy the goods and who has taken delivery of them but to whom property (title) has not yet passed and who sells and delivers them (or the documents of title) to a buyer who receives them in good faith and without notice of the rights of the original seller (Sale of Goods Act 1979 s.25). The latter exception (in s.25) does not apply where the contract under which the seller had acquired the goods was a hire-purchase agreement, because in that case the seller is not a "buyer", i.e. someone who has "bought or agreed to buy", *Helby v Matthews* [1895] A.C. 471, *Close Asset Finance v Care Graphics Machinery Ltd* [2000] C.C.L.R. 43. Nor does this exception apply where the contract under which the seller had acquired the goods is a conditional sale agreement which is a consumer credit agreement within the meaning of the Consumer Credit Act 1974 (Sale of Goods Act 1979 s.25(2)).

There is a further exception (in the Hire Purchase Act 1964 s.27) which applies only to the sale of motor vehicles. This applies where the seller is someone who is hiring the vehicle under a hire-purchase agreement or buying it under a conditional sale agreement and who, before he acquires title, sells the vehicle to a "private purchaser" who is bona fide and unaware of any relevant hire-purchase or conditional sale agreement. In that case the innocent private purchaser obtains good title to the vehicle (or, more accurately, such title as belonged to the person from whom the seller had acquired the vehicle on hire-purchase or conditional sale terms). A buyer who is aware only of a hire purchase agreement under which all the payments have been made is still an innocent purchaser (*Barker v Bell* 1 W.L.R. 983) as also is a buyer who originally had suspicions but whose suspicions had at the time he bought the car been laid to rest, *Dodds v Yorkshire Bank Finance Ltd* [1992] C.C.L.R. 92, CA. Someone who is carrying on business in the motor trade (whether as dealer or as finance house) is not a private purchaser—and that is so even if he is buying for his private (and not his business) purposes, *Stevenson v Beverley Bentinck* [1976] 1 W.L.R. 483 and see also *G.E. Capital Bank Ltd v Rushton and Jenking* [2005] EWCA Civ 1556; [2006] 1 W.L.R. 899. Where the purchaser is not a private purchaser and then himself sells the vehicle, then the first private purchaser who buys the vehicle thereafter will, providing he is bona fide and without notice, acquire title by virtue of the Hire Purchase Act 1964 s.27. Notwithstanding that an innocent private purchaser obtains good title to the vehicle by virtue of s.27, he still has the same right to reject the vehicle (and reclaim all money paid) as if s.27 did not apply (*Barber v NWS Bank* [1996] 1 W.L.R. 641). This is because nothing in s.27 exonerates the seller from any liability he would have been under apart from the section (s.27(3)).

*Subsection (2)* —Where the seller supplies goods which involve an infringement of the trade mark rights of a third party, that will amount to a breach of the condition in s.12(1) and also of the warranty of quiet possession, *Niblett Ltd v Confectioners' Materials*

***Paragraph numbers marked with a "+" can be found online and on CD.***

*Co* [1921] 3 K.B. 387. Where after the sale a third party obtained a patent and brought patent proceedings against the buyers to enforce the patent, the sellers were not in breach of the condition in s.12(1) which related to the time of the sale but were in breach of the warranty that "the buyer *will* enjoy quiet possession", *Microbeads v Vinhurst Road Markings* [1975] 1 W.L.R. 218.

*Subsection (3)* —A seller might, for example, acknowledge that he has only a limited title where he has found the goods which he is selling—a finder having only a limited, possessory, title.

#### Exclusion

3H-603 It is not possible to contract out of liability for breach of the undertakings under s.12 where the liability is a business liability, see ss.1(3) and 6(1) of the Unfair Contract Terms Act 1977.

## Sale by description

3H-604 **13.**—(1) Where there is a contract for the sale of goods by description, there is an implied term that the goods will correspond with the description.

(1A) As regards England and Wales and Northern Ireland, the term implied by subsection (1) above is a condition.

(2) If the sale is by sample as well as by description it is not sufficient that the bulk of the goods corresponds with the sample if the goods do not also correspond with the description.

(3) A sale of goods is not prevented from being a sale by description by reason only that, being exposed for sale or hire, they are selected by the buyer.

(4) Paragraph 4 of Schedule 1below applies in relation to a contract made before 18 May 1973.

3H-605 *Note* —Subsection (1) amended and subs.(1A) inserted by the Sale and Supply of Goods Act 1994 s.7, Sch.2, para.5(4).

#### By description

3H-606 It is a sale by description if the item is sold as corresponding to a description and the buyer placed some (but not necessarily exclusive) reliance upon the description, *Grant v Australian Knitting Mills* [1936] A.C. 85; *Beale v Taylor* [1967] 1 W.L.R. 1193. If it is not within the reasonable contemplation of the parties that the buyer is relying on the description, then it is not a sale by description, *Harlingdon & Leinster Enterprises Ltd v Christopher Hull Fine Art Ltd* [1991] 1 Q.B. 564 (painting attributed by seller to a painter of the German impressionist school when both seller and buyer knew that the buyer had, and the seller did not have, expertise and knowledge of the German expressionist school). If some of the goods supplied are outside the contract description, then that amounts to a breach of the condition, *Pinnock Bros. v Lewis & Peat* [1923] 1 K.B. 690 (castor oil included in goods supplied under contract to sell "copra cake"). The fact that the goods are of poor quality does not of itself indicate a failure to correspond with description. The key to the concept of description is "identification", not "quality", *Ashington Piggeries v Hill* [1972] A.C. 441. An expression in the contract which refers to quality (e.g. "fair average quality for the season"), though usually not part of the description and therefore not relevant to a claim under s.13, will nevertheless amount to an express term (albeit probably only a warranty and not a condition) of the contract.

#### Exclusion and remedies

3H-607 For the buyer's rights of rejection and to claim damages, see ss.11, 15A, 35, 35A and 53. For restrictions on the ability to exclude or limit the seller's liability, see Unfair Contract Terms Act 1977 ss.1– 6.

***Paragraph numbers marked with a "+" can be found online and on CD.***

## Implied terms about quality or fitness

**14.**—(1) Except as provided by this section and section 15below and subject to any other enactment, there is no implied term about the quality or fitness for any particular purpose of goods supplied under a contract of sale. 3H–608

(2) Where the seller sells goods in the course of a business, there is an implied term that the goods supplied under the contract are of satisfactory quality.

(2A) For the purposes of this Act, goods are of satisfactory quality if they meet the standard that a reasonable person would regard as satisfactory, taking account of any description of the goods, the price (if relevant) and all the other relevant circumstances.

(2B) For the purposes of this Act, the quality of goods includes their state and condition and the following (among others) are in appropriate cases aspects of the quality of goods—

- (a) fitness for all the purposes for which goods of the kind in question are commonly supplied.
- (b) appearance and finish,
- (c) freedom from minor defects,
- (d) safety, and
- (e) durability.

(2C) The term implied by subsection (2) above does not extend to any matter making the quality of goods unsatisfactory—

- (a) which is specifically drawn to the buyer's attention before the contract is made,
- (b) where the buyer examines the goods before the contract is made, which that examination ought to reveal, or
- (c) in the case of a contract for sale by sample, which would have been apparent on a reasonable examination of the sample.

(2D) If the buyer deals as consumer or, in Scotland, if a contract of sale is a consumer contract, the relevant circumstances mentioned in subsection (2A) above include any public statements on the specific characteristics of the goods made about them by the seller, the producer or his representative, particularly in advertising or on labelling.

(2E) A public statement is not by virtue of subsection (2D) above a relevant circumstance for the purposes of subsection (2A) above in the case of a contract of sale, if the seller shows that—

- (a) at the time the contract was made, he was not, and could not reasonably have been, aware of the statement,
- (b) before the contract was made, the statement had been withdrawn in public or, to the extent that it contained anything which was incorrect or misleading, it had been corrected in public, or
- (c) the decision to buy the goods could not have been influenced by the statement.

(2F) Subsections (2D) and (2E) above do not prevent any public statement from being a relevant circumstance for the purposes of subsection (2A) above (whether or not the buyer deals as consumer or, in Scotland, whether or not the contract of sale is a consumer contract) if the statement would have been such a circumstance apart from those subsections.

(3) Where the seller sells goods in the course of a business and the buyer, expressly or by implication, makes known—

(a) to the seller, or

(b) where the purchase price or part of it is payable by instalments and the goods were previously sold by a credit-broker to the seller, to that credit-broker,

any particular purpose for which the goods are being bought, there is an implied term that the goods supplied under the contract are reasonably fit for that purpose, whether or not that is a purpose for which such goods are commonly supplied, except where the circumstances show that the buyer does not rely, or that it is unreasonable for him to rely, on the skill or judgment of the seller or credit-broker:

(4) An implied term about quality or fitness for a particular purpose may be annexed to a contract of sale by usage.

(5) The preceding provisions of this section apply to a sale by a person who in the course of a business is acting as agent for another as they apply to a sale by a principal in the course of a business, except where that other is not selling in the course of a business and either the buyer knows that fact or reasonable steps are taken to bring it to the notice of the buyer before the contract is made.

(6) As regards England and Wales and Northern Ireland, the terms implied by subsection (2) and (3) above are conditions.

(7) Paragraph 5 of Schedule 1below applies in relation to a contract made on or after 18 May 1973 and before the appointed day, and paragraph 6in relation to one made before 18 May 1973.

(8) In subsection (7) above and paragraph 5 of Schedule 1 below references to the appointed day are to the day appointed for the purposes of those provisions by an order of the Secretary of State made by statutory instrument.

**3H–609** *Note* —Subsections (3) and (4) amended, subss.(2)–(2C) substituted for original subs.(2) and subs.(6) inserted by the Sale and Supply of Goods Act 1994 ss.1(1), 7, Sch.2, para.5(5); subss.(2D)–(2F) inserted by SI 2002/3045.

**Goods supplied in the course of a business**

**3H–610** The implied terms apply to second hand as well as new goods. They apply also not only to the goods bought but also to other goods "supplied", e.g. a returnable bottle, even though the ownership in those goods is not to transfer to the buyer, *Geddling v Marsh* [1920] 1 K.B. 668. Apparently, in the case of a book or computer disk they apply not only to the tangible item but also to the information or program within it, *obiter* in *St Albans DC v ICL* [1996] 4 All E.R. 481, CA. The expression "in the course of a business" includes all sales of goods made by businesses, whether or not the sale of such goods was the regular trade of that business, *Stevenson v Rogers* [1999] Q.B. 1028; [1999] 2 W.L.R. 1064; [1999] 1 All E.R. 613 (distinguishing *R & B Customs Brokers Co Ltd v United Dominions Trust* [1988] 1 W.L.R. 321, a case decided under Unfair Contract Terms Act 1977 s.12).

*Subsection (5)* —where the (selling) agent is acting in the course of a business and the principal (seller) is not selling in the course of a business and the buyer is unaware of the latter fact and reasonable steps have not been taken to bring it to the buyer's attention, the buyer is entitled to rely on s.14 to bring proceedings against the principal (the seller), *Boyter v Thomson* [1995] 2 A.C. 628.

***Paragraph numbers marked with a "+" can be found online and on CD.***

**Satisfactory quality**

The Sale and Supply of Goods Act 1994 implemented recommendations in the Law Commission Final Report, *Sale and Supply of Goods* (1987), (Law Com. No.160 Cm. 137). Subsections 14(2) to (2C) replaced the previous subs.(2) thereby substituting "satisfactory quality" for the old expression "merchantable quality" and introducing the revised definition in subss.14(2A) and 14(2B). This refers to the goods' fitness for the purposes for which such goods are commonly supplied. In the case of a motor vehicle those purposes include not merely the purpose of driving it from place to place but of doing so with the appropriate degree of comfort, ease of handling and pride in the vehicle's outward and interior appearance: *Rogers v Parish (Scarborough) Ltd* [1987] Q.B. 933 (decided under the old definition of "merchantable quality" but still authoritative). The relative weight to be attached to the different characteristics of the vehicle depends on the market at which it is aimed. On a vehicle sold as new, the performance and finish to be expected are those of a model of average standard with no mileage—and no less is expected of a vehicle sold with a manufacturer's warranty. The same general approach is to be taken in the case of a second hand vehicle, though defects unacceptable on a new car, might be acceptable on a second hand model. It is a matter of degree, bearing in mind various factors including especially the price. Examples are: *Lee v York Coach and Marine* [1977] R.T.R. 35 (car unmerchantable when brakes were in such a state that they would have failed if driver had to perform an emergency stop); *Bartlett v Sydney Marcus* [1965] 1 W.L.R. 1013 (car not unmerchantable when one month after purchase it required new clutch—buyer had turned down seller's offer at time of sale to supply the car with new clutch fitted if buyer agreed to pay £25 extra); *Shine v General Guarantee Finance .Co Ltd* [1988] 1 All E.R. 911 (20 month old Fiat held unmerchantable because, unknown to the buyer, it had been treated as a "write off" after being submerged in water for over 24 hours); *Crowther v Shannon* [1975] 1 W.L.R. 30 (eight year old Jaguar with 82,000 miles on clock, seized up after three weeks and 2,300 miles—held unfit for purpose under subs.14(3)); *Bramhill v Edwards* [2004] EWCA Civ 403, [2004] 2 Lloyd's Rep. 653 (American motorhome 102 inches wide sold for use on UK roads where it was illegal to use such a vehicle exceeding 100 inches in width, held to be of satisfactory quality in the light of evidence that the authorities turned a blind eye to such illegality and that such motorhomes were used by enthusiasts who knew of their non-compliance with the regulations). For an extended discussion of the requirement of satisfactory quality in relation to a contract to supply a computer system comprising hardware and software to a business, see *Anglo Group Plc v Winther Browne & Co Ltd* (2000) 144 S.J.L.B. 197; [2000] I.T.C.L.R. 559, available on the Court Service website. 3H–611

*Subsection (2C)* —(a) where the defect is drawn to the buyer's attention but he is reasonably of the (erroneous) opinion that the defect can and will be rectified at no cost to himself, then the implied term may well not be excluded, per Neill L.J. in *R & B Customs Brokers Co Ltd v United Dominions Trust* [1988] 1 W.L.R. 321. (b) The buyer cannot complain of defects he should have discovered during any examination he made of the goods. Apparently, if the buyer made no examination, then this provision does not apply.

*Subsections (2D) to (2F)* —added by the Sale and Supply of Goods to Consumers Regulations 2002, these subsections implement art.2 of Directive on Certain Aspects of Sale of Goods and Consumer Guarantees (1999/44), which provides for the seller to be made liable for public statements made by the seller, the producer or his representative. Similar amendments were at the same time made to the Supply of Goods and Services Act 1982 ss.4 and 9 and to the Supply of Goods (Implied Terms) Act 1973 s.10. For the latter, see paras 3H–527 and 3H–536+ above.

**Fitness for purpose**

For the condition to be implied the buyer must make known to the seller the particular purpose for which the goods are required. The buyer may have made known a particular purpose (e.g. that he wants a garment to wear) but failed to indicate some particular idiosyncrasy of his intended use of them (e.g. that his skin is abnormally sensitive to contracting dermatitis). There is no breach of the term as to fitness for purpose where the failure of the goods to meet the intended purpose arises from an abnormal feature or idiosyncrasy, not made known to the seller, in the buyer or in the 3H–612

***Paragraph numbers marked with a "+" can be found online and on CD.***

circumstances of the use of the goods by the buyer, *Slater v Finning* [1997] A.C. 473. That is so even if the buyer was himself unaware of the abnormal feature or idiosyncrasy.

Subsection (3)(b) applies to the situation where the buyer acquires the goods on conditional sale or credit sale terms in the typical triangular transaction, i.e. where the dealer (the credit broker) sells the goods to a finance company (the seller) which then contracts to supply them to the buyer on the aforesaid instalment terms; it is sufficient that the buyer has informed the dealer of the particular purpose. This is so irrespective of whether the resulting contract is a consumer credit agreement regulated by the Consumer Credit Act 1974. If, however, the resulting contract is one of hire-purchase, then the Sale of Goods Act does not apply to it but it will instead contain virtually identical terms (similar to those in ss.12–15 of the Sale of Goods Act) implied by the Supply of Goods (Implied Terms) Act 1973 ss.8– 11.

Where goods are to be made to a specification supplied by the buyer, the buyer will still be placing reliance on the seller's skill and judgment in some respects (e.g. in regard to matters not covered by the specification). If the goods' subsequent unfitness for their intended purpose relates to the sphere of reliance placed upon the seller, the buyer will have a claim, *Cammell Laird & Co Ltd v Manganese Bronze & Brass Co Ltd* [1934] A.C. 402.

The implied term requires the goods to continue to be fit for the intended purpose for a reasonable period after delivery, so long as they remain in the same apparent state and condition as when they were delivered, apart from normal wear and tear, *Lambert v Lewis* [1982] A.C. 225. Often in practice, where goods are being put to a conventional use, there is little, if any, distinction between liability under s.14(3) and s.14(2), see e.g. *Crowther v Shannon*, above. Liability is strict and does not depend upon proof of negligence, *Frost v Aylesbury Dairy Co* [1905] 1 K.B. 608.

### Exclusion and remedies

3H–613 For the buyer's rights of rejection and to claim damages, see ss.11, 15A, 35, 35A and 53. For restrictions on the ability to exclude or limit the seller's liability, see Unfair Contract Terms Act 1977 ss.1– 6.

## *SALE BY SAMPLE*

### Sale by sample

3H–614 **15.**—(1) A contract of sale is a contract for sale by sample where there is an express or implied term to that effect in the contract.

(2) In the case of a contract for sale by sample there is an implied term—

(a) that the bulk will correspond with the sample in quality;

(b) [...]

(c) that the goods will be free from any defect, making their quality unsatisfactory, which would not be apparent on reasonable examination of the sample.

(3) As regards England and Wales and Northern Ireland, the term implied by subsection (2) above is a condition.

(4) Paragraph 7 of Schedule 1below applies in relation to a contract made before 18 May 1973.

3H–615 *Note* —Subsection (2) amended and subs.(3) substituted by the Sale and Supply of Goods Act 1994 ss.1(2), 7, Sch.2, para.5(6), Sch.3.

**[THE NEXT PARAGRAPH IS 3H–617.]**

## *MISCELLANEOUS*

### Modification of remedies for breach of condition in non-consumer cases

3H–617 **15A.**—(1) Where in the case of a contract of sale—

(a) the buyer would, apart from this subsection, have the right to reject goods by reason of a breach on the part of the seller of a term implied by section 13, 14 or 15 above, but

(b) the breach is so slight that it would be unreasonable for him to reject them,

then, if the buyer does not deal as consumer, the breach is not to be treated as a breach of condition but may be treated as a breach of warranty.

(2) This section applies unless a contrary intention appears in, or is to be implied from, the contract.

(3) It is for the seller to show that a breach fell within subsection (1)(b) above.

(4) This section does not apply to Scotland.

*Note*—Section 15A was added with effect from January 3, 1995 by the Sale and Supply of Goods Act 1994, which implemented the recommendations in the Law Commission Final Report, *Sale and Supply of Goods* (1987), (Law Com. No.160 Cm. 137). "Dealing as a consumer" has the same meaning as in the Unfair Contract Terms Act 1977 s.12 (see s.61(5A) of the Sale of Goods Act 1979, as inserted by the Sale and Supply of Goods Act 1994). For s.12 of the 1977 Act see para.3H–573 above. **3H–618**

**For ss.15B to 33 of the Sale of Goods Act 1979 (see Arrangement) plus any related commentary see paragraphs 3H–619+ to 3H–648+ on White Book on Westlaw UK or the Civil Procedure CD.**

## Buyer's right of examining goods

**34.**—(1) Unless otherwise agreed when the seller tenders delivery of the goods to the buyer, he is bound on request to afford the buyer a reasonable opportunity of examining the goods for the purpose of ascertaining whether they are in conformity with the contract and, in the case of a contract for sale by sample, of comparing the bulk with the sample. **3H–649**

*Note*—Amended with effect from January 3, 1995 by the Sale and Supply of Goods Act 1994. See further the commentary to s.35. **3H–650**

## Acceptance

**35.**—(1) The buyer is deemed to have accepted the goods subject to subsection (2) below— **3H–651**

(a) when he intimates to the seller that he has accepted them, or

(b) when the goods have been delivered to him and he does any act in relation to them which is inconsistent with the ownership of the seller.

(2) Where goods are delivered to the buyer, and he has not previously examined them, he is not deemed to have accepted them under subsection (1) above until he has had a reasonable opportunity of examining them for the purpose—

(a) of ascertaining whether they are in conformity with the contract, and

(b) in the case of a contract for sale by sample, of comparing the bulk with the sample.

(3) Where the buyer deals as consumer or (in Scotland) the contract of sale is a consumer contract, the buyer cannot lose his right to rely on subsection (2) above by agreement, waiver or otherwise.

(4) The buyer is also deemed to have accepted the goods when after the lapse of a reasonable time he retains the goods without intimating to the seller that he has rejected them.

(5) The questions that are material in determining for the purposes of subsection (4) above whether a reasonable time has elapsed include whether the buyer has had a reasonable opportunity of examining the goods for the purpose mentioned in subsection (2) above.

(6) The buyer is not by virtue of this section deemed to have accepted the goods merely because—(a) he asks for, or agrees to, their repair by or under an arrangement with the seller, or (b) the goods are delivered to another under a sub-sale or other disposition.

(7) Where the contract is for the sale of goods making one or more commercial units, a buyer accepting any goods included in a unit is deemed to have accepted all the goods making the unit; and in this subsection "commercial unit" means a unit division of which would materially impair the value of the goods or the character of the unit.

(8) Paragraph 10 of Schedule 1 below applies in relation to a contract made before 22 April 1967 or (in the application of this Act to Northern Ireland) 28 July 1967.

**3H-652** *Note*—Amended, and subs.(7) added, with effect from January 3, 1995 by the Sale and Supply of Goods Act 1994.

**Acceptance**

**3H-653** Acceptance of the goods (within the meaning of s.35) removes any right the buyer might have to reject the goods for breach of condition (see s.11(4) above). Loss of that right still leaves the buyer with a claim for damages, see s.53. In *Bernstein v Pamson Motors (Golders Green) Ltd* [1987] 2 All E.R. 220, it was held, at first instance, that acceptance occurred after lapse of a length of time which was reasonable for the buyer to try out the goods generally, which in that case was held to be less than three weeks after the buyer took delivery of a new car. That decision, however, no longer represents the law: *Clegg v Andersson* (below). One purpose of the amendments made by the 1994 Act was to allow the buyer an opportunity to check the goods to see if they conform to the contract, before the buyer is deemed to have lost his right to reject the goods for breach of condition. It is quite possible that long, perhaps months or years, after the buyer examined them for conformity and (let us assume) was unable to find any suggestion of non-conformity, the goods might prove not to have been of satisfactory quality. A reasonable period of time will not necessarily last years, however. An opportunity to examine the goods for conformity is not a guarantee that such an examination will necessarily be capable of discovering any non-conformity. Another purpose of the 1994 amendments was to encourage informal attempts at cure. Thus the buyer is now not taken to have accepted the goods simply because he asks for or agrees to their repair: s.35(6). Similarly he is entitled to a reasonable period to ascertain what would be required for modification or repair. In *Clegg v Andersson* [2003] EWCA Civ 320; [2003] 2 Lloyd's Rep. 32, the buyers had contracted to buy a new yacht costing £236,000, which when they took delivery had a keel which was dangerously overweight. The buyers returned the vessel to the seller after a few days and were not prepared to agree to repairs/modifications proposed by the seller until (a) the seller had first supplied them with details (with drawings and calculations) as to what was proposed and (b) the buyers had been able to take professional advice in the light of that information. When after approximately a further six months the seller supplied the information, the buyers took less than three weeks to reject the yacht. The Court held that the buyers had not accepted the yacht and had validly rejected it. A buyer is entitled to a reasonable period to ascertain what is required for modification or repair and in this case time had not begun to run until the buyers were given the requested information which was necessary for them to make a decision. There is, however, no general rule that acceptance cannot take place whilst the buyer is seeking information about possible alleged breaches of contract and possible cures for them: see *Jones v Callagher* [2004] EWCA Civ 10; [2004] 1 Lloyd's Rep.377, an ordinary case, where the defects in the goods (kitchen fitments) were obvious needing no expert to identify them and where a purported rejection five months after delivery was held to be too late. *Truk (UK) Ltd v Tokmakidis GmbH* [2000] 1 Lloyd's Rep. 543 involved a contract between two businesses for the sale and fitting of some lifting equipment to be paid for six months after delivery. The equipment was to be fitted to, and form part of, a towing vehicle which the buyer was then going to resell. Approximately six months after delivery the buyer was informed by a potential purchaser of the towing vehicle that the equipment was defective. The buyer immediately informed the seller and refused to pay the price pending investigation (by an appropriate company). About three months later, promptly upon receipt of the result of the investigation which confirmed the allegation, the buyer unequivocally rejected the goods. The judge held as follows. Where goods are sold for resale, a reasonable time in which to give notice of rejection should normally be the time actually taken to resell the goods, together with an additional period in which they can be inspected and tried out (by the sub-purchaser). Where the price is payable at a date after delivery, that reasonable period of time should normally last at least until the date for payment. The reasonable time had not expired when about six months after delivery, the buyer first questioned compliance. The buyer was entitled to a further period in which to investigate that issue. Accordingly the buyer had not accepted the goods when he validly rejected them nine months after delivery.

In *J & H Ritchie Ltd v Lloyd Ltd* [2007] 1 W.L.R. 670 (HL), s.35(6)(a) meant that the buyer's agreement to have faulty goods inspected and, if possible, repaired was not deemed an acceptance. It was an implied term of the inspection and repair agreement that during its currency the buyer would not exercise his right of rejection. It not being immediately obvious what was the nature of the defect or what could be done to correct it, it was a further implied term of the inspection and repair agreement that the seller would, if requested, provide information to enable the buyer to make an informed decision as to whether to accept the goods after they had been repaired. Failing provision of that information, the buyer was entitled to reject the goods.

### Commercial Unit

Subsection (7) creates an exception to the rule in s.35A which rule allows the buyer to accept conforming goods without losing the right to reject non-conforming goods. For example, accepting volume A to M of a two volume dictionary would amount to acceptance of the other volume and thus prevent the buyer being able to reject either volume. Whether a three-piece suite amounts to a commercial unit would be a nice question of fact. **3H–654**

## Right of partial rejection

**35A.**—(1) If the buyer— **3H–655**

(a) has the right to reject the goods by reason of a breach on the part of the seller that affects some or all of them, but

(b) accepts some of the goods, including, where there are any goods unaffected by the breach, all such goods,

he does not by accepting them lose his right to reject the rest.

(2) In the case of a buyer having the right to reject an instalment of goods, subsection (1) above applies as if references to the goods were references to the goods comprised in the instalment.

***Paragraph numbers marked with a "+" can be found online and on CD.***

(3) For the purposes of subsection (1) above, goods are affected by a breach if by reason of the breach they are not in conformity with the contract.

(4) This section applies unless a contrary intention appears in, or is to be implied from, the contract.

3H-656 *Note*—Inserted by the Sale and Supply of Goods Act 1994 ss.3(1), 8(2).

**Right of partial rejection**

3H-657 The amendments made by the 1994 Act were designed, amongst other things, to enable the buyer to accept conforming goods without thereby losing the right to reject goods which did not conform to the contract. Where the contract is not severable and the buyer accepts some *but not all* of the *conforming* goods, then subs.(1) will not apply, with the result that, applying s.11(4), the buyer will have lost the right to reject any of the goods whether conforming or not. Acceptance of part of a "commercial unit" amounts to acceptance of all of it, see s.35(7).

## Buyer not bound to return rejected goods

3H-658 **36.** Unless otherwise agreed, where goods are delivered to the buyer, and he refuses to accept them, having the right to do so, he is not bound to return them to the seller, but it is sufficient if he intimates to the seller that he refuses to accept them.

3H-659 *Note*—The buyer is entitled to claim reasonably incurred storage expenses, if the seller fails to collect goods which the buyer has rightly rejected, *Kolfor Plant Ltd v Tilbury Plant Ltd* (1977) 121 S.J. 390. The buyer has no lien over rejected goods to enforce the return of the purchase price, *Lyons v May & Baker* [1923] 1 K.B. 695.

**For ss.37 to 48 of the Sale of Goods Act 1979 (see Arrangement) plus any related commentary see paragraphs 3H-660+ to 3H-672+ on White Book on Westlaw UK or the Civil Procedure CD.**

# PART 5A

# ADDITIONAL RIGHTS OF BUYER IN CONSUMER CASE

3H-673 *Note*—Inserted by SI 2002/3045.

## Introductory

3H-674 **48A.**—(1) This section applies if—

(a) the buyer deals as consumer or, in Scotland, there is a consumer contract in which the buyer is a consumer, and

(b) the goods do not conform to the contract of sale at the time of delivery.

(2) If this section applies, the buyer has the right—

(a) under and in accordance with section 48B below, to require the seller to repair or replace the goods, or

(b) under and in accordance with section 48C below—

(i) to require the seller to reduce the purchase price of the goods to the buyer by an appropriate amount, or

(ii) to rescind the contract with regard to the goods in question.

*Paragraph numbers marked with a "+" can be found online and on CD.*

(3) For the purposes of subsection (1)(b) above goods which do not conform to the contract of sale at any time within the period of six months starting with the date on which the goods were delivered to the buyer must be taken not to have so conformed at that date.

(4) Subsection (3) above does not apply if—

(a) it is established that the goods did so conform at that date;

(b) its application is incompatible with the nature of the goods or the nature of the lack of conformity.

*Note*—Part 5A of the Act comprises ss.48A to 48F and was added with effect from March 31, 2003 by the Sale and Supply of Goods to Consumers Regulations 2002 (SI 2002/3045). **3H–675**

**Consumer's additional rights for non-conformity**

The Sale and Supply of Goods to Consumers Regulations 2002 implemented the Directive on Aspects of Sale of Goods and Consumer Guarantees (1999/44). They introduced additional remedies for a buyer dealing as a consumer where there has been any breach of an express term of the contract or of the statutory implied terms as to description, satisfactory quality, fitness for purpose and sample. Those additional remedies are set out in ss.48A to 48F. They include the right to require the goods to be repaired or replaced (if that is not a disproportionate remedy) and, failing that, to rescind the contract or obtain a reduction in the price. These rights are entirely additional and do not take away any right (e.g. to reject the goods for breach of condition and/or to claim damages for consequential loss) which the buyer has independently of ss.48A to 48F. If, however, the buyer chooses to require repair or replacement, he cannot reject the goods and terminate the contract without allowing the seller a reasonable time to comply with his request. Section 61(5A) of the Sale of Goods Act provides that "dealing as a consumer" has the same meaning as in s.12 of the Unfair Contract Terms Act 1977. For the latter, see para.3H–573 above. Similar provisions to those in ss.48A to 48F were added to the Supply of Goods and Services Act 1982 (s.11M to s.11S). Under the latter, the goods will also be non-conforming (and the buyer will thus be entitled to require repair or replacement) if, in installing the goods, the supplier has been in breach of the implied term that he will use reasonable care and skill. For the term as to reasonable care and skill, see Supply of Goods and Services Act 1982 s.13 at para.3H–818 below. **3H–676**

*"The time of delivery"*—is normally when the goods are physically handed over to the buyer. Where the buyer deals as a consumer and the seller is authorised or required to send the goods to the buyer, delivery of the goods to a carrier does not constitute delivery: s.32(4). In that case delivery will occur only when the carrier delivers to the buyer.

## Repair or replacement of the goods

**48B.**—(1) If section 48A above applies, the buyer may require the seller— **3H–677**

(a) to repair the goods, or

(b) to replace the goods.

(2) If the buyer requires the seller to repair or replace the goods, the seller must—

(a) repair or, as the case may be, replace the goods within a reasonable time but without causing significant inconvenience to the buyer;

(b) bear any necessary costs incurred in doing so (including in particular the cost of any labour, materials or postage).

***Paragraph numbers marked with a "+" can be found online and on CD.***

(3) The buyer must not require the seller to repair or, as the case may be, replace the goods if that remedy is—

(a) impossible, or

(b) disproportionate in comparison to the other of those remedies, or

(c) disproportionate in comparison to an appropriate reduction in the purchase price under paragraph (a), or rescission under paragraph (b), of section 48C(1) below.

(4) One remedy is disproportionate in comparison to the other if the one imposes costs on the seller which, in comparison to those imposed on him by the other, are unreasonable, taking into account—

(a) the value which the goods would have if they conformed to the contract of sale,

(b) the significance of the lack of conformity, and

(c) whether the other remedy could be effected without significant inconvenience to the buyer.

(5) Any question as to what is a reasonable time or significant inconvenience is to be determined by reference to—

(a) the nature of the goods, and

(b) the purpose for which the goods were acquired.

3H-678 *Note*—Inserted by SI 2002/3045.

**Repair or replacement of the goods**

3H-679 See note and commentary to s.48A above.

## Reduction of purchase price or rescission of contract

3H-680 **48C.**—(1) If section 48A above applies, the buyer may—

(a) require the seller to reduce the purchase price of the goods in question to the buyer by an appropriate amount, or

(b) rescind the contract with regard to those goods,

if the condition in subsection (2) below is satisfied.

(2) The condition is that—

(a) by virtue of section 48B(3) above the buyer may require neither repair nor replacement of the goods; or

(b) the buyer has required the seller to repair or replace the goods, but the seller is in breach of the requirement of section 48B(2)(a) above to do so within a reasonable time and without significant inconvenience to the buyer.

(3) For the purposes of this Part, if the buyer rescinds the contract, any reimbursement to the buyer may be reduced to take account of the use he has had of the goods since they were delivered to him.

3H-681 *Note*—Inserted by SI 2002/3045.

**Reduction of purchase price or rescission of contract**

3H-682 See note and commentary to s.48A above

## Relation to other remedies etc

**48D.**—(1) If the buyer requires the seller to repair or replace the goods the buyer must not act under subsection (2) until he has given the seller a reasonable time in which to repair or replace (as the case may be) the goods. 3H–683

(2) The buyer acts under this subsection if—

(a) in England and Wales or Northern Ireland he rejects the goods and terminates the contract for breach of condition;

(b) in Scotland he rejects any goods delivered under the contract and treats it as repudiated;

(c) he requires the goods to be replaced or repaired (as the case may be).

*Note* —Inserted by SI 2002/3045. 3H–684

### Reasonable time for repair or replacement of goods

See note and commentary to s.48A above. 3H–685

## Powers of the court

**48E.**—(1) In any proceedings in which a remedy is sought by virtue of this Part the court, in addition to any other power it has, may act under this section. 3H–686

(2) On the application of the buyer the court may make an order requiring specific performance or, in Scotland, specific implement by the seller of any obligation imposed on him by virtue of section 48B above.

(3) Subsection (4) applies if—

(a) the buyer requires the seller to give effect to a remedy under section 48B or 48C above or has claims to rescind under section 48C, but

(b) the court decides that another remedy under section 48B or 48C is appropriate.

(4) The court may proceed—

(a) as if the buyer had required the seller to give effect to the other remedy, or if the other remedy is rescission under section 48C;

(b) as if the buyer had claimed to rescind the contract under that section.

(5) If the buyer has claimed to rescind the contract the court may order that any reimbursement to the buyer is reduced to take account of the use he has had of the goods since they were delivered to him.

(6) The court may make an order under this section unconditionally or on such terms and conditions as to damages, payment of the price and otherwise as it thinks just.

*Note* —Inserted by SI 2002/3045. 3H–687

### Powers of the court

See note and commentary to s.48A above. 3H–688

## Conformity with the contract

3H-689 **48F.** For the purposes of this Part, goods do not conform to a contract of sale if there is, in relation to the goods, a breach of an express term of the contract or a term implied by section 13, 14 or 15 above.

3H-690 *Note* —Inserted by SI 2002/3045.

**Conformity with the contract**

3H-691 See note and commentary to s.48A above.

**For ss.49 to 52 of the Sale of Goods Act 1979 (see Arrangement) plus any related commentary see paragraphs 3H-692+ to 3H-695+ on White Book on Westlaw UK or the Civil Procedure CD.**

## Remedy for breach of warranty

3H-696 **53.**—(1) Where there is a breach of warranty by the seller, or where the buyer elects (or is compelled) to treat any breach of a condition on the part of the seller as a breach of warranty, the buyer is not by reason only of such breach of warranty entitled to reject the goods; but he may—

(a) set up against the seller the breach of warranty in diminution or extinction of the price, or

(b) maintain an action against the seller for damages for the breach of warranty.

(2) The measure of damages for breach of warranty is the estimated loss directly and naturally resulting, in the ordinary course of events, from the breach of warranty.

(3) In the case of breach of warranty of quality such loss is prima facie the difference between the value of the goods at the time of delivery to the buyer and the value they would have had if they had fulfilled the warranty.

(4) The fact that the buyer has set up the breach of warranty in diminution or extinction of the price does not prevent him from maintaining an action for the same breach of warranty if he has suffered further damage.

(5) This section does not apply to Scotland.

3H-697 *Note* —Subsection (5) inserted by the Sale and Supply of Goods Act 1994 ss.7(1), 8(2), Sch.2, para.5.

**For ss.53A to 64 of and Schs 1 to 4 to the Sale of Goods Act 1979 (see Arrangement) plus any related commentary see paragraphs 3H-698+ to 3H-757+ on White Book on Westlaw UK or the Civil Procedure CD.**

## Supply of Goods and Services Act 1982

3H-758 (S.I. 1982 c.29)

ARRANGEMENT OF SECTIONS

PART I



***Paragraph numbers marked with a "+" can be found online and on CD.***

**Paragraph numbers marked with a "+" denote content that is available on White Book on Westlaw UK or the Civil Procedure CD.**

**For ss.1 to 11S of the Supply of Goods and Services Act 1982 (see Arrangement) plus any related commentary see paragraphs 3H–759+ to 3H–815+ on White Book on Westlaw UK or the Civil Procedure CD.**

### Implied terms as to description, quality and sample

Terms as to title, description, quality and sample are implied in contracts of sale of **3H–816**

***Paragraph numbers marked with a "+" can be found online and on CD.***

goods by the Sale of Goods Act 1979 ss.12– 15. Similar terms are implied by the Supply of Goods and Service Act 1982 in: contracts of barter or exchange, contracts whereby goods are exchanged for trading stamps and contracts for services under which the property is to pass (ss.1– 5A); contracts of hire (other than hire-purchase) (ss.6–11). These terms apply only to the goods supplied, not to the services. As with the terms implied by the Sale of Goods Act, any clause purporting to exclude or limit liability in respect of them is subject to the provisions of the Unfair Contract Terms Act 1977 (in this case, in particular, s.7 of that Act.) Sections 12–16 imply into contracts for the supply of services (whether or not the contract is one of sale of goods) terms which relate to the services provided—terms as to care and skill, time for performance and the remuneration.

**Consumer's additional rights for non-conformity**

**3H–817** Amendments to the Sale of Goods Act 1979 by the Sale and Supply of Goods to Consumer Regulations 2002 (SI 2002/3045) are mirrored by similar amendments to the Supply of Goods and Services Act 1982. Sections 48A to 48F of the former Act give the buyer additional rights in relation to non-conforming goods (including the right to require repair or replacement of the goods), see para.3H–674 above. The Supply of Goods and Services Act 1982 contains, in ss.11M to 11S, provisions which are, with one exception, identical apart from necessary changes of wording. The exception is as follows. Whereas under both Acts the goods will be non-conforming if there is a breach of any of the statutory implied terms as to description, satisfactory quality, fitness for purpose or sample, under the Supply of Goods of Services Act the goods will also be non-conforming if, in installing the goods, the supplier has been in breach of the implied term in s.13 that he will use reasonable care and skill. For s.13 see below.

# PART II

# SUPPLY OF SERVICES

## The contracts concerned

**3H–818** **12.**—(1) In this Act a "contract for the supply of a service" means-,subject to subsection (2) below, a contract under which a person ("the supplier") agrees to carry out a service.

(2) For the purposes of this Act, a contract of service or apprenticeship is not a contract for the supply of a service.

(3) Subject to subsection (2) above, a contract is a contract for the supply of a service for the purposes of this Act whether or not goods are also—

(a) transferred or to be transferred, or

(b) bailed or to be bailed by way of hire,

under the contract, and whatever is the nature of the consideration for which the services is to be carried out.

(4) The Secretary of State may by order provide that one or more of sections 13 to 15 below shall not apply to services of a description specified in the order, and such an order may make different provision for different circumstances.

(5) The power to make an order under subsection (4) above shall be exercisable by statutory instrument subject to annulment in pursuance of a resolution of either House of Parliament.

**"Contracts for the supply of a service"**

**3H–819** This concept will include not only contracts of which the substance is the provision of a service, but also a contract of sale of goods under which a service is also to be provided (e.g. the sale and installation of a washing machine).

## Implied term about care and skill

**13.** In a contract for the supply of a service where the supplier is acting in the course of a business, there is an implied term that the supplier will carry out the service with reasonable care and skill. 3H–820

**Implied term about care and skill**

For exclusion of liability see s.16. For case law on "in the course of a business", see commentary to Sale of Goods Act 1979 s.14. For the other party's right to require repair or replacement of goods where the supplier is in breach of the implied term as to care and skill in installing goods, see para.3H–817. 3H–821

## Implied term about time for performance

**14.**—(1) Where, under a contract for the supply of a service by a supplier acting in the course of a business, the time for the service to be carried out is not fixed by the contracts, left to be fixed in a manner agreed by the contract or determined by the course of dealing between the parties, there is an implied term that the supplier will carry out the service within a reasonable time. 3H–822

(2) What is a reasonable time is a question of fact.

**Time for performance**

A related requirement appears in the Consumer Protection (Distance Selling) Regulations 2000 (SI 2000/2334), which implemented the Distance Selling Directive (97/7) and are set out at para.3H–906. By reg.19(1), in the case of a "distance contract" which is not an "excepted contract", the supplier must, unless the parties agree otherwise, perform the contract within a period of 30 days, which period begins when the consumer forwarded his order to the supplier. Regulation 19(1) does not apply to any excepted contract, nor to timeshare agreements (within the meaning of the Timeshare Act 1992), nor to the following agreements: contracts for food, beverages or other goods used for everyday consumption supplied to the consumer at his residence or workplace by regular roundsmen; contracts for accommodation, catering, transport or leisure services where the supplier undertakes to supply the services on a specific date or within a specific period. Where reg.19(1) does apply and the supplier is unable to supply the goods or services ordered, reg.19(7) allows the supplier to supply substitute goods or services of equivalent price and quality, if the contract provided for that possibility. Apart from that possibility, if reg.19(1) applies and the supplier is unable, because the goods or services are not available, to perform the contract within the 30 days or such other period as the parties agree, reg.19(2) to (6) come into play. These contain consequential provisions: the supplier is required to reimburse any sum paid by or on behalf of the consumer, including any sum paid by a creditor under a personal credit agreement with the consumer; the contract shall be treated as if never made (except for any rights or remedies arising from the non-performance); any security provided in relation to the contract is to be treated as if never having had any effect. 3H–823

## Implied term about consideration

**15.**—(1) Where, under a contract for the supply of a service, the consideration for the service is not determined by the contract, left to be determined in a manner agreed by the contract or determined by the course of dealing between the parties, there is an implied term that the party contracting with the supplier will pay a reasonable charge. 3H–824

(2) What is a reasonable charge is a question of fact.

## Exclusion of implied terms, etc.

**16.**—(1) Where a right, duty or liability would arise under a 3H–825 contract for the supply of a service by virtue of this Part of this Act, it may (subject to subsection (2) below and the 1977 Act) be negatived or varied by express agreement, or by the course of dealing between the parties, or by such usage as binds both parties to the contract.

(2) An express term does not negative a term implied by this Part of this Act unless inconsistent with it.

(3) Nothing in this Part of this Act prejudices—

(a) any rule of law which imposes on the supplier a duty stricter than that imposed by section 13 or 14 above; or

(b) subject to paragraph (a) above, any rule of law whereby any term not inconsistent with this Part of this Act is to be implied in a contract for the supply of a service.

(4) This Part of this Act has effect subject to any other enactment which defines or restricts the rights, duties or liabilities arising in connection with a service of any description.

**Exclusion of implied terms**

**3H–826** The 1977 Act referred to in subs.(1) is the Unfair Contract Terms Act 1977. Liability for breach of the implied term as to care and skill in s.13 is negligence liability within the meaning of the 1977 Act and thus any attempt to exclude such liability is subject to s.2 of the 1977 Act. If the recipient of the services contracts as a consumer or the exclusion clause is a standard term of the service provider, s.3 of the 1977 Act will apply as well.

**For ss.17–20 of and Sch.1 to the Supply of Goods and Services Act 1982 (see Arrangement) plus any related commentary see paragraphs 3H–827+ to 3H–835+ on White Book on Westlaw UK or the Civil Procedure CD.**

## The Package Travel, Package Holidays and Package Tours Regulations 1992

**3H–836** (S.I. 1992 No. 3288)

ARRANGEMENT OF SECTIONS



***Paragraph numbers marked with a "+" can be found online and on CD.***

**General note**

These regulations implemented the EC Directive on Package Travel, Package Holidays and Package Tours 90/314. In various respects they enhance holiday makers' rights compared with what they would or might otherwise be. The ordinary law of contract and tort continues to apply to any holiday which is outside the regulations (i.e. if it is not a "package" within reg.2). Similarly, even where the holiday is a package within the regulations, the common law continues to apply in relation to matters not covered by the regulations. Thus, the regulations being silent on the matter, the assessment of damages is to be determined by decisions based on *Jarvis v Swans Tours Ltd* [1973] Q.B. 233. **3H–837**

As an alternative to court action, the ABTA (Association of British Travel Agents) arbitration scheme administered by the Chartered Institute of Arbitrators allows a claim for up to £5,000 (or £15,000 per booking) to be referred to arbitration if it is against an ABTA member.

For an authoritative account of this area of the law, see *Holiday Law* by Grant and Mason (3rd edn, Sweet and Maxwell, 2003).

## Citation and commencement

**1.** These Regulations may be cited as the Package Travel, Package Holidays and Package Tours Regulations 1992 and shall come into force on the day after the day on which they are made. **3H–838**

## Interpretation

**2.**—(1) In these Regulations– **3H–839**

"brochure" means any brochure in which packages are offered for sale;

"contract" means the agreement linking the consumer to the organiser or to the retailer, or to both, as the case may be;

"the Directive" means Council Directive 90/314/EEC on package travel, package holidays and package tours;

"member State" means a member State of the European Community or another State in the European Economic Area;

"offer" includes an invitation to treat whether by means of advertising or otherwise, and cognate expressions shall be construed accordingly;

"organiser" means the person who, otherwise than occasionally, organises packages and sells or offers them for sale, whether directly or through a retailer;

"the other party to the contract" means the party, other than the consumer, to the contract, that is, the organiser or the retailer, or both, as the case may be;

"package" means the pre-arranged combination of at least two of the following components when sold or offered for sale at an inclusive price and when the service covers a period of more than twenty-four hours or includes overnight accommodation:–

(a) transport;

(b) accommodation;

(c) other tourist services not ancillary to transport or accommodation and accounting for a significant proportion of the package, and

*Paragraph numbers marked with a "+" can be found online and on CD.*

(i) the submission of separate accounts for different components shall not cause the arrangements to be other than a package;

(ii) the fact that a combination is arranged at the request of the consumer and in accordance with his specific instructions (whether modified or not) shall not of itself cause it to be treated as other than pre-arranged; and

"retailer" means the person who sells or offers for sale the package put together by the organiser.

(2) In the definition of "contract" in paragraph (1) above, "consumer" means the person who takes or agrees to take the package ("the principal contractor") and elsewhere in these Regulations "consumer" means, as the context requires, the principal contractor, any person on whose behalf the principal contractor agrees to purchase the package ("the other beneficiaries") or any person to whom the principal contractor or any of the other beneficiaries transfers the package ("the transferee").

**3H–840** *Note*—Definition of "member state" added by the Package Travel, Package Holidays and Package Tours (Amendment) Regulations 1995 (SI 1995/1648).

**"contract"**

**3H–841** This definition is taken from the Directive. It would appear that it is possible for an agreement to fall within this definition even though it is not what would at common law be recognised as a contract. Thus a travel agent might on a given occasion arrange for the consumer (a) flights with an airline and (b) accommodation with an hotel. That would constitute a "package" and the travel agent would be the "organiser", see para.3H–842 below. Yet the contracts for flights and accommodation may well have been between the consumer and, respectively, the airline and the hotel. In this situation, it can perhaps be said that there was an "agreement" between the travel agent and the consumer which was a "contract" within the meaning of the regulations, albeit it may not have been a contract at common law, the agreement being that the travel agent would make, or try to make, the arrangements which the consumer wanted.

**"the other party to the contract"**

**3H–842** This expression is not derived from the Directive. In the usual situation the tour operator will be "the other party to the contract"", the travel agent having been merely an agent to bring about a contract between the consumer and tour operator. The definition clearly contemplates, however, that the travel agent (the retailer) can also, either alone or as well as the tour operator, be "the other party to the contract". The vagueness created by the words "as the case may be" leaves a great deal of scope for judicial interpretation. It allows the courts to determine who is (or are) the other party(ies) to the contract according to the facts of different cases. It also leaves open the possibility that the identity of "the other party to the contract" may vary according to which of the substantive regulations is in point. According to Goldring J. in *ABTA v Civil Aviation Authority* [2006] EWHC 13 (Admin), at para.161, "[T]he [regulations] do not exclude the application of the English law of contract . . .[W]hether the agreement links the consumer to the organiser or retailer or both depends upon the application of the English law of contract, in particular the law of agency. So too do decisions as to whether the organiser or retailer or both are parties to the contract or whether under regulation 15, the organiser or retailer or both are liable under it."

**"Package"**

**3H–843** Only those holidays which are "packages" are affected by the regulations.

*"Pre-arranged combination"*—In *Club-Tour Viagens e Turismo SA v Lobo Goncalves Garrido (C400/00)* [2002] E.C.R. I-4051, the ECJ, in interpreting the Directive, determined

***Paragraph numbers marked with a "+" can be found online and on CD.***

two things: (i) arrangements put together by a travel agent at the request of, and according to the specifications of, a consumer (or defined group of consumers) can fall within the definition of a package; (ii) "pre-arranged combination" must be interpreted so as to include combinations of tourist services put together at the time when the contract is concluded between the travel agency and the consumer. Thus, where a travel agent had arranged both (a) a holiday at the destination resort and (b) the flights to reach the destination, that was a package within the regulations and, apparently, the travel agent was an "organiser" within the meaning of the regulations.

*"Inclusive price"* —The arrangement is not a package unless it is sold or offered "at an inclusive price". Thus an optional excursion which the consumer buys from the tour operator only after arrival at his holiday resort would not be part of the package. It would, however, be part of the package it if it was arranged (and the cost included) at the time the holiday was booked. In *Rechberger v Austria (C140/97)* [1999] E.C.R. I-3499; [2000] 2 C.M.L.R. 1, trips including travel and accommodation were offered (as part of an advertising campaign) to subscribers to a newspaper. The lucky travellers were to pay only airport taxes and, if they travelled alone, a single supplement. The price was held to be "inclusive", even though it did not equal the value of either the travel or the accommodation. Thus the trips were held to be "packages". According to Goldring J. in *ABTA v Civil Aviation Authority* [2006] EWHC 13 (Admin), at para.156:

> "[T]he words 'inclusive price' should be given their ordinary and natural meaning.If the substance of a transaction is the sale by the travel agent of separate and discrete components of ... a holiday, with no one part being connected with or dependent upon any other part (other than that they are sold together), ... the resultant price ... is no more an 'inclusive price' than is the total of goods at the checkout of a supermarket. For the sale of a package at an inclusive price the relationship between the component parts of the package must be such as to mean that the consumer is buying and paying for them as a whole; that the sale or offer for sale of one component part is in some way connected with or dependent on the sale or offer for sale of the others."

*"Accommodation"* —*Administrative Proceedings Concerning AFS Intercultural Programs Finland RY (C237/97)* [1999] E.C.R. I-825; [2000] 1 C.M.L.R. 845 involved a student exchange arrangement whereby students would be sent from Finland to study in another country for a period of six months or more, lodging with families which put them up free of charge. AFS Finland organised the exchange by: arranging transport, selecting the host family, arranging the school to be attended by students during their visit abroad, preparing documentation relating to the host country and organising a preparatory course for the students and their families. The ECJ held that the combination of all three of the following factors meant that the lodging with the families was not "accommodation" within the meaning of the Directive: (i) the lodging was free, (ii) it was not in a hotel or similar establishment, and (iii) it was for a long time.

*"Other tourist services. ."* —In the *AFS Finland* case (see "Accommodation" above), it was held that AFS Finland did not organise "other tourist services" within the meaning of the Directive, because: (i) selecting the school for the exchange student to attend was not a tourist service, since its specific purpose was education of the student; (ii) selection of the host family, if it was a tourist service, was ancillary to accommodation; (iii) preparation of the documentation and the courses followed by the students and parents prior to departure, though within the definition of "tourist services", did not account for a significant proportion of the package.

**"Organiser" and "retailer"**

A tour operator, whether it markets its package holidays directly or via travel **3H–844**
agents, is clearly an "organiser". A travel agent who sells such a package holiday will be a "retailer" but not normally an "organiser". However, in two situations a travel agent might be an "organiser". The first is where, in addition to selling the conventional package holiday and as part of that same transaction, the travel agent himself arranges transport to the hotel or the airport, *c.f.* the *Club-Tour* case at para.3H–841 above. Whilst the package travel company remains an "organiser" and the travel agent remains a "retailer" of the conventional package, the travel agent

would appear to be "organiser" of the whole package, i.e. including the additional transport. The second situation is where in selling the package, the travel agent has acted as an undisclosed agent, i.e. held himself out, whether or not intentionally, as principal: *Hone v Going Places Leisure Travel Ltd* (QBD, Nov 16, 2000, confirmed in the Court of Appeal—see para.3H–866 below).

*Paragraph (2)*—the definition of "consumer", coupled with the provisions of substantive regulations (including in particular reg.15), means that the common law rule of privity of contract is effectively abrogated. The consumer, whether that be the purchaser of the package or someone else in the party, can proceed against "the other party to the contract" in respect of any improper performance of the contract. Where the regulations apply, therefore, the consumer will not need to rely on the Contracts (Rights of Third Parties) Act 1999. Re "transferee", see reg.10 below.

### Application of Regulations

**3H–845** **3.**—(1) These Regulations apply to packages sold or offered for sale in the territory of the United Kingdom.

(2) Regulations 4 to 15 apply to packages so sold or offered for sale on or after 31st December 1992.

(3) Regulations 16 to 22 apply to contracts which, in whole or part, remain to be performed on 31st December 1992.

#### Application of the regulations

**3H–846** Subsection (3) is an example of very sloppy drafting. It is generally accepted that regs 16 to 22 apply to "contracts" sold after December 31, 1992 as well as to those which had been made previously and on that date still remained to be fully performed.

### Descriptive matter relating to packages must not be misleading

**3H–847** **4.**—(1) No organiser or retailer shall supply to a consumer any descriptive matter concerning a package, the price of a package or any other conditions applying to the contract which contains any misleading information.

(2) If an organiser or retailer is in breach of paragraph (1) he shall be liable to compensate the consumer for any loss which the consumer suffers in consequence.

#### Misleading information

**3H–848** Where the only remedy claimed is damages, this regulation makes unnecessary any consideration of whether the misleading information amounted to either (a) an actionable misrepresentation or (b) a term of the contract. In *Mawdsley v Cosmosair Plc* [2002] EWCA Civ 587, the claimant and her husband booked a holiday for themselves and their two children. The defendant tour operator had advertised in its brochure that the hotel had "Lifts (in main building)". The restaurant, however, could be reached only via stairs because it was located on a mezzanine floor not served by the lifts. Whilst the claimant and her husband were descending the stairs carrying their baby daughter in a pushchair, the claimant lost her footing, fell and suffered injuries. It was held that "Lifts (in main building)" was a representation that all levels in the main building, including the restaurant, could be accessed by lift. That was "misleading information" for the purposes of Regulation 4, "with the result that [the defendant] is liable under that Regulation for all consequent damage", per Jonathan Parker L.J. at para.45. His Lordship continued: "Since Regulation 6 ... provides that particulars in the brochure are implied warranties in the contract, it follows that [the defendant] was also in breach of contract in that respect." There was a sufficient causal link between the misrepresentation that the restaurant could be accessed by lift and the accident which occurred on the stairs. There had been no novus actus interveniens since the claimant and her husband had behaved perfectly reasonably in taking their daughter in her pushchair in the way that they had (*Quinn v Burch Bros (Builders) Ltd* [1966] 2 Q.B. 370 distinguished).

***Paragraph numbers marked with a "+" can be found online and on CD.***

### Requirements as to brochures

**5.** [Regulation 5 creates criminal offences in relation to brochures which do not include the price and information on the matters specified in Sch. 1 to the regulations.] **3H-849**

### Circumstances in which particulars in brochure are to be binding

**6.**—(1) Subject to paragraphs (2) and (3) of this regulation, the particulars in the brochure (whether or not they are required by regulation 5(1) above to be included in the brochure) shall constitute implied warranties (or, as regards Scotland, implied terms) for the purposes of any contract to which the particulars relate. **3H-850**

(2) Paragraph (1) of this regulation does not apply–

(a) in relation to information required to be included by virtue of paragraph 9 of Schedule 1 to these Regulations; or

(b) where the brochure contains an express statement that changes may be made in the particulars contained in it before a contract is concluded and changes in the particulars so contained are clearly communicated to the consumer before a contract is concluded.

(3) Paragraph (1) of this regulation does not apply when the consumer and the other party to the contract agree after the contract has been made that the particulars in the brochure, or some of those particulars, should not form part of the contract.

#### Brochure contents as terms of the contract

*Mawdsley v Cosmosair Plc* [2002] EWCA Civ 587 provides an example of the application of reg.6(1)—see para.3H-848 above. **3H-851**

The information "required to be included by virtue of paragraph 9 of Schedule 1" is information about "the arrangements for security for money paid over and for the repatriation of the consumer in the event of insolvency".

### Information to be provided before contract is concluded

**7.** [Regulation 7 creates criminal offences for a failure by "the other party to the contract" to provide certain information to the intending consumer before the contract is made, namely information regarding: passport and visa requirements; health formalities; arrangements for security of money paid over and repatriation of the consumer in the event of insolvency.] **3H-852**

### Information to be provided in good time

**8.** [Regulation 8 creates criminal offences for a failure by "the other party to the contract" to provide certain information to the consumer before the start of the journey, namely information regarding: transport arrangements, connections, accommodation en route, contact details of local representatives, holiday/travel insurance.] **3H-853**

### Contents and form of contract

**9.**—(1) The other party to the contract shall ensure that– **3H-854**

(a) depending on the nature of the package being purchased, the contract contains at least the elements specified in Schedule 2 to these Regulations;

***Paragraph numbers marked with a "+" can be found online and on CD.***

(b) subject to paragraph (2) below, all the terms of the contract are set out in writing or such other form as is comprehensible and accessible to the consumer and are communicated to the consumer before the contract is made; and

(c) a written copy of these terms is supplied to the consumer.

(2) Paragraph (1)(b) above does not apply when the interval between the time when the consumer approaches the other party to the contract with a view to entering into a contract and the time of departure under the proposed contract is so short that it is impracticable to comply with the sub-paragraph.

(3) It is an implied condition (or, as regards Scotland, an implied term) of the contract that the other party to the contract complies with the provisions of paragraph (1).

(4) In Scotland, any breach of the condition implied by paragraph (3) above shall be deemed to be a material breach justifying rescission of the contract.

### Transfer of bookings

3H–855 **10.**—(1) In every contract there is an implied term that where the consumer is prevented from proceeding with the package the consumer may transfer his booking to a person who satisfies all the conditions applicable to the package, provided that the consumer gives reasonable notice to the other party to the contract of his intention to transfer before the date when departure is due to take place.

(2) Where a transfer is made in accordance with the implied term set out in paragraph (1) above, the transferor and the transferee shall be jointly and severally liable to the other party to the contract for payment of the price of the package (or, if part of the price has been paid, for payment of the balance) and for any additional costs arising from such transfer.

#### Transfer of bookings

3H–856 This regulation will sometimes enable a consumer to avoid having to pay cancellation charges by transferring his booking to someone else. It applies, however, only where the consumer is "prevented" from proceeding. It is not enough that the consumer has simply changed his mind.

### Price revision

3H–857 **11.**—(1) Any term in a contract to the effect that the prices laid down in the contract may be revised shall be void and of no effect unless the contract provides for the possibility of upward or downward revision and satisfies the conditions laid down in paragraph (2) below.

(2) The conditions mentioned in paragraph (1) are that–

(a) the contract states precisely how the revised price is to be calculated;

(b) the contract provides that price revisions are to be made solely to allow for variations in:–

(i) transportation costs, including the cost of fuel,

(ii) dues, taxes or fees chargeable for services such as landing taxes or embarkation or disembarkation fees at ports and airports, or

(iii) the exchange rates applied to the particular package; and

(3) Notwithstanding any terms of a contract,

(i) no price increase may be made in a specified period which may not be less than 30 days before the departure date stipulated; and

(ii) as against an individual consumer liable under the contract, no price increase may be made in respect of variations which would produce an increase of less than 2%, or such greater percentage as the contract may specify, ("non-eligible variations") and that the non-eligible variations shall be left out of account in the calculation.

**Significant alterations to essential terms**

**12.** In every contract there are implied terms to the effect that– **3H–858**

(a) where the organiser is constrained before the departure to alter significantly an essential term of the contract, such as the price (so far as regulation 11 permits him to do so), he will notify the consumer as quickly as possible in order to enable him to take appropriate decisions and in particular to withdraw from the contract without penalty or to accept a rider to the contract specifying the alterations made and their impact on the price; and

(b) the consumer will inform the organiser or the retailer of his decision as soon as possible.

**Withdrawal by consumer pursuant to regulation 12 and cancellation by organiser**

**13.**—(1) The terms set out in paragraphs (2) and (3) below are implied in every contract and apply where the consumer withdraws from the contract pursuant to the term in it implied by virtue of regulation 12(a), or where the organiser, for any reason other than the fault of the consumer, cancels the package before the agreed date of departure. **3H–859**

(2) The consumer is entitled–

(a) to take a substitute package of equivalent or superior quality if the other party to the contract is able to offer him such a substitute; or

(b) to take a substitute package of lower quality if the other party to the contract is able to offer him one and to recover from the organiser the difference in price between the price of the package purchased and that of the substitute package; or

(c) to have repaid to him as soon as possible all the monies paid by him under the contract.

***Paragraph numbers marked with a "+" can be found online and on CD.***

(3) The consumer is entitled, if appropriate, to be compensated by the organiser for non-performance of the contract except where–

(a) the package is cancelled because the number of persons who agree to take it is less than the minimum number required and the consumer is informed of the cancellation, in writing, within the period indicated in the description of the package; or

(b) the package is cancelled by reason of unusual and unforeseeable circumstances beyond the control of the party by whom this exception is pleaded, the consequences of which could not have been avoided even if all due care had been exercised.

(4) Overbooking shall not be regarded as a circumstance falling within the provisions of sub-paragraph (b) of paragraph (3) above.

**Pre-departure cancellation**

3H–860 The regulations are silent as to the position where the consumer cancels the contract other than in the situations covered in reg.12 (a price increase or other alteration to an essential term of the contract). Thus the consumer who cancels in any other situation will fall liable to pay the cancellation charges stated in the contract, unless they are challengeable under the Unfair Terms in Consumer Contracts Regulations 1999 (see para.3H–886) or are inconsistent with the terms of a code (e.g. ABTA) subscribed to by the tour organiser. For post-departure cancellation, see regulation 14.

*Para.(3)(b)* —The wording here follows exactly that of the Directive in its definition of "force majeure". Sometimes the "unusual and unforeseeable circumstances" will amount to what at common law would be a frustrating event (e.g. the destination resort is completed destroyed by fire). Nevertheless, it seems clear that the contract will not be frustrated but rather the consumer, though not entitled to compensation, will be entitled to the appropriate remedy under para.(2).

## Significant proportion of services not provided

3H–861 **14.**—(1) The terms set out in paragraphs (2) and (3) below are implied in every contract and apply where, after departure, a significant proportion of the services contracted for is not provided or the organiser becomes aware that he will be unable to procure a significant proportion of the services to be provided.

(2) The organiser will make suitable alternative arrangements, at no extra cost to the consumer, for the continuation of the package and will, where appropriate, compensate the consumer for the difference between the services to be supplied under the contract and those supplied.

(3) If it is impossible to make arrangements as described in paragraph (2), or these are not accepted by the consumer for good reasons, the organiser will, where appropriate, provide the consumer with equivalent transport back to the place of departure or to another place to which the consumer has agreed and will, where appropriate, compensate the consumer.

**Force majeure**

3H–862 This regulation contains no exception for force majeure and thus it applies whatever may be the reason that a significant proportion of the services cannot be, or are not, provided. Thus it seems clear that a post-departure event which would otherwise have frustrated the contract at common law will not do so in the case of a package to

*Paragraph numbers marked with a "+" can be found online and on CD.*

which the regulations apply. For the position regarding a pre-departure event, see commentary to reg.13.

**Compensation**

Paragraphs (2) and (3) state that compensation is to be paid "where appropriate". It is submitted that this regulation is to be read together with reg.15 and that payment of compensation under reg.14 will not be "appropriate" where the failure to provide the services falls within paras (a) to (c) of reg.15(2) and is not due to the fault of the organiser (or of another supplier of services). Similarly compensation would not be appropriate to the extent that liability to pay it is limited by an exclusion clause which is reasonable within the meaning of para.(4) of reg.15. **3H–863**

## Liability of other party to the contract for proper performance of obligations under contract

**15.**—(1) The other party to the contract is liable to the consumer for the proper performance of the obligations under the contract, irrespective of whether such obligations are to be performed by that other party or by other suppliers of services but this shall not affect any remedy or right of action which that other party may have against those other suppliers of services. **3H–864**

(2) The other party to the contract is liable to the consumer for any damage caused to him by the failure to perform the contract or the improper performance of the contract unless the failure or the improper performance is due neither to any fault of that other party nor to that of another supplier of services, because–

(a) the failures which occur in the performance of the contract are attributable to the consumer;

(b) such failures are attributable to a third party unconnected with the provision of the services contracted for, and are unforeseeable or unavoidable; or

(c) such failures are due to–

(i) unusual and unforeseeable circumstances beyond the control of the party by whom this exception is pleaded, the consequences of which could not have been avoided even if all due care had been exercised; or

(ii) an event which the other party to the contract or the supplier of services, even with all due care, could not foresee or forestall.

(3) In the case of damage arising from the non-performance or improper performance of the services involved in the package, the contract may provide for compensation to be limited in accordance with the international conventions which govern such services.

(4) In the case of damage other than personal injury resulting from the non-performance or improper performance of the services involved in the package, the contract may include a term limiting the amount of compensation which will be paid to the consumer, provided that the limitation is not unreasonable.

(5) Without prejudice to paragraph (3) and paragraph (4) above, liability under paragraphs (1) and (2) above cannot be excluded by any contractual term.

(6) The terms set out in paragraphs (7) and (8) below are implied in every contract.

(7) In the circumstances described in paragraph (2)(b) and (c) of this regulation, the other party to the contract will give prompt assistance to a consumer in difficulty.

(8) If the consumer complains about a defect in the performance of the contract, the other party to the contract, or his local representative, if there is one, will make prompt efforts to find appropriate solutions.

(9) The contract must clearly and explicitly oblige the consumer to communicate at the earliest opportunity, in writing or any other appropriate form, to the supplier of the services concerned and to the other party to the contract any failure which he perceives at the place where the services concerned are supplied.

**"Proper performance of the contract"**

**3H–865** Regulation 15 does not impose strict liability in all cases. Whether there has been proper performance "can only be determined by reference to the terms of the contract. There may be absolute obligations, e.g. as to the existence of a swimming-pool or any other matter, but, in the absence of the assumption of an absolute obligation, the implication will be that reasonable skill and care will be used in the rendering of the relevant service. There will thus be no improper performance of the air carriage unless there is an absence of reasonable skill and care in the provision of that service": per Longmore L.J. in *Hone v Going Places Leisure Travel Ltd* [2001] EWCA Civ 947 at para.15.

The duty of reasonable care and skill requires, in the case of a hotel abroad, that the hotel complies with local safety regulations rather than British safety standards; compliance with local safety standards does not, however, preclude other possible breaches of the duty of care: *Codd v Thomson Tour Operators Ltd* [2000] CA transcripts 1470/2000, cited in *Evans v Kosmar Villa Holidays* [2007] EWCA Civ 1003; [2008] 1 W.L.R. 297. It was held in the latter case, applying *Tomlinson v Congelton* [2003] UKHL 47; [2004] 1 A.C. 46, that there was no duty to give a holiday maker, who was of full capacity and able to make an informed decision, a warning about the risks of diving into the shallow end of a small swimming pool at his holiday apartment complex.

**The "other party to the contract"**

**3H–866** Regulation 15 ensures that the other party to the contract (usually the tour operator) is responsible for the proper performance of the contract by those supplying the relevant service, whether transport, accommodation or another service, irrespective of whoever it is that actually performs that service. In the conventional package holiday situation, the tour operator will be the other party to the contract. Query whether reg.15 imposes liability on a travel agent who, in addition to selling a tour operator's conventional package holiday and as part of that same transaction, himself arranges transport to the hotel or the airport. In that situation there are two "organisers", the tour operator and the agent, but arguably only the tour operator is the other party to the contract—see the commentary to reg.2 above. Where the travel agent has held himself out as principal (i.e. as the tour operator), he will on ordinary principles of the law of agency be liable as if he were the other party to the contract: see the High Court decision in *Hone v Going Places Leisure Travel Ltd* (QBD, November 16, 2000, Manchester District Registry, No.MA993390, confirmed on appeal at [2001] EWCA Civ 947). In *Hone*, the consumer had viewed the defendant travel agent's teletext advertisement, which had failed to make clear that the travel agent was merely an agent for the tour operator, and had then booked the package by phone to the defendant travel agent.

**"Damage"**

**3H–867** It is thought that nothing hangs on the use of the different words "loss" and "damage" in regs 4 and 15 respectively. The latter certainly includes more than personal injuries (see reg.14(4)) and would appear to include any type of loss for which damages can be awarded for breach of contract. On assessment, see the General Note at the start of these regulations.

### Exclusion clauses

An exclusion clause is not effective except to the extent allowed under paras (3) and (4). The international conventions referred to in para.(3) include, but are not limited to: the Warsaw Convention on Carriage by Air; the Berne Convention on Carriage by Rail; the Athens Convention on Carriage by Sea; the Paris Convention on Liability of Hotel Keepers. Paragraph (4) allows a limitation (except in relation to personal injuries) which "is not unreasonable". This appears to involve a test similar to the requirement of reasonableness in s.11 of the Unfair Contract Terms Act 1977. **3H–868**

### Unfair Contract Terms

Regulation 15 (apart from para.(9)) deals with the contractual liability of the other party to the contract (usually the tour operator) and not with that of the consumer. The regulations are silent as regards contractual obligations which can be said to be unfair to the consumer, e.g. a clause imposing unreasonably high cancellation charges. Such obligations are, however, challengeable under the Unfair Terms in Consumer Contracts Regulations 1999, see below. **3H–869**

### Regulations 16–26

[Regulations 16–22 require arrangements to be in place to cover the risk of the tour operator becoming insolvent, so that there is security for the refund of money paid over and for the repatriation of the consumer. **3H–870**

Regulations 23–26 (and also Schs 1 and 3) contain provisions relating to the criminal offences created by the regulations.]

* * * *

## Saving for civil consequences

**27.** No contract shall be void or unenforceable, and no right of action in civil proceedings in respect of any loss shall arise, by reason only of the commission of an offence under regulations 5, 7, 8, 16 or 22 of these Regulations. **3H–871**

## Terms implied in contract

**28.** Where it is provided in these Regulations that a term (whether so described or whether described as a condition or warranty) is implied in the contract it is so implied irrespective of the law which governs the contract. **3H–872**

* * * *

**REGULATION 9**

## SCHEDULE 2

ELEMENTS TO BE INCLUDED IN THE CONTRACT IF RELEVANT TO THE PARTICULAR PACKAGE

1. The travel destination(s) and, where periods of stay are involved, the relevant periods, with dates. **3H–873**

2. [Repealed by the Enterprise Act 2002 (Part 8 Notice to OFT of Intended Prosecution Specified Enactments, Revocation and Transitional Provision) Order (SI 2003 No. 1376), art.3.]

3. Where the package includes accommodation, its location, its tourist category or degree of comfort, its main features and, where the accommodation is to be provided in a member State, its compliance with the rules of that member State.

4. The meals which are included in the package.

5. Whether a minimum number of persons is required for the package to take place and, if so, the deadline for informing the consumer in the event of cancellation.

6. The itinerary.

7. Visits, excursions or other services which are included in the total price agreed for the package.

8. The name and address of the organiser, the retailer and, where appropriate, the insurer.

9. The price of the package, if the price may be revised in accordance with the term which may be included in the contract under regulation 11, an indication of the possibility of such price revisions, and an indication of any dues, taxes or fees chargeable for certain services (landing, embarkation or disembarkation fees at ports and airports and tourist taxes) where such costs are not included in the package.

10. The payment schedule and method of payment.

11. Special requirements which the consumer has communicated to the organiser or retailer when making the booking and which both have accepted.

12. The periods within which the consumer must make any complaint about the failure to perform or the inadequate performance of the contract.

## Contracts (Rights of Third Parties) Act 1999

3H–874 1999 c.31

ARRANGEMENT OF SECTIONS



**Paragraph numbers marked with a "+" denote content that is available on White Book on Westlaw UK or the Civil Procedure CD.**

## Unfair Terms in Consumer Contracts Regulations 1999

3H–886 (S.I. 1999 No. 2083)

ARRANGEMENT OF SECTIONS



**General note**

3H–887 The European Directive on Unfair Terms in Consumer Contracts (93/13) was first implemented in the UK by the Unfair Terms in Consumer Contracts Regulations 1994, which came into effect on July 1, 1995. Those regulations therefore apply to contracts entered on or after that date and before October 1, 1999 when the present regulations came into force. The present regulations replicate most of what was in the 1994 regulations with some relatively minor modifications to reflect more closely the wording of the Directive.

### Contracts affected

The regulations apply to contracts concluded between on the one hand a seller or supplier who is acting for purposes related to his trade, business or profession (whether publicly or private owned) and on the other a consumer who is a natural person (not a corporate body) acting for purposes which are outside his trade business or profession (whether publicly or private owned) and on the other a consumer who is a natural person (not a corporate body) acting for purposes which are outside his trade business or profession. In *Evans v Cherry Tree Finance Ltd* [2008] EWCA Civ 331; [2008] C.C.L.R. 5, the defendant owned premises used largely for the purposes of his business. He took out a loan, secured on those premises, in order (as the loan application made clear) to provide finance to pay off his divorce settlement. He was acting in the capacity of a consumer, i.e. for purposes outside his trade business or profession. Accordingly the terms of the agreement were assessable for fairness under the regulations. Similarly, where a wealthy professional couple, who did not earn their living from the investment industry, entered into foreign exchange contracts in the hope of making profitable use of their disposable income, these contracts were (despite the large amounts invested) made for purposes outside their trade, business or profession: *Standard Bank London Ltd v Apostolakis* [2002] C.L.C. 933 (High Ct). **3H–888**

The regulations overlap with other enactments, including particularly the Consumer Credit Act 1974 and the Unfair Contract Terms Act 1977. A term of a regulated consumer credit agreement could, for example, form the basis of a claim (under s.140B of the 1974 Act) that there was an unfair relationship between the creditor and the debtor and could also be rendered ineffective by the regulations. The range of contracts subject to the regulations is, in one respect, wider and, in another respect, narrower than those regulated by the Consumer Credit Act. It is wider in that it includes contracts involving all sorts of subject matter, and not just credit and hire agreements. It is narrower in that it does not cover contracts where the customer is making the contract for the purposes of his trade or profession. The scope of the two is the same in one respect, namely neither applies where the customer is a corporate body.

The overlap with the Unfair Contract Terms Act is that an exclusion clause could be rendered ineffective by either, or both of the regulations and the 1977 Act. Unlike the Act, the regulations do not apply (e.g. to standard form exclusion clauses) where both parties are acting for business purposes. On the other hand, where the regulations do apply to a contract, they apply, not just to exclusion clauses but also to other terms that may be unfair.

### Effect of the regulations

- All written terms are required to be in plain and intelligible language; if there is a doubt, the interpretation most favourable to the consumer applies (reg.7). **3H–889**
- Any terms which (a) are not core terms, (b) have not been individually negotiated and, (c) are unfair, are not binding on the consumer (reg.8). The validity of the rest of the contract is not affected, provided it is capable of continuing in existence without the unfair term. The test of unfairness is stated in reg.5 and a non-exhaustive indicative list of unfair terms is given in Sch.2.
- In so far as they are in plain and intelligible language, the core terms of the contract (i.e. those relating to the definition of the main subject matter of the contract or the adequacy of the price or remuneration) are not subject to the requirement to be fair (reg.6).

Regulations 10 to 15 and Sch.1 which are not reproduced here, deal with the powers and duties of the Director General of Fair Trading (now the Office of Fair Trading) and other bodies under the regulations. Under the 1994 Regulations the Director General was given a duty to consider any complaint that a contract term drawn up for general use was unfair and was given a power to ask the court for an injunction to prohibit its use. The 1999 Regulations re-enact those provisions and extend the power to seek an injunction to a range of other regulatory bodies and to trading standards departments. They also extend the power to seek an injunction to the Consumers' **3H–890**

Association. Pursuant to the 1994 and the 1999 Regulations, the Office of Fair Trading periodically publishes bulletins giving information on complaints received and undertakings taken from traders to change or abandon the use of particular clauses.

### Case law

3H–891 The regulations have no express exclusion for land transactions and thus do apply to tenancy agreements between tenants and a local authority: *Khatun v Newham LBC* [2005] Q.B. 37; [2004] 3 W.L.R. 417. The protection provided for consumers by the Directive (which the regulations implement) entails the court being able of its own motion to determine whether a term of a contract (which is before the court) is unfair, when making its preliminary assessment as to whether to allow a claim to proceed, C–240/98 *Oceano Grupo Editorial SA v Rocio Murciano Qunitero*, June 27, 2000, ECJ. That case involved a number of contracts by a company which had its principal place of business in Barcelona, each such contract being a contract to sell, on instalment credit terms, an encyclopedia to a consumer domiciled in another part of Spain. Each contract contained a clause, not individually negotiated, giving exclusive jurisdiction to the Barcelona courts, which is where the seller commenced proceedings against consumers who had defaulted on their repayments. It was held that the Barcelona court should of its own motion (a) determine whether the jurisdiction clause was fair and (b) it being unfair, decline the jurisdiction it conferred.

For an example of a successful challenge under the 1994 Regulations to the terms of a mortgage loan agreement, see *Falco Finance Ltd v Gough* [1999] C.C.L.R. 16, noted in the commentary to the Consumer Credit Act 1974 s.138 (at para.3H–320, above). In *Director General of Fair Trading v First National Bank Plc* [2002] 1 A.C. 48; [2003] C.C.L.R. 8, HL, the Director General sought an injunction (under the 1994 Regulations) in respect of a clause in the standard form loan agreement used by the defendant Bank. The contractual rate of interest was stated and was variable in accordance with changes in the Bank's Base Lending rate. Clause 3 of the agreement provided that that rate of interest was to be charged on a day to day basis on the outstanding balance and debited to the account in arrears. Clause 8 provided that the same rate of interest would be charged on arrears until payment. It further provided that interest would continue to be charged at the same rate after judgment, until the debt was paid. Clause 3 and the other contract provisions which fixed the contractual rate of interest were core terms (concerned with the adequacy of the remuneration) which could not be challenged as unfair under the regulations (see now reg.6 of the 1999 Regulations). Clause 8, however was assessable for fairness. It was part of the Director General's case that not infrequently a borrower, against whom the Bank had brought proceedings to recover the outstanding balance, would agree to a consent order being made, such judgment being for the balance to be payable by instalments over an extended period. The effects of clause 8 were: (i) to reverse the common law rule that the right to interest merged with the judgment debt and thus evaporated after judgment; (ii) to oust the application of the County Court (Interest on Judgments) Order 1991 (under which no interest is payable on judgments for money due under regulated consumer credit agreements). The House of Lords held that clause 8 was not unfair within the 1994 Regulations. The problems for consumers (debtors) arose from the fact that debtors were unaware of the reliefs which the court could give them at the default stage. Those reliefs included: (i) re-opening an extortionate agreement (under s.139 of the Consumer Credit Act 1974); and (ii) reducing the rate of interest (under s.136 when granting a time order under s.128 of the 1974 Act). It was, however, not customary (nor was it a statutory requirement) that the debtor be given notice of those possible reliefs when the contract was made. Clause 8 was not rendered unfair by the absence of procedural safeguards for the debtor at the default stage. Such procedural safeguards, subsequently introduced by the Consumer Credit Act 2006, are now to be found in ss.86A to 86F of the Consumer Credit Act 1974. Section 86F prevents more than simple interest being payable on "default sums". *Cf. Bairstow Eves London Central v Smith* [2004] EWHC 263; [2004] E.G. 118, (QB), where the contract provided for an estate agent to be paid commission of 1.5 per cent of the purchase price. A clause entitling the estate agent to claim commission at 3 per cent if the commission was not paid in full within 10 days of completion of the sale, was held, (a) not to fall within reg.6(2) and thus to be assessable for fairness and, (b) to be unfair.

### Arbitration agreements

3H–892 A term of an agreement which amounts to an arbitration agreement is unfair within the meaning of the regulations in so far as it relates to a claim for a pecuniary remedy which does not exceed £5000: Arbitration Act 1996 s.91(1)—see para.2E–324+. This provision can be seen as a more precise statement of a more vaguely worded provision in para.(q) of Schedule 2 to the Regulations. Also it applies even where the "consumer" is a legal person as well as when he is a natural person: Arbitration Act, s.90.

### Citation and commencement

**1.** These Regulations may be cited as the Unfair Terms in Consumer Contracts Regulations 1999 and shall come into force on 1st October 1999. **3H–893**

### Revocation

**2.** The Unfair Terms in Consumer Contracts Regulations 1994 are hereby revoked. **3H–894**

### Interpretation

**3.**—(1) In these Regulations— **3H–895**

"the Community" means the European Community;

"consumer" means any natural person who, in contracts covered by these Regulations, is acting for purposes which are outside his trade, business or profession;

"court" in relation to England and Wales and Northern Ireland means a county court or the High Court, and in relation to Scotland, the Sheriff or the Court of Session;

"Director" means the Director General of Fair Trading;

"EEA Agreement" means the Agreement on the European Economic Area signed at Oporto on 2nd May 1992 as adjusted by the protocol signed at Brussels on 17th March 1993;

"Member State" means a State which is a contracting party to the EEA Agreement;

"notified" means notified in writing;

"qualifying body" means a person specified in Schedule 1;

"seller or supplier" means any natural or legal person who, in contracts covered by these Regulations, is acting for purposes relating to his trade, business or profession, whether publicly owned or privately owned;

"unfair terms" means the contractual terms referred to in regulation 5.

(1A) The references—

(a) in regulation 4(1) to a seller or a supplier, and

(b) in regulation 8(1) to a seller or supplier,

include references to a distance supplier and to an intermediary.

(1B) In paragraph (1A) and regulation 5(6) "distance supplier" means—

(a) a supplier under a distance contract within the meaning of the Financial Services (Distance Marketing) Regulations 2004, or

(b) a supplier of unsolicited financial services within regulation 15 of those Regulations; and

"intermediary" has the same meaning as in those Regulations.

*Paragraph numbers marked with a "+" can be found online and on CD.*

(2) In the application of these Regulations to Scotland for references to an "injunction" or an "interim injunction" there shall be substituted references to an "interdict" or "interim interdict" respectively.

3H-896 *Note* —Paragraphs (1A) and (1B) were added by the Financial Services (Distance Marketing) Regulations 2004 (SI 2004/2095). "Consumer"—In *Evans v Cherry Tree Finance Ltd* [2008] EWCA Civ 331; [2008] C.C.L.R. 5, the debtor who had applied for a loan stating the purpose to be "to pay equity to divorced wife and pay off existing mortgage" was held to have been acting for purposes outside his trade business or profession. For other cases on the meaning of "consumer", see *Benincasa v Dentalkit* [1997] E.C.R. I-3767 and *Standard Bank London Ltd v Apostolakis* [2002] C.L.C. 933.

### Terms to which these Regulations apply

3H-897 **4.**—(1) These Regulations apply in relation to unfair terms in contracts concluded between a seller or a supplier and a consumer.

(2) These Regulations do not apply to contractual terms which reflect—

(a) mandatory statutory or regulatory provisions (including such provisions under the law of any Member State or in Community legislation having effect in the United Kingdom without further enactment);

(b) the provisions or principles of international conventions to which the Member States or the Community are party.

### Unfair Terms

3H-898 **5.**—(1) A contractual term which has not been individually negotiated shall be regarded as unfair if, contrary to the requirement of good faith, it causes a significant imbalance in the parties' rights and obligations arising under the contract, to the detriment of the consumer.

(2) A term shall always be regarded as not having been individually negotiated where it has been drafted in advance and the consumer has therefore not been able to influence the substance of the term.

(3) Notwithstanding that a specific term or certain aspects of its in a contract has been individually negotiated, these Regulations shall apply to the rest of a contract if an overall assessment of it indicates that it is a pre-formulated standard contract.

(4) It shall be for any seller or supplier who claims that a term was individually negotiated to show that it was.

(5) Schedule 2 to these Regulations contains an indicative and non-exhaustive list of the terms which may be regarded as unfair.

(6) Any contractual term providing that a consumer bears the burden of proof in respect of showing whether a distance supplier or an intermediary complied with any or all of the obligations placed upon him resulting from the Directive and any rule or enactment implementing it shall always be regarded as unfair.

(7) In paragraph (6)—

"the Directive" means Directive 2002/65/EC of the European Parliament and of the Council of 23 September 2002 concerning the distance marketing of consumer financial services and amending Council Directive 90/619/EEC and Directives 97/7/EC and 98/27/EC; and

"rule" means a rule made by the Financial Services Authority under the Financial Services and Markets Act 2000 or by a designated professional body within the meaning of section 326(2) of that Act.

*Note* —Paragraphs (6) and (7) were added by the Financial Services (Distance Marketing) Regulations 2004 (SI 2004/2095). See, generally, case law mentioned in the general note at the start of these Regulations. **3H–899**

## Assessment of unfair terms

**6.**—(1) Without prejudice to regulation 12, the unfairness of a contractual term shall be assessed, taking into account the nature of the goods or services for which the contract was concluded and by referring, at the time of conclusion of the contract, to all the circumstances attending the conclusion of the contract and to all the other terms of the contract or of another contract on which it is dependent. **3H–900**

(2) In so far as it is in plain intelligible language, the assessment of fairness of a term shall not relate—

(a) to the definition of the main subject matter of the contract, or

(b) to the adequacy of the price or remuneration, as against the goods or services supplied in exchange.

*Note* —See case law mentioned in the general note at the start of these Regulations. **3H–901**

*Subsection (2)* —A default charge is not part of the price or remuneration for the goods or services purchased: *Director General of Fair Trading v First National Bank Plc* [2001] UKHL 52; [2002] 1 A.C. 481. The identification of the price or remuneration (as opposed to a default charge) is a matter of objective interpretation for the court: *Office of Fair Trading v Abbey National Plc* [2009] UKSC 6; [2009] 3 W.L.R. 1215. See, for example *Bairstow Eves London Central v Smith* [2004] EWHC 263; [2004] E.G. 118 (QB) (para.3H–891 above), approved in the *Abbey National* case just cited. **3H–901.1**

In the Abbey National case, the Supreme Court considered the charges made by banks for unauthorised overdrafts, i.e. the charge made by a bank when a customer with a current account causes his bank to make a payment which is not covered by either sufficient funds in the account or an agreed overdraft facility. It held that these charges, a significant part of the revenue stream of the banks and an important part of the banks' charging structure, were part of the price or remuneration paid by a customer for the package of services provided by the bank to the customer. Accordingly these charges fell within reg.6(2)(b) and, being in plain and intelligible language, were excluded from assessment for fairness. Their Lordships observed that various expressions had been used to describe contractual terms which are subject to assessment for fairness, including "ancillary", "subordinate", "incidental", "non-core" and "collateral". Such expressions should be treated with caution; terms as to the price or remuneration were excluded from assessment for fairness. In *Office of Fair Trading v Foxtons (No.2)* [2009] EWHC 1681 (Ch), Mann J. gave two reasons for holding that renewal fees in contracts between letting agents and consumer landlords were not assessable for fairness: (i) they would not have been understood as part of the "core bargain" by the typical consumer landlord, and (ii) they were not in plain and intelligible language. After the decision of the Supreme Court in the *Abbey National* case, the first of those reasons now seems questionable and the case is now the subject of an appeal.

## Written contracts

**7.**—(1) A seller or supplier shall ensure that any written term of a contract is expressed in plain, intelligible language. **3H–902**

(2) If there is no doubt about the meaning of a written term, the interpretation which is most favourable to the consumer shall prevail but this rule shall not apply in proceedings brought under regulation 12.

**Effect of unfair term**

3H–903 **8.**—(1) An unfair term in a contract concluded with a consumer by a seller or supplier shall not be binding on the consumer.

(2) The contract shall continue to bind the parties if it is capable of continuing in existence without the unfair term.

**Choice of law clauses**

3H–904 **9.** These Regulations shall apply notwithstanding any contract term which applies or purports to apply the law of a non-Member State, if the contract has a close connection with the territory of the Member States.

* * * *

SCHEDULES

**REGULATION 5(5)** SCHEDULE 2

INDICATIVE AND NON-EXHAUSTIVE LIST OF TERMS WHICH MAY BE REGARDED AS UNFAIR

3H–905 1. Terms which have the object or effect of—

(a) excluding or limiting the legal liability of a seller or supplier in the event of the death of a consumer or personal injury to the latter resulting from an act or omission of that seller or supplier;

(b) inappropriately excluding or limiting the legal rights of the consumer *vis-à-vis* the seller or supplier or another party in the event of total or partial non-performance or inadequate performance by the seller or supplier of any of the contractual obligations, including the option of offsetting a debt owed to the seller or supplier against any claim which the consumer may have against him;

(c) making an agreement binding on the consumer whereas provision of services by the seller or supplier is subject to a condition whose realisation depends on his own will alone;

(d) permitting the seller or supplier to retain sums paid by the consumer where the latter decides not to conclude or perform the contract, without providing for the consumer to receive compensation of an equivalent amount from the seller or supplier where the latter is the party cancelling the contract;

(e) requiring any consumer who fails to fulfil his obligation to pay a disproportionately high sum in compensation;

(f) authorising the seller or supplier to dissolve the contract on a discretionary basis where the same facility is not granted to the consumer, or permitting the seller or supplier to retain the sums paid for services not yet supplied by him where it is the seller or supplier himself who dissolves the contract;

(g) enabling the seller or supplier to terminate a contract of indeterminate duration without reasonable notice except where there are serious grounds for doing so;

(h) automatically extending a contract of fixed duration where the consumer does not indicate otherwise, when the deadline fixed for the consumer to express his desire not to extend the contract is unreasonably early;

(i) irrevocably binding the consumer to terms with which he had no real opportunity of becoming acquainted before the conclusion of the contract;

(j) enabling the seller or supplier to alter the terms of the contract unilaterally without a valid reason which is specified in the contract;

(k) enabling the seller or supplier to alter unilaterally without valid reason any characteristics of the product or service to be provided;

(l) providing for the price of goods to be determined at the time of delivery or allowing a seller of goods or supplier of services to increase their price without in both cases giving the consumer the corresponding right to cancel the contract if the final price is too high in relation to the price agreed when the contract was concluded;

(m) giving the seller or supplier the right to determine whether the goods or services supplied are in conformity with the contract, or giving him the exclusive right to interpret any term of the contract;

(n) limiting the seller's or supplier's obligation to respect commitments undertaken by his agents or making his commitments subject to compliance with a particular formality;

(o) obliging the consumer to fulfil all his obligations where the seller or supplier does not perform his;

(p) giving the seller or supplier the possibility of transferring his rights and obligations under the contract, where this may serve to reduce the guarantees for the consumer, without the latter's agreement;

(q) excluding or hindering the consumer's right to take legal action or excercise any other legal remedy, particularly by requiring the consumer to take disputes exclusively to arbitration not covered by legal provisions, unduly restricting the evidence available to him or imposing on him a burden of proof which, according to the acpplicable law, should lie with another party to the contract.

2. Scope of paragraphs 1(g), (j) and (l)

(a) Paragraph 1(g) is without hindrance to terms by which a supplier of financial services reserves the right to terminate unilaterally a contract of indeterminate duration without notice where there is a valid reason, provided that the supplier is required to inform the other contracting party or parties thereof immediately.

(b) Paragraph 1(j) is without hindrance to terms under which a supplier of financial services reserves the right to alter the rate of interest payable by the consumer or due to the latter, or the amount of other charges for financial services without notice where there is a valid reason, provided that the supplier is required to inform the other contracting party or parties thereof at the earliest opportunity and that the latter are free to dissolve the contract immediately.

Paragraph 1(j) is also without hindrance to terms under which a seller or supplier reserves the right to alter unilaterally the conditions of a contract of indeterminate duration, provided that he is required to inform the consumer with reasonable notice and that the consumer is free to dissolve the contract.

(c) Paragraphs 1(g), (j) and (l) do not apply to:

- transactions in transferable securities, financial instruments and other products or services where the price is linked to fluctuations in a stock exchange quotation or index or a financial market rate that the seller or supplier does not control;
- contracts for the purchase or sale of foreign currency, traveller's cheques or international money orders denominated in foreign currency.

(d) Paragraph 1(1) is without hindrance to price indexation clauses, where lawful, provided that the method by which prices vary is explicitly described.

## The Consumer Protection (Distance Selling) Regulations 2000

3H–906 (S.I. 2000 No. 2344)

ARRANGEMENT OF REGULATIONS



**Paragraphs numbers marked with a "+" denote content that is available on White Book on Westlaw UK or the Civil Procedure CD.**

## Sale and Supply of Goods to Consumers Regulations 2002

3H–954 (S.I. 2002 No. 3045)

ARRANGEMENT OF REGULATIONS



**General note**

3H–955 These regulations implemented the Directive on Certain Aspects of Sale of Goods and Consumer Guarantees (1999/44/EC). They made the seller liable for public statements made by the seller, the producer or his representative; they extended the range of remedies available to a consumer in the case of goods which fail to comply with statutory implied terms; they provide, in regulation 15, that a consumer guarantee takes effect as a contractual obligation. Regs 2 and 15 are the only free-standing provisions in the regulations. The other provisions all operate by making amendments to existing Acts, namely: Supply of Goods (Implied Terms) Act 1973; Supply of Goods and Services Act 1982; Unfair Contract Terms Act 1977; Sale of Goods Act 1979. See commentaries to ss.14(2D) and 48A of the Sale of Goods Act 1979 above.

**Interpretation**

**2.** In these Regulations— 3H-956

"consumer" means any natural person who, in the contracts covered by these Regulations, is acting for purposes which are outside his trade, business or profession;

"consumer guarantee" means any undertaking to a consumer by a person acting in the course of his business, given without extra charge, to reimburse the price paid or to replace, repair or handle consumer goods in any way if they do not meet the specifications set out in the guarantee statement or in the relevant advertising;

"court" in relation to England and Wales and Northern Ireland means a county court or the High Court, and in relation to Scotland, the sheriff or the Court of Session;

"enforcement authority" means the Director General of Fair Trading, every local weights and measures authority in Great Britain and the Department of Enterprise, Trade and Investment for Northern Ireland; "goods" has the same meaning as in section 61 of the Sale of Goods Act 1979;

"guarantor" means a person who offers a consumer guarantee to a consumer; and

"supply" includes supply by way of sale, lease, hire or hire-purchase.

* * * *

**Consumer guarantees**

**15.**—(1) Where goods are sold or otherwise supplied to a consumer which are offered with a consumer guarantee, the consumer guarantee takes effect at the time the goods are delivered as a contractual obligation owed by the guarantor under the conditions set out in the guarantee statement and the associated advertising. 3H-957

(2) The guarantor shall ensure that the guarantee sets out in plain intelligible language the contents of the guarantee and the essential particulars necessary for making claims under the guarantee, notably the duration and territorial scope of the guarantee as well as the name and address of the guarantor.

(2A) The guarantor shall also ensure that the guarantee contains a statement that the consumer has statutory rights in relation to the goods which are sold or supplied and that those rights are not affected by the guarantee.

*Paragraph numbers marked with a "+" can be found online and on CD.*

(3) On request by the consumer to a person to whom paragraph (4) applies, the guarantee shall within a reasonable time be made available in writing or in another durable medium available and accessible to him.

(4) This paragraph applies to the guarantor and any other person who offers to consumers the goods which are the subject of the guarantee for sale or supply.

(5) Where consumer goods are offered with a consumer guarantee, and where those goods are offered within the territory of the United Kingdom, then the guarantor shall ensure that the consumer guarantee is written in English.

(6) If the guarantor fails to comply with the provisions of paragraphs (2) or (5) above, or a person to whom paragraph (4) applies fails to comply with paragraph (3) then the enforcement authority may apply for an injunction or (in Scotland) an order of specific implement against that person requiring him to comply.

(7) The court on application under this Regulation may grant an injunction or (in Scotland) an order of specific implement on such terms as it thinks fit.

**3H–957.1** *Note*—Amended by SI 2008/1277.

**Extended warranties on electrical goods**

**3H–958** In addition to the protection given under reg.15 above, a consumer who buys an extended guarantee (usually one lasting more than a year) relating to an electrical product may have further protection by virtue of the Supply of Extended Warranties on Domestic Electrical Goods Order 2005 (SI 2005/37). The 2005 Order does not apply to a warranty unless the consumer gives a monetary consideration for it and thus does not apply where a warranty or guarantee comes free with the goods. Nor does it apply to extended warranties that are distance contracts. It is designed to deal with the situation where a consumer buys an electrical item (usually making the purchase in-store) and also (for an additional amount) buys an extended warranty (usually one lasting more than one year after purchase of the goods). The Order requires, where an extended warranty is available for purchase at the same time as electrical goods are bought, that in-store (or in-catalogue) information be displayed, close to where the goods are displayed (or advertised) clearly indicating that purchase of the extended guarantee is optional and stating its duration and price.The Order makes it unlawful for the trader to supply the consumer with an extended warranty lasting more than a year unless the consumer is allowed certain cancellation and termination rights. As regards cancellation, the consumer must be allowed, for 45 days after purchasing the warranty (and provided no claim has been made under it), to give notice, either written or oral, to cancel it and to obtain a complete refund of the price of it. As regards termination, the consumer must be allowed, regardless of whether a claim has been made under the warranty, to give oral or written notice to terminate it after the 45 day period and to obtain a pro-rata refund. Where the price of the warranty exceeds £20, the supplier must give the consumer written notice of the consumer's rights of cancellation and termination.

# 3I DISCRIMINATION



## PRACTICE DIRECTION—PROCEEDINGS UNDER ENACTMENTS RELATING TO DISCRIMINATION

### Scope and Interpretation

**1.1** This Practice Direction applies to certain county court proceedings under the enactments defined in paragraph 1.2. **3I–1**

**1.2** In this Practice Direction—

(1) 'the 1975 Act' means the Sex Discrimination Act 1975[1];

(2) 'the 1976 Act' means the Race Relations Act 1976[2];

(3) 'the 1995 Act' means the Disability Discrimination Act 1995[3];

(4) 'the 2006 Act' means the Equality Act 2006[4]

(5) 'the Religion or Belief Regulations' means the Employment Equality (Religion or Belief) Regulations 2003[5];

(6) 'the Sexual Orientation Regulations 2003' means the Employment Equality (Sexual Orientation) Regulations 2003[6];

(7) 'the Age Regulations' means the Employment Equality (Age) Regulations 2006[7];

(8) 'the Sexual Orientation Regulations 2007' means the Equality Act (Sexual Orientation) Regulations 2007[8].

**1.3** In this Practice Direction—

(a) a reference to 'the Commission', in relation to proceedings under a particular enactment is a reference to the Commission for Equality and Human Rights;

(b) where it applies to proceedings under the 1976 Act, 'court' means a designated county court under section 67(1) of that Act.

### Commission to be given notice of claims

**2.1** This paragraph applies to claims under— **3I–2**

(a) section 66 of the 1975 Act;

(b) section 57 of the 1976 Act;

(c) section 25 of the 1995 Act;

(d) section 66 of the 2006 Act;

(e) regulation 39 of the Age Regulations;

(f) regulation 31 of the Religion or Belief Regulations;

(g) regulation 31 of the Sexual Orientation Regulations 2003; or

---

[1] 1975 c.65.
[2] 1976 c.74.
[3] 1995 c.50.
[4] 2006 c.3.
[5] S.I. 2003/1660.
[6] S.I. 2003/1661.
[7] S.I. 2006/1031
[8] S.I. 2007/1263.

*Paragraph numbers marked with a "+" can be found online and on CD.*

(h) regulation 20 of the Sexual Orientation Regulations 2007.

**2.2** When a claim to which this paragraph applies is commenced, the claimant must—

(a) give notice of the commencement of the proceedings to the Commission;

(b) file a copy of that notice.

### Assessors

3I–3 **3.** Rule 35.15 has effect in relation to an assessor who is to be appointed in proceedings under section 66 (1) of the 1975 Act.

### Admissibility of Evidence

3I–4 **4.1** This paragraph applies where a claimant in a claim alleging discrimination has questioned the defendant under—

(a) section 74 of the 1975 Act;

(b) section 65 of the 1976 Act;

(c) section 56 of the 1995 Act;

(d) regulation 41 of the Age Regulations;

(e) regulation 33 of the Religion or Belief Regulations; or

(f) regulation 33 of the Sexual Orientation Employment Regulations 2003.

(g) section 70 of the 2006 Act; or

(h) regulation 24 of the Sexual Orientation Regulations 2007.

**4.2** Either party may apply to the court to determine whether the question or any reply is admissible under that section.

(Part 23 contains general rules about making applications).

**4.3** Rule 3.4 (power to strike out a statement of case) applies to the question and any answer as it applies to a statement of case.

### Exclusion of persons from certain proceedings

3I–5 **5.1** In a claim—

(1) brought under section 66(1) of the 1975 Act;

(2) brought under section 57(1) of the 1976 Act;

(3) alleging discrimination under the 1995 Act;

(4) brought under section 66 of the 2006 Act; or

(5) brought under regulation 20 of the Sexual Orientation Regulations 2007,

the court may, where it considers it expedient in the interests of national security—

(a) exclude from all or part of the proceedings—

(i) the claimant;

(ii) the claimant's representatives; or

(iii) any assessors

(Section 67(4) of the 1976 Act allows an assessor to be appointed in proceedings under that Act);

(b) permit a claimant or representative to make a statement to the court before the start of the proceedings (or the part of the proceedings) from which he is excluded; or

(c) take steps to keep secret all or part of the reasons for its decision in the claim.

**5.2** In this paragraph, a 'special advocate' means a person appointed under—

(1) section 66B(2) of the 1975 Act;
(2) section 67A(2) of the 1976 Act;
(3) section 59A(2) of the 1995 Act;
(4) section 71(2) of the 2006 Act; or
(5) regulation 25(2) of the Sexual Orientation Regulations 2007.

**5.3** In proceedings to which this paragraph refers, where the claimant or his representatives have been excluded from all or part of the proceedings—

(a) the court will inform the Attorney General of the proceedings; and
(b) the Attorney General may appoint a special advocate to represent the claimant in respect of those parts of the proceedings from which he or his representative have been excluded.

**5.4** In exercise of its powers under paragraph 5.1(c), the court may order the special advocate not to communicate (directly or indirectly) with any persons (including the excluded claimant)—

(a) on any matter discussed or referred to; or
(b) with regard to any material disclosed,

during or with reference to any part of the proceedings from which the claimant or his representative are excluded.

**5.5** Where the court makes an order referred to in paragraph 5.4 (or any similar order), the special advocate may apply to the court for directions enabling him to seek instructions from, or otherwise to communicate with an excluded person.

### Expenses of Commission

**6.1** This paragraph applies where the Commission has, in respect of a claim, provided a claimant with assistance under section 28 of the 2006 Act. **3I–6**

**6.2** If the Commission claims a charge for expenses incurred by it in providing such assistance, it must give notice of the claim to—

(a) the court; and
(b) the claimant

within 14 days of determination of the proceedings.

**6.3** If notice is given to the court under paragraph 6.2—

(a) money paid into court for the benefit of the claimant that relates to costs and expenses must not be paid out unless this is permitted by an order of the court; and
(b) the court may order the expenses incurred by the Commission to be assessed as if they were costs payable by the claimant to his own solicitor for work done in connection with the proceedings.

**6.4** The court may either—

(a) make a summary assessment of the expenses; or

(b) order detailed assessment of the expenses by a costs officer.

**Editorial note**

3I–7 Proceedings for unlawful sex and race discrimination may be brought under the Sex Discrimination Act 1975 and the Race Relations Act 1976. Part VII of the former Act and Part VIII of the latter contain provisions dealing with (amongst other things) the bringing of civil proceedings for discrimination. Those provisions are set out below (see paras. 3I–9 *et seq.* to 3I–27). Extended commentary on these Parts then follows (see para.3I–41 *et seq.*). Proceedings for discrimination may also be brought under the Disability Discrimination Act 1995, the Employment Equality (Religion or Belief) Regulations 2003 (SI 2003/1660) and the Employment Equality (Sexual Orientation) Regulations 2003 (SI 2003/1661). Selected provisions relating to the bringing of proceedings under the Disability Discrimination Act 1995 are set out in paras 3I–47 *et seq.*, followed by commentary (para.3I–50). Part 2 of the Equality Act 2006 has also introduced provisions addressing religion and belief discrimination comparable to that made in the Sex Discrimination Act 1975 and the Race Relations Act 1976, including in relation to enforcement (ss.65–71). These provisions came into force on April 30, 2007. Selected provisions are set out in paras 3I–26 *et seq.* Part 3 of the Equality Act gives the Secretary of State power to introduce regulations "about discrimination or harassment on grounds of sexual orientation" and "in particular make provision of a kind similar to Part 2" of the Equality Act 2006 (s.81). Regulations have been made and brought into force with effect from April 30, 2007 (Equality Act (Sexual Orientation) Regulations 2007 (SI 2007/1263)). These Regulations contain measures prohibiting discrimination on grounds of sexual orientation in the provision of goods, facilities and services, education, the use and disposal of premises and the exercise of public functions. Their enforcement provisions mirror those provided for in the other anti discrimination enactments. Part 1 of the Equality Act 2006 establishes the Equality and Human Rights Commission ("EHRC"). From October 1, 2007, the EHRC has taken over the functions of the Commission for Racial Equality, the Equal Opportunities Commission and the Disability Rights Commission. The relevant provisions of the Equality Act are referred to in the notes below. As is indicated in the commentary, rules of court relating to proceedings under the legislation referred to above are found in CPR, Sch.2 CCR O.49, r.17 (see Vol.1, para.cc49.17).

## Sex Discrimination Act 1975

3I–8 (1975 c.65)

ARRANGEMENT OF SECTIONS

PART VII

ENFORCEMENT



***Paragraph numbers marked with a "+" can be found online and on CD.***

# PART VII

## ENFORCEMENT

### GENERAL

**Restriction of proceedings for breach of Act**

**62.**—(1) Except as provided by this Act no proceedings, whether civil or criminal, shall lie against any person in respect of an act by reason that the act is unlawful by virtue of a provision of this Act. **3I–9**

(2) Subsection (1) does not preclude the making of an order of certiorari, mandamus or prohibition.

(3) [...]

* * * *

### ENFORCEMENT OF PART III

**Claims under Part III**

**66.**—(1) A claim by any person ("the claimant") that another person ("the respondent")— **3I–10**

(a) has committed an act of discrimination or harassment against the claimant which is unlawful by virtue of Part III other than section 35A or 35B, or

(b) is by virtue of section 41 or 42 to be treated as having committed such an act of discrimination or harassment against the claimant,

may be made the subject of civil proceedings in like manner as any other claim in tort or (in Scotland) in reparation for breach of statutory duty.

(2) Proceedings under subsection (1)—

(a) shall be brought in England and Wales only in a county court, and

(b) shall be brought in Scotland only in a sheriff court,

but all such remedies shall be obtainable in such proceedings as, apart from this subsection and section 62(1), would be obtainable in the High Court or the Court of Session, as the case may be.

(3) As respects an unlawful act of discrimination falling within section 1(1)(b) ... no award of damages shall be made if the respondent proves that the requirement or condition in question was not applied with the intention of treating the claimant unfavourably on the ground of his sex.

(3A) Subsection (3) does not affect the award of damages in respect of an unlawful act of discrimination falling within section 1(2)(b).

(4) For the avoidance of doubt it is hereby declared that damages in respect of an unlawful act of discrimination or harassment may

include compensation for injury to feelings whether or not they include compensation under any other head.

(5) Civil proceedings in respect of a claim by any person that he has been discriminated against, or subjected to harassment, in contravention of section 22 or 23 by a body to which section 25(1) applies shall not be instituted unless the claimant has given notice of the claim to the Secretary of State and either the Secretary of State has by notice informed the claimant that the Secretary of State does not require further time to consider the matter, or the period of two months has elapsed since the claimant gave notice to the Secretary of State; but nothing in this subsection applies to a counterclaim.

(6) For the purposes of proceedings under subsection (1)—

(a) section 63(1) (assessors) of the County Courts Act 1984 shall apply with the omission of the words "on the application of any party", and

(b) [...]

(7) [...]

(8) A county court or sheriff court shall have jurisdiction to entertain proceedings under subsection (1) with respect to an act done on a ship, aircraft or hovercraft outside its district, including such an act done outside Great Britain.

3I–11 *Note*—Amended by SI 2005/2467.

### Burden of proof: county and sheriff courts

3I–12 **66A.**—(1) This section applies to any claim brought under section 66(1) in a county court in England and Wales or a sheriff court in Scotland.

(2) Where, on the hearing of the claim, the claimant proves facts from which the court could, apart from this section, conclude in the absence of an adequate explanation that the respondent—

(a) has committed an act of discrimination or harassment against the claimant which is unlawful by virtue of—

(i) section 29, 30 or 31, or

(ii) any other provision of Part 3 so far as it applies to vocational training, or

(b) is by virtue of section 41 or 42 to be treated as having committed such an act of discrimination [or harassment] against the claimant,

the court shall uphold the claim unless the respondent proves that he did not commit, or, as the case may be, is not to be treated as having committed, that act.]

3I–13 *Note*—Amended by SI 2005/2467 and SI 2008/963.

### National security

3I–14 **66B.**—(1) Rules of court may make provision for enabling a county court or sheriff court in which a claim is brought under section 66(1), where the court considers it expedient in the interests of national security—

(a) to exclude from all or part of the proceedings—
(i) the claimant;
(ii) the claimant's representatives;
(iii) any assessors;
(b) to permit a claimant or representative who has been excluded to make a statement to the court before the commencement of the proceedings, or the part of the proceedings, from which he is excluded;
(c) to take steps to keep secret all or part of the reasons for the court's decision in the proceedings.

(2) The Attorney General or, in Scotland, the Advocate General for Scotland, may appoint a person to represent the interests of a claimant in, or in any part of, proceedings from which the claimant or his representatives are excluded by virtue of subsection (1).

(3) A person may be appointed under subsection (2) only—
(a) in relation to proceedings in England and Wales, if he has a general qualification (within the meaning of section 71 of the Courts and Legal Services Act 1990 (c. 41)), or
(b) in relation to proceedings in Scotland, if he is—
(i) an advocate, or
(ii) qualified to practice as a solicitor in Scotland.

(4) A person appointed under subsection (2) shall not be responsible to the person whose interests he is appointed to represent.

*Note* —Inserted by the Equality Act 2006 s.87, with effect from April 18, 2006 (SI 2006/1082). **3I–15**

* * * *

### HELP FOR PERSONS SUFFERING DISCRIMINATION

## Help for aggrieved persons in obtaining information etc

**74.**—(1) With a view to helping a person ("the person aggrieved") who considers he may have been discriminated against or subjected to harassment in contravention of this Act to decide whether to institute proceedings and, if he does so, to formulate and present his case in the most effective manner, the Minister shall by order prescribe— **3I–16**
(a) forms by which the person aggrieved may question the respondent on his reasons for doing any relevant act, or on any other matter which is or may be relevant;
(b) forms by which the respondent may if he so wishes reply to any questions.

(2) Where the person aggrieved questions the respondent (whether in accordance with an order under subsection (1) or not)—
(a) the question, and any reply by the respondent (whether in accordance with such an order or not) shall, subject to

the following provisions of this section, be admissible as evidence in the proceedings;

(b) if it appears to the court or tribunal that the respondent deliberately, and without reasonable excuse, omitted to reply within the period applicable under subsection (2A) or that his reply is evasive or equivocal, the court or tribunal may draw any inference from that fact that it considers it just and equitable to draw, including an inference that he committed an unlawful act.

(2A) The period applicable for the purposes of subsection (2)(b) is—

(a) eight weeks beginning with the day when the question was served on the respondent, if the question relates to discrimination under—

(i) any provision of Part 2,

(ia) section 29, 30 or 31, except in so far as it relates to an excluded matter,

(ii) section 35A or 35B, or

(iii) any other provision of Part 3, so far as it applies to vocational training;

(b) a reasonable period, as regards any other question.

(3) The Minister may by order—

(a) prescribe the period within which questions must be duly served in order to be admissible under subsection (2)(a), and

(b) prescribe the manner in which a question, and any reply by the respondent, may be duly served.

(4) Rules may enable the court entertaining a claim under section 66 to determine, before the date fixed for the hearing of the claim, whether a question or reply is admissible under this section or not.

(5) This section is without prejudice to any other enactment or rule of law regulating interlocutory and preliminary matters in proceedings before a county court, sheriff court or employment tribunal, and has effect subject to any enactment or rule of law regulating the admissibility of evidence in such proceedings.

(6) In this section "respondent" includes a prospective respondent and "rules"—

(a) in relation to county court proceedings, means county court rules;

(b) in relation to sheriff court proceedings, means sheriff court rules.

**3I–17** *Note*.—Amended by SI 2005/2467, SI 2007/2914 and SI 2008/963.

* * * *

*PERIOD WITHIN WHICH PROCEEDINGS TO BE BROUGHT*

## Period within which proceedings to be brought

**3I–18** **76.**—(1) [...]

***Paragraph numbers marked with a "+" can be found online and on CD.***

(2) A county court or a sheriff court shall not consider a claim under section 66 unless proceedings in respect of the claim are instituted before the end of

(a) the period of six months beginning when the act complained of was done; or

(b) in a case to which section 66(5) applies, the period of eight months so beginning.

(2A) Where in England and Wales—

(a) proceedings or prospective proceedings under section 66 relate to the act or omission of a qualifying institution, and

(b) the dispute concerned is referred as a complaint under the student complaints scheme before the end of the period of six months mentioned in subsection (2)(a),

the period allowed by subsection (2)(a) shall be extended by three months.

(2B) In subsection (2A)—

"qualifying institution" has the meaning given by section 11 of the Higher Education Act 2004;

"the student complaints scheme" means a scheme for the review of qualifying complaints, as defined by section 12 of that Act, that is provided by the designated operator, as defined by section 13(5)(b) of that Act.

(2C) The period allowed by subsection (2)(a) or (b) shall be extended by three months in the case of a dispute which is referred for conciliation in pursuance of arrangements under section 27 of the Equality Act 2006 (unless the period is extended under subsection (2A)).

(3) [...]

(4) [...]

(5) A court or tribunal may nevertheless consider any such complaint or claim which is out of time if, in all the circumstances of the case, it considers that it is just and equitable to do so.

(6) For the purposes of this section—

(a) where the inclusion of any term in a contract renders the making of the contract an unlawful act that act shall be treated as extending throughout the duration of the contract, and

(b) any act extending over a period shall be treated as done at the end of that period, and

(c) a deliberate omission shall be treated as done when the person in question decided upon it,

and in the absence of evidence establishing the contrary a person shall be taken for the purposes of this section to decide upon an omission when he does an act inconsistent with doing the omitted act or, if he has done no such inconsistent act, when the period expires within which he might reasonably have been expected to do the omitted act if it was to be done.

*Note* —Amended by the Higher Education Act 2004 s.19(1). Subsection (2A) was **3I–19**

***Paragraph numbers marked with a "+" can be found online and on CD.***

amended so as to extend the period from two months to three months, by the Equality Act 2006 s.40, Sch.3, paras 6, 14(1), (2) from October 1, 2007 (the Equality Act 2006 (Commencement No.3 and Savings) Order 2007 SI 2007/2603). Subsection (2C), providing for an extension of time where a complaint has been referred for conciliation pursuant to arrangements made under s.27 of the Equality Act 2006, was inserted by the Equality Act 2006 s.40, Sch.3, paras 6, 14(1), (3) from October 1, 2007 (the Equality Act 2006 (Commencement No.3 and Savings) Order 2007 SI 2007/2603. Subsection (3) is repealed by the Equality Act 2006 s.40, Sch.3, paras 6, 14(1), (4), Sch.4 from October 1, 2007 (the Equality Act 2006 (Commencement No.3 and Savings) Order 2007 SI 2007/2603. In subsection (5) the words "complaint, claim or application" were repealed and replaced with replaced with the words "complaint or claim" by the Equality Act 2006 s.40, Sch.3, paras 6, 14(1), (5), from October 1, 2007 (the Equality Act 2006 (Commencement No.3 and Savings) Order 2007 SI 2007/2603.

## Public authorities: general statutory duty

3I–20 **76A.**—(1) A public authority shall in carrying out its functions have due regard to the need—

(a) to eliminate unlawful discrimination and harassment, and

(b) to promote equality of opportunity between men and women.

(2) In subsection (1)—

(a) "public authority" includes any person who has functions of a public nature (subject to subsections (3) and (4)),

(b) "functions" means functions of a public nature, and

(c) the reference to unlawful discrimination shall be treated as including a reference to contravention of terms of contracts having effect in accordance with an equality clause within the meaning of section 1 of the Equal Pay Act 1970 (c. 41).

(3) The duty in subsection (1) shall not apply to—

(a) the House of Commons,

(b) the House of Lords,

(c) the Scottish Parliament,

(ca) the National Assembly for Wales,

(d) the General Synod of the Church of England,

(e) the Security Service,

(f) the Secret Intelligence Service,

(g) the Government Communications Headquarters,

(h) a part of the armed forces of the Crown which is, in accordance with a requirement of the Secretary of State, assisting the Government Communications Headquarters, or

(i) a person specified for the purpose of this paragraph by order of the Minister (and a person may be specified generally or only in respect of specified functions).

(4) The duty in subsection (1) shall not apply to the exercise of—

(a) a function in connection with proceedings in the House of Commons or the House of Lords,

*Paragraph numbers marked with a "+" can be found online and on CD.*

(b) a function in connection with proceedings in the Scottish Parliament (other than a function of the Scottish Parliamentary Corporate Body),

(ba) a function in connection with proceedings in the National Assembly for Wales (other than a function of the National Assembly for Wales Commission),

(c) a judicial function (whether in connection with a court or a tribunal),

(d) a function exercised on behalf of or on the instructions of a person exercising a judicial function (whether in connection with a court or a tribunal), or

(e) a function specified for the purpose of this paragraph by order of the Minister.

(5) Subsection (1)(b) is without prejudice to the effect of any exception to or limitation of the law about sex discrimination.

(6) A failure in respect of performance of the duty under subsection (1) does not confer a cause of action at private law.

*Note*—Inserted by the Equality Act 2006 s.84, with effect from April 18, 2006 (for certain purposes) and April 6, 2007 (for remaining purposes) (see SI 2006/1082); amended by SI 2007/1388 and SI 2007/2914. **3I–21**

## Specific duties

**76B.**—(1) The Minister may by order impose on a person to whom the duty in section 76A(1) applies, or in so far as that duty applies to a person, a duty which the Minister thinks will ensure better performance of the duty under section 76A(1). **3I–22**

(2) Before making an order under subsection (1) the Minister shall consult the Commission.

(3) The Minister—

(a) must consult the Welsh Ministers before making an order under subsection (1) in respect of a person exercising functions in relation to Wales, and

(b) may not, without the consent of the Welsh Ministers, make an order under subsection (1) in respect of a person all of whose functions are public functions in relation to Wales.

(4) A failure in respect of performance of a duty imposed under subsection (1) does not confer a cause of action at private law.

*Note*—Inserted by the Equality Act 2006 s.85, with effect from April 18, 2006 (for certain purposes) and April 6, 2007 (for remaining purposes) (see SI 2006/1082); amended by SI 2007/1388 and SI 2007/2914. For subordinate legislation see, Sex Discrimination Act 1975 (Public Authorities) (Statutory Duties) Order 2006 (SI 2006/2930) (made under subs.(1)). **3I–23**

## Specific duties: Scotland

**76C.**—(1) Section 76B(1) shall not apply in relation to a person who is a relevant Scottish authority or a cross-border authority. **3I–24**

(2) The Minister may by order impose on a cross-border authority to whom the duty under section 76A(1) applies, or in so far as

that duty applies to the cross-border authority, a duty which the Minister thinks will ensure better performance of the duty under section 76A(1), to the extent that the cross-border authority's functions are not Scottish functions.

(3) The Scottish Ministers may by order impose on a relevant Scottish authority to whom the duty under section 76A(1) applies, or in so far as that duty applies to the relevant Scottish authority, a duty which the Scottish Ministers think will ensure better performance of the duty under section 76A(1).

(4) The Scottish Ministers may by order impose on a cross-border authority to whom the duty under section 76A(1) applies, or in so far as that duty applies to the cross-border authority, a duty which the Scottish Ministers think will ensure better performance of the duty under section 76A(1), to the extent that the cross-border authority's functions are Scottish functions.

(5) Before making an order under any of subsections (2) to (4) the person making the order shall consult the Commission.

(6) Before making an order under subsection (2) the Minister shall consult the Scottish Ministers.

(7) Before making an order under subsection (4) the Scottish Ministers shall consult the Minister.

(8) A failure in respect of performance of a duty imposed under this section does not confer a cause of action at private law.

(9) In this section—

"relevant Scottish authority" means—

(a) a member of the Scottish executive or a junior Scottish Minister;

(b) the Registrar General of Births, Deaths and Marriages for Scotland, the Keeper of the Registers of Scotland or the Keeper of the Records of Scotland;

(c) any office of a description specified in an Order in Council under section 126(8)(b) of the Scotland Act 1998 (other non-ministerial office in the Scottish Administration); or

(d) a public body, public office or holder of a public office—

(i) which (or who) is not a cross-border authority or the Scottish Parliamentary Corporate Body;

(ii) whose functions are exercisable only in or as regards Scotland; and

(iii) some at least of whose functions do not (within the meaning of the Scotland Act 1998) relate to reserved matters;

"cross-border authority" means a cross-border public authority within the meaning given by section 88(5) of the Scotland Act 1998;

"Scottish functions" means functions which are exercisable in or as regards Scotland and which do not (within the meaning of the Scotland Act 1998) relate to reserved matters;

3I–25 *Note* —Inserted by the Equality Act 2006, s.85, with effect from April 18, 2006 (for certain purposes) and April 6, 2007 (for remaining purposes) (see SI 2006/1082); amended by SI 2007/2914. For subordinate legislation see, (for the UK) Sex Discrimination Act 1975 (Public Authorities) (Statutory Duties) Order 2006 (SI 2006/2930) (made under subs.(2)) and (for Scotland) the Sex Discrimination (Public Authorities) (Statutory Duties) (Scotland) Order 2007 (SSI 2007/32) (made under subs.(3)). For enforcement of the duties by the EHRC, see ss.31 and 32 of the Equality Act 2006 (repealing earlier provision in the Sex Discrimination Act 1975; see the Equality Act 2006 ss.40, 91, Sch.3, paras 6, 16 and Sch.4 as from October 1, 2007).

## Race Relations Act 1976

(1976 c.74) **3I–26**

ARRANGEMENT OF SECTIONS

PART VIII

ENFORCEMENT



## PART VIII

## ENFORCEMENT

### Restriction of proceedings for breach of Act

**53.**—(1) Except as provided by this Act or the Special Immigration Appeals Commission Act 1997 or Part 5 of the Nationality, Immigration and Asylum Act 2002 no proceedings, whether civil or criminal, shall lie against any person in respect of an act by reason that the act is unlawful by virtue of a provision of this Act. **3I–27**

(2) Subsection (1) does not preclude the making of an order of certiorari, mandamus or prohibition.

(3) [...]

(4) Subsections (2) and (3) do not, except so far as provided by section 76, apply to any act which is unlawful by virtue of section 76(5) or (9) or by virtue of section 76(10)(b), (11) and (11B).

* * * *

### Claims under Part III etc

**57.**—(1) A claim by any person ("the claimant") that another person ("the respondent")— **3I–28**

(a) has committed an act against the claimant which is unlawful by virtue of Part III other than, in relation to

*Paragraph numbers marked with a "+" can be found online and on CD.*

discrimination on grounds of race or ethnic or national origins, or harassment, section 26A or 26B; or

(b) is by virtue of section 32 or 33 to be treated as having committed such an act against the claimant,

may be made the subject of civil proceedings in like manner as any other claim in tort or (in Scotland) in reparation for breach of statutory duty.

(2) Proceedings under subsection (1)—

(a) shall, in England and Wales, be brought only in a designated county court; and

(b) [...]

but all such remedies shall be obtainable in such proceedings as, apart from this subsection and section 53(1), would be obtainable in the High Court or the Court of Session, as the case may be.

(3) Asrespects an unlawful act of discrimination falling within section 1(1)(b), no award of damages shall be made if the respondent proves that the requirement or condition in question was not applied with the intention of treating the claimant unfavourably on racial grounds.

(4) For the avoidance of doubt it is hereby declared that damages in respect of an unlawful act of discrimination may include compensation for injury to feelings whether or not they include compensation under any other head.

(4A) As respects an act which is done, or by virtue of section 32 or 33 is treated as done, by a person in carrying out public investigator functions or functions as a public prosecutor and which is unlawful by virtue of section 19B, no remedy other than—

(a) damages; or

(b) a declaration or, in Scotland, a declarator;

shall be obtainable unless the court is satisfied that the remedy concerned would not prejudice a criminal investigation, a decision to institute criminal proceedings or any criminal proceedings.

(4B) In this section—

"criminal investigation" means —

(a) any investigation which a person in carrying out functions to which section 19B applies has a duty to conduct with a view to it being ascertained whether a person should be charged with, or in Scotland prosecuted for, an offence, or whether a person charged with or prosecuted for an offence is guilty of it;

(b) any investigation which is conducted by a person in carrying out functions to which section 19B applies and which in the circumstances may lead to a decision by that person to institute criminal proceedings which the person has power to conduct; or

(c) any investigation which is conducted by a person in carrying out functions to which section 19B applies and which in the circumstances may lead to a decision by that person to make a report to the procurator fiscal for the purpose of enabling him to determine whether criminal proceedings should be instituted; and

"public investigator functions" means functions of conducting criminal investigations or charging offenders;

and in this subsection "offence" includes any service offence within the meaning of the Armed Forces Act 2006 (and "offender" shall be construed accordingly).

(4C) Subsection (4D) applies where a party to proceedings under subsection (1) which have arisen by virtue of section 19B has applied for a stay or sist of those proceedings on the grounds of prejudice to—

(a) particular criminal proceedings;

(b) a criminal investigation; or

(c) a decision to institute criminal proceedings.

(4D) The court shall grant the stay or sist unless it is satisfied that the continuance of the proceedings under subsection (1) would not result in the prejudice alleged.

(5) Civil proceedings in respect of a claim by any person that he has been discriminated against in contravention of section 17 or 18 by a body to which subsection (5A) applies shall not be instituted unless the claimant has given notice of the claim to the Secretary of State.

(5A) This subsection applies to—

(a) local education authorities in England and Wales;

(b) [...]

(c) any body which is a responsible body in relation to an establishment falling within paragraph 3, 3B or 7B of the table in section 17.

(6) [...]

(7) This section has effect subject to section 57A.

## Burden of proof: County and Sheriff Courts

**57ZA.**—(1) This section applies where a claim is brought under section 57 and the claim is that the respondent— 3I–29

(a) has committed an act of discrimination, on grounds of race or ethnic or national origins, which is unlawful by virtue of any provision referred to in section 1(1B)(b) to (d), or Part IV in its application to those provisions, or

(b) has committed an act of harassment.

(2) Where, on the hearing of the claim, the claimant proves facts from which the court could, apart from this section, conclude in the absence of an adequate explanation that the respondent—

(a) has committed such an act of discrimination or harassment against the claimant, or

(b) is by virtue of section 32 or 33 to be treated as having committed such an act of discrimination or harassment against the claimant,

*Paragraph numbers marked with a "+" can be found online and on CD.*

the court shall uphold the claim unless the respondent proves that he did not commit or, as the case may be, is not to be treated as having committed, that act.

3I–29.1 *Note*—See, in relation to the modificationof subs.(4B) above so as to include reference to an SDA offence: the Armed Forces Act 2006 (Transitional Provisions etc) Order 2009 SI 2009/1059 reg.205 Sch.1 para.16(1).

* * * *

### *HELP FOR PERSONS SUFFERING DISCRIMINATION*

## Help for aggrieved persons in obtaining information etc

3I–30 **65.**—(1) With a view to helping a person ("the person aggrieved") who considers he may have been discriminated against or subjected to harassment in contravention of this Act to decide whether to institute proceedings and, if he does so, to formulate and present his case in the most effective manner, the Minister shall by order prescribe—

(a) forms by which the person aggrieved may question the respondent on his reasons for doing any relevant act, or on any other matter which is or may be relevant; and

(b) forms by which the respondent may if he so wishes reply to any questions.

(2) Where the person aggrieved questions the respondent (whether in accordance with an order under subsection (1) or not)—

(a) the question, and any reply by the respondent (whether in accordance with such an order or not) shall, subject to the following provisions of this section, be admissible as evidence in the proceedings;

(b) if it appears to the court or tribunal that the respondent deliberately, and without reasonable excuse, omitted to reply within a reasonable period or, where the question relates to discrimination on grounds of race or ethnic or national origins, or to harassment, the period of eight weeks beginning with the day on which the question was served on him or that his reply is evasive or equivocal, the court or tribunal may draw any inference from that fact that it considers it just and equitable to draw, including an inference that he committed an unlawful act.

(3) The Minister may by order—

(a) prescribe the period within which questions must be duly served in order to be admissible under subsection (2)(a); and

(b) prescribe the manner in which a question, and any reply by the respondent, may be duly served.

(4) Rules may enable the court entertaining a claim under section 57 to determine, before the date fixed for the hearing of the claim, whether a question or reply is admissible under this section or not.

(4A) In section 19B proceedings, subsection (2)(b) does not apply in relation to a failure to reply, or a particular reply, if the conditions specified in subsection (4B) are satisfied.

(4B) Those conditions are that—

(a) at the time of doing any relevant act, the respondent was carrying out public investigator functions or was a public prosecutor; and

(b) he reasonably believes that a reply or (as the case may be) a different reply would be likely to prejudice any criminal investigation, any decision to institute criminal proceedings or any criminal proceedings or would reveal the reasons behind a decision not to institute, or a decision not to continue, criminal proceedings.

(4C) For the purposes of subsections (4A) and (4B)—

"public investigator functions" has the same meaning as in section 57;

"section 19B proceedings" means proceedings in respect of a claim under section 57 which has arisen by virtue of section 19B.

(5) This section is without prejudice to any other enactment or rule of law regulating interlocutory and preliminary matters in proceedings before a county court, sheriff court or employment tribunal, and has effect subject to any enactment or rule of law regulating the admissibility of evidence in such proceedings.

(6) In this section "respondent" includes a prospective respondent and "rules"

(a) in relation to county court proceedings, means county court rules;

(b) [...]

(7) This section does not apply in relation to any proceedings under—

(a) the Special Immigration Appeals Commission Act 1997; or

(b) Part 5 of the Nationality, Immigration and Asylum Act 2002.

*Note*—Amended by SI 2007/2914. 3I–30.1

* * * *

## Period within which proceedings to be brought

**68.**—(1) [...] 3I–31

(2) Subject to subsection (2A) a county court or a sheriff court shall not consider a claim under section 57 unless proceedings in respect of the claim are instituted before the end of—

(a) the period of six months beginning when the act complained of was done;

(b) [...]

(2A) In relation to an immigration claim within the meaning of section 57A, the period of six months mentioned in subsection (2)(a) begins on the expiry of the period during which, by virtue of section 57A(1)(a), no proceedings may be brought under section 57(1) in respect of the claim.

(3) [...]

(3A) Where in England and Wales—

(a) proceedings or prospective proceedings by way of a claim under section 57 relate to the act or omission of a qualifying institution,

(b) the dispute concerned is referred as a complaint under the student complaints scheme before the end of the period of six months mentioned in subsection (2), and

(c) subsection (3) does not apply,

the period allowed by subsection (2) for instituting proceedings in respect of the claim shall be extended by two months.

(3B) In subsection (3A)—

"qualifying institution" has the meaning given by section 11 of the Higher Education Act 2004;

"the student complaints scheme" means a scheme for the review of qualifying complaints, as defined by section 12 of that Act, that is provided by the designated operator, as defined by section 13(5)(b) of that Act.

(4) An employment tribunal, county court or sheriff court shall not consider an application under section 63(2)(a) unless it is made before the end of the period of six months beginning when the act to which it relates was done; and a county court or sheriff court shall not consider an application under section 63(4) unless it is made before the end of the period of five years so beginning.

(5) An employment tribunal shall not consider a complaint under section 64(1) unless it is presented to the tribunal before the end of the period of six months beginning when the act complained of was done.

(6) A court or tribunal may nevertheless consider any such complaint, claim or application which is out of time if, in all the circumstances of the case, it considers that it is just and equitable to do so.

(7) For the purposes of this section—

(a) when the inclusion of any term in a contract renders the making of the contract an unlawful act, that act shall be treated as extending throughout the duration of the contract; and

(b) any act extending over a period shall be treated as done at the end of that period; and

(c) a deliberate omission shall be treated as done when the person in question decided upon it;

and in the absence of evidence establishing the contrary a person shall be taken for the purposes of this section to decide upon an omission when he does an act inconsistent with doing the omitted act or, if he has done no such inconsistent act, when the period expires within which he might reasonably have been expected to do the omitted act if it was to be done.

*Note* — Subsection (3) has been repealed by the Equality Act 2006 ss.40, 91, Sch.3, paras 21, 29(1), (2) and Sch.4 from October 1, 2007. Subsection (3A)(c) has been repealed by the Equality Act 2006 ss.40, 91, Sch.3, paras 21, 29(1), (3A) and Sch.4 from October 1, 2007 (the Equality Act 2006 (Commencement No.3 and Savings) Order 2007 SI 2007/2603. Subsection (3A) is amended so as to extend the period from two months to three months, by the Equality Act 2006 s.40, Sch.3, paras 21, 29(1) and (3)(b) from October 1, 2007 (the Equality Act 2006 (Commencement No.3 and Savings) Order 2007 SI 2007/2603. Subsection (3C), providing for an extension of time where a complaint has been referred for conciliation pursuant to arrangements made under s.27 of the Equality Act 2006, was inserted by the Equality Act 2006 s.40, Sch.3, paras 21, 29(1) and (4) from October 1, 2007 (the Equality Act 2006 (Commencement No.3 and Savings) Order 2007 SI 2007/2603. Subsection (4) and (5) have been repealed by the Equality Act 2006 ss.40, 91, Sch.3, paras 21, 29(1), (5), Sch.4 from October 1, 2007 (the Equality Act 2006 (Commencement No.3 and Savings) Order 2007 SI 2007/2603. In subs.(6) the words "complaint, claim or application" have been repealed and replaced with the words "complaint or claim" by the Equality Act 2006 s.40, Sch.3, paras 21, 29(1) and (6), from October 1, 2007 (the Equality Act 2006 (Commencement No.3 and Savings) Order 2007 SI 2007/2603. **3I–32**

DISCRIMINATION

* * * *

## Specified authorities: general statutory duty

**71.**—(1) Every body or other person specified in Schedule 1A or of a description falling within that Schedule shall, in carrying out its functions, have due regard to the need— **3I–33**

(a) to eliminate unlawful racial discrimination; and

(b) to promote equality of opportunity and good relations between persons of different racial groups.

(2) The Minister may by order impose, on such persons falling within Schedule 1A as he considers appropriate, such duties as he considers appropriate for the purpose of ensuring the better performance by those persons of their duties under subsection (1).

(3) An order under subsection (2)—

(a) may be made in relation to a particular person falling within Schedule 1A, any description of persons falling within that Schedule or every person falling within that Schedule;

(b) may make different provision for different purposes.

(4) Before making an order under subsection (2), the Minister shall consult the Commission.

(5) The Minister may by order amend Schedule 1A; but no such order may extend the application of this section unless the Secretary of State considers that the extension relates to a person who exercises functions of a public nature.

(6) An order under subsection (2) or (5) may contain such incidental, supplementary or consequential provision as the Minister considers appropriate (including provision amending or repealing provision made by or under this Act or any other enactment).

(7) This section is subject to section 71A and 71B and is without prejudice to the obligation of any person to comply with any other provision of this Act.

*Note* —Substituted, together with ss.71A–71E for original s.71 by the Race Relations **3I–34**

***Paragraph numbers marked with a "+" can be found online and on CD.***

(Amendment) Act 2000 s.2(1), with effect from April 2, 2001 (SI 2001/566); amended by SI 2007/2914. For subordinate legislation made under subss.(2), (3)) see, (for the UK) Race Relations Act 1976 (Statutory Duties) Order 2001 (SI 2001/3458); Race Relations Act 1976 (Statutory Duties) Order 2003 (SI 2003/3006); Race Relations Act 1976 (Statutory Duties) Order 2004 (SI 2004/3125); Race Relations Act 1976 (Statutory Duties) Order 2006 (SI 2006/2471) and (for Scotland) Race Relations Act 1976 (Statutory Duties) (Scotland) Order 2002 (SSI 2002/62); Race Relations Act 1976 (Statutory Duties) (Scotland) Amendment Order 2003 (SSI 2003/566); Race Relations Act 1976 (Statutory Duties) (Scotland) Amendment Order 2004 (SSI 2004/521); Race Relations Act 1976 (Statutory Duties) (Scotland) Amendment Order 2006 (SSI 2006/467).

## General statutory duty: special cases

3I–35 **71A.**—(1) In relation to the carrying out of immigration and nationality functions (within the meaning of section 19D(1)), section 71(1)(b) has effect with the omission of the words "equality of opportunity and".

(2) Where an entry in Schedule 1A is limited to a person in a particular capacity, section 71(1) does not apply to that person in any other capacity.

(3) Where an entry in Schedule 1A is limited to particular functions of a person, section 71(1) does not apply to that person in relation to any other functions.

3I–36 *Note*—Substituted, together with ss.71, 71B–71E for original s.71 by the Race Relations (Amendment) Act 2000 s.2(1), with effect from April 2, 2001 (SI 2001/566).

## General statutory duty: Scotland and Wales

3I–37 **71B.**—(1) For the purposes of the Scotland Act 1998, subsections (2) to (4) of section 71 (and sections 71(6) and 74 so far as they apply to the power conferred by subsection (2) of section 71) shall be taken to be pre-commencement enactments within the meaning of that Act.

(2) Before making an order under section 71(2) in relation to functions exercisable in relation to Wales by a person who is not a Welsh public authority, the Secretary of State shall consult the Welsh Ministers.

(3) The Secretary of State shall not make an order under section 71(2) in relation to functions of a Welsh public authority except with the consent of the Welsh Ministers.

(4) In this section "Welsh public authority" means any person whose functions are exercisable only in relation to Wales and includes—

(a) the National Assembly for Wales Commission;

(b) the Welsh Ministers, the First Minister for Wales and the Counsel General to the Welsh Assembly Government.

3I–38 *Note*—Substituted, together with ss.71, 71A, 71C–71E for original s.71 by the Race Relations (Amendment) Act 2000 s.2(1), with effect from April 2, 2001 (SI 2001/566); amended by SI 2007/1388, with effect from May 25, 2007.

## General statutory duty: codes of practice

3I–39 **71C.** [...]

***Paragraph numbers marked with a "+" can be found online and on CD.***

*Note*—Substituted, together with ss.71, 71A, 71B, 71D, 71E for original s.71 by the Race Relations (Amendment) Act 2000, s.2(1), with effect from April 2, 2001 (SI 2001/566); repealed by the Equality Act 2006 s.40, s.91, Sch.3, paras 21, 31 and Sch.4 with effect from October 1, 2007. For enforcement of the duties by the EHRC, see ss.31 and 32 of the Equality Act 2006. 3I–40

**Notes on Part VII of the Sex Discrimination Act 1975 and Part VIII the Race Relations Act 1976**

Part VII of the Sex Discrimination Act 1975 (SDA) and Part VIII of the Race Relations Act 1976 (RRA) address enforcement and the evidential and procedural issues peculiar to the SDA and RRA. 3I–41

**Rules of court (CPR Sch.2, CCR O.49, r.17)**

When the 1975 Act and the 1976 Act came into effect the County Court Rules 1984 were amended by the addition of r.17 to O.49 for the purpose of providing necessary rules of court. When the CPR came into effect, those provisions were carried forward into Sch.2 (see Vol.1, para.cc49.17). That rule has been amended from time to time, principally for the purpose of taking account of changes in primary legislation. The practice direction relating to discrimination proceedings (Practice Direction—Proceedings Under Enactments Relating To Discrimination) is at para.3I–1. 3I–42

**Jurisdiction and Proceedings**

Proceedings in respect of the unlawful acts created by the SDA and RRA may be brought only in the way provided for by the Acts themselves (SDA s.62; RRA s.53). Nothing in the SDA or RRA prevents an application being made in judicial review (SDA s.62; RRA s.53; see *Secretary of State for Defence v Elias* [2006] EWCA Civ 1293; [2006] 1 W.L.R. 3213). However (outside the employment and related fields), jurisdiction is in the main exclusively conferred on the county courts. Where appropriate, proceedings may be brought by way of a defence and/or counter claim (e.g. in defence of a possession action, see *Manchester City Council v Romano* [2004] EWCA Civ 834, June 29, 2004, unrep., CA, paras 63–64; *Lewisham LBC v Malcolm (Equality and Human Rights Commission intervening)* [2008] 1 A.C. 1399). In England and Wales proceedings under Pt III of the RRA (alone) may only be brought in a "designated" County Court (RRA s.57(2), as to which see RRA s.67; see too, s.57A for claims arising in certain immigration cases). In addition, by s.67(4) of the RRA, the judge hearing such a claim "shall, unless with the consent of the parties he sits without assessors, be assisted by two assessors". Assessors have a wide role (*Ahmed v Governing Body of the University of Oxford* [2002] EWCA Civ 1907; [2003] 1 W.L.R. 995, CA). They assist the judge in the broadest sense of helping him or her "evaluate the evidence in the area of race relations". They may therefore be involved in fact finding though the judge remains responsible for actually deciding the facts and the "ultimate decision has to be for the judge" (*ibid.* para.32). The fact that the assessors' primary role is in the decision making process, "militates against any general obligation of disclosure prior to judgment" but there may be circumstances where disclosure of their views will be necessary, "for example where a point arises as a result of the assistance of the assessors which the parties clearly did not have in mind and which they should be entitled to address". Furthermore assessors, despite their primary role, may provide a piece of information akin to expert evidence, and here, once again, disclosure should be made (*ibid.*, para.34). The judge must ensure that it is apparent from his or her judgment that s.67(4) has been complied with and the assistance of his assessors has been used in reaching conclusions on issues relating to possible racism (*ibid.*, para.35). Where the judge accepts the evaluation of the assessors it will normally form part of the reasoning for the conclusion ultimately reached and this aspect should be recorded in the judgment (*ibid.*, para.36). Disagreement between the judge and the assessors on issues relating to racism should be rare, at least if the assessors themselves are agreed (*ibid.*, para.37). Where there is disagreement between the judge and the assessors as to an important matter, this should be recorded in the judgment with the judge explaining his reasons for taking a different view or, where the assessors are not agreed, preferring the advice of one assessor rather than the other (*ibid.*, paras 38–39). In addition, the SDA makes specific provision allowing for the appointment of assessors under s.63 of the County Courts Act 1984 (SDA s.66(6)). Certain claims (but not counter claims) 3I–43 under the education provisions of the SDA and RRA may only be instituted after the Claimant has given notice of the claim to the Secretary of State (SDA s.66(5) and RRA s.57(5)–(5A)) and, in the case of claims under the SDA, two months has elapsed since notice has been given or the Secretary of State has indicated that no further time is required (the same requirement in the RRA was removed by the Race Relations (Amendment) Act 2000). Where proceedings are brought under RRA, s.19B (public authorities) and a party has applied for a stay of the proceedings on the grounds of prejudice to, particular criminal proceedings; a criminal investigation or a decision to institute criminal proceedings then the stay must be granted unless the court is satisfied that the continuance of the proceedings would not result in the prejudice alleged (RRA s.57(4C) and (4D)). The SDA makes comparable provision in respect of proceedings under s.21A (public authorities) (SDA s.21A(6)).

The SDA has been recently amended by the Employment Equality (Sex Discrimination) Regulations 2005 SI 2005/2467 so as to, amongst other things, introduce a statutory tort of harassment into certain parts of the SDA (already found in the RRA and Disability Discrimination Act 1995) and to move the unlawful acts applicable to the treatment of barristers, pupils and advocates from the jurisdiction of the County Court to the Employment Tribunals. These changes took effect from October 1, 2005 though the jurisdictional changes do not apply to proceedings where the act complained of took place before that date (see transitional provisions in regs 1(1) and 2(1)). The effect of these Regulations has been modified by the Sex Discrimination Act 1975 (Amendment) Regulations 2008 SI 2008/656, following *Equal Opportunities Commission v Secretary of State for Trade and Industry* [2007] I.C.R. 1234; [2007] I.R.L.R. 327 in which it was held that they were in part defective. The SDA has been further amended by the Sex Discrimination (Amendment of Legislation) Regulations 2008 SI 2008/963 to give effect to Council Directive 2004/113 EC ("the Gender Goods and Services Directive") so as to, amongst other things, extend the new meaning of discrimination, including harassment, to the unlawful acts outside the employment field.

Further, the SDA, the RRA and the DDA contain general duties upon public authorities to, amongst other things, have due regard to the need to eliminate unlawful discrimination and promote equality of opportunity (SDA s.76A; RRA s.71 and DDA s.49A) and pursuant to subordinate legislation made under the Acts, specific duties are imposed on certain public authorities. The duties may be enforced by way of judicial review (see *Secretary of State for Defence v Elias (CRE Intervening)* [2005] EWHC 1435 (Admin); [2006] EWCA Civ 1293; *R (on the application of C (A Minor, by his litigation friend MS)) v Secretary of State for Justice* [2008] EWCA Civ 882) and by the CEHR (EA s.32).

The Equality Act 2006 made a number of changes to the enforcement provisions of the SDA and RRA (s.40 and Sch.3, s.91 and Sch.4). These changes came into force on October 1, 2007 and give the EHRC power to "assess" the extent to which or manner in which a public authority has complied with a general or specific equality duty under the SDA, RRA (Equality Act 2006 s.31 and Sch.2) and the EHRC has power to issue compliance notices in respect of a breach of the general statutory duties (but only after an "assessment" has been carried out and only where the notice relates to the results of the "assessment") as well as the specific statutory duties (Equality Act 2006 s.32).

### Time limits

3I–44 Proceedings under Pts III of the SDA and RRA must be instituted within six months of when the act complained was done (SDA s.76(2)(a); RRA s.68(2), and see s.68(2A) for a modification in relation to certain immigration claims under RRA s.19B). In cases falling under ss.22 and 23 of the SDA (education) proceedings must be instituted within eight months of when the act complained of was done (SDA s.76(2)(b)). In cases where the dispute involves a higher education institution and the complaint has been referred as a complaint under the "student complaints scheme" the time limit for instituting proceedings is extended by three months (SDA s.76(2A); RRA s.68(3A). As to when time begins to run, see SDA s.76(6); s.68(7) RRA.The circumstances in which an act might be said to "extend over a period" (usually described as a "continuing act") for the purposes of the time limits have proved problematic and controversial. A policy, rule or practice, in accordance with which decisions are taken from time to time, might constitute a "continuing act" for these purposes, even where such policy is unwritten and informal (*Owusu v London Fire and Civil Defence Authority* [1995] I.R.L.R.

574, EAT; *Cast v Croydon College* [1998] I.C.R. 500, CA). Likewise a continuing state of affairs may constitute a continuing act for these purposes (*Hendricks v MPC* [2003] I.R.L.R. 96, even where the individual acts relied upon are done by different persons and are done at different places). In addition, in each case, a claim may be considered notwithstanding that it has been instituted outside of the time limit where it would be "just and equitable" to do so (SDA s.76(5); RRA s.68(6)); as to the factors which are likely to be relevant, see *Anderson v Rover Group* (1999) 1426/99, EAT; *British Coal Corporation v Keeble* [1997] I.R.L.R. 336, EAT, at 338, and *London Borough of Southwark v Afolabi* [2003] I.R.L.R. 220, presented nearly nine years after the expiry of the statutory time limit). Each case is likely to turn very much on its own facts.

**Enforcement and Remedies**

The unlawful acts created by the SDA and RRA are statutory torts and in general terms the Courts have addressed their enforcement and remedies in relation to them in much the same way as with any other statutory tort. Thus, where an award of compensation is made in respect of joint tortfeasors, the award will be distributed according to what is just and equitable having regard to the extent of that person's responsibility for the damage in question (Civil Liability (Contribution) Act 1978; see *Prison Service v Johnson* [1997] I.C.R. 275). Further, where a person has a cause of action under the SDA and RRA that cause of action survives his or her death for the benefit of his estate (Law Reform (Miscellaneous Provisions) Act 1934; *Lewisham and Guys Mental Health NHS Trust v Harris* [2000] I.C.R. 707, CA). As to remedies under the SDA and RRA the county courts may make any order as would be available in the High Court (in England and Wales) and the Court of Session (in Scotland) and in particular awards of compensation, including an award for injury to feelings (*Vento v Chief Constable of West Yorkshire Police* [2002] EWCA Civ 1871; [2003] I.C.R. 318), and declarations may be made (SDA s.66(1)–(2) and (4) and RRA s.57(1)–(2) and (4)). In determining whether any particular losses are recoverable the test to be applied is whether such losses are caused by (or arise naturally and directly from) the discrimination found proved. There is no requirement of foreseeabilty (*Essa v Laing Ltd* [2004] EWCA Civ 2; [2004] I.C.R. 746, CA). In relation to many claims of indirect sex discrimination outside the employment field and certain claims of indirect race discrimination outside the employment field, no award of damages may be made if the defendant proves that the requirement or condition in question was not applied with the intention of treating the claimant unfavourably (SDA s.66(3); RRA s.57(3)) but a court may infer that a defendant had the requisite intention where he knew when he applied the offending requirement or condition that the discriminatory consequences would follow (*London Underground Limited v Edwards* [1995] IRLR 355, EAT; *JH Walker Ltd v Hussain* [1996] ICR 291, EAT). **3I–45**

The Equality Act 2006 gives the EHRC power to make arrangements for the provision of conciliation services for disputes in respect of which proceedings have been or could be brought under the SDA or RRA (Equality Act 2006 s.27). By s.27(3), information communicated to a person providing conciliation services in accordance with such arrangements may not be adduced in legal proceedings without the consent of the person who communicated the information. Certain persons are excluded from participating in the provision of such conciliation services (including EHRC Commissioners and staff; see s.27(6) of the Equality Act 2006).

**Proving discrimination and the burden of proof**

There is much guidance from the appellate courts on proving the different forms of discrimination provided for under the SDA and RRA (see, for example, *Anya v University of Oxford* [2001] EWCA Civ 405; [2001] I.C.R. 847, CA, at pp 851–855, *per* Sedley L.J.; *Qureshi v Victoria University of Manchester* [2001] I.C.R. 863, EAT, for the very helpful guidance of Mummery L.J.; *Shamoon v Chief Constable of the Royal Ulster Constabulary* [2003] UKHL 11; [2003] ICR 337, HL; *Chief Constable of the West Yorkshire Police v Khan* [2001] UKHL 48; [2001] I.C.R. 1065, HL). In addition, the SDA and RRA now make specific provision shifting the burden of proof in certain circumstances. Where a claimant proves facts from which a court could conclude in the absence of an adequate explanation that the defendant has committed an unlawful act, a court must uphold the complaint unless the defendant proves that he did not so act (SDA s.63A and s.66A; RRA s.54A and s.57ZA). This shift applies only in relation to certain of the **3I–46** unlawful acts created by the SDA and RRA (and does not apply to victimisation under the RRA; *Oyarce v Cheshire County Council (Equality and Human Rights Commission intervening)* [2008] EWCA Civ 434; [2008] I.C.R. 1179), as the provisions themselves make clear. As to the impact of these provisions, see *Igen Ltd (formerly Leeds Careers Guidance) v. Wong* [2005] EWCA Civ 142; [2005] I.C.R. 931;*EB v BA* [2006] EWCA Civ 132; [2006] I.R.L.R. 471 and *Madarassy v Nomura International Plc* [2007] I.R.L.R 246. The SDA and RRA also make provision for the service of "questionnaires" (SDA s.74 and RRA s.65; see too, Sex Discrimination (Questions and Replies) Order 1975 (SI 1975/2048); Race Relations (Questions and Replies) Order 1977 (SI 1977/842)). Time limits are prescribed for the purposes of serving and replying to such questionnaires and provision is made allowing for adverse inferences to be drawn in cases where a questionnaire is not replied to or not replied to within the time limit prescribed for so doing (SDA s.74 and RRA s.65). Carefully crafted questions can assist a complainant in properly identifying his complaints and in proving them, as can be seen from the guidance in *Igen*, above(and see *West Midlands Passenger Transport Executive v Singh* [1988] I.R.L.R. 186, CA). The statutory Codes of Practice also provide valuable guidance as to the proving of discrimination.

## Disability Discrimination Act 1995

3I–47 (1995 c.50)

ARRANGEMENT OF SECTIONS

PART IV

EDUCATION



## PART IV

## EDUCATION

### Enforcement, remedies and procedure

3I–48 **28V.**—(1) A claim by a person—

(a) that a responsible body has discriminated against him, or subjected him to harassment in a way which is unlawful under this Chapter,

(b) that a responsible body is by virtue of section 57 or 58 to be treated as having done so, or

(c) that a person is by virtue of section 57 to be treated as having done so,

may be made the subject of civil proceedings in the same way as any other claim in tort or (in Scotland) in reparation for breach of statutory duty.

(1A) Where—

(a) a claim is brought under subsection (1), and

(b) the claimant (or pursuer, in Scotland) proves facts from which the court could, apart from this subsection, conclude in the absence of an adequate explanation that the defendant (or defender, in Scotland) has acted in a way which is unlawful under this Chapter,

the court shall uphold the claim unless the defendant (or defender, in Scotland) proves that he did not so act.

(2) For the avoidance of doubt it is hereby declared that damages in respect of discrimination in a way which is unlawful under this Chapter may include compensation for injury to feelings whether or not they include compensation under any other head.

(3) Proceedings in England and Wales may be brought only in a county court.

(4) Proceedings in Scotland may be brought only in a sheriff court.

(5) The remedies available in such proceedings are those which are available in the High Court or (as the case may be) the Court of Session.

(6) The fact that a person who brings proceedings under this Part against a responsible body may also be entitled to bring proceedings against that body under Part 2 is not to affect the proceedings under this Part.

(7) Part 4 of Schedule 3 makes further provision about the enforcement of this Part and about procedure.

*Note*—Amended by SI 2006/1721. **3I–49**

**Notes on Part IV of the Disability Discrimination Act 1995**

When the 1995 Act came into effect the CCR O.49, r.17 was amended for the purpose of providing necessary rules of court; see now Sch. 2 CCR O.49, r.17 (Vol.1, para.cc49.17). In 2004, that rule was amended to take account of the coming into effect of the Disability Rights Commission Act 1999. **3I–50**

Part IV, Chapters 1 and 2, of the Disability Discrimination Act 1995 (DDA) was inserted by the Special Educational Needs and Disability Act 2001 and it creates a number of unlawful acts in relation to schools and local education authorities in relation to pupils (ss.28A–C and 28F); in relation to further and higher education (s.28R to s.28T) and in relation to certain providers of statutory youth and community services including adult education in relation to students (s.28U and Sch.4C DDA). The provisions addressing discrimination by further and higher education institutions were amended by the Disability Discrimination Act 1995 (Amendment) (Further and Higher Education) Regulations 2006 (SI 2006/1721) which create certain new unlawful acts, including by outlawing harassment. Claims under Part IV, Chapter 1 (discrimination in relation to pupils) are heard in Special Educational Need and Disability Tribunals (s.28I). Claims under Part IV Chapter 2 (discrimination in relation to students) are heard in the county courts (s.28V).

There are many similarities between the DDA, on the one hand, and the SDA and RRA on the other, but significant differences also. However, the DDA addresses remedies and enforcement in a similar way in respect of those unlawful acts it creates and, in particular, in respect of those justiciable in the county courts under Part III and IV DDA (Sch.3, paras. 2(1)–(2), 5(1)–(2), 9(1)–(2) and 12(1)–(2); ss.25(1), (2), (5) and 28V(1)–(5)). In addition the DDA provides for a shift in the burden of proof in respect of certain of the unlawful acts (s.17A(1C), s.25(7)–(9) and 28V(1A)); provides for a questionnaire procedure (s.56 DDA and Disability Discrimination (Questions and Replies) Order 2004 (SI 2004/1168)); addresses vicarious and secondary liability (ss.57–58 and s.64A DDA) and time limits (Sch. 3, paras. 6 and 13) and the guidance provided by the courts on these matters in relation to the SDA and the RRA should be taken as applying equally to proceedings under the DDA. The Equality Act 2006 gives

***Paragraph numbers marked with a "+" can be found online and on CD.***

the EHRC power to make arrangements for the provision of conciliation services for disputes in respect of which proceedings have been or could be brought under the DDA (s.27 of the Equality Act 2006). By s.27(3), information communicated to a person providing conciliation services in accordance with such arrangements may not be adduced in legal proceedings without the consent of the person who communicated the information. Certain persons are excluded from participating in the provision of such conciliation services (including EHRC Commissioners and staff; see s.27(6) of the Equality Act 2006).

* * * *

## Part 5A

## Public Authorities

### General Duty

3I–51 **49A.**—(1) Every public authority shall in carrying out its functions have due regard to—

(a) the need to eliminate discrimination that is unlawful under this Act;

(b) the need to eliminate harassment of disabled persons that is related to their disabilities;

(c) the need to promote equality of opportunity between disabled persons and other persons;

(d) the need to take steps to take account of disabled persons' disabilities, even where that involves treating disabled persons more favourably than other persons;

(e) the need to promote positive attitudes towards disabled persons; and

(f) the need to encourage participation by disabled persons in public life.

(2) Subsection (1) is without prejudice to any obligation of a public authority to comply with any other provision of this Act.

3I–52 *Note*.—Inserted by the Disability Discrimination Act 2005 s.3, with effect from December 5, 2005 (subs.(1), for the purpose only of regulations under s. 49D) and December 4, 2006 (subs.(1) remaining purposes, subs.(2)); see SI 2005/2774.

### Meaning of "public authority" in Part 5A

3I–53 **49B.**—(1) In this Part "public authority"—

(a) includes any person certain of whose functions are functions of a public nature; but

(b) does not include—

(i) any person mentioned in section 21B(3);

(ii) the Scottish Parliament;

(iii) a person, other than the Scottish Parliamentary Corporate Body, exercising functions in connection with proceedings in the Scottish Parliament.

(iv) the National Assembly for Wales; or

(v) a person, other than the National Assembly for

Wales Commission, exercising functions in connection with proceedings in the National Assembly for Wales.

(2) In relation to a particular act, a person is not a public authority by virtue only of subsection (1)(a) if the nature of the act is private.

(3) Regulations may provide for a person of a prescribed description to be treated as not being a public authority for the purposes of this Part.

*Note* —Inserted by the Disability Discrimination Act 2005, s.3, with effect from December 5, 2005 (SI 2005/2774); amended by SI 2007/1388. **3I–54**

## Exceptions from section 49A(1)

**49C.**—(1) Section 49A(1) does not apply to— **3I–55**

(a) a judicial act (whether done by a court, tribunal or other person); or

(b) an act done on the instructions, or on behalf, of a person acting in a judicial capacity.

(2) Section 49A(1) does not apply to any act of, or relating to, making or approving an Act of Parliament, an Act of the Scottish Parliament, a Measure or Act of the National Assembly for Wales or an Order in Council.

(3) Section 49A(1)(c) and (d) do not apply to—

(a) an act done in connection with recruitment to any of the naval, military or air forces of the Crown; or

(b) an act done in relation to a person in connection with service by him as a member of any of those forces.

(4) Regulations may provide for one or more specified paragraphs of section 49A(1) not to apply to an act of a prescribed description.

*Note* —Inserted by the Disability Discrimination Act 2005 s.3, with effect from December 5, 2005 (SI 2005/2774); amended by the Equality Act 2006 s.88(1); and by SI 2007/1388, with effect from May 25, 2007. **3I–56**

## Power to impose specific duties

**49D.**—(1) The Secretary of State may by regulations impose on a public authority, other than a relevant Scottish authority or a cross-border authority, such duties as the Secretary of State considers appropriate for the purpose of ensuring the better performance by that authority of its duty under section 49A(1). **3I–57**

(2) The Secretary of State may by regulations impose on a cross-border authority such duties as the Secretary of State considers appropriate for the purpose of ensuring the better performance by that authority of its duty under section 49A(1) so far as relating to such of its functions as are not Scottish functions.

(3) The Scottish Ministers may by regulations impose on a relevant Scottish authority such duties as the Scottish Ministers consider appropriate for the purpose of ensuring the better performance by that authority of its duty under section 49A(1).

(4) The Scottish Ministers may by regulations impose on a cross-

border authority such duties as the Scottish Ministers consider appropriate for the purpose of ensuring the better performance by that authority of its duty under section 49A(1) so far as relating to its Scottish functions.

(5) Before making regulations under any of subsections (1) to (4), the person making the regulations shall consult the Commission for Equality and Human Rights.

(6) Before making regulations under subsection (1) or (2) in relation to functions exercisable in relation to Wales by a public authority that is not a relevant Welsh authority, the Secretary of State shall consult the Welsh Ministers.

(7) The Secretary of State shall not make regulations under subsection (1) or (2) in relation to a relevant Welsh authority except with the consent of the Welsh Ministers.

(8) Before making regulations under subsection (2), the Secretary of State shall consult the Scottish Ministers.

(9) Before making regulations under subsection (4), the Scottish Ministers shall consult the Secretary of State.

(10) In this section—

"relevant Scottish authority" means—

(a) a member of the Scottish executive or a junior Scottish Minister;

(b) the Registrar General of Births, Deaths and Marriages for Scotland, the Keeper of the Registers of Scotland or the Keeper of the Records of Scotland;

(c) any office of a description specified in an Order in Council under section 126(8)(b) of the Scotland Act 1998 (other non-ministerial office in the Scottish Administration); or

(d) a public body, public office or holder of a public office—

(i) which (or who) is not a cross-border authority or the Scottish Parliamentary Corporate Body;

(ii) whose functions are exercisable only in or as regards Scotland; and

(iii) some at least of whose functions do not (within the meaning of the Scotland Act 1998) relate to reserved matters;

"cross-border authority" means a cross-border public authority within the meaning given by section 88(5) of the Scotland Act 1998;

"Scottish functions" means functions which are exercisable in or as regards Scotland and which do not (within the meaning of the Scotland Act 1998) relate to reserved matters;

"relevant Welsh authority" means—

(a) the National Assembly for Wales Commission; or

(aa) the Welsh Ministers, the First Minister for Wales or the Counsel General to the Welsh Assembly Government; or

(b) a public authority whose functions are exercisable only in relation to Wales.

*Note*—Inserted by the Disability Discrimination Act 2005, s.3, with effect from June 30, 2005 (SI 2005/1676); amended by SI 2007/1388, with effect from May 25, 2007. For subordinate legislation made under subss.(1)–(4) see, (for the UK) Disability Discrimination (Public Authorities) (Statutory Duties) Regulations 2005 (SI 2005/2966); Disability Discrimination (Public Authorities) (Statutory Duties) (Amendment) Regulations 2007 (SI 2007/618) and (for Scotland) Disability Discrimination (Public Authorities) (Statutory Duties) (Scotland) Regulations 2005 (SSI 2005/565); Disability Discrimination (Public Authorities) (Statutory Duties) (Scotland) Amendment Regulations 2007 (SSI 2007/195). For enforcement of the duties by the EHRC, see ss.31 and 32 of the Equality Act 2006 (repealing earlier provision in the Disability Discrimination Act 1995; see the Equality Act 2006 ss.40, 91, Sch.3, paras 41, 49, Sch.4 as from October 1, 2007). 3I–58

# Equality Act 2006

(2006 c.3) 3I–59

ARRANGEMENT OF SECTIONS

PART 2

DISCRIMINATION ON GROUNDS OF RELIGION OR BELIEF

*ENFORCEMENT*



## PART 2

## DISCRIMINATION ON GROUNDS OF RELIGION OR BELIEF

### *ENFORCEMENT*

### Restriction of proceedings

**65.**—(1) Except as provided by this Act, no proceedings, whether criminal or civil, may be brought against a person on the grounds that an act is unlawful by virtue of this Part. 3I–60

(2) But subsection (1) does not prevent—

(a) an application for judicial review,

(b) proceedings under the Immigration Acts,

(c) proceedings under the Special Immigration Appeals Commission Act 1997 (c. 68), or

(d) in Scotland, the exercise of the jurisdiction of the Court of Session to entertain an application for reduction or suspension of an order or determination or otherwise to consider the validity of an order or determination, or to require reasons for an order or determination to be stated.

### Claim of unlawful action

**66.**—(1) A claim that a person has done anything that is unlawful 3I–61 by virtue of this Part may be brought in a county court (in England and Wales) or in the sheriff court (in Scotland) by way of proceedings in tort (or reparation) for breach of statutory duty.

(2) Proceedings in England and Wales alleging that any of the following bodies has acted unlawfully by virtue of section 49 or 51 may not be brought unless the claimant has given written notice to the Secretary of State; and those bodies are—

(a) a local education authority, and
(b) the responsible body of an educational establishment listed in the Table in section 49.

(3) Proceedings in Scotland alleging that any of the following bodies has acted unlawfully by virtue of section 49 or 51 may not be brought unless the pursuer has given written notice to the Scottish Ministers; and those bodies are—

(a) an education authority, and
(b) the responsible body of an educational establishment listed in the Table in section 49.

(4) In subsection (1) the reference to a claim that a person has done an unlawful act includes a reference to a claim that a person is to be treated by virtue of this Part as having done an unlawful act.

(5) In proceedings under this section, if the claimant (or pursuer) proves facts from which the court could conclude, in the absence of a reasonable alternative explanation, that an act which is unlawful by virtue of this Part has been committed, the court shall assume that the act was unlawful unless the respondent (or defender) proves that it was not.

## Immigration

3I–62 **67.**—(1) Proceedings may not be brought under section 66 alleging that a person has acted unlawfully by virtue of section 52 if the question of the lawfulness of the act could be raised (and has not been raised) in immigration proceedings (disregarding the possibility of proceedings brought out of time with permission).

(2) If in immigration proceedings a court or tribunal has found that an act was unlawful by virtue of section 52, a court hearing proceedings under section 66 shall accept that finding.

(3) In this section "immigration proceedings" means proceedings under or by virtue of—

(a) the Immigration Acts, or
(b) the Special Immigration Appeals Commission Act 1997 (c. 68).

## Remedies

3I–63 **68.**—(1) This section applies to proceedings under section 66.

(2) A court may, in addition to any remedy available to it in proceedings for tort, grant any remedy that the High Court could grant in proceedings for judicial review.

(3) A court may not award damages in proceedings in respect of an act that is unlawful by virtue of section 45(3) if the respondent

*Paragraph numbers marked with a "+" can be found online and on CD.*

proves that there was no intention to treat the claimant unfavourably on grounds of religion or belief.

(4) A court may award damages by way of compensation for injury to feelings (whether or not other damages are also awarded).

(5) In the application of this section to proceedings in Scotland—

(a) a reference to the High Court shall be taken as a reference to the Court of Session,

(b) a reference to tort shall be taken as a reference to reparation,

(c) a reference to the respondent shall be taken as a reference to the defender, and

(d) a reference to the claimant shall be taken as a reference to the pursuer.

(6) This section is subject to section 52(5).

## Timing

**69.**—(1) Proceedings under section 66 may be brought only— **3I–64**

(a) within the period of six months beginning with the date of the act (or last act) to which the proceedings relate, or

(b) with the permission of the court in which the proceedings are brought.

(2) In relation to immigration proceedings within the meaning of section 67, the period specified in subsection (1)(a) above shall begin with the first date on which proceedings under section 66 may be brought.

## Information

**70.**—(1) In this section— **3I–65**

(a) a reference to a claimant is a reference to a person who has brought proceedings under this Part,

(b) reference to a potential claimant is a reference to a person who—

(i) thinks he may have been the subject of an act that is unlawful by virtue of this Part, and

(ii) wishes to consider whether to bring proceedings under this Part, and

(c) a person questioned by a potential claimant for the purpose of considering whether to bring proceedings is referred to as a potential respondent.

(2) The Minister shall by order prescribe—

(a) forms by which a claimant or potential claimant may question the respondent or a potential respondent about the reasons for an action or about any matter that is or may be relevant, and

(b) forms by which a respondent or potential respondent may reply (if he wishes).

(3) A claimant's or potential claimant's questions, and a respondent or potential respondent's replies, (in each case whether or not put by a prescribed form) shall be admissible as evidence in proceed-

ings in respect of the act to which the questions relate if (and only if) the questions are put—

(a) within the period of six months beginning with the date of the act (or last act) to which they relate, and

(b) in such manner as the Minister may prescribe by order.

(4) A court may draw an inference from—

(a) a failure to reply to a claimant's or potential claimant's questions (whether or not put by a prescribed form) within the period of eight weeks beginning with the date of receipt, or

(b) an evasive or equivocal reply to a claimant's or potential claimant's questions (whether or not put by a prescribed form).

(5) The Minister may by order amend subsection (3)(a) so as to substitute a new period for that specified.

(6) In the application of this section to Scotland—

(a) a reference to a claimant or potential claimant shall be taken as a reference to a pursuer or potential pursuer, and

(b) a reference to a respondent or potential respondent shall be taken as a reference to a defender or potential defender.

(7) An order under this section—

(a) shall be made by statutory instrument, and

(b) shall be subject to annulment in pursuance of a resolution of either House of Parliament.

(8) This section is subject to section 52(6).

**3I–65.1** *Note*—Amended by SI 2007/2914.

## National security

**3I–66** **71.**—(1) Rules of court may make provision for enabling a county court or sheriff court in which a claim is brought under section 66, where the court considers it expedient in the interests of national security—

(a) to exclude from all or part of the proceedings

(i) the claimant;

(ii) the claimant's representatives;

(iii) any assessors;

(b) to permit a claimant or representative who has been excluded to make a statement to the court before the commencement of the proceedings, or the part of the proceedings, from which he is excluded;

(c) to take steps to keep secret all or part of the reasons for the court's decision in the proceedings.

(2) The Attorney General or, in Scotland, the Advocate General for Scotland, may appoint a person to represent the interests of a claimant in, or in any part of, proceedings from which the claimant or his representatives are excluded by virtue of subsection (1).

(3) A person may be appointed under subsection (2) only—

(a) in relation to proceedings in England and Wales, if he has a general qualification (within the meaning of section 71 of the Courts and Legal Services Act 1990 (c. 41)), or

(b) in relation to proceedings in Scotland, if he is—

(i) an advocate, or

(ii) qualified to practice as a solicitor in Scotland.

(4) A person appointed under subsection (2) shall not be responsible to the person whose interests he is appointed to represent.

## The Equality Act (Sexual Orientation) Regulations 2007

(S.I. 2007 No. 1263) **3I–67**

ARRANGEMENT OF REGULATIONS



### Restriction of proceedings

**19.**—(1) Except as provided by these Regulations, no proceedings, whether criminal or civil, may be brought against a person on the grounds that an act is unlawful by virtue of these Regulations. **3I–68**

(2) But paragraph (1) does not preclude—

(a) proceedings by the Commission under Part 1 of the 2006 Act,

(b) an application for judicial review,

(c) proceedings under the Immigration Acts,

(d) proceedings under the Special Immigration Appeals Commission Act 1997, or

(e) in Scotland, the exercise of the jurisdiction of the Court of Session to entertain an application for reduction or suspension of an order or determination or otherwise to consider the validity of an order or determination, or to require reasons for an order or determination to be stated.

### Claims of unlawful action

**20.**—(1) A claim that a person has done anything that is unlawful by virtue of these Regulations may be brought— **3I–69**

(a) in England and Wales, in a county court, by way of proceedings in tort, or

(b) in Scotland, in the sheriff court, by way of proceedings in reparation,

for breach of statutory duty.

*Paragraph numbers marked with a "+" can be found online and on CD.*

(2) Proceedings in England and Wales alleging that a local education authority or the responsible body of an educational establishment listed in Schedule 3 has acted unlawfully by virtue of regulation 7 or 8 may not be brought unless the claimant has given written notice to the Secretary of State.

(3) Proceedings in Scotland alleging that an education authority or the responsible body of an educational establishment listed in Schedule 3 has acted unlawfully by virtue of regulation 7 or 8 may not be brought unless the pursuer has given written notice to the Scottish Ministers.

(4) In paragraph (1) the reference to a claim that a person has done an unlawful act includes a reference to a claim that a person is to be treated by virtue of these Regulations as having done an unlawful act.

(5) In proceedings under this regulation, if the claimant (or pursuer) proves facts from which the court could conclude, in the absence of a reasonable alternative explanation, that an act which is unlawful by virtue of these Regulations has been committed, the court shall assume that the act was unlawful unless the respondent (or defender) proves that it was not.

**Claims of unlawful action: immigration cases**

3I–70 **21.**—(1) Proceedings may not be brought under regulation 20 alleging that a person has acted unlawfully by virtue of regulation 8 if the question of the lawfulness of the act could be raised (and has not been raised) in immigration proceedings (disregarding the possibility of proceedings brought out of time with permission).

(2) If in immigration proceedings a court or tribunal has found that an act was unlawful by virtue of regulation 8, a court hearing proceedings under regulation 20 shall accept that finding.

(3) In this regulation "immigration proceedings" means proceedings under or by virtue of—

(a) the Immigration Acts, or
(b) the Special Immigration Appeals Commission Act 1997.

**Remedies for unlawful action**

3I–71 **22.**—(1) In proceedings under regulation 20, the court (subject to paragraph (2))—

(a) (in addition to granting any remedy available to it in proceedings for tort) may grant any remedy that the High Court could grant in proceedings for judicial review,
(b) may award damages by way of compensation for injury to feelings (whether or not other damages are also awarded),
(c) may not award damages in proceedings in respect of an act that is unlawful by virtue of regulation 3(5) if the respondent proves that there was no intention to treat the claimant unfavourably on grounds of sexual orientation,

(2) In respect of a contravention of regulation 8, the court—

(a) shall not grant an injunction unless satisfied that it will not prejudice criminal proceedings or a criminal investigation, and

(b) shall grant any application to stay the proceedings under regulation 20 on the grounds of prejudice to criminal proceedings or to a criminal investigation, unless satisfied that the proceedings or investigation will not be prejudiced.

(3) In the application of this regulation to Scotland—

(a) a reference to the court shall be taken as a reference to the sheriff,

(b) a reference to the High Court shall be taken as a reference to the Court of Session,

(c) a reference to tort shall be taken as a reference to reparation,

(d) a reference to the claimant shall be taken as a reference to the pursuer,

(e) a reference to the respondent shall be taken as a reference to the defender,

(f) a reference to an injunction shall be taken as a reference to an interdict, and

(g) a reference to staying proceedings shall be taken as a reference to sisting proceedings.

**Claims of unlawful action: timing**

**23.**—(1) Proceedings under regulation 20 may be brought only— **3I–72**

(a) within the period of six months beginning with the date of the act (or the last act) to which the proceedings relate, or

(b) with the permission of the court in which the proceedings are brought.

(2) In relation to immigration proceedings (as defined in regulation 21) the period specified in paragraph (1)(a) shall begin with the first date on which proceedings under regulation 20 may be brought.

**Claims of unlawful action: information**

**24.**—(1) A claimant or a potential claimant may question a respondent or a potential respondent about the reasons for an action or about any matter that is or may be relevant and may do so— **3I–73**

(a) in the form set out in Part 1 of Schedule 2, or

(b) in a form to the like effect with such variation as the circumstances require.

(2) A respondent or potential respondent may reply (if he so wishes) to questions served under paragraph (1)—

(a) in the form set out in Part 2 of Schedule 2, or

(b) in a form to the like effect with such variation as the circumstances require.

(3) A claimant's or potential claimant's questions (whether or not put in a form mentioned in paragraph (1)), and a respondent or

*Paragraph numbers marked with a "+" can be found online and on CD.*

potential respondent's replies shall be admissible as evidence in proceedings in respect of the action or about any matter that is or may be relevant, to which the questions relate if (and only if) the questions are served—

(a) within the period of six months beginning with the date of the action (or last action) to which they relate, and

(b) in accordance with paragraph (4).

(4) A question may be served on a respondent or potential respondent and a reply may be served on a claimant or potential claimant—

(a) by delivering it to him,

(b) by sending it by post to him at his usual or last known residence or place of business,

(c) where the person to be served is acting by a solicitor, by delivering it at, or by sending it by post to, the solicitor's address for service,

(d) where the person to be served is a claimant or potential claimant, by delivering the reply, or sending it by post, to him at his address for reply as stated by him in the document containing the questions, or if no address is so stated, at his usual or last known residence, or

(e) where the person to be served is a body corporate or is a trade union or employers' association within the meaning of the Trade Union and Labour Relations (Consolidation) Act 1992, by delivering it to the secretary or clerk of the body, union or association at its registered or principal office, or by sending it by post to the secretary or clerk at that office.

(5) A court may draw an inference from—

(a) a failure to reply to a claimant's or potential claimant's questions within the period of eight weeks beginning with the date the questions were served, or

(b) an evasive or equivocal reply to such questions (whether or not put in a form mentioned in paragraph (1)).

(6) In this regulation—

(a) "claimant" means a person who has brought proceedings under these Regulations,

(b) "potential claimant" means a person who—

(i) thinks he may have been the subject of an act that is unlawful by virtue of these Regulations, and

(ii) wishes to consider whether to bring proceedings under these Regulations,

(c) "potential respondent" means a person questioned by a potential claimant for the purpose of considering whether to bring proceedings under these Regulations

(7) In the application of this regulation to Scotland—

(a) a reference to a claimant or potential claimant shall be taken as a reference to a pursuer or potential pursuer, and

(b) a reference to a respondent or potential respondent shall be taken as a reference to a defender or potential defender.

(8) Paragraph (5) does not apply in relation to a reply, or a failure to reply, to a question—

(a) if the respondent or potential respondent reasonably asserts that to have replied differently or at all might have prejudiced criminal proceedings or a criminal investigation,

(b) if the respondent or potential respondent reasonably asserts that to have replied differently or at all would have revealed the reason for not instituting or not continuing criminal proceedings, or

(c) if the respondent or potential respondent reasonably asserts that to have replied differently or at all would have frustrated the purpose of national security.

**National security**

**25.**—(1) Rules of court may make provision for enabling a county court or sheriff court in which a claim is brought under regulation 20, where the court considers it expedient in the interests of national security— **3I–74**

(a) to exclude from all or part of the proceedings—

(i) the claimant,

(ii) the claimant's representatives, or

(iii) any assessors,

(b) to permit a claimant or representative who has been excluded to make a statement to the court before the commencement of the proceedings, or the part of the proceedings, from which he is excluded;

(c) to take steps to keep secret all or part of the reasons for the court's decision in the proceedings.

(2) The Attorney General or, in Scotland, the Advocate General for Scotland, may appoint a person to represent the interests of a claimant in, or in any part of, proceedings from which the claimant or his representatives are excluded by virtue of paragraph (1).

(3) A person may be appointed under paragraph (2) only—

(a) in relation to proceedings in England and Wales, if he has a general qualification (within the meaning of section 71 of the Courts and Legal Services Act 1990), or

(b) in relation to proceedings in Scotland, if he is—

(i) an advocate, or

(ii) qualified to practise as a solicitor in Scotland.

(4) A person appointed under paragraph (2) shall not be responsible to the person whose interests he is appointed to represent.

**Note**

For subordinate legislation, see Act of Sederunt (Ordinary Cause, Summary Ap- **3I–75** plication, Summary Cause and Small Claim Rules) Amendment (Equality Act (Sexual Orientation) Regulations 2007) 2007 SSI 2007/339.

Part 2 of the Equality Act 2006 and the Equality Act (Sexual Orientation) Regulations 2007 (SI 2007/1263) (made under Pt.3 of the Equality Act 2006) outlaw discrimination connected to religion and belief and sexual orientation, respectively. Sections 65–71 of the Equality Act 2006 and regs 19–25 of the Equality Act (Sexual Orientation) Regulations 2007 (SI 2007/1263) address enforcement of the unlawful acts. In the main they reflect the enforcement provisions found in the SDA, RRA and DDA and the differences do not appear to have been intended to be material.

The Equality Act 2006 gives the EHRC power to make arrangements for the provision of conciliation services for disputes in respect of which proceedings have been or could be brought under the Equality Act and the Equality Act (Sexual Orientation) Regulation 2007 (s.27 of the Equality Act 2006). By s.27(3), information communicated to a person providing conciliation services in accordance with such arrangements may not be adduced in legal proceedings without the consent of the person who communicated the information. Certain persons are excluded from participating in the provision of such conciliation services (including EHRC Commissioners and staff: see s.27(6) of the Equality Act 2006). For the lawfulness of certain of the analogue Regulations enacted for Northern Ireland (Equality Act (Sexual Orientation) Regulation (Northern Ireland) 2006) addressing sexual orientation discrimination, see *The Christian Institute v Office of the First Minister and Deputy First Minister* [2007] NIQB 66.

# 3J DIRECTORS DISQUALIFICATION PROCEEDINGS

## PRACTICE DIRECTION—DIRECTORS DISQUALIFICATION PROCEEDINGS

*Editorial note*



**Purposes of the Company Directors Disqualification Act 1986 ("the Act")**

The Directors Disqualification Proceedings Practice Direction ("the Practice Direction") needs to be interpreted and applied in the context of the underlying legislation. The Act was introduced as part of the substantial re-casting of the insolvency legislation in the mid-1980s, and came into force on December 29, 1986. Its main provisions were originally introduced under the Insolvency Act 1985, which was brought into force on April 28, 1986. Although earlier insolvency legislation also made provision for disqualification of directors in certain circumstances, the 1986 changes were such that earlier case law is largely (though not entirely) redundant. The court's approach to Parliament's intention in introducing the Act is summarised in the judgment of Henry L.J. in *Re Grayan Building Services Ltd* [1995] Ch. 241, at 257: **3J–1**

> "The concept of limited liability and the sophistication of our corporate law offers great privileges and great opportunities for those who wish to trade under that regime. But the corporate environment carries with it the discipline that those who avail themselves of those privileges must accept the standards laid down and abide by the regulatory rules and disciplines in place to protect creditors and shareholders. ... The parliamentary intention to improve managerial safeguards and standards for the long term good of employees, creditors and investors is clear."

See also Sir Donald Nicholls V.-C. in *Re Swift 736 Ltd* [1993] B.C.C. 312 at 315:

> "Limited liability is a valuable tool in the promotion of trade and business, but it must not be misused. Those who make use of limited liability must do so with a proper sense of responsibility. The directors' disqualification procedure is an important sanction introduced by Parliament to raise standards in this regard."

On a closely related point, it has been frequently said that the primary purpose of the Act is to protect the public. This phrase is used in both a narrow and a wide sense. Even where the director no longer needs to be kept "off the road", the "wider interests of protecting the public" in making a disqualification order include a deterrent element in relation to both the director himself and as far as other directors are concerned: see the comments of Lord Woolf M.R. in *Re Westmid Packing Services Ltd* [1998] 2 All E.R. 124, at 131–2.

The court has also made clear that the disqualification jurisdiction is intended to be a summary jurisdiction, and has deprecated over-elaboration in the preparation and hearing of cases, and a technical approach to admissibility of evidence. "What is required and what the court should confine the parties to is sufficient evidence to enable the court to adopt a broad brush approach.": see Lord Woolf M.R. in *Westmid*, at 134–5. That is consistent with the "jury question" at the heart of most cases under s.6 of the Act (under which the vast majority of applications for disqualification orders are made), namely whether the person concerned is "unfit to be concerned in the management of a company" (s.6(1)(b) of the Act). Nevertheless, the summary approach is tempered by the fact that the court also recognises that in practice a disqualification order can represent "a serious interference with the freedom of an individual" (see Sir Donald Nicholls V.-C. in *Re Rex Williams Leisure Plc* [1994] Ch. 1, at 14. Further, breach of a disqualification order or undertaking can lead to criminal sanctions, of up to two years in prison and a fine (see s.11 of the Act).

**Application of the CPR**

In a number of places the Practice Direction makes specific provision that a certain aspect of the CPR shall or shall not apply. This can be a trap for the unwary. It should **3J–2** be emphasised that the rules which primarily govern disqualification proceedings are the Insolvent Companies (Disqualification of Unfit Directors) Rules 1987 (as amended by the Insolvent Companies (Disqualification of Unfit Directors) Proceedings (Amendment) Rules 1999) and by the Insolvent Companies (Disqualification of Unfit Directors Proceedings (Amendment) Rules 2001) (as amended, "the Disqualification Rules"), which were made under the rule-making power contained in s.21 of the Act and s.411 of the Insolvency Act 1986. By r.2(1), the CPR and any relevant practice directions are applied to disqualification proceedings, "except where these Rules make provision to inconsistent effect". This is equivalent to the position in relation to proceedings under the Insolvency Act 1986: see r.7.51 of the Insolvency Rules 1986. Thus, for example, service out of the jurisdiction under r.5(2) of the Disqualification Rules is not subject to the regime set out in Pt 6 of the CPR (though the court may in its discretion apply parts of it by analogy): see *Re Seagull Manufacturing Co Ltd (No.2)* [1994] Ch. 91.

**Companies Court Practice**

3J–3 The large bulk of disqualification proceedings are brought in the Companies Court, part of the Chancery Division of the High Court in London, and practice elsewhere tends to reflect Companies Court practice. The notes to the Practice Direction make reference, where appropriate, to the practice of the Companies Court.

## *Part I*

### 1. Application and interpretation

3J–4 **1.1** In this practice direction:

(1) "the Act" means the Company Directors Disqualification Act 1986 (as amended);

(2) "the Disqualification Rules" means the rules for the time being in force made under section 411 of the Insolvency Act 1986 in relation to disqualification proceedings.[1]

(3) "the Insolvency Rules" means the rules for the time being in force made under sections 411 and 412 of the Insolvency Act 1986 in relation to insolvency proceedings;

(4) "CPR" means the Civil Procedure Rules 1998 and "CPR" followed by "Part" or "Rule" and a number means the part or Rule with that number in those Rules;

(5) "disqualification proceedings" has the meaning set out in paragraph 1.3 below;

(6) "a disqualification application" is an application under the Act for the making of a disqualification order;

(7) "registrar" means any judge of the High Court or the county court who is a registrar within the meaning of the Insolvency Rules;

(8) "companies court registrar" means any judge of the High Court sitting in the Royal Courts of Justice in London who is a registrar within the meaning of the Insolvency Rules.

(9) except where the context otherwise requires references to;

[1] The current rules are the Insolvent Companies (Disqualification of Unfit Directors) Proceedings Rules 1987. For convenience relevant references to the Insolvent Companies (Disqualification of Unfit Directors) Proceedings Rules 1987, which apply to disqualification applications under ss.7, 8 and 9A of the Act (see rule 1(3)), are set out in footnotes to this Practice Direction. This Practice Direction applies certain provisions contained in the Insolvent Companies (Disqualification of Unfit Directors) Proceedings Rules 1987 to disqualification proceedings other than applications under ss.7, 8 and 9A of the Act.

(a) "company" or "companies" shall include references to "partnership" or "partnerships" and to "limited liability partnership" and to "limited liability partnerships";
(b) "director" shall include references to an "officer" of a partnership and to a "member" of a limited liability partnership;
(c) "shadow director" shall include references to a "shadow member" of a limited liability partnership and in appropriate cases, the forms annexed to this practice direction shall be varied accordingly;

(10) "disqualification order" has the meaning set out in section 1 of the Act and "disqualification undertaking" has the meaning set out in section 1A or section 9B of the Act (as the context requires);"; and

(11) a "section 8A application"is an application under section 8A of the Act to reduce the period for which a disqualification undertaking is in force or to provide for it to cease to be in force;

(12) "specified regulator" has the meaning set out in section 9E(2) of the Act".

**1.2** This practice direction shall come into effect on April 26, 1999 and shall replace all previous practice directions relating to disqualification proceedings.

**1.3** This practice direction applies to the following proceedings ("disqualification proceedings"):

(1) disqualification applications made:
(a) under section 2(2)(a) of the Act (after the person's conviction of an indictable offence in connection with the affairs of a company);
(b) under section 3 of the Act (on the ground of persistent breaches of provisions of companies legislation);
(c) under section 4 of the Act (on the ground of fraud etc);
(d) by the Secretary of State or the official receiver under section 7(1) of the Act (on the ground that the person is or has been a director of a company which has at any time become insolvent and his conduct makes him unfit to be concerned in the management of a company);
(e) by the Secretary of State under section 8 of the Act (on it appearing to the Secretary of State from investigative material that it is expedient in the public interest that a disqualification order should be made); or
(f) by the Office of Fair Trading or a specified regulator under section 9A of the Act (on the ground of breach of competition law by an undertaking and unfitness to be concerned in the management of a company);

(2) any application made under sections 7(2) or 7(4) of the Act;

(3) any application for permission to act made under section 17

of the Act for the purposes of any of sections 1(1)(a), 1A(1)(a) or 9B(4), or made under section 12(2) of the Act;

(4) any application for a court order made under CPR Part 23 in the course of any of the proceedings set out in sub-paragraphs (1) to (3) above.

(5) any application under the Act to the extent provided for by subordinate legislation[1];

(6) any section 8A application.

#### Definition of "Director"

3J-5 Paragraph 1.1(9)(b) has been inserted to make it clear how the Practice Direction is to be interpreted where proceedings are brought arising out of the affairs of insolvent partnerships and limited liability partnerships. The statutory definition of director is found in s.22(4) of the Act, which states that director "includes any person occupying the position of director, by whatever name called". Broadly speaking, directors within the meaning of the Act fall into three categories: (a) properly appointed (or "*de jure*") directors, who will normally be registered at Companies House; (b) "de facto" directors (i.e. those who, as a matter of fact after all the circumstances are considered, are treated as directors by the court); and (c) "shadow directors", namely persons in accordance with whose directions or instructions the directors of the company are accustomed to act (see s.22(5) of the Act).

#### Restrictions imposed by Disqualification Orders and Disqualification Undertakings

3J-6 A disqualification order is an order that, for a specified period, the specified person (a) "shall not be a director of a company, act as a receiver of a company's property or in any way, whether directly or indirectly, be concerned or take part in the promotion, formation or management of a company unless (in each case) he has the leave of the court", and (b) "shall not act as an insolvency practitioner" (see s.1 of the Act).

A disqualification undertaking is an undertaking, offered by a person and accepted by the Secretary of State for Business, Innovation and Skills (formerly the Secretary of State for Business, Enterprise and Regulatory Reform (before that known as the Secretary of State for Trade and Industry)), in effect to be subject for a specified period to the restrictions found in a Disqualification Order. The Act originally contained no mechanism whereby the parties to proceedings could compromise, because a finding of unfitness could only be made by the court, and accordingly the statutory consequences of an order would not flow from any private agreement between the parties. This led to (a) the court developing the *Carecraft* procedure (see the notes after para.13 of the Practice Direction below), and (with the particular encouragement of Sir Richard Scott V.-C. (see for example Practice Note [1996] 1 All E.R. 442)) (b) the amendments to the Act introduced in the Insolvency Act 2000 (in force since April 2, 2001) which created the statutory undertakings regime.

#### Date of commencement of proceedings

3J-7 The limitation period for the bringing of s.6 cases is found in s.7(2), which provides: "Except with the leave of the court, an application for the making under that section of a disqualification order against any person shall not be made after the end of the period of two years beginning with the day on which the company of which that person is or has been a director became insolvent". Although the general rule is that proceedings are started on the date of issue entered on a claim form by the court (see CPR r.7.2(1)–(2), which apply as set out in para.3J–2 above), that position is displaced where the provision at issue is a limitation provision, in which case proceedings are "brought" on the date on which the form is stamped as received at the court (see para.7PD.5.1.2). Thus, where a draft claim form was stamped as received on April 26, 2004, the two year limitation period expired on May 7, 2004, and the claim form was issued on May 17, 2004, it was held that proceedings had been brought in time: *Secretary of State v Vohora* [2007] EWHC 2656 (Ch); [2009] B.C.C. 369.

[1] Current subordinate legislation includes the Insolvent Partnerships Order 1994 and the Limited Liability Partnerships Regulations 2001.

### 2. Multi-track

**2.1** All disqualification proceedings are allocated to the multi-track. The CPR relating to allocation questionnaires and track allocation shall not apply. 3J–8

### 3. Rights of audience

**3.1** Official receivers and deputy official receivers have right of audience in any proceedings to which this Practice Direction applies, including cases where a disqualification application is made by the Secretary of State or by the official receiver at his direction, and whether made in the High Court or a county court.[1] 3J–9

#### Rights of audience

It is occasionally assumed that because official receivers and deputy official receivers have rights of audience, the court will take a more flexible approach to directors being represented by accountants or insolvency advisers. This assumption is incorrect, and the general practice of the Companies Court is to require strict observance of the relevant statutory provisions as to rights of audience. 3J–10



## *Part II*

## *Disqualification applications*

### 4. Commencement

**4.1** Sections 2(2)(a), 3(4), 4(2), 6(3), 8(3) and 9E(3) of the Act identify the civil courts which have jurisdiction to deal with disqualification applications. 3J–11

**4.1A** A disqualification application must be commenced by a claim form issued:

(1) in the case of a disqualification application under section 9A of the Act, in the High Court out of the office of the companies court registrar at the Royal Courts of Justice;

(2) in any other case,

(a) in the High Court out of the office of the companies court registrar or a chancery district registry; and

(b) in the county court, out of a county court office.

**4.2** Disqualification applications shall be made by the issue of a claim form in the form annexed hereto and the use of the procedure set out in CPR Part 8,[2] as modified by this practice direction and (where the application is made under sections 7, 8 or 9A of the Act) the Disqualification Rules CPR, rule 8.1(3) (power of the Court to order the application to continue as if the claimant had not used the Part 8 Procedure) shall not apply.

**4.3** When the claim form is issued, the claimant will be given a date for the first hearing of the disqualification application. This date

[1] Rule 10 of the Insolvent Companies (Disqualification of Unfit Directors) Proceedings Rules 1987.

[2] Rule 2(2) of the Insolvent Companies (Disqualification of Unfit Directors) Proceedings Rules 1987 as amended.

is to be not less than eight weeks from the date of issue of the claim form.[1] The first hearing will be before a registrar.

### Use of Pt 8 procedure

3J–12 The use of the Pt 8 procedure (and prior to 1999 the originating summons procedure under the RSC) is in some respects not entirely satisfactory, particularly in cases where a substantial amount of the factual evidence is disputed (a point indirectly alluded to by Sir Donald Nicholls V.-C. in *Re Rex Williams Leisure Plc* [1994] Ch. 1, at 9). However, use of the Pt 7 procedure with statements of case would be even less satisfactory, as the claimant's case (based on his conclusion that it is "expedient in the public interest that a disqualification order should be made") is not a cause of action which easily lends itself to being pleaded in the orthodox way (though the courts have recognised that the evidence in support of the application "has of necessity something of the character of a pleading": Laddie J. in *Re Finelist* [2003] EWHC 1780 (Ch); [2004] B.C.C 877 at [14]). The intention is that all the evidence deemed relevant by the parties can be put before the court, normally without the need for disclosure, so that (in the case of ss.6 to 9 of the Act) the court can decide the question of unfitness. Thus, although applications are occasionally made for an order that disqualification proceedings should proceed by way of statements of case, it is suggested that it will only be in the most exceptional circumstances that the court would consider it appropriate to make such an order.

### County Court Proceedings

3J–13 Most disqualification cases are issued in the High Court. By s.6(3) of the Act the only County Court which may make a disqualification order in relation to a director of a given lead company is the County Court which wound up the company, or had jurisdiction to do so. It has been held that the court has no jurisdiction to transfer a case from that County Court to a different one: see *Secretary of State v Shakespeare* [2005] B.C.C. 891. However, it should be noted that if proceedings are commenced in the wrong court they are not invalid, and they may be retained in that court: see s.6(3B) of the Act.

## 5. Headings

3J–14 **5.1** Every claim form by which an application under the Act is begun and all affidavits, notices and other documents in the proceedings must be entitled in the matter of the company or companies in question and in the matter of the Act. In the case of any disqualification application under section 7 or 9A of the Act it is not necessary to mention in the heading any company other than that referred to in section 6(1)(a) or 9A(2) of the Act (as the case may be).

## 6. The claim form

3J–15 **6.1** CPR, rule 8.2 does not apply. The claim form must state:

(1) that CPR Part 8 (as modified by this practice direction) applies, and (if the application is made under sections 7, 8 or 9A of the Act) that the disqualification application is made in accordance with the Disqualification Rules[2];

(2) that the claimant seeks a disqualification order, and the section of the Act pursuant to which the disqualification application is made;

(3) the period for which, in accordance with the Act, the court has power to impose a disqualification period.

[1] Rule 7(1) of the Insolvent Companies (Disqualification of Unfit Directors) Proceedings Rules 1987.

[2] Rule 4(a) of the Insolvent Companies (Disqualification of Unfit Directors) Proceedings Rules 1987.

The periods are as follows:—

(a) where the application is under section 2 of the Act, for a period of up to 15 years;

(b) where the application is under section 3 of the Act, for a period of up to 5 years;

(c) where the application is under section 4 of the Act, for a period of up to 15 years;

(d) where the application is under section 7 of the Act, for a period of not less than 2, and up to 15, years[1];

(e) where the application is under section 8 or 9A of the Act, for a period of up to 15 years.[2]

(4) in cases where the disqualification application is made under sections 7, 8 or 9A of the Act, that on the first hearing of the application, the court may hear and determine it summarily, without further or other notice to the defendant, and that, if the application is so determined, the court may impose a period of disqualification of up to 5 years but that if at the hearing of the application the court, on the evidence then before it, is minded to impose, in the case of any defendant, disqualification for any period longer than 5 years, it will not make a disqualification order on that occasion but will adjourn the application to be heard (with further evidence, if any) at a later date that will be notified to the defendant[3];

(5) that any evidence which the defendant wishes the court to take into consideration must be filed in court in accordance with the time limits set out in paragraph 9 below (which time limits shall be set out in the notes to the Claim Form).[4]



## 7. Service of the claim form

**7.1** Service of claim forms in disqualification proceedings will be the responsibility of the parties and will not be undertaken by the court. **3J–16**

**7.2** The claim form shall be served by the claimant on the defendant. It may be served by sending it by first class post to his last known address; and the date of service shall, unless the contrary is shown, be deemed to be the 7th day following that on which the claim form was posted.[5] CPR, r.6.7(1) shall be modified accordingly. Otherwise Sections I and II of CPR Part 6 apply.[6]

**7.3** Where any claim form or order of the court or other docu-

[1] Rule 4(b)(i) of the Insolvent Companies (Disqualification of Unfit Directors) Proceedings Rules 1987.

[2] Rule 4(b)(ii) of the Insolvent Companies (Disqualification of Unfit Directors) Proceedings Rules 1987.

[3] Rule 4(c) and (d) of the Insolvent Companies (Disqualification of Unfit Directors) Proceedings Rules 1987.

[4] Rule 4(e) of the Insolvent Companies (Disqualification of Unfit Directors) Proceedings Rules 1987.

[5] Rule 5(1) of the Insolvent Companies (Disqualification of Unfit Directors) Proceedings Rules 1987.

[6] Attention is drawn to CPR, r.6.14(2) regarding a certificate of service of the claim form.

ment is required under any disqualification proceedings to be served on any person who is not in England and Wales, the court may order service on him to be effected within such time and in such manner as it thinks fit,[1] and may give such directions as to acknowledgment of service as it thinks fit. Section III of CPR Part 6 shall not apply.

**7.4** The claim form served on the defendant shall be accompanied by an acknowledgement of service.

#### Service to be by the claimant

3J–17 One of the more substantial changes effected by the CPR to High Court practice was the provision (since October 1, 2008 to be found in CPR r.6.4) that service by the Court is the general rule. Rule 7.1 of the Disqualification Rules preserves the pre-1999 High Court practice for disqualification proceedings. There is a great deal of sense in this approach, in particular because of the very tight limitation period of two years following insolvency which applies in relation to applications under s.6 of the Act. Investigations into the conduct of directors can be very time-consuming, and many applications are only issued towards the end of the two year period. It is clearly appropriate that the burden of complying with the time limits should in such circumstances be the particular responsibility of the claimants, and not the court.

Service should always comprise service of the claim form, the evidence in support, and the acknowledgment of service.

NB—the reference in the footnote to r.6.14(2) is now obsolete. The provisions as to certificates of service are now found in CPR r.6.17.

#### Service to be at last known address

3J–18 It should be noted that the wording of para.7.2 is more flexible than r.5(1) of the Disqualification Rules (which states that "The claim form shall be served on the defendant by sending it by first class post to his last known address"). In the light of *Cranfield v Bridgegrove Ltd* [2003] EWCA Civ 656; [2003] 1 W.L.R. 2441 (inter alia dealing with the former CPR, r.6.5(6)), service at the last known address is good service, even when the claimant knows or believes the defendant no longer resides there.

#### Deemed service

3J–19 The phrase "unless the contrary is shown" contained in para.7.2 (and r.5(1) of the Disqualification Rules) means that deemed service in this context was significantly different to the deemed service provision found until October 1, 2008 in CPR r.6.7(1) (where the phrase was absent). The position on deemed service in general civil litigation reached as a result of *Anderton v Clwyd CC (No.2)* [2002] EWCA Civ 933; [2002] 1 W.L.R. 3174 therefore did not apply. The general provisions as to service were substantially recast with effect from October 1, 2008.

#### Service out of the jurisdiction

3J–20 As indicated above (see 3J–3, Application of the CPR), service out of the jurisdiction is governed by the discretion given to the court under r.5(2) of the Disqualification Rules (repeated as para.7.3 of the Practice Direction), rather than the provisions now found in CPR, Pt 6.

### 8. Acknowledgment of service

3J–21 **8.1** The form of acknowledgment of service is annexed to this practice direction. CPR, rule 8.3(2) and 8.3(3)(a) do not apply to disqualification applications.

**8.2** In cases brought under section 7, 8 or 9A of the Act, the form

[1] Rule 5(2) of the Insolvent Companies (Disqualification of Unfit Directors) Proceedings Rules 1987.

*Paragraph numbers marked with a "+" can be found online and on CD.*

of acknowledgment of service shall state that the defendant should indicate[1]:

(1) whether he contests the application on the grounds that, in the case of any particular company:—

(a) he was not a director or shadow director of that company at a time when conduct of his, or of other persons, in relation to that company is in question;

(b) his conduct as director or shadow director of that company was not as alleged in support of the application for a disqualification order;

(c) in the case of an application made under section 7 of the Act, the company has at no time become insolvent within the meaning of section 6; or

(d) in the case of an application under section 9A of the Act, the undertaking which is a company did not commit a breach of competition law within the meaning of that section.

(2) whether, in the case of any conduct of his, he disputes the allegation that such conduct makes him unfit to be concerned in the management of a company; and

(3) whether he, while not resisting the application for a disqualification order, intends to adduce mitigating factors with a view to reducing the period of disqualification.

**8.3** The defendant shall:

(1) (subject to any directions to the contrary given under paragraph 7.3 above) file an acknowledgment of service in the prescribed form not more than 14 days after service of the claim form; and

(2) serve the acknowledgment of service on the claimant and any other party.

**8.4** Where the defendant has failed to file an acknowledgment of service and the time period for doing so has expired, the defendant may attend the hearing of the application but may not take part in the hearing unless the court gives permission.

#### Filing and service of acknowledgments of service

Prior to 1999, there was simply a provision that the respondent (as the defendant was then called) had to file an acknowledgment of service with the court. Paragraph 8.3(2) of the Practice Direction has introduced the requirement that the defendant should also serve the acknowledgment on the claimant and other defendants. This has not worked entirely smoothly, as defendants and their advisers who intend to defend proceedings normally manage to file an acknowledgment at court, but not infrequently fail to serve a copy on the claimant or the other defendants. If finding out the stance of a particular defendant from whom an acknowledgment has not been received is important to any of the other parties, the only prudent course is to enquire of the court shortly before the first hearing date fixed for the claim. **3J–22**

Short of serious and deliberate flouting of court rules, it is difficult to imagine circumstances where at a first hearing the court will exercise the discretion given by

[1] Rule 5(4) of the Insolvent Companies (Disqualification of Unfit Directors) Proceedings Rules 1987.

*Paragraph numbers marked with a "+" can be found online and on CD.*

para.8.4 against hearing a defendant who has attended at court without having filed and served his acknowledgment. However, it should be noted that it is increasingly the practice of the Companies Court in such circumstances to order the filing of the acknowledgment of service as a condition of being permitted to file evidence.

## 9. Evidence

3J–23 **9.1** Evidence in disqualification applications shall be by affidavit, except where the official receiver is a party, in which case his evidence may be in the form of a written report (with or without affidavits by other persons) which shall be treated as if it had been verified by affidavit by him and shall be prima facie evidence of any matter contained in it.[1]

**9.2** In the affidavits or (as the case may be) the official receiver's report in support of the application, there shall be included:

(1) a statement of the matters by reference to which it is alleged that a disqualification order should be made against the defendant; and[2]

(2) a statement of the steps taken to comply with any requirements imposed by sections 16(1) and 9C(4) of the Act.

**9.3** When the claim form is issued:

(1) the affidavit or report in support of the disqualification application must be filed in court;

(2) exhibits must be lodged with the court where they shall be retained until the conclusion of the proceedings; and

(3) copies of the affidavit/report and exhibits shall be served with the claim form on the defendant.[3]

**9.4** The defendant shall, within 28 days from the date of service of the claim form[4]:

(1) file in court any affidavit evidence in opposition to the disqualification application that he or she wishes the court to take into consideration; and

(2) lodge the exhibits with the court where they shall be retained until the conclusion of the proceedings; and

(3) at the same time, serve upon the claimant a copy of the affidavits and exhibits.

**9.5** In cases where there is more than one defendant, each defendant is required to serve his evidence on the other defendant unless the court otherwise orders.

---

[1] Rule 3(2) of the Insolvent Companies (Disqualification of Unfit Directors) Proceedings Rules 1987. Section 441 of the Companies Act 1985 makes provision for the admissibility in legal proceedings of a certified copy of a report of inspectors appointed under Part XIV of the Companies Act 1985. Note that the requirements of paragraph 8.1(2)(c) and (d) of this practice direction are additional to the provisions in the said rule 5(4).

[2] Rule 3(3) of the Insolvent Companies (Disqualification of Unfit Directors) Proceedings Rules 1987.

[3] Rule 3(1) of the Insolvent Companies (Disqualification of Unfit Directors) Proceedings Rules 1987.

[4] Rule 6(1) of the Insolvent Companies (Disqualification of Unfit Directors) Proceedings Rules 1987.

**9.6** The claimant shall, within 14 days from receiving the copy of the defendant's evidence[1]:

(1) file in court any further affidavit or report in reply he wishes the court to take into consideration; and

(2) lodge the exhibits with the court where they shall be retained until the conclusion of the proceedings; and

(3) at the same time serve a copy of the affidavits/reports and exhibits upon the defendant.

**9.7** Prior to the first hearing of the disqualification application, the time for serving evidence may be extended by written agreement between the parties. After the first hearing, the extension of time for serving evidence is governed by CPR rules 2.11 and 29.5.

**9.8** So far as is possible all evidence should be filed before the first hearing of the disqualification application.



### Affidavits

Arguably one of the anomalous features of the disqualification jurisdiction is the continued requirement for affidavits by parties other than the official receiver. Advisers who are less familiar with the jurisdiction will often file and serve witness statements on behalf of their clients, and find their clients ordered by the court to re-file and re-serve the evidence in affidavit form. However, it should only be in rare circumstances that this procedural default should have substantial consequences for a defendant (aside from on the question of costs): in the ordinary case, where a litigant appears at trial to be cross-examined on his evidence, it should make no practical difference that the evidence in the court bundle (and to be adopted in the witness box) is in witness statement rather than affidavit form. **3J–24**

Notwithstanding that it might be thought that the wording of the last clause of para.9.1 of the Practice Direction implies that affidavit evidence must be first hand, it is conclusively established on the case law that there is an implied hearsay exception available to the claimant allowing affidavit evidence for use at trial to include hearsay: see, e.g. *Re Rex Williams Leisure Plc* [1994] Ch. 350, CA; and *Secretary of State v Ashcroft* [1998] Ch. 71, CA. Moreover, the Court of Appeal has held (*Secretary of State v Aaron* [2008] EWCA Civ 1146; [2009] B.C.C. 375) that the exception applies not only to the use of hearsay, but also to findings of fact and opinion when contained in investigatory material, i.e. reports or materials obtained under statutory powers—in *Aaron* the relevant report was an FSA report. By contrast, the Court of Appeal also held that there was no implied exception to the normal rules of evidence in respect of hearsay and conclusions of fact or opinion contained in other material on which the Secretary of State sought to rely which was not analogous to investigatory material (in that case, a decision of the Financial Ombudsman Service)—however, on the facts it was decided that the inadmissible material need not be excised, as the trial judge would simply be able to ignore it. Aside from the implied exception to the general rules of evidence, both claimants and defendants also take the benefit of the Civil Evidence Act 1995. The weight to be attached to hearsay evidence will of course be a matter for the court.

The claimant's evidence must include a statement of the matters by reference to which the defendant is alleged to be unfit ( r.3(3) of the Disqualification Rules). The Vice-Chancellor confirmed (in *Secretary of State v Andrews*, January 27, 2005, unrep.) that this does not mean that the claimant is required to put all its evidence in support of the claim: i.e., if the claimant adds to the evidence in on an allegation in evidence in reply which is filed after expiry of the two-year limitation period, that will not be a good ground to have the additional evidence excluded. Depending on the facts, though, it may be appropriate for the defendant to have the opportunity to file evidence in rejoinder (see further 3J–30 below).

If the Secretary of State decides not to proceed with an allegation, all he need do is

[1] Rule 6(2) of the Insolvent Companies (Disqualification of Unfit Directors) Proceedings Rules 1987.

to send a letter to that effect. The CPR notice of discontinuance procedure is not apt for this situation: see *Secretary of State v Blunt* [2006] B.C.C. 112.

#### Exhibits

3J–25 Notwithstanding the words of para.9.3(1), the Companies Court will often not require the lodging of the exhibits, because of pressures on court storage. If in doubt as to the practice, contact should be made with the court concerned.

#### Evidence timetable

3J–26 Rule 6 of the Disqualification Rules provides, in apparently mandatory terms, for a strict timetable for evidence in answer from the defendant, and evidence in reply from the claimant, subject only to the power in r.7(5) to make directions for further evidence if he adjourns the case for further consideration. Paragraph 9.8 of the Practice Direction recognises by implication that in practice this timetable will be hard to achieve.

It is entirely proper and understandable that the court should not wish to give encouragement to either claimants or defendants to think that the timetable contained in the rules should be ignored. Further, as the jurisdiction is intended to be a summary one, indulgent timetables for evidence would not be appropriate. However, as against that, the court is aware that disqualification proceedings are important regulatory proceedings, and fairness to the defendant, and to the public interest, may require extensions of time for evidence on both sides. Nevertheless, this flexibility is not intended to undermine the scheme of the rules, as confirmed by the Court of Appeal in *Rex Williams*, which is to advance the provision of evidence to well before trial. Thus, a party wishing to adduce affidavit evidence which should have been provided earlier will need to make a formal application to the court. In considering such an application, especially where it may lead to the delaying of a trial, it is suggested that the court will not only bear in mind the principles taken into account in late applications to amend statements of case under CPR Pt 17 (see para.17.3.5 above), but also (1) the particular public interest in dealing with disqualification cases expeditiously, (2) the scheme of the Disqualification Rules, and (3) the explanation proffered as to why the evidence was not provided earlier.

Further, where an earlier order has been breached, any application for relief from sanction will have to address the criteria in CPR r.3.9 in the normal way.

The parties will frequently agree, subject to the court, what directions are appropriate, and the court will normally be content to make the directions in the form agreed. The court will pay particular regard when considering the appropriate timetable to the need (which often arises) for defendants and their advisors to inspect company documents held by a liquidator.

### 10. The first hearing of the disqualification application

3J–27 **10.1** The date fixed for the hearing of the disqualification application shall not be less than 8 weeks from the date of issue of the claim form.[1]

**10.2** The hearing shall in the first instance be before the registrar.[2]

**10.3** The registrar shall either determine the case on the date fixed or give directions and adjourn it.[3]

**10.4** All interim directions should insofar as possible be sought at the first hearing of the disqualification application so that the disqualification application can be determined at the earliest possible date. The parties should take all such steps as they respectively can to avoid successive directions hearings.

---

[1] Rule 7(1) of the Insolvent Companies (Disqualification of Unfit Directors) Proceedings Rules 1987.

[2] Rule 7(2) of the Insolvent Companies (Disqualification of Unfit Directors) Proceedings Rules 1987.

[3] Rule 7(3) of the Insolvent Companies (Disqualification of Unfit Directors) Proceedings Rules 1987.

**10.5** In the case of a disqualification application made under sections 7, 8 or 9A of the Act, the registrar shall adjourn the case for further consideration if:—

(1) he forms the provisional opinion that a disqualification order ought to be made, and that a period of disqualification longer than 5 years is appropriate,[1] or

(2) he is of opinion that questions of law or fact arise which are not suitable for summary determination.[2]

**10.6** If the registrar adjourns the application for further consideration he shall—

(1) direct whether the application is to be heard by a registrar or by a judge.[3] This direction may at any time be varied by the court either on application or of its own initiative. If the court varies the direction in the absence of any of the parties, notice will be given to the parties;

(2) consider whether or not to adjourn the application to a judge so that the judge can give further directions;

(3) consider whether or not to make any direction with regard to fixing the trial date or a trial window;

(4) state the reasons for the adjournment.[4]



**The first hearing date**

The timetable for the first hearing date is fixed to allow the parties to comply with the evidence timetable in the Disqualification Rules. For the reasons given above, it is very rarely the case that both evidence in answer and evidence in reply will have been filed and served before the first hearing, and in the majority of cases evidence in answer will not have been served or filed. **3J–28**

**The hearing shall be before the registrar**

Surprisingly, para.10.2 omits reference to one of the procedural traps for those not familiar with the jurisdiction, as r.7(2) of the Disqualification Rules provides that the first hearing is before the registrar "in open court" (and therefore counsel and solicitors should be robed). The open court requirement had a practical consequence in terms of costs under the RSC, as chambers hearings would have had to have been certified fit for the attendance of counsel (a requirement which is not carried forward into the CPR). The principal residual significance of the rule is that the Companies Court general directions lists (in which all disqualification claims are listed for first hearing) normally include some cases which are to be disposed of by uncontested trial, and consistent with the continued general practice of the civil courts, these ought to be dealt with robed. The general lists are normally on a Monday, and it is not unusual to have a large number ofcases listed for directions or disposal. **3J–29**

**Directions as to evidence**

In most cases where the defendant has indicated an intention to contest, the first hearing is used as a directions hearing. If the defendant has not already filed and served his evidence in answer, the court will direct that the evidence is to be filed and served by a certain date. Depending on the circumstances, it is possible that the court **3J–30**

[1] Rule 7(4)(*a*) of the Insolvent Companies (Disqualification of Unfit Directors) Proceedings Rules 1987.

[2] Rule 7(4)(*b*) of the Insolvent Companies (Disqualification of Unfit Directors) Proceedings Rules 1987.

[3] Rule 7(5)(a) of the Insolvent Companies (Disqualification of Unfit Directors) Proceedings Rules 1987.

[4] Rule 7(5)(b) of the Insolvent Companies (Disqualification of Unfit Directors) Proceedings Rules 1987.

will give the directions on "unless" terms, but this is unusual at a first hearing. However, if by the date fixed for the second hearing the evidence still has not been provided, the court will normally only (absent special circumstances) grant a further extension of time on "unless" terms. The court takes a similar approach where claimants are concerned (though, consistent with the timetable set out in para.9 of the Practice Direction, claimants are normally allowed less time for evidence in reply than defendants are allowed for evidence in answer).

Although para.10.4 provides that all interim directions should as far as possible be dealt with at the first hearing, the court has found that a more flexible approach is required. Thus, in certain simple cases it will give fairly full directions at the first hearing, whereas in more complex cases it will normally only make provision for evidence in answer and evidence in reply and then direct that the matter come back for a second directions hearing.

In more complex cases, further rounds of evidence after evidence in reply are required, typically where the claimant has, as a result of further investigations, or as a result of the evidence in answer, decided to put forward further matters determining unfitness. One of the consequences of use of the Pt 8 procedure is that it is not realistic or sensible to order the claimant to amend his original evidence in support. Instead, any new matters by virtue of which it is alleged that the defendant is unfit (colloquially, "allegations") must be stated in the claimant's evidence in reply. Assuming no objection is taken to new matters being raised, the court will order a further evidential timetable so that the defendant can respond to the new allegations made. However, the court will normally be concerned to ensure that any directions given are not used as a cloak by either side to put in evidence which should have been provided before. Directions given by the Companies Court in these circumstances resort to the terminology used by the Court of Chancery to make this point explicit. Evidence from a defendant in response to new allegations is called evidence in rejoinder, and the claimant's response is called evidence in surrejoinder. Very occasionally new allegations are added by the claimant in surrejoinder, in which case the further two rounds of evidence are evidence in rebutter and evidence in surrebutter.

### Cross-examination

**3J–31** It will be noted that no specific reference is made to cross-examination of deponents to affidavits and reports. It is possible that when the Act and Disqualification Rules were in their formative stages it was envisaged that proceedings might in certain cases be dealt with by way of trials on paper (subject to the power of the court under the RSC to order cross-examination on affidavit). It has however long been the settled practice to order cross-examination in all contested cases. However, the form of the cross-examination direction has a number of aspects peculiar to the jurisdiction. First, the court may dispense with any attendance by the deponent of a purely formal affidavit, such as a Secretary of State's affidavit which lists the allegations and states that the view has been reached that it is expedient in the public interest that proceedings should be brought, but does no more. Secondly, in cases brought by the official receiver, the court may direct that "the official receiver, or his successor in office" attend. The rationale for this is that an official receiver normally has no first hand knowledge of the matters referred to in his report, and another official receiver will be just as well placed to speak to the evidence. If, however, the official receiver is making an allegation based on matters within his own knowledge (for instance, non-cooperation) then this approach may not be appropriate.

It should be noted that the court's power to control cross-examination can be invoked. This power is part of the court's inherent jurisdiction, as well as being set out in CPR, r.32.1(3). See *Secretary of State for Trade and Industry v Gill* [2004] EWHC 175 (Ch); [2005] B.C.C. 24 where, after refusing an application by the Secretary of State for permission to amend an allegation shortly before trial, Blackburne J. that cross-examination of the defendants' witnesses "must be properly confined to the complaint as it presently stands".

Subject to the above points, the standard cross-examination direction in the Companies Court is "All deponents to affidavits and reports to attend for cross-examination on 21 days' written notice, in default evidence not to be read without the permission of the court". It is sometimes not appreciated that this direction means that, unless the opposing party writes more than 21 days prior to the hearing requiring the attendance of a particular witness at trial for cross-examination, then that witness's evidence will be treated as unchallenged, and he will not need to go into the witness box (unless of course (a) an application is successfully made to the court for cross examination notwithstanding late notice, or (b) the other party waives the late notice and produces the witness for cross examination). The confusion may in part arise because the practice outside London has not always been consistent, with some courts using the Companies Court formulation, and others ordering witnesses to attend unless the opposing party indicates that no cross-examination is required.

#### Adjournment for further consideration

Paragraph 10.5(1) (which is taken from r.7 of the Disqualification Rules) occasionally throws up practical difficulties. The clear intention behind the five year rule is that it should operate to protect defendants. However, if a defendant has indicated an intention not to contest the proceedings, this might lead to unnecessary cost being incurred if the claimant, knowing the matter clearly required a disqualification period of more than five years, was required in all circumstances to present the case in full with a view to having the matter adjourned for uncontested hearing on another date. The Companies Court has accordingly developed the following settled practice: (1) the requirement that a provisional view be formed that a disqualification order ought to be made, and that a period of longer than five years is appropriate, is treated as only being applicable to a first hearing. Accordingly, (2) if the court does not form that preliminary view on the first hearing, but at the second hearing decides that a period of longer than five years is appropriate, the court is not precluded from making a disqualification order for longer than five years at that second hearing. Nevertheless, (3) the court will normally (if there is time) invite the claimant briefly to outline those first hearing cases where there is the possibility that an order of longer than five years will be appropriate, so that (if it thinks fit) a provisional opinion can be formed and recorded in the order for an adjournment (which will be served on the defendant). The court will also normally direct in such circumstances that the claimant send a letter to the defendant informing him in particular of the provisional opinion formed by the court. **3J–32**



#### Adjournment to the Judge

It is comparatively rare for disqualification cases to be adjourned to be heard by a Judge. Although there is no specific guidance in the Practice Direction, in *Secretary of State for Trade and Industry v Lewis* [2003] B.C.C. 567, Neuberger J. made certain observations when rejecting an application that a trial be heard by a High Court Judge rather than a registrar. He pointed to four particular relevant factors: **3J–33**

(1) The likely length of the hearing, a long hearing being probably more appropriate for a judge.
(2) Complex issues of fact or law would probably be another factor favouring a hearing before a judge.
(3) High profile, in the sense of public interest, would probably favour a hearing before a judge.
(4) The court should also take into account the likely hearing date, working on the principle that the earlier the hearing date, the better.

He also indicated that a case might have other special factors to be considered. However, he recorded his acceptance of the Secretary of State's submission that the fact that the consequence of disqualification may be serious for the director concerned was not in itself a relevant factor, as on that basis every disqualification application could or should be heard by a judge.

### 11. Case management

**11.1** On the first or any subsequent hearing of the disqualification application, the registrar may also give directions as to the following matters: **3J–34**

(1) the filing in court and the service of further evidence (if any) by the parties[1];
(2) the time-table for the steps to be taken between the giving of directions and the hearing of the application;
(3) such other matters as the registrar thinks necessary or expedient with a view to an expeditious disposal of the application or the management of it generally[2];
(4) the time and place of the adjourned hearing[3]; and
(5) the manner in which and the time within which notice of the adjournment and the reasons for it are to be given to the parties.[4]

**11.2** Where a case is adjourned other than to a judge, it may be heard by the registrar who originally dealt with the case or by another registrar.[5]

**11.3** If the companies court registrar adjourns the application to a judge, all directions having been complied with and the evidence being complete, the application will be referred to the Listing Office and any practice direction relating to listing shall apply accordingly.

**11.4** In all disqualification applications, the Court may direct a pre-trial review ('PTR'), a case management conference or pre-trial check lists (listing questionnaires) (in the form annexed to this practice direction) and will fix a trial date or trial period in accordance with the provisions of CPR Part 29: the Multi Track as modified by any relevant practice direction made thereunder.

**11.5** At the hearing of the PTR, the registrar may give any further directions as appropriate and, where the application is to be heard in the Royal Courts of Justice in London, unless the trial date has already been fixed, may direct the parties (by Counsel's clerks if applicable), to attend the Registrar at a specified time and place in order solely to fix a trial date. The court will give notice of the date fixed for the trial to the parties.

**11.6** In all cases, the parties must inform the court immediately of any material change to the information provided in a pre–trial checklist.

#### Case Management Directions

3J–35 One of the matters of greatest concern to the court over the years has been the number of disqualification cases set down for trial where a settlement (usually either by way of the acceptance of an undertaking or the *Carecraft* procedure) took place shortly before the date fixed for a hearing. Late settlement has historically caused significant wastage of judicial time. Partly with this in mind, and acknowledging that cost remained a significant factor cited as to why settlement took place, one of the direc-

[1] Rule 7(5)(c)(ii) of the Insolvent Companies (Disqualification of Unfit Directors) Proceedings Rules 1987.
[2] Rule 7(5)(c)(iii) of the Insolvent Companies (Disqualification of Unfit Directors) Proceedings Rules 1987.
[3] Rule 7(5)(c)(iv) of the Insolvent Companies (Disqualification of Unfit Directors) Proceedings Rules 1987.
[4] Rule 7(5)(c)(i) of the Insolvent Companies (Disqualification of Unfit Directors) Proceedings Rules 1987.
[5] Rule 7(6) of the Insolvent Companies (Disqualification of Unfit Directors) Proceedings Rules 1987.

tions formerly made as standard adopted and adapted s.4 of the Costs Practice Direction: prior to any PTR, the parties were ordered to serve on each other (a) a schedule of costs incurred to date, and (b) a schedule of likely costs up to and including trial. The intention was that if this was a factor of importance, it could be given early informed consideration by the respective clients. As the court now normally dispenses with PTRs (see 3J–39 below) these directions in relation to costs accordingly now rarely get made.

**Pre-trial checklist (listing questionnaire)**

Now that PTRs are normally dispensed with, pre-trial checklists are no longer, as a rule, sent out. **3J–36**

**Listing directions**

It will now normally be the case that Counsel's clerks will be ordered to attend before the Companies Court listing officer (or occasionally a Registrar) (with counsel's and witnesses' dates to avoid) on a fixed date to fix the trial date. This order was in the past normally given at the PTR, but is now generally given at the last direction hearing (i.e. the directions hearing at which the court is satisfied that there is no need for any further drections hearings). It should be noted that this procedure only applies if the trial is to be listed before a Registrar. If the case has been adjourned to the Judge for trial, then normal Chancery Division listing procedure should be followed. **3J–37**

**PTRs**

It was normally standard when the Practice Direction was first introduced for all disqualification cases in the Companies Court being listed for trial to be adjourned, after the directions hearings had been completed, to a day set aside for dealing exclusively with PTRs. After the introduction of undertakings, far fewer cases needed to be listed for trial, with the result that PTRs tended to be dealt with in the general Monday directions list. Recently, the court has moved to dispensing with PTRs in most cases, and this should now be regarded as a reserve provision, only to be used in complex or otherwise unusual cases. **3J–38**

## 12. The trial

**12.1** Trial bundles containing copies of:— **3J–39**

(1) the claim form;

(2) the acknowledgment of service;

(3) all evidence filed by or on behalf of each of the parties to the proceedings, together with the exhibits thereto;

(4) all relevant correspondence; and

(5) such other documents as the parties consider necessary;

shall be lodged with the court.

**12.2** Skeleton arguments should be prepared by all the parties in all but the simplest cases whether the case is to be heard by a registrar or a judge. They should comply with all relevant guidelines.

**12.3** The advocate for the claimant should also in all but the simplest cases provide: (a) a chronology; (b) a dramatis personae; (c) in respect of each defendant, a list of references to the relevant evidence.

**12.4** The documents mentioned in paragraph 12.1–12.3 above must be delivered to the court in accordance with any order of the court and/or any relevant practice direction.[1]

[1] Attention is drawn to the provisions of the Chancery Guide. Chapter 7 of that Guide dated September 2000 provides guidance on the preparation of trial bundles and skeleton arguments. Unless the Court otherwise orders, para.7.16 of the Chan-

(1) If the case is to be heard by a judge sitting in the Royal Courts of Justice, London, but the name of the judge is not known, or the judge is a deputy judge, these documents must be delivered to the Clerk of the Lists. If the name of the judge (other than a deputy judge) is known, these documents must be delivered to the judge's clerk;

(2) If the case is to be heard by a companies court registrar, these documents must be delivered to Room 409, Thomas More Building, Royal Courts of Justice. Copies must be provided to the other party so far as possible when they are delivered to the court;

(3) If the case is to be heard in the Chancery district registries in Birmingham, Bristol, Caernarfon, Cardiff, Leeds, Liverpool, Manchester, Mold, Newcastle upon Tyne or Preston, the addresses for delivery are set out in Annex 1;

(4) If the case is to be heard in a county court, the documents should be delivered to the relevant county court office.

**12.5** Copies of documents delivered to the court must, so far as possible, be provided to each of the other parties to the disqualification application.

**12.6** The provisions in paragraphs 12.1 to 12.5 above are subject to any order of the court making different provision.

#### Judgment

3J–40 The Companies Court Registrar may occasionally be in a position to give an *ex tempore* judgment after trial, but a reserved judgment will be normal. It will often be the case that, if unfitness is found, further submissions on the appropriate period of disqualification will be invited at the hand-down hearing if they have not been made at the conclusion of the trial.

The footnote to para.12.4 refers to the 2000 edition of the Chancery Guide. A new edition was published in November 2005 and was subsequently updated, and a further edition was published in October 2009—see para.1A–1 et seq. above.

### 13. Summary procedure

3J–41 **13.1** If the parties decide to invite the court to deal with the application under the procedure adopted in *Re Carecraft Construction Co Ltd* [1994] 1 W.L.R. 172, they should inform the court immediately and obtain a date for the hearing of the application.

**13.2** Whenever the *Carecraft* procedure is adopted, the claimant must:

(1) except where the court otherwise directs, submit a written statement containing in respect of each defendant any material facts which (for the purposes of the application) are either agreed or not opposed (by either party); and

(2) specify in writing the period of disqualification which the parties accept that the agreed or unopposed facts justify or the band of years (e.g. 4 to 6 years) or bracket (i.e. 2 to 5 years; 6 to 10 years; 11 to 15 years) into which they will submit the case falls.

---

cery Guide requires that the trial bundles be delivered to the Court seven days before trial and para.7.21 requires that skeleton arguments be delivered to the Court not less than two clear days before trial.

**13.3** Paragraph 12.4 of the above applies to the documents mentioned in paragraph 13.2 above unless the court otherwise directs.

**13.4** Unless the Court otherwise orders, a hearing under the *Carecraft* procedure will be held in private.

**13.5** If the Court is minded to make a disqualification order having heard the parties' representations, it will usually give judgment and make the disqualification order in public. Unless the Court otherwise orders, the written statement referred to in paragraph 13.2 shall be annexed to the disqualification order.

**13.6** If the Court refuses to make the disqualification order under the *Carecraft* procedure, the Court shall give further directions for the hearing of the application.

**Carecraft**

At the time of the introduction of the Practice Direction, the *Carecraft* procedure (named after the case in which its use was first approved) was in effect the only means by which proceedings could be compromised. The procedure was developed so that the parties could put before the court a series of facts on which they were not in dispute, a statement by the defendant that certain matters determining unfitness alleged by the claimant were undisputed, and an agreement based on the undisputed facts and allegations either as to what the appropriate period of disqualification might be, or within which range of years the court might consider it to lie. It was normal to include in the *Carecraft* statement a list of matters of mitigation which had been taken into account by the parties in reaching their suggestion as to the period of disqualification. The important factor to remember is that it remained for the court to decide, based on the *Carecraft* statement, whether (a) the defendant was unfit, and (b) if he was, what the court in its discretion believed the correct period of disqualification was. The first question was very rarely a difficulty, but it was not unknown that the court was unwilling to accept the parties' suggestion as to disqualification period. 3J–42

Since the introduction of disqualification undertakings, the use of the *Carecraft* procedure has largely dropped away, principally because undertakings have advantages in terms of reduced expense. However, it remains open for the parties to use, and certain defendants have preferred it, in particular because the opportunity to include matters of mitigation is not (as a matter of the Secretary of State's policy) available in respect of disqualification undertakings, but (at least as matters currently stand) is available in the *Carecraft* procedure.

The Secretary of State's discretion as to the form in which an undertaking will be accepted (i.e. with or without mitigation; with or without a schedule of unfit conduct) is unfettered: *Re Blackspur Group (No.4)* [2001] EWCA Civ 1595; [2004] B.C.C. 839.

## 14. Making and setting aside of disqualification order

**14.1** The court may make a disqualification order against the defendant, whether or not the latter appears, and whether or not he has completed and returned the acknowledgment of service of the claim form, or filed evidence.[1] 3J–43

**14.2** Any disqualification order made in the absence of the defendant may be set aside or varied by the court on such terms as it thinks just.[2]

**Making a disqualification order in the absence of a defendant**

In a large number of cases, no contact is received from the defendant. In such cir- 3J–44

[1] Rule 8(1) of the Insolvent Companies (Disqualification of Unfit Directors) Proceedings Rules 1987.

[2] Rule 8(2) of the Insolvent Companies (Disqualification of Unfit Directors) Proceedings Rules 1987.

*Paragraph numbers marked with a "+" can be found online and on CD.*

cumstances the claimant simply has to provide the court with a certificate of service confirming that the proceedings were served on the defendant at his last known address in accordance with r.5(1) of the Disqualification Rules, and the court will, if there is sufficient time, proceed to hear the claimant's case uncontested. It is normal for a short judgment to be given, setting out the salient matters which have caused the registrar to come to his conclusion, in particular on the questions of whether the defendant is unfit, and, if so, of what the appropriate period of disqualification is. If the defendant is disqualified, the claimant's costs will normally be summarily assessed.

There is no reported authority under the Disqualification Rules as to the circumstances in which the court would set aside or vary a disqualification order made in the absence of a defendant. Rule 8(2) (from which para.14.2 is taken) is similar in form to RSC O.35, r.2(1) which provided that "any judgment, order or verdict obtained where one party does not appear at the trial may be set aside by the Court, on the application of that party, on such terms as it thinks just". RSC O.35, r.2(2) provided that such an application had to be made within seven days after trial. RSC O.35, r.2 clearly dealt principally with the situation where a defendant had been involved in all steps up to trial, but had failed to attend the hearing: case law (see Supreme Court Practice 1999) built up on this footing. Although r.8(2) is wide enough to cover that situation, it is suggested that the principal concern underlying r.8(2) was the potential for injustice caused by the deemed service provisions in r.5(1) (for instance in circumstances where a defendant had moved abroad accidently leaving an incorrect forwarding address). That interpretation is consistent with no time limit for an application under r.8(2) being found in the Disqualification Rules: it might be months or years after the making of a disqualification order before such a defendant became aware of the proceedings, and it would be unjust if he were subject to a disqualification order which he had no opportunity to challenge. However, notwithstanding the substantial number of disqualification orders made in the absence of defendants, the lack of reported authority is indicative of there having been virtually no examples in practice of defendants seeking to avail themselves of this right. It is suggested that r8(2) should nevertheless be regarded as an important residual power, providing a wide and unfettered discretion to do what is just in potentially markedly varying circumstances. This is a view that was shared by Nicholas Warren Q.C. in *Official Receiver v Hodgkinson* (briefly reported at [2000] All E.R. (D) 1386).

### 15. Service of disqualification orders

3J–45 **15.1** Service of disqualification orders will be the responsibility of the claimant.

### 16. Commencement of disqualification order

3J–46 **16.1** Unless the court otherwise orders, the period of disqualification imposed by a disqualification order shall begin at the end of the period of 21 days beginning with the date of the order.[1]

## *Part III*

## *Applications under sections 7(2) and 7(4) of the Act*

### 17. Applications for permission to make a disqualification application after the end of the period of 2 years specified in section 7(2) of the Act

3J–47 **17.1** Such applications shall be made by Practice Form **N208** under CPR Part 8 save where it is sought to join a director or former director to existing proceedings, in which case such application shall be made by Application Notice under CPR Part 23 and Practice Direction 23A shall apply save as modified below.

[1] Section 1(2) of the Act (as amended).

### 18. Applications for extra information made under section 7(4) of the Act

**18.1** Such applications may be made: 3J–48

(1) by Practice Form **N208** under CPR Part 8;

(2) by Application Notice in existing disqualification claim proceedings; or

(3) by application under the Insolvency Rules in the relevant insolvency, if the insolvency practitioner against whom the application is made remains the officeholder.

### 19. Provisions applicable to applications under section 7(2) and 7(4) of the Act

**19.1 Headings:** Every claim form and notice by which such an application is begun and all witness statements, witness statements, affidavits, notices and other documents in relation thereto must be entitled in the matter of the company or companies in question and in the matter of the Act. 3J–49

**19.2 Service:**

(1) Service of claim forms and application notices seeking orders under section 7(2) or 7(4) of the Act will be the responsibility of the applicant and will not be undertaken by the court.

(2) Where any claim form, application notice or order of the court or other document is required in any application under section 7(2) or section 7(4) of the Act to be served on any person who is not in England and Wales, the court may order service on him to be effected within such time and in such manner as it thinks fit, may require such proof of service as it thinks fit, and may make such directions as to acknowledgment of service as it thinks fit. Section III of CPR Part 6 does not apply.

## *Part IV*

## *Applications for permission to act*

### 20. Commencing an application for permission to act

**20.1** This practice direction governs applications for permission to act made under: 3J–50

(1) section 17 of the Act for the purposes of any of sections 1(1)(a), 1A(1)(a) or 9B(4); and

(2) section 12(2) of the Act.

**20.2** Sections 12 and 17 of the Act identify the courts which have jurisdiction to deal with applications for permission to act. Subject to these sections, such applications may be made:

(1) by Practice Form **N208** under CPR Part 8; or

(2) by application notice in an existing disqualificiation application.

**20.3** In the case of a person subject to disqualification under section 12A or 12B of the Act (by reason of being disqualified in

Northern Ireland), permission to act notwithstanding disqualification can only be granted by the High Court of Northern Ireland.

**21. Headings**

3J–51 **21.1** Every claim form or application notice by which an application for permission to act is begun, and all affidavits, notices and other documents in the application must be entitled in the matter of the company or companies in question and in the matter of the Act.

**21.2** Every application notice by which an application for permission to act is made and all affidavits, notices and other documents in the application shall be entitled in the same manner as the heading of the claim form in the existing disqualification application.

**22. Evidence**

3J–52 **22.1** Evidence in support of an application for permission to act shall be by affidavit.

**23. Service**[1]

3J–53 **23.1** Where a disqualification application has been made under section 9A of the Act or a disqualification undertaking has been accepted under section 9B of the Act, the claim form or application notice (as appropriate), together with the evidence in support thereof, must be served on the Office of Fair Trading or specified regulator which made the relevant disqualification application or accepted the disqualification undertaking (as the case may be).

**23.2** In all other cases, the claim form or application notice (as appropriate), together with the evidence in support thereof, must be served on the Secretary of State.

**Applications for permission to act**

3J–54 Paragraph 23 is broad enough to cover free-standing applications for permission to act, but it should be emphasised that the preferable course is that applications should be heard by the tribunal which deals with the trial of the disqualification proceedings. "It is in everyone's interest that if [an application to act] is envisaged before the disqualification application comes on for hearing, and if the director has advice it will have been envisaged, then it should be heard at the same time because, from the point of view of the director, it is desirable that if he or she is going to be allowed to continue as director of that company there should be no time passing before the leave is granted": Dillon L.J. in *Re Dicetrade* [1994] B.C.C. 371, at 373.

The court has expressed the view that where the original disqualification was made as a result of the *Carecraft* procedure, the parties should normally be confined to the facts contained in the *Carecraft* statement as to the basis of the original disqualification, unless those facts need to be clarified: *Re TLL Realisations* [2000] B.C.C. 998.

[1] Addresses for service on government departments are set out in the List of Authorised Government Departments issued by the Cabinet Office under section 17 of the Crown Proceedings Act 1947, which is annexed to the Practice Direction supplementing Part 66.

*Part V*

*Applications*

### 24. Form of application

**24.1** CPR, Part 23 and the Practice Direction 23A (General Rules about Applications for Court Orders) shall apply in relation to applications governed by this practice direction (see paragraph 1.3(4) above) save as modified below. **3J–55**

#### Evidence in support of applications

The only point to be noted is that evidence in applications made within disqualification proceedings (other than applications for permission to act) will normally be expected to be in witness statement form, in accordance with the normal practice under CPR Pt 23. **3J–56**

### 25. Headings

**25.1** Every notice and all witness statements and witness statements and affidavits in relation thereto must be entitled in the same manner as the Claim Form in the proceedings in which the application is made. **3J–57**

### 26. Service

**26.1** Service of application notices in disqualification proceedings will be the responsibility of the parties and will not be undertaken by the court. **3J–58**

**26.2** Where any application notice or order of the court or other document is required in any application to be served on any person who is not in England and Wales, the court may order service on him to be effected within such time and in such manner as it thinks fit, and may also require such proof of service as it thinks fit. Section III of CPR Part 6 does not apply.

*Part VI*

*Disqualification proceedings other than in the Royal Courts of Justice*

**27.1** Where a disqualification application or a section 8A application is made by a claim form issued other than in the Royal Courts of Justice this practice direction shall apply with the following modifications: **3J–59**

(1) Upon the issue of the claim form the court shall endorse it with the date and time for the first hearing before a district judge. The powers exercisable by a registrar under this practice direction shall be exercised by a district judge.

(2) If the district judge (either at the first hearing or at any adjourned hearing before him) directs that the disqualification claim or a section 8A application is to be heard by a High Court judge or by an authorised circuit judge he will direct that the case be entered forthwith in the list for hearing by that judge and the court will allocate (i) a date for the hearing of the trial by that judge and (ii) unless the district judge directs otherwise a date for the hearing of a PTR by the trial judge.

***Paragraph numbers marked with a "+" can be found online and on CD.***

*Part VII*

*Disqualification undertakings*

**28. Costs**

3J–60 **28.1** The general rule is that the court will order the defendant to pay—

(1) the costs of the Secretary of State (and, in the case of a disqualification application made under section 7(1)(b) of the Act, the costs of the official receiver) if:
  (a) a disqualification application under section 7 or 8 of the Act has been commenced; and
  (b) that application is discontinued because the Secretary of State has accepted a disqualification undertaking under section 1A of the Act;

(2) the costs of the Office of Fair Trading or a specified regulator if:
  (a) a disqualification application under section 9A of the Act has been commenced; and
  (b) that application is discontinued because the Office of Fair Trading or specified regulator (as the case may be) has accepted a disqualification undertaking under section 9B of the Act.

**28.2** The general rule will not apply where the court considers that the circumstances are such that it should make another order.

**Costs where disqualification undertakings are given**

3J–61 Paragraph 28.1 is introduced to make it clear that the normal rule on discontinuance (that the claimant should pay the costs: see CPR, r.38.6 and r.44.12) is reversed where the claimant discontinues following acceptance of an undertaking.

**Disqualification undertakings generally**

3J–62 It will be noted that there is very little in the Practice Direction in relation to disqualification undertakings. This is because they are a matter between the claimant and the defendant, and (unlike the *Carecraft* procedure) do not require judicial sanction. Where proceedings are discontinued on the acceptance of an undertaking, it will not be normal for the undertaking to go on the court file.

The Court of Appeal has given consideration to the undertakings provisions in *Re Blackspur Group (No.4)* [2001] EWCA Civ 1595; [2004] B.C.C. 839, and has held that the Secretary of State has an unfettered discretion as to whether to accept an undertaking which has been offered, and is entitled to decide it would be inexpedient in the public interest to accept it without a schedule of unfit conduct.

*Applications under section 8A of the act to reduce the period for which a disqualification undertaking is in force or to provide for it to cease to be in force*

**29. Headings**

3J–63 **29.1** Every claim form by which a section 8A application is begun and all affidavits, notices and other documents in the proceedings must be entitled in the matter of a disqualification undertaking and its date and in the matter of the Act.

**Applications under section 8A of the Act**

3J–64 This procedure in effect mirrors the format of proceedings brought by the Secretary of State or the Official Receiver for a disqualification order, though with the important difference that the starting point should be (except in unusual circumstances) that the claimant accepts that he was properly disqualified pursuant to his undertaking. It is envisaged that making a successful application under s.8A may in practice prove very difficult for a disqualified director.

In *Re INS Realisations* [2006] EWHC 135 (Ch); [2006] 1 W.L.R. 3433, Hart J. expressed the view that the jurisdiction should only be sparingly exercised where the application was (e.g.) based on an assertion that the defendant had given the undertaking because he could not afford legal advice and assistance, or on the fact that at a subsequent trial other defendants received lesser periods of disqualification for the same misconduct. On the facts, the judge allowed an application that the undertaking should cease to be in force: he particularly took into account the fact that the undertaking had been given in relation to the director's omissions in relation to matters complained of, and the fact that proceedings against the director alleged to have caused those matters were subsequently discontinued.

It should be noted that an application cannot be made under s.8A where the period of disqualification has already expired: *Eastaway v Secretary of State* [2006] EWHC 299 (Ch); [2006] 2 B.C.L.C. 489 (the decision was appealed, but not on this point: *Eastaway v Secretary of State* [2007] EWCA Civ 425; [2007] B.C.C. 550).

Much of the commentary in the notes on paras 4 to 12 of the Practice Direction is also relevant to paras 29 to 34 of the Practice Direction. Reference should be made to those notes as appropriate.



### 30. Commencement: the claim form

**30.1** Section 8A(3) of the Act identifies the courts which have jurisdiction to deal with section 8A applications. **3J–65**

**30.1A** A section 8A application must be commenced by a claim form issued:

(1) in the case of a disqualification undertaking given under section 9B of the Act, in the High Court out of the office of the companies court registrar at the Royal Courts of Justice;

(2) in any other case,

(a) in the High Court out of the office of the companies court registrar or a chancery district registry; and

(b) in the county court, out of a county court office.

**30.2** A section 8A application shall be made by the issue of a Part 8 claim form, in the form annexed hereto and the use of the procedure set out in CPR Part 8, as modified by this practice direction. CPR rule 8.1(3)(power of the Court to order the application to continue as if the claimant had not used the Part 8 procedure) shall not apply.

**30.3** When the claim form is issued, the claimant will be given a date for the first hearing of the section 8A application. This date is to be not less than eight weeks from the date of the issue of the claim form. The first hearing will be before the registrar.

**30.4** CPR Rule 8.2 does not apply. The claim form must state:

(1) that CPR Part 8 (as modified by this practice direction) applies;

(2) the form of order the claimant seeks.

**30.5** In the case of a disqualification undertaking given under section 9B of the Act, the defendant to the section 8A application shall be the Office of Fair Trading or specified regulator which accepted the undertaking. In all other cases, the Secretary of State shall be made the defendant to the section 8A application.

**30.6** Service of claim forms in section 8A applications will be the responsibility of the claimant and will not be undertaken by the court. The claim form may be served by sending it by first class post and the date of service shall, unless the contrary is shown, be deemed to be the seventh day following that on which the claim form was posted. CPR r.6.7(1) shall be modified accordingly. Otherwise Sections I and II of CPR Part 6 apply.[1]

**30.7** Where any order of the court or other document is required to be served on any person who is not in England and Wales, the court may order service on him to be effected within such time and in such manner as it thinks fit and may require such proof of service as it thinks fit. Section III of CPR Part 6 shall not apply.

**30.8** The claim form served on the defendant shall be accompanied by an acknowledgement of service in the form annexed hereto.

**Service**

3J–66 Since October 1, 2008, the reference in the footnote has been obsolete. The provisions as certificates of service are now found in CPR r.6.17.

### 31. Acknowledgement of service

3J–67 **31.1** The defendant shall:

(1) file an acknowledgement of service in the relevant practice form not more than 14 days after service of the claim form; and

(2) serve a copy of the acknowledgement of service on the claimant and any other party.

**31.2** Where the defendant has failed to file an acknowledgement of service and the time period for doing so has expired, the defendant may nevertheless attend the hearing of the application and take part in the hearing as provided for by section 8A(2) or (2A) of the Act. However, this is without prejudice to the Court's case management powers and its powers to make costs orders.

### 32. Evidence

3J–68 **32.1** Evidence in section 8A applications shall be by affidavit. The undertaking (or a copy) shall be exhibited to the affidavit.

**32.2** When the claim form is issued:

(1) the affidavit in support of the section 8A application must be filed in court; and

(2) exhibits must be lodged with the court where thay shall be retained until the conclusion of the proceedings; and

(3) copies of the affidavit and exhibits shall be served with the claim form on the defendant.

**32.3** The defendant shall, within 28 days from the date of service of the claim form:

(1) file in court any affidavit evidence that he wishes the court to take into consideration on the application; and

[1] Attention is drawn to CPR, r.6.14(2) regarding a certificate of service of the claim form.

(2) lodge the exhibits with the court where they shall be retained until the conclusion of the proceedings; and

(3) at the same time, serve upon the claimant a copy of the affidavits and exhibits.

**32.4** The claimant shall, within 14 days from receiving the copy of the defendant's evidence:

(1) file in court any further affidavit evidence in reply he wishes the court to take into consideration; and

(2) lodge the exhibits with the court where they shall be retained until the conclusion of the proceedings; and

(3) at the same time serve upon the claimant a copy of the affidavits and exhibits upon the defendant.

**32.5** Prior to the first hearing of the section 8(2) application, the time for serving evidence may be extended by written agreement between the parties. After the first hearing, the extension of time for serving evidence is governed by CPR, rules 2.11 and 29.5.

**32.6** So far as is possible all evidence should be filed before the first hearing of the section 8A application.



#### Evidence in section 8A applications

In *Re INS Realisations* [2006] EWHC 135 (Ch); [2006] 1 W.L.R. 3433, Hart J. said that the agreement not to dispute certain facts embodied in the undertaking should be treated as binding in a s.8A application "unless either some ground is shown which would be sufficient to discharge a private law contract or some ground of public interest is shown which outweighs the importance of holding a party to his agreement". That evidential burden on the applicant is much heavier than (for instance) the burden associated with raising matters which have arisen since the undertaking was given. **3J–69**

### 33. Hearings and case management

**33.1** The date fixed for the first hearing of the section 8A application shall be not less than 8 weeks from the date of issue of the claim form. **3J–70**

**33.2** The hearing shall in the first instance be before the registrar.

**33.3** The registrar shall either determine the case on the date fixed or give directions and adourn it.

**33.4** All interim directions should insofar as possible be sought at the first hearing of the section 8A applications so that the section 8A application can be determined at the earliest possible date. The parties should take all such steps as they respectively can to avoid successive directions hearings.

**33.5** If the registrar adjourns the application for further considerations he shall:-

(1) direct whether the application is to be heard by a registrar or a judge. This direction may at any time be varied by the court either on application or of its own initiative. If the court varies the direction in the absence of any of the parties, notice will be given to the parties;

(2) consider whether or not to adjourn the application to a judge so that the judge can give further directions;

(3) consider whether or not to make any direction with regard to fixing the trial date or a trial window.

*Paragraph numbers marked with a "+" can be found online and on CD.*

**33.6** On the first or any subsequent hearing of the section 8A application, the registrar may also give directions as to the following matters:

(1) the filing in court and the service of further evidence (if any) by the parties;

(2) the time-table for the steps to be taken between the giving of directions and the hearing of the section 8A application;

(3) such other matters as the registrar thinks necessary or expedient with a view to an expeditious disposal of the section 8A application or the management of it generally;

(4) the time and place of the adjourned hearing.

**33.7** Where a case is adjourned other than to a judge, it may be heard by the registrar who originally dealt with the case or by another registrar.

**33.8** If the companies court registrar adjourns the application to a judge, all directions having been compiled with and the evidence being complete, the application will be referred to the Listing Office and any practice direction relating to listing shall apply accordingly.

**33.9** In all section 8A applications, the Court may direct a pre-trial review ('PTR'), a case management conference or pre-trial check lists (listing questionnaires) (in the form annexed to this practice direction) and will fix a trial date or trial period in accordance with the provisions of CPR Part 29: The Multi-Track, as modified by any relevant practice direction made thereunder.

**33.10** At the hearing of the PTR, the registrar may give any further directions as appropriate and, where the application is to be heard in the Royal Courts of Justice in London, unless the trial date has already been fixed, may direct the parties (by Counsel's clerks, if applicable) to attend the Registrar at a specified time and place in order solely to fix a trial date. The court will give notice of the date fixed for the trial to the parties.

**33.11** In all cases, the parties must inform the court immediately of any material change to the information provided in a pre–trial checklist.

### 34. The trial

3J–71 **34.1** Trial bundles containing copies of:-

(1) the claim form;

(2) the acknowledgement of service;

(3) all evidence filed by or on behalf of each of the parties to the proceedings, together with the exhibits thereto;

(4) all relevant correspondence; and

(5) such other documents as the parties consider necessary;

shall be lodged with the court.

**34.2** Skeleton arguments should be prepared by all the parties in all but the simplest cases whether the case is to be heard by a registrar or a judge. They should comply with all relevant guidelines.

**34.3** The advocate for the claimant should also in all but the simplest cases provide: (a) chronology; (b) dramatis personae.

***Paragraph numbers marked with a "+" can be found online and on CD.***

**34.4** The documents mentioned in paragraph 34.1 to 34.3 above must be delivered to the court in accordance with any order of the court and/or relevant practice direction.[1]

(1) If the case is to be heard by a judge sitting in the Royal Courts of Justice, London, but the name of the judge is not known, or the judge is a deputy judge, these documents must be delivered to the Clerk of the Lists. If the name of the judge (other than a deputy judge) is known, these documents must be delivered to the judge's clerk.

(2) If the case is to be heard by a companies court registrar, these documents must be delivered to Room 409, Thomas More Building, Royal Courts of Justice. Copies must be provided to the other party so far as possible when they are delivered to the court.

(3) If the case is to be heard in the Chancery district registries in Birmingham, Bristol, Caernarfon, Cardiff, Leeds, Liverpool, Manchester, Mold, Newcastle upon Tyne or Preston, the addresses for delivery are set out in Annex 1;

(4) If the case is to be heard in a county court, the documents should be delivered to the relevant county court office.

**34.5** Copies of documents delivered to the court must, so far as possible, be provided to each of the other parties to the claim.

**34.6** The provisions in paragraphs 34.1 to 34.5 above are subject to any order of the court making different provision.

**Chancery Guide**

The footnote to para.34.4 refers to the 2000 edition of the Chancery Guide. A new edition was published in November 2005 and was subsequently updated, and a further edition was published in October 2009—see para.1A–1 et seq. above. **3J–72**

## 35. Appeals

**35.1** Rules 7.47 and 7.49 of the Insolvency Rules, as supplemented by Part Four of the Insolvency Proceedings Practice Direction, apply to an appeal from, or review of, a decision made by the court in the course of: **3J–73**

(1) disqualification proceedings under any of sections 6 to 8A or 9A of the Act;

(2) an application made under section 17 of the Act for the purposes of any of sections 1(1)(a), 1A(1)(a) or 9B(4), for permission to act notwithstanding a disqualification order made, or a disqualification undertaking accepted, under any of sections 6 to 10.

Any such decision, and any appeal from it, constitutes 'insolvency

[1] Attention is drawn to the provisions of the Chancery Guide. Chapter 7 of that guide, dated September 2000 provides guidance on the preparation of trial bundles and skeleton arguments. Unless the Court otherwise orders, paragraph 7.16 of the Chancery Guide requires that trial bundles be delivered to the Court 7 days before trial, and paragraph 7.21 requires that skeleton arguments be delivered to the Court not less than 2 clear days before trial.

proceedings' for the purposes of the Insolvency Proceedings Practice Direction.[1]

**35.2** An appeal from a decision made by the court in the course of disqualification proceedings under any of sections 2(2)(a), 3 or 4 of the Act or on an application for permission to act notwithstanding a disqualification order made under any of those sections is governed by CPR Part 52 and Practice Direction 52.

**Appeals**

**3J–74** The view of the court has generally been that appeals from decisions of registrars in disqualification cases do not require permission, because disqualification proceedings are insolvency proceedings governed by the Insolvency Proceedings Practice Direction, which by the combined effect of paras 17.2 and 17.6 confirmed that no permission was required for a first appeal from a registrar. The correctness of this approach was confirmed by the Vice-Chancellor in *Secretary of State v Paulin* [2005] EWHC 888 (Ch); [2005] B.C.C. 927 at [13]–[19], though with a recommendation that the obscurity of the interrelationship of the various rules be looked at by the relevant rules committees. That led to the introduction of para.35 in September 2005.

However, the position has changed by virtue of the amendments to para.17 of the Insolvency Proceedings Practice Direction effective from October 2, 2006. Insolvency proceedings (and by extension disqualification proceedings) are brought into line with general civil litigation, with the imposition of a requirement for permission to make a first appeal (para.17.6 of the Insolvency Proceedings Practice Direction, as substituted). The time limit for appeal is, as of October 2, 2006, 21 days (para.17.11(2)(b) of the Insolvency Proceedings Practice Direction, as amended).

## Annex 1

**3J–75** *Birmingham:* The Chancery Listing Officer, The District Registry of the Chancery Division of the High Court, 33 Bull Street, Birmingham B4 6DS.

*Bristol:* The Chancery Listing Officer, The District Registry of the Chancery Division of the High Court, 3rd Floor, Greyfriars, Lewins Mead, Bristol BS1 2NR.

*Caernarfon:* The Chancery Listing Officer, The District Registry of the Chancery Division of the High Court, 1st Floor, Llanberis Road, Caernarfon, LL55 2DF.

*Cardiff:* The Chancery Listing Officer, The District Registry of the Chancery Division of the High Court, 1st Floor, 2 Park Street, Cardiff CF10 1ET.

*Leeds:* The Chancery Listing Officer, The District Registry of the Chancery Division of the High Court, Leeds Combined Court Centre, The Court House, 1 Oxford Row, Leeds LS1 3BG.

*Liverpool and Manchester:* The Chancery Listing Officer, The District Registry of the Chancery Division of the High Court, Manchester Courts of Justice, Crown Square, Manchester M60 9DJ.

*Mold:* The Chancery Listing Officer, The District Registry of the Chancery Division of the High Court, Law Courts, Civic Centre, Mold, CH7 1AE.

---

[1] CPR rule 2.1(2) and s.21(2) of the Act. See also rule 2(4) of the Insolvent Companies (Disqualification of Unfit Directors) Proceedings Rules 1987 and *Re Tasbian Limited, Official Receiver v Nixon* [1991] B.C.L.C. 59; [1990] B.C.C. 322; *Re Probe Data Systems Limited (No.3), Secretary of State for Trade and Industry v Desai* [1992] B.C.L.C.405; [1992] BCC 110 and *Re The Premier Screw & Repetition Company Ltd, Secretary of State for Trade and Industry v Paulin* [2005] EWHC 888 (Ch).

*Newcastle upon Tyne:* The Chancery Listing Officer, The District Registry of the Chancery Division of the High Court, The Law Courts, Quayside, Newcastle upon Tyne NE1 3LA.

*Preston:* The Chancery Listing Officer, The District Registry of the Chancery Division of the High Court, The Combined Court Centre, Ringway, Preston PR1 2LL.

**Editorial note**

The following forms which are annexed to this Practice Direction can be found in the *Civil Procedure Forms Volume*: **3J–76**

- **N500**
- **N500A**
- **N500B**
- **N501**
- **N501A**
- **N501B**
- **N502**
- **N503**
- **N504**

# 3K CIVIL RECOVERY PROCEEDINGS

## PRACTICE DIRECTION—CIVIL RECOVERY PROCEEDINGS

This Practice Direction was published in HMSO CPR Update 30, February 2003. It does not supplement any particular Part of the CPR, or Schedule rule, but is a consequence of the Proceeds of Crime Act 2002. See further Vol.1 para.sc115.0.2.1. **3K–1**

### Editorial note

The Practice Direction is concerned with powers under the Proceeds of Crime Act 2002 ("the 2002 Act") for the High Court to forfeit the proceeds of crime on application of certain government agencies. As originally enacted, only the Director of the Assets Recovery Agency could bring such an action. **3K–2**

On April 1, 2008, s.74 and Sch.8 of the Serious Crime Act 2007 ("the 2007 Act") came into force. These provisions abolished the Assets Recovery Agency and the office of the Director of the Assets Recovery Agency. The litigation functions of the Director under Pt 5 of the Proceeds of Crime Act 2002 were transferred to the Serious and Organised Crime Agency ("SOCA"). Consequently, all civil recovery proceedings in train as of April 1, 2008, were taken over by SOCA on that date and SOCA was empowered to bring proceedings.

Additionally, the 2007 Act conferred, for the first time, the power to bring civil recovery proceedings on the principal prosecuting authorities, namely the Director of Public Prosecutions (who is head of the Crown Prosecution Service), the Director of the Serious Fraud Office and the Director of the Revenue and Customs Prosecutions Office (the 2007 Act Sch.8, Pt 2, para.91).

### Part 5 powers—power to make a recovery order

The power in Pt 5 is for the High Court to make a "recovery order" against property if satisfied that the property is the proceeds of crime (see s.266(1) combined with ss.241, 242 and 304(1) of the 2002 Act). For whether property can properly be said to be the proceeds of crime (defined by 304(1) as property obtained "by or in return for" crime) see *Director of the Assets Recovery Agency v John* [2007] EWHC 360, QB; *Director of the Assets Recovery Agency v Olupitan* [2008] EWCA Civ 104; *R. (Greater Manchester Police) v Salford Magistrates' Court* [2008] EWHC 1651 (Admin); and *Serious Organised Crime Agency v Matthews* [2009] EWHC 1544 (Admin)). A recovery order is an order which forfeits the interests in the property to the State by vesting the property rights in a "trustee for civil recovery", a creature of the 2002 Act (see ss.266(2) and 267). Property may be traced and recovered from persons who did not carry out the crime, but there are various defences set out in Pt 5, the principal one of which is that the holder of the property is a good faith purchaser for value without notice of the unlawful origin of the property (s.308(1)). In domestic and European Convention of Human Rights law, civil recovery proceedings are civil proceedings, not criminal (*Charrington v Director of the Assets Recovery Agency* [2005] EWCA Civ 334; *Director of the Assets Recovery Agency v Ashton* [2006] EWHC 1064 (Admin)). The claimant does have to specify which *type* of crime generated the proceeds but does not have to identify a *particular* crime (*Director of Assets Recovery Agency v Green* [2005] EWHC 3168 (Admin)). In *Director of the Assets Recovery Agency v Olupitan* [2008] EWCA Civ 104 the Court of Appeal explained that to comply with the requirements identified in *Green* it was not necessary for the claimant to plead the facts in the same manner as in a civil case alleging fraud. All that was necessary was for the type of crime to be identified in the most general terms. The claimant may be able to allege money laundering. If so, he does not have to identify the type of crime which generated the proceeds which were laundered, provided he can establish an "irresistible inference" that they were criminally derived (*Serious Organised Crime Agency v Gale* [2009] EWHC 1015 (QB)). **3K–3**

The nature of the claim is neither proprietary nor in personam, but sui generis (*Director of the Assets Recovery Agency v Creaven* [2006] 1 W.L.R. 622).

The 2002 Act inserts s.27A into the Limitation Act 1980 providing for a limitation period of 12 years from when the recoverable property was first obtained. In *Director of the Assets Recovery Agency v Szepietowski* [2007] EWCA Civ 766 the Court of Appeal had to grapple with the applicability of s.32(1) of the Limitation Act 1980 to civil recovery cases. Section 32 has, so far as civil recovery case are concerned, two limbs. The first limb, s.32(1)(a), extends the period of time within which proceedings must be brought in causes of action based on fraud to begin when the fraud is, or should have been, discovered by the claimant. Moore-Bick L.J. took the view that this applied to civil recovery cases, Waller L.J. thought not and Wall L.J. was undecided. However, all the members of the court thought that s.32(1)(b) did apply. This subsection provides that where a defendant conceals facts necessary for a claim from the claimant, time does not begin to run until those facts are, or should have been, discovered. Thus concealment of facts, including the incidence of fraud (on the facts of *Szepietowski*) from the claimant resulted in the limitation period starting when those facts were, or should have been, discovered. *Szepietowski* was applied in *Serious Organised Crime Agency v Gale* [2009] EWHC 1015 (QB).

### Part 5 powers—procedure on application for a recovery order

**3K–4** The Practice Direction sets out how the claimant should make a claim for a recovery order (para.4). This must be read with the requirements in the Act. The claimant may bring proceedings against any person that it "thinks" holds recoverable property (s.243(1) of the 2002 Act). For the definition of "property" and holding property see s.316 of the 2002 Act. Such a person is called a "respondent" by the 2002 Act and the claim form must be served on that person (s.243(2) combined with s.316(1)). The claim form should also be served upon any person holding associated property, unless the court dispenses with service (s.243(2)). Associated property is property which is not itself recoverable property, but is another interest in recoverable property (s.245). The claim form should therefore be served on all persons with an interest in the property (*Director of the Assets Recovery Agency v Charrington* [2004] EWHC 2345 (Admin)). The proceedings "must be made using the Part 8 procedure" (PD para.4.1). This is a curious choice made by the draftsman of the Practice Direction as civil recovery proceedings almost always involve substantial disputes of fact. They are better suited to the Pt 7 procedure. This is recognised by the court which will order a case to proceed under Pt 7 where appropriate (*Director of the Assets Recovery Agency v Creaven* [2006] 1 W.L.R. 622; *Director of the Assets Recovery Agency v Szepietowski* [2007] EWCA Civ 766).

### Part 5 powers—making a recovery order

**3K–5** If the court makes a recovery order, then the court must appoint a trustee for civil recovery who will act under the direction and instructions of the claimant ss.266–267 of the 2002 Act). There are provisions in Pt 5 designed to protect the interests of innocent third parties, yet at the same time give effect to the intention to forfeit criminally obtained property to the State (see in particular ss.271 and 272). Express statutory provision is made for the parties to agree that the innocent person should retain the property on payment to the trustee for civil recovery of a sum relating to the criminally derived interest (s.271). The 2002 Act also permits the parties to enter into an order staying the proceedings on terms which the court thinks appropriate (s.276). These provisions do not represent the limit of the powers to settle proceedings. The CPR plainly applies to civil recovery proceedings as it does to any other statutory cause of action in the High Court and the parties may enter into any consent order the court is prepared to endorse, pursuant to CPRPt 40.6.

The court has power to enter summary judgment against the respondent pursuant to Pt 24, but Pt 24 must be applied properly taking care not to act merely on suspicion or on the basis of a reverse burden of proof (*Director of the Assets Recovery Agency v Woodstock* [2006] EWCA Civ 741).

### Part 5 powers—interim powers to preserve assets

**3K–6** In order to preserve the asset, Pt 5 of the 2002 Act provides for the High Court to make three types of statutory interim orders. The first is "a property freezing order", similar to a CPR Pt 25 freezing order (see s.245A of the 2002 Act, introduced by s.98 of the Serious Organised Crime and Police Act 2005). On January 1, 2006, the Practice Direction was amended to take into account this power.

The second type of interim order is for the appointment of a "civil recovery management receiver". This power is conferred by s.245E, inserted by s.83 of the Serious Crime Act 2007. Such a receiver is akin to a receiver appointed under the equitable jurisdiction of the High Court in civil litigation to manage assets and prevent dissipation. The powers which may be conferred on such a receiver are set out in s.245F of the 2002 Act. Such a receiver will be an officer of the court (as to which, in a different context, see *Re Andrews* [1999] 1 W.L.R. 1236).

The third type of order which the High Court may make is an "interim receiving order" (see s.245 of the 2002 Act). This is an order for detention, custody or preservation of the asset and for the appointment of a receiver. Unlike a court appointed receiver in civil proceedings or a receiver appointed under s.245E, an interim receiver has a statutory investigative function in relation to the source of the asset. The court must confer powers on the receiver to report to it and to the parties on his findings in relation to the status of the property (see ss.247, 252 and 255 of the 2002 Act).

These specific statutory interim powers are not the limit of the court's powers. The CPR applies and so any of the interim remedies in Pt 25 are available to the Court (see s.243(5) of the 2002 Act, inserted by Sch.6 of the Serious Organised Crime and Police Act 2005).

To obtain an interim order, the claimant must show that proceedings "may" be brought for the recovery of the property (s.245A/246 of the 2002 Act). The use of the word "may" indicates that the claimant need not have taken a final decision to commence such proceedings and does not have to give an undertaking to commence such proceedings within a particular time. So far, without the matter being tested, the court has not required the claimant to give such an undertaking as a condition of the grant of such an order and it is thought that this approach is correct. An application for a property freezing order or interim receiving order may be made without notice, if the giving of notice would "prejudice any right" of the claimant to obtain a recovery order (s.245A(3)/246(3)).

In all cases, the claimant must show "a good arguable case" the property is either recoverable property or "associated property" (s.245A(5)/246(6) of the 2002 Act). Associated property is property which is not, itself, recoverable property, but is some other interest in property which is recoverable (s.245 of the 2002 Act). In *Director of the Assets Recovery Agency v Szepietowski* [2007] EWCA Civ 766, Moore Bick L.J. took the view that in a case involving serious impropriety (as virtually all civil recovery cases will be), a good arguable case meant one which was beyond merely speculative, but stood a good prospect of success at trial.

CIVIL RECOVERY

**Varying and setting aside interim orders**

The 2002 Act contains specific provisions empowering affected persons to apply to vary or set aside a property freezing order or an interim receiving order (section s.245B/251). Such an interim order may be discharged against property if the good arguable case test is not satisfied in respect of it (*Director of the Assets Recovery Agency v Kean* [2007] EWHC 112 (Admin), although in *Director of Assets Recovery Agency v He and Chen* [2004] EWHC 3021 (Admin), Collins J. said that where an interim receiver is appointed the court should not normally accede to such an application on the basis that the property to which the application relates is not recoverable or associated property, until the receiver produces the report envisaged by the Act). **3K–6.1**

The receiver, any party or any person affected by action taken or proposed to be taken by the receiver may apply to the court for directions (s.251(1) of the 2002 Act). Before giving directions, all affected persons must be given an opportunity to be heard (s.252(2)). The Practice Direction sets out how such an application should be made (para.6) and by para.4 of the Practice Direction, Pt 69 of the CPR is applied. Consequently the receiver may apply for directions on uncontentious matters by letter (CPR Pt 69.8).

**Exclusions for legal costs**

As originally enacted, the 2002 Act permitted the court to exclude property from its ambit, in particular for living expenses and to permit businesses to trade, provided the right of the claimant to recover the property was not thereby "unduly prejudiced" (s.252 of the 2002 Act). However, the 2002 Act did not permit property to be excepted to pay legal costs (s.252(4)). Instead, the respondent was required to use other property or obtain community funding from the Legal Services Commission. **3K–6.2**

However the Serious Organised Crime and Police Act 2005, by Sch.6 para.14, amended s.252 of the 2002 Act by permitting legal expenses to be paid in accordance with regulations made by subordinate legislation. Such regulations have been made and came into force on the January 1, 2006. The 2002 Act and these regulations, the Proceeds of Crime Act 2002 (Legal Expenses in Civil Recovery Proceedings) Regulations 2005, permit property to be excepted from a property freezing order or an interim receiving order to pay legal costs under strict conditions. They have to be read with the provisions of the Practice Direction.

These provisions are dauntingly complex but their effect is as follows. If the court makes an interim receiving order or a property freezing order, it should normally "exclude" a sum of up to £3,000 to enable the respondent to take advice about the order, prepare a statement of assets for release of further sums to pay legal expenses and to apply to vary or set aside the order (PD para.5B). Such an exclusion should be made if there are other assets which might reasonably be expected to pay such costs (*Serious Organised Crime Agency v Szepietowski* [2009] EWHC 344 (Ch)).The court has power to exclude further sums but the exclusion must be limited to sums that are reasonably incurred (s.245C(5)/252(4)(a)), such an exclusion must specify the stage or stages in the proceedings to which it relates (reg.4(a)), the court must specify a maximum sum to be released for each stage (s.245C(5)/252(4)(b); reg.4B), an application by the respondent must be supported by a witness statement setting out his assets (PD paras 7A.2 and 7A.3) and the court will not make an order if the respondent has assets other than those subject to the interim receiving order or property freezing order from which he can reasonably be expected to meet legal costs (PD para.7A.4; *Serious Organised Crime Agency v Szepietowski* [2009] EWHC 344 (Ch)). The respondent's evidence for this exclusion must contain details of the stage or stages to which the costs apply, include an estimate of the costs incurred or to be incurred in the same form as Precedent H in the costs practice direction in CPR Pt 48 and, where the court has previously made an exclusion in relation to the stage concerned, an explanation of why the costs have exceeded the amount previously allowed and state whether the costs are agreed by the claimant (PD para.7.3).

An exclusion is not an order entitling the respondent's solicitors to be paid. It just ear-marks a piece of property by excluding it from a property freezing order or receivership.

Where the court makes an exclusion for legal costs, then in order for an excluded sum to be applied in satisfaction of legal costs, the respondent must obtain "release" of the sum by complying with Pt 3 of the regulations. These require the respondent to supply certain details of the work done to the claimant including evidence in support (reg.(8(1)). The respondent can only make one such request every two months and it must relate to work which has been carried out (reg.8(2)). If the claimant agrees the amount claimed, that amount may be applied in satisfaction of the costs (reg.10). In deciding whether to agree to the amount claimed, the claimant must have regard to the hourly rates in the table in reg.17 (reg.9(3)). The table has sliding scales of rates from £75 to £270 per hour for solicitors and £100 to £330 per hour for counsel. If the amount is not agreed, then only 65 per cent of the amount claimed may be paid and the whole amount is later subject to assessment in the event that a recovery order is made (regs 10, 11 and 13).

A release under Pt 3 of the regulations is not a final irreversible payment. If no recovery order is made, there is no possibility of such a release being reversed. But if a recovery order is made, that order should make provision for assessment of the respondent's costs, including those in respect of which a release has been ordered. If such an order is not made, the regulations seems to mean that the solicitors for the respondent must repay the amount released back to the trustee for civil recovery (regs 13 and 14; *Serious Organised Crime Agency v Szepietowski* [2009] EWHC 1560 (Ch) at [43]).

On an assessment of the respondent's legal costs (if there is one) post the making of a recovery order, the respondent's own client costs are assessed by application in accordance with CPR Pt 47. The application must be commenced within two months of the recovery order and the solicitor must file a request for a detailed assessment hearing within two months of the detailed assessment proceedings (reg.13(2)(a)). The costs are assessed on a standard basis in accordance with CPR Pt 44, but on the hourly rates set out in the table in reg.17 (regs 13 and 16). Any sums released but not allowed, must be paid by the solicitor for the respondent to the trustee for civil recovery (reg.14).

If there is a partial recovery order, it may be that the respondent will have assets released to him. If so the court could make an order for the reversal of exclusions and releases, if the assets released become reasonably available to the pay legal costs (*Serious Organised Crime Agency v Szepietowski* [2009] EWHC 1560 (Ch)).

## Scope and Interpretation

**1.1** Section I of this practice direction contains general provisions about proceedings in the High Court under Parts 5 and 8 of the Proceeds of Crime Act 2002 and Part 5 of the Proceeds of Crime Act 2002 (External Requests and Orders) Order 2005. **3K–7**

**1.2** Section II contains provisions about applications to the High Court under Part 5 of the Act and Part 5 of the Order in Council for—

(a) a recovery order;
(b) a property freezing order;
(c) an interim receiving order;
(d) a management receiving order; and
(e) the register of external orders.

**1.3** Section III contains provisions about applications to the High Court under Part 8 of the Act for any of the following types of order or warrant in connection with a civil recovery investigation or a detained cash investigation—

(a) a production order;
(b) a search and seizure warrant;
(c) a disclosure order;
(d) a customer information order; and
(e) an account monitoring order.

**1.4** Section IV of this practice direction contains further provisions about applications for each of the specific types of order and warrant listed in paragraph 1.3 above.

**1.5** In this practice direction—

(1) 'the Act' means the Proceeds of Crime Act 2002[1];

(1A) 'appropriate officer' has the meaning set out in section 378 of the Act;

(2) 'enforcement authority' has the meaning set out in section 316 of the Act;

(3) 'the Order in Council' means the Proceeds of Crime Act 2002 (External Requests and Orders) Order 2005;

(4) 'civil recovery proceedings' means proceedings under Part 5 of the Act or Part 5 of the Order in Council (as appropriate);

(4A) 'interim receiving order' has the meaning set out in section 246 of the Act;

(4B) 'management receiving order' means an order to appoint a receiver under section 245E of the Act;

[1] 2002 c. 29.

(4C) 'property freezing order' has the meaning set out in section 245A of the Act;

(5) 'the Regulations' means the Proceeds of Crime Act 2002 (Legal Expenses in Civil Recovery Proceedings) Regulations 2005;

(5A) 'relevant Director' has the meaning set out in section 352(5A) of the Act;

(5B) 'CPR' means the Civil Procedure Rules 1998; and

(6) other expressions used have the same meaning as in the Act or the Order in Council (as appropriate).

### *Section I—General Provisions*

#### Venue

3K–8 **2.1** A claim or application to the High Court under Part 5 or Part 8 of the Act or Part 5 of the Order in Council must be started in the Administrative Court.

**2.2** The Administrative Court may transfer the claim or application to the Queen's Bench Division Central Office or Chancery Chambers.

#### Use of pseudonyms by staff

3K–9 **3.1** If a member of the staff of the relevant Director gives written or oral evidence in any proceedings using a pseudonym in accordance with section 449 or section 449A of the Act—

(1) the court must be informed that the witness is using a pseudonym; and

(2) a certificate under section 449(3) or 449A(3) (as appropriate) of the Act must be filed or produced.

### *Section II—Civil Recovery Proceedings under Part 5 of the Act or Part 5 of the Order in Council*

#### Claim for a recovery order

3K–10 **4.1** A claim by the enforcement authority for a recovery order must be made using the CPR Part 8 procedure.

**4.2** In a claim for a recovery order based on an external order, the claim must include an application to register the external order.

**4.3** The claim form must—

(1) identify the property in relation to which a recovery order is sought;

(2) state, in relation to each item or description of property—

(a) whether the property is alleged to be recoverable property or associated property; and

(b) either—

(i) who is alleged to hold the property; or

(ii) where the enforcement authority is unable to identify who holds the property, the steps that have been taken to try to establish their identity;

(3) set out the matters relied upon in support of the claim;

(4) give details of the person nominated by the enforcement authority to act as trustee for civil recovery in accordance with section 267 of the Act or article 178 of the Order in Council; and

(5) in a claim which includes an application to register an external order, be accompanied by a copy of the external order.

**4.4** The evidence in support of the claim must include the signed, written consent of the person nominated by the enforcement authority to act as trustee for civil recovery if appointed by the court.

**4.5** In a claim which includes an application to register an external order, where—

(1) the sum specified in the external order is expressed in a currency other than sterling; and

(2) there are not funds held in the United Kingdom in the currency in which the sum specified is expressed sufficient to satisfy the external order,

the claim form, or particulars of claim if served subsequently, must state the sterling equivalent of the sum specified.

(Article 145(2) of the Order in Council provides that the sterling equivalent is to be calculated in accordance with the exchange rate prevailing at end of the day on which the external order is made.)

## Applications

**5.1** An application for a property freezing order, an interim receiving order or a management receiving order must be made— **3K–11**

(1) to a High Court judge; and

(2) in accordance with CPR Part 23.

**5.2** CPR rule 23.10(2) and Section I of CPR Part 25 do not apply to applications for property freezing orders, interim receiving orders and management receiving orders.

**5.3** The application may be made without notice in the circumstances set out in—

(1) section 245A(3) of the Act and article 147(3) of the Order in Council (in the case of an application for a property freezing order);

(2) section 246(3) of the Act and article 151(3) of the Order in Council (in the case of an application for an interim receiving order);

(3) section 245(E) of the Act and the Order in Council (in the case of an application for a management receiving order).

**5.4** An application for a property freezing order must be supported by written evidence which must—

(1) set out the grounds on which the order is sought; and

(2) give details of each item or description of property in respect of which the order is sought, including—

(a) an estimate of the value of the property; and

(b) the additional information referred to in paragraph 5.5(2).

**5.5** CPR Part 69 (court's power to appoint a receiver) and Practice Direction 69 apply to an application for an interim receiving order with the following modifications—

(1) paragraph 2.1 of Practice Direction 69 does not apply;

(2) the enforcement authority's written evidence must, in addition to the matters required by paragraph 4.1 of that practice direction, also state in relation to each item or description of property in respect of which the order is sought—

(a) whether the property is alleged to be—

(i) recoverable property; or

(ii) associated property,

and the facts relied upon in support of that allegation; and

(b) in the case of any associated property—

(i) who is believed to hold the property; or

(ii) if the enforcement authority is unable to establish who holds the property, the steps that have been taken to establish their identity; and

(3) the enforcement authority's written evidence must always identify a nominee and include the information in paragraph 4.2 of that practice direction.

**5.5A** Paragraph 2.1 of Practice Direction 69 does not apply to an application for a management receiving order.

**5.6** Where an application is made for an interim receiving order or management receiving order, a draft of the order which is sought must be filed with the application notice. This should if possible also be supplied to the court in an electronic form compatible with the word processing software used by the court.

### Property freezing order or interim receiving order made before commencement of claim for recovery order

3K–12 **5A.** A property freezing order or interim receiving order which is made before a claim for a recovery order has been commenced will—

(1) specify a period within which the enforcement authority must either start the claim or apply for the continuation of the order while he carries out his investigation; and

(2) provide that the order shall be set aside if the enforcement authority does not start the claim or apply for its continuation before the end of that period.

### Exclusions when making property freezing order or interim receiving order

3K–13 **5B.1** When the court makes a property freezing order or interim receiving order on an application without notice, it will normally make an initial exclusion from the order for the purpose of enabling the respondent to meet his reasonable legal costs so that he may—

(1) take advice in relation to the order;

(2) prepare a statement of assets in accordance with paragraph 7A.3; and

*Paragraph numbers marked with a "+" can be found online and on CD.*

(3) if so advised, apply for the order to be varied or set aside.

The total amount specified in the initial exclusion will not normally exceed £3,000.

**5B.2** When it makes a property freezing order or interim receiving order before a claim for a recovery order has been commenced, the court may also make an exclusion to enable the respondent to meet his reasonable legal costs so that (for example) when the claim is commenced—

(1) he may file an acknowledgment of service and any written evidence on which he intends to rely; or

(2) he may apply for a further exclusion for the purpose of enabling him to meet his reasonable costs of the proceedings.

**5B.3** Paragraph 7A contains general provisions about exclusions made for the purpose of enabling a person to meet his reasonable legal costs.

### Interim receiving order or management receiving order or management receiving order: application for directions

**6.1** An application for directions as to the exercise of the functions of— **3K–14**

(1) the interim receiver under section 251 of the Act or article 156 of the Order in Council, or

(2) the management receiver under section 245G of the Act or under the Order in Council,

may be made at any time by—

(a) the interim receiver or management receiver, as appropriate;

(b) any party to the proceedings; and

(c) any person affected by any action taken, or proposed to be taken, by the interim receiver or management receiver.

**6.2** The application must always be made by application notice, which must be served on—

(1) the interim receiver or management receiver as appropriate (unless he is the applicant);

(2) every party to the proceedings; and

(3) any other person who may be interested in the application.

### Application to vary or set aside an order

**7.1** An application to vary or set aside a property freezing order, an interim receiving order or a management receiving order (including an application for, or relating to, an exclusion from the order) may be made at any time by— **3K–15**

(1) the enforcement authority; or

(2) any person affected by the order.

**7.2** Unless the court otherwise directs or exceptional circumstances apply, a copy of the application notice must be served on—

(1) every party to the proceedings;

*Paragraph numbers marked with a "+" can be found online and on CD.*

(2) in the case of an application to vary or set aside an interim receiving order or management receiving order, the interim receiver or management receiver (as appropriate); and

(3) any other person who may be affected by the court's decision.

**7.3** The evidence in support of an application for an exclusion from a property freezing order or interim receiving order for the purpose of enabling a person to meet his reasonable legal costs must—

(1) contain full details of the stage or stages in civil recovery proceedings in respect of which the costs in question have been or will be incurred;

(2) include an estimate of the costs which the person has incurred and will incur in relation to each stage to which the application relates, substantially in the form illustrated in Precedent H in the Schedule of Costs Precedents annexed to the Costs Practice Direction;

(3) include a statement of assets containing the information set out in paragraph 7A.3 (unless the person has previously filed such a statement in the same civil recovery proceedings and there has been no material change in the facts set out in that statement);

(4) where the court has previously made an exclusion in respect of any stage to which the application relates, explain why the person's costs will exceed the amount specified in the exclusion for that stage; and

(5) state whether the terms of the exclusion have been agreed with the enforcement authority.

**Exclusions for the purpose of meeting legal costs: general provisions**

3K–16 **7A.1** Subject to paragraph 7A.2, when the court makes an order or gives directions in civil recovery proceedings it will at the same time consider whether it is appropriate to make or vary an exclusion for the purpose of enabling any person affected by the order or directions to meet his reasonable legal costs.

**7A.2** The court will not make an exclusion for the purpose of enabling a person to meet his reasonable legal costs, other than an exclusion to meet the costs of taking any of the steps referred to in paragraph 5B.1, unless that person has made and filed a statement of assets.

**7A.3** A statement of assets is a witness statement which sets out all the property which the maker of the statement owns, holds or controls, or in which he has an interest, giving the value, location and details of all such property. Information given in a statement of assets under this practice direction will be used only for the purpose of the civil recovery proceedings.

**7A.4** The court—

(1) will not make an exclusion for the purpose of enabling a

person to meet his reasonable legal costs (including an initial exclusion under paragraph 5B.1); and

(2) may set aside any exclusion which it has made for that purpose or reduce any amount specified in such an exclusion,

if it is satisfied that the person has property to which the property freezing order or interim receiving order does not apply from which he may meet those costs.

**7A.5** The court will normally refer to a costs judge any question relating to the amount which an exclusion should allow for reasonable legal costs in respect of proceedings or a stage in proceedings.

**7A.6** Attention is drawn to section 245C of the Act and article 149 of the Order in Council (in relation to exclusions from property freezing orders) and to section 252 of the Act and article 157 of the Order in Council (in relation to exclusions from interim receiving orders). An exclusion for the purpose of enabling a person to meet his reasonable legal costs must be made subject to the 'required conditions' specified in Part 2 of the Regulations.

**7A.7** An exclusion made for the purpose of enabling a person to meet his reasonable legal costs will specify—

(1) the stage or stages in civil recovery proceedings to which it relates;

(2) the maximum amount which may be released in respect of legal costs for each specified stage; and

(3) the total amount which may be released in respect of legal costs pursuant to the exclusion.

**7A.8** A person who becomes aware that his legal costs—

(1) in relation to any stage in civil recovery proceedings have exceeded or will exceed the maximum amount specified in the exclusion for that stage; or

(2) in relation to all the stages to which the exclusion relates have exceeded or will exceed the total amount that may be released pursuant to the exclusion,

should apply for a further exclusion or a variation of the existing exclusion as soon as reasonably practicable.

### Assessment of costs where recovery order is made

**7B.1** Where the court— **3K–17**

(1) makes a recovery order in respect of property which was the subject of a property freezing order or interim receiving order; and

(2) had made an exclusion from the property freezing order or interim receiving order for the purpose of enabling a person to meet his reasonable legal costs,

the recovery order will make provision under section 266(8A) of the Act or article 177(10) of the Order in Council (as appropriate) for the payment of those costs.

**7B.2** Where the court makes a recovery order which provides for the payment of a person's reasonable legal costs in respect of civil recovery proceedings, it will at the same time order the detailed assessment of those costs. Parts 4 and 5 of the Regulations, CPR Part 47 and Section 49A of the Costs Practice Direction apply to a detailed assessment pursuant to such an order.

### Registers

3K-18 **7C.** There will be kept in the Central Office of the Senior Courts at the Royal Courts of Justice, under the direction of the Senior Master, a register of external orders which the High Court has ordered to be registered.

*Section III—Applications under Part 8 of the Act in respect of Civil Recovery Investigations and Detained Cash Investigations*

### How to apply for an order or warrant

3K-19 **8.1** An application for an order or warrant under Part 8 of the Act in connection with a civil recovery investigation or (where applicable) a detained cash investigation must be made—

(1) to a High Court judge;

(2) by filing an application notice.

**8.2** The application may be made without notice.

### Confidentiality of court documents

3K-20 **9.1** CPR rules 5.4, 5.4B and 5.4C do not apply to an application under Part 8 of the Act, and paragraphs 9.2 and 9.3 below have effect in its place.

**9.2** When an application is issued, the court file will be marked 'Not for disclosure' and, unless a High Court judge grants permission, the court records relating to the application (including the application notice, documents filed in support, and any order or warrant that is made) will not be made available by the court for any person to inspect or copy, either before or after the hearing of the application.

**9.3** An application for permission under paragraph 9.2 must be made on notice to the appropriate officer in accordance with CPR Part 23.

(CPR rule 23.7(1) requires a copy of the application notice to be served as soon as practicable after it is filed, and in any event at least 3 days before the court is to deal with the application.)

### Application notice and evidence

3K-21 **10.1** The application must be supported by written evidence, which must be filed with the application notice.

**10.2** The evidence must set out all the matters on which the appropriate officer relies in support of the application, including any matters required to be stated by the relevant sections of the Act, and all material facts of which the court should be made aware.

**10.3** There must also be filed with the application notice a draft of the order sought. This should if possible also be supplied to the court on disk in a form compatible with the word processing software used by the court.

***Paragraph numbers marked with a "+" can be found online and on CD.***

### Hearing of the application

**11.1** The application will be heard and determined in private, unless the judge hearing it directs otherwise. **3K-22**

### Variation or discharge of order or warrant

**12.1** An application to vary or discharge an order or warrant may be made by— **3K-23**

(1) the appropriate officer; or

(2) any person affected by the order or warrant.

**12.2** An application under paragraph 12.1 to stop an order or warrant from being executed must be made immediately upon it being served.

**12.3** A person applying to vary or discharge a warrant must first inform the appropriate officer that he is making the application.

**12.4** The application should be made to the judge who made the order or issued the warrant or, if he is not available, to another High Court judge.

*Section IV—Further Provisions About Specific Applications Under Part 8 Of The Act*

### Production order

**13.1** The application notice must name as a respondent the person believed to be in possession or control of the material in relation to which a production order is sought. **3K-24**

**13.2** The application notice must specify—

(1) whether the application is for an order under paragraph (a) or (b) of section 345(4) of the Act;

(2) the material, or description of material, in relation to which the order is sought; and

(3) the person who is believed to be in possession or control of the material.

**13.3** An application under section 347 of the Act for an order to grant entry may be made either—

(1) together with an application for a production order; or

(2) by separate application, after a production order has been made.

**13.4** An application notice for an order to grant entry must—

(1) specify the premises in relation to which the order is sought; and

(2) be supported by written evidence explaining why the order is needed.

**13.5** A production order, or an order to grant entry, must contain a statement of the right of any person affected by the order to apply to vary or discharge the order.

### Search and seizure warrant

**14.1** The application notice should name as the respondent the occupier of the premises to be subject to the warrant, if known. **3K-25**

**14.2** The evidence in support of the application must state—

*Paragraph numbers marked with a "+" can be found online and on CD.*

(1) the matters relied on by the appropriate officer to show that one of the requirements in section 352(6) of the Act for the issue of a warrant is satisfied;

(2) details of the premises to be subject to the warrant, and of the possible occupier or occupiers of those premises;

(3) the name and position of the member of the staff of the appropriate officer who it is intended will execute the warrant.

**14.3** There must be filed with the application notice drafts of—

(1) the warrant; and

(2) a written undertaking by the person who is to execute the warrant to comply with paragraph 13.8 of this practice direction.

**14.4** A search and seizure warrant must—

(1) specify the statutory power under which it is issued and, unless the court orders otherwise, give an indication of the nature of the investigation in respect of which it is issued;

(2) state the address or other identification of the premises to be subject to the warrant;

(3) state the name of the member of the staff of the appropriate officer who is authorised to execute the warrant;

(4) set out the action which the warrant authorises the person executing it to take under the relevant sections of the Act;

(5) give the date on which the warrant is issued;

(6) include a statement that the warrant continues in force until the end of the period of one month beginning with the day on which it is issued;

(7) contain a statement of the right of any person affected by the order to apply to discharge or vary the order.

**14.5** An example of a search and seizure warrant is annexed to this practice direction. This example may be modified as appropriate in any particular case.

**14.6** CPR rule 40.2 applies to a search and seizure warrant.

(Rule 40.2 requires every judgment or order to state the name and judicial title of the person making it, to bear the date on which it is given or made, and to be sealed by the court.)

**14.7** Upon the issue of a warrant the court will provide to the appropriate officer—

(1) the sealed warrant; and

(2) a copy of it for service on the occupier or person in charge of the premises subject to the warrant.

**14.8** A person attending premises to execute a warrant must, if the premises are occupied produce the warrant on arrival at the premises, and as soon as possible thereafter personally serve a copy of the warrant and an explanatory notice on the occupier or the person appearing to him to be in charge of the premises.

**14.9** The person executing the warrant must also comply with any order which the court may make for service of any other documents relating to the application.

### Disclosure order

**15.1** The application notice should normally name as respondents the persons on whom the appropriate officer intends to serve notices under the disclosure order sought. **3K-26**

**15.2** A disclosure order must—

(1) give an indication of the nature of the investigation for the purposes of which the order is made;

(2) set out the action which the order authorises the appropriate officer to take in accordance with section 357(4) of the Act;

(3) contain a statement of—

(a) the offences relating to disclosure orders under section 359 of the Act; and

(b) the right of any person affected by the order to apply to discharge or vary the order.

**15.3** Where, pursuant to a disclosure order, the appropriate officer gives to any person a notice under section 357(4) of the Act, he must also at the same time serve on that person a copy of the disclosure order.

### Customer information order

**16.1** The application notice should normally (unless it is impracticable to do so because they are too numerous) name as respondents the financial institution or institutions to which it is proposed that an order should apply. **3K-27**

**16.2** A customer information order must—

(1) specify the financial institution, or description of financial institutions, to which it applies;

(2) state the name of the person in relation to whom customer information is to be given, and any other details to identify that person;

(3) contain a statement of—

(a) the offences relating to disclosure orders under section 366 of the Act; and

(b) the right of any person affected by the order to apply to discharge or vary the order.

**16.3** Where, pursuant to a customer information order, the appropriate officer gives to a financial institution a notice to provide customer information, he must also at the same time serve a copy of the order on that institution.

### Account monitoring order

**17.1** The application notice must name as a respondent the financial institution against which an account monitoring order is sought. **3K-28**

**17.2** The application notice must—

(1) state the matters required by section 370(2) and (3) of the Act; and

(2) give details of—

(a) the person whose account or accounts the application relates to;

(b) each account or description of accounts in relation to which the order is sought, including if known the number of each account and the branch at which it is held;

(c) the information sought about the account or accounts;

(d) the period for which the order is sought;

(e) the manner in which, and the frequency with which, it is proposed that the financial institution should provide account information during that period.

**17.3** An account monitoring order must contain a statement of the right of any person affected by the order to apply to vary or discharge the order.

# 3L DEVOLUTION ISSUES

For "Practice Direction—Devolution Issues" see paragraphs 3L–2+ to 3L–24+ on White Book on Westlaw UK or the Civil Procedure CD. **3L–1**

*Paragraph numbers marked with a "+" can be found online and on CD.*



DEVOLUTION

# SECTION 4

## SUPREME COURT OF THE UNITED KINGDOM AND JUDICIAL COMMITTEE OF THE PRIVY COUNCIL

# 4A SUPREME COURT OF THE UNITED KINGDOM APPEALS



**Editorial introduction**

The Constitutional Reform Act 2005 (c.4) received the Royal Assent in March 2005. (For text of this statute, see para.9A–962 below.) Provisions in Pt 3 of the Act (ss.23 to 53) dealing with the establishment of the Supreme Court of the United Kingdom came into effect on October 1, 2009. 4A–0.1

**Supreme Court Rules**

Section 45 of the 2005 Act gives the President of the Supreme Court power to make rules (to be known as Supreme Court Rules) governing the practice and procedure to be followed in the Court. Before making rules the President must consult the Lord Chancellor and the professional bodies referred to in s.45(4)). For the purpose of enabling rules to be enacted before the commencement date, this section was modified by the Constitutional Reform Act 2005 (Temporary Modifications) Order 2006 (SI 2006/227) to give the senior Law Lord power to make rules in the first instance. The procedure for the enactment in statutory instrument of rules made by the President is set out in s.45. The procedure for bringing Supreme Court Rules into effect differs from that which applies to the bringing into effect of Civil Procedure Rules (see Sect.12 para.12–3 below). The Lord Chancellor has no power to disallow or alter rules submitted to him by the President. The Supreme Court Rules 2009 (SI 2009/1603) were made by the senior Law Lord in June 2009 and the Lord Chancellor directed that they should come into effect on October 1, 2009. For transitional arrangements, see r.55. See further, commentary following r.2 below. 4A–0.2

**Practice Directions and Forms**

Practice directions are issued by the President of the Court (initially by the senior Law Lord) to supplement the Rules (see commentary following r.3 below) and to prescribe Forms (see r.4). 4A–0.3

The practice directions issued are as follows (see para.4A–56 et seq. below):

Practice Direction 1 (General Note and Jurisdiction)
Practice Direction 2 (The Registry of the Supreme Court)
Practice Direction 3 (Applications for Permission to Appeal)
Practice Direction 4 (Notice of Appeal)
Practice Direction 5 (Papers for the Appeal Hearing)
Practice Direction 6 (The Appeal Hearing)
Practice Direction 7 (Applications, Documents, Forms and Orders)
Practice Direction 8 (Miscellaneous Matters)
Practice Direction 9 (The Human Rights Act 1998)
Practice Direction 10 (Devolution Jurisdiction)
Practice Direction 11 (The European Court of Justice)
Practice Direction 12 (Criminal Proceedings)
Practice Direction 13 (Costs)
Practice Direction 14 (Filing Documents in the Registry of the Supreme Court by electronic means)

Practice Directions 2 to 11 and 13 and 14 govern civil proceedings. Practice Direction 12 is dedicated to criminal proceedings; Practice Directions 2 to 11 apply to criminal proceedings, subject to any modifications or additional provisions made by Practice Direction 12.

The Practice Directions are, in large part, based on the Directions and Standing Orders that formerly regulated judicial proceedings in the House of Lords. (Sometimes this provenance is revealed by the fact that terminology used follows those sources and not modern terminology used in the Rules). Generally the Practice Directions read rather more like a Court Guide than traditional practice directions. The great proportion of the material in them consists of re-statements of, or paraphrases of, provisions found in the Rules or in primary legislation governing the jurisdiction of the Court (but not infrequently the exact provision repeated is not acknowledged).

The prescribed Forms are published in Annex 1 to Practice Direction 7 (Applications, Documents, Forms and Orders) and are as follows:

Form 1 (Application for permission/notice of appeal);
Form 2 (Application form);
Form 3 (Notice of objection/acknowledgment by respondent).

For convenience these Forms are set out at paras 4A–197 to 4A–199 below.

**Jurisdiction of the Court**

4A–0.4 In para.1.1.1 of Practice Direction 1 it is explained that the jurisdiction of the Court corresponds to that formerly exercised by the House of Lords in its judicial capacity under the Appellate Jurisdiction Acts 1876 and 1888 (which are repealed) together with devolution matters under the Scotland Act 1998, the Northern Ireland Act 1998 and the Government of Wales Act 2006, which are transferred to the Supreme Court from the Judicial Committee of the Privy Council. The jurisdiction of the Supreme Court is defined by s.40 of, and Sch.9 to, the 2005 Act. By s.40(5) of the 2005 Act the Court has power to determine any question necessary to be determined for the purposes of doing justice in an appeal to it under any enactment (in effect, re-enacting s.4 of the 1876 Act as interpreted). The Court's jurisdiction is fully explained in Section 2 of Practice Direction 1.

## Supreme Court Rules 2009

4A–0 (S.I. 2009 No. 1603)

ARRANGEMENT OF RULES

PART 1

INTERPRETATION AND SCOPE



***Paragraph numbers marked with a "+" can be found online and on CD.***

## PART 1

## INTERPRETATION AND SCOPE

### Citation and commencement

**1. These Rules may be cited as the Supreme Court Rules 2009 and shall come into force on 1st October 2009.** 4A–1

*Paragraph numbers marked with a "+" can be found online and on CD.*

### Effect of rule

4A–1.1 These Rules came into effect on a date directed by the Lord Chancellor as provided by s.45 of the 2005 Act. The legislation establishing the Supreme Court came into effect on the same date. See further, Editorial introduction para.4A–0.2above.

The Rules apply, with any necessary modifications, to appeals which were proceeding, and petitions for leave which were lodged, in the House of Lords before the commencement date; see r.55 (Transitional arrangements).

### Scope and objective

4A–2 **2.—(1) These Rules apply to civil and criminal appeals to the Court and to appeals and references under the Court's devolution jurisdiction.**

**(2) The overriding objective of these Rules is to secure that the Court is accessible, fair and efficient.**

**(3) The Court must interpret and apply these Rules with a view to securing that the Court is accessible, fair and efficient and that unnecessary disputes over procedural matters are discouraged.**

### Effect of rule

4A–2.1 This rule reflects provisions in the 2005 Act.

*Scope*—The Rules govern the practice and procedure to be followed by the Court when exercising its jurisdiction (s.45(1) of the 2005 Act). The jurisdiction of the Court corresponds to that of the House of Lords in its judicial capacity, together with devolution matters. The Court's jurisdiction is summarised in Section 2 of Practice Direction 1. "Devolution jurisdiction" is defined in r.3(2). If any procedural question arises which is not dealt with by these Rules, the Court or the Registrar may adopt any procedure that is consistent with the overriding objective, the 2005 Act and these Rules (r.9(7)).

*Objective*—In the 2005 Act, subs.(3) of s.45 (Making of rules) states that the President of the Supreme Court must exercise the power to make Supreme Court Rules with a view to securing that (a) the Court is accessible, fair and efficient, and (b) the rules are both simple and simply expressed. This provision is reflected in para.(2) ("overriding objective") and in para.(3) of r.1. Apart from r.9(7) there is no express reference to the overriding objective in the Rules and none of operational significance in any of the Practice Directions.

### Interpretation

4A–3 **3.—(1) In these Rules—**

**"the Act" means the Constitutional Reform Act 2005;**

**"the Court" means the Supreme Court of the United Kingdom;**

**"Justice" means a judge of the Court and includes its President and Deputy President;**

**"the Registrar" means the Registrar of the Court;**

**"the Registry" means the Registry of the Court.**

**(2) In these Rules except where the context otherwise requires—**

**"appellant" means a person who files an application for permission to appeal or who files a notice of appeal;**

**"business day" means any day other than a Saturday, Sunday, Christmas Day, Good Friday or a bank holiday under the Banking and Financial Dealings Act 1971 [1], in England and Wales;**

**"certificate of service" means a certificate given under rule 6;**

[1] 1971 c.80.

"counsel" includes any person with the right to be heard as an advocate at a full hearing before the Court;

"court below" means the court from which an appeal (or application for permission to appeal) is made to the Court;

"court officer" means the Registrar or a member of the court staff;

"devolution jurisdiction" means the jurisdiction transferred to the Court by section 40 of, and Schedule 9 to, the Act;

"electronic means" means CD ROMs, memory sticks, email, fax or other means of electronic communication of the contents of documents;

"filing" means filing in the Registry in accordance with rule 7 and related expressions have corresponding meanings;

"form" and the "appropriate form" have the meanings given by rule 4;

"panel of Justices" means a panel of at least three Justices;

"party" means an appellant, a respondent and a person who has been given permission to intervene under rule 26;

"the relevant officer" means—

(a) in relation to proceedings in England and Wales, the Attorney General and, in relation to proceedings that particularly affect Wales, the Counsel General to the Welsh Assembly Government,

(b) in relation to proceedings in Scotland, the Advocate General for Scotland and the Lord Advocate; and

(c) in relation to proceedings in Northern Ireland, the Advocate General for Northern Ireland and (when section 22 of the Justice (Northern Ireland) Act 2002 comes into force [1]) the Attorney General for Northern Ireland;

"requisite number of copies" means the number of copies which are to be provided under the relevant practice direction or as directed by the Court;

"respondent" includes a respondent to an application for permission to appeal and means—

(a) a person other than the appellant who was a party to the proceedings in the court below and who is affected by the appeal; and

(b) a person who is permitted by the Court to be a party to the appeal;

"service" and related expressions have the meanings given by rule 6;

"solicitor" includes any person authorised to provide legal services other than as counsel in connection with proceedings before the Court.

(3) References in these Rules to a practice direction means a practice direction issued by the President of the Court.

[1] 2002 c. 26.

**(4) References in these Rules or in any form to a party's signing, filing or serving any document or taking any other procedural step include the signature, filing or service of that document or the taking of such other procedural step by the party's solicitor.**

**(5) Where any of these Rules or any practice direction requires a document to be signed, that requirement shall be satisfied if the signature is printed by computer or other mechanical means.**

**(6) Where these Rules require or permit the Court to perform an act of a formal or administrative character, that act may be performed by a court officer.**

### Effect of rule

**4A–3.1** The expressions referred to in r.3(1) are not subject to qualification. None of the expressions defined in the 2005 Act is of particular use in interpreting the Rules. Insofar as they do assist, Interpretation Act 1978 s.11 applies. The Rules must be interpreted by the Court with a view to securing the objective stated in r.2(3).

*"the Court"*—For obvious reasons, throughout the Rules there are many references to "the Court", but in some rules there are references to "the Supreme Court" (r.29). Throughout the practice directions the expression "Supreme Court" is more commonly used than "Court".

*"Justice"*— Section 40(6) of the 2005 Act states that the judges other than the President and Deputy President are to be styled "Justices of the Supreme Court". Within the Rules, "Justice" includes the President and the Deputy President (r.3(2)).

*"Registrar" and "Registry"*—The Registrar is an officer appointed by the President of the Court (s.49). For opening times of the Registry and postal and email addresses and telephone numbers, see Practice Direction 2 (The Registry of the Supreme Court). In the Rules, "court officer" means the Registrar or a member of the court staff (r.3(2)).

*Interpretation Act 1978*—Generally this Act applies to subordinate legislation and would therefore apply to the Rules.

### Interpretation of particular terms (r.3(2))

**4A–3.2** The terms and expressions listed in r.3(2) apply except where the context otherwise requires. The ones likely to be of most use in day-to-day practice are those relevant to the service and filing of Forms and documents. Expressions related to "filing" (which means filing in the Registry) would include "lodge" (r.54), and probably "submit" (r.48(1) and "provide" (r.7 and r.22). (For methods of filing, see r.7.) Methods of service are listed in r.6 and it is provided that "service and related expressions have the meanings given by rule 6". Related expressions would include submitting (r.22.2) and giving notice (rr.38(1), 40(1) and 49(4)). It may be noted that the expression "business day", which is referred to in r.6 (Service) and r.7 (Filing), is defined in accordance with legislation applicable in England and Wales (cf. CPR r.6.2). Throughout the practice directions there are numerous references to the filing and service of Forms and documents (most of them appearing where particular rules are restated or paraphrased, rather than where points of practice not expressly dealt with in the Rules are stipulated or explained).

### Practice Directions (r.3(3))

**4A–3.3** Practice directions are issued by the President of the Court (initially by the senior Law Lord) to supplement the Rules (1) to provide general guidance and assistance to parties and their legal representatives, and (2) to provide for the Forms (see r.4) to be used (Practice Direction 1 para.1.1.3).

### Procedural step by the party's solicitor (r.3(4))

**4A–3.4** "Solicitor" includes any person authorised to provide legal services other than as counsel in connection with proceedings before the Court. (r.3(2)). In certain circumstances, the signature of a party's counsel may be required; see Practice Direction 4 (Notice of Appeal) para.4.2.2.

### Signature of document by mechanical means (r.3(5))

**4A–3.5** This rule accords with CPR r.5.3 (see Vol.1, para.5.3). Rule 5.3 is helpfully supplemented by Practice Direction (Court Documents) para.1 (see Vol.1 para.5PD.1), but no comparable provision appears in the practice directions supplementing the SCR.

**Act of a formal or administrative character (r.3(6))**

This rule accords with CPR r.2.5(1) (see Vol.1, para.2.5.3). In terms it does not include acts required to be performed by practice directions. **4A–3.6**

## Forms

**4.—(1) In these Rules, a form means a form set out in a practice direction and a reference to the "appropriate form" means the form provided by the relevant practice direction for any particular case.** **4A–4**

**(2) The forms shall be used in the cases to which they apply, and in the circumstances for which they are provided by the relevant practice direction, but a form may be varied by the Court or a party if the variation is required by the circumstances of a particular case.**

**Effect of rule**

The Forms to be used in conjunction with the Rules are not prescribed by the Rules but are prescribed by practice direction. The Rules and the practice directions refer to a wide variety of documents other than the prescribed Forms. All documents placed before the Court must comply with the strictures stated in Practice Direction 5 (Papers for the Appeal Hearing) para.5.1.2. (Paragraphs 5.1.1 and 5.1.2 are repeated in Practice Direction 6 (The Appeal Hearing) paras 6.1.1 and 6.1.2.) Paragraph 7.2.1 of Practice Direction 7 (Applications, Documents, Forms and Orders) states that all formal documents for the Court must be produced on A4 paper, securely bound on the left, using both sides of the paper and warns that documents which are not legible or which are not produced in the authorised form or which are unsatisfactory for some other similar reason will not be accepted by the Registry. (Provisions to similar effect are found elsewhere in the practice directions; notably in Practice Direction 3 (Applications for Permission to Appeal) para.3.1.3, and Practice Direction (Notices of Appeal) para.4.2.1.) The Registrar may refuse to accept a document unless the relevant fee has been paid (r.45). **4A–4.1**

*Forms*—In para.1.1.5 of Practice Direction 1, r.4 is summarised and it is explained that three forms are set out in Annex 1 to Practice Direction 7 (Applications, Documents, Forms and Orders). They are: Form 1 (Application for permission/ notice of appeal), Form 2 (Application form), Form 3 (Notice of objection/acknowledgement by respondent) (see paras 4A–197 to 4A–199 below). As their titles suggest, Forms 1 and 3 may be used for more than one purpose. Form 2 is to be used in a variety of circumstances.

It is expressly provided that parties may consult the Registry at any stage of preparation of an application for permission to appeal or of a notice of appeal, and may submit applications and notices in draft for approval (Practice Direction 3 (Applications for Permission to Appeal) para.3.1.2, Practice Direction 4 (Notices of Appeal) para.4.2.1). Insofar as r.4(2) permits the variation of any Form by the Court or a party if the variation is required by the particular circumstances of the case it follows CPR r.4(2).

*Documents*—Throughout the Rules and practice directions there are references to various documents that may have to be produced during the appeal process and for which none of the prescribed Forms is appropriate. The principal documents falling into this category are: the statement of facts and issues, the appendix, the appellant's and respondent's cases, the core volumes and authorities volumes. to the Court for appeal hearings. Parties may if they wish follow the former practice in House of Lords appeals but are not required to do so. Where parties are in any doubt as to how documents should be presented they should consult the Registrar and discuss the practice which should be adopted. However, it should be noted that, despite the apparent

***Paragraph numbers marked with a "+" can be found online and on CD.***

generosity of what is said in paras 5.1.1 and 6.1.1, the practice directions contain some provisions applicable to the manner in which documents are presented to the Court which are quite prescriptive.

### Time limits

4A-5 **5.—(1) The Court may extend or shorten any time limit set by these Rules or any relevant practice direction (unless to do so would be contrary to any enactment).**

**(2) The Court may exercise these powers either on an application by one or more parties or without an application being made.**

**(3) The Registrar must notify the parties when a time limit is varied under this rule.**

**(4) An application for an extension of time may be granted after the time limit has expired.**

**(5) Where a party to a proposed appeal has applied for public funding and the Registrar is informed of the application, the time limits in rules 11 and 19 shall be extended until 28 days after the final determination of the application for public funding.**

**(6) When the period specified—**

**(a) by these Rules or a practice direction, or**

**(b) by any judgment or court order,**

**for doing any act at the Registry ends on a day on which the Registry is closed, that act shall be in time if done on the next day on which the Registry is open.**

#### Effect of rule

4A-5.1 The effects of this rule and provisions referred to in it are explained in Practice Direction 2 (The Registry of the Supreme Court) at para.2.1.12 et seq. The Registry may accept an application for permission to appeal or a notice of appeal which is out of time if the application sets out the reason(s) why it was not filed within the time limit and it is in order in all other respects (*ibid.* para.2.1.13). The Registrar may reject an application for permission to appeal solely on the ground that it is out of time (*ibid.* para.2.1.15).

In order to achieve indicative timetables for the expedited hearing of proceedings, the Court will set aside or vary the time limits and practice directions that normally apply to applications and appeals (see further Practice Direction 3 (Applications for Permission to Appeal) para.3.4.4 et seq.).

A decision made by the Court in exercise of powers conferred by r.5 is a procedural decision within r.9 and, generally, may be made by a single justice or the Registrar without an oral hearing.

#### Determination of public funding application (r.5(5))

4A-5.2 The Rule time limits automatically extended in the circumstances referred to in r.5(5) are for the filing of an application for permission to appeal (r.11) and for filing of a notice of appeal where permission is not required (r.19). The giving of notification to the Registrar of the public funding application is a pre-condition. Notification must be given far enough before the expiry of the original time limits to ensure that the appeal is not dismissed as being out of time; a copy of the order appealed from must be submitted by the applicant with the notification (Practice Direction 8 (Miscellaneous Matters) para.8.12.4). Note also *ibid.* para.8.12.5 (Effect of application by respondent for public funding/legal aid), and para.8.12.6 (Issue of public funding/legal aid certificate). Where r.5(5) takes effect, time is extended until 28 days after the determination of the application for public funding, including any appeals against a refusal of funding (*ibid.* para.8.12.3).

An appellant, a respondent and a person who has been given permission to

***Paragraph numbers marked with a "+" can be found online and on CD.***

intervene under r.26 may be "a party to a proposed appeal", unless the context otherwise requires (r.3(2)).

### Period for doing any act at the Registry (r.5(6))

For opening times of the Registry, see Practice Direction 2 (The Registry of the Supreme Court) para.2.1.3. **4A–5.3**

### Time limit set by Rules

These are set, not by weeks or months, but by number of days (except in r.48(1)). Principal time limits set by Rules for the taking of procedural steps after particular events in civil proceedings include: r.9(5) (14 days for filing application for review of Registrar's decision); r.11(1) (28 days for filing of application for permission to appeal); r.13(1) (14 days for respondent's objection to application for permission to appeal); r.14(2) (7 days for filing of further documents in support of application for permission to appeal); r.18(1)(c) (14 days for filing notice of intention to proceed with appeal); r.19(2) (42 days for filing notice of appeal where permission not required); r.21(1) (14 days for filing respondent's notice); r.22(1) (112 days for filing documents for appeal hearing); r.23 (filing of core volumes 14 days before date fixed for hearing); r.25(4) (42 days for filing notice of cross-appeal); r.30(4) (7 days for filing notice of objection to procedural application); r.39(2) (21 days for disposal of documents application). Time limits are imposed for various purposes in Rule provisions dealing with the making of orders for costs; see, r.48(1) (submission of claim for costs "within three months", r.48(4) and (5) (claim for costs), r.49(7) (assessment of costs), r.53(1) (appeal from assessment of costs). Other provisions impose time limits on actions to be taken by the Court or the Registrar, e.g. r.16(2) (invitation to parties to file written submissions as to grant of permission to appeal on terms), r.40(1) (notice to Crown where incompatibility issue arising), or particular parties, e.g. r.43(3) (notice of intention to appeal by Comptroller). **4A–5.4**

Prominent examples of time limits for the making of applications for permission to appeal being fixed, not by Rules, but by other enactments, include cases involving civil contempt of court (Administration of Justice Act 1960 s.2), and "leapfrog" appeals from the High Court (Administration of Justice Act 1969 s.13). See further, r.11 (Filing an application).

Provisions within the Rules and in other enactments affecting time limits for applying for permission to appeal and applications to extend such limits in criminal proceedings are explained in Practice Direction 12 (Criminal Proceedings) para.12.3. No extension may be granted in respect of an application for permission to appeal made under the Extradition Act 2003 ss.32 and 114.

### Time limit set by relevant practice direction

Throughout the practice directions, the many provisions in the Rules fixing time limits are restated (sometimes more than once). (In some instances, the Rule provenance of the time limit restated is not acknowledged.) Time limits fixed by practice direction provisions, and not by Rules (or any other enactment), are rare. **4A–5.5**

## Service

**6.—(1) A document may be served by any of the following methods—** **4A–6**

**(a) personal service;**

**(b) first class post (or an alternative service which provides for delivery on the next working day);**

**(c) (with the consent of the party to be served) through a document exchange;**

**(d) (with the consent of the party to be served or at the direction of the Registrar) by electronic means in accordance with the relevant practice direction.**

**(2) Where the address of the person on whom a document is to**

*Paragraph numbers marked with a "+" can be found online and on CD.*



SUPREME COURT

**be served is unknown, the Registrar may direct that service is effected by an alternative method of service.**

**(3) A document served by first-class post or through a document exchange will be taken to have been served on the second day after it was posted or left at the document exchange, as the case may be (not including days which are not business days).**

**(4) A certificate of service must give details of the persons served, the method of service used and must state the date on which the document was served personally, posted, delivered to the document exchange or sent electronically, as the case may be.**

#### Effect of rule

**4A-6.1** A number of provisions in the Rules stipulate that particular documents should be served by one party on another. Those relating to formal documents include: r.12 (application for permission to appeal), r.13(2) (respondent's notice of objection), r.15(2) (intervener's submissions), r.18(2) (re-sealed application for permission to appeal), r.20(1) (notice of appeal), r.21(2) (respondent's notice), r.25(4)(a) (notice of cross-appeal), r.30(3) (procedural application), r.30(4) (notice of objection to procedural application), r.48(3) (service of claim for costs on paying party), r.48(4) (service of points of dispute on receiving party), and r.48(5) (service of receiving party's response to points of dispute on paying party).

Rule 6 is not concerned with the questions as to which documents should be served upon whom and when, but with the "method" of service permitted. The methods stated are not exhaustive. (The methods of service listed in r.6(1) accord with the methods of filing listed in r.7(1).)

References in the Rules to a party's serving any document include service of that document by the party's solicitor (r.3(4)).

In r.3(2) it is provided that "service and related expressions have the meanings given by rule 6". Related expressions would include submitting (r.22.2) and giving notice (rr.38(1), 40(1) and 49(4)). Cf., r.15(4)(b) ("appellant must notify"); r.48(2) (receiving party "must supply").

In r.6(1)(b) "alternative service" has same meaning as "other service" in CPR r.6.3(1)(b). For explanation, see Vol.1, para.6.3.3. Rule 6(1)(b) refers to next working day (not next "business day").

#### Consent of party to be served (r.6(1))

**4A-6.2** Paragraph 2.1.23 of Practice Direction 2 (The Registry of the Supreme Court) states that a party or his solicitor will be taken to have consented to a particular method of service if, for example, their writing paper includes a fax number or a numbered box at a document exchange unless they have indicated in writing that they are not willing to accept service by that particular method. (Apart from that paragraph there is no practice direction provision dealing with service by electronic means inter partes.) The Registrar may direct that a document be served by electronic means. For meaning of "electronic means" see r.3(2) and commentary following r.7.

#### Time limits (r.6(3))

**4A-6.3** Some time limits imposed by provisions in the Rules for the taking of certain procedural steps are calculated from the date on which a formal document was served (e.g. rr.13(1), 21(1), 30(4)). For this reason (and others) it is important that the date of service should not be a matter for doubt. In cases where the method of service adopted is by first-class post or by a document exchange, r.6(3) fixes the date of service (which may not accord with the actual date upon which the document was received). It is important to note that, in the Rules, "business day", is defined in accordance with legislation applicable in England and Wales, and not with that applicable in other constituent parts of the United Kingdom (r.3(2)).

#### Certificate of service (r.6(4))

**4A-6.4** Provisions in the Rules stipulating that particular documents should be served by one party on another add the requirement that, when the document is filed, a certifi-

*Paragraph numbers marked with a "+" can be found online and on CD.*

cate of service (complying with r.6(4)) must be filed with it. The certificate must be included either in the original document and signed or a separate certificate of service must be provided (Practice Direction 2 (The Registry of the Supreme Court) para.2.1.24).

**Service before filing**

Documents such as applications for permission to appeal (r.12), notices of appeal (r.20), and interveners' applications (r.15) must be served on the persons referred to in the rules applicable, in accordance with r.6 or with any relevant statutory provisions (e.g. provisions in the Companies Acts 1985 and Companies Act 2006), before they are filed (see Practice Direction 2 (The Registry of the Supreme Court) para.2.1.23). Procedural applications (and objections thereto) must be served on the persons referred to in r.30 before filing. The Registry will not issue an application for permission to appeal or other document unless (amongst other things) it has been properly served on the respondents (*ibid.* para.2.1.11). **4A–6.5**

## Filing

**7.—(1) A document may be filed by any of the following methods—** **4A–7**

**(a) personal delivery;**

**(b) first class post (or an alternative service which provides for delivery on the next working day);**

**(c) through a document exchange;**

**(d) (with the consent of the Registrar) by electronic means in accordance with the relevant practice direction.**

**(2) A document filed by first-class post or through a document exchange will be taken to have been filed on the second day after it was posted or left at the document exchange, as the case may be (not including days which are not business days).**

**(3) Except with the consent of the Registrar, the contents of documents—**

**(a) filed in hard copy must also be provided to the Registry by electronic means, and**

**(b) filed by electronic means must also be provided to the Registry in hard copy,**

**in accordance with the relevant practice direction.**

**(4) A court officer must seal the following documents when they are filed—**

**(a) an application for permission to appeal,**

**(b) a notice of objection or acknowledgement by the respondent,**

**(c) a notice of appeal,**

**(d) an application form,**

**and may place the seal on the document by hand or by printing a facsimile of the seal on the document whether electronically or otherwise.**

**(5) A document purporting to bear the Court's seal shall be admissible in evidence without further proof.**

**Effect of rule**

A number of provisions in the Rules stipulate that particular documents should be filed. Except where the context otherwise requires, "filing" means filing in the Registry in accordance with r.7, and "related expressions" have corresponding meanings (r.3(2)). **4A–7.1**

*Paragraph numbers marked with a "+" can be found online and on CD.*



SUPREME COURT

Rule 7 is not concerned with questions as to which documents should be filed and when, or the form they should be in, but with the "method" of filing permitted. Paragraph (1) of r.7 is similar to para.(1) of r.6. Reference should be made to the commentary following r.6 accordingly.

In para.2.1.7 et seq. of Practice Direction 2 (The Registry of the Supreme Court) the effects of r.7 are re-stated and attention is drawn to the Registrar's power to refuse to accept a document under r.8(3) which does not comply with any provision in the Rules or any relevant practice direction.

In a number of instances, a fee is payable upon the filing of a document; see Annex 2 of Practice Direction 7 (Applications, Documents, Forms and Orders). The Registrar may refuse to accept a document (or refuse to allow a party to take any step) unless the relevant fee is paid (r.45).

#### Time limits (r.7(2))

4A–7.2 Provisions in the Rules (and in practice directions) requiring formal documents and other documents to be filed usually further require that they be filed within a particular time; e.g. r.11(1) (application for permission to appeal), r.16(2) (invited written submissions), r.18(1) (intention to proceed), r.14(2) (further documents in support of application), r.23 (core volumes).

Some time limits imposed by provisions in the Rules for the taking of certain procedural steps are calculated from the date on which a document was filed; e.g. r.22(1) (Documents for appeal hearing), r.25(4)(a) (Cross-appeal), r.26(1) (Intervention). Rule 7(2) is a deeming provision (similar to r.6(3)) having the effect of fixing the filing date in the circumstances to which it applied. See further commentary on r.6(3) above. Where a document is filed by electronic means the time and date of its receipt is fixed in accordance with para.14.4 of Practice Direction 14 (Filing Documents in the Registry of the Supreme or by electronic means).

#### Filing by electronic means (r.7.5(3))

4A–7.3 Except where the context otherwise requires, in the Rules "electronic means" means CD-ROMs, memory sticks, email, fax or other means of electronic communication of the contents of documents. The relevant practice direction referred to in r.7(1)(d) and r.7(2) is Practice Direction 14 (Filing Documents in the Registry of the Supreme Court by electronic means).

#### Sealing of filed documents (r.7(4))

4A–7.4 In terms, para.(4) of r.7 is similar to CPR r.2.6. For commentary on r.2.6, see Vol.1, para.2.6.1 et seq.

#### Sealed documents as evidence (r.7(5))

4A–7.5 Section 55(2) of the 2005 Act states that every document purporting to be sealed with the official seal of the Supreme Court is to be received in evidence in all parts of the United Kingdom without further proof. See further, "Sealed documents as evidence" Vol.1, para.2.6.3.

### Non-compliance with these Rules

4A–8 **8.—(1) Any failure by a party to comply with these Rules or any relevant practice direction shall not have the effect of making the proceedings invalid.**

**(2) Where any provision in these Rules or any relevant practice direction is not complied with, the Court may give whatever directions appear appropriate, having regard to the seriousness of the non-compliance and generally to the circumstances of the case.**

**(3) In particular, the Registrar may refuse to accept any document which does not comply with any provision in these Rules or any relevant practice direction and may give whatever directions appear appropriate.**

*Paragraph numbers marked with a "+" can be found online and on CD.*

**(4) Directions given under this rule may include the summary dismissal of an appeal or debarring a respondent from resisting an appeal.**

### Effect of rule

Paragraph (1) of r.8 demonstrates an abundance of caution. It has a similar effect to CPR r.3.10, the descendant of a rule introduced many years ago for the purpose of redressing the effects of an unfortunate line of authority that never applied to proceedings in the House of Lords (see Vol.1, para.3.10.1). **4A–8.1**

Paragraph (2) of r.8 is consistent with the statutory requirement that the Court's Rules should be "fair and efficient" (s.45(3) of the 2005 Act) and with the objective that unnecessary disputes over procedural matters (particularly those stimulated by excessive formalism) should be discouraged (r.1(3)).

Non-compliance with Rules and practice directions provisions is not to be encouraged. The Court's procedures have to be protected from abuse. The powers referred to in para.(3) of r.8 may have severe effects. Where an appellant is guilty of non-compliance, presumably the Court has power to stay the appeal.

Some rules have the effect of preventing a party from taking a procedural step to progress an appeal or from participating in a particular part of the appeal process without first having complied with certain conditions (e.g. r.13(3) and r.21(3)). In effect, such provisions contain their own sanctions.

In addition to the powers referred to in para.(3) of r.8, the Registrar has power under r.45 to refuse to accept a document for filing (or to refuse to allow a party to take any step) unless the relevant fee payable for filing a document is paid. The powers of the Registrar (including powers referred to in para.(3)) exercisable where an appellant has failed to comply with r.14(2) (filing of further documents in support of application for permission to appeal) are explained in para.3.2.3 of Practice Direction 3 (Applications for Permission to Appeal). Note also r.11(2)(c).

A decision made in exercise of the powers conferred by r.8 is a procedural decision within r.9 and, subject to r.9(2), may be made by a single justice or the Registrar without an oral hearing. Rule 9(2) states that any contested application for a direction under r.8(4) shall be referred to a panel of Justices who may hold an oral hearing.

## Procedural decisions

**9.—(1) Subject to paragraph (2), the powers of the Court under the following rules may be exercised by a single Justice or the Registrar without an oral hearing—** **4A–9**

**(a) rule 5 (time limits),**

**(b) rule 8 (non-compliance with Rules),**

**(c) rule 33 (change of interest),**

**(d) rule 34 (withdrawal of appeal),**

**(e) rule 35 (advocate to the Court and assessors),**

**(f) rule 36 (security for costs),**

**(g) rule 37 (stay of execution) and**

**(h) rule 41 (devolution jurisdiction).**

**(2) Any contested application—**

**(a) alleging contempt of the Court; or**

**(b) for a direction under rule 8 dismissing an appeal or debarring a respondent from resisting an appeal; or**

**(c) for security for costs,**

**shall be referred to a panel of Justices who shall, in a case of alleged contempt, and may, in any other case, hold an oral hearing.**

**(3) Where under these Rules any matter falls to be decided by a**

**single Justice, that Justice may, where it appears appropriate, direct an oral hearing or may refer the matter to a panel of Justices to be decided with or without an oral hearing.**

**(4) Where under these Rules any matter falls to be decided by the Registrar, the Registrar may—**

**(a) direct an oral hearing;**

**(b) refer the matter to a single Justice (and paragraphs (1) and (3) shall then apply);**

**(c) refer the matter to a panel of Justices to be decided with or without an oral hearing.**

**(5) A party may apply for a decision of the Registrar to be reviewed by a single Justice (in which case paragraphs (1) and (3) shall apply) and any application under this rule must be made in the appropriate form and be filed within 14 days of the Registrar's decision.**

**(6) Subject to rule 27, oral hearings on procedural matters must be heard in open court or in a place to which the public are admitted.**

**(7) If any procedural question arises which is not dealt with by these Rules, the Court or the Registrar may adopt any procedure that is consistent with the overriding objective, the Act and these Rules.**

### Effect of rule

4A–9.1 The principal effect of this rule is to allocate certain proceedings in which procedural decisions fall to be made and contested contempt proceedings for determination by the Registrar, a single Justice or a panel of Justices, and to indicate whether or not an oral hearing is required. Generally, procedural decisions are made in proceedings commenced by a procedural application as provided by r.30.

Paragraph (7) of r.9 stands alone and does not qualify other parts of the rule. It is an important provision, in effect enacting the inherent power of the Court to regulate its own processes. Though "procedural question" is not a term of art, its meaning is clear enough.

The terms of r.9 (excluding para.(7)) are re-stated in Section 3 of Practice Direction 1. The Registrar, when exercising powers under r.9(1), will normally make a decision without an oral hearing (*ibid.* para.1.3.5).

The appropriate form (r.9(5)) is Form 2. A fee is payable upon filing (Practice Direction 7 (Applications, Documents, Forms and Orders) Annex 2).

A panel of Justices (r.5(3) and r.5(4)) means a panel of at least three Justices (r.3(2)). The Registrar's jurisdiction does not extend to the contested applications referred to in r.9(2).

Rule 27 is concerned with oral hearings of appeals and not with oral hearings on procedural matters. The purpose of the reference to r.27 in r.9(6) would appear to be to make it clear that the Court, when holding an oral hearing under r.9, has the limiting powers referred to in r.27.

## PART 2

## APPLICATION FOR PERMISSION TO APPEAL

### Form of application

4A–10 **10.—(1) Every application to the Court for permission to appeal shall be made in the appropriate form.**

**(2) An application for permission to appeal must be made first to the court below, and an application may be made to the Supreme Court only after the court below has refused to grant permission to appeal.**

### Effect of rule

The provisions in Pt 2 (rr.10 to 17) apply to an application for permission to cross-appeal (r.25(3)). **4A–10.1**

Generally the Court's permission to appeal is required. Appeals in which the Court's permission is not required do not go through the Pt 2 process but are commenced by notice of appeal filed under r.19 (Form and filing of notice where permission is not required) and then proceed in accordance with the provisions of Pt 3 (Commencement and preparation of appeal).

Applications for permission to appeal are considered by a panel of (at least three) Justices, initially on paper and without a hearing (see r.16(1)). Throughout Practice Direction 3 (Applications for Permission to Appeal) and Practice Direction 13 (Costs), though not in the Rules in Pt 2, such a panel is referred to as an "Appeal Panel".

The rules in Pt 2 (rr.10 to 17) are supplemented by Practice Direction 3 (Applications for Permission Appeal).

Where permission to appeal is required, application must first be made to the court below (r.10(2)).

Rule 10 deals with the form of an application for permission to appeal. For form of a notice of appeal, see r.18 and r.19.

The appropriate form for an application for permission to appeal is Form 1 (see Practice Direction 7 (Applications, Documents, Forms and Orders) Annex 2). Detailed provisions as to the form and content of such applications are found in paras 3.1.1 to 3.1.5 of Practice Direction 3 (Applications for Permission to Appeal). The application should set out briefly the facts and points of law and include a summary why permission should be granted (*ibid.* para.3.1.2).

Where an appellant (or a respondent) seeks a declaration of incompatibility or seeks to challenge an act of a public authority under the Human Rights Act 1998, the practice in para.4.2.12 of Practice Direction 4 (Notices of Appeal) applies. See further r.40 and commentary following that rule.

If an appellant seeks a reference to the Court of Justice of the European Court of Justice, the practice in para.4.2.13 of Practice Direction 4 (Notices of Appeal) applies. See further r.42 and commentary following that rule.

For detailed information about the titles of cases in applications for permission to appeal, see Practice Direction 2 (The Registry of the Supreme Court) para.2.1.18 et seq.

### Anonymity and reporting restrictions

In any application concerning children, the parties, in addition to considering the case title to be used, should also consider whether it would be appropriate for the Court to make an order under the Children and Young Persons Act 1933 s.39 restricting the reporting of proceedings. The parties should always inform the Registry if such an order has been made by a court below. In such cases the Registrar will then make a further order imposing reporting restrictions. Any request for such an order to be made by the Court, and any objections to the making of such an order, should be made in writing, as soon as possible after the filing of an application for permission. Similar considerations apply to a request under the Contempt of Court Act 1981 s.4 (Contemporary reports of proceedings). **4A–10.1.1**

## Filing of application

**11.—(1) Subject to any enactment which makes special provision with regard to any particular category of appeal, an application for permission to appeal must be filed within 28 days from the date of the order or decision of the court below.** **4A–11**

**(2) The Registrar may refuse to accept any application on the ground that—**



SUPREME COURT

**(a) the Court does not have jurisdiction under section 40 of the Act to issue it;**

**(b) it contains no reasonable grounds; or**

**(c) it is an abuse of process,**

**and may give whatever directions appear appropriate.**

***(Section 2 of the Administration of Justice Act 1960 provides that an application for permission to appeal to the Supreme Court in a case involving civil contempt of court must be filed within 14 days, beginning with the date on which the application for permission is refused by the court below.)***

***(Section 13 of the Administration of Justice Act 1969 provides that an application for permission to appeal to the Supreme Court in a "leapfrog appeal" from the High Court must be filed within one month from the date on which the High Court judge grants a certificate under section 12.)***

### Effect of rule

4A–11.1 Rule 11(1) fixes (subject to any enactment) a time limit for the making of applications for permission to appeal. The application must be filed in the Court's Registry (see r.7 and commentary thereon). Before filing the application must be served as provided by r.12.

Time runs from the date of the order or decision of the court below. In proceedings to which the CPR apply, every judgment or order must bear the date on which it was given or made (CPR r.40(2)).

For fee payable on filing application for permission to appeal, see Practice Direction 7 (Practice Direction 7 (Applications, Documents, Forms and Orders) Annex 2.

When an application for permission to appeal is filed it will be sealed by a member of staff in the Registry (r.7(4)).

For provisions as to the documents to be filed in support of an application for permission to appeal, see r.14.

An application for permission to appeal, or any other document filed under these Rules, may be amended as provided by r.30(5); see commentary following r.30.

### Refusal of application for permission to appeal (r.11(2))

4A–11.2 The powers given to the Registrar by r.11(2) are strikingly wide. Decisions made by the Registrar under r.11(2) are not procedural decisions within r.9. Presumably, when refusing an application (or if minded to do so) the Registrar might under r.9(4) (which arguably applies to any matter and is not confined to procedural matters) direct that the matter be referred to a single Justice or to a panel of Justices. Presumably, also, the Registrar's decision to refuse an application under r.11(2) would be a decision reviewable at the instigation of a party by a single Justice under r.9(5).

In a given case, the Court's lack of jurisdiction under s.40 of the 2005 Act is likely to be clear enough, but lack of reasonable grounds or abuse of process will not always be obvious.

Presumably, the fact that the point of law raised in the application for permission to appeal was "hypothetical" or "academic", or the fact that an event had occurred depriving an appeal of practical significance to the parties (within r.33(d)), would provide grounds for refusal; see further commentary following r.33.

The most important restriction on the Court's jurisdiction under s.40, insofar as it extends to appeals to the Court from any order or judgment of the Court of Appeal in England and Wales in civil proceedings, is that imposed by s.54(4) of the Access to Justice Act 1999. That provision prevents the Court from entertaining an application for permission to appeal from a refusal by the Court of Appeal to grant leave to appeal to the Court of Appeal from a judgment or order of a lower court. (For other statutory restrictions, see Practice Direction 1 para.1.2.7.)

### Public funding of applicant

4A–11.3 Where a party to a proposed appeal has applied for public funding and the Registrar is informed of the application, the time limit in r.11(1) (and in r.19(2)) is extended until 28 days after the final determination of the application for public funding (r.5(5)). See further commentary following r.5.

A party to an appeal, including an applicant for permission to appeal, to whom a public funding or legal aid certificate has been issued must as soon as possible thereafter file a copy at the Registry; any emergency certificate and subsequent amendments and the authority for leading counsel must also be filed (Practice Direction 8 (Miscellaneous Matters) para.8.12.2).

### Extension of time for filing application for permission

The Court may extend any time limit set by these Rules, including that set by r.11(1) (and as extended by r.5(5)), unless to do so would be contrary to any enactment (r.5(1)). The time limits set by s.2 of the 1960 Act and s.13 of the 1969 Act (referred to in the signpost at the end of r.11) may be extended by the Court (see further commentary following r.5). **4A–11.4**

### Jurisdiction under s.40 (r.11(2))

The Court's jurisdiction under s.40 of the 2005 Act is summarised in Section 2 of Practice Direction 1. The Court's jurisdiction under the Administration of Justice Act 1960 s.2 (civil contempt appeals) is explained in para.1.2.8 and the jurisdiction under the Administration of Justice Act 1969 s.13 ("leapfrog" appeals) in para.1.2.17 et seq. of that practice direction (see further para.4A–59 below). The limited circumstances in which an appeal may be made to the Court against the refusal of the court below to grant permission to appeal to apply for judicial review are explained in paras 1.2.20 and 1.2.21. **4A–11.5**

Where the Court does not have jurisdiction, the Registrar will inform the appellant in writing accordingly (Practice Direction 1, para.1.2.6). An applicant may use that letter for the purpose satisfying the requirement, laid down by the European Convention on Human Rights art.35, that all domestic remedies must be exhausted before an appeal can be made to the European Court of Human Rights (*ibid.*).

### "Leapfrog" appeals

Under s.13 of the 1969 Act, before an application for permission to appeal is made to the Court a certificate of the High Court in England and Wales or Northern Ireland must first be obtained. For an explanation of the procedure and practice relating to the granting of the requisite judge's certificate by the court below, and for applying to the Court for permission to appeal direct to the Court, see Practice Direction 3 (Applications for Permission to Appeal) paras 3.6.2 to 3.6.16. **4A–11.6**

For issues arising where permission for a "leapfrog" appeal is granted on terms, see commentary following r.16.

Rule 43 and directions in Practice Direction 8 (Miscellaneous Matters) para.8.11 apply to leapfrog appeals from an order for the revocation of a patent made under s.32 or s.61 of the Patents Act 1949 or under s.72 of the Patents Act 1977. See further commentary following r.43.

### Appeals in habeas corpus proceedings

For the handling of applications for permission to appeal in habeas corpus proceedings, see Practice Direction 3 (Applications for Permission to Appeal) paras 3.6.7 and 3.6.8. **4A–11.7**

### Withdrawal of application for permission to appeal

An application for permission to appeal may be withdrawn with the written consent of all parties or with the permission of the Court; see r.34 and commentary following. **4A–11.8**

## Service of application

**12. Before the application is filed, a copy must be served—** **4A–12**

**(a) on every respondent, and**

**(b) on any person who was an intervener in the court below,**

**and, when the application is filed, the appellant must file a certificate of service.**

*Paragraph numbers marked with a "+" can be found online and on CD.*

#### Effect of rule

4A–12.1 For practice direction provisions relevant to service of an application for permission to appeal, see Practice Direction 2 (The Registry of the Supreme Court) para.2.1.23, and Practice Direction 3 (Applications for Permission to Appeal) para.3.1.6.

See further commentary following r.6 (Service), including commentary on certificates of service.

### Notice of objection by respondent

4A–13 **13.—(1) Each respondent who wishes to object to the application must, within 14 days after service, file notice of objection in the appropriate form together with a certificate of service.**

**(2) Before the notice is filed, a copy must be served on—**

**(a) the appellant,**

**(b) any other respondent, and**

**(c) any person who was an intervener in the court below.**

**(3) A respondent who does not file notice under this rule will not be permitted to participate in the application and will not be given notice of its progress.**

#### Effect of rule

4A–13.1 The terms of this rule are re-stated in Practice Direction 3 (Applications for Permission to Appeal) paras 3.1.8 to 3.1.10. When they file a notice of objection in accordance with r.13, respondents may submit written objections giving their reasons why permission to appeal should be refused; for details of practice to be followed, see *ibid.* para.3.3.6 et seq.

The appropriate form for a notice of objection is Form 3 (see Practice Direction 7 (Applications, Documents, Forms and Orders) Annex 1.

For fee payable on filing of notice of objection, see Practice Direction 7 (Applications, Documents, Forms and Orders) Annex 2.

For commentary on service of documents including notices of objection, see commentary following r.6 (Service), including commentary on certificates of service.

Where an oral hearing of an application for permission to appeal is directed under r.16(2), every respondent who has given notice under r.13 will be informed of the date of the oral hearing (r.17(1)). Where a respondent does not give such notice, r.13(3) applies (see also r.21(3)).

Subject to exceptions, a respondent who wishes to argue that the order appealed from should be varied must obtain permission to cross-appeal from the Court (r.25(2); see further Practice Direction 8 (Miscellaneous Matters) para.8.3.1.

#### Filing of notice of objection

4A–13.2 The original notice in Form 3 together with three copies must be filed at the Registry together with the prescribed fee. For the relevant fee, see Annex 2 to Practice Direction 7 (Applications, Documents, Forms and Orders). A certificate of service complying with r.6(4) must be included in Form 3 and signed or a separate certificate of service must be provided (Practice Direction 3 (Applications for Permission to Appeal) para.3.1.9).

When a notice of objection is filed, it will be sealed by a member of staff in the Registry (r.7(4)) (Practice Direction (Applications for Permission to Appeal) para.3.1.8).

#### Costs

4A–13.3 For costs of respondents' objections, see Practice Direction 3 (Applications for Permission to Appeal) para.3.5.1 et seq. An order for costs will not be made in favour of a respondent who has not given notice (Practice Direction 3 (Applications for Permission to Appeal) para.3.1.10).

### Documents in support of application

4A–14 **14.—(1) The requisite number of copies of the application must be filed together with—**

**(a) a copy of the order appealed from, and**

**(b) (if separate) a copy of any order refusing permission to appeal**

**and, if the order appealed from is not immediately available, the application should be filed without delay and the order filed as soon as it is available.**

**(2) The appellant must file the further documents required for the use of the Court within 7 days after filing the application.**

### Effect of rule

For detailed provisions relating to compliance with r.14(1) and 14(2), including provisions as to the form of presentation of documents, the number of copies to be filed, and applications for extension of time for complying with r.14, see Practice Direction 3 (Applications for Permission to Appeal) paras 3.1.7 and 3.2.1. Where the required papers are not filed within eight weeks after the filing of the application and no good reason is given for the delay, the Registrar may (a) refer the application to an Appeal Panel without the required accompanying papers, (b) dismiss the application, or (c) give such other directions as appear appropriate under r.8 (*ibid.* para.3.2.3). **4A-14.1**

Time limits for the filing of applications for permission to appeal are fixed by r.11(1). The purpose of the requirement in r.17 to the effect that applications "should be filed without delay" would seem to be that of making it clear that the non-availability of copies of the order appealed from should not delay filing of the documents required by r.14.

Documents filed under r.14 may be amended as provided by r.30(5); see commentary following r.30.

## Interventions in applications

**15.—(1) Any person and in particular—** **4A-15**

**(a) any official body or non-governmental organization seeking to make submissions in the public interest or**

**(b) any person with an interest in proceedings by way of judicial review,**

**may make written submissions to the Court in support of an application for permission to appeal and request that the Court takes them into account.**

**(2) Before the submissions are filed, a copy must be served on—**

**(a) the appellant,**

**(b) every respondent, and**

**(c) any person who was an intervener in the court below**

**and the requisite number of copies of the submissions must be filed together with a certificate of service.**

**(3) Any submissions which are made shall be referred to the panel of Justices which considers the application for permission to appeal.**

**(4) If permission to appeal is granted—**

**(a) a person whose submissions were taken into account by the panel will be notified but, if that person wishes to intervene in the appeal, an application must be made under rule 26;**

**(b) the appellant must notify any person who was an intervener in the court below whether or not that person made submissions under this rule.**

*Paragraph numbers marked with a "+" can be found online and on CD.*

#### Effect of rule

4A–15.1 This rule is re-stated in, and supplemented by, Practice Direction 3 (Applications for Permission to Appeal) para.3.3.17 et seq. Four copies of the submissions must be filed, together with a certificate of service (*ibid.* para.3.3.17).

For service of documents, including service of written submissions under r.15(2), see commentary following r.6, including commentary on certificates of service.

Where a person makes written submissions under r.15 and those submissions are taken into account under r.16, and permission to appeal is granted, the re-sealed application for permission standing as the notice of appeal should be served on that person by the appellant (r.18(2)). Further, in those circumstances that person may apply to the Court under r.26(1) for permission to intervene in the appeal.

### Consideration on paper

4A–16 **16.—(1) Every admissible application for permission to appeal (together with any submissions made under rule 15 and any respondent's notice of objection) shall be considered on paper without a hearing by a panel of Justices.**

**(2) The panel may—**

**(a) grant or refuse permission to advance all or any of the grounds of appeal;**

**(b) invite the parties to file written submissions within 14 days as to the grant of permission on terms (whether as to costs or otherwise); or**

**(c) direct an oral hearing.**

**(3) Where the panel has invited the parties' submissions as to terms, it shall reconsider the application on paper without a hearing and may refuse permission or grant permission (either unconditionally or on terms) to advance all or any of the grounds of appeal.**

**(4) Where the panel grants permission to advance limited grounds of appeal it shall (unless it directs otherwise) be taken to have refused permission to advance the other grounds.**

**(5) An order of the Court shall be prepared and sealed by the Registrar to record any decision made under this rule.**

#### Effect of rule

4A–16.1 The Court's practice in the several outcomes referred to in r.16(2) is amplified in Practice Direction 3 (Applications for Permission to Appeal) para.3.3.2 et seq.

Once the required papers under r.14 are filed at the Registry, the r.16 procedure is normally completed within eight sitting weeks (excluding any oral hearing). Requests for an expedited disposal of the application for permission to appeal and for an expedited hearing of the appeal in proceedings involving liberty of the subject, urgent medical intervention or the well-being of children, or under the Hague Convention etc, may be made in writing to the Registrar (r.31) (see further Practice Direction 3 (Applications for Permission to Appeal) paras 3.4.3 to 3.4.7, and note Practice Direction 4 (Notice of Appeal) para.4.8.1, and Practice Direction 6 (The Appeal Hearing) para.6.2.4).

The appellant, any recognised intervener and all respondents who have filed notice of objection under r.13, are sent a copy of the order sealed by the Registrar recording the decision of the panel of Justices (Practice Direction 3 (Applications for Permission to Appeal) para.3.3.19). (A person whose submissions were taken into account under r.15, or who was an intervener in the court below, may apply to the Court for permission to intervene in the appeal, should it proceed (see r.26).)

Where the panel of Justices grants permission for a "leapfrog" appeal on terms, and

*Paragraph numbers marked with a "+" can be found online and on CD.*

the prospective appellant declines to proceed on the basis of those terms, that party may instead pursue an appeal to the Court of Appeal in the usual way (*R. (Jones) v Ceredigion County Council v Jones (No.2)* [2007] UKHL 24; [2009] 1 W.L.R. 1400, HL) (see also Practice Direction 3 (Applications for Permission to Appeal) paras 3.3.11 and 3.6.16).

### Oral hearing of application

**17.—(1) Where the panel has directed an oral hearing, the appellant and every respondent who has given notice under rule 13 will be informed of the date of the oral hearing.** 4A–17

**(2) An order of the Court shall be prepared and sealed by the Registrar to record any decision made under this rule.**

#### Effect of rule

For Court's practice where the panel of Justices directs an oral hearing under r.16(2) and r.17 applies, see Practice Direction 3 (Applications for Permission to Appeal) para.3.3.12 et seq. Oral permission hearings usually last for 30 minutes. 4A–17.1

## PART 3

## COMMENCEMENT AND PREPARATION OF APPEAL

### Form and filing of notice where permission granted by the Court

**18.—(1) Where the Court grants permission to appeal, rules 19 and 20 shall not apply and** 4A–18

**(a) the application for permission to appeal shall stand as the notice of appeal;**

**(b) the grounds of appeal shall be limited to those on which permission has been granted;**

**(c) the appellant must, within 14 days of the grant by the Court of permission to appeal, file notice under this rule of an intention to proceed with the appeal.**

**(2) When notice is filed under rule 18(1)(c), the application for permission to appeal will be re-sealed and the appellant must then—**

**(a) serve a copy on each respondent and on any person who was an intervener in the court below or whose submissions were taken into account under rule 15; and**

**(b) file the requisite number of copies and a certificate of service.**

**(3) In any other case an appellant must file a notice of appeal under rule 19.**

#### Effect of rule

See commentary following r.20. 4A–18.1

### Form and filing of notice where permission not required

**19.—(1) Every notice of appeal shall be made in the appropriate form.** 4A–19

**(2) The notice of appeal together with the requisite number of copies must be filed within 42 days of the date of the order or decision of the court below.**

*Paragraph numbers marked with a "+" can be found online and on CD.*

**(3) The appellant must also file—**

**(a) a copy of the order appealed from and**

**(b) (if separate) a copy of the order granting permission to appeal and, if the order appealed from is not immediately available, the notice of appeal must be filed without delay and the order filed as soon as it is available.**

#### Effect of rule

4A-19.1 See commentary following r.20.

### Service of notice

4A-20 **20.—(1) Before the notice of appeal is filed, a copy must be served on each respondent and on any person who was an intervener in the court below.**

**(2) When the notice of appeal is filed, the appellant must file a certificate of service.**

#### Effect of rules 18 to 20

4A-20.1 Rules 19 and 20 apply where the applicant does not require permission to appeal from the Court. Rule 18 applies (and rr.19 and 20 do not) where the applicant did require permission to appeal and was granted such permission by the Court under the Pt 2 process.

#### Notice of intention to proceed (r.18(1))

4A-20.2 Where r.18 applies, the successful applicant, now the appellant, is not required to file a notice of appeal; the application for permission stands as the notice of appeal. But the applicant/appellant is required to file a notice of intention to proceed with the appeal; whereupon the application for permission to appeal is re-sealed. The appellant must then serve a copy of the re-sealed document (now in effect a notice of appeal) and otherwise comply with r.18(2). The rules as to service of documents as stated in r.6 apply to the service of the re-sealed document referred to in r.18(2).

For fee payable on filing of notice of intention to proceed with an appeal, see Practice Direction 7 (Applications, Documents, Forms and Orders) Annex 2.

In r.34 (Withdrawal etc of application for permission to appeal or of appeal, sub-r.(3) states that, in that rule "a notice of appeal" includes an application for permission to appeal which (under r.18) stands as a notice of appeal.

#### Complying with r.18(2)

4A-20.3 In para.3.4.1 of Practice Direction 3 (Applications for Permission to Appeal) the terms of r.18 are re-stated and it is explained that the original and three copies of the re-sealed document together with a certificate of service (complying with r.6(4)) must be filed. In para.3.4.2 it is further provided that, where an appellant is unable to file notice of an intention to proceed under r.18 within the time limit of 14 days, a formal application for an extension of time must be made in Form 2. The respondent's views on the extension of time should be sought and, if possible, those views should be communicated to the Registry. The application will be referred to the Registrar and, if it is granted, the appellant must then comply with r.18(2) and para.3.4.1. See also Practice Direction 4 (Notice of Appeal) para.4.3.3.

Within 112 days after the filing of the notice under r.18(1)(c) the appellant must file the documents referred to in r.22(1).

Each respondent who intends to participate in the appeal must, within 14 days after service under r.18(2)(a) file notice in the appropriate form with a certificate of service (see r.21(1)).

#### Complying with r.19

4A-20.4 The terms of r.19 are re-stated and amplified in paras 4.3.1 and 4.3.2 of Practice Direction 4 (Notice of Appeal). The number of documents to be filed is explained in para.4.3.1 (see also Practice Direction 7 (Applications, Documents, Forms and Orders) para.7.2.3).

The appropriate form for a notice of appeal is Form 1 (see Practice Direction 7 (Applications, Documents, Forms and Orders) Annex 1).

For fee payable on filing of notice of appeal, see Practice Direction 7 (Applications, Documents, Forms and Orders) Annex 2.

When a notice of appeal is filed it will be sealed by a member of staff in the Registry (r.7(4)).

A notice of appeal may be amended as provided by r.30(5); see commentary following r.30 and note Practice Direction 4 (Notice of Appeal) para.4.2.1.

Rule 19(2) states that time the 42 day time limit runs from the date of the order or decision of the court below. In proceedings to which the CPR apply, every judgment or order must bear the date on which it was given or made (CPR r.40(2)). Where a party to a proposed appeal has applied for public funding and the Registrar is informed of the application, the time limit in r.19(2) shall be extended until 28 days after the final determination of the application for public funding (r.5(5)).

The time limit in r.19(2) may be varied by the Court (r.5(1)). Paragraph 4.4.1 of Practice Direction 4 (Notice of Appeal) contains directions relating to applications for extension of this time limit.

Provisions in Pt 2 are designed to ensure that applicants for permission to appeal provide the Court and potential respondents with certain information. An appellant to whom r.19 applies, in effect, by-passes the Pt 2 process and commences proceedings by filing a notice of appeal. Provisions as to the form and content of notices of appeal are found in Practice Direction 4 (Notice of Appeal) paras 4.2.1 to 4.2.4. For obvious reasons the requirements of those provisions are similar to those applicable to applications for permission to appeal (see Practice Direction 3 (Applications for Permission to Appeal) paras 3.1.1 to 3.1.5).

Where an appellant seeks a declaration of incompatibility or seeks to challenge an act of a public authority under the Human Rights Act 1998, the notice of appeal should accord with the directions in para.4.2.12 of Practice Direction 4 (Notices of Appeal). See further r.40 and commentary following that rule.

Where an appellant seeks a reference to the Court of Justice of the European Court of Justice, the notice of appeal should accord with the directions in para.4.2.13 of Practice Direction 4 (Notices of Appeal) applies. See further r.42 and commentary following that rule.

### Service of notice of appeal (r.20)

Rule 20 is to be read together with r.19. Paragraph 4.2.15 of Practice Direction 4 (Notice of Appeal) re-states r.20 and, in relation to certificates of service, draws attention to r.6(4) and explains that such certificates must be included in Form 1 and signed or a separate certificate of service must be provided. See also Practice Direction 2 (The Registry of the Supreme Court) para.2.1.24. **4A–20.5**

The rules as to service of documents as stated in r.6 apply to the service of the copy of the notice of appeal as required by r.20(1).

Each respondent who intends to participate in the appeal must, within 14 days after service under r.20 file notice in the appropriate form with a certificate of service (r.21(1)).

### Cross-appeals

Where there is a cross-appeal the provisions of Pt 3, including rr.18 to r.20, apply with appropriate modifications. Rule 25(4)(a) (which is drafted with the circumstances envisaged by both r.18 and r.19 in mind) states that either the application for permission to cross-appeal to the Court shall stand as a notice of cross-appeal, or such a notice (in the appropriate form) shall be filed and served within 42 days of the grant by the Court of permission to appeal or of the filing of the notice of appeal. See further Practice Direction 8 (Miscellaneous Matters) para.8.3. **4A–20.6**

### Case titles

For detailed information about the titles of cases in applications for permission to appeal and in notices of appeal, see Practice Direction 2 (The Registry of the Supreme Court) para.2.1.18 et seq, and Practice Direction 4 (Notice of Appeal) para.4.2.5 et seq. **4A–20.7**

*Paragraph numbers marked with a "+" can be found online and on CD.*

**Requests for an expedited hearing of an appeal**

4A–20.8 In proceedings involving liberty of the subject, urgent medical intervention or the well-being of children, or under the Hague Convention, etc., such requests may be made in writing to the Registrar; see further Practice Direction 4 (Notice of Appeal) para.4.8.1, Practice Direction 6 (The Appeal Hearing) para.6.2.4, and commentary on r.31.

Requests for anonymity and reporting restrictions For directions concerning requests for orders under the Children and Young Persons Act 1933 s.39 and the Contempt of Court Act 1981, see Practice Direction 4 (Notice of Appeal) paras 4.2.10 and 4.2.11. Such request should be made as soon as possible after the appeal is commenced under Pt 3.

**Request for appointment of an advocate to the Court**

4A–20.9 See r.35 and commentary thereon.

**Request for attendance of assessor at hearing**

4A–20.10 See r.35 and commentary thereon.

**Request to record, film or broadcast proceedings**

4A–20.11 See Practice Direction 8 (Miscellaneous Matters) para.8.17.1.

## Acknowledgement by respondent

4A–21 **21.—(1) Each respondent who intends to participate in the appeal must, within 14 days after service under rule 18(2)(a) or 20, file notice in the appropriate form together with a certificate of service.**

**(2) Before the notice is filed, a copy must be served on—**

**(a) the appellant,**

**(b) any other respondent, and**

**(c) any person who was an intervener in the court below or whose submissions were taken into account under rule 15.**

**(3) A respondent who does not file notice under this rule will not be permitted to participate in the appeal and will not be given notice of its progress.**

**Effect of rule**

4A–21.1 The appropriate form is Form 3; see Practice Direction 3 (Applications for Permission to Appeal) Annex 1). For fee payable on filing notice of acknowledgement by respondent, see *ibid*. Annex 2.

Paragraphs 4.6.1, 4.6.2 and 4.6.4 of Practice Direction 4 (Notice of Appeal) re-state r.21 and, in relation to certificates of service, para.4.6.2 draws attention to r.6(4) and explains that such certificates must be included in Form 3 and signed or a separate certificate of service must be provided. See also Practice Direction 2 (The Registry of the Supreme Court) para.2.1.24.

The original respondent's acknowledgement notice together with three copies must be filed at the Registry (Practice Direction 4 (Notice of Appeal) para.4.6.3).

The rules as to service of documents as stated in r.6 apply to the service of the copy of the respondent's notice of acknowledgement as required by r.21(2).

A respondent may apply under r.5 for an extension of the time limit fixed by r.21(1).

An order for costs will not be made in favour of a respondent who has not given notice of acknowledgement under r.21 (Practice Direction 4 (Notice of Appeal) para.4.6.4.

## Documents for appeal hearing

4A–22 **22.—(1) Within 112 days after the filing of the notice under rule**

**18(1)(c) or the filing of the notice of appeal, the appellant must file—**

**(a) a statement of the relevant facts and issues; and**

**(b) an appendix (prepared in accordance with the relevant practice direction) of the essential documents which were in evidence before, or which record the proceedings in, the courts below.**

**(2) Both the statement and the appendix must be submitted to, and agreed with, every respondent before being filed.**

**(3) Within 7 days after the filing of the statement and the appendix, every party must—**

**(a) notify the Registrar that the appeal is ready for listing, and**

**(b) specify the number of hours that their respective counsel estimate to be necessary for their oral submissions**

**and the Registrar will subsequently inform the parties of the date fixed for the hearing.**

**(4) The appellant and every respondent (and any intervener and advocate to the Court) must then sequentially exchange their respective written cases and file them, and every respondent (and any intervener and advocate to the Court) must for the purposes of rule 23 provide copies of their respective written cases, in compliance with the relevant practice direction.**

### Effect of rule

Rules 22 to 24 go together. They are supplemented by Practice Direction 5 (Papers for the Appeal Hearing), and by Practice Direction 6 (The Appeal Hearing). **4A–22.1**

For fees for filing a statement of facts and issues and the appendix (referred to in r.22(1)), see Practice Direction 7 (Applications, Documents, Forms and Orders) Annex 2.

Documents filed under rr.22 to 24 may be amended as provided by r.30(5); see commentary following r.30.

With the consent of the Registrar, documents (including those referred to in rr.22 to 24) may be filed by electronic means in accordance with Practice Direction 14 (Filing Documents in the Registry of the Supreme Court by electronic means) (r.7(1)(d)).

If the appellant is unable to comply with a time limit imposed by r.22(1), an application for an extension of time must be made (r.5), and in that event paras 5.2.3 to 5.2.5 of Practice Direction 5 (Papers for the Appeal Hearing) apply.

All documents placed before the Court must comply with para.5.1.2 of Practice Direction 5 (Papers for the Appeal Hearing). Paragraphs (1) and (2) of r.22 refer to papers for the appeal hearing in the form of (a) a statement of the relevant facts and issues, and (b) an appendix of the essential documents. These documents must comply with paras 5.1.3 to 5.1.5. The number of copies of each of these papers to be filed is stated in para.5.2.6. For prescribed fees payable upon filing, see Practice Direction 7 (Applications, Documents, Forms and Orders) Annex 2.

A table summarising provisions found elsewhere dealing with the number of documents (including the several documents referred to in r.22) usually to be provided by the appellants, respondents and interveners for the Registry and "for other side" for the hearing of an appeal is found in Practice Direction 7 (Applications, Documents, Forms and Orders) para.7.2.3.

Rule 22(3) imposes certain duties on "every party". Rule 25(4)(c) states that, where there is a cross-appeal the appellant shall remain "primarily responsible" for the preparation of all of the papers for the appeal and for giving the Registrar notice of the matters referred to in r.22(3).

It would seem that, insofar as rr.22 to 24 and the practice directions supplementing them require parties to exchange documents or to provide documents one to another, the parties may consent to this being done by electronic means. This is because expressions such as "exchanging" or "providing" are expressions related to "service" (see r.3(2)) and therefore may be effected by the electronic means of service of documents permitted by r.6(1)(d). However, although r.6.1(d) anticipates it, there is no relevant practice direction dedicated to the service of documents by one party to an appeal upon another by "electronic means" (as defined in r.3(2)). However, para.2.1.23 of Practice Direction 2 (The Registry of the Supreme Court) does provide that a party or his solicitor will be taken to have consented to a particular method of service if, for example, their writing paper includes a fax number or a numbered box at a document exchange unless they have indicated in writing that they are not willing to accept service by that particular method.

In the period during which the procedural steps stated in rr.22 to 24 are taken it may become apparent to the Court or to the parties that a directions hearing should be held. In that event, the provisions of para.6.2.5 of Practice Direction 6 (The Appeal Hearing) apply.

#### Written cases

4A–22.2 The written case is the statement of a party's argument in the appeal. The Court does not prescribe any maximum length but the Court favours brevity and a case should be a concise summary of the submissions to be developed. Detailed directions concerning written cases (including information concerning form, exchange, filing and the number of copies to be filed) are given in Practice Direction 6 (The Appeal Hearing) para.6.3.1 et seq. These directions stipulate time limits for the filing and exchange of written cases. Rule 22(4) anticipates the duty imposed on the appellant by r.23 and para.6.3.11 of the practice direction states that, to enable the appellant to discharge that duty, the respondent and any other party who has filed a case must provide the appellant with a further 10 copies of their written case.

#### Exhibits

4A–22.3 Parties who require exhibits to be available for inspection at the hearing must apply to the Registrar for permission for the exhibits to be brought to the Court before the hearing (see Practice Direction 8 (Miscellaneous Matters) para.8.6.1, and Practice Direction 12 (Criminal Proceedings) para.12.14.1).

#### Fresh evidence

4A–22.4 See Practice Direction 6 (The Appeal Hearing) para.6.3.3.

#### Cross-appeals

4A–22.5 Where there is a cross-appeal, rr.22 to 24 (and the other rules in Pt 3) apply with appropriate modifications (r.25(4)). In particular, para.(b) of r.25(4) states that, where there is a cross-appeal, there shall be a single statement of facts and issues, a single appendix of essential documents (divided if necessary into parts) and a single case for each party in respect of the appeal and the cross-appeal (and each case should state clearly that it is in respect of both the appeal and the cross-appeal). Paragraph 8.3 of Practice Direction 8 (Miscellaneous Matters) includes directions as to the filing of documents (and numbers of copies) and relevant time limits where there is a cross-appeal.

#### Fixing the hearing date

4A–22.6 For directions supplementing r.22(3), including requests for expedited hearings (r.31), see Practice Direction 6 (The Appeal Hearing) paras 6.2.1 to 6.2.4 and paras 6.6.1 to 6.6.3. The Registrar will on request inform the parties of the intended constitution of the Court for the appeal hearing (para.6.6.7).

If a party wishes to have a stenographer present at the hearing or to obtain a full transcript of the hearing, he must notify the Registrar not less than 7 days before the hearing (para.6.6.6). (Any costs of the stenographer or of transcription must be borne by the party making such a request; *ibid.*).

### The core volumes

4A–23 **23. As soon as the parties' cases have been exchanged and in any event not later than 14 days before the date fixed for the hearing**

***Paragraph numbers marked with a "+" can be found online and on CD.***

**the appellant must file the requisite number of core volumes and, if necessary, additional volumes containing further parts of the appendix, in compliance with the relevant practice direction.**

### Effect of rule

This rule imposes duties on the appellant (to be discharged the assistance of other parties as required by r.22(4)). Detailed directions concerning core volumes (including information concerning form, party cooperation in preparation, filing and the number of copies to be filed) are given in Practice Direction 6 (The Appeal Hearing) para.6.4.1 et seq. (note also para.6.3.11). As to number of core volumes to be filed and exchanged, see also table following para.7.2.3 of Practice Direction 7 (Applications, Documents, Forms and Orders). **4A–23.1**

For filing of core volumes in electronic form, see Practice Direction 14 (Filing Documents in the Registry of the Supreme Court by electronic means).

See further, commentary following r.22 as relevant to r.23.

## Authorities

**24. The volumes of authorities that may be referred to during the hearing must be prepared in accordance with the relevant practice direction and the requisite number of copies of the volumes of authorities must be filed by the appellant at the same time as the core volumes.** **4A–24**

### Effect of rule

This rule imposes duties on the appellant. Detailed directions concerning volumes of authorities (including information concerning form, party cooperation in preparation, filing and the number of copies to be filed) are given in Practice Direction 6 (The Appeal Hearing) paras 6.5.1 to 6.5.8. Supplemental or additional volumes of authorities should be avoided. In order to produce the volumes of authorities, parties may download text from electronic sources; but the volumes of authorities must be filed in paper form (para.6.5.6). **4A–24.1**

As to number of volumes of authorities to be filed and exchanged, see also table following para.7.2.3 of Practice Direction 7 (Applications, Documents, Forms and Orders).

For filing of volumes of authorities in electronic form, see Practice Direction 14 (Filing Documents in the Registry of the Supreme Court by electronic means).

The cost of preparing the volumes of authorities falls to the appellants, but is ultimately subject to the decision of the Court as to the costs of the appeal (Practice Direction 6 (The Appeal Hearing) para.6.5.8).

See further, commentary following r.22 as relevant to r.24.

## Cross-appeals

**25.—(1) A respondent who wishes to argue that the order appealed from should be upheld on grounds different from those relied on by the court below, must state that clearly in the respondent's written case (but need not cross-appeal).** **4A–25**

**(2) Except where—**

**(a) leave is required from the Court of Session for an appeal from that court, or**

**(b) an appeal lies to the Court as of right,**

**a respondent who wishes to argue that the order appealed from should be varied must obtain permission to cross-appeal from the Court.**

**(3) Part 2 of these Rules shall apply (with appropriate modifica-**

*Paragraph numbers marked with a "+" can be found online and on CD.*

**tions) to an application to the Court for permission to cross-appeal and (if practicable) applications for permission to appeal and to cross-appeal shall be considered together by the same panel of Justices.**

**(4) Where there is a cross-appeal, this Part of these Rules shall apply with appropriate modifications and in particular—**

**(a) either the application for permission to cross-appeal to the Court shall stand as a notice of cross-appeal, or such a notice (in the appropriate form) shall be filed and served within 42 days of the grant by the Court of permission to appeal or of the filing of the notice of appeal;**

**(b) there shall be a single statement of facts and issues, a single appendix of essential documents (divided if necessary into parts) and a single case for each party in respect of the appeal and the cross-appeal (and each case should state clearly that it is in respect of both the appeal and the cross-appeal); and**

**(c) the appellant shall remain primarily responsible for the preparation of all the papers for the appeal and for notifying the Registrar under rule 22(3).**

#### Effect of rule

4A-25.1 The substance of r.25 is restated in para.8.3.1 of Practice Direction 8 (Miscellaneous Matters) and important and detailed directions as to practice follow thereafter, including directions as to the filing of documents (and numbers of copies) and relevant time limits. (See further commentary following r.22 (Documents for appeal hearing).) Where permission to cross-appeal is required, an application for permission may only be filed after permission to appeal has been granted to the original applicant for permission to appeal (*ibid.* para.8.3.2).

The provisions in Pt 2 (Application for permission to appeal) (rr.10 to 17) apply to an application for permission to cross-appeal (r.25(3)).

Where there is a cross-appeal, the provisions of Pt 3 (Commencement and preparation of appeal) (rr.18 to 26) apply with appropriate modifications (r.25(4)). See further commentary following r.20 and r.22.

For the purposes of r.34 (Withdrawal etc of application for permission to appeal or of appeal, "a notice of appeal" includes an application for permission to cross-appeal which (under r.25(4)(a)) stands as a notice of cross-appeal (r.34(3)).

No security for costs is required in cross-appeals (Practice Direction 4 (Notice of Appeal) para.4.7.4).

### Intervention

4A-26 **26.—(1) After permission to appeal has been granted by the Court or a notice of appeal has been filed, any person and in particular—**

**(a) any official body or non-governmental organization seeking to make submissions in the public interest,**

**(b) any person with an interest in proceedings by way of judicial review,**

**(c) any person who was an intervener in the court below or whose submissions were taken into account under rule 15,**

**may apply to the Court for permission to intervene in the appeal.**

**(2) An application under this rule must be made in the appropriate form and shall be considered on paper by a panel of Justices**

**who may refuse permission to intervene or may permit intervention—**

**(a) by written submissions only; or**

**(b) by written submissions and oral submissions**

**and any oral submissions may be limited to a specified duration.**

**(3) No permission is required—**

**(a) for an intervention by the Crown under section 5 of the Human Rights Act 1998, or**

**(b) for an intervention by the relevant officer in a case where the Court is exercising its devolution jurisdiction.**

***(For rules relating to Human Rights Act issues and the Court's devolution jurisdiction see rules 40 and 41.)***

### Effect of rule

A person who is not a party to an application for permission to appeal may apply for permission to intervene in accordance with r.15. (See further commentary following r.15.) A person who is not a party to an appeal may apply in accordance with r.26 for permission to intervene in the appeal. An intervener under r.15 who wishes to intervene in the appeal must make a formal application under r.26. The application should be made in Form 2. Rule 26 is supplemented by Practice Direction 6 (The Appeal Hearing) para.6.9. These directions include time limits for the making of applications to intervene. **4A–26.1**

Paragraph 8.8.2 of Practice Direction 8 (Miscellaneous Matters) draws attention to paras 2 and 3 of Lord Hoffmann's opinion in *E v Chief Constable of the Royal Ulster Constabulary* [2008] UKHL 66; [2008] 3 W.L.R. 1208, HL, where his Lordship (i) said that it is not the role of an intervener to be an additional counsel for one of the parties, (ii) stressed that an intervention is of no assistance if it merely repeats points which the appellant or respondent has already made, and (iii) expressed the hope that interveners "will avoid unnecessarily taking up the time of the House in this way".

Orders for costs will not normally be made in favour of or against interveners (see r.46(3), and note Practice Direction 6 (The Appeal Hearing) para.6.9.5).

In these Rules, except where the context otherwise requires, "party" includes a person who has been given permission to intervene under r.26 (r.3(2)). If an application for permission to appeal is granted, a person who has intervened in the application and whose submissions were taken into account will be notified, but if that person wishes to intervene in the appeal, an application must be made under r.26 (r.15(4)).

## PART 4

## HEARING AND DECISION OF APPEAL

### Hearing in open court

**27.—(1) Every contested appeal shall be heard in open court except where it is necessary in the interests of justice or in the public interest to sit in private for part of an appeal hearing.** **4A–27**

**(2) Where the Court considers it necessary for a party and that party's representative to be excluded from a hearing or part of a hearing in order to secure that information is not disclosed contrary to the public interest, the Court must conduct the hearing, or that part of it from which the party and the representative are excluded, in private but the Court may exclude a party and any representative only if a person who has been appointed as a special advocate to represent the interests of that party is present when the party and the representative are excluded.**

*Paragraph numbers marked with a "+" can be found online and on CD.*

**(3) Where the Court decides it is necessary for the Court to sit in private, it shall announce its reasons for so doing publicly before the hearing begins.**

**(4) Hearings shall be conducted in accordance with—**

**(a) the relevant practice direction, and**

**(b) any directions given by the Court**

**and directions given by the Court may limit oral submissions to a specified duration.**

#### Effect of rule

4A–27.1 Part 4 is concerned with appeal hearings, and not with hearings of procedural applications or of applications for permission to appeal. More specifically, para.(1) of r.27 is concerned with the hearing of contested appeals. Paragraph (2) of r.27 is concerned with special contingencies. Special advocates are likely to be appointed in proceedings under the Prevention of Terrorism Act 2005 or in financial restriction proceedings under the Counter-Terrorism Act 2008. (For provisions in the CPR comparable to r.27(2) and applying, respectively, to proceedings under the 2005 Act and 2008 Act, see CPR r.76.22 and 79.17(2); note also CPR r.39.2.)

Paragraph 6.6.4 of Practice Direction 6 (The Appeal Hearing) states that only in wholly exceptional circumstances will the Court consider sitting in private. Any request for the Court to sit in private should be addressed to the Registrar and should be copied to the other parties. The request should set out fully the reasons why it is made and the request together with any objections filed by the other parties will normally be referred to the presiding Justice.

The rule that oral hearings on procedural matters must be heard in open court or in a place to which the public are admitted (r.9(6)) is expressed as subject to r.27.

Detailed assessments of costs are conducted in public (Practice Direction 13 (Costs) para.1.3).

For requests for anonymity and reporting restrictions at contested appeal hearings or other oral hearings, see commentary following r.20.

#### Appeal hearings to be conducted in accordance with directions

4A–27.2 Paragraph (4) of r.27 is not concerned with the circumstances in which the Court may sit in private but with the conduct of the appeal hearing generally. Relevant practice direction provisions are found in para.6.6 of Practice Direction 6 (The Appeal Hearing). An example of a direction given by the Court would be a direction under r.32 as to the grouping of appeals for hearing together or consecutively.

#### New submissions after argument

4A–27.3 If, after the conclusion of the argument on an appeal, a party wishes to bring to the notice of the Court new circumstances which have arisen and which might affect the decision or order of the Court, the directions in para.8.9.1 of Practice Direction 8 (Miscellaneous Matters) apply.

## Judgment

4A–28 **28. A judgment may be—**

**(a) delivered in open court; or**

**(b) if the Court so directs, promulgated by the Registrar.**

#### Effect of rule

4A–28.1 Practice Direction 6 (The Appeal Hearing) para.6.8 supplements this rule and deals with the place and time of judgment, the attendance of counsel at handing down, and the conditions under which judgments are released in advance. It is expressly provided that where judgment is to be promulgated by the Registrar, copies will be made available for collection by counsel or a solicitor at the Registry on a day notified in advance (para.6.8.2).

## Orders

4A–29 **29.—(1) In relation to an appeal or a reference, the Supreme Court has all the powers of the court below and may—**

*Paragraph numbers marked with a "+" can be found online and on CD.*

**(a) affirm, set aside or vary any order or judgment made or given by that court;**

**(b) remit any issue for determination by that court;**

**(c) order a new trial or hearing;**

**(d) make orders for the payment of interest;**

**(e) make a costs order.**

**(2) An order of the Supreme Court may be enforced in the same manner as an order of the court below or of the appropriate superior court.**

**(3) For the purposes of paragraph (2) "the appropriate superior court" means—**

**(a) in the case of an appeal or reference from a court in England and Wales, the High Court;**

**(b) in the case of an appeal or reference from a court in Scotland—**

**(i) where the appeal or reference is in civil proceedings, the Court of Session; and**

**(ii) where the appeal or reference is in criminal proceedings, the High Court of Justiciary;**

**(c) in the case of an appeal or reference from a court in Northern Ireland, the High Court in Northern Ireland.**

**(4) In the case of references other than those mentioned in paragraph (3) "the appropriate superior court" in paragraph (2) means—**

**(a) where the reference is under the Scotland Act 1998, the Court of Session;**

**(b) where the reference is under the Northern Ireland Act 1998, the High Court in Northern Ireland; and**

**(c) where the reference is under the Government of Wales Act 2006, the High Court.**

**(5) Every order of the Court shall be prepared and sealed by the Registrar who may invite written submissions as to the form of the order.**

#### Effect of rule

Paragraph (1) of r.29 is to the same effect as CPR r.52.10(2) (Appeal court's powers). For the Court's powers as to costs and their exercise; see Pt 7 (Fees and Costs). **4A–29.1**

#### Enforcement of court's order (r.29(2))

For basic information as to the enforcement of the Court's orders in England and Wales, see Practice Direction 8 (Miscellaneous Matters) paras 8.18.1 to 8.18.3. For enforcement in Scotland or Northern Ireland, see *ibid.* para.8.18.4. **4A–29.2**

#### Order of the court (r.29(5))

Paragraph (5) of r.29 is supplemented by para.7.4 of Practice Direction 7 (Applications, Documents, Forms and Orders). In an order made under r.29 the amount of any assessed costs will be inserted, but if that order is drawn up before the assessment has been completed, the amount assessed will be certified by the Registrar (r.52). **4A–29.3**

*Paragraph numbers marked with a "+" can be found online and on CD.*

## PART 5

## FURTHER GENERAL PROVISIONS

### Procedural applications

4A–30 **30.—(1) Every procedural application to the Court must be made in the appropriate form for general procedural applications unless a particular form is provided for a specific case.**

**(2) An application must be made in the appropriate form and must—**

**(a) set out the reasons for making the application, and**

**(b) where necessary, be supported by written evidence.**

**(3) A copy of the application must be served on every other party before it is filed and, when the application is filed, the applicant must file a certificate of service.**

**(4) A party who wishes to oppose an application must, within 7 days after service, file notice of objection in the appropriate form and must (before filing) serve a copy on the applicant and any other parties.**

**(5) An application for permission to appeal, a notice of appeal or any other document filed under these Rules may be amended on application under this rule or with the permission of the Registrar on such terms as appear appropriate, and the Registrar may invite the parties' written submissions on any application to amend.**

#### Effect of rule

4A–30.1 Provisions in Practice Direction 7 (Applications, Documents, Forms and Orders) supplement paras (1) to (4) of this rule. An application should be made as soon as it becomes apparent that it is necessary or expedient (para.7.1.1). An application must be made in Form 2 (*ibid.* para.7.1.2) and should be served on all the other parties before it is filed (r.30(1)(3)). The original notice must bear a certificate of service on the other parties (para.7.1.7). The appropriate form for a notice of objection (r.30(4)) is Form 3 (para.7.1.4). For number of copies of application and any notice of objection to be filed, see para.7.1.7.

For fees for filing procedural applications, including an application for a decision of the Registrar to be reviewed and for permission to intervene in an appeal, and a notice of objection to a procedural application, see Practice Direction 7 (Applications, Documents, Forms and Orders) Annex 2.

Generally, procedural applications (including opposed applications) are dealt with without a hearing (para.7.1.6). In the event of an oral hearing of an opposed application by a Panel of Justices authorities are not normally cited (para.7.1.8).

#### Certificate of service

4A–30.2 A certificate of service is a certificate given under r.6 (r.3.1(2)). A certificate of service which complies with r.6(4) must be included either in the original procedural application and signed or a separate certificate of service must be provided (Practice Direction 2 (The Registry of the Supreme Court) para.2.1.24).

#### Evidence in support of application

4A–30.3 For directions as to the filing and serving of any evidence in support of an application, see Practice Direction 7 (Applications, Documents, Forms and Orders) para.7.1.3, and (where an oral hearing ordered) para.7.1.8. Parties to an application for a consent order must ensure that they provide any material needed to satisfy the Court that it is appropriate to make the order (para.7.1.5).

For guidance on documents which may need to be filed in support of an application, see Practice Direction 7 (Applications, Documents, Forms and Orders) para.7.1.3.

#### Amendment of filed document (r.30(5))

Paragraph (5) of r.30 is important. It is relevant to the amendment of a procedural application made in Form 2, but is not confined to such a document. For the exercise of the Registrar's power under r.30(5) to amend a document in the form of a notice of appeal, see Practice Direction 4 (Notice of Appeal) para.4.2.1. **4A–30.4**

### Requests for expedition

**31.—(1) Any request for urgent consideration of an application for permission to appeal or for an expedited hearing must be made to the Registrar.** **4A–31**

**(2) Wherever possible the views of all parties should be obtained before such a request is made.**

#### Effect of rule

For circumstances in which requests for expedition might be made and relevant practice, see Practice Direction 3 (Applications for Permission to Appeal) paras 3.4.3 to 3.4.7, Practice Direction 4 (Notice of Appeal) para.4.8.1, Practice Direction (The Appeal Hearing) para.6.2.4. **4A–31.1**

See, further, commentary following r.16 and r.20.

### Grouping appeals

**32. The Registrar may direct that appeals raising the same or similar issues shall be heard either together or consecutively by the Court constituted by the same Justices and may give any consequential directions that appear appropriate.** **4A–32**

#### Effect of rule

This rule is supplemented by Practice Direction 8 (Miscellaneous Matters) para.8.2. **4A–32.1**

### Change of interest

**33. The Court must be informed promptly of—** **4A–33**

**(a) the death or bankruptcy of any individual party;**

**(b) the winding up or dissolution of any corporate party;**

**(c) any compromise of the subject matter of an appeal;**

**(d) any event which does or may deprive an appeal of practical significance to the parties,**

**and the Court may give any consequential directions that appear appropriate.**

#### Effect of rule

A decision made in exercise of the Court's powers under r.33 is a procedural decision within r.9. **4A–33.1**

#### Death of party (r.33(a))

For practice where a party to an appeal dies before the hearing (including that relating to an application to substitute a new party in this circumstances), see Practice Direction 8 (Miscellaneous Matters) para.8.4. **4A–33.2**

#### Bankruptcy or winding up (r.33(a))

For practice where a party to an appeal is adjudicated bankrupt or a corporate **4A–33.3**

*Paragraph numbers marked with a "+" can be found online and on CD.*

party is ordered to be wound up before the hearing (including that relating to an application to pursue the appeal nonetheless), see Practice Direction 8 (Miscellaneous Matters) para.8.1.

#### Compromise (r.33(c))

4A-33.4 Paragraph 8.5.1 of Practice Direction 8 (Miscellaneous Matters) states that it is the duty of counsel and solicitors in any pending appeal, if an event occurs which arguably disposes of the dispute between the parties, either to ensure that the appeal is withdrawn by consent or, if there is no agreement on that course, to bring the facts promptly to the attention of the Registrar and to seek directions. See further r.34 and commentary thereon.

#### Event depriving appeal of practical significance (r.33(d))

4A-33.5 The Court must be informed of any event which does or may deprive an appeal of practical significance to the parties (r.33(c)). (There is no reason why "parties" in this context should not have the meaning given in r.3(2) and should therefore include an intervener.) An obvious such event would be where the parties consent to the appeal being withdrawn, see r.34. Another might be where an event had occurred that rendered "academic" or "hypothetical" the point of law raised by the appeal. For authorities on question whether appeal courts should decline jurisdiction in such circumstances (including House of Lords authority), see Vol.1 para.9A–77. The fact that an appeal has been deprived of its significance to the parties does not mean that it may not retain a wider significance.

### Withdrawal etc of application for permission to appeal or of appeal

4A-34 **34.—(1) An application for permission to appeal or a notice of appeal may be withdrawn with the written consent of all parties or with the permission of the Court on such terms as appear appropriate.**

**(2) The Court may set aside or vary the order appealed from by consent and without an oral hearing if satisfied that it is appropriate so to do.**

**(3) In this rule "a notice of appeal" includes an application for permission to appeal or cross-appeal which (under rule 18 or rule 25) stands as a notice of appeal or cross-appeal.**

#### Effect of rule

4A-34.1 A decision made in exercise of the Court's powers under r.34 is a procedural decision within r.9.

For practice where application is made to withdraw an application for permission to appeal, see Practice Direction 8 (Miscellaneous Matters) para.8.16.2.

For practice where application is made to withdraw an appeal that has not been listed, see *ibid*. para.8.16.3.

An appeal that has been listed for hearing may be withdrawn by order of the Court on application; for practice, see *ibid*. para.8.16.4.

### Advocate to the Court and assessors

4A-35 **35.—(1) The Court may request the relevant officer to appoint, or may itself appoint, an advocate to the Court to assist the Court with legal submissions.**

**(2) In accordance with section 44 of the Act the Court may, at the request of the parties or of its own initiative, appoint one or more independent specially qualified advisers to assist the Court as assessors on any technical matter.**

*Paragraph numbers marked with a "+" can be found online and on CD.*

**(3) The fees and expenses of any advocate to the Court or assessor shall be costs in the appeal.**

### Effect of rule

A decision made in exercise of the Court's powers under r.35 is a procedural decision within r.9. **4A–35.1**

### Assessors

Section 44(1) of the 2005 Act states that, if the Court thinks it expedient in any proceedings, it may hear and dispose of the proceedings wholly or partly with the assistance of one or more specially qualified advisers appointed by it. Rule 35(2) qualifies s.44(1) by adding that such advisers should be appointed "to assist the Court as assessors on any technical matter". Section 44(2) states that any remuneration payable to an adviser is to be determined by the Court unless agreed between the adviser and the parties to the proceedings, and s.44(3) states that any remuneration shall form part of the costs of the proceedings; r.35(3) states that an assessor's fees and expenses shall be costs in the appeal. **4A–35.2**

Specialist advisers provide assistance to the Court and are strictly independent of the parties to the appeal (Practice Direction 8 (Miscellaneous Matters) para.8.13.1). Any party to an appeal may apply in writing to the Registrar for specialist advisers appointed by the Court to attend the hearing (*ibid.*).

### Advocate to the Court

The "relevant officer" is, as provided by r.3(2), in relation to proceedings in England and Wales coming before the Court, the Attorney General. **4A–35.3**

A request for an advocate to the Court to be appointed in an appeal should be made in writing to the Registrar. Any request should indicate whether the other parties to the appeal support the request (Practice Direction 8 (Miscellaneous Matters) para.8.13.2).

For memorandum from the Lord Chief Justice and the Attorney General on requests for the appointment of an advocate to court in relation to proceedings in England and Wales, see Vol.1, para.39.8.1.

## Security for costs

**36.—(1) The Court may on the application of a respondent order an appellant to give security for the costs of the appeal and any order for security shall determine—** **4A–36**

**(a) the amount of that security, and**

**(b) the manner in which, and the time within which, security must be given.**

**(2) An order made under this rule may require payment of the judgment debt (and costs) in the court below instead of, or in addition to, the amount ordered by way of security for costs.**

### Effect of rule

A decision made in exercise of the Court's powers under r.36 is a procedural decision within r.9. **4A–36.1**

This rule is supplemented by Practice Direction 4 (Notice of Appeal) para.4.7.1 et seq. An application for security should be made in Form 2 (see Practice Direction 7 (Applications, Documents, Forms and Orders) para.7.1 and Annex 2).

As an application for security is a procedural application it should be made in accordance with r.30. The application should be made as soon as it becomes apparent that an application is necessary or expedient (Practice Direction 7 (Applications, Documents, Forms and Orders) para.7.1.1).

No security for costs is required in cross-appeals (*ibid.* para.4.7.2). No security for costs is required in criminal appeals (Practice Direction 12 (Criminal Proceedings) para.12.8.1). For payment of security, see Practice Direction 8 (Miscellaneous Matters) para.8.7.1.

Failure to provide security as required will result in the appeal being struck out by the Registrar although the appellant may apply to reinstate the appeal (Practice Direction 4 (Notice of Appeal) para.4.7.5.

For directions as to the deposit with the Court of security money (in cash or by cheque), see Practice Direction 8 (Miscellaneous Matters) para.8.7.1.

For payment out of any security for costs lodged with the Court, see r.54.

### Stay of execution

4A-37 **37. Any appellant who wishes to obtain a stay of execution of the order appealed from must seek it from the court below and only in wholly exceptional circumstances will the Court grant a stay.**

#### Effect of rule

4A-37.1 A decision made in exercise of the Court's powers under r.37 is a procedural decision within r.9. The rule assumes that the Court has power to order a stay. The Court has all the powers of the court below (r.29(1)) including, presumably, the power to order a stay pending an appeal.

Filing a notice of appeal or an application for permission to appeal does not in itself place a stay of execution on any order appealed from. A party seeking such a stay must apply to the court appealed from, not to the Court; the Court cannot stay an interlocutor of the Court of Session (Court of Session Act 1988 s.41(2)) (see Practice Direction 8 (Miscellaneous Matters) para.8.14.1).

### Change of solicitor and London agents

4A-38 **38.—(1) If a party for whom a solicitor is acting wishes to change solicitors, that party or the new solicitor must give the Registrar and the former solicitor written notice of the change.**

**(2) Until such notices are given the former solicitor shall continue to be treated as the party's solicitor.**

**(3) Solicitors practising outside London may appoint London agents and additional costs incurred by not appointing London agents may be disallowed.**

#### Effect of rule

4A-38.1 In this context, "solicitor" includes any person authorised to provide legal services other than as counsel in connection with proceedings before the Court (see r.3(2)).

Paragraph (3) of r.38 is restated in Practice Direction 4 (Notice of Appeal) para.4.2.14.

### Disposal of documents

4A-39 **39.—(1) All documents filed become the property of the Court and original documents must be retained in the records of the Registry.**

**(2) Other documents shall be destroyed unless the Registrar (on a written application made within 21 days of the end of the proceedings) directs otherwise.**

**(3) All documents held by the Court may be inspected by the press or members of the public on application to the Registrar but the Registrar may refuse an application for reasons of commercial confidentiality, national security or in the public interest.**

**(4) Before allowing an application for inspection under this rule, the Registrar may impose terms or conditions such as the**

**redaction of certain material where such a condition is necessary in the interests of justice or in the public interest.**

### Effect of rule

The heading to this rule is misleading. The rule deals with two quite distinct matters; disposal of documents by destruction, and inspection of documents by non-parties. **4A–39.1**

### Document disposal

Paragraph (2) of r.39 is supplemented by Practice Direction 7 (Applications, Documents, Forms and Orders) para.7.2.5. No documents submitted in connection with an application for permission to appeal can be returned (*ibid.*). Rule 29(2) states that an application to the Registrar should be made within 21 days of the end of proceedings; in para.7.2.5 it is stated that the application should be made within 14 days of judgment in the appeal. **4A–39.2**

### Inspection of documents held by the Court

Paragraph (3) of r.39 is amplified in Practice Direction 7 (Applications, Documents, Forms and Orders) para.7.2.6, where it is stated that non-parties inspecting documents must comply with any anonymity orders made in the proceedings, any data protection requirements, as well as with any conditions imposed by the Registrar under the rule. (Rule 39(3) may be contrasted with CPR r.5.4C (supply of documents to non-party from court records).) **4A–39.3**

For fees payable on requests for copies of documents, see Practice Direction 7 (Applications, Documents, Forms and Orders) Annex 2.

# PART 6

# PARTICULAR APPEALS AND REFERENCES

## Human Rights Act issues

**40.—(1) Where an appeal raises a question of incompatibility under section 4 of the Human Rights Act 1998[1] and the Crown is not already a party to the appeal, the Registrar shall give 21 days' notice of the question to the Crown.** **4A–40**

**(2) If notice is given that the Crown wishes to be joined, the appropriate Minister or other person shall be joined accordingly.**

**(3) If such a question arises for the first time during the course of an appeal hearing the Court will if necessary adjourn the proceedings to enable the Registrar to give notice under paragraph (1).**

### Effect of rule

It is explained in para.1.2.23 of Practice Direction 1 that the Human Rights Act 1998 applies to the Court and issues under that statute will often arise on appeals to the Court; but the Act does not confer any general right of appeal. **4A–40.1**

Rule 40 is supplemented by Practice Direction 9 (The Human Rights Act 1998), where detailed provisions as to practice and procedure are laid down, first for appeals involving declarations of incompatibility, and secondly, for other appeals under the 1998 Act.

## Devolution jurisdiction

**41.—(1) Appeals or references under the Court's devolution jurisdiction shall in general be dealt with in accordance with these** **4A–41**

[1] 1998 c. 42.

*Paragraph numbers marked with a "+" can be found online and on CD.*

SUPREME COURT

**Rules but the Court shall give special directions as and when necessary, and in particular as to—**

**(a) any question referred under section 33 of the Scotland Act 1998[1], section 11 of the Northern Ireland Act 1998[2] or section 96, 99 or 112 of the Government of Wales Act 2006[3],**

**(b) any reference of a devolution issue[4],**

**(c) any direct references under paragraph 33 or 34 of Schedule 6 to the Scotland Act 1998, paragraph 33 or 34 of Schedule 10 to the Northern Ireland Act 1998 or paragraph 29 or 30 of Schedule 9 to the Government of Wales Act 2006.**

**(2) A reference made by the relevant officer is made by filing the reference and by serving a copy on any other relevant officer who is not already a party and who has a potential interest in the proceedings.**

**(3) A reference must state the question or issue to be decided by the Court.**

**(4) The Registrar shall give notice of the question or issue to the appropriate relevant officer where that officer is not already a party to any proceedings.**

### Effect of rule

4A–41.2 The jurisdiction of the Court in devolution matters is explained in Practice Direction 1 para.1.2.24, and (in greater detail) in Practice Direction 10 (Devolution Jurisdiction) para.10.1. Rule 41(1) states that appeals or references under the Court's devolution jurisdiction shall in general be dealt with in accordance with the Rules. Practice Direction 10 restates r.41 and amplifies its provisions in certain respects. In addition it explains that devolution matters can reach the Court in four ways and contains directions as to each, some of which impose time limits for the taking of certain procedural steps (see paras 10.2 to 10.5 inclusive). In relation to the second way (appeals from UK superior courts) the practice direction briefly explains the normal effects of provisions in Pt 2 and Pt 3.

For meaning of "relevant officer", see r.3(2).

A decision made in exercise of the Court's powers under r.41 is a procedural decision within r.9.

For fees payable on references under the devolution jurisdiction, see Practice Direction 7 (Applications, Documents, Forms and Orders) Annex 2.

## Court of Justice of the European Communities

4A–42 **42.—(1) Where it is contended on an application for permission to appeal that it raises a question of Community law which should be the subject of a reference under Article 234 of the Treaty establishing the European Community and permission to appeal is refused, the panel of Justices will give brief reasons for its decision.**

---

[1] 1998 c. 46; section 33 provides for the scrutiny of proposed Acts of the Scottish Parliament by the Supreme Court.

[2] 1998 c. 47; section 11 provides for the scrutiny of proposed Acts of the Northern Ireland Assembly by the Supreme Court.

[3] 2006 c. 32; sections 96, 99 and 112 provide for the scrutiny of proposed Orders in Council, proposed Assembly Measures and proposed Acts of the National Assembly for Wales by the Supreme Court.

[4] A devolution issue is defined in Schedule 6 to the Scotland Act 1998, Schedule 10 to the Northern Ireland Act 1998 and Schedule 9 to the Government of Wales Act 2006.

*Paragraph numbers marked with a "+" can be found online and on CD.*

**(2) Where on an application for permission to appeal a panel of Justices decides to make a reference under Article 234 before determining the application, it will give consequential directions as to the form of the reference and the staying of the application (but it may if it thinks fit dispose of other parts of the application at once).**

**(3) Where at the hearing of an appeal the Court decides to make a reference under Article 234 it will give consequential directions as to the form of the reference and the staying of the appeal (but it may if it thinks fit dispose of other parts of the appeal at once).**

**(4) An order of the Court shall be prepared and sealed by the Registrar to record any decision made under this rule.**

#### Effect of rule

Community law requires that the Supreme Court (as the domestic court of last resort) should refer to the Court of Justice of the European Communities any doubtful questions of Community law necessary to its decision. **4A–42.1**

If an appellant seeks a reference to the Court of Justice, this should be stated clearly in the notice of appeal, and the appellant must notify the Registrar in writing (Practice Direction 4 (Notice of Appeal) para.4.2.13). In Section 7 of Form 1, which is to be used for applications for permission to appeal (as well as for notices of appeal), the applicant is required to state whether the Court is to be asked to make a reference to the Court of Justice.

Practice Direction 11 (The European Court of Justice) supplements r.42. This Practice Direction, in addition to amplifying r.42, contains provisions stating the practice and procedure to be followed if, after the Court of Justice has given judgment, a further hearing by the Court is required.

#### Costs of reference

The Court of Justice does not make orders for costs. The costs of the reference are included in the order of the Supreme Court disposing of the appeal; and, if necessary, are assessed by the Costs Officers of the Court (Practice Direction 11 (The European Court of Justice) para.11.1.10). **4A–42.2**

### Revocation of patents

**43.—(1) On any appeal under sections 12 and 13 of the Administration of Justice Act 1969[1] from an order for revocation of a patent the appellant must serve notice of the appeal on the Comptroller-General of Patents ("the Comptroller") as well as on every respondent.** **4A–43**

**(2) A respondent who decides not to oppose the appeal must serve notice of that decision on the Comptroller together with the relevant statements of case.**

**(3) The Comptroller shall within 14 days serve on the appellant and file a notice stating whether or not the Comptroller intends to appear on the appeal.**

**(4) Where notice is given under paragraph (3), the Comptroller may appear on the appeal.**

[1] 1969 c. 58; section 12 has been amended by the Courts Act 1971 (c.23), Schedule 11 Part IV, Judicature (Northern Ireland) Act 1978 (c.23) section 122(1)(2), Schedule 6 paragraph 13, Schedule 7, Part I and the Senior Courts Act 1981 (c.54), section 152(4), Schedule 7.

### Effect of rule

4A–43.1 This rule applies from where there is a direct ("leapfrog") appeal from the High Court from an order made by the High Court for the revocation of a patent made under the Patents Act 1949 s.32 or s.61, or the Patents Act 1977 s.72. The rule is re-stated, and directions are given, in Practice Direction 8 (Miscellaneous Matters) para.8.11. The 14 day time limit referred to in r.43(3) runs from the date on which the Comptroller receives notice of the respondent's decision (para.8.11.4). The Court may make such orders for the postponement or adjournment of the hearing of the appeal as may appear necessary for the purpose of giving effect to these provisions (para.8.11.6).

## Criminal appeals

4A–44 **44. The Court must apply in accordance with the relevant practice direction the code of practice for victims issued under section 32 of the Domestic Violence, Crime and Victims Act 2004.[1]**

### Effect of rule

4A–44.1 The jurisdiction of the Court in criminal proceedings is explained in Practice Direction 1 para.1.2. Appeals to the Court in criminal proceedings in England and Wales or Northern Ireland are subject to special restrictions limiting such appeals to cases of general public importance (para.1.2.10). There is no appeal in criminal proceedings from the High Court of Justiciary or any other court in Scotland, but issues relating to criminal proceedings in Scotland may come before the Supreme Court as devolution issues under the Scotland Act 1998 (*ibid.*).

Practice Direction 12 (Criminal Proceedings) contains detailed provisions for the handling of criminal appeals by the Court and affects a wide range of matters of procedure and practice. The Practice Directions governing civil proceedings (they are Practice Directions 1 to 11, 13 and 14) apply to criminal proceedings in the Court subject to any modifications or additional provisions made by Practice Direction 12 (*ibid.* para.12.1.2).

Although, in large part, Practice Direction 12 simply re-states the effects of particular Rules and provisions in other practice directions as they apply to criminal appeals, it also makes some modifications and additions. Consequently, care must be taken in reading its provisions alongside the Rules and other practice directions.

For practice relating to the giving effect, in criminal appeals to the Court, to the victims code of practice issued under the Domestic Violence, Crime and Victims Act 2004 s.42, see Practice Direction 12 (Criminal Proceedings) para.12.15.

# PART 7

# FEES AND COSTS

## Fees

4A–45 **45. Where a fee is prescribed by any order made under section 52 of the Act, the Registrar may refuse to accept a document or refuse to allow a party to take any step unless the relevant fee is paid.**

### Effect of rule

4A–45.1 The fees which are payable in the Court are prescribed by the Supreme Court Fees Order 2009 (SI 2009/2131) made under s.52 of the 2005 Act. For fees payable, see Annex 2 to Practice Direction 7 (Applications, Documents, Forms and Orders) (replicating Sch.1 to the 2009 Order). The Registry will not issue an application for permission to appeal or other document unless (amongst other things) the prescribed fee is paid

[1] 2004 c. 28.

*Paragraph numbers marked with a "+" can be found online and on CD.*

or a request for fee remission from court fees is made (Practice Direction 2 (The Registry of the Supreme Court) para.2.1.11).

Any fees paid are not refunded, even if it is decided that an application for permission to appeal is inadmissible or if an application or other proceeding is withdrawn (ibid para.2.1.31).

Payments of fees may be made in cash or by banker's draft or cheque made payable to "The Supreme Court of the United Kingdom" (Practice Direction 8 (Miscellaneous Matters) para 8.7.1).

### Fee waiver and remission

In circumstances where a party would suffer financial hardship by the payment of fees, the requirement to pay fees may be waived. Schedule 2 to the 2009 Order applies for the purpose of ascertaining whether a party is entitled to a remission or part remission of a prescribed fee. This Schedule is similar to Sch.2 to the Civil Proceedings Fees Order 2008 (see para.10–1 below), adjusted to take into account legislation applicable in Northern Ireland and Scotland, and with the Chief Executive of the Supreme Court authorised to remit fees in those particular circumstances in which the Lord Chancellor is so authorised under the 2008 Order (a variation that demonstrates the independence of the Court from the Executive branch of Government). **4A–45.2**

Any request for fee remission should be made to the Registrar (who is "the court officer" for the purposes of art.7 of Sch.2), supported by evidence of the party's means (Practice Direction 2 (The Registry of the Supreme Court) para.2.1.29). The Registrar may then grant full or part remission of the relevant fee. Remission of fees is usually granted where a remission of fees has been granted in the court below.

## Orders for costs

**46.—(1) The Court may make such orders as it considers just in respect of the costs of any appeal, application for permission to appeal, or other application to or proceeding before the Court.** **4A–46**

**(2) The Court's powers to make orders for costs may be exercised either at the final determination of an appeal or application for permission to appeal or in the course of the proceedings.**

**(3) Orders for costs will not normally be made either in favour of or against interveners but such orders may be made if the Court considers it just to do so (in particular if an intervener has in substance acted as the sole or principal appellant or respondent).**

### Effect of rules 46 to 53

In relation to an appeal or a reference, the Supreme Court has all the powers of the court below and may make a costs order (r.29(1)(e)). **4A–46.1**

Rules 46 to 53 are supplemented by Practice Direction 13 (Costs). This practice direction contains a comprehensive code dealing with the entitlement to costs of parties to cases dealt with by the Court, with the assessment of costs, and with the procedure for the detailed assessment of costs by Costs Officers appointed by the President of the Court under r.49. Subject to some minor variations, Practice Direction 13 follows in structure and in detail the Practice Directions Applicable to Judicial Taxations in the House of Lords (March 2007). Detailed provisions for the assessment of costs are contained in Section 1. Forms of bill of costs are set out in Section 2. Whereas the Judicial Taxation Directions contained two forms of the summary to be included in a completed bill of costs, one for general use and the other (requiring certain additional information) where costs are payable under a certificate of public funding or representation order, Section 3 of Practice Direction 13 contains a form for the summary adaptable to both circumstances, followed by the Allocatur form. Section 5 contains guideline figures for the provisional assessment of costs.

For the fees payable on the assessment of a bill of costs, see Annex 2 to Practice Direction 7 (Applications, Documents, Forms and Orders).

For provisions relevant to the award of costs where an application for permission to appeal in civil proceedings is determined by the Court, see Practice Direction 3 (Applications for Permission to Appeal) para.3.5.

For provisions relevant to the award of costs where an application for permission to appeal in criminal proceedings is determined by the Court, see Practice Direction 12 (Criminal Appeals) para.12.5.

#### Related provisions

4A-46.2 Some provisions found elsewhere in the Rules and in other supplementing practice directions deal with issues relating to costs. The principal ones (some of which are restated in Practice Direction 13) are outlined immediately below.

Conditional fee agreements may properly be made by parties to appeals before the Court (see Practice Direction 6 (The Appeal Hearing) para.6.7.2, and Practice Direction 13 (Costs) para.28.1).

An order for costs will not be made in favour of a respondent who has not given notice of acknowledgement under r.21 (Practice Direction 4 (Notice of Appeal) para.4.6.4).

Generally, only junior counsel's fees will be allowed for any stage of an application for permission to appeal (Practice Direction 3 (Applications for Permission to Appeal) para.3.4.8).

The fees of two counsel only for any party at an appeal hearing are allowed on assessment unless the Court orders otherwise on application at the hearing (Practice Direction 6 (The Appeal Hearing) para.6.3.7, and Practice Direction 13 (Costs) para.16.5).

Solicitors outside London who decide to appoint London agents may be disallowed on any assessment of costs any additional costs incurred as a result of that decision (r.38(3)).

The cost of preparing the volumes of authorities (r.24) falls to the appellants, but is ultimately subject to the decision of the Court as to the costs of the appeal (Practice Direction 6 (The Appeal Hearing) para.6.5.8).

A party requesting the services of a stenographer at an appeal hearing for the purpose of providing a transcript of the proceedings bears the costs involved (Practice Direction 6 (The Appeal Hearing) para.6.6.6).

### Submissions as to costs

4A-47 **47.—(1) If a party wishes to defer making submissions as to costs until after judgment, the Court must be informed of this not later than at the close of the oral argument.**

**(2) If the Court accedes to the request it will give such directions as appear appropriate and it may, in particular, give directions—**

- **(a) for the hearing of oral submissions as to costs immediately after judgment;**
- **(b) for the simultaneous or sequential filing of written submissions as to costs within a specified period after judgment;**
- **(c) for the hearing of oral submissions after the filing of written submissions.**

#### Effect of rule

4A-47.1 Where a party makes written submissions as to costs under r.47, the original and seven copies of the submissions must be filed at the Registry and copies should be sent to other parties to the appeal (Practice Direction 6 (The Appeal Hearing) para.6.7.1). Written costs submissions are considered on paper unless the Court gives directions for the hearing of oral submission.

### Claim for costs

4A-48 **48.—(1) Where the Court has made an order for costs, the claim**

**for costs must be submitted to the Registrar within three months beginning with the date on which the costs order was made.**

**(2) The form and contents of a claim for costs must comply with the relevant practice direction and the receiving party must supply such further particulars, information and documents as the Registrar may direct.**

**(3) The receiving party must serve a copy of a claim for costs on the paying party.**

**(4) Within 21 days beginning with the day on which a claim for costs is served, the paying party may (or, in the circumstances specified in the relevant practice direction, must) file points of dispute and, if so, must serve a copy on the receiving party.**

**(5) Within 14 days beginning with the day on which points of dispute are served, the receiving party may file a response and, if so, must serve a copy on the paying party.**

#### Effect of rule

For form and content of claim for cost, see Practice Direction 13 (Costs) Section 1 para.7. **4A–48.1**

The fee payable for filing a claim for costs is two-and-a-half per cent of the amount claimed (Sch.1 to the Supreme Court Fees Order 2009 (SI 2009/2131).

### Assessment of costs

**49.—(1) Every detailed assessment of costs shall be carried out by two costs officers appointed by the President and—** **4A–49**

**(a) one costs officer must be a Costs Judge (a Taxing Master of the Senior Courts), and**

**(b) the second may be the Registrar.**

**(2) A disputed assessment shall be dealt with at an oral hearing.**

**(3) An assessment may provide for the costs of the assessment procedure.**

**(4) The Registrar will give the receiving party and the paying party written notice of the date of the assessment.**

**(5) Where one of the parties so requests or in the circumstances specified in the relevant practice direction, the Registrar may make a provisional assessment of costs without the attendance of the parties.**

**(6) The Registrar must inform the parties in writing of the outcome of a provisional assessment and, if a party is dissatisfied with the outcome, or if points of disagreement cannot be resolved in correspondence, the Registrar shall appoint a date for an oral hearing.**

**(7) Any request for an oral hearing following a provisional assessment of costs must be made within 14 days of the receipt of the Registrar's decision on the assessment.**

#### Effect of rule

For directions as to provisional assessment, see Practice Direction 13 (Costs) Section 1 para.14. **4A–49.1**

Before s.59 of the 2005 Act came into force, the office of Taxing Master of the Senior Courts was the office of Taxing Master of the Supreme Court (see Pt II of Sch.2 to the 1981 Act).

### Basis of assessment

4A-50 **50.—(1) Where the Court is to assess the amount of costs it will assess those costs—**

**(a) on the standard basis, or**

**(b) on the indemnity basis,**

**in the manner specified by rule 51 or (where appropriate) on the relevant bases that apply in Scotland or Northern Ireland.**

**(2) Where—**

**(a) the Court makes an order about costs without indicating the basis on which the costs are to be assessed, or**

**(b) the Court makes an order for costs to be assessed on a basis other than one specified in paragraph (1),**

**the costs will be assessed on the standard basis.**

**(3) This rule applies subject to any order or direction to the contrary.**

#### Effect of rule

4A-50.1 See commentary following r.51.

### The standard basis and the indemnity basis

4A-51 **51.—(1) Costs assessed on the standard basis are allowed only if they are proportionate to the matters in issue and are reasonably incurred and reasonable in amount.**

**(2) Any doubt as to whether costs assessed on the standard basis are reasonably incurred and are reasonable and proportionate in amount will be resolved in favour of the paying party.**

**(3) Costs assessed on the indemnity basis are allowed only if they are reasonably incurred and reasonable in amount.**

**(4) Any doubt as to whether costs assessed on the indemnity basis are reasonably incurred and are reasonable in amount will be resolved in favour of the receiving party.**

#### Effect of rule

4A-51.1 For directions as to basis of assessment, see Practice Direction 13 (Costs) Section 1 para.10.

### Amount of assessed costs to be specified

4A-52 **52. The amount of any assessed costs will be inserted in the order made under rule 29 but, if that order is drawn up before the assessment has been completed, the amount assessed will be certified by the Registrar.**

#### Effect of rule

4A-52.1 The Court has all the powers of the court below and r.29(1)(e) expressly states that the Court may make a costs order.

For directions as to certificates, see Practice Direction 13 (Costs) Section 1 para.24. A fee of two-and-a-half per cent of the amount allowed on assessment is payable before the issue of a certificate (Sch.1 to the Supreme Court Fees Order 2009 (SI 2009/2131).

### Appeal from assessment

4A-53 **53.—(1) A party who is dissatisfied with the assessment of costs made at an oral hearing may apply for that decision to be reviewed**

**by a single Justice and any application under this rule must be made in the appropriate form and be filed within 14 days of the decision.**

**(2) The single Justice may (without an oral hearing) affirm the decision made on the assessment or may, where it appears appropriate, refer the matter to a panel of Justices to be decided with or without an oral hearing.**

**(3) An application may be made under this rule only on a question of principle and not in respect of the amount allowed on any item in the claim for costs.**

#### Effect of rule

An application for an appeal by way of review of an assessment decision is made in Form 2 under r.30. For relevant directions as to practice and procedure supplementing the provisions of r.53, see Practice Direction 13 (Costs) Section 1 para.18. **4A–53.1**

### Payment out of security for costs

**54. Any security for costs lodged by an appellant will be dealt with by the Registrar in accordance with the directions of the Court.** **4A–54**

#### Effect of rule

For deposit of security for costs, see r.36 and commentary following. **4A–54.1**

## PART 8

## TRANSITIONAL ARRANGEMENTS

### Transitional arrangements

**55.—(1) Unless the Court or the Registrar directs otherwise, these Rules shall apply, with any necessary modifications, to appeals which were proceeding, and petitions for leave which were lodged, in the House of Lords before 1st October 2009.** **4A–55**

**(2) The Court or the Registrar may give special directions, as and when necessary, in relation to appeals which were proceeding, and petitions for leave which were lodged, in the House of Lords before 1st October 2009 notwithstanding anything that was done in accordance with the Practice Directions and Standing Orders of the House of Lords.**

#### Effect of rule

The power to give directions exercisable by "the Court or the Registrar" under this rule do not fall under r.9 (Procedural decisions). Presumably, they are exercisable by a single Justice. **4A–55.1**

## PRACTICE DIRECTION 1—GENERAL NOTE AND THE JURISDICTION OF THE HIGH COURT

### *Section 1 The Supreme Court—General Note*

4A–56 **1.1.1** The Supreme Court of the United Kingdom was established by Part 3 of the Constitutional Reform Act 2005 ("the Act"), coming into force on 1st October 2009. Its jurisdiction corresponds to that of the House of Lords in its judicial capacity under the Appellate Jurisdiction Acts 1876 and 1888 (which are repealed) together with devolution matters under the Scotland Act 1998, the Northern Ireland Act 1998 and the Government of Wales Act 2006, which are transferred to the Supreme Court from the Judicial Committee of the Privy Council. The jurisdiction of the Supreme Court is defined by section 40 of, and Schedule 9 to, the Act.

**1.1.2** Under section 45 of the Act, the senior Lord of Appeal in Ordinary has, after consulting the Lord Chancellor, the General Council of the Bar of England and Wales, the Law Society of England and Wales, the Faculty of Advocates of Scotland, the Law Society of Scotland, the General Council of the Bar of Northern Ireland, the Law Society of Northern Ireland and other bodies likely to be affected by the Rules, made the Supreme Court Rules, which are published as S.I. 2009/1603. The Rules, which come into force on 1st October 2009, apply to civil and criminal appeals to the Court and to appeals and references under the Court's devolution jurisdiction.

**1.1.3** The overriding objective of the Supreme Court Rules is to secure that the Court is accessible, fair and efficient and the senior Lord of Appeal in Ordinary, the President of the Supreme Court, has issued these Practice Directions to supplement the Supreme Court Rules, to provide for the forms to be used in the Supreme Court and to provide general guidance and assistance to parties and their legal representatives.

#### Transitional arrangements

**1.1.4** Rule 55 of the Supreme Court Rules makes transitional arrangements for appeals and applications which were filed before 1st October 2009. Unless the Court or the Registrar directs otherwise, the Rules apply, with any necessary modifications, to any appeals and applications which were lodged in the House of Lords before 1st October 2009 and the Court or the Registrar may give special directions in these circumstances.

#### Forms

**1.1.5** The Practice Directions provide for a number of forms and a reference in the Supreme Court Rules or in these Practice Directions to a form by number means the form so numbered in the relevant practice direction. The forms are to be used in the cases to which they apply or in the particular circumstances for which they are provided but a form may be varied by the Court or a party if the variation is required by the circumstances of a particular case. The forms are set out in Annex 1 to Practice Direction 7.

#### Jurisdiction

**1.1.6** The jurisdiction of the Supreme Court corresponds to that of the House of Lords in its judicial capacity together with devolution matters and its jurisdiction is summarised in Section 2 of this Practice Direction.

### *Section 2 The Jurisdiction of the Supreme Court*

#### Civil Appeals

**1.2.1** The key provisions in relation to civil appeals are subsections (2) and (3) of section 40 of the Act: **4A–57**

(2) An appeal lies to the Court from any order or judgment of the Court of Appeal in England and Wales in civil proceedings.

(3) An appeal lies to the Court from any order or judgment of a court in Scotland if an appeal lay from that court to the House of Lords at or immediately before the commencement of this section.

**1.2.2** The principal provisions relating to civil appeals from Scotland are in section 40 of the Court of Session Act 1988 as amended by the Act. (But see also sections 24, 27 (5), 32(5), 41, 42, 43 and 52(3) as amended for further matters of detail.)

**1.2.3** The principal provisions relating to civil appeals from Northern Ireland are in section 42 of the Judicature (Northern Ireland) Act 1978 as amended by the Act. See also sections 43 (preserving leapfrog appeals), 44 (contempt) and 45 (habeas corpus), as amended.

**1.2.4** Schedule 9 of the Act also amends a large number of statutes which gave rights of appeal (often limited to issues of law) to the House of Lords; these are replaced by corresponding rights of appeal to the Supreme Court.

**1.2.5** Section 40(6) of the Act provides:

> An appeal under subsection (2) lies only with the per-mission of the Court of Appeal or the Supreme Court; but this is subject to provision under any other enactment restricting such an appeal.

The most important general restriction on rights of appeal is section 54(4) of the Access to Justice Act 1999.[1] The effect of this provision is that the Supreme Court may not entertain any appeal against an order of the Court of Appeal refusing permission for an appeal to the Court of Appeal from a lower court.

**1.2.6** Where the Supreme Court does not have jurisdiction, the Registrar will inform the appellant in writing that the Supreme Court does not have jurisdiction. The European Court of Human Rights accepts this letter as setting out the jurisdiction of the Supreme Court in the litigation, for the purpose of determining whether the appellant has satisfied the requirement, laid down by Article 35 of the European Convention on Human Rights, that all domestic remedies must be exhausted before an appeal can be made to the Strasbourg Court.

[1] Section 54 of the Access to Justice Act 1999 does not extend to Northern Ireland and the Civil Procedure Rules do not apply there, but the rule in *Lane v Esdaile* (see *Lane v Esdaile* [1891] AC 10) applies to Northern Ireland.

*Other statutory restrictions*

**1.2.7** There are other statutory restrictions on the Court's jurisdiction. The following are excluded from the Court's jurisdiction and are inadmissible–

(a) appeals from incidental decisions of the Court of Appeal which may be called into question by rules of court: see Senior Courts Act 1981, section 58 (as amended by Access to Justice Act 1999, section 60);

(b) applications brought by a person in respect of whom the High Court has made an order under section 42 of the Senior Courts Act 1981 (restriction of vexatious legal proceedings);[1]

(c) applications for permission to appeal from a decision of the Court of Appeal on any appeal from a county court in any probate proceedings;[2]

(d) applications for permission to appeal from a decision of the Court of Appeal on an appeal from a decision of the High Court on a question of law under Part III of the Representation of the People Act 1983 (legal proceedings);[3]

(e) applications for permission to appeal against the refusal by the Court of Appeal to reopen [4] a previously concluded appeal or application for permission to appeal.[5]

*Civil contempt of court cases*

**1.2.8** In cases involving civil contempt of court, an appeal may be brought under section 13 of the Administration of Justice Act 1960.[6] Permission to appeal is required and an application for permission must first be made to the court below. If that application is refused, an application for permission to appeal may then be made to the Supreme Court. Where the decision of the court below is a decision on appeal under the same section of the same Act, permission to appeal to the Supreme Court is only granted if the court below certifies that a point of law of general public importance is involved in that decision and if it appears to that court or to the Supreme Court, as the case may be, that the point is one that ought to be considered by the Supreme Court. Where the court below refuses to grant the certificate required, an application for permission to appeal is not accepted for filing in the Supreme Court.

*Time limit for applying for permission to appeal (civil appeals)*

**1.2.9** The time limit for applying for permission to appeal in civil cases (other than civil contempt of court or habeas corpus) is 28 days from the date of the order appealed from. The Supreme Court may extend this time limit.

---

[1] It is open to such a person to seek to appeal the section 42 order itself if that order was the subject of an appeal to the Court of Appeal.

[2] County Courts Act 1984 s 82.

[3] Representation of the People Act 1983 s 157(1).

[4] Under the rule in *Taylor v Lawrence* [2002] EWCA Civ 90 the Court of Appeal can in exceptional circumstances re-open an appeal or application for permission to appeal after it has given a final judgment.

[5] Civil Procedure Rules, r 52.17.

[6] Or, in Northern Ireland, under Judicature (Northern Ireland) Act 1978 s 44.

***Paragraph numbers marked with a "+" can be found online and on CD.***

**Criminal Appeals**

**1.2.10** Appeals to the Supreme Court in criminal proceedings in England and Wales or Northern Ireland are subject to special restrictions limiting such appeals to cases of general public importance. As before, there is no appeal in criminal proceedings from the High Court of Justiciary or any other court in Scotland, but issues relating to criminal proceedings in Scotland may come before the Supreme Court as devolution issues under the Scotland Act 1998. **4A-58**

**England and Wales (except courts-martial)**

**1.2.11** Appeals to the Supreme Court in criminal proceedings in England and Wales are regulated by sections 33 and 34 of the Criminal Appeal Act 1968 and sections 1 and 2 of the Administration of Justice Act 1960 as amended (in each case) by section 88 of the Courts Act 2003 and section 40 of, and Schedule 9 to, the Act. All such appeals may be made at the instance of the accused or the prosecutor. Section 13 of the Administration of Justice Act 1960 (as amended) extends the scope of sections 1 and 2, with some qualifications, to appeals relating to contempt of court (civil or criminal). Sections 36 to 38 of the Criminal Appeal Act 1968 (as amended) contain ancillary provisions about bail, detention and attendance at appeal hearings.

**1.2.12** Any appeal under these provisions requires the permission of the court below or the Supreme Court, which may be granted (except for a first appeal in a contempt of court matter) only if (i) the court below certifies that a point of general public importance is involved and (ii) it appears to the court below or to the Supreme Court that the point is one which ought to be considered by the Supreme Court.

**1.2.13** Section 36 of the Criminal Justice Act 1972 (as amended) permits the Court of Appeal to refer a point of law to the Supreme Court where (after an acquittal) the Attorney-General has referred the point of law to the Court of Appeal.

*Northern Ireland*

**1.2.14** Similar provisions apply to appeals in criminal proceedings in Northern Ireland: see sections 31 and 32 of the Criminal Appeal (Northern Ireland) Act 1980 and section 41 of, and Schedule 1 to, the Judicature (Northern Ireland) Act 1978 as amended (in each case) by section 105 of the Courts Act 2003 and section 40 of, and Schedule 9 to, the Act.

*Courts-Martial*

**1.2.15** Similar provisions apply to appeals from the Courts-Martial Appeal Court: see sections 39 and 40 of the Courts-Martial (Appeals) Act 1968 as amended by section 91 of the Courts Act 2003 and section 40 of, and Schedule 9 to, the Act.

*Time limit for applying for permission to appeal (criminal appeals)*

**1.2.16** As a result of amendments made by the Courts Act 2003 the time limit for applying for permission to appeal is 28 days from the

SUPREME COURT

date of the decision to be appealed from, or (if later) the date when reasons for the decision are given. The Supreme Court may extend time except in appeals under the Extradition Act 2003 (see sections 32 and 33 of that Act).

### Leapfrog appeals

4A–59 **1.2.17** Under sections 12 to 16 of the Administration of Justice Act 1969 as amended, appeals in civil matters may exceptionally be permitted to be made direct to the Supreme Court from (i) the High Court in England and Wales (ii) a Divisional Court in England and Wales and (iii) the High Court of Northern Ireland. These appeals are generally called leapfrog appeals.

**1.2.18** Such appeals are permitted only if (i) the judge certifies (immediately after judgment or on an application within 14 days) that the "relevant conditions" are satisfied, that a sufficient case has been made out to justify an application for permission to appeal to the Supreme Court, and that all parties consent; (ii) the Supreme Court (on an application made within one month, a time limit which may be extended by the Supreme Court) gives permission for the appeal and (iii) it is not a case of contempt of court or one in which an appeal to the Court of Appeal (or the Court of Appeal of Northern Ireland) (a) would not have lain even with permission or (b) would not have had leave granted for it.

**1.2.19** The "relevant conditions" (set out in section 12(3) of the Administration of Justice Act 1969) are that a point of general public importance is involved and that it either:

"(a) relates wholly or mainly to the construction of an enactment or of a statutory instrument, and has been fully argued in the proceedings and fully considered in the judgment of the judge in the proceedings, or

(b) is one in respect of which the judge is bound by a decision of the Court of Appeal or of the Supreme Court in previous proceedings, and was fully considered in the judgments given by the Court of Appeal or the Supreme Court (as the case may be) in those previous proceedings."

(In the case of leapfrog appeals from Northern Ireland the above references to the Court of Appeal must be read as references to the Court of Appeal of Northern Ireland.)

### Judicial review in England and Wales: civil matters

4A–60 **1.2.20** An application for permission to apply for judicial review is made to the Administrative Court (which is part of the Queen's Bench Division of the High Court). If the judge in the Administrative Court refuses the application without a hearing, an application can be made for the decision to be reconsidered at a hearing. Where permission to apply for judicial review has been refused by the Administrative Court after reconsideration at an oral hearing, the applicant may appeal against the refusal of permission. Such an appeal must be filed in the Court of Appeal within 7 days. For such an appeal to be successful, the applicant needs to be granted both i) permission to ap-

*Paragraph numbers marked with a "+" can be found online and on CD.*

peal against the Administrative Court's determination; and ii) permission to apply for judicial review.

**1.2.21** If the Court of Appeal refuses permission to appeal to it against the Administrative Court's refusal of permission to apply for judicial review, there is no appeal to the Supreme Court. The Supreme Court has no jurisdiction to entertain such an appeal: *R v Secretary of State for Trade and Industry, ex parte Eastaway* [2000] 1 WLR 2222 applying the principle in *Lane v Esdaile* [1891] AC 10. However, if the Court of Appeal (a) grants permission to appeal to it against the Administrative Court's refusal of permission to apply for judicial review, but then (b) itself refuses permission to apply for judicial review, the Supreme Court does have jurisdiction to hear an appeal against that refusal: *R v Hammersmith and Fulham LBC, ex parte Burkett* [2002] 1WLR 1593.

**1.2.22** Similar provisions apply in Scotland and Northern Ireland.

### Human Rights

**1.2.23** The Human Rights Act 1998 applies to the Supreme Court **4A–61**
and issues under that statute will often arise on appeals to the Supreme Court. But the Human Rights Act 1998 does not confer any general right of appeal beyond those mentioned in this Practice Direction. As to declarations of incompatibility, see rule 40 and Practice Direction 9 (Human Rights Act issues).

### Devolution Matters

**1.2.24** Devolution matters raise issues of constitutional importance **4A–62**
as to the purported or proposed exercise of a function by a member of the Scottish Executive, a Minister in Northern Ireland or a Northern Ireland department or the Welsh Ministers or as to the legislative competence of the Scottish Parliament under the Scotland Act 1998, the Northern Ireland Assembly under the Northern Ireland Act 1998, and the Welsh Assembly under the Government of Wales Act 2006. Under these Acts, as amended by Part 2 of Schedule 9 to the Act, the Supreme Court has an appellate jurisdiction in proceedings for the determination of a devolution issue and special statutory powers to consider referred questions, including questions referred by the relevant law officer or Ministers. The principal provisions are in sections 33 and 98 of, and paras 10, 11, 12, 13, 22, 23, 30, 31, 33 and 34 of Schedule 6 to, the Scotland Act 1998 (as amended by Part 2 of Schedule 9 to the Act); sections 11 and 79 of, and paras 9, 10, 19, 20, 28, 29, 30, 31, 33 and 34 of Schedule 10 to, the Northern Ireland Act 1998 (as amended by Part 2 of Schedule 9 to the Act), and section 96 of, and paras 10, 11, 18, 19, 20, 21, 27, 28, 29 and 30 of Schedule 9 to, the Government of Wales Act 2006.

See rule 41 and Practice Direction 10 (Devolution Issues).

### References under Art. 234

**1.2.25** Community law requires that the Supreme Court (as the **4A–63**
domestic court of last resort) should refer to the Court of Justice of the European Communities any doubtful questions of Community law necessary to its decision. See rule 42 and Practice Direction 11 (Court of Justice of the European Communities).

### *Section 3 The exercise of the Supreme Court's jurisdiction*

4A–64 **1.3.1** Some of the powers of the Court may be exercised by a single Justice and by the Registrar. Rule 9 makes specific provision for procedural decisions. If any procedural question arises which is not dealt with by the Rules, the Court or the Registrar may adopt any procedure that is consistent with the overriding objective, the Act and the Rules: rule 9(7).

**1.3.2** *Procedural Decisions* Except where rule 9(2) (see paragraph 1.3.4) applies, the powers of the Court under the following rules may be exercised by a single Justice or the Registrar without an oral hearing—

rule 5 (time limits),
rule 8 (non-compliance with Rules),
rule 11 (rejection of applications),
rule 33 (change of interest),
rule 34 (withdrawal of appeal),
rule 35 (advocate to the Court and assessors),
rule 36 (security for costs),
rule 37 (stay of execution) and
rule 41 (devolution jurisdiction).

**1.3.3** The single Justice may direct an oral hearing or may refer the matter to a panel of (at least three) Justices to be decided with or without an oral hearing: rule 9(3).

**1.3.4** A contested application

(a) alleging contempt of the Court; or
(b) for a direction under rule 8 dismissing an appeal or debarring a respondent from resisting an appeal; or
(c) for security for costs,

has to be referred to a panel of three Justices: rule 9(2). In a case of an alleged contempt, an oral hearing must be held; in any other case the Justices may hold an oral hearing.

**1.3.5** The Registrar will normally make a decision without an oral hearing but may direct an oral hearing. The Registrar may also refer the matter to a single Justice (and paragraphs 1.3.2 and 1.3.3 then apply) or to a panel of three Justices for decision.

**1.3.6** A party who is dissatisfied with a decision of the Registrar may apply for that decision to be reviewed by a single Justice. Any application must be made in Form 2 and must be filed within 14 days of the Registrar's decision: rule 9(5). A fee is payable and the procedure in paragraphs 1.3.2 and 1.3.3 applies. See paragraph 7.1 of Practice Direction 7 for applications and for the relevant fee see Annex 2 to Practice Direction 7.

**1.3.7** Oral hearings on procedural matters are normally heard in open court or in a place to which the public are admitted.

## PRACTICE DIRECTION 2—THE REGISTRY OF THE SUPREME COURT

**2.1.1** The Registry of the Supreme Court is situated on the ground floor of the building in Parliament Square which houses the Supreme Court, the former Middlesex Guildhall. The staff of the Registry act under the guidance and supervision of the Registrar. The Registry of the Judicial Committee of the Privy Council is situated in the same room and the staff of that Registry act under the guidance and supervision of the Registrar of the Privy Council. Where a member of staff of one Registry is not available, a member of staff of the other Registry will try to assist. **4A–65**

**2.1.2** The postal address of the Supreme Court is

The Supreme Court of the United Kingdom, Parliament Square, London SW1P 3BD DX 157230 Parliament Square 4.

The telephone numbers are 020 7960 1991, 1992.

The email address for the Registry is registry@supremecourt.gsi.gov.uk.

The Registry is open from 10.00 a.m. to 4.30 p.m. on Mondays to Thursdays during the law terms[1] and from 10 a.m. to 4.00 p.m. on Fridays and outside the law terms. During August the Registry is open from 10.00 a.m. to 2.00 p.m.

**2.1.3** The Registry is open on every day of the year except

(a) Saturdays and Sundays,

(b) the Thursday before Good Friday, Good Friday and the day after Easter Monday,

(c) during the Christmas vacation,

(d) Bank Holidays in England and Wales under the Banking and Financial Dealings Act 1971, and

(e) such other days as the Registrar, with the agreement of the President and the Chief Executive, may direct.

The "Christmas vacation" is the two week period over Christmas Day and New Year's Eve and in 2009, for example, starts on 21 December 2009 and ends on 2 January 2010. At a time when the Registry is closed, the Registrar can for urgent business be contacted via the Supreme Court switchboard on 020 7960-1900.

**2.1.4** Enquiries about fees and the filing of documents, papers and volumes should be addressed to Registry. The management of the Supreme Court's list is dealt with by the listing officer under the direction of the Registrar and enquiries about the listing of appeals should be addressed to the listing officer in the first instance. Enquiries about the assessment of costs should be addressed to the Registrar or the costs clerk.

**2.1.5** Cheques and drafts for fees should be made payable to "The Supreme Court of the United Kingdom".

**2.1.6** Cheques and drafts for security money should be made payable to "UK Supreme Court Security Fund Account".

[1] The law terms are the four terms of the year during which the Supreme Court holds its sittings see Practice Direction 6 paragraph 6.2.1.

### Filing Documents in the Registry of the Supreme Court

4A-66 **2.1.7** A document may be filed in the Registry "by any of the following methods—

(a) personal delivery;

(b) first class post (or an alternative service which provides for delivery on the next working day);

(c) through a document exchange;

(d) (with the consent of the Registrar) by electronic means in accordance with [...] practice direction" 14: rule 7(1).

When an application for permission to appeal, a notice of appeal, a notice of objection, an acknowledgement by a respondent or an application is filed, it will be sealed by a member of staff in the Registry: rule 7(4).

**2.1.8** A document filed by first-class post or through a document exchange will be taken to have been filed on the second day after it was posted or left at the document exchange, as the case may be (not including days which are not business days): rule 7(2). Business days are defined by rule 3(2) and mean any day other than a Saturday, Sunday, Christmas Day, Good Friday or a bank holiday under the Banking and Financial Dealings Act 1971, in England and Wales. Where a document is received on a business day at a time when the Registry is closed, the document will be taken to have been filed in time and the Registrar may give whatever consequential directions appear appropriate.

**2.1.9** Except with the consent of the Registrar, "the contents of documents (a) filed in hard copy must also be provided to the Registry by electronic means, and (b) filed by electronic means must also be provided to the Registry in hard copy," in accordance with the relevant practice direction: rule 7(3). See Practice Direction 14 for filing by electronic means.

**2.1.10** The Registrar may refuse to accept any document which is illegible or does not comply with any provision in the Rules or any relevant practice direction. On refusing to accept a document, the Registrar will give whatever directions appear appropriate. (See rule 8.)

**2.1.11** The Registry will not issue an application for permission to appeal or other document unless:

(a) it has been properly served on the respondents (see rule 6);

(b) all the required documents are supplied; and

(c) the prescribed fee is paid or a request for fee remission from court fees is made

(see paragraphs 2.1.28–2.1.30).

### Time limits

4A-67 **2.1.12** Rule 10(2) provides that an application for permission to appeal must be made first to the court below and an application may be made to the Supreme Court only after the court below has refused to grant permission to appeal. Where an application is made to the Supreme Court, the Rules provide for the following time limits to apply.

*Paragraph numbers marked with a "+" can be found online and on CD.*

(a) Except in cases of contempt of court and in leapfrog appeals, an application for permission to appeal must be filed "within 28 days from the date of the order or decision of the court below": rule 11. This period runs from the date of the substantive order appealed from, not from the date on which the order is sealed or the date of any subsequent procedural order (e.g. an order refusing permission to appeal).

(b) A notice of appeal must be filed within 42 days of the date of the order or decision of the court below: rule 19(2). This period runs from the date of the substantive order appealed from, not from the date on which the order is sealed or the date of any subsequent procedural order (e.g. an order granting permission to appeal).

(c) If an appellant has applied for public funding, the Registrar must be informed in writing within the original 28 or 42 day period that public funding has been applied for. The above periods are then extended to 28 days after the final determination of the application for funding, including any appeals. (See rules 5(2) and 11.)

**2.1.13** The Registry may accept an application for permission to appeal or a notice of appeal which is out of time if the application sets out the reason(s) why it was not filed within the time limit and it is in order in all other respects.

**2.1.14** The Justices or the Registrar may extend or shorten any time limit set by the Rules unless to do so would be contrary to any statutory provision. They may do so either on an application by one or both parties or without an application being made. An application for an extension of time may be granted after the time limit has expired. The Registrar will notify the parties when a time limit is varied. (See rule 5.)

**2.1.15** The Registrar may reject an application for permission to appeal solely on the ground that it is out of time. (See paragraphs 1.2.9 and 1.2.16 of Practice Direction 1 for general time limits for permission applications. For special cases see paragraph 2.1.16 and for notices of appeal see paragraph 4.3.1 of Practice Direction 4.)

### Special cases: contempt of court and leapfrog appeals

**2.1.16** An application for permission to appeal in **4A-68**

(a) a case involving civil contempt of court must be filed within 14 days, beginning with the date of the refusal of permission by the court below; and

(b) a "leapfrog appeal" from the High Court must be filed within one month from the date on which the High Court judge grants a certificate under section 12 of the Administration of Justice Act 1969.

### Form of application for permission to appeal and notice of appeal

**2.1.17** The form of an application for permission to appeal is dealt **4A-69** with in paragraphs 3.1.1–3.1.5 of Practice Direction 3. The form of a notice of appeal is dealt with in paragraphs 4.2.1–4.2.4 of Practice Direction 4.

*Paragraph numbers marked with a "+" can be found online and on CD.*

### Case title

**2.1.18** Applications for permission to appeal and appeals carry the same title as in the court below, except that the parties are described as appellant(s) and respondent(s). For reference purposes, the names of parties to the original proceedings who are not parties to the appeal should nevertheless be included in the title: their names should be enclosed in square brackets. The names of all parties should be given in the same sequence as in the title used in the court below.

**2.1.19** Applications for permission to appeal and appeals in which trustees, executors etc. are parties are titled in the short form, for example *Trustees of John Black's Charity (Respondents) v. White (Appellant)*.

**2.1.20** In any application or appeal concerning children or where in the court below the title used has been such as to conceal the identity of one or more parties to the proceedings, this fact should be clearly drawn to the attention of the Registry at the time of filing, so that the title adopted in the Supreme Court can take account of the need for anonymity. Applications involving children are normally given a title in the form B (Children).

**2.1.21** In case titles involving the Crown, the abbreviation "R" meaning "Regina" is used. "R" is always given first. So case titles using this abbreviation take the form R v Jones (Appellant) or R v Jones (Respondent) (as the case may be) or R (on the application of Jones) (Appellant) v Secretary of State for the Home Department (Respondent).

**2.1.22** Apart from the above, Latin is not used in case titles.

### Service

4A–70 **2.1.23** Documents such as applications for permission to appeal and notices of appeal must be served by the party or their solicitors on the respondents or their solicitors, in accordance with rule 6 or with any relevant statutory provisions,[1] before they are filed. A party or his solicitor will be taken to have consented to a particular method of service if, for example, their writing paper includes a fax number or a numbered box at a document exchange unless they have indicated in writing that they are not willing to accept service by that particular method.

**2.1.24** A certificate of service which complies with rule 6(4) by giving details of the persons served, the method of service used and the date on which the document was served personally, posted, delivered to the document exchange or sent electronically, must be included either in the original document and signed or a separate certificate of service must be provided.

### Supporting documents

4A–71 **2.1.25** See paragraph 3.1.7 of Practice Direction 3 for the documents which must be filed with an application for permission to appeal.

[1] The Companies Act 1985 and the Companies Act 2006 provide for the method of service on companies and limited liability partnerships.

**2.1.26** See paragraph 4.3.2 of Practice Direction 4 for the documents which must be filed with a notice of appeal.

**2.1.27** See paragraph 7.1.3 of Practice Direction 7 for guidance on documents which may need to be filed in support of an application.

**Fees**

**2.1.28** The fees which are payable in the Supreme Court are prescribed by an order made under section 52 of the Act and rule 45 allows the Registrar to refuse to accept a document or to allow a party to take any step unless the relevant fee is paid. **4A–72**

**2.1.29** In circumstances where a party would suffer financial hardship by the payment of fees, the requirement to pay fees may be waived (see the Supreme Court Fees Order 2009, S.I. 2009/2131). Any request for fee remission should be made to the Registrar, supported by evidence of the party's means. The Registrar may then grant full or part remission of the relevant fee. Remission of fees is usually granted where a remission of fees has been granted in the court below.

**2.1.30** For the fees payable in the Supreme Court see Annex 2 to Practice Direction 7.

**2.1.31** Any fees paid are not refunded, even if it is decided that an application for permission to appeal is inadmissible or if an application or other proceeding is withdrawn.

## PRACTICE DIRECTION 3—APPLICATIONS FOR PERMISSION TO APPEAL

### Form of application for permission to appeal

4A–73 **3.1.1** Applications for permission to appeal are considered by an Appeal Panel, consisting of at least three Justices. Applications are generally decided on paper, without a hearing, and it is essential that the application is in the correct form.

**3.1.2** An application for permission to appeal must be produced in Form 1 on A4 paper, securely bound on the left, using both sides of the paper. (See Annex 1 to Practice Direction 7 for Form 1.) The application should set out briefly the facts and points of law and include a summary of the reasons why permission should be granted. Applications which are not legible or which are not produced in the required form will not be accepted. Parties may consult the Registry at any stage of preparation of the application, and may submit applications in draft for approval. Amendments to applications are allowed where the Registrar is satisfied that this will assist the Appeal Panel and will not unfairly prejudice the respondents or cause undue delay. Any amendments must be served on the respondents (see paragraph 3.1.6).

**3.1.3** If an application for permission to appeal

(a) asks the Supreme Court to depart from one of its own decisions or from one made by the House of Lords;

(b) seeks a declaration of incompatibility under the Human Rights Act 1998; or

(c) seeks a reference to the Court of Justice of the European Communities,

this should be stated clearly in the application and full details must be given.

**3.1.4** An application for permission to appeal must be signed by the appellant or his agent.

**3.1.5** The application for permission to appeal should include the neutral citation of the judgment appealed against, the references of any law report in the courts below, and subject matter catchwords for indexing (whether or not the case has been reported). This can conveniently be done in Section 9 of Form 1.

*Service*

**3.1.6** A copy of the application (and any amendment to it) must be served on the respondents or their solicitors, and on any person who was an intervener in the court below in accordance with rule 6, before it is filed. A certificate of service (giving the full name and address of the respondents or their solicitors) must be included in the original application and signed or a separate certificate of service must be provided. See rule 6(4) and paragraph 2.1.24 of Practice Direction 2. Additional supporting documents other than those set out in paragraphs 3.1.7 and 3.2.1 (additional papers) are not normally accepted.

*Supporting documents*

**3.1.7** In order to comply with rule 14(1), the original application together with 3 copies must be filed at the Registry together with the prescribed fee, a copy of the order appealed against and, if separate, a copy of the order of the court below refusing permission to appeal. For the relevant fee see Annex 2 to Practice Direction 7. If the substantive order appealed against is not immediately available, the application should be filed within the required time limit, and the order filed as soon it is available. For the relevant time limits for filing an application for permission to appeal see paragraphs 2.1.12-2.1.16 of Practice Direction 2. Where an appellant is unable to file his permission application within the relevant time limit, an application for an extension of time must be made in Section 7 of Form 1. The respondent's views on the extension of time should be sought and, if possible, those views should be communicated to the Registry. The application for an extension of time will be referred to the Registrar and, if it is granted, the appellant must then comply with rule 14 and paragraph 3.2.1. When an application for permission to appeal is filed, it will be sealed by a member of staff in the Registry: rule 7(4).

**Objections by respondents**

**3.1.8** Each "respondent who wishes to object to the application must, within 14 days after service, file notice of objection" in Form 3 together with a certificate of service: rule 13(1). (See Annex 1 to Practice Direction 7 for Form 3.) The original notice together with 3 copies must be filed at the Registry together with the prescribed fee. For the relevant fee see Annex 2 to Practice Direction 7. When a notice of objection is filed, it will be sealed by a member of staff in the Registry: rule 7(4). **4A–74**

**3.1.9** Before filing, a respondent must serve a copy of the notice on the appellant, any other respondent and any person who was an intervener in the court below: rule 13(2). A certificate of service (giving the full name and address of the persons served) must be included in Form 3 and signed or a separate certificate of service must be provided. See rule 6(4) and paragraph 2.1.24 of Practice Direction 2.

**3.1.10** A respondent who files notice will be permitted to participate in the application and will be given notice of its progress: rule 13(3). An order for costs will not be made in favour of a respondent who has not given notice.

**Additional papers**

**3.2.1** To comply with rule 14(2), the following additional papers must be filed by the appellant for use by the Appeal Panel within 7 days after the filing of the application: **4A–75**

(a) **four** copies of the application;

(b) **four** copies of the order appealed against;

(c) if separate from the order at (b) above, **four** copies of the order of the court below refusing permission to appeal to the Supreme Court;

*Paragraph numbers marked with a "+" can be found online and on CD.*

(d) **four** copies of the official transcript of the judgment of the court below;[1]

(e) **four** copies of the final order(s) of all other courts below;

(f) **four** copies of the official transcript of the final judgment(s) of all other courts below;

(g) **four** copies of any unreported judgment(s) cited in the application or judgment of a court below;

(h) **four** copies of a document which sets out the history of the proceedings. (See rule 14.)

No other papers are required, and documents other than those listed above will not be accepted unless requested by the Appeal Panel. Documents which are not clearly legible or which are not in the required style or form (see paragraph 3.1.2) will not be accepted.

**3.2.2** The additional papers must be presented in the form required by paragraph 5.1.2 of Practice Direction 5.

**3.2.3** Where the required papers are not filed within 8 weeks after the filing of the application and no good reason is given for the delay, the Registrar may

(a) refer the application to an Appeal Panel without the required accompanying papers;

(b) dismiss the application, or

(c) give such other directions as appear appropriate under rule 8.

### Consideration on paper

4A-76 **3.3.1** The Appeal Panel decides first whether an application for permission to appeal is admissible (that is, whether the Court has jurisdiction to entertain an appeal). The Court's jurisdiction is summarised in section 2 of Practice Direction 1. If the Appeal Panel determines that an application is inadmissible, it will refuse permission on that ground alone and not consider the content of the application. The Appeal Panel gives a reason for deciding that the application is inadmissible.

**3.3.2** If the Appeal Panel decides that an application is admissible, rule 16 provides that the Panel may then:

(a) refuse permission (see paragraph 3.3.4);

(b) give permission (see paragraph 3.3.5);

(c) invite the parties to file written submissions as to the grant of permission on terms whether as to costs or otherwise (see paragraphs 3.3.6 - 3.3.11);

(d) direct an oral hearing (see paragraphs 3.3.12–3.3.16).

**3.3.3** Permission to appeal is granted for applications that, in the opinion of the Appeal Panel, raise an arguable point of law of general public importance which ought to be considered by the Supreme Court at that time, bearing in mind that the matter will already have

[1] If the judgment has been published in a report which is ordinarily received in court, copies of the report may be filed instead of transcripts. Transcripts of judgments marked "in draft" are not accepted without certification by the relevant court that the copy is the final version of the judgment.

been the subject of judicial decision and may have already been reviewed on appeal. An application which in the opinion of the Appeal Panel does not raise such a point of law is refused on that ground. The Appeal Panel gives brief reasons for refusing permission to appeal.

*Permission refused*

**3.3.4** If the Appeal Panel decides that permission should be refused, the parties are notified that the application is refused and they are sent a copy of the order sealed by the Registrar which records the Panel's decision.

*Permission given outright*

**3.3.5** If the Appeal Panel decides that an appeal should be entertained without further proceedings, it grants permission outright and the parties are sent a copy of the order sealed by the Registrar which records the Panel's decision.

*Respondents' objections*

**3.3.6** Respondents may submit written objections giving their reasons why permission to appeal should be refused when they file notice of objection in accordance with rule 13. Exceptionally a respondent could seek to file more fully reasoned objections or might be asked to do so by the Appeal Panel. In such circumstances further objections should be filed

(a) within 14 days of any invitation by the Appeal Panel to do so; or

(b) within 14 days of an application for permission to appeal being referred for an oral hearing.

**3.3.7** Respondents' objections should set out briefly the reasons why the application should be refused or make submissions as to the terms upon which permission should be granted (for example, on costs). One original and 4 copies of the respondents' written objections must be filed in the Registry. The objections must be produced on A4 paper, securely fastened, using both sides of the paper.

**3.3.8** A copy of the respondents' objections should be sent to the solicitors for the other parties. In certain circumstances the Appeal Panel may invite further submissions from the appellant in the light of the respondents' objections, but appellants do not have a right to comment on respondents' objections. Where the Appeal Panel does not require further submissions to make its decision, the parties are sent a copy of the order sealed by the Registrar which records the Panel's decision. Where the Appeal Panel proposes terms for granting permission, paragraph 3.3.11 applies.

**3.3.9** For the costs of respondents' objections, see paragraph 3.5.

**3.3.10** Respondents who are unable to meet the deadlines set out in paragraph 3.3.6 must write to the Registrar requesting an extension of time for filing their written objections.

***Paragraph numbers marked with a "+" can be found online and on CD.***

*Permission given on terms*

**3.3.11** If the Appeal Panel is considering granting permission to appeal on terms:

(a) the Panel proposes the terms and the parties have the right to make submissions on the proposed terms within 14 days of the date of the Panel's proposal;

(b) the Panel will then decide whether to grant permission (unconditionally or on terms);

(c) prospective appellants who are granted permission to appeal subject to terms that they are unwilling to accept may decline to pursue the appeal;

(d) in an application for permission to appeal under the "leapfrog" procedure (see paragraph 3.6.1), prospective appellants who decline to proceed on the basis of the terms proposed by the Appeal Panel may instead pursue an appeal to the Court of Appeal in the usual way [1]

*Application referred for oral hearing*

**3.3.12** In all cases where further argument is required, an application for permission to appeal is referred for an oral hearing.

**3.3.13** Respondents may seek to file more fully reasoned objections within 14 days of being informed that the application has been referred for a hearing (see paragraph 3.3.6(b)).

**3.3.14** When an application is referred for an oral hearing, the appellant and all respondents who have filed notice of objection under rule 13 are notified of the date of the hearing before the Appeal Panel. Parties may be heard before the Appeal Panel by counsel, by solicitor, or in person. If counsel are briefed, solicitors should ensure that the Registry is notified of their names. Only a junior counsel's fee is allowed on assessment (see paragraph 3.4.8).

**3.3.15** Oral permission hearings usually last for 30 minutes. The panel will normally give its decision orally at the end of the hearing.

**3.3.16** All the parties are sent a copy of the order sealed by the Registrar which records the Panel's decision.

**Interventions in applications for permission to appeal**

4A–77 **3.3.17** Any person (and in particular (i) any official body or non-governmental organization who seeks to make submissions in the public interest or (ii) any person with an interest in proceedings by way of judicial review) may make written submissions to the Court in support of an application for permission to appeal. See rule 15. Before the submissions are filed, a copy must be served on

(a) the appellant,

(b) every respondent and

(c) any person who was an intervener in the court below.

**Four copies** of the submissions must be filed together with a certificate of service.

**3.3.18** Any submissions which are made are referred to the panel

[1] *Ceredigion County Council v Jones and others* [2007] UKHL 24.

of Justices which considers the application for permission to appeal. Where the panel decides to take the submissions into account and grants permission to appeal, the person making them will be notified. If permission to appeal is granted, a formal application must be made under rule 26 if the intervener wishes to intervene in the appeal. See Practice Direction 7 - Applications.

### Sealed Orders

**3.3.19** The appellant, any recognised intervener and all respondents who have filed notice of objection under rule 13 are sent a copy of the order sealed by the Registrar which records the Panel's decision.

### Filing notice to proceed

**3.4.1** Where permission to appeal is granted by the Supreme Court, the application for permission to appeal will stand as the notice of appeal and the grounds of appeal are limited to those on which permission has been granted. The appellant must, within 14 days of the grant by the Court of permission to appeal, file notice under rule 18 that he wishes to proceed with his appeal. When the notice is filed, the application for permission to appeal will re-sealed and, in order to comply with rule 18(2), the appellant must then serve a copy on each respondent, on any recognised intervener (that is, an intervener whose submissions have been taken into account under rule 15) and on any person who was an intervener in the court below and file the original and 3 copies together with a certificate of service. See rule 6(4) and paragraph 2.1.24 of Practice Direction 2. **4A–78**

**3.4.2** Where an appellant is unable to file notice under rule 18 within the time limit of 14 days, a formal application for an extension of time must be made in Form 2: see paragraph 7.1 of Practice Direction 7 for applications. The respondent's views on the extension of time should be sought and, if possible, those views should be communicated to the Registry. The application will be referred to the Registrar and, if it is granted, the appellant must then comply with rule 18(2) and paragraph 3.4.1.

### Expedition

**3.4.3** Once the required papers are filed at the Registry (under paragraph 3.2.1), the procedure described above is normally completed within eight sitting weeks (excluding any oral hearing). In cases involving liberty of the subject, urgent medical intervention or the well-being of children (see paragraph 3.4.4), a request for expedition may be made in writing to the Registrar. See rule 31.

### Expedited hearing of proceedings under the Hague Convention etc

**3.4.4** The *Convention on the Civil Aspects of International Child Abduction* (the Hague Convention) deals with the wrongful removal and retention of children from their habitual country of residence. The **4A–79**

*Paragraph numbers marked with a "+" can be found online and on CD.*

Revised Brussels II Regulation also deals with these matters.[1] In the Supreme Court an expedited timetable applies. The parties must therefore inform the Registrar that the proceedings fall under the Convention or Regulation. The Court normally gives judgment within six weeks of the commencement of proceedings but this can only be achieved with the fullest co-operation of the parties.

**3.4.5** The following timetable may be taken as a general guideline:

(a) an application for permission to appeal is decided by an Appeal Panel within 7 days of being filed;

(b) an appeal is heard within 21 days of a decision to grant permission to appeal;

(c) the result of the appeal is given immediately after the end of the hearing with reasons given later or, if judgment is reserved, the result of the appeal and the reasons are given within 2 weeks of the end of the hearing.

**3.4.6** In order to achieve the above timetable the Court will set aside or vary the time limits and practice directions that normally apply to applications and appeals.

**3.4.7** Abridged procedures and special rules for the production of documents are applied to meet the circumstances of each application and appeal. The following timetable for the production of documents is therefore indicative only:

(a) the statement of facts and issues is filed within 7 days of the decision to grant permission to appeal;

(b) the appellant's case is filed within 10 days of the decision to grant permission to appeal (or, if the relevant day falls on a Saturday or Sunday, the following Monday);

(c) the respondent's case is filed within 14 days of the decision to grant permission to appeal;

(d) the core volumes (if required) and the volumes of authorities are filed within 17 days of the decision to grant permission to appeal (or, if the relevant day falls on a Saturday or Sunday, the following Monday).

### Counsel

4A–80 **3.4.8** Appellants and respondents to an application for permission to appeal may instruct leading or junior counsel, but on any assessment of costs only junior counsel's fees will be allowed for any stage of an application for permission to appeal, even if a public funding or legal aid certificate provides for leading counsel. The only exception to this practice is where leading counsel who conducted the case in the court below are instructed by the Legal Services Commission or legal aid authorities to advise on the merits of an appeal.

### Costs

4A–81 **3.5.1** Where an unsuccessful application for permission to appeal is determined without an oral hearing, costs may be awarded as follows:

[1] Council Regulation (EC) No 2201/2003.

(a) to a publicly funded or legally aided appellant, reasonable costs incurred in preparing papers for the Appeal Panel;
(b) to a publicly funded or legally aided respondent, only those costs necessarily incurred in attending the client, attending the appellant's agents, considering the application for permission to appeal, filing notice of objection under rule 13 and, where applicable, preparing respondent's objections to the application;
(c) to an unassisted respondent where the appellant is publicly funded or legally aided, payment out of the Community Legal Service Fund (pursuant to section 11 of the Access to Justice Act 1999 [1]) of costs as specified at (b) above;
(d) to a respondent where neither party is publicly funded or legally aided, costs as specified at (b) above.

**3.5.2** Where costs are sought under (c) or (d) above, the application may be made by letter addressed to the Registrar or may be included in a bill of costs filed in the Registry conditional upon the application being granted.

**3.5.3** Where an application for permission to appeal is referred for an oral hearing and is dismissed, application for costs must be made by the respondent at the end of the hearing. No order for costs will be made unless a request is made at that time.

**3.5.4** Where permission to appeal is granted, costs of the application for permission become costs in the appeal.

**3.5.5** The reasonable costs of objecting to an unsuccessful application for permission to appeal will normally be awarded to the respondent, subject to any order for costs made by the Appeal Panel. If permission to appeal is granted, the costs of respondent's objections become costs in the appeal.

**3.5.6** Bills of costs must be filed within three months from the date of the decision of the Appeal Panel or from the date on which an application for permission to appeal is withdrawn in accordance with rule 34. For the withdrawal of an application see paragraph 8.16.2 of Practice Direction 8. If an extension of the three month period is desired, application must be made in writing to the Registrar and copies of all such correspondence sent to all interested parties. In deciding whether to grant an application for an extension of time made after the expiry of the three month period, the Registrar takes into account the circumstances set out in paragraph 6 of Practice Direction 13.

**3.5.7** For the fees payable on the assessment of a bill of costs, see Annex 2 to Practice Direction 7. For the assessment of costs, see rules 48– 53 and Practice Direction 13. For security for costs see paragraph 4.7.1 of Practice Direction 4.

[1] Also pursuant to r 5(2) Community Legal Service (Cost Protection) Regulations 2000 and in accordance with the procedural requirements of rr 9, 10 Community Legal Service (Costs) Regulations 2000 (as amended); or Legal Aid Act 1988 s 18; or in Scotland pursuant to Legal Aid (Scotland) Act 1986 s 19; or in Northern Ireland pursuant to Legal Aid Advice and Assistance (N.I.) Order 1981 Article 16.

## Withdrawal of application for permission to appeal

**3.5.8** This is dealt with in paragraph 8.16.2 of Practice Direction 8.

## Leapfrog appeals

4A–82 **3.6.1** In certain cases an appeal lies direct from the High Court in England and Wales or in Northern Ireland to the Supreme Court see paragraph 1.2.17 of Practice Direction 1. A certificate of the High Court must first be obtained and the permission of the Supreme Court then given before the appeal may proceed.[1] Such appeals are known as "leapfrog" appeals.

### *Judge's certificate*

**3.6.2** An application for a certificate may be made by any of the parties to any civil proceedings in the High Court before a single judge or before a Divisional Court. The application should be made immediately after the trial judge gives judgment in the proceedings or, if no such application is made, within 14 days from the date on which judgment was given.

**3.6.3** The judge may grant a certificate under section 12 of the Administration of Justice Act 1969 if he is satisfied (a) that the relevant conditions are fulfilled; (b) that a sufficient case has been made to justify taking to the Supreme Court an application for permission; and (c) that all the parties to the proceedings consent to the grant of a certificate.

**3.6.4** The relevant conditions are that a point of law of general public importance is involved in the judge's decision, and that that point of law either (a) relates wholly or mainly to the construction of an enactment or of a statutory instrument and has been fully argued in the proceedings and fully considered in the judgment of the judge in the proceedings [2], or (b) is one in respect of which the judge is bound by a decision of the Court of Appeal, the House of Lords or the Supreme Court in previous proceedings and was fully considered in the judgments of the Court of Appeal, the House of Lords or Supreme Court in those previous proceedings.[3]

**3.6.5** The judge may not grant a certificate in cases where no appeal would lie (with or without permission) from the judge's decision to the Court of Appeal, apart from the provisions of the Administration of Justice Act 1969. Similarly, a certificate may not be granted where no appeal would lie (with or without permission) from the Court of Appeal on an appeal from the judge's decision. Where no appeal would lie from the judge's decision to the Court of Appeal except with the permission of the judge or the Court of Appeal, no certificate may be granted unless it appears to the judge that it would be a proper case for granting such permission.

**3.6.6** No certificate may be given where the judge's decision concerns punishment for contempt of court.

---

[1] Administration of Justice Act 1969 ss 12-15.
[2] Administration of Justice Act 1969 s 12(3)(a).
[3] Administration of Justice Act 1969 s 12(3)(b).

**3.6.7** No appeal lies against the grant or refusal of a certificate, but if a certificate is refused the applicant may appeal to the Court of Appeal from the High Court's decision in the normal way, once the time for applying for a certificate has expired.

*Application for permission to appeal direct from High Court*

**3.6.8** At any time within one month from the date on which the judge grants the certificate, or such extended time as the Supreme Court may allow, any of the parties may apply to the Supreme Court for permission to appeal.[1] Application is made in accordance with paragraph 3.1 of this Practice Direction. If any party to the proceedings in the High Court is not a party to the application, the application must be endorsed with a certificate of service on that party.

**3.6.9** One copy of the judge's certificate must be filed with the application. The application should indicate whether the judge's certificate was granted under section 12(3)(a) or section 12(3)(b) of the Administration of Justice Act 1969.

**3.6.10** The following additional papers for use by the Appeal Panel must be filed within seven days of the filing of the application:

(a) **four** additional copies of the application;

(b) **four** copies of the order of the High Court;

(c) **four** additional copies of the High Court's certificate, if not contained in the order; and

(d) **four** copies of the transcript of the judgment of the High Court.[2]

These additional papers must be presented in the form required by paragraph 5.1.2 of Practice Direction 5. No other papers are required, and documents other than those listed above will not be normally accepted.

**3.6.11** Applications for permission to appeal are normally determined by an Appeal Panel without a hearing.

**3.6.12** In applications where the certificate has been granted by the judge under section 12(3)(a) of the 1969 Act, the Appeal Panel only grants permission to appeal where:

(a) there is an urgent need to obtain an authoritative interpretation by the Supreme Court;

(b) the case is one in which permission to appeal to the Supreme Court would have been granted if it had not been brought direct to the Supreme Court and the judgment had been that of the Court of Appeal; and

(c) it does not appear likely that any additional assistance could be derived from a judgment of the Court of Appeal.

Similarly, where the certificate has been granted under section 12(3)(b) of the 1969 Act, the Appeal Panel only grants permission where:

SUPREME COURT

[1] Administration of Justice Act 1969 s 13(1).

[2] If the judgment has been published in a report which is ordinarily received in court, copies of the report may be filed in lieu of transcripts. Transcripts of judgments marked as in draft are not acceptable without certification by the relevant court that the copy is the final version of the judgment.

(i) the case is not distinguishable from the case that was the subject of the previous decision;
(ii) the previous case was fully considered in a previous judgment after argument that appears to have been adequate; and
(iii) the case is one in which permission to appeal to the Supreme Court would have been granted if it had not been brought direct to the Supreme Court and the judgment had been that of the Court of Appeal.

**3.6.13** The appellant and all respondents who have filed notice of objection under rule 13 are sent a copy of the order sealed by the Registrar which records the Panel's decision.

*Extensions of time*

**3.6.14** Where an appellant is unable to file his application within the time limit, an application for an extension of time must be made in Section 7 of Form 1. The respondent's views on the extension of time should be sought and, if possible, those views should be communicated to the Registry. The application for an extension of time will be referred to the Registrar or an Appeal Panel and, if it is granted, the appellant must then comply with rule 14 and paragraph 3.2.1.

*Proceedings after permission to appeal is granted or refused*

**3.6.15** If the Appeal Panel grants permission to appeal without terms, no appeal from the decision of the judge lies to the Court of Appeal but only to the Supreme Court. The appeal is brought in accordance with Practice Direction 4 and the usual requirements apply. However, an appeal does lie to the Court of Appeal from the judge's decision (i) where no application is made to the Supreme Court within the one month period after the judge has granted the certificate; or (ii) where permission to appeal direct to the Supreme Court has been refused by the Appeal Panel.

**3.6.16** Prospective appellants who decline to proceed on the basis of the terms proposed by the Appeal Panel may instead pursue an appeal to the Court of Appeal in the usual way.[1]

**Habeas corpus**

4A–83 **3.6.17** Proceedings for a writ of habeas corpus in England and Wales are subject to the procedures governing criminal appeals to the Supreme Court. These are set out in Practice Direction 12. In proceedings for a writ of habeas corpus, an appeal lies from the Queen's Bench Divisional Court to the Supreme Court at the instance of the defendant or prosecutor with the permission either of the Divisional Court or the Supreme Court. No certificate stating a point of law of general public importance is required.[2]

**3.6.18** Such an application is normally determined by an Appeal

[1] *Ceredigion County Council v Jones and others* [2007] UKHL 24.
[2] Administration of Justice Act 1969 ss 1, 15(3); Judicature (Northern Ireland) Act 1978, s 45(3).

***Paragraph numbers marked with a "+" can be found online and on CD.***

Panel without an oral hearing. The appellant and all respondents who have filed notice of objection under rule 13 are sent a copy of the order sealed by the Registrar which records the Panel's decision.

## PRACTICE DIRECTION 4—NOTICE OF APPEAL

### General note

4A–84 **4.1.1** The practice is that where permission to appeal is granted by the Supreme Court, the application for permission to appeal will stand as the notice of appeal and the grounds of appeal are limited to those on which permission has been granted: rule 18(1). The appellant must, within 14 days of the grant by the Court of permission to appeal, file notice under rule 18(1)(c) that he wishes to proceed with his appeal. When the notice is filed, the application for permission to appeal will be re-sealed and the appellant must then serve a copy on each respondent, on any recognized intervener (that is, an intervener whose submissions have been taken into account under rule 15) and on any intervener in the court below; and file the original and 3 copies: rule 18(2). In any other case an appellant must file a notice of appeal in Form 1. (See Annex 1 to Practice Direction 7 for Form 1.

### Form of notice of appeal

4A–85 **4.2.1** A notice of appeal must be produced in Form 1 on A4 paper, securely bound on the left, using both sides of the paper. (See Annex 1 to Practice Direction 7 for Form 1.) Notices which are not legible or which are not produced in the required form will not be accepted. Parties may consult the Registry at any stage of preparation of the notice, and may submit notices in draft for approval. Amendments to notices are allowed where the Registrar is satisfied that this will assist the Court and will not unfairly prejudice the respondents or cause undue delay. Any amendments must be served on the respondents (see paragraph 4.2.15).

**4.2.2** Where permission to appeal has been obtained, the notice of appeal must be signed by the appellants or their agents. In appeals where permission to appeal is not required (for example, in most Scottish appeals) the notice of appeal must be certified as reasonable by two counsel from the relevant jurisdiction and signed by them.[1] In Scottish appeals a certificate of difference of opinion must also be included where appropriate.

**4.2.3** The notice of appeal should include the neutral citation of the judgment appealed against, the references of any law report in the courts below, and subject matter catchwords for indexing (whether or not the case has been reported). This can conveniently be done in Section 9 of Form 1.

**4.2.4** If an appellant

(a) asks the Supreme Court to depart from one of its own decisions or from one made by the House of Lords;

(b) seeks a declaration of incompatibility under the Human Rights Act 1998; or

---

[1] In such cases, counsel's signatures are required even if the appellants propose to conduct the appeal in person. The term "counsel" is defined by rule 2 and, for the purposes of this provision, "counsel" includes an enrolled solicitor with a right of audience in the Supreme Court: see the Solicitors (Scotland) Act 1980, s.25A as amended by the Constitutional Reform Act 2005, Sch 9 para 32).

(c) seeks a reference to the Court of Justice of the European Communities,

this should be stated clearly in the notice of appeal and full details must be given.

*Case title*

**4.2.5** Notices of appeal to the Supreme Court carry the same title as in the court below, except that the parties are described as appellant(s) and respondent(s). For reference purposes, the names of parties to the original proceedings who are not parties to the appeal should nevertheless be included in the title: their names should be enclosed in square brackets. The names of all parties should be given in the same sequence as in the title used in the court below.

**4.2.6** Notices of appeal in which trustees, executors, etc. are parties are titled in the short form, for example *Trustees of John Black's Charity (Respondents) v. White (Appellant)*.

**4.2.7** In any notice of appeal concerning children or where in the court below the title used has been such as to conceal the identity of one or more parties to the proceedings, this fact should be clearly drawn to the attention of the Registry at the time the notice of appeal is filed, so that the title adopted in the Supreme Court can take account of the need for anonymity. Notices of appeal involving children are normally given a title in the form *B (Children)* (see also paragraph 4.2.10).

**4.2.8** In case titles involving the Crown, the abbreviation "R" meaning "Regina" is used. "R" is always given first. Case titles using this abbreviation take the form *R v Jones (Appellant)* or *R v Jones (Respondent)* (as the case may be) or *R (on the application of Jones) (Appellant) v Secretary of State for the Home Department (Respondent)*.

**4.2.9** Apart from the above, Latin is not used in case titles.

*Anonymity and reporting restrictions*

**4.2.10** In any appeal concerning children, the parties, in addition to considering the case title to be used, should also consider whether it would be appropriate for the Court to make an order under section 39 of the Children and Young Persons Act 1933 [1] (reporting restrictions). The parties should always inform the Registry if such an order has been made by a court below. A request for such an order to be made by the Court should be made in writing, preferably on behalf of all parties to the appeal, as soon as possible after the commencement of the appeal and not later than 14 days before the start of the hearing.

**4.2.11** Paragraph 4.2.10 also applies to a request for an order under section 4 of the Contempt of Court Act 1981 (contemporary reports of proceedings).

SUPREME COURT

[1] Extended to Scotland by the Children and Young Persons (Scotland) Act 1963, s 57(3).

*Human Rights Act 1998*

**4.2.12** Where an appellant or a respondent seeks a declaration of incompatibility or seeks to challenge an act of a public authority under the Human Rights Act 1998, the appropriate section of Form 1 or Form 3 must be completed. Parties should set out briefly in their cases the arguments involved and state whether the point was taken below. The Crown has a right to be joined as a party to the appeal where a question of incompatibility is raised (see rule 40 and Practice Direction 9).

*References to the European Court*

**4.2.13** If an appellant seeks a reference to the Court of Justice of the European Communities, this should be stated clearly in the notice of appeal and special provisions apply: see rule 42 and Practice Direction 11. The appellant must also notify the Registrar in writing.

*London agents*

**4.2.14** Solicitors outside London may appoint London agents. Those who decide not to do so should note that any additional costs incurred as a result of that decision may be disallowed on any assessment of costs.

*Service*

**4.2.15** A copy of the notice of appeal must be served on the respondents or their solicitors, on any recognized intervener (under rule 15) and on any person who was an intervener in the court below, in accordance with rule 6, before it is filed. A certificate of service (giving the full name and address of the respondents or their agents) must be included in Form 1 and signed or a separate certificate of service must be provided. See rule 6(4) and paragraph 2.1.24 of Practice Direction 2.

**Filing a notice of appeal**

4A–86 **4.3.1** A notice of appeal must be filed in the Registry within 42 days of the date of the order or decision of the court below (see rule 19). However, this time limit may be varied by the Court under rule 5. For other relevant time limits see paragraphs 2.1.12-2.1.16 of Practice Direction 2. When a notice of appeal is filed, it will be sealed by a member of staff in the Registry: rule 7(4).

**4.3.2 In order to comply with rule 19(2), the original notice of appeal together with 3 copies** must be filed at the Registry with the prescribed fee. For the relevant fee see Annex 2 to Practice Direction 7. If permission to appeal was granted by the court below, a copy of the order appealed from must also be filed and, if separate, a copy of the order granting permission to appeal to the Supreme Court: rule 19(3). If the order appealed from is not immediately available, *"the notice of appeal should be filed without delay and the order filed as soon as it is available"*: rule 19(3).

**Filing notice to proceed under rule 18**

4A–87 **4.3.3** Where under rule 18(1)(a) an application for permission to appeal stands as a notice of appeal, the appellant must, within 14 days of the grant by the Court of permission to appeal, file notice that he wishes to proceed with his appeal. See paragraph 3.4.1 of Practice Direction 3 for filing notice to proceed and paragraph 3.4.2 where an appellant is unable to file notice within the prescribed time limit.

### Out of time appeals

**4.4.1** Where an appellant is unable to file a notice of appeal within the relevant time limit, an application for an extension of time must be made in Section 7 of Form 1. The respondent's views on the extension of time should be sought and, if possible, those views should be communicated to the Registry. The application for an extension of time will be referred to the Registrar and, if it is granted, the appellant must comply with rule 19 and paragraph 4.3.2. **4A-88**

### Fees

**4.5.1** For the fees payable on filing a notice of appeal and on filing notice to proceed under rule 18 see Annex 2 to Practice Direction 7. **4A-89**

### Acknowledgement by respondent

**4.6.1** Each *"respondent who intends to participate in the appeal must, within 14 days after service under rule 18(2)(a) or rule 20, file notice"* in Form 3: rule 21(1). (See Annex 1 to Practice Direction 7 for Form 3.) (Where under rule 18(1)(a) an application for permission to appeal stands as a notice of appeal, the time limit for a respondent to give notice under rule 21 runs from the date on which he is served with a resealed copy of the application.) Form 3 must be produced on A4 paper, securely fastened, using both sides of the paper. **4A-90**

**4.6.2** Before filing, a respondent must serve a copy of Form 3 on the appellant, any other respondent and any person who was an intervener in the court below or whose submissions were taken into account under rule 15: see rule 21(2). A certificate of service (giving the full name and address of the persons served) must be included in Form 3 and signed or a separate certificate of service must be provided. See rule 6(4) and paragraph 2.1.24 of Practice Direction 2.

**4.6.3 The original notice together with 3 copies** must be filed at the Registry with the prescribed fee. For the relevant fee see Annex 2 to Practice Direction 7. When Form 3 is filed, it will be sealed by a member of staff in the Registry: rule 7(4).

**4.6.4** A respondent who does not give notice under rule 21 will not be permitted to participate in the appeal and will not be given notice of its progress: rule 21(3). An order for costs will not be made in favour of a respondent who has not given notice.

### Security for costs

**4.7.1** Orders for security for costs under rule 36 will be sparingly made but the Court may, on the application of a respondent, order an appellant to give security for the costs of the appeal and any order for security will determine **4A-91**

(a) the amount of that security, and
(b) the manner in which, and the time within which, security must be given.

*Paragraph numbers marked with a "+" can be found online and on CD.*

An application for security should be made in the general form of application, Form 2 (see paragraph 7.1 of, and Annex 1 to, Practice Direction 7). An order made under rule 36 may require payment of the judgment debt (and costs) in the court below instead of, or in addition to, the amount ordered by way of security for costs.

**4.7.2** For payment of security see paragraph 8.7.1 of Practice Direction 8.

**4.7.3** The following are generally not required to give security for costs:

(a) an appellant who has been granted a certificate of public funding/legal aid;

(b) an appellant in an appeal under the Child Abduction and Custody Act 1985;

(c) a Minister or Government department.

**4.7.4** No security for costs is required in cross-appeals.

**4.7.5** Failure to provide security as required will result in the appeal being struck out by the Registrar although the appellant may apply to reinstate the appeal. See paragraph 7.1 of Practice Direction 7.

### Expedition

4A–92 **4.8.1** In cases involving liberty of the subject, urgent medical intervention or the well-being of children (see paragraph 3.4.4 of Practice Direction 3), a request for expedition may be made in writing to the Registrar. See rule 31. Wherever possible the views of all parties should be obtained before a request for an expedited hearing is made.

## PRACTICE DIRECTION 5—PAPERS FOR THE APPEAL HEARING

### General note

**5.1.1** The Supreme Court does not wish to impose very detailed requirements as to the manner in which documents are presented to the Court for appeal hearings. Parties may if they wish follow the former practice in House of Lords appeals but are not required to do so. Where parties are in any doubt as to how documents should be presented they should consult the Registrar and discuss the practice which should be adopted. The provisions of paragraphs 5.1.2 to 5.1.5 must, however, be strictly complied with. **4A–93**

**5.1.2** All documents placed before the Court must be

(a) printed or reproduced (both as to font size and otherwise) so as to be easily legible;
(b) reproduced on paper of A4 size, printed on both sides; and
(c) (unless this causes great difficulty) presented in bound form, properly labelled and indexed.

Documents must be presented in a form which is robust, manageable and not excessively heavy. **Duplication of material must be avoided particularly where two or more appeals are heard together.** See Practice Direction 6 for core volumes, cases and authorities volumes.

**5.1.3 The statement of facts and issues** must be a single document, drafted initially by the appellant but "submitted to, and agreed with, every respondent before being filing": rule 22(2). The statement must set out the relevant facts and, if the parties cannot agree as to any matter, the statement should make clear what items are disputed. The statement should contain references to every law report of the proceedings below, and should state the duration of the proceedings below. It should be signed by counsel for all parties.

**5.1.4 The appendix** should contain only such material as is necessary for understanding the legal issues and the argument to be presented to the Supreme Court (see rule 22(2)). It should not contain documents which were not in evidence below, nor should it contain transcripts of the proceedings or evidence below unless they are essential to the legal argument. If necessary, the appendix should be prepared in several parts, only the most essential documents being included in Part 1; only Part 1 will be included in the core volumes. The appendix must be submitted to, and agreed with, every respondent before being filing: rule 22(2).

**5.1.5** Documents must be included in the appendix in the following order—

(a) the order appealed against;
(b) if separate from the order at (a) above, the order refusing permission to appeal to the Supreme Court;
(c) the official transcript of the judgment of the court below;[1]

[1] If the judgment has been published in a report which is ordinarily received in court, copies of the report may be filed instead of transcripts. Transcripts of judgments

*Paragraph numbers marked with a "+" can be found online and on CD.*



Supreme Court

(d) the final order(s) of all other courts below;
(e) the official transcript of the final judgment(s) of all other courts below;
(f) (where they are necessary for understanding the legal issues and the argument) the relevant documents filed in the courts below;
(g) (where they are necessary for understanding the legal issues and the argument) the relevant documents and correspondence relating to the appeal.

All documents must be numbered, and each part of the Appendix must include a list of its contents.

**Time limits**

4A-94 **5.2.1** The statement of facts and issues and the appendix must be filed by the appellant within 112 days after the filing of the notice under rule 18(1)(c) or the filing of the notice of appeal: rule 22(1).

**5.2.2** If the appellant is unable to comply with the relevant time limit, an application for an extension of time must be made. (See rule 5 and paragraph 5.2.3.)

*Extensions of time for filing the statement of facts and issues and the appendix*

**5.2.3** Appellants who are unable to complete preparation of the statement and appendix within the time limit may apply to the Registrar for an extension of that time under rule 5. Any application must be made in the general form of application, Form 2, (see Annex 1 to Practice Direction 7) and should explain the reason(s) why an extension is needed.

**5.2.4** The Registrar may grant an application for an extension of time, provided that it does not prejudice the preparation for the hearing or its proposed date. The time limits provided by the Rules are, however, generous and applicants for an extension of time must set out in some detail why they are unable to comply with any relevant time limit.

*Respondents' consent*

**5.2.5** Respondents are expected not to withhold unreasonably their consent to an application for an extension of time. Appellants are advised to communicate the views of respondents to the Registry since, if they raise no objection, the application may be dealt with on paper.

**Filing the Statement and Appendix**

4A-95 **5.2.6** When the statement and appendix are ready,

(a) **the original and 7 copies** of the statement,
(b) **eight copies** of Part 1 of the appendix and
(c) **10 copies** of Parts 2 etc. (if any)

marked "in draft" are not accepted without certification by the relevant court that the copy is the final version of the judgment.

must be filed at the Registry with the prescribed fee. (For the fee payable, see Annex 2 to Practice Direction 7.)

**5.2.7** Within 7 days after filing the statement and the appendix, the parties must comply with rule 22(3) by notifying the Registrar that the appeal is ready to list and providing a time estimate (see paragraph 6.2.1 of Practice Direction 6).

SUPREME COURT

*Paragraph numbers marked with a "+" can be found online and on CD.*

## PRACTICE DIRECTION 6—THE APPEAL HEARING

### General note

4A–96 **6.1.1** The Supreme Court does not wish to impose very detailed requirements as to the manner in which documents are presented to the Court for appeal hearings. Parties may if they wish follow the former practice in House of Lords appeals but are not required to do so. Where parties are in any doubt as to how documents should be presented they should consult the Registrar and discuss the practice which should be adopted. The provisions of paragraph 6.1.2 must, however, be strictly complied with.

**6.1.2** All documents placed before the Court must be

(a) reproduced or printed (both as to font size and otherwise) so as to be easily legible;

(b) reproduced on paper of A4 size, printed on both sides; and

(c) (unless this causes great difficulty) presented in bound form, properly labelled and indexed.

Documents must be presented in a form which is robust, manageable and not excessively heavy. Duplication of material must be avoided particularly where two or more appeals are heard together. See Practice Direction 5 for the statement of facts and issues and the appendix.

### Fixing the hearing date

4A–97 **6.2.1** Within 7 days after the filing of the statement of facts and issues and the appendix (see paragraphs 5.1.3 and 5.2.1 of Practice Direction 5), the parties must notify the Registrar that the appeal is ready to list and...specify the number of hours that their respective counsel estimate to be necessary for their oral submissions: rule 22(3). Time estimates must be as accurate as possible since, subject to the Court's discretion, they are used as the basis for arranging the Court's list. The sittings of the Court (or the 'law terms') are four in each year, that is to say:

(a) the Michaelmas sittings which begin on 1 October and end on 21 December;

(b) the Hilary sittings which begin on 11 January and end on the Wednesday before Easter Sunday;

(c) the Easter sittings which begin on the second Tuesday after Easter Sunday and end on the Friday before the spring holiday; and

(d) the Trinity sittings which begin on the second Tuesday after the spring holiday and end on 31 July.

The 'spring holiday' means the bank holiday falling on the last Monday in May or any day appointed instead of that day under section 1(2) of the Banking and Financial Dealings Act 1971.

**6.2.2** Subject to any directions by the Court before or at the hearing, counsel are expected to confine their submissions to the time indicated in their estimates. The Registrar **must** be informed at once of any alteration to the original estimate. Not more than two days are normally allowed for the hearing of an appeal and appeals are listed for hearing on this basis. Estimates of more than two days must be fully explained in writing to the Registrar and may be referred to the presiding Justice.

**6.2.3** The Registrar will subsequently inform the parties of the date fixed for the hearing. The appellant and every respondent (and any intervener or advocate to the Court) "must then sequentially exchange their respective written cases and file them", and every respondent (and any intervener or advocate to the Court) must provide copies of their respective written cases to the appellant for the preparation of the core volumes: rule 22(4). (See paragraph 6.3 for cases).

### Requests for expedition

**6.2.4** Any request for an expedited hearing should be made to the Registrar. Wherever possible the views of all parties should be obtained before a request is made. **4A–98**

### Directions hearings

**6.2.5** Where it considers it to be appropriate, the Court may decide that a directions hearing should be held. A directions hearing will normally be held before 3 Justices. Any request for a directions hearing should be made to the Registrar. Wherever possible the views of all parties should be obtained before a request is made. **4A–99**

### Appellants' and Respondents' cases

**6.3.1** The case is the statement of a party's argument in the appeal. The Court does not prescribe any maximum length but the Court favours brevity and a case should be a concise summary of the submissions to be developed. **4A–100**

**6.3.2** The case should be confined to the heads of argument that counsel propose to submit at the hearing and omit material contained in the statement of facts and issues (see paragraph 5.1.3 of Practice Direction 5).

**6.3.3** If either party is abandoning any point taken in the courts below, this should be made plain in their case. If they intend to apply in the course of the hearing for permission to introduce a new point not taken below, this should also be indicated in their case and the Registrar informed. If such a point involves the introduction of fresh evidence, application for permission must be made either in the case or by filing an application for permission to adduce the fresh evidence (see paragraph 7.1 of Practice Direction 7 for applications).

**6.3.4** If a party intends to invite the Court to depart from one of its own decisions or from a decision of the House of Lords, this intention must be clearly stated in a separate paragraph of their case, to which special attention must be drawn. A respondent who wishes to contend that a decision of the court below should be affirmed on grounds other than those relied on by that court must set out the grounds for that contention in their case.

**6.3.5** Transcripts of unreported judgments should only be cited when they contain an authoritative statement of a relevant principle of law not to be found in a reported case or when they are necessary for the understanding of some other authority.

**6.3.6** All cases must conclude with a numbered summary of the reasons upon which the argument is founded, and must bear the signature of at least one counsel for each party to the appeal who has appeared in the court below or who will be briefed for the hearing before the Court.

**6.3.7** The filing of a case carries the right to be heard by two counsel. The fees of two counsel only for any party are allowed on assessment unless the Court orders otherwise on application at the hearing. The Costs Officers have no discretion to allow fees for more than two counsel unless the Court has, on application at the hearing, made such an order: see paragraph 16.5 of Practice Direction 13.

*Separate cases*

**6.3.8** Parties whose interests in the appeal are passive (for example, stakeholders, trustees, executors, etc.) are not required to file a separate case but should ensure that their position is explained in one of the cases filed.

*Filing and exchange of cases*

**6.3.9** No later than five weeks before the proposed date of the hearing, the appellants must file at the Registry the original and 7 **copies** of their case and serve it on the respondents.

**6.3.10** No later than 3 weeks before the proposed date of the hearing, the respondents must serve on the appellants a copy of their case in response and file at the Registry the original and 7 **copies** of their case, as must any other party filing a case (for example, an intervener or advocate to the court).

**6.3.11** The number of copies of cases exchanged should be enough to meet the requirements of counsel and solicitors and should not usually exceed eight. To enable the appellants to file the core volumes, the respondents and any other party who has filed a case must also provide the appellants with **10** further copies of their case.

**6.3.12** Following the exchange of cases, further arguments by either side may not without permission be submitted in advance of the hearing.

*Form of cases*

**6.3.13** Cases must be produced on A4 paper, securely bound on the left, using both sides of the paper with:

(a) numbered paragraphs; and

(b) signatures of counsel at the end, above their printed names.

**The core volumes and authorities volumes**

4A–101 **6.4.1** As soon as the parties' cases have been exchanged and in any event not later than 14 days before the date fixed for the hearing the appellant must file core volumes in accordance with paragraph 6.4.3 and (if necessary) additional volumes containing further parts of the appendix.

**6.4.2** Copies of all authorities that may be referred to during the hearing must be filed by the appellant at the same time as the core volumes. See paragraph 6.5.1–6.5.8.

***Paragraph numbers marked with a "+" can be found online and on CD.***

**6.4.3** In addition to the documents already filed, the appellant must file 10 bound core volumes. Each core volume must contain in the following order:

(a) Form 1—a copy of the notice of appeal or the re-sealed application for permission to appeal;
(b) notice of cross-appeal (if any);
(c) statement of facts and issues;
(d) appellants' and respondents' cases, with cross-references to the Appendix and authorities volume(s);
(e) case of the advocate to the court or intervener, if any;
(f) Part 1 of the appendix; and
(g) index to the authorities volume(s).

*Form of core volumes*

**6.4.4** The core volumes:

(a) should be bound, preferably with plastic comb binding and with blue (or, for criminal appeals, red) card covers;
(b) should include tabs for each of the documents set out in paragraph 6.4.3, preferably with the name of the document on the tab;
(c) should show on the front cover a list of the contents and the names and addresses of the solicitors for all parties;
(d) must indicate (by e.g. a label (printed in landscape) attached to the plastic spine) the volume number (in roman numerals) and the short title of the appeal.

For volumes in electronic form see Practice Direction 14.

*Provision of documents*

**6.4.5** To enable the appellants to produce the core volumes, the respondents must provide the appellants' solicitors with a further 10 copies of the respondents' case in addition to the cases already exchanged.

**6.4.6** Respondents should arrange with the appellants' solicitors for the delivery to them of such core volumes as the respondents' counsel and agents require.

**Authorities**

**6.5.1 A joint set of authorities, jointly produced, should be complied for the appeal. Ten copies of the joint set of** authorities must be filed at the same time as the core volumes. The appellants have the initial responsibility for producing the authorities volumes and for filing them at the Registry but, to enable the appellants to file the volumes, the respondents must provide the appellants with 10 copies of any authorities which the respondents require but which the appellants do not, or arrange with the appellants for their photocopying. Respondents should arrange with the appellants for the delivery to them of such authorities volumes as the respondents' counsel and agents require. **Supplemental or additional volumes of authorities should be avoided.** 4A-102

SUPREME COURT

*Form and content of authorities volumes*

**6.5.2** The authorities should be collected together into one or more volumes or folders. The volumes of authorities should have a separate index and authorities should appear in alphabetical order. Authorities should (where appropriate) be further divided into the categories: domestic, Strasbourg, foreign and academic material. The volumes of authorities should

(a) be A4 size reproduced as one page per view (with any authorities smaller than A4 being enlarged);
(b) separate each authority by numbered dividers;
(c) contain an index to that volume; the first volume must also contain an index to all the volumes;
(d) be numbered consecutively on the cover and spine with numerals at least point 72 in size for swift identification of different volumes during the hearing;
(e) have printed clearly on the front cover the title of the appeal and the names of the solicitors for all parties;
(f) have affixed to the spine a sticker indicating clearly the volume number and short title of the appeal.

**6.5.3** In an appeal where there is a large number of volumes of authorities, it is helpful to produce an index of indexes, separate from the index contained in the first authorities volume.

**6.5.4** The volumes of authorities should be filed in the Registry preferably in separate containers from the core volumes.

**6.5.5** Where a case is not reported in the Law Reports or Session Cases, references to other recognised reports may be given. In Revenue appeals, Tax Cases or Simon's Tax Cases may be cited but, wherever possible, references to the case in the Law Reports or Session Cases should also be given.

**6.5.6** In order to produce the volumes of authorities, parties may download text from electronic sources; but the volumes of authorities must be filed in paper form. See Practice Direction 14 for provisions in relation to electronic volumes.

**6.5.7** In certain circumstances (for example, when during the hearing it becomes apparent that a particular authority is needed but is not in the volumes of authorities), the Supreme Court Library can arrange for copies of authorities to be made available at the hearing. Parties must themselves provide ten copies of any other authority or of unreported cases. They must similarly provide copies of any authority of which notice has not been given.

**6.5.8** The cost of preparing the volumes of authorities falls to the appellants, but is ultimately subject to the decision of the Court as to the costs of the appeal.

**The hearing**

4A–103 **6.6.1** The Registrar lists appeals taking into account the convenience of all the parties. Provisional dates are agreed with the parties well in advance of the hearing and every effort is made to keep to these dates. Counsel, solicitors and parties are, however, advised to hold themselves in readiness during the week before and the week

*Paragraph numbers marked with a "+" can be found online and on CD.*

following the provisional date given. Solicitors receive formal notification shortly before the hearing.

**6.6.2** Parties should inform the Registry as early as possible of the names of counsel they have briefed.

**6.6.3** The Court usually hears appeals on Mondays from 11.00am to 1pm and from 2pm to 4pm and on Tuesdays to Thursdays from 10.30am to 1pm and from 2 to 4pm.

**6.6.4** Only in wholly exceptional circumstances will the Court consider sitting in private. Any request for the Court to sit in private should be addressed to the Registrar and should be copied to the other parties. The request should set out fully the reasons why it is made and the request together with any objections filed by the other parties will normally be referred to the presiding Justice.

**6.6.5** No more than two counsel will be heard on behalf of a party (or a single counsel on behalf of an intervener permitted to make oral submissions).

**6.6.6** If a party wishes to have a stenographer present at the hearing or to obtain a full transcript of the hearing, he must notify the Registrar not less than 7 days before the hearing. Any costs of the stenographer or of transcription must be borne by the party making such a request.

**6.6.7** The Registrar will on request inform the parties of the intended constitution of the Court for the hearing of a forthcoming appeal; this will be subject to possible alteration. Counsel should assume that the Court will have read the printed cases and the judgment under appeal but not all the papers which have been filed.

**6.6.8** The Justices should be addressed as 'My Lord' or 'My Lady' as the case may be.

**6.6.9** Some hearings will be filmed and broadcast on television. See paragraph 8.17.1 of Practice Direction 8.

## Costs

**6.7.1** Rule 46 deals with orders for costs. If counsel seek an order **4A–104** other than that costs should be awarded to the successful party, they may make written submissions in accordance with rule 47 if the Court so directs. If a party wishes to defer making submissions as to costs until after judgment, the Court must be informed of this not later than at the close of the oral argument. If the Court

> "*accedes to the request it will give such directions as appear appropriate and it may, in particular, give directions—*
>
> (a) *for the hearing of oral submissions as to costs immediately after judgment;*
>
> (b) *for the simultaneous or sequential filing of written submissions as to costs within a specified period after judgment;*
>
> (c) *for the hearing of oral submissions after the filing of written submissions":* rule 47(2).

The original and 7 copies of any written submissions must be filed at the Registry. Copies should also be sent to the other parties to the appeal. Costs submissions are considered on paper.

***Paragraph numbers marked with a "+" can be found online and on CD.***

### Conditional fee agreements

4A-105 **6.7.2** Conditional fee agreements may properly be made by parties to appeals before the Supreme Court.[1] It is open to the officer assessing costs to reduce the percentage uplift recoverable under a conditional fee agreement if he considers it to be excessive. The costs officer decides questions of percentage uplift in accordance with the principles set out in *Designers Guild Limited v. Russell Williams (Textiles) Limited (trading as Washington DC)* [2003] 2 Costs LR 204. If a party appearing before the Court seeks a ruling that the percentage uplift provided for in a conditional fee agreement should be wholly disallowed on legal grounds, such a ruling should (unless otherwise ordered) be expressly sought from the Court before the end of the hearing. *This paragraph does not apply to appeals from Scotland or Northern Ireland.*

### Judgment

*Place and time of judgment*

4A-106 **6.8.1** Judgments are given on a day notified in advance. One week's notice is normally given. If judgment is to be handed down on a Wednesday, copies will be released on the previous Thursday. All corrections are to be submitted by midday on the following Monday.

*Attendance of counsel*

**6.8.2** One junior counsel for each party or group of parties who have filed a case may attend when judgment is delivered in open court, but the attendance of counsel is not required. If counsel do attend, they should be familiar with the subject matter of the appeal and with the options for its disposal. Where judgment is to be promulgated by the Registrar, copies will be made available for collection by counsel or a solicitor at the Registry on a day notified in advance.

*Conditions under which judgments are released in advance*

**6.8.3** The judgment of the Court is made available to certain persons before judgment is given. When, for example, judgment is given on a Wednesday morning, it is made available to counsel from 10.30 am on the previous Thursday morning. In releasing the judgment, the Court gives permission for the contents to be disclosed to counsel, solicitors (including solicitors outside London who have appointed London agents) and in-house legal advisers in a client Government department. The contents of the judgment and the result of the appeal may be disclosed to the client parties themselves 24 hours before the judgment is to be given unless the Court or the Registrar directs otherwise. A direction will be given where there is reason to suppose that disclosure to the parties would not be in the public interest.

[1] Conditional fee agreements are sanctioned by the Courts and Legal Services Act 1990, as amended by the Access to Justice Act 1999.

**6.8.4** It is the duty of counsel to check the judgment for typographical errors and minor inaccuracies. In the case of apparent error or ambiguity in the judgment, counsel are requested to inform the Head of Judicial Support as soon as possible. This should be done by e-mail to judicialsupport@supremecourt.gsi.gov.uk, no later than two working days before the date judgment is to be given. The purpose of disclosing the judgment is not to allow counsel to re-argue the case and attention is drawn to the opinions of Lord Hoffmann and Lord Hope in *R (Edwards) v Environment Agency* [2008] UKHL 22, [2008] 1WLR 1587.

**6.8.5** Accredited members of the media may also be given a copy of the judgment in advance. The contents of this document are subject to a strict embargo, and are not for publication, broadcast or use on club tapes before judgment has been delivered. The documents are issued in advance on the strict understanding that no approach is made to any person or organisation about their contents before judgment is given.

### Intervention

**6.9.1** A person who is not a party to an appeal may apply in accordance with rule 26 for permission to intervene in the appeal. An intervener under rule 15 who wishes to intervene in the appeal must make a formal application under rule 26. **4A–107**

**6.9.2** An application should be made in the general form of application, Form 2, (see paragraph 7.1 of Practice Direction 7 for applications) and should state whether permission is sought for both oral and written interventions or for written intervention only. The application should be filed with the prescribed fee and confirmation of the consent of the appellants and respondents in the appeal. If their consent is refused, the application must be endorsed with a certificate of service on them, with a brief explanation of the reasons for the refusal.

**6.9.3** Applications for permission to intervene should be filed at least 6 weeks before the date of hearing of the appeal. If permission is given, written submissions must be filed and also given to the appellants and respondents for incorporation into the core volumes at least 3 weeks before the hearing. Failure to meet these deadlines increases the burden on the parties in preparing their cases and the core volumes, and may delay the hearing of the appeal.

**6.9.4** All counsel instructed on behalf of an intervener with permission to address the Court should attend the hearing unless specifically excused.

**6.9.5** Subject to the discretion of the Court, interveners bear their own costs and any additional costs to the appellants and respondents resulting from an intervention are costs in the appeal. Orders for costs "will not normally be made either in favour of or against interveners but such orders may be made if the Court considers it just to do so (in particular if an intervener has in substance acted as the sole or principal appellant or respondent)": rule 46(3).



### Specialist advisers and advocates to the Court

**6.10.1** For a request for a specialist adviser or an advocate to the **4A–108**

Court to be appointed in an appeal see paragraphs 8.13.1 and 8.13.2 of Practice Direction 8.

*Paragraph numbers marked with a "+" can be found online and on CD.*

## PRACTICE DIRECTION 7—APPLICATIONS, DOCUMENTS, FORMS AND ORDERS

### Applications

**7.1.1** Applications are governed by rule 30. An application should be made as soon as it becomes apparent that an application is necessary or expedient. **4A–109**

**7.1.2** An application must be made in Form 2 and should be served on all the other parties before it is filed: rule 30(1)(3).

**7.1.3** An application must state what order the applicant is seeking and, briefly, why the applicant is seeking the order: see rule 30(2). Certain applications (e.g. for security) should be supported by written evidence. Although there may be no requirement to provide evidence in support, it should be borne in mind that, as a practical matter, the Court will often need to be satisfied by evidence of the facts that are relied on in support of or for opposing the application. Evidence must be filed as well as served on the respondents.

**7.1.4** A party *"who wishes to oppose an application must, within 7 days after service, file notice of objection"* in Form 3 and *"must (before filing) serve a copy on the applicant and any other parties"*: rule 30(4).

**7.1.5** The parties to an application for a consent order must ensure that they provide any material needed to satisfy the Court that it is appropriate to make the order.

**7.1.6** Applications will be dealt with without a hearing wherever possible. Unless the Registrar directs otherwise, opposed procedural applications are referred to a Panel of Justices and may be decided with or without an oral hearing.

**7.1.7 The original and 3 copies** of the application must be filed, with the prescribed fee. The original application must bear a certificate of service on the other parties and must clearly indicate whether the other parties consent or refuse to consent to the application. **The original and 3 copies** of the notice of objection must be filed, with the prescribed fee. The original notice must bear a certificate of service on the other parties.

**7.1.8** If the Panel of Justices orders an oral hearing, the parties may seek permission to adduce affidavits, witness statements and such other documents as they may wish. **Eight copies** are required. Copies of such documents must be served on the other parties before the oral hearing. Authorities are not normally cited before the Panel.

### Documents

*Preparation*

**7.2.1** All formal documents for the Supreme Court must be produced on A4 paper, securely bound on the left, using both sides of the paper. Documents which are not legible or which are not produced in the authorised form or which are unsatisfactory for some other similar reason are not accepted. **4A–110**

**7.2.2** See paragraph 7.2.4 for a list of the provisions governing the form of documents which are to be filed.

***Paragraph numbers marked with a "+" can be found online and on CD.***

*Number of documents required*

**7.2.3** The following table shows the numbers of documents usually required for the hearing of an appeal. The numbers shown are the minimum prescribed by the Rules. Actual requirements must be subject to agreement and depend on the number of parties, counsel and solicitors concerned, and on the special circumstances of each appeal. Copies for the use of the party originating the documents are not included in the numbers indicated.

The appellants must provide:

| Document | For Registry | For other side |
|---|---|---|
| Notice of appeal | Original and 3 copies on filing | One on service |
| Statement of facts and issues | Original and 7 copies | As arranged |
| Appendix Part 1 | 8 | One in advance otherwise as arranged |
| Appendix Part 2 and any subsequent Parts | 10 | One in advance otherwise as arranged |
| Case | Original and 7 copies no later than five weeks before the hearing | As arranged on exchange |
| Core volumes | 10 no later than two weeks before the hearing | As arranged |
| Authorities volumes | 10 no later than two weeks before the hearing | As arranged |

The respondents (and any interveners) must provide:

| Document | For Registry | For other side |
|---|---|---|
| Case | Original and 7 copies no later than three weeks before the hearing | As arranged on exchange; 10 for core volumes |
| Respondents' additional documents (if any) | 10 | As arranged |

*Form of documents*

**7.2.4** Reference should be made to the following Practice Directions for the form of documents—

For Statement of facts and issues: see Practice Direction 5 paragraph 5.1.3

For Appendix: see Practice Direction 5 paragraph 5.1.4

***Paragraph numbers marked with a "+" can be found online and on CD.***

For Cases: see Practice Direction 6 paragraph 6.3
For Core volumes: see Practice Direction 6 paragraph 6.4
For Volumes of authorities: see Practice Direction 6 paragraph 6.5.

*Disposal of documents*

**7.2.5** All forms and supporting documents which are filed become the property of the Court. No documents submitted in connection with an application for permission to appeal can be returned. Certain documents submitted in connection with an appeal may be returned, on application to the Registrar within 14 days of judgment in the appeal. Original documents are retained.

**7.2.6** Documents filed for the use of the Court may be inspected by persons who are not a party to the appeal on application under rule 39. Such persons must comply with any anonymity orders, data protection requirements and/or conditions imposed by the Registrar under rule 39.

**Forms**

**7.3.1** Rule 4 provides for the forms which are to be used in the Supreme Court. **4A–111**

**7.3.2** The following forms are set out in Annex 1 to this Practice Direction.

Form 1 Application for permission/notice of appeal
Form 2 Application form
Form 3 Notice of objection/acknowledgement by respondent

**Orders**

*Draft order*

**7.4.1** After the Court has given judgment, the Registrar will send a draft order to all parties who filed a case. The drafts must be returned to the Registrar within 7 days of the date of receipt (unless otherwise directed), either approved or with suggested amendments. If amendments are proposed, they must be submitted to the solicitors for the other parties, who should indicate their approval or disagreement both to the solicitors submitting the proposals and to the Registrar. **4A–112**

*Final order*

**7.4.2** A copy of the sealed final order is sent to the solicitors for all parties.

**Annex 1**

Form 1 Application for permission/notice of appeal **4A–113**
Form 2 Application form
Form 3 Notice of objection/acknowledgement by respondent

**Editorial note**

The Forms mentioned in the previous paragraph can be found at paras 4A–197 to 4A–199 below. **4A–113.1**



SUPREME COURT

## Annex 2

### Fees payable in the Supreme Court

4A-114 The fees set out in column (2) of the table below are payable in the Supreme Court in respect of the items described in column (1) of the table.

No fee in column (2) is payable in respect of criminal proceedings, other than the fee payable on submitting a claim for costs.

In relation to its devolution jurisdiction the fees set out in column (3) of the table are payable in respect of the items described in column (1) of the table.

| *(1)* *Number and description of fee* | *(2)* *Amount of fee* | *(3)* *Amount of fee* |
|---|---|---|
| **1 Application for permission to appeal** | | |
| 1.1 On filing an application for permission to appeal. | £800 | £400 |
| 1.2 On filing notice of objection to an application for permission to appeal. | £160 | £160 |
| **2 Appeals, etc** | | |
| 2.1 On filing notice under rule 18(1)(c) of the 2009 Rules of an intention to proceed with an appeal. | £800 | £400 |
| 2.2 On filing a notice of appeal. | £1600 | £400 |
| 2.3 On filing a reference under the Supreme Court's devolution jurisdiction. No fee is payable where the reference is made by a court. | n/a | £200 |
| 2.4 On filing notice under rule 21(1) of the 2009 Rules (acknowledgement by respondent). | £320 | £160 |
| 2.5 On filing a statement of relevant facts and issues and an appendix of essential documents. | £4820 | £800 |
| **3 Procedural applications** | | |
| 3.1 On filing an application for a decision of the Registrar to be reviewed. | £1500 | £200 |
| 3.2 On filing an application for permission to intervene in an appeal. | £800 | £200 |
| 3.3 On filing any other procedural application. | £350 | £200 |
| 3.4 On filing notice of objection to a procedural application. | £150 | £150 |
| **4 Costs** | | |
| 4.1 On submitting a claim for costs. | 2.5% of the sum claimed | 2.5% of the sum claimed |

| *(1)* *Number and description of fee* | *(2)* *Amount of fee* | *(3)* *Amount of fee* |
|---|---|---|
| 4.2 On certification by the Registrar under rule 52 of the 2009 Rules of the amount of assessed costs, or on receipt of an order showing the amount. | 2.5% of the sum claimed | 2.5% of the sum claimed |
| **5 Copying** | | |
| 5.1 On a request for a copy of a document (other than where fee 5.2 or 5.3 applies)— | | |
| (a) for ten pages or less; | £5 | £5 |
| (b) for each subsequent page. | 50p | 50p |
| **5.2 On a request for a copy of a document to be provided on a computer disk or in other electronic form, for each such copy.** | £5 | £5 |
| 5.3 On a request for a certified copy of a document. | £20 | £20 |

SUPREME COURT

## PRACTICE DIRECTION 8—MISCELLANEOUS MATTERS

### Bankruptcy or winding up

4A–115 **8.1.1** If a party to an appeal is adjudicated bankrupt or a corporate body is ordered to be wound up, their solicitor must give immediate notice in writing to the other parties and to the Registrar, who must also be provided with a certified copy of the bankruptcy or winding up order. The bankrupt party (or his trustee in bankruptcy) or the liquidator must file an application to pursue the appeal and the appeal cannot proceed until the application has been approved.

**8.1.2** An application to pursue the appeal must be filed within 42 days of the date of the notice.

**8.1.3** The form of application and the procedure for any supplemental case follows that for death of a party (see paragraph 8.4 below).

### Grouping or linking of appeals

4A–116 **8.2.1** The Registrar may direct that appeals raising the same or similar issues are heard either together or consecutively by the court constituted by the same Justices and may give any consequential directions that appear appropriate.

**8.2.2** The Registrar should be consulted on whether grouping or linking is likely to be appropriate. A principal consideration will be to avoid wherever possible separate representation by counsel and any duplication in the submissions made or in the documents produced for the hearing.

### Cross-appeals

4A–117 **8.3.1** A respondent who wishes to argue that the order appealed from should be upheld on grounds different from those relied on by the court below, must state that clearly in his written case but need not cross-appeal: rule 25(1). A respondent who wishes to argue that the order appealed from should be varied must obtain permission to cross-appeal except in cases where *"leave is required from the Court of Session for an appeal from that court or…an appeal lies…as of right"*:rule 25(2). Except in those cases, applications for permission to cross-appeal should be made by the respondents directly to the Supreme Court.

**8.3.2** Where permission to cross-appeal is required, an application for permission may only be filed after permission to appeal has been granted to the original applicant for permission to appeal. **The original and 3 copies** of the application for permission to cross-appeal must be filed. Where permission to cross-appeal is granted by the Supreme Court, the application for permission to cross-appeal will stand as the notice of appeal and the appellant must then comply with rule 18 and paragraph 3.4.1 of Practice Direction 3.

**8.3.3** If permission to cross-appeal is not required, the notice of cross-appeal must be filed with the prescribed fee within 42 days of the filing of the original appeal. **The original and 3 copies** of the notice of cross-appeal must be filed. In a notice of cross-appeal, the original appellant is designated as original-appellant/cross-respondent and the original respondent is designated as original-respondent/ cross-appellant.

**8.3.4** A cross-appeal may be presented out of time in accordance with paragraph 4.4.1 of Practice Direction 4. For the fees payable for cross-appeals see Annex 2 to Practice Direction 7.

**8.3.5** Argument in respect of a cross-appeal must be included by each party in their case in the original appeal. Such an inclusive case must clearly state that it is filed in respect of both the original and cross-appeals.

**8.3.6** In a cross-appeal, the cases on the original appeal must be filed 5 weeks before the hearing. The cross-appellants' case for the cross-appeal must be filed 3 weeks before the hearing as part of their reply to the original appellants' case. The original appellants/cross-respondents may reply to the case for the cross-appeal in their case filed in the core volumes.

**8.3.7** There is only one Appendix for the original appeal and cross-appeal, and documents in respect of the appeal and cross-appeal must be included in the same Appendix. The original-appellants/ cross-respondents are responsible for filing the Statement and Appendix and for notifying the Registrar that the appeal and cross-appeal are ready for listing (including payment of the fee).

**8.3.8** The provisions of the above paragraphs apply to appeals from Scotland with the appropriate modifications.

### Death of a party

**8.4.1** If a party to an appeal dies before the hearing, immediate notice of the death must be given in writing to the Registrar and to the other parties. The appeal cannot proceed until a new party has been appointed to represent the deceased person's interest. **4A-118**

**8.4.2** The application to substitute the new party must be filed with the prescribed fee within 42 days of the date of notice of death. It should explain the circumstances in which it is being filed. It must be endorsed with a certificate of service on all other parties.

**8.4.3** If the death takes place after the case for the deceased person has been filed but before the appeal has been heard, the appellants must file a supplemental case setting out the information about the newly-added parties.

### Dispute between parties settled

**8.5.1** It is the duty of counsel and solicitors in any pending appeal, if an event occurs which arguably disposes of the dispute between the parties, either to ensure that the appeal is withdrawn by consent or, if there is no agreement on that course, to bring the facts promptly to the attention of the Registrar and to seek directions. See further paragraph 8.16 below. **4A-119**

### Exhibits

**8.6.1** Parties who require exhibits to be available for inspection at the hearing must apply to the Registrar for permission for the exhibits to be brought to the Court before the hearing. **4A-120**

### Fees and security for costs

4A–121 **8.7.1** Payments of fees and deposits of security money may be made in cash or by banker's draft or cheque. If an appellant wishes to pay in cash, the Registry may only accept cash up to £10,000, in order to comply with money laundering regulations. Drafts and cheques for fees must be made payable to 'The Supreme Court of the United Kingdom'. Drafts and cheques for security money must be made payable to 'UK Supreme Court Security Fund Account'.

### Interveners

4A–122 **8.8.1** A person who is not a party to an application for permission to appeal may apply for permission to intervene in accordance with rule 15. See paragraph 3.3.17 of Practice Direction 3. A person who is not a party to an appeal may apply for permission to intervene in accordance with rule 26. See paragraph 6.9 of Practice Direction 6.

**8.8.2** Attention is drawn to paragraphs 2 and 3 of Lord Hoffmann's opinion in In *re E (a child) (Northern Ireland)* [2008] UKHL 66, (2008) Times, November 19, where he said this.

> "2. It may however be of some assistance in future cases if I comment on the intervention by the Northern Ireland Human Rights Commission. In recent years the House has frequently been assisted by the submissions of statutory bodies and non-governmental organisations on questions of general public importance. Leave is given to such bodies to intervene and make submissions, usually in writing but sometimes orally from the bar, in the expectation that their fund of knowledge or particular point of view will enable them to provide the House with a more rounded picture than it would otherwise obtain. The House is grateful to such bodies for their help.
>
> 3. An intervention is however of no assistance if it merely repeats points which the appellant or respondent has already made. An intervener will have had sight of their printed cases and, if it has nothing to add, should not add anything. It is not the role of an intervener to be an additional counsel for one of the parties. This is particularly important in the case of an oral intervention. I am bound to say that in this appeal the oral submissions on behalf of the NIHRC only repeated in rather more emphatic terms the points which had already been quite adequately argued by counsel for the appellant. In future, I hope that interveners will avoid unnecessarily taking up the time of the House in this way."

### New submissions

4A–123 **8.9.1** If, after the conclusion of the argument on an appeal, a party wishes to bring to the notice of the Court new circumstances which have arisen and which might affect the decision or order of the Court,

*Paragraph numbers marked with a "+" can be found online and on CD.*

application must be made without delay by letter to the Registrar for permission to make new submissions. The application should indicate the circumstances and the submissions it is desired to make, and a copy must be sent to the solicitors for the other parties to the appeal.

### Opposed procedural applications

**8.10.1** See paragraph 7.1 of Practice Direction 7 for applications. **4A–124**

### Patents

**8.11.1** This direction applies to any appeal direct from the High Court under sections 12 and 13 of the Administration of Justice Act 1969, from an order for the revocation of a patent made under section 32 or section 61 of the Patents Act 1949 or under section 72 of the Patents Act 1977. **4A–125**

**8.11.2** Notice of intention to file an appeal, with a copy of the notice of appeal, must be served on the Comptroller-General of Patents, Designs and Trade Marks, as well as on the respondents.

**8.11.3** If at any time before the hearing of the appeal the respondents decide not to file an acknowledgement to oppose the appeal, they must without delay serve notice of their decision on the Comptroller and on the appeal. Any such notice served on the Comptroller must be accompanied by a copy of the petition under section 32 of the 1949 Act or of the statements of case in the claim and the affidavits filed therein.

**8.11.4** The Comptroller must, within 14 days of receiving notice of the respondents' decision, serve on the appellant and file a notice stating whether or not he intends to file an acknowledgement.

**8.11.5** The Comptroller may appear and be heard in opposition to the appeal:

(a) in any case where he has given notice of his intention to appear, and
(b) in any other case (including in particular a case where the respondents withdraw opposition to the appeal during the hearing) if the Court so directs or allows.

**8.11.6** The Court makes such orders for the postponement or adjournment of the hearing of the appeal as may appear necessary for the purpose of giving effect to the provisions of this paragraph.

### Public funding and legal aid

**8.12.1** The Court does not provide public funding or legal aid. Application for public funding must be made in England and Wales to the Legal Services Commission, in Scotland to the Scottish Legal Aid Board, and in Northern Ireland to the Legal Aid Committee. **4A–126**

**8.12.2** A party to whom a public funding or legal aid certificate has been issued must as soon as possible thereafter file a copy at the Registry. Any emergency certificate and subsequent amendments and the authority for leading counsel must also be filed.

### Effect of application by appellant for public funding/legal aid

**8.12.3** Provided the Registrar and the other parties have been notified in writing, an application by an appellant for public funding

*Paragraph numbers marked with a "+" can be found online and on CD.*

or legal aid suspends the commencement of proceedings and the time limits in rules 11 and 19 are extended until 28 days after the determination of the application for public funding or legal aid (including any appeals against a refusal of funding).

**8.12.4** Notification must be given far enough before the expiry of the original time limits to ensure that the appeal is not dismissed as being out of time. A copy of the order appealed from must be submitted by the applicant with the notification.

### Effect of application by respondent for public funding/legal aid

**8.12.5** Where a respondent to an appeal has applied for public funding or legal aid, the Registrar should be informed within the original time limit for filing the statement and appendix.

### Issuing of public funding/legal aid certificate

**8.12.6** Where a public funding or legal aid certificate is granted, the relevant date for the purpose of calculation of time limits under paragraphs 8.12.4 and 8.12.5 is the date of issue of the certificate.

### Specialist advisers and advocates to the Court

**4A-127** **8.13.1** Any party to an appeal may apply in writing to the Registrar for specialist advisers to attend the hearing: rule 35.[1] Such advisers provide assistance to the Court and are strictly independent of the parties to the appeal.

**8.13.2** A request for an advocate to the Court to be appointed in an appeal should be made in writing to the Registrar. Any request should indicate whether the other parties to the appeal support the request.

### Stay of execution

**4A-128** **8.14.1** Filing a notice of appeal or an application for permission to appeal does not in itself place a stay of execution on any order appealed from. A party seeking such a stay must apply to the court appealed from, not to the Supreme Court. The Supreme Court cannot stay an interlocutor of the Court of Session.[2]

### Transcription

**4A-129** **8.15.1** See paragraph 6.6.6 of Practice Direction 6 for requests for stenographers and transcripts.

### Withdrawal of appeals and applications

**4A-130** **8.16.1** Attention is drawn to the provisions of rule 34.

*Applications for permission to appeal*

**8.16.2** An application for permission to appeal may be withdrawn by writing to the Registrar, stating that the parties have agreed how the costs should be settled. The respondents should notify the Registrar of their agreement.

---

[1] For Nautical Assessors, see also Supreme Court of Judicature Act 1891 s 3.
[2] Court of Session Act 1988 s 41(2).

*Appeals*

**8.16.3** An appeal that has not been listed for hearing may be withdrawn by writing to the Registrar, stating that the parties to the appeal have agreed the costs of the appeal. The nature of the agreement should be indicated. Where appropriate, the letter should also indicate how any security money should be disposed of. Written notification must also be given to the respondents who must notify the Registrar of their agreement to the withdrawal of the appeal and who must confirm that the costs have been agreed.

**8.16.4** An appeal that has been listed for hearing may only be withdrawn by order of the Court on application. (See paragraph 7.1 of Practice Direction 7 for applications.) An application for such an order should include submissions on costs and, where appropriate, indicate how any security money should be disposed of. The application must be submitted for their consent to those respondents who have filed an acknowledgement. The application should be filed with the prescribed fee.

### Broadcasting

**8.17.1** The President and the Justices of the Supreme Court will **4A–131** normally accede to a request to record, film or broadcast proceedings before the Court where the presence of cameras or recording equipment does not affect the administration of justice and the recording and broadcasting is conducted in accordance with the protocol [1] which has been agreed with representatives of the relevant broadcasting authorities. Permission to record, film or broadcast proceedings must be sought from the President or the presiding Justice on each occasion and requires his express approval. Where the President or the presiding Justice grants permission, he may impose such conditions as he considers to be appropriate including the obtaining of consent from all the parties involved in the proceedings.

### Enforcement of orders made by the Supreme Court

**8.18.1** The enforcement of orders made by the Supreme Court in **4A–132** England and Wales is dealt with in paragraph 13 of Practice Direction 40B which supplements Part 40 of the Civil Procedure Rules. This provides for an application to be made in accordance with CPR Part 23 for an order to make an order of the Supreme Court (or the House of Lords) an order of the High Court. The application should be made to the procedural judge of the Division, District Registry or court in which the proceedings are taking place and may be made without notice unless the court directs otherwise.

**8.18.2** The Part 23 application must be supported by the following:

(1) details of the order which was the subject of the appeal to the Supreme Court or the House of Lords;



[1] The protocol ensures that certain types of proceedings and some aspects of proceedings such as private discussions between parties and their advisers are not recorded, televised or filmed. It also regulates the use of extracts of proceedings and prevents their use in certain types of programmes (such as party political broadcasts) and in any form of advertising or publicity.

(2) details of the order of the Supreme Court or the House of Lords, with a copy annexed, and

(3) a copy of the certificate of the Registrar of the Supreme Court or of the Clerk of Parliaments of the assessment of the costs of the appeal to the Supreme Court or the House of Lords.

**8.18.3** The order to make an order of the Supreme Court or the House of Lords an order of the High Court should be in form no PF68.

**8.18.4** An order made by the Supreme Court is a UK judgment and enforcement of such an order in Scotland and Northern Ireland is dealt with in accordance with Schedule 6 to the Civil Jurisdiction and Judgments Act 1982. See Part 74 of the Civil Procedure Rules.

## PRACTICE DIRECTION 9—THE HUMAN RIGHTS ACT 1998

### Appeals involving declarations of incompatibility

**9.1.1** Where an appellant or a respondent seeks a declaration of incompatibility under the Human Rights Act 1998, the appropriate section of Form 1 or Form 3 must be completed and the provisions of the relevant Practice Direction must be complied with: see Practice Direction 4 paragraph 4.2.12. **4A–133**

**9.1.2** The Crown has the right to be joined as a party in any appeal where the Court is considering whether to declare that a provision of primary or subordinate legislation is incompatible with a Convention right: see rule 40. In any appeal where the Court is considering, or is being asked to consider, whether to make, uphold or reverse such a declaration, the Registrar must notify the appropriate Law Officer(s) [1] if the Crown (through a Minister, governmental body or other person defined in Human Rights Act 1998 s 5(2)) is not already a party to the appeal: rule 40(1).

**9.1.3** The person notified under paragraph 9.1.2 must within 21 days of receiving such notice, or such extended period as the Registrar may allow, serve on the parties and file a notice stating whether or not the Crown intends to intervene in the appeal; and the identity of the Minister or other person who is to be joined as a party to the appeal.[2]

**9.1.4** If a Minister or other person has already been joined to proceedings in the court below in accordance with the provisions of s 5 of the Human Rights Act 1998, the permission of the Court is not required for the continued intervention of the Crown.

**9.1.5** Once joined to the appeal, the case for the Minister or other person must be filed in accordance with Practice Direction 6, paragraph 6.3.

**9.1.6** The Court may order the postponement or adjournment of the hearing of the appeal for the purpose of giving effect to the provisions of this direction or the requirements of the Act.

### Other Human Rights Act appeals

**9.1.7** Where an appellant or a respondent seeks to challenge an act of a public authority under the Human Rights Act 1998, the appropriate section of Form 1 or Form 3 must be completed and the provisions of the relevant Practice Direction must be complied with: see Practice Direction 4 paragraph 4.2.12. **4A–134**

**9.1.8** Where an issue under the Human Rights Act is raised in respect of a judicial act,[3] the Registrar notifies the Crown through the Treasury Solicitor as agent for the Lord Chancellor.[4]



---

[1] The Registrar notifies: (i) in appeals from England, the Attorney-General; (ii) in appeals from Scotland, the Advocate General for Scotland and the Lord Advocate; (iii) in appeals from Wales, if appropriate, the Counsel General of the National Assembly for Wales; (iv) in appeals from Northern Ireland, the Attorney General for Northern Ireland.

[2] Human Rights Act 1998 ss 5(2) and 9(5).

[3] Human Rights Act 1998 ss 7, 9(3) and 9(4).

[4] In appeals from Scotland, the Registrar notifies the Solicitor to the Scottish Govern-

**9.1.9** Except as stated above, no special steps are required for other Human Rights Act appeals.

ment; in appeals from Northern Ireland, he notifies the Crown Solicitor and the Departmental Solicitor.

*Paragraph numbers marked with a "+" can be found online and on CD.*

## PRACTICE DIRECTION 10—DEVOLUTION JURISDICTION

### General note

**10.1.1** The Supreme Court has jurisdiction to hear and determine "devolution issues", that is questions relating to the powers and functions of the legislative and executive authorities established in Scotland and Northern Ireland by the Scotland Act 1998 and the Northern Ireland Act 1998 respectively, and questions as to the competence and functions of those established by the Government of Wales Act 2006, whether or not the issue arises in proceedings in England and Wales, Scotland or Northern Ireland. **4A–135**

**10.1.2** The Supreme Court can also be asked to scrutinise Bills of the Scottish Parliament (under section 33 of the Scotland Act), Bills of the Northern Ireland Assembly (under section 11 of the Northern Ireland Act) and proposed Orders in Council and proposed Assembly Measures and Bills under sections 96, 99 and 112 the Government of Wales Act 2006.

**10.1.3** Such cases can reach the Supreme Court in four ways.

(1) By way of a reference of a question by a relevant officer.

(2) By way of an appeal from certain superior courts of England and Wales, Scotland and Northern Ireland.

(3) By way of a reference of a devolution issue by certain appellate courts.

(4) By way of a direct reference of a devolution issue by a relevant officer whether or not the issue is the subject of litigation.

**10.1.4** Rule 3(2) defines "relevant officer" as meaning

(a) in relation to proceedings in England and Wales, the Attorney General and, in relation to proceedings that particularly affect Wales, the Counsel General to the Welsh Assembly Government,

(b) in relation to proceedings in Scotland, the Advocate General for Scotland and the Lord Advocate, and

(c) in relation to proceedings in Northern Ireland, the Advocate General for Northern Ireland and (when section 22 of the Justice (Northern Ireland) Act 2002 comes into force) the Attorney General for Northern Ireland.

**10.1.5** Rule 41 of the Supreme Court Rules provides in general for appeals or references under the Court's devolution jurisdiction (as defined by section 40 of, and Schedule 9 to, the Constitutional Reform Act 2005) to be dealt with in accordance with the Rules, but the Court will give special directions as and when necessary and in particular as to—

(a) any **question** referred under section 33 of the Scotland Act 1998, section 11 of the Northern Ireland Act 1998 or section 96, 99 or 112 of the Government of Wales Act 2006;

(b) any reference of a **devolution issue**;

(c) any **direct reference** under paragraph 33 or 34 of Schedule 6 to the Scotland Act 1998, paragraph 33 or 34 of Schedule 10 to the Northern Ireland Act 1998 or paragraph 29 or 30 of Schedule 9 to the Government of Wales Act 2006.

*Paragraph numbers marked with a "+" can be found online and on CD.*

As to **(a)** above, section 33 of the Scotland Act 1998 provides for the scrutiny of Bills of the Scottish Parliament by the Supreme Court. Section 11 of the Northern Ireland Act 1998 provides for the scrutiny of Bills of the Northern Ireland Assembly by the Supreme Court. Section 96, 99 or 112 of the Government of Wales Act 2006 provide for the scrutiny of proposed Orders in Council, proposed Assembly Measures and Bills of the National Assembly for Wales by the Supreme Court.

As to **(b)** above, a devolution issue is defined by Schedule 6 to the Scotland Act 1998, Schedule 10 to the Northern Ireland Act 1998 or Schedule 9 to the Government of Wales Act 2006. See paragraph 10.1.1 above. Under paragraphs 10, 11, 22 and 30 of Schedule 6 to the Scotland Act 1998, paragraphs 9, 19, 28 and 29 of Schedule 10 to the Northern Ireland Act 1998 or paragraphs 10, 18, 19 and 27 of Schedule 9 to the Government of Wales Act 2006, certain appellate courts may refer a devolution issue arising in proceedings to the Supreme Court.

As to **(c)** above, a relevant officer may make a direct reference of a devolution issue to the Supreme Court under paragraph 33 or 34 of Schedule 6 to the Scotland Act 1998, paragraph 33 or 34 of Schedule 10 to the Northern Ireland Act 1998 or paragraph 29 or 30 of Schedule 9 to the Government of Wales Act 2006 whether or not the issue is the subject of litigation.

### References of a question by a relevant officer

4A–136 **10.2.1** A reference of a question by a relevant officer is made by—

(a) filing the reference, and
(b) serving a copy on any other relevant officer who is not already a party and who has a potential interest in the proceedings,

within any time limits specified by the relevant statute.

**10.2.2** The reference should state—

(a) the question to be determined with respect to the proposed Order in Council, proposed Assembly Measure or Bill to which the reference relates;
(b) whether it applies to the whole Order in Council, Assembly Measure or Bill or to a provision of it,

and the reference shall have annexed to it a copy of the Order in Council, Assembly Measure or Bill to which it relates.

**10.2.3** Any relevant officer (other than the one making the reference) who wishes to participate in the proceedings shall within 7 days of service of the reference on him notify the Registrar and the other parties. Any relevant officer who gives notice automatically becomes a respondent to the proceedings.

**10.2.4** The relevant officer making the reference shall, within 7 days of filing the reference, file a case with respect to the question referred. The referring relevant officer's case should include a copy of any statement made in relation to the Order in Council, Assembly Measure or Bill in accordance with the relevant statute and any relevant extracts from the Official Report of proceedings in the Parliament or Assembly.

*Paragraph numbers marked with a "+" can be found online and on CD.*

**10.2.5** Any other relevant officer who is participating in the proceedings shall file a case with respect to the question referred within 7 days of the notice given under paragraph 10.2.3.

**10.2.6** The relevant officer making the reference shall also notify the relevant Assembly or Parliament which passed the Assembly Measure or Bill or approved the draft of the Order in Council, as the case may be, of the making of the reference.

## Appeals to the Supreme Court

### *(a) Permission to appeal*

**10.3.1** Part 2 of the Supreme Court Rules applies to applications for permission to appeal. Permission to appeal to the Supreme Court may be sought only if permission to appeal has been applied for and refused by the court below. The provisions of this section apply, with necessary modifications, to applications for permission to cross-appeal as they apply to applications for permission to appeal. For the procedure in cases where permission to appeal is not required, see paragraph 10.3.3. **4A–137**

**10.3.2** An application for permission to appeal shall—

(a) briefly set out the facts and points of law involved in the appeal;

(b) conclude with a summary of the reasons why permission to appeal should be granted; and

(c) not normally be accompanied by supporting documents except

(i) the order or interlocutor appealed from;

(ii) the judgment appealed from; and

(iii) if separate, the order or interlocutor of the court below refusing permission to appeal to the Supreme Court.

### *(b) Appeals*

**10.3.3** Rules 18 and 19 and the following paragraphs apply to a person who has obtained permission to appeal from the Supreme Court and in cases where permission to appeal is not required, for example, where a person desires to appeal to the Supreme Court against a determination of a devolution issue by the Inner House of the Court of Session on a reference under paragraph 7 or 8 of Schedule 6 to the Scotland Act 1998.

**10.3.4** A person who desires to appeal to the Supreme Court shall file Form 1 within 42 days of the date on which the order or interlocutor appealed from was made or permission to appeal was granted, as the case may be.

**10.3.5** A notice of appeal must be made in Form 1 and signed by the appellants or their counsel or solicitor.

**10.3.6** The appellant must also serve a copy of his Form 1 on any relevant officer who is not already a party and who has a potential interest in the proceedings. Any relevant officer who is so served may intervene in the proceedings on the appeal in the Supreme Court if within 14 days of service he notifies the Registrar and all other parties. Any relevant officer who gives notice automatically becomes a respondent to the proceedings.

### References by Courts

4A–138 **10.4.1** A reference by a court is made by the appropriate officer of the court—

(a) filing the reference,
(b) serving a copy of the reference on the parties, and
(c) serving a copy of the reference on any relevant officer who is not already a party and who has a potential interest in the proceedings.

**10.4.2** The reference shall set out—

(a) the question referred;
(b) the addresses of the parties;
(c) the name and address of any person who applied for or required the reference to be made;
(d) a concise statement of the background to the matter including—
  (i) the facts of the case, including any relevant findings of fact by the referring court or lower courts; and
  (ii) the main issues in the case and the contentions of the parties with regard to them;
(e) the relevant law, including the relevant provisions of the relevant statute;
(f) the reasons why an answer to the question is considered necessary for the purpose of disposing of the proceedings.

**10.4.3** All judgments and orders already given in the proceedings, including copies of any interlocutors and any notes attaching to such interlocutors, shall be annexed to the reference.

**10.4.4** Any party to the proceedings in the court making the reference who intends to participate in the proceedings in the Supreme Court shall within 14 days of service of the copy reference on him notify the Registrar and the other parties. Any relevant officer who is already a party to the proceedings automatically becomes a respondent to the proceedings.

**10.4.5** Any party who does not intend to participate shall give notice in writing to the Registrar and the other parties accordingly.

**10.4.6** Where notice has to be given under this section of this Practice Direction, it shall also be given to any relevant officer who is not already a party and who has a potential interest in the proceedings.

**10.4.7** Any relevant officer who is not already a party to the proceedings may intervene in the proceedings on the reference by giving notice to the Registrar, other relevant officers with a potential interest and the court making the reference.

**10.4.8** Unless the Supreme Court directs otherwise, once a final judgment has been given on a reference by a court the proceedings shall stand remitted to the court from which the reference came without further order, subject to the disposal of any outstanding issues as to the costs of the reference.

### Direct references by a relevant officer

**10.5.1** In a case where the devolution issue arises in proceedings before a court or tribunal to which the relevant officer is a party, a direct reference by the relevant officer is made by— **4A–139**

(a) filing the reference,

(b) serving a copy of the reference on the parties to those proceedings, and

(c) serving a copy of the reference on any other relevant officer who is not already a party to those proceedings and who has a potential interest.

**10.5.2** The reference shall set out—

(a) the question referred;

(b) the addresses of the parties;

(c) the name and address of any other person who applied for or required the reference to be made;

(d) a concise statement of the background to the matter including—

  (i) the facts of the case, including any relevant findings of fact by the court or tribunal; and

  (ii) the main issues in the case and the contentions of the parties with regard to them;

(e) the relevant law, including the relevant provisions of the relevant statute;

(f) the reasons why an answer to the question is considered necessary for the purpose of disposing of the proceedings.

**10.5.3** All judgments and orders already given in the proceedings, including copies of any interlocutors and any notes attaching to such interlocutors, shall be annexed to the reference.

**10.5.4** Any party to the proceedings in the court or tribunal who intends to participate in the proceedings in the Supreme Court shall within 14 days of service of the copy reference on him notify the Registrar and the other parties. Any relevant officer who gives notice automatically becomes a respondent to the proceedings.

**10.5.5** In a case where the devolution issue is not the subject of proceedings before a court or tribunal, a direct reference by the relevant officer is made by—

(a) filing the reference, and

(b) serving a copy of the reference on any other relevant officer who has a potential interest.

**10.5.6** Any relevant officer served with a copy of the reference may intervene in the proceedings on the reference by giving notice to the Registrar and the relevant officer making the reference.

**10.5.7** Where notice has to be given to any person under the Scotland Act 1998, the Northern Ireland Act 1998 or the Government of Wales Act 2006, as the case may be, the reference shall state the name and address of that person and when he was notified.

**10.5.8** A person who has to be notified under paragraph 35 of Schedule 6 to the Scotland Act 1998, paragraph 35 of Schedule 10 to the Northern Ireland Act 1998 or paragraph 30 of Schedule 9 to the

SUPREME COURT

Government of Wales Act 2006, as the case may be, but who does not intend to participate in the proceedings in the Supreme Court shall give notice in writing within 14 days to the Registrar and the other parties to the proceedings.

## PRACTICE DIRECTION 11—THE EUROPEAN COURT OF JUSTICE

**11.1.1** Article 234 of the Treaty establishing the European Community provides: **4A–140**

1. The Court of Justice shall have jurisdiction to give preliminary rulings concerning:
   (a) the interpretation of this Treaty;
   (b) the validity and interpretation of acts of the institutions of the Community and of the European Central Bank;
   (c) the interpretation of the statutes of bodies established by an act of the Council, where those statutes so provide.
2. Where such a question is raised before any court or tribunal of a Member State, that court or tribunal may, if it considers that a decision on the question is necessary to enable it to give judgment, request the Court of Justice to give a ruling thereon.
3. Where any such question is raised in a case pending before a court or tribunal of a Member State against whose decisions there is no judicial remedy under national law, that court or tribunal shall bring the matter before the Court of Justice.

**11.1.2** When the Court refuses permission to appeal where the application includes a contention that a question of Community law is involved, the Court gives additional reasons for its decision not to grant permission to appeal: rule 42(1). These reasons reflect the decision of the Court of Justice in *CILFIT v. Ministry of Health* (Case C-283/81) which laid down the categories of case where the Court of Justice considered that no reference should be made to it, namely:

(a) where the question raised is irrelevant;
(b) where the Community provision in question has already been interpreted by the Court of Justice;
(c) where the question raised is materially identical with a question which has already been the subject of a preliminary ruling in a similar case; and
(d) where the correct application of Community law is so obvious as to permission no scope for any reasonable doubt.

**11.1.3** The Court may order a reference to the Court of Justice before determining whether to grant permission to appeal. In such circumstances proceedings on the application for permission to appeal are stayed until the answer is received. The paragraphs below apply as appropriate.

**11.1.4** When the Court intends to make a reference, it will give consequential directions as to the form of the reference and the staying of the appeal (see rule 42(3)) and the parties are invited to submit an agreed draft of the question(s) to be referred. A further statement of facts and issues, for the use of the Court of Justice, may also be appropriate. The Court then makes the reference, with or without judgments. At this stage the appeal may also be disposed of in part.

**11.1.5** Within 28 days of the judgment of the Court of Justice, the parties must file written submissions on whether a further hearing before the Supreme Court is necessary or on how the appeal is to be disposed of.

### Further proceedings in the Supreme Court

4A–141 **11.1.6** If a further hearing is required before the Supreme Court, the parties may file supplemental cases.

**11.1.7** If supplemental cases are filed, then:

(a) no later than 5 weeks before the expected date of the further hearing, the appellants must file **the original and 7 copies** of their supplemental case and also serve it on the respondents;

(b) no later than 3 weeks before the expected date of the further hearing, the respondents must file **the original and 7 copies** of their supplemental case and also serve it on the appellants;

(c) no later than 3 weeks before the expected date of the further hearing, any other party filing a case (e.g. an intervener or advocate to the court) must file **the original and 7 copies** of their supplemental case, and also provide copies to the appellants and respondents.

**11.1.8** As soon as all the supplemental cases have been exchanged, and no later than 2 weeks before the date of the expected hearing, the appellants must file 10 additional sets of core volumes containing:

(a) appellants' and respondents' cases;

(b) cases of interveners etc, if any;

(c) judgment of the European Court of Justice;

(d) any additional authorities relied on that are not included in the original green authorities' volumes.

**11.1.9** The Registry supplies the Court with the original core volumes, appendices and authorities volumes.

### Costs

4A–142 **11.1.10** The Court of Justice does not make orders for costs. The costs of the reference are included in the order of the Supreme Court disposing of the appeal; and, if necessary, are assessed by the Costs Officers of the Court.

### Papers for the Court of Justice

4A–143 **11.1.11** Parties should be aware that the Court of Justice will not translate documents which are longer than 20 pages; only summaries are made.

# PRACTICE DIRECTION 12—CRIMINAL PROCEEDINGS

*Section 1 General Note and the Jurisdiction of the Supreme Court in Criminal Proceedings*

## 1. Introduction

**12.1.1** The procedure of the Supreme Court is regulated by statute, by the Supreme Court Rules and by the practice directions which supplement the Rules. Copies of these and other documents may be downloaded from *www.supremecourt.gov.uk*. **4A–144**

**12.1.2** Practice Directions 1-11 and 13 governing civil proceedings apply to criminal proceedings in the Supreme Court subject to any modifications or additional provisions made by this Practice Direction.

*Right of appeal*

**12.1.3** The right of appeal to the Supreme Court is regulated by statute and subject to statutory restrictions. The principal statutes for criminal appeals (as amended in most cases by section 40 of, and Schedule 9 to, the Act) are:

the Administration of Justice Act 1960;
the Criminal Appeal Act 1968;
the Courts-Martial (Appeals) Act 1968;
the Administration of Justice Act 1969;
the Judicature (Northern Ireland) Act 1978;
the Criminal Appeal (Northern Ireland) Act 1980;
the Proceeds of Crime Act 2002;
the Extradition Act 2003;
the Criminal Justice Act 2003;
the Serious Organised Crime and Police Act 2005.

Every applicant for permission to appeal must comply with the statutory requirements before the application can be considered by the Court. The Human Rights Act 1998 applies to the Court in its judicial capacity. But that Act does not confer any general right of appeal to the Court, or any right of appeal in addition to or superseding any right of appeal provided for in Acts passed before the coming into force of the Human Rights Act 1998.

*England and Wales and Northern Ireland*

**12.1.4** An appeal to the Supreme Court may only be brought with the permission of the court below or, if refused by that court, with the permission of the Supreme Court. Subject to paragraphs 12.2.2–12.2.4, in criminal matters such permission may not be granted unless the court below has issued the certificate referred to in paragraph 12.2.1.

**12.1.5** Subject to paragraphs 12.1.4 and 12.2.1-12.2.6, an application for permission to appeal to the Supreme Court in a criminal matter may be made by either the defendant or the prosecutor, as follows:

(a) from any decision of the Court of Appeal Criminal

Division in England and Wales on an appeal to that court[1];

(b) from any decision of the Courts-Martial Appeal Court on an appeal to that court[2];

(c) from any decision of the Court of Appeal in Northern Ireland on an appeal to that court by a person convicted on indictment[3];

(d) from any decision of the Court of Appeal in Northern Ireland in a criminal cause or matter on a case stated by a county court or magistrates' court[4];

(e) from any decision of the High Court of Justice in England and Wales in a criminal cause or matter;[5];

(f) from any decision of the High Court of Justice in Northern Ireland in a criminal cause or matter[6].

*Scotland*

**12.1.6** No appeal lies to the Supreme Court from criminal proceedings in the High Court of Justiciary in Scotland.

*Criminal contempt of court cases*

**12.1.7** In cases involving criminal contempt of court, an appeal lies to the Supreme Court at the instance of the defendant only and, in respect of an application for committal or attachment, at the instance of the applicant from any decision of the Court of Appeal Criminal Division, the Courts-Martial Appeal Court or the High Court [7].

### *Section 2 Applications for Permission*

### 2. Certificate of Point of Law

4A–145 **12.2.1** Subject to paragraphs 12.2.2–12.2.4, permission to appeal to the Supreme Court in a criminal matter may only be granted if it is certified by the court below that a point of law of general public importance is involved in the decision of that court, and it appears to that court or to the Supreme Court that the point is one that ought to be considered by the Supreme Court [8]. An application for permission to appeal without the required certificate may not be filed (paragraph 12.4.3), except as provided by paragraphs 12.2.2–12.2.4.

[1] Criminal Appeal Act 1968 s 33(1) (as amended); Criminal Justice Act 2003, Part 9.
[2] Courts-Martial (Appeals) Act 1968 s 39(1).
[3] Judicature (Northern Ireland) Act 1978 s 40(1)(b); Criminal Appeal (Northern Ireland) Act 1980 s 31(1) (as amended).
[4] Judicature (Northern Ireland) Act 1978 s 41(1)(b).
[5] Administration of Justice Act 1960 s 1(1)(a) (as amended); Extradition Act 2003 ss 32, 114.
[6] Judicature (Northern Ireland) Act 1978 s 41(1)(a); Extradition Act 2003 ss 32, 114.
[7] Administration of Justice Act 1960 s 13; Judicature (Northern Ireland) Act 1978 s 44. For appeals in cases involving civil contempt of court see Practice Direction 1 paragraph 2.1.8.
[8] Criminal Appeal Act 1968 s 33(2); Administration of Justice Act 1960 s 1(2); Courts-Martial (Appeals) Act 1968 s 39(2); Judicature (Northern Ireland) Act 1978 s 41(2); Criminal Appeals (Nothern Ireland) Act 1980 s 31(2); Extradition Act 2003 ss 32, 114; Proceeds of Crime Act (Appeals under Part 4) Order 2003, SI 2003/458.

**12.2.2** A certificate is not required for an appeal from a decision of the High Court in England and Wales or of the High Court in Northern Ireland on a criminal application for habeas corpus [1].

**12.2.3** A certificate is not required for an appeal by a minister of the Crown or a person nominated by him, a member of the Scottish Executive, a Northern Ireland minister or a Northern Ireland department when they have been joined as a party to any criminal proceedings, other than in Scotland, by a notice given under the Human Rights Act 1998 ss.5(1) and 5(2) and they wish to appeal under section 5(4) of that Act against any declaration of incompatibility made in those proceedings.

**12.2.4** A certificate is not required in contempt of court cases where the decision of the court below was not a decision on appeal [2].

**12.2.5** In cases where the court below has not certified a point of law of general public importance, the Registrar will at the request of an applicant provide a letter stating that no appeal lies to the Supreme Court. The European Court of Human Rights accepts this letter as setting out the jurisdiction of the Supreme Court in the litigation, for the purpose of determining whether the petitioner has satisfied the requirement, laid down by Article 35 of the European Convention on Human Rights, that all domestic remedies must be exhausted before an appeal can be made to the Strasbourg Court.

### *Judicial review: criminal matters*

**12.2.6** There is no appeal to the Court of Appeal from a refusal by a Divisional Court to grant permission to apply for judicial review in a criminal case [3]; and the Supreme Court has no jurisdiction to hear an appeal against a refusal by a Divisional Court of permission to apply for judicial review in a criminal case [4]. So, if a Divisional Court refuses permission to apply to it for judicial review in a criminal matter, there is no further remedy in the domestic courts. The only circumstances in which an application may be made to the Supreme Court for permission to appeal from a Divisional Court in a criminal judicial review matter are when the Divisional Court certifies that a point of law of general public importance arises from its decision.

## 3. Time Limits

### *Time within which to apply for permission to appeal*

**12.3.1** An application for permission to appeal to the Supreme Court in a criminal matter must first be made to the court below. If the court below refuses permission to appeal, application may then be made to the Supreme Court.

**12.3.2** An application to the Supreme Court for permission to ap-

[1] Administration of Justice Act 1960 s 15(3) (as amended); Judicature (Northern Ireland) Act 1978 s 45(3).

[2] Administration of Justice Act 1960 s 13(4); Judicature (Northern Ireland) Act 1978 s 44(4).

[3] Senior Courts Act 1981 s 18(1)(a).

[4] Administration of Justice Act 1960 s1(1) & (2) and the decisions of the House of Lords in Re Poh, Eastaway and Burkett.

peal is made in accordance with rule 10 and Practice Direction 3. An application for permission to appeal to the House of Lords

(a) from a decision of the Court of Appeal under s 33(1) of the Criminal Appeal Act 1968 or

(b) from a decision of a Divisional Court of the Queen's Bench Division in a criminal cause or matter under s 1(1)(a) of the Administration of Justice Act 1960

must be made within 28 days beginning with the date on which the application for permission was refused by the court below (and not the following day)[1]. This date is not necessarily that on which the point of law was certified. Where the time prescribed expires on a Saturday, Sunday, bank holiday or other day on which the Registry is closed, the application is accepted as being in time if it is received on the next day on which the Registry is open.

**12.3.3** An application for permission to appeal must be made within 14 days if made under one of the following provisions: ss 32(5), 114(5) of the Extradition Act 2003; ss 33, 44 and 66 of the Proceeds of Crime Act 2002[2]; and, ss 183, 193 and 214 of the Proceeds of Crime Act 2002[3]. A 14 day time limit also applies to an application to refer a case pursuant to the Attorney General's Reference procedure under s 36(5) of the Criminal Justice Act 1988[4].

*Application for extension of time to file application for permission*

**12.3.4** Subject to paragraph 12.3.5, the Supreme Court or the court below may, on application made at any time by the defendant and in certain limited circumstances the prosecutor[5], extend the time within which application for permission to appeal to the Supreme Court may be made to the Supreme Court or to that court[6]. Such an application to the Supreme Court is incorporated in the application for permission itself, and should set out briefly the reason(s) why the application is being presented outside the statutory period.

**12.3.5** No extension may be granted in respect of applications made under ss 32 and 114 of the Extradition Act 2003.

*Public funding and legal aid*

**12.3.6** Paragraph 8.12 of Practice Direction 8 applies to appeals in

[1] Criminal Appeal Act 1968 s 34(1) (as amended); Administration of Justice Act 1960 s 2(1) (as amended).

[2] Proceeds of Crime Act 2002 (appeals under Part 2) Order 2003 (SI 2003 No 82), Part 3, Article 12.

[3] Proceeds of Crime Act 2002 (appeals under Part 4) Order 2003 (SI 2003 No 483), Part 3, Article 12.

[4] Criminal Justice Act 1988 Sch 3, para 4.

[5] Criminal Appeal Act 1968, ss 33(1B), 34(2).

[6] Criminal Appeal Act 1968 s 34(2); Administration of Justice Act 1960 s 2(3); Courts-Martial (Appeals) Act 1968 s 40(2); Criminal Appeal (Northern Ireland) Act 1980 s 32(2); Judicature (Northern Ireland) Act 1978 Schedule 1, paragraph 1(2). Section 1A of the Geneva Conventions Act 1957 makes, in relation to protected prisoners, certain extensions to the time limits in the Administration of Justice Act 1960, the Criminal Appeal Act 1968, the Courts-Martial (Appeals) Act 1968 and the Criminal Appeal (Northern Ireland) Act 1968.

criminal proceedings. In criminal proceedings, depending on the route of appeal, application should be made to the court appealed from or, in Northern Ireland, to the Legal Aid Committee.

**12.3.7** A copy of the order appealed from must be submitted by the appellant with the notification of the application for funding. The period within which the application for permission to appeal or notice of appeal (as the case may be) must be filed is then extended to 28 days after the final determination of the application for funding, including any appeals. An extension may not be granted to an appellant under the Extradition Act 2003[1].

**12.3.8** A representation order will usually provide for junior counsel and solicitors at the permission stage with the addition of leading counsel if permission is granted.

## 4. Applications for Permission to Appeal

*Form of application*

**12.4.1** The provisions of Practice Direction 3 govern the form of applications for permission to appeal. **4A–146**

*Case title*

**12.4.2** In applications where a prosecuting authority is the appellant, the prosecuting authority should be described as follows: "Director of Public Prosecutions (*or other prosecuting authority*) (on behalf of Her Majesty)".

**12.4.3** Subject to paragraphs 12.2.2–12.2.4, the Registry cannot issue any application for permission to appeal that is not accompanied by the certificate from the court below required by statute, certifying a point of law of general public importance (see paragraph 12.2.1 above).

*Service*

**12.4.4** In habeas corpus appeals and/or in appeals concerning extradition, the application must be served on the government that is seeking extradition or on the Director of Public Prosecutions if he is acting for that government.

## 5. Costs

**12.5.1** Where an application for permission to appeal is determined without an oral hearing, costs may be awarded as follows: **4A–147**

(a) to a publicly funded or legally aided appellant, reasonable costs incurred in preparing papers for the Appeal Panel;

(b) to a publicly funded or legally aided respondent, only those costs necessarily incurred in attending the client, attending the appellant's solicitors, considering the application, filing notice of objection and, where applicable, preparing respondent's objections to the application;

(c) to an unassisted respondent where the appellant is publicly

[1] Extradition Act 2003 ss 32, 114

*Paragraph numbers marked with a "+" can be found online and on CD.*

funded or legally aided, payment out of the Community Legal Service Fund (pursuant to s 11 of the Access to Justice Act 1999[1])[2] of costs as specified at (b) above;

(d) to an appellant or respondent, payment out of central funds, pursuant to s 16 or s 17 of the Prosecution of Offences Act 1985, of costs incurred at (a) or (b) above, as the case may be;

(e) to a respondent where neither party is publicly funded or legally aided, costs as specified at (b) above to be paid by the appellant.

Where costs are sought under (c), (d) or (e) above, application may be made by letter addressed to the Registrar or may be included in a bill of costs filed in the Registry conditional upon the application being granted.

**12.5.2** Where an application for permission to appeal is referred for an oral hearing and is dismissed, application for costs must be made by the respondent at the end of the hearing. No order for costs will be made unless requested at that time.

**12.5.3** Where permission to appeal is granted, the costs of the permission application become costs in the appeal.

**12.5.4** Bills of costs for assessment must be filed within three months from the date of the decision of the Appeal Panel or the date on which an application for permission is withdrawn. If an extension of the three months period is desired, application must be made in writing to the Registrar and copies of all such correspondence sent to all interested parties. In deciding whether to grant an application for an extension of time made after the expiry of the three month period the Registrar takes into account the circumstances set out in paragraph 6.2 of Practice Direction 13.

### 6. Fees

**4A–148** **12.6.1** No fee is payable at any stage of an application for permission to appeal in a criminal matter. Fees are payable on the assessment of a bill of costs.

### *Section 3 Appeals*

### 7. Time Limits

**4A–149** **12.7.1** Apart from appeals under the Extradition Act 2003, a notice of appeal must be filed in accordance with rule 19.

**12.7.2** Appeals under the Extradition Act 2003 must be filed within 28 days of the grant of permission, starting with the day on which permission is granted. The time for doing so may not be extended[3].

---

[1] Also pursuant to r 5(2) Community Legal Service (Cost Protection) Regulations 2000 and in accordance with the procedural requirements of rr.9, 10 Community Legal Service (Costs) Regulations 2000 (as amended).

[2] Or s.18 Legal Aid Act 1988; or, in Scotland, pursuant to s.19 Legal Aid (Scotland) Act 1986 or, in Northern Ireland, pursuant to Article 16 Legal Aid Advice and Assistance (N.I.) Order 1981.

[3] Extradition Act 2003 ss 32, 114.

**8. Security for Costs**

**12.8.1** No security for costs is required in criminal appeals. **4A–150**

**9. Statement of Facts and Issues**

**12.9.1** The provisions of Practice Direction 5 apply to appeals in criminal proceedings. **4A–151**

**12.9.2** In any appeal under the Criminal Appeal Act 1968, the statement of facts and issues must state clearly whether any grounds of appeal have been left undetermined by the Court of Appeal (see also paragraph 12.11.2).

**10. Filing of Statement and Appendix**

*Respondents' consent*

**12.10.1** The provisions of Practice Direction 5 apply to appeals in criminal proceedings but it is not the practice in criminal appeals to require the consent of the respondents to applications for extension of time. **4A–152**

**11. Appellants' and respondents' cases**

**12.11.1** The provisions of Practice Direction 6 apply to appeals in criminal proceedings. **4A–153**

**12.11.2** In any appeal under the Criminal Appeal Act 1968 in which grounds of appeal have been left undetermined by the Court of Appeal (see paragraph 12.9.2), each party should include in their case submissions on the merits of those grounds and on how they would seek to have them disposed of by the Court.

**Core Volumes**

*Form of core volumes*

**12.12.1** The provisions of Practice Direction 6 apply to appeals in criminal proceedings. **4A–154**

**12.12.2** It is not necessary for the appellants' solicitors to produce additional volumes for the use of victims attending the hearing. The Registry provides the necessary documents from among the number produced for the use of the Court.

**13. Bail**

**12.13.1** The Supreme Court does not grant bail. Applications for bail should be made to the court below. Where bail is granted to a party to an appeal to the Court, the Registrar should be notified. **4A–155**

**12.13.2** The attendance of a party to an appeal who is in custody is not normally required or permitted. Where the attendance of a party in custody is required, his solicitors will be informed by the Registrar in writing.

**12.13.3** It should be noted that where a party was on bail pending the hearing of the appeal, surrender is usually required on the first day of the hearing.

**14. Exhibits**

**12.14.1** Parties who require exhibits to be available for inspection **4A–156**

at the hearing must apply to the Registrar for permission for the exhibits to be brought to the Court before the hearing.

**15. Victims' Code of Practice**

4A–157 **12.15.1** The Victims' Code of Practice governs the services to be provided in England and Wales to victims of criminal conduct that has occurred in England and Wales. The Code is issued by the Home Secretary under s 32 of the Domestic Violence, Crime and Victims Act 2004. The Court applies the Code.

**12.15.2** Accordingly, all applications for permission to appeal and all appeals are examined to establish whether a victim can be identified and, if so, to determine what services are required to be provided to the victim.

**12.15.3** In giving effect to paragraph 12.15.2 the Registrar may consult the Treasury Solicitor, the Court of Appeal Criminal Division and other relevant persons to obtain any necessary information.

**12.15.4** The Registry may either directly or through the joint police/CPS Witness Care Units contact victims to inform them that an application for permission to appeal or an appeal has been filed, to explain the appeals procedure, and to report progress on the application and/or appeal, including the date set for the hearing.

**12.15.5** Victims may attend the hearing of an appeal or application for permission to appeal or the handing down of judgment. The Registry arranges such attendance and provides the case papers.

**12.15.6** If permission to appeal is granted by an Appeal Panel, the Registrar notifies the joint police/CPS Witness Care Units no later than one working day after the day on which permission to appeal has been granted.

**12.15.7** The Registry notifies the joint police/CPS Witness Care Units of the result of the appeal no later than one working day after the day of the result.

# PRACTICE DIRECTION 13—COSTS

**Note**: enquiries about costs should be made to the Costs Clerk (tel: 020-7960 1990). Enquiries about fees should be made to the Registry (tel: 020-7960 1991, 1992). **4A–158**

Drafts and cheques for fees, including assessment fees, should be made payable to **'The Supreme Court of the United Kingdom'**.

Drafts and cheques for security money only should be made payable to 'UK Supreme Court Security Fund Account'.

*Section 1*

## 1. Introduction

**1.1** Detailed assessments of costs in the Supreme Court are conducted by Costs Officers appointed by the President: see rule 49. One Costs Officer will be the Senior Costs Judge (the Chief Taxing Master of the Senior Courts) or any Costs Judge nominated by him and the second may be the Registrar of the Supreme Court.

**1.2** The Costs Clerk is a court officer in the Registry of the Supreme Court who acts under the direction and supervision of the Costs Officers.

**1.3** Detailed assessments are conducted in public.

**1.4** The assessment of costs is governed by the relevant provisions of the Supreme Court Rules supplemented by this and the other Practice Directions issued by the President. To the extent that the Supreme Court Rules and Practice Directions do not cover the situation, the Rules and the Practice Directions which supplement Parts 43 to 48 of the Civil Procedure Rules are applied by analogy at the discretion of the Costs Officers, with appropriate modifications for appeals from Scotland and Northern Ireland. The legal principles applied are those also applicable to assessments between parties in the High Court and Court of Appeal in England and Wales[1].

**1.5** References in this Practice Direction to:

"the Costs Officer" include the plural;

"costs" and "bills of costs" include expenses and accounts of expenses in appeals from Scotland, and

"solicitor[2]" includes an agent or a costs draftsman.

## 2. Entitlement to costs

**2.1** Claims for costs or "*bills of costs*" may be filed in the Registry for assessment in the following circumstances: **4A–159**

(a) costs payable by appellants, respondents or other persons under an order for costs made by an Appeal Panel or by the Court;

(b) costs payable by the Legal Services Commission (LSC) or the

[1] Kuwait Airways Corporation v Iraqi Airways Company and others: Appeal Committee, 102nd Report (2001-02), paragraph 16, HL Paper 155.

[2] Rule 3 defines "solicitor" as including any person authorised to provide legal services other than as counsel in connection with proceedings before the Court.

*Paragraph numbers marked with a "+" can be found online and on CD.*

appropriate Legal Aid Board to appellants, respondents or other persons consequent upon an order for costs made by an Appeal Panel or by the Court to which section 11 of the Access to Justice Act 1999 or the equivalent provisions in the Legal Aid (Scotland) Act 1986 or the Legal Aid, Advice and Assistance (Northern Ireland) Order 1981 apply;

(c) costs payable by the Legal Services Commission (LSC) or the appropriate Legal Aid Board to solicitors, counsel or other legal representatives acting on behalf of a party whose legal proceedings in the Supreme Court were funded ("a publicly funded party").

**3. Orders under paragraph 3.5.1(d) of Practice Direction 3**

4A–160 **3.1** This paragraph applies to a respondent who is allowed to apply for his costs in accordance with paragraph 3.5(1)(d) of Practice Direction 3 (that is, in circumstances where an application for permission to appeal is refused).

**3.2** The application may be made by letter addressed to the Registrar or may be included in a bill of costs filed in the Registry conditional upon the application being granted.

**3.3** As a general rule the Registrar does not grant the application in any of the following cases:

(a) where the application for permission was not served on the respondent making the application;

(b) where the respondent making the application did not file notice of objection to the application for permission;

(c) where the application is made by one of two or more respondents and the Registrar is not satisfied that the applicant had an interest in the application for permission that required separate representation.

**4. Orders under section 11 of the Access to Justice Act 1999 etc.**

4A–161 **4.1** Any costs ordered to be paid by a publicly funded party must not exceed the amount which is a reasonable one for them to pay having regard to all the circumstances including

(a) the financial resources of all the parties to the proceedings; and

(b) their conduct in connection with the dispute to which the proceedings relate (Access to Justice Act 1999, section 11).

**4.2** Costs which were incurred by one party during a period when another party was publicly funded, and which are not recoverable from the publicly funded party only because of section 11 of the Access to Justice Act 1999, may, in certain circumstances, be payable by the LSC itself.

**4.3** The Community Legal Service (Costs) Regulations 2000 and the Community Legal Service (Cost Protection) Regulations 2000[1]

[1] SI 2000/441; SI 2000/824; SI 2001/822; SI 2001/823; SI 2001/3812; SI 2003/649; SI 2005/2006; and the equivalent provisions in the Legal Aid (Scotland) Act 1986 or the Legal Aid, Advice and Assistance (Northern Ireland) Order 1981.

are Regulations made under section 11 of the Access to Justice Act 1999 and provide a code governing orders for costs against publicly funded parties and against the LSC.

**4.4** A party who seeks costs against the LSC under section 11 of the Access to Justice Act 1999, or who may do so, depending upon the amount of costs payable by the publicly funded party, must file with his bill of costs copies of any documents (including a statement of resources and any notice served by him on the LSC) which he has served upon others in compliance with the Regulations[1].

**4.5** Within 21 days of being served with a bill of costs to which section 11 of the Access to Justice Act 1999 applies, a party who is or was publicly funded during any period covered by the bill must respond by filing in the Registry a statement of resources and serving a copy of it on the receiving party and, where relevant, on the LSC.

**4.6** The LSC may appear at any hearing relating to an order made against the LSC.

**4.7** References in this paragraph to the LSC and to section 11 of the Access to Justice Act 1999 are to be read as references to the appropriate Legal Aid Board and to the equivalent provisions in the Legal Aid (Scotland) Act 1986 and the Legal Aid, Advice and Assistance (Northern Ireland) Order 1981 in cases to which those provisions apply.

### 5. Filing

**5.1** Bills of costs for assessment must be filed within three months of: **4A–162**

(a) the date on which the final judgment in the appeal is handed down; or

(b) the date on which an application for permission to appeal is dismissed by an Appeal panel; or

(c) the date on which an application for permission or a notice of appeal is withdrawn.

### 6. Extension of time

**6.1** If an extension of the three month period for filing a bill is desired, application must be made in writing to the Registrar before the end of that period. Copies of all such correspondence must be sent to all interested parties. **4A–163**

**6.2** Applications for extensions of time may be made after the expiry of the three month period. In deciding whether to grant an application the Registrar takes into account all the circumstances, including:

(a) the interests of the administration of justice;

(b) whether the failure to file in time was intentional;

(c) whether there is a good explanation for the failure to file in time;

[1] There is a strict time limit for making an application under section 11 see *R v Secretary of State for the Home Dept ex parte Gunn* [2001] EWCA Civ 891 and the Guidance Notes issued by the Senior Costs Judge.

*Paragraph numbers marked with a "+" can be found online and on CD.*

(d) the effect which the delay has had on each party; and
(e) the effect which the granting of an extension of time would have on each party.

### 7. Form of bill

4A-164 **7.1** The items on a bill should be numbered consecutively as shown in Section 2 below and similarly worded where possible. Parties or their solicitors should adhere to the items shown so far as possible. The standard three column bill paper should be used. See paragraph 16.3 for items relating to counsel's fees.

**7.2** Where costs are to be assessed both as between the parties and under the Access to Justice Act 1999 or the Legal Aid (Scotland) Act 1986 or the Second Schedule to the Legal Aid, Advice and Assistance (Northern Ireland) Order 1981, a six column bill should be drawn.

### 8. Endorsement

4A-165 **8.1** The bill must be endorsed before filing with a certificate of service on the parties entitled to be represented at the assessment or their solicitors. Information about the date and time of the assessment is sent to all such parties or solicitors.

### 9. Documents

4A-166 **9.1** The following documents must be filed with the Costs Clerk:

(a) the bill **plus two copies**;
(b) Counsel's fee notes and, where counsel's fees exceed the guideline rates in paragraph 26.5, a detailed note explaining why;
(c) written evidence of any other disbursement which is claimed and which exceeds £500;
(d) certificates as to
 (i) accuracy,
 (ii) interest and payments,
 (iii) (where appropriate) interest of assisted person or funded client.

**9.2** Other papers on which parties intend to rely may be brought to the assessment hearing or filed with the Costs Clerk as he thinks appropriate. At least 4 copies of any such papers must be provided. Where a bill is complex or large, any papers which the Costs Officers will need to pre-read should be filed at least 7 days before the hearing.

### 10. Basis of assessment

4A-167 **10.1** Unless otherwise provided for by order or direction, costs in the Supreme Court are ordered to be assessed on the standard basis or on the indemnity basis in accordance with rules 50 and 51 of the Supreme Court Rules or the equivalent bases that apply in Scotland and Northern Ireland.

### 11. Fees for preparing applications for permission to appeal

4A-168 **11.1** The general rule is that a single fee is allowed for one junior counsel for preparing applications for permission to appeal. Rarely,

*Paragraph numbers marked with a "+" can be found online and on CD.*

if ever, are fees allowed for two counsel, but a fee may be allowed for a Queen's Counsel instead of junior counsel if this is held to be necessary because of the difficulty or complexity of the case or other good reason.[1]

**11.2** In a publicly funded application for permission to appeal, a fee for Queen's Counsel is not allowed unless permission has been given by the relevant funding authority.

**11.3** For guideline figures for fees on applications for permission to appeal, see paragraph 26.5.

### 12. Funded parties: applications for permission to appeal

**12.1** Where an applicant for permission to appeal is publicly funded and the application is dismissed without an oral hearing: **4A–169**

(a) reasonable costs may be awarded for preparing the applicant's papers for the Appeal panel;

(b) a publicly funded respondent may be awarded costs incurred in attending the client, filing notice of objection and, where applicable, preparing respondent's objections to the application;

(c) an unassisted respondent may be awarded costs similar to those at (b) above out of the Community Legal Service Fund pursuant to s ection 11 of the Access to Justice Act 1999 or the equivalent provisions in the Legal Aid (Scotland) Act 1986 and the Legal Aid, Advice and Assistance (Northern Ireland) Order 1981.

**12.2** If an application for permission to appeal is dismissed after an oral hearing, the costs of the hearing are allowable in addition to the costs at (a) to (c) above.

### 13. Respondents' Objections

**13.1** Respondents to an application for permission to appeal who submit objections under rule 13 may apply for costs in accordance with paragraphs 3 and 4 above. For guideline figures for preparing respondents' objections, see paragraph 26.5. **4A–170**

### 14. Provisional assessment

**14.1** A provisional assessment procedure exists for the assessment of costs involving public funding and in cases where the parties request a provisional assessment. In such cases a provisional assessment is conducted without the attendance of the parties, and the Registrar informs them in writing of the outcome: rule 49(6). If the result of this procedure proves unsatisfactory to the parties, or if points of disagreement cannot be resolved in correspondence, the Registrar appoints a date for a hearing. **4A–171**

**14.2** Large or complex bills, and bills to be assessed as between the parties, are not usually dealt with by provisional assessment procedure but at a hearing before the Costs Officers.

**14.3** Any request for a hearing following a provisional assessment

[1] As to "necessary", see Lord Woolf CJ, *Home Office v Lownds* [2002] EWCA Civ 365.

must be made within 14 days of the receipt of the letter from the Registrar: rule 49(6). Where an oral hearing is requested, it will take place before a Costs Judge and the Registrar.

**14.4** The Scottish Legal Aid Board will be informed of any provisional assessment in an appeal from Scotland in order that it may decide whether or not to intervene.

### 15. Assessment before Costs Officers

*Points of dispute*

4A–172 **15.1** A paying party may file points of dispute under rule 48 but, if the bill is above **£20,000**, the paying party must file points of dispute. Paying parties who file points of dispute must do so within 21 days of service of the bill upon them, and must at the same time serve a copy of the points of dispute on every other party. The points of dispute must be properly endorsed with a certificate of service. The receiving party may within 21 days from service of the points of dispute respond to the points if they think it appropriate to do so.

**15.2** Where the paying party does not file points of dispute and fails to attend an assessment, the Costs Officer may nevertheless assess the bill, but generally allows the bill to the extent that it appears reasonable and (if appropriate) proportionate.

*Date of assessment hearing*

**15.3** The Registrar gives at least 21 days' notice of the day and time appointed for assessment to all those entitled to be heard at the assessment.

*Attendance at assessments*

**15.4** The receiving party or their deputy must attend the assessment. Where additional papers are brought to the assessment, at least 4 copies must be provided. Only the parties or their solicitors who were responsible for the case in the Supreme Court or their deputies have a right to be heard. For the purpose of this paragraph, a deputy may be another member of the solicitor's firm, or the London agent, or the costs draftsman or counsel instructed for the purpose; but those attending must be fully conversant with the matters to be considered.

*Counsel*

**15.5** Where counsel's fees exceed the guideline rates in paragraph 26.5, a detailed note must accompany the bill, explaining why this is justified. Submissions on counsel's fees may be made at the assessment hearing or in writing to the Costs Officer on a provisional assessment.

### 16. Costs Officers' discretion (civil appeals)

4A–173 **16.1** The Costs Officers have discretion as to the amount to allow. In exercising this discretion they bear in mind the terms "unreasonably incurred" and "unreasonable in amount" in CPR 44.4, (or in appeals from Scotland the provisions of Rule 42.10 of the Rules of the

*Paragraph numbers marked with a "+" can be found online and on CD.*

Court of Session 1994) and in particular consider to what extent an item assisted the Court in determining the appeal. In the case of applications for permission to appeal, a major consideration is whether the application gave rise to a point of public importance.

**16.2** The length of a hearing, the complexity of the issues as indicated by the judgments delivered in the Court, and the general level of fees sought and allowed in the lower courts are taken into account.

**16.3** Counsel's fees are assessed in respect of each item of work counsel has undertaken. It is essential therefore in drawing a bill to apportion counsel's work according to the categories set out in paragraphs 26.5 and 26.7. The number of hours spent by counsel in preparation is rarely of assistance to the Costs Officers when assessing the quantum of counsel's fees at any stage of the proceedings.

**16.4** The Costs Officers have discretion to allow Queen's Counsel's fees for applications for permission to appeal (subject to paragraph 11).

**16.5** The Costs Officers have no discretion to allow fees for more than two counsel unless the Court has, on application at the hearing, made an order that the fees of more than two counsel may be allowed. See paragraph 6.3.7 of Practice Direction 6.

## 17. Costs Officers' discretion (criminal appeals)

**17.1** The Costs Officers do not generally take into account the hours spent by counsel in preparation. **4A-174**

**17.2** The Costs Officers have discretion to allow Queen's Counsel's fees for applications for permission to appeal (subject to paragraph 11).

**17.3** The Costs Officers have no discretion to allow fees for more than two counsel unless the Court has, on application at the hearing, made an order that the fees of more than two counsel may be allowed. See paragraph 6.3.7 of Practice Direction 6.

## 18. Appeals against assessment in the Supreme Court

*Appeals against assessment*

**18.1** Any party to an assessment who is dissatisfied with all or part of a decision of the Costs Officer may apply in accordance with rule 53 for that decision to be reviewed by a single Justice. **4A-175**

**18.2** An application may be made only on a question of principle and not in respect of the quantum allowed on any item. For applications see paragraph 7.1 of Practice Direction7.

**18.3** Any application must be made within 14 days after the decision of the Costs Officer or such longer period as may be fixed by him or by the Registrar.

*Written grounds of appeal*

**18.4** An application for a review must be accompanied by written submissions setting out the items or parts of items objected to and stating concisely in each case the nature and grounds of the

*Paragraph numbers marked with a "+" can be found online and on CD.*

objections. A copy of the grounds of appeal must be delivered to each party who attended the assessment of those items.

**18.5** Any party to whom a copy of the grounds of appeal is delivered may, within 14 days after delivery of the copy to them or such longer period as may be fixed by the Registrar, submit in writing to the Registrar their answers to the grounds of appeal. They should state concisely the reasons why they are opposed to a review of the item(s), and must at the same time deliver a copy of their answers to the party applying for review and to each party to whom a copy of the grounds of appeal has been delivered.

*Reference to a Single Justice*

**18.6** When he has received all the necessary documents, the Registrar refers the matter to a single Justice nominated by the presiding or senior Justice who heard the appeal or application for permission to appeal.

**18.7** The nominated single Justice decides whether the matter should be referred to an Appeal Panel and, before he makes a decision, he may consult other Justices who heard the appeal or application. If the single Justice is of the opinion that the matter should not be so referred, the decision of the Costs Officer is affirmed.

*Application to the Court*

**18.8** If the nominated single Justice decides that the matter should be referred to an Appeal panel, the party disputing the decision of the Costs Officer may, within 14 days of the date on which that decision is communicated to the parties, file an application in Form 2.

**18.9** The application will be referred to a Panel of Justices, which considers whether it should be referred for hearing.

### 19. Allocatur (Agreed Costs Figures)

4A–176 **19.1** Forms of allocatur are obtained from the Costs Clerk at the assessment hearing and must be returned by the receiving party to the Costs Clerk within one month, signed by all parties who attended the assessment, together with the completed bill and assessment fee. Specimen forms are set out in Section 3 below.

**19.2** If a paying party refuses to sign the form of allocatur, the signature of the receiving party will be sufficient, provided the Registrar is satisfied that the paying party has refused to sign without good reason.

### 20. Certificate of discharge

4A–177 **20.1** A certificate in the following form may be accepted as evidence of payment of any disbursement not exceeding £500 (other than fees to counsel) provided that the paying party does not object, and subject to any direction to the contrary that may be given by the Costs Officer:

We A.B. & Co.,

Hereby certify that all disbursements listed in the assessed bill in the matter of C. v. D. which individually do not exceed £500 (other than those relating to counsel's fees) have been duly discharged.

Signed A. B. & Co.

### 21. Vouching

**21.1** Counsel's fee notes must be receipted except in the case of publicly funded bills. **4A–178**

### 22. Summary

**22.1** The completed bill of costs must include a summary (see Section 3 below) showing the respective amounts of profit costs, counsel's fees, other disbursements and VAT allowed. **4A–179**

### 23. Fees

**23.1** Information about payment of assessment fees is set out in Section 4 below and the fees are set out in Annex 2 to Practice Direction 7. **4A–180**

**23.2** The receiving party is responsible for paying the filing fee and the assessment fee.

**23.3** The receiving party is responsible for paying the fee on a withdrawn bill.

**23.4** Reduced fees are payable when costs are agreed before assessment. Responsibility for informing the Registrar that agreement has been reached lies with the receiving party, but both parties must confirm the agreement in writing.

**23.5** Drafts and cheques for fees are payable to "**The Supreme Court of the United Kingdom**".

### 24. Certificates

*Civil*

**24.1** When the assessment fee has been paid, a certificate of assessment for the costs as allowed will be sent to the receiving party, except in the case of respondents whose costs can be wholly satisfied from money deposited as security for costs (see rules 36 and 54). **4A–181**

*Criminal*

**24.2** Where costs have been ordered to be paid out of Central Funds or where costs are paid under Legal Aid Orders issued by the Registrar of the Court of Appeal, Criminal Division, the certificate and counsel's fee notes are sent to the Senior Courts Fees Office to settle the certificated amounts with the parties or their agents and counsel direct.

*Courts-Martial*

**24.3** Where costs are payable to the Secretary of State for Defence in respect of an appeal from the Courts-Martial Appeal Court, the certificate is sent direct to the Ministry of Defence to settle as in 24.2 above.

*Criminal (Northern Ireland)*

**24.4** Where the costs are payable in accordance with section 41 of



SUPREME COURT

the Criminal Appeal (Northern Ireland) Act 1980 the certificates are sent to the Northern Ireland Office to settle as in 24.2 above.

## 25. Interest

4A–182 **25.1** Interest is chargeable on orders made in respect of costs assessed as between the parties and orders for costs in favour of successful unassisted parties. The rate of interest is in accordance with the provisions of the Judgments Act 1838, as amended, and interest accrues from the day on which the order of the Court is made or such other date as the Court may specify.

**25.2** It is within the discretion of the Costs Officer to vary the period for which interest is allowed in any case where the circumstances make it appropriate to do so.

## 26. Quantum: guidelines on fees allowed

*Solicitors practising in England and Wales*[1]

4A–183 **26.1** The guideline rates set out below are used. These are consolidated figures that include a mark-up for care and attention. No further mark-up is allowed for care and attention.

**26.2** The following table sets out the hourly rates and localities:

| *Grade of fee earner* | A | B | C | D |
|---|---|---|---|---|
| | £ | £ | £ | £ |
| City of London | 402 | 291 | 222 | 136 |
| Central London | 312 | 238 | 193 | 124 |
| Outer London | 225–263 | 169–225 | 162 | 119 |
| National 1 | 213 | 189 | 158 | 116 |
| National 2/3 | 198 | 174 | 144 | 109 |

An explanation of the grades and details of localities will be found in Section 5 below.

**26.3** Claims at the "A" rate must be justified.

**26.4** When travel and waiting is claimed, this is allowed at the rate agreed with the client, unless this is more than the hourly rate allowed on the assessment.

Letters and telephone calls are allowed at one tenth (1/10) of the hourly rate.

*Counsel*

**26.5** The following guideline figures are used in assessing payments to counsel:

[1] Consolidated rates based on those permitted in the respective jurisdictions are allowed for solicitors practising in Scotland or Northern Ireland.

*Applications for permission, civil and criminal*

| | Junior | QC (*subject to paragraph 11*) |
|---|---|---|
| Settling application | £1000 | £1250 |
| Advice (if any) for Legal Services Commission or Legal Aid Board in Scotland or Northern Ireland | £400 | £600 |
| Preparing respondents' objections | £700 | £1000 |
| Attending oral hearing by Appeal Panel | £1500 | £2000 |

**26.6** If an increase is sought on any of the above items, it must be explained in a detailed note from counsel which accompanies the bill. No other payments are allowed at the permission to appeal stage.

**26.7** The general rule is that only one counsel's fees are allowed on assessment for any stage of an application for permission to appeal, unless a public funding or legal aid certificate authorises two counsel (see paragraph 11).

*Appeals—civil and criminal*

| | Junior | QC |
|---|---|---|
| Settling notice of appeal | £100 | £100 |
| Statement of facts and issues | £2000 | £4000 |
| Authorities | £800 | £1600 |
| Conferences (each, up to a maximum of six) | £500 | £1000 |
| Advice | £900 | £1800 |
| Brief (based on a 1 day hearing) | £7000 | £14000 |
| Brief (based on a 2 day or longer hearing) | £9000 | £18000 |
| Refresher (from day two of the hearing) | £1500 | £3000 |

*Notes*

**26.8** Generally counsel for an appellant commands a higher fee than counsel for a respondent.

**26.9** The brief fee includes **all work on the brief, the case and the first day of attendance at the Court**.

***Paragraph numbers marked with a "+" can be found online and on CD.***

**26.10** The Costs Officers exercise discretion in instances where junior counsel has undertaken most of the work on a particular item.

**26.11** For settling a notice of appeal, only one counsel's fee is permitted. The Costs Officers have no discretion to allow fees for more than two counsel unless the Court has, on application at the hearing, made an order that the fees of more than two counsel may be allowed. See paragraph 6.3.7 of Practice Direction 6.

**26.12** These fees are intended as a guide. If counsel seek higher fees, they must explain in a detailed note which should accompany the bill.

## 27. Conditional Fee Agreements

4A-184 **27.1** Notification should be given to the opposing parties and to the Registry as soon as practicable after a conditional fee agreement has been entered into[1]. The Costs Officers decide questions of percentage uplift in accordance with the principles set out in *Designers' Guild Limited v Russell Williams (Textiles) Limited (Trading as Washington D.C.)* [2003] 2 Costs LR 20[2].

## 28. Costs of litigants in person

4A-185 **28.1** The amount allowed to a litigant in person may not exceed the loss actually sustained or, where no loss has been sustained, £9.25 for each hour reasonably spent, subject in either case to a maximum for any particular item of two thirds of the sum which in the opinion of the Costs Officer would have been allowed for that item if the litigant had been represented by a solicitor. The two thirds limit does not apply to out-of-pocket expenses which would be disbursements if incurred by a solicitor. (For further information see CPR 48.6 and section 52 of the Costs Practice Direction which supplements it.)

## 29. Costs of Drafting Bill for Assessment

4A-186 **29.1** By way of guidance for smaller bills, the following sums are usually justified:

| Amount of bill | Amount allowed |
|---|---|
| **Bills assessed at up to £2000 (excluding VAT)** | £300 |
| Bills assessed at £2001-£5000 (excluding VAT) | £500 |
| Bills assessed at £5001-£10000 (excluding VAT) | £700 |

[1] Notification is not generally needed in Scottish appeals where an agreement has been entered into under Rule 42.17 of the Rules of the Court of Session 1994 but it is helpful to the Costs Officers to be informed of any such agreement when the account of expenses is submitted for assessment.

[2] It is open to the Costs Officers to reduce the percentage uplift recoverable if it is considered to be excessive. A party who seeks a ruling that the percentage uplift should be disallowed on legal grounds should apply to the Court at the hearing for such a ruling.

**29.2** For a larger bill the amount allowed is a multiple of the relevant hourly rate for time reasonably spent in drafting the bill.

## SECTION 2: FORMS OF BILLS OF COSTS

4A–187 ***Note: the figures in the following forms are for illustrative purposes only***

**Form A: Respondent's bill of costs under paragraph 3.5.1(d) of Practice Direction 3**

**IN THE SUPREME COURT**

**ON APPEAL FROM HER MAJESTY'S COURT OF APPEAL (ENGLAND)**

BETWEEN

| | |
|---|---|
| AB | Claimant and Appellant |
| ~ and ~ | |
| CD | Defendant and Respondent |

**RESPONDENT'S BILL OF COSTS**

V.A.T. No. 33 5574 90

**Proceedings in the Courts below**

The appellant brought a claim in the High Court seeking compensation for personal injuries and other losses suffered in a road accident which occurred on 1st January 1999, as a result of which the respondent (the defendant in those proceedings) was later convicted of various offences including careless driving and driving under the influence of drink or drugs.

At the trial of the claim in July 2001 the appellant was awarded damages totalling £78,256.53 plus interest and costs. The respondent brought an appeal to the Court of Appeal relying upon several infringements of articles 6 and 8 of the Human Rights Act 1998 which had occurred at and before the trial. The appeal was successful. By its order dated 27 June 2002, the Court of Appeal set aside the trial award and awarded to the respondent her costs incurrred in the High Court and Court of Appeal.

**Proceedings in the Supreme Court**

The appellant sought permission to appeal against the Order of the Court of Appeal dated 27 June 2002. The application for permission was served on the respondent who then filed notice of objection. On 28 July 2003 permission to appeal was refused without a hearing and the respondent was allowed to apply for her costs in accordance with paragraph 3.5.1(d) of Practice Direction 3. The respondent respectfully requests the Registrar to accept this bill as constituting such an application.

**Fee earners and hourly rates**

The respondent first instructed T U V & Co in this matter in June 2002. The following rates were agreed

Partner - £195 per hour plus VAT
Assistant solicitor - £130 per hour plus VAT
Other fee earners - £95 per hour plus VAT
Routine letters and emails out and telephone calls – one tenth of the relevant hourly rate.

| Item No. | Description of work done | V.A.T. | Disbursements | Profit Costs |
|---|---|---|---|---|
| | **Attendances upon the Registry** | | | |
| | 18 July 2002 | | | |
| 1 | Filing notice of objection – Trainee solicitor 6 minutes | | | £ 9.50 |
| 2 | Travelling and waiting 1.3 hours | | | £ 123.50 |
| 3 | Paid fee | | £ 115.00 | |
| | **Attendances upon the respondent** | | | |
| 4 | Routine letters (5: assistant) | | | £ 65.00 |
| 5 | Routine telephone calls (7: assistant) | | | £ 91.00 |
| | **Attendances upon the appellant** | | | |
| 6 | Routine letters (5: assistant) | | | £ 65.00 |
| | **Communications with Registry** | | | |
| 7 | Routine letter (1: assistant) | | | £ 13.00 |
| | **Attendances upon documents** | | | |
| | 12 July 2002 considering the application for permission 24 mins partner | | | |
| | 28 July 2002 considering the ruling thereon 6 mins partner | | | |
| 8 | Total for partner 0.5 hours | | | £ 97.50 |
| | **Other work done** | | | |
| | Preparing and checking the bill | | | |
| 9 | Partner 24 mins | | | £ 78.00 |
| 10 | Costs draftsman 1.5 hours | | | £ 142.50 |
| | **Assessment of costs** | | | |
| | Preparing for and attending assessment (including perusal of any Points of Dispute served) | | | |
| 11 | Partner 0.5 hours (estimated) | | | £ 97.50 |
| 12 | Costs draftsman 1.5 hours (estimated) | | | £ 142.50 |
| 13 | Travel and waiting (costs draftsman) 1.5 hours (estimated) | | | £ 142.50 |
| 14 | VAT on total profit costs of £1,067.50 | | | £ 186.81 |
| 15 | Assessment fee (to be added) | | | |
| | **Grand totals** | | | |
| | Profit Costs £ 1,067.50 | | | |
| | VAT thereon £ 186.81 | | | |
| | Disbursements £ 115.00 | | | |
| | VAT thereon £ - | | | |
| | **Total costs claimed £ 1,369.31** | | | |

SUPREME COURT

*Paragraph numbers marked with a "+" can be found online and on CD.*

**Form B Appellant's bill for application for permission and appeal**

**IN THE SUPREME COURT**

**ON APPEAL FROM HER MAJESTY'S COURT OF APPEAL (ENGLAND)**

BETWEEN

AB Claimant and Appellant

~ and ~

CD Defendant and Respondent

**APPELLANT'S BILL OF COSTS**

V.A.T. No. 22 4462 80

**Proceedings in the Courts below**

The appellant brought a claim in the High Court seeking compensation for personal injuries and other losses suffered in a road accident which occurred on 1st January 1999, as a result of which the respondent (the defendant in those proceedings) was later convicted of various offences including careless driving and driving under the influence of drink or drugs.

At the trial of the claim in July 2001 the appellant was awarded damages totalling £78,256.53 plus interest and costs. The respondent brought an appeal to the Court of Appeal relying upon several infringements of articles 6 and 8 of the Human Rights Act 1998 which had occurred at and before the trial. The appeal was successful. By its order dated 27 June 2002, the Court of Appeal set aside the trial award and awarded to the respondent her costs incurrred in the High Court and Court of Appeal.

**Proceedings in the Supreme Court**

The appellant applied for permission to appeal against the Order of the Court of Appeal dated 27 June 2002. The application was heard on 28 October 2002 and was successful. The appellant then gave notice that he wishes to proceed with his appeal. It was not possible to agree the Statement of Facts and Issues within the time allowed and therefore, with the consent of the respondent, an application was made for an extension of time. In November 2002 an agreed Statement of Facts and Issues and an Appendix was filed and the Registrar was informed that the appeal was ready to list. The appeal then proceeded to a hearing before the Court on 18 July 2003 and, on 28 July 2003, Orders were made setting aside the Order of the Court of Appeal dated 27 June 2002 and restoring the Order of Mr Justice Alexander dated 26 July 2001. It was further ordered that the respondent should pay or cause to be paid to the appellant the costs incurred by the appellant in the proceedings in the Supreme Court and in the proceedings in the Court of Appeal.

**Fee earners and hourly rates**

The appellant first instructed E F & Co under a conditional fee agreement dated 8 July 2000 which applied to the claim and to the appeal brought in the Court of Appeal by the respondent. That agreement did not apply to the proceedings in the House of Lords and therefore a further conditional fee agreement dated 28 July 2001 was made which specifies the following base fees and success fees

Partner - £195 per hour plus VAT
Assistant solicitor - £144 per hour plus VAT
Success fee - 100% discounted to 25% if, before or within 2 weeks after the appeal is set down, the parties agree settlement terms which in effect restore the decision herein of Mr Justice Alexander.

Except where the contrary is stated the proceedings were conducted on behalf of the appellant by an assistant solicitor, admitted November 2001.

**Counsel's fees**

E F & Co instructed Counsel (Miss G H, called 1992) under a conditional fee agreement dated 28 July 2001, which specifies a success fee as defined in the agreement between solicitor and client and base fees, payable in various circumstances, of which the following are relevant

| | |
|---|---|
| Conferences | £250 plus £50 per half hour or part thereof, plus VAT |
| Brief for appeal (estimated duration 5 hours) | £2,750 plus VAT |
| Fee for second and subsequent days | £850 plus VAT |
| Judgment fee | £200 plus VAT |

SUPREME COURT

*Paragraph numbers marked with a "+" can be found online and on CD.*

| Item No. | Description of work done | V.A.T. | Disburse-ments | Profit Costs |
|---|---|---|---|---|
| | **APPLICATION FOR PERMISSION** | | | |
| | **Attendances at the Registry** | | | |
| | **8 July 2002** | | | |
| 1 | Filing the application 6 mins | | | £ 14.40 |
| 2 | Travelling and waiting 1.3 hours | | | £ 187.20 |
| 3 | Paid fee | | £ 570.00 | |
| | **Attending the Appeal Panel** | | | |
| | **28 October 2002** | | | |
| 4 | Attending Hearing 1.1 hours | | | £ 158.40 |
| 5 | Travel and waiting 1.8 hours | | | £ 259.20 |
| 6 | Counsel's base fee for hearing | | £ 750.00 | |
| | **Attendances upon the appellant** | | | |
| 7 | Routine letter (1: partner) | | | £ 19.50 |
| 8 | Routine letters (5: assistant) | | | £ 72.00 |
| 9 | Routine telephone calls (7: assistant) | | | £ 100.80 |
| 10 | Timed telephone calls (Schedule 1: total 1.7 hours) | | | £ 244.80 |
| | **Attendances upon the respondent** | | | |
| 11 | Routine letters (5) | | | £ 72.00 |
| | **Communications with Registry** | | | |
| 12 | Routine letters (5) | | | £ 72.00 |
| | **Communications with Counsel** | | | |
| 13 | Routine letters (2) | | | £ 28.80 |
| 14 | Routine telephone calls (6) | | | £ 86.40 |
| | **Attendances upon documents** (Schedule 2) | | | |
| 15 | Total for partner 1.1 hours | | | £ 214.50 |
| 16 | Total for assistant 36 minutes | | | £ 86.40 |
| | **NOTICE OF APPEAL** | | | |
| | **Attendances upon the Registry and Counsel** | | | |
| | **11 November 2002** | | | |
| 17 | Filing the notice 6 mins | | | £ 14.40 |
| 18 | Travelling and waiting 1.3 hours | | | £ 187.20 |
| 19 | Paid fee | | £ 570.00 | |
| | Carried forward- | £ - | £ 1,890.00 | £ 1,818.00 |

*Paragraph numbers marked with a "+" can be found online and on CD.*

| | | | | |
|---|---|---|---|---|
| | Conference with counsel | | | |
| 20 | Attending with client 1.5 hours | | | £ 216.00 |
| 21 | Travelling and waiting 1.2 hours | | | £ 172.80 |
| 22 | Counsel's base fee | | £ 400.00 | |
| | Application for extension of time (filed by post) | | | |
| 23 | Paid fee | | £ 230.00 | |
| | **15 January 2003** | | | |
| 24 | Filing Agreed Statement of Facts and Issues and Appendix 18 mins | | | £ 43.20 |
| 25 | Travelling and waiting 1.7 hours | | | £ 244.80 |
| 26 | Paid fee | | £ 3,420.00 | |
| | **Attending the Appeal** | | | |
| | **18 July 2003** | | | |
| 27 | Attending Hearing 4.7 hours | | | £ 676.80 |
| 28 | Travel and waiting 1.8 hours | | | £ 259.20 |
| 29 | Counsel's base fee for hearing | | £ 2,750.00 | |
| | **28 July 2003** | | | |
| 30 | Attending for Judgment 1.7 hours | | | £ 244.80 |
| 31 | Travel and waiting 1.8 hours | | | £ 259.20 |
| 32 | Counsel's Judgment fee | | £ 850.00 | |
| | **Attendances upon the appellant** | | | |
| 33 | Routine letter (7: partner) | | | £ 136.50 |
| 34 | Routine letters (35: assistant) | | | £ 504.00 |
| 35 | Routine telephone calls (27: assistant) | | | £ 388.80 |
| 36 | Timed telephone calls (Schedule 3: total 2.7 hours) | | | £ 388.80 |
| | **Attendances upon the respondent** | | | |
| 37 | Routine letters (15) | | | £ 216.00 |
| 38 | Routine telephone calls (27) | | | £ 388.80 |
| 39 | Timed telephone calls (Schedule 4: total 1.6 hours) | | | £ 230.40 |
| | **Communications with Registry** | | | |
| 40 | Routine letters (23) | | | £ 331.20 |
| | Carried forward - | £ - | £ 9,540.00 | £ 6,519.30 |

Page 4

| | | | | |
|---|---|---|---|---|
| 41 | Routine letters (22) | | | £ 316.80 |
| 42 | Routine telephone calls (16) | | | £ 230.40 |
| 43 | Timed telephone calls (Schedule 5: total 1.6 hours) | | | £ 230.40 |
| | **Attendances upon documents** (Schedule 6) | | | |
| 44 | Total for partner 3.1 hours | | | £ 604.50 |
| 45 | Total for assistant 18.7 hours | | | £ 2,692.80 |
| | **Other work done** | | | |
| | Preparing and checking the bill | | | |
| 46 | Partner 24 mins | | | £ 78.00 |
| 47 | Assistant 1.4 hours | | | £ 201.60 |
| 48 | Costs draftsman's fee | | £ 900.00 | |
| | Sub totals> | £ - | £ 10,440.00 | £ 10,873.80 |
| | **VAT and success fees** | | | |
| 49 | VAT on solicitors' base fees of £10,873.80 | £ 1,902.92 | | |
| 50 | Success fee on solicitors' base fees and VAT thereon | £ 1,902.92 | | £ 10,873.80 |
| 51 | VAT on counsel's base fees of £4,750 | £ 831.25 | | |
| 52 | Success fee on counsel's base fees and VAT thereon | £ 831.25 | £ 4,750.00 | |
| | **Assessment of costs** | | | |
| | Attending assessment including perusal of any points of dispute served | | | |
| 53 | Partner 1.5 hours (estimated) | | | £ 292.50 |
| 54 | Travel and waiting (Partner) 1.5 hours (estimated) | | | £ 292.50 |
| 55 | Success fee on estimated solicitors' charges (100%) | | | £ 585.00 |
| 56 | Costs draftsman's fee for attending the hearing and travel and waiting 3 hours (estimated) | £ 49.88 | £ 285.00 | |
| 57 | VAT on items 53 - 55 | £ 204.75 | | |
| 58 | Assessment fees (to be added) | | | |
| | Totals:- | £ 5,722.96 | £ 15,475.00 | £ 22,917.60 |
| | **Grand totals** | | | **£ 44,115.56** |
| | Profit Costs £ 22,917.60 | | | |
| | VAT thereon £ 4,010.58 | | | |
| | Disbursements £ 15,475.00 | | | |
| | VAT thereon £ 1,712.38 | | | |
| | **Total costs claimed £ 44,115.56** | | | |

Page 5

Form C: Respondent's bill of costs including separate accounts for Scottish and English agents

IN THE SUPREME COURT

ON APPEAL FROM THE COURT OF SESSION IN SCOTLAND

BETWEEN

| | |
|---|---|
| AB | Pursuer and Appellant |
| ~ and ~ | |
| CD | Defender and Respondent |

RESPONDENT'S BILL OF COSTS

**Proceedings in the Courts below**

The appellant brought a claim for compensation for personal injuries and other losses suffered in a road accident which occurred on 1st January 1999, as a result of which the respondent (the defender in those proceedings) was later convicted of various offences including careless driving and driving under the influence of drink or drugs.

The claim was heard by the Lord Ordinary (Lady X) in the Court of Session in July 2001 and was successful. The appellant was awarded damages totalling £78,256.53 plus interest and expenses. A reclaiming motion was marked by the respondent in which she relied upon several infringements of articles 6 and 8 of the Human Rights Act 1998 which had occurred at and before the trial. The reclaiming motion was heard by their lordships of the First Division of the Court of Session in June 2002. On 27 June 2002 the First Division allowed the reclaiming motion, set aside the trial award and awarded to the respondent her expenses incurrred in the proceedings before them and before the Lord Ordinary.

**Proceedings in the Supreme Court**

The notice of appeal was served on the respondent who filed an acknowledgement to it. In November 2002 a Statement of Facts and Issues and an Appendix were agreed. The appeal was proceeded to a hearing on 18 July 2003. On 28 July 2003, Orders were made dismissing the appeal and awarding the respondent her costs incurred in the Supreme Court.

**Fee earners and hourly rates**

**EDINBURGH AGENTS' ACCOUNT**
V.A.T. No. 43 9876 90
The respondent first instructed W X & Co in this matter in June 2002. The following rates were agreed
Partner - £190 per hour plus VAT
Assistant solicitor - £130 per hour plus VAT
Other fee earners - £95 per hour plus VAT
Routine letters and emails out and telephone calls – one tenth of the relevant hourly rate.

SUPREME COURT

**LONDON AGENTS' ACCOUNT**
V.A.T. No. 33 5574 90
By her solicitors W X & Co, the respondent instructed Y Z & Co and the following rates were agreed

Partner - £195 per hour plus VAT
Assistant solicitor - £144 per hour plus VAT
Routine letters and emails out and telephone calls – one tenth of the relevant hourly rate.

Except where the contrary is stated the proceedings were conducted on behalf of the appellant by an assistant solicitor, admitted November 2001.

| Item No. | Description of work done | V.A.T. | Disburse-ments | Profit Costs |
|---|---|---|---|---|
| | **PART 1 EDINBURGH AGENTS' ACCOUNT** | | | |
| | **NOTICE OF APPEAL** | | | |
| | **Attendances upon Counsel** | | | |
| | **5 December 2002** | | | |
| | Consultation with counsel | | | |
| 1 | Partner attending with client 1.5 hours | | | £ 285.00 |
| 2 | Travelling and waiting 1.2 hours | | | £ 228.00 |
| 3 | Counsel's fee | £ 78.75 | £ 450.00 | |
| 4 | Paid fee for certifying Appeal to the Supreme Court | | £ 97.00 | |
| | **Attending the Appeal** | | | |
| | **18 July 2003** | | | |
| 4 | Counsel's fee for hearing | £ 525.00 | £ 3,000.00 | |
| | **28 July 2003** | | | |
| 5 | Counsel's fee for judgment | £ 148.75 | £ 850.00 | |
| | **Attendances upon the respondent** | | | |
| | Personal attendances (Schedule 1) | | | |
| 6 | Total for partner 3.2 hours | | | £ 608.00 |
| 7 | Total for assistant 1.4 hours | | | £ 182.00 |
| 8 | Routine letters (15: Partner) | | | £ 285.00 |
| 9 | Routine letters (7: assistant) | | | £ 91.00 |
| 10 | Routine telephone calls (27: assistant) | | | £ 351.00 |
| | Timed telephone calls (Schedule 2) | | | |
| 11 | Total for partner 2.1 hours | | | £ 380.00 |
| 12 | Total for assistant 1.6 hours | | | £ 208.00 |
| | **Attendances upon the appellant** | | | |
| 13 | Routine letters (2: partner) | | | £ 38.00 |
| 14 | Routine letters (4: assistant) | | | £ 52.00 |
| | **Communications with Registry** | | | |
| 15 | Routine letters (8: assistant) | | | £ 104.00 |
| | **Communications with Counsel** | | | |
| 16 | Routine letters (12: partner) | | | £ 228.00 |
| 17 | Routine telephone calls (16: partner) | | | £ 304.00 |
| 18 | Timed telephone calls (Schedule 3: total 1.6 hours: partner) | | | £ 304.00 |
| | **Attendances upon documents** (Schedule 4) | | | |
| 19 | Total for partner 3.1 hours | | | £ 589.00 |
| 20 | Total for assistant 14.7 hours | | | £ 1,911.00 |
| | Carried forward | £ 752.50 | £ 4,397.00 | £ 6,148.00 |

SUPREME COURT

*Paragraph numbers marked with a "+" can be found online and on CD.*

| Item No. | Description of work done | V.A.T. | Disburse-ments | Profit Costs |
|---|---|---|---|---|
| | Brought forward | £ 752.50 | £ 4,397.00 | £ 6,148.00 |
| | **Other work done** | | | |
| | Preparing and checking the bill | | | |
| 21 | Partner 0.7 hours | | | £ 133.00 |
| 22 | Assistant 1.4 hours | | | £ 182.00 |
| 23 | Costs draftsman's fee | £ 94.50 | £ 540.00 | |
| | **Assessment of costs** | | | |
| | Preparing for assessment (including perusal of any Points of Dispute served) | | | |
| 24 | Partner 1.5 hours (estimated) | | | £ 285.00 |
| | Sub totals | £ 847.00 | £ 4,937.00 | £ 6,748.00 |

**Totals**

| | | |
|---|---|---|
| Profit Costs | £ | 6,748.00 |
| VAT thereon | £ | 1,180.90 |
| Disbursements | £ | 4,937.00 |
| VAT thereon | £ | 847.00 |
| **Total costs claimed in Part 1** | **£** | **13,712.90** |

*Paragraph numbers marked with a "+" can be found online and on CD.*

| Item No. | Description of work done | V.A.T. | Disburse-ments | Profit Costs |
|---|---|---|---|---|
| | PART 2 LONDON AGENTS' ACCOUNT | | | |
| | NOTICE OF APPEAL | | | |
| | **Attendances upon the Registry** | | | |
| | 18 July 2002 | | | |
| 25 | Presenting the notice of appeal 6 minutes | | | £ 14.40 |
| 26 | Travelling and waiting 1.3 hours | | | £ 187.20 |
| 27 | Paid fee | | £ 1,140.00 | |
| | **Attending the Appeal** | | | |
| | 18 July 2003 | | | |
| 28 | Attending Hearing 4.7 hours | | | £ 676.80 |
| 29 | Travel and waiting 1.8 hours | | | £ 259.20 |
| | 28 July 2003 | | | |
| 30 | Attending for Judgment 1.7 hours | | | £ 244.80 |
| 31 | Travel and waiting 1.8 hours | | | £ 259.20 |
| | **Attendances upon the respondent and her Edinburgh agents** | | | |
| 32 | Routine letters (35) | | | £ 504.00 |
| 33 | Routine telephone calls (27) | | | £ 388.80 |
| 34 | Timed telephone calls (Schedule 5: total 1.6 hours) | | | £ 230.40 |
| | **Attendances upon the appellant** | | | |
| 35 | Routine letters (25) | | | £ 360.00 |
| 36 | Routine telephone calls (27) | | | £ 388.80 |
| | **Communications with Registry** | | | |
| 37 | Routine letters (23) | | | £ 331.20 |
| | **Communications with Counsel** | | | |
| 38 | Routine letters (2) | | | £ 28.80 |
| 39 | Routine telephone calls (16) | | | £ 230.40 |
| | **Attendances upon documents** (Schedule 6) | | | |
| 40 | Total for partner 3.1 hours | | | £ 604.50 |
| 41 | Total for assistant 18.7 hours | | | £ 2,692.80 |
| | **Other work done** | | | |
| | Preparing and checking the bill | | | |
| 42 | Partner 24 mins | | | £ 78.00 |
| 43 | Assistant 1.4 hours | | | £ 201.60 |
| 44 | Costs draftsman's fee | £ 94.50 | £ 540.00 | |
| | Carried forward: | £ 94.50 | £ 1,680.00 | £ 7,680.90 |

SUPREME COURT

| Item No. | Description of work done | V.A.T. | Disbursements | Profit Costs |
|---|---|---|---|---|
| | Brought forward | £ 94.50 | £ 1,680.00 | £ 7,680.90 |
| | **Assessment of costs** | | | |
| | Preparing for and attending assessment (including perusal of any Points of Dispute served) | | | |
| 45 | Assistant 2.5 hours (estimated) | | | £ 360.00 |
| 46 | Travel and waiting 1.5 hours (estimated) | | | £ 216.00 |
| 47 | Costs draftsman's fee for attending the hearing and travel and waiting (estimated) | £ 52.50 | £ 300.00 | |
| 48 | Assessment fees (to be added) | | | |
| | Sub totals :- | £ 147.00 | £ 1,980.00 | £ 8,256.90 |

**Totals**

| | | |
|---|---|---|
| Profit Costs | £ | 8,256.90 |
| VAT thereon | £ | 1,444.96 |
| Disbursements | £ | 1,980.00 |
| VAT thereon | £ | 147.00 |
| **Total costs claimed in Part 2** | **£** | **11,828.86** |

**SUMMARY**

| | | |
|---|---|---|
| **Part 1** | **£** | **13,712.90** |
| **Part 2** | **£** | **11,828.86** |
| **TOTAL** | **£** | **25,541.76** |

4A–188

**SECTION 3: SUMMARY AND ALLOCATUR OF BILLS OF COSTS**

1 **Summary** for Bill

| Assessed Off | Value Added Tax[1] | Disbursements | Profit costs |
|---|---|---|---|

| Disbursements | Profit Costs |
|---|---|

Page 1 ... ... ...
Page 2 ... ... ...
Page 3 ... ... ...
Page 4 ... ... ...

Assessed off ... ... ....

Add profit costs ... ... ... ...

Add VAT on profit costs ... ... ... ...

Add counsel's fees ....

Add VAT on counsel's fees...

Other disbursements ... ... ...

Add VAT on other disbursements...

Total ... ... ... ...

Assessment fee 5%

(on total rounded up to next pound)

[1] Value Added Tax on disbursements as allowed.

SUPREME COURT

*Paragraph numbers marked with a "+" can be found online and on CD.*

Funded Summary

Profit costs (excluding costs of assessment) … … … … …

VAT on profit costs … ….

Counsel's fees … … … …

VAT on counsel's fees …

Other disbursements (excluding assessment fee) …

VAT on other disbursements … … …

Costs of assessment allowed against Community legal service fund (including assessment fee) … … … …

VAT thereon (excluding assessment fee) … … … …

*(or simple form if appropriate)*

3. **Allocatur**[2]

**IN THE SUPREME COURT**

BETWEEN

………………………

v.

………………………

APPELLANT'S/RESPONDENT/S* COSTS
*(Delete where applicable)*

Amount of profit costs and disbursements claimed ………………

Less assessed off disbursements and profit costs……………………

Total ………………………………………………………

Add VAT[3]

Total allowed……………………………………………

Assessment fee on total allowed[4]…………………………

Amount to be certified………………………………………

…………………………………………………Solicitor for the appellant

…………………………………………………Solicitor for the respondent

**REGISTRAR**
**SUPREME COURT**

[2] The return of this form together with the bill and the fee within one month of the assessment is the responsibility of the receiving party. The party must indicate their agreement to the castings in the bill by signing the allocatur.
[3] On amounts which attract VAT.
[4] Assessment fee payable to "the Supreme Court Fees Account".

## *SECTION 4: FEES*

For the relevant fees see the order made under section 52 of the Constitutional Reform Act 2005 on the website of the Supreme Court or Annex 2 to Practice Direction 7. Drafts and cheques for assessment fees are payable to 'The Supreme Court of the United Kingdom'. **4A–189**

***Paragraph numbers marked with a "+" can be found online and on CD.***

## SECTION 5: GUIDELINE FIGURES FOR THE PROVISIONAL ASSESSMENT OF COSTS

**4A–190** *Solicitors' hourly rates: England and Wales*

**1.** The guideline rates set out in paragraph 26 for solicitors are broad approximations. Rates include care and attention.

**2.** The grades of fee earner are those that have been agreed between representatives of the Senior Courts Costs Office, the Association of District Judges and the Law Society. The categories are as follows:

A. Solicitors with over eight years' post qualification experience including at least eight years litigation experience.

B. Solicitors, employed barristers and legal executives with over four years' post qualification experience including at least four years litigation experience.

C. Other solicitors, legal executives and fee earners of equivalent experience.

D. Trainee solicitors, para legals and fee earners of equivalent experience.

**3.** "Legal Executive" means a Fellow of the Institute of Legal Executives. Those who are not Fellows of the Institute are not entitled to call themselves legal executives and in principle are therefore not entitled to the same hourly rate as a legal executive.

**4.** Unqualified clerks who are fee earners of equivalent experience may be entitled to similar rates and in this regard it should be borne in mind that Fellows of the Institute of Legal Executives generally spend two years in a solicitor's office before passing their Section 1 general examinations, spend a further two years before passing the Section 2 specialist examinations and then complete a further two years in practice before being able to become Fellows. Fellows therefore possess considerable practical experience and academic achievement. Clerks without the equivalent experience of legal executives will be treated as being in the bottom grade of fee earner i.e. trainee solicitors and fee earners of equivalent experience. Whether or not a fee earner has equivalent experience is ultimately a matter for the discretion of the court.

***The National 1 rates apply to***

| |
|---|
| Aldershot, Farnham, Bournemouth (including Poole) |
| Birmingham Inner |
| Bristol |
| Cambridge City, Harlow |
| Canterbury, Maidstone, Medway & Tunbridge Wells |
| Cardiff (Inner) |
| Chelmsford South, Essex & East Suffolk |
| Chester |
| Fareham, Winchester |
| Hampshire, Dorset, Wiltshire, Isle of Wight |
| Kingston, Guildford, Reigate, Epsom |
| Leeds Inner (within 2 kilometers radius of the City Art Gallery) |
| Lewes |
| Liverpool, Birkenhead |
| Manchester Central |
| Newcastle—City Centre (within a 2 mile radius of St Nicholas Cathedral) |
| Norwich City |
| Nottingham City |
| Oxford, Thames Valley |
| Southampton, Portsmouth |
| Swindon, Basingstoke |
| Watford |

*Paragraph numbers marked with a "+" can be found online and on CD.*

***The National 2/3 rates apply to***

Bath, Cheltenham and Gloucester, Taunton, Yeovil
Bury
Chelmsford North, Cambridge County, Peterborough, Bury St E, Norfolk, Lowestoft
Cheshire & North Wales
Coventry, Rugby, Nuneaton, Stratford and Warwick
Exeter, Plymouth
Hull (City)
Leeds Outer, Wakefield & Pontefract
Leigh
Lincoln
Luton, Bedford, St Albans, Hitchin, Hertford
Manchester Outer, Oldham, Bolton, Tameside
Newcastle (other than City Centre)
Nottingham & Derbyshire
Sheffield, Doncaster and South Yorkshire
Southport
St Helens
Stockport, Altrincham, Salford
Swansea, Newport, Cardiff (Outer)
Southampton, Portsmouth
Wigan
Wolverhampton, Walsall, Dudley & Stourbridge
York, Harrogate

Birmingham Outer
Bradford (Dewsbury, Halifax, Huddersfield, Keighley & Skipton)
Cumbria
Devon, Cornwall
Grimsby, Skegness
Kidderminster
Northampton & Leicester
Preston, Lancaster, Blackpool, Chorley, Accrington, Burnley, Blackburn, Rawenstall & Nelson
Scarborough & Ripon
Stafford, Stoke, Tamworth
Teesside
Worcester, Hereford, Evesham and Redditch
Shrewsbury, Telford, Ludlow, Oswestry
South & West Wales

**LONDON BANDS**

| Grade | A | B | C | D |
|---|---|---|---|---|
| City of London: **EC1, EC2, EC3, EC4** | **£380** | **£274** | **£210** | **£129** |
| Central London: **W1, WC1, WC2, SW1** | **£292** | **£222** | **£181** | **£116** |
| Outer London: **(All other London post codes: W, NW, N, E, SE, SW and Bromley, Croydon, Dartford, Gravesend and Uxbridge)** | **£210-246** | **£158-210** | **£152** | **£111** |

*Scotland and Northern Ireland*

The Costs Officers bear in mind the guideline rates for England and Wales when determining appropriate rates in appeals from Scotland and Northern Ireland.

SUPREME COURT

## PRACTICE DIRECTION 14—FILING DOCUMENTS IN THE REGISTRY OF THE SUPREME COURT BY ELECTRONIC MEANS

### Introduction

4A-191 **14.1** The Supreme Court intends to take full advantage of the opportunities offered by modern information technology and rules 6(1)(d) and 7(1)(d) provide for the service and filing of documents "(with the consent of the party to be served or at the direction of the Registrar) by electronic means in accordance with the relevant practice direction". This Practice Direction makes the necessary provision.

### Filing of documents

4A-192 **14.2.1** Subject to paragraph 14.4.6, all documents must be filed electronically at the same time as hard copies are sent to the Registry. See rule 7(3) which provides that:

"Except with the consent of the Registrar, the contents of documents

(a) filed in hard copy must also be provided to the Registry by electronic means, and

(b) filed by electronic means must also be provided to the Registry in hard copy."

Other parties should be notified by the filing party that filing has taken place.

**14.2.2** Each electronic document must be named in accordance with the file naming convention published by the Registrar.

**14.2.3** In the event of a mistake being made, the Registry should be notified immediately.

### Submission of electronic documents to the Registry

4A-192.1 **14.3.1** Unless otherwise directed or permitted by the Registrar, or where the circumstances in paragraph 14.5.6 apply, the means of submitting electronic documents to the Registry is via e-mail at registry@supremecourt.gsi.gov.uk.

**14.3.2** Where the Registrar directs or permits, or in accordance with 14.5.6 below, the party should submit the electronic documents to the Registry on a memory stick, clearly marked or labelled with the title of the case and the identity of the party.

### General provisions

4A-193 **14.4.1** A document is not filed until the transmission is received and accepted by the Registry, whatever time it is shown to have been sent.

**14.4.2** The time of receipt of a transmission will be recorded electronically on the transmission as it is received.

**14.4.3** If a transmission is received after 4pm—

(1) the transmission will be treated as received; and

(2) any document attached to the transmission will be treated (if accepted) as filed, on the next day the Registry is open.

**14.4.4** A party sending an e-mail is responsible for ensuring that the transmission or any document attached to it is filed within any relevant time limits.

**14.4.5** The Registry will normally reply by e-mail where—

(1) the response is to a message transmitted electronically; and

(2) the sender has provided an e-mail address.

**14.4.6** Parties are advised not to transmit electronically any correspondence or documents of a confidential or sensitive nature, as security cannot be guaranteed.

**14.4.7** If a document transmitted electronically requires urgent attention, the sender should contact the court by telephone.

### Format of electronic documents

**14.5.1** Electronic documents must be in Portable Document Format (pdf). **4A–194**

**14.5.2** The electronic version, including pagination, must be identical to the hard copy.

**14.5.3** Unless otherwise directed or permitted by the Registrar, core volumes and volumes of authorities must be filed as a single pdf document and bookmarked in accordance with the index so that each individual document can be accessed directly by hypertext link both from the index page and from bookmarks on the left-hand side. Please see the example core volume and accompanying instructions on the Supreme Court website at http://www.supremecourt.gov.uk.

**14.5.4** Wherever possible, pdf documents within core volumes *and within volumes of authorities* and otherwise filed with the Court must be converted to pdf from their original electronic versions rather than scanned as images. Where documents are only available in hard copy and have to be scanned, the resultant pdf files should, where the quality of the scan allows, be subjected to a process of optical character recognition (OCR). This is to enable the documents to be text searchable and annotatable by the Court. Please see the example core volume and accompanying instructions on the Supreme Court website at http://www.supremecourt.gov.uk.

**14.5.5** Where electronic core volumes or other individual documents exceed 10 megabytes in size they must be submitted on memory stick, clearly marked or labelled with the title of the case and the identity of the party.

**14.5.6** The Registrar may permit filing in a different or additional format (e.g. Excel) for good reason.

### Hypertext linking within documents

**14.6.1** The Supreme Court does not intend at this stage to impose detailed requirements as to hypertext linking within documents. However, it wishes to encourage parties to employ hypertext links within documents. In particular, it would be helpful if hypertext links were introduced at the time the core volumes are produced to link: **4A–195**

(a) the statement of facts and issues to documents in the appendix;

(b) written cases to documents in the appendix and to the authorities;

(c) cases to the relevant law reports and to the index of authorities.

**14.6.2** The parties should seek to agree on the extent to which hypertext linking is to be used.

**Special directions**

4A–196 **14.7** The Registrar may give special directions for the filing of electronic documents to meet the requirements of particular cases or by way of experiment.

*FORMS*

**Form 1 (Application for permission/notice of appeal)**

**4A–197**

In the Supreme Court of the United Kingdom

# Notice of appeal

(or application for permission to appeal)

On appeal from

V

Appeal number

Date of filing

D D M M M Y Y Y Y

Appellant's solicitors

Respondent's solicitors

SC001 Notice of appeal (04.09)

## 1. Appellant

Appellant's full name

Original status
- ☐ Claimant ☐ Defendant
- ☐ Petitioner ☐ Respondent
- ☐ Pursuer ☐ Defender

**Solicitor**

Name

Address

Telephone no.

Fax no.

DX no.

Postcode

Ref.

Email

How would you prefer us to communicate with you?
- ☐ DX ☐ Email
- ☐ Post ☐ Other *(please specify)*

Is the appellant in receipt of public funding/legal aid?
☐ Yes ☐ No

If Yes, please give the certificate number

**Counsel**

Name

Address

Telephone no.

Fax no.

DX no.

Postcode

Email

Page 2

**SC001** Notice of appeal

**Counsel**

Name

Address

Telephone no.

Fax no.

DX no.

Postcode

Email

## 2. Respondent

Respondent's full name

Original status

- ☐ Claimant ☐ Defendant
- ☐ Petitioner ☐ Respondent
- ☐ Pursuer ☐ Defender

**Solicitor**

Name

Address

Telephone no.

Fax no.

DX no.

Postcode

Ref.

Email

How would you prefer us to communicate with you?

- ☐ DX ☐ Email
- ☐ Post ☐ Other *(please specify)*

Is the respondent in receipt of public funding/legal aid?

☐ Yes ☐ No

If Yes, please give the certificate number

Page 3

**SC001** Notice of appeal



*Paragraph numbers marked with a "+" can be found online and on CD.*

**Counsel**

Name

Address

Telephone no.

Fax no.

DX no.

Postcode

Email

**Counsel**

Name

Address

Telephone no.

Fax no.

DX no.

Postcode

Email

## 3. Decision being appealed

Name of Court

Names of Judges

Date of order/ interlocutor/decision

D D / M M M / Y Y Y Y

Page 4

**SC001** Notice of appeal

## 4. Permission to appeal

If you have permission to appeal complete **Part A** or complete **Part B** if you require permission to appeal.

PART A

Name of Court granting permission

Date permission granted

D D / M M M / Y Y Y Y

Conditions on which permission granted

PART B

☐ The appellant applies to the Supreme Court for permission to appeal.

Page 5

SC001 Notice of appeal

## 5. Information about the decision being appealed

Please set out

- Narrative of the facts
- Statutory framework
- Chronology of proceedings
- Orders made in the Courts below
- Issues before the Court appealed from
- Treatment of issues by the Court appealed from
- Issues in the appeal

Page 6

SC001 Notice of appeal

*Paragraph numbers marked with a "+" can be found online and on CD.*

## 6. Grounds of appeal

Counsel's name or signature:

Page 7

**SC001** Notice of appeal

SUPREME COURT

## 7. Other information about the appeal

Are you applying for an extension of time?

☐ Yes ☐ No

If Yes, please explain why

What order are you asking the Supreme Court to make?

Order being appealed ☐ set aside ☐ vary

Original order ☐ set aside ☐ restore ☐ vary

**Does the appeal raise issues under the:**

Human Rights Act 1998? ☐ Yes ☐ No

Are you seeking a declaration of incompatibility?

☐ Yes ☐ No

Are you challenging an act of a public authority?

☐ Yes ☐ No

If you have answered Yes to any of the questions above please give details below:

Court's devolution jurisdiction? ☐ Yes ☐ No

If Yes, please give details below:

Page 8

**SC001** Notice of appeal

*Paragraph numbers marked with a "+" can be found online and on CD.*

**Are you asking the Supreme Court to:**

depart from one of its own decisions or from one made by the House of Lords?

☐ Yes ☐ No

If Yes, please give details below:

make a reference to the European Court of Justice of the European Communities?

☐ Yes ☐ No

If Yes, please give details below:

Will you or the respondent request an expedited hearing?

☐ Yes ☐ No

If Yes, please give details below:

Page 9

**SC001** Notice of appeal

## 8. Certificate of Service

Either complete this section or attach a separate certificate

The date on which this form was served on the

1st Respondent ☐☐ / ☐☐☐ / ☐☐☐☐
D D M M M Y Y Y Y

2nd Respondent ☐☐ / ☐☐☐ / ☐☐☐☐
D D M M M Y Y Y Y

I certify that this document was served on

by

by the following method

Signature

## 9. Other relevant information

Neutral citation of the judgment appealed against e.g. [2009] EWCA Civ 95

References to Law Report in which any relevant judgment is reported.

Subject matter catchwords for indexing.

**Please return your completed form to:**

The Supreme Court of the United Kingdom, Parliament Square, London SW1P 3BD
DX 157230 Parliament Square 4
Telephone: 020 7960 1991/1992 Fax: 020 7960 1901
email: registry@supremecourt.gsi.gov.uk
www.supremecourt.gov.uk

Page 10

**SC001** Notice of appeal

Page 11

**SC001** Notice of appeal



*Paragraph numbers marked with a "+" can be found online and on CD.*

Page 12

SC001 Notice of appeal

**Form 2 (Application form)**

**4A–198**

In the Supreme Court of the United Kingdom

# Application form

THE SUPREME COURT

On appeal from

V

Appeal number

Date of filing

D D / M M M / Y Y Y Y

Applicant's solicitors

Appellant's solicitors

Respondent's solicitors

**SC002** Application form (04.09)

## 1. Details of the applicant

Applicant's full name

Original status
- Claimant
- Defendant
- Intervener
- Petitioner
- Respondent
- Pursuer
- Defender

**Solicitor**

Name

Address

Telephone no.

Fax no.

DX no.

Postcode

Ref.

Email

How would you prefer us to communicate with you?
- DX
- Email
- Post
- Other *(please specify)*

**Counsel**

Name

Address

Telephone no.

Fax no.

DX no.

Postcode

Email

Page 2

**SC002** Application form

Counsel

Name

Address

Telephone no.

Fax no.

DX no.

Postcode

Email

## 2. Nature of the application

The applicant applies for

- ☐ Extension of time
- ☐ Permission to intervene
- ☐ Security
- ☐ Order for substituted service
- ☐ Expedited hearing
- ☐ Review of Registrar's decision
- ☐ Other order *(please specify)*

Page 3

SC002 Application form

## 3. Grounds on which application made

On what grounds are you making this application?

Page 4

SC002 Application form

## 4. Consent to application

The following parties **consent** to this application

See attached letter(s) dated

The following parties **object** to this application

See attached letter(s) dated

## 5. Other relevant information

Page 5

SC002 Application form

SUPREME COURT

*Paragraph numbers marked with a "+" can be found online and on CD.*

## 6. Details of the appellant

Appellant's full name

Original status

- Claimant
- Defendant
- Petitioner
- Respondent
- Pursuer
- Defender

**Solicitor**

Name

Address

Telephone no.

Fax no.

DX no.

Postcode

Ref.

Email

**Counsel**

Name

Address

Telephone no.

Fax no.

DX no.

Postcode

Email

Page 6

SC002 Application form

**Counsel**

Name

Address

Telephone no.

Fax no.

DX no.

Postcode

Email

## 7. Details of the respondent

Respondent's full name

Original status

- ☐ Claimant
- ☐ Defendant
- ☐ Petitioner
- ☐ Respondent
- ☐ Pursuer
- ☐ Defender

**Solicitor**

Name

Address

Telephone no.

Fax no.

DX no.

Postcode

Ref.

Email

Page 7

SC002 Application form

**Counsel**

Name

Address

Telephone no.

Fax no.

DX no.

Postcode

Email

**Counsel**

Name

Address

Telephone no.

Fax no.

DX no.

Postcode

Email

## 8. Certificate of Service

Either complete this section or attach a separate certificate

On what date was this form served on the

Appellant D D / M M M / Y Y Y Y

Respondent D D / M M M / Y Y Y Y

I certify that this document was served on

by

by the following method

Signature

Page 8

SC002 Application form

### 9. Details of Registrar's order/decision being appealed

Date of order/decision [ ][ ] / [ ][ ][ ] / [ ][ ][ ][ ]
D D M M M Y Y Y Y

Page 9

SC002 Application form

Page 10

SC002 Application form

Supreme Court

*Paragraph numbers marked with a "+" can be found online and on CD.*

**Please return your completed form to:**

The Supreme Court of the United Kingdom, Parliament Square, London SW1P 3BD
DX 157230 Parliament Square 4
Telephone: 020 7960 1991/1992 Fax: 020 7960 1901
email: registry@supremecourt.gsi.gov.uk
www.supremecourt.gov.uk

**Form 3 (Notice of objection/acknowledgment by respondent)**

**4A–199**

In the Supreme Court of the United Kingdom

# Notice of objection/ Acknowledgement

V

Appeal number

Date of filing

D D / M M M / Y Y Y Y

Name of respondent

Respondent's solicitors

Name of appellant

Appellant's solicitors

**SC003** Notice of objection/Acknowledgement (04.09)

## 1. Respondent

Respondent's full name

The respondent was served with the

- application for permission to appeal
- notice of appeal
- application

On date __ __ / __ __ __ / __ __ __ __
D D M M M Y Y Y Y

The respondent intends to ask the Court to:

- refuse to grant permission to appeal
- order the appellant to give security for costs if permission to appeal is granted
- dismiss the appeal
- give the respondent permission to cross-appeal
- allow the appeal for reasons which are different from, or additional to, those given by the court below
- Other *(please specify)*

The respondent wishes to receive notice of any hearing date and to be advised of progress. The respondent's details are:

**Solicitor**

Name

Address

Telephone no.

Fax no.

DX no.

Postcode

Ref.

Email

How would you prefer us to communicate with you?

- DX
- Email
- Post
- Other *(please specify)*

Page 2

**SC003** Notice of objection/Acknowledgement

**Counsel**

Name

Address

Telephone no.

Fax no.

DX no.

Postcode

Email

**Counsel**

Name

Address

Telephone no.

Fax no.

DX no.

Postcode

Email

## 2. Certificate of Service

Either complete this section or attach a separate certificate

On what date was this form served on the

Appellant  D D / M M M / Y Y Y Y

Other  D D / M M M / Y Y Y Y

I certify that this document was served on

by

by the following method

Signature

Page 3

SC003 Notice of objection/Acknowledgement

SUPREME COURT

*Paragraph numbers marked with a "+" can be found online and on CD.*

## 3. Other information about the respondent

☐ The respondent is in receipt of public funding/legal aid

Certificate number

☐ The respondent is applying for public funding/legal aid

**Information about the respondent's case**

Set out here the respondent's grounds of appeal, reasons why permission to appeal should be refused or why the appeal should be allowed. Include information to explain what the respondent intends to ask the Court to do.

Page 4

**SC003** Notice of objection/Acknowledgement

Is the respondent seeking a declaration of incompatibility?

☐ Yes ☐ No

☐ The respondent will seek to raise issues under the Human Rights Act 1998 *(please give brief details)*

☐ The respondent will ask the court to make a reference to the European Court of Justice *(please give brief details)*

Page 5

SC003 Notice of objection/Acknowledgement

**Please return your completed form to:**

The Supreme Court of the United Kingdom, Parliament Square, London SW1P 3BD
DX 157230 Parliament Square 4

Telephone: 020 7960 1991/1992 Fax: 020 7960 1901

email: registry@supremecourt.gsi.gov.uk

www.supremecourt.gov.uk

Page 6

**SC003** Notice of objection/Acknowledgement

# 4B JUDICIAL COMMITTEE OF THE PRIVY COUNCIL APPEALS

### Editorial introduction

The Judicial Committee of the Privy Council is the court of final appeal for the UK overseas territories and Crown dependencies, and for those Commonwealth countries that have retained the appeal to Her Majesty in Council or, in the case of Republics, to the Judicial Committee. It also has other domestic jurisdiction in the United Kingdom. The Judicial Committee's devolution jurisdiction was transferred to the United Kingdom Supreme Court (see Section 4A above) by the Constitutional Reform Act 2005. For further details as to the Judicial Committee's jurisdiction, see Practice Direction 1 (referred to below). **4B–0.1**

The Registry of the Judicial Committee is situated in the building which houses the Supreme Court of the United Kingdom (Parliament Square, London SW1P 3BD). For contact information, see Practice Direction 2 (The Registry of the Judicial Committee) (referred to below).

The Judicial Committee's website address is: *http://www.privy-council.org.uk* [Accessed November 5, 2009].

### Judicial Committee (Appellate Jurisdiction) Rules 2009

For Rules, see para.4B–1+ below. **4B–0.2**

The Judicial Committee (Appellate Jurisdiction) Rules 2009 were enacted by art.2 and the Schedule to the Judicial Committee (Appellate Jurisdiction) Rules Order 2009 (SI 2009/224). These Rules govern the practice and procedure to be followed in relation to appeals to the Judicial Committee of the Privy Council. They came into effect on April 21, 2009. Article 3 of the Order provided that the Rules apply, with any necessary modifications, to appeals and modifications which were filed before that date. The text of the Rules is set out below (see para.4B–1+).

Article 4 (Revocations) of the 2009 Order revoked the Judicial Committee (General Appellate Jurisdiction) Rules Order 1982 (SI 1982/1676) and certain other statutory instruments. Article 4(2) revoked (with effect from October 1, 2009) the rules which regulated the exercise of the Judicial Committee's devolution jurisdiction since that jurisdiction was transferred to the United Kingdom Supreme Court by the Constitutional Reform Act 2005 s.40.

Article 5 (Partial Revocations) of the 2009 Order revoked a number of other Orders, but only so far as they relate to the powers of the Judicial Committee and the procedure to be adopted by it with respect to proceedings before it. The procedure which these Orders provide for proceedings in the various courts from which appeals lie to the Judicial Committee is not affected.

The Rules are divided in eight Parts (for Arrangement of Rules, see para.4B–0 below). In many respects, the Rules are very similar to the Supreme Court Rules 2009 (see Section 4A above). The contents of the several Parts are briefly described immediately below.

The rules in Pts 1 to 6 of the Rules and the practice directions which supplement them provide the procedure for civil and criminal appeals to the Judicial Committee of the Privy Council under its general appellate jurisdiction.

As is explained in the Explanatory Note attached to the 2009 Order, Pt 1 of the Rules (1) contains interpretation provisions (rr.2 and 3); (2) makes provision for forms (r.4); (3) contains rules about the service and filing of documents (rr.6 and r.7); (4) sets out what the Registrar may do in the event that the rules are not complied with (r.8); (5) sets out how and by whom procedural decisions will be made (r.9). Part 2 of the Rules contains the rules governing applications for permission to appeal and provides for the documents that are to be filed and the relevant time limits. Part 3 contains rules about commencement of, and preparation for, an appeal, providing for the documents that are to be filed and the relevant time limits. Part 4 contains rules about the hearing of appeals by the Judicial Committee. Part 5 contains miscellaneous rules such as for the making of incidental applications (r.31); for security for costs (r.37); for making an application to be treated as a financially assisted person (r.38).

The rule in Pt 7 of the Rules (r.53) applies to appeals to the Judicial Committee

***Paragraph numbers marked with a "+" can be found online and on CD.***

under the Veterinary Surgeons Act 1966 s.17; and the rule in Pt 8 (r.54) applies to appeals to the Judicial Committee under the Brunei (Appeals) Act 1989 s.1.

### Practice Directions

4B–0.3 For Practice Directions, see para.4B–56+ below.

Rule 3 states that any reference in these Rules to a practice direction means a practice direction issued by the Judicial Committee to supplement these Rules "to provide for the forms to be used in proceedings before the Judicial Committee and to provide general guidance and assistance for counsel, agents and the parties".

The practice directions issued are as follows:

- Practice Direction 1 (General Note and the Jurisdiction of the Judicial Committee)
- Practice Direction 2 (The Registry of the Judicial Committee)
- Practice Direction 3 (Applications for Permission to Appeal)
- Practice Direction 4 (Notice of Appeal)
- Practice Direction 5 (Papers for the Appeal Hearing)
- Practice Direction 6 (The Appeal Hearing)
- Practice Direction 7 (Miscellaneous Matters including Applications, Documents, Forms and Orders)
- Practice Direction 8 (Costs)

Practice Directions 3, 4, 5 and 6 are principally relevant to Pt 2 (Applications for permission to appeal) and Pt 3 (Commencement and preparation of appeal) of the Rules.

### Forms

4B–0.4 For Forms, see para.4B–75+ below.

Rule 4(1) states that in these Rules, a form means a form set out in a practice direction and a reference to the "appropriate form" means the form provided by the relevant practice direction for any particular case. The forms shall be used in the cases to which they apply, and in the circumstances for which they are provided by the relevant practice direction, but a form may be varied by the Judicial Committee or a party if the variation is required by the circumstances of a particular case (r.4(2)).

The prescribed Forms are published in Annex 1 to Practice Direction 7 (Miscellaneous Matters including Applications, Documents, Forms and Orders) and are as follows:

- Form 1 (Notice of appeal (or application for permission to appeal))
- Form 2 (Application form)
- Form 3 (Notice of objection/acknowledgment)

### Fees to be taken

4B–0.5 Rule 42 of the Rules states that, unless and except in so far as the fees are remitted or reduced because of the party's status as a financially assisted person, every party must pay fees in the amounts set out in the Appendix to the Rules (see para.4B–55+below) and also as Annex 2 to Practice Direction 7 (see para.4B–118+ below). The current fee levels (which were set in 2003) have been increased by the rate of inflation since 2003, and r.38 provides a procedure for appellants to claim exemption from the fees where this is justified by their circumstances or means.

### Costs

4B–0.6 The Judicial Committee may make such orders as it considers just in respect of the costs of any appeal, application for permission to appeal or other application to or proceeding before the Judicial Committee (r.43(1)). Part 6 of the Rules contains provisions in relation to costs. That part is supplemented by Practice Direction 8 (Costs).

***Paragraph numbers marked with a "+" can be found online and on CD.***

# Judicial Committee (Appellate Jurisdiction) Rules 2009

(S.I. 2009 No. 224) **4B–0**

ARRANGEMENT OF RULES

PART 1



***Paragraph numbers marked with a "+" can be found online and on CD.***

**Paragraph numbers marked with a "+" denote content that is available on White Book on Westlaw UK or the Civil Procedure CD.**

*Paragraph numbers marked with a "+" can be found online and on CD.*

# SECTION 5

## EUROPEAN JURISDICTION

# SECTION 5

## EUROPEAN JURISDICTION

# 5 EUROPEAN JURISDICTION

## GENERAL

### The Brussels Convention

When the EEC Treaty (now called the EC Treaty (as a result of the Treaty of Maastricht on European Union) and also referred to as the Treaty of Rome) was signed in 1957, the six original Member States agreed by art.220 that they would enter into negotiations with each other: 5–1

> "with a view to securing for the benefit of their nationals ... the simplification of formalities governing the reciprocal recognition and enforcement of judgments of courts or tribunals and of arbitration awards".

Subsequently, the Convention on Jurisdiction and Enforcement of Judgments in Civil and Commercial Matters was signed at Brussels on September 23, 1968 on behalf of these States (the Brussels Convention).

This Convention went beyond art.220 in that it was not confined to the recognition and enforcement of judgments, but also contained rules of jurisdiction applicable in all States. No provision was, however, made for the recognition of arbitration awards. In 1971 the Member States concluded a Protocol on the Interpretation of the 1968 Convention by the European Court of Justice (the 1971 Protocol). This provides for references for preliminary rulings on questions of interpretation of the Convention to be made to the Court by appellate courts of the Contracting States (see text of 1971 Protocol at para.5–140+ below).

The object of the Conventions is not to unify the rules of substantive law and of procedure of the different contracting states, but to determine which courts have jurisdiction in disputes relating to civil and commercial matters in relations between the contracting states and to facilitate enforcements of judgments (Case C–68/93 *Shevill v Presse Alliance* [1995] I.L.Pr. 267). However, the Conventions establish an enforcement procedure which constitutes an autonomous and complete system independent of the legal systems of the contracting states (*Société d'Informatique Realisation Organisation v Ampersand Software B.V.* [1995] All E.R. (EC) 783).

### Accession of United Kingdom

When the United Kingdom, together with Denmark and Ireland, joined the European Community, it undertook to accede to any Conventions provided for by art.220 of the Treaty of Rome and "to enter into negotiations with the original Member States in order to make the necessary adjustments thereto". The result was a Convention signed on October 9, 1978 amending the Brussels Convention and the 1971 Protocol and providing for the accession to them of the United Kingdom, Denmark and Ireland. In this instance, the amendments went well beyond mere "necessary adjustments". 5–2

### Civil Jurisdiction and Judgments Act 1982

This Act has as its main purpose the implementation of the Brussels Convention as amended by the 1978 Accession Convention and the 1971 Protocol. The Act gives the Conventions the force of law in the United Kingdom and requires judicial notice to be taken of them. They are set out, as s.2 states, for "convenience of reference" in the Act. Thus, the English text of the Brussels Convention (as it was at that time) is found in Sch.1, the 1971 Protocol in Sch.2 and the relevant provisions of the Accession Convention are in Sch.3. It is open to the UK islands and territories to ask that the Brussels Convention should be extended to them (see in this respect the Civil Jurisdiction and Judgments Act 1982 (Gibraltar) Order 1997) at para.5–164 below). 5–3

The Civil Jurisdiction and Judgments Act 1982 also contains rules of jurisdiction and rules for the enforcement of judgments as between the constituent parts of the United Kingdom, England and Wales, Scotland, and Northern Ireland. To this end, the Act sets out in Sch.4 a modified version of the jurisdictional rules found in the Brussels Convention and in addition contains a number of special provisions dealing with recognition and enforcement of judgments. It should be noted that the provisions of the 1982 Act, including the Brussels Convention and the 1971 Protocol (amended as explained below), contained in this Section of *Civil Procedure*, are confined to those dealing with the allocation of jurisdiction among the courts of the EC Member States. Schedule 4 of the 1982 Act contains provisions modelled on the Convention for

***Paragraph numbers marked with a "+" can be found online and on CD.***

the allocation business between the three separate jurisdictions within the UK. Its in terpretation is a matter solely within the jurisdiction of the United Kingdom national courts (Case C–346/93 *Kleinwort Benson Ltd v City of Glasgow District Council, The Times*, April 17, 1995).

The Civil Procedure Rules and the relevant Practice Directions give procedural effect to the provisions of the Act and the Conventions. The principal rules are CPR r.6.19 (service of Claim Form where the permission of the Court is not required), and PD 6B paras 1.1 to 1.3 (form of certificates on claim form when service abroad is to be effected without permission). See also Sch.1 and RSC O.71 (reciprocal enforcement of judgments under the Conventions) and the Practice Direction supplementing O.71. For applications under RSC O.71 the appropriate Practice Forms should be used: see **PF 157QB** to **PF 165QB**.

### Accession of Other States

5–4 Section 14(1) of the 1982 Act provides that the Act (including the texts of the Conventions in the Schedules) may be amended by Order in Council. The Civil Jurisdiction and Judgments Act 1982 (Amendment) Order 1989 (SI 1989/1346) modified the Act in consequence of a revision of the Brussels Convention and the 1971 Protocol occasioned by the accession to them of Greece by a Convention signed in Luxemburg on October 25, 1982. The Civil Jurisdiction and Judgments Act 1982 (Amendment) Order 1990 (SI 1990/2591) brought into effect in the UK revisions occasioned by the accession of Spain and Portugal as a result of the San Sebastian Convention signed on May 28, 1989 (as to ratification elsewhere, see para.5–6 below). The revisions made to the Brussels Convention on these occasions have not always been confined to what could be called "necessary adjustments" to cope with the accessions of new jurisdictions but in addition have included some changes thought necessary in the light of problems encountered in operating the provisions of the Convention over the years within the Member States.

### EC and EFTA—The 1988 and 2007 Lugano Conventions

5–5 On September 16, 1988, a Convention on jurisdiction and the enforcement of judgments in civil matters, known as "the Lugano Convention", was made between Member States of the EC and those of the European Free Trade Association (EFTA). (For convenience of reference, the English text of that Convention was set out in Sch.3C of the Civil Jurisdiction and Judgments Act 1988.) This Convention was replaced by the Convention on jurisdiction and the recognition and enforcement of judgments in civil and commercial matters agreed by the European Community, the Republic of Iceland, the Kingdom of Norway, the Swiss Confederation and the Kingdom of Denmark on October 30, 2007. The new Convention was ratified by the Council of Ministers on May 18, 2009 and entered into force for the European Community and Norway on January 1, 2010. (On that date it did not enter into force in relation to Switzerland and Iceland because those countries had not, as at that date, ratified it. In relation to those countries the 1988 Convention continues to apply until such time as those ratifications take place.)

Throughout the CPR, the expression "Lugano Convention" means this new, or revised version of the former Convention (see CPR r.6.31(j), r.12.11(6)(f) and r.74.1(5)(f)). The provisions of the new Convention are generally parallel in nature to those in the Judgments Regulation (the "Brussels I Regulation"), which operates within the EC (Council Regulation (EC) No.44/2001; see para.5–249 below). The commencement of the new Convention re-establishes the parallelism which had earlier existed between the 1988 Lugano Convention and the 1968 Brussels convention, and which had been disrupted by the commencement of the Brussels I Regulation in March 2002.

### Ratification

5–6 The San Sebastian Convention has been ratified by all Member States. (The UK ratified the San Sebastian Convention on September 13, 1991, with entry into force on December 1, 1991.) The Lugano Convention was ratified by all EC and EFTA Member States. (The UK ratified the Lugano Convention on February 5, 1992, with entry into force on May 1, 1992).

Up-to-date information as to the progress of ratification by EFTA Member States acceding to the Brussels Convention may be obtained from the Lord Chancellor's Department, International Division, 28 Old Queen Street, London SW1H 9HP, or from the International Litigation Procedure Reports. The information contained therein is updated monthly.

***Paragraph numbers marked with a "+" can be found online and on CD.***

# Civil Jurisdiction and Judgments Act 1982

## (1982 c.27) 5–7

ARRANGEMENT OF SECTIONS

PART I

IMPLEMENTATION OF THE CONVENTIONS

*MAIN IMPLEMENTING PROVISIONS*



***Paragraph numbers marked with a "+" can be found online and on CD.***

**Introductory note**

5–8 This Act incorporates into United Kingdom law the EC Convention on Jurisdiction and Enforcement of Judgments in Civil and Commercial Matters of 1968, known as the "Brussels Convention". As stated in s.2(2), "for convenience of reference" the English text of this Convention is set out in Sch.1 to the Act. For the Articles of the Convention relating to jurisdiction, see paras 5–24 *et seq.*

## PART I

## IMPLEMENTATION OF THE CONVENTIONS

### *MAIN IMPLEMENTING PROVISIONS*

### Interpretation of references to the Conventions and Contracting States

5–9 **1.**—(1) In this Act—

"the 1968 Convention" means the Convention on jurisdiction and the enforcement of judgments in civil and commercial matters (including the Protocol annexed to that Convention), signed at Brussels on 27th September 1968;

"the 1971 Protocol" means the Protocol on the interpretation of the 1968 Convention by the European Court, signed at Luxembourg on 3rd June 1971;

"the Accession Convention" means the Convention on the accession to the 1968 Convention and the 1971 Protocol of Denmark, the Republic of Ireland and the United Kingdom, signed at Luxembourg on 9th October 1978;

"the 1982 Accession Convention" means the Convention on the accession of the Hellenic Republic to the 1968 Convention and the 1971 Protocol, with the adjustments made to them by the Accession Convention, signed at Luxembourg on 25th October 1982;

"the 1989 Accession Convention" means the Convention on the accession of the Kingdom of Spain and the Portuguese Republic to the 1968 Convention and the 1971 Protocol, with the adjustments made to them by the Accession Convention and the 1982 Accession Convention, signed at Donostia—San Sebastián on 26th May 1989;

"the Brussels Conventions" means the 1968 Convention, the 1971 Protocol, the Accession Convention, the 1982 Accession Convention and the 1989 Accession Convention;

"the Lugano Convention" means the Convention on jurisdiction and the recognition and enforcement of judgments in civil and commercial matters, between the European Community and the Republic of Iceland, the Kingdom of Norway, the Swiss Confederation and the Kingdom of Denmark signed on behalf of the European Community on 30th October 2007.

"the Regulation" means Council Regulation (EC) No. 44/2001 of 22nd December 2000 on jurisdiction and the recognition and enforcement of judgments in civil and commercial matters, as

***Paragraph numbers marked with a "+" can be found online and on CD.***

amended from time to time and as applied by the Agreement made on 19th October 2005 between the European Community and the Kingdom of Denmark on jurisdiction and the recognition and enforcement of judgments in civil and commercial matters (OJ No. L 299 16.11.2005 at p62).

(2) In this Act, unless the context otherwise requires—

(a) references to, or to any provision of, the 1968 Convention or the 1971 Protocol are references to the Convention, Protocol or provision as amended by the Accession Convention, the 1982 Accession Convention and the 1989 Accession Convention; and

(b) any reference to a numbered Article without more is a reference—

(i) to the Article so numbered of the 1968 Convention, in so far as the provision applies in relation to that Convention, and

(ii) to the Article so numbered of the Lugano Convention, in so far as the provision applies in relation to that Convention,

and any reference to a sub-division of a numbered Article shall be construed accordingly.

(3) In this Act—

"Contracting State", without more, in any provision means—

(a) in the application of the provision in relation to the Brussels Conventions, a Brussels Contracting State; and

(b) in the application of the provision in relation to the Lugano Convention, a State bound by the Lugano Convention;

"Brussels Contracting State" means a state which is one of the original parties to the 1968 Convention or one of the parties acceding to that Convention under the Accession Convention, or under the 1982 Accession Convention, or under the 1989 Accession Convention, but only with respect to any territory—

(a) to which the Brussels Conventions apply; and

(b) which is excluded from the scope of the Regulation pursuant to Article 299 of the Treaty establishing the European Community;

"State bound by the Lugano Convention" in any provision, in the application of that provision in relation to the Lugano Convention has the same meaning as in Article 1(3) of that Convention;

"Regulation State" in any provision, in the application of that provision in relation to the Regulation, means a Member State.

(4) Any question arising as to whether it is the Regulation, any of the Brussels Conventions, or the Lugano Convention which applies in the circumstances of a particular case shall be determined as follows—

(a) in accordance with Article 64 of the Lugano Convention

(which determines the relationship between the Brussels Convention and the Lugano Convention); and

(b) in accordance with Article 68 of the Regulation (which determines the relationship between the Brussels Convention and the Regulation).

5–10 *Note* —Amended by the Civil Jurisdiction and Judgments Act 1982 (Amendment) Order 1989 (SI 1989/1346); the Civil Jurisdiction and Judgments Act 1982 (Amendment) Order 1990 (SI 1990/2591); the Civil Jurisdiction and Judgments Act 1991 s.2; the Civil Jurisdiction and Judgments Order 2001 (SI 2001/3929), Sch.2, para.1(c); the Civil Jurisdiction and Judgments Regulations 2007 (SI 2007/1655); and the Civil Jurisdiction and Judgments Regulations 2009 (SI 2009/3131) reg.3 (subject to savings contained in reg.48), with effect from January 1, 2010.

## The Conventions to have the force of law

5–11 **2.**—(1) The Brussels Conventions shall have the force of law in the United Kingdom, and judicial notice shall be taken of them.

(2) For convenience of reference there are set out in Schedules 1, 2, 3, 3A and 3B respectively the English texts of—

(a) the 1968 Convention as amended by Titles II and III of the Accession Convention, by Titles II and IIIof the 1982 Accession Convention and by Titles II and III of, and Annex I(d) to, the 1989 Accession Convention;

(b) the 1971 Protocol as amended by Title IV of the Accession Convention, by Title IV of the 1982 Accession Convention and by Title IV of the 1989 Accession Convention;

(c) Titles V and VI of the Accession Convention (transitional and final provisions) as amended by Title V of the 1989 Accession Convention;

(d) Titles V and VI of the 1982 Accession Convention (transitional and final provisions); and

(e) Titles VI and VII of the 1989 Accession Convention (transitional and final provisions),

(f) Titles V and VI of the 1996 Accession Convention (transitional and final provisions),

being texts prepared from the authentic English texts referred to in Articles 37 and 41 of the Accession Convention, in Article 17 of the 1982 Accession Convention and in Article 34 of the 1989 Accession Convention.

5–12 *Note* —Amended by the Civil Jurisdiction and Judgments Act 1982 (Amendment) Order 1989 (SI 1989/1346); the Civil Jurisdiction and Judgments Act 1982 (Amendment) Order 1990 (SI 1990/2591); the Civil Jurisdiction and Judgments Act 1991 s.3, Sch.2, para.1; and by the Civil Jurisdiction and Judgments Act 1982 (Amendment) Order 2000 (SI 2000/1824), art.6(e).

**"1968 Convention ... 1971 Protocol"**

5–13 This Convention, i.e. the Brussels Convention, and the attached 1971 Protocol are set out in, respectively, Sch.1 and 2 of the Act.

## Interpretation of the Conventions

5–14 **3.**—(1) Any question as to the meaning or effect of any provision of the Brussels Convention shall, if not referred to the European Court in accordance with the 1971 Protocol, be determined in accordance with the principles laid down by and any relevant decision of the European Court.

(2) Judicial notice shall be taken of any decision of, or expression of opinion by, the European Court on any such question.

(3) Without prejudice to the generality of subsection (1), the following reports (which are reproduced in the Official Journal of the Communities), namely—

(a) the reports by Mr P. Jenard on the 1968 Convention and the 1971 Protocol; and

(b) the report by Professor Peter Schlosser on the Accession Convention; and

(c) the report by Professor Demetrios I. Evrigenis and Professor K. D. Kerameus on the 1982 Accession Convention; and

(d) the report by Mr. Martino de Almeida Cruz, Mr. Manuel Desantes Real and Mr P. Jenard on the 1989 Accession Convention,

may be considered in ascertaining the meaning or effect of any provision of the Conventions and shall be given such weight as is appropriate in the circumstances.

*Note* —Amended by the Civil Jurisdiction and Judgments Act 1982 (Amendment) Order 1989 (SI 1989/1346); the Civil Jurisdiction and Judgments Act 1982 (Amendment) Order 1990 (SI 1990/2591); and the Civil Jurisdiction and Judgments Act 1991 s.3, Sch.2, para.1. **5–15**

## The Lugano Convention to have the force of law

**3A.** *[Repealed by the Civil Jurisdiction and Judgments Regulations 2009 (SI 2009/3131) reg.4 (subject to savings contained in reg.48), with effect from January 1, 2010.]* **5–16**

**[THE NEXT PARAGRAPH IS 5–18.]**

**"Lugano Convention"**

The text of this Convention is set out in Sch.3C of the Act as amended; it is not included in this Section of *The Supreme Court Practice*. The Lugano Convention is made between the Member States of the EC and those of the European Free Trade Association (EFTA). It is very closely modelled on the Brussels Convention. The amendments to the 1982 Act required to accommodate the Lugano Convention were introduced by the Civil Jurisdiction and Judgments Act 1991. See further, para.5–194 below. **5–18**

## Interpretation of the Lugano Convention

**3B.** *[Repealed by the Civil Jurisdiction and Judgments Regulations 2009 (SI 2009/3131) reg.4 (subject to savings contained in reg.48), with effect from January 1, 2010.]* **5–19**

**[THE NEXT PARAGRAPH IS 5–21.]**

***Paragraph numbers marked with a "+" can be found online and on CD.***

* * * *

### OTHER SUPPLEMENTARY PROVISIONS

## Allocation within UK of jurisdiction with respect to trusts and consumer contracts

5–21 **10.**—(1) The provisions of this section have effect for the purpose of allocating within the United Kingdom jurisdiction in certain proceedings in respect of which the 1968 Convention or the Lugano Convention confers jurisdiction on the courts of the United Kingdom generally and to which section 16 does not apply.

(2) Any proceedings which by virtue of Article 5(6) (trusts) are brought in the United Kingdom shall be brought in the courts of the part of the United Kingdom in which the trust is domiciled.

(3) Any proceedings which by virtue of the first paragraph of Article 14 of the 1968 Convention or Article 16(1) of the Lugano Convention (consumer contracts) are brought in the United Kingdom by a consumer on the ground that he is himself domiciled there shall be brought in the courts of the part of the United Kingdom in which he is domiciled.

5–22 *Note* —Amended by the Civil Jurisdiction and Judgments Act 1991 s.3 and Sch.2; and the Civil Jurisdiction and Judgments Regulations 2009 (SI 2009/3131) reg.11 (subject to savings contained in reg.48), with effect from January 1, 2010.

#### "To which section 16 does not apply"

5–23 Section 16 deals with the allocation within the UK of jurisdiction in certain civil proceedings. The provisions set out in Sch.4 to the Act (which contains a modified version of Title II of the Brussels Convention) have effect for determining, for each part of the UK, whether the courts of law of that part have jurisdiction.

* * * *

# PART IV

## MISCELLANEOUS PROVISIONS

### PROVISIONS RELATING TO JURISDICTION

## Interim relief and protective measures in cases of doubtful jurisdiction

5–24 **24.**—(1) Any power of a court in England and Wales or Northern Ireland to grant interim relief pending trial or pending the determination of an appeal shall extend to a case where—

(a) the issue to be tried, or which is the subject of the appeal, relates to the jurisdiction of the court to entertain the proceedings;

(b) the proceedings involve the reference of any matter to the European Court under the 1971 Protocol or

(c) the proceedings involve a reference of any matter relat-

*Paragraph numbers marked with a "+" can be found online and on CD.*

ing to the Regulation or the Lugano Convention to the European Court under Article 68 of the Treaty establishing the European Community.

(2) [*Applies to Scotland*]

(3) Subsections (1) and (2) shall not be construed as restricting any power to grant interim relief or protective measures which a court may have apart from this section.

*Note* —Subsection (1)(c) was added by the Civil Jurisdiction and Judgments Order 2001 (SI 2001/3929) Sch.2, para.9(b); amended by the Civil Jurisdiction and Judgments Regulations 2009 (SI 2009/3131) reg.16 (subject to savings contained in reg.48), with effect from January 1, 2010. **5–25**

**"The issue to be tried ... relates to the jurisdiction of the court"**

For example, where the issue is whether the court, or a court in a Contracting State, has jurisdiction under the Brussels Convention. See also art.24 of the Brussels Convention. **5–26**

## Interim relief in England and Wales and Northern Ireland in the absence of substantive proceedings

**25.**—(1) The High Court in England and Wales or Northern Ireland shall have power to grant interim relief where— **5–27**

(a) proceedings have been or are to be commenced in a Brussels Contracting State or a State bound by the Lugano Convention or a Regulation State other than the United Kingdom or in a part of the United Kingdom other than that in which the High Court in question exercises jurisdiction; and

(b) they are or will be proceedings whose subject-matter is either within the scope of the Regulation as determined by Article 1 of the Regulation or within the scope of the Lugano Convention as determined by Article 1 of the Lugano Convention (whether or not the Regulation or the Lugano Convention has effect in relation to the proceedings).

(2) On an application for any interim relief under subsection (1) the court may refuse to grant that relief if, in the opinion of the court, the fact that the court has no jurisdiction apart from this section in relation to the subject- matter of the proceedings in question makes it inexpedient for the court to grant it.

(3) Her Majesty may by Order in Council extend the power to grant interim relief conferred by subsection (1) so as to make it exercisable in relation to proceedings of any of the following descriptions, namely—

(a) proceedings commenced or to be commenced otherwise than in a Brussels or a State bound by the Lugano Convention or Regulation State;

(b) proceedings whose subject-matter is not within the scope either of the Regulation as determined by Article 1 of the Regulation or the Lugano Convention as determined by Article 1 of the Lugano Convention.

(c) [...]

(4) An Order in Council under subsection (3)—

(a) may confer power to grant only specified descriptions of interim relief;

(b) may make different provision for different classes of proceedings, for proceedings pending in different countries or courts outside the United Kingdom or in different parts of the United Kingdom, and for other different circumstances; and

(c) may impose conditions or restrictions on the exercise of any power conferred by the order.

(5) [...]

(6) Any Order in Council under subsection (3) shall be subject to annulment in pursuance of a resolution of either House of Parliament.

(7) In this section "interim relief", in relation to the High Court in England and Wales or Northern Ireland, means interim relief of any kind which that court has power to grant in proceedings relating to matters within its jurisdiction, other than—

(a) a warrant for the arrest of property; or

(b) provision for obtaining evidence.

**5–28** *Note* — Subsections (1)(a) and (3)(a) amended by the Civil Jurisdiction and Judgments Act 1991 s.3, Sch.2, para.12(a); subs.(1)(b) amended by para.12. Subss.(3)(c) and (5) repealed by the Arbitration Act 1996. The power to grant interim relief under subs.(1) has been extended by the Civil Jurisdiction and Judgments Act 1982 (Interim Relief) Order 1997 (see para.5–161 below). Subsections (1)(a), (b) and (3)(b) were further amended and by the Civil Jurisdiction and Judgments Order (SI 2001/3929), Sch.2, para.10(b)(ii). Subsections (1)(a) and (3)(a) amended by, and subss.(1)(b) and (3)(b) substituted by the Civil Jurisdiction and Judgments Regulations 2009 (SI 2009/3131) reg.17 (subject to savings contained in reg.48), with effect from January 1, 2010.

## Security in Admiralty proceedings in England and Wales or Northern Ireland in case of stay, etc.

**5–29** **26.**—(1) Where in England and Wales or Northern Ireland a court stays or dismisses Admiralty proceedings on the ground that the dispute in question should be submitted to the determination of the courts of another part of the United Kingdom or of an overseas country, the court may, if in those proceedings property has been arrested or bail or other security has been given to prevent or obtain release from arrest—

(a) order that the property arrested be retained as security for the satisfaction of any award or judgment which—

(i) is given in respect of the dispute in the legal proceedings in favour of which those proceedings are stayed or dismissed; and

(ii) is enforceable in England and Wales or, as the case may be, in Northern Ireland, or

(b) order that the stay or dismissal of those proceedings be conditional on the provision of equivalent security for the satisfaction of any such award or judgment.

***Paragraph numbers marked with a "+" can be found online and on CD.***

(2) Where the court makes an order under subsection (1), it may attach such conditions to the order as it thinks fit, in particular conditions with respect to the institution or prosecution of the relevant legal proceedings.

(3) Subject to any provision made by rules of court and to any necessary modifications, the same law and practice shall apply in relation to property retained in pursuance of an order made by a court under subsection (1) as would apply if it were held for the purposes of proceedings in that court.

*Note* —Amended by the Arbitration Act 1996. **5–30**

* * * *

## DOMICILE

### Proceedings in England and Wales or Northern Ireland for torts to immovable property

**30.**—(1) The jurisdiction of any court in England and Wales or Northern Ireland to entertain proceedings for trespass to, or any other tort affecting, immovable property shall extend to cases in which the property in question is situated outside that part of the United Kingdom unless the proceedings are principally concerned with a question of the title, or the right to possession of, that property. **5–31**

(2) Subsection (1) has effect subject to the 1968 Convention and the Lugano Convention and the Regulation and to the provisions set out in Schedule 4.

*Note* —Amended by the Civil Jurisdiction and Judgments Act 1991 s.3, Sch.2, para.13; and by the Civil Jurisdiction and Judgments Order (SI 2001/3929), Sch.2, para.13. **5–32**

* * * *

## PART V

## SUPPLEMENTARY AND GENERAL PROVISIONS

*Note* —Under the Brussels Convention, domicile rather than presence (or nationality), is the key to the allocation of jurisdiction among the courts of the Contracting States, see Arts 2 and 52, paras 5–50 and 5–122, below. Consequently, this Part of the Act, *inter alia*, enacts particular rules governing domicile. **5–33**

### Domicile of individuals

**41.**—(1) Subject to Article 52 (which contains provisions for determining whether a party is domiciled in a Contracting State), the following provisions of this section determine, for the purposes of the 1968 Convention and this Act, whether an individual is domiciled in the United Kingdom or in a particular part of, or place in, the United Kingdom or in a state other than a Contracting State. **5–34**

(2) An individual is domiciled in the United Kingdom if and only if—

(a) he is resident in the United Kingdom; and

(b) the nature and circumstances of his residence indicate that he has a substantial connection with the United Kingdom.

(3) Subject to subsection (5), an individual is domiciled in a particular part of the United Kingdom if and only if—

(a) he is resident in that part; and

(b) the nature and circumstances of his residence indicate that he has a substantial connection with that part.

(4) An individual is domiciled in a particular place in the United Kingdom if and only if he—

(a) is domiciled in the part of the United Kingdom in which that place is situated; and

(b) is resident in that place.

(5) An individual who is domiciled in the United Kingdom but in whose case the requirements of subsection (3)(b) are not satisfied in relation to any particular part of the United Kingdom shall be treated as domiciled in the part of the United Kingdom in which he is resident.

(6) In the case of an individual who—

(a) is resident in the United Kingdom, or in a particular part of the United Kingdom; and

(b) has been so resident for the last three months or more,

the requirements of subsection (2)(b) or, as the case may be, subsection (3)(b) shall be presumed to be fulfilled unless the contrary is proved.

(7) An individual is domiciled in a state other than a Contracting State if and only if—

(a) he is resident in that state; and

(b) the nature and circumstances of his residence indicate that he has a substantial connection with that state.

**5–35** *Note*—Subsection(1) amended by the Civil Jurisdiction and Judgments Act 1991 s.3 and Sch.2, para.16, and the Civil Jurisdiction and Judgments Regulations 2009 (SI 2009/3131) reg.18(1) (subject to savings contained in reg.48), with effect from January 1, 2010.

## Domicile of individuals for the purposes of the Lugano Convention

**5–35.1** **41A.**—(1) Subject to Article 59 of the Lugano Convention (which contains provisions for determining whether a party is domiciled in a State bound by the Lugano Convention), the following provisions of this section determine, for the purposes of the Lugano Convention, whether an individual is domiciled in the United Kingdom or in a particular part of, or place in, the United Kingdom or in a state other than a State bound by the Lugano Convention.

(2) An individual is domiciled in the United Kingdom if and only if—

(a) he is resident in the United Kingdom; and

(b) the nature and circumstances of his residence indicate that he has a substantial connection with the United Kingdom.

(3) Subject to subsection (5), an individual is domiciled in a particular part of the United Kingdom if and only if—

(a) he is resident in that part; and

(b) the nature and circumstances of his residence indicate that he has a substantial connection with that part.

(4) (4) An individual is domiciled in a particular place in the United Kingdom if and only if he—

(a) is domiciled in the part of the United Kingdom in which that place is situated; and

(b) is resident in that place.

(5) An individual who is domiciled in the United Kingdom but in whose case the requirements of subsection (3)(b) are not satisfied in relation to any particular part of the United Kingdom shall be treated as domiciled in the part of the United Kingdom in which he is resident.

(6) In the case of an individual who—

(a) is resident in the United Kingdom, or in a particular part of the United Kingdom; and

(b) has been so resident for the last three months or more,

the requirements of subsection (2)(b) or, as the case may be, subsection (3)(b) shall be presumed to be fulfilled unless the contrary is proved.

(7) An individual is domiciled in a state other than a State bound by the Lugano Convention if and only if—

(a) he is resident in that state; and

(b) the nature and circumstances of his residence indicate that he has a substantial connection with that state.

*Note* —Inserted by the Civil Jurisdiction and Judgments Regulations 2009 (SI 2009/ 3131) reg.18(2) (subject to savings contained in reg.48), with effect from January 1, 2010. **5–35.2**

## Domicile and seat of corporation or association

**42.**—(1) For the purposes of this Act the seat of a corporation or association (as determined by this section) shall be treated as its domicile. **5–36**

(2) The following provisions of this section determine where a corporation or association has its seat—

(a) for the purpose of Article 53 (which for the purposes of the 1968 Convention equates the domicile of such a body with its seat); and

(b) for the purposes of this Act other than the provisions mentioned in section 43(1)(b) and (c).

(3) A corporation or association has its seat in the United Kingdom if and only if—

(a) it was incorporated or formed under the law of a part of the United Kingdom and has its registered office or some other official address in the United Kingdom; or

(b) its central management and control is exercised in the United Kingdom.

(4) A corporation or association has its seat in a particular part of the United Kingdom if and only if it has its seat in the United Kingdom and—

(a) it has its registered office or some other official address in that part; or

(b) its central management and control is exercised in that part; or

(c) it has a place of business in that part.

(5) A corporation or association has its seat in a particular place in the United Kingdom if and only if it has its seat in the part of the United Kingdom in which that place is situated and—

(a) it has its registered office or some other official address in that place; or

(b) its central management and control is exercised in that place; or

(c) it has a place of business in that place.

(6) Subject to subsection (7), a corporation or association has its seat in a state other than the United Kingdom if and only if—

(a) it was incorporated or formed under the law of that state and has its registered office or some other official address there; or

(b) its central management and control is exercised in that state.

(7) A corporation or association shall not be regarded as having its seat in a Contracting State other than the United Kingdom if it is shown that the courts of that state would not regard it as having its seat there.

(8) In this section—

"business" includes any activity carried on by a corporation or association, and "place of business" shall be construed accordingly; "official address", in relation to a corporation or association, means an address which it is required by law to register, notify or maintain for the purpose of receiving notices or other communications.

5–37 *Note* — Subsection(2)(a) amended by the Civil Jurisdiction and Judgments Act 1991 s.3 and Sch.2, para.17; amended by the Civil Jurisdiction and Judgments Regulations 2009 (SI 2009/3131) reg.19 (subject to savings contained in reg.48), with effect from January 1, 2010.

### Seat of corporation or association for purposes of Article 16(2) and related provisions

5–38 **43.**—(1) The following provisions of this section determine where a corporation or association has its seat for the purposes of—

(a) Article 16(2) of the 1968 Convention (which confers

exclusive jurisdiction over proceedings relating to the formation or dissolution of such bodies, or to the decisions of their organs);

(b) Articles 5A and 16(2); in Schedule 4 and

(c) and Rules 2(12), 4(1)(b) in Schedule 8.

(2) A corporation or association has its seat in the United Kingdom if and only if—

(a) it was incorporated or formed under the law of a part of the United Kingdom; or

(b) its central management and control is exercised in the United Kingdom.

(3) A corporation or association has its seat in a particular part of the United Kingdom if and only if it has its seat in the United Kingdom and—

(a) subject to subsection (5), it was incorporated or formed under the law of that part; or

(b) being incorporated or formed under the law of a state other than the United Kingdom, its central management and control is exercised in that part.

(4) A corporation or association has its seat in a particular place in Scotland if and only if it has its seat in Scotland and—

(a) it has its registered office or some other official address in that place; or

(b) it has no registered office or other official address in Scotland, but its central management and control is exercised in that place.

(5) A corporation or association incorporated or formed under—

(a) an enactment forming part of the law of more than one part of the United Kingdom; or

(b) an instrument having effect in the domestic law of more than one part of the United Kingdom,

shall, if it has a registered office, be taken to have its seat in the part of the United Kingdom in which that office is situated, and not in any other part of the United Kingdom.

(6) Subject to subsection (7), a corporation or association has its seat in a Contracting State other than the United Kingdom if and only if—

(a) it was incorporated or formed under the law of that state; or

(b) its central management and control is exercised in that state.

(7) A corporation or association shall not be regarded as having its seat in a Contracting State other than the United Kingdom if—

(a) it has its seat in the United Kingdom by virtue of subsection 2(a); or

(b) it is shown that the courts of that other state would not regard it for the purposes of Article 16(2) as having its seat there.

***Paragraph numbers marked with a "+" can be found online and on CD.***

(8) In this section "official address" has the same meaning as in section 42.

5–39 *Note*—Subsection(1)(a) amended by the Civil Jurisdiction and Judgments Act 1991 s.3 and Sch.2, para.18; amended by the Civil Jurisdiction and Judgments Regulations 2009 (SI 2009/3131) reg.20(1) (subject to savings contained in reg.48), with effect from January 1, 2010.

## Seat of companies or other legal persons, or of associations, for the purposes of Article 22(2) of the Lugano Convention

5–39.1 **43A.**—(1) The following provisions of this section determine where a company, or other legal person or an association of natural or legal persons, has its seat for the purposes of Article 22(2) of the Lugano Convention (which confers exclusive jurisdiction over proceedings relating to the validity of the constitution, the nullity or the dissolution of such bodies, or to the validity of the decisions of their organs).

(2) A company, legal person or association has its seat in the United Kingdom if and only if—

(a) it was incorporated or formed under the law of a part of the United Kingdom; or

(b) its central management and control is exercised in the United Kingdom.

(3) Subject to subsection (4), a company, legal person or association has its seat in a State bound by the Lugano Convention other than the United Kingdom if and only if—

(a) it was incorporated or formed under the law of that state; or

(b) its central management and control is exercised in that state.

(4) A company, legal person or association shall not be regarded as having its seat in a State bound by the Lugano Convention other than the United Kingdom if—

(a) it has its seat in the United Kingdom by virtue of subsection (2)(a); or

(b) it is shown that the courts of that other state would not regard it for the purposes of Article 22(2) as having its seat there.

5–39.2 *Note*—Inserted by the Civil Jurisdiction and Judgments Regulations 2009 (SI 2009/3131) reg.20(2) (subject to savings contained in reg.48), with effect from January 1, 2010.

## Persons deemed to be domiciled in the United Kingdom for certain purposes

5–40 **44.**—(1) This section applies to—

(a) proceedings within Section 3 of Title II of the 1968 Convention (insurance contracts), and

(b) proceedings within Section 4 of Title II of either of those Conventions (consumer contracts).

(2) A person who, for the purposes of proceedings to which this section applies arising out of the operations of a branch, agency or

*Paragraph numbers marked with a "+" can be found online and on CD.*

other establishment in the United Kingdom, is deemed for the purposes of the 1968 Convention to be domiciled in the United Kingdom by virtue of—

(a) Article 8, second paragraph (insurers); or

(b) Article 13, second paragraph (suppliers of goods, services or credit to consumers),

shall, for the purposes of those proceedings, be treated for the purposes of this Act as so domiciled and as domiciled in the part of the United Kingdom in which the branch, agency or establishment in question is situated.

*Note* — Subsection(1) amended by the Civil Jurisdiction and Judgments Act 1991 s.3 and Sch.2, para.19; amended by the Civil Jurisdiction and Judgments Regulations 2009 (SI 2009/3131) reg.21 (subject to savings contained in reg.48), with effect from January 1, 2010. **5–41**

## Persons deemed to be domiciled in the United Kingdom for certain purposes of the Lugano Convention

**44A.**—(1) This section applies to— **5–41.1**

(a) proceedings within Section 3 of Title II of the Lugano Convention (insurance contracts);

(b) proceedings within Section 4 of Title II of the Lugano Convention (consumer contracts); and

(c) proceedings within Section 5 of Title II of the Lugano Convention (employment contracts).

(2) A person who, for the purposes of proceedings to which this section applies arising out of the operations of a branch, agency or other establishment in the United Kingdom, is deemed for the purposes of the Lugano Convention to be domiciled in the United Kingdom by virtue of—

(a) Article 9(2) (insurers); or

(b) Article 15(2) (suppliers of goods, services or credit to consumers); or

(c) Article 18(2) (employers),

shall, for the purposes of those proceedings, be treated as so domiciled and as domiciled in the part of the United Kingdom in which the branch, agency or establishment in question is situated.

*Note* —Inserted by the Civil Jurisdiction and Judgments Regulations 2009 (SI 2009/3131) reg.22 (subject to savingscontained in reg.48), with effect from January 1, 2010. **5–41.2**

## Domicile of trusts

**45.**—(1) The following provisions of this section determine, for the purposes of the 1968 Convention the Lugano Convention and this Act, where a trust is domiciled. **5–42**

(2) A trust is domiciled in the United Kingdom if and only if it is by virtue of subsection (3) domiciled in a part of the United Kingdom.

(3) A trust is domiciled in a part of the United Kingdom if and only if the system of law of that part is the system of law with which the trust has its closest and most real connection.

5–43 *Note* — Subsection (1) amended by the Civil Jurisdiction and Judgments Act 1991 s.3 and Sch.2, para.20.

### Domicile and seat of the Crown

5–44 **46.**—(1) For the purposes of this Act the seat of the Crown (as determined by this section) shall be treated as its domicile.

(2) The following provisions of this section determine where the Crown has its seat—

(a) for the purposes of the 1968 Convention (in which Article 53 equates the domicile of a legal person with its seat); and

(b) for the purposes of this Act.

(3) Subject to the provisions of any Order in Council for the time being in force under subsection (4)—

(a) the Crown in right of Her Majesty's government in the United Kingdom has its seat in every part of, and every place in, the United Kingdom; and

(aa) the Crown in right of the Scottish Administration has its seat in, and in every place in, Scotland; and

(b) the Crown in right of Her Majesty's government in Northern Ireland has its seat in, and in every place in, Northern Ireland.

(4) Her Majesty may by Order in Council provide that, in the case of proceedings of any specified description against the Crown in right of Her Majesty's government in the United Kingdom, the Crown shall be treated for the purposes of the 1968 Convention and this Act as having its seat in, and in every place in, a specified part of the United Kingdom and not in any other part of the United Kingdom.

(5) An Order in Council under subsection (4) may frame a description proceedings in any way, and in particular may do so by reference to the government department or officer of the Crown against which or against whom they fall to be instituted.

(6) Any Order in Council made under this section shall be subject to annulment in pursuance of a resolution of either House of Parliament.

(7) Nothing in this section applies to the Crown otherwise than in right of Her Majesty's government in the United Kingdom, the Scottish Administration or Her Majesty's government in Northern Ireland.

5–45 *Note* — Subsections (2)(a) & (4) amended by the Civil Jurisdiction and Judgments Act 1991 s.3 and Sch.2, para.21. Subsections (3) and (7) are amended by the Scotland Act 1998 (c.46) s.125 and Sch.8, para.18; amended by the Civil Jurisdiction and Judgments Regulations 2009 (SI 2009/3131) reg.23 (subject to savings contained in reg.48), with effect from January 1, 2010.

* * *

### Saving for powers to stay, sist, strike out or dismiss proceedings

5–46 **49.** Nothing in this Act shall prevent any court in the United

*Paragraph numbers marked with a "+" can be found online and on CD.*

Kingdom from staying, sisting, striking out or dismissing any proceedings before it, on the ground of forum non conveniens or otherwise, where to do so is not inconsistent with the 1968 Convention or, as the case may be, the Lugano Convention.

*Note* —Amended by the Civil Jurisdiction and Judgments Act 1991 s.3, Sch.2, para.24. **5–47**

**"Staying ... any proceedings"**

This section should be read in conjunction with the Senior Courts Act 1981 s.49(3), see paras 9A–168, 9A–176, 9A–177. **5–48**

* * * *

# SCHEDULES

**SECTION 2(2)(A)**

## SCHEDULE 1

### TEXT OF 1968 CONVENTION, AS AMENDED

*Note* —The text set out below is the version of the 1968 Convention as inserted in Sched.1 to the 1982 Act by the Civil Jurisdiction and Judgments Act 1982 (Amendment) Order 1990 (SI 1990/2591), art.12(1), Sch.1, following upon the accession to the European Community of Spain and Portugal. For the earlier version of the Convention inserted following the accession of Greece, see the Civil Jurisdiction and Judgments Act 1982 (Amendment) Order 1989 (SI 1989/1346), art.9(1), Sch.1. Section 3(3) of the 1982 Act, as amended, states that: **5–49**

> "the reports by Mr. P. Jenard on the 1968 Convention and the 1971 Protocol; and the reports by Professor Peter Schlosser, Professor Demetrios I. Evrigenis, Professor K.D. Kerameus, Mr. Martinho de Almedia Cruz, Mr. Manuel Desantes Real and Mr. P. Jenard on the various Accession Conventions between 1978 and 1989,"

may be considered in ascertaining the meaning or effect of any provision in the Convention and "shall be given such weight as is appropriate in the circumstances". These reports were published in the Official Journal of the European Communities. For a basic commentary on the text of Titles I and II see notes to RSC O.11 in SCP 1999, Vol.1 and particularly notes at Vol.1, paras 11/1/48 to 11/1/74. For a basic commentary on the text of Title III see notes to RSC O.71, rr.25–39 in SCP 1999, Vol.1. For more detailed analysis of the Convention see the leading textbooks, *e.g.* Dicey & Morris, *Conflict of Laws* (12th ed.), and Briggs & Rees, *Civil Jurisdiction and Judgments* (2nd ed.).

For commentary on the text of Title II see notes to O.11 in SCP 1999, Vol.1 and particularly notes at Vol.1, paras 11/4/48 to 11/1/74. For commentary on the text of Title III see notes to O.71 rr.25–39 in SCP 1999, Vol.1.

* * * *

### TITLE I

### SCOPE

*Article 1*

This Convention shall apply in civil and commercial matters whatever the nature of the court or tribunal. It shall not extend, in particular, to revenue, customs or administrative matters. **5–50**

The Convention shall not apply to—

1. The status or legal capacity of natural persons, rights in property arising out of a matrimonial relationship, wills and succession.

2. Bankruptcy, proceedings relating to the winding-up of insolvent companies or other legal persons, judicial arrangements, compositions and analogous proceedings.

***Paragraph numbers marked with a "+" can be found online and on CD.***

3. Social security.
4. Arbitration.

## TITLE II

## JURISDICTION

## SECTION 1

## GENERAL PROVISIONS

*Article 2*

5–51 Subject to the provisions of this Convention, persons domiciled in a Contracting State shall, whatever their nationality, be sued in the courts of that State.

Persons who are not nationals of the State in which they are domiciled shall be governed by the rules of jurisdiction applicable to nationals of that State.

**"Persons domiciled in a Contracting State"**

5–52 See ss.41–46 of the 1982 Act, paras 5–33 to 5–43, above.

*Article 3*

5–53 Persons domiciled in a Contracting State may be sued in the courts of another Contracting State only by virtue of the rules set out in Sections 2 to 6 of this Title.

In particular the following provisions shall not be applicable as against them—

. . .

—in the United Kingdom: the rules which enable jurisdiction to be founded on:

(a) the document instituting the proceedings having been served on the defendant during his temporary presence in the United Kingdom; or

(b) the presence within the United Kingdom of property belonging to the defendant; or

(c) the seizure by the plaintiff of property situated in the United Kingdom.

*Article 4*

5–54 If the defendant is not domiciled in a Contracting State, the jurisdiction of the courts of each Contracting State shall, subject to the provisions of Article 16, be determined by the law of that State.

As against such a defendant, any person domiciled in a Contracting State may, whatever his nationality, avail himself in that State of the rules of jurisdiction there in force, and in particular those specified in the second paragraph of Article 3, in the same way as the nationals of that State.

## SECTION 2

## SPECIAL JURISDICTION

*Article 5*

5–55 A person domiciled in a Contracting State may, in another Contracting State, be sued—

1. In matters relating to a contract, in the courts for the place of performance of the obligation in question; in matters relating to individual contracts of employment, this place is that where the employee habitually carries out his work, or if the employee does not habitually carry out his work in any one country, the employer may also be sued in the courts for the place where the business which engaged the employee was or is now situated.

2. In matters relating to maintainance, in the courts for the place where the maintenance creditor is domiciled or habitually resident or, if the matter is ancillary to proceedings concerning the status of a person, in the court which, according to its own

law, has jurisdiction to entertain those proceedings, unless that jurisdiction is based solely on the nationality of one of the parties.

3. In matters relating to tort, delict or quasi-delict, in the courts for the place where the harmful event occurred.

4. As regards a civil claim for damages or restitution which is based on an act giving rise to criminal proceedings, in the court seised of those proceedings, to the extent that that court has jurisdiction under its own law to entertain civil proceedings.

5. As regards a dispute arising out of the operations of a branch, agency or other establishment, in the courts for the place in which the branch, agency or other establishment is situated.

6. As settlor, trustee or beneficiary of a trust created by the operation of a statute, or by a written instrument, or created orally and evidenced in writing, in the courts of the Contracting State in which the trust is domiciled.

7. As regards a dispute concerning the payment of remuneration claimed in respect of the salvage of a cargo or freight, in the court under the authority of which the cargo or freight in question—

(a) has been arrested to secure such payment, or

(b) could have been so arrested, but bail or other security has been given;

provided that this provision shall apply only if it is claimed that the defendant has an interest in the cargo or freight or had such an interest at the time of salvage.

**"In matters relating to individual contracts of employment"**

In Point 1 these words and the text following were added by Civil Jurisdiction and Judgments Act 1982 (Amendment) Order 1990 at the time of the revision of the 1968 Convention upon the accession of Spain and Portugal. The opportunity was taken to make this modification in the light of experience. **5–56**

The corresponding Point in art.5.1 of the Lugano Convention reads:

"A person domiciled in a Contracting State may, in another Contracting State, be sued:

1. In matters relating to a contract, in the courts for the place of performance of the obligation in question; in matters relating to individual contracts of employments, this place is that where the employee habitually carries out his work, or if the employee does not habitually carry out his work in any one country, this place shall be the place of business through which he was engaged;".

*Article 6*

A person domiciled in a Contracting State may also be sued— **5–57**

1. Where he is one of a number of defendants, in the courts for the place where any one of them is domiciled.

2. As a third party in an action on a warranty or guarantee or in any other third party proceedings, in the court seised of the original proceedings, unless these were instituted solely with the object of removing him from the jurisdiction of the court which would be competent in his case.

3. On a counter-claim arising from the same contract or facts on which the original claim was based, in the court in which the original claim is pending.

4. In matters relating to a contract, if the action may be combined with an action against the same defendant in matters relating to rights in rem in immovable property, in the court of the Contracting State in which the property is situated.

**"In matters relating to a contract"**

Point 4 of this Article was added by Civil Jurisdiction and Judgments Act 1982 (Amendment) Order 1990 at the time of the revision of the 1968 Convention upon the accession of Spain and Portugal. The opportunity was taken to make this modification in the light of experience. **5–58**

*Article 6a*

5–59 Where by virtue of this Convention a court of a Contracting State has jurisdiction in actions relating to liability from the use or operation of a ship, that court, or any other court substituted for this purpose by the internal law of that State, shall also have jurisdiction over claims for limitation of such liability.

**"Relating to liability from"**

5–60 The corresponding Article in the Lugano Convention reads "relating to liability arising from".

## SECTION 3

## JURISDICTION IN MATTERS RELATING TO INSURANCE

*Article 7*

5–61 In matters relating to insurance, jurisdiction shall be determined by this Section, without prejudice to the provisions of Articles 4 and 5 point 5.

*Article 8*

5–62 An insurer domiciled in a Contracting State may be sued—

1. in the courts of the State where he is domiciled, or

2. in another Contracting State, in the courts for the place where the policy-holder is domiciled, or

3. if he is a co-insurer, in the courts of a Contracting State in which proceedings are brought against the leading insurer.

An insurer who is not domiciled in a Contracting State but has a branch, agency or other establishment in one of the Contracting States shall, in disputes arising out of the operations of the branch, agency or establishment, be deemed to be domiciled in that State.

*Article 9*

5–63 In respect of liability insurance or insurance of immovable property, the insurer may in addition be sued in the courts for the place where the harmful event occurred. The same applies if movable and immovable property are covered by the same insurance policy and both are adversely affected by the same contingency.

*Article 10*

5–64 In respect of liability insurance, the insurer may also, if the law of the court permits it, be joined in proceedings which the injured party had brought against the insured.

The provisions of Articles 7, 8 and 9 shall apply to actions brought by the injured party directly against the insurer, where such direct actions are permitted.

If the law governing such direct actions provides that the policy-holder or the insured may be joined as a party to the action, the same court shall have jurisdiction over them.

**"Injured party had brought"**

5–65 The corresponding Article in the Lugano Convention reads "injured party has brought".

*Article 11*

5–66 Without prejudice to the provisions of the third paragraph of Article 10, an insurer may bring proceedings only in the courts of the Contracting State in which the defendant is domiciled, irrespective of whether he is the policy-holder, the insured or a beneficiary.

The provisions of this Section shall not affect the right to bring a counterclaim in the court in which, in accordance with this Section, the original claim is pending.

*Article 12*

5–67 The provisions of this Section may be departed from only by an agreement on jurisdiction—

***Paragraph numbers marked with a "+" can be found online and on CD.***

1. which is entered into after the dispute has arisen, or

2. which allows the policy-holder, the insured or a beneficiary to bring proceedings in courts other than those indicated in this Section, or

3. which is concluded between a policy-holder and an insurer, both of whom are domiciled in the same Contracting State, and which has the effect of conferring jurisdiction on the courts of that State even if the harmful event were to occur abroad, provided that such an agreement is not contrary to the law of that State, or

4. which is concluded with a policy-holder who is not domiciled in a Contracting State, except in so far as the insurance is compulsory or relates to immovable property in a Contracting State, or

5. which relates to a contract of insurance in so far as it covers one or more of the risks set out in Article 12a.

**"Whom are domiciled in the same Contracting State"**

*Cf.*, art.15(3). The corresponding Article in the Lugano Convention (and in some earlier versions of the Brussels Convention) reads "whom are at the time of conclusion of the contract domiciled or habitually resident in the same Contracting State". **5–68**

*Article 12a*

The following are the risks referred to in point 5 of Article 12— **5–69**

1. Any loss of or damage to—

(a) sea-going ships, installations situated offshore or on the high seas, or aircraft, arising from perils which relate to their use for commercial purposes;

(b) goods in transit other than passengers' baggage where the transit consists of or includes carriage by such ships or aircraft.

2. Any liability, other than for bodily injury to passengers or loss of or damage to their baggage—

(a) arising out of the use or operation of ships, installations or aircraft as referred to in point 1(a) above in so far as the law of the Contracting State in which such aircraft are registered does not prohibit agreements on jurisdiction regarding insurance of such risks;

(b) for loss or damage caused by goods in transit as described in point 1(b) above.

3. Any financial loss connected with the use or operation of ships, installations or aircraft as referred to in point 1(a) above, in particular loss of freight or charter-hire.

4. Any risk or interest connected with any of those referred to in points 1 to 3 above.

## SECTION 4

## JURISDICTION OVER CONSUMER CONTRACTS

*Article 13*

In proceedings concerning a contract concluded by a person for a purpose which can be regarded as being outside his trade or profession, hereinafter called "the consumer", jurisdiction shall be determined by this Section, without prejudice to the provisions of Article 4 and point 5 of Article 5, if it is— **5–70**

1. a contract for the sale of goods on instalment credit terms, or

2. a contract for a loan repayable by instalments, or for any other form of credit, made to finance the sale of goods, or

3. any other contract for the supply of goods or a contract for the supply of services, and

(a) in the State of the consumer's domicile the conclusion of the contract was preceded by a specific invitation addressed to him or by advertising; and

(b) the consumer took in that State the steps necessary for the conclusion of the contract.

Where a consumer enters into a contract with a party who is not domiciled in a Contracting State but has a branch, agency or other establishment in one of the Contracting States, that party shall, in disputes arising out of the operations of the branch, agency or establishment, be deemed to be domiciled in that State.

***Paragraph numbers marked with a "+" can be found online and on CD.***

This Section shall not apply to contracts of transport.

*Article 14*

5–71 A consumer may bring proceedings against the other party to a contract either in the courts of the Contracting State in which that party is domiciled or in the courts of the Contracting State in which he is himself domiciled.

Proceedings may be brought against a consumer by the other party to the contract only in the courts of the Contracting State in which the consumer is domiciled.

These provisions shall not affect the right to bring a counter-claim in the court in which, in accordance with this Section, the original claim is pending.

*Article 15*

5–72 The provisions of this Section may be departed from only by an agreement—

1. which is entered into after the dispute has arisen, or

2. which allows the consumer to bring proceedings in courts other than those indicated in this Section, or

3. which is entered into by the consumer and the other party to the contract, both of whom are at the time of conclusion of the contract domiciled or habitually resident in the same Contracting State, and which confers jurisdiction on the courts of that State, provided that such an agreement is not contrary to the law of that State.

## SECTION 5

## EXCLUSIVE JURISDICTION

*Article 16*

5–73 The following courts shall have exclusive jurisdiction, regardless of domicile:

(a) in proceedings which have as their object rights *in rem* in immovable property or tenancies of immovable property, the courts of the Contracting State in which the property is situated;

(b) however, in proceedings which have as their object tenancies of immovable property concluded for temporary private use for a maximum period of six consecutive months, the courts of the Contracting State in which the defendant is domiciled shall also have jurisdiction, provided that the landlord and the defendant are natural persons and are domiciled in the same Contracting State.

2. In proceedings which have as their object the validity of the constitution, the nullity or the dissolution of companies or other legal persons or associations of natural or legal persons, or the decisions of their organs, the courts of the Contracting State in which the company, legal person or association has its seat.

3. In proceedings which have as their object the validity of entries in public registers, the courts of the Contracting State in which the register is kept.

4. In proceedings concerned with the registration or validity of patents, trade marks, designs, or other similar rights required to be deposited or registered, the courts of the Contracting State in which the deposit or registration has been applied for, has taken place or is under the terms of an international convention deemed to have taken place.

5. In proceedings concerned with the enforcement of judgments, the courts of the Contracting State in which the judgment has been or is to be enforced.

**"Tenancies of immovable property"**

5–74 Alterations to the circumstances in which concurrent jurisdiction would be enjoyed by the courts of Contracting States were made by Civil Jurisdiction and Judgments Act 1982 (Amendment) Order 1990 at the time of the revision of the 1968 Convention upon the accession of Spain and Portugal. The opportunity was taken to make this modification in the light of experience.

Article 6.1(b) in the Lugano Convention reads:

"however, in proceedings which have as their object tenancies of immovable property concluded for temporary private use for a maximum period of six consecutive months, the courts of the Contracting State in which the defendant is domiciled shall also have jurisdiction, provided that the tenant is a natural person and neither party is domiciled in the Contracting State in which the property is situated;".

## SECTION 6

### PROROGATION OF JURISDICTION

*Article 17*

If the parties, one or more of whom is domiciled in a Contracting State, have agreed that a court or the courts of a Contracting State are to have jurisdiction to settle any disputes which have arisen or which may arise in connection with a particular legal relationship, that court or those courts shall have exclusive jurisdiction. Such an agreement conferring jurisdiction shall be either— **5–75**

(a) in writing or evidenced in writing, or

(b) in a form which accords with practices which the parties have established between themselves, or

(c) in international trade or commerce, in a form which accords with a usage of which the parties are or ought to have been aware and which in such trade or commerce is widely known to, and regularly observed by, parties to contracts of the type involved in the particular trade or commerce concerned.

Where such an agreement is concluded by parties, none of whom is domiciled in a Contracting State, the courts of other Contracting States shall have no jurisdiction over their disputes unless the court or courts chosen have declined jurisdiction.

The court or courts of a Contracting State on which a trust instrument has conferred jurisdiction shall have exclusive jurisdiction in any proceedings brought against a settlor, trustee or beneficiary, if relations between these persons or their rights or obligations under the trust are involved.

Agreements or provisions of a trust instrument conferring jurisdiction shall have no legal force if they are contrary to the provisions of Articles 12 or 15, or if the courts whose jurisdiction they purport to exclude have exclusive jurisdiction by virtue of Article 16.

If an agreement conferring jurisdiction was concluded for the benefit of only one of the parties, that party shall retain the right to bring proceedings in any other court which has jurisdiction by virtue of this Convention.

In matters relating to individual contracts of employment an agreement conferring jurisdiction shall have legal force only if it is entered into after the dispute has arisen or if the employee invokes it to seise courts other than those for the defendant's domicile or those specified in article 5(1).

*Note*—The first paragraph of this Article was substantially amended by the Civil Jurisdiction and Judgments Act 1982 (Amendment) Order 1990 at the time of the revision of the 1968 Convention upon the accession of Spain and Portugal. The opportunity was taken to make this modification in the light of experience. O.10, r.3 (service of writ in pursuance of contract) provides that where a contract contains an agreement conferring jurisdiction to which the 1982 Act applies and the writ is served under O.11, r.1(2) the writ shall be deemed to have been duly served on the defendant. **5–76**

**"Individual contracts of employment"**

In the Lugano Convention the points within art.17 are numbered and the final point, numbered 5, reads as follows: "In matters relating to individual contracts of employment an agreement conferring jurisdiction shall have legal force only if it is entered into after the dispute has arisen." **5–77**

*Article 18*

Apart from jurisdiction derived from other provisions of this Convention, a court of a Contracting State before whom a defendant enters an appearance shall have jurisdiction. This rule shall not apply where appearance was entered solely to contest the jurisdiction, or where another court has exclusive jurisdiction by virtue of Article 16. **5–78**

***Paragraph numbers marked with a "+" can be found online and on CD.***

**"Enters an appearance"**

5–79 For relationship between "appearance" and "acknowledgement of service" as provided for in O.12, see Vol.1, para.12.0.1.

## SECTION 7

## EXAMINATION AS TO JURISDICTION AND ADMISSIBILITY

*Article 19*

5–80 Where a court of a Contracting State is seised of a claim which is principally concerned with a matter over which the courts of another Contracting State have exclusive jurisdiction by virtue of Article 16, it shall declare of its own motion that it has no jurisdiction.

*Article 20*

5–81 Where a defendant domiciled in one Contracting State is sued in a court of another Contracting State and does not enter an appearance, the court shall declare of its own motion that it has no jurisdiction unless its jurisdiction is derived from the provisions of the Convention.

The court shall stay the proceedings so long as it is not shown that the defendant has been able to receive the document instituting the proceedings or an equivalent document in sufficient time to enable him to arrange for his defence, or that all necessary steps have been taken to this end.

The provisions of the foregoing paragraph shall be replaced by those of Article 15 of the Hague Convention of 15th November 1965 on the service abroad of judicial and extrajudicial documents in civil or commercial matters, if the document instituting the proceedings or notice thereof had to be transmitted abroad in accordance with that Convention.

**"Provisions of the Convention"**

5–82 Would seem to mean "this" Convention, i.e. the Brussels Convention.

## SECTION 8

## LIS PENDENS—RELATED ACTIONS

*Article 21*

5–83 Where proceedings involving the same cause of action and between the same parties are brought in the courts of different Contracting States, any court other than the court first seised shall of its own motion stay its proceedings until such time as the jurisdiction of the court first seised is established.

Where the jurisdiction of the court first seised is established, any court other than the court first seised shall decline jurisdiction in favour of that court.

**"Stay its proceedings"**

5–84 This phrase and the words following it in the first paragraph of this Article were substituted for the words "decline jurisdiction in favour of that court". The substitution was made by the Civil Jurisdiction and Judgments Act 1982 (Amendment) Order 1990 at the time of the revision of the 1968 Convention upon the accession of Spain and Portugal. The opportunity was taken to make this modification in the light of experience.

*Article 22*

5–85 Where related actions are brought in the courts of different Contracting States, any court other than the court first seised may, while the actions are pending at first instance, stay its proceedings.

A court other than the court first seised may also, on the application of one of the parties, decline jurisdiction if the law of that court permits the consolidation of related actions and the court first seised has jurisdiction over both actions.

***Paragraph numbers marked with a "+" can be found online and on CD.***

For the purposes of this Article, actions are deemed to be related where they are so closely connected that it is expedient to hear and determine them together to avoid the risk of irreconcilable judgments resulting from separate proceedings.

*Article 23*

Where actions come within the exclusive jurisdiction of several courts, any court other than the court first seised shall decline jurisdiction in favour of that court. **5–86**

## SECTION 9

## PROVISIONAL, INCLUDING PROTECTIVE, MEASURES

*Article 24*

Application may be made to the courts of a Contracting State for such provisional, including protective, measures as may be available under the law of that State, even if, under this Convention, the courts of another Contracting State have jurisdiction as to the substance of the matter. **5–87**

* * * *

## TITLE III

## RECOGNITION AND ENFORCEMENT

*Article 25*

For the purposes of this Convention "judgment" means any judgment given by a court or tribunal of a Contracting State, whatever the judgment may be called, including a decree, order, decision or writ of execution, as well as the determination of costs or expenses by an officer of the court. **5–88**

## SECTION 1

## RECOGNITION

*Article 26*

A judgment given in a Contracting State shall be recognised in the other Contracting States without any special procedure being required. **5–89**

Any interested party who raises the recognition of a judgment as the principal issue in a dispute may, in accordance with the procedures provided for in Sections 2 and 3 of this Title apply for a decision that the judgment be recognised.

If the outcome of proceedings in a court of a Contracting State depends on the determination of an incidental question of recognition that court shall have jurisdiction over that question.

*Article 27*

A judgment shall not be recognised: **5–90**

1. if such recognition is contrary to public policy in the State in which recognition is sought;

2. where it was given in default of appearance, if the defendant was not duly served with the document which instituted the proceedings or with an equivalent document in sufficient time to enable him to arrange for his defence;

3. if the judgment is irreconcilable with a judgment given in a dispute between the same parties in the State in which recognition is sought;

4. if the court of the State of origin, in order to arrive at its judgment, has decided a preliminary question concerning the status or legal capacity of natural persons, rights in property arising out of a matrimonial relationship, wills or succession in a way that conflicts with a rule of the private international law of the State in which the recognition is sought, unless the same result would have been reached by the application of the rules of private international law of that State;

5. if the judgment is irreconcilable with an earlier judgment given in a non-contracting State involving the same cause of action and between the same parties, provided that this latter judgment fulfils the conditions necessary for its recognition in the state addressed.

*Article 28*

5–91 Moreover, a judgment shall not be recognised if it conflicts with the provisions of Sections 3, 4 or 5 of Title II, or in a case provided for in Article 59.

In its examination of the grounds if jurisdiction referred to in the foregoing paragraph, the court or authority applied to shall be bound by the findings of fact on which the court of the State of origin based its jurisdiction.

Subject to the provisions of the first paragraph, the jurisdiction of the court of the State of origin may not be reviewed; the test of public policy referred to in point 1 of Article 27 may not be applied to the rules relating to jurisdiction.

**Lugano Convention**

5–92 An additional paragraph has been inserted between paras 2 and 3 of this Article:

A judgment may furthermore be refused recognition in any case provided for in Article 54B(3) or 57(4).

**Application**

5–93 The mischief at which this Article is directed is the recognition and enforcement of a judgment of a court which did not have jurisdiction under Section 3, 4 or 5 of Title II to the Convention. It is not concerned with whether the foreign court had jurisdiction on an issue which would subsequently have fallen to be decided by the court of another Contracting State (*Berkeley Administration Inc. v McClelland (No.2)* [1995] I.L.Pr. 201).

*Article 29*

5–94 Under no circumstances may a foreign judgment be reviewed as to its substance.

*Article 30*

5–95 A court of a Contracting State in which recognition is sought of a judgment given in another Contracting State may stay the proceedings if an ordinary appeal against the judgment has been lodged.

A court of a Contracting State in which recognition is sought of a judgment given in Ireland or the United Kingdom may stay the proceedings if enforcement is suspended in the State of origin, by reason of an appeal.

## SECTION 2

## ENFORCEMENT

*Article 31*

5–96 A judgment given in a Contracting State and enforceable in that State shall be enforced in another Contracting State when, on the application of any interested party, it has been declared enforceable there.

However, in the United Kingdom, such a judgment shall be enforced in England and Wales, in Scotland, or in Northern Ireland when, on the application of any interested party, it has been registered for enforcement in that part of the United Kingdom.

*Article 32*

5–97 1. The application shall be submitted:

— in Belgium, to the tribunal de première instance or rechtbank van eerste aanleg,

— in Denmark, to the byret,

— in the Federal Republic of Germany, to the presiding judge of a chamber of the Landgericht,

***Paragraph numbers marked with a "+" can be found online and on CD.***

— in Greece, to the Μονομελεζ Πισωτοδιχειο,
— in Spain, to the Juzgado de Primera Instancia,
— in France, to the presiding judge of the tribunal de grande instance,
— in Ireland, to the High Court,
— in Italy, to the corte d'appello,
— in Luxembourg, to the presiding judge of the tribunal d'arrondissement,
— in the Netherlands, to the presiding judge of the arrondissementsrechtbank,
— in Portugal, to the Tribunal Judicial de Circulo,
— in the United Kingdom:

1. in England and Wales, to the High Court of Justice, or in the case of maintenance judgment to the Magistrates' Court on transmission by the Secretary of State;
2. in Scotland, to the Court of Session, or in the case of a maintenance judgment to the Sheriff Court on transmission by the Secretary of State;
3. in Northern Ireland, to the High Court of Justice, or in the case of a maintenance judgment to the Magistrates' Court on transmission by the Secretary of State.

2. The jurisdiction of local courts shall be determined by reference to the place of domicile of the party against whom enforcement is sought. If he is not domiciled in the State in which enforcement is sought, it shall be determined by reference to the place of enforcement.

**Lugano Convention**

The list of courts to which the application is made is supplemented in the Lugano Convention with courts of the additional Contracting States. **5–98**

*Article 33*

The procedure for making the application shall be governed by the law of the State in which enforcement is sought. **5–99**

The applicant must give an address for service of process within the area of jurisdiction of the court applied to. However, if the law of the State in which enforcement is sought does not provide for the furnishing of such an address, the applicant shall appoint a representative *ad litem*.

The documents referred to in Articles 46 and 47 shall be attached to the application.

*Article 34*

The court applied to shall give its decision without delay; the party against whom enforcement is sought shall not at this stage of the proceedings be entitled to make any submissions on the application. **5–100**

The application may be refused only for one of the reasons specified in Articles 27 and 28.

Under no circumstances may the foreign judgment be reviewed as to its substance.

*Article 35*

The appropriate officer of the court shall without delay bring the decision given on the application to the notice of the applicant in accordance with the procedure laid down by the law of the State in which enforcement is sought. **5–101**

*Article 36*

If enforcement is authorised, the party against whom enforcement is sought may appeal against the decision within one month of service thereof. **5–102**

If that party is domiciled in a Contracting State other than that in which the decision authorising enforcement was given, the time for appealing shall be two months and shall run from the date of service, either on him in person or at his residence. No extension of time may be granted on account of distance.

*Article 37*

5–103 1. An appeal against the decision authorising enforcement shall be lodged in accordance with the rules governing procedure in contentious matters:

— in Belgium, with the tribunal de première instance or rechtbank van eerste aanleg,
— in Denmark, with the landsret,
— in the Federal Republic of Germany, with the Oberlandesgericht,
— in Greece, with the Εφετειο,
— in Spain, with the Audiencia Provincial,
— in France, with the cour d'appel,
— in Ireland, with the High Court,
— in Italy, with the corte d'appello,
— in Luxembourg, with the Court supérieure de justice sitting as a court of civil appeal,
— in the Netherlands, with the arrondissementsrechtbank,
— in Portugal, with the Tribunal de Relação,
— in the United Kingdom:

(a) in England and Wales, with the High Court of Justice, or in the case of a maintenance judgment with the Magistrates' Court;
(b) in Scotland, with the Court of Session, or in the case of a maintenance judgment with the Sheriff Court;
(c) in Northern Ireland, with the High Court of Justice, or in the case of a maintenance judgment with the Magistrates' Court.

2. The judgment given on the appeal may be contested only:

— in Belgium, Greece, Spain, France, Italy, Luxembourg and in the Netherlands, by an appeal in cassation,
— in Denmark, by an appeal to the højesteret, with the leave of the Minister of Justice,
— in the Federal Republic of Germany, by a Rechtschwerde,
— in Ireland, by an appeal on a point of law to the Supreme Court,
— in Portugal, by an appeal on a point of law,
— in the United Kingdom, by a single further appeal on a point of law.

**Lugano Convention**

5–104 The list of courts to which the application shall be submitted is supplemented in the Lugano Convention with courts of the additional Contracting States.

*Article 38*

5–105 The court with which the appeal under Article 37(1) is lodged may, on the application of the appellant, stay the proceedings if an ordinary appeal has been lodged against the judgment in the State of origin or if the time for such an appeal has not yet expired; in the latter case, the court may specify the time within such an appeal is to be lodged.

Where the judgment was given in Ireland or the United Kingdom, any form of appeal available in the State of origin shall be treated as an ordinary appeal for the purposes of the first paragraph.

The court may also make enforcement conditional on the provision of such security as it shall determine.

**Lugano Convention**

5–106 The text of the first paragraph of art.38 differs and is set out below:

The court with which the appeal under the first paragraph of Article 37 is lodged may, on the application of the appellant, stay the proceedings if an ordinary appeal has been lodged against the judgment in the State of origin or if the time for such an appeal has not yet expired; in the latter case, the court may specify the time within which such an appeal is to be lodged.

*Article 39*

5–107 During the time specified for an appeal pursuant to Article 36 and until any such appeal has been determined, no measures of enforcement may be taken other than protective measures taken against the property of the party against whom enforcement is sought.

The decision authorising enforcement shall carry with it the power to proceed to any such protective measures.

*Article 40*

1. If the application for enforcement is refused, the applicant may appeal: **5–108**

— in Belgium, to the cour d'appel or hof van beroep,
— in Denmark, to the landsret,
— in the Federal Republic of Germany, to the Oberlandesgericht,
— in Greece, to the Εφετειο,
— in Spain, to the Audiencia Provincial,
— in France, to the court d'appel,
— in Ireland, to the High Court,
— in Italy, to the corte d'appello,
— in Luxembourg, to the Cour supérieure de justice sitting as a court of civil appeal,
— in the Netherlands, to the gerechtshof,
— in Portugal, to the Tribunal da Relação,
— in the United Kingdom,

(a) in England and Wales, to the High Court of Justice, or in the case of a maintenance judgment to the Magistrates' Court;
(b) in Scotland, to the Court of Session, or in the case of a maintenance judgment to the Sheriff Court,
(c) in Northern Ireland, to the High Court of Justice, or in the case of a maintenance judgment to the Magistrates' Court.

2. The party against whom enforcement is sought shall be summoned to appear before the appellate court. If he fails to appear, the provisions of the second and third paragraphs of Article 20 shall apply even where he is not domiciled in any of the Contracting States.

**Lugano Convention**

The list of courts to which the applicant may appeal is supplemented in the Lugano Convention with courts of the additional Contracting States. **5–109**

*Article 41*

A judgment given on an appeal provided for in Article 40 may be contested only: **5–110**

— in Belgium, Greece, Spain, France, Italy, Luxembourg and in the Netherlands, by an appeal in cassation,
— in Denmark, by an appeal to the højesteret, with the leave of the Minister of Justice,
— in the Federal Republic of Germany, by a Rechtsbeschwerde,
— in Ireland, by an appeal on a point of law to the Supreme Court,
— in Portugal, by an appeal on a point of law,
— in the United Kingdom, by a single further appeal on a point of law.

**Lugano Convention**

The list of courts to which a judgment on appeal may be contested is supplemented in the Lugano Convention with courts of the additional Contracting States. **5–111**

*Article 42*

Where a foreign judgment has been given in respect of several matters and enforcement cannot be authorised for all of them, the court shall authorise the enforcement for one or more of them. **5–112**

An applicant may request partial enforcement of a judgment.

*Article 43*

A foreign judgment which orders a periodic payment by way of a penalty shall be enforceable in the State in which enforcement is sought only if the amount of the payment has been finally determined by the courts of the State of origin. **5–113**

*Article 44*

5–114 An applicant who, in the State of origin has benefited from complete or partial legal aid or exemption from costs or expenses, shall be entitled, in the procedures provided for in Articles 32 to 35, to benefit from the most favourable legal aid or the most extensive exemption from costs or expenses provided for by the law of the State addressed.

However, an applicant who requests the enforcement of a decision given by an administrative authority in Denmark in respect of a maintenance order may, in the State addressed, claim the benefits referred to in the first paragraph if he presents a statement from the Danish Ministry of Justice to the effect that he fulfils the economic requirements to qualify for the grant of complete or partial legal aid or exemption from costs or expenses.

**Lugano Convention**

5–115 The text of the second paragraph of art.44 differs and is set out below:

However, an applicant who requests the enforcement of a decision given by an administrative authority in Denmark or in Iceland in respect of a maintenance order may, in the State addressed, claim the benefits referred to in the first paragraph if he presents a statement from, respectively, the Danish Ministry of Justice or the Icelandic Ministry of Justice to the effect that he fulfils the economic requirements to qualify for the grant of complete or partial legal aid or exemption from costs or expenses.

*Article 45*

5–116 No security, bond or deposit, however described, shall be required of a party who in one Contracting State applies for enforcement of a judgment given in another Contracting State on the ground that he is a foreign national or that he is not domiciled or resident in the State in which enforcement is sought.

## SECTION 3

## COMMON PROVISION

*Article 46*

5–117 A party seeking recognition or applying for enforcement of a judgment shall produce:

1. a copy of the judgment which satisfies the conditions necessary to establish its authenticity;

2. in the case of a judgment given in default, the original or a certified true copy of the document which establishes that the party in default was served with the document instituting the proceedings or with an equivalent document.

*Article 47*

5–118 A party applying for enforcement shall also produce:

1. documents which establish that, according to the law of the State of origin the judgment is enforceable and has been served;

2. where appropriate, a document showing that the applicant is in receipt of legal aid in the State of origin.

*Article 48*

5–119 If the documents specified in point 2 of Articles 46 and 47 are not produced, the court may specify a time for their production, accept equivalent documents or, if it considers that it has sufficient information before it, dispense with their production.

If the court so requires, a translation of the documents shall be produced; the translation shall be certified by a person qualified to do so in one of the Contracting States.

*Article 49*

5–120 No legalisation or other similar formality shall be required in respect of the documents referred to in Articles 46 or 47 or the second paragraph of Article 48, or in respect of a document appointing a representative *ad litem*.

***Paragraph numbers marked with a "+" can be found online and on CD.***

## TITLE IV

## AUTHENTIC INSTRUMENTS AND COURT SETTLEMENTS

### *Article 50*

A document which has been formally drawn up or registered as an authentic instrument and is enforceable in one Contracting State shall, in another Contracting State, be declared enforceable there, on application made in accordance with the procedures provided for in Article 31 *et seq*. The application may be refused only if enforcement of the instrument is contrary to public policy in the State addressed. **5–121**

The instrument produced must satisfy the conditions necessary to establish its authenticity in the State of origin.

The provisions of Section 3 of Title III shall apply as appropriate.

### *Article 51*

A settlement which has been approved by a court in the course of proceedings and is enforceable in the State in which it was concluded shall be enforceable in the State addressed under the same conditions as authentic instruments. **5–122**

## TITLE V

## GENERAL PROVISIONS

### *Article 52*

In order to determine whether a party is domiciled in the Contracting State whose courts are seised of a matter, the court shall apply its internal law. **5–123**

If a party is not domiciled in the State whose courts are seised of the matter, then, in order to determine whether the party is domiciled in another Contracting State, the court shall apply the law of that State.

*Note* —A third paragraph in this Article was omitted by the Civil Jurisdiction and Judgments Act 1982 (Amendment) Order 1990 at the time of the revision of the 1968 Convention upon the accession of Spain and Portugal. The opportunity was taken to make this modification in the light of experience. **5–124**

### *Article 53*

For the purposes of this Convention, the seat of a company or other legal person or association of natural or legal persons shall be treated as its domicile. However, in order to determine that seat, the court shall apply its rules of private international law. **5–125**

In order to determine whether a trust is domiciled in the Contracting State whose courts are seised of the matter, the court shall apply its rules of private international law.

## TITLE VI

## TRANSITIONAL PROVISIONS

### *Article 54*

The provisions of the Convention shall apply only to legal proceedings instituted and to documents formally drawn up or registered as authentic instruments after its entry into force in the State of origin and, where recognition or enforcement of a judgment or authentic instruments is sought, in the State addressed. **5–126**

However, judgments given after the date of entry into force of this Convention between the State of origin and the State addressed in proceedings instituted before that date shall be recognised and enforced in accordance with the provisions of Title III if jurisdiction was founded upon rules which accorded with those provided for either in Title II of this Convention or in a convention concluded between the State of origin and the State addressed which was in force when the proceedings were instituted.

If the parties to a dispute concerning a contract had agreed in writing before 1

June 1988 for Ireland or before 1 January 1987 for the United Kingdom that the contract was to be governed by the law of Ireland or of a part of the United Kingdom, the courts of Ireland or of that part of the United Kingdom shall retain the right to exercise jurisdiction in the dispute.

*Article 54a*

5–127 For a period of three years from 1 November 1986 for Denmark and from 1 June 1988 for Ireland, jurisdiction in maritime matters shall be determined in these States not only in accordance with the provisions of Title II, but also in accordance with the provisions of paragraphs 1 to 6 following. However, upon the entry into force of the International Convention relating to the arrest of sea-going ships, signed at Brussels on 10 May 1952, for one of these States, these provisions shall cease to have effect for that State.

1. A person who is domiciled in a Contracting State may be sued in the courts for one of the States mentioned above in respect of a maritime claim if the ship to which the claim relates or any other ship owned by him has been arrested by judicial process within the territory of the latter State to secure the claim, or could have been so arrested there but bail or other security has been given, and either:

(a) the claimant is domiciled in the latter State; or
(b) the claim arose in the latter State; or
(c) the claim concerns the voyage during which the arrest was made or could have been made; or
(d) the claim arises out of a collision or out of damage caused by a ship to another ship or to goods or persons on board either ship, either by the execution or non-execution of a manoeuvre or by the non-observance of regulations; or
(e) the claim is for salvage; or
(f) the claim is in respect of a mortgage or hypothecation of the ship arrested.

2. A claimant may arrest either the particular ship to which the maritime claim relates, or any other ship which is owned by the person who was, at the time when the maritime claim arose, the owner of the particular ship. However, only the particular ship to which the maritime claim relates may be arrested in respect of the maritime claims set out in (5)(o), (p) or (q) of this Article.

3. Ships shall be deemed to be in the same ownership when all the shares therein are owned by the same person or persons.

4. When in the case of a charter by demise of a ship the charterer alone is liable in respect of a maritime claim relating to that ship, the claimant may arrest that ship or any other ship owned by the charterer, but no other ship owned by the owner may be arrested in respect of such claim. The same shall apply to any case in which a person other than the owner of a ship is liable in respect of a maritime claim relating to that ship.

5. The expression "maritime claim" means a claim arising out of one or more of the following:

(a) damage caused by any ship either in collision or otherwise;
(b) loss of life or personal injury caused by any ship or occurring in connection with the operation on any ship;
(c) salvage;
(d) agreement relating to the use or hire of any ship whether by charterparty or otherwise;
(e) agreement relating to the carriage of goods in any ship whether by charterparty or otherwise;
(f) loss of or damage to goods including baggage carried in any ship;
(g) general average;
(h) bottomry;
(i) towage;
(j) pilotage;
(k) goods or materials wherever supplied to a ship for her operation or maintenance;
(l) construction, repair or equipment of any ship or dock charges and dues;

***Paragraph numbers marked with a "+" can be found online and on CD.***

(m) wages of masters, officers or crew;

(n) master's disbursements, including disbursements made by shippers, charterers or agents on behalf of a ship or her owner;

(o) dispute as to the title to or ownership of any ship;

(p) disputes between co-owners of any ship as to the ownership, possession, employment or earnings of that ship;

(q) the mortgage of hypothecation of any ship.

6. In Denmark, the expression "arrest" shall be deemed as regards the maritime claims referred to in 5(o) and (p) of this Article, to include a "forbud", where that is the only procedure allowed in respect of such a claim under Articles 646 to 653 of the law on civil procedure (lov om rettens pleje).

## TITLE VII

## RELATIONSHIP TO OTHER CONVENTIONS

### *Article 55*

Subject to the provisions of the second paragraph of Article 54, the Article 56, this Convention shall, for the States which are parties to it, supersede the following conventions concluded between two or more of them. **5–128**

— the Convention between Belgium and France on jurisdiction and the validity and enforcement of judgments, arbitration awards and authentic instruments, signed at Paris on 8th July, 1899,

— the Convention between Belgium and the Netherlands on jurisdiction, bankruptcy, and the validity and enforcement of judgments, arbitration awards and authentic instruments, signed at Brussels on 28th March, 1925,

— the Convention between France and Italy on the enforcement of judgments in civil and commercial matters, signed at Rome on 3rd June, 1930,

— the Convention between the United Kingdom and the French Republic providing for the reciprocal enforcement of judgments in civil and commercial matters, with Protocol, signed at Paris on 18th January, 1934,

— the Convention between the United Kingdom and the Kingdom of Belgium, providing for the reciprocal enforcement of judgments in civil and commercial matters, with Protocol, signed at Brussels on 2nd May, 1934,

— the Convention between Germany and Italy on the recognition and enforcement of judgments in civil and commercial matters, signed at Rome on 9th March, 1936,

— the Convention between the Federal Republic of Germany and the Kingdom of Belgium on the mutual recognition and enforcement of judgments, arbitration awards and authentic instruments in civil and commercial matters, signed at Bonn on 30th June, 1958,

— the Convention between the Kingdom of the Netherlands and the Italian Republic on the recognition and enforcement of judgments in civil and commercial matters, signed at Rome on 17th April, 1959,

— the Convention between the United Kingdom and the Federal Republic of Germany for the reciprocal recognition and enforcement of judgments in civil and commercial matters, signed at Bonn on 15th July, 1960,

— the Convention between the Kingdom of Greece and the Federal Republic of Germany for the reciprocal recognition and enforcement of judgments, settlements and authentic instruments in civil and commercial matters, signed in Athens on 4th November, 1961,

— the Convention between the Kingdom of Belgium and the Italian Republic on the recognition and enforcement of judgments and other enforceable instruments in civil and commercial matters, signed at Rome on 6th April, 1962,

— the Convention between the Kingdom of the Netherlands and the Federal Republic of Germany on the mutual recognition and enforcement of judgments and other enforceable instruments in civil and commercial matters, signed at The Hague on 30th August, 1962,

— the Convention between the United Kingdom and the Republic of Italy for the reciprocal recognition and enforcement of judgments in civil and commercial matters, signed at Rome on 7th February, 1964, with amending Protocol signed at Rome on 14th July, 1970,

— the Convention between the United Kingdom and the Kingdom of the Netherlands providing for the reciprocal recognition and enforcement of judgments in civil matters, signed at The Hague on 17th November, 1967,

— the Convention between Spain and France on the recognition and enforcement of judgment and arbitration awards in civil and commercial matters, signed at Paris on 28th May, 1969,

— the Convention between Spain and Italy regarding legal aid and the recognition and enforcement of judgments in civil and commercial matters, signed at Madrid on 22nd May, 1973,

— the Convention between Spain and the Federal Republic of Germany on the recognition and enforcement of judgments, settlements and enforceable authentic instruments in civil and commercial matters, signed at Bonn on 14th November, 1983.

and, in so far as it is in force:

— the Treaty between Belgium, the Netherlands and Luxembourg on jurisdiction, bankruptcy, and the validity and enforcement of judgments, arbitration awards and authentic instruments, signed at Brussels on 24th November, 1961.

*Article 56*

**5–129** The Treaty and the conventions referred to in Article 55 shall continue to have effect in relation to matters to which this Convention does not apply.

They shall continue to have effect in respect of judgments given and documents formally drawn up or registered as authentic instruments before the entry into force of this Convention.

*Article 57*

**5–130** 1. This Convention shall not affect any conventions to which the Contracting States are or will be parties and which in relation to particular matters, govern jurisdiction or the recognition or enforcement of judgments.

2. With a view to its uniform interpretation, paragraph 1 shall be applied in the following manner:

(a) this Convention shall not prevent a court of a Contracting State which is a party to a convention on a particular matter from assuming jurisdiction in accordance with that Convention, even where the defendant is domiciled in another Contracting State which is not a party to that Convention. The court hearing the action shall, in any event, apply Article 20 of this Convention;

(b) judgments given in a Contracting State by a court in the exercise of jurisdiction provided for in a convention on a particular matter shall be recognised and enforced in the other Contracting State in accordance with this Convention.

Where a convention on a particular matter to which both the State of origin and the State addressed are parties lays down conditions for the recognition or enforcement of judgments, those conditions shall apply. In any event, the provisions of this Convention which concern the procedure for recognition and enforcement of judgments may be applied.

3. This Convention shall not affect the application of provisions which, in relation to particular matters, govern jurisdiction or the recognition or enforcement of judgments and which are or will be contained in acts of the institutions of the European Communities or in national laws harmonised in implementation of such acts.

**Lis Pendens**

**5–131** When a specialised convention contains certain rules of jurisdiction but no provision as to *lis pendens*, Arts 21 and 22 of the Judgments Convention applies. The specialised convention will preclude the application of the Judgments Convention only in relation to questions governed by the specialised convention (*The Tatry* [1995] I.L.Pr. 81, E.C. Case No.406/92).

***Paragraph numbers marked with a "+" can be found online and on CD.***

*Article 58*

Until such time as the Convention on jurisdiction and the enforcement of judgments in civil and commercial matters, signed at Lugano on 16th September, 1988, takes effect with regard to France and the Swiss Confederation, this Convention shall not affect the rights granted to Swiss nationals by the Convention between France and the Swiss Confederation on jurisdiction and enforcement of judgments in civil matters, signed at Paris on 15th June, 1869. **5–132**

*Article 59*

This Convention shall not prevent a Contracting State from assuming, in a convention on the recognition and enforcement of judgments, an obligation towards a third State not to recognise judgments given in other Contracting States against defendants domiciled or habitually resident in the third State where, in cases provided for in Article 4, the judgment could only be founded on a ground of jurisdiction specified in the second paragraph of Article 3. **5–133**

However, a Contracting State may not assume an obligation towards a third State not to recognise a judgment given in another Contracting State by a court basing its jurisdiction on the presence within that State of property belonging to the defendant, or the seizure by the plaintiff of property situated there:

1. if the action is brought to assert or declare proprietary or possessory rights in that property, seeks to obtain authority to dispose of it, or arises from another issue relating to such property, or,
2. if the property constitutes the security for a debt which is the subject-matter of the action.

*Articles 61–63*

[...] **5–134**

*Article 64*

The Secretary-General of the Council of the European Communities shall notify the signatory State of: **5–135**

(a) the deposit of each instrument of ratification;
(b) the date of entry into force of this Convention;
(c) ...
(d) any declaration received pursuant to Article IV of the Protocol;
(e) any communication made pursuant to Article VI of the Protocol.

*Article 65*

The Protocol annexed to this Convention by common accord of the Contracting States shall form an integral part thereof. **5–136**

*Article 66*

This Convention is concluded for an unlimited period. **5–137**

*Article 67*

Any Contracting State may request the revision of this Convention. In this event, a revision conference shall be convened by the President of the Council of the European Communities. **5–138**

*Article 68*

*Note*—The annexed Protocol is not printed in this Section of *Civil Procedure*. **5–139**

* * * *

**SECTION 2(2)(B)**

## SCHEDULE 2

### TEXT OF 1971 PROTOCOL, AS AMENDED

*Note*—The text set out below is the version of the 1971 Protocol inserted in Sched.2 of the 1982 Act by the Civil Jurisdiction and Judgments Act 1982 (Amendment) Order **5–140**

***Paragraph numbers marked with a "+" can be found online and on CD.***

1990 (SI 1990/2591), art.12(2), Sched.2, following upon the accession to the European Community of Spain and Portugal. It has the force of law in the United Kingdom, see s.3(1) of the 1982 Act. Section 3(3) of the 1982 Act, as amended, states that the report by Mr. P. Jenard on the 1971 Protocol may be considered in ascertaining the meaning or effect of any provision in the 1971 Protocol and "shall be given such weight as is appropriate in the circumstances". This report was published in the *Official Journal of the European Communities* (O.J.) 1979, C.59) and is re-printed in various European law texts.

*Article 1*

**5–141** The Court of Justice of the European Communities shall have jurisdiction to give rulings on the interpretation of the Convention on jurisdiction and the enforcement of judgments in civil and commercial matters and of the Protocol annexed to that Convention, signed at Brussels on 27th September 1968, and also on the interpretation of the present Protocol.

**"Court of Justice"**

**5–142** For procedure for references to European Court of Justice by High Court and Court of Appeal, see O.114.

*Article 2*

**5–143** The following courts may request the Court of Justice to give preliminary rulings on questions of interpretation—

1. —... ...

— in the United Kingdom: the House of Lords and courts to which application has been made under the second paragraph of Article 37 or under Article 41 of the Convention.

2. The courts of the Contracting States when they are sitting in an appellate capacity.

3. In the case provided for in Article 37 of the Convention, the courts referred to in that Article.

*Article 3*

**5–144** 1. Where a question of interpretation of the Convention or of one of the other instruments referred to in Article 1 is raised in a case pending before one of the courts listed in point 1 of Article 2, that court shall, if it considers that a decision on the question is necessary to enable it to give judgment, request the Court of Justice to give a ruling thereon.

2. Where such a question is raised before any court referred to in point 2 or 3 of Article 2, that court may, under the conditions laid down in paragraph 1, request the Court of Justice to give a ruling thereon.

## SCHEDULE 4

### CHAPTER II OF THE REGULATION AS MODIFIED: RULES FOR ALLOCATION OF JURISDICTION WITHIN UK

*General*

**5–145** 1. Subject to the rules of this Schedule, persons domiciled in a part of the United Kingdom shall be sued in the courts of that part.

**5–146** 2. Persons domiciled in a part of the United Kingdom may be sued in the courts of another part of the United Kingdom only by virtue of rules 3 to 13 of this Schedule.

### SECTION 2

*Special jurisdiction*

**5–147** 3. A person domiciled in a part of the United Kingdom may, in another part of the United Kingdom, be sued—

(a) in matters relating to a contract, in the courts for the place of performance of the obligation in question;

***Paragraph numbers marked with a "+" can be found online and on CD.***

(b) in matters relating to maintenance, in the courts for the place where the maintenance creditor is domiciled or habitually resident or, if the matter is ancillary to proceedings concerning the status of a person, in the court which, according to its own law, has jurisdiction to entertain those proceedings, unless that jurisdiction is based solely on the nationality of one of the parties;

(c) in matters relating to tort, delict or quasi-delict, in the courts for the place where the harmful event occurred or may occur;

(d) as regards a civil claim for damages or restitution which is based on an act giving rise to criminal proceedings, in the court seised of those proceedings, to the extent that that court has jurisdiction under its own law to entertain civil proceedings;

(e) as regards a dispute arising out of the operations of a branch, agency or other establishment, in the courts for the place in which the branch, agency or other establishment is situated;

(f) as settlor, trustee or beneficiary of a trust created by the operation of a statute, or by a written instrument, or created orally and evidenced in writing, in the courts of the part of the United Kingdom in which the trust is domiciled;

(g) as regards a dispute concerning the payment of remuneration claimed in respect of the salvage of a cargo or freight, in the court under the authority of which the cargo or freight in question—

(i) has been arrested to secure such payment; or

(ii) could have been so arrested, but bail or other security has been given;

provided that this provision shall apply only if it is claimed that the defendant has an interest in the cargo or freight or had such an interest at the time of salvage;

(h) in proceedings—

(i) concerning a debt secured on immovable property; or

(ii) which are brought to assert, declare or determine proprietary or possessory rights, or rights of security, in or over movable property, or to obtain authority to dispose of movable property;

in the courts of the part of the United Kingdom in which the property is situated.

4. Proceedings which have as their object a decision of an organ of a company or other legal person or of an association of natural or legal persons may, without prejudice to the other provisions of this Schedule, be brought in the courts of the part of the United Kingdom in which that company, legal person or association has its seat. **5–148**

5. A person domiciled in a part of the United Kingdom may, in another part of the United Kingdom, also be sued— **5–149**

(a) where he is one of a number of defendants, in the courts for the place where any one of them is domiciled, provided the claims are so closely connected that it is expedient to hear and determine them together to avoid the risk of irreconcilable judgments resulting from separate proceedings;

(b) as a third party in an action on a warranty or guarantee or in any other third party proceedings, in the court seised of the original proceedings, unless these were instituted solely with the object of removing him from the jurisdiction of the court which would be competent in his case;

(c) on a counter-claim arising from the same contract or facts on which the original claim was based, in the court in which the original claim is pending;

(d) in matters relating to a contract, if the action may be combined with an action against the same defendant in matters relating to rights *in rem* in immovable property, in the court of the part of the United Kingdom in which the property is situated.

6. Where by virtue of this Schedule a court of a part of the United Kingdom has jurisdiction in actions relating to liability arising from the use or operation of a ship, **5–150**

***Paragraph numbers marked with a "+" can be found online and on CD.***

that court, or any other court substituted for this purpose by the internal law of that part, shall also have jurisdiction over claims for limitation of such liability.

## SECTION 4

### *Jurisdiction over consumer contracts*

5–151 7.—(1)In matters relating to a contract concluded by a person, the consumer, for a purpose which can be regarded as being outside his trade or profession, jurisdiction shall be determined by this rule and rules 8 and 9, without prejudice to rule 3(e) and (h)(ii), if—

(a) it is a contract for the sale of goods on instalment credit terms; or

(b) it is a contract for a loan repayable by instalments, or for any other form of credit, made to finance the sale of goods; or

(c) in all other cases, the contract has been concluded with a person who pursues commercial or professional activities in the part of the United Kingdom in which the consumer is domiciled or, by any means, directs such activities to that part or to other parts of the United Kingdom including that part, and the contract falls within the scope of such activities.

(2) This rule shall not apply to a contract of transport other than a contract which, for an inclusive price, provides for a combination of travel and accommodation, or to a contract of insurance.

5–152 8.—(1)A consumer may bring proceedings against the other party to a contract either in the courts of the part of the United Kingdom in which that party is domiciled or in the courts of the part of the United Kingdom in which the consumer is domiciled.

(2) Proceedings may be brought against a consumer by the other party to the contract only in the courts of the part of the United Kingdom in which the consumer is domiciled.

(3) The provisions of this rule shall not affect the right to bring a counter-claim in the court in which, in accordance with this rule and rules 7 and 9, the original claim is pending.

5–153 9. The provisions of rules 7 and 8 may be departed from only by an agreement—

(a) which is entered into after the dispute has arisen; or

(b) which allows the consumer to bring proceedings in courts other than those indicated in those rules; or

(c) which is entered into by the consumer and the other party to the contract, both of whom are at the time of conclusion of the contract domiciled or habitually resident in the same part of the United Kingdom, and which confers jurisdiction on the courts of that part, provided that such an agreement is not contrary to the law of that part.

### *Jurisdiction over individual contracts of employment*

5–154 10.—(1)In matters relating to individual contracts of employment, jurisdiction shall be determined by this rule, without prejudice to rule 3(e).

(2) An employer may be sued—

(a) in the courts of the part of the United Kingdom in which he is domiciled; or

(b) in the courts of the part of the United Kingdom where the employee habitually carries out his work or in the courts of that part where he last did so; or

(c) if the employee does not or did not habitually carry out his work in any one place, in the courts of the part of the United Kingdom where the business which engaged the employee is or was situated.

(3) An employer may bring proceedings only in the courts of the part of the United Kingdom in which the employee is domiciled.

(4) The provisions of this rule shall not affect the right to bring a counter-claim in the court in which, in accordance with this rule, the original claim is pending.

(5) The provisions of this rule may be departed from only by an agreement on jurisdiction—

(a) which is entered into after the dispute has arisen; or

***Paragraph numbers marked with a "+" can be found online and on CD.***

(b) which allows the employee to bring proceedings in courts other than those indicated in this rule.

(5) in proceedings concerned with the enforcement of judgments, the courts of the **part of the United Kingdom** in which the judgment has been or is to be enforced.

*Exclusive jurisdiction*

11. The following courts shall have exclusive jurisdiction, regardless of domicile:— **5–155**

(a) (i) in proceedings which have as their object rights *in rem* in immovable property or tenancies of immovable property, the courts of the part of the United Kingdom in which the property is situated;

(ii) however, in proceedings which have as their object tenancies of immovable property concluded for temporary private use for a maximum period of six consecutive months, the courts of the part of the United Kingdom in which the defendant is domiciled shall also have jurisdiction, provided that the tenant is a natural person and that the landlord and the tenant are domiciled in the same part of the United Kingdom;

(b) in proceedings which have as their object the validity of the constitution, the nullity or the dissolution of companies or other legal persons or associations of natural or legal persons, the courts of the part of the United Kingdom in which the company, legal person or association has its seat;

(c) in proceedings which have as their object the validity of entries in public registers, the courts of the part of the United Kingdom in which the register is kept;

(d) in proceedings concerned with the enforcement of judgments, the courts of the part of the United Kingdom in which the judgment has been or is to be enforced.

*Prorogation of jurisdiction*

12.—(1)If the parties have agreed that a court or the courts of a part of the United Kingdom are to have jurisdiction to settle any disputes which have arisen or which may arise in connection with a particular legal relationship, and, apart from this Schedule, the agreement would be effective to confer jurisdiction under the law of that part, that court or those courts shall have jurisdiction. **5–156**

(2) The court or courts of a part of the United Kingdom on which a trust instrument has conferred jurisdiction shall have jurisdiction in any proceedings brought against a settlor, trustee or beneficiary, if relations between these persons or their rights or obligations under the trust are involved.

(3) Agreements or provisions of a trust instrument conferring jurisdiction shall have no legal force if they are contrary to the provisions of rule 9, or if the courts whose jurisdiction they purport to exclude have exclusive jurisdiction by virtue of rule 11.

13.—(1)Apart from jurisdiction derived from other provisions of this Schedule, a court of a part of the United Kingdom before which a defendant enters an appearance shall have jurisdiction. **5–157**

(2) This rule shall not apply where appearance was entered to contest the jurisdiction, or where another court has exclusive jurisdiction by virtue of rule 11.

*Examination as to jurisdiction and admissibility*

14. Where a court of a part of the United Kingdom is seised of a claim which is principally concerned with a matter over which the courts of another part of the United Kingdom have exclusive jurisdiction by virtue of rule 11, it shall declare of its own motion that it has no jurisdiction. **5–158**

15.—(1)Where a defendant domiciled in one part of the United Kingdom is sued in a court of another part of the United Kingdom and does not enter an appearance, the court shall declare of its own motion that it has no jurisdiction unless its jurisdiction is derived from the provisions of this Schedule. **5–159**

(2) The court shall stay the proceedings so long as it is not shown that the defendant has been able to receive the document instituting the proceedings or an equiva-

***Paragraph numbers marked with a "+" can be found online and on CD.***

lent document in sufficient time to enable him to arrange for his defence, or that all necessary steps have been taken to this end.

*Provisional, including protective, measures*

5–160 16. Application may be made to the courts of a part of the United Kingdom for such provisional, including protective, measures as may be available under the law of that part, even if, under this Schedule, the courts of another part of the United Kingdom have jurisdiction as to the substance of the matter."

## Civil Jurisdiction and Judgments Act 1982 (Interim Relief) Order 1997

(S.I. 1997 No. 302)

5–161 **1.** This Order may be cited as the Civil Jurisdiction and Judgments Act 1982 (Interim Relief) Order 1997 and shall come into force on 1st April 1997.

5–162 **2.** The High Court in England and Wales or Northern Ireland shall have power to grant interim relief under section 25(1) of the Civil Jurisdiction and Judgments Act 1982 in relation to proceedings of the following descriptions, namely—

(a) proceedings commenced or to be commenced otherwise than in a Brussels Contracting State, a State bound by the Lugano Convention or a Regulation State;

(b) proceedings whose subject-matter is not within the scope of the Regulation as determined by Article 1 of the Regulation.

5–162.1 *Note* —Amended by the Civil Jurisdiction and Judgments Regulations 2009 (SI 2009/3131) reg.26 (subject to savings contained in reg.48), with effect from January 1, 2010.

## Civil Jurisdiction and Judgments Act 1982 (Gibraltar) Order 1997

(S.I. 1997 No. 2602)

5–163 **1.** This Order may be cited as the Civil Jurisdiction and Judgments Act 1982 (Gibraltar) Order 1997 and shall come into force on 1st February 1998.

**2.**

(a) Provision corresponding to that made by the provisions of the 1968 Convention specified in paragraph (b) shall apply, so far as relevant, for the purpose of regulating, as between the United Kingdom and Gibraltar, the jurisdiction of courts and the recognition and enforcement of judgments.

(b) Those provisions are—

(i) Titles I–V;

(ii) Articles 54 and 57; and

(iii) Article 65 and the Protocol referred to therein.

**3.** For the purpose stated in Article 2 above the United Kingdom and Gibraltar shall be treated as if each were a separate Contracting State and the relevant provisions of the 1968 Convention and the 1982 Act shall be construed accordingly.

***Paragraph numbers marked with a "+" can be found online and on CD.***

**4.** In determining any question as to the meaning or effect of the provision (or any part of the provision) made by Article 2 above—

(a) regard shall be had to any relevant principles laid down by the European Court in connection with Title II of the 1968 Convention and to any relevant decision of that court as to the meaning or effect of any provision of that Title; and

(b) without prejudice to the generality of paragraph (a), the reports mentioned in section 3(3) of the 1982 Act may be considered and shall, so far as relevant, be given such weight as is appropriate in the circumstances.

**5.** A judgment shall not be recognised under this Order if, had it been given in another Contracting State, recognition would be refused by virtue of an agreement to which Article 59 of the 1968 Convention applies.

**6.** This Order extends to Northern Ireland.

**[THE NEXT PARAGRAPH IS 5–165.]**

## Civil Jurisdiction and Judgments Act 1991

(1991 c.12) **5–165**

Arrangement of Sections



### Implementation and interpretation of the Lugano Convention

**1.**—(1) The Civil Jurisdiction and Judgments Act 1982 (in this Act referred to as "the 1982 Act") shall have effect with the insertion of the following after section 3— **5–166**

"**The Lugano Convention to have the force of law**

**3A.**—(1) The Lugano Convention shall have the force of law in the United Kingdom, and judicial notice shall be taken of it.

(2) For convenience of reference there is set out in Schedule 3C the English text of the Lugano Convention.

**Interpretation of the Lugano Convention**

**3B.**—(1) In determining any question as to the meaning or effect of a provision of the Lugano Convention, a court in the United Kingdom shall, in accordance with Protocol No. 2 to that Convention, take account of any principles laid down in any relevant decision delivered by a court of any other Lugano Contracting State concerning provisions of the Convention.

***Paragraph numbers marked with a "+" can be found online and on CD.***

(2) Without prejudice to any practice of the courts as to the matters which may be considered apart from this section, the report on the Lugano Convention by Mr P. Jenard and Mr G. Möller (which is reproduced in the Official Journal of the Communities of 28th July 1990) may be considered in ascertaining the meaning or effect of any provision of the Convention and shall be given such weight as is appropriate in the circumstances."

(2) In section 9 of that Act, after subsection (1) (which, as amended, will govern the relationship between other conventions and the 1968 and Lugano Conventions) there shall be inserted—

"(1A) Any question arising as to whether it is the Lugano Convention or any of the Brussels Conventions which applies in the circumstances of a particular case falls to be determined in accordance with the provisions of Article 54B of the Lugano Convention."

(3) After Schedule 3B to that Act there shall be inserted the Schedule 3C set out in Schedule 1 to this Act.

## Interpretation of the 1982 Act

5–167 **2.**—(1) Section 1 of the 1982 Act (interpretation of references to the Conventions and Contracting States) shall be amended in accordance with the following provisions of this section.

(2) In subsection (1), in the definition of "the Conventions", for the words "the Conventions" there shall be substituted the words "the Brussels Conventions".

(3) At the end of that subsection there shall be added—

"the Lugano Convention" means the Convention on jurisdiction and the enforcement of judgments in civil and commercial matters (including the Protocols annexed to that Convention) opened for signature at Lugano on 16th September 1988 and signed by the United Kingdom on 18th September 1989."

(4) In subsection (2), for paragraph (b) (citation of Articles) there shall be substituted—

"(b) any reference in any provision to a numbered Article without more is a reference—

(i) to the Article so numbered of the 1968 Convention, in so far as the provision applies in relation to that Convention, and

(ii) to the Article so numbered of the Lugano Convention, in so far as the provision applies in relation to that Convention,

and any reference to a sub-division of a numbered Article shall be construed accordingly."

(5) In subsection (3) (definition of "Contracting State") for the words "In this Act "Contracting State" means—" there shall be substituted the words—

"In this Act—

*Paragraph numbers marked with a "+" can be found online and on CD.*

"Contracting State", without more, in any provision means—

(a) in the application of the provision in relation to the Brussels Conventions, a Brussels Contracting State; and

(b) in the application of the provision in relation to the Lugano Convention, a Lugano Contracting State;

"Brussels Contracting State" means—".

(6) At the end of that subsection there shall be added—

""Lugano Contracting State" means one of the original parties to the Lugano Convention, that is to say—Austria, Belgium, Denmark, Finland, France, the Republic of Germany, the Hellenic Republic, Iceland, the Republic of Ireland, Italy, Luxembourg, the Netherlands, Norway, Portugal, Spain, Sweden, Switzerland and the United Kingdom, being a State in relation to which the Convention has taken effect in accordance with paragraph 3 or 4 of Article 61."

### Other amendments of the 1982 Act

**3.** The 1982 Act shall have effect with the amendments specified in Schedule 2 to this Act, which are either consequential on the amendments made by sections 1 and 2 above or otherwise for the purpose of implementing the Lugano Convention. **5–168**

### Application to the Crown

**4.** The amendments of the 1982 Act made by this Act bind the Crown in accordance with the provisions of section 51 of that Act. **5–169**

### Short title, interpretation, commencement and extent

**5.**—(1) This Act may be cited as the Civil Jurisdiction and Judgments Act 1991. **5–170**

(2) In this Act—

"the 1982 Act" means the Civil Juridiction and Judgments Act 1982;

"the Lugano Convention" has the same meaning as it has in the 1982 Act by virtue of section 2(3) above.

(3) This Act shall come into force on such day as the Lord Chancellor and the Lord Advocate may apopint in an order made by statutory instrument.

(4) This Act extends to Northern Ireland.

**For Schs 1 and 2 to the Civil Jurisdiction and Judgments Act 1991 (see Arrangement) plus any related commentary see paragraphs 5–171+ to 5–193+ on White Book on Westlaw UK or the Civil Procedure CD.**

## The Civil Jurisdiction and Judgments (Authentic Instruments and Court Settlements) Order 2001

(S.I. 2001 No. 3928)

**1.**—(1) This Order may be cited as the Civil Jurisdiction and **5–194**

Judgments (Authentic Instruments and Court Settlements) Order 2001 and shall come into force on 1st March 2002.

(2) In this Order—

"the Act" means the Civil Jurisdiction and Judgments Act 1982;

"the Regulation" means Council Regulation (EC) No. 44/2001 of 22nd December 2000 on jurisdiction and the recognition and enforcement of judgments in civil and commercial matters, as amended from time to time and as applied by the Agreement made on 19th October 2005 between the European Community and the Kingdom of Denmark on jurisdiction and the recognition and enforcement of judgments in civil and commercial matters;

"Regulation State" in any provision, in the application of that provision in relation to the Regulation, means a Member State;

"the 2001 Order" means the Civil Jurisdiction and Judgments Order 2001.

(3) In this Order—

(a) references to authentic instruments and court settlements are references to those instruments and settlements referred to in Chapter IV of the Regulation; and

(b) references to judgments and maintenance orders are references to judgments and maintenance orders to which the Regulation applies.

**5–195** *Note* —Amended by the Civil Jurisdiction and Judgments Regulations 2007 (SI 2007/1655).

Subsection 2 amended by the Civil Jurisdiction and Judgments Act 1991 (c.12) and by SI 1989/1346, SI 1990/2591, SI 1993/603 and SI 2000/1824.

*Article 2*

**5–196** **2.**—(1) Subject to the modifications specified in paragraphs (2) and (3), paragraphs 1 to 6 of Schedule 1 to the 2001 Order shall apply, as appropriate, to authentic instruments and court settlements which—

(a) do not concern maintenance as if they were judgments,

(b) concern maintenance as if they were maintenance orders.

(2) In the application of paragraph 2(2) of Schedule 1 to the 2001 Order to authentic instruments and court settlements, for the words "as if the judgment had been originally given" there shall be substituted "as if it was a judgment which had been originally given".

(3) In the application of paragraph 3(3) of Schedule 1 to the 2001 Order to authentic instruments and court settlements, for the words "as if the order had been originally made" there shall be substituted the words "as if it was an order which had been originally made".

(4) Paragraph 8 of Schedule 1 to the 2001 Order shall apply to authentic instruments as if they were judgments and in its application—

(a) for sub-paragraph (1)(b) there shall be substituted the following—

"(b) a certificate obtained in accordance with Article 57

and Annex VI shall be evidence, and in Scotland sufficient evidence, that the authentic instrument is enforceable in the Regulation State of origin.";

and

(b) for sub-paragraph (2) there shall be substituted the following—

"(2) A document purporting to be a copy of an authentic instrument drawn up or registered, and enforceable, in a Regulation State other than the United Kingdom is duly authenticated for the purposes of this paragraph if it purports to be certified to be a true copy of such an instrument by a person duly authorised in that Regulation State to do so.".

(5) Paragraph 8 of Schedule 1 to the 2001 Order shall apply to court settlements as if they were judgments and in its application for "Article 54" there shall be substituted "Article 58".

**3.** The disapplication of section 18 of the Act (enforcement of United Kingdom judgments in other parts of the United Kingdom) by section 18(7) will extend to authentic instruments and court settlements enforceable in a Regulation State outside the United Kingdom which will fall to be treated for the purposes of their enforcement as judgments of a court of law in the United Kingdom by virtue of registration under the Regulation. **5–197**

**4.** Section 48 of the Act (matters for which rules of court may provide) will apply to authentic instruments and court settlements as if they were judgments or maintenance orders, as appropriate, to which the Regulation applies. **5–198**

*Note* —Section 48 was amended by para.23 of Sch.2 to the Civil Jurisdiction and Judgments Act 1991 (c.12) and para.17 of Sch.2 of the Civil Jurisdiction and Judgments Order 2001 (SI 2001/3929). **5–198.1**

**[THE NEXT PARAGRAPH IS 5–201.]**

## The Civil Jurisdiction and Judgments Order 2001

(S.I. 2001 No. 3929)

### Citation and commencement

**1.** This Order may be cited as the Civil Jurisdiction and Judgments Order 2001 and shall come into force— **5–201**

(a) as to articles 1 and 2, paragraphs 1(a), 1(b)(ii) and 17 of Schedule 2 and, so far as it relates to those paragraphs, article 4, on 25th January 2002; and

(b) as to the remainder of this Order, on 1st March 2002.

### Interpretation

**2.**—(1) In this Order— **5–202**

"the Act" means the Civil Jurisdiction and Judgments Act 1982;

"the 2005 Agreement" means means the Agreement made on 19th October 2005 between the European Community and the Kingdom of Denmark on jurisdiction and the recognition and enforcement of judgments in civil and commercial matters;

*Paragraph numbers marked with a "+" can be found online and on CD.*

"the Regulation" means Council Regulation (EC) No. 44/2001 of 22nd December 2000 on jurisdiction and the recognition and enforcement of judgments in civil and commercial matters, as amended from time to time and as applied by the 2005 Agreement;

"Regulation State" in any provision, in the application of that provision in relation to the Regulation, means a Member State.

(2) In Schedule 2 to this Order, a section, Part, Schedule or paragraph referred to by number alone is a reference to the section, Part, Schedule or paragraph so numbered in the Act.

5-203 *Note*—Amended by the Civil Jurisdiction and Judgments Regulations 2007 (SI 2007/1655) reg.3.

### The Regulation

5-204 **3.** Schedule 1 to this Order (which applies certain provisions of the Act with modifications for the purposes of the Regulation) shall have effect.

### The 2005 Agreement

5-205 **3A.** The Regulation shall have effect as regards Denmark in accordance with the 2005 Agreement.

5-206 *Note*—Inserted by the Civil Jurisdiction and Judgments Regulations 2007 (SI 2007/1655) reg.3.

### Amendments to the Civil Jurisdiction and Judgments Act 1982

5-207 **4.** Schedule 2 to this Order (which makes amendments to the Act) shall have effect.

### Consequential amendments

5-208 **5.** Schedule 3 to this Order (which makes consequential amendments) shall have effect.

### Transitional provisions

5-209 **6.**—(1) Where proceedings are begun before 1st March 2002 in any part of the United Kingdom on the basis of jurisdiction determined in accordance with section 16 of, and Schedule 4 to, the Act, the proceedings may be continued as if the amendments made by paragraphs 3 and 4 of Schedule 2 to this Order had not been made and those amendments shall not apply in respect of any proceedings begun before that date.

(2) Where proceedings are begun before 1st March 2002 in any court in Scotland on the basis of jurisdiction determined in accordance with section 20 of, and Schedule 8 to, the Act, the proceedings may be continued as if the amendments made by paragraphs 6 and 7 of Schedule 2 to this Order had not been made and those amendments shall not apply in respect of any proceedings begun before that date.

**For Sch.1 to the Civil Jurisdiction and Judgments Order 2001 plus any related commentary see paragraphs 5-210+ to 5-221+ on White Book on Westlaw UK or the Civil Procedure CD.**

***Paragraph numbers marked with a "+" can be found online and on CD.***

## Council Regulations

## *Council Regulation (EC) No.1393/2007 of 13 November 2007 on the service in the Member States of judicial and extrajudicial documents in civil or commercial matters (service of documents), and repealing Council Regulation (EC) No.1348/2000*

**Editorial note**

The Council adopted the initial Regulation on the service in the Member States of judicial and extra-judicial documents in civil or commercial matters on May 29, 2000 ("the Service Regulation"). The Regulation was passed with the aim of improving efficiency and speed in judicial procedures in civil matters by providing for the transmission of judicial and extra-judicial documents by direct and rapid means by local bodies designated by Member States. The Regulation entered into force on May 31, 2001 and applies in civil and commercial matters where a judicial or extra-judicial document has to be transmitted from one Member State to another for service there (art.1(1)). **5–222**

The Regulation has two aims. First, it seeks to establish an efficient system for service of proceedings through agencies to be designated by each of the Member States, although there is also provision for service through diplomatic and consular channels and also by post, subject to the consent of and/or conditions imposed by the receiving state. Secondly, the Regulation tries to achieve consistency in the determination of the effective date of service, by identifying the system of law which governs that question. Generally, the law of the sending state is effective where under that system, the proceedings have to be served within a particular time. Otherwise, the law of the receiving state governs.

Each Member State shall designate the public officers, authorities or other persons competent for the transmission of judicial or extra-judicial documents to be served in another Member State ("transmitting agencies") (art.2(1)) and shall designate the public offices, authorities or other persons competent for the receipt of such documents (art.2(2)) ("receiving agencies"). Each Member State shall also designate a central body responsible for the following: supplying information to the transmitting agencies; seeking solutions to any difficulties which may arise during transmission of documents for service; and forwarding requests for service to the competent receiving agency (art.3). Article 4(1) provides that documents shall be transmitted "as soon as possible".

As to service, the receiving agency shall itself serve the document or have it served, either in accordance with the law of the Member State addressed, or by a particular form requested by the transmitting agency, unless such a method is incompatible with the law of that Member State (art.7(1)). Article 8 lays down certain circumstances in which the receiving agency may refuse to accept the document to be served. Notwithstanding the provisions of the Service Regulation, each Member State is free to effect service of judicial documents directly by post to persons residing in another Member State, and may specify the conditions under which it will accept such service (art.14).

There are particular provisions stipulating that where a document has been transmitted for the purpose of service and a defendant has not appeared, judgment shall not be given until certain conditions have been established (art.19).

According to art.23 of the service Regulation, the Member States shall communicate to the European Commission information referred to in certain of the Articles. This information (with the exception of the information referred to in art.17(a)) has been published in the Official Journal (O.J. C151 p.4.) and to date two updates have been published (O.J. C202, p.10 and O.J. C282 p.2).

A manual which contains the information provided by Member States concerning the names and addresses of the receiving agencies, the geographical areas in which they have jurisdiction, the means of receipt of documents available to them and the languages that may be used for the completion of the standard form has been compiled and published by the European Commission. A glossary which lists the documents in all the official languages of the European Union which may be served under the service Regulation has also been compiled and published. Both of these documents are updated regularly and may be found at: *http://ec.europa.eu* [Accessed March 28, 2007].

The operation of the Service Regulation is complicated by the fact that individual

***Paragraph numbers marked with a "+" can be found online and on CD.***

Member States are able to opt out of the Regulation for a transitional and potentially renewable period of up to fiveyears, the need to designate particular agencies, and the need to establish whether the receiving state allows service by post. Nevertheless, the service Regulation is important because of its impact on the date when proceedings are effectively commenced, which in some instances can be dispositive in determining which state has jurisdiction in a particular case.

Given the uncertainty surrounding this present state of implementation of the Regulation in Member States, it would generally be prudent to check a proposed method of service in the manual and with local lawyers in the receiving state.

## CHAPTER 1—GENERAL PROVISIONS

*Article 1*

### Scope

5–223 1. This Regulation shall apply in civil and commercial matters where a judicial or extrajudicial document has to be transmitted from one Member State to another for service there. It shall not extend in particular to revenue, customs or administrative matters or to liability of the State for actions or omissions in the exercise of state authority (*acta iure imperii*).

2. This Regulation shall not apply where the address of the person to be served with the document is not known.

3. In this Regulation, the term 'Member State' shall mean the Member States with the exception of Denmark.

*Article 2*

### Transmitting and receiving agencies

5–224 1. Each Member State shall designate the public officers, authorities or other persons, hereinafter referred to as 'transmitting agencies', competent for the transmission of judicial or extrajudicial documents to be served in another Member State.

2. Each Member State shall designate the public officers, authorities or other persons, hereinafter referred to as 'receiving agencies', competent for the receipt of judicial or extrajudicial documents from another Member State.

3. A Member State may designate one transmitting agency and one receiving agency, or one agency to perform both functions. A federal State, a State in which several legal systems apply or a State with autonomous territorial units shall be free to designate more than one such agency. The designation shall have effect for a period of five years and may be renewed at five-year intervals.

4. Each Member State shall provide the Commission with the following information:

(a) the names and addresses of the receiving agencies referred to in paragraphs 2 and 3;

(b) the geographical areas in which they have jurisdiction;

(c) the means of receipt of documents available to them; and

(d) the languages that may be used for the completion of the standard form set out in Annex I.

Member States shall notify the Commission of any subsequent modification of such information.

*Article 3*

### Central body

1. Each Member State shall designate a central body responsible for: **5–225**

(a) supplying information to the transmitting agencies;

(b) seeking solutions to any difficulties which may arise during transmission of documents for service;

(c) forwarding, in exceptional cases, at the request of a transmitting agency, a request for service to the competent receiving agency.

A federal State, a State in which several legal systems apply or a State with autonomous territorial units shall be free to designate more than one central body.

## CHAPTER II—JUDICIAL DOCUMENTS

### SECTION 1—TRANSMISSION AND SERVICE OF JUDICIAL DOCUMENTS

*Article 4*

### Transmission of documents

1. Judicial documents shall be transmitted directly and as soon as possible between the agencies designated pursuant to Article 2. **5–226**

2. The transmission of documents, requests, confirmations, receipts, certificates and any other papers between transmitting agencies and receiving agencies may be carried out by any appropriate means, provided that the content of the document received is true and faithful to that of the document forwarded and that all information in it is easily legible.

3. The document to be transmitted shall be accompanied by a request drawn up using the standard form set out in Annex I. The form shall be completed in the official language of the Member State addressed or, if there are several official languages in that Member State, the official language or one of the official languages of the place where service is to be effected, or in another language which that Member State has indicated it can accept. Each Member State shall indicate the official language or languages of the institutions of the European Union other than its own which is or are acceptable to it for completion of the form.

4. The documents and all papers that are transmitted shall be exempted from legalisation or any equivalent formality.

5. When the transmitting agency wishes a copy of the document to be returned together with the certificate referred to in Article 10, it shall send the document in duplicate.

*Article 5*

### Translation of documents

1. The applicant shall be advised by the transmitting agency to which he forwards the document for transmission that the addressee may refuse to accept it if it is not in one of the languages provided for in Article 8. **5–227**

2. The applicant shall bear any costs of translation prior to the transmission of the document, without prejudice to any possible subsequent decision by the court or competent authority on liability for such costs.

*Article 6*

**Receipt of documents by receiving agency**

5–228 1. On receipt of a document, a receiving agency shall, as soon as possible and in any event within seven days of receipt, send a receipt to the transmitting agency by the swiftest possible means of transmission using the standard form set out in Annex I.

2. Where the request for service cannot be fulfilled on the basis of the information or documents transmitted, the receiving agency shall contact the transmitting agency by the swiftest possible means in order to secure the missing information or documents.

3. If the request for service is manifestly outside the scope of this Regulation or if non-compliance with the formal conditions required makes service impossible, the request and the documents transmitted shall be returned, on receipt, to the transmitting agency, together with the notice of return using the standard form set out in Annex I.

4. A receiving agency receiving a document for service but not having territorial jurisdiction to serve it shall forward it, as well as the request, to the receiving agency having territorial jurisdiction in the same Member State if the request complies with the conditions laid down in Article 4(3) and shall inform the transmitting agency accordingly using the standard form set out in Annex I. That receiving agency shall inform the transmitting agency when it receives the document, in the manner provided for in paragraph 1.

*Article 7*

**Service of documents**

5–229 1. The receiving agency shall itself serve the document or have it served, either in accordance with the law of the Member State addressed or by a particular method requested by the transmitting agency, unless that method is incompatible with the law of that Member State.

2. The receiving agency shall take all necessary steps to effect the service of the document as soon as possible, and in any event within one month of receipt. If it has not been possible to effect service within one month of receipt, the receiving agency shall:

(a) immediately inform the transmitting agency by means of the certificate in the standard form set out in Annex I, which shall be drawn up under the conditions referred to in Article 10(2); and

(b) continue to take all necessary steps to effect the service of the document, unless indicated otherwise by the transmitting agency, where service seems to be possible within a reasonable period of time.

*Article 8*

**Refusal to accept a document**

5–230 1. The receiving agency shall inform the addressee, using the standard form set out in Annex II, that he may refuse to accept the document to be served at the time of service or by returning the document to the receiving agency within one week if it is not written in, or accompanied by a translation into, either of the following languages:

(a) a language which the addressee understands;

or

(b) the official language of the Member State addressed or, if there are several official languages in that Member State, the official language or one of the official languages of the place where service is to be effected.

2. Where the receiving agency is informed that the addressee refuses to accept the document in accordance with paragraph 1, it shall immediately inform the transmitting agency by means of the certificate provided for in Article 10 and return the request and the documents of which a translation is requested.

3. If the addressee has refused to accept the document pursuant to paragraph 1, the service of the document can be remedied through the service on the addressee in accordance with the provisions of this Regulation of the document accompanied by a translation into a language provided for in paragraph 1. In that case, the date of service of the document shall be the date on which the document accompanied by the translation is served in accordance with the law of the Member State addressed. However, where according to the law of a Member State, a document has to be served within a particular period, the date to be taken into account with respect to the applicant shall be the date of the service of the initial document determined pursuant to Article 9(2).

4. Paragraphs 1, 2 and 3 shall also apply to the means of transmission and service of judicial documents provided for in Section 2.

5. For the purposes of paragraph 1, the diplomatic or consular agents, where service is effected in accordance with Article 13, or the authority or person, where service is effected in accordance with Article 14, shall inform the addressee that he may refuse to accept the document and that any document refused must be sent to those agents or to that authority or person respectively.

*Article 9*

**Date of service**

1. Without prejudice to Article 8, the date of service of a document pursuant to Article 7 shall be the date on which it is served in accordance with the law of the Member State addressed. **5–231**

2. However, where according to the law of a Member State a document has to be served within a particular period, the date to be taken into account with respect to the applicant shall be that determined by the law of that Member State.

3. Paragraphs 1 and 2 shall also apply to the means of transmission and service of judicial documents provided for in Section 2.

*Article 10*

**Certificate of service and copy of the document served**

1. When the formalities concerning the service of the document have been completed, a certificate of completion of those formalities **5–232**

shall be drawn up in the standard form set out in Annex I and addressed to the transmitting agency, together with, where Article 4(5) applies, a copy of the document served.

2. The certificate shall be completed in the official language or one of the official languages of the Member State of origin or in another language which the Member State of origin has indicated that it can accept. Each Member State shall indicate the official language or languages of the institutions of the European Union other than its own which is or are acceptable to it for completion of the form.

*Article 11*

**Costs of service**

5–233 1. The service of judicial documents coming from a Member State shall not give rise to any payment or reimbursement of taxes or costs for services rendered by the Member State addressed.

2. However, the applicant shall pay or reimburse the costs occasioned by:

(a) recourse to a judicial officer or to a person competent under the law of the Member State addressed;

(b) the use of a particular method of service.

Costs occasioned by recourse to a judicial officer or to a person competent under the law of the Member State addressed shall correspond to a single fixed fee laid down by that Member State in advance which respects the principles of proportionality and nondiscrimination. Member States shall communicate such fixed fees to the Commission.

SECTION 2—OTHER MEANS OF TRANSMISSION AND SERVICE OF JUDICIAL DOCUMENTS

*Article 12*

**Transmission by consular or diplomatic channels**

5–234 Each Member State shall be free, in exceptional circumstances, to use consular or diplomatic channels to forward judicial documents, for the purpose of service, to those agencies of another Member State which are designated pursuant to Articles 2 or 3.

*Article 13*

**Service by diplomatic or consular agents**

5–235 1. Each Member State shall be free to effect service of judicial documents on persons residing in another Member State, without application of any compulsion, directly through its diplomatic or consular agents.

2. Any Member State may make it known, in accordance with Article 23(1), that it is opposed to such service within its territory, unless the documents are to be served on nationals of the Member State in which the documents originate.

*Article 14*

**Service by postal services**

5–236 Each Member State shall be free to effect service of judicial documents directly by postal services on persons residing in another

Member State by registered letter with acknowledgement of receipt or equivalent.

*Article 15*

**Direct service**

Any person interested in a judicial proceeding may effect service of judicial documents directly through the judicial officers, officials or other competent persons of the Member State addressed, where such direct service is permitted under the law of that Member State. **5–237**

### CHAPTER III—EXTRAJUDICIAL DOCUMENTS

*Article 16*

**Transmission**

Extrajudicial documents may be transmitted for service in another Member State in accordance with the provisions of this Regulation. **5–238**

### CHAPTER IV—FINAL PROVISIONS

*Article 17*

**Implementing rules**

Measures designed to amend non-essential elements of this Regulation relating to the updating or to the making of technical amendments to the standard forms set out in Annexes I and II shall be adopted in accordance with the regulatory procedure with scrutiny referred to in Article 18(2). **5–239**

*Article 18*

**Committee**

1. The Commission shall be assisted by a committee. **5–240**

2. Where reference is made to this paragraph, Article 5a(1) to (4), and Article 7 of Decision 1999/468/EC shall apply, having regard to the provisions of Article 8 thereof.

*Article 19*

**Defendant not entering an appearance**

1. Where a writ of summons or an equivalent document has had to be transmitted to another Member State for the purpose of service under the provisions of this Regulation and the defendant has not appeared, judgment shall not be given until it is established that: **5–241**

(a) the document was served by a method prescribed by the internal law of the Member State addressed for the service of documents in domestic actions upon persons who are within its territory; or

(b) the document was actually delivered to the defendant or to his residence by another method provided for by this Regulation;

and that in either of these cases the service or the delivery was effected in sufficient time to enable the defendant to defend.

*Paragraph numbers marked with a "+" can be found online and on CD.*

2. Each Member State may make it known, in accordance with Article 23(1), that the judge, notwithstanding the provisions of paragraph 1, may give judgment even if no certificate of service or delivery has been received, if all the following conditions are fulfilled:

(a) the document was transmitted by one of the methods provided for in this Regulation;

(b) a period of time of not less than six months, considered adequate by the judge in the particular case, has elapsed since the date of the transmission of the document;

(c) no certificate of any kind has been received, even though every reasonable effort has been made to obtain it through the competent authorities or bodies of the Member State addressed.

3. Notwithstanding paragraphs 1 and 2, the judge may order, in case of urgency, any provisional or protective measures.

4. When a writ of summons or an equivalent document has had to be transmitted to another Member State for the purpose of service under the provisions of this Regulation and a judgment has been entered against a defendant who has not appeared, the judge shall have the power to relieve the defendant from the effects of the expiry of the time for appeal from the judgment if the following conditions are fulfilled:

(a) the defendant, without any fault on his part, did not have knowledge of the document in sufficient time to defend, or knowledge of the judgment in sufficient time to appeal; and

(b) the defendant has disclosed a prima facie defence to the action on the merits.

An application for relief may be filed only within a reasonable time after the defendant has knowledge of the judgment.

Each Member State may make it known, in accordance with Article 23(1), that such application will not be entertained if it is filed after the expiry of a time to be stated by it in that communication, but which shall in no case be less than one year following the date of the judgment.

5. Paragraph 4 shall not apply to judgments concerning the status or capacity of persons.

*Article 20*

**Relationship with agreements or arrangements to which Member States are party**

**5–242** 1. This Regulation shall, in relation to matters to which it applies, prevail over other provisions contained in bilateral or multilateral agreements or arrangements concluded by the Member States, and in particular Article IV of the Protocol to the Brussels Convention of 1968 and the Hague Convention of 15 November 1965.

2. This Regulation shall not preclude individual Member States from maintaining or concluding agreements or arrangements to expedite further or simplify the transmission of documents, provided that they are compatible with this Regulation.

3. Member States shall send to the Commission:

(a) a copy of the agreements or arrangements referred to in

paragraph 2 concluded between the Member States as well as drafts of such agreements or arrangements which they intend to adopt; and

(b) any denunciation of, or amendments to, these agreements or arrangements.

*Article 21*

## Legal aid

This Regulation shall not affect the application of Article 23 of the Convention on civil procedure of 17 July 1905, Article 24 of the Convention on civil procedure of 1 March 1954 or Article 13 of the Convention on international access to justice of 25 October 1980 between the Member States party to those Conventions. **5–243**

*Article 22*

## Protection of information transmitted

1. Information, including in particular personal data, transmitted under this Regulation shall be used by the receiving agency only for the purpose for which it was transmitted. **5–244**

2. Receiving agencies shall ensure the confidentiality of such information, in accordance with their national law.

3. Paragraphs 1 and 2 shall not affect national laws enabling data subjects to be informed of the use made of information transmitted under this Regulation.

4. This Regulation shall be without prejudice to Directives 95/46/EC and 2002/58/EC.

*Article 23*

## Communication and publication

1. Member States shall communicate to the Commission the information referred to in Articles 2, 3, 4, 10, 11, 13, 15 and 19. Member States shall communicate to the Commission if, according to their law, a document has to be served within a particular period as referred to in Articles 8(3) and 9(2). **5–245**

2. The Commission shall publish the information communicated in accordance with paragraph 1 in the Official Journal of the European Union with the exception of the addresses and other contact details of the agencies and of the central bodies and the geographical areas in which they have jurisdiction.

3. The Commission shall draw up and update regularly a manual containing the information referred to in paragraph 1, which shall be available electronically, in particular through the European Judicial Network in Civil and Commercial Matters.

*Article 24*

## Review

No later than 1 June 2011, and every five years thereafter, the Commission shall present to the European Parliament, the Council and the European Economic and Social Committee a report on the application of this Regulation, paying special attention to the ef- **5–246** fectiveness of the agencies designated pursuant to Article 2 and to the practical application of Article 3(c) and Article 9. The report shall be accompanied if need be by proposals for adaptations of this Regulation in line with the evolution of notification systems.

*Article 24*

**Repeal**

5–246.1 1. Regulation (EC) No 1348/2000 shall be repealed as from the date of application of this Regulation.

2. References made to the repealed Regulation shall be construed as being made to this Regulation and should be read in accordance with the correlation table in Annex III.

*Article 26*

**Entry into force**

5–247

This Regulation shall enter into force on the 20th day following its publication in the Official Journal of the European Union.

It shall apply from 13 November 2008 with the exception of Article 23 which shall apply from 13 August 2008.

This Regulation shall be binding in its entirety and directly applicable in the Member States in accordance with the Treaty establishing the European Community.

**For Annex I to Council Regulation (EC) No.1393/2007 see paragraph 5–248+ on White Book on Westlaw UK or the Civil Procedure CD.**

*Council Regulation (EC) No.44/2001 of 22 December 2000 on jurisdiction and the recognition and enforcement of judgments in civil and commercial matters*

CHAPTER I—SCOPE

*Article 1*

5–249 1. This Regulation shall apply in civil and commercial matters whatever the nature of the court or tribunal. It shall not extend, in particular, to revenue, customs or administrative matters.

2. The Regulation shall not apply to:

(a) the status or legal capacity of natural persons, rights in property arising out of a matrimonial relationship, wills and succession;

(b) bankruptcy, proceedings relating to the winding-up of insolvent companies or other legal persons, judicial arrangements, compositions and analogous proceedings;

(c) social security;

(d) arbitration.

3. In this Regulation, the term "Member State" shall mean Member States with the exception of Denmark.

## CHAPTER II—JURISDICTION

### SECTION 1—GENERAL PROVISIONS

*Article 2*

1. Subject to this Regulation, persons domiciled in a Member State shall, whatever their nationality, be sued in the courts of that Member State. **5–250**

2. Persons who are not nationals of the Member State in which they are domiciled shall be governed by the rules of jurisdiction applicable to nationals of that State.

*Article 3*

1. Persons domiciled in a Member State may be sued in the courts of another Member State only by virtue of the rules set out in Sections 2 to 7 of this Chapter. **5–251**

2. In particular the rules of national jurisdiction set out in Annex I shall not be applicable as against them.

**Rules of national jurisdiction**

The rules of UK jurisdiction set out in Annex I are: rules which enable jurisdiction to be founded on (a) the document instituting the proceedings having been served on the defendant during his temporary presence in the United Kingdom; or (b) the presence within the United Kingdom of property belonging to the defendant; or (c) the seizure by the plaintiff of property situated in the United Kingdom. **5–251.1**

*Article 4*

1. If the defendant is not domiciled in a Member State, the jurisdiction of the courts of each Member State shall, subject to Articles 22 and 23, be determined by the law of that Member State. **5–252**

2. As against such a defendant, any person domiciled in a Member State may, whatever his nationality, avail himself in that State of the rules of jurisdiction there in force, and in particular those specified in Annex I, in the same way as the nationals of that State.

**Rules of jurisdiction**

For rules of United Kingdom jurisdiction relevant to art.4, see para.5–251.1 above. **5–252.1**

### SECTION 2—SPECIAL JURISDICTION

*Article 5*

A person domiciled in a Member State may, in another Member State, be sued: **5–253**

1.—(a) in matters relating to a contract, in the courts for the place of performance of the obligation in question;

(b) for the purpose of this provision and unless otherwise agreed, the place of performance of the obligation in question shall be:

- in the case of the sale of goods, the place in a Member State where, under the contract, the goods were delivered or should have been delivered,
- in the case of the provision of services, the place in a Member State where, under the contract, the services were provided or should have been provided,

(c) if subparagraph (b) does not apply then subparagraph (a) applies;

2. in matters relating to maintenance, in the courts for the place where the maintenance creditor is domiciled or habitually resident or, if the matter is ancillary to proceedings concerning the status of a person, in the court which, according to its own law, has jurisdiction to entertain those proceedings, unless that jurisdiction is based solely on the nationality of one of the parties;

3. in matters relating to tort, delict or quasi-delict, in the courts for the place where the harmful event occurred or may occur;

4. as regards a civil claim for damages or restitution which is based on an act giving rise to criminal proceedings, in the court seised of those proceedings, to the extent that that court has jurisdiction under its own law to entertain civil proceedings;

5. as regards a dispute arising out of the operations of a branch, agency or other establishment, in the courts for the place in which the branch, agency or other establishment is situated;

6. as settlor, trustee or beneficiary of a trust created by the operation of a statute, or by a written instrument, or created orally and evidenced in writing, in the courts of the Member State in which the trust is domiciled;

7. as regards a dispute concerning the payment of remuneration claimed in respect of the salvage of a cargo or freight, in the court under the authority of which the cargo or freight in question:

(a) has been arrested to secure such payment, or

(b) could have been so arrested, but bail or other security has been given;

provided that this provision shall apply only if it is claimed that the defendant has an interest in the cargo or freight or had such an interest at the time of salvage.

*Article 6*

**5–254** A person domiciled in a Member State may also be sued:

1. where he is one of a number of defendants, in the courts for the place where any one of them is domiciled, provided the claims are so closely connected that it is expedient to hear and determine them together to avoid the risk of irreconcilable judgments resulting from separate proceedings;

2. as a third party in an action on a warranty or guarantee or in any other third party proceedings, in the court seised of the original proceedings, unless these were instituted solely with the object of removing him from the jurisdiction of the court which would be competent in his case;

3. on a counter-claim arising from the same contract or facts on which the original claim was based, in the court in which the original claim is pending;

4. in matters relating to a contract, if the action may be combined with an action against the same defendant in matters relating to rights in rem in immovable property, in the court of the Member State in which the property is situated.

***Paragraph numbers marked with a "+" can be found online and on CD.***

*Article 7*

Where by virtue of this Regulation a court of a Member State has jurisdiction in actions relating to liability from the use or operation of a ship, that court, or any other court substituted for this purpose by the internal law of that Member State, shall also have jurisdiction over claims for limitation of such liability. **5–255**

## SECTION 3—JURISDICTION IN MATTERS RELATING TO INSURANCE

*Article 8*

In matters relating to insurance, jurisdiction shall be determined by this Section, without prejudice to Article 4 and point 5 of Article 5. **5–256**

*Article 9*

1. An insurer domiciled in a Member State may be sued: **5–257**

(a) in the courts of the Member State where he is domiciled, or

(b) in another Member State, in the case of actions brought by the policyholder, the insured or a beneficiary, in the courts for the place where the plaintiff is domiciled,

(c) if he is a co-insurer, in the courts of a Member State in which proceedings are brought against the leading insurer.

2. An insurer who is not domiciled in a Member State but has a branch, agency or other establishment in one of the Member States shall, in disputes arising out of the operations of the branch, agency or establishment, be deemed to be domiciled in that Member State.

*Article 10*

In respect of liability insurance or insurance of immovable property, the insurer may in addition be sued in the courts for the place where the harmful event occurred. The same applies if movable and immovable property are covered by the same insurance policy and both are adversely affected by the same contingency. **5–258**

*Article 11*

1. In respect of liability insurance, the insurer may also, if the law of the court permits it, be joined in proceedings which the injured party has brought against the insured. **5–259**

2. Articles 8, 9 and 10 shall apply to actions brought by the injured party directly against the insurer, where such direct actions are permitted.

3. If the law governing such direct actions provides that the policyholder or the insured may be joined as a party to the action, the same court shall have jurisdiction over them.

*Article 12*

1. Without prejudice to Article 11(3), an insurer may bring proceedings only in the courts of the Member State in which the defendant is domiciled, irrespective of whether he is the policyholder, the insured or a beneficiary. **5–260**

2. The provisions of this Section shall not affect the right to bring a counter-claim in the court in which, in accordance with this Section, the original claim is pending.

***Paragraph numbers marked with a "+" can be found online and on CD.***

*Article 13*

5–261 The provisions of this Section may be departed from only by an agreement:

1. which is entered into after the dispute has arisen, or

2. which allows the policyholder, the insured or a beneficiary to bring proceedings in courts other than those indicated in this Section, or

3. which is concluded between a policyholder and an insurer, both of whom are at the time of conclusion of the contract domiciled or habitually resident in the same Member State, and which has the effect of conferring jurisdiction on the courts of that State even if the harmful event were to occur abroad, provided that such an agreement is not contrary to the law of that State, or

4. which is concluded with a policyholder who is not domiciled in a Member State, except in so far as the insurance is compulsory or relates to immovable property in a Member State, or

5. which relates to a contract of insurance in so far as it covers one or more of the risks set out in Article 14.

*Article 14*

5–262 The following are the risks referred to in Article 13(5):

1. any loss of or damage to:

(a) seagoing ships, installations situated offshore or on the high seas, or aircraft, arising from perils which relate to their use for commercial purposes;

(b) goods in transit other than passengers' baggage where the transit consists of or includes carriage by such ships or aircraft;

2. any liability, other than for bodily injury to passengers or loss of or damage to their baggage:

(a) arising out of the use or operation of ships, installations or aircraft as referred to in point 1(a) in so far as, in respect of the latter, the law of the Member State in which such aircraft are registered does not prohibit agreements on jurisdiction regarding insurance of such risks;

(b) for loss or damage caused by goods in transit as described in point 1(b);

3. any financial loss connected with the use or operation of ships, installations or aircraft as referred to in point 1(a), in particular loss of freight or charter-hire;

4. any risk or interest connected with any of those referred to in points 1 to 3;

5. notwithstanding points 1 to 4, all "large risks" as defined in Council Directive 73/239/EEC, as amended by Council Directives 88/357/EEC and 90/618/EEC, as they may be amended.

SECTION 4—JURISDICTION OVER CONSUMER CONTRACTS

*Article 15*

5–263 1. In matters relating to a contract concluded by a person, the consumer, for a purpose which can be regarded as being outside his

***Paragraph numbers marked with a "+" can be found online and on CD.***

trade or profession, jurisdiction shall be determined by this Section, without prejudice to Article 4 and point 5 of Article 5, if:

(a) it is a contract for the sale of goods on instalment credit terms; or

(b) it is a contract for a loan repayable by instalments, or for any other form of credit, made to finance the sale of goods; or

(c) in all other cases, the contract has been concluded with a person who pursues commercial or professional activities in the Member State of the consumer's domicile or, by any means, directs such activities to that Member State or to several States including that Member State, and the contract falls within the scope of such activities.

2. Where a consumer enters into a contract with a party who is not domiciled in the Member State but has a branch, agency or other establishment in one of the Member States, that party shall, in disputes arising out of the operations of the branch, agency or establishment, be deemed to be domiciled in that State.

3. This Section shall not apply to a contract of transport other than a contract which, for an inclusive price, provides for a combination of travel and accommodation.

*Article 16*

1. A consumer may bring proceedings against the other party to a contract either in the courts of the Member State in which that party is domiciled or in the courts for the place where the consumer is domiciled. **5–264**

2. Proceedings may be brought against a consumer by the other party to the contract only in the courts of the Member State in which the consumer is domiciled.

3. This Article shall not affect the right to bring a counter-claim in the court in which, in accordance with this Section, the original claim is pending.

*Article 17*

The provisions of this Section may be departed from only by an agreement: **5–265**

1. which is entered into after the dispute has arisen; or

2. which allows the consumer to bring proceedings in courts other than those indicated in this Section; or

3. which is entered into by the consumer and the other party to the contract, both of whom are at the time of conclusion of the contract domiciled or habitually resident in the same Member State, and which confers jurisdiction on the courts of that Member State, provided that such an agreement is not contrary to the law of that Member State.

Section 5—Jurisdiction over individual contracts of employment

*Article 18*

1. In matters relating to individual contracts of employment, jurisdiction shall be determined by this Section, without prejudice to Article 4 and point 5 of Article 5. **5–266**

2. Where an employee enters into an individual contract of employment with an employer who is not domiciled in a Member State but has a branch, agency or other establishment in one of the Member States, the employer shall, in disputes arising out of the operations of the branch, agency or establishment, be deemed to be domiciled in that Member State.

*Article 19*

**5–267** An employer domiciled in a Member State may be sued:

1. in the courts of the Member State where he is domiciled; or

2. in another Member State:

(a) in the courts for the place where the employee habitually carries out his work or in the courts for the last place where he did so, or

(b) if the employee does not or did not habitually carry out his work in any one country, in the courts for the place where the business which engaged the employee is or was situated.

*Article 20*

**5–268** 1. An employer may bring proceedings only in the courts of the Member State in which the employee is domiciled.

2. The provisions of this Section shall not affect the right to bring a counter-claim in the court in which, in accordance with this Section, the original claim is pending.

*Article 21*

**5–269** The provisions of this Section may be departed from only be an agreement on jurisdiction:

1. which is entered into after the dispute has arisen; or

2. which allows the employee to bring proceedings in courts other than those indicated in this Section.

## SECTION 6—EXCLUSIVE JURISDICTION

*Article 22*

**5–270** The following courts shall have exclusive jurisdiction, regardless of domicile:

1. in proceedings which have as their object rights in rem in immovable property or tenancies of immovable property, the courts of the Member State in which the property is situated.

However, in proceedings which have as their object tenancies of immovable property concluded for temporary private use for a maximum period of six consecutive months, the courts of the Member State in which the defendant is domiciled shall also have jurisdiction, provided that the tenant is a natural person and that the landlord and the tenant are domiciled in the same Member State;

2. in proceedings which have as their object the validity of the constitution, the nullity or the dissolution of companies or other legal persons or associations of natural or legal persons, or of the validity of the decisions of their organs, the courts of the Member State in which the company, legal person or association has its seat. In order

to determine that seat, the court shall apply its rules of private international law;

3. in proceedings which have as their object the validity of entries in public registers, the courts of the Member State in which the register is kept;

4. in proceedings concerned with the registration or validity of patents, trade marks, designs, or other similar rights required to be deposited or registered, the courts of the Member State in which the deposit or registration has been applied for, has taken place or is under the terms of a Community instrument or an international convention deemed to have taken place.

Without prejudice to the jurisdiction of the European Patent Office under the Convention on the Grant of European Patents, signed at Munich on 5 October 1973, the courts of each Member State shall have exclusive jurisdiction, regardless of domicile, in proceedings concerned with the registration or validity of any European patent granted for that State;

5. in proceedings concerned with the enforcement of judgments, the courts of the Member State in which the judgment has been or is to be enforced.

## SECTION 7—PROROGATION OF JURISDICTION

### *Article 23*

1. If the parties, one or more of whom is domiciled in a Member **5–271** State, have agreed that a court or the courts of a Member State are to have jurisdiction to settle any disputes which have arisen or which may arise in connection with a particular legal relationship, that court or those courts shall have jurisdiction. Such jurisdiction shall be exclusive unless the parties have agreed otherwise. Such an agreement conferring jurisdiction shall be either:

(a) in writing or evidenced in writing; or

(b) in a form which accords with practices which the parties have established between themselves; or

(c) in international trade or commerce, in a form which accords with a usage of which the parties are or ought to have been aware and which in such trade or commerce is widely known to, and regularly observed by, parties to contracts of the type involved in the particular trade or commerce concerned.

2. Any communication by electronic means which provides a durable record of the agreement shall be equivalent to "writing".

3. Where such an agreement is concluded by parties, none of whom is domiciled in a Member State, the courts of other Member States shall have no jurisdiction over their disputes unless the court or courts chosen have declined jurisdiction.

4. The court or courts of a Member State on which a trust instrument has conferred jurisdiction shall have exclusive jurisdiction in any proceedings brought against a settlor, trustee or beneficiary, if relations between these persons or their rights or obligations under the trust are involved.

***Paragraph numbers marked with a "+" can be found online and on CD.***

5. Agreements or provisions of a trust instrument conferring jurisdiction shall have no legal force if they are contrary to Articles 13, 17 or 21, or if the courts whose jurisdiction they purport to exclude have exclusive jurisdiction by virtue of Article 22.

*Article 24*

5–272 Apart from jurisdiction derived from other provisions of this Regulation, a court of a Member State before which a defendant enters an appearance shall have jurisdiction. This rule shall not apply where appearance was entered to contest the jurisdiction, or where another court has exclusive jurisdiction by virtue of Article 22.

### SECTION 8—EXAMINATION AS TO JURISDICTION AND ADMISSIBILITY

*Article 25*

5–273 Where a court of a Member State is seised of a claim which is principally concerned with a matter over which the courts of another Member State have exclusive jurisdiction by virtue of Article 22, it shall declare of its own motion that it has no jurisdiction.

*Article 26*

5–274 1. Where a defendant domiciled in one Member State is sued in a court of another Member State and does not enter an appearance, the court shall declare of its own motion that it has no jurisdiction unless its jurisdiction is derived from the provisions of this Regulation.

2. The court shall stay the proceedings so long as it is not shown that the defendant has been able to receive the document instituting the proceedings or an equivalent document in sufficient time to enable him to arrange for his defence, or that all necessary steps have been taken to this end.

3. Article 19 of Council Regulation (EC) No 1348/2000 of 29 May 2000 on the service in the Member States of judicial and extrajudicial documents in civil or commercial matters shall apply instead of the provisions of paragraph 2 if the document instituting the proceedings or an equivalent document had to be transmitted from one Member State to another pursuant to this Regulation.

4. Where the provisions of Regulation (EC) No 1348/2000 are not applicable, Article 15 of the Hague Convention of 15 November 1965 on the Service Abroad of Judicial and Extrajudicial Documents in Civil or Commercial Matters shall apply if the document instituting the proceedings or an equivalent document had to be transmitted pursuant to that Convention.

### SECTION 9—LIS PENDENS—RELATED ACTIONS

*Article 27*

5–275 1. Where proceedings involving the same cause of action and between the same parties are brought in the courts of different Member States, any court other than the court first seised shall of its own motion stay its proceedings until such time as the jurisdiction of the court first seised is established.

2. Where the jurisdiction of the court first seised is established, any court other than the court first seised shall decline jurisdiction in favour of that court.

*Article 28*

1. Where related actions are pending in the courts of different Member States, any court other than the court first seised may stay its proceedings. **5–276**

2. Where these actions are pending at first instance, any court other than the court first seised may also, on the application of one of the parties, decline jurisdiction if the court first seised has jurisdiction over the actions in question and its law permits the consolidation thereof.

3. For the purposes of this Article, actions are deemed to be related where they are so closely connected that it is expedient to hear and determine them together to avoid the risk of irreconcilable judgments resulting from separate proceedings.

*Article 29*

Where actions come within the exclusive jurisdiction of several courts, any court other than the court first seised shall decline jurisdiction in favour of that court. **5–277**

*Article 30*

For the purposes of this Section, a court shall be deemed to be seised: **5–278**

1. at the time when the document instituting the proceedings or an equivalent document is lodged with the court, provided that the plaintiff has not subsequently failed to take the steps he was required to take to have service effected on the defendant, or.

2. if the document has to be served before being lodged with the court, at the time when it is received by the authority responsible for service, provided that the plaintiff has not subsequently failed to take the steps he was required to take to have the document lodged with the court.

## SECTION 10—PROVISIONAL, INCLUDING PROTECTIVE, MEASURES

*Article 31*

Application may be made to the courts of a Member State for such provisional, including protective, measures as may be available under the law of that State, even if, under this Regulation, the courts of another Member State have jurisdiction as to the substance of the matter. **5–279**

## CHAPTER III—RECOGNITION AND ENFORCEMENT

*Article 32*

For the purposes of this Regulation, "judgment" means any judgment given by a court or tribunal of a Member State, whatever the judgment may be called, including a decree, order, decision or writ of execution, as well as the determination of costs or expenses by an officer of the court. **5–280**

### SECTION 1—RECOGNITION

*Article 33*

5–281 1. A judgment given in a Member State shall be recognised in the other Member States without any special procedure being required.

2. Any interested party who raises the recognition of a judgment as the principal issue in a dispute may, in accordance with the procedures provided for in Sections 2 and 3 of this Chapter, apply for a decision that the judgment be recognised.

3. If the outcome of proceedings in a court of a Member State depends on the determination of an incidental question of recognition that court shall have jurisdiction over that question.

*Article 34*

5–282 A judgment shall not be recognised:

1. if such recognition is manifestly contrary to public policy in the Member State in which recognition is sought;

2. where it was given in default of appearance, if the defendant was not served with the document which instituted the proceedings or with an equivalent document in sufficient time and in such a way as to enable him to arrange for his defence, unless the defendant failed to commence proceedings to challenge the judgment when it was possible for him to do so;

3. if it is irreconcilable with a judgment given in a dispute between the same parties in the Member State in which recognition is sought;

4. if it is irreconcilable with an earlier judgment given in another Member State or in a third State involving the same cause of action and between the same parties, provided that the earlier judgment fulfils the conditions necessary for its recognition in the Member State addressed.

*Article 35*

5–283 1. Moreover, a judgment shall not be recognised if it conflicts with Sections 3, 4 or 6 of Chapter II, or in a case provided for in Article 72.

2. In its examination of the grounds of jurisdiction referred to in the foregoing paragraph, the court or authority applied to shall be bound by the findings of fact on which the court of the Member State of origin based its jurisdiction.

3. Subject to the paragraph 1, the jurisdiction of the court of the Member State of origin may not be reviewed. The test of public policy referred to in point 1 of Article 34 may not be applied to the rules relating to jurisdiction.

*Article 36*

5–284 Under no circumstances may a foreign judgment be reviewed as to its substance.

*Article 37*

5–285 1. A court of a Member State in which recognition is sought of a judgment given in another Member State may stay the proceedings if an ordinary appeal against the judgment has been lodged.

2. A court of a Member State in which recognition is sought of a judgment given in Ireland or the United Kingdom may stay the proceedings if enforcement is suspended in the State of origin, by reason of an appeal.

## SECTION 2—ENFORCEMENT

*Article 38*

1. A judgment given in a Member State and enforceable in that State shall be enforced in another Member State when, on the application of any interested party, it has been declared enforceable there. **5–286**

2. However, in the United Kingdom, such a judgment shall be enforced in England and Wales, in Scotland, or in Northern Ireland when, on the application of any interested party, it has been registered for enforcement in that part of the United Kingdom.

*Article 39*

1. The application shall be submitted to the court or competent authority indicated in the list in Annex II. **5–287**

2. The local jurisdiction shall be determined by reference to the place of domicile of the party against whom enforcement is sought, or to the place of enforcement.

**United Kingdom courts**

The UK courts listed in Annex II are: (a) in England and Wales, the High Court of Justice, or in the case of a maintenance judgment, the Magistrate's Court on transmission by the Secretary of State; (b) in Scotland, the Court of Session, or in the case of a maintenance judgment, the Sheriff Court on transmission by the Secretary of State; (c) in Northern Ireland, the High Court of Justice, or in the case of a maintenance judgment, the Magistrate's Court on transmission by the Secretary of State; (d) in Gibraltar, the Supreme Court of Gibraltar, or in the case of a maintenance judgment, the Magistrates' Court on transmission by the Attorney General of Gibraltar. **5–287.1**

*Article 40*

1. The procedure for making the application shall be governed by the law of the Member State in which enforcement is sought. **5–288**

2. The applicant must give an address for service of process within the area of jurisdiction of the court applied to. However, if the law of the Member State in which enforcement is sought does not provide for the furnishing of such an address, the applicant shall appoint a representative ad litem.

3. The documents referred to in Article 53 shall be attached to the application.

*Article 41*

The judgment shall be declared enforceable immediately on completion of the formalities in Article 53 without any review under Articles 34 and 35. The party against whom enforcement is sought shall not at this stage of the proceedings be entitled to make any submissions on the application. **5–289**

*Article 42*

1. The decision on the application for a declaration of enforceability shall forthwith be brought to the notice of the applicant in ac- **5–290**

cordance with the procedure laid down by the law of the Member State in which enforcement is sought.

2. The declaration of enforceability shall be served on the party against whom enforcement is sought, accompanied by the judgment, if not already served on that party.

*Article 43*

5–291 1. The decision on the application for a declaration of enforceability may be appealed against by either party.

2. The appeal is to be lodged with the court indicated in the list in Annex III.

3. The appeal shall be dealt with in accordance with the rules governing procedure in contradictory matters.

4. If the party against whom enforcement is sought fails to appear before the appellate court in proceedings concerning an appeal brought by the applicant, Article 26(2) to (4) shall apply even where the party against whom enforcement is sought is not domiciled in any of the Member States.

5. An appeal against the declaration of enforceability is to be lodged within one month of service thereof. If the party against whom enforcement is sought is domiciled in a Member State other than that in which the declaration of enforceability was given, the time for appealing shall be two months and shall run from the date of service, either on him in person or at his residence. No extension of time may be granted on account of distance.

**UK appeal courts**

5–291.1 The UK courts with which appeals referred to in art.43(2) and listed in Annex III may be lodged are the following: (a) in England and Wales, the High Court of Justice, or in the case of a maintenance judgment, the Magistrate's Court; (b) in Scotland, the Court of Session, or in the case of a maintenance judgment, the Sheriff Court; (c) in Northern Ireland, the High Court of Justice, or in the case of a maintenance judgment, the Magistrate's Court; (d) in Gibraltar, the Supreme Court of Gibraltar, or in the case of a maintenance judgment, the Magistrates' Court.

*Article 44*

5–292 The judgment given on the appeal may be contested only by the appeal referred to in Annex IV.

**Appeal**

5–292.1 In Annex IV it is stated that the appeals which may be lodged in the UK pursuant to art.44 is a single further appeal on a point of law.

*Article 45*

5–293 1. The court with which an appeal is lodged under Article 43 or Article 44 shall refuse or revoke a declaration of enforceability only on one of the grounds specified in Articles 34 and 35. It shall give its decision without delay.

2. Under no circumstances may the foreign judgment be reviewed as to its substance.

*Article 46*

1. The court with which an appeal is lodged under Article 43 or Article 44 may, on the application of the party against whom enforcement is sought, stay the proceedings if an ordinary appeal has been lodged against the judgment in the Member State of origin or if the time for such an appeal has not yet expired; in the latter case, the court may specify the time within which such an appeal is to be lodged. **5–294**

2. Where the judgment was given in Ireland or the United Kingdom, any form of appeal available in the Member State of origin shall be treated as an ordinary appeal for the purposes of paragraph 1.

3. The court may also make enforcement conditional on the provision of such security as it shall determine.

*Article 47*

1. When a judgment must be recognised in accordance with this Regulation, nothing shall prevent the applicant from availing himself of provisional, including protective, measures in accordance with the law of the Member State requested without a declaration of enforceability under Article 41 being required. **5–295**

2. The declaration of enforceability shall carry with it the power to proceed to any protective measures.

3. During the time specified for an appeal pursuant to Article 43(5) against the declaration of enforceability and until any such appeal has been determined, no measures of enforcement may be taken other than protective measures against the property of the party against whom enforcement is sought.

*Article 48*

1. Where a foreign judgment has been given in respect of several matters and the declaration of enforceability cannot be given for all of them, the court or competent authority shall give it for one or more of them. **5–296**

2. An applicant may request a declaration of enforceability limited to parts of a judgment.

*Article 49*

A foreign judgment which orders a periodic payment by way of a penalty shall be enforceable in the Member State in which enforcement is sought only if the amount of the payment has been finally determined by the courts of the Member State of origin. **5–297**

*Article 50*

An applicant who, in the Member State of origin has benefited from complete or partial legal aid or exemption from costs or expenses, shall be entitled, in the procedure provided for in this Section, to benefit from the most favourable legal aid or the most extensive exemption from costs or expenses provided for by the law of the Member State addressed. **5–298**

**Lugano Convention**

5-298.1 The texts of the articles in Chapter III of the Judgments Regulation and of the articles in Title III of the Lugano Convention are to the same effect. However, art.50 of the Lugano Convention contains an additional paragraph relating to applicants requesting the enforcement of a decision given by an administrative authority in Denmark, in Iceland, or in Norway.

*Article 51*

5-299 No security, bond or deposit, however described, shall be required of a party who in one Member State applies for enforcement of a judgment given in another Member State on the ground that he is a foreign national or that he is not domiciled or resident in the State in which enforcement is sought.

*Article 52*

5-300 In proceedings for the issue of a declaration of enforceability, no charge, duty or fee calculated by reference to the value of the matter at issue may be levied in the Member State in which enforcement is sought.

## SECTION 3—COMMON PROVISIONS

*Article 53*

5-301 1. A party seeking recognition or applying for a declaration of enforceability shall produce a copy of the judgment which satisfies the conditions necessary to establish its authenticity.

2. A party applying for a declaration of enforceability shall also produce the certificate referred to in Article 54, without prejudice to Article 55.

*Article 54*

5-302 The court or competent authority of a Member State where a judgment was given shall issue, at the request of any interested party, a certificate using the standard form in Annex V to this Regulation.

**Standard form of certificate (art.54)**

5-302.1 For the standard form of certificate as set out in Annex V, see para.5-329 below.

*Article 55*

5-303 1. If the certificate referred to in Article 54 is not produced, the court or competent authority may specify a time for its production or accept an equivalent document or, if it considers that it has sufficient information before it, dispense with its production.

2. If the court or competent authority so requires, a translation of the documents shall be produced. The translation shall be certified by a person qualified to do so in one of the Member States.

*Article 56*

5-304 No legalisation or other similar formality shall be required in respect of the documents referred to in Article 53 or Article 55(2), or in respect of a document appointing a representative ad litem.

## CHAPTER IV—AUTHENTIC INSTRUMENTS AND COURT SETTLEMENTS

*Article 57*

5-305 1. A document which has been formally drawn up or registered as an authentic instrument and is enforceable in one Member State shall, in another Member State, be declared enforceable there, on application made in accordance with the procedures provided for in Articles 38, et seq. The court with which an appeal is lodged under Article 43 or Article 44 shall refuse or revoke a declaration of enforceability only if enforcement of the instrument is manifestly contrary to public policy in the Member State addressed.

2. Arrangements relating to maintenance obligations concluded with administrative authorities or authenticated by them shall also be regarded as authentic instruments within the meaning of paragraph 1.

3. The instrument produced must satisfy the conditions necessary to establish its authenticity in the Member State of origin.

4. Section 3 of Chapter III shall apply as appropriate. The competent authority of a Member State where an authentic instrument was drawn up or registered shall issue, at the request of any interested party, a certificate using the standard form in Annex VI to this Regulation.

**Standard form of certificate (art.57)**

For the standard form of certificate as set out in Annex VI, see para.5–330 below. **5–305.1**

*Article 58*

A settlement which has been approved by a court in the course of proceedings and is enforceable in the Member State in which it was concluded shall be enforceable in the State addressed under the same conditions as authentic instruments. The court or competent authority of a Member State where a court settlement was approved shall issue, at the request of any interested party, a certificate using the standard form in Annex V to this Regulation. **5–306**

**Standard form of certificate (art.58)**

For the standard form of certificate as set out in Annex V, see para.5–329 below. **5–306.1**

## CHAPTER V—GENERAL PROVISIONS

*Article 59*

1. In order to determine whether a party is domiciled in the Member State whose courts are seised of a matter, the court shall apply its internal law. **5–307**

2. If a party is not domiciled in the Member State whose courts are seised of the matter, then, in order to determine whether the party is domiciled in another Member State, the court shall apply the law of that Member State.

*Article 60*

1. For the purposes of this Regulation, a company or other legal person or association of natural or legal persons is domiciled at the place where it has its: **5–308**

(a) statutory seat, or

(b) central administration, or

*Paragraph numbers marked with a "+" can be found online and on CD.*

(c) principal place of business.

2. For the purposes of the United Kingdom and Ireland "statutory seat" means the registered office or, where there is no such office anywhere, the place of incorporation or, where there is no such place anywhere, the place under the law of which the formation took place.

3. In order to determine whether a trust is domiciled in the Member State whose courts are seised of the matter, the court shall apply its rules of private international law.

*Article 61*

5–309 Without prejudice to any more favourable provisions of national laws, persons domiciled in a Member State who are being prosecuted in the criminal courts of another Member State of which they are not nationals for an offence which was not intentionally committed may be defended by persons qualified to do so, even if they do not appear in person. However, the court seised of the matter may order appearance in person; in the case of failure to appear, a judgment given in the civil action without the person concerned having had the opportunity to arrange for his defence need not be recognised or enforced in the other Member States.

*Article 62*

5–310 In Sweden, in summary proceedings concerning orders to pay (betalningsföreläggande) and assistance (handräckning), the expression "court" includes the "Swedish enforcement service" (kronofogdemyndighet).

*Article 63*

5–311 1. A person domiciled in the territory of the Grand Duchy of Luxembourg and sued in the court of another Member State pursuant to Article 5(1) may refuse to submit to the jurisdiction of that court if the final place of delivery of the goods or provision of the services is in Luxembourg.

2. Where, under paragraph 1, the final place of delivery of the goods or provision of the services is in Luxembourg, any agreement conferring jurisdiction must, in order to be valid, be accepted in writing or evidenced in writing within the meaning of Article 23(1)(a).

3. The provisions of this Article shall not apply to contracts for the provision of financial services.

4. The provisions of this Article shall apply for a period of six years from entry into force of this Regulation.

*Article 64*

5–312 1. In proceedings involving a dispute between the master and a member of the crew of a seagoing ship registered in Greece or in Portugal, concerning remuneration or other conditions of service, a court in a Member State shall establish whether the diplomatic or consular officer responsible for the ship has been notified of the dispute. It may act as soon as that officer has been notified.

2. The provisions of this Article shall apply for a period of six years from entry into force of this Regulation.

*Article 65*

1. The jurisdiction specified in Article 6(2), and Article 11 in actions on a warranty of guarantee or in any other third party proceedings may not be resorted to in Germany, Austria and Hungary. Any person domiciled in another Member State may be sued in the courts: 5–313

(a) of Germany, pursuant to Articles 68 and 72 to 74 of the Code of Civil Procedure (Zivilprozessordnung) concerning third-party notices,

(b) of Austria, pursuant to Article 21 of the Code of Civil Procedure (Zivilprozessordnung) concerning third-party notices.

(c) of Hungary, pursuant to Articles 58 to 60 of the Code of Civil Procedure (Polgári perrendtartás) concerning third-party notices.

2. Judgments given in other Member States by virtue of Article 6(2), or Article 11 shall be recognised and enforced in Germany, Austria and Hungary in accordance with Chapter III. Any effects which judgments given in these States may have on third parties by application of the provisions in paragraph 1 shall also be recognised in the other Member States.

## CHAPTER VI—TRANSITIONAL PROVISIONS

*Article 66*

1. This Regulation shall apply only to legal proceedings instituted and to documents formally drawn up or registered as authentic instruments after the entry into force thereof. 5–314

2. However, if the proceedings in the Member State of origin were instituted before the entry into force of this Regulation, judgments given after that date shall be recognised and enforced in accordance with Chapter III,

(a) if the proceedings in the Member State of origin were instituted after the entry into force of the Brussels or the Lugano Convention both in the Member State or origin and in the Member State addressed;

(b) in all other cases, if jurisdiction was founded upon rules which accorded with those provided for either in Chapter II or in a convention concluded between the Member State of origin and the Member State addressed which was in force when the proceedings were instituted.

## CHAPTER VII—RELATIONS WITH OTHER INSTRUMENTS

*Article 67*

This Regulation shall not prejudice the application of provisions governing jurisdiction and the recognition and enforcement of judgments in specific matters which are contained in Community instruments or in national legislation harmonised pursuant to such instruments. 5–315

*Article 68*

1. This Regulation shall, as between the Member States, supersede the Brussels Convention, except as regards the territories of the 5–316

***Paragraph numbers marked with a "+" can be found online and on CD.***

Member States which fall within the territorial scope of that Convention and which are excluded from this Regulation pursuant to Article 299 of the Treaty.

2. In so far as this Regulation replaces the provisions of the Brussels Convention between Member States, any reference to the Convention shall be understood as a reference to this Regulation.

*Article 69*

5–316.1 Subject to Article 66(2) and Article 70, this Regulation shall, as between Member States, supersede the following conventions and treaty concluded between two or more of them: [...]

**Superseded conventions, etc**

5–317.1 The list of 90 conventions, treaties and agreements made between Members States in the years 1899 to 1999 (being conventions, etc. superseded by the Judgments Regulation) as set out in art.69 (and referred to in art.70) has been omitted. Article 66(2) is a transitional provision.

*Article 70*

5–318 1. The Treaty and the Conventions referred to in Article 69 shall continue to have effect in relation to matters to which this Regulation does not apply.

2. They shall continue to have effect in respect of judgments given and documents formally drawn up or registered as authentic instruments before the entry into force of this Regulation.

*Article 71*

5–319 1. This Regulation shall not affect any conventions to which the Member States are parties and which in relation to particular matters, govern jurisdiction or the recognition or enforcement of judgments.

2. With a view to its uniform interpretation, paragraph 1 shall be applied in the following manner:

(a) this Regulation shall not prevent a court of a Member State, which is a party to a convention on a particular matter, from assuming jurisdiction in accordance with that convention, even where the defendant is domiciled in another Member State which is not a party to that convention. The court hearing the action shall, in any event, apply Article 26 of this Regulation;

(b) judgments given in a Member State by a court in the exercise of jurisdiction provided for in a convention on a particular matter shall be recognised and enforced in the other Member States in accordance with this Regulation.

Where a convention on a particular matter to which both the Member State of origin and the Member State addressed are parties lays down conditions for the recognition or enforcement of judgments, those conditions shall apply. In any event, the provisions of this Regulation which concern the procedure for recognition and enforcement of judgments may be applied.

*Article 72*

This Regulation shall not affect agreements by which Member States undertook, prior to the entry into force of this Regulation pursuant to Article 59 of the Brussels Convention, not to recognise judgments given, in particular in other Contracting States to that Convention, against defendants domiciled or habitually resident in a third country where, in cases provided for in Article 4 of that Convention, the judgment could only be founded on a ground of jurisdiction specified in the second paragraph of Article 3 of that Convention. **5–320**

## CHAPTER VIII—FINAL PROVISIONS

*Article 73*

No later than five years after the entry into force of this Regulation, the Commission shall present to the European Parliament, the Council and the Economic and Social Committee a report on the application of this Regulation. The report shall be accompanied, if need be, by proposals for adaptations to this Regulation. **5–321**

*Article 74*

1. The Member States shall notify the Commission of the texts amending the lists set out in Annexes I to IV. The Commission shall adapt the Annexes concerned accordingly. **5–322**

2. The updating or technical adjustment of the forms, specimens of which appear in Annexes V and VI, shall be adopted in accordance with the advisory procedure referred to in Article 75(2).

*Article 75*

1. The Commission shall be assisted by a committee. **5–323**

2. Where reference is made to this paragraph, Articles 3 and 7 of Decision 1999/468/EC shall apply.

3. The Committee shall adopt its rules of procedure.

*Article 76*

This Regulation shall enter into force on 1 March 2002. **5–324**

This Regulation is binding in its entirety and directly applicable in the Member States in accordance with the Treaty establishing the European Community.

Done at Brussels, 22 December 2000.

For the Council

The President

C. Pierret

*Annex I*

[*Text omitted*] **5–325**

*Annex II*

[*Text omitted*] **5–326**

*Annex III*

[*Text omitted*] **5–327**

*Annex IV*

[*Text omitted*] **5–328**

***Paragraph numbers marked with a "+" can be found online and on CD.***

*Annex V*

## Certificate referred to in Articles 54 and 58 of the Regulation on judgments and court settlements

(English, inglés, anglais, ingleses, ...)

5–329 1. Member State of origin
2. Court or competent authority issuing the certificate
   2.1. Name
   2.2. Address
   2.3. Tel./fax/email
3. Court which delivered the judgment/approved the court settlement (*)
   3.1. Type of court
   3.2. Place of court
4. Judgment/court settlement (*)
   4.1. Date
   4.2. Reference number
   4.3. The parties to the judgment/court settlement (*)
      4.3.1. Name(s) of plaintiff(s)
      4.3.2. Name(s) of defendant(s)
      4.3.3. Name(s) of other party(ies), if any
   4.4. Date of service of the document instituting the proceedings where judgment was given in default of appearance
   4.5. Text of the judgment/court settlement (*) as annexed to this certificate
5. Names of parties to whom legal aid has been granted

The judgment.court settlement (*) is enforceable in the Member State of origin (Articles 38 and 58 of the Regulation) against:

Name:

Done at .................................... date ....................................

Signature and/or stamp ....................................................................

(*) Delete as appropriate

*Annex VI*

## Certificate referred to in Article 57(4) of the Regulation on authentic instruments

(English, inglés, anglais, ingleses, ...)

5–330 1. Member State of origin
2. Competent authority issuing the certificate
   2.1. Name
   2.2. Address
   2.3. Tel./fax/email
3. Authority which has given authenticity to the instrument
   3.1. Authority involved in the drawing up of the authentic instrument (if applicable)
      3.1.1. Name and designation of authority
      3.1.2. Place of authority
   3.2. Authority which has registered the authentic instrument (if applicable)
      3.2.1. Type of authority
      3.2.2. Place of authority
4. Authentic instrument

***Paragraph numbers marked with a "+" can be found online and on CD.***

4.1. Description of the instrument
4.2. Date
4.2.1. on which the instrument was drawn up
4.2.2. if different: on which the instrument was registered
4.3. Reference number
4.4. Parties to the instrument
4.4.1. Name of the creditor
4.4.2. Name of the debtor
5. Text of the enforceable obligation as annexed to this certificate

The authentic instrument is enforceable against the debtor in the Member State of origin (Article 57(1) of the Regulation)

Done at .............................. date ..............................

Signature and/or stamp ..............................................................

## *Council Regulation (EC) No.1206/2001 of 28 May 2001 on cooperation between the courts of the Member States in the taking of evidence in civil or commercial matters*

### CHAPTER 1—GENERAL PROVISIONS

*Article 1*

#### Scope

1. This Regulation shall apply in civil or commercial matters where the court of a Member State, in accordance with the provisions of the law of that State, requests: **5–331**

(a) the competent court of another Member State to take evidence; or

(b) to take evidence directly in another Member State.

2. A request shall not be made to obtain evidence which is not intended for use in judicial proceedings, commenced or contemplated.

3. In this Regulation, the term "Member State" shall mean Member States with the exception of Denmark.

*Article 2*

#### Direct transmission between the courts

1. Requests pursuant to Article 1(1)(a), hereinafter referred to as "requests", shall be transmitted by the court before which the proceedings are commenced or contemplated, hereinafter referred to as the "requesting court", directly to the competent court of another Member State, hereinafter referred to as the "requested court", for the performance of the taking of evidence. **5–332**

2. Each Member State shall draw up a list of the courts competent for the performance of taking of evidence according to this Regulation. The list shall also indicate the territorial and, where appropriate, the special jurisdiction of those courts.

*Article 3*

#### Central body

1. Each Member State shall designate a central body responsible for: **5–333**

*Paragraph numbers marked with a "+" can be found online and on CD.*

(a) supplying information to the courts;

(b) seeking solutions to any difficulties which may arise in respect of a request;

(c) forwarding, in exceptional cases, at the request of a requesting court, a request to the competent court.

2. A federal State, a State in which several legal systems apply or a State with autonomous territorial entities shall be free to designate more than one central body.

3. Each Member State shall also designate the central body referred to in paragraph 1 or one or several competent authority(ies) to be responsible for taking decisions on requests pursuant to Article 17.

## CHAPTER II—TRANSMISSION AND EXECUTION OF REQUESTS

### SECTION 1—TRANSMISSION OF THE REQUEST

*Article 4*

**Form and content of the request**

5–334 1. The request shall be made using form A or, where appropriate, form I in the Annex. It shall contain the following details:

(a) the requesting and, where appropriate, the requested court;

(b) the names and addresses of the parties to the proceedings and their representatives, if any;

(c) the nature and subject matter of the case and a brief statement of the facts;

(d) a description of the taking of evidence to be performed;

(e) where the request is for the examination of a person:
- the name(s) and address(es) of the person(s) to be examined,
- the questions to be put to the person(s) to be examined or a statement of the facts about which he is (they are) to be examined,
- where appropriate, a reference to a right to refuse to testify under the law of the Member State of the requesting court,
- any requirement that the examination is to be carried out under oath or affirmation in lieu thereof, and any special form to be used,
- where appropriate, any other information that the requesting court deems necessary;

(f) where the request is for any other form of taking of evidence, the documents or other objects to be inspected;

(g) where appropriate, any request pursuant to Article 10(3) and (4), and Articles 11 and 12 and any information necessary for the application thereof.

2. The request and all documents accompanying the request shall be exempted from authentication or any equivalent formality.

3. Documents which the requesting court deems it necessary to enclose for the execution of the request shall be accompanied by a translation into the language in which the request was written.

Article 5

**Language**

The request and communications pursuant to this Regulation shall be drawn up in the official language of the requested Member State or, if there are several official languages in that Member State, in the official language or one of the official languages of the place where the requested taking of evidence is to be performed, or in another language which the requested Member State has indicated it can accept. Each Member State shall indicate the official language or languages of the institutions of the European Community other than its own which is or are acceptable to it for completion of the forms. **5–335**

Article 6

**Transmission of requests and other communications**

Requests and communications pursuant to this Regulation shall be transmitted by the swiftest possible means, which the requested Member State has indicated it can accept. The transmission may be carried out by any appropriate means, provided that the document received accurately reflects the content of the document forwarded and that all information in it is legible. **5–336**

SECTION 2—RECEIPT OF REQUEST

Article 7

**Receipt of request**

1. Within seven days of receipt of the request, the requested competent court shall send an acknowledgement of receipt to the requesting court using form B in the Annex. Where the request does not comply with the conditions laid down in Articles 5 and 6, the requested court shall enter a note to that effect in the acknowledgement of receipt. **5–337**

2. Where the execution of a request made using form A in the Annex, which complies with the conditions laid down in Article 5, does not fall within the jurisdiction of the court to which it was transmitted, the latter shall forward the request to the competent court of its Member State and shall inform the requesting court thereof using form A in the Annex.

Article 8

**Incomplete request**

1. If a request cannot be executed because it does not contain all of the necessary information pursuant to Article 4, the requested court shall inform the requesting court thereof without delay and, at the latest, within 30 days of receipt of the request using form C in the Annex, and shall request it to send the missing information, which should be indicated as precisely as possible. **5–338**

2. If a request cannot be executed because a deposit or advance is necessary in accordance with Article 18(3), the requested court shall inform the requesting court thereof without delay and, at the latest,

within 30 days of receipt of the request using form C in the Annex and inform the requesting court how the deposit or advance should be made. The requested Court shall acknowledge receipt of the deposit or advance without delay, at the latest within 10 days of receipt of the deposit or the advance using form D.

*Article 9*

**Completion of the request**

5–339 1. If the requested court has noted on the acknowledgement of receipt pursuant to Article 7(1) that the request does not comply with the conditions laid down in Articles 5 and 6 or has informed the requesting court pursuant to Article 8 that the request cannot be executed because it does not contain all of the necessary information pursuant to Article 4, the time limit pursuant to Article 10 shall begin to run when the requested court received the request duly completed.

2. Where the requested court has asked for a deposit or advance in accordance with Article 18(3), this time limit shall begin to run when the deposit or the advance is made.

SECTION 3—TAKING OF EVIDENCE BY THE REQUESTED COURT

*Article 10*

**General provisions on the execution of the request**

5–340 1. The requested court shall execute the request without delay and, at the latest, within 90 days of receipt of the request.

2. The requested court shall execute the request in accordance with the law of its Member State.

3. The requesting court may call for the request to be executed in accordance with a special procedure provided for by the law of its Member State, using form A in the Annex. The requested court shall comply with such a requirement unless this procedure is incompatible with the law of the Member State of the requested court or by reason of major practical difficulties. If the requested court does not comply with the requirement for one of these reasons it shall inform the requesting court using form E in the Annex.

4. The requesting court may ask the requested court to use communications technology at the performance of the taking of evidence, in particular by using videoconference and teleconference. The requested court shall comply with such a requirement unless this is incompatible with the law of the Member State of the requested court or by reason of major practical difficulties. If the requested court does not comply with the requirement for one of these reasons, it shall inform the requesting court, using form E in the Annex. If there is no access to the technical means referred to above in the requesting or in the requested court, such means may be made available by the courts by mutual agreement.

*Article 11*

**Performance with the presence and participation of the parties**

5–341 1. If it is provided for by the law of the Member State of the requesting court, the parties and, if any, their representatives, have the right to be present at the performance of the taking of evidence by the requested court.

2. The requesting court shall, in its request, inform the requested court that the parties and, if any, their representatives, will be present and, where appropriate, that their participation is requested, using form A in the Annex. This information may also be given at any other appropriate time.

3. If the participation of the parties and, if any, their representatives, is requested at the performance of the taking of evidence, the requested court shall determine, in accordance with Article 10, the conditions under which they may participate.

4. The requested court shall notify the parties and, if any, their representatives, of the time when, the place where, the proceedings will take place, and, where appropriate, the conditions under which they may participate, using form F in the Annex.

5. Paragraphs 1 to 4 shall not affect the possibility for the requested court of asking the parties and, if any their representatives, to be present at or to participate in the performance of the taking of evidence if that possibility is provided for by the law of its Member State.

*Article 12*

**Performance with the presence and participation of representatives of the requesting court**

1. If it is compatible with the law of the Member State of the requesting court, representatives of the requesting court have the right to be present in the performance of the taking of evidence by the requested court. **5–342**

2. For the purpose of this Article, the term "representative" shall include members of the judicial personnel designated by the requesting court, in accordance with the law of its Member State. The requesting court may also designate, in accordance with the law of its Member State, any other person, such as an expert.

3. The requesting court shall, in its request, inform the requested court that its representatives will be present and, where appropriate, that their participation is requested, using form A in the Annex. This information may also be given at any other appropriate time.

4. If the participation of the representatives of the requesting court is requested in the performance of the taking of evidence, the requested court shall determine, in accordance with Article 10, the conditions under which they may participate.

5. The requested court shall notify the requesting court, of the time when, and the place where, the proceedings will take place, and, where appropriate, the conditions under which the representatives may participate, using form F in the Annex.

*Article 13*

**Coercive measures**

Where necessary, in executing a request the requested court shall apply the appropriate coercive measures in the instances and to **5–343** the extent as are provided for by the law of the Member State of the requested court for the execution of a request made for the same purpose by its national authorities or one of the parties concerned.

*Article 14*

**Refusal to execute**

5–344 1. A request for the hearing of a person shall not be executed when the person concerned claims the right to refuse to give evidence or to be prohibited from giving evidence,

(a) under the law of the Member State of the requested court; or

(b) under the law of the Member State of the requesting court, and such right has been specified in the request, or, if need be, at the instance of the requested court, has been confirmed by the requesting court.

2. In addition to the grounds referred to in paragraph 1, the execution of a request may be refused only if:

(a) the request does not fall within the scope of this Regulation as set out in Article 1; or

(b) the execution of the request under the law of the Member State of the requested court does not fall within the functions of the judiciary; or

(c) the requesting court does not comply with the request of the requested court to complete the request pursuant to Article 8 within 30 days after the requested court asked it to do so; or

(d) a deposit or advance asked for in accordance with Article 18(3) is not made within 60 days after the requested court asked for such a deposit or advance.

3. Execution may not be refused by the requested court solely on the ground that under the law of its Member State a court of that Member State has exclusive jurisdiction over the subject matter of the action or that the law of that Member State would not admit the right of action on it.

4. If execution of the request is refused on one of the grounds referred to in paragraph 2, the requested court shall notify the requesting court thereof within 60 days of receipt of the request by the requested court using form H in the Annex.

*Article 15*

**Notification of delay**

5–345 If the requested court is not in a position to execute the request within 90 days of receipt, it shall inform the requesting court thereof, using form G in the Annex. When it does so, the grounds for the delay shall be given as well as the estimated time that the requested court expects it will need to execute the request.

*Article 16*

**Procedure after execution of the request**

5–346 The requested court shall send without delay to the requesting court the documents establishing the execution of the request and, where appropriate, return the documents received from the requesting court. The documents shall be accompanied by a confirmation of execution using form H in the Annex.

### SECTION 4—DIRECT TAKING OF EVIDENCE BY THE REQUESTING COURT

*Article 17*

**Direct taking of evidence by the requesting court Article 17**

1. Where a court requests to take evidence directly in another Member State, it shall submit a request to the central body or the competent authority referred to in Article 3(3) in that State, using form I in the Annex. **5–347**

2. Direct taking of evidence may only take place if it can be performed on a voluntary basis without the need for coercive measures. Where the direct taking of evidence implies that a person shall be heard, the requesting court shall inform that person that the performance shall take place on a voluntary basis.

3. The taking of evidence shall be performed by a member of the judicial personnel or by any other person such as an expert, who will be designated, in accordance with the law of the Member State of the requesting court.

4. Within 30 days of receiving the request, the central body or the competent authority of the requested Member State shall inform the requesting court if the request is accepted and, if necessary, under what conditions according to the law of its Member State such performance is to be carried out, using form J. In particular, the central body or the competent authority may assign a court of its Member State to take part in the performance of the taking of evidence in order to ensure the proper application of this Article and the conditions that have been set out. The central body or the competent authority shall encourage the use of communications technology, such as videoconferences and teleconferences.

5. The central body or the competent authority may refuse direct taking of evidence only if:

(a) the request does not fall within the scope of this Regulation as set out in Article 1;

(b) the request does not contain all of the necessary information pursuant to Article 4; or

(c) the direct taking of evidence requested is contrary to fundamental principles of law in its Member State.

6. Without prejudice to the conditions laid down in accordance with paragraph 4, the requesting court shall execute the request in accordance with the law of its Member State.

### SECTION 5—COSTS

*Article 18*

1. The execution of the request, in accordance with Article 10, shall not give rise to a claim for any reimbursement of taxes or costs. **5–348**

2. Nevertheless, if the requested court so requires, the requesting court shall ensure the reimbursement, without delay, of:

***Paragraph numbers marked with a "+" can be found online and on CD.***

– the fees paid to experts and interpreters, and

– the costs occasioned by the application of Article 10(3) and(4).

The duty for the parties to bear these fees or costs shall be governed by the law of the Member State of the requesting court.

3. Where the opinion of an expert is required, the requested court may, before executing the request, ask the requesting court for an adequate deposit or advance towards the requested costs. In all other cases, a deposit or advance shall not be a condition for the execution of a request. The deposit or advance shall be made by the parties if that is provided for by the law of the Member State of the requesting court.

## CHAPTER III—FINAL PROVISIONS

*Article 19*

### Implementing rules

5–349 1. The Commission shall draw up and regularly update a manual, which shall also be available electronically, containing the information provided by the Member States in accordance with Article 22 and the agreements or arrangements in force, according to Article 21.

2. The updating or making of technical amendments to the standard forms set out in the Annex shall be carried out in accordance with the advisory procedure set out in Article 20(2).

*Article 20*

### Committee

5–350 1. The Commission shall be assisted by a Committee.

2. Where reference is made to this paragraph, Articles 3 and 7 of Decision 1999/468/EC shall apply.

3. The Committee shall adopt its Rules of Procedure.

*Article 21*

### Relationship with existing or future agreements or arrangements between Member States

5–351 1. This Regulation shall, in relation to matters to which it applies, prevail over other provisions contained in bilateral or multilateral agreements or arrangements concluded by the Member States and in particular the Hague Convention of 1 March 1954 on Civil Procedure and the Hague Convention of 18 March 1970 on the Taking of Evidence Abroad in Civil or Commercial Matters, in relations between the Member States party thereto.

2. This Regulation shall not preclude Member States from maintaining or concluding agreements or arrangements between two or more of them to further facilitate the taking of evidence, provided that they are compatible with this Regulation.

3. Member States shall send to the Commission:

(a) by 1 July 2003, a copy of the agreements or arrangements maintained between the Member States referred to in paragraph 2;

(b) a copy of the agreements or arrangements concluded between the Member States referred to in paragraph 2 as well as drafts of such agreements or arrangements which they intend to adopt; and

(c) any denunciation of, or amendments to, these agreements or arrangements

*Article 22*

**Communication**

By 1 July 2003 each Member State shall communicate to the Commission the following: **5–352**

(a) the list pursuant to Article 2(2) indicating the territorial and, where appropriate, the special jurisdiction of the courts;

(b) the names and addresses of the central bodies and competent authorities pursuant to Article 3, indicating their territorial jurisdiction;

(c) the technical means for the receipt of requests available to the courts on the list pursuant to Article 2(2);

(d) the languages accepted for the requests as referred to in Article 5.

Member States shall inform the Commission of any subsequent changes to this information.

*Article 23*

**Review**

No later than 1 January 2007, and every five years thereafter, the Commission shall present to the European Parliament, the Council and the Economic and Social Committee a report on the application of this Regulation, paying special attention to the practical application of Article 3(1)(c) and 3, and Articles 17 and 18. **5–353**

*Article 24*

**Entry into force**

1. This Regulation shall enter into force on 1 July 2001. **5–354**

2. This Regulation shall apply from 1 January 2004, except for Articles 19, 21 and 22, which shall apply from 1 July 2001.

This Regulation shall be binding in its entirety and directly applicable in the Member States in accordance with the Treaty establishing the European Community. Done at Brussels, 28 May 2001.

For the Council
The President
T. Bodström

5–355

*ANNEX*

**FORM A**

Request for the taking of evidence

(Article 4 of Council Regulation (EC) No 1206/2001 of 28 May 2001 on cooperation between the courts of the Member States in the taking of evidence in civil or commercial matters (OJ L 174, 27.6.2001, p. 1))

1. Reference of the requesting court:
2. Reference of the requested court:
3. Requesting court:
    - 3.1. Name:
    - 3.2. Address:
        - 3.2.1. Street and No/PO box:
        - 3.2.2. Place and postcode:
        - 3.2.3. Country:
    - 3.3. Tel.
    - 3.4. Fax
    - 3.5. E-mail:
4. Requested court:
    - 4.1. Name:
    - 4.2. Address:
        - 4.2.1. Street and No/PO box:
        - 4.2.2. Place and postcode:
        - 4.2.3. Country:
    - 4.3. Tel.
    - 4.4. Fax
    - 4.5. E-mail:
5. In the case brought by the claimant/petitioner:
    - 5.1. Name:
    - 5.2. Address:
        - 5.2.1. Street and No/PO box:
        - 5.2.2. Place and postcode:
        - 5.2.3. Country:

5.3. Tel.

5.4. Fax

5.5. E-mail:

6. Representatives of the claimant/petitioner:

6.1. Name:

6.2. Address:

6.2.1. Street and No/PO box:

6.2.2. Place and postcode:

6.2.3. Country:

6.3. Tel.

6.4. Fax

6.5. E-mail:

7. Against the defendant/respondent:

7.1. Name:

7.2. Address:

7.2.1. Street and No/PO box:

7.2.2. Place and postcode:

7.2.3. Country:

7.3. Tel.

7.4. Fax

7.5. E-mail:

8. Representatives of defendant/respondent:

8.1. Name:

8.2. Address:

8.2.1. Street and No/PO box:

8.2.2. Place and postcode:

8.2.3. Country:

8.3. Tel:

8.4. Fax:

8.5. E-mail:

*Paragraph numbers marked with a "+" can be found online and on CD.*

9. Presence and participation of the parties:

9.1. Parties and, if any, their representatives will be present at the taking of evidence: ☐

9.2. Participation of the parties and, if any, their representatives is requested: ☐

10. Presence and participation of the representatives of the requesting court:

10.1. Representatives will be present at the taking of evidence: ☐

10.2. Participation of the representatives is requested: ☐

10.2.1. Name:

10.2.2. Title:

10.2.3. Function:

10.2.4. Task:

11. Nature and subject matter of the case and a brief statement of the facts (in annex, where appropriate):

12. Taking of evidence to be performed

12.1. Description of the taking of evidence to be performed (in annex, where appropriate):

12.2. Examination of witnesses:

12.2.1. Name and surname:

12.2.2. Address:

12.2.3. Tel.

12.2.4. Fax

12.2.5. E-mail:

12.2.6. Questions to be put to the witness or a statement of the facts about which they are to be examined (in annex, where appropriate):

12.2.7. Right to refuse to testify under the law of the Member State of the requesting court (in annex, where appropriate):

12.2.8. Please examine the witness:

12.2.8.1. under oath: ☐

12.2.8.2. on affirmation: ☐

12.2.9. Any other information that the requesting court deems necessary (in annex, where appropriate):

12.3. Other taking of evidence:

12.3.1. Documents to be inspected and a description of the requested taking of evidence (in annex, where appropriate):

12.3.2. Objects to be inspected and a description of the requested taking of evidence (in annex, where appropriate):

13. Please execute the request

13.1. In accordance with a special procedure (Article 10(3)) provided for by the law of the Member State of the requesting court and/or by the use of communications technology (Article 10(4)) described in annex:

13.2. Following information is necessary for the application thereof:

Done at:

Date:

| Notification of forwarding the request |
|---|
| Article 7(2) of Council Regulation (EC) No 1206/2001 of 28 May 2001 on cooperation between the courts of the Member States in the taking of evidence in civil or commercial matters (OJ L 174, 27.6.2001, p. 1). |

14. The request does not fall within the jurisdiction of the court indicated in point 4 above and was forwarded to

14.1. Name of the competent court:

14.2. Address:

14.2.1. Street and No/PO box:

14.2.2. Place and postcode:

14.2.3. Country:

14.3. Tel.

14.4. Fax

14.5. E-mail:

Done at:

Date:

**FORM B**

Acknowledgement of receipt of a request for the taking of evidence

(Article 7(1) of Council Regulation (EC) No 1206/2001 of 28 May 2001 on cooperation between the courts of the Member States in the taking of evidence in civil or commercial matters (OJ L 174, 27.6.2001, p. 1))

1. Reference of the requesting court:

2. Reference of the requested court:

3. Name of the requesting court:

4. Requested court:

4.1. Name:

4.2. Address:

4.2.1. Street and No/PO box:

4.2.2. Place and postcode:

4.2.3. Country:

4.3. Tel.

4.4. Fax

4.5. E-mail:

5. The request was received on … (date of receipt) by the court indicated in point 4 above.

6. The request cannot be dealt with because:

6.1. The language used to complete the form is not acceptable (Article 5): ☐

6.1.1. Please use one the following languages:

6.2. The document is not legible (Article 6): ☐

Done at:

Date:

**FORM C**

Request for additional information for the taking of evidence

(Article 8 of Council Regulation (EC) No 1206/2001 of 28 May 2001 on cooperation between the courts of the Member States in the taking of evidence in civil or commercial matters (OJ L 174, 27.6.2001, p. 1))

1. Reference of the requested court:
2. Reference of the requesting court:
3. Name of the requesting court:
4. Name of the requested court:
5. The request cannot be executed without the following additional information:
6. The request cannot be executed before a deposit or advance is made in accordance with Article 18(3). The deposit or advance should be made in the following way:

Done at:

Date:

**FORM D**

Acknowledgement of receipt of the deposit or advance

(Article 8(2) of Council Regulation (EC) No 1206/2001 of 28 May 2001 on cooperation between the courts of the Member States in the taking of evidence in civil or commercial matters (OJ L 174, 27.6.2001, p. 1))

1. Reference of the requesting court:

2. Reference of the requested court:

3. Name of the requesting court:

4. Name of the requested court:

5. The deposit or advance was received on ... (date of receipt) by the court indicated in point 4 above.

Done at:

Date:

**FORM E**

Notification concerning the request for special procedures and/or for the use of communications technologies

(Article 10(3) and (4) of Council Regulation (EC) No 1206/2001 of 28 May 2001 on cooperation between the courts of the Member States in the taking of evidence in civil or commercial matters (OJ L 174, 27.6.2001, p. 1))

1. Reference of the requested court:
2. Reference of the requesting court:
3. Name of the requesting court:
4. Name of the requested court:
5. The requirement for execution of the request according to the special procedure indicated in point 13.1 of the request (Form A) could not be complied with because:

   5.1. the required procedure is incompatible with the law of the Member State of the requested court: ☐

   5.2. the performance of the requested procedure is not possible by reason of major practical difficulties: ☐

6. The requirement for execution of the request for the use of communications technologies indicated in point 13.1 of the request (Form A) could not be complied with because:

   6.1. The use of communications technology is incompatible with the law of the Member State of the requested court ☐

   6.2. The use of the communications technology is not possible by reason of major practical difficulties ☐

Done at:

Date:

**FORM F**

| |
|---|
| Notification of the date, time, place of performance of the taking of evidence and the conditions for participation<br><br>(Articles 11(4) and 12(5) of Council Regulation (EC) No 1206/2001 of 28 May 2001 on cooperation between the courts of the Member States in the taking of evidence in civil or commercial matters (OJ L 174, 27.6.2001, p. 1)) |

1. Reference of the requesting court:

2. Reference of the requested court:

3. Requesting court

 3.1. Name:

 3.2. Address:

  3.2.1. Street and No/PO box:

  3.2.2. Place and postcode:

  3.2.3. Country:

 3.3. Tel.

 3.4. Fax

 3.5. E-mail:

4. Requested court

 4.1. Name:

 4.2. Address:

  4.2.1. Street and No/PO box:

  4.2.2. Place and postcode:

  4.2.3. Country:

 4.3. Tel.

 4.4. Fax

 4.5. E-mail:

5. Date and time of the performance of the taking of evidence:

6. Place of the performance of the taking of evidence, if different from that referred to in point 4 above:

7. Where appropriate, conditions under which the parties and, if any, their representatives may participate:

8. Where appropriate, conditions under which the representatives of the requesting court may participate:

Done at:

Date:

**FORM G**

Notification of delay

(Article 15 of Council Regulation (EC) No 1206/2001 of 28 May 2001 on cooperation between the courts of the Member States in the taking of evidence in civil or commercial matters (OJ L 174, 27.6.2001, p. 1))

1. Reference of the requested court:
2. Reference of the requesting court:
3. Name of the requesting court:
4. Name of the requested court:
5. The request can not be executed within 90 days of receipt for the following reasons:
6. It is estimated that the request will be executed by ... (indicate an estimated date)

Done at:

Date:

**FORM H**

Information on the outcome of the request

(Articles 14 and 16 of Council Regulation (EC) No 1206/2001 of 28 May 2001 on cooperation between the courts of the Member States in the taking of evidence in civil or commercial matters (OJ L 174, 27.6.2001, p. 1))

1. Reference of the requested court:

2. Reference of the requesting court:

3. Name of the requesting court:

4. Name of the requested court:

5. The request has been executed. ☐

   The documents establishing execution of the request are attached:

6. Execution of the request has been refused because:

   6.1. the person to be examined has claimed the right to refuse to give evidence or has claimed to be prohibited from giving evidence:

   6.1.1. under the law of the Member State of the requested court: ☐

   6.1.2. under the law of the Member State of the requesting court: ☐

   6.2. The request does not fall within the scope of this Regulation ☐

   6.3. Under the law of the Member State of the requested court, the execution of the request does not fall within the functions of the judiciary: ☐

   6.4. The requesting court has not complied with the request for additional information from the requested court dated ... (date of the request): ☐

   6.5. A deposit or advance asked for in accordance with Article 18(3) has not been made: ☐

Done at:

Date:

**FORM I**

Request for direct taking of evidence

(Article 17 of Council Regulation (EC) No 1206/2001 of 28 May 2001 on cooperation between the courts of the Member States in the taking of evidence in civil or commercial matters (OJ L 174, 27.6.2001, p. 1))

1. Reference of the requesting court:

2. Reference of the central body/competent authority:

3. Requesting court:

    3.1. Name:

    3.2. Address:

        3.2.1. Street and No/PO box:

        3.2.2. Place and postcode:

        3.2.3. Country:

    3.3. Tel.

    3.4. Fax

    3.5. E-mail:

4. Central body/competent authority of the requested State:

    4.1. Name:

    4.2. Address:

        4.2.1. Street and No/PO box:

        4.2.2. Place and postcode:

        4.2.3. Country:

    4.3. Tel.

    4.4. Fax

    4.5. E-mail:

5. In the case brought by the claimant/petitioner:

    5.1. Name:

    5.2. Address:

        5.2.1. Street and No/PO box:

        5.2.2. Place and postcode:

        5.2.3. Country:

5.3. Tel.:

5.4. Fax

5.5. E-mail:

6. Representatives of the claimant/petitioner:

6.1. Name:

6.2. Address:

6.2.1. Street and No/PO box:

6.2.2. Place and postcode:

6.2.3. Country:

6.3. Tel.

6.4. Fax

6.5. E-mail:

7. Against the defendant/respondent:

7.1. Name:

7.2. Address:

7.2.1. Street and No/PO box:

7.2.2. Place and postcode:

7.2.3. Country:

7.3. Tel.

7.4. Fax

7.5. E-mail:

8. Representatives of defendant/respondent:

8.1. Name:

8.2. Address:

8.2.1. Street and No/PO box:

8.2.2. Place and postcode:

8.2.3. Country:

8.3. Tel.

8.4. Fax

8.5. E-mail:

9. The taking of evidence shall be performed by:

   9.1. Name:

   9.2. Title:

   9.3. Function:

   9.4. Task:

10. Nature and subject matter of the case and a brief statement of the facts (in annex, where appropriate):

11. Taking of evidence to be performed:

   11.1. Description of the taking of evidence to be performed (in annex, where appropriate):

   11.2. Examination of witnesses:

      11.2.1. First names and surname:

      11.2.2. Address:

      11.2.3. Tel.

      11.2.4. Fax

      11.2.5. E-mail:

      11.2.6. Questions to be put to the witness or a statement of the facts about which they are to be examined (in the annex, where appropriate):

      11.2.7. Right to refuse to testify under the law of the Member State of the requesting court (in annex, where appropriate):

   11.3. Other taking of evidence (in annex, where appropriate):

12. The requesting court requests to take evidence directly by use of the following communications technology (in annex, where appropriate):

Done at:

Date:

**FORM J**

Information from the central body/competent authority

(Article 17 of Council Regulation (EC) No 1206/2001 of 28 May 2001 on cooperation between the courts of the Member States in the taking of evidence in civil or commercial matters (OJ L 174, 27.6.2001, p. 1))

1. Reference of the requesting court:

2. Reference of the central body/competent authority:

3. Name of the requesting court:

4. Central body/competent authority:

 4.1. Name:

 4.2. Address:

  4.2.1. Street and No/PO box:

  4.2.2. Place and postcode:

  4.2.3. Country:

 4.3. Tel.

 4.4. Fax

 4.5. E-mail:

5. Information from the central body/competent authority:

 5.1. Direct taking of evidence in accordance with the request is accepted: ☐

 5.2. Direct taking of evidence in accordance with the request is accepted under the following conditions (in annex, where appropriate): ☐

 5.3. Direct taking of evidence in accordance with the request is refused for the following reasons:

  5.3.1. The request does not fall within the scope of this Regulation: ☐

  5.3.2. The request does not contain all of the necessary information pursuant to Article 4: ☐

  5.3.3. The direct taking of evidence requested for is contrary to fundamental principles of law of the Member State of the central body/competent authority: ☐

Done at:

Date:

______________________________

## *Regulation (EC) No.805/2004 of the European Parliament and of the Council of 21 April 2004 creating a European Enforcement Order for uncontested claims*

5-356 **For Regulation (EC) No.805/2004 see paragraphs 5-357+ to 5-390+ on White Book on Westlaw UK or the Civil Procedure CD.**

## *Convention of 30th October 2007 on Jurisdiction and the Recognition and Enforcement of Judgments in Civil and Commercial Matters (Revised Lugano Convention)*

**For the Convention of 30th October 2007 on Jurisdiction and the Recognition and Enforcement of Judgments in Civil and Commercial Matters (Revised Lugano Convention) see paragraphs 5-392+ to 5-475+ on White Book on Westlaw UK or the Civil Procedure CD.**

*Paragraph numbers marked with a "+" can be found online and on CD.*

# SECTION 6

## ADMINISTRATION OF FUNDS, PROPERTY AND AFFAIRS

# 6A COURT FUNDS

## Senior Courts Act 1981

(1981 c.54)

### Accountant General of the Senior Courts 6A–1

**97.**—(1) There shall continue to be an Accountant General of, and an accounting department for, the Senior Courts.

(2) The Lord Chancellor shall appoint such person as he thinks fit to the office in the Senior Courts of Accountant General of the Senior Courts, and the person so appointed shall hold and vacate office in accordance with the terms of his appointment.

(3) The Accountant General shall be paid such salary or fees as the Lord Chancellor determines with the consent of the Treasury.

(4) If one person holds office both as the Accountant General and as the Public Trustee then, if he ceases to be the Public Trustee, he shall also cease to be the Accountant General unless the Lord Chancellor otherwise directs.

(5) If a vacancy occurs in the office of Accountant General or the person appointed to hold the office is for any reason unable to act for any period such person as the Lord Chancellor appoints as deputy in that office shall, during the vacancy or that period, perform the functions of that office (and any property vested in the Accountant General may accordingly be dealt with by the deputy in all respects as if it were vested in him instead).

*Note*—Amended by the Public Trustee and Administration of Funds Act 1986 Sch.3, para.5 and the Constitutional Reform Act 2005 s.59 and Sch.11, para.26 with effect from October 1, 2009 (SI 2009/1604). **6A–2**

**Court Funds Office**

The name of this office has replaced the former name of the Supreme Court Pay Office (see the Supreme Court Funds Rules 1975 r.3, paras 6A–26). This office is the office of the Accountant General of the Senior Courts (SCA 1981 s.97). The machinery of this office is governed by the Court Funds Rules 1987 made by the Lord Chancellor, with the concurrence of the Treasury, under the powers conferred by AJA 1982 s.38(2) and (7). Pt VI of the AJA 1982 was brought into force by the Public Trustee and Administration of Funds Act 1986. **6A–3**

## Administration of Justice Act 1982

(1982 c.53) **6A–4**

Arrangement of Sections

Part VI

Funds in Court



***Paragraph numbers marked with a "+" can be found online and on CD.***

## PART VI

## FUNDS IN COURT

### Management and investment of funds in court

6A–5 **38.**—(1) Subject to rules made under subsection (7) below, all sums of money, securities and effects paid and deposited in, or under the custody of—

(a) the High Court;

(b) a county court; or

(c) such other courts and tribunals as the Lord Chancellor may by rules made under that subsection prescribe,

shall be vested in the Accountant General.

(2) One or more accounts shall be opened and kept in the name of the Accountant General at such bank or banks as may be designated by the Lord Chancellor with the concurrence of the Treasury.

(3) Money and securities held by the Accountant General shall vest in his successor in office without any assignment or transfer.

(4) A sum of money paid and deposited in court may[...] be invested and reinvested by the Accountant General in any manner authorised by rules made under subsection (7) below.

(5) [...]

(6) The Accountant General may, in such cases as the Lord Chancellor may by rules made under subsection (7) below prescribe, apply to the court for an order for directions as to the manner in which a particular fund in court is to be dealt with.

(7) The Lord Chancellor, with the concurrence of the Treasury, may make provision as to the payment of interest on funds in court and may make rules as to the administration and management of funds in court including the deposit, payment, delivery and transfer in, into and out of any court of funds in court and regulating the evidence of such deposit, payment, delivery or transfer.

(8) Rules made under subsection (7) above may—

(a) provide for the discharge of the functions of the Accountant General under the rules by a person or persons appointed by him;

(b) provide for the transfer of money in court to and from the Commissioners;

(c) provide for money paid and deposited in a county court to be vested in, and accounted for by, a person other than the Accountant General;

(d) prescribe cases in which interest is to be paid on funds in court;

*Paragraph numbers marked with a "+" can be found online and on CD.*

(e) prescribe cases in which funds in court are to be invested;
(f) make provision for the transfer of funds in court from one court to another; and
(g) prescribe cases in which moneys payable under a judgment or order shall be paid into court.

(9) Any such rules may make different provision for different cases.

*Note*—Amended by Public Trustee and Administration of Funds Act 1986 s.4. **6A-6**



## Investment of money transferred to National Debt Commissioners

**39.**—(1) The Commissioners may invest, in such manner as may be prescribed by regulations made by the Treasury, money transferred to them in pursuance of rules made under section 38(7) above or section 82(1) of the Judicature (Northern Ireland) Act 1978 and the interest or dividends accruing on investments made under this subsection. **6A-7**

(2) If in any accounting year the aggregate of the sums of money received by the Commissioners by way of interest and dividends on investments made by them under subsection (1)above, after deduction of—

(a) any sum required by the Treasury to be set aside to provide for depreciation in the value of investments so made;
(b) such sum as the Lord Chancellor may with the concurrence of the Treasury direct to be paid to him in respect of the cost to him in that year of administering funds in court, and
(c) an amount equal to the expenses incurred by the Commissioners in that year in making investments under subsection (1) above and disposing of investments so made

exceeds the aggregate of the sums due to be paid or credited in respect of that year by way of interest on funds in court, the excess shall be paid into the Consolidated Fund.

(3) If in any accounting year the aggregate of the sums of money received as mentioned in subsection (2) above, after deduction of the sum or sums falling to be deducted under paragraphs (a) to (c) of that subsection, is less than the aggregate of the sums due as mentioned in that subsection, the deficiency shall be made good out of the Consolidated Fund.

(4) The Commissioners shall pay to the Lord Chancellor any sum deducted by them under subsection (2)(b) above; and any sum received by the Lord Chancellor under this subsection shall be paid into the Consolidated Fund.

(4A) Any sum deducted by the Commissioners under subsection (2)(c)above shall be applied as an appropriation in aid of moneys provided by Parliament for the expenses of the National Debt Commissioners; and, so far as not so applied, shall be paid into the Consolidated Fund.

(5) If at any time the Commissioners are unable to pay—

(a) to the Accountant General a sum due from them to him under rules made under section 38(7) above; or

(b) to the Accountant General of the Court of Judicature of Northern Ireland a sum due from them to him under rules made under section 82(1) of the Judicature (Northern Ireland) Act 1978,

the Treasury shall provide them with it out of the Consolidated Fund.

6A-8 *Note* —Amended by the Public Trustee and Administration of Funds Act 1986 s.5; and the Constitutional Reform Act 2005 Sch.11 para.27, with effect from October 1, 2009 (SI 2009/1604).

### Statutory deposits

6A-9 **40.**—(1) Where money or securities are deposited with the Accountant General under any enactment or subordinate legislation, whether passed or made before or after the commencement of this Part of this Act, they shall for the purposes of this Part of this Act be treated as if they were funds in court except in so far as—

(a) the enactment; or

(b) the subordinate legislation; or

(c) rules made under section 38(7) above,

provide to the contrary.

(2) In subsection (1) above "subordinate legislation" means Orders in Council, orders, rules, regulations and other instruments made or to be made under any Act.

### Transfer of funds in court to Official Custodian for Charities and Church Commissioners

6A-10 **41.**—(1) Any funds for the time being vested in the Accountant General and held by him in trust for any charity or in trust for any ecclesiastical corporation in the Church of England may, if the Accountant General on an application made in that behalf to him by the Charity Commission or the Church Commissioners thinks fit so to direct, be transferred to the Official Custodian for Charities or the Church Commissioners, as the case may be.

(2) Any funds transferred by virtue of a direction given under subsection (1) above shall be vested in and held by the Official Custodian for Charities or the Church Commissioners respectively in trust for the charity or ecclesiastical corporation upon the trusts upon which the funds were held before the transfer.

(3) In this section "ecclesiastical corporation" means a capitular body within the meaning of the Cathedrals Measure 1963 or the incumbent of a benefice.

6A-10.1 *Note* —Amended by the Charities Act 2006 s.75(1), Sch.8, para.67, with effect from February 27, 2007 (SI 2007/309).

### Common investment schemes

6A-11 **42.**—(1) The Lord Chancellor may continue to make schemes ("common investment schemes") establishing common investment funds for the purpose of investing funds in court and money held by any person who in accordance with subsection (5)(b) below may hold shares in common investment funds.

(2) A common investment scheme shall provide for the fund thereby established to be under the management and control of an investment manager appointed by the Lord Chancellor.

(3) A common investment scheme shall make provision for the investment by its investment manager in accordance with the provisions of this section of funds in court transferred to the fund under rules made by virtue of section 38(7) above and of any sums of money transferred to the fund by persons who in accordance with subsection (5)(b) below may hold shares in the fund.

(4) A common investment scheme shall make provision—

(a) for treating the fund established by it as being divided into shares; and

(b) for treating a sum invested in the fund as being represented by a number of shares determined by reference to that sum and the value of the fund at the time the investment was made.

(5) Shares in a common investment fund—

(a) shall be allotted to and held by the Accountant General and

(b) may be allotted to and held by the Accountant General of the Court of Judicature of Northern Ireland and any other person authorised by the Lord Chancellor.

(6) Where a person is authorised under subsection (5) above to hold shares in a common investment fund—

(a) he may invest trust money in shares in the fund without obtaining and considering advice on whether to make such an investment; and

(b) he may invest trust money in a common investment fund of which he is the investment manager.

(7) Moneys comprised in the fund established by a common investment scheme may, subject to the provisions of the scheme, be invested by the investment manager of the fund in any way in which he thinks fit, whether or not authorised by the general law in relation to trust funds.

(8) [...]

(9) The investment manager of a fund established by a common investment scheme shall not be required or entitled to take account of any trusts or equities affecting any share in the fund whether or not he is also a trustee of any such trust.

(10) The investment manager of a fund established by a common investment scheme shall be remunerated at such rates and in such manner as the Lord Chancellor shall with the concurrence of the Treasury determine.

(11) The salary or remuneration of an investment manager and his officers and such other expenses of executing his office or otherwise carrying this Part of this Act into effect as may be

sanctioned by the Treasury shall be paid out of moneys provided by Parliament.

(12) There shall be charged in respect of the running of a common investment scheme such fees, whether by way of percentage or otherwise, as the Lord Chancellor shall with the concurrence of the Treasury fix and such fees shall be collected and accounted for by such persons, and in such manner, and shall be paid to such account, as the Treasury direct.

(13) There shall be retained or paid out of a fund established by a common investment scheme any expenses which could be so retained or paid out of trust property if the investment manager of the fund were a trustee and such expenses shall be retained or paid in the same way as and in addition to fees charged in respect of the running of the scheme.

(14) Fees and expenses recovered under this section shall be paid into the Consolidated Fund.

(15) Money and securities held by an investment manager of a fund established by a common investment scheme shall vest in his successor in office without any assignment or transfer.

(16) The power conferred by subsection (1) above to make a common investment scheme shall include the power to vary or revoke such a scheme.

**6A-12** *Note*—Subsection 8 repealed by Financial Services Act 1986 s.212(3), Sch.17, Pt 1.

Subsection 6 amended by Trustee Act 2000, see SI 2001/49, art.2; and the Constitutional Reform Act 2005 Sch.11 para.27, with effect from October 1, 2009 (SI 2009/1604).

## Provision for making good defaults

**6A-13** **43.** If the Lord Chancellor, whether on a recommendation made to him by any person interested or not, certifies—

(a) that the Accountant General; or

(b) that the manager of a common investment fund,

has been guilty of any default with respect to any money, securities and effects for which he is responsible under this Part of this Act, such sum as may be certified by the Lord Chancellor to be necessary for making good the default shall be paid out of moneys provided by Parliament or, if and so far as it is not so paid, shall be charged on and issued out of the Consolidated Fund.

## Power to repeal and modify ss.42 and 43

**6A-14** **44.**—(1) Her Majesty may by Order in Council—

(a) repeal subsections (8), (10), (12), (14) and (15) of section 42 above and section 43 above; or

(b) make such modifications to those enactments as Her Majesty considers appropriate.

(2) Any Order in Council made under subsection (1) above shall be subject to annulment in pursuance of a resolution of either House of Parliament.

## Accounts

**6A-15** **45.**—(1) Accounts shall be prepared and shall at such times as the

Treasury shall direct be sent to the Comptroller and Auditor General—

(a) in respect of his transactions under section 38 above, by the Accountant General;

(b) in respect of their transactions under section 39 above, by the Commissioners; and

(c) in respect of transactions in a fund established by a common investment scheme, by the investment manager.

(2) The accounts shall be in such form and shall be prepared in respect of such periods as the Treasury may direct.

(3) The Comptroller and Auditor General shall examine, certify and report on accounts sent to him under subsection (1) above and lay copies of them and his report on them before each House of Parliament.



**Supplemental**

**46.**—(1) Any power conferred by this Part of this Act to make a scheme or rules or regulations shall be exercisable by statutory instrument which shall be subject to annulment in pursuance of a resolution of either House of Parliament. **6A–16**

(2) The following amendments shall have effect—

(a) the words "invested under section 38 of the Administration of Justice Act 1982" shall be substituted for the words "dealt with under section 6 of the Administration of Justice Act 1965" in each case where they occur in the following enactments—

(i) section 46 of the Chelsea and Kilmainham Hospitals Act 1826;

(ii) section 12 of the Ecclesiastical Houses of Residence Act 1842;

(iii) sections 70, 78 and 86 of the Lands Clauses Consolidation Act 1845; and

(iv) section 9 of the Tithe Act 1846;

(b) the words "section 42 of the Administration of Justice Act 1982" shall be substituted for the words " section 1 of the Administration of Justice Act 1965"—

(i) [...]

(ii) in section 20(1) of the Insurance Companies Act 1958;

(c) in section 7(1) of the Industrial Assurance Act 1923, for the words from the beginning of paragraph (a) to "1958" there shall be substituted—

"(a) the provision substituted by the Administration of Justice Act 1965 for section 19(1) of the Insurance Companies Act 1958 and the provision so substituted for section 20(1) of that Act, as amended by section 46(2)(c) of the Administration of Justice Act 1982,";

(d) [...]

(e) [...]

(f) [...]

(g) in section 9(7) of the Insurance Companies Act 1981 for the words " section 7 of the Administration of Justice Act 1965" there shall be substituted the words "section 38(7) of the Administration of Justice Act 1982".

6A–16.1 *Note*—Amended by Transport and Works Act 1992 s.68(1), and Sch.4, Income and Corporation Taxes Act 1988 s.844 and Sch.31 and Taxation of Chargeable Gains Act 1992 s.290(3) and Sch.12.

## Interpretation

6A–17 **47.** In this Part—

"Accountant General" means in relation to England and Wales, the Accountant General of the Senior Courts and, in relation to Northern Ireland, the Accountant General of the Court of Judicature;

"the Commissioners" means the National Debt Commissioners;

"a common investment scheme" means a scheme made under section 42 above;

"funds" or "funds in court" means—

(a) any money, securities or other investments (including foreign currency and assets) standing or to be placed to the account—

(i) of the Accountant General by virtue of section 38(1) above; or

(ii) of any other person by virtue of rules made under subsection (7) of that section;

(b) any effects deposited with the Accountant General by virtue of section 38(1) above; but does not include any statutory deposit referred to in section 40 above.

6A–17.1 *Note*—Amended by the Constitutional Reform Act 2005 Sch.11 para.27, with effect from October 1, 2009 (SI 2009/1604).

## Court Funds Rules 1987

6A–18 (S.I. 1987 No. 821)

ARRANGEMENT OF RULES

*PRELIMINARY*



***Paragraph numbers marked with a "+" can be found online and on CD.***

PART I

AUTHORITIES FOR LODGMENT, PAYMENT OUT, TRANSFER, ETC.



PART II

LODGMENT OF FUNDS IN COURT



PART III

APPROPRIATION



PART IV

PLACING OF MONEY ON DEPOSIT AND INVESTMENT OF FUNDS



PART V

RANGE OF INVESTMENTS



PART VI

DEALING WITH FOREIGN CURRENCIES



PART VII

PAYMENT, TRANSFER AND DELIVERY OF FUNDS OUT OF COURT



***Paragraph numbers marked with a "+" can be found online and on CD.***

**6A–19** *Note* —These Rules have been amended by the Court Funds (Amendment) Rules 1999 (SI 1999/1021). For "plaintiff" wherever it appears, substitute "claimant"; and for "proper officer" substitute "court officer".

## *Preliminary*

### Citation, commencement and revocation

**6A–20** **1.—(1)** These Rules may be cited as the Court Funds Rules 1987 and shall come into force on 1st June 1987.

(2) The Rules specified in the schedule to these Rules shall be hereby revoked, except that those Rules shall continue to apply to such extent as may be necessary for giving effect to any order or request made before 1st June 1987.

**6A–21** *Note* —Amended by SI 1997/177, and SI 1999/1021.

***Paragraph numbers marked with a "+" can be found online and on CD.***

**Interpretation**

**2.—(1)** Unless the context otherwise requires, expressions used in these Rules shall have the same meaning as in the Civil Procedure Rules 1998, and those Rules are referred to in these Rules as the "CPR". **6A–22**

(2) The following expressions shall have the following meanings:

"The 2005 Act" means the Mental Capacity Act 2005;

"Accountant General" means the Accountant General of the Senior Courts or an officer appointed by him under Rule 4;

"Appropriation" means where the whole or any part of money paid into court under a court order or in support of a defence of tender before claim—

(i) prior to 6th April 2007, was treated as a CPR Part 36 payment in accordance with CPR Part 37 as it was in force immediately prior to that date; and

(ii) on or after 6th April 2007, is used to satisfy a Part 36 offer in accordance with CPR Part 37.3, and the verb "appropriate" shall be construed accordingly;

"Authenticated" means authenticated with the impression of a stamp issued by the Accountant General;

"The Bank" means such bank or banks as may be designated by the Lord Chancellor with the concurrence of the Treasury;

"Bankers' Automated Clearing System" means the method of payment whereby funds are transferred from one bank in the United Kingdom to another by means of an automated system;

"Basic Account" means a deposit account bearing interest as established under Rule 26;

"Carry over" means to transfer a fund in Court or any part thereof from one account to another in the books of the Court Funds Office;

"Common Investment Fund" means a fund established by a scheme made under section 42(1) of the Administration of Justice Act 1982;

"Court" includes, unless otherwise specified, the following:—

The Senior Courts.

The Court of Protection.

Any county court.

The Employment Appeal Tribunal.

The Upper Tribunal;

"Any county court" means a judge or district judge exercising the powers of a county court in chambers as well as in open court;

"Court Funds Office account" means the cash account of the Accountant General at the Bank;

"Deputy" means, in relation to a person who lacks capacity, a person—

(i) appointed by the Court under section 16(2)(b) of the 2005 Act to make decisions on that person's behalf; or

*Paragraph numbers marked with a "+" can be found online and on CD.*

(ii) deemed to be so appointed by virtue of paragraph 1 of Schedule 5 to that Act (existing receivers);

"Effective date of appropriation" means, in relation to funds appropriated prior to 6th April 2007, the date on which a notice of appropriation was received by the Accountant General;

"Employment Appeal Tribunal" means the tribunal established by the Employment Tribunals Act 1996(a)[1];

"Foreign currency" means currency other than sterling;

"Holding" means the units in any one common investment fund purchased on any one valuation day and held in respect of a particular long-term investment account;

"Interest" means interest accruing on funds and includes dividends;

"Interest bearing account" means an account of funds established under Rule 26;

"International money transfer" means a method of payment by which funds are transferred from a bank in the United Kingdom to a bank outside the United Kingdom by means of an automated system;

"Lodge in court" means pay or transfer into court or deposit in court;

"Lodgment Schedule" means a schedule to an order directing funds to be lodged to the account of the Accountant General;

"Master" means a Master of the Senior Courts and includes the Admiralty Registrar, a District Judge, a Registrar in Bankruptcy and the Registrar of the Employment Appeal Tribunal;

"National Savings Stock" means stock registered on the National Savings Stock Register;

"Order" means a judgment or an order under the seal of the High Court or Court of Appeal or a county court, an order, certificate or direction under the seal of the Court of Protection, an order under the seal of the Employment Appeal Tribunal or an order under the seal of the UpperTribunal;

"Payment Schedule" means a schedule to an order directing the payment of funds from the account of the Accountant General;

"Person under a disability" means a person who is a child or a person who lacks capacity;

"Person who lacks capacity" means a person who—

(i) immediately before 1 October 2007, was a patient within the meaning of Part VII of the Mental Health Act 1983 (as that Act was in force immediately prior to that date); or

(ii) a court has found lacks capacity within the meaning of the 2005 Act and whose lack of capacity relates (directly or indirectly) to funds in court held (or to be held) on his behalf;

"Royal Courts of Justice" means the Senior Courts at the Royal Courts of Justice and does not include any District Registry

[1] 1996 c.17.

"Securities" includes units purchased and investments affected by placing money to special accounts;

"Special Account" means an investment account bearing interest as established under Rule 26;

"Transitional funds" means money which, less than 21 days prior to 6th April 2007, in satisfaction of a claim—

(i) had been paid into court in accordance with CPR Part 36; or

(ii) had been appropriated in accordance with CPR Part 37, as those Parts were in force immediately prior to 6th April 2007;

"Unit" means one of the shares into which a common investment fund is treated as being divided.

(2A) Where two or more deputies are appointed in relation to a person who lacks capacity, in these Rules—

(i) the word "deputy" is to be construed as a reference to those deputies acting jointly if and to the extent that joint action is required by the terms of their appointment; and

(ii) any rule permitting the Accountant General to refuse to—

(a) follow a direction given by; or

(b) undertake any other act at the request of,

a deputy includes a power, where more than one deputy has been appointed, to refuse to do so on the grounds that while the terms of appointment require the deputies to act jointly, the direction or request was not jointly made.

(3) Unless the context otherwise requires, a Rule, or Part referred to by number means the Rule or Part so numbered in these Rules.

*Note* —Definitions "Court" and "Order" amended by the Transfer of Tribunal Functions (Lands Tribunal and Miscellaneous Amendments) Order 2009, Sch.2, para.27 (SI 2009/1307, for transitional provisions see Sch.5) with effect from June 1, 2009. **6A–23**

There must be no liability upon any security to be lodged in court (*per*Selborne L.C., *Re Stephens* (1873) L.R. 86 Ch.App. 465).

Amended by SI 1988/817; SI 1991/1227; SI 1997/177; SI 1999/1008; SI 1999/1021; SI 2000/2918; SI 2001/703, SI 2003/375, SI 2007/729 and SI 2007/2617.

**[THE NEXT PARAGRAPH IS 6A–26.]**

### Court Funds Office

**3.** The office of the Accountant General shall continue to be known as the Court Funds Office. **6A–26**

### Discharge of Accountant General's functions

**4.—(1)** The functions of the Accountant General under these Rules may be discharged, to such extent as he may direct, by any officer appointed by him. **6A–27**

(2) The Accountant General, with the approval of the Treasury, may from time to time authorise in writing any officer to authenticate

*Paragraph numbers marked with a "+" can be found online and on CD.*

on his behalf any direction issued by him for the purpose of giving effect to these Rules and such authorisation may be either general or in respect of any particular class or classes of transaction.

**Power to authorise use of forms**

6A-28 **5.** [...]

6A-28.1 *Note* —Repealed by SI 1988/817 r.5(1)

PART I

AUTHORITIES FOR LODGMENT, PAYMENT OUT, TRANSFER, ETC.

**Lodgment Schedule or other authority to lodge**

6A-29 **6.—(1)** Subject to paragraph (1A), where lodgment of funds in court is directed by an order or authorised by a Master, the Accountant General shall not make such lodgment until he has received:—

(i) in proceedings in the Chancery Division, a lodgment schedule; or

(ii) in proceedings in the Queen's Bench Division, Family Division, or any other court or tribunal, a copy of the order.

but in the case of proceedings mentioned in sub-paragraph (ii) he may refuse to make such lodgment until he has received a lodgment schedule.

(1A) Paragraph (1) does not apply to proceedings in the Court of Protection.

(1B) Where, in proceedings in the Court of Protection, a person ("Person A") seeks to lodge funds in court on behalf of a person who lacks capacity ("Person B"), the Accountant General must not make such lodgment until he has received one of the following documents—

(i) a lodgment schedule;

(ii) where a deputy has not been appointed in relation to Person B, and the funds are required to be lodged by Person A by court order, a copy of that order;

(iii) where, prior to 1st October 2007, Person A had been appointed as Person B's receiver under Part VII of the Mental Health Act 1983 (as that part was in force immediately prior to that date), a copy of the order of the Court of Protection by which Person A was so appointed; or

(iv) a copy of the order of the Court of Protection appointing Person A as Person B's deputy.

(2) Where proceedings in which money has been lodged in court are ordered to be transferred to another court, the court officer of the transferring courts shall so advise the Accountant General in writing.

*Paragraph numbers marked with a "+" can be found online and on CD.*

*Note* —Amended by SI 1999/1021 and SI 2007/2617. With reference to 6(1)(i) and 6(1B) above, in the Chancery Division in respect of a person liable to account and in the Court of Protection Division, it is not necessary for the sum to be lodged to be specified; if this sum is not ascertainable at the time that the lodgment schedule is drawn up, any sum tendered in respect of the lodgment will be accepted by the Accountant General. **6A-30**

## Payment Schedule

**7.—(1)** Where an order directs the manner in which any fund in court is to be dealt with by the Accountant General, a payment schedule shall be lodged with him. **6A-31**

(2) Subject to paragraph (3) a payment schedule signed and authenticated by a court officer shall be sufficient authority to the Accountant General to deal with a fund in accordance with the schedule.

(3) Where money is lodged in court in proceedings under section 84 of the Law of Property Act 1925 and directions are given by the Upper Tribunalinstructing the Accountant General to deal with that fund, such directions shall be sufficient authority to the Accountant General to deal with the fund accordingly.

*Note* —Amended by SI 1999/1021 r.2(b). When the payment schedule directs payment, proof of the change may be furnished by proof of the change may be furnished by a certified copy of the instrument or authority under which the change has been made (Form 301). **6A-32**

When the payment schedule directs payment to a company and its name has been changed since the date of the Order, proof of change may be furnished by a copy of a certificate of the Registrar of Companies certified by the Company Secretary.

Where duty and costs are directed to be paid the first direction should be "Pay Duty".

The effect of opening a separate account in an action is to release it from the general questions in the suit, and to indicate in each heading the person interested in the fund placed to such separate account (*Edgar v Plomley* [1900] A.C. 431) but so long as the fund remains in Court it is under the control of the Court (*Cloutte v Storey* [1911] 1 Ch. 18, CA).

As to the payment and transfer of funds out of Court see Pt VII, rr.40–51.

Paragraph (3) amended by the Transfer of Tribunal Functions (Lands Tribunal and Miscellaneous Amendments) Order 2009, Sch.2, para.28 (SI 2009/1307, for transitional provisions see Sch.5) with effect from June 1, 2009.

## Preparation and amendment of Schedules

**8.—(1)** In any proceedings, other than proceedings in the Court of Protection, the Upper Tribunal or the Employment Appeal Tribunal, where an order is made for the lodgment of or dealing with funds in court, the party having carriage of the order shall prepare and submit the lodgment or payment schedule to the appropriate court office for authentication. **6A-33**

(2) Without prejudice to paragraph (1), the court officer of a court in which an order has been made for the lodgment of or dealing with funds in court, may prepare the lodgment or payment schedule where he considers it appropriate to do so.

(3) The court officer of the court in question shall sign and authenticate the lodgment or payment schedule and forward it to the Accountant General.

***Paragraph numbers marked with a "+" can be found online and on CD.***



COURT FUNDS

(4) Any amendment to a schedule needed to correct a clerical or accidental error or omission shall be signed by the court officer.

**6A-33.1** *Note*—Amended by SI 1999/1021 r.2(b) and by the Transfer of Tribunal Functions (Lands Tribunal and Miscellaneous Amendments) Order 2009 Sch.2, para.29 (SI 2009/1307, for transitional provisions see Sch.5) with effect from June 1, 2009.

### Regulations concerning the transmission of Schedules to the Accountant General

**6A-34** All schedules will be transmitted to the Accountant General immediately after they have been authenticated by the court using the stamp provided by the Accountant General.

It will be observed that in no case will a schedule ever be in the hands of the solicitor, and as a fact, the Accountant General will refuse to accept schedules by any other means than through official channels. In this way a complete record will be preserved of all schedules in the hands of the Accountant General.

All charging or stop orders affecting funds in Court or to be lodged must be produced to the Court Funds Office by the solicitors obtaining them. The Accountant General otherwise receives no notification of these orders. A copy of the Order should be supplied for retention in the Court Funds Office.

In the Queen's Bench and Family Divisions, although payment schedules are prepared by the solicitors having carriage of the Orders, they reach the Accountant General only through official channels (by post as appropriate). The practice is, however, different in the Admiralty Registry: payment schedules are always prepared by the Registry and transmitted direct to the Accountant General.

## Certificate of a Master or Taxing Master

**6A-35** **9.** [...]

**6A-36** *Note*—Revoked by SI 2007/2617.

## Particulars of interest ordered to be paid as directed in judgment or order

**6A-37** **10.** [...]

**6A-38** *Note*—Revoked by SI 2007/729.

## Regular payments

**6A-39** **11.** Where a payment schedule directs that regular payments (not being interest payable as it accrues due) are to be made by the Accountant General, the schedule shall state the dates on which payments are to be made.

**6A-40** *Note*—Amended by SI 2007/729.

## Funds on which duty is payable

**6A-41** **12.** [...]

**6A-42** *Note*—Revoked by SI 2007/729.

*Paragraph numbers marked with a "+" can be found online and on CD.*

## PART II

## LODGMENT OF FUNDS IN COURT

**Accountant General's directions for payment to the Bank**

**13.** Money shall not be paid directly to the Bank save on the direction of the Accountant General. **6A–43**

**Lodgment on receipt of a Lodgment Schedule or other authority to lodge**

**14.—(1)** Approval for the lodgment of funds in court shall be given by the Accountant General on receipt of a lodgment schedule in proceedings:— **6A–44**

(i) in the Employment Appeal Tribunal;

(ii) in the Chancery Division of the High Court, where the lodgment is:

(a) directed by a lodgment schedule;

(b) made under the Life Assurance (Payment into Court) Act 1896 or the Trustee Act 1925, and the lodgment schedule is accompanied by a copy of a witness statement or affidavit filed in accordance with CPR rule 37.4;

(iii) in a county court where money is paid into court under the Trustee Act 1925 in accordance with CPR rule 37.4, and the lodgment schedule has been authenticated by the court officer.

(1A) Where, in proceedings in the Court of Protection, a person ("Person A") seeks to lodge funds in court on behalf of a person who lacks capacity ("Person B"), the Accountant General must not make such lodgment until he has received one of the following documents

(i) a lodgment schedule;

(ii) where a deputy has not been appointed in relation to Person B, and the funds are required to be lodged by Person A by court order, a copy of that order;

(iii) where, prior to 1st October 2007, Person A had been appointed as Person B's receiver under Part VII of the Mental Health Act 1983 (as that part was in force immediately prior to that date), a copy of the order of the Court of Protection by which Person A was so appointed; or

(iv) a copy of the order of the Court of Protection appointing Person A as Person B's deputy.

(2) Where the Accountant General receives from a company a notice of claim after the making of the witness statement or affidavit required under CPR rule 37.4, he shall note the account accordingly.

*Note* —Amended by the Court Funds (Amendment) Rules 2003 (SI 2003/375), SI 2007/729 and SI 2007/2617. **6A–45**

***Paragraph numbers marked with a "+" can be found online and on CD.***

Where the amount of funds to be lodged is not ascertained at the date of the order, the lodgment schedule should describe them so far as possible and state how they are to be verified, e.g. by a certificate of the Master, by affidavit or certificate of the solicitor or of the person directed to make the lodgment.

The affidavit or certificate should quote the account title, date of order, description and amount of funds to be lodged, name of person lodging and the details concerning such lodgment mentioned in the schedule.

The authority for lodgment of proceeds of sale of any property directed by an order to be sold and of balances due from persons liable to account may be a lodgment schedule signed by a Master or judge, and it may contain a direction for investment and accumulation, and that the funds, whether capital or interest, or both, are not to be dealt with without notice.

Interest on securities directed to be lodged in Court, in cases other than in proceedings in the Court of Protection, which accrued due between the date of the order and the actual date of lodgment of the securities, will be payable into Court unless the order otherwise provides.

Stocks, shares, or bonds which cannot be accepted by the Accountant General, may be placed in a sealed packet or box, and a direction should then be inserted in the Schedule for the lodgment of such sealed packet or box, care being taken in the case of bonds with coupons to provide for the periodical delivery out and re-deposit of the box for the purpose of cutting off such coupons. See r.17(3) as to providing the Accountant General with an inventory of the contents of a sealed packet or box deposited in court.

**Security for costs of appeal**

**6A–46** When money is ordered to be lodged in Court as security for costs of an appeal from the Ch.D., the time limited for such lodgment should be stated in the lodgment schedule. When the time limited is short payment in should be by cash or banker's draft.

**6A–47** *Note*—The company shall not deduct any costs or expenses of or incidental to the payment into Court (Practice Direction (Miscellaneous Provisions About Payments Into Court) para.4.3, see Vol.1, para.37PD.4).

The draft lodgment schedule should be submitted to the Court Funds Office before the affidavit is sworn or witness statement drawn up. The lodgment schedule must be signed by the Commissioner for Oaths before whom the affidavit is sworn or the witness when a witness statement is submitted.

Boxes and other effects are not accepted under this rule.

If a trustee is in doubt as to who is entitled to a fund in his hands, CPR Pt 64, Section I is generally available for the purpose of getting the point decided, and this course should be followed instead of the fund being lodged in court under the Trustee Act (*Dix v Great Western Railway* (1886) 34 W.R. 712).

**"Witness statement or affidavit"**

**6A–48** See Practice Direction (Miscellaneous Provisions About Payment Into Court) para.6 (Vol.1, para.37PD.6).

The witness statement or affidavit may be made by one of several trustees (*Anon.* (1885) 1 Jur.N.S. 974; Trustee Act 1925 s.63); though, where reasonably possible, all should join.

If an affidavit is supplied the Schedule must be signed by the Commissioner for Oaths before whom the affidavit is sworn.

The witness statement or affidavit may be written or printed; only an office copy of the lodgment schedule to the witness statement or affidavit has to be left at the Court Funds Office.

The shares of several persons separately entitled may be lodged under a witness statement or an affidavit (*Re Wright* (1857) 3 K. & J. 419) but in the title of the account to be raised such shares must not be described as the "separate accounts of A.B. and C.D." A separate schedule should be used for each person's share where possible.

See notes to C.F.O. Form 103 as to the account title, statement as to duty and directions as to investment.

The beneficiary's name should appear first in the title, following the analogy of cases without affidavit where this form is compulsory.

Should the lodgment schedule require amendment or correction, a supplemental witness statement or affidavit may be filed with a corrected schedule. It is advisable before swearing trustee affidavits, to submit the draft schedule to the Court Funds Office for examination.

**Notice**

As to notice of payment into court, "filed in accordance with CPR rule 37.4" see Practice Direction (Miscellaneous Provisions About Payments Into Court), paras 4.5 and 6.3 (Vol.1, paras 37PD.4 and 37PD.6). **6A-49**

## Lodgment on receipt of a written request

**15.—(1)** Approval for the lodgment of funds in court shall be given by the Accountant General on receipt of a written request in proceedings:— **6A-50**

(i) in the Queen's Bench or Family Divisions of the High Court or in a county court where the request is accompanied by a sealed copy order directing the lodgment, or where in Admiralty proceedings the request is made by the Admiralty Marshal;

(ii) in the Chancery Division of the High Court where the lodgment is made in proceedings:—

(a) under section 84 of the Law of Property Act 1925; or

(b) under the Trustee Act 1925 where the written request is signed by or on behalf of the personal representative; or

(c) under any enactment other than those mentioned in Rule 14(1)(ii) or in this paragraph where it is accompanied by the appropriate document authorising lodgment where specific authority to lodge is required by the relevant enactment;

(iii) in any division of the High Court or in a county court where the lodgment is made under—

(a) [...]

(b) CPR, rule 37.2 (where the defendant wishes to rely on a defence of tender before claim) and the request is accompanied by a copy of the claim form and a copy of the defence;

(iv) in the Admiralty Registry if the request is sealed by the Registry.

(2) The Accountant General may give approval for lodgment of funds in court notwithstanding that a request is not accompanied by a sealed copy order directing lodgment in accordance with paragraph (1)(i), provided that he is satisfied that such an order has been made and the reason why a copy of the order does not accompany the request is stated in the request.

*Note* —Instructions as to lodgment will be given on application to the Court Funds Office. As to form of request for lodgment see C.F.O. Form 100 for High Court and **6A-51**

County Court lodgments, or C.F.O. Form 101 for Chancery lodgments except for lodgment under the Compulsory Purchase Act 1965 when a C.F.O. Form 102 should be used, and under the Trustee Act 1925 when a Form 103 should be used.

**[THE NEXT PARAGRAPH IS 6A–55.]**

6A–55 *Note*—Amended by the Court Funds (Amendment) Rules 1999 (SI 1999/1021) and SI 2007/729.

A lodgment of cash as security in QBD may be made on the authority of an order of certiorari under CPR, Pt 54, C.F.O. Form No.100.

**Security for costs of election petition**

6A–56 A lodgment of cash in QBD for costs of an election petition is made on the *fiat* of a Master on C.F.O. Form No.100. As there is a time limit of three days for payment in this should be by cash or banker's draft.

**Admiralty actions**

6A–57 See *British Shipping Laws*, Vol.1 (1964) paras 340 *et seq.*

The proceeds of the sale of a ship in U.S. dollars may be paid into court by the Admiralty Marshal without first converting them into sterling and placed in a dollar deposit account but an order of the court is necessary both for the payment into court of dollars and for placing them in a dollar deposit account (*The Halcyon the Great* [1975] 1 W.L.R. 515; [1975] 1 All E.R. 882).

**[THE NEXT PARAGRAPH IS 6A–59.]**

**Lodgment of money in court**

6A–59 **16.—(1)** Money to be lodged in accordance with Rules 14 or 15, except money representing the proceeds of sale or redemption of National Savings stock or money to be paid into court under rule 19, shall be paid directly into the Court Funds Office.

(2) [....]

(3) Where money is paid under paragraph (1), cheques or other instruments shall be made payable to the Accountant General of the Senior Courts.

(4) Money received in the Court Funds Office shall be paid into the Bank for the credit of the Accountant General's account as soon as practicable.

6A–60 *Note*—Amended by the Court Funds (Amendment) Rules 2003 (SI 2003/375) and SI 1999/1921.

The Accountant General can take no responsibility for any delays, losses, etc., where, for whatever reason, a cheque or payable instrument on presentation is returned by the Bank as unacceptable, i.e. insufficient funds, unauthorised signatory, etc. It is the responsibility of the payer to notify the other parties of any delays, non-compliance, etc.

6A–61 (5) Lodgments of money which are not required to be paid into the Court Funds Office under this rule to which rule 19 applies shall be made directly to the bank to the credit of the Accountant General's account.

(6) The effective date of lodgment of money lodged under paragraph (1) shall be—

(i) in the case of cash or a banker's draft, the date of its receipt in the Court Funds Office;

*Paragraph numbers marked with a "+" can be found online and on CD.*

(ii) in the case of a cheque or instrument other than a banker's draft the date of its receipt in the Court Funds Office or such later date as the Accountant General may determine;

(iii) in the case of a lodgment to which paragraph (5) applies, the date certified by the Bank as that on which the money was placed to an account of the Accountant General.

(7) Any person who desires or is directed to pay money into a District Registry or county court under any enactment, other than a payment to which rule 15 applies, and who has complied with the requirements of the relevant Civil Procedure Rules shall pay the money into the appropriate court office, by a cheque or other instrument made payable to the Accountant General of the Senior Courts which shall be forwarded to the Accountant General within one working day of the date of receipt.

(8) The effective date of lodgment of money paid in under paragraph (7) shall be the date of its receipt in the court office.

*Note* —Amended by SI 1988/817 and SI 1999/1021. 6A-62

**[THE NEXT PARAGRAPH IS 6A-64.]**

### Securities transferable by delivery and deposit of effects

**17.—(1)** The lodgment in the Senior Courts of securities transferable by delivery and the deposit of effects shall be made either by delivery to the Court Funds Office or, if the Accountant General so directs, by delivery to the Bank. 6A-64

(2) Where lodgment under paragraph (1) is made by delivery to the Bank:—

(i) effects so delivered shall be secured in locked boxes or otherwise to the satisfaction of the Bank, and any person delivering effects shall, if the Bank so requires, permit them to be inspected in his presence by an officer of the Bank; and

(ii) the Bank shall give a written receipt for the delivery of any securities or effects.

(3) Any person who deposits effects in court in accordance with these Rules shall provide the Accountant General with an inventory of those effects signed and certified by him as a true and accurate record.

(4) Any person who desires or is directed to deposit securities in a county court under any statute, and has complied with the requirements of the relevant Civil Procedure Rules, shall deposit the securities with the proper officer who shall give the depositor a receipt of the deposit and shall forward the security certificate or certificates to the Accountant General.

*Note* —Amended by the Court Funds (Amendment) Rules 1999 (SI 1999/1021).

### Return of lodgment directions

**18.—(1)** Where— 6A-65

(i) money lodged directly with the Bank has been received and credited to the Accountant General's account, or
(ii) securities transferable by delivery and effects have been delivered to the Bank, or
(iii) securities (other than those transferable by delivery) have been transferred into the Accountant General's name in the books of the Bank or in the books of a company,

the Bank or Company, as the case may be, shall certify on the lodgment direction issued under rule 14 that the funds have been lodged and shall send it to the Court Funds Office.

**Payment of money into a District Registry or county court**

6A-66 **19.—(1)** A litigant in person without a current account may pay money into a District Registry or a county court in accordance with paragraph (2).

(2) Where paragraph (1) applies payment shall be made—
(i) in cash;
(ii) at the appropriate court office during office hours on any day on which the office is open; and
(iii) the court officer shall give a receipt for it.

(3) Payments shall be forwarded to the Accountant General within one working day of the date of receipt.

(4) Money paid to a court office under rules 16(7) or 19(2) and which is remitted to the Accountant General in accordance with rules 16(7) or 19(3) must be accompanied by a notice stating the reason for the payment and its date.

*Note* —Amended by the Court Funds (Amendment) Rules 2003 (SI 2003/375), SI 1990/518 and SI 2007/729.

6A-66.1 **19A.** The effective date of lodgment paid in under rule 19 shall be the date of its receipt in the court office.

6A-66.2 **20.** [...]

6A-66.3 **21.** [...]

6A-66.4 **22.** An officer of a District Registry or county court who receives money under the process of the court shall give a written receipt for every sum so received in the form prescribed.

6A-66.5 **23.** [...]

6A-66.6 **24.** Where—
(a) money has been paid into court in a claim proceeding in the Royal Courts of Justice; and
(b) the claim is transferred to a District Registry or county court, the court officer of the court to which the claim is transferred shall notify the Accountant General.

PART III

APPROPRIATION

**Appropriation**

6A-67 **25.—(1)** Where—

*Paragraph numbers marked with a "+" can be found online and on CD.*

(i) a defendant has paid money into court under a court order or in support of a defence of tender before claim; and

(ii) a Part 36 offer is subsequently accepted without needing the permission of the court,

any request for payment lodged with the Accountant General by the claimant must include the written consent of the defendant that all, or part, of the money paid into court may be used to satisfy the offer (in whole or in part).

(2) Where, before the date on which a request for payment is received under paragraph (1), interest has accrued on the money in question, some or all of the accrued interest may be included in the amount used to satisfy the offer, and this rule applies to the interest in the same way as it applies to the money paid into court.

*Note*—Substituted by SI 2007/729. 6A–68

Where money lodged in court on or before March 31, 1983, and by that date had been directed by the court to be placed to short-term investment account, now special account, the money will remain so invested until the Accountant General receives a notice of appropriation under this rule or until alternative directions to deal with the money are received from the court. (See r.8(1) of SI 1983/290).

The defendant is entitled to any interest that has accrued on monies in court up to the date of the acceptance, unless he agrees that any such interest may be used to satisfy the amount offered. However, no interest will be payable after the date of acceptance.

Where this rule applies the claimant must submit both Form **201**, completed by them, and Form **202** completed by the defendant with the Court Funds Office in order to obtain payment out of monies in court.

PART IV

PLACING OF MONEY ON DEPOSIT AND INVESTMENT OF FUNDS

### Establishment of interest bearing accounts

**26.** There shall be established the following two interest bearing accounts, namely a basic account (that is to say, a deposit account) and a special account (that is to say, an investment account) to which shall accrue, in accordance with these Rules, interest derived from the transfer to, and investment by, the National Debt Commissioners of the money placed to all the accounts of those kinds. 6A–69

*Note*—This rule re-establishes the two interest bearing accounts under different names. Basic account and special account replace money on deposit and short term investment account respectively. 6A–70

### Interest on money placed to an interest bearing account

**27.—(1)** The rate at which interest on money placed to a basic account or a special account is to accrue shall be as prescribed from time to time by a direction made by the Lord Chancellor with the concurrence of the Treasury. 6A–71

***Paragraph numbers marked with a "+" can be found online and on CD.***

(2) Interest on money placed to a basic account or a special account shall accrue from day to day from the day on which the money is placed to the account until the day preceding its withdrawal from the account.

(3) Unless the Accountant General directs otherwise, accrued interest shall be credited:—

(i) on the capital sum when it is withdrawn from the account; or

(ii) on transfer of the capital sum from a basic account to a special account; and

(iii) on the last Friday in March and the last Friday in September each year in respect of money placed to a basic account and on the last Friday in May and the last Friday in November each year in respect of money placed to a special account.

(4) Accrued interest shall be credited without deduction of income tax.

**6A-72** *Note*—Amended by SI 1988/817 and SI 1999/1021.

### Time for placing money to an interest bearing account

**6A-73** **28.—(1)** Subject to the provisions of this part of the Rules and to any direction of the court, all money (including interest) shall be placed to a basic account or, in the case of a person under a disability, to a special account, on the day on which the schedule or other authority is received in the Court Funds Office or on the effective date of lodgment of the money, whichever is the later.

(2) Where judgment is given in favour of a person under a disability, or settlement of his claim is approved by the court the money to which he is entitled shall, subject to any directions of the court, be placed to a special account in his name as at the date of the judgment or on the effective date of lodgment of the money, whichever is the later, without further authority.

(3) Interest shall not accrue from a date earlier than that on which the money is placed to an interest bearing account in accordance with this Rule.

(4) This rule does not apply to transitional funds.

**6A-74** *Note*—Amended by the Court Funds (Amendment) Rules 1999 (SI 1999/1021) and SI 2007/729.

### Money not to be placed to a basic account

**6A-75** **29.** Money, including interest, shall not be placed to a basic account where the money:—

(i) has been directed by an order or another authority to be dealt with other than by being placed to a basic account; or

(ii) has been carried over to an account of unclaimed balances under Rule 57; or

***Paragraph numbers marked with a "+" can be found online and on CD.***

(iii) stood to the credit of a fund in court before 1st October 1965, without a request that it be placed on deposit; or

(iv) was paid into court in satisfaction of a claim before 1st April 1983, without a direction that it be placed on deposit; or

(v) amounts to a sum which is less than £10.

**Money to be placed to a special account**

**30.** Money, including interest, shall only be placed to a special account where the person entitled to it is under a disability, and it amounts to a sum which is not less than £10. **6A-76**



**Treatment of transitional funds**

**31.—(1)** Transitional funds must be placed to a basic account 21 days after the effective date of lodgment or the effective date of appropriation and interest accrues on those funds from the date of placement to that account. **6A-77**

(2) Paragraph (1) does not apply where a request for payment from the claimant is received in the Court Funds Office within the 21 days specified in that paragraph.

(3) Where the claimant is a person under a disability—

(i) paragraph (1) applies unless the court otherwise directs;

(ii) where the court directs that paragraph (1) does not apply, interest accrues on the funds in court from the date they are placed to a basic account; and

(iii) transitional funds placed to a basic account shall, unless the court otherwise directs, remain so placed until the claim is determined or the court approves a settlement, whether or not the claimant has indicated that he wishes to accept the payment or appropriation.

*Note* —Substituted by SI 2007/729. **6A-78**

When money has been lodged in court but interest has not started to accrue on it before April 1, 1983, any party may apply for such money to be placed to a basic account and where the court makes such an order the money will be treated thereafter in accordance with the provisions of these rules.

**Interest on payment out of money in court**

**32.—(1)** No interest accrues on money held in court in relation to a claim after the date on which the claimant serves notice on the Accountant General of acceptance of a Part 36 offer. **6A-79**

(2) Where—

(i) the permission of the court is not required to take money out of court; and

(ii) money lodged or appropriated by the defendant in satisfaction of a claim has been accepted by and paid to the claimant,

the Accountant General must pay any accrued interest remaining in court in respect of that claim to the defendant.

(3) Where the permission of the court is required to take money out of court, including where the court determines a claim or approves a settlement on behalf of a person under a disability, any interest which has accrued on the money in court must be dealt with as the court orders.

6A–79.1 *Note* —Substituted by SI 2007/729.

### Withdrawal of money from an interest bearing account

6A–80 **33.** Money shall only be withdrawn from an interest bearing account where the money, including any interest which has accrued at the time of withdrawal, is required to be withdrawn for the purpose of giving effect to a direction of the court or these Rules; provided that such interest shall not be used if directed by the court to be otherwise dealt with.

## PART V

## RANGE OF INVESTMENTS

### Range of Investments

6A–81 **34.—(1)** Subject to paragraph (5), money under the control of, or subject to an order of the court, may be invested or reinvested by the Accountant General in accordance with these Rules, in the following ways:—

(i) it may be placed to a basic account or; in the case of a person under a disability, to a special account;

(ii) it may be transferred to such of the funds established by common investment schemes as may be specified;

(iii) it may be invested in any manner specified in Part I, paragraphs 1 to 10 and 12 of Part II and paragraphs 2, 2A and 3 of Part III of Schedule 1 to the Trustee Investments Act 1961, as supplemented by the provisions of Part IV of that Schedule;

(iv) it may be invested in investment trust ordinary shares.

(2) Money subject to an order of the court may be invested or reinvested in accordance with instructions received from the Public Trustee.

(3) Paragraph (2) does not apply to money under the control of or subject to an order of the Court of Protection.

(4) In paragraphs (5) to (7), "investment manager" means a person appointed by a deputy to make decisions as to the investment of money held in court on behalf of a person who lacks capacity.

(5) Money under the control of or subject to an order of the Court of Protection may be invested or reinvested by the Accountant General in such investments—

(i) as the court may direct;

(ii) if a deputy has been appointed to make decisions in relation to that money on behalf of a person who lacks capacity, as the deputy may in writing direct; or

*Paragraph numbers marked with a "+" can be found online and on CD.*

(iii) if the deputy has appointed an investment manager, as the investment manager may in writing direct.

(6) If a deputy decides to appoint an investment manager for the purposes of this rule, he must send in writing to the Accountant General—

(i) contact details of the investment manager; and

(ii) authority for the investment manager to give directions for the investment of the funds held in court.

(7) The Accountant General may refuse to comply with a direction made under paragraph (5), if—

(i) in relation to a direction given by a deputy, it appears to him that the direction is not within the powers conferred on the deputy by the terms of his appointment;

(ii) in relation to an investment manager, it appears to him that—

(a) it was not within the powers of the deputy to appoint an investment manager;

(b) the deputy has not complied with paragraph (5); or

(c) it was not within the powers of the investment manager to give that direction; or

(iii) the court has made a contrary direction,

or for another good reason.



**Money lodged in court**

Where money has been lodged in court on or before March 31, 1983, and by that date had been directed by the court to be placed to short term investment account, now special account, the money will remain so invested until the Accountant General receives from the court alternative directions to deal with the money. **6A–82**

**[THE NEXT PARAGRAPH IS 6A–84.]**

*Note*—Amended by SI 1991/1227; SI 1997/177, SI 2003/720 and SI 2007/2617. **6A–84**

## Time for investment

**35.** Subject to the provisions of Part IV and this Part of the Rules and to any directions of the court, money, including interest, shall be invested as soon as it is available. **6A–85**

*Note*—A commission for a purchase of a security is passed to the brokers on the day following that on which the directions of the court have been received in the Court Funds Office or on which the money is available (whichever is the later). The security purchased will be credited to the beneficiary's account as soon as it is delivered by the brokers. **6A–86**

## Amount for investment

**36.—(1)** Notwithstanding Rule 34, no sum of money or interest shall be invested in any case where in the view of the Accountant General the cost of investment, by way of commission or otherwise, would be disproportionate to the amount of money involved. **6A–87**

(2) Any money which is not invested shall be placed, in the case of

*Paragraph numbers marked with a "+" can be found online and on CD.*

a person under a disability, to a special account and in all other cases to a basic account and shall be drawn from the account and invested when it, together with the interest credited to it, and further sums of money or interest credited to the account which are required to be invested in the same manner, amount to a sum in respect of which the cost of investment is not disproportionate.

### Investment in Common Investment Fund

6A–88 **37.—(1)** Where funds are required to be invested in Common Investment Fund units or such units are required to be realised, the purchases and sales shall be effected on the first available valuation day.

(2) Funds shall not be directed to be invested in Common Investment Fund Units unless the authority giving the direction is satisfied that the funds are likely to remain so invested for at least five years: provided that this paragraph shall not apply in any case where there is an express request for investment in Common Investment Fund Units by or on behalf of one or more of the persons interested in the fund, or, if no such person is ascertained or traceable, by the person who pays the funds into court.

**[THE NEXT PARAGRAPH IS 6A–90.]**

PART VI

DEALING WITH FOREIGN CURRENCIES

### Dealing with Foreign Currencies

6A–90 **38.—(1)** Foreign currency may only be lodged in court when:—

(i) [...]

(ii) the court so directs or permits.

(2) Foreign currency lodged in accordance with paragraph (1) shall be paid into court in the manner approved by the Accountant General.

6A–90.1 *Note*—Amended by SI 2007/729.

6A–91 **39.**—(1) Where foreign currency is lodged in court, the court may direct that it shall be placed in an interest bearing account in that currency or any other currency, and any interest shall accrue from the date of the order or the date of placing it in the account, whichever is the later; and the Accountant General shall deal with the interest as the court may direct.

(2) Any charges incurred by placing foreign currency to an account shall be deducted from the currency so placed or from the accrued interest, as may be appropriate.

(3) Where income from a security in court is received in a foreign currency, the court may give such direction as it thinks fit, and in the absence of such direction the foreign currency shall be converted

*Paragraph numbers marked with a "+" can be found online and on CD.*

into sterling and invested in accordance with the provisions of Part IV.

*Note*—Amended by the Court Funds (Amendment) Rules 1999 (SI 1999/1021). **6A–92**

Prior consultation is advisable with the Court Funds Office on all dealings with foreign currencies.

## PART VII

## PAYMENT, TRANSFER AND DELIVERY OF FUNDS OUT OF COURT



### Payments out of money by post and identification of payees

**40.—(1)** In this rule, the person entitled to the payment out of money lodged in court is referred to as the payee. **6A–93**

(2) Subject to paragraphs (4) to (9) below, the Accountant General may make payment out of money lodged in court by means of—

(i) the Bankers' Automated Clearing System to a bank in the United Kingdom; or

(ii) international money transfer to a bank outside the United Kingdom,

for the credit of the account of the payee at that bank..

(3) The Payment Schedule shall provide the necessary details of the payee's bank and account to enable a payment to be made under paragraph (2) above.

(4) In cases where:

(i) the Payment Schedule or supplementary authority is dated not more than one year prior to the date on which the Accountant General is able to make payment, he shall make payment as soon as is practicable;

(ii) the Payment Schedule or supplementary authority is dated more than one year prior to the date on which the Accountant General is able to make payment, he shall make payment on receipt of a written request from the payee.

(5) Subject to paragraph (5A), on receipt of a written request from a donee under a power of attorney given by the payee, the Accountant General may make payment by means of—

(i) the Bankers' Automated Clearing System (if the account is held at a bank in the United Kingdom); or

(ii) international money transfer (if the account is held at a bank outside the United Kingdom),

for the credit of the account of the payee at that bank.

(5A) The request for payment referred to in paragraph (5) must be accompanied by—

(i) an office copy of that power of attorney showing that it has been registered as required by the relevant Act in the case of—

(a) a lasting power of attorney made under section 9 of the 2005 Act; or

*Paragraph numbers marked with a "+" can be found online and on CD.*

(b) an enduring power of attorney (as defined in paragraph 2 of Schedule 4 to the 2005 Act) made before 1st October 2007 which was registered—

(aa) before that date under the Enduring Powers of Attorney Act 1985 (as that Act was in force immediately prior to that date); or

(ab) on or after that date under the 2005 Act; and

(ii) in all other cases, a copy of the power of attorney by which the donee was appointed, certified in accordance with the provisions of section 3 of the Powers of Attorney Act 1971.

(5B) The Accountant General may refuse to make the payment referred to in paragraph (5) if—

(i) the requirements of paragraph (5A) have not been met; or

(ii) he considers that the request for payment is not within the powers conferred on the donee by the power of attorney.

(6) Where the Accountant General does not make a payment by means of the Bankers' Automated Clearing System under paragraph (2) above, he shall make the payment by a cheque crossed "account payee" by post in accordance with paragraph (8).

(7) In cases where:

(i) the payee does not have an account which is suitable for the receipt of funds—

(a) (in respect of an account held at a bank in the United Kingdom) by Bankers' Automated Clearing System; or

(b) (in respect of an account held at a bank outside the United Kingdom) by international money transfer; or

(ii) there is a written request from the payee for the payment to be made by cheque;

the Accountant General shall make the payment by a cheque crossed "account payee".

(8) Where the Accountant General makes a payment under paragraph (6) or (7) above, it shall be sent by post as follows:

(i) where the address of the payee is stated in the Payment Schedule or supplementary authority and that schedule or authority is dated not more than one year prior to the date on which the Accountant General is able to make payment, he shall make payment to the payee at the address so stated;

(ii) where the Payment Schedule or supplementary authority is dated more than one year prior to the date on which the Accountant General is able to make payment, he shall make payment on receipt of a written request from the payee and, in a case where there has been a written request under paragraph (7)(ii) above, that request shall be sufficient for the purposes of this sub-paragraph.

(9) The Accountant General may, if he thinks fit:

(i) refuse to make a payment until he is satisfied as to the identity and entitlement of any person claiming to be the payee and may require the personal attendance of the payee at the Court Funds Office or a court office as a condition of payment;

(ii) refuse to make a payment by means of the Bankers' Automated Clearing System or international money transfer in any individual case if the Payment Schedule is not completed with sufficient information or for another good reason.

*Note* —Amended by SI 1997/177, SI 2007/729 and SI 2007/2617. **6A–94**

The Treasury has empowered the Accountant General at his discretion to dispense with evidence in the case of (1) holders of ecclesiastical benefices provided that remittance is made direct to *them;* (2) payment to treasurers and other officials of public bodies provided that the cheques are crossed to the accounts of the public bodies and remitted direct to their bankers; and (3) payments of dividends in Court of Protection matters.

As to the Form of Declaration by a person entitled to payment (Evidence of Life, etc.) see C.F.O. Form No.206.

In the Chancery Division, as to Notice of Creditors see C.F.O. Form No.207 and as to Notice to Security Holders see C.F.O. Form No.208.

As to form of Request for Remittance to Payee's Bank see C.F.O. Form No.205.

If payment is directed to be made to two or more payees the cheque will be remitted to the first named payee in the Schedule at his address stated therein.

When a request for payment is provided in accordance with para.(2):

If the payment is to one of the two persons, or to two or more of a large number, a postal request will be acted upon if signed by the required minimum number of the payees.

If the payees are executors or administrators, the request need only be signed by one of them. The cheque will be crossed to the account of the payees as executors or administrators as the case may be.

In the case of unincorporated trustees all must sign the request, and the cheque will be crossed to the trust account.

Special arrangements apply to payments in foreign currencies and prior consultation with the Court Funds Office is advisable.

**Payments to foreign companies under powers of attorney**

Powers of attorney executed by foreign companies should have attached thereto an affidavit made preferably by a notary public before a British consular official, proving:— **6A–95**

(1) that the company is duly constituted and registered in accordance with the local law of the foreign country;

(2) that A., B., and C. (the signatories) are respectively directors and secretary (as the case may be) of the said company, and that it has no common seal (if such is the case); and

(3) that the company is bound and engaged by the signature of A., B., and C., in accordance with the statutes (or articles of association) of the said company, and the local law.

**[THE NEXT PARAGRAPH IS 6A–97.]**

## Payment etc. after a change of name or style

**41.** Where a person entitled to payment of a fund in court changes **6A–97**

his name or style before the fund is paid, transferred or delivered to him, the Accountant General shall, except where payment is to be made to the person as deputy, require evidence of the change before dealing with the fund.

6A-98 *Note*—This rule enables the Accountant General to take proof of the marriage of a payee entitled to payment as legal personal representative or trustee as well as in her own right; there is now no limit to the amount that can be paid on proof of marriage. The rule further provides for the payment to a woman entitled as a deputy, who marries, upon her written request. On the marriage of a female child, payment to her guardian is continued unless the Court otherwise orders.

Amended by SI 2007/2617.

### Payment pursuant to direction of the Court of Protection

6A-99 **42.** Where a person who lacks capacity is entitled to a fund in court (other than pursuant to an order made under Part VII of the Mental Health Act 1983 as that Act was in force immediately prior to 1st October 2007, or under Part I of the 2005 Act) the Accountant General shall, on receipt of a direction from the Court of Protection, either—

(a) pay the money to the person's deputy; or

(b) carry it over to such account as that court may direct.

**Note**

6A-99.1 Amended by SI 2007/2617.

### Payment, etc. to representatives of deceased persons

6A-100 **43.—(1)** Where a person entitled to a fund in court either in his own right or as sole, or sole surviving, executor dies, the Accountant General may, where the fund exceeds £5,000, pay it to the personal representative of the deceased on production of a grant of probate or office copy thereof, or, where the deceased was entitled to the fund in his own right, letters of administration in respect of the deceased's estate.

(2) Where a person entitled to a fund in court in his own right dies intestate and no grant of administration has been issued, the Accountant General may, where the assets of the deceased (including the fund in court and after deduction of debts and funeral expenses) do not exceed £5,000, pay the fund to the person who appears to him to have the prior right to a grant of administration of the estate, on lodgment in the Court Funds Office of a written declaration of kinship.

(3) Where two or more persons were entitled to payment of a fund in court as personal representatives and any of them dies before the fund is dealt with, the Accountant General may pay the fund to the surviving personal representatives on proof of the death of the deceased personal representative; and where the fund does not exceed £5,000 the Accountant General may, unless a court otherwise directs, pay the fund to any one of them.

6A-100.1 *Note*—When monies are to be released under the rule the Court Funds Office also requires that a Form **209** (where assets in the estate are over £5,000) or a Form **210** (where assets are £5,000 or below) is completed and returned together with the grant or proof of death, as appropriate.

### Payment of funeral expenses out of funds in court

**43A.—(1)** In this rule and rule 43B, "the deceased" means a person— **6A–100.2**

(i) who immediately prior to his death was entitled to a fund in court in his own right;

(ii) in respect of whom—

(a) a deputy had been appointed; or

(b) where the person died before 1st October 2007, a receiver had been appointed under Part VII of the Mental Health Act 1983 (as that Act was in force immediately prior to that date); and

(iii) in respect of whose estate no grant of probate or administration has been issued.

(2) On the written request of the person who—

(i) is the executor of the deceased's will; or

(ii) if the deceased died intestate, arranged the deceased's funeral,

the Accountant General may, on receipt of an invoice issued by funeral directors, pay direct to those directors such amounts as have been reasonably incurred for the purposes of arranging and conducting the deceased's funeral.

(3) The Accountant General may, if he thinks fit, refuse to make the payment referred to in paragraph (2) in any individual case if—

(i) he has not received the invoice referred to in that paragraph;

(ii) the person requesting such payment fails to provide him with sufficient evidence as to his entitlement to make the request; or

(iii) the fund in court to which the deceased was entitled is insufficient to meet the cost of arranging and conducting the funeral,

or for another good reason.

### Payment of inheritance tax out of funds in court

**43B.—(1)** On the written request of the person who— **6A–100.3**

(i) is the executor of the deceased's will; or

(ii) if the deceased died intestate, appears to the Accountant General to have the prior right to a grant of administration of the estate,

the Accountant General may pay direct to Her Majesty's Revenue and Customs such funds as may be required to satisfy all, or any part, of the inheritance tax due on the deceased's estate.

(2) A request under paragraph (1) must be accompanied by—

(i) such information as Her Majesty's Revenue and Customs may require to be sent to financial institutions for the purposes of enabling those institutions to make direct payment of inheritance tax;

(ii) in the case of a request from the person mentioned in paragraph (1)(i), a certified copy of the will by which he was appointed; and

(iii) in the case of a request from the person mentioned in paragraph (1)(ii), a written declaration of kinship,

and the Accountant General may refuse to make payment if the requirements of this paragraph are not met, or for another good reason.

**Note**

6A–100.4 Rules 43A and 43B inserted by SI 2007/2617. For payment of funeral expenses or inheritance tax the Court Funds Office requires that a specific request for payment be completed in addition to the requirements above. The Form FE (for funeral expenses) and Form IHT (for inheritance tax) may be obtained from the Court Funds Office.

### Payment out without order of money lodged in satisfaction

6A–101 **44.—(1)** In this Rule[...] a person in respect of whose cause of action a sum has been paid into court in satisfaction, whether by way of claim or counterclaim, is referred to as a claimant and a person against whom such a cause of action lies is referred to as a defendant.

(2) Subject to paragraph (2B), the Accountant General shall, on receipt of a written request, pay:

(i) by cheque crossed "account payee" to the claimant,

(ii) to a bank in the United Kingdom by means of the Bankers' Automated Clearing System for the credit of the account of the claimant at the bank, or

(iii) to a bank outside the United Kingdom by means of international money transfer for the credit of the account of the claimant at that bank,

money lodged in court in satisfaction of a claim, or appropriated[...], and accepted by him in accordance with Rule of Court: provided that where a solicitor is acting for the claimant in the proceedings in which the money was lodged or appropriated by virtue of a certificate issued under the code approved under section 9 of the Access to Justice Act 1999 certifying a decision to fund services for the claimant as part of the Community Legal Service under sections 4 to 10 of that Act, the Accountant General shall pay the money to that solicitor, or to the Legal Services Commission if the claimant is no longer represented by the solicitor, but further provided that the Accountant General's obligation under this paragraph to pay the money to the solicitor or to the Legal Services Commission shall apply only to the extent that regulation 18(1) of the Community Legal Service (Costs) Regulations 2000 applies to that money.

(2A) The written request under paragraph (2) above shall, where payment is to be made under sub-paragraphs (ii) or (iii) of that paragraph, provide the necessary details of the claimant's bank and account.

*Paragraph numbers marked with a "+" can be found online and on CD.*

(2B) In cases where:

(i) the claimant does not have an account which is suitable for the receipt of funds—

(a) in respect of an account held at a bank in the United Kingdom, by Bankers' Automated Clearing System; or

(b) in respect of an account held at a bank outside the United Kingdom, by international money transfer; or

(ii) there is a written request from the claimant for the payment to be made by cheque;

the Accountant General shall make the payment by a cheque crossed "account payee", to the claimant by post.

(2C) The Accountant General may, if he thinks fit, refuse to make a payment by means of the Bankers' Automated Clearing System or international money transfer in any individual case if the claimant fails to provide him with sufficient information under paragraph (2A) above or for another good reason.

(3) [...]

(4) The Accountant General shall not make any payment under paragraph (2) where:—

(i) funds have been lodged or appropriated by one or more, but not all, of a number of defendants sued jointly or in the alternative, unless—

(a) the claimant discontinues the claim against all the other defendants;

(b) those defendants consent in writing to the payment; and

(c) a copy of the notice of discontinuance and the written consent of each consenting defendant is lodged with the Accountant General.

(ii) a defence of tender before claim has been pleaded, unless—

(a) a Part 36 offer is accepted without needing the permission of the court; and

(b) the written consent of the defendant that all, or part, of the money paid into court in support of that defence may be used to satisfy the offer (in whole or in part) is lodged with the Accountant General;

(iii) the claim is made by, or on behalf of, a person under a disability; or

(iv) money has been lodged in proceedings under the Fatal Accidents Act 1976 and the Law Reform (Miscellaneous Provisions) Act 1934, or under the first mentioned Act alone where more than one person is entitled to the money; or

(v) in respect of transitional funds—

*Paragraph numbers marked with a "+" can be found online and on CD.*

(a) the payment into court or appropriation was made less than 21 days prior to the start of the trial; or

(b) the claimant has not accepted the payment or appropriation within 21 days of the payment into court or appropriation; or

(vi) paragraphs 25(1)(i) and (ii) apply, unless the request for payment lodged with the Accountant General by the claimant includes the written consent of the defendant that all, or part, of the money paid into court may be used to satisfy the offer (in whole or in part).

(5) Rule 44(4)(v) does not apply where—

(i) at the time the request for payment is made the claimant certifies to the Accountant General that the parties have agreed liability for costs; or

(ii) less than 21 days prior to 6th April 2007—

(a) the defendant increased a Part 36 payment or appropriation by lodging further funds or by appropriating all or a further part of a sum lodged in court; and

(b) the increased payment or appropriation is accepted within 21 days of the effective date of lodgment or appropriation of the further funds.

**[THE NEXT PARAGRAPH IS 6A–104.]**

**6A–104** *Note*—Amended by SI 1997/177, SI 1999/1021, SI 2007/729 and SI 2007/2617.

### Payment out of interest

**6A–105** **45.** [...]

*Note*—Revoked by SI 2007/729.

### Payment out of interest on securities

**6A–106** **46.** Where securities are lodged in court under Rule 15 or money lodged under that Rule is invested, any interest which accrues shall (subject to any contrary provision contained in the relevant enactment) be paid by the Accountant General to the person in whose name the lodgment was made.

### Transfer or delivery of securities

**6A–107** **47.—(1)** Subject to paragraph (2) where pursuant to directions of the court or under these Rules the Accountant General is required to transfer or deliver any securities or effects held in his name he shall issue directions accordingly which shall be sufficient authority for the transfer or delivery and, in the case of a transfer of securities on sale, for the Bank to receive the proceeds of sale.

(2) The directions of the Accountant General shall not be required for the transfer of National Savings Stock, on sale or otherwise.

*Note*—Instructions as to transfer or delivery will be issued by the Court Funds Office on receipt of the appropriate payment schedule. **6A–108**

A transfer may be liable to Inland Revenue Stamp Duty and, now very occasionally, a company registration fee.

The transfers will be effected by the Court Funds Office who will, in due course, forward the new stock certificates to the solicitors on the record without any request or production of the order of court.

Delivery of bearer securities etc. requires the personal attendance of an identified solicitor or bank official at the Court Funds Office and the Royal Bank of Scotland.

## Charges on purchase or sale of securities

**48.** Except where Rule 34 applies and subject to any directions of the court:— **6A–109**

(i) where money in court is invested in the purchase of securities, the payment for the purchase shall include all applicable charges; and

(ii) where securities in court are sold, all applicable charges shall be deducted from the proceeds of sale:

provided that, if the schedule directing a purchase or sale also directs that charges are not to be deducted from the fund in court, the transaction shall not be completed until such charges have been paid either to the stockbroker or to the Accountant General, as the case may be.

*Note*—When a schedule directs a purchase or sale "without deducting any applicable charges" (i.e. that these deductions are not to be charged to the account, but otherwise provided for) the Court Funds Office will notify the solicitor having carriage of the order of the amount of these charges and inform him that the purchase or sale as the case maybe, cannot be completed until the total amount of the charges has been paid. **6A–110**

Sales are effected by the Accountant General when, and to the extent that, the proceeds thereof can be applied as directed.

A commission for a sale of a security is passed to a broker on the day following receipt of the payment schedule or other subsidiary document. The proceeds of the sale will usually be credited to the beneficiary's account approximately five working days afterwards.

## Application of funds dealt with before receipt of Payment Schedule

**49.** Unless otherwise directed by the court, where an order has been made dealing with a fund and, after the date of the order but before the Payment Schedule relating to it is received in the Court Funds Office, interest has accrued or money and interest have been dealt with in accordance with a previous direction of the court or under these Rules, the part of the fund attributable to accrued interest or to money or interest shall be treated as follows:— **6A–111**

(i) interest on securities directed to be transferred, delivered or carried over shall be dealt with as the securities are directed to be dealt with under the Payment Schedule;

(ii) interest which has accured on securities directed to be sold shall be dealt with as the proceeds of sale are directed to be dealt with under the Payment Schedule, except where the sale is to raise a specified sum of money, when the interest is included with the capital;

*Paragraph numbers marked with a "+" can be found online and on CD.*

(iii) where interest which has accrued on securities directed to be transferred, delivered or carried over has been invested in the purchase of further securities, the securities so purchased and any interest on them shall be dealt with as the original securities are directed to be dealt with;

(iv) where interest which has accrued on securities directed to be sold has been invested in the purchase of further securities, the securities so purchased shall be sold and the proceeds of sale added to the proceeds of the original securities;

(v) money or accrued interest which has been placed to a basic or special account shall be withdrawn and, together with any interest credited on withdrawal, applied as directed by the Payment Schedule: provided that where such money is directed to be invested, any interest credited on withdrawal shall be applied as interest accruing on the investment is directed to be applied.

**Payment of suitors' money out of a District Registry or county court**

6A–112 **50.** [...]

6A–112.1 *Note* —Revoked by SI 2003/375.

**Specially created account**

6A–113 **51.—(1)** In apportioning to any account the interest received in respect of securities the Accountant General shall exclude all fraction of one penny and shall carry over the aggregate of such fractions to a specially created account.

(2) The Accountant General shall from time to time transfer to the cash account of Her Majesty's Paymaster General, for the credit of the Administration of Justice: England and Wales (Lord Chancellor's Department) Vote all sums standing to the specially created account.

PART VIII

CONVERSION, ALLOTMENT AND WRITE-OFF OF SECURITIES

**Application to the court concerning conversion and allotment**

6A–114 **52.** Where a question has arisen as to an allotment or conversion of securities which have been paid into court under section 63 of the Trustee Act 1925, or in any other case in which he considers it appropriate because no application will otherwise be made, the Accountant General may apply to the court for directions as to how the securities should be dealt with.

**Conversion and allotment of securities**

6A–115 **53.—(1)** Where a security in court has been converted into another security the Accountant General shall write-off the original security from the account to which it is standing and shall place to that account the whole, or where appropriate a proportionate part, of the substituted security and shall, so far as practicable and unless otherwise directed by the court, deal with the substituted security and any interest on it in the same manner as the original security and interest.

(2) Where a security in court is paid off and the money received is invested or placed to an interest bearing account, the security purchased or money in the account and any interest on it shall, unless the court otherwise directs, be dealt with by the Accountant General in the same manner as the original security and interest.

(3) Where an allotment is made in respect of a security in court the Accountant General may:—

(i) credit the whole, or where appropriate a proportionate part, of the allotment to the account of the original security if the allotment is fully paid; or

(ii) sell the allotment and credit the whole, or a proportionate part, of the proceeds of sale to that account or otherwise as the Court may direct if the allotment is not fully paid; or

(iii) sell any non-apportionable shares and apportion such proceeds as nearly as practicable to the appropriate account.

*Note* —The usual brokerage and VAT are charged by the broker for a sale under this rule. **6A–116**

When a bearer security is allotted in lieu of interest it may be delivered to the person entitled to the interest.



### Arrangements with the Bank over paid off securities, etc.

**54.—(1)** Where bearer or similar bonds or securities deposited at the Bank to the credit of the Accountant General are being paid off, the Bank shall take the necessary steps to receive the principal money and interest due and shall inform the Accountant General in writing of the amounts of the securities paid off and of the principal money and interest received. **6A–117**

(2) Where the interest on securities in court is payable on the presentation of coupons in a series and the last coupon of any such series has been presented and paid, the Bank shall take the necessary steps to obtain a new series of coupons.

*Note* —Money received in respect of securities paid off will be placed to basic account (see r.28) except as provided by r.29, and interest received on such account may be dealt with in the same manner as the interest on the security paid off was dealt with, the basic account being regarded as a substituted security (see r.53(2)). **6A–118**

### Securities of dissolved companies

**55.** Where a company has been wound up and the Accountant General has received:— **6A–119**

***Paragraph numbers marked with a "+" can be found online and on CD.***

(i) written notice from the liquidator or from the Department of Trade that no assets are or will be distributable in respect of the securities of the company; and

(ii) written notice from the Registrar of the Companies Registration Office that the company has been dissolved;

he shall withdraw from the Bank the certificate representing any security in that company and shall write-off any such security from the account to which it stands.

## PART IX

## NATIONAL DEBT COMMISSIONERS

### National Debt Commissioners

6A–120 **56.—(1)** Where, in the opinion of the Accountant General, the cash balance in his account at the Bank exceeds the amount that he requires to satisfy current demands, he shall remit the excess to the National Debt Commissioners; and where, in his opinion the balance is insufficient to meet such demands, the Commissioners shall remit to that account such amount as the Accountant General may in writing request.

(2) As soon as practicable after half-yearly interest accruing on money placed to an interest bearing account has been credited to the appropriate account in accordance with these Rules, the Accountant General shall certify to the National Debt Commissioners the amount of the interest and the Commissioners shall credit that amount to the account kept by them of money received from the Accountant General.

## PART X

## UNCLAIMED FUNDS IN COURT

### Unclaimed funds

6A–121 **57.—(1)** Subject to the provisions of this Rule, the Accountant General may carry over an unclaimed fund in court to an account of unclaimed balances.

(2) [...] a fund shall be treated as unclaimed if:—

(i) subject to paragraph (3)it stands to the credit of an account which has not been dealt with for a period of ten years otherwise than by the continuous investment or placing on deposit of accrued interest, the compulsory conversion, redemption or acquisition of securities or the placing on deposit of any money arising therefrom; or

(ii) the Accountant General is, at any time, satisfied that although all reasonable steps have been taken to trace the person entitled to it and to pay it to him, that person cannot be traced.

*Paragraph numbers marked with a "+" can be found online and on CD.*

(3) Where a fund was lodged in court for the benefit of a child, the period of ten years mentioned in paragraph 2(i) shall not begin to run until the child's 18th birthday, or, if his date of birth is not known, until 18 years have elapsed since the account was opened.

(4) [...]

(5) [...]

(6) On receipt of a Payment Schedule directing a dealing with a fund carried over in accordance with this Rule, the Accountant General shall carry back the unclaimed balance to the appropriate account.

(7) Where a fund is carried back under paragraph (6) simple interest shall be credited to the fund in respect of the whole period during which the fund stood to an account of unclaimed balances at the rate of interest prescribed at the date when the fund is carried back, for money placed in a basic account.

*Note*—Amended by the Court Funds (Amendment) Rules 1999 (SI 1999/1021) r.2(b), SI 2000/2918, SI 2007/729 and SI 2007/2617. **6A–121.1**



### Lists of unclaimed funds

**58.—(1)** The Accountant General shall maintain a list of the accounts in respect of which funds have been carried over to an account of unclaimed balances under rule 57, which may be inspected at the Court Funds Office during normal office hours. **6A–122**

(2) The court officer of each county court shall maintain a list of unclaimed funds in the custody of that court, which may be inspected at the Court office; and he shall send to the Accountant General a copy of the list from time to time.

*Note*—Amended by the Court Funds (Amendment) Rules 1999 (SI 1999/1021) r.2(b). **6A–123**

The Accountant General may in his discretion supply information regarding an unclaimed fund in court on receipt of a written request from a person claiming to have a beneficial interest in the fund or from a solicitor acting on his behalf. Such information will not be given verbally in the Court Funds Office.

As to the nature of the information which the Accountant General can provide see notice in paras 6A–163 to 6A–170.

### Disposal of unclaimed effects in court

**59.—(1)** Where effects have been deposited in court on or after 3rd July 1978 and have been carried over to an account of unclaimed balances under Rule 57, the Accountant General may send to the court a copy of an inventory provided to him in accordance with Rule 17(3) in respect of such effects when 25 years have elapsed since he received the authority for such lodgment. **6A–124**

(2) On receipt of an inventory sent in accordance with paragraph (1) the court may:—

(i) cause enquiries to be made whether any party to the proceedings in which the effects were deposited wishes to make any application in respect of them, or whether any other person who may have an interest in the effects can be found; and

(ii) of its own motion and without reference to any party or person (other than a party or person who may have an interest and whose whereabouts or the whereabouts of whose personal representatives are known), order the final disposal of the effects by sale, realisation or otherwise; provided that the court shall not order the destruction of any effects unless it is satisfied that they have no realisable value.

(3) For the purpose of any reference to a party or other person who may have an interest in the effects in question it shall not be necessary to revive any proceedings which may have abated or to issue any summons unless the court so directs and an order for such final disposal may be made after oral or written communication with such party or person.

(4) The amount of the net proceeds of any sale or realisation under paragraph (2) should be certified by the court officer and placed to the credit of the unclaimed balance account in which the effects were held prior to the sale or realisation.

6A-124.1 *Note*—Amended by the Court Funds (Amendment) Rules 1999 (SI 1999/1021) r.2(b).

### Disposal of unclaimed securities in court

6A-125 **60.—(1)** Where any securities (including Common Investment Fund units) are carried over under Rule 57, or are standing to an account of unclaimed balances on 1st June 1987 the Accountant General shall sell the securities and pay the proceeds into the account of unclaimed balances.

(2) The Accountant General shall write-off any securities carried over under Rule 57 or standing to an account of unclaimed balances on 1st June 1987 which have no value.

(3) Where any sum carried over under Rule 57 stands to an interest bearing account the Accountant General shall withdraw the sum and place it to the account of unclaimed balances.

### Repayment of closed county court funds

6A-126 **61.—(1)** Where a fund in a county court has been closed a person may apply to the court at which the fund account was kept for repayment of all or part of the fund to him.

(2) Where the court is satisfied that the claimant is entitled to the whole or part of the fund, it may order the payment to him of money standing to the credit of the account as at the date of its closure or of a sum of money representing the value of the fund at the date of its closure.

(3) Where the Court makes an order under paragraph (2) the court officer shall send a sealed copy of the court's order to the Accountant General.

(4) On receipt of the order the Accountant General shall take such steps as may be necessary to give effect to it, and shall forward a remittance for the amount of the fund to the claimant.

*Note* —Amended by the Court Funds (Amendment) Rules 1999 (SI 1999/1021) r.2(b). **6A–127**

## Unclaimed money in county court

**62.** This part of these Rules shall apply, with such modifications as may be necessary, to unclaimed moneys in a county court which have not been dealt with for a period of one year immediately before the preceding 1st March. **6A–128**

*Note* —Amended by SI 1988/817. **6A–129**

The Court Manager of a court may in his discretion supply information regarding unclaimed money in that court on receipt of a written request from a person claiming to have a beneficial interest or from a solicitor acting on his behalf. Such information will not be given verbally.



# PART XI

# CERTIFICATES IN RESPECT OF FUNDS IN COURT

## Certificates of funds in court, copies of accounts, etc.

**63.—(1)** The Accountant General may, on receipt of a written request from a person appearing to him to be interested in a fund in court, issue to him a certificate as to lodgment in court, non-payment into court under an order, carry over of the fund to an account of unclaimed balances or any other dealing with the fund; and the certificate shall, where appropriate, state the account to which the fund has been placed, the amount standing to its credit, and particulars of any charges or restraints on the fund of which the Accountant General is aware. **6A–130**

(2) On receipt of a written request the Accountant General may issue to a person appearing to him to be interested in a fund in court a copy of the account relating to the fund, which shall be authenticated by the National Audit Office if that person so requires.

(3) The Accountant General shall supply an annual statement of any fund in court for the benefit of a child to that person or to his representàtive.

**[THE NEXT PARAGRAPH IS 6A–133.]**

*Note* —Amended by SI 2007/729. **6A–133**

**Date of Lodgment**

The date of lodgment is the date defined in r.16(6) and is not necessarily the date on which a cheque is received in the Court Funds Office.

**Copies of Accounts**

Copies of accounts will normally consist of computer produced copies and/or photocopies of the suitor's account and will be available within one week of the day on which they are applied for.

If the account was opened prior to the introduction of a mechanised accounting system, a transcript book must be provided to cover that earlier period. In these circumstances it may be necessary to extend the period for preparation beyond one week.

Copies of accounts for the use of Masters and other officers of the courts will have precedence.

*Paragraph numbers marked with a "+" can be found online and on CD.*

If so requested, the Accountant General will supply the prices at which securities have been purchased or realised with the copy of the account.

Should the copy of account require authentication, it may be sent by post to the National Audit Office, 157–197 Buckingham Palace Road, London SW1W 9SP. No fee is charged for the authentication.

As to the form of Request for Copy of Account see C.F.O. Form No.300.

## SCHEDULE

### RULES REVOKED

6A–134

| *Title* | | *Reference* |
|---|---|---|
| Supreme Court Funds | Rules 1975 | S.I. 1975/1803 |
| Supreme Court Funds (Amendment) | Rules 1976 | S.I. 1976/2235 |
| Supreme Court Funds (Amendment) | Rules 1979 | S.I. 1979/106 |
| Supreme Court Funds (Amendment No. 2) | Rules 1979 | S.I. 1979/1620 |
| Supreme Court Funds (Amendment) | Rules 1980 | S.I. 1980/1858 |
| Supreme Court Funds (Amendment) | Rules 1981 | S.I. 1981/1589 |
| Supreme Court Funds (Amendment) | Rules 1982 | S.I. 1982/123 |
| Supreme Court Funds (Amendment No. 2) | Rules 1982 | S.I. 1982/787 |
| Supreme Court Funds (Amendment) | Rules 1983 | S.I. 1983/290 |
| Supreme Court Funds (Amendment) | Rules 1984 | S.I. 1984/285 |
| Supreme Court Funds (Amendment) | Rules 1986 | S.I. 1986/1142 |
| County Court Funds (Amendment) | Rules 1982 | S.I. 1982/436 |
| County Court Funds (Amendment No. 2) | Rules 1982 | S.I. 1982/1140 |
| County Court Funds (Amendment No. 3) | Rules 1982 | S.I. 1982/1794 |
| County Court Funds (Amendment) | Rules 1983 | S.I. 1983/275 |
| County Court Funds (Amendment No. 2) | Rules 1983 | S.I. 1983/1716 |
| County Court Funds (Amendment) | Rules 1984 | S.I. 1984/576 |
| County Court Funds (Amendment No. 2) | Rules 1984 | S.I. 1984/878 |
| County Court Funds (Amendment) | Rules 1985 | S.I. 1985/566 |
| County Court Funds (Amendment No. 2) | Rules 1985 | S.I. 1985/1269 |
| County Court Funds (Amendment) | Rules 1986 | S.I. 1986/636 |
| County Court Funds (Amendment No. 2) | Rules 1986 | S.I. 1986/1189 |

6A–135 *Note*—The forms relating to Court Funds are reproduced in the *Civil Procedure Forms Volume*.

**[THE NEXT PARAGRAPH IS 6A–160.]**

# THE INVESTMENT OF FUNDS IN COURT

6A–160 *Note*—In addition to the investments authorised by CPR Pt 21; AJA 1982 Pt VI provides for the continuing methods of investment in the Senior Courts and the Court of Protection, namely

(a) investments in the common investment funds under the management and control of an investment manager appointed by the Lord Chancellor (as detailed below)—see the Court Funds Rules 1987 r.37;

(b) investments in a special investment account for persons under a disability (also detailed below)—see the Court Funds Rules 1987 rr.28 and 30.

### Common Investment Funds

6A–161 The Lord Chancellor has made a scheme (the Common Investment Funds Scheme

2004 (SI 2004/266)) under the powers conferred on him by the AJA 1982 Pt VI for the establishment of common investment funds. These funds are administered by a fund manager in a manner similar to a unit trust and are intended for money which is likely to remain invested for a period of 10 years or more.

**Special Investment Account (formerly short term investment account)**

Money is placed in a basic account but in the case of a person under disability, money is placed in a special investment account (see the Court Fund Rules 1987 r.28). The special account is particularly suitable for money which is unlikely to remain invested for a long time and which may have to be withdrawn, in whole or in part, at comparatively short notice. **6A–162**

The money is transferred by the court to the National Debt Commissioner and invested by them; the return of the capital is guaranteed £ for £ and this guarantee is backed by the Consolidated Fund.

The manner of crediting interest is set out in the Court Funds Rules 1987 r.27(1). Interest accruing to a special investment account is credited without the deduction of income tax.

The rate of interest on this investment is fixed by the Lord Chancellor and the Treasury.

The rate of interest changed to 0.5 per cent with effect from July 1, 2009. For further information on rate changes see the Court Funds Office's website at *http://www.courtfunds.gov.uk* [Accessed November 24, 2009].



**Dormant funds in court**

Dormant funds are generally cash accounts under the control of the court which have had no action on them for ten years. The majority are small accounts of under £150. **6A–163**

**Applications for information**

A search will be made on application in writing. The application should provide some evidence of beneficial interest. Whenever possible, the title of the court action or of an account title should be quoted and must relate solely to funds which have been, or are believed to have been, lodged in England and Wales. **6A–164**

It is unwise to send *original* documents such as certificates of birth, marriage or death with an application for search.

Applicants are notified of the results of searches and, when an account is traced, are given a statement of the funds credited to it and any other helpful information available.

The Court Funds Office is an accounting office which does not hold records of origin. It cannot answer queries regarding descent or relationship, or advise on the selection of legal advisers. It can only release a dormant fund, in an appropriate case,by an order of court and an order must initially be sought from the court of origin.

**Sources of information**

*The High Court of Justice*—Enquiries regarding orders and documents of the High Court in London should be made as follows: **6A–165**

(a) **Companies Winding Up Proceedings**
To inspect Orders, apply to:
Companies Court
Thomas More Building
Royal Courts of Justice
London WC2A 2LL

(b) **Chancery Chambers**
Apply in the first instance to:
Chancery Chambers
Royal Courts of Justice
London WC2A 2LL

***Paragraph numbers marked with a "+" can be found online and on CD.***

(c) **Court of Protection**
Apply to:
Archway Tower
2 Junction Road
London N19 5SZ

(d) **Family Division**
Apply to:
Principal Registry of the Family Division
First Avenue House
42–49 High Holborn
London WC1V 6NP

(e) **Other sources**
Wills, Probate and Letters of Administration
Principal Probate Registry
First Avenue House
42–49 High Holborn
London WC1V 6NP

(f) **Public Trustee Matters**
Apply in the first instance to:
The Official Solicitor and Public Trustee Office
81 Chancery Lane
London WC2A 1DD

(g) **Births, Marriages and Deaths**
Postal applications:
General Register Office
P.O. Box 2
Southport
Merseyside PR8 2JD
*http://www.gro.gov.uk*

(h) **Public Records**
The National Archives
Kew
Richmond
Surrey TW9 4DU

**6A–166** *Scotland* —Enquiries concerning Scottish estates which have fallen to the Crown in default of heirs should be made to: Queen's and Lord Treasurer's Remembrancer, Crown Office, 25 Chambers Street, Edinburgh, EH1 1LA.

Enquiries concerning funds lodged in the Court of Session and other unclaimed sums resulting from company liquidations, bankruptcies, judicial factories etc. are held by Accountant of Court, Parliament House, Parliament Square, Edinburgh EH1 1RQ for a period of seven years from the date of consignation. After this date, they are transferred to the Queen's and Lord Treasurer's Remembrancer at the address above.

Other enquiries may be made to the Keeper of the Records of Scotland, National Archives of Scotland, HM General Register House, 2, Princes Street, Edinburgh EH1 3YY or West Register House, Charlotte Square, Edinburgh EH2 4DJ.

**6A–167** *Republic of Ireland* —For funds under the control of the Supreme Court and High Court of Justice in Ireland write to the Accountant of the Courts of Justice, 3rd Floor, 15/24 Phoenix Street North, Smithfield, Dublin 7.

**6A–168** *Northern Ireland* —For funds lodged in Court in Northern Ireland, write to the Accountant General, Court Funds Office, Laganside House, 23-27 Oxford Street, Belfast BT1 3LA.

[For records prior to the institution of the Supreme Court in Northern Ireland in 1921 contact The Accountant of the Courts of Justice in Dublin].

**6A–169** *A caution* —You are cautioned against relying upon the statements of persons claiming to be "unclaimed money agents" at home or abroad, and to be able to recover money in Chancery on payment of fees or percentage, or to act on behalf of the "Court of Chancery". The Senior Courts have no such agents.

It is recommended that independent advice should be taken before making a payment to any agency in respect of money alleged to be in Court.

**6A–170** *Inspection of Orders of Court, etc.* —Orders, reports and certificates and affidavits prior to 1954 are kept, in the case of general Chancery proceedings, and in companies winding-up proceedings, if prior to 1949, at the Legal Room, The National Archives, Kew, Richmond, Surrey TW9 4DU. If the date and description of the documents and the title of the cause be given, copies may be obtained on application to the Secretary, but it must be understood that no search can be undertaken by the officials of the Public Record Office.

Access to old Chancery orders, certificates and affidavits is available in Room TM3.07, Thomas More Building. Old Queen's Bench orders, certificates and affidavits are retained at the Royal Courts of Justice (Room E07).

Applications to inspect orders in companies' winding-up proceedings from 1949 to the present time, may be made at the Companies Winding-up Department, Thomas More Building, Royal Courts of Justice, London WC2A 2LL.

Applications for permission to inspect orders in Court of Protection matters may be made at Archway Tower, 2 Junction Road, London N19 5SZ.

Inquiries respecting wills, probates and letters of administration may be made at the Principal Probate Registry, First Avenue House, 42–49 High Holborn, London WC1V 6NP. Such inquiries should state the full names and the date of death of the testator or intestate.

Records of births, marriages and deaths, since July 1, 1837, are kept at the General Register Office, P.O Box 2, Southport PR8 2JD.

The above records can be inspected during official hours or copies obtained on payment of the prescribed fees.

**Special and Basic rates from October 1, 1965** **6A–171**

Set out below are the interest rates which accrue on:

(a) the High Court and County Court Special Accounts, i.e. investment accounts, formerly the Short Term Investment accounts; and

(b) the High Court and County Court Basic accounts, i.e. deposit accounts, formerly the Money on Deposit accounts.

| *High Court Special (formerly S.T.I.)* | | | *High Court Basic (formerly M.O.D.)* | | |
|---|---|---|---|---|---|
| Date | Rate | SI | Date | Rate | SI |
| 1.10.65 | 5 | 65/1466 | 1.10.65 | 2 1/2 | 65/1466 |
| 1.9.66 | 5 1/2 | 66/876 | 1.4.71 | 3 1/2 | 71/259 |
| 1.3.68 | 6 | 68/106 | 1.4.73 | 4 | 73/231 |
| 1.3.69 | 6 1/2 | 69/206 | 1.2.77 | 5 | 76/2235 |
| 1.3.70 | 7 | 70/121 | 1.04.83 | 9 1/2 | 83/290 |
| 1.3.71 | 7 1/2 | 71/259 | 1.4.84 | 8 | 84/285 |
| 1.3.73 | 8 | 73/231 | 1.8.86 | 7 1/2 | 86/1142 |
| 1.3.74 | 9 | 74/207 | 1.1.87 | 8 1/2 | 86/2115 |
| 1.2.77 | 10 | 76/2235 | 1.12.87 | 8 | Lord Chancellor's direction d/d 23.11.87 |
| 1.3.79 | 12 1/2 | 79/106 | | | |
| 1.1.80 | 15 | 79/1620 | | | |
| 1.1.81 | 12 1/2 | 80/1858 | 1.5.88 | 7 1/2 | Lord Chancellor's direction d/d 22.4.88 |
| 1.12.81 | 15 | 81/1589 | | | |
| 1.3.82 | 14 | 82/123 | | | |
| 1.7.82 | 13 | 82/787 | 1.8.88 | 9 | Lord Chancellor's direction d/d 19.7.88 |
| 1.4.83 | 12 1/2 | 83/290 | | | |
| 1.4.84 | 12 | 84/285 | | | |
| 1.8.86 | 11 1/2 | 86/1142 | 1.11.88 | 10 1/4 | Lord Chancellor's direction d/d 22.10.88 |
| 1.1.87 | 12 1/4 | 86/2115 | | | |

***Paragraph numbers marked with a "+" can be found online and on CD.***

| *High Court Special (formerly S.T.I.)* | | | *High Court Basic (formerly M.O.D.)* | | |
|---|---|---|---|---|---|
| Date | Rate | SI | Date | Rate | SI |
| 1.4.87 | $11\frac{3}{4}$ | Lord Chancellor's direction d/d 30.3.87 | 1.01.89 | $10\frac{3}{4}$ | Lord Chancellor's direction d/d 21.12.88 |
| 1.11.87 | $11\frac{1}{4}$ | Lord Chancellor's direction d/d 19.10.87 | 1.11.89 | $11\frac{1}{4}$ | Lord Chancellor's direction d/d 27.10.89 |
| 1.12.87 | 11 | Lord Chancellor's direction d/d 23.11.87 | 1.4.91 | $9\frac{1}{2}$ | Lord Chancellor's direction d/d 25.3.91 |
| 1.5.88 | $9\frac{1}{2}$ | Lord Chancellor's direction d/d 22.4.88 | 1.10.91 | 8 | Lord Chancellor's direction d/d 20.9.91 |
| 1.8.88 | 11 | Lord Chancellor's direction d/d 19.7.88 | 1.2.93 | 6 | Lord Chancellor's direction d/d 27.1.93 |
| 1.11.88 | $12\frac{1}{4}$ | Lord Chancellor's direction d/d 22.10.88 | 1.8.99 | $5\frac{1}{4}$ | Lord Chancellor's direction d/d 14.7.99 |
| | | | 1.2.02 | 4 | Lord Chancellor's direction d/d 7.1.02 |
| 1.1.89 | 13 | Lord Chancellor's direction d/d 21.12.88 | | | |
| 1.11.89 | $14\frac{1}{4}$ | Lord Chancellor's direction d/d 27.10.89 | | | |
| 1.4.91 | 12 | Lord Chancellor's direction d/d 25.3.91 | | | |
| 1.10.91 | $10\frac{1}{4}$ | Lord Chancellor's direction d/d 20.9.91 | | | |
| 1.2.93 | 8 | Lord Chancellor's direction d/d 27.1.93 | | | |
| 1.8.99 | 7 | Lord Chancellor's direction d/d 14.7.99 | | | |

| *High Court Special (formerly S.T.I.)* | | | *High Court Basic (formerly M.O.D.)* | | |
|---|---|---|---|---|---|
| Date | Rate | SI | Date | Rate | SI |
| 1.2.02 | 6 | Lord Chancellor's direction d/d 7.1.02 | | | |

| *County Court Special (formerly S.T.I.)* | | | *County Court Basic (formerly M.O.D.)* | | |
|---|---|---|---|---|---|
| Date | Rate | SI | Date | Rate | SI |
| 1.10.65 | 5 | 65/1500 | 1.10.65 | 2½ | 65/1500 |
| 1.9.66 | 5½ | 66/875 | 1.3.71 | 3½ | 71/260 |
| 1.3.68 | 6 | 68/107 | 1.3.73 | 4 | 73/230 |
| 1.3.69 | 6½ | 69/204 | 1.3.77 | 5 | 76/2234 |
| 1.3.70 | 7 | 70/228 | 1.4.83 | 9½ | 83/291 |
| 1.3.71 | 7½ | 71/260 | 1.4.84 | 8 | 84/285 |
| 1.3.73 | 8 | 73/230 | 1.8.86 | 7½ | 86/1142 |
| 1.3.74 | 9 | 74/206 | 1.1.87 | 8½ | 86/2115 |
| 1.3.77 | 10 | 76/2234 | 1.12.87 | 8 | Lord Chancellor's direction d/d 23.11.87 |
| 1.3.79 | 12½ | 79/105 | | | |
| 1.1.80 | 15 | 79/1619 | | | |
| 1.1.81 | 12½ | 80/1857 | 1.5.88 | 7½ | Lord Chancellor's direction d/d 22.4.88 |
| 1.12.81 | 15 | 81/1588 | | | |
| 1.03.82 | 14 | 82/124 | | | |
| 1.7.82 | 13 | 82/786 | 1.8.88 | 9 | Lord Chancellor's direction d/d 19.7.88 |
| 1.4.83 | 12½ | 83/291 | | | |
| 1.4.84 | 12 | 84/285 | | | |
| 1.8.86 | 11½ | 86/1142 | 1.11.88 | 10¼ | Lord Chancellor's direction d/d 22.10.88 |
| 1.1.87 | 12¼ | 86/2115 | | | |
| 1.4.87 | 11¾ | Lord Chancellor's direction d/d 30.3.87 | | | |
| | | | 1.1.89 | 10¾ | Lord Chancellor's direction d/d 20.12.88 |

COURT FUNDS

***Paragraph numbers marked with a "+" can be found online and on CD.***

| *County Court Special (formerly S.T.I.)* | | | *County Court Basic (formerly M.O.D.)* | | |
|---|---|---|---|---|---|
| Date | Rate | SI | Date | Rate | SI |
| 1.11.87 | 11¼ | Lord Chancellor's direction d/d 19.10.87 | 1.11.89 | 11¼ | Lord Chancellor's direction d/d 27.10.89 |
| 1.12.87 | 11 | Lord Chancellor's direction d/d 23.11.87 | 1.4.91 | 9½ | Lord Chancellor's direction d/d 25.3.91 |
| 1.5.88 | 9½ | Lord Chancellor's direction d/d 22.4.88 | 1.10.91 | 8 | Lord Chancellor's direction d/d 20.9.91 |
| 1.8.88 | 11 | Lord Chancellor's direction d/d 19.7.88 | 1.2.93 | 6 | Lord Chancellor's direction d/d 27.1.93 |
| 1.11.88 | 12¼ | Lord Chancellor's direction d/d 22.10.88 | 1.8.99 | 5¼ | Lord Chancellor's direction d/d 14.7.99 |
| 1.1.89 | 13 | Lord Chancellor's direction d/d 21.12.88 | | | |
| 1.11.89 | 14¼ | Lord Chancellor's direction d/d 27.10.89 | 1.2.02 | 4 | Lord Chancellors' direction d/d 7.1.02 |
| 1.4.91 | 12 | Lord Chancellor's direction d/d 25.3.91 | | | |
| 1.10.91 | 10¼ | Lord Chancellor's direction d/d 20.9.91 | | | |
| 1.2.93 | 8 | Lord Chancellor's direction d/d 27.1.93 | | | |
| 1.8.99 | 7 | Lord Chancellor's direction d/d 14.7.99 | | | |
| 1.2.02 | 6 | Lord Chancellor's direction d/d 7.1.02 | | | |
| 1.2.09 | 3 | Lord Chancellor's direction d/d 8.12.08 | 1.2.09 | 2 | Lord Chancellor's direction d/d 8.12.08 |
| 1.6.09 | 1 | d/d 2.2.09 | 1.6.09 | 1.5 | d/d 2.2.09 |
| 1.7.09 | 0.5 | d/d 3.6.09 | 1.6.09 | 0.3 | d/d 3.6.09 |

***Paragraph numbers marked with a "+" can be found online and on CD.***

# 6B COURT OF PROTECTION

## GENERAL

### Mental Capacity Act 2005

(2005 c.9)

The Mental Capacity Act for England and Wales received Royal Assent on April 7, 2005 and came fully into effect on October 1, 2007. The Act affects everyone aged over 16 and provides a statutory framework for making decisions and acting on behalf of individuals who lack capacity to make those decisions for themselves. The Act enables people with capacity to make provision for a time in the future when they may lack the capacity to make some decisions by making a lasting power of attorney. **6B–1**

The Act covers major decisions about some ones property and affairs, healthcare treatment or where the person lives, as well as everyday decisions about personal care or what someone eats, where the person lacks capacity to make the decisions themselves. The Act aims to protect people but also aims to maximise their ability to make decisions or to participate in decision making as far as they are able to do so.

The Act has five statutory principles.

## The principles

**1.**—(1) The following principles apply for the purposes of this Act. **6B–2**

(2) A person must be assumed to have capacity unless it is established that he lacks capacity.

(3) A person is not to be treated as unable to make a decision unless all practicable steps to help him to do so have been taken without success.

(4) A person is not to be treated as unable to make a decision merely because he makes an unwise decision.

(5) An act done, or decision made, under this Act for or on behalf of a person who lacks capacity must be done, or made, in his best interests.

(6) Before the act is done, or the decision is made, regard must be had to whether the purpose for which it is needed can be as effectively achieved in a way that is less restrictive of the person's rights and freedom of action.

*Note* —The statutory principles aim to protect people who lack capacity and help them take part as much as possible in decisions that affect them. **6B–3**

Section 2 of the Act provides a two stage test of capacity, whist section 3 defines what it means to be unable to make a decision.

## People who lack capacity

**2.**—(1) For the purposes of this Act, a person lacks capacity in relation to a matter if at the material time he is unable to make a decision for himself in relation to the matter because of an impairment of, or a disturbance in the functioning of, the mind or brain. **6B–4**

(2) It does not matter whether the impairment or disturbance is permanent or temporary.

(3) A lack of capacity cannot be established merely by reference to—

(a) a person's age or appearance, or

*Paragraph numbers marked with a "+" can be found online and on CD.*

(b) a condition of his, or an aspect of his behaviour, which might lead others to make unjustified assumptions about his capacity.

(4) In proceedings under this Act or any other enactment, any question whether a person lacks capacity within the meaning of this Act must be decided on the balance of probabilities.

(5) No power which a person ("D") may exercise under this Act—

(a) in relation to a person who lacks capacity, or

(b) where D reasonably thinks that a person lacks capacity,

is exercisable in relation to a person under 16.

(6) Subsection (5) is subject to section 18(3).

## Inability to make decisions

6B–5 **3.**—(1) For the purposes of section 2, a person is unable to make a decision for himself if he is unable—

(a) to understand the information relevant to the decision,

(b) to retain that information,

(c) to use or weigh that information as part of the process of making the decision, or

(d) to communicate his decision (whether by talking, using sign language or any other means).

(2) A person is not to be regarded as unable to understand the information relevant to a decision if he is able to understand an explanation of it given to him in a way that is appropriate to his circumstances (using simple language, visual aids or any other means).

(3) The fact that a person is able to retain the information relevant to a decision for a short period only does not prevent him from being regarded as able to make the decision.

(4) The information relevant to a decision includes information about the reasonably foreseeable consequences of—

(a) deciding one way or another, or

(b) failing to make the decision.

6B–6 *Note*—One of the five principles of the act is that any act done for, or any decision made on behalf of a person who lacks capacity should be done in their best interests. Section 4 of the Act provides a checklist of things that the decision maker should consider when making a best interests decision.

## Best interests

6B–7 **4.**—(1) In determining for the purposes of this Act what is in a person's best interests, the person making the determination must not make it merely on the basis of—

(a) the person's age or appearance, or

(b) a condition of his, or an aspect of his behaviour, which might lead others to make unjustified assumptions about what might be in his best interests.

(2) The person making the determination must consider all the relevant circumstances and, in particular, take the following steps.

(3) He must consider—

(a) whether it is likely that the person will at some time have capacity in relation to the matter in question, and
(b) if it appears likely that he will, when that is likely to be.

(4) He must, so far as reasonably practicable, permit and encourage the person to participate, or to improve his ability to participate, as fully as possible in any act done for him and any decision affecting him.

(5) Where the determination relates to life-sustaining treatment he must not, in considering whether the treatment is in the best interests of the person concerned, be motivated by a desire to bring about his death.

(6) He must consider, so far as is reasonably ascertainable—
(a) the person's past and present wishes and feelings (and, in particular, any relevant written statement made by him when he had capacity),
(b) the beliefs and values that would be likely to influence his decision if he had capacity, and
(c) the other factors that he would be likely to consider if he were able to do so.

(7) He must take into account, if it is practicable and appropriate to consult them, the views of—
(a) anyone named by the person as someone to be consulted on the matter in question or on matters of that kind,
(b) anyone engaged in caring for the person or interested in his welfare,
(c) any donee of a lasting power of attorney granted by the person, and
(d) any deputy appointed for the person by the court,

as to what would be in the person's best interests and, in particular, as to the matters mentioned in subsection (6).

(8) The duties imposed by subsections (1) to (7) also apply in relation to the exercise of any powers which—
(a) are exercisable under a lasting power of attorney, or
(b) are exercisable by a person under this Act where he reasonably believes that another person lacks capacity.

(9) In the case of an act done, or a decision made, by a person other than the court, there is sufficient compliance with this section if (having complied with the requirements of subsections (1) to (7)) he reasonably believes that what he does or decides is in the best interests of the person concerned.

(10) "Life-sustaining treatment" means treatment which in the view of a person providing health care for the person concerned is necessary to sustain life.

(11) "Relevant circumstances" are those—
(a) of which the person making the determination is aware, and
(b) which it would be reasonable to regard as relevant.

## Restriction on deprivation of liberty

**4A.**—(1) This Act does not authorise any person ("D") to deprive any other person ("P") of his liberty. **6B–7.1**

***Paragraph numbers marked with a "+" can be found online and on CD.***

(2) But that is subject to—

(a) the following provisions of this section, and

(b) section 4B.

(3) D may deprive P of his liberty if, by doing so, D is giving effect to a relevant decision of the court.

(4) A relevant decision of the court is a decision made by an order under section 16(2)(a) in relation to a matter concerning P's personal welfare.

(5) D may deprive P of his liberty if the deprivation is authorised by Schedule A1 (hospital and care home residents: deprivation of liberty).

### Deprivation of liberty necessary for life-sustaining treatment etc

6B-7.2 **4B.**—(1) If the following conditions are met, D is authorised to deprive P of his liberty while a decision as respects any relevant issue is sought from the court.

(2) The first condition is that there is a question about whether D is authorised to deprive P of his liberty under section 4A.

(3) The second condition is that the deprivation of liberty—

(a) is wholly or partly for the purpose of—

(i) giving P life-sustaining treatment, or

(ii) doing any vital act, or

(b) consists wholly or partly of—

(i) giving P life-sustaining treatment, or

(ii) doing any vital act.

(4) The third condition is that the deprivation of liberty is necessary in order to—

(a) give the life-sustaining treatment, or

(b) do the vital act.

(5) A vital act is any act which the person doing it reasonably believes to be necessary to prevent a serious deterioration in P's condition.

6B-7.3 *Note*—Sections 4A and4B, and Sch.A1 (Hospital and Care Home Residents: Deprivation of Liberty) (referred to in s.4A(5)) were inserted in the 2005 Act by the Mental Health Act 2007 s.50 and Sch.7. Provisions in the 2005 Act affecting powers of the court in relation to Sch.A1 include s.16A (Section 16 powers: Mental Health Act patients etc) and s.21A (Powers of court in relation to Schedule A1) (also inserted by the 2007 Act). Schedule 1A (Persons Ineligible to be Deprived of Liberty by this Act) applies for the purposes of s.16A, and of Sch.A1 para.17 (The eligibility requirement).

#### The Code of Practice

6B-8 The legal framework provided by the Act is supported by the Code of Practice, which provides guidance and information about how the Act works in practice. The Code has statutory force and certain categories of people have a legal duty to have regard to it when working with or caring for adults who may lack capacity.

The Act does not impose a legal duty on anyone to comply with the Code but if they have not followed relevant guidance provided in it, they will be expected to give good reason why they have departed from it.

Categories of people who are legally required to have regard to relevant guidance in the Code include:

***Paragraph numbers marked with a "+" can be found online and on CD.***

1. attorneys appointed under Lasting Powers of Attorney,
2. deputies appointed by the Court of Protection,
3. anyone acting as an Independent Mental Capacity Advocate,
4. anyone acting in a professional capacity for, or in relation to, a person who lacks capacity, and
5. anyone being paid for acts for or in relation to a person who lacks capacity.

### The Public Guardian

The Public Guardian is a new statutory office holder created by s.57 of the Mental Capacity Act. The Office of the Public Guardian (OPG) replaces the Public Guardianship Office (PGO) and will provide support for attorneys of Lasting Powers of Attorney and for deputies appointed by the court to manage the affairs of those who lack the mental capacity to do so themselves. The relationship between the OPG and the Court differs from the relation ship that the old Court of Protection had with the PGO. The Public Guardian is governed by the Lasting Powers of Attorney, Enduring Powers of Attorney and Public Guardian Regulations 2007. **6B–9**

The OPG has offices at Archway Tower, London N19 and in Birmingham. All post should be sent to the OPG at PO Box 15118, Birmingham, B16 6GX. DX 744240 Birmingham 79. Further information on the Public Guardian and the OPG can be obtained from the website *http://www.publicguardian.gov.uk* [Accessed January 22, 2008].

### The Court of Protection Rules 2007

The Rules set out the practice and procedure to be followed in the Court of Protection. The processes set out in the Rules are more formal than the old Court of Protection. They adopt many of the provisions of the CPR along with certain rules relating to family proceedings as well as some of the rules of the former Court of Protection. **6B–10**

In the event that the Rules do not expressly provide for any case the default is to the CPR s.9 of the Court of Protection Rules. Hearings in the Court of Protection may be held in public or private, this is reflected in s.51(2) of the Act and in rr.90–93 of the Court of Protection Rules 2007. Practitioners are also referred to the decision in *Independent New Media Ltd v 'A'* [2009] EWHC 2858 (Fam).

### The Practice Directions

The practice directions accompany various parts of the Rules and provide more detailed practical guidance on the conduct of proceedings. They have been largely modelled on the relevant CPR practice directions, as well as procedure notes of the former Court of Protection. The practice directions are made pursuant to s.52 of the Act. Practice directions can be downloaded from the website: *http://www.hmcs.gov.uk* [Accessed October 8, 2007]. **6B–11**

### The forms

The practice directions supplementing Pt 8 (permission) and Pt 9 (How to start proceedings) provide details of the forms and evidence required to start applications in the court. **6B–12**

In general you will not need permission to apply to the court if the application relates to property and affairs; with the exception of cases involving the appointment or removal of trustees or applications relating to wills and gifts.

You will need permission if the application relates to personal welfare.

Copies of the forms and guidance notes are available by contacting the Customer Contact Centre at the Office of the Public Guardian on 0845 330 2900 or can be downloaded from the website: *http://www.hmcs.gov.uk* [Accessed September 20, 2007].

### The Court of Protection

Section 45 of the Mental Capacity Act creates a new Court of Protection. It is a superior court of record, able to establish precedent and build expertise in issues related to issues of capacity. It has the same rights, powers, privileges and authority as the High Court. The court can deal with property and affairs matters as well as serious decisions affecting healthcare and personal welfare matters previously dealt with by the High Court under its inherent jurisdiction. **6B–13**

***Paragraph numbers marked with a "+" can be found online and on CD.***

Sir Mark Potter has been appointed as the President of the Court and Sir Andrew Morritt as the Vice President. Denzil Lush is the Senior Judge.

Outside London, the work of the Court of Protection is administered in six regional registries: Birmingham, Bristol, Cardiff, Manchester, Newcastle-upon-Tyne and Preston. In London the work is administered in the central office and registry.

The work of the Court of Protection is governed by the Mental Capacity Act. Some of the Court's powers include:

1. decide whether a person has capacity to make a particular decision for themselves;
2. make declarations, decisions or orders on financial or welfare matters affecting people who lack capacity to make such decisions;
3. appoint deputies to make decisions for people lacking capacity to make those decisions;
4. decide whether a Lasting Power of Attorney or an Enduring Power of Attorney is valid;
5. remove deputies or attorneys who fail to carry out their duties.

### The Central Registry

6B–14 The Central Registry is situated at Archway Tower, 2 Junction Road, London, N19 5SZ. Tel: 0845 330 2900, DX: 141150 Archway 2, Fax: 020 7664 7705. The offices are open to the public between the hours of 10am and 4.30pm on working days, which are as prescribed in r.6 of the Court of Protection Rules 2007. All correspondence should be sent to the above address and the case number and any court reference on correspondence should be quoted.

### Out of hours applications

6B–15 In cases of emergency out of hours applications to the Court contact security at the Royal Courts of Justice on 020 7947 6000. Refer to Pt 10 of the Court Rules and the supplementary Practice Direction 10B for further information.

### The Judiciary

6B–16 Pursuant to s.46(1)–(4) of the Act, the Lord Chancellor has nominated various District, Circuit and High Court judges to deal with Court of Protection matters. Rule 86 of the Court of Protection Rules 2007 and the practice direction supplementing Pt 12 specifies the type of application which may be dealt with only by the president, the vice-President or one of the other judges nominated by virtue of s.46(2)(a) to (c) of the Act.

### Consideration of applications

6B–17 It is primarily a matter for country solicitors whether or not London agents are instructed in matters relating to the Court of Protection. Most applications are stamped on issue. Attendance not required unless notified. Attendance will therefore be required only when the judge so directs or the persons concerned wish to attend.

Where attendance at Court is required the hearings in most cases will be held at Archway Tower. Parties will be notified if the hearing is to be held in one of the Court of Protection regional registries.

### Court fees

6B–18 Court fees are set out in the Schedule to the Court of Protection Fees Order 2007. (the Court of Protection Fees Order 2007 (SI 2007/1745) has been amended by the Court of Protection Fees (Amendment) Order 2009 (SI 2009/513), with effect from April 1, 2009). Payment of fees may be made as follows:

(i) in cash at the Court of Protection, Archway Tower, 2 Junction Road, London N19 5SZ;

(ii) by cheque or postal order made payable to Her Majesty's Court Service and crossed and sent by post to the Court.

### Essential matter

6B–19 Before bringing any proceedings the applicant should think about the implications of doing so and consider whether the required outcome can be achieved in any other way.

***Paragraph numbers marked with a "+" can be found online and on CD.***

The starting point for the Mental Capacity Act is that a person is assumed to be able to make their own decisions unless it can be shown that they lack capacity to do so.

Section 5 of the Act provides protection for carers, healthcare and social care staff to carry out certain tasks without fear of liability; this may include personal care or treatment of people who lack capacity to consent to them.

In most matters regarding personal welfare the principles set out in the Act and in the Code of Practice will enable one to:

1. take action or make a decision in the best interests of someone who lacks capacity, and
2. find ways of settling disagreements about actions or decisions.

In certain situations informal decision-making is inappropriate and an application to the Court will be necessary. This may include:

1. difficult decisions,
2. disagreements that cannot be resolved, and
3. situations requiring ongoing personal welfare decisions.

**Adult Healthcare and Welfare cases**

Under the Act, healthcare and welfare proceedings begun in the High Court under the court's inherent jurisdiction before October 1, 2007 may continue to be dealt with in the High Court until a final decision is made— Mental Capacity Act 2005 (Transitional and Consequential Provisions) Order 2007. However from October 1, 2007 the principles of the Act and the Code of Practice will also apply to these cases. **6B–20**

Healthcare and welfare proceedings begun after October 1, 2007 must be made to the Court of Protection.

**Applications relating to serious medical treatment**

Serious medical treatment means treatment which involves providing, withdrawing or withholding treatment in circumstances where: **6B–21**

(a) in a case where a single treatment is being proposed, there is a fine balance between its benefits to P and the burdens and risks it is likely to entail for him;

(b) in a case where there is a choice of treatments, a decision as to which one to use is finely balanced; or

(c) the treatment, procedure or investigation proposed would be likely to involve serious consequences for P.

As part of its jurisdiction, under the Mental Capacity Act, the Court of Protection can now make decisions in relation to serious medical treatment. Applications to the Court should be made as outlined in Pt 9 of the Rules supplemented by Practice Direction 9E.

Members of the Official Solicitors staff are prepared to discuss applications in relation to serious medical treatment before an application is made. Enquiries should be addressed to a family and medical litigation lawyer. Email enquiries@offsol.gsi.gov.uk.

Unless the matter needs to be disposed of urgently, the court will list it for a first directions hearing. Practice Direction 10B sets out the procedure to be followed for urgent applications.

**Deprivation of Liberty**

The deprivation of liberty safeguards, in force from April 1, 2009, have been introduced to provide a legal framework around deprivation of liberty and to prevent breaches of the European Convention on Human Rights (ECHR) such as that identified by the case of *HL v United Kingdom* (2004) App. No.00045508/99—commonly known as the "Bournewood" judgment. **6B–21.1**

The case concerned an autistic man with learning disabilities who lacked capacity to decide whether he should be admitted to hospital for specific treatment. As he was compliant and did not resist detention, he was admitted for informal treatment under s.131(1) of the Mental Health Act 1983, but this decision was challenged by his carers.

To prevent similar breaches of the ECHR, the Mental Capacity Act 2005 has been amended to provide safeguards for people who lack capacity to consent to treatment or care in either a care home or a hospital, that in P's best interests can only be provided in circumstances that amount to a deprivation of liberty and where detention under the Mental Health Act 1983 is not appropriate for that person at that time. The term "care home" means a care home registered under the Care Standards Act 2000.

***Paragraph numbers marked with a "+" can be found online and on CD.***

Sections 49–51 of the Mental Health Act 2007 introduce additional safeguards into the Mental Capacity Act 2005, specifically in ss.4A and 4B and Schs A1 and 1A to the MCA. The safeguards can only be applied to people aged 18 and over. They cannot be applied to people while they are detained in hospital under the Mental Health Act 1983 (s.131(1)) but can be applied to a person who has previously been detained in hospital under the Mental Health Act 1983.

In order to deprive someone of their liberty a managing authority (the NHS authority responsible for the running of the hospital or the person registered/required to be registered under Pt 2 of the Care Standards Act 2000 must apply to the supervisory body either a Primary Care Trust (PCT) in England or the National Assembly for Wales via the Local Health Board (LHB).

### Type of authorisations

6B–21.2 There are two types of authorisation: standard and urgent. A managing authority should request a standard authorisation when it appears likely that within the next 28 days someone will be accommodated in a hospital or care home in circumstances that amount to a deprivation of liberty within the meaning of art.5 of the ECHR. If the deprivation is already occurring or about to occur then the managing authority must give itself an urgent authorisation and then obtain a standard authorisation within seven calendar days.

### The Code of Practice

6B–21.3 The legal framework provided by the new provisions in the Mental Capacity Act 2005 is supported by a Code of Practice (*Deprivation of Liberty Safeguards: Code of Practice to Supplement the Main Mental Capacity Act 2005 Code of Practice* (London: TSO, 2008)) which helps to explain how to identify when a person is, or is at risk of being deprived of their liberty and how deprivation of liberty may be avoided.

Like the main code, this Code has a statutory force and certain categories of people have a legal duty to have regard to it. The Code specifically focuses on providing guidance for people exercising functions relating to the deprivation of liberty safeguards and people acting as a relevant person's representative. A relevant person is a person who is, or may become,deprived of their liberty in accordance with the deprivation of liberty safeguards.

### Appeals to the Court of Protection

6B–21.4 Anybody deprived of their liberty in accordance with the safeguards is entitled to speedy access to a court to review the lawfulness of their deprivation. The Court of Protection is the court for this purpose.

A relevant person or someone acting on their behalf may apply to the court before a decision has been reached on an application for authorisation to deprive a person of their liberty. It is up to the court to decide whether or not to consider such an application in advance of the decision on authorisation.

Where a standard authorisation has been given, the Court of Protection can determine any question relating to:

1. whether the person meets any of the qualifying requirements/assessments;
2. the period for which it has been given;
3. the purpose for which it has been given; or
4. the conditions subject to which it has been given.

Once it has determined the question, the court may make an order varying or terminating the authorisation or ordering the supervisory body to vary or terminate it.

In the case of an urgent authorisation, the court may determine:

1. whether the urgent authorisation should have been given;
2. the period during which the urgent authorisation is to be in force
3. the purpose for which the urgent authorisation is given.

The court may make an order varying or terminating the urgent authorisation or ordering the managing authority of the relevant hospital or care home to vary or terminate the urgent authorisation.

There will usually be fee for applications to the court. Legal Aid will be available both for advice and representation before the court. Details of the fees charged by the Court and circumstances in which fees can be waived or remitted are available from the Office of the Public Guardian (*http://www.hmcs.gov.uk* [Accessed January 13, 2009]).

**Court of Protection Rules and Practice Directions**

The Court of Protection Rules 2007 have been amended by the Court of Protection (Amendment) Rules 2009 (SI 2009/582) with effect from April 1, 2009 in order to add supporting rules for the deprivation of liberty jurisdiction. A new part Pt 10A (Deprivation of Liberty matters) is inserted consisting of a new r.82A which provides the procedure for the applications is set out in the practice direction to that part. **6B–21.5**

**Minor (Infant) lacking capacity**

The Court of Protection has jurisdiction to deal with the property and affairs of a minor, and will do so in a proper case. Where damages are recovered on behalf of a minor the Court of Protection will accept jurisdiction to administer such damages if the minor is likely to survive until attaining his majority and is not likely to recover before then. **6B–22**

In cases relating to the healthcare and welfare of a minor s.21(a)(b) of the Act allows for the transfer of proceedings between the Court of Protection and a court having jurisdiction under the Children Act 1989 (c.41).

**Appeals**

See s.53 and rr.169– 182 and the supplemental Practice Direction 20A for Pt 20 of the Court of Protection Rules. Rules 172 and 173 set out the procedure for seeking the court's permission to appeal. Where an appeal lies to the Court of Appeal the CPR apply to such an appeal. **6B–23**

Unless the appeal is against an order for committal to prison, the court's permission is required to appeal. An appeal for permission may be made either to the judge at the hearing at which the decision being appealed was made (the first instance judge) or to an appeal judge, but refer to r.182, which sets out certain requirements in relation to second appeals.

**Service of notice**

Part 7 of the Court Rules and the supplemental practice direction set out the procedure to be followed where the adult "P" is to be given notice of any matter or document or provided (r.40) with any document. Part 7 does not apply when "P" becomes a party and service is to be effected in accordance with Pt 6 or as the Court may direct. In line with the principles of the Act, the information must be provided to "P" in a way that is appropriate to his/her circumstances for example using simple language, visual aids or any other means. **6B–24**

**Draft order and settlement**

Only in exceptional circumstances are draft orders now sent out for approval. The order is drafted and any additional information called for. It is then engrossed and dispatched to the solicitors having carriage of the order. **6B–25**

Where there is a lodgment and payment schedule to the order an additional copy of such schedule alone is prepared for the use of the Court Funds Office and is transmitted direct.

Note: If the order entails the execution of a deed, e.g. on a sale of land, an additional copy for placing with the title deeds should be requested.

**Security**

On the appointment of a financial deputy, the Court may direct that security be given to the Public Guardian. The question of the appropriate levels of security to be given by a professional deputy and the court's requirements was raised in *Re H*, an approved judgment of Her Honour Judge H. Marshall Q.C. **6B–26**

The methods of giving security are matters for the Public Guardian and are governed by the Lasting Powers of Attorney, Enduring Powers of Attorney and Public Guardian Regulations 2007 and in particular Pt 4 which outline the functions of the Public Guardian.

Security can be effected by one of two methods (Regulation 34(2)):

(a) an authorised insurance company; or

(b) an authorised deposit taker.

Should default be made in a case where security has been effected by bond, a certif-

*Paragraph numbers marked with a "+" can be found online and on CD.*

icate of default will issue which, under the term of the bond, is conclusive evidence against the deputy and the sureties.

### Lodgments in court

6B–27 With the implementation of the Mental Capacity Act, the court is now less likely to require the lodgement of stocks and shares into court.

Where stock or shares to be lodged stand in the name of "P" the lodgment is made by the proper officer of the company and where they stand in the joint names of "P" and another the lodgment is made by the proper officer of the company and that other; the lodgment will, usually, only be directed where "P" is solely entitled thereto. In cases where "P" holds securities either solely or jointly as trustee the question of appointing a new trustee in place "P" and obtaining any necessary vesting order would have to be considered.

Funds to be lodged are transferred into the name of the Accountant General, usually to the general credit of "P", but where any income is not required for maintenance or other necessary expenditure an accumulating fund is sometimes created, the Accountant General of the Supreme Court being directed to invest and accumulate the income. Accumulations are placed on Special Account pending investment.

### Application where "P" ceases to lack capacity

6B–28 Under r.202(1) of the Court of Protection Rules and on the Court being satisfied that "P" has the capacity to make decisions in relation to the property that the Court had previously appointed a deputy to administer, the Court may make an order to transfer the property in question back to "P". The application is to be made in accordance with Pt 10 of the Rules.

### Court of Protection Visitors

6B–28.1 Section 61 of the Act refers to Court of Protection Visitors. Court of Protection Visitors replace the Lord Chancellors Visitors created by the Mental Health Act 1983.

There are two types of Court Of Protection Visitor, General Visitor and Special Visitor. Special Visitors are registered medical practitioners with relevant expertise.

The Court or Public Guardian can send whichever type of Visitor is most appropriate to visit and interview a person who may lack capacity. Visitors can also interview Attorneys or Deputies and inspect any relevant healthcare or social care records.

## APPOINTMENT OF NEW TRUSTEES AND VESTING ORDERS

### Statutory jurisdiction

6B–29 The removal from his office of a trustee lacking mental capacity and the appointment, where necessary, of a new trustee in his place and the vesting of trust property are matters which may be effected out of court or may require relief either in the Court of Protection or the Chancery Division or county court, according to the circumstances.

The following enactments as amended or repealed by the Mental Capacity Act have special application:

(1) s.96(1)(k) of the Mental Health Act 1983—exercise of a patient's power of appointing new trustee or retiring from a trust with (if necessary) a vesting order under subs.(2);

(2) s.54(2) of the Trustee Act 1925—appointment by the Court of Protection of a new trustee in place of a patient with (if necessary) a vesting order.

(3) s.36(9) of the Trustee Act 1925—giving of leave to a continuing (or refusing or retiring) trustee to exercise his statutory power of appointment.

### Which method to adopt

6B–30 The practitioner should refer to the courts practice directions but with a view to assisting the practitioner to decide what is the appropriate course and procedure to be followed in any particular case, the following working rules are given:

(a) Where "P" is not a Trustee:

(1) Where "P" has no beneficial interest, and the assistance of the court is

***Paragraph numbers marked with a "+" can be found online and on CD.***

required, relief should be asked for in the Chancery Division (or county court, where appropriate; see Trustee Act 1925, s.67) but see note (4) below.

(2) s.54(2) of the Trustee Act 1925, does not apply.

(3) The only jurisdiction in the Court of Protection is under s.18(h)(j)) of the Mental Capacity Act, exercising a power of appointment (if any) vested in "P".

(4) Where "P" is the person nominated by the trust instrument to exercise the power of appointing new trustees, such power should be exercised in the Court of Protection if "P" is beneficially interested and a deputy has been appointed (see *Re Blake* [1887] W.N. 173); otherwise new trustees may be appointed out of court by any of the persons so empowered by s.36 of the Trustee Act 1925. Where, however, "P" was the settlor it is appropriate for the power to be exercised in the Court of Protection under note (3) above, whether or not "P" has a beneficial interest.

(5) If the power vested in "P" is purely statutory, and there is no other person with a power capable of exercising the same, application may be made to the Court of Protection to exercise the power.

(b) Where "P" is a Trustee:

(1) Where "P" has no beneficial interest and the assistance of the court is required, relief should be asked for in the Chancery Division (or other court, where appropriate; see Trustee Act 1925, s.67) but see note (5) below.

(2) If a vesting order is required and the matter is one coming within the scope of s.54 (2) of the Trustee Act 1925, proceed under that section for an order appointing and vesting. This course is advocated even where "P" or some other person (who would require to be an applicant) is the person nominated by the trust instrument to appoint new trustees, see note (5).

(3) There are four conditions which must be fulfilled if a case is to come within s.54 (2) of the Trustee Act 1925, namely:

(i) the trust is not subject to an order for administration in the Chancery Division;

(ii) the new trustees are to be appointed in place of "P";

(iii) a deputy is acting for "P" or an application for the appointment of a deputy is pending;

(iv) "P" is beneficially entitled to some interest in the trust property.

(4) If a vesting order is not required, new trustees should be appointed out of court by any of the persons so empowered by s.36 of the Trustee Act 1925, but where "P" has some beneficial interest in possession, and the appointment is being made by the continuing (or refusing or retiring) trustee, by virtue of subs.(1)(b) of that section, the prior leave of the Court of Protection is necessary under subs.(9).

(5) If "P" is the person nominated by the trust instrument to exercise the power of appointing new trustees and he is beneficially interested and there is a deputy, the appointment should be made in the Court of Protection: *Re Blake* [1887] W.N. 173) under s.18 of the Act, by exercising the power, and where "P" was the settlor, this course should be followed, even if he has no beneficial interest. If a vesting order is required it is preferable, where possible, to proceed under s.54(2) of the Trustee Act 1925 for an order appointing and vesting (see notes (2) and (3)).

(6) Where there is with "P" a capable trustee who wishes to retire, the matter does not fall within s.54(2) of the Trustee Act 1925, though there would be jurisdiction under s.18 of the Mental Capacity Act.

(7) Where it is desired that "P" shall retire from the trust under s.39 of the Trustee Act 1925, without a new trustee being appointed in his place, application can be made under s.18 of the Mental Capacity Act, for an order authorising the deputy to exercise the power with (if necessary) a vesting order under subs.(2) of that section.

Usually no vesting provisions are required, unless "P" is a trustee. Where there stand in the name of "P", either solely or jointly, mortgages or stocks or shares, etc. (see the Trustee Act 1925, s.40(4)) a vesting order is necessary, for, if the appointment of new trustees were made by deed either under s.18 of the Mental Capacity Act, or by the continuing trustee or other person empowered under s.36 of the Trustee Act 1925, such classes of property would not "follow the deed" under any express or implied vesting provisions under s.40 of the Trustee Act 1925.

Where, however, proceedings for appointment of new trustees are being taken under s.54 of the Trustee Act 1925 all property will be vested in the new trustees by or in pursuance of the order; there will be no deed of appointment.

Where new trustees are being appointed for the purposes of the Settled Land Act 1925, the order will not deal with the freehold and leasehold property (since if vested in him the legal estate remains in the tenant for life). Where land is vested in P as statutory owner (see the Settled Land Act 1925, s.23(1)(b)) the order will authorise the receiver to convey or join in conveying the land to the new statutory owners (see ibid., s.7(4)).

### Trustee Delegation Act 1999

6B–31 This Act came into effect on March 1, 2000 and all Enduring Powers of Attorney made on or after this date are subject to it.

An attorney of an EPA created on or after March 1, 2000 has acquired trustee functions under s.1(1) of the Trustee Delegation Act 1999 and can therefore exercise the Donor's trustee powers providing that:

(i) the Donor has a beneficial interest in the trust at the time when the function is exercised;
(ii) there is no indication that the Donor did not want the Attorney to exercise his/her trustee functions;
(iii) the trust consisted of land, the proceeds of sale of land or income from land. This includes appointing a new trustee if there is no continuing trustee or the attorney is the continuing trustee.

A new Section 22(3) was added to the Law of Property Act whereby the incapacitated trustee does not need to be replaced if there is an Attorney acting under an EPA.

The Trustee Delegation Act also allows a Donor to make EPAs specifically to deal with any trustee functions whether or not the Donor has a beneficial interest, but these are only valid for one year.

### Mode of application and applicants

6B–32 The application is made by way of formal application on form COP1.

### Documents and evidence

6B–33 The Practice Direction 9G provides full details of the information to be provided with the application form.

### The order

6B–34 Where an order is made under s.54(2) of the Trustee Act 1925, appointing new trustees and vesting the property, no deed of appointment is necessary; when the order is finally completed any necessary transfers in respect of stocks or shares, etc., should be executed by the new trustees. The order is drafted and settled in the usual way.

### Trustee Act 1925, s.36(9)

6B–35 This enactment, as amended by the Mental Capacity Act, provides that where a trustee is because of an impairment of or a disturbance in the functioning of, the mind or brain within the meaning of the Act, lacks capacity to exercise his functions as trustee and is also entitled in possession to some beneficial interest in the trust property, no appointment of a new trustee in his place shall be made unless sanctioned by the Court of Protection. A formal application must be issued. The practitioner is referred to Practice Direction 9G.

### Practice as to sale of land and house property

6B–36 An attorney under an enduring power of attorney (EPA) or a lasting power of attorney (LPA) may have authority to sell a property.

***Paragraph numbers marked with a "+" can be found online and on CD.***

Unless the financial deputy has already been authorised to sell the property in the Order, or an Interim Order for Sale has been issued, it will be necessary to make a formal application for an Order authorising the sale. Reference should be made to the practice direction supporting Pt 9 of the Rules. Once an order or direction for sale has been made the following points should be noted:

1. For a sale by private treaty. The court does not require to approve the terms of the contract itself, it being the responsibility of the solicitors acting in the sale to ensure that the contract is adequate in all respects. A contract (which should not contain any reference to mental incapacity) should be entered into by the vendor acting by the deputy (or other named person) pursuant to an order of the Court of Protection. Subject to any necessary adaptation, the following special conditions should be included:

(1) The amount of the deposit shall be £10 per cent of the purchase money and shall be paid to Messrs. . . . . . . . . . . . . [the solicitors in the matter] as stakeholders.

(2) The vendor as (beneficial owner) (tenant for life) is selling by his deputy pursuant to an order of the Court of Protection an LPA or EPA and a copy of the said order/LPA or EPA certified, or of the relevant portion thereof will be handed over on completion and shall be deemed to be conclusive evidence of such authority to sell and the purchaser(s) shall not require the production of or make any requisition or objection in relation to any evidence matter or thing referred to in the said order or otherwise relating thereto.

Notes:

(i) The court will rely entirely upon the solicitors for the accuracy and sufficiency of the contents of the contract and the draft particulars and conditions will not be settled or approved by the court.

(ii) The address of the vendor (if inserted) should be his home address or that of the deputy, never that of an institution.

(iii) Restrictive or other covenants. If the property is subject to any such covenants, the conditions should provide that the property will be sold and will be conveyed subject thereto and (unless it is clear that the vendor will not remain liable after parting with the property) that the purchaser shall in the conveyance enter into a covenant for indemnity in respect thereof.

2. Special condition on sale of leasehold property. In an assignment on sale of leasehold property by an assignor who is expressed to convey—as beneficial owner there is implied a covenant (inter alia) that all the covenants of the lease have been observed up to the time of the assignment; see the Law of Property Act 1925, Sch.II, Pt II; the Land Registration Act 1925, s.24(1)(a). It is, of course, notorious that covenants for repair and decoration are seldom completely performed at any given moment, and the purchaser is probably well aware of the actual condition of the property; but liability under the implied covenants depends not on knowledge of the grantee but on what is actually expressed in the conveyance. It is therefore important that the implied covenants should be restricted when it is known or suspected that there has been a breach of covenant.

In ordinary cases, therefore, every contract for the sale of leasehold property on behalf of P should contain a clause to the following effect: The purchaser shall in the assurance of the property covenant to indemnify the vendor and the vendor's estate and effects from and against all subsisting and future liabilities arising out of the state of repair and condition of the property and the assurance shall contain a declaration negativing any implied covenant by the vendor that the covenants contained in the said lease (underlease) and relating to the repair decoration painting or condition of the property have been performed.

3. For a sale by public auction. The sale may be advertised as being made by order of the Court of Protection. The particulars and conditions of sale must not contain any reference to a lack of capacity or the name of "P". Subject to any necessary adaptation the special conditions are set out in 1. above.

### Settlement and approval of the assurance

It is no longer necessary for draft deeds to be settled and approved by the court, the court relying on the solicitors for the accuracy and sufficiency of the contents. **6B–37**

### Entry to property prior to completion

It is not necessary to seek the court's permission to allow the purchaser: **6B–38**

*Paragraph numbers marked with a "+" can be found online and on CD.*

(i) to enter into occupation of the property prior to completion, provided that the contract contains a relevant condition similar to that in the National Conditions of Sale or the Law Society's General Conditions, and the solicitors for P take all necessary steps to safeguard "P" interest.

(ii) access to the property to effect repairs or decorations prior to completion, provided the contract contains a provision or there is a subsequent agreement by the purchasers to the effect that if for any reason whether due to the default of the vendor or not the contract is not completed, the purchaser shall not have any claim against the vendor in respect of work done and the purchaser shall make good at his own expense any damage to the property. Wherever possible, access by the buyer between exchange of contracts should be avoided.

### Purchase of property

6B–39 An attorney appointed to deal with property and financial affairs either by an LPA or EPA may have authority to purchase a property.

Unless the financial deputy has already been authorised by the court, he will need to apply to the court for an order authorising the purchase. Thereafter the procedure follows along similar lines as for a sale of property. If "P" is not an executing party, no reference should be made in the assurance to the fact that the purchaser a person under the jurisdiction of the court or that the purchase is proceeding pursuant to an order of the Court of Protection or that the purchaser is acting by a deputy.

On the completion of property purchased for "P", neither attorneys nor deputies should not seek to have the purchased registered in their own name. If "P" is an adult and has provided all the funds for the purchase, the property must be registered in his name. If the deputy has a concern that "P" may be influenced by a third party to deal with the property, the deputy could enter a restriction at the Land Registry requiring the deputy's consent to any dealing.

Where "P" is under 18, or where someone else is contributing to the purchase, it is necessary to have the property registered in the names of trustees (normally two). A suitable declaration of trust should be prepared but this will not require the approval of the court unless the court has directed that the declaration should be submitted for approval. A Land Registry restriction should also be entered.

### Estate agent's charges

6B–40 1. The charges of estate agents and auctioneers selling freehold or leasehold property pursuant to orders of the Chancery Division, Family Division, the Court of Protection, or divorce county courts will normally be considered reasonable by the court if they do not exceed the rate of commission which that agent would normally charge on a sole agency basis, and if they do not exceed 21/2 per cent of the sale price, exclusive of value added tax.

2. These charges are to include all commission, valuations, expenses and other disbursements, including making affidavits, the cost of advertising, and all other work except surveys.

### Joint tenant and tenant in common

6B–41 When "P" holds land with other co-owners upon trust for sale, a new trustee must be appointed in his place or he must be otherwise discharged from the trust before the legal estate is dealt with under the trust for sale or under the powers vested in the trustees for sale (s.22 (2) of the Law of Property Act 1925). By s.36(9) of the Trustee Act 1925, the leave of the court is required before any such appointment is made in a case by virtue of s.36(1)(b) where "P" has a beneficial interest in possession. In view of the undertaking required to be filed on the making of the application for leave to appoint a new trustee not to sell without first obtaining approval as to price and to deal with "P"s share of the proceeds as may be directed, directions must be obtained before any sale by the new trustees.

A sale of "P" beneficial interest in property (either as joint tenant or tenant in common) to a third party can, of course, be ordered at any time, but a new trustee in place of "P" will sometimes be required if the legal estate is not to remain outstanding. If, however, the purchaser is the co-owner it may also be possible to assure the "P" interest in the legal estate, inasmuch as it would not appear that such a transaction would be invalidated by s.22(2) of the Law of Property Act 1925.

**Tenant for life**

The jurisdiction to authorise the exercise of "P"s powers as tenant for life derives from s.18 the Mental Capacity Act In view of s.13 of the Settled Land Act 1925, the principal powers of the tenant for life cannot be exercised until the requisite vesting instrument has been executed. An authority under seal to procure the execution of the necessary vesting instrument will be issued. If execution of such instrument on behalf of "P" is unnecessary no reference to incapacity is to be made. Where the land is leasehold or freehold subject to a rent or covenants, and if execution on behalf "P" is required, the authority will authorise the deputy in the name and on behalf of "P" to execute. In either case the draft vesting instrument must be submitted to the court for approval. **6B–42**

The prior leave of the court is required before any notices under s.101 of the Settled Land Act 1925, can be given (*Re Ray's Settled Estates* (1884) L.R. 25 Ch.D. 464) where a sale of settled property is contemplated. The procedure to be followed is similar to that of a sale of "P" absolute property under a general order. That order will authorise the deputy to give all necessary notices required by s.101 of the Settled Land Act 1925. The proceeds will be received by the trustees as capital moneys who will also be responsible for the payment of the taxed costs of the application and order and of the sale.

**Business**

Under s.18(d) of the Mental Capacity Act 2005, the court may direct the carrying on by a suitable person of any profession trade or business owned by "P". **6B–43**

**Dissolution of partnership**

The Court of Protection may order the dissolution of a partnership of which "P" is a member (s.18 (1)(e) of the Mental Capacity Act 2005) but will only do so where there is a deputy and there are no partnership disputes; otherwise it may be necessary to apply in the Chancery Division. In any event the deputy may be authorised to give notice to dissolve, etc. **6B–44**

**Leases and surrenders**

The jurisdiction to authorise the granting of leases and accept surrenders derives from s.18(1)(b) of the Mental Capacity Act 2005. **6B–45**

**Performance of a contract**

The court may direct the carrying out of any contract entered into by "P", either prior to incapacity or during incapacity (s.18(1)(g) of the Mental Capacity Act 2005. The adoption of a voidable contract for the purchase (and semble, sale) of freehold property entered into prior to the proceedings works conversion as from the date of the contract (*Baldwyn v Smith* [1900] 1 Ch. 588). **6B–46**

See also s.54(2)(c) of the Trustee Act 1925.

**Exercise of power (including power to consent)**

Any such power may be exercised under s.18(1)(j) of the Mental Capacity Act 2005. **6B–47**

Among the powers exercisable under this provision are the powers of a "P" as tenant for life; the powers of a "P" as mortgagee; power to bar an entail (see *Re Pares* (1879) 12 Ch.D. 333; Re E. D. S. [1914] 1 Ch. 618, and *Re R. H. C.* [1963] 1 W.L.R. 1095); power to appoint in favour of children (*Re A.* [1904] 2 Ch. 328); powers of guardianship of an infant child (*Re L. H. B.* [1935] 1 Ch. 643); the exercise of a power to appoint trustee (*Re Fuller* [1900] 2 Ch. 551).

The question whether the Court of Protection could authorise a deputy, on behalf of "P", to give his consent under s.2(1)(d) of the Divorce Reform Act 1969 (now s.1(2)(d) of the Matrimonial Causes Act 1973) was raised in *Mason v Mason* [1972] Fam. 302; [1972] 3 All E.R. 315. The President declined to say whether the Court of Protection could give such authority. Section 27 of the Mental Capacity Act 2005 provides a list of family relationships where decisions cannot be made on behalf of "P".

It should be noted that powers of "P" as patron of a benefice may be discharged only by a person appointed by the court sch.4(10)(1-4) of the Mental Capacity Act 2005.

**Patient mortgagee**

Powers of a "P" as mortgagee are exercisable under s.18(1) (j) of the Mental Capa- **6B–48** city Act 2005. An application for an order or direction for the execution of a statutory receipt or reconveyance where "P" is beneficially entitled as mortgagee should be accompanied by the following undertaking: "We undertake to produce on the hearing of the application the mortgage referred to in the within written application and any transfer of the said mortgage." The application must be supported by:

(i) an affidavit by a solicitor dealing with "P's" title to the mortgage and who is entitled to give a receipt;

(ii) the title to the immediate equity of redemption and in whom vested;

(iii) who is entitled to receive the deeds bearing in mind any subsequent incumbrances; and

(iv) the amount due under the mortgage (capital and arrears of interest) bearing in mind any further advances, etc. or any moneys applied to protect the security.

The mortgagor should not be served, and if served is not entitled to his costs out of the patient's estate (*Re Phillips* (1869) L.R. 4 Ch.App. 629; and *Re Wheeler* (1852) 1 De G.M. & G. 434). The order or direction directs the deputy in the name and on behalf of "P" to execute the statutory receipt or to reconvey or transfer.

If "P" is one of several co-mortgagees and all of such mortgagees are living and each mortgagee is entitled to a definite amount of the mortgage money application can be made in the Court of Protection for "P" by his deputy to concur in the statutory receipt or transfer as the case may be, otherwise the appropriate proceedings must be taken for the appointment of a new trustee in place of the patient.

In a proper case an order will be made for the advance of the patient's money on mortgage. The application would have to be supported by evidence as to value and the proposed advance should not normally exceed two-thirds of such valuation.

An application for sale by "P" as mortgagee would proceed substantially in the same manner as an application for sale of property belonging "P" absolutely; it must be shown that the power of sale has arisen.

### P as mortgagor

**6B–49** When "P" is the mortgagor of any of his property the mortgagee should communicate with the deputy or his solicitor if the question arises of enforcing the mortgage or any of the covenants arising there under. Under s.18(1)(b) of the Mental Capacity Act 2005, the court can authorise the charging or other disposition of or dealing with any property of "P".

### Improvements

**6B–50** When "P" is tenant for life and it is desired to expend money on improvements upon the settled property application should be made for leave for the deputy in the name and on behalf of "P" tenant for life to execute the required improvement, to give a direction to the Settled Land Act trustees for payment pursuant to s.75 of the Settled Land Act 1925, and, if there are no capital moneys available in the hands of the Settled Land Act trustees, to raise the money required on the security of the settled land or of any part thereof by a legal mortgage (Settled Land Act 1925, s.71(1)); or the application could be made for the money required to be advanced out of "P"s capital and a mortgage given by the trustees to "P" to secure the amount advanced (Settled Land Act 1925, s.68).

### Preservation of interests in property disposed of on behalf of a person lacking capacity

**6B–51** This is now governed by Sch.4, ss.8 and 9 of the Mental Capacity Act 2005, to which reference should be made. Section 123(1) of the Lunacy Act 1890 which was replaced in the main by the Mental Health Act 1959, s.107, only applied to transactions wherein the element of conversion into money was present and did not apply, e.g. to the investment of money (*Walker, Re* [1921] 2 Ch. 63) purchase of property (*Searle, Re* [1912] 2 Ch. 365) and lodgment in court of funds in specie (*Palmer, Re* [1945] Ch. 8). The definition of "disposal" in subs.(3) nullifies the effect of these decisions.

The paramount consideration is the interest of "P", and the court pays no regard to those who come after, but in matters outside the ordinary course of management it is

*Paragraph numbers marked with a "+" can be found online and on CD.*

the duty of the court, so far as possible, not to alter the character of "P"s property or to interfere with any rights of succession (*Attorney General v Ailesbury* (1887) 12 L.R. App. Cas. 672).

As to proceeds of sale of real estate descending as realty, see *Re Matson* [1897] 2 Ch.509; *Re Tugwell* (1884) L.R. 27 Ch.D. 309; *Re Alston* [1917] 2 Ch. 226.

When it is desired to relieve a legatee from the incidence of duty upon freehold property which has been purchased out of personal property bequeathed to the legatee (his interest being automatically preserved under Sch 4.ss 8 and 9 the court can give a direction under Sch.4, s.8(3) The converse case of sale of real property and the acquisition in its place of personal property requires no direction of the court, and under Sch.4, s.8(4)(b) the property purchased would automatically be treated as real property.

As to devolution to the heir of a pre-1926 "P"s interest in realty on his death intestate, without having recovered his testamentary capacity, see Administration of Estates Act 1925, s.51(2).

**Creditors**

See s.18(1) (g) of the Mental Capacity Act 2005. During financial deputyship proceedings the creditors are without remedy. They cannot obtain any payment unless the court, in the exercise of its discretion, makes an order in their favour (*Re Seager Hunt* [1906] 2 Ch. 295). "P"s interest comes first, and if necessary the creditors will be ignored (*Re Plenderleith* [1893] 3 Ch. 332) or they can obtain a charging order under s.18(1)(b) of Mental Capacity Act 2005. After "P"s death the High Court, in administering his estate, will not be bound by any order of the Court of Protection directing payment of a dividend to creditors (*Re Seager Hunt* [1906] 2 Ch. 295); see also *Re Wheater* [1928] Ch. 223. A creditor who is entitled to interest is to have it at four per cent together with the costs of proving his claim (*Re Hunt* [1902] 2 Ch. 318). **6B–52**

Where the property "P" has become subject to the control of the Court of Protection by the appointment of a deputy, it cannot be seized under a writ of fi. fa. by an execution creditor of "P"; and the court will make an order dealing with his property, and for the payment thereout of costs and of an allowance for the maintenance of "P"—though not of his wife—in priority to any claim of the execution creditor; but subject to such allowance and to the costs incurred in relation to "P"s property, the order will be made without prejudice to any charge or priority which the creditor may have acquired by lodging his writ of fi. fa. with the sheriff (*Re Winkle* [1894] 2 Ch. 519, CA). An interim order has been made for the express purpose of protecting "P"s property from execution (*Re Pountain* (1888) L.R. 37 Ch.D. 609).

Nevertheless, the jurisdiction of the Court of Protection does not interfere with the common law or statutory rights of a judgment creditor over funds which have not been brought within the control of the Court of Protection (*Re Brown* [1900] 1 Ch. 489) or with the rights of creditors to seize and sell by legal process property of "P"which at the time of seizure is not in the custody of such court, and the issuing of an application in the Court of Protection does not withdraw the property of "P" from such legal process by a creditor until an order is made showing that the court has actually taken the property under its protection (*Re Charles Clarke* [1898] 1 Ch. 336, CA, distinguishing *Re Winkle*). Further, an order conferring on a person therein specified, to take possession or control of all of "P"s property and financial affairs and to exercise the same powers of management and investment as "P" has as the beneficial owner, does not affect rights against "P"s property at law or in equity (such as a vendor's lien for unpaid purchase money) previously acquired by third persons (*Davies v Thomas* [1900] 2 Ch. 462, explaining and distinguishing *Re Winkle*).

The Court of Protection will not normally pay statute barred debts (*Re Kenrick* [1907] 1 Ir. Ch. 480) but will recognise an honourable obligation on the part of "P", and will order payment by way of bounty (*Re Whitaker* (1889) L.R. 42 Ch.D. 119).

Debts properly incurred by a financial deputy under the direction of the court will be paid; such debts are the liability of "P"and not of the deputy, unless he expressly pledges his credit (*Plumpton v Burkinshaw* [1908] 2 K.B. 572; *Re E. G.* [1914] 1 Ch. 927).

**Charging order**

A charging order of the High Court under O.50 may be obtained against property **6B–53**

***Paragraph numbers marked with a "+" can be found online and on CD.***

of "P" in respect of a judgment for debts incurred before incapacity, and may be enforced against the estate of "P" after his death; for the effect of a charging order does not depend upon the capacity of the judgment debtor to give a valid charge but upon the validity of the judgment (*Re Leavesley* [1891] 2 Ch. 1, CA).

O.50 does not apply to Court of Protection charging orders made under s.18 (1)(b) of the Mental Capacity Act 2005 (*Re Cathcart* [1893] 1 Ch. 466, CA). It is now the normal practice, though discretionary, for charging orders of the Court of Protection to carry simple interest at the judgment rate (see current Judgment Debts (Rate of Interest) Order).

**Bankruptcy**

6B–54 The county court may, ex parte, and without notice appoint any person to act for "P". A person who lacks capacity, whether a financial deputy has been appointed or not, may be adjudicated bankrupt without the concurrence of the Court of Protection, but such adjudication and the appointment of a trustee in bankruptcy does not affect the direction and control of the debtor's property which may have already been assumed by the Court of Protection (*Re a Debtor (No.1 of 1941)* [1941] Ch. 487).

Where it is for "P"s benefit, the Court of Protection will authorise the necessary steps to be taken with a view to "P"s adjudication as a bankrupt (*Re Lee* (1883) L.R. 23 Ch.D. 216; and *Re Farnham* [1895] 2 Ch. 799) but the financial deputy, as such, should take no further steps than the Court of Protection may have authorised (*Re R.S.A.* [1901] 2 K.B. 32).

A person, who no longer lacks capacity to effectively manage his property and financial affairs, who does not apply to the Court under s.202 of the Court of Protection Rules 2007 to have his property transferred back to him, cannot set up the Court of Protection order as a defence against bankruptcy (*Re Belton* [1913] W.N. 63).

**Litigation by or against "P"**

6B–55 Under s.18(1)(k) of the Mental Capacity Act 2007, the Court of Protection may make orders and give directions and authorities for the conduct of legal proceedings in the name of "P"or on his behalf.

The deputy should before bringing or defending an action have the sanction of the Court of Protection, otherwise he will act at his own risk as to costs (*Re Nottley* (1839) 3 Jur. (o.s.) 719). To obtain such authority an application should be filed. Practitioners should have regard to part 17 of the Court of Protection Rules 2007 and the accompanying practice direction.

**Grant of administration**

6B–56 If "P" is entitled to apply for a grant of representation to the estate of a deceased person, authority may be given by the Court of Protection for the deputy to apply for a grant for the use and benefit of "P" during his incapacity.

**Damages recovered on behalf of a person lacking capacity**

6B–57 It is no longer a requirement that damages recovered for a person lacking capacity must be approved by the Court of Protection. The Civil Procedure (Amendment) Rules 2007 set out amendments to the CPR consequential to the Act. The key changes relating to civil damages settlements are listed below:

- before giving directions relating to how any settlement money should be dealt with, the court must first consider whether the "protected party" (the term which will replace the term "P" in relation to a party who lacks capacity to conduct the proceedings) is a "protected beneficiary" (a protected party who lacks capacity to manage or control any money recovered by them or on their behalf in the proceedings);
- the reference to approval by the Court of Protection in paragraph 13.4 of the practice direction supplementing Pt 52 of the Civil Procedure Rules has been removed; and
- there is a new practice direction supplementing Pt 21. Particular paragraphs to highlight are paras 5.6 and 6.5 which provide that only a Master, designated civil judge or his nominee should normally hear applications for the approval of a settlement or compromise involving a protected party. There are also amendments to paragraphs containing provisions about seeking of the court's

approval of settlements involving protected parties and investment of those funds (paras 5, 6, 8, 10 and 13).

Following the principles of the Mental Capacity Act, it is accepted that a person's lack of ability to give instructions to litigate does not automatically result in the person lacking the capacity to deal with their property and affairs as had been deemed in the past. Therefore the anticipation of a final award may not require the application to the Court of Protection for the appointment of a financial deputy.

## WHEN ARE SPECIAL NEEDS TRUSTS APPROPRIATE?

### Possible disadvantages

The Court of Protection will have to consider not only the possible financial advantages to "P" in terms of preserved eligibility for public funding, but also the various possible disadvantages. These disadvantages may include a loss of supervision by the Public Guardian, inflexibility, the imposition of a second layer of administration of "P"s affairs (which may be expensive), the difficulty of finding suitable trustees and, in the case of discretionary trusts, restricted access to the funds, the difficulty of finding alternative beneficiaries and possible tax disadvantages. Bare trusts are generally more straightforward. There may be no financial advantage in terms of preserved eligibility for public funding in setting up a trust if the income or capital are intended and used for an item of food, ordinary clothing or footwear, household fuel, rent in respect of which housing benefit is payable, council tax or water rate, even if paid to a third party as the regulations exclude such payments from the disregard (Income Support (General) Regulations 1987, Sch.9, para.15). **6B–58**

### Suitable cases

Normally, the Court of Protection will only approve the creation of a trust if this will result in some immediate and substantial benefit to "P" which will not accrue if the funds simply remain under a deputyship. Accordingly, it is not considered that all cases where a person is entitled to public funding prior to the receipt of an award of damages should give rise to an application for a trust; in some cases it may be more appropriate to continue to manage the funds under a deputyship. Also, if monies have been specifically received by "P" which will pay for all future care, these monies should generally remain available for that purpose. **6B–59**

The most suitable cases for settlement will therefore be those where such benefit to "P" can be demonstrated, and which also include one of the following features:

(i) the award is only small; or
(ii) in the case of a larger award, difficulties on liability or contributory negligence have resulted in substantially reduced damages; or
(iii) the award does not include the cost of future care as an element of damages.

### Timing

It is not to be assumed that time is of the essence, so far as creating a trust is concerned. It is now clear that it is not necessary to set up a trust as soon as the award is received. Provided the funds attributable to the personal injury compensation have been kept separate from other assets and remain identifiable, a trust can be set up at any time that the advantages to P of doing so become apparent. In some cases, it may be appropriate for the award to be held under normal receivership arrangements for a period of time to enable arrangements for the care of "P" to be developed and settle down into a pattern. **6B–60**

Solicitors advising the next friend are often concerned to ensure that any trust is created as early as possible. This is usually because they are concerned that "P" will otherwise be treated as possessing capital of which he has deprived himself for the purpose of securing entitlement to income support, overlooking the exception provided in reg.51(1) of the Income Support (General) Regulations 1987 (as amended by the Income Support (General) (Amendment No.3) Regulations 1990).

### Which method of setting up a trust should be chosen?

The separate methods of creating a trust have certain different consequences, which may sometimes influence the choice. **6B–61**

*Paragraph numbers marked with a "+" can be found online and on CD.*

**The accumulation period**

**6B–62** Trusts set up following an order of the High Court can only be done in the form of a declaration of trusts by the trustees, whereas trusts set up by an order of the Court of Protection will take the form of a settlement, with "P" being the settlor. In the former case, the period over which income can be accumulated by the trustees is restricted to 21 years, whereas, in the case of trusts set up by an order of the Court of Protection, provision can be made for income to be accumulated, if appropriate, for the lifetime of "P" as s.164(1)(a) of the Law of Property Act 1925 applies.

**Revocation**

**6B–63** Because of uncertainties about possible future changes in the benefits legislation, it is generally preferable for trusts to be revocable, to retain the flexibility to restore the capital to "P" absolutely, should this become desirable. There are, however, problems about including a power of revocation in trusts set up as part of the terms of compromise of a personal injury claim, as the award has never been the absolute property of "P" and it is accordingly arguable that exercising a power of revocation would restore the funds to the defendants.

**Inheritance tax**

**6B–64** All applications are expected to address the inheritance tax implications of the proposed settlement, where the relevant funds exceed the levels at which inheritance tax is charged. The method chosen to establish the trust may have an effect upon this.

Also, the tax implications of the form of trust should be considered. For example, there may in some cases be advantages in setting up a trust under the trusts for disabled persons regime, by virtue of which the trust will be treated for inheritance tax purposes as an income in possession trust and "P" as an income beneficiary even though there may be a power to accumulate income (Inheritance Tax Act 1984, s.89). Fully discretionary trusts will be liable to the ten-year charge and to the proportionate (or exit) charge on assets leaving the settlement at other times. When discretionary trusts are applied for, it will generally be necessary to demonstrate that, notwithstanding any tax disadvantages, such a trust is in "P" best interests.

**Settlement or gift of "P"'s property**

**6B–65** Under s.18(h) of the Mental Capacity Act 2007, the court may direct a settlement or gift to be made of any property of "P" with any consequential directions.

For reported cases, see *Re Freeman* [1927] 1 Ch. 479; *Re Greene* [1928] Ch. 528; *Re C. W. M.* [1951] 2 K.B. 714 and *Re C.* [1960] 1 W.L.R. 92. *Re C. E. F. D.* [1963] 1 W.L.R. 329 (costs); *Re R. H. C.* [1963] 1 W.L.R. 1095 (disentailing and resettlement). *Re D. M. L.* [1965] Ch. 1133 (meaning of family and persons for whom "P" might be expected to provide); *Re L. (W. J. G.)* [1966] Ch. 135 (disentailing and meaning of family, etc.); *Re T. B.* [1967] Ch. 247; [1966] 3 All E.R. 599 (settlement in favour of the illegitimate son of the patient).

**Statutory wills**

**6B–66** Under s.18 (i) of the Mental Capacity Act 2007 the court has jurisdiction to provide for the making of a will, or a codicil, for a person lacking capacity who does not possess testamentary capacity.

The court in drafting a will for "P" previously assumed that "P" is having a brief lucid interval at the time when the will is made. During that lucid interval "P" is assumed to have a full knowledge of the past, and a full realisation that as soon as the will is executed he will relapse into the mental state that previously existed. The court considers not a hypothetical "P" but the actual "P", with all the antipathies and affections he had while of full capacity, and seeks to make the will which he, acting reasonably, would have made "P" is to be envisaged during the hypothetical lucid interval as being advised by a competent solicitor and, in normal cases, "P" is to be envisaged as taking a broad brush to the claims on his bounty rather than an accountant's pen (*Re D. (J.)* [1982] Ch. 237; [1982] 2 All E.R. 37).

The above principle has been changed by the decision in *Re P* [2009] EWHC 163 (Ch) where Lewison J. held that the principles held prior to the implementation of the Mental Capacity Act no longer applied as the court must act in the best interests of the person taking into account all of the factors in s.4 of the Act. *Re P* also confirms that the court may authorise a statutory will for a person domiciled outside England and Wales in relation to land within the jurisdiction.

**Procedure on application for settlement, gift or statutory will**

Applications are by way of formal application to the court. Part 9 of the Court of Protection Rules and the supplementary Practice Direction 09F provide guidance. **6B–67**

## COSTS

**General note**

See the Court of Protection Rules 2007 rr.155–168. Where the proceedings concern P's property and affairs, the general rule is that the cost of the proceedings will be paid by P or charged to his estate (r.156). Where the proceedings concern P's personal welfare, the general rule is that there will be no order as to the costs of the proceedings (r.157). Where the proceedings concern both property and affairs and personal welfare, the court will apportion the costs between the respective issues, so far as is practicable (r.158). The court may depart from either of the general rules if the circumstances so justify (r.159). **6B–68**

Subject to the Court of Protection Rules and Civil Procedure Rules 1998, O.62 applies and the costs are assessed where required accordingly. They are awarded either on the indemnity basis (which is usually the case in deputyship proceedings) or on the standard basis, but the court will not in either case allow costs which have been unreasonably incurred or are unreasonable in amount.

On assessment on the indemnity basis the court will resolve any doubts which it may have as to whether costs were unreasonably incurred or were unreasonable in amount in favour of the receiving party.

On assessment of costs on the standard basis the court will: (a) only allow costs which are proportionate to the matters in issue; and (b) resolve any doubts which it may have as to whether costs were reasonably incurred or reasonable and proportionate in amount in favour of the paying party.

The rules against champerty (now obsolete) did not apply. A solicitor who fairly and properly conducts an objection to an application for the appointment of a deputy on a retainer from P ought to be allowed his costs in any event (see *Wentworth v Tubb* (1842) 7 Jur.(o.s.) 738). A solicitor will not be deprived of his costs merely because he represents P and other parties as well, but where there is a conflict of interest, and the solicitor acts on behalf of the other parties rather than P, the costs may be disallowed (*Re Weston* (1903) 116 L.T.J. 34).

The deputy acts as agent for P, and solicitors instructed by the deputy are entitled to look to P's estate for payment; the relationship of solicitor and client does not exist between the solicitor and the deputy (*Re E. G.* [1914] 1 Ch.927).

The costs of the notes of the judgment of the Lords Justices (in Lunacy) were allowed (*Re Cathcart*).

A surety is liable for costs directed to be paid by the deputy and which remain unsatisfied (*Re Graham* [1895] 1 Ch. 66).

If solicitors believe that an item in their bill is properly chargeable as work relating to financial affairs, but that contention is not accepted by the Supreme Court Costs Office, they should bring in objections and, if that is unsuccessful, take the question to appeal. The Court of Protection itself cannot assist by reinstating any costs disallowed by the Supreme Court Costs Office, since the function of deciding the quantum of costs belongs to them, by reason of r.160 of the Court of Protection Rules 2007 and the Civil Procedure Rules 1998.

If the deputy is a solicitor, costs are allowed for the whole range of deputyship duties, subject to detailed assessment. Accountant-deputies are allowed remuneration fixed by the court and their fees are not liable to detailed assessment. As regards visits by solicitor-deputies to "P", or attendances by solicitor-deputies at case conferences, it has become apparent that, with more clients living in the community, they may need a visit or require the deputy's help in connection with case conferences or similar attendances, which may be necessary in order to safeguard P's interests. In such cases the Supreme Court Costs Office will accept well-founded arguments that the costs should be allowed on detailed assessment.

***Paragraph numbers marked with a "+" can be found online and on CD.***

In Court of Protection matters, problems may arise for solicitors in knowing for whom they act. In the case of *Re EG* [1914] 1 Ch. 927, it is established that where a deputy has been appointed, the solicitor acting in the matter is acting for "P" and not for the deputy. The decision leaves undecided the question of who is "P"s solicitor in cases where more than one solicitor has been instructed to make an application for deputyship or where "P" himself wishes to instruct another solicitor for a particular area of his affairs, for example, where he remains of testamentary capacity and wishes to instruct a different solicitor to draw up a will for him. Where more than one solicitor has been instructed, perhaps each by a different member of "P"s family, this places the solicitors in a position of uncertainty as to who is acting for "P" on the principle of *Re EG*.

A further difficulty may arise as a result of the case of *Yonge v Toynbee* [1910] 1 K.B. 215, which decided that the retainer of a solicitor came to an end when "P" lost capacity (as an extension of the general rule that, except in the case of an enduring power of attorney or lasting power of attorney, the mental incapacity of the principal revokes any agency). Nevertheless, incapacitated people may need solicitors to act for them and them alone.

Assuming that "P" or donor is within the jurisdiction of the Court of Protection, the solicitor's authority to act for him can be expressly confirmed by the Court of Protection. Solicitors are also entitled to look upon themselves as acting for "P" or donor and not for the person who has given them instructions (if that is not "P" or donor) from the time that an application which is in order is received by the Court of Protection. This may, for example, be an application for the appointment of a deputy, for an order disposing of property where P ceases to lack capacity, for the appointment of a new deputy, for confirmation of the revocation of an enduring power of attorney, lasting power of attorney or for some other relief or authorisation. Where two or more solicitors have been instructed (expressly or by implication) to act for the same "P" or donor, preliminary directions should be sought from the court as to who will be deemed to be the solicitor in the matter.

A solicitor instructed by an applicant for deputyship or other order by the Court (or by an attorney) will be treated by the court as the P's (or donor's) solicitor until an objection to the application, or a competing application, is received by the court. As soon as this happens, the solicitor instructed by the first applicant must elect whether to continue representing "P"or to represent the first applicant. If the solicitor elects to represent the first applicant, then it is for the court to decide whether "P" needs separate representation and if so, to instruct a different private solicitor or the Official Solicitor (if he agrees) to act for him. If the solicitor elects to remain as the solicitor, then the first applicant will have to instruct another firm.

Solicitors will no doubt wish to make clear to the person from whom they take initial instructions relating to "P" or donors that their client will be "P" or donor and that the solicitors will have a duty of confidentiality to "P" or donor, even if the instructions come from somebody else.

In the case of applications for deputyship, the court would like applicants and solicitors to be aware that if a reference which is received by the court in respect of an applicant is not satisfactory, no further enquiry will be made as to the applicant's suitability but the applicant will not be appointed as deputy. This may be considered unfair to the applicant but in the court's view, the best interests of "P" must come first.

**Legal aid**

6B–69 Although a superior court of record, the Court of Protection is not part of the High Court. Advocacy bought before the court is not within the scope of Sch.2 to the Access to Justice Act 1999, however, the Lord Chancellor has issued an authorisation under s.6(8) of that Act bringing certain cases before the Court of Protection within the scope of CLS funding. The authorisation covers many of the cases which prior to October 1, 2007 would have been heard in the High Court for which CLS funding has always been available. Practitioners are advised to consult the Legal Services website *http://www.legalservices.gov.uk/civil/guidance/guidance_funding_decisions.asp* [Accessed January 22, 2008].

**Lodgment of order to assess, etc.**

6B–70 The solicitors having the carriage of an order which directs detailed assessment of

***Paragraph numbers marked with a "+" can be found online and on CD.***

costs should send to or leave at the Supreme Court Costs Office, Court of Protection Branch, Room 1–18, Cliffords Inn, Fetter Lane, London EC4A 1DQ, a copy of the order, a request for detailed assessment suitably amended and a statement showing the names and addresses of the parties (if any) appearing in person and of the solicitor of the parties (if any).

A statement of parties however is not required unless the costs clause directs the taxation of costs of a party separately represented or unless the costs are payable other than out of the estate of "P".

The copy order may be typed or photographed and should be properly endorsed with the title of the matter, the date of entry, and the name and address of the solicitor.

The following is the form of certificate which should be signed in the name of the firm:

'I/We hereby certify this to be a true copy of the Order dated as passed and entered.'
(Signed)

The Bill will be assessed and returned by post.

If desired an appointment for detailed assessment will be given.

#### Form of bill

Every bill of costs should be headed with the full title of the matter, also the name of the party and date of the order directing the assessment as under:— **6B–71**

IN THE COURT OF PROTECTION No.

In the matter of ...

The costs of the ...

to be assessed pursuant to Order dated ...

Bills of costs should be prepared on A4 paper bookwise, in accordance with Civil Procedure Rules 1998, Practice Direction supplementing Pt 43.

As the names of solicitors have to appear in all certificates of costs, it is essential that the full forenames of a single practitioner or the correct title of a firm should be endorsed on the bill. In agency matters, copies of orders and bills should show the name of the country solicitor.

Small bills of costs, for any type of business, are now accepted in summary form provided that the narrative is adequate for the work done and a summary of the number of personal attendances, telephone attendances and letters is provided. Care should be taken that in such bills all disbursements are included and summarised.

#### Documents to accompany bill

To facilitate the checking of the bills, before provisional assessment, all drafts of affidavits,deeds, orders, cases to counsel (if authorised) correspondence file, notes of attendances and vouchers should be lodged. In the case of sales of land the original contracts for sale, requisitions and draft transfers or conveyances should be lodged. **6B–72**

#### Prior costs

(a) If such costs are due to the Solicitor acting in the proceedings, they may be included in his bill without special mention in the Order. **6B–73**

(b) Should the prior costs be due to another Solicitor, particulars thereof should be forwarded to the court.

#### Deputyship general management costs

General management costs may be brought in for assessment at least every second year. **6B–74**

The bill and papers should be lodged with the Costs Office and the following request endorsed upon the front of the bill:

I/We request that the within bill of costs of general management may be assessed as provided for in the order dated...

(Signed)

(Dated)

Costs for income tax returns, recovering overpaid tax and the lodgment in court of any part of the balance on the account must be included in a bill of costs of general management.

**Short Form Bill of Costs**

6B–75 With effect from June 1, 2004 the Supreme Court Costs Office will accept a short form bill of costs where the amount of the bill does not exceed £3,000 excluding VAT and disbursements. A model form for a short form bill is printed hereunder. When lodging the request for assessment, the following should be submitted:

1. Short Form Bill.
2. Request for Assessment (Form N258B).
3. Fee of £100.
4. The document giving the right to detailed assessment.
5. A statement giving the name and address for service of any person having any financial interest in the outcome of the assessment.
6. The relevant papers in support of the bill including the correspondence and attendance file for the period covered by the claim in the bill. No duplicates should be lodged.
7. Any fee notes of counsel and receipts or accounts for other disbursements relating to items claimed.

## Model Short Form Bill

6B–76

IN THE COURT OF PROTECTION

**Model Short Form Bill**

Case No: - ..................

SCCO reference ..........................

IN THE MATTER OF
*(to be completed by the court)*

.......................................... (P's name )

Short form bill of costs of the deputy of *(e.g.) General Management for the period ....................to be assessed pursuant to the Order dated ..............*

<u>*Summary of work carried out*</u>

Fee earner category ........ Rate claimed ....................

| **Work done:-** | **Charge:-** |
|---|---|
| Time spent in personal attendances<br>*e.g. 22/9/02 45mins Upon patient* | ......... |
| Time spent in travel ............ | ......... |
| Letters Sent ............ | ......... |
| Telephone Calls ............ | ......... |
| Time spent on documents ............ | |
| Other work *(give details)*<br>..........................................<br>.......................................... | ......... |
| Sub Total | ......... |
| V.A.T. | |
| Disbursements (list below) | |
| Disbursements | ......... |
| V.A.T. | ......... |
| Grand Total | ......... |

I certify that this bill is both accurate and complete.

.................................(name and position)

*Name, address and reference of person filing bill*

**Short form bill of costs for use in Court of Protection assessments where the total costs claimed do not exceed £3000 excluding VAT and disbursements**

## Official Solicitor

Rule 163 of the Court of Protection Rules 2007 provides for the costs incurred by the Official Solicitor. **6B–77**

## Costs of preparing wills

Costs in respect of drawing wills for "P" during the course of the proceedings will normally only be allowed against the "P"s estate where the leave of the court has previously been obtained for the preparation of such will. **6B–78**

### Estate agents' fees

**6B–79** These should not be included in bills of costs as a disbursement. Solicitors do not need to obtain the Court's approval to the fees and should continue with the sale in the normal way and pay the fees.

Estate agents' fees will appear neither in the bill of costs nor, normally, in the deputy report form but in the completion statement which may be required to be produced to the court if it is necessary to seek directions regarding the net proceeds of sale.

The court will normally consider estate agent's charges reasonable if they do not exceed two and a half per cent of the sale price, to include all commission, expenses, etc. For full details of estate agent's charges solicitors should read the Practice Direction published jointly by the Chief Chancery Master, the Master of the Court of Protection, and the Senior Registrar of the Family Division, dated December 22, 1982, [1983] 1 All E.R. 160.

### Assessed bills of costs

**6B–80** A receipt will be issued when the assessed bill is lodged, stamped and completed in the Costs Office, and this receipt must be produced on any future enquiry: Direction dated November 1968 of Chief Taxing Master (Practice Direction (1968) 118 New L.J.1097).

### Certificate of costs

**6B–81** If the costs are payable out of the fund in court the office copy certificate of costs will be sent by the Costs Office direct to the Accountant General of the Supreme Court. London Solicitors must lodge with the Accountant General, Court Funds Office, 22 Kingsway, London, WC2B 6LE a form of postal request, but in country cases the Accountant General will forward this form direct to the solicitors.

Where the costs are not payable out of the fund in court the office copy certificate will be sent by post to the solicitors concerned.

### Fees on assessment

**6B–82** As from October 1, 1999, there shall be payable on the filing of a request for a detailed assessment of costs a fee of £200.

On an appeal against a decision made in a detailed assessment of costs or on an application to set aside a default costs certificate there shall be payable a fee of £60.

### Costs not assessed

**6B–83** Where an Order is referred for assessment and for any reason it is desired subsequently not to assess the costs, notification must be given to the Supreme Court Costs Office that an assessment will not take place. For precedents and Costs generally, see Heywood and Massey, Court of Protection Practice (12th edn, 1991), Ch.20.

### Fixed costs

**6B–84** Some items of costs may be dealt with in accordance with a Practice Note issued by the master on September 1, 1983 (see Practice Note (1983) 133 New L.J. 6121) whereby fixed costs were introduced by agreement with the Law Society in respect of certain Court of Protection work. Details of current fixed costs can be found on the website *http://www.publicguardian.gov.uk* [Accessed June 4, 2008].

**[THE NEXT PARAGRAPH IS 6B–86.]**

### Deeds, Forms, Recitals, etc.

**6B–86** Only the relevant part of the particular order or direction should be recited. The order appointing the deputy need only be recited where the deed is being executed under a sealed direction, as distinct from an order.

In deeds generally, such as conveyances, leases, etc., "P" is the "party" and is cited as A. B. ("P"s name, no address) acting by C.D. (the deputy) of etc. pursuant to the hereinafter recited Order (hereinafter called the Deputy). The fact of a lack of mental capacity should not appear in the description of "P". The actual wording of the direction contained in the order should wherever possible be strictly adhered to in the recital thereof, except that the recital is in the past tense.

**[THE NEXT PARAGRAPH IS 6B–88.]**

***Paragraph numbers marked with a "+" can be found online and on CD.***

### Usual form of conveyance when an order for sale has been made

Parties A.B. [no address required] (hereinafter called "the Vendor") acting by C.D. of ........... pursuant to the hereinafter recited (Order) (Direction) (hereinafter called "the Receiver") of one part and E.F. of ...... (hereinafter called "the Purchaser") of the other part. **6B–88**

Whereas:

(1) The Vendor is (seised in fee simple in possession [free from encumbrances]) (or as the case may be) of the property hereinafter described.

(2) By an (Order) (Direction) dated the ..................... day of ...... 20 . ... and made (in the Court of Protection) in the matter of the Vendor the deputy was authorised subject to the approval of the said Court in the name and on behalf of the Vendor to sell [the freehold/leasehold property belonging to the Vendor] [the said freehold/leasehold property] and for that purpose to receive and give a discharge for the purchase money and to execute such deeds as shall be necessary.

(3) (Pursuant to the said (Order) (Direction) and with such approval the deputy on behalf of the Vendor has agreed to sell the said property hereinafter described to the Purchaser at the price of £....) or (Pursuant to the said (Order) (Direction) and with such approval the said property was on the .... day of . 20 ........................................................................ put up for sale by public auction in [one] lot and at the said sale the Purchaser was the highest bidder for and was declared the Purchaser of the said property at the price of £..................................................................).

NOW THIS DEED WITNESSETH as follows:

In pursuance of the said (Order) (Direction) and agreement and in consideration of the sum of £......... now paid by the Purchaser to the Vendor acting by the deputy as aforesaid (the receipt whereof is hereby acknowledged) the Vendor as Beneficial Owner acting by the deputy as aforesaid hereby conveys unto the Purchaser (parcels) TO HOLD unto the Purchaser in fee simple [SUBJECT to etc.]

[If the property is subject to any restrictive or other covenants or conditions in respect of which the Vendor may remain liable after he has parted with the property, the usual covenant for indemnity by the purchaser should be inserted].

[Certificate of value in common form].

IN WITNESS whereof the parties hereto have hereunto set their hands the day and year first above written.

| | |
|---|---|
| Signed and delivered as a deed by the said A.B. | (A.B.) |
| by the said C.D. acting as aforesaid in the | by |
| presence of | (C.D.) |

*NOTE* No acknowledgment is required as regards production and delivery of copies of the recited Order of the Court of Protection. That is a document of record and the original is retained by the Court. The office copy thereof or of the relevant extracts therefrom handed over on completion is sufficient evidence of the contents of the original.

### Form of conveyance where an order for purchase has been made (necessary only where the Purchaser is an Executing Party)

Parties A.B. (hereinafter called "the Vendor") of the one part and C.D. (hereinafter called "the Purchaser") [acting by E.F. of ........... pursuant to the hereinafter recited order (hereinafter called "the deputy") of the other part. **6B–89**

(1) Recital of seisin.

(2) By an (Order) (Direction) dated the .... day of .... 20 .... made (in the Court of Protection) in the matter of the Purchaser the deputy was authorised in the name and on behalf of the Purchaser to purchase such property upon such terms as should be approved and to procure a conveyance/ assignment/transfer of the said property to the Purchaser and for that purpose to execute such deeds as shall be necessary.

***Paragraph numbers marked with a "+" can be found online and on CD.***

(3) (Pursuant to the said (Order) (Direction) and in consideration of the said sum of £ . ... now paid by [the deputy out of moneys in his hands belonging to] the Purchaser to the Vendor (the receipt whereof is hereby acknowledged) the Vendor as (Beneficial Owner) hereby conveys unto the Purchaser (parcels) to hold unto the Purchaser in fee simple. (Any covenants by the Purchaser should be expressed to the "by the Purchaser acting by the deputy as aforesaid-). [Certificate of Value in common form].

| | |
|---|---|
| Signed and delivered as a deed by the said C.D. | (C.D.) |
| by the said E.F. acting as aforesaid in the | by |
| presence of | (E.F.) |

## Statutory Receipt (on a Mortgage)

**6B–90** I A.B. of acting by C.D. of pursuant to an Order dated the made in the Court of Protection hereby acknowledge that pursuant to the said Order on the day of I have received the sum of £ representing the principal money (*or balance remaining owing in respect of the principal money if such is the case*) secured by the written mortgage by lodgment thereof in Court to my credit and that I have received all interest and costs, such lodgment and payment having been made by E.F.

In witness whereof I have hereunto set my hand this day of .

## Usual Form of Transfer of Registered Land

**6B–91** (County or County Borough)...

(District) ...

Title No. ...

Property ...

(Date ........... In consideration of ........... pounds (£........... the receipt whereof is hereby acknowledged (or paid to (names of Settled Land Act Trustees) I(P.) acting by R. of ........... pursuant to an (order) (direction) dated the ........... 20 ............... and made (in the Court of Protection) as Beneficial Owner (as Trustee) hereby transfer to X.Y. of etc. the land comprised in the title above mentioned (for the residue of the term granted by the registered Lease).

Add covenant for indemnity against restrictive covenants if required).

(Certificate of Value)

| | |
|---|---|
| Signed and delivered as a deed | (P) |
| by the said (P) by the said | by |
| (R) acting as aforesaid in the | (R) |
| presence of | (R) |

## Leave to appoint new trustees under s.36(9) of the Trustee Act 1925

**6B–92** And whereas the said A.B. has become incapable of acting in the trusts of the said (*trust*) and the appointor is desirous of appointing the said E.F. to be a trustee of the said (*trust*) in place of the said A.B.

And whereas pursuant to s.36(9) of the Trustee Act 1925, leave to make such appointment was given on the 20 by the Court of Protection as appears by the seal of the Court impressed in the margin hereof.

## Certificate of Examination of Engrossment of Deed

**6B–93** We Hereby Certify that this deed is an exact copy of the draft thereof as settled and approved by the Court.

Signed (*Solicitor*)
by (*person certifying*)
Date

***Paragraph numbers marked with a "+" can be found online and on CD.***

### *Statutory Will for Patient*

(This merely shows the manner in which the auhorised person makes the will and executes the same.) **6B–94**

THIS IS THE LAST WILL of me AB of etc. acting by CD the person authorised in that behalf by an Order dated the day of 20 made under the Mental Capacity Act 2005.

I hereby revoke all former Wills and Codicils made by me and declare this to be my last Will.

1. I appoint EF and GH to be Executors and Trustees of this my Will
2. I Give and Bequeath etc.

In witness whereof this Will is signed by me AB acting by CD pursuant to the said Order this day of .................................................. 20 .....................

Signed by the said AB by the said CD (authorised person) and by the AB .......... said CD with his (her) own name pursuant ....... CD (Authorised Person) to the said Order in our presence and attested by us in the presence of the said CD

(Names and addresses of witnesses)

Sealed with the official Seal of the Court of Protection this ............................................................ day of ............................................................................................................ 20

*Certificate of Examination of Statutory Will*

We Hereby Certify that this Will is an exact copy of the draft thereof as approved by the Court.

Signed (*Solicitor*)
by (*person certifying*)
Date

### *Affidavit proving death*

The court no longer requires such an affidavit to be filed as a matter of general practice. **6B–95**

## Court of Protection Rules 2007

## (S.I. 2007 No. 1744) **6B–96**

ARRANGEMENT OF RULES



***Paragraph numbers marked with a "+" can be found online and on CD.***



COURT OF PROTECTION

***Paragraph numbers marked with a "+" can be found online and on CD.***

***Paragraph numbers marked with a "+" can be found online and on CD.***

***Paragraph numbers marked with a "+" can be found online and on CD.***

**Paragraph numbers marked with a "+" denote content that is available on White Book on Westlaw UK or the Civil Procedure CD.**

**For rules 1 to 154 see paragraphs 6B–97+ to 6B–380+ on White Book on Westlaw UK or the Civil Procedure CD.**

***Paragraph numbers marked with a "+" can be found online and on CD.***



COURT OF PROTECTION

## PART 19

## COSTS

### Interpretation

6B–381 **155.—**(1) In this Part—

(a) "additional liability" means the percentage increase, the insurance premium, or the additional amount in respect of provision made by a membership organisation, as the case may be;

(b) "authorised court officer" means any officer of the Supreme Court Costs Office, whom the Lord Chancellor has authorised to assess costs;

(c) 'costs' include fees, charges, disbursements, expenses, reimbursement permitted to a litigant in person, any additional liability incurred under a funding arrangement and any fee or reward charged by a lay representative for acting on behalf of a party in proceedings;

(d) "costs judge" means a taxing Master of the Supreme Court;

(e) "costs officer" means a costs judge or an authorised court officer;

(f) "detailed assessment" means the procedure by which the amount of costs or remuneration is decided by a costs officer in accordance with Part 47 of the Civil Procedure Rules 1998 (which are applied to proceedings under these Rules, with modifications, by rule 160);

(g) 'fixed costs' are to be construed in accordance with the relevant practice direction;

(h) "fund" includes any estate or property held for the benefit of any person or class of persons and any fund to which a trustee or personal representative is entitled in his capacity as such;

(i) "funding arrangement" means an arrangement where a person has—

 (i) entered into a conditional fee agreement or a collective conditional fee agreement which provides for a success fee within the meaning of section 58(2) of the Courts and Legal Services Act 1990;

 (ii) taken out an insurance policy to which section 29 of the Access to Justice Act 1999 (recovery of insurance premiums by way of costs) applies; or

 (iii) made an agreement with a membership organisation to meet his legal costs;

(j) "insurance premium" means a sum of money paid or payable for insurance against the risk of incurring a costs liability in the proceedings, taken out after the event that is the subject matter of the claim;

(k) "membership organisation" means a body prescribed for the purposes of section 30 of the Access to Justice Act 1999 (recovery where body undertakes to meet costs liabilities);

(l) "paying party" means a party liable to pay costs;

(m) "percentage increase" means the percentage by which the amount of a legal representative's fee can be increased in accordance with a conditional fee agreement which provides for a success fee;

(n) "receiving party" means a party entitled to be paid costs;

(o) "summary assessment" means the procedure by which the court, when making an order about costs, orders payment of a sum of money instead of fixed costs or "detailed assessment".

(2) The costs to which the rules in this Part apply include—

(a) where the costs may be assessed by the court, costs payable by a client to his solicitor; and

(b) costs which are payable by one party to another party under the terms of a contract, where the court makes an order for an assessment of those costs.

(3) Where advocacy or litigation services are provided to a client under a conditional fee agreement, costs are recoverable under this Part notwithstanding that the client is liable to pay his legal representative's fees and expenses only to the extent that sums are recovered in respect of the proceedings, whether by way of costs or otherwise.

(4) In paragraph (3), the reference to a conditional fee agreement is to an agreement which satisfies all the conditions applicable to it by virtue of section 58 of the Courts and Legal Services Act 1990[1].



**Effect of Part**

Section 55 of the MCA 2005 states that, subject to Court of Protection Rules, the costs of and incidental to all proceedings in the Court are in its discretion. This provision has a similar effect to s.51 of the Senior Courts Act 1981. **6B–382**

**Civil Procedure Rules to apply with modifications**

Rule 160 states that the principal CPR provisions as to costs shall apply to proceedings in the Court of Protection, subject to modifications. **6B–383**

**Relevant practice direction (Pt 19)**

This Part is supplemented by Practice Direction 19A–Costs. This practice direction states that the practice direction supplementing CPR Pts 43 to 48 applies, insofar as those Parts apply to proceedings in the Court of Protection, with such modifications as are appropriate, together with modifications specified in the practice direction. **6B–384**

## Property and affairs—the general rule

**156.** Where the proceedings concern P's property and affairs the general rule is that the costs of the proceedings or of that part of the proceedings that concerns P's property and affairs, shall be paid by P or charged to his estate. **6B–385**

[1] Section 58 was substituted by s.27(1) of the Access to Justice Act 1999 (c. 22).

**Personal welfare—the general rule**

6B-386 **157.** Where the proceedings concern P's personal welfare the general rule is that there will be no order as to the costs of the proceedings or of that part of the proceedings that concerns P's personal welfare.

**Apportioning costs—the general rule**

6B-387 **158.** Where the proceedings concern both property and affairs and personal welfare the court, insofar as practicable, will apportion the costs as between the respective issues.

**Departing from the general rule**

6B-388 **159.—(1)** The court may depart from rules 156 to 158 if the circumstances so justify, and in deciding whether departure is justified the court will have regard to all the circumstances, including–

(a) the conduct of the parties;

(b) whether a party has succeeded on part of his case, even if he has not been wholly successful; and

(c) the role of any public body involved in the proceedings.

(2) The conduct of the parties includes–

(a) conduct before, as well as during, the proceedings;

(b) whether it was reasonable for a party to raise, pursue or contest a particular issue;

(c) the manner in which a party has made or responded to an application or a particular issue; and

(d) whether a party who has succeeded in his application or response to an application, in whole or in part, exaggerated any matter contained in his application or response.

(3) Without prejudice to rules 156 to 158 and the foregoing provisions of this rule, the court may permit a party to recover their fixed costs in accordance with the relevant practice direction.

**Rules about costs in the Civil Procedure Rules to apply**

6B-389 **160.—(1)** Subject to the provisions of these Rules, Parts 44, 47 and 48 of the Civil Procedure Rules 1998 ("the 1998 Rules") shall apply with the modifications in this rule and such other modifications as may be appropriate, to costs incurred in relation to proceedings under these Rules as they apply to costs incurred in relation to proceedings in the High Court.

(2) The provisions of Part 47 of the 1998 Rules shall apply with the modifications in this rule and such other modifications as may be appropriate, to a detailed assessment of the remuneration of a deputy under these Rules as they apply to a detailed assessment of costs in proceedings to which the 1998 Rules apply.

(3) Where the definitions in Part 43 (referred to in Parts 44, 47 and 48) of the 1998 Rules are different from the definitions in rule 155 of these Rules, the latter shall prevail.

(4) Rules 44.1, 44.3(1) to (5), 44.6, 44.7, 44.9, 44.10, 44.11. 44.12 and 44.12A of the 1998 Rules do not apply.

(5) In rule 44.17 of the 1998 Rules, the references to Parts 45 and 46 do not apply.

(6) In rule 47.3(1)(c) of the 1998 Rules, the words "unless the costs are being assessed under rule 48.5 (costs where money is payable to a child or a patient)" are removed.

(7) In rule 47.3(2) of the 1998 Rules, the words "or a district judge" are removed.

(8) Rule 47.4(3) and (4) of the 1998 Rules do not apply.

(9) Rules 47.9(4), 47.10 and 47.11 of the 1998 Rules do not apply where the costs are to be paid by P or charged to his estate.

(10) Rules 48.2, 48.3, 48.6A, and 48.10 of the 1998 Rules do not apply.

(11) Rule 48.1(1) of the 1998 Rules is removed and is replaced by the following: "This paragraph applies where a person applies for an order for specific disclosure before the commencement of proceedings".

**Detailed assessment of costs**

**161.—(1)** Where the court orders costs to be assessed by way of detailed assessment, the detailed assessment proceedings shall take place in the High Court. **6B–390**

(2) A fee is payable in respect of the detailed assessment of costs and on an appeal against a decision made in a detailed assessment of costs.

(3) Where a detailed assessment of costs has taken place, the amount payable by P is the amount which the court certifies as payable.

**Employment of a solicitor by two or more persons**

**162.** Where two or more persons having the same interest in relation to a matter act in relation to the proceedings by separate legal representatives, they shall not be permitted more than one set of costs of the representation unless and to the extent that the court certifies that the circumstances justify separate representation. **6B–391**

**Costs of the Official Solicitor**

**163.** Any costs incurred by the Official Solicitor in relation to proceedings under these Rules or in carrying out any directions given by the court and not provided for by remuneration under rule 167 shall be paid by such persons or out of such funds as the court may direct. **6B–392**

**Procedure for assessing costs**

**164.** Where the court orders a party, or P, to pay costs to another party it may either— **6B–393**

(a) make a summary assessment of the costs; or

(b) order a detailed assessment of the costs by a costs officer,

unless any rule, practice direction or other enactment provides otherwise.

### Costs following P's death

6B–394 **165.** An order or direction that costs incurred during P's lifetime be paid out of or charged on his estate may be made within 6 years after P's death.

### Costs orders in favour of or against non-parties

6B–395 **166.—(1)** Where the court is considering whether to make a costs order in favour of or against a person who is not a party to proceedings—

(a) that person must be added as a party to the proceedings for the purposes of costs only; and

(b) he must be given a reasonable opportunity to attend a hearing at which the court will consider the matter further.

(2) This rule does not apply where the court is considering whether to make an order against the Legal Services Commission.

### Remuneration of a deputy, donee or attorney

6B–396 **167.—(1)** Where the court orders that a deputy, donee or attorney is entitled to remuneration out of P's estate for discharging his functions as such, the court may make such order as it thinks fit, including an order that—

(a) he be paid a fixed amount;

(b) he be paid at a specified rate; or

(c) the amount of the remuneration shall be determined in accordance with the schedule of fees set out in the relevant practice direction.

(2) Any amount permitted by the court under paragraph (1) shall constitute a debt due from P's estate.

(3) The court may order a detailed assessment of the remuneration by a costs officer, in accordance with rule 164(b).

### Practice direction as to costs

6B–397 **168.** A practice direction may make further provision in respect of costs in proceedings.

**For rules 169 to 202 see paragraphs 6B–398+ to 6B–450+ on White Book on Westlaw UK or the Civil Procedure CD.**

## PRACTICE DIRECTION A—COSTS IN THE COURT OF PROTECTION

*This Practice Direction supplements Part 19 of the Court of Protection Rules 2007* **6B–451**

### *Modifications to the Civil Procedure Rules 1998*

**1** The practice direction supplementing Parts 43 to 48 of the Civil Procedure Rules 1998 ("the CPR Practice Direction") applies, insofar as those Parts apply to proceedings in the Court of Protection, with such modifications as are appropriate together with the modifications specified in this practice direction.

**2** The following paragraphs of the CPR Practice Direction do not apply: **6B–452**

6.4(1); 8.1 to 8.4; 13.2(1); 13.3; 13.4; 13.7(2); 13.11; 13.13(a); 15 to 17; 23.2A; 24 to 27; 28.1(2); 31; 49A; 50; and 51.

**3** In paragraphs 2.5 and 28.1(3) of the CPR Practice Direction, the words "or the parties may agree in writing" are removed. **6B–453**

**4** In paragraph 13.5(4) of the CPR Practice Direction, the words "any party against whom an order for payment of those costs is intended to be sought" are replaced with "all parties to the proceedings and any other person that the court may direct." **6B–454**

**5** In paragraph 19.2(1) of the CPR Practice Direction, the words "application form," are inserted after "includes". **6B–455**

**6** In paragraph 19.2(3)(b) of the CPR Practice Direction, the second and third sentences are removed. **6B–456**

**7** In paragraph 19.3(3) of the CPR Practice Direction, the words "of the Court of Protection Rules 2007" are inserted after "Part 6". **6B–457**

**8** In paragraph 21.19A of the CPR Practice Direction, the words "High Court or Country Court" are removed and replaced with "Court of Protection". **6B–458**

**9** The reference in paragraph 23.2 of the CPR Practice Direction to district registry or county court shall be read, in proceedings to which this Practice Direction applies, as a reference to the registry of the Court of Protection. **6B–459**

**10** In paragraph 23.18 of the CPR Practice Direction, the words "CPR Part 52 and CPR rule 47.20" are removed and replaced with "Part 20 of the Court of Protection Rules". **6B–460**

**11** The following paragraphs of the CPR Practice Direction are to be read as if the references in those paragraphs to a district judge were removed— **6B–461**

20.3(1); 21.19A; 22.1; 28.1(4)(a); 28.1(5); 30.1(3); 30.1(4); 36.3; 37.6(1); 38.1(2); and 38.3(2).

**12** In paragraph 33.1 of the CPR Practice Direction the words "under rule 2.11" are removed. **6B–462**

**13** In paragraph 33.2 of the CPR Practice Direction, the words "for an order under rule 3.1(2)(a)" are removed; and the words "that time" are removed and the following words are substituted: "the time specified by rule 47.7 for commencing the detailed assessment proceedings". **6B–463**

**14** Paragraph 35.1 of the CPR Practice Direction is replaced with **6B–464**

the following: "A party may apply to the appropriate officer for an order to shorten or extend the time for service of points of dispute".

6B–465 **15** In paragraph 37.4 of the CPR Practice Direction, the words "Rules 40.3" to "default costs certificate" are replaced with the words "rule 30 of the Court of Protection Rules 2007, which applies to the service of court orders".

6B–466 **16** In paragraph 38.1(1) of the CPR Practice Direction, the words "court officer" are replaced with "authorised court officer".

6B–467 **17** In rule 38.3(1) of the CPR Practice Direction, the following words are removed: "rule 3.1(3) (which enables the court when making an order to make it subject to conditions) and to".

6B–468 **18** In paragraphs 30.1(4), 36.2, 41.1(1), 42.6, 53.3, 53.7 and 53.8 of the CPR Practice Direction, the words "Part 23 (General Rules about Applications for Court Orders)" are removed and replaced with "Part 10 (Applications within proceedings)".

6B–469 **19** References in the CPR Practice Direction to "claimant" and "defendant" shall be read, in proceedings to which this Practice Direction applies, to "applicant" and "respondent" respectively.

6B–470 **20** The appropriate venue for detailed assessment of costs proceedings is the Supreme Court Costs Office, Clifford's Inn, Fetter Lane, London EC4A 1DQ.

## Court of Protection Fees Order 2007

(SI 2007 /1745)

6B–471 **For the Court of Protection Fees Order 2007 see paragraphs 6B–472+ to 6B–481+ on White Book on Westlaw UK or the Civil Procedure CD.**

## Mental Capacity Act 2005

6B–482 (2005 c.9)

Arrangement of Sections



### Fees

6B–483 **54.**—(1) The Lord Chancellor may with the consent of the Treasury by order prescribe fees payable in respect of anything dealt with by the court.

(2) An order under this section may in particular contain provision as to—

(a) scales or rates of fees;

(b) exemptions from and reductions in fees;

(c) remission of fees in whole or in part.

(3) Before making an order under this section, the Lord Chancellor must consult—

***Paragraph numbers marked with a "+" can be found online and on CD.***

(a) the President of the Court of Protection,
(b) the Vice-President of the Court of Protection, and
(c) the Senior Judge of the Court of Protection.

(4) The Lord Chancellor must take such steps as are reasonably practicable to bring information about fees to the attention of persons likely to have to pay them.

(5) Fees payable under this section are recoverable summarily as a civil debt.

## Costs

**55.**—(1) Subject to Court of Protection Rules, the costs of and incidental to all proceedings in the court are in its discretion. **6B–484**

(2) The rules may in particular make provision for regulating matters relating to the costs of those proceedings, including prescribing scales of costs to be paid to legal or other representatives.

(3) The court has full power to determine by whom and to what extent the costs are to be paid.

(4) The court may, in any proceedings—

(a) disallow, or
(b) order the legal or other representatives concerned to meet,

the whole of any wasted costs or such part of them as may be determined in accordance with the rules.

(5) "Legal or other representative", in relation to a party to proceedings, means any person exercising a right of audience or right to conduct litigation on his behalf.

(6) "Wasted costs" means any costs incurred by a party—

(a) as a result of any improper, unreasonable or negligent act or omission on the part of any legal or other representative or any employee of such a representative, or
(b) which, in the light of any such act or omission occurring after they were incurred, the court considers it is unreasonable to expect that party to pay.

## Fees and costs: supplementary

**56.**—(1) Court of Protection Rules may make provision— **6B–485**

(a) as to the way in which, and funds from which, fees and costs are to be paid;
(b) for charging fees and costs upon the estate of the person to whom the proceedings relate;
(c) for the payment of fees and costs within a specified time of the death of the person to whom the proceedings relate or the conclusion of the proceedings.

(2) A charge on the estate of a person created by virtue of subsection (1)(b) does not cause any interest of the person in any property to fail or determine or to be prevented from recommencing.

## The Mental Capacity Act 2005 (Transfer Of Proceedings) Order 2007

(S.I. 2007 No. 1899)

6B–486 **For The Mental Capacity Act 2005 (Transfer Of Proceedings) Order 2007 see paragraphs 6B–487+ to 6B–490+ on White Book on Westlaw UK or the Civil Procedure CD.**

## The Mental Capacity Act 2005 (Transitional and Consequential Provisions) Order 2007

(S.I. 2007 No. 1898)

6B–491 **For The Mental Capacity Act 2005 (Transitional and Consequential Provisions) Order 2007 see paragraphs 6B–492+ to 6B–497+ on White Book on Westlaw UK or the Civil Procedure CD.**

## The Lasting Powers of Attorney, Enduring Powers of Attorney and Public Guardian Regulations 2007

6B–498 (S.I. 2007 No. 1253)

Arrangement of Sections



***Paragraph numbers marked with a "+" can be found online and on CD.***

**Paragraph numbers marked with a "+" denote content that is available on White Book on Westlaw UK or the Civil Procedure CD.**

# 6C NON-CONTENTIOUS PROBATE

## Senior Courts Act 1981

(1981 c.54) 6C–1

Arrangement of Sections

Part II



**Paragraph numbers marked with a "+" denote content that is available on White Book on Westlaw UK or the Civil Procedure CD.**

## Non-Contentious Probate Rules 1987

(S.I. 1987 No. 2024)

[As amended by the Non-Contentious Probate (Amendment) Rules 1991 (S.I. 1991 No. 1876); the Non-Contentious Probate (Amendment) Rules 1998 (S.I. 1998 No. 1903); the Non-Contentious Probate (Amendment) Rules 1999 (S.I. 1999 No. 1015); the Non-Contentious Probate (Amendment) Rules 2003 (S.I. 2003 No. 185); and the Non-Contentious Probate (Amendment) Rules 2009 (S.I. 2009 No.1893).] 6C–68

Arrangement of Rules



***Paragraph numbers marked with a "+" can be found online and on CD.***



Non-Contentious Probate

***Paragraph numbers marked with a "+" can be found online and on CD.***

**Paragraph numbers marked with a "+" denote content that is available on White Book on Westlaw UK or the Civil Procedure CD.**

## Non-Contentious Probate Fees Order 2004

(S.I. 2004 No. 3120)

[This order replaces S.I. 1999 No 688 which was revoked by S.I. 2004 No.3123.] **6C–206**

**For Non-Contentious Probate Fees Order 2004 see paragraphs 6C–207+ to 6C–224+ on White Book on Westlaw UK or the Civil Procedure CD.**

# 6D TRUSTEES

## Judicial Trustees Act 1896

(1896 59 & 60 Vict. c.35) **6D–1**

Arrangement of Sections



**Paragraph numbers marked with a "+" denote content that is available on White Book on Westlaw UK or the Civil Procedure CD.**

## Judicial Trustee Rules 1983

(S.I. 1983 No. 370 (L.4)) **6D–15**

Arrangement of Rules



**Paragraph numbers marked with a "+" denote content that is available on White Book on Westlaw UK or the Civil Procedure CD.**

## Public Trustee Act 1906

(1906 6 Edw. 7, c.55) **6D–40**

Arrangement of Sections



***Paragraph numbers marked with a "+" can be found online and on CD.***

**Paragraph numbers marked with a "+" denote content that is available on White Book on Westlaw UK or the Civil Procedure CD.**

## Public Trustee Rules 1912

(S. R. & O. 1912 No. 348)

6D–91 **For the Public Trustee Rules 1912 see paragraphs 6D–92+ to 6D–149+ on White Book on Westlaw UK or the Civil Procedure CD.**

## Variation of Trusts Act 1958

6D–150 (1958 6 & 7 ELIZ. 2, c.53)

ARRANGEMENT OF SECTIONS



**Paragraph numbers marked with a "+"denote content that is available on White Book on Westlaw UK or the Civil Procedure CD.**

*Paragraph numbers marked with a "+" can be found online and on CD.*

# SECTION 7

## LEGAL REPRESENTATIVES—COSTS AND LITIGATION FUNDING

# 7A GENERAL

## INTRODUCTION

### Conditional fees

The Access to Justice Act 1999 has amended the law relating to conditional fee agreements between lawyers and their clients, in particular to allow the uplift payable in successful cases to be recovered from the other side. It also enables insurance premiums to be recovered and allows for third parties to establish funds to support litigation on a conditional basis. The Courts and Legal Services Act 1990 has been amended by the insertion of new ss.58 and 58A dealing with conditional fee agreements and s.58B dealing with Litigation Funding Agreements (this provision is not yet in force). Sections 29 and 30 of the Access to Justice Act provide for recovery of insurance premiums by way of costs and recovery where a membership organisation undertakes to meet costs liabilities. **7A–1**

After the introduction of Conditional Fees in 1995 the government extended the availability of Conditional Fees to all civil cases excluding family cases (in July 1998) following the decision of the Court of Appeal in *Thai Trading Co v Taylor* [1998] 3 All E.R. 65, CA that there were no longer public policy grounds to prevent lawyers agreeing to work for less than their normal fees in the event that they were unsuccessful, provided that they did not seek to recover more than their normal fees if they were successful. The Act and Regulations (now revoked) were drafted in such a way as to permit such agreements. Similarly the decision in *Bevan Ashford v Geoff Yeandle (Contractors) Limited* [1998] 3 All E.R. 238, Scott V.-C., confirmed that conditional fees could extend to a case which was to be resolved by arbitration, even though it was not court proceedings, provided that all the requirements specified by regulations as to the form and content of the conditional fee agreement were complied with.

It is now possible for an intending litigant to take out a policy of insurance to cover both the costs of the other party and his or her own legal costs (including the solicitors' fees if they are not subject to the conditional fee agreement). Premiums paid for such policies may be recovered as costs. The decision of the Court of Appeal in *Geraghty v Awad Awwad* [2001] Q.B. 570; [2000] 3 W.L.R. 1041; [2000] 1 All E.R. 608; [1999] N.P.C. 148, CA confirmed that contingency fee agreements entered into before the January 7, 1999 where champertous and unlawful. Although the law has now been clarified by the Access to Justice Act 1999 the decision is still of relevance because of the large number of conditional fee agreements entered into following the decision of the Court of Appeal in *Thai Trading* (above). The judgement rejected the possibility that such an agreement could be made at common law, and effectively outlawed all contingency fee agreements other than those authorised by statute.

## THE INDEMNITY PRINCIPLE

The Indemnity principle, as affirmed in *Gundry v Sainsbury* [1910] 1 K.B. 645 and referred to in many cases since, has been amended as a result of Government policy. The policy was announced in the Government's response to the Collective Conditional Fee Agreements Consultation Paper in September 2000 following extensive consultation with the profession. **7A–2**

Section 31 of the Access to Justice Act 1999 amends s.51 of the Senior Courts Act 1981 by inserting at the end of subs. (2) the words:

> "or for securing that the amount awarded to a party in respect of the costs to be paid by him to such representatives is not limited to what would have been payable by him to them if he had not been awarded costs".

The effect of this is to enable the court to disregard funding arrangements between solicitor and client when assessing the amount of costs to be recovered from a paying party.

Section 31 of the 1999 Act was brought into force on June 2, 2003 (Access to Justice Act 1999 (Commencement No.10) Order 2003 (SI 2003/1241)).

### Senior Courts Act Sections 51(1)–(7)

The following paragraphs do not apply, as regards a party to any proceedings in **7A–3**

*Paragraph numbers marked with a "+" can be found online and on CD.*

relation to which the party entered into a conditional agreement before April 1, 2000; or any proceedings arising out of the same cause of action. Section 27 of the Access Justice Act 1999 (dealing with conditional fee agreements) does not affect the validity of any conditional fee agreement entered into before April 1, 2000 and any such agreement continues to have effect after that date as if s.27 had not come into force. See para.9A–199.

## Courts and Legal Services Act 1990

7A–4 (1990 c.41)

Arrangement of Sections

Part II

Legal Services

*Miscellaneous*



## Part II

## Legal Services

### *Miscellaneous*

### Conditional fee agreements

7A–5 **58.**—(1) A conditional fee agreement which satisfies all of the conditions applicable to it by virtue of this section shall not be unenforceable by reason only of its being a conditional fee agreement; but (subject to subsection (5)) any other conditional fee agreement shall be unenforceable.

(2) For the purposes of this section and section 58A—

(a) a conditional fee agreement is an agreement with a person providing advocacy or litigation services which provides for his fees and expenses, or any part of them, to be payable only in specified circumstances; and

(b) a conditional fee agreement provides for a success fee if it provides for the amount of any fees to which it applies to be increased, in specified circumstances, above the amount which would be payable if it were not payable only in specified circumstances.

(3) The following conditions are applicable to every conditional fee agreement—

(a) it must be in writing;

(b) it must not relate to proceedings which cannot be the subject of an enforceable conditional fee agreement; and

(c) it must comply with such requirements (if any) as may be prescribed by the Lord Chancellor.

(4) The following further conditions are applicable to a conditional fee agreement which provides for a success fee—

(a) it must relate to proceedings of a description specified by order made by the Lord Chancellor;
(b) it must state the percentage by which the amount of the fees which would be payable if it were not a conditional fee agreement is to be increased; and
(c) that percentage must not exceed the percentage specified in relation to the description of proceedings to which the agreement relates by order made by the Lord Chancellor.

(5) If a conditional fee agreement is an agreement to which section 57 of the Solicitors Act 1974 (non-contentious business agreements between solicitor and client) applies, subsection (1) shall not make it unenforceable.

*Note* —Substituted, together with s.58A, by the Access to Justice Act 1999 s.27. Amended by SI 2003/1887; and SI 2005/3429. **7A–6**

All proceedings which can be the subject of an enforceable conditional fee agreement under s.58, other than proceedings under s.82 of the Environmental Protection Act 1990, are specified for the purposes of s.58(4)(a) by r.3 of the Conditional Fee Agreements Order 2000 (SI 2000/823).

With regards to subsection (4)(c), presently r.4 of the Conditional Fee Agreements Order 2000 (SI 2000/823) prescribes a maximum success fee of 100 per cent.

## Conditional fee agreements: supplementary

**58A.**—(1) The proceedings which cannot be the subject of an enforceable conditional fee agreement are— **7A–7**
(a) criminal proceedings; and
(b) family proceedings, apart from proceedings under section 82 of the Environmental Protection Act 1990.

(2) In subsection (1) "family proceedings" means proceedings under any one or more of the following—
(a) the Matrimonial Causes Act 1973;
(b) the Adoption and Children Act 2002;
(c) the Domestic Proceedings and Magistrates' Courts Act 1978;
(d) PartIII of the Matrimonial and Family Proceedings Act 1984;
(e) Parts I, II and IV of the Children Act 1989;
(f) Parts 4 and 4A of the Family Law Act 1996; and
(fa) Chapter 2 of Part 2 of the Civil Partnership Act 2004 (proceedings for dissolution etc of civil partnership);
(fb) Schedule 5 to the 2004 Act (financial relief in the High Court or a county court etc);
(fc) Schedule 6 to the 2004 Act (financial relief in magistrates' courts etc);
(fd) Schedule 7 to the 2004 Act (financial relief in England and Wales after overseas dissolution etc of a civil partnership); and
(g) the inherent jurisdiction of the High Court in relation to children.

(3) The requirements which the Lord Chancellor may prescribe under section 58(3)(c)—

(a) include requirements for the person providing advocacy or litigation services to have provided prescribed information before the agreement is made; and

(b) may be different for different descriptions of conditional fee agreements (and, in particular, may be different for those which provide for a success fee and those which do not).

(4) In section 58 and this section (and in the definitions of "advocacy services" and "litigation services" as they apply for their purposes) "proceedings" includes any sort of proceedings for resolving disputes (and not just proceedings in a court), whether commenced or contemplated.

(5) Before making an order under section 58(4), the Lord Chancellor shall consult—

(a) the designated judges;

(b) the General Council of the Bar;

(c) the Law Society; and

(d) such other bodies as he considers appropriate.

(6) A costs order made in any proceedings may, subject in the case of court proceedings to rules of court, include provision requiring the payment of any fees payable under a conditional fee agreement which provides for a success fee.

(7) Rules of court may make provision with respect to the assessment of any costs which include fees payable under a conditional fee agreement (including one which provides for a success fee).

**7A–8** *Note*—Inserted by the Access to Justice Act 1999 s.27; amended by SI 2003/1887; SI 2005/3429; the Adoption and Children Act 2002 s.139(1) and Sch.3, para.80; the Civil Partnership Act 2004 s.261(1) and s.261(4), Sch.27, para.138, Sch.30; and the Forced Marriage (Civil Protection) Act 2007 Sch.2, Pt.1, para.2, with effect from November 28, 2008.

## Litigation funding agreements

**7A–9** **58B.**—(1) A litigation funding agreement which satisfies all of the conditions applicable to it by virtue of this section shall not be unenforceable by reason only of its being a litigation funding agreement.

(2) For the purposes of this section a litigation funding agreement is an agreement under which—

(a) a person ("the funder") agrees to fund (in whole or in part) the provision of advocacy or litigation services (by someone other than the funder) to another person ("the litigant"); and

(b) the litigant agrees to pay a sum to the funder in specified circumstances.

(3) The following conditions are applicable to a litigation funding agreement—

(a) the funder must be a person, or person of a description, prescribed by the Lord Chancellor;

(b) the agreement must be in writing;
(c) the agreement must not relate to proceedings which by virtue of section 58A(1) and (2) cannot be the subject of an enforceable conditional fee agreement or to proceedings of any such description as may be prescribed by the Lord Chancellor;
(d) the agreement must comply with such requirements (if any) as may be so prescribed;
(e) the sum to be paid by the litigant must consist of any costs payable to him in respect of the proceedings to which the agreement relates together with an amount calculated by reference to the funder's anticipated expenditure in funding the provision of the services; and
(f) that amount must not exceed such percentage of that anticipated expenditure as may be prescribed by the Lord Chancellor in relation to proceedings of the description to which the agreement relates.

(4) Regulations under subsection (3)(a) may require a person to be approved by the Lord Chancellor or by a prescribed person.

(5) The requirements which the Lord Chancellor may prescribe under subsection (3)(d)—
(a) include requirements for the funder to have provided prescribed information to the litigant before the agreement is made; and
(b) may be different for different descriptions of litigation funding agreements.

(6) In this section (and in the definitions of "advocacy services" and "litigation services" as they apply for its purposes) "proceedings" includes any sort of proceedings for resolving disputes (and not just proceedings in a court), whether commenced or contemplated.

(7) Before making regulations under this section, the Lord Chancellor shall consult—
(a) the designated judges;
(b) the General Council of the Bar;
(c) the Law Society; and
(d) such other bodies as he considers appropriate.

(8) A costs order made in any proceedings may, subject in the case of court proceedings to rules of court, include provision requiring the payment of any amount payable under a litigation funding agreement.

(9) Rules of court may make provision with respect to the assessment of any costs which include fees payable under a litigation funding agreement.

*Note* — Prospectively inserted by the Access to Justice Act 1999 s.28, as from a date to be appointed. Amended by SI 2005/3429. **7A–10**

## Access to Justice Act 1999

7A–11 (1999 c.22)

ARRANGEMENT OF SECTIONS

PART II

OTHER FUNDING OF LEGAL SERVICES

*Costs*



## PART II

## OTHER FUNDING OF LEGAL SERVICES

### COSTS

### Recovery of insurance premiums by way of costs

7A–12 **29.** Where in any proceedings a costs order is made in favour of any party who has taken out an insurance policy against the risk of incurring a liability in those proceedings, the costs payable to him may, subject in the case of court proceedings to rules of court, include costs in respect of the premium of the policy.

7A–13 *Note* — For commentary on the recovery of insurance premiums as costs, see Vol.1, para.44.3A.3.

### Recovery where body undertakes to meet costs liabilities

7A–14 **30.**—(1) This section applies where a body of a prescribed description undertakes to meet (in accordance with arrangements satisfying prescribed conditions) liabilities which members of the body or other persons who are parties to proceedings may incur to pay the costs of other parties to the proceedings.

(2) If in any of the proceedings a costs order is made in favour of any of the members or other persons, the costs payable to him may, subject to subsection (3) and (in the case of court proceedings) to rules of court, include an additional amount in respect of any provision made by or on behalf of the body in connection with the proceedings against the risk of having to meet such liabilities.

(3) But the additional amount shall not exceed a sum determined in a prescribed manner; and there may, in particular, be prescribed as a manner of determination one which takes into account the likely cost to the member or other person of the premium of an insurance policy against the risk of incurring a liability to pay the costs of other parties to the proceedings.

(4) In this section "prescribed" means prescribed by regulations made by the Lord Chancellor by statutory instrument; and a statutory instrument containing such regulations shall be subject to annulment in pursuance of a resolution of either House of Parliament.

(5) Regulations under subsection (1) may, in particular, prescribe as a description of body one which is for the time being approved by the Lord Chancellor by a prescribed person.

*Note*—Amended by SI 2005/3429. **7A-15**

**Courts and Legal Services Act 1990, s.58 and The Access to Justice Act 1999, s.27**

Prior to the enactment of the Courts and Legal Services Act 1990 the historical position had been that conditional fee agreements were not lawful. A solicitor acting for a client in litigation was not entitled to agree with the client to accept a financial reward which varied according to the success of the case. See the Court of Appeal's judgment in *Thai Trading (A firm) v Taylor* [1998] Q.B. 781 for a summary of the early development of the law relating to Champerty and Maintenance. Following a policy review in 1988 and consultation, the original form of s.58 of the Courts and Legal Services Act 1990 was enacted, with Regulations following in 1995 to permit CFAs to be used in a fairly circumscribed range of six types of case. New regulations in 1998 extended the range of cases in which a CFA could be used but 'no win no fee' funding as it became known had to await developments in case law and statute before becoming commonplace. In early 1998 the Court of Appeal gave judgment in *Thai Trading (A firm) v Taylor* [1998] Q.B. 781, holding that an agreement between solicitor and client that the solicitor would charge no fee in the event of failure and only his normal fee in the event of success was no longer contrary to public policy and was not an unlawful agreement despite involving conduct by the solicitor which had been in breach of rule 8 of the then Solicitor's Practice Rules (which forbade conditional fee agreements). Thai Trading was initially not followed at Divisional Court level (*Hughes v Kingston upon Hull City Council* [1999] Q.B. 1193), on the basis that a dictum in the House of Lords case of *Swain v The Law Society* [1983] 1 AC 598, that the Solicitors' Practice rules "had the force of a statute" was incompatible with the *Thai Trading* decision and that *Swain* had not been considered in *Thai Trading*. Rule 8 of the Solicitor's Practice rules was then swiftly amended to permit CFA agreements to be entered into provided they were lawful either at common law or under statute. **7A-16**

In 1999 reform to the whole subject of litigation funding was considered by Parliament and the subject was placed on a new statutory footing in the guise of s.27 of the Access to Justice Act 1999 above, which wholly replaced s.58 of the Courts and legal Services Act 1990 and introduced s.58A. By these sections CFA agreements, provided they complied with the Act and any relevant regulations, are no longer unenforceable but any other forms of CFA are rendered unenforceable, a fact confirmed by the Court of Appeal in *Awwad v Geraghty & Co* [2001] Q.B. 570 to the effect that there was no longer scope for development of the Common Law in the area of CFA agreements.

**The Solicitors' Costs Information and Client Care Code 1999**

The Law Society published the Solicitors' Costs Information and Client Care Code in 1999 with the effect that solicitors were professionally obliged to provide to clients a wide range of information about charging and about funding options available to them, orally and in writing. This amendment to the Code was introduced in the light of the revocation in November 2005 of the Conditional Fees Regulations of 2000 and 2003. **7A-17**

**The developing role of professional rules and guidance as to conditional fee agreements**

The history of the courts' approach to the consequences of breach of Law Society's practice rules in relation to CFA's might give encouragement to litigators seeking to raise challenges to the new-form CFA agreements if there are departures from the Code. If the strict letter of the Code supplied by the Law Society is not followed it may be that a challenge could be founded upon that breach on the basis that the guidance is made pursuant to Law Society rules. It will be recalled that in *Thai Trading (A Firm) v Taylor* [1998] Q.B. 781, the Court of Appeal had regarded a breach of rule 8 of the Solicitor's practice rules as not affecting the enforceability or lawfulness of a fee agreement, but that the Divisional Court in *Hughes v Kingston upon Hull City Council* [1999] Q.B. 1193, in refusing to follow *Thai Trading*, relied upon a dictum in *Swain v The Law Society* [1983] 1 AC 598 that the Law Society's rules 'had the force of a statute ... just as **7A-18**

***Paragraph numbers marked with a "+" can be found online and on CD.***

much as if the rules, ... were set out in a Schedule to the Act' (per Lord Brightman in *Swain* at page 621G, cited in *Hughes*).

It appears however that more recent re-interpretation of Swain given by the Court of Appeal in *Garbutt v Edwards* [2005] EWCA Civ 1206 treats the Solicitors' Practice rules (in that instance rule 15) as a species of subordinate legislation the breach of which does not of itself necessarily render a funding contract unlawful and similarly decides that a breach of the Solicitors' Costs Information and Client Care Code does not necessarily have that consequence either. It is suggested that that is the correct approach, not least on the basis that to adopt too literal a reading of Lord Brightman's dictum in *Swain* quoted above might imply that the Law Society is empowered to create primary legislation. In a sense the *Thai Trading* public policy approach towards breaches of the Solicitors Practice rules has been revived, Per Arden L.J. at para.31 in *Garbutt v Edward*:

> "Estimates are required only by the Code (as defined above). The Code is made pursuant to Rule 15 of the Solicitors' Practice Rules. These Rules are made by the Council of the Law Society pursuant to section 31 of the 1974 Act (set out above). In making these Rules, the Council of the Law Society is acting in the public interest, and the Rules have the force of subordinate legislation: *Swain v Law Society* [1983] A.C. 598. The inference I would draw is that the Code is there to protect the legitimate interests of the client, and the administration of justice, rather than to relieve paying parties of their obligations to pay costs which have been reasonably incurred."

**The 2000 and 2003 Regulations**

**7A–19** The protections provided in the Solicitors' Costs Information and Client Care Code 1999 were joined by a series of arguably precipitate regulations in circumstances which were described at paras 25–30 of the Court of Appeal's judgment in the subsequent case of *Hollins v Russell* [2003] EWCA Civ 718. The Conditional Fee Agreements Regulations 2000 (SI 2000/692), the Collective Conditional Fee Agreements Regulations 2000 (SI 2000/2988), Conditional Fee Agreements (Miscellaneous Amendments) Regulations 2003 (SI 2003/1240), and the Conditional Fee Agreements (Miscellaneous Amendments) (No.2) Regulations 2003 (SI 2003/3344), were highly prescriptive and served to provide a technical battleground for challenges to CFA agreements by paying parties in the course of detailed assessment. The case history of technical challenges is lengthy: for a cross-section of challenges concerning the adherence to regulations see *Hollins v Russell* [2003] EWCA 718; *Sarwar v Alam* [2002] 1 W.L.R. 125; *Bowen v Bridgend BC*, March 25, 2004, unrep.; *Richards v Davis*, November 25, 2005, unrep.; *Hughes v Newham LBC* (2005) 102(34) L.S.G. 30; *Samonini v London General Transport Services Ltd* [2005] P.I.Q.R. P20; *Woods v Chaleff* [1999] C.L.Y. 500, and the numerous test and first instance cases which can be accessed through the Senior Courts Costs Office website at *http://www.hmcourts-service.gov.uk/infoabout/scco/transcripts/index.htm* [Accessed November 9, 2009].

The Court of Appeal, considering the words "or otherwise" in reg.3A(1) of the Conditional Fee Agreements (Miscellaneous Amendments) Regulations 2003, was not persuaded that those words were never intended to include insurance. When considering the actual terms of the CFA Waller L.J. expressed the view that he could see no reason why the court should not look at the whole package produced by the solicitor: the CFA, the Rule 15 letter explaining to the client the effect of the agreement and the insurance policy recommended by the solicitor. In that way it could be ascertained whether, as between client and solicitor, the proper understanding was that the client would not be liable for any own side's costs whatever the result of the proceedings, save to the extent that they could be recovered from the other side or under the insurance policy. As to whether the particular CFA was a "CFA lite" depended on the construction of the arrangement made between the solicitor and the client, including such arrangement as may have been made by the Rule 15 letter and by insurance. On the facts, the court found that the agreement was a CFA lite. The court also considered the extent to which the solicitors had an interest in recommending the particular policy. Had the court not found the agreement to be a CFA lite it would have held that there had been non-compliance with reg.4(2)(e) by the solicitors' failure to disclose their interest and the CFA would have been unenforceable. The solicitors were on the claims management company's panel and were required by the operations manual to use the company's precedents, i.e. the Rule 15 letter and CFA which included the recommendation of the company's own policy (*Jones v Wrexham BC* [2007] EWCA Civ 1356).

### Revocation of the 2000 and 2003 Regulations

In 2003 and 2004 the Government conducted consultation on the subject of the simplification of the regulatory legislation governing CFAs in the light of the state of affairs described above. The conclusion was that that the CFA regulations were not necessary or effective and to a large extent duplicated existing professional regulation and should be revoked so that the primary legislation in the form of s.27 of the Access to Justice Act 1999 would provide the basic legislative framework for the use of CFAs. The primary responsibility for client care, contractual and guidance aspects would be via the Law Society's Professional Rules and supporting guidance. The Conditional Fee Agreements (Revocation) Regulations 2005 (SI 2005/2305), reproduced in this section were the result, together with the Solicitors' Practice (Client Care) Amendment Rule [2005] and the Law Society's model CFA and guidance text for clients (see paras 7A–76 and 7A–77 for the model CFA and guidance). The entire new regime—effectively revoking the whole of the body of regulations governing the form and content of CFA agreements—came into force on November 1, 2005 and has been observed judicially as being intended by Parliament to prevent further technical challenges. See the judgment of the Senior Costs Judge in *Richards v Davis* 25/11/2005 SCCO case No.PTH0504722 at para.91: **7A–20**

> "...in revoking the CFA regulations Parliament's desire is clearly to prevent further technical challenges. Such challenges take up a disproportionate amount of court time and prevent the proper development of the CFA and ATE market. The client's protection has not simply been abandoned, but the regulation of the funding regime has been taken on by the professional bodies, in particular, by the Law Society which has passed the Solicitors' Practice (Amendment) Rule 2005."

Note that by reg.3 the 2000 and 2003 regulations continue to have effect in respect of agreements entered into before November 1, 2005, though there is presumably no reason in law why a client and solicitor cannot elect to enter into a new fee agreement under the new regime after that date by mutual agreement notwithstanding that they had earlier contracted under the old regime.

## The Conditional Fee Agreements Order 2000

(S.I. 2000 No. 823) **7A–21**

### Citation, commencement and interpretation

**1.**—(1) This Order may be cited as the Conditional Fee Agreements Order 2000 and shall come into force on 1st April 2000. **7A–22**

(2) In this Order "the Act" means the Courts and Legal Services Act 1990.

### Revocation of 1998 Order

**2.** The Conditional Fee Agreements Order 1998 is revoked. **7A–23**

### Agreements providing for success fees

**3.** All proceedings which, under section 58 of the Act, can be the subject of an enforceable conditional fee agreement, except proceedings under section 82 of the Environmental Protection Act 1990, are proceedings specified for the purposes of section 58(4)(a) of the Act. **7A–24**

### Amount of for success fees

**4.** In relation to all proceedings specified in article 3, the percentage specified for the purposes of section 58(4)(c) of the Act shall be 100%. **7A–25**

*Paragraph numbers marked with a "+" can be found online and on CD.*

## The Conditional Fee Agreements Regulations 2000

7A–26 (S.I. 2000 No. 692)

ARRANGEMENT OF REGULATIONS



*[The Conditional Fee Agreements Regulations 2000 have been revoked with effect from November 1, 2005 by the Conditional Fee Agreements (Revocation) Regulations 2005 (SI 2005/2305). The CFA Regulations 2000 continue to have effect for the purposes of a CFA agreement entered into before November 1, 2005.]*

### Citation, commencement and interpretation

7A–27 **1.**—(1) *These Regulations may be cited as the Conditional Fee Agreements Regulations 2000.*

(2) *These Regulations come into force on 1st April 2000.*

(3) *In these Regulations–*

*"client" includes, except where the context otherwise requires, a person who–*

(a) *has instructed the legal representative to provide the advocacy or litigation services to which the conditional fee agreement relates, or*

(b) *is liable to pay the legal representative's fees in respect of those services; and*

*"legal representative" means the person providing the advocacy or litigation services to which the conditional fee agreement relates.*

### Requirements for contents of conditional fee agreements: general

7A–28 **2.**—(1) *A conditional fee agreement must specify–*

(a) *the particular proceedings or parts of them to which it relates (including whether it relates to any appeal, counterclaim or proceedings to enforce a judgement or order),*

(b) *the circumstances in which the legal representative's fees and expenses, or part of them, are payable,*

(c) *what payment, if any, is due–*

(i) *if those circumstances only partly occur,*

(ii) *irrespective of whether those circumstances occur, and*

(iii) *on the termination of the agreement for any reason, and*

(d) *the amounts which are payable in all the circumstances and cases specified or the method to be used to calculate them and, in*

***Paragraph numbers marked with a "+" can be found online and on CD.***

*particular, whether the amounts are limited by reference to the damages which may be recovered on behalf of the client.*

(2) *A conditional fee agreement to which regulation 4 applies must contain a statement that the requirements of that regulation which apply in the case of that agreement have been complied with.*

### Requirements for contents of conditional fee agreements providing for success fees

**3.**—(1) *A conditional fee agreement which provides for a success fee–* **7A–29**

(a) *must briefly specify the reasons for setting the percentage increase at the level stated in the agreement, and*

(b) *must specify how much of the percentage increase, if any, relates to the cost to the legal representative of the postponement of the payment of his fees and expenses.*

(2) *If the agreement relates to court proceedings, it must provide that where the percentage increase becomes payable as a result of those proceedings, then–*

(a) *if–*

(i) *any fees subject to the increase are assessed, and*

(ii) *the legal representative or the client is required by the court to disclose to the court or any other person the reasons for setting the percentage increase at the level stated in the agreement,*

*he may do so,*

(b) *if–*

(i) *any such fees are assessed, and*

(ii) *any amount in respect of the percentage increase is disallowed on the assessment on the ground that the level at which the increase was set was unreasonable in view of facts which were or should have been known to the legal representative at the time it was set,*

*that amount ceases to be payable under the agreement, unless the court is satisfied that it should continue to be so payable, and*

(c) *if–*

(i) *sub-paragraph (b) does not apply, and*

(ii) *the legal representative agrees with any person liable as a result of the proceedings to pay fees subject to the percentage increase that a lower amount than the amount payable in accordance with the conditional fee agreement is to be paid instead,*

*the amount payable under the conditional fee agreement in respect of those fees shall be reduced accordingly, unless the court is satisfied that the full amount should continue to be payable under it.*

(3) *In this regulation "percentage increase" means the percentage by which the amount of the fees which would be payable if the agreement were not a conditional fee agreement is to be increased under the agreement.*

### Requirements where the client's liability is limited to sums recovered

**3A.**—(1) *This regulation applies to a conditional fee agreement under* **7A–30**

*which, except in the circumstances set out in paragraphs (5) and (5A), the client is liable to pay his legal representative's fees and expenses only to the extent that sums are recovered in respect of the relevant proceedings, whether by way of costs or otherwise.*

(2) *In determining for the purposes of paragraph (1) the circumstance in which a client is liable to pay his legal representative's fees and expenses only to the extent that sums are recovered in respect of the relevant proceedings, whether by way of costs or otherwise.*

(3) *Regulations 2, 3 and 4 do not apply to a conditional fee agreement to which this regulation applies.*

(4) *A conditional fee agreement to which this regulation applies must*

(a) *specify—*

(i) *the particular proceedings or parts of them to which it relates (including whether it relates to any appeal, counterclaim or proceedings to enforce a judgment or order); and*

(ii) *the circumstances in which the legal representative's fees and expenses, or part of them, are payable; and*

(b) *if it provides for a success fee—*

(i) *briefly specify the reasons for setting the percentage increase at the level stated in the agreement; and*

(ii) *provide that if, in court proceedings, the percentage increase becomes payable as a result of those proceedings and the legal representative or the client is ordered to disclose to the court or any other person the reasons for setting the percentage increase at the level stated in the agreement, he may do so.*

(5) *A conditional fee agreement to which this regulation applies may specify that the client will be liable to pay the legal representative's fees and expenses whether or not sums are recovered in respect of the relevant proceedings, if the client—*

(a) *fails to co-operate with the legal representative;*

(b) *fails to attend any medical or expert examination or court hearing which the legal representative reasonably requests him to attend;*

(c) *fails to give necessary instructions to the legal representative;*

(d) *withdraws instructions from the legal representative.*

(e) *is an individual who is adjudged bankrupt or enters into an arrangement or a composition with his creditors, or against whom an administration order is made; or*

(f) *is a company for which a receiver, administrative receiver or liquidator is appointed.*

(5A) *A conditional fee agreement to which this regulation applies may specify that, in the event of the client dying in the course of the relevant proceedings, his estate will be liable for the legal representative's fees and expenses, whether or not sums are recovered in respect of those proceedings.*

(6) *Before a conditional fee agreement to which this regulation applies is made, the legal representative must inform the client as to the circumstances in which the client or his estate may be liable to pay the legal representative's fees*

*and expenses, and provide such further explanation, advice or other information as to those circumstances as the client may reasonably require.*

*Note* —Amended by the Conditional Fee Agreements (Miscellaneous Amendments) (No.2) Regulations 2003 (SI 2003/3344)and the Conditional Fee Agreements (Miscellaneous Amendments) Regulations 2003 (SI 2003/1240).

### Information to be given before conditional fee agreements made

**4.**—(1) *Before a conditional fee agreement is made the legal representative must–* **7A–31**

(a) *inform the client about the following matters, and*

(b) *if the client requires any further explanation, advice or other information about any of those matters, provide such further explanation, advice or other information about them as the client may reasonably require.*

(2) *Those matters are–*

(a) *the circumstances in which the client may be liable to pay the costs of the legal representative in accordance with the agreement,*

(b) *the circumstances in which the client may seek assessment of the fees and expenses of the legal representative and the procedure for doing so,*

(c) *whether the legal representative considers that the client's risk of incurring liability for costs in respect of the proceedings to which agreement relates is insured against under an existing contract of insurance,*

(d) *whether other methods of financing those costs are available, and, if so, how they apply to the client and the proceedings in question,*

(e) *whether the legal representative considers that any particular method or methods of financing any or all of those costs is appropriate and, if he considers that a contract of insurance is appropriate or recommends a particular such contract–*

(i) *his reasons for doing so, and*

(ii) *whether he has an interest in doing so.*

(3) *Before a conditional fee agreement is made the legal representative must explain its effect to the client.*

(4) *In the case of an agreement where–*

(a) *the legal representative is a body to which section 30 of the Access to Justice Act 1999 (recovery where body undertakes to meet costs liabilities) applies, and*

(b) *there are no circumstances in which the client may be liable to pay any costs in respect of the proceedings,*

*paragraph (1) does not apply.*

(5) *Information required to be given under paragraph (1) about the matters in paragraph (2)(a) to (d) must be given orally (whether or not it is also given in writing), but information required to be so given about the matters in paragraph (2)(e) and the explanation required by paragraph (3) must be given both orally and in writing.*

(6) *This regulation does not apply in the case of an agreement between a legal representative and an additional legal representative.*

### Form of agreement

7A–32 **5.**—(1) *A conditional fee agreement must be signed by the client and the legal representative.*

(2) *This regulation does not apply in the case of an agreement between a legal representative and an additional legal representative.*

### Amendment of agreement

7A–33 **6.** *Where an agreement is amended to cover further proceedings or parts of them–*

(a) *regulations 2, 3, 3A and 5 apply to the amended agreement as if it were a fresh agreement made at the time of the amendment, and*

(b) *the obligations under regulation 4 apply in relation to the amendments in so far as they affect the matters mentioned in that regulation.*

### Revocation of 1995 Regulations

7A–34 **7.** *The Conditional Fee Agreements Regulations 1995 are revoked.*

#### Regulation 3(1)(b)

7A–35 The Regulation requires that the CFA must specify how much of the percentage increase relates to the cost of the legal representative of the postponement of the payment of his fees and expenses. This element of the success fee is not recoverable from a paying party. This continues the principle laid down by the Court of Appeal in a decision under the earlier rules, *Hunt v RM Douglas (Roofing) Ltd (Costs: Taxation)*, *The Times*, November 23, 1987, CA.

## The Collective Conditional Fee Agreements Regulations 2000

7A–36 (S.I. 2000 No. 2988)

ARRANGEMENT OF SECTIONS



*[The Collective Conditional Fee Agreements Regulations 2000 have been revoked with effect from November 1, 2005 by the Conditional Fee Agreements (Revocation) Regulations 2005 (SI 2005/2305). The CCFA Regulations 2000 continue to have effect for the purposes of a CFA agreement entered into before November 1, 2005.]*

### Citation, commencement and interpretation

7A–37 **1.**—(1) *These regulations may be cited as the Collective Conditional Fee*

***Paragraph numbers marked with a "+" can be found online and on CD.***

*Agreements Regulations 2000, and shall come into force on 30th November 2000.*

(2) *In these Regulations, except where the context requires otherwise—*

*"client" means a person who will receive advocacy or litigation services to which the agreement relates;*

*"collective conditional fee agreement" has the meaning given in regulation 3;*

*"conditional fee agreement" has the same meaning as in section 58 of the Courts and Legal Services Act 1990;*

*"legal representative" means the person providing the advocacy or litigation services to which the agreement relates.*

### Transitional provisions

**2.** *These Regulations shall apply to agreements entered into on or after 30th November 2000, and agreements entered into before that date shall be treated as if these Regulations had not come into force.* **7A–38**

### Definition of "collective conditional fee agreement"

**3.**—(1) *Subject to paragraph (2) of this regulation, a collective conditional fee agreement is an agreement which—* **7A–39**

(a) *disregarding section 58(3)(c) of the Courts and Legal Services Act 1990, would be a conditional fee agreement; and*

(b) *does not refer to specific proceedings, but provides for fees to be payable on a common basis in relation to a class of proceedings, or, if it refers to more than one class of proceedings, on a common basis in relation to each class.*

(2) *An agreement may be a collective conditional fee agreement whether or not—*

(a) *the funder is a client; or*

(b) *any clients are named in the agreement.*

### Requirements for contents of collective conditional fee agreements: general

**4.**—(1) *A collective conditional fee agreement must specify the circumstances in which the legal representative's fees and expenses, or part of them, are payable.* **7A–40**

(1A) *The circumstances referred to in paragraph (1) may include the fact that the legal representative's fees and expenses are payable only to the extent that sums are recovered in respect of the proceedings, whether by way of costs or otherwise.*

(2) *A collective conditional fee agreement must provide that, when accepting instructions in relation to any specific proceedings the legal representative must—*

(a) *inform the client as to the circumstances in which the client or his estate may be liable to pay the costs of the legal representative; and*

(b) *if the client requires any further explanation, advice or other information about the matter referred to in sub-paragraph (a), provide such further explanation, advice or other information about it as the client may reasonably require.*

(3) *Paragraph (2) does not apply in the case of an agreement between a legal representative and an additional legal representative.*

(4) *A collective conditional fee agreement must provide that, after accepting instructions in relation to any specific proceedings, the legal representative must confirm his acceptance of instructions in writing to the client.*

**Requirements for contents of collective conditional fee agreements providing for success fees**

**7A–41** **5.**—(1) *Where a collective conditional fee agreement provides for a success fee the agreement must provide that, when accepting instructions in relation to any specific proceedings the legal representative must prepare and retain a written statement containing—*

(a) *his assessment of the probability of the circumstances arising in which the percentage increase will become payable in relation to those proceedings ("the risk assessment");*

(b) *his assessment of the amount of the percentage increase in relation to those proceedings, having regard to the risk assessment; and*

(c) *the reasons, by reference to the risk assessment, for setting the percentage increase at that level.*

(2) *If the agreement relates to court proceedings it must provide that where the success fee becomes payable as a result of those proceedings, then—*

(a) *if—*

(i) *any fees subject to the increase are assessed, and*

(ii) *the legal representative or the client is required by the court to disclose to the court or any other person the reasons for setting the percentage increase at the level assessed by the legal representative,*

*he may do so,*

(b) *if—*

(i) *any such fees are assessed by the court, and*

(ii) *any amount in respect of the percentage increase is disallowed on the assessment on the ground that the level at which the increase was set was unreasonable in view of facts which were or should have been known to the legal representative at the time it was set*

*that amount ceases to be payable under the agreement, unless the court is satisfied that it should continue to be so payable, and*

(c) *if—*

(i) *sub-paragraph (b) does not apply, and*

(ii) *the legal representative agrees with any person liable as a result of the proceedings to pay fees subject to the percentage increase that a lower amount than the amount payable in accordance with the conditional fee agreement is to be paid instead,*

*the amount payable under the collective conditional fee agreement in respect of those fees shall be reduced accordingly, unless the court is satisfied that the full amount should continue to be payable under it.*

(3) *In this regulation "percentage increase" means the percentage by*

*which the amount of the fees which would have been payable if the agreement were not a conditional fee agreement is to be increased under the agreement.*

(4) *Sub-paragraphs (b) and (c) of paragraph (2) do not apply to a collective conditional fee agreement under which, except in the circumstances set out in paragraphs (6) and (7), the client is liable to pay his legal representative's fees and expenses only to the extent that sums are recovered in respect of the proceedings, whether by way of costs or otherwise.*

(5) *In determining for the purposes of paragraph (4) the circumstances in which a client is liable to pay his legal representative's fees and expenses, no account is to be taken of any obligation to pay costs in respect of the premium of a policy taken out to insure against the risk of incurring a liability in the relevant proceedings.*

(6) *A collective conditional fee agreement to which paragraph (4) applies may specify that the client will be liable to pay his legal representative's fees and expenses whether or not sums are recovered in respect of the relevant proceedings, if the client—*

(a) *fails to co-operate with the legal representative;*

(b) *fails to attend any medical or expert examination or court hearing which the legal representative reasonably requests him to attend;*

(c) *fails to give necessary instructions to the legal representative;*

(d) *withdraws instructions from the legal representative.*

(e) *is an individual who is adjudged bankrupt or enters into an arrangement or a composition with his creditors, or against whom an administration order is made; or*

(f) *is a company for which a receiver, administrative receiver or liquidator is appointed;*

(7) *A collective conditional fee agreement to which paragraph (4) applies may specify that, in the event of the client dying in the course of the relevant proceedings, his estate will be liable for the legal representative's fees and expenses, whether or not sums are recovered in respect of those proceedings.*

*Note* —Amended by the Conditional Fee Agreements (Miscellaneous Amendments) (No.2) Regulations 2003 (SI 2003/3344).

### Form and amendment of collective conditional fee agreement

**6.**—(1) *Subject to paragraph (2), a collective conditional fee agreement must be signed by the funder, and by the legal representative.* **7A–42**

(2) *Paragraph (1) does not apply in the case of an agreement between a legal representative and an additional legal representative.*

(3) *Where a collective conditional fee agreement is amended, regulations 4 and 5 apply to the amended agreement as if it were a fresh agreement made at the time of the amendment.*

### Amendment to the Conditional Fee Agreements Regulations 2000

**7.** *After regulation 7 of the Conditional Fee Agreements Regulations 2000 there shall be inserted the following new regulation:—* **7A–43**

### Exclusion of collective conditional fee agreements

**"8.** *These Regulations shall not apply to collective conditional fee agree-*

*ments within the meaning of regulation 3 of the Collective Conditional Fee Agreements Regulations 2000".*

## The Access to Justice (Membership Organisations) Regulations 2000

7A–44 (S.I. 2000 No. 693)

ARRANGEMENT OF REGULATIONS



*[The Access to Justice (Membership Organisation) Regulations 2000 have been revoked with effect from November 1, 2005 by the Access to Justice (Membership Organisation) Regulations 2005 (SI. 2005/2306). The 2000 Regulations continue to have effect for the purposes of arrangements entered into before November 1, 2005 as if the 2005 Regulations had not come into force. New simplified client care provisions are contained in the 2005 regulations for agreements entered into after November 1, 2005.]*

**Paragraph numbers marked with a "+" denote content that is available on White Book on Westlaw UK or the Civil Procedure CD.**

## The Access to Justice (Membership Organisations) Regulations 2005

7A–49 (S.I. 2005 No. 2306)

ARRANGEMENT OF REGULATIONS



**Paragraph numbers marked with a "+" denote content that is available on White Book on Westlaw UK or the Civil Procedure CD.**

## FUNDING ARRANGEMENTS

### CONDITIONAL FEES

7A–55 Conditional fee agreements (CFAs) cannot be used in respect of criminal and family proceedings. CFAs allow clients to agree with their lawyers that the lawyer will not receive all or part of their usual fees or expenses if the case is lost, but that if it is won the client will pay an uplift to the solicitor in addition to the usual fee. Prior to the coming into force of the Access to Justice Act 1999 CFAs had been allowed for a limited range of cases. The maximum uplift (which was not recoverable from an opposing party) was fixed at 100 per cent and the Law Society recommended that lawyers should voluntarily limit the uplift to a maximum of 25 per cent of the damages.

Following the decision of the Court of Appeal in *Thai Trading Co v Taylor* [1983] 3 All E.R. 65 CA, the Government accepted that there were no longer public policy grounds to prevent lawyers agreeing to work for less than their normal fees if they were successful. In *Bevan Ashford v Geoff Yeandle (Contractors) Ltd* [1998] 3 All E.R. 238

Scott V.-C., it was held that it was also lawful for a CFA to apply in a case which was to be resolved by arbitration even though they were not court proceedings, provided that all requirements specified by regulations were complied with. Section 58 of the Courts and Legal Services Act 1990 as substituted by the Access to Justice Act 1999 is sufficiently wide to include *Thai Trading* type agreements. Where solicitors entered into a retainer with a client seeking damages for personal injuries, and indicated in the retainer letter that if the claim was disputed by her opponent and she wished to pursue her claim "through litigation", the solicitors would discuss alternative methods of funding her case with her.

> "You may wish to enter into a conditional fee agreement with us and apply for after the event legal expenses insurance to cover your opponent's cost in litigation."

The retainer letter concluded:

> "If your claim is disputed by your opponent, and you decide not to pursue your claim, then we will not make a charge for the work we have done to date."

On detailed assessment the paying party challenged the retainer on the basis that it was itself a CFA and in breach of the statutory provisions, as a result of which the agreement was unenforceable and no costs were payable. The Costs Judge found that it was not a CFA and that there had been no intention to enter into such an agreement. On appeal to the Circuit Judge the court held that the retainer letter provided for the fees of the court to be payable only in certain circumstances and that accordingly it did constitute a CFA. On appeal to the Court of Appeal it was held, citing paras 100, 105 and 107 of *Hollins v Russell* [2003] EWCA Civ 718; [2003] 1 W.L.R. 2487, that the object of s.58 of the 1990 Act and the Regulations was to provide protection to clients, predicated on the assumption that the solicitor would in fact provide litigation or advocacy services:

> "13. ...If such services are not provided, the client has no need of protection. Section 58(2)(a) defines a CFA as an agreement with a person providing advocacy or litigation services, which provides for his fees and expenses for those services, or any of them, to be payable only in specified circumstances. The words that I have emphasised are critical to this appeal. A provision in an agreement as to the costs payable in respect of services which are not advocacy or litigation services as defined by section 119(1) is irrelevant to whether an agreement is a CFA. This is consistent with Regulation 1(3) of the Regulations which defines 'client' as including (except where the context otherwise provides) a person who '(a) has instructed the legal representative to provide advocacy or litigation services to which the conditional fee agreement relates'."

The court found, on the facts, that the wording of the retainer was an offer to waive fees for modest pre litigation services. The judgment continues:

> "17. Approaching it as a matter of construction, I would hold that the work done before a decision is made not to pursue the claim, pursuant to the last paragraph [of the retainer letter], is not the provision of litigation services. In my judgment, "contemplated proceedings" are proceedings of which it can be said that there is at least a real likelihood that they will be issued. Until the potential defendant disputes the claim, it is not possible to say that proceedings are contemplated. Advising a client as to whether he or she has a good prima facie case and writing a letter of claim are not enough to amount to litigation services.
>
> 18. ...A client who, having received limited pre litigation services, decides not to pursue a claim by litigation has no need for the panoply of protection afforded by the conditions stated in section 58(3) of the 1990 Act. In my view, it was not intended by Parliament that this statutory regime should apply to agreements to provide such limited services. This agreement is a far cry from the most obvious application of section 58(2)(a), namely a "no win, no [fee]" arrangement."

*Gaynor v Central West London Buses Ltd* [2006] EWCA Civ 1120; [2007] 1 W.L.R. 1045, CA.

Paragraph 32.7 of the Costs Practice Direction requires the receiving party to serve on the paying party various documents including a statement of the reasons for the percentage increase (success fee) in relation to a CFA. In a case where the receiving party declined to serve this information and sought an order restricting disclosure to solicitors, counsel and costs draftsmen for the paying party, because of concerns that it could be used for the purpose of criminal proceedings against him in Kuwait, the **7A–56** court held that it had inherent jurisdiction to restrict disclosure in an appropriate case. In order to warrant the exercise of the jurisdiction it was necessary to show a tangible risk of misuse of the information. Relief from the sanction for non disclosure was granted on condition that disclosure was made within ten days. The Costs Judge was directed to take into account the refusal to disclose in determining any claim for interest on the success fee: *Grupo Torras v Al-Sabah* [2003] EWHC 262 (QB); [2003] 2 Costs LR 294, Tracey J.

The defendant in libel proceedings argued that it was an abuse of process that such proceedings should be brought with a maximum 100 per cent success fee since this pre-supposed that lawyers would only take on cases with a prospect of success of at least 50 per cent. It further argued that the availability of CFAs in defamation cases had a potentially chilling effect on the activities of journalists, contrary to the European Convention right of freedom of speech. The court held that there was nothing inconsistent with the intention of the legislature in lawyers agreeing to support a claim by means of a CFA, even where a dispassionate assessment of the likely outcome would lead them to the conclusion the claim was unlikely to succeed. The application that the claimant should be ordered to make a payment into court unless ATE insurance was in place was rejected: *King v Telegraph* [2003] EWHC 1312 (QB) Eady J.

On appeal the court referred to *Olatawura v Abiloye* [2002] EWCA Civ 998 at [26] as setting out the principles relating to security for costs, and declined to make any different type of order to the one the judge at first instance had been asked to make. The appeal was accordingly dismissed. The court went on to consider the power of the court to keep the balance fairly between the interests of a claimant seekng to vindicate his/her reputation with the help of a CFA who cannot afford appropriate ATE cover and the interests of the media as the eyes and ears of the public. [55]. Brooke L.J. stated:

> "[94] It would be helpful if the senior master were to assign a particular master to case management applications in this specialist field of law because they demand a degree of practical experience that will not become available if they distributed generally among the masters. If the master considers that a budget or cap is required, he should refer the issue of imposing a cap to the costs judge. The costs judge should determine what sum is reasonable and proportionate to fix as the recoverable costs of the action. Similar arrangements should be made, if and when necessary, in district registaries of the High Court outside London".

*King v Telegraph Group Ltd* [2004] EWCA Civ 613; [2005] 1 W.L.R. 2282 CA.

The House of Lords has held that the scheme allowing success fees to be recovered from the losing party to an action for defamation is compatible with art.10 ECHR and it was not open to a defendant to argue that the threat of liability to pay a large sum by way of costs infringed its right to freedom of expression. Parliament was entitled to lay down a general rule that CFAs were open to everybody taking into account the impracticality of requiring a means test and the small number of individuals who would have sufficient resources to fund their own litigation. The financial position of the claimant was therefore not relevant in deciding whether it was appropriate to proceed with a CFA. The controls imposed by the court through costs capping and assessment, applying the test of reasonableness and proportionality were palliatives, and any perceived difficulty could only be resolved by legislation: *Campbell v MGN Ltd* [2005] UKHL 61; [2005] 4 All E.R. 793, HL.

For an explanation of the transitional provisions contained in the Access to Justice Act 1999 (Transitional Provisions) Order 1999 see *C v M* [2003] EWHC 250 (Fam) Sumner J. Where a claimant has entered into a CFA prior to April 1, 2000 no success fee is recoverable from the paying party.

Where a solicitor has moved firm taking an existing client with her to the new firm on a CFA, that agreement may lawfully be assigned to the new firm since the relationship between solicitor and client involves personal confidence and the trust and confidence that the client had in the solicitor was based upon her uninterrupted conduct of the proceedings. The CFA could therefore be assigned as an exception to the general rule: *Jenkins v Young Brothers Transport Ltd* [2006] EWHC 151 (QB); [2006] 1 W.L.R. 3189, Rafferty J.

**7A–57** Because of the difficulty caused by countless technical challenges to the enforceability of CFAs, legal representatives have on occasion resorted to deeds of rectification. There is, as yet, no definitive decision as to the effectiveness of such deeds. In relation to rectification generally the court has commented that it is not part of the court's jurisdiction, when exercising a rectifying function, to construct an agreement which the parties did not themselves make. *Platinum Investment Trust Plc v Knox D'Arcy Asset Management Ltd* [2006] EWHC 1893 (Ch), Pumfrey J. The Court has dealt with a backdated (rather than retrospective) CFA. In addition, a 25 per cent success fee had been inserted where previously it had been nil. It was accepted by the paying party and the court that there had been no impropriety. The paying party challenged the CFA on the ground that there were breaches of the regulations which together were material. The court found that the CFA was not retrospective, it was backdated:

> "19. ...a properly drafted agreement would have borne the date on which it was executed, but would have expressly provided for its application to work done from the prior date agreed by the parties..."

The judge went on to state:

> "23. ...I would emphasise, however, that the backdating of documents, as was done in this case, is generally wrong. It is wrong to seek to give an agreement retrospective effect by backdating it. If it is agreed that a written agreement should apply to work done before it is entered into, it should be correctly dated with the date on which it is signed and expressed to have retrospective effect, ie to apply to work done before its date. Backdating is liable to mislead third parties, and is liable to lead to the suspicion that it was done in order to mislead third parties, including a court before which the agreement is to be placed."
>
> "...backdating is, at best, due to incompetence or lack of thought, and at worst, to dishonesty. It should not be done.":

*Holmes v Alfred McAlpine Homes (Yorkshire) Ltd* [2006] EWHC 110 (QB), Stanley Burnton J.

Generally speaking parties are entitled to make, and often do make, an agreement which applies to the period before they made it. Section 59 of the Solicitors Act 1974, which permits a solicitor to make an agreement for remuneration in respect of contentious business "done or to be done by him" contemplates a retrospective agreement. The court went on to express the view that a retrospective success fee is not per se contrary to public policy,

> "There is, in my view, insufficient warrant for effectively precluding solicitor and client from making such an agreement. In some, perhaps many, circumstances a retrospective success fee, or its amount, may be unreasonable, either as between the parties or as between solicitor and client but this will not always be so. The court has, in my opinion, enough weapons in its armoury in the form of the criteria applicable on a detailed assessment and the provisions of the Costs Practice Direction and the Practice Direction on Protocols to disallow or reduce retrospective fees that are unreasonable ...". *Birmingham City Council v Forde* [2009] EWHC 12 (QB); [2009] 1 W.L.R. 2732, Christopher Clarke J (at para.[150]).

### Success fees

The Court of Appeal has dealt with the question of success fees in RTA claims arising out of accidents which took place before October 5, 2003 and which were therefore not covered by Pt 45 Sect.III. The court held: **7A–58**

> "49. ... In our judgment the guidance given by this court in *Callery v Gray* [see para.7A–62 below] can be applied by analogy to this case even though it was allocated to the multi track and settled for a sum exceeding £15,000. We consider that there are no factors here which could legitimately have taken the success fee over 20 per cent ... The only significant risk related to the possibility of the claimant accepting her solicitor's advice and then not beating a payment in. This is just one of the rare risks which justified a success fee set as high as 20 per cent in the simplest of claims."

The court continued:

> "Because there seems to be some lingering uncertainty about the combined effect of *Callery v Gray* and *Halloran v Delaney* we feel we ought to restate, for the benefit of District Judges and Costs Judges, the principles in cases governed by the old regime ... The reasonableness of the success fee has to be assessed as at the time the CFA was agreed. It is permissible for any CFA to include a two stage success fee and this is to be encouraged. In other words the success fee may be a

***Paragraph numbers marked with a "+" can be found online and on CD.***

higher percentage (up to 100 per cent in an appropriate case) in the event that a claim does not settle within the protocol period and a lower success fee (down to 5 per cent in the very simplest of cases) in claims which do settle within that period. Further statistical evidence is now available ... to which it will be legitimate for parties to refer in relation to success fees agreed in an old regime case after the date of this judgment whether it is permissible on the assessment of costs for a Judge to have recourse to paragraph 11.8(2) of the [Costs] Practice Direction and to set a two stage success fee when no such fee was contained in the CFA is an issue that will be determined by this court [in due course]."

52. It is not permissible simply to adopt the new CPR fixed rates for success fees when assessing the reasonableness of a success fee in an RTA case where the assessment of the CFA is not governed by the new rules. The reason for this is that the new CPR approach (informed by an industry wide agreement) does not take into account the individual effects of each particular case ...".

*Atak v Lee* [2004] EWCA Civ. 1712.

The Court of Appeal, in carrying out a summary assessment of costs with a success fee, found it hard to understand how responsible counsel could have agreed with responsible solicitors a success fee of 100 per cent in respect of an appeal, or how responsible solicitors could have agreed with their client a success fee of 70 per cent. Success fees negotiated at that level discredited and devalued the whole of the arrangements for conditional fee agreements. In *Callery v Gray* the House of Lords had expressed great concern about the new regime where success fees were in effect being negotiated between parties to the agreement and there was no direct financial incentive to drive the level of the success fee down. The court found that there was a small amount of risk in the litigation which would properly have been provided for by a success fee of 15 per cent: *Begum v Klarit* [2005] EWCA Civ 210.

The High Court has held, on a costs appeal, that the failure anywhere within the CFA to specify what percentage of the success fee related to postponement was fatal to the claimant's success. A letter sent to the claimant's next friend with the CFA for signature could not amount to a waiver, but in any event it did not say in terms that the postponement element amounted to 0 per cent as the solicitors submitted was the case. The letter did not have the clarity needed to remedy the potential prejudice of the un-apportioned element of the success fee (*Utting v McBain* [2007] EWHC 3293 (QB) Blake J.).

The Court of Appeal has considered the extent to which, whether, in a case where the CFA does not provide for variable success fees, the court has power to direct that a success fee is recoverable at different rates for different periods of the proceedings, including detailed assessment of costs. The court found:

"47. ...Once it is clear...that a CFA may only carry one success fee and that the task of a Costs Judge is to determine whether that success fee was a reasonable one in the light of the matters that the legal representative knew or should have known when it was made, there is simply no room for a Costs Judge to substitute different percentage increases for different items of costs, or for different periods when costs were incurred. He could only do this with the benefit of hindsight which is prohibited, and the Rules and the Regulations give him no power to remake the parties' agreement. His powers of interference are limited to altering the success fee to a more reasonable one when he considers the size of the additional liability the paying party should bear. This is because there is nothing in the statute or the regulations to suggest that he is required to do anything other than carry out his usual function of deciding whether an item on a bill is reasonable, and if he decides it is not, of substituting a reasonable amount or deleting the item altogether."

...

"49. It follows...that the court has no power to direct that a success fee is recoverable at different rates for different periods of the proceedings. In so far as paragraph 11.8(2) of the Costs Practice Direction suggests otherwise, it is wrong." *U v Liverpool City Council* [2005] EWCA Civ 475.

The Court of Appeal has dealt with the level of success fee to be allowed in cases where the CFA is entered into after the defendant has admitted liability. In the particular case on detailed assessment the District Judge had allowed a success fee of 70 per cent (against 83 per cent claimed). On appeal to the Circuit Judge this was reduced to

50 per cent. On appeal to the Court of Appeal the paying party argued that a success fee of 20 per cent and not more than 30 per cent would be apprqpriate. The court identified the real difficulty in the case as being the risk that the solicitors might lose the right to recover part of their fees as a result of their client's failure to beat a Pt 36 offer which she had rejected on their advice. The court considered the question, whether it can ever be reasonable for solicitors to enter into CFA when first instructed in a case where liability has been admitted. It pointed out that the legislation does no more than render it lawful to enter into an agreement for litigation services which provides for fees to be paid only in specified circumstances. Those circumstances are not defined:

> "when it comes to the detailed assessment of costs the receiving party must normally be able to justify as reasonable any success fee he seeks to recover from the paying party. ... The Costs Judge cannot refuse to award a success fee simply on the grounds that the difficulty of assessing the risks made it unreasonable to enter into a CFA at all; but if the receiving party cannot show that the success fee has been calculated in a way which reasonably reflects the risks that have been assumed he will not be able to satisfy the Costs Judge that it is recoverable.
>
> Having said that, I should make it clear that there is nothing unreasonable in my view in entering into a simple CFA at a time when liability has been admitted provided that the parties make a proper assessment of the inevitably much reduced risk of failure."

Having reappraised the risks the court allowed a success fee of 20 per cent: *C v W* [2008] EWCA Civ 1459; [2009] 4 All E.R. 1129, CA.

In a clinical negligence case, the court was persuaded that the solicitors for the claimant were, at the outset, faced with difficulties and the case had uncertain prospects. The court held that the solicitors knew when the CFA was made that it was one which could easily have been assessed as having chances of success lower than 50 per cent. The solicitor is entitled to enter into a CFA at an early stage. It follows inevitably from that entitlement that the solicitor will be in a position of ignorance compared with that when he has medical records and expert advice. But, given that he is likely to be experienced in the field and to have some knowledge of the claim, his ignorance is relative. A 100 per cent success fee was allowed: *Oliver v Whipps Cross University Hospital NHS Trust and Waltham Forest Primary Care Trust* [2009] EWHC 110 (QB), Jack J.

Where the CFA did not specify how much of the percentage increase, if any, related to the cost to the representative of the postponement of the payment of his fees and expenses, Burton J. held that if the postponement element was nil, there was no need for this to be specified unless doubt existed as to the construction of the agreement. In which event it would be necessary for the court to consider the full construction of the CFA. On the facts of the case the judge was satisfied that the position about postponement had been made sufficiently clear in the documents and the appeal was allowed: *Sidhu v Sandhu & Sandhu* [2009] EWHC 983 (QB), Burton J.

### Collective Conditional Fee Agreements

The Regulations governing CFAs and those governing CCFAs establish two mutually exclusive sets of requirements. (The Regulations have been revoked with effect from November 1, 2005. See paras 7A-26, 7A-36 and 7A-44). An obvious reason why the Regulations governing CCFAs are less exacting than those governing CFAs is that CCFAs involve bulk users of legal services who are less vulnerable than lay clients. Often these users will be contracting to purchase, at their own expense, legal services to be provided to litigants. In those circumstances the litigants will not be exposed to significant risk of liability to pay for the legal services provided to them. Sections 58 and 58A of the Courts and Legal Services Act 1990 and the Regulations are intended to give effect to fundamental changes to the manner in which litigation is funded in thisjurisdiction. The requirements of the Regulations are designed to protect those who enter into CFAs, and are of no legitimate concern to defendants. Furthermore where legal services are provided to a litigant under a CCFA by a trade union or other body, there is normally little need for such protection. The manifest object of having a different regime for CCFAs from that applying to CFAs is to simplify the formalities of supplying legal services. In a case in which a union agreed with their solicitors that they should represent a claimant under a CCFA (which was accepted to be valid), the **7A–59** union had agreed with the authority of the claimant. Alternatively the claimant had ratified the agreement reached by the union on his behalf by availing himself of the services of the solicitors. On either footing the contract pursuant to which he came under a liability to pay the solicitors for their services was a CCFA. The court confirmed that the agreement was not subject to the CFA Regulations: *Thornley v Lang* [2003] EWCA Civ 1484.

The natural and ordinary meaning of reg.5(1) of the 2000 Regulations was that there had to be provision in a CCFA that complied with the specification set out, but the Regulation did not additionally require the performance of the prescribed condition, ie the preparation and retention of risk assessments. Clause 5 of the agreement was neither a condition for the enforcement of the CCFA nor a condition precedent to the formation of an individual contract of retainer (see *Kitchen v Burwell Reed & Kinghorn Ltd* [2005] EWHC 1771 (QB)). The clause was in fact a term whose breach would give rise to a right to damages and a right to terminate the contract if the result of the breach had a serious adverse impact on the party: *Various Claimants v Gower Chemicals Ltd*, February 28, 2007, unrep., Field J.

Where a collective conditional fee agreement provided for a success fee of 100 per cent on basic charges of £145 per hour if the case was won and discounted charges of £95 per hour if the action was lost, the defendant argued on appeal that this provided the successful claimant's solicitors with a success fee of 290 per cent and that accordingly the CCFA was unenforceable. The court found that it is possible to have a CFA which provides for a discounted fee in the event of failure, and a success fee in the event of success. The correct interpretation of s.58(2)(b) is:

> "a conditional fee agreement provides for a success fee if it [the CFA] provides for the amount of any fees to which it [the CFA] applies to be increased in specified circumstances above the amount which would be payable if it [the amount of fees to which the success fee is applied] were not payable only in specified circumstances."

The appeal was dismissed (*Gloucestershire CC v Evans* [2008] EWCA Civ 21).

## INSURANCE PREMIUMS

**7A–60** The development of CFAs has gone hand in hand with major developments in the insurance products being offered in respect of litigation. It is now possible for a person contemplating litigation to take out an insurance policy to cover, in the event that the case is lost, both the costs of the other party and his or own legal costs (including the solicitor's fees if they are not subject to a CFA). Some of these policies were developed to support the use of CFAs but others are used to meet lawyers' fees in the traditional way. Section 29 of the 1999 Act makes premiums paid for After the Event (ATE) insurance recoverable in costs.

### Recoverability of Insurance Premiums

**7A–61** Whilst it is Government policy that damages awarded to a successful party are not "unreasonably eroded" (*Hansard*, December 12, 2000: David Lock, Parliamentary Secretary to the Lord Chancellor's Department), by unrecovered success fees or insurance premiums; putting that intention into effect depends on test cases dealing with the recoverability and level of insurance premiums and the interpretation of ss.29 and 30 of the Access to Justice Act 1999.

It was not the intention of Parliament when it enacted s.29 of the 1999 Act to overload the recoverable premium by adding to the costs customarily embraced by such a premium, the costs which a company providing personal injury claims handling services (including a costs indemnity in the event that a claimant's compensation clam was dismissed or discontinued), had to incur if insurers were to accept the risk at all. It was therefore permissible for the judge to consider what was actually being provided for the payment in order to identify what should truly be treated as premium: *Re Claims Direct Test Cases* [2003] EWCA Civ 136; [2003] 4 All E.R. 508, CA.

The Costs Judge had been correct to "deconstruct" the sum of money payable for legal costs insurance by claimant clients of The Accident Group to establish how much of that money was properly to be regarded as recoverable premium within the meaning of s.29 of the 1999 Act. The fee paid to AIL (an associate company) was a referral fee. It had not been properly payable by the panel solicitors and had not therefore

***Paragraph numbers marked with a "+" can be found online and on CD.***

been chargeable to their clients and was certainly not recoverable from the paying party. The arrangement viewed objectively was that the fee had been compulsory for any solicitor wishing to be sent cases by TAG: *Sharratt v London Central Bus Co & Other Cases (No.2), The Accident Group Test Cases* [2004] EWCA Civ 575; [2004] 3 All E.R. 325, CA.

**Recoverability of Success Fees and Insurance Premiums**

The Court of Appeal has considered four main questions: 7A-62

(i) the time at which it is appropriate to enter into a CFA and take out an ATE policy;

(ii) the reasonableness of the success fee when a claim is quickly resolved without the need for court proceedings;

(iii) whether the claimants are entitled to recover an ATE premium where there has been no need to commence proceedings;

(iv) the reasonableness of ATE premiums.

After a hearing at which representatives of interested bodies were also allowed to make representations the court found:

(i) it is in principle permissible for a claimant to enter into a CFA with a success fee and to take out ATE insurance when he first consults his solicitor and before the solicitor writes a letter of claim and receives the prospective defendant's response;

(ii) in relation to modest and straightforward claims for compensation resulting from road traffic accidents where a CFA is agreed at the outset, 20 0s the maximum uplift that can reasonably be agreed in such a case;

(iii) ATE premiums are in principle recoverable as part of a claimant's costs even though his claim is quickly resolved without the need for proceedings;

(iv) The court requested a Costs Judge to investigate and report on the reasonableness of ATE premiums.

The court also considered that it is open to a solicitor and to a client to agree a two stage success fee at the outset of proceedings. It gave an example of an uplift agreed at 100 per cent subject to a reduction to a maximum of 5 per cent should the claim settle before the end of the period fixed by a pre-action protocol. Such an uplift would normally reflect the risks of the individual case. The court suggested that once the necessary data becomes available consideration will need to be given to the question whether the requirement to act reasonably mandates the agreement of a two stage success fee in a case where a CFA with a success fee is agreed at the outset: *Callery v Gray* [2001] EWCA Civ. 1117; [2001] 3 All E.R. 833, CA. See now Pt 45, s.III with regard to success fees in RTA cases occurring after 2003.

The Court of Appeal subsequently held that the words "insurance against the risk of incurring a costs liability" in s.29 of the Access to Justice Act 1999 mean "insurance against the risk of incurring a costs liability that cannot be passed on to the opposite party". In the particular case the small element of cover for "own costs insurance" could be regarded as falling within the description of insurance against the risk of liability within s.29 and the premium of £350 was held to be reasonable.

The circumstances in which and the terms upon which "own costs" cover would be reasonable in relation to other policies so that the whole premium could be recovered as costs would have to be determined by the courts when dealing with individual cases. Other issues mentioned in the Costs Judge's Report would fall to be judicially determined as and when they arose in individual cases. A copy of the Report was annexed to the Court of Appeal judgment with the warning that the views expressed might be helpful but were not definitive: *Callery v Gray (No.2)* [2001] EWCA Civ 1244; [2001] 4 All E.R. 1, CA.

The decision of the Court of Appeal in *Callery v Gray* was upheld by the House of Lords: [2002] UKHL 28; [2002] 1 W.L.R. 2000; [2002] 3 All E.R. 417, HL. The Court of Appeal has again considered the question of success fees in simple claims which settle without the need for court proceedings. The court stated:

> "...it is now time to reappraise the appropriate level of success fee which should be recoverable on these simple claims when they are settled without the need for court proceedings ... we consider that Judges concerned with questions relating to the recoverability of a success fee in claims as simple as this which are settled

without the need to commence proceedings should now ordinarily decide to allow an uplift of 5% on the claimant's lawyers costs (including the costs of any costs only proceedings which are awarded to them) pursuant to their powers contained in CPD 11.8(2) unless persuaded that a higher uplift is appropriate in the particular circumstances of the case. This policy should be adopted in relation to all CFAs however they are structured which are entered into on and after 1 August 2001 when both Callery judgments had been published and the main uncertainties about costs recovery had been removed."

*Halloran v Delaney* [2002] EWCA Civ 1258.

The Court of Appeal in *Callery v Gray* (above) had been dealing with a case which involved success fees in simple claims. The court upheld the allowance of a success fee of 87 per cent in a claim by the widow of the original claimant in a mesothelioma case, in which the damages awarded were £185,000. The Court of Appeal held that advising on quantum was not straightforward, particularly in the instant case where there had been several factors affecting the final award. Whilst liability issues and quantum issues could be considered separately, ultimately a single success fee was to be arrived at on an assessment of the prospect of winning: *Smiths Dock Ltd v Edwards* [2004] EWHC 1116, (QBD) Crane J.

The Court of Appeal subsequently (in *Claims Direct Test Cases* [2003] EWCA Civ 136; [2003] 4 All E.R. 508 CA) explained that *Halloran* had been an extremely simple road traffic accident claim which was swiftly settled with a minimum of fuss and bother. The type of case to which the court was referring in *Halloran v Delaney* was a case similar to that in *Callery v Gray* and *Halloran v Delaney* in which the prospects of success are virtually 100 per cent. The two step fee advocated by the court in *Callery* is apt to allow a solicitor in such a case to cater for the wholly unexpected risk lurking below the limpid waters of the simplest of claims. It did not require any research evidence or submissions from other parties in the industry to persuade the court that in this type of extremely simple claim a success fee of over 5 per cent was no longer tenable in all the circumstances. The guidance given in the Halloran judgment was not intended to have any wider application. In the *Claims Direct Test Cases* (see above) the Court of Appeal held that, where a premium for litigation protection insurance includes sums other than for the underwriters' "risk for liability for the Claimant's" costs, those sums may not be recovered under a costs order. It was not the intention of Parliament, when enacting s.29, to overload the recoverable premium by adding to the costs customarily embraced by a premium, the costs which a company had to incur if underwriters were to accept the risk at all.

### Staged ATE insurance premiums

7A–63 The Court of Appeal dealt with the question of staged ATE premiums in a modest personal injury claim: *Rogers v Merthyr Tydfil County BC* [2006] EWCA Civ 1134; [2007] 1 W.L.R. 808; [2006] All E.R. 354, CA. It was the first time that the court had considered authoritatively the question of ATE premiums since *Callery v Gray (No.1)* [2001] EWCA Civ 1117; [2001] 1 W.L.R. 2113 and *Callery v Gray (No.2)* [2001] EWCA Civ 1246; [2001] 1 W.L.R. 2142. The main issues for decision in Rogers were:

"(i) What is the proper approach to proportionality in small personal injury cases where the ATE premium may appear large in comparison with the amount of the damages reasonably claimed?

(ii) What is the proper approach to evidence of reasonableness of the choice and of the amount of the ATE premium in such cases?

(iii) Are both stages (or stepped) premiums and single premiums for ATE insurance legitimate for the purposes of the recoverability of an ATE premium by a successful claimant, and is it reasonable that such premiums should be wholly or partially block rated?"

A subsidiary issue arose as to whether it was permissible for a recoverable premium to contain an element for the cost of self insuring the premium in the event of failure or only partial success. The court held that an affirmative answer to this question had already been given in *Callery v Gray (No.2)*. Having noted that an ATE premium may buy certain benefits not directly linked with the financial risk faced by the client who takes out an ATE policy the court held that it did not have sufficient material to deal with this issue fully on the instant appeal:

"119. ... Whether that element of the premium, if identifiable, should properly

***Paragraph numbers marked with a "+" can be found online and on CD.***

be chargeable to the unsuccessful defendant must await the outcome of a wider inquiry than has been possible to carry out within the four corners of the present appeal."

The appeal concerned a DAS 80e policy in respect of a claim for damages to a child which were eventually agreed in the sum of £3,105. The issue of liability was decided at trial and the costs were summarily assessed at £16,821 including the ATE premium of £4,860 plus IPT and a 100 per cent success fee.

The ATE policy had a three stage premium, £450 being payable at the outset, a further £900 when proceedings were issued and a further £3,510, 60 days before the trial. In subsequent policies the 60 day period has been reduced to 14 days or 21 days before trial depending on whether the claim is on the fast track or the multi track, in order to match up with provisions of Part 45.

On appeal to the Circuit Judge, it was held that the staged premium was excessive, given that other companies in the market appeared to be charging less than £1,800 for the whole proceedings. The recoverable premium was reduced to £900, a figure said to be in the middle of the range of policies quoted in the magazine Litigation Funding.

Because this was the first occasion on which the Court of Appeal had had the opportunity to consider ATE premiums since *Callery v Gray*, a number of interested parties, including ATE insurers and liability insurers, were invited to intervene. The court requested the Senior Costs Judge to investigate the submissions of the various interested parties and to report. In the time available it was only possible for the Senior Costs Judge to take evidence from the parties to the appeal, in order to prepare a report of the factual basis of the appeal upon which the Court of Appeal could proceed. The court also had before it submissions from the interveners and the Liability Insurers Group.

The court dealt first with proportionality (paragraphs 102 ff) stating in particular:

"105. ... If the court concludes that it was necessary to incur the staged premium, then as this court's judgment in Lownds shows, it should be adjudged a proportionate expense. Necessity here is, we think, not some absolute litmus test. It may be demonstrated by the application of strategic considerations which travel beyond the dictates of the particular case. Thus it may include, as we are persuaded it does, the unavoidable characteristics of the market in insurance of this kind. It does so because this very market is integral to the means of providing access to justice in civil disputes in what may be called the post-legal aid world.

106. It is important to recognise that this conclusion runs with, not across, the grain of the procedural reforms expressed in the CPR. The very recognition that justice requires a use of resources that is proportionate to what is at stake implies the rightness of a strategic approach. There can be no touchstone of a proportionate use of resources so understood, without an eye to the context in which any such resources are expended. Once it is concluded that the ATE staged premium here was necessarily incurred, principle and pragmatism together compel the conclusion that it was a proportionate expense ..........."

None of the parties suggested that a staged premium model was in itself an illegitimate way of rating the risk. Having considered the figures put before it, the court found that it was quite impossible to say that a total premium of £4,860 was unreasonable in all the circumstances. Indeed it was not fixed at a sufficiently high level to reflect the risk and to provide a contribution to the insurer's reasonable overheads and profit (para.110). The court went on to endorse what the Senior Costs Judge said about the material contained in Litigation Funding in *Re RSA Pursuit Test Cases* [2005] EWHC 9003 (Costs) (at para.235):

"235. As to the information contained in Litigation Funding and The Judge website, this is no more than an indication of policies which might be available in certain circumstances. ...the premiums on his website are 'indicative only' and the website contains further warnings. Litigation Funding has similar warnings and reservations. I can derive no firm data from these sources."

The court concluded that it is not legitimate to compare the total premium payable at the third stage of a three stage premium model, with the single premium under a single premium model that is payable throughout the progress of a claim to trial (paragraph 111). The court found that the solicitor had acted reasonably in selecting the particular product.

In respect of procedure to be followed in the future the court stated:

"116. During the course of argument it was accepted on all sides that a party who has an ATE insurance policy incorporating two or more staged premiums should inform its opponent that the policy is staged, and should set out accurately the trigger moments at which the second or later stages will be reached. This obligation should be undertaken in addition to the obligations set out in CPR 44.15(1) and in paras 19.1(1) and 19.4 of the Costs Practice Direction. If this is done, the opponent has been given fair notice of the staging, and unless there are features of the case that are out of the ordinary, his liability to pay at the second or third stage a higher premium than he would have had to pay if the claim had been settled at the first stage should not prove to be a contentious issue.

*Evidence justifying the ATE premium claimed*

117. If an issue arises about the size of a second or third stage premium, it will ordinarily be sufficient for a claimant's solicitor to write a brief note for the purposes of the costs assessment explaining how he came to choose the particular ATE product for his client, and the basis on which the premium is rated – whether block rated or individually rated. District judges and costs judges do not, as Lord Hoffmann observed in *Callery v Gray (Nos 1 and 2)* [2002] UKHL 28 at [44]; [2002] 1 WLR 2000, have the expertise to judge the reasonableness of a premium except in very broad brush terms, and the viability of the ATE market will be imperilled if they regard themselves (without the assistance of expert evidence) as better qualified than the underwriter to rate the financial risk the insurer faces. Although the claimant very often does not have to pay the premium himself, this does not mean that there are no competitive or other pressures at all in the market. As the evidence before this court shows, it is not in an insurer's interest to fix a premium at a level which will attract frequent challenges."

The appeal was accordingly allowed. Annexed to the judgment is an addendum by Janet Smith L.J. (paras 123 to 130) in which she expressed the view that the lack of rigour with which cases are reviewed by solicitors and insurers throughout their life is resulting in the system being more expensive (eventually to the premium paying public) than it should be.

### Before the event insurance

7A-64 The Court of Appeal, dealing with a simple road traffic accident in which a passenger was injured stated:

"45. In our judgment proper modern practice dictates that a solicitor should normally invite a client to bring to the first interview any relevant motor insurance policy, any household insurance policy and any stand alone BTE insurance policy belonging to the client and/or any spouse or partner living in same household of the client ..."

The court went on to say that if the motor accident claim is likely to be less than about £5,000 and there are no features of the cover which make it inappropriate, the solicitor should refer the client to the BTE insurer without further ado. The solicitor is not obliged to embark on a treasure hunt in case by chance an insurance policy belonging to a member of the client's family contains relevant BTE cover. The availability of ATE cover at a modest premium will inevitably restrict the extent to which it will be reasonable for a solicitor's time to be used in investigating alternative sources of insurance. On the facts of the case the Court of Appeal allowed the claimant to recover the ATE premium on the ground that the BTE policy did not provide him with appropriate cover in the circumstances of the case. Representation arranged by the insurer of the defendant to which the claimant had never been a party, and of which he had no knowledge at the time it was entered into and where the opposing insurer through its chosen representative reserved to itself the full conduct and control of the claim was not a reasonable alternative to representation by a lawyer of the claimant's own choice backed by an ATE policy (paragraphs 52 to 58). The position might be different if BTE insurers finance some transparently independent organisation to handle such claims and made it clear in the policy that this was what they were doing. The overriding principle is that the claimant assisted by his/her solicitor should act in a manner which is reasonable (paragraph 50): *Sarwar v Alam* [2001] EWCA Civ 1401; [2001] 4 All E.R. 541. See also para.7A–71 below.

**Clinical negligence**

In a straightforward case in which a dental patient swallowed a reamer but suffered no injury other than shock and upset and in which the claim settled quickly without proceedings having been commenced the success fee claimed at 50 per cent was allowed at 20 per cent: *Bensusan v Freedman* September 20, 2001, Senior Costs Judge. **7A–65**

The Court of Appeal in *Halloran v Delaney* [2002] EWCA Civ 1258 agreed with the comment of the Senior Costs Judge in relation to paragraphs 11.7 and 17.8(2) of the Costs Practice Direction: "The combined effect of these two paragraphs is to prevent the costs officer from using hindsight in arriving at the appropriate success fee and to prevent excessive claims for success fees in cases which settle without the need for proceedings when it was clear, or ought to have been clear from the outset, that the risk of having to commence proceedings was minimal."

**How long does the ATE policy remain in force?**

17. In deciding that the policy remained in force until the conclusion of costs only proceedings Master Hurst was influenced by the language of the Law Society model CFA which was also used in that case. This agreement expressly covered the claim and it also covered any proceedings taken to enforce a judgment, order or agreement ... in these circumstances Master Hurst accepted ... an argument by counsel for the claimant in these terms: **7A–66**

> "[counsel for the claimant], in support of his argument that costs only proceedings precede the conclusion [of the case], relies upon the duration of the conditional fee agreement which he submits covers enforcement proceedings. The assessment of costs is not an enforcement proceeding but, until costs are assessed, the agreement to pay costs cannot be enforced. By commencing costs only proceedings the claimant will obtain a detailed assessment of her costs which will result in a final certificate and that certificate will be enforceable in the same way as any other judgment for a civil debt."

18. Master Hurst went on to say: "...that, taken together, the insurance policy and the CFA made it clear that the insurance cover extended to all necessary steps in relation to resolving the claimant's claim, including her claim to be paid her reasonable costs. He therefore found that the ATE insurance policy was still in force, the case not yet having concluded. The case would be concluded when the costs were finally assessed.

19. We accept Master Hurst's conclusion and the reasons he gave". *Halloran v Delaney* [2002] EWCA Civ 1258 referring to *Tilby v Perfect Pizza Ltd* February 28, 2002, unrep.

**Enforceability of CFAs**

The provision in s.58 of the Courts and Legal Services Act 1990, that any conditional fee agreement which did not satisfy all of the conditions applicable to it should be unenforceable, led to paying parties taking every possible point on detailed assessment in an effort to demonstrate that the underlying CFA was unenforceable and that therefore by operation of the indemnity principle, no costs should be payable. Against this background six appeals came before the Court of Appeal (see *Hollins v Russell* below), and at the same time the Lord Chancellor introduced amendments to the Conditional Fee Agreement Regulations, making it possible for legal representatives to enter into conditional fee agreements with their clients under which the client is liable to pay the legal representatives fees and expenses, only to the extent that sums are recovered in respect of the relevant proceedings, whether by way of costs or otherwise. In respect of such agreements Regulations 2, 3 and 4 of the CFA Regulations are disapplied. Corresponding amendments were made to CPR r.43.2, similar provisions were inserted into the Collective Conditional Fee Agreements Regulations 2000 and s.31 of the Access to Justice Act 1999 amending s.51 of the Senior Courts Act 1981 was brought into force. **7A–67**

In *Hollins v Russell* (and five other appeals) [2003] EWCA Civ 718; [2003] 1 W.L.R. 2487 CA, *sub nom.Sharratt v London Central Bus Co Ltd* [2003] 4 All E.R. 590, CA the Court of Appeal dealt with a number of issues:

(i) The circumstances in which the court should put a receiving party in detailed assessment proceedings to its election so that it must choose whether to disclose its CFA to the paying party or to prove its claim by other means.

(ii) The proper construction of the words "satisfies all of the conditions applicable to it" in s.58(1) of the 1990 Act and whether any costs or disbursements are recoverable from a paying party in the event of non compliance with the CFA Regulations.

(iii) Whether on the particular facts the requirements contained in one or other of regs 2, 3 and 4 of the CFA Regulations were not complied with.

**7A-68** *Disclosure*—The court referred to the decision in *Bailey v IBC Vehichles Ltd* [1998] 3 All E.R. 570, CA stating (at paragraph 68):

"In our judgment the solicitor's certificate as to accuracy, important though it is, may not be sufficient, where the quality and quantity of the information served on the paying party about the success fee is less than would be made available in respect of the other aspects of the bill in the case on an assessment where there is no additional liability claimed."

The court declined to extend the decision in Bailey beyond the facts with which it was dealing, continuing (at 71):

> "... where there is a CFA a Costs Judge should normally exercise his discretion under the Costs Practice Direction and the Pamplin procedure [*Pamlin v Express Newspapers Ltd* [1985] 1 W.L.R. 689] so as to require the receiving parties (subject to their right of election preserved by paragraph 40.14 of the Costs Practice Direction and the Goldman case [*Goldman v Hesper* [1988] 1 W.L.R. 1238]) to produce a copy of their CFAs to the paying parties in order that they can see whether or not the Regulations were complied with and (where a CFA provides for a success fee) whether the liability of the receiving party to pay that success fee is indeed enforceable.
>
> * * * *
>
> 72. If the CFA contains confidential information which is not required to be disclosed for the purposes of fairly determining the receiving party's claim to costs ... the Costs Judge may permit that material to be redacted before service."

The court declined to decide whether or not a CFA is of itself privileged. The court approved Pumfrey J. in *South Coast Shipping Co Ltd v Havant BC* [2002] 3 All E.R. 779 when he found that there was no incompatibility of the European Convention on Human Rights.

*Satisfying the conditions in Section 58*

**7A-69** Under this head, having rehearsed the arguments, the court stated (paragraph 107):

> "The key question therefore is whether the conditions applicable to the CFA by virtue of section 58 of the 1990 Act have been sufficiently complied with in the light of their purposes. Costs Judges should accordingly ask themselves the following question: "Has the particular departure from a Regulation pursuant to section 58(3)(c) of the 1990 Act or a requirement in Section 58, either on its own or in conjunction with any other such departure in this case, had a materially adverse effect either upon the protection afforded to the client or upon the proper administration of justice?" If the answer is "yes" the conditions have not been satisfied. If the answer is "no" then the departure is immaterial and (assuming that there is no other reason to conclude otherwise) the conditions have been satisfied.
>
> 108. We would not draw any formal distinction between the conditions contained in the section itself and those contained in the Regulations. The meaning of "satisfies" must be the same in each case. However, it is more difficult to envisage questions of degree coming into the question whether the conditions in the section have been sufficiently met. Either the CFA relates to permissible proceedings or it does not. But one example might be that in section 58(4)(b), which requires that a CFA providing for a success fee "must state the percentage by which the amount of the fees which would be payable if it were not a conditional fee agreement is to be increased". Was that condition sufficiently met by agreement ... which left blank the percentage in the clause where it should have been filled in but stated it clearly in the risk assessment ...? The answer to that question is obviously "yes".
>
> 109. ... Sufficiency or materiality will depend upon the circumstances of each

***Paragraph numbers marked with a "+" can be found online and on CD.***

case. This is not to encourage paying parties to trawl through the facts of each case in order to try to discover a material breach. Quite the reverse. At the stage when the agreement has been made, acted upon, and success for the client has been achieved, it is most unlikely that any minor shortcoming which the paying party might discover in the agreement or the procedures leading up to its making will amount to a material breach of the requirements or mean that the applicable conditions have not been sufficiently met." —The court dealt with two other points under the heading of compliance which they felt could be of considerable importance in practice. First the recoverability of the ATE premium: "114. ...ATE insurance premiums are recoverable as costs in any proceedings, irrespective of whether or not there is a CFA between the receiving party and her legal representatives. The clients liability to pay the insurance premium arises from the contract of insurance, not from her contract with the legal representative. It arises whether or not there is a CFA and whether or not the CFA is enforceable. ... It would appear therefore that there is no bar to the recovery of the ATE insurance premium as costs whatever may be the bar to the recovery of the lawyers charges and success fee."

The second point which the court dealt with related to disbursements which the client has in fact paid to the solicitor either personally or by taking out a loan to do so:

> "115. ... The solicitor is required to retain this money on client's account until it is expended in accordance with the client's instructions. If the CFA fails, and the money has not been paid out, the solicitor would be required to pay it back to the client. If the money has been paid out, then this is money actually paid by the client. ... This should be recoverable by the client as costs. The costs claim is that of the client not of the solicitor. If the client has actually paid a debt to a third party, properly incurred in the conduct of the litigation, there seems no reason why this should not be recoverable from the paying party, insofar as it is reasonable and proportionate ... This is irrespective of whether the solicitor can enforce the CFA for this charges and success fee."

*Particular allegations of breach* —Dealing with reg.2(i)(d) the court stated (at para.118): **7A–70**

> "No difficulty will arise under regulation 2(i)(d) for solicitors who use the Law Society's model CFA which came into use in July 2000 ..."

On the facts of the particular appeals the court took the view that the effect of the CFA, read as a whole, was sufficiently clear and that the failure to specify the position accurately did not affect the protection given to the client or the administration of justice to any material degree. The result would have been different if the CFA was less clear as to its effect, that is, if it would not have been reasonably comprehensible to the lay person.

In respect of reg.3(1)(b), the point had been taken that the CFA did not specify how much of the percentage increase related to the cost to the legal representative of the postponement of the payment of fees and expenses. The court found this submission unattractive and unmeritorious. The court found that the language of Clause 32 of the CFA made the position clear. The reality being that despite what was said in the risk assessment calculation none of the recoverable success fee was attributable to the postponement in payment of the solicitor's fees. The court found that taken together Clause 32 and 33 prevailed over the risk assessment schedule and thus, on its true construction, the CFA complied with the regulations.

Under reg.4(2)(c), the paying parties argued that there was a breach because the client had not been informed that the risk of incurring a liability for costs in respect of proceedings to which the agreement related was insured against under an existing contract of insurance. The court found that attendance notes dealing with this issue should not ordinarily be disclosed. The court found that it was sufficient to satisfy s.58 that the solicitor had discussed the matter with the client and had formed a view on the funding options. The court pointed out that the recovery of the insurance premium is an entirely separate matter from the enforceability of the CFA.

The argument under reg.4(2)(e)(ii) was as to the meaning of "whether" and "whether or not". The court held (at 144):

> "... In this context there is no reason to construe 'whether' as meaning anything

***Paragraph numbers marked with a "+" can be found online and on CD.***

> other than 'if'. The language of the regulation ... mirrored the language of the Government's February 2000 paper ... The mischief which this regulation was introduced to remedy was the risk that the client's legal representative might induce the client to enter into insurance arrangements in which he had an interest. If he had no interest, then there was no identified mischief ..."

regulation 4(5) requires the legal representative to explain the effect of the CFA in writing to the client before she enters into it and in addition to explain it orally. In the particular case the client had received an oral explanation and a copy of the CFA, which itself had attached to it an explanation of its clauses. The court stated:

> "153. All these cases turn on their own facts. The regulatory intention is that the client should not be left in ... confusion ... If these documents had been in small print and as far removed from winning a prize for plain English as many documents of their type, then it is obvious that regulation 4(5) would have been breached ...
>
> 154. We therefore agree with the approach adopted by the Judge and also with his preference for a free standing explanatory letter, which may of course cross refer to any part of the Law Society conditions which sets out the effect of the CFA with clarity."

In the TAG Test Cases, the issue was whether the reg.4 information was given to the claimants by someone who qualified as "the legal representative" for the purposes of that regulation. The court, having extensively reviewed the argument, felt that it was not driven to the conclusion that the person who actually gave the reg.4 advice must inevitably be someone who was himself qualified to conduct litigation services. Parliament had not made this requirement and, in the context of the liberalising effect of Pt 2 of the 1990 Act, it would be wrong for the court to do so. The question therefore arose: if a wider degree of delegation is legally possible can a solicitor lawfully delegate his responsibility to an organisation like TAG, and can TAG sub-delegate it to one of their representatives? The court concluded (at 216):

> "...For the purposes [of this appeal] it is sufficient if we make it clear that it will be in theory permissible for a solicitors firm to delegate the performance of his regulation 4 duties to an organisation like TAG, and for TAG to sub-delegate to it representatives, provided that in so doing the solicitor is not abandoning the supervisory responsibilities required of him by Practice Rule 3.07 and the Guide to Professional Conduct. Whether the TAG scheme can and does provide properly for this is a matter for the fact finding trial.
>
> 217. Part 2 of the 1990 Act is concerned with the search for new or better ways of providing litigation services. A national organisation like TAG may be able to achieve economies of scale and standards of client service which simply are not available to an ordinary solicitor's firm. Quality control, however, is all important, and if a solicitor abjurs his duty to maintain supervisory responsibility, through an established framework for reporting and accountability, over the TAG representatives when they visit his client's home on his behalf, it is likely that it would be found that it was not he who gave the information he was required by regulation 4 to give and that the regulation has therefore been broken."

The court concluded by saying:

> "226. In future District Judges and Costs Judges must be equally astute to prevent satellite litigation about costs from being protracted by allegations about breaches of the CFA regulations where the breaches do not matter. They should remember that the law does not care about very little things, and that they should only declare a CFA unenforceable if the breach does matter and if the client could have relied on it successfully against his solicitor."

*Hollins v Russell* and other appeals [2003] EWCA Civ 718[2003] 1 W.L.R. 2487 CA *sub nom.Sharratt v London Central Bus Co Ltd* [2003] 4 All E.R. 590 CA.

See also *Myler & Mirror Group Newspapers v Williams* [2003] EWHC 1387 (QB), Crane J.

Where a CFA made no mention of the fee deferral element in its schedule, although the body of the agreement stated that this was set out in the schedule, the solicitors argued that s.58(1) of the Courts and Legal Services Act 1990 should be interpreted by inserting words such as "to the extent that it does not satisfy all requirements" so that the court could assess the effect of a particular breach. If the consequences were comparatively trivial this would penalise the solicitor far less than rendering the whole agreement unenforceable. The Court of Appeal rejected that argument pointing out that in *Hollins v Russell* the court had found: "there is no graduated response to different types of breach: it is all or nothing." The words "shall be unenforceable" mean what they say. The court held that Parliament had decided that unless a CFA satisfied all the conditions applicable to it, by virtue of s.58(1), it would not be exempt from the general rules as to the unenforceability of CFAs at common law: *Spencer v Wood (t/a Gordon's Tyres)* [2004] EWCA Civ 352.

A CFA with a contingent uplift as a success fee was held to be enforceable as the fact that an agreement was a conditional fee agreement under the Courts and Legal Services Act 1990 was sufficient to render it enforceable regardless of how the success fee was calculated: *Benaim (UK) Ltd v Davies Middleton & Davies Ltd* [2004] EWHC 737 (TCC) HHJ Rich Q.C..

**Subsequent Decisions**

A CCFA which stipulated a success fee of 120 per cent complied with s.58(4)(b) of the Courts and Legal Services Act 1990 in that it stated the percentage increase but was in breach of s.58(4)(c) in that the percentage exceeded the maximum specified increase, namely 100 per cent. The court held: **7A–71**

"35. A statement of 120% success fee is a stark departure from the 100% maximum specified in paragraph 4 of the Conditional Fee Agreements Order 2000. That maximum is plainly central to the regime on which terms the legislature has accepted the legality of CFAs. It being disregarded, even if in the result it could be shown that no-one would be the loser, is inimical to the administration of justice, ...

36. If we were to treat this violation as marginal, we should, in my judgment, be acting flat against the grain of the legislature's substantial policy objectives attained by section 58(1): that is to confine within the strict levels, specified by rule, the acceptability of costs arrangements of this kind."

per Laws L.J. in *Jones v Caradon Catnic Ltd* [2005] EWCA Civ 1821.

There is a distinction between total non compliance with a particular statutory provision in a CFA which is always fatal, and a partial non-compliance, which is capable of being insubstantial enough to permit the agreement to survive. The reasons for the percentage uplift under reg.3(2)(a) are obviously material to a consideration by a Costs Judge as to whether that uplift is reasonable. Accordingly that provision furthers the administration of justice, absence of such a provision in the CFA is material and substantial for the purpose of the Hollins test. Section 58(3)(a) of the 1990 Act requires that a CFA be in writing and signed by both parties. The omission of the client's signature from a letter agreed to form part of the agreement was fatal to its enforceability (*Fenton v Holmes* [2007] EWHC 2476 (Ch); [2008] 2 Costs L.R. 238 Mann J.).

The Court of Appeal has dealt with the requirement under reg.4(2)(e)(ii) of the CFA Regulations 2000 for the legal representative to inform the client if he considers that a contract of insurance is appropriate or recommends a particular such contract whether he has an interest in doing so. The court also considered the requirement in reg.4(2)(c) relating to the existence of before the event (BTE) insurance. Two appeals were heard together: *Garrett v Halton BC and Myatt v National Coal Board* [2006] EWCA Civ 1017; [2007] 1 W.L.R. 554; [2007] 1 All E.R. 147, CA. The court dealt first with the meaning of para.107 of the judgment in *Hollins v Russell* [2004] EWCA Civ 718; [2003] 1 W.L.R. 2487. The principle question which arose was, whether the test of materiality referred to in para.107 requires the court to consider whether the client has suffered actual prejudice as a result of an alleged failure to satisfy the conditions referred to in s.58(3) of the 1990 Act, and whether the enforceability of the CFA is to be judged by reference to the circumstances existing at the time when it was entered into, or by reference to the circumstances known to exist at the time when the question arises for decision. The court carried out a detailed analysis (paras 10 to 45) of the judgment in *Hollins*, in which they decided that the question before them had not already been decided in *Hollins* (para.22). The court stated:

"30. ...[Parliament] must be taken to have deliberately decided not to distinguish between cases of non compliance which are innocent and those which are negligent or committed in bad faith, nor between those which cause prejudice (in the sense of actual loss) and those which do not. It would have been open to Par-

***Paragraph numbers marked with a "+" can be found online and on CD.***

liament to distinguish between such cases but it chose not to do so. The conditions stated in section 58(3)(c) and in particular the requirements prescribed in the Regulations are for the protection of solicitors' clients. Parliament considered that the need to safeguard the interests of clients was so important that it should be secured by providing that if any of the conditions were not satisfied, the CFA would not be enforceable and the solicitor would not be paid ...

32. ...In our view it is fallacious to say that a breach is trivial or not material because it does not in fact cause loss to the client in the particular case. The scheme has the wider purpose of providing for client protection (as well as the proper administration of justice).

37. ...On the face of it the statutory scheme is straightforward. It provides that if a solicitor fails to comply with the obligation to inform the client of any of the matters set out in regulation 4(2), the CFA will be unenforceable. That is clear and stark. At first sight there is no room here for any consideration of the actual consequences of the failure to comply. To adopt language appropriate to a breach of contract, the statutory language refers only to breach, and not the causation or loss. Subject to the principle that the law is not concerned with very small things, a breach of contract is a breach even if it causes no loss.

39. ...In some cases, it may be helpful to have regard to what actually happened, because that may shed light on the potential consequences of a breach (if the matter is judged at the date of the CFA) and therefore on the extent to which the breach had a material adverse effect on the protection afforded to the client. In our view, however, in most cases the court should focus its attention principally on the terms of the CFA, and the advice and information given by the solicitor and other relevant circumstances, which existed at the date of the CFA, and make a judgment as to whether, in the light of that material, the departure from the requirement in question had a material adverse effect on the protection afforded to the client."

The court then referred to the decision in *Jones v Caradon Catnic Ltd* above which supported the view that the court was expressing. In relation to before the event insurance the court stated:

"45. At first sight it might seem odd that the fact that the client does not have BTE should not be taken into account. But once the relevance of that fact is understood, it becomes clear that [counsel for the claimant] wishes to rely on it for no other reason than that it shows that the breach has caused no loss to the client. It is not relied on as shedding any light on the gravity of the breach (which might be the result of a momentary lapse or a deliberate act taken to further the commercial interests of the solicitor). We have already explained why in our view the materiality of a breach is not judged by its consequences. For these reasons the fact that a client had no relevant BTE when a solicitor infringes regulation 4(2)(c) is irrelevant to the materiality of the breach."

With regard to the question of BTE insurance in Myatt the court found on the facts that the solicitors had asked the wrong question. They should not have asked the claimants to decide whether they had BTE insurance which would cover their risk as to costs in respect of their claims. Hence, since they asked the wrong question, they did not take reasonable steps to ascertain the true insurance position so as to enable them to inform their clients whether they considered that the risk was already insured. Although none of the four claimants had BTE insurance which would cover his claim, for the reasons already explained, the court held that there was a material breach of reg.4(2)(c).

The court went on to give guidance as to the steps that a solicitor should reasonably take to discharge his obligations under reg.4(2)(c):

"71. ... A number of factors are relevant. What follows is not intended to be an exhaustive list. We emphasise that what is reasonably required of a solicitor depends on all the circumstances of the case.

72. First, the nature of the client. If the client is evidently intelligent and has a real knowledge and understanding of insurance matters, it may be reasonable for the solicitor to ask him not only (i) whether he has credit cards, motor insurance or household insurance or is a member of a trade union, (ii) whether he has legal expenses insurance, but also (iii) the ultimate question of whether the legal expenses policy covers the proposed claim and, if so, whether it does so to a suf-

***Paragraph numbers marked with a "+" can be found online and on CD.***

ficient extent. Litigants such as the Myatt claimants and Ms Garrett plainly do not fall into this category: few litigants will. If the solicitor does ask such questions, he will have to form a view as to whether the client's answers to the questions can reasonably be relied upon.

73. Secondly, the circumstances in which the solicitor is instructed may be relevant to the nature of the enquiries that it is reasonable to expect the solicitor to undertake in order to establish the BTE position. A good example of the application of this factor is to be found in *Pratt v Bull*, which was one of the five cases that was heard together with *Hollins v Russell*. In that case, the 80 year old claimant was injured in a road accident. A solicitor visited her while she was in hospital and a CFA was made. At the assessment of her costs, it was argued on behalf of the defendant that the possibility of legal expenses insurance under her home insurance policy had not been fully explored. At para 138, the court said that there were limits to what can reasonably be expected of the interchange between solicitor and client in such circumstances: "It would be ridiculous to expect a solicitor dealing with a seriously ill old woman in hospital to delay making a CFA while her home insurance policy was found and checked." It was sufficient that the solicitor had discussed it with her and formed a view on the funding options.

74. Thirdly, the nature of the claim may be relevant. If the claim is one in respect of which it is unlikely that standard insurance policies would provide legal expenses cover, this may be a further reason why it may be reasonable for the solicitor to take fewer steps to ascertain the position than might otherwise be the case.

75. Fourthly, the cost of the ATE premium may be a relevant factor. This is the point made at para 50 of *Sarwar*. In our judgment, it is as relevant to a question of breach of regulation 4(2)(c) as to a question of the reasonableness of the premium for the purposes of an assessment of costs pursuant to CPR 44.4.

76. Fifthly, if the claim has been referred to solicitors who are on a panel, it may be relevant that the referring body has already investigated the question of the availability of BTE. Whether it is reasonable to rely on any conclusion already reached will be a matter on which the panel solicitor must exercise his own judgment.

77. It follows from the calibrated approach that we have suggested at paras 72–76 above that we do not consider that it is possible to give rigid guidance as to the questions a solicitor should ask in every case. In particular, in our judgment a solicitor is not required in every case to ask the client who says that he has a home, credit card or motor insurance or is a member of a trade union to send him the policy or trade union membership document (the first of the three approaches suggested by Mr McCue: see para.56 above). In some circumstances, it is reasonable for the solicitor to ask the further question whether the insurance covers legal expenses and to rely on the answer given by the client without further ado. In yet other cases, it is even reasonable to ask the client to answer what we have called the ultimate question.

78. We acknowledge that to require the solicitor to ask the client to send the policies in all cases has the merit of certainty and would minimise the risk of satellite litigation. In *Adair v Cullen*, Judge Holman said that the *Sarwar* approach should be adopted to breach of regulation cases and that it 'suggests a question along the lines of "Do you have motor insurance" and if the answer is "Yes", the next question is "can I see the policy document please?"' In some cases, such an approach is reasonable and necessary to enable the solicitor to discharge his regulation 4(2)(c) duty. But for the reasons that we have given, we do not accept that it is required in all cases.

79. What we have said in paras 71–78 should not be interpreted as giving encouragement to defendants to embark on fishing expeditions in the hope that, if they ask a sufficient number of questions, they may be able to show that the claimant's solicitor did not discharge his regulation 4(2)(c) duty. We refer to the salutary words of this court in *Hollins v Russell* at para 81 that the court should not require further disclosure unless there is a genuine issue as to whether there has been compliance with regulation 4."

In the case of *Garrett* the solicitors were panel members of a claims management company and had a financial interest in recommending a particular insurance contract to the claimant. The solicitors informed the client that they were panel members but stated that they did not have an interest in recommending the particular insurance agreement. The court found that there was a close relationship between the solicitors and the claims manager and that the indirect financial interest in maintaining a flow of work through the membership of a panel of solicitors was greater than the direct financial interest in commissions paid for insurance premiums. The advice to use the particular insurance product came in a CFA that the claims manager had supplied to its panel solicitors and which bore its livery. The court continued:

> "99. The statement that Websters had no interest in the insurance premium 'although we are on the AA panel' did not disclose to Ms Garrett that Websters had a financial interest in remaining on the panel which would be lost if she did not accept their recommendation that she enter into an ATE with NIG. She could not have known from what she was told that Websters were recommending the NIG policy because this was dictated by their financial interest.
>
> 101. ... In our judgment, by informing Ms Garrett that they were on the Ainsworth panel, the Websters representative did not disclose the real financial interest they had in recommending the NIG policy.
>
> 102. ... But even if clients rarely show any interest in these matters, that is not a good reason for not giving effect to the plain intention of Parliament."

**"Interest"**

**7A–71.1** The Court of Appeal further considered the question of "interest" and the duty to disclose it in *Tankard v John Fredricks Plastics Ltd* [2008] EWCA Civ 1375; [2009] 1 W.L.R. 1731; [2009] 4 All E.R. 526, CA. The court stated:

> "9. The meaning of 'interest', like the meaning of any other word or expression used in a statute or regulation depends upon the context in which it appears and thus upon the regulatory purpose of the regulations. The principal case in which this question had been considered is *Garrett* ... in which Dyson L.J. gave the judgment of the court.
>
> ...
>
> 13. . In the course of argument [in the *Tankard* case] Dyson L.J. suggested that a test along the following lines would be appropriate. For the purposes of Regulation 4, a solicitor has an interest if a reasonable person with knowledge of the relevant facts would think that the existence of the interest might affect the advice given by the solicitor to his client. We have considered the appropriate test in the light of the detailed submissions made to us and have concluded that such a test is appropriate because it is consistent with the language of Regulation 4 construed with due regard to the legislative pyrpose, which is identified in *Garrett* as being that of protecting the soiicitor's client. See also in this regard to [90] of Hollins and [101] of *Garrett*.
>
> 14. As to language Regulation 4 is concerned with giving the client who is considering entering into a CFA sufficient information and advice to enable him to take a properly informed considered decision. He can only do so if he is given information and advice which is not in any way affected by the solicitor's self interest ... As we see it the purpose of the regulation is to ensure that the solicitor acts and gives advice independently of his own interest."

The court distinguished the *Accident Line Protect (Tankard)* cases from other cases in which solicitors were members of a panel, stating:

> "20. . In our view, it is clear in all three cases now under appeal that the overriding consideration was the quality of the Accident Line ATE policy. That was why the solicitors subscribed to the scheme and recommended the policy to their clients. They kept the scheme under review and only renewed their membership of it if they regarded it as in their client's interest to do so.
>
> ...
>
> 24. There is, in our judgment, nothing in the ALP Scheme of a general nature which requires disclosure to the claimant on the ground that the solicitors have an interest of a kind which must be disclosed under Regulation 4(2)(e)(ii). That is because there is nothing which would lead a reasonable person with knowledge of the facts to think that the solicitor had an interest in the scheme that might affect the advice given to his or her client. Put another way, since there is nothing

in the arrangement which might affect the solicitor's advice or judgment in a manner adverse or potentially adverse to the client, disclosure byas not required. ..."

The court went on to consider whether it is sufficient for the solicitor simply to say that he has an interest in recommending the insurance which he recommends, or whether he is required at least to identify the nature of the interest. The court pointed out that the purpose of Regulation 4 is consumer protection: see *Hollins* at [25] ff. It must be construed in a way which gives adequate protection the client. The client needs to know more about the nature of the interest before being able to judge whether the solicitor has a motive for making his recommendation. The purpose of the sub-paragraph is to put the client in a position where he can make an informed decision.

Dealing with the submission that it is sufficient for a solicitor to disclose the fact that he is recommending the insurance because he is obliged to recommend the insurance in all eligible CFA cases, and if he does not do so he cannot remain a member of the ALP scheme, the Law Society intervening relied on the obiter dicta of the Court of Appeal at [103] in *Garrett*. The court held:

"44. In our judgment, the dicta at [103] of *Garrett* should not be followed. A solicitor who informs his client that he is recommending a policy because that is the only policy which he can recommend consistently with his membership of the panel tells the client nothing abqut the nature of the benefit that accrues to the solicitor through continuing membership of the panel. ... Take the facts of Garrett itself: as we have seen, Websters were 'dependent on Ainsworth for referrals of cases' (see [97]). The extent of the dependency was unclear on the evidence, but ... it is implicit in the decision that the dependency was substantial. It is difficult to see how the interest in such a benefit would be disclosed to the client by the mere statement that the policy was recommended because it was the only policy which, consistently with the solicitor's membership of the panel, he was allowed to recommend." *Tankard v John Fredricks Plastics Ltd* [2008] EWCA Civ 1375; [2009] 1 W.L.R. 1731; [2009] 4 All E.R. 526, CA.

### Maintenance and champerty

The mere fact that litigation services have been provided in return for a promise of a share of the proceeds is not of itself sufficient to justify that promise being held to be unenforceable. See *R. (on the application of Factortame) v Secretary of State for Transport* [2002] EWCA Civ 932; [2002] 3 W.L.R. 1104. In the particular case the claimant had entered into an agreement with another to supply his services as an investigator, in order to assist in the furtherance of that person's claim, in return for a sum equal to 1 per cent of the amount paid to conclude the action, together with a weekly charge. The claimant asserted that he had not received full payment and sued for the balance. At first instance the claim was struck out on the basis that the agreement was champertous and contrary to public policy. On appeal it was held that the agreement upon which the claimant had sued could not realistically be said to have a tendency to corrupt public justice. There was no direct relationship between the services supplied and any potential litigation. The agreement was not champertous and the claim ought not to have been struck out: *Mansell v Robinson* [2007] EWHC 101 (QB), Underhill J. **7A–72**

See note *Times Newspapers Ltd v Burstein (Costs: Champertous Retainer)* [2002] EWCA Civ 1739 at 47.14.3. The court's concern is with the nature of the contract of retainer and not with the behaviour of the solicitor subsequently, save in so far as it might throw light upon the true nature of the original agreement. What the court is concerned with is establishing the true nature of the contract entered into between the client and the solicitor. The court referred to the dictum of Lloyd J. in *R v Miller* and *R v Glennie* [1983] 1 W.L.R. 1056:

"... costs are incurred by a party if he is responsible or liable for those costs even though they are in fact paid by a third party, whether an employer insurance company, motoring organisation or trade union and even though the third party is also liable for those costs. It is only if it has been agreed that the client shall in no circumstances be liable for the costs that they cease to be costs incurred by him ..."

Whilst the client's impecuniosity may be relevant to determining what the true nature of the agreement was, the mere fact that the solicitor may have been conducting the action on credit or continuing an action in the knowledge of his client's lack of means does not justify a conclusion that he was unlawfully maintaining the action. The court went on to quote the judgment of Schiemann L.J. in *Awwad v Geraghty & Co* [2001]Q.B. 570, CA where he listed public policy arguments in favour of enforceability. At page 588F:

"6. If the lawyer's client has no assets then a conditional normal fee agreement merely gives legal form to what is a practical reality – the lawyer only gets paid if the client wins. Yet it is accepted as laudable for lawyers to act in such circumstances.

7. There is nothing improper in the lawyer agreeing to act for the client for his normal fee whilst having it in his mind, for reasons of friendship or wishing to foster future work from that client, not to exact his fee if the client should lose. It seems odd that an open contractual statement of what is unobjectionable in a solicitor's mind should render unenforceable an agreement which would have been enforceable had the solicitor not shared his thoughts with his client and promised not to change his mind."

The court went on to hold that the Deputy Costs Judge had been correct to refuse the paying party's application requiring the receiving party's solicitors to give full particulars of their dealings with the client both in relation to their original retention as his solicitors and the conditional fee agreement: *Times Newspapers Ltd v Burstein* [2002] EWCA Civ 1739.

### Costs orders relating to funding arrangements

**7A–73** Where a claimant entered into a conditional fee agreement with his solicitors and a conditional retainer agreement was entered into with counsel, and where, in the course of the proceedings, the claimant obtained certain pre-trial costs orders in his favour and the defendant obtained an order in their favour, the claimant sought to set off the opposing orders so as to extinguish any liability. The defendants argued that because of the CFA, no costs had become due and therefore nothing was recoverable by the claimant. The court held this argument to be wrong. The word "recover" was used in the agreement to mean obtain an order for payment as distinct from actually obtaining payment. The same applied to counsel's fees. "Winning" under the CFA included the client recovering costs during the litigation, thus, counsel and solicitors were entitled to their costs when the client obtained a pre-trial order for costs: *Arkin v Borchard Lines Ltd (Costs)* [2001] C.P. Rep. 108, QBD, Colman J.

## MEMBERSHIP ORGANISATIONS

**7A–74** Section 30 of the Access to Justice Act 1999 enables a membership organisation to recover, through a costs order made in favour of any of the members, an additional amount in respect of any provision made by or on behalf of the body in connection with the proceedings against the risk of having to meet the costs of the other parties to the proceedings. The additional amount recoverable must not exceed the likely cost of the premium of an insurance policy against the risk of incurring a liability to pay the costs of other parties to the proceedings.

The Lord Chancellor has the power to prescribe bodies as membership organisations for the purpose of s.30 of the 1999 Act. The organisations prescribed include most Trade Unions and Associations, as well as the Defence Police Federation, the Engineering Employers Federation, the Police Federation of England and Wales, the Automobile Association and RAC Motoring Services.

### Regulation of Claims Management Companies

**7A–75** Section 4 of the Compensation Act 2006 provides that a person may not provide claims management services unless he is authorised, exempt, the requirement for authorisation has been waived or he is an individual acting otherwise than in the course of a business. "Claims management services" means advice or other services in relation to the making of a claim. "Claim" means a claim for compensation, restitution, repayment or any other remedy or relief in respect of loss or damage or in respect of an obligation whether the claim is made or could be made:

(i) by way of legal proceedings;

(ii) in accordance with a scheme of regulation; or

(iii) in pursuance of a voluntary undertaking.
(Compensation Act 2006 s.4(2)).

The Compensation (Regulated Claims Management Services) Order 2006 (SI 2006/3319) prescribes the services which are regulated and the types of claim to which those services apply. The services include advertising for claimants, referral of claimants to legal practitioners, advice in relation to claims and investigation of claims (art.4(2)). The kinds of claim include: personal injury claims and criminal injuries compensation claims; employment related claims, such as claims for wages, unfair dismissal and discrimination; claims for housing disrepair; claims relating to financial products or services; and industrial injuries disability benefits (art.4(3)).

The Compensation (Specification of Benefits) Order 2006 (SI 2006/3321) specifies those benefits which are to be treated as a claim for the purposes of Part 2 of the Compensation Act 2006, namely: industrial injuries benefit under s.94 of the Social Security Contributions and Benefits Act 1992; any supplement, additional allowance or increase of benefit or allowance to which the recipient may be entitled under that or any other Act; and claims under certain older schemes (under Sch.8 to the 1992 Act); and benefit under the Pneumoconiosis, etc (Workers Compensation) Act 1979.

The Compensation (Claims Management Services) Regulations 2006 (SI 2006/3322) deals with, among other things, waiver of the requirement for authorisation (Pt 2). Members of certain professions whose professional conduct is already regulated (in particular barristers, solicitors and legal executives) and certain other classes of person that are regulated in other ways will be exempted from the requirements of Pt 2 of the 2006 Act by order of the Secretary of State. Not for profit organisations will also be exempted. The remainder of the Regulations deal with the grant of authorisation, fees, indemnity insurance, rules and codes of practice, complaints handling, audit investigation and cancellation, suspension and variation of authorisations. The regulator is required to prescribe, in writing, rules for the professional conduct of authorised persons (Reg.22).

## *Law Society Model Conditional Fee Agreement (2005) (Personal Injury and Clinical Negligence cases)*

**CFA**[1] 7A-76

For use in personal injury and clinical negligence cases only.

This agreement is a binding legal contract between you and your solicitor/s. Before you sign, please read everything carefully. This agreement must be read in conjunction with the Law Society document "What you need to know about a CFA".

**Agreement date**

[.........................................................................................]

**I/We, the solicitors/s** [............................................................................]

**You, the client**[...................................................................................]

**What is covered by this agreement**

- Your claim against [....................] for damages for personal injury suffered on [....................] ***(if either the name of the opponent or the date of the incident are unclear then set out here in as much detail as possible to give sufficient information for the client and solicitor to understand the basis of the claim being pursued)***
- Any appeal by your opponent.
- Any appeal you make against an interim order.
- Any proceedings you take to enforce a judgment, order or agreement.
- Negotiations about and/or a court assessment of the costs of this claim.

**What is not covered by this agreement**

- Any counterclaim against you.
- Any appeal you make against the final judgment order.

[1] This model Conditional Fee Agreement for use in Personal Injury and Clinical Negligence cases is reproduced with the kind permission of the Law Society.

***Paragraph numbers marked with a "+" can be found online and on CD.***

**Paying us**

If you win your claim, you pay our basic charges, our disbursements and a success fee. You are entitled to seek recovery from your opponent of part or all of our basic charges, our disbursements, a success fee and insurance premium as set out in the document "What you need to know about a CFA."

It may be that your opponent makes a Part 36 offer or payment which you reject on our advice, and your claim for damages goes ahead to trial where you recover damages that are less than that offer or payment. If this happens, we will ***[not add our success fee to the basic charges] [not claim any costs]*** for the work done after we received notice of the offer or payment.

If you receive interim damages, we may require you to pay our disbursements at that point and a reasonable amount for our future disbursements.

If you receive provisional damages, we are entitled to payment of our basic charges our disbursements and success fee at that point.

If you lose you remain liable for the other side's costs.

**The Success Fee**

The success fee is set at [........]% of basic charges, where the claim concludes at trial; or [ . . . . . . ...]% where the claim concludes before a trial has commenced. In addition [........]% relates to the postponement of payment of our fees and expenses and can not be recovered from your opponent. The Success fee inclusive of any additional percentage relating to postponement cannot be more than 100% of the basic charges in total.

**Other points**

The parties acknowledge and agree that this agreement is not a Contentious Business Agreement within the terms of the Solicitors Act 1974.

**Signatures**

**Signed by the solicitor(s):**..........................................................

**Signed by the client:** ..........................................................

## *Law Society Model CFA Agreement—Information for Clients (2005)*

7A–77 ***Conditional Fee Agreements: what you need to know***

Definitions of words used in this document and the accompanying CFA are explained at the end of this document.[1]

**What do I pay if I win?**

If you win your claim, you pay our basic charges, our disbursements and a success fee. The amount of these is not based on or limited by the damages. You can claim from your opponent part or all of our basic charges, our disbursements, a success fee and insurance premium.

It may be that your opponent makes a Part 36 offer or payment which you reject on our advice, and your claim for damages goes ahead to trial where you recover damages that are less than that offer or payment. Refer to the "Paying Us" section in the CFA document to establish costs we will be seeking for the work done after we received notice of the offer or payment.

If you receive interim damages, we may require you to pay our disbursements at that point as well as a reasonable amount for our future disbursements.

If you receive provisional damages, we are entitled to payment of our basic charges, our disbursements and success fee at that point.

If you win overall but on the way lose an interim hearing, you may be required to pay your opponent's charges of that hearing.

[1] This document is the Information for Clients document published by the Law Society and is copyright ©2005 The Law Society. It is reproduced with their kind permission.

If on the way to winning or losing you are awarded any costs, by agreement or court order, then we are entitled to payment of those costs, together with a success fee on those charges if you win overall.

### What do I pay if I lose?

If you lose, you pay your opponent's charges and disbursements. You may be able to take out an insurance policy against this risk. If you lose, you do not pay our charges but we may require you to pay our disbursements.

### Ending this agreement

If you end this agreement before you win or lose, you pay our basic charges and disbursements. If you go on to win, you also pay a success fee.

We may end this agreement before you win or lose.

### Basic charges

These are for work done from now until this agreement ends. These are subject to review.

### How we calculate our basic charges

These are calculated for each hour engaged on your matter. Routine letters and telephone calls will be charged as units of one tenth of an hour. Other letters and telephone calls will be charged on a time basis. The hourly rates are:

| Grade of Fee Earner | Hourly Rate |
|---|---|
| 1<br>Solicitors with over eight years post qualification experience including at least eight years litigation experience. | |
| 2<br>Solicitors and legal executives with over four years post qualification experience including at least four years litigation experience. | |
| 3<br>Other solicitors and legal executives and fee earners of equivalent experience | |
| 4<br>Trainee solicitors, para legals and other fee earners. | |

We review the hourly rate on [review date] and we will notify you of any change in the rate in writing.

### Road Traffic Accidents

[If your claim is settled before proceedings are issued, for less than £10,000, our basic costs will be £800; plus 20% of the damages agreed up to £5,000; and 15%of the damages agreed between £5,000 and £10,000.] [If you live in London, these costs will be increased by 12.5%]. These costs are fixed by the Civil Procedure Rules.

### Success fee

The success fee percentage set out in the agreement reflects the following:

(a) the fact that if you lose, we will not earn anything;

(b) our assessment of the risks of your case;

(c) any other appropriate matters;

(d) the fact that if you win we will not be paid our basic charges until the end of the claim;

(e) our arrangements with you about paying disbursements.

### Value added tax (VAT)

We add VAT, at the rate (now [......]%) that applies when the work is done, to the total of the basic charges and success fee.

***Paragraph numbers marked with a "+" can be found online and on CD.***

**The Insurance Policy**

In all the circumstances and on the information currently available to us, we believe, that a contract of insurance with [..........] is appropriate to cover your opponent's charges and disbursements in case you lose.

This is because

*You do not have an existing or satisfactory insurance that would cover the costs of making this claim. The policy we recommend will pay:*

(a) *the costs of the other party in the event that the claim fails, to a maximum of £X;*

(b) *all your disbursements if your claim fails.*

(c) *[add other key features where necessary such as, our costs and the other side's costs (without deduction from your damages) if you fail to beat an (Part 36) Offer to Settle your claim, which you rejected following our advice].*

or:

[We cannot identify a policy which meets your needs but our recommended policy is the closest that we can discover within the products that we have searched. It does not meet your needs in the following respects:

(a) *it has an excess of £Z*

(b) *the maximum cover is £ZZ*]

or:

*[We cannot obtain an insurance policy at this stage but we shall continue to look for one and if we are successful in our search then we shall advise you at that stage of the benefits of the policy and purchasing it]*

**[NB. The italicised reasons in set out are examples only. Your solicitor must consider your individual circumstances and set out the reasons that apply].**

**Law Society Conditions**

The Law Society Conditions below are part of this agreement. Any amendments or additions to them will apply to you. You should read the conditions carefully and ask us about anything you find unclear.

**Our responsibilities**

We must:

- always act in your best interests, subject to our duty to the court;
- explain to you the risks and benefits of taking legal action;
- give you our best advice about whether to accept any offer of settlement;
- give you the best information possible about the likely costs of your claim for damages.

**Your responsibilities**

You must:

- give us instructions that allow us to do our work properly;
- not ask us to work in an improper or unreasonable way;
- not deliberately mislead us;
- co-operate with us;
- go to any medical or expert examination or court hearing.

**Dealing with costs if you win**

- You are liable to pay all our basic charges, our disbursements and success fee.
- Normally, you can claim part or all of our basic charges, our disbursements success fee and insurance premium from your opponent.
- If we and your opponent cannot agree the amount, the court will decide how much you can recover. If the amount agreed or allowed by the court does not cover all our basic charges and our disbursements, then you pay the difference.
- You will not be entitled to recover from your opponent the part of the success fee that relates to the cost to us of postponing receipt of our charges and our disbursements. This remains payable by you.
- You agree that after winning, the reasons for setting the success fee at the amount stated may be disclosed:

***Paragraph numbers marked with a "+" can be found online and on CD.***

(i) to the court and any other person required by the court;

(ii) to your opponent in order to gain his or her agreement to pay the success fee.

- If the court carries out an assessment and reduces the success fee because the percentage agreed was unreasonable in view of what we knew or should have known when it was agreed, then the amount reduced ceases to be payable unless the court is satisfied that it should continue to be payable.
- If we agree with your opponent that the success fee is to be paid at a lower percentage than is set out in this agreement, then the success fee percentage will be reduced accordingly unless the court is satisfied that the full amount is payable.
- It may happen that your opponent makes an offer of one amount that includes payment of our basic charges and a success fee. If so, unless we consent, you agree not to tell us to accept the offer if it includes payment of the success fee at a lower rate than is set out in this agreement.
- If your opponent is receiving Community Legal Service funding, we are unlikely to get any money from him or her. So if this happens, you have to pay us our basic charges, disbursements and success fee.

As with the costs in general, you remain ultimately responsible for paying our success fee.

You agree to pay into a designated account any cheque received by you or by us from your opponent and made payable to you. Out of the money, you agree to let us take the balance of the basic charges; success fee; insurance premium; our remaining disbursements; and VAT.

You take the rest.

We are allowed to keep any interest your opponent pays on the charges.

*If your opponent fails to pay*

If your opponent does not pay any damages or charges owed to you, we have the right to take recovery action in your name to enforce a judgment, order or agreement. The charges of this action become part of the basic charges.

**Payment for advocacy**

The cost of advocacy and any other work by us, or by any solicitor agent on our behalf, forms part of our basic charges. We shall discuss with you the identity of any barrister instructed, and the arrangements made for payment.

*Barristers who have a conditional fee agreement with us*

If you win, you are normally entitled to recover their fee and success fee from your opponent. The barrister's success fee is shown in the separate conditional fee agreement we make with the barrister. We will discuss the barrister's success fee with you before we instruct him or her. If you lose, you pay the barrister nothing.

*Barristers who do not have a conditional fee agreement with us*

If you win, then you will normally be entitled to recover all or part of their fee from your opponent. If you lose, then you must pay their fee.

**What happens when this agreement ends before your claim for damages ends?**

*(a) Paying us if you end this agreement*

You can end the agreement at any time. We then have the right to decide whether you must:

- pay our basic charges and our disbursements including barristers' fees but not the success fee when we ask for them; or
- pay our basic charges, and our disbursements including barristers' fees and success fees if you go on to win your claim for damages.

*(b) Paying us if we end this agreement*

(i) We can end this agreement if you do not keep to your responsibilities. We then have the right to decide whether you must:

***Paragraph numbers marked with a "+" can be found online and on CD.***

- pay our basic charges and our disbursements including barristers' fees but not the success fee when we ask for them; or
- pay our basic charges and our disbursements including barristers' fees and success fees if you go on to win your claim for damages.

(ii) We can end this agreement if we believe you are unlikely to win. If this happens, you will only have to pay our disbursements. These will include barristers' fees if the barrister does not have a conditional fee agreement with us.

(iii) We can end this agreement if you reject our opinion about making a settlement with your opponent. You must then:

- pay the basic charges and our disbursements, including barristers' fees;
- pay the success fee if you go on to win your claim for damages.

If you ask us to get a second opinion from a specialist solicitor outside our firm, we will do so. You pay the cost of a second opinion.

(iv) We can end this agreement if you do not pay your insurance premium when asked to do so.

*(c) Death*

This agreement automatically ends if you die before your claim for damages is concluded. We will be entitled to recover our basic charges up to the date of your death from your estate.

If your personal representatives wish to continue your claim for damages, we may offer them a new conditional fee agreement, as long as they agree to pay the success fee on our basic charges from the beginning of the agreement with you.

**What happens after this agreement ends**

After this agreement ends, we may apply to have our name removed from the record of any court proceedings in which we are acting unless you have another form of funding and ask us to work for you.

We have the right to preserve our lien unless another solicitor working for you undertakes to pay us what we are owed including a success fee if you win.

**Explanation of words used**

*(a) Advocacy*

Appearing for you at court hearings.

*(b) Basic charges*

Our charges for the legal work we do on your claim for damages.

*(c) Claim*

Your demand for damages for personal injury whether or not court proceedings are issued.

*(d) Counterclaim*

A claim that your opponent makes against you in response to your claim.

*(e) Damages*

Money that you win whether by a court decision or settlement.

*(f) Our disbursements*

Payment we make on your behalf such as:

- court fees;
- experts' fees;
- accident report fees;
- travelling expenses.

*(g) Interim damages*

Money that a court says your opponent must pay or your opponent agrees to pay while waiting for a settlement or the court's final decision.

*(h) Interim hearing*

A court hearing that is not final.

***Paragraph numbers marked with a "+" can be found online and on CD.***

*(i) Lien*
Our right to keep all papers, documents, money or other property held on your behalf until all money due to us is paid. A lien may be applied after this agreement ends.

*(j) Lose*
The court has dismissed your claim or you have stopped it on our advice.

*(k) Part 36 offers or payments*
An offer to settle your claim made in accordance with Part 36 of the Civil Procedure Rules.

*(l) Provisional damages*
Money that a court says your opponent must pay or your opponent agrees to pay, on the basis that you will be able to go back to court at a future date for further damages if:

- you develop a serious disease; or
- your condition deteriorates;

in a way that has been proved or admitted to be linked to your personal injury claim.

*(m) Success fee*
The percentage of basic charges that we add to your bill if you win your claim for damages and that we will seek to recover from your opponent.

*(n) Trial*
The final contested hearing or the contested hearing of any issue to be tried separately and a reference to a claim concluding at trial includes a claim settled after the trial has commenced or a judgment.

*(o) Win*
Your claim for damages is finally decided in your favour, whether by a court decision or an agreement to pay you damages or in any way that you derive benefit from pursuing the claim.

'Finally' means that your opponent:

- is not allowed to appeal against the court decision; or
- has not appealed in time; or
- has lost any appeal.

# 7B BARRISTERS



## INTRODUCTION

A barrister may enter into a conditional fee agreement (CFA) with a solicitor as an "additional legal representative". The agreement is not with the lay client. A barrister in independent practice, whether or not acting for a fee, may supply legal services only if he or she is instructed by a professional client or by a BarDirect client or is appointed by the court. The barrister must not enter into a contract for the supply of legal services by him or her with any person other than a professional or a bar BarDirect client. A "professional client" means a solicitor or other professional person by whom a barrister in independent practice is instructed (See Code of Conduct of the Bar paragraphs 401 and 1001). **7B–1**

Although the solicitor will probably have a CFA (with a success fee) with the lay client, the agreements between counsel and solicitor and solicitor and client are entirely separate. The barrister and the solicitor will not necessarily seek the same level of success fee and the two success fees may be dealt with differently on assessment. When the solicitor bills the client there will be included in that bill an amount in respect of counsel's fees and any success fee due to counsel. Section 20 of the Costs Practice Direction deals with the procedure where the legal representative wishes to recover from the client an agreed percentage increase which has been disallowed or reduced on assessment (r.44.16).

Although counsel's fee and any success fee is separately recoverable by the solicitor from the client as a disbursement, counsel is unable to recover it separately. There is no direct relationship with the lay client, contractual or otherwise. Counsel is only able to recover fees from the solicitor who is personally liable for them. The Bar Council takes the view that barristers may enter into binding contracts for work under a CFA, but whether or not they do so depends upon the general law and the terms of the agreement used. APIL/PIBA have model forms of CFA which cover agreements which are non binding or binding contracts. The Chancery Bar Association's standard form of CFA contains an option for the agreement to be contractually binding. All License Access work has to be performed under contract.

## CONDITIONAL FEE AGREEMENTS

### *Bar Council Guidance for Barristers in relation to Conditional Fee Agreements (extract)*

The extract provided here, limited to ethical guidance from the Bar Council, is a part of the full material provided by the Bar Council in relation to CFAs and which is available from the Bar Council website free of charge at *http://www.barcouncil.org.uk* [Accessed February 5, 2009]. The publishers are grateful to the Bar Council for their permission to reproduce the ethical guidance part of their publication set out here. **7B–2**

**7B–3**

*[...] Ethical Guidance*

#### Introduction

1. This Part is intended to provide guidance only on the ethical problems which may arise from the operation of Conditional Fee Agreements ("CFAs"). It does not form part of the Bar's Code of Conduct. However, it is strongly advised that barristers should follow the advice set out here, which is intended to ensure compliance with the Code of Conduct. Any doubts felt by a barrister after reading this ethical guidance should be referred to the Bar Standards Board. The Practical Guidance section of the Bar Council's CFA Guidance should be referred to for guidance on practical matters.

#### General

2. Paragraph 405 of the Code of Conduct permits a barrister in independent practice to charge for any work undertaken by her/him (whether or not it involves an **7B–4**

*Paragraph numbers marked with a "+" can be found online and on CD.*

appearance in court) on any basis or by any method s/he thinks fit provided that such basis or method is permitted by law; and does not involve the payment of a wage or salary. It is the responsibility of any member of the Bar who enters into a CFA to ensure that:

(1) he or she is familiar with the statutory provisions and regulations and orders made thereunder (see Practical Guidance, and note in particular the distinction between "old" and "new" CFAs, and the different legislative regimes applicable thereto);

(2) **he or she at all times acts in accordance with the relevant extracts of which are included in part 3 of the Guidance. For example, the barrister, before entering a CFA, must bear in mind the provisions of paragraph 603, namely, that "A barrister must not accept any brief or instructions if to do so would cause him to be professionally embarrassed", and the subsequent sub paragraphs of the Code defining circumstances in which such professional embarrassment may arise. In particular, barristers who are asked to give CFA advice on a standard form must be satisfied that they have seen and had sufficient time to consider all relevant documents before giving the advice.**

(3) the terms of the CFA comply with the requirements of the law and the Code Compliance with the Code will be ensured if a Bar Council approved CFA is used.

### The "cab rank" rule

**7B–5** 3. **The "cab rank" rule** does not apply to CFAs. In other words, counsel cannot be compelled to accept instructions upon a CFA basis. See § 604 (c) of the Code.

### Internal agreements and arrangements between barristers

**7B–6** 4. Some barristers and some chambers will find it appropriate to enter into standing agreements with each other, or to establish practices whereby they will work under CFAs as a chambers or in groups. The main purpose of such arrangements will be to spread the risk of CFA work. This might include the sharing of fees to the extent of, for example, the payment of a proportion of success fees into a pool which is then used to compensate members for fees not recovered, or expenses incurred, in lost cases. There may also be arrangements the sole purpose of which relates to the return of work between barristers or chambers (see section 4.5 below), or for screening (see section 5 below). However, there are some barristers and sets of chambers who will not consider it appropriate to work under CFAs at all, or who will only consider it appropriate to work under them on a one off basis agreed for each particular CFA. The considerations to be taken into account when considering such internal arrangements are as follows:

(1) **It is important to ensure that no arrangement or agreement is entered into which compromises or appears to compromise a barrister's integrity or independence, which creates or may create a partnership, or which creates or appears to create a conflict of interest (see Code § § 104(a)(i), 301, 303, 306, 307(a), 603(e)).**

(2) The Professional Standards Committee (now the Bar Standards Board) in February 2002 gave guidance as follows in relation to fee-sharing agreements:

   (i) A simple fee sharing agreement would not of itself amount to a partnership, assuming that it does not involve sharing of responsibility for the work done.

   (ii) If fees are shared between a group of barristers, there are likely to be conflicts of interest between members of the group and their clients where members of the group are instructed for clients with opposing interests: a member of the group may have a financial interest in the success of his or her opposing fellow member. Such a conflict will arise in particular where (a) a member of the group is being paid on a conventional basis but the opponent is acting on a CFA, or (b) both are acting on a CFA, but the CFA of one is more advantageous (in terms of success fee) than the other.

   (iii) Whilst it is possible for barristers to act notwithstanding a conflict of

***Paragraph numbers marked with a "+" can be found online and on CD.***

interest provided that they have the fully informed consent of their clients, obtaining such fully informed consent will normally be fraught with difficulties, largely on grounds of confidentiality (see section 14 below): in particular, in order to give such consent, the client will need to know not only that the barrister on the opposing side is acting on a CFA, but also the terms of that agreement, including the success fee.

(iv) It will therefore be rare for it to be acceptable for members of a fee-sharing group to accept instructions on opposite sides. Although it is possible in principle for the members of such a group to agree that any cases in which members are on opposing sides shall fall outside the scope of the agreement, such a provision is fraught with practical difficulties, not least because a member accepting instructions on a CFA basis will not at that time know whether or not a fellow member will in due course be instructed for an opposing party.

(3) **However, quite apart from the position of the Bar Council, there remains a likelihood that a court or arbitral institution would conclude that such an arrangement created a conflict of interest or the appearance of such a conflict, such that counsel involved should not be permitted to act against each other in any case in which a member of the group is involved, or as judge or arbitrator in any case.**

(4) Although the above guidance of the Professional Standards Committee (now the Bar Standards Board) demonstrates that fee-sharing agreements are technically possible, the practical difficulties are such that the Bar Council CFA Panel advises against any fee- or profit-sharing agreement, or any agreement which provides for a subsidy to be paid by chambers or a CFA group to members in respect of lost CFA cases. In our view, the better policy is to reduce the financial risks of CFAs by proper risk assessment and screening procedures (see Practical Guidance).

(5) **Arrangements between counsel whereby they agree to accept each others' return CFA briefs and the question whether, in those circumstances, they would be precluded from acting against each other in any action to which such arrangements applied or from appearing in front of a counsel who was a party to such arrangements (acting as a judge or arbitrator) are more straightforward. It is not thought that such arrangements create a potential or actual conflict of interest.**

### Screening

5. If chambers operate a form of screening of CFA cases whereby one or more members of chambers read the papers in a case sent to another member with a view to deciding whether or not that case should be accepted on a CFA basis, the screener could not, in future, act on the other side, or as judge or arbitrator, in that case. Barristers acting as screeners should therefore keep records of the cases they have screened, and a record must be kept in each case of the identity of the screener. If screening would involve the disclosure of confidential information to the screener, consent to screening should be obtained in advance of the screening. **7B–7**

### Forms of CFAs

6. There is no form of CFA prescribed by the Bar Council or any other body or specialist association; but see the guidance relating to insurance and the BMIF in paragraph 7 below. Under the regime which existed prior to 1st November 2005, there were approved forms of CFA for use in personal injury and clinical negligence cases, in chancery cases, and employment cases. These forms of CFA were approved by the relevant specialist bar associations. A new form of CFA for use after 1st November 2005 in personal injury and clinical negligence cases has been agreed between PIBA and APIL (APIL/PIBA 6) and it can be found on the Bar Council website. It is for the barrister entering into a CFA to be satisfied that the form of agreement used is appropriate and lawful. In any case where a barrister proposes or is asked to enter into a CFA with a solicitor upon terms which materially depart from any form of agreement approved by a specialist bar association, the barrister should **7B–8**

ensure that such departure is lawful, fair to the lay client and reasonable in the particular circumstances of the case before agreeing to act on such terms. In particular, the barrister should ensure that no term increases or tends to increase pressure on the lay client to reach an inappropriate settlement.

There is no objection to barristers entering into contractually binding agreements. The barrister should ensure that the agreement does not contain any clause inconsistent with the Code.

### Insurance

**7B–9** 7. Under § § 204(b) and 402.1 of the Code, every barrister must be covered by insurance against claims for professional negligence, and be entered as a member with BMIF. Some standard form CFAs, including the APIL/PIBA model, provide for an indemnity in favour of the solicitor in the event that counsel's breach of duty causes the solicitor to suffer a loss of fees. The BMIF has agreed (subject to financial limits) to indemnify barristers against this type of claim, provided it has approved the form of the relevant agreement. A barrister will therefore not be insured against such a claim by the solicitor if he/she has entered into an agreement on a form not approved by the BMIF. Previously, the APIL/PIBA and Chancery Bar Association agreements have been approved by the BMIF; terms of the new APIL/PIBA 6 agreement have also been approved.

### Inducements

**7B–10** 8. The payment by barristers or their chambers of commissions or inducements is strictly prohibited by the Code: see § § 307(d) and (e). Paragraph 205 and 401(a) of the Code respectively prohibits the supply of legal services by barristers to the public through or on behalf of anyone other than solicitors, unless the Code requirements as to public access or Licensed access are complied with. Guidance was given on this topic by the Professional Standards Committee in May 2001.

Thus, for example:

(1) the payment of "introduction" or "administration" fees or charges to an insurer or claims organisation is not permissible;

(2) any scheme which requires barristers to pay for services provided outside chambers in order to accept work is likely to contravene § 307(e) and to involve a hidden commission contrary to § 307(e);

(3) a payment to the clerk of other chambers in return for forwarding work will be contrary to § 307(e);

(4) barristers are responsible for ensuring that their clerks do not receive or pay commission or inducements;

(5) barristers are responsible for their fee notes, which must be transparent and must not have the effect of misleading a court or any party; blank fee notes must not be sent out to be completed by third parties, nor must third parties be permitted to alter fee notes;

Barristers and their chambers should not accept or rely upon assurances from those promoting a CFA scheme that the scheme has received Bar Council approval: advice in respect of any such new scheme must be obtained from the Professional Standards Department of the Bar Council.

### Impartiality/conflicts of interest

**7B–11** 9. Having accepted instructions to act under a CFA, a barrister shall thereafter give impartial advice to the lay client at all times and take all reasonable steps to identify and declare to the lay client and to the instructing solicitor any actual or apparent conflict of interest between the barrister and the lay client.

### Advice and interests of lay client

**7B–12** 10. **Advice and interests of lay client.** During the currency of a CFA, the barrister should use his/her best endeavours to ensure that:

*Paragraph numbers marked with a "+" can be found online and on CD.*

(1) any advice given by the barrister in relation to the case is communicated and fully explained to the lay client;
(2) any offer of settlement is communicated to the lay client forthwith;
(3) the consequences of particular clauses in the solicitor/lay client and the solicitor/barrister agreement are explained to the client as and when they become relevant, particularly after an offer of settlement has been made.

This last obligation applies in particular to the financial consequences which may arise from the making of an offer to settle the case including consideration of (1) any increase in the offer of settlement; (2) "conventional" costs consequences; and (3) the success fees which are or may become payable.

### Advising on settlement

11. When advising on a settlement of the action the barrister should at all times have in mind his/ her obligation under paragraph 303 (a) of the Code to: **7B–13**

> "promote and protect fearlessly and by all proper and lawful means the lay client's best interests and do so without regard to his own interests or to any consequences to himself or to any other person (including any professional client or other intermediary or another barrister)".

The barrister's duty must be, when advising the client on a settlement or on a payment in or Part 36 offer, to advise as to the best course of action from the lay client's point of view only.

### Disagreement over Settlement

12. Difficulties may arise when the lawyers disagree about the wisdom of continuing the case or accepting an offer, whether that disagreement is: **7B–14**
(1) **between them on the one part and the lay client on the other; or**
(2) **between solicitor and counsel; or**
(3) **between leading and junior counsel.**

In such event careful consideration must be given to the lay client's interests. Every effort should be made to avoid unfairly putting the lay client in the position where having begun proceedings s/he is left without representation. However, where, for example, counsel has been misled about the true nature of the evidence or the lay client is refusing to accept firm advice as to the future conduct of the case, the terms of the CFA may permit counsel to withdraw. Before taking this serious step the barrister will have to check carefully whether s/he is entitled to withdraw.

### Withdrawal from the case

13. The barrister may withdraw from the case in any of the circumstances set out in the CFA agreement, but only if satisfied that s/he is permitted to withdraw pursuant to part VI - of the Code. In the event that the CFA agreement does not contain a term that the barrister may withdraw from the case in particular circumstances, but the Code requires the barrister to withdraw in those circumstances, the Code takes priority over the agreement. **7B–15**

### Disclosure of existence and terms of CFA

14. Disclosure of existence and terms of CFA. The fact that the action is funded by means of a CFA, and the terms of a CFA, should not be disclosed to the other parties to the action without the express written permission of the lay client, save insofar as such disclosure is required by the court, the CPR, statute, rule, order, or Practice Direction. **7B–16**

## Standard Form Conditional Fee Agreement between Solicitor and Counsel (APIL/PIBA 6)

7B-16.1 **For the "Standard Form Conditional Fee Agreement between Solicitor and Counsel (APIL/PIBA 6)" see paragraph 7B-17+ on White Book on Westlaw UK or the Civil Procedure CD.**

## APIL/PIBA Standard Terms and Conditions for CFAs between solicitor and counsel

7B-17.1 **For the "APIL/PIBA Standard Terms and Conditions for CFAs between solicitor and counsel" see paragraphs 7B-18+ to 7B-45+ on White Book on Westlaw UK or the Civil Procedure CD.**

*Paragraph numbers marked with a "+" can be found online and on CD.*

# 7C SOLICITORS ACT 1974

## Solicitors Act 1974

(1974 c.47) 7C–1

Arrangement of Sections

Part I

*Rights and privileges of solicitors*



***Paragraph numbers marked with a "+" can be found online and on CD.***

# PART I

## *RIGHTS AND PRIVILEGES OF SOLICITORS*

### Rights of practising and rights of audience

7C–2 **19.** [Repealed]

7C–3 *Note*—Repealed by the Legal Services Act 2007 Sch.16 para.24 Sch.23, with effect from January 1, 2010 (Legal Services Act 2007 (Commencement No.6, Transitory, Transitional and Saving Provisions) Order 2009 (SI 2009/3250)).

## *UNQUALIFIED PERSONS ACTING AS SOLICITORS*

### Unqualified person not to act as solicitor

7C–4 **20.**—(1) No unqualified person is to act as a solicitor.

(2) Any person who contravenes subsection (1) is guilty of an offence and liable on conviction on indictment to imprisonment for not more than 2 years or to a fine, or to both.

(3) [...]

(4) [...]

***Paragraph numbers marked with a "+" can be found online and on CD.***

**Note**

Substituted by the Legal Services Act 2007 Sch.16 para.25, with effect from January 1, 2010 (SI 2009/3250)). 7C–5

[THE NEXT PARAGRAPH IS 7C–7.]

## Unqualified person not to pretend to be a solicitor

**21.** Any unqualified person who wilfully pretends to be, or takes or uses any name, title, addition or description implying that he is, qualified or recognised by law as qualified to act as a solicitor shall be guilty of an offence and liable on summary conviction to a fine not exceeding the fourth level on the standard scale. 7C–7

*Note* —Amended by the Criminal Justice Act 1982; and the AJA 1985 Sch.1. 7C–8

## Unqualified person not to prepare certain instruments

**22.** [Repealed] 7C–9

*Note* —Repealed (subject to saving provision) by the Legal Services Act 2007 Sch.16 para.26 Sch.23, with effect from January 1, 2010 (Legal Services Act 2007 (Commencement No.6, Transitory, Transitional and Saving Provisions) Order 2009 (SI 2009/3250); saving provision contained in art.5). 7C–10

[THE NEXT PARAGRAPH IS 7C–12.]

## Powers of entry, etc., of local weights and measures authorities

**22A.** [Repealed] 7C–12

*Note* —Repealed (subject to saving provision) by the Legal Services Act 2007 Sch.16 para.26 Sch.23, with effect from January 1, 2010 (Legal Services Act 2007 (Commencement No.6, Transitory, Transitional and Saving Provisions) Order 2009 (SI 2009/3250); saving provision contained in art.5) 7C–13

## Unqualified person not to prepare papers for probate, etc.

**23.** [Repealed] 7C–14

*Note* —Repealed (subject to saving provision) by the Legal Services Act 2007 Sch.16 para.26 Sch.23, with effect from January 1, 2010 (Legal Services Act 2007 (Commencement No.6, Transitory, Transitional and Saving Provisions) Order 2009 (SI 2009/3250); saving provision contained in art.5) 7C–15

[THE NEXT PARAGRAPH IS 7C–17.]

## Application of penal provisions to body corporate

**24.**—(1) If any act is done by a body corporate, or by any director, officer or servant of a body corporate, and is of such a nature or is done in such a manner as to be calculated to imply that the body corporate is qualified or recognised by law as qualified to act as a solicitor— 7C–17

(a) the body corporate shall be guilty of an offence and liable on summary conviction to a fine not exceeding the fourth level on the standard scale, and

***Paragraph numbers marked with a "+" can be found online and on CD.***

(b) in the case of an act done by a director, officer or servant of the body corporate, he also shall be guilty of an offence and liable on summary conviction to a fine not exceeding the fourth level on the standard scale.

(2) For the avoidance of doubt it is hereby declared that in section 20 the reference to an unqualified person and the reference to a person both include a reference to a body corporate.

7C-18 *Note*—Amended by the Criminal Justice Act 1982; the AJA 1985 Sch.1; and (subject to saving provision) by the Legal Services Act 2007 Sch.16 para.27, with effect from January 1, 2010 (SI 2009/3250), saving provision contained in art.5).

### Costs where unqualified person acts as solicitor

7C-19 **25.**—(1) No costs in respect of anything done by any unqualified person acting as a solicitor shall be recoverable by him, or by any other person, in any action, suit or matter.

(2) Nothing in subsection (1) shall prevent the recovery of money paid or to be paid by a solicitor on behalf of a client in respect of anything done by the solicitor while acting for the client without holding a practising certificate in force if that money would have been recoverable if he had held such a certificate when so acting.

(3) [...]

7C-20 *Note*—Amended by the Courts and Legal Services Act 1990 Sch.18, para.12.

### Time limit for commencement of certain proceedings

7C-21 **26.** Notwithstanding anything in the Magistrates' Courts Act 1980, proceedings in respect of any offence under section 21 [.....] may be brought at any time before the expiration of two years from the commission of the offence or six months from its first discovery by the prosecutor, whichever period expires first.

7C-22 *Note*—Amended by the Magistrates' Courts Act 1980 Sch.7; and (subject to saving provision) by the Legal Services Act 2007 Sch.16 para.28 Sch.23, with effect from January 1, 2010 (SI 2009/3250), saving provision contained in art.5).

### Savings for persons authorised to conduct legal proceedings

7C-23 **27.** [Repealed]

7C-23.1 *Note*—Repealed by the Legal Services Act 2007 Sch.16 para.29 Sch.23, with effect from January 1, 2010 (Legal Services Act 2007 (Commencement No.6, Transitory, Transitional and Saving Provisions) Order 2009 (SI 2009/3250))

### Regulations

7C-24 **28.**—(1) The Society may make regulations [...] about the following matters, namely—

(a) admission as a solicitor;
(b) the keeping of the roll;
(c) practising certificates [...];
(ca) sole solicitor endorsements and applications for them,
(d) the keeping of the register under section 10A.

(2) [...]

***Paragraph numbers marked with a "+" can be found online and on CD.***

(3) Regulations about the keeping of the roll and of the register under section 9 may provide for the manner in which entries are to be made, altered and removed.

(3A) Regulations about the keeping of the roll may (among other things)—

(za) make provision about the form in which the roll is to be kept and the manner in which entries are to be made, altered and removed;

(a) provide for the Society, at such intervals as may be specified in the regulations, to enquire of solicitors of any class so specified whether they wish to have their names retained on the roll;

(b) require solicitors of any such class, at such intervals as aforesaid, to pay to the Society a fee in respect of the retention of their names on the roll of such amount as may be prescribed by the regulations; [...]

(c) authorise the Society to remove from the roll the name of any solicitor who—

(i) fails to reply to any enquiry made in pursuance of paragraph (a) or to pay any fee payable by virtue of paragraph (b), or

(ii) replies to any such enquiry by indicating that he does not wish to have his name retained on the roll;

(d) authorise the Society to remove from the roll the name of any solicitor who has died.

(e) require the information on the roll to be made available to the public;

(f) specify the manner in which information is to be made so available and require it to be made so available during office hours and without charge.

(3B) Regulations about practising certificates or sole solicitor endorsements may (among other things)—

(a) prescribe the form and manner in which applications for, or relating to, practising certificates or sole solicitor endorsements are to be made;

(b) prescribe information which must be included in or accompany such applications;

(c) make provision about time limits for dealing with such applications, and confer on a person power to extend or bring forward such a time limit in prescribed circumstances;

(d) prescribe the requirements which applicants for practising certificates must satisfy before they may be issued with a practising certificate;

(e) prescribe descriptions of applicants, and conditions in relation to them, for the purposes of section 10(2) (circumstances in which practising certificates must be issued subject to prescribed conditions);

*Paragraph numbers marked with a "+" can be found online and on CD.*

(f) prescribe descriptions of applicants, and conditions in relation to them, for the purposes of section 13ZA(5) (circumstances in which a practising certificate endorsed with a sole solicitor endorsement after it was issued must be made subject to prescribed conditions);

(g) prescribe circumstances for the purposes of section 10(3) (circumstances in which application may be refused etc in the public interest);

(h) make provision about when conditions imposed on practising certificates take effect (including provision conferring power on the Society to direct that a condition is not to have effect until the conclusion of any appeal in relation to it);

(i) make provision for the commencement, duration, replacement, withdrawal and expiry of practising certificates or sole solicitor endorsements;

(j) prescribe circumstances for the purposes of section 13A(2) (circumstances in which conditions can be imposed during period of practising certificate);

(k) require solicitors who hold practising certificates to notify the Society of such matters as may be prescribed, at such times, or in such circumstances as may be prescribed.

(3C) Regulations about the keeping of the register under section 10A may (among other things)—

(a) make provision about the form in which the register is to be kept and the manner in which entries are to be made, altered and removed;

(b) require information of a specified kind to be included in entries in the register;

(c) require information (or information of a specified description) on the register to be made available to the public;

(d) specify the manner in which it is to be made so available and require it to be made so available during office hours and without charge.

(3D) Regulations under this section may make provision for appeals to the High Court against decisions made by the Society under the regulations.

(3E) In relation to an appeal under regulations made by virtue of subsection (3D), the High Court may make such order as it thinks fit as to payment of costs.

(3F) The decision of the High Court on such an appeal shall be final.

(3G) Regulations under this section may—

(a) provide for a person to exercise a discretion in dealing with any matter;

(b) include incidental, supplementary and consequential provision;

(c) make transitory or transitional provision and savings;

(d) make provision generally or only in relation to specified cases or subject to specified exceptions;

(e) make different provision for different cases.

(4) [...]

(5) [...]

*Note* —Amended by the AJA 1985 Sch.1 and by the Secretary of State for Constitutional Affairs Order 2003 (SI 2003/1887), Sch.2, para.3; and (subject to transitional provisions) by the Constitutional Reform Act 2005 Sch.16 para.30 and Sch.23, with effect from July 1, 2009 (SI 2009/1365). **7C–25**

### Non-British subjects as solicitors

**29.** Nothing in section 3 of the Act of Settlement (which provides among other things that aliens are incapable of enjoying certain offices or places of trust) shall be taken to disqualify a person from becoming or practising as a solicitor of the Senior Courts or of the Court of Judicature. **7C–26**

*Note* —Amended by the Constitutional Reform Act 2005 s.59 and Sch.11, para 21(4), with effect from October 1, 2009 (SI 2009/1604). **7C–26.1**

### Evidence as to solicitors in Scotland

**30.** For the purposes of this Part, a letter purporting to be signed by or on behalf of the registrar of solicitors in Scotland— **7C–27**

(a) stating that a person specified in the letter is or is not a solicitor in Scotland shall be evidence that that person is or, as the case may be, is not a solicitor in Scotland;

(b) stating that a person specified in the letter did not at any time during a period so specified have in force a practising certificate as a solicitor in Scotland shall be evidence that that person was not during any part of that period a duly certified solicitor in Scotland.

## PART II

## PROFESSIONAL PRACTICE, CONDUCT AND DISCIPLINE OF SOLICITORS AND CLERKS

### *PRACTICE RULES*

### Rules as to professional practice, conduct and discipline

**31.**—(1) Without prejudice to any other provision of this Part the Society may make rules [.] for regulating in respect of any matter the professional practice, conduct, fitness to practice and discipline of solicitors and for empowering the Society to take such action as may be appropriate to enable the Society to ascertain whether or not the provisions of rules made; or if any code or guidance issued, by the Society are being, or have been, complied with. **7C–28**

(2) If any solicitor fails to comply with rules made under this section, any person may make a complaint in respect of that failure to the Tribunal.

***Paragraph numbers marked with a "+" can be found online and on CD.***

(3), (4) [...]

7C-29 *Note*—Amended by the Courts and Legal Services Act 1990 Sch.17, para.10; the Access to Justice Act 1999 Sch.7; and the Legal Services Act 2007 s.177 and Sch.16, Pt 1, para.31(2)(a) and (d) (with effect from March 7, 2008 (SI 2008/222)), Sch.16 Pt 1 para.31(2)(c) and (e) (with effect from March 31, 2009 (SI 2009/503)), Sch.16 Pt 1 para.31(2)(b), (3), (4), Sch.23, with effect from January 1, 2010 (SI 2009/3250).

### ACCOUNTS, ETC.

## Accounts rules and trust accounts rules

7C-30 **32.**—(1) The Society shall make rules [...]—

(a) as to the opening and keeping by solicitors of accounts at banks or with building societies for money within subsection (1A);

(aa) as to the operation by solicitors of accounts kept by their clients or other persons at banks or with building societies or other financial institutions;

(b) as to the keeping by solicitors of accounts containing information as to money received, held or paid by them for or on account of their clients or other persons (including money received, held or paid under a trust); and

(c) empowering the Society to take such action as may be necessary to enable it to ascertain whether or not the rules are being, or have been, complied with.

(1A) The money referred to in subsection (1) is money (including money held on trust) which is received, held or dealt with for clients or other persons.

(2) [...]

(3) If any solicitor fails to comply with rules made under this section, any person may make a complaint in respect of that failure to the Tribunal.

(4) The Society shall be at liberty to disclose a report on or information about a solicitor's accounts obtained in the exercise of powers conferred by rules made under subsection (1) for use in investigating the possible commission of an offence by the solicitor or any of his employees and for use in connection with any prosecution of the solicitor or any of his employees consequent on the investigation.

(5) Rules under this section may specify circumstances in which solicitors or any class of solicitors are exempt from the rules or a part of the rules.

7C-31 *Note*—Amended by the Building Societies Act 1986 Schs 18 and 19; and the Courts and Legal Services Act 1990 Sch.18, the Access to Justice Act 1999 Sch.15, Pt II and the Legal Services Act 2007 s.177, Sch.16, Pt 1, para.32(2)(a), (c)–(e), (3)–(7) and Sch.23, with effect from March 31, 2009 (SI 2009/503) and Sch.16, Pt 1, para.32(2)(b), Sch.23, with effect from January 1, 2010 (SI 2009/3250).

## Interest on clients' money

7C-32 **33.**—(1) Rules under section 32 may require a solicitor to pay interest, or sums in lieu of and equivalent to interest, to a client, any other person or any trust, for whom the solicitor holds money.

(2) The cases in which a solicitor may be required by the rules to act as mentioned in subsection (1) may be defined, among other things, by reference to the amount of any sum received or the period for which it is or is likely to be retained or both.

(3) Except as provided by the rules, a solicitor is not liable to account to any client, other person or trust for interest received by the solicitor on money held at a bank or building society in an account which is for money received or held for, or on account of—

(a) the solicitor's clients, other persons or trusts, generally, or

(b) that client, person or trust, separately.

(4) Rules under section 32 may—

(a) prescribe the circumstances in which a solicitor may make arrangements to limit or exclude an obligation imposed on the solicitor by rules made by virtue of this section, and

(b) prescribe the requirements to be met by and in relation to those arrangements.

*Note* —Amended by the Building Societies Act 1986 Sch.18 and the Legal Services Act 2007 s.177 and Sch.16, Pt 1, para.33 and Sch.23, with effect from March 31, 2009 (SI 2009/503). Subsection (4)(b) repealed by the Courts and Legal Services Act 1990 Sch.20. **7C–33**

## Inspection of practice bank accounts, etc.

**33A.**—(1) The Society may make rules [ .] empowering the Society to require a solicitor to produce documents relating to any account kept by him at a bank or with a building society— **7C–34**

(a) in connection with his practice; or

(b) in connection with any trust of which he is or formerly was a trustee,

for inspection by a person appointed by the Society pursuant to the rules.

(2) The Society shall be at liberty to disclose information obtained in exercise of the powers conferred by rules made under subsection (1) for use in investigating the possible commission of an offence by the solicitor and for use in connection with any prosecution of the solicitor consequent on the investigation.

*Note* —Inserted by the Access to Justice Act 1999 Sch.7 para.3 Sch.20; amended by the Legal Services Act 2007 s.177, Sch.16 Pt 1 para.34(2)(a) and (3), with effect from March 7, 2008 (SI 2008/222) and Sch.16 Pt 1 para.34(2)(b) Sch.23 with effect from January 1, 2010 (SI 2009/3250). **7C–35**

## Accountants' reports

**34.**—(1) The Society may make rules requiring solicitors to provide the Society with reports signed by an accountant (in this section referred to as an "accountant's report") at such times or in such circumstances as may be prescribed by the rules. **7C–36**

(2) The rules may specify requirements to be met by, or in relation to, an accountant's report (including requirements relating to the accountant who signs the report).

(3)–(5) [...]

(6) If any solicitor fails to comply with the provisions of any rules made under this section, a complaint in respect of that failure may be made to the Tribunal by or on behalf of the Society.

(7)–(8) [...]

(9) Where an accountant, during the course of preparing an accountant's report—

(a) discovers evidence of fraud or theft in relation to money held by a solicitor for a client or any other person (including money held on trust) or money held in an account of a client of a solicitor, or an account of another person, which is operated by the solicitor, or

(b) obtains information which the accountant has reasonable cause to believe is likely to be of material significance in determining whether a solicitor is a fit and proper person to hold money for clients or other persons (including money held on trust) or to operate an account of a client of the solicitor or an account of another person,

the accountant must immediately give a report of the matter to the Society.

(10) No duty to which an accountant is subject is to be regarded as contravened merely because of any information or opinion contained in a report under subsection (9).

**7C–37** *Note*—Amended by the AJA 1985 Sch.1 and the Legal Services Act 2007 s.177 and Sch.16, Pt 1, para.35 and Sch.23, with effect from March 31, 2009 (SI 2009/503)..

## SOLE SOLICITORS

### Employees of solicitors

**7C–37.1** **34A.**—(1) Rules made by the Society may provide for any rules made under section 31, 32, 33A or 34 to have effect in relation to employees of solicitors with such additions, omissions or other modifications as appear to the Society to be necessary or expedient.

(2) If any employee of a solicitor fails to comply with rules made under section 31 or 32, as they have effect in relation to the employee by virtue of subsection (1), any person may make a complaint in respect of that failure to the Tribunal.

(3) If any employee of a solicitor fails to comply with rules made under section 34, as they have effect in relation to the employee by virtue of subsection (1), a complaint in respect of that failure may be made to the Tribunal by or on behalf of the Society.

**7C–37.2** *Note*—Inserted by the Legal Services Act 2007 s.177 and Sch.16, Pt 1, para.36 with effect from March 31, 2009 (SI 2009/503).

### Employees of solicitors: accounts rules etc.

**7C–37.3** **34B.**—(1) Where rules made under section 32(1) have effect in relation to employees of solicitors by virtue of section 34A(1), section 85

***Paragraph numbers marked with a "+" can be found online and on CD.***

applies in relation to an employee to whom the rules have effect who keeps an account with a bank or building society in pursuance of such rules as it applies in relation to a solicitor who keeps such an account in pursuance of rules under section 32.

(2) Subsection (3) applies where rules made under section 32 —

(a) contain any such provision as is referred to in section 33(1), and

(b) have effect in relation to employees of solicitors by virtue of section 34A(1).

(3) Except as provided by the rules, an employee to whom the rules are applied is not liable to account to any client, other person or trust for interest received by the employee on money held at a bank or building society in an account which is for money received or held for, or on account of—

(a) clients of the solicitor, other persons or trusts, generally, or

(b) that client, person or trust, separately.

(4) Subsection (5) applies where rules made under section 33A(1) have effect in relation to employees of solicitors by virtue of section 34A(1).

(5) The Society may disclose a report on or information about the accounts of any employee of a solicitor obtained in pursuance of such rules for use—

(a) in investigating the possible commission of an offence by the solicitor or any employees of the solicitor, and

(b) in connection with any prosecution of the solicitor or any employees of the solicitor consequent on the investigation.

(6) Where rules made under section 34 have effect in relation to employees of solicitors by virtue of section 34A(1), section 34(9) and (10) apply in relation to such an employee as they apply in relation to a solicitor.

*Note* —Inserted by the Legal Services Act 2007 s.177 and Sch.16, Pt 1, para.36 with effect from March 31, 2009 (SI 2009/503). **7C–37.4**

* * * *

*INADEQUATE PROFESSIONAL SERVICES*

## Redress for inadequate professional services

**37A.** Schedule 1A shall have effect with respect to the provision by solicitors of services which are not of the quality which it is reasonable to expect of them. **7C–38**

*Note* —Added by the Courts and Legal Services Act 1990 s.93(2). **7C–39**

***Paragraph numbers marked with a "+" can be found online and on CD.***

* * * *

*IMPOSITION BY COUNCIL OF DISCIPLINARY SANCTIONS FOR INADEQUATE PROFESSIONAL SERVICES*

## Power of Council to impose sanctions for inadequate professional services

7C-40 **44A.** [...]

7C-41 *Note*—Repealed by Courts and Legal Services Act 1990 s.93(1) and (2).

Any case in which the final bill of costs was delivered to the client concerned before the commencement of s.93 (April 1, 1991) is not affected (Courts and Legal Services Act 1990 Sch.19).

* * * *

## Jurisdiction of Senior Courts over solicitors

7C-42 **50.**—(1) Any person duly admitted as a solicitor shall be an officer of the Senior Courts.

(2) Subject to the provisions of this Act, the High Court, the Crown Court and the Court of Appeal respectively, or any division or judge of those courts, may exercise the same jurisdiction in respect of solicitors as any one of the superior courts of law or equity from which the Senior Courts were constituted might have exercised immediately before the passing of the Supreme Court of Judicature Act 1873 in respect of any solicitor, attorney or proctor admitted to practise there.

(3) An appeal shall lie to the Court of Appeal from any order made against a solicitor by the High Court or the Crown Court in the exercise of its jurisdiction in respect of solicitors under subsection (2).

7C-43 *Note*—Amended by the Constitutional Reform Act 2005 s.59 and Sch.11, para.21(5) with effect from October 1, 2009 (SI 2009/1604).

### Subsection (2)

7C-44 The jurisdiction of the Court is frequently exercised, notwithstanding the existence of the Office for the Supervision of Solicitors. For the circumstances in which it will be exercised see *Gupta v Comer* [1991] 2 W.L.R. 494; *Holden & Co v Crown Prosecution Service* [1990] 1 All E.R. 368, CA.

## Procedure upon certain applications to High Court

7C-45 **51.**—(1) Where an application to strike the name of a solicitor off the roll or to require a solicitor to answer allegations contained in an affidavit is made to the High Court, then, subject to section 54, the following provisions of this section shall have effect in relation to that application.

(2) The court shall not entertain the application except on production of an affidavit proving that the applicant has served on the Society fourteen clear days' notice of his intention to make the application, together with copies of all affidavits intended to be used in support of the application.

***Paragraph numbers marked with a "+" can be found online and on CD.***

(3) The Society may appear by counsel on the hearing of the application and any other proceedings arising out of or in reference to the application, and may apply to the court—

(a) to make absolute any order nisi which the court may have made on the application;

(b) to make an order that the name of the solicitor be struck off the roll; or

(c) to make such other order as the court may think fit.

(4) The Court may order the costs of the Society of or relating to any of the matters mentioned in subsections (2) and (3) to be paid by the solicitor against whom, or by the person by whom, the application was made, or was intended to be made, or partly by one and partly by the other of them.



**Subsection (4)**

On a client's application to have a solicitor struck off, where the Law Society was not a party but appeared in the role of *amicus curiae*, it could not be made liable for costs (*Re A Solicitor* (1983) 80 L.S.G. 2998). **7C–46**

## Power of Society to draw up order of court

**52.** Where an order, whether nisi or absolute, is made by the High Court or the Court of Appeal on a motion to strike the name of a solicitor off the roll, or to require a solicitor to answer allegations contained in an affidavit, and that order is not drawn up by the applicant within one week of its being made, the Society may cause the order to be drawn up, and all future proceedings on the order shall be taken as if the motion had been made by the Society. **7C–47**

## Production of order of court to Society

**53.** Where an order is made by the High Court or the Court of Appeal that the name of a solicitor be struck off the roll, or that a solicitor be suspended from practice, the proper officer of the court shall forthwith send a copy of the order to the Society, and the Society shall enter a note of the order on the roll against the name of the solicitor and, where the order so directs, shall strike that name off the roll. **7C–48**

### *DISCIPLINARY PROCEEDINGS—GENERAL*

## Restrictions on powers to strike names off roll

**54.**—(1) No solicitor shall be liable to have his name struck off the roll on account of any failure to comply with the requirements with respect to persons seeking admission as solicitors of any training regulations or on account of any defect in his admission and enrolment, unless— **7C–49**

(a) the application to strike his name off the roll is made within twelve months of the date of his enrolment; or

(b) fraud is proved to have been committed in connection with the failure or defect.

(2) No solicitor shall be liable to have his name struck off the roll by reason only—

***Paragraph numbers marked with a "+" can be found online and on CD.***

(a) that a solicitor who undertook a training responsibility for him under training regulations neglected or omitted to take out a practising certificate; or

(b) that the name of a solicitor who undertook such a responsibility for a period has been removed from or struck off the roll after the end of that period.

7C–49.1 *Note*—Amended by the Legal Services Act 2007 s.177, Sch.16, Pt 1, para.53, with effect from March 7, 2008 (SI 2008/222).

### Applications to require solicitor to answer allegations

7C–50 **55.** For the avoidance of doubt it is hereby declared that an application by any person to require a solicitor to answer allegations contained in an affidavit, whether that application is made to the Tribunal or to the High Court, may be treated as an application to strike the name of that solicitor off the roll on the grounds of the matters alleged.

## PART III

## REMUNERATION OF SOLICITORS

### *NON-CONTENTIOUS BUSINESS*

### Orders as to remuneration for non-contentious business

7C–51 **56.**—(1) For the purposes of this section there shall be a committee consisting of the following persons—

(a) the Lord Chancellor;

(b) the Lord Chief Justice;

(c) the Master of the Rolls;

(d) the President of the Society;

(da) a member of the Legal Services Board nominated by that Board;

(e) a solicitor, being the president of a local law society, nominated by the Lord Chancellor to serve on the committee during his tenure of office as president; and

(f) for the purpose only of prescribing and regulating the remuneration of solicitors in respect of business done under the Land Registration Act 2002, the Chief Land Registrar appointed under that Act.

(2) The committee, or any three members of the committee (the Lord Chancellor being one) may make general orders prescribing and regulating in such manner as they think fit the remuneration of solicitors in respect of non-contentious business.

(3) The Lord Chancellor, before any order under this section is made, shall cause a draft of the order to be sent to the Society: and the committee shall consider any observations of the Society submitted to them in writing within one month of the sending of the draft, and may then make the order, either in the form of the draft or with such alterations or additions as they may think fit.

*Paragraph numbers marked with a "+" can be found online and on CD.*

(4) The principles prescribed by an order under this section may provide that solicitors should be remunerated—

(a) according to a scale of rates of commission or a scale of percentages, varying or not in different classes of business; or

(b) by a gross sum; or

(c) by a fixed sum for each document prepared or perused, without regard to length; or

(d) in any other mode; or

(e) partly in one mode and partly in another.

(5) The general principles prescribed by an order under this section may provide that the amount of such remuneration is to be determined by having regard to all or any of the following, among other, considerations, that is to say—

(a) the position of the party for whom the solicitor is concerned in the business, that is, whether he is vendor or purchaser, lessor or lessee, mortgagor or mortgagee, or the like;

(b) the place where, and the circumstances in which, the business or any part of it is transacted;

(c) the amount of the capital money or rent to which the business relates;

(d) the skill, labour and responsibility on the part of the solicitor, or any employee of his who is an authorised person, which the business involves;

(e) the number and importance of the documents prepared or perused without regard to length.

(6) An order under this section may authorise and regulate—

(a) the taking by a solicitor from his client of security for payment of any remuneration, to be ascertained by assessment or otherwise, which may become due to him under any such order; and

(b) the allowance of interest.

(7) So long as an order made under this section is in operation the assessment of bills of costs of solicitors in respect of non-contentious business shall, subject to the provisions of section 57, be subject to that order.

(8) Any order made under this section may be varied or revoked by a subsequent order so made.

(9) The power to make orders under this section shall be exercisable by statutory instrument which shall be subject to annulment in pursuance of a resolution of either House of Parliament; and the Statutory Instruments Act 1946 shall apply to a statutory instrument containing such an order in like manner as if the order had been made by a Minister of the Crown.

*Note*—For the definition of "non-contentious business" see s.87, para.7–137. Amended by the Land Registration Act 2002, Sch.11, para.12; the Legal Services Act 2007 s.177, Sch.16, Pt.1, para.54, with effect in part from March 7, 2008 (SI 2008/222), in part from June 30, 2008 (SI 2008/1436), in part from July 1, 2009 (SI 2009/1365) and in part from January 1, 2010 (SI 2009/3250). **7C–52**

**Subsection (7)**

7C–53 The Order now in force is the Solicitors' (Non-Contentious Business) Order 2009 (SI 2009/1931); see para.7C–241.1 below.

## Non-contentious business agreements

7C–54 **57.**—(1) Whether or not any order is in force under section 56, a solicitor and his client may, before or after or in the course of the transaction of any non-contentious business by the solicitor make an agreement as to his remuneration in respect of that business.

(2) The agreement may provide for the remuneration of the solicitor by a gross sum, or by reference to an hourly rate, or by a commission or percentage, or by a salary, or otherwise, and it may be made on the terms that the amount of the remuneration stipulated for shall or shall not include all or any disbursements made by the solicitor in respect of searches, plans, travelling, taxes, fees or other matters.

(3) The agreement shall be in writing and signed by the person to be bound by it or his agent in that behalf.

(4) Subject to subsections (5) and (7) the agreement may be sued and recovered on or set aside in the like manner and on the like grounds as an agreement not relating to the remuneration of a solicitor.

(5) If on any assessment of costs the agreement is relied on by the solicitor and objected to by the client as unfair or unreasonable, the taxing officer may enquire into the facts and certify them to the court, and if from that certificate it appears just to the court that the agreement should be set aside, or the amount payable under it reduced, the court may so order and may give such consequential directions as it thinks fit.

(6) Subsection (7) applies where the agreement provides for the remuneration of the solicitors to be by reference to an hourly rate.

(7) If, on the assessment of any costs, the agreement is relied on by the solicitor and the client objects to the amount of the costs (but is not alleging that the agreement is unfair or unreasonable), the costs officer may enquire into—

(a) the number of hours worked by the solicitor; and

(b) whether the number of hours worked by him was excessive.

7C–55 *Note*—Amended by the Courts and Legal Services Act 1990 s.98; and by the Legal Services Act 2007 Sch.16 para.55, with effect from January 1, 2010 (SI 2009/3250).

**Subsection (1)—"Non-contentious business"**

7C–56 See s.87 for the meaning of the term.

**Subsection (3)—"Agreement"**

7C–57 The agreement need not be signed by both parties, but only by the party to be charged (*Re Frape* [1893] 2 Ch. 284). As to what amounts to a signature, see *ibid*. All the terms of the agreement must be found in the document itself, which must sufficiently identify the costs (*Re Frape*). The solicitor cannot rely on an unwritten agreement (*Re West, King & Adams* [1892] 2 Q.B. 102 at 106) nor can the client (*Re A Solicitor (No.2)* [1956] 1 Q.B. 155) and a cash account signed by the client containing an item for "costs as agreed" pursuant to a verbal agreement only, is not a sufficient agreement in writing (*Re Baylis* [1896] 2 Ch. 107). An agreement to employ solicitors in work which might extend over a period of years and involve non-contentious business of various kinds, but for which it was contemplated that bills would be rendered and paid as matters proceeded, is not an entire contract, and the client can determine the retainer at any time on giving notice (*J. H. Milner and Son v Percy Bilton Ltd* [1966] 1 W.L.R. 1582; [1966] 2 All E.R. 894).

**Subsection (5)—"On any taxation of costs"**

Although the Court has power to refer an agreement within the section to the Costs Judge on the ground that it is unfair and unreasonable, yet such an order should not be made if unsupported by evidence leading to such conclusion. See *Re Palmer* (1890) L.R. 45 Ch.D. 291; *Re Frape* [1893] 2 Ch. 284. In *Re A & B* (1900) 44 S.J. 315, delivery of a bill was ordered after a delay of eight years, and the Costs Judge ordered to certify if the agreement was fair and reasonable, the agreed sum being prima facie unreasonable and no statute of limitations being applicable. In *Rutter v Sheridan-Young* [1958] 1 W.L.R. 44; [1958] 2 All E.R. 13, the Court of Appeal ordered delivery of an itemised bill and detailed assessment, where the agreement for a gross sum followed an erroneous statement by the solicitor as to the basis on which he was permitted to charge. On the other hand, in *Re Gray* (1886) 30 S.J. 551, the Court thought the matter more fit to be decided in an action than by a reference to the Costs Judge. **7C–58**

The amount payable under an agreement cannot be included in a cash account on the detailed assessment of other bills under an order of course (*Re Templeton and Cox* (1909) 101 L.T. 144, CA).

"Taxation of costs" is now referred to as detailed assessment of costs.

**Non-professional work**

Where an agreement has been made for the remuneration of a solicitor, and the solicitor alleges the remuneration was for non-professional work, the person chargeable cannot obtain the common order for delivery and detailed assessment of a bill of costs: the question of fact must first be decided (*Re Inderwick* (1884) L.R. 25 Ch D 279; *Re Fanshawe* [1905] W.N. 64). **7C–59**

For instances of unreasonable agreements, see *Re Montague Scott* [1889] W.N. 40; *Mearns v Knapp* (1889) 37 W.R. 585; and *cf. Re Haslam & Hier-Evans* [1902] 1 Ch. 765; and nn. to s.61, paras 7C–81 to 7C–85.

As to whether an agreement between a mortgagee or lessor and his solicitor is binding on the mortgagor or lessee, see *Hester v Hester* (1887) L.R. 34 Ch.D. 607 at 617; *Re Gray* [1901] 1 Ch. 239 at 245. See further para.7C–126.

An agreement by a mortgagor to pay a lump sum for mortgagor's and mortgagee's costs to a common solicitor is within the section (*Re Palmer* (1890) L.R. 45 Ch D 291).

**Interest**

See *Walton v Egan*, para.7C–241+. **7C–60**

## Remuneration of a solicitor who is a mortgagee

**58.**—(1) Where a mortgage is made to a solicitor, either alone or jointly with any other person, he or the firm of which he is a member shall be entitled to recover from the mortgagor in respect of all business transacted and acts done by him or them in negotiating the loan, deducing and investigating the title to the property, and preparing and completing the mortgage, such usual costs as he or they would have been entitled to receive if the mortgage had been made to a person who was not a solicitor and that person had retained and employed him or them to transact that business and do those acts. **7C–61**

(2) Where a mortgage has been made to, or has become vested by transfer or transmission in, a solicitor, either alone or jointly with any other person, and any business is transacted or acts are done by that solicitor or by the firm of which he is a member in relation to that

***Paragraph numbers marked with a "+" can be found online and on CD.***

mortgage or the security thereby created or the property thereby charged, he or they shall be entitled to recover from the person on whose behalf the business was transacted or the acts were done, and to charge against the security, such usual costs as he or they would have been entitled to receive if the mortgage had been made to and had remained vested in a person who was not a solicitor and that person had retained and employed him or them to transact that business and do those acts.

(3) In this section "mortgage" includes any charge on any property for securing money or money's worth.

### *CONTENTIOUS BUSINESS*

## Contentious business agreements

**7C–62** **59.**—(1) Subject to subsection (2) a solicitor may make an agreement in writing with his client as to his remuneration in respect of any contentious business done, or to be done, by him (in this Act referred to as a "contentious business agreement") providing that he shall be remunerated by a gross sum, or by reference to an hourly rate, or by a salary, or otherwise, and whether at a higher or lower rate than that at which he would otherwise have been entitled to be remunerated.

(2) Nothing in this section or in section 60 to 63 shall give validity to—

(a) any purchase by a solicitor of the interest, or any part of the interest, of his client in any action, suit or other contentious proceeding; or

(b) any agreement by which a solicitor retained or employed to prosecute any action, suit or other contentious proceeding, stipulates for payment only in the event of success in that action, suit or proceeding; or

(c) any disposition, contract, settlement, conveyance, delivery, dealing or transfer which under the law relating to bankruptcy is invalid against a trustee or creditor in any bankruptcy or composition.

**7C–63** *Note* —Amended by Courts and Legal Services Act 1990 s.98.

**"Contentious business"**

**7C–64** See s.87, para.7C–143.

**Subsection (1)**

**7C–65** *"Agreement in writing"* —The section enables solicitors to make binding agreements in writing. In *Chamberlain v Boodle & King* (1980) 124 S.J. 186, Smith J. held it was essential for the agreement to be in writing and must show all the terms of the bargain between the parties. This decision was upheld by the Court of Appeal [1982] 1 W.L.R. 1443; [1982] 3 All E.R. 188.

In *Martin Boston & Co v Levy* [1982] 1 W.L.R. 1434; [1982] 3 All E.R. 193, it was held that the client's rights under the Solicitors Act would not be defeated where solicitors sued on a dishonoured cheque received in payment of their account.

The fact that an agreement between a firm of solicitors and their client does not refer to itself as a contentious business agreement is not determinative of the issue as to whether it is in fact such an agreement. If the agreement fulfils the criteria for a contentious business agreement then that is what it is regardless of what the parties call it. The essence of a CBA is certainty: *In the matter of Wilson Properties UK Ltd (in liquidation) sub nom Pierre Wilson v The Specter Partnership, Official Receiver, and Joint Liquidators of Wilson Properties UK Ltd* [2007] EWHC 133 (Ch), Mann J.

**Cross claims and account stated**

The solicitor cannot rely on a parol agreement (*Re Russell, Son & Scott* (1885) 30 Ch D 114) yet where there is a claim for costs and a cross-claim, and an account stated, but not in writing, showing a balance in favour of the solicitor, he can sue for it without delivering a signed bill (*Turner v Willis* [1905] 1 K.B. 468). **7C–66**

**Agreement for security**

The section has no application to an agreement by a client to give his solicitor security for such costs as he may become entitled to, whether the security be by cash cover, or charge upon or assignment of part of a fund to be received by the solicitor, and such agreement may be oral (*Re Jackson* [1915] 1 K.B. 371; *Jonesco v Evening Standard* [1932] 2 K.B. 340, CA). **7C–67**

**Bill of exchange**

A solicitor cannot evade his obligations under the Act by taking a bill of exchange (*Ray v Newton* [1913] 1 K.B. 249, CA). **7C–68**

**Signature by client**

The agreement may be enforced by the solicitor though signed by the client alone (*Re Thompson* [1894] 1 Q.B. 462; *Re Jones* [1895] 2 Ch. 719; *Beake v French (No.2)* [1907] 2 Ch. 215). **7C–69**

**"Gross sum ... hourly rate ... or salary or otherwise"**

Contingency fee agreements are not enforceable in English law, but s.58 of the Courts and Legal Services Act 1990, introduced conditional fees subject to appropriate orders being made by the Lord Chancellor. See the Conditional Fee Agreements Order 2000 para.7A–21, and the Conditional Fee Agreements Regulations 2000 para.7A–26. The 1974 Act is not intended to legalise champertous agreements (*Anon.* (1875) 1 Ch D 573) as to the nature of which see *Simpson v Lamb* (1856) 7 El. & Bl. 84; *Davis v Freethy* (1890) L.R. 24 Q.B.D. 519 at 523; *Pittman v Prudential Deposit Bank* (1896) 13 T.L.R. 110; *Re a Solicitor* [1912] 1 K.B. 302. So, a solicitor who receives a proper retainer subsequently varied so as to be champertous, cannot recover his fees (*Wild v Simpson* [1919] 2 K.B. 544; *Awwad v Geraghty &Co* [2001] Q.B. 570, CA). This includes disbursements as well as profit costs (*Re Trepca Mines Ltd* [1963] Ch. 199, CA). Similarly, an agreement for the collection of rents, interest, or debts, the remuneration for which is to be a percentage of the amount recovered, and which contemplates litigation, would be an infringement of the law against champerty and illegal; but such an agreement, if it excludes the taking of legal proceedings, is neither unprofessional nor objectionable. *Wallersteiner v Moir (No.2)* [1975] Q.B. 373; [1975] 1 All E.R. 849, CA and see *AXA Equity & Law Life Assurance Society Plc (No.2), Re*; *Axa Sun Life Plc, Re* [2001] 1 All E.R. (Comm) 1010. **7C–70**

**Salaried solicitor**

A solicitor can be remunerated by salary for contentious as well as non-contentious business (see *Galloway v Corporation of London* (1867) L.R. 4 Eq. 90) and the client can recover usual costs from his opponent in litigation unless the latter can show that such costs would exceed the appropriate amount of the salary (see s.60(2), para.7C–75 and *Henderson v Merthyr Urban DC* [1900] 1 Q.B. 434). See also *Re Eastwood (dec'd), Lloyds Bank Ltd v Eastwood* [1975] Ch. 112; [1974] 3 All E.R. 607, CA and *Maes Finance Ltd v W.G. Edwards & Partners*, February 11, 200, unrep., QBD. Reaffirmed: *Cole v British Telecommunications Plc* [2000] 2 Costs L.R. 310, CA. **7C–71**

**Lump sum where no agreement**

See s.64. **7C–72**

**Bankruptcy**

A solicitor may retain moneys paid under an agreement before notice of an act of bankruptcy, though the services are rendered later, *Re Charlwood* [1894] 1 Q.B. 643). **7C–73**

**Subsection (2)**

7C–74 This section merely provides that nothing in the Act shall give validity to arrangements of the kind specified. The Act does not legitimise any arrangements which would otherwise be unlawful but neither does it made them unlawful if they are otherwise lawful. The Court of Appeal found nothing in the 1974 Act which prohibits the charging of contingent fees. The fact that the Solicitors Practice Rules 1990 made it professional misconduct for a solicitor to enter into any agreement, even for his normal fee, where this was dependent on achieving a successful result in litigation, did not of itself make the practice contrary to law (following *Picton Jones & Co v Arcadia Developments Ltd* [1989] 1 E.G.L.R. 42). The Court found that the rules were based on a perception of public policy derived from judicial decisions which were flawed, *Thai Trading Co v Taylor* [1998] 2 W.L.R. 893, CA. In *Hughes v Kingston Upon Hull City Council* [1999] 2 All E.R. 49, DC, the Divisional Court decided that *Thai Trading* (above) had been decided per incuriam because *Swain v The Law Society* [1983] 1 A.C. 598, HL decided that the (Solicitors Practice Rules 1990 r.8) had the force of statute (see also *Leeds City Council v Carr*; *Wells v Barnsley MBC*, *The Times*, November 12, 1999, DC). Since that decision the Solicitors' Practice Rules 1990 have been altered (with effect from January 7, 1999) to forbid contingency fee agreements save those permitted under statute or by the common law. In *Awwad v Geraghty &Co*, [2001] Q.B. 570, CA, the Court of Appeal held that all contingency fee agreements other than those permitted by statute are unlawful; i.e. there can be no lawful contingency fee agreement under the common law. The decision in *Thai Trading* has thus been reversed and the only valid contingency fee agreements are those which accord with statute (see Conditional Fee Agreements Order 2000, para.7A–21, and Conditional Fee Agreements Regulations 2000, para.7A–26). The Access to Justice Act 1999 ss.27–31 brings all types of fee agreements into one statutory framework backed up by statutory instrument.

## Effect of contentious business agreements

7C–75 **60.**—(1) Subject to the provisions of this section and to sections 61 to 63, the costs of a solicitor in any case where a contentious business agreement has been made shall not be subject to assessment or (except in the case of an agreement which provides for the solicitor to be remunerated by reference to an hourly rate) to the provisions of section 69.

(2) Subject to subsection (3) a contentious business agreement shall not affect the amount of, or any rights or remedies for the recovery of, any costs payable by the client to, or to the client by, any person other than the solicitor, and that person may, unless he has otherwise agreed, require any such costs to be assessed according to the rules for their assessment for the time being in force.

(3) A client shall not be entitled to recover from any other person under an order for the payment of any costs to which a contentious business agreement relates more than the amount payable by him to his solicitor in respect of those costs under the agreement.

(4) A contentious business agreement shall be deemed to exclude any claim by the solicitor in respect of the business to which it relates other than—

(a) a claim for the agreed costs; or

(b) a claim for such costs as are expressly excepted from the agreement.

(5) A provision in a contentious business agreement that the solicitor shall not be liable for his negligence, or that of any employee of his, shall be void if the client is a natural person who, in entering that agreement, is acting for purposes which are outside his trade, business or profession.

(6) A provision in a contentious business agreement that the solicitor shall be relieved from any responsibility to which he would otherwise be subject as a solicitor shall be void.

*Note*—Amended by the Courts and Legal Services Act 1990 s.98; and the Legal Services Act 2007 s.177, Sch.16, Pt.1, para.56(c), with effect from June 30, 2008 (SI 2008/1436) and Sch.16 Pt 1 para.56(a), (b) with effect from January 1, 2010 (SI 2009/3250). **7C–75.1**

**"Contentious business"**

See s.87, para.7C–143. **7C–76**

**Subsection (2)**

See *Henderson v Merthyr Urban DC* [1900] 1 Q.B. 434. **7C–77**

**Subsection (3)**

Subsection (3) does no more than express the common law doctrine under which costs are given to the successful party by way of indemnity only. A claimant therefore who has an oral agreement with his solicitor to pay no costs cannot recover any from the defendant (*Gundry v Sainsbury* [1910] 1 K.B. 99 at 645, CA) *aliter* if he is merely indemnified by another (*Baillie v Neville* (1920) 149 L.T.J. 300) or is a member of a trade union and he and the union are both liable for the costs (*Adams v London, etc., Builders* [1921] 1 K.B. 495 or where an employer is indemnified by an insurance Company. (*Cornish v Lynch* (1910) 3 B.W.C.C. 343, CA) and see *R. v Miller and Glennie* [1983] 1 W.L.R. 1056; [1983] 3 All E.R. 186. **7C–78**

The words "any costs" in the phrase "an order for the payment of any costs" in s.60(3) relate not to costs at large or to the costs payable by the receiving party to his own solicitor but to the costs and items of costs to be identified on the detailed assessment between the parties as the proper and recoverable costs. The words "costs" clearly refer to the same costs.

The operation of the cap then becomes readily intelligible. Where applicable the figures in the contentious business agreement provide both a measure and a ceiling for each recoverable item of costs. Per Sir Brian Neill in *General of Berne Insurance Co, The v Jardine Reinsurance Management Ltd* [1998] 2 All E.R. 301, CA.

When solicitors realised that the opposing party was intent on mounting a challenge to the enforceability of a CFA they entered into a contentious business agreement with the clients who had signed the CFA. In the event the CFA was found to be valid. The judge was asked to consider giving guidance as to the efficacy of the contentious business agreement seeking to put right any defect in a CFA. The judge declined to give guidance but stated that he would be hesitant to conclude that any CBA entered into by a claimant after an adverse costs order had been made against the defendant in favour of a claimant who had signed a potentially defective CFA could be held to alter retrospectively the rights and obligations as between claimant and solicitor: *Birmingham City Council v Crook* [2007] EWHC 1415 (QB) Irwin J.

Where solicitors had acted for a limited company in litigation and shortly before trial went on the record as acting for both the limited company and the director a dispute arose as to the extent of the retainer. The director was unable to produce any evidence of a separate retainer between himself and the solicitors and there was no separate retainer letter. The court held that where the solicitors had placed themselves on the record as acting for a client the existence of a retainer might be implied unless there was evidence to the contrary. Evidence that the limited company had paid the solicitors' bills was not sufficient on the balance of probabilities to displace the inference of a retainer between the solicitors and the director: *Bulmer v Owlett*, unrep., Briggs J.

Where a firm of solicitors acted for certain members of the management committee of a charity, in respect of a dispute between members of the management committee which was resolved by litigation and ultimately by mediation, the mediated agreement did not deal with all aspects of costs. The solicitors acting for the claimants sued the charity for their costs and disbursements in respect of the work which they had undertaken. The defendant charity argued that the solicitors did not have a proper retainer from it and that the charity's funds should not be used to pay the costs. The

***Paragraph numbers marked with a "+" can be found online and on CD.***



SOLICITORS

court found that although the solicitors had not been instructed by the charity's chief executive or by any formal resolution, there was a letter from the chairman suggesting that the charity's resources would be involved in the proceedings. In any event the costs incurred represented the price of getting the charity's governance back into order. The solicitors' instructions, despite their imperfections and incompleteness should be treated as having been ratified by the charity so that the solicitors were entitled to be paid (*Harding (t/a Hardings Solicitors) v The Davenant Centre Ltd* July 30, 2008, unrep. (Ch), Robin Knowles Q.C.).

## Enforcement of contentious business agreements

7C-79 **61.**—(1) No action shall be brought on any contentious business agreement, but on the application of any person who—

(a) is a party to the agreement or the representative of such a party; or

(b) is or is alleged to be liable to pay, or is or claims to be entitled to be paid, the costs due or alleged to be due in respect of the business to which the agreement relates,

the court may enforce or set aside the agreement and determine every question as to its validity or effect.

(2) On any application under subsection (1) the court—

(a) if it is of the opinion that the agreement is in all respects fair and reasonable, may enforce it;

(b) if it is of the opinion that the agreement is in any respect unfair or unreasonable, may set it aside and order the costs covered by it to be assessed as if it had never been made;

(c) in any case, may make such order as to the costs of the application as it thinks fit.

(3) If the business covered by a contentious business agreement (not being an agreement to which section 62 applies) is business done, or to be done, in any action, a client who is a party to the agreement may make application to a costs officer of the court for the agreement to be examined.

(4) A costs officer before whom an agreement is laid under subsection (3) shall examine it and may either allow it, or, if he is of the opinion that the agreement is unfair or unreasonable, require the opinion of the court to be taken on it, and the court may allow the agreement or reduce the amount payable under it, or set it aside and order the costs covered by it to be assessed as if it had never been made.

(4A) Subsection (4B) applies where a contentious business agreement provides for the remuneration of the solicitor to be by reference to an hourly rate.

(4B) If on the assessment of any costs the agreement is relied on by the solicitor and the client objects to the amount of the costs (but is not alleging that the agreement is unfair or unreasonable), the costs officer may enquire into—

(a) the number of hours worked by the solicitor; and

(b) whether the number of hours worked by him was excessive.

(5) Where the amount agreed under any contentious business

agreement is paid by or on behalf of the client or by any person entitled to do so, the person making the payment may at any time within twelve months from the date of payment, or within such further time as appears to the court to be reasonable, apply to the court, and, if it appears to the court that the special circumstances of the case require it to be re-opened, the court may, on such terms as may be just, re-open it and order the costs covered by the agreement to be assessed and the whole or any part of the amount received by the solicitor to be repaid by him.

(6) In this section and in sections 62 and 63 "the court" means—

(a) in relation to an agreement under which any business has been done in any court having jurisdiction to enforce and set aside agreements, any such court in which any of that business has been done;

(b) in relation to an agreement under which no business has been done in any such court and under which not more than £50 is payable, the High Court;

(c) in relation to an agreement under which no business has been done in any such court and under which not more than £50 is payable, any county court which would, but for the provisions of subsection (1) prohibiting the bringing of an action on the agreement, have had jurisdiction in any action on it;

and for the avoidance of doubt it is hereby declared that in paragraph (a) "court having jurisdiction to enforce and set aside agreements" includes a county court.

*Note* — Subsections (4A) and (4B) added by the Courts and Legal Services Act 1990 s.98; and by the Legal Services Act 2007 Sch.16 para.57, with effect from January 1, 2010 (SI 2009/3250). **7C–80**

**Subsection (1)—"No action"**

An action for damages for breach of such an agreement is not precluded by this section (*Rees v Williams* (1874–75) L.R. 10 Ex. 200). **7C–81**

**"Representative"**

For the right of a trustee in bankruptcy to go behind an agreement made before bankruptcy, see *Re Van Laun* [1907] 1 K.B. 155, affirmed [1907] 2 K.B. 23 and see the Insolvency Act 1986 ss.283–291. **7C–82**

**Subsection (2)—"Fair and reasonable"**

For the meaning of the expression, see *Re Stuart, Ex p. Cathcart* [1893] 2 Q.B. 201, CA. An agreement to pay 5 per cent on all amounts deducted from a bill is not reasonable (*Re Stuart* [1893] 2 Q.B. 201). An agreement to pay a percentage on the amount recovered otherwise than by action is legitimate (*Re Hoggart's Settlement* (1912) 56 S.J. 415). A one-sided provision inserted by solicitors into the contract between them and the client justified the construction of ambiguous provisions in that contract *contra proferentem* (*Re A Debtor (No.1594 of 1992), The Times*, December 8, 1992 Knox J.). **7C–83**

**Subsection (3)—"Examined"**

The allowance of the agreement by the costs officer under this section does not preclude an independent application under subs.(1) to set it aside, or under subs.(5) to reopen it (*Re Stuart* [1893] 2 Q.B. 201; *Re Simmons & Politzer* [1954] 2 Q.B. 296). **7C–84**

The costs officer cannot go into such an agreement and deal with the amount payable under it as an item in the solicitor's cash account in assessing other bills (*Re Templeton and Cox* (1909) 101 L.T. 144, CA).

***Paragraph numbers marked with a "+" can be found online and on CD.***

In taking accounts in a foreclosure action which involved the validity of such an agreement, the Court referred the agreement to the Cost Judge (*Bake v French (No.2)* [1907] 2 Ch. 215).

**Subsection (5)—"Within 12 months after payment"**

7C-85 Payment within the meaning of this subsection "must be made under such circumstances as to show that the client understands that in making the payment he is carrying out the terms of the agreement and ratifying it" (*Re Jackson* [1915] 1 K.B. 371 at 381, 383).

## Contentious business agreements by certain representatives

7C-86 **62.**—(1) Where the client who makes a contentious business agreement makes it as a representative of a person whose property will be chargeable with the whole or part of the amount payable under the agreement, the agreement shall be laid before a costs officer of the court before payment.

(2) A costs officer before whom an agreement is laid under subsection (1) shall examine it and may either allow it, or, if he is of the opinion that it is unfair or unreasonable, require the opinion of the court to be taken on it, and the court may allow the agreement or reduce the amount payable under it, or set it aside and order the costs covered by it to be assessed as if it had never been made.

(3) A client who makes a contentious business agreement as mentioned in subsection (1) and pays the whole or any part of the amount payable under the agreement without it being allowed by the officer or by the court shall be liable at any time to account to the person whose property is charged with the whole or any part of the amount so paid for the sum so charged, and the solicitor who accepts the payment may be ordered by the court to refund the amount received by him.

(4) A client makes a contentious business agreement as the representative of another person if he makes it—

(a) as his guardian,

(b) as a trustee for him under a deed or will,

(c) as his receiver appointed under Part VII of the Mental Health Act 1983, or

(d) as a person other than a receiver authorised under that Part of that Act to act on his behalf.

7C-87 *Note* —Amended by the Mental Health Act 1983 s.148, Sch.4; and by the Mental Capacity Act 2005 s.67(1), Sch.6, para.22, with effect from October 1, 2007 (SI 2007/1897); and by the Legal Services Act 2007 Sch.16, para.58, with effect from January 1, 2010 (SI 2009/3250).

## Effect on contentious business agreement of death, incapability or change of solicitor

7C-88 **63.**—(1) If, after some business has been done under a contentious business agreement but before the solicitor has wholly performed it—

(a) the solicitor dies, or becomes incapable of acting; or

(b) the client changes his solicitor (as, notwithstanding the agreement, he shall be entitled to do) any party to, or the representative of any party to, the agreement may apply to the court, and the court shall have the same jurisdiction as to enforcing the agreement so far as it has been performed, or setting it aside, as the court would have had if the solicitor had not died or become incapable of acting, or the client had not changed his solicitor.

(2) The court, notwithstanding that it is of the opinion that the agreement is in all respects fair and reasonable, may order the amount due in respect of business under the agreement to be ascertained by assessment, and in that case—

(a) the costs officer, in ascertaining that amount, shall have regard so far as may be to the terms of the agreement; and

(b) payment of the amount found by him to be due may be enforced in the same manner as if the agreement had been completely performed.

(3) If in such a case as is mentioned in subsection (1)(b) an order is made for the assessment of the amount due to the solicitor in respect of the business done under the agreement, the court shall direct the costs officer to have regard to the circumstances under which the change of solicitor has taken place, and the costs officer, unless he is of the opinion that there has been no default, negligence, improper delay or other conduct on the part of the solicitor, or any of his employees, affording the client reasonable ground for changing his solicitor, shall not allow to the solicitor the full amount of the remuneration agreed to be paid to him.

*Note*—Amended by the Legal Services Act 2007 s.177 and Sch.16, Pt.1, para.59, with effect in part (subject to transitory provisions) from March 31, 2009 (SI 2009/503; and with effect in part from January 1, 2010 (SI 2009/3250). **7C–88.1**

### Form of bill of costs for contentious business

**64.**—(1) Where the remuneration of a solicitor in respect of contentious business done by him is not the subject of a contentious business agreement, then, subject to subsections (2) to (4) the solicitor's bill of costs may at the option of the solicitor be either a bill containing detailed items or a gross sum bill. **7C–89**

(2) The party chargeable with a gross sum bill may at any time—

(a) before he is served with a writ or other originating process for the recovery of costs included in the bill, and

(b) before the expiration of three months from the date on which the bill was delivered to him,

require the solicitor to deliver, in lieu of that bill, a bill containing detailed items; and on such a requirement being made the gross sum bill shall be of no effect.

(3) Where an action is commenced on a gross sum bill, the court shall, if so requested by the party chargeable with the bill before the expiration of one month from the service on that party of the writ or other originating process, order that the bill be assessed.

(4) If a gross sum bill is assessed, whether under this section or otherwise, nothing in this section shall prejudice any rules of court

*Paragraph numbers marked with a "+" can be found online and on CD.*

with respect to assessment, and the solicitor shall furnish the costs officer with such details of any of the costs covered by the bill as the costs officer may require.

7C–89.1 *Note*—Amended by the Legal Services Act 2007 Sch.16, para.60, with effect from January 1, 2010 (SI 2009/3250).

7C–90 *Note*—Solicitors delivered a gross sum bill to their client in respect of wardship proceedings. The client, after the expiration of three months, asked for a detailed bill, which was greater than the gross sum bill. In *Carlton v Theodore Goddard & Co* [1973] 1 W.L.R. 623; [1973] 2 All E.R. 877, Megarry J. ordered the gross sum bill to be assessed and refused an application by the solicitors for leave to substitute the detailed bill for the gross sum bill. See also notes to s.69, paras 7C–103 *et seq.*

Where a bill has been delivered to a client, that bill may be withdrawn later and substituted by a second bill if the client consents or with the leave of the court. The first bill is not conclusive evidence of the reasonableness of the amounts charged in it although it may be relevant evidence. Detailed assessment of the second bill would be valid and not without jurisdiction. *Rezvi v Brown Cooper* (1997) 1 Costs L.R. 109 (Newman J.).

## Security for costs and termination of retainer

7C–91 **65.**—(1) A solicitor may take security from his client for his costs, to be ascertained by assessment or otherwise, in respect of any contentious business to be done by him.

(2) If a solicitor who has been retained by a client to conduct contentious business requests the client to make a payment of a sum of money, being a reasonable sum on account of the costs incurred or to be incurred in the conduct of that business and the client refuses or fails within a reasonable time to make that payment, the refusal or failure shall be deemed to be a good cause whereby the solicitor may, upon giving reasonable notice to the client, withdraw from the retainer.

7C–91.0 *Note*—Amended by the Legal Services Act 2007 Sch.16, para.61, with effect from January 1, 2010 (SI 2009/3250).

7C–91.1 Where solicitors acted for a client on two matters, one being a statutory appeal to the Administrative Court. The solicitors advised the client against pursuing the appeal but he insisted on proceeding. The solicitors terminated their retainer and formally came off the record at a late stage. At first instance it was held that the solicitors did not have just cause to terminate the retainer even though the instructions given by the client were doomed to failure. The Costs Judge found that because they had failed to carry out the client's instructions they were not entitled to charge him fees in the matter since they had been retained for the entire contract. On appeal it was argued by the solicitors that although, in principle, the nature of a solicitor's retainer is one of an entire contract, in the particular case that worked unfairness and operated harshly against solicitors' interests and should accordingly be modified. The judge reviewed the law (i.e. *Underwood Son & Piper v Lewis* (1894) 2 Q.B. 306 (CA); *Warmingtons v McMurray* (1936) 2 All E.R. 745, Goddard J.). On the facts the Costs Judge had been entitled to find that there was no just cause for termination. The argument that the Court of Appeal authority was elderly and should be applied more flexibly in modern conditions was rejected (*Richard Buxton v Mills-Owens* [2008] EWHC 1831 (QB), Mackay J.)

## Assessments with respect to contentious business

7C–92 **66.** Subject to the provisions of any rules of court, on every assessment of costs in respect of any contentious business, the costs officer may—

(a) allow interest at such rate and from such time as he thinks just on money disbursed by the solicitor for the client, and on money of the client in the hands of, and improperly retained by, the solicitor or an employee of the solicitor; and

(b) in determining the remuneration of the solicitor, have regard to the skill, labour and responsibility involved in the business done by him or by any employee of his who is an authorised person (within the meaning of section 56(5A)).

*Note* —Amended by the Legal Services Act 2007 s.177 and Sch.16, Pt.1, para.62, with effect in part from March 31, 2009 (SI 2009/503) and in part from January 1, 2010 (SI 2009/3250). **7C–92.1**



**Interest**

The power to allow interest relates only to disbursements by the solicitor and, in respect of money belonging to the client, only if it is in the hands of and improperly retained by the solicitor. There is no power to allow interest on profit charges and the Act applies only as between the solicitor and his client and not to the detailed assessment of costs to be paid out of a fund in Court belonging wholly or partly to persons other than the client. The solicitor cannot appropriate payments to costs so as to leave disbursements unpaid and therefore bearing interest (*Hartland v Murrell* (1873) L.R. 16 Eq. 285, 43 L.J. Ch. 94). Nor does the section apply to accounts between a London agent and his country solicitor client (*Ward v Eyre* (1880) L.R. 15 Ch D 130, 49 L.J. Ch. 657; *Re Savery* (1851) 15 Beav. 58). **7C–93**

A contentious business agreement which includes a provision that the client should pay interest on costs would appear to be binding if it is valid in all other respects (*Re Fanshawe* (1905) 59 S.J. 404). A solicitor who sues on his bill of costs and recovers judgment is entitled to interest upon the amount recovered from the time of signing judgment. The rate of interest is fixed periodically. (Currently 8 per cent, Judgment Debts (Rates of Interest) Order 1993.)

The mere receipt of clients' money by his solicitor does not entitle the client to receive interest but as soon as the demand is made by the client for payment, which is not complied with within a reasonable time, interest becomes payable (*Barclay v Harris & Cross* (1915) 85 L.J.K.B. 115, 112 L.T. 1134). A credit in favour of the client produced only by a reduction of the solicitors' bill on detailed assessment does not automatically carry interest (*Wright v Southwood* (1827) 1 Y & J 527).

In detailed assessment proceedings of a solicitors' bill to their client, the client claimed interest on one of four alternative bases:

(a) s.35(A) of the Senior Courts Act 1981;

(b) the general equitable jurisdiction of the courts;

(c) s.66(a) of the Solicitors Act 1974; and

(d) reg.25 of the Solicitors' Accounts Rules 1998.

The court held that s.35(A) could not apply because the claim was not one for a debt or damages. So far as the equitable jurisdiction of the court was concerned following *Wright v Southwood* (above) no such claim was permissible in the circumstances of the case. The court held that, so far as s.66(a) of the Solicitors Act 1974 was concerned, the money was not "improperly retained" by the solicitor since the money had been retained pending the decision of the Costs Judge as to whether or not the bills were payable in full or in part. Finally the court held that the Solicitors Accounts Rules applied only to money held in a client account, whereas in the particular case the money had been paid direct into the office account because it was paid in settlement of bills. In any event the solicitors' terms of business expressly excluded the right of the claimant to interest *Argonaut Property Development Ltd v Collyer-Bristow* October 16, 2001 QB, Nelson J.

The House of Lords in *Hunt v Douglas (R.M.) (Roofing)* [1988] 3 W.L.R. 975; [1988] 2 All E.R. 823, ruled that a litigant who has been awarded costs is entitled to interest from the date upon which judgment is pronounced rather than the date of the costs officer's certificate. The rate of interest will be the rate prescribed for judgment debts.

This judgment does not of itself make any difference to the interest position on a detailed assessment between solicitor and client, but if the solicitor sues the client for his fees, it would seem that the costs of reference could carry interest from the date of judgment in the solicitor's favour, notwithstanding that the amount of the judgment is to be ascertained on detailed assessment.

## REMUNERATION—GENERAL

### Inclusion of disbursements in bill of costs

7C–94 **67.** A solicitor's bill of costs may include costs payable in discharge of a liability properly incurred by him on behalf of the party to be charged with the bill (including counsel's fees) notwithstanding that those costs have not been paid before the delivery of the bill to that party; but those costs—

(a) shall be described in the bill as not then paid; and

(b) if the bill is assessed, shall not be allowed by the costs officer unless they are paid before the assessment is completed.

7C–94.1 *Note* —Amended by the Legal Services Act 2007 Sch.16, para.63, with effect from January 1, 2010 (SI 2009/3250).

#### "Costs payable in discharge of a liability properly incurred by the solicitor on behalf of the party to be charged with the bill"

7C–95 These words define the "disbursements" which may be included as costs. They are those payments only which are made in pursuance of the professional duty undertaken by the solicitor, and which he is bound to perform whether kept in funds by his client or not, or payments which are sanctioned as professional payments by the established custom and practice of the profession (*Re Remnant* (1849) 11 Beav. 603) such as court fees (*Langridge v Lynch* (1876) 34 L.T. 695)) counsel's fees, payments to witnesses (*Franklin v Featherstonhaugh* (1834) 1 Ad. & El. 475) deposit on presentation of bankruptcy petition (*Re Grant Bulcraig & Co* [1906] 1 Ch. 124) stamp duties on deeds, printer's charges and fees for certificates of birth, etc. Payments for photographs are usually reckoned in this class even though the solicitor be not personally liable for them (*Wakefield v Duckworth* [1915] 1 K.B. 218). Such disbursements are properly placed in the bill even though actually paid by the client (*Re Metcalf* (1862) 30 Beav. 406; *Re Seal* (1893) 37 S.J. 685 at 842; *Devereaux v White* (1896) 41 S.J. 67) or though security has been taken for them (*Re Bedson (No.1)* (1845) 9 Beav. 5). Since these disbursements form part of the bill and the law implies authority to make them from the solicitor's character as solicitor, it follows that where that character is wanting (e.g. where the solicitor is uncertificated) the disbursements as well as the charges are disallowed (*Fowler v Monmouthshire Ry.* (1879) 4 Q.B.D. 334; *Kent v Ward* (1894) 70 L.T. 612; *Browne v Barber* [1913] 2 K.B. 553).

But payments which neither law nor custom required the solicitor himself to make, such as purchase-money (*Re Remnant* (1849) 11 Beav. 603) deposit for security for costs (*Re Buckwell* [1902] 2 Ch. 596) payments to other parties' solicitors (except for copy documents, etc.) (*Re Fletcher & Dyson* [1903] 2 Ch. 688) debt and costs paid to opponents (*Prothero v Thomas* (1815) 6 Taunt. 196; *Woollison v Hodgson* (1834) 2 Dowl. 360) capital duty on registering a company (*Re Blair & Girling* [1906] 2 K.B. 131) are not properly charged in the bill, but should appear in the cash account. Agents' charges should not appear as a disbursement in either (*Re Pomeroy & Tanner* [1897] 1 Ch. 284) though the charges of other solicitors for service of process or answering inquiries are generally treated as professional disbursements.

#### "Shall be described as not then paid"

7C–96 For a case in which there were defects in the original bill and leave was given for delivery of a fresh bill, see paras 7C–109 and 7C–110.

In *Tearle & Company (a firm) v Sherring*, October 29, 1993, unrep., Wright J. in chambers, reviewed the law surrounding s.67 and concluded that he had the power to permit the solicitors to amend their original bill of costs to include the necessary words (i.e. "not paid"). Furthermore, relying on the judgment of Farwell J. in *Re Grant Bulcraig & Co* [1906] 1 Ch. 124, stated *obiter* that it might have been within the power of a Costs Judge or District Judge to do likewise if the application had been made during the course of a hearing.

## Power of court to order solicitor to deliver bill, etc.

**68.**—(1) The jurisdiction of the High Court to make orders for the delivery by a solicitor of a bill of costs, and for the delivery up of, or otherwise in relation to, any documents in his possession, custody or power, is hereby declared to extend to cases in which no business has been done by him in the High Court. **7C–97**

(2) A county court shall have the same jurisdiction as the High Court to make orders making such provision as is mentioned in subsection (1) in cases where the bill of costs or the documents relate wholly or partly to contentious business done by the solicitor in that county court.

(3) In this section and in sections 69 to 71 "solicitor" includes the executors, administrators and assignees of a solicitor.



### Orders for the delivery of a bill of costs

It is a matter for the discretion of the Court whether it will order the delivery of a bill in a given set of circumstances (*Re A Solicitor* [1953] Ch. 480; at 487 [1953] 2 All E.R. 23 at 26). For example, the delivery of a bill can be waived (*Re Van Laun* [1907] 1 K.B. 162, affirmed [1907] 2 K.B. 23, CA). A valid agreement dispenses with delivery (*Re Chapman* (1903) 20 T.L.R. 3, CA); and if a third party has paid a sum in settlement of costs, the client is not entitled to an order for delivery *ibid.* Nor will a solicitor who refuses to make a charge be ordered to deliver a bill (see *Re Griffith* (1891) 7 T.L.R. 268) though he may be ordered to deliver a cash account (*Re Landor* [1899] 1 Ch. 818). It is an answer to the application that the solicitor has already delivered his bill, but not if it was a mere constructive delivery (*Re Robertson* (1889) 42 Ch D 553) or if the delivery was to a third person not shown to be an authorised agent (*Re Layton Steele & Co* (1890) 38 W.R. 652). **7C–98**

### Practice

The application is under CPR Pt 8 (see Costs Practice Direction s.56). **7C–99**

### Application for delivery of a cash account or securities or the payment of moneys

If no costs are due to or from the solicitor, there is no jurisdiction under the Act to order an account of monetary transactions between him and his client (see *Re Landor* [1899] 1 Ch. 818). **7C–100**

## Action to recover solicitor's costs

**69.**—(1) Subject to the provisions of this Act, no action shall be brought to recover any costs due to a solicitor before the expiration of one month from the date on which a bill of those costs is delivered in accordance with the requirements mentioned in subsection (2); but if there is probable cause for believing that the party chargeable with the costs— **7C–101**

(a) is about to quit England and Wales, to become bankrupt or to compound with his creditors, or

(b) is about to do any other act which would tend to prevent or delay the solicitor obtaining payment,

the High Court may, notwithstanding that one month has not

*Paragraph numbers marked with a "+" can be found online and on CD.*

expired from the delivery of the bill, order that the solicitor be at liberty to commence an action to recover his costs and may order that those costs be assessed.

(2) The requirements referred to in subsection (1) are that the bill must be—

(a) signed in accordance with subsection (2A), and
(b) delivered in accordance with subsection (2C).

(2A) A bill is signed in accordance with this subsection if it is—

(a) signed by the solicitor or on his behalf by an employee of the solicitor authorised by him to sign, or
(b) enclosed in, or accompanied by, a letter which is signed as mentioned in paragraph (a) and refers to the bill.

(2B) For the purposes of subsection (2A) the signature may be an electronic signature.

(2C) A bill is delivered in accordance with this subsection if—

(a) it is delivered to the party to be charged with the bill personally,
(b) it is delivered to that party by being sent to him by post to, or left for him at, his place of business, dwelling-house or last known place of abode, or
(c) it is delivered to that party—
   (i) by means of an electronic communications network, or
   (ii) by other means but in a form that nevertheless requires the use of apparatus by the recipient to render it intelligible,

and that party has indicated to the person making the delivery his willingness to accept delivery of a bill sent in the form and manner used.

(2D) An indication to any person for the purposes of subsection (2C)(c)—

(a) must state the address to be used and must be accompanied by such other information as that person requires for the making of the delivery;
(b) may be modified or withdrawn at any time by a notice given to that person.

(2E) Where a bill is proved to have been delivered in compliance with the requirements of subsections (2A) and (2C), it is not necessary in the first instance for the solicitor to prove the contents of the bill and it is to be presumed, until the contrary is shown, to be a bill bona fide complying with this Act.

(2F) A bill which is delivered as mentioned in subsection (2C)(c) is to be treated as having been delivered on the first working day after the day on which it was sent (unless the contrary is proved).

(3) Where a bill of costs relates wholly or partly to contentious business done in a county court and the amount of the bill does not exceed £5,000, the powers and duties of the High Court under this section and sections 70 and 71 in relation to that bill may be exercised

and performed by any county court in which any part of the business was done.

(4) [...]

(5) In this section references to an electronic signature are to be read in accordance with section 7(2) of the Electronic Communications Act 2000 (c.7).

(6) In this section—

"electronic communications network" has the same meaning as in the Communications Act 2003 (c.21).

"working day" means a day other than a Saturday, a Sunday, Christmas Day, Good Friday or a bank holiday in England and Wales under the Banking and Financial Dealings Act 1971 (c.80).



*Note* —Amended by the Administration of Justice Act 1982; the County Courts Jurisdiction Order 1981 (SI 1981/1123); and the High Court and County Courts Jurisdiction Order 1991 (SI 1991/724); the Legal Services Act 2007 s.177, Sch.16, Pt 1, para.64(3) and (4), with effect from March 7, 2008 (SI 2008/222) and para.64(2), with effect from January 1, 2010 (SI 2009/3250). **7C–102**

**Subsection (1)—"No action shall be brought"**

Therefore equally no counterclaim lies (see *Spencer v Watts* [1889] W.N. 121). But even without delivering a signed bill the solicitor may sue on an account stated (*Turner v Willis* [1905] 1 K.B. 468) or a promissory note given on account of costs (*Jeffreys v Evans* (1845) 14 M. & W. 210) or to foreclose a mortgage given to secure them (*Thomas v Cross* (1864) 11 L.T. 430); and they may be the subject of a set-off (*Harrison v Turner* (1847) 10 L.J. Q.B. 482; *Ex p. Cooper* (1854) 14 C.B. 663; *Brown v Tibbits* (1862) 11 C.B. N.S. 855) provided they are not statute-barred (*Smith v Betty* [1903] 2 K.B. 317 at 323) or of a proof in bankruptcy (*Eicke v Nokes* (1829) Moo. 8 M. 303; *Re Howell* (1812) 1 Rose 312; and see *Ex p. Peacock* (1873) L.R. 8 Ch. 682). **7C–103**

The service of a statutory demand for payment of solicitor's costs does not constitute the bringing of an action. Accordingly, a statutory demand may be served before the expiration of a month from the date of the delivery of the bill (*Re A Debtor (No.88 of 1991)* [1992] 4 All E.R. 301).

A claim by a solicitor for his fees is a liquidated claim for the purposes of section 28(5) of the Limitation Act 1980: *Byatt v Nash* [2002] All E.R. (D.) 254, Mr J Crowley Q.C.

**"To recover any costs"**

See definition of costs (s.87) as including "fees, charges, disbursements, expenses and remuneration", and for disbursements see s.67 n. This section only applies to an action for work done in a professional capacity (*Bush v Martin* (1863) 2 H. & C. 311; *Re Inderwick* (1884) L.R. 25 Ch D 279). See, for example, as to a solicitor acting as election agent. *Re Osborne* (1858) 25 Beav. 353; *Re Oliver* (1866) 36 L.J.Ch. 261: as parliamentary agent. *Baker & Lees* [1903] 1 K.B. 189, CA: as rent collector. *Re Shilson & Co* [1904] 1 Ch. 837. **7C–104**

It is non performance of a contract to provide legal services by a solicitor, where a firm of solicitors is asked to provide a solicitor and, without telling the client that the adviser is not a solicitor, provides such an adviser. Accordingly, the firm of solicitors was not entitled to recover anything by way of costs (*Pilbrow v Pearless de Rugemont & Co* [1999] 3 All E.R. 355, CA).

In *Pilbrow* (above) the client did not receive what he thought he was receiving because of a mistake within the solicitor's firm. The decision was followed where the client was fraudulently deceived into believing that he was being advised by a qualified solicitor: *Adrian Alan Ltd v Fuglers* [2002] EWCA Civ 1655. Where solicitors sued their former client for their fees, the client asserted that the firm had been engaged on the express basis that the client would have the services of a qualified solicitor and that it had never been explained that the person who dealt with the work was an unadmitted

***Paragraph numbers marked with a "+" can be found online and on CD.***

clerk. It was submitted that this was a fundamental breach of duty and that the solicitors were not entitled to recover any fees. The court held that although the client care letter had described the clerk as a partner, the firm had subsequently communicated to the client that the clerk was not qualified and that superseded the client's request for a "solicitor". It was the clerk's standard practice to give new clients his business card and the firm's brochure, which stated that he was not admitted and gave an explanation of his position within the firm. There was no special reason why he should have departed from his usual practice. It was not uncommon for managing clerks to conduct major litigation and if the clerk was regarded by the solicitors as competent to handle the case there was no reason why the firm would necessarily have questioned it. The court was satisfied that the bills had been signed by a partner. *Manches LLP v Green* [2008] EWHC 917 (QB), Underhill J.

It is inconsistent with the duty of a solicitor that the solicitor should be entitled to a period of time during which they continued to take instructions and run up costs while they gathered information in relation to the contemplated proceedings and only once the gathering of that information had prompted them to consider that their client might be eligible for legal aid were they obliged to act.

> "A solicitor must be bound at the outset to consider the question whether a client might be eligible for legal aid. There are various reasons why that must be so. First, it would be quite wrong to incur substantial expenditure chargeable privately to the client if public funding was available. Second, a client is in more difficulties changing firms of solicitors if work has been done and a relationship built up, before advice is given that a different firm could become involved."
>
> *Truex v Kitchin* [2007] EWCA Civ 618.

Where a claimant, represented by solicitors, sued a firm of accountants for professional negligence and did not wish to accept the Pt 36 payment made by the defendants, but could not afford to continue with the action with his current solicitors, the claimant entered into a retainer with new solicitors and new counsel on the basis of what the court described as "some fairly novel proposals as to their own remuneration". A retainer letter was drafted stipulating the payment of enhanced fees to the lawyers (excluding Queens Counsel). It was also proposed that the lawyers should be given shares in a new company to be formed by the client with the assistance of and capital from the third party.

At trial the claimant was successful but the damages were limited to £5. His solicitors claimed payment of their fees saying that the retainer letter was the entire agreement between the parties. The defendant however argued that the letter was a sham and that in fact the agreement was that he would be liable for no more fees unless he won. It was clear that the negotiations as to the terms of remuneration had kept going beyond the date of the retainer letter. The Judge disagreed with the Master's refusal to award summary judgment and allowed the appeal. After the draft judgment had been circulated, but before the approved judgment was handed down, those representing the defendant client sought to open substantive arguments on the basis that the retainer letter was in fact a conditional fee agreement and that the client should not be liable for the fees claimed. This argument was held to be "inappropriate" because it had not been actively pursued at the substantive hearing. The Judge refused to allow the hearing to be re-opened. *McFaddens Solicitors v Chandrasekaran* [2006] EWHC 1357 (QB), Irwin J.

**"One month from the date on which a bill is delivered"**

**7C–105** The following cases were decided on the somewhat different wording of s.68 of the Solicitors Act 1957 and its predecessors. This is a calendar month (Interpretation Act 1978 Sch.1) and excludes the day of delivery of the bill and the day of the commencement of the action (*Blunt v Heslop* (1838) 4 A. & E. 577). If the bill is sent by post, delivery for this purpose is on the day on which in the ordinary course of post it would be delivered, and the month excludes that day (*Browne v Black* [1912] 1 K.B. 316, CA).

Prima facie the right to deliver a bill arises on completion of the work for which the solicitor was retained (for example, the termination of the suit: *Harris v Osbourn* (1834) 2 Cr. & M. 629; *Re Romer & Haslam* [1893] 2 Q.B. 286) and therefore the Limitation Act runs from that time, and not from the expiry of the month (*Coburn v Colledge* [1897] 1 Q.B. 702). And if an appeal is brought and the same solicitor retained for it, there is a continuance of the contract so that it includes the appeal, and postpones the commencement of the period of limitation (*Harris v Quine* (1868–69) L.R. 4 Q.B. 653). But the circumstances may give rise to a right to deliver a bill at stages in the work (*Re Romer & Haslam* [1893] 2 Q.B. 286; *Re Hall & Barker* (1878) L.R. 9 Ch D 538; *Harris v Osbourn*, above) and a bill may be a final bill, though one of a series (*ibid.* and *Re Hudson* [1904] W.N. 32): and see *Davidsons v Jones-Fenleigh* (1980) 124 S.J. 204, where the Court of Appeal held that as three of a series of four bills had been paid more than 12 months prior to the application each was complete and final in its own right and only the fourth fell to be assessed; but see *Chamberlain v Boodle & King* [1982] 1 W.L.R. 1443; [1982] 3 All E.R. 188; where the Court of Appeal held that a series of bills were rendered as part of a current account in the same matter and should be treated as one bill. Before obtaining an acknowledgment of the debt so as to take it out of the operation of the Limitation Act, it may be the duty of the solicitor to advise his client as to his rights (*Lloyd v Coote & Ball* [1915] 1 K.B. 242).

A Costs Judge held that certain bills sent by a solicitor to its client were interim bills not statute bills and that the client was entitled to detailed assessment. The Costs Judge further held that if the bills were not interim bills there were special circumstances, within the meaning of s.70(3) Solicitors Act 1974, that justified assessment of the bills including that the letter of retainer between the parties failed to deal with the calculation of legal costs, the disparity between the estimated legal costs and the costs as billed. Permission to appeal was refused by the single Judge and the application to rely on fresh evidence was refused since the evidence was available at the time of the hearing before the Costs Judge. *Nigel Adams & Co v Al Malick Carpets Ltd* [2003] EWHC (QB) December 4, 2003 Fulford J.

**Subsection (2)—The bill**

It must be a complete bill containing sufficient information to enable the client to obtain advice as to its detailed assessment (*Haigh v Ousey* (1857) 7 El. & Bl. 578 at 582; *Eversheds v Osman*, April 7, 1998, unrep., CA) and the Costs Judge to assess it (*Slingsby v Attorney General* [1918] P. 236; *Waller v Lacey* (1840) 1 M. & Gr. 54). Otherwise there is no "bill" (*Duffet v McEvoy* (1885) 10 App.Cas. 300 at 302; *Re Baylis* [1896] 2 Ch. 107; *Cobbett v Wood* [1908] 2 K.B. 420; *Lomas v Joseph* (1909) 53 S.J. 271). So, if costs between the parties have been assessed and paid by the opponent, or disbursements paid by the client, they must yet be included in the client's bill (*Cobbett v Wood* [1908] 2 K.B. 420, CA; *Re Osborne and Osborne* [1913] 3 K.B. 862, CA); and the same applies to the items of charges of a London agent, if they form a substantial portion of the charges of a country solicitor (*Re Pomeroy & Tanner* [1897] 1 Ch. 284). If, by reason of the absence of details, there is no "bill", an itemised bill may be delivered (*cf. Re Russell* (1886) 55 L.T. 71). If the work is not ordinary professional work of a solicitor it must not be included in the bill (see notes to subs.(1)). **7C–106**

This note must be read in conjunction with the Solicitors' (Non-Contentious Business) Remuneration Order 2009 (SI 2009/1931), and where appropriate, with the Solicitors' (Non-Contentious Business) Remuneration Order 1994 (SI 1994/2616).

For an extensive examination of the authorities relating to the information properly to be contained in a solicitor's bill see *Ralph Hulme Gary (A Firm) v Gwillim* [2002] EWCA Civ 1500. Ward L.J. stated:

> "63. I accept the principle … that the defendant who undertakes to prove that the bill is not a bona fide compliance with the act cannot found an objection upon want of information in the bill if it appears that he is already in possession of that information.
>
> …
>
> 64. Thus I would accept the proper principle to be that the there must be something in the written bill to indicate the ambit of the work but that inadequacies of description of that work may be redressed by accompanying documents … or by other information already in possession of the client. That it seems to me would serve the purpose of the Act to give the client the knowledge he reasonably needs in order to decide whether to insist on taxation. If the solicitor satisfies that then the bill is one bona fide complying with the Act.
>
> …
>
> 70. This review of the legislation and the case law leads me to conclude that the burden on the client under section 69(2) to establish that a bill for a gross sum in

> contentious business will not be a bill 'bona fide complying with the Act' is satisfied if the client shows; (i) that there is no sufficient narrative in the bill to identify what it is he is being charged for; and (ii) that he does not have sufficient knowledge from other documents in his possession or from what he has been told reasonably to take advice whether or not to apply for that bill to be taxed. The sufficiency of the narrative and the sufficiency of his knowledge will vary from case to case, and the more he knows, the less the bill may need to spell it out for him. The interests of justice require that the balance be struck between protection of the client's right to seek taxation and the solicitor's right to recover not being defeated by opportunistic resort to technicality."

Ward L.J. went on to suggest that a copy of the solicitor's computer print-out containing a description of the fee earner, the rate of charging and some description of the work done, adjusted to remove items recorded for administrative purposes but not chargeable to the client, could easily be rendered to a client and thus avoid the problems which had arisen in the instant case "in these days where there seems to be a need for transparency in all things, is a print out not the least a client is entitled to expect?".

The court found on the facts that two solicitors letters requesting full payment of costs incurred did not amount to a termination of retainer disentitling the firm from claiming its costs in respect of work done. The first bill was found to be consistent with an interim statute bill rather than a request for payment on account so that the solicitor was entitled to recover the costs without instigating fresh proceedings. A second letter demanding full payment on account did not amount to the termination of retainer disentitling the solicitors from claiming costs in respect of work properly done. Although the solicitors sought to charge 20 per cent in excess of the proper fee this had not automatically terminated the retainer so that it was unable to recover any part of the costs it had incurred. Even if this was a breach of contract it was not one such as to disentitle the solicitors to reasonable costs for work properly carried out: *Wilson v Williams Sturges & Co* [2006] EWHC 792 (QB) Nelson J.

### Signature of bill

**7C–107** The bill may be signed by the solicitor, or one of the firm of solicitors, in his own name or in the name in which the practice is carried on (*Goodman v Eban Ltd* [1954] 1 Q.B. 550). It may also be signed by the executors or administrators of the solicitor (s.67(3)), or by an assignee (*ibid.*) even if he is a layman (*Ingle v McCutchan* (1884) 12 Q.B.D. 518; *Penley v Anstruther* (1883) 52 L.J.Ch. 367; *M'Lean v. Weaver* (1924) 41 T.L.R. 47, CA; *Medlicott v Emery* (1933) 49 T.L.R. 427). Signature by a clerk is not enough (cf. *Angell v Tratt* (1883) 1 Cab. & El. 118). In respect of bills delivered after March 7, 2008, s.69 of the Solicitors Act 1974 was amended to state, at s.69(2A):

> "A bill is signed in accordance with this subsection, if it is—
>
> (a) signed by the solicitor, or on his behalf by an employee of the solicitor authorised by him to sign…"

Before, a former requirement that the bill had to be signed by a partner was accordingly directory and not mandatory. In the particular case the bills had been signed by a non-practising barrister: *Magantic Services Ltd v Dorsey & Whitney* [2008] EWHC 2662 (QB), Irwin J. The signature may be by a facsimile representation by stamp affixed by the solicitor, though this is not desirable (*Goodman v Eban Ltd*, above). But the client may preclude himself by his acts from objecting that the bill is unsigned (*Re Pender* (1846) 2 Ph. 69; *Re Gedge* (1851) 14 Beav. 56; *Young v Walker* (1847) 16 M. & W. 446). See *Bartletts de Reya v Byrne*, *The Times*, January 14, 1983; (1983) 127 S.J. 69; where the Court of Appeal considered a contraction of the firm's name was sufficient but thought it sensible if the full name was used. An unsigned bill, if delivered, may be assessed (*Ex p. D'Aragon* (1887) 3 T.L.R. 815) and may be a paid bill within s.69 (*Re Sutton* (1883) 11 Q.B.D. 377) and cannot be withdrawn without leave (*Re Jones* (1886) 54 L.T. 648).

### Delivery of bill

**7C–108** The bill may be delivered to an agent authorised for the purpose (*Re Bush* (1844) 8 Beav. 66; *Daubney v Phipps* (1849) 18 L.J.Q.B. 337) or to a servant at his dwelling-house (*Macgregor v Keily* (1849) 3 Ex. 794). If actually delivered, it does not matter that it was misdirected (*Welsh v Sitwell* (1847) 11 Jur. 471). Delivery to the client's new solicitor is not enough (*Re Abbott* (1861) 4 L.T. (n.s.) 576; see *Re Kellock* (1887) 56 L.T. (n.s.) 887, p.890), unless in accordance with the clients' direction or authority (*Spier v Barnard* (1863) 8 L.T. (n.s. 396) or an order of the Court (*Vincent v Slaymaker* (1810) 12 East 372). Delivery to one of a number of persons jointly liable is delivery to each (*Crowder v Shee* (1808) 1 Camp. 437; *Finchett v Howe* (1809) 2 Camp. 275; *Mant v Smith* (1859) 4 Hurl. & N. 324; and cf. *Edwards v Lawless* (1848) 6 C.B. 329; *Blandy v De Burgh* (1848) 6 C.B. 623).

**Delivery of a fresh bill**

The court has a wide discretion to deal with the circumstances which arise in any particular case, per Newman J., *Rezvi v Brown Cooper (a firm)*, January 12, 1996, unrep., Open Court. If a bill has been delivered it cannot be substituted by a new bill without the consent of the parties or an order of the court, the grant of which is a matter of discretion (*Polak v Marchioness of Winchester* [1956] 1 W.L.R. 819; [1956] 2 All E.R. 660, CA, and cases there cited; see also *Chappel v Mehta* [1981] 1 All E.R. 349 where the Court of Appeal upheld an order allowing a detailed assessment to be set aside, for bills to be withdrawn and fresh ones submitted to include counsel's fees; and even where certain items in a bill have been struck out by consent, the Court has held that the bill to be assessed must be a bill as delivered (*Re Heather* (1870) L.R. 5 Ch. 694; *Sadd v Griffin* [1908] 2 K.B. 512, per Farwell L.J. at 512). Where an action has been brought on the basis of a Bill of Costs which fails to comply with the statutory requirements or which contains erroneous items the Court is not bound to dismiss the action but can consider the merits of the case and if appropriate allow the solicitor to withdraw the bill and deliver another one *Zuliani v Veira* [1994] 1 W.L.R. 1149, PC. The one-fifth rule in s.70(9) governing the incidence of the costs of detailed assessment, relates to the amount of the whole bill. But a bill may be delivered subject to a condition, if it is lawful and fair and the situation is clearly stated to the client (*Re Thompson* (1885) L.R. 30 Ch D 441, CA; *Re Jones* (1886) 54 L.T. 648). Arithmetical errors can be corrected on assessment (*Re Grant* [1906] 1 Ch. 124). The general rule stated above only applies to a detailed assessment under the Solicitors Act and not to an assessment between parties (*Davis v Dysart (No.2)* (1855) 21 Beav. 124) nor to a reference to a costs officer by order of a court to fix the reasonable charge for the work done (*Lumsden v Shipcote Land Co* [1906] 2 K.B. 433; and *Rollinson v Eversheds Hepworth and Chadwick*, May 11, 1993, unrep., CA). **7C–109**

The court confirmed the guidance given in *Polak v Marchioness of Winchester* [1956] 1 W.L.R. 818, CA that permission to amend a bill, or to allow a bill to be withdrawn and substituted with a correct bill, should be granted only in exceptional circumstances. In the instant case the court found that the proposed amendment (an uplift of £50,000) was objectionable. Firstly, because it was in breach of the terms of the retainer; secondly, it purported to charge an uplift in respect of earlier bills, all of which were final; and thirdly, it purported to charge an uplift in respect of contentious business. This showed a serious disregard of the solicitor's contract with the client, and the relevant provisions of the Solicitors Act 1974. Henderson J. stated:

> "49. I emphasise that this is not just a matter of discipline for its own sake. It is essential that the terms upon which a solicitor charges his client should be recorded in writing, and that a solicitor should not attempt to charge fees which are contrary to the terms of his retainer. It is also sensible that in all save exceptional circumstances the client should be able to rely on the accuracy, both factual and legal, of the bills which he receives from his solicitors. The particular mischief in the present case is that the firm sought to charge an unspecified success fee of £50,000 in circumstances where it was clear that the client had not agreed to this." (*Bilkus v Stockler Brunton* [2009] EWHC 1957 (Ch) Henderson J.)

**Subsections (3) and (4): county court**

Although references to "the county court limit" have been removed, the situation has not altered since 1981 when the limit was £5,000. **7C–110**

A county court has jurisdiction under ss.69, 70 and 71 of the Act where a bill of costs relates wholly or partly to contentious business done in a county court and the amount of the bill does not exceed £5,000 (High Court and County Court Jurisdiction Order 1991 (SI 1991/724)).

## Assessment on application of party chargeable or solicitor

**70.**—(1) Where before the expiration of one month from the **7C–111**

*Paragraph numbers marked with a "+" can be found online and on CD.*

delivery of a solicitor's bill an application is made by the party chargeable with the bill, the High Court shall, without requiring any sum to be paid into court, order that the bill be assessed and that no action be commenced on the bill until the assessment is completed.

(2) Where no such application is made before the expiration of the period mentioned in subsection (1) then, on an application being made by the solicitor or, subject to subsections (3) and (4) by the party chargeable with the bill, the court may on such terms, if any, as it thinks fit (not being terms as to the costs of the assessment) order—

(a) that the bill be assessed; and

(b) that no action be commenced on the bill, and that any action already commenced be stayed, until the assessment is completed.

(3) Where an application under subsection (2) is made by the party chargeable with the bill—

(a) after the expiration of 12 months from the delivery of the bill, or

(b) after a judgment has been obtained for the recovery of the costs covered by the bill, or

(c) after the bill has been paid, but before the expiration of 12 months from the payment of the bill,

no order shall be made except in special circumstances and, if an order is made, it may contain such terms as regards the costs of the assessment as the court may think fit.

(4) The power to order assessment conferred by subsection (2) shall not be exercisable on an application made by the party chargeable with the bill after the expiration of 12 months from the payment of the bill.

(5) An order for the assessment of a bill made on an application under this section by the party chargeable with the bill shall, if he so requests, be an order for the assessment of the profit costs covered by the bill.

(6) Subject to subsection (5) the court may under this section order the assessment of all the costs, or of the profit costs, or of the costs other than profit costs and, where part of the costs is not to be assessed, may allow an action to be commenced or to be continued for that part of the costs.

(7) Every order for the assessment of a bill shall require the costs officer to assess not only the bill but also the costs of the assessment and to certify what is due to or by the solicitor in respect of the bill and in respect of the costs of the assessment.

(8) If after due notice of any assessment either party to it fails to attend, the officer may proceed with the assessment ex parte.

(9) Unless—

(a) the order for assessment was made on the application of the solicitor and the party chargeable does not attend the assessment, or

(b) the order for assessment or an order under subsection (10) otherwise provides, the costs of an assessmentshall be paid according to the event of the assessment, that is to say, if the amount of the bill is reduced by one fifth, the solicitor shall pay the costs, but otherwise the party chargeable shall pay the costs.

(10) The costs officer may certify to the court any special circumstances relating to a bill or to the assessment of a bill, and the court may make such order as respects the costs of the assessment as it may think fit.

(11) [...]

(12) In this section "profit costs" means costs other than counsel's fees or costs paid or payable in the discharge of a liability incurred by the solicitor on behalf of the party chargeable, and the reference in subsection (9) to the fraction of the amount of the reduction in the bill shall be taken, where the assessment concerns only part of the costs covered by the bill, as a reference to that fraction of the amount of those costs which is being assessed.

*Note*—Amended by the Legal Services Act 2007 Sch.16, para.65, Sch.23, with effect from January 1, 2010 (SI 2009/3250). **7C-111.1**

**Subsection (1)—"One month"**

This is a calendar month (Interpretation Act 1978 Sch.1). **7C-112**

**"The party chargeable therewith"**

Where the retainer is joint all the clients ought to concur in the application, but the bill may be ordered to be assessed on the application of one if the others refuse to join (*Lockhart v Hardy* (1841) 4 Beav. 224; and see *Re Hair* (1847) 10 Beav. 187; *Re Lewin* (1853) 16 Beav. 608). If the retainer is not joint, each client may have the bill assessed, but the Court will, if possible, order one detailed assessment and the application should be served on all (*Re Salaman* [1894] 2 Ch. 201). The application may be made by a personal representative (*Jefferson v Warrington* (1840) 7 M. & W. 137) or trustee in bankruptcy (*Re Allingham* (1886) L.R. 32 Ch D 36, CA); or liquidator (*Re Foss, Bilborough & Co* [1912] 2 Ch. 261; *Re Palace Restaurants* [1914] 1 Ch. 492); or a country solicitor in respect of his London agent's costs (*Re William Wilde* [1910] 1 Ch. 100). The co-trustee of a solicitor may assess the latter's bill for work done as a solicitor for the trust (*Re H. P. Davies & Son* [1917] 1 Ch. 216). **7C-113**

As to the power of a solicitor, on reasonable notice, to determine the retainer of a client who fails to pay a reasonable amount on account of costs incurred or to be incurred, see s.65(2).

A dispute arose as to whether a solicitor, whose practice had been intervened by the Law Society, was the "party chargeable" with the bill for the purposes of s.70(3) or a third party under s.71. The Costs Judge hearing the application ordered detailed assessment of all the bills delivered to the Law Society without deciding the status of the solicitor but ordering as a condition of assessment the payment of £50,000 on account. If the solicitor was found to be the party chargeable with the bill then time ran only from when the bills were served upon him, his application would have been within the one month prescribed by s.70(1) and the court would have no power to impose any condition. On appeal the court found that the "person chargeable with the bill" was the person to whom the solicitor was contractually entitled to look for payment and if necessary to sue for payment of the bill. On the facts of the case that could only be the Law Society. The intervened solicitor was therefore a third party with rights under s.71 of the Act. Permission to appeal was refused and the associated challenge under the Human Rights Act also failed: *MacPherson v Bevan Ashford* [2003] EWHC 636 (Ch), Patten J.

**The application**

Applications are made by CPR Pt 8 claim form or, if the claim is made in existing proceedings, by application notice in accordance with Pt 23. A claim in the High Court **7C-114**



SOLICITORS

under Pt III of the 1974 Act may be determined by a High Court Judge; a Master, a Costs Judge or a District Judge of the Principal Registry of the Family Division; or a District Judge if the costs are for:

(i) contentious business done in proceedings in the District Registry of which he is the District Judge;

(ii) contentious business done in proceedings in a County Court within the district of that District Registry; or

(iii) non contentious business (Pt 47, r.67.3(3)).

A claim for an order under Part III of the Act for the assessment of costs payable to a solicitor by his client, which relates to contentious business done in a County Court; and is within the financial limit of the County Court's jurisdiction specified in s.69(3) of the Act, may be made in that County Court. In every other case the application must be made in the High Court (r.67.3(1)).

Where an application was made by a client and the claim form contained a list of bills, a clear statement that the bills were disputed, the grounds upon which they were disputed, a proper identification of the parties and a duly signed statement of truth—the solicitors argued that the Part 8 claim form contained a number of discrepancies which meant that s.70 of the 1974 Act had not been satisfied. The court held that although there were defects in the claim form they did not affect the proper interpretation of the document as a whole, the effect of which was to convey to the solicitors the message that the client wanted the bills to be assessed within the statutory period and that she had commenced proceedings to do so. Once it was established that the claim form sufficiently identified the claim for it to have been taken to have commenced the proceedings, there was no basis upon which the court could decline to make a formal order. the client's cause of action was an indefeasible statutory right to have bills assessed and there was no defence on the merits of the claim: *Szekeres v Alan Smeath & Co* [2005] EWHC 1733, Ch, Pumfrey J.

If the order to assess is insufficient for the client's purpose—for example where the bill does not relate to any professional business (*Baker & Lees & Co* [1903] 1 K.B. 189, CA; *Re Landor* [1899] 1 Ch. 818) or where the retainer is wholly disputed (*Re Inderwick* (1884) L.R. 25 Ch D 279; *Re Ames* (1883) 25 Ch D 73; *Re Hulbert* (1894) 71 L.T. 748); or there is an agreement, the client must bring an action (*Re Lymn* (1910) 130 L.T.J. 9).

**Disputed retainer**

7C-115 In the absence of special provision in the order for detailed assessment, if made at the instance of the client, he would be entitled to dispute particular items on the ground of want of retainer, but not the whole bill (*Re Herbert* (1887) 34 Ch D 504; *Re Frape* [1894] 2 Ch. 290. Where the order includes several bills, the same rule applies to each bill (*Re Frape*). If there is any dispute as to whether the solicitor was in fact retained, an ex parte order ought not to be obtained (*Re Inderwick* (1884) L.R. 25 Ch D 279). But where the solicitor obtains the order to assess, the client, having made no admission, can object to the whole bill for want of a retainer (*Re Jones* (1887) 36 Ch D 105; *Re Graham & Wigley* (1908) 52 S.J. 684; *Re Wingfield & Blew* (1904) 2 Ch. 665 at 675).

In a case where retainer was disputed Mr Justice Butterfield quoted with approval the judgment of Denning L.J. in *Griffiths v Evans* [1953] 2 All E.R. 1364 at 1369:

> "On this question of retainer, I would observe that where there is difference between a solicitor and his client on it, the courts have said for the last 100 years or more that the word of the client is to be preferred to the word of the solicitor, or, at any rate, more weight is to be given to it: see *Crossley v Crowther* per Sir George J. Turner V.-C.; *re Paine* per Warrington J. The reason is plain. It is because the client is ignorant and the solicitor is, or should be, learned. If the solicitor does not take the precaution of getting a written retainer, he has only himself to thank for being at variance with his client over it and must take the consequences." *Moy v Pettman Smith (A Firm)* [2002] EWCA Civ 875.

The insertion by solicitors of a one-sided provision into a contract between them and a client justified the construction of ambiguous provisions in that contract *contra proferentem*, that is in the client's favour (*Re A Debtor (No.1594 of 1992), The Times*, December 9, 1992).

**Solicitor to give credit**

7C-116 For the meaning of the clause in the common order, directing the solicitor to give

*Paragraph numbers marked with a "+" can be found online and on CD.*

credit for all moneys received for or on account of his client, see *Re Le Brasseur & Oakley* [1896] 2 Ch. 487 at 493; *Re Templeton & Cox* (1909) 101 L.T. 144.

**Subsection (2)—Statutory Demand**

It would place solicitors in an intolerable position if a debtor could apply to have a statutory demand set aside on the basis that it was intended to have the bill assessed under the 1974 Act. Per Vinelott J., *Re A Debtor (Nos. 833 and 834 of 1993)* 1994 N.P.C. 82. **7C–117**

A sum which had not been judicially assessed or determined was not a claim for a liquidated sum that could be the subject of a bankruptcy petition under s.267 of the Insolvency Act 1986, even if the period for challenging the claim under the 1974 Act had expired. The court considered *Re a Debtor (Nos 833 and 834 of 1993)* (above) but held that if public policy required the client to be able to seek assessment of a solicitor's bill, even after having reached an otherwise binding agreement, that was merely a reason why the court ought not to make a bankruptcy order on a petition likely to be the subject of an assessment under the 1974 Act. The availability of assessment did not prevent an otherwise binding agreement converting what had previously been a solicitor's mere estimate of proper costs, into a liquidated sum capable of founding a petition under s.267 of the 1986 Act: *Truex v Toll* [2009] EWHC 396 (Ch); [2009] 4 All E.R. 419, Proudman J.

Where a solicitor was instructed to act in liquidation proceedings by the liquidator, bills were delivered but remained unpaid. The solicitor sued for non payment of fees and the liquidator counterclaimed seeking an account and inquiry in respect of the bills. The court held that this was sufficient to enable it to order assessment under s.70(2) even though no formal written application and been made. The order was made on the implicit application under s.70(2) and/or under the relevant jurisdiction of the court: *Connolly v Harrington* May 17, 2002, unrep., QB, H.H.J. Chapman.

**Subsection (3)—"Except in special circumstances"**

There is no hard and fast rule as to what are special circumstances; each case must stand on its own circumstances, and the Court of Appeal will not lightly interfere with the exercise of the Judge's discretion (*Re Cheeseman* [1891] 2 Ch. 289, CA; *Re Ward, Bowie & Co* (1910) 102 L.T. 881, CA). "Special circumstances" are "those which appear to the Judge exercising such discretion so special and exceptional as to justify [detailed assessment]", and are not confined to misconduct or fraud, as laid down in some earlier cases *Re Hirst & Capes* [1908] 1 K.B. 982, CA, affirmed [1908] A.C. 416). The client should point to items of overcharge (*Boycott, Re* (1885) L.R. 29 Ch D 571; *Re A Solicitor* [1961] Ch. 491; [1961] 2 All E.R. 321). Charges may be unreasonably large (*Re Norman* (1885–86) L.R. 16 Q.B.D. 673) or such as to call for explanation (*Re Robinson* (1867) L.R. 3 Ex. 4) or there may be gross blunders in the bill (*Re Norman*). Payment of the bill with an express reservation of the right to assess has been held, in all the circumstances of the case, to be a "special circumstance" (*Re Tweedie* [1909] W.N. 110; *Re Solicitors* (1934) 50 T.L.R. 327) and so has the delivery of the bill with the reservation of the right to deliver a further bill (*Harris v Yarm* [1960] Ch. 256 at 259); and so have overcharges by mistake under the then Solicitors' Remuneration Order 1883 (*Re G.* (1909) 53 S.J. 469; *Re N.* (1912) 56 S.J. 520). The fact that there was an agreement that the bill should be assessed was as powerful a special circumstances as it is possible to conceive for ordering detailed assessment. Although there had been unexplained delay there was no evidence of significant prejudice to the defendants as a result of that delay and detailed assessment was ordered accordingly: *Arrowfield Services Ltd v BP Collins (A Firm)* [2003] EWHC 830 (Ch) (Michael Briggs Q.C.). The fact that the solicitor has not paid disbursements before delivery of the bill was held not to be a "special circumstance" (*Re Massey* (1909) 101 L.T. 517; 26 T.L.R. 68). Whether or not payment with a reservation was alone sufficient to constitute special circumstances it was an important factor which, together with the exercise by the solicitors of their lien over the papers while asking to be relieved of their retainer and evidence pointing to substantial overcharging in the bills, were sufficient to justify the court in ordering detailed assessment (*Sanders v Isaacs* [1971] 1 W.L.R. 240; [1971] 1 All E.R. 755). **7C–118**

A client queried the bill sent to her by her solicitors and requested that it be assessedpursuant to the Solicitors Act 1974. The solicitor wrote stating that it was for the client to apply for the assessment and that since over a month had passed since the bill

***Paragraph numbers marked with a "+" can be found online and on CD.***



SOLICITORS

had been delivered any order for assessment would be conditional upon her paying 40 per cent of the bill into court. Eleven months after delivery of the bill the solicitor served a statutory demand for payment. At first instance the Costs Judge found that there were no special circumstances within the meaning of s.70(3) of the 1974 Act justifying assessment more than 12 months after delivery of the bill. On appeal the court found that the purpose of the solicitor's letter was to induce payment, it was not merely inaccurate and a misrepresentation, but, given the inequality of the parties, exerted pressure that was capable of amounting to special circumstances. The appeal was allowed: *Kundrath v Harry Kwatia & Gooding* [2004] EWHC 2852 (QB) Beatson J.

Solicitors acting for a limited company in litigation which went into creditors voluntary liquidation delivered fourteen bills in respect of work done, and the company applied for detailed assessment under s.70. The two most recent bills had not been paid and were ordered to be assessed. Six were delivered and paid after the company had gone into liquidation, and six were delivered and paid before the company went into liquidation. The court held that apart from the two most recent bills, all the statute bills had all been paid within 12 months of the application for assessment. The application could only succeed if special circumstances were shown. The level of fees was high but this was explicable by virtue of the particular expertise of the solicitors and each had been paid without any major complaint. The high level of fees did not amount to special circumstances (*Winchester Commodities Group Ltd v R. D. Black & Co* [2000] B.C.C. 310, Mr John Martin Q.C.

**If 12 months have expired from the delivery of the bill**

**7C–119** When a series of bills have been delivered, which the Court regards as one, the time runs from the delivery of the last bill. The distinction is between a retainer to perform an entire contract (e.g. to conduct an action) and a retainer to act for the client generally (e.g. to get him out of his difficulties, see *Warmingtons v McMurray* [1937] 1 All E.R. 565). In regard to an application to assess by a company in liquidation, the 12 months are counted back from the date of the winding-up (*Re James* (1850) 4 De G. & Sm. 183; *Re Foss, Bilborough & Co* [1912] 2 Ch. 261). The 12 months run from the delivery of a complete bill (*Re Pomeroy & Tanner* [1897] 1 Ch. 284). After 12 months from payment detailed assessment can only be ordered under the inherent jurisdiction of the Court, and not under the Act, and the one-fifth rule as to costs does not apply (*Re Park* (1889) 41 Ch D 326.

Subsection (3)(c) applies also to an application for detailed assessment by a third party under subs.(1). Where payment had been made by deduction with the consent of a mortgagor company which since had a compulsory winding-up order made against it, no order for detailed assessment on the application of the liquidator more than 12 months after the deduction could be made (*Forsinard Estate Ltd v Dykes* [1971] 1 W.L.R. 232; [1971] 1 All E.R. 1018). See also subs.(4).

Where a client applied for a remuneration certificate from the Law Society under the provisions of the Solicitors' (Non-Contentious Business) Remuneration Order 1994 it was held that the fact that the remuneration certificate procedure occupied more than twelve months from the delivery of the bill, was a special circumstance enabling the Court to order a detailed assessment under s.70(3) (*Riley v Dibb Lupton Alsop* June 5, 1997, unrep., Sedley J.)).

Where parties came before the court on an application for an order for detailed assessment under s.70(3), where there subsisted an agreement that there should be such an assessment (albeit that the client had delayed making any application), that was as powerful a special circumstance as it was possible to conceive for ordering the detailed assessment. The solicitors had not been caused any prejudice by the delay and accordingly the court exercised its discretion and ordered detailed assessment: *Arrowfield Services Ltd v BP Collins (A Firm)* [2003] EWHC 830, Mr M. Briggs Q.C.

**Payment of the bill**

**7C–120** As a general rule, there can be no "payment" before delivery of the bill *Re Foster* [1920] 3 K.B. 306). Mere retainer by the solicitor of the amount of the costs, coupled with an oral agreement as to the amount (*Re Frape* [1893] 2 Ch. 284) or a settled account (*Re Baylis* [1896] 2 Ch. 107, CA) is not payment if no bill has been delivered (*Re Foss, Bilborough & Co* [1912] 2 Ch. 261 contrast *Re Webb* [1894] 1 Ch. 73, CA, where there was a settled account in writing and the expiry of the period of limitation, the

***Paragraph numbers marked with a "+" can be found online and on CD.***

solicitors were also trustees, and no error in the account shown). If a bill has been delivered, the retention of moneys by the solicitors is no payment unless there has been a settlement of account (*ibid.*); mere acquiescence is not enough (*Re Ingle* (1855) 25 L.J.Ch. 169; *Re West, King & Adams* [1892] 2 Q.B. 102) but retention with the client's express assent may amount to payment (*Re David* (1861) 30 Bav. 278; *Hitchcock v Stretton* [1892] 2 Ch. 343; *Re Thompson* [1894] 1 Q.B. 462; *Re Baylis*). Retention under an invalid agreement to charge a lump sum is not payment (*Re West, King & Adams*). Contrast *Re Thompson*, where there was a valid agreement in writing. There may be a good payment where the bill of costs is delivered subsequently to the payment or retention, if the payment or retention can be referred to the bill (*Re Thompson*, and cases there cited; *Re Baylis*; *Smith v Betty* [1903] 2 K.B. 317, CA) but not if the business is "business done, or to be done, in any action" (see s.61(3) and *Re Simmons & Politzer* [1954] 2 Q.B. 296).

The giving of a negotiable instrument is prima facie only payment of a debt if it is honoured, and the same applies when it is given in payment of a bill of costs (*Sayer v Wagstaff* (1844) 14 L.J.Ch. 116) and the date of payment is the date when the instrument is honoured (*Re Harries* (1844) 13 M. & W. 2; *Re Romer & Haslam* [1893] 2 Q.B. 286, CA; *Ray v Newton* [1913] 1 K.B. 249, CA; but the facts may show that the instrument is given by way of unconditional payment (*Re Harries*; *Re Romer & Haslam*). If payment is made of less than the full amount, it is only a payment on account unless there is accord and satisfaction (*Re Woodard* (1869) 18 W.R. 37; *Re Callis* (1901) 49 W.R. 316).

The transfer of funds from an estate into the solicitor's account amounted to satisfaction of the bill with the consent of the payers. The solicitors, one of whom was executor, had completed the administration of the estate and presented a final bill to the principal beneficiary which was then paid by way of transfer with the knowledge and consent of the trustees. The beneficiary made no application for detailed assessment until more than 12 months had expired, the application for detailed assessment was therefore struck out. The fact that one of the executors was a partner in the firm of solicitors was of no relevance to the issue of payment (*Gough v Chivers & Jordan*, *The Times*, July 15, 1996, CA).

A firm of solicitors consisting of three partners rendered a bill to their client relating to the administration of an estate. A number of charities who were residuary beneficiaries of the estate sought detailed assessment because sums equal to the full amount of the bill had already been paid to them to one of the partners before he joined the firm. They sought repayment of any amounts found on assessment to have been overpaid. The partner to whom the money was originally paid had since disappeared. The Costs Judge found that the remaining partners were bound by representations made by the partner who had disappeared, even though the representations were made before the partnership was formed. The court rejected the suggestion that there was a novation which had the effect of rendering the firm liable for matters arising in the course of the prior retainer. The court also rejected the argument that the partners were estopped from denying that there had been a novation, nor was it persuaded that there was any statutory liability to pay under ss.70 and 71 of the Solicitors Act 1974. The continuing partners were therefore held to be not liable to repay any sum by which the bill was reduced, the only person being so liable being the partner who had disappeared: *Marsden v Guide Dogs for the Blind Association* [2004] EWHC 593 (Ch); [2004] 3 All E.R. 222, also known as *Burton Marsden Douglas (A Firm), Re*, Lloyd J.

**"After a judgment has been obtained"**

If the solicitor sues on the bill, and before verdict or judgment an order is made to assess it, it usually directs detailed assessment according to the Solicitors Act and applies the one-fifth rule as to costs (*Smith v Edwardes* (1889) L.R. 22 Q.B.D. 10, and see *Smith v Howes* [1922] 1 K.B. 590; *Lumley v Brookes* (1889) 41 Ch.D. 323; *Hirst & Capes v Fox* [1908] 1 K.B. 982). But a detailed assessment after verdict or judgment can only be ordered under the Act in "special circumstances". Yet the Court has inherent jurisdiction to refer the bill to a Costs Judge to fix the proper amount of remuneration, in which case the one-fifth rule would not apply (*Lumsden v Shipcote* [1906] 2 K.B. 433; *Hirst & Capes v Fox* [1908] 1 K.B. 982). **7C–121**

**Inherent jurisdiction to order detailed assessment**

Even more than 12 months after payment of the bill, though there is no jurisdiction **7C–122**

***Paragraph numbers marked with a "+" can be found online and on CD.***

under the Act to order detailed assessment, the Court retains its inherent jurisdiction to do so (*Re A Solicitor* [1961] Ch. 591). In *Symbol Park Lane Ltd v Steggles Palmer* [1985] 1 W.L.R. 668; [1985] 2 All E.R. 167, the Court of Appeal held that inherent jurisdiction should only be invoked to avoid a clear injustice and that the clearest descriptions of the three jurisdictions were set out in *Re Park*, para.7C–119 above. But in *Harrison v Tew* [1988] 2 W.L.R. 1; [1987] 3 All E.R. 865, the Court of Appeal by a majority overruled *Re A Solicitor* [1961] Ch. 591 and held that the preservation of the inherent powers over solicitors expressed in s.50 of the Solicitors Act 1974 was subject to the provisions of s.70(4) and therefore detailed assessment of a bill of costs could not be ordered on an application made after the expiration of 12 months from payment of the bill. The House of Lords held that the Courts' inherent jurisdiction was displaced by s.70(4) of the 1974 Act and upheld the Court of Appeal decision (*Harrison v Tew* [1990] 2 W.L.R. 210).

Where solicitors sued for their costs and the defendant counterclaimed for negligence, all of which allegations failed, the court (the time for applying for detailed assessment having expired) nonetheless made an order that the solicitors' bill should be examined.

> "Where a quantum meruit is claimed for work done, the benefit of which has been obtained under a contract, but where the contract sum has not been agreed, there may be an order for judgment for the claimant with the quantum to be assessed. The judicial assessment should be carried out by a Costs Judge. It is the Costs Judges that have the requisite expertise for that purpose", per Sir Richard Scott, *Thomas Watts & Co v Smith* (1998) 2 Costs L.R. 59, CA.

Where solicitors delivered five bills which the client paid, and the solicitors then issued proceedings claiming a further £67,000 said to be outstanding, the client sought detailed assessment of the bills on the basis that they were interim requests for payment. The application for detailed assessment was refused on the basis that 12 months had expired since the payment of the bills. The solicitors for their part applied for summary judgment. The Court of Appeal held on the facts that the bills were not statute bills and that the solicitors were not entitled to summary judgment because the client was entitled to defend the solicitors' claim on the ground that the fees claimed were unreasonably high, even though the time for assessment under s.70 of the 1974 Act had expired. The statutory right to claim detailed assessment in accordance with s.70 does not exclude any other common law right to challenge the bill. See *Re Park* (1889) 41 Ch D 326; *Jones v Whitehouse* [1918] 2 K.B. 61; *Thomas Watts & Co v Smith* (1998) 2 Costs L.R. 59; *Turner & Co v O. Palomo SA* [1999] 4 All E.R. 353, CA.

#### Subsection (9)—"One-fifth of the amount of the bill"

**7C–123** The rule is imperative that the solicitor shall pay the costs if one-fifth of the amount is disallowed; except that if the costs officer certifies "special circumstances" under proviso (ii) the Court has power to relax the rule (see *Re Richards* [1912] 1 Ch. 49). An offer made before the last projected day of a hearing is not an offer to which any real weight can be given. It cannot be a special circumstance within the meaning of s.70(10) of the 1974 Act. A clear without prejudice offer made in proper time and in proper form can be a special circumstance which might otherwise reverse the statutory presumption in s.70(9) (*Angel Airlines (in Liquidation)* v Dean & Dean [2008] EWHC 1513 (QB) Coulson J.). The amount, on which one-fifth is taken, includes disbursements (*Re Haigh* (1849) 12 Beav. 307) and costs already assessed and paid by the opposite party (*Re Osborne & Osborne* [1913] 3 K.B. 861, CA). It includes the total of the bills ordered to be assessed by one order, but not other bills delivered under the same retainer (*Devereaux v White* (1896) 13 T.L.R. 52). It includes the full amount of the bill, and disregards the added expression "say £X" (*Re Carthew* (1884) 27 Ch D 485; *Re Mackenzie* (1894) 69 L.T. 751) or the fact that a lesser figure is alone claimed (*Re Paull* (1884) 27 Ch D 485). It includes in the lessor's solicitor's bill the costs of the concurring parties' solicitors, if he has included them (*Re Fletcher & Dyson* [1903] 2 Ch. 688). On the other hand the amount, on which one-fifth is taken, excludes items in the cash account (*Re Haigh*) and excludes items struck out of the bill for want of retainer (*Re Taxation of Costs*; *Re a Solicitor* [1936] 1 K.B. 523).

In calculating whether one-fifth of a bill is taxed off, VAT is ignored for the purpose of the calculation.

#### County courts

**7C–124** See note at para.7C–110.

***Paragraph numbers marked with a "+" can be found online and on CD.***

## Assessment on application of third parties

**71.**—(1) Where a person other than the party chargeable with the bill for the purposes of section 70 has paid, or is or was liable to pay, a bill either to the solicitor or to the party chargeable with the bill, that person or his executors, administrators or assignees may apply to the High Court for an order for the assessment of the bill as if he were the party chargeable with it, and the court may make the same order (if any) as it might have made if the application had been made by the party chargeable with the bill. **7C–125**

(2) Where the court has no power to make an order by virtue of subsection (1) except in special circumstances it may, in considering whether there are special circumstances sufficient to justify the making of an order, take into account circumstances which affect the applicant but do not affect the party chargeable with the bill.

(3) Where a trustee, executor or administrator has become liable to pay a bill of a solicitor, then, on the application of any person interested in any property out of which the trustee, executor or administrator has paid, or is entitled to pay, the bill, the court may order—

(a) that the bill be assessed on such terms, if any, as it thinks fit; and

(b) that such payments, in respect of the amount found to be due to or by a solicitor and in respect of the costs of the taxation, be made to or by the applicant, to or by the solicitor, or to or by the executor, administrator or trustee, as it thinks fit.

(4) In considering any application under subsection (3) the court shall have regard—

(a) to the provisions of section 70 as to applications by the party chargeable for the assessment of a solicitor's bill so far as they are capable of being applied to an application made under that subsection;

(b) to the extent and nature of the interest of the applicant.

(5) If an applicant under subsection (3) pays any money to the solicitor, he shall have the same right to be paid that money by the trustee, executor or administrator chargeable with the bill as the solicitor had.

(6) Except in special circumstances, no order shall be made on an application under this section for the assessment of a bill which has already been taxed.

(7) If the court on an application under this section orders a bill to be assessed, it may order the solicitor to deliver to the applicant a copy of the bill on payment of the costs of that copy.

*Note* —Amended by the Legal Services Act 2007 Sch.16, para.66, with effect from January 1, 2010 (SI 2009/3250). **7C–125.1**

#### Subsection (1)—"Person other than ... the party chargeable with the bill"

Examples are—a mortgagee, the trustee in bankruptcy of a mortgagor, the liquidator of a company, a subsequent encumbrancer, a lessee in respect of his lessor's costs, a *cestui que trust*, a party liable to pay the costs of the umpire's solicitor (*Re Collyer-Bristow* **7C–126**

***Paragraph numbers marked with a "+" can be found online and on CD.***

*& Co* [1901] 2 K.B. 839, CA) a third person who, as a term of an agreement of compromise, agrees to pay costs as between solicitor and client (*Re Grundy, Kershaw & Co* (1881) 17 Ch D 108; *Re Chapman* (1903) 20 T.L.R. 3). In the latter case, if there is a question as to the construction of the agreement, the Costs Judge has jurisdiction to determine it for the purposes of the detailed assessment (*Re Hirst & Capes* [1908] A.C. 416) though not exclusive jurisdiction (*Mosley v Kitson* (1912) 57 S.J. 12). The following have been held not to be entitled to detailed assessment—a volunteer who pays the costs (*Re Becke & Flower* (1843) 5 Beav. 406; *Langford v Nott* (1820) 1 Jac. & W. 291; *Re Cookson* (1886) 30 S.J. 305); ratepayers where the bill has been paid by a surveyor of highways (*Re Barber* (1845) 14 M. & W. 720); a party who agrees to pay the opposite party a fixed sum for costs on discontinuing proceedings (*Re Morris* (1872) 27 L.T. 554; *Ex p. Docker, Re Heritage* (1878) 3 Q.B.D. 726; *Re Grundy, Kershaw & Co*, above).

**"As if he were the party chargeable"**

**7C–127** The detailed assessment at the instance of the third person is to proceed on the same principles of allowance as though it were at the instance of the party chargeable (see *Re Wells* (1845) 8 Beav. 416; *Re Holliday & Godlee* (1888) 58 L.T. 301; *Re Massey* (1865) 34 L.J.Ch. 492).

Where a third party's liability is dependent on a contract, express or implied, to pay costs the fact that he obtains an order for detailed assessment under this section does not alter the nature or enlarge or extend the scope of that liability which will be determined on a proper construction of that contract. Nor can he dispute the amount properly payable as between the solicitor and his client.

The Law Society instructed solicitors to intervene in another solicitor's practice. The intervening solicitor submitted five bills to the Law Society for their professional charges. The Society paid the bills and sought reimbursement from the solicitor whose practice had been intervened. That solicitor applied for detailed assessment of the bills under s.71. The Court of Appeal held that the bills clearly were solicitors bills within the meaning of s.70(1) of the 1974 Act and that para.13 of Pt 2 of Sch.I to the Act did not override or exclude the right conferred by s.71. Section 71 was of general application, it recognised that the person chargeable with the bill might not be ultimately liable to pay the costs thereby claimed. Its evident purpose was to confer on one with a secondary liability for those costs a right comparable to that possessed by the person primarily liable: *Pine v The Law Society* [2002] EWCA Civ 175; [2002] 2 All E.R. 658; [2002] 1 W.L.R. 2189, CA.

**Subsection (3)—"Any person interested in any property"**

**7C–128** This includes a creditor who has obtained a judgment in an administration action, and he can assess a bill of costs paid by the deceased (*Re Jones & Everett* [1904] 2 Ch. 363). For the rights of a *cestui que trust* in respect of a bill delivered to his trustee, see *Re Downes* (1844) 5 Beav. 425; *Re Brown* (1867) L.R. 4 Eq. 464). A trustee in bankruptcy is not such a "trustee" as to enable the bankrupt to obtain detailed assessment (*Re Leadbitter* (1878–79) L.R. 10 Ch D 388).

**Subsection (4)—"The provisions of section 70"**

**7C–129** So, if the bill has already been paid, no order will be made in the absence of "special circumstances" (*Re Wellborne* [1901] 1 Ch. 312); and see nn. to s.69, paras 7C–103 *et seq.*

The court allowed a beneficiary under a will to apply to have assessed solicitors' bills which had been discharged out of the estate even though some had been paid more than twelve months before the application, and in respect of others there were no special circumstances. The court held that the power under s.71(3) of the Act was a separate power and although s.70(3) had to be taken into account under s.71(4), it was not determinative of the application. It was for the applicant to persuade the court that it should, in all the circumstances, order assessment: *McIlwraith v McIlwraith and Stevens & Bolton* [2002] EWHC Ch, July 24, 2002, HHJ, Rich Q.C.

**The application**

**7C–130** As to the application see para.7C–114.

**County courts**

**7C–131** See note at para.7C–110.

***Paragraph numbers marked with a "+" can be found online and on CD.***

## Supplementary provisions as to assessments

**72.**—(1) Every application for an order for the assessment of a solicitor's bill or for the delivery of a solicitor's bill and for the delivery up by a solicitor of any documents in his possession, custody or power shall be made in the matter of that solicitor. **7C–132**

(2) Where a costs officer is in the course of assessing a bill of costs, he may request the costs officer of any other court to assist him in assessing any part of the bill, and the costs officer so requested shall assess that part of the bill and shall return the bill with his opinion on it to the costs officer making the request.

(3) Where a request is made as mentioned in subsection (2) the costs officer who is requested to assess part of a bill shall have such powers, and may take such fees, in respect of that part of the bill, as he would have or be entitled to take if he were assessing that part of the bill in pursuance of an order of the court of which he is an officer; and the costs officer who made the request shall not take any fee in respect of that part of the bill.

(4) The certificate of the costs officer by whom any bill has been assessed shall, unless it is set aside or altered by the court, be final as to the amount of the costs covered by it, and the court may make such order in relation to the certificate as it thinks fit, including, in a case where the retainer is not disputed, an order that judgment be entered for the sum certified to be due with costs.

*Note*—Amended by the Legal Services Act 2007 Sch.16, para.67, with effect from January 1, 2010 (SI 2009/3250). **7C–132.1**

### Subsection (1)—"Every application"

See Notes to ss.68–70. **7C–133**

### Non-compliance with order

For non-compliance by the solicitor with the common order for detailed assessment in failing to pay the amount certified to be due, the remedy is by attachment of the solicitor as an officer of the Court (*Re Wilde* [1910] W.N. 128, CA). **7C–134**

## Charging orders

**73.**—(1) Subject to subsection (2) any court in which a solicitor has been employed to prosecute or defend any suit, matter or proceeding may at any time— **7C–135**

(a) declare the solicitor entitled to a charge on any property recovered or preserved through his instrumentality for his assessed costs in relation to that suit, matter or proceeding; and

(b) make such orders for the assessment of those costs and for raising money to pay or for paying them out of the property recovered or preserved as the court thinks fit;

and all conveyances and acts done to defeat, or operating to defeat, that charge shall, except in the case of a conveyance to a bona fide purchaser for value without notice, be void as against the solicitor.

(2) No order shall be made under subsection (1) if the right to recover the costs is barred by any statute of limitations.

***Paragraph numbers marked with a "+" can be found online and on CD.***

7C-135.1 *Note*—Amended by the Legal Services Act 2007 Sch.16, para.68, with effect from January 1, 2010 (SI 2009/3250).

**"taxed costs"**

7C-136 The court has jurisdiction to make a charging order over costs recoverable in an action by a client company where that company has become dormant and incapable of acting or unwilling to act further, even though the order for costs contains no direction that the costs be assessed and the costs have not been assessed.

The court is not bound to order that the costs in question be assessed as between solicitor and client (*Fairfold Properties Ltd v Exmouth Docks Company Ltd (No.2)* [1993] 2 W.L.R. 241).

"Taxed costs" in this context must refer to costs which have been assessed by detailed assessment.

The provisions of s.73(1) are plainly directed to cases in which the court has made an order for costs; where the question of costs was dealt with in a compromise agreement there was therefore no power to continue a freezing order or to make a declaration under s.73(1): *Al-Abbas v Al-Dabbagh* [2002] EWCA Civ 1962.

The taking of a legal charge by a firm of solicitors over the property of former clients to secure legal costs does not necessarily waive the rights of the firm under the Solicitors Act 1974, s.73. Although it is well established that in certain circumstances the taking of security by a solicitor would be treated as a waiver of his right to a common law lien, the court had not been referred to any case indicting that the taking of a charge on an unrelated asset was inconsistent with a possessory lien or a solicitor's right to apply for a charge on different property. It was at least arguable that the grant of the legal charge was not inconsistent or incompatible with the exercise by the solicitors of its right to apply for a charge under s.73. *Clifford Harris & Co v Solland International Ltd* [2004] EWHC 2488, (Ch),Richards J.

7C-137 In proceedings for infringement of a patent the claimant was unsuccessful in respect of part of the claim and a declaration of non infringement was made in favour of the defendant. The claimant paid £75,000 costs into a joint account of the parties' solicitors pending appeal. The defendant subsequently went into administrative receivership. The defendants' solicitors obtained a charging order over the £75,000 under s.73 of the Solicitors Act 1974 in order to protect their fees. The claimants' appeal was dismissed but the claimant then sought judgment in default and costs in respect of the defendant's non compliance with the court's directions in respect of the remaining part of the claim. The claimants sought to set off those costs against the £75,000 held in the joint account. Although the court gave judgment in default to the claimants it did not allow set off of the cost to be awarded so as to defeat the charging order. Whilst there was no direct prejudice to the defendant in allowing a set off, the existence of the charging order meant there would be prejudice to the defendant's solicitors. The protection afforded by the charging order should be upheld unless there were good reasons to come to a contrary decision: *Rhom & Hass Co v Collag Ltd* [2001] EWHC (Ch) November 14, 2001, Pumfrey J.

7C-138 Where a district judge of the County Court granted a charging order over land which had been the subject of litigation for costs to be assessed by the court it was held that the detailed assessment had to take place at the SCCO since the bill fell outside the parameters laid down in s.69(3): *Jones v Twinsectra Ltd* [2002] EWCA Civ 668, April 16, 2002.

Where solicitors took out a charge on the freehold property of their clients as security for fees and disbursements, the question arose whether, in taking the charge, the solicitors had waived their rights under s.73 of the Solicitors Act 1974 as the security was inconsistent with the original lien. The court held that the taking of any alternative security by a solicitor would not necessarily waive his lien, the lien was only waived if the security taken was inconsistent with it. The solicitor could not enforce a stipulation for interest markedly higher than would ever be allowed by the court under s.35A of the Senior Courts Act 1981 unless he established that the client had been informed that the law would not otherwise enable the solicitor to claim interest at that rate. A solicitor who took security confirming a right to interest that he did not otherwise possess, waived his right to a lien unless it was expressly reserved. The same principle applied to the solicitors in the present case and their rights under s.73 which they had waived by taking the charge. Once the rights were waived there had to be a fresh

***Paragraph numbers marked with a "+" can be found online and on CD.***

agreement between solicitor and client that the rights were to be exercisable thereafter. The solicitors could not revive their s.73 right simply by making it clear to the client that they expected to look to any recoveries under the settlement. If, however, the client was able to have the security avoided then the solicitors s.73 rights would revive, as they would be entitled to be put back in the same position they would have been in had the security never been granted. On the facts the court found that there was an equitable charge over the settlement monies in favour of the solicitors: *Clifford Harris & Co v Solland International Ltd* [2005] EWHC 141; [2005] 2 All E.R. 34, Christopher Nugee Q.C.

## Special provisions as to contentious business done in county courts

**74.**—(1) The remuneration of a solicitor in respect of contentious business done by him in a county court shall be regulated in accordance with sections 59 to 73, and for that purpose those sections shall have effect subject to the following provisions of this section. **7C–139**

(2) The district judge of a county court shall be the costs officer of that court but any assessment of costs by him may be reviewed by a judge assigned to the county court district, or by a judge acting as a judge so assigned, on the application of any party to the assessment.

(3) The amount which may be allowed on the assessment of any costs or bill of costs in respect of any item relating to proceedings in a county court shall not, except in so far as rules of court may otherwise provide, exceed the amount which could have been allowed in respect of that item as between party and party in those proceedings, having regard to the nature of the proceedings and the amount of the claim and of any counterclaim.

*Note*—Amended by the Legal Services Act 2007 Sch.16, para.69, with effect from January 1, 2010 (SI 2009/3250). **7C–139.1**

*Note*—Section 74(3) does not operate to limit what is allowed between solicitor and client in County Court proceedings to that which has already been allowed on an assessment between the parties. All it does is limit the solicitor's own client costs to what is reasonably recoverable in principle between the parties in the County Court: *Lynch v Paul Davidson Taylor* [2004] EWHC 89 (QB), Hughes J. **7C–140**

## Saving for certain enactments

**75.** [...] **7C–141**

*Note* —Repealed by the Statute Law (Repeals) Act 1989; and the Legal Aid Act 1988 Sch.6. **7C–142**

# PART IV

# MISCELLANEOUS AND GENERAL

### *SUPPLEMENTARY*

* * * *

## Rules

**86A.**—(1) Rules made by the Society under this Act may— **7C–143.0**

(a) make provision generally or subject to exceptions or only in relation to specified cases;

(b) make different provision for different cases or circumstances or for different purposes.

(2) Without prejudice to the generality of subsection (1), any rules prescribing a fee may provide for that fee to be reduced or waived in such circumstances as may be specified in the rules.

7C–143.0.1 *Note*—Inserted by the Legal Services Act 2007 s.177 and Sch.16, Pt.1, para.74, with effect from March 31, 2009 (SI 2009/503).

## Interpretation

7C–143 **87.**—(1) In this Act, except where the context otherwise requires,—

[...]

"authorised insurer" means a person who—

(a) is permitted under the Insurance Companies Act 1982 to carry on insurance business of class 13 in Schedule 2 to that Act or, being an insurance company the head office of which is in a member State, is permitted under the law of a member State other than the United Kingdom to carry on business of a corresponding class; or

(b) is permitted under the Insurance Companies Act 1982 to carry on insurance business of classes 1, 2, 14, 15, 16 and 17 in that Schedule or, being an insurance company the head office of which is in a member State, is permitted under the law of a member State other than the United Kingdom to carry on insurance business of corresponding classes.

"bank" means—

(a) the Bank of England, the Post Office, in the exercise of its power to provide banking services, or an institution authorised under the Banking Act 1987.

(b) [...]

(c) [...]

"building society" means a building society within the meaning of the Building Societies Act 1986; [...]

"the Charter" means the Royal Charter dated 26th February 1845, whereby the Society was incorporated, together with the Royal Charters supplemental to it dated respectively, 26th November 1872, 4th June 1903, 2nd June 1909 and 10th March 1954;

"client"— includes

(a) in relation to contentious business, any person who as principal or on behalf of another person retains or employs, or is about to retain or employ, a solicitor, and any person who is or may be liable to pay a solicitor's costs;

(b) in relation to non-contentious business, any person

who, as a principal or on behalf of another, or as a trustee or executor, or in any other capacity, has power, express or implied, to retain or employ, and retains or employs or is about to retain or employ a solicitor, and any person for the time being liable to pay to a solicitor for his services any costs;

"client account" means an account "client account" means an account subject to rules under section 32(1)(a);

"contentious business" means business done, whether as solicitor or advocate, in or for the purposes of proceedings begun before a court or before an arbitrator, not being business which falls within the definition of non-contentious or common form probate business contained in section 128 of the Senior Courts Act 1981;

"contentious business agreement" means an agreement made in pursuance of section 59;

"costs" includes fees, charges, disbursements, expenses and remuneration;

"the Council" means the Council of the Society elected in accordance with the provisions of the Charter and this Act;

[...]

[...]

[...]

"local law society" means a society which is for the time being recognised by the Council as representative of solicitors in some particular part of England and Wales;

"non-contentious business" means any business done as a solicitor which is not contentious business as defined by this subsection;

"practising certificate" has the meaning assigned to it by section 1;

[...]

"the roll" means the list of solicitors of the Senior Courts kept by the Society under section 6;

"Secretary" of the Society includes any deputy or person appointed temporarily to perform the duties of that office;

"the Society" means the Law Society, that is to say, the Society incorporated and regulated by the Charter;

"sole solicitor" means a solicitor who is the sole principal in a practice;

"sole solicitor endorsement" has the same meaning as in section 1B;

"solicitor" means solicitor of the Senior Courts;

"solicitor in Scotland" means a person enrolled or deemed to have been enrolled as a solicitor in pursuance of the Solicitors (Scotland) Act 1933;

[...]

"training regulations" means regulations under section 2;

"the Tribunal" means the Solicitors Disciplinary Tribunal;

*Paragraph numbers marked with a "+" can be found online and on CD.*

"trust" includes an implied or constructive trust and a trust where the trustee has a beneficial interest in the trust property, and also includes the duties incident to the office of a personal representative, and "trustee" shall be construed accordingly;

"unqualified person" means a person who is not qualified under section 1 to act as a solicitor.

In this Act "authorised insurer" means

(a) a person who has permission under Part 4 of the Financial Services and Markets Act 2000 to effect or carry out contracts of insurance of a relevant class;

(b) a person who carries on an insurance market activity, within the meaning of section 316(3) of that Act;

(c) an EEA firm of the kind mentioned in paragraph 5(d) of Schedule 3 to that Act, which has permission under paragraph 15 of that Schedule (as a result of qualifying for authorisation under paragraph 12 of that Schedule) to effect or carry out contracts of insurance of a relevant class; or

(d) a person who does not fall within paragraph (a), (b) or (c) and who may lawfully effect or carry out contracts of insurance of a relevant class in a member state other than the United Kingdom.

(1B) A contract of insurance is of a relevant class for the purposes of subsection (1A) if it insures against risks arising from

(a) accident;
(b) credit;
(c) legal expenses;
(d) general liability to third parties;
(e) sickness;
(f) suretyship;
(g) miscellaneous financial loss.

(1C) The definition of "bank" in subsection (1) and subsections (1A) and (1B) must be read with—

(a) section 22 of the Financial Services and Markets Act 2000;
(b) any relevant order under that section; and
(c) Schedule 2 to that Act.

(2) In this Act—

(a) references to the removal of a solicitor's name from the roll are references to its removal at his own request or in pursuance of regulations under section 28(3A);
(b) references to striking a solicitor's name off the roll are references to striking it off as a disciplinary sanction; and
(c) references to removal or striking off include references to deleting an entry made by means of a computer by whatever means are appropriate.

(3) In this Act, except where otherwise indicated—

(a) a reference to a numbered Part, section or Schedule is a reference to the Part or section of, or the Schedule to, this Act so numbered;
(b) a reference in a section to a numbered subsection is a reference to the subsection of that section so numbered;
(c) a reference in a section, subsection or Schedule to a numbered paragraph is a reference to the paragraph of that section, subsection or Schedule so numbered; and
(d) a reference in a paragraph to a numbered sub-paragraph is a reference to the sub-paragraph of that paragraph so numbered.

(4) Except where the context otherwise requires, references in this Act to any enactment shall be construed as references to that enactment as amended or applied by or under any other enactment, including this Act.

*Note*—Amended by the Finance (No.2) Act 1975 s.74; Banking Act 1979 Sch.6; the Insurance Companies Act 1981 Sch.4; the Trustee Savings Banks Act 1981 Sch.6; the Insurance Companies Act 1982 Sch.5; the Trustee Savings Banks Act 1985 Sch.4; the Administration of Justice Act 1985 Sch.1; the Building Societies Act 1986; the Banking Act 1987 s.108 Sch.6, para.5; the Courts and Legal Services Act 1990 Sch.18; the Insurance Companies (Amendment) Regulations 1992 (SI 1992/2890); the Statute Law (Repeals) Act 1993; the Arbitration Act 1996 Sch.4; the Access to Justice Act 1999 Sch.15, Pt II; the Financial Services and Markets Act 2000 (Consequential Amendments and Repeals) Order 2001 (SI 2001/3649), art.286(4); and the Legal Services Act 2007 s.177, Sch.16, Pt 1, para.75 and Sch.23, with effect in part from March 7, 2008 (SI 2008/222), in part from March 31, 2009 (SI 2009/503), in part from July 1, 2009 (SI 2009/1365) and in part from January 1, 2010 (SI 2009/3250) (remaining amendments not yet in force) and the Constitutional Reform Act 2005 s.59 and Sch.11, para 21(6) with effect from October 1, 2009 (SI 2009/1604). **7C–144**

## Saving for solicitors to public departments and City of London

**88.**—(1) Nothing in this Act shall prejudice or affect any rights or privileges of the solicitor to the Treasury, any other public department, the Church Commissioners or the Duchy of Cornwall, or require any such officer or any clerk or officer appointed to act for him to be admitted or enrolled or to hold a practising certificate in any case where it would not have been necessary for him to be admitted or enrolled or to hold such a certificate if this Act had not been passed. **7C–145**

(1A) The exemption from the requirement to hold a practising certificate conferred by subsection (1) above shall not apply to solicitors who are Crown Prosecutors.

(2) Sections 31 and 32(1) shall not apply to, and nothing in this Act shall prejudice or affect any rights or privileges which immediately before the commencement of this Act attach to the office of, the Solicitor of the City of London.

### Subsection (1A)

Added by the Prosecution of Offences Act 1985 s.4. **7C–146**

## Consequential amendments, repeals, savings, etc.

**89.**—(1) The enactments specified in Schedule 3 shall have effect **7C–147**

*Paragraph numbers marked with a "+" can be found online and on CD.*

subject to the amendments there specified, being amendments consequential upon the provisions of this Act.

(2) The enactments specified in Schedule 4 are hereby repealed to the extent specified in the third column of that Schedule.

(3) In so far as any instrument or other document made, issued, served or kept or treated as having been or having effect as if made, issued, served or kept, or other thing done or treated as having been or having effect as if done, under or for the purposes of any of the enactments repealed by this Act (in this section referred to as "the repealed enactments") could have been made, issued, served, kept or done under or for the purposes of a corresponding provision of this Act, it shall not be invalidated by the repeal but shall have effect as if made, issued, served, kept or done under or for the purposes of that corresponding provision; and anything begun under any of the repealed enactments may be continued under any corresponding provision of this Act as if begun under that provision.

(4) Any enactment or other document referring to any of the repealed enactments shall, so far as may be necessary for preserving its effect, be construed as referring to this Act or to the corresponding provision of this Act.

(5) References in any enactment or instrument to the disciplinary committee constituted under section 46 of the Solicitors Act 1957 shall be construed as references to the Tribunal.

(6) References in any enactment to solicitors, attorneys or proctors, or to the registrar of attorneys and solicitors or the registrar of solicitors, shall be construed as references to solicitors and to the Society respectively.

(7) […]

(8) Nothing in this Act shall be taken as prejudicing the operation of […] (which relates to the effect of repeals).

7C–148 *Note* —Amended by the Interpretation Act 1978 s.25(2)); and by the Legal Services Act 2007 Sch.16, para.76, Sch.23, with effect from January 1, 2010 (SI 2009/3250).

## Short title, commencement and extent

7C–149 **90.**—(1) This Act may be cited as the Solicitors Act 1974.

(2) This Act shall come into force on such day as the Lord Chancellor may by order made by statutory instrument appoint, not being earlier than the first day on which all the provisions of the Solicitors (Amendment) Act 1974 are in force.

(3) If any order made under section 19(7) of the Solicitors (Amendment) Act 1974 makes any savings from the effect of any provision of that Act which it brings into force, the order under subsection (2) may make corresponding savings from the effect of the corresponding provisions of this Act.

(4) The provisions of this Act extend to England and Wales only, with the exception of—

(a) section 4(4) and the repeal of section 5(3) of the Solicitors Act 1957, which extend to Scotland;

(b) section 29 and the repeal of section 1 of the Solicitors (Amendment) Act 1974, which extend to Northern Ireland;

***Paragraph numbers marked with a "+" can be found online and on CD.***

(c) sections 5(3) and 86 [...] and the repeals of section 5(2) of the Solicitors Act 1957 and paragraphs 1 and 5 of Schedule 2 to the Solicitors (Amendment) Act 1974, all of which extend both to Scotland and to Northern Ireland.

*Note*—Amended by the House of Commons Disqualification Act 1975 Sch.3. **7C–150**

# SCHEDULES
# SCHEDULE 1A

## INADEQUATE PROFESSIONAL SERVICES

*Circumstances in which Council's powers may be exercised*

1.—(1) The Council may take any of the steps mentioned in paragraph 2 ("the steps") with respect to a solicitor where it appears to them that the professional services provided by him in connection with any matter in which he or his firm have been instructed by a client have, in any respect, not been of the quality which it is reasonable to expect of him as a solicitor. **7C–151**

(2) The Council shall not take any steps unless they are satisfied that in all the circumstances of the case it is appropriate to do so.

(3) In determining in any case whether it is appropriate to take any of the steps, the Council may—

(a) have regard to the existence of any remedy which it is reasonable to expect to be available to the client in civil proceedings; and

(b) where proceedings seeking any such remedy have not been begun by him, have regard to whether it is reasonable to expect him to begin them.

*Directions which may be given*

2.—(1) The steps are— **7C–152**

(a) determining that the costs to which the solicitor is entitled in respect of his services ("the costs") are to be limited to such amount as may be specified in the determination and directing him to comply, or to secure compliance, with such one or more of the permitted requirements as appear to the Council to be necessary in order for effect to be given to their determination;

(b) directing him to secure the rectification, at his expense or at that of his firm, of any such error, omission or other deficiency arising in connection with the matter in question as they may specify;

(c) directing him to pay such compensation to the client as the Council sees fit to specify in the direction;

(d) directing him to take, at his expense or at that of his firm, such other action in the interests of the client as they may specify.

(2) The "permitted requirements" are—

(a) that the whole or part of any amount already paid by or on behalf of the client in respect of the costs be refunded;

(b) that the whole part of the costs be remitted;

(c) that the right to recover the costs be waived, whether wholly or to any specified extent.

(3) The power of the Council to take any such steps is not confined to cases where the client may have a cause of action against the solicitor for negligence.

*Compensation*

3.—(1) The amount specified in a direction by virtue of paragraph 2(1)(c) shall not exceed £15,000. **7C–153**

(2) The Secretary of State may by order made by statutory instrument amend sub-paragraph (1) by substituting for the sum of £1000 such other sum as he considers appropriate.

***Paragraph numbers marked with a "+" can be found online and on CD.***

(3) Before making any such order the Secretary of State shall consult the Law Society.

(4) Any statutory instrument made under this paragraph shall be subject to annulment in pursuance of a resolution of either House of Parliament.

7C-154 *Note* —Amended by Solicitors (Compensation for Inadequate Professional Services) Order 2005 (SI 2005/2749).

*Taxation of costs*

7C-155 4.—(1) Where the Council have given a direction under paragraph 2(1)(a), then—

(a) for the purposes of any taxation of a bill covering the costs, the amount charged by the bill in respect of them shall be deemed to be limited to the amount specified in the determination; and

(b) where a bill covering the costs has not been taxed, the client shall, for the purposes of their recovery (by whatever means and notwithstanding any statutory provision or agreement) be deemed to be liable to pay in respect of them only the amount specified in the determination.

(2) Where a bill covering the costs has been taxed, the direction shall, so far as it relates to the costs, cease to have effect.

*Failure to comply with direction*

7C-156 5.—(1) If a solicitor fails to comply with a direction given under this Schedule, any person may make a complaint in respect of that failure to the Tribunal; but no other proceedings whatever shall be brought in respect of it.

(2) On the hearing of such a complaint the Tribunal may, if it thinks fit (and whether or not it makes any order under section 47(2)), direct that the direction be treated, for the purpose of enforcement, as if it were contained in an order made by the High Court.

*Fees*

7C-157 6.—(1) The Council may, by regulations made with the concurrence of the Secretary of State and the Master of the Rolls, make provision for the payment, by any client with respect to whom the Council are asked to consider whether to take any of the steps, of such fee as may be prescribed.

(2) The regulations may provide for the exemption of such classes of client as may be prescribed.

(3) Where a client pays the prescribed fee it shall be repaid to him if the Council take any of the steps in the matter with respect to which the fee was paid.

(4) In this paragraph "prescribed" means prescribed by the regulations.

*Costs*

7C-158 7. Where the Council take any of the steps with respect to a solicitor they may also direct him to pay to the Council—

(a) the amount of the fee repayable by the Council to the client under paragraph 6(3); and

(b) an amount which is calculated by the Council as the cost to them of dealing with the complaint, or which in their opinion represents a reasonable contribution towards that cost.

*Duty of Tribunal*

7C-159 8. Where the Tribunal—

(a) is considering, or has considered, an application or complaint with respect to a solicitor; and

(b) is of the opinion that the Council should consider whether to take any of the steps with respect to that solicitor,

it shall inform the Council.

*Interpretation*

7C-160 9. The Council's powers under this Schedule are exercisable in relation to a person even though his name has been removed from, or struck off, the roll and references to

***Paragraph numbers marked with a "+" can be found online and on CD.***

a solicitor in this Schedule, so far as they relate to the exercise of those powers, shall be construed accordingly.

*Note* —Added by Courts and Legal Services Act 1990 s.93(3) and Sch.15. Amended by the Secretary of State for Constitutional Affairs Order 2003 (SI 2003/1887), Sch.2, para.3. **7C-161**

Where the Complaints Bureau makes a finding of failure to provide adequate professional services it is not necessary for prejudice to a client or the possibility of prejudice to have been established (*R. v The Law Society, Ex p. Singh & Choudry (a firm), The Times*, April 1, 1994, DC).



## THE SOLICITORS' CODE OF CONDUCT 2007

**Contents** **7C-162**



***Paragraph numbers marked with a "+" can be found online and on CD.***

***Paragraph numbers marked with a "+" can be found online and on CD.***

*Paragraph numbers marked with a "+" can be found online and on CD.*

***Paragraph numbers marked with a "+" can be found online and on CD.***

***Paragraph numbers marked with a "+" can be found online and on CD.***

***Paragraph numbers marked with a "+" can be found online and on CD.***

*Paragraph numbers marked with a "+" can be found online and on CD.*

*Paragraph numbers marked with a "+" can be found online and on CD.*

*Paragraph numbers marked with a "+" can be found online and on CD.*



SOLICITORS

***Paragraph numbers marked with a "+" can be found online and on CD.***

SOLICITORS

*Paragraph numbers marked with a "+" can be found online and on CD.*

***Paragraph numbers marked with a "+" can be found online and on CD.***

Rules dated 10 March 2007 commencing 1 July 2007 made under Part II of the Solicitors Act 1974 and section 9 of the Administration of Justice Act 1985 with the concurrence of the Master of the Rolls under that section and the approval of the Secretary of State for Constitutional Affairs under Schedule 4 to the Courts and Legal Services Act 1990, regulating the conduct of solicitors, registered European lawyers, registered foreign lawyers and recognised bodies.

The guidance printed with these rules is not mandatory and does not form part of the Solicitors' Code of Conduct.

[Rules reproduced as amended]



## Rule 1—Core duties

**1.01 Justice and the rule of law**

You must uphold the rule of law and the proper administration of justice. 7C–163

**1.02 Integrity**

You must act with integrity.

**1.03 Independence**

You must not allow your independence to be compromised.

**1.04 Best interests of clients**

You must act in the best interests of each client.

**1.05 Standard of service**

You must provide a good standard of service to your clients.

**1.06 Public confidence**

You must not behave in a way that is likely to diminish the trust the public places in you or the profession.

**For the Guidance to rule 1 see paragraph 7C–164+ on White Book on Westlaw UK or the Civil Procedure CD.**

## Rule 2—Client relations

### INTRODUCTION

Rule 2 is designed to help both you and your clients understand each other's expectations and responsibilities. In particular, the purpose of 2.02 (Client care) and 2.03 (Information about the cost) is to ensure that clients are given the information necessary to enable them to make appropriate decisions about if and how their matter should proceed. Under rule 5 (Business management) a principal in a firm, a director of a recognised body which is a company and a member of a recognised body which is an LLP, must effect supervision and put in place management arrangements to provide 7C–165

*Paragraph numbers marked with a "+" can be found online and on CD.*

for compliance with rule 2. The rule does not apply to your overseas practice but you must comply with 15.02.

**2.01 Taking on clients**

(1) You are generally free to decide whether or not to take on a particular client. However, you must refuse to act or cease acting for a client in the following circumstances:

(a) when to act would involve you in a breach of the law or a breach of the rules of professional conduct;

(b) where you have insufficient resources or lack the competence to deal with the matter;

(c) where instructions are given by someone other than the client, or by only one client on behalf of others in a joint matter, you must not proceed without checking that all clients agree with the instructions given; or

(d) where you know or have reasonable grounds for believing that the instructions are affected by duress or undue influence, you must not act on those instructions until you have satisfied yourself that they represent the client's wishes.

(2) You must not cease acting for a client except for good reason and on reasonable notice.

**2.02 Client care**

(1) You must:

(a) identify clearly the client's objectives in relation to the work to be done for the client;

(b) give the client a clear explanation of the issues involved and the options available to the client;

(c) agree with the client the next steps to be taken; and

(d) keep the client informed of progress, unless otherwise agreed.

(2) You must, both at the outset and, as necessary, during the course of the matter:

(a) agree an appropriate level of service;

(b) explain your responsibilities;

(c) explain the client's responsibilities;

(d) ensure that the client is given, in writing, the name and status of the person dealing with the matter and the name of the person responsible for its overall supervision; and

(e) explain any limitations or conditions resulting from your relationship with a third party (for example a funder, fee sharer or introducer) which affect the steps you can take on the client's behalf.

(3) If you can demonstrate that it was inappropriate in the circumstances to meet some or all of these requirements, you will not breach 2.02.

**2.03 Information about the cost**

(1) You must give your client the best information possible about the likely overall cost of a matter both at the outset and, when appropriate, as the matter progresses. In particular you must:

(a) advise the client of the basis and terms of your charges;

(b) advise the client if charging rates are to be increased;

(c) advise the client of likely payments which you or your client may need to make to others;

(d) discuss with the client how the client will pay, in particular:

(i) whether the client may be eligible and should apply for public funding; and

(ii) whether the client's own costs are covered by insurance or may be paid by someone else such as an employer or trade union;

***Paragraph numbers marked with a "+" can be found online and on CD.***

(e) advise the client that there are circumstances where you may be entitled to exercise a lien for unpaid costs;

(f) advise the client of their potential liability for any other party's costs; and

(g) discuss with the client whether their liability for another party's costs may be covered by existing insurance or whether specially purchased insurance may be obtained.

(2) Where you are acting for the client under a conditional fee agreement, (including a collective conditional fee agreement) in addition to complying with 2.03(1) above and 2.03(5) and (6) below, you must explain the following, both at the outset and, when appropriate, as the matter progresses:

(a) the circumstances in which your client may be liable for your costs and whether you will seek payment of these from the client, if entitled to do so;

(b) if you intend to seek payment of any or all of your costs from your client, you must advise your client of their right to an assessment of those costs; and

(c) where applicable, the fact that you are obliged under a fee sharing agreement to pay to a charity any fees which you receive by way of costs from the client's opponent or other third party.

(3) Where you are acting for a publicly funded client, in addition to complying with 2.03(1) above and 2.03(5) and (6) below, you must explain the following at the outset:

(a) the circumstances in which they may be liable for your costs;

(b) the effect of the statutory charge;

(c) the client's duty to pay any fixed or periodic contribution assessed and the consequence of failing to do so; and

(d) that even if your client is successful, the other party may not be ordered to pay costs or may not be in a position to pay them.

(4) Where you agree to share your fees with a charity in accordance with 8.01(k) you must disclose to the client at the outset the name of the charity.

(5) Any information about the cost must be clear and confirmed in writing.

(6) You must discuss with your client whether the potential outcomes of any legal case will justify the expense or risk involved including, if relevant, the risk of having to pay an opponent's costs.

(7) If you can demonstrate that it was inappropriate in the circumstances to meet some or all of the requirements in 2.03(1) and (5) above, you will not breach 2.03.

**2.04 Contingency fees**

(1) You must not enter into an arrangement to receive a contingency fee for work done in prosecuting or defending any contentious proceedings before a court of England and Wales, a British court martial or an arbitrator where the seat of the arbitration is in England and Wales, except as permitted by statute or the common law.

(2) You must not enter into an arrangement to receive a contingency fee for work done in prosecuting or defending any contentious proceedings before a court of an overseas jurisdiction or an arbitrator where the seat of the arbitration is overseas except to the extent that a lawyer of that jurisdiction would be permitted to do so.

**2.05 Complaints handling**

(1) If you are a principal in a firm you must ensure:

(a) that the firm has a written complaints procedure and that complaints are handled promptly, fairly and effectively in accordance with it;

(b) that the client is told, in writing, at the outset:

(i) that, in the event of a problem, the client is entitled to complain; and

***Paragraph numbers marked with a "+" can be found online and on CD.***

(ii) to whom the client should complain;

(c) that the client is given a copy of the complaints procedure on request; and

(d) that once a complaint has been made, the person complaining is told in writing:

(i) how the complaint will be handled; and

(ii) within what timescales they will be given an initial and/or substantive response.

(2) If you can demonstrate that it was inappropriate in the circumstances to meet some or all of these requirements, you will not breach 2.05.

(3) You must not charge your client for the cost of handling a complaint.

**2.06 Commissions**

If you are a principal in a firm you must ensure that your firm pays to your client commission received over £20 unless the client, having been told the amount, or if the precise amount is not known, an approximate amount or how the amount is to be calculated, has agreed that your firm may keep it.

**2.07 Limitation of civil liability by contract**

If you are a principal in a firm you must not exclude or attempt to exclude by contract all liability to your clients. However, you may limit your liability, provided that such limitation:

(a) is not below the minimum level of cover required by the Solicitors' Indemnity Insurance Rules for a policy of qualifying insurance;

(b) is brought to the client's attention; and

(c) is in writing.

**For the Guidance to rule 2 see paragraph 7C–166+ on White Book on Westlaw UK or the Civil Procedure CD.**

# Rule 3—Conflict of interests

7C–167 **Introduction**

Rule 3 sets out provisions for dealing with conflicts of interests. Conflicts between the duty of confidentiality and duty of disclosure owed by an individual or a firm to two or more clients are dealt with in rule 4 (Confidentiality and disclosure).

Subrules 3.01 to 3.03 deal with conflicts generally.

Subrules 3.04 to 3.06 deal with conflicts in particular high risk situations—gifts from clients, public offices and appointments leading to conflict, and alternative dispute resolution (ADR).

Subrules 3.07 to 3.22 deal with conflicts in conveyancing. Note the special meaning of "you" in 3.07 to 3.15 (acting for seller and buyer) and 3.16 to 3.22 (acting for lender and borrower). See also 18.03 which sets out additional requirements which apply to the provision of property selling services.

Subrule 3.23 sets out that there is no power to waive 3.01 to 3.05.

Subrules 3.07 to 3.22 do not apply to your overseas practice unless the land conveyed is situated in England and Wales.

**3.01 Duty not to act**

(1) You must not act if there is a conflict of interests (except in the limited circumstances dealt with in 3.02).

(2) There is a conflict of interests if:

(a) you owe, or your firm owes, separate duties to act in the best interests of two or more clients in relation to the same or related matters, and those duties conflict, or there is a significant risk that those duties may conflict; or

(b) your duty to act in the best interests of any client in relation to a matter conflicts, or there is a significant risk that it may conflict, with your own interests in relation to that or a related matter.

(3) For the purpose of 3.01(2), a related matter will always include any other matter which involves the same asset or liability.

**3.02 Exceptions to duty not to act**

(1) You or your firm may act for two or more clients in relation to a matter in situations of conflict or possible conflict if:

(a) the different clients have a substantially common interest in relation to that matter or a particular aspect of it; and

(b) all the clients have given in writing their informed consent to you or your firm acting.

(2) Your firm may act for two or more clients in relation to a matter in situations of conflict or possible conflict if:

(a) the clients are competing for the same asset which, if attained by one client, will make that asset unattainable to the other client(s);

(b) there is no other conflict, or significant risk of conflict, between the interests of any of the clients in relation to that matter;

(c) the clients have confirmed in writing that they want your firm to act in the knowledge that your firm acts, or may act, for one or more other clients who are competing for the same asset; and

(d) unless the clients specifically agree, no individual acts for, or is responsible for the supervision of, more than one of those clients.

(3) When acting in accordance with 3.02(1) or (2) it must be reasonable in all the circumstances for you or your firm to act for all those clients.

(4) If you are relying on the exceptions in 3.02(1) or (2), you must:

(a) draw all the relevant issues to the attention of the clients before agreeing to act or, where already acting, when the conflict arises or as soon as is reasonably practicable, and in such a way that the clients concerned can understand the issues and the risks involved;

(b) have a reasonable belief that the clients understand the relevant issues; and

(c) be reasonably satisfied that those clients are of full capacity.

**3.03 Conflict when already acting**

If you act, or your firm acts, for more than one client in a matter and, during the course of the conduct of that matter, a conflict arises between the interests of two or more of those clients, you, or your firm, may only continue to act for one of the clients (or a group of clients between whom there is no conflict) provided that the duty of confidentiality to the other client(s) is not put at risk.

**3.04 Accepting gifts from clients**

Where a client proposes to make a lifetime gift or a gift on death to, or for the benefit of:

(a) you;

(b) any principal, owner or employee of your firm;

(c) a family member of any of the above,

and the gift is of a significant amount, either in itself or having regard to the size of the client's estate and the reasonable expectations of the prospective beneficiaries, you must advise the client to take independent advice about the gift, unless the client is a member of the beneficiary's family. If the client refuses, you must stop acting for the client in relation to the gift.

**3.05 Public office or appointment leading to conflict**

You must decline to act where you, a member of your family, or a principal, owner or employee of your firm holds some public office or appointment as a result of which:

(a) a conflict of interests, or a significant risk of a conflict, arises;

(b) the public might reasonably conclude that you, or your firm, had been

*Paragraph numbers marked with a "+" can be found online and on CD.*

able to make use of the office or appointment for the advantage of the client; or

(c) your ability to advise the client properly and impartially is inhibited.

**3.06 Alternative dispute resolution (ADR)**

If you provide ADR services you must not:

(a) advise or act for any party in respect of a dispute in which you or any person within your firm is acting, or has acted, as mediator;

(b) provide ADR services in connection with a matter in which you or any person within your firm has acted for any party; or

(c) provide ADR services where you or any person within your firm has acted for any of the parties in issues not relating to the mediation, unless that has been disclosed to the parties and they consent to your acting.

**3.07 Acting for seller and buyer in conveyancing, property selling and mortgage related services**

(1) 3.07 to 3.15 apply to the transfer of land for value, and the grant or assignment of a lease or some other interest in land for value. Both commercial and residential conveyancing transactions are covered. The terms "seller" and "buyer" include a lessor and lessee. "You" is defined in 23.01, but is to be construed in 3.07 to 3.15 as including an associated firm (see rule 24 (Interpretation) for the meaning of "associated firms").

(2) You must not act for more than one party in conveyancing, property selling or mortgage related services other than as permitted by, and in accordance with, 3.08 to 3.15. "Property selling" means negotiating the sale for the seller. "Mortgage related services" means advising on or arranging a mortgage, or providing mortgage related financial services, for a buyer. "Mortgage" includes a remortgage.

**3.08 Conveyancing transactions not at arm's length**

Subject to the prohibition in 10.06(3) and (4), you may act for seller and buyer when the transaction between the parties is not at arm's length, provided there is no conflict or significant risk of conflict.

**3.09 Conveyancing transactions at arm's length**

Subject to the prohibition in 10.06(3) and (4), you may act for seller and buyer if the conditions set out in 3.10 below are satisfied and one of the following applies:

(a) both parties are established clients;

(b) the consideration is £10,000 or less and the transaction is not the grant of a lease; or

(c) seller and buyer are represented by two separate offices in different localities.

**3.10 Conditions for acting under 3.09**

In order to act for seller and buyer under 3.09 above, the following conditions must be met:

(a) the written consent of both parties must be obtained;

(b) no conflict of interests must exist or arise;

(c) the seller must not be selling or leasing as a builder or developer; and

(d) when the seller and buyer are represented by two separate offices in different localities:

(i) different individuals (either solicitors or RELs qualified to do conveyancing under regulation 12 of the European Communities (Lawyer's Practice) Regulations 2000 (SI 2000/1119)) who normally work at each office, conduct or supervise the transaction for seller and buyer; and

(ii) no office of the firm (or an associated firm) referred either client to the office conducting the transactions.

**3.11 Property selling and mortgage related services**

Subject to the prohibition in 10.06(3) and (4), you may act for seller and buyer if the conditions set out in 3.13 below are satisfied and one of the following applies:

(a) the only way in which you are acting for the buyer is in providing mortgage related services; or

(b) the only way in which you are acting for the seller is in providing property selling services through a Solicitors' Estate Agency Limited (SEAL).

**3.12 SEALs and participating firms**

A SEAL means a recognised body which:

(a) does not undertake conveyancing;

(b) is owned jointly by at least four participating firms which are not associated firms and none of which has majority control;

(c) is conducted from accommodation physically divided from, and clearly differentiated from that of any participating firm; and

(d) a "participating firm" means a firm one or more of whose principals (or members if it is an LLP, or owners if it is a company) is part owner of the SEAL.

**3.13 Conditions for acting under 3.11**

In order to act for seller and buyer under 3.11 above, the following conditions must be met:

(a) the written consent of both parties must be obtained;

(b) no conflict of interests must exist or arise;

(c) the seller must not be selling or leasing as a builder or developer;

(d) different individuals must conduct the work for the seller and the work for the buyer and, if these individuals need supervision, they must be supervised by different solicitors or RELs who are qualified to do conveyancing under regulation 12 of the European Communities (Lawyer's Practice) Regulations 2000 (SI 2000/1119);

(e) you must inform the seller in writing, before accepting instructions to deal with the property selling, of any services which might be offered to a buyer, whether through the same firm or any associated firm; and

(f) you must explain to the buyer, before the buyer gives consent to the arrangement:

(i) the implications of a conflict of interests arising;

(ii) your financial interest in the sale going through; and

(ii) if you propose to provide mortgage related services to the buyer through a SEAL which is also acting for the seller, that you cannot advise the buyer on the merits of the purchase.

**3.14 Special circumstances in property selling and conveyancing**

If any of the circumstances set out in 3.09 apply (established clients; consideration of £10,000 or less; representation by two separate offices), you may sell the property, provide mortgage related services, and act for seller and buyer in the conveyancing, subject to the prohibition in 10.06(3) and (4) and compliance with the conditions set out in 3.10 and 3.13 as appropriate.

**3.15 Conflict arising when acting for seller and buyer**

If a conflict arises during the course of a transaction in which you are acting for more than one party, you may continue to act for one of the parties only if the duty of confidentiality to the other party is not at risk.

**3.16 Acting for lender and borrower in conveyancing transactions**

(1) 3.16 to 3.22 cover the grant of a mortgage of land and are intended to avoid conflicts of interests. "Mortgage" includes a remortgage. Both commercial and residential conveyancing transactions are covered. "You" is defined in 23.01, but is to be construed in 3.16 to 3.22 as including an associated firm (see rule 24 (Interpretation) for the meaning of "associated firms").

***Paragraph numbers marked with a "+" can be found online and on CD.***

(2) You must not act for both lender and borrower on the grant of a mortgage of land:

(a) if a conflict of interests exists or arises;

(b) on the grant of an individual mortgage of land at arm's length;

(c) if, in the case of a standard mortgage of property to be used as the borrower's private residence only, the lender's mortgage instructions extend beyond the limitations contained in 3.19 and 3.21, or do not permit the use of the certificate of title required by 3.20; or

(d) if, in the case of any other standard mortgage, the lender's mortgage instructions extend beyond the limitations contained in 3.19 and 3.21.

**3.17 Standard and individual mortgages**

(1) A mortgage is a "standard mortgage" where:

(a) it is provided in the normal course of the lender's activities;

(b) a significant part of the lender's activities consists of lending; and

(c) the mortgage is on standard terms.

(2) A mortgage will not be on standard terms if material terms in any of the documents relating to the mortgage transaction are negotiated between the lender's and borrower's lawyers or licensed conveyancers contemporaneously with effecting the mortgage. In commercial transactions, the element of negotiation will often relate to the facility letter or facility agreement rather than the mortgage deed itself.

(3) Provided there has been no contemporaneous negotiation of material terms between the parties' lawyers or licensed conveyancers, a mortgage will be on standard terms where the lender uses a prescribed form of mortgage deed. Minor variations, such as the usual clause limiting the liability of trustee mortgagors, are not regarded as material and do not alter the nature of these terms as standard.

(4) In addition to its normal standard terms, a lender may have a different set or sets of standard terms applicable to specialised types of borrower, such as registered social landlords. Provided these terms are applied by the lender to all equivalent specialist borrowers or have been agreed between the lender and a specialist borrower as applicable to all transactions between them, they will constitute standard terms for the purposes of 3.16 to 3.22.

(5) The lender and the borrower must be separately represented on the grant of an individual mortgage at arm's length (see 3.16(2)(b)). 3.16 to 3.22 are not then applicable.

(6) You may act for both lender and borrower in a standard mortgage (see 3.16(2)(c) to (d)), provided:

(a) there is no conflict of interests;

(b) the mortgage instructions do not go beyond the limits set out in 3.19; and

(c) in the case of a property to be used solely as the borrower's private residence, the approved certificate of title set out in the annex to rule 3 is used.

(7) The limitations of 3.19 also apply to a standard mortgage where the lender and the borrower are separately represented (see 3.22(1) which includes certificates of title). However, 3.22(2) allows the borrower's lawyer or licensed conveyancer, in a transaction where the property is not to be used solely as the borrower's private residence, to give a certificate of title in any form recognised by the Board of the Solicitors Regulation Authority. You also remain free to give any other form of certificate which complies with this rule.

(8) There may be cases where the lapse of time between the mortgage offer and completion (for example, when new properties are added) results in use of an earlier edition of a recognised certificate. That is acceptable.

**3.18 Notification of certain circumstances to lender**

(1) If you wish to act for both lender and borrower on the grant of a standard mortgage of land, you must first inform the lender in writing of the circumstances if:

(a) the prospective borrower is:

(i) a principal in the firm (or a member if the firm is an LLP, or owner or director if the firm is a company), or a member of their immediate family;

(ii) a principal in an associated firm (or a member if the firm is an LLP, or owner or director if the firm is a company), or a member of their immediate family; and/or

(iii) the solicitor or REL conducting or supervising the transaction, or a member of their immediate family; or

(b) you propose to act for seller, buyer and lender in the same transaction.

(2) "Immediate family" means spouse, children, parents, brothers and sisters.

**3.19 Types of instruction which may be accepted**

If acting for both lender and borrower in a standard mortgage, you and the individual solicitor or REL conducting or supervising the transaction may only accept or act upon instructions from the lender which are limited to the following matters:

(a)

(i) taking reasonable steps to check the identity of the borrower (and anyone else required to sign the mortgage deed or other document connected with the mortgage) by reference to a document or documents, such as a passport, precisely specified in writing by the lender;

(ii) following the guidance given by the Law Society or the Solicitors Regulation Authority on property fraud and on money laundering;

(iii) checking that the seller's conveyancers (if unknown to you) appear in a current legal directory or hold practising certificates issued by their professional body; and

(iv) in the case of a lender with no branch office within reasonable proximity of the borrower, carrying out the money laundering checks precisely specified in writing by the lender;

(b) making appropriate searches relating to the property in public registers (for example, local searches, commons registration searches, mining searches), and reporting any results specified by the lender or which you consider may adversely affect the lender; or effecting search insurance;

(c) making enquiries on legal matters relating to the property reasonably specified by the lender, and reporting the replies;

(d) reporting the purchase price stated in the transfer and on how the borrower says that the purchase money (other than the mortgage advance) is to be provided; and reporting if you will not have control over the payment of all the purchase money (other than a deposit paid to an estate agent or a reservation fee paid to a builder or developer);

(e) reporting if the seller or the borrower (if the property is already owned by the borrower) has not owned or been the registered owner of the property for at least six months;

(f) if the lender does not arrange insurance, confirming receipt of satisfactory evidence that the buildings insurance is in place for at least the sum required by the lender and covers the risks specified by the lender; giving notice to the insurer of the lender's interest and requesting confirmation that the insurer will notify the lender if the policy is not renewed or is cancelled; and supplying particulars of the insurance and the last premium receipt to the lender;

(g) investigating title to the property and appurtenant rights; reporting any defects revealed, advising on the need for any consequential statutory declarations or indemnity insurance, and approving and effecting indemnity cover if required by the lender; and reporting if you are aware of any rights needed for the use or enjoyment of the property over other land;



SOLICITORS

(h) reporting on any financial charges (for example, improvement or repair grants or Housing Act discounts) secured on the property revealed by your searches and enquiries which will affect the property after completion of the mortgage;

(i) in the case of a leasehold property:

(i) confirming that the lease contains the terms stipulated by the lender and does not include any terms specified by the lender as unacceptable;

(ii) obtaining a suitable deed of variation or indemnity insurance if the terms of the lease are unsatisfactory;

(iii) enquiring of the seller or the borrower (if the property is already owned by the borrower) as to any known breaches of covenant by the landlord or any superior landlord and reporting any such breaches to the lender;

(iv) reporting if you become aware of the landlord's absence or insolvency;

(v) making a company search and checking the last three years' published accounts of any management company with responsibilities under the lease;

(vi) if the borrower is required to be a shareholder in the management company, obtaining the share certificate, a blank stock transfer form signed by the borrower and a copy of the memorandum and articles of association;

(vii) obtaining any necessary consent to or prior approval of the assignment and mortgage;

(viii) obtaining a clear receipt for the last payment of rent and service charge; and

(ix) serving notice of the assignment and mortgage on the landlord;

(j) in the case of a commonhold unit:

(i) confirming receipt of satisfactory evidence that common parts insurance is in place for at least the sum required by the lender and covers the risks specified by the lender;

(ii) confirming that the commonhold community statement contains the terms specified by the lender and does not include any restrictions on occupation or use specified by the lender as unacceptable;

(iii) enquiring of the seller (or the borrower if the property is already owned by the borrower) and the commonhold association as to any known breaches of the commonhold community statement by the commonhold association or any unit-holder, and reporting any such breaches to the lender;

(iv) making a company search to verify that the commonhold association is in existence and remains registered, and that there is no registered indication that it is to be wound up;

(v) obtaining the last three years' published accounts of the commonhold association and reporting any apparent problems with the association to the lender;

(vi) obtaining a commonhold unit information certificate; and

(vii) serving notice of the transfer and mortgage of the commonhold unit on the commonhold association;

(k) if the property is subject to a letting, checking that the type of letting and its terms comply with the lender's requirements;

(l) making appropriate pre-completion searches, including a bankruptcy search against the borrower, any other person in whom the legal estate is vested and any guarantor;

(m) receiving, releasing and transmitting the mortgage advance, including asking for any final inspection needed and dealing with any retentions and cashbacks;

***Paragraph numbers marked with a "+" can be found online and on CD.***

(n) procuring execution of the mortgage deed and form of guarantee as appropriate by the persons whose identities have been checked in accordance with any requirements of the lender under (a) above as those of the borrower, any other person in whom the legal estate is vested and any guarantor; obtaining their signatures to the forms of undertaking required by the lender in relation to the use, occupation or physical state of the property; and complying with the lender's requirements if any document is to be executed under a power of attorney;

(o) asking the borrower for confirmation that the information about occupants given in the mortgage instructions or offer is correct; obtaining consents in the form required by the lender from existing or prospective occupiers of the property aged 17 or over specified by the lender, or of whom you are aware;

(p) advising the borrower on the terms of any document required by the lender to be signed by the borrower;

(q) advising any other person required to sign any document on the terms of that document or, if there is a conflict of interests between that person and the borrower or the lender, advising that person on the need for separate legal advice and arranging for them to see an independent conveyancer;

(r) obtaining the legal transfer of the property to the mortgagor;

(s) procuring the redemption of:

  (i) existing mortgages on property the subject of any associated sale of which you are aware; and

  (ii) any other mortgages secured against a property located in England or Wales made by an identified lender where an identified account number or numbers or a property address has been given by the lender;

(t) ensuring the redemption or postponement of existing mortgages on the property, and registering the mortgage with the priority required by the lender;

(u) making administrative arrangements in relation to any collateral security, such as an endowment policy, or in relation to any collateral warranty or guarantee relating to the physical condition of the property, such as NHBC documentation;

(v) registering the transfer and mortgage;

(w) giving legal advice on any matters reported on under 3.19, suggesting courses of action open to the lender, and complying with the lender's instructions on the action to be taken;

(x) disclosing any relationship specified by the lender between you and the borrower;

(y) storing safely the title deeds and documents pending registration and delivery to or as directed by the lender; and

(z) retaining the information contained in your conveyancing file for at least six years from the date of the mortgage.

**3.20 Using the approved certificate of title**

In addition, if acting for both lender and borrower in a standard mortgage of property to be used as the borrower's private residence only:

(a) you must use the certificate of title set out in the annex to rule 3 (below) ("the approved certificate"); and

(b) unless the lender has certified that its mortgage instructions are subject to the limitations contained in 3.19 above and 3.21 below, you must notify the lender on receipt of instructions that the approved certificate will be used, and that your duties to the lender are limited to the matters contained in the approved certificate.

***Paragraph numbers marked with a "+" can be found online and on CD.***

### 3.21 Terms of rule to prevail

The terms of 3.16 to 3.20 above will prevail in the event of any ambiguity in the lender's instructions, or discrepancy between the instructions and 3.19 above or the approved certificate.

### 3.22 Anti-avoidance

(1) Subject to (2) below, if acting only for the borrower in a standard mortgage of property you must not accept or act upon any requirements by way of undertaking, warranty, guarantee or otherwise of the lender, the lender's solicitor or other agent which extend beyond the limitations contained in 3.19.

(2) Provided the property is not to be used solely as the borrower's private residence, (1) above does not prevent you from giving any form of certificate of title recognised from time to time by the Council of the Law Society (a "recognised certificate"). Additions or amendments which arise from the individual transaction may be made to the text of a recognised certificate but, to the extent to which they create an increased or additional obligation, must not extend beyond the limitations contained in 3.19.

### 3.23 Waivers

In spite of 22.01(1) (Waivers), the Board of the Solicitors Regulation Authority shall not have power to waive any of the provisions of 3.01 to 3.05.

**ANNEX**

**Certificate of title**

Details box

TO: (Lender)

Lender's Reference or Account No:

The Borrower:

Property:

Title Number:

Mortgage Advance:

Price stated in transfer:

Completion Date:

Conveyancer's Name & Address:

Conveyancer's Reference:

Conveyancer's bank, sort code and account number:

Date of instructions:

**WE THE CONVEYANCERS NAMED ABOVE CERTIFY** as follows:

(1) If so instructed, we have checked the identity of the Borrower (and anyone else required to sign the mortgage deed or other document connected with the mortgage) by reference to the document or documents precisely specified in writing by you.

(2) Except as otherwise disclosed to you in writing:

(i) we have investigated the title to the Property, we are not aware of any other financial charges secured on the Property which will affect the Property after completion of the mortgage and, upon completion of the mortgage, both you and the mortgagor (whose identity has been checked in accordance with paragraph (1) above) will have a good and marketable title to the Property and to appurtenant rights free from prior mortgages or charges and from onerous encumbrances which title will be registered with absolute title;

(ii) we have compared the extent of the Property shown on any plan provided by you against relevant plans in the title deeds and/or the description of the Property in any valuation which you have supplied to us, and in our opinion there are no material discrepancies;

(iii) the assumptions stated by the valuer about the title (its tenure, easements, boundaries and restrictions on use) in any valuation which you have supplied to us are correct;

(iv) if the Property is leasehold the terms of the lease accord with your instructions, including any requirements you have for covenants by the

*Paragraph numbers marked with a "+" can be found online and on CD.*

Landlord and/or a management company and/or by a deed of mutual covenant for the insurance, repair and maintenance of the structure, exterior and common parts of any building of which the Property forms part, and we have or will obtain on or before completion a clear receipt for the last payment of rent and service charge;

(v) if the Property is a commonhold unit, the commonhold community statement contains the terms specified by you and does not include any restrictions on occupation or use specified by you as unacceptable, and we have or will obtain on or before completion a commonhold unit information certificate;

(vi) we have received satisfactory evidence that the buildings insurance is in place, or will be on completion, for the sum and in the terms required by you;

(vii) if the Property is to be purchased by the Borrower:

(a) the contract for sale provides for vacant possession on completion;

(b) the seller has owned or been the registered owner of the Property for not less than six months; and

(c) we are not acting on behalf of the seller;

(viii) we are in possession of:

(a) either a local search or local search insurance; and

(b) such other searches or search insurance as are appropriate to the Property, the mortgagor and any guarantor, in each case in accordance with your instructions;

(ix) nothing has been revealed by our searches and enquiries which would prevent the Property being used by any occupant for residential purposes; and

(x) neither any principal nor any other solicitor or registered European lawyer in the firm giving this certificate nor any spouse, child, parent, brother or sister of such a person is interested in the Property (whether alone or jointly with any other) as mortgagor.

**WE:**

(a) undertake, prior to use of the mortgage advance, to obtain in the form required by you the execution of a mortgage and a guarantee as appropriate by the persons whose identities have been checked in accordance with paragraph (1) above as those of the Borrower, any other person in whom the legal estate is vested and any guarantor; and, if required by you:

(i) to obtain their signatures to the forms of undertaking required by you in relation to the use, occupation or physical state of the Property;

(ii) to ask the Borrower for confirmation that the information about occupants given in your mortgage instructions or offer is correct; and

(iii) to obtain consents in the form required by you from any existing or prospective occupier(s) aged 17 or over of the Property specified by you or of whom we are aware;

(b) have made or will make such Bankruptcy, Land Registry or Land Charges Searches as may be necessary to justify certificate no. (2)(i) above;

(c) will within the period of protection afforded by the searches referred to in paragraph (b) above:

(i) complete the mortgage;

(ii) arrange for the issue of a stamp duty land tax certificate if appropriate;

(iii) deliver to the Land Registry the documents necessary to register the mortgage in your favour and any relevant prior dealings; and

(iv) effect any other registrations necessary to protect your interests as mortgagee;

(d) will despatch to you such deeds and documents relating to the Property as you require with a list of them in the form prescribed by you within ten working days of receipt by us of the title information document from the Land Registry;

(e) will not part with the mortgage advance (and will return it to you if required) if it shall come to our notice prior to completion that the Property will at completion be occupied in whole or in part otherwise than in accordance with your instructions;

(f) will not accept instructions, except with your consent in writing, to prepare any lease or tenancy agreement relating to the Property or any part of it prior to despatch of the title information document to you;

(g) will not use the mortgage advance until satisfied that, prior to or contemporaneously with the transfer of the Property to the mortgagor, there will be discharged:

(i) any existing mortgage on property the subject of an associated sale of which we are aware; and

(ii) any other mortgages made by a lender identified by you secured against a property located in England or Wales where you have given either an account number or numbers or a property address;

(h) will notify you in writing if any matter comes to our attention before completion which would render the certificate given above untrue or inaccurate and, in those circumstances, will defer completion pending your authority to proceed and will return the mortgage advance to you if required; and

(i) confirm that we have complied, or will comply, with your instructions in all other respects to the extent that they do not extend beyond the limitations contained in the Solicitors' Code of Conduct 2007, 3.19 (Conflict of interests—types of instruction which may be accepted).

**OUR** duties to you are limited to the matters set out in this certificate and we accept no further liability or responsibility whatsoever. The payment by you to us (by whatever means) of the mortgage advance or any part of it constitutes acceptance of this limitation and any assignment to you by the Borrower of any rights of action against us to which the Borrower may be entitled shall take effect subject to this limitation.

Signature box
SIGNED on behalf of
THE CONVEYANCERS ...................................................
NAME of
Authorised Signatory ...................................................
QUALIFICATION
of Authorised Signatory ...................................................
DATE of Signature ...................................................

**For the Guidance to rule 3 see paragraph 7C–168+ on White Book on Westlaw UK or the Civil Procedure CD.**

# Rule 4—Confidentiality and disclosure

7C–169 **Introduction**

Rule 4 sets out provisions for dealing with the protection of clients' confidential information and the duty of disclosure owed to clients.

**4.01 Duty of confidentiality**

You and your firm must keep the affairs of clients and former clients confidential except where disclosure is required or permitted by law or by your client (or former client).

**4.02 Duty of disclosure**

You must disclose to a client all information of which you are aware which is material to that client's matter regardless of the source of the information, subject to:

(a) the duty of confidentiality in 4.01 above, which always overrides the duty to disclose; and

(b) the following where the duty does not apply:

***Paragraph numbers marked with a "+" can be found online and on CD.***

(i) where such disclosure is prohibited by law;
(ii) where it is agreed expressly that no duty to disclose arises or a different standard of disclosure applies; or
(iii) where you reasonably believe that serious physical or mental injury will be caused to any person if the information is disclosed to a client.

**4.03 Duty not to put confidentiality at risk by acting**

If you hold, or your firm holds, confidential information in relation to a client or former client, you must not risk breaching confidentiality by acting, or continuing to act, for another client on a matter where:

(a) that information might reasonably be expected to be material; and
(b) that client has an interest adverse to the first-mentioned client or former client,

except where proper arrangements can be made to protect that information in accordance with 4.04 and 4.05 below.

**4.04 Exception to duty not to put confidentiality at risk by acting—with clients' consent**

(1) You may act, or continue to act, in the circumstances otherwise prohibited by 4.03 above with the informed consent of both clients but only if:

(a) the client for whom you act or are proposing to act knows that your firm, or a member of your firm, holds, or might hold, material information (in circumstances described in 4.03) in relation to their matter which you cannot disclose;
(b) you have a reasonable belief that both clients understand the relevant issues after these have been brought to their attention;
(c) both clients have agreed to the conditions under which you will be acting or continuing to act; and
(d) it is reasonable in all the circumstances to do so.

(2) "Both clients" in the context of 4.04(1) means:

(a) an existing or former client for whom your firm, or a member of your firm, holds confidential information; and
(b) an existing or new client for whom you act or are proposing to act and to whom information held on behalf of the other client is material (in circumstances described in 4.03 above).

(3) If you, or you and your firm, have been acting for two or more clients in compliance with rule 3 (Conflict of interests) and can no longer fulfil its requirements you may continue to act for one client with the consent of the other client provided you comply with 4.04.

**4.05 Exception to duty not to put confidentiality at risk by acting—without clients' consent**

You may continue to act for a client on an existing matter, or on a matter related to an existing matter, in the circumstances otherwise prohibited by 4.03 above without the consent of the client for whom your firm, or a member of your firm, holds, or might hold, confidential information which is material to your client (in circumstances described in 4.03) but only if:

(a) it is not possible to obtain informed consent under 4.04 above from the client for whom your firm, or a member of your firm, holds, or might hold, material confidential information;
(b) your client has agreed to your acting in the knowledge that your firm, or a member of your firm, holds, or might hold, information material to their matter which you cannot disclose;
(c) any safeguards which comply with the standards required by law at the time they are implemented are put in place; and
(d) it is reasonable in all the circumstances to do so.

**4.06 Waivers**

*Paragraph numbers marked with a "+" can be found online and on CD.*

In spite of 22.01(1) (Waivers), the Board of the Solicitors Regulation Authority shall not have power to waive any of the provisions of this rule.

**For the Guidance to rule 4 see paragraph 7C–170+ on White Book on Westlaw UK or the Civil Procedure CD.**

# Rule 5—Business management in England and Wales

## INTRODUCTION

7C–171 Rule 5 deals with the supervision and management of a firm or in-house practice, the maintenance of competence, and the internal business arrangements essential to the proper delivery of services to clients. "Supervision" and "management" refer, respectively, to the professional overseeing of staff and clients' matters; and to the overall direction and development of the firm or in-house practice and its day-to-day administration. The rule does not apply to your overseas practice but you must comply with 15.05.

Broadly, the rule aims to set out:

(a) responsibility for the overall supervision and management framework of your firm or in-house practice;
(b) the minimum requirements to be met in order to be "qualified to supervise";
(c) the minimum standards applying to supervision of clients' matters; and
(d) the minimum requirements in relation to those business arrangements considered to be essential to good practice and integral to compliance with supervision and other duties to clients.

### 5.01 Supervision and management responsibilities

(1) If you are a principal in a firm, a director of a recognised body which is a company, or a member of a recognised body which is an LLP, you must make arrangements for the effective management of the firm as a whole, and in particular provide for:

(a) compliance with the duties of a principal, in law and conduct, to exercise appropriate supervision over all staff, and ensure adequate supervision and direction of clients' matters;
(b) compliance with the money laundering regulations, where applicable;
(c) compliance by the firm and individuals with key regulatory requirements such as certification, registration or recognition by the Solicitors Regulation Authority, compulsory professional indemnity cover, delivery of accountants' reports, and obligations to co-operate with and report information to the Authority;
(d) the identification of conflicts of interests;
(e) compliance with the requirements of rule 2 (Client relations) on client care, costs information and complaints handling;
(f) control of undertakings;
(g) the safekeeping of documents and assets entrusted to the firm;
(h) compliance with rule 6 (Equality and diversity);
(i) the training of individuals working in the firm to maintain a level of competence appropriate to their work and level of responsibility;
(j) financial control of budgets, expenditure and cashflow;
(k) the continuation of the practice of the firm in the event of absences and emergencies, with the minimum interruption to clients' business; and
(l) the management of risk.

(2) If you are a solicitor or REL employed as the head of an in-house legal department, you must effect supervision and management arrangements within your department to provide for:

(a) adequate supervision and direction of those assisting in your inhouse practice;

***Paragraph numbers marked with a "+" can be found online and on CD.***

(b) control of undertakings; and

(c) identification of conflicts of interests.

**5.02 Persons who must be "qualified to supervise"**

(1) The following persons must be "qualified to supervise":

(a) a sole principal;

(b) one of the partners of a partnership;

(c) one of the members of a recognised body which is an LLP;

(d) one of the directors of a recognised body which is a company;

(e) one of the solicitors or RELs employed by a law centre; or

(f) one in-house solicitor or in-house REL in any department where solicitors and/or RELs, as part of that employment:

(i) do publicly funded work; or

(ii) exercise or supervise the exercise of any right of audience or right to conduct litigation when advising or acting for members of the public.

(2) To be "qualified to supervise" under this paragraph a person:

(a) must have completed the training specified from time to time by the Solicitors Regulation Authority for this purpose; and

(b) must have been entitled to practise as a lawyer for at least 36 months within the last ten years; and must be able to demonstrate this if asked by the Solicitors Regulation Authority.



**5.03 Supervision of work for clients and members of the public**

(1) If you are a principal in a firm, you must ensure that your firm has in place a system for supervising clients' matters.

(2) If you are an in-house solicitor or in-house REL and you are required to be "qualified to supervise" under 5.02(1)(e) or (f) above, you must ensure that your law centre or in-house legal department has in place a system for supervising work undertaken for members of the public.

(3) The system for supervision under 5.03(1) and (2) must include appropriate and effective procedures under which the quality of work undertaken for clients and members of the public is checked with reasonable regularity by suitably experienced and competent persons within the firm, law centre or in-house legal department.

**For the Guidance to rule 5 see paragraph 7C–172+ on White Book on Westlaw UK or the Civil Procedure CD.**

# Rule 6—Equality and diversity

## INTRODUCTION

Rule 6 is designed to prevent discrimination within your firm or in-house practice. **7C–173**
The rule does not apply to overseas practice but solicitors practising overseas must comply with 15.06 (Equality and diversity) and 1.02 (Integrity). The duties contained in this rule are in addition to, and not in substitution for, your obligations to comply with anti-discrimination legislation.

## Rule 6—Equality and diversity

**6.01 Duty not to discriminate**

(1) You must not in your professional dealings with employees, partners, members, directors, barristers, other lawyers, clients or third parties discriminate, without lawful cause, against any person, nor victimise or harass them on the grounds of:

(a) race or racial group (including colour, nationality and ethnic or national origins);

***Paragraph numbers marked with a "+" can be found online and on CD.***

(b) sex (including marital status, gender reassignment, pregnancy, maternity and paternity);
(c) sexual orientation (including civil partnership status);
(d) religion or belief;
(e) age; or
(f) disability.

(2) You must take such steps, and make such adjustments, as are reasonable in all the circumstances in order to prevent any of your employees, partners, members, directors or clients who are disabled from being placed at a substantial disadvantage in comparison with those who are not disabled.

**6.02 Evidence of breach**

Where there has been a decision of a court or tribunal of the United Kingdom in proceedings to which you are a party, that you have committed, or are to be treated as having committed, an unlawful act of discrimination then that finding shall be treated as evidence of a breach of this rule.

**6.03 Equality and diversity policy**

If you are a principal in a firm, or a member or a director of a recognised body, you must adopt and implement an appropriate policy for preventing discrimination and harassment and promoting equality and diversity within your firm. You must take all reasonable steps to ensure that all employees, partners, members and directors are aware of, and act in compliance with, its provisions and that it is made available to clients, the Solicitors Regulation Authority and other relevant third parties where required.

**6.04 In-house practice**

If you have management responsibilities in in-house practice you must use all reasonable endeavours to secure the adoption and implementation of an appropriate policy for preventing discrimination and promoting equality and diversity within your department. You must take all reasonable steps to ensure that all staff within that department are aware of, and act in accordance with, its provisions.

**6.05 Waivers**

In spite of 22.01(1), the Board of the Solicitors Regulation Authority shall not have power to waive any of the provisions of this rule.

**6.06 Meaning of terms**

For the avoidance of doubt, unless otherwise defined in the rules, the terms used in this rule shall have the meanings assigned to them in law.

**For the Guidance to rule 6 see paragraph 7C–174+ on White Book on Westlaw UK or the Civil Procedure CD.**

# Rule 7—Publicity

## INTRODUCTION

7C–175 You are generally free to publicise your practice as a solicitor, REL or RFL, subject to the requirements of this rule. The rule as it applies to your overseas practice is modified by 15.07.

## Rule 7—Publicity

**7.01 Misleading or inaccurate publicity**

Publicity must not be misleading or inaccurate.

**7.02 Clarity as to charges**

Any publicity relating to your charges must be clearly expressed. In relation to practice from an office in England and Wales it must be clear whether disbursements and VAT are included.

**7.03 Unsolicited visits or telephone calls**

(1) You must not publicise your practice by making unsolicited visits or telephone calls to a member of the public.

(2) "Member of the public" does not include:

(a) a current or former client;

(b) another lawyer;

(c) an existing or potential professional or business connection; or

(d) a commercial organisation or public body.

**7.04 International aspects of publicity**

Publicity intended for a jurisdiction outside England and Wales must comply with:

(a) the provisions of rule 7 (and 15.07, if applicable); and

(b) the rules in force in that jurisdiction concerning lawyers' publicity.

Publicity intended for a jurisdiction where it is permitted will not breach 7.04 through being incidentally received in a jurisdiction where it is not permitted.

**7.05 Responsibility for publicity**

You must not authorise any other person to conduct publicity for your practice in a way which would be contrary to rule 7 (and 15.07, if applicable).

**7.06 Application**

(1) Rule 7 applies to any publicity you or your firm conduct(s) or authorise(s) in relation to:

(a) your practice;

(b) any other business or activity carried on by you or your firm; or

(c) any other business or activity carried on by others.

(2) 7.01 to 7.05 apply to all forms of publicity including the name or description of your firm, stationery, advertisements, brochures, websites, directory entries, media appearances, promotional press releases, and direct approaches to potential clients and other persons, and whether conducted in person, in writing, or in electronic form.

**7.07 Letterhead**

(1) The letterhead of a firm must bear the words "regulated by the Solicitors Regulation Authority".

(2) (a) The letterhead of:

(i) a sole principal must include the name of the sole principal;

(ii) a partnership of 20 or fewer persons must include a list of the partners; and

(iii) a recognised body which is a company with a sole director must include the name of the director, identified as director.

(b) The letterhead of:

(i) a partnership of more than 20 persons must include either a list of the partners;

(ii) a recognised body which is an LLP must include either a list of the members, identified as members; and

(iii) a recognised body which is a company with more than one director must include either a list of the directors, identified as directors,

or a statement that the list is open to inspection at the office.

(c) (i) On the letterhead of a recognised body which is an unlimited company; or

(ii) in the list of partners referred to in 7.07(2)(a) or (b) if a partnership has an unlimited company as a member; or

***Paragraph numbers marked with a "+" can be found online and on CD.***

(iii) in the list of members referred to in 7.07(2)(b) if an LLP has an unlimited company as a member,

it must be stated, either as part of the unlimited company's name or otherwise, that the unlimited company is a body corporate.

(3) In a firm, if the partners (or directors in the case of a company, or members in the case of an LLP) comprise both solicitors and foreign lawyers, the list referred to in 7.07(2)(a) or (b) must:

(a) identify any solicitor as a solicitor;

(b) in the case of any lawyer or notary of an Establishment Directive state other than the UK;

(i) identify the jurisdiction(s)—local or national as appropriate—under whose professional title the lawyer or notary is practising;

(ii) give the professional title(s), expressed in an official language of the Establishment Directive state(s) concerned; and

(iii) if the lawyer is an REL, refer to that lawyer's registration with the Solicitors Regulation Authority; and

(c) indicate the professional qualification(s) as a lawyer and the country or jurisdiction of qualification of any RFL not included in (b) above.

(4) Whenever an REL is named on the letterhead used by any firm or inhouse practice, there must be compliance with 7.07(3)(b).

(5) In 7.07, "letterhead" includes a fax heading.

**For the Guidance to rule 7 see paragraph 7C–176+ on White Book on Westlaw UK or the Civil Procedure CD.**

# Rule 8—Fee sharing

7C–177 **Introduction**

Rule 8 restricts the persons and businesses with whom or with which you can share your professional fees. Broadly, you may not share fees with a nonlawyer unless the fee sharing is with an employee or, in the case of overseas practice, a partner, or in the strictly defined circumstances set out in this rule. Its purpose is to protect your independence and professional judgement in these situations for the ultimate public benefit.

## Rule 8—Fee sharing

### 8.01 Fee sharing with lawyers and colleagues

Except as permitted under 8.02 below you may only share or agree to share your professional fees with the following persons:

(a) practising members of legal professions covered by the Establishment Directive (other than a member of the English Bar practising in England and Wales);

(b) practising members of other legal professions (other than a person who is struck off or suspended from the register of foreign lawyers);

(c) bodies corporate wholly owned and directed by lawyers within (a) and (b) above for the purpose of practising law;

(d) your partner as permitted by rule 12 (Framework of practice), your retired partner or predecessor, or the dependants or personal representatives of your deceased partner or predecessor;

(e) in the case of a recognised body, a retired director, member or shareowner, or the dependants or personal representatives of a deceased director, member or shareowner;

(f) your genuine employee (this does not allow you to disguise as "employment" what is in fact a partnership which rule 12 prohibits);

(g) a body corporate through which you practise as permitted by rule 12;

***Paragraph numbers marked with a "+" can be found online and on CD.***

(h) your employer, if you are employed by a firm permitted under rule 12, or if you are practising in-house and acting in accordance with rule 13 (In-house practice) or 15.13 (In-house practice overseas);

(i) a law centre or advice service operated by a charitable or similar non-commercial organisation if you are working as a volunteer and receive fees or costs from public funds or recovered from a third party; or

(j) an estate agent who is your sub-agent for the sale of a property; or

(k) a charity (as defined in rule 24 (Interpretation)), provided:

(i) you remain in compliance with 1.02 (Integrity), 1.03 (Independence) and 1.04 (Best interests of clients);

(ii) if requested by the Solicitors Regulation Authority to do so, you supply details of all agreements to share fees with a charity;

(iii) the operation of any such agreement does not result in a partnership;

(iv) any such agreement does not involve a breach of rule 9 (Referrals of business); and

(v) if you are employed in-house, you remain in compliance with 13.04 (Pro bono work).



**8.02 Fee sharing with other non-lawyers**

(1) Except in relation to European cross-border practice, you may share your professional fees with another person or business ("the fee sharer") if:

(a) the purpose of the fee sharing arrangement is solely to facilitate the introduction of capital and/or the provision of services to your firm;

(b) neither the fee sharing agreement nor the extent of the fees shared permits any fee sharer to influence or constrain your professional judgement in relation to the advice which you give to any client;

(c) the operation of the agreement does not result in a partnership prohibited by rule 12 (Framework of practice);

(d) if requested by the Solicitors Regulation Authority to do so, you supply details of all agreements which you have made with fee sharers and the percentage of your firm's annual gross fees which has been paid to each fee sharer; and

(e) your fee sharing agreement does not involve a breach of rule 9 (Referrals of business) or 15.09 (Overseas practice—referrals of business).

(2) "Fee sharer" means a person or business who or which shares your fees in reliance on (1) above and the expression includes any person or business connected to or associated with the fee sharer.

**For the Guidance to rule 8 see paragraph 7C-178+ on White Book on Westlaw UK or the Civil Procedure CD.**

# Rule 9—Referrals of business

**Introduction** 7C-179

Rule 9 applies when you receive referrals of business from, or make referrals to, third parties. Its purpose is to protect your independence. Additional provisions apply when you have a financial arrangement with an introducer. The rule does not apply to your overseas practice but you must comply with 15.09.

## Rule 9—Referrals of business

**9.01 General**

(1) When making or receiving referrals of clients to or from third parties you must do nothing which would compromise your independence or your ability to act and advise in the best interests of your clients.

*Paragraph numbers marked with a "+" can be found online and on CD.*

(2) You must draw the attention of potential introducers to this rule and to the relevant provisions of rule 7 (Publicity).

(3) This rule does not apply to referrals between lawyers.

(4) You must not, in respect of any claim arising as a result of death or personal injury, either:

(a) enter into an arrangement for the referral of clients with; or

(b) act in association with,

any person whose business, or any part of whose business, is to make, support or prosecute (whether by action or otherwise, and whether by a solicitor or agent or otherwise) claims arising as a result of death or personal injury, and who, in the course of such business, solicits or receives contingency fees in respect of such claims.

(5) The prohibition in 9.01(4) shall not apply to an arrangement or association with a person who solicits or receives contingency fees only in respect of proceedings in a country outside England and Wales, to the extent that a local lawyer would be permitted to receive a contingency fee in respect of such proceedings.

(6) In 9.01(4) and (5) "contingency fee" means any sum (whether fixed, or calculated either as a percentage of the proceeds or otherwise howsoever) payable only in the event of success in the prosecution or defence of any action, suit or other contentious proceedings.

**9.02 Financial arrangements with introducers**

The following additional requirements apply when you enter into a financial arrangement with an introducer:

(a) The agreement must be in writing and be available for inspection by the Solicitors Regulation Authority.

(b) The introducer must undertake, as part of the agreement, to comply with the provisions of this rule.

(c) You must be satisfied that clients referred by the introducer have not been acquired as a result of marketing or publicity or other activities which, if done by a person regulated by the Solicitors Regulation Authority, would be in breach of any of these rules.

(d) The agreement must not include any provision which would:

(i) compromise, infringe or impair any of the duties set out in these rules; or

(ii) allow the introducer to influence or constrain your professional judgement in relation to the advice given to the client.

(e) The agreement must provide that before making a referral the introducer must give the client all relevant information concerning the referral, in particular:

(i) the fact that the introducer has a financial arrangement with you; and

(ii) the amount of any payment to the introducer which is calculated by reference to that referral; or

(iii) where the introducer is paying you to provide services to the introducer's customers:

(A) the amount the introducer is paying you to provide those services; and

(B) the amount the client is required to pay the introducer.

(f) If you have reason to believe that the introducer is breaching any of the terms of the agreement required by this rule, you must take all reasonable steps to ensure that the breach is remedied. If the introducer continues to breach it you must terminate the agreement.

(g) Before accepting instructions to act for a client referred under 9.02 you must, in addition to the requirements contained in 2.02 (Client care), 2.03 (Information about the cost) or 2.05 (Complaints handling), give the client, in writing, all relevant information concerning the referral, in particular:

(i) the fact that you have a financial arrangement with the introducer;

(ii) the amount of any payment to the introducer which is calculated by reference to that referral; or

(iii) where the introducer is paying you to provide services to the introducer's customers:

(A) the amount the introducer is paying you to provide those services; and

(B) the amount the client is required to pay the introducer;

(iv) a statement that any advice you give will be independent and that the client is free to raise questions on all aspects of the transaction; and

(v) confirmation that information disclosed to you by the client will not be disclosed to the introducer unless the client consents; but that where you are also acting for the introducer in the same matter and a conflict of interests arises, you might be obliged to cease acting.

(h) You must not enter into a financial arrangement with an introducer for the referral of clients in respect of criminal proceedings or any matter in which you will act for the client with the benefit of public funding.

(i) For the purpose of this rule:

(i) "financial arrangement" includes:

(A) any payment to a third party in respect of referrals; and

(B) any agreement to be paid by a third party introducer to provide services to the third party's customers; and

(ii) "payment" includes any other consideration but does not include normal hospitality, proper disbursements or normal business expenses.



**9.03 Referrals to third parties**

(1) If you recommend that a client use a particular firm, agency or business, you must do so in good faith, judging what is in the client's best interests.

(2) You must not enter into any agreement or association which would restrict your freedom to recommend any particular firm, agency or business.

(3) (2) above does not apply to arrangements in connection with any of the following types of contracts:

(a) regulated mortgage contracts;

(b) general insurance contracts; or

(c) pure protection contracts.

(4) The terms "regulated mortgage contracts", "general insurance contracts" and "pure protection contracts" in (3) above have the meanings given in 19.01(4).

(5) Where you refer a client to a firm, agency or business that can only offer products from one source, you must notify the client in writing of this limitation.

(6) If a client is likely to need an endowment policy, or similar life insurance with an investment element, you must refer them only to an independent intermediary authorised to give investment advice.

**For the Guidance to rule 9 see paragraph 7C–180+ on White Book on Westlaw UK or the Civil Procedure CD.**

# Rule 10—Relations with third parties

**Introduction** 7C–181

Rule 10 draws together a variety of obligations linked by the need to deal with third parties in a proper manner. The rule as it applies to your overseas practice is modified by 15.10.

***Paragraph numbers marked with a "+" can be found online and on CD.***

# Rule 10—Relations with third parties

### 10.01 Not taking unfair advantage

You must not use your position to take unfair advantage of anyone either for your own benefit or for another person's benefit.

### 10.02 Agreeing costs with another party

When negotiating the payment of your client's costs by another firm's client or a third party, you must give sufficient time and information for the amount of your costs to be agreed or assessed.

### 10.03 Administering oaths

You can administer oaths or affirmations or take declarations if you are a solicitor or an REL. You must not do so where you or your firm is acting for any party in the matter.

### 10.04 Contacting other party to a matter

You must not communicate with any other party who to your knowledge has retained a lawyer or licensed conveyancer to act in a matter, except:

(a) to request the name and address of the other party's lawyer or licensed conveyancer;

(b) where it would be reasonable to conclude that the other party's lawyer or licensed conveyancer has refused or failed for no adequate reason either to pass on messages to their client or to reply to correspondence, and has been warned of your intention to contact their client direct;

(c) with that lawyer or licensed conveyancer's consent; or

(d) in exceptional circumstances.

### 10.05 Undertakings

(1) You must fulfil an undertaking which is given in circumstances where:

(a) you give the undertaking in the course of practice;

(b) you are a principal in a firm, and any person within the firm gives the undertaking in the course of practice;

(c) you give the undertaking outside the course of practice, but as a solicitor; or

(d) you are an REL based at an office in England and Wales, and you give the undertaking within the UK, as a lawyer of an Establishment Directive state, but outside your practice as an REL.

(2) You must fulfil an undertaking within a reasonable time.

(3) If you give an undertaking which is dependent upon the happening of a future event, you must notify the recipient immediately if it becomes clear that the event will not occur.

(4) When you give an undertaking to pay another's costs, the undertaking will be discharged if the matter does not proceed unless there is an express agreement that the costs are payable in any event.

### 10.06 Dealing with more than one prospective buyer in a conveyancing transaction

(1) Each time a seller of land, other than in a sale by auction or tender, either:

(a) instructs you to deal with more than one prospective buyer; or

(b) to your knowledge:

(i) deals directly with another prospective buyer (or their conveyancer); or

(ii) instructs another conveyancer to deal with another prospective buyer;

you must, with the client's consent, immediately inform the conveyancer of each prospective buyer, or the prospective buyer if acting in person.

(2) If the seller refuses to agree to such disclosure, you must immediately stop acting in the matter.

*Paragraph numbers marked with a "+" can be found online and on CD.*

(3) You must not act for both the seller and any of the prospective buyers.
(4) You must not act for more than one of the prospective buyers.

**10.07 Fees of lawyers of other jurisdictions**

(1) If in the course of practice you instruct a lawyer of another jurisdiction you must, as a matter of professional conduct, pay the lawyer's proper fees unless the lawyer is practising as a solicitor or barrister of England and Wales; or
   (a) you have expressly disclaimed that responsibility at the outset, or at a later date you have expressly disclaimed responsibility for any fees incurred after that date;
   (b) the lawyer is an REL or is registered with the Bar of England and Wales under the Establishment Directive; or
   (c) the lawyer is an RFL based in England and Wales and practising in a firm.
(2) If in the course of practice you instruct a business carrying on the practice of a lawyer of another jurisdiction you must, as a matter of professional conduct, pay the proper fees for the work that lawyer does, unless:
   (a) you have expressly disclaimed that responsibility at the outset, or at a later date you have expressly disclaimed responsibility for any fees incurred after that date; or
   (b) the business is a firm.

**For the Guidance to rule 10 see paragraph 7C–182+ on White Book on Westlaw UK or the Civil Procedure CD.**

SOLICITORS

# Rule 11—Litigation and advocacy

**Introduction** 7C–183

Rule 11 imposes additional duties on you if you are a solicitor, an REL or an RFL whenever you exercise a right to conduct litigation or act as an advocate. "Court" in this rule has a wide meaning—see rule 24 (Interpretation). References to appearing or acting as an advocate apply when you are exercising rights of audience before any court, not just if you have been granted rights of audience in the higher courts. The rule only applies in a modified form to overseas practice—see 15.11.

## Rule 11—Litigation and advocacy

**11.01 Deceiving or misleading the court**

(1) You must never deceive or knowingly or recklessly mislead the court.
(2) You must draw to the court's attention:
   (a) relevant cases and statutory provisions;
   (b) the contents of any document that has been filed in the proceedings where failure to draw it to the court's attention might result in the court being misled; and
   (c) any procedural irregularity.
(3) You must not construct facts supporting your client's case or draft any documents relating to any proceedings containing:
   (a) any contention which you do not consider to be properly arguable; or
   (b) any allegation of fraud unless you are instructed to do so and you have material which you reasonably believe establishes, on the face of it, a case of fraud.

**11.02 Obeying court orders**

You must comply with any court order requiring you or your firm to take, or refrain from taking, a particular course of action.

*Paragraph numbers marked with a "+" can be found online and on CD.*

**11.03 Contempt of court**

You must not become in contempt of court.

**11.04 Refusing instructions to act as advocate**

(1) You must not refuse to act as an advocate for any person on any of the following grounds:

(a) that the nature of the case is objectionable to you or to any section of the public;

(b) that the conduct, opinions or beliefs of the prospective client are unacceptable to you or to any section of the public; or

(c) that the source of any financial support which may properly be given to the prospective client for the proceedings is unacceptable to you.

(2) You are not required to act as an advocate:

(a) under a conditional fee agreement; or

(b) if you reasonably consider that you are not being offered a proper fee having regard to:

(i) the circumstances of the case;

(ii) the nature of your practice; or

(iii) your experience and standing.

**11.05 Appearing as an advocate**

If you are appearing as an advocate:

(a) you must not say anything which is merely scandalous or intended only to insult a witness or any other person;

(b) you must avoid naming in open court any third party whose character would thereby be called into question, unless it is necessary for the proper conduct of the case;

(c) you must not call into question the character of a witness you have cross-examined unless the witness has had the opportunity to answer the allegations during cross-examination; and

(d) you must not suggest that any person is guilty of a crime, fraud or misconduct unless such allegations:

(i) go to a matter in issue which is material to your client's case; and

(ii) appear to you to be supported by reasonable grounds.

**11.06 Appearing as a witness**

You must not appear as an advocate at a trial or act in the litigation if it is clear that you, or anyone within your firm, will be called as a witness, unless you are satisfied that this will not prejudice your independence as an advocate, or litigator, or the interests of your client or the interests of justice.

**11.07 Payments to witnesses**

You must not make, or offer to make, payments to a witness dependent upon the nature of the evidence given or upon the outcome of the case.

**11.08 Recordings of child witnesses' evidence**

If you are acting in the defence or prosecution of an accused and you have in your possession a copy of an audio or video recording of a child witness which has been identified as having been prepared to be admitted in evidence at a criminal trial in accordance with the relevant provisions of the Criminal Justice Act 1991 or the Youth Justice and Criminal Evidence Act 1999, you must:

(a) not make or permit any person to make a copy of the recording;

(b) not release the recording to the accused;

(c) not make or permit any disclosure of the recording or its contents to any person except when, in your opinion, it is necessary in the course of preparing the prosecution, defence or appeal against conviction and/or sentence;

(d) ensure that the recording is always kept in a locked, secure container when not in use; and

***Paragraph numbers marked with a "+" can be found online and on CD.***

(e) return the recording when you are no longer instructed in the matter.

**For the Guidance to rule 11 see paragraph 7C–184+ on White Book on Westlaw UK or the Civil Procedure CD.**

# Rule 12—Framework of practice

## INTRODUCTION

This rule sets out the types of business through which solicitors, RELs, RFLs and recognised bodies may practise under the regulation of the Solicitors Regulation Authority. The restrictions are necessary to ensure that members of the public receiving services from solicitors, RELs and their firms have all the client protections provided under the current statutory framework, and so that the Authority can adequately regulate the firm within its current statutory powers. The guidance signposts the reader to other rules which deal with particular types of business in more detail. **7C–185**

## Rule 12—Framework of practice

### 12.01 Solicitors

*Practice from an office in England and Wales*

(1) You may practise as a solicitor from an office in England and Wales in the following ways only:

(a) as a sole principal;

(b) as a partner in a partnership consisting of:

(i) solicitors, with or without RELs and/or recognised bodies;

(ii) solicitors and RFLs, with or without RELs;

(iii) solicitors, RELs and non-registered European lawyers, with or without RFLs; or

(iv) solicitors, RELs, non-registered European lawyers and recognised bodies;

(c) as a director, member or shareowner of a company which is a recognised body;

(d) as a member of an LLP which is a recognised body;

(e) in the employment of any firm in which a solicitor or an REL would be permitted to participate under this rule as a sole principal, partner, director, member or shareowner, for practice from an office in England and Wales; or

(f) in any other employment, provided that you undertake work only for your employer, or as permitted by rule 13 (In-house practice).

(2) You must not, as a solicitor:

(a) be a partner in a partnership which has a separate legal identity, if the partnership has an office in England and Wales; or

(b) be a director, member or owner of a body corporate which has an office in England and Wales and is not a recognised body, unless you do so as an in-house solicitor.

*Practice from an office outside England and Wales*

(3) You may practise as a solicitor from an office outside England and Wales in the following ways only:

(a) as a sole principal;

(b) as a partner in a partnership consisting of:

(i) practising lawyers; and/or

(ii) bodies corporate wholly owned and directed by lawyers for the purpose of practising law; and/or

(iii) partnerships which have separate legal identity, whose partners are all lawyers;

(c) as a partner in a partnership consisting of persons under (b) above, together with other persons, provided that:

(i) the partnership has no office in England and Wales;

(ii) a controlling majority of the partners are persons under (b) above;

(iii) the involvement of non-lawyers in the partnership does not put the lawyers in breach of any applicable local rules; and

(iv) if the partnership has an office in an Establishment Directive state, the rules applying in that jurisdiction would permit local lawyers to enter into a partnership with similar involvement of non-lawyers;

(d) as a director or owner of a body corporate wholly owned and directed, for the purpose of practising law, by:

(i) practising lawyers; and/or

(ii) bodies corporate wholly owned and directed by lawyers for the purpose of practising law; and/or

(iii) partnerships which have separate legal identity, whose partners are all lawyers;

(e) as a director or owner of a body corporate wholly owned and directed, for the purpose of practising law, by persons under (d) above, together with other persons, provided that:

(i) the body corporate has no office in England and Wales;

(ii) a controlling majority of the directors and of the owners are persons under (d) above;

(iii) the involvement of non-lawyers in the body corporate does not put the lawyer directors or owners in breach of any applicable local rules; and

(iv) if the body corporate has an office in an Establishment Directive state, the rules applying in that jurisdiction would permit local lawyers to practise through a body corporate with similar involvement of non-lawyers;

(f) in the employment of any firm in which a solicitor or an REL would be permitted to participate under this rule as a sole principal, partner, director or owner, for practice as a solicitor from an office outside England and Wales or as a lawyer of an Establishment Directive state from an office in Scotland or Northern Ireland; or

(g) in any other employment, provided that you undertake work only as permitted by 15.13 (In-house practice overseas).

**12.02 RELs**

If you are an REL:

*Practice from an office in England and Wales*

(1) You may practise as a lawyer of an Establishment Directive state from an office in England and Wales in the following ways only:

(a) as a sole principal;

(b) as a partner in a partnership consisting of:

(i) RELs, with or without solicitors and/or recognised bodies;

(ii) RELs and RFLs, with or without solicitors;

(iii) RELs and non-registered European lawyers, with or without solicitors and/or RFLs; or

(iv) RELs, non-registered European lawyers and recognised bodies, with or without solicitors;

(c) as a director, member or shareowner of a company which is a recognised body;

***Paragraph numbers marked with a "+" can be found online and on CD.***

(d) as a member of an LLP which is a recognised body;

(e) in the employment of any firm in which an REL or a solicitor would be permitted to participate under this rule as a sole principal, partner, director, member or shareowner, for practice from an office in England and Wales; or

(f) in any other employment, provided that you undertake work only for your employer, or as permitted by rule 13 (In-house practice).

(2) You must not, as a lawyer of an Establishment Directive state:

(a) be a partner in a partnership which has a separate legal identity, if the partnership has an office in England and Wales; or

(b) be a director, member or owner of a body corporate which has an office in England and Wales and is not a recognised body, unless you do so as an in-house lawyer.

*Practice from an office in Scotland or Northern Ireland*

(3) You may practise as a lawyer of an Establishment Directive state from an office in Scotland or Northern Ireland in the following ways only:

(a) as a sole principal;

(b) as a partner in a partnership consisting of:

(i) practising lawyers; and/or

(ii) bodies corporate wholly owned and directed by lawyers for the purpose of practising law; and/or

(iii) partnerships which have separate legal identity, whose partners are all lawyers;

(c) as a partner in a partnership consisting of persons under (b) above, together with other persons, provided that:

(i) the partnership has no office in England and Wales;

(ii) a controlling majority of the partners are persons under (b) above;

(iii) the involvement of non-lawyers in the partnership does not put the lawyers in breach of any applicable local rules; and

(iv) the rules applying in that jurisdiction would permit local lawyers to enter into a partnership with similar involvement of non-lawyers;

(d) as a director or owner of a body corporate wholly owned and directed, for the purpose of practising law, by:

(i) practising lawyers; and/or

(ii) bodies corporate wholly owned and directed by lawyers for the purpose of practising law; and/or

(iii) partnerships which have separate legal identity, whose partners are all lawyers;

(e) as a director or owner of a body corporate wholly owned and directed, for the purpose of practising law, by persons under (d) above, together with other persons, provided that:

(i) the body corporate has no office in England and Wales;

(ii) a controlling majority of the directors and of the owners are persons under (d) above;

(iii) the involvement of non-lawyers in the body corporate does not put the lawyer directors or owners in breach of any applicable local rules; and

(iv) the rules applying in that jurisdiction would permit local lawyers to practise through a body corporate with similar involvement of non-lawyers;

(f) in the employment of any firm in which an REL or a solicitor would be permitted to participate under this rule as a sole principal, partner, director, or owner, for practice as a lawyer of an Establishment Directive state from an office in Scotland or Northern Ireland or as a solicitor from an office outside England and Wales; or

(g) in any other employment, provided that you undertake work only as permitted by 15.13 (In-house practice overseas).

**12.03 RFLs**

*Practice in the capacity of an RFL*

(1) In these rules, practice as a foreign lawyer in the capacity of an RFL is confined to:

(a) practice as a partner in an MNP which has an office in England and Wales and which consists of:

(i) solicitors and/or RELs, together with RFLs; or

(ii) RELs, RFLs and non-registered European lawyers, with or without solicitors;

(b) practice as a director of a company which is a recognised body; and

(c) practice as a member of an LLP which is a recognised body,

and if you practise in that capacity you will be subject to these rules and to regulation by the Solicitors Regulation Authority.

*Practice in another capacity than as an RFL*

(2) If you provide services as a foreign lawyer in any of the following ways, you will not be practising in the capacity of an RFL:

(a) as a sole principal;

(b) as a partner in a partnership in which none of the partners is a solicitor, or an REL;

(c) as a director of a company, or a member of an LLP, which is not a recognised body; or

(d) as the employee of a business which is not the practice of a solicitor, an REL or a recognised body,

and you must not be held out or described in that context as an RFL, or as regulated by or registered with the Law Society or the Solicitors Regulation Authority.

(3) You must not be held out or described as an RFL, or as regulated by or registered with the Law Society or the Solicitors Regulation Authority, in the context of:

(a) employment in the practice of a solicitor, an REL or a recognised body; or

(b) participation in any firm which operates wholly outside England and Wales.

(4) If you have a practice under (1) above, and another business under (2) above, the latter is a "separate business" for the purpose of these rules and you must therefore comply with rule 21 (Separate businesses).

*Scope of practice of an RFL*

(5) Whether practising in your capacity as an RFL or not, you must not:

(a) undertake work which you are not qualified or entitled to undertake by the law of England and Wales; or

(b) appear as advocate before any court or tribunal in England and Wales in which you have no right of audience.

**12.04 Recognised bodies**

*Practice from an office in England and Wales*

(1) A recognised body may practise from an office in England and Wales in the following ways only:

(a) as a stand-alone firm;

(b) as a body corporate wholly owned by, and providing services in conjunction with:

***Paragraph numbers marked with a "+" can be found online and on CD.***

(i) the practice of a solicitor or an REL as a sole principal;

(ii) a partnership consisting of:

(A) solicitors and/or RELs and/or recognised bodies;

(B) solicitors and/or RELs together with RFLs;

(C) RELs and non-registered European lawyers, with or without solicitors and/or RFLs; or

(D) RELs, non-registered European lawyers and recognised bodies, with or without solicitors;

(iii) another recognised body;

(c) as a partner in a partnership consisting of:

(i) recognised bodies, with or without solicitors and/or RELs; or

(ii) recognised bodies, RELs and non-registered European lawyers, with or without solicitors; or

(d) as a member or shareowner of another recognised body.

(2) A recognised body must not practise as:

(a) a partner in a partnership which has a separate legal identity, if the partnership has an office in England and Wales; or

(b) a director, member or owner of a body corporate which has an office in England and Wales and is not a recognised body.

*Practice from an office outside England and Wales by a recognised body incorporated in England and Wales*

(3) A recognised body which is incorporated in England and Wales may practise from an office outside England and Wales in the following ways only:

(a) as a stand-alone firm;

(b) as a partner in a partnership consisting of:

(i) practising lawyers; and/or

(ii) bodies corporate wholly owned and directed by lawyers for the purpose of practising law; and/or

(iii) partnerships which have separate legal identity, whose partners are all lawyers;

(c) as a partner in a partnership consisting of persons under (b) above together with other persons, provided that:

(i) the partnership has no office in England and Wales;

(ii) a controlling majority of the partners are persons under (b) above;

(iii) the involvement of non-lawyers in the partnership does not put the lawyers in breach of any applicable local rules; and

(iv) if the partnership has an office in an Establishment Directive state, the rules applying in that jurisdiction would permit local lawyers to enter into a partnership with similar involvement of non-lawyers;

(d) as a member or shareowner of another recognised body;

(e) as a director or owner of a body corporate which is wholly owned and directed, for the purpose of practising law, by:

(i) practising lawyers; and/or

(ii) bodies corporate wholly owned and directed by lawyers for the purpose of practising law; and/or

(iii) partnerships which have separate legal identity, whose partners are all lawyers; or

(f) as a director or owner of a body corporate wholly owned and directed, for the purpose of practising law, by persons under (e) above, together with other persons, provided that:

(i) the body corporate has no office in England and Wales;

(ii) a controlling majority of the directors and of the owners are persons under (e) above;

(iii) the involvement of non-lawyers in the body corporate does not put the lawyer directors or owners in breach of any applicable local rules; and

(iv) if the body corporate has an office in an Establishment Directive state, the rules applying in that jurisdiction would permit local lawyers to practise through a body corporate with similar involvement of non-lawyers.

*Practice from an office outside England and Wales by a recognised body incorporated outside England and Wales*

(4) (a) In relation to practice from an office outside England and Wales, a recognised body incorporated outside England and Wales is not subject to these rules except as specified in this paragraph.

(b) The recognised body is subject to:

(i) this paragraph;

(ii) 1.06 (Public confidence);

(iii) rule 14 (Incorporated practice); and

(iv) rule 15 (Overseas practice), but only to the extent that rule 15 specifically applies any provision of these rules to a recognised body incorporated outside England and Wales.

(c) If a provision of these rules does not apply to a recognised body incorporated outside England and Wales, 14.01(4) will not apply to a director, member or shareowner of the recognised body or a person employed to work in the practice of the recognised body, in relation to that rule.

**12.05 Definition of "lawyer" in this rule**

In this rule, "lawyer" means a member, and entitled to practise as such, of:

(a) a legal profession covered by the Establishment Directive, including a solicitor and a barrister of England and Wales; or

(b) a legal profession not covered by the Establishment Directive, but excluding a lawyer whose registration under section 89 of the Courts and Legal Services Act 1990 is suspended or whose name has been struck off the register.

**For the Guidance to rule 12 see paragraph 7C–186+ on White Book on Westlaw UK or the Civil Procedure CD.**

# Rule 13—In-house practice

## INTRODUCTION

7C–187 If you are a solicitor or an REL you may practise from an office in England and Wales as the employee of a business which is not the practice of a solicitor, an REL or a recognised body (rule 12 (Framework of practice)). The rule, except for 13.04, does not apply to your overseas practice, but you must comply with 15.13 (In-house practice).

## Rule 13—In-house practice

**13.01 Conditions applying at all times**

(1) You must not act for a client other than your employer under 13.02 to 13.12 if to do so would compromise:

(a) your professional independence or integrity;

(b) your duty to act in the best interests of that client;

(c) your duty to comply with rule 3 (Conflict of interests);

(d) your duty to keep information about that client's affairs confidential from your employer (unless the other client consents to disclosure, or you are acting under 13.11 as the employee of a foreign law firm); or

(e) your ability to discharge any other duty owed to that client under these rules.

(2) (a) In order to act for a client other than your employer under 13.04, 13.07, 13.09 and 13.11, you must have professional indemnity insurance cover.

(b) In all other cases you must consider whether your employer has appropriate indemnity insurance or funds to meet any award made as a result of a claim in professional negligence against you, for which your employer might be vicariously liable. If not, you must inform the client in writing that you are not covered by the compulsory insurance scheme.

**13.02 Fellow employees**

(1) Subject to the provisos in 13.02(2), you may act for a person who is, or was formerly:

(a) a fellow employee;

(b) a director, the company secretary, a board member or (if the employer is an LLP) a member of your employer;

(c) an employee, a director, the company secretary, a board member, a trustee or (if the related body is an LLP) a member of a related body of the employer within the meaning of 13.03(1) or 13.08(c); or

(d) a contributor to a programme or periodical publication, broadcast or published by your employer (or by a related body within the meaning of 13.03(1) or 13.08(c)), but only where the contributor is a defendant or potential defendant in a defamation case.

(2) You may act under (1) above only if:

(a) the matter relates to or arises out of the work of the employee, director, company secretary, board member, trustee, member or contributor in that capacity;

(b) the matter does not relate to a claim arising as a result of a personal injury to the employee, director, company secretary, board member, trustee, member or contributor;

(c) you are satisfied that the employee, director, company secretary, board member, trustee, member or contributor does not wish to instruct some other lawyer or qualified conveyancer; and

(d) no charge is made for your work unless those costs are recoverable from another source.

(3) Where acting in a conveyancing transaction under (1)(a) to (c) above you may also act for a joint owner/buyer and for a mortgagee.

**13.03 Related bodies**

(1) You may act for:

(a) the employer's holding, associated or subsidiary company;

(b) a partnership, syndicate, LLP or company by way of joint venture in which the employer and others have an interest;

(c) a trade association of which the employer is a member; or

(d) a club, association, pension fund or other scheme operated for the benefit of employees of the employer.

(2) If you are employed in local government, (1)(a) and (b) above do not apply.

(3) For the purpose of 13.04 to 13.07 references to your employer include related bodies of your employer as set out in (1) above, and "employment" and "employed" must be construed accordingly.

**13.04 Pro bono work**

(1) You may, in the course of your employment, conduct work on a pro bono basis for a client other than your employer provided:

(a) the work is covered by an indemnity reasonably equivalent to that required under the Solicitors' Indemnity Insurance Rules; and

(b) either:

(i) no fees are charged; or

***Paragraph numbers marked with a "+" can be found online and on CD.***

(ii) a conditional fee agreement is used and the only fees charged are those which you receive by way of costs from your client's opponent or other third party and pay to a charity under a fee sharing agreement.

(2) (1) above does not permit you to conduct work on a pro bono basis in conjunction with services provided by your employer under 13.05 (Associations), 13.06 (Insurers), 13.07 (Commercial legal advice services) or 13.11 (Lawyers of other jurisdictions).

**13.05 Associations**

If you are employed by an association you may act for a member provided:

(a) the membership of the association is limited to persons engaged or concerned in a particular trade, occupation or activity or otherwise having a community of interest;

(b) the association is one formed bona fide for the benefit of its members and not formed directly or indirectly for your benefit or primarily for securing assistance in legal proceedings; and

(c) there is no charge to the member in non-contentious matters, and in contentious matters the association indemnifies the member in relation to your costs and disbursements insofar as they are not recoverable from any other source.

**13.06 Insurers**

(1) If you are employed by an insurer subrogated to the rights of an insured in respect of any matter you may act on behalf of the insurer in relation to that matter in the name of the insured, and also:

(a) act on behalf of the insured in relation to uninsured losses in respect of the matter;

(b) act in proceedings both for the insured and for a defendant covered by another insurer where the insurers have agreed an apportionment of liability; and/or

(c) act in the matter on behalf of the employer and another insurer in the joint prosecution of a claim.

(2) If you are employed by a legal expenses insurer you may, provided that the insured has given specific consent, act for an insured in any proceedings which are covered by the legal expenses insurance policy, provided that the proceedings do not include:

(a) a personal injury claim (whether made by or for the insured); or

(b) a civil claim for damages which:

(i) exceeds the small claims limit from time to time in operation in the county court; and/or

(ii) is allocated or re-allocated to the fast track or the multi-track.

**13.07 Commercial legal advice services**

If you are employed by a commercial organisation providing a telephone legal advice service you may advise enquirers, provided:

(a) the advice comprises telephone advice only, together with a follow up letter to the enquirer when necessary; and

(b) you are satisfied that there is indemnity cover reasonably equivalent to that required under the Solicitors' Indemnity Insurance Rules.

**13.08 Local government**

If you are employed in local government you may act:

(a) for another organisation or person to which or to whom the employer is statutorily empowered to provide legal services, subject to the conditions in (b) to (g) below;

(b) for a member or former member of the local authority, provided that:

(i) the matter relates to or arises out of the work of the member in that capacity;

(ii) the matter does not relate to a claim arising as a result of a personal injury to the member;

***Paragraph numbers marked with a "+" can be found online and on CD.***

(iii) you are satisfied that the member does not wish to instruct some other lawyer; and

(iv) no charge is made for your work unless those costs are recoverable from some other source;

(c) for a company limited by shares or guarantee of which:

(i) the employer or nominee of the employer is a shareholder or guarantor; or

(ii) you are, or an officer of the employer is, appointed by the employer as an officer of the company,

provided the employer is acting in pursuance of its statutory powers;

(d) for lenders in connection with new mortgages arising from the redemption of mortgages to the local authority, provided:

(i) neither you nor any other employee acts on behalf of the borrowers; and

(ii) the borrowers are given the opportunity to be independently advised by a qualified conveyancer of their choice;

(e) for a charity or voluntary organisation whose objects relate wholly or partly to the employer's area, provided that there is no charge to the charity or voluntary organisation in non-contentious matters, and in contentious matters the employer indemnifies the charity or voluntary organisation in relation to your costs in so far as they are not recoverable from any other source;

(f) for a patient who is the subject of a Court of Protection Order where you are acting for a fellow employee (under 13.02 above) who is appointed as receiver for the patient; or

(g) for a child or young person subject to a Care Order in favour of the employer on an application to the Criminal Injuries Compensation Authority.



**13.09 Law centres, charities and other non-commercial advice services**

(1) If you are employed by a law centre or advice service operated by a charitable or similar non-commercial organisation you may give advice to and otherwise act for members of the public, provided:

(a) no funding agent has majority representation on the body responsible for the management of the service, and that body remains independent of central and local government;

(b) no fees are charged save:

(i) where the client is publicly funded; or

(ii) where the organisation indemnifies the client in relation to your costs in so far as they are not recoverable from any other source;

(c) all fees you earn and costs you recover are paid to the organisation for furthering the provision of the organisation's services;

(d) the organisation is not described as a law centre unless it is a member of the Law Centres Federation; and

(e) the organisation effects indemnity cover reasonably equivalent to that required under the Solicitors' Indemnity Insurance Rules.

(2) (1) above does not apply to an association formed for the benefit of its members.

**13.10 The Crown, non-departmental public bodies, and the Legal Services Commission**

If you are employed by the Crown, a non-departmental public body, or the Legal Services Commission (or any body established or maintained by the Legal Services Commission), you may give legal advice to, and act for, other persons if in doing so you are carrying out the lawful functions of the employer.

**13.11 Lawyers of other jurisdictions**

(1) You may provide legal services to your employer's clients, subject to the conditions set out in (2) below, if you are a solicitor or an REL employed by:

(a) a practising lawyer of another jurisdiction who:

(i) is not struck off or suspended from the register of foreign lawyers or the register of European lawyers; and

(ii) is not practising in that context as a solicitor or as an REL; or

(b) a business (including a body corporate) whose principals (or owners and directors) are all practising through that business as lawyers of jurisdictions other than England and Wales, but do not include any principal, owner or director who:

(i) is struck off or suspended from the register of foreign lawyers or the register of European lawyers; or

(ii) is practising through or in the context of that business as a solicitor or as an REL.

(2) You must meet the following conditions if acting for anyone other than your employer.

(a) Even if you are qualified to do such work for your employer, you must not do, or supervise or assume responsibility for doing any of the following:

(i) drawing or preparing any instrument or papers, or making any application or lodging any document relating to litigation reserved to qualified persons by the Solicitors Act 1974;

(ii) exercising any right of audience, or right to conduct litigation, for which a solicitor would have to rely on his or her qualification as a solicitor; or

(iii) providing any immigration advice or immigration services, unless the employer, or a senior fellow employee, is registered with the Immigration Services Commissioner.

(b) You must ensure that the work is covered by professional indemnity insurance reasonably equivalent to that required under the Solicitors' Indemnity Insurance Rules.

(c) You must inform your client that your employer is not regulated by the Solicitors Regulation Authority and that the Authority's compulsory insurance scheme does not apply; and either give or confirm this information in writing, if you are a solicitor, and you are held out to a client as a solicitor (or as an English or Welsh lawyer) in connection with work you are doing for that client.

(d) You must ensure that if you are identified on the notepaper as a solicitor (or as an English or Welsh lawyer) the notepaper also states that your employer is not regulated by the Solicitors Regulation Authority.

(3) (2)(c) and (d) above should also be read as referring to an REL being held out or identified as a lawyer, or under the REL's home title.

**13.12 Regulatory bodies**

If you are employed by a regulatory body you may in carrying out the function of the employer give legal advice to other persons and in the case of statutory functions may act generally for such persons.

**For the Guidance to rule 13 see paragraph 7C–188+ on White Book on Westlaw UK or the Civil Procedure CD.**

# Rule 14—Incorporated practice

## INTRODUCTION

**7C–189** Under the Solicitors Act 1974 a body corporate—that is, a company or an LLP—may not carry on the practice of a solicitor unless it is a recognised body. A solicitor or an REL may only practise from an office in England and Wales through a body corporate if it is a recognised body.

Rule 14 sets out the requirements which apply specifically to a recognised body and its members, directors, shareowners and employees. There are provisions which

*__Paragraph numbers marked with a "+" can be found online and on CD.__*

exclude non-lawyers from being directors, members or shareowners of a recognised body. These are necessary because section 9 of the Administration of Justice Act 1985 restricts the management and control of recognised bodies to lawyers.

# Rule 14—Incorporated practice

## 14.01 General

*Compliance duties*

(1) A recognised body must:

(a) comply with rule 14; and

(b) so far as possible ensure that its directors, members and shareowners comply with 14.03, 14.04 and 14.05.

(2) A director of a recognised body which is a company must so far as possible ensure that the body complies with rule 14.

(3) A member of a recognised body which is an LLP must take all reasonable steps to ensure that the body complies with rule 14.

(4) A director, member or shareowner of a recognised body and a person employed to work in the practice of a recognised body must not cause, instigate or connive at any breach of these rules.

*Mental Health Act equivalents*

(5) In rule 14, references to a "patient" as defined by section 94 of the Mental Health Act 1983, a person made the subject of emergency powers, and a receiver appointed under that Act include equivalents in other Establishment Directive states.

## 14.02 Scope of practice

*General business of a recognised body*

(1) The business of a recognised body may consist only of professional services of the sort provided by individuals practising as solicitors and/or lawyers of other jurisdictions.

*Conveyancing and probate*

(2) A recognised body must not undertake any work which includes a conveyancing or probate service reserved to qualified persons by the Solicitors Act 1974, unless:

(a) if the recognised body is a company, at least one director is a solicitor with a practising certificate or an REL qualified to provide that service under regulation 12 or 13 of the European Communities (Lawyer's Practice) Regulations 2000 (SI 2000/1119); and, if the company is a societas Europaea with a two-tier system, at least one member of both the management organ and the supervisory organ is such a person; or

(b) if the recognised body is an LLP, at least one member is a solicitor with a practising certificate, an REL qualified to provide that service under regulation 12 or 13 of the European Communities (Lawyer's Practice) Regulations 2000 (SI 2000/1119), or a recognised body qualified to undertake the work under (a) above.

## 14.03 Directors of a company

*Persons who may be directors*

(1) A recognised body which is a company must ensure that at all times:

(a) all the directors are solicitors with practising certificates, RELs, RFLs and/or non-registered European lawyers; and

(b) at least one director is a solicitor with a practising certificate or an REL, and, if the company is a societas Europaea with a two-tier system, at least one member of both the management organ and the supervisory organ is a solicitor with a practising certificate or an REL.

***Paragraph numbers marked with a "+" can be found online and on CD.***

*Death of director*

(2) If a director dies and this would put a company in breach of (1)(b) above, the company must ensure that a director who is a solicitor with a practising certificate or an REL is appointed within 14 days. If this is done the company will be deemed to have remained in compliance with (1)(b) above, and to that extent will not be liable to have its recognition revoked under regulation 7.1(b) of the Solicitors' Recognised Bodies Regulations.

*Director incapacitated, abandoning the practice, etc.*

(3) If the company's only, or last remaining, director who is a solicitor with a practising certificate or an REL or, if the company is a societas Europaea with a two-tier system, the only or last remaining member of either the management organ or the supervisory organ who is a solicitor with a practising certificate or an REL:

- (a) is committed to prison in civil or criminal proceedings;
- (b) becomes and continues to be unable to attend to the practice of the company because of incapacity caused by illness, accident or age;
- (c) becomes and continues to be a "patient" as defined by section 94 of the Mental Health Act 1983 or is made the subject of powers exercised under section 98 of that Act and continues to be subject to those powers;
- (d) abandons the practice of the company; or
- (e) the director's practising certificate or registration is made subject to a condition which would be breached by continuing as a director,

the company must ensure that an additional or replacement director who is a solicitor with a practising certificate or an REL is appointed within 14 days.

### 14.04 Members and shareowners of a company

*Persons who may be members or shareowners*

(1) A recognised body which is a company must ensure that all members and all shareowners are:

- (a) solicitors with practising certificates;
- (b) RELs;
- (c) RFLs;
- (d) non-registered European lawyers;
- (e) recognised bodies; and/or
- (f) European corporate practices.

(2) A recognised body which is a company with shares must have at least one shareowner who is a solicitor with a practising certificate, an REL, a recognised body, or a European corporate practice which is at least partly owned by a solicitor with a practising certificate or an REL.

(3) A recognised body which is a company without shares must have at least one member who is a solicitor with a practising certificate, an REL, a recognised body, or a European corporate practice which is at least partly owned by a solicitor with a practising certificate or an REL.

*Prohibition on creating third party interests*

(4) A member or shareowner must not create any charge or other third party interest over his or her interest in the company, except by holding a share as nominee for a non-member shareowner who is eligible to be a member or shareowner under (1) above.

*Record of non-member shareowners*

(5) (a) A recognised body which is a company with shares must keep a record of any non-member shareowners, and retain the record for at least three years after their ownership ceases; and

(b) A member who holds a share as nominee for a non-member shareowner must keep the recognised body informed of all facts necessary to keep an accurate and up-to-date record.

***Paragraph numbers marked with a "+" can be found online and on CD.***

*Death of member or shareowner of a company*

(6) (a) If a member or shareowner of a company with shares dies and is eligible to be a member or shareowner at the date of death, then, whether or not the personal representatives are themselves eligible to be members or shareowners, the personal representatives may replace the deceased member or shareowner in their capacity as personal representatives, provided that:

(i) no vote may be exercised by or on behalf of a personal representative (and no such vote may be accepted) unless all the personal representatives are eligible to be members or shareowners;

(ii) no personal representative may hold or own a share in that capacity for longer than 12 months from the date of death;

(iii) within 12 months of the death the recognised body must cancel or acquire the shares or ensure that they are held and owned by persons eligible to be members and shareowners, but without this resulting in RFLs being the only shareowners; and

(iv) no vote may be exercised by or on behalf of any personal representative (and no such vote may be accepted) after the 12-month period has expired.

(b) If, following the death of a member or shareowner, a company meets the requirements of (a) above the company will be deemed to have remained in compliance with (1) above as to membership and share ownership, and to that extent will not be liable to have its recognition revoked under regulation 7.1(b) of the Solicitors' Recognised Bodies Regulations.

*Member or shareowner ceasing to be eligible to be a member or shareowner*

(7) (a) If a member or shareowner of a recognised body which is a company with shares ceases to be eligible to be a member or shareowner, or ceases to exist as a body corporate, then:

(i) no vote may be exercised or accepted on the shares held by or on behalf of that member or shareowner;

(ii) in the case of a member or shareowner becoming ineligible, a trustee in bankruptcy or liquidator may (whether or not eligible to be a member or shareowner) replace that member or shareowner in the capacity of trustee or liquidator for a period which must not exceed six months from the date the member or shareowner became ineligible; and

(iii) the company must cancel or acquire the shares within six months, or within that time ensure that the shares are held and owned by persons eligible to be members and shareowners, but without this resulting in RFLs being the only shareowners.

(b) If (a) above applies and a company meets its requirements, the company will be deemed to have remained in compliance with (1) above as to membership and share ownership, and to that extent will not be liable to have its recognition revoked under regulation 7.1(b) of the Solicitors' Recognised Bodies Regulations.

*Member or shareowner becoming insolvent but not ineligible*

(8) (a) If a member or shareowner of a recognised body which is a company with shares becomes insolvent but remains eligible to be a member or shareowner, then the trustee in bankruptcy or liquidator (whether eligible or not) may replace the insolvent member or shareowner in the capacity of trustee in bankruptcy or liquidator, provided that:

(i) no vote may be exercised by or on behalf of a trustee in bankruptcy or liquidator (and no such vote may be accepted) unless the trustee or liquidator is eligible to be a member or shareowner;

(ii) no trustee in bankruptcy or liquidator may hold or own a share in that capacity for longer than six months from the date of the insolvency;

(iii) within six months of the insolvency the company must cancel or acquire the shares or ensure that they are held and owned by persons eligible to be members and shareowners, and without this resulting in RFLs being the only shareowners; and

(iv) no vote may be exercised by or on behalf of any trustee in bankruptcy or liquidator (and no such vote may be accepted) after the six-month period has expired.

(b) If (a) above applies and a company meets its requirements, the company will be deemed to have remained in compliance with (1) above as to membership and share ownership, and to that extent will not be liable to have its recognition revoked under regulation 7.1(b) of the Solicitors' Recognised Bodies Regulations.

*Mental health receiver for a member or shareowner in a company*

(9) (a) A receiver appointed under the Mental Health Act 1983 may be a member or shareowner in that capacity, without breach of these rules, provided that:

(i) the "patient" (as defined in the Mental Health Act 1983) remains eligible to be a member or shareowner; and

(ii) if the receiver is not eligible to be a member or shareowner, no vote is exercised or accepted on the shares.

(b) If (a) above applies and a company meets its requirements, the company will be deemed to have remained in compliance with (1) above as to membership and share ownership, and to that extent will not be liable to have its recognition revoked under regulation 7.1(b) of the Solicitors' Recognised Bodies Regulations.

*Proxies and corporate representatives*

(10) Only a solicitor with a practising certificate, an REL, an RFL or a nonregistered European lawyer may be appointed as a proxy or corporate representative for the purpose of attending and voting at meetings.

**14.05 Members of an LLP**

*Persons who may be members*

(1) A recognised body which is an LLP must ensure that all the members are:

(a) solicitors with practising certificates;

(b) RELs;

(c) RFLs;

(d) non-registered European lawyers;

(e) recognised bodies; and/or

(f) European corporate practices.

(2) (a) A recognised body which is an LLP must have at least two members.

(b) If a death results in an LLP having fewer than two members, but a person within (1) above becomes a member within six months, the LLP will be deemed to have remained in compliance with (a) above and to that extent will not be liable to have its recognition revoked under regulation 7.1(b) of the Solicitors' Recognised Bodies Regulations.

(3) (a) A recognised body which is an LLP must have at least one member who is:

(i) a solicitor with a practising certificate;

(ii) an REL;

(iii) a recognised body which is a company with a director who is a solicitor with a practising certificate or an REL; or

(iv) a recognised body which is an LLP with a member who is a solicitor with a practising certificate or an REL.

(b) If a member dies and this would put the company in breach of (a) above, but a person within (a) above becomes a member within 14 days, the LLP will be deemed to have remained in compliance with (a) above as to membership, and to that extent will not be liable to have its recognition revoked under regulation 7.1(b) of the Solicitors' Recognised Bodies Regulations.

***Paragraph numbers marked with a "+" can be found online and on CD.***

*Member incapacitated, abandoning the practice, etc.*

(4) If the last remaining solicitor or REL within (3)(a) above:

(a) is committed to prison in civil or criminal proceedings;

(b) becomes and continues to be unable to attend to the practice of the LLP because of incapacity caused by illness, accident or age;

(c) becomes and continues to be a "patient" as defined by section 94 of the Mental Health Act 1983 or is made the subject of powers exercised under section 98 of that Act and continues to be subject to those powers;

(d) abandons the practice of the LLP; or

(e) the member's practising certificate or registration (or director's, as the case may be) is made subject to a condition which would be breached by continuing as a member or director,

the LLP must ensure that an additional or replacement solicitor with a practising certificate or REL within (3)(a) above is in place within 14 days.

*Prohibition on creating third party interests*

(5) A member must not create any charge or other third party interest over the member's interest in the LLP.



**14.06 Practising address and registered office of a recognised body**

(1) A recognised body must have at least one practising address in England and Wales.

(2) A recognised body must have its registered office at a practising address in England and Wales if the recognised body is registered in England and Wales:

(a) under Part I of the Companies Act 1985;

(b) under the Limited Liability Partnerships Act 2000; or

(c) as a societas Europaea.

**14.07 Information and documentation**

(1) A recognised body must supply any information and documentation relating to the ownership, structure, directors, members or shareowners of the recognised body as and when requested to do so by the Solicitors Regulation Authority.

(2) A recognised body must notify the Solicitors Regulation Authority immediately of any change to:

(a) its name;

(b) its registered office and/or any of its practising addresses; or

(c) its directors, members and/or shareowners.

(3) A recognised body must notify the Solicitors Regulation Authority immediately if it is an unlimited company and it is re-registered as limited under the Companies Act 1985.

(4) If a recognised body's recognition expires automatically under regulation 8.2 of the Solicitors' Recognised Bodies Regulations, the directors (if it is a company) or the members (if it is an LLP) must notify the Solicitors Regulation Authority immediately.

(5) If a recognised body which is an oversea company or a societas Europaea registered outside England, Wales and Scotland is subject to an event in its country of incorporation analogous to a winding-up order or administration order under Part II of the Insolvency Act 1986, a resolution for voluntary winding-up, or the appointment of an administrative receiver, the directors must notify the Solicitors Regulation Authority immediately.

**For the Guidance to rule 14 see paragraph 7C–190+ on White Book on Westlaw UK or the Civil Procedure CD.**

# Rule 15—Overseas practice

## INTRODUCTION

Rule 15 is specific to overseas practice, which is defined in rule 24 (Interpretation) **7C–191**

***Paragraph numbers marked with a "+" can be found online and on CD.***

to mean the practice of a solicitor or a recognised body from an office or offices outside England and Wales; and the practice of an REL from an office or offices in Scotland or Northern Ireland.

Rule 15 applies the provisions of these rules to your overseas practice. Sometimes rule 15 disapplies one of these rules, or a provision in one of the rules, and in some cases substitutes alternative provisions.

Rule 15 also makes specific provisions in relation to accounts, deposit interest and professional indemnity, because the equivalent domestic rules do not apply to your overseas practice.

The purpose of applying different provisions to overseas practice is to ensure similar protection for clients but by way of rules which are more adaptable to conditions in other jurisdictions.

# Rule 15—Overseas practice

### 15.01 Core duties (rule 1) application, and conflicts of rules

*The core duties*

(1) Rule 1 (Core duties) applies to your overseas practice.

*Application, and conflicts of rules*

(2) These rules and the principles of professional conduct apply to the practice of a solicitor or a recognised body from an office outside England and Wales, and to the practice of an REL from an office in Scotland or Northern Ireland, with the following exceptions:

(a) a recognised body incorporated outside England and Wales is subject only to the following of these rules in relation to its practice outside England and Wales:

(i) 1.06 (Public confidence);

(ii) 12.04(4) (Framework of practice);

(iii) rule 14 (Incorporated practice); and

(iv) if a controlling majority of the owners are, or are controlled by, solicitors, 15.07(b)(ii) (letterhead), 15.15 (Deposit interest), 15.27 (Accounts), and rule 20 (Requirements of practice);

(b) if this rule states that a rule or a provision of these rules does not apply to your overseas practice, you may disregard that rule or provision in relation to your overseas practice, but you must comply with any alternative provision which is substituted by this rule; and

(c) if compliance with any provision of these rules would result in your breaching local law, you may disregard that provision to the extent necessary to comply with that local law.

(3) In this rule, in relation to practice from an office in Scotland or Northern Ireland:

(a) references to a firm with a controlling majority of partners or owners who are, or which are controlled by, solicitors must be read as referring to a controlling majority of partners or owners who are, or which are controlled by, solicitors and/or RELs;

(b) references to a solicitor sole principal must be read as referring to a solicitor or REL sole principal; and

(c) references to lawyers of England and Wales must be read as including lawyers registered in England and Wales under the Establishment Directive.

### 15.02 Client relations (rule 2)

(1) Rule 2 (Client relations) does not apply to your overseas practice but you must comply with (2) to (4) below.

(2) (a) You must pay to your clients any commission received, unless:

(i) the client, having been told the amount of the commission (or an approximate amount if the precise amount is not known) has agreed that you or your firm may keep the commission; or

(ii) in all the circumstances it is not reasonable to pay the commission to the client.

(b) In deciding whether it is reasonable to pay a commission to your client you must have regard to all the circumstances, including the law governing the retainer and the prevailing custom of lawyers in the jurisdiction in which you are practising.

(3) If you are a principal in a firm you must not exclude or attempt to exclude by contract all liability to your clients. However, you may limit your liability, provided that such limitation:

(a) is not below the minimum level of cover you would need in order to comply with 15.26 below;

(b) is brought to the client's attention; and

(c) is in writing.

(4)(a) (i) You must not enter into an arrangement to receive a contingency fee for work done in prosecuting or defending any contentious proceedings before a court of England and Wales, a British court martial or an arbitrator where the seat of the arbitration is in England and Wales, except as permitted by statute or the common law.

(ii) If you enter into a conditional fee agreement with a client in relation to such proceedings, you must explain, both at the outset and, where appropriate, as the matter progresses:

(A) the circumstances in which your client may be liable for your costs, and whether you will seek payment of these from the client, if entitled to do so; and

(B) if you intend to seek payment of any or all of your costs from your client, you must advise your client of their right to an assessment of those costs.

(b) You must not enter into an arrangement to receive a contingency fee for work done in prosecuting or defending any contentious proceedings before a court of an overseas jurisdiction or an arbitrator where the seat of the arbitration is overseas except to the extent that a lawyer of that jurisdiction would be permitted to do so.

**15.03 Conflict of interests (rule 3)**

Rule 3 (Conflict of interests) applies to your overseas practice, except that you do not have to comply with 3.07 to 3.22 (provisions relating to conveyancing of land) if the land in question is situated outside England and Wales.

**15.04 Confidentiality (rule 4)**

Rule 4 (Confidentiality and disclosure) applies to your overseas practice.

**15.05 Business management (rule 5)**

(1) Rule 5 (Business management in England and Wales) does not apply to your overseas practice but you must comply with (2) and (3) below.

(2) (a) You must not set up as a solicitor sole principal unless you have been entitled to practise as a lawyer for a minimum of 36 months within the last 10 years.

(b) If you are:

(i) a partner in a partnership with a controlling majority of partners who are, or which are controlled by, solicitors; or

(ii) a director of a body corporate with a controlling majority of owners who are, or which are controlled by, solicitors,

you must ensure that the partnership has at least one partner, or the body corporate has at least one director if it is a company, or at least one member if it is an LLP, who has been entitled to practise as a lawyer for a minimum of 36 months within the last 10 years.

(3) If you are:

(a) a solicitor sole principal;

(b) a partner in a partnership with a controlling majority of partners who are, or which are controlled by, solicitors; or

(c) a director of a company or a member of an LLP with a controlling majority of owners who are, or which are controlled by, solicitors,

you must ensure that the firm is managed and supervised with a view to ensuring that its affairs are properly conducted at all times; and that clients' matters receive proper attention, and are supervised so as to ensure that the quality of the work is checked with reasonable regularity by suitably experienced and competent persons within the firm.

**15.06 Equality and diversity (rule 6)**

Rule 6 (Equality and diversity) does not apply to your overseas practice, but rule 1 (Core duties) will always apply.

**15.07 Publicity (rule 7)**

Rule 7 (Publicity) applies to your overseas practice, except that:

(a) rule 7 does not apply to the website, e-mails, text messages or similar electronic communications of any practice you conduct from an office in an EU state other than the UK; and

(b) 7.07 (Letterhead) does not apply, but:

(i) if an REL is named on the letterhead (including a fax heading) of an office in Scotland or Northern Ireland, the letterhead must also identify:

(A) the European jurisdiction(s)—local or national as appropriate—under whose professional title the REL is practising;

(B) the REL's professional title(s), expressed in an official language of the European state concerned; and

(C) the fact that the REL is registered with the Solicitors Regulation Authority of England and Wales; and

(ii) if you are a partner in a partnership with a controlling majority of partners who are, or which are controlled by, solicitors, or a director of a company or member of an LLP with a controlling majority of owners who are, or which are controlled by, solicitors, you must make clear on the firm's letterhead (including a fax heading) that it is the letterhead of a law firm.

**15.08 Fee sharing (rule 8)**

Rule 8 (Fee sharing) applies to your overseas practice.

**15.09 Referrals of business (rule 9)**

(1) Rule 9 (Referrals of business) does not apply to your overseas practice, but you must comply with (2) below.

(2) When you accept referrals of business from other persons and when you refer business to other persons, you must ensure that there is no breach of rule 1 (Core duties) or any other applicable provision of these rules.

**15.10 Relations with third parties (rule 10)**

(1) Rule 10 (Relations with third parties) applies to your overseas practice except as provided in (2) and (3) below.

(2) 10.05 (Undertakings) does not apply, but:

(a) you must fulfil an undertaking which you give:

(i) in the course of practice;

(ii) outside the course of practice, but as a "solicitor"; or

(iii) if you are an REL based at an office in Scotland or Northern Ireland, and you give the undertaking within the UK, outside your practice as an REL, but as a lawyer of an Establishment Directive state;

(b) you must fulfil an undertaking within a reasonable time; and

(c) if you give an undertaking which is dependent upon the happening of a future event, you must notify the recipient immediately if it becomes clear that the event will not occur; and

(3) 10.06 (Dealing with more than one prospective buyer in a conveyancing transaction) applies only if the land in question is situated in England and Wales.

***Paragraph numbers marked with a "+" can be found online and on CD.***

**15.11 Litigation and advocacy (rule 11)**

Rule 11 (Litigation and advocacy) applies to your overseas practice in relation to litigation or advocacy conducted before a court, tribunal or inquiry in England and Wales or a British court martial. Rule 11 does not apply to your overseas practice in relation to litigation or advocacy conducted before a court or tribunal in another jurisdiction, but rule 1 (Core duties) will always apply.

**15.12 Framework of practice (rule 12)**

Rule 12 (Framework of practice) applies to your overseas practice.

**15.13 In-house practice (rule 13)**

(1) 13.04 (Pro bono work) applies to your overseas practice. The other provisions of rule 13 (In-house practice) do not apply to your overseas practice, but you must comply with (2) below.

(2) (a) Subject to (b) below, you may act as an in-house lawyer, but only for:

(i) your employer;

(ii) a company or organisation controlled by your employer or in which your employer has a substantial measure of control;

(iii) a company in the same group as your employer;

(iv) a company which controls your employer; or

(v) an employee (including a director or a company secretary) of a company or organisation under (i) to (iv) above, provided that the matter relates to or arises out of the work of that company or organisation, does not relate to a claim arising as a result of a personal injury to the employee, and no charge is made for your work unless those costs are recoverable from another source.

(b) If you are a solicitor registered in another state under the Establishment Directive with the professional body for a local legal profession you may practise in-house to the extent that a member of that legal profession is permitted to do so.

**15.14 Incorporated practice (rule 14)**

(1)(a) Rule 14 (Incorporated practice) applies to a recognised body in relation to the recognised body's overseas practice.

(b) Rule 14 applies to the overseas practice of the directors, members and shareowners of a recognised body, but 14.01(4) applies in relation to a recognised body incorporated outside England and Wales only where the provision in question is specifically applied to the recognised body by 15.01(2)(a).

(2) If you are a solicitor or an REL you are not required to comply with rule 14 in order to practise through a body corporate which has no office in England and Wales, but you must comply with 12.01(3) or 12.02(3).

**15.15 Deposit interest**

(1) You must comply with (2) below, if:

(a) you have held client money as a sole principal; or

(b) you are a partner in a partnership which has held client money and:

(i) the partnership has no separate legal identity and either a controlling majority of partners are, or are controlled by, solicitors, or lawyers of England and Wales form the national group of lawyers with the largest share of control of the partnership, either as partners or by controlling partners; or

(ii) the partnership has a separate legal identity and a controlling majority of partners are or are controlled by solicitors; or

(c) you are a director or owner of a body corporate which is not a recognised body and which has held client money, and a controlling majority of the owners are, or are controlled by, solicitors.

(2) If interest ought, in fairness, to be earned for the client on client money held under (1) above, you must ensure that:

(a) the client money is dealt with so that proper interest is earned upon it, and that the interest is paid to the client;

(b) the client is paid a sum equivalent to the interest that would have been earned if the client money had earned proper interest; or

(c) any alternative written agreement with the client setting out arrangements regarding the payment of interest on that money is carried out.

(3) In deciding whether interest ought, in fairness, to be earned for a client on client money, you must have regard to all the circumstances, including:

(a) the amount of the money;

(b) the length of time for which you are likely to hold the money; and

(c) the law and prevailing custom of lawyers practising in the jurisdiction in which you are practising.

**15.16 European cross-border practice (rule 16)**

Rule 16 (European cross-border practice) applies to your overseas practice, to the extent that such practice is European cross-border practice as defined in 16.01(1).

**15.17 Insolvency practice (rule 17)**

Rule 17 (Insolvency practice) does not apply to your overseas practice except in relation to appointments appertaining to orders made in the courts of England and Wales.

**15.18 Property selling (rule 18)**

Rule 18 (Property selling) applies to your practice from offices in Scotland or Northern Ireland but not to your practice from offices outside the UK.

**15.19 Financial services (rule 19)**

(1) Rule 19 (Financial services) does not apply to your overseas practice except as provided in (2) below.

(2) Rule 19 applies to regulated activities you conduct:

(a) from an office in Scotland or Northern Ireland; or

(b) into the UK from an office outside the UK.

**15.20 Requirements of practice (rule 20)**

Rule 20 (Requirements of practice) applies to your overseas practice.

**15.21 Separate businesses (rule 21)**

(1) (a) Rule 21 (Separate businesses) applies to you if you practise from an office in England and Wales and you have a separate business, wherever the separate business is situated.

(b) If you do not practise from an office in England and Wales but you practise from an office outside England and Wales and you have a separate business, rule 21 does not apply but you must comply with (2) below; wherever the separate business is situated.

(2) In relation to your separate business:

(a) you must do nothing in the course of practice, or in the course of making referrals to the business or accepting referrals from the business, which would contravene rule 1 (Core duties);

(b) you must not allow the separate business to be held out or described in such a way as to suggest that it is carrying on the practice of a lawyer regulated by the Solicitors Regulation Authority;

(c) you must ensure that all paperwork, documents, records or files relating to the separate business and its customers are kept separate from those of any firm or in-house practice, even where a customer of the separate business is also a client of the firm or inhouse practice;

(d) you must not allow the client account used for any firm or in-house practice to be used to hold money for the separate business, or for customers of the separate business in their capacity as such; and

(e) you must ensure that if you or your firm refer(s) a client to the separate

***Paragraph numbers marked with a "+" can be found online and on CD.***

business, the client is first informed of your interest in the separate business, that the separate business is not regulated by the Solicitors Regulation Authority of England and Wales, and that the statutory protections attaching to clients of a lawyer regulated by the Authority are not available to clients of the separate business.

**15.22 Waivers (rule 22)**

Rule 22 (Waivers) applies to your overseas practice.

**15.23 Application (rule 23)**

Rule 23 (Application of these rules) applies to your overseas practice.

**15.24 Interpretation (rule 24)**

Rule 24 (Interpretation) applies to your overseas practice.

**15.25 Commencement and repeals (rule 25)**

Rule 25 (Commencement and repeals) applies to your overseas practice.

**15.26 Professional indemnity**

(1) You must comply with (2) below in relation to your overseas practice, unless you are practising only in-house in compliance with 15.13.

(2) (a) You must ensure that in relation to your overseas practice you are at all times covered by insurance or other indemnity against professional liabilities.

(b) The extent and amount of the insurance or other indemnity need not exceed the current requirements of the Solicitors' Indemnity Insurance Rules or any other current rules made under section 37 of the Solicitors Act 1974 but must be reasonable having regard to:

(i) the nature and extent of the risks you incur in your overseas practice;

(ii) the local conditions in the jurisdiction in which you are practising; and

(iii) the terms upon which insurance or other indemnity is available.

**15.27 Accounts**

(1) You must comply with (3) to (5) below if you have held or received client money or controlled trust money:

(a) as the sole principal in a firm which has held or received client money or controlled trust money;

(b) as a named trustee; or

(c) as a partner in a partnership which has held or received client money or controlled trust money, if the partnership has no separate legal identity and:

(i) a majority of the partners are or are controlled by solicitors; or

(ii) lawyers of England and Wales form the national group of lawyers with the largest share of control of the partnership, either as partners or by controlling partners.

(2) You must also comply with (3) to (5) below as if you have held or received client money or controlled trust money as a principal, if you are:

(a) a director or owner of a body corporate which is not a recognised body and which has held or received client money or controlled trust money, if a controlling majority of the body's owners are or are controlled by solicitors; or

(b) a partner in a partnership with separate legal identity which has held or received client money or controlled trust money, if a controlling majority of the partners are or are controlled by solicitors.

*Dealings with client money*

(3) In all dealings with client money, you must ensure that:

***Paragraph numbers marked with a "+" can be found online and on CD.***

(a) it is kept separate from money which is not client money or controlled trust money in a client account;

(b) on receipt, it is paid without delay into a client account and kept there, unless the client has expressly or by implication agreed that the money shall be dealt with otherwise;

(c) it is not paid or withdrawn from a client account except on the specific authority of the client or where the payment or withdrawal is properly required:

(i) for a payment to or on behalf of the client;

(ii) for or towards payment of a debt due to the firm from the client or in reimbursement of money expended by the firm on behalf of the client; or

(iii) for or towards payment of costs due to the firm from the client, provided that a bill of costs or other written intimation of the amount of the costs incurred has been delivered to the client and it has thereby (or otherwise in writing) been made clear to the client that the money held will be applied in payment of the costs due;

(d) accounts are kept at all times, whether by written, electronic, mechanical or other means, to:

(i) record all dealings with client money in any client account;

(ii) show all client money received, held or paid, distinct from any other money, and separately in respect of each client; and

(iii) ensure that the firm is able at all times to account, without delay, to each and every client for all money received, held or paid on that client's behalf; and

(e) all accounts, books, ledgers and records kept in relation to the firm's client account(s) are preserved for at least six years from the date of the last entry therein.

*Dealings with controlled trust money*

(4) If you hold or receive money subject to a controlled trust of which you are a trustee, you must:

(a) keep it separate from money which is not client money or controlled trust money in a client account;

(b) pay controlled trust money without delay into a client account and keep it there, unless you pay it straight over to a third party in the execution of the trust;

(c) make no payment or withdrawal of controlled trust money out of a client account, except in proper execution of the trust under which it is held;

(d) keep accounts at all times, whether by written, electronic, mechanical or other means, to:

(i) show all your dealings with money received, held or paid on account of controlled trusts;

(ii) record all your dealings separately in respect of each controlled trust of which you are a trustee; and

(iii) distinguish money you have received, held or paid subject to a controlled trust from money you have received, held or paid for some other reason,

and either keep such accounts together, centrally, or maintain a central register of controlled trusts of which you are a trustee; and

(e) preserve all accounts, books, ledgers and records of your dealings with money you receive, hold or pay which is subject to a controlled trust for at least six years from the date of the last entry therein.

*Accountants' reports*

(5) (a) You must deliver an accountant's report in respect of any period during which:

(i) you or your firm have held or received client money or controlled trust money and you were subject to (3) or (4) above; or

(ii) you have been a director of a company, or a member of an LLP, which, as a recognised body was subject to (3) or (4) above.

(b) The accountant's report must be signed by the reporting accountant, who must be an accountant qualified in England and Wales or in the overseas jurisdiction where your office is based, or by such other person as the Solicitors Regulation Authority may think fit. The Authority may for reasonable cause disqualify a person from signing accountants' reports.

(c) The accountant's report must be based on a sufficient examination of the relevant documents to give the reporting accountant a reasonable indication whether or not you have complied with (3) and/or (4) above, as appropriate, during the period covered by the report, and must include the following:

(i) your name, practising address(es) and practising style and the name(s) of your partner(s), and those details for a body corporate through which you practise if relevant;

(ii) the name, address and qualification of the reporting accountant;

(iii) an indication of the nature and extent of the examination the reporting accountant has made of the relevant documents;

(iv) a statement of the total amount of money held at banks or similar institutions on behalf of clients and controlled trusts, and of the total liabilities to clients and controlled trusts, on any date selected by the reporting accountant (including the last day), falling within the period under review; and an explanation of any difference between the total amount of money held for clients and controlled trusts and the total liabilities to clients and controlled trusts;

(v) if the reporting accountant is satisfied that (so far as may be ascertained from the examination) you have complied with (3) and/or (4) above, as appropriate, during the period covered by the report, except for trivial breaches, or situations where you have been bound by a local rule not to comply, a statement to that effect; and

(vi) if the reporting accountant is not sufficiently satisfied to give a statement under (v) above, details of any matters in respect of which it appears to the reporting accountant that you have not complied with (3) and/or (4) above, as appropriate.

(d) You need not deliver an accountant's report until after the end of any period of 12 months, ending 31 October, during which you or your firm first held or received client money or controlled trust money subject to (3) or (4) above, if you, or your firm, had not held or received any such money in the 12 months immediately preceding that period, provided that the accountant's report then delivered includes the period when such money was first held or received.

**For the Guidance to rule 15 see paragraph 7C–192+ on White Book on Westlaw UK or the Civil Procedure CD.**

# Rule 16—European cross-border practice

## INTRODUCTION

The purpose of rule 16 is to apply the provisions of the CCBE Code to European cross-border practice. This is necessary to provide a system of mutual professional understanding for professional relations between lawyers of different CCBE states. Although the CCBE Code contains a large number of requirements, rule 16 contains only those requirements which are not replicated elsewhere in these rules. **7C–193**

# Rule 16—European cross-border practice

## 16.01 Definition and application

*Definition*

(1) (a) European cross-border practice is:

(i) any professional activity in a CCBE state other than the UK, whether or not you are physically present in that CCBE state; and

(ii) any professional contact with a lawyer of a CCBE state other than the UK.

(b) For the purposes of this rule professional contacts and professional activities taking place within a firm or in-house legal department are not European cross-border practice.

*Application of this rule*

(2)(a) If you are a solicitor this rule applies to your European crossborder practice from an office in, or outside, England and Wales.

(b) If you are an REL this rule applies to your European cross-border practice from an office within the UK.

(c) If you are an RFL and you are a partner in an MNP, a director of a recognised body which is a company, or a member of a recognised body which is an LLP, this rule applies to your European cross-border practice from an office in England and Wales.

(d) This rule applies to a recognised body incorporated in England and Wales in relation to its European cross-border practice from an office in, or outside, England and Wales; and

(e) This rule applies to a recognised body incorporated outside England and Wales in relation to its European cross-border practice from an office in England and Wales.

## 16.02 Occupations considered incompatible with legal practice

(1) If you act in legal proceedings or proceedings before public authorities in a CCBE state other than the UK, you must, in that state, comply with any rules regarding occupations incompatible with the practice of law, as if you were a lawyer of that state, whether or not you are based at an office in that state.

(2) If you are a solicitor based at an office in a CCBE state other than the UK, you must respect any rules regarding participation in commercial or other activities not connected with the practice of law, as they are applied to lawyers of that state.

## 16.03 Fee sharing with non-lawyers

(1) You must not share your professional fees with a non-lawyer situated in a CCBE state other than the UK except:

(a) within a firm which is permitted under rule 12 (Framework of practice); or

(b) with your retired partner or predecessor, or the dependants or personal representatives of your deceased partner or predecessor; or, in the case of a body corporate, a retired director, member or shareowner, or the dependants or personal representatives of a deceased director, member or shareowner.

(2) If you are practising from an office in a CCBE state other than the UK, whether or not you are physically present at that office, you must not share your professional fees from that practice with a non-lawyer, except:

(a) within a firm which is permitted under rule 12 (Framework of practice); or

(b) with your retired partner or predecessor, or the dependants or personal representatives of your deceased partner or predecessor; or, in the case of a body corporate, a retired director, member or shareowner, or the

*Paragraph numbers marked with a "+" can be found online and on CD.*

dependants or personal representatives of a deceased director, member or shareowner.

**16.04 Co-operation between lawyers of different CCBE states**

(1) If you are approached by a lawyer of a CCBE state other than the UK to undertake work which you are not competent to undertake, you must assist that lawyer to obtain the information necessary to find and instruct a lawyer capable of providing the service asked for.

(2) When co-operating with a lawyer of a CCBE state other than the UK you must take into account the differences which may exist between your respective legal systems and the professional organisations, competencies and obligations of lawyers in your respective states.

**16.05 Correspondence between lawyers in different CCBE states**

(1) If you are practising from an office in a CCBE state and you want to send to a lawyer in a different CCBE state (with the exception of the UK) a communication which you wish to remain "confidential" or "without prejudice", you must, before sending the communication, clearly express your intention in order to avoid misunderstanding, and ask if the lawyer is able to accept the communication on that basis. When you send the communication you must express your intention clearly at the head of the communication or in a covering letter.

(2) If you are the intended recipient of a communication from a lawyer in another CCBE state which is stated to be "confidential" or "without prejudice", but which you are unable to accept on the basis intended by that lawyer, you must inform the sender accordingly without delay. If the communication has already been sent you must return it unread without revealing the contents to others. If you have already read the communication and you are under a professional duty to reveal it to your client you must inform the sender of this immediately.

**16.06 Paying referral fees to non-lawyers**

You must not pay a fee, commission or any other compensation to a nonlawyer as a consideration for referring a client to you:

(a) if the non-lawyer is situated in a CCBE state other than the UK; or

(b) if you are practising from an office in a CCBE state other than the UK, whether or not you are physically present at that office.

**16.07 Disputes between lawyers in different member states**

(1) If you consider that a lawyer in a CCBE state other than the UK has acted in breach of a rule of professional conduct you must draw the breach to the other lawyer's attention.

(2) Before commencing any form of proceedings against the other lawyer, you must inform the Law Society and the other lawyer's bar or law society in order to allow them an opportunity to assist in resolving the matter.

**For the Guidance to rule 16 see paragraph 7C–194+ on White Book on Westlaw UK or the Civil Procedure CD.**

# Rule 17—Insolvency practice

## INTRODUCTION

If you are a solicitor or an REL, and an insolvency practitioner in a firm, rule 17 applies to you when you accept appointments and act as an appointment holder. Rule 17 should be read in conjunction with The Practice of Insolvency: a Guide to Professional Conduct and Ethics produced by the Joint Insolvency Committee and adopted by all recognised professional bodies (RPBs) including the Solicitors Regulation Authority. The purpose of this Guide is to ensure your independence and objectivity when acting as an appointment holder and that you can identify and avoid conflicts of interest. The rule does not apply to your overseas practice except in relation to appointments appertaining to orders made in the courts of England and Wales. **7C–195**

***Paragraph numbers marked with a "+" can be found online and on CD.***

## Rule 17—Insolvency practice

**17.01**

If you are a solicitor or an REL you must, when accepting an appointment or acting as an appointment holder as an insolvency practitioner, comply with The Practice of Insolvency: a Guide to Professional Conduct and Ethics produced by the Joint Insolvency Committee and adopted by the Board of the Solicitors Regulation Authority.

**For the Guidance to rule 17 see paragraph 7C–196+ on White Book on Westlaw UK or the Civil Procedure CD.**

# Rule 18—Property selling

### INTRODUCTION

7C–197 This rule sets out requirements for providing property selling services through your firm. Requirements for providing property selling services through a separate business are dealt with under rule 21 (Separate businesses).

The seller is your client, and any property selling work you do is, in addition to this rule, subject to the same law and professional rules binding on you in relation to your other work.

The rule applies to your overseas practice from offices in Scotland or Northern Ireland but not to your overseas practice from offices outside the UK.

## Rule 18—Property selling

**18.01 Standards of property selling services**

(1) When providing property selling services through your firm, you must:

(a) ensure that you, or the relevant staff, are competent to carry out the work;

(b) not seek from any prospective buyer a pre-contract deposit in excess of any prescribed limit; and

(c) promptly send to your client written accurate details of any offer you have received from a prospective buyer in respect of an interest in the property (other than those of a description which your client has indicated in writing that they do not want to receive).

(2) If you are the person who is responsible for marketing a residential property you must comply with any Home Information Packs regulations made under the Housing Act 2004.

(3)

(a) In 18.01(1) above:

(i) "competent" includes meeting any standards of competence set by the Secretary of State under section 22 of the Estate Agents Act 1979; and

(ii) "prescribed limit" means any limit prescribed by the Secretary of State under section 19 of the Estate Agents Act 1979.

(b) In 18.01(2) "the person who is responsible for marketing a residential property" has the meaning used in ss.151–153 of the Housing Act 2004.

**18.02 Statement on the cost**

(1) When accepting instructions to act in the sale of a property, you must, at the outset of communication between you and the client, or as soon as is reasonably practicable, and before the client is committed to any liability towards you, give the client a written statement setting out your agreement as to:

(a) the identity of the property;

(b) the interest to be sold;

(c) the price to be sought;

(d) the amount of your fee or the method of its calculation;
(e) the circumstances in which your fee is to become payable;
(f) regarding any payments to be made to others, and charged separately:
(i) the amount, or the method by which they will be calculated; and
(ii) the circumstances in which they may be incurred; and
(g) the incidence of VAT.

(2) You must also, within the written statement:
(a) state whether or not you are to have "sole agency" or "sole selling rights". The statement must also include a clear explanation of the intention and effect of those terms, or any similar terms used; and
(b) if the statement refers to a "ready, willing and able" buyer (or similar term), include a clear explanation of the term.



**18.03 Conflict of interests**

(1) In addition to your duties under rule 3 (Conflict of interests), when selling property you must comply with the following requirements.
(a) If you or any connected person has, or is seeking to acquire, a beneficial interest in the property or in the proceeds of sale of any interest in the property, you must promptly inform your client in writing.
(b) If you act in the sale of property, even if not in the conveyancing, you must not act for the buyer in the negotiations.
(c) If a prospective buyer makes an offer for a client's property, you must promptly inform the client in writing if, to your knowledge, you or any connected person has been instructed, or is to be instructed by the buyer to sell an interest in land, and that sale is necessary to enable the buyer to buy from the client or results from that prospective purchase.
(d) If you have, or to your knowledge any connected person has, a beneficial interest in a property or in the proceeds of sale of any interest in it, you must promptly inform in writing any person negotiating to acquire or dispose of any interest in that property. You must make this disclosure before entering into any negotiations with a prospective buyer.
(e) You must not discriminate against a prospective buyer because they are unlikely to instruct you to sell an interest in land, which sale is necessary to enable the buyer to buy from your client or results from that prospective purchase.
(f) When acting for a seller, you must restrict communication with the buyer to your property selling function. In particular:
(i) you must communicate about legal matters so far as possible only through the buyer's solicitor; and
(ii) you must not lead the buyer to believe that they are receiving legal advice from you.
(g) When acting for a seller, if you arrange for a mortgage to be available on the property in order to facilitate the sale, you may inform prospective buyers of the availability of the mortgage (subject to the buyer's status) but, unless exempted by rule 3 (Conflict of interests) you must also inform prospective buyers in writing:
(i) that you cannot advise or act for the prospective buyer in respect of the mortgage;
(ii) that the mortgage may not be the only one available; and
(iii) that the prospective buyer should consult their own lawyer or licensed conveyancer.

(2) In 18.03(1) above:
(a) "connected person" means:
(i) spouse, former spouse, reputed spouse, brother, sister, uncle, aunt, nephew, niece, direct descendant, parent or other direct ancestor;
(ii) any employee of your firm, and any member of your employee's family;

***Paragraph numbers marked with a "+" can be found online and on CD.***

(iii) any owner or employee of an associated firm defined in rule 24 (Interpretation) or any member of their families;

(iv) any company of which you are a director or employee, or any LLP of which you are a member or employee, or any company in which you, either alone or with any other connected person or persons are entitled to exercise, or control the exercise of, one-third or more of the voting power at any general meeting;

(v) any company of which any of the persons mentioned in (i) to (iii) above is a director or employee, or any LLP of which any of them is a member or employee, or any company in which any of them, either alone or with any other connected person or persons, is entitled to exercise, or control the exercise of, one-third or more of the voting power at any general meeting; and

(vi) any other "associate" as defined in section 32 of the Estate Agents Act 1979; and

(b) "you" includes anyone with whom you carry on a joint property selling practice, and owners of an associated firm as defined in rule 24 (Interpretation).

**18.04 Waivers**

In spite of 22.01(1) (Waivers), the Board of the Solicitors Regulation Authority shall not have power to waive any of the provisions of this rule.

**For the Guidance to rule 18 see paragraph 7C–198+ on White Book on Westlaw UK or the Civil Procedure CD.**

# Rule 19—Financial services

## INTRODUCTION

7C–199 This rule sets out the requirements for ensuring that your independence is preserved when acting in connection with the provision of financial services for clients, both through your firm and through a separate business.

The rule applies to your overseas practice in relation to regulated activities you conduct from an office in Scotland or Northern Ireland and to regulated activities you conduct into the UK from an office outside the UK.

## Rule 19—Financial services

**19.01 Independence**

(1) You must not, in connection with any regulated activity:

(a) be an appointed representative; or

(b) have any arrangement with other persons under which you could be constrained to recommend to clients or effect for them (or refrain from doing so) transactions:

(i) in some investments but not others;

(ii) with some persons but not others; or

(iii) through the agency of some persons but not others; or

(c) have any arrangement with other persons under which you could be constrained to introduce or refer clients or other persons with whom you deal to some persons but not others.

(2) You must not have any active involvement in a separate business which is an appointed representative, unless it is the appointed representative of an independent financial adviser.

(3) (1)(b) and (c) above shall not apply to arrangements in connection with any of the following types of investments:

(a) regulated mortgage contracts;

(b) general insurance contracts; or

(c) pure protection contracts.

(4) In this rule:

***Paragraph numbers marked with a "+" can be found online and on CD.***

(a) "appointed representative" has the meaning given in the Financial Services and Markets Act 2000;

(b) "general insurance contract" is any contract of insurance within Part I of Schedule 1 to the Financial Services and Markets Act 2000 (Regulated Activities) Order 2001 (SI 2001/544);

(c) "investment" means any of the investments specified in Part III of the Financial Services and Markets Act 2000 (Regulated Activities) Order 2001 (SI 2001/544);

(d) "pure protection contract" has the meaning given in rule 8(1) of the Solicitors' Financial Services (Scope) Rules 2001;

(e) "regulated activity" means an activity which is specified in the Financial Services and Markets Act 2000 (Regulated Activities) Order 2001 (SI 2001/544); and

(f) "regulated mortgage contract" has the meaning given by article 61(3) of the Financial Services and Markets Act 2000 (Regulated Activities) Order 2001 (SI 2001/544).

**For the Guidance to rule 19 see paragraph 7C–200+ on White Book on Westlaw UK or the Civil Procedure CD.**



# Rule 20—Requirements of practice

## INTRODUCTION

Rule 20 sets out the requirements for certification, the types of work which you are permitted to do, and co-operation with, and provision of information to, the Solicitors Regulation Authority. **7C–201**

## Rule 20—Requirements of practice

### 20.01 Practising certificates

(1) If you are practising as a solicitor you must:

(a) have in force a practising certificate issued by the Solicitors Regulation Authority; or

(b) be exempt under section 88 of the Solicitors Act 1974 from holding a practising certificate.

(2) You will be practising as a solicitor if you are involved in legal practice and:

(a) your involvement in the firm or the work depends on your being a solicitor;

(b) you are held out explicitly or implicitly as a practising solicitor;

(c) you are employed explicitly or implicitly as a solicitor; or

(d) you are deemed by section 1A of the Solicitors Act 1974 to be acting as a solicitor.

(3) In (2) above "legal practice" includes not only the practice of law but also the provision of business services such as are provided by solicitors.

(4) If you are a solicitor who was formerly an REL, and you are practising from an office in the UK as a lawyer of an Establishment Directive state, you must have in force a practising certificate issued by the Solicitors Regulation Authority, even if you are not practising as a solicitor.

### 20.02 Reserved work

A firm may undertake activities reserved to solicitors under the Solicitors Act 1974 relating to the conveyancing of land or the administration of a deceased's estate only if:

(a) the firm has a principal who is:

(i) a solicitor;

(ii) an REL qualified to provide that service under regulation 12 or 13 of the Establishment Directive Regulations; or

(iii) a recognised body qualified to provide that service under (b) below; or

(b) the firm is a recognised body which is:

(i) a company with a director who is a solicitor, or an RFL qualified to provide that service under regulation 12 or 13 of the Establishment Directive Regulations; or

(ii) an LLP with a member who is:

(A) a solicitor;

(B) an REL qualified to provide that service under regulation 12 or 13 of the Establishment Directive Regulations;

(C) a recognised body which is a company with a director who is a solicitor, or an REL qualified to provide that service under regulation 12 or 13 of the Establishment Directive Regulations; or

(D) a recognised body which is an LLP with a member who is a solicitor, or an REL qualified to provide that service under regulation 12 or 13 of the Establishment Directive Regulations.

**20.03 Duty to co-operate with the Solicitors Regulation Authority and the Legal Complaints Service**

(1) You must deal with the Solicitors Regulation Authority and the Legal Complaints Service in an open, prompt and co-operative way.

(2) You must:

(a) provide the Solicitors Regulation Authority with information necessary in order to issue you with a practising certificate, or deal with renewal of registration or renewal of recognition, as appropriate; and

(b) during the period your practising certificate, registration or recognition is in force, notify the Authority of any changes to relevant information about you or your firm or in-house practice.

**20.04 Reporting serious misconduct and serious financial difficulty**

You must (subject, where necessary, to your client's consent) report to the Solicitors Regulation Authority if:

(a) you become aware of serious misconduct by a solicitor, an REL, an RFL or a firm;

(b) you are a principal in a firm, and you become aware of serious misconduct by an employee of the firm;

(c) you have reason to doubt the professional integrity of a solicitor, an REL or an RFL; or

(d) you have reason to believe that a solicitor, an REL, an RFL or a firm is in serious financial difficulty which could put the public at risk.

**20.05 Obstructing complaints**

(1) You must not try to hinder or prevent a person who wishes to report your conduct to the Solicitors Regulation Authority or the Legal Complaints Service from doing so.

(2) You must not victimise a person for reporting your conduct to the Solicitors Regulation Authority or the Legal Complaints Service.

(3) You must not on your own or on your clients' behalf enter into an agreement which would attempt to preclude the Solicitors Regulation Authority or the Legal Complaints Service from investigating any actual or potential allegation of professional misconduct.

(4) Unless you can properly allege malice, you must not issue defamation proceedings in respect of a complaint to the Solicitors Regulation Authority or the Legal Complaints Service.

**20.06 Production of documents and information**

(1) You must promptly comply with a notice served by the Solicitors Regulation Authority in accordance with (2) below for the purpose of ascertaining whether a solicitor, an REL, an RFL or a recognised body is complying with or has complied with any provision of these rules, or of any other rules, codes or

mandatory guidance made or issued by the Board of the Solicitors Regulation Authority.

Such notice will be to the effect that you must produce for inspection by the appointee of the Solicitors Regulation Authority all documents held by you or held under your control and all information and explanations requested:

(a) in connection with your practice; or

(b) in connection with any trust of which you are, or formerly were, a trustee;

and you must promptly comply with any notice served under (2) below.

(2) Notice served under this rule:

(a) must be in writing;

(b) must be left at, or sent by registered post or recorded delivery to, the most recent address held by the Solicitors Regulation Authority, or delivered by the Authority's appointee; and

(c) will be deemed to have been received upon proof of its having been delivered at your practising address or last known practising address (or, in the case of a recognised body, its registered office) 48 hours (excluding Saturdays, Sundays and Bank Holidays) after posting.

(3) You must provide any necessary permissions for information to be given so as to enable the appointee of the Solicitors Regulation Authority to:

(a) prepare a report on the documents produced under (1) above; and

(b) seek verification from clients, staff and the banks, building societies or other financial institutions used by you.

(4) (a) You must comply with all requests from the Solicitors Regulation Authority or its appointee as to:

(i) the form in which you produce any documents you hold electronically; and

(ii) photocopies of any documents to take away.

(b) The Authority's appointee is not entitled under 20.06 to take original documents away.

**20.07 Dealing with claims**

(1) If you are a principal in a firm, a director of a recognised body which is a company, a member of a recognised body which is an LLP or a recognised body, and you discover an act or omission which could give rise to a claim, you must inform your client.

(2) If a client makes a claim against you, or notifies an intention to do so, or if you discover an act or omission which could give rise to a claim, you must:

(a) inform your client that independent advice should be sought (unless your client's loss, if any, is trivial and you promptly remedy that loss);

(b) consider whether a conflict of interests has arisen, and if so not act further for your client in the matter giving rise to the claim; and

(c) notify the qualifying insurer or the Assigned Risks Pool (ARP) Manager in accordance with the terms of the policy or, if appropriate, the Solicitors Indemnity Fund Ltd (SIF).

**For the Guidance to rule 20 see paragraph 7C–202+ on White Book on Westlaw UK or the Civil Procedure CD.**

# Rule 21—Separate businesses

## Introduction

A "separate business" is a business which is not regulated by the Solicitors Regulation Authority but which provides "solicitor-like" services. The purpose of rule 21 is to ensure that members of the public are not confused or misled into believing that a business carried on by a solicitor or REL is regulated by the Solicitors Regulation **7C–203**

Authority when it is not. The rule as it applies to your overseas practice is modified by 15.21.

# Rule 21—Separate businesses

### 21.01 General

(1) If you are practising from an office in England and Wales as a solicitor or an REL, or as an RFL who is a partner in an MNP, a director of a recognised body which is a company or a member of a recognised body which is an LLP, you must comply with the provisions of this rule in relation to:

(a) services which may not be provided through a separate business;

(b) services which may be provided through a separate business or (subject to these rules) through a firm or in-house practice; and

(c) services which fall outside the scope of a solicitor's practice but which may be provided in conjunction with a firm or in-house practice.

(2) This rule applies to your involvement in any separate business whether the separate business is in England and Wales or outside the jurisdiction.

(3) This rule also applies to a recognised body in relation to an interest held in another body corporate which is not a recognised body.

(4) For the avoidance of doubt, in this rule "practising" includes practising as an in-house solicitor or an in-house REL.

### 21.02 Services which may not be provided through a separate business

(1) Subject to (2) below, you must not provide any of the following services through a separate business:

(a) the conduct of any matter which could come before a court, tribunal or inquiry, whether or not proceedings are started;

(b) advocacy before a court, tribunal or inquiry;

(c) instructing counsel in any part of the UK;

(d) immigration advice or immigration services;

(e) any activity in relation to conveyancing, applications for probate or letters of administration, or drawing trust deeds or court documents, which is reserved to solicitors and others under the Solicitors Act 1974;

(f) drafting wills;

(g) acting as nominee, trustee or executor in England and Wales;

(h) legal advice not included above; or

(i) drafting legal documents not included above.

*Exceptions*

(2) The provisions of (1) above do not apply to prohibit you from providing services through a separate business:

(a) which carries on your practice as a lawyer of another jurisdiction;

(b) which carries on your business as a trade mark agent, patent agent or European patent attorney;

(c) which carries on your business as a parliamentary agent;

(d) which is a wholly owned nominee company operated as a subsidiary but necessary part of the work of a separate business providing financial services;

(e) which provides legal advice and/or drafts legal documents within (1)(h) and/or (i) above, as a subsidiary but necessary part of some other service which is one of the main services of the separate business; or

(f) which has no office in England and Wales, does not receive customers directly or indirectly referred from any firm through which you carry on your practice in England and Wales, or from any in-house practice you have in England and Wales, does not provide any services in relation to the UK; and does not provide executor, trustee or nominee services anywhere.

***Paragraph numbers marked with a "+" can be found online and on CD.***

However, you must comply with the requirements of 21.05 in relation to any such separate business.

**21.03 Services which may be provided in conjunction with a firm or inhouse practice**

(1) The following services extend beyond, or fall outside, the scope of a solicitor's practice but you may provide such services in conjunction with a firm or in-house practice:

(a) practice as a qualified notary public;

(b) educational activities; and

(c) authorship, journalism or publishing.

(2) A service provided in conjunction with a firm or in-house practice of a solicitor, an REL, an MNP or a recognised body is not provided through a separate business.

**21.04 Services which may be provided (subject to these rules) either through a firm or in-house practice, or through a separate business**

(1) You may provide the following services either (subject to these rules) through a firm or in-house practice, or through a separate business:

(a) alternative dispute resolution;

(b) financial services (except those that cannot form part of a solicitor's practice);

(c) estate agency;

(d) management consultancy;

(e) company secretarial services;

(f) acting as a parliamentary agent;

(g) acting as a trade mark agent, patent agent or European patent attorney;

(h) practising as a lawyer of another jurisdiction;

(i) acting as a bailiff;

(j) acting as nominee, trustee or executor outside England and Wales; or

(k) providing any other business, advisory or agency service which could be provided (subject to these rules) through a firm or inhouse practice but is not included in 21.02.

(2) If you provide any service listed in (1) above through a separate business you must comply with 21.05.

**21.05 Safeguards in relation to a separate business**

(1) If you provide services through a separate business you must do nothing in the course of practice, or in the course of making referrals to the business or accepting referrals from the business, which would breach rule 1 (Core duties).

(2) You must ensure that the following safeguards are in place in relation to a separate business which offers or provides any of the services listed in 21.04(1):

(a) the separate business must not be held out or described in such a way as to suggest that the separate business is carrying on a practice regulated by the Solicitors Regulation Authority, or that any lawyer connected with your firm is providing services through the separate business as a practising lawyer regulated by the Solicitors Regulation Authority;

(b) all paperwork, documents, records or files relating to the separate business and its customers must be kept separate from those of any firm or in-house practice, even where a customer of the separate business is also a client of the firm or in-house practice;

(c) the client account used for any firm or in-house practice must not be used to hold money for the separate business, or for customers of the separate business in their capacity as such;

(d) if the separate business shares premises, office accommodation or reception staff with any firm or in-house practice:

(i) the areas used by the firm or in-house practice must be clearly differentiated from the areas used by the separate business; and

***Paragraph numbers marked with a "+" can be found online and on CD.***

(ii) all customers of the separate business must be informed that it is not regulated by the Solicitors Regulation Authority and that the statutory protections attaching to clients of a lawyer regulated by the Authority are not available to them as customers of that business;

(e) if you or your firm refer(s) a client to the separate business, the client must first be informed of your interest in the separate business, that the separate business is not regulated by the Solicitors Regulation Authority, and that the statutory protections attaching to clients of a lawyer regulated by the Authority are not available to clients of the separate business; and

(f) if the separate business is an estate agency, then without prejudice to the provisions of these rules regarding conflicts of interests, neither you nor any firm through which you practise as a principal may act in the conveyance for the buyer of any property sold through the estate agency unless:

(i) the firm shares ownership of the estate agency with at least one other business in which neither you nor the firm have any financial interest;

(ii) neither you nor anyone else in the firm is dealing with or has dealt with the sale of the seller's property for the separate business; and

(iii) the buyer has given written consent to you or the firm acting, after your financial interest in the sale going through has been explained to the buyer.

**For the Guidance to rule 21 see paragraph 7C–204+ on White Book on Westlaw UK or the Civil Procedure CD.**

# Rule 22—Waivers

**22.01**

**7C–205** (1) In any particular case or cases the Board of the Solicitors Regulation Authority shall have power to waive in writing the provisions of these rules for a particular purpose or purposes expressed in such waiver, to place conditions on and to revoke such waiver.

(2) In spite of (1) above, the Board of the Solicitors Regulation Authority shall not have power to waive any of the provisions of the following rules:

(a) rule 1 (Core duties);

(b) 3.01 to 3.05 (conflict of interests, excluding provisions relating to alternative dispute resolution, conveyancing and property selling);

(c) rule 4 (Confidentiality and disclosure);

(d) rule 6 (Equality and diversity);

(e) 15.01, 15.03, 15.04, 15.18, 15.22, 15.23 and 15.24 (overseas practice provisions which apply provisions that cannot be waived for practice in England and Wales);

(f) rule 18 (Property selling);

(g) rule 22 (Waivers);

(h) rule 23 (Application); and

(i) rule 24 (Interpretation).

**For the Guidance to rule 22 see paragraph 7C–206+ on White Book on Westlaw UK or the Civil Procedure CD.**

# Rule 23—Application of these rules

**23.01**

Subject to 23.03 below these rules apply to you (and "you" must be construed ac- 7C–207
cordingly) if you are:

(a) a solicitor, in relation to practice as a solicitor from offices in England and Wales and outside England and Wales;
(b) an REL, in relation to practice as a lawyer of an Establishment Directive state from offices in England and Wales, Northern Ireland and Scotland;
(c) a recognised body incorporated in England and Wales, in relation to practice from offices in England and Wales and outside England and Wales;
(d) a recognised body incorporated in an Establishment Directive state but outside England and Wales:
    (i) in relation to practice from offices in England and Wales; and
    (ii) in relation to practice from offices outside England and Wales, but only to the following extent:
        (A) 1.06 (Public confidence);
        (B) 12.04(4) (Framework of practice);
        (C) rule 14 (Incorporated practice); and
        (D) rule 15 (Overseas practice), but only to the extent that rule 15 specifically applies any provision of these rules to a recognised body incorporated outside England and Wales;
(e) an RFL, in relation to practice as a foreign lawyer from offices in England and Wales, as:
    (i) a partner in an MNP as defined in rule 24 (Interpretation);
    (ii) a director of a recognised body which is a company; or
    (iii) a member of a recognised body which is an LLP; and
(f) a solicitor who was formerly an REL, in relation to practice as a lawyer of an Establishment Directive state from offices in the UK;

but see also 3.07(1) in relation to acting for seller and buyer, and 3.16(1) in relation to acting for lender and borrower.

**23.02**

The following apply in relation to other forms of practice, and outside practice:

(a) 1.06 (Public confidence);
(b) 10.01:
    (i) if you are a solicitor, in England and Wales and overseas; and
    (ii) if you are an REL, within the UK;
(c) 10.05(1)(c) and (d), (2) and (3), and 15.10(2)(a)(ii) and (iii), (b) and (c);
(d) 12.03(2) and 12.03(3).

**23.03**

The provisions of rules 1 to 14 and 16 to 25 of these rules will only apply to your overseas practice if specifically applied by rule 15 (Overseas practice).

**For the Guidance to rule 23 see paragraph 7C–208+ on White Book on Westlaw UK or the Civil Procedure CD.**

# Rule 24—Interpretation

**24.01**

In these rules, unless the context otherwise requires, all references to legislation 7C–209
include existing and future amendments to that legislation and:

*Paragraph numbers marked with a "+" can be found online and on CD.*

| | |
|---|---|
| "arrangement" | in relation to financial services, fee sharing and the introduction of clients, means any express or tacit agreement between you and another person, whether contractually binding or not; |
| "associated companies" | means two companies which are subsidiary companies of the same holding company; |
| "associated firms" | means two or more partnerships with at least one partner in common; two or more companies without shares with at least one member in common; two or more LLPs with at least one member in common; two or more companies with shares with at least one owner in common, or any combination of these; |
| "CCBE" | means the Council of the Bars and Law Societies of Europe; |
| "CCBE Code" | means the CCBE's Code of Conduct for European Lawyers; |
| "CCBE state" | means any state whose legal profession is a full member or an observer member of the CCBE; |
| "charity" | has the same meaning as in section 96(1) of the Charities Act 1993; |
| "client account" | in rule 15 (Overseas practice), means an account at a bank or similar institution, subject to supervision by a public authority, which is used only for the purpose of holding client money and/or controlled trust money, and the title or designation of which indicates that the funds in the account belong to the client or clients of a solicitor or REL or are held subject to a trust;<br>(for the definition of "client account" in relation to practice from an office in England and Wales, see the Solicitors' Accounts Rules 1998); |
| "client money" | in rule 15 (Overseas practice), means money you receive or hold for or on behalf of a client;<br>(for the definition of "client money" in relation to practice from an office in England and Wales, see the Solicitors' Accounts Rules 1998); |
| "company" | in rule 14 (Incorporated practice), means a company registered under Part I of the Companies Act 1985, or an overseas company incorporated in an Establishment Directive state and registered under section 690A or 691 of the Companies Act 1985, or a societas Europaea; |
| "contentious proceedings" | is to be construed in accordance with the definition of "contentious business" in section 87 of the Solicitors Act 1974; |
| "contingency fee" | except in 9.01(4) to (6), means any sum (whether fixed, or calculated either as a percentage of the proceeds or otherwise) payable only in the event of success; |
| "controlled trust" | in rule 15 (Overseas practice), means a trust of which:<br>(a) you are the sole trustee; or<br>(b) you are co-trustee only with one of more of your, or your firm's, employees, partners; officers (in the case of a company, including a recognised body); or members (in the case of an LLP, including a recognised body); or<br>(c) you are co-trustee only with your firm (in the case of a partnership with a separate legal identity, a company or LLP, including a recognised body);<br>(for the definition of "controlled trust" in relation to practice from an office in England and Wales, see the Solicitors' Accounts Rules 1998); |
| "controlled trust money" | in rule 15 (Overseas practice), means money which is subject to a controlled trust of which you are a trustee;<br>(for the definition of "controlled trust" in relation to practice from an office in England and Wales, see the Solicitors' Accounts Rules 1998); |

| | |
|---|---|
| "corporate firm" | means a body corporate which carries on the practice of a solicitor or an REL but is not an in-house practice; |
| "court" | in rule 11 (Litigation and advocacy) means any court, tribunal or enquiry of England and Wales, or a British court martial, or any court of another jurisdiction; |
| "director" | means a director of a company, and includes the director of a recognised body which is a company; and in relation to a societas Europaea includes:<br>(a) in a two-tier system, a member of the management organ and a member of the supervisory organ; and<br>(b) in a one-tier system, a member of the administrative organ; |
| "documents" | in rule 20 (Requirements of practice) includes documents, whether written or electronic, relating to the solicitor's client and office accounts; |
| "eligible to be a member and eligible to be a shareowner" | in rule 14 (Incorporated practice), mean a person who falls within one of the following categories:<br>(a) a solicitor with a practising certificate;<br>(b) a registered European lawyer;<br>(c) a registered foreign lawyer;<br>(d) a non-registered European lawyer;<br>(e) a recognised body; or<br>(f) a European corporate practice;<br>and "ineligible" must be construed accordingly; |
| "employee" | except in rule 6 (Equality and diversity) includes, in the case of a solicitor or an REL:<br>(a) a solicitor or REL who is a director of a company;<br>(b) a solicitor or REL who is engaged under a contract of service (for example, an assistant solicitor); or<br>(c) a solicitor or REL who is engaged under a contract for services (for example, a consultant or a locum);<br>and "employer" and "employment" must be construed accordingly |
| "Establishment Directive" | means the Establishment of Lawyers Directive 98/5/EC; |
| "Establishment Directive Regulations" | means the European Communities (Lawyer's Practice) Regulations 2000 (SI 2000/1119); |
| "Establishment Directive state" | means a state to which the Establishment of Lawyers Directive 98/5/EC applies —currently all the states of the EU plus Iceland, Liechtenstein, Norway and Switzerland; |
| "EU" | means the European Union; |
| "European corporate practice" | means a lawyers' practice incorporated in or formed under the law of an Establishment Directive state, which does not have an office in England and Wales, and is either:<br>(a) a body corporate wholly owned (whether directly or indirectly) and directed by RELs and/or non-registered European lawyers, or by such persons together with solicitors with practising certificates, RFLs and/or barristers of England and Wales; or<br>(b) a lawyers' partnership with separate legal identity whose partners are all RELs and/or non-registered European lawyers, or such persons together with solicitors with practising certificates, RFLs and/or barristers of England and Wales. |
| "European cross-border practice" | has the meaning assigned by 16.01(1); |

***Paragraph numbers marked with a "+" can be found online and on CD.***

| | |
|---|---|
| "firm" | means any business which carries on the practice of a solicitor or an REL, except in-house practice; |
| "foreign lawyer" | means a person who is not a solicitor or barrister of England and Wales, but who is a member, and entitled to practise as such, of a legal profession regulated within a jurisdiction outside England and Wales; |
| "holding company" | has the meaning assigned by the Companies Act 1985; |
| "in-house practice" | means:<br>(a) a solicitor's employment in England and Wales as a solicitor, or an REL's employment in England and Wales as a lawyer of an Establishment Directive state, by any business which is not:<br>(i) the business of a solicitor or an REL practising as a sole principal;<br>(ii) a recognised body; or<br>(iii) a partnership with at least one partner who is:<br>(A) a practising solicitor;<br>(B) an REL practising as such; or<br>(C) a recognised body; and<br>(b) a solicitor's employment outside England and Wales as a solicitor, or an REL's employment in Scotland or Northern Ireland as a lawyer of an Establishment Directive state, by any business which is not:<br>(i) the business of a lawyer practising as a sole principal;<br>(ii) a partnership of lawyers, or of lawyers together with other persons, within rule 12; or<br>(iii) a body corporate wholly owned, for the purpose of practising law, by lawyers, or by lawyers together with other persons, within rule 12; |
| "lawyer" | except in rule 12 (Framework of practice), means a member of one of the following professions, entitled to practise as such:<br>(a) the profession of solicitor, barrister or advocate of the UK;<br>(b) a legal profession of an Establishment Directive state other than the UK;<br>(c) a legal profession which has been approved by the Solicitors Regulation Authority for the purpose of multinational partnerships in England and Wales; or<br>(d) any other regulated legal profession which is recognised as such by the Solicitors Regulation Authority;<br>(for the definition of "lawyer" for the purpose of rule 12 (Framework of practice) see 12.05); |
| "lawyer of an Establishment Directive state" | means a member, and entitled to practise as such, of a legal profession which is covered by the Establishment of Lawyers Directive 98/5/EC, and includes a solicitor or a barrister of England and Wales; |
| "legal profession" | means a profession whose members are lawyers as defined in this rule; |
| "LLP" | means a limited liability partnership formed by being incorporated under the Limited Liability Partnerships Act 2000; |
| "member" | in relation to a recognised body, means:<br>(a) a person who has agreed to be a member of a company and whose name is entered in the company's register of members; or<br>(b) a member of an LLP; |
| "MNP" | means a multi-national partnership as defined in section 89(9) of the Courts and Legal Services Act 1990; |

***Paragraph numbers marked with a "+" can be found online and on CD.***

| | |
|---|---|
| "non-lawyer" | means:<br>(a) an individual who is not a lawyer as defined in this rule; or<br>(b) a body corporate which includes an individual who is not a lawyer as defined in this rule; or<br>(c) a partnership which includes as a partner an individual who is not a lawyer as defined in this rule; |
| "non-registered European lawyer" | means a lawyer of an Establishment Directive state who is based at an office or offices outside England and Wales and who is not:<br>(a) a solicitor, REL or RFL; or<br>(b) a barrister of England and Wales, Northern Ireland or the Irish Republic, or a Scottish advocate; |
| "officer" | in relation to a company, means a director or the company secretary; |
| "overseas" | means in or of a jurisdiction other than England and Wales; |
| "overseas practice" | means:<br>(a) the practice of a solicitor or a recognised body from an office or offices outside England and Wales; and<br>(b) the practice of an REL from an office or offices in Scotland or Northern Ireland; |
| "owner" | in relation to a body corporate, means a person with any ownership interest in the body corporate; |
| "partner" | includes both an equity partner and a salaried partner in a partnership; |
| "partnership" | means an unincorporated body falling within the definition of partnership in section 1 of the Partnership Act 1890, and does not include an LLP; |
| "person" | includes an individual, a body corporate, or other legal person; |
| "practice" | means:<br>(a) the activities of a solicitor, in that capacity;<br>(b) the activities of an REL in the capacity of lawyer of an Establishment Directive state, from an office or offices within the UK;<br>(c) the activities of an RFL from an office or offices in England and Wales as:<br>(i) a partner in an MNP;<br>(ii) a director of a recognised body which is a company; or<br>(iii) a member of a recognised body which is an LLP; and<br>(d) the activities of a recognised body;<br>and "practise" and "practising" should be construed accordingly; |
| "practice from an office" | includes practice carried on:<br>(a) from an office at which you are based; or<br>(b) from an office of a firm in which you are a principal, director, member or an owner, even if you are not based there;<br>and "practising from an office in England and Wales", etc. should be construed accordingly; |
| "practice through a body corporate" | includes having an ownership interest in a body corporate or being a director of a company, even if you yourself undertake no work for clients of the body corporate;<br>and "practising through a body corporate" should be construed accordingly; |
| "principal" | means a sole practitioner or a partner in a partnership; |

| | |
|---|---|
| "principal in a firm" | means:<br>(a) a solicitor or recognised body practising either as a sole principal or as partner;<br>(b) an REL practising in the UK either as a sole principal or as a partner; or<br>(c) an RFL practising from an office in England and Wales as a partner in an MNP; |
| "providing a service through a separate business" | means having any active involvement in a separate business which provides that service, and includes:<br>(a) any substantial ownership in the business;<br>(b) any direct control over the business, and any indirect control through another person such as a spouse; and<br>(c) any active participation in the business or the provision of its services to customers;<br>(being a non-executive director or providing services under rule 13 (In-house practice) does not, on its own, constitute active involvement); |
| "publicity" | includes all promotional material and activity, including the name or description of your firm, stationery, advertisements, brochures, websites, directory entries, media appearances, promotional press releases, and direct approaches to potential clients and other persons, whether conducted in person, in writing, or in electronic form, but does not include press releases prepared on behalf of a client; |
| "recognised body" | means a body corporate (which can be a company or an LLP) for the time being recognised by the Solicitors Regulation Authority under section 9 of the Administration of Justice Act 1985 and the Solicitors' Recognised Bodies Regulations 2007; |
| "REL (registered European lawyer)" | means an individual registered with the Solicitors Regulation Authority under regulation 17 of the Establishment Directive Regulations; |
| "register of European lawyers" | means the register of European lawyers maintained by the Solicitors Regulation Authority under regulation 15 of the Establishment Directive Regulations; |
| "RFL (registered foreign lawyer)" | means an individual registered with the Solicitors Regulation Authority under section 89 of the Courts and Legal Services Act 1990; |
| register of foreign lawyers | means the register of foreign lawyers maintained by the Solicitors Regulation Authority under the Courts and Legal Services Act 1990; |
| "right of audience and right to conduct litigation" | are to be construed in accordance with Part II and section 119 of the Courts and Legal Services Act 1990; |
| "separate business" | means a business which does not carry on the practice of a solicitor, REL or recognised body but which offers a service or services that could properly be offered by a solicitor, REL or recognised body in the course of practice; |
| "shareowner" | means:<br>(a) a member of a recognised body which is a company with a share capital, who owns a share in the body; or<br>(b) a person who is not a member of a company with a share capital, but owns a share in the body, which is held by a member as nominee; |
| "societas Europaea" | means a European public limited liability company within the meaning of article 1 of Council Regulation 2157/2001/EC; |

| | |
|---|---|
| "Solicitors' Recognised Bodies Regulations" | means the Solicitors' Recognised Bodies Regulations 2007 |
| "subsidiary company" | has the meaning assigned by the Companies Act 1985; |
| "UK" | means United Kingdom; and |
| "undertaking" | in 10.05 and 15.10, means a statement made by you or your firm to someone who reasonably relies upon it, that you or your firm will do something or cause something to be done, or refrain from doing something. The undertaking can be given orally or in writing and need not include the words "undertake" or "undertaking". |

SOLICITORS

## Rule 25—Commencement and repeals

**25.01**

(1) These rules, together with the Solicitors' Recognised Bodies Regulations 2007, shall come into force on the first day of the fourth month commencing after notification of the approval of the Secretary of State for Constitutional Affairs under Schedule 4 to the Courts and Legal Services Act 1990. **7C–210**

(2) The following provisions are repealed by these rules:

(a) the Solicitors' Practice Rules 1990;
(b) the Solicitors' Publicity Code 2001;
(c) the Solicitors' Introduction and Referral Code 1990;
(d) the Employed Solicitors Code 1990;
(e) the Solicitors' Separate Business Code 1994;
(f) the Solicitors' Costs Information and Client Care Code 1999;
(g) the Law Society's Code for Advocacy;
(h) the Solicitors' Anti-Discrimination Rules 2004;
(i) the Solicitors' Overseas Practice Rules 1990; and
(j) the Solicitors' Incorporated Practice Rules 2004.

(3) These rules also replace the conduct obligations imposed by virtue of The Guide to the Professional Conduct of Solicitors (1999) and Guide Online.

(4) For the avoidance of doubt, the following will remain in force after the coming into force of these rules:

(a) the Solicitors' Accounts Rules;
(b) the Solicitors' Indemnity Insurance Rules;
(c) the Solicitors' Indemnity (Enactment) Rules;
(d) the Solicitors' Financial Services (Scope) Rules;
(e) the Solicitors' Financial Services (Conduct of Business) Rules;
(f) the Solicitors' Compensation Fund Rules; and
(g) the Solicitors' Compensation Fund (Foreign Lawyers' Contributions) Rules.

**For the Guidance to rule 25 see paragraph 7C–211+ on White Book on Westlaw UK or the Civil Procedure CD.**

*Paragraph numbers marked with a "+" can be found online and on CD.*

# Solicitors' Recognised Bodies Regulations 2007

7C-212 Rules dated 10 March 2007 commencing 1 July 2007 made with the concurrence of the Master of the Rolls under section 9(2) of the Administration of Justice Act 1985, making provision as to the form and manner of applications relating to recognition of a recognised body, and as to the list of recognised bodies, the duration of recognition and revocation of recognition.

**Regulation 1—Applications for recognition and for renewal of recognition**

1.1 Applications for initial recognition and for renewal of recognition must be made on the prescribed form, and accompanied by the prescribed fee and such information and documentation as the Solicitors Regulation Authority may require.

1.2 A recognised body wishing to continue in practice after the renewal date must send its application for renewal of recognition so as to be received by the Solicitors Regulation Authority on or before the renewal date.

1.3 A recognised body not wishing to renew its recognition must notify the Solicitors Regulation Authority on or before the renewal date that it does not seek renewal of recognition.

**Regulation 2—Discretion to grant or refuse applications**

2.1 The Solicitors Regulation Authority may grant an application for initial recognition or renewal of recognition, if satisfied that the applicant body corporate:

(a) is registered under the Companies Act 1985 or the Limited Liability Partnerships Act 2000 either in England and Wales or in Scotland, or registered outside England, Wales and Scotland as a societas Europaea;

(b) complies with rule 14 (Incorporated practice) of the Solicitors' Code of Conduct in relation to its internal structure, direction and ownership;

(c) has a name that complies with rule 7 (Publicity) of the Solicitors' Code of Conduct; and

(d) complies with or is exempt from the Solicitors' Indemnity Insurance Rules as to qualifying insurance and top-up insurance.

2.2 The Solicitors Regulation Authority may refuse an application for initial recognition or renewal of recognition if:

(a) the Authority is satisfied that a director, member or shareowner is not a suitable person to be engaged in the direction or ownership of a recognised body, by reason of that person's character, conduct or associations; or

(b) for any other reason the Authority thinks it proper in the public interest not to recognise the body.

**Regulation 3—Appeals**

3.1 If the Solicitors Regulation Authority refuses an application for initial recognition or renewal of recognition, the applicant is entitled to receive notice in writing of the grounds for refusal, and may appeal to the Master of the Rolls under paragraph 2 of Schedule 2 to the Administration of Justice Act 1985.

3.2 If the Solicitors Regulation Authority neither grants nor refuses recognition within three months of the date an application was received, the applicant may appeal to the Master of the Rolls under paragraph 2 of Schedule 2 to the Administration of Justice Act 1985 as if the application had been refused.

**Regulation 4—Duration of recognition and renewal date**

4.1 Recognition lasts for three years and continues in force until it is revoked.

4.2 Renewal of recognition commences on the day following the renewal date.

4.3 The renewal date following initial recognition is the last day of the last calendar month of the three-year period; and thereafter, the day before the end of each subsequent three-year period of recognition.

**Regulation 5—The list of recognised bodies**

5.1 The Solicitors Regulation Authority shall keep a list of recognised bodies.

***Paragraph numbers marked with a "+" can be found online and on CD.***

5.2 The list of recognised bodies may be kept in electronic form and must contain, for each recognised body:

(a) the recognised body's name;

(b) the recognised body's registered office;

(c) all the recognised body's practising addresses; and

(d) whether it is a company limited by shares, a company limited by guarantee, an unlimited company, an oversea company registered in England and Wales, an oversea company registered in Scotland, a societas Europaea, or an LLP.

5.3 The Solicitors Regulation Authority must make a copy of any entry in the list available for inspection on request by any member of the public.

**Regulation 6—Certificates of recognition**

6.1 Once a body is granted initial recognition or its recognition is renewed, the Solicitors Regulation Authority shall issue a certificate of recognition.

6.2 Each certificate of recognition shall state, in respect of the recognised body:

(a) its name;

(b) its registered office (or its principal practising address in England and Wales, if it is a company or LLP incorporated in Scotland, an oversea company, or a societas Europaea registered outside England and Wales);

(c) whether it is a company limited by shares, a company limited by guarantee, an unlimited company, an oversea company registered in England and Wales, an oversea company registered in Scotland, a societas Europaea, or an LLP;

(d) that it is recognised by the Solicitors Regulation Authority as suitable to provide legal services;

(e) the date from which recognition is granted or renewed; and

(f) the next renewal date.

**Regulation 7—Revocation of recognition**

7.1 Recognition may be revoked at any time, if:

(a) the Solicitors Regulation Authority is satisfied that recognition was granted as a result of error or fraud; or

(b) the Authority is satisfied that the body would not be eligible to be recognised if it were at that time applying for initial recognition.

**Regulation 8—Expiry of recognition**

8.1 Recognition will automatically expire if a recognised body ceases to be registered, either:

(a) under Part I of the Companies Act 1985 as an unlimited company, a company limited by shares or a company limited by guarantee;

(b) under section 690A or 691 of the Companies Act 1985 as an oversea company incorporated in an Establishment Directive state;

(c) under the Limited Liability Partnerships Act 2000 as an LLP; or

(d) as a societas Europaea.

8.2 Recognition will automatically expire if a winding-up order or administration order is granted under Part II of the Insolvency Act 1986, or a resolution is passed for voluntary winding-up, or an administrative receiver is appointed, in respect of a recognised body.

8.3 Recognition will expire if:

(a) the renewal date stated on the last certificate of recognition has passed;

(b) the Solicitors Regulation Authority has not received an application for renewal of recognition and all required fees, information and documentation; and

(c) the Solicitors Regulation Authority has decided that recognition will not be renewed.

**Regulation 9—Interpretation**

9.1 All terms in these regulations are to be interpreted in accordance with rule 24 (Interpretation) of the Solicitors' Code of Conduct.

***Paragraph numbers marked with a "+" can be found online and on CD.***

**Regulation 10—Waivers**

10.1 In any particular case or cases the Board of the Solicitors Regulation Authority shall have power to waive in writing the provisions of these regulations for a particular purpose or purposes expressed in such waiver, and to revoke such waiver.

## Solicitors' Accounts Rules 1998

(JULY 22, 1998) (UPDATED AUGUST 30, 2005)

### Receipt and transfer of costs

7C-213 **19.—(1)** A *solicitor* who receives money paid in full or part settlement of the *solicitor's* bill (or other notification of *costs*) **must follow one of the following four options**:

(a) **determine the composition of the payment *without delay*, and deal with the money accordingly:**

(i) if the sum comprises *office money* only, it must be placed in an *office account*;

(ii) if the sum comprises only *client money* (for example an unpaid *professional disbursement*—see rule 2(2)(s), and note (v) to rule 2), the entire sum must be placed in a *client account*;

(iii) if the sum includes both *office money* and *client money* (such as unpaid *professional disbursements*; purchase money; or payments in advance for court fees, stamp duty land tax, Land Registry registration fees or telegraphic transfer fees), the *solicitor* must follow rule 20 (receipt of mixed payments); **or**

(b) **ascertain that the payment comprises only *office money*, and/or *client money* in the form of *professional disbursements* incurred but not yet paid, and deal with the payment as follows:**

(i) place the entire sum in an *office account* at a *bank* or *building society* branch (or head office) in England and Wales; and

(ii) by the end of the second working day following receipt, either pay any unpaid *professional disbursement*, or transfer a sum for its settlement to a *client account*; **or**

(c) **pay the entire sum into a *client account* (regardless of its composition), and transfer any *office money* out of the *client account* within 14 days of receipt; or**

(d) **on receipt of *costs* from the Legal Aid Board, follow the option in rule 21(1)(b).**

(2) A *solicitor* who properly requires payment of his or her *fees* from money held for the *client* or *controlled trust* in a *client account* must first give or send a bill of *costs*, or other written notification of the *costs* incurred, to the *client* or the paying party.

(3) Once the *solicitor* has compiled with paragraph (2) above, the

money earmarked for *costs* becomes *office money* and must be transferred out of the *client account* within 14 days.

(4) A payment on account of *costs* generally is *client money*, and must be held in a *client account* until the *solicitor* has complied with paragraph (2) above. (For an exception in the case of legal aid payments, see rule 21(1)(a)).

(5) A payment for an *agreed fee* must be paid into an *office account*. An "agreed fee" is one that is fixed—not a *fee* that can be varied upwards, nor a *fee* that is dependent on the transaction being completed. An *agreed fee* must be evidenced in writing.



* * * *

**Treatment of payments to legal aid practitioners**

**21. Payments from the Legal Services Commission** **7C–214**

(1) Two special dispensations apply to payments (other than regular payments) from the Legal Services Commission:

(a) An advance payment in anticipation of work to be carried out, although *client money*, may be placed in an *office account*, provided the Commission instructs in writing that this may be done.

(b) A payment for *costs* (interim and/or final) may be paid into an *office account* at a *bank* or *building society* branch (or head office) in England and Wales, regardless of whether it consists wholly of *office money*, or is mixed with *client money* in the form of:

(i) advance payments for *fees* or *disbursements*; or

(ii) money for unpaid *professional disbursements*;

provided all money for payment of *disbursements* is transferred to a *client account* (or the *disbursements* paid) within 14 days of receipt.

(2) The following provisions apply to *regular payments* from the Legal Services Commission:

(a) "Regular payments" (which are office money) are:

(i) standard monthly payments paid by the Commission under the civil legal aid contracting arrangements;

(ii) monthly payments paid by the Commission under the criminal legal aid contracting arrangements; and

(iii) any other payments for work done or to be done received from the Commission under an arrangement for payments on a regular basis.

(b) *Regular payments* must be paid into an *office account* at a *bank* or *building society* branch (or head office) in England and Wales.

(c) A *solicitor* must within 28 days of submitting a report to the Commission, notifying completion of a matter, either:

(i) pay any unpaid *professional disbursement(s)*, or

(ii) transfer to a *client account* a sum equivalent to the amount of any unpaid *professional disbursement(s)*,

relating to that matter.

(d) In cases where the Commission permits solicitors to submit reports at various stages during a matter rather than only at the end of a matter, the requirement in paragraph (c) above applies to any unpaid *professional disbursement(s)* included in each report so submitted.

**Payments from a third party**

(3) If the Legal Services Commission has paid any costs to a *solicitor* or a previously nominated *solicitor* in a matter (advice and assistance or legal help *costs*, advance payments or interim *costs*), or has paid *professional disbursements* direct, and costs are subsequently settled by a third party:

(a) The entire third party payment must be paid into a *client account*.

(b) A sum representing the payments made by the Commission must be retained in the *client account*.

(c) Any balance belonging to the *solicitor* must be transferred to an *office account* within 14 days of the *solicitor* sending a report to the Commission containing details of the third party payment.

(d) The sum retained in the client account as representing payments made by the Commission must be:

**(i) either recorded in the individual *client's* ledger account, and identified as the Commission's money;**

**(ii) or recorded in a ledger account in the Commission's name, and identified by reference to the *client* or matter;**

**and kept in the *client account* until notification from the Commission that it has recouped an equivalent sum from subsequent payments due to the *solicitor*. The retained sum must be transferred to an *office account* within 14 days of notification.**

**Withdrawals from a client account**

7C–215 **22.—(1)** *Client money* may only be withdrawn from a *client account* when it is:

(a) properly required for a payment to or on behalf of the *client* (or other person on whose behalf the money is being held);

(b) properly required for payment of a *disbursement* on behalf of the *client*;

(c) properly required in full or partial reimbursement of money spent by the *solicitor* on behalf of the *client*;

(d) transferred to another *client account*;

(e) withdrawn on the *client's* instructions, provided the instructions are for the *client's* convenience and are given in writing, or are given by other means and confirmed by the *solicitor* to the *client* in writing;
(f) a refund to the *solicitor* of an advance no longer required to fund a payment on behalf of a *client* (see rule 15(2)(b));
(g) money which has been paid into the account in breach of the rules (for example, money paid into the wrong *separate designated client account*)—see paragraph (4) below; or
(h) money not covered by (a) to (g) above, withdrawn from the account on the written authorisation of the *Society*. The *Society* may impose a condition that the *solicitor* pay the money to a charity which gives an indemnity against any legitimate claim subsequently made for the sum received.

(2) *Controlled trust money* may only be withdrawn from a *client account* when it is:

(a) properly required for a payment in the execution of the particular *trust*, including the purchase of an investment (other than money) in accordance with the *trustee's* powers;
(b) properly required for payment of a *disbursement* for the particular *trust*;
(c) properly required in full or partial reimbursement of money spent by the *solicitor* on behalf of the particular *trust*;
(d) transferred to another *client account*;
(e) transferred to an account other than a *client account* (such as an account outside England and Wales), but only if the *trustee's* powers permit, or to be properly retained in cash in the performance of the *trustee's* duties;
(f) a refund to the *solicitor* of an advance no longer required to fund a payment on behalf of a *controlled trust* (see rule 15(2)(b));
(g) money which has been paid into the account in breach of the rules (for example, money paid into the wrong *separate designated client account*)—see paragraph (4) below; or
(h) money not covered by (a) to (g) above, withdrawn from the account on the written authorisation of the *Society*. The *Society* may impose a condition that the *solicitor* pay the money to a charity which gives an indemnity against any legitimate claim subsequently made for the sum received.

(3) *Office money* may only be withdrawn from a *client account* when it is:

(a) money properly paid into the account to open or maintain it under rule 15(2)(a);

***Paragraph numbers marked with a "+" can be found online and on CD.***

(b) properly required for payment of the *solicitor's costs* under rule 19(2) and (3);

(c) the whole or part of a payment into a *client account* under rule 19(1)(c);

(d) part of a *mixed payment* placed in a *client account* under rule 20(2)(b); or

(e) money which has been paid into a *client account* in breach of the rules (for example, interest wrongly credited to a *general client account*)—see paragraph (4) below.

(4) Money which has been paid into a *client account* in breach of the rules must be withdrawn from the *client account* promptly upon discovery.

(5) Money withdrawn in relation to a particular *client* or *controlled trust* from a *general client account* must not exceed the money held on behalf of that *client* or *controlled trust* in all the *solicitor's general client accounts* (except as provided in paragraph (6) below).

(6) A *solicitor* may make a payment in respect of a particular *client* or *controlled trust* out of a *general client account*, even if no money (or insufficient money) is held for that *client* or *controlled trust* in the *solicitor's general client account(s)*, provided:

(a) sufficient money is held for that *client* or *controlled trust* in a *separate designated client account*; and

(b) the appropriate transfer from the *separate designated client account* to a *general client account* is made immediately.

(7) Money held for a *client* or *controlled trust* in a *separate designated client account* must not be used for payments for another *client* or *controlled trust*.

(8) A *client account* must not be overdrawn, except in the following circumstances:

(a) A *separate designated client account* for a *controlled trust* can be overdrawn if the *controlled trustee* makes payments on behalf of the *trust* (for example, inheritance tax) before realising sufficient assets to cover the payments.

(b) If a sole practitioner dies and his or her *client accounts* are frozen, the *solicitor*-manager can operate *client accounts* which are overdrawn to the extent of the money held in the frozen accounts.

**Method of and authority for withdrawals from client account**

7C–216 **23.—(1)** A withdrawal from a *client account* may be made only after a specific authority in respect of that withdrawal has been signed by at least one of the following:

(a) a *solicitor* who holds a current practising certificate or a *registered European lawyer*;

(b) a Fellow of the Institute of Legal Executives of at least three years standing who is employed by such a *solicitor*, a *registered European lawyer* or a *recognised body*;

(c) in the case of an office dealing solely with conveyancing, a licensed conveyancer who is employed by such a *solicitor*, a *registered European lawyer* or a *recognised body*; or

(d) a *registered foreign lawyer* who is a *partner* in the practice, or who is a director of the practice (if it is a company), or who is a member of the practice (if it is a limited liability partnership).

(2) There is no need to comply with paragraph (1) above when transferring money from one *general client account* to another *general client account* at the same *bank* or *building society*.

(3) A withdrawal from a *client account* in favour of the *solicitor* or the practice must be either by way of a cheque to the *solicitor* or practice, or by way of a transfer to the *office account* or to the *solicitor's* personal account. The withdrawal must not be made in cash.



PART C

INTEREST

**When interest must be paid**

**24.—(1)** When a *solicitor* holds money in a *separate designated client account* for a *client*, or for a person funding all or part of the *solicitor's fees*, the *solicitor* must account to the *client* or that person for all interest earned on the account. **7C–217**

(2) When a *solicitor* holds money in a *general client account* for a *client*, or for a person funding all or part of the *solicitor's fees* (or if money should have been held for a *client* or such other person in a *client account* but was not), the *solicitor* must account to the *client* or that person for a sum in lieu of interest calculated in accordance with rule 25.

(3) A *solicitor* is not required to pay a sum in lieu of interest under paragraph (2) above:

(a) if the amount calculated is £20 or less;

(b)

(i) if the solicitor holds a sum of money not exceeding the amount shown in the left hand column below for a time not exceeding the period indicated in the right hand column:

| *Amount* | *Time* |
|---|---|
| £1,000 | 8 weeks |
| £2,000 | 4 weeks |
| £10,000 | 2 weeks |
| £20,000 | 1 week |

(ii) if the solicitor holds a sum of money exceeding £20,000 for one week or less, unless it is fair and reasonable to account for a sum in lieu of interest having regard to all the circumstances;

(c) on money held for the payment of counsel's fees, once counsel has requested a delay in settlement;

(d) on money held for the Legal Services Commission;

(e) on an advance from the *solicitor* under rule 15(2)(b) to fund a payment on behalf of the *client* in excess of funds held for that *client*; or

(f) if there is an agreement to contract out of the provisions of this rule under rule 27.

(4) If sums of money are held intermittently during the course of acting, and the sum in lieu of interest calculated under rule 25 for any period is £20 or less, a sum in lieu of interest should still be paid if it is fair and reasonable in the circumstances to aggregate the sums in respect of the individual periods.

(5) If money is held for a continuous period, and for part of that period it is held in a *separate designated client account*, the sum in lieu of interest for the rest of the period when the money was held in a *general client account* may as a result be £20 or less. A sum in lieu of interest should, however, be paid if it is fair and reasonable in the circumstances to do so.

(6)

(a) If a *solicitor* holds money for a *client* (or person funding all or part of the *solicitor's fees*) in an account opened on the instructions of the *client* (or that person) under rule 16(1)(a), the *solicitor* must account to the *client* (or that person) for all interest earned on the account.

(b) If a *solicitor* has failed to comply with instructions to open an account under rule 16(1)(a), the *solicitor* must account to the *client* (or the person funding all or part of the *solicitor's fees*) for a sum in lieu of any net loss of interest suffered by the *client* (or that person) as a result.

(7) This rule does not apply to *controlled trust money*.

### Amount of interest

7C–218 **25.—(1)** *Solicitors* must aim to obtain a reasonable rate of interest on money held in a *separate designated client account*, and must account for a fair sum in lieu of interest on money held in a *general client account* (or on money which should have been held in a *client account* but was not). The sum in lieu of interest need not necessarily reflect the highest rate of interest obtainable but it is not acceptable to look only at the lowest rate of interest obtainable.

**(2) The sum in lieu of interest** for money held in a *general client account* (or on money which should have been held in a *client account* but was not) **must be calculated**

- **on the balance or balances held over the whole period for which cleared funds are held**
- **at a rate not less than (whichever is the higher of) the following**

(i) the rate of interest payable on a *separate designated client account* for the amount or amounts held, or

(ii) the rate of interest payable on the relevant amount or amounts if placed on deposit on similar terms by a member of the business community

- **at the *bank* or *building society* where the money is held.**

(3) If the money, or part of it, is held successively or concurrently in accounts at different *banks* or *building societies*, the relevant *bank* or *building society* for the purpose of

***Paragraph numbers marked with a "+" can be found online and on CD.***

paragraph (2) will be whichever of those *banks* or *building societies* offered the best rate on the date when the money was first held.

(4) If, contrary to the rules, the money is not held in a *client account*, the relevant *bank* or *building society* for the purpose of paragraph (2) will be a clearing bank or *building society* nominated by the *client* (or other person on whose behalf *client money* is held).

### Interest on stakeholder money

**26.** When a *solicitor* holds money as stakeholder, the *solicitor* must pay interest, or a sum in lieu of interest, on the basis set out in rule 24 to the person to whom the stake is paid. **7C–219**



### Contracting out

**27.—(1)** In appropriate circumstances a *client* and his or her *solicitor* may by a written agreement come to a different arrangement as to the matters dealt with in rule 24 (payment of interest). **7C–220**

(2) A *solicitor* acting as stakeholder may, by a written agreement with his or her own *client* and the other party to the transaction, come to a different arrangement as to the matters dealt with in rule 24.

### Interest certificates

**28.** Without prejudice to any other remedy: **7C–221**

(a) any *client*, including one of joint *clients*, or a person funding all or part of a *solicitor's fees*, may apply to the *Society* for a certificate as to whether or not interest, or a sum in lieu of interest, should have been paid and, if so, the amount; and

(b) if the *Society* certifies that interest, or a sum in lieu of interest, should have been paid, the *solicitor* must pay the certified sum.

* * * *

## PART G

## COMMENCEMENT

### Commencement

**50.—(1)** These rules must be implemented not later than May 1, 2000; until a practice implements these rules, it must continue to operate the Solicitors' Accounts Rules 1991. **7C–222**

(2) Practices opting to implement these rules before May 1, 2000 must implement them in their entirety, and not selectively.

(3) Part F of the rules (accountants' reports) will apply to:

(a) reports covering any period of time after April 30, 2000; and also

(b) reports covering any earlier period of time for which a practice has opted to operate these rules.

(4) The Accountant's Report Rules 1991 will continue to apply to:

(a) reports covering any period of time before July 22, 1998; and also

(b) reports covering any period of time after July 21, 1998 and before May 1, 2000 during which a practice continued to operate the Solicitors' Accounts Rules 1991.

(5) If a practice operated the Solicitors' Accounts Rules 1991 for part of an *accounting period*, and these rules for the rest of the *accounting period*, the practice may, in respect of that *accounting period* ("the transitional accounting period") either:

(a) deliver a single accountant's report covering the whole of the transitional accounting period, made partly under the Accountant's Report Rules 1991 and partly under Part F of these rules, as appropriate; or

(b) deliver a separate accountant's report for each part of the transitional accounting period, one under the Accountant's Report Rules 1991 and the other under Part Fof these rules; or

(c) deliver a report under the Accountant's Report Rules 1991 to cover that part of the transitional accounting period during which the practice operated the Solicitors' Accounts Rules 1991; and subsequently a report under Part F of these rules to cover the remaining part of the transitional accounting period plus the whole of the next *accounting period*; or

(d) deliver a report under the Accountant's Report Rules 1991 to cover the last complete *accounting period* during which the practice operated the Solicitors' Accounts Rules 1991 plus that part of the transitional accounting period during which the practice continued to operate those rules; and subsequently a report under Part F of these rules to cover the remaining part of the transitional accounting period.

## Solicitors' (Non Contentious Business) Remuneration Order 1994

(S.I. 1994 No. 2616)

7C–223 **For the Solicitors' (Non Contentious Business) Remuneration Order 1994 plus any related commentary see paragraphs to 7C–224+ to 7C–241+ on the White Book on Westlaw UK or the Civil Procedure CD.**

## The Solicitors' (Non-Contentious Business) Remuneration Order 2009

(S.I. 2009 No. 1931)

7C–241.1 **For the Solicitors' (Non Contentious Business) Remuneration Order 2009 plus any related commentary see paragraphs to 7C–241.2+ to 7C–241.7+ on the White Book on Westlaw UK or the Civil Procedure CD.**

## NOTES ON THE GENERAL LAW RELATING TO SOLICITORS

7C–242 **For "Notes on the General Law Relating to Solicitors" see paragraphs 7C–243+ to 7C–277+ on the White Book on Westlaw UK or the Civil Procedure CD.**

***Paragraph numbers marked with a "+" can be found online and on CD.***

# 7D LSC FUNDED PROCEEDINGS

## GENERAL INTRODUCTION

The Access to Justice Act 1999 established the Legal Services Commission ("LSC"), which replaced the Legal Aid Board. The Commission itself has responsibility for two separate schemes for the provision of public funding for legal services, the Community Legal Service (the "CLS") and the Criminal Defence Service. Both the LSC and the CLS came into being on April 1, 2000. **7D–1**

The scheme for public funding and the establishment of the CLS under the 1999 Act mark a radical change from the funding of legal services under former legal aid schemes. The public funding of civil cases is no longer permitted by Parliament to be demand-led, but is subject to priorities which seek to balance competing needs and allocate money within a finite budget.

As to the commencement provisions which brought the relevant sections of Pt I of the 1999 Act into force, these are contained in the Access to Justice Act 1999 (Commencement No.3 Transitional Provisions and Savings) Order 2000 (SI 2000/774). This Order, read together with Pt I of Sch.15 of the 1999 Act, largely repealed and revoked the Legal Aid Act 1988.

A number of cases are still before the Courts (in particular on assessment proceedings) under the old legal aid regime governed by the 1988 Act. This is by reason of art.5 of the Transitional Provisions and Savings Order 2000, the most significant effect of which has been the preservation of the 1988 Act system in respect of cases where funding was applied for prior to April 1, 2000 and the application reached the Board before May 2, 2000. The 1988 Act scheme is also preserved for a residual category of other matters. For such cases the old regulations must be consulted and these are set out in the *Legal Aid Handbook 1998/99* (Sweet & Maxwell).

Since April 1, 2001 solicitors have only been able to provide services funded by the CLS if they have been licensed by contract. In respect of certificates granted before that date in non-contracted areas, art.4, the Community Legal Service (Funding) Order 2000 (SI 2000/627) also provides that provisions under the Civil Legal Aid (General) Regulations (as amended) apply.

Save for the cases referred to in the previous two paragraphs, therefore, the provision of public funding in respect of civil cases and consequential costs rules are governed by the 1999 Act and regulations made thereunder.

This section of the *White Book Service* summarises the main parts of the current regime insofar as they concern civil (non-family) representation. In particular these include the following:

- the statutory charge and the right of set-off under a Lockley order (s.10(7), Access to Justice Act 1999 and Pt III, the Community Legal Service (Financial) Regulations 2000 (SI 2000/516))
- security for costs (reg.6, the Community Legal Service (Costs) Regulations 2000 (SI 2000/441))
- costs protection and orders for costs against funded clients and the LSC (s.11, Access to Justice Act 1999 and Pt II, the Community Legal Service (Costs) Regulations 2000 (SI 2000/441) and the Community Legal Service (Cost Protection) Regulations 2000 (SI 2000/824).

The commentary to the Act will detail the services which may be funded under the 1999 Act, (s.6), the financial eligibility requirements of funded clients (s.7) and the Funding Code (s.8). The Funding Code is at the heart of the new public funding scheme and seeks to set out the criteria by which decisions are to be made about which cases are to be funded by public money.

### Contempt proceedings

Contempt committed by an individual in the face of the court is covered by s.12(1)(f), Access to Justice Act 1999 and funded by the Criminal Defence Service. Any court, whether civil or criminal can grant a Representation Order so long as the interests of justice criteria contained in para.5 of Sch.3 to the Act are satisfied (see s.14). Any solicitor or barrister can provide representation where a Representation Order has been made (s.15). A judge, before dealing with a contempt in the face of the **7D–2**

***Paragraph numbers marked with a "+" can be found online and on CD.***



LSC

court has a duty to inform the alleged contemnor of the right to legal advice and public funding (see further, Pt 11 of PD—Committal Applications at scpd 52.7).

## Access to Justice Act 1999

7D–3 (1999 c.22)

ARRANGEMENT OF SECTIONS

PART I

LEGAL SERVICES COMMISSION



## PART I

## LEGAL SERVICES COMMISSION

### Community Legal Service

7D–4 **4.**—(1) The Commission shall establish, maintain and develop a service known as the Community Legal Service for the purpose of promoting the availability to individuals of services of the descriptions specified in subsection (2) and, in particular, for securing (within the resources made available, and priorities set, in accordance with this Part) that individuals have access to services that effectively meet their needs.

[…]

* * * *

### Services which may be funded

7D–5 **6.**—(1) […]

(2) Subject to that (and to subsection (6)), the services which the Commission may fund as part of the Community Legal Service are those which the Commission considers appropriate.

[…]

(6) The Commission may not fund as part of the Community Legal Service any of the services specified in Schedule 2.

(7) Regulations may amend that Schedule by adding new services or omitting or varying any services.

(8) The Lord Chancellor—

(a) may by direction require the Commission to fund the provision of any of the services specified in Schedule 2 in circumstances specified in the direction, and

(b) may authorise the Commission to fund the provision of

*Paragraph numbers marked with a "+" can be found online and on CD.*

any of those services in specified circumstances or, if the Commission request him to do so, in an individual case.

*Note* —Amended by SI 2005/3429. Subsections 6(1) and 6(3) of the 1999 Act (which are not reproduced) require the LSC to set priorities for the funding of services and prescribe the means by which services may be funded. The remainder of s.6 must be read in conjunction with Sch.2, which specifies which services may not be funded. Some services, however, are brought back into the scope of the Act either by way of directions from the Secretary of State (formerly the Lord Chancellor) (see s.6(8)(a)), or where an express authorisation has been granted to the Commission (under s.6(8)(b)). See para.7D–17 below. **7D–6**

The only way that funding may be provided if it relates to services that are excluded by Sch.2 and cannot be funded within the Lord Chancellor's directions on scope is by way of exceptional funding under s.6(8)(b).Chapter 27 of the Funding Code contains guidance as to "Exceptional Funding", and by para.27.1 this allows exceptional funding to be granted to cover two types of application, namely (i) applications for funding individual excluded cases under s.6(8)(b) of the Access to Justice Act 1999; and (ii) applications to cover representation in inquest proceedings pursuant to the Lord Chancellor's direction on inquest funding. In such cases the Commission itself cannot grant legal aid, it is only able to recommend a grant of funding to the Lord Chancellor. The final decision to fund an individual excluded case rests with the Lord Chancellor (in practice the Minister for Legal Aid). In *R.(on the application of Main) v Minister for Legal Aid* [2007] EWHC 742 (Admin), Owen J. allowed an application for judicial review of the Minister's decision not to fund advocacy at an inquest, holding that she had been wrong not to take the view that representation would serve the wider public interest and would be necessary in order to ensure an effective investigation for the purposes of European Convention on Human Rights art2.

The applicant has to be able to show that there are either exceptional factual or legal issues which demonstrate that representation is required at the inquest in order to ensure an effective investigation (see also *R. (on the application of Andrew Jones) v Legal Services Commission* [2007] EWHC 2106 (Admin), James Goudie QC).

* * * *

## Individuals for whom services may be funded

**7.**—(1) The Commission may only fund services for an individual as part of the Community Legal Service if his financial resources are such that, under regulations, he is an individual for whom they may be so funded. **7D–7**

[...]

*Note* —The eligibility criteria which must be satisfied before funding can be granted are set out in Pt II, the Community Legal Service (Financial) Regulations 2000 (SI 2000/516). Part D of the Funding Code (see para.7D–10 below) contains the LSC's Guide to Assessing Financial Eligibility. **7D–8**

## Code about provision of funded services

**8.**—(1) The Commission shall prepare a code setting out the criteria according to which it is to decide whether to fund (or continue to fund) services as part of the Community Legal Service for an individual for whom they may be so funded and, if so, what services are to be funded for him. **7D–9**

[...]

*Note* —The Funding Code (which runs to about 700 pages) is an attempt to ensure that decision-makers who are to determine whether an individual should obtain public **7D–10**

***Paragraph numbers marked with a "+" can be found online and on CD.***



LSC

funding for legal services make their decisions both consistently and with the ultimate objective of appropriately allocating the money which is made available to fund the CLS.

Part A of the Funding Code establishes levels of services which will be funded by the CLS, of which two are particularly relevant in civil proceedings. The first is "legal representation" which includes litigation and advocacy services in current and contemplated proceedings. The second is "support funding" which is a means for the partial funding of proceedings which are to be pursued under a CFA.

In order to obtain funding the individual concerned must be able to satisfy the specified criteria set out in Pt A of the Code, which are likely to include an application of a costs-benefit matrix unless some wider public interest is at stake.

Specific criteria apply to High Cost Cases (handled by the Special Cases Unit), judicial review, claims against public authorities, clinical negligence, housing, family, mental health and immigration. Separate rules govern multi-party actions.

Part C of the Funding Code sets out detailed guidance on making decisions about the Funding Code criteria. As the Code says, it "is a flexible set of Rules which seeks to direct the resources available to areas of work where the need is greatest and the priority highest".

* * * *

## Terms of provision of funded services

7D-11 **10.**—(1) An individual for whom services are funded by the Commission as part of the Community Legal Service shall not be required to make any payment in respect of the services except where regulations otherwise provide.

[...]

(7) Except so far as regulations otherwise provide, where services have been funded by the Commission for an individual as part of the Community Legal Service—

(a) sums expended by the Commission in funding the services (except to the extent that they are recovered under section 11), and

(b) other sums payable by the individual by virtue of regulations under this section,

shall constitute a first charge on any property recovered or preserved by him (whether for himself or any other person) in any proceedings or in any compromise or settlement of any dispute in connection with which the services were provided.

7D-12 *The Statutory Charge—General Note* —Section 10(7) substantially reproduces s.16(6) of the Legal Aid Act 1988. Section 10(8) allows regulations to be made which "make provision about the charge" and these are contained in Pt III, the Community Legal Service (Financial) Regulations 2000 (SI 2000/441) (the relevant provisions of which are reproduced in full below), reg.21, the Community Legal Service (Costs) Regulations 2000 (release of purchase money on the postponement of the statutory charge). In *Cassidy v (1) Stephensons, (2) Legal Services Commission* [2009] EWHC 1562 (QB); [2009] EWHC 1562 (QB), it was held that the reference to "any proceedings" in s.10(7) of the Access to Justice Act 1999 was wider than the reference to "the proceedings" in s.16(6) of the 1988 Act. However, the words used in the 1999 Act were held not to be so clearly different as to have had the effect of rendering costs paid to solicitors who acted in original clinical negligence proceedings subject to a statutory charge in subsequent professional negligence proceedings against the same firm. This meant that when the claimant succeeded in the professional negligence proceedings against the solicitors, the LSC was wrong to have considered that it was entitled to a statutory charge over those costs.

***Paragraph numbers marked with a "+" can be found online and on CD.***

These regulations substantially reproduce their equivalents in regs.93–99, Civil Legal Aid (General) Regulations 1999. The main differences are that the LSC may waive the statutory charge in cases which have a significant wider interest (reg.47 of the Costs Regulations 2000) and a funded client is not obliged to agree that interest shall accrue to the benefit of the LSC if the enforcement of the charge is to be postponed in respect of money recovered in family proceedings for the purpose of purchasing a home (reg.21 of the Costs Regulations).

*"Recovered or preserved" (s.10(7))* —Whether property has been recovered or preserved is a matter of fact (and not of theoretical risk) based on an examination of the pleadings and the evidence. It has been recovered by the claimant if it has been the subject of a successful claim, and preserved to the respondent if the claim fails. (See *Hanlon v Law Society* [1981] A.C. 124 as applied in *Till v Till* [1974] Q.B. 558, *Manley v Law Society* [1981] 1 W.L.R. 335 and *Curling v Law Society* [1985] 1 W.L.R. 470 as applied in *McPherson v Legal Services Commission* [2008] EWHC 2865 (Ch)). The charge has been held to extend to the costs allowed in respect of all proceedings to which a certificate relates, and not just to the application in which the property was recovered or preserved (*Watkinson v Legal Aid Board* [1991] 1 W.L.R. 419).

*"Compromise or settlement" (s.10(7))* —In *Van Hoorn v Law Society* [1985] Q.B. 106 it was held that any rights under a compromise arrived at to avoid the proceedings were encompassed by the statutory charge even though the property which was subject to the compromise had not been "recovered or preserved" in the proceedings within the meaning of the test set out in *Hanlon's* case (see above).

*Set-Off* —Section 16(8) of the Legal Aid Act 1988 expressly preserved the right of set-off notwithstanding the existence of the statutory charge. A "Lockley Order" was commonplace by which an unassisted party was entitled to set off against any sum it might be ordered to pay to an assisted party costs which it was to receive from the assisted party (*Lockley v National Blood Transfusion Service* [1992] 1 W.L.R. 492). Section 16(8) has not been reproduced into s.10 of the 1999 Act. In *R. (on the application of Burkett) v Hammersmith and Fulham LBC (Costs)* [2004] EWCA Civ 1342, s.16(8) was described as mere surplusage, and it was made clear that the discretionary power to make a Lockley Order (which exists by virtue of s.51, Senior Courts Act 1981) is not affected by the new statutory framework.

* * * *

## Costs in funded cases

**11.**—(1) Except in prescribed circumstances, costs ordered against an individual in relation to any proceedings or part of proceedings funded for him shall not exceed the amount (if any) which is a reasonable one for him to pay having regard to all the circumstances including— **7D–13**

(a) the financial resources of all the parties to the proceedings, and

(b) their conduct in connection with the dispute to which the proceedings relate;

and for this purpose proceedings, or a part of proceedings, are funded for an individual if services relating to the proceedings or part are funded for him by the Commission as part of the Community Legal Service.

(2) In assessing for the purposes of subsection (1) the financial resources of an individual for whom services are funded by the Commission as part of the Community Legal Service, his clothes and household furniture and the tools and implements of his trade shall not be taken into account, except so far as may be prescribed.

***Paragraph numbers marked with a "+" can be found online and on CD.***



LSC

(3) Subject to subsections (1) and (2), regulations may make provision about costs in relation to proceedings in which services are funded by the Commission for any of the parties as part of the Community Legal Service.

**General Note**

7D-14 *Costs Protection and the Funded Party*—Section 11 contains costs protection provisions which were found previously in ss.12, 13, 17, 18 and 34(2)(b) of the Legal Aid Act 1988. The former position which existed in relation to the liability of an assisted party who enjoyed civil legal aid is preserved (see s.17 of the 1988 Act), namely that a funded client cannot be compelled to pay more than an amount which is reasonable given all the circumstances, including the financial resources of all of the parties and their conduct in connection with the dispute.

Notwithstanding the general rule as to costs protection set out in s.11(1), reg.3, the Community Legal Service (Costs Protection) Regulations 2000 prohibits the application of costs protection in most cases of Help at Court, Litigation Support and Legal Help (as defined by the Funding Code made under s.6). Regulation 3 also sets out additional prescribed circumstances in which costs protection does or does not apply.

*Costs Orders against the Commission*—This is a limited provision for a non-funded party to obtain an order for costs against the LSC. Where such an application is made the court must always be satisfied that it is just and equitable for costs to be paid out of public funds (reg.5(3)(d), the Costs Protection Regulations 2000). In cases in which applications for public funding were made prior to December 3, 2001, the court must also be satisfied in relation to costs incurred in a court of first instance that the non-funded party will suffer 'severe' financial hardship (reg.5(3)(c)). Since December 3, 2001 only an individual can recover costs against the LSC in respect of his costs incurred in a court of first instance.

*Procedures for Ordering Costs against Funded Clients and the Commission*—This topic is comprehensively dealt with in the Guidance notes on the Application of s.11 Access to Justice Act 1999 issued by the Senior Costs Judge and approved by the Master of the Rules (see paras 48.14.9 *et seq.*).

The Costs Practice Direction ss.21 to 23 (44PD.15 – 44PD.17) sets out the Procedure to be followed.

*"the amount ...which is a reasonable one...to pay having regard to all the circumstances" (s.11(1))*—What is a "reasonable amount" in all the circumstances has been considered for instance in *Nolan v C & C Marshall Ltd* [1954] 2 Q.B. 42, *Crystall v Crystall* [1963] 1 W.L.R. 574, *Godfrey v Smith* [1955] 1 W.L.R. 692, *Mercantile Credit Co Ltd v Cross* [1965] 2 Q.B. 205, *Chaggar v Chaggar* [1997] 1 All E.R. 104. The basis of which an appeal court is likely to interfere is set out in *Gooday v Gooday* [1969] P.1.

* * * *

## Guidance

7D-15 **23.**—(1) The Lord Chancellor may give guidance to the Commission as to the manner in which he considers it should discharge its functions.

(2) The Commission shall take into account any such guidance when considering the manner in which it is to discharge its functions.

(3) Guidance may not be given under this section in relation to individual cases.

7D-16 *Note*—Amended by SI 2005/3429.

***Paragraph numbers marked with a "+" can be found online and on CD.***

**General Note on the scope of the Community Legal Service Fund and on Guidance and Directions which affect what can be funded**

Whilst Sch.2 to the 1999 Act excludes certain categories of case from the scope of the CLS Fund, the effect of various Directions and Guidance is to enable some otherwise excluded matters to be funded. **7D–17**

Four directions have been made to date under s.6(8), Access to Justice Act 1988. These include Lord Chancellor's Direction—Exceptions to the Exclusions, reproduced below. All Directions must be read in conjunction with the various Guidances issued under s.23 of the 1999 Act and Guidance issued by the LSC itself.

"Lord Chancellor's Direction—Exceptions to the exclusions

1. This is a direction by the Lord Chancellor under Section 6(8)of the Access to Justice Act 1999 authorising the Legal Services Commission to fund in specified circumstances services generally excluded from the scope of the Community Legal Service Fund by paragraph 1 of Schedule 2 to the Act. In this direction "excluded services" means services which would, but for this direction, be excluded under that paragraph. **7D–18**
2. In this direction descriptions of types of case and other terms should be interpreted in accordance with definitions contained in the Act and in the Funding Code. For convenience, separate rules are given below in relation to the main levels of service under the Code. For the avoidance of doubt, nothing in this direction authorises the Commission to fund conveyancing services or the making of wills save where the direction specifically authorises this. Applications for funding under this direction must still satisfy all relevant criteria in the Funding Code and regulations.

* * * *

**Part 2—Legal Representation**

*Case Categories* **7D–18.1**

7. The Lord Chancellor authorises the Commission to fund Legal Representation, including excluded services, in any of the following types of case:
   (a) Proceedings under section 7 of the Code (Judicial Review), subject to the restrictions set out at paragraph 8 below.
   (b) Proceedings under section 8 of the Code (Proceedings against public authorities concerning serious wrongdoing, abuse of position or power, or significant breach of human rights).
   (c) Proceedings under section 10 of the Code (Housing) subject to the restrictions set out in paragraph 9 below.
   (d) Proceedings under section 11 of the Code (Family Proceedings).
   (e) Professional negligence proceedings, save where the alleged negligence relates to services provided to the client's business.
   (f) Personal insolvency proceedings.
8. Paragraph 7(a) above does not authorise the Commission to fund judicial review proceedings which arise out of the carrying on of the client's business unless those proceedings concern the serious wrongdoing, abuse of position or power or significant breach of human rights by a public authority.
9. Paragraph 7(c) above does not authorise the Commission to fund housing proceedings relating to business tenancies or otherwise arising out of the carrying on of the client's business, save where possession of the client's home is in issue in those proceedings.

*Public Interest Cases*

10. The Lord Chancellor authorises the Commission to fund excluded services in Legal Representation in proceedings which have a significant wider public interest, other than proceedings arising out of the carrying on of the client's business.

*Liberty of the client*

11. The Lord Chancellor authorises the Commission to fund excluded services in Legal Representation in relation to hearings at which the liberty of the client is in issue.

***Paragraph numbers marked with a "+" can be found online and on CD.***



LSC

*Scope of specific exclusions*

12. The following paragraphs limit the scope specific subparagraphs of paragraph 1 of Schedule 2 of the Act. Cases which benefit from paragraphs 13 to 16 below may still be excluded under any other subparagraph of paragraph 1 of Schedule 2. For example, a case concerning a constructive trust would still be excluded if the case arose out of the carrying on of a business.
13. Paragraph 1(b) conveyancing. Where the Commission is funding Legal Representation in proceedings, the Lord Chancellor authorises the Commission to fund conveyancing services as part of Legal Representation where this is necessary to give effect to a court order made in those proceedings. Where the Commission is funding Legal Representation in family proceedings the Lord Chancellor authorises the Commission to fund conveyancing services as part of Legal Representation where this is necessary to give effect to an agreement reached, with the help of funded services, to settle or avoid those proceedings.
14. Paragraph 1(e) matters of trust law. The Lord Chancellor authorises the Commission to fund services relating to matters of trust law as part of Legal Representation where the matters of trust law concern implied, resulting or constructive trusts, trusts arising when a person dies intestate or where matters of trust law arise in cases under section 14 of the Trusts for Land and Appointment of Trustees Act 1996 concerning the ownership or possession of the client's home.
15. Paragraph (g) matters of company or partnership law. The Lord Chancellor authorises the Commission to fund services relating to matters of partnership law as part of Legal Representation where the Commission is satisfied that the client needs to rely on partnership law only in order to dispute whether a partnership existed, for example in order to contest liability on the grounds of undue influence.
16. Paragraph (h) other matters arising out of the carrying on of a business. The Lord Chancellor authorises the Commission to fund services in relation to matters arising out of the carrying on a business as part of Legal Representation where the Commission is satisfied that the client is reasonably disputing whether he or she was carrying on a business, for example where the client is contesting liability on the grounds of undue influence.

*Mixed Cases*

17. The Lord Chancellor authorises the Commission to fund excluded services in Legal Representation when the excluded services relate to issues which are only minor or incidental to the main purpose of the proceedings.
18. The Lord Chancellor authorises the Commission to fund Legal Representation in partially excluded proceedings where any of the following conditions apply:
    (a) The client is a defendant or third party in proceedings brought against him or her by an opponent.
    (b) The excluded issues were introduced into existing proceedings by an opponent.
    (c) The client is bringing the proceedings but it is or would have been impracticable for the client to bring proceedings without also covering the excluded services.
19. In paragraph 18 above "partially excluded proceedings" means proceedings which (apart from this direction) are mostly within scope but which also include specific issues or causes of action which are excluded under paragraph 1 of Schedule 2 of the Act.

* * * *

**Part 4—Support Proceedings**

**7D–18.2** (21) The Lord Chancellor authorises the Commission to fund Investigative Support in relation to personal injury claims which satisfy the funding criteria for Investigative Support set out in the General Funding Code.

(22) The Lord Chancellor authorises the Commission to fund Litigation Support in relation to personal injury claims which satisfy the funding criteria for Litigation Support set out in the General Funding Code.

(23) The Lord Chancellor authorises the Commission to fund Investigative Support

***Paragraph numbers marked with a "+" can be found online and on CD.***

or Litigation Support in relation to personal injury claims which have a significant wider public interest.

Date: April 2, 2001

Signed: Irvine of Lairg"

**"Proceedings against public authorities concerning serious wrongdoing" (para.7(b))**

In *R. (on the application of G) v Legal Services Commission* [2004] EWHC 276 (an action **7D–19** for personal injuries) Pitchford J. gave the Court's guidance as to the meaning of "proceedings against public authorities concerning serious wrongdoing, abuse of position or power, or significant breach of Human Rights" (see 7D–18 paras 8 and 9). Criteria were set out by which "serious wrongdoing by a public authority" ought generally to be considered, including: "(1) the nature of the duty owed; (2) the purpose of that duty, [which] will involve a consideration to whom and to what class of person was the duty owed, and the protection the duty was designed to afford; (3) the quality of the acts and omissions which are alleged to constitute the serious wrongdoing, and the circumstances in which those acts or omissions occur; (4) the harm or risk of harm which the breach occasioned; and (5) the public dimension of the duty and the breach which informs the priority for funding Legal Representation".

## The Community Legal Service (Financial) Regulations 2000

(S.I. 2000 No. 516)

### Interpretation

**2.**—(1) In these Regulations, unless the context requires otherwise: **7D–20**

"the Act" means the Access to Justice Act 1999;

[...]

'assessing authority' means the Commission, except where under contract or under the Funding Code the Commission has delegated this function to the supplier;

"asylum claim" means a claim that it would be contrary to the United Kingdom's obligations under the Convention relating to the Status of Refugees done at Geneva on 28th July 1951 and the protocol to the Convention or to Article 3 of the Convention for the Protection of Human Rights and Fundamental Freedoms, agreed by the Council of Europe at Rome on 4th November 1950, for the claimant to be removed from or required to leave the United Kingdom;

"certificate" means a certificate issued under the Funding Code certifying a decision to fund services for the client;

"client" means an individual who applies for or receives funded services and, in the case of actual or contemplated proceedings, is a party or prospective party to the proceedings;

[...]

"family proceedings" means proceedings which arise out of family relationships, including proceedings in which the welfare of children is determined. Family proceedings also include all proceedings under any one or more of the following:

(a) the Matrimonial Causes Act 1973;

(b) the Inheritance (Provision for Family and Dependants) Act 1975;

(c) the Adoption Act 1976;

(d) the Domestic Proceedings and Magistrates' Courts Act 1978;

***Paragraph numbers marked with a "+" can be found online and on CD.***



LSC

(e) Part III of the Matrimonial and Family Proceedings Act 1984;

(f) Parts I to V of the Children Act 1989;

(g) Part IV of the Family Law Act 1996

(ga) the Adoption and Children Act 2002; and

(gb) the Civil Partnership Act 2004; and

(h) the inherent jurisdiction of the High Court in relation to children.

7D–21 *Note* —Amended by SI 2005/3504, SI 2006/713, SI 2006/2363, SI 2007/906 and SI 2007/2442.

7D–22 **40.**—(1) […]

(2) The net cost of the funded services means the cost paid by the Commission less any costs recovered by the Commission from another party.

(3) Where funding is provided by the Commission under a contract which does not differentiate between the remuneration for the client's case and remuneration for other cases, or require the cost of individual cases to be assessed, the reference in paragraph (2) to the cost paid by the Commission shall be construed as a reference to such part of the remuneration payable under the contract as may be specified in writing by the Commission.

(4) For the purposes of this regulation and regulation 43, where a certificate is discharged the cost of any assessment proceedings under CPR Part 47 or of taxation in the Supreme Court shall not be included as part of the cost of the funded services, and the cost of drawing up a bill is not part of the cost of assessment proceedings.

7D–22.1 *Note* —Amended by the Constitutional Reform Act 2005 (Consequential Amendments) Order 2009 (SI 2009/2468) with effect from October 1, 2009.

## PART III

## THE STATUTORY CHARGE

7D–23 **42.** In regulations 43 to 53:

"relevant dispute" means the dispute in connection with which funded services are provided;

"relevant proceedings" means proceedings in connection with which funded services are provided;

"recovered", in relation to property or money, means property or money recovered or preserved by a client, whether for himself or for any other person;

"settlement fee"means the separate fee payable in addition to the standard fee which a supplier may claim in accordance with the unified contract where a case settles under Family Help (Lower);

"standard fee" means the basic fee payable for the relevant category of law in accordance with the unified contract;

"statutory charge" means the charge created by section 10(7) of the Act in respect of the amount defined in regulation 43; and

*Paragraph numbers marked with a "+" can be found online and on CD.*

"success fee" is defined in accordance with section 58 of the Courts and Legal Services Act 1990;

"supplier" means a party to the unified contract other than the Commission;

"unified contract" means the contract between the Commission and a supplier for the provision of funded services which consists of the contract document, the schedule, the contract standard terms and the specification.

*Note* —Amended by SI 2007/2442.

**43.**—(1) Subject to paragraphs (3), (4), (4A); and (5), where any money or property is recovered for a client in a relevant dispute or proceedings, the amount of the statutory charge shall be the aggregate of the sums referred to in section 10(7)(a) and (b) of the Act. **7D–24**

(2) For the purposes of this regulation:

(a) the sum referred to in section 10(7)(a) shall be defined in accordance with regulation 40(2) to (4), less any contribution paid by the client;

(b) the sum referred to in section 10(7)(b) shall include:

(i) any interest payable under regulation 52; and

(ii) any sum which the client has agreed to pay only in specific circumstances under section 10(2)(c) of the Act.

(3) Subject to paragraphs (4) or (4A), the amount of the statutory charge must not include sums expended by the Commission in funding any of the following services—

(a) Legal Help;

(b) Help at Court;

(c) Family Mediation; or

(d) Family Help (Lower).

(4) Where the client receives Family Help (Higher) or Legal Representation in connection with a dispute or proceedings for which Legal Help, Help at Court or Family Help (Lower) was also granted, the amount of the statutory charge—

(a) will include the sums expended by the Commission under paragraph (3)(a), (b) or (d);

(b) will not include any settlement fee paid in relation to family proceedings.

(4A) Where the cost of the funded services provided for a client under Family Help (Lower) exceeds the level which would otherwise have qualified for a standard fee, the amount of the statutory charge—

(a) will include the sums expended by the Commission under paragraph (3)(a) and (d) which exceed the level which would otherwise have qualified for a standard fee;

(aa) will include disbursements;

(b) will not include any settlement fee paid in relation to family proceedings.

(5) The amount of the charge created by section 10(7) of the Act shall not include reasonable costs incurred by the supplier in accor-

dance with his statutory obligations under the Disability Discrimination Act 1995.

7D–25 *Note*—Amended by SI 2003/650, SI 2005/1793, SI 2007/906, SI 2007/2442 and SI 2008/658.

7D–26 **44.**—(1) The charge created by section 10(7) of the Act shall not apply to any of the following:

(a) any periodical payment of maintenance;

(aa) any sum or sums ordered to be paid under sections 25B(4) or 25C of the Matrimonial Causes Act 1973;

(b) other than in circumstances which are exceptional having regard in particular to the quantity or value of the items concerned, the client's clothes or household furniture or the tools or implements of his trade;

(c) any sum or sums ordered to be paid under section 5 of the Inheritance (Provision for Family and Dependants) Act 1975 or Part IV of the Family Law Act 1996;

(d) […]

(e) one-half of any redundancy payment within the meaning of Part XI of the Employment Rights Act 1996 recovered by the client;

(f) […]

(g) where the statutory charge is in favour of the supplier, the client's main or only dwelling; or

(h) any sum, payment or benefit which, by virtue of any provision of or made under an Act of Parliament, cannot be assigned or charged.

(2) […]

(4) In paragraph (1)(a), "maintenance" means money or money's worth paid towards the support of a former partner, child or any other person for whose support the payer has previously been responsible or has made payments.

7D–27 *Note*—Amended by SI 2001/3663, SI 2005/589 and SI 2007/906.

7D–28 **45.**—(1) Subject to paragraph (2), the statutory charge shall be in favour of the Commission.

(2) Subject to paragraph (3), where it relates to the cost of Legal Help, Help at Court or Family Help (Lower), the statutory charge shall be in favour of the supplier.

(3) Where Legal Help or Help at Court has been provided, the statutory charge shall be in favour of the Commission if it attaches to money or property recovered after a certificate has been granted in relation to the same matter.

7D–28.1 *Note*—Amended by SI 2007/2442.

7D–29 **46.**—(1) This regulation applies only where the statutory charge is in favour of the supplier.

(2) The Commission may grant a supplier authority, either in respect of individual cases or generally, to waive either all or part of the amount of the statutory charge where its enforcement would

cause grave hardship or distress to the client or would be unreasonably difficult because of the nature of the property.

**47.**—(1) [...] **7D–30**

(2) Paragraph (3) applies where:

(a) [...]

(b) the Commission considers it cost-effective to fund those services for a specified claimant or claimants, but not for other claimants or potential claimants who might benefit from the litigation.

(3) Where this paragraph applies, the Commission may, if it considers it equitable to do so, waive some or all of the amount of the statutory charge.

*Note* —Amended by SI 2001/3663; and SI 2005/1793. **7D–31**

**48.** Regulations 49 to 53 apply only in relation to a statutory charge in favour of the Commission. **7D–32**

**49.**—(1) Where a certificate has been revoked or discharged, section 10 (7) of the Act shall apply to any money or property recovered as a result of the client continuing to pursue the relevant dispute or take, defend or be a party to the relevant proceedings. **7D–33**

(2) In paragraph (1), "client" means the person whose certificate has been revoked or discharged, or, as the case may be, his personal representatives, trustee in bankruptcy or the Official Receiver.

**50.**—(1) Paragraph (2) applies where any money recovered by a client in any proceedings is ordered to be paid into or remain in court and invested for the benefit of the client. **7D–34**

(2) Where this paragraph applies, the statutory charge shall attach only to such part of the money as, in the opinion of the Commission, will be sufficient to safeguard the interests of the Commission, and the Commission shall notify the court in writing of the amount so attached.

**51.** Subject to regulation 52, the Commission may enforce the statutory charge in any manner which would be available to a charge in respect of a charge given between parties. **7D–35**

**52.**—(1) Where the condition in regulation 52A is satisfied the Commission may postpone the enforcement of the statutory charge where: **7D–36**

(a) by order of the court or agreement it relates to property to be used as a home by the client or his dependants, or, where the relevant proceedings were family proceedings, to money to pay for such a home;

(b) the Commission is satisfied that the property in question will provide such security for the statutory charge as it considers appropriate; and

(c) as soon as it is possible to do so, the Commission registers a charge under the Land Registration Act 2002 to secure the amount in regulation 43 or, as appropriate, takes equivalent steps (whether in England and Wales or in

LSC

any other jurisdiction) to protect its interest in the property.

(2) Where the client wishes to purchase a property in substitution for the property over which a charge is registered under paragraph (1)(c), the Commission may release the charge if the conditions in paragraph (1)(b) and (c) are satisfied.

(3) Where the enforcement of the statutory charge is postponed, interest shall accrue for the benefit of the Commission in accordance with regulation 53.

(4) Without prejudice to the provisions of the Land Registration Act 2002 and the Land Charges Act 1972, all conveyances and acts done to defeat, or operating to defeat, any charge shall, except in the case of a bona fide purchaser for value without notice, be void as against the Commission.

**7D–37** *Note*—Amended by SI 2005/589; and SI 2005/1793.

**7D–38** **52A.** The Commission may only postpone enforcement of the statutory charge if it appears to the Commission that it would be unreasonable for the client to repay the amount of the charge.

**7D–39** *Note*—Inserted by SI 2005/1793.

**7D–40** **52B.**—(1) The Commission may review any decision to postpone enforcement of the charge at any time and, unless it appears to the Commission that it would be unreasonable for the client to repay the amount of the charge which has been postponed, it shall either—

(i) proceed to enforce the charge; or

(ii) where the conditions in regulation 52(1) (a) to (c) are satisfied continue to postpone enforcement of the charge, in which case the provisions of regulation 52(3) shall also continue to apply.

(2) If the Commission continues to postpone enforcement under paragraph (1) (ii) it may do so on such terms or conditions as to repayment of the amount of the charge by way of interim payments of either capital or interest or both, or otherwise, as appear to the Commission to be appropriate.

**7D–41** *Note*—Inserted by SI 2005/1793.

**7D–42** **53.**—(1) Where interest is payable by the client under regulation 52, that interest shall continue to accrue until the amount of the statutory charge is paid.

(2) The client may make interim payments of interest or capital in respect of the outstanding amount of the statutory charge, but no interim payment shall be used to reduce the capital outstanding while any interest remains outstanding.

(3) Where interest is payable by the client under regulation 52:

(a) it shall run from the date when the charge is first registered;

(b) the applicable rate shall be:

*Paragraph numbers marked with a "+" can be found online and on CD.*

(i) 8% per annum until 31st March 2002;
(ii) 5% per annum from 1st April 2002 until 30th September 2005;
(iii) 8% per annum from 1st October 2005;

(c) [...]
(d) [...]
(e) the capital on which it is calculated shall be the lesser of:
(i) the amount of the statutory charge outstanding from time to time, less any interest accrued by virtue of regulation 52(3), or
(ii) the value of the property recovered at the time of such recovery.

*Note* —Amended by SI 2001/3663; and SI 2005/589. **7D–43**

**[THE NEXT PARAGRAPH IS 7D–45.]**

**The Community Legal Service (Costs) Regulations 2000**

(S.I. 2000 No. 441) **7D–45**

PART I

GENERAL

LSC

### Citation and commencement

**1.** These Regulations may be cited as the Community Legal Service (Costs) Regulations 2000 and shall come into force on 1st April 2000. **7D–46**

### Interpretation

**2.** In these Regulations: **7D–47**

"the Act" means the Access to Justice Act 1999;

"certificate" means a certificate issued under the Funding Code certifying a decision to fund services for the client;

"child" means a person under 18;

"client" means an individual who receives funded services;

"Commission" means the Legal Services Commission established under section 1 of the Act;

"costs judge" has the same meaning as in the CPR;

"costs order" means an order that a party pay all or part of the costs of proceedings;

"costs order against the Commission" means an order, made under regulation 5 of the Community Legal Service (Cost Protection) Regulations 2000 (but not one under regulation 6 of those Regulations), that the Commission pay all or part of the costs of a party to proceedings who has not received funded services in relation to those proceedings under a certificate, other than a certificate which has been revoked;

***Paragraph numbers marked with a "+" can be found online and on CD.***

"cost protection" means the limit on costs awarded against a client set out in section 11(1) of the Act;

"court" includes any tribunal having the power to award costs in favour of, or against, a party;

"CPR" means the Civil Procedure Rules 1998, and a reference to a Part or rule, prefixed by "CPR", means the Part or rule so numbered in the CPR;

"Director" means any Director appointed by the Commission in accordance with the Funding Code and any other person authorised to act on his behalf, except a supplier;

"Financial Regulations" means the Community Legal Service (Financial) Regulations 2000;

"Funding Code" means the code approved under section 9 of the Act;

"full costs" means , where a section 11(1) costs order is made against a client, the amount of costs which that client would, but for section 11(1) of the Act, have been ordered to pay;

"funded services" means services which are provided directly for a client and funded for that client by the Commission as part of the Community Legal Service under sections 4 to 11 of the Act;

"litigation friend" has the meaning given by CPR Part 21;

"partner", in relation to a party to proceedings, means a person with whom that party lives as a couple, and includes a person with whom the party is not currently living but from whom he is not living separate and apart;

"patient" means a person who by reason of mental disorder within the meaning of the Mental Health Act 1983 is incapable of managing and administering his own affairs;

"proceedings" include proceedings in any tribunal which is a court, as defined, in this paragraph;

"receiving party" means a party in favour of whom a costs order is made;

"rules of court", in relation to a tribunal, means rules or regulations made by the authority having power to make rules or regulations regulating the practice and procedure of that tribunal and, in relation to any court, includes practice directions;

"section 11(1) costs order" means a costs order against a client where cost protection applies;

"solicitor" means solicitor or other person who is an authorised litigator within the meaning of section 119(1) of the Courts and Legal Services Act 1990;

"statement of resources" means :

(a) a statement, verified by a statement of truth, made by a party to proceedings setting out:

(i) his income and capital and financial commitments during the previous year and, if applicable, those of his partner;

***Paragraph numbers marked with a "+" can be found online and on CD.***

(ii) his estimated future financial resources and expectations and, if applicable, those of his partner; and

(iii) a declaration stating whether he, and if applicable his partner, has deliberately foregone or deprived himself of any resources or expectations, together (if applicable and as far as is practical) with details of those resources or expectations and the manner in which they have been foregone or deprived;

(iv) particulars of any application for funding made by him in connection with the proceedings; and

(v) any other facts relevant to the determination of his resources; or

(b) a statement, verified by a statement of truth, made by a client receiving funded services, setting out the information provided by the client under regulation 6 of the Financial Regulations, and stating that there has been no significant change in the client's financial circumstances since the date on which the information was provided or, as the case may be, details of any such change;

"statement of truth" has the same meaning as in CPR Part 22;

"supplier" means any person or body providing funded services to the client, including any authorised advocate (within the meaning of section 119(1) of the Courts and Legal Services Act 1990) engaged by the client's solicitor to act in proceedings.

LSC

*Note*—Amended by SI 2001/823, SI 2005/2006 and SI 2007/2444. **7D–48**

**Effect of these Regulations**

**3.** Nothing in these Regulations shall be construed, in relation to proceedings where one or more parties are receiving, or have received, funded services, as: **7D–49**

(a) requiring a court to make a costs order where it would not otherwise have made a costs order; or

(b) affecting the court's power to make a wasted costs order against a legal representative.

**Termination of retainer where funding is withdrawn**

**4.**—(1) The following paragraphs of this regulation apply where funding is withdrawn by revoking or discharging the client's certificate. **7D–50**

(2) Subject to paragraphs (3) and (4), on the revocation or discharge of the client's certificate, the retainer of any supplier acting under that certificate shall terminate immediately.

(3) Termination of retainers under paragraph (2) shall not take effect unless and until any procedures under the Funding Code for

review of the decision to withdraw the client's funding are concluded, and confirm the decision to withdraw funding.

(4) The solicitor's retainer shall not terminate until he has complied with any procedures under the Funding Code that require him to send or serve notices.

## PART II

## COSTS ORDERS AGAINST CLIENT AND AGAINST COMMISSION

*Application of regulations 6 to 13*

7D–51 **5.** Regulations 6 to 13 apply only where cost protection applies.

**Security for costs**

7D–52 **6.** Where in any proceedings a client is required to give security for costs, the amount of that security shall not exceed the amount (if any) which is a reasonable one having regard to all the circumstances, including the client's financial resources and his conduct in relation to the dispute to which the proceedings relate.

7D–53 *Note*—In the absence of special circumstances an order for security for costs should not be made against a funded client (*Conway v George Wimpey & Co Ltd (No.1)* [1951] 1 All E.R. 56). Special circumstances which may justify such an order were considered on *Wyld v Silver (No.2)* [1962] 1 W.L.R. 863, *Jackson v John Dickinson & Co (Bolton)* [1952] 1 All E.R. 104, *Friedmann v Austay (London), Ltd* [1954] 1 W.L.R. 466 and *Bampton v Cook* [1954] 1 W.L.R. 450.

7D–54 **7.**—(1) The first £100,000 of the value of the client's interest in the main or only dwelling in which he resides shall not be taken into account in having regard to the client's resources for the purposes of section 11(1) of the Act.

(2) Where, but only to the extent that, the court considers that the circumstances are exceptional, having regard in particular to the quantity or value of the items concerned, the court may take into account the value of the client's clothes and household furniture, or the tools and implements of his trade, in having regard to the client's resources for the purposes of section 11(1) of the Act.

(3) Subject to paragraph (4), in having regard to the resources of a party for the purposes of section 11(1) of the Act, the resources of his partner shall be treated as his resources.

(4) The resources of a party's partner shall not be treated as that party's resources if the partner has a contrary interest in the dispute in respect of which the funded services are provided.

(5) Where a party is acting in a representative, fiduciary or official capacity, the court shall not take the personal resources of the party into account for the purposes of section 11(1) of the Act, but shall have regard to the value of any property or estate, or the amount of any fund out of which he is entitled to be indemnified, and may also have regard to the resources of the persons, if any, including that party where appropriate, who are beneficially interested in that property, estate or fund.

(6) For the purposes of section 11(1) of the Act, where a party is acting as a litigation friend to a client who is a child or a patient, the court shall not take the personal resources of the litigation friend into account in assessing the resources of the client.

### *Statements of resources*

**8.**—(1) Any person who is a party to proceedings in which another party is a client may make a statement of resources, and file it with the court. **7D–55**

(2) A person making and filing a statement of resources under paragraph (1) shall serve a copy of it on the client.

(3) Where a copy of a statement of resources has been served under paragraph (2) not less than seven days before the date fixed for a hearing at which the amount to be paid under a section 11(1) costs order falls, or may fall, to be decided, the client shall also make a statement of resources, and shall produce it at that hearing.

### *Procedures for ordering costs against client and Commission*

**9.**—(1) Where the court is considering whether to make a section 11(1) costs order, it shall consider whether, but for cost protection, it would have made a costs order against the client and, if so, whether it would, on making the costs order, have specified the amount to be paid under that order. **7D–56**

(2) If the court considers that it would have made a costs order against the client, but that it would not have specified the amount to be paid under it, the court shall, when making the section 11(1) costs order:

(a) specify the amount (if any) that the client is to pay under that order if, but only if:

(i) it considers that it has sufficient information before it to decide what amount is, in that case, a reasonable amount for the client to pay, in accordance with section 11(1) of the Act; and

(ii) it is satisfied that, if it were to determine the full costs at that time, they would exceed the amount referred to in sub-paragraph (i);

(b) otherwise, it shall not specify the amount the client is to pay under the section 11(1) costs order.

(3) If the court considers that it would have made a costs order against the client, and that it would have specified the amount to be paid under it, the court shall, when making the section 11(1) costs order:

(a) specify the amount (if any) that the client is to pay under that order if, but only if, it considers that it has sufficient information before it to decide what amount is, in that case, a reasonable amount for the client to pay, in accordance with section 11(1) of the Act;

(b) otherwise, it shall not specify the amount the client is to pay under the section 11(1) costs order.

(4) Any order made under paragraph (3) shall state the amount of the full costs.

***Paragraph numbers marked with a "+" can be found online and on CD.***



LSC

(5) The amount (if any) to be paid by the client under an order made under paragraph (2)(b) or paragraph (3)(b), and any application for a costs order against the Commission, shall be determined in accordance with regulation 10, and at any such determination following an order made under paragraph (2)(b), the amount of the full costs shall also be assessed.

(6) Where the court makes a section 11(1) costs order that does not specify the amount which the client is to pay under it, it may also make findings of fact, as to the parties' conduct in the proceedings or otherwise, relevant to the determination of that amount, and those findings shall be taken into consideration in that determination.

**7D–57** **10.**—(1) The following paragraphs of this regulation apply where the amount to be paid under a section 11(1) costs order, or an application for a costs order against the Commission, is to be determined under this regulation, by virtue of regulation 9(5).

(2) The receiving party may, within three months after a section 11(1) costs order is made, request a hearing to determine the costs payable to him.

(3) A request under paragraph (2) shall be accompanied by:

(a) if the section 11(1) costs order does not state the full costs, the receiving party's bill of costs, which shall comply with any requirements of relevant rules of court relating to the form and content of a bill of costs where the court is assessing a party's costs;

(b) unless the conditions set out in paragraph (3A) are satisfied, a statement of resources; and

(c) if the receiving party is seeking, or, subject to the determination of the amount to be paid under the section 11(1) costs order, may seek, a costs order against the Commission, written notice to that effect.

(3A) The conditions referred to in paragraph (3)(b) above are that—

(a) the court is determining an application for a costs order against the Commission;

(b) the costs were not incurred in a court of first instance.

(4) The receiving party shall file the documents referred to in paragraph (3) with the court and at the same time serve copies of them:

(a) on the client, if a determination of costs payable under section 11(1) of the Act is sought; and

(b) on the Director, if notice has been given under paragraph (3)(c).

(5) Where documents are served on the client under paragraph (4)(a), the client shall make a statement of resources.

(6) The client shall file the statement of resources made under paragraph (5) with the court, and serve copies of it on the receiving party and, if notice has been given under paragraph (3)(c), on the Director, not more than 21 days after the client receives a copy of the receiving party's statement of resources.

(7) The client may, at the same time as filing and serving a state-

ment of resources under paragraph (6), file, and serve on the same persons, a statement setting out any points of dispute in relation to the bill of costs referred to in paragraph (3)(a).

(8) If the client, without good reason, fails to file a statement of resources in accordance with paragraph (6), the court shall determine the amount which the client shall be required to pay under the section 11(1) costs order (and, if relevant, the full costs), having regard to the statement made by the receiving party, and the court need not hold an oral hearing for such determination.

(9) If the client files a statement of resources in accordance with paragraph (6), or the period for filing such notice expires, or if the costs payable by the client have already been determined, the court shall set a date for the hearing and, at least 14 days before that date, serve notice of it on:

(a) the receiving party;
(b) the client (unless the costs payable by the client have already been determined); and
(c) if a costs order against the Commission is or may be sought, the Director.

(10) The court's functions under this regulation may be exercised:

(a) in relation to proceedings in the Supreme Court, by such officers as may be appointed by the President;
(b) in relation to proceedings in the Court of Appeal, High Court or a county court, a costs judge or a district judge;
(c) in relation to proceedings in a magistrates' court, by a single justice or by the justices' clerk;
(d) in relation to proceedings in the Employment Appeal Tribunal, by the Registrar of that Tribunal.

(11) The amount of costs to be determined under this regulation may include the costs incurred in relation to a request made under this regulation.

*Note* —Amended by SI 2007/2444 and by the Constitutional Reform Act 2005 (Consequential Amendments) Order 2009 (SI 2009/2468) with effect from October 1, 2009.

**10A.**—(1) Subject to paragraph (2), where the court makes a section 11(1) costs order but does not specify the amount which the client is to pay under it, the court may order the client to pay an amount on account of the costs which are the subject of the order. **7D–58**

(2) The court may order a client to make a payment on account of costs under this regulation only if it has sufficient information before it to decide the minimum amount which the client is likely to be ordered to pay on a determination under regulation 10.

(3) The amount of the payment on account of costs shall not exceed the minimum amount which the court decides that the client is likely to be ordered to pay on such a determination.

(4) Where the court orders a client to make a payment on account of costs—

(a) it shall order the client to make the payment into court; and

LSC

(b) the payment shall remain in court unless and until the court—

(i) makes a determination under regulation 10 of the amount which the client should pay to the receiving party under the section 11(1) costs order, and orders the payment on account or part of it to be paid to the receiving party in satisfaction or part satisfaction of the client's liability under that order; or

(ii) makes an order under paragraph (5)(b) or (5)(c) of this regulation that the payment on account or part of it be repaid to the client.

(5) Where a client has made a payment on account of costs pursuant to an order under paragraph (1) of this regulation—

(a) the receiving party shall request a hearing under regulation 10 to determine the amount of costs payable to him;

(b) if the receiving party fails to request such a hearing within the time permitted by regulation 10(2), the payment on account shall be repaid to the client;

(c) if upon the hearing under regulation 10 the amount of costs which it is determined that the client should pay is less than the amount of the payment on account, the difference shall be repaid to the client.

*Appeals, etc*

7D–59 **11.**—(1) Subject to the following paragraphs of this regulation, and to regulation 12, any determination made under regulation 9 or regulation 10 shall be final.

(2) Any party with a financial interest in an assessment of the full costs may appeal against that assessment, if and to the extent that that party would, but for these Regulations, be entitled to appeal against an assessment of costs by the court in which the relevant proceedings are taking place.

(3) Where, under regulation 9(2)(a), the court has specified the amount which a client is required to pay under a section 11(1) costs order, the client may apply to the court for a determination of the full costs and if, on that determination, the amount of the full costs is less than the amount which the court previously specified under regulation 9(2)(a), the client shall instead be required to pay the amount of the full costs.

(4) The receiving party or the Commission may appeal, on a point of law, against the making of a costs order against the Commission (including the amount of costs which the Commission is required to pay under the order), or against the court's refusal to make such an order.

*Variation and late determination of amount of costs*

7D–60 **12.**—(1) The following paragraphs of this regulation apply where the court makes a section 11(1) costs order.

(2) Where the amount (if any) which the client is required to pay

under the section 11(1) costs order, together with the amount which the Commission is required to pay under any costs order against the Commission, is less than the full costs, the receiving party may, on the ground set out in paragraph (4)(a), apply to the court for an order varying the amount which the client is required to pay under the section 11(1) costs order.

(3) Where the court has not specified the amount to be paid under the section 11(1) costs order, and the receiving party has not, within the time limit in regulation 10(2), applied to have that amount determined in accordance with regulation 10, the receiving party may, on any of the grounds set out in paragraph (4), apply for a determination of the amount that the client is required to pay.

(4) The grounds referred to in paragraphs (2) and (3) are the grounds that:

- (a) there has been a significant change in the client's circumstances since the date of the order;
- (b) material additional information as to the client's financial resources is available, and that information could not with reasonable diligence have been obtained by the receiving party in time to make an application in accordance with regulation 10; or
- (c) there were other good reasons justifying the receiving party's failure to make an application within the time limit in regulation 10(2).

(5) Any application under paragraph (2) or (3) shall be made by the receiving party within six years from the date on which the section 11(1) costs order is first made.

(6) On any application under paragraph (2), the order may be varied as the court thinks fit, but the amount of costs ordered (excluding any costs ordered to be paid under paragraph (9)) shall not exceed the amount of the full costs as stated in any previous order of the court.

(7) When the amount which the client is required to pay under the section 11(1) costs order has been determined under regulation 9(2)(a), and the receiving party applies under paragraph (2) for an order varying that amount:

- (a) the receiving party shall file with the application under paragraph (2) his bill of costs, which shall comply with any requirements of relevant rules of court relating to the form and content of a bill of costs where the court is assessing a party's costs; and
- (b) the court shall, when determining the application, assess the full costs.

(8) Where the receiving party has received funded services in relation to the proceedings, the Commission may make an application under paragraph (2) or paragraph (3), and:

- (a) when making the application the Commission shall file with the court a statement of the receiving party's costs or, if those costs have not been assessed, the receiving party's bill of costs; and

*Paragraph numbers marked with a "+" can be found online and on CD.*

LSC

(b) paragraphs (4) to (6) shall apply to that application as if "the Commission" were substituted for "the receiving party" in those paragraphs.

(9) The amount of costs to be determined under this regulation may include the costs incurred in relation to an application made under this regulation.

*Rights to appear*

**7D–61** **13.**—(1) The Director may appear at:

(a) any hearing in relation to which notice has been given under regulation 10(3)(c);

(b) the hearing of any appeal under regulation 11(4); or

(c) the hearing of any application under regulation 12(8).

(2) The Director may, instead of appearing under paragraph (1), give evidence in the form of a written statement to the court, verified by a statement of truth.

(3) The Director shall file with the court any statement under paragraph (2), and serve a copy on the receiving party, not less than seven days before the hearing to which it relates.

**7D–61.1** *Note* —Amended by SI 2007/2444.

## The Community Legal Service (Cost Protection) Regulations 2000

**7D–62** (S.I. 2000 No. 824)

Arrangement of Regulations

Reg.



### Citation and commencement

**7D–63** **1.** These Regulations may be cited as the Community Legal Service (Cost Protection) Regulations 2000 and shall come into force on 1st April 2000.

### Interpretation

**7D–64** **2.**—(1) In these Regulations:

"the Act" means the Access to Justice Act 1999;

"certificate" means a certificate issued under the Funding Code certifying a decision to fund services for the client and "emergency certificate" means a certificate certifying a decision to fund Legal Representation for the client in a case of emergency;

"client" means an individual who receives funded services;

"Commission" means the Legal Services Commission established under section 1 of the Act;

***Paragraph numbers marked with a "+" can be found online and on CD.***

"costs judge" has the same meaning as in the Civil Procedure Rules 1998;

"costs order" means an order that a party pay all or part of the costs of proceedings;

"cost protection" means the limit on costs awarded against a client set out in section 11(1) of the Act;

"court" includes any tribunal having the power to award costs in favour of, or against, a party;

'family proceedings' means –

(a) all proceedings under any one or more of the following—

(i) the Matrimonial Causes Act 1973;

(ii) the Domestic Proceedings and Magistrates' Courts Act 1978;

(iii) Part III of the Matrimonial and Family Proceedings Act 1984;

(iv) the Child Abduction and Custody Act 1985;

(v) Parts I and II of and Schedule 1 to the Children Act 1989;

(vi) section 53 of and Schedule 7 to the Family Law Act 1996; and

(b) proceedings which arise out of family relationships under either or both of the following—

(i) the Inheritance (Provision for Family and Dependants) Act 1975;

(ii) the Trusts of Land and Appointment of Trustees Act 1996;

'family relationships' has the same meaning as in the Funding Code which came into force on 1st April 2000 and the Funding Code Guidance published on 1st April 2000 by the Commission for the purpose of making decisions under the Funding Code;

"full costs" means, where a section 11(1) costs order is made against a client, the amount of costs which that client would, but for section 11(1) of the Act, have been ordered to pay;

"funded proceedings" means proceedings (including prospective proceedings) in relation to which the client receives funded services or, as the case may be, that part of proceedings during which the client receives funded services;

"funded services" means services which are provided directly for a client and funded for that client by the Commission as part of the Community Legal Service under sections 4 to 11 of the Act;

"Funding Code" means the code approved under section 9 of the Act;

"non-funded party" means a party to proceedings who has not received funded services in relation to those proceedings under a certificate, other than a certificate which has been revoked;

"partner" means a person with whom the person concerned

LSC

*Paragraph numbers marked with a "+" can be found online and on CD.*

lives as a couple, and includes a person with whom the person concerned is not currently living but from whom he is not living separate and apart;

"proceedings" include proceedings in any tribunal which is a court, as defined in this paragraph;

"receiving party" means a party in favour of whom a costs order is made;

"section 11(1) costs order" means a costs order against a client where cost protection applies;

"solicitor" means a solicitor or another person who is an authorised litigator within the meaning of section 119(1) of the Courts and Legal Services Act 1990.

(2) References to the levels of service listed in paragraph (3) shall be construed as references to the receipt or provision of those levels of service granted in accordance with the Funding Code.

(3) The levels of service referred to in paragraph (2) are:

(a) Legal Help;
(b) Help at Court;
(c) Legal Representation;
(d) General Family Help and Help with Mediation
(e) [...]
(f) [...]

7D-65 *Note*—Amended by SI 2001/823; and SI 2005/2006.

**Cost protection**

7D-66 **3.**—(1) Cost protection shall not apply in relation to such parts of proceedings, or prospective proceedings, as are funded for the client by way of:

(a) Help at Court;
(b) [...]
(c) subject to paragraph (2), Legal Help.
(d) General Family Help and Help with Mediation in family proceedings;
(e) Legal Representation in family proceedings.

(2) Subject to paragraph (4), where the client receives Legal Help, but later receives Legal Representation or General Family Help or Help with Mediation in respect of the same dispute, other than Legal Representation in family proceedings or General Family Help or Help with Mediation in family proceedings, cost protection shall apply, both in respect of:

(a) the costs incurred by the receiving party before the commencement of proceedings which, as regards the client, are funded proceedings by virtue of the client's receipt of Legal Help, and
(b) the costs incurred by the receiving party in the course of proceedings which, as regards the client, are funded proceedings by virtue of the client's receipt of Legal Rep-

*Paragraph numbers marked with a "+" can be found online and on CD.*

resentation, General Family Help or Help with Mediation.

(3) Subject to paragraph (4), cost protection shall apply only to costs incurred by the receiving party in relation to proceedings which, as regards the client, are funded proceedings, and:

(a) where work is done before the issue of a certificate, cost protection shall (subject to paragraphs (2) and (5)) apply only to costs incurred after the issue of the certificate;

(b) where funding is withdrawn by discharging the client's certificate, cost protection shall apply only to costs incurred before the date when funded services under the certificate ceased to be provided.

(4) Where funding is withdrawn by revoking the client's certificate, cost protection shall not apply, either in respect of work done before or after the revocation.

(5) Cost protection shall apply to work done immediately before the grant of an emergency certificate, other than an emergency certificate granted in relation to family proceedings, if:

(a) no application for such a certificate could be made because the Commission's office was closed; and

(b) the client's solicitor applies for an emergency certificate at the first available opportunity, and the certificate is granted.

*Note*—Amended by SI 2005/2006. **7D-67**



### Enforcement of costs order against client

**4.** Where, in a case where costs protection applies, for the purpose of enforcing a costs order against a client (alone or together with any other judgment or order), a charging order under section 1 of the Charging Orders Act 1979 is made in respect of the client's interest in the main or only dwelling in which he resides: **7D-68**

(a) that charging order shall operate to secure the amount payable under the costs order (including, without limitation, any interest) only to the extent of the amount (if any) by which the proceeds of sale of the client's interest in the dwelling (having deducted any mortgage debts) exceed £100,000; and

(b) an order for the sale of the dwelling shall not be made in favour of the person in whose favour the charging order is made.

*Note*—Amended by SI 2005/2006. **7D-69**

### Costs order against Commission

**5.**—(1) The following paragraphs of this regulation apply where: **7D-70**

(a) funded services are provided to a client in relation to proceedings;

(b) those proceedings are finally decided in favour of a non-funded party; and

(c) cost protection applies.

***Paragraph numbers marked with a "+" can be found online and on CD.***

(2) The court may, subject to the following paragraphs of this regulation, make an order for the payment by the Commission to the non-funded party of the whole or any part of the costs incurred by him in the proceedings (other than any costs that the client is required to pay under a section 11(1) costs order).

(3) An order under paragraph (2) may only be made if all the conditions set out in sub-paragraphs (a), (b), (c) and (d) are satisfied:

(a) a section 11(1) costs order is made against the client in the proceedings, and the amount (if any) which the client is required to pay under that costs order is less than the amount of the full costs;

(b) unless there is a good reason for the delay, the non-funded party makes a request under regulation 10(2) of the Community Legal Service (Costs) Regulations 2000 within three months of the making of the section 11(1) costs order;

(c) as regards costs incurred in a court of first instance, the proceedings were instituted by the client, the non-funded party is an individual, and the court is satisfied that the non-funded party will suffer financial hardship unless the order is made; and

(d) in any case, the court is satisfied that it is just and equitable in the circumstances that provision for the costs should be made out of public funds.

(3A) An order under paragraph (2) may be made—

(a) in relation to proceedings in the House of Lords, by the Clerk to the Parliaments;

(b) in relation to proceedings in the Court of Appeal, High Court or a county court, by a costs judge or a district judge;

(c) in relation to proceedings in a magistrates' court, by a single justice or by the justices' clerk;

(d) in relation to proceedings in the Employment Appeal Tribunal, by the Registrar of that tribunal.

(4) Where the client receives funded services in connection with part only of the proceedings, the reference in paragraph (2) to the costs incurred by the non-funded party in the relevant proceedings shall be construed as a reference to so much of those costs as is attributable to the part of the proceedings which are funded proceedings.

(5) Where a court decides any proceedings in favour of the non-funded party and an appeal lies (with or without permission) against that decision, any order made under this regulation shall not take effect:

(a) where permission to appeal is required, unless the time limit for applications for permission to appeal expires without permission being granted;

(b) where permission to appeal is granted or is not required, unless the time limit for appeal expires without an appeal being brought.

(6) Subject to paragraph (7), in determining whether the conditions in paragraph (3)(c) and (d) are satisfied, the court shall have regard to the resources of the non-funded party and of his partner.

(7) The court shall not have regard to the resources of the partner of the non-funded party if the partner has a contrary interest in the funded proceedings.

(8) Where the non-funded party is acting in a representative, fiduciary or official capacity and is entitled to be indemnified in respect of his costs from any property, estate or fund, the court shall, for the purposes of paragraph (3), have regard to the value of the property, estate or fund and the resources of the persons, if any, including that party where appropriate, who are beneficially interested in that property, estate or fund.

**"Costs incurred by him in the proceedings" (reg.5(2))**

The costs "incurred…in the proceedings" include costs incurred before the successful party himself received a grant of public funding (see *H (Minors) (Abduction: Custody Rights) (No.2), Re* [1992] 2 A.C. 303). **7D–71**

**"A court of first instance" (reg.5(3)(c))**

The Divisional Court has been held to be a court of first instance where a decision under review was that of a body other than a court or tribunal (*R. v Greenwich LBC Ex p. Lovelace (No.2)* [1992] Q.B. 155). **7D–72**

**"Severe financial hardship" (reg.5(3)(c))**

Whether or not financial hardship is severe is a question of fact and degree in the particular circumstances of the case (see *Kelly v London Transport Executive* [1982] 1 W.L.R. 1055; *Hanning v Maitland (No.3)* [1970] 1 Q.B. 580 and *Stewart v Stewart* [1974] 1 W.L.R. 877). A local authority or some other large body must be able to show by evidence that it would sustain "some real impairment of the ability to function normally" (*R. v Greenwich LBC Ex p. Lovelace (No.2)* [1992] Q.B. 155). **7D–73**

LSC

**"Just and equitable in all the circumstances" (reg.5(3)(d))**

In *Gallie v Lee* [1971] A.C. 1039 Lord Reid stated that this is one composite phrase which should not be separated and which is to be applied broadly (at p.1047G). This dictum has been approved by the House of Lords in *Davies v Taylor (No.2)* [1974] A.C. 225 and *Din (Taj) v Wandsworth LBC (No.2)* [1982] 1 W.L.R. 418, and has been followed, for instance in *Maynard v Osmond (No.2)* [1979] 1 W.L.R. 31. **7D–74**

**"representative, fiduciary or official capacity" (reg.5(8))**

Regulation 5(3) and (8), and in particular the meaning of the expression "representative, fiduciary or official capacity" in reg.5(8) were considered in *Aehmed v Legal Services Commission* [2009] EWCA Civ 572. The Court of Appeal held that all three categories were cases where a person was "acting in a capacity on behalf of another body or bodies, or other person or persons, where that person is entitled to be indemnified in respect of his costs from any property, estate or fund" (*R. v Chester and North Wales Legal Aid Area Office (No.12) Ex p Floods of Queensferry Ltd* (1998) 1 W.L.R. 1496 CA (Civ Div) applied). This meant that "a person who is acting on his own behalf is not acting in an official capacity within the meaning of regulation 5(8) merely because he is a party to the proceedings by virtue of the office whichhe holds. He must be acting on behalf of another or others in an official capacity." This had the consequence that an officer of the Labour Party who was a party to electoral proceedings did not fall within the definition. **7D–74.1**

## Orders for costs against Commission — Litigation Support

**6.—** […] **7D–75**

*Note* —Regulation 6 revoked by SI 2005/2006.

***Paragraph numbers marked with a "+" can be found online and on CD.***

**Effect of these Regulations**

**7D–76** **7.**—(1) No order to pay costs in favour of a non-funded party shall be made against the Commission in respect of funded proceedings except in accordance with these Regulations, and any costs to be paid under such an order shall be paid out of the Community Legal Service Fund.

(2) Nothing in these Regulations shall be construed, in relation to proceedings where one or more parties are receiving, or have received, funded services, as:

(a) requiring a court to make a costs order where it would not otherwise have made a costs order; or
(b) affecting the court's power to make a wasted costs order against a legal representative.

# SECTION 8

## LIMITATION

# 8 LIMITATION

## Limitation Act 1980

(1980 c.58)

**Northern Ireland.** With a minor exception this Act does not apply; see s.41(4) post. **8–1**

Arrangement of Sections

Part I

Ordinary Time Limits for Different Classes of Action



***Paragraph numbers marked with a "+" can be found online and on CD.***



LIMITATION

**Paragraph numbers marked with a "+" denote content that is available on White Book on Westlaw UK or the Civil Procedure CD.**

***Paragraph numbers marked with a "+" can be found online and on CD.***

# PART I

## ORDINARY TIME LIMITS FOR DIFFERENT CLASSES OF ACTION

### Time limits under Part I subject to extension or exclusion under Part II

**1.**—(1) This Part of this Act gives the ordinary time limits for bringing actions of the various classes mentioned in the following provisions of this Part. **8–2**

(2) The ordinary time limits given in this Part of this Act are subject to extension or exclusion in accordance with the provisions of Part II of this Act.

#### Scope and operation of the Act

The Act is a consolidating Act, not a codifying or reforming measure. It embodies substantively without amendment the relevant provisions of the Limitation Acts of 1939, 1963 and 1975 and the Limitation Amendment Act 1980, and some other statutory provisions dealing with limitation periods (e.g. limitation periods for recovery of contribution). **8–3**

The Limitation Act 1963 was designed to mitigate the injustice caused to a plaintiff who did not know that he had suffered injury until after the expiry of the current period of limitation and thus had his claim barred without knowing that he had a claim (see *Cartledge v Jopling (E.) and Sons Ltd* [1963] A.C. 758).

There have been introduced, by amendment into the Act, further important provisions extending the time limit for bringing actions for negligence causing latent damage and not involving personal injuries: see s.14A, below which was added by the Latent Damage Act 1986, and s.14B which provides for finality after 15 years. Such new statutory provision for extension has reversed the effect of cases such as *Pirelli General Cable Works Ltd v Faber (Oscar) and Partners* [1983] 2 A.C. 1, HL. Furthermore by s.3 of the Latent Damage Act, 1986, provision is now made, subject to the terms of that section, for accrual of a fresh cause of action to successive purchasers of property suffering from latent damage. By the transitional provisions of the Latent Damage Act 1986, some actions will continue to be governed by the law applicable before the introduction of the Act (see s.4). Thus, the new provisions will not enable any action to be brought which was already barred before the new Act came into force; or affect any action commenced before such time. The Act came into force on September 18, 1986 (see s.5(3)).

In applying the Limitation Act 1980, there are three points which need, subject to the above, to be borne in mind.

First, the Act is a consolidating statute. The previous case-law relating to the earlier statutory provisions replaced without amendment by the Act still remain binding and authoritative, subject of course to the overriding judicial power in applying earlier decisions to the instant case. Further, an accrued right to plead a six year time bar under s.2(1) of the Limitation Act 1939, prior to its amendment by the Law Reform (Limitation of Actions, etc.) Act 1954, is not overcome by the operation of the Limitation Act 1975: *Arnold v Central Electricity Generating Board* [1988] A.C. 228, applied in *McDonnell v Congregation of Christian Brothers Trustees (formerly Irish Christian Brothers)* [2003] UKHL 63; [2004] 1 A.C. 1101, HL.

Second, the requirement of the rules of pleading that any relevant statute of limitation must be specifically pleaded also remains binding and must be complied with (see, Practice Direction 16, para.13.1, see Vol.1, para.16PD.13).

Third, following the introduction of the CPR, whilst the court has a very wide power to strike out proceedings as being an abuse of process it may always wish to have regard to the fact that the limitation period is still on foot and that future proceedings might be brought on the same cause of action within the limitation period. It is submitted that a ready use of the power to impose conditions upon the bringing of a new claim, whether on the occasion of striking out the existing claim, or

***Paragraph numbers marked with a "+" can be found online and on CD.***



LIMITATION

upon any new claim being made, and including an order that such new claim be not brought or pursued without permission of the court, is to be expected: see, e.g. CPR 3.1(3) and 3.4(4) and (5).

It should be further observed that the 1980 Act applies to arbitrations as it applies to actions in the High Court (see s.34).

### *ACTIONS FOUNDED ON TORT*

## Time limit for actions founded on tort

8–4 **2.** An action founded on tort shall not be brought after the expiration of six years from the date on which the cause of action accrued.

### Accrual of cause of action

8–5 A commentary on the principles relevant to the ascertainment of the date of accrual of a cause of action founded on tort is contained in McGee, *Limitation Periods*, (2002) 4th ed., Ch.5. In relation to the particular tort of negligence, the principles are summarised in the judgment of the Court of Appeal in *Polley v Warner Goodman & Streat (a firm)* [2003] EWCA Crim 1013; [2003] P.N.L.R. 40, at paras 15 and 16 of the judgment.

### "Shall not be brought"

8–6 With respect to these particular words it has been held that the expiry of the limitation period bars the remedy by action and does not extinguish the right: see, in relation to the limitation period in contract, *Royal Norwegian Government v Constant & Constant* [1960] 2 Lloyd's Rep. 431 at 442, per Diplock J. See also, in relation to tort, *Horton v Sadler* [2006] UKHL 27; [2006] 3 All E.R. 1182, HL, per Lord Bingham of Cornhill at 1182:

> "Despite the language used, this has not been taken to mean that the bringing of an action after that time is prohibited but that the defendant has a statutory defence of time-bar in such a case."

Accordingly, it is for the defendant to take the point of limitation and, furthermore, by PD 16 para.13.1, the defendant must give details of the expiry of any relevant limitation period relied on.

## Time limit in case of successive conversions and extinction of title of owner of converted goods

8–7 **3.**—(1) Where any cause of action in respect of the conversion of a chattel has accrued to any person and, before he recovers possession of the chattel, a further conversion takes place, no action shall be brought in respect of the further conversion after the expiration of six years from the accrual of the cause of action in respect of the original conversion.

(2) Where any such cause of action has accrued to any person and the period prescribed for bringing that action has expired and he has not during that period recovered possession of the chattel, the title of that person to the chattel shall be extinguished.

## Special time limit in case of theft

8–8 **4.**—(1) The right of any person from whom a chattel is stolen to bring an action in respect of the theft shall not be subject to the time limits under sections 2 and 3(1) of this Act, but if his title to the chattel is extinguished under section 3(2) of this Act he may not bring an action in respect of a theft preceding the loss of his title, unless the theft in question preceded the conversion from which time began to run for the purposes of section 3(2).

***Paragraph numbers marked with a "+" can be found online and on CD.***

(2) Subsection (1) above shall apply to any conversion related to the theft of a chattel as it applies to the theft of a chattel; and, except as provided below, every conversion following the theft of a chattel before the person from whom it is stolen recovers possession of it shall be regarded for the purposes of this section as related to the theft.

If anyone purchases the stolen chattel in good faith neither the purchase nor any conversion following it shall be regarded as related to the theft.

(3) Any cause of action accruing in respect of the theft or any conversion related to the theft of a chattel to any person from whom the chattel is stolen shall be disregarded for the purpose of applying section 3(1) or (2) of this Act to his case.

(4) Where in any action brought in respect of the conversion of a chattel it is proved that the chattel was stolen from the plaintiff or anyone through whom he claims it shall be presumed that any conversion following the theft is related to the theft unless the contrary is shown.

(5) In this section "theft" includes—

(a) any conduct outside England and Wales which would be theft if committed in England and Wales; and

(b) obtaining any chattel (in England and Wales or elsewhere) by—

(i) blackmail (within the meaning of section 21 of the Theft Act 1968),

(ii) fraud (within the meaning of the Fraud Act 2006);

and references in this section to a chattel being "stolen" shall be construed accordingly.

*Note* —Amended by the Fraud Act 2006 s.14(1), Sch.1, para.18, with effect from January 15, 2007 (SI 2006/3200).

## Time limit for actions for defamation or malicious falsehood

**4A.** The time limit under section 2 of this Act shall not apply to an action for— **8–9**

(a) libel or slander, or

(b) slander of title, slander of goods or other malicious falsehood,

but no such action shall be brought after the expiration of one year from the date on which the cause of action accrued.

*Note* —Added by the Administration of Justice Act 1985 s.57(2), 69(2) and Sch.9, para.14. Substituted, in relation to causes of action arising after September 4, 1996, by the Defamation Act 1996 s.5(2). **8–10**

### ACTIONS FOUNDED ON SIMPLE CONTRACT

## Time limit for actions founded on simple contract

**5.** An action founded on simple contract shall not be brought after the expiration of six years from the date on which the cause of action accrued. **8–11**

**"Shall not be brought"**

8–12 See the note at para.8–6 above.

## Special time limit for actions in respect of certain loans

8–13 **6.**—(1) Subject to subsection (3) below, section 5 of this Act shall not bar the right of action on a contract of loan to which this section applies.

(2) This section applies to any contract of loan which—

(a) does not provide for repayment of the debt on or before a fixed or determinable date; and

(b) does not effectively (whether or not it purports to do so) make the obligation to repay the debt conditional on a demand for repayment made by or on behalf of the creditor or on any other matter;

except where in connection with taking the loan the debtor enters into any collateral obligation to pay the amount of the debt or any part of it (as, for example, by delivering a promissory note as security for the debt) on terms which would exclude the application of this section to the contract of loan if they applied directly to repayment of the debt.

(3) Where a demand in writing for repayment of the debt under a contract of loan to which this section applies is made by or on behalf of the creditor (or, where there are joint creditors, by or on behalf of any one of them) section 5 of this Act shall thereupon apply as if the cause of action to recover the debt had accrued on the date on which the demand was made.

(4) In this section "promissory note" has the same meaning as in the Bills of Exchange Act 1882.

## Time limit for actions to enforce certain awards

8–14 **7.** An action to enforce an award, where the submission is not by an instrument under seal, shall not be brought after the expiration of six years from the date on which the cause of action accrued.

**Application for leave to enforce award**

8–15 It was common ground in *Good Challenger Navegante SA v Metalexportimport SA (The "Good Challenger")* [2003] EWCA Civ 1668; [2004] 1 Lloyd's Rep. 67, CA that when an ex parte application for leave to enforce award was made under s.26 of the Arbitration Act 1950, an action was brought for the purposes of s.7 above. This was because such an application was an alternative to proceeding by way of writ or originating summons.

**Accrual of cause of action**

8–16 It was also common ground in the above case that time runs, not from the date upon which the award is made or published, but from the date when the paying party is in breach of its implied obligation to pay the award.

*GENERAL RULE FOR ACTIONS ON A SPECIALTY*

## Time limit for actions on a specialty

8–17 **8.**—(1) An action upon a specialty shall not be brought after the expiration of twelve years from the date on which the cause of action accrued.

***Paragraph numbers marked with a "+" can be found online and on CD.***

(2) Subsection (1) above shall not affect any action for which a shorter period of limitation is prescribed by any other provision of this Act.

**Claims to recover money**

See the note to s.9 below. **8–18**

*ACTIONS FOR SUMS RECOVERABLE BY STATUTE*

## Time limit for actions for sums recoverable by statute

**9.**—(1) An action to recover any sum recoverable by virtue of any enactment shall not be brought after the expiration of six years from the date on which the cause of action accrued. **8–19**

(2) Subsection (1) above shall not affect any action to which section 10 of this Act applies.

**Claim to recover money**

The reference in subsection (1) to any sum is not limited to claims for liquidated sums of money. The scheme of the Act is to impose a 6 year limitation period on claims for money under an enactment, thus constituting an exception to the general rule as regards specialties: *Rowan Companies Inc v Lambert Eggink Offshore Transport Consultants V.O.F.* [1999] 2 Lloyd's Rep 443. **8–20**

## Special time limit for claiming contribution

**10.**—(1) Where under section 1 of the Civil Liability (Contribution) Act 1978 any person becomes entitled to a right to recover contribution in respect of any damage from any other person, no action to recover contribution by virtue of that right shall be brought after the expiration of two years from the date on which that right accrued. **8–21**

(2) For the purposes of this section the date on which a right to recover contribution in respect of any damage accrues to any person (referred to below in this section as "the relevant date") shall be ascertained as provided in subsections (3) and (4) below.

(3) If the person in question is held liable in respect of that damage—

(a) by a judgment given in any civil proceedings; or

(b) by an award made on any arbitration;

the relevant date shall be the date on which the judgment is given, or the date of the award (as the case may be).

For the purposes of this subsection no account shall be taken of any judgment or award given or made on appeal in so far as it varies the amount of damages awarded against the person in question.

(4) If, in any case not within subsection (3) above, the person in question makes or agrees to make any payment to one or more persons in compensation for that damage (whether he admits any liability in respect of the damage or not), the relevant date shall be the earliest date on which the amount to be paid by him is agreed between him (or his representative) and the person (or each of the persons, as the case may be) to whom the payment is to be made.

(5) An action to recover contribution shall be one to which sections 28, 32 and 35 of this Act apply, but otherwise Parts II and III

*Paragraph numbers marked with a "+" can be found online and on CD.*

of this Act (except sections 34, 37 and 38) shall not apply for the purposes of this section.

**Operation of this section**

8–22 This section is derived from para.6 of Schedule I to the Civil Liability (Contribution) Act 1978. It prescribes the time limit within which a claim to recover contribution may be brought under s.1 of that Act against any other person as defined by s.6(1). Section 10 provides that the claim to recover contribution must not be brought more than two years from the date upon which that right accrued. That date is referred to in s.10 as "the relevant date." It has been held that the judgment or award referred to in s.10(3) as setting the relevant date for the running of time against a tortfeasor who seeks contribution under the 1978 Act is a judgment or award which ascertains the quantum, and not merely the existence, of the tortfeasor's liability: *Aer Lingus Plc v Gildacroft Ltd* [2006] EWCA Civ 4; [2006] 2 All E.R. 290, CA.

If the right to recover contribution arises from a judgment or award then the relevant date is the date of judgment or award. If the amount of the judgment or award is varied on appeal the relevant date remains the date of the judgment at first instance or the original award. Presumably, if no right to contribution arose until the decision on appeal then the date of judgment of the higher court would be the relevant date.

If the right to recover contribution arises from an agreement to settle (whether liability be admitted or not) then the relevant date is the date of agreement, *not* the date of payment. *Semble*, if payment into court (now a Part 36 offer) is made and accepted, the relevant date would be the date of acceptance.

The two year period may be extended where the person claiming contribution is under a disability (s.28) or under s.32 where fraud, concealment or mistake are present.

And, by subs.(5), an action for contribution is one by definition to which s.35 applies; i.e. the same rules as to the date of bringing of third party proceedings, set-offs and counterclaims as are laid down by s.35 in the case of actions generally are also to apply to actions for contribution.

This section sets a time limit for the bringing of the contribution proceedings themselves. There remains the question of the effect on contribution proceedings of the expiry of the period of limitation applicable between the person who has suffered the damage and the person claiming contribution. The effect of s.1(2) of the Civil Liability (Contribution) Act 1978 appears to be that the running of time as between such person and the person claiming contribution does not affect the entitlement to recover contribution provided that immediately before the person claiming contribution made or was ordered or agreed to make the payment in respect of which contribution is sought, he (i.e. the person claiming) was liable in respect of the damage. Thus, he will not be entitled to recover where, for example, the claim against him by the person who has suffered the damage is settled at a time when an action brought upon that claim would be statute-barred. The drafting of s.1 of the 1978 Act is not without its difficulties and for a full commentary see Current Law Statutes Annotated 1978, Chap. 47.

*ACTIONS IN RESPECT OF WRONGS CAUSING PERSONAL INJURIES OR DEATH*

## Special time limit for actions in respect of personal injuries

8–23 **11.**—(1) This section applies to any action for damages for negligence, nuisance or breach of duty (whether the duty exists by virtue of a contract or of provision made by or under a statute or independently of any contract or any such provision) where the damages claimed by the plaintiff for the negligence, nuisance or breach of duty consist of or include damages in respect of personal injuries to the plaintiff or any other person.

(1A) This section does not apply to any action brought for damages under section 3 of the Protection from Harassment Act 1997.

***Paragraph numbers marked with a "+" can be found online and on CD.***

(2) None of the time limits given in the preceding provisions of this Act shall apply to an action to which this section applies.

(3) An action to which this section applies shall not be brought after the expiration of the period applicable in accordance with subsection (4) or (5) below.

(4) Except where subsection (5) below applies, the period applicable is three years from—

(a) the date on which the cause of action accrued; or

(b) the date of knowledge (if later) of the person injured.

(5) If the person injured dies before the expiration of the period mentioned in subsection (4) above, the period applicable as respects the cause of action surviving for the benefit of his estate by virtue of section 1 of the Law Reform (Miscellaneous Provisions) Act 1934 shall be three years from—

(a) the date of death, or

(b) the date of the personal representative's knowledge;

whichever is the later.

(6) For the purposes of this section "personal representative" includes any person who is or has been a personal representative of the deceased, including an executor who has not proved the will (whether or not he has renounced probate) but not anyone appointed only as a special personal representative in relation to settled land; and regard shall be had to any knowledge acquired by any such person while a personal representative or previously.

(7) If there is more than one personal representative, and their dates of knowledge are different, subsection (5)(b) above shall be read as referring to the earliest of those dates.

*Note* — Subsection (1A) was added by the Protection from Harassment Act 1997 s.6. **8–24**
For notes on ss.11 to 14 of this Act see commentary which follows s.14, below.

## Actions in respect of defective products

**11A.**—(1) This section shall apply to an action for damages by **8–25**
virtue of any provision of Part I of the Consumer Protection Act 1987.

(2) None of the time limits given in the preceding provisions of this Act shall apply to an action to which this section applies.

(3) An action to which this section applies shall not be brought after the expiration of the period of ten years from the relevant time, within the meaning of section 4 of the said Act of 1987; and this subsection shall operate to extinguish a right of action and shall do so whether or not that right of action had accrued, or time under the following provisions of this Act had begun to run, at the end of the said period of ten years.

(4) Subject to subsection (5) below, an action to which this section applies in which the damages claimed by the plaintiff consist of or include damages in respect of personal injuries to the plaintiff or any other person or loss of or damage to any property, shall not be brought after the expiration of the period of three years from whichever is the later of—

(a) the date on which the cause of action accrued; and



LIMITATION

(b) the date of knowledge of the injured person or, in the case of loss of or damage to property, the date of knowledge of the plaintiff or (if earlier) of any person in whom his cause of action was previously vested.

(5) If in a case where the damages claimed by the plaintiff consist of or include damages in respect of personal injuries to the plaintiff or any other person the injured person died before the expiration of the period mentioned in subsection (4) above, that subsection shall have effect as respects the cause of action surviving for the benefit of his estate by virtue of section 1 of the Law Reform (Miscellaneous Provisions) Act 1934 as if for the reference to that period there were substituted a reference to the period of three years from whichever is the later of—

(a) the date of death; and

(b) the date of the personal representative's knowledge.

(6) For the purposes of this section "personal representative" includes any person who is or has been a personal representative of the deceased, including an executor who has not proved the will (whether or not he has renounced probate) but not anyone appointed only as a special personal representative in relation to settled land, and regard shall be had to any knowledge acquired by any such person while a personal representative or previously.

(7) If there is more than one personal representative and their dates of knowledge are different, subsection (5)(b) above shall be read as referring to the earliest of those dates.

(8) Expressions used in this section or section 14 of this Act and in Part I of the Consumer Protection Act 1987 have the same meanings in this section or that section as in that Part; and section 1(1) of that Act (Part I to be construed as enacted for the purpose of complying with the product liability Directive) shall apply for the purpose of construing this section and the following provisions of this Act so far as they relate to an action by virtue of any provision of that Part as it applies for the purpose of construing that Part.

**8–26** *Note*—Added by the Consumer Protection Act 1987 s.6, s.50(2) and Sch.1, para.1.

For notes on ss.11 to 14 of this Act see commentary which follows s.14, below.

For a case deciding that the 10-year long-stop provision under s.11A(3) is a period of limitation for the purposes of s.35(3) of the Act, and that the court had a discretion pusuant to s.35 and to CPR r.19.5 to allow substitution of the defendant after the expiry of such time limit, see *Horne-Roberts vSmithKline Beecham Plc* [2001] EWCA Civ 2006.

## Special time limit for actions under Fatal Accidents legislation

**8–27** **12.**—(1) An action under the Fatal Accidents Act 1976 shall not be brought if the death occurred when the person injured could no longer maintain an action and recover damages in respect of the injury (whether because of a time limit in this Act or in any other Act, or for any other reason). Where any such action by the injured person would have been barred by the time limit in section 11 or 11A of this Act, no account shall be taken of the possibility of that time limit being overridden under section 33 of this Act.

(2) None of the time limits given in the preceding provisions of this Act shall apply to an action under the Fatal Accidents Act 1976, but no such action shall be brought after the expiration of three years from—

(a) the date of death; or

(b) the date of knowledge of the person for whose benefit the action is brought;

whichever is the later.

(3) An action under the Fatal Accidents Act 1976 shall be one to which sections 28, 33 and 35 of this Act apply, and the application to any such action of the time limit under subsection (2) above shall be subject to section 39; but otherwise Parts II and III of this Act shall not apply to any such action.

*Note*—Amended by the Consumer Protection Act 1987 s.6(6), 50(2) and Sch.1, para.2. **8–28**

For notes on ss.11 to 14 of this Act see commentary which follows s.14, below.

## Operation of time limit under section 12 in relation to different dependants

**13.**—(1) Where there is more than one person for whose benefit an action under the Fatal Accidents Act 1976 is brought, section 12(2)(b) of this Act shall be applied separately to each of them. **8–29**

(2) Subject to subsection (3) below, if by virtue of subsection (1) above the action would be outside the time limit given by section 12(2) as regards one or more, but not all, of the persons for whose benefit it is brought, the court shall direct that any person as regards whom the action would be outside that limit shall be excluded from those for whom the action is brought.

(3) The court shall not give such a direction if it is shown that if the action were brought exclusively for the benefit of the person in question it would not be defeated by a defence of limitation (whether in consequence of section 28 of this Act or an agreement between the parties not to raise the defence, or otherwise).

*Note*—For notes on ss.11 to 14 of this Act see commentary which follows s.14, below. **8–30**

## Definition of date of knowledge for purposes of sections 11 and 12

**14.**—(1) Subject to subsection (1A) below, in sections 11 and 12 of this Act references to a person's date of knowledge are references to the date on which he first had knowledge of the following facts— **8–31**

(a) that the injury in question was significant; and

(b) that the injury was attributable in whole or in part to the act or omission which is alleged to constitute negligence, nuisance or breach of duty; and

(c) the identity of the defendant, and

(d) if it is alleged that the act or omission was that of a person other than the defendant, the identity of that person and the additional facts supporting the bringing of an action against the defendant;

and knowledge that any acts or omissions did or did not, as a matter of law, involve negligence, nuisance or breach of duty is irrelevant.

(1A) In section 11A of this Act and in section 12 of this Act so far as that section applies to an action by virtue of section 6(1)(a) of the Consumer Protection Act 1987 (death caused by defective product) references to a person's date of knowledge are references to the date on which he first had knowledge of the following facts—

(a) such facts about the damage caused by the defect as would lead a reasonable person who had suffered such damage to consider it sufficiently serious to justify his instituting proceedings for damages against a defendant who did not dispute liability and was able to satisfy a judgment; and

(b) that the damage was wholly or partly attributable to the facts and circumstances alleged to constitute the defect; and

(c) the identity of the defendant;

but, in determining the date on which a person first had such knowledge there shall be disregarded both the extent (if any) of that person's knowledge on any date of whether particular facts or circumstances would or would not, as a matter of law, constitute a defect and, in a case relating to loss of or damage to property, any knowledge which that person had on a date on which he had no right of action by virtue of Part I of that Act in respect of the loss or damage.

(2) For the purposes of this section an injury is significant if the person whose date of knowledge is in question would reasonably have considered it sufficiently serious to justify his instituting proceedings for damages against a defendant who did not dispute liability and was able to satisfy a judgment.

(3) For the purposes of this section a person's knowledge includes knowledge which he might reasonably have been expected to acquire—

(a) from facts observable or ascertainable by him, or

(b) from facts ascertainable by him with the help of medical or other appropriate expert advice which it is reasonable for him to seek;

but a person shall not be fixed under this subsection with knowledge of a fact ascertainable only with the help of expert advice so long as he has taken all reasonable steps to obtain (and, where appropriate, to act on) that advice.

**8–32** *Note*—Subsection (1A) inserted by the Consumer Protection Act 1987 s.6(6), s.50(2) and Sch.1, para.3.

**Actions for damages for personal injuries or death**

**8–33** Sections 11–14 and 28 and 33 re-enact the provisions of the Limitation Act 1975.

The main changes introduced by the Act of 1975, and embodied in the provisions of the Act of 1980, may be summarised as follows:

***Paragraph numbers marked with a "+" can be found online and on CD.***

(1) the introduction of new time limits for commencing

(a) actions for personal injuries (s.11);

(b) actions under the Law Reform (Miscellaneous Provisions) Act 1934 (see s.11(5)); and

(c) actions under the Fatal Accidents Act 1976 (see ss.12, 13).

(2) the introduction of a new time limit for commencing such actions, namely, "the date of knowledge" if later than the date of actual accrual of the cause of action. "Date of knowledge" is defined by s.14; and see paras 8–29, 8–30 and 8–31 below.

(3) the introduction of a power conferred on the court to "override" or "disapply" the time limits provided, in the sense that an action may be allowed to proceed notwithstanding the expiry of such time limits; see s.33, below (para.8–88).

(4) the abolition of the need for obtaining the leave of the court for the purposes of the Limitation Act 1963.

(5) the exclusion of the limitation period in case of disability (see s.28 of the 1980 Act).

These statutory provisions of the 1980 Act, embodying those of the 1975 Act, do not envisage the need for rules of court to govern their operation, and no such rules have been made; nevertheless, they will inevitably have a great influence on the conduct of actions for personal injuries or death. See for the practice in relation to the pleading of matters arising under ss.11–14, SCP 1999, Vol.1, paras 18/8/23 to 18/8/26 *et seq*.

The statutory provisions do not affect periods of limitation prescribed by other enactments, e.g. Merchant Shipping Act 1995, Carriage by Air Act 1961, Nuclear Installations Act 1965, and the International Transport Conventions Act 1983 (see 1980 Act s.39).

The defendant may, in a case where the cause of action arose sufficiently long ago, be entitled to rely on accrued limitation defences under the regime of the unamended Limitation Act 1939: see *Arnold v Central Electricity Generating Board*, applied in *McDonnell v Congregation of Christian Brothers Trustees*, both cited at para.8–3 above.

**Time limits for actions for personal injuries**

For the purposes of s.11, an action for personal injuries includes any action for damages for negligence, nuisance or breach of duty (whether the duty exists by virtue of a contract or of a provision made by or under a statute or independently of any contract or any such provision) where the damages claimed by the plaintiff for the negligence, nuisance or breach of duty consist of or include damages in respect of personal injuries to the plaintiff or any other person (subs.(1)); and personal injuries include any disease and any impairment of a person's physical or mental condition; and "injury" and cognate expressions are to be construed accordingly (s.38(1)). **8–34**

The definition of personal injuries (*cf*. O.1, r.4) is wide enough to cover all proceedings, whether in tort or contract or under statute, in which a claim is made for personal injuries. In its judgment *A v Hoare* delivered on January 30, 2008 the House of Lords has departed from its decision in *Stubbings v Webb* and has held that claims for damages for trespass to the person causing personal injury including claims for sexual abuse fall within s.11(1) as being actions for damages for negligence, nuisance or breach of duty reaffirming the law as laid down in *Letang v Cooper* [1965] 1 Q.B. 232, CA. Accordingly, whilst the primary limitation period is three years from accrual of the cause of action, extension is possible under s.14 (three years from date of knowledge); and exclusion of the period is possible under s.33 (discretionary power of the court).

It should be noted that the other ground on which *Letang v Cooper* was decided, namely that no cause of action in trespass to the person lies for negligent driving, was held by *Stubbings v Webb* to be correct.

A claim by a daughter against her mother for breach of her duty as a parent to protect her against the risk of foreseeable injury from sexual abuse by her father was not a claim for trespass to the person. Distinguishing *Stubbings v Webb* it was held that the action fell within section 11. Subject to the primary limitation period, extensions were possible under both ss.14 and 33; *S. v W.* [1995] 1 F.L.R. 862 [1995] P.I.Q.R. 470, CA.

***Paragraph numbers marked with a "+" can be found online and on CD.***



LIMITATION

It has been held at first instance that a claim under s.2(2) of the Animals Act 1971 is not a claim for "negligence, nuisance or breach of duty" within s.11: *Clarke v Barber* [2002] 5 C.L. 70.

Although a failed sterilisation operation is not itself a personal injury within the meaning of s.38(1), the subsequent unwanted pregnancy is such an injury, in the sense of an "impairment". The whole claim for damages, including economic loss, was barred by the three year rule under s.11 (*Walkin v S. Manchester HA* [1995] 1 W.L.R. 1543; [1995] 1 W.L.R. 1543, CA). *Walkin* was applied, subject to a ruling under s.33, in *Godfrey v Gloucestershire Royal Infirmary NHS Trust* [2003] Lloyd's Rep. Med. 398 (a case of alleged negligent advice leading to failure to terminate a pregnancy in the case of an injured child).

A claim for damages in respect of a failure to address a dyslexic's difficulties in reading and writing so as to ameliorate the effects of that condition was a claim for personal injuries and thus subject to the provisions of ss.11 and 14: *Adams v Bracknell Forest BC* [2004] UKHL 29; [2004] 3 W.L.R. 89, HL.

A cause of action for *Francovich* damages against the Government for failing to implement a relevant Directive, whereby a claim for damages for personal injuries was less valuable than it should have been, accrued at the date of the accident notwithstanding that the loss could not be quantified at that point (*Spencer v Secretary of State for Work and Pensions; Moore v same* [2008] EWCA Civ 750, CA). In *Moore* the court held that the case could not be regarded as one in which there was a continuous breach by the Government.

The question whether an action is for damages in respect of personal injuries is one of substance, not a matter of pleading (*Walkin's* case, applying *Howe v David Brown Tractors (Retail) Ltd* [1991] 4 All E.R. 30, CA).

A claim containing claims for both damages for personal injuries and for damages for economic loss which is time-barred under s. 11 may be amended by permission by deletion of the claim for personal injuries if the remaining claim would not have been barred if raised in new proceedings commenced at the time of the hearing of the application to amend. In a proper case, the amendment may be allowed under CPR r.17.4(2) where the new claim can be regarded as arising "out of the same facts or substantially the same facts": *Shade v The Compton Partnership* [2000] Lloyd's Rep. P.N. 81, CA. The court went further in *Pounds v Eckford Rands* [2003] Lloyd's Rep. P.N. 195, holding that a claim for damages for personal injuries and financial loss as a result of negligence might be amended by excising the claim for personal injuries when each element of the claim would have been time-barred at the date of application for permission to amend. The remaining, narrowed, claim was not a new claim; even if it was, it fell squarely within CPR 17.4(2).

Section 11(1) does not apply to an action for breach of contract against insurance brokers to arrange cover for a passenger who suffers personal injuries (*Ackbar v C.F. Green & Co Ltd* [1975] Q.B. 582).

A claim for damages against a solicitor for negligence in permitting an action by the plaintiff for damages for personal injury to be struck out for want of prosecution is not itself a claim for damages in respect of personal injury. See *Hopkins v MacKenzie* [1995] 6 Med.L.R. 26, CA. Nor is a claim by an employee against his employers for failing to advise him as to the benefits to which he was entitled on suffering personal injury in the course of his employment: *Gould v Leeds HA, The Times*, May 14, 1999, CA. But a claim against solicitors for alleged mishandling of a case, causing clinical depression, is a claim which includes damages for personal injuries: *Bennett v Greenland Houchen & Co* [1998] P.N.L.R. 458, CA.

An action will include a claim "in respect of personal injuries to the plaintiff or any other person" where a firm claims damages for loss of profits by reason of injury to one of its partners (*Howe v David Brown Tractors (Retail) Ltd* [1991] 4 All E.R. 30, CA).

On the other hand, s.11, which provides the time limit for actions for personal injuries, does not apply to actions under the Fatal Accidents Act, as to which a separate limitation period is provided (see s.12).

For actions for personal injuries (except for claims for the benefit of the estate of a deceased under the Law Reform (Misc. Prov.) Act 1934 s.1) the limitation period for commencing such actions runs from:

(a) the date on which the cause of action accrued; or

(b) the date (if later) of the plaintiff's knowledge (s.11(3) and (4)).

Thus, for such actions, s.11 of the 1980 Act has preserved unchanged the existing period of three years and it has also preserved the general rule that this limitation period will run from the date on which the cause of action accrued, including presumably the rule that in an action in tort the cause of action accrues at the date on which the injury was suffered, whether or not it was then apparent (see *Cartledge v Jopling* [1963] A.C. 758). On the other hand if "the date of knowledge" of the plaintiff is later than the date on which the cause of action accrued, the limitation period will run from such date of knowledge. As to what is the "date of knowledge," see s.14(1)–(3).

The use of the expression in ss.11(3) and 12(1) that "an action ... shall not be brought" has not altered the law that an action may be brought without the leave of the court after the expiry of the limitation periods, leaving the defendant, if he so wishes, to raise the defence of the limitation period (see *Dawkins v Lord Penrhyn* (1878) 4 App.Cas. 51, per Earl Cairns L.C. at 59; *Dismore v Milton* [1938] 3 All E.R. 762, CA).

**Time limits for actions under Law Reform (Misc. Prov.) Act 1934 s.1**

In an action under the Law Reform (Misc. Prov.) Act 1934 s.1, by or on behalf of **8–35** the estate of an injured person who dies, e.g. a claim for loss of expectation of life (so far as such an action may still survive: see ss.1 and 73 of the Administration of Justice Act 1982), the limitation period is three years from (a) the date of his death or (b) the date of knowledge of his personal representative, whichever is the later (s.11(5)) or if there is more than one personal representative and their dates of knowledge are different, from the earliest date of knowledge of any of them (s.11(7)). Such an action will lie where an action has been started by him in his lifetime and continued by his personal representatives or the action is started by his personal representatives within three years of his death or within three years of the earliest date of knowledge of any one of them whichever is the later (s.11(5) of the Act). On the other hand, such an action will be barred if the injured person dies *after* the expiration of the period in which he could have brought the action during his own lifetime (*ibid.*); but in such a case the court has power to override the time-limits under s.33 (see subss.(4) and (5)). If however the deceased has brought an action in his own lifetime, a claim by his estate under the 1943 Act may be barred under the *Walkley* principle. The estate is in no better position in this respect than the deceased: *Young (Deceased) v Western Power Distribution (South West) Plc* [2003] EWCA Civ 1034, CA.

**Time limits under the Fatal Accidents Act**

In an action under the Fatal Accidents Act 1976, the limitation period is three years **8–36** from (a) the date of death or (b) the date of knowledge of the persons for whose benefit the action is brought, whichever is the later (s.12(2)). If, however, an action brought under the Fatal Accidents Acts is out of time by virtue of this provision, the court may nevertheless allow the action to proceed in the exercise of its discretion under s.33 of the Act.

On the other hand, an action under the Fatal Accidents Act may not be brought if at the time of his death the injured person could no longer maintain an action and recover damages in respect of the injury, whether because of a time limit in the Act (see *Williams v Mersey Docks and Harbour Board* [1905] 1 K.B. 804) or in any other Act or for any other reason, e.g. because he had settled his claim, s.12(1). And if the action by the injured person would have been barred by the time limit in s.11 of the Act, no account may be taken of the possibility that such time limit may be overridden by the court under s.33 of the Act, though the court still has power to exercise its discretion under s.33 of the Act in an action under the Fatal Accidents Act in favour of the *dependants* of the deceased.

In the case of a dependant under disability in an action under the Fatal Accidents Act 1976, the period of limitation is extended to within three years of the disability ceasing (see ss.12(3) and 28).

Where, in an action under the Fatal Accidents Act, there are a number of dependants whose dates of knowledge differ, the date of knowledge from which the limitation period is to be calculated must be applied separately to each of them (see s.13(1) of the Act) and if one or more of them, but not all, are debarred, any person so debarred will be excluded from those for whom the action is brought unless it is shown that if the action were brought exclusively for the benefit of that person, it would not be defeated by a defence of limitation whether in consequence of s.28 of the

Act or an agreement between the parties not to raise the defence or otherwise, e.g. where such dependant could rely on s.33 (s.13(3)).

### Time limits for actions from date of knowledge

8–37 The House of Lords has delivered a judgment on January 30, 2008 in *A v Hoare* [2008] UKHL 6 which has significant effect on the proper construction of s.14(2) of the Act, holding that the test in s.14(2) is an entirely impersonal standard. The cases cited in the text in paras 8–37 to 8–39must be considered in the light of this decision. An essential feature of this Act re-enacting the Limitation Act 1975 is the extension of the limitation period from the "date of knowledge" of the relevant person, if this is later than the date of the accrual of the cause of action. This fundamental development in the law relating to actions for personal injuries or death was designed to overcome the rule that in actions in tort the cause of action accrues when the damage first occurs and not when the plaintiff first discovers the same, by which time his action may already have become statute-barred (see *Cartledge v E. Jopling & Sons Ltd* [1963] A.C. 758; *Higgins v Arfon BC* [1975] 1 W.L.R. 524; [1975] 2 All E.R. 589; see also *Pirelli General Cable Works Ltd v Oscar Faber & Partners* [1983] 2 A.C. 1; [1983] 1 All E.R. 65).

The date of knowledge as the date from which, in a proper case, the limitation period runs applies both to actions for personal injuries (see s.11(4)(b)) including claims under the Law Reform (Misc. Prov.) Act 1934 (see s.11(5)(b)) and to actions under the Fatal Accidents Act 1976 (see s.12(2)(b)).

For the purposes of both ss.11 and 12 of the Act, a person's date of knowledge is defined (see s.14 of the 1980 Act) as a reference to the date on which he had knowledge of the four following facts, namely,

(a) that the injury in question was significant; and
(b) that the injury was attributable in whole or in part to the act or omission which is alleged to constitute negligence, nuisance or breach of duty; and
(c) the identity of the defendant; and
(d) if it is alleged that the act or omission was that of a person other than the defendant, the identity of that person and the additional facts supporting the bringing of an action against the defendant. These four facts are stated conjunctively. The plaintiff must have knowledge of them all. But they are exhaustive (*Dobbie v Medway HA* [1994] 1 W.L.R. 1234, CA).

It has been held that, for the purposes of s.14(1)(b), "attributable" means capable of being attributed to rather than caused by: see *Wilkinson v Ancliff (B.L.T.) Ltd* [1986] 1 W.L.R. 1352, CA, adopted in *Dobbie v Medway HA* [1994] 1 W.L.R. 1234, above, in which it was pointed out that the words of subs.(1)(b) are "that the injury *was* attributable ... to the act or omission which *is* alleged to constitute negligence ..." (emphasis added by the court). Attributability does not mean legal responsibility. It can only refer to causation; per Steyn L.J. at 1247.

It is specifically provided that ignorance of matters of law as to whether any act or omission involved negligence, nuisance or breach of duty is not relevant in determining whether a person had knowledge (see s.14(1)).

A person's knowledge includes knowledge which he might reasonably have been expected to acquire:

(a) from facts observable or ascertainable by him; or
(b) from facts ascertainable by him with the help of medical or other appropriate expert advice which it is reasonable for him to seek (see s.14(3)).

Nevertheless a person is not fixed with knowledge of a fact ascertainable only with the help of expert advice so long as he has taken all reasonable steps to obtain (and where appropriate, to act on) that advice (*ibid.*).

8–38 The plaintiff will not be fixed with knowledge which he might reasonably have been expected to ascertain with the help of a solicitor if that knowledge would not itself have been ascertained by a solicitor acting reasonably on his behalf (*Nash v Eli Lilly & Co* [1991] 2 Med.L.R. 169; *Hepworth v Kerr* [1995] 6 Med.L.R. 135). However, the name of a party liable for a wrongdoing is not, save in exceptional circumstances, a fact ascertainable only with the help of expert advice, and accordingly a claimant may, under ss.14(1)(c) and 14(3)(a), be fixed with constructive knowledge of the identity of the defendant which his advisers, as reasonably competent legal representatives, ought to have acquired: *Henderson v Temple Pier Co Ltd* [1998] 1 W.L.R. 1540; [1998] 3 All E.R. 324, CA.

The questions which the court may have to decide in any case involving the plaintiff's knowledge under s.14(1), (2) and (3) were fully considered by the Court of Appeal in *Nash v Eli Lilly & Co* [1993] 1 W.L.R. 782, [1993] 4 All E.R. 383, CA. In particular, the court's judgment, delivered by Purchas L.J., is addressed to the questions of "significant injury" under s.14(1)(a) and (2), "attributability" for the purposes of s.14(1)(b), and "constructive knowledge" for the purposes of s.14(3). It was held at p.796 that:

(a) "Knowledge" in the meaning of s.14 is a state of mind experienced by the plaintiff actually existing or which might have existed had the plaintiff, acting reasonably, acquired knowledge from the facts observable or ascertainable by him or which he could have acquired with the help of medical or other appropriate expert advice which it was reasonable for him to obtain.

(b) The period of limitation begins to run when the plaintiff can first be said to have knowledge of the nature of his injury to justify the particular plaintiff taking the preliminary steps for the institution of proceedings against the person or persons whose act or omission has caused the significant injury concerned.

(c) By s.14(3) "knowledge" for the purposes of s.14(1) includes knowledge reasonably expected to be acquired. There will be cases in which a firmly held belief actually held by the plaintiff precluded consideration of any further steps which he might reasonably have taken to acquire from knowledge of further facts before initiating proceedings. In other cases the state of the plaintiff's belief would make it reasonable for him to make the further inquiries envisaged in s.14(3). The temporal and circumstantial span of reasonable inquiry will depend on the factual context of the case and the subjective characteristics of the individual plaintiff involved.

(d) It is to be noted that a firm belief held by the plaintiff that his injury was attributable to the act or omission of the defendant, but in respect of which he thought it necessary to obtain reassurance or confirmation from experts, medical or legal, or others, would not be regarded as knowledge until the result of his inquiries was known to him or, if he delayed in obtaining that confirmation, until the time at which it was reasonable for him to have got it. If negative expert advice is obtained, that fact must be considered in combination with all other relevant facts in deciding when, if ever, the plaintiff had knowledge. If no inquiries were made, then, if it were reasonable for such inquiries to have been made, and if the failure to make them is not explained, constructive knowledge within the terms of s.14(3) must be considered. If the plaintiff held a firm belief which was of sufficient certainty to justify the taking of the preliminary steps for proceedings by obtaining advice about making a claim for compensation, then such belief is knowledge and the limitation period would begin to run.

(e) Finally it is important to remember where the onus of proof lies. If the writ is not issued within three years of the date when the cause of action arose (s.11(4)(a)), the onus is on the plaintiff to plead and prove a date within the three years preceding the date of the issue of the writ (s. 11(4)(b)). If the defendant wishes to rely on a date prior to the three year period immediately preceding the issue of the writ, the onus is on the defendant to prove that the plaintiff had or ought to have had knowledge by that date.

The passage cited above on the onus of proof has been subject to comment by Mance, J. (as he then was) in *Crocker v British Coal Corp* [1996] 29 B.M.L.R. 159 at 172 and 173. The judge held that there cannot be opposing legal onuses on opposite parties on the single issue whether there was or was not knowledge within the three year period. He held that the legal burden rests throughout on the claimant, whether the issue is when the cause of action accrued or when the claimant first had knowledge of the facts in the sense identified in s.14. An issue as to constructive knowledge arising under s.14(3) is however apt to involve an evidential burden on a defendant, at all events if there is nothing in the claimant's own case or evidence to raise the issue, although in some respects, for example in relation to the words "so long as he had taken all reasonable steps to obtain (and, where appropriate, to act on) that advice" in the proviso where they became material, it may be easy to envisage both the legal and an evidential burden on a claimant.

Further, the dictum in (c) above, that the enquiry will depend on the subjective

***Paragraph numbers marked with a "+" can be found online and on CD.***

characteristics of the individual claimant involved, has been disapproved by the House of Lords in *Adams v Bracknell Forest BC* [2004] UKHL 29; [2004] 3 W.L.R. 89, HL: see the commentary in para.8–39 below.

In relation to the question of "attributability" the court held, at p.799, "it was not, in our judgment, the intention of Parliament to require for the purposes of s.11 and s.14 of the Act proof of knowledge of the terms in which it will be alleged that the act or omission of the defendants constituted negligence or breach of duty. What is required is knowledge of the essence of the act or omission to which the injury is attributable".

This view has been reinforced by the Court of Appeal in *Broadley v Guy Clapham & Co.* [1994] 4 All E.R. 439, CA, where it was held that there was nothing in s.14 of the Limitation Act 1980 to suggest that the plaintiff must have known that the defendant's act or omission was capable of being attributed to some fault on his part, and the words "which is alleged to constitute negligence, nuisance or breach of duty" were intended to identify the facts of which the plaintiff had knowledge, without implying that she needed to know that there was some breach of rule.

This decision was followed in *Fennan v Anthony Hodari & Co* [2001] Lloyd's Rep. PN 183, CA (a case where the claimant did not know that the defendant's omission to tell her the nature and effect of a document amounted to a breach of duty of care). See further, as to the issue of attributability, the authorities cited in the note to s.14A, at para.8–43 below.

Furthermore, the court has firmly rejected the argument that the plaintiff must know that he has a possible cause of action (*Dobbie v Medway HA* [1994] 1 W.L.R. 1234, aboveat p.1248). Likewise, in *Whitfield v North Durham HA* [1995] 6 Med L.R. 32, CA, it was held that the court must look at the essence of a complaint and enquire how far the plaintiff had knowledge in broad terms of the facts on which it was based. It was erroneous to seek to anticipate how the case might ultimately be put—in terms of positive act or negligent omission. The issue of an earlier writ claiming damages for the negligence alleged may itself not be determinative of the plaintiff's state of knowledge.

**Significant injury**. The test for the purpose of deciding knowledge of significant injury under s.14(2) was explained by Geoffrey Lane L.J. in *McCafferty v Receiver for the Metropolitan Police District* [1977] 1 W.L.R. 1073, CA at 1081 as follows:

> "... it is clear that the test is partly a subjective test, namely: 'would this plaintiff have considered the injury sufficiently serious?' And partly an objective test, namely: 'would he have been reasonable if he did not regard it as sufficiently serious?' It seems to me that the subsection is directed at the nature of the injury as known to the plaintiff at that time. Taking that plaintiff, with that plaintiff's intelligence, would he have been reasonable in considering the injury not sufficiently serious to justify instituting proeedings for damages?"

Such a test was followed by the Court of Appeal in *Nash v Eli Lilly & Co*, above, and in *KR v Bryn Alyn Community (Holdings) Ltd* [2003] EWCA Civ 85; [2003] Q.B. 1441; [2003] 3 W.L.R. 107; [2004] 2 All E.R. 716, CA. It has been held more recently that the test under s.14(2) to determine when a person would reasonably have considered an injury to be sufficiently serious to justify him instituting proceedings for damages is an objective one. That a person was inhibited by the injury from instituting proceedings is a factor to be taken into account: *Young v Catholic Care (Diocese of Leeds)* [2006] EWCA Civ 1534, CA, following *Adams v Bracknell Forest BC* [2004] UKHL 29; [2005] 1 A.C. 76, HL and doubting *KR v Bryn Alyn*, above.

The requirement that the injury of which a plaintiff has knowledge should be "significant" is directed solely to the quantum of the injury and not to the plaintiff's evaluation of its cause, nature or usualness. Time does not run against a plaintiff if he would reasonably have considered it insufficiently serious to justify proceedings against a creditworthy defendant (*Dobbie v Medway HA* [1994] 1 W.L.R. 1234, above at p.1241).

A claimant's contention that he did not have knowledge of a significant injury until he was aware that the physical side effects of the prescibed drug were not justified by its therapeutic value was rejected. Knowledge of significant injury is not determined by such an equation: *Briggs v Pitt-Payne* [1999] Lloyd's Rep. Med. 1, CA.

**8–39** Each case must of course depend on its own facts, but it is thought that the following two cases may provide useful examples of the court's approach when considering questions under s.14. In a case where the plaintiff had been told by a doctor what had happened in the first operation and that a second operation had put things right she was held to have the necessary knowledge even though the precise terms of what had gone wrong were not known to her (*Hendy v Milton Keynes HA* [1992] 3 Med.L.R. 114). Compare *Driscoll-Varley v Parkside HA* [1991] 2 Med.L.R. 346, in which it was held reasonable for the plaintiff not to initiate proceedings while she was still undergoing a long and complex course of treatment at the hands of those persons against whom any action would be directed. She had not known that her injury was attributable to the acts alleged to constitute negligence until she had sought the advice of another surgeon. The burden was on the defendants to establish the constructive knowledge required by s.14(3) and they had failed to do so.

Knowledge was shown where the plaintiff was sufficiently clear in her own mind to establish a causal link between the negligence and her injury. It was not necessary to ask what would have been the reasonable layman's state of mind without seeking expert confirmation (*Spargo v N. Esse HA* [1997] 8 Med.L.R. 125, CA). Applying the third principle in *Spargo* it is necessary to distinguish between a claimant who has a firm belief that he has a significant injury, attributable to his working conditions, especially one which takes him to a solicitor for advice about a claim, a belief which he retains whatever contrary advice he receives, and a claimant who believes that he may have or even probably has, a significant injury which is attributable to his working conditions, but is not sure and feels it necessary to have expert advice on those questions: *Sniezek v Bundy (Letchworth) Ltd* [2000] P.I.Q.R. 213, CA.

In *Forbes v Wandsworth HA* [1997] Q.B. 402; [1996] 3 W.L.R. 1108; [1996] 4 All E.R. 881, CA, the Court of Appeal expressed difficulty with the proposition in *Nash v Eli Lilley & Co*, above at [1993] 1 W.L.R. p.799, that the standard of reasonableness for the purposes of s.14(3) must be qualified by the position, circumstances and character of a particular plaintiff. It was held, by a majority, that a reasonable man of moderate intelligence, such as the deceased in that case, if he thought about the matter, would say that the lack of success of the operation was:

> "Either just one of those things, a risk of the operation or something may have gone wrong and there may have been a want of care; I do not know which, but if I am ever to make a claim, I must find out."

Constructive knowledge was found and the action held statute-barred.

In *Smith v Leicestershire HA* (1996) 36 B.M.L.R. 23 May J. (as he then was) held that the court was bound by the majority decision in *Forbes v Wandsworth HA* [1997] Q.B. 402 to adopt an objective test when applying s. 14(3). His judgment contains a useful review of the leading decisions on the question of knowledge. The Court of Appeal in *Smith* at [1998] Lloyd's Rep. Med. 77, whilst overruling the judge's decision on the facts, held that it was free to decide which of the two conflicting decisions in *Nash* and *Forbes v Wandsworth HA* [1997] Q.B. 402 it should follow. It expressly approved the observations Evans L.J. in *Forbes v Wandsworth HA* [1997] Q.B. 402 that the test of objectivity and reasonableness should be applied. It posed this question "what would the reasonable person have done placed in the situation of the plaintiff?" Moreover, the reasoning in *Forbes* has received the support of the House of Lords. In determining under s.14(3) whether a claimant had knowledge which he might reasonably have been expected to acquire the court was to consider how a reasonable person in the situation of the claimant would have acted, save that (per Lord Hoffmann, Lord Phillips of Worth Matravers and Lord Scott of Foscote) aspects of character or intelligence peculiar to the claimant were to be disregarded: *Adams v Bracknell Forest BC* [2004] UKHL 29; [2004] 3 W.L.R. 89, HL.

Where a plaintiff knows that his injury is attributable to the defendant's act or omission and the injury is sufficiently serious in the eyes of a reasonable man to justify bringing an action, the time limit will not be extended simply because the injury subsequently becomes worse (*Miller v London Electrical Manufacturing Co Ltd* [1976] 2 Lloyd's Rep. 284, applying *Goodchild v Greatness Timber Co Ltd* [1968] 2 Q.B. 37, CA).

**Different injuries.** *KR v Bryn Alyn Community (Holdings) Ltd* [2003] EWCA Civ 85; [2003] Q.B. 1441; [2003] 3 W.L.R. 107; [2004] 2 All E.R. 716, CA, (where the claimants as minors had suffered immediate physical injury and long-term psychiatric injury by reason of sexual abuse) is authority on the impact of s.14 in cases where the claimant's knowledge of the injuries occurs at different times: see in particular paras 37 to 58 of the judgment. In *AB v Ministry of Defence* [2009] EWHC 1225 (QB); *The Times* June 9, 2009 it was held in relation to a claim involving multiple injuries, and to the reference in s.14 (1)(a) to "the injury in question", that the defendant's submission that the first significant injury in time was necessarily the relevant one for the purpose of fixing the date of knowledge could not be applied: *KR v Bryn Alyn* did not lay down a universal proposition of law to that effect. It was an issue of fact to be resolved in each individual case.

**Vicarious liability.** In circumstances where a defendant is held vicariously liable for acts of deliberate abuse by his employee, but not liable by reason of his own negligence, the deliberate abuse does not fall within s.11, and is therefore governed by a non-extendable six years period of limitation rather than an extendable three years period: *KR v Bryn Alyn Community (Holdings) Ltd*, above, at para.108 of the judgment.

As regards the question of knowledge which may, in any particular case, be imputed to the plaintiff only with the help of medical or other appropriate expert advice (see s.14(3)), it should be noted that knowledge of facts which are capable of giving rise to a claim is not knowledge of facts ascertainable only with the help of expert advice (*Halford v Brookes* [1991] 1 W.L.R. 428, CA, where the plaintiff, who realised that her daughter's death was capable of being attributed to the defendants or one or other of them, was held to have the necessary knowledge without recourse to legal advice). Further, only in exceptional circumstances would the name of a party liable for a wrongdoing be a fact ascertainable "only with the help of expert advice": *Henderson v Temple Pier Co Ltd* [1998] 1 W.L.R. 1540; [1998] 3 All E.R. 324, CA.

Where a severely disabled person, dependent on his parents, has brought proceedings after attaining his majority, the question has arisen at first instance whether the knowledge of the parents is attributable to the paintiff for the purposes of ss.11 and 14. Compare, e.g. *Parry v Clwyd HA* [1997] P.I.Q.R. 1 with *O'Driscoll v Dudley HA* [1998] Lloyd's Rep. Med. 210. It is submitted that the decision in *Parry*, that the court is to look exclusively to the knowledge of the plaintiff, is to be preferred on this point. The relevance of a parent's knowledge was treated in *Bates v Leicester HA* [1998] Lloyd's Rep. Med. 93 as related to the information which the plaintiff would have acquired from his parents on the assumption that he ought reasonably to have pressed them for more information. The judge's decision in *O'Driscoll v Dudley HA* [1998] Lloyd's Rep. Med. 210 on constructive knowledge was reversed by the Court of Appeal on the facts: see [1998] Lloyd's Rep. Med. 210, CA. See also *Appleby v Walsall HA* [1999] Lloyd's Rep. 154 in which *Parry v Clwyd HA* was followed.

While in any case a plaintiff may fail the objective test of his knowledge for the purposes of s.11(4)(b) he may nonetheless succeed in an application under s.33 (see para.8–88) to disapply the relevant time limit applying the proper tests under that section (see, e.g. *Brookes v J. & P. Coates (UK) Ltd* [1984] I.C.R. 158).

As regards the identity of the defendant where at the time of his injury the plaintiff did not know the exact identity of his employers (they were described in the statement given to him as "Norwest Holst Group" which did not identify any legal entity) and he learnt of their precise identity only at a later date, it was held that since the action for damages for personal injuries started within three years of such later date, the action was not barred (*Simpson v Norwest Holst Southern Ltd* [1980] 1 W.L.R. 968; [1980] 2 All E.R. 471, CA; and if it were, it would be a case, having regard to all the circumstances, to make it equitable to allow the action to proceed under s.33 of the Act (*ibid.*). See also *Eidi v Dowell Schlumberger SA* [1990] 3 C.L. 269. See further, in relation to cases where the identity of the employer is uncertain or even wrongly stated to the employee, *Cressey v E Timm & Son Ltd* [2005] EWCA Civ 763, CA.

In relation to the pleading of any question of knowledge under s.14 of the Act, and of any right to relief under s.33 thereof, see SCP 1999, Vol.1, para.18.8.25.

8–40 *Note* — **Section 11(3): "shall not be brought"** For the date at which a claim is "brought" having regard to the delivery of a claim form to the court, see *Barnes v St Helen's MBC* [2006] EWCA Civ 1372, CA.

### *ACTIONS IN RESPECT OF LATENT DAMAGE NOT INVOLVING PERSONAL INJURIES*

## Special time limit for negligence actions where facts relevant to cause of action are not known at date of accrual

8–41 **14A.**—(1) This section applies to any action for damages for negligence, other than one to which section 11 of this Act applies, where the starting date for reckoning the period of limitation under subsection (4)(b) below falls after the date on which the cause of action accrued.

(2) Section 2 of this Act shall not apply to an action to which this section applies.

(3) An action to which this section applies shall not be brought after the expiration of the period applicable in accordance with subsection (4) below.

(4) That period is either—

(a) six years from the date on which the cause of action accrued; or

(b) three years from the starting date as defined by subsection (5) below, if that period expires later than the period mentioned in paragraph (a) above.

(5) For the purposes of this section, the starting date for reckoning the period of limitation under subsection (4)(b) above is the earliest date on which the plaintiff or any person in whom the cause of action was vested before him first had both the knowledge required for bringing an action for damages in respect of the relevant damage and a right to bring such an action.

(6) In subsection (5) above "the knowledge required for bringing an action for damages in respect of the relevant damage" means knowledge both—

(a) of the material facts about the damage in respect of which damages are claimed; and

(b) of the other facts relevant to the current action mentioned in subsection (8) below.

(7) For the purposes of subsection (6)(a) above, the material facts about the damage are such facts about the damage as would lead a reasonable person who had suffered such damage to consider it sufficiently serious to justify his instituting proceedings for damages against a defendant who did not dispute liability and was able to satisfy a judgment.

(8) The other facts referred to in subsection (6)(b) above are—

(a) that the damage was attributable in whole or in part to the act or omission which is alleged to constitute negligence; and

(b) the identity of the defendant; and

(c) if it is alleged that the act or omission was that of a person other than the defendant, the identity of that person and the additional facts supporting the bringing of an action against the defendant.

(9) Knowledge that any acts or omissions did or did not, as a matter of law, involve negligence is irrelevant for the purposes of subsection (5) above.

(10) For the purposes of this section a person's knowledge includes knowledge which he might reasonably have been expected to acquire—

(a) from facts observable or ascertainable by him; or



LIMITATION

(b) from facts ascertainable by him with the help of appropriate expert advice which it is reasonable for him to seek;

but a person shall not be taken by virtue of this subsection to have knowledge of a fact ascertainable only with the help of expert advice so long as he has taken all reasonable steps to obtain (and, where appropriate, to act on) that advice.

8–42 *Note*—Added by the Latent Damage Act 1986 s.1

**Knowledge of plaintiff in negligence actions**

8–43 This section was added by the Latent Damage Act 1986 s.1. See para.8–3 above. The plain purpose of the reform was to avoid the injustice which might occur where a cause of action accrued by reason of the existence of damage without the plaintiff being aware of it. In such a case, lapse of a period of six years from the actual occurrence of damage would, ordinarily, bar the right to bring an action. See *Pirelli General Cable Works Ltd v Faber (Oscar) & Partners* [1983] 2 A.C. 1, HL. By the transitional provisions of the Latent Damage Act 1986, some actions will continue to be governed by the law applicable before the introduction of the Act (see s.4). Thus, the new provisions will not enable any action to be brought which was already barred before the new Act came into force; or affect any action commenced before such time. The Act came into force on September 18, 1986 (see s.5(3)). For a full commentary on the provisions of the Act, and on the law as it stood when the Act was passed, see *Current Law Statutes*, Latent Damage Act 1986.

The section applies only to actions for negligence. It has been held that the negligence referred to is negligence in tort only, and that the section does not apply to claims for breach of duty of care arising out of contract: see *Iron Trades Mutual Insurance Co Ltd v J. K. Buckenham Ltd* [1990] 1 All E.R. 808, where the action, so far as it was framed in contract, was struck out as statute-barred. This decision was approved in *Société Commerciale de Réassurance v ERAS (International) Ltd* [1992] 2 All E.R. 82; [1992] 1 Lloyd's Rep. 570, CA, deciding that s.14A is limited to actions for negligence where the duty of care, the breach of which constitutes the negligence relied on, arises solely in tort. In *West Bromwich Building Society v Mander Hadley & Co*, *The Times*, March 9, 1998, CA (a case where the plaintiff wished to guard against future unascertained claims against it outside the limitation period by issuing protective writs claiming contribution) Millett L.J. observed that it was not clear why Parliament had confined the operation of s. 14A so that it was not available for claims in negligence framed in contract; nor why Parliament had not provided that a contingent cause of action should not be treated for limitation purposes as accruing before the contingency occurred. But it was not for the courts to extend the limitation period in hard cases by permitting writs to be issued at a time when the plaintiff was unaware of any valid basis for the claim.

It has been held that the scope of the Latent Damage Act 1986 extends to cover negligent misstatements by professional advisers after the construction of a building; and that, for the purposes of the commencement of the three year period under s.14A, "damage" was the single cause of action suffered by the plaintiff when she bought the house: *Horbury v Craig Hall and Rutley* [1991] E.G.C.S. 81. This decision has been approved in the Court of Appeal in *Hamlin v Edwin Evans*, *The Times*, July 15, 1996, CA. Where the tort complained of was negligence by error or omission in a survey there could only be one cause of action which accrued when the damage was suffered. It made no difference that the damage was multiple or single or whether, if multiple, it came to light at varying times with varying degrees of gravity. Thus, where a claim for lesser defects had been settled but more serious defects were discovered later, it was held that time for the purposes of s.14A ran from the date of knowledge regarding the lesser defects and that a writ issued some two years after discovery of the serious defects was out of time. It has however been held that knowledge of facts relating to a cause of action not relied on by the plaintiff in his claim, being a cause of action truly separate from that on which he does rely, will not enable the defence of limitation to succeed: *Birmingham Midshires Building Society v Wretham* [1999] 07 E.G. 138, a case where the differing nature of the various duties of a solicitor acting for a purchaser or mortgagee is discussed.

***Paragraph numbers marked with a "+" can be found online and on CD.***

The section itself does not provide any definition of when the cause of action accrues: see subs.(4)(a). *Pirelli General Cable Works v Faber (Oscar) & Partners* [1983] 2 A.C. 1, above, and cases decided subsequently thereto (see *Current Law Statutes*, Latent Damage Act 1986), will continue to govern the resolution of this question.

In addition, the extended period provided by subs.(4)(b) arises only where that period itself expires after the period of six years from accrual of the cause of action. In these circumstances, it will in many cases be necessary to determine when the cause of action accrued in order to ascertain whether or not the three year rule under subs.(4)(b) applies. For a full commentary on the question when, for the purposes of the Limitation Act 1980, a cause of action in tort is held to accrue, see McGee, *Limitation Periods* (2002) 4th edn., Chap. 5; and in particular, in relation to that question in the tort of negligence causing either physical damage or economic loss (where recoverable), see *Islander Trucking Ltd v Hogg Robinson & Gardner Mountain (Marine) Ltd* [1990] 1 All E.R. 826.

In *Graham v Entec Europe Ltd* [2003] EWCA Civ 1177; [2003] 4 All E.R. 1345, CA it was held that, in relation to a subrogated claim, the nominal claimant is fixed with the knowledge of the insurer for whose benefit the action was brought; it was appropriate to construe the words "the plantiff" in s.14A(5) as meaning/extending to a plaintiff whether suing in his own name or the name of another by way of subrogation. Further the knowledge of a loss adjuster acting on behalf of insurers for the purpose of pursuing a subrogated claim by the insurers was to be treated as the knowledge of the insurers for the purposes of s.14A(5). Subs.(10) was not engaged.

The provisions of subss.(6)–(10), which relate to ascertaining whether the plaintiff had the requisite knowledge are closely modelled on those of s.14, which relate to actions for personal injuries (see paras 8–29, 8–30 and 8–31 above).

In applying the test propounded in *Nash v Eli Lilly & Co* [1993] 1 W.L.R. 782 (see paras 8–29, 8–30 and 8–31) it is necesssary to ask what a reasonable person placed in the situation of the plaintiff and having his character and intelligence would or would not have done. A reasonable man was one who obeyed the law. Thus a plaintiff seeking to rely upon an extended time-limit under s.14A could not rely on his fear of being exposed as an illegal immigrant as a reason for not seeking professional advice so as to acquire constructive knowledge under s.14A(10) (*Coban v Allen*, *The Times*, October 14, 1996, CA).

Section 14A (8)(a) requires that the act or omission of which the claimant must have knowledge must be that which is causally relevant for the purposes of an allegation of negligence. Section 14A is based on ss.11 and 14, and the authorities decided under s.14(1)(b) were equally applicable to s.14A(8)(a). The claimant did not have to know that he had a cause of action or that the defendant's acts could be characterised as negligent. But the words "which is alleged to constitute negligence" served to identify the facts of which the claimant must have knowledge: *Hallan-Eames v Merrett Syndicates Ltd* [2001] Lloyd's Rep. P.N. 178; [1996] 7 Med. L.R. 122, CA, applying *Broadley v Guy Clapham & Co* [1994] 4 All E.R. 439; [1993] 4 Med. L.R. 328, CA. It was held in *HF Pension Trustees Ltd v Ellison* [1999] Lloyd's Rep. P.N. 489 that the claimants had knowledge for the purposes of s.14A at the time when they made payments under a transfer even though they did not know, and could not have known at the time, that the transfer would subsequently be held unlawful. Mere ignorance that the known facts might give rise to a claim in law could not postpone the running of time. The above case was distinguished in *Haward v Fawcetts* [2004] EWCA Civ 240; [2004] P.N.L.R. 34, CA, in which Jonathan Parker LJ reviewed the authorities, under both s.14 and s.14A, on the issue of attributability.

The decision of the Court of Appeal in *Haward v Fawcetts* has been reversed in the House of Lords [2006] UKHL 9, Lord Nicholls of Birkenhead holding that the relevant date in the application of s.14A(8)(a) was when the claimant first knew enough to justify setting about investigating the possibility that the defendant's advice was defective. The claimant had the burden of proving that this was within three years of bringing the claim. The difficulties of the application of s.14A are well illustrated in the case, Lord Walker of Gestingthorpe, Lord Brown of Eaton-under-Heywood, and Lord Mance doubting the decision of the Court of Appeal in *HF Pension Trustees Ltd v Ellison*, above. As to the test of knowledge of seriousness of the damage to be applied under s.14A(7), see *3M United Kingdom Plc v Linklaters & Paines* [2006] EWCA Civ 530, CA. The decision in that case at first instance also includes the question of knowledge by officers of a corporate claimant: see [2005] P.N.L.R. 46.

***Paragraph numbers marked with a "+" can be found online and on CD.***

It has been held at first instance that the burden of proving the necessary facts to establish the extended time limit under s.14A falls on the plaintiff (*Iron Trades Mutual Insurance Co Ltd v J.K. Buckenham Ltd* [1990] 1 All E.R. 808 at 824). In a case under s.14, rather than s.14A, the Court of Appeal has held that if the writ is not issued within three years of the date when the cause of action arose (see s.11(4)(a)), the onus is on the plaintiff to plead and prove a date within the three years preceding the date of issue of the writ (see s.11(4)(b)). If the defendant wishes to rely on a date prior to the three year period immediately preceding the issue of the writ, the onus is on the defendant to prove that the plaintiff had or ought to have had knowledge by that date (*Nash v Eli Lilly & Co* [1993] 4 All E.R. 383 at 396, CA). See however *Crocker v British Coal Corp* [1996] BMLR 159 at 172 and 173 per Mance J.

Where the question whether the plaintiff did or did not have the requisite knowledge turns on disputed questions of fact it will be inappropriate to decide the matter on an application by the defendant to strike out the cause of action. The issue must be tried, either at trial or by way of preliminary issue (*Iron Trades Mutual Insurance Co Ltd, ibid.*, at 824).

Where the plaintiff seeks to amend to add a new defendant, and the date of the plaintiff's knowledge for the purposes of determining the starting date of the secondary period of limitation is in issue, the court does not lack jurisdiction to decide whether to allow the amendment. The issue may be tried as a preliminary issue in the action (*Busby v Cooper, The Times*, April 15, 1996, CA, approving the note to this effect in the preceding paragraph.

**Deliberate concealment**

8–44 It is expressly provided that s.14A shall not apply to any action to which s.32(1)(b) of the Act applies, i.e. where any fact relevant to the plaintiff's right of action has been deliberately concealed from him by the defendant. To achieve that purpose Parliament, by s.2(2) of the Latent Damage Act 1986, introduced a new subs.(5) into s.32. This ensures that in cases of deliberate concealment the provisions of ss.14A and 14B, with their respective provisions for an extended period of three years from the date of knowledge, and a long stop of 15 years, do not apply. Thus the period of limitation is that laid down by s.2 of the Limitation Act, with the beginning of the period postponed by virtue of s.32 until the plaintiff has discovered the concealment, or could with reasonable diligence have discovered it. See paras 8–63 and 8–64. For a commentary on the provisions of s.32(1)–(4) relating to fraud, concealment or mistake, see *Current Law Statutes*, Limitation Act 1980.

## Overriding time limit for negligence actions not involving personal injuries

8–45 **14B.**—(1) An action for damages for negligence, other than one to which section 11 of this Act applies, shall not be brought after the expiration of fifteen years from the date (or, if more than one, from the last of the dates) on which there occurred any act or omission—

(a) which is alleged to constitute negligence; and

(b) to which the damage in respect of which damages are claimed is alleged to be attributable (in whole or in part).

(2) This section bars the right of action in a case to which subsection (1) above applies notwithstanding that—

(a) the cause of action has not yet accrued; or

(b) where section 14A of this Act applies to the action, the date which is for the purposes of that section the starting date for reckoning the period mentioned in subsection (4)(b) of that section has not yet occurred;

before the end of the period of limitation, prescribed by this section.

8–46 *Note*—Added by the Latent Damage Act 1986 s.1

***Paragraph numbers marked with a "+" can be found online and on CD.***

Section 14B provides a long stop period of 15 years after the day of the negligence relied on; and this even though the cause of action has not yet accrued (e.g. by reason of the absence of any damage) or the starting date for the three year period under s.14A(5), if applicable, has not yet occurred.

It has been held that s.14B is procedural in effect. It was not intended to extinguish the claimant's rights rather than bar his remedy: *Financial Services Compensation Scheme Ltd v Larnell (Insurances) Ltd* [2006] P.N.L.R. 13, CA.

**Deliberate concealment**

See commentary to s.14A above. **8–47**

In *Gwembe Valley Development Co Ltd v Koshy (No.3)* [2004] 1 B.C.L.C. 131, CA, the distinction drawn in *Paragon* , above, between the two classes of case in relation to trusts was applied to cases of breach of fiduciary duty. That distinction was also applied by Lewison J. in *JD Wetherspoon PLC v Van de Berg & Co Ltd* [2007] EWHC 1044; [2007] EWHC 1044; [2007] PNLR 28.

In *Cattley v Pollard* [2006] EWHC 3130 (Ch); [2007] 3 W.L.R. 317 it was held that the second paragraph of s.21(3) of the Act had the effect, where a trustee was suing for beneficiaries where intent had not fallen into possession, that time had not begun to run. The case also applied the decisions in *Paragon* , above, and in *Dubai Aluminium Co Ltd v Salaam* [2002] UKHL 48; [2003] AC 366, HL to claim for dishonest assistance in a fraudulent breach of trust.

## *ACTIONS TO RECOVER LAND AND RENT*

### Time limit for actions to recover land

**15.**—(1) No action shall be brought by any person to recover any land after the expiration of twelve years from the date on which the right of action accrued to him or, if it first accrued to some person through whom he claims, to that person. **8–48**

(2) Subject to the following provisions of this section, where—

(a) the estate or interest claimed was an estate or interest in reversion or remainder or any other future estate or interest and the right of action to recover the land accrued on the date on which the estate or interest fell into possession by the determination of the preceding estate or interest; and

(b) the person entitled to the preceding estate or interest (not being a term of years absolute) was not in possession of the land on that date;

no action shall be brought by the person entitled to the succeeding estate or interest after the expiration of twelve years from the date on which the right of action accrued to the person entitled to the preceding estate or interest or six years from the date on which the right of action accrued to the person entitled to the succeeding estate or interest, whichever period last expires.

(3) Subsection (2) above shall not apply to any estate or interest which falls into possession on the determination of an entailed interest and which might have been barred by the person entitled to the entailed interest.

(4) No person shall bring an action to recover any estate or interest in land under an assurance taking effect after the right of action to recover the land had accrued to the person by whom the assurance was made or some person through whom he claimed or some

*Paragraph numbers marked with a "+" can be found online and on CD.*

person entitled to a preceding estate or interest, unless the action is brought within the period during which the person by whom the assurance was made could have brought such an action.

(5) Where any person is entitled to any estate or interest in land in possession and, while so entitled, is also entitled to any future estate or interest in that land, and his right to recover the estate or interest in possession is barred under this Act, no action shall be brought by that person, or by any person claiming through him, in respect of the future estate or interest, unless in the meantime possession of the land has been recovered by a person entitled to an intermediate estate or interest.

(6) Part I of Schedule 1 to this Act contains provisions for determining the date of accrual of rights of action to recover land in the cases there mentioned.

(7) Part II of that Schedule contains provisions modifying the provisions of this section in their application to actions brought by, or by a person claiming through, the Crown or any spiritual or eleemosynary corporation sole.

8–48.1 *Note*—It has been held that the right of a mortgagee to recover land by virtue of the mortgage was extinguished 12 years after a demand for payment under the mortgage. There was no reason in principle why time should not run from the date when the mortgagee was entitled to possession, whether he unequivocally demanded possession on that date or forbore from doing so while attempting to persuade the mortgagor to pay up: *Ashe v National Westminster Bank* [2007] EWHC 494 (Ch); [2007] B.P.I.R. 988; affirmed on appeal [2008] EWCA Civ 55; [2008] B.P.I.R. 1.

### Time limit for redemption action

8–49 **16.** When a mortgagee of land has been in possession of any of the mortgaged land for a period of twelve years, no action to redeem the land of which the mortgagee has been so in possession shall be brought after the end of that period by the mortgagor or any person claiming through him.

### Extinction of title to land after expiration of time limit

8–50 **17.** Subject to—

(a) section 18 of this Act;

(b) [...]

at the expiration of the period prescribed by this Act for any person to bring an action to recover land (including a redemption action) the title of that person to the land shall be extinguished.

8–51 *Note*—Amended by the Land Registration Act 2002, Sch.13, para.1.

### Settled land and land held on trust

8–52 **18.**—(1) Subject to section 21(1) and (2) of this Act, the provisions of this Act shall apply to equitable interests in land [...] as they apply to legal estates. Accordingly a right of action to recover the land shall, for the purposes of this Act but not otherwise, be treated as accruing to a person entitled in possession to such an equitable interest in the like manner and circumstances, and on the same date, as it would accrue if his interest were a legal estate in the land (and any

*Paragraph numbers marked with a "+" can be found online and on CD.*

relevant provision of Part I of Schedule 1 to this Act shall apply in any such case accordingly).

(2) Where the period prescribed by this Act has expired for the bringing of an action to recover land by a tenant for life or a statutory owner of settled land—

(a) his legal estate shall not be extinguished if and so long as the right of action to recover the land of any person entitled to a beneficial interest in the land either has not accrued or has not been barred by this Act; and

(b) the legal estate shall accordingly remain vested in the tenant for life or statutory owner and shall devolve in accordance with the Settled Land Act 1925;

but if and when every such right of action has been barred by this Act, his legal estate shall be extinguished.

(3) Where any land is held upon trust [...] and the period prescribed by this Act has expired for the bringing of an action to recover the land by the trustees, the estate of the trustees shall not be extinguished if and so long as the right of action to recover the land of any person entitled to a beneficial interest in the land [...] either has not accrued or has not been barred by this Act; but if and when every such right of action has been so barred the estate of the trustees shall be extinguished.

(4) Where—

(a) any settled land is vested in a statutory owner; or

(b) any land is held upon trust [...];

an action to recover the land may be brought by the statutory owner or trustees on behalf of any person entitled to a beneficial interest in possession in the land [...] whose right of action has not been barred by this Act, notwithstanding that the right of action of the statutory owner or trustees would apart from this provision have been barred by this Act.

*Note* —Amended by the Trusts of Land and Appointment of Trustees Act 1996 s.25(2) and Sch.4. **8–53**

## Time limit for actions to recover rent

**19.** No action shall be brought, or distress made, to recover arrears of rent, or damages in respect of arrears of rent, after the expiration of six years from the date on which the arrears became due. **8–54**

## Actions for breach of commonhold duty

**19A.** An action in respect of a right or duty of a kind referred to in section 37(1) of the Commonhold and Leasehold Reform Act 2002 (enforcement) shall not be brought after the expiration of six years from the date on which the cause of action accrued. **8–55**

*Note* —This section was added by the Commonhold and Leasehold Reform Act 2002 (c.15), s.68 and Sc. Regulations made under s.37(1) confer on the courts certain jurisdiction in relation to the enforcement of particular rights and duties arising under Part 1 (Commonhold) of the Act. **8–56**

*Paragraph numbers marked with a "+" can be found online and on CD.*

*ACTIONS TO RECOVER MONEY SECURED BY A MORTGAGE OR CHARGE OR TO RECOVER PROCEEDS OF THE SALE OF LAND*

## Time limit for actions to recover money secured by a mortgage or charge or to recover proceeds of the sale of land

8–57 **20.**—(1) No action shall be brought to recover—

(a) any principal sum of money secured by a mortgage or other charge on property (whether real or personal); or

(b) proceeds of the sale of land;

after the expiration of twelve years from the date on which the right to receive the money accrued.

(2) No foreclosure action in respect of mortgaged personal property shall be brought after the expiration of twelve years from the date on which the right to foreclose accrued.

But if the mortgagee was in possession of the mortgaged property after that date, the right to foreclose on the property which was in his possession shall not be treated as having accrued for the purposes of this subsection until the date on which his possession discontinued.

(3) The right to receive any principal sum of money secured by a mortgage or other charge and the right to foreclose on the property subject to the mortgage or charge shall not be treated as accruing so long as that property comprises any future interest or any life insurance policy which has not matured or been determined.

(4) Nothing in this section shall apply to a foreclosure action in respect of mortgaged land, but the provisions of this Act relating to actions to recover land shall apply to such an action.

(5) Subject to subsections (6) and (7) below, no action to recover arrears of interest payable in respect of any sum of money secured by a mortgage or other charge or payable in respect of proceeds of the sale of land, or to recover damages in respect of such arrears shall be brought after the expiration of six years from the date on which the interest became due.

(6) Where—

(a) a prior mortgagee or other incumbrancer has been in possession of the property charged; and

(b) an action is brought within one year of the discontinuance of that possession by the subsequent incumbrancer;

the subsequent incumbrancer may recover by that action all the arrears of interest which fell due during the period of possession by the prior incumbrancer or damages in respect of those arrears, notwithstanding that the period exceeded six years.

(7) Where—

(a) the property subject to the mortgage or charge comprises any future interest or life insurance policy, and

(b) it is a term of the mortgage or charge that arrears of interest shall be treated as part of the principal sum of money secured by the mortgage or charge;

*Paragraph numbers marked with a "+" can be found online and on CD.*

interest shall not be treated as becoming due before the right to recover the principal sum of money has accrued or is treated as having accrued.

*Note*—In *West Bromwich Building Society v Wilkinson* [2005] UKHL 44; [2005] 1 W.L.R. 2303, the House of Lords held that the cause of action for a debt secured on a mortgage arose, on the construction of the deed, one month after default in payment of a monthly instalment. The subsequent exercise of the power of sale by the mortgagee did not stop time running. Nor did s.20 cease to apply when the security was subsequently realised. **8–58**

## *ACTIONS IN RESPECT OF TRUST PROPERTY OR THE PERSONAL ESTATE OF DECEASED PERSONS*

### Time limit for actions in respect of trust property

**21.**—(1) No period of limitation prescribed by this Act shall apply to an action by a beneficiary under a trust, being an action— **8–59**

(a) in respect of any fraud or fraudulent breach of trust to which the trustee was a party or privy; or

(b) to recover from the trustee trust property or the proceeds of trust property in the possession of the trustee, or previously received by the trustee and converted to his use.

(2) Where a trustee who is also a beneficiary under the trust receives or retains trust property or its proceeds as his share on a distribution of trust property under the trust, his liability in any action brought by virtue of subsection (1)(b) above to recover that property or its proceeds after the expiration of the period of limitation prescribed by this Act for bringing an action to recover trust property shall be limited to the excess over his proper share.

This subsection only applies if the trustee acted honestly and reasonably in making the distribution.

(3) Subject to the preceding provisions of this section, an action by a beneficiary to recover trust property or in respect of any breach of trust, not being an action for which a period of limitation is prescribed by any other provision of this Act, shall not be brought after the expiration of six years from the date on which the right of action accrued.

For the purposes of this subsection, the right of action shall not be treated as having accrued to any beneficiary entitled to a future interest in the trust property until the interest fell into possession.

(4) No beneficiary as against whom there would be a good defence under this Act shall derive any greater or other benefit from a judgment or order obtained by any other beneficiary than he could have obtained if he had brought the action and this Act had been pleaded in defence.

#### Section 21—actions for breach of trust and actions for breach of fiduciary duty

*Paragon Finance Plc v Thakerar & Co* [1999] 1 All E.R. 400; (1998) 95(35) L.S.G. 36, CA elucidates the true nature of the distinction between two different classes of persons described as constructive trustees, namely (1) those holding on trust by virtue of tak- **8–60**

*Paragraph numbers marked with a "+" can be found online and on CD.*

ing possession of property on trust for or on behalf of others before the occurrence of the transaction impeached, and (2) those to whom the description applies only by reason of that transaction. It was held that, arguably, s.21 of the 1980 Act, and its predecessor s.19 of the Limitation Act 1939, have not abrogated that distinction and that s.21 is intended to apply only to trustees of the first description. The limitation period applicable to those of the second description, whether the case against them be put in damages for fraud at common law or by a corresponding claim in equity "for an account as constructive trustee", is six years, though the start of the period may be deferred in such latter cases. Likewise, a claim against an agent for an account in equity, absent any trust, was subject to the statutes of limitation. His liability to account for more than six years before the issue of the writ depended on whether he was, not merely a fiduciary (for every agent owes fiduciary duties to his principal), but a trustee, i.e. on whether he owed fiduciary duties *in relation to the money* (*Nelson v Rye* [1996] 2 All E.R. 186 disapproved). See also *Coulthard v Disco Mix Club Ltd* [1999] 2 All E.R. 457, following *Paragon*. *Paragon* was also followed in *Halton International Inc (Holdings) SARL v Guernroy Ltd* [2006] EWCA Civ 801; [2006] W.T.L.R. 1241, CA where it was held that there were two kinds of constructive trust: those where the defendant had assumed the duties of a trustee by a lawful transaction that was independent of and preceded the breach of trust and was not impeached by the claimant (class 1); and those where the trust obligation arose as a direct consequence of the unlawful transaction that was impeached by the claimant (class 2). Only class I was treated as a trust for the purposes of the exception for trust property in s.21(1) of the Act. In the instant case the new shares came into existence by reason of the transaction impeached. Therefore s.21(1) did not apply and the action was statute-barred.

In *Gwembe Valley v Development Co v Koshy (No.3)* [2004] 1 B.C.L.C. 131, CA, the distinction drawn in *Paragon* above, between the two classes of case in relation to trusts was applied to cases of breach of fiduciary duty. That distinction was also applied by Lewison J. in *J.D. Wetherspoon Plc v Van de Berg & Co Ltd* [2007] EWHC 1044; [2007] P.N.L.R. 28.

In *Cattley v Pollard* [2006] EWHC 3130 (Ch); [2007] 3 W.L.R. 317 it was held that the second paragraph of s.21(3) of the Act had the effect, where a trustee was suing for beneficiaries whose interest had not fallen into possession, that time had not begin to run. The case was applied to the decisions in *Paragon*, above, and in *Dubai Aluminium Co Ltd v Salaam* [2003] 2 A.C. 366, HL to a claim for dishonest assistance in a fraudulent breach of trust.

For a decision on the application of the statute by analogy to claims for equitable damages for breach of fiduciary duty, see *Companha de Seguros Imperio v Heath (REBX) Ltd* [2000] 2 All E.R. (Comm) 787, CA.

On the question of the extent to which an *executor de son tort* is in the same position as a trustee for the purposes of s.21(1)(b), see *James v Williams* [1999] 3 W.L.R. 451, CA.

## Time limit for actions claiming personal estate of a deceased person

8–61 **22.** Subject to section 21(1) and (2) of this Act—

(a) no action in respect of any claim to the personal estate of a deceased person or to any share or interest in any such estate (whether under a will or on intestacy) shall be brought after the expiration of twelve years from the date on which the right to receive the share or interest accrued; and

(b) no action to recover arrears of interest in respect of any legacy, or damages in respect of such arrears, shall be brought after the expiration of six years from the date on which the interest became due.

### *ACTIONS FOR AN ACCOUNT*

## Time limit in respect of actions for an account

8–62 **23.** An action for an account shall not be brought after the expiration of any time limit under this Act which is applicable to the claim which is the basis of the duty to account.

MISCELLANEOUS AND SUPPLEMENTAL

## Time limit for actions to enforce judgments

**24.**—(1) An action shall not be brought upon any judgment after the expiration of six years from the date on which the judgment became enforceable. **8–63**

(2) No arrears of interest in respect of any judgment debt shall be recovered after the expiration of six years from the date on which the interest became due.

### Time limit for actions to enforce judgments

The House of Lords has held that proceedings to execute a judgment debt (in that case by charging and garnishee orders) were not an action upon a judgment within the meaning of s.24(1) and were not barred after six years by that subsection. Action meant a fresh action. But, as to subs.(2), the ordinary meaning of the words barred recovery of arrears of interest in respect of *all* judgments after six years, whether recovery was sought by a fresh action or by execution on the original judgment. Nor did s.32 of the Act apply to extend such period, since the recovery of interest by way of execution was not a "right of action" within the meaning of s.32(1)(b): *Lowsley v Forbes* [1998] 3 W.L.R. 501, HL. Further, an action upon any judgment within the meaning of s.24(1) does not include insolvency proceedings, whether by winding up petition or bankruptcy petition, brought by a judgment creditor: *Ridgeway Motors (Isleworth) Ltd v ALTS Ltd* [2005] EWCA Civ 92; [2005] 2 All E.R. 304, CA, following *WT Lamb & Sons v Rider* [1948] 2 K.B. 331 CA, in which the statutory predecessor of s.24(1) was construed as applying only to suing for a judgment upon a judgment. **8–64**

## Time limit for actions to enforce advowsons and extinction of title to advowsons

**25.** [...] **8–65**

*Note* —Repealed by the Patronage (Benefices) Measure 1986 s.4(3). **8–66**

## Administration to date back to death

**26.** For the purposes of the provisions of this Act relating to actions for the recovery of land and advowsons an administrator of the estate of a deceased person shall be treated as claiming as if there had been no interval of time between the death of the deceased person and the grant of the letters of administration. **8–67**

## Cure of defective disentailing assurance

**27.**—(1) This section applies where— **8–68**

(a) a person entitled in remainder to an entailed interest in any land makes an assurance of his interest which fails to bar the issue in tail or the estates and interests taking effect on the determination of the entailed interest, or fails to bar those estates and interests only, and

(b) any person takes possession of the land by virtue of the assurance.

(2) If the person taking possession of the land by virtue of the as-

***Paragraph numbers marked with a "+" can be found online and on CD.***



LIMITATION

surance, or any other person whatsoever (other than a person entitled to possession by virtue of the settlement) is in possession of the land for a period of twelve years from the commencement of the time when the assurance could have operated as an effective bar, the assurance shall thereupon operate, and be treated as having always operated, to bar the issue in tail and the estates and interests taking effect on the determination of the entailed interest.

(3) The reference in subsection (2) above to the time when the assurance could have operated as an effective bar is a reference to the time at which the assurance, if it had then been executed by the person entitled to the entailed interest, would have operated, without the consent of any other person, to bar the issue in tail and the estates and interests taking effect on the determination of the entailed interest.

### Actions for recovery of property obtained through unlawful conduct etc.

8–69 **27A.**—(1) None of the time limits given in the preceding provisions of this Act applies to any proceedings under Chapter 2 of Part 5 of the Proceeds of Crime Act 2002 (civil recovery of proceeds of unlawful conduct).

(2) Proceedings under that Chapter for a recovery order in respect of any recoverable property shall not be brought after the expiration of the period of twelve years from the date on which the relevant person's cause of action accrued.

(3) Proceedings under that Chapter are brought when—

(aa) an application is made for a property freezing order, or

(a) a claim form is issued, or

(b) an application is made for an interim receiving order,

whichever is the earliest.

(4) The relevant person's cause of action accrues in respect of any recoverable property—

(a) in the case of proceedings for a recovery order in respect of property obtained through unlawful conduct, when the property is so obtained,

(b) in the case of proceedings for a recovery order in respect of any other recoverable property, when the property obtained through unlawful conduct which it represents is so obtained.

(5) If—

(a) a person would (but for the preceding provisions of this Act) have a cause of action in respect of the conversion of a chattel, and

(b) proceedings are started under that Chapter for a recovery order in respect of the chattel,

section 3(2) of this Act does not prevent his asserting on an application under section 281 of that Act that the property belongs to him, or the court making a declaration in his favour under that section.

(6) If the court makes such a declaration, his title to the chattel is to be treated as not having been extinguished by section 3(2) of this Act.

(7) Expressions used in this section and Part 5 of that Act have the same meaning in this section as in that Part.

(8) In this section "relevant person" means—

(a) the Serious Organised Crime Agency,

(b) the Director of Public Prosecutions,

(c) the Director of Revenue and Customs Prosecutions, or

(d) the Director of the Serious Fraud Office.

*Note* —Inserted by the Proceeds of Crime Act 2002 s.288(1); amended by the Serious Organised Crime and Police Act 2005 s.109, Sch.6, para.2; and by the Serious Crime Act 2007 s.74, Sch.8, Pt.7, para.147, with effect from April 1, 2008 (SI 2008/755). **8–70**

### Actions for recovery of property for purposes of an external order

**27B.**—(1) None of the time limits given in the preceding provisions of this Act applies to any proceedings under Chapter 2 of Part 5 of the Proceeds of Crime Act 2002 (External Requests and Orders) Order 2005 (civil proceedings for the realisation of property to give effect to an external order). **8–71**

(2) Proceedings under that Chapter for a recovery order in respect of any recoverable property shall not be brought after the expiration of the period of twelve years from the date on which the relevant person's cause of action accrued.

(3) Proceedings under that Chapter are brought when—

(a) a claim form is issued, or

(b) an application is made for a property freezing order, or

(c) an application is made for an interim receiving order,

whichever is the earliest.

(4) The relevant person's cause of action accrues in respect of any recoverable property—

(a) in the case of proceedings for a recovery order in respect of property obtained, or believed to have been obtained, as a result of or in connection with criminal conduct, when the property is so obtained,

(b) in the case of proceedings for a recovery order in respect of any other recoverable property, when the property obtained, or believed to have been

*Paragraph numbers marked with a "+" can be found online and on CD.*

LIMITATION

obtained, as a result of or in connection with criminal conduct which it represents is so obtained.

(5) If—

(a) a person would (but for the preceding provisions of this Act) have a cause of action in respect of the conversion of a chattel, and

(b) proceedings are started under that Chapter for a recovery order in respect of the chattel,

section 3(2) of this Act does not prevent his asserting on an application under section 281 of that Act that the property belongs to him, or the court making a declaration in his favour under that section.

(6) If the court makes such a declaration, his title to the chattel is to be treated as not having been extinguished by section 3(2) of this Act.

(7) In this section—

(a) "criminal conduct" is to be construed in accordance with section 447(8) of the Proceeds of Crime Act 2002, and

(b) expressions used in this section which are also used in Part 5 of the Proceeds of Crime Act 2002 (External Requests and Orders) Order 2005 have the same meaning in this section as in that Part.

(8) In this section "relevant person" means—

(a) the Serious Organised Crime Agency,

(b) the Director of Public Prosecutions,

(c) the Director of Revenue and Customs Prosecutions, or

(d) the Director of the Serious Fraud Office.

**8–72** *Note*—Inserted by SI 2005/3181; amended by SI 2008/302.

## PART II

## EXTENSION OR EXCLUSION OF ORDINARY TIME LIMITS

### *DISABILITY*

#### Extension of limitation period in case of disability

**8–73** **28.**—(1) Subject to the following provisions of this section, if on the date when any right of action accrued for which a period of limitation is prescribed by this Act, the person to whom it accrued was under a disability, the action may be brought at any time before the expiration of six years from the date when he ceased to be under a disability or died (whichever first occurred) notwithstanding that the period of limitation has expired.

(2) This section shall not affect any case where the right of action first accrued to some person (not under a disability) through whom the person under a disability claims.

(3) When a right of action which has accrued to a person under a disability accrues, on the death of that person while still under a disability, to another person under a disability, no further extension of time shall be allowed by reason of the disability of the second person.

(4) No action to recover land or money charged on land shall be brought by virtue of this section by any person after the expiration of thirty years from the date on which the right of action accrued to that person or some person through whom he claims.

(4A) If the action is one to which section 4A of this Act applies, subsection (1) above shall have effect—

(a) in the case of an action for libel or slander, as if for the words from "at any time" to "occurred)" there were substituted the words "by him at any time before the expiration of one year from the date on which he ceased to be under a disability"; and

(b) in the case of an action for slander of title, slander of goods or other malicious falsehood, as if for the words "six years" there were substituted the words "one year".

(5) If the action is one to which section 10 of this Act applies, subsection (1) above shall have effect as if for the words "six years" there were substituted the words "two years".

(6) If the action is one to which section 11 or 12(2) of this Act applies, subsection (1) above shall have effect as if for the words "six years" there were substituted the words "three years".

(7) If the action is one to which section 11A of this Act applies or one by virtue of section 6(1)(a) of the Consumer Protection Act 1987 (death caused by defective product), subsection (1) above—

(a) shall not apply to the time limit prescribed by subsection (3) of the said section 11A or to that time limit as applied by virtue of section 12(1) of this Act; and

(b) in relation to any other time limit prescribed by this Act shall have effect as if for the words "six years" there were substituted the words "three years".

*Note* — Subsection (4A) added by the Administration of Justice Act 1985 s.57; substituted by the Defamation Act 1996 s.5(3). Subsection (7) added by the Consumer Protection Act 1987 Sch.1. **8–74**

**Effect of this section**

This section extends the limitation period in case of a person under disability, i.e. during the period he is a minor or of unsound mind (see s.38(2), (3) and (4)) and in this respect it follows s.2(1) of the Act of 1975. Thus if a young child of two-and-a-half years of age is injured and an action is brought to recover damages within the primary period of limitation, but there is prolonged and inexcusable delay in the conduct of the action causing serious prejudice to the defendant, nevertheless the court will not, under the doctrine of *Birkett v James* [1978] A.C. 297, dismiss the action for want of prosecution, since the limitation period for the plaintiff to bring his action for damages is still current and will not expire until three years from the date when he ceases to be a minor (*Tolley v Morris* [1979] 1 W.L.R. 592; [1979] 2 All E.R. 561, HL). Likewise, an action by a plaintiff under permanent disability will not be struck out for want of prosecution since a fresh action might be issued at any time; nor, it was held, should a condition be imposed on the continued progress of such an action (*Turner v W.H. Malcolm Ltd, The Times*, August 24, 1992, CA). **8–75**

In *Headford v Bristol and District HA* [1995] 6 Med. L.R. 1, CA, an appeal was al-



LIMITATION

lowed against an order striking out the claim of a person under disability, the action having been brought 28 years after the events complained of. It was held that, whilst there was an inherent jurisdiction to strike out an action as an abuse of process even though the plaintiff remained under disability (see *Hogg v Hamilton* [1993] 4 Med. L.R. 369, CA), in this case the facts did not warrant such a course. Section 28 conferred a right in general to bring proceedings in negligence during the period of disability. Section 28 contained no provision comparable with that in s.33 for carrying out a balancing exercise as to prejudice. Section 28(1) contained no longstop, in contrast to s.28(4). And, in permitting an action to be started within six years of the end of the disability, Parliament had expressly contemplated that, in the case of one well-known and substantial group of persons under disability, namely minors, an action might not be started until 24 years after the conduct complained of.

It is of course clear that a person under a disability may bring his action for damages while he is still under disability; the section is intended to extend the period of limitation, not to compel proceedings to await the cessation of disability.

Subs.(4) provides a long stop period of 30 years from accrual of the cause of action for bringing an action to recover land or money charged on land seemingly notwithstanding that the person entitled is or has been for the whole or part of such period under disability. For the ordinary time limits applicable to such actions, see ss.15 and 20 of the Act.

Among the factors to be regarded when considering whether to override any time limit in respect of actions for personal injuries is the duration of any disability of the plaintiff *arising after* the date of accrual of the cause of action (see s.33(3)(d)). This suggests that while regard is to be had to disability subsequently arising, regard will not necessarily be had, under that section, to disability existing at or continuing after the accrual of the cause of action. In such a case the plaintiff should be prompt to exercise his rights within the extended period provided under s.28.

Subs.(4A) in its original terms was inserted by the Administration of Justice Act 1985 s.57. It was totally replaced, with respect to causes of action arising after September 4, 1996, by the Defamation Act 1996 s.5(3). By the new subsection, as set out above, the extension of the limitation period in libel or slander in cases of disability is now one year after the plaintiff ceases to be under a disability. In actions for malicious falsehood the limitation period (now one year by virtue of s.4A of this Act) is extended in cases of disability by one year from the date on which the plaintiff ceases to be under a disability or dies.

## Extension for cases where the limitation period is the period under section 14A(4)(b)

8–76 **28A.**—(1) Subject to subsection (2) below, if in the case of any action for which a period of limitation is prescribed by section 14A of this Act—

(a) the period applicable in accordance with subsection (4) of that section is the period mentioned in paragraph (b) of that subsection;

(b) on the date which is for the purposes of that section the starting date for reckoning that period the person by reference to whose knowledge that date fell to be determined under subsection (5) of that section was under a disability; and

(c) section 28 of this Act does not apply to the action;

the action may be brought at any time before the expiration of three years from the date when he ceased to be under a disability or died (whichever first occurred) notwithstanding that the period mentioned above has expired.

(2) An action may not be brought by virtue of subsection (1) above after the end of the period of limitation prescribed by section 14B of this Act.

***Paragraph numbers marked with a "+" can be found online and on CD.***

*Note*—Section 28A added by Latent Damage Act 1986 s.2, see Current Law Statutes, Latent Damage Act 1986. Subsection (1) had the effect, in cases where the person whose knowledge is relevant for determining the starting date under s.14A is under disability *on that date*, of extending the limitation period until three years after cessation of disability or three years after his death. The long stop period under s.14B still remains. **8–77**

### ACKNOWLEDGMENT AND PART PAYMENT

## Fresh accrual of action on acknowledgment or part payment

**29.**—(1) Subsections (2) and (3) below apply where any right of action (including a foreclosure action) to recover land or an advowson or any right of a mortgagee of personal property to bring a foreclosure action in respect of the property has accrued. **8–78**

(2) If the person in possession of the land, benefice or personal property in question acknowledges the title of the person to whom the right of action has accrued—

(a) the right shall be treated as having accrued on and not before the date of the acknowledgment; and

(b) in the case of a right of action to recover land which has accrued to a person entitled to an estate or interest taking effect on the determination of an entailed interest against whom time is running under section 27 of this Act, section 27 shall thereupon cease to apply to the land.

(3) In the case of a foreclosure or other action by a mortgagee, if the person in possession of the land, benefice or personal property in question or the person liable for the mortgage debt makes any payment in respect of the debt (whether of principal or interest) the right shall be treated as having accrued on and not before the date of the payment.

(4) Where a mortgagee is by virtue of the mortgage in possession of any mortgaged land and either—

(a) receives any sum in respect of the principal or interest of the mortgage debt; or

(b) acknowledges the title of the mortgagor, or his equity of redemption;

an action to redeem the land in his possession may be brought at any time before the expiration of twelve years from the date of the payment or acknowledgment.

(5) Subject to subsection (6) below, where any right of action has accrued to recover—

(a) any debt or other liquidated pecuniary claim; or

(b) any claim to the personal estate of a deceased person or to any share or interest in any such estate;

and the person liable or accountable for the claim acknowledges the claim or makes any payment in respect of it the right shall be treated as having accrued on and not before the date of the acknowledgment or payment.

(6) A payment of a part of the rent or interest due at any time

shall not extend the period for claiming the remainder then due, but any payment of interest shall be treated as a payment in respect of the principal debt.

(7) Subject to subsection (6) above, a current period of limitation may be repeatedly extended under this section by further acknowledgments or payments, but a right of action, once barred by this Act, shall not be revived by any subsequent acknowledgment or payment.

8–79 *Note* — In *Bradford & Bingley Plc v Rashid* [2006] UKHL 37 it was held by the House of Lords that acknowledgments within the meaning of s.29(5) were not confined to admissions of debts that were indisputable as to quantum as well as to liability. See also that case as to the lack of application of the without prejudice rule to apparently open communications that were designed only to discuss the repayment of an admitted liability rather than to negotiate and compromise a disputed liability.

## Formal provisions as to acknowledgments and part payments

8–80 **30.**—(1) To be effective for the purposes of section 29 of this Act, an acknowledgment must be in writing and signed by the person making it.

(2) For the purposes of section 29, any acknowledgment or payment—

(a) may be made by the agent of the person by whom it is required to be made under that section; and

(b) shall be made to the person, or to an agent of the person, whose title or claim is being acknowledged or, as the case may be, in respect of whose claim the payment is being made.

### Without prejudice acknowledgment

8–81 For a case turning on the question of privilege attaching to a without prejudice acknowledgment of liability see *Cadle Co v Hearley* [2002] 1 Lloyd's Rep. 143.

### Signature

8–82 As a matter of general principle, a document is signed by the maker of it when his name or mark is attached to it in a manner which indicates, objectively, his approval of the contents. The typed name of the sender at the end of a telex not only identifies the maker but leads to the inference that he has approved the contents: the typed name therefore constitutes his signature: *Good Challenger Navegante SA v Metalexportimport SA (The "Good Challenger")* [2003] EWCA Civ 1668; [2004] 1 Lloyd's Rep. 67, CA, approving the judgment of the court below.

## Effect of acknowledgment or part payment on persons other than the maker or recipient

8–83 **31.**—(1) An acknowledgment of the title to any land, benefice, or mortgaged personalty by any person in possession of it shall bind all other persons in possession during the ensuing period of limitation.

(2) A payment in respect of a mortgage debt by the mortgagor or any other person liable for the debt, or by any person in possession of the mortgaged property, shall, so far as any right of the mortgagee to foreclose or otherwise to recover the property is concerned, bind all other persons in possession of the mortgaged property during the ensuing period of limitation.

***Paragraph numbers marked with a "+" can be found online and on CD.***

(3) Where two or more mortgagees are by virtue of the mortgage in possession of the mortgaged land, an acknowledgment of the mortgagor's title or of his equity of redemption by one of the mortgagees shall only bind him and his successors and shall not bind any other mortgagee or his successors.

(4) Where in a case within subsection (3) above the mortgagee by whom the acknowledgment is given is entitled to a part of the mortgaged land and not to any ascertained part of the mortgage debt the mortgagor shall be entitled to redeem that part of the land on payment, with interest, of the part of the mortgage debt which bears the same proportion to the whole of the debt as the value of the part of the land bears to the whole of the mortgaged land.

(5) Where there are two or more mortgagors, and the title or equity of redemption of one of the mortgagors is acknowledged as mentioned above in this section, the acknowledgment shall be treated as having been made to all the mortgagors.

(6) An acknowledgment of any debt or other liquidated pecuniary claim shall bind the acknowledgor and his successors but not any other person.

(7) A payment made in respect of any debt or other liquidated pecuniary claim shall bind all persons liable in respect of the debt or claim.

(8) An acknowledgment by one of several personal representatives of any claim to the personal estate of a deceased person or to any share or interest in any such estate, or a payment by one of several personal representatives in respect of any such claim, shall bind the estate of the deceased person.

(9) In this section "successor", in relation to any mortgagee or person liable in respect of any debt or claim, means his personal representatives and any other person on whom the rights under the mortgage or, as the case may be, the liability in respect of the debt or claim devolve (whether on death or bankruptcy or the disposition of property or the determination of a limited estate or interest in settled property or otherwise).

*FRAUD, CONCEALMENT AND MISTAKE*

## Postponement of limitation period in case of fraud, concealment or mistake

**32.**—(1) Subject to subsections (3) and (4A) below, where in the case of any action for which a period of limitation is prescribed by this Act, either— **8–84**

(a) the action is based upon the fraud of the defendant; or

(b) any fact relevant to the plaintiff's right of action has been deliberately concealed from him by the defendant; or

(c) the action is for relief from the consequences of a mistake;

the period of limitation shall not begin to run until the plaintiff has discovered the fraud, concealment or mistake (as the case may be) or could with reasonable diligence have discovered it.

***Paragraph numbers marked with a "+" can be found online and on CD.***

References in this subsection to the defendant include references to the defendant's agent and to any person through whom the defendant claims and his agent.

(2) For the purposes of subsection (1) above, deliberate commission of a breach of duty in circumstances in which it is unlikely to be discovered for some time amounts to deliberate concealment of the facts involved in that breach of duty.

(3) Nothing in this section shall enable any action—

(a) to recover, or recover the value of, any property; or

(b) to enforce any charge against, or set aside any transaction affecting, any property;

to be brought against the purchaser of the property or any person claiming through him in any case where the property has been purchased for valuable consideration by an innocent third party since the fraud or concealment or (as the case may be) the transaction in which the mistake was made took place.

(4) A purchaser is an innocent third party for the purposes of this section—

(a) in the case of fraud or concealment of any fact relevant to the plaintiff's right of action, if he was not a party to the fraud or (as the case may be) to the concealment of that fact and did not at the time of the purchase know or have reason to believe that the fraud or concealment had taken place; and

(b) in the case of mistake, if he did not at the time of the purchase know or have reason to believe that the mistake had been made.

(4A) Subsection (1) above shall not apply in relation to the time limit prescribed by section 11A(3) of this Act or in relation to that time limit as applied by virtue of section 12(1) of this Act.

(5) Sections 14A and 14B of this Act shall not apply to any action to which subsection (1)(b) above applies (and accordingly the period of limitation referred to in that subsection, in any case to which either of those sections would otherwise apply, is the period applicable under section 2 of this Act).

**8–85** *Note* —Section 11A of the Act, referred to in subs.(4A) above, imposes special time limits for actions for damages in respect of defective products, and was introduced by the Consumer Protection Act 1987.

Subsection (1) was amended by the Consumer Protection Act 1987 s.6(6), s.50(2) and Sch.1, para.5(a). Subsection (4A) was added by the Consumer Protection Act 1987 s.6(6), s.50(2) and Sch.1, para.5(b).

The new subs.(5) of s.32 above was added by s.2(2) of the Latent Damage Act 1986. It ensures, in cases of deliberate concealment by the defendant within the meaning of s.32(1)(b), that ss.14A and 14B, with their respective provisions for an extended period of three years from the date of knowledge and a long stop of 15 years, do not apply. Thus the period of limitation is that laid down by s.2 (six years), with the beginning of the period postponed by virtue of s.32 until the plaintiff has discovered the concealment, or could with reasonable diligence have discovered it. For a commentary on the provisions of s.32(1)–(4) relating to fraud, concealment or mistake, see *Current Law Statutes*, Limitation Act 1980.

The House of Lords has held that on its true construction s.32(1)(b) operated to postpone the running of time in every case where there was deliberate concealment by the defendant of facts relevant to the plaintiff's cause of action, regardless of whether such concealment was contemporaneous with or subsequent to the accrual of the cause of action. In the case of subsequent concealment time did not begin to run until the concealment was or should have been discovered (*Sheldon v RHM Outhwaite (Underwriting Agencies) Ltd* [1996] 1 A.C. 102; [1995] 2 W.L.R. 570; [1995] 2 All E.R. 558, HL). Where, however, the claimant was aware of the relevant facts during a period preceding the alleged concealment, no subsequent act on the part of the defendent can have concelaed them from him: see at [1996] 1 A.C., p.144, applied in *Ezekiel v Lehrer* [2002] Lloyd's Rep. P.N. 260 at pp. 268, 270.

Section 32(1)(b) is not to be construed as a statutory enactment of the equitable doctrine of concealed fraud: *Sheldon*, above, at p.145.

It has been held that deliberate concealment for the purposes of s.32(1)(b) and s.32(2) does not include failure to disclose a negligent breach of duty that the actor was not aware of committing: see *Cave v Robinson Jarvis & Rolf* [2002] 2 W.L.R. 1107, HL (overruling *Brocklesbury v Armitage & Guest* [2002] 1 W.L.R. 598, CA and *Liverpool Roman Catholic Archdiocese Trustees Inc v Goldberg* [2001] 1 All E.R. 182. On the other hand, deliberate concealment by the defendant of the fact that he had been negligent satisfies the test in s.32(1)(b): *Williams v Fanshaw Porter & Hazelhurst* [2004] EWCA Civ. 157; [2004] 2 All E.R. 616, CA.

It was held in *Skerratt v Linfax Ltd* [2003] EWCA Civ 695; [2004] P.I.Q.R. 124, CA, a case where the claimant had signed a disclaimer before the accident, that it was difficult to conceive of a case of concealment unless the concealment took place either at the very time that the cause of action was accruing, or it took place after the cause of action had accrued, i.e. unless the defendant took some steps to deliberately conceal a fact relevant to the cause of action. Further, without deciding the point, there was some doubt whether the existence or otherwise of a cause of action was a fact relevant to the claimant's right of action on any view.

The normal rule is that, where there is a dispute as to whether a claim is time-barred, the claimant has to commence a fresh action in which the viability of the limitation defence can be determined (*Welsh Development Agency v Redpath Dorman Long Ltd* [1994] 1 W.L.R. 1409; [1999] 4 All E.R. 10, CA). It has been held at first instance that this rule does not apply where there is an issue under s.32(2) whether any fact relevant to the claimant's right of action has been deliberately concealed and the deliberateness of the breach is an essential element of the new cause of action: *Mortgage Corp v Alexander Johnson*, *The Times*, September 22, 1999.

In relation to the words in s.32(1)(b) "any fact relevant to the plaintiff's right of action", it has been held that the relevant facts are those which the plantiff has to prove to establish a *prima facie* case: see *C v Mirror Group Newspapers Ltd* [1997] 1 W.L.R. 131, CA at p.138 G, followed in *Cohen v Kingsley Napley* [2005] EWHC 899; [2005] P.N.L.R. 37, holding that a cause of action in contract or the tort of negligence is complete whether or not the omission complained of is deliberate.

The expression "breach of duty" in s.32(2) has been held to include legal wrongdoing of a kind wider than breach of duty in a tortious or contractual sense, and to apply to a claim under s.423 of the Insolvency Act 1986: the authority is *Giles v Rhind* [2008] EWCA Civ 118, CA.

LIMITATION

## Discretionary exclusion of time limit for actions for defamation or malicious falsehood

**32A.**—(1) If it appears to the court that it would be equitable to allow an action to proceed having regard to the degree to which— **8–86**

(a) the operation of section 4A of this Act prejudices the plaintiff or any person whom he represents, and

(b) any decision of the court under this subsection would prejudice the defendant or any person whom he represents,

the court may direct that that section shall not apply to the action or shall not apply to any specified cause of action to which the action relates.

***Paragraph numbers marked with a "+" can be found online and on CD.***

(2) In acting under this section the court shall have regard to all the circumstances of the case and in particular to—

(a) the length of, and the reasons for, the delay on the part of the plaintiff;

(b) where the reason or one of the reasons for the delay was that all or any of the facts relevant to the cause of action did not become known to the plaintiff until after the end of the period mentioned in section 4A—

(i) the date on which any such facts did become known to him, and

(ii) the extent to which he acted promptly and reasonably once he knew whether or not the facts in question might be capable of giving rise to an action; and

(c) the extent to which, having regard to the delay, relevant evidence is likely—

(i) to be unavailable, or

(ii) to be less cogent than if the action had been brought within the period mentioned in section 4A.

(3) In the case of an action for slander of title, slander of goods or other malicious falsehood brought by a personal representative—

(a) the references in subsection (2) above to the plaintiff shall be construed as including the deceased person to whom the cause of action accrued and any previous personal representative of that person; and

(b) nothing in section 28(3) of this Act shall be construed as affecting the court's discretion under this section.

(4) In this section "the court" means the court in which the action has been brought.

8–87 *Note*—Added by the Administration of Justice Act 1985 s.57. Substituted by the Defamation Act 1996 s.5.

Essentially, the reforms brought about by s.5 include the reduction of the limitation period in libel and slander cases from three years to one year (see amended s.4A of the 1980 Act), but with a discretionary power of exclusion, rather than extension, of that time limit where the court considers that it would be equitable to make an order. The new section applies as well to actions in malicious falsehood.

The limitation period is deliberately short in defamation cases because a Claimant is expected vigorously to pursue a claim. Where no explanation for a 15 month delay was given, the judge was justified in refusing to exercise his discretion to make a direction under s.32A: *Steedman v BBC* [2001] EWCA Civ 1534; *The Times*, 13 December 2001, CA.

The phrase "facts relevant to that cause of action" in the old section, which corresponds with the similar phrase in subs(2)(b) of the new section, is to be construed narrowly and relates only to those facts which the plaintiff has to plead and prove to establish a prima facie case. It does not extend to facts which are capable of rebutting possible defences as, for example, facts relevant to privilege in a libel action (*C v Mirror Group Newspapers* [1996] E.M.L.R. 518, CA, following *Johnson v Chief Constable of Surrey* [1992] T.L.R. 551, CA, a decision under s.32(1)(b) of the Act).

A cause of action in libel acrrues at the date of publication. If knowledge of the identity of a defendant were required, s.32A would not be necessary. An order joining the author as a defendant after the expiry of the limitation period was rightly set aside on the ground that such order had proceeded on the mistaken basis that the added defendant would be left with a limitation defence: *Edwards v Golding* [2007] EWCA Civ 416, CA and see para. 17.4.2 of Vol.1 and paras 8–85 and 8–86 of Vol.2.

## Discretionary exclusion of time limit for actions in respect of personal injuries or death

**33.**—(1) If it appears to the court that it would be equitable to allow an action to proceed having regard to the degree to which— **8–88**

(a) the provisions of section 11 or 11A or 12 of this Act prejudice the plaintiff or any person whom he represents; and

(b) any decision of the court under this subsection would prejudice the defendant or any person whom he represents;

the court may direct that those provisions shall not apply to the action, or shall not apply to any specified cause of action to which the action relates.

(1A) The court shall not under this section disapply—

(a) subsection (3) of section 11A; or

(b) where the damages claimed by the plaintiff are confined to damages for loss of or damage to any property, any other provision in its application to an action by virtue of Part I of the Consumer Protection Act 1987.

(2) The court shall not under this section disapply section 12(1) except where the reason why the person injured could no longer maintain an action was because of the time limit in section 11 or subsection (4) of section 11A.

If, for example, the person injured could at his death no longer maintain an action under the Fatal Accidents Act 1976 because of the time limit in Article 29 in Schedule 1 to the Carriage by Air Act 1961, the court has no power to direct that section 12(1) shall not apply.

(3) In acting under this section the court shall have regard to all the circumstances of the case and in particular to—

(a) the length of, and the reasons for, the delay on the part of the plaintiff;

(b) the extent to which, having regard to the delay, the evidence adduced or likely to be adduced by the plaintiff or the defendant is or is likely to be less cogent than if the action had been brought within the time allowed by section 11, by section 11A or (as the case may be) by section 12;

(c) the conduct of the defendant after the cause of action arose, including the extent (if any) to which he responded to requests reasonably made by the plaintiff for information or inspection for the purpose of ascertaining facts which were or might be relevant to the plaintiff's cause of action against the defendant;

(d) the duration of any disability of the plaintiff arising after the date of the accrual of the cause of action;

(e) the extent to which the plaintiff acted promptly and reasonably once he knew whether or not the act or omission of the defendant, to which the injury was attributable, might be capable at that time of giving rise to an action for damages;

(f) the steps, if any, taken by the plaintiff to obtain medical, legal or other expert advice and the nature of any such advice he may have received.

(4) In a case where the person injured died when, because of section 11, or subsection (4) of section 11A he could no longer maintain an action and recover damages in respect of the injury, the court shall have regard in particular to the length of, and the reasons for, the delay on the part of the deceased.

(5) In a case under subsection (4) above, or any other case where the time limit, or one of the time limits, depends on the date of knowledge of a person other than the plaintiff, subsection (3) above shall have effect with appropriate modifications, and shall have effect in particular as if references to the plaintiff included references to any person whose date of knowledge is or was relevant in determining a time limit.

(6) A direction by the court disapplying the provisions of section 12(1) shall operate to disapply the provisions to the same effect in section 1(1) of the Fatal Accidents Act 1976.

(7) In this section "the court" means the court in which the action has been brought.

(8) References in this section to section 11 or 11A include references to that section as extended by any of the preceding provisions of this Part of this Act or by any provision of Part III of this Act.

**8–89** *Note*—Amended by the Consumer Protection Act 1987 Sch.1, para.6.

#### Discretionary power to override time limits in actions for personal injuries or death

**8–90** Section 33, which is derived verbatim from s.2D of the 1939 Act, provides a most important and substantial change in the law of limitation relating to actions for personal injuries or death. It does so by conferring on the court a discretionary power to direct that the provisions of ss.11 or 12 shall not apply to the action or shall not apply to any specified cause of action to which the action relates (s.33(1)). The court may not however disapply s.12(1), i.e. that provision which prevents dependants from recovering, where at the date of his death the deceased could not have maintained an action, except where the only reason why the deceased could not have recovered was the time bar under s.11. Accordingly, the court may still, in that particular case, exercise its jurisdiction in favour of the dependants to disapply s.11 (see s.33(2) and (4)). Similar provisions have now been added in relation to s.11A (see the Consumer Protection Act 1987 Sch.1).

#### The abolition of a former preclusion from the exercise of discretion

**8–91** In *Horton v Sadler* [2006] UKHL 27; [2006] 3 All E.R. 1177, HL, the House of Lords has refused to follow the reasoning of its decision in *Walkley v Precision Forgings Ltd* [1979] 2 All E.R. 548; [1979] 1 W.L.R. 606, HL, namely that the prejudice to a claimant whose first action, brought within the limitation period, had been disissued or discontinued is caused not by s.11 but by his own self inflicted wounds, and that the court was therefore precluded from exercising its powers under s.33 in a second action, brought outside the limitation period. The question for the court under s.33, as held in *Horton v Sadler*, is always whether it is equitable or inequitable as between the two parties to override the time bar, which if relied upon by the defendant, would, unless disapplied by order of the court, defeat the action which the claimant had ex hypothesis brought out of time. The fine distinctions drawn in cases subsequent to

*Walkley*, necessitated by the decision in that case, and considered in the text of earlier editions of the *White Book* and in particular at paras 8–70 and 8–71 of Volume 2 of the 2006 edition, no longer arise.

In *Horton v Sadler* the House of Lords confirmed the exercise of the judge's discretion in favour of the claimant under s.33 in the event that he had been permitted to exercise such discretion: see [2006] 3 All E.R. 1177 at pp.1191–2. Lord Bingham of Cornhill held at p.1191:

> "In resolving an application under section 33 the court must make a decision of which the inevitable effect is either to deprive the defendant of an accrued statute-bar defence or to stifle the claimant's action against the tortfeasor who caused his personal injuries. In choosing between these outcomes the court must be guided by what appears to it to be equitable, which I take to mean no more (but also no less) than fair, and it must have regard to all the circumstances of the case and in particular the six matters listed in subsection (3)."

In *Cain v Francis; McKay v Hamlani* [2008] EWCA Civ 1451 the Court of Appeal has further considered, in cases where there is no defence to liability on the merits, whether the loss of a limitation defence constitutes prejudice to a defendant within the meaning of s.33(1)(g). After reviewing the earlier authorities, including the speech of Diplock L.J. in *Thompson v Brown* [1981] 1 W.L.R. 744, HL, Smith L.J. held, at para.69:

> "In my view, the words of section 33 must be construed against that background. The context is that the claimant had the right to pursue his cause of action which he has lost by the operation of section 11. The defendant, on the other hand, had an obligation to pay the damages due; his right was the right to a fair opportunity to defend himself against the claim. The operation of section 11 has given him a complete procedural defence which removes his obligation to pay. In fairness and justice, he only deserves to have that obligation removed if the passage of time has significantly diminished his opportunity to defend himself (on liability and/or quantum). So the making of a direction, which would restore the defendant's obligation to pay damages, is only prejudicial to him if his right to a fair opportunity to defend himself has been compromised."

**Discretion to disapply relevant limitation period**

The House of Lords delivered judgment on January 30, 2008 in *A v Hoare* [2008] UKHL 6 holding that the question whether an actual claimant, taking into account his psychological state in consequence of the injury, could reasonably have been expected to start proceedings, was to be dealt with under s.33 and not under s.14 (2) of the Act. The wording of the section is to empower the court to direct that the provisions of s.11 or s.12 shall not apply to the action or to any specified cause of action to which the action relates, and this enabling power may be exercised if it appears to the court that it would be equitable to allow the action to proceed having regard both (a) to the degree to which the provisions of these sections prejudice the plaintiff and (b) to the extent to which a decision to allow the action to proceed would prejudice the defendant (s.33(1)). It would seem that such a direction may be given at the trial of an action, but nevertheless it is right that this issue should be decided at a preliminary stage and if the court is satisfied that it has all the circumstances of the case before it, there is no reason why it should not determine the issue at any interlocutory stage (see *Firman v Ellis* (1978)) or preliminary hearing or upon a preliminary issue whether before or at the trial. See *Buck v English Electric Co Ltd* [1977] 1 W.L.R. 806; [1978] 1 All E.R. 271; *Davies v British Insulated Callender's Cables Ltd* (1977) 121 S.J. 203. **8-92**

The Act of 1980 does not lay down any specific procedure whereby the statutory power under s.33 ("to override time limits") is to be invoked. In order to preclude any undue prolongation of an action which it may not be equitable to permit to proceed and in seeking to limit the burden of costs which may be imposed on the defendant, an application by him to stay the claim under CPR r.3.1(f) would, provided that the plaintiff has given due notice of his intention to rely on the section, serve to initiate the investigation contemplated by s.33. In a clear case, the defendant may apply for summary judgment under CPR r.24.2(a)(i), though in some situations the substantive issues may be so intimately and inextricably bound up with the questions arising under s.33 as to make any summary resolution of the question impracticable (see per Shaw L.J. in *Walkley v Precision Forgings Ltd* [1979] 1 W.L.R. 606 at 1238; [1979] 1 All E.R. 102, CA). It has however been observed that there is a "danger in the section 33

LIMITATION

exercise of putting the cart before the horse, that is, determining the claim and relying on that determination in undertaking the balance of prejudice as to whether the claim should have preceded at all": see *KR v Bryn Alyn Community (Holdings) Ltd* [2003] EWCA Civ 85; [2003] Q.B. 1441; [2003] 3 W.L.R. 107; [2004] 2 All E.R. 7116, CA, at paras 74(viii) and 309. It was also held at para.74(vi), that "Whenever the judge considers it feasible to do so, he should decide the limitation point by a preliminary hearing by reference to the pleading and written witness statements and, importantly, the extent and content of discovery ... It may not always be feasible or produce savings in time and cost for the parties to deal with the matter by way of preliminary hearing, but a judge should strain to do so whenever possible."

The discretion conferred on the court by s.33 requires that the court must have regard to all the circumstances of the case (s.33(3)). This entitles the judge to take account of the ultimate prospects of success, and it has been emphasised in *Davis v Jacobs* [1999] Lloyd's Rep. Med. 72, CA that it is incumbent on the judge to take great care when deciding to do so; he must specifically take care that all matters which might be taken into account are in fact considered. The court however must have regard to certain matters in particular which may provide guidelines when deciding whether to override a defence of limitation although in *Donovan v Gwentoys Ltd* [1990] 1 W.L.R. 472; and [1990] 1 All E.R. 1018, HL. Lord Griffiths emphasised that these specific considerations are not intended to place any fetter on the court's general discretion. These are:

(a) the length and reasons for delay on the part of the plaintiff;
(b) the effect of any delay on the cogency of the evidence;
(c) the conduct of the defendant;
(d) the duration of any disability of the plaintiff arising after accrual of the cause of action;
(e) the conduct of the plaintiff;
(f) the diligence on the part of the plaintiff in obtaining medical, legal or other expert advice.

The outcome of the balancing exercise under s.33 is not to be determined on comparative scales of hardship (though hardship can never be irrelevant in a jurisdiction where all circumstances are to be taken into account). The overriding question is one of equity: would it be equitable for the action to be allowed to proceed on a balance of prejudice weighed with due regard to all the circumstances and to the specific factors mentioned in the section?

Again, in *Nash v Eli Lilly & Co* [1993] 1 W.L.R. 782, it was emphasised by the Court of Appeal that subs.(1) establishes the balancing exercise in considering, from an equitable point of view, the prejudice to the plaintiff if he is deprived of his right of action as against the prejudice to the defendant if the action is permitted to continue. Subs.(3) provides that the court in carrying out this exercise must have regard to "all the circumstances of the case" and particularly to the considerations set out in paras (a) to (f). Subject to acting judicially, the discretion of the court is entirely unfettered. The specific matters set out in subs.(3) are exemplary and not definitive (*Nash v Eli Lilly & Co* [1993] 4 All E.R. 383 at 402, CA).

The burden of showing that it is equitable to disapply the limitation period is on the claimant. The court must take account of all the circumstances including the ability to have a fair trial. Where the claimant failed to disclose all the relevant circumstances of his medical history the judge's exercise of discretion in his favour was set aside even though liability had been established: *Long v Tolchard and Sons Ltd*, *The Times*, January 5, 2000, CA. The burden is a heavy one. Another way of putting it is that it is an exceptional indulgence to a claimant to be granted only where equity between the parties demands it: see *KR v Bryn Alyn Community (Holdings) Ltd (In Liquidation)* [2003] EWCA Civ 85, at para.74(ii), referring to the dicta of Lord Diplock in *Thompson v Brown Construction Ltd (t/a George Albert Brown (Builders) & Co)* [1981] 1 W.L.R. 744, CA, at 750C and 752E–F; and at para.92. It has however been observed that this particular passage in *KR v Bryn Alyn* no longer sits happily with the subsequent House of Lords decisions in *Horton v Sadler* and *A v Hoare*, above, as to the approach now to be adopted in exercising the wholly unfettered discretion under this section: *Leeson v Marsden* [2008] EWHC 1011 (QB); [2008] 103 B.M.L.R. 49 at p.79. In *D v Harrow B.C* [2008] EWCH 3048 (QB); [2009] 1 F.L.R. 719 it was held by Eady J, applying *A v Hoare*, that although the discretion was unfettered and had to be addressed in the light of all the circumstances, the court should never lose sight of the public policy considerations on limitation periods. There was a public interest in legal certainty and finality that should not lightly be discounted.

In cases of claims for damages for negligence in education in failing to address dyslexia, it has been held that the courts should be slow to find that the balance of prejudice under s.33 is in favour of the claimant: see *Robinson v St.Helens Metropolitan BC* [2003] P.I.Q.R. 128, CA at 139–140, approved by the House of Lords in *Adams v Braknell Forest BC* [2004] UKHL 29; [2004] 3 W.L.R. 89; at 103; and applied in *Smith v Hampshire CC* [2007] EWCA Civ 246; [2007] E.L.R. 321, CA.

There are no grounds for limiting the exercise of the court's discretion in group actions for reasons of public policy (*ibid.*, p.409).

For the purposes of s.33(3)(b), cogency is directed to the degree to which either party is prejudiced in the presentation of the claim or defence because the evidence is either no longer available or has been adversely affected by the passage of time. Consideration of cogency in the context of the plaintiff's delay under s.33(3)(a) must not be confused with the overall discretion which is to be exercised under subs.(1) (*ibid.*, p.406).

The factors to be taken into account under s.33(3)(b) may include potential prejudice to the defendant in relation to contribution proceedings: see *Buckler v Sheffield City Council* [2004] EWCA Civ. 920; [2005] P.I.Q.R. P3 at p.36, CA.

The test to be applied under s.33(3)(a) to the reasons for the plaintiff's delay is a subjective test and not an objective one (*Coad v Cornwall and Isles of Scilly HA* [1997] 8 Med.L.R. 154, CA).

Section 33(3)(c) relates to the conduct of the defendant after the cause of action arose. A health authority with a policy of destroying patients' X-rays after three years, even those of patients known to be contemplating actions in negligence and whose solicitors had requested notes, would have any prejudice pleaded in a limitation defence significantly discounted: *Hammond v West Lancashire HA*, [1998] Lloyd's Rep. Med. 146, CA.

In cases of claims for damages for negligence in education in failing to address dyslexia, it has been held that the courts should be slow to find that the balance of prejudice under s.33 is in favour of the claimant; see *Robinson v St. Helens Metropolitan BC* [2004] UKHL 29; [2004] 3 W.L.R. 89 at p.103; and in *Smith v Hampshire CC* [2007] EWCA Civ 246; [2007] E.L.R. 321,CA.

Where the defendant is insured, the defendant and his insurers are to be treated as one composite unit. Thus, if the delay has seriously prejudiced the ability to defend, and the action would have been discounted by the court if the defendant had not been insured, no regard should be paid to the fact that he is insured (*Kelly v Bastible*, *The Times*, November 15, 1996, CA). **8–93**

In *Yates v Thakeham Tiles Ltd* [1995] P.I.Q.R. 135, CA, it was held that, for the purpose of s.33(3)(d), "disability" was limited to the context of a person under disability by reason of being an infant or a patient under the Mental Health Act 1983. The judge had erroneously taken physical disability into account under s.33(3)(d). He was however entitled to take it into account in the overall exercise of his discretion under s.33 (see also *Davis v Jacobs*, above) and the fact that he had taken it into account under subs.(3)(d) did not detract from that. It was observed that the very breadth of the discretion afforded to the judge under the section made an attack on its exercise inherently difficult. Again, in *Thomas v Plaistow*, *The Times*, May 19, 1997, CA, it was held that the word "disability" clearly had the same meaning in s.33(3)(d) as in section 28. The rationale was that while section 28 conferred mandatory extension of time in the case of existing disability, supervening disability should be dealt with as an exercise of the court's discretion.

It was emphasised in a pre-CPR case that the exercise of discretion under s.33 differed in two vital respects from that in applications to strike out for want of prosecution. Firstly, in a striking out application the onus was on the defendant to prove not merely delay but that he had been prejudiced by it. In an application under s.33 the onus was on the plaintiff. Secondly, under s.33(3) there were six criteria to which the court must have regard. Whilst it was not essential for the judge to go through the criteria referring to each, i.e. to use the section as a checklist, nevertheless it was a useful exercise to do so (*Barrand v British Cellophane Plc*, *The Times*, February 16, 1995, CA).

***Paragraph numbers marked with a "+" can be found online and on CD.***

The court held in *Nash v Eli Lilly & Co* [1993] 1 W.L.R. 782, above, that if it is shown that the claim is a poor case lacking in merit, there may be significant and relevant prejudice to the defendant if the limitation provisions are disapplied: *ibid.*, at pp. 403–404, considering *Hartley v Birmingham City DC* [1992] 1 W.L.R. 968; [1992] 2 All E.R. 213, CA, where the Court of Appeal, whose leading judgment was delivered by Parker L.J., expressed the view that "as the prejudice resulting from the loss of the limitation defence will always or almost always be balanced by the prejudice to the plaintiff from the operation of the limitation provision, the loss of the defence *as such* will be of little importance. What is of paramount importance is the effect of the delay on the defendant's ability to defend". In the later case (*Nash v Eli Lilly & Co*), the court held that it could not accept that in every case where the ability of a defendant to defend on the issue of liability has not been affected by the delay, the benefit of the limitation defence must be regarded as a "windfall" (*ibid.*, p.403).

The court has refused to lay down a guideline that, in the absence of fault on the part of the defendant, the limitation period will be enforced unless the delay has been minimal, especially if the plaintiff has a good claim against his solicitors. Such a guideline would lead to litigation as to what constitutes minimal delay (*Ramsden v Lee* [1992] 2 All E.R. 204, CA).

In considering whether the plaintiff had received legal advice and the nature of any such advice, the court will have regard to the character of the advice in so far as it is relevant to the question whether the plaintiff had acted promptly and reasonably after he had knowledge of the information which might give rise to the cause of action; therefore, the court should know whether the advice was favourable to the plaintiff's alleged cause of action (*Jones v G. D. Searle & Co Ltd* [1979] 1 W.L.R. 101; [1978] 3 All E.R. 654, CA).

The test to be applied under s.33(3)(e) in deciding whether the plaintiff has acted reasonably in bringing the case late is an objective one: what would a reasonable man in the position of the plaintiff have done? A trade union member could usually be said to act reasonably if he followed union advice (*Dale v British Coal Corp (No.2) The Times*, July 2, 1992, CA). It was further held that where, as in this case, both notice of the existence of the claim and sufficient particulars were given so late that it was virtually impossible for a defendant to investigate, the defendant was gravely prejudiced, and it would take exceptional circumstances to disapply the limitation period. The test to be applied under s.33(3)(a), rather than (3)(e), is however a subjective one (*Coad v Cornwall and Isles of Scilly HA* [1997] 8 Med.L.R. 154, CA, distinguishing *Dale's* case, above. And, it has been held, the person whose conduct is relevant to consider under (3)(e) is the claimant himself, and not his advisers: *Davis v Jacobs* above.

In *Smith v Leicestershire HA* (1996) 36 B.M.L.R. 23 negligence and causation were found by the trial judge in favour of the plaintiff. But the question arose how s.33(3)(b) should operate in light of the fact that the plaintiff had succeeded in 1996 but might not have done so had the trial taken place even 20 years earlier. The Court of Appeal, at [1998] Lloyd's Rep. Med. 77, CA, overruling the judge's decision, held that causation does not change with the passage of time and allowed the action to proceed.

**8–94** In terms of evidence required on an application under s.33, where it was necessary for the plaintiff's case to show that a prudent employer should have taken precautions to protect an employee at special risk, expert evidence should normally be advanced on the application (*Dale v BCC (No.2)* above).

The court may permit an action to proceed under s.33 where the plaintiff, in ignorance of his legal rights has delayed in suing, and cannot be criticised for doing so, even though he knew facts on which a claim was available (*Halford v Brookes* [1991] 1 W.L.R. 428, CA). See also *Das v Ganju, The Times*, May 4, 1999, CA, in which the claimant was permitted to proceed where the delay was caused by the fault of her lawyers and where she herself could not be criticised.

*Das v Ganju* has established that there is no rule of law that a solicitor's faults are to be visited on the claimant: *Corbin v Penfold Metallising Co Ltd, The Times*, May 2, 2000, CA. See also *Steeds v Peverel Management Services Ltd, The Times*, May 16, 2001, CA.

On an application for a direction to disapply the relevant limitation period, the length of and reasons for delay which are required to be considered by the court under s.33(3)(a) are those which had occurred between the expiry of the limitation period and the issue of the writ, and *not* between the beginning of the limitation period and the issue of the writ (*Eastman v London County Bus Services Ltd, The Times*, November

2, 1985, applying *Thompson v Brown* [1981] 1 W.L.R. 751, per Lord Diplock). Lord Diplock's dictum was approved in *Donovan v Gwentoys Ltd* (above), although in that case, the House of Lords held that the court should look at all the circumstances including those arising within the limitation period. Thus it was specifically held that prejudice caused to a defendant by the plaintiff's delay in notifying him of the claim during the limitation period is relevant and that this was a significant factor in weighing the relative prejudice to the plaintiff and defendant as required by s.33(1)(a) and (b) (per Lord Griffiths, at [1990] 1 W.L.R. 478–479; and [1990] 1 All E.R. 1024).

In deciding whether to exercise its discretion under s.33 to disapply the time limit it would not be proper to apply different principles for the ordinary single case and for multi-party litigation: *Nash v Eli Lilly* [1991] 2 Med.L.R. 169, per Hidden J).

The overriding discretion of the court arises if the court considers it "equitable" to allow an action to proceed. This is the widest term that the legislature could have used to confer this discretion on the court (see per Lord Cowper L.C. in *Dudley (Lord) v Dudley (Lady)* (1705) Prec.Ch. 241 at 244, cited in Vol.2, "Words & Phrases", p.173) and such discretion may be exercised to override the technical defence of limitation and to enable the court to sustain the action if it would be fair and just in all the circumstances of the case to do so as between the plaintiff and defendant. Moreover, where a person has been added as a defendant after the expiry of the primary period of limitation against him the court will not exercise its discretion to extend such period under s.33 of the Act where the plaintiff is not prejudiced because he has a cast-iron case against the original defendant and the Motor Insurers' Bureau would be required to satisfy any judgment against that defendant. Their presence in the case is one of the circumstances to which the court is required to have regard under s.33(3) of the Act of 1980 (*Liff v Peasley* [1980] 1 W.L.R. 781; [1980] 1 All E.R. 623, CA). Furthermore, the court was entitled to have regard to the fact that a plaintiff was impecunious and legally aided and that the defendant would have little prospect of recovering his costs (*Lye v Marks and Spencer Plc, The Times*, February 15, 1988, CA).

Opposition by a defendant to an application to extend time under s.33 will not be upheld solely on the ground that the cause of action itself is to be regarded as inequitable. The question posed by s.33 is not whether the claim is equitable, but whether it was equitable to allow it to proceed (*Ward v Foss, The Times*, November 29, 1993, CA (claim for damages for loss of earnings during the "lost years" after death arising out of a fatal accident in 1982. The Administration of Justice Act 1982 s.4(2), which was not retrospective, abolished such claims where the cause of action accrued on or after January 1, 1983)).

The jurisdiction of the court under s.33 of the 1980 Act to direct that the time limits in actions for personal injuries or death shall not apply to an action or to any specified cause of action, may be exercised by a judge, Master or District Judge: CPR r.2.4.

#### Dissolution of a company defendant

In relation to s.651 of the Companies Act 1985 it has been held that a cause of action against a company restored to the register accrued on the date on which it would otherwise have accrued but for this dissolution. It followed in that case that in the absence of a limitation direction the action was statute-barred. On the hearing of an application for restoration under s.651 the court should not normally make a direction that the period between dissolution and restoration be discounted for limitation purposed unless: **8–95**

(a) notice of the application has been given to all parties who might be expected to oppose including the Company's insurers and

(b) the court is satisfied

 (i) that it has before it all the evidence that the parties would wish to adduce on an application under s.33 and

 (ii) that an application under s.33 is bound to succeed. If those conditions are not met, the applicant should seek relief under section 33: *Smith v White Knight Laundry* [2001] 3 All. E.R 862, CA, approving *Workvale Ltd, Re* [1992] 2 All E.R. 627; [1992] 1 W.L.R. 416, CA.

#### Appeal

Under the CPR it will be necessary to decide, for the purposes of establishing the **8–96**

***Paragraph numbers marked with a "+" can be found online and on CD.***

correct route of appeal, whether a determination under s.33 disapplying the time limits under s.11 is a final decision on a decision other than final. The routes of appeal are shown in PD 52 para.2A.1 and the meaning of final decision for the purposes of the route of appeal is sent out in paras 2A.2 and 2A.3. It is apparent that, in so far as a determination under s.33 would not finally determine the entire proceedings whichever way the court decided the issues before it, such determination is not to be regarded as a final decision.

#### Alternative dispute resolution

8–97 It has been held that a waiver by a defendant of its right to rely in an ADR scheme on limitation defences did not extend, after the termination of that scheme, to litigation (*Blytheway v British Steel Corp Plc* [1997] 9 C.L. 103, CA).

#### Scope of s.33 in relation to other Statutes

8–98 Section 33 has been held not to apply to cases where a time limit imposed by statute under the Merchant Shipping Act 1979 arises (2 year limit under the Athens Convention). The terms of the Convention provided for "suspension or interruption" of limitation periods but, unlike s.32, s.33 was concerned not with suspension or interruption but with exclusion altogether of a time period which had already run its course. Further, it was not possible to construe s.33, which refers expressly to the provisions of ss.11 and 12 of this Act, as extending to the Convention (*Higham v Stena Sealink Ltd* [1996] 1 W.L.R. 1107, CA).

#### Article 6 of the ECHR

8–99 The Court of Appeal did not accept that, whilst the *Walkley* principle continued to hold good under domestic law, the UK was to be regarded as violating the Art.6 rights of those affected by it: *Young (Deceased) v Western Power Distribution (South West) Plc* [2003] EWCA Civ 1034 at para.55. See, however, para.8–91above.

## PART III

## MISCELLANEOUS AND GENERAL

### Application of Act and other limitation enactments to arbitrations

8–100 **34.** [...]

8–101 *Note* —Repealed by the Arbitration Act 1996 Sch.4.

### New claims in pending actions: rules of court

8–102 **35.**—(1) For the purposes of this Act, any new claim made in the course of any action shall be deemed to be a separate action and to have been commenced—

(a) in the case of a new claim made in or by way of third party proceedings, on the date on which those proceedings were commenced; and

(b) in the case of any other new claim, on the same date as the original action.

(2) In this section a new claim means any claim by way of set-off or counterclaim, and any claim involving either—

(a) the addition or substitution of a new cause of action; or

(b) the addition or substitution of a new party;

and "third party proceedings" means any proceedings brought in the course of any action by any party to the action against a person

***Paragraph numbers marked with a "+" can be found online and on CD.***

not previously a party to the action, other than proceedings brought by joining any such person as defendant to any claim already made in the original action by the party bringing the proceedings.

(3) Except as provided by section 33 of this Act or by rules of court, neither the High Court nor any county court shall allow a new claim within subsection (1)(b) above, other than an original set-off or counterclaim, to be made in the course of any action after the expiry of any time limit under this Act which would affect a new action to enforce that claim.

For the purposes of this subsection, a claim is an original set-off or an original counterclaim if it is a claim made by way of set-off or (as the case may be) by way of counterclaim by a party who has not previously made any claim in the action.

(4) Rules of court may provide for allowing a new claim to which subsection (3) above applies to be made as there mentioned, but only if the conditions specified in subsection (5) below are satisfied, and subject to any further restrictions the rules may impose.

(5) The conditions referred to in subsection (4) above are the following—

(a) in the case of a claim involving a new cause of action, if the new cause of action arises out of the same facts or substantially the same facts as are already in issue on any claim previously made in the original action; and

(b) in the case of a claim involving a new party, if the addition or substitution of the new party is necessary for the determination of the original action.

(6) The addition or substitution of a new party shall not be regarded for the purposes of subsection (5)(b) above as necessary for the determination of the original action unless either—

(a) the new party is substituted for a party whose name was given in any claim made in the original action in mistake for the new party's name; or

(b) any claim already made in the original action cannot be maintained by or against an existing party unless the new party is joined or substituted as plaintiff or defendant in that action.

(7) Subject to subsection (4) above, rules of court may provide for allowing a party to any action to claim relief in a new capacity in respect of a new cause of action notwithstanding that he had no title to make that claim at the date of the commencement of the action.

This subsection shall not be taken as prejudicing the power of rules of court to provide for allowing a party to claim relief in a new capacity without adding or substituting a new cause of action.

(8) Subsections (3) to (7) above shall apply in relation to a new claim made in the course of third party proceedings as if those proceedings were the original action, and subject to such other modifications as may be prescribed by rules of court in any case or class of case.

(9) [...]

*Note*—Repealed by the Senior Courts Act 1981 Sch.7. **8–103**

***Paragraph numbers marked with a "+" can be found online and on CD.***

**Scope and operation of this section**

8–104 This section re-enacts s.8 of the Limitation Amendment Act 1980, which had not been brought into force and which had replaced s.28 of the Limitation Act 1939, relating to set-off and counterclaims. It deals in the scope of one section with a number of disparate procedural problems and it is a mix of both substantive and procedural law, with the added complication that it authorises rules of court to be made but only within the limits laid down by the section itself. The connecting thread which runs through the section and which may justify its form is that it is dealing with "new claims in pending actions."

The matters which are dealt with by this section may be summarised as follows:

(1) definition of "new claims" in pending actions;

(2) time limits for third party proceedings;

(3) time limits for a set-off or counterclaim;

(4) amendments in pending actions after the expiry of a current period of limitation:

(a) to add or substitute a new cause of action;

(b) to add or substitute a new party;

(c) to add a claim for relief in a new capacity;

(5) powers under rules of court to make such amendments.

It should be noted that s.35, with its provisions which are intended to permit, or refuse, as the case may be, new claims in pending actions in the light of statutory limitation periods under this Act, has no application where a contractual or substantive time-limit, such as in the Hague Rules, has expired and the action has ceased to exist: *Payabi v Armstel Shipping Corp* [1992] Q.B. 907; [1992] 2 W.L.R. 898.

**Nature of new claims in pending actions**

8–105 For the purposes of the 1980 Act s.35 provides that any new claim made in the course of any action, i.e. while the action is pending or in being, is deemed to be "a separate action" (subs.(1)).

For this purpose a "new claim" means or includes:

(a) a claim made in or by way of third party proceedings (see s.35(1)(a));

(b) any claim made by way of set-off or counterclaim (see s.35(2));

(c) any claim involving the addition or substitution of a new cause of action (see s.35(2)(a));

(d) any claim involving the addition or substitution of a new party (see s.35(2)(b)).

For the analysis of the meaning of a "new claim" within s.35(2)(a) or (b) see *Yorkshire Regional HA v Fairclough Building Ltd* [1996] 1 All E.R. 519, CA. The two paragraphs of the subsection are to be regarded as mutually exclusive, para.(a) being confined to claims involving a new cause of action but not the addition or substitution of a new party, and para.(b) being applicable to the addition or substitution of a new party, whether or not that involved a new cause of action.

It is not clear whether a claim for relief in a new capacity under s.35(7) is a "new claim," though it probably is if the relief is sought in respect of a new cause of action, but not if it is sought without the addition or substitution of a new cause of action.

**Time limits for third party proceedings**

8–106 In the case of a new claim made in or by way of third party proceedings, the separate action, which such claim is deemed to be, is deemed to have commenced on the date on which those proceedings were commenced (see s.35(1)(a)).

For this purpose, "third party proceedings" are defined as meaning any proceedings brought in the course of any action by any party to the action against a party not previously a party to the action, other than proceedings brought by joining any such person as defendant to any claim already made in the action by the party bringing the proceedings. Accordingly, an amendment made, or sought to be made, in existing proceedings by the addition of a new defendant to an existing claim falls to be treated as a new claim under subs.(1)(b), (i.e. proceedings deemed to have been commenced on the same date as the original action) whereas the addition by a defendant of a new party in the form of a third party falls to be dealt with under subs.(1)(a) (proceedings deemed to have been commenced on date of commencement of third party proceedings): and see *Kennett v Brown* [1988] 1 W.L.R. 582, CA. In that case the party making the new claim was in fact the first defendant who sought, out of time, to recover by contribution notice against the second defendant damages for his own injuries incurred in the accident. It was held that these were not third party proceedings within the meaning of s.35(1). Any claim or issue within the former O.16, r.1(1) was a third party proceeding, but claims and issues between co-defendants under the former O.16, r.8 were not "third party proceedings" for the purposes of this section.

Of course, third party proceedings for the purposes of this section include fourth and subsequent party proceedings.

The former Rule of Court (RSC O.16) providing procedural machinery for the bringing and conduct of third party proceedings has been repealed. Indeed, the description "third party proceedings" is not now used in the CPR, the description being "Part 20 claim" and the relevant Rule being CPR Pt 20. As under RSC O.16, Part 20 does not itself contain any provision dealing with limitation. The matter is left to s.35 of the Act.

The provision that third party proceedings are deemed to have been commenced on the date on which those proceedings are begun is a provision of great importance. It is to be contrasted with the provision in s.35(1)(b) whereby other new claims in an action are deemed to have been commenced on the same date as the original action. Accordingly, in third party proceedings there is no backdating. However, the question still arises when, for the purposes of third party proceedings, does the relevant cause of action as between the defendant and third party accrue? In many cases the question may be of little relevance, for the third party proceedings will be grounded on a right to recover contribution for damage for which the defendant is liable to the plaintiff. In procedural terms, such right is plainly granted by CPR Pt 20. In substantive terms, the right arises under s.1 of the Civil Liability (Contribution) Act 1978. The limitation period in such cases is that set by s.10 of the Limitation Act 1980, i.e. two years from the date when the right to recover contribution accrued, as defined by s.10(3) and (4). Accordingly, the defendant seeking contribution will have two years from the date when he is ordered, or agrees, to make payment. And, it appears, the running of time as between the plaintiff and the person claiming contribution does not affect the entitlement to recover contribution provided that immediately before the person claiming contribution made or was ordered or agreed to make the payment in respect of which contribution is sought he (i.e. the person claiming contribution) was liable in respect of the damage: see para.8–15 above. In other cases, however, where, for example, the defendant relies on a right of indemnity under contract against a third party, or where the defendant seeks to recover against the third party damages for damage suffered by himself, and is entitled to bring third party proceedings in respect thereof (see CPR Pt 20), the primary limitation periods imposed by the Limitation Act 1980 will apply to the defendant's cause of action. In such cases, the defendant will need to be diligent, especially if the claimant's proceedings against him are commenced towards the end of the limitation period, to commence the third party proceedings in time. It appears that, in view of the fact that subs.(1) deems that the new claim is to be a separate action, a defendant in such a position is to be regarded as claimant for the purposes of the Limitation Act 1980 and that accordingly, in appropriate circumstances in a personal injury action, such a defendant could apply to the court to override the bar of limitation under s.33 of the Act.

The section does not define the date when third party proceedings will be treated as having been commenced. The better view under the former RSC was that such proceedings were commenced only when the third party notice itself was issued (pursuant to leave if such leave was required). The issue of a third party notice took effect from its being sealed by an Officer of the Court out of which it was issued (see *College Street Market Gardens v Short*, October 5, 1989, unrep. per Saville J.).

The position under the Civil Procedure Rules is that a Pt 20 claim is made when the court issues the Pt 20 claim form: see CPR r.20.7(1)– (5).

**Time limits for set-off or counterclaim**

A claim by way of set-off or counterclaim is a separate action and is deemed to have been commenced on the same date as the original action (see s.35(1)(b)). This provision repeats the former law as prescribed by s.28 of the Limitation Act 1939. **8–107**

***Paragraph numbers marked with a "+" can be found online and on CD.***

In *Westdeutsche Landesbank v Islington B.C.* [1994] 4 All E.R. 890, the meaning of the term "set off" in s.35 of this Act, and s.28 of the Limitation Act 1939, was considered. It was held, applying Lord Denning's judgment in *Henriksens Rederi A/S v PHZ Rolimpex* [1974] Q.B. 233; [1973] 3 All E.R. 589, CA, that the time bars arising out of s.28 and s.35 did not apply to equitable set-offs in the nature of a defence but only to legal set-offs, properly so called, by way of cross-claim (see *Westdeutsche*, above at pp.944–945.

A party may of course seek to make a claim by way of set-off or counterclaim in an existing action. If he is a party who has not previously made any claim in the action such set-off or counterclaim will be regarded as "original" for the purposes of s.35(3) and may be allowed to be made after the expiry of the current period of limitation which would affect a new action to enforce that claim (*ibid.*).

It has been held under the former RSC that while O.15 permits the bringing of a counterclaim by the defendant against one or more of the plaintiffs by whom he has been sued and section 35 permits such counterclaim to be treated as having been brought on the same date as the original action, the discretion of the court might be exercised against the defendant to say that the counterclaim shall be brought as a separate action. In the instant case the counterclaim should be struck out with the result that a separate action would be statute barred. Mutuality of the subject-matter of the claim and counterclaim are not necessary, but want of mutuality may be a weighty factor in exercising discretion. In the ordinary case procedural convenience is the primary consideration and limitation consequences are at best only secondary (*Ernst & Young v Butte Mining Plc* [1997] 2 All E.R. 471).

See also *JFS (UK) Ltd v Dwr Cymru Cyf*, *The Times*, October 10, 1998, CA, in which the word "claim" for the purposes of s.35(3) was held to mean a claim for relief rather than an averment by way of defence.

**8–108** *Amendments in pending actions after the expiry of a current period of limitation—power under Rules of Court to make such amendments*—Subsection (3) of s.35 is of cardinal importance in considering the power of the court. It is enacted that, except as provided by s.33 or by rules of court, the court shall not allow a new claim within subs.(1)(b) "other than an original set-off or counterclaim" to be made after the expiry of a time limit which would affect a new action to enforce such claim. A new claim within subs.(1)(b) is any new claim other than third party proceedings (which are themselves limited by the rule that they are deemed to have been commenced on the date of commencement of the third party proceedings).

The purpose of this subsection is, subject to the qualifications stated, to bar new and additional causes of action being litigated outside the period of limitation and to prevent new and additional parties being sued outside such period. But set-offs and counterclaims, if they are "original," may be relied on. The subsection defines an original set-off and an original counterclaim as a claim by way of set-off or by way of counterclaim made by a party who has not previously made any claim in the action. Thus, a defendant served with a writ which has been issued before the end of the limitation period may claim once by way of set-off or counterclaim even though his set-off or counterclaim is not pleaded until after the limitation period has expired. See *Lloyds Bank Plc v Wojcik*; *Independent*, January 19, 1998 (C.S.), CA. But he may not do so again in the action, for his set-off or counterclaim would not then be "original." A defendant should in such circumstances make sure that he includes all claims on which he may wish to rely in his original pleading. A claim by way of set-off is treated as a new claim even though a set-off operates by way of defence. Accordingly, it would not appear to be open to a defendant, who has pleaded a set-off only, to seek to add (outside the limitation period) a counterclaim; though, if he has previously made no claim at all, he may do so. If, however, the new counterclaim arises out of the same or substantially the same facts as those upon which the set-off was based, the defendant may bring himself within s.35(5), and accordingly add a counterclaim.

In *Law Society v Wemyss* [2009] 1 All E.R. 752, Norris J. held that on its true construction s.35(3), in referring to "an original … counterclaim", was referring to any cause of action that might be asserted by an existing defendant against a claimant. The nature of the cause of action was not integral to the concept of "counterclaim". All that mattered was that all the parties requisite to assert the cause of action were on one side of the record and one of the parties against whom the cause of action could be asserted

***Paragraph numbers marked with a "+" can be found online and on CD.***

was on the other side of the record. Permission to amend would not however be given on the facts.

The word "claim" in s.35(3) should be construed as a claim for relief. Accordingly, where a defendant had previously pleaded a defence stating that the plaintiff had extended time for payment of a debt, that was not a claim in the legal sense. There was power under s.35(3) to grant leave to amend to plead a counterclaim even though it was founded on a cause of action which was statute-barred: *JFS (UK) Ltd v Dwr Cymru Cyf*, *The Times*, October 10, 1998, CA.

In *Kennett v Brown* [1988] 1 W.L.R. 582, CA, where a first defendant sought by contribution notice against a second defendant to recover damages for his own injuries incurred in the accident, it was held that this was not an original set-off or counterclaim within the meaning of subs.(3), Lord Donaldson M.R. construing these words, at p.585, as meaning "a set-off or counterclaim by an original defendant against an original plaintiff."

The further decision in *Kennett v Brown* [1988] 1 W.L.R. 582 that s.35(3) does not automatically bar a new claim but presents a procedural bar for the defendant to raise if he wishes, has been expressly overruled in *Welsh Development Agency v Redpath Dorman Long Ltd* [1994] 1 W.L.R. 1409 below. The onus was on the plaintiff to show that the amendment came within s.35(5) and the former O.20, r.5(5).

**Relationship of s.35 with the Civil Procedure Rules 1998**

It is important when considering the various matters for which this section makes provision to refer to the particular Civil Procedure Rules which apply in relation to that provision. Indeed, s.35(4) provides that rules of court may provide for allowing a new claim to be made outside the limitation period but only if the conditions of s.35(5) are satisfied and subject to any further restrictions the rules may impose. Those rules may be enumerated under the following headings: **8–109**

*(1) Addition of a new cause of action* —Section 35(5)(a) applies, together with CPR 17.4(1) and (2). These provisions are correspondingly restrictive, though the Act refers to the addition of a "new cause of action", while the Rule refers to the addition of a "new claim". In each case, the addition must arise out of the same facts or substantially the same facts. The Act qualifies these words with the words "as are already in issue on any claim previously made in the original action". The words of restriction in the Rule are "as a claim in respect of which the party applying for permission has already claimed a remedy in the proceedings". The Rule may thus be regarded as imposing an additional restriction, but this is expressly envisaged by s.35(4). In *Law Society v Wemyss* [2009] 1 All E.R. 752, it was held by Norris J. that the fact that the words of the section were less restrictive than the words of the rule did not assist the applicant for permission to amend. The rule required that the applicant should have already claimed a remedy, which it had not. **8–110**

Useful guidance as to whether a claim gives rise to a new cause of action and, if so, whether it arises out of the same or substantially the same facts is to be found in the decision of the Court of Appeal in *Smith v Henniker-Major & Co* [2002] EWCA Civ 762; [2003] Ch. 182, CA, and of Blackburne J. in *Finlan v Eyton Morris Winfield* [2007] EWHC 914 (Ch); [2007] 4 All E.R. 143.

As the Court of Appeal emphasised in *Lloyds Bank plc v Rogers* [1999] 3 E.G.L.R. 83, per Auld L.J. at p.85, "It is important to note that what makes a 'new claim' as defined in s.35(2) is not the newness of the claim according to the type or quantum of remedy sought, but the newness of the cause of action that it involves. The formula employed in s.35(2)(a) and (5) is 'a claim involving ... the addition or substitution of a new cause of action'." Auld L.J.'s judgment was applied in *Aldi Stores Ltd v Holmes Buildings plc* [2005] P.N.L.R. 9, CA. *Aldi*, and the cases cited therein of *Gordon v JB Wheatley & Co* [2000] Lloyd's Rep. P.N. 605 and *Stock v London Underground Ltd*, *The Times*, August 13, 1999, CA are examples, on their facts, of what may or may not amount to a new cause of action.

Amendment of a case to add a new cause of action after the expiry of a limitation period was governed under the former rules of the Supreme Court by Order 20, rule 5. That rule may be compared with CPR r.17.4(2). In *Welsh Development Agency v Redpath Dorman Long Ltd* [1994] 1 W.L.R. 1409 and [1994] 4 All E.R. 10, CA, the Court of Appeal made it clear that in cases where s.35(1) does, or may well, give the plaintiff an

***Paragraph numbers marked with a "+" can be found online and on CD.***

advantage the correct test to apply is that leave to amend by adding a new claim should not be given unless the claimant could show that the defendant did not have a reasonably arguable case on limitation which would be prejudiced by the new claim, or could bring himself within Order 20, rule 5. The court held that the onus was on the plaintiff to show that the amendment came within s.35(5), and that s.35(3) was a mandatory direction to a court dealing with an application to amend by adding a new claim: commenting on *Grimsby Cold Stores Ltd v Jenkins & Potter* (1985) 1 Const. L.J. 362, CA, and on *Leicester Wholesale Fruit Market Ltd v Grundy* [1990] 1 W.L.R. 107; [1990] 1 All E.R. 442, CA, and stating that the decision in *Holland v Yates Building Co Ltd*, *The Times*, December 5, 1989, CA was one which should not be followed.

The court in *Welsh Development Agency* [1994] 1 W.L.R. 1409 further held that on a true construction of s.35, unless a new claim came within one of the exceptions provided by the rules of court, leave to amend could not be given where the limitation period had expired at the time when the court was considering the matter, even if it had not expired at the time when application for leave was made, since the relevant date was the date on which the amendment was actually made, which by definition must be no earlier than the date on which leave was granted: p.1421.

The decision in *Welsh Development Agency* [1994] 1 W.L.R. 1409, by preventing an amendment being permitted where limitation is arguable, may make it incumbent on a claimant to issue fresh proceedings asserting the new cause of action, whilst preserving the defendant's right to argue (including by way of an application to strike out) limitation as a defence in those proceedings. In appropriate circumstances, an order for consolidation might be made of the fresh proceedings with the original claim.

Under s.35(5)(a) it will often be necessary to consider whether the amended claim involves a new cause of action. While it is not appropriate to construe the original pleading unduly literally or pedantically, a pleading is a formal document and cannot be held to include a cause of action which its language does not adequately express (*Balfour Beatty Construction v Parsons Brown and Newton* (1991) 7 Const.L.J. 205, CA).

In a case where an allegation in the statement of claim had, in further and better particulars, not been pursued, it was permissible as a matter of discretion, by amendment of the particulars after the expiry of the limitation period, to resuscitate the allegation. Such did not constitute the pleading of a new cause of action (*Burton v MBC (Builders–Ashingdon) Ltd* (1995) 69 P.&C.R. 496, CA). Further, a writ might be amended out of time to include a new case of action which had been pleaded within time in the statement of claim but had been inadvertently omitted from the writ (*Phelps v Spon Smith & Co (Amendment of Writ)*, *The Times*, November 26, 1999).

An existing statement of claim pleading negligent acts may not enable a plaintiff wishing to amend by alleging negligent statements to say that the new factual material arises out of the same or substantially the same facts as are already in issue (*Hydrocarbons Great Britain v Cammell Laird Shipbuilders* (1991) 25 Con.L.R. 131).

A statement of claim which originally disclosed no sustainable cause of action might in a proper case be amended with leave of the court despite the expiry of the limitation period, so that a cause of action based on the same or substantially the same facts could be introduced (*Sion v Hampstead HA* [1994] 5 Med. L.R. 170, June 10, CA). But where the court has refused an amendment to plead a new cause of action on the ground that the same is arguably time-barred, it may similarly refuse an amendment to plead a yet further new cause of action arising out of the same facts: *Goose v Wilson Sandford and Co*, *The Times*, May 10, 1994, per Harman J.

Section 35(5)(a) enables a new cause of action to be asserted if it arises out of the same or substantially the same facts as are already in issue. This exception may, contrary to the general rule, permit a cause of action to be pleaded which did not exist at the date of the writ, as where the original proceedings were brought by an injured plaintiff and amendment is sought after his death to introduce his widow's claim under the Fatal Accidents Act after the expiry of the limitation period under that Act (*Booker v Associated British Ports* [1995] P.I.Q.R. 375, CA).

Section 35(5)(a) will also permit, subject to the exercise of the court's discretion, a new claim to be made by way of amendment to a counterclaim to plead a claim in libel after the expiry of the limitation period in relation to that claim if by the same application an amendment is permitted to plead a contractual claim within the limitation period and if the two claims are based on substantially the same facts. The court will

***Paragraph numbers marked with a "+" can be found online and on CD.***

treat the new claim within the limitation period as a claim previously made in the original action for the purposes of s.35(5)(a) (*Lloyd's Bank Plc v Rogers The Times*, April 11, 1996; affirmed in the Court of Appeal, *The Times*, March 24, 1997, CA).

An amendment to allege intentional wrongdoing by pleading fraud where previously only negligence had been alleged amounts to the introduction of a new cause of action: *Paragon Finance plc v D.B. Thakerar & Co* [1999] 1 All E.R. 400, CA.

For amendment of a claim containing claims both for damages for personal injuries and for damages for economic loss by deletion of the claim for personal injuries, see *Shade v The Compton Partnership* [2000] Lloyd's Rep. P.N. 81, CA, and *Pounds v Eckford Rands* [2003] Lloyd's Rep. P.N. 195, cited also in the note to section 11, below.

*(2) Addition or substitution of parties* —Here, s.35(5)(b) and s.35(6) apply, together with CPR Pt 19. Amendment may be allowed after the expiry of the limitation period only in restricted circumstances. Thus, by s.35(5)(b) the amendment must be necessary for the determination of the action. And, by s.35(6)(b), apart from mistake, such amendment shall not be regarded as necessary unless a claim already made cannot be maintained by or against an existing party unless the new party is joined or substituted. Likewise, by CPR r.19.4(3)(b) the restriction is that the claim cannot be properly carried on by or against the original party unless the new party is added or substituted. **8–111**

The rationale of the restriction is that, by s.35(1)(b), the new claim, if permitted, is deemed to have commenced on the same date as the original action. It is for this reason of relation back that, on an application to add a new party, unless the court is satisfied that the question of limitation is unarguable, permission should be refused: *c.f. Welsh Development Agency* [1994] 1 W.L.R. 1409, above, where the application to amend related to the addition of a new cause of action.

It should be noted however that the restriction does not apply where substitution is necessary by reason of the original party having died or having had a bankruptcy order made against him and of his interest or liability having passed to the new party: CPR r.19.4(3)(c). This reflects the former RSC Ord.15, r.7(1) which is preserved by CPR Sch.1. In *Yorkshire Regional HA v Fairclough Building Ltd* [1996] 1 W.L.R. 210, CA it was held that the restrictive effect of the former Ord.15, r.6(5) and (6) did not apply in cases falling under the former r.7, which provided for substitution of a party by reason of assignment, transmission or devolution of interest or liability. It was held that the substitution of a new party unless Ord.15, r.7 did not involve the making of a new claim as defined in s.35(2) of the Limitation Act 1980. There were two entirely different kinds of substitution provided by the rules, one where the party substituted had succeeded to a claim or liability already represented in the action, and one where he had not. It would be outside the scope of the 1980 Act to alter the law relating to the former kind of substitution, which involved no question of limitation. It is to be observed, in relation to this decision, that the former Order 15, rule 7 has survived only in respect of r.7(1) (death and bankruptcy): see CPR Schedule 1; and further that CPR r.19.1(4) permits a new party to be substituted if the existing party's interest or liability has passed and it is *desirable* to substitute the new party. It is not clear to what extent CPR r.19.4(3) will be held restrictive of the general power in CPR r.19.1(4) but it is to be hoped that the reasoning in *Yorkshire Regional HA v Fairclough Building* [1996] 1 W.L.R. 210 will survive. A further respect in which the restrictions of s.35(5)(b) will not apply arises where a claim is made to add a defendant in a personal injuries claim and the claimant relies on s.33 of the Limitation Act 1980. This is recognised by the combined operation of s.35(3) and CPR r.19.5(4). The rule provides that the new party may be added either where the court directs that ss.11 or 12 of the Act shall not apply or where it directs that that issue shall be determined at trial: see *Howe v David Brown Tractors (Retail) Ltd* [1991] 4 All E.R. 30, CA, where it was held that the party whom it is sought to add could be heard on the question, even before he had become a party. And see *Bridgeman v Brown* [2000] 12 C.L. 48, CA, per Hale L.J., where it was held that arrangements should be made for the trial of issues of identity, limitation and joinder of an added defendant to be heard together.

The relevant authorities on the substitution of a claimant bringing a new claim where this is necessary for the determination of the original action were reviewed and explained by the Court of Appeal in *Parkinson Engineering Plc v Swan* [2009] EWCA Civ 1366, December 21, 2009, CA, unrep. (substitution of a company liquidator as claimant, bringing (with permission) a new claim under the Insolvency Act 1986 s.212

against former administrators of the company, allowed in proceedings originally brought (at the instigation of the liquidator) against them in the name of the company for breach of duty).

8–112 *(3) Mistake in name of party* —Section 35(6)(a) of the Act applies so as to permit the substitution of a new party for a party whose name was given in any claim made in the original action in mistake for the new party's name. Section 35(4) provides that rules of court may provide for allowing a new claim in such circumstances and subject to any further restrictions the rules may impose. CPR 19.5 is made under such power and the words of the rule, including CPR 19.5(3)(a), should be noted. Further, the distinction between CPR 17.4(3) (power to allow amendment to correct a mistake as to the name of a party) and CPR 19.5(3)(a) (power to allow a new party to be substituted for a party who was named in the claim form in mistake for the new party) should be noted. See the commentary on each of the two rules in Vol.1. And see *Horne-Roberts v Smithkline Beecham PLC* [2001] EWCA Civ 2006; [2002] 1 W.L.R. 1662; [2002] C.P. Rep. 20; (2002) 65 BMLR 79, CA.

In *Evans Constructions Co Ltd v Charrington & Co Ltd* [1983] Q.B. 810; [1983] 2 W.L.R. 117; [1983] 1 All E.R. 310, CA, Griffiths L.J. held at p.825 in relation to the former RSC Order 20, r.5(3),

> "The wording of the rule makes it clear that it is not the identity of the person sued that is crucial, but the identity of the person intended to be sued, which is a very different matter."

The court permitted an amendment to be made to substitute as intended the name of the current landlord as defendant. This was applied in *The Sardinia Sulcis* [1991] 1 Lloyd's Rep. 201, CA, Lloyd L.J. holding, at p.207,

> "In all these cases it was possible to identify the intending plaintiff or intended defendant by reference to a description which was more or less specific to the particular case;"

and Stocker L.J. holding, at p.209,

> "can the intending plaintiff or defendant be identified by reference to a description which is specific to the particular case— e.g. landlord, employer, owners or shipowners?"

The view was also expressed at p.208, without argument, that the amendmentrelated back to the date of the writ, and that the writ was accordingly not a nullity by reason of the non-existence of the plaintiff. However, s.35 of the Act has no application where a substantive or contractual time limit, such as that in the Hague Rules, has expired and the action has ceased to exist: *Payabi v Armstel Shipping Corp* [1992] Q.B. 907; [1992] 2 W.L.R. 898; [1992] 3 All E.R. 329; [1992] 2 Lloyd's Rep. 62, per Hobhouse J. The reasoning in the *Sardinia Sulcis*, above was applied in *International Bulk Shipping and Services Ltd v Mineral and Metals Trading Corp of India* [1996] 1 All E.R. 1017, CA, in which orders made under the former RSC after the expiry of the limitation period to substitute as plaintiff the trustee in bankruptcy of the plaintiffs' assets were set aside, and applications to amend the names of the plaintiffs to the trustee's name were dismissed, where the actions were a nullity at their commencement in that the plaintiff companies had been dissolved and ceased to exist and where the amendments would be to correct the identity of the person intending to sue rather than a mistake in the name of such person.

The above cases were considered, after the introduction of the CPR, in *Horne-Roberts v SmithKline Beecham Plc*, cited above, where the manufacture of a vaccine had been wrongly attributed to the person named as defendant. Substitution of the true manufacturer as defendant was permitted under s.35 of the Act and CPR 19.5. See also the commentary under s.11A of the Act, above.

It has also been held, in *Parsons v George* [2004] EWCA Civ 912; [2004] 3 All E.R. 633, CA, that the conditions of CPR 19.5(3)(a) were satisfied where the tenants had always intended to sue the persons who answered the description of competent landlord.

The true construction of s.35(4)–(6) of the Act, having regard to CPR 19.5(3)(a), is that where the new party was to be substituted for a party whose name had been given in a claim in the original action in mistake for the new party's name, substitution was to be regarded as necessary for the determination of the original action: *O'Byrne v Aventis Pasteur MSD Ltd* [2006] EWHC 2562, [2006] 92 BMLR 130.

*(4) Claim in a new capacity*—Subject to the restrictive provisions of s.35(4), Rules of Court may authorise a party to claim relief in a new capacity in respect of a new cause of action notwithstanding that he had no title to make that claim at the commencement of the action. Indeed he will be allowed in appropriate circumstances to claim relief in a new capacity without adding or substituting a new cause of action: see s.35(7) and CPR r.17.4(4). **8–113**

**Service on new party**

Practice Direction 19, para.3.3 provides that a new defendant does not become a party to the proceedings until the amended claim form has been served on him. Service of a writ which had been amended to add a new defendant was the subject, under the former Rules, of O.15, r.8(4). The new defendant did not become a party until the writ had been amended and served on him. And that must take place before the expiry of the limitation period (*Bank of America National Trust and Savings Association v Christmas, The Kyriaki* [1993] 1 Lloyd's Rep. 137). Hirst J. rejected the argument that under s.35(3) all that was required was an order within the limitation period giving leave to amend. He held that O.15, r.8(4) was directly applicable, and that since s.35(3)–(5) enacted the principle that joinder of a new defendant related back to the date of issue of the writ, Lord Keith's statement in *Ketteman v Hansel Properties Ltd* [1987] A.C. 189, HL, that, if that theory applied it would be unjust to join a new defendant at a time when limitation had run in his favour, because to do so would have the effect of depriving him of a valid defence, was fully applicable under s.35. Service on the new defendant out of time was set aside. It was also held that O.2, r.1, with its provisions for correcting an irregularity in failing to draw in time an order granting leave to amend, was subordinate to s.35 and to those provisions of O.15, rr.6 and 8 which implement that section, and that there was no jurisdiction to grant an extension of time for making the amendment so as to allow the action to be brought against the new defendant by service after the expiry of the limitation period. The decision in *The Kyriaki* has been expressly approved by the CA in *Welsh Development Agency v Redpath Dorman Long Ltd* [1994] 1 W.L.R. 1409, above. **8–114**

## Equitable jurisdiction and remedies

**36.**—(1) The following time limits under this Act, that is to say— **8–115**

(a) the time limit under section 2 for actions founded on tort;

(aa) the time limit under section 4A for actions for libel or slander, or for slander of title, slander of goods or other malicious falsehood;

(b) the time limit under section 5 for actions founded on simple contract;

(c) the time limit under section 7 for actions to enforce awards where the submission is not by an instrument under seal;

(d) the time limit under section 8 for actions on a specialty;

(e) the time limit under section 9 for actions to recover a sum recoverable by virtue of any enactment; and

(f) the time limit under section 24 for actions to enforce a judgment;

shall not apply to any claim for specific performance of a contract or for an injunction or for other equitable relief, except in so far as any such time limit may be applied by the court by analogy in like manner as the corresponding time limit under any enactment repealed by the Limitation Act 1939 was applied before 1st July 1940.

(2) Nothing in this Act shall affect any equitable jurisdiction to refuse relief on the ground of acquiescence or otherwise.

***Paragraph numbers marked with a "+" can be found online and on CD.***

8–116 *Note*—Subsection (1), para.(aa) was added by the Administration of Justice Act 1985 s.57; substituted, in regard to causes of action arising after September 4, 1996, by the Defamation Act 1996 s.5.

8–117 *Time limits in breach of fiduciary duty*—In cases where the claimant had a cause of action for intentional breach of fiduciary duty independently of causes of action in contract or tort, the limitation periods in ss.2 and 5 of the Act are not directly applicable. Whilst there is no reference in the 1980 Act to breach of fiduciary duty, a claim for equitable damages for breach of such duty is a claim for equitable relief. Accordingly section 36 applies. In applying it, the court is not looking to see whether a limitation period was actually applied to a dishonest breach of fiduciary duty by analogy before July 1, 1940, but looking to see whether it would have been applied. Where the facts to support the claim for breach of fiduciary duty are the same as those relied on to support breach of contract, the statute will be applied by analogy. Even where equity was acting in its exclusive, as opposed to its concurrent, jurisdiction, the statute might be applied by analogy: *Cia de Seguros Imperio v Heath (REBX) Ltd (formerly CE Heath &Co (America) Ltd)* [2001] 1 W.L.R. 112, CA. The cited case of *Cia de Seguros* was applied, where the claimant alleged breach of contract and claimed specific performance, in *P & O Nedlloyd BV vArab Metals Co* [2005] EWHC 1276; [2005] 1 W.L.R. 3733.

## Application to the Crown and the Duke of Cornwall

8–118 **37.**—(1) Except as otherwise expressly provided in this Act, and without prejudice to section 39, this Act shall apply to proceedings by or against the Crown in like manner as it applies to proceedings between subjects.

(2) Notwithstanding subsection (1) above, this Act shall not apply to—

(a) any proceedings by the Crown for the recovery of any tax or duty or interest on any tax or duty;

(b) any forfeiture proceedings under the customs and excise Acts (within the meaning of the Customs and Excise Management Act 1979); or

(c) any proceedings in respect of the forfeiture of a ship.

In this subsection "duty" includes any debt due to Her Majesty under section 16 of the Tithe Act 1936, and "ship" includes every description of vessel used in navigation not propelled by oars.

(3) For the purposes of this section, proceedings by or against the Crown include—

(a) proceedings by or against Her Majesty in right of the Duchy of Lancaster;

(b) proceedings by or against any Government department or any officer of the Crown as such or any person acting on behalf of the Crown; and

(c) proceedings by or against the Duke of Cornwall.

(4) For the purpose of the provisions of this Act relating to actions for the recovery of land and advowsons, references to the Crown shall include references to Her Majesty in right of the Duchy of Lancaster; and those provisions shall apply to lands and advowsons forming part of the possessions of the Duchy of Cornwall as if for the references to the Crown there were substituted references to the Duke of Cornwall as defined in the Duchy of Cornwall Management Act 1863.

(5) For the purposes of this Act a proceeding by petition of right (in any case where any such proceeding lies, by virtue of any saving in section 40 of the Crown Proceedings Act 1947, notwithstanding the general abolition by that Act of proceedings by way of petition of right) shall be treated as being commenced on the date on which the petition is presented.

(6) Nothing in this Act shall affect the prerogative right of Her Majesty (whether in right of the Crown or of the Duchy of Lancaster) or of the Duke of Cornwall to any gold or silver mine.

## Interpretation

**38.**—(1) In this Act, unless the context otherwise requires— **8–119**

"action" includes any proceeding in a court of law, including an ecclesiastical court;

"land" includes corporeal hereditaments, tithes and rentcharges and any legal or equitable estate or interest therein [...] but except as provided above in this definition does not include any incorporeal hereditament;

"personal estate" and "personal property" do not include chattels real;

"personal injuries" includes any disease and any impairment of a person's physical or mental condition, and "injury" and cognate expressions shall be construed accordingly;

"rent" includes a rentcharge and a rentservice;

"rentcharge" means any annuity or periodical sum of money charged upon or payable out of land, except a rent service or interest on a mortgage on land;

"settled land", "statutory owner" and "tenant for life" have the same meanings respectively as in the Settled Land Act 1925;

"trust" and "trustee" have the same meanings respectively as in the Trustee Act 1925; and

[...]

(2) For the purposes of this Act a person shall be treated as under a disability while he is an infant, or of unsound mind.

(3) [...]

(4) [...]

(5) Subject to subsection (6) below, a person shall be treated as claiming through another person if he became entitled by, through, under, or by the act of that other person to the right claimed, and any person whose estate or interest might have been barred by a person entitled to an entailed interest in possession shall be treated as claiming through the person so entitled.

(6) A person becoming entitled to any estate or interest by virtue of a special power of appointment shall not be treated as claiming through the appointor.

(7) References in this Act to a right of action to recover land shall include references to a right to enter into possession of the land or, in the case of rentcharges and tithes, to distrain for arrears of rent or tithe, and references to the bringing of such an action shall include references to the making of such an entry or distress.



LIMITATION

(8) References in this Act to the possession of land shall, in the case of tithes and rentcharges, be construed as references to the receipt of the tithe or rent, and references to the date of dispossession or discontinuance of possession of land shall, in the case of rentcharges, be construed as references to the date of the last receipt of rent.

(9) References in Part II of this Act to a right of action shall include references to—

(a) a cause of action;
(b) a right to receive money secured by a mortgage or charge on any property;
(c) a right to recover proceeds of the sale of land; and
(d) a right to receive a share or interest in the personal estate of a deceased person.

(10) References in Part II to the date of the accrual of a right of action shall be construed—

(a) in the case of an action upon a judgment, as references to the date on which the judgment became enforceable, and
(b) in the case of an action to recover arrears of rent or interest, or damages in respect of arrears of rent or interest, as references to the date on which the rent or interest became due.

**8-120** *Note* —Amended by the Trusts of Land and Appointment of Trustees Act 1996 Sch.4 and, with respect to references in subss.(3) and (4) to the Mental Health Act 1959, by the Mental Health Act 1983 Sch.4, para.55; the Care Standards Act 2000 Sch.4, para.8; and the Mental Capacity Act 2005 s.67, Sch.6, para.25, Sch.7, with effect from October 1, 2007 (SI 2007/1897).

### Saving for other limitation enactments

**8-121** **39.** This Act shall not apply to any action or arbitration for which a period of limitation is prescribed by or under any other enactment (whether passed before or after the passing of this Act) or to any action or arbitration to which the Crown is a party and for which, if it were between subjects, a period of limitation would be prescribed by or under any such other enactment.

### Transitional provisions, amendments and repeals

**8-122** **40.**—(1) Schedule 2 to this Act, which contains transitional provisions, shall have effect.

(2) The enactments specified in Schedule 3 to this Act shall have effect subject to the amendments specified in that Schedule, being amendments consequential on the provisions of this Act; but the amendment of any enactment by that Schedule shall not be taken as prejudicing the operation of section 17(2) of the Interpretation Act 1978 (effect of repeals).

(3) The enactments specified in Schedule 4 to this Act are hereby repealed to the extent specified in column 3 of that Schedule.

### Short title, commencement and extent

**8-123** **41.** This Act may be cited as the Limitation Act 1980.

(2) This Act, except section 35, shall come into force on 1st May 1981.

(3) Section 35 of this Act shall come into force on 1st May 1981 to the extent (if any) that the section substituted for section 28 of the Limitation Act 1939 by section 8 of the Limitation Amendment Act 1980 is in force immediately before that date; but otherwise section 35 shall come into force on such day as the Lord Chancellor may by order made by statutory instrument appoint, and different days may be appointed for different purposes of that section (including its application in relation to different courts or proceedings).

(4) The repeal by this Act of section 14(1) of the Limitation Act 1963 and the corresponding saving in paragraph 2 of Schedule 2 to this Act shall extend to Northern Ireland, but otherwise this Act does not extend to Scotland or to Northern Ireland.

**For Schs 1 to 4 to the Limitation Act 1980 (see Arrangement) plus any related commentary see paragraph 8–124+ to 8–130+ on White Book on Westlaw UK or the Civil Procedure CD.**

## Foreign Limitation Periods Act 1984

(1984 c.16) 8–131

ARRANGEMENT OF SECTIONS

SECT.



**Paragraph numbers marked with a "+" denote content that is available on the White Book on Westlaw UK Service or the Civil Procedure CD.**

LIMITATION

# SECTION 9

## JURISDICTIONAL AND PROCEDURAL LEGISLATION

# 9A MAIN STATUTES

## Senior Courts Act 1981

(1981 c.54) 9A–0

ARRANGEMENT OF SECTIONS

PART I



***Paragraph numbers marked with a "+" can be found online and on CD.***



MAIN STATUTES

***Paragraph numbers marked with a "+" can be found online and on CD.***

THE HIGH COURT

*DISTRIBUTION OF BUSINESS*



***Paragraph numbers marked with a "+" can be found online and on CD.***

**Paragraph numbers marked with a "+" denote content that is available on White Book on Westlaw UK or the Civil Procedure CD.**

### Introductory note

**9A–1** This Act repealed and replaced the Supreme Court of Judicature (Consolidation) Act 1925 as well as the whole or parts of several other statutes, some ancient, obsolete or unnecessary and others more recent, which had dealt with the administration of justice in the Supreme Court in England and Wales. It also made consequential amendments in many other similar enactments and introduced several amendments.

The Act came into force on January 1, 1982 (s.153(2) (para.20A–566) except for ss.72, 143 and 152(2) which came into force on the day the Act received Royal Assent, July 28, 1981).

***Paragraph numbers marked with a "+" can be found online and on CD.***

By the Constitutional Reform Act 2005 s.59 and Sch.11 Pt I para.1(1) the Senior Courts Act 1981 is re-titled the Senior Courts Act 1981 and throughout the 1981 Act "Senior Courts" is substituted for "Supreme Court". Certain other amendments are also made by the 2005 Act to the 1981 Act, in particular amendments made necessary by the transfer of the judicial functions of the House of Lords to the Supreme Court of the United Kingdom (see s.40 and Sch.9 para.36 of the 2005 Act).

**Interpretation**

Whereas the JA 1925 was a consolidating statute, the SCA 1981 is not a mere consolidating statute but is, as expressly stated in its preamble, an Act "to consolidate with amendments" the JA 1925 and other enactments. A major consequence of this fact is that, in interpreting the provisions of the 1981 Act the Court will not be bound to apply the presumption, applicable to the construction of a consolidating statute that Parliament did not intend to alter but simply to reproduce or repeat the existing law; nor will the Court be bound by the presumption that the words used in the 1981 Act should have the same meaning as they had at the time the Act was passed (see Bennion, *Statutory Interpretation* (3rd edn, 1997) Sect.211, and authorities cited there). The Court will bear in mind that these presumptions are rebuttable, and will lean towards giving effect to the overriding intention of Parliament to provide an efficient and effective system for the administration of justice, both civil and criminal. **9A–2**

**Continuity of procedure**

Whereas the JA 1925 contained an express provision for the saving of the former practice and procedure (see s.103 which replaced s.73 of the JA 1873), the SCA 1981 omits this provision (note also the JA 1925 s.32 was repealed but not replaced by the 1981 Act). Nevertheless, there are to be found scattered through the Act provisions which recall and reimpose those as to jurisdiction, practice and procedure which prevailed before the passing of the Act and which may, in some instances, refer back to the jurisdiction, practice and procedure prevailing before J.A.s 1873—1875 (see, e.g. s.15(2)(b) (jurisdiction, civil and criminal of the Court of Appeal); s.19(2)(b) (jurisdiction, civil and criminal exercisable by the High Court); s.28(3)(b) (jurisdiction of the High Court to determine appeals from Crown Court and inferior courts); s.29(1) (orders of mandamus, prohibition and certiorari); s.44 (extraordinary functions of Judges of High Court); s.49(2) (jurisdiction as to the current administration of law and equity to be exercised "as hitherto"); s.84(2) (powers to make rules of court); s.96(2) (business of the Central Office). **9A–3**

**Impact of Constitutional Reform Act 2005**

The Constitutional Reform Act 2005 (c.4) modifies the office of Lord Chancellor and makes provision relating to the functions of that office. The Act also (1) establishes a Supreme Court of the United Kingdom and abolishes the appellate jurisdiction of the House of Lords, and (2) makes provision about the jurisdiction of the Judicial Committee of the Privy Council. In addition the Act makes provision about the judiciary (their appointment and discipline). The Act is being brought into force over a period of time. It alters in many respects the Senior Courts Act 1981 (and other legislation printed in Section 9 of *The White Book*). At the time of going to press, only a few of the provisions in the 2005 Act had been brought into force. Those provisions having an impact on the SCA 1981 are referred to in commentary where relevant and some (but not all) of the prospective amendments are also noted. Provisions in the Courts Act 2003 (c.39) also amended sections in the 1981 Act. Some of those provisions are September 19, 2007. When they are they will take effect as amended (if at all) by the 2005 Act. Further provisions in the Constitutional Reform Act 2005 altering provisions in the Senior Courts Act 1981 were brought into force with effect from April 3, 2006, by the Constitutional Reform Act 2005 (Commencement No.5) Order 2006 (SI 2006/1014). Included among them was s.13 of the 2005 Act which deals with, to give directions. Other provisions brought into force by that Order affect provisions relating to the organisation of the courts but most are a consequence of the transfer of functions from the Lord Chancellor to the Lord Chief Justice. **9A–4**

**For ss.1 to 8 of the Senior Courts Act 1981 (see Arrangement) plus any related commentary see paragraphs 9A–5+ to 9A–29+ on White Book on Westlaw UK or the Civil Procedure CD.**

***Paragraph numbers marked with a "+" can be found online and on CD.***

OTHER PROVISIONS

## Assistance for transaction of judicial business of Senior Courts

9A–30 **9.**—(1) A person within any entry in column 1 of the following Table may subject to the proviso at the end of that Table at any time, at the request of the appropriate authority, act—

(a) as a judge of a relevant court specified in the request; or

(b) if the request relates to a particular division of a relevant court so specified, as a judge of that court in that division.

9A–31

| | 1 *Judge or ex-judge* | 2 *Where competent to act on request* |
|---|---|---|
| 1. | A judge of the Court of Appeal. | The High Court and the Crown Court. |
| 2. | A person who has been a judge of the Court of Appeal. | The Court of Appeal, the High Court and the Crown Court. |
| 3. | A puisne judge of the High Court. | The Court of Appeal. |
| 4. | A person who has been a puisne judge of the High Court. | The Court of Appeal, the High Court and the Crown Court. |
| 5. | A Circuit judge. | The High Court and the Court of Appeal. |
| 6. | A Recorder. | The High Court. |

The entry in column 2 specifying the Court of Appeal in relation to a Circuit judge only authorises such a judge to act as a judge of a court in the criminal division of the Court of Appeal.

(1A) A person shall not act as a judge by virtue of subsection (1) after the day on which he attains the age of 75.

(2) In subsection (1)

"the appropriate authority"—

(a) the Lord Chief Justice or a judicial office holder (as defined in section 109(4) of the Constitutional Reform Act 2005) nominated by him to exercise his functions under this section, or

(b) at any time when the Lord Chief Justice or the nominated judicial office holder is unable to make such a request himself, or there is a vacancy in the office of Lord Chief Justice, the Master of the Rolls;

"relevant court", in the case of a person within any entry in column 1 of the Table, means a court specified in relation to that entry in column 2 of the Table.

(2A) The power of the appropriate authority to make a request under subsection (1) is subject to subsections (2B) to (2D).

(2B) In the case of a request to a person within entry 1, 3, 5 or 6 in column 1 of the Table, the appropriate authority may make the request only after consulting the Lord Chancellor.

(2C) In any other case the appropriate authority may make a request only with the concurrence of the Lord Chancellor.

(2D) In the case of a request to a Circuit judge or Recorder to act as a judge of the High Court, the appropriate authority may make the request only with the concurrence of the Judicial Appointments Commission.

(3) In the case of—

(a) a request under subsection (1) to a Lord Justice of Appeal to act in the High Court; or

(b) any request under that subsection to a puisne judge of the High Court or a Circuit judge,

it shall be the duty of the person to whom the request is made to comply with it.

(4) Without prejudice to section 24 of the Courts Act 1971 (temporary appointment of deputy Circuit judges and assistant Recorders), if it appears to the Lord Chief Justice, after consulting the Lord Chancellor, that it is expedient as a temporary measure to make an appointment under this subsection in order to facilitate the disposal of business in the High Court or the Crown Court, he may appoint a person qualified for appointment as a puisne judge of the High Court to be a deputy of the High Court during such period or on such occasions as the Lord Chief Justice, after consulting the Lord Chancellor, thinks fit; and during the period or on the occasions for which a person is appointed as a deputy judge under this subsection, he may act as a puisne judge of the High Court.

(4A) No appointment of a person as a deputy judge of the High Court shall be such as to extend beyond the day on which he attains the age of 70, but this subsection is subject to section 26(4) to (6) of the Judicial Pensions and Retirement Act 1993 (Lord Chancellor's power to authorise continuance in office up to the age of 75).

(5) Every person while acting under this section shall, subject to subsections (6) and (6A), be treated for all purposes as, and accordingly may perform any of the functions of, a judge of the court in which he is acting.

(6) A person shall not by virtue of subsection (5)—

(a) be treated as a judge of the court in which he is acting for the purposes of section 98(2) or of any statutory provision relating to—

(i) the appointment, retirement, removal or disqualification of judges of that court;

(ii) the tenure of office and oaths to be taken by such judges; or

(iii) the remuneration, allowances or pensions of such judges; or

(b) subject to section 27 of the Judicial Pensions and Retirement Act 1993, be treated as having been a judge of a court in which he has acted only under this section.

(6A) A Circuit judge or Recorder shall not by virtue of subsection (5) exercise any of the powers conferred on a single judge by sections 31, 31B, 31C and 44 of the Criminal Appeal Act 1968 (powers of single judge in connection with appeals to the Court of Appeal and appeals from the Court of Appeal to the Supreme Court).

(7) […]

(8) Such remuneration and allowances as the Lord Chancellor may, with the concurrence of the Minister for the Civil Service, determine may be paid out of money provided by Parliament—

(a) to any person who has been—

(i) a judge of the Supreme Court; or

(ii) a judge of the Court of Appeal; or

(iii) a judge of the High Court,

and is by virtue of subsection (1) acting as mentioned in that subsection;

(b) to any deputy judge of the High Court appointed under subsection (4).

(9) The Lord Chief Justice may nominate a judicial office holder (as defined in section 109(4) of the Constitutional Reform Act 2005) to exercise his functions under subsection (4).

9A-32 *Note* —Amended by the Administration of Justice Act 1982 s.58; the Judicial Pensions and Retirement Act 1993 ss.26 and 31; Schs 6 and 9; the Criminal Justice and Public Order Act 1994 s.52; the Courts Act 2003 s.109(1), Sch.8, para.260; the Constitutional Reform Act 2005 s.15(1), Sch.4, para.121 and by the 2005 Act, ss 40, 59, Sch.9, para.36(2), Sch.11, para.26, Sch 17, para 22(3), with effect from October 1, 2009 (SI 2009/1604).

**Judicial assistance**

9A-33 The most interesting feature of this section is that it provides for circumstances in which puisne judges of the High Court may sit in the Court of Appeal and in which circuit judges may sit in the High Court or in the Court of Appeal. This facilitates the flexibile deployment of judge power and has other advantages. This section gathers together in simplified language and with the use of a table, scattered provisions from several enactments enabling judicial assistance to be obtained for the business of the Supreme Court, see the JA 1925 ss.3, 7 and 8; the A.J. (M.P.) A. 1933 s.2(1); the Criminal Appeal Act 1966 s.1(3); and the Courts Act 1971 ss.4(3), 23 and 24.

Under the common law doctrine of de facto authority, the acts of a circuit judge in dealing with a High Court case, though not authorised to do so under s.9, may be upheld (*Fawdry & Co v Murfitt* [2002] EWCA Civ 643; [2002] 3 W.L.R. 1354, CA; see also *Baldock v Webster* [2004] EWCA Civ 1869, CA; *Coppard v Customs and Excise Commissioners* [2003] EWCA Civ 511; [2003] 2 W.L.R. 1618, CA). Note also s.68 (Exercise of High Court jurisdiction otherwise than by judges of that court). Where the necessary judicial authority of a judge is provided by the de facto authority doctrine, the judge constitutes a tribunal established by law within the meaning of art.6 of the Convention, as the doctrine validates the judge's office as well as his acts (*Coppard v Customs and Excise Commisioners* [2003] EWCA Civ 511; [2003] 2 W.L.R. 1618, CA).

**Subsection (1)**

9A-34 Item 6 in the table was added by the AJA 1982 s.58.

**For ss.10 to 13 of the Senior Courts Act 1981 (see Arrangement) plus any related commentary see paragraphs 9A-35+ to 9A-45+ on White Book on Westlaw UK or the Civil Procedure CD.**

## Power of judge of Senior Courts to act in cases relating to rates and taxes

9A-46 **14.**—(1) A judge of the Senior Courts or of the Crown Court shall

***Paragraph numbers marked with a "+" can be found online and on CD.***

not be incapable of acting as such in any proceedings by reason of being, as one of a class of ratepayers, taxpayers or persons of any other description, liable in common with others to pay, or contribute to, or benefit from, any rate or tax which may be increased, reduced or in any way affected by those proceedings.

(2) In this section "rate or tax" means any rate, tax, duty or liability, whether public, general or local, and includes—

(a) any fund formed from the proceeds of any such rate, tax, duty or liability; and

(b) any fund applicable for purposes the same as, or similar to, those, for which the proceeds of any such rate, tax, duty or liability are or might be applied.

*Note* —Derived from the JA 1925 s.17. Amended by the Constitutional Reform Act 2005 s.59 and Sch.11, para.26 with effect from October 1, 2009 (SI 2009/1604). **9A-47**

### Judicial bias—"incapable" and "apparent"

Under the Human Rights Act 1998 Sch.1, Pt 1, art.6.1 (right to a fair trial), in the determination of his civil rights and obligations, everyone is entitled to a fair hearing by an independent and impartial tribunal (see para.3D-76 above). The requirement that the tribunal should be independent and impartial is one that has long been recognised by English common law. An appellate or reviewing court will set aside a decision affected by bias. **9A-48**

On the matter of impartiality, the decided cases draw a distinction between "actual bias" and "apparent bias" (*Director General of Fair Trading v Proprietary Association of Great Britain* [2001] 1 W.L.R. 700, CA, para.38). The phrase "actual bias" has been applied to the situation (1) where a judge has been influenced by partiality or prejudice in reaching his decision and (2) where it has been demonstrated that a judge is actually prejudiced in favour of or against a party. Findings of actual bias on the part of a judge are rare.

The phrase "apparent bias" describes the situation where circumstances exist which give rise to a reasonable apprehension that the judge may have been, or may be, biased. After *R. v Bow Street Metropolitan Stipendiary Magistrate Ex p. Pinochet Ugarte (No.2)* [1999] 2 W.L.R. 272, HL, allegations of apparent bias in the court became increasingly prevalent (in particular, allegations against part-time professional judges and against full-time judges recruited from the solicitors' branch of the legal profession). In *Locabail (UK) Ltd v Bayfield Properties Ltd* [2000] QB 451, CA, after hearing a number of appeals at the same time, the Court of Appeal sought to give guidance as to the principles which should be applied. Subsequently, in *Porter v Magill* [2001] UKHL 67; [2002] 2 A.C. 357, HL, the House of Lords approved the following test formulated in the *Re Medicaments* case: "The court must first ascertain all the circumstances which have a bearing on the suggestion that the judge was biased. It must then ask whether those circumstances would lead a fair-minded and informed observer to conclude that there was a real possibility or a real danger, the two being the same, that the tribunal was biased". The fair-minded observer is not unduly sensitive or suspicious (*Helow v Secretary of State for the Home Department* [2008] UKHL 62; [2008] 1 W.L.R. 2416, HL). Actual or apparent bias against a witness is as serious as bias against or in favour of a party (*Phillips v Symes* [2003] EWCA Civ 1769; December 5, 2003, CA, unrep.).

In *Helow v Secretary of State for the Home Department* [2008] UKHL 62; [2008] 1 W.L.R. 2416, HL, an application by a Palestinian asylum-seeker for the review of a removal order was refused by a judge of the Scottish Court of Session. The applicant's appeal to the Inner House, made on the ground of apparent bias, in particular on the ground that the judge was a member of a voluntary association (the International Association of Jewish Lawyers and Jurists) in whose publications pro-Israel sentiments expressed by the association's president had been published, was dismissed. The House of Lords dismissed the applicant's further appeal. It was held that, in the absence of evidence that the judge had read the material complained of, or endorsed the views expressed thereon, a fair-minded and informed observer would not have concluded that there was a real possibility of bias.

Conceivably, cases may arise in which judges have to decide questions as to the raising and levying of rates and taxes, the outcome of which may affect their interests as rate payers or tax payers. The Senior Courts Act 1981 s.14 states that a judge shall not be "incapable of acting" by reason of that interest.

On application or on his own motion a judge may recuse himself on the ground of bias. Applications for recusal go to the heart of the administration of justice and must be raised as soon as is practicable (*Baker v Quantum Clothing Group* [2009] EWCA Civ 566; June 6, 2009, CA, unrep.). As an impartial judge is a fundamental prerequisite of a fair trial a judicial officer should not hesitate to recuse himself if there are reasonable grounds on the part of a litigant for apprehending that the judicial officer, for whatever reason, was not or will not be impartial (*Locabail (UK) Ltd v Bayfield Properties Ltd, op. cit.*, at p.479). The reasonableness of the apprehension must be assessed in the light of the oath of office taken by the judges to administer justice without fear or favour; and their ability to carry out that oath by reason of their training and experience. It must be assumed that they can disabuse their minds of any irrelevant personal beliefs or predispositions. They must take into account the fact that they have a duty to sit in any case in which they are not obliged to recuse themselves (*ibid.*). Where, following trial, an application is made by a party for a costs order against a non-party under CPR r.48.2, the application should normally be determined by the trial judge who could give effect to any views he had expressed as to the conduct of the non-party without constituting bias or the appearance of bias (*Thomson v Berkhamsted Collegiate School* [2009] EWHC 2374 (QB), October 2, 2009, unrep. (Blake J.)). The circumstances in which an application to a trial judge under CPR r.48.2 for a costs order against a non-party arise may be such as to cause the judge to consider whether he should recuse himself on the grounds of apparent bias (*Bahai v Rashidian* [1985] 1 W.L.R. 1337, CA, *Symphony Group Plc v Hodgson* [1994] QB 179; [1993] 3 W.L.R. 830, CA, *Phillips v Symes (No.2)* [2004] EWHC 2330; 154 New L.J. 1615, (Ch) (Peter Smith J.)). In a case where proceedings are brought to commit a person for contempt in the face of the court, the judge should, if there is a risk of the appearance of bias, ask another judge to hear the committal application (Practice Direction (Committal Applications) para.13(6); see Vol.1, para.scpd52.7). It is not a breach of art.6 of the ECHR for the judge to deal with the contempt himself (*Wilkinson v S.* [2003] EWCA Civ 95; [2003] 1 W.L.R. 1254, CA, (see further Vol.1, para.sc52.1.17).

As to the risk of apparent bias in an appeal, where the appeal court is constituted by several judges, of whom one had dealt with the application for permission to appeal on paper (both generally and where that judge has specialist experience in the area of law involved), see *Sengupta v Holmes* [2002] EWCA Civ 1104; *The Times* August 19, 2002, CA, and *Dŵr Cymru Cyfyngedig v Albion Water* [2008] EWCA Civ 97, January 14, 2008, unrep. CA; and note commentary in Vol.1 para. 52.3.18. See also *Desmond v Bower* [2009] EWCA Civ 857; July 20, 2009, CA, unrep. (at permission stage, appeal panel judge recusing himself where a possible consequence of allowing an appeal against an admissibility of evidence decision would be that a person known to the judge would become a trial witness).

The disqualification of a judge for apparent bias is not a discretionary matter; either there is a real possibility of bias or there is not. A real danger of bias might well be thought to arise where the judge was closely acquainted with a member of the public involved in the case, whether or not that person was to give evidence. Judicial impartiality is the fundamental principle of justice (both at common law and under art.6 of the Convention). Consequently, a judge's concerns about the prejudicial effect that his withdrawal would have on the parties and on the administration of justice (delays, costs, listing problems) are not relevant, as efficiency and convenience are not the determinative legal values in this context (*AWG Group Limited v Morrison* [2006] EWCA Civ 6; [2006] 1 W.L.R. 1163, CA (appeal allowed where, shortly before trial, assigned judge realising that a prospective witness was known to him but dismissing defendant's application for recusal)).

Other English cases on apparent bias coming to attention since the Locabail case include: *Hampshire CC v Gillingham* April 5, 2000, unrep., CA; *Taylor v Lawrence* [2001] EWCA Civ 119; January 25, 2001, unrep., CA; *Re Bank of Credit and Commerce International (SA)* (2001) 151 New L.J. 1852, (Lawrence Collins J.); *Taylor v Lawrence*

[2002] EWCA Civ 90; [2002] 2 All E.R. 353, CA; *Taylor v Williamsons* [2002] EWCA Civ 1380, *The Times*, August 9, 2002, CA; *Sengupta v Holmes* [2002] EWCA Civ 1104; *The Times*, August 19, 2002, CA; *Berg v I.M.L. London Ltd* [2002] 1 W.L.R. 3271; [2002] 4 All E.R. 87 (Stanley Burnton J.) (Master dealing with application for summary judgment seeing "without prejudice" correspondence); *Hart v Relentless Records Ltd* [2002] EWHC 1984 (Jacob J.) (corridor meeting between judge and counsel in which judge indicated case was weak and parties should reconsider settlement). See also *Geveran Trading Co Ltd v Skjevesland* [2002] EWCA Civ 1567; [2003] 1 W.L.R. 912, CA (test of apparent bias not relevant to application to prevent an advocate from acting); *Garratt v Saxby (Practice Note)* [2004] EWCA Civ 341; [2004] 1 W.L.R. 2152, CA (offer to settle inadvertently disclosed to judge); *Foenander v Foenander* [2004] EWCA Civ 1675, (judges formerly in same chambers as counsel); *Birmingham City Council v Yardley*, [2004] EWCA Civ 1756, CA (part-time judge and counsel belonging to same chambers); *Howell v Lees Millais* [2007] EWCA Civ 720, July 4, 2007, CA (judge ought to have recused himself from dealing with application in which partner of firm of solicitors involved where alleged he had had personal dealings with another partner in the same firm); *Amjad v Steadman-Byrne* [2007] EWCA Civ 625; *The Times* July 30, 2007, CA, (before presentation of defence case, judge meeting privately with counsel and expressing various views on the progress of the case and giving opinion on the effectiveness of the defendant's cross examination of the claimants' witnesses); *Thompson v Collins* [2009] EWCA Civ 525; April 6, 2009, CA, unrep. (solicitor for one party contacting part-time judge directly when parties unable to resolve issues required to be agreed in accordance with judge's order); *Baker v Quantum Clothing Group* [2009] EWCA Civ 566; June 6, 2009, CA, unrep. (website links between claimant's solicitors and voluntary organisation of which appeal panel judge was honorary president and which provided self-help for persons afflicted by the particular disability suffered by the claimant as a result of the defendants' alleged negligence); *Desmond v Bower* [2009] EWCA Civ 857; July 20, 2009, CA, unrep. (at permission stage, appeal panel judge recusing himself where a possible consequence of allowing an appeal against an admissibility of evidence decision would be that a person known to the judge would become a trial witness). In *OFT v Abbey National plc* [2009] EWCA Civ 116; [2009] 2 W.L.R. 1286, CA, each of the three lord justices sitting to hear an appeal in a case involving a number of banks was a customer of one or more of them, but (as their lordships noted) none of the parties to the appeal suggested that they should not continue to sit (*ibid* at [3]). In the Scottish case of *Davidson v Scottish Ministers (No.2)* [2004] UKHL 34; *The Times* July 16, 2004, HL, it was held that a risk of apparent bias is liable to arise where a judge who had participated in the drafting or promotion of legislation during the parliamentary process is called upon to rule judicially on the effect of the legislation. But the fact that a judge has been a member of a government is not enough to disqualify that judge in respect of decisions made by that government; there must be a nexus between the issue before the court and the role of the judge while he was a minister (*R. (Ewing) v Secretary of State for Justice* [2008] EWHC 3416 (Admin); December 19, 2008, unrep. (Beatson J.)). A party may be taken to have waived his right to object to a particular judge hearing his case on grounds of apparent bias provided he was given a fair opportunity to reach an unpressured decision and did so freely and in full knowledge of the facts giving rise to an appearance of bias (*Smith v Kvaerner Cementation Foundations Ltd* [2006] EWCA Civ 242; [2006] 3 All E.R. 593, CA (re-trial before different judge ordered where claimant's decision assisted by counsel's advice did not amount to waiver of right to complain of bias)).

In *Locabail (UK) Ltd v Bayfield Properties Ltd, op. cit.*, Lord Bingham C.J., stated that, among the factors which were likely to give rise to a soundly based objection of apparent (or perceived) bias, was personal friendship between, or close acquaintance with, the judge and any member of the public involved in the case. If the credibility of a judge's friend or acquaintance is an issue to be decided by him, the judge should be readier to recuse himself. In *Grant v Teacher's Appeal Tribunal* [2006] UKPC 59, December 7, 2006, PC, unrep., the Privy Council dismissed an appeal from the Court of Appeal of Jamaica in part based on this factor. In doing so the Board recognised the special problems that judges in small communities face where parties and witnesses are known, and not infrequently well known, to judges assigned to sit.

Circumstances may arise where it would be improper for a judge to sit (1) to hear an application in, or (2) to try a particular issue arising for determination in, particular proceedings because of his earlier involvement in those proceedings or in related

MAIN STATUTES

proceedings. An obvious example would be where, in the course of managing a case, a judge who was to try the case necessarily had communicated to him the fact that Pt 36 payment had been made (see r.36.13(2)). There are less obvious examples not specifically dealt with by extant legal provisions (such as r.36.13(2)). Under the CPR case management system, the risks of a judge sitting for certain purposes knowing of matters that in fairness he should not are increased. Such difficulties have arisen in a number of post-CPR cases. Examples are: *Thomson Directories Ltd v Planet Telecom Plc* [2003] EWHC 1882 (Ch); July 4, 2003, unrep. (Laddie J.) (inquiry as to damages after trial of preliminary issue); *ALM Manufacturing v Black & Decker* [2003] EWHC 1646 (Ch); May 21, 2003, unrep. (Pumfrey J.) (without prejudice communication between defendant and third party); *GE Capital Commercial Finance Ltd v Sutton* [2003] EWHC 1648 (QB); July 4, 2003, unrep. (McCombe J.) (evidence ruling on material obtained by improper means); *Smithkline Beecham Plc v Generics (UK) Ltd* [2003] EWCA Civ 1109, *The Times*, August 25, 2003, CA (confidential documents where claims tried together). The handling of judicial review claims (especially those involving nationality and asylum issues) in which a judge is required to look at particular documents for interlocutory purposes may pose particular hazards in this respect. In such circumstances, the judge may think it right not to take part in a determination of the merits; all depends upon the circumstances (*R. (AHK & FM) v Secretary of State for the Home Department* [2009] EWCA Civ 287, April 2, 2009, CA, at para.20). In *Mireskandari v The Law Society* [2009] EWCA Civ 864; July 8, 2009, CA, unrep., the Court of Appeal noted that, where a recusal application is made to a judge managing a case and, whilst that application is pending, the judge makes case management directions, questions of the status of those directions may arise (should orders made in the meantime be set aside as of right?, or is there a more general discretion and, if so, in accordance with what principles should it be exercised?). In this case, the judge granted the claimant's recusal application, not on a ground alleged in the claimant's initial application (all of which the judge rejected), but on a single ground (relating to the judge's trial of an action 12 years previously in which the applicant was a witness) of which the judge became aware after he had refused the claimant's application for an extension of time for complying with an unless order. The Court of Appeal held that, in these circumstances, there was no principle pursuant to which it could be said that the judge was under a duty to stop giving case management directions or that he erred in principle in continuing to do so; accordingly, no question as to the status of those directions arose.

A judge to whom a case has been assigned for trial has to be very careful, in ruling on pre-trial applications, not to pre-judge any matter that will be argued and decided at trial, and not to pre-empt any decision that will be made on that occasion (*Hammond v Pro-Fit USA Limited* [2007] EWHC 2941 (Ch), June 28, 2007, unrep. (Morgan J.) (defendant's application for disclosure raising issue whether, on ground of fraud, claimant unable to claim document privileged); *Bank of Tokyo-Mitsubishi UFJ Ltd v Baskan Gida Sanayi Ve Pazarlama AS* [2008] EWHC 659 (Ch), April 9, 2008, unrep. (Briggs J.) (minor defendant's application in heavy proceedings for summary judgment on single conspiracy claim against him)). A judge's role in actively managing a case or group of cases (whether subject to a group litigation order or not) may require the judge to further consider or re-consider issues that have already arisen for determination, either at a case management hearing, or on an interlocutory application (e.g. for an interim injunction) or at a trial (e.g. of a preliminary issue). Obviously, circumstances may arise in which a judge assigned at an early stage to a particular case or group of cases should recuse himself from hearing particular matters; e.g. where successive applications are made in relation to the same interim injunction (e.g. one for continuation and another for variation) and fairness dictates that the same judge should not hear each (*Dadourian Group International Inc v Simms (Practice Note)* [2006] EWCA Civ 399; [2006] 1 W.L.R. 2499; [2006] 3 All E.R. 48, CA, at para.66 per Arden L.J.), or where, in ruling on a question whether part of a claim has been compromised, an assigned judge has seen documents he would not have seen were he trying the case (*Baris Ltd v Kasima Construction Europe (UK) Ltd* [2006] EWHC 31 (TCC), January 20, 2006, unrep.), or where, in dealing with a case management issue a judge to whom a case had been assigned for trial expressed the opinion that the claim was exaggerated (*Stallwood v David* [2006] EWHC 2600 (QB); October 25, 2006, unrep.), or where on a pre-trial application in a libel claim the parties wished to refer to matters which could not be mentioned to the designated judge (managing the case and due to try it) (*Adel-*

*son v Associated Newspapers Ltd* [2007] EWHC 997 (QB); *The Times* May 10, 2007). However, to characterise too readily a judge's conduct in this role as conduct at risk of being perceived as apparent bias would subvert the proactive management of cases expected of judges under the CPR (*A-B v British Coal Corp* [2006] EWCA Civ 172, January 24, 2006, unrep., CA, per Auld L.J.).

In the Family Proceedings Rules 1991, the procedural code for the handling of applications for ancillary relief under the Matrimonial Causes Act 1973 includes, in r.2.61A et seq, provisions for the hearing by a judge of a "Financial Dispute Resolution appointment", a meeting held for the purposes of discussion and negotiation, and in r.2.61E(2) it is expressly provided that, subject to exceptions, the judge "must have no further involvement with the application" (for purpose and ambit of this restriction and dicta on question whether it may be waived by party agreement, see *Myerson v Myerson* [2008] EWCA Civ 1376; *The Times* January 7, 2009, CA).

Cases have arisen in which, after trial, it has been argued that the appearance of bias was given by the way in which the judge conducted himself during the trial. The dictum of Lord Greene M.R. in *Yuill v Yuill* [1945] P. 15, about the judge who "descends into the arena and is liable to have his vision clouded by the dust of the conflict" has been much-quoted. The cases that have caused concern are those in which judges' interventions have taken the form, either of dealing brusquely with counsel, arguably frustrating the development of submissions, or of pointed and regular questioning of witnesses, arguably preventing the witness from giving of his best, or both (e.g. *Southwark LBC v Kofi-Adu* [2006] EWCA Civ 281; *The Times*, June 1, 2006, CA). Such behaviour causes concern, not simply because the judge has abandoned his traditional passive role, but because the manner in which he has chosen to play a more active role threatens the fairness of the trial. Most commonly, the connection between the judge's behaviour and the possibility of unfairness is the impression that the judge had pre-judged the issues he was required to try. Thus the argument has been that a fair-minded lay observer might reasonably apprehend from the judge's interventions that he had pre-judged the very questions he was to decide and therefore might not bring an impartial and unprejudiced mind to the resolution of those questions. Such pre-judgment may form the basis for a challenge of apparent bias (or, indeed, of actual bias). However, not every case in which it is contended that a trial was unfair because of excessive judicial intervention should be analysed in terms of apparent bias (*Opportunity Equity Partners Ltd v Almeida* [2006] UKPC 44, October 3, 2006, unrep., PC).

The surest means by which a judge might avoid any allegations of apparent bias on the grounds that he pre-judged issues would be for him to remain silent throughout the proceedings, giving no hint of his thought processes, listening to advocates without interruption, asking no question and voicing no opinion until breaking his silence to give judgment. In a number of cases (most of them involving allegations of bias against members of tribunals) the impracticality of such passive judicial behaviour and the advantages of judges engaging in dialogue with parties and counsel, whilst avoiding premature expressions of factual conclusions or anything which may prematurely indicate a closed mind, have been noted and explained (see *Arab Monetary Fund v Hashim* (1993) 6 Admin. L.R. 348, CA, and authorities referred to in *Southwark LBC v Jiminez* [2003] EWCA Civ 502; [2003] I.C.R. 1176, CA). At a trial a judge may legitimately give assistance to the parties by telling them about the views that he is forming in his mind as the evidence goes along, but it is not acceptable for a judge to form (or to give the impression of having formed) a firm view in favour of one side's credibility when the other side has not yet called evidence which is intended to impugn it (*Amjad v Steadman-Byrne* [2007] EWCA Civ 625; *The Times* July 30, 2007, CA). A judge who intervenes to suggest new lines of argument to counsel risks being accused of entering into the arena on behalf of one side, especially where for good reasons unknown to the court experienced counsel has chosen not to utilise them (*W.X. Investments Ltd v Bragg* [2002] EWHC 925 (Ch); [2002] 1 W.L.R. 2849 (Patten J.). On the other hand, where counsel fail to refer the judge to the law relevant to the determination of a procedural application it is proper for the judge to direct their attention to it and to invite submissions (*James v London Borough of Havering* [2007] EWHC 2168 (QB), September 26, 2007 (Keith J.) (application to lift automatic stay).

As to bias in arbitrators, see *Save and Prosper Pensions Ltd v Homebase Ltd* [2001] L. & T.R. 11; *AT&T Corp v Saudi Cable Co* [2000] 2 Lloyd's Rep. 127, CA.

***Paragraph numbers marked with a "+" can be found online and on CD.***

As to bias in tribunal, see *Harada Ltd v Turner* [2001] EWCA Civ 599; April 6, 2001, unrep., CA; *Bennett v London of Southwark* [2002] EWCA Civ 223; February 21, 2002, unrep., CA; *Lawal v Northern Spirit Limited* [2003] UKHL 35; [2003] I.C.R. 856, HL (part-time tribunal member acting as advocate); *Bennett v London Borough of Southwark* [2002] EWCA Civ 223; February 21, 2002, unrep., CA (whether industrial tribunal should have recused itself when claimant's lay representative accused it of racism); *Jones v DAS Legal Expenses Insurance Co Ltd* [2003] EWCA Civ 1071 (chairman of tribunal related to barrister in chambers routinely receiving cases from defendants); *ASM Shipping Ltd of India v TTMI Ltd of England* [2005] EWHC 2238 (Comm); [2006] 1 Lloyd's Rep. 375 (Morison J.); *Ansar v Lloyds Bank TSB Plc* [2006] EWCA Civ 1462, October 9, 2006, CA, unrep. (allegations of bias and misconduct made against tribunal chairman by claimant in previous proceedings); *Ezsias v North Glamorgan NHS Trust* [2007] EWCA Civ 330, March 7, 2007, CA, unrep. (premature expression of concluded view).

# PART II

# JURISDICTION

## *THE COURT OF APPEAL*

### General jurisdiction of Court of Appeal

9A–49 **15.**—(1) The Court of Appeal shall be a superior court of record.

(2) Subject to the provisions of this Act, there shall be exercisable by the Court of Appeal—

(a) all such jurisdiction (whether civil or criminal) as is conferred on it by this or any other Act; and

(b) all such other jurisdiction (whether civil or criminal) as was exercisable by it immediately before the commencement of this Act.

(3) For all purposes of or incidental to—

(a) the hearing and determination of any appeal to the civil division of the Court of Appeal; and

(b) the amendment, execution and enforcement of any judgment or order made on such an appeal,

the Court of Appeal shall have all the authority and jurisdiction of the court or tribunal from which the appeal was brought.

(4) It is hereby declared that any provision in this or any other Act which authorises or requires the taking of any steps for the execution or enforcement of a judgment or order of the High Court applies in relation to a judgment or order of the civil division of the Court of Appeal as it applies in relation to a judgment or order of the High Court.

#### Criminal and Civil Divisions of the Court of Appeal

9A–50 The Court of Appeal is divided into the Criminal Division and the Civil Division. For the provisions governing distribution of business between the Divisions see s.53 below.

#### Appeals in civil matters

9A–51 For procedure regulating appeals to the Court of Appeal (Civil Division), see CPR Pt 52 and the practice direction supplementing that Part. The courts and tribunals from which the Court of Appeal hears appeals in civil matters include:

***Paragraph numbers marked with a "+" can be found online and on CD.***

(1) *High Court*—Subject to exceptions, appeal lies to the Court of Appeal from all Divisions of the High Court (s.16); see para.9A–59 below and note (5) below (bankruptcy appeals).
(2) *County courts*—Subject to exceptions, appeal lies to the Court of Appeal from decisions of the county courts in civil matters, including matrimonial proceedings (County Courts Act 1984 s.77); see para.9A–568.
(3) *Employment Appeal Tribunal*—Appeal lies to the Court of Appeal from the EAT, but only with the leave of the EAT or the Court of Appeal (Employment Protection (Consolidation) Act 1978 s.136(4)).
(4) *Patents Court*—Appeal lies to the Court of Appeal from decisions of the Patents Court (see the SCA 1981 s.6 (which provides that the Patents Court is part of the Chancery Division of the High Court) and the Patents Act 1977 s.97(3) (which sets out the requirements concerning leave to appeal)).
(5) *Bankruptcy*—An appeal lies from a decision made by a county court or by a registrar in bankruptcy of the High Court to a single judge of the High Court and an appeal lies from a decision of that judge with his leave or the leave of the Court of Appeal (Insolvency Act 1986 s.375(2)).
(6) *Lands Tribunal*—Appeal lies to the Court of Appeal from decisions of the Lands Tribunal Act 1949 s.3(4)). Section 4(1) of the 1949 Act was amended by the Civil Procedure (Modification of Enactments) Order 2000 (SI 2000/941), with the result that the requirement that appeals from the Lands Tribunal on points of law should be by case stated was removed. Such appeals are now governed by CPR Pt 52, with permission to appeal being required in every case (*Practice Direction (Lands Tribunal: Appeals: Applications)* [2000] R.V.R. 223).
(7) *Social Security Commissioners*—Appeal lies to the Court of Appeal from decisions of the Social Security Commissioners, with the leave of the Commissioner or the Court of Appeal (Social Security Act 1980 s.14). Although s.55(1) of the Access to Justice Act 1999, s.55(1) (Second appeals) does not apply to these appeals, a robust attitude to the "prospect of success" criterion (CPR r.52.3(6)) should be adopted in these cases (*Cooke v Secretary of State for Social Security* [2001] EWCA Civ 734, April 25, 2001, unrep., CA).
(8) *Upper Tribunal* —By the Tribunal, Courts and Enforcement Act 2007 s.13 (para 9B–994 below), where the Court of Appeal is "the relevant appeal court" (see s.13(13), an appeal lies to that Court, with permission, on a point of law arising from a decision made by the Upper Tribunal, other than an "excluded decision" (as defined, see s. 3(8)). Permission to appeal to the Court of Appeal shall not be granted unless the Upper Tribunal, or where the Upper Tribunal refuses permission, the Court, considers that (a) the proposed appeal would raise some important point of principle or practice, or (b) there is some other compelling reason to hear the appeal (Appeals from the Upper Tribunal to the Court of Appeal Order 2008 (SI 2008/2834)).

For appeals to the Court of Appeal from the Pathogens Access Appeal Commission, and from the Proscribed Organisations Appeal Commission established, respectively, by the Anti-terrorism, Crime and Security Act 2001, and the Terrorism Act 2000, see respectively, Court of Appeal (Appeals from Pathogens Access Appeal Tribunal) Rules 2002 (SI 2002/1844) and the Court of Appeal (Appeals from Proscribed Organisations Appeal Commission) Rules 2002 (SI 2002/1843).

The Court of Appeal has no jurisdiction to hear an appeal from Immigration Appeal Tribunal decision on appeal from a special adjudicator sitting in Scotland; in these circumstances, appeal lies to the Court of Session (*Gardi v Secretary of State for the Home Department (No.2)* [2002] EWCA Civ 1560; [2002] 1 W.L.R. 3282, CA).

**"all purposes of or incidental to"**

In judicial review proceedings, the High Court has an inherent jurisdiction to make ancillary orders temporarily releasing an applicant from detention, and by virtue of s.15(3), on appeal in those proceedings, the Court of Appeal could make like order (*R. (Sezek) v Secretary of State for the Home Department*, *The Times*, June 20, 2001, CA). **9A–52**

**Application of High Court enforcement provisions to Court of Appeal judgments**

The purpose of the declaration in s.15(4) to the effect that provisions for the enforcement of High Court judgment or orders (which are legion) apply to the enforcement **9A–53**

***Paragraph numbers marked with a "+" can be found online and on CD.***

by the High Court of judgments and orders of the Court of Appeal (Civil Division) is obvious. The County Courts Act 1984 contains no similar provision. However, in *Ager v Ager* [1998] 1 W.L.R. 1074, CA, it was held that the jurisdiction conferred on the High Court by s.15(4) constituted a "general principle of practice" within the meaning of s.76 of the 1984 Act which could be adopted and applied in proceedings in a county court.

**Jurisdiction where appeal raising "academic" or "hypothetical" point of law**

9A-54 See para.9A-77 below.

**Inherent jurisdiction of Court of Appeal**

9A-55 Circumstances have arisen in which, under its inherent jurisdiction, procedural innovations relating, not only to its own procedures, but also to procedures affecting the lower courts, have been initiated by the Court; see *YD (Turkey) v Secretary of State for the Home Department* [2006] EWCA Civ 52; [2006] 1 W.L.R. 1646, CA (Court's power to suspend removal directions pending determination of application for extension of time for appealing in asylum-seeker case), and illustrations given there.

**Appeals from Court of Appeal to House of Lords**

9A-56 The Administration of Justice (Appeals) Act 1934 s.1(3) states that no appeal shall lie from any order or judgment made or given by the Court of Appeal except with the leave of that Court or of the House of Lords. That provision does not affect any other restriction that may exist apart from that imposed by s.1(3) on the bringing of appeals from the Court of Appeal to the House of Lords.

## Appeals from High Court

9A-57 **16.**—(1) Subject as otherwise provided by this or any other Act (and in particular to the provision in section 13(2)(a) of the Administration of Justice Act 1969 excluding appeals to the Court of Appeal in cases where leave to appeal from the High Court directly to the Supreme Court is granted under Part II of that Act) or as provided by any order made by the Lord Chancellor under section 56(1) of the Access to Justice Act 1999, the Court of Appeal shall have jurisdiction to hear and determine appeals from any judgment or order of the High Court.

(2) An appeal from a judgment or order of the High Court when acting as a prize court shall not be to the Court of Appeal, but shall be to Her Majesty in Council in accordance with the Prize Acts 1864 to 1944.

9A-57.1 *Note*—Amended by the Constitutional Reform Act 2005 s.40 and Sch.9, para.36(3) with effect from October 1, 2009 (SI 2009/1604).

**Appeals directly from the High Court to the Supreme Court—"leap-frog" petitions**

9A-58 See the AJA 1969 s.13 (para.9B-33 below) and Section 4 paras 4.1.5 and 4.5.9 above.

**Jurisdiction to hear appeals from High Court**

9A-59 The general rule is that the Court of Appeal shall have jurisdiction "to hear and determine appeals from any judgment or order of the High Court" (s.16(1)). Two exceptions (provided for in s.16) are "leap-frog" appeals to the Supreme Court of the United Kingdom (formerly to the House of Lords) and Prize Court appeals. The general rule is further qualified by the Access to Justice Act 1999. Section 56(1) of that Act states that the Lord Chancellor may by order provide that appeals "which would otherwise lie to the Court of Appeal", for example, appeals falling within the general rule stated above, shall lie instead to the High Court (see para.9A-775 below). Accordingly, the power of the Lord Chancellor by order to affect the jurisdiction of the Court of Appeal in relation to appeals from the High Court was added to s.16(1) by the Access to Justice Act 1999 (Destination of Appeals) Order 2000 (SI 2000/1071) art.7. Provisions exercising this power in relation to appeals to the Court of Appeal from the High Court are found in arts 2, 4 and and 5 of that statutory instrument. Article 2 states that, where the decision to be appealed is a decision made by (inter alia) a Master or a district judge, then, subject to two exceptions, the appeal shall not go according to the general rule (i.e. from the High Court to the Court of Appeal) but shall go to a judge of the High Court. In this context, "decision" includes any judgment, order or direction. The two exceptions are: (1) where the decision is a final decision in a claim allocated to the multi-track under CPR rr.12.7, 14.8 or 26.5, or is made in "specialist proceedings" provided for by CPR Pt 49 (e.g. proceedings in the Commercial Court, the Patents Court, or the Technology and Construction Court) (see art.4); and (2) where the decision appealed was itself a decision made on appeal (other than from the decision of an officer of the court authorised to assess costs) (so-called "second appeals") (see art.5). In this context, "final decision" means any decision that would finally determine (subject to any possible appeal or detailed assessment of costs) the entire proceedings whichever way the court decided the issues before it (*ibid.*, art.1(2)(c)). Certain decisions, though not strictly falling within this definition, are to be treated as final decisions (*ibid.*, art.1(3)) (see further *Roerig v Valiant Trawlers Ltd* [2002] EWCA Civ 21; [2002] 1 W.L.R. 2304, CA, and authorities referred to therein).

The Access to Justice Act 1999, s.57 (see para.9A–848 below) states that, where in any proceedings in a county court or the High Court a person seeks permission to make an appeal which, but for the operation of the alternative destination of appeals provisions explained above, would go to the Court of Appeal, the Master of the Rolls or the court from which or to which the appeal is made, or from which permission to appeal is sought, may direct that the appeal shall be heard instead by the Court of Appeal. Where this power is exercised, in effect the alternative destination provisions are overridden. In the case of *Re Claims Direct Test Cases* [2002] EWCA Civ 428; *The Times*, April 4, 2002, CA, it was held that this procedure could not be used to "leapfrog" the requirement that an application for permission to appeal should be made.

No appeal shall lie to the Court of Appeal: (1) from any order, judgment or decision of the High Court which is final, or (2) from any order of the High Court allowing an extension of time for appealing from a judgment or order (paras (b) and (c) of s.18(1); see para.9A–62 below).

No appeal shall lie from a decision of the High Court refusing leave required by s.42 (Restriction of vexatious legal proceedings) (see para.9A–148 below).

As to appeals to the Court of Appeal against an order of the High Court refusing permission to appeal, see *Foenander v Bond Lewis & Co* [2001] EWCA Civ 759; [2001] 2 All E.R. 1019, CA. In those circumstances where there is no appeal to the Court of Appeal without the permission of the High Court, generally, where such permission is refused, that refusal cannot be reviewed by the Court of Appeal. But the Court of Appeal has a residual discretion to permit an appeal, despite the lower court's refusal of permission, where that refusal can be challenged on the grounds of unfairness pursuant to art.6 of the Convention on Human Rights (*CGU International Insurance plc v Astrazeneca Insurance Co Ltd* [2006] EWCA Civ 1340; *The Times*, November 3, 2006, CA (leave required by *The Times*, November 3, 2006, Arbitration Act 1996 s.68(6) refused)).

For rules of court affecting appeals from the High Court to the Court of Appeal, see CPR Pt 52, and for further information as to the jurisdiction of the Court of Appeal in relation to appeals from the High Court, see notes on the rules in Pt 52 (Vol.1, paras 52.0.1 *et seq*).

Section 13(2)(a) of the Administration of Justice Act 1969 provides that where a trial judge grants a certificate unders.12 of that Act and permission is given for an appeal from the High Court directly to the House of Lords, no appeal from "the decision of the judge" as to which the certificate relates shall lie to the Court of Appeal (see paras 9B–33 and 9B–35 below).

MAIN STATUTES

## Applications for new trial

**17.**—(1) Where any cause or matter, or any issue in any cause or matter, has been tried in the High Court, any application for a new trial thereof, or to set aside a verdict, finding or judgment therein, **9A–60**

shall be heard and determined by the Court of Appeal except where rules of court made in pursuance of subsection (2) provide otherwise.

(2) As regards cases where the trial was by a judge alone and no error of the court at the trial is alleged, or any prescribed class of such cases, rules of court may provide that any such application as is mentioned in subsection (1) shall be heard and determined by the High Court.

(3) Nothing in this section shall alter the practice in bankruptcy.

**Effect of the section**

9A–61 See CPR Pt 52 and notes thereto (see para.52.1).

## Restrictions on appeals to Court of Appeal

9A–62 **18.**—(1) No appeal shall lie to the Court of Appeal—

(a) except as provided by the Administration of Justice Act 1960, from any judgment of the High Court in any criminal cause or matter;

(b) from any order of the High Court or any other court or tribunal allowing an extension of time for appealing from a judgment or order;

(c) from any order, judgment or decision of the High Court or any other court or tribunal which, by virtue of any provision (however expressed) of this or any other Act, is final;

(d) from a decree absolute or nullity of marriage, by a party who, having had time and opportunity to appeal from the decree nisi on which that decree was founded, has not appealed from the decree nisi;

(dd) from a divorce order;

(e) [...]

(f) [...]

(fa) from a dissolution order, nullity order or presumption of death order under Chapter 2 of Part 2 of the Civil Partnership Act 2004 that has been made final, by a party who, having had time and opportunity to appeal from the conditional order on which that final order was founded, has not appealed from the conditional order;

(g) except as provided by Part I of the Arbitration Act 1996, from any decision of the High Court under that Part;

(h) [...]

(1A) [...]

(1B) [...]

(2) [...]

9A–63 *Note*—Amended by the Children Act 1989 Sch.13; the Courts and Legal Services Act 1990 s.7(2) and s.125(7); the Arbitration Act 1996 Sch.3; the Family Law Act 1996 Sch.8, para.30 and Sch.10; the Civil Procedure Act 1997 Sch.2; the Access to Justice Act 1999 s.106, Sch.15, Pt III; and the Civil Partnership Act 2004 s.261(1), Sch.27, para.68.

**Restrictions on appeals**

9A–64 Section 18(1) indicates that, in certain circumstances, no appeal shall lie to the

Court of Appeal. The legislative basis for the requirement that an appeal may not be made to the Court of Appeal without permission (i.e. without leave) was removed from s.18 and is now found in the Access to Justice Act 1999 s.54; note also ss.55 to 58 of that Act (see para.9A–843). The effect of other statutory provisions (either in this Act or elsewhere) may be to restrict appeals to the Court of Appeal. For example, s.28A of this Act (para.9A–93 below) provides that certain decisions of the High Court are final. For powers of High Court in relation to arbitrations, see Arbitration Act 1996 ss.66 to 71 (para.2E–241 *et seq.*); for appeals to Court of Appeal, see section 69 and notes thereto and note *Inco Europe Ltd v First Choice Distribution* [2000] 1 W.L.R. 586, HL; *Henry Boot Construction (UK) Ltd v Malmaison Hotel (Manchester) Ltd* [2001] 1 All E.R. 193, CA; [2000] 2 Lloyd's Rep. 625, CA.

The leading House of Lords authority on the phrase "in any criminal cause or matter" is *Amand v Home Secretary and Minister of Defence of Royal Netherlands Government* [1943] A.C. 147, HL, see *United States Government v Montgomery* [2001] UKHL 3; [2001] 1 W.L.R. 196, HL, where the Amand case and other authorities are examined. In *R. (South West Yorkshire Mental Health NHS Trust) v Crown Court at Bradford* [2003] EWCA Civ 1857; [2004] 1 W.L.R. 1664, CA, it was held that, although an order made by the Crown Court upon a verdict being entered was made under a statute empowering the court to make a custodial order in the absence of conviction (in this instance, the Criminal Procedure (Insanity) Act 1964 s.5(2)(a)), the order did not for that reason cease to be an order in a criminal cause or matter. In determining whether an appeal is in a criminal cause or matter it is appropriate for the court to take an overall view and not to enter into a detailed order by order analysis.

The Magistrates' Courts Act 1980 s.111 is an important example of a statutory provision, other than one found in the 1981 Act, providing that a decision of the High Court in a non-criminal cause or matter will be final and ousting the jurisdiction of the Court of Appeal (*Westminster City Council v O'Reilly* [2003] EWCA Civ 1007; *The Times*, August 21, 2003, CA (decision of High Court on appeal by way of cased stated from magistrates' court in licensing matter final)).

The effect of the various restrictions on appeals contained in this section is discussed in detail in notes to CPR Pt 52 (see Vol.1, para.52.1). See also para.9A–59 above.

## THE HIGH COURT

### *GENERAL JURISDICTION*

#### General jurisdiction of High Court

**19.**—(1) The High Court shall be a superior court of record. **9A–65**

(2) Subject to the provisions of this Act, there shall be exercisable by the High Court—

(a) all such jurisdiction (whether civil or criminal) as is conferred on it by this or any other Act; and

(b) all such other jurisdiction (whether civil or criminal) as was exercisable by it immediately before the commencement of this Act (including jurisdiction conferred on a judge of the High Court by any statutory provision).

(3) Any jurisdiction of the High Court shall be exercised only by a single judge of that court, except in so far as it is—

(a) by or by virtue of rules of court or any other statutory provision required to be exercised by a divisional court; or

(b) by rules of court made exercisable by a master, registrar or other officer of the court, or by any other person.

(4) The specific mention elsewhere in this Act of any jurisdiction

*Paragraph numbers marked with a "+" can be found online and on CD.*

covered by subsection (2) shall not derogate from the generality of that subsection.

9A–66 *Note*—Derived from the JA 1925 s.18.

**Jurisdiction exercisable by the High Court**

9A–67 By s.16 of the Judicature Act 1873, the High Court of Justice was created as a superior court of record and the jurisdiction which, at the commencement of that Act, was vested in or capable of being exercised by, certain courts of common law and equity, and certain other courts, was transferred to and vested in the High Court. The courts so merged in the High Court included, for example, the High Court of Chancery and the Court of Queen's Bench. Thus the jurisdiction of the High Court was co-extensive with the aggregate of the jurisdictions of the courts from whom jurisdiction was transferred, subject to legislative changes made by the 1873 Act itself (and by subsequent legislation) (see *Re Mill's Estate* (1886) 34 Ch.D. 24, at 33 per Cotton L.J.; *Bow, McLachlan and Co v Ship Camosun* (1909) 101 L.T. 167, PC, at 170, per Lord Gorell).

In the main, questions as to the extent of the jurisdiction of the High Court had to be answered by investigating the extent of the jurisdictions of the courts from whom jurisdiction was transferred and, as is indicated by s.19(1)(b), to an important degree, this remains the position to the present day. Obviously, the jurisdiction of the High Court has been affected by legislation coming into force after 1873 (see s.19(1)(a)) and by case law. Section 19(1)(b) states that the High Court shall have all such jurisdiction "as was exercisable by it immediately before the commencement of this Act". Comparable provisions were found in the predecessors to the 1981 Act, the successive Judicature Acts (e.g. s.18(2) of the JA 1925). In effect, the cumulative effect of these provisions has been to keep alive s.16 of the 1873 Act referred to above.

Section 19 confers jurisdiction on the High Court in general terms. It is expressed as "subject to the provisions of this Act". Provisions following s.19 deal with particular fields of jurisdiction, e.g. ss.20 to 24 (Admiralty), s.25 (probate), etc.

The general jurisdiction defined in s.19 is vested in all the Judges of the High Court, irrespective of the Division to which they are attached (see subs.(4), ss.4(3) and 5(5)).

**Inherent jurisdiction of High Court**

9A–68 The provision in s.19(2)(b), that there shall be exercisable by the High Court "all such other jurisdiction (whether civil or criminal) as was exercisable by it immediately before the commencement of the Act" of 1981, subsumes and incorporates "the inherent jurisdiction of the court". Such jurisdiction has been exercisable by the superior courts from the earliest days of the common law (see e.g. *Metropolitan Bank v Pooley* (1885) 10 App.Cas. 210, HL, at 220—221 per Lord Blackburn).

The court may execute its inherent jurisdiction even in respect of matters which are regulated by statute or by rules of court (see *Willis v Earl Beauchamp* (1886) 11 P.D. 59, at 63 per Bowen L.J., *Davey v Bentick* [1893] 1 Q.B. 185, CA, at 187 per Lord Esher M.R., *Stewart Charting v C. & O. Managements SA, The Venus Destiny* [1980] 1 W.L.R. 460, [1980] 1 All E.R. 718 (Goff J.)).

An important practical illustration of the Court's inherent jurisdiction is the Court's power to stay proceedings. The power may be exercised in various contexts (e.g. on abuse of process grounds); see s.49(3) below and notes thereto.

The powers which may said to be "inherent" in the High Court's jurisdiction cannot be stated succinctly. It has been said by the highest authority that there can be no doubt that a court which is endowed with a particular jurisdiction has powers "which are necessary to enable it to act effectively within such jurisdiction" and that a court must enjoy such powers "in order to enforce its rules of practice and to suppress any abuse of its process and to defeat any attempted thwarting of its processes" (*Connelly v DPP* [1964] A.C. 1254, HL, at 1301 per Lord Morris). It has also been said that it would be "conducive to legal clarity" if the use of the expressions "inherent power" and "inherent jurisdiction" were confined "to the doing by the court of acts which it needs must have power to do in order to maintain its character as a court of justice" (*Bremer Vulkan Schiffbau und Maschinenfabrik v South India Shipping Corp Ltd* [1981] A.C. 909, HL, at 971 per Lord Diplock). See, further, Jacob, "The Inherent Jurisdiction of the Court" (1970) 23 *Current Legal Problems* 27, and authorities cited there.

***Paragraph numbers marked with a "+" can be found online and on CD.***

The overriding features of the inherent jurisdiction of the court are that it is a part of procedural law, both civil and criminal and not part of substantive law: it is exercisable by summary process, without a plenary or full trial; it may be invoked not only in relation to parties in pending proceedings, but in relation to anyone, whether a party or not, and in relation to matters not raised in the litigation between the parties; it must be distinguished from the exercise of judicial discretion; and it may be exercised even in circumstances governed by rules of court (see *Jacob*, *ibid*.).

The Court of Appeal exercises its own inherent jurisdiction, e.g. the power to strike out a notice of appeal where the appeal is frivolous, vexatious or an abuse of the process of the court (*Burgess v Stafford Hotel Ltd* [1990] 1 W.L.R. 1215; [1990] 3 All E.R. 222, CA; *Aviagents Ltd v Balstravest Investments Ltd* [1966] 1 W.L.R. 150; [1966] 1 All E.R. 450, CA).

A county court has inherent jurisdiction to regulate its own procedures (*Langley v North West Water Authority* [1991] 1 W.L.R. 697; [1991] 3 All E.R. 610, CA); but note County Courts Act 1984 s.74A.

In *Tombstone Limited v Raja* [2008] EWCA Civ 1444, December 17, 2008, CA, unrep., one of the questions arising was whether the judge at first instance was right to dispose of a matter that fell for his determination by exercising a discretion derived from provisions found in the CPR in circumstances where it was arguable that he ought to have dealt with the matter by exercising the court's inherent jurisdiction. The Court of Appeal stated that the position pre-CPR was that "the inherent powers of the court could not be invoked to do something which was inconsistent with a rule", and the same position has applied since the introduction of the CPR. The court held that, where the subject matter of an application is governed by rules in the CPR, it should be dealt with by the court in accordance with the rules, and not by exercising the court's inherent jurisdiction (para.78).

For modern illustrations of reliance by court on its inherent jurisdiction, see the following Court of Appeal cases: *Rocksteady Services Ltd, Re* [2001] C.P. Rep. 1 (court can decline to proceed with a trial which it feels it can no longer conduct fairly because of delay caused by the court); *Woodford & Ackroyd v Burgess*, [2000] C.P. Rep. 79, CA (admissibility of an alleged expert's evidence); *C.J. Hurst (Lickfold) Ltd v Belchamber*, November 20, 1998, unrep., CA (county court's power to restrain a litigant from making further applications without leave, a "*Grepe v Loam*" order); *DowlesManor Properties Ltd v Bank of Namibia* [1999] C.P.L.R. 259, January 19, 1999, unrep., CA (dismissing action for claimant's failure adequately to comply with an "unless" order requiring exchange of witness statements within particular period); *Riniker v University College London, The Times* April 17, 1999, CA (backdating issue of writ from date when actually issued to date when received by the court for purpose of ensuring that action brought within relevant limitation period, see now CPR r.7.2(2) and Practice Direction (How to Start Proceedings—The Claim Form), para.5.1); *Reichhold Norway A.S.A. v Goldman Sachs International* [2000] 1 W.L.R. 173; [2000] 2 All E.R. 679, CA (stay of English proceedings in favour of foreign arbitration); *Mainwaring v Encyclopedia Britannica International Ltd*, June 21, 1999, unrep., CA (jurisdiction (acknowledged in CPR r.3.1) to strike out appeal, even though no "unless" order has been made); *Al-Naimi v Islamic Press Agency Inc* [2000] 1 Lloyd's Rep. 522, CA (jurisdiction to stay in addition to power under Arbitration Act 1996 s.9); *Walsh v Misseldine*, February 29, 2000, unrep., CA (residual inherent abuse of process jurisdiction and power to strike out under CPR r.3.4(2)); *R. (Sezek) v Secretary of State for the Home Department (Bail Application)*, [2001] EWCA Civ 795, CA (ancillary order in judicial review proceedings temporarily releasing an applicant from detention). Note also, *Harley v McDonald* [2001] UKPC 18; [2001] 2 W.L.R. 1749, PC (jurisdiction to award costs personally against practitioner where serious dereliction of duty); and *Orton v Collins* [2007] EWHC 803 (Ch); [2007] 1 W.L.R. 2953 (Mr. Peter Prescott Q.C.) (jurisdiction to enforce terms of offer to settle), and *Grupo Torras SA v Al-Sabah (Costs)* [2003] EWHC 262 (Treacy J.) (jurisdiction to restrict disclosure to paying party of reasons for success fee in receiving party's conditional fee agreement).

The court has inherent power to control its own process and it is entitled to bring argument to a close when it concludes that its process is being abused and that nothing of value will be lost by ending it (*Attorney General v Scriven* February 4, 2000, unrep., CA, courts are "not required to listen to litigants, whether represented or not, for as long as they like", per Simon Brown L.J.).

Where a winding up petition is dismissed, and the whole purpose of presenting it had been to obtain payment of a debt, the starting of fresh proceedings by the petitioner or his assignees to recover the same debt without paying the costs of the petition was an abuse of process (*Investment Invoice Financing Ltd v Limehouse Board Mills* [2006] EWCA Civ 9; [2006] 1 W.L.R. 985, CA).

See also authorities referred to in notes following s.42 (Restriction on vexatious legal proceedings) (paras 9A–149 *et seq.* below).

The court has no power under the Family Law Reform Act 1969 s.21 or the inherent jurisdiction to enforce compliance with an order requiring samples to be taken of a child's blood for the purposes of determining paternity (In *Re O. (Minor) (Blood Tests: Constraint)* [2000] 2 W.L.R. 1284; [2000] 2 All E.R. 29).

### Jurisdiction to be exercised by single judge

**9A–69** Subsection (3)(a) requires that the jurisdiction of the High Court should be exercised only by a single Judge of the Court except where such jurisdiction is required by virtue of rules of court or other statutory provision to be exercised by a Divisional Court, constituted under s.66 (see s.151(1)) i.e. consisting of not less than two Judges. A Divisional Court consisting of two judges has no jurisdiction to deal with a matter or proceeding which the Act confers on the High Court (see, e.g. In *Re Fletcher, The Times*, June 12, 1984, where held that a Divisional Court had no jurisdiction to make a civil proceedings order under s.42).

Subsection (3)(b) requires that the jurisdiction of the High Court should be exercised only by a single Judge of the Court except where such jurisdiction "by or by virtue of rules of court" is made exercisable by a master, district judge or other officer of the Court or by any other person. CPR r.2.4 provides that where the Civil Procedure Rules provide for the Court "to perform any act" masters and district judges may exercise any function of the High Court except where an enactment, rule or practice direction provides otherwise. Practice Direction (Allocation of Cases to Levels of Judiciary) sets out the matters over which masters and district judges do not have jurisdiction or which they may deal with only on certain conditions, but does not affect jurisdiction conferred by other enactments.

### Ouster of jurisdiction

**9A–70** The general principle is that parties cannot by agreement between themselves oust the jurisdiction of the High Court. Such an agreement is void, as contrary to public policy (*Czarnikow v Roth & Co* [1922] 2 K.B. 478, CA; *Re Davstone Estates Ltd's Leases, Manprop Ltd v O'Dell* [1969] 2 Ch. 378). There are important exceptions. An agreement to refer to arbitration, or that the ascertainment of facts by the arbitrator is to be a condition precedent to the exercise of jurisdiction does not oust the jurisdiction of the court, and is valid (*Scott v Avery* (1856) 5 H.L.Cas. 811; *Atlantic Co v Dreyfus* [1922] 2 A.C. 250; *Cipriani v Burnett* [1933] A.C. 83). An agreement that disputes shall be referred to a foreign tribunal equally does not oust the jurisdiction of the English Courts and is valid, and prima facie the English Courts will stay proceedings instituted in this country in breach of such agreement (*The Fehmarn* [1958] 1 W.L.R. 159; [1958] 1 All E.R. 333, CA). As to agreement to seek to settle a dispute by mediation, see *Halifax Financial Services Ltd v Intuitive Systems Ltd*, December 21, 1998 (unrep.) (McKinnon J.).

The parties to an agreement may validly provide, expressly or impliedly, that it shall be an agreement of honour only and not enforceable at law (*Balfour v Balfour* [1919] 2 K.B. 571; *Rose & Frank Co v Crompton* [1923] 2 K.B. 261; *Jones v Vernon's Pools Ltd* [1938] 2 All E.R. 626; *Appleson v Littlewood Ltd* [1939] 1 All E.R. 464, CA).

A settlor is not entitled to make any power or discretion exercisable with consent of the Ch.D. or a Judge thereof except in the event of trustees failing or refusing to exercise such discretion (*Re H.'s Settlement* [1939] W.N. 318).

### Ouster of jurisdiction by statute

**9A–71** Many statutes depute to other tribunals, or to officials, or other bodies, the right to determine questions of various kinds, and often give finality to such determination; e.g. *Joseph Crosfield & Sons Ltd v Manchester Ship Canal Co* (1904) 90 L.J. 557. Unless the statute in clear terms deprives the claimant of his remedy at law, the jurisdiction of the Court is not ousted (*Lowther v Clifford* [1927] 1 K.B. 130, CA, *cf. R. & W. Paul v Wheat*

*Commission* [1937] A.C. 139). In such cases, subject to exceptions that need not be canvassed here, the High Court has no jurisdiction to interfere by way of appeal, judicial review or otherwise.

Under the Housing Act 1985 s.110, certain jurisdiction under Pt IV of that Act is conferred on county courts (see Vol.2 para.3A–443), but this provision does not oust the jurisdiction of the High Court (*Fletcher v Sheffield City Council* [2007] EWHC 419 (Ch), January 12, 2007, unrep. (Lewison J.) (High Court has power, when dismissing a secured tenant's appeal against the refusal of application to vary an order for possession forthwith, to suspend the date of possession or stay or suspend execution of the order)).

**Want of jurisdiction—waiver**

It is sometimes a question of difficulty whether a proceeding is void for want of jurisdiction or whether there has been merely an irregularity in procedure which has been waived; see *Smythe v Wiles* [1921] 2 K.B. 66; *Shrager v Dighton* [1924] 1 K.B. 274; *Pringle v Hales* [1925] 1 K.B. 573; *Key v Bastin* [1925] 1 K.B. 650; *Wyndham v Jackson* [1937] W.N. 291. See also CPR r.3.10 (General power of the court to rectify matters where there has been an error of procedure). Want of jurisdiction cannot be cured by consent, see *Papadopoulos v Papadopoulos* [1930] P. 44; *Simons v Simons* [1939] 1 K.B. 490; *Rothman of Pall Mall (Overseas) Ltd v Saudi Arabia Airlines Corp* [1981] Q.B. 368; [1980] 3 All E.R. 359, CA. **9A–72**

**Bail**

The High Court has an inherent jurisdiction to grant bail. This jurisdiction extends to the grant of bail to persons under remand but does not extend to the grant of bail to persons who have been tried and convicted (In *Re L.* (1944) 61 T.L.R. 180, *Ex p. Speculand* [1946] K.B. 48). The jurisdiction has been affected by, and is exercised in accordance with, legislative provisions. See, further, Archbold, Criminal Pleading, Evidence and Practice (2001), paras 3—186 to 3—194. For relevant rules of court, see CPR Sch.1, RSC O.79 (Criminal Proceedings), r.9 (Bail) (see Vol.1, para.sc79.9). **9A–73**

**Benefice**

Order to admit against bishop (*Notley v Bp. of Birmingham* [1930] W.N. 110; [1931] 1 Ch. 529). **9A–74**

**Domestic forum**

The Court cannot interfere with the decision of a "domestic tribunal" if made bona fide, in accordance with its rules, and not contrary to the elementary principles of justice (*Catt v Wood* [1910] A.C. 404; *Leeson v General Council of Medical Education* (1890) L.R. 43 Ch.D. 366; *Maclean v Workers' Union* [1929] 1 Ch. 602; *Cotter v N.U.S.* [1929] 2 Ch. 58). **9A–75**

**Foreign state or sovereign**

See "Parties generally," The Supreme Court Practice 1999, Vol.2,23 paras 17B—23 *et seq.* **9A–76**

**Jurisdiction where proceedings raising "academic" or "hypothetical" point of law**

In *Ainsbury v Millington (Note)* [1987] 1 W.L.R. 379, HL, Lord Bridge said (at 381) that it has always been a fundamental feature of the English judicial system that the courts, whether first instance or appellate, "decide disputes betwen the parties before them" and that they do not "pronounce on abstract questions of law where there is no dispute to be resolved". In a number of reported cases it has been argued that the court either lacked jurisdiction on the ground that the proceedings raised an "academic" or "hypothetical" point of law, or should decline to exercise its jurisdiction on that ground. Generally, the issue has arisen in courts exercising appellate or review jurisdiction (see, e.g. *Sun Life Assurance Co of Canada v Jervis* [1944] A.C. 111, HL, at 113 per Viscount Simon L.C., and *R. v Secretary of State for the Home Department, Ex p. Wynne* [1993] 1 W.L.R. 115, HL, at 120 per Lord Goff). In some cases, the outcome of this question of jurisdiction has turned on the question whether the point of law raised was truly "academic" or "hypothetical" (e.g. *R. v Canons Park Mental Health Review Tribunal Ex p. A* [1995] Q.B. 60, CA). **9A–77**

***Paragraph numbers marked with a "+" can be found online and on CD.***

A live issue between parties may become "academic" or "hypothetical" for various reasons. Generally, it is inappropriate for parties seeking to resolve a dispute between them as to costs to seek to do so by litigating to a conclusion a substantive issue that has become "academic" (*R. v Holderness BC Ex p. James Robert Developments Ltd* [1993] L.G.R. 643, *R. v Hackney London BC, Ex p. Jarram*, June 14, 1999 (unrep.)), *R. (Tshikangu) v Newham LBC*, [2001] EWHC Admin 92 (Stanley Burnton J.).

In *Ainsbury v Millington* [1987] 1 W.L.R. 379, *op. cit.* Lord Bridge conceded that the court may entertain proceedings where, although there was no *lis* to be determined directly affecting the parties' rights and obligations *inter se*, the proceedings could be described as a "friendly action" and, conceivably, where the proceedings were instituted specifically as a "test" case (*ibid.*, 381).

In modern times, the appellate courts have indicated a greater willingness to entertain proceedings which raise points of law which, although "academic" or "hypothetical", are points of general public interest (see cases cited arguendo in *R. v Canons Park Mental Health Review Tribunal Ex p. A* [1995] Q.B. 60, *op. cit.* at 63) but no general principle to this effect has emerged (see also *Don Pasquale v Customs & Excise* [1990] 1 W.L.R. 1108, CA; *Watford BC v Simpson*, February 10, 2000, unrep., CA; *Prudential Assurance Co Ltd v McBains Cooper* [2000] 1 W.L.R. 2000, CA; *Callery v Gray (No.2)* [2001] EWCA Civ 1246; [2001] 1 W.L.R. 2142, CA (Court deciding not to resolve hypothetical questions as to recovery of insurance premiums as costs)). The law is not settled. In *R. v Secretary of State for the Home Department Ex p. Salem* [1999] 2 W.L.R. 483, HL, it was held that the House of Lords has a discretion, to be exercised sparingly, to hear an appeal on an "academic" issue of public law involving a public authority where there was good reason in the public interest for doing so. Note also *R. v Secretary of State for Health, Ex p. Imperial Tobacco Ltd* [2001] 1 W.L.R. 127, HL; *R. v Secretary of State for Employment Ex p. Equal Opportunities Commission* [1995] 1 A.C. 1, HL; *R. (Barron) v Surrey CC* [2002] EWCA Civ 713; May 7, 2002, unrep., CA (and cases cited therein); *Pridding v Secretary of State for Work and Pensions* [2002] EWCA Civ 306; *R. (Customs and Excise Commissioners) v Canterbury Crown Court*, 2002 S.L.T. 834 (court declaring that Crown Court judge had no jurisdiction to make order even though matter had become academic); *R. (W.) v Commissioner of Police for the Metropolis* [2006] EWCA Civ 458; [2006] All E.R. (D.) 144 (May), CA (Court determining meaning and effect of statutory provision affecting powers of police). It is not unusual for the Court of Appeal, especially in public law proceedings, to give permission to appeal in a case raising a short point of some practical importance set in a context in which there is some uncertainty as to related issues with the intention that the court should not only determine the short point, but also should carry out an authoritative review of the whole position and give guidance on matters which are (strictly speaking) academic (e.g. *R. (Davey) v Aylesbury Vale DC* [2007] EWCA Civ 1166; *The Times*, November 21, 2007, CA (successful respondent's recovery of pre-permission costs in judicial review proceedings)).

In *R. (Bushell) v Newcastle Licensing Justices* [2006] UKHL 7; [2006] 1 W.L.R. 496, HL, licensing justices granted the application of a company for the transfer of a licence from premises sold to the local authority to new premises. The objectors successfully applied for judicial review, arguing that the justices had no jurisdiction under the relevant statute, and this decision was affirmed by the Court of Appeal. The House of Lords granted the company permission to appeal, but by the time the appeal came on, by legislative reform, licences of the variety held by the company had ceased to exist unless converted within a particular time limit which had expired. Thus the subject matter of the appeal had ceased to exist and the point of law raised was no longer of general public importance. The House rejected the submission of the objectors that the appeal should be dismissed without a hearing because it had become moot. The appeal was not moot because its outcome could have practical consequences for the parties. In particular, it would affect the company's outstanding claim for damages on a cross-undertaking given by the objectors on the company's undertaking not to commence trading at the new premises until after the judicial review application had been determined. If the appeal was successful that claim had prospects of success, but if it failed it would have none. (The House also held that there is no rule of law or practice that the House would not proceed with an appeal because of a change of circumstances as a result of which the issues between the parties were no longer of general public importance.) On the merits, the House allowed the appeal, granting the company their costs of the appeal and below. In expressing his own opinion, Lord Simon Brown said (at paras 23 and 28) it would not be proper for the House to give permission to appeal "if the only reason for doing so was to determine what had become a purely academic point just so as to see whether the Court of Appeal had decided it correctly and thus made the right costs order below"; the present appeal was not to be regarded "as any kind of precedent for this House to decide points of law for no purpose other than to determine who should be liable for past costs".

In *Bowman v Fels* [2005] EWCA Civ 226; [2005] 1 W.L.R. 3083, CA, a county court judge made an order in a private law claim (involving a dispute as to the beneficial interest in property) requiring the claimant to make certain disclosures to the defendant. The claimant appealed. The appeal raised important issues as to the application to the legal profession of certain provisions in the Proceeds of Crime Act 2002. The Bar Council, The Law Society and the National Criminal Intelligence Service appeared as intervening parties in the appeal. By the time the appeal came on the substantive litigation between the parties had been settled. The Court held that, nevertheless, the Court had jurisdiction to hear the appeal. The Court said that, had this been a public law claim, the Court would readily have found that it had jurisdiction on the basis of *R. v Secretary of State for the Home Department Ex p. Salem*, *op. cit.* The difficulty was that the underlying proceedings sounded in private law and not in public law. However, the question at the heart of this appeal was an issue of public law of very great importance and all of the parties involved in the appeal wished the appeal to proceed. The Court said (para.10): "To send them away empty-handed on an issue of such importance seemed to be not only churlish but also in breach of the overriding objective which illuminates all civil practice today". Instances have occurred in which the Court of Appeal has taken the opportunity to give detailed guidance intended to be authoritative on procedural points in appeals in which, in the event, no issue as to the particular point arose; e.g. *King v Telegraph Group Ltd (Practice Note)* [2004] EWCA Civ 613; [2005] 1 W.L.R. 2282, CA (guidance on costs capping orders).

In *Gawler v Raettig* [2007] EWCA Civ 1560, December 12, 2007, CA, unrep., the Court of Appeal stated (para.34) that the conclusion to be drawn from *Bowman v Fels* [2005] EWCA Civ 226; [2005] 1 W.L.R. 3083, CA, is that, even in cases where the litigation is private, the court may entertain an appeal if it is in the public interest to do so. However, such cases are likely to be very rare. They are likely to have a number of characteristics in addition to the critical requirement that an academic appeal is in the public interest. They include the necessity that all sides of the argument will be fully and properly put. In the vast majority of such cases, this must involve counsel being instructed by solicitors instructed by those with a real interest in the outcome of the appeal. Further, before giving permission the court will wish to consider what the other options are and how the proposed issues could otherwise be resolved without doing so by way of academic appeal. All will depend upon the facts of the particular case.

In public law cases, a declaration on a point which, though moot, may have public interest benefits. In *R. v Oxfordshire CC Ex p. Pittick* [1996] E.L.R. 153, Laws J. said (at p.157): "A decision to refuse [a remedy] as a matter of discretion on the footing that the claim is academic ought not in my view to be made without some appreciation of the force of those arguments. In a public law case, [a claimant] may have an important point to bring to the court's attention whose resolution might be required in the public interest, even if [the claimant] himself has suffered no perceptible prejudice as a result of the decision in question". In *R. (Couronne) v Crawley BC* [2007] EWCA Civ 1086; November 2, 2007, unrep., CA, a judicial review claim brought by British citizens against a decision refusing them exemption from the legislative "habitual residence" test for determining entitlement to certain state benefits was unsuccessful. By the time the appeal came on it was clear that, as the claimants had become habitually resident, the determination in their favour of the point of law on which the decision was based, would be of very little practical effect to them. However, partly for the reason that the question whether the test was discriminatory raised a point of principle that might affect others, and with the defendants not submitting that the appeal should be dismissed on the ground that it was academic, the Court of Appeal proceeded to hear and determine the appeal (holding that the test was not discriminatory). See also *Levy v The Environment Agency* [2002] EWHC 1663 (Admin), July 30, 2002, unrep., per Silber J. (at para.127). However, although judicial review

MAIN STATUTES

proceedings may often serve to clarify issues of wider importance than the particular concerns of the parties, it is important not to forget the interest of the person or group in whose name the case is being brought. The court decides issues between parties, not issues in the abstract (*R. (England) v Tower Hamlets London Borough Council* [2006] EWCA Civ 1742; December 20, 2006, unrep., CA (refusing application for permission to appeal (for purpose of raising question of European law) by unsuccessful applicant for judicial review of planning decision for development involving demolition of building made after the building had been demolished and practical purpose of the proceedings had gone)).

See further s.31(2) (declarations in judicial review proceedings), Human Rights Act 1998 s.4 (declarations of incompatibility), and CPR r.40.20 (Binding declarations) and commentary following that rule. For other authorities on question whether court should make a declaration on a question that is or has become academic, see The Supreme Court Practice 1999, Vol.1, paras 15/16/2 and 15/16/3.

In *A v B plc* [2002] EWCA Civ 337; [2003] QB 195, CA, the Court of Appeal, having apparently come to the conclusion that the defendant's appeal should be allowed on the merits, but reserving judgment, declined to hear oral argument on another ground of appeal. That other ground was not related to the merits, but raised the procedural issue whether the judge acted properly in acceding to an application to re-consider his judgment. In the light of the court's conclusions on the merits that issue had become academic. Nevertheless, in its reserved judgment the court gave a decision on the procedural appeal, having been urged to do so by the parties on the bases that the points involved raised issues of principle and could be relevant on the question of costs.

In *Fawdry & Co v Murfitt* [2002] EWCA Civ 643; [2003] Q.B. 104, CA, the Court of Appeal, having held that a case had been validly transferred from the Queen's Bench Division for trial in the Technology and Construction Court, gave an extended judgment on the question (though it had become academic) whether, had the transfer not been valid, the circuit judge would have had de facto authority at common law. The point was of jurisdictional significance and the Court had heard full argument, including submissions from counsel for the Lord Chancellor intervening.

In *Williams v Devon CC* [2003] EWCA Civ 365; [2003] CP Rep. 47, CA, a two-judge court of the Court of Appeal, having disposed an appeal in a personal injuries case on the ground that the trial judge erred in finding that the claimant was guilty of contributory negligence, gave an extended judgment on a point (though it had become academic) concerning the costs implications of Pt 36 payments where social security benefits were recoverable. The point was of practical significance and the Court had heard full argument, including submissions from the Secretary of State.

In *Ebert v Official Receiver (No.2)* [2001] EWCA Civ 340, [2002] 1 W.L.R. 320, CA, the Court of Appeal gave a considered judgment on the question whether a High Court judge's refusal to grant a vexatious litigant leave to apply to the Court of Appeal for permission to appeal infringed his rights under art.6 of the Convention even though the point was moot as the judge had in fact granted such leave. In *Poole BC v Hambridge* [2007] EWCA Civ 990; September 25, 2007, unrep., CA, the court held that the appellant's appeal had no prospects of success and refused permission to appeal on that ground, but gave a considered judgment (which was expressly released for citation) on the question (which had become academic and was conceded) whether as a matter of law the appellant did not require permission.

As to appropriate order for costs where the subject-matter of proceedings becomes academic during the course of proceedings, leaving costs as the only issue, see Vol.1, para.44.3.5.1.

For authorities concerning the issue of justiciability in the Court of Appeal, see notes to CPR Pt 52, Vol.1, para.52.1.

**Rent for foreign property**

**9A-78** See *St. Pierre v S. American Stoves Ltd* [1936] 1 K.B. 382, CA.

**For ss.20 to 27 of the Senior Courts Act 1981 (see Arrangement) plus any related commentary see paragraphs 9A-79+ to 9A-89+ on White Book on Westlaw UK or the Civil Procedure CD.**

## Appeals from Crown Court and inferior courts

**9A-90** **28.**—(1) Subject to subsection (2), any order, judgment or other

***Paragraph numbers marked with a "+" can be found online and on CD.***

decision of the Crown Court may be questioned by any party to the proceedings, on the ground that it is wrong in law or is in excess of jurisdiction, by applying to the Crown Court to have a case stated by that court for the opinion of the High Court.

(2) Subsection (1) shall not apply to—

(a) a judgment or other decision of the Crown Court relating to trial on indictment; or

(b) any decision of that court by the Local Government (Miscellaneous Provisions) Act 1982 which, by any provision of any of those Acts, is to be final.

(3) Subject to the provisions of this Act and to rules of court, the High Court shall, in accordance with section 19(2), have jurisdiction to hear and determine—

(a) any application, or any appeal (whether by way of case stated or otherwise), which it has power to hear and determine under or by virtue of this or any other Act; and

(b) all such other appeals as it had jurisdiction to hear and determine immediately before the commencement of this Act.

(4) In subsection (2)(a) the reference to a decision of the Crown Court relating to trial on indictment does not include a decision relating to an order under section 17 of the Access to Justice Act 1999.

*Note*—Derived from the JA 1925 s.24; and the Courts Act 1971 s.10. Amended by the Local Government (Miscellaneous Provisions) Act 1982 s.3, Sch.3, para.27(6); the Access to Justice Act 1999 s.24 and Sch.4, para.22; the Licensing Act 2003 s.99 and Sch.7; and the Gambling Act 2005 s.356(4), Sch.17, with effect from September 1, 2007 (SI 2006/3272), rules of court. For the procedure, see CPR, Pt 52. **9A–91**

*"rules of court"*—For the procedure, see CPR Pt 52. **9A–92**

## Proceedings on case stated by magistrates' court or Crown Court

**28A.**—(1) This section applies where a case is stated for the opinion of the High Court— **9A–93**

(a) by a magistrates' court under section 111 of the Magistrates' Courts Act 1980; or

(b) by the Crown Court under section 28(1) of this Act.

(2) The High Court may, if it thinks fit, cause the case to be sent back for amendment and, where it does so, the case shall be amended accordingly.

(3) The High Court shall hear and determine the question arising on the case (or the case as amended) and shall—

(a) reverse, affirm or amend the determination in respect of which the case has been stated; or

(b) remit the matter to the magistrates' court, or the Crown Court, with the opinion of the High Court,

and may make such other order in relation to the matter (including as to costs) as it thinks fit.

***Paragraph numbers marked with a "+" can be found online and on CD.***

(4) Except as provided by the Administration of Justice Act 1960 (right of appeal to the Supreme Court in criminal cases), a decision of the High Court under this section is final."

9A–94 *Note*—Amended by the Access to Justice Act 1999 s.61 and the Constitutional Reform Act 2005 s.40 and Sch.9 para.36(6) with effect from October 1, 2009 (SI 2009/1604).

**"decision of the High Court ... is final"**

9A–95 In *Westminster City Council v O'Reilly* [2003] EWCA Civ 1007; [2004] 1 W.L.R. 195, CA, the Court of Appeal held that a decision of the High Court on an appeal by way of case stated is indeed a decision that is final, and therefore, whatever may have been the position under the statutory antecedents of s.28A, its effect (at least when read with s.18) is to provide that no appeal from such a decision lies to the Court of Appeal.

In *Farley v Secretary of State for Work and Pensions (No.2)* [2005] EWCA Civ 869; *The Times*, June 30, 2005, CA, this point was overlooked and the Court of Appeal entertained and allowed the defendant's appeal from the decision of a High Court judge on case stated. The claimants petitioned the House of Lords for leave to appeal. Subsequently, when the Court's lack of jurisdiction was drawn to the attention of the Court by the parties the Court exercised its exceptional jurisdiction to re-open the appeal and set aside the decision (see r.52.17). However, by adopting considerable procedural ingenuity, the Court was able to retrieve the position for the parties (both of whom were anxious to have the important point upon which the case turned authoritatively determined). The Court noted that, had the judge's decision been made on an application for judicial review, the Court would have had jurisdiction to entertain an appeal. Accordingly, the Court ruled that, on the defendant's undertaking to make an application to the Court for permission to apply for judicial review the Court (a) first sitting as a court of first instance, would dismiss the application, but (b) then sitting as an appellate court, would allow the defendant's appeal against that refusal (issuing a declaration in the terms of the Court's previous decision made without jurisdiction). The claimants could then pursue their petition for leave to appeal to the House of Lords. The Court was satisfied that it had jurisdiction to proceed in this manner but stressed that, in doing so, it was exercising a wholly exceptional jurisdiction. In any usual circumstances the procedure would amount to an abuse of process.

## Mandatory, prohibiting and quashing orders

9A–96 **29.**—(1) The orders of mandamus, prohibition and certiorari shall be known instead as mandatory, prohibiting and quashing orders respectively.

(1A) The High Court shall have jurisdiction to make mandatory, prohibiting and quashing orders in those classes of case in which, immediately before 1st May 2004, it had jurisdiction to make orders of mandamus, prohibition and certiorari.

(2) Every such order shall be final, subject to any right of appeal therefrom.

(3) In relation to the jurisdiction of the Crown Court, other than its jurisdiction in matters relating to trial on indictment, the High Court shall have all such jurisdiction to make mandatory, prohibiting and quashing orders as the High Court possesses in relation to the jurisdiction of an inferior court.

(3A) The High Court shall have no jurisdiction to make mandatory, prohibiting and quashing orders in relation to jurisdiction of a court-martial in matters relating to—

(a) trial by court martial for an offence, or

(b) appeals from a Standing Civilian Court;

***Paragraph numbers marked with a "+" can be found online and on CD.***

and in this subsection "court-martial" means a court martial under the Army Act 1955, the Air Force Act 1955 or the Naval Discipline Act 1957.

(4) The power of the High Court under any enactment to require justices of the peace or a judge or officer of a county court to do any act relating to the duties of their respective offices, or to require a magistrates' court to state a case for the opinion of the High Court, in any case where the High Court formerly had by virtue of any enactment jurisdiction to make a rule absolute, or an order, for any of those purposes, shall be exercisable by mandatory order.

(5) In any statutory provision —

(a) references to mandamus or to a writ or order of mandamus shall be read as reference to a mandatory order;

(b) references to prohibition or to a writ or order of prohibition shall be read as reference to a prohibiting order;

(c) references to certiorari or to a writ or order of certiorari shall be read as reference to a quashing order; and

(d) references to the issue or award of a writ of mandamus, prohibition and certiorari shall be read as references to the making of the corresponding mandatory, prohibiting or quashing order.

(6) In subsection (3) the reference to Crown Court's jurisdiction in matters relating to trial on indictment does not include if jurisdiction relating to orders under section 17 of the Access to Justice Act 1999.

*Note* —Derived from the A.J. (M.P.) A. 1938 ss.7 and 8; and the Courts Act 1971 s.10. Amended by the Access to Justice Act 1999 s.24 and Sch.4, para.23. Amended by the Armed Forces Act 2001 (c.19) s.23. With effect from May 1, 2004, amended by the Civil Procedure (Modification of Senior Courts Act 1981) Order 2004 (SI 2004/1033), so as to provide that orders of mandamus, prohibition and certiorari should be known instead as mandatory, prohibiting and quashing orders respectively. **9A–97**

**Matters relating to trial on indictment**

The Crown Court is a superior court. Nevertheless, the High Court may make orders of mandamus, prohibition or certiorari in relation to the jurisdiction of the Crown Court "other than its jurisdiction in matters relating to trial on indictment" (subs.(3)) (see also s.28(1)). This provision first appeared as s.10(5) of the Courts Act 1971 and was designed to ensure that such jurisdiction as the High Court then had over the jurisdiction of the courts of quarter sessions (whether civil or criminal) absorbed by the Crown Court, when the latter superior court was created and the former inferior courts were abolished by the 1971 Act, was preserved. In the years since, the meaning of the phrase "relating to trial on indictment" has fallen for determination on a number of occasions and the provision has been extended beyond the circumstances for which it was originally intended. The many authorities were referred to, in argument if not in speeches, in *R. v DPP, Ex p. Kebilene* [1999] 3 W.L.R. 972, HL; see also *R. v Maidstone Crown Court Ex p. Harrow LBC* [1999] 3 All E.R. 542; *The Times*, May 14, 1999, DC (whether order under Criminal Procedure (Insanity) Act 1964 s.5, a matter relating to trial on indictment); see also *R. v Canterbury Crown Court Ex p. Regentford Ltd*, *The Times*, February 6, 2001, DC, and *R. v Leicester Crown Court Ex p. Commissioners for Customs and Excise*, *The Times*, February 23, 2001, DC; *R. (Kenneally) v Crown Court at Snaresbrook* [2002] EWHC 968 (Admin); [2002] 2 W.L.R. 1430; *R. (Sullivan) v Maidstone Crown Court* [2002] EWHC 967 (Admin); [2002] 4 All E.R. 427, DC; *R. (H.) v Crown Court at Wood Green* [2006] EWHC 2683 (Admin); [2007] 1 W.L.R. **9A–98**

MAIN STATUTES

1670, DC; *R. (Faithfull) v Ipswich Crown Court* [2007] EWHC 2763; [2008] 1 W.L.R. 1636, DC

### Injunctions to restrain persons from acting in offices in which they are not entitled to act

**9A-99** **30.**—(1) Where a person not entitled to do so acts in an office to which this section applies, the High Court may—

(a) grant an injunction restraining him from so acting; and

(b) if the case so requires, declare the office to be vacant.

(2) This section applies to any substantive office of a public nature and permanent character which is held under the Crown or which has been created by any statutory provision or royal charter.

**9A-100** *Note* —Derived from the AJ (MP) A 1938 s.9, which had abolished informations in the nature of *quo warranto*.

### Application for judicial review

**9A-101** **31.**—(1) An application to the High Court for one or more of the following forms of relief, namely—

(a) a mandatory, prohibiting or quashing order,

(b) a declaration or injunction under subsection (2); or

(c) an injunction under section 30 restraining a person not entitled to do so from acting in an office to which that section applies,

shall be made in accordance with rules of court by a procedure to be known as an application for judicial review.

(2) A declaration may be made or an injunction granted under this subsection in any case where an application for judicial review, seeking that relief, has been made and the High Court considers that, having regard to—

(a) the nature of the matters in respect of which relief may be granted by mandatory, prohibiting and quashing orders;

(b) the nature of the persons and bodies against whom relief may be granted by such orders; and

(c) all the circumstances of the case,

it would be just and convenient for the declaration to be made or the injunction to be granted, as the case may be.

(3) No application for judicial review shall be made unless the leave of the High Court has been obtained in accordance with rules of court; and the court shall not grant leave to make such an application unless it considers that the applicant has a sufficient interest in the matter to which the application relates.

(4) On an application for judicial review the High Court may award to the applicant damages, restitution or the recovery of a sum due if—

(a) the application includes a claim for such an award arising from any matter to which the application relates; and

(b) the court is satisfied that such an award would have been made if the claim had been made in an action begun by the applicant at the time of making the application.

(5) If, on an application for judicial review, the High Court quashes the decision to which the application relates, it may in addition—

(a) remit the matter to the court, tribunal or authority which made the decision, with a direction to reconsider the matter and reach a decision in accordance with the findings of the High Court, or

(b) substitute its own decision for the decision in question.

(5A) But the power conferred by subsection (5)(b) is exercisable only if

(a) the decision in question was made by a court or tribunal,

(b) the decision is quashed on the ground that there has been an error of law, and

(c) without the error, there would have been only one decision which the court or tribunal could have reached.

(5B) Unless the High Court otherwise directs, a decision substituted by it under subsection (5)(b) has effect as if it were a decision of the relevant court or tribunal.

(6) Where the High Court considers that there has been undue delay in making an application for judicial review, the court may refuse to grant—

(a) leave for the making of the application; or

(b) any relief sought on the application,

if it considers that the granting of the relief sought would be likely to cause substantial hardship to, or substantially prejudice the rights of, any person or would be detrimental to good administration.

(7) Subsection (6) is without prejudice to any enactment or rule of court which has the effect of limiting the time within which an application for judicial review may be made.

*Note*—For relevant rules of court, see CPR Pt 54 (Judicial Review); see Vol.1, paras 54.0.1 *et seq.* With effect from May 1, 2004, subss.(1), (2) and (5) amended, and subs.(4) substituted, by the Civil Procedure (Modification of Senior Courts Act 1981) Order 2004 (SI 2004/1033), as a consequence of amendments to s.31, see para.9A–97 above. Subsection (4) provided that, on an application for judicial review, in certain circumstances the High Court should have power to award damages. As substituted, the subs.(4) provides that the Court has, in addition to the power to award damages, power to award restitution or the recovery of a sum due. Subsections (5) and (5A) are substituted for original subs.(5) by the Tribunals Courts and Enforcement Act 2007 s.141, with effect from April 6, 2008 (SI 2008/749). **9A–102**

## Transfer of judicial review applications to Upper Tribunal

**31A.**—(1) This section applies where an application is made to the High Court— **9A–102.1**

(a) for judicial review, or

(b) for permission to apply for judicial review.

(2) If Conditions 1, 2, 3 and 4 are met, the High Court must by order transfer the application to the Upper Tribunal.

(3) If Conditions 1, 2 and 4 are met, but Condition 3 is not, the High Court may by order transfer the application to the Upper Tribunal if it appears to the High Court to be just and convenient to do so.

(4) Condition 1 is that the application does not seek anything other than—

(a) relief under section 31(1)(a) and (b);
(b) permission to apply for relief under section 31(1)(a) and (b);
(c) an award under section 31(4);
(d) interest;
(e) costs.

(5) Condition 2 is that the application does not call into question anything done by the Crown Court.

(6) Condition 3 is that the application falls within a class specified under section 18(6) of the Tribunals, Courts and Enforcement Act 2007.

(7) Condition 4 is that the application does not call into question any decision made under—

(a) the Immigration Acts,
(b) the British Nationality Act 1981 (c. 61),
(c) any instrument having effect under an enactment within paragraph (a) or (b), or
(d) any other provision of law for the time being in force which determines British citizenship, British overseas territories citizenship, the status of a British National (Overseas) or British Overseas citizenship.

**9A–102.2** *Note*—Inserted by the Tribunals, Courts and Enforcement Act 2007 s.19, with effect from November 3, 2008 (SI 2008/2696).

### *POWERS*

## Orders for interim payment

**9A–103** **32.**—(1) As regards proceedings pending in the High Court, provision may be made by rules of court for enabling the court, in such circumstances as may be prescribed, to make an order requiring a party to the proceedings to make an interim payment of such amount as may be specified in the order, with provision for the payment to be made to such other party to the proceedings as may be so specified or, if the order so provides, by paying it into court.

(2) Any rules of court which make provision in accordance with subsection (1) may include provision for enabling a party to any proceedings who, in pursuance of such an order, has made an interim payment to recover the whole or part of the amount of the payment in such circumstances, and from such other party to the proceedings, as may be determined in accordance with the rules.

(3) Any rules made by virtue of this section may include such incidental, supplementary and consequential provisions as the rule-making authority may consider necessary or expedient.

*Paragraph numbers marked with a "+" can be found online and on CD.*

(4) Nothing in this section shall be construed as affecting the exercise of any power relating to costs, including any power to make rules of court relating to costs.

(5) In this section "interim payment", in relation to a party to any proceedings, means a payment on account of any damages, debt or other sum (excluding any costs) which that party may be held liable to pay to or for the benefit of another party to the proceedings if a final judgment or order of the court in the proceedings is given or made in favour of that other party.

*Note* —Derived from the AJA 1969 s.20. See also County Courts Act 1984 s.50. **9A–104**

**Rules of court**

Rules of court are found in CPR rr.25.6 to 25.9, and note Practice Direction (Interim Payments) (see Vol.1, para.25BPD.1). For additional commentary on interim payments, see s.15 (Interim Remedies) Sub-sect.D (Vol.2, para.15–94). **9A–105**

**Exclusion of costs**

Subsection (5) expressly excludes "costs" from the definition of "interim payment", so that rules of court cannot be made to authorise a payment on account of costs which one party had been held liable to pay another. **9A–106**

## Orders for provisional damages for personal injuries

**32A.**—(1) This section applies to an action for damages for personal injuries in which there is proved or admitted to be a chance that at some definite or indefinite time in the future the injured person will, as a result of the act or omission which gave rise to the cause of action, develop some serious disease or suffer some serious deterioration in his physical or mental condition. **9A–107**

(2) Subject to subsection (4) below, as regards any action for damages to which this section applies in which a judgment is given in the High Court, provision may be made by rules of court for enabling the court, in such circumstances as may be prescribed, to award the injured person—

(a) damages assessed on the assumption that the injured person will not develop the disease or suffer the deterioration in his condition; and

(b) further damages at a future date if he develops the disease or suffers the deterioration.

(3) Any rules made by virtue of this section may include such incidental, supplementary and consequential provisions as the rule-making authority may consider necessary or expedient.

(4) Nothing in this section shall be construed—

(a) as affecting the exercise of any power relating to costs, including any power to make rules of court relating to costs; or

(b) as prejudicing any duty of the court under any enactment or rule of law to reduce or limit the total damages which would have been recoverable apart from any such duty.

*Note* —Added by the AJA 1982 s.6(1). Referred to in the Social Security (Recovery **9A–108** of Benefits) Act 1997 s.11(4), and in the Damages Act 1996 s.3. See also County Courts Act 1984 s.51 (para.9A–497 below).

**"rules of court"**

9A–109 For rules of court under this section, see CPR Pt 41.

## Powers of High Court exercisable before commencement of action

9A–110 **33.**—(1) On the application of any person in accordance with rules of court, the High Court shall, in such circumstances as may be specified in the rules, have power to make an order providing for any one or more of the following matters, that is to say—

(a) the inspection, photographing, preservation, custody and detention of property which appears to the court to be property which may become the subject-matter of subsequent proceedings in the High Court, or as to which any question may arise in any such proceedings; and

(b) the taking of samples of any such property as is mentioned in paragraph (a), and the carrying out of any experiment on or with any such property.

(2) On the application, in accordance with rules of court, of a person who appears to the High Court to be likely to be a party to subsequent proceedings in that court, the High Court shall, in such circumstances as may be specified in the rules, have power to order a person who appears to the court to be likely to be a party to the proceedings and to be likely to have or to have had in his possession, custody or power any documents which are relevant to an issue arising or likely to arise out of that claim—

(a) to disclose whether those documents are in his possession, custody or power; and

(b) to produce such of those documents as are in his possession, custody or power to the applicant or, on such conditions as may be specified in the order—

(i) to the applicant's legal advisers; or

(ii) to the applicant's legal advisers and any medical or other professional adviser of the applicant; or

(iii) if the applicant has no legal adviser, to any medical or other professional adviser of the applicant.

9A–111 *Note* —Derived from the AJA 1969 s.21(1); and the AJA 1970 s.31. Subsection (2) amended by Civil Procedure Act 1997 s.8 and the Civil Procedure (Modification of Enactments) Order 1998 (SI 1998/2940) art.5(a). See also County Courts Act 1984 s.52.

**"rules of court"**

9A–112 For rules of court under this section, see CPR Pt 25 and commentary in Vol.1, paras 25.1.26 and 25.1.27; CPR rr.31.16 and 48.1. For provisions supplementing s.33, see s.35 below.

**Powers exercisable before action commenced**

9A–113 The powers referred to in subs.(1) and subs.(2) may be exercised by the High Court after proceedings have been commenced (*Arsenal Football Club Plc v Elite Sports Distribution Ltd (No.1)*, [2002] EWHC 3057 (Mr Geoffrey Vos Q.C.)). The significance of this section is that it provides that, in accordance with rules of court, application may be made to the Court for those powers to be exercised before proceedings have been commenced. Initially, subs.(2) was confined to proceedings in which a claim in respect of personal injuries to a person, or in respect of a person's death, was likely to be made. That restriction was removed by an amendment coming into effect on April 25, 1999. (For discussion of changed arrangements, see *Black v Sumito Corp* [2001] EWCA Civ 1819; [2002] 1 W.L.R. 1562, CA.) Subsection (2), in its amended form, binds the Crown. However, in its application to the Crown subs.(1) is limited to property which may be the subject-matter of proceedings involving a claim for personal injuries or death (see s.35(4), para.9A-118 below).

Section 35 (below) contains provisions supplementary to this section.

**Persons to whom documents to be produced**

Under subs.(2) the Court may order that relevant documents should be produced to the applicant. Alternatively, the Court may order, on such conditions as may be specified in the order, that they should be produced to the applicant's legal adviser and any medical or other professional adviser of the applicant. In the latter event, the Court may impose a condition that the contents of a document should not be disclosed by the legal, medical or other adviser to the applicant (see *Dunning v United Liverpool Hospitals' Board of Governors* [1973] 1 W.L.R. 586; [1973] 2 All E.R. 454, CA; *cf. McIvor v Southern Health and Social Services Board* [1978] 1 W.L.R. 757; [1978] 2 All E.R. 625, HL). **9A–114**

## Power of High Court to order disclosure of documents, inspection of property etc. in proceedings for personal injuries or death

**34.**—(1) [...] **9A–115**

(2) On the application, in accordance with rules of court, of a party to any proceedings, the High Court shall, in such circumstances as may be specified in the rules, have power to order a person who is not a party to the proceedings and who appears to the court to be likely to have in his possession, custody or power any documents which are relevant to an issue arising out of the said claim—

(a) to disclose whether those documents are in his possession, custody or power; and

(b) to produce such of those documents as are in his possession, custody or power to the applicant or, on such conditions as may be specified in the order—

(i) to the applicant's legal advisers; or

(ii) to the applicant's legal advisers and any medical or other professional adviser of the applicant; or

(iii) if the applicant has no legal adviser, to any medical or other professional adviser of the applicant.

(3) On the application, in accordance with rules of court, of a party to any proceedings, the High Court shall, in such circumstances as may be specified in the rules, have power to make an order providing for any one or more of the following matters, that is to say—

(a) the inspection, photographing, preservation, custody and detention of property which is not the property of, or in the possession of, any party to the proceedings but

*Paragraph numbers marked with a "+" can be found online and on CD.*



MAIN STATUTES

which is the subject-matter of the proceedings or as to which any question arises in the proceedings;

(b) the taking of samples of any such property as is mentioned in paragraph (a) and the carrying out of any experiment on or with any such property.

(4) The preceding provisions of this section are without prejudice to the exercise by the High Court of any power to make orders which is exercisable apart from those provisions.

9A-116 *Note*—Derived from the AJA 1970 s.32. Subsection (1) omitted and subss.(2) and (3) amended by the Civil Procedure (Modification of Enactments) Order 1998 (SI 1998/2940) art.5(b) made by the Lord Chancellor in exercised of powers conferred by Civil Procedure Act 1997 s.4. The section is referred to in CPR rr.25.1, 25.5, 31.17 and 48.1.

**"rules of court"**

9A-117 See CPR Pt 25 and commentary in Vol.1, paras 25.1.28 and 25.1.29. For provision supplementing s.34, see s.35 below.

## Provisions supplementary to ss.33 and 34

9A-118 **35.**—(1) The High Court shall not make an order under section 33 or 34 if it consider that compliance with the order, if made, would be likely to be injurious to the public interest.

(2) Rules of court may make provision as to the circumstances in which an order under section 33 or 34 can be made; and any rules making such provision may include such incidental, supplementary and consequential provisions as the rule-making authority may consider necessary or expedient.

(3) Without prejudice to the generality of subsection (2), rules of court shall be made for the purpose of ensuring that the costs of and incidental to proceedings for an order under section 33(2) or 34 incurred by the person against whom the order is sought shall be awarded to that person unless the court otherwise directs.

(4) Sections 33(2) and 34 and this section bind the Crown; and section 33(1) binds the Crown so far as it relates to property as to which it appears to the court that it may become the subject-matter of subsequent proceedings involving a claim in respect of personal injuries to a person or in respect of a person's death.

In this subsection references to the Crown do not include references to Her Majesty in Her private capacity or to Her Majesty in right of Her Duchy of Lancaster or to the Duke of Cornwall.

(5) In sections 32A, 33 and 34 and this section—

"property" includes any land, chattel or other corporeal property of any description;

"personal injuries" includes any disease and any impairment of a person's physical or mental condition.

9A-119 *Note*—Derived from the AJA 1969 s.21; and the AJA 1970 ss.32 and 33, 35; amended by AJA 1982 s.6(2).

**"rules of court"**

9A-120 See CPR Pt 25 and paras 9A-112 and 9A-133+.

**"personal injuries"**

9A-121 See further commentary on meaning of "claim for personal injuries" in CPR r.2.3(1) (Vol.1, para.2.3.6).

***Paragraph numbers marked with a "+" can be found online and on CD.***

## Power of High Court to award interest on debts and damages

**35A.**—(1) Subject to rules of court, in proceedings (whenever instituted) before the High Court for the recovery of a debt or damages there may be included in any sum for which judgment is given simple interest, at such rate as the court thinks fit or as rules of court may provide, on all or any part of the debt or damages in respect of which judgment is given, or payment is made before judgment, for all or any part of the period between the date when the cause of action arose and— 9A-122

(a) in the case of any sum paid before judgment, the date of the payment; and

(b) in the case of the sum for which judgment is given, the date of the judgment.

(2) In relation to a judgment given for damages for personal injuries or death which exceed £200 subsection (1) shall have effect—

(a) with the substitution of "shall be included" for "may be included"; and

(b) with the addition of "unless the court is satisfied that there are special reasons to the contrary" after "given," where first occurring.

(3) Subject to rules of court, where—

(a) there are proceedings (whenever instituted) before the High Court for the recovery of a debt; and

(b) the defendant pays the whole debt to the plaintiff (otherwise than in pursuance of a judgment in the proceedings),

the defendant shall be liable to pay the plaintiff simple interest at such rate as the court thinks fit or as rules of court may provide on all or any part of the debt for all or any part of the period between the date when the cause of action arose and the date of the payment.

(4) Interest in respect of a debt shall not be awarded under this section for a period during which, for whatever reason, interest on the debt already runs.

(5) Without prejudice to the generality of section 84, rules of court may provide for a rate of interest by reference to the rate specified in section 17 of the Judgments Act 1838 as that section has effect from time to time or by reference to a rate for which any other enactment provides.

(6) Interest under this section may be calculated at different rates in respect of different periods.

(7) In this section "plaintiff" means the person seeking the debt or damages and "defendant" means the person from whom the plaintiff seeks the debt or damages and "personal injuries" includes any disease and any impairment of a person's physical or mental condition.

(8) Nothing in this section affects the damages recoverable for the dishonour of a bill of exchange.

*Note*—Inserted by the AJA 1982 s.15(1), Sch.1, Pt I. 9A-123

***Paragraph numbers marked with a "+" can be found online and on CD.***

### Power to award interest on debts and damages

9A–124 Section 35A together with s.69 of the County Courts Act 1984 superseded ss.3 and 22 of the L.R.(M.P.) A. 1934 and the words from "and section 22" onwards in s.34(3) of the AJA 1969, so far as the provisions of those sections apply to the High Court and county courts (see the AJA 1982 s.15(4)(5)). The result is that s.3 of the Act of 1934 (see para.9B–1218+ below) remains in force so far as courts of record, other than the High Court and county courts are concerned, e.g. the Court of Appeal (Civil Division) when it gives a judgment on appeal for debt or damages.

Various important amendments to provisions in the RSC were made after s.35A came into force. Where necessary, these provisions were carried forward into the Civil Procedure Rules. Rules in the CPR relating to the award of interest include r.12.6 (Interest on default judgment), r.14.14 (Interest where admission), r.16.4 (Contents of particulars of claim), and r.40.8 (Time from which interest begins to run). For detailed notes on the award of interest, see Vol.1, paras 7.0.9 to 7.0.23 and paras 40.8.1 to 40.8.16. As to (1) reducing the period for which interest is payable on an award, or (2) altering the rate at which interest is calculated, or both, as a procedural sanction, see Vol.1, para.3.1.6.

It has been held at first instance that CPR r.36.21(2), which grants the court power to award interest on damages awarded to a claimant in case where he recovers more than he proposed in his Pt 36 offer, is not ultra vires the rule-making power and that "interest" within r.36.21 is not the same as "interest" within s.35A (*All-in-One Design & Build Ltd v Motcomb Estates Ltd* (2000) 144 S.J.L.B. 219).

There are some significant points of difference between s.35A of the 1981 Act and s.3 of the 1934 Act. Under s.35A interest is to be included in any judgment for debt or damages whether or not the proceedings have been "tried" (as required by s.3). Thus, the court may award interest on default judgments, summary judgments and judgments given in admissions (see, generally, CPR Pts 12, 14 and 24). Section 35A provides for interest to be included in the judgment, not only in respect of the debt or damages for which judgment is given but also in respect of any sum paid before the judgment up to the date of payment (see subs.(1)) thereby negativing the effect of *The Medina Princess* [1962] 2 Lloyd's Rep. 17. Section 35A provides that the defendant will be liable to pay simple interest in respect of the debt paid in full after proceedings are instituted, at such rate as the Court thinks fit or rules of court provide on all or part of the debt for the whole or part of the period from the date the cause of action arose and up to the date of payment. Section 35A provides for rates of interest to be fixed by rules of court by reference to the rate specified in s.17 of the Judgments Act 1838 as that section has effect from time to time. Section 35A makes awards of interest under that section "subject to rules of court".

Other significant points in the provisions of s.35A which should be emphasised are as follows.

(a) The award of interest in actions for personal injuries is mandatory unless the Court is satisfied that there are special reasons to the contrary.
(b) Except in the case of claims for damages for personal injuries or death, the award of interest under s.35A as it is under s.3 of the Act of 1934 is in the discretion of the Court which may award interest at such rate as it thinks fit on all or any part of the debt or damages in respect of which judgment is given or payment is made before judgment for all or any part of the period between the date when the cause of action arose and the date of payment or the date of judgment whichever is the earlier (see s.35A(1) (6)). The interest may be awarded at different rates in respect of different periods (see s.35A(6)), but interest will not be awarded under s.35A for a period during which, for whatever reason, interest on the debt already runs, e.g. under a contract (see s.35A(4), *cf.* proviso (b) of s.3 of the Act of 1934).
(c) The award of interest under s.35A must be for "simple interest" which is perhaps similar to the prohibition contained in proviso (a) to s.3 of the Act of 1934 against "the giving of interest upon interest" (see *Bushwall Properties Ltd v Vortex Properties Ltd* [1975] 1 W.L.R. 1659; [1975] 2 All E.R. 214).
(d) As in the case of s.3 of the Act of 1934 under proviso (c), s.35A does not affect the damages recoverable for the dishonour of a bill of exchange (see s.35A(8)).

As to calculation of s.35A interest and of judgment interest where (1) defendant making installment payments under interim payment order, and (2) before all install-

***Paragraph numbers marked with a "+" can be found online and on CD.***

ments paid, claimant granted unopposed final judgment for same sum, see *Kuwait Airways Corp v Kuwait Insurance Co (No.3)* [2000] 1 All E.R. (Comm) 972, April 19, 2000, unrep. (where held by Langley J. that judgment interest on s.35A interest should not be backdated). Where interest is entered under the Arbitration Act 1996 s.66 in terms of an arbitration award, the court has no power to grant interest under s.35A on the sum awarded but remaining unpaid after the award (*Walker v Rowe* [2000] 1 Lloyd's Rep. 116, (Aikens J.)

In *Cookson v Knowles* [1979] A.C. 556, HL, it was stated that interest on damages for loss of financial dependency under the Fatal Accidents Act 1976 should be awarded at one half of the special account rate, and only on that part of the loss arising between the date of death and the date of trial. In *Fletcher v A Train & Sons Ltd* [2008] EWCA Civ 413; [2008] 4 All E.R. 699, CA, the trial judge (sitting in a county court) made an award of interest at the full rate (17.5 per cent) for that period upon the whole of the sum of the damages claim, including future loss. The Court of Appeal allowed the defendant's appeal, holding there were no special circumstances and the judge's exercise of discretion (in this instance, not under s.35A of the 1981 Act, but under the equivalent provisions in s.69 of the 1984 Act) was contrary to binding authority as to the principle upon which such discretion should be exercised.

Under English conflict of laws rules and the Private International Law (Miscellaneous Provisions) Act 1995 s.11, the assessment of damages in tort is a procedural matter and, therefore, is governed by the law of the forum, but the right to claim interest by way of damages in a claim in tort depends on the proper law and is not in any sense a procedural question for the law of the forum. Section 35A does not create a substantive legal right to interest, but merely gives the court a discretionary power to award interest on damages as a remedy in appropriate cases; the power is to be classified as procedural rather than as substantive and, therefore, is a matter for the lex fori. However, in exercising that power, the factors to be taken into account by the English court may well include any relevant provisions of the proper law relating to the recovery of interest on damages (including, for example, provisions as to rate of interest) (*Maher v Groupama Grand Est* [2009] EWCA Civ 1191, November 12, 2009, CA, unrep.).

## Subpoena issued by High Court to run throughout United Kingdom

**36.**—(1) If in any cause or matter in the High Court it appears to the court that it is proper to compel the personal attendance at any trial of a witness who may not be within the jurisdiction of the court, it shall be lawful for the court, if in the discretion of the court it seems fit so to do, to order that a writ of subpoena ad testificandum or writ of subpoena duces tecum shall issue in special form commanding the witness to attend the trial wherever he shall be within the United Kingdom; and the service of any such writ in any part of the United Kingdom shall be as valid and effectual for all purposes as if it had been served within the jurisdiction of the High Court. **9A–125**

(2) Every such writ shall have at its foot a statement to the effect that it is issued by the special order of the High Court, and no such writ shall issue without such a special order.

(3) If any person served with a writ issued under this section does not appear as required by the writ, the High Court, on proof to the satisfaction of the court of the service of the writ and of the default, may transmit a certificate of the default under the seal of the court or under the hand of a judge of the court—

(a) if the service was in Scotland, to the Court of Session at Edinburgh; or

(b) if the service was in Northern Ireland, to the High Court of Justice in Northern Ireland at Belfast;

*Paragraph numbers marked with a "+" can be found online and on CD.*

and the court to which the certificate is sent shall thereupon proceed against and punish the person in default in like manner as if that person had neglected or refused to appear in obedience to process issued out of that court.

(4) No court shall in any case proceed against or punish any person for having made such default as aforesaid unless it is shown to the court that a reasonable and sufficient sum of money to defray—

(a) the expenses of coming and attending to give evidence and of returning from giving evidence; and

(b) any other reasonable expenses which he has asked to be defrayed in connection with his evidence,

was tendered to him at the time when the writ was served upon him.

(5) Nothing in this section shall affect—

(a) the power of the High Court to issue a commission for the examination of witnesses out of the jurisdiction of the court in any case in which, notwithstanding this section, the court thinks fit to issue such a commission; or

(b) the admissibility at any trial of any evidence which, if this section had not been enacted, would have been admissible on the ground of a witness being outside the jurisdiction of the court.

(6) In this section references to attendance at a trial include references to attendance before an examiner or commissioner appointed by the High Court in any cause or matter in that court, including an examiner or commissioner appointed to take evidence outside the jurisdiction of the court.

**9A–126** *Note*—Derived from the JA 1925 s.49, which replaced the Attendance of Witnesses Act 1854 as amended by the JA 1884 s.16; and the Arbitration Act 1889 s.18 as regards references by oath.

Subsection (4) amended by the Courts and Legal Services Act 1990 Sch.17. Subsection (6) is derived from s.4 of the Evidence (Proceedings in Other Jurisdictions) Act 1975.

#### Channel Islands and the Isle of Man

**9A–127** The Interpretation Act 1978 s.5, Sch.1 provides that in every Act the expression "British Islands" shall mean the United Kingdom, the Channel Islands, and the Isle of Man. By inference, these islands are not part of the United Kingdom. A High Court subpoena cannot be issued in the Islands as they are outside the jurisdiction. The Court has power under this section to give leave to issue a subpoena to Scotland or Northern Ireland, but it has no power to give such leave in respect of the Channel Islands or the Isle of Man. As to the Isle of Man, see also *Davison v Farmer* (1851) 6 Exch. 242; *Re Brown* (1864) 33 L.J.Q.B. 193.

### Powers of High Court with respect to injunctions and receivers

**9A–128** **37.**—(1) The High Court may by order (whether interlocutory or final) grant an injunction or appoint a receiver in all cases in which it appears to the court to be just and convenient to do so.

(2) Any such order may be made either unconditionally or on such terms and conditions as the court thinks just.

(3) The power of the High Court under subsection (1) to grant an interlocutory injunction restraining a party to any proceedings from removing from the jurisdiction of the High Court, or otherwise dealing with, assets located within that jurisdiction shall be exercisable in cases where that party is, as well as in cases where he is not, domiciled, resident or present within that jurisdiction.

(4) The power of the High Court to appoint a receiver by way of equitable execution shall operate in relation to all legal estate and interests in land, and that power—

(a) may be exercised in relation to an estate or interest in land whether or not a charge has been imposed on that land under section 1 of the Charging Orders Act 1979 for the purpose of enforcing the judgment, order or award in question; and

(b) shall be in addition to, and not in derogation of, any power of any court to appoint a receiver in proceedings for enforcing such a charge.

(5) Where an order under the said section 1 imposing a charge for the purpose of enforcing a judgment, order or award has been, or has effect as if, registered under section 6 of the Land Charges Act 1972, subsection (4) of the said section 6 (effect of non-registration of writs and orders registrable under that section) shall not apply to an order appointing a receiver made either—

(a) in proceedings for enforcing the charge; or

(b) by way of equitable execution of the judgment, order or award or, as the case may be, of so much of it as requires payment of moneys secured by the charge.

*Note* —Derived from the JA 1925 s.45; and the AJA 1956 s.36. Amended by the Charging Orders Act 1979 s.7. **9A–129**

### Effect of this section

This section restates the law and practice governing the power of the Court with respect to injunctions and receivers. The section does not, in terms, fetter the court's power in any way (*Motorola Credit Corp v Uzan (No.6)* [2003] EWCA Civ 752, CA), and neither does Civil Jurisdiction and Judgments Act 1982 s.25 (interim relief in absence of substantive proceedings) (*ibid*). Section 37(3) makes it clear (if it was a matter for doubt) that a Mareva injunction, described in the CPR as a "freezing" injunction (see CPR r.25.1(1)), may be granted against a party domiciled, resident or present within the jurisdiction. The phrase "or otherwise dealing with" in s.37(3) confirms that a freezing injunction may be granted where there is a danger that assets of the defendant or judgment debtor within the jurisdiction may be dissipated by disposal sale or charge or otherwise "salted away" or placed out of the reach of the plaintiff or judgment creditor (see *Z Ltd v A-Z and AA-LL* [1982] Q.B. 558; [1982] 1 All E.R. 796, CA; *C.B.S. United Kingdom v Lambert* [1983] Ch. 37; [1982] 3 All E.R. 237, CA). **9A–130**

The power to prosecute legal proceedings granted to local authorities by the Local Government Act 1972 s.222 (see para.3A–57.2 above) includes a power in some circumstances to bring proceedings for relief in the form of an injunction under s.37(1). Section 222 does not give authorities substantive powers. It is simply a procedural provision which gives them powers formerly vested only in the Attorney-General (*Birmingham City Council v Shafi* [2008] EWCA Civ 1186; [2009] 1 W.L.R. 1961, CA, at [21] to [25]) (see further paras 3A–57.2 and 3A–57.4 above).

### Application for injunctions

See CPR r.25.1 and commentary thereto. The words in brackets in s.37(1) "whether interlocutory or final" are thought to be mere words of description of the practice **9A–131** prevailing before the passing of the Act and are not apt to create a new or extended jurisdiction to grant an injunction. It should, however, be explained that the power to grant an injunction may be exercised not only before judgment but also after judgment in order to assist the process of the enforcement of the judgment. This is specially important in relation to a freezing injunction (see *Stewart-Chartering Ltd v C. & O. Managements SA* [1982] 1 W.L.R. 460; [1980] 1 All E.R. 718; *Faith Panton Property Plan v Hodgetts* [1981] 1 W.L.R. 927; [1981] 2 All E.R. 877, CA). The words "whether interlocutory or final" do not have the effect of removing or diminishing this power.

The Human Rights Act 1998 s.3 and art.6 of the ECHR do not require that insofar as section 37 confers jurisdiction to grant an anti-suit injunction it should be read more narrowly than heretofore (*O.T. Africa Line Ltd v Hijazy (The Kribi)*, [2001] 1 Lloyd's Rep. 76, Aikens J.). The 1998 Act requires that a marginally higher threshold test than that which applied previously should apply in all applications for interlocutory injunctions likely to affect freedom of expression (*Imutran Ltd v Uncaged Campaigns Ltd* [2001] 2 All E.R. 385, Sir Andrew Morritt V.-C.).

**Appointment of receiver**

9A-132 See CPR Sch.1, RSC O.30 (Receivers); and RSC O.51 (Receivers; equitable execution).

**For s.38 of the Senior Courts Act 1981 (see Arrangement) plus any related commentary see paragraphs 9A-133+ to 9A-135+ on White Book on Westlaw UK or the Civil Procedure CD.**

## Execution of instrument by person nominated by High Court

9A-136 **39.**—(1) Where the High Court has given or made a judgment or order directing a person to execute any conveyance, contract or other document, or to indorse any negotiable instrument, then, if that person—

(a) neglects or refuses to comply with the judgment or order; or

(b) cannot after reasonable inquiry be found,

the High Court may, on such terms and conditions, if any, as may be just, order that the conveyance, contract or other document shall be executed, or that the negotiable instrument shall be indorsed, by such person as the court may nominate for that purpose.

(2) A conveyance, contract, document or instrument executed or indorsed in pursuance of an order under this section shall operate, and be for all purposes available, as if it had been executed or indorsed by the person originally directed to execute or indorse it.

9A-137 *Note*—Derived from the JA 1925 s.47, replacing the JA 1884, s.14.

**Powers of the court**

9A-138 An order under this section should not be made in anticipation of a failure to execute unless the defendant has already shown by his conduct that he refuses and will refuse to execute (*Savage v Norton* [1908] 1 Ch. 290).

Once an order has been made under this section the document executed by the appointed person has the same effect as if it had been executed by the person originally directed to execute it (see subs.(2), and *Savage v Norton* [1908] 1 Ch. 290).

There is no limitation on the class of document in relation to which the powers accorded by this section might be invoked nor on the purpose for which a document executed in accordance with those powers might be used, and accordingly the court has jurisdiction to order a party to execute an essential document by a specified time on a specified date, failing which to order a Master of the Queen's Bench Division to sign such document even though the execution of such document would be to fulfil the

***Paragraph numbers marked with a "+" can be found online and on CD.***

requirement of a contract other than the parties immediately before the court (*Astro Exito Navegacion SA v Southland Enterprise Co Ltd (No.2)* [1983] 2 A.C. 787; [1983] 2 All E.R. 725, HL).

The section applies where an order has been made for payment of costs to compel obedience (*Re Cathcart* [1893] 1 Ch. 466; and see *Re Lumley* [1893] W.N. 13).

Where a wife was granted a writ of sequestration over the matrimonial home and the court had ordered the husband to transfer the title to the sequestrators, the court had the power under s.39(1) to order that, if such transfer was refused, the necessary conveyance be executed (*Mir v Mir* [1992] Fam. 79; [1992] 2 W.L.R. 225; [1992] 1 All E.R. 765).

#### Person nominated by the court

Cases have arisen in which masters and district judges have been nominated by the court to execute instruments (see *Re Edwards* (1885) 33 W.R. 578) or in the Family Division the District Judge of the Principal Registry (*Howarth v Howarth* (1886) 11 P.D. 68) and in which court officers have been nominated in vacations (see *Hoare v Gray* (1887) 31 S.J. 744). In protection cases the Official Solicitor has been appointed (*Re Cathcart* [1893] 1 Ch. 466). In *Hood-Barrs v Cathcart* (1895) 39 S.J. 639, the Bank of England was ordered to execute, the Bank being given leave to move to discharge the order. **9A-139**

#### Practice

Application is normally made by application notice. The court has made an order under the section on an application for attachment for refusal to execute pursuant to an order to do so. **9A-140**

For form of order, see *Savage v Norton* [1908] 1 Ch. 290, at 301.

#### Alternative procedure

Before applying for an order under this section, consideration should be given to the advantages of an application for a vesting order (see *Jones v Davies* [1940] W.N. 174) or for an order appointing a person to convey pursuant to the TA 1925 s.50, or the AEA 1925 s.43(2), which give to a third person the protection of the TA 1925 s.66. **9A-141**

## Attachment of debts

**40.**—(1) Subject to any order for the time being in force under subsection (4), this section applies to any deposit account, and any withdrawable share account, with a deposit-taker. **9A-142**

(2) In determining whether, for the purposes of the jurisdiction of the High Court to attach debts for the purpose of satisfying judgments or orders for the payment of money, a sum standing to the credit of a person in an account to which this section applies is a sum due or accruing to that person and, as such, attachable in accordance with rules of court, any condition mentioned in subsection (3) which applies to the account shall be disregarded.

(3) Those conditions are—

(a) any condition that notice is required for any money or share is withdrawn;

(b) any condition that a personal application must be made before any money or share is withdrawn;

(c) any condition that a deposit book or share-account book must be produced before any money or share is withdrawn; or

(d) any other prescribed condition.

(4) The Lord Chancellor may by order make such provision as he thinks fit, by way of amendment of this section or otherwise, for all or any of the following purposes, namely—

***Paragraph numbers marked with a "+" can be found online and on CD.***



MAIN STATUTES

(a) including in, or excluding from, the accounts to which this section applies accounts of any description specified in the order;

(b) excluding from the accounts to which this section applies all accounts with any particular deposit-taker so specified or with any deposit-taker of a description so specified.

(5) Any order under subsection (4) shall be made by statutory instrument subject to annulment in pursuance of a resolution of either House of Parliament.

(6) "Deposit-taker" means a person who may, in the course of his business, lawfully accept deposits in the United Kingdom.

(7) Subsection (6) must be read with—

(a) section 22 of the Financial Services and Markets Act 2000;

(b) any relevant order under that section; and

(c) Schedule 2 to that Act.

**9A–143** *Note*—Derived from the AJA 1956 s.38. Amended by the Banking Act 1987 s.108(1), Sch.6. Subsections (1), (4)(b) and (6) were amended by subs.(7), added by, the Financial Services and Markets Act 2000 (Consequential Amendments and Repeals) Order 2001 (SI 2001/3649) art.290. As to garnishee proceedings, see CPR Sch.1, RSC O.49.

## Administrative and clerical expenses of garnishees

**9A–144** **40A.**—(1) Where an interim third party debt order made in the exercise of the jurisdiction mentioned in subsection (2) of the preceding section is served on a deposit-taker, it may, subject to the provisions of this section, deduct from the relevant debt or debts an amount not exceeding the prescribed sum towards its administrative and clerical expenses in complying with the order; and the right to make a deduction under this subsection shall be exercisable as from the time the interim third party debt order is served on it.

(1A) In subsection (1) "the relevant debt or debts," in relation to an interim third party debt order served on a deposit taker, means the amount, as at the time the order is served on it, of the debt or debts of which the whole or a part is expressed to be attached by the order.

(1B) A deduction may be made under subsection (1) in a case where the amount referred to in subsection (1A) is insufficient to cover both the amount of the deduction and the amount of the judgment debt and costs in respect of which the attachment was made, notwithstanding that the benefit of the attachment to the creditor is reduced as a result of the deduction.

(2) An amount may not in pursuance of subsection (1) be deducted or, as the case may be, retained in a case where, by virtue of section 346 of the Insolvency Act 1986 or section 183 of the Insolvency Act 1986 or otherwise, the creditor is not entitled to retain the benefit of the attachment.

(3) In this section—

"deposit-taker" has the meaning assigned to it by section 40(6); and "prescribed" means prescribed by an order made by the Lord Chancellor.

(4) An order under this section—

(a) may make different provision for different cases;

(b) without prejudice to the generality of paragraph (a) of this subsection, may prescribe sums differing according to the amount due under the judgment or order to be satisfied.

(c) may provide for this section not to apply to deposit-takers of any prescribed description.

(5) Any such order shall be made by statutory instrument subject to annulment in pursuance of a resolution of either House of Parliament.

*Note*—Added by the AJA 1982 s.55, Sch. 4, Pt 1. Amended by the Companies Consolidation (Consequential Provisions) Act 1985 s.32, Sch.2; the Insolvency Act 1985 s.235, Sch.8, para.35; the Insolvency Act 1986 s.439(2), Sch.14. The AJA 1985 s.52, replaced subs.(1) and added subss.(1A) and (1B). Subsections (1), (1A), (3) and (4)(c) amended by the Financial Services and Markets Act 2000 (Consequential Amendments and Repeals) Order 2001 (SI 2001/3649), art.291. Referred to in the Attachment of Debts (Expenses) Order 1996 (SI 1996/3098) art.2. In subss.(1) and (1A), with effect from March 23, 2002, "interim third party debt order" was substituted for "order nisi" by the Civil Procedure (Modification of Enactments) Order 2002 (SI 2002/439); see further CPR Pt 72 (Third Party Debt Orders). **9A–145**

## Wards of court

**41.**—(1) Subject to the provisions of this section, no minor shall be made a ward of court except by virtue of an order to that effect made by the High Court. **9A–146**

(2) Where an application is made for such an order in respect of a minor, the minor shall become a ward of court on the making of the application, but shall cease to be a ward of court at the end of such period as may be prescribed unless within that period an order has been made in accordance with the application.

(2A) Subsection (2) does not apply with respect to a child who is the subject of a care order (as defined by section 105 of the Children Act 1989).

(3) The High Court may, either upon an application in that behalf or without such an application, order that any minor who is for the time being a ward of court shall cease to be a ward of court.

*Note*—Derived from the LR (M.P.) A 1949 s.9. Amended by the Children Act 1989 Sch.13. **9A–147**

## Restriction of vexatious legal proceedings

**42.**—(1) If, on an application made by the Attorney General under this section, the High Court is satisfied that any person has habitually and persistently and without any reasonable ground— **9A–148**

(a) instituted vexatious civil proceedings, whether in the High Court or any inferior court, and whether against the same person or against different persons; or

(b) made vexatious applications in any civil proceedings,

*Paragraph numbers marked with a "+" can be found online and on CD.*

whether in the High Court or any inferior court, and whether instituted by him or another; or

(c) instituted vexatious prosecutions (whether against the same person or different persons),

the court may, after hearing that person or giving him an opportunity of being heard, make a civil proceedings order, a criminal proceedings order or an all proceedings order.

(1A) In this section—

"civil proceedings order" means an order that—

(a) no civil proceedings shall without the leave of the High Court be instituted in any court by the person against whom the order is made;

(b) any civil proceedings instituted by him in any court before the making of the order shall not be continued by him without the leave of the High Court; and

(c) no application (other than one for leave under this section) shall be made by him, in any civil proceedings instituted in any court by any person, without the leave of the High Court;

"criminal proceedings order" means an order that—

(a) no information shall be laid before a justice of the peace by the person against whom the order is made without the leave of the High Court; and

(b) no application for leave to prefer a bill of indictment shall be made by him without the leave of the High Court; and

"all proceedings order" means an order which has the combined effect of the two other orders.

(2) An order under subsection (1) may provide that it is to cease to have effect at the end of a specified period, but shall otherwise remain in force indefinitely.

(3) Leave for the institution or continuance of, or for the making of an application in, any Civil proceedings by a person who is the subject of an order for the time being in force under subsection (1) shall not be given unless the High Court is satisfied that the proceedings or application are not an abuse of the process of the court in question and that there are reasonable grounds for the proceedings or application.

(3A) Leave for the laying of an information or for an application for leave to prefer a bill of indictment by a person who is the subject of an order for the time being in force under subsection (1) shall not be given unless the High Court is satisfied that the institution of the prosecution is not an abuse of the criminal process and that there are reasonable grounds for the institution of the prosecution by the applicant.

(4) No appeal shall lie from a decision of the High Court refusing leave required by virtue of this section.

(5) A copy of any order made under subsection (1) shall be published in the London Gazette.

*Note* —Amended by the Prosecution of Offences Act 1985 s.24. 9A–149

### Effect of section

The section gives the High Court power, on the application of the Attorney General, to make orders having the effects described in para.(1A). This power should be distinguished from the power which the court has to make a civil restraint order (CRO), as provided for by CPR r.3.11, and elsewhere (see Vol.1 para.3.11.1). For an account of the court's inherent jurisdiction to prevent abuse of process by "protective measures", of which the power to make orders under s.42 and under the several CPR provisions relating to CROs are examples, see the judgments of the Court of Appeal in *Ebert v Venvil* [2000] Ch. 484, CA, and *Bhamjee v Forsdick* [2003] EWCA Civ 1113; [2004] 1 W.L.R. 88, CA. 9A–150

In recent years the courts have become more conscious of the extent to which vexatious proceedings represent a drain on the resources of the court itself, which of necessity are not infinite (*Attorney-General v Jones* [1990] 1 W.L.R. 859, CA, at p.865 per Staughton L.J.; *Attorney-General v Ebert* [2000] EWHC Admin 286, July 7, 2000, DC, at para.50 per Laws L.J.; *Bhamjee v Forsdick* [2003] EWCA Civ 1113; [2004] 1 W.L.R. 88, CA, at para 8).

See also Vol.1, para.52.0.16.

### Application for an order (s.42(1))

An application by the Attorney-General for an order under s.42 is made in accordance with CPR Pt 8 procedure and is heard and determined by a Divisional Court. The claim form (accompanied by a witness statement) must be filed at the Administrative Court (Practice Direction—Alternative Procedure for Claims, para.16; see Vol.1, para.8PD.16. The claim form should be served on the person against whom the order is sought (*ibid*). 9A–151

### Interlocutory injunction

Where an application for an order under s.42 has been lodged in the Administrative Court Office on behalf of the Attorney General, but there is no prospect of an early hearing, the court has power to grant an interlocutory injunction under s.37(1) of the Senior Courts Act 1981 to prevent the allegedly vexatious litigant from instituting, taking any further step or making any application in any civil proceeding until the application for the order under s.42 has been heard (*Re Blackstone* [1995] C.O.D. 105, DC). 9A–152

The court will only grant an interlocutory injunction in proceedings under s.42 where (a) a strong case for the granting of final relief is made out, (b) there is likely to be substantial delay before the matter can be finally heard and (c) there is a probability that, unless restrained by an interlocutory injunction, the respondent will resort to further allegedly vexatious proceedings. It is always open to a litigant, where an interim injunction is granted, to apply for leave under s.42(3) to institute, continue or make any applications in such proceedings (*Attorney General v Campbell* [1997] C.O.D. 249, DC).

### Conditions to be satisfied (s.42(1))

An order may be made where the court is satisfied as to the matters stated in s.42(1). The appropriate standard of proof is the civil standard having due regard to the seriousness of the issue at stake, and not the criminal standard (*Attorney-General v Hayward* , November 10, 1995, unrep., CA). Where the court is so satisfied it has a discretion to make an order, but is not obliged to do so. 9A–152.1

*Vexatious legal proceedings* —In *Attorney-General v Barker* [2000] 1 F.L.R. 759, DC, it was stated (at para.19) by Lord Bingham C.J. that the hallmark of a "vexatious" proceeding is (1) that it has little or no basis in law (or at least no discernible basis), (2) that whatever the intention of the proceeding may be, its effect is to subject the defendant to inconvenience, harassment and expense out of all proportion to any gain likely to accrue to the claimant, and (3) that it involves an abuse of the process of the court, meaning by that a use of the court process for a purpose or in a way which is significantly different from the ordinary and proper use of the court process. 9A–152.2

**9A–152.3** *Instituted or made "habitually and persistently"* —In *Attorney-General v Barker* op. cit. Lord Bingham C.J. stated (at para.22) that the distinguishing features of the behaviour of a claimant whose conduct may be found to fall within s.42(1) are that the claimant: (1) sues the same party repeatedly in reliance on essentially the same cause of action, perhaps with minor variations, after it has been ruled upon, thereby imposing on defendants the burden of revisiting claim after claim; (2) relies on essentially the same cause of action, perhaps with minor variations, after it has been ruled upon, in actions against successive parties who, if they were to be sued at all should be joined in the same action; (3) automatically challenges every adverse decision on appeal, and (4) refuses to take any notice of or give any effect to orders of the court. His lordship added: "The essential vice of habitual and persistent litigation is keeping on and on litigating when earlier litigation has been unsuccessful and when on any rational and objective assessment the time has come to stop". It is necessary to look at the whole picture. It is the cumulative effect of the claimant's activities, both against the individuals who are drawn into the proceedings and on the administration of justice generally that has to be taken into account (*Attorney General v Covey* [2001] EWCA Civ 254, February 19, 2001, CA, unrep., at para.61 per Lord Woolf CJ).

**9A–152.4** *"whether in the High Court or any inferior court"* —Section 42(1) states that the court must be satisfied that vexatious legal proceedings have habitually, etc. been brought in the High Court "or any inferior court". The terms of s.42(1) in this respect are not co-extensive with s.42(1A) (see further para.9A–152.5 below). In *Attorney General v British Broadcasting Corp* [1981] A.C. 303, HL, in a different context (committals for contempt of court), the principles to be applied in deciding whether a body exercising judicial functions is an "inferior court" were the subject of examination (see also *Peach Grey & Co v Sommers* [1995] I.C.R. 549, DC).

### Effect of civil proceedings order (s.42(1A))

**9A–152.5** A person against whom an order is made may not, without leave, "in any court" institute, or continue, or (subject to the obvious qualification in s.41(1A)(c)) make an application in, "civil proceedings". Where a person subject to a civil proceedings order commences, or seeks to commence, proceedings before a body that is not obviously a "court" as popularly understood, the meanings, in this context, of "in any court" and "civil proceedings" may have to be determined; e.g. *In re Ewing* [2002] EWHC 3169, December 12, 2002, unrep. (Davis J.) (appeal to Information Tribunal); *Ewing v Security Service* December 10, 2008, unrep. (Douglas Brown J.) (complaint to Investigatory Powers Tribunal); *R. (Oakes) v The Information Commissioner* [2007] EWHC 2956 (Admin), November 28, 2007, unrep. (Sullivan J.) (appeal to Information Tribunal).

### Period of order (s.42(2))

**9A–152.6** Unless the court orders otherwise, an order under s.42 will remain in force indefinitely. Generally, in the first instance, orders should be for an unlimited period. The object of an order is to prevent the person subject to it from bringing vexatious proceedings. Persons who would be put to the inconvenience of defending proceedings if the order were not effective should not be put in a position where, because of the expiry of a specified period, they should be again exposed to unjustified proceedings (*Attorney General v Covey*, op cit., at para.64 per Lord Woolf). The court always has a jurisdiction, in the light of entirely new circumstances, to vary orders which have been made (*ibid*).

Where an order for a limited period is sought the court, having first concluded that a civil proceedings order is necessary, will then go on to consider whether there is any logical or rational basis for such a limitation (*Attorney General v Benton* [2004] EWHC 1952 (Admin)).

### Application for leave by person subject of an order (s.42(3))

**9A–152.7** A Master or district judge may not make orders or grant interim remedies in applications under s.42 by a person subject to an order under that section for permission to start or continue proceedings (Practice Direction—Allocation of Cases to Levels of Judiciary, para.3.1(f) (see Vol.1 para.2BPD.3)).

For practice and procedure relating to such applications for permission, see Practice Direction—Striking out a Statement of Case, para.7, and commentary thereon (see Vol.1 paras 3.4.9 and 3PD.7).

In *R. (Ewing) v Secretary of State for Justice* [2008] EWHC 3416 (Admin); December 19, 2008, unrep. (Beatson J.), it was explained that, where a person subject to an order under s.42(1A) wishes to apply, under s.42(3), for leave to apply, under CPR r.54.4, for permission to proceed with a claim for judicial review, it may, depending on the circumstances, be appropriate for the High Court to consider the applications together or in stages; see also Vol.1 para. 54.4.1.

**No appeal from decision refusing leave (s.42(4))**

The restriction on appeal in s.42(4) does not infringe Convention rights or any provision of the Human Rights Act 1998 (*Ebert v Official Receiver* [2001] EWCA Civ 340; [2002] 1 W.L.R. 320, CA). In the circumstances where a judge (1) gives a person subject to a civil proceedings order leave to make an application, but (2) refuses that substantive application, and (3) also refuses that person's application to him for permission to appeal to the Court of Appeal, then (3) by virtue of s.42(4) there is no appeal against that decision (*ibid*). **9A–152.8**

## Power of High Court to vary sentence on application for quashing order

**43.**—(1) Where a person has been sentenced for an offence— **9A–153**

(a) by a magistrates' court; or

(b) by the Crown Court after being convicted of the offence by a magistrates' court and committed to the Crown Court for sentence; or

(c) by the Crown Court on appeal against conviction or sentence,

applies to the High Court in accordance with section 31 for a quashing order to remove the proceedings of the magistrates' court or the Crown Court into the High Court, then, if the High Court determines that the magistrates' court or the Crown Court had no power to pass the sentence, the High Court may, instead of quashing the conviction, amend it by substituting for the sentence passed any sentence which the magistrates' court or, in a case within paragraph (b), the Crown Court, has power to impose.

(2) Any sentence passed by the High Court by virtue of this section in substitution for the sentence passed in the proceedings of the magistrates' court or the Crown Court shall, unless the High Court otherwise directs, begin to run from the time when it would have begun to run if passed in those proceedings; but in computing the term of the sentence, any time during which the offender was released on bail in pursuance of section 37(1)(d) of the Criminal Justice Act 1948 shall be disregarded.

(3) Subsections (1) and (2) shall, with the necessary modifications, apply in relation to any order of a magistrates' court or the Crown Court which is made on, but does not form part of, the conviction of an offender as they apply in relation to a conviction and sentence.

*Note* —Derived from the AJA 1960 s.16. Amended by the Courts Act 1971 Sch.8, para.40; and the Bail Act 1976 Sch.2. With effect from May 1, 2004, amended by the Civil Procedure (Modification of Senior Courts Act 1981) Order 2004 (SI 2004/1033), as a consequence of amendments to s.31, see para.9A–97 above. **9A–154**

**Effect of this section**

This section extends the powers of the High Court when an application for an order of certiorari is made in an application for judicial review under CPR Pt 54 (Judicial **9A–155**

Review) to remove proceedings from a magistrates' court or the Crown Court on the ground that the court has no power to pass the sentence it imposed. In such case, the High Court is empowered, instead of quashing the conviction, to amend by substituting for the sentence passed any sentence which the magistrates' court or the Crown Court, as the case may be, has power to impose.

### Power of High Court to vary committal in default

9A-156 **43ZA.**—(1) Where the High Court quashes the committal of a person to prison or detention by a magistrates' court or the Crown Court for—

(a) a default in paying a sum adjudged to be paid by a conviction; or

(b) want of sufficient distress to satisfy such a sum,

the High Court may deal with the person for the default or want of sufficient distress in any way in which the magistrates' court or Crown Court would have power to deal with him if it were dealing with him at the time when the committal is quashed.

(2) If the High Court commits him to prison or detention, the period of imprisonment or detention shall, unless the High Court otherwise directs, be treated as having begun when the person was committed by the magistrates' court or the Crown Court (except that any time during which he was released on bail shall not be counted as part of the period).

9A-157 *Note* —This section was inserted after s.43 by the Access to Justice Act 1999 s.62. The section extends the powers of the High Court in the circumstances referred to in the section in a manner which avoids the necessity of proceedings being remitted to the Crown Court or a magistrates' court.

### Specific powers of arbitrator exercisable by High Court

9A-158 **43A.** In any cause or matter proceeding in the High Court in connection with any contract incorporating an arbitration agreement which confers specific powers upon the arbitrator, the High Court may, if all parties to the agreement agree, exercise any such powers.

9A-159 *Note* —Added by the Courts and Legal Services Act 1990 s.100.

The addition of s.43A restores the law to the position existing before the decision of the Court of Appeal in *Northern Regional Health Authority v Crouch (Derek) Construction Co* [1984] 1 Q.B. 644, CA, in so far as that case decided that the powers referred to in the new section were only exercisable under the contract by the arbitrator. The Court of Appeal's decision in Crouch was overruled by the House of Lords in *Beaufort Developments (NI) Ltd v Gilbert Ash NI Ltd* [1999] 1 A.C. 266, HL As a result the utility of s.43A is now less obvious.

**For ss.44 to 46A and 48 of the Senior Courts Act 1981 (see Arrangement) plus any related commentary see paragraphs 9A-160+ to 9A-167+ on White Book on Westlaw UK or the Civil Procedure CD.**

## GENERAL PROVISIONS

### *LAW AND EQUITY*

### Concurrent administration of law and equity

9A-168 **49.**—(1) Subject to the provisions of this or any other Act every court exercising jurisdiction in England and Wales in any civil cause or matter shall continue to administer law and equity on the basis that, wherever there is any conflict or variance between the rules of equity and the rules of the common law with reference to the same matter, the rules of equity shall prevail.

(2) Every court shall give the same effect as hitherto—

(a) to all equitable estates, titles, rights, reliefs, defences and counterclaims, and to all equitable duties and liabilities; and

(b) subject thereto, to all legal claims and demands and all estates, titles, rights, duties, obligations and liabilities existing by the common law or by any custom or created by any statute,

and, subject to the provisions of this or any other Act, shall so exercise its jurisdiction in every cause or matter before it as to secure that, as far as possible, all matters in dispute between the parties are completely and finally determined, and all multiplicity of legal proceedings with respect to any of those matters is avoided.

(3) Nothing in this Act shall affect the power of the Court of Appeal or the High Court to stay any proceedings before it, where it thinks fit to do so, either of its own motion or on the application of any person, whether or not a party to the proceedings.

*Note* —Derived from the JA 1925 ss.36–44. **9A–169**

**Effect of section**

This section is derived from the JA 1925 ss.36– 44. It lies at the heart of the administration of civil justice in England and Wales, since it embodies, in a concentrated form, the fundamental objectives of the Judicature Acts 1873—1875 (see *C.E. Heath Plc v Ceram Holding Co* [1988] 1 W.L.R. 1219, CA, at 1229, per Neill L.J.), namely: **9A–170**

(a) to bring about the concurrent jurisdiction of law and equity in all civil causes and matters in all civil courts on the basis that in any matter where there is a conflict or variance between the rules of equity and the rules of the common law, the rules of equity shall prevail; and at the same time;

(b) to secure that the Court will be empowered to determine finally all matters in dispute between the parties and to avoid all multiplicity of proceedings.

The three subsections of this section deal with three different aspects of the concurrent administration of law and equity:

(a) rules of equity to prevail where conflict or variance (subs.(1)) (see paras 9A–172 to 9A–174 below).

(b) final determination and avoidance of multiplicity of proceedings (subs.(2)) (see paras 9A–175).

(c) stay of proceedings (subs.(3)) (paras 9A–176 to 9A–194).

Notes on these aspects of the three subsections, taken in turn, are set out below (see paras 9A–172 *et seq.*).

**CPR Pt 20 claims (counterclaims and third party proceedings)**

Section 49(2) is derived, in part, from the Judicature Act 1925 s.39, which in turn was derived from the Judicature Act 1873 s.24(3). Those earlier provisions had the effect of empowering the court to hear, in the same action (1) a counterclaim of any kind by the defendant against the plaintiff; (2) a counterclaim by the defendant against the plaintiff along with any other persons, claiming relief relating to or connected with the original subject-matter; (3) third party proceedings; (4) a counterclaim by the third party, brought in by third party proceedings, against the party bringing him in; (5) a counterclaim by the plaintiff to the defendant's counterclaim, in so far as it is merely **9A–171** intended as a protection against it. The legislative basis for these proceedings is now found in s.49(2). The significance of s.49(2) in this respect for the jurisdiction of the courts goes without notice. Very occasionally, cases arise in which the effect of the subsection, in the light of its history, falls for consideration; a recent example is *Coca Cola Financial Corp v Finsat International Ltd* [1998] Q.B. 43; [1996] 2 Lloyd's Rep. 274, CA.

Rules of court relating to counterclaims and third party proceedings are now found in Pt 20 of the CPR and are compendiously described as "Part 20 claims".

**CPR r.16.6 (Defence of set-off)**

**9A–171.1** In the case of *Re Kaupthing Singer and Friedlander Ltd* [2009] EWHC 740 (Ch); [2009] 2 Lloyd's Rep. 154, Sir Andrew Morritt C. explained that the effects of pre-1873 legislation creating legal set-off rights was continued by subsequent legislation and are now enshrined in s.49(2)(a) of the 1981 Act and CPR r.16.6 (Defence of set-off) and surveyed relevant authorities.

## *A. Section 49(1)*

**Rules of equity to prevail where conflict or variance**

**9A–172** The Judicature Acts of 1873 and 1875 did not in any way alter the nature of legal and equitable rights. These Acts did not "fuse" law and equity. They did not abolish the distinctions between law and equity, nor between legal and equitable principles nor between legal and equitable interests or estates (see per Cotton L.J. in *Joseph v Lyons* (1884–85) L.R. 15 Q.B.D. 280 at 286, and see *Manchester Brewery Co v Coombs* [1901] 2 Ch. 608 at 617). The distinct identity of the two systems of law was preserved and this has remained the case. However, the legislation did achieve the union of the administration of the two systems of law.

Section 49(1) states that, subject to the provisions of the 1981 Act itself or any other Act, every court exercising jurisdiction "in any civil cause or matter" shall administer law and equity on the basis that, wherever there is any conflict or variance between the rules of equity and the rules of the common law "with reference to the same matter", the rules of equity shall prevail. If there is no "conflict or variance" the subsection does not apply (*The Bernina* (1887) 12 P.D. 58 at 95; *Manners v Mew* (1885) L.R. 29 Ch.D. 725 at 735; *Re Terry* (1886) 32 Ch.D. 14 at 23).

Section 49(1) may be traced to the Judicature Act 1873 s.25. That section endeavoured to remove a number of cases of conflict between law and equity which had occasioned difficulty beforehand. Subsections (1) to (10) dealt with ten particular matters of difficulty and then came subs.(11) which stated: "Generally in all matters not hereinbefore particularly mentioned in which there is any conflict or variance between the rules of equity and the rules of common law with reference to the same matter, the rules of equity shall prevail". Section 25(11) was re-enacted as s.44 of the Judicature Act 1925, and again as s.49(1) of the 1981 Act.

It may be noted that s.49(1) and its statutory ancestors, refers to "rules" of equity and "rules" of common law and it may be concluded from this that its effect is confined to matters of substantive law and does not extend to rules of practice, though equitable practice should be followed when it results from the adoption of equitable doctrines (*La Grange v McAndrew* (1878–79) L.R. 4 Q.B.D. 210; *Poyser v Minors* (1880–81) L.R. 7 Q.B.D. 329, at 335 per Lush J.; *Dalrymple v Leslie* (1881–82) L.R. 8 Q.B.D. 5; *Harrison v Rutland* [1893] 1 Q.B. 142 at 149). At an early date the Court of Appeal said that, in cases where no rule of practice was laid down by the rules of court enacted with the Judicature Acts, and there was a variance in the old practice of the Chancery and Common Law courts, "that practice is to prevail which is considered by the Court most convenient" (*Newbiggin-by-the-Sea Gas Co v Armstrong* (1879) 13 Ch.D. 310, CA).

**9A–173** *Particular illustrations of conflict or variance*—Editions of the Supreme Court Practice and the Annual Practice made reference to many of the late nineteenth century and early twentieth century cases in which issues concerning conflict or variance between particular rules of equity and rules of common law were determined. Virtually all of these cases were concerned with matters of substantive law. A few of them had implications for procedural law. For example, some of them established the rule of equity that children and patients cannot make binding admissions (at common law it seems to have been otherwise as to children). One consequence of this was the practice of not allowing interrogatories to be administered to a minor (*Mayor v Collins* (1890) L.R. 24 Q.B.D. 361; *Curtis v Mundy* [1892] 2 Q.B. 178). In the light of the rule derived from equity, admissions, discovery and interrogatories by minors and patients came to be regulated by rules of court, and that remains the case. The rule of equity that children and patients cannot make binding admissions is now reflected in CPR r.14.1(3).

Other illustrations of the consequences for practice and procedure of rules of equity prevailing over rules of common law which were in conflict or at variance could be given.

*Giving effect to all equitable and legal rights and duties etc.* —Section 49(2) of the Act provides (in part) that every court shall give the same effect as hitherto to each of the matters specified in sub-paragraphs (a) and (b). In this respect, the subsection replaced, in shortened and simplified form, the following provisions of the Judicature Act 1925: **9A–174**

s.37 (Equities of plaintiff)
s.38 (Equitable defences)
s.39 (Counterclaims and third parties)
s.40 (Equities appearing incidentally)
s.42 (Common law and statutory rights and duties).

In the process of shortening and simplifying these provisions of the 1925 Act, much that throws light on what those provisions (and their predecessors in the 1873 legislation) were designed to effect was lost. However, it would seem that no change in the law was intended.

## B. Section 49(2)

### Final determination and avoidance of multiplicity of proceedings

Section 49(2) of Act provides (in part) that, subject to the provisions of the 1981 Act itself or any other Act, every court shall so exercise its jurisdiction in every cause or matter before it as to secure that: **9A–175**

(a) as far as possible, all matters in dispute between the parties are completely and finally determined, and
(b) as far as possible, all multiplicity of legal proceedings with respect to any of those matters is avoided.

In this respect, the subsection replaced s.43 of the 1925 Act. However, it may be noted that s.43 was primarily concerned with remedies. The section said that the court, in exercising its jurisdiction in every cause or matter pending before it, shall grant, whether absolutely or on such terms and conditions as it thinks just, "all such remedies whatsoever as any the parties thereto may appear to be entitled in respect of any legal or equitable claim properly brought forward by them in the cause or matter". The section went on to state that the court shall grant all remedies (legal or equitable) to which the parties were entitled so that, as far as possible, all matters in controversy between the parties "may be completely and finally determined, and all multiplicity of legal proceedings concerning any of those matters is avoided". The section was to be read as subject to any other Act (see s.36 of the 1925 Act).

Before the concurrent administration of law and equity was fully achieved by the Judicature Acts of 1873 and 1875, there was a risk that parties bringing proceedings before a superior court might find that, in the event, the court was restricted in the remedies it could grant, and, therefore, could not grant remedies in relation to all of the matters in dispute between the parties. Consequently, in order to obtain full relief parties faced the prospect of having to bring separate proceedings in separate courts. The Judicature Acts solved this problem. The statutory provision under discussion here reinforced the solution by enjoining courts to exercise their power to grant all remedies whether legal or equitable to which parties appeared to be entitled and to do so for the purpose of ensuring that, as far as possible, all matters in dispute between the parties are completely and finally determined, and all multiplicity of legal proceedings with respect to any of those matters is avoided. In early cases it was said of this provision that "every remedy necessary for doing complete justice in an action in any division of the High Court" is provided for by it (*Serrao v Noel* (1884–85) L.R. 15 Q.B.D. 549, CA, per Baggallay L.J.) and that it was in the spirit of the "whole tenor of the Judicature Acts" which was "to require all proceedings as far as possible to be taken in one action" (*Searle v Choat* (1884) L.R. 25 Ch.D. 723 at 727 per Cotton L.J.; see also *Harmer v Armstrong* [1934] Ch. 65).

The principles (1) that all matters in dispute should be completely and finally determined, and (2) that multiplicity of legal proceedings should be avoided are deeply embedded in the law and s.49(2) is but one manifestation of them. In most instances, finality and avoidance of multiplicity will be compatible goals. However, they can be in conflict; for example, where case management rules require swift movement to finality at the expense of the uncovering of, and further development of, matters in dispute between the parties. It may be noted that the principle that all matters in dispute should be completely and finally determined is not the same as the principle that there should be finality in litigation. In some instances, the application of the latter principle will involve a violation of the former (e.g. where proceedings are brought to an end in the knowledge that some matters remain in dispute, at least in the opinion of one party). It may also be noted that there is a relationship between the principles stated in s.49(2) and the rule in *Henderson v Henderson* (1843) 3 Hare 100 which holds that a party may be estopped from pursuing in subsequent proceedings issues that ought to have been pursued and determined in former proceedings; the link is illustrated by *Beoco Ltd v Alfa Laval Co Ltd* [1995] Q.B. 137; [1994] 4 All E.R. 464, CA. The relationship between the rule in *Henderson v Henderson* and the court's inherent jurisdiction to protect its processes from abuse was examined in *Johnson v Gore Wood & Co (No.1)* [2002] 2 A.C. 1, HL. See further Vol.1, paras 1.4.15 and 3.4.3 above.

The application of the principles, stated in s.49(2), (1) that all matters in dispute should be completely and finally determined, and (2) that multiplicity of legal proceedings should be avoided, may be seen at work in various parts of the law of procedure. A good example is provided by the rules relating to the amendment of statements of case (formerly pleadings). Traditionally, these rules have been generously applied for the purpose of ensuring that the real matters in dispute between the parties are reached and dealt with completely and finally, thereby avoiding further proceedings (assuming they are not statute barred). In some amendment cases, express reference has been made to s.49(2); see e.g. *Easton v Ford Motor Co Ltd* [1993] 1 W.L.R. 1511, CA; [1993] 4 All E.R. 257, CA; in *Re Therm-a-Stor Ltd* [1996] 3 All E.R. 228. Under the case management principles implemented by the CPR this generosity is unlikely to extend to the granting of amendments where the consequence will be that a trial date will have to be abandoned.

Other aspects of practice and procedure in which the principles stated in s.49(2) may be seen at work include: the transfer of proceedings from one court to another, the consolidation of proceedings, the trial or two or more claims on the same occasion, the addition and substitution of parties, the joinder of claims, and counterclaims and other additional claims (see CPR seriatim and note, in particular, r.19.3 (provisions applicable where two or more persons are jointly entitled to a remedy), and r.20.9 (whether a Pt 20 claim should be separate from main claim). In *Dadourian Group International Inc v Simms (Practice Note)* [2006] EWCA Civ 399; [2006] 1 W.L.R. 2459, CA, the Court of Appeal stated that a major reason for requiring an applicant for a worldwide freezing order to undertake not to enforce it in another jurisdiction without the court's permission is to protect the defendant from a multiplicity of suits. In *Knauf UK GmbH v British Gypsum Ltd* [2001] EWCA Civ 1570, *The Times*, November 15, 2001, CA, the claimants were granted permission to serve their claim form out of the jurisdiction on a second defendant under CPR r.6.8, partly for the purpose of ensuring that all disputes between all parties were determined in the same set of proceedings. The Court of Appeal found that the claimant's main objective was to render their claim immune from jurisdictional attack under the Brussels Convention and set aside service on the second defendants.

The terms of s.49(2) indicate that the court is to exercise its jurisdiction in a manner designed to secure the two principles discussed above "in every cause or matter". In former versions of the subsection the court was enjoined to secure the application of the principles "in every pending cause or matter". In the early cases the question of the point at which a cause or matter ceased to be "pending" and the court's duty to ensure that all matters in dispute between the parties were completely and finally determined no longer obtained. The question remains important (*Charlesworth v Relay Roads Ltd (No.2)* [2000] 1 W.L.R. 230).

***Paragraph numbers marked with a "+" can be found online and on CD.***

In various ways procedures under the CPR seek to avoid a multiplicity of proceedings. An example is provided by the particular aspect of the court's duty to manage cases that requires the court to deal with as many aspects of the case as it can on the same occasion (CPR r.1.4); see Vol.1, para.1.4.15 (final determination and avoidance of multiplicity of proceedings).

## *C. Section 49(3)*

### Stay of proceedings

Section 49(3) states that nothing in the 1981 Act shall affect the power of either the Court of Appeal or the High Court "to stay any proceedings before it". The subsection suggests that provisions may be found in the 1981 Act which give the Court of Appeal and the High Court power to restrain pending proceedings and that it is necessary for it to be made clear that any such provisions do not affect the power of those courts to exercise their inherent jurisdiction to stay proceedings. The need for such a saving was apparent in 1873, when conflicts between common law and equity powers to restrain proceedings had to be ameliorated, and was found in s.24(5) of the Judicature Act 1873. The saving was re-enacted in the Judicature Act 1925 s.41. In its original form the section forbad the pre-1873 practice of restraint of actions by prohibition or injunction subject to the saving that any person who would formerly have been entitled to apply to any court to restrain the prosecution of any action could apply to the High Court for a stay of proceedings in the action (*Gore v Van Der Lann* [1967] 2 Q.B. 31, CA, at 43 per Harman L.J.). The manner in which the saving is preserved in s.49(3) of the 1981 Act is confusing and may be regarded as an excess of caution. **9A–176**

In terms, s.49(3) takes the form, not of conferring a power on the Court of Appeal and High Court to order a stay of proceedings, but of statutorily recognising an inherent power which the courts already possess and exercise, and which it is said they exercised from "the earlier times" (*Metropolitan Bank v Pooley* (1884—5) L.R. 10 App. Cas. 210 at 220—221 per Lord Blackburn). It has been said that the subsection applies to county court proceedings by virtue of the County Courts Act 1984 s.76 (*Gore v Van Der Lann* [1967] 2 Q.B. 31, CA).

This subsection needs to be read in parallel with s.49 of the Civil Jurisdiction and Judgments Act 1982, which also provides for the saving of the powers of the Court to stay, strike out or dismiss any proceedings before it on the ground of forum non conveniens or otherwise, where to do so is not inconsistent with the 1968 Convention, i.e. the EEC Convention on Jurisdiction and the Enforcement of Judgments.

The extent of the court's inherent jurisdiction to stay proceedings cannot be stated exactly, certainly not in a short compass. Perhaps the best known manifestation of the jurisdiction is the court's power stay proceedings to prevent its procedures being abused. This jurisdiction is said to be extensive (*Ebert v Birch* [2000] Ch. 484, CA). As there is a public interest in the finality of litigation, proceedings may be stayed on the grounds that they are an abuse of process to prevent a defendant from being vexed twice in the same matter (*Johnson v Gore Wood & Co (No.1)* [2002] 2 A.C. 1, HL); but whether an action should be stayed on this basis should be judged broadly on the merits, taking account of all public and private interests involved and all the facts of the case, the crucial question being whether the claimant was in all the circumstances misusing or abusing the process of the court (*ibid.*). See also, *Stevens v School of Oriental and African Studies, The Times*, February 2, 2001 (Pumfrey J.) (a stay to prevent, what was in substance, a re-litigation of earlier proceedings, was, in the circumstances, a reasonable exercise of the court's inherent jurisdiction and did not infringe the Human Rights Act 1998 Sch.1, art.6). Another common circumstance in which a stay of proceedings may be ordered is where a party has not complied with an order for security for costs (e.g. *CIBC Mellon Trust Co v Mora Hotel Corp NV* [2002] EWCA Civ 1688, CA; *Aoun v Bahri* [2002] EWCA Civ 1141, July 31, 2002, CA). See further para.9A–178 below.

As to court's power under its inherent jurisdiction or statute to stay proceedings where parties have agreed to arbitrate their dispute, see para.9A–177 below.

As to whether court has inherent jurisdiction, and if so whether it should exercise it, to stay legal proceedings where there is an agreement between the parties to negotiate or mediate (albeit an agreement that is lacking in the certainty traditionally regarded as necessary for enforceability and perhaps even non-binding), see *Cable &*

MAIN STATUTES

***Paragraph numbers marked with a "+" can be found online and on CD.***

*Wireless Plc v IBM United Kingdom Ltd* [2002] EWHC 2059 (Colman J.) and authorities referred to there; *cf., Halifax Financial Services Ltd v Intuitive Systems Ltd* [1999] 1 All E.R. (Comm) 303 (McKinnon J.). See also Vol.1, para.1.4.11 above.

Where a civil proceedings order is made against a person under the Senior Courts Act 1981 s.42, or where a civil restraint order is made against a person (see CPR r.3.11), depending on the circumstances the effects may include imposing a stay of proceedings.

A distinction is to be drawn between the situation (a) where no progress is made in proceedings because they have been stayed, and (b) where no progress is made because the court has made an order absolving the parties from the duty to take further steps in the proceedings (being steps that they would otherwise be required to take in accordance with rules, directions or orders) (*Simms v The Law Society* [2005] EWCA Civ 849, July 12, 2005, unrep., CA).

**9A–177** *Stay under particular statutes*—Further powers to stay proceedings or execution are conferred by particular statutes, e.g. to stay an action brought contrary to agreement to arbitrate (Arbitration Act 1950 s.4, Arbitration Act 1996 s.9); to stay proceedings against a debtor after presentation of bankruptcy petition (Insolvency Act 1986 s.285); to stay actions or proceedings against a company after the presentation of winding-up petition or in a voluntary winding up (Insolvency Act 1986 s.126); to prevent institution or continuance of proceedings by vexatious litigant (SCA 1981 s.42); to stay execution of judgment for delivery of possession of mortgaged property (Administration of Justice Act 1970 s.36(2)(b); to stay execution of possession orders in certain proceedings (Housing Act 1985 s.85(2)). Sometimes a clause in a statute conferring jurisdiction to grant a stay of proceedings in particular circumstances is intended to be, and takes effect as, a complete bar to proceedings (e.g. the Lunacy Act section considered in *Shackleton v Swift* [1913] 2 K.B. 304, CA). In effect, such provisions are substantive and not procedural and, where applied, should lead to the dismissal of the claim.

For the stay of proceedings to which the Convention on Jurisdiction and Enforcement of Judgments in Civil and Commercial Matters applies, see para.9A–186 below.

The question whether an action should be stayed under some special Act "is a very different thing ... to the case of a question under the Judicature Act and the Rules whether an action ought to be stayed or not" (per Vaughan Williams L.J. in *Shackleton v Swift* [1913] 2 K.B. 304 at 312, a case decided under the Lunacy Act 1890 s.330, and see the Mental Health Act 1983 s.139).

The court has, in addition to the power granted under the Arbitration Act 1996 s.9 (see para.2E–104 above), an inherent jurisdiction to stay proceedings, and this jurisdiction may be exercised if good sense and litigation management make it desirable for the matter to be referred to arbitration (*Al-Naimi v Islamic Press Agency Inc* [2000] 1 Lloyd's Rep. 522, CA).

Domestic insolvency law does not apply to foreign insolvency proceedings and accordingly does not give the court power to stay English proceedings against a company on the ground that it is subject to insolvency proceedings in Germany (*Mazur MediaLtd v Mazur Media GmbH* [2004] EWHC 1566 (Ch); [2004] 1 W.L.R. 2966 (Lawrence Collins J.).

The Housing Act 1990 s.89 states that an order for possession must take effect not later than 14 days after the making of the order and six weeks from the order in cases of exceptional hardship (see para. 3A–292 above). In *Admiral Taverns (Cygnet) Ltd v Daniel* [2008] EWCA Civ 1501; [2009] 3 All E.R. 71, CA, the landlord's submission that the court's power to stay under r.3.1(2)(f) and under its inherent jurisdiction are subject to this section was rejected on their appeal to the High Court (see [2008] EWHC 1688 (QB)) and, on a second appeal, to the Court of Appeal. It was held (1) generally, that a court has an inherent jurisdiction (not changed by the CPR) to arrange its appeal business, and when so doing to suspend an order if necessary, and (2) particularly that s.89(1)(a) is to be read as restricting the jurisdiction of the court granting the order, and not as directed to an appellate court considering the exercise of its inherent jurisdiction to stay execution pending an appeal, and (b) does not restrict the exercise of that inherent jurisdiction (though in considering whether to grant a stay, an appeal court will have in mind the purposes of that provision). Consequently, an appellate court that had either granted permission to appeal form an order for possession, or was still considering permission, could stay the order pending determination of the appeal or application for permission to appeal.

*Stay under the CPR*—The rules of court found in the CPR apply to proceedings in the Court of Appeal, in the High Court, and also to proceedings in the county courts. **9A-178**

In r.3.1(2)(f) the power to "stay the whole of part of any proceedings either generally or until a specified event or date" is listed among the court's "general powers of case management" which may be exercised except where the CPR provide otherwise. The several powers listed in r.3.1(2) are in addition to any powers (including powers to stay proceedings) given to the court by any other rule or practice direction or by any other enactment or any power it may otherwise have (e.g. the inherent power to stay proceedings). The discretion to stay granted by r.3.1(2)(f) is only available for a procedural reason and should not be exercised where (1) a stay under a particular statutory provision (e.g. Administration of Justice Act 1970 s.36(2)(a)) is refused and (2) such reason does not exist (*State Bank of New South Wales v Harrison* [2002] EWCA Civ 363; March 8, 2002, unrep., CA)).

In the Glossary attached to the CPR it is stated as follows: "A stay imposes a halt on proceedings, apart from taking any steps allowed by the Rules or the terms of the stay. Proceedings can be continued if the stay is lifted."

Specific provisions found in the "core" provisions in the CPR to stay orders, claims or proceedings include:

- r.3.3(5) (Application by party to stay order made by court of its own initiative without hearing parties or giving opportunity for representations)
- r.3.4(4) (Staying second claim until costs of first claim paid)
- r.11(6)(d) (Staying proceedings where court declaring it has no jurisdiction)
- r.14.5(5) (Where admission of part of claim for a specified amount money, claim stayed if claimant does not file notice)
- r.15.10(3)(4) (Where defence is that money claim has been paid, claim stayed if claimant does not file notice) [specific reference to application to lift in r.15.10(4)]
- r.15.11(1) (Claim stayed where claimant has not applied for default judgment or summary judgment after specified time) [specific reference to application to lift in r.15.11(2)]
- r.26.4 (Stay to allow for settlement of the case) (see also r.26.5(1)(b))
- r.36.11(1) (Stay where Pt 36 offer accepted) (see also r.36.13(3)
- r.38.8 (Stay of remainder of partly discontinued proceedings where costs not paid)
- r.40.6 (Consent judgments to stay proceedings or enforcement of a judgment)
- r.52.7 (Appeals to Court of Appeal - stay of order of lower court)
- r.52.9 (Stay pending discharge of conditions imposed on appeal to Court of Appeal)
- r.54.10 (Stay of judicial review claim)
- r.68.4 (Stay where reference to European Court for preliminary ruling)
- r.74.33 (Stay under art.23 of EEO Regulation)

Existing proceedings that did not come before a judge between April 26, 1999, and April 25, 2000, were stayed by operation of CPR r.51.1 and Practice Direction (Transitional Arrangements), para.19(1). Any party to those proceedings may apply for the stay to be lifted (para.19(2) (see Vol.1, paras 51.1.2 and 51PD.19).

Practice Direction (Case Management-Preliminary Stage: Allocation and Reallocation), para.12.2 states that where the court, in certain circumstances, has given a judgment or made an order requiring an amount of money, to be decided by the court, to be paid by one party to another, the court will give directions. The circumstances include such judgment or order obtained, for example, by default or on a summary judgment application. It is expressly provided that the directions which the court may give include a direction staying the claim while the parties try to settle the case by alternative dispute resolution or other means (para.12.2(1)(d)).

In the former RSC and CCR rules now re-enacted in, respectively, Schs 1 and 2 of the CPR, references to the stay of proceedings (by order or by rule) are found in a number of places (especially in provisions concerned with enforcement of judgments and execution). Such references include (the list is not exhaustive):

RSC O.17 (Interpleader), r.5 (Power to stay proceedings)
RSC O.47, r.1 (Power to stay execution by writ of *fieri facias*)

***Paragraph numbers marked with a "+" can be found online and on CD.***

RSC O.45 (Enforcement of judgments and orders: general), r.11 (Matters occurring after judgment: stay of execution, etc.)

The court has power to stay an action where a party is funded by a non-party who would not or could not satisfactorily accept liability to pay a successful opponent's costs (*Abraham v Thompson* [1997] 4 All E.R. 362, CA; *StoczniaSA v Latvian Shipping Co (No.2)* [1999] 3 All E.R. 822).

A defendant may be entitled to a stay of proceedings against him until the claimant satisfies an order for costs made against him and in favour of the defendant in previous proceedings (*Hines v Birbeck College (No.2)* [1991] 3 W.L.R. 557; [1991] 4 All E.R. 450, CA).

The court's power referred to in CPR r.3.4(4) to stay subsequent proceedings pending payment of costs, ordered when a statement of case (which, as defined, does not include a winding-up petition) was struck out in previous proceedings, does not have the effect of limiting the court's general power to stay proceedings (see para.9A-161) or its inherent jurisdiction (see para.9A-59) to stay proceedings to prevent abuse of its process (*Investment Invoice Financing Ltd v Limehouse Board Mills* [2006] EWCA Civ 9; [2006] 1 W.L.R. 985, CA).

Modern examples of instances in which proceedings have been stayed until the claimant complied with procedural rules or orders include the following cases: *Dunn v British Coal Corp*, *The Times*, March 5, 1993, CA (disclosure of medical records), *Jackson v Mirror Group Newspapers Ltd*, *The Times*, March 29, 1994, CA (submission to medical examination), *Jackson v Pinchbeck* [1998] 3 All E.R. 97, CA ("unless" order requiring filing of statement of special damages). See also *Westminster City Council v Porter* [2002] EWHC 1589 (Ch), July 16, 2002, unrep. (Hart J.) (judgment debtor's application for stay of execution of judgment pending application to European Court of Human Rights refused). See further para.9A–176 above.

As to stay of judicial review claim, see CPR r.54.10 and Vol.1, paras 54.10.2 *et seq.*

As to circumstances relevant to question whether a stay may be ordered for the purpose of enabling parties to comply with, or to complete, pre-action protocol procedures, see *Alfred McAlpine Capital Projects Ltd v SIAC Construction (UK) Ltd* [2005] EWHC 3139 (TCC); [2006] B.L.R. 139 (Jackson J.); *Orange Personal Communications Services Limited v Hoare Lea* [2008] EWHC 223 (TCC), February 12, 2008, unrep. (Akenhead J.).

As to stay of order or decision of lower court pending appeal to the Court of Appeal, see CPR r.52.7 and commentary thereto (Vol.1, para.52.7.1).

**9A–178.1** *Stay pending arbitration or ADR* —Even before the Arbitration Act 1996 s.9 (Stay of legal proceedings) (see para 2E–104 above) came into effect it was clear that the court has an inherent, albeit discretionary power to stay proceedings brought before it in breach of an agreement to decide a dispute by arbitration (*Channel Tunnel Group Ltd v Balfour Beatty Construction Ltd* [1993] A.C. 334, HL). In reliance on this inherent power it has been held that the court may stay legal proceedings pending adjudication under the Housing Grants, Construction and Regeneration Act 1996 (*DGT Steel and Cladding Limited v Cubitt Building and Interiors Limited* [2007] EWHC 1584 (TCC) (Judge Coulson Q.C.)), and pending reference of dispute to an expert for determination as provided by contract between the parties (*Cott (UK) Limited v F.E. Barber Ltd* [1997] 3 All E.R. 540).

As to the court's power to stay proceedings pending the determination of arbitration proceedings elsewhere in circumstances where no issue of forum non conveniens arises (that is to say, purely on case management grounds), see *Reichhold Norway ASA v Goldman Sachs International* [2000] 1 W.L.R.173, CA and *Equitas Limited v Allstate Insurance Company* [2008] EWHC 1671 (Comm), July 17, 2008, unrep. (Beatson J.).

**9A–179** *Court staying proceedings of its own motion* —Section 49(3) recognises that the court's power to stay proceedings is exercisable, either (a) of its own motion or (b) on the application of any person, whether (i) a party to the proceedings or (ii) not a party to the proceedings. In CPR r.3.3 it is expressly provided that, subject to conditions, the court may exercise its power to stay the whole or part of any proceedings (see r.3.1(2)(f)) on an application or of its own initiative. Where the court stays proceedings by an order made of its own initiative, without hearing the parties or giving them an opportunity to make representations, a party affected by the order may apply to have it set aside, varied or stayed (r.3.3(5)).

*Nature or effect of a stay of proceedings* —In *Cohens v Virginia* (1871) 6 Wheat. 264, Marshall C.J. said (at p.404, speaking for the United States Supreme Court): "We have no more right to decline the exercise of jurisdiction which is given, than to usurp that which is not given". When, for whatever reason, proceedings are stayed, in effect the court is declining to exercise its jurisdiction. That is a strong thing (*Shackleton v Swift* [1913] 2 K.B. 304, CA, at 312 per Vaughan Williams L.J.). Obviously, jurisdiction should not be declined except for very good reason. In *Abraham v Thompson* [1997] 4 All E.R. 363, CA, Potter L.J. said (at p.374) that, "where a stay is sought in circumstances which are not provided for by statute or rules of court, the starting point is the fundamental rule that an individual who is not under a disability, a bankrupt or a vexatious litigant, is entitled to untrammelled access to a court of first instance in respect of a bona fide claim based on a properly pleaded cause of action". **9A–180**

With the emergence of modern case management practices (exemplified by many of the provisions of the CPR), the jurisdiction to stay proceedings has become a useful procedural sanction, available to ensure compliance by parties with rules of court, practice directions, and procedural orders. Nowadays, more than ever before, "good reason" justifying the exercise of the jurisdiction to stay proceedings includes the achievement of case management goals in individual cases (see, further, "Stay under the CPR", para.9A–178 above).

For considerations relevant to the question whether a stay should take effect forthwith or at a later stage in the development of the proceedings (e.g. after the disclosure of documents and exchange of witness statements had been completed), see *Synstar Computer Service (UK Ltd v I.C.L. (Sorbus) Ltd, The Times*, May 1, 2001 (Lightman J.).

In giving the opinion of the Judicial Committee in *Minister of Foreign Affairs, Trade & Industry v Vehicles and Supplies Ltd* [1991] 1 W.L.R. 550, PC, [1991] 4 All E.R. 65, PC, Lord Oliver said (at p.556 and p.71): "A stay of proceedings is an order which puts a stop to the further conduct of proceedings in court or before a tribunal at the stage which they have reached, the object being to avoid the hearing or trial taking place". Whilst the stay endures, "the relevant court or tribunal cannot ... effectively entertain any further proceedings except for the purpose of lifting the stay". In general, "anything done prior to the lifting of the stay will be ineffective, although such an order would not, if imposed to enforce the performance of a condition by a plaintiff (e.g. to provide security for costs), prevent a defendant from applying to dismiss the action if the condition is not fulfilled". His lordship further explained that a stay order is not an order enforceable by proceedings for contempt because it is not, in its nature, capable of being "breached" by a party to the proceedings or anyone else.

By definition, a stay takes effect on proceedings which are on foot; that is to say, on claims (or other proceedings) within which some proceedings may still be taken. Section 49(3) speaks of the jurisdiction of the court to stay proceedings "before it", and earlier legislation spoke of "pending" proceedings. Thus, a stay may be imposed after judgment as well as before, and execution proceedings may be stayed.

The early authorities as to the nature and effect of a stay of proceedings were reviewed by Neill L.J. in *Rofa Sport Management A.G. v D.H.L. International (UK) Ltd* [1989] 1 W.L.R. 902; [1989] 2 All E.R. 743, CA. His lordship noted that, historically speaking, it was possible to draw a distinction between an "absolute" order to stay, which was equivalent to a discontinuance or dismissal, and a "conditional" order to stay, which by its terms contemplated the continuance of the action if the condition was fulfilled. However, his lordship concluded that, nowadays, it would not be satisfactory to seek to draw a line between the two and to equate "absolute" stays with orders for dismissal or discontinuance. In his lordship's judgment, for the sake of clarity and certainty the word "stay" in an order should not be treated as a possible equivalent of a dismissal or a discontinuance, no matter how unlikely it is that the stay will be lifted by an order of the court enabling the case to "resume its active life"; e.g. where the proceedings are stayed by consent following a compromise (*Cooper v Williams* [1963] 2 Q.B. 567; [1963] 2 All E.R. 282, CA; *Green v Rozen* [1955] 1 W.L.R. 741; [1955] 2 All E.R. 797). It is submitted that the same result should follow (unless expressly provided otherwise) where proceedings are stayed, not by court order, but by operation of legislation (including rules of court).

Where proceedings are settled by agreement and stayed by a Tomlin order, the stay does not operate to deny the court jurisdiction to determine an application by the claimant for a wasted costs order against he defendant's solicitors (such an application being wholly tangential to the stayed proceedings and not affecting the defendant's rights in any way) (*Wagstaff v Colls* [2003] EWCA Civ 469; *The Times*, April 17, 2003, CA).

The question whether costs incurred during a stay are allowable depends upon whether the work in respect of which they are charged was premature (*Pècheries Ostendaises v Merchant's Marine Insurance Co* [1928] 1 K.B. 750).

**9A–181** *Costs, stay pending payment or security for* —The court has jurisdiction to stay proceedings until payment of costs in an interlocutory matter which have been ordered to be paid. In the early cases, such a stay was ordered where the party in default was acting vexatiously in withholding payment (*Re Wickham* (1887) L.R. 35 Ch.D. 272; *Graham v Sutton, Carden & Co* [1897] 2 Ch. 367). A second application for the same relief as in a previous application which had been dismissed with costs will be stayed unless and until those costs are paid or a reasonable sum to cover those costs is paid into court, if the costs are unquantified (*Thames Investment and Securities v Benjamin* [1984] 1 W.L.R. 1381; [1984] 3 All E.R. 393). Where an order is made requiring a party to provide security for costs, it may be further ordered that proceedings be stayed pending the provision of security (e.g. *Clive Brooks & Co Ltd v Baynard, The Times*, April 30, 1998, CA). As to stay of second claim where order for costs of first claim not paid, see CPR r.3.4(4)). See further CPR Pt 25, Sect.II (Security for costs).

**9A–182** *Stay pending changes in law* —It is possible that, after proceedings have been commenced, but before they are tried, legislative changes in the law affecting the respective positions of the parties to the proceedings may come into effect. Judges trying cases apply the law as it stands at the time of trial. It is also conceivable that, before proceedings are tried, it will become apparent that legislative changes in the law are to be anticipated. In those circumstances it may be argued that the proceedings should be stayed so as to ensure that they are not tried before the changes come into effect. In *Willow Wren Canal Carrying Co Ltd v British Transport Commission* [1956] 1 W.L.R. 213; [1956] 1 All E.R. 567, legislation which would have given the defendants immunity from the plaintiff's claim was going through Parliament. The defendants applied to stay the proceedings long enough to gain the benefit of the legislation. If granted, the stay would have had the effect of preventing the case from going to trial. The application was refused. (See also *Wilson v Dagnall* [1972] 1 Q.B. 509, CA.) In *Sparks v Harland* [1997] 1 W.L.R. 143, the plaintiff's action was brought outside the limitation period and the defendant applied to have them dismissed on that ground. There was a prospect (depending on the likely response of the legislature to the outcome of other proceedings pending in the European Court of Human Rights) of retrospective legislation being enacted which would have the effect of removing the time bar from the plaintiff's claim. It was held that, in the circumstances, the plaintiff's action should not be struck out, but should be stayed.

It is conceivable that, in the course of the hearing of a case, it may become apparent that issues of law arising in the proceedings have arisen in other cases and are presently subject to appellate proceedings or references to the E.C.J. in those cases in which it is expected that the issues of law will be authoritatively determined. In those circumstances it may be argued that the hearing should be adjourned pending the outcome of the appeal or the reference (see *Re Yates' Settlement Trusts* [1954] 1 All E.R. 619, CA; *Sprote v Commissioner of Police of the Metropolis, The Times*, August 6, 1991, EAT; *Green v Skandia Life Assurance Co Ltd* [2006] EWHC 1626 (Ch); July 7, 2006, unrep. (Mr. Edward Nugee Q.C.)). An adjournment of a hearing is not the same as a stay of proceedings. The question whether proceedings which have not reached the point of trial should be stayed (whether by consent or otherwise) where it has become apparent that issues of law arising in the proceedings have arisen in other cases which are presently subject to appellate proceedings or references to the E.C.J. raises different considerations. At trial a first instance judge is bound by the doctrine of precedent to apply the law as laid down in a decision of the Court of Appeal, even if there is a possibility that that decision may be reversed. But the same is not necessarily the case where a judge is dealing with an application to strike out a claim or to give summary judgment before a trial. Then the judge can take into account the possibility that the Court of Appeal's decision may be reversed on appeal and may dispose of the application by refusing to strike it out or to give summary judgment accordingly, especially where it is known that in other proceedings the Court of Appeal's decision is to be tested in a pending appeal to the House of Lords (*Derby v Weldon (No.5)* [1989] 1 W.L.R. 1244). But in such circumstances it may be a more proportionate use of the parties' and the court's resources to stay the application pending the determination of the appeal instead of dismissing it (*Green v Skandia Life Assurance Co Ltd, op. cit.*).

In *Johns v Solent SD Ltd* [2008] EWCA Civ 790; *The Times* June 27, 2008, CA, the facts were that a particular regulation included in UK Regulations implementing an EU Directive provided the defendant employers with a complete defence to an age discrimination claim brought against them in an employment tribunal by a former employee. On the ground that in reference proceedings pending in the ECJ, and arising in another jurisdiction, the validity of a similar provision was being tested, the EAT ordered that the employee's claim should not be struck out but should be stayed pending the outcome of that reference. The Court of Appeal held that the balance of prejudice weighed heavily in favour of staying the claim and dismissed the employers' appeal.

The question whether, in the handling of a claim, either at trial or before trial, the further pursuit of, or the determination of, a particular matter disputed by the parties should be stayed (or otherwise put aside) pending the expected clarification by the Court of Appeal of the relevant law has arisen is cases where the court was required to consider whether the damages awarded for future pecuniary loss to a claimant in a personal injuries claim should be awarded in the form of periodical payments (as provided by the Damages Act 1996 s.2 and CPR r.41.8). In these cases, the particular point on which clarification was awaited was the correct approach to be adopted by the judge as to the selection of the appropriate form of indexation, should a periodical payments order be made (a matter likely to have a significant impact on the total amount recovered by the claimant). In the event, clarification was provided by the Court of Appeal in *Thompstone v Tameside & Glossop Acute Services NHS Trust* [2008] EWCA Civ 5; [2008] 1 W.L.R. 2207; [2008] 2 All E.R. 553, CA; see further Vol.1, para. 41.8.2.1.

*Concurrent civil proceedings* —When civil proceedings are commenced, they proceed according to rules of practice and procedure, including case management rules designed to ensure that cases proceed with despatch. **9A–183**

Circumstances can arise in which it becomes apparent that two (or possibly more) separate sets of proceedings (perhaps in the same court, perhaps in different courts) are related in some material way and that it is just and convenient that one (or some) should be stayed pending the final determination of the other (or others). One set of proceedings may be "the senior of the two" in the sense that it was commenced before, or had reached a later stage of pre-trial development than, the other (*J. BollingerSA v Goldwell Ltd* [1971] R.P.C. 412 at 423 per Megarry J.). All of the parties involved may agree that one set of proceedings (not necessarily "the senior") should be stayed by consent pending the outcome of the other. The court may readily agree to the stay. However, despite the agreement amongst the parties, in the interests of effective case management the court may refuse to order a stay by consent and, instead, order (for example) that the claims should be consolidated, tried together, or one tried immediately after the other.

In the absence of agreement amongst the parties to the effect that one set of proceedings should be stayed whilst another proceeds, the question may arise whether, on the application of a party (or parties) or of its own initiative, the court should order such a stay. The question may arise in many different circumstances and procedural settings. Consequently, it is not possible to state general principles as to the exercise of the discretionary jurisdiction to stay proceedings in this context. Further, special considerations may arise in particular jurisdictions (especially in arbitration, bankruptcy, insolvency, and patents). Where a company is placed in the hands of receivers, concurrent proceedings may arise in the form of (1) proceedings against a director under the Company Directors Disqualification Act 1986, and (2) a claim challenging the receivership, leading to an application by the director for a stay of the disqualification proceedings. The authorities on the exercise of the discretion to stay proceedings in these circumstances were examined in *Secretary of State for Trade and Industry v Woolf* [2005] EWHC 3074 (Ch), November 29, 2005, unrep.

The concurrent (or "parallel") proceedings may be disciplinary proceedings against one of the parties to the civil proceedings in which the stay is sought (e.g. *Wakefield v Channel Four Television Corporation* [2005] EWHC 2410 (QB), November 4, 2005, unrep. (Eady J.)). The burden lies upon the applicant seeking a stay to demonstrate, through cogent evidence, that there are sound reasons for a stay *(ibid.)*.

Perhaps the clearest example of a situation in which the court might be persuaded to order a stay would be where the several sets of proceedings involve the same parties and raise the same issues (*Slough Estates Ltd v Slough BC* [1968] Ch. 299; [1967] 2 All E.R. 270). The advantages to be gained in avoiding a duplication of proceedings are obvious; they include the avoidance of unnecessary costs and delays and of a party being vexed more than once with, in effect, the same claim. (It may be noted that the need to avoid "all multiplicity of legal proceedings" with respect to all matters in dispute between the same parties is referred to in s.49(2); see para.9A–175 above.) The case for a stay is less strong where there is merely a considerable degree of common ground between the two claims (*J. Bollinger SA v Goldwell Ltd*, *op. cit.*).

Some of the early authorities suggest a stay will not be granted if the issues in the several proceedings are not the same (*Adamson v Tuff* (1881) 44 L.T. 420; *Higgins v Woodhall* (1890) 6 T.L.R. 1; *Perry v Croydon BC* [1938] 3 All E.R. 670) but this cannot be stated as a strict rule. If there are two courts faced with substantially the same question or issue, it is desirable that the question or issue should be determined in only one of those two courts if by that means justice can be done, and the court will if necessary stay one of the actions (*Royal Bank of Scotland Ltd v Citrusdal Investments Ltd* [1971] 1 W.L.R. 1469; [1971] 3 All E.R. 558, applying *Thames Launches Ltd v Trinity House Corp (Deptford Strond)* [1961] Ch. 197; [1961] 1 All E.R. 26). A second action dealing with the same events as in the first action but alleging a different contract with different terms will not be stayed (*Hardy v Elphick* [1974] Ch. 65; [1973] 2 All E.R. 914, CA).

Where there are multiple sets of proceedings against the same defendant raising the same issues one may be selected as a "test" case and the other proceedings stayed pending the outcome of that case (*Ashmore v British Coal Corp* [1990] 2 W.L.R. 1437; [1990] 2 All E.R. 981, CA).

Where an action founded on a certain cause of action is in existence, albeit stayed, it is an abuse of process to bring new proceedings founded upon that same cause of action; the second action will be struck out and the proper course would be to apply for the stay to be removed in respect of the first action (*Buckland v Palmer* [1984] 1 W.L.R. 1109; [1984] 3 All E.R. 554, CA). See further CPR rr.19.11(ii) and 19.15.

Where one set of proceedings has been stayed but another set has proceeded to final determination, the question may then arise as to whether the stay on the former proceedings should be lifted. The considerations relevant to this question need not be considered here. However, it may be noted that, depending on the circumstances, as a result of the determination of the latter proceedings, pleas of *res judicata* or issue estoppel may become relevant in the former proceedings and affect the question whether the stay should be lifted. Further, the rule stated in *Henderson v Henderson* (1843) 3 Hare 100 (which holds that a party may be estopped from pursuing in subsequent proceedings issues that ought to have been pursued and determined in former proceedings) may also become relevant.

Many of the earlier authorities were referred to in editions of the Supreme Court Practice; see SCP 1991, Vol.2, paras 20A—357 (Concurrent actions), 20A—363 (Cross actions in respect of same subject-matter), 20A—389 (Test actions), and 20A—394 (Two actions or proceedings for same matter).

Recent authorities on the matters referred to above include: *Re B (Minors: Abduction), The Times*, November 6, 1992; *Chorion Plc v Lane, The Times*, April 7, 1999; *Steans Fashions Ltd v Legal and General Assurance Society Ltd, The Times*, December 31, 1994, CA. See further authorities referred to in para.9A–176 above.

Where several proceedings "give rise to common or related issues of fact or law", for purposes of case management they may be made subject to a Group Litigation Order (GLO) under the rules of court found in CPR Pt 19, Sect.III and the practice direction supplementing those rules. The authorities referred to above are relevant to the exercise of the court's jurisdiction to stay cases subject to a GLO, but as the CPR provisions are to be applied in accordance with the overriding objective (stated in r.1.1) they perhaps cannot be regarded as binding.

*Concurrent civil and criminal proceedings* —Where there are concurrent civil and criminal proceedings against the same defendant arising out of the same subject-matter, there is no principle of law that the claimant in the civil proceedings is to be debarred from pursuing the action in accordance with the normal rules merely because so to do would or might result in the defendant, if he wished to defend the action, having to disclose his defence by taking some necessary procedural step, and so give an indication of what his defence was likely to be in contemporaneous criminal proceedings, but the civil court has a discretion to stay the proceedings if it appeared to the Court that justice between the parties so required having regard to concurrent criminal proceedings arising out of the same subject matter and taking into account the defendant's "right of silence" in the criminal proceedings (*Jefferson Ltd v Bhetcha* [1979] 1 W.L.R. 898; [1979] 2 All E.R. 1108, CA). In *Barnet London BC v Hurst* [2002] EWCA Civ 1009; [2002] 4 All E.R. 457, CA, upon the defendant giving undertakings, the judge adjourned the hearing of a local authority's application to commit the defendant for breach of anti-social behaviour injunction pending the completion of criminal proceedings against the defendant. **9A–184**

The discretion to stay civil proceedings until criminal proceedings have been determined is a power which has to be exercised with great care and only where there is a real risk of serious prejudice which may lead to injustice (*R. v Panel on Takeovers and Mergers Ex p. Fayed* [1992] B.C.C. 524, CA). What has to be shown is the causing of unjust prejudice by the continuance of the civil proceedings (*Panton v Financial Institutions Services Ltd* [2003] UKPC 86, December 12, 2003, unrep., PC). See also *Zambia v Meer Care & Desai* [2006] EWCA Civ 390, March 7, 2006, CA, unrep. (where a stay of English civil proceedings pending the completion of foreign criminal proceedings was refused).

There is no overriding right based on the privilege against self incrimination, to have a civil action stayed pending the conclusion of criminal proceedings. It is for a defendant to seek to avail himself of the privilege to take specific objection on an application at some point in the interlocutory stages of a civil action (*Guinness plc v Saunders, The Times*, October 18, 1988, CA). See also the comments of Millett J. in *Re D.P.R. Futures Ltd* [1989] 1 W.L.R. 778, CA.

Where civil proceedings in the form of an application under the Directors Disqualification Act 1986 were stayed pending the outcome of a related criminal proceedings, and, after the completion of the criminal proceedings, the Secretary of State applied to restore the application, the civil proceedings were not barred by the doctrine of double recovery, and the continuation of the civil proceedings was not an abuse of process (*Re Cedarwood Productions Ltd, The Times*, July 12, 2001, CA). See also *Secretary of State for Trade and Industry v Crane, The Times* June 4, 2001 (Ferris J.), and note *R. v Panel on Takeovers and Mergers Ex p. Fayed* [1992] B.C.C. 524.

*Lis alibi pendens, forum non conveniens and foreign jurisdiction clauses* —The court has an inherent jurisdiction to stay proceedings in England, or to restrain by injunction the institution or continuation of proceedings in a foreign court, whenever it is necessary to do so in order to prevent injustice. **9A–185**

Thus, where simultaneous proceedings are pending in England and in a foreign country between the same parties and involving the same or similar issues (*lis alibi pendens*), the English proceedings may be stayed. Further, in certain circumstances, although there is no *lis alibi pendens* English proceedings may be stayed on forum *non conveniens* grounds where there is a foreign forum to whose jurisdiction the defendant is amenable.

Also, pending English proceedings may be stayed where the parties have agreed by contract that all disputes between them shall be referred to the jurisdiction of a foreign tribunal (foreign jurisdiction clause).

The jurisdiction to grant stays of English proceedings in the circumstances mentioned above is highly discretionary and is exercised with extreme caution. The relevant law is complicated and extensive and need not be explained here.

The jurisdiction to stay proceedings on forum *non conveniens* grounds or otherwise is recognised by the Civil Jurisdiction and Judgments Act 1982 s.49).

For the stay of proceedings to which the Convention on Jurisdiction and Enforcement of Judgments in Civil and Commercial Matters applies, see para.9A–186 below.

9A–186 *EC Convention actions* —An action brought in an English court which is within the scope of the EC Conventions on Jurisdiction and the Enforcement of Judgments, which have been given the force of law by s.2 of the Civil Jurisdiction and Judgments Act 1982 set out in s.7 may be stayed and in some instances must be stayed or dismissed in the following classes or cases:

9A–187 *(i) Exclusive jurisdiction* —(a) where the claim is principally concerned with a matter over which the courts of another Member State of the EC have exclusive jurisdiction under art.16, the English Court must declare of its own motion that it has no jurisdiction (see art.19), and presumably for this purpose the Court will make an order staying or dismissing the action; (b) where the English Court is not the court first seised of an action which comes within the exclusive jurisdiction of several Courts, it must decline jurisdiction in favour of the Court first seised (art.23).

9A–188 *(ii) Agreement conferring jurisdiction* —(a) where an agreement is concluded between parties one or more of whom is domiciled in a Member State of the EC, that a Court or the Courts of a specified Member State are to have jurisdiction to settle disputes between them, that Court will have exclusive jurisdiction and presumably the Courts of another Member State must decline jurisdiction; (b) where such agreement is concluded between parties, one of whom is domiciled in a Member State of the EEC, the Courts of the contracting states will have no jurisdiction over their disputes, unless the Courts chosen have declined jurisdiction; (c) if a trust instrument has conferred jurisdiction on the Court or Courts of a Member State, that Court or Courts will have exclusive jurisdiction in proceedings brought against a settlor, trustee or beneficiary (see art.17).

9A–189 *(iii) Default of acknowledgment of service* —where a defendant is domiciled in another Member State of the EC but is sued in England and does not acknowledge service of process, the English Court must declare of its own motion that it has no jurisdiction, unless its jurisdiction is derived from other provisions of the EC Conventions (art.20) and in any event, in such case, the Court must stay the proceedings so long as it is not shown that the defendant had been able to receive the originating document or its equivalent in sufficient time to arrange for his defence or that all necessary steps have been taken to this end (art.20).

9A–190 *(iv) Lis pendens* —where the English Court is not the Court first seised of proceedings involving the same cause of action between the same parties which are brought in the Courts of different Member States of the EC, it must of its own motion declare jurisdiction in favour of the Court first seised (art.21), although if the jurisdiction of that Court is contested, it may stay the proceedings pending the outcome of that contest (art.21).

9A–191 *(v) Related actions* —where the English Court is not the Court first seised of related actions which are brought in the Courts of different Member States of the EC, it may stay the proceedings while the actions are pending at first instance (art.22). It may also, on the application of one of the parties decline jurisdiction if the law of the court first seised permits the consolidation of related actions and that Court has jurisdiction over both actions (art.22). For this purpose, actions are deemed to be related where they are so closely connected that it is expedient to hear and determine them together to avoid the risk of irreconcilable judgments resulting from separate proceedings (art.22).

9A–192 *EC Jurisdiction Regulation* —Council Regulation 44/2001 was implemented by the Civil Jurisdiction Order 2001 (SI 2001/3929) (see para. 5–200 above). In this Regulation, arts 23 to 29 correspond, respectively, with arts 17 to 23 of the Brussels Convention. Under the Regulation, where (a) proceedings involving the same cause of action and between the same parties are brought in the courts of different Member States (lis pendens), or (b) where related actions are pending in the courts of different Member States (related actions), or (b) where actions come within the exclusive juris-

***Paragraph numbers marked with a "+" can be found online and on CD.***

diction of several courts, and the English court has to determine whether it should stay proceedings because another court was first seised of the proceedings, reference has to be made to art.30 (see para. 5–278 above). That article has no counterpart on the Brussels Convention and is designed to overcome certain difficulties that have arisen under the Convention (e.g. *Dresser UK Ltd v Falcongate Freight Management Ltd (The Duke of Yare)* [1992] Q.B. 502, CA.)

*European Commission investigation*—Where a defendant alleges that he has a defence by reason of a breach of the Rome Treaty and makes a complaint to the EC Commission the Court may order a stay pending investigation by the Commission of the plaintiff's action upon terms providing some protection as to costs and damages (*British Leyland Motor Corp Ltd v Wyatt Interpart Co Ltd* [1979] F.S.R. 583; [1979] 3 C.M.L.R. 77 and further hearing [1980] F.S.R. 18). Paragraph 5.3 of Practice Direction (Competition Law, Etc) provides that, where the court is seised of competition claim and is aware that the Commission is contemplating adopting a decision in relation to proceedings that it has initiated, the court shall consider whether to stay the claim pending the Commission's decision (see Vol.1, para.B9–005+). **9A–193**

*Cases illustrating exercise of jurisdiction to stay proceedings*—In successive editions of the Supreme Court Practice, many cases illustrating the exercise of jurisdiction to stay proceedings in particular contexts were given; see SCP 1999, Vol.2, paras 20A–337 *et seq.* In the above paragraphs, no effort is made to reproduce all of the information formerly found in the Supreme Court Practice. Significant omissions include the information found in the following paragraphs of Vol.2 of the 1999 edition: para.20A–251 (Bankruptcy), paras 20A–53 and 20A–354 (Company winding-up), para.20A–355 (Company—stay of petition and order). **9A–194**

*Parallel EPO patent proceedings*—In *Glaxo Group Limited v Genentech Inc* [2008] EWCA Civ 23; [2008] F.S.R. 83, CA, a pharmaceutical company (D) was granted a patent by the European Patent Office (EPO). Another company brought opposition proceedings in the EPO, and, in addition, brought an action in the Patents Court for revocation. The judge refused D's application for a stay of the English proceedings. In dismissing D's appeal the Court of Appeal stated that the traditional approach of the court to the stay of proceedings where there are concurrent proceedings in commercial cases is not appropriate in these circumstances and gave guidance on the exercise of the discretion to stay in this context. See also *Interdigital Technology Corporation v Nokia Corporation* [2008] EWHC 736 (Pat), April 8, 2008, unrep. (Floyd J.) and *GlaxoSmithKline Biologicals SA v Sanofi Pasteur SA* [2006] EWHC 2333 (Pat), July 28, 2006, unrep. (Kitchin J.). **9A–195**

## Power to award damages as well as, or in substitution for, injunction or specific performance

**50.** Where the Court of Appeal or the High Court has jurisdiction to entertain an application for an injunction or specific performance, it may award damages in addition to, or in substitution for, an injunction or specific performance. **9A–196**

*Note*—Derived from the Chancery Amendment Act 1858 s.2; and the JA 1925 ss.18 and 26. **9A–197**

**Effect of this section**

The purpose of this section was to make it possible for a claimant to claim both damages and an injunction in the same proceedings, whether those proceedings were brought in the Queen's Bench Division or the Chancery Division. **9A–198**

CPR r.16.2(1) states that the claim form must (amongst other things) specify the remedy which the claimant seeks. Accordingly, if the claimant seeks damages in addition to an injunction or specific performance the claim form should state accordingly.

Since s.50 was enacted (initially in Lord Cairn's Act 1858), most of the case law on the provision has been concerned with the question whether the claimant should be required (as contended by the defendant) to make do with damages as a remedy in

***Paragraph numbers marked with a "+" can be found online and on CD.***

substitution for an injunction against the continuation of a wrongful act. The leading modern cases on the matter are *Jaggard v Sawyer* [1995] 1 W.L.R. 269, CA; *Regan v Paul Properties Ltd* [2006] EWCA Civ 1391; [2007] Ch. 135, CA (both reviewing and largely confirming propositions stated in *Shelfer v City of London Electric Lighting Co.* [1895] 1 Ch. 287, CA); see also *Chiron Corp v Organon Teknika Ltd (No.10)* [1995] F.S.R. 325 (Aldous J.); *Watson v Croft Promo-Sport Ltd* [2009] EWCA Civ 15; [2009] 3 All E.R. 249, CA (where the relevant authorities are reviewed).

In the *Jaggard* case, Sir Thomas Bingham M.R. stated (at p.288):

> "Reported cases are merely illustrations of circumstances in which particular judges have exercised their discretion, in some cases by granting an injunction, and in others by awarding damages instead. Since they are all cases on the exercise of discretion, none of them is binding authority on how the discretion should be exercised."

It has been held at first instance that, since the coming into effect of the Human Rights Act 1998 Sch.1, Pt 1, damages for future infringements of a claimant's rights may be awarded under s.50 in lieu of an injunction (*Marcic v Thames Water Utilities Ltd* [2001] 3 All E.R. 698 (Judge Richard Havery Q.C.)).

## COSTS

### Costs in civil division of Court of Appeal, High Court and county courts

9A–199 **51.**—(1) Subject to the provisions of this or any other enactment and to rules of court, the costs of and incidental to all proceedings in—

(a) the civil division of the Court of Appeal;
(b) the High Court, and
(c) any county court,

shall be in the discretion of the court.

(2) Without prejudice to any general power to make rules of court, such rules may make provision for regulating matters relating to the costs of those proceedings including, in particular, prescribing scales of costs to be paid to legal or other representatives or for securing that the amount awarded to a party in respect of the costs to be paid by him to such representatives is not limited to what would have been payable by him to them if he had not been awarded costs.

(3) The court shall have full power to determine by whom and to what extent the costs are to be paid.

(4) In subsections (1) and (2) "proceedings" includes the administration of estates and trusts.

(5) Nothing in subsection (1) shall alter the practice in any criminal cause, or in bankruptcy.

(6) In any proceedings mentioned in subsection (1), the court may disallow, or (as the case may be) order the legal or other representative concerned to meet, the whole of any wasted costs or such part of them as may be determined in accordance with rules of court.

(7) In subsection (6), "wasted costs" means any costs incurred by a party—

(a) as a result of any improper, unreasonable or negligent act or omission on the part of any legal or other representative or any employee of such a representative; or
(b) which, in the light of any such act or omission occurring

after they were incurred, the court considers it is unreasonable to expect that party to pay.

(8) Where—

(a) a person has commenced proceedings in the High Court; but

(b) those proceedings should, in the opinion of the court, have been commenced in a county court in accordance with any provision made under section 1 of the Courts and Legal Services Act 1990 or by or under any other enactment,

the person responsible for determining the amount which is to be awarded to that person by way of costs shall have regard to those circumstances.

(9) Where, in complying with subsection (8), the responsible person reduces the amount which would otherwise be awarded to the person in question—

(a) the amount of that reduction shall not exceed 25 per cent; and

(b) on any taxation of the costs payable by that person to his legal representative, regard shall be had to the amount of the reduction.

(10) The Lord Chancellor may by order amend subsection (9)(a) by substituting, for the percentage for the time being mentioned there, a different percentage.

(11) Any such order shall be made by statutory instrument and may make such transitional or incidental provision as the Lord Chancellor considers expedient.

(12) No such statutory instrument shall be made unless a draft of the instrument has been approved by both Houses of Parliament.

(13) In this section "legal or other representative", in relation to a party to proceedings, means any person exercising a right of audience or right to conduct litigation on his behalf.

*Note* —Substituted by the Courts and Legal Services Act 1990 s.4. Amended by the Access to Justice Act 1999 s.31. **9A-200**

**Effect of this section**

This section came into its present form as a result of the Courts and Legal Services Act 1990 s.4(1). In its amended form the section implemented recommendations made in the Report of the Review Body on Civil Justice (Cm. 394, 1988), including the recommendation that there should be a single costs regime for the High Court and the county courts, subject to an exception for county court cases below £3,000. As amended, the section provides statutory bases for awarding costs, not only for proceedings in the Court of Appeal (Civil Division) and the High Court, but for the county courts also. Rules of court relating to costs are found in the CPR made by the rule committee established under the Civil Procedure Act 1997 s.2. Section 51 is referred to specifically in CPR rr.48.2 and 48.7. In s.51(2), the words "or for securing" onwards were added by the Access to Justice Act 1999. This addition makes it possible for rules of court to provide that a successful party may recover by way of *inter partes* costs a sum in excess of his liability to his own legal representative (*cf. Gundry v Sainsbury* [1910] 1 K.B. 645). This addition was brought into effect on June 2, 2003, by the Access to Justice Act 1999 (Commencement No.10) Order 2002 (SI 2003/1241), making possible amendments to CPR r.43.2 brought about by the Civil Procedure (Amendment No.2) Rules 2003 (SI 2003/1242) and coming into effect on the same date. Note **9A-201**

***Paragraph numbers marked with a "+" can be found online and on CD.***

also, Access to Justice Act 1999 s.29 (recovery of insurance premium by way of costs) (see para.9A–826+).

**"costs ... shall be in the discretion of the court"**

**9A–202** Subject to the provisions of the 1981 Act or any other enactment and to rules of court, the costs of and incidental to all proceedings shall be in the discretion of the court and the court shall have full power to determine by whom and to what extent the costs are to be paid (subss.(1) and (3)). This general principle applies in all forums. It is re-stated in CPR r.44.3 and the exercise of the discretion is regulated by the many detailed provisions found in Pts 44 to 48 of the CPR and supplementing practice directions.

The breadth of the discretion was emphasised by the House of Lords in *Aiden Shipping Co Ltd v Interbulk Ltd* [1986] A.C. 965, HL, where it was held that it includes a power to award costs against a person who is not a party to the proceedings. In modern times, the jurisdiction to order that costs should be paid by a person who, though not actually a party to the proceedings, is sufficiently involved in them in support of a losing party for it to be appropriate for the court to order that they should bear at least some or a proportion of the winning party's costs (see further para.9A–203 below), has been explained and developed in a number of cases. Significant authorities include the following: *Symphony Group Plc v Hodgson* [1994] Q.B. 179, CA; *Tharros Shipping Co Ltd v Bias Shipping Ltd (The Griparion) (No.3)* [1995] 1 Lloyd's Rep. 541; *Murphy v Young & Co's Brewery Plc* [1997] 1 W.L.R. 1591, CA; *Faryab v Smyth (Stay of Appeal: Champerty)* [1998] C.L.Y. 411; *Pendennis Shipyard Ltd v Magrathea (Pendennis) Ltd* [1998] 1 Lloyd's Rep. 315; *TGA Chapman Ltd v Christopher* [1998] 1 W.L.R. 12, CA; *Gloucestershire HA v MA Torpy & Partners Ltd (t/a Torpy & Partners) (No.2)* [1999] Lloyd's Rep. I.R. 303; *Globe Equities Ltd v Globe Legal Services Ltd, The Times*, April 14, 1999, unrep., CA; *Fulton Motors Ltd v Toyota (G.B.) Ltd* July 23, 1999, unrep., CA.; *Stocznia Gdanska SA v Latreefers Inc*, [1999] 1 B.C.L.C. 271, CA; *Cormack v Washbourne (formerly t/a Washbourne & Co)*, [1999] Lloyd's Rep. P.N. 389, CA; *Secretary of State for Trade and Industry v Aurum Marketing Ltd*, [1999] 2 B.C.L.C. 498, CA; *North West Holdings Plc (In Liquidation) (Costs), Re*, [2001] EWCA Civ 67, CA; *Hamilton v Al Fayed (No.2)* [2002] EWCA Civ 665; [2002] 3 All E.R. 641, CA, *Gulf Azov Shipping Co Ltd v Idisi (Costs)* [2004] EWCA Civ 292; March 15, 2004, CA.

The approach of the courts to the making of an award of costs against a non-party has had to accommodate the change in public policy which has recognised that access to justice can properly be procured by giving those who provide legal services an interest in the outcome of litigation through conditional fee agreements (*Gulf Azov Shipping Co Ltd v Idisi (Costs), op cit.*).

The courts' general discretion as to costs referred to in s.51 includes a power to order that one order for costs should be set-off against another. In *R. (Burkett) v London Borough of Hammersmith and Fulham* [2004] EWCA Civ 1342; *The Times* October 20, 2004, CA, where the Court of Appeal was concerned with the set-off of costs against costs (and not against damages) in the same proceedings (and not in different proceedings) the law as to set-off in this context and its history were explained in detailed (see para.38 *et seq*).

Normally, orders made by the court in the exercise of the discretion to award costs referred to in s.51(1) are made at the end of the proceedings to which they relate (whether interlocutory, final or appeal). However the discretion is wide enough to enable the court to make an order for costs in advance, based on assumptions as to the possible outcomes (and, therefore, the possible costs liabilities) of the proceedings. Depending on the circumstances, such orders may be aptly described as "prospective", "pre-emptive" or "protective" costs orders. The clearest example is where the court makes an order that a party involved in legal proceedings in the capacity of trustee should be entitled to his own costs out of the fund and should be indemnified by the fund against any award for costs which may be made against him (*Re Beddoe, Downes v Cottam* [1893] 1 Ch. 547, CA) (CPR r. 64.2 and Practice Direction (Estates, Trusts and Charities) para.6.1; see Vol.1 paras 48.1.5 and 64APD.6). In certain circumstances the costs protection enjoyed by trustees may be extended to beneficiaries (*Re Buckton, Buckton v Buckton* [1907] 2 Ch. 406; *D'Abo v Paget (No.1)*, [2002] B.C.C. 31). The protection has also been extended to minority shareholders (*Wallersteiner v Moir (No.2)* [1975] Q.B. 373), to beneficiaries under pension funds (*McDonald v Horn* [1995] 1 All

***Paragraph numbers marked with a "+" can be found online and on CD.***

E.R. 961, CA; *Machin v National Power Plc*, July 31, 1998, unrep. (Carnwarth J.)), and to insurance policy-holders (*AXA Equity & Law Life Assurance Society Plc (No.1), Re*, [2001] 2 B.C.L.C. 447 (Evans-Lombe J.)). In modern times, pre-emptive costs orders have been sought in circumstances quite different to the trust and trust-related circumstances noted above, in particular in judicial review applications where organisations acting in the public interest are involved. It has been held that, in exceptional circumstances, pre-emptive costs orders may be granted in such "public interest challenge" cases; see *R. v Lord Chancellor Ex p. Child Poverty Action Group*, [1999] 1 W.L.R. 347 (Dyson J.); *R. v Hammersmith and Fulham LBC Ex p. CPRE London Branch*, October 26, 1999, unrep. (Richards J.); *R. v Secretary of State for the Environment, Transport and the Regions Ex p. O'Byrne (Application for Jo)*, [2000] C.P. Rep. 9 (Hooper J.); *cf. Hodgson v Imperial Tobacco Ltd* [1998] 1 W.L.R. 1056, CA. In giving the judgment of the Court of Appeal in *Gulf Azov Shipping Co Ltd v Idisi (Costs)* [2004] EWCA Civ 292, CA March 15, 2004, unrep., Lord Phillips M.R. said (at para.34) it was unfortunate that the application for costs against a non-party funder was heard, not by the judge who had dealt with the principal proceedings giving rise to the application, or by any other judge of the Commercial Court who had been involved with the litigation, but by a deputy High Court judge who had had no previous connection with the proceedings.

**Costs order in favour of or against non—parties**

The procedure to be followed where the court is considering whether to exercise its **9A–203**
discretion under s.51 to make a costs order in favour or against a person who is not a party to the proceedings is stated in CPR r.48.2. For information on the exercise of the discretion in this manner, see commentary following that rule (Vol 1, para.48.2.1).

**"court may disallow, or ... order ... wasted costs"**

Subsections (6) and (7) deal with liability for "wasted costs". The court may disallow **9A–204**
such costs, or it may make the the legal or other representatives (see subs.(11)) concerned personally liable for such costs. Subsection (6) applies, not only in the Court of Appeal (Civil Division), the High Court and county courts, but also in relation to any civil proceedings in the Crown Court (s.52(1A)). The definition of "wasted costs" given in subs.(7) does not require a showing of misconduct or gross neglect, but is, at its lowest, a negligence test. The provisions and the rules of court elaborating on them were designed to deal with doubts which had arisen under former legislation and rules of court (for background, see White Paper on Legal Services Cm 740, 1989). The inherent jurisdiction to penalise in costs remains. Relevant rules of court are found in CPR r.44.14 (Court's powers in relation to misconduct) (see Vol.1, para.44.14) and r.48.7 (Personal liability of legal representative for costs) (see Vol.1, para.48.7). For explanation, see commentaries following those rules.

**Costs sanction for bringing proceedings in High Court**

In its amended form, the section introduced a modified costs sanction to discourage **9A–205**
litigants from bringing in the High Court proceedings that could have been brought in a county court (subss.(8) to (12)). The statutory provisions which formerly provided the basis for this costs sanction were repealed. The power to impose such sanction is reflected in provisions found in the CPR and supplementing practice directions.

**For s.52 of the Senior Courts Act 1981 (see Arrangement) plus any related commentary see paragraphs 9A–206+ to 9A–207+ on White Book on Westlaw UK or the Civil Procedure CD.**



## PART III

## PRACTICE AND PROCEDURE

### THE COURT OF APPEAL

### *DISTRIBUTION OF BUSINESS*

## Distribution of business between civil and criminal divisions

**53.**—(1) Rules of court may provide for the distribution of business **9A–208**

in the Court of Appeal between the civil and criminal divisions, but subject to any such rules business shall be distributed in accordance with the following provisions of this section.

(2) The criminal division of the Court of Appeal shall exercise—

(a) all jurisdiction of the Court of Appeal under Parts I and II of the Criminal Appeal Act 1968;

(b) the jurisdiction of the Court of Appeal under section 13 of the Administration of Justice Act 1960 (appeals in cases of contempt of court) in relation to appeals from orders and decisions of the Crown Court;

(c) all other jurisdiction expressly conferred on that division by this or any other Act; and

(d) the jurisdiction to order the issue of writs of venire de novo.

(3) The civil division of the Court of Appeal shall exercise the whole of the jurisdiction of that court not exercisable by the criminal division.

(4) Where any class of proceedings in the Court of Appeal is by any statutory provision assigned to the criminal division of that court, rules of court may provide for any enactment relating to—

(a) appeals to the Court of Appeal under Part I of the Criminal Appeal Act 1968; or

(b) any matter connected with or arising out of such appeals,

to apply in relation to proceedings of that class or, as the case may be, to any corresponding matter connected with or arising out of such proceedings, as it applies in relation to such appeals or, as the case may be, to the relevant matter within paragraph (b), with or without prescribed modifications in either case.

9A–209 *Note*—The effect of ss.18 and 53 is that the Civil Division of the Court of Appeal has no jurisdiction to hear appeals in any criminal cause or matter.

### COMPOSITION OF COURT

**Court of civil division**

9A–210 **54.**—(1) This section relates to the civil division of the Court of Appeal; and in this section "court", except where the context otherwise requires, means a court of that division.

(2) Subject as follows, a court shall be duly constituted for the purpose of exercising any of its jurisdiction if it consists of one or more judges.

(3) The Master of the Rolls may, with the concurrence of the Lord Chancellor, give (or vary or revoke) directions about the minimum number of judges of which a court must consist if it is to be duly constituted for the purpose of any description of proceedings.

(4) The Master of the Rolls, or any Lord Justice designated by him, may (subject to any directions under subsection (3)) determine the number of judges of which a court is to consist for the purpose of any particular proceedings.

(4A) The Master of the Rolls may give directions as to what is to happen in any particular case where one or more members of a court which has partly heard proceedings are unable to continue.

(5) Where—

(a) an appeal has been heard by a court consisting of an even number of judges; and

(b) the members of the court are equally divided,

the case shall, on the application of any party to the appeal, be re-argued before and determined by an uneven number of judges not less than three, before any appeal to the Supreme Court.

(6) […]

(7) […]

(8) Subsections (1) and (2) of section 70 (assessors in the High Court) shall apply in relation to causes and matters before the civil division of the Court of Appeal as they apply in relation to causes and matters before the High Court.

(9) Subsections (3) and (4) of section 60 (scientific advisers to assist the Patents Court in proceedings under the Patents Act 1949 and the Patents Act 1977) shall apply in relation to the civil division of the Court of Appeal and proceedings on appeal from any decision of the Patents Court in proceedings under those Acts as they apply in relation to the Patents Court and proceedings under those Acts.

(10) […]

*Note* —Amended by the Courts and Legal Services Act 1990 s.7 and the Access to Justice Act 1999 ss.59, 106, Sch.15, Pt III. See para.9A–4 above. Further amended by the Constitutional Reform Act 2005 Sch.9 para.36 with effect from October 1, 2009 (SI 2009/1604). **9A–211**

### Composition of the Court of Appeal

By operation of the Access to Justice 1999, s.59, subss.(2) to (4A) were substituted for subs.(2) to (4) and subss.(6), (7) and (10) were repealed. Previously, the basic rule was that, in order to be properly constituted, a court of the Division had to consist of "an uneven number of judges not less than three". **9A–212**

In exceptional cases, provided for in s.54 and regulations, a court of the Division was duly constituted for certain purposes if it consisted of two judges. In its amended form, subs.(2) states the basic rule that a court shall be duly constituted "for the purpose of exercising any of its jurisdiction if it consists of one or more judges". The circumstances in which a court of the Division should consist of two or more judges is provided for by directions given under subss.(3) and (4). Subsections (4A) states that the Master of the Rolls may give directions as to what is to happen in any particular case where one or more members of a court which has partly heard proceedings are unable to continue. This replaces former subs.(3) which stated that a court would remain duly constituted so long as the number of judges was not reduced to less than three. Where an appeal has been heard by a court consisting of an even number of judges, and the members of the court are eqully divided, subs.(5) applies. As a consequence of the amendments made by the 1999 Act, the Court of Appeal (Civil Division) Order 1982 (SI 1982/543) will be repealed.

### Assessors and scientific advisers

Subss.(8) and (9) extend to the Court of Appeal the provisions of s.70 concerning assessors and scientific advisers (see para.9A–261 below). **9A–213**

**For s.55 of the Senior Courts Act 1981 (see Arrangement) plus any related commentary see paragraphs 9A–214+ to 9A–215+ on White Book on Westlaw UK or the Civil Procedure CD.**

***Paragraph numbers marked with a "+" can be found online and on CD.***

### Judges not to sit on appeal from their own judgments, etc.

9A–216 **56.**—(1) No judge shall sit as a member of the civil division of the Court of Appeal on the hearing of, or shall determine any application in proceedings incidental or preliminary to, an appeal for a judgment or order made in any case by himself or by any court of which he was a member.

(2) No judge shall sit as a member of the criminal division of the Court of Appeal on the hearing of, or shall determine any application in proceedings incidental or preliminary to, an appeal against—

(a) a conviction before himself or a court of which he was a member; or

(b) a sentence passed by himself or such a court.

9A–217 *Note*—The fact that a judge in the Court of Appeal is a judge of the Division of the High Court in which the proceedings under appeal were brought does not preclude him from being a member of the Court of Appeal hearing the appeal, provided of course that he has himself taken no part in the making of the order appealed against (*Fisher v Val de Travers Asphalte Co* (1875) 1 C.P.D. 259).

**For s.56B of the Senior Courts Act 1981 (see Arrangement) plus any related commentary see paragraphs 9A–218+ to 9A–219+ on White Book on Westlaw UK or the Civil Procedure CD.**

## *SITTINGS AND VACATIONS*

### Sittings and vacations

9A–220 **57.**—(1) Sittings of the Court of Appeal may be held, and any other business of the Court of Appeal may be conducted, at any place in England or Wales.

(2) Subject to rules of court—

(a) the places at which the Court of Appeal sits outside the Royal Courts of Justice; and

(b) the days and times at which the Court of Appeal sits at any place outside the Royal Courts of Justice,

shall be determined in accordance with directions given by the Lord Chancellor after consulting the Lord Chief Justice.

(3) Rules of court may make provision for regulating the vacations to be observed by the Court of Appeal and in the offices of that court.

(4) Rules of Court—

(a) may provide for securing such sittings of the civil division of the Court of Appeal during vacation as the Master of the Rolls may with the concurrence of the Lord Chancellor determine;

(b) without prejudice to paragraph (a), shall provide for the transaction during vacation by judges of the Court of Appeal of all such business in the civil division of that court as may require to be immediately or promptly transacted; and

(c) shall providing for securing sittings of the criminal division of that court during vacation if necessary.

(5) The Lord Chief Justice may nominate a judicial office holder (as defined in section 109(4) of the Constitutional Reform Act 2005) to exercise his functions under this section.

*Note* —Amended by the Constitutional Reform Act 2005 s.15(1), Sch.4, para.128 (see para.9A–4 above). **9A–221**

**Directions as to sittings**

Paragraph 10.8 of *Practice Direction (Court of Appeal (Civil Division))*, [1999] 1 W.L.R. 1027, CA (*sub nom Practice Note (Court of Appeal: Procedure)* 2 All E.R. 490, CA) states that the Court of Appeal will sit in vacation on such days as the Master of the Rolls may direct and may hear such appeals and applications as the Court may direct. Details of the number of courts sitting in August and September will be published each year, normally before Easter. See further, Practice Direction (Court Sittings), supplementing CPR Pt 39. **9A–222**

## OTHER PROVISIONS

## Calling into question of incidental decisions in civil division

**58.**—(1) Rules of court may provide that decisions of the Court of Appeal which— **9A–223**

(a) are taken by a single judge or any officer or member of staff of that court in proceedings incidental to any cause or matter pending before the civil division of that court; and

(b) do not involve the determination of an appeal or of an application for permission to appeal,

may be called into question in such manner as may be prescribed.

(2) No appeal shall lie to the Supreme Court from a decision which may be called into question pursuant to rules under subsection (1).

*Note* —Amended by the Access to Justice Act 1999 s.60. See para.9A–4 above. Further amended by the Constitutional Reform Act 2005 Sch.9 para.36 with effect from October 1, 2009 (SI 2009/1604). **9A–224**

**Jurisdiction of a single judge or any officer or member of court staff to hear incidental applications**

Subsection (1) makes provision for any application incidental to any cause or matter pending before the Civil Division of the Court of Appeal to be heard by a single judge, or of any officer or member of court staff, so far as provided in rules of court. (The office of Registrar of Civil Appeals, formerly referred to in s.58, was abolished by the Access to Justice 1999, s.70.) **9A–225**

See CPR Pt 52, Sect.II. In *Perotti v Watson*, February 2, 2000, unrep., CA, it was held that by operation of s.58 and former RSC O.59, r.2B (see now CPR r.52.16) a single Lord Justice may vary a procedural order for the conduct and management of a substantive appeal previously made by the Court constituted by two Lord Justices.

## Form of judgment of court of criminal division

**59.** Any judgment of a court of the criminal division of the Court of Appeal on any question shall, except where the judge presiding over the court states that in his opinion the question is one of law on which it is convenient that separate judgments should be pronounced by the members of the court, be pronounced by the judge presiding over the court or by such other member of the court as he directs **9A–226**

and, except as aforesaid, no judgment shall be separately pronounced on any question by any member of the court.

### Rules of court, and decisions of Court of Appeal, as to whether judgment or order is final or interlocutory

9A–227 **60.**—(1) Rules of court may provide for orders or judgments of any prescribed description to be treated for any prescribed purpose connected with appeals to the Court of Appeal as final or as interlocutory.

(2) No appeal shall lie from a decision of the Court of Appeal as to whether a judgment or order is, for any purpose connected with an appeal to that court, final or interlocutory.

9A–228 *Note*.—The significance of the distinction between final and interlocutory orders in relation to the jurisdiction and procedure of the Court of Appeal (Civil Division) is not as important as it was. Former RSC O.59, r.1A elaborated on the distinction, principally for the purpose of distinguishing between those cases where leave to appeal was required under O.59, r.1B and where not. See now CPR Pt 52, Sect.II.

## THE HIGH COURT

### *DISTRIBUTION OF BUSINESS*

### Distribution of business among Divisions

9A–229 **61.**—(1) Subject to any provision made by or under this or any other Act (and in particular to any rules of court made in pursuance of subsection (2) and any order under subsection (3)), business in the High Court of any description mentioned in Schedule 1, as for the time being in force, shall be distributed among the Divisions in accordance with that Schedule.

(2) Rules of court may provide for the distribution of business in the High Court among the Divisions; but any rules made in pursuance of this subsection shall have effect subject to any orders for the time being in force under subsection (3).

(3) Subject to subsection (5), the Lord Chief Justice may, with the concurrence of the Lord Chancello, by order—

(a) direct that any business in the High Court which is not for the time being assigned by or under this or any other Act to any Division be assigned to such Division as may be specified in the order;

(b) if at any time it appears to the Lord Chief Justice and the Lord Chancellor desirable to do so with a view to the more convenient administration of justice, direct that any business for the time being assigned by or under this or any other Act to any Division be assigned to such other Division as may be specified in the order; and

(c) amend Schedule 1 so far as may be necessary in consequence of provision made by order under paragraph (a) or (b).

(4) The powers conferred by subsection (2) and subsection (3)

include power to assign business of any description to two or more Divisions concurrently.

(5) No order under subsection (3)(b) relating to any business shall be made without the concurrence of the senior judge of—

(a) the Division or each of the Divisions to which the business is for the time being assigned; and

(b) the Division or each of the Divisions to which the business is to be assigned by the order.

(6) Subject to rules of court, the fact that a cause or matter commenced in the High Court falls within a class of business assigned by or under this Act to a particular Division does not make it obligatory for it to be allocated or transferred to that Division.

(7) Without prejudice to subsections (1) to (5) and section 63, rules of court may provide for the distribution of the business (other than business required to be heard by a divisional court) in any Division of the High Court among the judges of that Division.

(8) Any order under subsection (3) shall be made by statutory instrument, which shall be laid before Parliament after being made.

(9) The Lord Chief Justice may nominate a judicial office holder (as defined in section 109(4) of the Constitutional Reform Act 2005) to exercise his functions under subsection (3).

*Note* —Derived from the JA 1925 ss.55–57, and the AJA 1970 s.1, Sch.1; amended by the Constitutional Reform Act 2005 s.15(1), Sch.4, para.129 (see para.9A–4 above). **9A–230**

**Effect of section**

This section should be read closely with s.5, which provides for the constitution of three Divisions of the High Court, and with Sch.1 which provides for the distribution of the business of the High Court among the three Divisions. Such distribution of the business is intended to achieve a more convenient system of the administration of civil justice and a more effective machinery for the despatch of business. It reflects the high degree of specialisation which exists among the members of the legal profession, as well as to some extent of the judiciary. It is not intended to create, and does not have the effect of creating separate or self-contained Courts nor of distributing among the Divisions the jurisdiction and power of the High Court, which in spite of appearing to be fragmented into Divisions still remains a single, integrated Court. This section should also be read in conjunction with s.19(2)(b) which empowers the High Court to exercise all such other jurisdiction as was exercisable by it before the commencement of the Act. **9A–231**

The Admiralty, Commercial, and Administrative Courts are not separate Divisions within the High Court but are designated as courts within the Queen's Bench Division of the High Court, in the case of the first two mentioned, by s.6 of this Act (see para.9A–23+ above), and in the case of the last-mentioned, by *Practice Direction (Administrative Court: Establishment)* [2000] 1 W.L.R. 1654. The Patents Court is designated as a court within the Chancery Division of the High Court by s.6. See further s.62 below.

For considerations relevant to the proper distribution of business between the Administrative Court, on the one hand, and the Family Division of the High Court on the other, see *DC v B MBC* [2002] EWHC 1438 (Fam), (Butler-Sloss P.); *R. (on the application of P) v Secretary of State for the Home Department*, [2001] EWHC Admin 357, and *A v A Health Authority* [2002] EWHC 866 (Admin); [2002] 3 W.L.R. 24 (Munby J.).

**Jurisdiction exercisable by all Divisions**

"There is but one High Court" (*Re Hastings (No.3)* [1959] Ch. 368, at 379, per Vaisey J.). Section 5(5) expressly provides that all jurisdiction vested in the High Court under the Act belongs to all Divisions alike. This principle is further underscored by **9A–232**

***Paragraph numbers marked with a "+" can be found online and on CD.***

the direction issued by the Lord Chancellor that any Division of the High Court to which a cause or matter is assigned has jurisdiction to grant any remedy or relief arising out of or related to or connected with any claim made in that cause or matter notwithstanding that proceedings for such remedy or relief are assigned to another Division of the Court (*Practice Direction (High Court: Division)* [1973] 1 W.L.R. 627; [1973] 2 All E.R. 233.

A judge of one Division may decline to exercise his jurisdiction over a matter which is properly assignable to another Division, to which he may transfer the matter (see s.65 below). Equally, however, the judge may, in his discretion, decide to retain a matter which is properly assignable to another Division (*Russian Commercial and Industrial Bank v British Bank for Foreign Trade Ltd* [1921] 2 A.C. 438; *Midland Bank Ltd v Stamps* [1978] 1 W.L.R. 635; [1978] 3 All E.R. 1).

As to transfer of proceedings from one Division to another, see s.65 below.

Various CPR provisions stipulate that certain proceedings should be commenced, or applications made, in particular Divisions of the High Court. See e.g. r.7.1 and Practice Direction How to Start Proceedings—The Claim Form), paras 2.1 *et seq.* (see Vol.1, para.7PD.2), and Practice Direction (Interim Injunctions), para.8.5 (all applications in intellectual property cases to be made in Chancery Division).

**Re-distribution of business**

**9A–233** The distribution of business among the Divisions of the High Court in accordance with Sch.1 to the Act is not fixed or unalterable but is capable of addition, amendment or variation by orders made by the Lord Chancellor under s.61(3) and (5), under which he may direct that any business in the High Court not already assigned by the Act of 1981 or any other Act to any Division be assigned to a specified Division, and that any business already assigned by the Act of 1981 or any other Act to any Division be assigned to another specified Division, and for these purposes, he may amend Sch.1 to the Act under s.61(3)(c); and the Lord Chancellor has power to assign any business to two or more Divisions concurrently (s.61(4)). Such orders must be made with the concurrence of the senior Judge of the Division or Divisions concerned, and they must be made by statutory instrument (see s.61(8)). Amendments were made to Sch.1 of the Act concerning the distribution of business to the Family Division by the High Court (Distribution of Business) Order 1991 (SI 1991/1210) and High Court (Distribution of Business) Order 1993 (SI 1993/622).

## Business of Patents, Admiralty and Commercial Courts

**9A–234** **62.**—(1) The Patents Court shall take such proceedings relating to patents as are within the jurisdiction conferred on it by the Patents Act 1977, and such other proceedings relating to patents or other matters as may be prescribed.

(2) The Admiralty Court shall take Admiralty business, that is to say causes and matters assigned to the Queen's Bench Division and involving the exercise of the High Court's Admiralty jurisdiction or its jurisdiction as a prize court.

(3) The Commercial Court shall take such causes and matters as may in accordance with rules of court be entered in the commercial list.

**9A–235** *Note* —Derived from the AJA 1970 ss.2 and 3; and the Patents Act 1977 s.96. See also s.6.

**Procedure**

**9A–236** Procedure before these specialised courts within the High Court is governed by the CPR. However, the procedures for each of the courts mentioned in s.62 is subject to considerable elaboration and variation in Parts of the CPR specially dedicated to them; see Pt 58 (Commercial Court), Pt 61 (Admiralty Claims), Pt 63 (Patents and Other Intellectual Property Claims) and the practice directions supplementing those Parts.

## Business assigned to specially nominated judges

**9A–237** **63.**—(1) Any business assigned, in accordance with this or any other Act or rules of court, to one or more specially nominated judges of the High Court may—

(a) during vacation; or

(b) during the illness or absence of that judge or any of those judges; or

(c) for any other reasonable cause,

be dealt with by any judge of the High Court named for that purpose by the Lord Chief Justice after consulting the Lord Chancellor.

(2) If at any time it appears to the Lord Chief Justice, after consulting the Lord Chancellor, desirable to do so with a view to the more convenient administration of justice, he may by order direct that business of any description which is for the time being assigned, in accordance with this or any other Act or rules of court, to one or more specially nominated judges of the High Court shall cease to be so assigned and may be dealt with by any one or more judges of the High Court.

(3) An order under subsection (2) shall not be made in respect of any business without the concurrence of the senior judge of the Division to which the business is for the time being assigned.

(4) The Lord Chief Justice may nominate a judicial office holder (as defined in section 109(4) of the Constitutional Reform Act 2005) to exercise his functions under subsection (1) or (2).

*Note*—Derived from the JA 1925 s.60A. See also s.61(7). Amended by the Constitutional Reform Act 2005 s.15(1), Sch.4, para.130 (see para.9A–4 above). **9A–238**

## Choice of Division by plaintiff

**64.**—(1) Without prejudice to the power of transfer under section 65, the person by whom any cause or matter is commenced in the High Court shall in the prescribed manner allocate it to whichever Division he thinks fit. **9A–239**

(2) Where a cause or matter is commenced in the High Court, all subsequent interlocutory or other steps or proceedings in the High Court in that cause or matter shall be taken in the Division to which the cause or matter is for the time being allocated (whether under subsection (1) or in consequence of its transfer under section 65).

*Note*—Derived from the JA 1925 s.58. **9A–240**

### Choice of Division

This section confers on the plaintiff the initiative to choose the Division in which he thinks fit to commence his proceedings. However, this is subject to the power of the Court to order the transfer of proceedings from one Division to another, or to or from a specialist list (see s.65 and CPR r.30.5). The choice of the Division in which an action is commenced has the consequence that all subsequent interlocutory or other steps or proceedings must be taken in that Division. If the action is subsequently transferred to another Division, all further interlocutory or other steps or proceedings must be taken in the Division to which it has been transferred (s.64(2)), but the validity of the interlocutory or other steps or proceedings taken in the Division originally chosen will not be affected by the transfer (s.65(2)). **9A–241**

## Power of transfer

**65.**—(1) Any cause or matter may at any time and at any stage **9A–242**

thereof, and either with or without application from any of the parties, be transferred, by such authority and in such manner as rules of court may direct, from one Division or judge of the High Court to another Division or judge thereof.

(2) The transfer of a cause or matter under subsection (1) to a different Division or judge of the High Court shall not affect the validity of any steps or proceedings taken or order made in that cause or matter before the transfer.

**9A-243** *Note* —Derived from the JA 1925 s.59.

**Transfer to another Division**

**9A-244** This section should be read with s.64. For rules of court as to transfer, see CPR r.30.5. The power of transfer from one Division or Judge of the High Court to another Division or Judge may be exercised either on the application of a party or by the Court of its own motion, s.65(1). A party bringing his action in the wrong Division may be ordered to pay all costs incurred thereby (see *Re Pollard* (1888) L.R. 20 Q.B.D. 656, CA).

The Judge has an absolute discretion whether to transfer to the appropriate Division a matter assigned to his Division or to deal with it. In *DBS Management Plc v Excess Insurance Co Ltd*, April 25, 1994, unrep., CA, it was said that the test for transfer from one Division to another is whether it is inappropriate for the case to be tried in the Division in which it was begun because that Division lacked a special expertise needed for the just and expeditious disposal of the case; the same test applies for transfers from the QB general list and the commercial list. Other modern authorities include: *Boobyer v David Holman & Co Ltd* [1992] 2 Lloyd's Rep. 436; *Deeny v Littlejohn & Co (A Firm), The Times*, January 19, 1995; *O'Brien v Hughes-Gibb & Co Ltd, The Times*, October 20, 1993.

See further, CPR r.30.5 and notes following (see Vol.1, para.30.5).

## DIVISIONAL COURTS

## Divisional courts of the High Court

**9A-245** **66.**—(1) Divisional courts may be held for the transaction of any business in the High Court which is, by or by virtue of rules of court or any other statutory provisions, required to be heard by a divisional court.

(2) Any number of divisional courts may sit at the same time.

(3) A divisional court shall be constituted of not less than two judges.

(4) Every judge of the High Court shall be qualified to sit in any divisional court.

(5) The judge who is, according to the order of precedence under this Act, the senior of the judges constituting a divisional court shall be the president of the court.

**9A-246** *Note* —Derived from the JA 1925 s.63; and the AJA 1977 s.9.

**Disagreement between two judges**

**9A-247** There is authority for the proposition that whenever there is an appeal to two judges in a Divisional Court who differ, the judgment appealed from should stand (*Metropolitan Water Board v Johnson & Co* [1913] 3 K.B. 900 at 904 per Channel J.; see also *Bradford Corp v Myers* [1916] 1 A.C. 242; *Barron v Potter* [1915] 3 K.B. 593; *Cheater v Cater* [1918] 1 K.B. 247). As to disagreement between equal numbers of the members of the Court of Appeal, see s.54(5) and notes following s.54 above (para.9A-212). It is

***Paragraph numbers marked with a "+" can be found online and on CD.***

thought that, wherever possible, the provisions relating to disagreement between members of the Court of Appeal will be applied, by analogy, to disagreement between two judges in a Divisional Court.

## *MODE OF CONDUCTING BUSINESS*

## Proceedings in court and in chambers

**67.** Business in the High Court shall be heard and disposed of in court except in so far as it may, under this or any other Act, under rules of court or in accordance with the practice of the court, be dealt with in chambers. **9A–248**

*Note* —Derived from the JA 1925 s.61. **9A–249**

### Business to be conducted "in court" and "in public"

In this section, the expression "in court" means in open court, in open view, in public, in a court to which the public and the press are entitled to be admitted (see as to the meaning of "open court" *R. v Lewes Prison (Governore) Ex p. Doyle* [1917] 2 K.B. 254 at 271 per Lord Reading C.J.). **9A–250**

Article 6 of the European Convention on Human Rights, incorporated in the Human Rights Act 1998 Sch.1, states that in the determining of his civil rights "everyone is entitled to a fair and public hearing". Article 6 further states that, in certain circumstances, the press and public may be excluded "from all or part of the trial", for example, where publicity would prejudice the interests of justice.

CPR r.39.2(1) states that the general rule is that "a hearing must be in public". Further, r.32.2(1) states that, where any facts needs to be proved by the evidence of witnesses at trial, it is to be proved "by their oral evidence given in public".

In early cases it was said that the obligation of the Court to hear and determine any proceeding in public is a mere matter of procedure, the departure from which is a mere irregularity and does not render the proceedings or the decision null and void (see *McPherson v McPherson* [1936] A.C. 177, PC, applying *Dimes v Proprietors of the Grand Junction Canal* (1852) 3 H.L.C. 750).

### Business may be dealt with "in chambers" and "in private"

The expression "in chambers"used in this section in contrast to "in court", means in private, for example, in the judge's private room. The parties and their advisers are entitled to be present. Formerly, it was the practice that the public or the press were automatically excluded, unless invited to be present with the consent of the parties or the court. However, in *Hodgson v Imperial Tobacco Ltd* [1998] 1 W.L.R. 1056, CA; [1998] 2 All E.R. 673, CA, the Master of the Rolls said, generally, the public has no right to attend hearings in chambers because of the nature of the work transacted and because of the physical restrictions on the room available, but if requested permission to attend may be granted if this is practical. Disclosure of proceedings in chambers is not a breach of confidence or amount to contempt so long as comment thereon does not substantially prejudice the administration of justice (for circumstances in which publication of information relating to proceedings before any court sitting in private may be contempt, see Administration of Justice Act 1960 s.12, see para.9B–15). Proceedings in chambers are not confidential and any judgment or order will be made available on request (*ibid.*, see also *Forbes v Smith* [1998] 1 All E.R. 973). **9A–251**

Section 67 states that business in the High Court may be dealt with in chambers, to the extent that this is permitted by the 1981 Act, any other Act, or rules of court. Whereas the expression "in chambers" was used throughout the RSC, in the CPR it is not used. After stating the general rule that a hearing is to be in public, r.39.2 goes on to state that, in certain circumstances, a hearing, or any part of it, may be "in private". Numerous provisions in the CPR state that particular proceedings shall be "in private". The result is that, nowadays, hearings "in chambers" (in so far as that expression is still apt) are not ipso facto hearings in private. See further, commentary on r.39.2 (Vol 1, paras 39.2.1 *et seq.*).

### Business conducted in camera

Section 67 does not have the effect of derogating from the inherent jurisdiction of **9A–252**

***Paragraph numbers marked with a "+" can be found online and on CD.***

the Court to order that the hearing of the proceedings should be in camera, that is, in private, so that the court, when sitting in circumstances in which normally the press and public ought to be admitted, may be closed or cleared and the public and the press excluded (see *Scott v Scott* [1913] A.C. 417, HL). The underlying principle that the public should be excluded is "that the administration of justice would be rendered impracticable by their presence" (*ibid.* at 446 per Earl Loreburn; see also *R. v Lewes Prison (Governor) Ex p. Doyle* [1917] 2 K.B. 254, at 271 per Lord Reading C.J., and *R. v Chief Registrar of Friendly Building Societies Ex p. New Cross Building Society* [1984] Q.B. 227; [1984] 2 All E.R. 27, CA). (See also authorities referred to in S.C.P. 1999, Vol.1, para.33/4/6.) This power may be exercised in relation to the whole or only part of the proceedings, or to the whole or part of the evidence (e.g. *Hallam-Eames v Merrett Syndicates Ltd*, *The Times*, June 16, 1995), even perhaps the evidence of one witness. The limits of this power, perhaps wisely have not been precisely defined. Most, if not all, of the circumstances justifying the Court's sitting in camera are covered by CPR r.39.2. The exercise of the inherent jurisdiction is subject to art.6 of the Convention (see above).

Hearings in camera may be authorised by statute, see e.g. Matrimonial Causes Act 1973 s.48(2)).

## Exercise of High Court jurisdiction otherwise than by judges of that court

9A–253 **68.**—(1) Provision may be made by rules of court as to the cases in which jurisdiction of the High Court may be exercised by—

(a) such Circuit judges, deputy Circuit judges or Recorders as the Lord Chief Justice may, with the concurrence of the Lord Chancellor, from time to time nominate to deal with official referees' business; or

(b) special referees.

(2) Without prejudice to the generality of subsection (1), rules of court may in particular—

(a) [...]

(b) authorise any question arising in any cause or matter to be referred to a special referee for inquiry and report.

(3) Rules of court shall not authorise the exercise of power of attachment and committal by a special referee or any officer or other staff of the court.

(4) Subject to subsection (5), the decision of—

(a) any such person as is mentioned in subsection (1); or

(b) any officer or other staff of the court,

may be called in question in such manner as may be prescribed by rules of court, whether by appeal to the Court of Appeal, or by an appeal or application to a divisional court or a judge in court or a judge in chambers, or by an adjournment to a judge in court or a judge in chambers.

(5) Rules of court may provide either generally or to a limited extent for decisions of persons nominated under subsection (1)(a) being called in question only by appeal on a question of law.

(6) The cases in which jurisdiction of the High Court may be exercised by person nominated under subsection (1)(a) shall be known as "official referees' business"; and, subject to rules of court, the distribution of official referees' business among persons so nominated shall be determined in accordance with directions given by the Lord Chief Justice after consulting the Lord Chancellor.

(7) Any reference to an official referee in any enactment, whenever passed, or in rules of court of any other instrument or document, whenever made, shall, unless the context otherwise requires, be construed as, or (where the context requires) as including, a reference to a person nominated under subsection (1)(a).

(8) The Lord Chief Justice may nominate a judicial office holder (as defined in section 109(4) of the Constitutional Reform Act 2005) to exercise his functions under subsection (1)(a) and (6).

*Note* —Derived from the AJA 1956 s.15, and the Courts Act 1971 s.25. Amended by the AJA 1982 s.59; the Civil Procedure Act 1997 Sch.2; and the Constitutional Reform Act 2005 s.15(1), Sch.4, para.131 (see para.9A–4 above). **9A–254**

**Effect of section**

Paragraph 2 of Sch.1 to the Civil Procedure Act 1997 states that Civil Procedure Rules may provide for the exercise of the jurisdiction of the High Court by officers of the Court or other staff of the Court. CPR r.2.4 states that, where those Rules provide for the court "to perform any act" provided for by the CPR (an important qualification) then, except where an enactment, rule or practice direction provides otherwise, the act may be performed, in relation to proceedings in the High Court, by any judge, Master or district judge of that Court. The circumstances in which jurisdiction may be exercised only by a judge need not be listed here. However, it may be noted that s.68(3) states that rules of court shall not authorise the exercise of power of attachment and committal by any officer of the court or other staff of the court. Further, s.68(4) provides that the decision of any officer or other staff of the court may be called in question (e.g. by appeal) in such manner as may be prescribed by rules of court. The rules so prescribing need not be listed here. **9A–255**

Section 68 is principally concerned with the nomination of judges to deal with official referees' business and the handling of such business. Under the CPR, this business is described as Technology and Construction Court business; see CPR Pt 60 (Technology and Construction Court Claims) (see CPR Pt 60 para.2C–1 above).

The section also preserves the exercise of High Court jurisdiction, in accordance with rules of court, by "special referees". Trial by a special referee was provided for by former RSC O.36, r.10 but no comparable provision appears in the CPR. The former rules made no provision for the appointment of special referees; nor do the CPR.

Under s.9 of this Act (see para.9A–30 above) certain persons who are not judges of the High Court may act as judges of the Court on request.

## Trial by jury

**69.**—(1) Where, on the application of any party to an action to be tried in the Queen's Bench Division, the court is satisfied that there is in issue— **9A–256**

(a) a charge of fraud against that party; or

(b) a claim in respect of libel, slander, malicious prosecution or false imprisonment; or

(c) any question or issue of a kind prescribed for the purposes of this paragraph,

the action shall be tried with a jury, unless the court is of opinion that the trial requires any prolonged examination of documents or accounts or any scientific or local investigation which cannot conveniently be made with a jury.

(2) An application under subsection (1) must be made not later than such time before the trial as may be prescribed.

(3) An action to be tried in the Queen's Bench Division which does not by virtue of subsection (1) fall to be tried with a jury shall be

tried without a jury unless the court in its discretion orders it to be tried with a jury.

(4) Nothing in subsections (1) to (3) shall affect the power of the court to order, in accordance with rules of court, that different questions of fact arising in any action be tried by different modes of trial; and where any such order is made, subsection (1) shall have effect only as respects questions relating to any such charge, claim, question or issue as is mentioned in that subsection.

(5) Where for the purpose of disposing of any action or other matter which is being tried in the High Court by a judge with a jury it is necessary to ascertain the law of any other country which is applicable to the facts of the case, any question as to the effect of the evidence given with respect to that law shall, instead of being submitted to the jury, be decided by the judge alone.

**9A–257** *Note*—Derived from the A.J.(M.P.) A. 1938 s.6; and the and JA 1925 s.102.

**"application ... not later than such time before trial as may be prescribed"**

**9A–258** For an account of the matters to be considered by the court in determining whether an action to which this section relates should not be tried with a jury, see *Aitken v Preston* [1997] E.M.L.R. 415, CA, and *Gentoo Group Ltd v Hanratty* [2008] EWHC 2328 (QB), October 8, 2008, unrep. (Eady J.).

Since the coming into effect of the CPR, the meaning of "in accordance with rules of court" in s.69(4) is not clear (*Armstrong v Times Newspapers Ltd* [2005] EWHC 2816 (QB), December 7, 2005, unrep. (Eady J.)).

CPR r.26.11 states that an application for a claim to be tried with a jury must be made within 28 days of the defence. In *Oliver v Calderdale MBC, The Times*, July 7, 1999, CA, a case decided under the old rules, it was held that an application made wholly out of time could be rejected on the grounds that it was unreasonable.

It is necessary to be wary of any tension between case management powers under the CPR (e.g. r.3.1(2)(m)) and statutory issues of jurisdiction arising under statute (e.g. s.69). If there is no jurisdiction by virtue of s.69 such a gap cannot readily be filled by case management powers (*Armstrong v Times Newspapers Ltd, op cit.*).

Subject to the terms of s.69(l), either party to a defamation action has a right to trial by jury, and the power to make procedural rules under Civil Procedure Act 1997 s.4 does not permit the restriction of that fundamental right; consequently, although in terms CPR r.24.2 makes no exception for defamation cases, summary judgment should not be granted where one party was entitled to exercise his right to jury trial and wished to do so (*Safeway Stores Plc v Tate* [2001] 2 W.L.R. 1377, CA; see also *Elite Model Management Corp v British Broadcasting Corp* March 14, 2001, unrep., Eady J.).

If there is a material issue of fact in a libel case, s.69(l) entitles a party to have that issue determined by a jury; however it is for the judge to decide whether there really is such an issue (*Alexander v Arts Council of Wales, The Times*, April 27, 2001, CA). Where the judge comes to the conclusion that the evidence, taken at its highest, is such that a jury properly directed could not properly reach a necessary factual conclusion, it is his duty, upon a submission being made, to withdraw that issue from the jury; but where there is a risk that the judge's view on a particular issue might be overturned on appeal it is desirable that it should be left to the jury (*ibid.*).

Where appropriate, in the same proceedings the court may in the exercise of powers listed in CPR r.3.1(2) order that certain issued be tried by judge alone and others by judge and jury (s.69(4)). However, where it is clear that some issues could not conveniently be tried with a jury it may be more appropriate for the whole case to be tried by judge alone (e.g. where questions of credibility are universally relevant) (*Phillips v Commissioner of Police of the Metropolis* [2003] EWCA Civ 382; *The Times*, April 2, 2003, CA; *Armstrong v Times Newspapers Ltd, op cit.*).

In defamation proceedings it may be appropriate for certain issues to be tried by the judge sitting with a jury and others by the judge sitting alone (*Gregson v Channel Four Television Corp* [2002] EWCA Civ 941). Where a libel action is to be tried by a judge without a jury, the first part of s.69(4) taken alone gives the court a discretion to order that the issue of meaning, being a question of fact, is to be tried with a jury. That conclusion is not affected or moderated by the second part of s.69(4). The discretion is an open discretion which does not start with any leaning towards any particular mode of trial (*Armstrong v The Times Newspapers Ltd (No.2)* [2006] EWCA Civ 519; [2006] 1 W.L.R. 2462, CA (judge's decision (over defendant's objection) to try issue of meaning without jury where parties had agreed that action should be tried by judge alone upheld)).

#### Questions of foreign law to be decided by judge

As to evidence of foreign law, see Civil Evidence Act 1972 s.4 (see para.9B–1063 below). **9A–259**

The trial judge is entitled to construe a statutory provision of foreign law put in evidence by an expert in that law (*Sharif v Azad* [1967] 1 Q.B. 605; [1966] 3 All E.R. 785, CA). This is especially so where there is a conflict in the evidence between the expert witnesses as to the foreign law (*Parkasho v Singh* [1968] P. 233; [1967] 1 All E.R. 737, DC).

#### Discharge of jury or of juror

The trial judge has a discretion to continue the trial where a juror has to be discharged (e.g. by reason of ill health), thereby reducing the number of jurors to eleven (*Hamilton v Al-Fayed (Costs)*, *The Times*, July 25, 2001). Where the interests of justice make it appropriate for him to do so, a judge in civil proceedings may allow a discharged jury to make alterations to its verdict (*Igwemma v Chief Constable of Greater Manchester Police* [2001] EWCA Civ 953; [2001] 4 All E.R. 751, CA. **9A–260**

## Assessors and scientific advisers

**70.**—(1) In any cause or matter before the High Court the court may, if it thinks it expedient to do so, call in the aid of one or more assessors specially qualified, and hear and dispose of the cause or matter wholly or partially with their assistance. **9A–261**

(2) The remuneration, if any, to be paid to an assessor for his services under subsection (1) in connection with any proceedings shall be determined by the court, and shall form part of the costs of the proceedings.

(3) Rules of court shall make provision for the appointment of scientific advisers to assist the Patents Court in proceedings under the Patents Act 1949 and Patents Act 1977 and for regulating the functions of such advisers.

(4) The remuneration of any such adviser shall be determined by the Lord Chancellor with the concurrence of the Minister for the Civil Service and shall be defrayed out of money provided by Parliament.

*Note*—Derived from the JA 1925 s.98; and the Patents Act 1977 s.96(4). **9A–262**

#### Assessors and scientific advisers

Where assessors are called in aid to assist the court in hearing and disposing of any cause or matter, the provisions of CPR r.35.15 apply. **9A–263**

As to nautical assessors in Admiralty proceedings, see CPR r.61.13 (para.2D–83 above).

As to appointment of scientific advisers in patent actions, see CPR r.35.15 (replacing former O.114, r.15).

As to assessors in the Court of Appeal, see s.54(8) above.

In *Esso Petroleum Co Ltd v Southport Corp* [1956] A.C. 218, Devlin J. said that he had appointed assessors to advise him after the hearing and stated that, in future, especially having regard to his earlier experience in *Waddle v Wallsend Shipping Co Ltd* [1925] 2 Lloyd's Rep. 105, he would, if necessary, adjourn the court so that an assessor might be present during the hearing.

In *Ahmed v University of Oxford* [2002] EWCA Civ 1907; [2003] 1 All E.R. 915, unrep., CA, the Court of Appeal examined the role of assessors appointed in various contexts, including under s.70 of this Act and the County Courts Act 1984 s.63 (see para.9A–537 below), but particularly under the Race Relations Act 1976 s.67(4). Note also *Sutton v Tesco Stores Plc*, July 30, 2002, unrep. (Mr Michael Yelton Q.C.) (at directions hearing the judge making order under s.70 appointing an assessor to assist the court on the psychiatric evidence in the case). In *Bow Spring (Owners) v Manzanillo II (Owners) (Note)* [2004] EWCA Civ 1007; [2004] 4 All E.R. 899, CA, the Court of Appeal held (partly on art.6 grounds) that the practice of the Admiralty judge putting questions to assessors after discussion with counsel should be complemented by a practice of disclosing their answers to counsel in order that any appropriate submission could be made as to whether the judge should accept their advice. In *Appiah v. Bishop Douglas Roman Catholic High School* [2007] EWCA Civ 10, January 26, 2007, CA, the Court of Appeal found in a Race Relations Act 1976 case that judge had fallen into error in treating the assessors "as part of the decision making team" but held that, in the circumstances, this was not a material error. See further CPR r.35.15, and commentary following that rule.

The principles relevant to appointment of assessors in TCC building disputes were explained in *Balcombe Group Plc v London Development Agency* [2008] EWHC 1392 (TCC), June 24, 2008, unrep. (Coulson J.) (application to call in aid assessor specially qualified in relation to relevant compensation code for trial of quantum refused).

On appointing assessors to assist court under s.70 as alternative to practice of referring of fixing of remuneration of provisional liquidators to costs judge, see *Re Independent Insurance Company Limited* [2002] EWHC 1577 (Ch), July 25, 2002, unrep. (Ferris J.).

### *SITTINGS AND VACATIONS*

## Sittings and vacations

9A–264 **71.**—(1) Sittings of the High Court may be held, and any other business of the High Court may be conducted, at any place in England or Wales.

(2) Subject to rules of court—

(a) the places at which the High Court sits outside the Royal Courts of Justice; and

(b) the days and times when the High Court sits at any place outside the Royal Courts of Justice,

shall be determined in accordance with directions given by the Lord Chancellor after consulting the Lord Chief Justice.

(3) Rules of court may make provision for regulating the vacations to be observed by the High Court and in the offices of that court.

(4) Rules of court—

(a) may provide for securing such sittings of any Division of the High Court during vacation as the senior judge of that Division may with the concurrence of the Lord Chancellor determine; and

(b) without prejudice to paragraph (a), shall provide for the transaction during vacation by judges of the High Court of all such business in the High Court as may require to be immediately or promptly transacted.

(5) Different provision may be made in pursuance of subsection (3) for different parts of the country.

(6) The Lord Chief Justice may nominate a judicial office holder (as defined in section 109(4) of the Constitutional Reform Act 2005) to exercise his functions under this section.

*Note*—Derived as to subss.(1) and (2) from the Courts Act 1971 s.2 and as to subs.(3) and (4) from the JA 1925 ss.53– 54; amended by the Constitutional Reform Act 2005 s.15(1), Sch.4, para.132 (see para.9A–4 above). **9A–265**

**Sittings of High Court**

Directions as to the location of sittings of the High Court under the power now found in s.71(2) were first given by the Lord Chancellor in 1971 when the "court centres" system recommended by the Beeching Commission was implemented within a revised system of court circuits. Within each of the six circuits, court centres were classified as first-, second- or third-tier centres, and High Court business was taken at first-tier centres. These directions, indicating the places outside the Royal Courts of Justice at which the Lord Chancellor has directed sittings of the High Court shall be held, have been modified from time to time. There are four sittings in every year (see para.1.1 of Practice Direction (Court Sittings), supplementing CPR Pt 39 above). **9A–266**

For sitting outside London of Chancery Division, see Chancery Guide para.12.1 and practice direction referred to there (see para.1–91).

For provisions about where a claim for judicial review may be started, administered and heard, see Practice Direction 54D (Administrative Court (Venue)) (Vol.1, para 54DPD.1).

For power of Lord Chancellor to direct places at which district registries of the High Court shall be located, see s.99 below.

**Vacations of High Court**

Provisions as to sittings of the High Court in vacations are found in paras 3.1 to 3.3 of Practice Direction (Court Sittings), the practice direction supplementing CPR Pt 39 (see Vol.1, para.39BPD.1). **9A–267**

**"at any place in England and Wales"**

The taking of evidence abroad under procedures that enable that to be done in cases proceeding in the High Court does not constitute a sitting of the High Court outside England and Wales. Accordingly, s.71(1) does not prevent a High Court judge from appointing himself to be a special examiner under CPR r.34.13(4) for the purpose of taking a deposition from a person out of the jurisdiction (*Peer International Corp v Termidor Music Publishers Ltd* [2005] EWHC 1048 (Ch), May 25, 2005, unrep. (Lindsay J.)). **9A–268**

### *OTHER PROVISIONS*

## Withdrawal of privilege against incrimination of self or spouse in certain proceedings

**72.**—(1) In any proceedings to which this subsection applies a person shall not be excused, by reason that to do so would tend to expose that person, or his or her spouse or civil partner, to proceedings for a related offence for the recovery of a related penalty— **9A–269**

(a) from answering any question put to that person in the first-mentioned proceedings; or

(b) from complying with any order made in those proceedings.

(2) Subsection (1) applies to the following civil proceedings in High Court, namely—

*Paragraph numbers marked with a "+" can be found online and on CD.*

MAIN STATUTES

(a) proceedings for infringement of rights pertaining to any intellectual property or for passing off;
(b) proceedings brought to obtain disclosure of information relating to any infringement of such rights or to any passing off; and
(c) proceedings brought to prevent any apprehended infringement of such rights or any apprehended passing off.

(3) Subject to subsection (4), no statement or admission made by a person—

(a) in answering a question put to him in any proceedings to which subsection (1) applies; or
(b) in complying with any order made in any such proceedings,

shall, in proceedings for any related offence or for the recovery of any related penalty, be admissible in evidence against that person (unless they married or became civil partners after the making of the statement or admission) against the spouse or civil partner of that person.

(4) Nothing in subsection (3) shall render any statement or admission made by a person as there mentioned inadmissible in evidence against that person in proceedings for perjury or contempt of court.

(5) In this section—

"intellectual property" means any patent, trade mark, copyright, design rights, registered design, technical or commercial information or other intellectual property;

"related offence", in relation to any proceedings to which subsection (1) applies, means—

(a) in the case of proceedings within subsection (2)(a) or (b)—
  (i) any offence committed by or in the course of the infringement or passing off to which those proceedings relate; or
  (ii) any offence committed by or in the course of the infringement or passing off to which those proceedings relate; or
(b) in the case of proceedings within subsection (2)(c), any offence revealed by the facts on which the plaintiff relies in those proceedings;

"related penalty", in relation to any proceedings to which subsection (1) applies means—

(a) in the case of proceedings within subsection (2)(a) or (b), any penalty incurred in respect of anything done or omitted in connection with the infringement or passing off to which those proceedings relate;
(b) in the case of proceedings within subsection (2)(c), any penalty incurred in respect of any act or omission revealed by the facts on which the plaintiff relies in those proceedings.

(6) Any reference in this section to civil proceedings in the High Court of any description includes a reference to proceedings on appeal arising in the High Court of that description.

*Note* —Amended by the Copyright, Designs and Patents Act 1988 Sch.7, para.28; and the Civil Partnership Act 2004 s.261(1), Sch.27, para.69. **9A–270**

**Effect of section**

In legal proceedings, a person (or that person's spouse) may refuse to answer any question or produce any document or thing if to do so would tend to expose that person to proceedings for an offence or for the recovery of a penalty (*Rank Film Distributors Ltd v Video Information Centre* [1982] A.C. 380, HL). By operation of the Civil Evidence Act 1968 s.14, in legal proceedings other than criminal proceedings, that privilege is confined to the risk of exposure to proceedings and penalties under the law of any part of the UK. The privilege may be withdrawn by statute (*ibid.*, s.14(3)). **9A–271**

This section withdraws the privilege in proceedings relating to the infringement of industrial property rights. It provides that it does not excuse a person (or that person's spouse) (a) from answering any question in such proceedings, or (b) from complying with any order made in those proceedings, for example, an order to disclose documents, a freezing injunction (formerly a Mareva injunction) or a search order (formerly Anton Piller order). The section is not limited to a case where criminal procedings have not yet been commenced (*Charles of the Ritz Group Ltd v Jory* [1986] F.S.R. 14).

In *C. Plc v P.* [2007] EWCA Civ 493; [2007] 3 W.L.R. 437, CA, the question of the extent of the privilege arose where the respondent to a search order asserted it in relation to material stored electronically. In the course of executing the order, the applicant's independent computer expert discovered material (highly objectionable images of children) which he believed incriminated the respondent. On the expert's application the judge directed that the material be passed to the police, and in doing so held that, as a result of the coming into effect of theHuman Rights Act 1998, it is open to the court to modify the privilege to provide that it dos not extend to disclosed documents and other material evidence in civil proceedings in addition to those provided for by s.72 ([2006] EWHC 1226 (Ch); [2006] Ch. 549). The Court of Appeal dismissed the respondent's appeal, the majority holding (1) that although, by virtue of the orders made by the judge, the offending material had to be disclosed to the solicitor supervising the search and to the expert, there was no privilege in that material itself, (2) the material existed independently of the order, (3) the privilege can be invoked to refuse to disclose matters (including documents or other things) which are ordinarily discoverable, (4) but independent matters coming to light in the course of executing a proper order of the court are in an altogether different category.

In Practice Direction (Interim Injunctions) para.9, in the context of provisions dealing with applications for search orders, the proceedings in which by statute (including s.72) the privilege against self-incrimination is withdrawn are listed (see Vol.1, para.23APD.7).

**For ss.73 to 82, 84, 86 to 93, 95 to 100, 102, 104 to 135 of the Senior Courts Act 1981 (see Arrangement) plus any related commentary see paragraphs 9A–272+ to 9A–378+ on White Book on Westlaw UK or the Civil Procedure CD.**

## Production of documents filed in, or in custody of, Senior Courts

**136.**—(1) Rules may be made in accordance with Part 1 of Schedule 1 to the Constitutional Reform Act 2005 for providing that, in any case where a document filed in, or in the custody of, any office of the Senior Courts is required to be produced to any court or tribunal (including an umpire or arbitrator) sitting elsewhere than at the Royal Courts of Justice— **9A–379**

(a) it shall not be necessary for any officer, whether served

***Paragraph numbers marked with a "+" can be found online and on CD.***

with a subpoena in that behalf or not, to attend for the purpose of producing the document; but

(b) the document may be produced to the court or tribunal by sending it to the court or tribunal, in the manner prescribed in the rules, together with a certificate, in the form so prescribed, to the effect that the document has been filed in, or is in the custody of, the office;

and any such certificate shall be prima facie evidence of the facts stated in it.

(2) Rules under this section may contain—

(a) provisions for securing the safe custody and return to the proper office of the Senior Courts of any document sent to a court or tribunal in pursuance of the rules; and

(b) such incidental and supplementary provisions as appear to the person making the rules to be necessary or expedient.

**9A-380** *Note* —Derived from the JA 1925 s.220 as amended by the A.J.(M.P.) A. 1938. Amended by the Constitutional Reform Act 2005 s.59(5), Sch.11, para.26 (see para.9A-4 above). Subsections (1) and (2) amended and subs.(3) repealed by the Constitutional Reform Act 2005 ss.12(2) and 146 and Sch.1, Pt 2, para.13 and Sch.18, Pt 1 and, with effect from October 1, 2009, by s.59 and Sch.11, para.26 (SI 2009/1604).

**"sending ... in the manner prescribed"**

**9A-381** The principal purpose behind the granting to the Lord Chancellor of power to make rules prescribing the manner in which court documents are to be produced to any court or tribunal is to facilitate production by post. The rule-making power as contained in JA 1925 s.220, the predecessor of s.136, insofar as it applied to production by post was confined to the making of rules permitting production by registered post. Rules to this effect were found in the Supreme Court Documents (Production) Rules 1926 (S.R. & 0) No.461). After the coming into force of the Recorded Delivery Service Act 1962 those Rules, insofar as they permitted production by registered post, were to be read as also permitting production by recorded delivery service. The 1926 Rules were superseded by Practice Direction (Court Documents), para.5.6 (see Vol.1, para.5PD.5). In terms, sub-para.(4) of para.5.6 follows the 1926 Rules and permits production by the court by registered post. However, by virtue of the 1962 Act (referred to above) production by recorded delivery service is permitted. See further, Vol.1, para.5.1.4.

**For ss.137 and 139 of the Senior Courts Act 1981 (see Arrangement) plus any related commentary see paragraphs 9A-382+ to 9A-385+ on White Book on Westlaw UK or the Civil Procedure CD.**

## Enforcement of fines and forfeited recognizances

**9A-386** **140.**—(1) Payment of a fine imposed, or sum due under a recognizance forfeited, by the High Court or the civil division of the Court of Appeal may be enforced upon the order of the court—

(a) in like manner as a judgment of the High Court for the payment of money; or

(b) in like manner as a fine imposed by the Crown Court.

(2) Where payment of a fine or other sum falls to be enforced as mentioned in paragraph (a) of subsection (1) upon an order of the High Court or the civil division of the Court of Appeal under that subsection—

*Paragraph numbers marked with a "+" can be found online and on CD.*

(a) the court shall, if the fine or other sum is not paid in full forthwith or within such time as the court may allow, certify to Her Majesty's Remembrancer the sum payable; and

(b) Her Majesty's Remembrancer shall thereupon proceed to enforce payment of that sum as if it were due to him as a judgment debt.

(3) Where payment of a fine or other sum falls to be enforced as mentioned in paragraph (b) of subsection (1) upon an order of the High Court or the civil division of the Court of Appeal under that subsection, the provisions of sections 139 and 140 of the Powers of Criminal (Sentencing) Act 2000 shall apply to that fine or other sum as they apply to a fine imposed by the Crown Court.

(4) Where payment of a fine or other sum has become enforceable by Her Majesty's Remembrancer by virtue of this section or section 16 of the Contempt of Court Act 1981, any payment received by him in respect of that fine or other sum shall be dealt with by him in such manner as the Lord Chancellor may direct.

(5) In this section, and in sections 139 and 140 of the Powers of Criminal Courts (Sentencing) Act 2000 as extended by this section, "fine" includes a penalty imposed in civil proceedings.

*Note* —Amended by the Powers of Criminal Courts (Sentencing) Act 2000 (c.6) s.165, Sch.9, para.88. See para.9A–4 above. **9A–387**

**For ss.142 and 150 of the Senior Courts Act 1981 (see Arrangement) plus any related commentary see paragraphs 9A–388+ to 9A–390+ on White Book on Westlaw UK or the Civil Procedure CD.**

## Interpretation of this Act, and rules of construction for other Acts and documents

**151.**—(1) In this Act, unless the context otherwise requires— **9A–391**

"action" means any civil proceedings commenced by writ or in any other manner prescribed by rules of court;

"appeal", in the context of appeals to the civil division of the Court of Appeal, includes—

(a) an application for a new trial, and

(b) an application to set aside a verdict, finding or judgment in any cause or matter in the High Court which has been tried, or in which any issue has been tried, by a jury;

"arbitration agreement" has the same meaning as it has in Part I of the Arbitration Act 1996;

"cause" means any action or any criminal proceedings;

"Division", where it appears with a capital letter, means a division of the High Court;

"judgment" includes a decree;

"jurisdiction" includes powers;

"matter" means any proceedings in court not in a cause;

"party", in relation to any proceedings, includes any person who pursuant to or by virtue of rules of court or any other statutory provision has been served with notice of, or has intervened in, those proceedings;

*Paragraph numbers marked with a "+" can be found online and on CD.*

"prescribed" means—

(a) except in relation to fees, prescribed by rules of court;

(b) [...]

"senior judge", where the reference is to the senior judge of a Division, means—

(a) in the case of the Chancery Division, the Vice-Chancellor;

(b) in any other case, the president of the Division in question;

"senior judge", where the reference is to the senior judge of a Division, means the president of that Division;

"solicitor" means a solicitor of the Senior Courts;

"statutory provision" means any enactment, whenever passed, or any provision contained in subordinate legislation (as defined in section 21(1) of the Interpretation Act 1978), whenever made;

"this or any other Act" includes an Act passed after this Act.

(2) Section 128 contains definitions of expressions used in Part V and in the other provisions of this Act relating to probate causes and matters.

(3) Any reference in this Act to rules of court under section 84 includes a reference to rules of court in relation to the Senior Courts under any provision of this or any other Act which confers on the Civil Procedure Rule Committee or the Crown Court Rule Committee power to make rules of court.

(4) Except where the context otherwise requires, in this or any other Act—

"divisional court" (with or without capital letters) means a divisional court constituted under section 66;

"judge of the Senior Courts" means—

(a) a judge of the Court of Appeal other than an ex-officio judge within paragraph (b) or (c) of section 2(2), or

(b) a judge of the High Court, and accordingly does not include, as such, a judge of the Crown Court "official referees' business" has the meaning given by section 68(6);

"official referees' business" has the meaning given by section 68(6);

(5) The provisions of Schedule 4 (construction of references to superseded courts and officers) shall have effect.

**9A–392** *Note*—Derived from the JA 1925 s.225. Amended by the Courts and Legal Services Act 1990 Sch.18; the Arbitration Act 1996 Sch.3; the Civil Procedure Act 1997 Sch.2; SI 2004/2035; the Constitutional Reform Act 2005 s.15(1) and Sch.4 para.146 and with effect from October 1, 2009 the 2005 Act s.59 and Sch.11 para.1 (SI 2009/1604).

#### "Action" "Cause" "Matter"

**9A–393** These words are terms of art. They were used throughout the Rules of the Supreme Court in their technical senses. Their meanings and the differences between them were important and, in some respects, of practical significance. However, in the Civil Procedure Rules they are not used. The result is that there is now a lack of consistency between the language of the primary legislation governing the jurisdiction, practice and procedure of the High Court and the Court of Appeal and the language of the rules of court applicable in those Courts and some distinctions which had a practical usefulness have been lost.

### Judgment

The definition of "judgment" as including a "decree" is not a general definition, but one for the purposes of the SCA 1981 only, per Chitty J. *Burrows v Holley* (1887) L.R. 35 Ch.D. 123; per M.R., *Re Binstead* [1893] 1 Q.B. 199 at 203, in which case it was held that a decree made in a suit for divorce was not a final judgment within s.4(1)(g) of the B.A. 1883. **9A–394**

Judgments and orders are kept distinct by the SCA 1981 (as they were under the JA 1925), although they may be enforced in the same manner (*Ex p. Chinery* (1884) 12 Q.B.D. 342 at 345; see Vol.1, para.40.2.3, "Orders Enforceable like Judgments"). In *Joyne v MacCabe*, [1899] 1 Ir.R. 104, it was held that a consent order staying proceedings could not be registered as a "judgment"; and *cf. Shaw v Hertford CC* [1899] 2 Q.B. 282.

For the purposes of an appeal a judgment means a decision obtained in an action, and every other decision is an order (*Onslow v Commissioners etc.* (1890) 25 Q.B.D. 465 at 466, adopting judgment in *Ex p. Chinery*; *Austin Friars, etc. Co v Strack* [1906] 2 K.B. 499, CA). And see *Tata Co v Bombay C.R.A.* (1923) 39 T.L.R. 268.

**For ss.152 and 153 of the Senior Courts Act 1981 (see Arrangement) plus any related commentary see paragraphs 9A–395+ to 9A–397+ on White Book on Westlaw UK or the Civil Procedure CD.**

## SCHEDULE 1

### DISTRIBUTION OF BUSINESS IN HIGH COURT

*Chancery Division*

1. To the Chancery Division are assigned all causes and matters relating to— **9A–398**
   (a) the sale, exchange or partition of land, or the raising of charges on land;
   (b) the redemption of foreclosure of mortgages;
   (c) the execution of trusts;
   (d) the administration of the estates of deceased persons;
   (e) bankruptcy;
   (f) the dissolution of partnership or the taking of partnership or other accounts;
   (g) the rectification, setting aside or cancellation of deeds or other instruments in writing;
   (h) probate business, other than non-contentious or common form business;
   (i) patents, trade marks, registered designs, copyright or design right;
   (j) the appointment of a guardian of a minor's estate,and all causes and matters involving the exercise of the High Court's jurisdiction under the enactments relating to companies.

*Queen's Bench Division*

2. To the Queen's Bench Division are assigned— **9A–399**
   (a) applications for writs of habeas corpus, except applications made by a parent or guardian of a minor for such a writ concerning the custody of the minor;
   (b) applications for judicial review;
   (ba) all control order proceedings (within the meaning of the Prevention of Terrorism Act 2005);
   (bb) all financial restrictions proceedings within the meaning of Chapter 2 of Part 6 of the Counter-Terrorism Act 2008 (see section 65 of that Act);
   (c) all causes and matters involving the exercise of the High Court's Admiralty jurisdiction or its jurisdiction as a prize court; and
   (d) all causes and matters entered in the commercial list.

*Family Division*

9A–400 3. To the Family Division are assigned—

(a) all matrimonial causes and matters (whether at first instance or on appeal);

(b) all causes and matters (whether at first instance or on appeal) relating to—

(i) legitimacy;

(ii) the exercise of the inherent jurisdiction of the High Court with respect to minors, the maintenance of minors and any proceedings under the Children Act 1989, except proceedings solely for the appointment of a guardian of a minor's estate;

(iii) adoption;

(iv) non-contentious or common form probate business;

(c) applications for consent to the marriage of a minor or for a declaration under section 27B(5) of the Marriage Act 1949;

(d) proceedings on appeal under section 13 of the Administration of Justice Act 1960 from an order or decision made under section 63(3) of the Magistrates' Courts Act 1980 to enforce an order of a magistrates' court made in matrimonial proceedings or proceedings under Part IV of the Family Law Act 1996 or with respect to guardianship of a minor.

(e) proceedings under the Children Act 1989;

(ea) proceedings under section 79 of the Childcare Act 2006;

(f) all proceedings under:—

(i) Part IV or 4A of the Family Law Act 1996;

(ii) the Child Abduction and Custody Act 1985;

(iii) the Family Law Act 1986;

(iv) section 30 of the Human Fertilisation and Embryology Act 1990;

(v) Council Regulation (EC) No 2201/2003 of 27th November 2003 concerning jurisdiction and the recognition and enforcement of judgments in matrimonial matters and matters of parental responsibility, so far as that Regulation relates to jurisdiction, recognition and enforcement in parental responsibility matters;

(fa) all proceedings relating to a debit or credit under section 29(1) or 49(1) of the Welfare Reform and Pensions Act 1999;

(g) all proceedings for the purpose of enforcing an order made in any proceedings of a type described in this paragraph.

(h) all proceedings under the Child Support Act 1991.

(i) all proceedings under section 6 and 8 of the Gender Recognition Act 2004.

(i) all civil partnership causes and matters (whether at first instance or on appeal);

(j) applications for consent to the formation of a civil partnership by a minor or for a declaration under paragraph 7 of Schedule 1 to the Civil Partnership Act 2004;

(k) applications under section 58 of that Act (declarations relating to civil partnerships).

9A–401 *Note*—Amended by the Marriage (Prohibited Degrees of Relationship) Act 1986 s.5; the Family Law Reform Act 1987 Sch.4; the Children Act 1989 Schs 11 and 13; SI 1991/1210; SI 1993/622; the Family Law Act 1986 s.68(1), Sch.1; the Copyright, Designs and Patents Act 1988 s.303(1), Sch.7; the Family Law Act 1996 Sch.8, para.51; SI 2004/3418; SI 2005/265; the Civil Partnership Act 2004 s.261(1), Sch.27, para.70 (for certain purposes only: see SI 2005/1112); the Prevention of Terrorism Act 2005 s.11, Sch.1 para.10; the Childcare Act 2006 Sch.2 para.3; Forced Marriage (Civil Protection) Act 2007 Sch.2 para.1; and the Counter-Terrorism Act 2008 s.71.

**For Schs 2 and 6 to the Senior Courts Act 1981 (see Arrangement) plus any related commentary see paragraphs 9A–402+ to 9A–407+ on White Book on Westlaw UK or the Civil Procedure CD.**

# County Courts Act 1984

(1984 c.28)

9A–408

ARRANGEMENT OF SECTIONS

PART I



***Paragraph numbers marked with a "+" can be found online and on CD.***

MAIN STATUTES

***Paragraph numbers marked with a "+" can be found online and on CD.***

***Paragraph numbers marked with a "+" can be found online and on CD.***

MAIN STATUTES

**Paragraph numbers marked with a "+" denote content that is available on White Book on Westlaw UK or the Civil Procedure CD.**

### Introductory note

9A–409 The County Courts Act 1984 replaced the County Courts Act 1959 and a number of other provisions set out in Sch.4 to the Act. By operation of the Civil Procedure Act 1997 s.10 and Sch.2, para.2(2) throughout this Act, for "county court rules", wherever occurring, there is substituted "rules of court" and for "rule committee" there is substituted " Civil Procedure Rule Committee".

### Jurisdiction of county courts

9A–410 Formerly, in many sections in Pt II of this Act the jurisdiction of the county courts was determined by reference to "the county court limit" as defined in s.147(1). Since the coming into effect of Courts and Legal Services Act 1990 and the High Court and County Courts Jurisdiction Order 1991 the significance of this limit is very much reduced. Where it remains relevant in the sections printed below, e.g. s.23 (equity jurisdiction), the applicable "county court limit" has been inserted in brackets in the printed text. The effect of the 1990 Act and 1991 Order was to increase greatly the jurisdiction of the county courts. In relation to some proceedings, the Order places financial restrictions on the county court jurisdiction.

A county court has no jurisdiction to hear any action in which the title to any toll, fair, market or franchise is in question or any action for libel or slander (s.15(2)) and no action shall be brought in a county court on any judgment of the High Court (s.36). Further, a county court has no jurisdiction to hear any application for judicial review (Courts and Legal Services Act 1990 s.1(10)) (see para.9B–102 below), or to grant relief prescribed by the County Court Remedies Regulations 1991 reg.2 (see para.9B–78 below). In relation to certain proceedings, the county court jurisdiction is restricted by, for example, provisions in High Court and County Courts Jurisdiction Order 1991 and by "the county court limit" where it remains operative. In some instances exclusions and restrictions on jurisdiction may be overridden by agreement of the parties under s.18. Note also s.17 (Abandonment of part of claim to give court jurisdiction).

A county court claim commenced by a single plaint is a single action, irrespective of the number of plaintiffs to the claim, and the total amount to be recovered by all the plaintiffs in such action cannot exceed the relevant county court limit; a failure expressly to limit a county court claim to such limit is an irregularity, but does not deprive the county court of jurisdiction to hear and determine the claim and to award judgment up to such limit (*Doyle v Talbot Motor Co Ltd* [1988] 1 W.L.R. 980, CA).

**For ss.1 to 6, 8 to 9, and 11 to 13 of the County Courts Act 1984 (see Arrangement) plus any related commentary see paragraphs 9A–411+ to 9A–434+ on White Book on Westlaw UK or the Civil Procedure CD.**

## Penalty for assaulting officers

**14.**—(1) If any person assaults an officer of a court while in the execution of his duty, he shall be liable— **9A–435**

(a) on summary conviction, to imprisonment for a term not exceeding 3 months or to a fine of an amount not exceeding level 5 on the standard scale, or both; or

(b) on an order made by the judge in that behalf, to be committed for a specified period not exceeding 3 months to prison or to such a fine as aforesaid, or to be so committed and to such a fine,

and a bailiff of the court may take the offender into custody, with or without warrant, and bring him before the judge.

(2) The judge may at any time revoke an order committing a person to prison under this section and, if he is already in custody, order his discharge.

(3) A district judge, assistant district judge or deputy district judge shall have the same powers under this section as a judge.

*Note* —Amended by the Statute Law (Repeals) Act 1986; and the Courts and Legal Services Act 1990 s.74. **9A–436**

## PART II

## JURISDICTION AND TRANSFER OF PROCEEDINGS

### *ACTIONS OF CONTRACT AND TORT*

## General jurisdiction in actions of contract and tort

**15.**—(1) Subject to subsection (2), a county court shall have jurisdiction to hear and determine any action founded on contract or tort. **9A–437**

(2) A county court shall not, except as in this Act provided, have jurisdiction to hear and determine—

(a) [...]

***Paragraph numbers marked with a "+" can be found online and on CD.***

(b) any action in which the title to any toll, fair, market or franchise is in question; or

(c) any action for libel or slander.

9A–438 *Note*—Amended by the High Court and County Courts Jurisdiction Order (SI 1991/724) art.2(8) and Sch., Pt I.

**"any action founded on contract or tort"**

9A–439 Before the High Court and County Courts Jurisdiction Order 1991 came into force on July 1, 1991, this general jurisdiction was limited to £5,000. Now the jurisdiction of county courts in claims for money is governed by the 1991 Order (para.9B–928 below). As to whether a particular claim is an action "founded on contract", see *Hutchings v Islington LBC* [1998] 3 All E.R. 445, CA.

## Money recoverable by statute

9A–440 **16.** A county court shall have jurisdiction to hear and determine an action for the recovery of a sum recoverable by virtue of any enactment for the time being in force, if—

(a) it is not provided by that or any other enactment that such sums shall only be recoverable in the High Court or shall only be recoverable summarily;

(b) [...]

9A–441 *Note*—Amended by the High Court and County Courts Jurisdiction Order (SI 1991/724) art.2(8) and Sch., Pt I.

## Abandonment of part of claim to give court jurisdiction

9A–442 **17.**—(1) Where a plaintiff has a cause of action for more than a county court limit in which, if it were not for more than the county court limit, a county court would have jurisdiction, the plaintiff may abandon the excess, and thereupon a county court shall have jurisdiction to hear and determine the action, but the plaintiff shall not recover in the action an amount exceeding the county court limit.

(2) Where the court has jurisdiction to hear and determine an action by virtue of this section, the judgment of the court in the action shall be in full discharge of all demands in respect of the cause of action, and entry of the judgment shall be made accordingly.

## Jurisdiction by agreement in certain actions

9A–443 **18.** If the parties to any action, other than an action which, if commenced in the High Court, would have been assigned to the Chancery Division or to the Family Division or have involved the exercise of the High Court's Admiralty jurisdiction, agree, by a memorandum signed by them or by their respective legal representatives, that a county court specified in the memorandum shall have jurisdiction in the action, that court shall have jurisdiction to hear and determine the action accordingly.

9A–444 *Note*—Amended by the Courts and Legal Services Act 1990 Sch.18, para.49(3).

The exclusions mentioned in s.15(2) may be overridden by an agreement under this section. This section applies only to actions which could be brought in the QBD. See s.24, para.9A–453 for a similar provision relating to certain equity proceedings.

*RECOVERY OF LAND AND CASES WHERE TITLE IN QUESTION*

## Actions for recovery of land and actions where title is in question

**21.**—(1) A county court shall have jurisdiction to hear and determine any action for the recovery of land. **9A-445**

(2) A county court shall have jurisdiction to hear and determine any action in which the title to any hereditament comes into question.

(3) Where a mortgage of land consists of or includes a dwelling-house and no part of the land is situated in Greater London then, subject to subsection (4), if a county court has jurisdiction by virtue of this section to hear and determine an action in which the mortgagee under that mortgage claims possession of the mortgaged property, no court other than a county court shall have jurisdiction to hear and determine that action.

(4) Subsection (3) shall not apply to an action for foreclosure or sale in which a claim for possession of the mortgaged property is also made.

(5) [...]

(6) [...]

(7) In this section—

"dwelling-house" includes any building or part of a building which is used as a dwelling;

"mortgage" includes a charge and "mortgagor" and "mortgagee" shall be construed accordingly;

"mortgagor" and "mortgagee" includes any person deriving title under the original mortgagor or mortgagee.

(8) The fact that part of the premises comprised in a dwelling-house is used as a shop or office for business, trade or professional purposes shall not prevent the dwelling-house from being a dwelling-house for the purposes of this section.

(9) This section does not apply to a mortgage securing an agreement which is a regulated agreement within the meaning of the Consumer Credit Act 1974.

*Note* —Amended by the High Court and County Courts Jurisdiction Order (SI 1991/724) art.2(8) and Sch., Pt I. **9A-446**

**"title to any hereditament"**

Section 147 (Interpretation) states that "hereditament" includes both a corporeal and an incorporeal hereditament. **9A-447**

*EQUITY PROCEEDINGS*

## Equity jurisdiction

**23.** A county court shall have all jurisdiction of the High Court to hear and determine— **9A-448**

(a) proceedings for the administration of the estate of a deceased person, where the estate does not exceed in amount or value the county court limit £30,000,

***Paragraph numbers marked with a "+" can be found online and on CD.***

(b) proceedings—

(i) for the execution of any trust, or

(ii) for a declaration that a trust subsists, or

(iii) under section 1 of the Variation of Trusts Act 1958,

where the estate or fund subject, or alleged to be subject, to the trust does not exceed in amount or value the county court limit £30,000;

(c) proceedings for foreclosure or redemption of any mortgage or for enforcing any charge or lien, where the amount owing in respect of the mortgage charge or lien does not exceed the county court limit £30,000;

(d) proceedings for the specific performance, or for the rectification, delivery up or cancellation, of any agreement for the sale, purchase or lease of any property, where, in the case of a sale or purchase, the purchase money, or in the case of a lease, the value of the property, does not exceed the county court limit £30,000;

(e) proceedings relating to the maintenance or advancement of a minor, where the property of the minor does not exceed in amount or value the county court limit £30,000;

(f) proceedings for the dissolution or winding-up of any partnership (whether or not the existence of the partnerships is in dispute), where the whole assets of the partnership do not exceed in amount or value the county court limit £30,000;

(g) proceedings for relief against fraud or mistake, where the damage sustained or the estate or fund in respect of which relief is sought does not exceed in amount or value the county court limit £30,000.

9A-449 *Note* —The text of this section has been amended so as to indicate that, for the purposes of the equity jurisdiction, the County Court limit is £30,000 (see County Courts Jurisdiction Order 1981).

9A-449.1 *"proceedings for foreclosure"* —Although county courts have an unlimited jurisdiction to make charging orders, their jurisdiction to enforce them by orders for sale is restricted by s.23(c) to proceedings in which the amount owing does not exceed the county court limit (see further Vol.1 para. 73.10.1). However, the High Court's power to transfer proceedings to a county court as provided for by s.40 of this Act includes power to transfer an application for an order for sale to enforce a final charging order for a sum in excess of that limit (*National Westminster Bank plc v King* [2008] EWHC 280 (Ch); *The Times* April 14, 2008, (David Richards J.)).

## Jurisdiction by agreement in certain equity proceedings

9A-450 **24.**—(1) If, as respects any proceedings to which this section applies, the parties agree, by a memorandum signed by them or by their respective legal representatives or agents, that a county court specified in the memorandum shall have jurisdiction in the proceedings, that court shall, notwithstanding anything in any enactment, have jurisdiction to hear and determine the proceedings accordingly.

(2) Subject to subsection (3), this section applies to any proceedings in which a county court would have jurisdiction by virtue of—

(a) section 113(3) of the Settled Land Act 1925,

(b) section 63A of the Trustee Act 1925,

(c) sections 3(7), 49(4), 66(4), 89(7), 90(3), 91(8), 92(2), 136(3), 181(2), 188(2) of, and paragraph 3A of Part III and paragraph 1(3A) and (4A) of Part IV of Schedule 1 to, the Law of Property Act 1925,

(d) sections 17(2), 38(4), 41(1A) and 43(4) of the Administration of Estates Act 1925,

(e) section 6(1) of the Leasehold Property (Repairs) Act 1938,

(f) sections 1(6A) and 5(11) of the Land Charges Act 1972, and

(g) section 23 of this Act,

but for the limits of the jurisdiction of the court provided in those enactments.

(3) This section does not apply to proceedings under section 1 of the Variation of Trusts Act 1958.

*Note*—Amended by the Courts and Legal Services Act 1990 Sch.18, para.49(3); the High Court and County Courts Jurisdiction Order (SI 1991/724) art.2(8) and Sch., Pt I and the Statute Law (Repeals) Act 2004 Sch.1, Pt 1, Group 4. **9A–451**

### *FAMILY PROVISION PROCEEDINGS*

## Jurisdiction under Inheritance (Provisions for Family and Dependants) Act 1975

**25.** A county court shall have jurisdiction to hear and determine any application for an order under section 2 of the Inheritance (Provision for Family and Dependants) Act 1975 (including any application for permission to apply for such an order and any application made, in the proceedings on an application for such an order under any other provision of that Act). **9A–452**

*Note*—Amended by the High Court and County Courts Jurisdiction Order (SI 1991/724) art.2(8) and Sch., Pt I. **9A–453**

**For ss.26 to 28, 30 to 33, 35 to 38 of the County Courts Act 1984 (see Arrangement) plus any related commentary see paragraphs 9A–454+ to 9A–471+ on White Book on Westlaw UK or the Civil Procedure CD.**

* * * *

### *TRANSFER OF PROCEEDINGS*

## Transfer of proceedings to county court

**40.**—(1) Where the High Court is satisfied that any proceedings before it are required by any provision of a kind mentioned in subsection (8) to be in a county court it shall— **9A–472**

***Paragraph numbers marked with a "+" can be found online and on CD.***

(a) order the transfer of the proceedings to a county court; or

(b) if the court is satisfied that the person bringing the proceedings knew, or ought to have known, of that requirement, order that they be struck out.

(2) Subject to any such provision, the High Court may order the transfer of any proceedings before it to a county court.

(3) An order under this section may be made either on the motion of the High Court itself or on the application of any party to the proceedings.

(4) Proceedings transferred under this section shall be transferred to such county court as the High Court considers appropriate, having taken into account the convenience of the parties and that of any other persons likely to be affected and the state of business in the courts concerned.

(5) The transfer of any proceedings under this section shall not affect any right of appeal from the order directing the transfer.

(6) Where proceedings for the enforcement of any judgment or order of the High Court are transferred under this section—

(a) the judgment or order may be enforced as if it were a judgment or order of a county court; and

(b) subject to subsection (7), it shall be treated as a judgment or order of that court for all purposes.

(7) Where proceedings for the enforcement of any judgment or order of the High Court are transferred under this section—

(a) the powers of any court to set aside, correct, vary or quash a judgment or order of the High Court, and the enactments relating to appeals from such a judgment or order, shall continue to apply; and

(b) the powers of any court to set aside, correct, vary or quash a judgment or order of a county court, and the enactments relating to appeals from such a judgment or order, shall not apply.

(8) The provisions referred to in subsection (1) are any made—

(a) under section 1 of the Courts and Legal Services Act 1990; or

(b) by or under any other enactment.

(9) This section does not apply to family proceedings within the meaning of Part V of the Matrimonial and Family Proceedings Act 1984.

**9A-473** *Note* —Substituted by the Courts and Legal Services Act 1990 s.2(1).

**"Transfer of the proceedings"**

**9A-474** For the practice in relation to transfer, see CPR Pt 30, Vol.1, para.30.0.1. For procedure for appeal against order of transfer, see Practice Direction (Transfer), para.5.1, Vol.1, para.30PD.5. For transfer of Chancery work from the High Court to a county court and patents county court, see Chancery Guide Chs 13 and 23 (paras 1A-128 and 1A-174 above). For observations on time when transfer takes effect, see *Kings Quality Homes Ltd v AJ Paints Ltd* [1998] 1 W.L.R. 124, CA (jurisdiction of county court judge to hear appeal from order made by district judge before proceedings transferred from High Court to a county court).

**"order that they be struck out"**

Where, under s.40(1), the Court is satisfied that any proceedings before it are required to be in a county court the Court is not required to strike out the proceedings but may, and should normally, order their transfer to a county court (*Restick v Crickmore* [1994] 1 W.L.R. 420; [1994] 2 All E.R. 112, CA. Presumably the same construction should be applied to s.42(1). **9A–475**

**"provisions ... made"**

The provision made under s.1 of the 1990 Act is the High Court and County Courts Jurisdiction Order 1991 (see para.9B–928 below). **9A–476**

**Second application for transfer**

An order refusing the transfer of an action can never be final because circumstances can change. Nevertheless, if a party attempts but fails to obtain a transfer, and does not appeal against the refusal to transfer, but thereafter makes a second application, he will ordinarily be held to be guilty of an abuse of process unless there has been a material change of circumstances, or new grounds have arisen or new evidence has come to light; for to do otherwise would be oppressive or unjust to the party opposing the first application (*Habib Bank AG Zurich v Mindi Investment Ltd* (1987) 131 S.J. 1455; *The Times*, October 9, 1987, CA). See further Vol.1, para.23.0.14 "Successive applications for same relief". See Vol.1, paras 23.0.14 and 23.0.15 **9A–477**

**Subsection (8), Courts and Legal Services Act 1990 s.1**

Provisions made under this section are found in the High Court and County Courts Jurisdiction Order 1991 (SI 1991/724) (see para.9B–928 below). **9A–478**

For transfer of proceedings under the Arbitration Act 1996, see the High Court and County Courts (Allocation of Arbitration Proceedings) Order 1996 art.5 (see para.2E–379).

## Transfer to High Court by order of High Court

**41.**—(1) If at any stage in proceedings commenced in a county court or transferred to a county court under section 40, the High Court thinks it desirable that the proceedings, or any part of them, should be heard and determined in the High Court, it may order the transfer to the High Court of the proceedings or, as the case may be, of that part of them. **9A–479**

(2) The power conferred by subsection (1) is without prejudice to section 29 of the Senior Courts Act 1981 (power of High Court to issue prerogative orders) but shall be exercised in relation to family proceedings (within the meaning of Part V of the Matrimonial and Family Proceedings Act 1984) in accordance with any direction given under section 37 of that Act (directions as to distribution and transfer of family business and proceedings).

(3) The power conferred by subsection (1) shall be exercised subject to any provision made—

(a) under section 1 of the Courts and Legal Services Act 1990; or

(b) by or under any other enactment.

*Note* —Subsection (2) was amended by the Matrimonial and Family Proceedings Act 1984 Sch.1, para.31; subs.(3) was added by the Courts and Legal Services Act 1990 s.2(2). Amended by the Constitutional Reform Act 2005 s.59 and Sch.11, para.1 with effect from October 1, 2009 (SI 2009/1604). **9A–480**

**Subsection (3), Courts and Legal Services Act 1990 s.1**

Provisions made under this section are found in the High Court and County Courts **9A–481**

***Paragraph numbers marked with a "+" can be found online and on CD.***

Jurisdiction Order 1991 (SI 1991/724) (see para.9B–928). In *McLaughlin v British Coal Corp, The Times*, December 16, 1992, CA, the defendants applied to a county court judge to have proceedings transferred to the High Court where other proceedings raising similar issues were pending. It was held the plaintiffs were entitled to have their action treated separately and that the judge applied art.7 of the 1991 Order correctly in refusing to transfer the proceedings.

For transfer of proceedings under the Arbitration Act 1996, see the High Court and County Courts (Allocation of Arbitration Proceedings) Order 1996 art.5, see para.2E–379 above.

For rules of court, see CPR Pt 30, Vol.1, para.30.0.1.

For transfer of proceedings from a county court to the High Court in insolvency proceedings, see *Bullard & Taplin Ltd, Re* [1996] B.C.C. 973 (Knox J.), *Licence Holder, Re* [1997] B.C.C. 666 (Carnwath J.), *Debtors (No.13-MISC-2000 and No.14-MISC-2000), Re, The Times*, April 10, 2000 (Neuberger J.).

## Transfer to High Court by order of a county court

9A–482 **42.**—(1) Where a county court is satisfied that any proceedings before it are required by any provision of a kind mentioned in subsection (7) to be in the High Court, it shall—

(a) order the transfer of the proceedings to the High Court; or

(b) if the court is satisfied that the person bringing the proceedings knew, or ought to have known, of that requirement, order that they be struck out.

(2) Subject to any such provision, a county court may order the transfer of any proceedings before it to the High Court.

(3) An order under this section may be made either on the motion of the court itself or on the application of any party to the proceedings.

(4) The transfer of any proceedings under this section shall not affect any right of appeal from the order directing the transfer.

(5) Where the proceedings for the enforcement of any judgment or order of a county court are transferred under this section—

(a) the judgment or order may be enforced as if it were a judgment or order of the High Court; and

(b) subject to subsection (6), it shall be treated as a judgment or order of that court for all purposes.

(6) Where proceedings for the enforcement of any judgment or order of a county court are transferred under this section—

(a) the powers of any court to set aside, correct, vary or quash a judgment or order of a county court, and the enactments relating to appeals from a judgment or order, shall continue to apply; and

(b) the powers of any court to set aside, correct, vary or quash a judgment or order of the High Court, and the enactments relating to appeals from such a judgment or order, shall not apply.

(7) The provisions referred to in subsection (1) are any made—

(a) under section 1 of the Courts and Legal Services Act 1990; or

(b) by or under any other enactment.

***Paragraph numbers marked with a "+" can be found online and on CD.***

(8) This section does not apply to family proceedings within the meaning of Part V of the Matrimonial and Family Proceedings Act 1984.

*Note* —Substituted by the Courts and Legal Services Act 1990 s.2(3). 9A–483

**Subsection (7), Courts and Legal Services Act 1990 s.1**

The provision made under s.1 of the 1990 Act is the High Court and County Courts Jurisdiction Order 1991 (see para.9B–928). An example of "any other enactment" concerning transfer to the High Court by order of a county court is the Copyright, Designs and Patents Act 1988 s.289, discussed in *Chaplin Patents Holdings Company Plc v Group Lotus Plc, The Times*, January 12, 1994, CA. 9A–484

**Transfer of proceedings to High Court**

Under this section, depending on the circumstances, county court proceedings may or must be transferred to the High Court. The jurisdiction of the county courts to deal with freezing orders is restricted (see para.9A–471+ above). Where an application for a freezing order is wrongly issued in a county court in connection with a claim properly brought in that court, that application (as distinct from the claim to which it is incidental) does not constitute free-standing "proceedings" within the meaning of s.42. Consequently, a county court judge has no power or duty under sub-s.(1) or (2) of s.42 to transfer the application to the High Court (*Schmidt v Wong (Practice Note)* [2005] EWCA Civ 1506; [2005] 1 W.L.R. 561, CA). 9A–485

For transfer of proceedings under the Arbitration Act 1996, see the High Court and County Courts (Allocation of Arbitration Proceedings) Order 1996 art.5, see para.2E–379 above.

For rules of court, see CPR Pt 30.

* * * *

## Costs in transferred cases

**45.**—(1) Where an action, counterclaim or matter is ordered to be transferred— 9A–486

(a) from the High Court to a county court; or

(b) from a county court to the High Court; or

(c) from one county court to another county court,

the costs of the whole proceedings both before and after the transfer shall, subject to any order of the court which ordered the transfer, be in the discretion of the court to which the proceedings are transferred; and that court shall have power to make orders with respect to the costs, and the costs of the whole proceedings shall be taxed in that court.

(2) […]

*Note* —Amended by the Courts and Legal Services Act 1990 Sch.20. 9A–487

## PART III

## PROCEDURE

### *PARTIES*

## Proceedings by the Crown

**46.**—(1) Subject to the provisions of any enactment limiting the ju- 9A–488

***Paragraph numbers marked with a "+" can be found online and on CD.***

risdiction of a county court, whether by reference to the subject matter of the proceedings to be brought or the amount sought to be recovered in the proceedings or otherwise, proceedings by the Crown may be instituted in a county court.

(2) Subject to section 40(5), all rules of law and enactments regulating the removal or transfer of proceedings from a county court to the High Court and the transfer of proceedings in the High Court to a county court shall apply respectively to the removal or transfer of proceedings in the High Court to a county court shall apply respectively to the removal or transfer of proceedings by the Crown in a county court and to the transfer of proceedings by the Crown in the High Court.

(3) Nothing in this section shall apply to proceedings affecting Her Majesty in Her private capacity.

**Proceedings by the Crown**

9A–489 Subsection (1) states that proceedings may be instituted *by the Crown* in a county court. For statutory basis for proceedings *against the Crown* in a county court, see the Crown Proceedings Act 1947 s.15 (para.9B–1125+). Rules of court for proceedings by and against the Crown whether in a county court of High Court are found in CPR Pt 66 (Crown proceedings).

Subsection (2) is expressed as being "subject to section 40(5)". Section 40 (Transfer of proceedings to county court) was substituted by the Courts and Legal Services Act 1990 s.2(1). Before the substitution, s.40(5) stated that an order for the transfer to a county court of any proceedings by or against the Crown in the High Court "shall not be made without the consent of the Crown". No such provision appears in s.40 as substituted by the 1990 Act (see paras 9A–475 above). However, the High Court and County Courts Jurisdiction Order 1991 art.11 stated (see para.9B–928) that, for a period of two years from the date upon which the Order came into force (i.e. until July 1, 1993), no order should be made transferring proceedings in the High Court to which the Crown is a party to a county court except (a) when the proceedings are set down to be tried or heard, or (b) with the consent of the Crown. Section 20(1) of the Crown Proceedings Act 1947, which gave the Attorney General power to require that proceedings against the Crown instituted in a county court be transferred to the High Court, was revoked when Pt 66 was inserted in the CPR by the Civil Procedure (Amendment No.3) Rules 2005 (SI 2005/2292). (At the same time, s.19 of the 1947 Act (Venue and related matters) was also revoked.) For provisions as to transfer of proceedings involving the Crown, whether from a county to the High Court or vice versa, insofar as they differ from provisions applying to proceedings where the Crown is not involved, see Pt 66 and the practice direction supplementing that Part.

* * * *

## Persons jointly liable

9A–490 **48.**—(1) Where a plaintiff has a demand recoverable under this Act against two or more persons jointly liable, it shall be sufficient to serve any of those persons with process, and judgment may be obtained and execution issued against any person so served, notwithstanding that others jointly liable may not have been served or sued or may not be within the jurisdiction of the court.

(2) Where judgment is so obtained against any person by virtue of subsection (1) and is satisfied by that person, he shall be entitled to recover in the court contribution from any other person jointly liable with him.

***Paragraph numbers marked with a "+" can be found online and on CD.***

**Persons jointly liable**

Two or more persons may be joined together in one action as defendants see CPR r.7.3 (see Vol.1, para.7.3). Formerly, it was expressly provided by rules of court that no action or matter shall be defeated by reason of the non-joinder of any party as defendant (see CCR O.5, r.4 and note RSC O.15, r.6(1)); but no comparable provision is included in the CPR. At common law, where two (or more) persons were jointly liable for the payment of a debt or damages and the plaintiff proceeded to judgment against one only, the other was released from his obligations ("release by judgment"), even if the judgment remained unsatisfied. The result was that the plaintiff could not proceed against the other person. Further, the judgment debtor could not bring proceedings against him for a contribution. The "release by judgment" rule was removed by the Law Reform (Married Women and Tortfeasors) Act 1935 and the Civil Liability (Contribution) Act 1978. Section 48 also alters the effect of the rule but this provision has a much earlier provenance as it first appeared as the County Courts Act 1846 s.68. The section makes it clear that a defendant with a right to contribution from another person is not entitled, for the purpose of protecting that right, to a stay of proceedings until that other is joined as a defendant by the plaintiff. The plaintiff may proceed to judgment and the defendant's right to recover contribution against the other person is preserved. Whilst "demands recoverable under this Act" were limited to cases involving small sums, the impact on the release by judgment rule of the legislation now found in s.48 was slight. By the time those limits were significantly altered the rule had been abolished by the legislation referred to above. **9A-491**

## Bankruptcy of plaintiff

**49.**—(1) The bankruptcy of the plaintiff in any action in a county court which the trustee might maintain for the benefit of the creditors shall not cause the action to abate if, within such reasonable time as the court orders, the trustee elects to continue the action and to give security for the costs of the action. **9A-492**

(2) The hearing of the action may be adjourned until such an election is made.

(3) Where the trustee does not elect to continue the action and to give such security as is mentioned in subsection (1) within the time limited by the order, the defendant may avail himself of the bankruptcy as a defence to the action.

**Bankruptcy of plaintiff**

In proceedings in the High Court, the implications of the bankruptcy of a plaintiff are dealt with by CPR r.19.2. The most significant feature of s.49 is that it states that, upon the bankruptcy of the plaintiff, his cause of action shall not abate provided, within such reasonable time as the court orders, the trustee elects to continue the action "and to give security for the costs thereof". Generally, a plaintiff, whether bringing proceedings as a trustee or not, and whether bankrupt or not, cannot be required to give security for costs (CPR r.25.13). Section 49 creates an exception in county court proceedings. It would seem that where proceedings are transferred from the High Court to a county court and, before the transfer takes effect, by order made in the High Court under CPR r.19.2 a trustee becomes plaintiff, the county court has no jurisdiction under this section to require the trustee to give security for costs (*Hemming v Davies* [1898] 1 Q.B. 660). **9A-493**

### *INTERIM PAYMENTS IN PENDING PROCEEDINGS*

## Orders for interim payment

**50.**—(1) Provision may be made by rules of court for enabling the court, in such circumstances as may be prescribed, to make an order requiring a party to the proceedings to make an interim payment of **9A-494**

MAIN STATUTES

such amount as may be specified in the order, with provision for the payment to be made to such other party to the proceedings as may be so specified or, if the order so provides, by paying it into court.

(2) Any rules of court which make provision in accordance with subsection (1) may include provision for enabling a party to any proceedings who, in pursuance of such an order, has made an interim payment to recover the whole or part of the amount of the payment in such circumstances, and from such other party to the proceedings, as may be determined in accordance with the rules.

(3) Any rules made by virtue of this section may include such incidental, supplementary and consequential provisions as the rule committee may consider necessary or expedient.

(4) Nothing in this section shall be construed as affecting the exercise of any power relating to costs, including any power to make rules of court relating to costs.

(5) In this section "interim payment", in relation to a party to any proceedings, means a payment on account of any damages, debt or other sum (excluding any costs) which that party may be held liable to pay to or for the benefit of another party to the proceedings if a final judgment or order of the court in the proceedings is given or made in favour of that other party; and any reference to a party to any proceedings includes a reference to any person who for the purposes of the proceedings acts as next friend or guardian of a party to the proceedings.

**9A–495** *Note* —Amended by the Civil Procedure Act 1997 Sch.2, para.2(2).

**Orders for interim payment**

**9A–496** The jurisdictions of the High Court and the county courts to order interim payments may be traced to the Administration of Justice Act 1969 s.20. The Senior Courts Act 1981 s.32 is in similar terms to s.50.

For rules of court, see CPR rr.25.6 *et seq.*

### *PROVISIONAL DAMAGES FOR PERSONAL INJURIES*

## Orders for provisional damages for personal injuries

**9A–497** **51.**—(1) This section applies to an action for damages for personal injuries in which there is proved or admitted to be a chance that at some definite or indefinite time in the future the injured person will, as a result of the act or omission which gave rise to the cause of action, develop some serious disease or suffer some serious deterioration in his physical or mental condition.

(2) Subject to subsection (4), as regards any action for damages to which this section applies in which a judgment is given in the county court, provision may be made by rules of court for enabling the court, in such circumstances as may be prescribed, to award the injured person—

(a) damages assessed on the assumption that the injured person will not develop the disease or suffer the deterioration in his condition; and

(b) further damages at a future date if he develops the disease or suffers the deterioration.

(3) Any rules made by virtue of this section may include such incidental, supplementary and consequential provisions as the rule committee may consider necessary or expedient.

(4) Nothing in this section shall be construed—

(a) as affecting the exercise of any power relating to costs, including any power to make rules of court relating to costs; or

(b) as prejudicing any duty of the court under any enactment or rule of law to reduce or limit the total damages which would have been recoverable apart from any such duty.

(5) In this section "personal injuries" includes any disease and any impairment of a person's physical or mental condition.

*Note* —Amended by the Civil Procedure Act 1997 Sch.2, para.2(2). See also the Senior Courts Act 1981 s.32A (para.9A–107 above). **9A–498**

**Orders for provisional damages for personal injuries**

The jurisdictions of the High Court and the county courts to order provisional damages may be traced to the Administration of Justice Act 1968. The Senior Courts Act 1981 s.32A (para.9A–107) is in similar terms to s.51. **9A–499**

For rules of court, see CPR Pt 41.

As to appeal against a "certificate of total benefit" given by the Secretary of State in accordance with the Social Security Administration Act 1992 Pt IV, where an award of provisional damages has been made under s.51(2)(a) (or under the Senior Courts Act 1981 s.32A(2)), see s.98(3) of the 1992 Act. See also the Damages Act 1996 s.3; the Social Security (Recovery of Benefits) Act 1997; and *Willson v Ministry of Defence* [1991] 1 All E.R. 638; [1991] I.C.R. 595; and *Curi v Colina, The Times*, October 14, 1998, CA.

### *DISCOVERY AND RELATED PROCEDURES*

## Powers of court exercisable before commencement of action

**52.**—(1) On the application of any person in accordance with rules of court, a county court shall, in such circumstances as may be prescribed, have power to make an order providing for any one or more of the following matters, that is to say— **9A–500**

(a) the inspection, photographing, preservation, custody and detention of property which appears to the court to be property which may become the subject-matter of subsequent proceedings in the court, or as to which any question may arise in any such proceedings; and

(b) the taking of samples of any such property as is mentioned in paragraph (a) and the carrying out of any experiment on or with any such property.

(2) On the application, in accordance with rules of court, of a person who appears to a county court to be likely to be a party to subsequent proceedings in that court, the county court shall in such circumstances as may be prescribed, have power to order a person who appears to the court to be likely to be a party to the proceedings and to be likely to have or to have had in his possession, custody or power any documents which are relevant to an issue arising or likely to arise out of that claim—

MAIN STATUTES

(a) to disclose whether those documents are in his possession, custody or power; and

(b) to produce such of those documents as are in his possession, custody or power to the applicant or, on such conditions as may be specified in the order—

(i) to the applicant's legal advisers; or

(ii) to the applicant's legal advisers and any medical or other professional adviser of the applicant; or

(iii) if the applicant has no legal adviser, to any medical or other professional adviser of the applicant.

(3) This section is subject to any provision made under section 38.

9A-501 *Note* —Subsection (3) added by the Courts and Legal Services Act 1990 s.125(3), Sch.18, para.43. Amended by the Civil Procedure (Modification of Enactments) Order 1998 (SI 1998/2940) art.6(b) and by the Civil Procedure Act 1997 Sch.2, para.2(2).

**Powers of court exercisable before commencement of action**

9A-502 By order made under the Civil Procedure Act 1997 s.8, the Lord Chancellor may amend subs.(2) of this section for the purposes mentioned there (see para.9A-753). By the Civil Procedure (Modification of Enactments) Order 1998 (SI 1998/2940) para.6(b), subs.(2) was amended with the effect that the court's power to make an order under this section is no longer restricted to proceedings in which a claim in respect of personal injuries to a person, or in respect of a person's death, is likely to be made. It may be noted that the 1998 Order was made, not under s.8 of the 1997 Act, but under s.4(2) of that Act.

The comparable provision to s.52(2) in the Senior Courts Act 1981 is s.33(3), which was also amended by the 1998 Order (see para.9A-110).

*subs.(1)* —The powers of the High Court and the county courts to order inspection, etc., and taking of samples, etc., before commencement of action may be traced to the Administration of Justice Act 1969 s.21. The Senior Courts Act 1981 s.33(1) (para.9A-110) is in similar terms to s.52(1).

9A-503 *subs.(2)* —The powers of the High Court and the county courts to order disclosure and inspection of documents before commencement of action may be traced to the Administration of Justice Act 1970 s.31. The Senior Courts Act 1981 s.33(2) (para.9A-110) is in similar, terms to s.52(2).

9A-504 *subs.(3)* —Generally, s.52 gives the county court the same powers as those enjoyed by the High Court in relation to the matters dealt with in subss.(1) and (2). Section 38 states that, subject to that section and regulations made under it, in any in a county court the court may make any order which could be made in the High Court if the proceedings were in the High Court. Any restrictions so imposed apply to the powers granted by this section.

**Rules of court**

9A-505 The orders that a court may make under s.52 are listed among the interim remedies referred to in CPR r.25.1; see further Vol.1, paras 25.1.26 and 25.1.27.

## Power of court to order disclosure of documents, inspection of property, etc., in proceedings for personal injuries or death

9A-506 **53.**—(1) [...]

(2) On the application, in accordance with county court rules, of a party to any proceedings, a county court shall, in such circumstances

as may be prescribed, have power to order a person who is not a party to the proceedings and who appears to the court to be likely to have in his possession, custody or power any documents which are relevant to an issue arising out of the said claim—

(a) to disclose whether those documents are in his possession, custody or power; and

(b) to produce such of those documents as are in his possession, custody or power to the applicant or, on such conditions as may be specified in the order—

(i) to the applicant's legal advisers; or

(ii) to the applicant's legal advisers and any medical or other professional adviser of the applicant; or

(iii) if the applicant has no legal adviser, to any medical or other professional adviser of the applicant.

(3) On the application, in accordance with county court rules, of a party to any proceedings, a county court shall, in such instances as may be prescribed, have power to make an order providing for any one or more of the following matters, that is to say—

(a) the inspection, photographing, preservation, custody and detention of property which is not the property of, or in the possession of, any party to the proceedings but which is the subject-matter of the proceedings or as to which any question arises in the proceedings;

(b) the taking of samples of any such property as is mentioned in paragraph (a) and the carrying out of any experiment on or with any such property.

(4) The preceding provisions of this section are without prejudice to the exercise by a county court of any power to make orders which is exercisable apart from those provisions.

(5) This section is subject to any provision made under section 38.

*Note* —Subsection (5) added by the Courts and Legal Services Act 1990 s.125(3), Sch.18, para.44. Subsection (1) and subss.(2) and (3) amended by the Civil Procedure (Modification of Enactments) Order 1998 (SI 1998/2940) art.6(b). **9A–507**

**Power of court to order disclosure of documents, inspection of property, etc., in proceedings for personal injuries or death**

The powers of the High Court and the county courts to order, what could be called, "third party discovery" may be traced to the Administration of Justice Act 1970 s.32. **9A–508**

This section was amended by the Civil Procedure (Modification of Enactments) Order 1998 (SI 1998/2940) para.6(c), made under the Civil Procedure Act 1997 s.4(2), with the effect that the court's power to make an order under this section is no longer restricted to proceedings in which a claim in respect of personal injuries to a person, or in respect of a person's death, is likely to be made. In terms, the 1998 Order did not amend the title to s.53 which reads "Power of court to order disclosure of documents, inspection of property, etc., *in proceedings for personal injuries or death*". Obviously, the words in italics are no longer apposite.

The comparable provision to s.53 in the Senior Courts Act 1981 is s.34, which was also amended by the 1998 Order (see para.9A–115).

This section is subject to s.38 (see commentary to s.52(3), above).

**Rules of Court**

The orders that a court may make under section 53 are listed among the interim **9A–509** remedies referred to in CPR r.25.1; see further Vol.1, paras 25.1.28 and 25.1.29. Note also CPR rr.25.5, 31.17 and 48.1.

## Provisions supplementary to sections 52 and 53

9A–510 **54.**—(1) A county court shall not make an order under section 52 or 53 if it considers that compliance with the order, if made, would be likely to be injurious to the public interest.

(2) Rules of court may make provision as to the circumstances in which an order under section 52 or 53 can be made; and any rules making such provision may include such incidental, supplementary and consequential provisions as the Civil Procedure Rule Committee may consider necessary or expedient.

(3) Without prejudice to the generality of subsection (2), rules of court shall be made for the purpose of ensuring that the costs of and incidental to proceedings for an order under section 52(2) or 53 incurred by the person against whom the order is sought shall be awarded to that person unless the court otherwise directs.

(4) Sections 52(2) and 53 and this section bind the Crown; and section 52(1) binds the Crown so far as it relates to property as to which it appears to the court that it may become the subject-matter of subsequent proceedings involving a claim in respect of personal injuries to a person or in respect of a person's death.

In this subsection references to the Crown do not include references to Her Majesty in Her private capacity or to Her Majesty in right of Her Duchy of Lancaster or to the Duke of Cornwall.

(5) In sections 52 and 53 and this section—

"property" includes any land, chattel or other corporeal property of any description;

"personal injuries" includes any disease and any impairment of a person's physical or mental condition.

(6) This section is subject to any provision made under section 38.

9A–511 *Note* —Subsection (6) added by the Courts and Legal Services Act 1990 s.125(3), Sch.18, para.45. Amended by the Civil Procedure Act 1997 Sch.2, para.2(2).

### Provisions supplementary to sections 52 and 53

9A–512 This section is in similar terms to the Senior Courts Act 1981 s.35 (para.9A–118). This section is subject to s.38 (see commentary to s.52(3), above).

### *WITNESSES AND EVIDENCE*

## Penalty for neglecting or refusing to give evidence

9A–513 **55.**—(1) Subject to subsections (2) and (3), any person who—

(a) having been summoned in pursuance of rules of court as a witness in a county court refuses or neglects, without sufficient cause, to appear or to produce any documents required by the summons to be produced; or

(b) having been so summoned or being present in court and being required to give evidence, refuses to be sworn or give evidence,

*Paragraph numbers marked with a "+" can be found online and on CD.*

shall forfeit such fine as the judge may direct.

(2) A judge shall not have power under subsection (1) to direct that a person shall forfeit a fine of an amount exceeding £1000.

(3) No person summoned in pursuance of rules of court as a witness in a county court shall forfeit a fine under this section unless there has been paid or tendered to him at the time of the service of the summons such sum in respect of his expenses (including, in such cases as may be prescribed, compensation for loss of time) as may be prescribed for the purposes of this section.

(4) The judge may at his discretion direct that the whole or any part of any such fine, after deducting the costs, shall be applicable towards indemnifying the party injured by the refusal or neglect.

(4A) A district judge, assistant district judge or deputy district judge shall have the same powers under this section as a judge.

(5) This section does not apply to a debtor summoned to attend by a judgment summons.

*Note* —Amended by the Courts and Legal Services Act 1990 s.74; and the Criminal Justice Act 1991 s.17(3), Sch.4. Amended by the Civil Procedure Act 1997 Sch.2, para.2(2). **9A–514**

#### Penalty for neglecting or refusing to give evidence

For procedure for summoning witnesses, see CPR Pt 34. Notice to show cause why a fine should not be imposed (or should not have been imposed) under this section may be served on the witness (CPR Sch.2; CCR O.34, r.2). The limit of £1,000 in subs.(2) was set by the Criminal Justice Act 1991 s.17(3)(a), Sch.4, Pt I, and this figure may be altered by order made under the Magistrates' Courts Act 1980 s.143(1). **9A–515**

## Examination of witnesses abroad

**56.** The High Court shall have the same power to issue a commission, request or order to examine witnesses abroad for the purpose of proceedings in a county court as it has for the purpose of an action or matter in the High Court. **9A–516**

#### Examination of witnesses abroad

For powers of High Court, see CPR r.34.13. The power conferred on the High Court by this section is exercised by the Senior Master of the Queen's Bench Division (Practice Direction Depositions and Attendance by Witnesses), para.5.5 (see Vol.1, para.34APD.6). **9A–517**

## Evidence of prisoners

**57.**—(1) Subject to subsection (2), in any proceedings pending before a county court, the judge may, if he thinks fit, upon application on affidavit by any party, issue an order under his hand for bringing up before the court any person (in this section referred to as a "prisoner") confined in any place under any sentence or following the transfer of proceedings against him for trial or otherwise, to be examined as a witness in the proceedings. **9A–518**

(2) No such order shall be made with respect to a person confined under process in any civil action or matter.

(3) Subject to subsection (4), the prisoner mentioned in any such order shall be brought before the court under the same custody, and shall be dealt with in the same manner in all respects, as a prisoner

*Paragraph numbers marked with a "+" can be found online and on CD.*

required by a writ of habeas corpus to be brought before the High Court and examined there as a witness.

(4) The person having the custody of the prisoner shall not be bound to obey the order unless there is tendered to him a reasonable sum for the conveyance and maintenance of a proper officer or officers and of the prisoner in going to, remaining at, and returning from, the court.

9A-519 *Note*—Amended by the Criminal Justice and Public Order Act 1994 s.44, Sch.4.

**Evidence of prisoners**

9A-520 For procedure for application for habeas corpus to bring up a prisoner to give evidence in the High Court, see CPR Sch.1; RSC O.54, r.9. Provisions in the Criminal Justice and Public Order Act 1994 amending this section (see s.44(3) Sch.4, Pt II, para.57) were never brought into force and those provisions were omitted from the 1994 Act by the Criminal Procedure and Investigations Act 1996 s.44.

## Persons who may take affidavits for use in county courts

9A-521 **58.**—(1) An affidavit to be used in a county court may be sworn before—

(a) the judge or registrar of any court; or

(b) any justice of the peace; or

(c) an officer of any court appointed by the judge of that court for the purpose,

as well as before a commissioner for oaths or any other person authorised to take affidavits under the Commissioners for Oaths Acts 1889 and 1891 [...].

(2) An affidavit sworn before a judge or registrar or before any such officer may be sworn without the payment of any fee.

9A-522 *Note*—Amended by the Administration of Justice Act 1985 s.67, Schs 7 and 8.

**Persons who may take affidavits for use in county courts**

9A-523 The Family Proceedings Rules 1991 r.10.13 provides that in relation to family proceedings pending or treated as pending in a divorce county court an affidavit may be sworn before certain other persons in addition to those listed in s.58(1).

**For s.59 of the County Courts Act 1984 (see Arrangement) plus any related commentary see paragraphs 9A-524+ to 9A-526+ on White Book on Westlaw UK or the Civil Procedure CD.**

*RIGHT OF AUDIENCE*

## Right of audience

9A-527 **60.**—(1) [...]

(2) Where an action is brought in a county court by a local authority for either or both of the following—

(a) the recovery of possession of a house belonging to the authority;

(b) the recovery of any rent, mesne profits, damages or other sum claimed by the authority in respect of the occupation by any person of such a house,

***Paragraph numbers marked with a "+" can be found online and on CD.***

then, in so far as the proceedings in the action are heard by the registrar, any officer of the authority authorised by the authority in that behalf, not being a person entitled to address the court by virtue of subsection (1), may address the registrar as if he were a person so entitled.

(3) In this section—

"local authority" means a county council, a district council, the Broads Authority, any National Park Authority, a London borough council, a Police authority established under section 3 of the Police Act 1996, the Metropolitan Police Authority, a joint authority established by Part IV of the Local Government Act 1985, an authority established for an area in England by an order under section 207 of the Local Government and Public Involvement in Health Act 2007 (joint waste authorities), the London Fire and Emergency Planning Authority, or the Common Council of the City of London; and

"local authority" means a county council, a district council, the Broads Authority, any National Park Authority, a London borough council, a Police authority established under section 3 of the Police Act 1996, the Metropolitan Police Authority, a joint authority established by Part IV of the Local Government Act 1985, an authority established for an area in England by an order under section 207 of the Local Government and Public Involvement in Health Act 2007 (joint waste authorities), the London Fire and Emergency Planning Authority, or the Common Council of the City of London; and

"house" includes a part of a house, a flat or any other dwelling and also includes any yard, garden, outhouse or appurtenance occupied with a house or part of a house or with a flat or other dwelling; and

any reference to the occupation of a house by a person includes a reference to anything done by that person, or caused or permitted by him to be done, in relation to the house as occupier of the house, whether under a tenancy or licence or otherwise.

*Note*—Amended by the Local Government Act 1985 ss.82 and 102, Schs 14 and 17; the Norfolk and Suffolk Broads Act 1988 s.21, Sch.6; the Education Reform Act 1988 s.237, Sch.13; the Courts and Legal Services Act 1990 s.125(7), Sch.20; the Police and Magistrates' Courts Act 1994 s.43, Sch.4; the Environment Act 1995 s.78, Sch.10, the Police Act 1996 s.103 and Sch.7, Pt I, para.1, the Police Act 1997 s.134 and Sch.9, para.45. The definition of "local authority" in subs.(3) was amended by the Criminal Justice and Police Act 2001 (c.16), s.128 and Sch.6, para.66, and s.137and Sch.7, Pt 5 and the Local Government and Public Involvement in Health Act 2007 s.209, Sch.13, Pt 2, para.40, with effect from April 1, 2008 (SI 2008/917). The references in this section to "registrar" should be construed as references to "district judge": Courts and Legal Services Act 1990 s.74. **9A–528**

**Right of audience**

See commentary to s.61, below. **9A–529**

## Rights of audience etc of employees of housing management bodies

**60A.**—(1) An employee of a housing management body who is authorised by that body for the purposes of this section has— **9A–530**

MAIN STATUTES

***Paragraph numbers marked with a "+" can be found online and on CD.***

(a) a right of audience in relation to any proceedings to which this section applies, and

(b) a right to conduct litigation in relation to any such proceedings.

(2) This section applies to relevant housing proceedings in a county court before a district judge which are brought—

(a) in the name of a local housing authority, and

(b) by the housing management body in the exercise of functions of that local housing authority delegated to that body under a housing management agreement.

(3) "Relevant housing proceedings" are—

(a) proceedings under section 82A of the Housing Act 1985 (demotion because of anti-social behaviour);

(b) proceedings for possession of a dwelling-house subject to a secure tenancy, where possession is sought on ground 2 in Part 1 of Schedule 2 to that Act (anti-social behaviour);

(c) proceedings for possession of a dwelling-house subject to a demoted tenancy;

(d) proceedings for a suspension order under section 121A of the Housing Act 1985 (suspension of right to buy);

(e) proceedings under section 153A, 153B or 153D of the Housing Act 1996 (injunctions against anti-social behaviour);

(f) proceedings for the attachment of a power of arrest to an injunction by virtue of section 91(2) of the Anti-social Behaviour Act 2003 or section 27(2) of the Police and Justice Act 2006 (proceedings under section 222 of the Local Government Act 1972: power of arrest attached to injunction);

(g) at a hearing at which a decision is made in relation to proceedings within paragraphs (a) to (f), proceedings for permission to appeal against that decision;

(h) such other proceedings as the Lord Chancellor may prescribe by order.

(4) An authorisation for the purposes of this section must be in writing.

(5) The power to make an order under subsection (3)(h) is exercisable by statutory instrument subject to annulment by resolution of either House of Parliament.

(6) In subsection (3)(e) the reference to section 153A of the Housing Act 1996 is a reference to that section—

(a) as inserted by section 13 of the Anti-social Behaviour Act 2003, or

(b) as substituted by section 26 of the Police and Justice Act 2006.

(7) In this section—

"dwelling-house" has the same meaning as in Part 4 of the Housing Act 1985;

"housing management agreement" means an agreement under section 27 of the Housing Act 1985 (including an agreement to which section 27B(2) or (3) of that Act applies);

"housing management body" means a person who exercises management functions of a local housing authority by virtue of a housing management agreement;

"local housing authority" has the same meaning as in section 27 of the Housing Act 1985;

"right of audience" means the right to appear before and address a court, including the right to call and examine witnesses;

"right to conduct litigation" means the right—

(a) to issue proceedings before any court in England and Wales,

(b) to commence, prosecute and defend such proceedings, and

(c) to perform any ancillary functions in relation to such proceedings (such as entering appearances to actions);

"secure tenancy" has the same meaning as in Part 4 of the Housing Act 1985.

*Note* —Inserted by the Legal Services Act 2007 s.191. For commentary on effect of this provision, see Section 13 (Rights of Audience) para.13–6, below. **9A–531**

## Right of audience by direction of Lord Chancellor

**61.**—(1) The Lord Chancellor may, with the concurrence of the Lord Chief Justice, at any time direct that such categories of persons in relevant legal employment as may be specified in the direction may address the court in any proceedings in a county court, or in proceedings in a county court of such description as may be so specified. **9A–532**

(2) In subsection (1), "relevant legal employment" means employment which consists of or includes giving assistance in the conduct of litigation to a legal representative whether in private practice or not.

(3) A direction under this section may be given subject to such conditions and restrictions as appear to the Lord Chancellor to be necessary or expedient, and may be expressed to have effect as respects every county court or as respects a specified county court or as respects one or more specified places where a county court sits.

(4) The power to give directions conferred by this section includes a power to vary or rescind any direciton given under this section.

(5) The Lord Chief Justice may nominate a judicial office holder (as defined in section 109(4) of the Constitutional Reform Act 2005) to exercise his functions under this section.

*Note* —Amended by the Courts and Legal Services Act 1990 s.125(3), Sch.18, **9A–533** para.49and the Constitutional Reform Act 2005 s.15(1), Sch.4, para.168 (see para.9A–4 above).

**Right of audience by direction of Lord Chancellor**

9A–534 Under various statutory provisions, including this section, rights of audience before county courts and other courts may be granted; see further Section 13 (Rights of Audience) para.13–6, below.).

## *MODE OF TRIAL*

### General power of judge to determine questions of law and fact

9A–535 **62.** Subject to the provisions of this Act and of county court rules, the judge of a county court shall be the sole judge in all proceedings brought in the court, and shall determine all questions of fact as well as of law.

**Judge to determine all questions of law and fact**

9A–536 Other "provisions of the Act" includes the sections immediately following. Where the rules found in the CPR provide for a county court to "perform any act", that act may be performed, not only by any judge, but also by any district judge. In terms, r.3.4 is subject to any enactment, rule or practice direction that provides otherwise. What is meant in this context by "perform any act" provided for by the CPR is not free from doubt. Practice Direction (Allocation of Cases to Levels of Judiciary) sets out the matters over which district judges do not have jurisdiction or which they may deal with only on certain conditions (see Vol.1, 2BPD.1). Circuit judges and district judges have concurrent jurisdiction to hear trials of cases allocated to the fast track. For the jurisdiction of district judges to deal with trials and assessments of damages in multi-track cases, see Practice Direction (Allocation of Cases to Levels of Judiciary), para.4.1.

### Assessors

9A–537 **63.**—(1) In any proceedings the judge may, if he thinks fit, summon to his assistance, in such manner as may be prescribed, one or more persons of skill and experience in the matter to which the proceedings relate who may be willing to sit with the judge and act as assessors.

(2) [...]

(3) Subject to subsection (4), the remuneration of assessors for sitting under this section shall be determined by the judge and shall be costs in the proceedings unless otherwise ordered by the judge.

(4) Where one or more assessors are summoned for the purposes of assisting the judge in reviewing the taxation by the district judge of the costs of any proceedings the remuneration of any such assessor—

(a) shall be at such rate as may be determined by the Lord Chancellor with the approval of the Treasury; and

(b) shall be payable out of moneys provided by Parliament.

(5) Where any person is proposed to be summoned as an assessor, objection to him, either personally or in respect of his qualification, may be taken by any party in the prescribed manner.

9A–538 *Note* —Subsections (1), (3) and (4) were amended by, and subs.(2) omitted by, the Civil Procedure (Modification of Enactments) Order 1998 (SI 1998/2940) art.6(d).

***Paragraph numbers marked with a "+" can be found online and on CD.***

Amendments previously made to s.63 by the Courts and Legal Services Act 1990 s.14 were never brought into force.

**Assessors summoned to assist judge**

The comparable provision in the Senior Courts Act 1981 is s.70 (see para.9A–328). For rules of court relevant to the use of assessors generally see CPR r.35.15 (this rule does not apply to proceedings allocated to the small claims track, see r.27.2(1)(e)); see also Practice Direction (Experts and Assessors), para.6 (see Vol.1, para.35PD.6). For provisions as to the use of assessors in certain landlord and tenant proceedings, see Landlord and Tenant Act 1954 s.63, and CPR Sch.2, CCR O.43, r.13 (see Vol.1, para.cc43.13). **9A–539**

In *Ahmed v University of Oxford* [2002] EWCA Civ 1907; [2003] 1 W.L.R. 995; [2003] 1 All E.R. 915, CA, unrep., the Court of Appeal examined the role of assessors appointed in various contexts, including under s.63 of this Act and the Senior Courts Act 1981 s.70 (see para.9A–261 above), but particularly under the Race Relations Act 1976 s.67(4). See further CPR r.35.15, and commentary following that rule.

## Reference to arbitration

**64.**—(1) Rules of court— **9A–540**

(a) may prescribe cases in which proceedings are (without any order of the court) to be referred to arbitration, and

(b) may prescribe the manner in which and the terms on which cases are to be so referred, and

(c) may, where cases are so referred, require other matters within the jurisdiction of the court in dispute between the parties also to be referred to arbitration.

(2) Rules of court—

(a) may prescribe cases in which proceedings may be referred to arbitration by order of the court, and

(b) may authorise the court also to order other matters in dispute between the parties and within the jurisdiction of the court to be so referred.

(2A) Rules of court may prescribe the procedures and rules of evidence to be followed on any reference under subsection (1) or (2).

(2B) Rules made under subsection (2A) may, in particular, make provision with respect to the manner of taking and questioning evidence.

(3) On a reference under subsection (1) or (2) the award of the arbitrator, arbitrators or umpire shall be entered as the judgment in the proceedings and shall be as binding and effectual to all intents, subject to subsection (4), as if it had been given by the judge.

(4) The judge may, if he thinks fit, on application made to him within such time as may be prescribed, set aside the award, or may, with the consent of the parties, revoke the reference or order another reference to be made in the manner specified in this section.

(5) In this section "award" includes an interim award.

*Note*—Subsections (2A) and (2B) added by the Courts and Legal Services Act 1990 s.6. Amended by the Civil Procedure Act 1997 Sch.2, para.2(2). **9A–541**

**Rules of court prescribing reference to arbitration**

Before the CPR came into force, rules of court found in CCR O.19, Pt I and made under s.64 provided for two forms of reference to arbitration by the court. They were (1) reference on application by a party to proceedings, and (2) automatic reference by **9A–542**

*Main Statutes*

rule of proceedings falling within the "small claims" jurisdiction of the court. Under the CPR, the second form of reference has been replaced by the procedure for the allocation to the small claims track of minor claims. The relevant rules of court are found in CPR Pts 26 and 27. In these provisions, no use is made of the word "arbitration" for the purpose of describing the summary procedures used by the court for the handling and trial of small claims. It would seem that it would not be appropriate to describe the allocation of a claim to the small claims track as a reference to a form of statutory arbitration. Consequently, the significance of the Arbitration Act 1996 s.92, which states that nothing in Pt I of that Act applies to arbitrations under s.64 is diminished.

There are no express provisions in the CPR comparable to those formerly found in CCR O.19, Pt I for the first form of reference of county court proceedings to arbitration mentioned above, that is to say, a reference on the application of a party. However, r.1.4(2)(e) states that the court's duty to manage cases includes encouraging the parties "to use an alternative dispute resolution procedure if the court considers that appropriate and facilitating the use of such procedure". (In the Glossary attached to the CPR, "alternative dispute resolution" is described in terms sufficiently wide to include arbitration.) Further, r.26.4 states that, in certain circumstances, the court may stay proceedings whilst parties try to settle the case "by alternative dispute resolution or other means". It would seem, therefore, that the court has power under the CPR to refer proceedings to arbitration on the application of a party. However, it is doubtful whether the rules from which such power may be derived are rules of court of the express type envisaged by s.64. Further, it is doubtful whether a reference to arbitration on the application of a party (if it is permissible) could be described as a reference under s.64 (see above observations on the Arbitration Act 1996 s.92).

### Power of judge to refer to district judge or referee

**9A–543** **65.**—(1) Subject to rules of court, the judge may refer to the registrar or a referee for inquiry and report—

(a) any proceedings which require any prolonged examination of documents or any scientific or local investigation which cannot, in the opinion of the judge, conveniently be made before him;

(b) any proceedings where the question in dispute consists wholly or in part of matters of account;

(c) with the consent of the parties, any other proceedings;

(d) subject to any right to have particular cases tried with a jury, any question arising in any proceedings.

(2) In such cases as may be prescribed by, and subject to, rules of court the registrar may refer to a referee for inquiry and report any question arising in any proceedings.

(3) Where any proceedings or question are referred under subsection (1) or (2), the judge or, as the case may be, the registrar may direct how the reference shall be conducted, and may remit any report for further inquiry and report, and on consideration of any report or further report may give such judgment or make such order in the proceedings as may be just.

(4) The judge may, after deciding or reserving any question of liability, refer to the registrar any mere matter of account which is in dispute between the parties and, after deciding the question of liability, may give judgment on the registrar's report.

**9A–544** *Note* —Amended by Civil Procedure Act 1997 Sch.2, para.2(2). The Courts and Legal Services Act 1990 s.74 states that any reference in any enactment to the offices of registrar, etc., shall be construed as a reference to the office of district judge.

**Reference for inquiry and report**

This section is comparable to the Senior Courts Act 1981 s.68, the provision upon which what was once called "official referees' business" was based. Before the CPR came into force, rules of court made in pursuance of s.65 were found in CCR O.19, Pt II (reference for inquiry and report). Initially, no comparable rules were found in the CPR, but official referees' business, now known as "Technology and Construction Court Business" was treated as a form of "specialist proceedings" under CPR Pt 49. This ceased to be the case when, subsequently, provisions dealing with such Business (whether arising in the High Court or in a county court) were inserted in the CPR as Pt 60 (Proceedings in the Technology and Construction Court) (see para.2C-1 above). **9A-545**

### *JURIES*

## Trial by jury

**66.**—(1) In the following proceedings in a county court the trial shall be without a jury— **9A-546**

(a) Admiralty proceedings;

(b) proceedings arising—

(i) under Part I of the Rent (Agriculture) Act 1976, or

(ii) under any provision of the Rent Act 1977 other than a provision contained in Part V, sections 103 to 106 or Part IX, or

(iii) under Part I of the Protection from Eviction Act 1977; or

(iv) under Part I of the Housing Act 1988.

(c) any appeal to the county court under the Housing Act 1985;

(2) In all other proceedings in a county court the trial shall be without a jury unless the court otherwise orders on an application made in that behalf by any party to the proceedings in such manner and within such time before the trial as may be prescribed.

(3) Where, on any such application, the court is satisfied that there is in issue—

(a) a charge of fraud against the party making the application; or

(b) a claim in respect of libel, slander, malicious prosecution or false imprisonment; or

(c) any question or issue of a kind prescribed for the purposes of this paragraph,

the action shall be tried with a jury, unless the court is of the opinion that the trial requires any prolonged examination of documents or accounts of any scientific or local investigation which cannot conveniently be made with a jury.

(4) There shall be payable, in respect of the trial with a jury of proceedings in a county court, such fees as may be prescribed by an order under section 92 of the Courts Act 2003 (fees).

*Note*—Amended by the Housing (Consequential Provisions) Act 1985 Sch.2, para.57; and the Housing Act 1988 Sch.17, para.35; subs.(4) amended by the Courts Act 2003 s.109(1), Sch.8, para.271(a). **9A-547**

***Paragraph numbers marked with a "+" can be found online and on CD.***

**Trial by jury**

9A–548 The general rule is that the judge shall determine all questions of fact as well as of law (s.62). The circumstances in which proceedings may be tried with a jury are stated in this section. (The section may be contrasted with the Senior Courts Act 1981 s.69). As to impanelling of jury, see s.67.

The structure of this section may be stated as follows. (1) The proceedings listed in subs.(1) may not be tried with a jury. (2) All other proceedings shall be without a jury unless the court, in the exercise of discretion, otherwise orders on application (subs.(2)). However, (3) on such application the court shall order jury trial if it is satisfied that an issue of the type listed in subs.(3) exists, unless (4) such trial would be inconvenient for any of the reasons stated in that subsection.

The discretion to grant jury trial is rarely exercised; the circumstances must be wholly exceptional (*H. v Ministry of Defence* [1991] 2 W.L.R. 1192, CA).

Where a "charge of fraud" is an issue in the proceedings the party against whom it is made (but no other party) has a right to jury trial (subject to any inconvenience). A mere allegation of fraud does not raise a "charge of fraud" as an issue; such an issue must involve an allegation of actionable deceit (*Grant v Travellers Cheque Associates Ltd*, *The Times*, April 19, 1995, CA, applying *Barclays Bank Ltd v Cole* [1967] 2 Q.B. 738, CA; see also *Parsons v Provincial Insurance Plc*, February 20, 1988, unrep., CA).

Where a claim in respect of libel, slander, malicious prosecution or false imprisonment is an issue in the proceedings a right to jury trial arises (subject to any inconvenience). In these circumstances, any application for jury trial is likely to be made by the party making the claim. An action against police for damages for assault and battery does not raise an issue of a claim for false imprisonment although the facts pleaded might bear the inference that the plaintiff was briefly falsely imprisoned (*Hendry v Chief Constable of Lancashire Constabulary*, December 7, 1993, unrep., CA).

Where an issue of the type listed in subs.(3) exists, nevertheless, jury trial may be refused where the court is of opinion that the trial requires "prolonged examination of documents, etc." which cannot conveniently be made with a jury. For principles to be applied and relevant considerations in these circumstances, see *Aitken v Preston*, *The Times*, May 21, 1997, CA, and *Taylor v Anderton* [1995] 1 W.L.R. 447, CA. See further notes following Senior Courts Act 1981 s.69 (para.9A–256 above).

**Application made in such manner and within such time "as may be prescribed"**

9A–549 Section 66(2) states that the trial of certain proceedings shall be without jury and that in all other proceedings trial should be without a jury unless the court otherwise orders "on an application made in that behalf by any party to the proceedings in such manner and within such time before the trial *as may be prescribed*", which means, as prescribed by rules of court (see County Courts Act 1984 s.147(1)) (see also Senior Courts Act 1981 s.69(2)). CPR r.26.11 states that an application for a claim to be tried by a jury must be made within 28 days of service of the defence. This rule was inserted in the CPR by the Civil Procedure (Amendment No.4) Rules 2000 (SI 2000/2092). In *Oliver v Calderdale Metropolitan BC*, *The Times*, July 7, 1999, CA, a case decided under the old rules, it was held that an application made wholly out of time could be rejected on the ground that it was unreasonable.

## Impanelling and swearing of jury

9A–550 **67.** At any county court where proceedings are to be tried with a jury, eight jurymen shall be impanelled and sworn as occasion requires to give their verdicts in the proceedings brought before them, and being once sworn need not be re-sworn in each trial.

**Impanelling and swearing of jury**

9A–551 By tradition, a jury consists of twelve persons, but the number may be reduced by statute. By virtue of this provision juries in county court proceedings consist of eight persons. Any party to county court proceedings to be tried by jury has the same right of challenge to all or some of the jurors as he would in the High Court (Juries Act 1974 s.12(2)). Challenge in the High Court is governed by the common law as modified statute (see *ibid.*, s.12). A jury's verdict need not be unanimous if seven agree on it.

***Paragraph numbers marked with a "+" can be found online and on CD.***

However, a court should only accept a majority verdict if it is satisfied that the jury had such period of time for deliberation as the court thinks reasonable having regard to the nature and complexity of the case (*ibid.*, s.17(2), (4)). As to majority verdict in High Court cases, see *ibid.*, s.17(1).

## Duty of judge to determine foreign law in jury trials

**68.** Where, for the purpose of disposing of any proceedings which are being tried in a county court by the judge with a jury, it is necessary to ascertain the law of any other country which is applicable to the facts of the case, any question as to the effect of the evidence given with respect to that law shall, instead of being submitted to the jury, be decided by the judge alone. **9A–552**

### Duty of judge to determine foreign law in jury trials

This section is in same terms of the Senior Courts Act 1981 s.69(5) (para.9A–256). As to evidence of foreign law, see the Civil Evidence Act 1972 s.4 (para.9B–1063). **9A–553**

*INTEREST ON DEBTS AND DAMAGES*

## Power to award interest on debts and damages

**69.**—(1) Subject to rules of court, in proceedings (whenever instituted) before a county court for the recovery of a debt or damages there may be included in any sum for which judgment is given simple interest, at such rate as the court thinks fit or as may be prescribed, on all or any part of the debt or damages in respect of which judgment is given, or payment is made before judgment, for all or any part of the period between the date when the cause of action arose and— **9A–554**

(a) in the case of any sum paid before judgment, the date of the payment; and

(b) in the case of the sum for which judgment is given, the date of the judgment.

(2) In relation to a judgment given for damages for personal injuries or death which exceed £200 subsection (1) shall have effect—

(a) with the substitution of "shall be included" for "may be included"; and

(b) with the addition of "unless the court is satisfied that there are special reasons to the contrary" after "given", where first occurring.

(3) Subject to rules of court, where—

(a) there are proceedings (whenever instituted) before a county court for the recovery of a debt; and

(b) the defendant pays the whole debt to the plaintiff (otherwise than in pursuance of a judgment in the proceedings),

the defendant shall be liable to pay the plaintiff simple interest, at such rate as the court thinks fit or as may be prescribed, on all or any part of the debt for all or any part of the period between the date when the cause of action arose and the date of the payment.

(4) Interest in respect of a debt shall not be awarded under this



MAIN STATUTES

section for a period during which, for whatever reason, interest on the debt already runs.

(5) Interest under this section may be calculated at different rates in respect of different periods.

(6) In this section "plaintiff" means the person seeking the debt or damages and "defendant" means the person from whom the plaintiff seeks the debt or damages and "personal injuries" includes any disease and any impairment of a person's physical or mental condition.

(7) Nothing in this section affects the damages recoverable for the dishonour of a bill of exchange.

(8) In determining whether the amount of any debt or damages exceeds that prescribed by or under any enactment, no account shall be taken of any interest payable by virtue of this section except where express provision to the contrary is made by or under that or any other enactment.

**9A–555** *Note*—Subsection (8) substituted by the Courts and Legal Services Act 1990 s.125(3), Sch.18, para.46.

**Power to award interest on debts and damages**

**9A–556** With the exception of subs.(8), this section is in similar terms to the Senior Courts Act 1981 s.35A (para.9A–122 and commentary thereto). A claim for interest under this section should be included in the particulars of claim (CPR r.16.4(2)). Judgment by default in a claim for a specified amount of money may include interest claimed under this section in the circumstances provided by CPR r.12.6. For interest on judgment under CPR r.14.4 (admission of whole of claim for specified amount of money) where interest claimed under s.69, see CPR r.14.14. Subsection (8) was substituted by the Courts and Legal Services Act 1990 Sch.18, para.46. Some of the provisions for the allocation of business for commencement and trial between the High Court and the county courts found in the High Court and County Court Jurisdiction Order 1991 and in Practice Direction (How to Start Proceedings—The Claim Form), paras 2.1 *et seq.* turn on the "value" of the action. art.9 of the Order states that in determining the value of an action for these purposes claims for interest shall be disregarded (see para.9B–164+ below). In the exercise of its discretion, the court may reduce the rate at which interest on an award of damages is payable or reduce the period for which interest is payable. Since the coming into effect of the CPR, this power has been increasingly used by the courts as a sanction where parties fail to comply with procedural rules, practice directions and case management orders. The Court of Appeal has encouraged the use of this sanction as an alternative to more serious sanctions (e.g. striking out); see, e.g. *Biguzzi v Rank Leisure Plc* [1999] 1 W.L.R. 1926, CA; *Baron v Lovell, The Times*, September 14, 1999, CA; *Abbahall Ltd v Smee* [2002] EWCA Civ 1831; January 24, 2000, unrep., CA; *Walsh v Misseldine*, February 29, 2000, unrep., CA, *UYB Ltd v British Railways Board, The Times*, November 15, 2000, CA; *Adcock v Co-operative Insurance Society Ltd* [2000] Lloyd's Rep. I.R. 657, CA; note also Practice Direction (Protocols), para.2.3 (see Vol.1, para.C1–002).

### *JUDGMENTS AND ORDERS*

## Finality of judgments and orders

**9A–557** **70.** Every judgment and order of a county court shall, except as provided by this or any other Act or as may be prescribed, be final and conclusive between the parties.

**Finality of judgments and orders**

**9A–558** Originally, this section formed the first part of the County Courts Act 1846 s.93. A later part of the old provision went on to state that the judge should have a discretionary power to order a new trial in every case. The relationship between the two parts created difficulties and was subject to a considerable amount of case law. Subsequently, the power to order a new trial was removed from primary legislation, put into rules of court and substantially altered. Until it was revoked by the Civil Procedure (Amendment No.4) Rules 2002 (SI 2002/2058) the relevant rule was CPR Sch.2, RSC O.37, r.1. Consequently, since 1934 this section has stated the simple general proposition that, except as provided by legislation or as may be prescribed, "every judgment and order of a county court shall be final and conclusive between the parties". The general proposition is unimpeachable. When considering s.93 of the 1846 Act, Willes J. said: "The very object of instituting courts of justice is that litigation should be decided, and decided finally" (*Great Northern Railway Co v Mossop* (1855) 17 C.B. 130 at 1022).

The exceptions to the general proposition are important and inherently difficult; the power to order a rehearing is but one. Another example is the power to set aside a judgment given in a party's absence (CPR r.39.3(3)). Obviously, the various provisions as to appeals from particular judgments and orders must also be regarded as exceptions.

Under some statutes it is expressly provided that the decision of a court shall be "final" in the sense that no appeal shall lie. This is recognised by the County Courts Act 1984 s.79(1) (and by the Senior Courts Act 1981 s.18(1)(c)). Before CPR Pt 52 (Appeals) came into effect, the distinction between "final" and 'interlocutory" appeals was important in appeal procedure (see Senior Courts Act 1981 s.60 and notes following, para.9A–227 above). In s.70, the word "final" is used in a different sense. A judgment or order takes effect from the day when it is given or made, or such later date as the court may specify (CPR r.40.7). In any system of adjudication there must come a point when a judgment or order rendered (particularly at the end of a trial) is final in the sense that it will not be re—considered by the court or other tribunal pronouncing it. The authorities show that a judgment becomes final in this sense, not when it is pronounced, but when the order giving it effect has been drawn up, registered or perfected (*R. v Cripps Ex p. Muldoon* [1984] Q.B. 686, CA, at p.695 Sir John Donaldson M.R.; see also *Preston Banking Co v William Allsupp & Sons* [1895] 1 Ch. 141, CA, at p.145 per A.L. Smith L.J.). After this point, a party's remedy lies, not in attempting to persuade the court which rendered the judgment to change its mind, but in challenging the judgment on appeal. Before this point, the court has jurisdiction in limited circumstances to recall the judgment for further consideration. Authority for this is provided by *Barrell Enterprises, Re* [1973] 1 W.L.R. 19, CA, where it was said that the jurisdiction should not be exercised "save in the most exceptional circumstances" (see also *Pittalis v Sherefettin* [1986] Q.B. 868, CA, at p.882 Dillon L.J. and authorities referred to there). In modern times, pressures to reduce costs and delays in civil proceedings, coupled with the desire to discourage parties from mounting appeals and the new restrictions on access to appellate courts, have focussed attention on the circumstances in which the Barrell jurisdiction may and should be exercised (see further Vol.1, para.40.2.2 and cases referred to there). Since the coming into effect of the CPR, the extent of the jurisdiction has been considered at first instance in the High Court (see *Charlesworth v Relay Road Ltd*, [2000] 1 W.L.R. 230, [1999] 4 All E.R. 397, Neuberger J.; *Spice Girls Ltd v Aprilia World Service BV (Permission to Appeal), The Times*, September 12, 2000, Arden J.; *Mamidoil-Jetoil Greek Petroleum SA v Okta Crude Oil Refinery AD (No.2)* [2001] 1 Lloyd's Rep. 591, Thomas J.; *Compagnie Noga d'Importation et d'Exportation SA v Abacha* [2001] 3 All E.R. 513, Rix L.J.) and by the Court of Appeal in *Stewart v Engel* [2000] 1 W.L.R. 2268; [2000] 3 All E.R. 518, CA, where their lordships were agreed that the Barrell jurisdiction has survived the CPR, but were not agreed on the question whether the jurisdiction remains subject to the "exceptional circumstances" requirement as understood before the CPR came into effect; see also *Royal Brompton Hospital NHS Trust v Hammond* [2001] EWCA Civ 778.

In *Roche v Chief Constable of Greater Manchester Police* [2005] EWCA Civ 1454; *The Times*, November 10, 2005, CA, the Court of Appeal held that, where an order carrying into effect a judgment is perfected, in dealing with an appeal made on the basis that the judge failed to make findings on particular issues, the circumstances may be such as to make it appropriate for the appeal court to take into consideration a subsequent supplementary judgment by the judge dealing with those issues where that judgment did not in any way alter the perfected order, rather than to remit the matter for further consideration by the trial court (see Vol.1, para.40.2.1 above). In so holding that Court said that neither s.70, nor the general provisions about finality of judgment, precluded the Court from considering the second judgment in the course of this appeal.

Under rules of court which, on occasion, have been rather generously applied, clerical mistakes in judgments or orders or errors arising therein from any accidental slip or omission may at any time be corrected by the court (CPR r.40.12 and Practice Direction (Judgments and Orders), paras 4.1 *et seq.*, Vol.1, para.40BPD.4).

## Satisfaction of judgments and orders for payment of money

9A-559 **71.**—(1) Where a judgment is given or an order is made by a county court under which a sum of money of any amount is payable, whether by way of satisfaction of the claim or counterclaim in the proceedings or by way of costs or otherwise, the court may, as it thinks fit, order the money to be paid either—

(a) in one sum, whether forthwith or within such period as the court may fix; or

(b) by such instalments payable at such times as the court may fix.

(2) If at any time it appears to the satisfaction of the court that any party to any proceedings is unable from any cause to pay any sum recovered against him (whether by way of satisfaction of the claim or counterclaim in the proceedings or by way of costs or otherwise) or any instalment of such a sum, the court may, in its discretion, suspend or stay any judgment or order given or made in the proceedings for such time and on such terms as the court thinks fit, and so from time to time until it appears that the cause of inability has ceased.

### Satisfaction of judgments and orders for payment of money

9A-560 The general rule is that where judgment is given or an order is made for the payment of money, including costs, the money shall be payable at the expiration of 14 days from the date of the judgment or order (CPR r.40.11). Obviously, if a day for payment is specified in the judgment or order, then the money shall be payable on that date. The significance of subs.(1) is that it makes it clear that the court has power to order that a money judgment or order should be paid, not in a lump sum in 14 days or on a particular date, but by instalments. Subsection (2) gives the court power to suspend or stay a money judgment or order against a party, whether requiring payment in a lump sum or by instalments, where the court is satisfied that the party is unable to pay. For practice where payment by instalments is ordered, see Practice Direction (Judgments and Orders), para.12.

## Set-off in cases of cross judgments in county courts and High Court

9A-561 **72.**—(1) Where one person has obtained a judgment or order in a county court against another person, and that other person has obtained a judgment or order against the first-mentioned person in the same or in another county court or in the High Court, either such person may, in accordance with rules of court, give notice in writing to the court or the several courts as the case may be, and may apply to the court or any of the said courts in accordance with rules of court for leave to set off any sums, including costs, payable under several judgments or orders.

*Paragraph numbers marked with a "+" can be found online and on CD.*

(2) Upon any such application, the set-off may be allowed in accordance with the practice for the time being in force in the High Court as to the allowance of set-off and in particular in relation to any solicitor's lien for costs.

(3) Where the cross judgments or orders have not been obtained in the same court, a copy of the order made on any such application shall be sent by the proper officer of the court to which the application is made to the proper officer of the other court.

**Set-off in cases of cross judgments in county courts and High Court**

A set-off is a monetary cross-claim which is also a defence to the claim made in the action. The right of a party to plead a set-off avoids the need to commence a separate action for the purpose of asserting the claim. A party may plead a previous judgment as a set-off. (In these circumstances, unless the previous judgment is a foreign judgment, the alternative course of commencing a separate action does not exist). This section is concerned, not with the setting off of a previous judgment as a defence to a claim (see CPR r.16.6), but with such set-off against a judgment debt. **9A–562**

The section states that where, in the High Court or a county court, X has obtained judgment against Y and Y has obtained judgment against X in other proceedings, either in the same or a different county court or in the High Court, for a lesser sum, Y may apply for permission to set-off his judgment against X's judgment. The section requires Y to make application "to the court or any of the said courts in accordance with rules of court". It is necessary to be clear as to what these rules of court might be.

An order of the Supreme Court Costs Office requiring the Revenue to pay costs awarded to a duty payer by the VAT and Duties Tribunal is an order in the High Court to which s.72 applies; accordingly, it was open to the High Court to order that the Revenue's costs liability should be set off against the duty payer's liability to the Revenue under a county court judgment for unpaid tax and insurance contributions (*Revenue & Customs Commissioners v Xicom Systems Ltd* [2008] EWHC 1945 (Ch), September 4, 2008, unrep.).

Where the several judgments have been obtained in a county court, or several county courts, CPR Sch.2, O.22, r.11 applies and Y should make application to one of the relevant county courts in accordance with the provisions of that rule. That rule states that where X's judgment was obtained in one county court and Y's in another, Y may make application to either county court on notice (with notice also being given to the proper officer of the other county court) (r.11(3)). Where the several judgments were obtained in the same county court application should be made on notice to that court; however, if the application is made "on the day when the last judgment or order is obtained" notice is not required provided both parties are present (r.11(2)).

Where the several judgments have been obtained in the High Court it would seem that application must be made to the High Court but rules of court expressly dedicated to such applications are contained in the CPR. Accordingly, it seems that an application on notice pursuant to CPR Pt 23 is required (though by analogy with CPR Sch.2, CCR O.22, r.11(2), perhaps an application could be made without notice to the court "on the day when the last judgment or order is obtained" if both parties are present).

An anomaly still remains. Where X has obtained judgment against Y in a county court and Y has obtained judgment against X in the High Court for a lesser sum and Y wishes to apply for permission to set-off his High Court judgment against X's county court judgment, the provisions of CPR Sch.2, CCR O.22, r.11 do not apply. Prior to the CPR such applications were made to the High Court and were governed by RSC O.107, r.4. Order 107 is not replicated in the CPR. Consequently, the proper procedure is now a matter for doubt. As CPR Sch.2, CCR O.22, r.11 clearly does not apply it is submitted that application should be made to the High Court on notice pursuant to CPR Pt 23. CPR Sch.2, CCR O.22, r.11(8) clearly envisages such order being made in the High Court and directs the county court officer as to how he should proceed.

The section does not give a right to set-off (the application is for "leave" to do so). Section 72(2) expressly requires a county court to approach the application in accordance with the practice for the time being in force in the High Court and "in particular in relation to any solicitor's lien for costs".

An order of the Supreme Court Costs Office for the Revenue and Customs Commissioners to pay costs awarded to a taxpayer by the VAT and Duties Tribunal is an order in the High Court to which s.72 applies and it was open to the High Court to set-off the commissioners' liability to the taxpayer under the costs order against the taxpayer's liability to the commissioners under a county court judgment (*Revenue and Customs Commissioners v Ximon Systems Ltd* [2008] EWHC 1945 (Ch)).

* * * *

## Interest on judgment debts, etc.

9A-563 **74.**—(1) The Lord Chancellor may by order made with the concurrence of the Treasury provide that any sums to which this subsection applies shall carry interest at such rate and between such times as may be prescribed by the order.

(2) The sums to which subsection (1) applies are—

(a) sums payable under judgments or orders given or made in a county court, including sums payable by instalments; and

(b) sums which by virtue of any enactment are, if the county court so orders, recoverable as if payable under an order of that court, and in respect of which the county court has so ordered.

(3) The payment of interest due under subsection (1) shall be enforceable as a sum payable under the judgment or order.

(4) The power conferred by subsection (1) includes power—

(a) to specify the descriptions of judgment or order in respect of which interest shall be payable;

(b) to provide that interest shall be payable only on sums exceeding a specified amount;

(c) to make provision for the manner in which and the periods by reference to which the interest is to be calculated and paid;

(d) to provide that any enactment shall or shall not apply in relation to interest payable under subsection (1) or shall apply to it with such modifications as may be specified in the order; and

(e) to make such incidental or supplementary provisions as the Lord Chancellor considers appropriate.

(5) Without prejudice to the generality of subsection (4), an order under subsection (1) may provide that the rate of interest shall be the rate specified in section 17 of the Judgments Act 1838 as that enactment has effect from time to time.

(5A) The power conferred by subsection (1) includes power to make provision enabling a county court to order that the rate of interest applicable to a sum expressed in a currency other than sterling shall be such rate as the court thinks fit (instead of the rate otherwise applicable).

(6) The power to make an order under subsection (1) shall be exerciseable by statutory instrument subject to annulment in pursuance of a resolution of either House of Parliament.

*Note* —Subsection (5A) added by the Private International Law (Miscellaneous Provisions) Act 1995 s.2. **9A–564**

**Interest on judgment debts, etc.**

The County Court (Interest on Judgment Debts) Order 1991 (SI 1991/1184) (as amended) was made by the Lord Chancellor in exercise of powers conferred by this section. For rate of interest specified from time to time under the Judgments Act 1838 s.17; see further Vol.1, para.40.8.1, and note CPR rr.40.8, 44.12, 47.8 and 47.14. **9A–565**

Subsection (5A) was added by the Private International Law (Miscellaneous Provisions) Act 1995 s.2 and the additional powers granted by it were exercised in the 1996 amendment to the 1991 Order. For comparable provision to subs.(5A) applicable to High Court judgments, see the Administration of Justice Act 1970 s.44A (inserted by s.1 of the 1974 Act) (see para.9B–49+).

* * * *

## Application of practice of High Court

**76.** In any case not expressly provided for by or in pursuance of this Act, the general principles of practice in the High Court may be adopted and applied to proceedings in a county court. **9A–566**

**Application of practice of High Court**

This section says that the general principles of High Court practice may be adopted and applied to proceedings in a county court where there is, as it were, a "gap" in county court practice and procedure because the matter is "not expressly provided for by or in pursuance of this Act", that is to say, provided for by sections in the Act or in delegated legislation made under the Act, including, principally, rules of court. Before the CPR came into force, the CCR were made under s.75 of the Act (now omitted) and the rules found therein were significantly different in many respects to those found in the RSC and, generally, much simpler. In these circumstances, s.76 was occasionally brought into play to deal with "gaps" apparent in the CCR. CCR O.1, r.6 said that where by virtue of s.76 provisions of the RSC were applied in relation to proceedings in a county court, that provision "shall have effect with the necessary modifications". The CPR govern county court and High Court proceedings and, in the main, the procedures for both levels of court are the same. Nevertheless, some differences do remain and this leaves open the possibility that "gaps" in county court practice will continue to emerge and that s.76 may still have a role to play (e.g. *Ager v Ager* [1998] 1 W.L.R. 1074, CA, where it was held that the jurisdiction conferred on the High Court by the Senior Courts Act 1981 s.15(4) could be conferred on county courts by operation of s.76). Further, there remains the possibility that, in county court proceedings to which rules in Sch.2 of the CPR apply (viz., former CCR rules), rules in Sch.1 (viz., former RSC rules) may be applied by operation of s.76. This prospect is specifically acknowledged by CCR O.1, r.6 (referred to above) which has survived in the CPR as one of the "schedule rules" (see Vol.1, para.cc1.6) (see *Jephson Homes Housing Association Ltd v Moisejevs* [2001] 2 All E.R. 901, CA, application to set aside warrant for possession). **9A–567**



# PART IV

# APPEALS ETC.

### *APPEALS*

## Appeals: general provisions

**77.**—(1) Subject to the provisions of this section and the following provisions of this Part of this Act, and to any order made by the Lord **9A–568**

Chancellor under section 56(1) of the Access to Justice Act 1999, if any party to any proceedings in a county court is dissatisfied with the determination of the judge or jury, he may appeal from it to the Court of Appeal in such manner and subject to such conditions as may be provided by Civil Procedure Rules.

(1A) Without prejudice to the generality of the power to make rules of court under section 75, such rules may make provision for any appeal from the exercise by a district judge, assistant district judge or deputy district judge of any power given to him by virtue of any enactment to be to a judge of a county court.

(2) [...]

(3) [...]

(4) [...]

(5) Subject to the provision of this section and the following provisions of this Part of this Act, where an appeal is brought under subsection (1) in any action, an appeal may be brought under that subsection in respect of any claim or counterclaim in the action notwithstanding that there could have been no such appeal if that claim had been the subject of a separate action.

(6) In proceedings in which either the plaintiff or the defendant is claiming possession of any premises this section shall not confer any right of appeal on any question of fact if by virtue of—

(a) section 13(4) of the Landlord and Tenant Act 1954; or

(b) Cases III to IX in Schedule 4 to the Rent (Agriculture) Act 1976; or

(c) section 98 of the Rent Act 1977, as it applies to Cases 1 to 6 and 8 and 9 and Schedule 15 to that Act, or that section as extended or applied by any other enactment; or

(d) section 69 of the Rent Act 1977, as it applies to Cases 1 to 6 and 9 in Schedule 15 to that Act; or

(e) section 84(2)(a) of the Housing Act 1985; or

(ee) section 7 of the Housing Act 1988, as it applies to the grounds in Part II of Schedule 2 to that Act; or

(f) any other enactment,

the court can only grant possession on being satisfied that it is reasonable to do so.

(7) This section shall not—

(a) confer any right of appeal from any judgment or order where a right of appeal is conferred by some other enactment; or

(b) take away any right of appeal from any judgment or order where a right of appeal is so conferred,

and shall have effect subject to any enactment other than this Act.

(8) In this section—

"enactment" means an enactment whenever passed;

9A–569 *Note* —Amended the by Housing (Consequential Provisions) Act 1985 Sch.2, para.57(2); the Housing Act 1988 Sch.17, para.35(2); the Civil Procedure Act 1997 Sch.2.; the Access to Justice (Destination of Appeals) Order 2000 (SI 2000/1071).

Subsection (1A) added by the Courts and Legal Services Act 1990 Sch.17, para.15. Subsections (2) to (4) repealed by, and subs.(8) amended by, the Access to Justice Act 1999 Sch.15, Pt III. Section 75, referred to in subs.(1A) of this section, was repealed by the Civil Procedure Act 1997 Sch.2, para.2(6).

**Appeal from county court determination to Court of Appeal**

The procedural rules relating to the proper routes for appeals from decisions made in proceedings in a county court, whether to the Court of Appeal or to some other forum, are complicated. In Sect.I of Practice Direction (Appeals), supplementing CPR Pt 52, an effort is made to summarise the position in tabular form. **9A–570**

The Court of Appeal has all such jurisdiction as is conferred on it by the Senior Courts Act 1981 or any other Act, including the County Courts Act 1984 (Senior Courts Act 1981 s.15(2), see para.9A–49 above). Section 77(1) of the 1984 Act states that the general rule is that any party to any proceedings in a county court who is "dissatisfied with the determination of the judge or jury" may appeal from it to the Court of Appeal (see para.9A–568 below). This general rule is subject to the provisions of paras (1A) *et seq.* of s.77 (which, amongst other things, provide for appeals from a district judge to a judge of a county court) and other provisions in Pt IV of the 1984 Act. The general rule is further qualified by the Access to Justice Act 1999. Section 56(1) of that Act states that the Lord Chancellor may by order provide that appeals "which would otherwise lie to the Court of Appeal", for example, appeals falling within the general rule stated above, shall lie instead to the High Court or to a county court (see para.9A–845 below). Accordingly, the power of the Lord Chancellor by order to affect the jurisdiction of the Court of Appeal in relation to appeals from the High Court was added to s.77(1) by the Access to Justice Act 1999 (Destination of Appeals) Order 2000 (SI 2000/1071) art.7. Provisions exercising this power in relation to appeals to the Court of Appeal from a county court are found in arts 3, 4 and 5 of that statutory instrument. art.3(1) states that, subject to two exceptions, an appeal from a decision of a county court shall not go according to the general rule (i.e. from a county court to the Court of Appeal) but shall go to the High Court. And art.3(2) states that, subject to the same exceptions, where the decision to be appealed is a decision made by a district judge, the appeal shall go to a judge of a county court. In this context, "decision" includes any judgment, order or direction. The two exceptions are (1) where the decision is a final decision made in a mercantile claim dealt with in a county court (art.4(b), note also the exception provided for by 4(a)); and (2) where the decision appealed was itself a decision made on appeal (other than from the decision of an officer of the court authorised to assess costs) (so-called "second appeals") (see art.5). In this context, "final decision" means any decision that would finally determine (subject to any possible appeal or detailed assessment of costs) the entire proceedings whichever way the court decided the issues before it (*ibid.* art.(2)(c)).

No appeal shall lie to the Court of Appeal: (1) from any order, judgment or decision of a county court which is final, or (2) from any order of a county court allowing an extension of time for appealing from a judgment or order (paras (b) and (c) of s.18(1); see para.9A–62 below).

For rules of court affecting appeals from a county court to the Court of Appeal, see CPR Pt 52, and for further information as to the jurisdiction of the Court of Appeal in relation to appeals from a county court, see notes on the rules in Pt 52 (Vol.1, paras 52.0.1 *et seq.*).

**For s.78 of the County Courts Act 1984 (see Arrangement) plus any related commentary see paragraph 9A–571+ on White Book on Westlaw UK or the Civil Procedure CD.**

## Agreement not to appeal

**79.**—(1) No appeal shall lie from any judgment, direction, decision or order of a judge of county courts if, before the judgment, direction, decision or order is given or made, the parties agree, in writing signed by themselves or their legal representatives or agents, that it shall be final. **9A–572**

(2) [...]

***Paragraph numbers marked with a "+" can be found online and on CD.***

9A-573 *Note*—Amended by the Courts and Legal Services Act 1990 s.125(3) and Sch.18, para.49(3); and the Statute Law (Repeals) Act 1986 Sch.1.

## Judge's note on appeal

9A-574 **80.**—(1) At the hearing of any proceedings in a county court in which there is a right of appeal or from which an appeal may be brought with leave, the judge shall, at the request of any party, make a note—

(a) of any question of law raised at the hearing; and

(b) of the facts in evidence in relation to any such question; and

(c) of his decision on any such question and of his determination of the proceedings.

(2) Where such a note has been taken, the judge shall (whether notice of appeal has been served or not), on the application of any party to the proceedings, and on payment by that party of such fee as may be prescribed by an order under section 92 of the Courts Act 2003 (fees), furnish him with a copy of the note, and shall sign the copy, and the copy so signed shall be used at the hearing of the appeal.

9A-575 *Note*—Subsection (2) amended by the Courts Act 2003 s.109(1), Sch.8, para.271(b).

### Judge's note in small claim

9A-576 Practice Direction (Small Claims Track), para.5.1 *et seq.* provides for the recording of evidence and the giving of reasons. Nothing in that direction affects the duty of the judge under s.80 (*ibid.* para.5.8, see Vol.1, para.27PD.5).

## Powers of Court of Appeal on appeal from county court

9A-577 **81.**—(1) On the hearing of an appeal, the Court of Appeal may draw any inference of fact and either—

(a) order a new trial on such terms as the court thinks just; or

(b) order judgment to be entered for any party; or

(c) make a final or other order on such terms as the court thinks proper to ensure the determination on the merits of the real question in controversy between the parties.

(2) Subject to Civil Procedure Rules on any appeal from a county court the Court of Appeal may reverse or vary, in favour of a party seeking to support the judgment or order of the county court in whole or in part, any determinations made in the county court on questions of fact, notwithstanding that the appeal is an appeal on a point of law only, or any such determinations on points of law, notwithstanding that the appeal is an appeal on a question of fact only.

(3) Subsection (2) shall not enable the Court of Appeal to reverse or vary any determination, unless the party dissatisfied with the determination would have been entitled to appeal in respect of it if aggrieved by the judgment or order.

9A-578 *Note*—Amended by the Civil Procedure Act 1997 Sch.2.

## Decision of Court of Appeal on probate appeals to be final

**82.** No appeal shall lie from the decision of the Court of Appeal on any appeal from a county court in any probate proceedings. **9A–579**

*CERTIORARI AND PROHIBITION*

## Stay of proceedings in case of certiorari or prohibition

**83.**—(1) The grant by the High Court of leave to make an application for an order of certiorari or prohibition to a county court shall, if the High Court so directs, operate as a stay of the proceedings in question until the determination of the application, or until the High Court otherwise orders. **9A–580**

(2) Where any proceedings are so stayed, the judge of the county court shall from time to time adjourn the hearing of the proceedings to such day as he thinks fit.

## Prohibition

**84.**—(1) Where an application is made to the High Court for an order or prohibition addressed to any county court, the matter shall be finally disposed of by order. **9A–581**

(2) Upon any such application, the judge of the county court shall not be served with notice of it, and shall not, except by the order of a judge of the High Court—

(a) be required to appear or be heard; or

(b) be liable to any order for the payment of the costs of the application;

but the application shall be proceeded with and hear in the same manner in all respects as an appeal duly brought from a decision of the judge, and notice of the application shall be given to or served upon the same parties as in the case of an order made or refused by a judge in a matter within his jurisdiction.

# PART V

## ENFORCEMENT OF JUDGMENTS AND ORDERS

*EXECUTION AGAINST GOODS*

## Execution of judgments or orders for payment of money

**85.**—(1) Subject to Article 8 of the High Court and County Courts Jurisdiction Order 1991, any sum of money payable under a judgment or order of a county court may be recovered, in case of default or failure of payment, forthwith or at the time or times and in the manner thereby directed, by execution against the goods of the party against whom the judgment or order was obtained. **9A–582**

(2) The district judge, on the application of the party prosecuting any such judgment or order, shall issue a warrant of execution in the nature of a writ of *fieri facias* whereby the district judge shall be

MAIN STATUTES

empowered to levy or cause to be levied by distress and sale of the goods, wherever they may be found within the district of the court, the money payable under the judgment or order and the costs of the execution.

(3) The precise time of the making of the application to the district judge to issue such a warrant shall be entered by him in the record prescribed for the purpose under section 12 and on the warrant.

(4) It shall be the duty of every constable within his jurisdiction to assist in the execution of every such warrant.

#### Execution of judgments or orders for payment of money

9A–583 Execution by means of a warrant of execution is one of the principal means of enforcing a judgment. Important procedural rules are contained in CPR Sch.2, CCR O.25 and O.26. Broadly speaking, a warrant of execution in a county court is the equivalent of a writ of *fieri facias* in the High Court. Warrants in the county court are executed by county court bailiffs.

Section 85 imposes certain functions on the "registrar", an office now abolished by s.74 of the Courts and Legal Services Act 1990 and replaced by the district judge. By CPR Sch.2, CCR O.26, r.1(1A) these functions are now discharged by the "court officer".

The "precise time" referred to in s.85(3) is important for establishing priority of warrants (see also s.99, below).

Article 8 of the 1991 Order imposes restrictions on the circumstances in which a judgment or order of a county court for the payment of a sum of money which it is sought to enforce wholly or partly by execution against goods may be enforced in the High Court (see para. 9B–939 below). Coinciding with the substitution of CPR r.70.5 (Enforcement of decisions of bodies other than the High Court and county courts and compromises enforceable by enactment) by SI 2008/3327, significant amendments to art.8 were made by SI 2009/577.

### Execution of orders for payment by instalments

9A–584 **86.**—(1) Where the court has made an order for payment of any sum of money by instalments, execution on the order shall not be issued until after default in payment of some instalment according to the order.

(2) Rules of court may prescribe the cases in which execution is to issue if there is any such default and limit the amounts for which and the times at which execution may issue.

(3) Except so far as may be otherwise provided by county court rules made for those purposes, execution or successive executions may issue if there is any such default for the whole of the said sum of money and costs then remaining unpaid or for such part as the court may order either at the time of the original order or at any subsequent time; but except so far as may be otherwise provided by such rules, no execution shall issue unless at the time when it issues the whole or some part of an instalment which has already become due remains unpaid.

9A–585 *Note*—Amended by the Civil Procedure Act 1997 Sch.2, para.2(2).

#### Execution of orders for payment by instalments

9A–586 A county court has power under s.71 to order a sum of money payable under a judgment to be paid by instalments. In such cases warrants of execution may only be granted on default of the instalment order. The judgment creditor can issue a warrant

***Paragraph numbers marked with a "+" can be found online and on CD.***

for the whole or part of the debt (CPR Sch.2, CCR O.26, r.1(2)). The minimum sum for which a warrant may be issued is £50, or the amount of one monthly instalment or four weekly instalments, whichever is greater. See generally, CPR Sch.2, CCR O.26 and commentary to CPR Sch.2, CCR O.26, r.11 on suspension of part warrants.

In *Ropaigealach v Allied Irish Bank Plc* [2001] EWCA Civ 1790; November 12, 2001, CA, unrep., an instalment order had been made and the Court held that, for the purposes of s.86, "execution" by charging order is "issued" when it is issued nisi. As, in this case, the order nisi had been obtained before the instalment order was made, the court had jurisdiction to make the charging order absolute. The Court explained that the existence of an instalment order is one of the circumstances to be considered by the court in exercising its discretion. In many circumstances it may be entirely sensible and satisfactory from both parties' points of view for an instalment order and an order absolute to co-exist, particularly where a long-running instalment order is made.

## Execution to be superseded on payment

**87.**—(1) In or upon every warrant of execution issued from a county court against the goods of any person, the district judge shall cause to be inserted or indorsed the total amount to be levied, inclusive of the fee for issuing the warrant but exclusive of the fees for its execution. **9A-587**

(2) If the person against whom the execution is issued, before the actual sale of the goods, pays or causes to be paid or tendered to the district judge of the court from which the warrant is issued, or to the bailiff holding the warrant, the amount inserted in, or indorsed upon, the warrant under subsection (1), or such part as the person entitled agrees to accept in full satisfaction, together with the amount stated by the officer of the court to whom the payment or tender is made to be the amount of the fees for the execution of the warrant, the execution shall be superseded, and the goods shall be discharged and set at liberty.

### Execution to be superseded on payment

This section states the obvious rule that the warrant of execution is to be superseded on payment of the amount for which the warrant is issued or such other sum as the judgment creditor accepts in full satisfaction of the warrant. Indeed sales under warrants of execution (see ss.93—98) follow only a small proportion of warrants issued. **9A-588**

## Power to stay execution

**88.** If at any time it appears to the satisfaction of the court that any party to any proceedings is unable from any cause to pay any sum recovered against him (whether by way of satisfaction of the claim or counterclaim in the proceedings or by way of costs or otherwise), or any instalment of such a sum, the court may, in its discretion, stay any execution issued in the proceedings for such time and on such terms as the court thinks fit and so from time to time it appears that the cause of inability has ceased. **9A-589**

### Power to stay execution

The district judge exercises the jurisdiction to stay execution of warrants (CPR Sch.2, CCR O.25, r.8). See also s.71(2) for a similar provision on suspension and stay of judgments. **9A-590**

*Seizure and Custody of Goods, etc.*

## Goods which may be seized

**89.**—(1) Every bailiff or officer executing any warrant of execution **9A-591**

issued from a county court against the goods of any person may by virtue of it seize—

(a) any of that person's goods except—

(i) such tools, books, vehicles and other items of equipment as are necessary to that person for use personally by him in his employment, business or vocation;

(ii) such clothing, bedding, furniture, household equipment and provisions as are necessary for satisfying the basic domestic needs of that person and his family;

(b) any money, banknotes, bills of exchange, promissory notes, bonds, specialties or securities for money belonging to that person.

(2) Any reference to the goods of an execution debtor in this Part of this Act includes a reference to anything else of his that may lawfully be seized in execution.

(3) [...]

**9A-592** *Note* —Amended by the Courts and Legal Services Act 1990 ss.15 and 125(7), Sch.20.

**Goods which may be seized**

**9A-593** This section permits execution against the judgment debtor's "goods" and money, etc., but exempts certain goods from subjection to execution. See the detailed commentary to CPR Sch.1, RSC O.45.

For the device of "walking possession" see commentary to s.90, below.

## Custody of goods seized

**9A-594** **90.** Goods seized in execution under process of a county court shall, until sale—

(a) be deposited by the bailiff in some fit place; or

(b) remain in the custody of a fit person approved by the district judge to be put in possession by the bailiff; or

(c) be safeguarded in such other manner as the district judge directs.

**Custody of goods seized**

**9A-595** If goods are actually removed they must be deposited in a "fit place" such as a warehouse or compound. An inventory must be made and notice of the time and place of the sale served on the judgment debtor (CPR Sch.2, CCR O.26, r.12).

To avoid some of the administrative inconvenience of actual removal, the device of "walking possession" is frequently used whereby the judgment debtor signs an agreement that in consideration of the bailiff not removing the goods, the judgment debtor undertakes not to remove the goods and agrees that the bailiff may re-enter, using force if necessary, at any time to seize the goods.

## Disposal of bills of exchange, etc., seized

**9A-596** **91.** The district judge shall hold any bills of exchange, promissory notes, bonds, specialties or other securities for money seized in execution under process of a county court as security for the amount directed to be levied by the execution, or for so much of that amount as has not been otherwise levied or raised, for the benefit of the plaintiff, and the plaintiff may sue in the name of the defendant, or in the name of any person in whose name the defendant might have sued, for the recovery of the sum secured or made payable thereby, when the time of payment arrives.

**Disposal of bills of exchange, etc., seized**

A "bill of exchange" includes a cheque (see the Bills of Exchange Act 1882 s.73). **9A–597**

## Penalty for rescuing goods seized

**92.**—(1) If any person rescues or attempts to rescue any goods seized in execution under process of a county court, he shall be liable— **9A–598**

(a) on summary conviction, to imprisonment for a term not exceeding one month or to a fine of an amount not exceeding level 4 on the standard scale, or both; or

(b) on an order made by the judge in that behalf, to be committed for a specified period not exceeding one month to prison or to a fine of an amount not exceeding level 4 on the standard scale or to be so committed and to such a fine,

and a bailiff of the court may take the offender into custody, with or without warrant, and bring him before the judge.

(2) The judge may at any time revoke an order committing a person to prison under this section and, if he is already in custody, order his discharge.

*Note*—Amended by the Statute Law (Repeals) Act 1986. **9A–599**

**Penalty for rescuing goods seized**

This section enables the county court to punish any person who rescues or attempts to rescue goods seized in execution. Compare s.14. The procedure is the same under ss.14 and 92 (see CPR Sch.2, CCR O.34, r.1). **9A–600**

The "standard scale" is provided for by s.37 of the Criminal Justice Act 1982. Level 4 is currently £2,500.

### *SALE OF GOODS SEIZED*

## Period to elapse before sale

**93.** No goods seized in execution under process of a county court shall be sold for the purpose of satisfying the warrant of execution until the expiration of a period of at least 5 days next following the day on which the goods have been so seized unless— **9A–601**

(a) the goods are of a perishable nature; or

(b) the person whose goods have been seized so requests in writing.

## Goods not to be sold except by brokers or appraisers

**94.** No goods seized in execution under process of a county court shall be sold for the purpose of satisfying the warrant of execution except by one of the brokers or appraisers appointed under this Part of this Act. **9A–602**

*Paragraph numbers marked with a "+" can be found online and on CD.*

## Appointment of brokers, appraisers, etc.

9A-603 **95.**—(1) The registrar may from time to time as he thinks fit appoint such number of persons for keeping possession, and such number of brokers and appraisers for the purpose of selling or valuing any goods seized in execution under process of the court, as appears to him to be necessary.

(2) The registrar may direct security to be taken from any broker, appraiser or other person so appointed for such sum and in such manner as he thinks fit for the faithful performance of his duties without injury or oppression.

(3) The judge or registrar may dismiss any broker, appraiser or other person so appointed.

(4) There shall be payable to brokers and appraisers so appointed in respect of their duties, out of the produce of goods distrained or sold, such fees as may be prescribed by an order under section 92 of the Courts Act 2003 (fees).

9A-604 *Note*—Subsection (4) amended by the Courts Act 2003 s.109(1), Sch.8, para.271(c).

#### Registrar

9A-605 By the Courts and Legal Services Act 1990 s.74, the office of registrar became that of district judge and references in any enactment to "registrar" are to be construed as a reference to that office in its new name.

## Power to appoint bailiffs to act as brokers and appraisers

9A-606 **96.**—(1) The judge may appoint in writing any bailiff of the court to act as a broker or appraiser for the purpose of selling or valuing any goods seized in execution under process of the court.

(2) A bailiff so appointed may, without other licence in that behalf, perform all the duties which brokers or appraisers appointed under section 95 may perform under this Act.

## Sales under executions to be public unless otherwise ordered

9A-607 **97.**—(1) Where any goods are to be sold under execution for a sum exceeding £20 (including legal incidental expenses), the sale shall, unless the court from which the warrant of execution issued otherwise orders, be made by public auction and not by bill of sale or private contract, and shall be publicly advertised by the registrar on, and during 3 days next preceding, the day of sale.

(2) Where any goods are seized in execution and the registrar has notice of another execution or other executions, the court shall not consider an application for leave to sell privately until the prescribed notice has been given to the other execution creditor or creditors, who may appear before the court and be heard upon the application.

#### Sales under executions to be public unless otherwise ordered

9A-608 See generally CPR Sch.2, CCR O.26, and in particular, rr.12, 13 and 15. Where goods are sold under an execution, the proper officer shall furnish the debtor with a detailed account in writing of the sale and of the application of the proceeds (see CPR Sch.2, CCR O.26, r.13).

***Paragraph numbers marked with a "+" can be found online and on CD.***

A sale not in conformity with s.97 will be voidable rather than void (*Crawshaw v Harrison* [1894] 1 Q.B. 79; (1893) L.J.Q.B. 94).

## Protection of district judge selling goods under execution without notice of claim by third party

**98.**—(1) Where any goods in the possession of an execution debtor at the time of seizure by a district judge or other officer charged with the enforcement of a warrant or other process of execution issued from a county court are sold by that district judge or other officer without any claims having been made to them— **9A–609**

(a) the purchaser of the goods so sold shall acquire a good title to those goods; and

(b) no person shall be entitled to recover against the district judge or other officer, or anyone lawfully acting under his authority—

(i) for any sale of the goods, or

(ii) for paying over the proceeds prior to the receipt of a claim to the goods,

unless it is proved that the person from whom recovery is sought had notice, or might by making reasonable inquiry have ascertained, that the goods were not the property of the execution debtor.

(2) Nothing in this section shall affect the right of any claimant, who may prove that at the time of sale he had a title to any goods so seized and sold, to any remedy to which he may be entitled against any person other than the district judge or other officer.

(3) The provisions of this section have effect subject to those of sections 183, 184 and 346 of the Insolvency Act 1986.

*Note* —Subsection (3) substituted by the Insolvency Act 1986 s.439(2), Sch.14; subs.(1)(b) substituted by the Courts Act 2003 s.109(1), Sch.8, para.273. **9A–610**

**Protection of district judge selling goods under execution without notice of claim by third party**

For the anomalous position of the district judge in relation to execution, see the commentary to s.123, below. In the county court the "high bailiff" (i.e. nowadays, the district judge) has the same liabilities as the sheriff in the High Court. **9A–611**

Section 98 protects the district judge in the same way as s.138B of the SCA 1981 protects the sheriff.

### *CLAIMS IN RESPECT OF GOODS SEIZED*

## Effects of warrants of execution

**99.**—(1) Subject **9A–612**

(a) to subsection (2); and

(b) to section 103(2),

a warrant of execution against goods issued from a county court shall bind the property in the goods of the execution debtor as from the time at which application for the warrant was made to the district judge of the county court.

(2) Such a warrant shall not prejudice the title to any goods of the execution debtor acquired by a person in good faith and for valuable consideration unless he had at the time when he acquired his title—

*Paragraph numbers marked with a "+" can be found online and on CD.*

MAIN STATUTES

(a) notice that an application for the issue of a warrant of execution against the goods of the execution debtor had been made to the district judge or a county court and that the warrant issued on the application either—

(i) remained unexecuted in the hands of the district judge of the court from which it was issued; or

(ii) had been sent for execution to, and received by, the district judge of another county court, and remained unexecuted in the hands of the district judge of that court; or

(b) notice that a writ of fieri facias or other writ of execution by virtue of which the goods of the execution debtor might be seized or attached had been delivered to an enforcement officer or other officer charged with the execution of the writ and remained unexecuted in the hands of that person.

(3) It shall be the duty of the district judge (without fee) on application for a warrant of execution being made to him to endorse on its back the hour, day, month and year when he received the application.

(4) For the purposes of this section—

(za) "enforcement officer" means an individual who is authorised to act as an enforcement officer under the Courts Act 2003;

(a) "property" means the general property in goods, and not merely a special property;

(b) [...]

(c) a thing shall be treated as done in good faith if it is in fact done honestly whether it is done negligently or not.

**Effects of warrants of execution**

9A–613 This section corresponds with s.138 of the SCA 1981 (see commentary thereto) which replaced the only section in the Sale of Goods Act 1893 not consolidated into the Sale of Goods Act 1979 because it belonged in a statute concerned with the administration of justice.

In *Woodland v Fuller* (1840) 11 Ad. & El. 859; [1835–42] All E.R. Rep. 343, it was held that where goods are sold, the phrase "binds the property in goods" does not prevent the property from passing but constitutes the execution of a charge on the goods.

See also s.103(2) which deals with execution of warrants outside the jurisdiction of the issuing court.

With effect from March 15, 2004, subsections (2)(b) and (4) were amended by the Courts Act 2003 s.109(1) and Sch.8, para.274(3)(a).

## Sale of goods to which claim is made

9A–614 **100.**—(1) Where a claim is made to or in respect of any goods seized in execution under process of a county court, the claimant may—

(a) deposit with the bailiff either—

(i) the amount of the value of the goods claimed; or

(ii) the sum which the bailiff is allowed to charge as

*Paragraph numbers marked with a "+" can be found online and on CD.*

costs for keeping possession of the goods until the decision of the judge can be obtained on the claim; or

(b) give the bailiff in the prescribed manner security for the value of the goods claimed.

(2) For the purpose of this section, the amount of the value of the goods claimed shall, in the case of dispute, be fixed by appraisement, and where that amount is deposited it shall be paid by the bailiff into court to abide the decision of the judge upon the claim.

(3) Subject to subsection (4), in default of the claimant's complying with this section, the bailiff shall sell the goods as if no such claim had been made, and shall pay into court the proceeds of the sale to abide the decision of the judge.

(4) The goods shall not be sold if the district judge decides that, in all the circumstances, the decision of the judge on the claim made to or in respect of them ought to be awaited.

#### Sale of goods to which claim is made

This section is concerned with situations where there is a dispute as to title to the goods and spells out the action required of the person claiming the goods. Disputes will usually be resolved by interpleader proceedings. See generally CPR Sch.2, CCR O.33 and commentary thereto and s.101, below. **9A-615**

## Interpleader by district judge

**101.**—(1) If a claim is made to or in respect of any goods seized in execution under process of a county court, or in respect of the proceeds or value of any such goods, the district judge may, as well before as after any action brought against him, issue a summons calling before the court the party at whose instance the process issued and the party making the claim. **9A-616**

(2) Upon the issue of the summons, any action brought in any county court or other court in respect of the claim or of any damage arising out of the execution of the warrant shall be stayed.

(3) On the hearing of the summons, the judge shall adjudicate upon the claim, and shall also adjudicate between the parties or either of them and the district judge upon any claim to damages arising or capable of arising out of the execution of the warrant by the district judge, and shall make such order in respect of any such claim and the costs of the proceedings as he thinks fit.

#### Interpleader by district judge

Interpleader is a process for determining rival claims to goods. This section enables the circuit judge (not the district judge) to adjudicate upon the rival claims where the goods have been seized in execution. The procedure is governed by CPR Sch.2, CCR O.33 (see commentary thereto). The district judge cannot determine an interpleader relating to execution in the county court (*cf.* the High Court; see CPR Sch.1, RSC O.17) because of his anomalous position as "high bailiff" (see commentary to s.123, below). **9A-617**

MAIN STATUTES

## Claims for rent where goods seized in execution

**102.**—(1) Section 1 of the Landlord and Tenant Act 1709 shall not apply to goods seized in execution under process of a county court, but the following provisions of this section shall apply in substitution. **9A-618**

(2) The landlord of any tenement in which any goods are seized may claim the rent of the tenement in arrear at the date of the seizure, at any time within the 5 days next following that date, or before the removal of the goods, by delivering to the bailiff or officer making the levy a claim in writing, signed by himself or his agent, stating—

(a) the amount of rent claimed to be in arrear; and

(b) the period in respect of which the rent is due.

(3) Where such a claim is made, the bailiff or officer making the levy shall in addition distrain for the rent so claimed and the cost of the distress, and shall not, within 5 days next after the distress, sell any part of the goods seized, unless—

(a) the goods are of a perishable nature; or

(b) the person whose goods have been seized so requests in writing.

(4) The bailiff shall afterwards sell under the execution and distress such of the goods as will satisfy—

(a) first, the costs of and incidental to the sale;

(b) next, the claim of the landlord not exceeding—

(i) in a case where the tenement is let by the week, 4 weeks' rent;

(ii) in a case where the tenement is let for any other term less than a year, the rent of two terms of payment;

(iii) in any other case, one year's rent; and

(5) If any replevin is made of the goods seized, the bailiff shall nevertheless sell such portion of them as will satisfy the costs of and incidental to the sale under the execution and the amount for which the warrant of execution issued.

(6) In any event the surplus of the sale, if any, and the residue of the goods shall be returned to the execution debtor.

(7) The fees of the district judge and broker for keeping possession, appraisement and sale under any such distress shall be the same as would have been payable if the distress had been an execution of the court, and no other fees shall be demanded or taken in respect thereof.

(8) Nothing in this section affects section 346 of the Insolvency Act 1986.

**9A–619** *Note*—Subsection (8) substituted by the Insolvency Act 1986 s.439(2), Sch.14.

### Claims for rent where goods seized in execution

**9A–620** Subsection (8) of this section refers to s.346 of the Insolvency Act 1986 but this is clearly an error and should be a reference to s.347 which is titled "Distress, etc.".

Sections 6 and 7 of the Landlord and Tenant Act 1709 should be distinguished from s.1 of that Act. The former apply only to cases *between* landlord and tenant, whereas s.1 applies in other cases. Section 102(2) to (8) of the County Courts Act 1984 applies only in substitution for s.1 of the 1709 Act.

On replevin see s.144 and Sch.1, below.

*EXECUTION OUT OF JURISDICTION OF COURT*

## Execution out of jurisdiction of court

**9A–621** **103.**—(1) Where a warrant of execution has been issued from a county court (hereafter in this section referred to as a "home court") against the goods of any person and the goods are out of the jurisdiction of that court, the district judge of that court may send the warrant of execution to the district judge of any other county court within the jurisdiction of which the goods are or are believed to be, with a warrant endorsed on it or annexed to it requiring execution of the original warrant.

(2) The original warrant shall bind the property in goods of the execution debtor which are within the jurisdiction of the court to which it is sent as from the time when it is received by the district judge of that court.

(3) It shall be the duty of the district judge of the court to which the warrant is sent (without fee) on receipt of the warrant to endorse on its back the hour, day, month and year when he received it.

(4) On the receipt of the warrant, the district judge of the other county court shall act in all respects as if the original warrant of execution had been issued by the court of which he is district judge and shall within the prescribed time—

(a) report to the district judge of the home court what he has done in the execution of the warrant; and

(b) pay over all moneys received in pursuance of the warrant.

(5) Where a warrant of execution is sent by the district judge of a home court to the district judge of another court for execution under this section, that other court shall have the same power as the home court of staying the execution under section 88 as respects any goods within the jurisdiction of that other court.

(6) Rules of court may make provision for the suspension of any judgment or order, on terms, in connection with any warrant issued with respect to any instalment payable under the judgment or order.

*Note* —Subsection (6) added by the Courts and Legal Services Act 1990 s.125(2), Sch.17, para.16. Amended by the Civil Procedure Act 1997 Sch.2, para.2(2). **9A–622**

**Execution out of jurisdiction of court**

The judge of one county court has no authority to order execution in the area of another county court because the jurisdiction of county courts is limited geographically. This section overcomes the difficulties this presents by adopting a procedure of reciprocal enforcement between county courts. **9A–623**

The functions of the district judge under s.103 are discharged by the "court officer" pursuant to CPR Sch.2, CCR O.26, r.1(1A).

## Information as to writs and warrants of execution

**104.**—(1) Where a writ against the goods of any person issued from the High Court is delivered to an enforcement officer who is under a duty to execute the writ or to a sheriff, then on demand from the district judge of a county court that person shall— **9A–624**

(a) in the case of an enforcement officer, by writing signed by that officer or a person acting under his authority, and

(b) in the case of a sheriff, by writing signed by any clerk in the officer of the under-sheriff, inform the district judge of the precise time the writ was delivered to him.

(2) A bailiff of a county court shall on demand show his warrant to any enforcement officer, any person acting under the authority of an enforcement officer and any sheriff's officer.

(3) Any writing purporting to be signed as mentioned in subsection (1) and the endorsement on any warrant issued from a county court shall respectively be sufficient justification to any district judge, or enforcement officer or sheriff, acting on it.

(4) In this section "enforcement officer" means an individual who is authorised to act as an enforcement officer under the Courts Act 2003.

#### Information as to writs and warrants of execution

9A–625 The purpose of this section is to facilitate the exchange of information concerning the enforcement of judgments between county courts and the High Court. This section was substituted by the Courts Act 2003 s.109(1) and Sch.8, para.275, with effect from March 15, 2004.

* * * *

*RECEIVERS AND ATTACHMENT OF DEBTS*

### Receivers

9A–626 **107.**—(1) The power of the county court to appoint a receiver by way of equitable execution shall operate in relation to all legal estates and interests in land.

(2) The said power may be exercised in relation to an estate or interest in land whether or not a charge has been imposed on that land under section 1 of the Charging Orders Act 1979 for the purpose of enforcing the judgment, decree, order or award in question, and the said power shall be in addition to and not in derogation of any power of any court to appoint a receiver in proceedings for enforcing such a charge.

(3) Where an order under section 1 of the Charging Orders Act 1979 imposing a charge for the purpose of enforcing a judgment, decree, order or award has been registered under section 6 of the Land Charges Act 1972, subsection (4) of that section (which provides that, amongst other things, an order appointing a receiver and any proceedings pursuant to the order or in obedience to it, shall be void against a purchaser unless the order is for the time being registered under that section) shall not apply to an order appointing a receiver made either in proceedings for enforcing the charge or by way of equitable execution of the judgment, decree, order or award or, as the case may be, of so much of it as requires payment of moneys secured by the charge.

#### Receivers

9A–627 The procedure for the appointment of a receiver is governed by CPR Pt 69 (Court's Power to Appoint Receiver).

### Attachment of debts

9A–628 **108.**—(1) Subject to any order for the time being in force under subsection (4), this section applies to any deposit account, and any withdrawable share account, with a deposit-taker.

(2) In determining whether, for the purposes of the jurisdiction of the county court to attach debts for the purpose of satisfying judgments or orders for the payment of money, a sum standing to the credit of a person in an account to which this section applies is a sum due or accruing to that person and, as such, attachable in accordance with rules of court, any condition mentioned in subsection (3) which applies to the account shall be disregarded.

(3) Those conditions are—

(a) any condition that notice is required before any money or share is withdrawn;

(b) any condition that a personal application must be made before any money or share is withdrawn;

(c) any condition that a deposit book or share-account book must be produced before any money or share is withdrawn; or

(d) any other prescribed condition.

(4) The Lord Chancellor may by order make such provision as he thinks fit, by way of amendment of this section or otherwise, for all or any of the following purposes, namely—

(a) including in, or excluding from, the accounts to which this section applies accounts of any description specified in the order;

(b) excluding from the accounts to which this section applies all accounts with any particular deposit-taker so specified or with any deposit-taker of a description so specified.

(5) An order under subsection (4) shall be made by statutory instrument subject to annulment in pursuance of a resolution of either House of Parliament.

*Note* —Amended by the Civil Procedure Act 1997 Sch.2, para.2(2). Subsections (1) and (4)(b) amended by the Financial Services and Markets Act 2000 (Consequential Amendments and Repeals) Order 2001 (SI 2001/3649) art.294. **9A–629**

**Attachment of debts**

This section re-enacts amendments made to the CCA. 1959 by the SCA. 1981. The purpose of the section is to enable attachment of any deposit account or withdrawable share account of any deposit-taking institution. Deposit-taking institutions include banks, the National Savings Bank, building societies, trustee savings banks, and even credit unions. Proceedings for orders for the attachment of debts, formerly known as "garnishee orders" but now known as "third party debt orders", are governed by CPR Pt 72. **9A–630**

Note the provisions for amendment in subss.(4) and (5). The section can be compared with s.40 of the SCA 1981.

It is not possible under this section to attach wages or salary but see instead the Attachment of Earnings Act 1971 and CPR Sch.2, CCR O.27.



## Administrative and clerical expenses of garnishees

**109.**—(1) Where an interim third party debt order made in the exercise of the jurisdiction mentioned in subsection (2) of the preceding section is served on a deposit-taker, it may, subject to the provi- **9A–631**

sions of this section, deduct from the relevant debt or debts an amount not exceeding the prescribed sum towards its administrative and clerical expenses in complying with the order; and the right to make a deduction under this subsection shall be exercisable as from the time the interim third party debt order is served on it.

(1A) In subsection (1) "the relevant debt or debts", in relation to an interim third party debt order served on a deposit-taker, means the amount, as at the time the order is served on it, of the debt or debts of which the whole or a part is expressed to be attached by the order.

(1B) A deduction may be made under subsection (1) in a case where the amount referred to in subsection (1A) is insufficient to cover both the amount of the deduction and the amount of the judgment debt and costs in respect of which the attachment was made, notwithstanding that the benefit of the attachment to the creditor is reduced as a result of the deduction.

(2) An amount may not in pursuance of subsection (1) be deducted or, as the case may be, retained in a case where by virtue of section 346 of the Insolvency Act 1986 or section 325 of the Companies Act 1948 or otherwise, the creditor is not entitled to retain the benefit of the attachment.

(3) In this section "prescribed" means prescribed by an order made by the Lord Chancellor.

(4) An order under this section—

(a) may make different provision for different cases;

(b) without prejudice to the generality of paragraph (a) may prescribe sums differing according to the amount due under the judgment or order to be satisfied;

(c) may provide for this section not to apply to deposit-taker of any prescribed description.

(5) Any such order shall be made by statutory instrument subject to annulment in pursuance of a resolution of either House of Parliament.

9A-632 *Note* —Amended by the Administration of Justice Act 1985 ss.52 and 67(2), Sch.8; and the Insolvency Act 1986 s.439(2), Sch.14. Subsections (1), (1A) and (4)(c) were amended by the Financial Services and Markets Act 2000 (Consequential Amendments and Repeals) Order 2001 (SI 2001/3649) art.295. In subss.(1) and (1A), with effect from March 23, 2002, "interim third party debt order" was substituted for "order nisi" by the Civil Procedure (Modification of Enactments) Order 2002 (SI 2002/439); see further CPR Pt 72 (Third Party Debt Orders).

#### Administrative and clerical expenses of garnishees

9A-633 The purpose of this section is to enable the "deposit-taking institution" (see s.108) to recover, from the judgment debtor's account, a "prescribed sum" towards its expenses of complying with the garnishee order. The "prescribed sum" is varied from time to time by statutory instrument and is currently £55 (see Attachment of Debts (Expenses) Order (SI 1996/3098)).

### *MISCELLANEOUS PROVISIONS AS TO ENFORCEMENT OF JUDGMENTS AND ORDERS*

## Penalty for non-attendance on judgment summons

9A-634 **110.**—(1) If a debtor summoned to attend a county court by a judgment summons fails to attend on the day and at the time fixed for any hearing of the summons, the judge may adjourn or further adjourn the summons to a specified time on a specified day and order the debtor to attend at that time on that day.

(2) If—

(a) a debtor, having been ordered under subsection (1) to attend at a specified time on a specified day, fails to do so;

(b) [...]

the judge may make an order committing him to prison for a period not exceeding 14 days in respect of the failure or refusal.

(3) In any case where the judge has power to make an order of committal under subsection (2) for failure to attend, he may in lieu of or in addition to making that order, order the debtor to be arrested and brought before the court either forthwith or at such time as the judge may direct.

(4) A debtor shall not be committed to prison under subsection (2) for having failed to attend as required by an order under subsection (1) unless there was paid to him at the time of the service of the judgment summons, or paid or tendered to him at the time of the service of the order, such sum in respect of his expenses as may be prescribed for the purposes of this section.

(5) The judge may at any time revoke an order committing a person to prison under this section and, if he is already in custody, order his discharge.

### Penalty for non-attendance on judgment summons

"Judgment summons" is defined in s.147. Under s.5 of the Debtors Act 1869, a judge, sitting in open court, can commit to prison, for a term not exceeding six weeks, where it is proved that the judgment debtor has, or has had since the date of the judgment, the means to pay and has refused or neglected to do so. The procedure is governed by CPR Sch.2, CCR O.28 (see generally the commentary thereto). The judgment summons was once a very common method of enforcement but its availability was restricted by s.11 of the AJA 1970. **9A–635**

This section deals not with committal for failure to pay the judgment debt but with committal for failure to attend the hearing of the judgment summons. As to securing the debtor's attendance, see CPR Sch.2, CCR O.28, r.4.

On travelling expenses (see s.110(4)) the sum prescribed is "a sum reasonably sufficient to cover [the judgment debtor's] expenses" (see CPR Sch.2, CCR O.28, r.2(4) on tendering such expenses on service of the judgment summons, and CPR Sch.2, CCR O.28, r.10(2) on recovery of the sum).

Paragraph (b) was omitted from subs.(2) by the Civil Procedure (Modification of Enactments) Order 2002 (SI 2002/439) with effect from March 23, 2002.

## Provisions as to warrants of possession

**111.**—(1) For the purpose of executing a warrant to give possession of any premises, it shall not be necessary to remove any goods from those premises. **9A–636**

(2) The duration of any warrant of possession issued by a county court to enforce a judgment or order for the recovery of land or for the delivery of possession of land shall be such as may be fixed by or in accordance with rules of court.

*Note*—Amended by the Civil Procedure Act 1997 Sch.2, para.2(2). **9A–637**

***Paragraph numbers marked with a "+" can be found online and on CD.***

**Provisions as to warrants of possession**

9A–638 The procedure on warrants of possession is prescribed by CPR Sch.2, CCR O.26, r.17.

## PART VI

## ADMINISTRATION ORDERS

### Power to make administration order

9A–639 **112.**—(1) Where a debtor—

(a) is unable to pay forthwith the amount of a judgment obtained against him, and

(b) alleges that his whole indebtedness amounts to a sum not exceeding the county court limit, inclusive of the debt for which the judgment was obtained;

a county court may make an order providing for the administration of his estate.

(2) In this Part of this Act

"administration order" means an order under this section; and

"the appropriate court", in relation to an administration order, means the court which has the power to make the order.

(3) Before an administration order is made, the appropriate court shall, in accordance with rules of court, send to every person whose name the debtor has notified to the appropriate court as being a creditor of his, a notice that that person's name has been so notified.

(4) So long as an administration order is in force, a creditor whose name is included in the schedule to the order shall not, without the leave of the appropriate court, be entitled to present, or join in, a bankruptcy petition against the debtor unless—

(a) his name was so notified; and

(b) the debt by virtue of which he presents, or joins in, the petition, exceeds £1,500; and

(c) the notice given under subsection (3) was received by the creditor within 28 days immediately preceding the day on which the petition is presented.

(5) An administration order shall not be invalid by reason only that the total amount of the debts is found at any time to exceed the county court limit, but in that case the court may, if it thinks fit, set aside the order.

(6) An administration order may provide for the payment of the debts of the debtor by instalments or otherwise, and either in full or to such extent as appears practicable to the court under the circumstances of the case, and subject to any conditions as to his future earnings or income which the court may think just.

(7) The Secretary of State may by regulations increase or reduce the sum for the time being specified in subsection (4)(b); but no such increase in the sum so specified shall affect any case in which the bankruptcy petition was presented before the coming into force of the increase.

(8) The power to make regulations under subsection (7) shall be exercisable by statutory instrument; and no such regulations shall be made unless a draft of them has been approved by resolution of each House of Parliament.

*Note* —Amended by the Insolvency Act 1985 s.220 and by the Civil Procedure Act 1997 Sch.2, para.2(2). **9A–640**

**Power to make administration order**

Substantial amendments were made to s.112 by s.13 of the Courts and Legal Services Act 1990. In addition to amending s.112, new ss.112A and 112B were inserted into the CCA 1984. However, these amendments have not yet been brought into force and it is now uncertain whether they ever will be. Accordingly, the text is reproduced here in its unamended form as currently in force. **9A–641**

Detailed rules on administration orders are in CPR Sch.2, CCR O.39.

Administration orders are a means of consolidating debts where there are multiple debt problems. The effect of an order is to release the debtor from the burden of dealing with the debts (and arrangements with creditors) on an individual basis. The debtor under an administration order makes regular payments to the court which are then distributed among the scheduled creditors. The total debts must not exceed £5,000.

## Notice of order and proof of debts

**113.** Where an administration order has been made— **9A–642**

(a) notice of the order—

(i) [...]

(ii) shall be posted in the office of the county court for the district in which the debtor resides, and

(iii) shall be sent to every person whose name the debtor has notified to the appropriate court as being a creditor of his or who has proved;

(b) any creditor of the debtor, on proof of his debt before the district judge, shall be entitled to be scheduled as a creditor of the debtor for the amount of his proof;

(c) any creditor may object in the prescribed manner to any debt scheduled, or to the manner in which payment is directed to be made by instalments;

(d) any person who, after the date of the order, becomes a creditor of the debtor shall, on proof of his debt before the district judge, be scheduled as a creditor of the debtor for the amount of his proof, but shall not be entitled to any dividend under the order until the creditors who are scheduled as having been creditors before the date of the order have been paid to the extent provided by the order.

*Note* —Amended by the Administration of Justice Act 1985 s.67(2), Sch.8. **9A–643**

**Notice of order and proof of debts**

"Dividend" is the term used for the sums distributed to scheduled creditors. The practice is to wait until a sufficient sum has been paid into court to justify payment of dividends (see CPR Sch.2, CCR O.39, r.17). **9A–644**

Objection by a creditor before the order is made is governed by CPR Sch.2, CCR O.39, r.6, and objection after the order by CPR Sch.2, CCR O.39, r.10.

### Effect of administration order

9A-645 **114.**—(1) Subject to sections 115 and 116, when an administration order is made, no creditor shall have any remedy against the person or property of the debtor in respect of any debt—

(a) of which the debtor notified the appropriate court before the administration order was made; or

(b) which has been scheduled to the order,

except with the leave of the appropriate court, and on such terms as that court may impose.

(2) Subject to subsection (3), any county court in which proceedings are pending against the debtor in respect of any debt so notified or scheduled shall, on receiving notice of the administration order, stay the proceedings, but may allow costs already incurred by the creditor, and such costs may, on application, be added to the debt.

(3) The requirement to stay proceedings shall not operate as a requirement that a county court in which proceedings in bankruptcy against the debtor are pending shall stay those proceedings.

9A-646 *Note*—Amended by the Civil Procedure Act 1997 Sch.2, para.2(2).

**Effect of administration order**

9A-647 See commentary to s.116, below.

### Execution by district judge

9A-648 **115.**—(1) Where it appears to the district judge of the appropriate court at any time while an administration order is in force that property of the debtor exceeds in value the minimum amount, he shall, at the request of any creditor, and without fee, issue execution against the debtor's goods.

(1A) In subsection (1) above "the minimum amount" means £50 or such other amount as the Lord Chancellor may by order specify instead of that amount or the amount for the time being specified in such an order; and an order under this subsection shall be made by statutory instrument subject to annulment in pursuance of a resolution of either House of Parliament.

(2) Section 89 applies on an execution under this section as it applies on an execution under Part V.

9A-649 *Note*—Amended by the Insolvency Act 1985 s.22.

**Execution by district judge**

9A-650 See commentary to s.116, below.

### Right of landlord to distrain notwithstanding order

9A-651 **116.** A landlord or other person to whom any rent is due from a debtor in respect of whom an administration order is made, may at any time, either before or after the date of the order, distrain upon the goods or effects of the debtor for the rent due to him from the debtor, with this limitation, that if the distress for rent is levied after the date of the order, it shall be available only for six months' rent accrued due prior to the date of the order and shall not be available

***Paragraph numbers marked with a "+" can be found online and on CD.***

for rent payable in respect of any period subsequent to the date when the distress was levied, but the landlord or other person to whom the rent be due from the debtor may prove under the order for the surplus due for which the distress may not have been available.

**Right of landlord to distrain notwithstanding order**

An important protection afforded to the judgment debtor by an administration order is that no creditor may, without leave of the court and on conditions imposed by the court, take any enforcement action against the debtor. Unless the administration order is revoked under CPR Sch.2, O.39, r.14, a creditor will not get leave to issue execution for the purpose of the order is to secure equal treatment of creditors and proportionate distribution among them (*Re Frank* [1894] 1 Q.B. 9). **9A–652**

Two important exceptions to the non-execution rule are:

(1) that a district judge, who considers that the judgment debtor has goods exceeding £50 in value (after discounting protected goods—see s.89) must, at the request of a creditor and without fee, levy execution and distribute the proceeds among all the scheduled creditors, and

(2) a landlord may distrain for rent in accordance with s.116.

## Appropriation of money paid under order and discharge of order

**117.**—(1) Money paid into court under an administration order shall be appropriated— **9A–653**

(a) first in satisfaction of the costs of administration (which shall not exceed 10 pence in the pound on the total amount of the debts); and

(b) then in liquidation of debts in accordance with the order.

(2) Where the amount received is sufficient to pay—

(a) each creditor scheduled to the order to the extent provided by the order;

(b) the costs of the plaintiff in the action in respect of which the order was made; and

(c) the costs of the administration,

the order shall be superseded, and the debtor shall be discharged from his debts to the scheduled creditors.

# PART VII

# COMMITTALS

## Power to commit for contempt

**118.**—(1) If any person— **9A–654**

(a) wilfully insults the judge of a county court, or any juror or witness, or any officer of the court during his sitting or attendance in court, or in going to or returning from the court; or

(b) wilfully interrupts the proceedings of a county court or otherwise misbehaves in court;

any officer of the court, with or without the assistance of any other person, may, by order of the judge, take the offender into custody and detain him until the rising of the court, and the judge may, if he thinks fit,—

(i) make an order committing the offender for a specified period not exceeding one month to prison; or

(ii) impose upon the offender, for every offence, a fine of an amount not exceeding £2,500, or may both make such an order and impose such a fine.

(2) The judge may at any time revoke an order committing a person to prison under this section, and if he is already in custody, order his discharge.

(3) A district judge, assistant district judge or deputy district judge shall have the same powers under this section in relation to proceedings before him as a judge.

9A–655 *Note* —Amended by the Statute Law (Repeals) Act 1986; the Courts and Legal Services Act 1990 s.74; and the Criminal Justice Act 1991 s.17(3), Sch.4.

#### Power to commit for contempt

9A–656 Section 118 is concerned with contempt "in the face of the court" and does not apply, for example, to committal for breach of an order or undertaking (as to which see CCR O.29). However, the time-honoured expression "in the face of the court" is not literally construed and includes contempt "in going to or returning from the court". See *Manchester City Council v McCann* [1999] 2 W.L.R. 590, CA.

Generally, a county court can commit for a fixed term not exceeding two years (Contempt of Court Act 1981; County Courts (Penalties for Contempt) Act 1983) but specific statutory provisions (such as s.118) often provide a lesser maximum.

Contempt of court in connection with county court proceedings which was neither contempt in the face of the court nor disobedience of an order of a county court is punishable only by an order of committal made in the Queen's Bench Division (In *Re G (A Child) (Contempt: Committal)*, *The Times*, May 5, 2003, CA).

The procedure for dealing with a contempt in the face of the court is set out in Part II of Practice Direction—Committal Applications which can be found in Vol.1 at scpd52.7. This PD is clearly distilled from a series of Court of Appeal decisions and should be regarded as authoritative.It is not a breach of art.6 of the ECHR for a judge to deal with a contempt of his own court (*Wilkinson v S* [2003] 1 W.L.R. 1254) provided it is dealt with pursuant to the PD.

## Issue and execution of orders of committal

9A–657 **119.**—(1) Whenever any order or warrant for the committal of any person to prison is made or issued by a county court (whether in pursuance of this or any other Act or of rules of court), the order or warrant shall be directed to the district judge of the court, who shall thereby be empowered to take the body of the person against whom the order is made or warrant issued.

(2) It shall be the duty of every constable within his jurisdiction to assist in the execution of every such order or warrant.

(3) The governor of the prison mentioned in any such order or warrant shall be bound to receive and keep the person mentioned in it until he is lawfully discharged.

9A–658 *Note* —Amended by the Civil Procedure Act 1997 Sch.2, para.2(2).

#### Issue and execution of orders of committal

9A–659 This section is of general application and covers all situations in which committal to prison is a remedy available in the county court (see further CPR Sch.2, CCR O.29).

***Paragraph numbers marked with a "+" can be found online and on CD.***

## Prisons to which committals may be made

**120.** Any person committed to prison by the judge of any county court, in pursuance of this or any other Act or of rules of court, shall be committed to such prison as may from time to time be directed in the case of that court by order of the Secretary of State. **9A–660**

*Note* —Amended by the Civil Procedure Act 1997 Sch.2, para.2(2). **9A–661**

## Power of judge to order discharge

**121.** If at any time it appears to the satisfaction of a judge of a county court that any debtor arrested or confined in prison by order of the court is unable from any cause to pay any sum recovered against him (whether by way of satisfaction of a claim or counterclaim or by way of costs or otherwise), or any instalments thereof, and ought to be discharged, the judge may order his discharge upon such terms (including liability to re-arrest if the terms are not complied with) as the judge thinks fit. **9A–662**

## Execution of committal orders out of jurisdiction of court

**122.**—(1) Where any order or warrant for the committal of any person to prison has been made or issued (whether in pursuance of this or any other Act or of county court rules) by a county court (hereafter in this section referred to as a "home court") and that person is out of the jurisdiction of that court, the district judge may send the order or warrant to the district judge of any other county court within the jurisdiction of which that person is or is believed to be, with a warrant endorsed on it or annexed to it requiring execution of the original order or warrant. **9A–663**

(2) On receipt of the warrant, the district judge of the other county court shall act in all respects as if the original order or warrant had been issued by the court of which he is district judge and shall within the prescribed time—

(a) report to the district judge of the home court what he has done in the execution of the order or warrant; and
(b) pay over all moneys received in pursuance of the order or warrant.

(3) Where a person is apprehended under the order or warrant, he shall be forthwith conveyed, in custody of the officer apprehending him, to the prison of the court within the jurisdiction of which he was apprehended and kept there, unless sooner discharged by law, until the expiration of the period mentioned in the order or warrant.

(4) It shall be the duty of every constable within his jurisdiction to assist in the execution of every such order or warrant.

(5) Where an order of committal—

(a) under the Debtors Act 1869; or
(b) under section 110,

is sent by the district judge of a home court to the district judge of another court for execution under this section, the judge of that other court shall have the same powers to order the debtor's discharge as the judge of the home court would have under section 110 or 121.

**Execution of committal orders out of jurisdiction of court**

9A-664 The jurisdiction of a county court is limited geographically. This section overcomes the difficulties this presents by adopting a procedure of reciprocal execution of committal orders between county courts. This section parallels the power of execution out of the jurisdiction of a county court contained in s.103.

# PART VIII

# RESPONSIBILITY AND PROTECTION OF OFFICERS

## District judge to have same responsibilities as sheriff

9A-665 **123.** Every district judge shall be responsible for the acts and defaults of himself and of the bailiffs appointed to assist him in like manner as the sheriff of any county in England or Wales is responsible for the acts and defaults of himself and his officers.

**District judge to have same responsibilities as sheriff**

9A-666 Section 123 in its present form (March 1998) is an historical anomaly and is due for repeal. Under the County Courts Act 1846 the "high bailiff" was responsible for the acts and defaults of bailiffs in the same way as, in the High Court, the sheriff is responsible for the acts and defaults of sheriff's officers. Subsequently, the office of high bailiff was merged with that of the county court registrar. The office of "registrar" was abolished by s.74 of the Courts and Legal Services Act 1990 and replaced by the "district judge". Hence the anomaly that the district judge is now liable for the acts and defaults of county court bailiffs (see also s.124). For the duties of the sheriff, see Vol.1, para.sc45.1.10.

For discussion of the liabilities of the "high bailiff" (see above) see *Smith v Pritchard* (1849) 8 K.B. 565; (1849) L.J.C.P. 53; and *Burton v Le Gros* (1864) 34 L.J.Q.B. 91.

## Liability of bailiff for neglect to levy execution

9A-667 **124.**—(1) Where a bailiff of a county court, being employed to levy any execution against goods, loses the opportunity of levying the execution by reason of neglect, connivance or omission, any party aggrieved thereby may complain to the judge of that court.

(2) On any such complaint the judge, if the neglect, connivance or omission is proved to his satisfaction, shall order the bailiff to pay such damages as it appears that the complainant has sustained by reason of it, not exceeding in any case the sum for which the execution issued.

**Liability of bailiff for neglect to levy execution**

9A-668 The purpose and terms of this section are self-explanatory. For the procedure see CPR Sch.2, CCR O.34, r.1.

## Irregularity in executing warrants

9A-669 **125.**—(1) No officer of a county court in executing any warrant of a court, and no person at whose instance any such warrant is executed, shall be deemed a trespasser by reason of any irregularity or informality—

(a) in any proceeding on the validity of which the warrant depends; or

(b) in the form of the warrant or in the mode of executing it;

but any person aggrieved may bring an action for any special damage sustained by him by reason of the irregularity or informality against the person guilty of it.

(2) No costs shall be recovered in such an action unless the damages awarded exceed £2.

## Actions against bailiffs acting under warrants

**126.**—(1) No action shall be commenced against any bailiff for anything done in obedience to a warrant issued by the district judge, unless— **9A-670**

(a) a demand for inspection of the warrant and for a copy of it is made or left at the office of the bailiff by the party intending to bring the action, or his legal representative or agent; and

(b) the bailiff refuses or neglects to comply with the demand within six days after it is made.

(2) The demand must be in writing and signed by the person making it.

(3) If an action is commenced against a bailiff in a case where such a demand has been made and not complied with, judgment shall be given for the bailiff if the warrant is produced or proved at the trial, notwithstanding any defect of jurisdiction or other irregularity in the warrant; but the district judge who issued the warrant may be joined as a defendant in the action, and if the district judge is so joined and judgment is given against him, the costs to be recovered by the plaintiff against the district judge shall include such costs as the plaintiff is liable to pay to the bailiff.

(4) In this section (except in paragraph (a) of subsection (1)) "bailiff" includes any person acting by the order and in aid of a bailiff.

*Note*—Amended by the Courts and Legal Services Act 1990 s.125(3), Sch.18. **9A-671**

**Actions against bailiffs acting under warrants**

See commentary to s.123 for an explanation of how the district judge became included in this provision. Section 147 defines "bailiff" to include "registrar" (now to be construed as "district judge" (Courts and Legal Services Act 1990 s.74)). It follows that the district judge is protected by s.126. **9A-672**

## Warrants evidence of authority

**127.** In any action commenced against a person for anything done in pursuance of this Act, the production of the warrant of the county court shall be deemed sufficient proof of the authority of the court previous to the issue of the warrant. **9A-673**

* * * *

## Enforcement of fines

**129.** Payment of any fine imposed by any court under this Act may be enforced upon the order of the judge in like manner— **9A-674**

(a) as payment of a debt adjudged by the court to be paid may be enforced under this Act; or

***Paragraph numbers marked with a "+" can be found online and on CD.***

(b) as payment of a sum adjudged to be paid by a conviction of a magistrates' court may be enforced under the Magistrates' Courts Act 1980 (disregarding section 81(*1*) of that Act).

### Payment and application of fees, fines, etc.

9A–675 **130.**—(1) Subject to subsection (2), all fees, forfeitures and fines payable under this Act and any penalty payable to an officer of a county court under any other Act shall be paid to officers designated by the Lord Chancellor and dealt with by them in such manner as the Lord Chancellor, after consultation with the Treasury, may direct.

(2) Subsection (1) does not apply to fines imposed on summary conviction or to so much of a fine as is applicable under section 55(4) to indemnify a party injured.

(3) The Lord Chancellor, with the concurrence of the Treasury, shall from time to time make such rules as he thinks fit for securing the balances and other sums of money in the hands of any officers of a county court, and for the due accounting for and application of those balances and sums.

### Appointment of auditors and other officers

9A–676 **131.** The Lord Chancellor may, subject to the consent of the Treasury as to numbers and salaries, appoint as officers in his department such auditors and other officers as he may consider necessary for the purpose of controlling the accounts of county courts.

### Payment of salaries and expenses

9A–677 **132.** There shall be paid out of money provided by Parliament—

(a) all salaries, remuneration and other sums payable under Part I of this Act or under section 131;

(b) the expenses of supplying the courts and offices with law and office books and stationery and postage stamps;

(c) expenses incurred in conveying to prison persons committed by the courts; and

(d) all other expenses arising out of any jurisdiction for the time being conferred on the courts of any officer of the courts.

## *SUMMONSES AND OTHER DOCUMENTS*

### Proof of service of summonses, etc.

9A–678 **133.**—(1) Where any summons or other process issued from a county court is served by an officer of a court, the service may be proved by a certificate in a prescribed form showing the fact and mode of the service.

(2) Any officer of a court wilfully and corruptly giving a false certificate under subsection (1) in respect of the service of a summons or other process shall be guilty of an offcence and on conviction thereof, shall be removed from office and shall be liable—

***Paragraph numbers marked with a "+" can be found online and on CD.***

(a) on conviction on indictment, to imprisonment for any term not exceeding 2 years; or

(b) on summary conviction, to imprisonment for any term not exceeding 6 months or to a fine not exceeding the statutory maximum or to both such imprisonment and fine.

*Note*—Subsection (1) amended by the Civil Procedure (Modification of Enactments) Order 1998 (SI 1998/2940) art.6(e). **9A-679**

**Proof of service of summonses, etc.**

On service of documents generally, CPR Pt 6. As to certification of service, see CPR r.6.10. **9A-680**

* * * *

## Penalty for falsely pretending to act under authority of court

**135.** Any person who— **9A-681**

(a) delivers or causes to be delivered to any other person any paper falsely purporting to be a copy of any summons or other process or a county court, knowing it to be false; or

(b) acts or professes to act under any false colour or pretence of the process or authority of a county court;

shall be guilty of an offence and shall for each offence be liable on conviction on indictment to imprisonment for a term not exceeding 7 years.

## Penalty for falsely representing document to have been issued from county court

**136.**—(1) It shall not be lawful to deliver or cause to be delivered to any person any document which was not issued under the authority of a county court but which, by reason of its form or contents or both, has the appearance of having been issued under such authority. **9A-682**

(2) If any person contravenes this section, he shall for each offence be liable on summary conviction to a fine of an amount not exceeding level 3 on the standard scale.

(3) Nothing in this section shall be taken to prejudice section 135.

## Lessee to give notice of summons for recovery of land

**137.**—(1) Every lessee to whom there is delivered any summons issued from a county court for the recovery of land demised to or held by him, or to whose knowledge any such summons comes, shall forthwith give notice of the summons to his lessor or his bailiff or receiver. **9A-683**

(2) If a lessee fails to give notice as required by subsection (1), he shall be liable to forfeit to the person of whom he holds the land an amount equal to the value of 3 years' improved or rack rent of the land to be recovered by action in any county court or other court having jurisdiction in respect of claims for such an amount.

**For ss.138 to 140 of the County Courts Act 1984 (see Arrangement) plus any re-**

***Paragraph numbers marked with a "+" can be found online and on CD.***

**lated commentary see paragraphs 9A–684+ to 9A–703+ on White Book on Westlaw UK or the Civil Procedure CD.**

* * * *

## Power to enforce undertakings of solicitors

9A–704 **142.** A county court shall have the same power to enforce an undertaking given by a solicitor in relation to any proceedings in that court as the High Court has to enforce an undertaking so given in relation to any proceedings in the High Court.

### Power to enforce undertakings of solicitors

9A–705 An undertaking is a promise. In the old books "undertaker" means a promisor (1 Salk. 27). "Undertaking" is today usually used in the sense of a promise given in the course of proceedings by a party or his solicitor or counsel.

Where a solicitor gives an undertaking he is bound as a matter of professional etiquette to implement it. Furthermore, a solicitor is, of course, a "solicitor of the Supreme Court" and consequently the High Court may exercise jurisdiction over solicitors (see also s.50 of the Solicitors Act 1974 see para.7C–42).

Section 142 of the CCA. 1984 enables the county court to enforce an undertaking given by a solicitor in that court in the same way as could the High Court. For the powers of the High Court see *"Summary Jurisdiction of the Court over solicitors"* at SCP 1999, Vol.2, para 15G—1, and in particular "Jurisdiction to enforce undertakings given by solicitors" at SCP 1999, Vol.2, para.15G—6.

## Prohibition on persons other than solicitors receiving remuneration for business done in county courts

9A–706 **143.**—(1) No person other than—

(a) a legal representative; or

(b) a person exercising a right of audience or a right to conduct litigation by virtue of an order made under section 11 of the Courts and Legal Services Act 1990 (representation in county courts),

shall be entitled to have or recover any fee or reward for acting on behalf of a party in proceedings in a county court.

(2) [...]

9A–707 *Note* —Amended by the Courts and Legal Services Act 1990 s.125(3), (7), Schs 8 and 20.

*REPLEVIN*

## Replevin

9A–708 **144.** Schedule 1 to this Act shall have effect.

*POWER TO RAISE MONETARY LIMITS*

## Power to raise monetary limits

9A–709 **145.**—(1) If it appears to Her Majesty in Council—

(a) that the county court limit for the purposes of any enactment referring to that limit, or

***Paragraph numbers marked with a "+" can be found online and on CD.***

(b) that the higher limit or the lower limit referred to in section 20 of this Act,

should be increased, Her Majesty may by Order in Council direct that the limit in question shall be such amount as may be specified in the Order.

(2) An Order under subsection (1) may contain such incidental or transitional provisions as Her Majesty considers appropriate.

(2A) It is for the Lord Chancellor to recommend to Her Majesty the making of an Order under subsection (1).

(3) No recommendation shall be made to Her Majesty in Council to make an Order under this section unless a draft of the Order has been laid before Parliament and approved by resolution of each House of Parliament.

*Note*—No Order has been made under this section. See further, commentary to s.147(1). Amended by the Constitutional Reform Act 2005 s.15(1), Sch.4, para.170 (see para.9A–4 above). **9A–710**

**For s.146 of the County Courts Act 1984 (see Arrangement) plus any related commentary see paragraph 9A–711+ on White Book on Westlaw UK or the Civil Procedure CD.**

## Interpretation

**147.**—(1) In this Act, unless the context otherwise requires— **9A–712**

"action" means any proceedings in a county court which may be commenced as prescribed by plaint;

"Admiralty county court" means a county court appointed to have Admiralty jurisdiction by order under this Act;

"Admiralty proceedings" means proceedings in which the claim would not be within the jurisdiction of a county court but for sections 26 and 27;

"bailiff" includes a registrar;

"the county court limit" means—

(a) in relation to any enactment contained in this Act for which a limit for the time being specified by an Order under section 145, that limit,

(b) [...]

(c) in relation to any enactment contained in this Act and not within paragraph (a), the county court limit for the time being specified by any other Order in Council or order defining the limit of county court jurisdiction for the purposes of that enactment;

"court" and "county court" mean a court held for a district under this Act;

"deposit-taking institution" means a person who may, in the course of his business, lawfully accept deposits in the United Kingdom;

"district" and "county court district" mean a district for which a court is to be held under section 2;

"hearing" includes trial, and "hear" and "heard" shall be construed accordingly;

*Paragraph numbers marked with a "+" can be found online and on CD.*

"hereditament" includes both a corporeal and incorporeal hereditament;
"judge", in relation to a county court, means a judge assigned to the district of that court under subsection (1) of section 5 and any person sitting as a judge for that district under subsection (3) or (4) of that section;
"judgment summons" means a summons issued on the application of a person entitled to enforce a judgment or order under section 5 of the Debtors Act 1869 requiring a person, or where two or more persons are liable under the judgment or order, requiring any one or more of them, to attend court;
"landlord", in relation to any land, means the person entitled to the immediate reversion or, if the property therein is held in joint tenancy, any of the persons entitled to the immediate reversion;
"legal representative" means an authorised advocate or authorised litigator, as defined by section 119(1) of the Courts and Legal Services Act 1990;
"matter" means every proceeding in a county court which may be commenced as prescribed otherwise than by plaint;
"officer", in relation to a court, means any district judge or deputy district judge assigned to that court and any clerk, bailiff, usher or messenger in the service of that court;
"part-time registrar" and "part-time assistant registrar" have the meaning assigned to them by section 10(3);
"party" includes every person served with notice of, or attending, any proceeding, whether named as a party to that proceeding or not;
"prescribed" means prescribed by rules of court;
"probate proceedings" means proceedings brought in a county court by virtue of section 32 or transferred to that court under section 40;
"proceedings" includes both actions and matters;
"registrar" and "registrar of a county court" mean a registrar appointed for a district under this Act, or in a case where two or more registrars are appointed jointly, either or any of those registrars;
"return day" means the day appointed in any summons or proceeding for the appearance of the defendant or any other day fixed for the hearing of any proceedings;
"ship" includes any description of vessel used in navigation;
"solicitor" means solicitor of the Senior Courts.

(1A) The definition of "deposit-taking institution" in subsection (1) must be read with—

(a) section 22 of the Financial Services and Markets Act 2000;
(b) any relevant order under that section; and
(c) Schedule 2 to that Act.

(2) [...]

(3) [...]

*Note*—Subsection (1) amended by the Courts and Legal Services Act 1990 s.125(3) and Sch.18, para.49; the Matrimonial and Family Proceedings Act 1984 s.46(3) and Sch.3; the High Court and County Courts Jurisdiction Order 1991 (SI 1991/724); the Statute Law (Repeals) Act 1993; and the Civil Procedure Act 1997 Sch.2, paras 2(2) and 2(9). **9A–713**

Subsections (2) and (3) of this section were repealed by the Local Government Finance (Repeals, Savings and Consequential Amendments) Order 1990 (SI 1990/776).

The definition of "judgment summons" in s.147(1) was amended by the Civil Procedure (Modification of Enactments) Order 2002 (SI 2002/439) with effect from March 23, 2002.

The definition "deposit-taking institution" in s.147(1) was added by, and subs.(1A) were inserted by, the Financial Services and Markets Act 2000 (Consequential Amendments and Repeals) Order 2001 (SI 2001/3649) art.296.

The definition "solicitor" was amended by the Constitutional Reform Act 2005 Sch.11 para.4 with effect from October 1, 2009 (SI 2009/1604).

The definition "officer" was amended by the Tribunals, Courts and Enforcement Act 2007 s.56 and Sch.11, para.8, with effect from July 19, 2007.

**"The county court limit"**

No order has been made under s.145. See further "Jurisdiction of county courts" para.9A–410 above. **9A–714**

**Registrar, etc.**

By the Courts and Legal Services Act 1990 s.74, the office of registrar became that of district judge and references in any enactment to registrar are to be construed as a reference to that office by its new name. **9A–715**

**For ss.148 to 151 of and Sch.1 to 2 to the County Courts Act 1984 (see Arrangement) plus any related commentary see paragraphs 9A–716+ to 9A–722+ on White Book on Westlaw UK or the Civil Procedure CD.**

**SECTION 148(2)**

## SCHEDULE 3

### TRANSITORY AND TRANSITIONAL PROVISIONS AND SAVINGS

*Section 21 of this Act*

1. [...] **9A–723**

*Section 51 of this Act*

2. [...] **9A–724**

*Sections 105(1) and 106 of this Act*

3. [...] **9A–725**

*Administration Orders*

4.—(1) Any reference in Part VI of this Act to an administration order includes a reference to an administration order made under an enactment repealed by this Act. **9A–726**

2. [...]

*County Court*

5. References in any enactment or document to a county court constituted under the County Courts Act 1888 or the County Courts Act 1934 or the County Courts Act 1959 shall be construed as references to a county court constituted under this Act and anything done or proceedings taken in respect of any action or matter whatsoever before the commencement of this Act in a county court under any of the enactments mentioned above shall be deemed to have been done or taken in a county court constituted under this Act. **9A–727**

***Paragraph numbers marked with a "+" can be found online and on CD.***

*Former enactments*

**9A–728** 6. Any document referring to any former enactment relating to county courts shall be construed as referring to the corresponding enactment in this Act. In this paragraph "former enactment relating to county courts" means any enactment repealed by the County Courts Act 1959, by the County Courts Act 1934 or by the County Courts Act 1888.

*High bailiffs*

**9A–729** 7. References to a high bailiff in any enactment, Order in Council, order, rule, regulation or any document whatsoever shall be construed as a reference to a registrar.

*Periods of time*

**9A–730** 8. Where a period of time specified in an enactment repealed by this Act is current at the coming into force of this Act shall have effect as if the corresponding provision of it had been in force when that period began to run.

*Offences*

**9A–731** 9. Nothing in this Act renders a person liable to punishment by way of fine or imprisonment for an offence committed before the coming into force of this Act which differs from the punishment to which he would have been liable if this Act had not been passed.

*Saving for certain provisions of the County Courts Act 1959*

**9A–732** 10. [...]

*General*

**9A–733** 11. Without prejudice to any express amendment made by this Act, a reference in an enactment or other document, whether express or implied, to an enactment repealed by this Act shall, unless the context otherwise requires, be construed as, or as including, a reference to this Act or to the corresponding provisions of this Act.

12. Nothing in this Schedule shall be taken as prejudicing the operation of the provisions of the Interpretation Act 1978 as respects the effects of repeals.

**9A–734** *Note*—Schedule 3 repealed in part by the Statute Law (Repeals) Act 1989.

**SECTION 148(3)**

## SCHEDULE 4

REPEALS

**9A–735** [The text of Schedule 4 is not reproduced here.]

## Civil Procedure Act 1997

**9A–736** (1997 c.12)

ARRANGEMENT OF SECTIONS

*RULES AND DIRECTIONS*

SECT.



***Paragraph numbers marked with a "+" can be found online and on CD.***

**Introductory note**

The provisions in this Act, with the exception of s.7 (which has a different provenance), paved the way for the implementation of the recommendations contained in the Report by Lord Woolf to the Lord Chancellor on the civil justice system in England and Wales: "Access to Justice Final Report" (July 1996). **9A–737**

Section 11 came into effect on February 27, 1997. Sections 1 to 9 and Sch.1 were brought into force on April 27, 1997, by the Civil Procedure Act 1997 (Commencement No.1) Order 1997 (SI 1997/841). That statutory instrument also brought into force on that date some of the minor and consequential amendments contained in Sch.2. The remaining provisions of the Act were brought into force by the Civil Procedure Act 1997 (Commencement No.2) Order 1999 (SI 1999/1009).

For further notes on this Act, see *Current Law Statutes Annotated* (London: Sweet & Maxwell, 1997) Vol.1.

Amendments to the Act were made by the Courts Act 2003 and by the Constitutional Reform Act 2005. Some of the amending provisions in the 2003 Act were in turn amended by the 2005 Act before being brought into force.

## *RULES AND DIRECTIONS*

## Civil Procedure Rules

**1.**—(1) There are to be rules of court (to be called "Civil Procedure Rules") governing the practice and procedure to be followed in— **9A–738**

(a) the civil division of the Court of Appeal,

(b) the High Court, and

(c) county courts.

(2) Schedule 1 (which makes further provision about the extent of the power to make Civil Procedure Rules) is to have effect.

(3) Any power to make Civil Procedure Rules is to be exercised with a view to securing that—

(a) the system of civil justice is accessible, fair and efficient, and

(b) the rules are both simple and simply expressed.

**Civil Procedure Rules**

For extended commentary on the process for making Civil Procedure Rules, see Section 12 (CPR: Application, Amendment and Interpretation) paras 12–38 *et seq*, below. **9A–739**

## Rule Committee

**2.**—(1) Civil Procedure Rules are to be made by a committee known as the Civil Procedure Rule Committee, which is to consist of the following persons — **9A–740**

(a) the Head of Civil Justice,

***Paragraph numbers marked with a "+" can be found online and on CD.***

(b) the Deputy Head of Civil Justice (if there is one),
(c) the persons currently appointed in accordance with subsections (1A) and (1B).

(1A) The Lord Chief Justice must appoint the persons falling within paragraphs (a) to (d) of subsection (2).

(1B) The Lord Chancellor must appoint the persons falling within paragraphs (e) to (g) of subsection (2).

(2) The persons to be appointed in accordance with subsections (1A) and (1B) are

(a) either two or three judges of the Senior Courts,
(b) one Circuit judge,
(c) either one or two district judges,
(d) one person who is a Master referred to in Part II of Schedule 2 to the Senior Courts Act 1981,
(e) three persons who have a Senior Courts qualification (within the meaning of section 71 of the Courts and Legal Services Act 1990), including at least one with particular experience of practice in county courts,
(f) three persons who have been authorised by a relevant approved regulator to conduct litigation in relation to all proceedings in the Senior Courts, including at least one with particular experience of practice in county courts,
(g) two persons with experience in and knowledge of the lay advice sector and consumer affairs.

(2A) In subsection (2)(f) "relevant approved regulator" is to be construed in accordance with section 20(3) of the Legal Services Act 2007.

(3) Before appointing a person in accordance with subsection (1A), the Lord Chief Justice must consult the Lord Chancellor.

(4) Before appointing a person in accordance with subsection (1B), the Lord Chancellor must consult the Lord Chief Justice and, if the person falls within paragraph (e) or (f) of subsection (2), must also consult any body which—

(a) has members who are eligible for appointment under that paragraph, and
(b) is an authorised body for the purposes of section 27 or 28 of the Courts and Legal Services Act 1990.

(5) The Lord Chancellor may reimburse the members of the Civil Procedure Rule Committee their travelling and out-of-pocket expenses.

(6) […]

(7) […]

(8) […]

(9) The Lord Chief Justice may nominate a judicial office holder (as defined in section 109(4) of the Constitutional Reform Act 2005) to exercise his functions under this section.

(9) If the Lord Chancellor disallows rules under subsection (8), he must give the Civil Procedure Rule Committee written reasons for doing so.

*Note*—Amended by the Constitutional Reform Act 2005 s.59 and Sch.11, paras 1, 4 with effect from October 1, 2009 (SI 2009/1604); and by the Legal Services Act 2007 Sch.21, para.122, with effect from January 1, 2010 (SI 2009/3250). **9A–740.1**

**Effect of rule**

This section establishes the Civil Procedure Rule Committee and deals with its membership. Provisions in the Senior Courts Act 1981 and the County Courts Act 1984 dealing with the constitution of the former two Rule Committees were repealed when the 1997 Act came into force. In its original form, s.2 dealt with various matters now dealt with in s.3. **9A–741**

Section 2 was substantially amended by the Constitutional Reform Act 2005 Sch.4, para.263. Further, subss.(6), (7) and (8) of the section were to be omitted by the Courts Act 2003 s.85(1). However, s.85(1) was never brought into effect. However, Sch.4, para.385 of the 2005 Act brought into force on April 4, 2006, amendments to several statutory provisions "repealed or amended otherwise than by this Act" and among such statutory provisions was s.85(1) of the 2003 Act. So by this convoluted route, subss.(6), (7) and (8) of the s.2 appear to have been omitted. It seems that this was intended because the roles played by these subsections are now played, respectively, by s.3(1), s.1(3) and s.3(2) and (3). Curiously, other amendments made by the 2005 Act consisted of two sub-sections numbered (9), inserted by paras 263(6) and 385(2) of Sch.4 to the Act. The first of these insertions is subs.(9) as printed above. The second is to the same effect as s.3(4). Presumably this duplication was not intended (and this casts doubt on the legislative effect of para.385 generally, and on the question whether subss.(6), (7) and (8) have in fact been omitted from s.2). Accordingly, this latter version of subs.(9) is omitted from the version of s.2 as printed above. Subsection (2)(c) was amended by the Civil Procedure Act 1997 (Amendment) Order 2006 (SI 2006/1847), increasing to two the number of district judges that may be appointed to the Committee.

Courts Act 2003 s.62 provides for the appointment of the Head and Deputy Head of Civil Justice, referred to in s.2(1).

For the process to be adopted by the Committee in making Rules, see s.3 below. One of the functions of the Civil Justice Council is to refer proposals for changes in the civil justice system to the Committee (see s.6(3)).

## Power to change certain requirements relating to Committee

**2A.**—(1) The Lord Chancellor may by order— **9A–742**

(a) amend section 2(2), (3) or (4), and,

(b) make consequential amendments in any other provision of section 2.

(2) The Lord Chancellor may make an order under this section only with the concurrence of the Lord Chief Justice.

(2A) Before making an order under this section the Lord Chancellor must consult the following persons—

(a) the Head of Civil Justice,

(b) the Deputy Head of Civil Justice (if there is one),

(2B) The Lord Chief Justice may nominate a judicial office holder (as defined in section 109(4) of the Constitutional Reform Act 2005) to exercise his functions under this section.

(3) The power to make an order under this section is exercisable by statutory instrument.

(4) A statutory instrument containing such an order is subject to annulment in pursuance of a resolution of either House of Parliament.

*Note*—This section was inserted by the Courts Act 2003 s.84, and came into effect on January 24, 2004, and was amended by the Constitutional Reform Act 2005 Sch.4, **9A–743**



MAIN STATUTES

para.264 with effect from April 3, 2006. The power given to the Lord Chancellor under the section was exercised by the Civil Procedure Act 1997 (Amendment) Order 2006 (SI 2006/1847) for the purpose of amending s.2(2)(c), see para.9A-741 above.

## Process for making Civil Procedure Rules

9A–744 **3.**—(1) The Civil Procedure Rule Committee must, before making Civil Procedure Rules—

(a) consult such persons as they consider appropriate, and
(b) meet (unless it is inexpedient to do so).

(2) Rules made by the Civil Procedure Rule Committee must be—

(a) signed by a majority of the members of the Committee, and
(b) submitted to the Lord Chancellor.

(3) The Lord Chancellor may allow, disallow or alter rules so made.

(4) If the Lord Chancellor disallows Rules he must give the Committee written reasons for doing so.

(5) Rules so made, as allowed or altered by the Lord Chancellor—

(a) come into force on such day as the Lord Chancellor directs, and
(b) are to be contained in a statutory instrument to which the Statutory Instruments Act 1946 applies as if the instrument contained rules made by a Minister of the Crown.

(6) A statutory instrument containing Civil Procedure Rules is subject to annulment in pursuance of a resolution of either House of Parliament.

(7) [...]

9A–745 *Note* —This section was substituted by the Courts Act 2003 s.85(2), but that provision was not brought into force. However, Constitutional Reform Act 2005 Sch.4, para.265 states that s.3 "as amended by section 85 of the Courts Act 2003" is to be amended in certain respects, and para.265 was brought into effect on April 6, 2006. By this route, s.3 as substituted by the s.85(2) of the 2003 Act, and as further amended by Sch.4, para.265 of the 2005 Act, came into force in the form printed above. The section contains in amended form provisions that were previously found in the former s.3 and in s.2 before it was amended (as is explained in para.9A–741 above).

### Rule-making process

9A–746 The rule-making process is outlined in s.3. For extended commentary on the process for making Civil Procedure Rules, see Section 12 (CPR: Application, Amendment and Interpretation) paras 12–3 and 12–38, below. A significant feature of s.3, when compared with the provisions it replaces, is that it states that, if the Lord Chancellor disallows Rules, he must give the Committee written reasons for doing so (s.3(4)). In practice, the matters considered by the Civil Procedure Rule Committee are matters brought to their attention by the Civil Justice Council (see s.6(3) below) or, more commonly, by the Department for Constitutional Affairs. The Lord Chancellor may give the Rule Committee notice requiring rules to be made to achieve a specified purpose (see s.3A below). In *YD (Turkey) v Secretary of State for the Home Department* [2006] EWCA Civ 52; [2006] 1 W.L.R. 1646, CA, Brooke L.J. said (at para.22) that the Civil Procedure Act 1997 and the Civil Procedure Rules 1998 "have changed the landscape" enabling the Court, by case law, to initiate innovative ways of regulating procedure, safe in the knowledge that the Rule Committee would move swiftly to codify or extend the new procedures the judges had so introduced by making appropriate amendments to the CPR. His lordship gave illustrations of desirable changes which would never have been made, or not made so swiftly, "if the judges had not been ready to take the lead" (*ibid.*). Practice directions are not made by the Rule Committee (see s.5 below and commentary following).

Section 72 of the Counter-Terrorism Act 2008 states that, in certain circumstances and for particular statutory proceedings, Civil Procedure Rules may, in the first instance, be made by the Lord Chancellor by a process which, in effect, by-passes the s.3 process but subject to safeguards enacted in such statutory provisions. In November 2008, in exercise of these powers Pt 79 (Financial Restrictions Proceedings Under the Counter-Terrorism Act 2008) was inserted in the CPR (see further, Vol.2, para.12–3 below, and commentary on CPR Pt 79 in Vol.1).

The Lord Chancellor's power under this section is a protected function within the Constitutional Reform Act 2005 s.19 and Sch.7.

## Rules to be made if required by Lord Chancellor

**3A.**—(1) This section applies if the Lord Chancellor gives the Civil Procedure Committee written notice that he thinks it is expedient for Civil Procedure Rules to include provision that would achieve a purpose specified in the notice. **9A–747**

(2) The Committee must make such Rules as it considers necessary to achieve the specified purpose.

(3) Those Rules must be—

(a) made within a reasonable period after the Lord Chancellor gives notice to the Committee;

(b) made in accordance with section 3.

*Note* —Section 3A inserted by the Constitutional Reform Act 2005 s.15(1), Sch.4, para.265, (see para.9A–4 above). **9A–748**

## Power to make consequential amendments

**4.**—(1) The Lord Chancellor may, after consulting the Lord Chief Justice, by order amend, repeal or revoke any enactment to the extent he considers necessary or desirable in consequence of— **9A–749**

(a) section 1 or 2, or

(b) Civil Procedure Rules.

(2) The Lord Chancellor may by order amend, repeal or revoke any enactment passed or made before the commencement of this section to the extent he considers necessary or desirable in order to facilitate the making of Civil Procedure Rules.

(3) Any power to make an order under this section is exercisable by statutory instrument.

(4) A statutory instrument containing an order under subsection (1) shall be subject to annulment in pursuance of a resolution of either House of Parliament.

(5) No order may be made under subsection (2) unless a draft of it has been laid before and approved by resolution of each House of Parliament.

(6) The Lord Chief Justice may nominate a judicial office holder (as defined in section 109(4) of the Constitutional Reform Act 2005) to exercise his functions under subsection (1) or (2).

#### Power to make consequential and other amendments to enactments

With effect from April 3, 2006, subs.(6) was added to this section, and the require- **9A–750**

*Paragraph numbers marked with a "+" can be found online and on CD.*



MAIN STATUTES

ment that the Lord Chancellor should consult the Lord Chief Justice was inserted in subss.(1) and (2), by the Constitutional Reform Act 2005 Sch.4, para.267. Curiously, para.267 states that these amendments should be made to s.4 "as amended by s.85 of the Courts Act 2003"; however, s.85 made no amendments at all to s.4.

See further, Section 12 (CPR: Application, Amendment and Interpretation) para.12–42, below.

## Practice directions

9A–751 **5.**—(1) Practice directions may be given in accordance with Part 1 of Schedule 2 to the Constitutional Reform Act 2005.

(2) Practice directions given otherwise than under subsection (1) may not be given without the approval of—

(a) the Lord Chancellor, and

(b) the Lord Chief Justice.

(3) Practice directions (whether given under subsection (1) or otherwise) may provide for any matter which, by virtue of paragraph 3 of Schedule 1, may be provided for by Civil Procedure Rules.

(4) The power to give practice directions under subsection (1) includes power—

(a) to vary or revoke directions given by any person;

(b) to give directions containing different provision for different cases (including different areas);

(c) to give directions containing provision for a specific court, for specific proceedings or for a specific jurisdiction.

(5) Subsection (2)(a) does not apply to directions to the extent that they consist of guidance about any of the following—

(a) the application or interpretation of law;

(b) the making of judicial decisions.

(6) Subsection (2)(a) does not apply to directions to the extent that they consist of criteria for determining which judges may be allocated to hear particular categories of case; but the directions may, to that extent be given only—

(a) after consulting the Lord Chancellor, and

(b) the Lord Chief Justice.

### Effect of section

9A–752 See further, Section 12 (CPR: Application, Amendment and Interpretation) para.12–17, below.

*CIVIL JUSTICE COUNCIL*

## Civil Justice Council

9A–753 **6.**—(1) The Lord Chancellor is to establish and maintain an advisory body, to be known as the Civil Justice Council.

(2) The Council must include—

(a) members of the judiciary,

(b) members of the legal professions,

(c) civil servants concerned with the administration of the courts,

***Paragraph numbers marked with a "+" can be found online and on CD.***

(d) persons with experience in and knowledge of consumer affairs,

(e) persons with experience in and knowledge of the lay advice sector, and

(f) persons able to represent the interests of particular kinds of litigants (for example, businesses or employees).

(2A) The Lord Chancellor must decide the following questions, after consulting the Lord Chief Justice—

(a) how many members of the Council are to be drawn from each of the groups mentioned in subsection (2);

(b) how many other members the Council is to have.

(2B) It is for—

(a) the Lord Chief Justice to appoint members of the judiciary to the Council, after consulting the Lord Chancellor;

(b) the Lord Chancellor to appoint other persons to the Council.

(3) The functions of the Council are to include—

(a) keeping the civil justice system under review,

(b) considering how to make the civil justice system more accessible, fair and efficient,

(c) advising the Lord Chancellor and the judiciary on the development of the civil justice system,

(d) referring proposals for changes in the civil justice system to the Lord Chancellor and the Civil Procedure Rule Committee, and

(e) making proposals for research.

(4) The Lord Chancellor may reimburse the members of the Council their travelling and out-of-pocket expenses.

(5) The Lord Chief Justice may nominate a judicial office holder (as defined in section 109(4) of the Constitutional Reform Act 2005) to exercise his functions under this section.

*Note* —Amended by the Constitutional Reform Act 2005 s.15(1), Sch.4, para.268, (see para.9A–4 above). **9A–754**

**Civil Justice Council**

In the report by Lord Woolf to the Lord Chancellor on the civil justice system in England and Wales: "Access to Justice Final Report" (July 1996), it was recommended that a Civil Justice Council should be established as an advisory body to keep the civil justice system under review. This section carries that recommendation into effect. The Council is to include judges, lawyers, Lord Chancellor's Department staff and others including those representing consumer, advice sector, business and other interests. The Lord Chancellor's power under this section is a protected function within the Constitutional Reform Act 2005 s.19 and Sch.7. **9A–755**



## COURT ORDERS

### Power of courts to make orders for preserving evidence, etc.

**7.**—(1) The court may make an order under this section for the purpose of securing, in the case of any existing or proposed proceedings in the court— **9A–756**

(a) the preservation of evidence which is or may be relevant, or

(b) the preservation of property which is or may be the subject-matter of the proceedings or as to which any question arises or may arise in the proceedings.

(2) A person who is, or appears to the court likely to be, a party to proceedings in the court may make an application for such an order.

(3) Such an order may direct any person to permit any person described in the order, or secure that any person so described is permitted—

(a) to enter premises in England and Wales, and

(b) while on the premises, to take in accordance with the terms of the order any of the following steps.

(4) Those steps are—

(a) to carry out a search for or inspection of anything described in the order, and

(b) to make or obtain a copy, photograph, sample or other record of anything so described.

(5) The order may also direct the person concerned—

(a) to provide any person described in the order, or secure that any person so described is provided, with any information or article described in the order, and

(b) to allow any person described in the order, or secure that any person so described is allowed, to retain for safe keeping anything described in the order.

(6) An order under this section is to have effect subject to such conditions as are specified in the order.

(7) This section does not affect any right of a person to refuse to do anything on the ground that to do so might tend to expose him or his spouse or civil partner to proceedings for an offence or for the recovery of a penalty.

(8) In this section—

"court" means the High Court, and

"premises" includes any vehicle;

and an order under this section may describe anything generally, whether by reference to a class or otherwise.

**9A–757** *Note*—Amended by the Civil Partnership Act 2004 s.261(1), Sch.27, para 154.

**Effect of section**

**9A–758** This section puts on a statutory footing the High Court's powers to grant orders aimed at securing the preservation of evidence for the purposes of civil proceedings. It does not implement recommendations made in "Access to Justice Final Report" (July 1996), but has a different provenance.

In a report prepared by a committee of judges appointed by the Judges' Council and published in 1992, the uncertainty of the basis of the Court's jurisdiction to grant Anton Piller orders was noted. Some judges had suggested that the jurisdiction may be based on the general power to grant injunctions found in the Senior Courts Act 1981 s.37(1); others preferred to say that it is based on the Court's inherent jurisdiction to make interlocutory orders for a securing a just and proper trial of the issues joined between the parties. The committee recommended that the legal basis for the making of these orders should be laid down in primary legislation which should also make provision for covering the principal features of the remedy (see "Anton Piller Orders: A Consultation Paper" (LCD 1992), para.3.2).

Such legislation is now found in this section. The person against whom the order is made is required to comply with the order so as to permit entry to premises, to facilitate inspection of matters specified in the court order and to permit the removal of items for safe keeping. It may be noted that this provision preserves the privilege against self-incrimination. In the 1992 report it was recommended that s.72 of the 1981 Act should be extended so that the privilege should no longer apply to civil proceedings generally. This recommendation raised wider issues which still await official attention. See further para.9A–271aboveand para.15–93 below.

For limits on jurisdiction of county courts in relation to grant relief of the type referred to in s.7, see County Court Remedies Regulations (SI 1991/1222) reg.2(a) (para.9B–78).

## Disclosure etc. of documents before action begun

**8.**—(1) The Lord Chancellor may by order amend the provisions of section 33(2) of the Senior Courts Act 1981, or section 52(2) of the County Courts Act 1984 (power of court to order disclosure etc. of documents where claim may be made in respect of personal injury or death), so as to extend the provisions— **9A–759**

(a) to circumstances where other claims may be made, or

(b) generally.

(2) The power to make an order under this section is exercisable by statutory instrument which shall be subject to annulment in pursuance of a resolution of either House of Parliament.

*Note* —Amended by the Constitutional Reform Act 2005 s.59 and Sch.11, para.1 with effect from October 1, 2009 (SI 2009/1604). **9A–759.1**

### Senior Courts Act 1981 s.33(2) and the County Courts Act 1984 s.52(2)

This section provides an order-making power to extend the circumstances in which courts have power to order disclosure of documents before legal proceedings commence. Before 1970, where proceedings had been commenced an order for discovery of documents could be made under rules of court against a party to those proceedings but an order could not be made (1) before proceedings had been commenced, or (2) if they had been commenced, against a person, who was not a party. These two restrictions on, respectively, "pre-action" discovery and "third party" discovery were modified by statute. Nowadays, the power to order "pre-action" discovery is derived from the Senior Courts Act 1981 s.33(2) and the County Courts Act 1984 s.52(2) (see paras 9A–110 and 9A–503). The power to order "third party" discovery is derived from the Senior Courts Act 1981 s.34(2) and the County Courts Act 1984 s.53(2) (see paras 9A–115 and 9A–508). **9A–760**

In the "Access to Justice Final Report" (July 1995), no recommendation was made concerning "third party" discovery, but it was recommended that "pre-action" discovery under s.33(2) of the 1981 Act and s.52(2) of the 1984 Act should be altered in two respects. It was recommended, first, that "pre-action" discovery should no longer be limited to situations in which personal injury and wrongful death proceedings are in prospect (*ibid.*, paras 47 *et seq.*), and secondly, that it should be possible where a personal injury or wrongful death action is in prospect for an application to be made against a person who is not likely to be a party (*ibid.*, paras 51 *et seq.*).

### Effect of section

This section provides legislation necessary for carrying those two recommendations into effect. The Lord Chancellor is given power to amend s.33(2) and s.52(2) by statutory instrument (subject to negative resolution) so as to extend the provisions of those subsections (a) to circumstances where other claims may be made, or (b) generally. Amendments to s.33(2) and s.52(2), sufficient to carry into effect the first (but not the **9A–761**

*Paragraph numbers marked with a "+" can be found online and on CD.*

second) of these recommendations, were made by the Civil Procedure (Modification of Enactments) Order 1998 (SI 1998/2940) paras 5(a) and 6(b). (It may be noted that this Order was made, not under s.8, but under s.4(2) of this Act.) In the "Access to Justice Final Report" it was not specifically recommended that s.33(2) and s.52(2) should be amended so as to enable that courts to grant "pre-action" orders for discovery against third parties where claims for other than personal injury and wrongful death are likely to be made in subsequent proceedings. It may be noted, however, that the powers given to the Lord Chancellor by this section are wide enough to enable him to amend s.33(2) and s.52(2) to accomplish such a change in the law.

As explained above, once proceedings are commenced, the court has power under s.34 of the 1981 Act and s.53 of the 1984 Act, in accordance with rules of court, to make an order requiring a person who is not a party to the proceedings to give disclosure of documents (and to permit inspection of property and the taking of samples). It is convenient to note here that, as a result of amendments to these sections made by the Civil Procedure (Modification of Enactments) Order 1998 (SI 1998/2940) paras 5(b) and 6(c), that power is not restricted to proceedings in respect of personal injuries or wrongful death.

*GENERAL*

### Interpretation

9A-762 **9.**—(1) A court the practice and procedure of which is governed by Civil Procedure Rules is referred to in this Act as being "within the scope" of the rules; and references to a court outside the scope of the rules are to be read accordingly.

(2) In this Act—

"enactment" includes an enactment contained in subordinate legislation (within the meaning of the Interpretation Act 1978), and

"practice directions" means directions as to the practice and procedure of any court within the scope of Civil Procedure Rules.

### Minor and consequential amendments

9A-763 **10.** Schedule 2 (which makes minor and consequential amendments) is to have effect.

### Short title, commencement and extent

9A-764 **11.**—(1) This Act may be cited as the Civil Procedure Act 1997.

(2) Sections 1 to 10 are to come into force on such day as the Lord Chancellor may by order made by statutory instrument appoint, and different days may be appointed for different purposes.

(3) This Act extends to England and Wales only.

**SECTION 1** SCHEDULE 1

CIVIL PROCEDURE RULES

*Matters dealt with by the former rules*

9A-765 1. Among the matters which Civil Procedure Rules may be made about are any matters which were governed by the former Rules of the Supreme Court or the former county court rules (that is, the Rules of the Supreme Court (Revision) 1965 and the County Court Rules 1981).

***Paragraph numbers marked with a "+" can be found online and on CD.***

*Exercise of jurisdiction*

2. Civil Procedure Rules may provide for the exercise of the jurisdiction of any court within the scope of the rules by officers or other staff of the court. **9A–766**

*Removal of proceedings*

3.—(1) Civil Procedure Rules may provide for the removal of proceedings at any stage— **9A–767**

(a) within the High Court (for example, between different divisions or different district registries), or

(b) between county courts.

(2) In sub-paragraph (1)—

(a) "provide for the removal of proceedings" means—

(i) provide for transfer of proceedings, or

(ii) provide for any jurisdiction in any proceedings to be exercised (whether concurrently or not) elsewhere within the High Court or, as the case may be, by another county court without the proceedings being transferred, and

(b) "proceedings" includes any part of proceedings.

*Evidence*

4. Civil Procedure Rules may modify the rules of evidence as they apply to proceedings in any court within the scope of the rules. **9A–768**

*Application of other rules*

5.—(1) Civil Procedure Rules may apply any rules of court which relate to a court which is outside the scope of Civil Procedure Rules. **9A–769**

(2) Any rules of court, not made by the Civil Procedure Rule Committee, which apply to proceedings of a particular kind in a court within the scope of Civil Procedure Rules may be applied by Civil Procedure Rules to other proceedings in such a court.

(3) In this paragraph "rules of court" includes any provision governing the practice and procedure of a court which is made by or under an enactment.

(4) Where Civil Procedure Rules may be made by applying other rules, the other rules may be applied—

(a) to any extent,

(b) with or without modification, and

(c) as amended from time to time.

*Practice directions*

6. Civil Procedure Rules may, instead of providing for any matter, refer to provision made or to be made about that matter by directions. **9A–770**

*Different provision for different cases etc.*

7. The power to make Civil Procedure Rules includes power to make different provision for different cases or different areas, including different provision— **9A–771**

(a) for a specific court or specific division of a court, or

(b) for specific proceedings, or a specific jurisdiction, specified in the rules.

*Note* —For explanation of paragraphs in this Schedule, see notes to s.1 above. **9A–772**

**SECTION 10**

## SCHEDULE 2

### MINOR AND CONSEQUENTIAL AMENDMENTS

*Note* —By this Schedule, minor and consequential amendments were made to the Senior Courts Act 1981, the County Courts Act 1984, the Courts and Legal Services Act 1990, and the Matrimonial and Family Proceedings Act 1984. The first three of these Acts are printed elsewhere in this volume and, where necessary, the amendments made by this Schedule have been incorporated. **9A–773**

***Paragraph numbers marked with a "+" can be found online and on CD.***

# Access to Justice Act 1999

9A–774 (1999 c.22)

ARRANGEMENT OF SECTIONS

PART I



PART II



PART IV

APPEALS, COURTS, JUDGES AND COURT PROCEEDINGS

*APPEALS*



*JUDGES ETC.*



***Paragraph numbers marked with a "+" can be found online and on CD.***

**Paragraph numbers marked with a "+" denote content that is available on White Book on Westlaw UK or the Civil Procedure CD.**

*Note*—The functions of the Secretary of State for Constitutional Affairs under Pts 1 to 3 and Pt 7 of this Act, so far as relating to any provisions of those Parts, were transferred to the Lord Chancellor by The Transfer of Functions (Lord Chancellor and Secretary of State) Order 2005 (SI 2005/3429) with effect from January 12, 2006. **9A–775**

**For ss.1 to 30, 44 to 47 and 51 to 53 of the Access to Justice Act 1999 (see Arrangement) plus any related commentary see paragraphs 9A–776+ to 9A–840+ on White Book on Westlaw UK or the Civil Procedure CD.**

*Section —*

## PART IV

## APPEALS, COURTS, JUDGES AND COURT PROCEEDINGS

*APPEALS*

### Permission to appeal

**54.**—(1) Rules of court may provide that any right of appeal to— **9A–841**

(a) a county court,

(b) the High Court, or

(c) the Court of Appeal,

may be exercised only with permission.

(2) This section does not apply to a right of appeal in a criminal cause or matter.

(3) For the purposes of subsection (1) rules of court may make provision as to—

(a) the classes of case in which a right of appeal may be exercised only with permission,

(b) the court or courts which may give permission for the purposes of this section,

(c) any considerations to be taken into account in deciding whether permission should be given, and

(d) any requirements to be satisfied before permission may be given,

and may make different provision for different circumstances.

(4) No appeal may be made against a decision of a court under this section to give or refuse permission (but this subsection does not affect any right under rules of court to make a further application for permission to the same or another court).

(5) For the purposes of this section a right to make an application to have a case stated for the opinion of the High Court constitutes a right of appeal.

(2) The power conferred by subsection (1)(b) shall be subject to rules of court.

9A-848.1 *Note* —Amended by the Constitutional Reform Act 2005 Sch.9 para.68 with effect from October 1, 2009 (SI 2009/1604).

9A-849 * * * *

*JUDGES ETC.*

## Judges holding office in European or international courts

**68.**—(1) A holder of a United Kingdom judicial office may hold office in a relevant international court without being required to relinquish the United Kingdom judicial office.

(2) In this section—

"United Kingdom judicial office" means the office of—

(a) Lord Justice of Appeal, Justice of the High Court or Circuit Judge, in England and Wales,

(b) judge of the Court of Session or sheriff, in Scotland, or

(c) Lord Justice of Appeal, judge of the High Court or county court judge, in Northern Ireland, and

"relevant international court" means—

(a) any court established for any purposes of the European Communities, or

(b) any international court (apart from the European Court of Human Rights) which is designated in relation to the holder of a United Kingdom judicial office by the appropriate Minister.

(3) A holder of a United Kingdom judicial office who also holds office in a relevant international court is not required to perform any duties as the holder of the United Kingdom judicial office but does not count as holding the United Kingdom judicial office—

(a) for the purposes of section 12(1) to (6) of the [1981 c. 54.], Senior Courts Act 1981 section 9(1)(c) or (d) of the [1973 c. 15.] Administration of Justice Act 1973, section 18 of the [1971 c. 23.] Courts Act 1971, section 14 of the [1907 c. 51.] Sheriff Courts (Scotland) Act 1907 or section 106 of the [1959 c. 25(N.I.).] County Courts Act (Northern Ireland) 1959 (judicial salaries),

(b) for the purposes of, or of any scheme established by and in accordance with, the [1993 c. 8.] Judicial Pensions and Retirement Act 1993, the [1981 c. 20.] Judicial Pensions Act 1981, the [1961 c. 42.] Sheriffs' Pensions (Scotland) Act 1961 or the County Courts Act (Northern Ireland) 1959 (judicial pensions), or

(c) for the purposes of section 2(1) or 4(1) of the Senior Courts Act 1981 1981, section 1(1) of the [1988 c. 36.] Court of Session Act 1988 or section 2(1) or 3(1) of the [1978 c. 23.] Judicature (Northern Ireland) Act 1978 (judicial numbers).

(4) If the sheriff principal of any sheriffdom also holds office in a relevant international court, section 11(1) of the [1971 c. 58.] Sheriff Courts (Scotland) Act 1971 (temporary appointment of sheriff principal) applies as if the office of sheriff principal of that sheriffdom were vacant.

(5) The appropriate Minister may be order made by statutory instrument make in relation to a holder of a United Kingdom judicial office who has ceased to hold office in a relevant international court such transitional provision (including, in particular, provision for a temporary increase in the maximum number of judges) as he considers appropriate.

(6) In this section "the appropriate Minister" means—

(a) in relation to any United Kingdom judicial office specified in paragraph (a) or (c) of the definition in subsection (2), the Lord Chancellor, and

(b) in relation to any United Kingdom judicial office specified in paragraph (b) of that definition, the Secretary of State.

(7) A statutory instrument containing an order made under subsection (5) shall be subject to annulment in pursuance of a resolution of either House of Parliament.

(8) The Lord Chancellor may exercise functions under this section in relation to the holder of a United Kingdom judicial office specified in paragraph (a) of the definition in subsection (2) only after consulting the Lord Chief Justice of England and Wales.

(9) The Lord Chancellor may exercise functions under this section in relation to the holder of a United Kingdom judicial office specified in paragraph (c) of the definition in subsection (2) only after consulting the Lord Chief Justice of Northern Ireland.

(10) The Lord Chief Justice of England and Wales may nominate a judicial office holder (within the meaning of section 109(4) of the Constitutional Reform Act 2005) to exercise his functions under subsection (8).

(11) The Lord Chief Justice of Northern Ireland may nominate any of the following to exercise his functions under subsection (9)—

(a) the holder of one of the offices listed in Schedule 1 to the Justice (Northern Ireland) Act 2002;

(b) a Lord Justice of Appeal (as defined in section 88 of that Act).

*Note*—Amended by the Constitutional Reform Act 2005 s.15(1), Sch.4, para.281, and s.59 and Sch.11, para.1 with effect from October 1, 2009 (SI 2009/1604). **9A-850**

* * * * **9A-851**

**Vice-president of Queen's Bench Division.**

**69.**—(1) The Lord Chancellor may appoint one of the ordinary judges of the Court of Appeal as vice-president of the Queen's Bench Division; and any person so appointed shall hold that office in accordance with the terms of his appointment.

(1A) The Lord Chief Justice may nominate a judicial office holder

MAIN STATUTES

***Paragraph numbers marked with a "+" can be found online and on CD.***

(as defined in section 109(4) of the Constitutional Reform Act 2005) to exercise his functions under subsection (1).

(2) In section 4 of the Senior Courts Act 1981 (composition of High Court)—

(a) in subsection (1) (membership), after the words "the Senior Presiding Judge;" insert—

"(ddd) the vice-president of the Queen's Bench Division;"

, and

(b) in subsection (6) (vacancy in offices not to affect constitution), at the end insert "and whether or not an appointment has been made to the office of vice-president of the Queen's Bench Division".

(3) In section 5 of that Act (divisions of High Court), in subsection (1)(b) (Queen's Bench Division), after "thereof," insert "the vice-president of the Queen's Bench Division".

9A-852 *Note* —Amended by the Constitutional Reform Act 2005 s.15(1) and Sch.4 para.282, and with effect from October 1, 2009 by s.59 and Sch.11 para.1 (SI 2009/1604).

## *SCHEDULES*

**For Schs 1 to 3 and 8 to the Access to Justice Act 1999 (see Arrangement) plus any related commentary see paragraphs 9A–853+ to 9A–895+ on White Book on Westlaw UK or the Civil Procedure CD.**

## Access to Justice Act 1999 (Destination of Appeals) Order 2000

9A-896 (S.I. 2000 No. 1071) (L.10)

### Introductory note

9A-897 See also CPR Pt 52.

This Order was made under the Access to Justice Act 1999 s.56, and came into effect on May 2, 2000. That section gives the Lord Chancellor power to provide by Order that appeals which would lie to (a) a county court, (b) the High Court, or (c) the Court of Appeal, shall lie instead to another of those courts, as specified in the Order.

The references to CPR Pts 57 to 62 were added to para.(b) of art.4 of this Order by the Civil Procedure (Modification of Enactments) Order 2002 (SI 2002/439) with effect from March 23, 2002. The heading to art.2 is misleading, as it is concerned, not with appeals from, but with appeals to, the High Court.

art.4 was amended by the Civil Procedure (Modification of Enactments) Order 2003 (SI 2003/490) with effect from April 1, 2003.

### Citation, commencement and interpretation

9A-898 **1.**—(1) This Order may be cited as the Access to Justice Act 1999 (Destination of Appeals) Order 2000 and shall come into force on 2nd May 2000.

(2) In this Order—

(a) "decision" includes any judgment, order or direction of the High Court or a county court;

(b) "family proceedings" means proceedings which are business of any description which in the High Court is for the time being assigned to the Family Division and to no other Division by or under section 61 of (and Schedule 1 to) the Senior Courts Act 1981; and

(c) "final decision" means a decision of a court that would finally determine (subject to any possible appeal or detailed assessment of costs) the entire proceedings whichever way the court decided the issues before it.

(3) A decision of a court shall be treated as a final decision where it—

(a) is made at the conclusion of part of a hearing or trial which has been split into parts; and

(b) would, if made at the conclusion of that hearing or trial, be a final decision under paragraph (2)(c).

(4) Articles 2 to 6—

(a) do not apply to an appeal in family proceedings; and

(b) are subject to—

(i) any enactment that provides a different route of appeal (other than section 16(1) of the Senior Courts Act 1981 or section 77(1) of the County Courts Act 1984); and

(ii) any requirement to obtain permission to appeal.

*Note* —Amended by the Constitutional Reform Act 2005 s.59 and Sch.11, para.1 with effect from October 1, 2009 (SI 2009/1604). **9A–898.1**

**Appeals from the High Court**

**2.** Subject to articles 4 and 5, an appeal shall lie to a judge of the High Court where the decision to be appealed is made by— **9A–899**

(a) a person holding an office referred to in Part II of Schedule 2 to the Senior Courts Act 1981;

(b) a district judge of the High Court; or

(c) a person appointed to act as a deputy for any person holding such an office as is referred to in sub-paragraphs (a) and (b) or to act as a temporary additional officer in any such office.

*Note* —Amended by the Constitutional Reform Act 2005 s.59 and Sch.11, para.1 with effect from October 1, 2009 (SI 2009/1604). **9A–899.1**

**Appeals from a county court**

**3.**—(1) Subject to articles 4 and 5 and to paragraph (2), an appeal shall lie from a decision of a county court to the High Court. **9A–900**

(2) Subject to articles 4 and 5, where the decision to be appealed is made by a district judge or deputy district judge of a county court, an appeal shall lie to a judge of a county court.



**Appeals in a claim allocated to the multi-track or in specialist proceedings**

**4.** An appeal shall lie to the Court of Appeal where the decision to be appealed is a final decision— **9A–901**

(a) in a claim made under Part 7 of the Civil Procedure Rules 1998 and allocated to the multi-track under those Rules, or

(b) made in proceedings under the Companies Act 1985 or the Companies Act 1989 or to which Sections I, II or III of Part 57 or any of Parts 58 to 63 of the Civil Procedure Rules 1998 apply.

**Appeals where decision was itself made on appeal**

9A–902 5. Where—

(a) an appeal is made to a county court or the High Court (other than from the decision of an officer of the court authorised to assess costs by the Lord Chancellor); and

(b) on hearing the appeal the court makes a decision,

an appeal shall lie from that decision to the Court of Appeal and not to any other court.

**Transitional provisions**

9A–903 6. Where a person has filed a notice of appeal or applied for permission to appeal before 2nd May 2000—

(a) this Order shall not apply to the appeal to which that notice or application relates; and

(b) that appeal shall lie to the court to which it would have lain before 2nd May 2000.

**Consequential amendments**

9A–904 7. In section 16(1) of the Senior Courts Act 1981, before "the Court of Appeal" the second time it appears, insert "or as provided by any order made by the Lord Chancellor under section 56(1) of the Access to Justice Act 1999".

9A–904.1 *Note* —Amended by the Constitutional Reform Act 2005 s.59 and Sch.11, para.1 with effect from October 1, 2009 (SI 2009/1604).

9A–905 8. In section 77(1) of the County Courts Act 1984, after "Act" insert "and to any order made by the Lord Chancellor under section 56(1) of the Access to Justice Act 1999".

## Courts Act 2003

9A–906 (2003 c.39)

ARRANGEMENT OF SECTIONS

PART 1

SECT.



***Paragraph numbers marked with a "+" can be found online and on CD.***

**Paragraph numbers marked with a "+" denote content that is available on White Book on Westlaw UK or the Civil Procedure CD.**

## Constitutional Reform Act 2005

(2005 c.4) 9A–962

Arrangement of Sections



***Paragraph numbers marked with a "+" can be found online and on CD.***

**Paragraph numbers marked with a "+" denote content that is available on White Book on Westlaw UK or the Civil Procedure CD.**

## Tribunals, Courts and Enforcement Act 2007

9A–994

(2007 c.15)

ARRANGEMENT OF SECTIONS

PART 1

CHAPTER 1



***Paragraph numbers marked with a "+" can be found online and on CD.***

***Paragraph numbers marked with a "+" can be found online and on CD.***



MAIN STATUTES

***Paragraph numbers marked with a "+" can be found online and on CD.***

***Paragraph numbers marked with a "+" can be found online and on CD.***

**For ss.1 to 12 of the Tribunals, Courts and Enforcement Act 2007 (see Arrangement) plus any related commentary see paragraphs 9A–995+ to 9A–1006+ on White Book on Westlaw UK or the Civil Procedure CD.**

## Right to appeal to Court of Appeal etc.

9A–1007 **13.**—(1) For the purposes of subsection (2), the reference to a right of appeal is to a right to appeal to the relevant appellate court on any point of law arising from a decision made by the Upper Tribunal other than an excluded decision.

(2) Any party to a case has a right of appeal, subject to subsection (14).

(3) That right may be exercised only with permission (or, in Northern Ireland, leave).

(4) Permission (or leave) may be given by—

(a) the Upper Tribunal, or

(b) the relevant appellate court,

on an application by the party.

(5) An application may be made under subsection (4) to the relevant appellate court only if permission (or leave) has been refused by the Upper Tribunal.

(6) The Lord Chancellor may, as respects an application under subsection (4) that falls within subsection (7) and for which the relevant appellate court is the Court of Appeal in England and Wales or the Court of Appeal in Northern Ireland, by order make provision for permission (or leave) not to be granted on the application unless the Upper Tribunal or (as the case may be) the relevant appellate court considers—

(a) that the proposed appeal would raise some important point of principle or practice, or

(b) that there is some other compelling reason for the relevant appellate court to hear the appeal.

(7) An application falls within this subsection if the application is for permission (or leave) to appeal from any decision of the Upper Tribunal on an appeal under section 11.

(8) For the purposes of subsection (1), an "excluded decision" is—

(a) any decision of the Upper Tribunal on an appeal under section 28(4) or (6) of the Data Protection Act 1998 (c. 29) (appeals against national security certificate),

(b) any decision of the Upper Tribunal on an appeal under section 60(1) or (4) of the Freedom of Information Act 2000 (c. 36) (appeals against national security certificate),

(c) any decision of the Upper Tribunal on an application under section 11(4)(b) (application for permission or leave to appeal),

(d) a decision of the Upper Tribunal under section 10—

(i) to review, or not to review, an earlier decision of the tribunal,

(ii) to take no action, or not to take any particular action, in the light of a review of an earlier decision of the tribunal, or

(iii) to set aside an earlier decision of the tribunal,

(e) a decision of the Upper Tribunal that is set aside under section 10 (including a decision set aside after proceedings on an appeal under this section have been begun), or

(f) any decision of the Upper Tribunal that is of a description specified in an order made by the Lord Chancellor.

(9) A description may be specified under subsection (8)(f) only if—

(a) in the case of a decision of that description, there is a right to appeal to a court from the decision and that right is, or includes, something other than a right (however expressed) to appeal on any point of law arising from the decision, or

(b) decisions of that description are made in carrying out a function transferred under section 30 and prior to the transfer of the function under section 30(1) there was no right to appeal from decisions of that description.

(10) Where—

(a) an order under subsection (8)(f) specifies a description of decisions, and

(b) decisions of that description are made in carrying out a function transferred under section 30,

the order must be framed so as to come into force no later than the time when the transfer under section 30 of the function takes effect (but power to revoke the order continues to be exercisable after that time, and power to amend the order continues to be exercisable after that time for the purpose of narrowing the description for the time being specified).

(11) Before the Upper Tribunal decides an application made to it under subsection (4), the Upper Tribunal must specify the court that is to be the relevant appellate court as respects the proposed appeal.

(12) The court to be specified under subsection (11) in relation to a proposed appeal is whichever of the following courts appears to the Upper Tribunal to be the most appropriate—

(a) the Court of Appeal in England and Wales;

(b) the Court of Session;

(c) the Court of Appeal in Northern Ireland.

(13) In this section except subsection (11), "the relevant appellate court", as respects an appeal, means the court specified as respects that appeal by the Upper Tribunal under subsection (11).

(14) The Lord Chancellor may by order make provision for a person to be treated as being, or to be treated as not being, a party to a case for the purposes of subsection (2).

(15) Rules of court may make provision as to the time within which an application under subsection (4) to the relevant appellate court must be made.

### Proceedings on appeal to Court of Appeal etc.

9A–1008 **14.**—(1) Subsection (2) applies if the relevant appellate court, in deciding an appeal under section 13, finds that the making of the decision concerned involved the making of an error on a point of law.

(2) The relevant appellate court—

(a) may (but need not) set aside the decision of the Upper Tribunal, and

(b) if it does, must either—

(i) remit the case to the Upper Tribunal or, where the decision of the Upper Tribunal was on an appeal or reference from another tribunal or some other person, to the Upper Tribunal or that other tribunal or person, with directions for its reconsideration, or

(ii) re-make the decision.

(3) In acting under subsection (2)(b)(i), the relevant appellate court may also—

(a) direct that the persons who are chosen to reconsider the case are not to be the same as those who—

(i) where the case is remitted to the Upper Tribunal, made the decision of the Upper Tribunal that has been set aside, or

(ii) where the case is remitted to another tribunal or person, made the decision in respect of which the appeal or reference to the Upper Tribunal was made;

(b) give procedural directions in connection with the reconsideration of the case by the Upper Tribunal or other tribunal or person.

(4) In acting under subsection (2)(b)(ii), the relevant appellate court—

(a) may make any decision which the Upper Tribunal could make if the Upper Tribunal were re-making the decision or (as the case may be) which the other tribunal or person could make if that other tribunal or person were re-making the decision, and

(b) may make such findings of fact as it considers appropriate.

(5) Where—

(a) under subsection (2)(b)(i) the relevant appellate court remits a case to the Upper Tribunal, and

(b) the decision set aside under subsection (2)(a) was made by the Upper Tribunal on an appeal or reference from another tribunal or some other person,

the Upper Tribunal may (instead of reconsidering the case itself) remit the case to that other tribunal or person, with the directions given by the relevant appellate court for its reconsideration.

(6) In acting under subsection (5), the Upper Tribunal may also—

(a) direct that the persons who are chosen to reconsider the case are not to be the same as those who made the decision in respect of which the appeal or reference to the Upper Tribunal was made;

(b) give procedural directions in connection with the reconsideration of the case by the other tribunal or person.

(7) In this section "the relevant appellate court", as respects an appeal under section 13, means the court specified as respects that appeal by the Upper Tribunal under section 13(11).

### Upper Tribunal's "judicial review" jurisdiction

9A-1009 **15.**—(1) The Upper Tribunal has power, in cases arising under the law of England and Wales or under the law of Northern Ireland, to grant the following kinds of relief—

(a) a mandatory order;
(b) a prohibiting order;
(c) a quashing order;
(d) a declaration;
(e) an injunction.

(2) The power under subsection (1) may be exercised by the Upper Tribunal if—

(a) certain conditions are met (see section 18), or
(b) the tribunal is authorised to proceed even though not all of those conditions are met (see section 19(3) and (4)).

(3) Relief under subsection (1) granted by the Upper Tribunal—

(a) has the same effect as the corresponding relief granted by the High Court on an application for judicial review, and
(b) is enforceable as if it were relief granted by the High Court on an application for judicial review.

(4) In deciding whether to grant relief under subsection (1)(a), (b) or (c), the Upper Tribunal must apply the principles that the High Court would apply in deciding whether to grant that relief on an application for judicial review.

(5) In deciding whether to grant relief under subsection (1)(d) or (e), the Upper Tribunal must—

(a) in cases arising under the law of England and Wales apply the principles that the High Court would apply in deciding whether to grant that relief under section 31(2) of the Senior Courts Act 1981 (c. 54) on an application for judicial review, and
(b) in cases arising under the law of Northern Ireland apply the principles that the High Court would apply in deciding whether to grant that relief on an application for judicial review.

(6) For the purposes of the application of subsection (3)(a) in relation to cases arising under the law of Northern Ireland—

(a) a mandatory order under subsection (1)(a) shall be taken to correspond to an order of mandamus,
(b) a prohibiting order under subsection (1)(b) shall be taken to correspond to an order of prohibition, and
(c) a quashing order under subsection (1)(c) shall be taken to correspond to an order of certiorari.

### Application for relief under section 15(1)

9A-1010 **16.**—(1) This section applies in relation to an application to the Upper Tribunal for relief under section 15(1).

(2) The application may be made only if permission (or, in a case arising under the law of Northern Ireland, leave) to make it has been obtained from the tribunal.

(3) The tribunal may not grant permission (or leave) to make the application unless it considers that the applicant has a sufficient interest in the matter to which the application relates.

(4) Subsection (5) applies where the tribunal considers—

(a) that there has been undue delay in making the application, and

(b) that granting the relief sought on the application would be likely to cause substantial hardship to, or substantially prejudice the rights of, any person or would be detrimental to good administration.

(5) The tribunal may—

(a) refuse to grant permission (or leave) for the making of the application;

(b) refuse to grant any relief sought on the application.

(6) The tribunal may award to the applicant damages, restitution or the recovery of a sum due if—

(a) the application includes a claim for such an award arising from any matter to which the application relates, and

(b) the tribunal is satisfied that such an award would have been made by the High Court if the claim had been made in an action begun in the High Court by the applicant at the time of making the application.

(7) An award under subsection (6) may be enforced as if it were an award of the High Court.

(8) Where—

(a) the tribunal refuses to grant permission (or leave) to apply for relief under section 15(1),

(b) the applicant appeals against that refusal, and

(c) the Court of Appeal grants the permission (or leave),

the Court of Appeal may go on to decide the application for relief under section 15(1).

(9) Subsections (4) and (5) do not prevent Tribunal Procedure Rules from limiting the time within which applications may be made.

**Quashing orders under section 15(1): supplementary provision**

**17.**—(1) If the Upper Tribunal makes a quashing order under section 15(1)(c) in respect of a decision, it may in addition— **9A-1011**

(a) remit the matter concerned to the court, tribunal or authority that made the decision, with a direction to reconsider the matter and reach a decision in accordance with the findings of the Upper Tribunal, or

(b) substitute its own decision for the decision in question.

(2) The power conferred by subsection (1)(b) is exercisable only if—

(a) the decision in question was made by a court or tribunal,
(b) the decision is quashed on the ground that there has been an error of law, and
(c) without the error, there would have been only one decision that the court or tribunal could have reached.

(3) Unless the Upper Tribunal otherwise directs, a decision substituted by it under subsection (1)(b) has effect as if it were a decision of the relevant court or tribunal.

### Limits of jurisdiction under section 15(1)

9A-1012 **18.**—(1) This section applies where an application made to the Upper Tribunal seeks (whether or not alone)—

(a) relief under section 15(1), or
(b) permission (or, in a case arising under the law of Northern Ireland, leave) to apply for relief under section 15(1).

(2) If Conditions 1 to 4 are met, the tribunal has the function of deciding the application.

(3) If the tribunal does not have the function of deciding the application, it must by order transfer the application to the High Court.

(4) Condition 1 is that the application does not seek anything other than—

(a) relief under section 15(1);
(b) permission (or, in a case arising under the law of Northern Ireland, leave) to apply for relief under section 15(1);
(c) an award under section 16(6);
(d) interest;
(e) costs.

(5) Condition 2 is that the application does not call into question anything done by the Crown Court.

(6) Condition 3 is that the application falls within a class specified for the purposes of this subsection in a direction given in accordance with Part 1 of Schedule 2 to the Constitutional Reform Act 2005 (c. 4).

(7) The power to give directions under subsection (6) includes—

(a) power to vary or revoke directions made in exercise of the power, and
(b) power to make different provision for different purposes.

(8) Condition 4 is that the judge presiding at the hearing of the application is either—

(a) a judge of the High Court or the Court of Appeal in England and Wales or Northern Ireland, or a judge of the Court of Session, or
(b) such other persons as may be agreed from time to time between the Lord Chief Justice, the Lord President, or the Lord Chief Justice of Northern Ireland, as the case may be, and the Senior President of Tribunals.

*Paragraph numbers marked with a "+" can be found online and on CD.*

(9) Where the application is transferred to the High Court under subsection (3)—

(a) the application is to be treated for all purposes as if it—

(i) had been made to the High Court, and

(ii) sought things corresponding to those sought from the tribunal, and

(b) any steps taken, permission (or leave) given or orders made by the tribunal in relation to the application are to be treated as taken, given or made by the High Court.

(10) Rules of court may make provision for the purpose of supplementing subsection (9).

(11) The provision that may be made by Tribunal Procedure Rules about amendment of an application for relief under section 15(1) includes, in particular, provision about amendments that would cause the application to become transferrable under subsection (3).

(12) For the purposes of subsection (9)(a)(ii), in relation to an application transferred to the High Court in Northern Ireland—

(a) an order of mandamus shall be taken to correspond to a mandatory order under section 15(1)(a),

(b) an order of prohibition shall be taken to correspond to a prohibiting order under section 15(1)(b), and

(c) an order of certiorari shall be taken to correspond to a quashing order under section 15(1)(c).

**For ss.20 to 149 and Schs 1 to 23 of the Tribunals, Courts and Enforcement Act 2007 (see Arrangement) plus any related commentary see paragraphs 9A–1014+ to 9A–1232+ on White Book on Westlaw UK or the Civil Procedure CD.**

# 9B OTHER STATUTES AND REGULATIONS

**For a list of the statutes and regulations published in Section 9B, see the contents list preceding Section 9A (Main Statutes).**

## Administration of Justice (Miscellaneous Provisions) Act 1933

(1933 23 & 24 Geo. 5 c.36) **9B–0**

Arrangement of Sections



**Paragraph numbers marked with a "+" denote content that is available on the White Book on Westlaw UK Service or the Civil Procedure CD.**

## Administration of Justice Act 1925

(1925 15 & 16 Geo. 5 c.28) **9B–6.1**

Arrangement of Sections



**Paragraph numbers marked with a "+" denote content that is available on the White Book on Westlaw UK Service or the Civil Procedure CD.**

## Administration of Justice Act 1960

(1960 8 & 9 Eliz. 2 c.65) **9B–14**

Arrangement of Sections

*Contempt of Court, Habeas Corpus and Certiorari*



### *Contempt of Court, Habeas Corpus and Certiorari*

### Publication of information relating to proceedings in private

**12.**—(1) The publication of information relating to proceedings before any court sitting in private shall not of itself be contempt of court except in the following cases, that is to say— **9B–15**

(a) where the proceedings—

(i) relate to the exercise of the inherent jurisdiction of the High Court with respect to minors;

***Paragraph numbers marked with a "+" can be found online and on CD.***

(ii) are brought under the Children Act 1989 or the Adoption and Children Act 2002; or

(iii) otherwise relate wholly or mainly to the maintenance or upbringing of a minor;

(b) where the proceedings are brought under the Mental Capacity Act 2005 or under any provision of the Mental Health Act 1983, or under any provision of the Act authorising an application or reference to be made to the First-tier Tribunal, the Mental Health Review Tribunal for Wales or to a county court;

(c) where the court sits in private for reasons of national security during that part of the proceedings about which the information in question is published;

(d) where the information relates to a secret process, discovery or invention which is in issue in the proceedings;

(e) where the court (having power to do so) expressly prohibits the publication of all information relating to the proceedings or of information of the description which is published.

(2) Without prejudice to the foregoing subsection, the publication of the text or a summary of the whole or part of an order made by a court sitting in private shall not of itself be contempt of court except where the court (having power to do so) expressly prohibits the publication.

(3) In this section references to a court include references to a judge and to a tribunal and to any person exercising the functions of a court, a judge or tribunal; and references to a court sitting in private include references to a court sitting in camera or in chambers.

(4) Nothing in this section shall be construed as implying that any publication is punishable as contempt of court which would not be so punishable apart from this section (and in particular where the publication is not so punishable by reason of being authorised by rules of court).

**9B–16** *Note*—Part VIII of the Mental Health Act 1959 was replaced by Pt VII of the Mental Health Act 1983. Amended by the Children Act 1989 Sch.13; the Children Act 2004 s.62(2). Amended by the Children Act 1989 Sch.13; the Adoption and Children Act 2002 s.101(2); and the Children Act 2004 s.62(2); the Mental Capacity Act 2005 s.67(1) and Sch.6 para.10; and SI 2008/2833.

**"court sitting in private"**

**9B–17** Traditionally, legal proceedings have been conducted either "in court" or "in chambers" (see Senior Courts Act 1981 s.67). Nowadays, it is common to draw a distinction between courts sitting "in public" or "in private" (see CPR r.39.2). It is expressly provided that, in s.12 references to a court "sitting in private" include a court sitting "in court" but in camera, or a court sitting "in chambers" (s.12(3)). This would suggest that the section was drafted on the assumption that, contrary to the modern position, a court sitting "in chambers" was *ipso facto* a court sitting "in private". These pairings are not co-terminous; at least, a court sitting "in chambers" is not necessarily a court sitting "in private". See further paras 9A–315 to 9A–319 above, and Vol.1, para.39.2.1.

When enacted, s.12 was remedial in the sense that it had the effect of making it clear that the publication of information relating to proceedings "in private" is not necessarily contempt. The section sets out the circumstances in which, subject to exceptions, it shall be a contempt of court to publish information given in private proceedings. The stated exceptions are not exhaustive. For a recent review of the relevant law, see *Clibbery v Allan* [2002] EWCA Civ 45; [2002] 2 W.L.R. 1511, CA, a case involving specifically the confidentiality of documents disclosed in, and the publication of information relating to, proceedings in the Family Division conducted in private.

## Appeal in cases of contempt of court

**13.**—(1) Subject to the provisions of this section, an appeal shall lie under this section from any order or decision of a court in the exercise of jurisdiction to punish for contempt of court (including criminal contempt); and in relation to any such order or decision the provisions of this section shall have effect in substitution for any other enactment relating to appeals in civil or criminal proceedings. **9B–18**

(2) An appeal under this section shall lie in any case at the instance of the defendant and, in the case of an application for committal or attachment, at the instance of the applicant; and the appeal shall lie—

(a) from an order or decision of any inferior court not referred to in the next following paragraph, to the High Court;

(b) from an order or decision of a county court or any other inferior court from which appeals generally lie to the civil division of the Court of Appeal, and from an order or decision (other than a decision on an appeal under this section) of a single judge of the High Court, or of any court having the powers of the High Court or of a judge of that court, to the civil division of the Court of Appeal;

(bb) from an order or decision of the Crown Court to the Court of Appeal;

(c) from a decision of a single judge of the High Court on an appeal under this section, from an order or decision of a Divisional Court or the civil division of the Court of Appeal (including a decision of either of those courts on an appeal under this section) and from an order or decision of the criminal division of the Court of Appeal or the Courts-Martial Appeal Court, to the Supreme Court.

(3) The court to which an appeal is brought under this section may reverse or vary the order or decision of the court below, and make such other order as may be just; and without prejudice to the inherent powers of any court referred to in subsection (2) of this section, provision may be made by rules of court for authorising the release on bail of an appellant under this section.

(4) Subsections (2) to (4) of section one and section two of this Act shall apply to an appeal to the Supreme Court under this section as they apply to an appeal to that House under the said section one, except that so much of the said subsection (2) as restricts the grant of leave to appeal shall apply only where the decision of the court below is a decision on appeal to that court under this section.

*Paragraph numbers marked with a "+" can be found online and on CD.*

(5) In this section "court" includes any tribunal or person having power to punish for contempt; and references in this section to an order or decision of a court in the exercise of jurisdiction to punish for contempt of court include references—

(a) to an order or decision of the High Court, the Crown Court or a county court under any enactment enabling that court to deal with an offence as if it were contempt of court;

(b) to an order or decision of a county court, under section 14, 92 or 118 of the County Courts Act 1984;

(c) to an order or decision of a magistrates' court under subsection (3) of section 63 of the Magistrates' Courts Act 1980,

but do not include references to order under section five of the Debtors Act 1869, or under any provision of the Magistrates' Courts Act 1980, or the County Courts Act 1984, except those referred to in paragraphs (b) and (c) of this subsection and except sections 38 and 142 of the last mentioned Act so far as those sections confer jurisdiction in respect of contempt of court.

(6) This section does not apply to a conviction or sentence in respect of which an appeal lies under Part I of the Criminal Appeal Act 1968, or to a decision of the criminal division of the Court of Appeal under that Part of that Act.

9B–19 *Note* —Amended by the Courts Act 1971 Sch.8, para.40(1) and Sch.11; and the Criminal Appeal Act 1968 Sch.5; the Senior Courts Act 1981 s.152(4) and Sch.7 the County Courts Act 1984 Sch.2, the Access to Justice Act 1999 s.64 and Sch.15, Pt III and the Constitutional Reform Act 2005, s.40 and Sch.9, para.13, with effect from October 1, 2009 (SI 2009/1604).

**Destination of appeals against orders punishing for contempt**

9B–20 In *Barnett LBC v Hurst* [2002] EWCA Civ 1009; 152 New L.J. 1275 (2002), CA, the Court of Appeal explained the appropriate routes for appeals from decisions made in committal proceedings by judges exercising county court jurisdiction. See further CPR Pt 52.

## Procedure on application for habeas corpus

9B–21 **14.**—(1) [...]

(2) Notwithstanding anything in any enactment or rule of law, where a criminal or civil application for habeas corpus has been made by or in respect of any person, no such application shall again be made by or in respect of that person on the same grounds, whether to the same court or judge or to any other court or judge, unless fresh evidence is adduced in support of the application ...

(3) In every case where the person by or in respect of whom an application for habeas corpus is made is restrained as a person liable, or treated by virtue of any enactment as liable, to be detained in pursuance of an order or direction under Part V of the Mental Health Act 1959 (otherwise than by virtue of paragraph (e) or paragraph (f) of subsection (2) of section seventy-three of that Act) the application shall be deemed for the purposes of his section and of

any appeal in the proceedings to constitute a criminal cause or matter.

*Note*—In subs.(3) see now the Mental Health Act 1983 s.48. Amended by the Access to Justice Act 1999 Sch.15, Pt III; and the Constitutional Reform Act 2005 ss.15(1) and 146, and Sch.4, para 52, Sch.18 (see para.9A–4.1 above). **9B–22**

#### Further application for habeas corpus

The applicant for habeas corpus must put forward on his initial application the whole of the case then fairly available to him, and the doctrine of *res judicata*, whereby it is an abuse of the process to raise in subsequent proceedings matters which could have been litigated in earlier proceedings, applies to subsequent proceedings for habeas corpus; and moreover, to constitute "fresh evidence" in support of a subsequent application within the meaning of s.14(2) the evidence must not be merely additional to or different from that which was adduced before the Court on the first application but evidence which the applicant could not have, or could not reasonably have been expected to, put forward on the first application (*Re Tarling* [1979] 1 W.L.R. 1417; [1979] 1 All E.R. 981, DC). **9B–23**

### Appeal in habeas corpus proceedings

**15.**—(1) Subject to the provisions of this section, an appeal shall lie, in any proceedings upon application for habeas corpus, whether civil or criminal, against an order for the release of the person restrained as well as against the refusal of such an order. **9B–24**

(2) [...]

(3) In relation to a decision of the High Court on a criminal application for habeas corpus, section one of this Act shall have effect as if so much of subsection (2) as restricts the grant of leave to appeal were omitted.

(4) Except as provided by section five of this Act in the case of an appeal against an order of the High Court on a criminal application, an appeal brought by virtue of this section shall not affect the right of the person restrained to be discharged in pursuance of the order under appeal and (unless an order under subsection (1) of that section is in force at the determination of the appeal) to remain at large regardless of the decision on appeal.

* * * *

*Note*—Subsection (2) repealed by the Access to Justice Act 1999 Sch.15, Pt III. **9B–25**

#### Release on bail pending appeal

In proceedings on application for habeas corpus in criminal matters, where the prosecutor is granted, or gives notice that he intends to apply for, leave to appeal to the House of Lords from the Divisional Court, the fugitive should not be released unconditionally, but only on bail pending the appeal to the House of Lords (*Government of USA v McCaffery* [1984] 1 W.L.R. 867; [1984] 2 All E.R. 570, HL, applying *DPP v Merriman* [1974] 3 All E.R. 42). **9B–26**

## SUPPLEMENTARY

### Interpretation

**17.**—(1) In this Act any reference to the defendant shall be construed— **9B–27**

(a) in relation to proceedings for an offence, and in relation to an application for an order of mandamus, prohibition or certiorari in connection with such proceedings, as a reference to the person who was or would have been the defendant in those proceedings;

(b) in relation to any proceedings or order for or in respect of contempt of court, as a reference to the person against whom the proceedings were brought or the order was made;

(c) in relation to a criminal application for habeas corpus, as a reference to the person by or in respect of whom that application was made,

and any reference to the prosecutor shall be construed accordingly.

(2) In this Act "application for habeas corpus" means an application for a writ of habeas corpus *ad subjiciendum* and references to a criminal application or civil application shall be construed according as the application does or does not constitute a criminal cause or matter.

(3) In this Act any reference to the court below shall, in relation to any function of a Divisional Court, be construed as a reference to the Divisional Court or to a judge according as the function is by virtue of rules of court exercisable by the Divisional Court or a judge.

(4) An appeal under section one of this Act shall be treated for the purposes of this Act as pending until any application for leave to appeal is disposed of and, if leave to appeal is granted, until the appeal is disposed of; and for the purposes of this Act an application for leave to appeal shall be treated as disposed of at the expiration of the time within which it may be made, if it is not made within that time.

(5) [...]

(6) Any reference in this Act to any other enactment is a reference thereto as amended by or under any other enactment, including this Act.

**9B–28** *Note*—Subsection (5) repealed by the Criminal Appeal Act 1995 Sch.3.

## Administration of Justice Act 1969

**9B–29** (1969 c.58)

ARRANGEMENT OF SECTIONS

PART II

APPEAL FROM HIGH COURT TO SUPREME COURT



***Paragraph numbers marked with a "+" can be found online and on CD.***

## Part II

## Appeal from High Court to Supreme Court

### Grant of certificate by trial Judge

**12.**—(1) Where on the application of any of the parties to any proceedings to which this section applies the judge is satisfied— **9B–30**

(a) that the relevant conditions are fulfilled in relation to his decision in those proceedings, and

(b) that a sufficient case for an appeal to the Supreme Court under this Part of this Act has been made out to justify an application for leave to bring such an appeal, and

(c) that all the parties to the proceedings consent to the grant of a certificate under this section,

the judge, subject to the following provisions of this Part of this Act, may grant a certificate to that effect.

(2) This section applies to any civil proceedings in the High Court which are either—

(a) proceedings before a single judge of the High Court, or

(b) [...]

(c) proceedings before a Divisional Court.

(3) Subject to any Order in Council made under the following provisions of this section, for the purposes of this section the relevant conditions, in relation to a decision of the judge in any proceedings, are that a point of law of general public importance is involved in that decision and that that point of law either—

(a) relates wholly or mainly to the construction of an enactment or of a statutory instrument, and has been fully argued in the proceedings and fully considered in the judgment of the judge in the proceedings, or

(b) is one in respect of which the judge is bound by a decision of the Court of Appeal or of the Supreme Court in previous proceedings, and was fully considered in the judgments given by the Court of Appeal or the Supreme Court (as the case may be) in those previous proceedings.

(4) Any application for a certificate under this section shall be made to the judge immediately after he gives judgment in the proceedings:

Provided that the judge may in any particular case entertain any such application made at any later time before the end of the period of fourteen days beginning with the date on which that judgment is given or such other period as may be prescribed by rules of court.

(5) No appeal shall lie against the grant or refusal of a certificate under this section.

(6) Her Majesty may by Order in Council amend subsection (3) of this section by altering, deleting, or substituting one or more new paragraphs for, either or both of paragraphs (a) and (b) of that subsection, or by adding one or more further paragraphs.

(7) Any Order in Council made under this section shall be subject to annulment in pursuance of a resolution of either House of Parliament.

(8) In this Part of this Act "civil proceedings" means any proceedings other than proceedings in a criminal cause or matter, and "the judge," in relation to any proceedings to which this section applies, means the judge or commissioner referred to in paragraph (a) of subsection (2) of this section, or the Divisional Court referred to in paragraph (c) of that subsection, as the case may be.

**9B-31** *Note* —Part II heading amended by the Constitutional Reform Act 2005 s.40 and Sch.9, para.20(2), with effect from October 1, 2009 (SI 2009/1604).

Amended by the Senior Courts Act 1981 s.152(4), Sch.7; the Courts Act 1971 s.56 and Sch.11 and the Constitutional Reform Act 2005 s.40 and Sch.9 para.20(3), with effect from October 1, 2009 (SI 2009/1604).

**Certificate for appeal from High Court to House of Lords**

**9B-32** For a case where a certificate under this section has been granted, see *Ealing London Borough Council v Race Relations Board* [1970] 1 W.L.R. 1599.

For a review of the general operation of this section, see *Inland Revenue Commissioners v Church Commissioners for England* [1975] 1 W.L.R. 251; [1974] 3 All E.R. 529). Even where the requirements of the section are satisfied, the judge has a discretion whether or not to grant the certificate, as where he considers that the case does not fall within the spirit, as distinct from the letter, of the section (*ibid.*).

In *Gawler v Raettig* [2007] EWCA Civ 1560, December 3, 2007, unrep., CA, a High Court judge granted a defendant in a road accident personal injury case a certificate under this section on the basis that his decision was one in which he was bound by the decision of the Court of Appeal in *Froom v Butcher* [1976] Q.B. 286, CA, where it was held that failure to wear a seat belt was contributory negligence. (The judge refused the defendant's application for permission to appeal to the Court of Appeal, but extended time for the making of such an application to that court pending a petition to the House Lord). A curiosity of this case is that the defendant applicant's submission under s.12 was made, not on the basis that the point of law in *Froom v Butcher* had been wrongly decided, but on the basis that the judge was not bound by the guidance given in that case as to the circumstances in which a reduction in the victim's damages would be appropriate and the proportion thereof. (In the event, the defendant was refused permission to appeal by the House of Lords, and subsequently, by the Court of Appeal.)

## Leave to appeal to Supreme Court

**9B-33** **13.**—(1) Where in any proceedings the judge grants a certificate under section 12 of this Act, then, at any time within one month from the date on which that certificate is granted or such extended time as in any particular case the Supreme Court may allow, any of the parties to the proceedings may make an application to the Supreme Court under this section.

(2) Subject to the following provisions of this section, if on such an application it appears to the Supreme Court to be expedient to do so, the Supreme Court may grant leave for an appeal to be brought directly to the Supreme Court; and where leave is granted under this section—

(a) no appeal from the decision of the judge to which the certificate relates shall lie to the Court of Appeal, but

(b) an appeal shall lie from that decision to the Supreme Court.

(3) Applications under this section shall be determined without a hearing.

(4) [...]

(5) Without prejudice to subsection (2) of this section, no appeal shall lie to the Court of Appeal from a decision of the judge in respect of which a certificate is granted under section 12 of this Act until—

(a) the time within which an application can be made under this section has expired, and

(b) where such an application is made, that application has been determined in accordance with the preceding provisions of this section.

*Note* —Amended by the Constitutional Reform Act 2005 s.40 and Sch.9, para.20(4), with effect from October 1, 2009 (SI 2009/1604). **9B–33.1**

**No appeal to Court of Appeal**

In *R. (Jones) v Ceredigion CC* [2007] UKHL 24; May 23, 2007, unrep., HL, a High Court judge determined an application for judicial review in favour of the claimant and quashed a decision made by the defendant local authority, The judge granted the defendants a certificate under s.12(1) to apply for permission to appeal to the House of Lords and, in addition, granted the defendants permission to appeal to the Court of Appeal if, in the event, the Lords did not grant permission. The House of Lords granted the defendants permission to appeal to them in relation to one of three issues on which the defendants sought to appeal. Subsequently, the defendants withdrew that appeal (in effect, abandoning the point), and applied for permission to appeal to the Court of Appeal on one of the two issues on which the House of Lords had refused permission. The claimant contended that, by virtue of s.13(2)(a), the defendants were precluded from bringing an appeal to the Court of Appeal. The Court held (by majority) that it did have jurisdiction to entertain the appeal, rejecting the argument that "decision" in s.13(2) could, in the circumstances of this case, refer only to the quashing order made by the judge ([2005] EWCA Civ 986; [2005] 1 W.L.R. 3626, CA). The House of Lords dismissed the claimant's further appeal, but for reasons different to that given by the Court of Appeal. The House explained and stated: (1) it is open to the Appeal Committee in response to an application for leave under s.13 to indicate that it will not receive argument on a particular point, (2) in accordance with the practice stated in para.4.15 of the Practice Directions Applicable to Civil Appeals (see para. 4A–31 above), where (as here) the Committee decides that leave to appeal should be given (in this case, restricting argument to one only of the issues appealed), it proposes such terms to the parties and invites submissions, (3) in this case, the defendants made such submissions which the Committee considered before confirming its order in the terms previously communicated, but the defendants then rejected what was proposed by exercising their option to withdraw the appeal, (4) in s.13(2) the words "leave is granted" must be understood to refer (a) to an unconditional grant of leave, or (b) to a grant of leave subject to conditions which are accepted or not unequivocally rejected; only then does the applicant lose his right to proceed in the Court of Appeal, (5) as the Committee's order in this case fell into neither category, the defendants were free to pursue a full appeal in the Court of Appeal. The Committee further explained that the defendants appreciated that the terms put forward by the Committee were proposals which it resisted, but they did not invite the Committee to refuse leave to appeal if minded to adhere to them; had the defendants done so the Committee doubtless would have accepted the invitation to refuse leave and then it would have been clear that they were free to pursue an appeal on all points to the Court of Appeal. **9B–34**

As a result of the transfer of the jurisdiction formerly exercised by the House of Lords to the Supreme Court of the United Kingdom, para.4.15 of Practice Directions Applicable to Civil Appeals is replaced by r.16 of the Supreme Court Rules 2009.

## Appeal where leave granted

**14.** *[Repealed by the Constitutional Reform Act 2005 s.40 and Sch.9, para.20(5), with effect from October 1, 2009 (SI 2009/1604).]* **9B–35**

***Paragraph numbers marked with a "+" can be found online and on CD.***

### Cases excluded from section 12

9B–36 **15.**—(1) No certificate shall be granted under section 12 of this Act in respect of a decision of the judge in any proceedings where by virtue of any enactment, apart from the provisions of this Part of this Act, no appeal would lie from that decision to the Court of Appeal, with or without the leave of the judge or of the Court of Appeal.

(2) No certificate shall be granted under section 12 of this Act in respect of a decision of the judge where—

(a) [...]

(b) by virtue of any enactment, apart from the provisions of this Part of this Act, no appeal would (with or without the leave of the Court of Appeal or of the Supreme Court) lie from any decision of the Court of Appeal on an appeal from the decision of the judge.

(3) Where by virtue of any enactment, apart from the provisions of this Part of this Act, no appeal would lie to the Court of Appeal from the decision of the judge except with the leave of the judge or of the Court of Appeal, no certificate shall be granted under section 12 of this Act in respect of that decision unless it appears to the judge that apart from the provisions of this Part of this Act it would be a proper case for granting such leave.

(4) No certificate shall be granted under section 12 of this Act where the decision of the judge, or any order made by him in pursuance of that decision, is made in the exercise of jurisdiction to punish for contempt of court.

9B–37 *Note*—Subsection (2)(a) repealed by the Administration of Justice Act 1977 s.32(4), Sch.5. Amended by the Constitutional Reform Act 2005 s.40 and Sch.9 para.20(6), with effect from October 1, 2009 (SI 2009/1604).

**[THE NEXT PARAGRAPH IS 9B–39]**

## Administration of Justice Act 1970

9B–39 (1970 c.31)

ARRANGEMENT OF SECTIONS



***Paragraph numbers marked with a "+" can be found online and on CD.***

**Paragraph numbers marked with a "+" denote content that is available on White Book on Westlaw UK or the Civil Procedure CD.**

## Administration of Justice Act 1985

(1985 c.61) 9B–57

ARRANGEMENT OF SECTIONS

PART IV



**Paragraph numbers marked with a "+" denote content that is available on White Book on Westlaw UK or the Civil Procedure CD.**

* * * *

## The County Courts (Interest on Judgment Debts) Order 1991

(S.I. 1991 No.1184)

### Citation, commencement, interpretation and savings

**1.**—(1) This Order may be cited as the County Courts (Interest on Judgment Debts) Order 1991 and shall come into force on 1st July 1991. 9B–70

(2) In this Order, unless the context otherwise requires,—

"administration order" means an order under section 112 of the 1984 Act;

"given", in relation to a relevant judgment, means "given or made";

"judgment creditor" means the person who has obtained or is entitled to enforce the relevant judgment and "debtor" means the person against whom it was given;

"judgment debt" means a debt under a relevant judgment;

"relevant judgment" means a judgment or order of a county court for the payment of a sum of money (a) of not less than £5,000 or (b) in respect of a debt which is a qualifying debt for the purposes of the Late Payment of Commercial Debts (Interest) Act 1998 and, in relation to a judgment debt, means the judgment or order which gives rise to the judgment debt.

"the 1984 Act" means the County Courts Act 1984.

(3) Where in accordance with the provisions of this Order inter-

*Paragraph numbers marked with a "+" can be found online and on CD.*

est ceases to accrue on a specified day, interest shall cease to accrue at the end of that day.

(4) Nothing in this Order shall apply where the relevant judgment is given before 1st July 1991.

**The general rule**

**9B–71** **2.**—(1) Subject to the following provisions of this Order, every judgment debt under a relevant judgment shall, to the extent that it remains unsatisfied, carry interest under this Order from the date on which the relevant judgment was given.

(2) In the case of a judgment or order for the payment of a judgment debt, other than costs, the amount of which has to be determined at a later date, the judgment debt shall carry interest from that later date.

(3) Interest shall not be payable under this Order where the relevant judgment—

(a) is given in proceedings to recover money due under an agreement regulated by the Consumer Credit Act 1974;

(b) grants—

(i) the landlord of a dwelling house, or

(ii) the mortgagee under a mortgage of land which consists of or includes a dwelling house,

a suspended order for possession.

(4) Where the relevant judgment makes financial provision for a spouse or a child, interest shall only be payable on an order for the payment of not less than £5,000 as a lump sum (whether or not the sum is payable by instalments).

For the purposes of this paragraph, no regard shall be had to any interest payable under section 23(6) of the Matrimonial Causes Act 1973.

**Interest where payment deferred**

**9B–72** **3.** Where under the terms of the relevant judgment payment of a judgment debt—

(a) is not required to be made until a specified date, or

(b) is to be made by instalments,

interest shall not accrue under this Order—

(i) until that date, or

(ii) on the amount of any instalment, until it falls due,

as the case may be.

**Interest and enforcement or other proceedings**

**9B–73** **4.**—(1) Where a judgment creditor takes proceedings in a county court to enforce payment under a relevant judgment, the judgment debt shall cease to carry interest thereafter, except where those proceedings fail to produce any payment from the debtor in which case interest shall accrue as if those proceedings had never been taken.

(2) For the purposes of this article "proceedings to enforce pay-

*Paragraph numbers marked with a "+" can be found online and on CD.*

ment under a relevant judgment"include any proceeding for examining or summoning a judgment debtor or attaching a debt owed to him, but do not include proceedings under the Charging Orders Act 1979;

(3) Where an administration order or an attachment of earnings order is made, interest shall not accrue during the time the order is in force.

### Rate of interest

**5.**—(1) Subject to paragraph (2), where a judgment debt carries interest the rate of interest shall be the rate for the time being specified in section 17 of the Judgments Act 1838. **9B–74**

(2) Where a judgment debt carries interest and has been given for a sum expressed in a currency other than sterling, a county court may order that the rate of interest shall be such rate as the court thinks fit (instead of the rate otherwise applicable under paragraph (1)) and, where the court makes such an order, section 17 of the Judgments Act 1838 shall have effect in relation to the judgment debt as if the rate specified in the order were substituted for the rate specified in that section.

### Appropriation of interest

**6.**—(1) Where the debtor is indebted to the same judgment creditor under two or more judgments or orders, money paid by him shall be applied to satisfy such of the judgments as the debtor may stipulate or, where no such stipulation is made, according to their priority in time. **9B–75**

(2) Money paid by the debtor in respect of any judgment debt shall be appropriated first to discharge or reduce the principal debt and then towards the interest.

**[THE NEXT PARAGRAPH IS 9B–77.]**

## County Court Remedies Regulations 1991

(S.I. 1991 No. 1222)

(As amended by S.I. 1995 No. 206) **9B–77**

#### Introductory note

See also CPR Pt 25.

The effect of the amendments to these Regulations brought about by the County Court Remedies (Amendment) Regulations 1995 (SI 1995/206) is to give the nominated judge jurisdiction to grant freezing injunctions restraining parties from removing assets from the jurisdiction of the High Court or dealing with assets in proceedings which are to be handled by, or are being handled by, a Mercantile Court (see CPR Pt 59 (Mercantile Courts)).

**1.** These Regulations may be cited as the County Court Remedies Regulations 1991 and shall come into force on 1st July 1991. **9B–78**

**2.** In these Regulations, "prescribed relief" means relief of any of the following kinds—

(a) an order requiring a party to admit any other party to premises for the purpose of inspecting or removing documents or articles which may provide evidence in any proceedings, whether or not the proceedings have been commenced;

(b) an interlocutory injunction—

(i) restraining a party from removing from the jurisdiction of the High Court assets located within that jurisdiction; or

(ii) restraining a party from dealing with assets whether located within the jurisdiction of the High Court or not.

**3.**—(1) Subject to the following provisions of this regulation, a county court shall not grant prescribed relief or vary or revoke an order made by the High Court granting such relief.

(2) Paragraph (1) shall not apply to—

(a) any county court held by a judge of the Court of Appeal or judge of the High Court sitting as a judge for any county court district;

(b) a patents county court held by a person nominated under section 291 of the Copyright, Designs and Patents Act 1988 to sit as a judge of that court.

(3) A county court may grant relief of a kind referred to in regulation 2(b)—

(a) when exercising jurisdiction in family proceedings within the meaning of Part V of the Matrimonial and Family Proceedings Act 1984;

(b) for the purpose of making an order for the preservation, custody or detention of property which forms or may form the subject matter of proceedings,

(c) in aid of execution of a judgment or order made in proceedings in a county court to preserve assets until execution can be levied upon them, or

(d) where proceedings are to be or are included in the Central London County Court Mercantile List and the application is made to a Circuit judge nominated by the Senior Presiding Judge.

(3A) In paragraph (3)(d)—

"the Central London County Court Mercantile List" means the Mercantile Court established at the Central London County Court pursuant to Part 59 of the Civil Procedure Rules 1998; and

"the Senior Presiding Judge" means the judge appointed as such under section 72(2) of the Courts and Legal Services Act 1990.

(4) Paragraph (1) shall not—

(a) affect or modify powers expressly conferred on a county court by or under any enactment other than section 38 of the County Courts Act 1984; or

(b) prevent a county court from varying an order granting prescribed relief where all the parties are agreed on the terms of the variation.

**4.** An application to the High Court for relief of a kind referred to in regulation 2(a) in county court proceedings shall be deemed to include an application for transfer of the proceedings to the High Court.

**5.**—(1) After an application for prescribed relief has been disposed of by the High Court, the proceedings shall, unless the High Court orders otherwise, be transferred to a county court if—

(a) they were transferred to the High Court; or

(b) apart from these Regulations, they should have been commenced in a county court.

(2) Where an order is made on an ex parte application, the application shall not be treated as disposed of for the purposes of paragraph (1) until any application to set aside or vary the order has been heard, or until the expiry of 28 days (or such other period as the Court may specify) during which no such application has been made.

## Courts Act 1971

(1971 c.23) **9B–79**

Arrangement of Sections

Part III



**Paragraph numbers marked with a "+" denote content that is available on White Book on Westlaw UK or the Civil Procedure CD.**

## Courts and Legal Services Act 1990

(1990 c.41) **9B–100**

Arrangement of Sections

Part I

Procedure etc. in Civil Courts

*Allocation and Transfer of Business*



***Paragraph numbers marked with a "+" can be found online and on CD.***

***Paragraph numbers marked with a "+" can be found online and on CD.***

**Paragraph numbers marked with a "+" denote content that is available on White Book on Westlaw UK or the Civil Procedure CD.**

**Introductory note**

For detailed commentary on this Act, see Courts and Legal Services Act 1990, Current Law Statutes Annotated 1991. **9B–101**

The functions of the Lord Chancellor under Pts 2 and 4 and ss.113 and 125, and s.124 (Commencement) so far as relating to any of the provisions, were transferred to the Secretary of State for Constitutional Affairs by the Secretary of State for Constitutional Affairs Order 2003 (SI 2003/1887) with effect from August 19, 2003.

## PART I

## PROCEDURE ETC. IN CIVIL COURTS

### *ALLOCATION AND TRANSFER OF BUSINESS*

### Allocation of business between High Court and county courts

**1.**—(1) The Lord Chancellor may by order make provision— **9B–102**

(a) conferring jurisdiction on the High Court in relation to proceedings in which county courts have jurisdiction;
(b) conferring jurisdiction on county courts in relation to proceedings in which the High Court has jurisdiction;
(c) allocating proceedings to the High Court or to county courts;
(d) specifying proceedings which may be commenced only in the High Court;
(e) specifying proceedings which may be commenced only in a county court;
(f) specifying proceedings which may be taken only in the High Court;
(g) specifying proceedings which may be taken only in a county court.

(1A) An order under subsection (1)(a) or (b) may be made only with the concurrence of the Lord Chief Justice.

(2) Without prejudice to the generality of section 120(2), any such order may differentiate between categories of proceedings by reference to such criteria as the Lord Chancellor sees fit to specify in the order.

(3) The criteria so specified may, in particular, relate to—

(a) the value of an action (as defined by the order);
(b) the nature of the proceedings;
(c) the parties to the proceedings;

*Paragraph numbers marked with a "+" can be found online and on CD.*

(d) the degree of complexity likely to be involved in any aspect of the proceedings; and

(e) the importance of any question likely to be raised by, or in the course of, the proceedings.

(4) An order under subsection (1)(b) (e) or (g) may specify one or more particular county courts in relation to the proceedings so specified.

(5) Any jurisdiction exercisable by a county court, under any provision made by virtue of subsection (4), shall be exercisable throughout England and Wales.

(6) Rules of court may provide for a matter—

(a) which is pending in one county court; and

(b) over which that court has jurisdiction under any provision made by virtue of subsection (4),

to be heard and determined wholly or partly in another county court which also has jurisdiction in that matter under any such provision.

(7) Any such order may—

(a) amend or repeal any provision falling within subsection (8) and relating to—

(i) the jurisdiction, practice or procedure of the Senior Courts; or

(ii) the jurisdiction, practice or procedure of any county court,

so far as the Lord Chancellor considers it to be necessary, or expedient, in consequence of any provision made by the order; or

(b) make such incidental or transitional provision as the Lord Chancellor considers necessary, or expedient, in consequence of any provision made by the order.

(8) A provision falls within this subsection if it is made by any enactment other than this Act or made under any enactment.

(9) Before making any such order the Lord Chancellor shall consult the Lord Chief Justice, the Master of the Rolls, the President of the Queen's Division, the President of the Family Division, the Chancellor of the High Court and the Senior Presiding Judge (appointed under section 72).

(10) No such order shall be made so as to confer jurisdiction on any county court to hear any application for judicial review.

(11) For the purposes of this section the commencement of proceedings may include the making of any application in anticipation of any proceedings or in the course of any proceedings.

(12) [...]

(13) The Lord Chief Justice may nominate a judicial office holder (as defined in section 109(4) of the Constitutional Reform Act 2005) to exercise his functions under this section.

**9B–103** *Note*—Amended by the Courts Act 2003 s.109(1), (3), Sch.8, para.348, Sch.10; and the Constitutional Reform Act 2005 s.15(1), Sch.4, para.212; and subs.(7) amended by the Constitutional Reform Act 2005 s.59 and Sch.11, para.4, with effect from October 1, 2009 (SI 2009/1604).

Subsection (9) amended by the Constitutional Reform Act 2005 s.15, Sch.4, para.212(3). subss (1A) and (13). This section empowers the Lord Chancellor, after consulting senior judges (see subs.(9)), by order to make provision for the allocation of business between the High Court and the county courts (subs.(1)). The powers given by this section are very wide. An order made under this section may amend or repeal existing provisions, including primary legislation and delegated legislation such as rules of court, on the jurisdiction, practice or procedure of the Supreme Court or of the county courts but may not amend or repeal any provision of this Act (subss.(7) (8)). By order, jurisdiction may be conferred on the High Court in relation to proceedings in which county courts have jurisdiction and vice versa; further, it may be specified that proceedings falling within the jurisdiction of the High Court should be commenced in a county court and vice versa (as to "commencement of proceedings," see subs.(11)); furthermore it may be specified that proceedings may be taken only in the High Court or only in a county court. The power is broad enough to enable provision to be made for the transfer of particular proceedings from one court to another at different stages of case progress, for example, for trial or enforcement. The exclusive jurisdiction of the High Court to hear applications for judicial review is preserved (subs.(10)). In conferring jurisdiction in relation to a particular type of proceeding on the county courts the Lord Chancellor may choose one or more county courts to exercise that jurisdiction rather than to confer such jurisdiction on all county courts (subss.(4),(5) and (6)). (Such an arrangement would parallel the Copyright, Designs and Patents Act 1988 Pt VI which empowers the Lord Chancellor to confer patent jurisdiction on one or more particular county courts.)

The first exercise of the powers given by this section was the High Court and County Courts Jurisdiction Order 1991 (SI 1991/724), see below, paras 9B–928 *et seq.*

As a result of the amendment of s.120(4) of this Act by the Civil Procedure Act 1997 s.10 and Sch.2, para.4, instruments made by the Lord Chancellor under s.1(1) are now subject, not to approval by both Houses of Parliament, but merely to annulment in pursuance of a petition of both Houses (s.120(6)).

* * * *

## *EVIDENCE*

### Witness statements

**5.**—(1) Rules of court may make provision— 9B–104

(a) requiring, in specified circumstances, any party to civil proceedings to serve on the other parties a written statement of the oral evidence which he intends to adduce on any issue of fact to be decided at the trial;

(b) enabling the court to direct any party to civil proceedings to serve such a statement on the other party; and

(c) prohibiting a party who fails to comply with such a requirement or direction from adducing oral evidence on the issue of fact to which it relates.

(2) Where a party to proceedings has refused to comply with such a requirement or direction, the fact that his refusal was on the ground that the required statement would have been a document which was privileged from disclosure shall not affect any prohibition imposed by virtue of subsection (1)(c).

(3) This section is not to be read as prejudicing in any way any other power to make rules of court.

*Note*—This section provides the power for Rules of Court to require pre-trial exchange of non-expert witness statements throughout the High Court and the county 9B–105 courts. (Henceforth, the bases of such rule-making power will not have to be found in the Senior Courts Act 1981 ss.85 and 87 or in the County Courts Act 1984 s.75). This provision makes it clear that rules of court may override the legal professional privilege attaching to witness statements prepared with a view to proceedings (subs.(2)) (*cf.*, the Civil Evidence Act 1972 s.2(3)) dealing with privilege and the disclosure of experts' evidence).

This section clarifies the rule-making authority underpinning CPR, r.32.4 (Requirement to serve witness statements for use at trial).

* * * *

### APPEALS

## Powers of Court of Appeal to award damages

9B–106 **8.**—(1) In this section "case" means any case where the Court of Appeal has power to order a new trial on the ground that damages awarded by a jury are excessive or inadequate.

(2) Rules of court may provide for the Court of Appeal, in such classes of case as may be specified in the rules, to have power, in place of ordering a new trial, to substitute for the sum awarded by the jury such sum as appears to the court to be proper.

(3) This section is not to be read as prejudicing in any way any other power to make rules of court.

9B–107 *Note* —This section was designed to meet concerns about excessively high jury awards in defamation cases. It enables Rules of Court to confer on the Court of Appeal the power to substitute its own award of damages for the sum awarded by a jury in the court of first instance instead of ordering a new trial and to do so in classes of cases as may be specified in the rules (subs.(2)). This rule-making power was first exercised by RSC (Amendment No.3) 1990 (SI 1990/2599) reg.13, amending CPR Sch.1, RSC O.59, r.11.

#### Proper award

9B–108 In *Rantzen v Mirror Group Newspapers Ltd* [1993] 3 W.L.R. 953, CA, in reducing a jury's award in a defamation case, the Court considered the operation of s.8(2) and O.52.10(3). See also *Clark v Chief Constable of Cleveland* [2000] C.P. Rep. 22; *Thompson v Commissioner of Police of the Metropolis* [1998] Q.B. 498, CA; *Bennett v Chief Constable of West Yorkshire* April 24, 1998, unrep. CA; *John v MGN Ltd* [1997] Q.B. 586 CA; *Kiam v M.G.N Ltd* [2002] EWCA Civ 43; [2002] 2 All E.R. 219, CA.

**For ss.9 and 11 of the Courts and Legal Services Act 1990 (see Arrangement) plus any related commentary see paragraphs 9B–109+ to 9B–114+ on White Book on Westlaw UK or the Civil Procedure CD.**

* * * *

## Enforcement

9B–115 **15.**—(1) [...]

(2) [...]

(3) Where a person takes steps to enforce a judgment or order of the High Court or a county court for the payment of any sum due, the costs of any previous attempt to enforce that judgment shall be recoverable to the same extent as if they had been incurred in the taking of those steps.

***Paragraph numbers marked with a "+" can be found online and on CD.***

(4) Subsection (3) shall not apply in respect of any costs which the court considers were unreasonably incurred (whether because the earlier attempt was unreasonable in all the circumstances of the case or for any other reason).

*Note*—Subsection (1) repealed by the Courts Act 2003 s.109(3), Sch.10. **9B–116**

**For ss.21 to 26, 31B, 31C, 54 to 58B and 60 to 62 of the Courts and Legal Services Act 1990 (see Arrangement) plus any related commentary see paragraphs 9B–117+ to 9B–149+ on White Book on Westlaw UK or the Civil Procedure CD.**

## Legal professional privilege

**63.** [Repealed] **9B–150**

*Note*—Repealed by the Legal Services Act 2007 Sch.21, para.91, with effect from January 1, 2010 (SI 2009/3250). **9B–151**

**For ss.66, 69 to 76, 78, and 89 of the Courts and Legal Services Act 1990 (see Arrangement) plus any related commentary see paragraphs 9B–152+ to 9B–168+ on White Book on Westlaw UK or the Civil Procedure CD.**

# Part VI

# Miscellaneous and Supplemental

### *Miscellaneous*

* * * *

## Administration of oaths and taking of affidavits

**113.** [Repealed] **9B–169**

*Note*—Repealed (subject to savings) by the Legal Services Act 2007 Sch.21, para.96, Sch.23, with effect from January 1, 2010 (SI 2009/3250; for savings see art.9). **9B–170**

* * * *

## Law reports

**115.** A report of a case made by a person who is not a barrister but who is a solicitor or has a Senior Courts qualification (within the meaning of section 71) shall have the same authority as if it had been made by a barrister. **9B–171**

*Note*—Amended by the Constitutional Reform Act 2005 s.59 and Sch.11, para.4, with effect from October 1, 2009 (SI 2009/1604). **9B–171.1**

### *Supplemental*

## Interpretation

**119.**—(1) In this Act— **9B–172**

"advocacy services" means any services which it would be reasonable to expect a person who is exercising, or contemplating

*Paragraph numbers marked with a "+" can be found online and on CD.*

exercising, a right of audience in relation to any proceedings, or contemplated proceedings, to provide;

[...]

"conveyancing services" means the preparation of transfers, conveyances, contracts and other documents in connection with, and other services ancillary to, the disposition or acquisition of estates or interests in land;

"designated judge" means the Lord Chief Justice, the Master of the Rolls, the President of the Queen's Division, the President of the Family Division or the Chancellor of the High Court;

"litigation services" means any services which it would be reasonable to expect a person who is exercising, or contemplating exercising, a right to conduct litigation in relation to any proceedings, or contemplated proceedings, to provide;

"the OFT" means the Office of Fair Trading;

"probate services" means the drawing or preparation of any papers on which to found or oppose a grant of probate or a grant of letters of administration and the administration of the estate of a deceased person;

"prescribed" means prescribed by regulations under this Act;

"proceedings" means proceedings in any court;

"right of audience" means the right to appear before and address a court including the the right to call and examine witnesses;

"right to conduct litigation" means the right—

(a) issue proceedings before any court in England and Wales;

(aa) to commence, prosecute and defend such proceedings; and

(b) to perform any ancillary functions in relation to proceedings (such as entering appearances to actions);

(2) and (3) [...]

**9B–173** *Note*—This interpretation section has been reduced so as to exclude definitions not relevant to the selected sections of the Act printed above. Amended by the Access to Justice Act 1999 Sch.6, para.10(3) and the Enterprise Act 2002, Sch.25, para.23(9)(b); definition of "designated judge" amended by the Constitutional Reform Act 2005 s.15, Sch.4, para.216; and amended by the Legal Services Act 2007 Sch.21, para.97, Sch.23, with effect from January 1, 2010 (SI 2009/3250).

**For s.120 of and Schs 3, 4 (Parts I to IV), 9, 11, 14 (Parts I and II), 17, 18, and 19 to the Courts and Legal Services Act 1990 (see Arrangement) plus any related commentary see paragraphs 9B–174+ to 9B–355+ on White Book on Westlaw UK or the Civil Procedure CD.**

## Legal Services Act 2007

**9B–356** (2007 c.29)

ARRANGEMENT OF SECTIONS

PART 1

THE REGULATORY OBJECTIVES



***Paragraph numbers marked with a "+" can be found online and on CD.***

***Paragraph numbers marked with a "+" can be found online and on CD.***

***Paragraph numbers marked with a "+" can be found online and on CD.***

***Paragraph numbers marked with a "+" can be found online and on CD.***

***Paragraph numbers marked with a "+" can be found online and on CD.***

**Paragraph numbers marked with a "+" denote content that is available on White Book on Westlaw UK or the Civil Procedure CD.**

**General Note**

Sections 208(2) to (5), 211, 212 and 214 came into force on the date of Royal Assent, October 30, 2007 (see s.211). As at the date of publication, the following Commencement Orders have been made in relation to this Act: **9B–356.1**

Legal Services Act 2007 (Commencement No.1 and Transitory Provisions) Order 2008 (SI 2008/222), bringing into force with effect from March 7, 2008 certain provisions of the Act which inter alia establish the Legal Services Board ("the Board") and the Office for Legal Complaints ("the OLC"), and allow the Lord Chancellor to modify the functions of legal services regulators pending the establishment of the new regulatory regime under the 2007 Act.

***Paragraph numbers marked with a "+" can be found online and on CD.***

Legal Services Act 2007 (Commencement No.2 and Transitory Provisions) Order 2008 (SI 2008/1436) bringing into force with effect from June 30, 2008 and October 1, 2008 certain provisions of the Act which inter alia permits a charity to be prescribed for the receipt of payments in respect of pro bono representation and allows the Law Society to determine whether indemnity rules have been broken.

Legal Services Act 2007 (Commencement No.3 and Transitory Provisions) Order 2008 (SI 2008/3149) bringing further provisions into force on January 31, 2009.

Legal Services Act 2007 (Commencement No.4, Transitory and Transitional Provisions and Appointed Day) Order 2009 (SI 2009/503) bringing further provisions into force on March 31, 2009. Legal Services Act 2007 (Commencement No.5, Transitory and Transitional Provisions) Order 2009 (SI 2009/1365) bringing provisions into force on July 1, 2009.

Legal Services Act 2007 (Commencement No.6, Transitory, Transitional and Saving Provisions) Order 2009 (SI 2009/3250) bringing provisions into force (subject to transitory and transitional provisions) on January 1, 2010.

We have reproduced below those provisions currently in force with relevant commencement notes. Where provisions or (in schedules) paragraphs are partially brought into force, the whole provision/paragraph is reproduced for ease of reference.

## PART 1

## THE REGULATORY OBJECTIVES

### The regulatory objectives

9B–357 **1.**—(1) In this Act a reference to "the regulatory objectives" is a reference to the objectives of—

(a) protecting and promoting the public interest;
(b) supporting the constitutional principle of the rule of law;
(c) improving access to justice;
(d) protecting and promoting the interests of consumers;
(e) promoting competition in the provision of services within subsection (2);
(f) encouraging an independent, strong, diverse and effective legal profession;
(g) increasing public understanding of the citizen's legal rights and duties;
(h) promoting and maintaining adherence to the professional principles.

(2) The services within this subsection are services such as are provided by authorised persons (including services which do not involve the carrying on of activities which are reserved legal activities).

(3) The "professional principles" are—

(a) that authorised persons should act with independence and integrity,
(b) that authorised persons should maintain proper standards of work,
(c) that authorised persons should act in the best interests of their clients,
(d) that persons who exercise before any court a right of audience, or conduct litigation in relation to proceedings in any court, by virtue of being authorised persons

should comply with their duty to the court to act with independence in the interests of justice, and

(e) that the affairs of clients should be kept confidential.

(4) In this section "authorised persons" means authorised persons in relation to activities which are reserved legal activities.

*Commencement note* —Brought into force (subject to transitional provisions) by the Legal Services Act 2007 (Commencement No.1 and Transitory Provisions) Order 2008 (SI 2008/222), with effect from March 7, 2008. The transitional provisions contained in art.7(1) are as follows: **9B–357.1**

"Until section 13 (Entitlement to carry on a reserved legal activity) comes into force a reference to an authorised person in section 1 and in the definition of 'consumers' in section 207 is to be treated as a reference to a person who will be an authorised person on the coming into force of section 13."

**For ss.2 to 11 of the Legal Services Act 2007 (see Arrangement) plus any related commentary see paragraphs 9B–358+ to 9B–367+ on White Book on Westlaw UK or the Civil Procedure CD.**

# PART 3

# RESERVED LEGAL ACTIVITIES

## *RESERVED LEGAL ACTIVITIES*

### Meaning of "reserved legal activity" and "legal activity"

**12.**—(1) In this Act "reserved legal activity" means— **9B–368**

(a) the exercise of a right of audience;

(b) the conduct of litigation;

(c) reserved instrument activities;

(d) probate activities;

(e) notarial activities;

(f) the administration of oaths.

(2) Schedule 2 makes provision about what constitutes each of those activities.

(3) In this Act "legal activity" means—

(a) an activity which is a reserved legal activity within the meaning of this Act as originally enacted, and

(b) any other activity which consists of one or both of the following—

(i) the provision of legal advice or assistance in connection with the application of the law or with any form of resolution of legal disputes;

(ii) the provision of representation in connection with any matter concerning the application of the law or any form of resolution of legal disputes.

(4) But "legal activity" does not include any activity of a judicial or quasi-judicial nature (including acting as a mediator).

(5) For the purposes of subsection (3) "legal dispute" includes a

dispute as to any matter of fact the resolution of which is relevant to determining the nature of any person's legal rights or liabilities.

(6) Section 24 makes provision for adding legal activities to the reserved legal activities.

9B-368.1 *Commencement note*—Brought into force for certain purposes by the Legal Services Act 2007 (Commencement No.1 and Transitory Provisions) Order 2008 (SI 2008/222), with effect from March 7, 2008. The purposes (contained in art.3) for which s.12 comes into force are in so far as it defines the term "Reserved legal activity" for the purpose of the following provisions:

- Section 1;
- The definition of "consumers" in s.207;
- Section 69(4) as modified by the Order;
- Paragraph 2(3) to (5) of Sch.1;
- Paragraph 2(3) and (4) of Sch.15;
- Paragraph 2(6) and 2(7)(b) of Sch.22.

Brought into force for certain purposes by the Legal Services Act 2007 (Commencement No.4, Transitory and Transitional Provisions and Appointed Day) Order 2009 (SI 2009/503), with effect from March 31, 2009. The purposes (contained in art.3) for which s.12 comes into force are in so far as it defines the term 'Reserved legal activity' for the purpose of ss.9 and 32A of the Administration of Justice Act 1985.

### *CARRYING ON THE ACTIVITIES*

## Entitlement to carry on a reserved legal activity

9B-369 **13.**—(1) The question whether a person is entitled to carry on an activity which is a reserved legal activity is to be determined solely in accordance with the provisions of this Act.

(2) A person is entitled to carry on an activity ("the relevant activity") which is a reserved legal activity where—

(a) the person is an authorised person in relation to the relevant activity, or

(b) the person is an exempt person in relation to that activity.

(3) Subsection (2) is subject to section 23 (transitional protection for noncommercial bodies).

(4) Nothing in this section or section 23 affects section 84 of the Immigration and Asylum Act 1999 (c. 33) (which prohibits the provision of immigration advice and immigration services except by certain persons).

**Commencement note**

9B-369.1 Brought into force (subject to transitory and transitional provisions) by the Legal Services Act 2007 (Commencement No.6, Transitory, Transitional and Saving Provisions) Order 2009 (SI 2009/3250), with effect from January 1, 2010; for transitory and transitional provisions see arts 3–6.

### *OFFENCES*

## Offence to carry on a reserved legal activity if not entitled

9B-370 **14.**—(1) It is an offence for a person to carry on an activity ("the relevant activity") which is a reserved legal activity unless that person is entitled to carry on the relevant activity.

(2) In proceedings for an offence under subsection (1), it is a defence for the accused to show that the accused did not know, and could not reasonably have been expected to know, that the offence was being committed.

(3) A person who is guilty of an offence under subsection (1) is liable—

(a) on summary conviction, to imprisonment for a term not exceeding 12 months or a fine not exceeding the statutory maximum (or both), and

(b) on conviction on indictment, to imprisonment for a term not exceeding 2 years or a fine (or both).

(4) A person who is guilty of an offence under subsection (1) by reason of an act done in the purported exercise of a right of audience, or a right to conduct litigation, in relation to any proceedings or contemplated proceedings is also guilty of contempt of the court concerned and may be punished accordingly.

(5) In relation to an offence under subsection (1) committed before the commencement of section 154(1) of the Criminal Justice Act 2003 (c. 44), the reference in subsection (3)(a) to 12 months is to be read as a reference to 6 months.

**Commencement note**

Brought into force (subject to transitory and transitional provisions) by the Legal Services Act 2007 (Commencement No.6, Transitory, Transitional and Saving Provisions) Order 2009 (SI 2009/3250), with effect from January 1, 2010; for transitory and transitional provisions see arts 3–6. **9B–370.1**

**For ss.15 to 17 of the Legal Services Act 2007 (see Arrangement) plus any related commentary see paragraphs 9B–371+ to 9B–373+ on White Book on Westlaw UK or the Civil Procedure CD.**

*INTERPRETATION*

## Authorised persons

**18.**—(1) For the purposes of this Act "authorised person", in relation to an activity ("the relevant activity") which is a reserved legal activity, means— **9B–374**

(a) a person who is authorised to carry on the relevant activity by a relevant approved regulator in relation to the relevant activity (other than by virtue of a licence under Part 5), or

(b) a licensable body which, by virtue of such a licence, is authorised to carry on the relevant activity by a licensing authority in relation to the reserved legal activity.

(2) A licensable body may not be authorised to carry on the relevant activity as mentioned in subsection (1)(a).

(3) But where a body ("A") which is authorised as mentioned in subsection (1)(a) becomes a licensable body, the body is deemed by virtue of this subsection to continue to be so authorised from that time until the earliest of the following events—

(a) the end of the period of 90 days beginning with the day on which that time falls;

***Paragraph numbers marked with a "+" can be found online and on CD.***

(b) the time from which the relevant approved regulator determines this subsection is to cease to apply to A;

(c) the time when A ceases to be a licensable body.

(4) Subsection (2) is subject to Part 2 of Schedule 5 (by virtue of which licensable bodies may be deemed to be authorised as mentioned in subsection (1)(a) in relation to certain activities during a transitional period).

(5) A person other than a licensable body may not be authorised to carry on the relevant activity as mentioned in subsection (1)(b).

(6) But where a body ("L") which is authorised as mentioned in subsection (1)(b) ceases to be a licensable body, the body is deemed by virtue of this subsection to continue to be so authorised from that time until the earliest of the following events—

(a) the end of the period of 90 days beginning with the day on which that time falls;

(b) the time from which the relevant licensing authority determines this subsection is to cease to apply to L;

(c) the time when L becomes a licensable body.

**Commencement note**

9B–374.1 Subsection (1)(a) brought into force (subject to transitory and transitional provisions) by the Legal Services Act 2007 (Commencement No.6, Transitory, Transitional and Saving Provisions) Order 2009 (SI 2009/3250), with effect from January 1, 2010; for transitory and transitional provisions see arts 3–6. Specifically, art.3(1) states that until s.18(2) comes into force, s.18(1)(a) is to be read as if the words "(other than by virtue of a licence under Part 5), or" were omitted.

## Exempt persons

9B–375 **19.** In this Act, "exempt person", in relation to an activity ("the relevant activity") which is a reserved legal activity, means a person who, for the purposes of carrying on the relevant activity, is an exempt person by virtue of—

(a) Schedule 3 (exempt persons), or

(b) paragraph 13 or 18 of Schedule 5 (additional categories of exempt persons during transitional period).

**Commencement note**

9B–375.1 Brought into force (subject to transitory and transitional provisions) by the Legal Services Act 2007 (Commencement No.6, Transitory, Transitional and Saving Provisions) Order 2009 (SI 2009/3250), with effect from January 1, 2010; for transitory and transitional provisions see arts 3–6.

**For ss.20 to 175 of the Legal Services Act 2007 (see Arrangement) plus any related commentary see paragraphs 9B–376+ to 9B–531+ on White Book on Westlaw UK or the Civil Procedure CD.**

# PART 8

# MISCELLANEOUS PROVISIONS ABOUT LAWYERS ETC

### *DUTIES OF REGULATED PERSONS*

## Duties of regulated persons

9B–532 **176.**—(1) A person who is a regulated person in relation to an approved regulator has a duty to comply with the regulatory arrangements of the approved regulator as they apply to that person.

(2) A person is a regulated person in relation to an approved regulator if the person—

(a) is authorised by the approved regulator to carry on an activity which is a reserved legal activity, or

(b) is not so authorised, but is a manager or employee of a person who is so authorised.

(3) This section applies in relation to the Board in its capacity as a licensing authority and its licensing rules, as it applies in relation to an approved regulator and its regulatory arrangements.

**For ss.177 to 180 of the Legal Services Act 2007 (see Arrangement) plus any related commentary see paragraphs 9B–533+ to 9B–536.1+ on White Book on Westlaw UK or the Civil Procedure CD.**

*OTHER LAWYERS*

## Unqualified person not to pretend to be a barrister

**181.**—(1) It is an offence for a person who is not a barrister— 9B–537

(a) wilfully to pretend to be a barrister, or

(b) with the intention of implying falsely that that person is a barrister to take or use any name, title or description.

(2) A person who is guilty of an offence under subsection (1) is liable—

(a) on summary conviction, to imprisonment for a term not exceeding 12 months or a fine not exceeding the statutory maximum (or both), and

(b) on conviction on indictment, to imprisonment for a term not exceeding 2 years or a fine (or both).

(3) In relation to an offence under subsection (1) committed before the commencement of section 154(1) of the Criminal Justice Act 2003 (c. 44), the reference in subsection (2)(a) to 12 months is to be read as a reference to 6 months.

**For ss.182 to 187 of the Legal Services Act 2007 (see Arrangement) plus any related commentary see paragraphs 9B–538+ to 9B–543.1+ on White Book on Westlaw UK or the Civil Procedure CD.**

*ADVOCATES AND LITIGATORS*

## Duties of advocates and litigators

**188.**—(1) This section applies to a person who— 9B–544

(a) exercises before any court a right of audience, or

(b) conducts litigation in relation to proceedings in any court,

by virtue of being an authorised person in relation to the activity in question.

(2) A person to whom this section applies has a duty to the court in question to act with independence in the interests of justice.

*Paragraph numbers marked with a "+" can be found online and on CD.*

(3) That duty, and the duty to comply with relevant conduct rules imposed on the person by section 176(1), override any obligations which the person may have (otherwise than under the criminal law) if they are inconsistent with them.

(4) "Relevant conduct rules" are the conduct rules of the relevant authorising body which relate to the exercise of a right of audience or the conduct of litigation.

(5) The relevant authorising body is—

(a) the approved regulator by which the person is authorised to exercise the right of audience or conduct the litigation, or

(b) where the person is authorised to exercise the right of audience or conduct the litigation by the Board in its capacity as a licensing authority, the Board.

**Commencement note**

9B–544.1 Brought into force (subject to transitory and transitional provisions) by the Legal Services Act 2007 (Commencement No.6, Transitory, Transitional and Saving Provisions) Order 2009 (SI 2009/3250), with effect from January 1, 2010; for transitory and transitional provisions see arts 3–6.

## Employed advocates

9B–545 **189.**—(1) This section applies where an authorised person in relation to the exercise of a right of audience is employed as a Crown Prosecutor or in any other description of employment.

(2) Qualification regulations or conduct rules of the approved regulator by whom the person is authorised to carry on that activity which relate to the right of audience do not have effect in relation to the person if—

(a) they—

(i) limit the courts before which, or proceedings in which, that activity may be carried on by persons who are employed, or

(ii) limit the circumstances in which that activity may be carried on by persons who are employed by requiring such persons to be accompanied by some other person when carrying on that activity, and

(b) they do not impose the same limitation on persons who are authorised persons in relation to the activity in question but are not employed.

**Commencement note**

9B–545.1 Brought into force (subject to transitory and transitional provisions) by the Legal Services Act 2007 (Commencement No.6, Transitory, Transitional and Saving Provisions) Order 2009 (SI 2009/3250), with effect from January 1, 2010; for transitory and transitional provisions see arts 3–6.

*LEGAL PROFESSIONAL PRIVILEGE*

## Legal professional privilege

9B–546 **190.**—(1) Subsection (2) applies where an individual ("P") who is not a barrister or solicitor—

(a) provides advocacy services as an authorised person in relation to the exercise of rights of audience,

(b) provides litigation services as an authorised person in relation to the conduct of litigation,

(c) provides conveyancing services as an authorised person in relation to reserved instrument activities, or

(d) provides probate services as an authorised person in relation to probate activities.

(2) Any communication, document, material or information relating to the provision of the services in question is privileged from disclosure in like manner as if P had at all material times been acting as P's client's solicitor.

(3) Subsection (4) applies where—

(a) a licensed body provides services to a client, and

(b) the individual ("E") through whom the body provides those services—

(i) is a relevant lawyer, or

(ii) acts at the direction and under the supervision of a relevant lawyer ("the supervisor").

(4) Any communication, document, material or information relating to the provision of the services in question is privileged from disclosure only if, and to the extent that, it would have been privileged from disclosure if—

(a) the services had been provided by E or, if E is not a relevant lawyer, by the supervisor, and

(b) at all material times the client had been the client of E or, if E is not a relevant lawyer, of the supervisor.

(5) "Relevant lawyer" means an individual who is—

(a) a solicitor;

(b) a barrister;

(c) a solicitor in Scotland;

(d) an advocate in Scotland;

(e) a solicitor of the Court of Judicature of Northern Ireland;

(f) a member of the Bar of Northern Ireland;

(g) a registered foreign lawyer (within the meaning of section 89 of the Courts and Legal Services Act 1990 (c. 41));

(h) an individual not within paragraphs (a) to (g) who is an authorised person in relation to an activity which is a reserved legal activity; or

(i) a European lawyer (within the meaning of the European Communities (Services of Lawyers) Order 1978 (S.I. 1978/1910)).

(6) In this section—

"advocacy services" means any services which it would be reasonable to expect a person who is exercising, or contemplating exercising, a right of audience in relation to any proceedings, or contemplated proceedings, to provide;

"litigation services" means any services which it would be reasonable to expect a person who is exercising, or contemplating exercising, a right to conduct litigation in relation to any proceedings, or contemplated proceedings, to provide;

"conveyancing services" means the preparation of transfers, conveyances, contracts and other documents in connection with, and other services ancillary to, the disposition or acquisition of estates or interests in land;

"probate services" means the preparation of any papers on which to found or oppose a grant of probate or a grant of letters of administration and the administration of the estate of a deceased person.

(7) This section is without prejudice to any other enactment or rule of law by virtue of which a communication, a document, material or information is privileged from disclosure.

**Commencement note**

9B–546.1 Brought into force (subject to transitory and transitional provisions) by the Legal Services Act 2007 (Commencement No.6, Transitory, Transitional and Saving Provisions) Order 2009 (SI 2009/3250), with effect from January 1, 2010; for transitory and transitional provisions see arts 3–6.

**For s.191 of the Legal Services Act 2007 (see Arrangement) plus any related commentary see paragraph 9B–547+ on White Book on Westlaw UK or the Civil Procedure CD.**

*SAVINGS*

## Powers of court in respect of rights of audience and conduct of litigation

9B–548 **192.**—(1) Nothing in this Act affects the power of any court in any proceedings to refuse to hear a person (for reasons which apply to that person as an individual) who would otherwise have a right of audience before the court in relation to those proceedings.

(2) Where a court refuses to hear a person as mentioned in subsection (1), it must give its reasons for refusing.

(3) Where—

(a) immediately before the commencement of section 13 (entitlement to carry on reserved legal activities), or

(b) by virtue of any provision made by or under an enactment passed subsequently,

a court does not permit the appearance of advocates, or permits the appearance of advocates only with leave, no person may exercise a right of audience before the court, in relation to any proceedings, solely by virtue of being entitled to do so under this Act.

(4) But a court may not limit the right to appear before the court in any proceedings to only some of those who are entitled to exercise that right by virtue of this Act.

(5) A court may not limit the right to conduct litigation in relation

to proceedings before the court to only some of those who are entitled to exercise that right by virtue of this Act.

(6) In this section "advocate", in relation to any proceedings, means a person exercising a right of audience as a representative of, or on behalf of, any party to the proceedings.

**Commencement note**

Brought into force (subject to transitory and transitional provisions) by the Legal Services Act 2007 (Commencement No.6, Transitory, Transitional and Saving Provisions) Order 2009 (SI 2009/3250), with effect from January 1, 2010; for transitory and transitional provisions see arts 3–6. **9B–548.1**

## Solicitors to public departments and the City of London

**193.**—(1) Nothing in this Act is to prejudice or affect any rights or privileges of— **9B–549**

(a) the Treasury Solicitor,

(b) the solicitor to any other public department,

(c) the solicitor to the Church Commissioners, or

(d) the solicitor to the Duchy of Cornwall.

(2) Nothing in this Act requires a person to whom subsection (1) applies, or any clerk or officer appointed to act for such a person, to be entitled to carry on an activity which is a reserved legal activity in any case where, by virtue of section 88(1) of the Solicitors Act 1974 (c. 47), it would not have been necessary for that person to be admitted and enrolled and to hold a practising certificate under that Act if this Act had not been passed.

(3) Nothing in this Act is to prejudice or affect any rights or privileges which immediately before the commencement of this Act attached to the office of Solicitor of the City of London.

(4) Nothing in section 17 (offence to pretend to be entitled) applies to a person to whom subsection (1) applies, or any clerk or officer appointed to act for such a person, or to the Solicitor of the City of London.

(5) A person who—

(a) exercises before any court a right of audience, or

(b) conducts litigation in relation to proceedings in any court,

by virtue of this section has a duty to the court in question to act with independence in the interests of justice.

(6) That duty overrides any obligations which the person may have (otherwise than under the criminal law) if it is inconsistent with them.

**Commencement note**

Brought into force (subject to transitory and transitional provisions) by the Legal Services Act 2007 (Commencement No.6, Transitory, Transitional and Saving Provisions) Order 2009 (SI 2009/3250), with effect from January 1, 2010; for transitory and transitional provisions see arts 3–6. **9B–549.1**

### *PRO BONO REPRESENTATION*

## Payments in respect of pro bono representation

**194.**—(1) This section applies to proceedings in a civil court in which— **9B–550**

*Paragraph numbers marked with a "+" can be found online and on CD.*

(a) a party to the proceedings ("P") is or was represented by a legal representative ("R"), and
(b) R's representation of P is or was provided free of charge, in whole or in part.

(2) This section applies to such proceedings even if P is or was also represented by a legal representative not acting free of charge.

(3) The court may order any person to make a payment to the prescribed charity in respect of R's representation of P (or, if only part of R's representation of P was provided free of charge, in respect of that part).

(4) In considering whether to make such an order and the terms of such an order, the court must have regard to—
(a) whether, had R's representation of P not been provided free of charge, it would have ordered the person to make a payment to P in respect of the costs payable to R by P in respect of that representation, and
(b) if it would, what the terms of the order would have been.

(5) The court may not make an order under subsection (3) against a person represented in the proceedings if the person's representation was at all times within subsection (6).

(6) Representation is within this subsection if it is—
(a) provided by a legal representative acting free of charge, or
(b) funded by the Legal Services Commission as part of the Community Legal Service.

(7) Rules of court may make further provision as to the making of orders under subsection (3), and may in particular—
(a) provide that such orders may not be made in civil proceedings of a description specified in the rules;
(b) make provision about the procedure to be followed in relation to such orders;
(c) specify matters (in addition to those mentioned in subsection (4)) to which the court must have regard in deciding whether to make such an order, and the terms of any order.

(8) "The prescribed charity" means the charity prescribed by order made by the Lord Chancellor.

(9) An order under subsection (8) may only prescribe a charity which—
(a) is registered in accordance with section 3A of the Charities Act 1993 (c. 10), and
(b) provides financial support to persons who provide, or organise or facilitate the provision of, legal advice or assistance (by way of representation or otherwise) which is free of charge.

(10) In this section—

"legal representative", in relation to a party to proceedings, means a person exercising a right of audience or conducting litigation on the party's behalf;

"civil court" means the civil division of the Court of Appeal, the High Court, or any county court;

"free of charge" means otherwise than for or in expectation of fee, gain or reward.

(11) The court may not make an order under subsection (3) in respect of representation if (or to the extent that) it is provided before this section comes into force.

*Commencement note*—Subsections (8) and (9), and definition "free of charge" in subs.(10) brought into force with effect from June 30, 2008, and remaining subsections and the remainder of subs.(10) brought into force with effect from October 1, 2008, by the Legal Services Act 2007 (Commencement No.2 and Transitory Provisions) Order 2008 (SI 2008/1436). **9B–550.1**

**For ss.195 to 214 of and Sch.1 to the Legal Services Act 2007 (see Arrangement) plus any related commentary see paragraphs 9B–551+ to 9B–586.1+ on White Book on Westlaw UK or the Civil Procedure CD.**

# SCHEDULE 2

## THE RESERVED LEGAL ACTIVITIES

### *Introduction*

1. This Schedule makes provision about the reserved legal activities. **9B–587**

2. In this Schedule "the appointed day" means the day appointed for the coming into force of section 13 (entitlement to carry on reserved legal activities).

### *Rights of audience*

3.—(1) A "right of audience" means the right to appear before and address a court, including the right to call and examine witnesses. **9B–588**

(2) But a "right of audience" does not include a right to appear before or address a court, or to call or examine witnesses, in relation to any particular court or in relation to particular proceedings, if immediately before the appointed day no restriction was placed on the persons entitled to exercise that right.

### *Conduct of litigation*

4.—(1) The "conduct of litigation" means— **9B–589**

(a) the issuing of proceedings before any court in England and Wales,

(b) the commencement, prosecution and defence of such proceedings, and

(c) the performance of any ancillary functions in relation to such proceedings (such as entering appearances to actions).

(2) But the "conduct of litigation" does not include any activity within paragraphs (a) to (c) of sub-paragraph (1), in relation to any particular court or in relation to any particular proceedings, if immediately before the appointed day no restriction was placed on the persons entitled to carry on that activity.

**For Sch.2, paras 5 to 8, to the Legal Services Act 2007 (see Arrangement) plus any related commentary see paragraphs 9B–590+ to 9B–593+ on White Book on Westlaw UK or the Civil Procedure CD.**

*Commencement note*—Schedule 2 brought into force for certain purposes by the Legal Services Act 2007 (Commencement No.1 and Transitory Provisions) Order 2008 (SI 2008/222), with effect from March 7, 2008. The purposes (contained in art.3) for which Schedule 2 comes into force are in so far as it defines the term 'Reserved legal activity' for the purpose of the following provisions: **9B–593.1**

- Section 1;
- The definition of "consumers" in s.207;
- Section 69(4) as modified by this Order;

***Paragraph numbers marked with a "+" can be found online and on CD.***

- Paragraph 2(3) to (5) of Sch.1;
- Paragraph 2(3) and (4) of Sch.15;
- Paragraph 2(6) and 2(7)(b) of Sch.22.

Schedule 2 brought into force for certain purposes by the Legal Services Act 2007 (Commencement No.4, Transitory and Transitional Provisions and Appointed Day) Order 2009 (SI 2009/503), with effect from March 31, 2009. The purposes (contained in art.3) for which Sch.2 comes into force are in so far as it defines the term "Reserved legal activity" for the purpose of ss.9 and 32A of the Administration of Justice Act 1985.

Brought into force for remaining purposes (subject to transitory and transitional provisions) by the Legal Services Act 2007 (Commencement No.6, Transitory, Transitional and Saving Provisions) Order 2009 (SI 2009/3250), with effect from January 1, 2010; for transitory and transitional provisions see arts 3–6.

## SCHEDULE 3

### EXEMPT PERSONS

**Rights of audience**

**9B–594** 1.—(1) This paragraph applies to determine whether a person is an exempt person for the purpose of exercising a right of audience before a court in relation to any proceedings (subject to paragraph 7).

(2) The person is exempt if the person—
- (a) is not an authorised person in relation to that activity, but
- (b) has a right of audience granted by that court in relation to those proceedings.

(3) The person is exempt if the person—
- (a) is not an authorised person in relation to that activity, but
- (b) has a right of audience before that court in relation to those proceedings granted by or under any enactment.

(4) The person is exempt if the person is the Attorney General or the Solicitor General and—
- (a) the name of the person is on the roll kept by the Law Society under section 6 of the Solicitors Act 1974 (c. 47), or
- (b) the person has been called to the Bar by an Inn of Court.

(5) The person is exempt if the person is the Advocate General for Scotland and is admitted—
- (a) as a solicitor in Scotland under section 6 of the Solicitors (Scotland) Act 1980 (c. 46), or
- (b) to practise as an advocate before the courts of Scotland.

(6) The person is exempt if the person—
- (a) is a party to those proceedings, and
- (b) would have a right of audience, in the person's capacity as such a party, if this Act had not been passed.

(7) The person is exempt if—
- (a) the person is an individual whose work includes assisting in the conduct of litigation,
- (b) the person is assisting in the conduct of litigation—
  - (i) under instructions given (either generally or in relation to the proceedings) by an individual to whom sub-paragraph (8) applies, and
  - (ii) under the supervision of that individual, and
- (c) the proceedings are being heard in chambers in the High Court or a county court and are not reserved family proceedings.

(8) This sub-paragraph applies to—
- (a) any authorised person in relation to an activity which constitutes the conduct of litigation;
- (b) any person who by virtue of section 193 is not required to be entitled to carry on such an activity.

(9) The person is an exempt person in relation to the exercise of a right of audience in proceedings on an appeal from the Comptroller-General of Patents, Designs and Trade Marks to the Patents Court under the Patents Act 1977 (c. 37), if the person is a solicitor of the Court of Judicature of Northern Ireland.

(10) For the purposes of this paragraph—

"family proceedings" has the same meaning as in the Matrimonial and Family Proceedings Act 1984 (c. 42) and also includes any other proceedings which are family proceedings for the purposes of the Children Act 1989 (c. 41);

"reserved family proceedings" means such category of family proceedings as the Lord Chancellor may, after consulting the President of the Law Society and with the concurrence of the President of the Family Division, by order prescribe;

and any order made under section 27(9) of the Courts and Legal Services Act 1990 (c. 41) before the day appointed for the coming into force of this paragraph is to have effect on and after that day as if it were an order made under this sub-paragraph.

## Conduct of litigation

2.—(1) This paragraph applies to determine whether a person is an exempt person for the purpose of carrying on any activity which constitutes the conduct of litigation in relation to any proceedings (subject to paragraph 7). **9B-595**

(2) The person is exempt if the person—

(a) is not an authorised person in relation to that activity, but

(b) has a right to conduct litigation granted by a court in relation to those proceedings.

(3) The person is exempt if the person—

(a) is not an authorised person in relation to that activity, but

(b) has a right to conduct litigation in relation to those proceedings granted by or under any enactment.

(4) The person is exempt if the person—

(a) is a party to those proceedings, and

(b) would have a right to conduct the litigation, in the person's capacity as such a party, if this Act had not been passed.

(5) The person is an exempt person in relation to any activity which is carried on in or in connection with proceedings on an appeal from the Comptroller-General of Patents, Designs and Trade Marks to the Patents Court under the Patents Act 1977 (c. 37), if the person is a solicitor of the Court of Judicature of Northern Ireland.

**For Sch.3, paras 3 to 6, to the Legal Services Act 2007 (see Arrangement) plus any related commentary see paragraphs 9B-596+ to 9B-599+ on White Book on Westlaw UK or the Civil Procedure CD.**

### European lawyers

7. A European lawyer (within the meaning of the European Communities (Services of Lawyers) Order 1978 (S.I. 1978/1910)) is an exempt person for the purposes of carrying on an activity which is a reserved legal activity and which the European lawyer is entitled to carry on by virtue of that order. **9B-600**

**For Sch.3, paras 8 and 9, and Schs 4 to 24 to the Legal Services Act 2007 (see Arrangement) plus any related commentary see paragraphs 9B-601+ to 9B-927+ on White Book on Westlaw UK or the Civil Procedure CD.**

# High Court and County Courts Jurisdiction Order 1991

(S.I. 1991 No. 724)

### Introductory note

The Order was made by the Lord Chancellor in exercise of powers granted by the Courts and Legal Services Act 1990 s.1 (see para.9B-102, above). **9B-928**

The Lord Chancellor may by order make provision (a) allocating proceedings under the Arbitration Act 1996 to the High Court or to county courts, or (b) specifying proceedings under that Act which may be commenced or taken only in the High Court or in a county court (s.105(2)). The High Court and County Courts (Allocation of Arbitration Proceedings) Order 1996 (SI 1996/3215) (see para.2E–375) was made in exercise of this power.

This Order has been amended by the following statutory instruments: High Court and County Courts Jurisdiction (Amendment) Order 1993 (SI 1993/1407), High Court and County Courts Jurisdiction (Amendment) Order 19954 (SI 1995/205), High Court and County Courts Jurisdiction (Amendment) Order 1996 (SI 1996/3141), High Court and County Courts Jurisdiction (Amendment) Order 1999 (SI 1999/1014), High Court and County Courts Jurisdiction (Amendment) Order 2001 (SI 2001/1387), High Court and County Courts Jurisdiction (Amendment No.2) Order 2001 (SI 2001/2685), High Court and County Courts Jurisdiction (Amendment) Order 2005 (SI 2005/587), High Court and County Courts Jurisdiction (Amendment) Order 2008 (SI 2008/2934); High Court and County Courts Jurisdiction (Amendment) Order 2009 (SI 2009/577) (making amendments to arts 4A, 5(1) and 9 consequential upon amendments to the CPR relating to fast track claims made by SI 2008/3327 which came into force on April 6, 2009, but haseffect only in relation to proceedings issued before that date, and other amendments). The 1999 Order provides, amongst other things, that for the word "plaintiff", wherever it appears in the 1991 Order, there should be substituted the word "claimant".

### Title and commencement

9B–929 **1.** This Order may be cited as the High Court and County Courts Jurisdiction Order 1991 and shall come into force on 1st July 1991.

### Interpretation

9B–929.1 **1A.** In this Order—

(a) "the EOP Regulation" means Regulation (EC) No 1896/2006 of the European Parliament and of the Council of 12 December 2006 creating a European order for payment procedure; and

(b) "the ESCP Regulation" means Regulation (EC) No 861/2007 of the European Parliament and of the Council of 11 July 2007 establishing a European small claims procedure.

### Jurisdiction

9B–930 **2.**—(1) A county court shall have jurisdiction under—

(a) sections 146 and 147 of the Law of Property Act 1925,
(b) [...]
(c) section 26 of the Arbitration Act 1950,
(d) section 63(2) of the Landlord and Tenant Act 1954,
(e) section 28(3) of the Mines and Quarries (Tips) Act 1969,
(f) section 66 of the Taxes Management Act 1970,
(g) section 41 of the Administration of Justice Act 1970,
(h) [Revoked]
(i) section 13 of the Torts (Interference with Goods) Act 1977,
(j) section 87 of the Magistrates' Courts Act 1980,
(k) sections 19 and 20 of the Local Government Finance Act 1982,
(l) sections 15, 16, 21, 25 and 139 of the County Courts Act 1984,
(m) section 39(4) of, and paragraph 3(1) of Schedule 3 to, the Legal Aid Act 1988,

(n) sections 99, 102(5), 114, 195, 204, 230, 231 and 235(5) of the Copyright, Designs and Patents Act 1988,

(o) section 40 of the Housing Act 1988,

(p) sections 13 and 14 of the Trusts of Land and Appointment of Trustees Act 1996.

(q) the EOP Regulation,

(r) the ESCP Regulation,

whatever the amount involved in the proceedings and whatever the value of any fund or asset connected with the proceedings.

(2) A county court shall have jurisdiction under—

(a) section 10 of the Local Land Charges Act 1975, and

(b) section 10(4) of the Rentcharges Act 1977,

where the sum concerned or amount claimed does not exceed £5,000.

(3) A county court shall have jurisdiction under the following provisions of the Law of Property Act 1925 where the capital value of the land or interest in land which is to be dealt with does not exceed £30,000:

(a) sections 3, 49, 66, 181, and 188;

(b) proviso (iii) to paragraph 3 of Part III of Schedule 1;

(c) proviso (v) to paragraph 1(3) of Part IV of Schedule 1;

(d) provisos (iii) and (iv) to paragraph 1(4) of Part IV of Schedule 1.

(4) A county court shall have jurisdiction under sections 89, 90, 91 and 92 of the Law of Property Act 1925 where the amount owing in respect of the mortgage or charge at the commencement of the proceedings does not exceed £30,000.

(5) A county court shall have jurisdiction under the proviso to section 136(1) of the Law of Property Act 1925 where the amount or value of the debt or thing in action does not exceed £30,000.

(6) A county court shall have jurisdiction under section 1(6) of the Land Charges Act 1972—

(a) in the case of a land charge of Class C(i), C(ii) or D(i), if the amount does not exceed £30,000;

(b) in the case of a land charge of Class C(iii), if it is for a specified capital sum of money not exceeding £30,000 or, where it is not for a specified capital sum, if the capital value of the land affected does not exceed £30,000;

(c) in the case of a land charge of Class A, Class B, Class C(iv), Class D(ii), Class D(iii) or Class E, if the capital value of the land affected does not exceed £30,000;

(d) in the case of a land charge of Class F, if the land affected by it is the subject of an order made by the court under section 1 of the Matrimonial Homes Act 1983 or an application for an order under that section relating to that land has been made to the court;

(e) in a case where an application under section 23 of the Deeds of Arrangement Act 1914 could be entertained by the court.

*Paragraph numbers marked with a "+" can be found online and on CD.*

(7) A county court shall have jurisdiction under sections 69, 70 and 71 of the Solicitors Act 1974 where a bill of costs relates wholly or partly to contentious business done in a county court and the amount of the bill does not exceed £5,000.

(7A) A patents county court and the county courts listed in paragraph (7B) shall have jurisdiction under the following provisions of the Trade Marks Act 1994—

(a) sections 15, 16, 19, 23(5), 25(4)(b), 30, 31, 46, 47, 64, 73 and 74;
(b) paragraph 12 of Schedule 1;
(c) paragraph 14 of Schedule 2,

to include jurisdiction to hear and determine any claims or matters ancillary to, or arising from proceedings brought under such provisions.

(7B) For the purposes of paragraph (7A), the county courts at—

(a) Birmingham;
(b) Bristol;
(c) Cardiff;
(d) Leeds;
(e) Liverpool
(f) Manchester; and
(g) Newcastle upon Tyne,

shall have jurisdiction.

(8) The enactments and statutory instruments listed in the Schedule to this Order are amended as specified therein, being amendments which are consequential on the provisions of this article.

**9B–931** *Note*—Amended by the High Court and County Courts Jurisdiction (Amendment) Order 1996 (SI 1996/3141) the High Court and County Courts Jurisdiction (Amendment) Order 2005 (SI 2005/587), and the High Court and County Courts Jurisdiction (Amendment) Order 2008 (SI 2008/2934).

#### Effect

**9B–932** The amendments made by SI 1996/3141 to the 1991 Order grant county courts jurisdiction in proceedings under the Trusts of Land and Appointment of Trustees Act 1996 ss.13 and 14 (art.2(1)), reduce to £1,000 (from £2,000) the value-limit for enforcement by execution against goods, above which judgment debts may be transferred from a county court to the High Court (art.8(1)), and make consequential amendments to take account of extension to areas outside London of statutory scheme for enforcement through county courts of certain road traffic debts. The amendments made by SI 2005/587 altered the jurisdictions of a patents county court and certain county courts in relation to proceedings under the Trade Marks Act 1994 (see paras (7A) and (7B) of art.2). Sub-paras (q) and (r) were added to art. 2(1) by SI 2008/2934.

### Injunctions

**9B–933** **3.** The High Court shall have jurisdiction to hear an application for an injunction made in the course of or in anticipation of proceedings in a county court where a county court may not, by virtue of regulations under section 38(3)(b) of the County Courts Act 1984 or otherwise, grant such an injunction.

#### "Regulations under s.38(3)(b)"

**9B–934** See the County Court Remedies Regulations 1991 (SI 1991/1222), para.9B–77, above.

***Paragraph numbers marked with a "+" can be found online and on CD.***

**Allocation—Commencement of proceedings**

**4.** Subject to articles 5, 6, 6A and 6B, proceedings in which both the county courts and the High Court have jurisdiction may be commenced either in a county court or in the High Court. **9B–935**

**4A.** Except for proceedings to which article 5 applies, a claim for money in which the county courts have jurisdiction may only be commenced in the High Court if the value of the claim is more than £25,000.

**5.**—(1) Proceedings which include a claim for damages in respect of personal injuries may only be commenced in the High Court if the value of the claim is £50,000 or more.

(2) In this article "personal injuries" means personal injuries to the plaintiff or any other person, and includes disease, impairment of physical or mental condition, and death.

(3) This article does not apply to proceedings which include a claim for damages in respect of an alleged breach of duty of care committed in the course of the provision of clinical or medical services (including dental or nursing services).

**6.** Applications and appeals under section 19 of the Local Government Finance Act 1982 and appeals under section 20 of that Act shall be commenced in the High Court.

**6A.** Applications under section 1 of the Access to Neighbouring Land Act 1992 shall be commenced in a county court.

**6B.** Applications under article 4 of the ESCP Regulation must be commenced in a county court.

*Note* —Amended by the High Court and County Courts Jurisdiction (Amendment) Order 1993 (SI 1993/1407); and the Access to Neighbouring Land Act 1992 s.7(2). Article 6B was inserted by SI 2008/2934. Article 4A was substituted and art.5(1) was amended in relation to proceedings issued on or after April 6, 2009 by the High Court and County Courts Jurisdiction (Amendment) Order 2009 (SI 2009/577). **9B–936**

**Allocation—Trial**

**7.** [...] **9B–937**

*Note* —Repealed by SI 1999/1014. **9B–938**

**Enforcement**

**8.**—(1) Subject to paragraph (1A) a judgment or order of a county court for the payment of a sum of money which it is sought to enforce wholly or partially by execution against goods— **9B–939**

(a) shall be enforced only in the High Court where the sum which it is sought to enforce is £5,000 or more;

(b) shall be enforced only in a county court where the sum which it is sought to enforce is less than £600.

(1A) A judgment of order of a county court for the payment of a sum of money in proceedings arising out of an agreement regulated by the Consumer Credit Act 1974 shall be enforced only in a county court.

(2) *[amends the County Courts Act 1984, s.85(1)]*

(2) Subject to paragraph (3), where—

***Paragraph numbers marked with a "+" can be found online and on CD.***

(a) an enactment provides that a sum of money shall be or may be recoverable as if it were payable under a county court order; and

(b) the recovery of that sum is sought wholly or partially by execution against goods, payment of that sum shall be enforced in accordance with paragraphs (1)(a) to (c).

(3) Paragraph (1)(b) does not apply to the enforcement of—

(a) a sum of money recoverable under section 15(1) of the Employment Tribunals Act 1996; or

(b) a compromise sum which is recoverable under section 19A(3) of that Act.

9B–940 *Note*—Amended by SI 1993/1407; SI 1995/205 art.5, SI 1996/3141 and new paras (2) and (3) inserted in relation to proceedings issued on or after April 6, 2009 by SI 2009/577.

**Transfer to the High Court for execution**

9B–941 The amendments made by SI 1996/3141 to the 1991 Order reduce to £1,000 (from £2,000) the value-limit for enforcement by execution against goods, above which judgment debts may be transferred from a county court to the High Court (art.8(1)).

**"enforced ... in the High Court"**

9B–942 For procedure and practice where transfer of county court judgment or order to High Court for enforcement, see CPR Pt 30.

Where county court judgments between £2,000 and £5,000 are transferred to the High Court for enforcement interest is earned from the date of transfer.

The amendments brought about by SI 1995/205 make clear that judgments given in proceedings arising out of the Consumer Credit Act 1974 may only be enforced in a county court, whatever the enforcement chosen (whether execution against grounds or some other method).

## Enforcement of traffic penalties

9B–943 **8A.**—(1) Proceedings for the recovery of—

(a) increased penalty charges provided for in charge certificates issued under—

(i) paragraph 6 of Schedule 6 to the 1991 Act[1];

(ii) paragraph 8 of Schedule 1 to the London Local Authorities Act 1996[2]

(iii) regulation 17 of the Road User Charging (Enforcement and Adjudication) (London) Regulations 2001;

(iv) regulation 21 of the Civil Enforcement of Parking Contraventions (England) General Regulations 2007; and

(v) regulation 13 of the Civil Enforcement of Parking Contraventions (Penalty Charge Notices, Enforcement and Adjudication) (Wales) Regulations 2008;

[1] The Road Traffic Act 1991 (c.40).

[2] 1996 c.ix; para.8 of Sch.1 was amended by para.7 of Sch.2 to the London Local Authorities Act 2000 (c. vii) and Sch.1 is repealed by Sch.31 to the Transport Act 2000 (c.38) on such day as the Secretary of State may by order provide.

(b) amounts payable by a person other than a local authority under an adjudication of a parking adjudicator pursuant to section 73 of the 1991 Act

(c) amounts payable by a person other than a local authority under an adjudication pursuant to—

(i) the Road User Charging (Enforcement and Adjudication) (London) Regulations 2001;

(ii) the Civil Enforcement of Parking Contraventions (England) Representations and Appeals Regulations 2007; and

(iii) the Civil Enforcement of Parking Contraventions (Representations and Appeals) (Wales) Regulations 2008; and

(d) increased fixed penalties referred to in—

(i) regulation 17(6) of the Road Traffic (Vehicle Emissions) (Fixed Penalty) (England) Regulations 2002; and

(ii) regulation 17(6) of the Road Traffic (Vehicle Emissions) (Fixed Penalty) (Wales) Regulations 2003,

shall be taken in Northampton County Court

(2) In this article, "the 1991 Act" means the Road Traffic Act 1991.

(3) In this article, "a local authority" means—

(a) in England, a London borough council, the Common Council of the City of London, Transport for London,, a county or district council or the Council of the Isles of Scilly; and

(b) in Wales, a county or county borough council.

*Note* —Amended by the High Court and County Courts Jurisdiction (Amendment) Order 1993 (SI 1993/1407), the High Court and County Courts Jurisdiction (Amendment) Order 1995 (SI 1995/205), the High Court and County Courts Jurisdiction (Amendment) Order 2001 (SI 2001/1387) and (in relation to proceedings issued on or after April 6, 2009) the High Court and County Courts Jurisdiction (Amendment) Order 2009 (SI 2009/577). **9B–944**

**Road traffic debts**

The Road Traffic Act 1991 introduced a new regime for the enforcement of parking charges in London removing the enforcement proceedings from the jurisdiction of magistrates' courts. CPR Sch.2, CCR O.48B, introduced into the CCR in 1993, enables local authorities to issue county court orders to recover certain parking charges and to enforce such orders. This article gives Cardiff County Court exclusive jurisdiction to deal with the initial processing of orders. **9B–945**

## Enforcement of possession orders against trespassers

**8B.**—(1) A judgment or order of a county court for possession of land made in a possession claim against trespassers may be enforced in the High Court or a county court. **9B–946**

(2) In this article "a possession claim against trespassers" has the same meaning as in Part 55 of the Civil Procedure Rules 1998.

*Note* —Paragraph 8B was added to the Order by the High Court and County **9B–947**

Courts Jurisdiction (Amendment No.2) Order 2001 (SI 2001/2685). CPR Pt 55 (Possession Claims) came into force on October 15, 2001. For transitional provisions relating to Pt 55, see Vol.1, para.51.1.4.

### Value of claim

9B–948 **9.** For the purposes of Articles 4A, and 5, the value of the claim shall be calculated in accordance with rule 16.3(6) of the Civil Procedure Rules 1998.

9B–948.1 *Note* —Amended in relation to proceedings issued on or after April 6, 2009 by the High Court and County Courts Jurisdiction (Amendment) Order 2009 (SI 2009/577).

#### CPR r.16.3(6)

9B–949 This provision states that, in calculating how much he expects to recover, certain sums that the claimant might possibly recover in addition to the basic claim should be disregarded (e.g. interest and costs). Further, the possibility that the amount claimed may in the event be reduced by certain factors (e.g. a set-off included in the defence) should also be disregarded. In addition to CPR, r.16.3(6), note also Practice Direction (How to Start Proceedings—The Claim Form) para.2.2 (Vol.1, para.7PD.2).

9B–950 **10.** [...]

9B–951 *Note* —Repealed by SI 1999/1014.

### Crown proceedings—transitional provisions

9B–952 **11.** For a period of two years from the date upon which this Order comes into force no order shall be made transferring proceedings in the High Court to which the Crown is a party to a county court, except—

(a) when the proceedings are set down to be tried or heard; or

(b) with the consent of the Crown.

### Savings

9B–953 **12.** This Order shall not apply to:

(a) family proceedings within the meaning of Part V of the Matrimonial and Family Proceedings Act 1984;

(b) [...]

## Attachment of Earnings Act 1971

9B–954 (1971 c.32)

ARRANGEMENT OF SECTIONS

*CASES IN WHICH ATTACHMENT IS AVAILABLE*



***Paragraph numbers marked with a "+" can be found online and on CD.***

## *CASES IN WHICH ATTACHMENT IS AVAILABLE*

### Courts with power to attach earnings

**1.**—(1) The High Court may make an attachment of earnings order to secure payments under a High Court maintenance order. **9B–955**

(2) A county court may make an attachment of earnings order to secure—

(a) payments under a High Court or a county court maintenance order;

***Paragraph numbers marked with a "+" can be found online and on CD.***

(b) the payment of a judgment debt, other than a debt of less than £5 or such other sum as may be prescribed by county court rules; or

(c) payments under an administration order.

(3) A magistrates' court may make an attachment of earnings order to secure—

(a) payments under a magistrates' court maintenance order; or

(b) [...]

(c) the payment of any sum required to be paid by an order under section 17(2) of the Access to Justice Act 1999 or under regulations under section 17A(1) of that Act.

(4) The following provisions of this Act apply, except where otherwise stated, to attachment of earnings orders made, or to be made, by any court.

(5) Any power conferred by this Act to make an attachment of earnings order includes a power to make such an order to secure the discharge of liabilities arising before the coming into force of this Act.

9B–956 *Note*—Amended by the Access to Justice Act 1999 Sch.4, para.8; SI 2006/1737; and the Criminal Defence Service Act 2006 s.4(1).

## Orders to which this Act applies

9B–957 **1A.** The following provisions of this Act apply, except where otherwise stated, to attachment of earnings orders made, or to be made, by any court under this Act or under Schedule 5 to the Courts Act 2003, or by a fines officer under that Schedule.

9B–958 *Note*—Inserted by SI 2006/1737, with effect from July 3, 2006.

## Principal definitions

9B–959 **2.** In this Act—

(a) "maintenance order" means any order specified in Schedule 1 to this Act and includes such an order which has been discharged if any arrears are recoverable thereunder;

(b) "High Court maintenance order", "county court maintenance order" and "magistrates' court maintenance order" mean respectively a maintenance order enforceable by the High Court, a county court and a magistrates' court;

(c) "judgment debt" means a sum payable under—

(i) a judgment or order enforceable by a court in England and Wales (not being a magistrates' court);

(ii) an order of a magistrates' court for the payment of money recoverable summarily as a civil debt; or

(iii) an order of any court which is enforceable as if it were for the payment of money so recoverable,

but does not include any sum payable under a maintenance order or an administration order;

(d) "the relevant adjudication", in relation to any payment secured or to be secured by an attachment of earnings order, means the conviction, judgment, order or other adjudication from which there arises the liability to make the payment; and

(e) "the debtor", in relation to an attachment of earnings order, or to proceedings in which a court has power to make an attachment of earnings order, or to proceedings arising out of such an order, means the person by whom payment is required by the relevant adjudication to be made.

## Application for order and conditions of court's power to make it

**3.**—(A1) This section shall not apply to an attachment of earnings order to be made under Schedule 5 to the Courts Act 2003. **9B-960**

(1) The following persons may apply for an attachment of earnings order:—

(a) the person to whom payment under the relevant adjudication is required to be made (whether directly or through an officer of any court);

(b) where the relevant adjudication is an administration order, any one of the creditors scheduled to the order;

(c) without prejudice to paragraph (a) above, where the application is to a magistrates' court for an order to secure maintenance payments, and there is in force an order under section 59 of the Magistrates' Courts Act 1980 or section 19(2) of the Maintenance Orders Act 1950, that those payments be made to the designated officer for a magistrates' court, that officer;

(d) in the following cases the debtor—

(i) where the application is to a magistrates' court; or

(ii) where the application is to the High Court or a county court for an order to secure maintenance payments.

(2) [...]

(3) Subject to subsection (3A) below, for an attachment of earnings order to be made on the application of any person other than the debtor it must appear to the court that the debtor has failed to make one or more payments required by the relevant adjudication.

(3A) Subsection (3) above shall not apply where the relevant adjudication is a maintenance order.

(3B) [...]

(3C) [...]

(4) Where proceedings are brought—

(a) in the High Court or a country court for the enforcement of a maintenance order by committal under section 5 of the Debtors Act 1869; or

(b) in a magistrates' court for the enforcement of a maintenance order under section 76 of the Magistrates' Courts Act 1980 (distress or committal),

then, the court may make an attachment of earnings order to secure payments under the maintenance order, instead of dealing with the case under section 5 of the said Act of 1869 or, as the case may be, section 76 of the said Act of 1980.

(5) [...]

(6) Where proceedings are brought in a county court for an order of committal under section 5 of the Debtors Act 1869 in respect of a judgment debt for any of the taxes, contributions premiums or liabilities specified in Schedule 2 to this Act, the court may, in any circumstances in which it has power to make such an order, make instead an attachment of earnings order to secure the payment of the judgment debt.

(7) A county court shall not make an attachment of earnings order to secure the payment of a judgment debt if there is in force an order or warrant for the debtor's committal, under section 5 of the Debtors Act 1869, in respect of that debt; but in any such case the court may discharge the order or warrant with a view to making an attachment of earnings order instead.

**9B–961** *Note*—Amended by the Social Security Act 1973 Sch.27; the Magistrates' Courts Act 1980 Sch.7; and the Maintenance Enforcement Act 1991 Sch.2; the Criminal Procedure and Investigations Act 1996 s.53; the Powers of Criminal Courts (Sentencing) Act 2000 Sch.9, para.44; the Courts Act 2003 s.109(1), Sch.8, para.141; and SI 2006/1737.

*ADMINISTRATION ORDERS IN THE COUNTY COURT*

## Extension of power to make administration order

**9B–962** **4.**—(1) Where, on an application to a county court for an attachment of earnings order to secure the payment of a judgment debt, it appears to the court that the debtor also has other debts, the court—

(a) shall consider whether the case may be one in which all the debtor's liabilities should be dealt with together and that for that purpose an administration order should be made; and

(b) if of opinion that it may be such a case, shall have power (whether or not it makes the attachment of earnings order applied for), with a view to making an administration order, to order the debtor to furnish to the court a list of all his creditors and the amounts which he owes to them respectively.

(2) If, on receipt of the list referred to in subsection (1)(b) above, it appears to the court that the debtor's whole indebtedness amounts to not more than the amount which for the time being is the county court limit for the purposes of section 112 of the County Courts Act 1984 (limit of total indebtedness governing county court's power to make administration order on application of debtor), the court may make such an order in respect of the debtor's estate.

(2A) Subsection (2) above is subject to section 112(3) and (4) of the County Courts Act 1984 (which require that, before an administration order is made, notice is to be given to all the creditors and thereafter restricts the right of any creditor to institute bankruptcy proceedings).

(3) [...]

(4) Nothing in this section is to be taken as prejudicing any right of a debtor to apply, under section 112 of the County Courts Act 1984, for an administration order.

*Note*—Amended by the Insolvency Act 1976 s.13, Sch.3; and the County Court Act 1984 s.148, Sch.2. **9B–963**

## Attachment of earnings to secure payments under administration order

**5.**—(1) Where a county court makes an administration order in respect of a debtor's estate, it may also make an attachment of earnings order to secure the payments required by the administration order. **9B–964**

(2) At any time when an administration order is in force a county court may (with or without an application) make an attachment of earnings order to secure the payments required by the administration order, if it appears to the court that the debtor has failed to make any such payment.

(3) The power of a county court under this section to make an attachment of earnings order to secure the payments required by an administration order shall, where the debtor is already subject to an attachment of earnings order to secure the payment of a judgment debt, include power to direct that the last-mentioned order shall take effect (with or without variation under section 9 of this Act) as an order to secure the payments required by the administration order.

### *CONSEQUENCES OF ATTACHMENT ORDER*

## Effect and contents of order

**6.**—(1) An attachment of earnings order shall be an order directed to a person who appears to the court, or as the case may be the fines officer, making the order to have the debtor in his employment and shall operate as an instruction to that person— **9B–965**

(a) to make periodical deductions from the debtor's earnings in accordance with Part I of Schedule 3 to this Act; and

(b) at such times as the order may require, or as the court, or where the order is made under Schedule 5 to the Courts Act 2003 as the court or the fines officer as the case may be, may allow, to pay the amounts deducted to the collected officer of the court, as specified in the order.

(2) For the purposes of this Act, the relationship of employer and employee shall be treated as subsisting between two persons if one of them, as a principal and not as a servant or agent, pays to the other any sums defined as earnings by section 24 of this Act.

(3) An attachment of earnings order shall contain prescribed particulars enabling the debtor to be identified by the employer.

(4) Except where it is made to secure maintenance payments, the order shall specify the whole amount payable under the relevant adjudication (or so much of that amount as remains unpaid), including any relevant costs.

(5) Subject to subsection (5A) below, the order shall specify—

(a) the normal deduction rate, that is to say, the rate (expressed as a sum of money per week, month or other period) at which the court thinks it reasonable for the debtor's earnings to be applied to meeting his liability under the relevant adjudication; and

(b) the protected earnings rate, that is to say the rate (so expressed) below which, having regard to the debtor's resources and needs, the court thinks it reasonable that the earnings actually paid to him should not be reduced.

(5A) If the order is made under Schedule 5 to the Courts Act 2003 then it shall specify the percentage deduction rate in accordance with fines collection regulations made under that Schedule.

(6) In the case of an order made to secure payments under a maintenance order (not being an order for the payment of a lump sum), the normal deduction rate—

(a) shall be determined after taking account of any right or liability of the debtor to deduct income tax when making the payments; and

(b) shall not exceed the rate which appears to the court necessary for the purpose of—

(i) securing payment of the sums falling due from time to time under the maintenance order, and

(ii) securing payment within a reasonable period of any sums already due and unpaid under the maintenance order.

(7) For the purposes of an attachment of earnings order, the collecting officer of the court shall be (subject to later variation of the order under section 9 of this Act)—

(a) in the case of an order made by the High Court, either—

(i) the proper officer of the High Court, or

(ii) the appropriate officer of such county court as the order may specify;

(b) in the case of an order made by a county court, the appropriate officer of that court; and

(c) in the case of an order made by a magistrates' court, the designated officer for that court or for another magistrates' court specified in the order.

(8) In subsection (7) above "appropriate officer" means an officer designated by the Lord Chancellor.

(9) The Lord Chancellor may by order make such provision as he considers expedient (including transitional provisions) with a view to providing for the payment of amounts deducted under attachment of earnings orders to be made to such officers as may be designated by the order rather than to collecting officers of the court.

(10) Any such order may make such amendments in this Act, in relation to functions exercised by or in relation to collecting officers of the court as he considers expedient in consequence of the provision made by virtue of subsection (9) above.

(11) The power to make such an order shall be exercisable by statutory instrument.

(12) Any such statutory instrument shall be subject to annulment in pursuance of a resolution of either House of Parliament.

*Note* —Amended by the Administration of Justice Act 1977 s.19; Courts Act 2003 s.109(1), Sch.8, para.142; and SI 2006/1737; subss.(9)–(12) prospectively inserted by the Courts and Legal Services Act 1990 s.125(2), Sch.17, para.5, as from a date to be appointed. **9B–966**

## Compliance with order by employer

**7.**—(1) Where an attachment of earnings order has been made, the employer shall, if he has been served with the order, comply with it; but he shall be under no liability for non-compliance before seven days have elapsed since the service. **9B–967**

(2) Where a person is served with an attachment of earnings order directed to him and he has not the debtor in his employment, or the debtor subsequently ceases to be in his employment, he shall (in either case), within ten days from the date of service or, as the case may be, the cesser, give notice of that fact to the court.

(3) Part II of Schedule 3 to this Act shall have effect with respect to the priority to be accorded as between two or more attachment of earnings orders directed to a person in respect of the same debtor.

(4) On any occasion when the employer makes, in compliance with the order, a deduction from the debtor's earnings—

(a) he shall be entitled to deduct, in addition, £1.00, or such other sum as may be prescribed by order made by the Lord Chancellor, towards his clerical and administrative costs; and

(b) he shall give to the debtor a statement in writing of the total amount of the deduction.

(5) An order of the Lord Chancellor under subsection (4)(a) above—

(a) may prescribe different sums in relation to different classes of cases;

(b) may be varied or revoked by a subsequent order made under that paragraph; and

(c) shall be made by statutory instrument subject to annulment by resolution of either House of Parliament.

*Note* —Amended by the Attachment of Earnings (Employer's Deduction) Order 1991 (SI 1991/356). **9B–968**

## Interrelation with alternative remedies open to creditors

**8.**—(1) Where an attachment of earnings order has been made to secure maintenance payments, no order or warrant of commitment shall be issued in consequence of any proceedings for the enforcement of the related maintenance order begun before the making of the attachment of earnings order. **9B–969**

(2) Where a county court has made an attachment of earnings order to secure the payment of a judgment debt—

*Paragraph numbers marked with a "+" can be found online and on CD.*

(a) no order or warrant of commitment shall be issued in consequence of any proceedings for the enforcement of the debt begun before the making of the attachment of earnings order; and

(b) so long as the order is in force, no execution for the recovery of the debt shall issue against any property of the debtor without the leave of the county court.

(3) An attachment of earnings order made to secure maintenance payments shall cease to have effect upon the making of an order of commitment or the issue of a warrant of commitment for the enforcement of the related maintenance order, or upon the exercise for that purpose of the power conferred on a magistrates' court by section 77(2) of the Magistrates' Courts Act 1980 to postpone the issue of such a warrant.

(4) An attachment of earnings order made to secure the payment of a judgment debt shall cease to have effect on the making of an order of commitment or the issue of a warrant of commitment for the enforcement of the debt.

(5) An attachment of earnings order made to secure—

(a) any payment mentioned in section 1(3)(c) of this Act; or

(b) the payment of any sum mentioned in paragraph 1 of Schedule 5to the Courts Act 2003, shall cease to have effect on the issue of a warrant committing the debtor to prison for default in making that payment.

**9B–970** *Note*—Amended by the Magistrates' Courts Act 1980 s.154, Sch.7; and SI 2006/1737.

*SUBSEQUENT PROCEEDINGS*

## Variation, lapse and discharge of orders

**9B–971** **9.**—(1) The court, or where an attachment of earnings order is made under Schedule 5 to the Courts Act 2003 the court or the fines officer as the case may be, may make an order discharging or varying an attachment of earnings order.

(2) Where an order is varied, the employer shall, if he has been served with notice of the variation, comply with the order as varied; but he shall be under no liability for non-compliance before seven days have elapsed since the service.

(3) Rules of court may make provision—

(a) as to the circumstances in which an attachment of earnings order may be varied or discharged by the court of its own motion;

(aa) as to the circumstances in which an attachment of earnings order made under Schedule 5 to the Courts Act 2003 may be varied or discharged by the court or the fines officer of its or his own motion;

(b) in the case of an attachment of earnings order made by a magistrates' court, for enabling a single justice, on an application made by the debtor on the ground of a material change in his resources and needs since the order was made or last varied, to vary the order for a period of not more than four weeks by an increase of the protected earnings rate.

(4) Where an attachment of earnings order has been made and the person to whom it is directed ceases to have the debtor in his employment, the order shall lapse (except as respects deduction from earnings paid after the cesser and payment to the collecting officer of amounts deducted at any time) and be of no effect unless and until the court, or where the order was made under Schedule 5 to the Courts Act 2003 unless and until the court or the fines officer as the case may be, again directs it to a person (whether the same as before or another) who appears to the court or the fines officer (as the case may be), or where the order was made under Schedule 5 to the Courts Act 2003 unless and until the court or the fines officer as the case may be, again directs it to a person (whether the same as before or another) who appears to the court or the fines officer (as the case may be) to have the debtor in his employment.

(5) The lapse of an order under subsection (4) above shall not prevent its being treated as remaining in force for other purposes.

*Note*—Amended by SI 2006/1737. **9B–972**

## Normal deduction rate to be reduced in certain cases

**10.**—(1) The following provisions shall have effect, in the case of an attachment of earnings order made to secure maintenance payments, where it appears to the collecting officer of the court that— **9B–973**

(a) the aggregate of the payments made for the purposes of the related maintenance order by the debtor (whether under the attachment of earnings order or otherwise) exceeds the aggregate of the payments required up to that time by the maintenance order; and

(b) the normal deduction rate specified by the attachment of earnings order (or, where two or more such orders are in force in relation to the maintenance order, the aggregate of the normal deduction rates specified by those orders) exceeds the rate of payments required by the maintenance order; and

(c) no proceedings for the variation or discharge of the attachment of earnings order are pending.

(2) In the case of an order made by the High Court or a county court, the collecting officer shall give the prescribed notice to the person to whom he is required to pay sums received under the attachment of earnings order, and to the debtor; and the court shall make the appropriate variation order, unless the debtor requests it to discharge the attachment of earnings order, or to vary it in some other way, and the court thinks fit to comply with the request.

(3) In the case of an order made by a magistrates' court, the collecting officer shall apply to the court for the appropriate variation order; and the court shall grant the application unless the debtor appears at the hearing and requests the court to discharge the attach-

ment of earnings order, or to vary it in some other way, and the court thinks fit to comply with the request.

(4) In this section, "the appropriate variation order" means an order varying the attachment of earnings order in question by reducing the normal deduction rate specified thereby so as to secure that that rate (or, in the case mentioned in subsection (1)(b) above, the aggregate of the rates therein mentioned)—

(a) is the same as the rate of payments required by the maintenance order; or

(b) is such lower rate as the court thinks fit having regard to the amount of the excess mentioned in subsection (1)(a).

### Attachment order in respect of maintenance payments to cease to have effect on the occurrence of certain events

9B-974 **11.**—(1) An attachment of earnings order made to secure maintenance payments shall cease to have effect—

(a) upon the grant of an application for registration of the related maintenance order under section 2 of the Maintenance Orders Act 1958 (which provides for the registration in a magistrates' court of a High Court or county court maintenance order, and for registration in the High Court of a magistrates' court maintenance order);

(b) where the related maintenance order is registered under Part I of the said Act of 1958, upon the giving of notice with respect thereto under section 5 of that Act (notice with view to cancellation of registration);

(c) subject to subsection (3) below, upon the discharge of the related maintenance order while it is not registered under Part I of the said Act of 1958;

(d) upon the related maintenance order ceasing to be registered in a court in England or Wales, or becoming registered in a court in Scotland or Northern Ireland, under Part II of the Maintenance Orders Act 1950.

(2) Subsection (1)(a) above shall have effect, in the case of an application for registration under section 2(1) of the said Act of 1958, notwithstanding that the grant of the application may subsequently become void under subsection (2) of that section.

(3) Where the related maintenance order is discharged as mentioned in subsection (1)(c) above and it appears to the court discharging the order that arrears thereunder will remain to be recovered after the discharge, that court may, if it thinks fit, direct that subsection (1) shall not apply.

### Termination of employer's liability to make deductions

9B-975 **12.**—(1) Where an attachment of earnings order ceases to have effect under section 8 or 11 of this Act, the proper officer of the prescribed court shall give notice of the cesser to the person to whom the order was directed.

***Paragraph numbers marked with a "+" can be found online and on CD.***

(2) Where, in the case of an attachment of earnings order made otherwise than to secure maintenance payments, the whole amount payable under the relevant adjudication has been paid, and also any relevant costs, the court shall give notice to the employer that no further compliance with the order is required.

(3) Where an attachment of earnings order—

(a) ceases to have effect under section 8 or 11 of this Act; or

(b) is discharged under section 9,

the person to whom the order has been directed shall be under no liability in consequence of his treating the order as still in force at any time before the expiration of seven days from the date on which the notice required by subsection (1) above or, as the case may be, a copy of the discharging order is served on him.

*Administrative provisions*

## Application of sums received by collecting officer

**13.**—(1) Subject to subsection (3) below, the collecting officer to whom a person makes payments in compliance with an attachment of earnings order shall, after deducting such court fees, if any, in respect of proceedings for or arising out of the order, as are deductible from those payments, deal with the sums paid in the same way as he would if they had been paid by the debtor to satisfy the relevant adjudication. **9B–976**

(2) Any sums paid to the collecting officer under an attachment of earnings order made to secure maintenance payments shall, when paid to the person entitled to receive those payments, be deemed to be payments made by the debtor (with such deductions, if any, in respect of income tax as the debtor is entitled or required to make) so as to discharge—

(a) first, any sums for the time being due and unpaid under the related maintenance order (a sum due at an earlier date being discharged before a sum due at a later date); and

(b) secondly, any costs incurred in proceedings relating to the related maintenance order which were payable by the debtor when the attachment of earnings order was made or last varied.

(3) Where a county court makes an attachment of earnings order to secure the payment of a judgment debt and also, under section 4(1) of this Act, orders the debtor to furnish to the court a list of all his creditors, sums paid to the collecting officer in compliance with the attachment of earnings order shall not be dealt with by him as mentioned in subsection (1) above, but shall be retained by him pending the decision of the court whether or not to make an administration order and shall then be dealt with by him as the court may direct.

## Power of court to obtain statement of earnings, etc.

**14.**—(1) Where in any proceedings a court has power to make an **9B–977**

attachment of earnings order, under this Act or under Schedule 5 to the Courts Act 2003 or a fines officer has power under that Schedule, to make an attachment of earnings order, the court or the fines officer, as the case may be, may—

(a) order the debtor to give to the court, or the fines officer, as the case may be, within a specified period, a statement signed by him of—

(i) the name and address of any person by whom earnings are paid to him;

(ii) specified particulars as to his earnings and anticipated earnings, and as to his resources and needs; and

(iii) specified particulars for the purpose of enabling the debtor to be identified by any employer of his;

(b) order any person appearing to the court or the fines officer, as the case may be,to have the debtor in his employment to give to the court or the fines officer, as the case may be, within a specified period, a statement signed by him or on his behalf of specified particulars of the debtor's earnings and anticipated earnings.

(2) Where an attachment of earnings order has been made, the court or the fines officer, as the case may be, may at any time thereafter while the order is in force

(a) make such an order as is described in subsection 1(a) or (b)above; and

(b) order the debtor to attend before the court on a day and at a time specified in the order to give the information described in subsection 1(a) above.

(3) In the case of an application to a magistrates' court for an attachment of earnings order, or for the variation or discharge of such an order, the power to make an order under subsection (1) or (2) above shall be exercisable also, before the hearing of the application, by a single justice.

(4) Without prejudice to subsections (1) to (3) above, rules of court may provide that where notice of an application for an attachment of earnings order is served on the debtor, it shall include a requirement that he shall give to the court, within such period and in such manner as may be prescribed, a statement in writing of the matters specified in subsection (1)(a) above and of any other prescribed matters which are, or may be, relevant under section 6 of this Act to the determination of the normal deduction rate and the protected earnings rate to be specified in any order made on the application. This subsection does not apply to an attachment of earnings order to be made under Schedule 5 to the Courts Act 2003.

(5) In any proceedings in which a court has power under this Act or under Schedule 5 to the Courts Act 2003 or a fines officer has power under that Schedule,to make an attachment of earnings order, and in any proceedings for the making, variation or discharge of such an order, a document purporting to be a statement given to the court or the fines officer, as the case may be, in compliance with an

order under subsection (1)(a) or (b) above, or with any such requirement of a notice of application for an attachment of earnings order as is mentioned in subsection (4) above, shall, in the absence of proof to the contrary, be deemed to be a statement so given and shall be evidence of the facts stated therein.

*Note*—Amended by the Administration of Justice Act 1982 s.53; and SI 2006/1737. **9B–978**

## Obligation of debtor and his employers to notify changes of employment and earnings

**15.**—(1) While an attachment of earnings order is in force— **9B–979**

(a) the debtor shall from time to time notify the court in writing of every occasion on which he leaves any employment, or becomes employed or re-employed, not later (in each case) than seven days from the date on which he did so;

(b) the debtor shall, on any occasion when he becomes employed or re-employed, include in his notification under paragraph (a) above particulars of his earnings and anticipated earnings from the relevant employment; and

(c) any person who becomes the debtor's employer and knows that the order is in force and by, or (if the order was made by a fines officer), which court what court it was made shall, within seven days of his becoming the debtor's employer or of acquiring that knowledge (whichever is the later) notify that court in writing that he is the debtor's employer, and include in his notification a statement of the debtor's earnings and anticipated earnings.

(2) In the case of an attachment of earnings order made by a fines officer, the reference to "the court" in subsection (1)(a) above shall mean the court for which that order was made.

*Note*—Amended by SI 2006/1737. **9B–980**

## Power of court to determine whether particular payments are earnings

**16.**—(1) Where an attachment of earnings order is in force, the court shall, on the application of a person specified in subsection (2) below, determine whether payments to the debtor of a particular class or description specified by the application are earnings for the purposes of the order; and the employer shall be entitled to give effect to any determination for the time being in force under this section. **9B–981**

(2) The persons referred to in subsection (1) above are—

(a) the employer;

(b) the debtor.

(c) the person to whom payment under the relevant adjudication is required to be made (whether directly or through an officer of any court); and

(d) without prejudice to paragraph (c) above, where the application is in respect of an attachment of earnings order made to secure payments under a magistrates' court maintenance order, the collecting officer.

(3) Where an application under this section is made by the employer, he shall not incur any liability for non-compliance with the order as respects any payments of the class or description specified by the application which are made by him to the debtor while the application, or any appeal in consequence thereof, is pending; but this subsection shall not, unless the court otherwise orders, apply as respects such payments if the employer subsequently withdraws the application or, as the case may be, abandons the appeal.

## Consolidated attachment orders

9B–982 **17.**—(1) The powers of a county court under sections 1 and 3 of this Act shall include power to make an attachment of earnings order to secure the payment of any number of judgment debts; and the powers of a magistrates' court under those sections or under Schedule 5 to the Courts Act 2003, and the powers of a fines officer under that Schedule, shall include power to make an attachment of earnings order to secure the discharge of any number of such liabilities as are specified in section 1(3)of this Act and paragraph 1 of Schedule 5 to the Courts Act 2003.

(2) An attachment of earnings order made by virtue of this section shall be known as a consolidated attachment order.

(3) The power to make a consolidated attachment order shall be exercised subject to and in accordance with rules of court; and rules made for the purposes of this section may provide—

(a) for the transfer from one court to another or (where Schedule 5 to the Courts Act 2003 applies) from a court or a fines officer, as the case may be, acting in one local justice area, to a court or a fines officer, as the case may be, acting in another local justice area—

(i) of an attachment of earnings order, or any proceedings for or arising out of such an order; and

(ii) of functions relating to the enforcement of any liability capable of being secured by attachment of earnings;

(b) for enabling a court or a fines officer, as the case may be, to which or to whom any order, proceedings or functions have been transferred under the rules to vary or discharge an attachment of earnings order made by another court or fines officer and to replace it (if the court, or fines officer as the case may be, thinks fit) with a consolidated attachment order;

(c) for the cases in which any power exercisable under this section or the rules may be exercised by a court of its or a fines officer, as the case may be, of its or hisown motion or on the application of a prescribed person;

(d) for requiring the clerk or registrar of a court who

*Paragraph numbers marked with a "+" can be found online and on CD.*

receives payments made to him in compliance with an attachment of earnings order, instead of complying with section 13 of this Act, to deal with them as directed by the court or the rules; and

(e) for modifying or excluding provisions of this Act of Part III of the Magistrates' Courts Act 1980, but only so far as may be necessary or expedient for securing conformity with the operation of rules made by virtue of paragraphs (a) to (d) of this subsection

*Note* —Amended by the Magistrates Courts Act 1980 s.154, Sch.7; and SI 2006/1737. **9B–983**

*SPECIAL PROVISIONS WITH RESPECT TO MAGISTRATES' COURTS*

## Certain action not to be taken by collecting officer except on request

**18.**—(1) A designated officer for a magistrates' court who is entitled to receive payments under a maintenance order for transmission to another person shall not— **9B–984**

(a) apply for an attachment of earnings order to secure payments under the maintenance order; or

(b) except as provided by section 10(3) of this Act, apply for an order discharging or varying such an attachment of earnings order; or

(c) apply for a determination under section 16 of this Act,

unless he is requested in writing to do so by a person entitled to receive the payments through him.

(2) Where the designated officer for a magistrates' court is so requested—

(a) he shall comply with the request unless it appears to him unreasonable in the circumstances to do so; and

(b) the person by whom the request was made shall have the same liabilities for all the costs properly incurred in or about any proceedings taken in pursuance of the request as if the proceedings has been taken by that person.

(3) For the purposes of subsection (2)(b) above, any application made by the designated officer for a magistrates' court as required by section 10(3) of this Act shall be deemed to be made on the request of the person in whose favour the attachment of earnings order in question was made.

*Note* —Amended by the Courts Act 2003 s.109(1), Sch.8, para.143.

## Procedure on applications

**19.**—(1) Subject to rules of court made by virtue of the following subsection, an application to a magistrates' court for an attachment of earnings order, or an order discharging or varying an attachment of earnings order, shall be made by complaint. **9B–985**

***Paragraph numbers marked with a "+" can be found online and on CD.***

(2) Rules of court may make provision excluding subsection (1) in the case of such an application as is referred to in section 9(3)(b) of this Act.

(3) An application to a magistrates' court for a determination under section 16 of this Act shall be made by complaint.

(4) For the purposes of section 51 of the Magistrates' Courts Act 1980 (which provides for the issue of a summons directed to the person against whom an order may be made in pursuance of a complaint)—

(a) the power to make an order in pursuance of a complaint by the debtor for an attachment of earnings order, or the discharge or variation of such an order, shall be deemed to be a power to make an order against the person to whom payment under the relevant adjudication is required to be made (whether directly or through an officer of any court); and

(b) the power to make an attachment of earnings order, or an order discharging or varying an attachment of earnings order, in pursuance of a complaint by any other person (including a complaint in proceedings to which section 3(4)(b) of this Act applies) shall be deemed to be a power to make an order against the debtor.

(5) A complaint for an attachment of earnings order may be heard notwithstanding that it was made within the six months allowed by section 127(1) of the Magistrates' Courts Act 1980.

**9B-986** *Note* —Amended by the Magistrates' Court Act 1980 s.154, Sch.7.

## Jurisdiction in respect of persons residing outside England and Wales

**9B-987** **20.**—(1) It is hereby declared that a magistrates' court has jurisdiction to hear a complaint by or against a person residing outside England and Wales for the discharge or variation of an attachment of earnings order made by a magistrates' court to secure maintenance payments; and where such a complaint is made, the following provisions shall have effect.

(2) If the person resides in Scotland or Northern Ireland, section 15 of the Maintenance Orders Act 1950 (which relates to the service of process on persons residing in those countries) shall have effect in relation to the complaint as it has effect in relation to the proceedings therein mentioned.

(3) Subject to the following subsection, if the person resides outside the United Kingdom and does not appear at the time and place appointed for the hearing of the complaint, the court may, if it thinks it reasonable in all the circumstances to do so, proceed to hear and determine the complaint at the time and place appointed for the hearing, or for any adjourned hearing, in like manner as if the person had then appeared.

(4) Subsection (3) above shall apply only if it is proved to the satisfaction of the court, on oath or in such other manner as may be

prescribed, that the complainant has taken such steps as may be prescribed to give to the said person notice of the complaint and of the time and place appointed for the hearing of it.

### Costs on application under s.16

**21.**—(1) On making a determination under section 16 of this Act, a magistrates' court may in its discretion make such order as it thinks just and reasonable for payment by any of the persons mentioned in subsection (2) of that section of the whole or any part of the costs of the determination (but subject to section 18(2)(b) of this Act). **9B–988**

(2) Costs ordered to be paid under this section shall—

(a) in the case of costs to be paid by the debtor to the person in whose favour the attachment of earnings order in question was made, be deemed—

(i) if the attachment of earnings order was made to secure maintenance payments, to be a sum due under the related maintenance order, and

(ii) otherwise, to be a sum due to the designated officer for the magistrates' court; and

(b) in any other case, be enforceable as a civil debt.

*Note*—Amended by the Courts Act 2003 s.109(1), Sch.8, para.144.

*MISCELLANEOUS PROVISIONS*

### Persons employed under the Crown

**22.**—(1) The fact that an attachment of earnings order is made at the suit of the Crown shall not prevent its operation at any time when the debtor is in the employment of the Crown. **9B–989**

(2) Where a debtor is in the employment of the Crown and an attachment of earnings order is made in respect of him, then for the purposes of this Act—

(a) the chief officer for the time being of the department, office or other body in which the debtor is employed shall be treated as having the debtor in his employment (any transfer of the debtor from one department, office or body to another being treated as a change of employment); and

(b) any earnings paid by the Crown or a Minister of the Crown, or out of the public revenue of the United Kingdom, shall be treated as paid by the said chief officer.

(3) If any question arises, in proceedings for or arising out of an attachment of earnings order, as to what department, office or other body is concerned for the purposes of this section, or as to who for those purposes is the chief officer thereof, the question shall be referred to and determined by the Minister for the Civil Service; but that Minister shall not be under any obligation to consider a reference under this subsection unless it is made by the court.

(4) A document purporting to set out a determination of the said Minister under subsection (3) above and to be signed by an official of the Office of Public Service shall, in any such proceedings as are mentioned in that subsection, be admissible in evidence and be deemed to contain an accurate statement of such a determination unless the contrary is shown.

(5) This Act shall have effect notwithstanding any enactment passed before 29th May 1970 and preventing or avoiding the attachment or diversion of sums due to a person in respect of service under the Crown, whether by way of remuneration, pension or otherwise.

9B–990 *Note* —Amended by the Transfer of Functions (Minister for the Civil Service and Treasury) Order 1981 (SI 1981/1670); the Transfer of Functions (Minister for the Civil Service and Treasury) Order 1987 (SI 1987/2039); the Transfer of Functions (Science) Order 1992 (SI 1992/1296); and the Transfer of Functions (Science) Order 1995 (SI 1995/2985).

## Enforcement provisions

9B–991 **23.**—(1) If, after being served with notice of an application to a county court for an attachment of earnings order or for the variation of such an order or with an order made under section 14(2)(b) above, the debtor fails to attend on the day and at the time specified for any hearing of the application or specified in the order, the court may adjourn the hearing and order him to attend at a specified time on another day; and if the debtor—

(a) fails to attend at that time on that day; or

(b) attends, but refuses to be sworn or give evidence,

he may be ordered by the judge to be imprisoned for not more than fourteen days.

(1A) In any case where the judge has power to make an order of imprisonment under subsection (1) for failure to attend, he may, in lieu of or in addition to making that order, order the debtor to be arrested and brought before the court either forthwith or at such time as the judge may direct.

(2) Subject to this section, a person commits an offence if—

(a) being required by section 7(1) or 9(2) of this Act to comply with an attachment of earnings order, he fails to do so; or

(b) being required by section 7(2) of this Act to give a notice for the purposes of that subsection, he fails to give it, or fails to give it within the time required by that subsection; or

(c) he fails to comply with an order under section 14(1) of this Act or with any such requirement of a notice of application for an attachment of earnings order as is mentioned in section 14(4), or fails (in either case) to comply within the time required by the order or notice; or

(d) he fails to comply with section 15 of this Act; or

(e) he gives a notice for the purposes of section 7(2) of this Act, or a notification for the purposes of section 15, which he knows to be false in a material particular, or recklessly gives such a notice or notification which is false in a material particular; or

(f) in purported compliance with section 7(2) or 15 of this Act, or with an order under section 14(1), or with any such requirement of a notice of application for an attachment of earnings order as is mentioned in section 14(4), he makes any statement which he knows to be false in a material particular, or recklessly makes any statement which is false in a material particular.

(3) Where a person commits an offence under subsection (2) above in relation to proceedings in, or to an attachment of earnings order made by, the High Court or a county court, he shall be liable on summary conviction to a fine of not more than level 2 on the standard scale or he may be ordered by a judge of the High Court or the county court judge (as the case may be) to pay a fine of not more than £250 or, in the case of an offence specified in subsection (4) below, to be imprisoned for not more than fourteen days; and where a person commits an offence under subsection (2) otherwise than as mentioned above in this subsection, he shall be liable on summary conviction to a fine of not more than level 2 on the standard scale.

(4) The offences referred to above in the case of which a judge may impose imprisonment are—

(a) an offence under subsection (2)(c) or (d), if committed by the debtor; and

(b) an offence under subsection (2)(e) or (f), whether committed by the debtor or any other person.

(5) It shall be a defence—

(a) for a person charged with an offence under subsection (2)(a) above to prove that he took all reasonable steps to comply with the attachment of earnings order in question;

(b) for a person charged with an offence under subsection (2)(b) to prove that he did not know, and could not reasonably be expected to know, that the debtor was not in his employment, or (as the case may be) had ceased to be so, and that he gave the required notice as soon as reasonably practicable after the fact came to his knowledge.

(6) Where a person is convicted or dealt with for an offence under subsection (2)(a), the court may order him to pay, to whoever is the collecting officer of the court for the purposes of the attachment of earnings order in question, any sums deducted by that person from the debtor's earnings and not already paid to the collecting officer.

(7) Where under this section a person is ordered by a judge of the High Court or a county court judge to be imprisoned, the judge may at any time revoke the order and, if the person is already in custody, order his discharge.

(8) Any fine imposed by a judge of the High Court under subsection (3) above and any sums ordered by the High Court to be paid

under subsection (6) above shall be recoverable in the same way as a fine imposed by that court in the exercise of its jurisdiction to punish for contempt of court; section 129 of the County Courts Act 1984 (enforcement of fines) shall apply to payment of a fine imposed by a county court judge under subsection (3) and of any sums ordered by a county court judge to be paid under subsection (6); and any sum ordered by a magistrates' court to be paid under subsection (6) shall be recoverable as a sum adjudged to be paid on a conviction by that court.

(9) For the purposes of section 13 of the Administration of Justice Act 1960 (appeal in cases of contempt of court), subsection (3) above shall be treated as an enactment enabling the High Court or a county court to deal with an offence under subsection (2) above as if it were contempt of court.

(10) In this section references to proceedings in a court are to proceedings in which that court has power to make an attachment of earnings order or has made such an order.

(11) A district judge, assistant district judge or deputy district judge shall have the same powers under this section as a judge of a county court.

9B–992 *Note*—Amended by the Contempt of Court Act 1981 Sch.2; the Criminal Justice Act 1982 Sch.4; the Administration of Justice Act 1982 s.53; the County Courts Act 1984 Sch.2; the Court and Legal Services Act 1990 Sch.17; and the Criminal Justice Act 1991 Sch.4.

## Meaning of "earnings"

9B–993 **24.**—(1) For the purposes of this Act, but subject to the following subsection, "earnings" are any sums payable to a person—

(a) by way of wages or salary (including any fees, bonus, commission, overtime pay or other emoluments payable in addition to wages or salary or payable under a contract of service);

(b) by way of pension (including an annuity in respect of past services, whether or not rendered to the person paying the annuity, and including periodical payments by way of compensation for the loss, abolition or relinquishment, or diminution in the emoluments, of any office or employment);

(c) by way of statutory sick pay.

(2) The following shall not be treated as earnings:—

(a) sums payable by any public department of the Government of Northern Ireland or of a territory outside the United Kingdom;

(b) pay or allowances payable to the debtor as a member of Her Majesty's forces other than pay or allowances payable by his employer to him as a special member of a reserve force (within the meaning of the Reserve Forces Act 1996);

(ba) a tax credit (within the meaning of the Tax Credits Act 2002);

*Paragraph numbers marked with a "+" can be found online and on CD.*

(c) pension, allowances or benefit payable under any enactment relating to social security;
(d) pension or allowances payable in respect of disablement or disability;
(e) except in relation to a maintenance order wages payable to a person as a seaman, other than wages payable to him as a seaman of a fishing boat;
(f) guaranteed minimum pension within the meaning of the Pension Schemes Act 1993.

(3) In subsection (2)(e) above:

"fishing boat" means a vessel of whatever size, and in whatever way propelled, which is for the time being employed in sea fishing or in the sea-fishing service;

"seaman" includes every person (except masters and pilots) employed or engaged in any capacity on board any ship; and

"wages" includes emoluments.

*Note* —Amended by the Social Security Pensions Act 1975 Sch.4; the Merchant Shipping Act 1979 s.39; the Social Security Act 1985 Sch.4; the Social Security Act 1986 Sch.10; the Pension Schemes Act 1993 Sch.8; the Merchant Shipping Act 1995 Sch.13, para.46; the Reserve Forces Act 1996 (Consequential Provisions, etc.) Regulations 1998 (SI 1998/3086) reg.6; and by the Tax Credits Act 2002 Sch.3, para.1. **9B–994**

## General interpretation

**25.**—(1) In this Act, except where the context otherwise requires— **9B–995**

"administration order" means an order made under, and so referred to in, Part VI of the County Courts Act 1984;

"the court", in relation to an attachment of earnings order, means the court which made the order, subject to rules of court as to the venue for, and the transfer of, proceedings in county courts and magistrates' courts;

"debtor" and "relevant adjudication" have the meanings given by section 2 of this Act;

"the employer", in relation to an attachment of earnings order, means the person who is required by the order to make deductions from earnings paid by him to the debtor;

"the fines officer", in relation to a debtor who is subject to a collection order made under Schedule 5 to the Courts Act 2003, means any fines officer working at the fines office specified in that order;

"judgment debt" has the meaning given by section 2 of this Act;

"maintenance order" has the meaning given by section 2 of this Act;

"maintenance payments" means payments required under a maintenance order;

"prescribed" means prescribed by rules of court;

and, in relation to a magistrates' court, references to a single justice are to a justice of the peace acting for the same petty sessions area as the court.

(2) Any reference in this Act to sums payable under a judgment

or order, or to the payment of such sums, includes a reference to costs and the payment of them; and the references in sections 6(4) and 12(2) to relevant costs are to any costs of the proceedings in which the attachment of earnings order in question was made, being costs which the debtor is liable to pay.

(3) References in sections 6(5)(b), 9(3)(b) and 14(1)(a) of this Act to the debtor's needs include references to the need of any person for whom he must, or reasonably may, provide.

(4) [...]

(5) Any power to make rules which is conferred by this Act is without prejudice to any other power to make rules of court.

(6) This Act, so far as it relates to magistrates' courts, and Part III of the Magistrates' Courts Act 1980 shall be construed as if this Act were contained in that Part.

(7) References in this Act to any enactment include references to that enactment as amended by or under any other enactment, including this Act.

**9B–996** *Note*—Amended by the Legal Aid Act 1974 Sch.4; the Magistrates. Courts Act ss.144, 154, Sch.7; the County Courts Act 1984 s.148, Sch.2; the Legal Aid Act 1988 s.45, Sch.5; the Dock Work Act 1989 Sch.1; the Access to Justice Act 1999 Sch.15; the Courts Act 2003 Sch.10, para.1; and SI 2006/1737.

*General*

### Transitional provision

**9B–997** **26.**—(1) As from the appointed day, an attachment of earnings order made before that day under Part II of the Maintenance Orders Act 1958 (including an order made under that Part of that Act as applied by section 46 or 79 of the Criminal Justice Act 1967) shall take effect as an attachment of earnings order made under the corresponding power in this Act, and the provisions of this Act shall apply to it accordingly, so far as they are capable of doing so.

(2) Rules of court may make such provision as the rule-making authority considers requisite—

(a) for enabling an attachment of earnings order to which subsection (1) above applies to be varied so as to bring it into conformity, as from the appointed day, with the provisions of this Act, or to be replaced by an attachment of earnings order having effect as if made under the corresponding power in this Act;

(b) to secure that anything required or authorised by this Act to be done in relation to an attachment of earnings order made thereunder is required or, as the case may be, authorised to be done in relation to an attachment of earnings order to which the said subsection (1) applies.

(3) In this section "the appointed day" means the day appointed under section 54 of the Administration of Justice Act 1970 for the coming into force of Part II of that Act.

### Consequential amendment of enactments

**9B–998** **27.**—(1) In consequence of the repeals effected by this Act, section

*Paragraph numbers marked with a "+" can be found online and on CD.*

20 of the Maintenance Orders Act 1958 (which contains certain provisions about magistrates' courts and their procedure), except subsection (6) of that section (which amends section 52(3) of the Magistrates' Courts Act 1952), shall have effect as set out in Schedule 5 to this Act.

(2) [...]

(3) [...]

*Note*—Amended by the Insolvency Act 1976 Sch.3. 9B–999

**28.** [...] 9B–1000

*Note*—Repealed with savings by the Northern Ireland Constitution Act 1973 s.42 , Sch.6. 9B–1001

## Citation, repeal, extent and commencement

**29.**—(1) This Act may be cited as the Attachment of Earnings Act 1971. 9B–1002

(2) The Enactments specified in Schedule 6 to this Act are hereby repealed to the extent specified in the third column of that Schedule.

(3) This Act, except section 20(2), does not extend to Scotland and, except sections 20(2) ... does not extend to Northern Ireland.

(4) This Act shall come into force on the day appointed under section 54 of the Administration of Justice Act 1970 for the coming into force of Part II of that Act.

*Note*—Amended by the Northern Ireland Constitution Act 1973 s.42, Sch.6. 9B–1003

## SCHEDULE 1

### Maintenance Orders to Which This Act Applies

1. An order for alimony, maintenance or other payments made, or having effect as if made, under Part II of the Matrimonial Causes Act 1965 (ancillary relief in actions for divorce etc.). 9B–1004

2. An order for payments to or in respect of a child, being an order made, or having effect as if made, under Part III of the said Act of 1965 (maintenance of children following divorce, etc.).

3. An order for periodical or other payments made, or having effect as if made, under Part II of the Matrimonial Causes Act 1973.

4. An order for maintenance or other payments to or in respect of a spouse or child, being an order made under Part I of the Domestic Proceedings and Magistrates' Court Act 1978.

5. An order for periodical or other payments made or having effect as if made under Schedule 1 to the Children Act 1989.

6. [...]

7. An order under paragraph 23 of Schedule 2 to the Children Act 1989... section 23 of the Ministry of Social Security Act 1966 ... section 18 of the Supplementary Benefits Act 1976 ... or section 106 of the Social Security Administration Act 1992 (various provisions for obtaining contributions from a person whose dependants are assisted or maintained out of public funds).

8. An order under section 43 of the National Assistance Act 1948 (recovery of costs of maintaining assisted person).

9. An order to which section 16 of the Maintenance Orders Act 1950 applies by virtue of subsection (2)(b) or (c) of that section (that is to say an order made by a court in Scotland or Northern Ireland and corresponding to one of those specified in the

foregoing paragraphs) and which has been registered in a court in England and Wales under Part II of that Act.

10. A maintenance order within the meaning of the Maintenance Orders (Facilities for Enforcement) Act 1920 (Commonwealth orders enforceable in the United Kingdom) registered in, or confirmed by, a court of England and Wales under that Act.

11. A maintenance order within the meaning of Part I of the Maintenance Orders (Reciprocal Enforcement) Act 1972 registered in a magistrates' court under the said Part I.

12. An order under section 34(1)(b) of the Children Act 1975 (payments of maintenance in respect of a child to his custodian).

13. A maintenance order within the meaning of Part I of the Civil Jurisdiction and Judgments Act 1982 which is registered in a magistrates' court under that Part.

14. A maintenance judgment within the meaning of Council Regulation (EC) No. 44/2001 of 22nd December 2000 on jurisdiction and the recognition and enforcement of judgments in civil and commercial matters, as amended from time to time and as applied by the Agreement made on 19th October 2005 between the European Community and the Kingdom of Denmark on jurisdiction and the recognition and enforcement of judgments in civil and commercial matters (OJ No. L 299 16.11.2005 at p62) which is registered in a magistrates' court under that Regulation.

15. An order made under Schedule 5 to the Civil Partnership Act 2004 (financial relief in the High Court or a county court etc), for periodical or other payments.

16. An order made under Schedule 6 to the 2004 Act (financial relief in magistrates' courts etc), for maintenance or other payments to or in respect of a civil partner or child.

**9B–1005** *Note*—Amended by the Maintenance Orders (Reciprocal Enforcement) Act 1972; Sch.; the Matrimonial Causes Act 1973 Sch.2; Guardianship Act 1973 s.9; the Children Act 1975 Sch.3; the Supplementary Benefits Act 1976 Sch.7; the Domestic Proceedings and Magistrates. Courts Act 1978 s.89, Sch.2; the Child Care Act 1980 Sch.5; the Civil Jurisdiction and Judgments Act 1982 s.15, Sch.12; the Social Security Act 1986 Sch.10; the Family Law Reform Act 1987 s.33, Schs 2, 4; the Children Act 1989 s.108, Sch.3; the Courts and Legal Services Act 1990 Sch.16; the Social Security (Consequential Provisions) Act 1992 Sch.2; SI 2001/3929; the Civil Partnership Act 2004 s.261(1), Sch.27, para.35; and the Civil Jurisdiction and Judgments Regulations 2007 (SI 2007/1655) Schedule, para.7.

**SECTION 3**

## SCHEDULE 2

### TAXES, SOCIAL SECURITY CONTRIBUTIONS ETC RELEVANT FOR PURPOSES OF SECTION 3(6)

**9B–1006** 1. Income tax or any other tax or liability recoverable under section 65, 66 or 68 of the Taxes Management Act 1970.

2. [...]

3. Contributions equivalent premiums under Part III of the Pension Schemes Act 1993.

3A. Class 1, 2 and 4 contributions under Part I of the Social Security Contributions and Benefits Act 1992.

4. [...]

**9B–1007** *Note*—Amended by the Social Security Act 1973 Sch.28; the Social Security (Consequential Provisions) Act 1975 Sch.2; the Social Security Pensions Act 1975 Sch.4; the Statute Law (Repeals) Act 1989 s.1, Sch.1; the Social Security (Consequential Provision) Act 1992 Sch.2; the Pension Schemes Act 1993 Sch.8; and the Pensions Act 1995 Sch.5.

SECTIONS 6 AND 7

# SCHEDULE 3

## DEDUCTIONS BY EMPLOYER UNDER ATTACHMENT OF EARNINGS ORDER

## PART I

## SCHEME OF DEDUCTIONS

*Preliminary definitions*

1. The following three paragraphs have effect for defining and explaining, for purposes of this Schedule, expressions used therein. 9B–1008

2. "Pay-day", in relation to earnings paid to a debtor, means an occasion on which they are paid.

3. "Attachable earnings", in relation to a pay-day, are the earnings which remain payable to the debtor on that day after deduction by the employer of—

(a) income tax;

(b) ...

(bb) primary Class 1 contributions under Part I of the Social Security Act 1975.

(c) amounts deductible under any enactment, or in pursuance of a request in writing by the debtor, for the purposes of a superannuation scheme, namely any enactment, rules, deed or other instrument providing for the payment of annuities or lump sums—

(i) to the persons with respect to whom the instrument has effect on their retirement at a specified age or on becoming incapacitated at some earlier age, or

(ii) to the personal representatives or the widows, relatives or dependants of such persons on their death or otherwise, whether with or without any further or other benefits.

4.—(1) On any pay-day—

(a) "the normal deduction" is arrived at by applying the normal deduction rate (as specified in the relevant attachment of earnings order) with respect to the relevant period; and

(b) "the protected earnings" are arrived at by applying the protected earnings rate (as so specified) with respect to the relevant period.

(2) For the purposes of this paragraph the relevant period in relation to any pay-day is the period beginning—

(a) if it is the first pay-day of the debtor's employment with the employer, with the first pay-day of the employment; or

(b) if on the last pay-day earnings were paid in respect of a period falling wholly or partly after that pay-day, with the first day after the end of that period; or

(c) in any other case, with the first day after the last pay-day, and ending—

(i) where earnings are paid in respect of a period falling wholly or partly after the pay-day, with the last day of that period; or

(ii) in any other case, with the pay-day.

*Employer's deduction (judgment debts and administration orders)*

5. In the case of an attachment of earnings order made to secure the payment of a judgment debt or payments under an administration order, the employer shall on any pay-day— 9B–1009

(a) if the attachable earnings exceed the protected earnings, deduct from the attachable earnings the amount of the excess or the normal deduction, whichever is the less;

(b) make no deduction if the attachable earnings are equal to, or less than, the protected earnings.

*Employer's deduction (other cases)*

6.—(1) The following provision shall have effect in the case of an attachment of earnings order to which paragraph 5 above and paragraph 6A below do does not apply. 9B–1010

***Paragraph numbers marked with a "+" can be found online and on CD.***

(2) If on a pay-day the attachable earnings exceed the sum of—

(a) the protected earnings; and

(b) so much of any amount by which the attachable earnings on any previous pay-day fell short of the protected earnings as has not been made good by virtue of this sub-paragraph on another previous pay-day,

then, in so far as the excess allows, the employer shall deduct from the attachable earnings the amount specified in the following sub-paragraph.

(3) The said amount is the sum of—

(a) the normal deduction; and

(b) so much of the normal deduction on any previous pay-day as was not deducted on that day and has not been paid by virtue of this sub-paragraph on any other previous pay-day.

(4) No deduction shall be made on any pay-day when the attachable earnings are equal to, or less than, the protected earnings.

(6A) In the case of an attachment of earnings order made under Schedule 5 to the Courts Act 2003, the employer shall make deductions from the debtor's earnings in accordance with fines collection regulations made under that Schedule.

## PART II

## PRIORITY AS BETWEEN ORDERS

**9B–1011** 7. Where the employer is required to comply with two or more attachment of earnings orders in respect of the same debtor, all or none of which orders are made to secure either the payment of judgment debts or payments under an administration order, then on any pay-day the employer shall, for the purpose of complying with Part I of this Schedule—

(a) deal with the orders according to the respective dates on which they were made, disregarding any later order until an earlier one has been dealt with;

(b) deal with any later order as if the earnings to which it relates were the residue of the debtor's earnings after the making of any deduction to comply with any earlier order.

8. Where the employer is required to comply with two or more attachment of earnings orders, and one or more (but not all) of those orders are made to secure either the payment of judgment debts or payments under an administration order, then on any pay-day the employer shall, for the purpose of complying with Part I of this Schedule—

(a) deal first with any order which is not made to secure the payment of a judgment debt or payments under an administration order (complying with paragraph 7 above if there are two or more such orders); and

(b) deal thereafter with any order which is made to secure the payment of a judgment debt or payments under an administration order as if the earnings to which it relates were the residue of the debtor's earnings after the making of any deduction to comply with an order having priority by virtue of sub-paragraph (a) above; and

(c) if there are two or more orders to which sub-paragraph (b) above applies, comply with paragraph 7 above in respect of those orders.

**9B–1012** *Note* —Amended by the Social Security (Consequential Provisions) Act 1975 Sch.2; the Wages Councils Act 1979 Sch.6; the Administration of Justice Act 1982 s.54; the Wages Act 1986, Sch.4; and the Employment Rights Act 1996, Sch.1, para.3; and SI 2006/1737.

**SECTION 24**

## SCHEDULE 4

### ENACTMENTS PROVIDING BENEFITS WHICH ARE NOT TO BE TREATED AS DEBTOR'S EARNINGS

**9B–1013** [...]

**9B–1014** *Note* —Repealed by the Social Security Act 1986 s.86, Sch.11.

***Paragraph numbers marked with a "+" can be found online and on CD.***

SECTION 27

## SCHEDULE 5

SECTION 20 OF MAINTENANCE ORDERS ACT 1958 AS HAVING EFFECT IN CONSEQUENCE OF THIS ACT

*Special provisions as to magistrates' courts*

20.—(1) Notwithstanding anything in this Act, the clerk of a magistrates' court who is entitled to receive payments under a maintenance order for transmission to another person shall not apply for the registration of the maintenance order under Part I of this Act or give notice in relation to the order in pursuance of subsection (1) of section five thereof unless he is requested in writing to do so by a person entitled to receive the payments through him; and where the clerk is requested as aforesaid— **9B–1015**

(i) he shall comply with the request unless it appears to him unreasonable in the circumstances to do so;

(ii) the person by whom the request was made shall have the same liabilities for all the costs properly incurred in or about any proceedings taken in pursuance of the request as if the proceedings had been taken by that person.

(2) An application to a magistrates' court by virtue of subsection (2) of section four of this Act for the variation of a maintenance order shall be made by complaint.

(3)–(7) [*Not reproduced here*]

(8) For the avoidance of doubt it is hereby declared that a complaint may be made to enforce payment of a sum due and unpaid under a maintenance order notwithstanding that a previous complaint has been made in respect of that sum or a part thereof and whether or not an order was made in pursuance of the previous complaint.

# Charging Orders Act 1979

(1979 c.53) **9B–1016**

ARRANGEMENT OF SECTIONS

*CHARGING ORDERS*



## CHARGING ORDERS

### Charging orders

**1.**—(1) Where, under a judgment or order of the High Court or a county court, a person (the "debtor") is required to pay a sum of money to another person (the "creditor") then, for the purpose of enforcing that judgment or order, the appropriate court may make an order in accordance with the provisions of this Act imposing on any such property of the debtor as may be specified in the order a charge for securing the payment of any money due or to become due under the judgment or order. **9B–1017**

(2) The appropriate court is—

(a) in a case where the property to be charged is a fund in court, the court in which that fund is lodged;

(b) in a case where paragraph (a) above does not apply and the order to be enforced is a maintenance order of the High Court, the High Court or a county court;

(c) in a case where neither paragraph (a) nor paragraph (b) above applies and the judgment or order to be enforced is a judgment or order of the High Court for a sum exceeding the county court limit, the High Court or a county court; and

(d) in any other case, a county court.

In this section "county court limit" means the county court limit for the time being specified in an Order in Council under section 145 of the County Courts Act 1984, as the county court limit for the purposes of this section and "maintenance order" has the same meaning as in section 2(a) of the Attachment of Earnings Act 1971.

(3) An order under subsection (1) above is referred to in this Act as a "charging order".

(4) Where a person applies to the High Court for a charging order to enforce more than one judgment or order, that court shall be the appropriate court in relation to the application if it would be the appropriate court, apart from this subsection, on an application relating to one or more of the judgments or orders concerned.

(5) In deciding whether to make a charging order the court shall consider all the circumstance of the case and, in particular, any evidence before it as to—

(a) the personal circumstances of the debtor, and

(b) whether any other creditor of the debtor would be likely to be unduly prejudiced by the making of the order.

9B-1018 *Note*—Amended by the County Courts Jurisdiction Order 1981 (SI 1981/1123); the Administration of Justice Act 1982 ss.34, 37, Sch.3; and the County Courts Act 1984 Sch.2.

**"the county court limit"**

9B-1019 The limit is £5,000. See para.9B-1020 below.

**"appropriate court may make an order"**

9B-1020 In a case where a High Court judgment or order is to be enforced and neither paras (a) nor (b) of s.1(2) applies, generally the appropriate court to make a charging order will be a county court. Where the amount required to be paid exceeds a statutory sum, the appropriate court will be the High Court or a county court. Originally, the statutory sum was fixed at £2,000. Subsequently it was set at the same level as "the county court limit" (s.1(2)(c)). By operation of the County Court Jurisdiction Order 1981 (SI 1981/1123) that limit currently stands at £5,000.

## Property which may be charged

9B-1021 **2.**—(1) Subject to subsection (3) below, a charge may be imposed by a charging order only on—

(a) any interest held by the debtor beneficially—

(i) in any asset of a kind mentioned in subsection (2) below, or

*Paragraph numbers marked with a "+" can be found online and on CD.*

(ii) under any trust; or

(b) any interest held by a person as trustee of a trust ("the trust"), if the interest is in such an asset or is an interest under another trust and—

(i) the judgment or order in respect of which a charge is to be imposed was made against that person as trustee of the trust, or

(ii) the whole beneficial interest under the trust is held by the debtor unencumbered and for his own benefit, or

(iii) in a case where there are two or more debtors all of whom are liable to the creditor for the same debt, they together hold the whole beneficial interest under the trust unencumbered and for their own benefit.

(2) The assets referred to in subsection (1) above are—

(a) land,

(b) securities of any of the following kinds—

(i) government stock,

(ii) stock of any body (other than a building society) incorporated within England and Wales,

(iii) stock of any body incorporated outside England and Wales or of any state or territory outside the United Kingdom, being stock registered in a register kept at any place within England and Wales,

(iv) units of any unit trust in respect of which a register of the unit holders is kept at any place within England and Wales, or

(c) funds in court.

(3) In any case where a charge is imposed by a charging order on any interest in an asset of a kind mentioned in paragraph (b) or (c) of subsection (2) above, the court making the order may provide for the charge to extend to any interest or dividend payable in respect of the asset.

## Provisions supplementing sections 1 and 2

**3.**—(1) A charging order may be made either absolutely or subject to conditions as to notifying the debtor or as to the time when the charge is to become enforceable, or as to other matters. **9B–1022**

(2) The Land Charges Act 1972 and the Land Registration Act 2002 shall apply in relation to charging orders as they apply in relation to other orders or writs issued or made for the purpose of enforcing judgments.

(3) [...]

(4) Subject to the provisions of this Act, a charge imposed by a charging order shall have the like effect and shall be enforceable in the same courts and in the same manner as an equitable charge created by the debtor by writing under his hand.

(5) The court by which a charging order was made may at any time, on the application of the debtor or of any person interested in any property to which the order relates, make an order discharging or varying the charging order.

(6) Where a charging order has been protected by an entry registered under the Land Charges Act 1972 or the Land Registration Act 2002, an order under subsection (5) above discharging the charging order may direct that the entry be cancelled.

(7) The Lord Chancellor may be order made by statutory instrument amend section 2(2) of this Act by adding to, or removing from, the kinds of asset for the time being referred to there, any asset of a kind which in his opinion ought to be so added or removed.

(8) Any order under subsection (7) above shall be subject to annulment in pursuance of a resolution of either House of Parliament.

9B–1023 *Note*—Amended by the Land Registration Act 2002 Sch.11, para.15.

* * * *

*STOP ORDERS AND NOTICES*

## Stop orders and notices

9B–1024 **5.**—(1) In this section—

"stop order" means an order of the court prohibiting the taking, in respect of any of the securities specified in the order, of any of the steps mentioned in subsection (5) below;

"stop notice" means a notice requiring any person or body on whom it is duly served to refrain from taking, in respect of any of the securities specified in the notice, any of those steps without first notifying the person by whom, or on whose behalf, the notice was served; and

"prescribed securities" means securities (including funds in court) of a kind prescribed by rules of court made under this section.

(2) The power to make rules of court under section 1 of, and Schedule 1 to, the Civil Procedure Act 1997 shall include power by any such rules to make provision—

(a) for the High Court to make a stop order on the application of any person claiming to be entitled to an interest in prescribed securities; and

(b) for the service of a stop notice by any person claiming to be entitled to an interest in prescribed securities.

(3) [...]

(4) Rules of court made by virtue of subsection (2) above shall prescribe the person or body on whom a copy of any stop order or a stop notice is to be served.

(5) The steps mentioned in subsection (1) above are—

(a) the registration of any transfer of the securities;

(b) in the case of funds in court, the transfer, sale, delivery out, payment or other dealing with the funds, or of the income thereon;

(c) the making of any payment by way of dividend, interest or otherwise in respect of the securities; and

(d) in the case of a unit trust, any acquisition of or other dealing with the units by any person or body exercising functions under the trust.

(6) Any rules of court made by virtue of this section may include such incidental, supplemental and consequential provisions as the authority making them consider necessary or expedient, and may make different provision in relation to different cases or classes of case.

*Note*—Amended by the Senior Courts Act 1981 s.153 and Sch.5; and the County Courts Act 1984 s.148, Sch.2. Section 75 of the County Courts Act 1984 (referred to in subs.(3)) was omitted by, and s.84 of the Senior Courts Act 1981 (referred to in subs.(2)) was amended by, the Civil Procedure Act 1997 Sch.2, paras 1(4) and 2(6). **9B–1025**

SUPPLEMENTAL

**Interpretation**

**6.**—(1) In this Act— **9B–1026**

"building society" has the same meaning as in the Building Societies Act 1986;

"charging order" means an order made under section 1(1) of this Act;

"debtor" and "creditor" have the meanings given by section 1(1) of this Act;

"dividend" includes any distribution in respect of any unit of a unit trust;

"government stock" means any stock issued by her Majesty's government in the United Kingdom or any funds of, or annuity granted by, that government;

"stock" includes shares, debentures and any securities of the body concerned, whether or not constituting a charge on the assets of that body;

"unit trust" means any trust established for the purpose, or having the effect, of providing, for persons having funds available for investment, facilities for the participation by them, as beneficiaries under the trust, in any profits or income arising from the acquisition, holding management or disposal of any property whatsoever.

(2) For the purposes of section 1 of this Act references to a judgment or order of the High Court or a county court shall be taken to include references to a judgment, order, decree or award (however called) of any court or arbitrator (including any foreign court or arbitrator) which is or has become enforceable (whether wholly or to a limited extent) as if it were a judgment or order of the High Court or a county court.

*Paragraph numbers marked with a "+" can be found online and on CD.*

(3) References in section 2 of this Act to any securities include references to any such securities standing in the name of the Accountant General.

9B–1027 *Note*—Amended by the Building Societies Act 1986 ss.54, 120, Sch.18.

## Consequential amendment, repeals and transitional provisions

9B–1028 **7.**—(1) [...]

(2) [...]

(3) Any order made or notice given under any enactment repealed by this Act or under any rules of court revoked by rules of court made under this Act (the "new rules") shall, if still in force when the provisions of this Act or, as the case may be, the new rules come into force, continue to have effect as if made under this Act or, as the case may be, under the new rules.

(4) [...]

9B–1029 *Note*—Amended by the Senior Courts Act 1981 Sch.7; the County Courts Act 1984 s.148, Sch.4; and by the Land Registration Act 2002 Sch.13, para.1.

## Short title, commencement and extent

9B–1030 **8.**—(1) This Act may be cited as the Charging Orders Act 1979.

(2) This Act comes into force on such day as the Lord Chancellor may appoint by order made by statutory instrument.

(3) This Act does not extend to Scotland or Northern Ireland.

# Civil Evidence Act 1968

9B–1031 (1968 c.64)

ARRANGEMENT OF SECTIONS

PART II

MISCELLANEOUS AND GENERAL

*CONVICTIONS, ETC. AS EVIDENCE IN CIVIL PROCEEDINGS*



# PART II

## MISCELLANEOUS AND GENERAL

### *CONVICTIONS, ETC. AS EVIDENCE IN CIVIL PROCEEDINGS*

## Convictions as evidence in civil proceedings

9B–1032 **11.**—(1) In any civil proceedings the fact that a person has been

*Paragraph numbers marked with a "+" can be found online and on CD.*

convicted of an offence by or before any court in the United Kingdom or by a court-martial there or elsewhere shall (subject to subsection (3) below) be admissible in evidence for the purpose of proving, where to do so is relevant to any issue in those proceedings, that he committed that offence, whether he was so convicted upon a plea of guilty or otherwise and whether or not he is a party to the civil proceedings; but no conviction other than a subsisting one shall be admissible in evidence by virtue of this section.

(2) In any civil proceedings in which by virtue of this section a person is proved to have been convicted of an offence by or before any court in the United Kingdom or by a court-martial there or elsewhere—

(a) he shall be taken to have committed that offence unless the contrary is proved; and

(b) without prejudice to the reception of any other admissible evidence for the purpose of identifying the facts on which the conviction was based, the contents of any document which is admissible as evidence of the conviction, and the contents of the information, complaint, indictment or charge-sheet on which the person in question was convicted, shall be admissible in evidence for that purpose.

(3) Nothing in this section shall prejudice the operation of section 13 of this Act or any other enactment whereby a conviction or a finding of fact in any criminal proceedings is for the purposes of any other proceedings made conclusive evidence of any fact.

(4) Where in any civil proceedings the contents of any document are admissible in evidence by virtue of subsection (2) above, a copy of that document, or of the material part thereof, purporting to be certified or otherwise authenticated by or on behalf of the court or authority having custody of that document shall be admissible in evidence and shall be taken to be a true copy of that document or part unless the contrary is shown.

(5) Nothing in any of the following enactments, that is to say—

(a) section 1C of the Powers of Criminal Courts Act 1973 (under which a conviction leading to discharge is to be disregarded except as therein mentioned);

(b) section 191 of the Criminal Procedure (Scotland) Act 1975 (which makes similar provision in respect of convictions on indictment in Scotland); and

(c) section 8 of the Probation Act (Northern Ireland) 1950 (which corresponds to the said section 12) or any corresponding enactment of the Parliament of Northern Ireland for the time being in force,

shall affect the operation of this section; and for the purposes of this section any order made by a court of summary jurisdiction in Scotland under section 383 or section 384 of the said Act of 1975 shall be treated as a conviction.

(6) In this section "court-martial" means a court-martial constituted under the Army Act 1955, the Air Force Act 1955 or the Naval

***Paragraph numbers marked with a "+" can be found online and on CD.***

Discipline Act 1957 and in relation to a court-martial "conviction" means a finding of guilty which is, or falls to be treated as, the finding of the court, and "conviction" shall be construed accordingly.

#### Effect of rule

9B–1033 This section came into force on December 2, 1968 (Civil Evidence Act 1968 (Commencement No.1) Order 1968 (SI 1968/1734)). Amended by the Powers of Criminal Courts Act 1973 s.56(1); Sch.5; the Criminal Justice Act 1991 Sch.11; the Armed Forces Act 1996 Sch.1, para.100, Sch.7, Pt II; and by the Armed Forces Act 2001 Sch.7, para.1.

This section, and ss.12 and s.13, provide statutory exceptions to a rule established in *Hollington v Hewthorn* [1943] 1 K.B. 587, CA. The rule, insofar as it survives, has the effect of rendering inadmissible in civil proceedings findings in other, earlier proceedings (not being earlier criminal or matrimonial proceedings covered by ss.11 to 13). The rule has been subject to judicial criticism. For explanation, see *Secretary of State for Business Enterprise & Regulatory Reform v Aaron* [2008] EWCA Civ 1146, October 16, 2008, CA, unrep. (where held that findings in report of company investigators appointed under statute not rendered inadmissible by the rule in disqualification proceedings). In English criminal proceedings, evidence is admissible of convictions before any UK court in earlier proceedings (Police and Criminal Evidence Act 1984 s.73). In *Director of the Assets Recovery Agency v Virtosu* [2008] EWHC 149 (QB); [2008] 3 All E.R. 637 (Tugendhat J.), the question arose whether, in English civil recovery proceedings, evidence of the defendant's previous conviction, not in a UK court (as s.11(1) provides), but in a foreign court, was admissible. Under Pt 5 of the Proceeds of Crime Act 2002, an order may be made for the recovery of property obtained through "unlawful conduct". Such conduct is defined as including conduct occurring in a country outside the UK which is unlawful under the criminal law of that country, provided it would also be criminal conduct within the UK (s.241). In this case, in discharging the burden of proving such conduct, the claimant relied on evidence of the defendant's conviction in a French court of people trafficking offences, including a summary of the matters found proved by that court. The judge rejected the submission that the evidence was rendered inadmissible by the rule in *Hollington v Hewthorn*.

#### Subsection (1): "Admissible in evidence"

9B–1034 The effect of admitting the conviction in evidence is in civil proceedings to shift on to the convicted person the burden of proving that he is innocent. This should be contrasted with the effect of s.13, below.

#### "A subsisting one"

9B–1035 A conviction which has been quashed on appeal cannot be "subsisting"; nor, it is thought, can it be "subsisting" if a free pardon has been granted. Moreover, although a conviction as to which an appeal is pending is "subsisting", a court cannot enter judgment in reliance upon it in a civil action, since the conviction may be quashed on appeal (*Re Raphael Dec'd, Raphael v D'antin* [1973] 1 W.L.R. 998).

### Findings of adultery and paternity as evidence in civil proceedings

9B–1036 **12.**—(1) In any civil proceedings—

(a) the fact that a person has been found guilty of adultery in any matrimonial proceedings; and

(b) the fact that a person has been found to be the father of a child in relevant proceedings before any court in England and Wales or Northern Ireland or has been adjudged to be the father of a child in affiliation proceedings before any court in the United Kingdom,

shall (subject to subsection (3) below) be admissible in evidence for the purpose of proving, where to do so is relevant to any issue in

*Paragraph numbers marked with a "+" can be found online and on CD.*

those civil proceedings, that he committed the adultery to which the finding relates or, as the case may be, is (or was) the father of that child, whether or not he offered any defence to the allegation of adultery or paternity and whether or not he is a party to the civil proceedings; but no finding or adjudication other than a subsisting one shall be admissible in evidence by virtue of this section.

(2) In any civil proceedings in which by virtue of this section a person is proved to have been found guilty of adultery as mentioned in subsection (1)(a) above or to have been found or adjudged to be the father of a child as mentioned in subsection (1)(b) above—

(a) he shall be taken to have committed the adultery to which the finding relates or, as the case may be, to be (or have been) the father of that child, unless the contrary is proved; and

(b) without prejudice to the reception of any other admissible evidence for the purpose of identifying the facts on which the finding or adjudication was based, the contents of any document which was before the court, or which contains any pronouncement of the court, in the other proceedings in question shall be admissible in evidence for that purpose.

(3) Nothing in this section shall prejudice the operation of any enactment whereby a finding of fact in any matrimonial or affiliation proceedings is for the purposes of any other proceedings made conclusive evidence of any fact.

(4) Subsection (4) of section 11 of this Act shall apply for the purposes of this section as if the reference to subsection (2) were a reference to subsection (2) of this section.

(5) In this section—

"matrimonial proceedings" means any matrimonial cause in the High Court or a county court in England and Wales or in the High Court in Northern Ireland, any consistorial action in Scotland, or any appeal arising out of any such cause or action;

"relevant proceedings" means—

(a) proceedings on a complaint under section 42 of the National Assistance Act 1948 or section 26 of the Social Security Act 1986;

(b) proceedings under the Children Act 1989;

(c) proceedings which would have been relevant proceedings for the purposes of this section in the form in which it was in force before the passing of the Children Act 1989;

"affiliation proceedings" means, in relation to Scotland, any action of affiliation and aliment;

and in this subsection "consistorial action" does not include an action of aliment only between husband and wife raised in the Court of Session or an action of interim aliment raised in the sheriff court.

*Note*—This section came into force on December 2, 1968 (Civil Evidence Act 1968 **9B-1037**

(Commencement No.1) Order 1968 (SI 1968/1734)). It has been amended by the Family Law Reform Act 1987 s.29; the Children Act 1989 Sch.13; the Courts and Legal Services Act 1990 Sch.16; and the Children (Northern Ireland Consequential Amendments) Order 1995 (SI 1995/756).

**Subsection (1): "Found guilty of adultery"**

**9B-1038** See Practice Direction [1969] 1 W.L.R. 1192.

## Conclusiveness of convictions for purposes of defamation actions

**9B-1039** **13.**—(1) In an action for libel or slander in which the question whether the plaintiff did or did not commit a criminal offence is relevant to an issue arising in the action, proof that, at the time when that issue falls to be determined, he stands convicted of that offence shall be conclusive evidence that he committed that offence; and his conviction thereof shall be admissible in evidence accordingly.

(2) In any such action as aforesaid in which by virtue of this section the plaintiff is proved to have been convicted of an offence, the contents of any document which is admissible as evidence of the conviction, and the contents of the information, complaint, indictment or charge-sheet on which he was convicted, shall, without prejudice to the reception of any other admissible evidence for the purpose of identifying the facts on which the conviction was based, be admissible in evidence for the purpose of identifying those facts.

(2A) In the case of an action for libel or slander in which there is more than one plaintiff—

(a) the references in subsections (1) and (2)above to the plaintiff shall be construed as references to any of the plaintiffs, and

(b) proof that any of the plaintiffs stands convicted of an offence shall be conclusive evidence that he committed that offence so far as that fact is relevant to any issue arising in relation to his cause of action or that of any other plaintiff.

(3) For the purposes of this section a person shall be taken to stand convicted of an offence if but only if there subsists against him a conviction of that offence by or before a court in the United Kingdom or by a court-martial there or elsewhere.

(4) Subsections (4) to (6) of section 11 of this Actshall apply for the purposes of this section as they apply for the purposes of that section, but as if in the said subsection (4) the reference to subsection (2) were a reference to subsection (2) of this section.

(5) The foregoing provisions of this section shall apply for the purposes of any action begun after the passing of this Act, whenever the cause of action arose, but shall not apply for the purposes of any action begun before the passing of this Act or any appeal or other proceedings arising out of any such action.

**9B-1040** *Note*—Amended by the Defamation Act 1996 s.12.

**Subsection (1): "Shall be conclusive"**

**9B-1041** This should be contrasted with the effect of s.11 above. It is of course elementary

*Paragraph numbers marked with a "+" can be found online and on CD.*

that an *acquittal* in a criminal trial of the plaintiff is no bar to a plea of justification by a defendant in defamation proceedings.

## PRIVILEGE

### Privilege against incrimination of self or spouse

**14.**—(1) The right of a person in any legal proceedings other than criminal proceedings to refuse to answer any question or produce any document or thing if to do so would tend to expose that person to proceedings for an offence or for the recovery of a penalty— **9B–1042**

(a) shall apply only as regards criminal offences under the law of any part of the United Kingdom and penalties provided for by such law; and

(b) shall include a like right to refuse to answer any question or produce any document or thing if to do so would tend to expose the spouse or civil partner of that person to proceedings for any such criminal offence or for the recovery of any such penalty.

(2) In so far as any existing enactment conferring (in whatever words) powers of inspection or investigation confers on a person (in whatever words) any right otherwise than in criminal proceedings to refuse to answer any question or give any evidence tending to incriminate that person, subsection (1) above shall apply to that right as it applies to the right described in that subsection; and every such existing enactment shall be construed accordingly.

(3) In so far as any existing enactment provides (in whatever words) that in any proceedings other than criminal proceedings a person shall not be excused from answering any question or giving any evidence on the ground that to do so may incriminate that person, that enactment shall be construed as providing also that in such proceedings a person shall not be excused from answering any question or giving any evidence on the ground that to do so may incriminate the husband or wife of that person.

(4) Where any existing enactment (however worded) that—

(a) confers powers of inspection or investigation; or

(b) provides as mentioned in subsection (3) above,

further provides (in whatever words) that any answer or evidence given by a person shall not be admissible in evidence against that person in any proceedings or class of proceedings (however described, and whether criminal or not) that enactment shall be construed as providing also that any answer or evidence given by that person shall not be admissible in evidence against the husband or wife of that person in the proceedings or class of proceedings in question.

(5) In this section "existing enactment" means any enactment passed before this Act; and the references to giving evidence are references to giving evidence in any manner, whether by furnishing information, making discovery, producing documents or otherwise.

*Note* —Amended by the Civil Partnership Act 2004 s.261(1), Sch.27, para.30. **9B–1043**

**Effect of section**

9B–1044 Section 72 of the Senior Courts Act 1981 (see para.9A–335 above) withdraws the privilege against incrimination of self or spouse in certain proceedings. The effect of s.14 is confined to the risk of exposure to proceedings and penalties under the law of any part of the UK in legal proceedings other than criminal proceedings. In subs.(1) of s.14 "penalty" is apt to include a fine under the EC Treaty (*Rio Tinto Zinc Corporation v Westinghouse Electrical Corporation*, [1978] A.C. 547, HL), or a fine imposed by a civil court as a penalty for contempt (*Bhimji v Chatwani (No.2)* [1992] 1 W.L.R. 1158). The phrase "proceedings for an offence" does not include proceedings in respect of a contempt of court (*Garvin v Domus Publishing* [1989] Ch. 335). In *C. Plc v P.* [2007] EWCA Civ 493; [2007] 3 W.L.R. 437, CA, the privilege was asserted by a respondent to a search order, generally and specifically in relation to incriminating material found on computer discs. In dismissing the respondent's appeal the Court of Appeal held that the privilege can be invoked to refuse to disclose matters (including documents or other things) which are ordinarily discoverable, but material existing independently of the order and coming to light in the course of executing a proper order of the court are in an altogether different category (see further para.9A–271 above).

**"Under the law of any part of the United Kingdom"**

9B–1045 For an example of a case in which consideration was given to the risk of incrimination by reference to foreign law, see *Arab Monetary Fund v Hashim* [1989] 1 W.L.R. 565.

9B–1045.1 **15.** [...]

9B–1045.2 *Note* —Repealed by the Patents Act 1977 s.132 and Sch.6. See ibid., ss.103–105.

## Abolition of certain privileges

9B–1046 **16.**—(1) The following rules of law are hereby abrogated except in relation to criminal proceedings, that is to say—

(a) the rule whereby, in any legal proceedings, a person cannot be compelled to answer any question or produce any document or thing if to do so would tend to expose him to a forfeiture; and

(b) the rule whereby, in any legal proceedings, a person other than a party to the proceedings cannot be compelled to produce any deed or other document relating to his title to any land.

(2) The rule of law whereby, in any civil proceedings, a party to the proceedings cannot be compelled to produce any document relating solely to his own case and in no way tending to impeach that case or support the case of any opposing party is hereby abrogated.

(3) Section 3 of the Evidence (Amendment) Act 1853 (which provides that a husband or wife shall not be compellable to disclose any communication made to him or her by his or her spouse during the marriage) shall cease to have effect except in relation to criminal proceedings.

(4) In section 43(1) of the Matrimonial Causes Act 1965 (under which the evidence of a husband or wife is admissible in any proceedings to prove that marital intercourse did or did not take place between them during any period, but a husband or wife is not compellable in any proceedings to give evidence of the matters aforesaid) the words from "but a husband or wife" to the end of the subsection shall cease to have effect except in relation to criminal proceedings.

(5) A witness in any proceedings instituted in consequence of

adultery, whether a party to the proceedings or not, shall not be excused from answering any question by reason that it tends to show that he or she has been guilty of adultery; and accordingly the proviso to section 3 of the Evidence (Further Amendment) Act 1869 and, in section 43(2) of the Matrimonial Causes Act 1965, the words from "but" to the end of the subsection shall cease to have effect.

### Consequential amendments relating to privilege

**17.**—(1) In relation to England and Wales— **9B–1047**

(a) [...]

(b) section 8(5) of the Parliamentary Commissioner Act 1967 (which provides that, subject as there mentioned, no person shall be compelled for the purposes of an investigation under that Act to give any evidence or produce any document which he could not be compelled to give or produce in proceedings before the High Court) shall have effect as if before the word "proceedings" there were inserted the word "civil";

and, so far as it applies to England and Wales, any other existing enactment, however framed or worded, which in relation to any tribunal, investigation or inquiry (however described) confers on persons required to answer questions or give evidence any privilege described by reference to the privileges of witnesses in proceedings before any court shall, unless the contrary intention appears, be construed as referring to the privileges of witnesses in civil proceedings before that court.

(2) [...]

(3) Without prejudice to the generality of subsection (2) to (4) of section 14 of this Act, the enactments mentioned in the Schedule to this Act shall have effect subject to the amendments provided for by that Schedule (being verbal amendments to bring those enactments into conformity with the provisions of that section).

(4) Subsection (5) of section 14 of this Act shall apply for the purposes of this section as it applies for the purposes of that section.

*Note*—Subsection (2) repealed by the Evidence (Proceedings in Other Jurisdictions) Act 1975 s.8(2), Sch.2; subs.(1)(a) repealed by the Inquiries Act 2005 s.49(2), Sch.3. **9B–1048**

## GENERAL

### General interpretation, and savings

**18.**—(1) In this Act "civil proceedings" includes, in addition to civil proceedings in any of the ordinary courts of law— **9B–1049**

(a) civil proceedings before any other tribunal, being proceedings in relation to which the strict rules of evidence apply; and

(b) an arbitration or reference, whether under an enactment or not,

but does not include civil proceedings in relation to which the strict rules of evidence do not apply.

(2) In this Act—

"court" does not include a court-martial, and, in relation to an arbitration or reference, means the arbitrator or umpire and, in relation to proceedings before a tribunal (not being one of the ordinary courts of law) means the tribunal;

"legal proceedings" includes an arbitration or reference, whether under an enactment or not;

and for the avoidance of doubt it is hereby declared that in this Act, and in any amendment made by this Act in any other enactment, references to a person's husband or wife do not include references to a person who is no longer married to that person.

(3) Any reference in this Act to any other enactment is a reference thereto as amended, and includes a reference thereto as applied, by or under any other enactment.

(4) Nothing in this Act shall prejudice the operation of any enactment which provides (in whatever words) that any answer or evidence given by a person in specified circumstances shall not be admissible in evidence against him or some other person in any proceedings or class of proceedings (however described).

In this subsection the reference to giving evidence is a reference to giving evidence in any manner, whether by furnishing information, making discovery, producing documents or otherwise.

(5) Nothing in this Act shall prejudice—

(a) any power of a court, in any legal proceedings, to exclude evidence (whether by preventing questions from being put or otherwise) at its discretion; or

(b) the operation of any agreement (whenever made) between the parties to any legal proceedings as to the evidence which is to be admissible (whether generally or for any particular purpose) in those proceedings.

(6) It is hereby declared that where, by reason of any defect of speech or hearing from which he is suffering, a person called as a witness in any legal proceedings gives his evidence in writing or by signs, that evidence is to be treated for the purposes of this Act as being given orally.

**9B–1050** *Note* —Committal proceedings for contempt of court in the course of civil litigation are not criminal but remain civil proceedings for the purposes of s.18, and although they were unreasoned or extraordinary because of possible penal consequences and thus the proof required was the criminal standard of proof that did not convert such proceedings (*Savings and Investment Bank Ltd v Gasco Investments (Netherlands) BV (No.2)* [1988] Ch. 422, CA).

**Subsection (1): "Proceedings in relation to which the strict rules of evidence apply"**

**9B–1051** Some courts and tribunals, notably coroners', election and prize courts, are not bound by the rules of evidence (*R. v Deputy Industrial Injuries Commissioner, Ex p. Moore* [1965] 1 Q.B. 456; and *Wednesbury Corporation v Ministry of Housing and Local Government (No.2)* [1966] 2 Q.B. 275).

* * * *

## Short title, repeals, extent and commencement

**9B–1052** **20.**—(1) This Act may be cited as the Civil Evidence Act 1968.

(2) Sections 1, 2, 6(1)(except the words from "Proceedings" to "references") and 6(2)(b) of the Evidence Act 1938 are hereby repealed.

(3) This Act shall not extend to Scotland or to Northern Ireland.

(4) The following provisions of this Act, namely sections 13 to 19, this section (except subsection (2)) and the Schedule, shall come into force on the day this Act is passed, and the other provisions of this Act shall come into force on such day as the Lord Chancellor may by order made by statutory instrument appoint; and different days may be so appointed for different purposes of this Act or for the same purposes in relation to different courts or proceedings or otherwise in relation to different circumstances.

*Note*—Amended by the Northern Ireland Constitution Act 1973 Sch.6. **9B–1053**

**[THE NEXT PARAGRAPH IS 9B–1055.]**

## Civil Evidence Act 1972

(1972 c.30) **9B–1055**

ARRANGEMENT OF SECTIONS

SECT.



**Note**

This Act is concerned with (1) evidence of opinion, and (2) foreign evidence. **9B–1056** Initially, s.5 (Interpretation, application to arbitration, etc.) stated that the provisions of the Act applied to "civil proceedings" and in "courts" as defined in the Civil Evidence Act 1968 s.18 (see para.9B–1049 above). This provision, in combination with Commencement Orders issued in 1973 and 1974, restricted the application of the Act to certain civil proceedings in certain courts. However, s.5(1) was amended by the Civil Evidence Act 1995 and now states (see para.9B–1064 below) that "civil proceedings" means civil proceedings "before any tribunal in relation to which the strict rules of evidence apply, whether as a matter of law or by agreement between the parties" (e.g. an arbitration agreement); references to "court" should be construed accordingly (note also s.5(2)).

* * * *

### Rules of court with respect to expert reports and oral expert evidence

**2.**—(1) [...] **9B–1057**

(2) [...]

(3) Notwithstanding any enactment or rule of law by virtue of which documents prepared for the purpose of pending or contemplated civil proceedings or in connection with the obtaining or giving of legal advice are in certain circumstances privileged from disclosure, provision may be made by rules of court—

(a) for enabling the court in any civil proceedings to direct, with respect to medical matters or matters of any other class which may be specified in the direction, that the parties or some of them shall each by such date as may be so specified (or such later date as may be permitted or agreed in accordance with the rules) disclose to the other or others in the form of one or more expert reports the expert evidence on matters of that class which he proposes to adduce as part of his case at the trial; and

(b) for prohibiting a party who fails to comply with a direction given in any such proceedings under rules of court made by virtue of paragraph (a) above from adducing in evidence except with the leave of the court, any statement (whether of fact or opinion) contained in any expert report whatsoever in so far as that statement deals with matters of any class specified in the direction.

(4) Provision may be made by rules of court as to the conditions subject to which oral expert evidence may be given in civil proceedings.

(5) Without prejudice to the generality of subsection (4) above, rules of court made in pursuance of that subsection may make provision for prohibiting a party who fails to comply with a direction given as mentioned in subsection (3)(b) above from adducing, except with the leave of the court, any oral expert evidence whatsoever with respect to matters of any class specified in the direction.

(6) Any rules of court made in pursuance of this section may make different provisions for different classes of cases, for expert reports dealing with matters of different classes, and for other different circumstances.

(7) References in this section to an expert report are references to a written report by a person dealing wholly or mainly with matters on which he is (or would if living be) qualified to give expert evidence.

(8) [...]

**9B–1058** *Note*—Amended by the MCA 1980 s.154, Sch.7; the Senior Courts Act 1981 s.152(4), Sch.7; the County Courts Act 1984 s.148(1), Sch.2; the Civil Evidence Act 1995 s.15(2), Sch.2; the Courts Act 2003 s.109(1), (3), Sch.8, para.165, Sch.10.

**Subsection (2): "Documents"**

**9B–1059** This word is apt to include a letter (*Carlish v East Ham Corporation and Edwards* [1948] 3 K.B. 380; a tape-recording: *Grant v South-Western and County Properties* [1975] Ch. 185; or a film: *Senior v Holdsworth Ex p. Independent Television* [1976] Q.B. 23).

## Admissibility of expert opinion and certain expressions of non-expert opinion

**9B–1060** **3.**—(1) Subject to any rules of court made in pursuance of this Act, where a person is called as a witness in any civil proceedings, his opinion on any relevant matter on which he is qualified to give expert evidence shall be admissible in evidence.

(2) It is hereby declared that where a person is called as a witness in any civil proceedings, a statement of opinion by him on any relevant matter on which he is not qualified to give expert evidence, if made as a way of conveying relevant facts personally perceived by him, is admissible as evidence of what he perceived.

(3) In this section "relevant matter" includes an issue in the proceedings in question.

*Note* —Amended by the Civil Evidence Act 1995 s.15(2), Sch.2. **9B–1061**

**"shall be automatically given in evidence"**

An expert' report is not automatically admissible solely by virtue of its coming within s.3; it must also be helpful to the court in arriving at its conclusions where the court accepted that there existed a recognised expertise (*Barings Plc (In Liquidation) v Coopers & Lybrand (No.2)* [2001] Lloyd's Rep. Bank. 85; [2001] Lloyd's Rep. P.N. 379; [2001] P.N.L.R. 22; (2001) 98(13) L.S.G. 40 (Evans-Lombe J.)). **9B–1062**

## Evidence of foreign law

**4.**—(1) It is hereby declared that in civil proceedings a person who is suitably qualified to do so on account of his knowledge or experience is competent to give expert evidence as to the law of any country or territory outside the United Kingdom, or of any part of the United Kingdom other than England and Wales, irrespective of whether he has acted or is entitled to act as a legal practitioner there. **9B–1063**

(2) Where any question as to the law of any country or territory outside the United Kingdom, or of any part of the United Kingdom other than England and Wales, with respect to any matter has been determined (whether before or after the passing of this Act) in any such proceedings as are mentioned in subsection (4) below, then in any civil proceedings (not being proceedings before a court which can take judicial notice of the law of that country, territory or part with respect to that matter)—

(a) any finding made or decision given on that question in the first-mentioned proceedings shall, if reported or recorded in citable form, be admissible in evidence for the purpose of proving the law of that country, territory or part with respect to that matter; and

(b) if that finding or decision, as so reported or recorded, is adduced for that purpose, the law of that country, territory or part with respect to that matter shall be taken to be in accordance with that finding or decision unless the contrary is proved:

Provided that paragraph (b) above shall not apply in the case of a finding or decision which conflicts with another finding or decision on the same question adduced by virtue of this subsection in the same proceedings.

(3) Except with the leave of the court, a party to any civil proceedings shall not be permitted to adduce any such finding or decision as is mentioned in subsection (2) above by virtue of that subsection unless he has in accordance with rules of court given to every other party to the proceedings notice that he intends to do so.

(4) The proceedings referred to in subsection (2) above are the following, whether civil or criminal, namely—

(a) proceedings at first instance in any of the following courts, namely the High Court, the Crown Court, a court of quarter sessions, the Court of Chancery of the county palatine of Lancaster and the Court of Chancery of the county palatine of Durham;

(b) appeals arising out of any such proceedings as are mentioned in paragraph (a) above;

(c) proceedings before the Judicial Committee of the Privy Council on appeal (whether to Her Majesty in Council or to the Judicial Committee as such) from any decision of any court outside the United Kingdom.

(5) For the purposes of this section a finding or decision on any such question as is mentioned in subsection (2) above shall be taken to be reported or recorded in citable form if, but only if, it is reported or recorded in writing in a report, transcript or other document which, if that question had been a question as to the law of England and Wales, could be cited as an authority in legal proceedings in England and Wales.

## Interpretation, application to arbitrations, etc., and savings

9B–1064 **5.**—(1) In this Act "civil proceedings" means civil proceedings, before any tribunal, in relation to which the strict rules of evidence apply, whether as a matter of law or by agreement of the parties; and references to "the court" shall be construed accordingly.

(2) The rules of court made for the purposes of the application of sections 2 and 4 of this Act to proceedings in the High Court apply, except in so far as their application is excluded by agreement, to proceedings before tribunals other than the ordinary courts of law, subject to such modifications as may be appropriate.

Any question arising as to what modifications are appropriate shall be determined, in default of agreement, by the tribunal.

(3) Nothing in this Act shall prejudice—

(a) any power of a court, in any civil proceedings, to exclude evidence (whether by preventing questions from being put or otherwise) at its discretion; or

(b) the operation of any agreement (whenever made) between the parties to any civil proceedings as to the evidence which is to be admissible (whether generally or for any particular purpose) in those proceedings.

9B–1065 *Note* —Subsections (1) and (2) substituted by the Civil Evidence Act 1995 s.15(1), Sch.1, para.7.

## Short title, extent and commencement

9B–1066 **6.**—(1) This Act may be cited as the Civil Evidence Act 1972.

(2) This Act shall not extend to Scotland or Northern Ireland.

(3) This Act, except sections 4(2) to (5) shall come into force on 1st January 1973, and sections 4(2) to (5) shall come into force on such day as the Lord Chancellor may by order made by statutory instrument appoint; and different days may be so appointed for different purposes or for the same purposes in relation to different courts or proceedings or otherwise in relation to different circumstances.

*Note*—Amended by the Civil Evidence Act 1995 s.15(2), Sch.2. 9B-1067

## Civil Evidence Act 1995

(1995 c.38) 9B-1068

Arrangement of Sections



### Introduction

The Civil Evidence Act 1995 received the Royal Assent on November 8, 1995, and, with the single exception of s.10 (Ogden Tables), came into force on January 31, 1997 (SI 1996/3217). Essentially, it: 9B-1069

(1) Abolishes the principle excluding evidence on the ground that it is hearsay.
(2) Creates provisions governing the receiving of such evidence.
(3) Preserves certain Common Law rules relating to hearsay.
(4) Provides for the manner of proving documents and records.
(5) Applies to any proceedings in England and Wales to which the strict rules of evidence apply.
(6) Does not apply to cases started before January 31, 1996 (but see below, "Important note").
(7) Repeals the Civil Evidence Act 1968 Pt I.

### Editorial comment

For rules of court, see CPR Pt 33. In 1998, the Lord Chancellor decided not to bring s.10 into force, pending further consideration. 9B-1070

*Admissibility of Hearsay Evidence*

### Admissibility of hearsay evidence

**1.**—(1) In civil proceedings evidence shall not be excluded on the ground that it is hearsay. 9B-1071

(2) In this Act—

***Paragraph numbers marked with a "+" can be found online and on CD.***

(a) "hearsay" means a statement made otherwise than by a person while giving oral evidence in the proceedings which is tendered as evidence of the matters stated; and

(b) references to hearsay include hearsay of whatever degree.

(3) Nothing in this Act affects the admissibility of evidence admissible apart from this section.

(4) The provisions of sections 2 to 6 (safeguards and supplementary provisions relating to hearsay evidence) do not apply in relation to hearsay evidence admissible apart from this section, notwithstanding that it may also be admissible by virtue of this section.

*SAFEGUARDS IN RELATION TO HEARSAY EVIDENCE*

## Notice of proposal to adduce hearsay evidence

9B–1072 **2.**—(1) A party proposing to adduce hearsay evidence in civil proceedings shall, subject to the following provisions of this section, give to the other party or parties to the proceedings—

(a) such notice (if any) of that fact, and

(b) on request, such particulars of or relating to the evidence,

as is reasonable and practicable in the circumstances for the purpose of enabling him or them to deal with any matters arising from its being hearsay.

(2) Provision may be made by rules of court—

(a) specifying classes of proceedings or evidence in relation to which subsection (1) does not apply, and

(b) as to the manner in which (including the time within which) the duties imposed by that subsection are to be complied with in the cases where it does apply.

(3) Subsection (1) may also be excluded by agreement of the parties; and compliance with the duty to give notice may in any case be waived by the person to whom notice is required to be given.

(4) A failure to comply with subsection (1), or with rules under subsection (2)(b), does not affect the admissibility of the evidence but may be taken into account by the court—

(a) in considering the exercise of its powers with respect to the course of proceedings and costs, and

(b) as a matter adversely affecting the weight to be given to the evidence in accordance with section 4.

## Power to call witness for cross-examination on hearsay statement

9B–1073 **3.** Rules of court may provide that where a party to civil proceedings adduces hearsay evidence of a statement made by a person and does not call that person as a witness, any other party to the proceedings may, with the leave of the court, call that person as a witness and cross-examine him on the statement as if he had been called by the first-mentioned party and as if the hearsay statement were his evidence in chief.

## Considerations relevant to weighing of hearsay evidence

**4.**—(1) In estimating the weight (if any) to be given to hearsay evidence in civil proceedings the court shall have regard to any circumstances from which any inference can reasonably be drawn as to the reliability or otherwise of the evidence. **9B–1074**

(2) Regard may be had, in particular, to the following—

(a) whether it would have been reasonable and practicable for the party by whom the evidence was adduced to have produced the maker of the original statement as a witness;

(b) whether the original statement was made contemporaneously with the occurrence or existence of the matters stated;

(c) whether the evidence involves multiple hearsay;

(d) whether any person involved has any motive to conceal or misrepresent matters;

(e) whether the original statement was an edited account, or was made in collaboration with another or for a particular purpose;

(f) whether the circumstances in which the evidence is adduced as hearsay are such as to suggest an attempt to prevent proper evaluation of its weight.

*SUPPLEMENTARY PROVISIONS AS TO HEARSAY EVIDENCE*

## Competence and credibility

**5.**—(1) Hearsay evidence shall not be admitted in civil proceedings if or to the extent that it is shown to consist of, or to be proved by means of, a statement made by a person who at the time he made the statement was not competent as a witness. For this purpose "not competent as a witness" means suffering from such mental or physical infirmity, or lack of understanding, as would render a person incompetent as a witness in civil proceedings; but a child shall be treated as competent as a witness if he satisfies the requirements of section 96(2)(a) and (b)of the Children Act 1989 (conditions for reception of unsworn evidence of child). **9B–1075**

(2) Where in civil proceedings hearsay evidence is adduced and the maker of the original statement, or of any statement relied upon to prove another statement, is not called as a witness—

(a) evidence which if he had been so called would be admissible for the purpose of attacking or supporting his credibility as a witness is admissible for that purpose in the proceedings; and

(b) evidence tending to prove that, whether before or after he made the statement, he made any other statement inconsistent with it is admissible for the purpose of showing that he had contradicted himself.

Provided that evidence may not be given of any matter of which, if he had been called as a witness and had denied that matter in cross-examination, evidence could not have been adduced by the cross-examining party.

## Previous statements of witnesses

9B-1076 **6.**—(1) Subject as follows, the provisions of this Act as to hearsay evidence in civil proceedings apply equally (but with any necessary modifications) in relation to a previous statement made by a person called as a witness in the proceedings.

(2) A party who has called or intends to call a person as a witness in civil proceedings may not in those proceedings adduce evidence of a previous statement made by that person, except—

(a) with the leave of the court, or

(b) for the purpose of rebutting a suggestion that his evidence has been fabricated.

This shall not be construed as preventing a witness statement (that is, a written statement of oral evidence which a party to the proceedings intends to lead) from being adopted by a witness in giving evidence or treated as his evidence.

(3) Where in the case of civil proceedings section 3, 4 or 5of the Criminal Procedure Act 1865applies, which make provision as to—

(a) how far a witness may be discredited by the party producing him,

(b) the proof of contradictory statements made by a witness, and

(c) cross-examination as to previous statements in writing,

this Act does not authorise the adducing of evidence of a previous inconsistent or contradictory statement otherwise than in accordance with those sections.

This is without prejudice to any provision made by rules of court under section 3 above (power to call witness for cross-examination on hearsay statement).

(4) Nothing in this Act affects any of the rules of law as to the circumstances in which, where a person called as a witness in civil proceedings is cross-examined on a document used by him to refresh his memory, that document may be made evidence in the proceedings.

(5) Nothing in this section shall be construed as preventing a statement of any description referred to above from being admissible by virtue of section 1 as evidence of the matters stated.

## Evidence formerly admissible at common law

9B-1077 **7.**—(1) The common law rule effectively preserved by section 9(1) and (2)(a) of the Civil Evidence Act 1968 (admissibility of admissions adverse to a party) is superseded by the provisions of this Act.

(2) The common law rules effectively preserved by section 9(1)

*Paragraph numbers marked with a "+" can be found online and on CD.*

and (2)(b) to (d) of the Civil Evidence Act 1968, that is, any rule of law whereby in civil proceedings—

(a) published works dealing with matters of a public nature (for example, histories, scientific works, dictionaries and maps) are admissible as evidence of facts of a public nature stated in them,

(b) public documents (for example, public registers, and returns made under public authority with respect to matters of public interest) are admissible as evidence of facts stated in them, or

(c) records (for example, the records of certain courts, treaties, Crown grants, pardons and commissions) are admissible as evidence of facts stated in them.

shall continue to have effect.

(3) The common law rules effectively preserved by section 9(3) and (4) of the Civil Evidence Act 1968, that is, any rule of law whereby in civil proceedings—

(a) evidence of a person's reputation is admissible for the purpose of proving his good or bad character, or

(b) evidence of reputation or family tradition is admissible—

(i) for the purpose of proving or disproving pedigree or the existence of a marriage, or

(ii) for the purpose of proving or disproving the existence of any public or general right or of identifying any person or thing,

shall continue to have effect in so far as they authorise the court to treat such evidence as proving or disproving that matter.

Where any such rule applies, reputation or family tradition shall be treated for the purposes of this Act as a fact and not as a statement or multiplicity of statements about the matter in question.

(4) The words in which a rule of law mentioned in this section is described are intended only to identify the rule and shall not be construed as altering it in any way.

*OTHER MATTERS*

## Proof of statements contained in documents

**8.**—(1) Where a statement contained in a document is admissible as evidence in civil proceedings, it may be proved— **9B–1078**

(a) by the production of that document, or

(b) whether or not that document is still in existence, by the production of a copy of that document or of the material part of it,

authenticated in such manner as the court may approve.

(2) It is immaterial for this purpose how many removes there are between a copy and the original.

## Proof of records of business or public authority

**9.**—(1) A document which is shown to form part of the records of a **9B–1079**

*Paragraph numbers marked with a "+" can be found online and on CD.*

business or public authority may be received in evidence in civil proceedings without further proof.

(2) A document shall be taken to form part of the records of a business or public authority if there is produced to the court a certificate to that effect signed by an officer of the business or authority to which the records belong.

For this purpose—

(a) a document purporting to be a certificate signed by an officer of a business or public authority shall be deemed to have been duly given by such an officer and signed by him; and

(b) a certificate shall be treated as signed by a person if it purports to bear a facsimile of his signature.

(3) The absence of an entry in the records of a business or public authority may be proved in civil proceedings by affidavit of an officer of the business or authority to which the records belong.

(4) In this section—

"records" means records in whatever form;

"business" includes any activity regularly carried on over a period of time, whether for profit or not, by any body (whether corporate or not) or by an individual;

"officer" includes any person occupying a responsible position in relation to the relevant activities of the business or public authority or in relation to its records; and

"public authority" includes any public or statutory undertaking, any government department and any person holding office under Her Majesty.

(5) The court may, having regard to the circumstances of the case, direct that all or any of the above provisions of this section do not apply in relation to a particular document or record, or description of documents or records.

### Admissibility and proof of Ogden Tables

9B–1080 **10.**—(1) The actuarial tables (together with explanatory notes) for use in personal injury and fatal accident cases issued from time to time by the Government Actuary's Department are admissible in evidence for the purpose of assessing, in an action for personal injury, the sum to be awarded as general damages for future pecuniary loss.

(2) They may be proved by the production of a copy published by Her Majesty's Stationery Office.

(3) For the purposes of this section—

(a) "personal injury" includes any disease and any impairment of a person's physical or mental condition; and

(b) "action for personal injury" includes an action brought by virtue of the Law Reform (Miscellaneous Provisions) Act 1934 or the Fatal Accidents Act 1976.

GENERAL

### Meaning of "civil proceedings"

9B–1081 **11.** In this Act "civil proceedings" means civil proceedings, before any tribunal, in relation to which the strict rules of evidence apply, whether as a matter of law or by agreement of the parties. References to "the court" and "rules of court" shall be construed accordingly.

## Provisions as to rules of court

**12.**—(1) Any power to make rules of court regulating the practice or procedure of the court in relation to civil proceedings includes power to make such provision as may be necessary or expedient for carrying into effect the provisions of this Act. **9B–1082**

(2) Any rules of court made for the purposes of this Act as it applies in relation to proceedings in the High Court apply, except in so far as their operation is excluded by agreement, to arbitration proceedings to which this Act applies, subject to such modifications as may be appropriate.

Any question arising as to what modifications are appropriate shall be determined, in default of agreement, by the arbitrator or umpire, as the case may be.

## Interpretation

**13.** In this Act— **9B–1083**

"civil proceedings" has the meaning given by section 11 and "court" and "rules of court" shall be construed in accordance with that section;

"document" means anything in which information of any description is recorded, and "copy", in relation to a document, means anything onto which information recorded in the document has been copied, by whatever means and whether directly or indirectly;

"hearsay" shall be construed in accordance with section 1(2);

"oral evidence" includes evidence which, by reason of a defect of speech or hearing, a person called as a witness gives in writing or by signs;

"the original statement", in relation to hearsay evidence, means the underlying statement (if any) by—

(a) in the case of evidence of fact, a person having personal knowledge of that fact, or

(b) in the case of evidence of opinion, the person whose opinion it is; and

"statement" means any representation of fact or opinion, however made.

## Savings

**14.**—(1) Nothing in this Act affects the exclusion of evidence on grounds other than that it is hearsay. This applies whether the evidence falls to be excluded in pursuance of any enactment or rule of law, for failure to comply with rules of court or an order of the court, or otherwise. **9B–1084**

(2) Nothing in this Act affects the proof of documents by means other than those specified in section 8 or 9.

*Paragraph numbers marked with a "+" can be found online and on CD.*

(3) Nothing in this Act affects the operation of the following enactments—

(a) section 2 of the Documentary Evidence Act 1868 (mode of proving certain official documents);

(b) section 2 of the Documentary Evidence Act 1882 (documents printed under the superintendence of Stationery Office);

(c) section 1 of the Evidence (Colonial Statutes) Act 1907 (proof of statutes of certain legislatures);

(d) section 1 of the Evidence (Foreign, Dominion and Colonial Documents) Act 1933 (proof and effect of registers and official certificates of certain countries);

(e) section 5 of the Oaths and Evidence (Overseas Authorities and Countries) Act 1963 (provision in respect of public registers of other countries).

### Consequential amendments and repeals

9B–1085 **15.**—(1) The enactments specified in Schedule 1 are amended in accordance with that Schedule, the amendments being consequential on the provisions of this Act.

(2) The enactments specified in Schedule 2 are repealed to the extent specified.

### Short title, commencement and extent

9B–1086 **16.**—(1) This Act may be cited as the Civil Evidence Act 1995.

(2) The provisions of this Act come into force on such day as the Lord Chancellor may appoint by order made by statutory instrument, and different days may be appointed for different provisions and for different purposes.

(3) Subject to subsection (3A), the provisions of this Act shall not apply in relation to proceedings begun before commencement.

(3A) Transitional provisions for the application of the provisions of this Act to proceedings begun before commencement may be made by rules of court or practice directions.

(4) This Act extends to England and Wales.

(5) Section 10 (admissibility and proof of Ogden Tables) also extends to Northern Ireland.

As it extends to Northern Ireland, the following shall be substituted for subsection (3)(b)—

"(b) "action for personal injury" includes an action brought by virtue of the Law Reform (Miscellaneous Provisions) (Northern Ireland) Act 1937 or the Fatal Accidents (Northern Ireland) Order 1977."

(6) The provisions of Schedules 1 and 2(consequential amendments and repeals) have the same extent as the enactments respectively amended or repealed.

9B–1087 *Note*—Subsection (3) was replaced by, and subs.(3A) was added by, the Civil Procedure (Modification of Enactments) Order 1999 (SI 1999/1217) art.4. These modifications enabled the 1995 Act and the CPR provisions related to it to be applied to cases begun before the original commencement date of the Act (i.e. before January 31, 1997) (see further Vol.1, para.33.0.2).

## Civil Liability (Contribution) Act 1978

(1978 c.47) 9B–1088

Arrangement of Sections

*Proceedings for contribution*



### *Section 1—Entitlement to contribution*

### *Proceedings for contribution*

### Entitlement to contribution

**1.**—(1) Subject to the following provisions of this section, any person liable in respect of any damage suffered by another person may recover contribution from any other person liable in respect of the same damage (whether jointly with him or otherwise). 9B–1089

(2) A person shall be entitled to recover contribution by virtue of subsection (1) above notwithstanding that he has ceased to be liable in respect of the damage in question since the time when the damage occurred, provided that he was so liable immediately before he made or was ordered or agreed to make the payment in respect of which the contribution is sought.

(3) A person shall be liable to make contribution by virtue of subsection (1) above notwithstanding that he has ceased to be liable in respect of the damage in question since the time when the damage occurred, unless he ceased to be liable by virtue of the expiry of a period of limitation or prescription which extinguished the right on which the claim against him in respect of the damage was based.

(4) A person who has made or agreed to make any payment in bona fide settlement or compromise of any claim made against him in respect of any damage (including a payment into court which has been accepted) shall be entitled to recover contribution in accordance with this section without regard to whether or not he himself is or ever was liable in respect of the damage, provided, however, that he would have been liable assuming that the factual basis of the claim against him could be established.

(5) A judgment given in any action brought in any part of the United Kingdom by or on behalf of the person who suffered the damage in question against any person from whom contribution is sought under this section shall be conclusive in the proceedings for contribution as to any issue determined by that judgment in favour of the person from whom the contribution is sought.

(6) References in this section to a person's liability in respect of any damage are references to any such liability which has been or could be established in an action brought against him in England and Wales by or on behalf of the person who suffered the damage; but it is immaterial whether any issue arising in any such action was or would be determined (in accordance with the rules of private international law) by reference to the law of a country outside England and Wales.

**9B–1090** *Note*—The words "any person liable in respect of any damage suffered by another person ... *in respect of the same damage*" means the damage suffered by the same person (*Birse Construction Ltd v Haiste Ltd* [1996] 1 W.L.R. 675; [1996] 2 All E.R. 1, CA). See also *Howkins & Harrison v Taylor* [2001] Lloyd's Rep. PN 1, and *Eastgate Group Ltd v Lindsey Morden Group Inc* (2001) 151 N.L.J. 458. In *Royal Brompton Hospital NHS Trust v Hammond* [2002] UKHL 14; [2002] 1 W.L.R. 1397, HL, it was said that, although the purpose of the 1978 Act was to enlarge the category of causes of action capable of giving rise to claims for contribution, the requirement of a shared, or common, liability among contributors remains the root of the contribution principle. The word "payment" in s.1(4) includes a payment in kind, at any rate where the payment in kind is capable of valuation in monetary terms. There is no suggestion in s. 1(1) of a limit or restriction on the right of a person to claim contribution from another person liable in respect of the same damage. Subsections (2) to (4) of s. 1 were designed, not to restrict such right, but to remove restrictions or defences that might otherwise be raised (*Baker & Davies plc v Leslie Wilks* [2005] EWHC 1179 (TCC); [2005] 3 All E.R. 603).

Section 6(1) states that a party is a person "liable in respect of any damage" within s.1(1) if the person who suffered the damage "is entitled to recover compensation from him in respect of that damage" (s.6(1)). In *Charter plc v City Index Ltd Charter plc v City Index Ltd* [2007] EWCA Civ 1382; [2008] 2 W.L.R. 950, CA the authorities on these provisions were examined, a case in which a claim was made for "knowing receipt" and the defendants sought contribution from the claimant's auditors. It was held (affirming the trial judge in this respect) that the claimant's remedy was compensatory (even if it could also be described as restitutionary), and the Pt 20 claim satisfied ss.1 and 6. In this case the trial judge further held that, as the overriding cause of the claimant's loss was that the defendants, having knowingly received money, paid it away in bad faith, it would not be just or equitable to require the auditors to contribute to the defendants' liability, and summarily dismissed the defendants' contribution claim on this ground (see [2006] EWHC 2508 (Ch), [2007] 1 W.L.R. 26). The Court of Appeal reversed the judge and allowed the defendants' appeal on this ground, holding that there was no rule of law or practice (at least on the facts of this case) that the knowing recipient should bear 100 per cent of the loss. Such a rule would place an unjustified restriction on the wide scope of the court's discretion under s.2. The extent of the claimant's loss depended on the facts which could only be assessed at trial. A party (X) is liable in respect of any damage within the meaning of these provisions if another party (Y) was entitled to recover compensation from X in respect of that damage, whatever the legal basis of X's liability (*BRB (Residuary) Ltd v Connex South Eastern Ltd* [2008] EWHC 1172 (QB); [2008] 1 W.L.R. 2867 (Cranston J.) where X, under the mistaken belief that they were contractually obliged to indemnify a third party (Z) in respect of Y's damage and had suffered judgment on liability to be entered against them, were subsequently allowed, on the basis that they and Z were liable in respect of the same damage, to bring a contribution claim against Z).

The Compensation Act 2006 s.3(3) expressly preserves a defendant's right to claim contribution from another in mesothelioma cases in the circumstances covered by that provision.

***Paragraph numbers marked with a "+" can be found online and on CD.***

Claims for contribution are subject to a special time limit for limitation purposes (Limitation Act 1980 s.10, see para.8–21 above).

## Assessment of contribution

**2.**—(1) Subject to subsection (3) below, in any proceedings for contribution under section 1 above the amount of the contribution recoverable from any person shall be such as may be found by the court to be just and equitable having regard to the extent of that person's responsibility for the damage in question. **9B–1091**

(2) Subject to subsection (3) below, the court shall have power in any such proceedings to exempt any person from liability to make contribution, or to direct that the contribution to be recovered from any person shall amount to a complete indemnity.

(3) Where the amount of the damages which have or might have been awarded in respect of the damage in question in any action brought in England and Wales by or on behalf of the person who suffered it against the person from whom the contribution is sought was or would have been subject to—

(a) any limit imposed by or under any enactment or by any agreement made before the damage occurred;

(b) any reduction by virtue of section 1 of the Law Reform (Contributory Negligence) Act 1945 or section 5 of the Fatal Accidents Act 1976; or

(c) any corresponding limit or reduction under the law of a country outside England and Wales;

the person from whom the contribution is sought shall not by virtue of any contribution awarded under section 1 above be required to pay in respect of the damage a greater amount than the amount of those damages as so limited or reduced.

*Note*—The similarity in the language used in s.2(1) and in the Law Reform (Contributory Negligence) Act 1945 s.1(1) (see para.9B–1198.1 below) is striking and there is no reason why the principles applicable under the two provisions should be different in cases where the facts are themselves similar (*J (A Child) v Wilkins* [2001] R.T.R. 19). An apportionment made under s.2(1) by a trial judge will only be interfered with on appeal where it is clearly wrong or there has been an error of principle or mistake of fact (*ibid.*). As the discretion as to costs granted by the Senior Courts Act s.51 is not limited so as to exclude an order in contribution proceedings in respect of a sum paid to the original claimants in respect of their costs, the court is entitled to order a contribution in respect of the full sum paid by the person applying for contribution inclusive of any part referable to costs (*B.I.C.C. Ltd v Cumbrian Industrials Ltd* [2001] EWCA Civ 1621; October 30, 2001, unrep., CA). **9B–1092**

For an illustration of circumstances where, because the defendant had assigned his contribution claim against his co-defendant to the claimant on terms that did not extinguish the defendant's liability entirely, the court held that it was not possible in the proceedings on the assigned claim to identify the just and equitable proportion of the claim for which the defendant was liable, see *Abbey National Bank Plc v Matthews & Son* [2003] EWHC 925 (Mr Simon Berry Q.C.).

Section 2(1) requires the court to have regard to the parties' responsibility for the damage. The personal innocence of a person vicariously liable for the wrongful act of his employee or partner is not relevant for the purposes of determining contribution proceedings between that person and another wrongdoer, even in cases of dishonesty (*Dubai Aluminium Co Ltd v Salaam*, [2002] UKHL 48 [2003] 1 All E.R. 97, H.L.).

*PROCEEDINGS FOR THE SAME DEBT OR DAMAGE*

### Proceedings against persons jointly liable for the same debt or damage

9B–1093 **3.** Judgment recovered against any person liable in respect of any debt or damage shall not be a bar to an action, or to the continuance of an action, against any other person who is (apart from any such bar) jointly liable with him in respect of the same debt or damage.

### Successive actions against persons liable (jointly or otherwise) for the same damage

9B–1094 **4.** If more than one action is brought in respect of any damage by or on behalf of the person by whom it was suffered against persons liable in respect of the damage (whether jointly or otherwise) the plaintiff shall not be entitled to costs in any of those actions, other than that in which judgment is first given, unless the court is of the opinion that there was reasonable ground for bringing the action.

*SUPPLEMENTAL*

### Application to the Crown

9B–1095 **5.** Without prejudice to section 4(1) of the Crown Proceedings Act 1947 (indemnity and contribution) this Act shall bind the Crown, but nothing in this Act shall be construed as in any way affecting Her Majesty in Her private capacity (including in right of Her Duchy of Lancaster) or the Duchy of Cornwall.

### Interpretation

9B–1096 **6.**—(1) A person is liable in respect of any damage for the purposes of this Act if the person who suffered it (or anyone representing his estate or dependants) is entitled to recover compensation from him in respect of that damage (whatever the legal basis of his liability whether tort, breach of contract, breach of trust or otherwise).

(2) References in this Act to an action brought by or on behalf of the person who suffered any damage include references to an action brought for the benefit of his estate or dependants.

(3) In this Act "dependants" has the same meaning as in the Fatal Accidents Act 1976.

(4) In this Act, except in section 1(5) above, "action" means an action brought in England and Wales.

### Savings

9B–1097 **7.**—(1) Nothing in this Act shall affect any case where the debt in question became due or (as the case may be) the damage in question occurred before the date on which it comes into force.

(2) A person shall not be entitled to recover contribution or liable to make contribution in accordance with section 1 above by reference to any liability based on breach of any obligation assumed by him before the date on which this Act comes into force.

***Paragraph numbers marked with a "+" can be found online and on CD.***

(3) The right to recover contribution in accordance with section 1 above supersedes any right, other than an express contractual right, to recover contribution (as distinct from indemnity) otherwise than under this Act in corresponding circumstances; but nothing in this Act shall affect—

(a) any express or implied contractual or other right to indemnity; or

(b) any express contractual provision regulating or excluding contribution;

which would be enforceable apart from this Act (or render enforceable any agreement for indemnity or contribution which would not be enforceable apart from this Act).

### Consequential amendments and repeals

**9.**—(1) The enactments specified in Schedule 1 to this Act shall have effect subject to the amendments set out in that Schedule, being amendments consequential on the preceding provisions of this Act. **9B–1098**

(2) The enactments specified in Schedule 2 to this Act are hereby repealed to the extent specified in column 3 of that Schedule.

* * * *

## Crown Proceedings Act 1947

(1947 10 & 11 GEO. 6 C.44) **9B–1099**

ARRANGEMENT OF SECTIONS

PART I



***Paragraph numbers marked with a "+" can be found online and on CD.***

**Paragraph numbers marked with a "+" denote content that is available on the White Book on Westlaw UK Service or the Civil Procedure CD.**

### Introduction

9B–1100 Part I of this Act contains provisions broadening the liability of the Crown. Provisions in other Parts of the Act concern matters relating to the jurisdiction of the High Court and the county courts in civil proceedings brought by or against the Crown and to the procedures to be adopted in such cases.

The broad intention of the 1947 Act is that proceedings by and against the Crown should be taken in the same circumstances and in the same way as proceedings between subjects. However, procedurally speaking, in a significant number of ways (and usually for obvious reasons) the Crown as a party is in a special position and enjoys advantages not extended to the ordinary party in civil proceedings. Some of these advantages are granted expressly by particular provisions in the 1947 Act (supplemented by rules of court). Others are granted indirectly by s.35(1) of the Act. That sub-section states that any power to make rules of court may contain provisions to have effect in Crown proceedings "in substitution for or by way of addition to any of the provisions of the Rules applying to proceedings between subjects". In relation to the procedural matters listed in s.35(2), rules conferring on the Crown procedural advantages not available to ordinary parties must be made (e.g. as to default judgment, summary judgment, and interrogatories).

Before the CPR came into effect, rule making powers granted by the 1947 Act were exercised principally through the provisions of RSC O.77 and CCR O.42. Both of these Orders were carried forward into the CPR. They were revoked by the Civil Procedure (Amendment No.3) Rules 2005 (SI 2005/2292) and, with effect from October 1, 2005, replaced by CPR Pt 66 (Crown Proceedings). In the new provisions, the effects of some of the rules formerly found in RSC O.77 and CCR O.42 were retained. But to an extent the new provisions altered the effects of former provisions by removing or limiting some of the advantages enjoyed by the Crown as a party. Inevitably, certain of the new rule provisions conflicted with statutory provisions in the 1947 Act. Accordingly, by the Civil Procedure (Modification of Crown Proceedings Act 1947) Order 2005 (SI 2005/2712), the Lord Chancellor has exercised his powers under the Civil Procedure Act 1997 s.4(2) (see Vol.2, para.9A–749), for the purpose of making necessary changes to sections in the 1947 Act that placed the Crown in a special position. The principal modifications were: the repeal of s.19 (Venue and related matters) and s.20(1) (Removal and transfer of proceedings), and the substantial amendment of s.35(2) (removing statutory requirements placing the Crown in a special position as to default judgment, summary judgment, and interrogatories).

### "The Crown"

9B–1101 An agency or person carrying out functions of executive government on behalf of the Crown, such as a health board established under legislation relating to the National Health Service, is not itself or himself "the Crown"; the general purpose of the Act is to make it easier rather than more difficult for a subject to sue the Crown, and to hold that the Act had clothed with immunity from proceedings a body which prior to its passing would have enjoyed no such immunity would be to run wholly counter to its spirit (*British Medical Association v Greater Glasgow Health Board* [1989] A.C. 1211; [1989] 1 All E.R. 984, HL).

**For ss.1 to 4, 11, 13 to 18 and 20 to 23 of the Crown Proceedings Act 1947 (see Arrangement) plus any related commentary see paragraphs 9B–1102+ to 9B–1146+ on White Book on Westlaw UK or the Civil Procedure CD.**

## PART III

## JUDGMENTS AND EXECUTION

### Interest on debts, damages and costs

**24.**—(1) Section 17 of the Judgments Act 1838 (which provides that a judgment debt shall carry interest) and section 44A of the Administration of Justice Act 1970 (which enables the court to order an appropriate rate for a judgment debt expressed in a currency other than sterling) shall apply to judgment debts due from or to the Crown. 9B–1147

(2) Where any costs are awarded to or against the Crown in the High Court, interest shall be payable upon those costs unless the Court otherwise orders, and any interest so payable shall be at the same rate as that at which interest is payable upon judgment debts due from or to the Crown.

(3) Section 35A of the Senior Courts Act 1981 and section 69 of the County Courts Act 1984 (which respectively empower the High Court and county courts to award interest on debts and damages) see section 3 of the Law Reform (Miscellaneous Provisions) Act 1934 (which empowers other courts of record to do so) shall apply to judgments given in proceedings by and against the Crown.

*Note*—Amended by the Administration of Justice Act 1982 s.15, Sch.1, Pt III; the County Courts Act 1984 Sch.2; the Statute Law (Repeals) Act 1993; the Private International Law (Miscellaneous Provisions) Act 1995 s.4; and the Constitutional Reform Act 2005 s.59 and Sch.11, para.1 with effect from October 1, 2009 (SI 2009/1604). 9B–1148

### Satisfaction of orders against the Crown

**25.**—(1) Where in any civil proceedings by or against the Crown, or in any proceedings on the Crown side of the King's Bench Division, or in connection with any arbitration to which the Crown is a party, any order (including an order for costs) is made by any Court in favour of any person against the Crown or against a Government department or against an officer of the Crown as such, the proper officer of the Court shall, on an application in that behalf made by or on behalf of that person at any time after the expiration of twenty-one days from the date of the order or, in case the order provides for the payment of costs and the costs require to be taxed, at any time after the costs have been taxed, whichever is the later, issue to that person a certificate in the prescribed form containing particulars of the order: Provided that, if the Court so directs, a separate certificate shall be issued with respect to the costs (if any) ordered to be paid to the applicant. 9B–1149

***Paragraph numbers marked with a "+" can be found online and on CD.***

(2) A copy of any certificate issued under this section may be served by the person in whose favour the order is made upon the person for the time being named in the record as the solicitor, or as the person acting as solicitor, for the Crown or for the Government department or officer concerned.

(3) If the order provides for the payment of any money by way of damages or otherwise, or of any costs, the certificate shall state the amount so payable, and the appropriate Government department shall, subject as hereinafter provided, pay to the person entitled or to his solicitor the amount appearing by the certificate to be due to him together with the interest, if any, lawfully due thereon:

Provided that the Court by which any such order as aforesaid is made or any Court to which an appeal against the order lies may direct that, pending an appeal or otherwise, payment of the whole of any amount so payable, or any part thereof, shall be suspended, and if the certificate has not been issued may order any such directions to be inserted therein.

(4) Save as aforesaid no execution or attachment or process in the nature thereof shall be issued out of any Court for enforcing payment by the Crown of any such money or costs as aforesaid, and no person shall be individually liable under any order for the payment by the Crown, or any Government department, or any officer of the Crown as such of any such money or costs.

**9B–1150** *Note*—Amended by the Statute (Repeals) Act 1993.

**Orders, etc., against the Crown**

**9B–1151** See CPR r.66.6(1).

## Execution by the Crown

**9B–1152** **26.**—(1) Subject to the provisions of this Act, any order made in favour of the Crown against any person in any civil proceedings to which the Crown is a party may be enforced in the same manner as an order made in an action between subjects, and not otherwise.

(2) Sections four and five of the Debtors Act 1869 (which provide respectively for the abolition of imprisonment for debt, and for saving the power of committal in case of small debts) shall apply to sums of money payable and debts due to the Crown:

Provided that for the purpose of the application of the said section four to any sum of money payable or debt due to the Crown, the section shall have effect as if there were included among the exceptions therein mentioned default in payment of any sum payable in respect of death duties.

(3) Nothing in this section shall affect any procedure which immediately before the commencement of this Act was available for enforcing an order made in favour of the Crown in proceedings brought by the Crown for the recovery of any fine or penalty, or the forfeiture or condemnation of any goods, or the forfeiture of any ship or any share in a ship.

**9B–1153** *Note*—Amended by the Statute (Repeals) Act 1993; and the Finance Act 1972 s.134, Sch.28.

**Section 5**

Since the abolition by the Senior Courts Act 1981 s.141 of the writ of *capias ad satisfaciendum*, the only special method of enforcing Crown debts which remains is the very limited power of committal under s.5 preserved to the county court by the Access to Justice Act 1970 s.11; it extends only to income tax and certain other social security and tax payments (see Access to Justice Act 1970 Sch.4). **9B–1154**

## Attachment of moneys payable by the Crown

**27.**—(1) Where any money is payable by the Crown to some person who, under any order of any Court, is liable to pay any money to any other person, and that other person would, if the money so payable by the Crown were money payable by a subject, be entitled under Rules of Court to obtain an order for the attachment thereof as a debt due or accruing due, or an order for the appointment of a sequestrator or receiver to receive the money on his behalf, the High Court may, subject to the provisions of this Act and in accordance with Rules for receiving that money, and directing payment thereof to that other Court, make an order restraining the first-mentioned person from receiving that money and directing payment thereof to that other person, or to the sequestrator or receiver: Provided that no such order shall be made in respect of:— **9B–1155**

(a) any wages or salary payable to any officer of the Crown as such;

(b) any money which is subject to the provisions of any enactment prohibiting or restricting assignment or charging or taking in execution.

(2) The provisions of the preceding subsection shall, so far as they relate to forms of relief falling within the jurisdiction of a county court, have effect in relation to county courts as they have effect in relation to the High Court.

(3) In their application to England and Wales the preceding provisions of this section shall have effect subject to any order for the time being in force under section 139(2) of the Senior Courts Act 1981.

*Note* —Amended by the Post Office Act 1969 Sch.6; the Senior Courts Act 1981 ss.139(1), 152(4), Sch.7; and SI 2005/2712 and the Constitutional Reform Act 2005 s.59 and Sch.11, para.1 with effect from October 1, 2009 (SI 2009/1604). **9B–1156**

**Orders, etc., against the Crown**

See CPR r.66.7. **9B–1157**

# PART IV

# MISCELLANEOUS AND SUPPLEMENTAL

### *MISCELLANEOUS*

## Discovery

**28.**—(1) Subject to and in accordance with Rules of Court:— **9B–1158**

(a) in any civil proceedings in the High Court or a county

court to which the Crown is a party, the Crown may be required by the Court to make discovery of documents and produce documents for inspection; and

(b) in any such proceedings as aforesaid, the Crown may be required by the Court to answer interrogatories:

Provided that this section shall be without prejudice to any rule of law which authorities or requires the withholding of any document or the refusal to answer any question on the ground that the disclosure of the document or the answering of the question would be injurious to the public interest.

Any order of the Court made under the powers conferred by paragraph (b) of this subsection shall direct by what officer of the Crown the interrogatories are to be answered.

(2) Without prejudice to the proviso to the preceding subsection, any Rules made for the purposes of this section shall be such as to secure that the existence of a document will not be disclosed if, in the opinion of a Minister of the Crown, it would be injurious to the public interest to disclose the existence thereof.

*Note* —Amended by SI 2005/2712.

**Discovery in proceeding by or against the Crown**

9B–1159 See CPR r.66.3. See also CPR r.31.19(1) as to Crown privilege and "Documents privileged on the ground that production would be injurious to the public interest," Vol.1, para.31.3.33.

**For ss.29, 31 to 33, 35, 38, 40, 52 and 54 of and Sch.1 to the Crown Proceedings Act 1947 (see Arrangement) plus any related commentary see paragraphs 9B–1160+ to 9B–1177+ on White Book on Westlaw UK or the Civil Procedure CD.**

## Evidence (Proceedings in Other Jurisdictions) Act 1975

9B–1178 (1975 c.34)

ARRANGEMENT OF SECTIONS

*EVIDENCE FOR CIVIL PROCEEDINGS*

SECT.



**"General"**

9B–1179 The Act enables a foreign or international court to obtain an order from specified courts of the United Kingdom requiring evidence to be given in the United Kingdom

***Paragraph numbers marked with a "+" can be found online and on CD.***

for purposes of proceedings before the requesting court. See, generally, O.70 and notes thereto.

*EVIDENCE FOR CIVIL PROCEEDINGS*

## Application to United Kingdom court for assistance in obtaining evidence for civil proceedings in other court

**1.** Where an application is made to the High Court, the Court of Session or the High Court of Justice in Northern Ireland for an order for evidence to be obtained in the part of the United Kingdom in which it exercises jurisdiction, and the court is satisfied— **9B–1180**

(a) that the application is made in pursuance of a request issued by or on behalf of a court or tribunal ("the requesting court") exercising jurisdiction in any other part of the United Kingdom or in a country or territory outside the United Kingdom; and

(b) that the evidence to which the application relates is to be obtained for the purposes of civil proceedings which either have been instituted before the requesting court or whose institution before that court is contemplated,

the High Court, Court of Session or the High Court of Justice in Northern Ireland, as the case may be, shall have the powers conferred on it by the following provisions of this Act.

*Note*—For relevant rules of court, see Sect.II of CPR Pt 34, replacing CPR Sch.1, RSC O.70 with effect from December 2, 2002. **9B–1181**

## Power of United Kingdom court to give effect to application for assistance

**2.**—(1) Subject to the provisions of this section, the High Court, the Court of Session and the High Court of Justice in Northern Ireland shall each have power, on any such application as is mentioned in section 1 above, by order to make such provision for obtaining evidence in the part of the United Kingdom in which it exercises jurisdiction as may appear to the court to be appropriate for the purpose of giving effect to the request in pursuance of which the application is made; and any such order may require a person specified therein to take such steps as the court may consider appropriate for that purpose. **9B–1182**

(2) Without prejudice to the generality of subsection (1) above but subject to the provisions of this section, an order under this section may, in particular, make provision—

(a) for the examination of witnesses, either orally or in writing;

(b) for the production of documents;

(c) for the inspection, photographing, preservation, custody or detention of any property;

(d) for the taking of samples of any property and the carrying out of any experiments on or with any property;

(e) for the medical examination of any person;

***Paragraph numbers marked with a "+" can be found online and on CD.***

(f) without prejudice to paragraph (e) above, for the taking and testing of samples of blood from any person.

(3) An order under this section shall not require any particular steps to be taken unless they are steps which can be required to be taken by way of obtaining evidence for the purposes of civil proceedings in the court making the order (whether or not proceedings of the same description as those to which the application for the order relates); but this subsection shall not preclude the making of an order requiring a person to give testimony (either orally or in writing) otherwise than on oath where this is asked for by the requesting court.

(4) An order under this section shall not require a person—

(a) to state what documents relevant to the proceedings to which the application for the order relates are or have been in his possession, custody or power; or

(b) to produce any documents other than particular documents specified in the order as being documents appearing to the court making the order to be, or to be likely to be, in his possession, custody or power.

(5) A person who, by virtue of an order under this section, is required to attend at any place shall be entitled to the like conduct money and payment for expenses and loss of time as on attendance as a witness in civil proceedings before the court making the order.

**9B–1183** *Note*—See notes to CPR Sch.1, RSC O.70, Vol.1, para.sc70.6.1. For discussion of this section, see *Refco Capital Markets Ltd v Credit Suisse (First Boston) Ltd* [2001] EWCA Civ 1733; *The Times*, December 7, 2001, CA, and *Commerce and Industry Insurance Co of Canada v Certain Underwriters at Lloyd's of London* [2002] 1 W.L.R. 1323 (Moore-Bick J.). For relevant rules of court, see Sect.II of CPR Pt 34, replacing CPR Sch.1, RSC O.70 with effect from December 2, 2002.

## Privilege of witnesses

**9B–1184** **3.**—(1) A person shall not be compelled by virtue of an order under section 2 above to give any evidence which he could not be compelled to give—

(a) in civil proceedings in the part of the United Kingdom in which the court that made the order exercises jurisdiction; or

(b) subject to subsection (2) below, in civil proceedings in the country or territory in which the requesting court exercises jurisdiction.

(2) Subsection (1)(b) above shall not apply unless the claim of the person in question to be exempt from giving the evidence is either—

(a) supported by a statement contained in the request (whether it is so supported unconditionally or subject to conditions that are fulfilled); or

(b) conceded by the applicant for the order;

and where such a claim made by any person is not supported or conceded as aforesaid he may (subject to the other provisions of this section) be required to give the evidence to which the claim relates but that evidence shall not be transmitted to the requesting court if that court, on the matter being referred to it, upholds the claim.

(3) Without prejudice to subsection (1) above, a person shall not be compelled by virtue of an order under section 2 above to give any evidence if his doing so would be prejudicial to the security of the United Kingdom; and a certificate signed by or on behalf of the Secretary of State to the effect that it would be so prejudicial for that person to do so shall be conclusive evidence of that fact.

(4) In this section references to giving evidence include references to answering any question and to producing any document and the reference in subsection (2) above to the transmission of evidence given by a person shall be construed accordingly.

*Note*—See CPR r.34.20, replacing CPR Sch.1, RSC O.70, r.6 (with effect from December 2, 2002). **9B–1185**

## Extension of powers of High Court, etc., in relation to obtaining evidence for proceedings in that court

**4.** The Attendance of Witnesses Act 1854 (which enables the Court of Session to order the issue of a warrant of citation in special form throughout the United Kingdom, for the attendance of a witness at trial) shall have effect as if references to attendance at a trial included references to attendance before an examiner or commissioner appointed by the court or a judge thereof in any cause or matter in that court, including an examiner or commissioner appointed to take evidence outside the jurisdiction of the court. **9B–1186**

*Note*—Amended by the Judicature (Northern Ireland) Act 1978 s.122(2) and Sch.7; and the Senior Courts Act 1981 s.152(4) and Sch.7. **9B–1187**

* * * *

*EVIDENCE FOR INTERNATIONAL PROCEEDINGS*

## Power of United Kingdom court to assist in obtaining evidence for international proceedings

**6.**—(1) Her Majesty may by Order in Council direct that, subject to such exceptions, adaptations or modifications as may be specified in the Order, the provisions of sections 1 to 3 above shall have effect in relation to international proceedings of any description specified in the order. **9B–1188**

(2) An Order in Council under this section may direct that section 1(4) of the Perjury Act 1911 or Article 3(4) of the Perjury (Northern Ireland) Order 1979 shall have effect in relation to international proceedings to which the Order applies as it has effect in relation to a judicial proceeding in a tribunal of a foreign state.

(3) In this section "international proceedings" means proceedings before the International Court of Justice or any other court, tribunal, commission, body or authority (whether consisting of one or more persons) which in pursuance of any international agreement or any resolution of the General Assembly of the United Nations, exercises any jurisdiction or performs any functions of a judicial nature or by way of arbitration, conciliation or inquiry or is appointed (whether

permanently or temporarily) for the purpose of exercising any jurisdiction or performing any such functions.

9B–1189 *Note*—Amended by SI 1979/1714.

*SUPPLEMENTARY*

## Rules of court

9B–1190 **7.** Civil Procedure Rules or rules of court under section 7 of the Northern Ireland Act 1962 shall include power to make rules of court—

(a) as to the manner in which any such application as is mentioned in section 1 above is to be made;

(b) subject to the provisions of this Act, as to the circumstances in which an order can be made under section 2 above; and

(c) as to the manner in which any such reference as is mentioned in section 3(2) above is to be made;

and any such rules may include such incidental, supplementary and consequential provision as the authority making the rules may consider necessary or expedient.

9B–1191 *Note*—Amended by the Senior Courts Act 1981 s.152(4) and Sch.7; and by the Courts Act 2003 s.109(1), Sch.8, para.177(a).

With effect from December 2, 2002, the provisions in Sect.II of CPR Pt 34 replaced RSC O.70 (Obtaining Evidence for Foreign Courts, Etc.) as the rules of court authorised by this section.

## Consequential amendments and repeals

9B–1192 **8.**—(1) The enactments mentioned in Schedule 1 to this Act shall have effect subject to the amendments there specified, being amendments consequential on the provisions of this Act.

(2) The enactments mentioned in Schedule 2 to this Act are hereby repealed to the extent specified in the third column of that Schedule.

(3) Nothing in this section shall affect—

(a) any application to any court or judge which is pending at the commencement of this Act;

(b) any certificate given for the purposes of any such application;

(c) any power to make an order on such an application; or

(d) the operation or enforcement of any order made on such an application.

(4) Subsection (3) above is without prejudice to section 38(2) of the Interpretation Act 1889 (effect of repeals).

## Interpretation

9B–1193 **9.**—(1) In this Act—

"civil proceedings", in relation to the requesting court, means proceedings in any civil or commercial matter;

"requesting court" has the meaning given in section 1 above;

"property" includes any land, chattel or other corporeal property of any description;

"request" includes any commission, order or other process issued by or on behalf of the requesting court.

(2) In relation to any application made in pursuance of a request issued by the High Court under section 56 of the County Courts Act 1984 or the High Court of Justice in Northern Ireland under Article 43 of the County Courts (Northern Ireland) Order 1980, the reference in section 1(b) above to proceedings instituted before the requesting court shall be construed as a reference to the relevant proceedings in the county court.

(3) Any power conferred by this Act to make an Order in Council includes power to revoke or vary any such Order by a subsequent Order in Council.

(4) Nothing in this Act shall be construed as enabling any court to make an order that is binding on the Crown or on any person in his capacity as an officer or servant of the Crown.

(5) Except so far as the context otherwise requires, any reference in this Act to any enactment is a reference to that enactment as amended or extended by or under any other enactment.

*Note* —Amended by the County Courts Act 1984 s.148(1) and Sch.2. **9B–1194**

**"Civil or commercial matters"**

The words "civil or commercial matters" in the Act of 1975 cannot be construed with reference to any internationally acceptable meaning but equally they are not to be given a restricted construction derived from the distinction between public and private law in civil law systems and accordingly the definition extends to relevant proceedings in a civil or commercial matter in both the United Kingdom and the requesting state, e.g. proceedings in the foreign court challenging a tax assessment made by a foreign tax authority (*Re State of Norway's Application (Nos 1 and 2)* [1990] 1 A.C. 723; [1989] 2 W.L.R. 458, HL(E), affirming [1987] Q.B. 433). **9B–1195**

## Short title, commencement and extent

**10.**—(1) This Act may be cited as the Evidence (Proceedings in Other Jurisdictions) Act 1975. **9B–1196**

(2) This Act shall come into operation on such day as Her Majesty may by Order in Council appoint.

(3) Her Majesty may by Order in Council make provision for extending any of the provisions of this Act (including section 6 or any Order in Council made thereunder) with such exceptions, adaptations or modifications as may be specified in the Order, to any of the Channel Islands, the Isle of Man, any colony (other than a colony for whose external relations a country other than the United Kingdom is responsible) or any country or territory outside Her Majesty's dominions in which Her Majesty has jurisdiction in right of Her Majesty's Government in the United Kingdom.

**Commencement**

The Act was brought into force on May 4, 1976, by SI 1976/429. **9B–1197**

# Law Reform (Contributory Negligence) Act 1945

(1945 8 & 9 Geo. 6 c.28) **9B–1198**

Arrangement of Sections

***Paragraph numbers marked with a "+" can be found online and on CD.***

## Apportionment of liability in case of contributory negligence

**1.**—(1) Where any person suffers damage as the result partly of his own fault and partly of the fault of any other person or persons, a claim in respect of that damage shall not be defeated by reason of the fault of the person suffering the damage, but the damages recoverable in respect thereof shall be reduced to such extent as the Court thinks just and equitable having regard to the claimant's share in the responsibility for the damage: Provided that—

(a) this subsection shall not operate to defeat any defence arising under a contract;

(b) where any contract or enactment providing for the limitation of liability is applicable to the claim, the amount of damages recoverable by the claimant by virtue of this subsection shall not exceed the maximum limit so applicable.

(2) Where damages are recoverable by any person by virtue of the foregoing subsection subject to such reduction as is therein mentioned, the Court shall find and record the total damages which would have been recoverable if the claimant had not been at fault.

(3) [...]

(4) [...]

(5) Where, in any case to which subsection (1) of this section applies, one of the persons at fault avoids liability to any other such person or his personal representative by pleading the Limitation Act 1939, or any other enactment limiting the time within which proceedings may be taken, he shall not be entitled to recover any damages from that other person or representative by virtue of the said subsection.

(6) [...]

(7) [...]

**9B–1199** *Note*—Amended by the Carriage by Air Act 1961 Sch.2, the Fatal Accidents Act 1976 s.6 and Sch.6 and the Civil Liability (Contribution) Act 1978 s.9(2) and Sch.2; see now Limitation Act 1980 Vol.2, Section 8.

**9B–1200** *Note*—Where the plaintiff brings a claim in tort and the defendant makes a counterclaim in contract, both claims being attributable to two concurrent causes contemporaneously, the apportionment of liability cannot be solved by applying the Act of 1945 but can only be resolved by assessing the recoverable damages per each claim on the basis of causation (*Tenant Radiant Heat Ltd v Warrington Development Corp* (1988) 11 E.G. 71, CA, distinguishing *Forsikringsaktielskapet Vesta v Butcher* [1988] 3 W.L.R. 565, CA, apportionment of liability between two claims in contract).

In the case of a claimant "fault" in this context means "negligence, breach of statutory duty or other act or omission"(see s.4) which gives rise, at common law, to a defence of contributory negligence (*Standard Chartered Bank v Pakistan National Shipping Corporation (No.2)* [2002] UKHL 43; [2003] 1 All E.R. 173, HL (there is no common law defence of contributory negligence in the case of fraudulent misrepresentation)).

* * * *

## Saving for Maritime Conventions Act 1911, and past cases

**9B–1201** **3.**—(1) This Act shall not apply to any claim to which section one of the Maritime Conventions Act 1911, applies and that Act shall have effect as if this Act had not passed.

(2) This Act shall not apply to any case where the acts or omissions giving rise to the claim occurred before the passing of this Act.

## Interpretation

**4.** The following expressions have the meanings hereby respectively assigned to them, that is to say— **9B–1202**

"Court" means, in relation to any claim, the Court or arbitrator by or before whom the claim falls to be determined;

"damage" includes loss of life and personal injury;

"fault" means negligence, breach of statutory duty or other act or omission which gives rise to a liability in tort or would, apart from this Act, give rise to the defence of contributory negligence;

*Note* —Meaning of "dependant" repealed by the Fatal Accidents Act 1976. **9B–1203**

Meaning of "employer" and "workman" repealed by the National Insurance (Industrial Injuries) Act 1946.

**Law Reform (Miscellaneous Provisions) Act 1934**

(1934 24 & 25 GEO. 5 C.41) **9B–1204**

ARRANGEMENT OF SECTIONS



## Effect of death on certain causes of action

**1.**—(1) Subject to the provisions of this section, on the death of any person after the commencement of this Act all causes of action subsisting against or vested in him shall survive against, or, as the case may be, for the benefit of his estate: Provided that this subsection shall not apply to causes of action for defamation.

(1A) The right of a person to claim under section 1A of the Fatal Accidents Act 1976 (bereavement) shall not survive for the benefit of his estate on his death.

(2) Where a cause of action survives as aforesaid for the benefit of the estate of a deceased person, the damages recoverable for the benefit of the estate of that person:—

(a) shall not include—

(i) any exemplary damages;

(ii) any damages for loss of income in respect of any period after that person's death;

(b) [...]

(c) where the death of that person has been caused by the act or omission which gives rise to the cause of action, shall be calculated without reference to any loss or gain to his estate consequent on his death, except that a sum in respect of funeral expenses may be included.

***Paragraph numbers marked with a "+" can be found online and on CD.***

(3) [...]

(4) Where damage has been suffered by reason of any act or omission in respect of which a cause of action would have subsisted against any person if that person had not died before or at the same time as the damage was suffered, there shall be deemed, for the purposes of this Act, to have been subsisting against him before his death such cause of action in respect of that act or omission as would have subsisted if he had died after the damage was suffered.

(5) The rights conferred by this Act for the benefit of the estates of deceased persons shall be in addition to and not in derogation of any rights conferred on the dependants of deceased persons by the Fatal Accidents Acts 1846to 1908, and so much of this Act as relates to causes of action against the estates of deceased persons shall apply in relation to causes of action under the said Acts as it applies in relation to other causes of action not expressly excepted from the operation of subsection (1) of this section.

(6) In the event of the insolvency of an estate against which proceedings are maintainable by virtue of this section, any liability in respect of the cause of action in respect of which the proceedings are maintainable shall be deemed to be a debt provable in the administration of the estate, notwithstanding that it is a demand in the nature of unliquidated damages arising otherwise than by a contract, promise or breach of trust.

**9B–1205** *Note* —Amended by the Statute Law Revision Act 1950; the Law Reform (Miscellaneous Provisions) Act 1970 Sch.; the Proceedings Against Estates Act 1970; and the Administration of Justice Act 1982 ss.4, 41 and 75, Sch.9. Subsection (5) extended by the Fatal Accidents Act 1976 s.6(1), Sch.1.

* * * *

## Power of Courts of Record to award interest on debts and damages

**9B–1206** **3.**—(1) In any proceedings tried in any Court of Record for the recovery of any debt or damages, the Court may, if it thinks fit, order that there shall be included in the sum for which judgment is given interest at such rate as it thinks fit on the whole or any part of the debt or damages for the whole or any part of the period between the date when the cause of action arose and the date of the judgment: Provided that nothing in this section—

(a) shall authorise the giving of interest upon interest; or

(b) shall apply in relation to any debt upon which interest is payable as of right whether by virtue of any agreement or otherwise; or

(c) shall affect the damages recoverable for the dishonour of a bill of exchange.

(1A) Where in any such proceedings as are mentioned in subsection (1) of this section judgment is given for a sum which (apart from interest on damages) exceeds £200 and represents or includes damages in respect of personal injuries to the plaintiff or any other person, or in respect of a person's death, then (without prejudice to the exercise of the power conferred by that subsection in relation to any part of that sum which does not represent such damages) the court shall exercise that power so as to include in that sum interest on those damages or on such part of them as the court considers appropriate, unless the court is satisfied that there are special reasons why no interest should be given in respect of those damages.

(1B) Any order under this section may provide for interest to be calculated at different rates in respect of different parts of the period for which interest is given, whether that period is the whole or part of the period mentioned in subsection (1) of this section.

(1C) For the avoidance of doubt it is hereby declared that in determining, for the purposes of any enactment contained in the County Courts Act 1959, whether an amount exceeds, or is less than, a sum specified in that enactment, no account shall be taken of any power exercisable by virtue of this section or of any order made in the exercise of such a power.

(1D) In this section "personal injuries" includes any disease and any impairment of a person's physical or mental condition.

*Note*—Amended by the Statute Law Revision Act 1950 and the Administration of Justice Act 1969 s.22. **9B–1207**

By the AJA 1982 s.15(4) and (5), the provisions of this section have ceased to have effect in relation to the High Court and the county courts, but they remain in force and operation in relation to other Courts of Record, e.g. the Court of Appeal (Civil Division), so that on the hearing of an appeal, where that Court gives judgment for any debt or damages, it may also award interest under this section. It would seem that the hearing of an appeal will be regarded as coming within the word "tried", since the Court will have made a judicial decision (see *per* Lord Denning M.R. in *Wallersteiner v Moir (No.2)* [1975] Q.B. 373 at 387).

For the power to award interest on any debt or damages in the High Court, see SCA 1981 s.35A; in the county courts see C.C.A. 1984, s.69; in arbitration proceedings, see Arb. A. 1950 s.19A. See also AJA 1982 s.15; and by the Statute Law (Repeals) Act 2004 Sch.1, Part 1, Group 4.

## Short title and extent

**4.**—(1) This Act may be cited as the Law Reform (Miscellaneous Provisions) Act 1934. **9B–1208**

(2) This Act shall not extend to Scotland or Northern Ireland.

# Litigants in Person (Costs and Expenses) Act 1975

(1975 c.47) **9B–1209**

ARRANGEMENT OF SECTIONS



## Costs or expenses recoverable

**1.**—(1) Where, in any proceedings to which this subsection applies, any costs of a litigant in person are ordered to be paid by any other party to the proceedings or in any other way, there may, subject to rules of court, be allowed on the taxation or other determination of those costs sums in respect of any work done, and any expenses and **9B–1210**

losses incurred, by the litigants in or in connection with the proceedings to which the order relates. This subsection applies to civil proceedings—

(a) in a county court, in the Senior Courts, in the Court of Judicature or in the Supreme Court on appeal from the High Court or the Court of Appeal,
(b) before [...] the Lands Tribunal for Northern Ireland, or
(ba) before the First-tier Tribunal or the Upper Tribunal, or
(c) in or before any other court or tribunal specified in an order made under this subsection by the Lord Chancellor.

(2) Where, in any proceedings to which this subsection applies, any costs or expenses of a party litigant are ordered to be paid by any other party to the proceedings or in any other way, there may, subject to rules of court, be allowed on the taxation or other determination of those costs or expenses sums in respect of any work done, and any outlays and losses incurred, by the litigant or in connection with the proceedings to which the order relates.

This subsection applies to civil proceedings—

(a) in the sheriff court, the Scottish Land Court, the Court of Session or the Supreme Court on appeal from the Court of Session.
(b) before the Lands Tribunal for Scotland, or
(ba) before the First-tier Tribunal or the Upper Tribunal, or
(c) in or before any other court or tribunal specified in an order made under this subsection by the Lord Advocate.

(3) An order under subsection (1) or (2) above shall be made by statutory instrument and shall be subject to annulment in pursuance of the resolution of either House of Parliament.

(4) In this section "rules of court"—

(a) in relation to [...] the Lands Tribunal for Scotland, means rules made under section 3 of the Lands Tribunal Act 1949,
(b) in relation to the Lands Tribunal for Northern Ireland means rules made under section 9 of the Lands Tribunal and Compensation Act (Northern Ireland) 1964, and
(ba) in relation to the First-tier Tribunal or the Upper Tribunal, means Tribunal Procedure Rules, and
(c) in relation to any other tribunal specified in an order made under subsection (1) or (2) above, shall have the meaning given by the order as respects that tribunal.

(5) In the application of subsection (1) above to Northern Ireland, the expression "county court," "the High Court" and "the Court of Appeal" shall have the meanings respectively assigned to them by section 29(1) of the Northern Ireland Act 1962.

**9B–1210.1** *Note*—Amended by the Tribunals, Courts and Enforcement Act 2007 Sch.8 para.6, with effect from November 3, 2008; by SI 2009/1307, with effect from June 1, 2009; and by the Constitutional Reform Act 2005 s.59 and Sch.11 para.22 with effect from October 1, 2009 (SI 2009/1604).

## Short title, commencement and extent

**2.**—(1) This Act may be cited as the Litigants in Person (Costs and Expenses) Act 1975. **9B–1211**

(2) [...]

(3) [...]

*Note* —See also CPR r.48.6. **9B–1212**

This Act applies to all costs incurred after April 1, 1976, and was partially brought into force on that day by the Litigants in Person (Costs and Expenses) Act 1975 Commencement Order 1976 (SI 1976/364) and the residue by (Commencement No.2) Order 1980 (SI 1980/1158). The scope of the Act was extended to the Employment AppealTribunal by the Litigants in Person (Costs and Expenses) Order 1980 (SI 1980/1159) and to civil proceedings in magistrates' courts by the Litigants in Person (Costs and Expenses) (Magistrates' Courts) Order 2001 (SI 2001/3438).

There is no provision for the costs of litigants in person in criminal proceedings.

For notes on costs and expenses which are recoverable see Vol.1, paras 48.6.1 and for rights of audience see para.47.14.7 *et seq.*

Subsections (2) and (3) repealed by the Statute Law (Repeals) Act 2004 Sch.1, Pt 1, Group 4.

# Oaths Act 1978

(1978 c.19) **9B–1213**

ARRANGEMENT OF SECTIONS

PART I



* * * *

**Paragraph numbers marked with a "+" denote content that is available on the White Book on Westlaw UK Service or the Civil Procedure CD.**

# The High Court Enforcement Officers Regulations 2004

(S.I. 2004 No. 400) **9B–1224**

ARRANGEMENT OF SECTIONS

PART 1



***Paragraph numbers marked with a "+" can be found online and on CD.***

**Paragraph numbers marked with a "+" denote content that is available on the White Book on Westlaw UK Service or the Civil Procedure CD.**

## The Proceeds of Crime Act 2002 (Legal Expenses in Civil Recovery Proceedings) Regulations 2005

9B–1246 (S.I. 2005 No. 3382)

ARRANGEMENT OF REGULATIONS



*Paragraph numbers marked with a "+" can be found online and on CD.*

BASIS OF ASSESSMENT OF LEGAL EXPENSES



* * * *

## PART 1

## INTRODUCTION

### Citation and commencement

**1.** These Regulations may be cited as the Proceeds of Crime Act 2002 (Legal Expenses in Civil Recovery Proceedings) Regulations 2005 and shall come into force on 1st January 2006.

### Interpretation

**2.**—(1) In these Regulations— **9B–1247**

"the 1990 Act" means the Courts and Legal Services Act 1990;

"the 2002 Act" means the Proceeds of Crime Act 2002;

"CPR" means the Civil Procedure Rules 1998;

"the Order in Council" means the Proceeds of Crime Act 2002 (External Requests and Orders) Order 2005;

"RSC (NI)" means the Rules of the Supreme Court (Northern Ireland) 1980;

"civil recovery proceedings" means proceedings under Part 5 of the 2002 Act or Part 5 of the Order in Council;

"notice" means notice in writing;

"relevant enforcement authority" means the enforcement authority which is conducting the civil recovery proceedings concerned;

"solicitor" means a solicitor of the Supreme Court and, in relation to England and Wales, includes any other person who is an authorised litigator within the meaning of section 119(1) of the 1990 Act.

(2) Any reference in these Regulations to the assessment of legal expenses by the court shall, in relation to Northern Ireland, be interpreted as referring to the taxation of those expenses by the Master (Taxing Office).

*Note*—Amended by SI 2008/523. **9B–1247.1**

## PART 2

## REQUIRED CONDITIONS: GENERAL

### Effect of this part

**3.** This Part specifies the required conditions for the purposes of sections 245C(5) and 252(4) of the 2002 Act and articles 149(5) and 157(4) of the Order in Council. **9B–1248**

***Paragraph numbers marked with a "+" can be found online and on CD.***

**Condition relating to work covered by exclusion**

9B–1249 **4.** An exclusion from a property freezing order or interim receiving order must specify—

(a) the stage or stages in civil recovery proceedings to which it relates; and

(b) the maximum amount which may be released in respect of legal expenses for each stage to which it relates.

**Condition relating to notification**

9B–1250 **5.** If the solicitor acting for the person to whose legal expenses the exclusion relates becomes aware that—

(a) that person's legal expenses in respect of any stage in civil recovery proceedings have exceeded or will exceed the maximum amount specified in the exclusion for that stage; or

(b) that person's total legal expenses in respect of all the stages to which the exclusion relates have exceeded or will exceed the total amount that may be released pursuant to the exclusion,

the solicitor must give notice to the relevant enforcement authority and the court as soon as reasonably practicable.

9B–1250.1 *Note* —Amended by SI 2008/523.

**Condition relating to payment of expenses**

9B–1251 **6.** Where a person has incurred legal expenses in relation to a stage in civil recovery proceedings specified in an exclusion—

(a) during any period when the property freezing order or interim receiving order has effect, a sum may only be released in respect of those expenses in accordance with Part 3;

(b) where the court makes a recovery order which provides for the payment of that person's reasonable legal expenses in respect of civil recovery proceedings, the sum payable in respect of his legal expenses shall be determined in accordance with Part 4, regardless of whether a sum has been released in respect of any of those expenses under Part 3.

PART 3

REQUIRED CONDITIONS: RELEASE OF INTERIM PAYMENTS

**Effect of this Part**

9B–1252 **7.** This Part applies where, during a period when a property freezing order or interim receiving order has effect, a person to whose property the order applies seeks the release of a sum in respect of his legal expenses pursuant to an exclusion from the order.

**Request for relevant enforcement authority's agreement to release of interim payment**

9B–1253 **8.**—(1) A request for the relevant enforcement authority's agreement to the release of a sum in respect of legal expenses pursuant to an exclusion must be made in writing to that authority by the person to whose expenses the exclusion relates.

(2) The request must—

(a) describe the stage or stages in the civil recovery proceedings in relation to which the legal expenses were incurred;

(b) summarise the work done in connection with each stage;

(c) be accompanied by any invoices, receipts or other documents which are necessary to show that the expenses have been incurred; and

(d) identify any item or description of property from which the person making the request wishes the sum to be released.

(3) A person may not make a request under this regulation—

(a) in respect of legal expenses which he has not yet incurred; or

(b) more than once in any 2 month period.

*Note* —Amended by SI 2008/523. **9B–1253.1**

**Relevant enforcement authority's response to request**

**9.**—(1) Not later than 21 days after it receives the request, the relevant enforcement authority must give notice to the person who made the request stating— **9B–1254**

(a) whether it agrees to the release of the requested sum; and

(b) if it does not agree to the release of the requested sum—

(i) the amount (if any) which it agrees may be released; and

(ii) the reasons for its decision.

(2) Where an interim receiving order applies to the property from which it is proposed that the requested sum should be released, the relevant enforcement authority must at the same time send copies of the request and the notice referred to in paragraph (1) to the interim receiver.

(3) In determining the amount which may be released in respect of legal expenses with its agreement, the relevant enforcement authority must have regard to the provisions of Part 5 which would apply on the assessment of those expenses by the court.

*Note* —Amended by SI 2008/523. **9B–1254.1**

**Release of interim payment**

**10.**—(1) The sum which may be released pursuant to the exclusion is the greater of— **9B–1255**

(a) the amount which the relevant enforcement authority agrees may be released; and

(b) 65% of the requested sum.

(2) The sum may only be released to—

*Paragraph numbers marked with a "+" can be found online and on CD.*

(a) the solicitor who is instructed to act in the civil recovery proceedings for the person to whose legal expenses the exclusion relates; or

(b) where appropriate, to the solicitor who was so instructed when the legal expenses to which the sum relates were incurred.

9B–1255.1 *Note* —Amended by SI 2008/523.

PART 4

AGREEMENT OR ASSESSMENT OF EXPENSES AT CONCLUSION OF CIVIL RECOVERY PROCEEDINGS

### Effect of this Part

9B–1256 **11.** This Part specifies the procedure for determining the amount payable in respect of a person's reasonable legal expenses in civil recovery proceedings, where the court has made a recovery order which provides for the payment of those expenses.

### Agreement of expenses by the relevant enforcement authority

9B–1257 **12.**—(1) This regulation applies where a person seeks the relevant enforcement authority's agreement to the payment of a sum in respect of its legal expenses pursuant to section 266(8B)(a) of the 2002 Act or article 177(11)(a) of the Order in Council.

(2) In determining the amount which may be paid in respect of legal expenses with its agreement, the relevant enforcement authority must have regard to the provisions of Part 5 which would apply on the assessment of those expenses by the court.

(3) Where the relevant enforcement authority agrees to the payment of the sum which a person seeks in respect of his legal expenses—

(a) it shall give that person and the trustee for civil recovery notice of the agreed sum; and

(b) the sum payable in respect of those expenses shall be the agreed sum.

9B–1257.1 *Note* —Amended by SI 2008/523.

### Expenses to be assessed if not agreed

9B–1258 **13.**—(1) Unless the relevant enforcement authority agrees to the payment of the sum which a person seeks in respect of his legal expenses pursuant to provision made in a recovery order, that person must commence proceedings for the assessment of those expenses in accordance with paragraph (2).

(2) Where paragraph (1) requires a person to commence proceedings for the assessment of his legal expenses—

(a) in relation to civil recovery proceedings in England and Wales, he must commence proceedings for the detailed assessment of those expenses in accordance with CPR Part 47, subject to the modifications that—

(i) rule 47.7 shall have effect as if it provided that he must commence those proceedings not later than 2 months after the date of the recovery order; and

(ii) rule 47.14(2) shall have effect as if it provided that he must file a request for a detailed assessment hearing not later than 2 months after the expiry of the period for commencing the detailed assessment proceedings;

(b) in relation to civil recovery proceedings in Northern Ireland, he must begin proceedings for the taxation of those expenses in accordance with RSC (NI) Order 62, subject to the modification that rule 29(1) shall have effect as if it provided that he must begin those proceedings not later than 4 months after the date of the recovery order.

(3) The court will assess the person's legal expenses in accordance with the provisions of Part 5 and the relevant rules of court, and the sum payable in respect of those expenses shall be the assessed amount.

*Note*—Amended by SI 2008/523. **9B–1258.1**

**Payment of expenses**

**14.**—(1) Where the sum payable in respect of a person's legal expenses— **9B–1259**

(a) exceeds the total amount which has been released in respect of those expenses in accordance with Part 3, the trustee for civil recovery must pay the balance out of the sums referred to in section 280(1) of the 2002 Act or article 191(1) of the Order in Council;

(b) is less than the total amount which has been released in respect of those expenses in accordance with Part 3, the person to whose expenses the sum relates must repay the balance to the trustee.

(2) The trustee for civil recovery may only make a payment in respect of a person's legal expenses to—

(a) the solicitor who is instructed to act for that person; or

(b) where appropriate, the solicitor who was so instructed when the legal expenses to which the sum relates were incurred.

PART 5

BASIS OF ASSESSMENT OF LEGAL EXPENSES

**Effect of this Part**

**15.** This Part sets out the basis on which the court must assess the amount payable in respect of a person's reasonable legal expenses of civil recovery proceedings pursuant to provision made in a recovery order. **9B–1260**

### General principles

9B–1261 **16.**—(1) Subject to regulation 17, the court will assess a person's legal expenses on the standard basis.

(2) The court must give effect to—

(a) any provision made in the recovery order for the purpose of enabling the person to meet his reasonable legal expenses of civil recovery proceedings; and

(b) subject to sub-paragraph (a), the terms of any exclusion made for the purpose of enabling that person to meet those legal expenses (including the required conditions).

(3) In paragraph (1), "the standard basis" has the meaning given in—

(a) CPR rule 44.4 in relation to proceedings in England and Wales;

(b) RSC (NI) Order 62 rule 12 in relation to proceedings in Northern Ireland.

### Rates of remuneration

9B–1262 **17.**—(1) Subject to the following paragraphs of this regulation, remuneration for work done by a legal representative may only be allowed at the appropriate hourly rate shown in the Table below.

(2) The higher hourly rates specified in the third column of the Table may only be allowed where the case involves substantial novel or complex issues of law or fact.

(3) The rates specified in the Table will be increased by—

(a) 20% for legal representatives whose offices are situated in Central London; and

(b) 10% for legal representatives whose offices are situated in Outer London.

(4) In paragraph (3)—

(a) "Central London" means postcode districts EC1—4, SW1, W1 and WC1—2;

(b) "Outer London" means all other postcode districts in postcode areas BR, CR, DA, E, N, NW, SE, SW, UB and W.

and "postcode area" and "postcode district" shall be construed in accordance with the Postcode Address File within the meaning given in section 116 of the Postal Services Act 2000.

TABLE:

TABLE: RATES OF REMUNERATION FOR LEGAL REPRESENTATIVES

| *Category of fee earner*[(1)] | *Standard hourly rate (excluding VAT)* | *Higher hourly rate (excluding VAT)* |
|---|---|---|
| **Solicitors and their employees** | | |
| Senior solicitor (of at least 8 years' standing) | £187.50 | £225.00 |

*Paragraph numbers marked with a "+" can be found online and on CD.*

| *Category of fee earner*[(1)] | *Standard hourly rate (excluding VAT)* | *Higher hourly rate (excluding VAT)* |
|---|---|---|
| Solicitor (of at least 4 years' and less than 8 years' standing) | £150.00 | £187.50 |
| Junior solicitor (of less than 4 years' standing) | £107.50 | £131.25 |
| Trainee solicitor, paralegal or other fee earner | £75.00 | £93.75 |
| **Counsel** | | |
| Queen's Counsel | — | £275.00 |
| Senior junior counsel (of at least 10 years' standing) | £150.00 | £225.00 |
| Junior counsel (of less than 10 years' standing) | £100.00 | £150.00 |
| (1)In relation to England and Wales, a reference to a number of years' standing as a solicitor or counsel to be interpreted as referring to that number of years' general qualification (within the meaning of section 71 of the 1990 Act). | | |

## Blood Tests (Evidence of Paternity) Regulations 1971

(S.I. 1971 No. 1861)

[As amended by the Transfer of Functions (Magistrates' Court and Family Law) Order 1992 (SI 1992/709), the Blood Tests (Evidence of Paternity) (Amendment) Regulations 2001 (SI 2001/773), the Blood Tests (Evidence of Paternity) (Amendment) Regulations 2004 (SI 2004/596), the Blood Tests (Evidence of Paternity) (Amendment) Regulations 2008 (SI 2008/972), the Health Professions (Operating Department Practitioners and Miscellaneous Amendments) Order 2004 (SI 2004/2033) and the Tests (Evidence of Paternity) (Amendment) Regulations 2008 (SI 2008/972).] 9B–1263

ARRANGEMENT OF SECTIONS



**Paragraph numbers marked with a "+" denote content that is available on White Book on Westlaw UK or the Civil Procedure CD.**

***Paragraph numbers marked with a "+" can be found online and on CD.***

## Reserve and Auxiliary Forces (Protection of Civil Interests) Act 1951

9B–1276.1 1951 (14 AND 15 GEO. 6 C.65)

ARRANGEMENT OF SECTIONS

PART I PROVISIONS AGAINST CERTAIN LEGAL REMEDIES



**Paragraph numbers marked with a "+" denote content that is available on White Book on Westlaw UK or the Civil Procedure CD.**

## Late Payment of Commercial Debts (Interest) Act 1998

9B–1325 (1998 C.20)

ARRANGEMENT OF SECTIONS

PART I

STATUTORY INTEREST ON QUALIFYING DEBTS



***Paragraph numbers marked with a "+" can be found online and on CD.***

*Introduction* —This Act applies where both contracting parties are acting in the course of business. Its aim is to encourage prompt payment in such cases but in pursuit of this aim uses the "stick" rather than the "carrot" by providing for payment of a fixed sum plus statutory interest at a penal rate in the event of late payment. Anti-avoidance provisions prevent contracting out.The Act was brought into force gradually by a series of statutory instruments and has been fully in force from August 7, 2002 (SI 2002/1673), and this applies to all commercial contracts (unless exempt—see below).

# PART I

## STATUTORY INTEREST ON QUALIFYING DEBTS

### Statutory interest

**1.**—(1) It is an implied term in a contract to which this Act applies that any qualifying debt created by the contract carries simple interest subject to and in accordance with this Part. **9B–1326**

(2) Interest carried under that implied term (in this Act referred to as "statutory interest") shall be treated, for the purposes of any rule of law or enactment (other than this Act) relating to interest on debts, in the same way as interest carried under an express contract term.

(3) This Part has effect subject to Part II (which in certain circumstances permits contract terms to oust or vary the right to statutory interest that would otherwise be conferred by virtue of the term implied by subsection (1)).

#### "implied term"/"express term"

The principle of the Act is to imply a term into commercial contracts but the implied term is then treated as an express term. **9B–1327**

***Paragraph numbers marked with a "+" can be found online and on CD.***

**"statutory interest"**

9B–1328 When suing for a debt which is covered by the Act the particulars of the claim should include a claim for:

> "statutory interest pursuant to the Late Payment of Commercial Debts (Interest) Act at [appropriate rate—see below] amounting to £x as at the date hereof and continuing at £y per day from today until judgment or sooner payment."

## Contracts to which Act applies

9B–1329 **2.**—(1) This Act applies to a contract for the supply of goods or services where the purchaser and the supplier are each acting in the course of a business, other than an excepted contract.

(2) In this Act "contract for the supply of goods or services" means—

(a) a contract of sale of goods; or

(b) a contract (other than a contract of sale of goods) by which a person does any, or any combination, of the things mentioned in subsection (3) for a consideration that is (or includes) a money consideration.

(3) Those things are—

(a) transferring or agreeing to transfer to another the property in goods;

(b) bailing or agreeing to bail goods to another by way of hire or, in Scotland, hiring or agreeing to hire goods to another; and

(c) agreeing to carry out a service.

(4) For the avoidance of doubt a contract of service or apprenticeship is not a contract for the supply of goods or services.

(5) The following are excepted contracts—

(a) a consumer credit agreement;

(b) a contract intended to operate by way of mortgage, pledge, charge or other security.

(6) [...]

(7) In this section—

"business" includes a profession and the activities of any government department or local or public authority;

"consumer credit agreement" has the same meaning as in the Consumer Credit Act 1974;

"contract of sale of goods" and "goods" have the same meaning as in the Sale of Goods Act 1979;

"government department" includes any part of the Scottish Administration;

"property in goods" means the general property in them and not merely a special property.

9B–1330 *Note*—Amended by the Late Payment of Commercial Debts (Scotland) Regulations 2002 (SSI 2002/335), reg.2(2).

**"in the course of a business"**

9B–1331 Only contracts where both supplier and purchaser are acting in the course of a business are covered by this Act. All such contracts are covered unless specifically exempted.

***Paragraph numbers marked with a "+" can be found online and on CD.***

**"excepted contracts"**

Excepted contracts include mortgage and contracts governed by the Consumer Credit Act 1974. **9B–1332**

*Note*—Section 2A applies to Scotland and is not reproduced here. **9B–1333**

## Qualifying debts

**3.**—(1) A debt created by virtue of an obligation under a contract to which this Act applies to pay the whole or any part of the contract price is a "qualifying debt" for the purposes of this Act, unless (when created) the whole of the debt is prevented from carrying statutory interest by this section. **9B–1334**

(2) A debt does not carry statutory interest if or to the extent that it consists of a sum to which a right to interest or to charge interest applies by virtue of any enactment (other than section 1 of this Act).

This subsection does not prevent a sum from carrying statutory interest by reason of the fact that a court, arbitrator or arbiter would, apart from this Act, have power to award interest on it.

(3) A debt does not carry (and shall be treated as never having carried) statutory interest if or to the extent that a right to demand interest on it, which exists by virtue of any rule of law, is exercised.

*Note*—Amended by the Late Payment of Commercial Debts (Scotland) Regulations, reg.2.(4) **9B–1335**

**"qualifying debt"**

The Act applies to a "qualifying debt" as defined. By s.3(1) it applies both to contracts providing for a lump sum payment and to those providing for stage payments. The Act is intended to deal with contracts not already subject to a different statutory regime: hence s.3(2). **9B–1336**

## Period for which statutory interest runs

**4.**—(1) Statutory interest runs in relation to a qualifying debt in accordance with this section (unless section 5 applies). **9B–1337**

(2) Statutory interest starts to run on the day after the relevant day for the debt, at the rate prevailing under section 6 at the end of the relevant day.

(3) Where the supplier and the purchaser agree a date for payment of the debt (that is, the day on which the debt is to be created by the contract), that is the relevant day unless the debt relates to an obligation to make an advance payment.

A date so agreed may be fixed one or may depend on the happening of an event or the failure of an event to happen.

(4) Where the debt relates to an obligation to make an advance payment, the relevant day is the day on which the debt is treated by section 11 as having been created.

(5) In any other case, the relevant day is the last day of the period of 30 days beginning with—

(a) the day on which the obligation of the supplier to which the debt relates is performed; or

(b) the day on which the purchaser has notice of the amount

*Paragraph numbers marked with a "+" can be found online and on CD.*

of the debt or (where that amount is unascertained) the sum which the supplier claims is the amount of the debt, whichever is the later.

(6) Where the debt is created by virtue of an obligation to pay a sum due in respect of a period of hire of goods, subsection (5)(a) has effect as if it referred to the last day of that period.

(7) Statutory interest ceases to run when the interest would cease to run if it were carried under an express contract term.

(8) In this section "advance payment" has the same meaning as in section 11.

#### When does the statutory interest start to run?

9B–1338 The question posed in this sub-heading is answered by s.4. Interest runs from the day after the "relevant day" as defined. Where a date has been agreed for payment that is the relevant day (s.4(3)). Where the contract provides for an advance payment see s.11. In other cases the relevant day is 30 days after the date specified in s.4(5).

### Remission of statutory interest

9B–1339 **5.**—(1) This section applies where, by reason of any conduct of the supplier, the interests of justice require that statutory interest should be remitted in whole or part in respect of a period for which it would otherwise run in relation to a qualifying debt.

(2) If the interests of justice require that the supplier should receive no statutory interest for a period, statutory interest shall not run for that period.

(3) If the interests of justice require that the supplier should receive statutory interest at a reduced rate for a period, statutory interest shall run at such rate as meets the justice of the case for that period.

(4) Remission of statutory interest under this section may be required—

(a) by reason of conduct at any time (whether before or after the time at which the debt is created); and

(b) for the whole period for which statutory interest would otherwise run or for one or more parts of that period.

(5) In this section "conduct" includes any act or omission.

#### Discretion

9B–1340 The effect of s.5 is to give the court a discretion to withhold statutory interest where the interests of justice so require. For example, interest may be awarded for a period less than that of the relevant day to the day of the judgment where the claimant has unreasonably delayed in either issuing or prosecuting the claim.

### Compensation arising out of late payment

9B–1341 **5A.**—(1) Once statutory interest begins to run in relation to a qualifying debt, the supplier shall be entitled to a fixed sum (in addition to the statutory interest on the debt).

(2) That sum shall be—

(a) for a debt less than £1,000, the sum of £40;

(b) for a debt of £1,000 or more, but less than £10,000, the sum of £70;

(c) for a debt of £10,000 or more, the sum of £100.

(3) The obligation to pay an additional fixed sum under this section in respect of a qualifying debt shall be treated as part of the term implied by section 1(1) in the contract creating the debt.

*Note* —Amended by the Late Payment of Commercial Debts (Scotland) Regulations (SSI 2002/335) reg.2(5). **9B–1342**

#### Compensation payment

In addition to statutory interest at a penal rate (see below) the claimant is entitled to a fixed sum as provided for by s.5A(2). **9B–1343**

### Rate of statutory interest

**6.**—(1) The Secretary of State shall by order made with the consent of the Treasury set the rate of statutory interest by prescribing— **9B–1344**

(a) a formula for calculating the rate of statutory interest; or

(b) the rate of statutory interest.

(2) Before making such an order the Secretary of State shall, among other things, consider the extent to which it may be desirable to set the rate so as to—

(a) protect suppliers whose financial position makes them particularly vulnerable if their qualifying debts are paid late; and

(b) deter generally the late payment of qualifying debts.

#### "rate of statutory interest"

The rate of statutory interest prescribed pursuant to s.6 is currently that set out in the Late Payment of Commercial Debts (Rate of Interest) (No.3) Order 2002 (SI 2002/1675). The rate is eight per cent above the official bank rate. For all relevant rates see Vol.1 para. 7.0.17(h). Paragraph 4 of SI 2002/1675 provides that the rate is eight per cent above the official bank rate in force on the June 30 (in respect of interest which starts to run between July 1 and December 31) or on the December 31 (in respect of interest which starts to run between January 1 and June 30) immediately before the day on which statutory interest starts to run. **9B–1345**

SI 2002/1675 refers to "the official dealing rate" but this is the rate now known as the official bank rate, as set out at para. 7.0.17(h). (Somewhat unhelpfully the statutory instrument's "explanatory note" mentions the "repo" rate which is no longer in use.)

#### Editorial note

Sections 7 to 10 set out the anti-avoidance provisions of the Act, but see also ss.12 and 14. **9B–1346**

## PART II

## CONTRACT TERMS RELATING TO LATE PAYMENT OF QUALIFYING DEBTS

### Purpose of Part II

**7.**—(1) This Part deals with the extent to which the parties to a contract to which this Act applies may by reference to contract terms oust or vary the right to statutory interest that would otherwise apply when a qualifying debt created by the contract (in this Part referred to as "the debt") is not paid. **9B–1347**

*Paragraph numbers marked with a "+" can be found online and on CD.*

(2) This Part applies to contract terms agreed before the debt is created; after that time the parties are free to agree terms dealing with the debt.

(3) This Part has effect without prejudice to any other ground which may affect the validity of a contract term.

#### Forbearance

9B–1348 The anti-avoidance provisions are intended to prevent a commercial contract excluding the provisions of the Act. Thus Pt II applies to contract terms agreed before the debt is created and by s.7(2), does not apply to later terms agreed by the parties dealing with the debt e.g. a term whereby the creditor later agrees to forego interest if payment is made by a new agreed date.

### Circumstances where statutory interest may be ousted or varied

9B–1349 **8.**—(1) Any contract terms are void to the extent that they purport to exclude the right to statutory interest in relation to the debt, unless there is a substantial contractual remedy for late payment of the debt.

(2) Where the parties agree a contractual remedy for late payment of the debt that is a substantial remedy, statutory interest is not carried by the debt (unless they agree otherwise).

(3) The parties may not agree to vary the right to statutory interest in relation to the debt unless either the right to statutory interest as varied or the overall remedy for late payment of the debt is a substantial remedy.

(4) Any contract terms are void to the extent that they purport to—

(a) confer a contractual right to interest that is not a substantial remedy for late payment of the debt, or

(b) vary the right to statutory interest so as to provide for a right to statutory interest that is not a substantial remedy for late payment of the debt,

unless the overall remedy for late payment of the debt is a substantial remedy.

(5) Subject to this section, the parties are free to agree contract terms which deal with the consequences of late payment of the debt.

#### Limited contracting out

9B–1350 Section 8, the key anti-avoidance provision, renders void any contract term which merely purports to exclude the right to statutory interest. Contracting parties are free to agree an alternative to statutory interest provided that it is a "substantial remedy".

### Meaning of "substantial remedy"

9B–1351 **9.**—(1) A remedy for the late payment of the debt shall be regarded as a substantial remedy unless—

(a) the remedy is insufficient either for the purpose of compensating the supplier for late payment or for deterring late payment; and

(b) it would not be fair or reasonable to allow the remedy to be relied on to oust or (as the case may be) to vary the right to statutory interest that would otherwise apply in relation to the debt.

(2) In determining whether a remedy is not a substantial remedy, regard shall be had to all the relevant circumstances at the time the terms in question are agreed.

(3) In determining whether subsection (1)(b) applies, regard shall be had (without prejudice to the generality of subsection (2)) to the following matters—

(a) the benefits of commercial certainty;

(b) the strength of the bargaining positions of the parties relative to each other;

(c) whether the term was imposed by one party to the detriment of the other (whether by the use of standard terms or otherwise); and

(d) whether the supplier received an inducement to agree to the term.

**"substantial remedy"**

Any term purporting to exclude the right to statutory interest is void (see s.8 above) **9B–1352**
but a "substantial remedy" can be agreed instead. To be "substantial" the remedy must fulfil the Act's primary aim of deterring late payment or, alternatively be sufficient to compensate for late payment. Additionally, it must be fair and reasonable to allow the remedy to be relied on to deny, or vary, the right to statutory interest. In deciding this all the circumstances at the time the contract was agreed are relevant (see s.9(2)) and, without prejudice to this, the factors in s.9(3) will be considered.

## Interpretation of Part II

**10.**—(1) In this Part— **9B–1353**

"contract term" means a term of the contract creating the debt or any other contract term binding the parties (or either of them);

"contractual remedy" means a contractual right to interest or any contractual remedy other than interest;

"contractual right to interest" includes a reference to a contractual right to charge interest;

"overall remedy", in relation to the late payment of the debt, means any combination of a contractual right to interest, a varied right to statutory interest or a contractual remedy other than interest;

"substantial remedy" shall be construed in accordance with section 9.

(2) In this Part a reference (however worded) to contract terms which vary the right to statutory interest is a reference to terms altering in any way the effect of Part I in relation to the debt (for example by postponing the time at which interest starts to run or by imposing conditions on the right to interest).

(3) In this Part a reference to late payment of the debt is a reference to late payment of the sum due when the debt is created (excluding any part of that sum which is prevented from carrying statutory interest by section 3).

***Paragraph numbers marked with a "+" can be found online and on CD.***

# PART III

## GENERAL AND SUPPLEMENTARY

### Treatment of advance payments of the contract price

9B–1354 **11.**—(1) A qualifying debt created by virtue of an obligation to make an advance payment shall be treated for the purposes of this Act as if it was created on the day mentioned in subsection (3), (4) or (5) (as the case may be).

(2) In this section "advance payment" means a payment falling due before the obligation of the supplier to which the whole contract price relates ("the supplier's obligation") is performed, other than a payment of a part of the contract price that is due in respect of any part performance of that obligation and payable on or after the day on which that part performance is completed.

(3) Where the advance payment is the whole contract price, the debt shall be treated as created on the day on which the supplier's obligation is performed.

(4) Where the advance payment is a part of the contract price, but the sum is not due in respect of any part performance of the supplier's obligation, the debt shall be treated as created on the day on which the supplier's obligation is performed.

(5) Where the advance payment is a part of the contract price due in respect of any part performance of the supplier's obligation, but is payable before that part performance is completed, the debt shall be treated as created on the day on which the relevant part performance is completed.

(6) Where the debt is created by virtue of an obligation to pay a sum due in respect of a period of hire of goods, this section has effect as if—

(a) references to the day on which the supplier's obligation is performed were references to the last day of that period; and

(b) references to part performance of that obligation were references to part of that period.

(7) For the purposes of this section an obligation to pay the whole outstanding balance of the contract price shall be regarded as an obligation to pay the whole contract price and not as an obligation to pay a part of the contract price.

**"advance payment"**

9B–1355 The Act applies not merely to a conventional contract, e.g. where goods are supplied and payment is then due, but also to contracts where some or all of the payment is to be made in advance. The right to statutory interest arises where the advance payment is not made and s.11 defines the date when the debt is deemed to have been created for the purpose of statutory interest.

### Conflict of laws

9B–1356 **12.**—(1) This Act does not have effect in relation to a contract governed by the law of a part of the United Kingdom by choice of the parties if—

*Paragraph numbers marked with a "+" can be found online and on CD.*

(a) there is no significant connection between the contract and that part of the United Kingdom; and

(b) but for that choice, the applicable law would be a foreign law.

(2) This Act has effect in relation to a contract governed by a foreign law by choice of the parties if—

(a) but for that choice, the applicable law would be the law of a part of the United Kingdom; and

(b) there is no significant connection between the contract and any country other than that part of the United Kingdom.

(3) In this section—

"contract" means a contract falling within section 2(1); and

"foreign law" means the law of a country outside the United Kingdom.

**"conflict of laws"**

Although s.12 has the title "conflict of laws", s.12(2) is in reality an anti-avoidance provision. It prevents the Act being disapplied by a term stating that the contract is governed by a foreign law when in reality the contract has no connection with the foreign country and would otherwise be governed by the law of a part of the United Kingdom. Section 12(1) operates the other way round to disapply the Act in contracts expressed to be governed by the law of a part of the United Kingdom but which otherwise have no connection with the United Kingdom and the applicable law would be a foreign law. **9B–1357**

## Assignments, etc.

**13.**—(1) The operation of this Act in relation to a qualifying debt is not affected by— **9B–1358**

(a) any change in the identity of the parties to the contract creating the debt; or

(b) the passing of the right to be paid the debt, or the duty to pay it (in whole or in part) to a person other than the person who is the original creditor or the original debtor when the debt is created.

(2) Any reference in this Act to the supplier or the purchaser is a reference to the person who is for the time being the supplier or the purchaser or, in relation to a time after the debt in question has been created, the person who is for the time being the creditor or the debtor, as the case may be.

(3) Where the right to be paid part of a debt passes to a person other than the person who is the original creditor when the debt is created, any reference in this Act to a debt shall be construed as (or, if the context so requires, as including) a reference to part of a debt.

(4) A reference in this section to the identity of the parties to a contract changing, or to a right or duty passing, is a reference to it changing or passing by assignment or assignation, by operation of law or otherwise.

**"change in identity of the parties"**

The effect of the Act is not affected by a change in the identity of the parties (e.g. by assignment under a factoring agreement). **9B–1359**

## Contract terms relating to the date for payment of the contract price

9B-1360 **14.**—(1) This section applies to any contract term which purports to have the effect of postponing the time at which a qualifying debt would otherwise be created by a contract to which this Act applies.

(2) Sections 3(2)(b) and 17(1)(b) of the Unfair Contract Terms Act 1977 (no reliance to be placed on certain contract terms) shall apply in cases where such a contract term is not contained in written standard terms of the purchaser as well as in cases where the term is contained in such standard terms.

(3) In this section "contract term" has the same meaning as in section 10(1).

### Postponing payment

9B-1361 Section 14 is in reality another anti-avoidance provision. Any term purporting to have the effect of postponing the time at which a qualifying debt would otherwise have been created is subject to s.3(2)(b) and 17(1)(b) of the Unfair Contract Terms Act 1977 (see para. 3H-555).

## Orders and regulations

9B-1362 **15.**—(1) Any power to make an order or regulations under this Act is exercisable by statutory instrument.

(2) Any statutory instrument containing an order or regulations under this Act, other than an order under section 17(2), shall be subject to annulment in pursuance of a resolution of either House of Parliament.

## Interpretation

9B-1363 **16.**—(1) In this Act—

"contract for the supply of goods or services" has the meaning given in section 2(2);

"contract price" means the price in a contract of sale of goods or the money consideration referred to in section 2(2)(b) in any other contract for the supply of goods or services;

"purchaser" means (subject to section 13(2)) the buyer in a contract of sale or the person who contracts with the supplier in any other contract for the supply of goods or services;

"qualifying debt" means a debt falling within section 3(1);

"statutory interest" means interest carried by virtue of the term implied by section 1(1); and

"supplier" means (subject to section 13(2)) the seller in a contract of sale of goods or the person who does one or more of the things mentioned in section 2(3) in any other contract for the supply of goods or services.

(2) In this Act any reference (however worded) to an agreement or to contract terms includes a reference to both express and implied terms (including terms established by a course of dealing or by such usage as binds the parties).

## Short title, commencement and extent

9B-1364 **17.**—(1) This Act may be cited as the Late Payment of Commercial Debts (Interest) Act 1998.

(2) This Act (apart from this section) shall come into force on such day as the Secretary of State may by order appoint; and different days may be appointed for different descriptions of contract or for other different purposes.

An order under this subsection may specify a description of contract by reference to any feature of the contract (including the parties).

(3) The Secretary of State may by regulations make such transitional, supplemental or incidental provision (including provision modifying any provision of this Act) as the Secretary of State may consider necessary or expedient in connection with the operation of this Act while it is not fully in force.

(4) This Act does not affect contracts of any description made before this Act comes into force for contracts of that description.

(5) This Act extends to Northern Ireland.

# SECTION 10

# 10 COURT FEES



## The Civil Proceedings Fees Order 2008

2008 1053 (L. 5)

CITATION AND COMMENCEMENT

**1.**—(1) This Order may be cited as the Civil Proceedings Fees Order 2008 and shall come into force on 1st May 2008. **10–1**

(2) In this Order—

(a) "CCBC" means County Court Bulk Centre;

(b) "the CPR" means the Civil Procedure Rules 1998;

(c) "LSC" means the Legal Services Commission established under section 1 of the Access to Justice Act 1999[1];

(d) expressions also used in the CPR have the same meaning as in those Rules.

*Note*—Amended by the Civil Proceedings Fees (Amendment) Order 2008 (SI 2008/2853). **10–1.1**

FEES PAYABLE

**2.** The fees set out in column 2 of Schedule 1 are payable in the Supreme Court and in county courts in respect of the items described in column 1 in accordance with and subject to the directions specified in that column. **10–2**

**3.** No fee is payable in respect of— **10–3**

(a) non-contentious probate business;

(b) the enrolment of documents;

(c) criminal proceedings (except proceedings on the Crown side of the Queen's Bench Division to which the fees in Schedule 1 are applicable);

(d) proceedings by sheriffs, under-sheriffs, deputy-sheriffs or other officers of the sheriff; or

(e) family proceedings in the High Court or in a county court.

**4.** Where by any convention entered into by Her Majesty with any foreign power it is provided that no fee is required to be paid in respect of any proceedings, the fees specified in this Order are not payable in respect of those proceedings. **10–4**

REMISSIONS AND PART REMISSIONS

**5.** Schedule 2 applies for the purpose of ascertaining whether a party is entitled to a remission or part remission of a fee prescribed by this Order. **10–5**

REVOCATIONS

**6.** The instruments listed in column 1 of the table in Schedule 3 (which have the references listed in column 2) are revoked. **10–6**

---

[1] Sections 1 and 9 were amended by S.I. 2005/3429.

ARTICLE 2

## SCHEDULE 1

FEES TO BE TAKEN

10–7

| *Column 1*<br>*Number and description of fee* | *Column 2*<br>*Amount of fee* |
|---|---|
| **1 Starting proceedings (High Court and county court)** | |
| 1.1 On starting proceedings (including proceedings issued after permission to issue is granted but excluding Claim Production Centre cases brought by Centre users or cases brought by Money Claim OnLine users) to recover a sum of money where the sum claimed— | |
| (a) does not exceed £300; | £30 |
| (b) exceeds £300 but does not exceed £500; | £45 |
| (c) exceeds £500 but does not exceed £1,000; | £65 |
| (d) exceeds £1,000 but does not exceed £1,500; | £75 |
| (e) exceeds £1,500 but does not exceed £3,000; | £85 |
| (f) exceeds £3,000 but does not exceed £5,000; | £108 |
| (g) exceeds £5,000 but does not exceed £15,000; | £225 |
| (h) exceeds £15,000 but does not exceed £50,000; | £360 |
| (i) exceeds £50,000 but does not exceed £100,000; | £630 |
| (j) exceeds £100,000 but does not exceed £150,000; | £810 |
| (k) exceeds £150,000 but does not exceed £200,000; | £990 |
| (l) exceeds £200,000 but does not exceed £250,000; | £1,170 |
| (m) exceeds £250,000 but does not exceed £300,000; | £1,350 |
| (n) exceeds £300,000 or is not limited. | £1,530 |
| 1.2 On starting proceedings to recover a sum of money in Claim Production Centre cases brought by Centre users, where the sum claimed— | |
| (a) does not exceed £300; | £15 |
| (b) exceeds £300 but does not exceed £500; | £30 |
| (c) exceeds £500 but does not exceed £1,000; | £55 |
| (d) exceeds £1,000 but does not exceed £1,500; | £65 |
| (e) exceeds £1,500 but does not exceed £3,000; | £75 |
| (f) exceeds £3,000 but does not exceed £5,000; | £85 |
| (g) exceeds £5,000 but does not exceed £25,000; | £190 |
| (h) exceeds £25,000 but does not exceed £50,000; | £310 |
| (i) exceeds £50,000 but does not exceed £100,000. | £550 |
| 1.3 On starting proceedings to recover a sum of money brought by Money Claim OnLine users where the sum claimed— | |
| (a) does not exceed £300; | £25 |
| (b) exceeds £300 but does not exceed £500; | £35 |
| (c) exceeds £500 but does not exceed £1,000; | £60 |
| (d) exceeds £1,000 but does not exceed £1,500; | £70 |
| (e) exceeds £1,500 but does not exceed £3,000; | £80 |
| (f) exceeds £3,000 but does not exceed £5,000; | £100 |
| (g) exceeds £5,000 but does not exceed £25,000; | £210 |

| *Column 1*<br>*Number and description of fee* | *Column 2*<br>*Amount of fee* |
|---|---|
| (h) exceeds £25,000 but does not exceed £50,000; | £340 |
| (i) exceeds £50,000 but does not exceed £100,000. | £595 |
| Fees 1.1, 1.2 and 1.3.<br>Where the claimant is making a claim for interest on a specified sum of money, the amount on which the fee is calculated is the total amount of the claim and the interest. | |
| 1.4 On starting proceedings for the recovery of land— | |
| (a) in the High Court; | £400 |
| (b) in the county court, other than where fee 1.4(c) applies; | £150 |
| (c) using the Possession Claims Online website. | £100 |
| 1.5 On starting proceedings for any other remedy (including proceedings issued after permission to issue is granted)— | |
| — in the High Court | £400 |
| — in the county court | £150 |
| Fees 1.1, 1.4 and 1.5. Recovery of land or goods.<br>Where a claim for money is additional or alternative to a claim for recovery of land or goods, only fee 1.4 or 1.5 is payable. | |
| Fees 1.1and 1.5. Claims other than recovery of land or goods.<br>Where a claim for money is additional to a non money claim (other than a claim for recovery of land or goods), then fee 1.1 is payable in addition to fee 1.5. | |
| Where a claim for money is alternative to a non money claim (other than a claim for recovery of land or goods), only fee 1.1 is payable in the High Court, and, in the county court, whichever is greater of fee 1.1 or fee 1.5 is payable. | |
| Fees 1.1 and 1.5.<br>Where more than one non money claim is made in the same proceedings, fee 1.5 is payable once only, in addition to any fee which may be payable under fee 1.1. | |
| Fees 1.1 and 1.5 are not payable where fee 1.8(b), fee 1.9(a), fee 10.1 or fee 3 applies. | |
| Fees 1.1 and fee 1.5. Amendment of claim or counterclaim.<br>Where the claim or counterclaim is amended, and the fee paid before amendment is less than that which would have been payable if the document, as amended, had been so drawn in the first instance, the party amending the document must pay the difference. | |
| 1.6 On the filing of proceedings against a party or parties not named in the proceedings. | £40 |

***Paragraph numbers marked with a "+" can be found online and on CD.***

| *Column 1*<br>*Number and description of fee* | *Column 2*<br>*Amount of fee* |
|---|---|
| Fee 1.6 is payable by a defendant who adds or substitutes a party or parties to the proceedings or by a claimant who adds or substitutes a defendant or defendants. | |
| 1.7 On the filing of a counterclaim. | The same fee as if the remedy sought were the subject of separate proceedings |
| No fee is payable on a counterclaim which a defendant is required to make under rule 57.8 of the CPR (requirement to serve a counterclaim if a defendant makes a claim or seeks a remedy in relation to a grant of probate of a will, or letters of administration of an estate, of a deceased person). | |
| 1.8 (a) On an application for permission to issue proceedings. | £40 |
| (b) On an application for an order under Part 3 of the Solicitors Act 1974 for the assessment of costs payable to a solicitor by a client or on starting costs-only proceedings. | £40 |
| 1.9(a) On starting proceedings for judicial review. | £50 |
| Where the court has made an order giving permission to proceed with a claim for judicial review, there is payable by the claimant within 7 days of service on the claimant of that order: | |
| 1.9(b) if the judicial review procedure has been started. | £180 |
| 1.9(c) if the claim for judicial review was started otherwise than by using the judicial review procedure. | £50 |
| **2 General Fees (High Court and county courts)** | |
| 2.1 On the claimant filing an allocation questionnaire; or | |
| where the court dispenses with the need for an allocation questionnaire, within 14 days of the date of despatch of the notice of allocation to track; or<br>where the CPR or a Practice Direction provide for automatic allocation or provide that the rules on allocation do not apply, within 28 days of the filing of the defence (or the filing of the last defence if there is more than one defendant), or within 28 days of the expiry of the time permitted for filing all defences if sooner— | |
| (a) if the case is on the small claims track and the claim exceeds £1,500; | £35 |
| (b) if the case is on the fast track or multi-track. | £200 |
| Fee 2.1 is payable by the claimant except where the action is proceeding on the counterclaim alone, when it is payable by the defendant—<br>— on the defendant filing an allocation questionnaire; or | |

*Paragraph numbers marked with a "+" can be found online and on CD.*

| *Column 1* *Number and description of fee* | *Column 2* *Amount of fee* |
|---|---|
| — where the court dispenses with the need for an allocation questionnaire, within 14 days of the date of despatch of the notice of allocation to track; or<br>— where the CPR or a Practice Direction provide for automatic allocation or provide that the rules on allocation do not apply, within 28 days of the filing of the defence to the counterclaim (or the filing of the last defence to the counterclaim if there is more than one party entitled to file a defence to the counterclaim), or within 28 days of the expiry of the time permitted for filing all defences to the counterclaim if sooner.<br>Where fee 2.1 is payable on the filing of an allocation questionnaire, by the claimant or the defendant as the case may be, the fee payable is based on the track for the case specified in the allocation questionnaire. If the case is subsequently allocated to a track which attracts a higher fee then the difference in fee is payable, by the party liable to pay the fee, within 14 days of the date of despatch of notice of allocation to track. If the case is allocated to a track which attracts a lower fee the difference in fee will be refunded. | |
| 2.2 On the claimant filing a pre-trial check list (listing questionnaire); or where the court fixes the trial date or trial week without the need for a pre-trial check list, within 14 days of the date of despatch of the notice (or the date when oral notice is given if no written notice is given) of the trial week or the trial date if no trial week is fixed. | £100 |
| Fee 2.2 is payable by the claimant except where the action is proceeding on the counterclaim alone, when it is payable by the defendant—<br>— on the defendant filing a pre-trial check list; or<br>— where the court fixes the trial date or trial week without the need for a pre-trial check list, within 14 days of the date of despatch of the notice (or the date when oral notice is given if no written notice is given) of the trial week or the trial date if no trial week is fixed. | |
| Fees 2.1 and 2.2 in the High Court and the county court.<br>Fees 2.1 and 2.2 are payable as appropriate where the court allocates a case to track for a trial of the assessment of damages.<br>Fees 2.1 and 2.2 are not payable in relation to claims managed under a Group Litigation Order after that Order is made.<br>Fees 2.1 and 2.2 are payable once only in the same proceedings. | |

***Paragraph numbers marked with a "+" can be found online and on CD.***

| *Column 1*<br>*Number and description of fee* | *Column 2*<br>*Amount of fee* |
|---|---|
| Fee 2.1 is not payable where the procedure in Part 8 of the CPR is used.<br>Fee 2.2 is not payable where the court fixed the hearing date on the issue of the claim. | |
| Fees 2.1 and 2.2 in the county court.<br>Fee 2.1 is not payable in proceedings where the only claim is a claim to recover a sum of money and the sum claimed does not exceed £1,500.<br>Fee 2.2 is not payable in respect of a case on the small claims track. | |
| 2.3 On the occasion of fee 2.2 becoming payable; or where the claim is on the small claims track, within 14 days of the date of despatch of the notice (or the date when oral notice is given if no written notice is given) of the trial week or the trial date if no trial week is fixed a fee payable for the hearing of— | |
| (a) a case on the multi-track; | £1,000 |
| (b) a case on the fast track; | £500 |
| (c) a case on the small claims track where the sum claimed— | |
| (i) does not exceed £300; | £25 |
| (ii) exceeds £300 but does not exceed £500; | £50 |
| (iii) exceeds £500 but does not exceed £1,000; | £75 |
| (iv) exceeds £1,000 but does not exceed £1,500; | £100 |
| (v) exceeds £1,500 but does not exceed £3,000; | £150 |
| (vi) exceeds £3,000. | £300 |
| Fee 2.3 is payable by the claimant except where the action is proceeding on the counterclaim alone, when it is payable by the defendant—<br>— on the defendant filing a pre-trial check list; or<br>— where the claim is on the small claims track or the court fixes the trial date or trial week without the need for a pre-trial check list, within 14 days of the date of despatch of the notice (or the date when oral notice is given if no written notice is given) of the trial week or the trial date if no trial week is fixed.<br>Where a case is on the multi-track or fast track and, after a hearing date has been fixed, the court receives notice in writing from the party who paid the hearing fee that the case has been settled or discontinued then the following percentages of the hearing fee will be refunded—<br>(i) 100% if the court is notified more than 28 days before the hearing;<br>(ii) 75% if the court is notified between 15 and 28 days before the hearing; | |

| *Column 1*<br>*Number and description of fee* | *Column 2*<br>*Amount of fee* |
|---|---|
| (iii) 50% if the court is notified between 7 and 14 days before the hearing.<br>Where a case is on the small claims track and, after a hearing date has been fixed, the court receives notice in writing from the party who paid the hearing fee, at least 7 days before the date set for the hearing, that the case has been settled or discontinued the hearing fee will be refunded in full.<br>Fee 2.3 is not payable in respect of a case where the court fixed the hearing date on the issue of the claim. | |
| 2.4 In the High Court on filing—<br>— an appellant's notice, or<br>— a respondent's notice where the respondent is appealing or wishes to ask the appeal court to uphold the order of the lower court for reasons different from or additional to those given by the lower court. | £200 |
| 2.5 In the county court on filing—<br>— an appellant's notice, or<br>— a respondent's notice where the respondent is appealing or wishes to ask the appeal court to uphold the order of the lower court for reasons different from or additional to those given by the lower court— | |
| (a) in a claim allocated to the small claims track; | £100 |
| (b) in all other claims. | £120 |
| Fees 2.4 and 2.5 do not apply on appeals against a decision made in detailed assessment proceedings. | |
| 2.6 On an application on notice where no other fee is specified. | £75 |
| 2.7 On an application by consent or without notice where no other fee is specified. | £40 |
| For the purpose of fee 2.7 a request for a judgment or order on admission or in default does not constitute an application and no fee is payable.<br>Fee 2.7 is not payable in relation to an application by consent for an adjournment of a hearing where the application is received by the court at least 14 days before the date set for that hearing. | |
| Fees 2.6 and 2.7 is not payable when an application is made in an appeal notice or is filed at the same time as an appeal notice. | |
| 2.8 On an application for a summons or order for a witness to attend court to be examined on oath or an order for evidence to be taken by deposition, other than an application for which fee 7.2 or 8.3 is payable. | £35 |
| 2.9 On an application to vary a judgment or suspend enforcement, including an application to suspend a warrant of possession. | |

***Paragraph numbers marked with a "+" can be found online and on CD.***

| *Column 1*<br>*Number and description of fee* | *Column 2*<br>*Amount of fee* |
|---|---|
| Where more than one remedy is sought in the same application only one fee is payable. | £35 |
| 2.10 Register of judgments, orders and fines kept under section 98 of the Courts Act 2003 — | |
| On a request for the issue of a certificate of satisfaction. | £15 |
| **3 Companies Act 1985, Companies Act 2006 and Insolvency Act 1986 (High Court and county court)** | |
| 3.1 On entering a bankruptcy petition— | |
| (a) if presented by a debtor or the personal representative of a deceased debtor; | £150 |
| (b) if presented by a creditor or other person. | £190 |
| 3.2 On entering a petition for an administration order. | £150 |
| 3.3 On entering any other petition. | £190 |
| One fee only is payable where more than one petition is presented in relation to a partnership. | |
| 3.4(a) On a request for a certificate of discharge from bankruptcy. | £60 |
| (b) and after the first certificate, for each copy. | £5 |
| 3.5 On an application under the Companies Act 1985, the Companies Act 2006 or the Insolvency Act 1986 other than one brought by petition and where no other fee is specified. | £130 |
| Fee 3.5 is not payable where the application is made in existing proceedings. | |
| 3.6 On an application for the conversion of a voluntary arrangement into a winding up or bankruptcy under Article 37 of Council Regulation (EC) No 1346/2000. | £130 |
| 3.7 On an application, for the purposes of Council Regulation (EC) No 1346/2000, for an order confirming creditors' voluntary winding up (where the company has passed a resolution for voluntary winding up, and no declaration under section 89 of the Insolvency Act 1986 has been made). | £30 |
| 3.8 On filing—<br>— a notice of intention to appoint an administrator under paragraph 14 of Schedule B1 to the Insolvency Act 1986 or in accordance with paragraph 27 of that Schedule; or<br>— a notice of appointment of an administrator in accordance with paragraphs 18 or 29 of that Schedule. | £30 |
| Where a person pays fee 3.8 on filing a notice of intention to appoint an administrator, no fee is payable on that same person filing a notice of appointment of that administrator. | |
| 3.9 On submitting a nominee's report under section 2(2) of the Insolvency Act 1986. | £30 |

***Paragraph numbers marked with a "+" can be found online and on CD.***

| *Column 1* *Number and description of fee* | *Column 2* *Amount of fee* |
|---|---|
| 3.10 On filing documents in accordance with paragraph 7(1) of Schedule A1 to the Insolvency Act 1986. | £30 |
| 3.11 On an application by consent or without notice within existing proceedings where no other fee is specified. | £30 |
| 3.12 On an application with notice within existing proceedings where no other fee is specified. | £60 |
| 3.13 On a search in person of the bankruptcy and companies records, in a county court. | £40 |
| Requests and applications with no fee. No fee is payable on a request or on an application to the Court by the Official Receiver when applying only in the capacity of Official Receiver to the case (and not as trustee or liquidator), or on an application to set aside a statutory demand. | |
| **4 Copy Documents** (Court of Appeal, High Court and county court) | |
| 4.1 On a request for a copy of a document (other than where fee 4.2 applies)— | |
| (a) for ten pages or less; and | £5 |
| (b) for each subsequent page. | 50p |
| Note: The fee payable under fee 4.1 includes— • where the court allows a party to fax to the court for the use of that party a document that has not been requested by the court and is not intended to be placed on the court file. • where a party requests that the court fax a copy of a document from the court file. • the court provides a subsequent copy of a document which it has previously provided. | |
| 4.2 On a request for a copy of a document on a computer disk or in other electronic form, for each such copy. | £5 |
| **5 Determination of costs** (Supreme Court and county court) Fee 5 does not apply to the determination in the Supreme Court of costs incurred in the Court of Protection. | |
| 5.1 On the filing of a request for detailed assessment where the party filing the request is legally aided or is funded by the LSC and no other party is ordered to pay the costs of the proceedings. | £140 |
| 5.2 On the filing of a request for detailed assessment in any case where fee 5.1 does not apply; or on the filing of a request for a hearing date for the assessment of costs payable to a solicitor by a client pursuant to an order under Part 3 of the Solicitors Act 1974 where the amount of the costs claimed— | |
| (a) does not exceed £25,000; | £300 |
| (b) exceeds £25,000 but does not exceed £50,000; | £600 |

***Paragraph numbers marked with a "+" can be found online and on CD.***

| *Column 1* *Number and description of fee* | *Column 2* *Amount of fee* |
|---|---|
| (c) exceeds £50,000 but does not exceed £100,000; | £900 |
| (d) exceeds £100,000 but does not exceed £150,000; | £1,200 |
| (e) exceeds £150,000 but does not exceed £200,000; | £1,500 |
| (f) exceeds £200,000 but does not exceed £300,000; | £2,250 |
| (g) exceeds £300,000 but does not exceed £500,000; | £3,750 |
| (h) exceeds £500,000. | £5,000 |
| Where there is a combined party and party and legal aid, or a combined party and party and LSC, or a combined party and party, legal aid and LSC determination of costs, fee 5.2 will be attributed proportionately to the party and party, legal aid, or LSC (as the case may be) portions of the bill on the basis of the amount allowed. | |
| 5.3 On a request for the issue of a default costs certificate. | £60 |
| 5.4 On an appeal against a decision made in detailed assessment proceedings. | £200 |
| 5.5 On applying for the court's approval of a certificate of costs payable from the Community Legal Service Fund. | £50 |
| Fee 5.5 is payable at the time of applying for the court's approval and is recoverable only against the Community Legal Service Fund. | |
| 5.6 On a request or application to set aside a default costs certificate. | £100 |
| **6 Determination in the Supreme Court of costs incurred in the Court of Protection** | |
| 6.1 On the filing of a request for detailed assessment— | |
| (a) where the amount of the costs to be assessed (excluding VAT and disbursements) does not exceed £3,000; | £100 |
| (b) in all other cases. | £200 |
| 6.2 On an appeal against a decision made in detailed assessment proceedings. | £60 |
| 6.3 On a request or application to set aside a default costs certificate. | £60 |
| **7 Enforcement in the High Court** | |
| 7.1 On sealing a writ of execution/possession/delivery. | £50 |
| Where the recovery of a sum of money is sought in addition to a writ of possession and delivery, no further fee is payable. | |
| 7.2 On an application for an order requiring a judgment debtor or other person to attend court to provide information in connection with enforcement of a judgment or order. | £50 |
| 7.3(a) On an application for a third party debt order or the appointment of a receiver by way of equitable execution. | £100 |
| (b) On an application for a charging order. | £100 |

***Paragraph numbers marked with a "+" can be found online and on CD.***

| *Column 1* *Number and description of fee* | *Column 2* *Amount of fee* |
|---|---|
| Fee 7.3(a) is payable in respect of each third party against whom the order is sought. Fee 7.3(b) is payable in respect of each charging order applied for. | |
| 7.4 On an application for a judgment summons. | £100 |
| 7.5 On a request or application to register a judgment or order, or for permission to enforce an arbitration award, or for a certificate or a certified copy of a judgment or order for use abroad. | £50 |
| **8 Enforcement in the county court** | |
| 8.1 On an application for or in relation to enforcement of a judgment or order of a county court or through a county court, by the issue of a warrant of execution against goods except a warrant to enforce payment of a fine — | |
| (a) in cases other than CCBC cases; | £100 |
| (b) in CCBC cases. | £70 |
| 8.2 On a request for a further attempt at execution of a warrant at a new address following a notice of the reason for non-execution (except a further attempt following suspension and CCBC cases brought by Centre users). | £25 |
| 8.3 On an application for an order requiring a judgment debtor or other person to attend court to provide information in connection with enforcement of a judgment or order. | £50 |
| 8.4(a) On an application for a third party debt order or the appointment of a receiver by way of equitable execution. | £100 |
| (b) On an application for a charging order. | £100 |
| Fee 8.4(a) is payable in respect of each third party against whom the order is sought. Fee 8.4(b) is payable in respect of each charging order applied for. | |
| 8.5 On an application for a judgment summons. | £100 |
| 8.6 On the issue of a warrant of possession or a warrant of delivery. | £95 |
| Where the recovery of a sum of money is sought in addition, no further fee is payable. | |
| 8.7 On an application for an attachment of earnings order (other than a consolidated attachment of earnings order) to secure payment of a judgment debt. | £100 |
| Fee 8.7 is payable for each defendant against whom an order is sought. Fee 8.7 is not payable where the attachment of earnings order is made on the hearing of a judgment summons. | |
| 8.8 On a consolidated attachment of earnings order or on an administration order. | For every £1 or part of a £1 of the money paid into court in respect of debts due to creditors — 10p |

*Paragraph numbers marked with a "+" can be found online and on CD.*

| *Column 1* *Number and description of fee* | *Column 2* *Amount of fee* |
|---|---|
| Fee 8.8 is calculated on any money paid into court under any order at the rate in force at the time when the order was made (or, where the order has been amended, at the time of the last amendment before the date of payment). | |
| 8.9 On an application for the enforcement of an award for a sum of money or other decision made by any court, tribunal, body or person other than the High Court or a county court. | £35 |
| 8.10 On a request for an order to recover a sum that is— | |
| — a specified debt within the meaning of the Enforcement of Road Traffic Debts Order 1993[1] as amended from time to time; or<br>— pursuant to an enactment, treated as a specified debt for the purposes of that Order. | £5 |
| No fee is payable on—<br>— an application for an extension of time to serve a statutory declaration or a witness statement in connection with any such order; or<br>— a request to issue a warrant of execution to enforce any such order. | |
| **8A Service in the county court** | |
| 8A.1 On a request for service by a bailiff of an order to attend court for questioning | £100 |
| **9 Sale** (county court only) | |
| 9.1 For removing or taking steps to remove goods to a place of deposit. | The reasonable expenses incurred |
| Fee 9.1 is to include the reasonable expenses of feeding and caring for any animals. | |
| 9.2 For advertising a sale by public auction pursuant to section 97 of the County Courts Act 1984. | The reasonable expenses incurred |
| 9.3 For the appraisement of goods. | 5p in the £1 or part of a £1 of the appraised value |
| 9.4 For the sale of goods (including advertisements, catalogues, sale and commission and delivery of goods). | 15p in the £1 or part of a £1 on the amount realised by the sale or such other sum as the district judge may consider to be justified in the circumstances |

[1] As amended by S.I. 2001/1386.

| *Column 1*<br>*Number and description of fee* | *Column 2*<br>*Amount of fee* |
|---|---|
| 9.5 Where no sale takes place by reason of an execution being withdrawn, satisfied or stopped. | (a) 10p in the £1 or part of a £1 on the value of the goods seized, the value to be the appraised value where the goods have been appraised or such other sum as the district judge may consider to be justified in the circumstances; and in addition (b) any sum payable under fee 9.1, 9.2 or 9.3 |
| **FEES PAYABLE IN HIGH COURT ONLY** | |
| **10 Miscellaneous proceedings or matters** | |
| **Bills of Sale** | |
| 10.1 On filing any document under the Bills of Sale Acts 1878 and the Bills of Sale Act (1878) Amendment Act 1882 or on an application under section 15 of the Bills of Sale Act 1878 for an order that a memorandum of satisfaction be written on a registered copy of the bill. | £25 |
| **Searches** | |
| 10.2 For an official certificate of the result of a search for each name, in any register or index held by the court; or in the Court Funds Office, for an official certificate of the result of a search of unclaimed balances for a specified period of up to 50 years. | £40 |
| 10.3 On a search in person of the bankruptcy and companies records, including inspection, for each 15 minutes or part of 15 minutes. | £5 |
| **Judge sitting as arbitrator** | |
| 10.4 On the appointment of— | |
| (a) a judge of the Commercial Court as an arbitrator or umpire under section 93 of the Arbitration Act 1996; or | £1,800 |
| (b) a judge of the Technology and Construction Court as an arbitrator or umpire under section 93 of the Arbitration Act 1996. | £1,400 |
| 10.5 For every day or part of a day (after the first day) of the hearing before— | |
| (a) a judge of the Commercial Court; or | £1,800 |
| (b) a judge of the Technology and Construction Court, so appointed as arbitrator or umpire. | £1,400 |
| Where fee 10.4 has been paid on the appointment of a judge of the Commercial Court or a judge of the Technology and Construction Court as an arbitrator or umpire but the arbitration does not proceed to a hearing or an award, the fee will be refunded. | |
| **11 Fees payable in Admiralty matters** | |
| In the Admiralty Registrar and Marshal's Office— | |

***Paragraph numbers marked with a "+" can be found online and on CD.***

| *Column 1*<br>*Number and description of fee* | *Column 2*<br>*Amount of fee* |
|---|---|
| 11.1 On the issue of a warrant for the arrest of a ship or goods. | £200 |
| 11.2 On the sale of a ship or goods— | |
| Subject to a minimum fee of £200— | |
| (a) for every £100 or fraction of £100 of the price up to £100,000; | £1 |
| (b) for every £100 or fraction of £100 of the price exceeding £100,000. | 50p |
| Where there is sufficient proceeds of sale in court, fee 11.2 will be payable by transfer from the proceeds of sale in court. | |
| 11.3 On entering a reference for hearing by the Registrar. | £50 |
| **FEES PAYABLE IN HIGH COURT AND COURT OF APPEAL ONLY** | |
| **12 Affidavits** | |
| 12.1 On taking an affidavit or an affirmation or attestation upon honour in lieu of an affidavit or a declaration except for the purpose of receipt of dividends from the Accountant General and for a declaration by a shorthand writer appointed in insolvency proceedings—<br>— for each person making any of the above. | £10 |
| 12.2 For each exhibit referred to in an affidavit, affirmation, attestation or declaration for which fee 12.1 is payable. | £2 |
| **FEES PAYABLE IN COURT OF APPEAL ONLY** | |
| **13 Fees payable in appeals to the Court of Appeal** | |
| 13.1(a) Where in an appeal notice permission to appeal or an extension of time for appealing is applied for (or both are applied for)—<br>— on filing an appellant's notice, or<br>— where the respondent is appealing, on filing a respondent's notice. | £200 |
| 13.1(b) Where permission to appeal is not required or has been granted by the lower court—<br>— on filing an appellant's notice, or<br>— on filing a respondent's notice where the respondent is appealing. | £400 |
| 13.1(c) On the appellant filing an appeal questionnaire (unless the appellant has paid fee 13.1(b), or on the respondent filing an appeal questionnaire (unless the respondent has paid fee 13.1(b)). | £400 |
| 13.2 On filing a respondent's notice where the respondent wishes to ask the appeal court to uphold the order of the lower court for reasons different from or additional to those given by the lower court. | £200 |

***Paragraph numbers marked with a "+" can be found online and on CD.***

| *Column 1*<br>*Number and description of fee* | *Column 2*<br>*Amount of fee* |
|---|---|
| 13.3 On filing an application notice. | £200 |
| Fee 13.3 is not payable for an application made in an appeal notice. | |

*Note* —Amended by SI 2008/2853 and SI 2009/1498. **10–7.1**

**ARTICLE 4**

# SCHEDULE 2

## REMISSIONS AND PART REMISSIONS

**Interpretation**

1.—(1)In this Schedule— **10–8**

"child" means a child or young person in respect of whom a party is entitled to receive child benefit in accordance with section 141, and regulations made under section 142, of the Social Security Contributions and Benefits Act 1992;

"child care costs" has the meaning given in the Criminal Defence Service (Financial Eligibility) Regulations 2006[1];

"couple" has the meaning given in section 3(5A) of the Tax Credits Act 2002[2];

"disposable monthly income" has the meaning given in paragraph 5;

"excluded benefits" means—

(a) any of the following benefits payable under the Social Security Contributions and Benefits Act 1992—

(i) attendance allowance paid under section 64;

(ii) severe disablement allowance;

(iii) carer's allowance;

(iv) disability living allowance;

(v) constant attendance allowance paid under section 104 or paragraph 4 or 7(2) of Schedule 8 as an increase to a disablement pension;

(vi) council tax benefit;

(vii) any payment made out of the social fund;

(viii) housing benefit;

(b) any direct payment made under the Community Care, Services for Carers and Children's Services (Direct Payments) (England) Regulations 2003 or the Community Care, Services for Carers and Children's Services (Direct Payments) (Wales) Regulations 2004;

(c) a back to work bonus payable under section 26 of the Jobseekers Act 1995;

(d) any exceptionally severe disablement allowance paid under the Personal Injuries (Civilians) Scheme 1983

(e) any pension paid under the Naval, Military and Air Forces etc (Disablement and Death) Service Pension Order 2006;

(f) any payment made from the Independent Living Funds; and

(g) any financial support paid under an agreement for the care of a foster child;

"the Funding Code" means the code approved under section 9 of the Access to Justice Act 1999;

[1] To which there are amendments not relevant to this Order.

[2] Section 3(5A) was inserted by paragraph 144 of Schedule 24 to the Civil Partnership Act 2004 (c.33).

***Paragraph numbers marked with a "+" can be found online and on CD.***

"gross annual income" means total annual income, for the 12 months preceding the application for remission or part remission, from all sources other than receipt of any of the excluded benefits;

"gross monthly income" means total monthly income, for the month in which the application for remission or part remission is made, from all sources other than receipt of any of the excluded benefits;

"the Independent Living Funds" has the meaning given in the Criminal Defence Service (Financial Eligibility) Regulations 2006;

"partner" means a person with whom the party lives as a couple and includes a person with whom the party is not currently living but from whom the party is not living separate and apart;

"party" means the individual who would, but for this Schedule, be liable to pay the fee required under this Order;

"restraint order" means—

(h) an order under section 42(1A) of the Senior Courts Act 1981[1]; or

(i) a civil restraint order under rule 3.11 of the Civil Procedure Rules 1998[2] or a practice direction made under that rule.

(2) Paragraphs 2, 3 and 4—

(a) do not apply to a party who is in receipt of funding provided by the LSC for the purposes of the proceedings for which a certificate has been issued under the Funding Code; and

(b) are subject to the provisions of paragraphs 10 (vexatious litigants) and 11 (exception).

**10–8.1** *Note*—Amended by SI 2008/2853, SI 2009/1498 and the Constitutional Reform Act 2005, s.59 and Sch.11, para.1 with effect from October 1, 2009 (SI 2009/1604).

### Full remission of fees—qualifying benefits

**10–9** 2.—(1)No fee is payable under this Order if, at the time when a fee would otherwise be payable, the party is in receipt of a qualifying benefit.

(2) The following are qualifying benefits for the purposes of sub-paragraph (1)—

(a) income support under the Social Security Contributions and Benefits Act 1992;

(b) working tax credit, provided that no child tax credit is being paid to the party;

(c) income-based jobseeker's allowance under the Jobseekers Act 1995; and

(d) guarantee credit under the State Pension Credit Act 2002; and

(e) income-related employment and support allowance under the Welfare Reform Act 2007.

**10–9.1** *Note*—Amended by SI 2008/2853.

### Full remission of fees—gross annual income

**10–10** 3.—(1)No fee is payable under this Order if, at the time when the fee would otherwise be payable, the party has the number of children specified in column 1 of the following table and—

(a) if the party is single, the gross annual income of the party does not exceed the amount set out in the appropriate row of column 2; or

(b) if the party is one of a couple, the gross annual income of the couple does not exceed the amount set out in the appropriate row of column 3.

[1] Section 42(1A) was inserted by section 24 of the Prosecution of Offences Act 1985 (c.23).

[2] Amended by S.I.2004/2072; there are other amending instruments but none is relevant.

***Paragraph numbers marked with a "+" can be found online and on CD.***

| *Column 1* *Number of children of party paying fee* | *Column 2* *Single* | *Column 3* *Couple* |
|---|---|---|
| no children | £13,000 | £18,000 |
| 1 child | £15,930 | £20,930 |
| 2 children | £18,860 | £23,860 |
| 3 children | £21,790 | £26,790 |
| 4 children | £24,720 | £29,720 |

(2) If the party paying the fee has more than 4 children then the relevant amount of gross annual income is the amount specified in the table for 4 children plus the sum of £2,930 for each additional child.

*Note* —Amended by SI 2009/1498. **10–10.1**

**Full and part remission of fees—disposable monthly income**

4.—(1)No fee is payable under this Order if, at the time when the fee would otherwise be payable, the disposable monthly income of the party is £50 or less. **10–11**

(2) The maximum amount of fee payable is—

(a) if the disposable monthly income of the party is more than £50 but does not exceed £210, an amount equal to one-quarter of every £10 of the party's disposable monthly income up to a maximum of £50; and

(b) if the disposable monthly income is more than £210, an amount equal to £50 plus one-half of every £10 over £200 of the party's disposable monthly income.

(3) Where the fee that would otherwise be payable under this Order is greater than the maximum fee which a party is required to pay as calculated in sub-paragraph (2), the fee will be remitted to the amount payable under that sub-paragraph.

**Disposable monthly income**

5.—(1)A party's disposable monthly income is the gross monthly income of the party for the month in which the fee becomes payable ("the period") less the deductions referred to in sub-paragraphs (2) and (3). **10–12**

(2) There are to be deducted from the gross monthly income—

(a) income tax paid or payable in respect of the period;

(b) any contributions estimated to have been paid under Part 1 of the Social Security Contributions and Benefits Act 1992 in respect of the period;

(c) either—

(i) monthly rent or monthly payment in respect of a mortgage debt or hereditable security, payable in respect of the only or main dwelling of the party, less any housing benefit paid under the Social Security Contributions and Benefits Act 1992; or

(ii) the monthly cost of the living accommodation of the party;

(d) any child care costs paid or payable in respect of the period;

(e) if the party is making bona fide payments for the maintenance of a child who is not a member of the household of the party, the amount of such payments paid or payable in respect of the period; and

(f) any amount paid or payable by the party, in respect of the period, in pursuance of a court order.

(3) There will be deducted from the gross monthly income an amount representing the cost of living expenses in respect of the period being—

(a) £315; plus

(b) £244 for each child of the party; plus

(c) £159, if the party has a partner.

**Resources of partners**

6.—(1)For the purpose of determining whether a party is entitled to the remission or part remission of a fee in accordance with this Schedule, the income of a partner, if any, is to be included as income of the party. **10–13**

***Paragraph numbers marked with a "+" can be found online and on CD.***

(2) The receipt by a partner of a qualifying benefit does not entitle a party to remission of a fee.

**Application for remission or part remission of fees**

10–14 7.—(1)An application for remission or part remission of a fee must be made to the court officer at the time when the fee would otherwise be payable.

(2) Where a claim for full remission of fees is made, the party must provide documentary evidence of, as the case may be—

(a) entitlement to a qualifying benefit; or

(b) gross annual income and, if applicable, the children included for the purposes of paragraph 3.

(3) Where a claim for full or part remission of fees under paragraph 4 is made, the party must provide documentary evidence of—

(a) such of the party's gross monthly income as is derived from—

(i) employment;

(ii) rental or other income received from persons living with the party by reason of their residence in the party's home;

(iii) a pension; or

(iv) a state benefit, not being an excluded benefit; and

(b) any expenditure being deducted from the gross monthly income in accordance with paragraph 5(2).

**Remission in exceptional circumstances**

10–15 8. Where it appears to the Lord Chancellor that the payment of any fee prescribed by this Order would, owing to the exceptional circumstances of the particular case, involve undue financial hardship, the Lord Chancellor may reduce or remit the fee in that case.

**Refunds**

10–15.1 9.—(1)Subject to sub-paragraph (3), where a party has not provided the documentary evidence required by paragraph 7 and a fee has been paid at a time when, under paragraphs 2, 3 or 4, it was not payable, the fee will be refunded if documentary evidence relating to the time when the fee became payable is provided at a later date.

(2) Subject to sub-paragraph (3), where a fee has been paid at a time where the Lord Chancellor, if all the circumstances had been known, would have reduced or remitted the fee under paragraph 8,the fee or the amount by which the fee would have been reduced, as the case may be, will be refunded.

(3) No refund will be made under this paragraph unless the party who paid the fee applies within 6 months of paying the fee.

(4) The Lord Chancellor may extend the period of 6 months mentioned in sub-paragraph (3) if the Lord Chancellor considers that there is a good reason for an application being made after the end of the period of 6 months.

**Vexatious Litigants**

10–15.2 10.—(1)This paragraph applies where—

(a) a restraint order is in force against a party; and

(b) the party makes an application for permission to—

(i) issue proceedings or take a step in proceedings as required by the restraint order;

(ii) apply for amendment or discharge of the order; or

(iii) appeal the order.

(2) The fee prescribed for the application by Schedule 1 is payable in full.

(3) If the court grants the permission requested the applicant will be refunded the difference between—

(a) the fee paid; and

(b) the fee that would have been payable if this Schedule had been applied without reference to this paragraph.

**Exception**

10–15.3 11. This Schedule does not apply to fee 8.8 (fee payable on a consolidated attachment of earnings order or an administration order).

*Paragraph numbers marked with a "+" can be found online and on CD.*

*Note*—Amended by SI 2008/2853 and SI 2009/1498. 10–15.3.1

**ARTICLE 8**

## SCHEDULE 3

### REVOCATIONS

10–15.4

| Article 8 | |
|---|---|
| ***Column 1*** ***Title*** | ***Column 2*** ***Reference*** |
| The Civil Proceedings Fees Order 2004 | S.I. 2004/3121 |
| The Civil Proceedings Fees (Amendment) Order 2005 | S.I. 2005/473 |
| The Civil Proceedings Fees (Amendment No. 2) Order 2005 | S.I. 2005/3445 |
| The Civil Proceedings Fees (Amendment) Order 2006 | S.I. 2006/719 |
| The Civil Proceedings Fees (Amendment) Order 2007 | S.I. 2007/680 |
| The Civil Proceedings Fees (Amendment) (No. 2) Order 2007 | S.I. 2007/2176 |
| The Civil Proceedings Fees (Amendment) (No. 2) (Amendment) Order 2007 | S.I. 2007/2801 |
| The Civil Proceedings Fees (Amendment) Order 2008 | S.I. 2008/116 |

*Editorial note*—The Civil Proceedings Fees Order 2008 came into effect on May 1, 2008. 10–15.5

## The Non-Contentious Probate Fees Order 2004

(S.I. 2004 No. 3120)

**For The Non-Contentious Probate Fees Order 2004 plus any related commentary see paragraphs 10–17+ to 10–29+ on White Book on Westlaw UK or the Civil Procedure CD.** 10–16

## The Enrolment of Deeds (Fees) Regulations 1994

(S.I. 1994 No. 601)

**For The Enrolment of Deeds (Fees) Regulations 1994 plus any related commentary see paragraphs 10–31+ to 10–32+ on White Book on Westlaw UK or the Civil Procedure CD.** 10–30

## The Insolvency Proceedings (Fees) Order 2004

(S.I. 2004 No. 593)

**For the Insolvency Proceedings (Fees) Order 2004 plus any related commentary see paragraphs 10–34+ to 10–53+ on White Book on Westlaw UK or the Civil Procedure CD.** 10–33

***Paragraph numbers marked with a "+" can be found online and on CD.***

# SECTION 11

## OVERRIDING OBJECTIVE OF CPR

11

# 11 OVERRIDING OBJECTIVE OF CPR

CONTENTS





## A. INTRODUCTION

In March 1994, the Lord Mackay L.C. appointed Lord Woolf (then a Lord of Appeal in Ordinary) to review the current rules and procedures of the civil courts in England and Wales. The aims of the review were to improve access to justice and reduce the costs of litigation; to reduce the complexity of the rules and modernise terminology; to remove unnecessary distinctions of practice and procedure. Lord Woolf conducted the "Access to Justice" inquiry over a period of two and a quarter years, assisted by a panel of assessors and the staff of the Lord Chancellor's Department. He consulted widely with judges, members of the legal profession, academic lawyers and court users throughout the country. Public seminars, chaired by Lord Woolf, were held at several major universities. Lord Woolf's conclusions from his inquiry were set out in two "Access to Justice" reports, namely the Interim Report (June 1995) and the Final Report (July 1996). **11–2**

In his two reports, Lord Woolf recommended that the existing Rules of the Supreme Court (RSC) and the County Court Rules (CCR) should be revoked; that they should be replaced by a single statutory instrument, containing rules of court applicable both to the High Court and the county courts. Lord Woolf annexed a first draft of these rules to his Final Report. That draft did not cover all of the matters of practice and procedure covered by the RSC and the CCR, but focused on those matters in relation to which Lord Woolf had made firm reform proposals. After a considerable amount of further work on that draft, including the addition of a lot of material dealing with matters either not covered in the draft or not adequately dealt with there (but covered by the RSC and the CCR) the Civil Procedure Rules 1998 (SI 1998/3132) emerged.

A novel feature of Lord Woolf's draft was the inclusion of provisions setting out the "overriding objective" of the rules. It was intended that these provisions should state the basic principles (a) upon which the procedural rules were founded, and (b) which should influence civil courts in exercising their numerous discretions under the rules, and should commit the courts and parties to them. In the Final Report it was said (at p.274) that, ultimately, the purpose of rules of court "is to guide the court and the litigants towards the just resolution of the case". Rules of court contain detailed directions for the steps which must be taken. The effectiveness of those steps "depends upon the spirit in which they are carried out". That, in turn, "depends on an understanding of the fundamental purpose of the rules and of the underlying system of procedure". It was further said in the Final Report (ibid) that the "overriding objective", as stated in r.1.1 and r.1.2, encapsulates that fundamental purpose. The CPR are deliberately not designed expressly to answer every question which could arise.

***Paragraph numbers marked with a "+" can be found online and on CD.***

The statement of the overriding objective in those rules "provides a compass to guide courts and litigants and legal advisers as to their general course' (Final Report, p.275).

The provisions as to the "overriding objective", as set out in the draft rules annexed to the Final Report, were duly adopted and became Pt 1 of the CPR.

# B. CPR PT1

11–3 Part 1 of the CPR (Overriding Objective) contains four provisions. Rule 1.1 states that the Rules are a new procedural code "with the overriding objective of dealing with cases justly". In para.(2) of that provision, the overriding objective is elaborated. Rules 1.2 and 1.4 stipulate that the court should give effect to the overriding objective in applying and interpreting the rules, and by actively managing cases. Rule 1.4 states that parties are required to help the court to further the overriding objective.

Part 76 of the CPR (Prevention of Terrorism Act 2005) contains rules about control order proceedings in the High Court and appeals to the Court of Appeal against an order of the High Court in such proceedings. CPR Pt 79 (Financial Restrictions Proceedings Under the Counter-Terrorism Act 2008) contains rules about financial restriction proceedings in the High Court and appeals to the Court of Appeal against an order of the High Court in such proceedings. In those Parts, respectively, r.76.2 and r.79.2 impose on the court a duty to ensure that information is not disclosed contrary to the public interest. And those rules further provide that in proceedings to which the Parts apply, the overriding objective in Pt 1, and so far as relevant any other rule, must be read and given effect in a way which is compatible with that duty.

The texts of these rules with annotations are found in Vol.1 para.1.1 *et seq*. Extended commentaries on the various aspects of these rules, in particular on the provisions in para.(2) of r.1.1, are found in what follows in this Section of the White Book.

# C. GIVING EFFECT TO THE "OVERRIDING OBJECTIVE"—GENERALLY (RR.1.1 AND 1.2)

11–4 The assertion in r.1.1(1) to the effect that the CPR "are a new procedural code" did not appear in Lord Woolf's draft of the terms of the overriding objective. For commentary on the significance of the assertion, see Vol.2 Section 12 (CPR:Application, Amendments and Interpretation, para.12–56).

## 1. EXPRESS REFERENCES TO "OVERRIDING OBJECTIVE" IN CPR

11–5 The CPR overriding objective is a more elaborate version of the first of the "general principles" stated in the Arbitration Act 1996 s.1. Provisions similar to r.1.1 have found their way into other procedural rules governing courts and tribunals to which the CPR do not apply; notably the Criminal Procedure Rules 2005 (SI 2005/384) Pt 1, the Employment Tribunals (Constitution and Rules of Procedure) Regulations 2001 (SI 2001/1171) reg.10, the Court of Protection Rules 2007 (SI 2007/1744) r.3, and the Tribunal Procedure (Upper Tribunal) Rules 2008 (SI 2008/2698) r.2.

In some instances the sentiments reflected in the overriding objective have been invoked in cases which were not only not subject to the CPR but which involved a procedural regime which did not contain a provision similar to s.1.1; e.g. *Mobile Export 365 Ltd v Revenue and Customs Commissioners* [2007] EWHC 1737 (Ch), July 20, 2007, unrep. (Lightman J.) (Value Added Tax Tribunal Rules 1986).

As to the effect of the overriding objective on proceedings in the Lands Tribunal, see Vol.2 Section 12 (CPR: Application, Amendments and Interpretation, para.12–14).

Express references to the overriding objective are found in some specific provisions in the CPR and related practice directions (e.g. r.19.7(2) and Practice Direction (Disclosure and Inspection), para.5.4, see Vol.1, para.31PD.5).

The court must give effect to the overriding objective when it exercises any power given to it by the CPR (r.1.2(a)). It will not always be obvious whether a particular "power" which the court is being invited to exercise, or which the court proposes to exercise, is a power "given to it by the Rules". (The point is that many of the court's powers, including some of the "general powers of management" listed in r.3.1, are not given to the court by the CPR but are derived from elsewhere.) Among the more obvious and frequently recurring circumstances where the court will have at the forefront of its mind the requirement that it should seek to give effect to the overriding objective when exercising a power to give it by the CPR are where extensions of time for taking procedural steps are sought (e.g. r.3.1(2)(a)), and where relief is sought from procedural sanctions (r.3.9) (e.g. *Sayers v Clarke Walker (Practice Note)* [2002] EWCA Civ 645; [2002] 1 W.L.R. 3095, CA; *Tarling v Wabara* [2003] EWHC 450 (QB); March 5, 2003, unrep. (Gray J.); *IBS Technologies Ltd v APM Technologies SA*, April 7, 2003, unrep. (Mr Michael Briggs Q.C.)).The courts are likely to call in aid the overriding objective (either in specific or general terms) when justifying the broad exercise of a particular discretion, especially where it arises in a context in which the relevant CPR rules were intended to mark a significant departure from previous rules; e.g. *Capital Bank plc v Stickland* [2004] EWCA Civ 1677, December 10, 2004, unrep., CA (court's discretion under r.36.5(6)(b)(ii) to permit acceptance of Pt 36 offer should be as wide as possible so as to advance the overriding objective); *National Amusements (UK) Ltd v White City (Shepherds Bush) LLP* [2009] EWHC 2524 (TCC), October 16, 2009, unrep. (Akenhead J.) (court's discretion under r.30.5 (Transfer) not constrained by pre-CPR "appropriateness" test but to be exercised flexibly in accordance with the overriding objective). On several occasions, the Court of Appeal has stressed that it is important for judges making case management decisions to have in mind the overriding objective to deal with cases justly; e.g. *Roberts v Williams* [2005] EWCA Civ 1086, May 18, 2005, unrep., CA (on second appeal, defendants' late application to amend statement of case, to adduce new witness statement, and to vacate trial date granted).

Further, the court must give effect to the overriding objective when it interprets any rule (presumably, any rule in the CPR) (r.1.2(b)); see Vol.2 Section 12 (CPR: Application, Amendments and Interpretation, para.12–45).

When Pt 76 (Proceedings under the Prevention of Terrorism Act 2005) was inserted in the CPR by the Civil Procedure (Amendment No.2) Rules 2005 (SI 2005/656), r.1.2 was amended by the addition at the end of the words "subject to rule 76.2". When the High Court is dealing with proceedings to which Pt 76 applies, it "must ensure that information is not disclosed contrary to the public interest" (r.76.2(2)). Rule 76.2(1) states that, where Pt 76 applies, the overriding objective in Pt 1, and so far as relevant any other rule, must be read and given effect to in a way which is compatible with that duty.

Increasingly the courts refer to the objective that they should "deal with cases justly" in circumstances where the overriding objective stated in r.1.1 is not applied by r.1.2, that is to say, in circumstances where the court is not exercising any power given to it by the CPR or interpreting any rule (e.g. *Clarkson v Gilbert (Rights of Audience)* [2000] C.P. Rep. 58, CA (application by claimant's spouse for right of audience under the Courts and Legal Services Act 1990 s.27(2)(c)); *Igwemma v Chief Constable of Greater Manchester Police* [2001] EWCA Civ 953; [2001] 4 All E.R. 751, CA (permitting jury to alter verdict after discharge); *Bentley v Jones Harris & Co* [2001] EWCA Civ 1724; November 2, 2001, unrep., CA (acceding to submission of no case to answer without putting defendant to election); *Compagnie Noga d'Importation et d'Exploration SA v Australia and New Zealand Banking Group Ltd* [2002] EWCA Civ 1142; July 31, 2002, CA (judge structuring judgment order in manner having effect of imposing on party need to obtain permission to appeal in circumstances where he would not otherwise require it); *London Borough of Southwark v Kofi-Adu* [2006] EWCA Civ 281, March 23, 2006, unrep., CA (conduct of judge raising apparent judicial bias concerns leading to retrial); *I.D. v Home Office* [2005] EWCA Civ 38; [2006] 1 W.L.R. 1003, CA (whether bringing claim for damages in a county court instead of making application for judicial review an abuse of process); *Bowman* v Fels [2005] EWCA Civ 226; [2005] 1 W.L.R. 3083, CA (jurisdiction of appeal court to hear "hypothetical" appeal). This stretching of the overriding objective beyond its intended boundaries has been aided by the approximation of some of the language in CPR r.1.1 with that used in relation to Art.6 of the Convention (right to fair trial) and in the abuse of process jurisprudence, aided by dicta asserting that the principles in the rule "are now central to determining what is due process" (*Clark v University of Lincolnshire and Humberside* [2000] 1 W.L.R. 1988, CA, at para.39 per Lord Woolf M.R.). There are some remarkable illustrations of the overriding objective being pressed into service in the determination of issues to which it clearly does not in terms apply and, indeed, which are better categorised as jurisdictional rather than procedural. A good illustration is the issue whether the Court of Appeal should refuse permission to appeal on the ground that the point raised is "academic (or "hypothetical") (e.g. *Gawler v Raettig* [2007] EWCA Civ 1560, December 3, 2007, CA, unrep.); see further para.9A–77 above).

Rule 1.4(1) states that the court must further the overriding objective by "actively managing cases" and active case management includes exercising the various judicial powers listed in r.1.4(2) on a case by case basis as appropriate. Paragraph (h) of r.1.4(2) refers to the court's power to consider whether the likely benefits of taking a particular step justify the cost of taking it. It seems clear that the court has jurisdiction to dismiss a pre-trial application summarily on the ground that it is not an appropriate application to make because it is likely to add to the costs without any significant benefit to the conduct of the case, and is therefore contrary to the overriding objective (*Norwich Union Linked Life Assurance Ltd v Mercantile Credit Co Ltd* [2003] EWHC 3064 (Ch); December 19, 2003, unrep. (David Richards J.)).

In a number of practice directions, it is expressly stated that the court should take the overriding objective into account before making particular decisions (e.g. Practice Direction (Applications), para.3 (applications without notice) (see Vol.1, para.23APD.3), Practice Direction (Case Management—Preliminary Stage: Allocation and Re-Allocation), para.4.1 (court's general approach to allocation of proceedings to case management track) (see Vol.1, para.26PD.4), Practice Direction (The Multi-Track), para.5.1 (directions at case management conference) (see Vol.1, para.29PD.5), and Practice Direction (Disclosure and Inspection), para.5.4 (order for specific disclosure) (see Vol.1, para.31PD.5). (Note also, Practice Direction (General Rules About Applications), para.3 (applications without notice possible where overriding objective best furthered), see Vol.1, para.23APD.3)).

Practice Direction (Protocols), para.4 states that, in cases not covered by any approved pre-action protocol, the court will expect the parties, in accordance with the overriding objective and the matters referred to in paras (a), (b) and (c) of r.1.1(2), to act reasonably in exchanging information and documents relevant to the claim and generally in trying to avoid the necessity for the start of proceedings (see Vol.1, para.C1–003).

In r.3.1, which lists various "general powers" of case management, it is provided that the court may "take any other step or make any other order for the purpose of managing the case and furthering the overriding objective" (r.3.1(2)(m)).

## 2. GENERAL APPLICATION OF "OVERRIDING OBJECTIVE" AS DEMONSTRATED IN DECIDED CASES

**11–6** The particular objectives of the overriding objective as listed in r.1.1(2), to be implemented "so far as is practicable", are not mutually exclusive and, in a given situation, a course taken by the court to meet one objective may yield a different result to a course taken to meet another. In some cases, in reaching a particular conclusion, courts have drawn attention generally to the matters listed in r.1.1(2) when clearly having only some of those matters in mind as considerations relevant to the exercise of a particular power in circumstances where other considerations might suggest a different conclusion to that preferred (e.g. *O'Brien v Chief Constable of South Wales* [2005] UKHL 26; [2005] 2 A.C. 534, HL (court's power under r.32.1(2) to exclude admissible evidence)). In other cases the courts have been able to draw attention to the r.1.1(2) criteria without there being any such obvious conflict (e.g. *Independiente Ltd v Music Trading On-Line (HK) Ltd* [2003] EWHC 470 (Ch); March 13, 2003, unrep. (Sir Andrew Morritt V.-C.) (whether representative parties have same interest under r.19.6)). Instances have arisen where the court, in rejecting a submission in which substantial reliance was placed on one aspect of the overriding objective (e.g. r.1.1(2)(d)), has underpinned its decision by reference to another aspect (e.g. r.1.1(2)(e)) (see e.g. (*R. (Johnson) v Secretary of State for Health* [2006] EWHC 288 (Admin), February 23, 2006, unrep. (Silber J.)).

It is not uncommon for a court, in disposing of a procedural issue, to derive support for its conclusion from a broad range of the particular objectives in r.1.1(2). A good example is provided by *Palfrey v Wilson* [2007] EWCA Civ 94; *The Times* March 5, 2007, CA, a case in which, in order to upset the order under appeal, the appellant had to succeed on two grounds. The Court of Appeal, having heard argument on one and reserved judgment on it, declined to hear argument on the other. The court said it may take such a course in the interest of saving expense, dealing with cases proportionately and expeditiously, and allocating judicial resources appropriately.

Before the CPR came into force, in arriving at decisions on the scope and application of procedural law, frequently the courts were influenced by matters listed in r.1.1(2), particularly the need to do justice in the individual case, to be fair, and to avoid delays and unnecessary costs. Nowadays, the courts can draw out and focus attention upon these matters by reference to the overriding objective. Inevitably, in some cases attention has been drawn to the fact that, in certain circumstances, considerations which governed the exercise of particular powers in accordance with rules of court replaced by the CPR are consistent with considerations encapsulated by the overriding objective as stated in r.1.1; e.g. the discretion to order inspection of document where party resisting on ground of risk of prosecution abroad (r.31.19) (*Morris v Banque Arabe et Internationale d'Investissement SA (No.1)* [2000] C.P. Rep. 65 (Neuberger J.)); the power to strike out for want of prosecution petitions presented under the Companies Act 1985 s.459 (*Gerrard v Whitworth*, January 28, 2000, unrep., CA); the power to recall judgments (*Stewart v Engel* [2000] 1 W.L.R. 2268; [2000] 3 All E.R. 518, CA).

In *Colley v Council for Licensed Conveyancers* [2001] EWCA Civ 1137; [2002] 1 W.L.R. 160, CA, the Court of Appeal said (para.45) there is a tension between the principle stated by Lord Bingham in *R. (Daly) v Secretary of State for the Home Department* [2001] UKHL 26; [2001] 2 A.C. 532, HL, that the right of access to a court may only be curtailed by clear and precise terms, and the provisions of CPR r.1.2.

Paragraph (d) of r.1.1(2) states that, dealing with a case justly includes, so far as is practicable, ensuring that it is dealt with expeditiously and fairly. There is an obvious tension between, on the one hand justice and fairness (see para.11–8 below) and the avoidance of delay on the other (see para.11–9 below) and occasionally this is remarked upon by judges endeavouring to ensure that the overriding objective is taken into account (e.g. *Nesheim v Kosa* [2007] EWHC 2710 (Ch), October 4, 2006, unrep. (Briggs J.) (retrospective permission to serve out of jurisdiction)). In *Holmes v S.G.B. Services Plc* [2001] EWCA Civ 354, the judge granted C's application (1) vacating trial date, (2) giving C leave to amend his particulars of claim, and (3) permitting parties to re-instruct the expert on particular issues. The judge said that there is a tension between (a) rules emphasising the maintaining of trial dates and (b) the interests of justice in achieving a fair trial and under r.52.3(6) gave D permission to appeal on the basis that the possibility that the Court of Appeal would resolve the tension in favour of (a) rather than (b) gave D real prospects of success or provided a compelling reason for hearing the appeal. In dismissing D's appeal, the Court of Appeal noted the elements of the overriding objective and doubted whether the tension existed. Buxton L.J. said, in making a case management decision, the court has to balance all of the criteria identified in r.1.1 without giving any one of them undue weight. Striking the balance was a matter for the judge and it would be wrong for the Court of Appeal to give, or for judges to seek, any direction suggesting that one or other of those criteria was more or less important.

The overriding objective is not applicable where legal rights are involved (*Dicker v Scammell* [2003] EWHC 1601), and it cannot confer jurisdiction if manifestly there is none (*Russell-Cooke Trust Co v Prentis* [2002] EWHC 1435 (Ch); January 21, 2003, unrep. (Lindsay J.)). Further, the CPR being rules of court, cannot (neither by means of the overriding objective provisions in them nor by any other provision) extend the jurisdiction of the court from that which the law provides (*Jaffray v The Society of Lloyds* [2007] EWCA Civ 586, June 20, 2007, unrep., CA).

The requirement that the court should give effect to the overriding objective when exercising any power does not affect the established principles as stated in the authorities as to the inadvertent disclosure of documents subject to legal professional privilege (e.g. *Guinness Peat Properties Ltd v Fitzroy Robinson Partnership* [1987] 1 W.L.R. 1027, CA; *Breeze (Disclosure) v John Stacey & Sons Ltd* (2000) C.P. Rep. 77, CA). The court's approach to striking out in defamation claims is based on a long line of authority predating the CPR and reflecting matters of substance inherent in such claims (*Best v Charter Medical of England Ltd* [2001] EWCA Civ 1588). The overriding objective provides no basis upon which the court can prevent a party from instructing the legal representative of his choice (*Maltez v Lewis The Times* May 4, 1999). There is nothing in r.1.1 to suggest that, if a defendant failed to give an explanation for delay, that failure could be relied upon by the other party to show that the court should exercise its discretion to set aside a default judgment in a certain way (*MacDonald v Thorn Plc The Times*,

***Paragraph numbers marked with a "+" can be found online and on CD.***

October 15, 1999, CA). The limits imposed by *Re Barrell Enterprises* [1973] 1 W.L.R. 19, CA, on the jurisdiction of a judge to recall a judgment before it is sealed or otherwise perfected are based on considerations consistent with those stated in r.1.1(2) (*Stewart v Engel* [2000] 1 W.L.R. 2268, CA; *Mamidoil-Jetoil Greek Petroleum SA v Okta Crude Oil Refinery AD (No.2)* [2001] 1 Lloyd's Rep. 591 (Thomas J.); *Compagnie Noga d'Importation et d'Exploration SA v Abacha* [2001] 3 All E.R. 513, Rix L.J.; *Royal Brompton Hospital NHS Trust v Hammond* [2001] EWCA Civ 778). Where an application is made for the recall for reconsideration of a judgment granting an interim injunction it has to be decided on its merits, as to which the only guidance which is required is that contained in the overriding objective (*A v B (A Company)* [2002] EWCA Civ 337; [2002] 2 All E.R. 545, CA). It has been said that the guidance as to the production of fresh evidence in the Court of Appeal given in *Ladd v Marshall* [1954] 1 W.L.R. 1489, CA, fits exactly into the statement of the overriding objective in r.1.1, including the need to make efficient use of the court's resources (*R. (Amraf Training Plc) v Department of Education and Employment* [2001] EWCA Civ 914, para.30 per Buxton L.J.; see also *Hertfordshire Investments Ltd v Bubb* [2000] 1 W.L.R. 2318, CA; *Gloyne v Richardson* [2001] EWCA Civ 716; May 18, 2001, unrep., CA; *Aylwen v Taylor Johnson Garrett* [2001] EWCA Civ 1171; July 3, 2001, unrep., CA; *J.J. Harrison (Properties) v Harrison* [2001] EWCA Civ 1295; July 16, 2001, unrep., CA; *Taylor v Lawrence* [2002] EWCA Civ 53; [2002] 2 All E.R. 353, CA; *Shaker v Al-Bedrawi* [2002] EWCA Civ 1452; October 18, 2002, unrep., CA). Before the rules as to payments into court were changed, it was said that, although nowadays the courts may incline to a more flexible approach when considering applications for the withdrawal of a payment into court, the traditional "change of circumstance" test was consistent with the overriding objective (*MRW Technologies v Cecil Holdings Ltd* June 22, 2001, unrep. (Garland J.); *Marsh v Frenchay Healthcare NHS Trust The Times*, March 13, 2001). The requirement that a statement of case must be verified by a statement of truth does not prevent a claimant from being given permission to amend his statement of case to plead his claim on an alternative and inconsistent basis, where that alternative was suggested by the defence, for to do so would be contrary to the overriding objective (*Binks v Securicor Omega Express Ltd* [2003] EWCA Civ 993; July 16, 2003, unrep., CA). In a case where a defendant is in danger of losing his home, the overriding objective does not require that his pleaded admission to the effect that the claimant had served the required statutory notice (though the fact was otherwise) should be disregarded (*Loveridge v Healey* [2004] EWCA Civ 173, CA).

It has been said that, in the exercise of discretion the court may suspend the rule that a defendant should be called upon to elect before submitting that there is no case to answer where the overriding objective would be better served by such a course (*Mullan v Birmingham City Council The Times*, July 29, 1999; *Worsley v Tambrands Ltd* December 3, 1999, unrep., (Ebsworth J.); cf. *Landare Investments Ltd v Welsh Development Agency* November 25, 1999, unrep. (McKinnon J.)). But the jurisdiction to suspend the rule that a defendant should be called upon to elect before submitting that there is no case to answer should be exercised with considerable caution (*Boyce v Wyatt Engineering* [2001] EWCA Civ 692, CA); see further on this point, Vol.1, para.32.1.6. For further illustrations of circumstances in which the courts, in exercising powers given to them by the CPR and in interpreting rules, have called in aid specific aspects of the overriding objective as listed in r.1.1(2); see paras 11–8 to 11–12 below.

The court will also have to have regard to its obligation to ensure a fair trial arising from Art.6 of the European Convention on Human Rights. See further Vol.2 Section 12 (CPR: Application, Amendments and Interpretation, para.12–58).

## 3. RISK OF OVER-RELIANCE ON CPR (R.1.1)

**11–7** In some instances, references in reported judgments to r.1.1 simply draw attention to the overriding objective in general terms. For example, in *Powell v Pallisers of Hereford Ltd* [2002] EWCA Civ 959; July 1, 2002, unrep., CA, Chadwick L.J. said (para.32) that reported cases and the overriding objective require that the Court of Appeal should "exercise a proper degree of self-discipline by respecting case management decisions made by judges in cases which they are to try". More commonly, attention is drawn to specific aspects of r.1.1(2).There is a risk that the particular objectives listed in r.1.1(2) will be subjected to over-elaborate analysis. There is also a risk that the particular objectives will be used selectively and merely for the purpose of giving added

***Paragraph numbers marked with a "+" can be found online and on CD.***

weight to particular exercises of powers given to the court by the CPR and to preferred interpretations of rules.

In a number of cases decided shortly after the implementation of the CPR the courts drew attention to the significance of Pt 1 under the new procedural regime. In some cases they did so, it is submitted, in circumstances where it was neither necessary nor helpful to do so. Further, in some cases advocates have urged that the dominant if not exclusive considerations for resolving certain procedural issues were to be found in r.1.1. These tendencies have given rise to a risk of over-reliance on the overriding objective (e.g. *Law v St Margarets Insurances Ltd* January 18, 2001, unrep., CA (overriding objective used to support wholly unsustainable result that default judgment entered against wrong defendant should not be set aside)). It is probably true to say that, in almost any circumstance in which the court exercises a power given to it by the CPR, it would be possible to justify (at least in part) the particular manner in which the power is exercised in the light of one or other of the aspects of the overriding objective as listed in r.1.1(2). However, usually, the law (perhaps not only procedural but also substantive), derived from relevant legislation (e.g. the Senior Courts Act 1981, the County Courts Act 1984, the Limitation Act 1981), CPR rules and practice directions (and, possibly, other rules and directions), authorities and usual practice, to be applied and taken into account in determining whether and how a particular power given to the court by the CPR should be exercised will be clear, principled and specifically tailored for the exercise of that power. Obviously, such relevant law and practice, which will often have its own objectives (not inconsistent with the overriding objective) designed to do justice expressly or impliedly "built-in", should be given its full and proper effect and, in being applied, should not be distorted or diminished by strained attempts to bring into consideration selected aspects of the overriding objective as listed in r.1.1(2). Premature and unnecessary recourse to the overriding objective may lead to inadequate legal analysis of important procedural issues (thus hindering the proper development of the law), to radical provisions in the CPR not being consistently applied as intended, and to an erratic "palm tree justice" approach to interlocutory work (leading to inconsistent treatment of like situations) and, it is submitted, for these reasons should be avoided, even in those cases (which will be the great majority) where simple reliance on selected aspects of the overriding objective and proper legal analysis will tend to yield the same result.

OVERRIDING OBJECTIVE OF CPR

## D. GIVING EFFECT TO THE "OVERRIDING OBJECTIVE"—PARTICULAR OBJECTIVES

### 1. JUSTICE AND FAIRNESS (RR.1.1(1) AND 1.1(2)(d))

It is perhaps obvious that the fundamental purpose of civil procedure should be to **11–8**
r.1.3.3 enable the court "to deal with cases justly" (r.1.1(1)) and, so far as is practicable, "fairly" (r.1.1(2)(d)). The classic explanation of the role of civil procedure is that it should be the "handmaiden of justice" (*Coles and Ravenshear Arbitration, Re* [1907] 1 K.B. 1, per Collins M.R.). However, these sentiments cannot be allowed to hide the fact that procedural rules are not "value free". They are based on policy choices, they have their own objectives and, in the adversary context, for good reason individual rules may reflect a bias towards one party or another. Further, in a given situation, what is just and what is fair may be a matter on which reasonable persons may reasonably differ. Clearly, the overriding consideration must be the doing of justice in the individual case and the application of the several aspects of the overriding objective as particularised in r.1.1(2) is subject to that consideration.

Instances in which it has been said expressly that powers should be exercised in accordance with the overriding objective of dealing with cases justly include the following: the power to exclude admissible evidence (r.32.1) (*Grobbelaar v Sun Newspapers Ltd The Times*, August 12, 1999, CA); the power to grant permission to amend a notice of appeal (r.52.8) (*Crane v Sky In Home Ltd* [2008] EWCA Civ 978, July 3, 2008, CA, unrep.); the power to set aside a witness summons (r.34.3(4)) (*Harrison v Bloom Camillin* May 12, 1999, unrep.); the exercise of the discretion to join parties (r.19.4) (*Messier-Dowty Ltd v Sabena SA* [2000] 1 Lloyd's Rep. 428, CA); setting aside order for summary judgment made in absence of defendant (*Stock v Stock* October 17, 2000, unrep., CA;

***Paragraph numbers marked with a "+" can be found online and on CD.***

granting permission to amend a claim form or statement of case (r.17.1(2)) (*Thurrock BC v Secretary of State for the Environment, Transport and the Regions (No.1)* [2001] C.P. Rep. 55, CA); striking out claim form for non-compliance with rules (r.3.4(2)(c)) (*Hannigan v Hannigan* [2000] 2 F.C.R. 650); requiring party to give additional information in relation to matter in dispute (r.18.1) (*Toussaint v Mattis* [2001] C.P. Rep. 61, May 22, 2000, unrep., CA); the power to grant permission to amend a notice on appeal (r.52.8 (*Crane v Sky In-Home Ltd* [2008] EWCA Civ 978, July 3, 2008, unrep., CA)), the power to set aside a grant of permission of appeal or to impose conditions on an appeal (r.52.9), though not made promptly (*Mamidoil-Jetoil Greek Petroleum Company S.A. v Okta Crude Oil Refinery A.D.* [2003] EWCA Civ 617; [2003] 2 Lloyd's Rep. 645, CA); the power to require defamation defendant to permit inspection of documents under r.31.12 (*Rigg v Associated Newspapers* [2003] EWHC 710 (QB); April 7, 2003, unrep.); joinder of additional defendant to oppose claimant's application for summary judgment (r.19.2) (*Chubb Insurance Company of Europe S.A. v Davies* [2004] EWHC 2138, (Comm), September 23, 2004, unrep. (Langley J.). In *Cala Homes (South) Ltd v Chichester DC (Time Limits)* [2000] C.P. Rep. 28, it was held that where, instead of filing a claim form in the Crown Office in accordance with Sch.1, RSC O.94, r.2(1), an applicant by mistake filed it in another office or division of the High Court, the court had a discretion, either to strike out the claim or to transfer it to the Crown Office, to be exercised in a manner which enabled the case to be dealt with justly (see also *R. v Secretary of State for the Environment Ex p. National Farmers' Union* November 24, 1999, unrep.). In *Infantino v MacLean* [2001] 3 All E.R. 802, where the claimant failed to serve his claim form before the expiry of the period for validity for service, Douglas Brown J. held at first instance that it would be consistent with the overriding objective of enabling the court to deal with cases justly to dispense with service under r.6.9 (a course disapproved in *Godwin v Swindon BC* [2001] EWCA Civ 641; [2001] 4 All E.R. 641, CA, and then approved in certain circumstances in *Wilkey v BBC* [2002] EWCA Civ 1561, but without express reliance on the overriding objective).

Before the CPR came into effect, the courts tended to allow interlocutory applications that would inevitably result in delay in case progress. Frequently, ensuring that a respondent party adversely affected by the granting of the application was compensated in costs was the only real concern of the court. Such compensation may be classified as a fairness concern. However, the overriding objective requires that cases should be dealt with expeditiously as well as fairly (see para.11–9 below). Whether expedition should weigh more heavily in the balance than fairness is a dilemma lying at the heart of the CPR case management system (but not one readily acknowledged, see e.g. *Holmes v S.G.B. Services Plc* [2001] EWCA Civ 354; February 19, 2001, unrep., CA). Inevitably, its resolution may be affected by the particular procedural or case management issue confronting the court. It has been said that, generally, amendments to statements of case required to permit the real dispute between the parties to be adjudicated should be allowed, provided the respondent party can be compensated in costs and "the public interest in the efficient administration of justice is not significantly harmed" (*Cobbold v Greenwich LBC* August 9, 1999, unrep., per Peter Gibson L.J.; see also *Sumitomo Corporation v Credit Lyonnais Rousse Ltd* [2003] EWHC 833 (Comm); April 8, 2003, unrep., per Cooke J.). On the other hand, the Court of Appeal has stressed that judges must be astute to correct sloppy practice and to avoid at all costs "slipping back to the bad old days when courts took a relaxed attitude to the need for compliance with rules and court orders", and has suggested that, for the purpose of achieving justice and fairness, when granting applications the courts should be more ready to exercise their powers to impose conditions having the effect of limiting the applicant's claim or defence (r.3.1(3)), rather than merely saying "yes" or "no" to the application (*Southern and District Finance Ltd v Turner* [2003] EWCA Civ 1574 at para.34, per Brooke L.J. (defendant's application out of time to amend counterclaim to plead further issues allowed subject to condition that any recovery on those issues should not include losses incurred before a particular date)).

## 2. COST AND DELAY (RR.1.1(2)(b) AND (d))

**11–9** The "Access to Justice" Reports were concerned to recommend cures for the time-honoured twin scourges of civil justice; they are cost and delay. Paragraphs (b) and (d) of r.1.1(2) state that the furthering of the overriding objective of dealing with a case justly includes "so far as is practicable", amongst other things, saving expense and

***Paragraph numbers marked with a "+" can be found online and on CD.***

ensuring that it is dealt with expeditiously and fairly. The matter of expense is also referred to in para.(c)(iv) which requires the court to deal with the case in ways which take account of the financial position of each party (see further "Proportionality", para.11–10 below). The cost and delay elements of the overriding objective are reflected in r.1.4 (Court's duty to manage cases) where it is stated that active case management includes, amongst other things, considering whether the likely benefits of taking a particular step justify the cost of taking it, and giving directions to ensure that the trial of a case proceeds quickly and efficiently. And these objectives are expressly re-stated in particular contexts in the CPR; e.g. Practice Direction (Possession Claims), para.3.3 (court to consider what steps are needed finally to determine "as quickly as reasonably practicable" possession claim where assault and property damage threatened) (see Vol.1, para.55APD.6); and Practice Direction (Small Claims), para.2.5 (in deciding whether to order an exchange of witness statements court to have regard to the need for the parties "to have access to justice without undue formality, cost or delay") (see Vol.1, para.27PD.2). In these respects r.1.1 echoes the Arbitration Act 1996 s.1. That section states that the provisions of Pt 1 of that Act are founded on certain principles "and shall be construed accordingly". One of the principles is that "the object of arbitration is to obtain the fair resolution of disputes by an impartial tribunal without unnecessary delay or expense". Rule 1.1(2) also reflects Art.6 of the Convention (right to a fair trial) and the Strasbourg and British jurisprudence thereon (see the Human Rights Act 1998, Sch.1, art.6).



Well before the CPR came into effect, the courts expressed their determination to clamp down on unnecessary delay. For example, when issuing *Practice Direction (HC: Civil Litigation: Case Management)* [1995] 1 W.L.R. 262, the Lord Chief Justice and the Chancellor of the High Court said the courts "have over the years been too ready to allow those who are litigating to dictate the pace at which cases proceed". Since the CPR came into effect it has been explained that "in contrast to the old regime the court will determine the length of the trial and what is to happen at the trial" (*Loveridge v Healey* [2004] EWCA Civ 173, at para.30 per Buxton L.J.).

The courts have shown a willingness to avoid the costs inherent in, and the delays that are a consequence of, oral hearings, by requesting parties to make submissions in writing. This is apparent, not only where the rules expressly allow the court to deal with particular applications without a hearing, but also where they do not; e.g. where at the conclusion of the time allocated for a hearing, or upon circulating a written judgment before handing down, the court requests the parties to make further submissions, or submissions on post-trial matters, in writing. A striking illustration is *Simms v The Law Society* [2005] EWCA Civ 849, July 12, 2005, unrep., CA, where, after the conclusion of oral argument, the Court of Appeal invited the parties to make written submissions on an important issue as to indemnity costs. See also *Baris Ltd v Kajima Construction Europe (UK) Ltd* [2006] EWHC 31 (TCC), January 20, 2006, unrep. (Judge Peter Coulson Q.C.) (claim by claimant for interest where defendant's pre-action offer of lump sum had been accepted by claimant), and *Redhead v Rawcliffe* [2006] EWHC 2695 (QB), October 31, 2006, unrep. (Keith J.) (post-judgment submissions as to calculation of figure for final lump sum award). The procedural device of dealing with matters on paper and without a hearing has obvious cost and delay reducing advantages and is available to the court in a number of circumstances (e.g. *Baris Ltd v Kasima Construction Europe (UK) Ltd* [2006] EWHC 31 (TCC), January 20, 2006, unrep. (with consent of parties, trial judge dealing with contested application on paper)). The Court of Appeal has had this very much in mind in giving guidance as to the form of conditional orders (*Bristol City Council v Hassan* [2006] EWCA Civ 656, May 23, 2006, unrep., CA).

One of the principal ways in which the CPR seek to reduce costs and delays is by providing incentives for parties to make, and to take seriously, offers to settle (see CPR Pt 36), for example, by rules exposing parties rejecting offers to penalties in certain circumstances. It has been suggested that, for the purpose of enhancing the efficacy of these rules, they should be interpreted in the light of the "saving expense" objective stated in r.1.1(2)(b) (*Little v George Little Sebrie & Co The Times*, November 17, 1999).

Another principal way in which the CPR seek to reduce costs and delays is by providing for the summary disposal of claims and issues within claims (see CPR Pt 24). In r.1.4(2) this is identified as one of the elements of "active case management". It has been said that in exercising these powers the court saves expense and achieves expedition (*Swain v Hillman* [2001] 1 All E.R. 91, CA; *Puma AG Rudolf Dassler Sport v Sports Soccer Ltd* [2003] EWHC 2705 (Etherton J.)).

Under the CPR, for the purpose of ensuring that cases are dealt with expeditiously, greater emphasis than previously is placed on the keeping of procedural time limits. The clearest reflection of this is the unqualified power the court has to strike out a statement of case where there has been a failure to comply with a rule, practice direction or court order (r.3.4(2)(c)) (*Biguzzi v Rank Leisure Plc* [1999] 1 W.L.R. 1926, CA).

Frequently, in exercising powers given to them by the CPR the courts make specific reference to the objectives of dealing with cases expeditiously and saving expense (e.g. *Spice Girls Ltd v Aprilia World Service BV (Permission to Appeal) The Times*, September 12, 2000 (correcting errors of fact in judgment on quantum before order drawn); *Sohal v Sohal* [2002] EWCA Civ 1297; July 30, 2002, unrep., CA (whether party losing at trial alleging judgment obtained by fraud should be required to challenge judgment by separate action rather than by appeal)).

In *A v B (A Company)* [2002] EWCA Civ 337; [2002] 2 All E.R. 545, CA, the Court of Appeal laid down guidelines to assist first instance judges when dealing with applications for interim injunctions restraining publication in breach of confidence claims. The guidelines state the effect of the voluminous case law and, generally, make it unnecessary for parties to refer judges to the copious authorities; a practice that can add hugely to the costs of litigation and also can create great problems for judges hearing such applications, particularly in view of the urgency with which they have to be dealt. The Court said that the guidelines were made in discharge of the Court's obligations under the overriding objective and are intended to ensure that the majority of applications for this form of interim relief are dealt with "in a more appropriate manner". The Court added that the need for control of the excessive citation of authority should be borne in mind in deciding questions of costs "since it leads to disproportionate expense which can in turn make litigation beyond the means of ordinary person". In considering the well known recent Strasbourg jurisprudence on freedom of expression and its impact on the English law of defamation there were a growing number of cases making the same point in similar language and there was a danger of over citation.

A claimant is not obliged to include in his pleaded case all the claims which he could arguably advance against a defendant (though there are risks in failing to do so), and may legitimately limit his claim for the purpose of reducing costs and ensuring that it is dealt with proportionately (*Khiaban v Beard* [2003] EWCA Civ 358 (court has no power under r.16.3 or r.26.8(1)(a) to require claimant to increase value of a claim or to include items of claim which he has chosen not to include, and it is no part of the judicial function to force a claimant to claim more than he wishes to claim in order to maximise court fees)).

The court's general powers of case management include the power to direct that particular issues arising in any proceeding should be dealt with before others (see Vol.1, para.1.4.8). Necessarily, when this is done, the disposal of the other issues is delayed. In personal injury and wrongful death cases it is quite common for issues of liability to be tried before issues of damages. In the interests of bringing finality in litigation, it is the court's function to make a single award for damages, making the best assessment possible of future loss. The inherent difficulty in doing this, which is only partly overcome by the court's power to order interim payment of damages (CPR r.25.6), provisional damages, or payment of damages by periodical payments (CPR Pt 41), and the risk of doing injustice if the assessment is seriously wrong, encourages delays in concluding the assessment of damages hearing. It is not uncommon for the assessment of damages in such cases to be postponed for quite a long time after the conclusion of the liability trial, particularly where the claimant has suffered catastrophic injuries; see e.g. *Parkin v Bromley Hospital NHS Trust* October 4, 2001, unrep., (Buckley J.) (assessment hearing adjourned for eight months, principally for purpose of enabling accurate estimate to be made of costs of home (rather then institutional) care for the claimant). It may well be in the interests of justice that a final award of damages should not be made until sufficient time has elapsed for a reliable prognosis to be made of the claimant's medical condition, and it is possible to envisage a case where the nature of the damage and the likelihood that it will be incurred is clear, but yet quantification cannot yet be meaningfully assessed. In such a case, it may well serve the interests of all concerned to postpone the quantification until all the necessary evidence becomes available (*Adan v Securicor Custodial Services Ltd* [2004] EWHC 394,

***Paragraph numbers marked with a "+" can be found online and on CD.***

(QB), (Eady J.) (after accident claimant developing psychotic symptoms and detained under mental health legislation)). It is important that courts should continue to manage cases that are, for these reasons, subject to necessary delays before final disposition.

Those aspects of the CPR that are aimed at reducing delays in the handling of civil proceedings assist in preventing violations of Convention rights, in particular violations of Art.6. The Human Rights Act 1998 Sch.1, Pt 1, Art.6(1) states that, in the determination of his civil rights and obligations, everyone is entitled to a fair and public hearing "within a reasonable time" (see Vol.2, para.3D–76). In *Davies v United Kingdom (Application No.42007/98)* (2002) 35 E.H.R.R. 29, proceedings under the Company Directors Disqualification Act 1986 s.6 were commenced against D in July 1992, but were not completed until January 1998. The European Court of Human Rights found that the State was responsible for the greater part of the delay and held that, in the circumstances, the proceedings were not pursued with the diligence required by Art.6(1). The reasonableness of the length of proceedings has to be assessed in the light of the circumstances in each case, having regard in particular to its complexity, the conduct of the parties, and of the relevant authorities (*Robins v United Kingdom* (1998) 26 E.H.R.R. 527; *Reid v United Kingdom (Application No.50272/99)* (2003) 37 E.H.R.R. 9; 14 B.H.R.C. 41. In *Eastaway v United Kingdom (74976/01)* (2005) 40 E.H.R.R. 17, following the collapse in 1990 of group of companies, proceedings brought by Secretary of State against a former company director under the 1986 Act were commenced on July 1, 1992, and completed on June 4, 2001. The ECtHR held that, in all the circumstances, the proceedings were not pursued with the diligence required by Art.6, and there had been a violation of Art.6 in that director's civil rights and obligations were not determined within a reasonable time. In *Mitchell v United Kingdom (Application No.44808/98)* (2003) 36 E.H.R.R. 52; 14 B.H.R.C. 431 there was a delay of in excess of ten years between the commencement of a substantial and complex action in 1988 and the conclusion of enforcement proceedings, including a delay of 30 months, for which the parties were not responsible, between the date when the case was set down for trial and the trial. Because of the delays before and after trial, the enforcement proceedings were concluded on terms less favourable to the judgment creditors than would otherwise have been the case. The Court found that in the circumstances judgment creditors Art.6 rights had been violated by failures by the State to arrange its civil procedure legal system so as to prevent undue delay. In *Ceskoslovenska Obchodni Banka AS v Nomura International Plc* [2003] I.L.Pr. 20 (Mr Jonathan Sumption Q.C.), in rejecting a submission that foreign proceedings in a non-EU jurisdiction should be stayed on the ground that substantial justice would not be done, the judge noted that delays were not unusual in the courts of many modern European states despite potentially being capable of constituting a breach of Art.6. It may be commented that, even though the English courts are now relieved of the problem of applying the complex law that formerly applied to applications to strike out for want of prosecution, there is now a risk that they will become burdened with an equally complex task of considering whether claims should be struck out, or judgments set aside, for breaches of Art.6, on the ground that proceedings will not be, or were not, determined within a reasonable time. Note also in *McHugh Southern Ltd (In Liquidation), Re* [2002] EWHC 3069 (Art.6(1) requires civil proceedings to be struck out only where it is no longer possible for the defendant to receive a fair trial). See further Vol.2 Section 12 (CPR: Application, Amendments and Interpretation, para.12–58).

## 3. PROPORTIONALITY (R.1.1(2)(c))

See also "Ensuring parties on equal footing" at para.11–11 below. **11–10**

Rule 1.1(2)(c) introduces one of the most important principles underlying the new approach to civil procedure heralded by the bringing into force of the CPR, that is, the principle of proportionality. Dealing justly with a case (i.e. furthering the overriding objective) includes, so far as is practicable, dealing with the case in ways which are proportionate (i) to the amount of money involved, (ii) to the importance of the case, (iii) to the complexity of the issues, and (iv) to the financial position of each party.

There is nothing new in the concept of proportionality. Civil procedures have always been designed in a manner which took account of the fact that cases vary enormously in these respects. However, as a practical matter, in important respects the mechanisms that existed for matching claims with appropriate procedures and for ensuring that procedures designed for the heavier cases were not routinely used in ordinary cases were ineffective. In the "Report of the Civil Justice Review Body" (Cm. 394, 1988) it was said (p.14) that the cost of litigation was often quite disproportionate to the amount of the claim, that too many cases were dealt with according to High Court procedures when county court procedures would suffice, and that procedures for handling smaller cases (including debts, other small claims and many housing cases) were disproportionately complex. These findings were confirmed in the "Access to Justice" Reports.

To a significant extent, the principle of proportionality is implemented by the procedure for allocation of cases to one or other of the three case management tracks, the small claims track, the fast track, and the multi-track (see CPR Pts 26 to 29). Allocation is controlled by the court. The procedures applied in the several tracks are significantly different. The procedures applicable to cases on the small claims track are similar to those which formerly applied in cases referred to arbitration under former CCR O.19, Pt I. (In Practice Direction (Case Management—Preliminary Stage: Allocation and Re-Allocation), para.8.1 (see Vol.1, para.26PD.8) it is said that the small claims track is intended to provide "proportionate procedure" for such claims). The fast track is designed to accommodate cases in the middle range. The procedures applicable to cases proceeding on this track are limited and in this way proportionality is assured. Nothing comparable to the fast track existed in the rules formerly applicable to actions proceeding in the High Court or the county courts. (Historically speaking, the county courts were meant to offer procedures which were proportionate to smaller cases but meaningful distinctions between High Court and county court procedures disappeared as the jurisdictional limits on the county courts were raised for the purpose of relieving the High Court of business. The introduction of the fast track may be seen as an effort to re-invent the county courts). The multi-track is designed to accommodate the heavier cases and the full range of procedures is available. At this level proportionality is assured by the court's power to control the development of the case by directions given in exercise of the powers given to the court by rules of court and practice directions (all of which should be exercised with the overriding objective, and therefore the need for proportionality, in mind). Rule 26.8 states the matters which the court should take into account when deciding whether to allocate a case to one track or another. As would be expected, paras (i) to (v) of r.1.1(2)(c) are reflected in that provision. Paragraphs (i) to (v), or some of them, are referred to, either expressly or impliedly, in a number of other provisions in the CPR; e.g. r.30.3 (Criteria for transfer order), r.31.3 (Right of inspection of a disclosed document), r.31.7 (Duty of search), r.44.4 (Basis of assessment of costs), and r.44.5 (Matters to be taken into account in deciding the amount of costs); note also Practice Direction (Costs), Section 11.1 (see Vol.1, para.44PD.5). Further, express references to proportionality are found in some of the supplementing practice directions (e.g. Practice Direction (Disclosure and Inspection), para.2 (see Vol.1, para.31PD.2), Practice Direction (Costs), para.13.13 (court will not endorse agreed costs if disproportionate and unreasonable) (see Vol.1, para.44PD.4) and Practice Direction (Protocols), para.4 (Pre-action behaviour in cases not covered by approved protocol) (see Vol.1, para.C1–003). The financial position of each party is a relevant factor where the court is considering whether to exercise its discretion under r.44.3(8) to order an amount to be paid on account before costs are assessed (*Mars UK Ltd v Teknowledge Ltd (Costs)* [1999] 2 Costs L.R. 44). Applicants for wasted costs orders must bear in mind the principle of proportionality (*Re Merc Property Ltd The Times*, May 19, 1999). In *Contractreal Ltd v Davies* [2001] EWCA Civ 928; May 17, 2001, unrep., CA, Arden L.J. said (para.64) that, in the context of costs awards:

> "proportionality is a more complex exercise than simply comparing the amount of the costs with the amount that was recovered and scaling down the costs accordingly."

See also *SCT Finance Ltd v Bolton* [2002] EWCA Civ 56; [2003] 3 All E.R. 434, CA (whether, in interests of proportionality, ceiling may be placed on paying party's costs where costs to be assessed on standard basis).

The Court of Appeal has held that it is essential that courts should attach the appropriate significance to the requirement of proportionality when making orders for costs and when assessing costs (*Lownds v Secretary of State for the Home Department* [2002] EWCA Civ 365; [2002] 1 W.L.R. 2450, CA; *Voice and Script International Ltd v Alghafar* [2003] EWCA Civ 736; May 8, 2003, unrep., CA). The Court has stressed that, in modern litigation, with the emphasis on proportionality, "costs budgeting" is required in cases where it is recognised at the outset that the proceedings could easily result in disproportionate costs being incurred. The legal representatives for the parties should make an assessment of the likely value of the claim and its importance and complexity, and then plan the necessary legal work needed. This involves determining in advance the appropriate amount of time to be spent on the various stages of the proceedings and to be spent overall, and estimating the likely costs overall (ibid., see also *Jefferson v National Freight Carriers Ltd* [2001] EWCA Civ 2082; [2001] Costs L.R. 313, CA.

In para.1.1(2)(c) the word "proportionate" is used in a technical sense. In some CPR rule and practice direction provisions the words "proportionate" and "disproportionate" are used in a general sense and not for the specific purpose of drawing attention to this aspect of the overriding objective. Examples are Practice Direction (Further Information), para.1.2 (requests to be confined to matters "which are reasonably necessary and proportionate" and para.4.2 (objection to request on ground of "disproportionate expense") (see Vol.1, paras 18PD.1 and 18PD.4). Some provisions state that remuneration awarded by the court should be proportionate (e.g. CPR r.69.7 (Receiver's remuneration)). Increasingly the words are used by judges in their judgments (e.g. *Malgar Ltd v RE Leach (Engineering) Ltd* [2000] C.P. Rep. 39 (Sir Richard Scott V.-C.) (application to commit for contempt disproportionate in all the circumstances); *Secretary of State for Trade and Industry v Staton* [2001] C.P. Rep. 1; [2001] B.C.C. 467, CA (application to dismiss claim under r.3.4(2) where delay caused by the court's mistake), Keith v CPM Field Marketing Ltd [2001] C.P. Rep. 35, CA (order barring defendant from defending claim disproportionate); Price v Price [2003] EWCA Civ 888; [2003] 3 All E.R. 911, CA (time for extending service of particulars of claim extended on conditions where alternative of striking out claim disproportionate)) but it is not always clear whether they are being used in their technical or general senses.

The concept of proportionality is also relevant to the taking of appeals, both from interlocutory and final orders; see *Piglowska v Piglowski* [1991] 1 W.L.R. 1360, HL (wisdom of granting successive permissions to appeal important point of principle at expense of parties with very limited resources doubted by Lord Hoffmann) and *Walker v Home Office* April 16, 1999, unrep., CA (permission to appeal striking out order refused where point of principle trivial in circumstances).

The requirement that, so far as is practicable, the court should exercise powers given to it by the CPR "in ways which are proportionate" has been referred to in various procedural contexts. For example, whether permission should be given to reamend a statement of case (*McPhilemy v Times Newspapers Ltd* [1999] 3 All E.R. 775, CA); whether expert evidence should be admitted (*Gumpo v Church of Scientology Religious Education College Inc.* July 26, 1999, unrep.; *Mann v Chetty & Patel* [2001] C.P. Rep. 24); whether a party should be committed for technical breach of complex order in circumstances where breach trivial and non-blameworthy (*Adam Phones Ltd v Goldschmidt* [1999] 4 All E.R. 486); whether a pre-emptive costs order should be made in favour of an economically weak party bringing proceedings in the public interest (*R. v Hammersmith and Fulham LBC Ex p. C.P.R.E. London Branch* October 26, 1999, unrep. (Richards J.)); whether a second respondent should be joined in judicial review proceedings on the basis that the applicant, if unsuccessful, would not be liable for that respondent's costs (*R. v Secretary of State for the Environment, Transport and the Regions Ex p. O'Byrne (Application for Jo)* [2000] C.P. Rep. 9); whether wasted costs order should be granted (*Merc Property Ltd, Re The Times*, May 19, 1999); whether further evidence should be received under CPR Sch.1, RSC O.55, r.7(2) (see now r.52.11(2)) in trade mark appeal (*CLUB EUROPE Trade Mark* [2000] R.P.C. 329); whether a party dissatisfied with the report of a single joint expert should be permitted to instruct another expert (*Daniels v Walker* [2000] 1 W.L.R. 1382, CA); whether personal injuries claim should be stayed until claimant submitted to expert examination designed to investigate medical issue relevant to one of several heads of damage (*James v Baily Gibson & Co* [2002] EWCA Civ 1690); whether application for summary assessment of costs should be refused because of applicant's failure to serve schedule of costs 24 hours before hearing (*MacDonald v Taree Holdings Ltd* [2001] C.P.L.R. 439 (Neuberger J.)), whether permission to appeal should be subject to the condition (see r.52.3(7)) that the appellant should pay all the costs of the appeal irrespective of the outcome of the proceedings (*Morris v Wrexham CBC* [2001] EWHC Admin 697; May 18, 2001, unrep. (Jackson J.)); whether issues of liability and quantum should be tried separately (*DHL Air Ltd v Wells* [2003] EWCA Civ 1743; *The Times*, November 14, 2003, CA; whether summary judgment application should be stayed pending determination of appeal in another case likely to clarify relevant law (*Green v Skandia Life Assurance Co Ltd* [2006] EWHC 1626 (Ch), July 7, 2006, unrep.). In *Flynn v Robin Thompson & Partners* (2000) 80 P. & C.R. 419, CA, the Court had recourse to the principle of proportionality when holding that it was not reasonable to allow to go to trial an allegation that a partnership was liable under the Partnership Act 1890 s.10 for an assault perpetrated by one of its members as a result of which no loss was sustained.

Beyond the CPR, concepts of proportionality are found in European Law and in the law relating to Convention rights, and they have effects on English substantive and procedural law in a number of respects. More detailed explanation of the impact of these concepts is beyond the scope of this commentary. It suffices to say that there is plenty of room for confusion. The case of *Campbell v M.G.N. Ltd (No.2)* [2005] UKHL 61; [2005] 1 W.L.R. 3394, HL, provides an illustration. Here the unsuccessful defendants in a libel claim argued on appeal that the costs they were obliged to pay the winning claimant, who had the benefit of a conditional fee agreement with her legal advisers incorporating a success fee, was necessarily disproportionate because the award of costs was more than (and up to twice as much as) the amount which, under the ordinary assessment rules, a costs judge would consider reasonable and proportionate. Lord Hoffmann said this argument was flawed because it confused two different concepts of proportionality. On the one hand there is the concept of proportionality within the CPR costs rules, which is concerned with whether expenditure on litigation was proportionate to the amount at stake, the interests of the parties, the complexity of the issues, and so forth. On the other hand there is the concept of proportionality used for testing whether a party's rights under Art.10 of the Convention (freedom of expression) were infringed. In relation to the latter his lordship pointed out that it was settled that the statutory CFA scheme, under which unsuccessful defendants may be required to pay, not only the reasonable and proportionate costs of their adversary, but also to contribute to funding of other litigation, was a proportionate measure to provide those other litigants with access to justice.

## 4. ENSURING PARTIES ON EQUAL FOOTING (R.1.1(2)(a))

**11–11** Dealing with a case justly includes, so far as is practicable, "ensuring that the parties are on an equal footing" (r.1.1(2)(a)). Obviously, this aspect of the overriding objective is closely related to that of dealing with a case in ways which are proportionate "to the financial position of each party" (r.1.1(2)(c)(iv)). However, equality is not limited to the respective capacities of the parties to finance the litigation in which they are involved.

In the "Access to Justice" Reports it was said that one of the defects in the civil justice system was the "lack of equality" between the powerful, wealthy litigant and the under-resourced litigant and amongst the specific objectives of the reforms proposed in those Reports was the need to establish "equality of arms" between the parties involved in civil cases so as to ensure, so far as possible, that there should be "a level playing field between litigants of unequal financial or other resources" (see Final Report, pp.2 and 146 and Interim Report, p.26). It was said that financially stronger and more experienced parties could exploit rules of court so as to intimidate weaker parties by spinning out proceedings and escalating costs. In the Interim Report it was said that the overriding objective should include "making allowances for any inequality between the parties" (p.216) but in the Final Report this formula was abandoned in favour of that now found in r.1.1(2)(a) (p.274).

The procedures introduced by the CPR are simpler than those which previously prevailed and their application in individual cases is subject to supervision by the court through the case management system. Consequently, the scope for a wealthy or experienced party using intimidatory tactics against a party weaker in either or both of those respects is now reduced. Thus, the overall system goes a long way towards ensuring that in individual cases the parties are "on an equal footing".

Practice Direction (Protocols), para.4 states that, in cases not covered by any approved pre-action protocol, the court will expect the parties to act reasonably in exchanging information and documents relevant to the claim and generally in trying to avoid the necessity for the start of proceedings. This paragraph refers generally to the overriding objective and expressly to the equal footing objective stated in r.1.1(2)(a) (see Vol.1, para.C1–003).

The exercise of the court's discretion to allow a witness to give evidence through a video link (r.32.3), which relates to the furthering of the overriding objective (r.1.1) by making use of technology (r.1.4(2)(k)) in the active management of cases, has been seen as a means by which the court may seek to ensure that the parties are on an equal footing (*Rowland v Bock* [2002] EWHC 692 (QB); [2002] 4 All E.R. 370 (Newman J.)).

The provisions introduced by the CPR as to costs should have the effect of reducing the burden on a party who is financially weaker than his opponent. In fast track cases the costs recoverable by a successful party are limited. As this limitation accrues to the benefit of both financially strong and financially weak losing parties it has been suggested that it may have the effect of favouring the stronger party and introducing inequality. However, fast track cases are subject to limited procedures and to strict timetables and this reduces both the scope for a strong party to push up the amount of work required by his weaker opponent and the extent to which the strong party will be able to spend money extravagantly on his own case (see Final Report, pp.28 and 45).



The "equal footing" aspect of the overriding objective (together with the need to deal with cases in ways which are proportionate to the financial position of each party) may be relevant where the costs payable to a successful litigant in person fall to be assessed (*R. (Wulfsohn) v Legal Services Commission* [2002] EWCA Civ 250; February 8, 2002, unrep., CA), where an application is made for an order for costs against non-party (*Hamilton v Al-Fayed* [2002] EWCA Civ 665; *The Times*, June 17, 2002, CA, at para.65 per Chadwick L.J.) and when the court is considering whether it should exercise its powers to make a pre-emptive costs order in favour of the economically weaker party (*R. v Hammersmith and Fulham LBC Ex p. C.P.R.E. London Branch* October 26, 1999, unrep. (Richards J.); *R. v Secretary of State for the Environment, Transport and the Regions Ex p. O'Byrne* [2000] C.P. Rep. 9 (Hooper J.); *R. (Campaign for Nuclear Disarmament) v Prime Minister (Costs)* [2002] EWHC 2712 (Admin); *Henry v BBC (Qualified Privilege)* [2005] EWHC 2503 (Gray J.)).

Where one party can afford to instruct a large firm of experienced and expensive solicitors, whereas the other can afford only small and relatively inexperienced advisers, the court may make orders designed to rectify this imbalance; for example, orders allowing the smaller firm more time to carry out necessary work, or requiring the larger firm to prepare bundles of documents needed for court hearings (*Maltez v Lewis The Times*, May 4, 1999). However, the court has no power, either under r.1.1(2) or under any other provision, to prevent a party from instructing the legal representatives of his choice, simply on the ground that he is able to afford more powerful representation than his opponent.

A potential source of inequality between parties may lie in their respective access to expert evidence. Some of the provisions as to experts now found in Pt 35 (particularly r.35.8) are designed to remedy this imbalance; e.g. *ES v Chesterfield & North Derbyshire Royal Hospital NHS Trust* [2003] EWCA Civ 1284; [2004] Lloyd's Med. Rep. 90, CA (on "equality of arms" grounds, infant claimant granted permission to call second expert witness in serious medical negligence claim); *Kearsley v Klarfeld* [2005] EWCA Civ 1510; [2006] 2 All E.R. 303, CA (further expert permitted on issue on which current opinion divided); *Radu v Houston* [2006] EWHC 231 (QB), March 7, 2006, unrep. (Eady J.) (permitting expert evidence on prospects for enforcement of judgment in foreign jurisdiction on application for security for costs); see also Final Report, p.146.

There is no absolute rule that, in every case, parties must be limited to the same number of expert witnesses. Although "equality of arms" in this respect should be the general rule, there may be circumstances in which it should give way for the sake of achieving the overriding objective of dealing with cases justly (*Kirkman v Euro Exide Corporation (CMP Batteries Ltd)* [2007] EWCA Civ 66 *The Times* February 6, 2007, CA).

When deciding the track for a claim, the matters to which the court should have regard include "the circumstances of the parties" (r.26.8(1)(i)), and that would include inequality in their circumstances.

It has been said that a factor that may weigh against allowing a party's application to amend his statement of case made when trial is imminent is that such amendment would create a risk of prejudice and embarrassment to his opponent with the effect that the parties would not be on an equal footing (*Woods v Chaleff* May 28, 1999, unrep., CA). Circumstances may arise where a refusal to order security for costs for an appeal would result in the appeal being pursued on an unequal footing, an outcome which should be avoided (*Federal Bank of the Middle East v Hadkinson The Times*, December 7, 1999, CA).

The objective of ensuring that parties are on an equal footing may be a relevant consideration where the court is considering whether it should exercise such powers as it may have to require a party to provide his opponent with information to enable the latter to make a realistic Pt 36 payment and to respond to a Pt 36 offer (*Gnitrow Ltd v Cape Plc* [2000] 3 All E.R. 763, CA) or to make an order for an interim payment following judgment on liability (*Harmon CFEM Facades (UK) Ltd v Corporate Officer of the House of Commons (Interim Payment)* [2001] C.P. Rep. 20). The "equal footing" aspect of the overriding objective was stressed as a reason for not ordering a re-trial in a defamation case where the defendant newspaper argued on appeal, contrary to their argument at trial, that a particular question should not have been left to the jury (*McPhilemy v Times Newspapers Ltd (No.3) The Times*, June 19, 2001, CA).

In *Geveran Trading Co Ltd v Skjevesland* [2002] EWCA Civ 1567; [2003] 1 W.L.R. 912, CA, the question arising was whether an advocate who is or was acquainted socially with the litigant against whom he is instructed to appear or a close member of that litigant's family should be prevented from acting. The bearing of the equality of arms principle on this issue figured in the submissions of the parties but was not emphasised by the Court in the reasoning underlying its judgment.

As to the right to equality of arms under Art.6 of the European Convention on Human Rights, see further Vol.2 Section 12 (CPR: Application, Amendments and Interpretation, para.12–58).

## 5. COURT'S RESOURCES (R.1.1(2)(e))

**11–12** Dealing with a case justly includes, so far as is practicable, "allotting to it an appropriate share of the court's resources, while taking into account the need to allot resources to other cases" (r.1.1(2)(e)). This provision is inelegant, but its meaning is tolerably clear. An underlying theme in the "Access to Justice" Reports is that the harmful impacts of excessive and disproportionate costs, and of delays brought about by the behaviour of parties, are not confined to the parties themselves. The burden of costs can fall on publicly provided funds and can harm the economic health of businesses. Where delays occur in one case, parties in other cases can be inconvenienced, subject to delays not of their own making, and put to additional expense. Further, court resources can be wasted where parties make successive applications for the same interim relief (see Vol.1, para.1.4.14), or make unnecessary applications, or where time is taken up by hearings provoked or made necessary by one party's failure to comply with court rules or orders.

In modern times, concerns about these wider effects have influenced decisions made by the courts in cases involving applications for late adjournments, to extend time (including time for appealing), to relieve from the normal consequences of defaults of various kinds (including failures to comply with "unless" orders), and to strike out for want of prosecution or abuse of process (e.g. *Mortgage Corporation Ltd v Sandoes The Times*, December 27, 1996, CA; *Hytec Information Systems Ltd v Coventry City Council* [1997] 1 W.L.R. 1666, CA; and *Arbuthnot Latham Bank Ltd v Trafalgar Holdings Ltd The Times*, December 29, 1997, CA) (for further illustrations, see below).

Rule 1.1(2)(e) recognises that court resources are limited, that demand is always likely to outstrip supply, that justice has to be "rationed". The overall scheme of the CPR and the case management system in particular is designed to ensure that each case is allotted its "appropriate share of the court's resources" (see further "Proportionality", para.11–10 above). The significance of r.1.1(2)(e) is that it states that, in allotting each case its share of resources, the court should take into account "the need to allot resources to other cases". It would seem that what is meant by determining the share of court resources which should be allotted to a case is determining what is the appropriate form of management for that case. This is not confined to determining the appropriate case management track but also includes the manner in which all of the other powers which the court has to control the development of the case (including the power to impose sanctions for procedural failures) is exercised. In determining the appropriate form of management the court should have regard to the need to prevent any one case being conducted in a way that interferes with the resolution of other disputes and wastes the resources of the court (see Interim Report,

***Paragraph numbers marked with a "+" can be found online and on CD.***

p.39); see e.g. *W.L. Gore & Associates GmbH v Geox SpA* [2008] EWHC 462 (Pat), March 5, 2008, unrep. (Lewison J.) (on application to advance trial date, account taken of effects that granting application would have on parties in other cases awaiting trial). Litigants and their advisers should recognise that any delay which occurs will be assessed, not only from the point of view of the prejudice caused in their case, but also in relation to other litigants and the prejudice which is caused to the due administration of justice (*Arbuthnot Latham Bank Ltd v Trafalgar Holdings Ltd*, op. cit., per Lord Woolf M.R.).

An important aspect of case management is the allocation of cases to judges who have specialist expertise. There is an understandable tendency to assume that a case raising complicated issues in a highly specialised area of the law would be dealt with more efficiently and effectively if it were handled and tried by a judge whose skill, training and experience matched the demands of the case (especially where there is serious conflict of esoteric expert evidence). To an extent this is accomplished by the mechanisms by which cases are allocated to particular "courts" and "lists" (especially within the High Court) with nominated judges. Directions given by the court in a particular case that the proceedings be assigned to a specialist judge, whether in accordance with a system habitually adhered to by the court or ad hoc (and whether on the application of parties or not), can be seen as a practice designed to ensure, so far as is practicable, that cases are allotted an appropriate share of the court's resources. See e.g. *InterDigital Technology Corporation v Nokia Corporation* [2008] EWHC 297 (Ch), February 19, 2008, unrep, (Floyd J.) (system of allocating patent cases to judges (including "career patent judges") according to their technical complexity described as a practice designed to make maximum use of judicial time). Usually, planning by the court to ensure that particular cases can be dealt with by particular specialist judges takes place months in advance of the trials themselves. The postponement of dates fixed for trial and the adjournment of trials can affect the resources which the court may have available at any given time (*Fitzpatrick Contractors Ltd v Tyco Fire Integrated Solutions (UK) Ltd* [2008] EWHC 1927 (TCC), July 25, 2008, unrep. (Coulson J.)).

Under the Senior Courts Act 1981 s.42 (Restriction of vexatious legal proceedings), on the application of the Attorney General the court has power to make a civil proceedings order restraining a person from bringing or continuing legal proceedings. In modern times, the need to ensure that the resources of the courts are husbanded has figured increasingly prominently in the cases in which the scope of this power has been explained. For example, in *Attorney General v Foden* [2005] EWHC 1281 (Admin), April 7, 2005, DC, unrep., the court said that a person alleged to be a vexatious litigant had "perpetrated a waste of scarce judicial resources needed for the determination of proper claims". In *Attorney General v Miles* [2007] EWHC 1729 (Admin), June 19, 2006, DC, unrep., the court referred to the need "to protect scarce judicial resources from being wasted by the pursuit of hopeless and repetitive litigation". It has also figured in the development of the power of the court to make civil restraint orders (see r.3.11), a power based on the court's inherent jurisdiction to prevent abuse of process. To an extent, the procedures supporting this jurisdiction themselves are designed are to protect the court's resources by providing that certain applications must be made on paper and may be dealt with without a hearing.

It has been said that by exercising its powers of summary disposal under Pt 24 the court gives effect to the particular objective stated in r.1.1(2)(e) by "avoiding the court's resources being used up on cases where it would serve no purpose" (*Swain v Hillman* [2001] 1 All E.R. 91, CA).

It has been said that, where an application is made to strike out a claim as an abuse of process under r.3.4(2)(b), on the ground that the claim is indistinguishable from a previous claim which was not proceeded with, the application may be granted on the basis that permitting the claim to continue would involve an inappropriate allocation of a share of the court's resources (*Securum Finance Ltd v Ashton (No.1)* [2001] Ch. 29; [2000] 3 W.L.R. 1400, CA).

Even in an important case where the amount at stake is very large, the issues are very complex, and where both parties appear to have very substantial resources at their command, the judge is nevertheless under a duty to manage the case in a manner that, so far as is practicable, allots to it an appropriate share of the court's resources, while taking into account the need to allot resources to other cases (*Morris v Bank of America National Trust* December 21, 1999, unrep., CA (where parties' estimates of needed trial time varied from three months to 12 months)).

The need to ensure that cases are allocated an appropriate share of the court's resources and that those resources are not wasted has been emphasised in cases where a party has requested the court to exercise its discretion to re-consider a judgment before it is sealed or otherwise perfected (*Compagnie Noga d'Importation et d'Exploration S.A. v Abacha (No.2)* (2001) 151 New L.J. 693; *Royal Brompton Hospital NHS Trust v Hammond (No.8)* [2001] EWCA Civ 778); it has been used as a justification for making orders striking out moribund claims entirely instead of subjecting them to indefinite stays leaving open "the possibility of applications being made to resurrect them from time to time" (*Astaldi S.p.A. v Generali-Kent Sigorta A.S.* June 25, 2002, unrep.(Judge Dean Q.C.)); as a justification in part for refusing an application to substitute a party as claimant in circumstances not directly provided for by the rules (*R. (Johnson) v Secretary of State for Health* [2006] EWHC 288 (Admin), February 23, 2006, unrep. (Silber J.), or to remit to a costs judge an application for a prospective costs order (Willis v *Nicolson* [2007] EWCA Civ 199, March 13, 2007, CA, unrep,); for refusing to substitute a new party as claimant in judicial review proceedings (ibid); as an additional reason for holding that permission to make an appeal was required where that might be a matter for doubt (*Compagnie Noga d'Importation et d'Exploration S.A. v Australia and New Zealand Banking Group Ltd* [2002] EWCA Civ 1142; July 31, 2002, unrep., CA); as a consideration weighing against the granting of an application for an adjournment of the hearing of an application made at the start of the hearing (*Albon v Naza Motor Trading Sdn Bhd* [2007] EWHC 2613 (Ch); 157 New L.J. 1615 (2007) (Lightman J.)); for enabling an appeal court to decline to hear submissions one ground of appeal when minded to find against the appellant on another ground in circumstances in which he had to succeed on both in order to upset the order under appeal (*Palfrey v Wilson* [2007] EWCA Civ 94; *The Times* March 5, 2007, CA) (see also *A. v B. Plc*, referred to above), or to refuse an application to set aside permission to appeal made at the start of the substantive appeal after the court had devoted preparation time to the case (*Tradigrain SA v Intertek Testing Services*[2007] EWCA Civ 154; *The Times* March 20, 2007, CA); as a consideration relevant in determining whether a TCC claim should continue to be handled through its pre-trial stages by a senior circuit judge at a provincial court centre or transferred to the RCJ (*Neath Port Talbot BC v Currie & Brown Project Management Ltd* [2008] EWHC 1508 (TCC), June 16, 2008, unrep.). The Court of Appeal has been critical of parties who waste court resources by contesting applications unnecessarily, especially where they had no standing to do so (*Folks v Faizey* [2006] EWCA Civ 381, April 6, 2006, unrep., CA (defendant opposing claimant's application for appointment of litigation friend)). In *Aldi Stores Ltd v WSP Group Plc* [2007] EWCA Civ 1260, November 28, 2007, unrep, CA, a judge sitting in the Technology and Construction Court granted the defendant's application to strike out a claim against them on abuse of process grounds and did so partly for the reasons that that the claim should have been raised in an earlier action, and that the resources of the TCC should not be devoted, for a second time, to trying the same allegations. In allowing the appeal the Court of Appeal stated that, if a litigant's claim can be properly brought, he cannot be denied the right to bring it on the basis that he could have acted differently, and so made more efficient use of the court's resources.

The allocation to a case of an appropriate share of the court's resources may also be a consideration in the handling of appeals by the Court of Appeal (*Adoko v Jemal The Times*, July 8, 1999, CA; *Stephenson (S.B.J.) Ltd v Mandy The Times*, July 21, 1999, CA); and in dealing with applications for re–trials (*Coflexip SA v Stolt Comex Seaway MS Ltd* July 31, 2000, unrep., CA). In *A v B plc.* [2002] EWCA Civ 337; [2003] Q.B. 195, CA, the Court of Appeal, having apparently come to the conclusion that the defendant's appeal against an interim injunction should be allowed on the merits, but reserving judgment, declined to hear oral argument on another ground of appeal (not related to the merits, but raising a procedural issue). The Court pointed out that the time allocated for the appeal was exhausted in considering the substantive appeal, and full argument on the procedural issue (which had become academic) would have extended the hearing by two days. In *Irving v Penguin Books Ltd* [2001] EWCA Civ 935, CA, very shortly before the date fixed for the commencement of a hearing before a particular panel of the Court of Appeal in a libel appeal, and after the members of the panel had done a considerable amount of preparation for the hearing, the appellant (acting in person) applied for a 21-day adjournment. In dismissing the application the Court stressed inconvenience to the Court and the waste of resources that would result should the application be granted. In *Anufrijeva v Southwark London BC* [2003] EWCA

Civ 1406; [2004] Q.B. 1124, CA, the judges of the Court of Appeal undertook much more pre-reading in preparation for the appeal than usual and did this for the purpose of reducing, by using court resources in this way, the number of days needed for the oral hearing, and thereby reducing the costs incurred by the publicly funded parties. An appeal court's resources may be wasted, not only when a hearing overruns its estimate, but also when it is concluded well within it in circumstances where counsel should have appreciated that that would happen (e.g. *Wilson v Jaymarke Estates Ltd* [2007] UKHL 29; *The Times* June 28, 2007, H.L.). In *Hunte v E. Bottomley and Sons Ltd* October 16, 2007, unrep., CA, for purposes of reducing costs and avoiding waste of court resources, the court gave guidance on manner in which parties (1) should present plans, maps, diagrams and photographs relied on, and (2) relate them to skeleton arguments, for use by court in pre-reading and at hearing.

Particular provisions in the CPR impose duties on parties to keep the court informed of case developments which may affect the efficient administration of the court's business (e.g. claimant's duty under r.26.4(4) to inform court if settlement is reached where stay ordered).

It is the duty of the parties and of their professional advisers to inform the court (whether first instance or appeal) immediately they become aware of any development which might make it unnecessary for judgment to be delivered; the foundation of this duty is the requirement (derived from r.1.1(2)(e)) that the court's resources should be properly and efficiently deployed (*HFC Bank Plc v HSBC Bank Plc (formerly Midland Bank Plc)* [2000] F.S.R. 176, CA; *Gurney Consulting Engineers v Gleeds Health and Safety Limited* [2006] EWHC 536 (TCC); *The Times*, April 24, 2006).). Similarly, for the purpose of ensuring that judge's do not waste time pre-reading and preparing for hearings, parties must promptly advise the court if a listed case is not proceeding (*Tasyurdu v Secretary of State for the Home Department* [2003] EWCA Civ 447; [2003] C.P. Rep. 61, CA); *Red River UK Ltd v Sheikh [2009] EWCA Civ 643*; *The Times* May 6, 2009, CA. The court's resources are likely to be used inefficiently if parties do not assist the court by complying with practice directions relating to the presentation and filing of documents for an appeal and for the citation of authorities (*Bank of Scotland v Henry Butcher & Co* [2003] EWCA Civ 67; [2004] 2 All E.R. (Comm) 557, CA) or if an application is withdrawn on the day of hearing where it has become unarguable because the point had been overtaken by another case of which counsel was, or ought to have been, aware much earlier (*Gahie v Immigration Appeal Tribunal* [2003] EWCA Civ 611; *The Times*, March 20, 2003, CA). If, on an appeal to the Court of Appeal, a party wishes to file a replacement skeleton argument making an expanded case requiring additional time for argument, counsel should at the earliest date give the court full deals making entirely clear what is wanted and why it is wanted (*AIC Ltd v ITS Testing Service (UK) Ltd* [2006] EWCA Civ 1601; [2007] 1 Lloyd's Rep. 555, CA (rules as to supplementary skeleton arguments explained)).

It should be noted, however, that, save in exceptional circumstances, structural deficiencies, including those arising from a shortage of resources, cannot be a reason for denying the right to a fair trial guaranteed under Art.6(1) of the European Convention on Human Rights: *Bucholz v Germany* (1981) 3 E.H.R.R. 597. In *Berry Trade Ltd v Moussavi* [2002] EWCA Civ 477; [2002] 1 W.L.R. 1910, CA, the court held that, in the circumstances of this case, the judge's refusal to grant a defendant's application for a further adjournment of a committal hearing violated the defendant's Convention rights. The court said affording the defendant a proper opportunity to exercise those rights should outweigh other considerations, such as the use of court resources and the convenience of other parties.

## 6. MAKING USE OF TECHNOLOGY (R.1.4(2)(k))

Rule 1.4(1) states that the court must further the overriding objective by actively managing cases and "active case management" is described as including (amongst other things) making use of technology. This aspect of the overriding objective (though appearing in r.1.4) is related to the allocation of court resources element stated in r.1.1(2)(e). **11–13**

In the "Access to Justice" Reports, much was made of the importance of using computer-assisted technology to improve the efficiency of the administration of civil justice at all levels (see Interim Report, pp.82 *et seq.* and Final Report, pp.284 *et seq.*). Such technology may be used to advantage:

***Paragraph numbers marked with a "+" can be found online and on CD.***

(1) by practitioners to assist them in the management of their cases,
(2) by courts
 (a) for the purpose of recording information about individual cases, tracking their progress and ensuring deadlines are met, and
 (b) for the purpose of providing management information about pending business to aid forward planning of sittings and listing, and
(3) by courts and parties to aid communication between one another.

In addition, technology may be used in the court room itself to facilitate the presentation of evidence and argument. It could be argued that the very success of the reforms introduced by the CPR depends on technology, particularly on court-based technology to facilitate case management. (In *Heyward v Plymouth Hospital N.H.S. Trust* [2005] EWCA Civ 939, June 20, 2005, unrep., CA, the Master of the Rolls regretted the fact that, because of lack of funding, the Court Service had not been able to introduce electronic case files to facilitate the handling of cases in the civil courts.)

The objective (stated in r.1.4(1)(k)) of furthering the overriding objective (of enabling the court to deal with cases justly) by "making use of technology" for the purpose of "actively managing cases", is carried forward by rules and practice directions. Where a document is required to be signed, that requirement may be satisfied if the signature is "printed by computer or other mechanical means" (r.5.3). The court's general powers of case management include the power to hold a hearing and receive evidence by telephone or by using any other method of direct oral communication (except where the rules provide otherwise) (r.3.1(2)(d)). As to telephone hearings of applications to the court and video conferencing, see Practice Direction (Applications) paras 6 and 7 (see Vol.1, paras 23APD.6 and 23APD.7). In *Heyward v Plymouth Hospital N.H.S. Trust* [2005] EWCA Civ 939, June 20, 2005, unrep., CA, the Master of the Rolls commended the practice of carrying out case management conferences or other interlocutory matters by telephone where it is appropriate but added that, where this done, it is important that the judge who is conducting the hearing should have available before him the appropriate documentary material in a form which the parties to the proceedings are able to duplicate so that their submissions are readily intelligible. A further illustration of the use of technology is provided by r.32.3 which states that the court may allow a witness to give evidence through a video link or by other means (see further, Practice Direction (Written Evidence), para.29.1 and the "Video Conferencing Guide" annexed thereto (see Vol.1, para.32PD.29), and note *Practice Direction (Family Division: Video Conferencing)* [2002] 1 W.L.R. 406). A list of sites which are available for videoconferencing can be found on Her Majesty's Court Service website at *http://www.hmcourtsservice.gov.uk* [Accessed November 22, 2007]. Legal representatives situated in provincial centres have been urged to use the videoconferencing facilities available for making applications to the Court of Appeal sitting at the Royal Courts of Justice (*Babbings v Kirklees Metropolitan BC* (2004) 101(45) L.S.G. 32; *The Times* November 4, 2004, CA). In *Black v Pastouna* [2005] EWCA Civ 1389, October 31, 2005, unrep., CA, the Court of Appeal stated that, in every case involving an application to the court which is likely to last half an hour or less, parties should consider whether VCF would be desirable, and warned that, if the Court is not satisfied that there are any features of the application which warrant an oral hearing with the applicant or his advisers present in court, it may direct that any recoverable costs may be limited to the cost of conducting the hearing by video conference, if these are likely to be less than the cost of attending court and any associated travel expenses. Practice Direction (Third Party Debt Orders), para.5.5 expressly provides that, where, in a case of exceptional urgency, an application without notice to a judgment creditor for a hardship payment order is made by a judgment debtor subject to interim third party debt order, the judge where possible will normally direct that the judgment creditor be informed of the application and give him the opportunity to make representations "by telephone, fax or other appropriate method of communication". See also Practice Direction (Costs), para.40.9(2) (notice to court by fax of settlement of detailed assessment proceedings) (see Vol.1, para.47PD.13), Practice Direction (Further Information), para.1.7 (preliminary request for further information or clarification to be served by email if reasonably practicable) (para.18PD.1 below), and Practice Direction (Third Party Debt Orders), para.5.5 (judgment creditor to be given opportunity to make representations by telephone, fax or other appropriate method of communication) (see Vol.1, para.72PD.5).

Where legal representatives refuse service of a document which the legal representatives of their client's opponent in an emergency purported to serve on them by electronic means where such service is not expressly permitted by the rules, they are likely to have difficulty in resisting any application by the opponent for relief from sanctions imposed as a result of the defective service (*R.C. Residuals Ltd v Linton Fuel Oils Ltd* [2002] EWCA Civ 911; [2002] 1 W.L.R. 2782, CA (service of expert evidence by email attachment)).

Rule 5.5 (Filing and sending documents) was added to the CPR by the Civil Procedure (Amendment) Rules 2002 (SI 2002/2058) and came into effect on December 2, 2002. This rule states that a practice direction may make provision for documents to be filed or sent to the court by (a) facsimile, or (b) other electronic means. Rule 5.5 is supplemented by Practice Direction (Communication and Filing of Documents by E-mail), see para.5BPD.1 below). Further new CPR provisions allowing for the greater use of technology to facilitate the service of documents civil proceedings may be expected as a result of the "Modernising Justice" initiative.

Claim forms in certain county court proceedings may be issued through the Production Centre. The Centre provides a facility which, through the use of information technology, enables claim forms to be issued in any county court. The facility requires the modification of the CPR in certain respects (Practice Direction (Production Centre), see Vol.1, para.7CPD.1. Rule 75.4 provides for the electronic delivery of certain documents in county court proceedings under Pt 75 (Traffic Penalties). Rule 55.10A and Practice Direction (Possession Claims Online) make provision for a claimant to start certain types of possession claim in certain courts by requesting the issue of a claim form electronically.

It is expressly provided that where an oral hearing is held on an application for a European order for payment, or on an application under art.8 of the ESCP Regulation, it may take place by telephone or video conference; Practice Direction—European Order for Payment and European Small Claims Procedures paras 6.2 and 17.2 (see Vol.1, paras 78PD.6 and 78PD.17).

As to use of information technology in the Chancery Division, see Chancery Guide, Chap.14 (Vol.2, para.1A–130); see also *Morris v Bank of America National Trust* December 21, 1999, unrep., CA (observations on opportunities for use of information technology in complex case).

As to information technology in the Queen's Bench Division, see Queen's Bench Guide, para.2.7 (Vol.2, para.1B–15); Admiralty and Commercial Cruts Guide Section J.4 (Vol.2, para.2A–109); Technology and Construction Court Guide paras 4.5 and 4.6 (Vol.2, paras 2C–62 and 2C–63).

## E. DUTY OF THE PARTIES (R.1.3)

As is explained in the commentary to CPR r.1.3 (see Vol.1 para.1.3.8), the structure **11–14** of the rules in Pt 1 suggests that it is the duty of the court to give effect to the overriding objective in particular proceedings. The rules are designed to enable "the court" to deal with cases justly (r.1.1), it is "the court" that must seek to give effect to the overriding objective (r.1.2), and it is "the court" that must further that objective by actively managing cases (r.1.4). (Note also CPR r.3.1(2)(m)). No such duty is directly imposed on the parties. However, r.1.3 states that the parties are required "to help the court" to further the overriding objective (r.1.3).

In *Albon v Naza Motor Trading Sdn Bhd* [2007] EWHC 2613 (Ch), (2007) 157 N.L.J. 1615 (Lightman J.), where the late request of an applicant (who had been remiss in complying with directions) for an adjournment of the hearing of his application was refused, the judge said that it is necessary, if the court is to deal with cases justly, that the parties and their legal representatives act justly, responsibly and in accordance with any directions of the court.

Rule 1.3 may be contrasted with the Arbitration Act 1996 s.40 which is expressed in rather more forceful and pointed language and states that the parties "shall do all things necessary for the proper and expeditious conduct of the arbitral proceedings". This includes:

> "complying without delay with any determination of the tribunal as to procedural or evidential matters, or with any order or directions of the tribunal".

In the final draft of the CPR (and in previous drafts), r.1.3 stated that parties were

***Paragraph numbers marked with a "+" can be found online and on CD.***

"expected" rather than "required" to help the court further the overriding objective. Civil proceedings in the courts differ from arbitration proceedings (and other ADR procedures) in that they are not optional but mandatory. If parties agree to arbitrate they know that the Arbitration Act 1996 s.40 will apply and therefore it is not unreasonable to expect that they will conduct themselves accordingly. If a party is brought into civil proceedings in the courts against his wishes and interests he will find that the procedural rules to which the proceedings are subject provide plenty of sanctions to ensure that he cannot frustrate the process. It may not be unreasonable for rules of court to say that, in addition to being exposed to such penalties, he is also "expected" to help the court in furthering the overriding objective. But to say that he is "required" to do so may be regarded as excessive and unnecessary.

Although, in terms, r.1.3 imposes a duty on "the parties" it is readily assumed that this includes their legal advisers, including advocates (*Geveran Trading Co Ltd v Skjevesland* [2002] EWCA Civ 1567; [2003] 1 W.L.R. 912, CA), but an advocate's duty to the court is not confined to any duties that may be derived from r.1.3 and may override his duty to his client (ibid. para.37). An advocate's duty to assist the court in ensuring that a case is dealt with fairly does not require him to place his own client at a substantial disadvantage by acting contrary to his interests, as whatever the scope of r.1.3 may be, it cannot extend so far as to imposed upon counsel a duty in conflict with his proper duty to his client (*Khudados v Hayden* [2007] EWCA Civ 1316, December 13, 2007, unrep., CA, rejecting submission that defendant's counsel ought to have brought to court's attention, when determining at outset of trial absent claimant's request for an adjournment (made by letter), evidence relating to that party's reasons for failing to attend). It has been stated that, where a judge has handed down or delivered judgment in a complex case, for the purpose of avoiding the delay and costs of an appeal an advocate ought immediately draw the judge's attention to any material omission of which he is then aware or then believes exists and that, in many cases, the advocate ought to raise the matter with the judge "in pursuance with his duty to assist the court to achieve the overriding objective" under r.1.3 (*In re T. (A Child) (Contact: Alienation: Permission to Appeal)* [2002] EWCA Civ 1736; [2003] 1 F.L.R. 531, CA, at para.50 per Arden L.J.).

Shortly after the CPR came into effect, Hale L.J. noted that under r.1.3 both parties are required to help the court to further the overriding objective, and stated that it may, therefore, no longer always be appropriate:

> "for defendants to sit back and wait for the claimant to do nothing when there are several steps that they themselves could have taken to have the matter disposed of earlier" (*Khilili v Bennett* May 19, 2000, unrep., CA at para 46).

In some cases, where issues have arisen as to whether a claimant has effected service of originating process, judges have been attracted to the submission that a defendant is in breach of his duty under r.1.3 where his solicitor, when requested to do so by the claimant, refuses to confirm that he has instructions to accept service or prevaricates about the matter, but the point has not been endorsed on appeal (see *Kuenyehia v International Hospitals Group Ltd* [2006] EWCA Civ 21, January 25, 2006, unrep., CA, at paras 8, 11 and 34; *Collier v Williams* [2006] EWCA Civ 20, January 25, 2006, unrep., CA, at para.54). This reluctance is consistent with the view that the duty imposed on a party by the rule is to the court, and not to other parties.

One important way in which parties can assist the court in furthering the objective of dealing with cases fairly and expeditiously is by cooperating with the court in the fixing of trial dates, particularly by providing timely and accurate information as to the availability of expert witnesses (*Matthews v Tarmac Bricks &Tiles Ltd* [1999] C.P.L.R. 463, CA).

The furthering of the overriding objective by the court is not likely to be helped where parties fail to comply with rules, practice directions or court orders. Generally, inaction of a party's legal representative must be treated as inaction by the party himself (*Training in Compliance Ltd v Dewse* [2001] C.P. Rep. 46, per Peter Gibson L.J.; *Dowles Manor Properties Ltd v Bank of Namibia* [1999] C.P.L.R. 259, CA; but considerations in asylum cases are different (see *BR (Iran) v Secretary of State for the Home Department* [2007] EWCA Civ 198; [2007] 1 W.L.R. 2278, CA, at para.18, and authorities referred to there). Rule 3.9(1)(f) states that, where a party applies under r.3.9 for relief from a procedural sanction imposed for failure to comply with any rule, practice direction or court order, the circumstance that the failure was caused by the legal representative, rather than by the party, is to be considered. No such express provision is to be found in r.13.3 (Cases where the court may set aside default judgment) and none should be read into it (*Mullock v Price* [2009] EWCA Civ 1222, October 15, 2009, CA, unrep.).

The requirement that the parties should help the court to further the overriding objective (r.1.3) extends to helping the court to achieve the particular objective of allotting a case an appropriate share of the court's resources (r.1.1(2)(e)) (*Mlauzi v Secretary of State for the Home Department* [2005] EWCA Civ 128 *The Times* February 15, 2005, CA). And it also extends to helping the court actively to manage cases (r.1.4). A party would not be helping the court where, for example, by his conduct, he frustrated the court in its endeavour to actively manage a case by (as r.1.4(2)(a) states) "encouraging the parties to co-operate with each other in the conduct of proceedings"; for example, by deliberately refraining from explaining to his opponent the exact nature of a technical procedural error which the opponent had unwittingly committed (e.g. *Hertsmere Primary Care Trust v Rabindra-Anandh [2005] EWHC 320 (Ch) The Times* April 25, 2005, Lightman J. (judge disapproving of party's failure to respond to opponent's request for him to explain to them in what respect he asserted that their offer did not comply with the provisions of Pt 36)). Cf. *Estates Acquisitions and Development Ltd v Wiltshire* [2006] EWCA Civ 533 *The Times*, June 12, 2006, CA(parties in a continuing legal relationship (e.g. landlord and tenant) not obliged to ensure that they have in place a system for ensuring that, in the event of legal proceedings being invoked, they receive communications relating to them (e.g. a system for forwarding post from deemed service addresses) to facilitate compliance with CPR service of documents provisions). There is no duty on an employer to assist a claimant to serve proceedings on an employee who is a potential defendant; further the latter should not make life difficult for the claimant, but he is not obliged to help by giving positive assistance and he certainly is not under any obligation to forego his legal rights (*Drury v British Broadcasting Corporation* [2007] EWCA Civ 497; *The Times*, June 11, 2007, CA, at para.45 per Smith L.J. (where libel claim brought against employee and employer, but claimant failing to effect service on former)).

The obligation of a party to help the court to further the overriding objective, in particular to assist the court to save expense and to deal with the case proportionately (r.1.1(2)), requires that a publicly funded party should meet his continuing obligation to keep the Legal Services Commission informed of any information which may be relevant to the continuance of his certificate or contract (*R. (Murray) v Hampshire CC (No.2)* [2003] EWCA Civ 760; May 14, 2003, unrep., CA).

For the duty of the parties and their professional representatives to keep the court advised of developments that may enable judges to abandon or re-schedule pre-reading or the completion of written judgments, see para.11–12 above. Note also Vol.1. para.52.12.9(Notification of settlement of appeal).

# SECTION 12

## CPR: APPLICATION, AMENDMENTS AND INTERPRETATION

# 12 CPR: APPLICATION, AMENDMENTS AND INTERPREATION

CONTENTS



*Paragraph numbers marked with a "+" can be found online and on CD.*

# A. INTRODUCTION

**12–2** In March 1994, the Lord Chancellor appointed Lord Woolf to review the current rules and procedure of the civil courts in England and Wales. The aims of the review were to improve access to justice and reduce the costs of litigation; to reduce the complexity of the rules and modernise terminology; to remove unnecessary distinctions of practice and procedure. Lord Woolf conducted the "Access to Justice" inquiry over a period of two and a quarter years, assisted by a panel of assessors and the staff of the Lord Chancellor's Department. He consulted widely with judges, members of the legal profession, academic lawyers and court users throughout the country. Public seminars, chaired by Lord Woolf, were held at several major universities. Lord Woolf's conclusions from his inquiry were set out in two reports, namely the Interim Report (June 1995), and the Final Report (July 1996).

In his two reports, Lord Woolf recommended a wide range of substantial reforms of the law relating to procedure and practice governing the handling of civil proceedings (not including family proceedings) at first instance. Included among them was the recommendation that a single, uniform set of rules of court should be enacted (as had been recommended in 1988 in the Report of the Review Body on Civil Justice (Cm. 394, 1988)). In particular it was recommended that the existing Rules of the Supreme Court (RSC) and the County Court Rules (CCR) should be revoked; that they should be replaced by a single statutory instrument, containing rules of court applicable both to the High Court and the county courts. Lord Woolf annexed a first draft of these rules to his Final Report (entitled there as the "Civil Proceedings Rules"). After a considerable amount of further work on that draft, the Civil Procedure Rules 1998 (SI 1998/3132) (CPR) emerged. The Civil Procedure Act 1997 paved the way for the enactment of these rules.

The CPR deal with procedural matters previously covered by provisions in the RSC and the CCR. To a considerable extent the CPR do no more than re-enact (usually in updated language) provisions formerly found in the RSC and the CCR. But many of the provisions in the CPR implement highly innovative recommendations made in the "Access to Justice" reports and mark significant changes to the practice and procedure that formerly applied in the Court of Appeal (Civil Division), the High Court and in the county courts. Among the striking features of the "Access to Justice" reports were the recommendations that, once commenced, the progress of civil proceedings should be managed by the court (rather than left entirely in the hands of the parties) and that, at an early stage, each case should be allocated to one of several case management "tracks".

The CPR have had to take account of developments in practice and procedure coming about, not only as a result of innovative recommendations made in the "Access to Justice" reports, but also of reforms having different provenances. In particular, the introduction of conditional fee agreements between parties and their legal representatives and changes to arrangements for the funding of civil proceedings generally, the implementation of EU Council Regulations (concerning civil jurisdiction, the service of documents, and the enforcement of judgments), and reforms relating to civil appeals. So, although the CPR arose out of the "Access to Justice" reports, the background to the content of most of the provisions in this set of rules is found elsewhere.

# B. EXTENT AND APPLICATION OF CPR

## 1. SOURCE OF POWER TO MAKE CPR

**12–3** Section 1(1) of the Civil Procedure Act 1997 states that there are to be rules of court called "Civil Procedure Rules" (CPR) and provides that the CPR shall govern the practice and procedure to be followed in the civil division of the Court of Appeal, the High Court, and county courts. This is reflected in CPR r.2.1 which states that, subject to exceptions, the CPR shall apply "to all proceedings" in those courts. Schedule 1 of the 1997 Act (brought into effect by s.1(2)) makes further provision about the extent of the power to make such rules. The CPR are to be made by statutory instrument (s.3). Accordingly, the Civil Procedure Rules 1998 were made in 1998 (see SI 1998/3132) and came into force on April 24, 1999. Before coming into force, the CPR were amended by the Civil Procedure (Amendment) Rules 1999 (SI 1999/1008).

***Paragraph numbers marked with a "+" can be found online and on CD.***

The power to make Civil Procedure Rules (CPR) is to be exercised with a view to securing (a) that "the civil justice system is accessible, fair and efficient" and (b) that rules which are both simple and simply expressed" (s.1(3)). The rules are to be made by a rule committee (see s.2); see further "The process for making Civil Procedure Rules", para.12–38 et seq below).

Before the Civil Procedure Act 1997 came into effect, s.84 and s.85 of the Senior Courts Act 1981 stated that the making of rules of court for the purpose of regulating and prescribing the practice and procedure to be followed in the High Court and the civil division of the Court of Appeal, should be delegated to "the Supreme Court Rule Committee" as constituted under s.85. The Rules of the Supreme Court (Revision) 1965 were brought into being under comparable statutory provisions found in the Supreme Court of Judicature Act 1925, and from time to time were amended subsequently. Section 75 of the County Courts Act 1984 stated that rules of court for regulating the practice and procedure in county courts were to be made by a rule committee as provided for by that section. The County Court Rules 1981 were brought into being under a comparable provision in the County Courts Act 1959, and from time to time were amended subsequently.

Nowadays there is one rule committee, a standing body created by s.2 of the 1997 Act, known as "the Civil Procedure Rule Committee" and empowered to make rules of court known as "Civil Procedure Rules" (CPR).Section 1 and Sch.1 of the 1997 Act are not the sole legislative source of the rule-making power. Examples of other statutory provisions authorising the making of rules (some coming into being before the CPR were enacted, and some after) are: Limitation Act 1980 s.35 (new claims in pending actions), Senior Courts Act 1981 s.32 (interim payments), s.32A (orders for provisional damages for personal injuries) and s.58 (rules of court affecting Court of Appeal), Damages Act 1996 s.2A (periodical payments), Access to Justice Act 1999 s.54 (permission to appeal). Such statutory provisions may impose conditions as to how the rule-making power is to be exercised in certain contexts. The amending of the CPR is not a matter lying exclusively in the hands of the Rule Committee. For example, powers exercised by a Secretary of State under the Regulatory Reform Act 2001 may have the consequential effect of amending CPR provisions. Note also, powers exercisable by the Lord Chancellor under the European Communities Act 1972 (see "European Law and the CPR", para.12–67 below).

It should be noted that s.84 of the 1981 Act (power to make rules of court), though substantially amended by the 1997 Act remains. As amended, it had the effect of providing authority for the making of rules of court in relation to the Crown Court (which became a component part of the Supreme Court in 1971) and the Court of Appeal (Criminal Division). Such rules were made by the Crown Court Rule Committee set up under s.86 of 1981 Act. The Courts Act 2003 completely restructured the arrangements for the making of rules of court for those courts. Provisions granting power to make rules for proceedings in the Court of Appeal (Criminal Division) and, when dealing with any criminal cause or matter, in the Crown Court and in magistrates' courts, and establishing the Criminal Procedure Rule Committee with authority to make such rules, are now found in Pt 7 of that Act. In order to give full effect to those provisions, the scope of s.84 was further restricted by the Courts Act 2003 (Consequential Amendments) Order 2004 (SI 2004/2035) so as to provide authority for the making of rules of court regulating and prescribing the practice and procedure to be followed in the Court of Appeal (Criminal Division) and the Crown Court other than "in relation to criminal causes or matters"; that is to say, in relation to proceedings that might be described as civil proceedings. The Crown Court Rule Committee established under s.86 of this Act continues to make rules for the small number of civil matters that are dealt with by those courts.

It should also be noted that the County Courts Act 1981 s.75 (Application of practice of High Court) was unaffected by the 1997 Act. This section does not confer a power to make rules but says that "the general principles of High Court practice" may be adopted and applied to proceedings in a county court where there is, as it were, a "gap" in county court practice and procedure because the matter is "not expressly provided for by or in pursuance of this Act", that is to say, provided for by sections in the Act or in delegated legislation made under the Act, including, principally, rules of court. Before the CPR came into force, the CCR were made under s.75 of the Act (now omitted) and the rules found therein were significantly different in many respects to those found in the RSC and, generally, much simpler. In these circumstances, s.76 was occasionally brought into play to deal with "gaps" apparent in the CCR. CCR O.1, r.6 said that where by virtue of s.76 provisions of the RSC were applied in relation to proceedings in a county court, that provision "shall have effect with the necessary modifications". The CPR govern county court and High Court proceedings and, in the main, the procedures for both levels of court are the same. Nevertheless, some differences do remain and this leaves open the possibility that "gaps" in county court practice will continue to emerge and that s.76 may still have a role to play (e.g. *Ager v Ager* [1998] 1 W.L.R. 1074, CA, where it was held that the jurisdiction conferred on the High Court by the Senior Courts Act 1981 s.15(4) could be conferred on county courts by operation of s.76). Further, there remains the possibility that, in county court proceedings to which rules in Sch.2 of the CPR apply (viz., former CCR rules), rules in Sch.1 (viz., former RSC rules) may be applied by operation of s.76. This prospect is specifically acknowledged by CCR O.1, r.6 (referred to above) which has survived in the CPR as one of the "schedule rules" (see Vol.1, para.cc1.6, and commentary thereon) (see *Jephson Homes Housing Association Ltd v Moisejevs* [2001] 2 All E.R. 901, CA, application to set aside warrant for possession).

Under UN terrorism orders, HM Treasury has exceptional powers under which, without prior court order, it may make decisions freezing the assets of individuals and organisations. Further, HM Treasury may also make an asset freezing order by way of statutory instrument under Pt 2 of the Anti-terrorism, Crime and Security Act 2001. In Ch.6 of the Counter-Terrorism Act 2008, s.63 provides that any person affected by a decision of HM Treasury under the UN terrorism orders, or by a freezing order under Pt 2 of the 2001 Act, may apply to the High Court to set aside the decision or order. Proceedings on an application under s.63, or on a claim arising from any matter to which such an application relates, are known as "financial restrictions proceedings". Such proceedings are brought in the High Court, and are assigned to the Queen's Bench Division (s.71); specifically, an application must be started and heard in the Administrative Court (r.79.4). Other sections in Ch.6 provide for the making of rules of court relating to such proceedings. Among them is s.72 which states that rules made for the first time after the passing of the 2008 Act (November 26, 2008) may be made, not by the Civil Procedure Rule Committee, but by the Lord Chancellor (after consultation with the Lord Chief Justice). However, unlike rules made by the Rule Committee, any such rules made by the Lord Chancellor are subject to positive resolution by each House of Parliament. (Accordingly, s.3(6) of the Civil Procedure Act 1997 is expressly disapplied; see para.9A–746 above.) In exercise of this power by the Lord Chancellor, CPR Pt 79 (Financial Restrictions Proceedings Under the Counter-Terrorism Act 2008) was inserted in the CPR by the Civil Procedure (Amendment No.2) Rules 2008 (SI 2008/3085) (see further, commentary on CPR Pt 79 in Vol.1).

## 2. EXTENT OF POWER TO MAKE CPR

**12–4** Section 1(1) of the Civil Procedure Act 1997 states that the CPR is to consist of rules of court "governing the procedure and practice to be followed". Section 1(2) brings into effect Schedule 1 to the Act.

Paragraph 1 of Sch.1 states that the CPR may deal with matters which were governed by the former RSC and CCR. Section 84 of the 1981 Act stated that the former Supreme Court Rule Committee was empowered to make rules of court "for the purpose of regulating and prescribing ... practice and procedure" including all such matters regulated by rules of court before the 1981 Act came into force (see also the County Courts Act 1984 s.75(4)) and certain particular matters for which rules of court might provide were listed in sub-ss.(1) and (2) of s.87. It should be noted that neither the RSC nor the CCR covered all proceedings which, conceivably, could come within the jurisdiction of, on the one hand, the High Court, and on the other, the county courts (e.g. proceedings covered by the Family Proceedings Rules (made under the Matrimonial and Family Proceedings Act 1984 s.40) and by the Insolvency Rules (made under the Insolvency Act 1986 s.411)).

Paragraph 2 of Sch.1 states that the CPR may provide for the exercise of the jurisdiction of any court within the scope of the rules (that is to say, the civil division of the Court of Appeal, the High Court, and county courts) by officers or other court staff. In modern times, increasingly the discharge of certain judicial tasks has been devolved to court staff, particularly in the county courts. Usually, this was accomplished by expanding the definition of "proper officer" in CCR O.1, r.3 to include the court manager (or an officer acting on his behalf in accordance with directions given by the Lord Chancellor), and by further rule amendments increasing the range of matters that could be dealt with by the proper officer. (See now CPR r.2.5.) Paragraph 2 makes it clear (as did the County Courts Act 1984 s.75(3)) that rules devolving judicial responsibilities in this way are not ultra vires.

The language of s.1(1) and Sch.1 raises the questions: what is the scope of "practice and procedure", and what is the scope of "matters governed by" the former RSC and CCR. In practice, these questions are unlikely to arise; where the second arises, considerable historical research may be involved (as in *Masri v Consolidated Contractors International (UK) Ltd (No.4)* [2009] UKHL 43; [2009] 3 W.L.R. 385, H.L., at [10] et seq per Lord Mance (rejecting submission that rule-making power in respect of extraterritorial jurisdiction limited to matters covered by specific statutory authority)).

Paragraph 3 of Sch.1 states that the CPR may provide for the transfer of proceedings (or any part of proceedings) within the High Court, for example, between different divisions or different district registries. Similar rules may be made for the transfer of proceedings (or part) from one county court to another (as permitted by s.75(3)(b) and rules in the CCR made thereunder). In addition, rules may provide for any jurisdiction in any proceedings (or in any part of proceedings) to be exercised (whether concurrently or not) elsewhere within the High Court without the proceedings being transferred. Similar rules may provide for any jurisdiction in any proceedings (or part) to be exercised (whether concurrently or not) by another county court without the proceedings being transferred (cf., Courts and Legal Services Act 1990 s.1(6)). The allocation of business between the High Court and the county courts is not a matter to be dealt with by the CPR legislation regulating the allocation of business is found in the Courts and Legal Services Act 1990 s.1 and in Orders made by the Lord Chancellor under that section (see the High Court and County Courts Jurisdiction Order 1991, as amended). The power to make rules of court contained in s.1(6) of the 1990 Act may be exercised in the CPR.

Paragraph 4 of Sch.1 states that the CPR "may modify the rules of evidence" as they apply to proceedings in the civil division of the Court of Appeal, the High Court, and county courts. The scope of this paragraph is not immediately apparent. The RSC and the CCR contain provisions dealing with the taking of evidence. In some instances the authority for such rules comes from the general power to make rules as to practice and procedure, in other instances they are derived from particular statutory provisions, for example, the Civil Evidence Act 1968 s.8 (hearsay) and the Courts and Legal Services Act 1990 s.5 (service of witness statements). The County Courts Act 1984 s.64 states that in relation to proceedings referred to arbitration rules of court may prescribe "the rules of evidence" to be followed and may make provision with respect to the taking and questioning of evidence. Generally, in the past it has been accepted that what could be called the substantive law of evidence, in particular the exclusionary rules rendering inadmissible relevant and material evidence, lay outside the rule-making power. The reform of the exclusionary hearsay rule was accomplished by primary legislation in the form of the Civil Evidence Act 1995. In terms, para.4 seems to make the whole of the law of evidence susceptible to changes wrought by rules of court but, presumably, it does not extend to matters that cannot be regarded as mere rules of evidence (e.g. rules of law relating to claims of privilege).

Paragraph 5 of Sch.1 states that the CPR may apply any rules of court which relate to courts "outside the scope of" the CPR, that is to say, courts other than the civil division of the Court of Appeal, the High Court and, the county courts (see s.9(1)). Consequently, for example, rules made for the criminal division of the Court of Appeal or the Crown Court, could be applied by the CPR to the civil division of the Court of Appeal, the High Court and, the county courts (just as, in the past, the CCR could apply rules relating to the practice and procedure of courts other than county courts: see s.75(6A)(a) of the 1984 Act). Paragraph 5 further states that any rules of court not made by the Civil Procedure Rules Committee (see s.2), but which apply to particular proceedings in the civil division of the Court of Appeal, the High Court and, the county courts, for example, the Family Proceedings Rules and the Insolvency Rules, may be applied by the CPR to other proceedings in those courts.

Paragraph 6 states that the CPR may, instead of providing for any matter, refer to

***Paragraph numbers marked with a "+" can be found online and on CD.***

provision made or to be made about that matter by directions. The giving of practice directions is regulated by s.5 (as substituted in the Act by the Constitutional Reform Act 2005).

Paragraph 7 of Sch.1 states that the power to make CPR includes the power to make different provision for different cases "including different provision ... for specific proceedings, or a specific jurisdiction" (e.g. mercantile courts sitting at district registries). To that extent para.7 is unremarkable. However, the paragraph also states that different provision may be made for different areas, "including different provision ... for a specific court or specific division of a court" (see also s.5). This aspect of the rule making power opens up the possibility that, in relation to proceedings which are indistinguishable, rules of practice and procedure may vary from court centre to court centre, perhaps for the purpose of taking account of the state of business at particular centres (cf., s.40(4) of the 1984 Act). It may be noted that in the Matrimonial and Family Proceedings Act 1984 s.40, the section containing the rule making power for the Family Proceedings Rules, is amended (see Sch.2, para.3) so that different provision may be made for different cases, etc., in those rules also.

In a number of cases it has been argued at first instance that particular provisions in the CPR are outside the rule-making power as stated in s.1 and Sch.1 of the 1997 Act. In *All-in-One Design & Build Ltd v Motcomb Estates Ltd* (2000) 144 S.J.L.B. 219, r.36.21(2) (power of court to award interest on damages awarded to a claimant in case where he recovers more that he proposed in his Pt 36 offer) was held to be intra vires. In *General Mediterranean Holdings SA v Patel* [2000] 1 W.L.R. 272, r.48.7(3) (power of court to order disclosure of privileged documents on wasted costs application) was held to be ultra vires (subsequently the paragraph in Practice Direction (Pt 48—Costs—Special Cases) Section II, drawing attention to r.48.7(3), was revoked). In *Safeway Stores Plc v Tate* [2001] 2 W.L.R. 1377, CA, it was said that the power to make procedural rules under s.4 does not permit the restriction of a party's right to trial by jury in a defamation claim (cf. *Alexander v Arts Council of Wales*, *The Times*, April 27, 2001, CA). In 2006, amendments to CPR r.5.4C, as inserted by the Civil Procedure (Amendment) Rules 2006, were challenged in judicial review proceedings. The proceedings were settled on the basis that the rule should be amended so as to prevent its retrospective operation and the necessary amendment was accomplished by the Civil Procedure (Amendment No.2) Rules 2006.

## 3. APPLICATION OF THE CPR

### (a) Application to proceedings issued before April 26, 1999

**12-5** CPR r.51.1 states that a practice direction "shall make provision for the extent to which these Rules shall apply to proceedings issued before 26 April 1999". The practice direction supplementing this rule is Practice Direction (Transitional Arrangements). These provisions have the effect of limiting the application of the CPR. For detailed explanation, see "Application of CPR to proceedings issued before April 26, 1999 (CPR Pt 51)" para.12–35 below.

### (b) Proceedings to which CPR do not apply (CPR r.2.1)

**12-6** CPR r.2.1 reflects s.1(1) of the 1997 Act and states that, subject to exceptions, the CPR shall apply "to all civil proceedings" in county courts, the High Court and the Civil Division of the Court of Appeal. The exceptions are as stated in para.(2) of r.2.1 and the table therein.

Proceedings of the type referred to in the first column of the Table in r.2.1(2) may be taken either in the High Court or a county court (sometimes exclusively one or the other) and in the Court of Appeal. Such proceedings may be subject to rules of court made under the enactments referred to in the second column (see further below).

Paragraph (2) states that the CPR "do not apply to proceedings of the kinds specified in the first column" of the Table, except to the extent that they are applied "by another enactment". This formulation follows that formerly found in RSC O.2, r.2 (cf. CCR O.1, r.2). Enactments applying the CPR (at least to some extent) to proceedings referred to in r.2.1 are referred to in the notes following.

#### (i) Insolvency proceedings

**12-7** The CPR do not apply, and the former RSC did not apply, to insolvency proceedings. This is not because such proceedings are not civil proceedings, but "because they are specialised proceedings which need special rules" (*Stubbs v Gonzales (Practice Note)* [2005] 1 W.L.R. 2730, PC, at para.5). Under the Insolvency Act 1986 s.411 rules may be made in relation to England and Wales by the Lord Chancellor with the concurrence of the Secretary of State for the purposes of giving effect to Pts I to VIII of that Act (company insolvency and companies winding-up), and under s.412 for the purpose of giving effect to Pts VII to IX (insolvency of individuals, bankruptcy). Nothing in the Insolvency Act s.411 or s.412 prejudices any power to make rules of court. The Lord Chancellor is required to consult the Insolvency Rules Committee before making any rules under s.411 or s.412 of the 1986 Act. The Insolvency Rules 1986 (SI 1986/1925) were made under the Insolvency Act s.411 and s.412; numerous other sets of rules have been made, or are deemed to have been made, under s.411. Although CPR r.2.1 states that the CPR do not apply to insolvency proceedings, r.7.51 of the Insolvency Rules 1986 (SI 1986/1925), as amended by the Insolvency (Amendment) (No.2) Rules 1999 (SI 1999/1022) (and as subsequently amended), provides that the CPR, the practice and procedure of the High Court and of the county courts (including any practice direction) apply to insolvency proceedings "with any necessary modifications, except so far as inconsistent with the Rules".

The 1999 amending statutory instrument made a number of substantial changes to the 1986 Rules specifically for the purposes of bringing them into line with innovative provisions in the CPR and making them consistent with CPR terminology. Certain provisions in the 1986 Rules expressly incorporate CPR provisions; see e.g. those falling for consideration in the case of *In re T. & N. Ltd (No.3)* (Practice Note) [2006] EWHC 842 (Ch); [2006] 1 W.L.R. 2831 (service of documents). In insolvency proceedings, the High Court has power under rr.7.7 and 7.60 of the 1986 Rules to order disclosure of documents and information and to order cross-examination, but the 1986 Rules do not provide for disclosure akin to the procedure under the CPR (*Highberry Ltd v Colt Telecom Group Plc* [2002] EWHC 2503 (Ch); November 25, 2002, unrep. (Lawrence Collins J.)). The procedure and practice for a first appeal to the High Court brought under s.375 of the 1986 Act are governed by the Insolvency Rules 1986 r.7.49 (as amended) which imports the procedure and practice of the Court of Appeal under CPR Pt 52 and its Practice Direction. An application for the disqualification of a director of an insolvent company as being unfit to run a company can, for certain purposes, properly be characterised as insolvency proceedings (*Secretary of State for Trade and Industry v Paulin* [2005] EWHC 888 (Ch); *The Times*, May 26, 2005 (Sir Andrew Morritt V.-C.), (permission not required for appeal from decision of registrar to single judge of High Court)).

### *(ii) Probate proceedings*

Probate rules may be made under the Senior Courts Act 1981 s.127 for regulating **12–8** and prescribing the practice and procedure of the High Court with respect to non-contentious or common form probate business. The Non-contentious Probate Rules 1987 (SI 1987/2024) were made in exercise of this power (see Vol.2, para.6C–68).

### *(iii) Prize Court proceedings*

Under the Prize Courts Act 1894 s.3, rules of court may be made for regulating, **12–9** subject to the provisions of the Naval Prize Act 1864 and the 1894 Act, the procedure and practice of prize courts; see the Prize Court Rules 1939 (S.R. & O. No.1466).

### *(iv) Court of Protection proceedings*

The CPR do not apply to proceedings before the Court of Protection, being **12–10** proceedings for which rules may be made under the Mental Capacity Act 2005, expect to the extent that they are applied to those proceedings "by another enactment". The Court of Protection is a court of record created by s.45 of the 2005 Act. In effect, the Court took over the responsibilities under the Mental Health Act 1983 formerly discharged by an office of the Supreme Court (called "the Court of Protection") but its jurisdiction is greater than that exercised under that Act. Section 51(1) states that rules of court may be made "with respect to the practice and procedure" of the Court. Rules of court and supplementing practice directions are made under s.51 and s.52 of the

2005 Act as, respectively, amended by and substituted by, the Lord Chancellor (Transfer of Functions and Supplementary Provisions) (No.2) Order 2006 (SI 2006/1016) Sch.1 para.35. Sections in the 2005 Act expressly providing for the making of rules of court dealing with particular matters include (in addition to s.51) the following: s.49(5) (reports to the Court), s.50(2) (permission to apply to Court), s.53(2) (permission to appeal), s.55 (costs), and s.56 (payment of fees and costs). The Court of Protection Rules 2007 (SI 2007/1744) (CtPrR) were made in exercise of these powers and constitute a comprehensive set of rules covering the practice and procedure of this Court. Rule 3 (The Overriding Objective) is similar to r.1.1 of the CPR. Rule 9 states that, in any case not expressly provided by the CtPrR or the practice directions made under them, the CPR (including any practice directions made under them) may be applied with any necessary modifications, insofar as it is necessary to further the overriding objective. In various places, provisions in the CPR are expressly incorporated in the CtPrR by reference (with any necessary modifications and disapplications). Notable examples are: r.25(7) (security for costs), r.111 (court examiners), r.160 (costs), and r.184 (enforcement).

### *(v) Family proceedings*

**12–11** Upon the coming into effect of the CPR, the Family Proceedings (Miscellaneous Amendments) Rules (SI 1999/1012) provided for the RSC and CCR generally to continue to apply in the FPR subject to the exception that the CPR provisions as to assessment of costs should apply. The significance of this preservation of RSC and CCR rules was lessened when the reformed procedures for applications for ancillary relief were introduced by theFamily Proceedings (Amendment No.2) Rules 1999 (SI 1999/3491).

The Matrimonial and Family Proceedings Act 1984 s.40 gives power to make rules of court for the purposes of family proceedings in the High Court or county courts. The Family Proceedings Rules 1991 (SI 1991/1247) were made in exercise of this power. Rule 1.3 of the FPR states that, subject to the provisions of those rules and any enactment, the CCR and the RSC shall apply, with the necessary modifications, to family proceedings in a county court and the High Court respectively. Further, for these purposes, any provision of the FPR authorising or requiring anything to be done in family proceedings shall be treated as if it were, in the case of proceedings pending in a county court, a provision of the CCR and, in the case of proceedings pending in the High Court, a provision of the RSC. In *Norris v Norris* [2003] EWCA Civ 1084; *The Times* August 26, 2003, CA (a case raising issues as to costs in ancillary relief cases where offers to settle without prejudice to costs were made) the Court referred to the desirability of working towards the "harmonious integration" of the CPR and the FPR.

The making of practice directions in relation to family proceedings is dealt with by the Courts Act 2003 s.81 and it is expressly provided there that such directions may provide for any matter which, by virtue of the Civil Procedure Act 1997 Sch.1 para.3, may be provided for by CPR. With effect from April 3, 2006, the Family Proceedings (Amendment) Rules 2006 (SI 2006/352) amended the FPR making significant changes to the court's power to make costs orders in ancillary relief cases and, as a consequence, adjustments were made to the manner in which certain provisions in CPR Practice Direction (Costs) (supplementing CPR Pts 43 to 48) apply in such cases; see *Practice Direction (Ancillary Relief: Costs)* [2006] 1 W.L.R. 634, and other directions referred to therein.

CPR r.57.15(2) states that the CPR apply to proceedings under the Inheritance (Provision for Family and Dependants) Act 1975 (which are brought in the Family Division of the High Court), except that the provisions of the Family Proceedings Rules 1991 (SI 1991/1247) relating to the drawing up and service of orders apply instead of the provisions of CPR Pt 40 and its practice direction.

### *(vi) Adoption proceedings*

**12–12** The Adoption Act 1976 was a consolidating measure, bringing together the law of adoption as found in several Acts of Parliament, including the Adoption Act 1958. Section 9 of the 1958 Act consolidated several former rule-making powers and provided that Adoption Rules shall be made by the Lord Chancellor; see now s.66 of the 1976

Act. Former CCR O.1, r.2(2) stated that, in relation to proceedings of a particular kind in county courts (e.g. adoption proceedings), the CCR should have effect subject to any rules made by an authority other than the County Rules Committee (e.g. the Adoption Rules). As a result of the Civil Procedure (Amendment) Rules 1999 (SI 1999/1008) r.2, the effect of that provision was preserved by the addition, by the Civil Procedure (Amendment) Rules 1999, of a reference to adoption proceedings and to the Adoption Act 1976 s.66 in the Table attached to r.2.1(2). The 1976 Act was overtaken by the Adoption and Children Act 2002 and, as a consequence, by the Civil Procedure (Amendment No.4) Rules 2005. A reference to s.141 of that Act was substituted in the Table.

#### *(vii) Election petitions in the High Court*

Provisions of the Representation of the People Act 1983 and the Election Petition Rules 1960 take priority over the CPR (*Ullah v Pagel* [2002] EWCA Civ 1793; December 12, 2002, CA, unrep. (failure to comply with requirements of the 1983 Act and 1960 Rules not curable irregularity)). Accordingly, by the Civil Procedure (Amendment No.2) Rules 2003 (SI 2003/1242), proceedings in the form of election petitions in the High Court under the 1983 Act were added to the table following r.2. This makes it clear that the CPR do not apply directly to such proceedings, although they apply indirectly with modifications by virtue of r.2(4) of the 1960 Rules. **12–13**

### *(c) Lands Tribunal proceedings*

Procedure in the Lands Tribunal is governed, not by the CPR, but by the Lands Tribunal Rules 1996 (SI 1996/1022) made under the Lands Tribunal Act 1949. Practice directions issued from time to time by the President of the Lands Tribunal contain information on the way in which procedure contained in the 1996 Rules is operated. In a practice direction issued on April 5, 2001, the President confirmed that the CPR have no application in the Lands Tribunal. Nevertheless, in following its procedures the Tribunal does so "on the basis of the same overriding objective as that in the CPR" (para.2.1). Further, costs are in the discretion of the Tribunal and this discretion "will usually be exercised in accordance with the principles applied in the High Court and county courts" (para.19.2). In *Purfleet Farms Ltd v Secretary of State for Transport, Local Government and the Regions* [2002] EWCA Civ 1430; October 15, 2002, CA, unrep., the Court of Appeal considered the principles underlying the award of costs in a Lands Tribunal compulsory purchase claim and doubted whether they are or should be the same as those applicable in ordinary civil litigation under the CPR. **12–14**

### *(d) Proceedings to which CPR apply with necessary modifications*

European order for payment applications (see CPR Pt 78 Section I) are primarily governed by the EOP Regulation. Practice Direction—European Order for Payment and European Small Claims Procedures para.1.1 states that where that Regulation "is silent", the CPR "apply with necessary modifications" (see Vol.1 para.78PD.1 above). Where the EOP Regulation is silent on service, the Service Regulation and the CPR "apply as appropriate" (*ibid* para.4). **12–14.1**

Claims under the European small claims procedure (see CPR Pt 78 Section II) are primarily governed by the ESCP Regulation. Practice Direction—European Order for Payment and European Small Claims Procedures para.10 states that where that Regulation "is silent", the CPR "apply with necessary modifications"; in particular, CPR Pt 52 applies to any appeals (see Vol.1 para.78PD.10 above). Where the ESCP Regulation is silent on service, the Service Regulation and the CPR "apply as appropriate" (*ibid* para.15).

It may be noted that Sections I and II of CPR Pt 78 contain detailed rules of court applying to, respectively, applications for EOPs and claims under the ESCP (in some instances, disapplying particular CPR provisions). Presumably, the statement in paras 1.1 and 10 of the practice direction supplementing that Part, to the effect that the CPR only apply where the respective Regulations are silent and then only with necessary modifications, is not meant to derogate from those detailed rules.

## C. STRUCTURE OF CPR

12-15 The CPR consists of rules of court made by statutory instrument. Many of the rules are supplemented by practice directions. Schedules attached to the CPR include some rules formerly found in the RSC and in the CCR (see Pt 50). Other former RSC and CCR provisions, dealing with "specialist proceedings", were not re-enacted in that way but were converted to practice directions. In what follows, comment on this structure is made under the three principal headings indicated above.

### 1. RULES AND PRACTICE DIRECTIONS

#### *(a) Generally*

12-16 The CPR is divided into Parts (originally 51 of them), each dealing with a discrete matter of practice or procedure, and each containing rules of court. The CPR are made by a rule committee established by the Civil Procedure Act 1997 s.2. In part, the power to make rules of court is governed by Sch.3 to the 1997 Act. Since their enactment in 1998, the CPR have been subject to many amending statutory instruments. (These are listed below in para.12–31 where their commencement dates are noted, and in paras 12–32 to 12–34 any transitional provisions within them are explained.) The process of amending the CPR to take account of new forms of work coming before the courts and to effect improvements is unending. In some significant respects amendments have been made to put into rules of court form procedural innovations emanating from the Court of Appeal in cases decided by that Court since the CPR came into effect (see e.g. *YD (Turkey) v Secretary of State for the Home Department* [2006] EWCA Civ 52; [2006] 1 W.L.R. 1646, CA, per Brooke L.J. at para.22).

Paragraph 6 of Sch.3 to the 1997 Act states that CPR "may, instead of providing for any matter, refer to provisions made or to be made about that matter by directions". Section 9(2) of the 1997 Act states that in that Act "practice directions" means directions as to the practice and procedure "of any court within the scope of the Civil Procedure Rules". For the purpose of distinguishing them from other directions (being directions not within the scope of the CPR but nevertheless dealing with the practice and procedure for the handling of civil proceedings), such directions could be called "CPR Practice Directions" (but this is not a term of art). Most Parts of the CPR are supplemented by practice directions as provided for by para.6. The CPR practice directions apply (as do the rules themselves) to proceedings in the Queen's Bench Division and the Chancery Division of the High Court, and in the county courts (other than family proceedings). Where relevant they also apply to appeals to the Court of Appeal (Civil Division).

The extent to which rules in particular CPR Parts make express reference to practice direction provisions supplementing rules varies. Where reference is made, generally the practice direction referred to will be one supplementing the Part wherein the rule is found; but this will not always be the case (e.g. r.26.2(6) refers to the practice direction supplementing r.7.10). Where a rule refers, simply, to "the practice direction", what is meant is the practice direction supplementing the Part wherein the rule is situated (e.g. r.69.2 and r.75.1(1)). (There are, of course, many other practice directions of a different provenance (some pre-dating the CPR) which affect the administration of civil justice in the courts.)

By stating that practice directions "may provide for any matter" which might be provided for by rules in the CPR, in a given case para.6 of Sch.1 may provide the basis for the contention that a particular practice direction provision is ultra vires because it purports to deal with a matter that cannot be dealt with by such rules (e.g. *R. (Ewing) v Department for Constitutional Affairs* [2006] 2 All E.R. 993 (Sullivan J.), where a practice direction enabling an application by a vexatious litigant to be dismissed without a hearing was unsuccessfully challenged).

Practice directions supplementing CPR provisions differ from rules in the CPR in that (a) in general they provide guidance that should be followed, but do not have binding effect, and (b) they should yield to rules in the CPR where there is a clear conflict between them (*R. (Mount Cook Land Limited) v Westminster City Council* op. cit., at para.68 per Auld L.J.). They are "at best a weak aid to the interpretation of the rules themselves" (*Godwin v Swindon BC* [2001] EWCA Civ 1478; [2002] 1 W.L.R. 997, CA, at para.11 per May L.J.). For further information on practice directions as aids to

***Paragraph numbers marked with a "+" can be found online and on CD.***

the interpretation of CPR provisions, see commentary below under heading "Practice directions as aids to interpretation" at para.12-47.

### (b) Process for making or giving practice directions

The power to make practice directions is regulated by s.5 of the 1997 Act. That section was substituted by the Constitutional Reform Act 2005 s.13(2) and Pt 2 of Sch.2, and came into effect on April 3, 2006 (see Constitutional Reform Act 2005 (Commencement No.5) Order 2006 (SI 2006/1014) art.7 and Sch.1, para.7). The provisions in Pt 1 of Sch.2 to the 2005 Act referred to in s.5(1) set out the process for making practice directions. Under the County Courts Act 1984 s.74A (as inserted by the Civil Procedure Act 1997s.5(2)), directions as to the practice and procedure of county courts were made by the Lord Chancellor or any person authorised by him to act on his behalf. That provision was revoked by s.15(1) and Sch.4, Pt 1, para.169 of the 2005 Act. The substitution of s.5 and the omitting of s.74A came about as a result of the change of status of the Lord Chancellor and the working out of the Concordat. **12-17**

Within s.5, "practice directions" means directions as to the practice and procedure "of any court within the scope of the Civil Procedure Rules" (see s.9(2)). Section 5(1) states that practice directions may be given in accordance with the process set out in Pt 1 of Sch.2 to the 2005 Act. The power to give practice directions by this process include the supplementary powers referred to in s.5(4). That is to say, it includes the power (a) to vary or revoke directions given by any person, (b) to give directions containing different provision for different cases (including different areas), (c) to give directions containing provision for a specific court, for specific proceedings or for a specific jurisdiction.

Section 5(2) indicates that CPR Practice Directions may be made otherwise than in accordance with the process set out in Pt 1 of Sch.2 to the 2005 Act. And s.5(3) expressly states that directions falling into that category may include directions providing for any matter which, by virtue of para.3 of Sch.1 to the 1997 Act, may be provided for by CPR; that is to say, for the removal of proceedings (either by providing for the transfer of proceedings from one court to another, or for the exercise of jurisdiction by one court over proceedings in another court without those proceedings being transferred for that purpose).

Generally, under the process set out in Pt 1 of Sch.2 to the 2005 Act, CPR Practice Directions are made by the Lord Chief Justice. The Lord Chief Justice, with the agreement of the Lord Chancellor, may nominate another judicial office holder to exercise his power to make practice directions. In relation to the making of CPR Practice Directions, with effect from April 3, 2006, the Master of the Rolls was so nominated. (Before that date, the powers of the Master of the Rolls in this respect were confined to the making of directions for the Court of Appeal (Civil Division), and comparable powers for the Queen's Bench and Chancery Divisions of the High Court were exercised by, respectively, the Lord Chief Justice and the Vice-Chancellor.) Subject to certain exceptions, the Lord Chief Justice or his nominee may make or give practice directions only with the agreement of the Lord Chancellor. The exceptions are stated in sub-paras (2) and (3) of para.3 in Pt 1 of Sch.2 to the 2005 Act.

As indicated above, practice directions may be made otherwise than under the process set out in Pt 1 of Sch.2 to the 2005 Act. There is nothing in the 1997 Act or the 2005 Act to indicate how or by whom any such alternative process may be used or invoked. However, s.5(2) states that practice directions given otherwise than under the process set out in Pt 1 of Sch.2 to the 2005 Act may not be given without the approval of the Lord Chancellor and the Lord Chief Justice. But the approval of the Lord Chancellor is not required in the circumstances referred to in subs.(5) of s.5. Further, the approval of the Lord Chancellor is not required in the circumstances referred to in subs.(6) of s.5, but in those circumstances the Lord Chancellor must be consulted.

In *Bovale Ltd v Secretary of State for the Communities and Local Government* [2009] EWCA Civ 171; March 11, 2009, unrep., CA, in amplification of what is said above, the Court of Appeal explained (at para.23) that, after the amendments to s.5 of the 1997 Act made by the 2005 Act came into effect, it became the custom for new practice directions or amendments to existing practice directions affecting civil proceedings to be issued only after consideration by the Civil Procedure Rule Committee (see para. 12-3 above). That Committee is chaired by the Master of the Rolls with persons from the Lord Chancellor's department (the Ministry of Justice) in attendance. After such consideration, practice directions are then issued by the Master of the Rolls (as the nominee of the Lord Chief Justice) and "with the agreement of the Lord Chancellor" (see Sch.2, Pt 1, para.3(1) of the 2005 Act).

In a Note issued with TSO CPR Update 42 (September 2006) it was stated that, since the coming into force of the 2005 Act:

> "the power to make practice directions for the civil courts falls to the Lord Chief Justice (with the approval of the Lord Chancellor in most instances)."

This statement is true insofar as it relates to practice directions that are made under the process set out in Pt 1 of Sch.2 to the 2005 Act, but it fails to take account of practice directions affecting civil proceedings not made under that process.

Before the coming into effect of the changes to the statutory provisions dealing with the making of practice directions brought about by the 2005 Act, the powers to make CPR Practice Directions and other directions affecting civil proceedings were examined by the courts in several cases; e.g. *In re C. (Legal Aid: Preparation of Bill of Costs)* [2001] 1 F.L.R. 602, CA; *Leigh v Michelin Tyre Plc* [2003] EWCA Civ 1766; [2004] 1 W.L.R. 846, CA; *R. (Mount Cook Land Limited) v Westminster City Council* [2003] EWCA Civ 1346; [2004] C.P. Rep. 12, CA; *R. (Ewing) v DCA* [2006] 2 All E.R. 993 (Sullivan J.)).

After the coming into effect of those provisions, in *Bovale Ltd v Secretary of State for the Communities and Local Government*, op cit, the Court of Appeal traced the history of the inherent power of the court to make practice directions and explained the restrictions on that power imposed, first by provisions in the 1997 Act, and secondly by provisions in the 2005 Act. In this appeal the Court held that the lead judge of the Administrative Court, by giving standard directions in a judgment handed down in a particular case ([2008] EWHC 2143 (Admin)), had exceeded his powers. A majority of the judges on the appeal regarded it as significant that, in doing so, the judge did not simply provide guidance as to the interpretation and application of the rules and practice directions applicable to cases of a particular type coming before his court or fill in a gap apparent therein, but attempted to vary them.

Practice directions for the Court of Protection are made under the Mental Capacity Act 2005 s.52, as substituted by the Lord Chancellor (Transfer of Functions and Supplementary Provisions) (No.2) Order 2006 (SI 2006/1016) art.2, Sch.1, para.35.

### *(c) Modification or disapplication of rules or practice directions—pilot schemes*

**12-18** Paragraph 7 of Sch.1 to the Civil Procedure Act 1997 states that the power to make Civil Procedure Rules includes the power to make different provision for different cases or different areas, including different provision (a) for a specific court or specific division of a court, or (b) for specific proceedings, or a specific jurisdiction, specified in the rules.

And, as was noted above, the power to give practice directions by the process stated in s.5(1) of the 1997 Act includes the power to give directions containing different provision for different cases (including different areas), or to give directions containing provision for a specific court, for specific proceedings or for a specific jurisdiction.

The result is that rules and practice directions apparently of general application may be modified or disapplied in particular contexts. A good example of the disapplication of rules is provided by CPR r.27.2 which states that several Parts of the CPR shall not apply to proceedings allocated to the small claims track.

CPR r.51.2 states that practice directions may modify or disapply "any provisions of these rules" for specified periods and in relation to proceedings in specified courts during the operation of pilot schemes for assessing the use of new practices and procedures in connection with proceedings. Obviously, there must be a good justification for this. One of the basic themes of justice is that like cases should be treated alike, both procedurally and substantively. The justification given in r.51.2 is the purpose of assessing by pilot schemes the use of new practices and procedures. The mechanism for effecting the modification or disapplication of CPR provisions for such purpose is practice directions made under the rule. This makes it possible for a pilot scheme to be mounted, and in the course of its operation, modified, without it being necessary to enact by statutory instrument amendments to the CPR.

Advantage of r.51.2 was first taken for the purpose of making directions for a pilot scheme enabling parties to conduct certain aspects of money claims electronically through the Court Service website; see Practice Direction (Pilot Schemes for Money Claims). This practice direction was issued by HMSO CPR Update 25 (December 2001) and supplemented CPR Pt 7. This practice direction was replaced by Practice Direction (Pilot Scheme for Money Claims Online), issued by HMSO CPR Update 29 (October 2002) extending the scheme to January 31, 2004. After completion of the pilot scheme, these arrangements were firmed up and inserted in the CPR as Practice Direction—Money Claim Online, one of the practice directions supplementing Pt 7 (see Vol.1, para.7EPD.1 above). The next practice direction made under r.51.2 was Practice Direction (Pilot Scheme for Small Claims) which introduced "the small claims pilot scheme". Under this scheme, in the county courts at Lincoln, Wandsworth and Wigan, by the device of disapplying rr.26.3, 26.4 and 26.5 (and subject to certain exceptions), claims may be allocated by the court to the small claims track without the need for the court to serve allocation questionnaires or to make any orders dispensing with them. This practice direction was issued by HMSO CPR Update 28 (June 3, 2002) and supplements Pt 27 (The Small Claims Track). The original scheme came to an end on December 31, 2002, but in October 2002 the scheme was extended to a further four county courts for the period November 11, 2002, to February 21, 2003. After r.5.5 (Filing and sending documents) was added to the CPR with effect from December 2, 2002 (see para.5.5.1 above), further advantage was taken of r.51.2 by the issuing by HMSO CPR Update 29 (October 2002) of Practice Direction (Pilot Scheme for Communication and Filing of Documents by E-mail), supplementing r.5.5, and subsequently the title of this practice direction was changed, deleting any reference to it as a "pilot scheme" (see para.5BPD.1 above), and by the issuing by HMSO CPR Update 32 (May 2003) of Practice Direction (Pilot Scheme for Telephone Hearings), supplementing Pt 23 (see para.23BPD.1 above). Another pilot scheme that made the transition from temporary measure to permanent feature of the CPR was Practice Direction (Pilot Scheme for Detailed Assessment by the SCCO of Costs of Civil Proceedings in London County Courts); see now Practice Direction (Costs) para.31.1A. By TSO CPR Update 36 (August 2004) additions were made to Practice Direction (Anti-Social Behaviour and Harassment) (supplementing Pt 65) introducing a pilot scheme restricted to certain county court under which applications might be under the Crime and Disorder Act 1998 s.1B to join children to principal proceedings. Practice Direction—Automatic Orders Pilot Scheme was inserted in the CPR, as a practice direction supplementing Pt 51, by TSO CPR Update 47 (September 2008) and extended by TSO Update 50 (October 2009) (see Vol.1, para.51BPD.1). It allows for a pilot study to run in five county courts for (in the first instance) one year (from October 1, 2008) to assess the effect of amending CPR provisions (in particular in Pts 26 and 28) to allow certain orders to be made administratively (see further Vol.1 para.51.1.5).

Practice Direction (Electronic Working Pilot Scheme) was brought into effect for the period April 1, 2009, to March 31, 2010. (This practice direction was first published in TSO CPR Update 50 (October 1, 2009).) With effect from April 1, 2010, this pilot scheme was superseded by a permanent scheme introduced by Practice Direction 5C (Electronic Working Scheme), supplementing CPR r r.5.5 and 7.12. See further Vol.1 paras 5.5.1, 5CPD.0 and 51.1.6.

## 2. SPECIALIST PROCEEDINGS (CPR PT 49)

In the light of the Report of the Civil Justice Review Body and the "Access to Justice" reports, it was expected that the CPR would constitute "a single procedural code" making provision, not only for "general High Court and county court business", but also for "specialist jurisdictions and procedures" in each court. When the CPR were enacted in 1998, rules of court dedicated to "specialist proceedings" previously dealt with in dedicated Orders in the RSC and the CCR were not included. Instead, by operation of CPR Pt 49 (Specialist Proceedings) these proceedings were dealt with in practice directions made and brought into effect with the CPR. In r.49(1) it is stated that "these Rules" shall apply to each of the proceedings designated as "specialist proceedings" listed in r.49(2) subject to the provisions of the "relevant practice direction" which applies to those proceedings. (Presumably, "these Rules" means the provisions of CPR Parts and Schedule rules.) **12–19**

Listed below are the several types of specialist proceedings originally referred to in r.49(2) (seven in all) followed in each case by the relevant practice direction made and brought into effect with the CPR. The title of each practice direction is followed by a note indicating the former RSC and CCR provisions which it replaced. It may be noted that applications for judicial review are not included amongst the list of specialist proceedings. Rules of court relating to these applications were found in RSC O.53. The survival of the provisions found there was secured by the inclusion of that Order (with some modifications) in the CPR among the Schedule rules (see further below), and not as a specialist proceedings practice direction.

*Admiralty proceedings*

Practice Direction—Admiralty (replacing with modifications RSC O.75)

*Arbitration proceedings*

Practice Direction—Arbitrations (replacing with modifications RSC O.73)

*Commercial and mercantile actions*

Practice Direction—Commercial Court (replacing with modifications RSC O.72)

Practice Direction—Mercantile Courts and Business Lists (replacing with modifications CCR O.48C and several practice directions establishing mercantile courts in provincial cities)

*Patents Court business*

Practice Direction—Patents Etc. (replacing with modifications RSC O.104, O.100 and O.93, r.24 and CCR O.48A and O.49, r.4A)

*Technology and Construction Court business*

Practice Direction—Technology and Construction Court (replacing with modifications RSC O.36)

*Proceedings under the Companies Acts (RSC O.102)*

Practice Direction—Applications Under the Companies Act 1985 and the Insurance Companies Act 1982 (replacing with modifications RSC O.102 and CCR O.49, r.3)

*Contentious probate proceedings*

Practice Direction—Contentious Probate (replacing RSC O.76 and CCR O.41)

Since the coming into effect of the CPR in April 1999, the practice directions relating to all but one of the seven types of specialist proceedings listed in r.49(2) have been withdrawn and replaced by new provisions inserted in the CPR by statutory instruments. By 2007, the sole specialist proceedings were proceedings under legislation relating to companies, for which there was one relevant practice direction. Following changes in relevant primary legislation, r.49(2) was recast by the Civil Procedure (Amendment) Rules 2007 (SI 2007/2204) r.17, with effect from October 1, 2007, and again (as a consequence of remaining provisions of the Companies Act 2006 being brought into force) by the Civil Procedure (Amendment) Rules 2009 (SI 2009/2092) r.9, with effect from October 1, 2009. The effect of these amendments was to replace the sole remaining variety of specialist proceedings with three discrete (but related) forms of such proceedings: viz proceedings under (a) the Companies Act 1985, (b) the Companies Act 2006 and (c) other legislation relating to companies and limited liability partnerships. The relevant practice directions which apply to these proceedings, as published in TSO CPR Update 50, and coming into effect on October 1, 2009 (replacing with amendments the two practice directions published in TSO CPR Update 45, and which came into effect on October 2, 2007), are: Practice Direction 49A—Applications under the Companies Acts and Related Legislation (see Vol.2 Section 2G), and Practice Direction 49B—Order Under Section 127 Insolvency Act 1986 (ibid).

For a detailed explanation of CPR amendments that have had the effect of replacing specialist proceedings practice directions, see para.12–30 below.

The CPR is concerned with the procedures to be followed in the courts to which they apply, and they are not concerned with the jurisdiction of those courts. However, the facts (1) that express provision is not made in the CPR for particular proceedings brought under statute, in circumstances where such provision could have been made (as it is made for specialist proceedings) and might have been expected, and (2) that express provision is made in rules governing procedure in another forum, may lend weight to the submission that the court lacked jurisdiction (*R. (A) v Director of Establishments of the Security Service* [2009] EWCA Civ 24; [2009] 3 W.L.R. 717, CA, at [48] and [49] per Dyson L.J. (whether High Court was, within the Human Rights Act 1998 s.7(1)(a), "the appropriate court or tribunal" in which proceedings should be brought against a particular public authority where it was alleged that the authority acted in a way which was made unlawful by s.6(1) of that Act)).

## 3. SCHEDULES (CPR PT 50)

### (a) Schedule rules

To a considerable extent the CPR do no more than re-enact (in re-arranged form and usually in updated language) provisions formerly found in the Rules of the Supreme Court (RSC) and the County Court Rules (CCR) and which, before the CPR came into effect, dealt with practice and procedure in civil proceedings. It was intended that the CPR should be a uniform set of rules, bringing together (but with some substantial amendments) provisions formerly found in the RSC and CCR. When the CPR were enacted in 1998, the task of drafting a uniform set of rules had not been completed (and ten years later is still not completed). The solution adopted was to attach to the CPR (which, as enacted, consisted of 51 Parts) two Schedules enacting those RSC and CCR provisions that were still required but which had not been redrawn and included in the main body of the CPR. Schedule 1 contains the RSC provisions and Schedule 2 the CCR provisions. **12–20**

The position of the Schedules in the CPR is explained in CPR Pt 50. Rule 50(1) states that the Schedules set out, with modifications, certain provisions previously contained in the RSC and the CCR. Rule 50(2) states: "These Rules apply in relation to the proceedings to which the Schedules apply subject to the provisions in the Schedules and the relevant practice directions".

RSC O.116 (The Criminal Procedure and Investigations Act 1996) was added to the RSC by the Civil Procedure (Amendment) Rules 1999 and is included in Sch.1. CCR O.48D (Enforcement of Fixed Penalties, etc) was added by the same statutory instrument and was included in Sch.2 until it was revoked by the Civil Procedure (Amendment No.4) Rules 2003 (SI 2003/2113).

In the period since the CPR came into effect, as a consequence of the insertion of new Parts and provisions in the CPR dealing with matters covered by "Schedule rules", several of the RSC and CCR provisions contained in the Schedules have been omitted. Eventually, the CPR will be a true set of uniform of rules and the "Schedule rules" will disappear (but that day is still some way off).

### (b) Content of the Schedules

Generally, Schs 1 and 2 include former RSC and CCR Orders dealing with procedural matters that had not been subjected to reform recommendations arising from the "Access to Justice" reports, or from elsewhere. Various general comments on the content of the Schedules are made immediately below. In the years since the CPR were enacted most of the RSC and CCR provisions included in the Schedules have been revoked. Those surviving in Schs 1 and 2 are listed in paras 12–31 and 12–32 below. **12–21**

#### *(i) Enforcement of judgments*

Many of the former RSC and CCR Orders included in Schs 1 and 2 when the CPR were enacted dealt with the enforcement of judgments and orders. It was expected then that, in due course, the rules relating to the enforcement of domestic judgments would be reformed and that some proposals would emerge which would enable many of the provisions re-enacted in the two Schedules to be represented as a single coherent code in new Parts to be included in the CPR. That has not yet been accomplished, but a start was made when, with effect from March 25, 2002, Pts 70 to 73 were inserted in the CPR by the Civil Procedure (Amendment No.4) Rules (SI 2001/2792). This facilitated the omission from Schs 1 and 2 of a number of former RSC and CCR provisions (in particular RSC 0.48, 49 and 50, and CCR O.30 and 31). **12–22**

By the Civil Procedure (Amendment) Rules 2002 (SI 2002/2058), with effect from December 2, 2002, Pt 74 (Enforcement of Judgments in Different Jurisdictions) was added to the CPR. This Part deals with (1) the enforcement in England and Wales of judgments from abroad, (2) the enforcement abroad of judgments of courts in England

***Paragraph numbers marked with a "+" can be found online and on CD.***



CPR: APPLICATION

and Wales, (3) the enforcement in England and Wales, Scotland and Northern Ireland of judgments made in other jurisdictions, and (4) the enforcement of European Community judgments. As a consequence, Sch.1, RSC O.71 was revoked.

The Civil Procedure (Amendment) Rules 2007 (SI 2007/2204), which came into effect on October 1, 2007, inserted Section IV (Statutory Rights of Appeal) into CPR Pt 52 (Appeals) and, at the same time, significant additions were made to Practice Direction (Alternative Procedure for Claims) (supplementing CPR Pt 8). As a consequence, Sch.1, RSC O.93, 94 and 95, and Sch.2 CCR O.45 were revoked.

*(ii) Statutory Proceedings*

**12–23** A number of the former RSC and CCR Orders included in Schs 1 and 2 when the CPR were enacted dealt with the proceedings under particular Acts of Parliament. There are many statutes under which proceedings in the High Court or the county courts (or both) can be taken and for which it was thought special provision had to be made in separate Orders found in the RSC from O.74 onwards and in the CCR in O.49 (Miscellaneous statutes). Most of these provisions still remain in the Schedules, but some have been revoked, either because they became redundant or because separate arrangements are now made in CPR Parts.

*(iii) Uniform process for applications*

**12–24** Many of the former RSC and CCR rules re-enacted in the Schedules to the CPR contained, either within themselves or by cross-reference to other RSC and CCR Orders, provisions regulating the manner in which applications may be made to the court. Many of these rules incorporated by reference (sometimes with modifications) provisions found in former RSC O.32 (Applications and proceedings in chambers) and CCR O.13 (Applications and orders in the course of proceedings). In the CPR RSC O.32 and CCR O.13 are in effect replaced by Pt 23 (General rules about applications for court orders). Consequently, references to former RSC O.32 and CCR O.13 in the RSC and CCR provisions re-enacted in the Schedules to the CPR have been replaced with references to Pt 23.

*(iv) Specialist jurisdictions (judicial review applications)*

**12–25** It was expected that the CPR would constitute "a single procedural code" making provision, not only for "general High Court and county court business", but also for "specialist jurisdictions and procedures" in each court. The RSC contained a number of particular Orders containing rules of court dedicated to specialist jurisdictions. As is explained elsewhere, those several Orders were brought into the CPR, not as rules, but as practice directions connected to the CPR by Pt 49 (Specialist Proceedings). However, it may be noted that the rules contained RSC O.53, the Order dealing with specialist proceedings in the form of applications for judicial review, were not brought into the CPR by this method. Instead, when the CPR were introduced in April 1999, this Order was re-enacted (with some significant modifications) in Sch.1. With effect from October 2, 2000, O.53 was revoked and replaced by CPR Pt 54 (Judicial Review) inserted in the CPR by Civil Procedure (Amendment No.4) Rules 2000 (SI 2000/2092). By this statutory instrument RSC O.57 (Divisional Court Proceedings, Etc.: Supplementary Provisions), which also had been re-enacted in Sch.1 and which contained rules relevant to judicial review proceedings, was also revoked. Consequently, neither O.53 nor O.57 are now included in Sch.1.

### (c) Schedule rules remaining in effect

**12–26** As is explained elsewhere, as a result of amendments made to the CPR since they came into effect in 1999, a number of the RSC and CCR provisions included in the Schedules have been revoked. The list below indicates the provisions that have not been revoked and which remain in effect.

*(i) Schedule 1—RSC provisions*

Order 17 (Interpleader) **12–27**

Order 45 (Enforcement of judgments and orders: general), rr.2, 3, 4, 5, 6, 7, 8, 11 and 12

Order 46 (Writs of execution: general)

Order 47 (Writs of fieri facias)

Order 52 (Committal)

Order 54 (Applications for writ of habeas corpus)

Order 64 (Sittings, vacations and office hours), r.4

Order 79 (Criminal proceedings)

Order 109 (The Administration of Justice Act 1960)

Order 110 (Environmental Control Proceedings)

Order 113 (Summary proceedings for possession of land), r.7

Order 115 (Confiscation and forfeiture in connection with criminal proceedings)

Order 116 (The Criminal Procedure and Investigations Act 1996)

*(ii) Schedule 2—CCR provisions*

Order 1, r.6 (Application of RSC to county court proceedings) **12–28**

Order 16 (Transfer of proceedings), r.7 (Interpleader proceedings under execution)

Order 22 (Judgments and orders), rr.8, 10, 11 and 13

Order 24 (Summary proceedings for the recovery of land) r.6

Order 25 (Enforcement of judgments and orders: General), rr.1, 6, 7, 8 and 13

Order 26 (Warrants of execution, delivery and possession)

Order 27 (Attachment of earnings)

Order 28 (Judgment summonses)

Order 29 (Committal for breach of order or undertaking)

Order 33 (Interpleader proceedings), excluding r.12

Order 34 (Penal and disciplinary provisions), excluding r.5

Order 39 (Administration orders)

Order 44 (The Agricultural Holdings Act 1986), r.4

Order 46 (The Legitimacy Act 1976)

Order 49 (Miscellaneous Statutes) rr.7, 12, 18A and 19

# D. STATUTORY INSTRUMENTS AMENDING CPR

## 1. INTRODUCTION

Since the CPR were enacted in 1998, they have been amended by a steady stream of statutory instruments. These instruments (together with their commencement dates) are listed below in para.12–31 (in chronological order) and the transitional provisions contained in them (if any) are set out in paras 12–32 to 12–34. **12–29**

The significant changes made to the CPR by these statutory instruments have been, in the main, those that have introduced new provisions replacing (a) practice directions dealing with the several specialist proceedings listed in r.49(2), and (b) RSC and CCR Orders re-enacted in Schs 1 and 2 of the CPR.

## 2. AMENDMENTS TO CPR PARTS AFFECTING SPECIALIST PROCEEDINGS AND SCHEDULE RULES

Since the CPR came into effect in April 1999, by a series of statutory instruments significant additions have been made to certain CPR Parts and some new Parts have been added. In some instances, these additions have consisted of the insertion of new Parts replacing practice directions dealing with "specialist proceedings" connected to the CPR by Pt 49, with the relevant practice direction being withdrawn as a **12–30** consequence. In other instances, the additions have consisted of the insertion of new rules in existing Parts or the insertion of entirely new Parts dealing with matters previously dealt with by RSC and CCR provisions found in Schs 1 and 2, with such provisions being revoked or amended accordingly (subject to relevant transitional provisions).

New Parts added to the CPR and replacing practice directions dealing with "specialist proceedings" connected to the CPR by Pt 49, include: Pt 57 (Probate and Inheritance), Pt 58 (Commercial Court), Pt 59 (Mercantile Courts), Pt 60 (Proceedings in the Technology and Construction Court), Pt 61 (Admiralty Claims), Pt 62 (Arbitration Claims), Pt 63 (Patents and Other Intellectual Property Claims).

Other new Parts added to the CPR include the following (most, but not all of them, have had the revocation or amendment of Schedule rules as a consequence): Pt 52 (Appeals), Pt 53 (Defamation Claims), Pt 54 (Judicial Review), Pt 55 (Possession Claims), Pt 56 (Landlord and Tenant Claims and Miscellaneous Provisions about Land), Pt 57 (Probate Claims: Rectification of Wills: Substitution and Removal of Personal Representatives), Pt 64 (Estates, Trusts and Charities), Pt 65(Proceedings Relating to Anti-Social Behaviour and Harassment), Pt 66 (Crown Proceedings), Pt 67 (Proceedings Relating to Solicitors), Pt 68 (References to the European Court), Pt 69 (Court's Power to Appoint a Receiver), Pt 70 (General Rules about Enforcement of Judgments and Orders), Pt 71 (Orders to Obtain Information from Judgment Debtors), Pt 72 (Third Party Debt Order), Pt 73 (Charging Orders, Stop Orders and Stop Notices), Pt 74 (Enforcement of Judgments in Different Jurisdictions), Pt 75 (Traffic Enforcement) and Pt 76 (Proceedings Under the Prevention of Terrorism Act 2005).

Significant additions to certain Parts of the CPR which have resulted in the revoking of Schedule rules include: Pt 6, Section III (Special Provisions About Service Out of the Jurisdiction) and Section IV (Service of Foreign Process), Pt 19, Sections II and III (Representative Parties and Group Litigation), Pt 25, Section II (Security for Costs), Pt 34, Section II (Evidence for Foreign Courts), Pt 55, Section III (Interim Possession Orders), Pt 57, Section IV (Claims under the Inheritance (Provision for Family and Dependants) Act 1975)). When Sch.1 RSC O.81 (Partners) and Sch.2 CCR O.25, rr.9 and 10 (Enforcement against firm or between firm members) were revoked, with some modifications their effects were continued by amendments to several existing CPR Parts and practice directions, including provisions in Pts 7, 70, 72 and 73. In some instances, since the coming into effect of the CPR, Schedule rules have been revoked, not because they have been replaced by new Parts inserted in the CPR or by additions to existing Parts, but by new CPR practice directions; e.g. by TSO CPR Update 42 (October 2006), Sch.1 RSC O.112 (Applications for Use of Scientific Tests) and Sch.2 CCR O.47, r.5 (Family Law Reform Act 1969) were replaced by Practice Direction (Applications Under Particular Statutes), a practice direction supplementing Pt 23, and Sch.2 CCR O.49, r.17 (Sex Discrimination Act 1975 etc) was replaced by Practice Direction (Proceedings Under Enactments Relating to Discrimination), a free-standing CPR practice direction.

When the CPR came into force in April 1999, provisions in CCR O.6 (Particulars of claim) dealing with claims for the recovery of land (r.3), claims by mortgagees (rr.5 and 5A), and claims for delivery of goods let on hire purchase (r.6) survived in Sch.2. Subsequently, when CPR Pt 55 (Possession Claims) and Pt 56 (Landlord and Tenant Claims and Miscellaneous Provisions About Land) were brought into effect on October 1, 2001, by Civil Procedure (Amendment No.2) Rules 2001 (SI 2001/256), rr.3, 5 and 5A were revoked. Rule 6 was always surplus to requirements; see Practice Direction (How to Make Claims in Schedule Rules and Other Claims) para.6.1 (formerly para.7.1) (supplementing CPR Pt 16). It was belatedly revoked by Civil Procedure (Amendment No.2) Rules 2003 (SI 2003/1242) with effect from June 2, 2003.

Further revocations of Schedule rules were made by the Civil Procedure (Amendment) Rules 2002 (SI 2002/2058) rr.35 and 36 and Sch.10. By that statutory instrument, with effect from December 2, 2002, Section IV to Pt 6, Section II to Pt 34, Section III to Pt 55, Section IV to Pt 57, and new Pts 64, 68, 69, 74 and 75, were added to the CPR. As a consequence, seventeen RSC and CCR Orders in Schs 1 and 2 were wholly revoked and four in part, thus reducing considerably the number of Schedule rules.

## 3. COMMENCEMENT DATES FOR STATUTORY INSTRUMENTS AMENDING CPR

**12–31** The Civil Procedure Rules 1998 (SI 1998/3132) were made on December 10, 1998, and came into force on the appointed day, April 26, 1999. These Rules have been amended on a number of occasions. Amendments made by the Civil Procedure (Amendment) Rules 1999 (SI 1999/1008) also came into force on the appointed day.

Civil Procedure (Amendment) Rules 2000 (SI 2000/221)—February 28 and May 2, 2000

Civil Procedure (Amendment No.2) Rules 2000 (SI 2000/940)—May 2, 2000

Civil Procedure (Amendment No.3) Rules 2000 (SI 2000/1317)—July 3, 2000

Civil Procedure (Amendment No.4) Rules 2000 (SI 2000/2092)—October 2, 2000

Postal Services Act 2000 (Consequential Modifications No.1) Order 2001 (SI 2001/ 1149)—March 26, 2001

Civil Procedure (Amendment) Rules 2001 (SI 2001/256)—March 26, April 1, 2001, and October 15, 2001

Civil Procedure (Amendment No.2) Rules 2001 (SI 2001/1388)—May 31, June 1, and October 15, 2001

Civil Procedure (Amendment No.3) Rules 2001 (SI 2001/1769)—May 31, and October 15, 2001

Civil Procedure (Amendment No.4) Rules 2001 (SI 2001/2792)—October 15, 2001 and March 25, 2002

Civil Procedure (Amendment No.5) Rules 2001 (SI 2001/4015)—January 14, March 1 and 25, 2002

Civil Procedure (Amendment No.6) Rules 2001 (SI 2001/4016)—December 20, 2001

Civil Procedure (Amendment) Rules 2002 (SI 2002/2058)—December 2, 2002

Civil Procedure (Amendment No.2) Rules 2002 (SI 2002/3219)—April 1, 2003

Civil Procedure (Amendment) Rules 2003 (SI 2003/364)—April 1, 2003

Civil Procedure (Amendment No.2) Rules 2003 (SI 2003/1242)—June 2, 2003

Civil Procedure (Amendment No.3) Rules 2003 (SI 2003/1329)—June 9, 2003

Civil Procedure (Amendment No.4) Rules 2003 (SI 2003/2113)—October 10, 2003, January 1 and April 1, 2004

Civil Procedure (Amendment No.5) Rules 2003 (SI 2003/3361)—February 1, March 1, April 1 and May 1, 2004

Civil Procedure (Amendment) Rules 2004 (SI 2004/1306)—June 1 and June 30, 2004

Civil Procedure (Amendment No.2) Rules 2004 (SI 2004/2072)—September 1 and October 1, 2004

Civil Procedure (Amendment No.3) Rules 2004 (SI 2004/3129)— April 1, 2005

Civil Procedure (Amendment No.4) Rules 2004 (SI 2004/3419)—April 1, 2005

Civil Procedure (Amendment) Rules 2005 (SI 2005/352)—April 4, 2005

Courts Act 2003 (Consequential Provisions) (No.2) Order 2005 (SI 2005/ 617)—April 1, 2005

Civil Procedure (Amendment No.2) Rules 2005 (SI 2005/656)—March 11, 2005

Civil Procedure (Amendment No.3) Rules 2005 (SI 2005/2292)—October 1 and 21, 2005, and April 6, 2006

Civil Procedure (Amendment No.4) Rules 2005 (SI 2005/3515)—April 6, 2006

Civil Procedure (Amendment) Rules 2006 (SI 2006/1689)—October 2, 2006

Regulatory Reform (Agricultural) Tenancies (England and Wales) Order 2006 (SI 2006/2805)—December 10, 2006

Civil Procedure (Amendment No.2) Rules (SI 2006/3132)—December 18, 2006

***Paragraph numbers marked with a "+" can be found online and on CD.***

Civil Procedure (Amendment No.3) Rules 2006 (SI 2006/3435)—April 6, 2007

Civil Jurisdiction and Judgments Regulations 2007 (SI 2007/1655)—July 1, 2007

Civil Procedure (Amendment) Rules 2007 (SI 2007/2204)—October 1, 2007

Civil Procedure (Amendment No.2) Rules 2007 (SI 2007/3543)—March 31 and April 6, 2008

Civil Procedure (Amendment) Rules 2008 (SI 2008/2178)—October 1, 2008, December 12, 2008 and January 1, 2009

Civil Procedure (Amendment No.2) Rules 2008 (SI 2008/3085)—December 4, 2008

Civil Procedure (Amendment No.3) Rules 2008 (SI 2008/3327)—April 6, 2009

Civil Procedure (Amendment) Rules 2009 (SI 2009/2092)—August 31, 2009 and October 1, 2009

Civil Jurisdiction and Judgments Regulations 2009 (SI 2009/ 3131)—January 1, 2010

Civil Procedure (Amendment No.2) Rules 2009 (SI 2009/3390)—February 1 and 15, and April 6, 2010

## 4. TRANSITIONAL ARRANGEMENTS IN AMENDING STATUTORY INSTRUMENTS

**12–32** In some instances, special transitional arrangements were made for bringing into force amendments to the CPR taking effect after April 26, 1999. These provisions are as follows.

### *(a) 2000 to 2004*

**12–33** Part 52 (Appeals) was added to the CPR byCivil Procedure (Amendment) Rules 2000 r.19. Rule 39 of that statutory instrument (as amended by Civil Procedure (Amendment No.2) Rules 2000 r.2) states:

> "Where a person has filed a notice of appeal or applied for permission to appeal before 2nd May 2000—
>
> (a) rule 19 of these Rules shall not apply to the appeal to which that notice or application relates; and
>
> (b) the rules of court relating to appeals in force immediately before 2nd May 2000 shall apply to that appeal as if they had not been revoked."

See further, para.52.0.14 (Transitional provisions) below, and note also the Access to Justice Act 1999 (Destination of Appeals Order 2000) (SI 2000/1071) art.6.

Following the establishment of the Legal Services Commission by the Access to Justice Act 1999 (replacing the Legal Aid Board) and the introduction of new funding arrangements for legal proceedings, amendments were made to the CPR (principally to the Parts dealing with costs) by the Civil Procedure (Amendment No.3) Rules 2000 and took effect on July 3, 2000. Rule 39(1) and (2) of this statutory instrument states:

> "(1) This rule applies where a person has—
>
> (a) entered into a funding arrangement, and
>
> (b) started proceedings in respect of a claim the subject of that funding arrangement, before the date on which these Rules came into force.
>
> (2) Any requirement imposed—
>
> (a) by any provisions of the Civil Procedure Rules 1998 amended by these Rules, or
>
> (b) by a practice direction,
>
> in respect of that funding arrangement may be complied with within 28 days of the coming into force of these Rules, and that compliance shall be treated as compliance with the relevant rule or practice direction."

"Funding arrangement" is defined in r.39(3) in terms similar to those found in CPR r.43.2(1)(k) (see para.43.2 above).

Rules 27.12 and 27.13 dealt with appeals against orders made in cases dealt with in

***Paragraph numbers marked with a "+" can be found online and on CD.***

the small claims track. These provisions were revoked by the Civil Procedure (Amendment No.4) Rules 2000 with effect from October 2, 2000, and thereafter provisions in Pt 52 applied to such appeals (for text of these revoked rules, see Civil Procedure 2000, Vol.1, paras 27.12 and 27.13). Rule 29 of that statutory instrument states:

"Where a person has, before 2nd October 2000, filed a notice of appeal in a claim allocated to the small claims track—

(a) Part 52 shall not apply to the appeal to which that notice relates; and

(b) rules 27.12 and 27.13 shall apply to that appeal as if they had not been revoked."

Part 54 (Judicial Review) was added to the CPR by Civil Procedure (Amendment No.4) Rules 2000 with effect from October 2, 2000, and replaced various provisions formerly found in Sch.1, principally RSC O.53. Rule 30 of that statutory instrument states:

"Where a person has, before 2nd October 2000, filed an application for permission to make an application for judicial review in accordance with RSC Order 53—

(a) Part 54 shall not apply to that application for permission or the application for judicial review to which it relates; and

(b) RSC Order 53 shall apply to those applications as if it had not been revoked."

For text of RSC O.53, see Civil Procedure 2000, Vol.1 paras sc53.0.1 et seq.

Part 55 (Possession claims) and Pt 56 (Landlord and tenant claims and Miscellaneous provisions about land) were added the CPR by the Civil Procedure (Amendment) Rules 2001 (SI 2001/256) with effect from October 15, 2001. As a consequence, various provisions in CPR Schs 1 and 2 were amended or revoked. The principal revocations were RSC O.88 (Mortgage Claims), RSC O.97 (The Landlord and Tenant Acts, etc.), RSC O.113 (Summary Proceedings for Possession of Land) (with the exception of r.7), CCR O.24 (Summary Proceedings for the Recovery of Land) (with the exception of r.6), CCR O.43 (The Landlord and Tenant Acts, etc.), and certain provisions in CCR O.49 (Miscellaneous Statutes). The transitional provisions in the statutory instrument state (r.31):

"Where a claim form—

(a) relates to proceedings to which Part 55 or Part 56 would apply if it was issued on or after [October 15, 2001], but

(b) is issued before that date, those rules shall not apply, and the rules of court in force immediately before that date shall apply as if they had not been amended or revoked."

Part 57 (Probate Claims: Rectification of Wills: Substitution and Removal of Personal Representatives) was added to the CPR was added to the CPR by the Civil Procedure (Amendment No.2) Rules 2001 (SI 2001/1388) with effect from October 15, 2001. Previously, contentious probate claims were designated as "specialist proceedings" by r.49(2)(g) (see para.49.0.1 above) and the relevant practice direction (see r.49(1)) was Practice Direction (Contentious Probate Proceedings). By this statutory instrument r.49(2)(g) is omitted and Sch.1 RSC O.93, r.20 (substitution and removal of personal representatives) is revoked. The transitional provisions in the statutory instrument provide (see r.19):

"Where a claim form—

(a) relates to proceedings to which Part 57 would apply if it was issued on or after 15 October 2001, but

(b) is issued before that date,

that Part shall not apply to the proceedings, and the rules of court in force immediately before that date shall apply as if they had not been amended or revoked."

Part 70 (General Rules About Enforcement of Judgments and Orders), Pt 71 (Orders to Obtain Information from Judgment Debtors), Pt 72 (Third Party Debt Orders), and Pt 73 (Charging Orders, Stop Orders and Stop Notices), were added to the CPR by the Civil Procedure (Amendment No.4) Rules 2001 (SI 2001/2792) with effect from March 25, 2002. The transitional provisions in that statutory instrument state (r.24):

(1) Parts 70 to 73 shall not apply to any enforcement proceedings specified in paragraph (2) which are issued before 25th March 2002, and the rules of court

in force immediately before that date shall apply to those proceedings as if they had been amended or revoked.

(2) The enforcement proceedings to which this rule applies are—

(a) an application for an oral examination;
(b) an application for a garnishee order;
(c) an application by a judgment credit for an order for the payment to him of money standing in court to the credit of a judgment debtor;
(d) an application for a charging order;
(e) a claim for the enforcement of a charging order by sale of the property charged; and
(f) an application for a stop order."

Certain amendments to CPR provisions dealing with fixed costs were made by the Civil Procedure (Amendment No.5) Rules 2001 (SI 2001/4015). As a consequence, the transitional provisions stated immediately above (i.e. r.24 of the Civil Procedure (Amendment No.4) Rules 2001), have to be read with the transitional and savings provisions found in r.43 of the later statutory instrument.

Rule 43 states:

"Where a claim form—

(1) Where proceedings for possession of land are issued before March 25, rule 42(b) [which amends Pt II of App. B to CCR O.38] shall not apply, and CCR Order 38 shall apply as if it had not been amended.

(2) Where on or after 25th March 2002 fixed costs are to be awarded in enforcement proceedings which, pursuant to rule 24 of the Civil Procedure (Amendment No.4) Rules 2000, continue to be governed by rules in Sch.1 or Schedule 2 to the Civil Procedure Rules 1998 rather than rules in Pts 70 to 73, the rules governing enforcement costs in force immediately before March 25, 2002 shall continue to apply as if they had not been revoked."

The CPR amendments made by the Civil Procedure (Amendment) Rules 2002 (SI 2002/2058), including the amendments to r.48.6 (Litigants in person), come into effect on December 2, 2002. Rule 34 of that statutory instrument states that, where before that date proceedings have begun under r.47.6(1) for the detailed assessment of the costs of a litigant in person, r.48.6 shall continue to apply to those proceedings as if it had not been amended.

Civil Procedure (Amendment) Rules 2003 (SI 2003/364), which came into effect on April 1, 2003, contain no transitional provisions.

Civil Procedure (Amendment No.2) Rules 2003 (SI 2003/1242), which came into effect June 2, 2003 in r.6 provided that paras (3) and (4) of CPR r.43.2 (application of costs rules), inserted in the CPR by that statutory instrument have effect only where the conditional fee agreement which is in issue was entered into on or after June 2, 2003.

Civil Procedure (Amendment No.3) Rules 2003 (SI 2003/1329), which came into effect on June 9, 2003, contain no transitional provisions.

Civil Procedure (Amendment No.4) Rules 2003 (SI 2003/2113), which came into effect on October 10, 2003, January 1 and April 1, 2004 in r.18 provides that the provisions of CPR Pt 45 (Fixed Costs) Section II inserted in the CPR by that statutory instrument shall not apply to any cost-only proceedings arising out of a dispute, where the road traffic accident which gave rise to he dispute occurred before October 6, 2003.

The Civil Procedure (Amendment No.5) Rules 2003 (SI 2003/3361), which came into effect on February 1, March 1, April 1 and May 1, 2004, contain no transitional provisions.

The Civil Procedure (Amendment) Rules 2004 (SI 2004/1306) made changes to CPR Pt 56 (Landlord and Tenant Claims, Etc.) as a result of the coming into effect of amendments made to the Landlord and Tenant Act 1954 by the Regulatory Reform (Business Tenancies) (England and Wales) Order 2003. In particular, r.15 amended r.56.2 and r.16 substituted r.56.3. These amendments came into effect on June 1, 2004. Rule 20(1) of these Rules contains transitional provisions and states:

"In the circumstances where article 29(1) or (4) of the Regulatory Reform (Business Tenancies) (England and Wales) Order 2003 applies—

(a) the amendments to Part 56 made by rules 15 and 16 of these Rules shall not apply; and

(b) Part 56 shall continue to apply on and after 1st June, 2004, as if those amendments had not been made."

Further, the Civil Procedure (Amendment) Rules 2004 also amended the CPR by inserting Pt 65 (Proceedings Relating to Anti-Social Behaviour and Harassment) and, as a consequence, revoking Sch.2 CCR O.49, r.6B. These amendments came into effect on June 30, 2004. Rule 20(2) of these Rules contains transitional provisions and states:

"Where an application for an injunction under Chapter III or Part V of the Housing Act 1996 has been issued before 30th June 2004:

(a) Section I of Part 65 shall not apply in relation to that application; and

(b) CCR Order 49, rule 6B shall continue to apply on and after 30th June as if it had not been revoked."

Furthermore, it should be noted CPR Pt 45, Section III (Fixed Percentage Increase in Road Traffic Claims), added by the Civil Procedure (Amendment) Rules 2004, with effect from June 1, 2004, does not apply where the accident occurred before October 6, 2003 (r.45.15(4)(c)).

The Civil Procedure (Amendment No.2) Rules 2004 (SI 2004/2072), which came into effect on September 1 and October 1, 2004, contain no transitional provisions. But it should be noted that CPR Pt 45, Section IV (Fixed Percentage Increase in Employers Liability Claims), added to the CPR by these Rules with effect from October 1, 2004, does not apply where the dispute relates to an injury sustained before that date (r.45.20(2)(a)).

Civil Procedure (Amendment No.3) Rules 2004 (SI 2004/3129), which came into effect on April 1, 2005, contains no transitional provisions.

Civil Procedure (Amendment No.4) Rules 2004 (SI 2004/3419), which came into effect on April 1, 2005, contains no transitional provisions.

### *(b) 2005 to date*

The Civil Procedure (Amendment) Rules 2005 (SI 2005/352), which came into effect on April 4, 2005, inserted a new Section III of CPR Pt 54 containing rules about applications to the High Court under the Nationality, Immigration and Asylum Act 2002 s.103A, and made consequential amendments to Section II of that Part. The Section II provisions continue in their unamended form for certain purposes. Rule 9 of SI 2005/352, which incorporates by reference Orders made under the Asylum and Immigration (Treatment of Claimants, etc.) Act 2004 s.48(3)(a), contains transitional provisions. **12–34**

The Courts Act 2003 (Consequential Provisions) (No.2) Order 2005 (SI 2005/617), which came into effect on April 1, 2005, contains no transitional provisions, insofar as that statutory instrument amended the CPR.

The Civil Procedure (Amendment No.2) Rules 2005 (SI 2005/656), which came into effect on March 11, 2005, contain no transitional provisions.

The Civil Procedure (Amendment No.3) Rules 2005 (SI 2005/2292), which came into effect on October 1 and 21, 2005, and April 6, 2006, contain no transitional provisions.

The Civil Procedure (Amendment No.4) Rules 2005 (SI 2005/3515), which came into effect on April 6, 2006, contain no transitional provisions.

The Civil Procedure (Amendment) Rules 2006 (SI 2006/1689), which came into effect on October 2, 2006, contain no transitional provisions.

The Regulatory Reform (Agricultural) Tenancies (England and Wales) Order 2006 (SI 2006/2805), which came into effect on December 10, 2006, contains no transitional provisions.

The Civil Procedure (Amendment No.2) Rules (SI 2006/3132), which came into effect on December 18, 2006, contain no transitional provisions.

The Civil Procedure (Amendment No.3) Rules 2006 (SI 2006/3435) came into effect on April 6, 2007. This statutory instrument substituted Pt 36 (Offers to Settle) and Pt 37 (Miscellaneous Provisions About Payments Into Court). In r.7 the statutory instrument made transitional arrangements in relation to Pt 36 for the purpose of providing that the rules of court contained in Pt 36 as it was in force before April 6, 2007, for certain purposes should continue to apply in circumstances where Pt 36 offers and Pt 36 payments had been made before that use date. A practice direction supplementing Pt 36 as substituted explains how the new rules otherwise apply to offers and payments into court made before that date. The statutory instrument also made amendments to Pt 14 (Admissions), principally for the purpose of dealing with pre-action admissions by inserting r.14.1A (Admissions made before commencement of proceedings) in that Part. Rule 5 of the statutory instrument states that r.14.1A "will not apply to an admission made before April 6, 2007".

The Civil Jurisdiction and Judgments Regulations 2007 (SI 2007/1655) which came into effect on July 1, 2007, contain no transitional provisions.

The Civil Procedure (Amendment) Rules 2007 (SI 2007/2204) came into effect on October 1, 2007. Amongst other things, these rules amend r.19.9 and insert new rules 19.9A to 19.9F to take account of new procedures for derivative claims under the Companies Act 2006. (As is explained below, under transitional provisions the replaced rules remain in effect for a certain period; for convenience those rules are included in Practice Direction (Derivative Claims) (19CPD)). Further r.46.2 and r.46.3 are amended to make provision for the increase to the amount of fast track trial costs which the court may award where the fast track trial commences on or after October 1, 2007. Transitional provisions relating to these amendments to Pt 19 and Pt 46 are contained, respectively, in r.21 and r.22 of this statutory instrument. Those rules state as follows:

"**21.**—(1) The amendments to Part 19 made by rule 7 of these Rules apply as follows—

(a) rule 19.9 and rule 19.9A apply only to a derivative claim issued on or after 1st October 2007;

(b) rule 19.9B applies to the taking over of a derivative claim only where the relevant application for permission to take over the claim is filed on or after 1st October 2007;

(c) rule 19.9C—

(i) applies to a derivative claim issued on or after the date, and

(ii) applies to the taking over of a derivative claim only where the relevant application for permission to take over the claim is filed on or after 1st October 2007;

(d) rule 19.9D applies to a derivative claim that arises in the course of other proceedings only if—

(i) rule 19.9A would apply to the claim if it were brought, or

(ii) rule 19.9B or rule 19.9C would apply to the taking over of the claim; and

(e) rule 19.9E and rule 19.9F apply to a derivative claim only if rule 19.9A, rule 19.9B or rule 19.9C also applies to the claim.

(2) The rules of court relating to a derivative claim (within the meaning of those rules) in force immediately before 1st October, 2007, apply as if they had not been amended to any derivative claim in respect of which the claim form was issued before that date 1st October, 2007."

"**22.**—(1) The amendments to Part 46 only apply where the hearing of the fast track trial commences on or after 1st October, 2007.

(2) Where the hearing of the fast track trial commences before 1st October 2007, the rules of court relating to the amount of fast track trial costs which the court may award that were in force immediately before 1st October 2007 apply as if they had not been amended."

Among the amendments made by the Civil Procedure (Amendment No.2) Rules 2007 (SI 2007/3543) were amendments to CPR Pt 75 (Traffic Enforcement). Those particular amendments were made by r.9 of the statutory instrument and came into effect on March 31, 2008. Rule 13 of this statutory instrument contained transitional provisions relating to some of those amendments and stated as follows:

"**13.** The amendments made by rule 9(c)(iii) and (iv) of these Rules to rule 75.3(4) and (5) and the omission of rule 75.3(6) by rule 9(c)(v) of these Rules do not apply to proceedings where the authority filed a request pursuant to rule 75.3(1) before 31st March 2008 and the rules of court in force immediately before that date will continue to apply to those proceedings as if they had not been amended or revoked."

The Civil Procedure (Amendment No.2) Rules 2007 (SI 2007/3543) came into effect on April 6, 2008, with the exception of the amendments made by r.9 of that statutory instrument to CPR Pt 75 (Traffic Enforcement). Rule 9 amended paras (4) and (5) of r.75.3 and omitted para.(6). Rule 13 contained transitional provisions affecting these particular changes and state that they do not apply to proceedings where the authority filed a request pursuant to r.75.3(1) before March 31, 2008, and the rules of court in force immediately before that date will continue to apply to those proceedings as if the had not been amended or revoked.

The Civil Procedure (Amendment) Rules 2008 (SI 2008/2178) generally, including the rules substituting CPR Pt 6 (Service of Documents) and making related and consequential amendments in other Parts, came into effect on October 1, 2008. Amongst other things, this statutory instrument inserted in the CPR (and brought into effect at later dates) a new Part, Part 78 (European order for payment and European small claims procedures). Section I of Part 78 contains rules about European orders for payment made under Regulation (EC) No 1896/2006 of the European Parliament and of the Council of 12 December 2006 creating a European order for payment procedure. Section II of Part 78 contains rules about the European small claims procedure under Regulation (EC) No 861/2007 of the European Parliament and of the Council of 11 July 2007 establishing a European small claims procedure. Rule 1(3) of the statutory instrument provided that the provisions in Section I should come into force on December 12, 2008, and those in Section II on January 1, 2009. The Civil Procedure (Amendment No.2) Rules 2008 (SI 2008/3085), which came into effect on December 4, 2008, contained no transitional provisions.

The Civil Procedure (Amendment No.3) Rules 2008 (SI 2008/3327), which came into effect on April 6, 2009, contained no transitional provisions.

The Civil Procedure (Amendment) Rules 2009 (SI 2009/2092) came into effect on October 1, 2009 (with the exception of rules adding Section VI to CPR Pt 65, which came into effect on August 31, 2009). Amongst other things, this statutory instrument (by r.7) inserted r.44.12B (Costs-only proceedings—costs in respect of insurance premium in publication cases) in CPR Pt 44, subject to a transitional provision (r.23) which stated that that new rule and amendments related to it do not apply to proceedings where the insurance policy was taken out before October 1, 2009, and provided that Pt 44 as in force immediately before that date will continue to apply to those provisions as if that Part had not been amended. Other important effects of this statutory instrument included amendments to Pt 35 (Experts and Assessors) and the substitution of Pt 63 (Intellectual Property Claims).

The Civil Jurisdiction and Judgments Regulations 2009 (SI 2009/3131) came into effect on January 1, 2010, and contained provisions making amendments of a minor and technical nature to the CPR (and other legislation) following ratification of a new Lugano Convention. Regulation 48 states that the legislation affected shall continue to have effect as if not amended for the purposes of proceedings, judgments and authentic instruments to which the 1988 Convention continues to apply pursuant to art.63 of the 2007 Lugano Convention (transitional provision).

The Civil Procedure (Amendment No.2) Rules 2009 (SI 2009/3390), which came into effect on February 1 and 15, and April 6, 2010, contained no express transitional provisions. However, rules in Pts 52 and 54 revoked and replaced by that statutory instrument as a consequence of the abolition of the Asylum and Immigration Tribunal, survived (together with some related practice direction provisions) for certain purposes; see Section IV of Practice Direction 52 (Appeals).

## E. APPLICATION OF CPR TO PROCEEDINGS ISSUED BEFORE APRIL 26, 1999 (CPR PT 51)

Rule 51.1 states that a practice direction shall make provision for the extent to which these Rules shall apply to proceedings issued before April 26, 1999. The practice direction supplementing this rule is Practice Direction—Transitional Arrangements. It is necessary to distinguish proceedings coming before judge before April 26, 2000, from those that do not. **12–35**

*Paragraph numbers marked with a "+" can be found online and on CD.*

## 1. PROCEEDINGS COMING BEFORE JUDGE BEFORE APRIL 26, 2000

12–36 The transitional arrangements are directed at proceedings issued before April 26, 1999, and not automatically stayed by the operation of para.19(1) of the practice direction (see Vol.1, para.51PD.19). That is to say, they are directed at proceedings (a) which were started before that date and (b) which came before a judge, at a hearing or on paper, between April 26, 1999, and April 25, 2000. Consequently, the commentary that follows is now out of date. However, as is explained in para.12–37 below, from time to time the courts still have to deal with applications under para.19(2) to lift automatic stays imposed by para.19(1), thereby allowing the transitional arrangements to have their effects. To that extent the commentary may remain useful.

The general scheme of the transitional arrangements is to apply the CPR to defended cases. When a new step has to be taken it is to be taken under the CPR. The overriding objective (see Pt 1) applies. In particular, when existing proceedings come before a judge for the first time (whether at a hearing or on paper) after April 26, 1999 he is to direct how the CPR will apply to the proceedings from then on. These principles are simple to state but have proved to be very difficult and time consuming to apply in practice. It is never easy to change horses in mid-stream. Every case requires an individualised order according to the type of case, the steps taken so far and the steps now needed to get the case ready for trial. In many cases insufficient time has been allowed to enable the court to consider how to apply the CPR to the pending case.

Solicitors should ensure that a sufficient time estimate is given to allow the court to deal with the matter which has caused the application and then additionally to give directions pursuant to the Practice Direction which supplements Pt 51 and, of course, the assessment of costs. Wherever possible the necessary directions should be agreed with the other side and submitted for the court's approval. It is suggested that, for cases commenced prior to April 26, 1999, the following matters need to be addressed:

(1) Allocation to track (consider Pt 26)
(2) Statements of Case (consider Pts 7, 8, 15, 16, 17 and 18)
(3) Disclosure and Inspection of Documents (consider Pt 31)
(4) Expert Evidence (consider Pt 35)
(5) Exchange of witness statements (consider Pt 32)
(6) Other outstanding matters
(7) Likely length of trial and proposed trial "window".

It may be helpful to complete Listing Questionnaires (Pre-Trial Check lists).

In *McPhilemy v Times Newspapers Ltd* [1999] 3 All E.R. 775, CA, it was explained that in an appeal to the Court of Appeal from an interlocutory decision made before April 26, 1999, (1) if the decision would not have been regarded as wrong before that date the Court will not interfere, (2) if it would have been regarded as wrong the Court will take into account the CPR (in particular, the provisions of Pt 1) when deciding what order should be made for the future.

The requirement (stated in r.1.2) that the court must seek to give effect to the overriding objective (r.1.1) when it exercises any power given to it by the CPR or interprets any rule applies to the exercise of powers under the transitional provisions in Pt 51 (*Hamblin v Field The Times*, April 26, 2000, CA).

After the appointed day, issues concerning the application of the transitional arrangements arose in various contexts and some differences of view as to whether CPR provisions should or should not be applied emerged. For example, where the question was whether an application by a defendant for relief under RSC O.18, r.19, made before the appointed day but coming before a judge after, should be dealt with under CPR r.24.2(a)(i) (an innovative provision) (*Whincup v Barclays Bank Plc* January 14, 2000, unrep.).

In *Doncaster Metropolitan BC v Kelly* April 26, 2001, unrep. (Gray J.), judgment was entered in June 1996 against a tenant in possession proceedings following a trial which the tenant did not attend. The landlord took no steps to enforce the order for arrears until after the CPR came into effect in April 1999. In December 2000, the recorder granted the defendant's application to set aside the judgment. In doing so, the recorder did not apply the tests stated in CPR r.39.3(5), under which the tenant's ap-

***Paragraph numbers marked with a "+" can be found online and on CD.***

plication would surely have failed, but dealt with the application in accordance with the former law, in particular the provisions of CCR O.37, r.2 and the principles stated in *Shocked v Goldschmidt* [1998] 1 All E.R. 372, CA. In dismissing the landlord's appeal the judge considered para.15(1) and (2) of the Practice Direction (see Vol.1, para.51PD.15) and held that the recorder, although not dealing with the proceedings "for the first time" after the coming into effect of the CPR, had jurisdiction to direct that the CPR should not apply to the tenant's application.

Under para.18(2) a party has a right to recover any costs incurred before April 26, 1999, if such costs would have been allowed on a taxation under former RSC O.62 (*Joseph v Boyd & Hutchison* [2003] EWHC 413 (Ch); The Times, April 28, 2003 (Patten J. and assessors), where held that a solicitor with a limited practice, who had no indemnity cover and was not permitted to charge for her time, could not be regarded as a practising solicitor within the meaning of O.62 r.18(6) and was therefore entitled to charge for her time as a solicitor).

## 2. STAY OF EXISTING PROCEEDINGS AFTER ONE YEAR

Paragraph 19(1) of the Practice Direction (see Vol.1, para.51PD.19) states that, if any "existing proceedings" have not "come before a judge" at "a hearing on paper" between April 26, 1999, and April 25, 2000, those proceedings "shall be stayed". Paragraph 19(3) states that certain proceedings will not be stayed as a result of para.19(1). Those proceedings are: (a) where the case has been given a fixed trial date which is after April 25, 2000, (b) personal injury cases where there is no issue on liability but the proceedings have been adjourned by court order to determine the prognosis, (c) where the court is dealing with the continuing administration of an estate or a trust or a receivership (applied in *Ministry of Defence v Foxley* [2007] EWHC 2874 (Admin), December 12, 2007, unrep.), (d) applications relating to funds in court (this last was added in March 1999). For these purposes, proceedings will not be "existing proceedings" once final judgment has been given (see para.19(4), a provision added in May 2000). Any party to such existing proceedings may apply for the stay to be lifted (para.19(2)). As was to be expected, with every passing year, the number of such applications decreases. **12–37**

As April 25, 2000, approached it became clear that a significant number of cases were exposed to the risk of an automatic stay and the courts were faced with many applications, some by defendants under CPR r.3.4(2)(c) to strike out claims against them (*Cheng I Food Co Ltd v Theotoko Maritime Inc* July 21, 2000, unrep. Toulson J.), but more by claimants making applications of various types (often applications for case management conferences) principally for the purpose of ensuring that the proceedings came before a judge before the trigger date. Administrative guidance was given by the courts. In *Reliance National Insurance Co (Europe) Ltd v Ropner Insurance Services Ltd* [2001] 1 Lloyd's Rep. 477, CA, the Court of Appeal referred to the guidance given by the Admiralty and Commercial Court Registry. The particular question arising in this case was whether it can be said that proceedings have come before a judge "on paper" (and therefore were not stayed by operation of para.19(1)) where the judge, upon receiving a letter from the claimant asking that para.19(1) be disapplied, simply perused the file or correspondence relating to the proceedings and reached the view that the automatic stay should apply. The Court said that para.19 has to be read in the context of paras 14 and 15 and held that the phrase "comes before a judge ... on paper" in para.19(1) denotes an occasion on which, on the application of a party (perhaps made in circumstances where the court permits the application to be made by letter; see r.23.3(2)(b)) that is dealt with without a hearing (see r.23.8), a judge considers exercising his powers in accordance with the CPR. The phrase also denotes an occasion on which the court, having proposed to make an order in the proceedings on its own initiative (perhaps having been provoked into doing so by a letter received from a party), makes an order without hearing the parties (r.3.3(1) and (4)).

The effects of sub-paras (1) and (4) of para.19 were considered by the Court of Appeal in *National Westminster Bank Plc v Feeney* [2003] EWCA Civ 950, June 11, 2003, CA, unrep. In that case, in April 1998, a bank (C) commenced proceedings against property owners (D) to enforce a charge over the property executed by D as security for debts to C. D put in a defence and made a counterclaim alleging misrepresentation by C as to the creditworthiness of a third party who had become indebted to D. In March 1999, D's defence was struck out and C obtained an order for possession on

***Paragraph numbers marked with a "+" can be found online and on CD.***

their claim. Over the course of the following 18 months, C issued a warrant for possession and D made a series of applications to suspend the warrant, each of which met with a degree of success. Eventually, in February 2001, C's claim was settled on terms that enabled D to remain in possession. In November 2002, a district judge ruled that, by operation of para.19(1), proceedings on D's counterclaim had been stayed with effect from April 26, 2000. The Court of Appeal upheld this decision. The Court held that the possession order of March 1999 was a "final judgment" within the meaning of para.19(4). Consequently, it was not possible for D to argue that their applications to suspend the warrant, made during the year following April 26, 1999, were instances of "existing proceedings" coming "before a judge at a hearing" during that period. After the order of March 1999, D's counterclaim became, in effect, a freestanding claim susceptible to being stayed by operation of para.19(1).

In *Neo Investments Inc v Cargill International SA* [2001] 2 Lloyd's Rep. 33 (Aikens J.), it was conceded that where a stay is automatically imposed by operation of para.19(1), in effect a procedural sanction has been imposed for failure to comply with a rule, practice direction or court order. Consequently, an application for such a stay to be lifted should be made under CPR r.3.9, and the circumstances listed in that rule become relevant. In this case, after considering those circumstances the judge refused the claimant's application to lift the stay and granted the defendant's application to strike out the claim under r.3.4. In the judge's view, were the defendant's application not granted the claim would have still existed "in a rather ghostly fashion", a state of affairs that should not be permitted unless there are very special reasons. However, where a defendant's case is that the stayed proceedings should be struck out on the basis of para.(b) or (c) of r.3.4(2) the question to be asked is whether a fair trial is impossible or there is a considerable risk that it will not be possible (*Taylor v Anderson* [2002] EWCA Civ 1680; *The Times*, November 22, 2002, CA; see also *Oxnard Financing S.A. v Rahn* February 22, 2001, unrep. (Mr A Boswood Q.C.); *Fay v Chief Constable of Bedfordshire Police* [2003] EWHC 673 (QB); *The Times*, February 13, 2003 (Davies J.); *Leckstein v Menon* [2003] EWHC 90, (QB) January 30, 2003, unrep. (Eady J.)). Even in cases of inordinate and inexcusable delay, the court should only strike out a claim as an abuse of process where there is a real risk that the matter can no longer be fairly tried and the interest of justice so requires (*Fay v Chief Constable of Bedfordshire Police* [2003] EWHC 673 (QB); *The Times*, February 13, 2003 (Davies J.)). It is conceivable that, in applying that test the court will conclude that the proceedings should not be struck, whilst at the same time, applying the r.3.9 criteria, will conclude that the stay should not be lifted.

In *Hansom v E Rex Makin & Co* [2003] EWCA Civ 1801, the question was: to what extent should the court, when considering the circumstances listed in r.3.9(1) and the requirement to "consider all the circumstances" on an application under para.19(2) to lift an automatic stay, attach importance to the possibility that there could still be a fair trial? The Court concluded that there will be many cases where the possibility or otherwise of a fair trial will be highly important to the exercise of discretion under r.3.9, but it does not follow that, where a fair trial is still possible, relief will necessarily be granted under that rule. In giving the principal judgment of the court in this case, Mance L.J. explained (para.12) that r.3.9 was not specifically crafted for the purpose of dealing with applications to lift an automatic stay imposed by para.19(1) as both the imposing of such a stay and the need for an application to lift it are transitional phenomena. In applications to lift an automatic stay, the circumstances listed in r.3.9(1) that focus on procedural "failures" have to applied with care. It is the effect of the sanction (that is, of the indefinite stay), as much as if not more than that of the "failure" that is likely to be of interest. The underlying situation after an automatic stay may be more akin to that which used to exist under the former rules where a plaintiff failed to prosecute his claim with due expedition. The length of the delay in applying to lift the stay and the effect of such delay become of primary interest (see paras (b) and (i) of r.3.9(1)).

In *Audergon v La Baguette Ltd* [2002] EWCA Civ 10; *The Times*, January 31, 2002, CA, the Court of Appeal held that the automatic stay imposed by para.19(1) of Practice Direction (Transitional Arrangements) falls to be treated as a sanction "imposed for a failure to comply with any rule, practice direction or court order" within the meaning of CPR r.3.9 (see also *Stanford v Stanford* [2001] EWCA Civ 1289); see also *Bank of Credit and Commerce International SA v Bugshan* March 14, 2001, unrep. (David Steel J.).

***Paragraph numbers marked with a "+" can be found online and on CD.***

Rule 3.9 instructs the court to consider all the circumstances of the particular case, including the nine items listed in sub-rule (1). In *Woodhouse v Consignia plc* [2002] EWCA Civ 275; March 7, 2002, CA, the court said (at [41]–[42]), when dealing with applications under para.19(2), judges should submit themselves to the discipline of considering each of the matters listed in r.3.9 which appear to them to be relevant to the case they have to decide. If they fail to do so, there may be a serious danger that an appeal court may overturn their decision for omitting to take a material consideration into account. They must carry out the necessary balancing exercise methodically and explain how they reached their ultimate decision. They must remember that if a stay remains in place, they are depriving the claimant of access to the court, a concept which now has particular resonance under ECHR, art.6.

In *Flaxman-Binns v Lincolnshire CC* [2004] EWCA Civ 424; [2004] 1 W.L.R. 2232, CA, a circuit judge dismissed a student's (C) application under para.19(2) for the automatic stay to be lifted on his negligence claim against a local education authority (D), first brought when C was a child. In allowing C's appeal the Court of Appeal said (1) no criticism should attach to C for taking no step to prevent the operation of the automatic stay as (a) at that stage he was a litigant in person and (b) until Autumn 2000 decisions of the House of Lords relevant to C's claim were pending, (2) on the evidence (including additional evidence), the judge was wrong to assume that during the period of further delay, for which C's solicitor accepted full responsibility, no efforts were made by or on behalf of C to chase the solicitor, (3) D had not sought to advance a positive case by appropriate evidence of significant prejudice to the conduct of the defence caused to them by the additional delay.

In *B v B* [2005] EWCA Civ 237, March 10, 2005, CA, unrep., a claim commenced in July 1997 by an adult daughter against a parent for abuse was stayed, by operation of para.19(1), on April 25, 2000. In May 2005, the Court of Appeal, applying the r.3.9 criteria, granted the claimant's appeal against a lower court dismissal of her application under para.19(2) to lift the stay. The Court said the overriding concern was that the claimant's undetermined claims should be justly tried.

In *James v London Borough of Havering*, [2007] EWHC 2168 (QB), September 26, 2007, unrep. (Keith J.) a claim in which a default judgment had been obtained in September 1995 was automatically stayed by operation of para.19(2). The claimant's application under para.19(2) to lift the stay was refused. Upon investigating the circumstances, the judge found that if the stay were lifted (1) the default judgment would be set aside as it was irregular, and (2) the claim would be struck out under r.3.4(2)(c) for the claimant's failure to comply with rules, practice directions and court orders. The judge was guided by the principle that it would hardly be unjust to prevent the claimant's case from proceeding if the claims were doomed to fail; conversely, it could well be unjust for the claims not to be permitted to continue (despite the inordinate and largely unexplained delay) if the claims had every chance of succeeding.

Instances have arisen in which the court has lifted an automatic stay but imposed conditions restricting the claims that may be pursued (e.g. *Dar v Taylor* May 17, 2001, unrep. (Eady J.) (stay on libel claim lifted on condition that claim is confined to one for general damages and the claims for special damages are withdrawn).

Normally, an application under para.19(2) to lift a stay automatically imposed by para.19(1) will be made by a claimant. Where such an application fails the stay on the proceedings remains in place. There is no absolute bar to the claimant's making a second application. A further application may succeed, even where material relevant to the exercise of the court's discretion under r.3.9 is relied on which was not produced at the earlier application though it could and should have been. The interests of justice may demand that a second application should succeed, with the failure to deploy the material earlier being reflected by suitable orders for costs and (if appropriate) interest. The failure to produce supporting material timeously is in itself relevant to the exercise of the court's discretion under r.3.9 (*Woodhouse v Consignia Plc* [2002] EWCA Civ 275; [2002] 1 W.L.R. 2558, CA, at paras [55]–[57]).

In a case where a stay is not lifted, it may be possible for the claimant to commence fresh proceedings. However, if a claimant pursues this course, there is a likelihood that his new claim will be stayed or struck out as an abuse of process. This possibility was a significant factor in *Overseas and Commercial Developments Ltd v Cox* [2002] EWCA Civ 635; April 25, 2002, CA, unrep. where the claim was for possession of land and the effect of the stay was to leave unresolved the question of title, with the result that

***Paragraph numbers marked with a "+" can be found online and on CD.***

the land's saleability and value was adversely affected. On the claimant's appeal the Court of Appeal lifted the stay imposed by operation of para.19(1). The Court found that the consequences of not lifting the stay probably would be to commit both parties to further proceedings involving yet more delay and cost. The Court held that, in considering and applying the r.3.9(1) criteria, it was necessary (a) to form a realistic appreciation of the extent of the risk that fresh proceedings would be struck out as an abuse, and (b) to take it into account in considering the effect which lifting the stay would have on each party.

# F. THE PROCESS FOR MAKING CIVIL PROCEDURE RULES

## 1. INTRODUCTION

**12–38** The source of the power to make Civil Procedure Rules, the objectives and the extent and application of such rules, have been explained above. In what follows comment is made on the statutory provisions in the Civil Procedure Act 1997 concerning the process for making CPR. Provisions in that Act states that Civil Procedure Rules are to be made by a statutory committee, and are to be enacted by statutory instrument. The objectives to be achieved are set out in s.1 and the process for making and enacting such rules is set out in s.3. The first enactment was the Civil Procedure Rules 1998 (SI 1998/3132). Although the primary legislation does not spell the matter out, the making of Civil Procedure Rules is a continuing process. The original statutory instrument may be (and has been) amended by subsequent ones, all made in accordance with the process stipulated in s.3.

## 2. THE RULE COMMITTEE (S.2)

**12–39** Section 2 of the 1997 Act states that the statutory committee charged with the responsibility for making CPR is to be known as the "Civil Procedure Rule Committee". In terms familiar to those in government, the Rule Committee is an NDPB, that is, a Non-Departmental Public Body. Section 3(1)(a) of the 1997 Act states that the Committee has a statutory duty to "consult such persons as they consider appropriate" when making rules of court (see para.9A–744 above). The constitution of that committee and the methods by which its members are to be appointed are dealt with in that section. Section 2A states that certain provisions in s.2 may be changed by statutory instrument. Provisions in the Senior Courts Act 1981 and the County Courts Act 1984 dealing with the constitution of the former two Rule Committees were repealed when the 1997 Act came into force. In its original form, s.2 dealt with various matters now dealt with in s.3. Section 2 was substantially amended by the Constitutional Reform Act 2005 Sch.4, para.263.

## 3. RULE-MAKING PROCESS (S.3)

**12–40** The rule-making process is outlined in s.3. A significant feature of that section, when compared with the provisions it replaced, is that it states that, if the Lord Chancellor disallows Rules, he must give the Committee written reasons for doing so (s.3(4)). In practice, the matters considered by the Civil Procedure Rule Committee are matters brought to their attention by the Civil Justice Council (see s.6(3)) or, more commonly, by the Department for Constitutional Affairs. The Lord Chancellor may give the Rule Committee notice requiring rules to be made to achieve a specified purpose (see s.3A below). In *YD (Turkey) v Secretary of State for the Home Department* [2006] EWCA Civ 52; [2006] 1 W.L.R. 1646, CA, Brooke L.J. said (at para.22) that the Civil Procedure Act 1997 and the Civil Procedure Rules 1998 "have changed the landscape" enabling the Court, by case law, to initiate innovative ways of regulating procedure, safe in the knowledge that the Rule Committee would move swiftly to codify or extend the new procedures the judges had so introduced by making appropriate amendments to the CPR. His lordship gave illustrations of desirable changes which would never have been made, or not made so swiftly, "if the judges had not been ready to take the lead" (*ibid.*). But judicial leadership in this respect has its limits. In the case of *Willis v Nicolson* [2007] EWCA Civ 199; March 13, 2007, CA, unrep., where the claimant had suffered catastrophic injuries and the defendant applied (in advance of trial of quantum) for an order capping the claimant's costs, the Court of Appeal declined an invitation to give general guidance on costs capping in personal injuries cases, taking the view that this was a matter that should be dealt with by the Civil Procedure Rule Committee after extensive consultation (as it subsequently was, see Vol.1, para.44.18.1). Practice directions are not made by the Rule Committee.

Section 3 was amended by the Courts Act 2003, but before those amendments were brought into effect was again amended by the Constitutional Reform Act 2005.

### 4. RULES TO BE MADE IF REQUIRED (S.3A)

In the making of Civil Procedure Rules, the members of the Rule Committee are **12–41** not entirely free to act as they think best in achieving the objectives stipulated in s.1. Section 3A states that the Lord Chancellor may give the Rule Committee notice "that he thinks it is expedient for Civil Procedure Rules to include provision that it would achieve a purpose specified in the notice". This reflects the fact that the Lord Chancellor has certain responsibilities for court administration and therefore has a legitimate interest in matters provided for by rules of court and in how rules operate in practice. Where such notice is given, within a reasonable period the Rule Committee must make such Rules as it considers necessary to achieve the specified purpose" (s.3A(2)). Section 3A was inserted in the 1997 Act by the Constitutional Reform Act 2005.

### 5. POWER TO MAKE CONSEQUENTIAL AMENDMENTS (S.4)

Subsection (1) of s.4 states that the Lord Chancellor may by order (subject to the **12–42** negative resolution procedure) amend, repeal or revoke any enactment (whenever passed or made) to the extent he considers it necessary or desirable (a) in consequence of Civil Procedure Rules or (b) in consequence of s.1 or s.2 of this Act.

Subsection (2) of s.4 states that the Lord Chancellor may by order (subject to the positive resolution procedure) amend, repeal or revoke any enactment (passed or made before this section was brought into force on April 27, 1997) to the extent he considers it necessary or desirable to facilitate the making of Civil Procedure Rules. This subsection is not confined to amendments, etc., which are merely consequential. Thus, where a particular rule is proposed which is inconsistent with an enactment in force at commencement, the Lord Chancellor may amend, etc., the enactment by order. Where a particular rule is proposed which is inconsistent with an enactment in force subsequently, necessary or desirable amendments, etc., cannot be made to the enactment under this subsection as it stands.

This section may be contrasted with s.87(3) of the Senior Courts Act 1981 and s.75(6A)(b) of the County Courts Act 1984. Those sections provided that rules in the RSC and CCR could amend or repeal any statutory provision relating to the practice or procedure of the courts concerned "so far as may be necessary in consequence of any provision made by the rules". Such consequential amendments cannot be accomplished by provisions in the CPR but the same result may be achieved by the exercise by the Lord Chancellor of powers given by s.4.

For examples of the exercise of the power to make consequential amendments granted by s.4, see Civil Procedure (Modification of Enactments) Order 1998 (SI 1998/2940), Civil Procedure (Modification of Enactments) Order 1999 (SI 1999/1217), Civil Procedure (Modification of Enactments) Order 2000 (SI 2000/941), Civil Procedure (Modification of Enactments) Order 2001 (SI 2001/2717), Civil Procedure (Modification of Enactments) Order 2002 (SI 2002/439), Civil Procedure (Modification of Senior Courts Act 1981) Order 2004 (SI 2004/1033), Civil Procedure (Modification of Crown Proceedings Act 1947) Order 2005 (SI 2005/2712). Note also (amending CPR) Postal Services Act 2000 (Consequential Modifications No.1) Order 2001 (SI 2001/1149).

## G. CONSTRUCTION AND INTERPRETATION OF RULES

### 1. THE PURPOSIVE METHOD OF INTERPRETATION

In the Access to Justice Interim Report it was said (at p.215) that the exercise of **12–43** drafting the single procedural code involved three specific objectives. They were: (a) to identify the core propositions in the rules and to cut down the number of interconnecting provisions which are used; (b) to provide procedures which apply to the

*Paragraph numbers marked with a "+" can be found online and on CD.*

broadest possible range of cases and to reduce the number of instances in which a separate regime is provided for a special type of case; and (c) to reduce the size of the rules and the number of propositions contained in them, to remove verbiage and to adopt a simpler and plainer style of drafting. The Interim Report said (at p.215) that these specific objectives can only be fully achieved if a new approach is taken by the judges applying the rules under a managed system of litigation. Instead of the over-technical way the rules have been applied in the past:

> "the new rules will have to be used in a different way: they will have to be read as a whole, not dissected and viewed word by word under a microscope."

The new rules have been deliberately framed so that the approach of those construing them can be more purposive and less technical. It will thus be the responsibility of the judiciary to make the new system work.

In the Access to Justice Final Report it was said (at p.275) that the CPR are deliberately not designed expressly to answer every question which could arise. The statement of the overriding objective in those rules "provides a compass to guide courts and litigants and legal advisers as to their general course" (see further "Interpretation to give effect to overriding objective", para.12–45 below).

The construction of the CPR, like the construction of any legislation, primary or delegated, requires the application of ordinary canons of construction (*Vinos v Marks & Spencer Plc* [2001] 3 All E.R. 784, CA at [26] per Peter Gibson L.J.). In *James Buchanan & Co Ltd v Babco Forwarding and Shipping (UK) Ltd* [1977] Q.B. 208, Lord Denning M.R. explained that under the purposive method of interpretation the judges do not go by the literal meaning of the words or by the grammatical structure of the sentence. They go by the design or purpose behind it. When they come upon a situation which is to their minds within the spirit but not the letter of the legislation, they solve the problem by looking at the effect it was sought to achieve.

> "They then interpret the legislation so as to produce the desired effect. This means they fill in gaps, quite unashamedly, without hesitation. They ask simply: what is the sensible way of dealing with this situation so as to give effect to the presumed purpose of the legislation?"

In *Collier v Williams* [2006] EWCA Civ 20; [2006] 1 W.L.R. 1945, C.A., the Court of Appeal stated that the rules should, if possible, be interpreted in a practical way which permits certainty and minimises the risk of satellite litigation. However, this does not warrant re-writing rules "so as to make them bear a meaning which they plainly do not have".

A feature of the CPR (subject to very few exceptions) is that each discrete rule is given a heading. A rule heading may be considered in interpreting the rule to which it relates, provided due account is taken of the fact that the function of a heading is to provide a brief and therefore a necessarily inexact guide to the material to which it applies (*Brown v Innovatorone Plc.* [2009] EWCA Civ 1376 (Comm); June 19, 2009, unrep. (Andrew Smith J.) at [17] (examining provisions in CPR Pt 6, and contrasting interpretive value of headings in primary and delegated legislation)).

Rights and obligations created by international treaties have no effect in UK domestic law unless legislation is in force giving effect to them. Where legislation intended to bring a treaty into effect is ambiguous or discretionary, there is in English law a presumption (based on the principle that Parliament cannot have intended to act in breach of international obligations) that the legislation is to be construed so as to avoid a conflict with international law. The presumption applies to delegated legislation and circumstances may arise where it comes into play in interpreting and applying CPR provisions (*Morgan v Hinton Organics (Wessex) Ltd* [2009] EWCA Civ 107; [2009] Env. L.R. 30, C.A. (relevance of Aarhus Convention to CPR costs in private nuisance proceedings); see further para.12–59 below).

## 2. THE ACCESS TO JUSTICE REPORTS AS AIDS TO INTERPRETATION

**12–44** Many of the provisions in the CPR carry into effect reform proposals made in the Access to Justice Reports. It would be expected, therefore, that judges and lawyers would have recourse to those Reports, for the purpose of better understanding the meaning and application of such provisions. Numerous examples may be given of cases in which the courts have relied (sometimes quite heavily) on passages from the

Access to Justice Reports (both Interim and Final) for the purposes of informing and supporting their decisions on rules relating to innovative aspects of the CPR; e.g. *Trustees of Stokes Pension Fund v Western Power Distribution (South West) Plc* [2005] EWCA Civ 854; [2005] 1 W.L.R. 3595, CA (exercise of discretion as to costs where offer to settle a money claim not made in accordance with Pt 36), *ES v Chesterfield and North Derbyshire Royal Hospital NHS Trust* [2003] EWCA Civ 1284; [2004] Lloyd's Med. Rep. 90, CA ("equality of arms" in relation to expert witnesses); *Hawley v Luminar Leisure Plc* [2006] EWCA Civ 30; *The Times* February 14, 2006, CA (offers to settle). However, it must be remembered that a number of the recommendations in the Access to Justice Reports that were implemented underwent considerable revision following further consultation and deliberation before enactment by the Rule Committee in 1998 and some have been subject to significant revisions since and the value of the Reports as aids to the proper interpretation of the CPR has been reduced. The same may be said of other Reports leading to major changes in the CPR; e.g. the Bowman Report (see *George Wimpey UK Ltd v Tewkesbury BC* [2008] EWCA Civ 12; [2008] 1 W.L.R. 1649, CA).

Other reports produced by various sources, and forming at least background to the implementation of additions and amendments to the CPR, have been dealt with variously by the courts as aids to interpretation; see e.g. *Jirehouse Capital v Beller* [2008] EWCA Civ 908, July 30, 2008, CA, unrep., at para.16 per Arden L.J. (DCA Consultation Paper "Civil Procedure Rules—Security for Costs" provided no assistance and not admissible as an aid to interpretation of r.25.3(2)(c)); *Digicel (St Lucia) Ltd* v Cable & Wireless Plc [2008] EWHC 2522 (Ch), October 23, 2008, unrep. (Morgan J.) at para.37 (Cresswell Report on subject of electronic disclosure referred to in determining application of r.31.7 as supplemented by Practice Direction (Disclosure and Inspection) para.2A).

## 3. INTERPRETATION TO GIVE EFFECT TO OVERRIDING OBJECTIVE

The overriding objective is stated in r.1.1. It is specifically provided (subject to the exceptional modification imposed by r.76.2) that the court must seek to give effect to the overriding objective, not only when it exercises any power given to it by the CPR, but also when it interprets any rule (r.1.2(b)). In the Final Report it was said (at p.274) that every word in the rules of court should have a purpose, but every word cannot be given "a minutely exact meaning". Civil procedure involves more judgment and knowledge than rules can directly express. Ultimately their purpose is to guide the court and litigants towards the just resolution of the case. Although rules of court can offer detailed directions for the technical steps to be taken, the effectiveness of those steps depends upon the spirit in which they are carried out. That in turn depends on an understanding of the fundamental purpose of the rules and of the underlying system of procedure. The use of the word "seek" in r.1.2(b) acknowledges that, in giving effect to the overriding objective when interpreting any rule, the court can only do what is possible. The express words of a particular rule falling for interpretation may be so clear in what it commands or orders that the court cannot use the overriding objective to give effect to, what the court may otherwise consider to be, the just way of dealing with the case (*Vinos v Marks & Spencer Plc* [2001] 3 All E.R. 784, CA, at para.26 per Peter Gibson L.J., and *Totty v Snowden* [2001] EWCA Civ 1415; [2001] 4 All E.R. 577, CA, para.34 per Simon Brown L.J.). The court should avoid the slavish application of individual rules, practice directions and Pre-Action Protocols if such application undermines the overriding objective (*Orange Personal Communications Services Ltd v Hoare Lea* [2008] EWHC 223 (TCC), February 12, 2008, unrep. (Akenhead J.)). CPR Pt 76 contains provisions dealing with proceedings under the Prevention of Terrorism Act 2005. Rule 76.2(2) imposes a duty on the court in such proceedings to ensure that information is not disclosed contrary to the public interest. Rule 76.2(1) states that, where Pt 76 applies, the overriding objective in Pt 1, and so far as relevant, any other rule, must be read and given effect in a way which is compatible with that duty. 12–45

For extended commentary on the ways in which the courts have made use of the various elements of the overriding objective when interpreting CPR rules (and when exercising powers given to them by the CPR), see Section 11—The Overriding Objective, paras 11–4 to 11–6. Note also below at para.12–56 (Significance of CPR as "a new procedural code"), and para.12–57 (Reliance on pre-CPR authorities).

***Paragraph numbers marked with a "+" can be found online and on CD.***

## 4. INTERPRETATION ACT 1978

12-46 Former RSC O.1, r.3 stated that the 1978 Act should apply to the interpretation of those rules. The CPR contain no such provision but, for the reasons which follow, the effect is the same. The provisions of the 1978 Act, except ss.1 to 3 and 4(b), apply, so far as applicable and unless the contrary intention appears, to subordinate legislation made after January 1, 1979 (s.23(1)). In this context, "subordinate legislation" includes rules made under any Act (s.21(1)). Consequently, those provisions in the 1978 Act apply to the CPR. Section 5 of the Act states that, in any Act (or subordinate legislation), unless the contrary intention appears, words and expressions listed in Sch.1 to the Act are to be construed according to that Schedule. Several words and expressions in Sch.1 are relevant to matters of practice and procedure dealt with by the CPR. Note also s.7 (references to service by post).

Section 11 of the 1978 Act states that, where an Act confers power to make subordinate legislation, expressions used in that legislation have, unless the contrary intention appears, the meaning which they bear under the Act. By operation of this section, expressions used in the CPR have, unless the contrary intention appears, the meaning which they bear under the Civil Procedure Act 1997. It would seem that the Interpretation Act 1978 s.11 does not have the effect of incorporating into the CPR meanings assigned to expressions found in the Senior Courts Act 1981 (particularly by s.151) in the County Courts Act 1984 (particularly by s.147).

## 5. MEANING OF PARTICULAR WORDS AND EXPRESSIONS—GLOSSARY (CPR RR.2.2 AND 2.3)

12-47 The former RSC and CCR contained provisions of general application giving definitions of particular expressions (see former RSC O.1, r.4 and CCR O.1, r.3) and particular expressions were specially defined in the context of particular rules. Further, definitions were incorporated by reference from the Senior Courts Act 1981 and the County Courts Act 1984. The CPR follows a similar pattern.

The definitions given in r.2.3 (Interpretation) apply throughout the CPR. Other words and phrases are defined in context. For example, in the text of Pt 23 (General rules about applications for court orders) "application notice" and "respondent" are defined in r.23.1 and in Pt 31 (Disclosure and Inspection of Documents) "document" and "copy" of a document are defined. Further, many of the Parts added to the CPR since they came into effect in April 1999 have "local" interpretation provisions (sometimes quite extensive), defining certain words and phrases in the context of particular Parts or Sections of Parts; e.g. r.52.1(3) (appeals), r.54.1(2) (judicial review), r.54.21 (statutory review), r.55.1 (possession claims), r.57.1(2) (probate claims), r.58.1(2) (commercial claims), r.62.2(1) (arbitration claims), and rr.70.1(2) and 74.2(1) (enforcement of judgments). Where such Parts or Sections of Parts are dedicated to the purpose of providing procedures to support particular statutory schemes with their own terms of art, such "local" interpretation provisions are unavoidable.

An innovative feature of the CPR is the Glossary at the end. It contains a number of legal expressions, some of which were defined in rules found in the former RSC and CCR. In r.2.2 it is stated that the meanings given for the expressions listed in the Glossary are meant as guides only and do not give those expressions "any meaning in the Rules which they do not have in law generally". The Civil Procedure Act 1997 s.1(3) (as amended) states that the rule committee when making rules must "try to make rules which are both simple and simply expressed". The Glossary may be seen as an attempt to discharge that duty.

For commentaries on the particular words and phrases listed in para.(1) of r.2.3, see commentary following that rule in Vol.1.

## 6. PRACTICE DIRECTIONS AS AIDS TO INTERPRETATION

12-48 In relation to many matters relevant to the handling of cases by the civil courts, a complete understanding of the relevant practice and procedure may involve reference to, what has been called, a "somewhat cumbrous and confusing three-tier hierarchy of rules and guidance" consisting of statutory provisions, rules of court, and practice directions (*R. (Mount Cook Land Limited) v Westminster City Council* [2003] EWCA Civ 1346; [2004] C.P. Rep. 12, CA at para.67 per Auld L.J.). And to that structure may be added a fourth and a fifth tier, pre-actions protocols and court guides. One source

***Paragraph numbers marked with a "+" can be found online and on CD.***

(e.g. practice directions) can aid the interpretation of another (e.g. rules of court); but there is a potential for conflict between them.

A broad distinction may be drawn between practice directions supplementing the CPR and other practice directions affecting civil proceedings in the Court of Appeal (Civil Division), the High Court and the county courts (whether made before or after the coming into effect of the CPR). Statutory provisions dealing with powers to make practice directions of both varieties are found in the Civil Procedure Act 1997, particularly s.5 and Sch.1. These provisions were amended and supplemented by the Constitutional Reform Act 2005 to take account of changes in the role of the Lord Chancellor in relation to the administration of justice. A process for making practice directions is set out in Pt 1 of Sch.2 to the 2005 Act and is incorporated by reference in s.5, as amended, but that process does not apply to the making of all practice directions that may be made affecting civil proceedings in jurisdictions to which the CPR apply. One of the changes brought about by the 2005 Act was the revoking of the County Courts Act 1984 s.74A. Under that section the Lord Chancellor or a person authorised by him to act on his behalf (in practice, a Lord Justice of Appeal) had power to make directions as to the practice and procedure of county courts.

The CPR are made by the Civil Procedure Rule Committee under statutory powers (Civil Procedure Act 1997 s.2). Practice directions may provide for any matter which, by virtue of Sch.1 para.3 of the 1997 Act, may be provided for by the CPR (*ibid.* s.5(1)). Practice directions are not the responsibility of the Rule Committee. However, the CPR may, instead of providing for any matter, refer to provisions made about that matter by directions (*ibid.* Sch.1, para.6) (e.g. r.56.1(2) states that a practice direction may set out special provisions with regard to any particular category of landlord and tenant claim). Thus, practice directions are subordinate to the CPR. There is no necessary clash where a practice direction provision spells out explicitly what is implicit in a broad power conferred on the court by a rule (*Leigh v Michelin Tyre Plc* [2003] EWCA Civ 1766; [2004] 1 W.L.R. 846, CA). In *Hormel Foods Corp v Antilles Landscape Investment* [2003] EWHC 1912 (Ch); July 7, 2003, unrep., Lindsay J. refused to strike out a defendant's statement of case for failure to comply with a mandatory rule where the defendant could be said to have complied with a permissive provision in a practice direction supplementing the rule but apparently in conflict with it. In *Binks v Securicor Omega Express Ltd* [2003] EWCA Civ 993; July 16, 2003, CA, where there was an apparent clash between r.22.1(2) (reverification of amended statement of case) and Practice Direction (Amendments to Statements of Case) para.1.4, the Court of Appeal said precedence should be given to the rule. In *Godwin v Swindon BC* [2001] EWCA Civ 1478; [2002] 1 W.L.R. 997, CA, May L.J. expressed the opinion that practice directions supplementing the CPR (i.e. of the former variety referred to above) are "at best a weak aid to the interpretation of the rules themselves" (*ibid.* at para.11). It has been argued that, where a rule is capable of two possible constructions, then the relevant practice direction may be a legitimate aid to interpretation (*Van Aken v London Borough of Camden* [2002] EWCA Civ 1724; October 11, 2002, unrep., CA at para.36). In the *Mount Cook* case (op. cit.) Auld L.J. said (para.68) that it is important that all involved in civil proceedings ought to be able to rely on practice directions as indicating the normal practice of the courts unless and until amended. However, the practice directions supplementing CPR provisions differ from rules in the CPR in that (a) in general they provide guidance that should be followed, but do not have binding effect, and (b) they should yield to rules in the CPR where there is a clear conflict between them. Where there is a conflict between a CPR rule and a practice direction provision, it is the rule that must apply (*Harlow & Milner Ltd v Teasdale* [2006] EWHC 1708 (TCC), July 7, 2006, unrep. (Judge Peter Coulson Q.C.); *Brennan v ECO Composting Ltd* [2006] EWHC 3153 (QB); [2007] 1 W.L.R. 773 (Silber J.)). Where rules of court implement a statutory provision a supplementing practice direction may prove to be an aid to the construction of the primary legislation (e.g. *St Helens MBC v Barnes* [2006] EWCA Civ 1372; October 25, 2006, unrep., CA).

Rule 49(1) states that the CPR shall apply to certain listed proceedings subject to the provisions of "the relevant practice direction which applies to those proceedings". Thus, within the CPR, the expression "relevant practice direction" is a term of art.The expression is found in various places (e.g. r.6.7 (Deemed service)). A "relevant practice direction" is not the same as a practice direction supplementing a particular CPR Part. Since the CPR came into effect, the number of "relevant practice directions" has been

***Paragraph numbers marked with a "+" can be found online and on CD.***

steadily reduced and, eventually, all will disappear as new Parts are inserted in the CPR.

Examples may be found of rules within the CPR which provide that, for certain purposes, practice directions may modify or disapply particular CPR rules; e.g. r.55.10A (Electronic issue of certain possession claims). In r.66.2 (Application of CPR to civil proceedings to which the Crown is a party) it is expressly stated that CPR rules and their practice directions apply to civil proceedings by or against the Crown and to other civil proceedings to which the Crown is a party unless Pt 66, a practice direction or any other enactment provides otherwise. Obviously, in a given case, provisions such these may affect the interpretation of CPR.

Unfortunately, before 2010, no consistent style for giving titles to supplementing practice directions or for referring to them in cross-references within the CPR had been developed. The result was that it was not always the case that the number of the Part to which it related was included in the title of a supplementing practice direction, and sometimes no clue was given is given in the title as to whether it was the sole, or one of several, practice directions supplementing the Part. Further, forms of citation for cross-references varied. (The confusion was reflected in judgments and in legal writing.) During 2009 and 2010, in statutory instruments amending rules and in TSO CPR Updates amending practice directions, steps were taken to remedy this problem. However, it remains the case that the system for citing practice directions in cross-references within the CPR now in place gives the reader no clue as to the subject matter of the practice direction. For example, although a reader coming across the citation "Practice Direction 25B" will now know that that is a reference to the second practice direction supplementing Pt 25, he or she is unlikely to know, without looking it up expressly, that Pt 25 is concerned with the subjects of interim remedies and security for costs, and that the second practice supplementing that Part contains provisions dealing with interim payments.

## 7. COURT GUIDES

**12–49** In modern times, various "Court Guides" have been published (both before and after the coming into effect of the CPR), e.g. Chancery Guide (see Vol.2, para.1.1), Queen's Bench Guide (see Vol.2, para.1A.1), and Commercial Court Guide (see Vol.2, para.2B.18). To a large extent, these guides consist of narrative accounts of rules of court found in the CPR and practice directions (of various varieties), together with additional guidance on practice approved by judges. Much of the material is concerned with pre-trial applications (see commentary on CPR Pt 23 in Vol.1). In some instances, parts of these narrative accounts have not always been in accord with the rules and practice directions on which they were based (this was particularly true of the Commercial Court Guide). However, it is clear that the effect of rules and directions cannot be suspended or disapplied by what may be said in Court Guides. They are not sources of law. But in matters not covered by the CPR (or other sources of law) the Guides should be carefully observed (see Practice Statement (Admiralty and Commercial Courts: Procedure), *The Times*, April 2, 2002). Where ambiguity exists in the primary sources, the Guides may assist as aids to interpretation.

## 8. CROSS-REFERENCES AS AIDS TO INTERPRETATION

**12–50** One feature of the CPR which distinguishes them from the RSC and CCR is that, in various places, the texts of particular rules are interleaved with bracketed cross-references (or "signposts") to other CPR provisions. For example, r.2.11 contains cross references to r.3.8, r.28.4 and r.29.5. In the "Access to Justice" Final Report (July 1996) it was explained that the purpose of this system of cross-referring is to avoid duplication where it makes sense to do so by referring in the text of one rule to other contextually relevant rules in such a way as to make it clear what those other rules do (*ibid.* Chap.20, paras 18 to 22). In the Stationery Office version of the CPR, as published in early 1999 shortly before the CPR came into effect (and regularly updated subsequently), there were attached to certain rules a number of additional cross-references, most of them drawing attention to provisions found in Schs 1 and 2 of the CPR. Thus there appeared to be a distinction between, what could be called, "formal" and "informal" (or "non-statutory") cross-references. The provenance of the informal cross-references (which were amended from time to time) was unclear; certainly they had never formed part of the CPR as enacted by statutory instrument. By HMSO CPR Update 29, 2002, these informal cross-references were removed from the Stationery Office version of the CPR (many had become out-of-date as Schedule rules became revoked). Curiously, Civil Procedure (Amendment) Rules 2002 (SI 2002/ 2058) rr.12(d)(i) and 13 purported to omit cross-references from r.34.15 and r.40.4 despite the fact that they were informal cross-references and never appeared in the Civil Procedure Rules 1998 as enacted (see SI 1998/3132). It is obvious that many of the cross-references appended to particular CPR rules do not have any force, as opposed to being mere guidance to the reader as to where to find matters elsewhere in the rules. Formal cross-references of this type may be seen as efforts by the Rule Committee to discharge its statutory duty "to try to make rules which are both simple and simply expressed" (Civil Procedure Act 1997 s.1(3)). But some other cross-references (particularly of the formal variety) appear to have been inserted in particular rules for the purpose of making clear what the rule means where there might otherwise be room for doubt. In a number of cases, the question of the status of cross-references as aids to interpretation of the CPR rules to which they are attached has arisen; see e.g. *Re Casserly* , October 23, 2000, unrep. (Johnson J.) (cross-reference to r.7.5 in r.8.2); *Anderton v Clwyd County Council* July 25, 2001, unrep. (McCombe J.) (cross-reference to r.2.8 in r.6.7(1)); *Montrose Investments Ltd v Orion Nominees* July 19, 2001, unrep. (Sir Donald Rattee) (cross-reference to r.15.4 in r.11(4)). In *Godwin v Swindon BC* [2001] EWCA Civ 1478; [2001] 4 All E.R. 641, CA, the approach adopted by the judge in the *Anderton* case was approved (*ibid.* at paras [37] and [47] per May L.J.). In the *Montrose* case, the judge did not accept the proposition that the setting of words referring to other CPR provisions in parentheses deprived them of any effect that they would otherwise have. What matters is, not whether the words are in brackets, but what they say. In *Anderton v Clwyd County Council* [2002] EWCA Civ 933; [2002] 3 All E.R. 813, CA, Mummery L.J. said (para.44) the fact that the express mention "by way of seemingly informal cross-reference in brackets" of r.2.8 in r.6.7(1) was, in the circumstances, beside the point as what mattered is "the language of r.2.8, whether in or out of brackets, and whether it is apt to apply to r.6.7". The cross-reference in r.6.7(1) was removed by the Civil Procedure (Amendment No.3) Rules 2005 (SI 2005/2292).

See further "The significance of the CPR as 'a new procedural code'" para.12–56, and "Reliance on pre-CPR authorities" para.12–57, below.

## 9. CPR CHECK-LISTS AND JUDGE-MADE CHECK-LISTS

In *Biguzzi v Rank Leisure Plc* [1999] 1 W.L.R. 1926, CA, Lord Woolf M.R. referred **12–51** to the wide powers that the courts have under the CPR to enable them to respond to procedural defaults on the part of parties and said (at p.1934) "judges have to be trusted to exercise the wide discretion which they have fairly and justly in all circumstances". It is to be expected that a judge, in giving a reasoned judgment explaining how he has gone about exercising his broad discretion in a particular procedural context (whether or not it is one involving a procedural default), will be anxious to demonstrate that he has proceeded in a principled way and directed himself properly, especially where the consequences of his decision are serious for the parties involved. He is likely therefore to itemise at a reasonable level of abstraction in a "check-list" style the considerations that seem to him to be relevant, particularly where the considerations laid down by rules or practice directions are obviously incomplete, sketchy, bland or non-existent, and then to apply them to the case in hand. Doubtless, in doing so he will draw inspiration from, amongst other sources, the judgments of other judges similarly placed, bearing in mind that judgments in cases dealt with before the CPR came into effect should be treated with caution. All this sounds like a perfectly innocent, indeed commendable, judicial exercise. However, it should be noted that the Court of Appeal has gone out of its way to discourage the reliance of judges on check-lists made by other judges when interpreting and applying CPR provisions.

An example of the Court of Appeal's position on this matter is provided by *Audergon v La Baguette Ltd* [2002] EWCA Civ 10; *The Times*, January 31, 2002, CA. In this case the judge refused an application to lift an automatic stay imposed on proceedings by Practice Direction (Transitional Arrangements), para.19(1) and, in coming to that decision, was guided by the matters listed by Neuberger J. in *Annodeus Ltd v Gibson*, *The Times*, March 3, 2000, as being relevant considerations. In allowing the appeal, the

***Paragraph numbers marked with a "+" can be found online and on CD.***

Court expressed the opinion that the value of relying on judicially created check-lists, which do not appear in the CPR provision being applied, is doubtful; inherent in such an approach is the danger that a body of "satellite authority" might be built up leading in effect to the re-writing of the provision through the medium of judicial authority (as occurred in relation to dismissal for want of prosecution under the former RSC). The point has been reinforced by the Court of Appeal in subsequent cases. (It may be noted that, despite the Court's strictures, in applications to strike out under r.3.4, judges have continued to refer to the list of considerations adumbrated by Neuberger J. in the *Annodeus Ltd* case; e.g. *McLoughlin v Grovers* [2005] EWHC 803 (QB), February 17, 2005, unrep. (Simon J.) and *Sweetman v Shepherd* [2007] EWHC 137 (QB), February 2, 2007, unrep. (Irwin J.).)

The Court's attitude to this matter is not so much based on a hostility to judge-made check-lists as such, but to the growth of procedural case law generally. In *Woodhouse v Consignia Plc* [2002] EWCA Civ 275; [2002] 1 W.L.R. 2558, CA, Brooke L.J. explained (at para.32) that one of the great demerits of the former procedural regimes was that simple rules "got barnacled with case-law". Under the CPR regime, in various procedural contexts, the draftsman has sought to dispense with the need for litigants to be familiar with judge-made case-law by drawing together in one place the most common of the considerations a court must take into account when making its procedural decision. In *Anglo-Eastern Trust Ltd v Kermanshahchi* [2002] EWCA Civ 198; [2002] C.P. Rep. 36, CA, Brooke L.J. said that Practice Direction (Summary Judgment) para.4 is clearly intended to set out a new code of practice which could be understood without the need to refer to case law. The clearest illustration of a rule-made check-list designed to be applied unencumbered by case law glosses is the list of considerations set forth in r.3.9 (Relief from sanctions), and it was this rule that was the centre of attention in both the *Audergon* case and the *Woodhouse* case. It is a rule that has been pressed into service in circumstances for which, arguably, it was not designed. The Court of Appeal has even gone so far as to hold that it should be used in a context in which, as the court admitted, it clearly does not in terms apply (see *Sayers v Clarke Walker (Practice Note)* [2002] EWCA Civ 645; [2002] 1 W.L.R. 3095, CA (application for extension of time for appealing); cf., *Cottrell v General Cologne Re UK Ltd* [2004] EWHC 2402, (Comm), October 20, 2004, unrep. (Morison J.) (r.3.9 does not apply where breach of r.33.2(4)(a)). This may suggest that there is perhaps a shortage in the CPR of rules and practice directions setting out in a codified form the various matters that the court should take into account when deciding how to exercise its discretion, and that a market for judge-made check-lists exists. But the fear that particular CPR provisions may be re-written through the medium of judicial authority, leading to the kind of over-elaboration that occurred following *Birkett v James* and the consequences of that, is still very real. So the Court of Appeal's discouragement of judge-made check-lists and preference for rule-made check-lists is understandable, if perhaps a little heavy-handed. In *Hashtroodi v Hancock* [2004] EWCA Civ 652; [2004] 1 W.L.R. 3206, CA, the Court of Appeal noted, and regarded as significant, the fact that r.7.6 (extension of time for serving a claim form), unlike r.3.9 (see above), contains no checklist of relevant factors to be taken into account by the court when exercising its discretion. Instances can arise in which parties to appeals to the Court of Appeal request the Court to give "guidance" on particular procedural matters and, in effect, to design a check-list (usually to guide the exercise of discretion). For example, in *Glaxo Group Limited v Genentech Inc* [2008] EWCA Civ 23; *The Times* February 21, 2008, CA, the court acknowledged that a check-list "is a convenient way of making sure that the court has all the information it needs and of collating the information" and endeavoured to give guidance as to the factors to be taken into account by a judge in determining, in the exercise of discretion, an application for a stay of patent proceedings.

## 10. CASE LAW AS AID TO CONSTRUCTION

**12–52** In the Interim Report it was said (at p.217) that it would be of fundamental importance that the new rules "are not hidebound by previous authorities on the old rules". It was also said that the procedural innovations in the CPR "will make most of the old authorities redundant". Doubtless that is an exaggeration. However, to the extent that provisions in the CPR are shorter and more clearly expressed than the provisions in the RSC and CCR they replace, they ought to have made the task of the judge and practitioner easier. Furthermore, the plainer, simpler form of drafting of the new rules should have meant "that there should be less need to seek instructions from the courts on what the rules mean" (Interim Report, p.217). It is clear that many provisions in the CPR have been drafted on the assumption that previous case law will continue to apply. This is particularly true of provisions that simply re-enact in simpler language procedural rules which drew no criticism in the "Access to Justice" Reports. It is also largely true of the case law on former RSC and CCR provisions incorporated in Schs 1 and 2 of the CPR. It would be expected that pre-CPR authorities most likely to be treated as redundant in those circumstances where the CPR rules falling for examination are provisions that were drafted and included in the CPR for the purpose of overcoming known difficulties in previous procedural rules; e.g. *Akram v Adam* [2004] EWCA Civ 1601; [2005] 1 W.L.R. 2762, CA (service by post at last known address). The Court of Appeal has said that the thinking behind the CPR, especially behind the innovative provisions as to costs, was that they would "speak for themselves" and that courts would not have to refer to an ever increasing body of authority in order to apply them (see *ABCI v Banque Franco-Tunisienne* [2003] EWCA Civ 295, at para.68, and *Somatra Ltd v Sinclair Roche & Temperley (No.2)* [2003] EWCA Civ 1474; October 23, 2003, CA, unrep., at para.86). However, it has to be said that, for various reasons, certain CPR provisions have proved to be difficult to apply and quite naturally and properly case law has been expected to supply the deficiencies. Indeed, in some respects innovative aspects of the CPR have generated an enormous amount of case law, complicating the work of judges considerably. For example, in *Rackham v Sandy (Costs)* [2005] EWHC 1354 (Gray J.), the judge ruefully noted that in dealing with an issue as to the apportionment of costs in libel proceedings he was faced with a joint bundle of 24 authorities and skeleton argument totalling 49 pages. Where particular provisions have become encrusted with case law the explanation lies in the fact that the subject matter has inherent difficulties that cannot all be anticipated and resolved in rules that are meant to be simply expressed or that the response of the courts has been uncertain. Further, as is increasingly recognised, references to former RSC and CCR rules and the authorities decided under them may be instructive, but will not necessarily be determinative, of the meaning and effect of CPR provisions (*S.T. Dupont v E.I. du Pont de Nemours & Co* [2003] EWCA Civ 1368; October 10, 2003, CA, unrep., at para.86 per May L.J.).



## 11. DOCTRINE OF PRECEDENT AND RESTRICTIONS ON CITATION

Rules of court, being a form of legislation, have to be read and applied in the light **12–53** of relevant case law. In procedural law (whether derived from rules of court or other sources), as well as in substantive law, the doctrine of precedent applies and lower courts are obliged to apply the decisions of higher courts. Uncertainty in the law, whether procedural or substantive, can exacerbate costs and delays in individual cases. The rules that make up the doctrine of precedent seek to avoid uncertainty and their effects in the field of procedural law are justified as much by judicial administration and case management considerations as by any others.

In modern times, courts have complained about the tendency of legal representatives to over-burden legal submissions (1) by citing several authorities where one would do, (2) by citing authorities that (a) are not relevant, or only marginally so, or (b) are as no value as precedents. As a consequence, efforts have been made to restrict the "over-citation" of authority by lawyers handling civil proceedings.

### *(a) Doctrine of precedent*

Only the outlines of the precedent rules need to be explained here. The Court of **12–54** Appeal regards itself as being bound by its own previous decisions. For an explanation of the per incuriam exception to this rule, see *Desnousse v Newham London BC* [2006] EWCA Civ 547; [2006] Q.B. 831, CA, at paras 70 to 77 per Lloyd L.J. This self-denying ordinance applies as strictly to decisions on procedural law as to substantive law. It also applies equally to decisions of two-judge and three-judge courts made on an appeal (as distinct from an application for permission to appeal) (*Langley v North West Water Authority* [1991] 1 W.L.R. 697, CA, at p.697 per Lord Donaldson M.R.; see also *Limb v Union Jack Removals Ltd* [1998] 1 W.L.R. 1354, CA, at para.34). (The position may have been otherwise in the days when the division of work between two-judge and three-judge courts was determined by whether there was a need for other than brief argument or the point was of minimal importance other than to the immediate parties; see *Welsh Development Agency v Redpath Dorman Long* [1994] 1 W.L.R. 1409, CA at p.1423 per Glidewell L.J.). In *Actavis UK Ltd v Merck and Co Inc* [2008] EWCA Civ 444, May 21, 2008, unrep., CA, the Court of Appeal held that it was free to depart from its own previous decision where it was satisfied that the EPO Boards of Appeal had formed a settled view of European patent law which was inconsistent with that earlier decision. Generally, where higher authority does not bind, a Divisional Court will follow an earlier decision of another Divisional Court of the High Court, and will do so as a matter of judicial comity unless convinced that the previous judgment is wrong (*R. v Greater Manchester Coroner, Ex p. Tal* [1985] 1 Q.B. 67, DC). Similarly, a High Court judge, whether sitting at first instance or as an appeal court, will follow an earlier decision by a High Court judge (*ibid.*) (for an example of a previous decision on a procedural issue not being followed, see *Ansari v Puffin Investment Co Ltd* [2002] EWHC 1243).

Decisions of the High Court, whether made on appeal or at first instance (and whether made by a High Court judge or a deputy High Court judge) are binding on a county court. Further, for these purposes a decision of the High Court does not cease to be a decision of a higher court binding on a county court when it is made in the exercise of the same first instance jurisdiction as is conferred on the latter court (*Howard de Walden Estates Ltd v Aggio* [2007] EWCA Civ 499; [2007] 3 W.L.R. 542, CA).

The problem of the over-citation of authorities in skeleton arguments in cases in which submissions related to procedural issues are made (especially as to costs) appears to be a perennial problem, continuing despite regular pleas from the Court of Appeal and from judges sitting at first instance for legal representatives to be more discriminating (see e.g. *Cel Group Ltd v Nedlloyd Lines UK Ltd* [2003] EWCA Civ 1716; [2004] 1 Lloyd's Rep. 388, CA, at para.23 per Carnwath L.J.; *Hedrich v Standard Bank Ltd* [2008] EWCA Civ 905, July 30, 2008, CA, unrep., at para.40 per Ward L.J.).

Where there is an apparent conflict of authority between two previous decisions of the Court of Appeal, it is not unknown for the matter to be argued before a full court of the Court, as the decision of such a court holds greater weight (*Young v Bristol Aeroplane Co* [1944] K.B. 718, CA at p.728). In modern times, the Court has resorted to this device for the purpose of clarifying aspects of procedural law (e.g. *Taylor v Lawrence* [2002] EWCA Civ 90; [2003] Q.B. 528, CA (power of Court of Appeal to reopen appeal)).

It is conceivable that a judge sitting in the High Court or in a county court may find himself confronted with Court of Appeal decisions on procedural questions which, though apparently binding on him, are contradictory or, at best, not ad idem. The rule of precedent seems to be that a judge finding himself in this predicament should prefer the later decision if it was reached after full consideration of the earlier; otherwise he should follow one or the other (*Minister of Pensions v Higham* [1948] 2 K.B. 153). In *Colchester Estates (Cardiff) v Carlton Industries Plc* [1984] 3 W.L.R. 693, Nourse J. stated that, where a High Court judge is confronted with two High Court authorities, one conflicting with the other, the later decision is to be preferred if it was reached after full consideration of the earlier decision, unless the judge is convinced that the second was wrong in not following the first. In the case of *In re Taylor (A Bankrupt)* [2006] EWHC 3029 (Ch); [2007] 2 W.L.R. 148, this dictum was doubted by Judge Kershaw Q.C., who preferred the view that, as decisions of co-ordinate courts are persuasive and not binding, the judge should make his decision on the merits of the submissions, giving appropriate weight but no more to the conflicting authorities, especially when the issue is one of jurisdiction rather than the exercise of discretion.

As a practical matter, in many instances decisions made by judges and courts on procedural issues (both at first instance and on appeal) involve the exercise of discretion. A long time ago it was said that, in a question of discretion "authorities are not of much value", as no two cases are exactly alike, and even if they were, the court cannot be bound by a previous decision to exercise its discretion in a particular way (because that would be in effect putting an end to the discretion) (*Jenkins v Bushby* [1891] 1 Ch. 484, CA at p.495 per Kay L.J.). Certainly, it is dangerous for a court, in the exercise of a discretion in a case, to take a reported case as a guide for that exercise (*Bragg v Crossville Motor Services Ltd* [1959] 1 W.L.R. 324, CA at p.236 per Hodson L.J.). Much of the modern judicial criticism levelled at legal representatives for their "over-citation" of authorities (see further below) is derived from the fact that, all too frequently, they attempt to use decisions illustrating the exercise of discretion and dicta therein as persuasive authorities, rather than as mere inspiration for forensic argument (*Koller v Secretary of State for the Home Department* [2001] EWCA Civ 1267; July 26, 2001, CA, unrep. at para.21).

The operation of the doctrine of precedent is affected by the Human Rights Act 1998. Section 6 of that Act makes it unlawful for a court "to act in a way which is incompatible with a Convention right". Section 2 provides that, in determining any question concerning a Convention right (e.g. the right to a fair trial granted by art.6) a court "must take into account" the Strasbourg jurisprudence. If an English court (at any level) concludes that, in the s.6 sense, it would be acting unlawfully should it follow a previous decision apparently binding on it, then it should apply the ECHR rule rather than that decision. (As to the effects of the 1998 Act on the application of the rules of statutory interpretation, see para.12–58 below).

Frequently, judges dealing with interlocutory applications and applications for permissions to appeal are faced with the problem of giving definitive interpretations of rules of court. Sometimes such applications may be unopposed or attended by one party only, with the result that any value the decision may have as a binding or persuasive authority is weakened for that reason alone.

### *(b) Citation of previous authority—restrictions on*

When it comes to the citation of previous authorities (in skeleton arguments and legal submissions), whether of binding or persuasive authority, and whether on procedural or substantive issues, *Practice Direction (Citation of Authorities)* [2001] 1 W.L.R. 1001, must be borne in mind. Paragraphs 6.1 and 6.2 of this Practice Direction provide that (1) judgments given on applications attended by one party only, (2) applications for permission to appeal, and (3) decisions given on applications that only decide that the application is arguable, may not in future be cited before any court "unless it clearly indicates that it purports to establish a new principle or to extend the present law". To be citable, decisions rendered after April 9, 2001, must have an express statement to that effect. **12–55**



Decisions on procedural issues containing such express statement include: *Napp Pharmaceutical Holdings Ltd v Director General of Fair Trading* [2002] EWCA Civ 796; [2002] 4 All E.R. 376, CA; *Seray-Wurie v Hackney London BC* [2002] EWCA Civ 909; [2003] 1 W.L.R. 257, CA; [2002] 3 All E.R. 490; *Sayers v Clarke Walker (Practice Note)* [2002] EWCA Civ 645; [2002] 1 W.L.R. 3095, CA; *Sohal v Sohal* [2002] EWCA Civ 1297; July 30, 2002, CA; *Gregory v Turner* [2003] EWCA Civ 183; [2003] 2 All E.R. 114, CA; *Bhamjee v Forsdick (Application for Permission to Appeal)* [2003] EWCA Civ 799; May 14, 2003, CA, unrep.; *Jeyapragash v Secretary of State for the Home Department* [2004] EWCA Civ 1260; [2005] All E.R. 412, CA; *Uphill v B.R.B. (Residuary) Ltd* [2005] EWCA Civ 60; [2005] 1 W.L.R. 2070, CA; *Perotti v Westminster City Council* [2005] EWCA Civ 581; *The Times*, May 30, 2005, unrep., CA; *Black v Pastouna* [2005] EWCA Civ 1389, October 31, 2005,,unrep., CA; *YD (Turkey) v Secretary of State for the Home Department* [2006] EWCA Civ 52, [2006] 1 W.L.R. 1646, CA; *R. (Pereira) v Inner South London Coroner* [2007] EWHC 1723 (Admin); *The Times*, June 22, 2007, DC; *R. (England) v Tower Hamlets LBC* [2006] EWCA Civ 1742, December 20, 2006, unrep., CA; *Boyland & Son Ltd v Rand* [2006] EWCA Civ 1860; *The Times* January 18, 2007, CA; *Jaffray v The Society of Lloyds* [2007] EWCA Civ 586, June 20, 2007, CA, unrep.; *Poole BC v Hambridge* [2007] EWCA Civ 990, September 25, 2007, CA, unrep.; *Gawler v Raettig* [2007] EWCA Civ 1560, December 12, 2007, unrep., CA; *Jackson v Marina Homes Ltd* [2007] EWCA Civ 1404, November 13, 2007, CA, unrep. An important judgment not containing an express statement releasing for citation, when surely it ought to have done, is the judgment of the Court of Appeal in *George Wimpey UK Ltd v Tewkesbury BC* [2008] EWCA Civ 12; [2008] 1 W.L.R. 1649, CA (applicant, not party to proceedings below (in which the claimant succeeded), added as party for purposes of bringing appeal).

Further, county court cases may not be cited in any court unless (1) cited in order to illustrate the conventional measure of damages in a personal injury case, or (2) cited in a county court in order to demonstrate current authority at that level on an issue in respect of which no decision at a higher level of authority is available. On a number of occasions the courts have had cause to stress the importance of complying with the practice direction (see e.g. *Jennings v Cairns* [2003] EWCA Civ 1935; [2004] W.T.L.R. 361, CA). In *Mandrake Holdings Ltd v Countrywide Assured Group Plc* [2005] EWHC 311

(Ch), March 8, 2005, unrep., the defendants, in resisting the claimants' application to add an additional head of damage, alleged that the new claim was bad in law, and cited in support of that submission a pre-April 9, 2001, decision given by the Court of Appeal when granting an application for permission to appeal. The judge (Lightman J.) ruled that the bar on citation had been breached, because there was no indication present in, or clearly deductible from, the language used in the judgment that the decision "purports to establish a new principle or to extend the present law". The judge concluded that, in these circumstances, he was precluded from relying on the judgment, even though it had been published in an established and respected series of law reports.

Usually, any express statement to the effect that a decision purports to establish a new principle or to extend the present law (freeing a case for citation) will be made at the time when the decision is given. However, that is not necessary; e.g. *Smith v Brough* [2005] EWCA Civ 261, February 22, 2005, CA, unrep. (decision on extension of time for applying for permission to appeal freed for citation several months after made).

The problem of the over-citation of authorities on interlocutory applications to the court was referred to in *A v B Plc* [2002] EWCA Civ 337; [2003] Q.B. 195, CA. In this case, the Court of Appeal laid down guidelines according to which judges at first instance should direct themselves when hearing applications for interim injunctions restraining publication in breach of confidence claims, and did so, not only for the purpose of clarifying the law, but also for the purpose of making it possible generally for judges to ignore other authorities, even if referred to them by the parties. The Court said that the pursuit of the latter purpose was consistent with the duty of courts under the overriding objective, in particular, the saving of cost and dealing with cases in ways which are proportionate. In a number of cases where Convention rights issues have arguably arisen on procedural applications, the courts have criticised the tendency towards the over-citation by parties of authorities on the impact on English law of the Strasbourg jurisprudence in areas where a growing number of cases make the same point in similar language (e.g. *Chase v News Group Newspapers Ltd* [2002] EWHC 1101, QB (Eady J.)).

In the Court of Appeal, if a case referred to by a party has been reported in the official Law Reports published by the Incorporated Council of Law Reporting for England and Wales, that report should be cited. If a case is not, or not yet reported in the official Law Reports, but has been reported in the Weekly Law Reports or the All England Law Reports, that report should be cited. Otherwise cases may be cited as provided by *Practice Direction (Court of Appeal: Citation of Authority)* [1995] 1 W.L.R. 1096, CA (superseding para.5 of *Practice Direction (Court of Appeal: Presentation of Argument)* [1989] 1 W.L.R. 281, CA); see further *Bank of Scotland v Henry Butcher & Co* [2003] EWCA Civ 67; [2003] 2 All E.R. (Comm) 557. Where it is necessary for a party to give evidence of an authority referred to in the Human Rights Act 1998 s.2 (Strasbourg jurisprudence), para.8.1 of Practice Direction (Miscellaneous Provisions Relating to Hearings (supplementing CPR Pt 39) applies. The authority to be cited should be an authoritative and complete report, and the party must give to the court and any other party a list of authorities he intends to cite and copies of the reports not less than three days before the hearing.

## 12. THE SIGNIFICANCE OF THE CPR AS "A NEW PROCEDURAL CODE"

**12–56** In CPR r.1.1(1), it is asserted that the CPR "are a new procedural code". This concept was not referred to in the penultimate draft of the CPR published in July 1998. The purpose and significance of this very late addition were not immediately clear as it is obvious that the CPR do not constitute a "code" in any technical sense understood by lawyers, and much of the content of the CPR is far from "new". Further, it is doubtful whether anyone closely involved in the very long gestation period of the CPR ever thought of them as such. The bulk of the CPR consists of former RSC and CCR provisions, in most instances revised and expressed in modern language. The Civil Procedure Act 1997 s.1(3) (as amended) enjoins the rule committee to try "to make rules which are both simple and simply expressed". This, of course, is a counsel of perfection. The risk is, that in attempting to express rules in modern, and preferably simple, language, important distinctions may be lost. In *Société Eram Shipping Co Ltd v Compagnie Internationale de Navigation* [2003] UKHL 30; [2004] 1 A.C.

260, HL, Lord Millett (para.112) drew attention to the fact that certain provisions of CPR Pt 72 (which replaced RSC O.49) are unsatisfactory in this respect, and cannot easily be understood without a knowledge of their history and antecedents. Lack of understanding as to the provenance (found in the former CCR) of CPR Pt 14 (Admissions) created problems in relation to the question whether a party may resile from a pre-action admission which had to be rectified by amendment to the CPR (*Sowerby v Charlton* [2005] EWCA Civ 1610; [2006] 1 W.L.R. 568, CA).

Nevertheless, as apparently they have been trained to do, the judges have stressed the concept of the CPR as "a new procedural code" in many cases. It appears that the courts may place emphasis on the concept for various reasons, including (1) adding force to the fact that the court must seek to give effect to the overriding objective when it exercises any power given to it by the Rules or interprets any rule (r.1.2), (2) ensuring that the truly innovative provisions in the CPR are given their full and proper intended effects and are not limited by practices and attitudes that attached to the former rules of court which they supplant, and (3) making it clear that provisions in the CPR plainly based on provisions formerly found in the RSC and CCR will not necessarily be interpreted and applied in accordance with the case law that had been built up around those provisions over the years. Reference to the assertion that the CPR constitutes "a new procedural code" in these circumstances does no harm. However, it is submitted that the assertion should not be relied upon as an excuse for dealing with important procedural issues as matters of first impression rather than as matters requiring rigorous legal analysis (in their historical context, if necessary).

In some cases, for the purpose of maintaining that the CPR do constitute a new procedural code introducing greater flexibility into the law, the courts have tended to caricature certain pre-CPR rules, portraying them as being much more rigid in application than they really were (e.g. *Warren v Secretary of State for Trade and Industry* [2006] EWHC 1992 (Ch), June 14, 2006, unrep. (admissibility of additional evidence on appeal)). On occasion, the lengths that the Court of Appeal has gone to in order to avoid having to have recourse to well-settled and accepted pre-CPR principles for the purpose of solving particular procedural problems not clearly or adequately dealt with by the CPR, have been extreme (e.g. *Nelson v Clearsprings (Management) Ltd* [2006] EWCA Civ 1252, *The Times* October 5, 2006, CA(setting aside irregular judgment)).

The requirement, stated in r.1.2, that the court must seek to give effect to the overriding objective when it exercises any power given to it by the CPR, or interprets any rule, can readily provide a basis upon which a judge may proceed on the basis that pre-CPR authorities do not govern. For further explanation and examples, see Section 11—The Overriding Objective, para.11–5 above.

In cases where the courts have necessarily been driven to pre-CPR authorities for the purpose of understanding and properly applying particular provisions in the CPR, the bald assertion in r.1.1(1) that the CPR "are a new procedural code" is either studiously ignored (e.g. *Drinkall v Whitwood* [2003] EWCA Civ 1547; [2004] 1 W.L.R. 462, CA), or gamely acknowledged with some such qualification made as "generally speaking" cases decided under the former rules "are not helpful in interpreting the new code" or "will only occasionally provide assistance" (e.g. *Flynn v Scougall (Practice Note)* [2004] EWCA Civ 873; [2004] 1 W.L.R. 3069, CA, at para.23, per May L.J.; *Parsons v George* [2004] EWCA Civ 912; [2004] 1 W.L.R. 3264, CA, at para.41, per Dyson L.J.). Often the courts are more positive and, whilst accepting that recourse to earlier authorities is inappropriate, frankly admit that they "provide valuable guidance", especially where this is common ground (*Ultraframe (U.K.) Ltd v Eurocell Building Plastics Ltd* [2005] EWHC 2111 (Ch), August 26, 2005, unrep. (Pumfrey J.)). Where pre-CPR authorities were used to fill serious gaps in the RSC, they have also been relied upon for the purpose of filling such gaps surviving in the CPR, and instances have arisen of such authorities being incorporated in the CPR without embarrassment through the exercise of the court's power under r.3.10 (General power to rectify matters where there has been an error of procedure) (e.g. *Nesheim v Kosa* [2006] EWHC 2710 (Ch), October 10, 2006, unrep. (Briggs J.) (retrospective permission to serve claim form out of jurisdiction)). In some instances the courts have seized on the freedom given by the CPR and have relished the opportunity to ignore certain well-established pre-CPR authorities; e.g. *Morgan Est (Scotland) Ltd v Hanson Concrete Products Ltd* [2005] EWCA Civ 134; [2005] 1 W.L.R. 2557, CA (mistaken service on wrong party where claim statute barred). Paradoxically, sometimes recourse to pre-CPR authorities is justified on the ground that that is required by the court's duty to deal with cases justly in accordance with the overriding objective, so far as is practicable (r.1.1); e.g. *Humber Work Boats Ltd v Owners of the Selby Paradigm* [2004] EWHC 1804 (Admlty), (2004) (David Steel J.). Obviously, whatever significance may be given to the CPR being "a new procedural code", necessarily the requirement that the court must seek to give effect to the overriding objective when it exercises any power given to it by the CPR or interprets any rule (r.1.2) may loosen the hold that pre-CPR authority may have in particular contexts (see para.12–45). For examples of the application of pre-CPR authorities for purpose of applying particular CPR provisions, see below.

## 13. RELIANCE ON PRE-CPR AUTHORITIES

**12–57** Despite the fact that it is asserted in r.1.1(1) that the CPR constitutes "a new procedural code", most of the provisions in the CPR have been copied from former RSC and CCR provisions, often virtually word-for-word, but mostly with some modest attempt at simplifying the language. Instances have arisen of the Court of Appeal holding that phrases found in pre-CPR rules, but which have been omitted from their leaner CPR analogues, should be read into the latter (e.g. *Bailey v Warren* [2006] EWCA Civ 51; *The Times* February 20, 2006, C.A., (words found in RSC O.80, r.11 (Approval of settlement), to be read into CPR r.21.10 (Compromise etc. by or on behalf child or patient)). Where former RSC and CCR provisions were to the same effect, though differently expressed, a tendency to use CCR rather than RSC formulations is apparent (see e.g. *Anderton v Clwyd CC (No.2)* [2003] EWCA Civ 933; [2002] 1 W.L.R. 3174, CA, explaining CPR service out of jurisdiction rules). Where they were not to the same effect a choice had to be made. Since the CPR have come into effect, in interpreting and applying CPR provisions where their provenance in the RSC and CCR is obvious, the courts have routinely relied on, and re-affirmed, case law relating to the former provisions in those circumstances where, by doing so, the key case management policies introduced by the CPR are not undermined. Illustrations of this are legion.

A few examples arising recently are as follows: *Riyad Bank v Ahli United bank (UK) Plc* [2005] EWCA Civ 1419, November 23, 2005, C.A., unrep. (test for admissibility of additional evidence on appeal); *Independiente Ltd v Music Trading On-Line (HK) Ltd* [2003] EWHC 470 (Ch); March 13, 2003, (Sir Andrew Morritt V.-C.) (whether representative parties have same interest under r.19.6); *Bentley Skinner (Bond Street Jewellers) Ltd v Searchmap Ltd* [2003] EWHC 1621 (Ch); July 8, 2003, unrep. (Lightman J.) (evidence on appeal as to matters occurring after trial); *Drinkall v Whitwood* [2003] EWCA Civ 1547; [2004] 1 W.L.R. 462, CA (proper construction of r.21.10 where offer to settle infant's claim); *Hackney LBC v Driscoll* [2003] EWCA Civ 1037; [2003] 1 W.L.R. 2602, CA (granting application under r.39.5 where party failed to attend trial); *Rosen v Rose* [2003] EWHC 309 (QB); January 27, 2003, unrep. (Fulford J.) (evidence in freezing injunction application); *Flynn v Scougall (Practice Note)* [2004] EWCA Civ 873; [2004] 1 W.L.R. 3069, CA (payments into court); *Parsons v George*, [2004] EWCA Civ 912; [2004] 1 W.L.R. 3264, CA (substitution of party under r.19.5 after expiry of limitation period); *Humber Work Boats Ltd v Owners of the Selby Paradigm* [2004] EWHC 1804 (Admlty) (David Steel J.) (joinder of defendant's insurers under r.19.2 after default judgment against defendant); *University of East London Higher Education Corp v Barking and Dagenham LBC* [2004] EWHC 2908; *The Times*, January 3, 2005, (Ch) (Lightman J.) (payment of costs where party joined in claim for declaration against existence of adverse rights); *Mersey Docks Properties v Kilgour* [2004] EWHC 1638 (TCC), June 25, 2004, unrep. (Judge Toulmin Q.C.) (service at last known place of business); *Red Bull GmbH v Mean Fiddler Music Group Plc* [2004] EWHC 3330 (Ch), December 13, 2004, unrep. (Evans Lombe J.) (enforcement of judgment to abstain from doing any act); *Tajik Aluminium Plant v Hydro Aluminium AS* [2005] EWCA Civ 1218; [2005] 4 All E.R. 1232, CA (identification of documents in witness summons to produce documents); *TSP Group Ltd v Globemark (UK) Ltd* [2005] EWHC 2396(QB); *The Times*, November 30, 2005 (Roderick Evans J.) (summary disposal of interpleader issue); *Edwards v Golding* [2006] EWHC 1684 (QB), July 12, 2006, unrep. (Tugendhat J.) (test for setting aside judgment in default of defence); *Fairmays v Palmer* [2006] EWHC 96 (Ch), January 31, 2006, unrep. (Evans Lombe J.) (fundamental rule that defendant may be served with originating process within jurisdiction only if he is present in the jurisdiction at the time of service unaffected by CPR); *Adelson v Associated Newspapers*

*Ltd* [2007] EWCA Civ 701, [2007] 4 All E.R. 330, CA(substitution of claimant on grounds of mistake after expiry of limitation period); *Rubin v Expandable Ltd* [2008] EWCA Civ 59; [2008] 1 W.L.R. 1099, CA (withholding from inspection on ground of privilege document mentioned in witness statement); *Lexi Holdings Plc v Luqman* October 22, 2007, unrep. (Briggs J.) (service by post of claim form on one partner at his last known address is good service on firm); *Fiona Trust and Holding Corporation v Privalov* [2007] EWHC 39 (Comm), January 19, 2007, unrep. (David Steel J.) (disclosure of documents for purpose of interlocutory proceedings); *L'Oreal v Bellure N.V.* [2006] EWHC 1503 (Ch), May 24, 2006, unrep. (Peter Smith J.) (implied undertakings as to collateral use of disclosed documents); *Kamali v City & County Properties Ltd* [2006] EWCA Civ 1879, July 24, 2006, CA (effect of service by post whilst defendant out of jurisdiction); *Dunwoody Sports Marketing v Prescott (Practice Note)* [2007] EWCA Civ 461; [2007] 1 W.L.R. 2343, CA (substitution of parties after judgment); *Marcan Shipping (London) Ltd v Kefalas* [2007] EWCA Civ 643; [2007] 1 W.L.R. 1864, CA (automatic dismissal of claim by consent order); *Capewell v Revenue and Customs Commissioners* [2007] UKHL 2; [2007] 1 W.L.R. 386, HL (indemnity of receiver in respect of costs and expenses); *Moat Housing Group-South Ltd v Harris* [2007] EWHC 3092 (QB); 158 New L.J. 67 (2008) (Christopher Clarke J.) (detailed assessment proceedings where two solicitors representing receiving party); *Kostic v Chaplin* [2007] EWHC 2909 (Ch); *The Times* January 11, 2008 (Henderson J.) (costs in contentious probate claim)"; *Phillips v Nussberger* [2008] UKHL 1; [2008] 1 W.L.R. 180, HL (application of authorities on RSC O.2, r.1, to CPR r.3.10);*West London Pipeline & Storage Ltd v Total UK Ltd* [2008] EWHC 1296 (Comm), June 9, 2008, unrep. (David Steel J.) (providing of additional information in relation to liability insurance arrangements); *Harris v Society of Lloyd's* [2008] EWHC 1433 (Comm), July 1, 2008, unrep. (David Steel J.) (court's power to order disclosure for the purpose of interlocutory proceedings); *Emerald Supplies Ltd v British Airways plc* [2009] EWHC 741 (Ch); [2009] 3 W.L.R. 1200 (Sir Andrew Morritt C.) (whether "other persons" whom the claimant sought to represent had "the same interest" within r.19.6(1)).

It is often said that one of the advantages that follows from the CPR's being a new procedural code is that enables the courts to apply rules flexibly for the primary purpose of giving effect to the overriding objective. In cases where it can be strongly argued that a particular provision should be interpreted or applied in a certain manner, and that manner happens to yield a more restrictive result than the comparable pre-CPR rules and the authorities thereon would have yielded, the courts do not shrink from reverting to the earlier position (see *George Wimpey UK Ltd v Tewkesbury BC* [2008] EWCA Civ 12; [2008] 1 W.L.R. 1649, CA, where authorities on RSC O.59, r.3 relied on in holding that CPR r.52.1 countenanced appeal by party not a party to the proceedings below).

Cases have arisen where the failure of counsel to recognise that pre-CPR authorities continue to be of considerable persuasive force (if not strictly binding) have caused avoidable confusion and lead to unnecessary appeals (e.g. *Garratt v Saxby* [2004] EWCA Civ 341; [2004] 1 W.L.R. 2152, CA (inadvertent disclosure of defendant's payment into court)). In *Drinkall v Whitwood* [2003] EWCA Civ 1547; [2003] EWCA Civ 1547; [2004] 1 W.L.R. 462, CA, relevant pre-CPR authority dealing conclusively with the procedural point in issue came to light only after permission to appeal to the Court of Appeal had been given.

In *Nomura International Plc v Granada Group Ltd* [2007] EWHC 642 (Comm), March 23, 2007, unrep., Cooke J. neatly summarised points made above (and in para.1.3.9), by noting that whereas, on the one hand, there are numerous authorities stressing that detailed reference to decisions on particular rules in the RSC are of little value in interpreting provisions of the CPR where the wording and the substance of a particular provision are different, there are, on the other, numerous instances where the courts have drawn upon decisions relating to the RSC where the new rule under the CPR follows the same form and appears to have the same underlying intention.

## 14. HUMAN RIGHTS ACT 1998 AND THE CPR

The Human Rights Act 1998 gives further effect to rights and freedoms guaranteed under the European Convention on Human Rights (see Vol.2, para.3D–1). The Act came into effect on October 2, 2000. Section 1(1) states that, under the Act, "Convention rights" means the rights and fundamental freedoms set out in arts 2 to 12 and 14 **12–58**

***Paragraph numbers marked with a "+" can be found online and on CD.***

of the Convention, arts 1 to 3 of the First Protocol, and arts 1 and 2 of the Sixth Protocol, as read with arts 16 to 18 of the Convention. The Convention articles, the First Protocol articles, and the Sixth Protocol articles referred to in this definition are set out, respectively, in Pts I, II and III of Sch.1 to the Act.

Section 2 of the Act states that a court, in determining a question which has arisen under the Act in connection with a Convention right, must take into account judgments of the European Court of Human Rights and certain other related sources of law, for convenience sometimes compendiously and colloquially described as "the Strasbourg jurisprudence". Section 3 states that, so far as it is possible to do so, primary legislation and subordinate legislation must be read and given effect in a way which is compatible with the Convention rights. Section 4 states that, in certain circumstances, a court may make a declaration that a provision of primary or subordinate legislation is incompatible with a Convention right. Section 6 states that it is unlawful for a "public authority" to act in a way which is incompatible with a Convention right. In this context, "public authority" includes a court.

Guidance on the approach which the courts should adopt to the difficult task of interpreting primary legislation and subordinate legislation in a manner which is compatible with Convention rights was given by the House of Lords in *R. v A. (No.2)* [2001] UKHL 251; [2001] 2 W.L.R. 1546, HL. In that case Lord Steyn said (at para.[44]) that the interpretative obligation under s.3 of the 1998 Act is a strong one. It applies even if there is no ambiguity in the language in the sense of the language being capable of two different meanings. The section places on the court a duty to strive to find a possible interpretation compatible with Convention rights. In complying with the will of Parliament as expressed in s.3, it will sometimes be necessary for a court to adopt an interpretation which linguistically may appear strained. The techniques to be used will not only involve the reading down of express language in a statutory provision but also their implications. A declaration of incompatibility is a measure of last resort.

The Convention rights most likely to find their voice (either separately or in conjunction) in relation (1) to questions concerning the proper interpretation of primary and subordinate legislation affecting (what broadly could be called) civil procedural law, or (2) to questions about whether certain aspects of such law should be declared incompatible with Convention rights, are arts 6(1) and 8 of the Convention (right to a fair trial and right to respect for private life) and art.1 of the First Protocol (right to property) (see Vol.2, paras 3D–76, 3D–78 and 3D–87). Other Convention rights may also come into play, but perhaps less frequently. The potential applicability of each of these rights is considered in more detail in the notes to individual CPR rules. As to the circumstances where art.6 may be said to have been violated by delays in completing proceedings, see Section 11—The Overriding Objective para.11–8.

The European Court of Human Rights has recognised the legitimacy of certain restrictions on the right of access to a court guaranteed by art.6. The governing test, set out in the judgment of the court in *Ashingdane v UK* (1985) 7 E.H.R.R. 528, is that such restrictions must not impair the essence of the right of access; they must have a legitimate aim, and the means used must be reasonably proportionate to the aim sought to be achieved. In applying this test, the Court has recognised that the enactment of limitation periods represents the pursuit of a legitimate aim (see *Stubbings v UK* (1996) 23 E.H.R.R. 524). Other examples are restrictions placed on the bringing of proceedings by vexatious litigants and by persons under disability, and procedural rules providing for the striking out of actions for want of prosecution.

In recent times, the Court of Appeal has dealt with cases in which it has been argued that, in discharge of their obligation under s.3 of the 1998 Act, the Court was required to interpret primary legislation and subordinate legislation on limitation of actions in a manner that was compatible with a party's art.6 Convention rights. Examples are: *Cachia v Faluyl* [2001] EWCA Civ 998; [2001] 1 W.L.R. 1966, CA (Fatal Accidents Act 1976 s.2(3)); *Goode v Martin* [2001] EWCA Civ 1899; December 13, 2001, CA, unrep. (Limitation Act 1980 s.35 and CPR r.17.4); *A. v Hoare* [2006] EWCA Civ 395; *The Times*, April 28, 2006, CA (s.3 cannot be applied retrospectively for the purpose of depriving a defendant of his accrued rights under the Limitation Act 1980 s.2).

It has been said that it should be remembered that the CPR "were drafted with the ECHR in the background and were clearly intended to be compliant with it" (*Less v*

***Paragraph numbers marked with a "+" can be found online and on CD.***

*Benedict* [2005] EWHC 1643 (Ch), July 25, 2005, unrep. (Warren J.). It is clear from r.1.1 that the overriding objective of the CPR is to enable courts to do justice in the individual case. This aim is consistent with the purpose of art.6(1). The overriding requirement of a fair hearing under art.6(1) places the court under a duty "to conduct a proper examination of the submissions, arguments and evidence adduced by the parties, without prejudice to its assessment of whether they are relevant to its decision": *Kraska v Switzerland* (1994) 18 E.H.R.R. 188, para.30, ECtHR. The Court of Appeal has stated that art.6 does no more than reflect the approach of the common law as indicated in *R. v Lord Chancellor, ex. p. Witham* [1998] Q.B. 575, DC; *Ebert v Birch* [2000] Ch. 484, CA.

In *Bow Spring (Owners) v Manzanillo II (Owners) (Note)* [2004] EWCA Civ 1007; [2004] 4 All E.R. 899, CA, the Court of Appeal said that the fairness required by both the common law and by art.6 requires that the parties should have knowledge of, and be able to comment on, all evidence adduced or observations filed with a view to influencing the court's decision, and held that, where the Admiralty judge sits with assessors (see CPR r.61.13), the practice of the judge putting questions to the assessors after discussion with counsel should be complemented by a practice of disclosing their answers to counsel, either orally or in writing, in order that any appropriate submission could be made as to whether the judge should accept their advice.

In *Secretary of State for Health v Norton Healthcare Ltd* (2003) 100(36) L.S.G. 41; *The Times*, August 26, 2003, where witnesses were unavailable to the defendants because of outstanding criminal charges against them, the defendants were unsuccessful in arguing that, on equality of arms grounds, the trial proceedings against them should be stayed.

The fairness of a trial is assessed by reference to the proceedings as a whole, including any appeal: *Dombo Beheer BV v Netherlands* (1994) 18 E.H.R.R. 213, para.31, ECtHR; *Official Receiver v Stern* [2000] 1 W.L.R. 2230, CA; *Daisystar Limited v Woolwich Plc*, March 16, 2000, unrep., CA. A fair hearing before an appeal court may "cure" breaches of ECHR, art.6(1) at the first instance: *Edwards v United Kingdom (A/247B)* (1993) 15 E.H.R.R. 417, and *De Cubber v Belgium* (1985) 7 E.H.R.R. 236, ECtHR. See also *R. (on the application of Holding & Barnes Plc) v Secretary of State for the Environment, Transport and the Regions* [2001] UKHL 23, HL.

The rights which the ECHR has found to be inherent in art.6(1) include the following:

(a) The right to equality of arms, under which each party must be afforded a reasonable opportunity to present his case under conditions which do not place him at a substantial disadvantage vis-à-vis his opponent: *De Haes v Belgium* (1998) 25 E.H.R.R. 1. This principle is echoed in the r.1.1(2)(a) principle of ensuring that the parties are on an equal footing.

(b) The right of access to a court: *Golder v United Kingdom (A/18)* (1979–80) 1 E.H.R.R. 524, para.35, ECtHR. This concept is now familiar to English law: *R. v Lord Chancellor Ex p. Witham* [1998] Q.B. 575, DC. This right is not absolute, and may be circumstanced by procedural rules, provided that such rules do not restrict court access to such an extent that the "very essence of the right is impaired": *Ashingdane v UK* (1985) 7 E.H.R.R. 528, para.57, ECtHR. See also *Kreuz v Poland* (28249/95) 11 B.H.R.C. 456, ECtHR, 1st section (excessive court fees unduly restricted right of access to court). A practical and effective right of access to a court may require the provision of legal assistance or representation in certain cases, depending on their complexity or the importance of what is at stake for the individual: *Airey v Ireland* (1979) 2 E.H.R.R. 305, ECtHR. The test is whether a claimant has had a reasonable opportunity of putting his or her case. Legal assistance may be required where its absence would make assertion of a civil claim practically impossible or lead to an obvious unfairness: *R. (Jarrett) v Legal Services Commission* [2001] EWHC Admin 389. The fact that the Legal Services Commission has refused funding may be a significant factor in support of the contention that ECHR, art.6(1) has not been breached: R. v Secretary of State for the *Environment, Transport and the Regions Ex p. Challenger* June 15, 2000, unrep., QBD. See also *Simon John Pine v Law Society, sub nom Re a Solicitor* [2001] EWCA Civ 1574.

(c) The right to a properly adversarial procedure. This entails the right of a



***Paragraph numbers marked with a "+" can be found online and on CD.***

party not only to have the opportunity to make known any evidence needed for his claims to succeed, but also to have knowledge of and to comment on all evidence adduced or observations submitted with a view to influencing the court's decision: *Mantovanelli v France* (1997) 24 E.H.R.R. 370, para.33, ECtHR. See also *Pellegrini v Italy (30882/96)* (2002) 35 E.H.R.R. 2.

Section 6 of the Human Rights Act 1998 provides that it is unlawful for a court to act in a way which is incompatible with a Convention right (see Vol.2, para.3D–23). In *Jones v Warwick University* [2003] EWCA Civ 151, CA, the question was whether the court, by not excluding evidence unlawfully obtained by the defendant's agents in breach of the claimant's art.8 rights (right to respect for private and family life), had properly exercised its discretion under r.32.1 (power of court to control evidence). Lord Woolf C.J. said that, once a court had decided upon the order that it should make for the purpose of exercising, in accordance with the overriding objective (r.1.1), its discretion under r.32.1, then it was required or was necessary for the court to make that order and there was no breach of the claimant's art.8 rights by the court.

## 15. EUROPEAN LAW AND THE CPR

**12–59** In certain circumstances and for various reasons, the national courts of member states of the European Union, as a consequence of the effects of EU law in the member states, may have to adapt their rules of civil procedure. Areas of law that may properly be described as procedural (at least in common law if not civilian jurisdictions), and which have been affected in this way, include limitation periods, and other time limits, monetary limits to awards of compensation, interest and costs, and rules of evidence. (Obviously, areas of English procedural law that may be so affected are not confined to matters dealt with by the CPR or to proceedings to which the CPR extends.) In *Autologic Holdings Plc v Inland Revenue Commissioners* [2005] UKHL 54; [2005] 3 W.L.R. 339, HL, where the question was whether disputes between the taxpayer and the Revenue should be resolved, not by proceedings in the High Court, but by appeals brought in the first instance to the General or Special Commissioners, the taxpayer's submissions relied on certain general principles of EU law (viz., the principle of effectiveness, the principle of equivalence, and the principle of certainty). In that case, Lord Walker explained (para.95) the correct general approach to be adopted by national courts to these issues. Depending on the circumstances, a national court may be able to achieve the necessary adapting of their procedural law to EU law requirements by adopting one interpretation of a rule rather than another. But it may be necessary to go beyond interpretation and, in effect, to re-write the national law for the purposes of achieving compliance.

In *Morgan v Hinton Organics (Wessex) Ltd* [2009] EWCA Civ 107; March 2, 2009, unrep., CA, where it was noted that the presumption that legislation is to be construed so as to avoid conflict with international law may apply where domestic legislation intended to bring a treaty into effect is ambiguous, the Court of Appeal held that the State's treaty obligation under art.9(4) of the Aarhus Convention to provide remedies that are not "prohibitively expensive" (albeit one adopted by the EC for certain purposes) was not a rule of law directly binding on the English court and in the circumstances of that case was, at most, a matter potentially relevant to the judge's exercise of discretion as to costs under CPR r.44.3. In *Football Association Premier League Ltd v QC Leisure* [2008] EWHC 2897 (Ch); November 13, 2008, unrep. (Kitchin J.), the question was whether an application for the joinder of additional parties under CPR r.19.2 should be granted where the application was made after a question raised in the proceedings had been referred to the ECJ for preliminary ruling under r.68.2. In granting the application on terms the judge took into account not only the overriding objective but also the duty of sincere co-operation enshrined in EC Treaty art.10.

Various EU Conventions and EU Regulations have come into being expressly for the purpose of harmonising procedural rules applied by courts throughout the Member States. The most obvious examples are the Judgments Regulation and the Service Regulation. Insofar as necessary, such Conventions and Regulations are carried into effect through the CPR, usually bringing with them definition clauses. See further CPR r.6.18 and commentary following. Note also, the effect of the Civil Jurisdiction and Judgments Act 1982 ss.3 and 3B on the use of extrinsic materials to assist interpretation of Conventions (see Vol.1, para.6.19.6).

Under the European Communities Act 1972 s.2 and Sch.2 para.1A, the Lord

Chancellor has power, for the purposes stated in s.2 (e.g. implementing any Community obligation of the UK) and in the circumstances provided for in para.1A (e.g. updating references to amended Community instruments where that is necessary or expedient), to amend by subordinate legislation CPR provisions. For example, CPR rr.6.18, 12.11, 74.1 and 74.2 (wherein references are made to various such instruments) were amended by consequential provisions in the Civil Jurisdiction and Judgments Regulations 2007 (SI 2007/1655).

# SECTION 13

## RIGHTS OF AUDIENCE

# 13 RIGHTS OF AUDIENCE

CONTENTS



## A. QUALIFICATION OR ENTITLEMENT TO ACT AS AN ADVOCATE

Part 3 of the Legal Services Act 2007 came into force on January 1, 2010. This Act **13–2** provides for a new regulatory framework for the provision of legal services. Part 3 lists and defines reserved legal activities and who may carry them out. The regime is not "profession based" (e.g. "barrister" or "solicitor") but qualification based. Approved regulators (whose functions are set out in Pt 4, also in force from January 1, 2010) will authorise and regulate persons to carry on reserved legal activities which, of course, includes advocacy.

Practice Direction 39 (Miscellaneous Provisions Relating to Hearings) para.5.1 states that, at any hearing, a written statement containing the following information should be provided for the court: (1) the name and address of each advocate, (2) his qualification or entitlement to act as an advocate, and (3) the party for whom he so acts (see Vol.1, para.39APD.5). This provision skates over the question of what is meant by acting as an advocate for a party. Further, it indicates that a person may not act as such unless appropriately qualified but, of course, does not attempt to explain what those qualifications might be. The use of the expression "qualification or entitlement" should be noted because it indicates that an advocate's right of audience may be derived from a qualification that he holds, but he may be entitled to a such right for other reasons.

At common law, nobody had a right to act as an advocate without the leave of the court which, as part of its power to regulate its own proceedings, had a discretion to control who addressed it. Nevertheless, by ancient usage in the superior courts barristers and others similarly qualified could not be prevented from acting as advocates (*Paragon Finance Plc v Noueiri (Practice Note)* [2001] 1 W.L.R. 2357; CA, at para.52 per Brooke L.J.).

Before the Courts and Legal Services Act 1990 barristers enjoyed rights of audience in all courts for all proceedings (subject to regulations of the General Council of the Bar), but solicitors, though having rights of audience for all proceedings in county courts and magistrates' courts, had only restricted rights of audience in the High

***Paragraph numbers marked with a "+" can be found online and on CD.***

Court (in particular they had no right of audience in trials). Under various statutory dispensations, persons other than barristers (including solicitors) had rights of audience before particular courts for particular purposes. (For a summary of the different rules which previously governed rights of audience in the various courts, see White Paper "Legal Services: a Framework for the future" Cm 740 July 1989.)

Part II of the 1990 Act introduced a new statutory scheme for defining and regulating rights of audience before any court. The scheme preserved the positions of those who had rights of audience previously. Subsequently, Pt II was amended and enhanced by provisions in Pt III of the Access to Justice Act 1999 (as was explained in *Gregory v Turner* [2003] EWCA Civ 183; [2003] 1 W.L.R. 1149, CA, at para.50 et seq per Brooke L.J.).

The principal effect of part of the 1990 Act was to make it possible for solicitors to attain rights of audience in the higher courts by completing prescribed courses of training and assessment after admission to practice administered by the Law Society. By the 1999 Act, the means by which the Law Society could regulate the granting of higher rights of audience to solicitors were changed.

Another important effect of the statutory scheme was that it made it possible for other professional groups (apart from barristers and solicitors) to be designated by statutory instrument as bodies authorised to grant rights of audience to their members for particular purposes. Professional bodies that have taken advantage of this opportunity include the Institute of Legal Executives (SI 1999/1077), the Chartered Institute of Patent Agents (SI 1999/3137), the Institute of Trade Mark Attorneys (SI 2005/240), and the Association of Law Costs Draftsmen (SI 2006/3333).

The Legal Services Act 2007 established the Legal Services Board (LSB). In part, the LSB's function is to regulate those professional bodies ("approved regulators") that are permitted to grant rights of audience (and rights to carry on other legal activities) to their members. That is to say, to regulate in this respect, in addition to the four bodies authorised to grant rights of audience mentioned in the previous paragraph, The Law Society and the General Council of the Bar. The 2007 Act contains a new statutory framework replacing that in the 1990 Act. The position of persons having rights of audience before the 2007 Act came not effect are preserved.

Where rights of audience are granted under the statutory scheme, they are exercisable in accordance with the qualification regulations and rules of conduct of the authorised body as approved under the scheme.

The commentary which follows is based on provisions in the 2007 Act.

## B. AUTHORISED PERSONS AND EXEMPT PERSONS

13–3 In the 2007 Act the term "legal activities" is used to describe generally activities which consist of the provision of legal advice or assistance or of representation, and the term "reserved legal activities" is used to describe some particular activities, including the exercise of a right of audience (s.12(1)). A "right of audience" means the right to appear before and address a court, including the right to call and examine witnesses (s.12 and Sch.2 para.3(1)).

Section 13(1) of the 2007 Act states that the question whether a person is entitled to carry on an activity which is "a reserved legal activity" is to be determined solely in accordance with the provisions of this Act.

Section 13(2) states that a person is entitled to carry on an activity ("the relevant activity") which is a reserved legal activity where (a) the person is an authorised person in relation to the relevant activity, or (b) the person is an exempt person in relation to that activity. In this context, an "authorised person" is a person able to exercise rights of audience (whether limited to particular courts and proceedings or unlimited) in accordance with regulations of an authorised body under the statutory scheme. An "exempt person" (see s.19) is a person determined as such by para.1 of Sch.3 to the 2007 Act. By this provision, the 2007 Act recognises (as did the 1990 Act) that, in certain circumstances, a person who is not authorised in accordance with the statutory scheme to exercise rights of audience (a reserved legal activity) may nevertheless do so.

In particular proceedings, the question may arise as to whether an authorised person's rights of audience (being rights that are limited) extend to those proceedings. But, as a practical matter, the question that is more likely to arise is whether a person (not being an authorised person) falls into one of the categories of exempt person and has a right of audience in those proceedings, or should be granted such right, by that route. So para.1 of Sch.3 to the 2007 Act is a key provision. It should be noted that it plays a similar role to that formerly played by s.27 of the 1990 Act, a provision that has figured in the case law on the granting of rights audience to persons not authorised to exercise such rights under the statutory scheme.

The principal categories of persons who are exempt for the purpose of exercising a right of audience before a court in relation to any proceedings are:

- A person who has a right of audience before that court in relation to those proceedings granted by or under any enactment (para.1(3));
- A person whose work includes assisting in the conduct of litigation (para.1(7));
- A person who is a European lawyer (para.7);
- A person who is a party to those proceedings and would have a right of audience, in the person's capacity as such a party, if the 2007 Act had not been passed (para.1(6));
- A person who has a right of audience granted by that court in relation to those proceedings (para.1(2) of Sch.3 of 2007 Act).

For commentary on these various categories of exempt person, see below.

Under the Senior Courts Act 1981 s.51, the court may order a "legal or other representative" to meet wasted costs as may be determined by rules of court (see CPR r.44.14 and r.48.7). In this context "legal or other representative", in relation to a party to proceedings, means any person exercising a right of audience (or a right to conduct litigation) on his behalf (s.51(13)). Thus, a person qualified or entitled to exercise a right of audience on any of the bases described in following paragraphs may be exposed to liability for a wasted costs order in appropriate circumstances.

It is an offence for a person to carry on a reserved legal activity (including an activity in the form of the exercise of a right of audience) (ss.14 to 17 of the 2007 Act).

It is an offence for a person who is not a barrister (a) wilfully to pretend to be a barrister, or (b) with the intention of implying falsely that that person is a barrister to take or use any name, title or description (s.181). It is an offence for an unqualified person to act as a solicitor (Solicitors Act 1974 s.20).

## C. RIGHT OF AUDIENCE GRANTED BY OR UNDER ANY ENACTMENT

Certain provisions granting rights of audience are considered below. **13–4**

It should be noted that various other provisions enable persons who are not parties to proceedings "to appear" "to appear and be heard" or "to appear and make representations" in particular circumstances. It is not always clear whether such dispensations give the person a right of audience in the sense of enabling him to address the court and call and examine witnesses. Some examples are: Orders for the Delivery of Documents (Procedure) Regulations 2000 (SI 2000/2875) reg.7 (Commissioners entitled to appear and be heard at hearing of taxpayer's application to resolve dispute as to legal privilege in documents); Practice Direction 8 para.15A.6 (Civil Aviation Authority entitled to be heard in application to amend aircraft mortgages register); Community Legal Service (Costs) Regulations 2000 (SI 2000/441) reg.13 (LSC Regional Director and any other person authorised to act on his behalf, given right to appear at certain hearings where issues as to costs payable by a funded client or the LSC—see Vol.2, para.7D–61).

It should also be noted that CPR r.52.12A states that, in a statutory appeal, any person may apply for permission "to make representations" at the appeal hearing. Further, CPR r.54.17 makes similar provision in relation to hearings for judicial review claims.

### 1. LAY REPRESENTATIVES IN SMALL CLAIMS (S.11 OF 1990 ACT)

An exempt person includes a person who is not an authorised person in relation to **13–5**
the reserved legal activity, meaning, the exercise of a right of audience, but who has a

right of audience "in relation to those proceedings granted by or under any enactment" (para.1(3) of Sch.3 of the 2007 Act.

One example of an enactment granting a right of audience is the Courts and Legal Services Act 1990 s.11 (Representation in certain county court cases). This provision was not affected by the 2007 Act. It states that the Lord Chancellor may (with the concurrence of the Lord Chief Justice) by Order provide that there shall be no restriction on the persons who may exercise rights of audience "in relation to proceedings in a county court of such a kind as may be specified in the Order". For these purposes "right of audience" means the right to exercise all or any of the functions of appearing before and addressing a court including the calling and examining of witnesses as defined (s.119(1) of the 1990 Act). The Lay Representatives (Rights of Audience) Order 1999 (SI 1999/1225) was made in exercise of this power and has the effect of enabling lay representatives to exercise rights of audience in proceedings dealt with as small claims in accordance with rules of court (see further Vol.1 para.27.8.2). Article 3(2) of the Order provides that this right of audience may not be exercised (a) where the lay representative's client does not attend the hearing, (b) at any stage after judgment, or (c) on any appeal brought against any decision made by the district judge in the proceedings. Read literally, this would appear to exclude any discretion to allow appearance by a lay representative where those conditions are not met. However, para.3.2 of Practice Direction 27 (Small Claims Track) recites Art.3(2) and further states that the court "exercising its general discretion to hear anybody" may hear a lay representative even in circumstances excluded by the Order (see Vol.1 para.27PD.3). The "general discretion" referred to here is that referred to in para.1(2) of Sch.3 of the 2007 Act (formerly s.27(2)(c) of the 1990 Act; see further below). (This confirms the view that s.11 is intended to widen rights of audience which would otherwise be available, and therefore does not detract from the general discretion; see *Gregory v Turner*, op cit.) Provisions in s.11 give the court various powers to restrict a lay representative in the exercise of his right of audience where he behaves in an unruly manner or intentionally misleads to court or otherwise demonstrates that he is unsuitable to exercise that right.

## 2. HOUSING AUTHORITY OFFICERS AND EMPLOYEES OF HOUSING MANAGEMENT BODIES (SS.60 & 60A OF 1984 ACT)

**13–6** Other examples of enactments granting a right of audience are the County Courts Act 1984 s.60 and s.60A.

Section 60 (Right of audience) states that, where certain housing claims are brought in a county court by a local authority then, in so far as the proceedings in the claim are heard by a district judge:

> "any officer of the authority authorised by the authority in that behalf ... may address the district judge as if he were a person so entitled".

This is a long-standing provision of some practical importance. It may be noted that a right of audience would embrace rather more forensic functions than a mere right to "address the judge".

The modern tendency is for local housing authorities to contract out their responsibilities to non-government agencies (known as Arm's Length Management Organisations (ALMOs)). Section 60 is restricted to local authority officers; employees of such agencies do not fall within it. This restriction created certain practical difficulties which have been met by the insertion in the 1984 Act, by s.191 of the 2007 Act, of a new provision, s.60A (Rights of audience etc of employees of housing management bodies).

Section 60A provides that in certain housing proceedings in a county court before a district judge, brought (a) in the name of a local housing authority and (b) by the housing management body in the exercise of functions of the authority delegated to that body under a housing management agreement, an authorised employee of the body has a right of audience (including a right to call an examine witnesses). The type of housing proceedings to which this dispensation applies are stated in s.60A(3) and (6). The authorisation must be in writing (s.60A(4)). ("Housing management agreement" and "housing management body) are defined in s.60A(7).)

## 3. REPRESENTATION AT TRIAL OF CORPORATIONS (CPR R.39.6)

Before the CPR came into effect, RSC O.5, r.6 stated that "any person ... may begin and carry on proceedings in the High Court by a solicitor or in person", but, except as expressly provided by or under any enactment, "a body corporate may not begin or carry on any such proceedings otherwise than by a solicitor". Thus, a person duly authorised to act on its behalf (e.g. a director or an employee) could not conduct proceedings for the inanimate corporation. The rules provided some exceptions to this general prohibition; for example, a body corporate, including a limited liability company, was expressly empowered itself to acknowledge service of a writ and to give notice of its intention to defend by a person duly authorised to act on its behalf, instead of acting by a solicitor (see RSC O.12, r.1(2)). In the Access to Justice—Final Report (July 1996) it was recommended (1) that rules of court should no longer require a company to act by a solicitor, (2) that the court should normally exercise its discretion in favour of allowing an employee of a company to take any steps on behalf of the company which a litigant in person could take in High Court or county court proceedings, (3) that the employee would have to show, if required, that he was duly authorised to act by the company, (4) that a practice direction should indicate the considerations relevant to the exercise of the court's discretion (*ibid* Ch.12, paras 61 to 72). **13–7**

The first of these recommendations was quite clear and was carried into effect by not re-enacting RSC in the CPR. The other recommendations were muddled, as it was not clear what court discretion was being alluded to in them; in particular, whether it was a discretion as to the conduct of litigation or as to rights of audience.

As noted (above or below) a litigant in person may, by virtue of his being a party, exercise rights of audience on his own behalf, both at a trial hearing and at other hearings. On its own, the abolition of the rule that a body corporate may not begin or carry on proceedings otherwise than by a solicitor did not confer on persons duly authorised to act on behalf of corporate parties rights of audience at court hearings of any variety.

The general rule (subject to the important exception mentioned below) is that a corporate body can only be represented at a court hearing by its legal advisers with appropriate rights of audience. It has no right, comparable to the right that a litigant in person enjoys, to represent itself. However, the court may be prepared to exercise its discretion to relax this rule. This was demonstrated in cases decided before the CPR came into effect. For example, it was held that a director of a company might appear as an advocate on its behalf where the company's assets were frozen by a freezing order so that it could not instruct solicitors (*Arbuthnot Leasing International Ltd v Havelet Leasing Ltd* [1991] 1 All E.R. 591), or where the director and his company were both parties to proceedings the court might allow the director to appear in person for purposes which were those also of the company (*Radford v Samuel* [1993] B.C.C. 870, CA).

An important exception to this general rule is provided by CPR r.39.6. That rule states that the court may give permission for a company or other corporation "to be represented at trial" by an employee if the employee has been authorised by the company to appear at trial on its behalf. In effect, the rule enacts what had been a quite common practice in county courts but its practical usefulness in those courts has been diminished by the expansion of the small claims jurisdiction. Practice Direction 39 (Miscellaneous Provisions Relating to Hearings) para.5 states that r.39.6 "is intended to enable a company or other corporation to represent itself as a litigant in person" and goes on to state that permission should be given "unless there is some particular or sufficient reason why it should be withheld". Presumably, therefore, the employee representing the company at trial may, in addition to appearing before and addressing the court, call and examine witnesses. Paragraph 5 further states that the court's permission should be obtained in advance of the hearing and may be obtained informally and without notice to the other parties, and also describes some of the considerations relevant to the grant or refusal of permission (Vol.1, paras 39.6.1 and 39APD.5). The rule opens up the possibility that a company may be represented at a trial by in-house counsel (possibly one already the holder of restricted rights of audience not extending to trials). In the Admiralty and Commercial Courts Guide para.M3.1, it is said that, because of the complexity of most cases in the Commercial Court, permission under r.39.6 is likely to be given only in unusual circumstances (Vol.2 para.2A–128). See also the Chancery Guide (Vol.2 para.1A–139). For examples of applications of r.39.6, see *Watson v Bluemoor Properties Ltd* [2002] EWCA Civ 1875; *Tamglass Limited OY v Luoyang North Glass Technology Company Limited* [2006] EWHC 65 (Ch); January 27, 2006, unrep. (Mann J.) (employee of defendant foreign company permitted to represent company in patent action); cf. *Milne v Kennedy The Times*, February 11, 1999, CA.

CPR r.39.6 is confined to the representation of companies or other corporations by their duly authorised employees at trial. In terms, the rule does not confer on such employees rights of audience in relation to other hearings.

### 4. OFFICIAL RECEIVERS

**13–8** Rule 7.52 of the Insolvency Rules 1986 (SI 1986/1925) states that official receivers have right of audience in insolvency proceedings, whether in the High Court or a county court.

Para.3.1 of Practice Direction (Directors Disqualification Proceedings) states that official receivers and deputy official receivers have a right of audience in any proceedings to which the Practice Direction applies. The right extends to cases where a disqualification application is made under the Company Directors Disqualification Act 1986 by the Secretary of State or by the official receiver at his direction, and whether made in the High Court or a county court. For further information on the effect of this provision, see commentary on para.3.1 (para.3J–12).

### 5. DETAILED ASSESSMENT PROCEEDINGS

**13–9** For an account of the persons who may exercise rights of audience in detailed assessment proceedings, including assessments involving litigants in person, see Vol.1 paras 47.14.7 and 47.14.7.

## D. PERSON ASSISTING IN THE CONDUCT OF LITIGATION OR ENGAGED IN LEGAL EMPLOYMENT

**13–10** The combined effect of s.13, s.19, and para.1(7) of Sch.3 of the 2007 Act, is to provide that in certain circumstances a person "whose work includes assisting in the conduct of litigation" is an exempt person for the purpose of exercising a right of audience. Before the Courts and Legal Services Act 1990 came into effect, solicitors' general rights of audience in the High Court and county courts when sitting in chambers, extended to their responsible representatives; in particular to solicitors' clerks and legal executives, and to persons providing clerk's services and who were not employed but acted under instructions. There was no such right in open court although, in the exercise of a discretion, a judge could grant this. These statutory provisions were designed to preserve that position and must be seen against that background. (Before the Association of Law Costs Draftsmen became an authorised body the rights of audience of the Association's members in detailed assessment proceedings rested on a fiction that they were employed by the solicitors who engaged them.)

Paragraph 1(7) of Sch.3 states that a right of audience accrues to such a person when that person is acting under instructions given (either generally or in relation to the proceedings) and under supervision, and the proceedings are being heard in chambers in the High court or a county court and are not reserved family proceedings (see paras 1(7)(b) and 1(8), referring to s.193). Thus the person giving instructions and providing supervision includes practising solicitors and solicitors to certain public departments and the City of London.

In the case of *In re HS (Minors) (Chambers Proceedings: Right of Audience)* [1998] 1 F.L.R. 868, CA, it was held that, where a person satisfies the criteria (then stated in s.27(2)(e) and now in para.1(7) of Sch.3), the court retains no discretion to refuse right of audience.

The County Courts Act 1984 s.61 states that the Lord Chancellor may, with the concurrence of the Lord Chief Justice, direct that such categories of persons in "relevant legal employment" as may be specified in the direction "may address the court" in proceedings in a county court of such description as may be specified. This provi-

***Paragraph numbers marked with a "+" can be found online and on CD.***

sion (which could be exercised in favour of legal executives) has been overtaken by the statutory scheme for granting rights of audience first introduced in Pt II of the 1990 Act and now found in the 2007 Act. The section is restricted to entitling an unqualified person in legal employment to "address the court".

## E. EUROPEAN LAWYERS (PARA.7 OF SCH.3)

Paragraph 1 of Sch.3 to the 2007 Act is expressed as being "subject to paragraph 7". Paragraph 7 states that a European lawyer (within the meaning of the European Communities (Services of Lawyers) Order 1978 (SI 1978/1910) is an exempt person "for the purposes of carrying on an activity which is a reserved legal activity and which the European lawyer is entitled to carry on by virtue of that order". (See also Council Directive No.77/249/EEC of 22 March 1977.) **13–11**

In *Masri v Consolidated Contractors International (UK) Ltd* [2007] EWCA Civ 702; June 12, 2007, unrep., CA, on an application in an appeal to the Court of Appeal a single lord justice permitted an advocate of the Brussels bar, being a person who lacked a right of audience but who was an "EEC lawyer" within Art.5 of the 1978 Order, to address the court on the appellant's behalf and to speak to a note prepared by him on issues arising in the appeal.

## F. RIGHT OF AUDIENCE FOR PARTIES ACTING IN PERSON (SCH.3, PARA.1(6) (S.27(2)(d))

It is recognised by s.19 and paras 1 and 2 of Sch.3 to the 2007 Act that a party acting in person has the right to represent himself in the proceedings to which he is a party, and that carries with it the right to exercise the functions included in the right to conduct litigation (para.2(4)), and in the right of audience (para.1(6)) (*Clarkson v Gilbert* [2000] 2 F.L.R. 839, CA, at para.10 per Lord Woolf C.J.). It is conceivable (but perhaps unlikely) that a party may be assisted in the proceedings by a person with rights to conduct litigation (and to that extent will not be acting in person) whilst exercising himself the right of audience (and to that extent will be acting in person). It is also possible that a party to legal proceedings will be a lawyer with rights of audience that would in any event entitle him to act as an advocate in those proceedings. **13–12**

The combined effect of s.13, s.19, and para.1(6) of Sch.3 of the 2007 Act, is to provide that a person who is "a party" to proceedings, and would have had a right of audience, "in the person's capacity as such a person", if the Act had not been passed is an exempt person, and is therefore entitled to carry on that particular reserved legal activity though not an authorised person in relation to that activity. These provisions play the same role in the 2007 Act as did s.27(2)(d) of the 1990 Act. Throughout it has been the rule that an individual could appear in his own case in any court, regardless of his qualifications. A "party" in this context does not include a party's agent (*Gregory v Turner* [2003] EWCA Civ 183; [2003] 1 W.L.R. 1149, CA (a party may not by power of attorney confer on another the right to appear in court as his lay advocate)).

Presumably, where a party retains a qualified advocate to act on his behalf at a hearing, that party's personal right of audience derived from para.1(6) of Sch.3 of the 2007 Act lies in abeyance for the period during which the advocate remains instructed. Therefore, the party has no right to top-up (as it were) the assistance of his advocate by speaking either before or after him or by interrupting him. (This was the conclusion reached in a modern New South Wales case where early English authorities on the point were examined; see *Malouf v Malouf* (2006) 65 N.S.W.L.R. 449.)

## G. RIGHT OF AUDIENCE GRANTED BY THE COURT IN RELATION TO THE PROCEEDINGS (SCH.3 PARA.1(2)) (S.27(2)(c))

### 1. THE SOURCE OF THE COURT'S DISCRETION

It was explained above that, among the principal categories of person who are exempt for the purpose of exercising a right of audience before a court in relation to **13–13**

*Paragraph numbers marked with a "+" can be found online and on CD.*

any proceedings, is "a person who has a right of audience granted by that court in relation those proceedings" (see para.1(2) of Sch.3 of 2007 Act, replicating s.27(2)(c) of 1990 Act).

This provision proceeds on the assumption that a court has power to grant a person (what might be called for the purposes of exposition here) a "special right" of audience for particular proceedings before it. But in terms the legislation does not grant the court such power or attempt to indicate its scope. It assumes that the courts do have a power to grant a right of audience to a person in a particular case, being a person who is not an authorised person. Nevertheless, in *D. v S. (Rights of Audience)* [1997] 1 F.L.R. 724, CA, the Court of Appeal held that it is clear that this provision, when read in the context of the terms of Pt II of the 1990 Act, gives the court a discretionary power to grant a special right of audience in particular proceedings before it to a person who does not have an appropriate right of audience derived from some other source for those proceedings. It is a power designed to be exercised on a case by case basis, but there is no reason why the same person, having benefited from it in one case, should not benefit from it in others.

It is odd that, in cases decided since the 1990 Act came into force, the courts should not have explained, what was s.27(2)(c) of that Act and what is now para.1(2) of Sch.3 of the 2007 Act, simply on the basis that that provision acknowledged the existence of, and the survival of, a long-standing discretion, which was capable of being exercised in a variety of circumstances, and which in practice for good reasons was exercised more liberally in some circumstances than in others. There was plenty of pre-1990 authority establishing that, as part of the inherent power of courts to regulate their own procedures, a judge in an individual case has power to permit any advocate to appear for a litigant (see *A.L.I. Finance Ltd v Havelet Leasing Ltd* [1992] 1 W.L.R. 455, and authorities referred to there).

The statutory scheme for the granting of rights of audience by authorised bodies, formerly set out in Pt II of the 1990 Act and now found in the 2007 Act, is designed with a view to maintaining the proper and efficient administration of justice, but it will always be susceptible to the criticism that it is in some respects too restrictive. The inherent discretionary power acknowledged in para.1(2) of Sch.3 may be seen as the frontier on which, on a case by case basis, the defences of the scheme are constantly probed. The provision has given rise to a good deal of case law in which a clash can be observed between, on the one hand, the need to preserve the integrity of the statutory scheme (and other arrangements for granting rights of audience), and on the other, the need to do justice in individual cases to parties acting in person, and to provide the court in such cases with at least some of the assistance that it might normally except to receive from a qualified advocate. In dealing with applications for the granting of rights of audience on this basis the courts have stressed that the statutory scheme is in the public interest, enabling those engaged in legal proceedings to know that they are briefing a person who has been properly trained and approved by an appropriate professional body, and it provides judges with the assurance that they can rely on the professionalism and integrity of advocates appearing before them. It has been said that to permit any person unknown to the court with no legal training and no professional accreditation to represent a party "may be unfair to the litigant, unfair to the other parties, and unfair to the court" (*Izzo v Philip Ross & Co* [2002] B.P.I.R. 310; *The Times* August 9, 2001 (Neuberger J.)).

## 2. THE CONTEXT FOR EXERCISE OF THE DISCRETION

**13–14** In *Clarkson v Gilbert* [2000] 2 F.L.R. 839, CA, Lord Woolf C.J. explained that, normally, there are two options open to a person bringing or defending civil proceedings. First, a lawyer who has the appropriate rights of audience can be instructed to appear on his behalf. Secondly, he can act in person. If a party chooses the second option he has, by operation of law, a right of audience which he may exercise personally (para.1(6) of Sch.3, formerly s.27(2)(d)), but which he may not delegate (*Gregory v Turner* [2003] EWCA Civ 183; [2003] 1 W.L.R. 1149, CA). If a party, having chosen the second option, does not want himself to exercise the right of audience that accrues to him, but wants somebody who is not an advocate and who has no rights of audience to appear on his behalf, instead of someone who has the appropriate right of audience, he may request the court to exercise its inherent discretion acknowledged in para.1(2) of Sch.3 and grant that person a special right of audience in relation to the proceedings.

***Paragraph numbers marked with a "+" can be found online and on CD.***

The reported cases show that, as a practical matter, the persons for whom rights of audience have been sought in this way (sometimes successfully, sometimes not) fall into various categories. They include, for example, a member of the party's family or a personal friend (perhaps a work colleague), or a person acting as his McKenzie friend or as his lay representative in small claim proceedings. (It is possible that a person falling into one of these categories may have some legal qualifications; e.g. a person who has completed his training as a barrister but has not undergone pupilage.) The categories also include a person exercising on behalf of the party a right to conduct litigation, or enjoying restricted rights of audience not broad enough to cover the instant proceedings (an illustration is given in the Chancery Guide para.15.17, see Vol.2 para.1A–141), or a person who is a member of a professional or other body that has not attained the status of a body authorised to grant rights of audience under the statutory scheme, but which may reasonably aspire to such accreditation. A person appointed as a party's litigation friend under CPR Pt 21 does not, by virtue of that appointment, have a right of audience, but there is no reason why he should not apply for a special right (*Gregory v Turner*, op cit., para.64 per Brooke L.J.). The important point to notice is that the exercise by a court of the inherent discretionary power acknowledged in para.1(2) of Sch.3 to grant a special right of audience is not confined to granting a special right of audience to holders of restricted rights, but may be exercised to enable a lay person to act as advocate for a party acting in person.

## 3. APPLICATION PRACTICE

In *Clarkson v Gilbert*, op cit, Waller L.J. said that the normal time for the making of an application by a party in person for the exercise of the court's discretion is at the first inter partes hearing with the party in person and the other side present. Normally it will be wrong to deal with the matter on an ex parte application. The person for whom the special right of audience is sought should also be present, at least where that person is a lay person, as it is only in those circumstances that the court can make a fully informed decision. The application is the application of the party acting in person, and not the person that that party wishes to have as his advocate. (There is, of course, a chicken and egg problem here, and as a practical matter it may be the latter who will address the court on the application.) **13–15**

## 4. EXERCISE OF THE DISCRETION

Before the 1990 Act came into force, the determination of the circumstances in which the court may exercise the discretionary power to grant a special right of audience for particular proceedings gave rise to occasional difficulty. As has been explained above, the statutory scheme and other legislative initiatives have extended rights of audience significantly. This has taken pressure off the discretionary power, but, on the other hand, countervailing pressures have emerged; in particular the increase in the number of parties acting in person caused by the run down in the availability of legal aid. In any event, since 1990 arguments about the tests to be applied and about the circumstances in which the discretion should be exercised have persisted. **13–16**

### *(a) Generally*

Some guidance (but not a lot) may be gained from reported decisions of the Court of Appeal made before the 2007 Act came into force. Just as the context of s.27(2)(c) (now para.1(2) of Sch.3), as provided by other provisions of Pt II of the 1990 Act, was called in aid to justify the existence of the discretionary power (see "The source of the court's discretion" above"), so too was it called in aid to illuminate the manner in which it should be exercised. In particular, in *D. v S.* (Rights of Audience), op cit, and subsequent cases the Court of Appeal called attention to the "statutory objective" and the "general principle for the development of legal services" as stated in s.17 of the 1990 Act, and to the "statutory duty" to adhere to them imposed by s.18 of that Act on "any person" called upon to exercise any functions which were conferred by Pt II "with respect to . . . the granting of rights of audience". In addition, after it was added to s.27 in 1999, the Court drew attention to the duties imposed on advocates by s.27.2(a). It is obvious that the provisions of s.17 and s.18 applied to persons engaged in operating the statutory scheme as it existed under Pt II of the 1990 Act for the granting of rights of audience by authorised bodies; for example, the members of the **13–17** consultative panel established by the Act and the designated judges (institutions that do not figure in the statutory scheme in the 2007 Act). But it is much less obvious that they applied to an individual judge confronted with an application under s.27(2)(c) for the grant of a special right of audience for particular proceedings. (The point being that he is to be regarded as "any person" within s.18.) And it has to be said, that the calling in aid of s.17 and s.18 originated in cases where the Court was anxious to stress that s.27(2)(c) should not be habitually relied on by unqualified persons for the purpose of setting themselves up as providers of advocacy services (whether for reward or not) for parties acting in person (particularly in family law proceedings). That, according to Lord Woolf M.R., would be "monstrously inappropriate", and totally out of accord with the spirit of the 1990 Act, having regard to the stringent requirements as to training and conduct imposed upon those who gain normal rights of audience from authorised bodies (*D. v S. (Rights of Audience)*, op cit).

It has to be noted that, since the replacement of the statutory scheme as found in Pt II of the 1990 Act with that now found in the 2007 Act, the usefulness of much of this contextual analysis (repeated by the court in *Clarkson v Gilbert*, see below) as a guide to the exercise of the discretion is diminished. That is because, although s.27.2(a) of the 1990 Act is re-enacted in the 2007 Act (see s.188 and note, s.1(3)(d)), s.17 (The statutory objective and the general principle) and s.18 (The statutory duty) are not. Nevertheless, it is submitted that Lord Woolf's concluding point still holds good. (Section 1(1) of the 2007 Act states a series of "regulatory objectives" which includes promoting and maintaining adherence by authorised persons to "the professional principles" elaborated in s.1(3). The contexts in which the regulatory objectives are referred to in the Act do not include that of a court considering an application for a special right of audience.)

It is submitted that where an application is made in ordinary civil proceedings to grant a right of audience to a person who is not authorised to exercise it the judge should take as his starting point the judgment of the Court of Appeal in *Clarkson v Gilbert* [2000] 2 F.L.R. 839, CA In that case, Lord Woolf C.J. said that if a party, having chosen to act in person, wants somebody who is not an advocate and who has no rights of audience to appear on his behalf, instead of someone who has rights of audience, that has to be justified; the party acting in person must satisfy the court that that is appropriate. This was a case in which a claimant in person made allegations of conspiracy, inducement to breach of contract, and libel, and wished to have, as her advocate throughout the proceedings, her husband (a man who had completed the Bar finals but had not been called to the Bar). Here the Court held (overruling the judge) that a special right of audience should be granted to the party's husband. The Court accepted that for reason of ill-health the claimant was unable to conduct the proceedings herself and needed assistance. If the separate judgments of Lord Woolf and Clarke L.J. (with whom Waller L.J. agreed) are put side by side it can been seen that the Court was of the opinion (1) that (what is now) para.1(2) of Sch.3 in no way fetters the discretion, (2) that "all will depend on the circumstances" of the case, (3) that here there was "good reason on the facts" to permit the husband to speak on behalf of the claimant and it was "just to permit him to do so", (4) that the fact that the husband could not comply with (what is now s.188) did not mean that he should not be allowed to act as his wife's advocate. The Court expressly rejected the contention that the discretion could be exercised only in "exceptional circumstances" (see further "Unqualified advocates providing advocacy services" below).

In *Harris v Society of Lloyd's* [2008] EWHC 1433 (Comm), July 1, 2008, unrep. (David Steel J.), on the commencement of the hearing of the defendant's application for summary judgment, an application was made on behalf of a claimant in person (represented in previous interlocutory proceedings by spouse) for permission for that claimant to be represented by a person who, though not an unqualified advocate purporting to offer advocacy services, was a person closely concerned with the events out of which the proceedings arose and who had made witness statements used in parallel proceedings. The judge refused the application and in doing so relied, not on the *Clarkson* test, but on the "exceptional circumstances" test.

In *Zappia Middle East Construction Co Ltd v Clifford Chance* [2001] EWCA Civ 1383; August 30, 2001, unrep., CA, in an application to the Court of Appeal for an extension of time for complying with an order for security for costs, the appellant contended that counsel of his choice were unavailable and applied for permission to enable his so-

***Paragraph numbers marked with a "+" can be found online and on CD.***

licitor to act as advocate. The Court found that no good reason had been shown, and dismissed the application. In *Cooper v Rhuscott Estates Ltd* [2004] EWCA Civ 673, February 19, 2004, CA, a single lord justice permitted the brother of a litigant in person address the Court on his behalf on an application for permission to appeal. In *R. (England) v Tower Hamlets London BC* [2006] EWCA Civ 1742, December 20, 2006, CA, the Court of Appeal permitted a solicitor lacking the appropriate rights of audience to make a renewed application to the court for permission to appeal in circumstances where it was not clear whether his client had an interest in continuing judicial review proceedings. In *Huntingdon Life Sciences Group Plc v Stop Huntingdon Animal Cruelty* [2005] EWHC 2233 (QB); [2005] 4 All E.R. 899 (Mackay J.), a judge hearing an appeal against a third party debt order, made against an unincorporated association in an harassment claim in which the association was one of several defendants, permitted an unqualified person to represent the association (apparently acting on the instruction of a person who was one of the other defendants in the proceedings). For an example of a court permitting a litigation friend to make representations on behalf of an unrepresented defendant, see *SmithKline Beecham Plc v Avery* [2007] EWHC 948 (QB); April 27, 2007, unrep. (Teare J.) (hearing of claimant's application to continue interim injunction made without notice).

### *(b) Unqualified advocates providing advocacy services*

In *Clarkson v Gilbert*, the Court of Appeal confirmed, as it had held in *D. v S. (Rights of Audience)*, that in a case where the proposed advocate is a person who has set **13–18**
himself up as an unqualified advocate and holds himself out as providing advocacy services, whether for reward or not, the discretion of the court is wide enough to enable a court to grant him a special right of audience in the proceedings. However, in these circumstances, the court will only make an order in exceptional circumstances. The courts should pause long before granting rights of audience to individuals who do not meet the stringent requirements laid down in the statutory scheme now found in the 2007 Act and who make a practice of seeking to represent otherwise unrepresented parties. This was confirmed by the Court of Appeal in *Paragon Finance Plc v Noueiri (Practice Note)* [2001] EWCA Civ 1402; [2001] 1 W.L.R. 2357, CA, a case going well beyond that issue and in which the Court said there was a need for the development of an administrative system to help courts identify such individuals. (It should be explained that, in some instances, these individuals have been experienced and frequently obsessive litigants in their own causes, often subject to civil restraint or civil proceedings orders, making their services available to others as a matter of course. Obviously, a court should be very reluctant to permit a litigant in person to speak through someone whose attitude to his own litigation has justified a court in making such order against him; see *Izzo v Philip Ross & Co* [2002] B.P.I.R. 310; *The Times* August 9, 2001 (Neuberger J.)).

The key feature of the Court's decision in *Clarkson v Gilbert* was the holding that the judge erred in acting on the assumption that in all applications for the exercise of the court's discretion to grant a right of audience in particular proceedings to a person not authorised to exercise the right the test to be applied was the "exceptional circumstances" test. In some cases, the facts will be such as to make it apparent that the proposed advocate is a person who has set himself up as an unqualified advocate and is holding himself out as providing advocacy services, whether for reward or not, and therefore that the court should apply the "exceptional circumstances" test. But it is interesting to note that in some cases dealt with since *Clarkson v Gilbert* and *Paragon Finance Plc v Noueiri* the courts have continued to apply the "exceptional circumstances" test in situations that do not fall clearly into the "unqualified advocate holding himself out" category. For example, *Official Receiver v Mullarkey* [2003] EWCA Civ 404; [2003] C.P. Rep. 59, CA (forensic accountant with professional relationship with party acting in person and suffering from ill-health granted special right for application for permission to appeal in director's disqualification case); see also *Gregory v Turner*, op cit., at para.57. In *Clarkson v Gilbert*, Lord Woolf C.J. stressed that his reference to the "exceptional circumstances" test in *D. v S. (Rights of Audience)* was confined to the circumstances in that case.

Some unqualified persons who offer advocacy services describe themselves as "solicitor's agents". This is a misleading term in this context as it implies an authority which does not exist. "Solicitor's agent" is not a term used in the 2007 Act.

***Paragraph numbers marked with a "+" can be found online and on CD.***

The practice of solicitors using other solicitors as local agents is well established (though the practice has declined since telephone hearings were introduced by the CPR). Rather than attend a short hearing in a distant city, a solicitor would instruct a solicitor in that city to attend as an agent. This practice is still recognised in rules of court (see, e.g. r.38(3) of the Supreme Court Rules 2009 at para.4–38). Indeed the pre-CPR High Court writ included space for an agent's name and address. The key point is that the agent is also a solicitor, or an employee of that solicitor for whom the solicitor is responsible.

There is no independent profession of "solicitor's agent" but this is a term regularly used by unqualified persons offering advocacy services. Such persons are generally self-employed and obtain work through an agency. Being unqualified they are not subject to the disciplinary process of any profession. Importantly, they are not "authorised persons" within s.18 of the 2007 Act nor "exempt persons" within s.19 and Sch.3. Consequently, they do not have a right of audience. See further the comment of Lord Woolf M.R. (para.13–17 above) that s.27(2)(c) of the Courts and Legal Services Act 1990 (now para.1(2) of Sch.3 of the 2007 Act) should not be habitually relied on by unqualified persons for the purpose of setting themselves up as providers of advocacy services.

### *(c) McKenzie friend*

**13–19** The court may permit any person to attend an unrepresented party before the court as a friend and to assist him by taking notes, by quietly making suggestions and giving advice (*McKenzie v McKenzie* [1971] P. 33; CA, *R. v Bow County Court Ex p. Pelling* [1999] 1 W.L.R. 1807; [1999] 1 W.L.R. 1807, CA. The practice of permitting a party in person to have the assistance of a "McKenzie friend" first emerged in county court family proceedings and spread into ordinary civil proceedings. It became more important when the jurisdiction of county courts was significantly increased in the 1990s, and spread to the higher courts. Generally, permission should be given unless the court is satisfied that fairness and the interests of justice do not require it. In family proceedings it has been held that art.6 of the Convention is engaged in any request for such assistance, and there is a strong presumption in favour of allowing assistance (*Re O. (Children) (Hearing in Private: Assistance)* [2005] EWCA Civ 759; [2005] 3 W.L.R. 1191, CA). It is still the cases that there is a "slightly more relaxed" attitude to "McKenzie friends" in the family jurisdiction (per Wall L.J. *J (a child)* [2009] EWCA Civ 1210). In *Re N (A Child)* [2008] EWHC 2042 (Fam) Munby J. held that there was no general principle that the court could only grant a right of audience to a McKenzie friend in exceptional circumstances when granting such a right to a family friend to represent a mother in children proceedings. Following this decision the President of the Family Division issued *Practice Note (Family Courts; McKenzie Friends) (No.2)* [2008] 1 W.L.R. 2757. Although, strictly, it applies only to family proceedings the guidance given could be applied generally and is likely to be so treated particularly by judges who deal with both family and civil proceedings. The Practice Note restates the principle that a litigant who is not legally represented has the right to have reasonable assistance from a lay person. (This guidance supersedes that given in previous cases and practice notes).

The court can prevent the assistant from continuing to act as such where the assistance given is inimical to the efficient administration of justice, for example, where he is indirectly running the case using the litigant as a puppet (*Paragon Finance Plc v Noueiri* (Practice Note), op cit, at para.56 per Brooke L.J.), where his assistance results in the wasting of court time, or where he is unruly (*R. v Leicester City Justice, Ex p. Barrow* [1991] 2 Q.B. 260, DC).

Once a party acting in person is allowed to have the assistance of a "McKenzie friend", the question might then arise whether the court should exercise its discretion under para.1(2) of Sch.3 and grant the assistant a right of audience. Statements may be found to the effect that this is an "exceptional course" and one that the court "should be very slow to permit" (see e.g. Chancery Guide para.15.12 above)). However, it seems that the cases in which such views have been expressed have been cases in which the courts were dealing with a McKenzie friend in the form of a person who was attempting to set himself up as an unqualified advocate providing advocacy services. As has been explained above, there is authority for the proportion that, although a special right of audience may be granted to such a person, the court will only make an order in exceptional circumstances. It is submitted that, where the circumstances are otherwise, and a party acting in person wishes that the person who happens to be serving as his McKenzie friend should have a right of audience under para.1(2) of Sch.3, then the party need not show that there are exceptional circumstances. This view is supported by the decision of Munby J. in *Re N (a child)* [2008] EWHC 2042 (Fam) which, it is submitted, is of general application and is not confined to family proceedings.

In *Practice Note (Family Courts: McKenzie Friends) (No.2)* [2008] 1 W.L.R. 2757, Fam D, it is stated that, in family proceedings, the court should be slow to grant an application under s.27(2)(c) of the 1990 Act (i.e. Sch.3 para.1(2)(b) of the 2007 Act) for a McKenzie friend be granted a special right of audience. In the case of *In re N. (A Child) (McKenzie Friend: Rights of Audience) (Practice Note)* [2008] EWHC 2042 (Fam); [2008] 1 W.L.R. 2743 (Munby J.) it was held that it is not the law that an application by a party in person for that party's McKenzie friend to be granted a right of audience in the proceedings may be granted only in exceptional circumstances, although there may be a general principle that a "professional" McKenzie friend should not be granted such a right except in such circumstances.

In the case of *In re D. (A Child)* [2005] EWCA Civ 347; March 15, 2005, unrep., CA, a party's McKenzie friend was a solicitor who had been struck from the Rolls by the Solicitors Disciplinary Tribunal. On the hearing of the party's application for permission to appeal the Court refused his application under s.27(2)(c) for the McKenzie friend to be granted a special right of audience. The party's argument that the friend was better able to put her case did not amount to an exceptional circumstance.

On the disadvantages that can accrue if a McKenzie friend is not granted a special right of audience where that is requested by the litigant in person, see *Izzo v Philip Ross & Co* [2002] B.P.I.R. 310; *The Times* August 9, 2001 (Neuberger J.).

## 5. WITHDRAWAL OF SPECIAL RIGHT

Section 27(4) of the 1990 Act acknowledged that the court has power: **13–20**

> "in any proceedings to refuse to hear a person (for reasons which apply to him as an individual) who would otherwise have a right of audience before the court in those proceedings".

This provision as re-enacted in s.192(1) of the 2007 Act is to the same effect and states that nothing in that Act shall affect the power. By s.192(2) it is provided that, where a court in exercise of this power refuses to hear a person it must give its reasons for refusing. The power may be exercised in relation to a person who has been granted a right of audience in the circumstances under consideration here (as well as to persons exercising such rights with a different provenance). The circumstances in which a court would be justified in having recourse to the power cannot be shortly stated; but among them would be the situation where the advocate repeatedly took hopeless points and advanced completely futile arguments (see further *Paragon Finance Plc v Noueiri (Practice Note)*, op cit, and authorities referred to therein, in particular *Mensah v Islington London BC* December 1, 2000, unrep., CA).

## 6. MISCELLANEOUS OBSERVATIONS

Various points relevant to what has been said above about the special right of audience (some gleaned from first instance judgments), but which would have complicated **13–21**
the narrative had they been dealt with there (possibly to the point of causing confusion in the mind of the reader), may now be explained briefly (in no particular order).

It is clear that a special right of audience cannot be conferred on a person by the consent of the parties to the proceedings (*D. v S. (Rights of Audience)* [1997] 2 F.L.R. 458, CA). Even though it may be a matter of no importance to the parties, the court has to be mindful of the need to protect the integrity of the statutory scheme and the other legislation and their several objectives. However, the fact that the party acting in person's opponent (whether himself represented or not) is prepared to consent to permission being granted may weigh with the court.

The situation where a party in person makes an application at a hearing at which his opponent does not appear is different to that where the opponent does appear and does object to the application (*In re D. (A Child)* [2005] EWCA Civ 347; March 15, 2005, unrep., CA).

The fact that a party in person's opponent is represented by an advocate may be a factor to be taken into account in the exercise of the discretion. This can cut two ways. The court's estimation of the opponent's advocate's ability and willingness to conduct the case in a manner that shows the cases of both parties in their best light may go against the exercise of discretion. On the other hand, fairness and level playing field considerations may suggest otherwise. Allowance has to be made for the fact that it is an advocate's duty to promote and protect fearlessly and by all proper means his client's best interests, and he would fail in that duty were he to supplement deficiencies as to evidence in the case of his client's unrepresented opponent (*Khudados v Hayden* [2007] EWCA Civ 1316, December 13, 2007, unrep., CA). (For duties of advocate for a represented party when that party's opponent is a litigant in person, see Admiralty and Commercial Courts Guide para.M2, Vol.2 para.2A–126.)

The functions embraced by a right of audience include all of the activities traditionally associated with advocacy. In a given case, the full range of those activities may be deployed including the making of opening and closing speeches, putting legal and factual submissions, and examining and cross-examining witnesses. It would be unrealistic not to admit that in many cases where the party in person wishes to have a lay person as his advocate the exercise by the court of its discretionary power is influenced by the court's expectation of the extent to which that person might take advantage of the special right if it were granted. It might be anticipated that the court is likely to be yielding where the party in person simply wishes to have someone else "speak on his behalf", as the party himself would do but feels he cannot do adequately without assistance (perhaps because of language difficulties), and perhaps less yielding where there is bad blood between the parties (perhaps shared by the proffered advocate) and heated cross-examination likely.

The court's estimation of the proffered advocate's capacity to cope with the complexity of the issues arising in the proceedings in a manner which does not impair proper and efficient administration of justice is a matter to be considered. Courts are familiar with the way in which court resources can be wasted where a litigant in person, in acting as his own advocate, performs erratically and is impervious to guidance from the bench (and perhaps deaf to help offered by his opponent's qualified advocate). The same thing can happen where the discretion to grant a special right of audience is exercised unwisely. The possibility that the party may be a better advocate than the person he says he wishes to have act for him should not be overlooked.

Where a court grants a special right of audience it may do so in terms that restricts that right to a particular hearing. The extent to which a person, were he granted a special right of audience, might take advantage of such right is related to the nature of the hearing for which the right is sought. It seems that courts are more willing to grant special rights of audience for the hearing of interlocutory matters than for trials (reflecting the fact that rights of audience granted by authorised bodies sometimes draw a similar distinction), in particular contested trials. And it is not uncommon for a right granted for one hearing to be extended for a later hearing. However, neither the party acting in person nor his chosen and approved advocate should be misled into thinking that because a special grant was made for a hearing early on in the proceedings that further grants will be made for later hearings as the case develops.

Where a lay representative acts as advocate for a party acting in person in a small claim (see "Lay representatives in small claims (s.11)" above), his right of audience may not be exercised where his client does not attend the hearing. Presumably, where a court is minded to grant a person a special right of audience in any proceedings it may do so on the understanding that the client will attend the hearings at which his advocate appears. In *Clarkson v Gilbert*, op cit., Lord Woolf stressed (at para.21) it is the client who has the conduct of the proceedings and normally he would be expected to be present on occasions where matters directly affecting his interests were involved.

When the court exercises any power given to it by provisions in the CPR, or interprets any rule, the court must seek to give effect to the overriding objective (r.1.2). The court is not exercising such power when it grants or refuses an application by a litigant in person to grant a right of audience to a person who is not authorised to exercise it, nor does the task of determining such application involve the interpretation of a rule. Nevertheless, it is not uncommon for courts to call the overriding objective in aid when ruling on an application (e.g. *Mensah v Islington London BC* December 1, 2000, unrep., CA; *Izzo v Philip Ross & Co* [2002] B.P.I.R. 310; *The Times* August 9, 2001 (Neuberger J.)).

***Paragraph numbers marked with a "+" can be found online and on CD.***

# SECTION 14

## ALTERNATIVE DISPUTE RESOLUTION

# 14 ALTERNATIVE DISPUTE RESOLUTION

CONTENTS 14–1



## A. INTRODUCTION

### 1. NEGOTIATION, MEDIATION AND OTHER DISPUTE RESOLUTION PROCEDURES

By definition, disputes between parties are adversarial (or at least bi-polar) in the sense that one party is opposed to another. A large proportion of the business of the courts (but by no means all) consists of the adjudication of disputes. Adjudication involves the intervention of a third party in the form of a judge. Adjudication takes place according to law (substantive, jurisdictional and adjectival). (Unfortunately, this proper use of the term "adjudication" has been rendered ambiguous, and discourse on ADR made more difficult, by the special statutory form of adjudication by experts in disputes arising under construction contracts introduced by the Housing Grants, Construction and Regeneration Act 1996 s.108.) **14–2**

Disputes may be, and usually are, resolved by the parties themselves, and this is so even where legal proceedings have been commenced by one party or another. Broadly speaking, where the culmination of the adjudicative process (i.e. a trial at law) is avoided, whether in the course of trial, on the steps of the court, or at some earlier stage, it is because the parties negotiated a resolution to their dispute. Procedural law encourages resolution by negotiation. Indeed, the pre-trial process (though preparatory to trial) can be regarded as an alternative method to trial for the resolution of disputes (and a highly effective one).

Negotiation is a dispute resolution procedure and it is the principal "alternative" method to adjudication by the courts. It is a method which may, or may not, involve the assistance of others, for example, legal representatives of the parties. In modern times, increasing attention has been given to dispute resolution procedures alternative to adjudication by the courts (ADR) and involving third parties, for example, mediators. Such methods are many and various. Some are very much akin to negotiation and others are virtually informal forms of adjudication. As dispute resolution methods, they have some attributes not shared, on the one hand, by simple negotiation between the parties, and, on the other, by adjudication by the courts (and attendant pre-trial procedures). Not least of these attributes are the possibility of reducing the costs incurred by parties and the potential for relieving the courts of business.

In the "Access to Justice" Interim Report it was said that the range and availability

***Paragraph numbers marked with a "+" can be found online and on CD.***

of ADR procedures should be increased. In the "Access to Justice" Final Report it was explained that, for some time before the CPR came into force, resort by parties involved in litigation to ADR methods had been encouraged by the courts in various ways (p.11). The CPR and the practice directions build on those earlier developments. Further, the pre-action protocols, which outline the steps parties in dispute should take to seek information from, and to provide information to, each other before one or other of them starts civil proceedings by issuing originating process, have as one of their objectives the avoiding of litigation by settlement through negotiation (see further below).

The benefits that can accrue from the adoption by parties of ADR procedures in a given case are various (see further below). The main justification given by judges for encouraging parties to do so is the saving of costs. From the court's perspective, one of the principal justifications must be the avoiding of expenditure of court resources on cases where it seems obvious (at least to the court) that an assisted settlement would be reached through ADR procedures. (Indeed, it may be suspected that much lawyer resistance to ADR procedures, such as it is, could be ascribed to an over-emphasis on this justification, particularly at a time when court resources for the handling of civil claims appear to be declining in real terms.)

### 2. APPELLATE JUDGES' STATEMENTS AND SPEECHES ON ADR

14-3 Recent statements made by judges in the Court of Appeal strongly urging practitioners and parties to make greater use of alternative forms of dispute resolution (in particular mediation) are found in dicta of Ward L.J. in *Burchell v Bullard* [2005] EWCA Civ 358, April 8, 2004, unrep., CA (at para.42), and in *Egan v Motor Services (Bath) Ltd* [2007] EWCA Civ 1002, October 18, 2007, unrep., CA (at para.50), and of Longmore L.J. in *Vahidi v Fairstead House School Trust Ltd* [2005] EWCA Civ 765, June 9, 2005, unrep., CA (at para.27), and in *Painting v University of Oxford* [2005] EWCA Civ 161, February 3, 2005, unrep., CA (at para.27) and of Mummery LJ in Bradford v James [2008] EWCA Civ 837 (at para.1).

Additionally, between 2007 and 2009, Lightman J., Lord Phillips C.J. and Sir Anthony Clarke M.R. each delivered speeches, out of court, all of which were predicated on the greater use of ADR. They will be referred to collectively below as the "Judicial Speeches" and the speech on May 8, 2008 will be referred to as the "Master of the Rolls' Birmingham Speech". The speeches are available at *http://www.judiciary.gov.uk/docs/speeches/berwins_mediation.pdf* [Accessed October 27, 2009] (Lightman J.); *http://www.judiciary.gov.uk/docs/speeches/lcj_adr_india_290308.pdf* [Accessed October 27, 2009] (Lord Phillips C.J.); *http://www.judiciary.gov.uk/docs/speeches/mr_apil_ann_conf_2008.pdf* [Accessed October 27, 2009] (Sir Anthony Clarke M.R., Brighton);*http://www.judiciary.gov.uk/docs/speeches/mr_mediation_conference_may08.pdf* [Accessed October 27, 2009] (Sir Anthony Clarke M.R., Birmingham); *http://www.judiciary.gov.uk/docs/speeches/mr-littleton-chambers-080609.pdf* [Accessed October 27, 2009] (Lord Clarke of Stone-Cum-Ebony M.R.).

## B. ADR IN THE CONTEXT OF THE CPR

### 1. CASE MANAGEMENT

#### *(a) ADR as integral to our litigation culture*

14-4 In May 2008 Sir Anthony Clarke MR, delivering a major speech on ADR at a Civil Mediation Council Conference, said that ADR "must become an integral part of our litigation culture. It must become such a well established part of it that when considering the proper management of litigation it forms as intrinsic and as instinctive a part of our lexicon and of our thought processes, as standard considerations like what, if any expert evidence is required and whether a Part 36 Offer ought to made and at what level." (The Master of the Rolls' Birmingham Speech. See para.14-3 above.)

### (b) Encouragement to negotiate and use other dispute resolution processes

Once legal proceedings are commenced, the rules of court which apply, and the case management powers available to the court, in various ways encourage settlement by simple negotiation between the parties. There is a belief that the quality of settlements might be improved and the incidence of settlements increased if recourse was had to ADR procedures during the pre-trial process. Accordingly, r.1.4(2)(e) states that active case management includes the court's encouragement of the parties to use ADR procedures "if the court considers that appropriate". Such encouragement may be given at various points in the procedure laid down in the CPR and related practice directions and may be given, either on the court's own initiative, or in response to an initiative of the parties (as to the latter, see r.26.4). The Glossary attached to the CPR explains that ADR is a collective description of methods of resolving disputes "otherwise than through the normal trial process". In terms, this includes simple negotiation between the parties not involving third parties (apart from the parties' legal representatives). However, it would seem that the purpose of r.1.4(2)(e) is to draw attention to methods other than simple negotiation. **14–5**

The process most often used, apart from negotiation, is mediation. Although it is a process that may take time and can be expensive, in difficult cases a skilled mediator can oil the wheels of settlement in ways that are likely to be more effective than the normal process of negotiation by discussion and offer and counter-offer (*Hickman v Blake Lapthorn* [2006] EWHC 12 (QB), January 17, 2006, unrep. (Jack J.)) Another dispute resolution process is known as Med-Arb and in *IDA Ltd v Southampton University* [2006] EWCA Civ 145; *The Times* March 31, 2006, CA, the Court of Appeal stated that this process (where a mediator trusted by both sides is given authority to decide the terms of a binding settlement agreement) is particularly apt for the resolution of disputes about entitlements to patents. Also note that Early Neutral Evaluation is referred to in the Admiralty and Commercial Court Guide and the Commercial Court working party report on long trials referred to at para.14–22 below.

### (c) Voluntary v compulsory/mandatory ADR and case management

It is often said that the hallmark of ADR procedures, and perhaps the key to their effectiveness in individual cases, is that they are processes voluntarily entered into by the parties in dispute with outcomes, if the parties so wish, which are non-binding. Indeed, it is also a popular view that the voluntary nature of mediation lies at the very heart of mediation and that compulsory mediation is an oxymoron. Authoritative commentators such as Lord Phillips of Worth Matravers, Lord Chief Justice and Professor Dame Hazel Genn, have remarked that compulsory mediation has always been a controversial subject that promotes strong views and more than a little confusion. It is, however, clear beyond doubt, and this was noted in the Judicial Speeches referred to in para.14–3 above, that some jurisdictions (with more experience than our own in the deployment of ADR) do use compulsory mediation. Also, the fact that compulsory mediation is used in Europe can be inferred from the EU Mediation Directive 2008 which includes a provision that nothing in the Directive should prejudice a Member State making the use of mediation compulsory. (Directive 2008/52/EC of the European Parliament and of the Council of May 21, 2008 on certain aspects of mediation in civil and commercial matters, para.(14) of the preamble: *http://eur-lex.europa.eu/LexUriServ/LexUriServ.do?uri=OJ:L:2008:136:0003:0008:EN:PDF* [Accessed October 27, 2009]). More information about how and where compulsory mediation is used may be obtained from a most comprehensive review of ADR in the "Consultation Paper on Alternative Dispute Resolution" published by the Law Reform Commission in Ireland in July 2008. (See *http://www.lawreform.ie/publications/consultpapers.htm* [Accessed October 27, 2009]). One of the most controversial aspects of compulsory mediation is whether it is successful. There is evidence to suggest that compulsory mediation schemes can (fairly obviously) increase the rate of take up of mediation, but that this is at the expense of lowering both the success rate in relation to settlements and the client satisfaction rate in the process (see "Twisting arms: court referred and court linked mediation under judicial pressure." *http://www.justice.gov.uk/docs/Twisting-arms-part1.pdf* [Accessed October 27, 2009]). Against that, however, the Lord Chief Justice has commented that "Statistics show that settlement rates in relation to parties who have been compelled to mediate are just about as high as they are in the case of those who resort **14–6**

***Paragraph numbers marked with a "+" can be found online and on CD.***

to mediation of their own volition." (See the Judicial Speeches referred to in para.14–3 above.) The Irish Consultation Paper (see above) assists our understanding of these issues by suggesting that the issue of "voluntary" or "compulsory" is not an "either, or" choice but that there is a range of options along a spectrum. The options identified by the Commission were:

1. The parties themselves propose the idea for mediation as an option;
2. The court encourages the parties to consider mediation;
3. The court encourages the parties to consider mediation and warns of the possible imposition of cost sanctions for an unreasonable refusal to consider ADR;
4. Access to court is denied, where mediation has not first been attempted.

It is useful to keep this spectrum in mind when examining how the court carries out its duty under r.1.4(2)(e), to encourage the parties to use an alternative dispute resolution procedure. Further, the following brief review of how judicial encouragement to use ADR has evolved since the introduction of the CPR may assist in understanding how this aspect of active case management is likely to be dealt with today.

### *(d) Active case management in relation to ADR after the introduction of the CPR*

**14–7** It is clear from the Access to Justice reports and cases such as *Thompson v Commissioner of Police of the Metropolis* [1998] Q.B. 498 and *Robert Alan Dyson and John Watson Field (Executors of the Estate of Lawrence Twohey, Deceased) v Leeds City Council* [2000] C.P. Rep. 42 (November 22, 1999, CA) that Lord Woolf was always of the view that encouragement to use ADR was to be robust and reinforced by the teeth of costs sanctions. As the CPR became established it was also clear that the courts' interpretation of the CPR on this issue was that parties could be ordered to use ADR. In *Cable & Wireless Plc v IBM UK Ltd* [2002] EWHC 2059 (Comm); [2002] 2 All E.R. (Comm) 1041; [2003] B.L.R. 89 Coleman J., faced with parties who resisted ADR, said: "Occasionally, the circumstances of a dispute may appear to the court so strongly to demand a reference to ADR that, even in the face of objections from both parties, [ADR orders] have been made and have led to settlements much to the surprise of the parties concerned." In *Shirayama Shokusan v Danovo Ltd* [2003] EWHC 3006 (Ch) Blackburn J. concluded that the court did have jurisdiction to direct ADR even though one party may not be willing. This was on the basis that the provisions of the CPR were not confined to cases where the parties jointly wished to use alternative dispute resolution procedures. Similar first instance authorities suggesting that a party might be ordered to submit his dispute to mediation against his will are *Kinstreet Ltd v Balmargo Corporation Ltd* [2000] C.P. Rep. 62 (Arden J.); *Muman v Nagasena* [2000] 1 W.L.R. 299, CA and *Guinle v Kirreh Ch D* [2000] C.P. Rep. 62; 1999 WL 1399987. *Dunnett v Railtrack Plc* [2002] EWCA Civ 303; [2002] 2 All E.R. 850, CA, came to be regarded as the high water mark of judicial encouragement. Notwithstanding advice from the court that the parties use ADR, the defendants failed to agree to mediation, with the consequence that, despite succeeding before the Court of Appeal, they failed to recover their costs.

### *(e) Halsey*

**14–8** In *Halsey v Milton Keynes General NHS Trust* [2004] EWCA Civ 576; [2004] 1 W.L.R. 3002, CA, the Court of Appeal expressly adopted the proposition about voluntary mediation stated in the first sentence of para.14–6 above. It also took the view that r.1.4(2)(e) does not expressly permit the court to direct that such ADR procedures be used, but may merely encourage and facilitate. The court heard argument on the question whether the court has power to order parties to submit their disputes to mediation against their will. The court said it was likely that compulsion of ADR would be regarded as an unacceptable constraint on the right to access to the court and, therefore, a violation of art.6 of the European Convention on Human Rights (see further below), and even if (contrary to the court's view) the court does have jurisdiction to order unwilling parties to refer their disputes to mediation the court found it difficult to conceive of circumstances in which it would be appropriate to exercise it. It should also be mentioned, however, that, in terms of case management, the Court of Appeal made it clear that it was in favour of robust encouragement of ADR. Dyson L.J.

referred to the type of order known an "Ungley Order" (see para.14–13) and said: "We can see no reason why such an order should not also routinely be made at least in general personal injury litigation, and perhaps in other litigation too. A party who refuses even to consider whether a case is suitable for ADR is always at risk of an adverse finding at the costs stage of litigation, and particularly so where the court has made an order requiring the parties to consider ADR."

### *(f) Judicial speeches—ADR case management post Halsey—power to direct ADR*

The Judicial Speeches referred to in para.14–3 above were delivered between 2007 and 2009 and, for the main part, focused on *Halsey*. One of several criticisms levelled at the Court of Appeal by Lightman J. concerned the art.6 point referred to immediately above. In the Judicial Speeches all three judges noted the use of compulsory mediation in other jurisdictions (which the Court of Appeal had been unaware of?) and felt that such compulsion did not, of itself, give rise to a violation of art.6 or equivalent legislation. Sir Anthony Clarke M.R. concluded that there may well be grounds for suggesting that Halsey was wrong on this point. The Master of the Rolls added the caveat that this point was not investigated in detail in *Halsey*, might have to be reviewed by the Court of Appeal, in which case the point would be fully argued, and could also be the subject of a rule change. A closely related question was addressed by these speeches: whether the court had power to direct the parties to use an ADR process. The Lord Chief Justice felt there should be built into the litigation process "a stage at which the court can require (the parties) to attempt mediation". The Master of the Rolls, however, argued that the court already has power to direct ADR. He said that, despite *Halsey*, "it is at least strongly arguable that the court retains a jurisdiction to require parties to enter into mediation" and went on to say "that the court has sufficient powers at present routinely to direct the parties to take part in a mediation process ...". Sir Anthony reasoned that such power exists under a combination of the court's case management powers under r.1.4 (2)(e) (encouraging the parties to use an alternative dispute resolution procedure)' and r.3.1 (2)(m) (which enables the court to take any step in managing a case to further the overriding objective). He added that exercising case management in this way requires the power to be applied consistently with the duty under r.1.1 (2)(e) (which requires the court to take account of the needs of all litigants and the court in furthering the overriding objective). Sir Anthony added that there was no compunction on the parties to settle through mediation but the "parties must assist the court in furthering the overriding objective by taking proper part in the mediation process." (Reverting to the range of options listed in para.14–6 above, it would seem that the Master of the Rolls' approach would be placed between options 3 and 4.) In terms of understanding how the court is likely to exercise its case management powers today, we are in the slightly unusual position of having a leading Court of Appeal decision, namely *Halsey*, which should now presumably be read in the context of the speeches referred to. **14–9**

As a footnote to the above it is clear that some courts do take the view that they have power to direct mediation. For example, in *Honda Giken Kogyo Kabushiki Kaisha (A Firm) v Neesam* [2009] EWHC 1213 (Pat) 2009 WL 1504398 Judge Fysh Q.C. concluded an application for a trial of preliminary issues saying, " In summary, then, I shall dismiss the application and direct that both parties use their best endeavours to ensure that a mediation is heard before (date)."

### *(g) Case management and the duty of the parties*

The encouragement and facilitating of ADR by the court is an aspect of active case management which in turn is an aspect of achieving the overriding objective. The parties have a duty to help the court in furthering that objective and, therefore, they have a duty to consider seriously the possibility of ADR procedures being utilised for the purpose of resolving their claim or particular issues within it, particularly when encouraged by the court to do so. The discharge of the parties' duty in this respect may be relevant to the question of costs because, when exercising its discretion as to costs, the court must have regard to all the circumstances, including the conduct of all the parties (r.44.3(4), see too r.44.5). In *Dunnett v Railtrack Plc* [2002] EWCA Civ 303; [2002] 2 All E.R. 850, CA at [12]–[15], Brooke L.J. quoted the foregoing commentary **14–10** with approval and said that parties and their legal representatives should be alert to the possibility that, if they "turn down out of hand" the chance of ADR when suggested by the court they may have to face "uncomfortable costs consequences". See further below.

### (h) Case management and cost sanctions

14–11 The two paragraphs immediately above might, without more, lead one to expect to see parties regularly seeking cost sanctions against other parties for failing to use ADR. The Master of the Rolls' Birmingham Speech, however, strongly discouraged satellite litigation on this topic and forecast that parties would only in exceptional circumstances be penalised for not taking part in mediation. The expectation seems to be that active case management will render mediation part of the normal pre-trial case management process, so it should not be necessary for the courts to make frequent use of cost sanctions. As the Lord Chief Justice noted: "Experience shows that where a court directs the parties to attempt mediation they usually comply." (See Judicial Speeches in para.14.3) Perhaps in future the emphasis will be on sanctions for failure to follow case management directions, rather than sanctions for failure to mediate per se. The Master of the Rolls further discouraged satellite litigation on costs sanctions by expressly approving the finding in *Halsey* that the burden of showing unreasonableness in refusing mediation is on the losing party. He sympathised with the party who says: 'I have a cast iron case and I decline to mediate because there is no point' and who subsequently wins at trial and is appalled when it is suggested that he should be penalised in costs for refusing to mediate. He also noted that cast iron cases were relatively rare. See also *Earl of Malmesbury v Strutt & Parker* [2008] EWHC 424 (QB) and the Master of the Rolls comments thereon in para.14–19 below regarding costs sanctions in relation to conduct at a mediation. Costs sanctions were imposed in circumstances where one party unilaterally cancelled an imminent pre-action mediation: *Roundstone Nurseries Ltd v Stephenson Holdings Ltd* [2009] EWHC 1431 (TCC), 2009 WL 2392342. Further information on costs sanctions is given in para.14–17.

### (i) Case management: facilitation of ADR procedures and criteria for referral to ADR

14–12 The overriding objective in the CPR requires the court to encourage the use of an ADR procedure, in appropriate cases, and to facilitate the use of such procedure, as one of the elements of active case management (r.1.4(2)(e)). The manner in which the court may facilitate the use of an ADR procedure includes the following:

(i) By ensuring that the opportunity to explore ADR prospects is not prejudiced by the rigours of case management procedures generally.

(ii) By acting as a source of information about professional and commercial bodies providing ADR services (for example, see *http://www.nationalmediationhelpline.com* [Accessed October 27, 2009] and paras 14–24 and 14–27 below).

(iii) By verbally encouraging the parties to consider ADR at a hearing or telephone conference, such as a case management conference or a pre-trial review.

(iv) By ordering a stay of the whole or part of the proceedings, for mediation or some other ADR procedure, pursuant to the application of the parties or one of them (r.3.1(2)(f) and r.3.3(1) and see para.14–13 below).

(v) By ordering such a stay of its own initiative (r.3.1(2)(f) and r.3.3(1)). An appropriate time to make such an order might be upon perusal of the parties' statements about ADR in their Allocation Questionnaires. (See para.14–13 below.)

(vi) By making an order, whether on directions for allocation or a later stage, of the type referred to in the Multi-Track Practice Direction (sometimes referred to as an "Ungley Order"). (29PD4.10(9) and see para.14–13 below.)

(vii) By making an ADR order on the basis of the draft in App.7 to the Admiralty and Commercial Courts Guide (see para.14–22). The draft order includes the following paragraph: "4. The parties shall take such serious steps as they may be advised to resolve their disputes by ADR procedures before the neutral individual or panel so chosen by no later than [*]." See para.14–9 above regarding the issue of the court's power to order parties to take part in a mediation process.

***Paragraph numbers marked with a "+" can be found online and on CD.***

(viii) By making an ADR order on the basis of the draft order in App.E to and Section 7 of the Technology and Construction Court Guide (see para.14–22). Although these Guides refer to their particular courts there appears to be no reason why the type of ADR orders made in these courts could not be made, where appropriate, in other courts. Again, see para.14–9 above regarding the issue of the court's power to order parties to take part in a mediation process. See also paras. 14–22 and 14–23 below regarding ADR in the Commercial Court and the Technology and Construction Court.

(ix) By arranging, in the Admiralty and Commercial Court or the Technology and Construction Court, for the court to provide Early Neutral Evaluation (see the references to the respective Court Guides in sub-paras (vii) and (viii) immediately above). Further, in the Technology and Construction Court the court can provide a judge to act as a mediator; further information about this, and a reference to nine cases having been mediated to date, can be found at *http://www.tecsa.org.uk/mediation_adr-1328.htm* [Accessed October 27, 2009].

(x) By, in a case which is suitable to be resolved by an ADR procedure except for one sticking point, ordering the hearing of that point as a preliminary issue with a view to the case then being referred to ADR (see s.8 of the Technology and Construction Court Guide, para.14–22, although, again, there is no reason why the approach taken by the Technology and Construction Court cannot be taken by other courts, where appropriate).

(xi) By referring a Small Claim to the Small Claims Mediation Service (see para.14–24).

(xii) By making an appropriate costs order (or advising that such an order might be made in the future) in respect of failure to give adequate consideration to ADR prior to the commencement of proceedings (para.14–21) or during proceedings (see para.14–17).

Criteria for referral to mediation is given in Guidance on Judicial Referral to Mediation issued to members of the judiciary in 2007: see para.14–28 below. The Guidance deals with the type of cases suitable for mediation and the indicators and counter indicators for referral.

### *(j) Case management: the stages at which ADR may be encouraged*

The issue of timing, as in when is the best stage of a case to use an ADR procedure, is often a complex question. It is dealt with in the *Guidance on Judicial Referral to Mediation* referred to in para.14–2 above (see paras 14–28 and 14–31). In *Nigel Witham Ltd v Smith* [2008] EWHC 12, TCC Judge Peter Coulson Q.C. offered general guidance saying that a premature mediation simply wasted time and could sometimes lead to a hardening of positions on both sides whereas, conversely, a delay in any mediation until after full particulars and documents had been exchanged could mean that the costs that had been incurred to get to that point became themselves the principal obstacle to a successful mediation. He added: **14–13**

> "The trick in many cases was to identify the happy medium: the point when the detail of the claim and the response were known to both sides, but before the costs that had been incurred in reaching that stage were so great that a settlement was no longer possible."

The first main opportunity the court has to consider ADR is at the allocation stage. One of the matters a court may then consider, in the context of ADR, is whether the parties have complied with the ADR provisions of any relevant pre-action protocol (see para.14–21 below). The court will also consider the parties' allocation questionnaire forms. (See Form N150 (Allocation Questionnaire), Section A). CPR r.26.4 provides that a party, when completing the allocation questionnaire required by r.26.3, may make a written request for the proceedings to be stayed while the parties try to settle the case by alternative dispute resolution or other means. The allocation questionnaire form was amended in 2008 and now offers parties the facility of the court to arranging a mediation appointment through the National Mediation Helpline (see para.14–24 below). It also asks about the steps that have been taken regarding settlement and requires the parties to state (if such is the case) why they consider it inappropriate to try and settle the claim at this stage.

Practice Direction (Case Management. Preliminary Stage: Allocation and Reallocation), para.12.2 states that, where the court in certain circumstances has given a judgment or made an order requiring an amount of money, to be decided by the court, to be paid by one party to another, the court will give directions (e.g., a direction listing the claim for a disposal hearing). It is expressly provided that the directions may include a direction staying the claim while the parties try to settle the case by alternative dispute resolution or other means. (para.12.2(1)(d)).

CPR r.29.2 states that, when it allocates a case to the multi-track, the court will give case management directions. This provision is supplemented by paras 4.1 to 4.11 of Practice Direction (The Multi-Track) (see Vol.1, para.29PD.4). Paragraph 4.10 states the general approach that the court will adopt where it gives directions on its own initiative without holding a case management conference and is not aware of any steps taken by the parties other that the exchange of statements of case. Sub-paragraph (9) of para.4.10 states that a direction requiring the parties to consider ADR is included among the directions that the court may give in these circumstances and sets out the form of Order, known as an "Ungley Order" which may be made; this is as follows:

> "The parties shall by [the date determined by the court] consider whether the case is capable of resolution by ADR. If any party considers that the case is unsuitable for resolution by ADR, that party shall be prepared to justify that decision at the conclusion of the trial, should the judge consider that such means of resolution were appropriate, when he is considering the appropriate costs order to make. The party considering the case unsuitable for ADR shall, not less than 28 days before the commencement of the trial, file with the court a witness statement without prejudice, save as to costs, giving reasons upon which they rely for saying that the case was unsuitable".

### *(k) Case management: where a public authority is a party*

**14–14** In *R. (Cowl) v Plymouth City Council (Practice Note)* [2001] EWCA Civ 1935; [2002] 1 W.L.R. 803, CA, the Court of Appeal noted that, in disputes between public authorities and members of the public for whom they were responsible, insufficient attention is being paid to the paramount importance of saving cost and reducing delay by avoiding recourse to the application for judicial review procedure. The court said that the High Court should scrutinise extremely carefully such applications and should use its powers to ensure that the parties tried to resolve their dispute with the minimum involvement of the court. To achieve that objective, the court might have to hold (of its own initiative) a hearing at which the parties could explain what steps they had taken to resolve or reduce their dispute by means alternative to the procedure. In Practice Statement (Administrative Court: Listing and Urgent Cases) [2002] 1 W.L.R. 810, QBD (sub nom Practice Statement (Administrative Court: Annual Statement) [2002] 1 All E.R. 633), the lead judge of the Administrative Court drew attention to the Cowl case and stated that the judges of that court "were fully committed to resolving disputes by alternative means where appropriate and are exploring ways of promoting this". It has since been suggested, in *Halsey*, that the issue of public money is not a special factor and that the list of factors outlined in *Halsey* determine when it is reasonable to refuse ADR.

A rather different picture is painted by "Mediation and Judicial Review: An empirical research study" published in 2009 by the Public Law Project (see *http://www.publiclawproject.org.uk/documents/MediationandJudicialReview.pdf* [Accessed October 27, 2009]).This detailed research paper does not contemplate mediation as having a significant role in this area. One of its conclusions is:

> "Any exploration of the role of mediation in judicial review would therefore be likely to focus on the small percentage of unresolved cases that proceed beyond the permission stage and in which both parties have an interest in reaching a settlement but are unable to do so because negotiations have become 'stuck'" (page 35).

### *(l) Case management: miscellaneous*

**14–15** CPR r.3.1(2) states that the court's general powers of case management include the power to order that a party or a party's legal representative be required to attend the court. Such an order may be made with a view to making an ADR order (though the attendance of any party is not required for this purpose) or to otherwise facilitate settlement, but should not be made for the purpose of putting pressure on the party to discontinue the proceedings (*Tarajan Overseas Ltd v Kaye* [2001] EWCA Civ 1859; *The Times*, January 22, 2002, CA).

Although the court has jurisdiction to order that parties should be adequately represented at a mediation, it has no jurisdiction to order that a particular person should attend, especially where that person was not a party to the proceedings (*Shirayama Shokusan Co Ltd v Danovo Ltd* (2004) 101(13) L.S.G. 34; *The Times*, March 22, 2004 (Blackburne J.) (D applying for order staying proceedings until conclusion of mediation attended by a third party (X) as a representative of C, where D contending that X's presence was essential to meaningful mediation)).

In a housing dispute, it would be wrong for a social landlord to use recourse to mediation as a delaying tactic having the effect of causing a tenant to lose priority status for housing (*Robinson v Hammersmith and Fulham London BC* [2006] EWCA Civ 1122; *The Times* September 5, 2006, unrep., CA).

As to ADR in the Court of Appeal, see below, and CPR Pt 52.

For use of ADR procedures for purpose of resolving conflict of expert evidence in lease renewal claims, see commentary in para.56PD.7F.1.

For information on references to ADR in pre-action protocols and court guides, see below.

## 2. PREDOMINANCE OF MEDIATION AS AN ADR PROCEDURE

In relation to disputes of the varieties that might result in legal proceedings being threatened or commenced in a county court or in the High Court, the form of alternative process most likely to be suggested to a party is mediation. Many lawyers have received training in acting as mediators and in representing parties engaged in mediation. It is the ADR process with which judges are most familiar. It is the process most frequently urged on parties by judges managing cases who have become concerned about the direction that particular proceedings are taking (especially where costs look like far outstripping what is at stake). **14–16**

In most instances, where parties are working their way through pre-action protocols or endeavouring to comply with what rules, practice directions, and court guides say about ADR procedures, the particular procedure to which their attention will be led is mediation.

The Civil Justice Council has issued a document entitled "Judicial Referral to Mediation", see further para.14–28 below.

## 3. COSTS WHERE ADR DECLINED

The question as to when the court should impose a costs sanction against a successful litigant on the grounds that he has refused to take part in an alternative dispute resolution (ADR), referred to in *Dunnett v Railtrack Plc*, op cit, was considered by the Court of Appeal in *Halsey v Milton Keynes General NHS Trust* [2004] EWCA Civ 576; [2004] 1 W.L.R. 3002, CA. The court said the fundamental principle is that departure from the general rule (that the unsuccessful party should be ordered to pay the costs of the successful party) is not justified unless it is shown (the burden being on the unsuccessful party) that the successful party acted unreasonably in refusing to agree to ADR. The court gave guidance (see especially para.16) as to the factors that should be considered by the court in deciding whether a refusal to agree to ADR is unreasonable. See also *Reed Executive Plc v Reed Business Information Ltd* [2004] EWCA Civ 887; [2004] 1 W.L.R. 3026, CA; *Wills v Mills & Co Solicitors* [2005] EWCA Civ 591, May 3, 2005, unrep., CA; *Daniels v Commissioner of Police of the Metropolis* [2005] EWCA Civ 1312; *The Times*, October 28, 2005, CA; *Hickman v Blake Lapthorn* [2006] EWHC 12 (QB), January 17, 2006, unrep. (Jack J.) (reviewing the authorities and summarising the principles). This matter is dealt with in commentary following r.44.3 (court's discretion and circumstances to be taken into account when exercising discretion as to costs), in particular in para.44.3.13. In a given case it is quite conceivable that, before legal proceedings were commenced, the parties may have made a genuine but unsuccessful attempt to reach agreement on an ADR procedure or, indeed, may have participated in such a procedure in an unsuccessful (or only partly successful) effort to settle their dispute. The failures in these respects should not blind the parties or the court to the possibility that an opportunity may arise during the pre-trial process (or even on appeal) when an ADR procedure might yet be used to good effect. **14–17**

In *Société Internationale de Telecommunications Aeronautiques S.C. v Wyatt Co (UK) Ltd* [2002] EWHC 2401 (Ch)(Park J.) it was held that, in the circumstances, it was reasonable for a Pt 20 defendant to refuse to participate in a mediation between the claimant and the defendant (which led to a compromise), or a mediation between themselves and the claimant, offered by the claimant shortly before trial of the Pt 20 claim at which judgment was given in their favour, and therefore they should not be deprived of any part of their costs. Other cases in which the imposing of a costs sanction on a party for his failure to take up an offer of mediation was countenanced, and in some instances effected, include: *Hurst v Leeming* [2002] EWHC 1051 (Ch); [2003] 1 Lloyd's Rep. 379 (Lightman J.); *R. (Cowl) v Plymouth City Council* [2001] EWCA Civ 1935; [2002] 1 W.L.R. 803, CA; *Leicester Circuits Ltd v Coates Brothers Plc* [2003] EWCA Civ 333, March 5, 2003, unrep., CA. In *Reed Executive Plc v Reed Business Information Ltd* [2004] EWCA Civ 159 the Court of Appeal invited submissions on the relevance to the question of costs of the defendants' refusal of a number of offers to go to mediation. After noting that the defendants had engaged in serious settlement negotiations, Jacob L.J. said (para.167) that such negotiations were not the same as mediation as "a good and tough mediator can bring about a sense of commercial reality to both sides which their own lawyers, however good, may not be able to convey".

The Master of the Rolls' Birmingham Speech (see para.14–3, above) touched on a number of the points dealt with immediately above. The Master of the Rolls, commenting extensively on *Halsey*, argued that the court had power routinely to direct the parties to take part in mediation (see para.14–9 above). Additionally, he discouraged satellite litigation in respect of refusal to mediate cost penalties and expressly approved the finding in *Halsey* that the burden of showing that a successful party's refusal to mediate was unreasonable fell on the unsuccessful party (see para.14–11 above).

In *Vale of Glamorgan Council v Roberts* [2008] EWHC 2911 an unsuccessful litigant claimed costs against the successful defendant local authority. His application did not succeed. The court noted that the defendant had not positively suggested mediation and said that it would be going too far to disallow costs incurred by a local authority because that authority did not initiate suggestions for a mediation.

In *S v Chapman* [2008] EWCA Civ 800; [2008] E.L.R. 603; (2008) 152 S.J.L.B. 29 the court found that the defendant was entitled to await the outcome of its application to strike out before deciding whether or not it was either necessary or advantageous to enter into mediation of the substantive issues with the claimant. There was no reason to depart from the normal principle that costs followed the event.

It is often the case, where a party has refused mediation, that the court has a number of factors to consider, in relation to r.44.3(4)(a) and the parties' conduct, rather than (as in *Halsey*) the single issue of whether refusal was unreasonable. The overall nature of the court's discretion on costs can be seen in *Multiplex Construction (UK) Ltd v Cleveland Bridge (UK) Ltd* [2008] EWHC 2280, TCC where Jackson J. made a comprehensive review of costs authorities from which he derived (at para.72) eight principles. These included

> "(v) In many cases the judge can and should reflect the relative success of the parties on different issues by making a proportionate costs order"

and

> "(vi) In considering the circumstances of the case the judge will have regard not only to any part 36 offers made but also to each party's approach to negotiations (insofar as admissible) and general conduct of the litigation."

In two cases, *Whitecap Leisure Ltd v John H. Rundle Ltd* [2008] EWCA Civ 1026 and *Shah v Joshi* [2008] EWHC 1766 the court's overall approach to costs was seen. Features of the parties' conduct included the following. In *Whitecap*, the conduct of each party was described as having been as bad as the other, although one party's obdurate attitude was more striking than the other's conduct, and an offer of mediation was rejected as was a very favourable Pt 36 offer. In *Shah*, mediation was proposed but flatly rejected, as was a Calderbank offer. The parties did undertake mediation shortly before trial, but it was unsuccessful. On the first day of the trial, the judge emphasised to the parties the extreme desirability of a settlement but despite giving an extended adjournment to facilitate a settlement no agreement was reached. In *Whitecap* the court came to deal with costs and ordered that one party should recover only 80 per cent of its costs of the appeal and that the costs of the claim and the costs of the appeal should be set off against each other. In *Shah* an application for indemnity costs in respect of a successful claims and counterclaim was only granted in part; the court took into account all the circumstances, including the losing party's attitude at the time when the other party first proposed mediation. These cases perhaps demonstrate that if a party rejects an offer of mediation, or fails to give ADR adequate consideration when following a pre-action protocol or completing the allocation questionnaire, it will run the risk of an adverse costs order when costs are dealt with and the court considers the overall conduct of the litigation.

This was in fact the approach taken by the Court of Appeal in *Bray (t/a Building Co) v Bishop* 2009 WL 1657212 when it considered conduct in relation to costs and took into account a number of factors, including one party's rejection of a Pt 36 offer and the other's refusal to engage with a suggestion of mediation.

In *Roundstone Nurseries Ltd v Stephenson Holdings Ltd* [2009] EWHC 1431 (TCC); 2009 WL 2392342 mediation was not declined initially but one party unilaterally cancelled an imminent pre-action mediation. The TCC held that this was wrong, that it was an agreed part of the pre-action process in which that party was obliged to participate, and that the other party was entitled to its costs thrown away by the late cancellation (albeit on a standard, not indemnity, basis).

## 4. CONFIDENTIALITY, WITHOUT PREJUDICE AND "MEDIATION PRIVILEGE" IN RELATION TO MEDIATION

### (a) Privacy is important, but not without exceptions

It is very important, for reasons of public policy, that communications between parties to a mediation, and between those parties and the mediator, remain private and confidential. The courts will, generally, be ready to reinforce the cloak of confidentiality under which settlements are reached; **14–18**

> "communications made with a view to an amicable settlement ought to be held very sacred; for if parties were to be afterwards prejudiced by their efforts to compromise, it would be impossible to attempt an amicable arrangement of differences." (per Lord Scott, quoting Romilly M.R. in *Hoghton v Hoghton* (1852) 15 Beav 278, 321 when discussing the "without prejudice" rule in *Ofulue v Bossert* [2009] UKHL 16; [2009] 2 W.L.R. 749).

In the context of ADR, Dyson L.J. said in *Halsey v Milton Keynes General NHS Trust* [2004] EWCA Civ 576; [2004] 1 W.L.R. 3002 (at para.14):

> "...parties are entitled in an ADR to adopt whatever position they wish and if, as a result the dispute is not settled, that is not a matter for the court . . . . if the integrity and confidentiality of the process is to be respected, the court should not know, and therefore should not investigate, why the process did not result in agreement."

This statement is reinforced by Toulson and Phipps on Confidentiality (at para.15–016):

> "... it would destroy the basis of mediation if, in the case of the mediation failing, either party could publicise matters which had passed between themselves or between either of them and the mediator for the purposes of mediation ........."

Finally, in *Cumbria Waste Management Ltd and Lakeland Waste Management Ltd v Baines Wilson* [2008] EWHC 786 (QB), H.H.J. Kirkham said: "... the court should support the mediation process by refusing, in normal circumstances, to order disclosure of documents and communications within a mediation."

There are different ways in which mediation communications are protected and, as the cases mentioned below demonstrate, it can be important to differentiate between the concepts of confidentiality, "without prejudice", legal professional privilege, and (if it exists) "mediation privilege". The cloak of confidentiality is, in fact, multi-layered.

These cases will also demonstrate that, and again this is for reasons of public policy, confidentiality is not absolute and there are exceptions whereby a court may wish to examine mediation matters that usually remain private and confidential. Such exceptions are limited in nature and guarded by the court. Essentially, when considering whether matters in relation to a particular mediation should remain confidential, the court will usually be involved in a careful public policy balancing act, weighing the importance of encouraging parties to settle against, for example, some kind of impropriety.

The final paragraph in this section mentions some less obvious aspects relating to confidentiality.

Issues that relate to confidentiality in its broadest sense are of importance in various ways; they are relevant, for example, to lawyers advising a party before a mediation, to mediation providers when drafting agreements to mediate, to lawyers and mediators in relation to the conduct of a mediation and to lawyers and the courts when there are applications, post mediation, that the court should explore what took place at a mediation.

### *(b) Farm Assist 2*

14–18.1 In *Farm Assist Limited (in liquidation) v The Secretary of State for the Environment, Food and Rural Affairs (No.2)* [2009] EWHC 1102 (TCC) ("Farm Assist 2") the court gave guidance on these matters. It did so in the context of an application by a mediator to set aside a witness summons that was intended to require her to give evidence about what had taken place at a mediation. Having reviewed the authorities Ramsey J. gave the following summary of the different concepts or principles that are applied in the protection of the privacy of mediation:

> "(1) Confidentiality: The proceedings (at a mediation) are confidential both as between the parties and as between the parties and the mediator. As a result even if the parties agree that matters can be referred to outside the mediation, the mediator can enforce the confidentiality provision. The court will generally uphold that confidentiality but where it is necessary in the interests of justice for evidence to be given of confidential matters, the Courts will order or permit that evidence to be given or produced.
>
> (2) Without Prejudice Privilege: The proceedings are covered by without prejudice privilege. This is a privilege which exists as between the parties and is not a privilege of the mediator. The parties can waive that privilege.
>
> (3) Other Privileges: If another privilege attaches to documents which are produced by a party and shown to a mediator, that party retains that privilege and it is not waived by disclosure to the mediator or by waiver of the without prejudice privilege."

These three concepts of privilege will be explored in more detail below.

The mediator's application in this case to set aside the witness summons was dismissed for a number of reasons: the parties had, as they were entitled to do, waived the without prejudice privilege and, although the mediator was on the face of it entitled to enforce the confidentiality provision in the Mediation Agreement, it was held that this was "... a case where, as an exception, the interests of justice lie strongly in favour of evidence being given of what was said and done (at the mediation)." These findings, however, had no practical consequences as the mediator did not have any relevant notes or any recall of the issues; further, the case went on to settle in any event. *Farm Assist 2* has attracted the attention of mediators and has resulted in the publication by the Civil Mediation Council of "Civil Mediation Council Guidance Note No.1 Mediation Confidentiality" (see *http://www.civilmediation.org* [Accessed October 27, 2009]).

### *(c) Confidentiality*

14–18.2 As in *Farm Assist 2*, most agreements to mediate include clauses providing that, in addition to the mediation being conducted on a without prejudice basis, the parties and the mediator are required to treat the proceedings as confidential. In *Farm Assist 2* Ramsey J. also found that the confidentiality would have been implied, even if the mediation agreement had not agreed it expressly.

In concluding that the court can override such confidentiality, where it is necessary in the interests of justice, the court in *Farm Assist 2* took into account on the following passage in *Confidentiality* by Toulson and Phipps:

> "Generally speaking, confidentiality is not a bar to disclosure of documents or information in the process of litigation, but the court will only compel such disclosure if it considers it necessary for the fair disposal of the case: see. . . . *British Steel Corporation v Granada Television Ltd* [1981] A.C. 1096 " (para.17–001).

***Paragraph numbers marked with a "+" can be found online and on CD.***

If there is an explicit agreement on confidentiality it will, as with any other type of agreement, fall to be construed by the court. In *Farm Assist 2* the confidentiality provisions were narrowly drawn and not as wide as the mediator might have wished.

Another particular point clarified by this case was the finding that the mediator could enforce the provisions relating to confidentiality, as against the parties. This means that where, as in *Farm Assist 2*, the parties have waived without prejudice privilege the mediator may nevertheless be able to require that confidentiality will be maintained.

Where there is a risk that a party may act in breach of the agreement that proceedings at a mediation be kept confidential he may be restrained by an injunction (*Venture Investment Placement Ltd v Hall* [2005] EWHC 1227 (Ch); [2005] All E.R. (D) 224 and *David Instance v Denny Brothers Printing Ltd* [2000] F.S.R. 869.

### (d) Without Prejudice

It is apparent, from the analysis in *Farm Assist 2*, that part of the mediation cloak of confidentiality is based on without prejudice privilege, and that such privilege can be waived by the parties. For a fuller statement of the without prejudice rule or concept see *Cutts v Head* [1984] Ch. 290; [1984] 1 All E.R. 597, CA; *Unilever plc v The Proctor & Gamble Co* [2000] 1 W.L.R. 2436; [2001] 1 All E.R. 783;*Muller v Linsley & Mortimer* [1996] P.N.L.R. 74 and Vol.1, para.31.3.40 below. There are, however, exceptions to this privilege (helpfully summarised by Robert Walker L.J. in *Unilever* [2000] 1 W.L.R. 2444) which are of importance in the context of mediation and ADR. A number of these exceptions, which are largely based on public policy and the better administration of justice, appear in the following cases. **14–18.3**

In *Muller*, the claimant's initial claim had been against his fellow shareholders in a private company following his dismissal as a director of that company. He settled that claim following without prejudice correspondence. Subsequently, he sued the solicitors who had advised him in the initial claim, alleging negligence. It was held that the without prejudice correspondence in the initial claim was disclosable in the subsequent claim. The public policy reasons that would have applied to prevent disclosure in the initial claim did not apply in the context of the subsequent claim: any without prejudice statements or offers made in the initial claim were kept from the court, in that claim, lest they be treated as an admission of liability. Once that claim has been concluded, however, that reason fell away. (See Vol.1, para.35.12.3 and also *Bradford and Bingley v Rashid* [2006] 1 W.L.R. 2066).

The decision in *Muller* seems applicable in circumstances where there is a subsequent claim following an earlier claim and there are relevant mediation communications in the earlier claim that do, on the face of it, appear to be subject to without prejudice privilege. This was the finding in *Cattley v Pollard* [2007] EWHC 1310 (Ch). There the claimants in the initial action were the executors of an estate who sued various defendants, including the solicitors acting in the estate, for misappropriation of estate funds. A settlement was reached at a successful mediation involving some of the defendants. A subsequent action was bought by the claimants against one of the defendants in the initial action who had not been involved in the mediated settlement. The defendant in this subsequent action was concerned about the issue of double recovery by the claimants and sought disclosure of mediation documents. The defendants resisted disclosure, arguing that mediations will not succeed if confidentiality is broken. The court held, following *Muller* and taking account of the overriding objective to deal justly with cases, that there should be disclosure limited to such parts of the mediation bundle as were factually material to the defendant's argument relating to double recovery.

In *Cumbria Waste Management Ltd and Lakeland Waste Management Ltd v Baines Wilson* [2008] EWHC 786 (QB), however, the court found that Muller did not apply and refused to order disclosure of confidential mediation documents for the purposes of a subsequent action. The parties to the mediation did not waive privilege and the court held that the documents should remain privileged, both on the basis that they were subject to without prejudice privilege and were confidential by virtue of the agreement to mediate. H.H.J. Kirkham said that the court should support the mediation process by refusing, in normal circumstances, to order disclosure of documents and communications within a mediation. The court found that the disclosure sought here did not fall within the exception to the without prejudice rule set out in *Muller* and, further, noted that the court in *Muller* gave no consideration to the position of third parties.

ADR

***Paragraph numbers marked with a "+" can be found online and on CD.***

*Muller* and the applicability of the without prejudice rule fell to be considered by the House of Lords in *Ofulue v Bossert* [2009] UKHL 16; [2009] 2 W.L.R. 749. This property case concerned two sets of proceedings between the same parties and, in particular, without prejudice negotiations between the parties during the first set of proceedings. The House of Lords said that the without prejudice rule was based on both the public policy of encouraging the negotiated settlement of actions and the express or implied agreement of the parties that communications in the course of such negotiations should not be admissible in evidence. It was held that the rule did extend to without prejudice negotiations conducted during earlier proceedings involving an issue which was still unresolved. The court further found that, although there were exceptions to the rule where justice required it, as where it was necessary to prevent the rule being used to further impropriety, reasons of legal and practical certainty made it inappropriate to create a further exception to limit the protection to identifiable admissions. Lord Hope referred to Ormrod J.'s words in *Tomlin v Standard Telephones & Cables Ltd* [1969] 1 W.L.R. 1378 when he said that the court should be very slow to lift the without prejudice umbrella unless the case for doing so is absolutely plain. Lord Neuberger explained that if the House of Lords created further exceptions to the without prejudice rule this would severely risk hampering the freedom parties should feel when entering into settlement negotiations.

Another well established exception to the without prejudice rule is that it does not prevent the admission in evidence of what parties said to one another when the issue is whether or not such communications resulted in a concluded settlement agreement (see Vol.1, para.31.3.40 below). At the trial of such issue, the fact that such communications took place between the parties at a mediation does not confer on them a status distinct from any other without prejudice communications sufficient to take them outside the scope of the exception or otherwise to render them inadmissible (*Brown v Rice and Patel* [2007] EWHC 625 (Ch).

As seen in *Farm Assist 2*, parties can waive their entitlement to without prejudice confidentiality and did so in *Chantry Vellacott v Convergence Group* [2007] EWHC 1774 and *Earl of Malmesbury v Strutt & Parker* [2008] EWHC 424 (QB). In the latter case Jack J. made adverse findings in relation to a party's recovery of costs on the basis of that party's conduct during a mediation. He said that " . the claimant's position at the mediation was plainly unrealistic and unreasonable" and found that, had they made an offer which truly reflected their position, the mediation might have succeeded. Subsequently, however, the Master of the Rolls seemed to disapprove of this approach on the basis that it might lead to satellite litigation (see para.19 of the Master of the Rolls' Birmingham Speech referred to in para.14–3 above.)

Note, however, that without prejudice privilege is effectively regarded as a joint privilege and cannot be waived by one party alone (see *Somatra Ltd v Sinclair Roche & Temperley* [2000] 1 W.L.R. 2453; [2000] 2 Lloyd's Rep. 673, referred to in Vol.1 at para.31.3.40).

In *Smiths Group v Weiss* [2002] LTL 22/3/2002, the court followed *Somatra* (see above) when considering whether material, prepared for a mediation that did not result in a settlement, should retain its without prejudice status. It was held that the material should remain without prejudice save in clear and unequivocal circumstances. The court had to consider whether in all the circumstances it was fair and just to allow a party to rely on the material.

Where the court directs under r.35.12 that there should be a discussion between experts and that they must prepare a statement for the court, any such statement is available for use in the proceedings and is not protected by the without prejudice privilege (see Vol.1, para.35.12.3 below). Consequently, where a mediation takes place after such order, it cannot be argued in subsequent proceedings before the court that the statement cannot be referred to, even though the direction was made by the court with an eye to assisting a contemplated mediation (*Aird v Prime Meridian Ltd* [2006] EWCA Civ 1866; *The Times*, February 14, 2007 CA).

In *Farm Assist Ltd v Secretary of State* [2008] EWHC 3079 (the precursor to *Farm Assist 2*) the issue concerned legal advice privilege rather than the without prejudice concept. Party 1 sought to set aside the agreement resulting from a mediation on account of duress by party 2. Party 2 said that, as the allegations about duress went to party 1's state of mind, it should be able to see the (usually privileged) documents containing the legal advice to party 1. It was held that disclosure be refused, there having been no waiver of legal advice privilege.

### (e) Mediation Privilege

In *Farm Assist 2* Ramsey J., having considered "other privileges" (see (3) in 14–18.1 above), noted that in Brown & Marriott *ADR Principles and Practice* the authors discuss the possible existence of and desirability for a distinct privilege attaching to the mediation process: **14–18.4**

> "It remains to be resolved definitively by the English Courts (if not by the legislature) whether there is a privilege attaching to the whole mediation process, including all communications passing within that process, whether the mediation relates to family matters, civil or commercial disputes or any other kind of issue" (para.22–088, 2nd edition).

He went on to canvass the "… the need for a further 'privilege' which arises other than the Mediator's right to confidentiality in relation to the mediation proceedings." In *Brown v Rice* [2007] EWHC 625 the court commented, although it did not have to make a finding on the point, that: "It may be in the future that the existence of a distinct mediation privilege will require to be considered by either the legislature or the courts …"

Mr Justice Briggs has written on "Mediation Privilege?" in an authoritative two part review in the New Law Journal (159 N.L.J. 506 and 159 N.L.J. 550). Having reviewed the various concepts of privilege in relation to mediation he goes on to develop a potential common law solution. This is based on a distinction between the facts that:

> "a mediator will act as a conduit for the sharing of such information between the parties as is commonly shared in without prejudice negotiations: (shared information)"

and

> "the important part of the mediator's facilitative role (which) is to encourage the parties to share with him or her information, views, hopes and fears about the dispute which the party communicating them does not wish the other party to know, and which the mediator agrees to keep secret from the other party (mediator secrets)."

His thesis likens Mediator Secrets to legal professional privilege, on the basis that parties to disputes should be able to unburden themselves with absolute frankness to a mediator in the same way as with their legal advisers, and to argue that public policy may justify a new privilege strictly limited to Mediator Secrets. He adds that such a privilege would not be likely to interfere with the application to Shared Information in mediation of the recognised exceptions to the without prejudice principle, as occurred in both *Brown* and *Cattley*. Mr Justice Briggs supports the idea of a new privilege by referring to the ability of the common law to recognise a new form of privilege, where, in a new context, the public interest so requires, pointing out that a distinct form of non-status based privilege, in connection with matrimonial conciliation relating to children, has recently been recognised: see *Re D (Minors) (Conciliation: Disclosure of Information)* [1993] Fam 231 at 238. He concludes:

> "There is in principle therefore good reason why the courts should now recognise that the undoubted public interest in facilitating the process of mediation as a desirable and often preferable means of dispute resolution, by comparison with the full panoply of a trial, justifies the identification of a narrow form of mediator secret privilege of the type described above. There is no reason why a party to a mediation should not be encouraged to be as frank with the mediator as with his or her legal adviser. The similarity with the underlying justification for legal professional privilege is therefore very close."

Mr Justice Briggs' call for a development in this area is made all the more timely by virtue of the fact that the EU Mediation Directive (Directive 2008/52/EC of the European Parliament and of the Council of 21 May 2008 on certain aspects of mediation in civil and commercial matters) carries the requirement that it be complied with by May 2011. By art.7 of the Directive member states must ensure that, with reference to cross-border mediation, mediators must not be compellable to give evidence in civil proceedings or arbitration regarding information arising out of or in connection with a mediation, except where overriding considerations of public policy otherwise require, or where disclosure of the content of the mediation settlement agreement is necessary in order to implement or enforce it.

***Paragraph numbers marked with a "+" can be found online and on CD.***

### (f) Other aspects relating to confidentiality

**14–18.5** There are other ways in which mediation confidentiality may be called into question and a number of these are dealt with in "Mediator Confidentiality—Conduct and Communications" by Burnley and Lascelles (see *http://www.cedr.co.uk/library/articles/Mediator_confidentiality_SJBerwin.pdf* [Accessed October 27, 2009]).These include, for example, money laundering (Proceeds of Crime Act 2002), breaches of professional conduct, insolvency proceedings in circumstances where the court reserves the power to veto settlement agreements and, arguably, a mediation settlement involving a minor where court approval is required. Other examples might possibly include applications of the Data Protection Act and the Freedom of Information Act.

## 5. MEDIATION COSTS—RECOVERABILITY

**14–19** There are three important points regarding the recoverability of mediation costs (both the fees paid to the mediator and the costs and disbursements in preparing for and attending mediation) that need to be considered before a mediation takes place. The first concerns the provisions regarding costs in the mediation agreement (that is, the agreement which forms the contractual basis under which the mediation takes place), the second relates to recoverability generally and the third is concerned with the costs of mediations which take place pre-proceedings.

The costs provisions in a mediation agreement were considered in *National Westminster Bank Plc v Thomas Feeney and Linda Feeney* [2006] EWHC 90066 (Costs) and [2007] (Costs Appeal). Eady J. held that the successful party could not recover the mediator's costs or its costs for preparing for and attending at the mediation because: (a) the mediation agreement entered in to by the parties on the mediation provider's standard terms was on the basis that the mediator's fee would be borne equally by the parties who would bear their own costs; (b) the Tomlin Order agreed when settlement was reached did not deal explicitly with the costs of the mediation; and (c) it was held that the Tomlin Order did not alter the mediation agreement. This approach was followed in *Lobster Group Ltd v Heidelberg Graphic Equipment Ltd* [2008] EWHC 413.

Subject to the provisions of the mediation agreement, mediation costs are, on the face of it, recoverable. In *Feeney*, Eady J. said that: "as a matter of general principle, costs incurred in a mediation would form part of the costs of the action just as any reasonable costs of negotiation would (see Costs Practice Direction para.4.6(8))."

Whether mediation costs are recoverable in pre proceedings mediations, however, appears to depend on both the provisions of the mediation agreement (see above) and whether or not the mediation took place as part of the pre-action protocol work.This is important, because, in accordance with the pre-action protocols, mediations are increasingly carried out pre-proceedings. The cases dealing with this issue have involved the construction of s.51 of the Senior Courts Act 1981. In *Lobster* Coulson J. was considering mediation costs as one aspect of an application for security for costs and he put forward a number of reasons for his view that the costs of the pre-action mediation were not recoverable:

> "16. First, unlike the costs incurred in a pre-action protocol, I do not believe that the costs of a separate pre-action mediation can ordinarily be described as 'costs of and incidental to the proceedings' (pursuant to s.51 of the Senior Courts Act 1981). On the contrary, it seems to me clear that they are not. They are the costs incurred in pursuing a valid method of alternative dispute resolution. Those costs were incurred in a form of dispute resolution which had no connection to these proceedings, and which here took place 2.5 years before the proceedings even started."

In *McGlinn v Waltham Contractors Ltd* [2005] EWHC 1419 (TCC); [2005] All E.R. 1126 Judge Peter Coulson Q.C. had also considered s.51 of the Senior Courts Act. He held that, although costs in respect of claims dropped by a claimant prior to the commencement of proceedings were not, in unexceptional circumstances, capable of amounting to costs "incidental" to the proceedings, the costs incurred in complying with a Pre-Action Protocol may be recoverable as costs "incidental to" any subsequent proceedings. Further, in *Roundstone Nurseries Ltd v Stephenson Holdings Ltd* [2009] EWHC 1431 (TCC); 2009 WL 2392342 the court, noting that a pre proceedings mediation was treated by the parties as an integral part of the pre-action protocol work, applied *McGlinn* and held that, as a matter of principle, costs incurred during

***Paragraph numbers marked with a "+" can be found online and on CD.***

the pre-action protocol process could be recovered as costs incidental to the litigation. The court did confirm that the costs of a separate, stand-alone pre-proceedings mediation or ADR process would not usually form part of the costs of, or incidental to, litigation and would not, therefore, be recoverable.

See also *Earl of Malmesbury v Strutt & Parker* [2008] EWHC 424 (QB) and the comments thereon in paras 14–11 and 14–18 above regarding costs sanctions in relation to conduct at a mediation.

### 6. MISCELLANEOUS MATTERS

Where the parties freely consent to arbitration there is unlikely to be a denial of access to a court within the meaning of ECHR, art.6(1): *Deweer v Belgium* (1979–1980) 2 E.H.R.R. 439; *Axelsson v Sweden* No.11960/86, decision of July 13, 1990, unrep., EComHR; *Pastore v Italy* No.46483/99, May 25, 1999, unrep., ECtHR, 2nd chamber. The key is the absence of restraint: *ibid*. Where the court was excessively forceful in its encouragement of the use of ADR, ECHR art.6(1) might be engaged. Any waiver of art.6 rights must be unequivocal: *Zumtobel v Austria* (1994) 17 E.H.R.R. 116; *Rolf Gustafson v Sweden* (1998) 25 E.H.R.R. 623. **14–20**

For the enforcement of a contractual ADR clause and comparison with an arbitration clause, see *Cable & Wireless Plc v IBM United Kingdom Ltd* [2003] EWHC 316; [2002] All E.R. (D) 277 (Colman J.).

Routinely, the courts will exercise their inherent jurisdiction to stay legal proceedings where there is an extant arbitration clause, in effect enforcing the agreement to arbitrate the dispute. It would appear that the English courts may be edging towards the position that they should exercise their jurisdiction to stay legal proceedings where there is an agreement between the parties to negotiate or mediate (albeit an agreement that is lacking in the certainty traditionally regarded as necessary for enforceability and perhaps even non-binding) (ibid.; cf., *Halifax Financial Services Ltd v Intuitive Systems Ltd* [1999] 1 All E.R. (Comm) 303 (McKinnon J.)). See further Vol.2, paras 9A–176 to 9A–177. See also *Ardentia Ltd v British Telecommunications Plc* [2008] EWHC 2111 where one of the parties commenced proceedings before a tiered dispute resolution procedure had been exhausted. The procedure made an exception to the bar on commencing proceedings where, as was the case, interim relief was sought from the court. The court, however, having granted interim relief, then stayed the matter to enable the other issues between the parties to be dealt with under the procedure.

## C. ADR IN PRE-ACTION PROTOCOLS AND COURT GUIDES

### 1. ADR IN PROTOCOLS

Pre-action conduct is dealt with by Practice Direction—Pre-Action Conduct, as amended in April 2009 (para.C1–001) and the various pre-action protocols listed below. Section II of the Practice Direction is general in its application, whereas Section III deals with the conduct of cases that are not subject to a pre-action protocol (paras 2.3 and 2.4). The Practice Direction reinforces the role of ADR. The aims of the Practice Direction are stated, in para.1, to include enabling the parties to settle without needing to commence proceedings. Parties are to be encouraged to do this by exchanging information and considering using a form of ADR. Paragraph 4 (which falls within Section II and is therefore of general application) deals with parties' compliance with both the Practice Direction and the pre-action protocols and goes on, at para.4.3, to state that one example of non-compliance is a party's unreasonable refusal to consider ADR. **14–21**

The new para.8 (which falls within Section III and therefore deals with the cases that are not subject to a pre-action protocol) commences with the mantra that starting proceedings should usually be a step of last resort and is one that should not normally be taken when settlement is being actively explored. Parties are warned that the court may require evidence that parties considered some form of ADR (paras 8.1 and 4.4(3)). ADR is defined (para.8.2) so as to include discussion and negotiation, mediation, early neutral evaluation and arbitration. Parties are also reminded that the duty to consider the possibility of reaching a settlement at all times is a continuing one that applies af-

***Paragraph numbers marked with a "+" can be found online and on CD.***



ADR

ter the commencement of proceedings and up to and during any final hearing (para.8.4).

The several pre-action protocols all refer to ADR. In each of them (with two exceptions), reference is made to the LSC booklet entitled "Alternatives to Court" available at *http://www.communitylegaladvice.org.uk/media/656/13/leaflet23e.pdf* [Accessed October 27, 2009] (see also Practice Direction (Protocols) para.4.7) (see further below).

Also, in each of them (again with two exceptions) it is stated and emphasised as follows: "It is expressly recognised that no party can or should be forced to mediate or enter into any form of ADR". (This "health-warning" reflects the decision of the Court of Appeal in *Halsey v Milton Keynes General NHS Trust* [2004] EWCA Civ 576; [2004] 1 W.L.R. 3002, CA although this should now be read in conjunction with the Master of the Rolls' Birmingham Speech (see paras 14–3 and 14–9 above)).

The several protocols are distinguished by the fact that each covers distinctive forms of civil proceedings. Obviously, parties in person and the legal representatives of parties engaged in such proceedings are well advised to read carefully what is said about ADR in the appropriate protocol. (In some forms of proceedings arising out of commercial transactions methods of pre-action resolution are well established and habitually used by parties falling into dispute and the relevant pre-action protocols take account of that.)

The references to ADR in the several protocols are as follows (for complete texts, see Vol.1, Section C (Pre-Action Protocols)):

- *Pre-Action Protocol for Personal Injury Claims*, paras 2.16 to 2.19;
- *Pre-Action Protocol for the Resolution of Clinical Disputes*, paras 5.1 to 5.4;
- *Pre-Action Protocol for Construction and Engineering Disputes*, paras 5.1 to 5.7;
- *Pre-Action Protocol for Defamation*, paras 3.7 to 3.9;
- *Professional Negligence Pre-action Protocol*, paras B6.1 to B6.4 and C3.1 to C3.3;
- *Pre-Action Protocol for Judicial Review*, paras 3.1 to 3.4;
- *Pre-action Protocols for Disease and Illness Claims*, paras 2A.1 to 2A.4;
- *Pre-Action Protocol for Housing Disrepair Claims*, para.4.1;
- *Pre-Action Protocol for Possession Claims Based on Rent Arrears*, para.11;
- *Pre-Action Protocol for Possession Claims (Mortgage)*, paras 7 and 8.

### 2. ADR IN COURT GUIDES

**14–22** Several Court Guides make reference to ADR procedures. To an extent the Guides repeat what is said in CPR provisions and in practice directions. Necessarily, the Court Guides are more broadly focussed than the pre-action protocols and refer to the application of ADR procedures in claims falling across the court's jurisdiction. However, parties in person and the legal representatives of parties engaged in proceedings before those courts that have issued Court Guides are well advised to read carefully what is said about ADR, particularly if they are unfamiliar with the subject. The jurisdiction of the TCC is more specific than the other courts and the coverage of ADR procedures in that Guide is rather more detailed than that provided in the other Guides (see further "ADR in Technology and Construction Court", below). References to ADR in the Court Guides are as follows (for complete texts, see Section 1 (Court Guides) and Section 2 (Specialist Proceedings) above):

- *Chancery Guide*, Ch.17 (Alternative Dispute Resolution) paras 17.1 to 17.6;
- *Queen's Bench Guide*, Section 6 (Preliminary Case Management) para.6.6 (ADR);
- *Admiralty and Commercial Courts Guide*, Section G1 (Alternative Dispute Resolution), G2 (Early neutral evaluation), and App.7 Draft ADR Order. See also the Commercial Court working party report on long trials, which includes a number of provisions about ADR at *http://www.judiciary.gov.uk/docs/rep_comm_wrkg_party_long_trials.pdf* [Accessed October 27, 2009];
- *Technology and Construction Court Guide*, Section 7 (Alternative Dispute Resolution and ENE) paras 7.1 to 7.5), Section 8 (Preliminary Issues) para.8.5 (Use of PI (Preliminary Issues) as an adjunct to ADR), and App.E (Draft ADR Order).

## D. ADR IN PARTICULAR COURTS

### 1. ADR IN TECHNOLOGY AND CONSTRUCTION COURT

**14–23** Proceedings in the TCC are governed by the CPR and the practice directions supplementing those rules. Consequently, provisions in those legal sources relating to ADR apply to proceedings in the TCC. CPR Pt 60 and the practice direction supplementing that Part, that is, Practice Direction—Technology and Construction Court Claims (60PD), deal specifically with the practice and procedure of the TCC but contain no express provisions concerning ADR. However, in Section A of the Case Management Information Sheet (CM1), attached to 60PD as Appendix A, the parties are asked whether they wish there to be a one month stay to settle the claim either by informal discussion or ADR (see CPR r.26.4) and the Notes for this section refer parties to the LSC Leaflet for further information on ADR.

The Pre-Action Protocol for Construction and Engineering Disputes (see Vol.1, para.C5–001) provides for a pre-action meeting of the parties for the purpose of determining the main issues between them and to consider whether, and if so, how the issues might be resolved without recourse to litigation (para.5.2). In respect of each issue, the parties should consider whether some form of ADR procedure would be more suitable than litigation, and if so, endeavour to agree which form to adopt (para.5.4). In itself, this meeting may be regarded as a form of ADR as it provides an opportunity for the parties to negotiate a settlement.

Section 7 of the Technology and Construction Court Guide (see para.2C–85 above) is rather more forthcoming on the matter of ADR than are the rules, the practice direction or the pre-action protocol. That Section contains detailed information on the likely approach that the court will take in a given case in an attempt to encourage the parties to use ADR and to facilitate the use of such procedure (CPR r.1.4(2)(e)). The Section also contains information about early neutral evaluation (ENE). A draft order for ADR or ENE is attached to this Court Guide as Appendix E. In para.7.2.2 it is explained that, where a pre-action meeting has been held in accordance with the Protocol, the court will not necessarily grant a one month stay of proceedings upon demand.

In Section 8 of the Guide (Preliminary Issues) reference is made to, and guidance is given on, the situation in which the parties wish to resolve their dispute by ADR, but there is one major issue which is a sticking point in any negotiation or mediation and upon which the parties wish to obtain the court's decision in the expectation that, after that, they will be able to resolve their difference without further recourse to the court.

Paragraph 7.3.4 of the Guide states that parties and their advisers may obtain information as to the types of ADR procedures available, and about third parties able to undertake such procedures, from some TCC court centres outside London, and, in addition, from certain organisations. Three organisations are mentioned; viz. the Technology & Construction Solicitors Association (TeCSA), the Technology & Construction Bar Association (TECBAR), and the Civil Mediation Council (CMC) (see further "ADR Providers" at para.14–27 below).

In 2006, the TCC introduced as a pilot scheme involving TCC judges in London, a process, known as the Court Settlement Process, for those situations where a case managing judge feels, either of his own volition or following a request from parties, that the parties should be able to achieve an amicable settlement and that the judge is particularly able to assist in achieving that settlement. In effect, under the process judges are able to offer their services as mediators. (For further information and a reference to nine cases having been mediated, see *http://www.tecsa.org.uk/mediation_adr-1328.htm* [Accessed October 27, 2009]). (Under the Arbitration Act 1996 s.93(1) TCC judges may act as arbitrators; see further Court Guide Section 18.)

## 2. MEDIATION IN COUNTY COURTS

When court-based mediation began to be introduced in some of the larger county courts (such as Central London and Birmingham), it was targeted at cases in the fast and multi tracks, where parties are generally represented and legal costs likely to be significant. In developing court based schemes, Her Majesty's Courts Service (HMCS) worked in partnership with a number of commercial mediation providers to set up time-limited and relatively low cost mediation services. **14–24**

However, it became clear to HMCS that only the largest courts would be able to establish their own mediation schemes—many courts were simply too small to be able to provide the administrative support necessary to manage a court-based scheme. Consequently, towards the end of 2004, HMCS set up the National Mediation Helpline (NMH). The NMH provides court users (and members of the public) with access to information about mediation. The service is accessed by telephone (0845 603 0809) or by the website (*http://www.nationalmediationhelpline.com* [Accessed October 27, 2009]).

From April 2006, the National Mediation Helpline was reconfigured into 42 area panels to coincide with the then 42 HMCS geographical areas. Each of those area panels was served by a mix of local, regional as well as national mediation providers who had been accredited by the Civil Mediation Council. (Civil Mediation Council accredited providers are listed at: *http://www.civilmediation.org/files/pdf/List%20of%20Organisations.pdf* [Accessed October 27, 2009].) Using the structure that the Helpline provided, HMCS then developed a best-practice Mediation Service Toolkit. This Toolkit enables courts to offer a mediation service to all court users—it has all the benefits of an individual court scheme, but with real economies of scale achieved through centralising much of the administration.

While the above services are primarily aimed at fast and multi track disputes, the vast majority of hearings in the courts are small claims below £5000. HMCS took the view that since it can cost as little as £30 to issue a small claim in the courts, it was unrealistic to expect small claims users to pay for mediation. HMCS therefore piloted a number of potential new mediation services—aimed at lower cost disputes—that were free to users. A number of different pilots were set up and evaluated in 2005/06. The in-house mediation service at Manchester County Court was shown to be the most effective, demonstrating the highest levels of both settlement and customer satisfaction. HMCS extended the service, now called the Small Claims Mediation Service, to all court users during 2007/2008. The service has become the largest single mediation service in the UK, with 5,097 mediations conducted in the year to July 2008, and was recognised in the 2008 CEDR Awards for Excellence. A survey in 2008 found that 98 per cent of users were satisfied with the professionalism and helpfulness of the mediators. 94 per cent of users said that they would use the service again.

### 3. COURT OF APPEAL MEDIATION SCHEME (CAMS)

**14–25** Information about mediation in cases pending or proceeding in the Court of Appeal (Civil Division) is found on the Court of Appeal website (*http://www.hmcourts-service.gov.uk/cms/civilappeals.htm*) [Accessed October 27, 2009]; click on "Mediation".

It is explained there that the court has a mediation scheme for non-family work administered by CEDR Solve (Centre for Effective Dispute Resolution: *http://www.cedr.com* [Accessed October 27, 2009]). The scheme was introduced in March 2003, following upon the decision of the court in *Dunnett v Railtrack Plc* [2002] EWCA Civ 303; [2002] 1 W.L.R. 2434, CA, and replaced a previous scheme initiated in 1996.

When an application is made to the court for permission to appeal, the single lord justice considers whether the matter is suitable for mediation. If so, the Head of the Civil Appeals Office, sends details of the case to CEDR. The full court may also propose mediation where there are outstanding issues and a possibility of further court proceedings. It is requested that, where a recommendation for ADR is given at an oral hearing, the appropriate Case Lawyer in the court could be informed as soon as possible so that the recommendation can be taken forward by the court's relevant Case Management Group.

Under the scheme, upon being informed, CEDR writes directly to the parties seeking agreement to arrange a mediation hearing. Participation in the scheme is voluntary and a mediation will only proceed if all parties agree. Parties are offered a choice from three mediators suggested by CEDR and selected from a panel. The court remains responsible for the composition of the panel. The panel includes mediators from a varied range of disciplines including Commercial, Personal Injury, Insurance, Shipping, Employment, Intellectual Property, etc. If the mediation proceeds, CEDR is responsible for preparing the mediation agreement and liaising with the parties over the mediation arrangements. Parties are free to terminate the mediation by informing the Civil Appeals Office or CEDR at any time without giving any reason.

The court is also responsible for any adjustment to the fees payable to mediators. Fees for mediation and case management are paid for by those using the scheme but, where a party cannot afford the fees, the service is provided pro bono.

Family mediations are administered and monitored by the Civil Appeals Office which will appoint a suitable mediator from mediation panels provided by the Law Society and Resolution.

# E. ACCESS TO MEDIATION ADVICE AND SERVICES

## 1. ADVICE ON MEDIATION—WHEN DOES MEDIATION WORK?

Much has been written about (1) the circumstances in which the resolution of a particular dispute might be better pursued through a process other than that of commencing civil proceedings in a county court or in the High Court, and (2) the circumstances in which the whole or part of a claim proceeding in a trial court or an appeal court might be referred to an alternative process. **14–26**

There was a time when advice to, and information for, parties in person, or for their advisers and representatives (legal and otherwise) assisting them, as to whether, when and how, a particular dispute or part thereof might be referred to an alternative process rather than further pursued through court processes, was difficult to come by. Nowadays, the reverse is true. There is a surfeit of such information. However, this abundance has brought its own problems.

Sometimes, the advice available to parties and their advisers and representatives is couched in terms of answers, usually in the forms of lists, to crude questions that, conceivably, a party or representative might ask. In relation to mediation such questions are, for example, when does (does not) mediation work?, what are the advantages (disadvantages) of using (not using) mediation?, what kinds of disputes are appropriate (inappropriate) for mediation? The difficulty with these accounts is that they try to say too much. The range of civil proceedings that can be brought in the county courts and the High Court is enormous, and the extent to which the legal and factual complexities of cases, and the issues at stake (both in terms of amount and importance) in them, can differ hugely. Further, not all disputes are static; even in a case of moderate complexity, what the parties are arguing about today might bear little resemblance to what they were at odds about three months ago (raising the vexed question of "timing"). This means that, in relation to one particular dispute when contrasted with another similar in certain respects (e.g. both might be a dispute damages for breach of contract), quite different answers to the questions above might be given.

For parties in person, and advisers and representatives (both legal and other) to parties, in need of introductory advice on the suitability of ADR procedures, in particular mediation, for the particular matter in which they are engaged are themselves best advised to consult an Internet website dedicated to providing such help. The following may be suggested (see further "Mediation service providers" below):

- ***Her Majesty's Courts Service*** *http://www.hmcourts-service.gov.uk/cms/7770.htm* [Accessed October 27, 2009];
- ***ADRnow*** *http://www.adrnow.org.uk* [Accessed October 27, 2009].

## 2. MEDIATION SERVICE PROVIDERS

There are many organisations holding themselves out as willing and able to provide mediation services. Indeed, there is a bewildering array of them. There are some organisations that limit their activities to providing guidance on the attributes of service providers. Parties in person, and advisers and representatives (both legal and other) to parties, wishing to investigate the possibility of engaging the services of a mediator will need to be assured that they are engaging a suitably qualified person, on the right terms, and that the mediation will administered properly. **14–27**

Paragraph 4.7 of Practice Direction (Protocols) and the several Pre-Action Protocols refer to CLS Direct Information Leaflet 23 "Alternatives to Court" (Aug 06), principally (it would seem) for directing parties contemplating legal proceedings and making use of the Protocols to organisations that provide ADR services. See *http://www.communitylegaladvice.org.uk/en/legalhelp/leaflet23_15.jsp* [Accessed October 27, 2009].

This leaflet covers a very wide range of disputes which may afflict the ordinary member of the public, and contains a lot of information about the various forms of dispute resolution and special schemes for particular kinds of dispute, including many that are very unlikely to result in court proceedings. The information on providers of dispute resolution services is not particularly well-suited for parties who are involved in legal disputes of the type covered by the Protocols and who have reached the point where engaging in mediation should be considered seriously.

***Paragraph numbers marked with a "+" can be found online and on CD.***

In the Admiralty and Commercial Courts Guide, para.G1.9, and in the Queen's Bench Guide, para.6.6.3, it is explained that the Clerk to the Commercial Court keeps some published information on individuals and bodies that offer ADR and arbitration services. The same point is made in the Chancery Guide (para.17.6) where it is further said that, if the parties are unable to agree upon a neutral individual, or panel of individuals for ADR, they may refer to the judge for assistance, though the court will not recommend any particular body or individual to act as mediator or arbitrator.

Organisations willing and able to provide mediation services, or to direct inquires to such organisations, and which are referred to in information provided by Her Majesty's Courts Service and in Court Guides (some of which have been referred to already above) are listed below.

- ***National Mediation Helpline (NMH)*** *http://www.nationalmediationhelpline.com* [Accessed October 27, 2009]

  See further, "Mediation in county courts", at para.14–24 above.
- ***ADRnow*** *http://www.adrnow.org.uk* [Accessed October 27, 2009]

  On July 8, 2004, the Advice Services Alliance (ASA) (an umbrella organisation for independent advice services in the UK) launched ADRnow, a website devoted to ADR. This site contains information about all kinds of ADR processes, and has links to mediation providers and ombudsmen schemes throughout the UK. The aim of the website is to provide an independent overview of a wide range of ADR options. The information is directed, not only at parties who may or might be engaged in legal proceedings, but also at their advisers and representatives.
- ***Civil Mediation Council*** *http://www.civilmediation.org* [Accessed October 27, 2009]

  The CMC was founded in April 2003 to represent the common interests of mediation providers and mediators in promoting mediation, setting standards for mediators, accrediting training providers, and liaising with Government on matters of mutual concern, such as the running of the NMH.
- ***Clinical Disputes Forum*** *http://www.clinical-disputes-forum.org.uk* [April 11, 2009]

  This resource is referred to in the Pre-Action Protocol for the Resolution of Clinical Dispute, paras 5.1 to 5.4 (see Vol.1, para.C3–018)
- ***Technology & Construction Solicitors Association (TeCSA)*** *http://www.tecsa.org.uk* [Accessed October 27, 2009]

  See "ADR in Technology and Construction Court", above.
- ***Technology & Construction Bar Association (TECBAR)*** *http://www.tecbar.org* [Accessed October 27, 2009]

  See "ADR in Technology and Construction Court", at para.14–23 above.

# F. JUDICIAL REFERRAL TO MEDIATION

### Editorial note

14–28 In an internal HMCS Document entitled "Civil Court Mediation Service Manual" guidance is given on judicial referral to mediation. That guidance was approved by the ADR Committee of the Civil Justice Council and by the Judicial Studies Board, and in May and June 2007 was issued to all district judges and designated civil judges. The guidance is reproduced below with the kind permission of HMCS.

### The Legal Background

14–29 The overriding objective of the Civil Procedure Rules encourages the use of alternative dispute resolution (ADR):

Rule 1.4(1) obliges the court to further the overriding objective of enabling the court to deal with cases justly by actively managing cases;

Rule 1.4(2)(e) defines "active case management" as including "encouraging the parties to use an alternative dispute resolution procedure if the court considers that appropriate and facilitating the use of such procedure".

Rule 26.4(1) provides that "a party may, when filing the completed allocation questionnaire, make a written request for the proceedings to be stayed while the parties try to settle the case by alternative dispute resolution or other means". The court/judiciary can also stay the case if considered appropriate.

***Paragraph numbers marked with a "+" can be found online and on CD.***

Rule 44.5(3)(a)(ii) requires the court, in deciding the amount of costs to be awarded, to have regard to the conduct of the parties, including in particular "the efforts made, if any, before and during the proceedings in order to try to resolve the dispute".

The pre-action protocols contain standard wording on ADR, to the effect that:

> "The parties should consider whether some form of alternative dispute resolution procedure would be more suitable than litigation, and if so, endeavour to agree which form to adopt. Both the Claimant and Defendant may be required by the Court to provide evidence that alternative means of resolving their dispute were considered. The Courts take the view that litigation should be a last resort, and that claims should not be issued prematurely when a settlement is still actively being explored. Parties are warned that if this paragraph is not followed then the court must have regard to such conduct when determining costs."

The courts have also given strong support for the use of ADR in general, and mediation in particular, in cases such as *R (Cowl) v Plymouth City Council* [2001] EWCA Civ 1935, [2002] 1 W.L.R. 803; *Dunnett v Railtrack Plc* [2002] EWCA Civ 303; [2002] 1 W.L.R. 2434 and *Hurst v Leeming* [2001] EWHC 1051 (Ch), [2003] 1 Lloyds Rep. 379.

In addition, in *Halsey v Milton Keynes General NHS Trust* [2004] EWCA Civ 576, the court identified six factors, which might be considered as justifying refusal to mediate when determining costs issues:

- **The nature of the dispute**, as to which the court warned that "most cases are not, by their very nature, unsuitable for mediation."
- **The merits of the case**, by which a party which reasonably believes it has a strong case might make refusal of mediation reasonable.
- **Other settlement methods have been attempted**, though the court noted that "mediation often succeeds where other settlement attempts have failed".
- **Costs of mediation would be disproportionately high**.
- **Delay** to a trial date.
- **Whether mediation had a reasonable prospect of success**, the burden of showing which lies with the unsuccessful party who proposed mediation, and not with the successful party who refused.

### Judicial Encouragement

At the local level a key factor in the success of any court mediation scheme is the commitment of the Designated Civil Judge and District Judges. The judicial role is essential, driving the change process and encouraging parties to mediate—as well as recommending other members of the judiciary to take an active role. **14–30**

Judges can give careful consideration to cases at the allocation stage, case management conferences or even at late stages such as the pre-trial review to see if there is scope for the case being diverted towards mediation. The participation of District Judges, who can act as a single point of contact for all mediation queries and referrals, is vitally important for the success of mediation.

Evidence from the evaluation of court-based mediation schemes in England and Wales (in particular the Automatic Referral to Mediation pilot at Central London County Court), indicates that voluntary mediation is more likely to achieve higher settlement rates when compared to compulsory mediation. Mediation is by its very nature a consensual process and works best when parties come to mediation willingly or of their own volition.

However, if court-based mediation is to rely entirely on parties requesting mediation, the demand for it is likely to remain small.

Research shows that it works best when there is some form of judicial encouragement, and that such encouragement can be quite robust. But referral is a delicate balance. On the one hand, a "push" or gentle encouragement from the judge could possibly be viewed as a relief where the parties might not want to suggest mediation for fear of losing face. On the other hand, if the judge is too forceful, it could lead to unwilling parties going to mediation. Similarly, if a judge is overenthusiastic about mediation, unsuitable or over-complex cases could be referred to mediation, which might be unlikely to settle, particularly where the mediation is time-limited to three hours.

In addition, the vast majority of litigants, and many legal professionals—even if they know the term 'mediation'—probably know relatively little about the potential of mediation in settling disputes. There is therefore a clear need for good information about mediation—both on what mediation is, as well as its potential for settling specific cases. This information should, wherever possible, be made available to the parties themselves, because research shows that parties represented by a lawyer choose mediation significantly less often than unrepresented parties. See H. Brown and A. Marriott, *ADR Principles and Practice*, 32 (1999); H. Genn, University College of London, Faculty of Laws, Research Series, The Central London County Court Pilot Mediation Scheme (1998). Judges should therefore make independent judgments on suitability and no be over-influenced by attitudes of lawyers or clients without significant experience of mediation. Over time and with experience both judges and lawyers will find it easier to identify cases and timing.

**The Timing of Mediation**

**14–31** There are different opinions about the most favourable time to refer parties to mediation. One school of thought believes that the choice should be made as quickly as possible, before parties have become entrenched and dug in their heels. Others believe that the dispute needs to have reached a certain stage of maturity before parties decide to turn away from the courtroom and go back to the negotiating table.

However, it is generally agreed, that even in conflicts that run aground, a stage can be reached at which the parties realise the futility of more legal action and return to the original underlying basis of the conflict. But, there will always be some who let things escalate to the point where they would rather go to trial almost regardless of the outcome.

Overall though, one of the real benefits of mediation, when set against the court process, is that it can and should be quicker. Under the National Mediation Helpline arrangements—which in the future, will provide for all court mediation services in the fast and multi track—providers are required to undertake a mediation within 28 days of being referred a case. At the same time, judges are expected to stay the case for no longer than six weeks. In the small claims mediation service at Manchester County Court, the in-house mediator takes an average of fiveweeks from allocation to mediation settlement—compared to an average of 12–13 weeks for a small claims hearing.

**Case Types**

**14–32** Most mediation providers suggest that nearly all cases are suitable for mediation. However, as a general rule, the following cases are generally regarded as inappropriate for mediation and should therefore not be considered for mediation at allocation stage:

- where a legal precedent is needed to clarify the law or inform policy;
- where settlement would not be in the public interest; or because of a party's past conduct;
- where protective proceedings are required, such as injunctions; or
- where summary judgment is appropriate.

Some examples of types of case that are suitable include:

Contracts for goods and services

- Printing, electrical work, carpet fitting, double glazing, beauty treatment and therapy contracts—between businesses and between businesses and consumers;

Contracts for services

- Holiday companies and customers;
- Non-payment of professional fees—solicitors and architects;

Landlord and Tenant

- Non-payment of rent;

Land disputes

- Developers and adjacent landowners;

Clinical negligence

Insurance disputes

Building disputes

**Personal Injury**

**14–33** There is an ongoing discussion about whether personal injury cases are suitable for

***Paragraph numbers marked with a "+" can be found online and on CD.***

mediation. During the Automatic Referral to Mediation Scheme at Central London County Court, a common reason for opting-out of mediation in personal injury cases, was that the case would settle anyway, and so mediation was unnecessary. As a result, over the year of the pilot fewer than 10 per cent of the personal injury referrals actually resulted in a mediation. However, of those that did mediate the settlement rate was 59 per cent—significantly higher than the settlement rate of non-PI cases (47 per cent). Indeed, in the 40 PI cases where both parties accepted the referral to mediation from the outset, and proceeded to a mediation, the settlement rate was as high as 65 per cent.

Consequently, there should be no automatic assumption that PI cases will fail to mediate successfully. Judges should feel free therefore to refer suitable PI cases to mediation. But this should be on the understanding that if a party objects to mediation, it would probably not be worthwhile attempting to persuade them to change their mind.

#### Indicators and Counter Indicators for Referral and Selection of Cases for Referral

While it is important that the judge, in making the referral, is sure that the case in question is suitable for mediation, there are other criteria that are just as important in indicating the success of mediation. See H. Brown and A. Marriott, *ADR Principles and Practice*, 32 (1999); H.Genn, University College of London, Faculty of Laws, Research Series, The Central London County Court Pilot Mediation Scheme (1998). While research has shown that there are no uniform criteria for making referrals to mediation, there are what could generally be termed "referral indicators". **14–34**

The key indicator is the willingness of the parties to negotiate. Experienced mediators agree that it is not the type of case that determines the chances of successful mediation, but the attitudes and insights of the parties themselves. They have to be prepared for and capable of discussing a solution to their conflicts while also being able to develop an eye for their mutual interests. However, good mediators can frequently overcome unwillingness to help parties in problem-solving and risk assessment of their case, even if parties are initially reluctant to get around a table.

The other most critical indicator is the presence of room for negotiation, for example, mediation may not be suitable for a simple debt recovery action.

Research shows that these two fundamental conditions need to be met—otherwise the other indicators (see below) can be ignored.

Table 1 below gives a general outline of the indicators and counter-indicators.

**Table 1**

**14–35**

| **Indicators** |
|---|
| A result other than that possible through a court ruling is desirable<br>Speedy solution is desired<br>'Legal proceedings fatigue'<br>Long-term relationship (family, neighbours, business contact, company, long-term contract, etc.)<br>Common future interest(s)<br>More litigation or more conflicts than presented in the proceedings<br>Importance of confidential treatment, with possibility of separate interviews<br>More parties involved in the conflict than just the parties in the proceedings<br>A longstanding solution is essential |
| **Counter indicators** |
| Earlier mediation attempt failed<br>Parties have allowed conflict to escalate too much (i.e., they are comfortable with their conflict)<br>A precedent is desired<br>Public decision is desired<br>Too great a power imbalance<br>Parties with a cultural background which has no place for mediation<br>Legal procedure in which only a court ruling can bring about a solution |

ADR

# SECTION 15

## INTERIM REMEDIES

# 15 INTERIM REMEDIES

CONTENTS



## A. INTERIM INJUNCTIONS

In CPR r.25.1(1) it is noted that the court may grant various interim remedies, including an interim injunction (para.(a)). This power has to be seen in the context of the court's power to grant injunctions generally. A freezing injunction is a particular variety of interim injunction best understood against the background of the law and practice relating to interim injunctions generally. For practice and procedure, see commentary on CPR r.25.1(1)(a) in Vol.1. **15–2**

***Paragraph numbers marked with a "+" can be found online and on CD.***

## 1. JURISDICTION

15–3 It is necessary to distinguish English proceedings, foreign proceedings, and proceedings in other UK jurisdictions.

### (a) English proceedings

15–4 Sub-sections (1) and (2) of s.37 of the Senior Courts Act 1981 state that the High Court may by order (whether interlocutory or final) grant an injunction in all cases in which it appears to the court "just and convenient" to do so, and any such order may be made either unconditionally or on such terms as the court thinks just. The court's powers in these respects are not derived from this section but rather confirmed by it (*Fourie v Le Roux* [2007] UKHL 1; [2007] 1 W.L.R. 320, HL, at para.25, per Lord Scott). The section is traceable to the Supreme Court of Judicature Act 1873 s.25(8). Initially it was confined to interlocutory orders but was in terms extended to final orders on the basis that whatever a court could do by the former orders it could surely also do by the latter. The 1873 legislation conferred on the High Court the jurisdiction vested in, or capable of being exercised by, various courts, including courts of equity. In courts of equity the jurisdiction to grant injunctions:

> "has always been without limit, and could indeed be exercised either in support of any legal right, or in the creation of a new equitable right, as the court thought fit in the application of equitable principles" (Spry, *The Principles of Equitable Remedies*, 5th edn (1997) p.331).

It follows from this that, insofar as the High Court has thought it fit not to exercise its equitable jurisdiction to grant injunctions (either interlocutory or final), and has customarily refused relief, it has done so, not because it lacked jurisdiction or power, but as a matter of discretion. However, this analysis has not always carried the day. Some confusion has been caused by different assumptions about what is meant by the court not having "jurisdiction" to grant an injunction. As Lord Scott explained in *Fourie v Le Roux* (*ibid*), used in its strict sense it means (1) that the court has no power to deal with and decide the dispute as to the subject-matter before it, no matter in what form or by whom it is raised, but in another sense it means (2) that, although the court has power to decide the question, it will not according to its settled practice do so except in a certain way and under certain circumstances. (In a given case, the determination of the question whether the court has jurisdiction in the latter sense does not in the lease involve a review of the area of discretion available to any judge who is asked to grant injunctive relief.)

In *Siskina v Distos Compania Naviera SA (The Siskina)* [1979] A.C. 210, HL, Lord Diplock referred to (what is now) s.37(1) and said that the reference therein to interlocutory orders "presupposes the existence of a cause of action, actual or potential, claiming substantive relief which the High Court has jurisdiction to grant". Put the other way around, this proposition holds that an applicant may not be granted an interlocutory injunction where there is no cause of action over which the Court has jurisdiction. Where a respondent opposing an application for an interlocutory injunction contends that such cause of action does not exist it is necessary to be clear about what is meant by the Court not having "jurisdiction" to grant substantive relief. In *Fourie v Le Roux* (*op cit*) (a case concerning the grant of a freezing order) the House of Lords held that the authorities following *The Siskina* show that the court has jurisdiction in the strict sense, and therefore has power to decide the question whether an interlocutory injunction should be granted, where it has *in personam* jurisdiction over the person against whom the injunction is sought. But, although the court has power to decide the question, the circumstances may be such that, according to its settled practice it will not do so. And those circumstances may include the fact that there is no cause of action over which the court has jurisdiction. Whether or not this is a critical circumstance affecting the court's exercise of jurisdiction (in the other than strict sense referred to above) will depend on the law relating to the particular nature of the interlocutory relief sought. For discussion on this point in relation to interim relief in the form of a freezing injunction, see para.15–67 below (see also para.15–55).

Under the Arbitration Act 1996 s.44 (Court powers exercisable in support of arbitral proceedings) the court has for the purposes of, and in relation to, arbitral proceedings the same power of making orders about certain matters stated therein as it has for the purposes of, and in relation to, legal proceedings. Such orders include orders made for the purpose of preserving evidence or assets. For a discussion of the question as to the circumstances in which, in exercise of the power stated in this section, the court may grant interim injunctions, including the circumstances in which it may grant freezing injunctions ex parte, see *Cetelem S.A. v Roust Holdings Ltd* [2005] EWCA Civ 618; [2005] 1 W.L.R. 3555, CA; *Mobil Cerro Negro Ltd v Petroleos de Venezuela SA* [2008] 1 Lloyd's Rep. 684 (Walker J.) at para.120.

### (b) Foreign proceedings

Before 1982, the court could not grant interlocutory relief when the substantive proceedings were taking place abroad (*Siskina v Distos Compania Naviera SA (The Siskina), op cit*). However, the Civil Jurisdiction and Judgments Act 1982 s.25(1) conferred power on the High Court to grant interim relief (as defined) when the substantive proceedings were pending in a Brussels or Lugano Contracting State and the subject-matter of the proceedings was within the scope of the Brussels of Lugano Conventions. Council Regulation (EC) No.44/2001 (Judgments Regulation) replaced the Conventions. Article 31 of the Judgments Regulation states that an application may be made to the courts of a Member State "for such provisional, including protective, measures" as may be available under the law of that State even if, under the Regulation, the courts of another Member State "have jurisdiction as to the substance of the matter". This provision authorises but does not require the courts of a Contracting State to make protective orders in support of substantive proceedings which are pending in another Contracting State. The principle underlying it is that each Member State should be willing to assist the courts of another by providing such interim relief as would be available if its own courts were seised of the substantive proceedings (*Refco Inc v Eastern Trading Company* [1999] 1 Lloyd's Rep. 159, CA). In deciding the proper scope of any interim relief it is necessary for the English court to have regard to the nature of the substantive proceedings and their possible outcome (*Kensington International Ltd v Republic of Congo* [2007] EWCA Civ 1128; [2008] 1 Lloyd's Rep. 161, CA (rejecting respondent's submission that foreign proceedings should be characterised as equivalent to English third party debt order proceedings and interim relief restricted accordingly)). (By s.25(7) "interim relief" means interim relief of any kind which the court has power to grant in proceedings relating to matters within its jurisdiction, other than (a) a warrant for the arrest of property, or (b) provision for obtaining evidence.) **15–5**

By the Civil Jurisdiction and Judgments Act 1982 (Interim Relief) Order 1997 (SI 1997/302), made under s.25(3), the effect of s.25(1) was extended to non-Convention countries and to proceedings outside the scope of the Conventions.

By these provisions, the position was reached where the High Court has power to grant interim relief in aid of substantive proceedings elsewhere of whatever kind and wherever taking place (*Credit Suisse Trust S.A. v Cuoghi* [1998] Q.B. 818, CA, at p.825, per Millett L.J.).

Section 25(1) of the 1982 Act was enacted in order to prevent the rule established in *The Siskina* from preventing English courts from giving effect to (what now is) art.31 of the Judgments Regulation. See *Fourie v Le Roux, op cit*, at para.31 per Lord Scott.

Section 25(2) of the 1982 Act states that, on any application for interim relief under s.25(1), the court may refuse to grant that relief if, in the opinion of the court, "the fact that the court has no jurisdiction apart from this section in relation to the subject-matter of the proceedings in question makes it inexpedient for the court to grant it". (In *Motorola Credit Corporation v Uzan (No.2)* [2003] EWCA Civ 752; [2004] 1 W.L.R. 113, CA, the Court of Appeal identified a number of particular considerations to be borne in mind when considering the question of inexpediency; see also *Banco Nacional de Comercio Exterior SNC v Empresa de Telecommunicationes de Cuba SA* [2007] EWCA Civ 662; [2007] 2 Lloyd's Rep. 484, CA. It would rarely if ever be appropriate or expedient for the English court to assume jurisdiction under s.25 where the relevant defendant had no connection with the jurisdiction and the relevant assets were not located in England (*Belletti v Morici* [2009] EWHC 2316 (Comm), September 24, 2009, unrep. (Flaux J.)).)

The extent of the English court's jurisdiction to grant applications for interim injunctions in support of foreign proceedings includes granting relief in the form of an injunction freezing the respondent's assets. It is, of course, one thing for the English court in these circumstances to grant relief in the form of an injunction freezing the respondent's assets within the jurisdiction (a "domestic" freezing injunction), and quite another for the court to grant relief in the form of an injunction freezing the respondent's assets outside the English jurisdiction (a "worldwide" freezing injunction). However, it is clear that the jurisdiction to grant applications for interim injunctions in support of foreign proceedings extends to the latter circumstance, but special considerations may inhibit its exercise (see further, "Worldwide" Freezing Injunctions, para.15–81 below).

Where a claim is made for an interim remedy under s.25(1), provision for application for service out of the jurisdiction is made by PD6B (Service Out of the Jurisdiction) para.3.1(5).

See further commentary following CPR r.25.4 (Application for an interim remedy where there is no related claim); Vol.1 para.25.4.2.

### *(c) UK proceedings*

15–6 Scotland, Northern Ireland, and England and Wales, form three constituent parts of the United Kingdom as a political entity but are separate legal jurisdictions. Relations between the three jurisdictions in civil and commercial matters are regulated by a modified version the Judgments Regulation found in Sch.4 of the 1982 Act. Article 16 of that modified version is in terms comparable to art.31 of the Judgments Regulation. In this context, the proposition derived from *The Siskina* is again superseded with the result that the English court has jurisdiction to grant interim relief where jurisdiction over the applicant's claim lies, not with the English court, but with a court in Scotland or Northern Ireland. Section 25(2) applies to such application.

## 2. PRINCIPLES AND GUIDELINES TO BE APPLIED (AMERICAN CYANAMID CO. CASE)

15–7 The grant of an interlocutory injunction is a very important matter as a defendant can be sent to prison for breach (*Rochdale BC v Anders* [1988] 3 All E.R. 490). When an application is made for an order granting such relief, the court has a very difficult jurisdiction to exercise. It is sometimes impossible to make an order which may not do some injustice to one party or the other (*Thompson v Park* [1944] 1 K.B. 408, CA at 411, per du Parcq L.J.).

The procedure to be adopted by the court in hearing an application for an interlocutory injunction, and the tests to be applied, were laid down by the House of Lords in *American Cyanamid Co v Ethicon Ltd* [1975] A.C. 396; [1975] 2 W.L.R. 316, HL.

According to the *American Cyanamid Co* case, when an application is made for an interlocutory injunction, in the exercise of the court's discretion an initial question falls for consideration. That is:

(1) Is there a serious question to be tried?

If the answer to that question is, "yes", then two further related questions arise; they are:

(2) Would damages be an adequate remedy for a party injured by the court's grant of, or its failure to grant, an injunction?

(3) If not, where does the "balance of convenience" lie?

The first question indicates a threshold requirement. It marked a departure from the law that applied before the decision of the House of Lords in the *American Cyanamid Co* case. Guidance on the manner on which the court should approach the second and third questions is provided in guidelines derived from that case (to be applied in two stages). These guidelines have been much discussed in later decisions. A full account is given below. But first further comment is made on the principles that underpin the three questions.

### *(a) Principles—a serious question to be tried*

15–8 The key principles derived from the speech of Lord Diplock in *American Cyanamid Co v Ethicon Ltd* [1975] A.C. 396, HL, at pp 406–409, may be listed as follows:

(1) The grant of an interlocutory injunction is a remedy that is both temporary and discretionary.

(2) The evidence available to the court at the hearing of the application for an interlocutory injunction is incomplete. It is given in written evidence and has not been tested by oral cross-examination.

***Paragraph numbers marked with a "+" can be found online and on CD.***

(3) It is no part of the court's function at this stage of the litigation to try to resolve conflicts of evidence on the written evidence as to facts on which the claims of either party may ultimately depend nor to decide difficult questions of law which call for detailed argument and mature considerations. These are matters to be dealt with at the trial.
(4) When an application for an interlocutory injunction to restrain a defendant from doing acts alleged to be in violation of the claimant's legal right is made upon contested facts, the decision whether or not to grant an interlocutory injunction has to be taken at a time when ex hypothesi the existence of the right or the violation of it, or both, is uncertain and will remain uncertain until final judgment is given in the action.
(5) It was to mitigate the risk of injustice to the claimant during the period before that uncertainty could be resolved that the practice arose of granting him relief by way of interlocutory injunction.
(6) But (at least since the middle of the 19th century) this has been made subject to the claimant's undertaking to pay damages to the defendant for any loss sustained by reason of the injunction if it should be held at the trial that the claimant had not been entitled to restrain the defendant from doing what he was threatening to do.
(7) The object of the interlocutory injunction is to protect the claimant against injury by violation of his right for which he could not be adequately compensated in damages recoverable in the action if the uncertainty were resolved in his favour at the trial; but the claimant's need for such protection must be weighed against the corresponding need of the defendant to be protected against injury resulting from his having prevented from exercising his own legal rights for which he could not be adequately compensated under the claimant's undertaking in damages if the uncertainty were resolved in the defendant's favour at the trial.
(8) The court must weigh one need against another and determine where, "the balance of convenience" lies.
(9) There is no rule of law or practice to the effect that the court is not entitled to take any account of the balance of convenience unless it has first been satisfied that upon the evidence adduced by both the parties on the hearing of the application the applicant had satisfied the court that on the balance of probabilities the acts of the other party sought to be enjoined would, if committed, violate the applicant's legal rights. The purpose sought to be achieved by giving to the court discretion to grant interlocutory injunctions would be stultified if the discretion were clogged by such a technical rule.
(10) However, the court must be satisfied that the claim is not frivolous or vexatious; in other words, that there is a serious question to be tried.
(11) So, unless the material available to the court at the hearing of the application for an interlocutory injunction fails to disclose that the claimant has any real prospect of succeeding in his claim for a permanent injunction at the trial, the court should go on to consider whether the balance of convenience lies in favour of granting or refusing the interlocutory relief that is sought.
(12) It would be most exceptional for the House of Lords to give leave to appeal in a case which turned upon where the balance of convenience lay.

In the context in which they were stated (though they may not be confined to it), these principles are based on the assumption that a trial is in fact likely to take place, in the sense that the applicant's case shows that he is genuinely concerned to pursue his claim to trial, and that he is seeking the injunction as a means of a "holding operation" pending the trial. Where the contest about the grant or refusal of an interlocutory injunction is effectively the only contest between the parties, and it is clear that the action would never proceed to trial, additional considerations arise (see *N.W.L. Ltd v Woods* [1979] 1 W.L.R. 1294, HL and *Cayne v Global Natural Resources Plc* [1984] 1 All E.R. 225, CA, at p 234 per Kerr L.J.) (see further para.15–17 below).

The main significance of the *American Cyanamid* case lies in principles (9) and (10). Those principles were controversial when announced by the House of Lords in 1975, and have remained so since then. The case establishes that it is not necessary, as a threshold requirement, for the court to be satisfied that on the balance of probabilities the acts of the other party sought to be enjoined would, if committed, violate the applicant's legal rights. Previously the question was whether the applicant had made out a prima facie case of succeeding at trial and this often required "trial in miniature" involving a detailed investigation of the claimant's prospects of success as revealed by the (often conflicting) affidavit evidence and the weighing of them to see whether they were greater than his prospects of failure. The *American Cyanamid* case substituted a lower threshold test (see further below). This approach is consistent with the "great object" of the court in hearing an application for an interlocutory injunction which is to abstain from expressing any opinion on the merits of the case until the hearing (see *American Cyanamid Co v Ethicon Ltd*, *op cit*, at p.408 per Lord Diplock, citing *Wakefield v Duke of Buccleuch* (1865) 12 L.T. 628 at 629). It is also consistent with the view that, in the interest of husbanding scarce judicial resources, the court should not be expected to devote an inordinate amount of time to the hearing of applications for interlocutory injunctions. Further, the approach should have the effect of discouraging interlocutory appeals, because, as a practical matter, a respondent party is likely to find it more difficult to upset on appeal a judge's finding arrived at by applying a lower threshold test.

In the *American Cyanamid* case, in expounding the principles Lord Diplock said that, in addressing the threshold test, it is sufficient if the court asks itself: is the applicant's action "not frivolous or vexatious"? Is there "a serious question to be tried" (principle (10))? Is there "a real prospect that he will succeed in his claim for a permanent injunction at the trial" (principle (11))?. These may appear to be three subtly different questions. It has been said that they are intended to state the same test (see *Smith v Inner London Education Authority* [1978] 1 All E.R. 411, CA, at p 419 per Browne L.J.).

The decision of the House in this respect changed established previous practice based on highly persuasive if not binding authority (see *J.T. Stratford v Lindley* [1965] A.C. 269, HL and *F. Hoffmann-La Roche A.G. v Secretary of State for Trade and Industry* [1975] A.C. 295, HL, at p.360 per Lord Diplock). A period of adaptation in the face of a degree of judicial resistance was necessary (*Lawrence David Ltd v Ashton* [1989] I.C.R. 123, CA, at p 131 per Balcombe L.J.). A certain amount of ingenuity was displayed in efforts to sustain the "prima facie case" threshold test. For example, the arguments that the lower threshold test was confined to actions in which disputes on matters of fact were apparent on the affidavits, and that it did not apply in cases where the final order would not include an injunction, both received some judicial support (*Alfred Dunhill Ltd v Sunoptic SA* [1979] F.S.R. 337, CA, at p.369 per Browne L.J.). Further, for some time it was widely believed that the prima facie case test survived in actions to enforce contractual obligations in restraint of trade (see the judgments of Lord Denning M.R. in *Fellowes & Son v Fisher* [1976] Q.B. 122, CA, and *Office Overload Ltd v Gunn* [1977] F.S.R. 39, CA). However, it was later made clear that these cases were not in a special category (see *Lawrence David Ltd v Ashton*, supra, *Dairy Crest Ltd v Pigott* [1989] I.C.R. 92, CA, and *John Michael Design Plc v Cooke* [1987] F.S.R. 402, CA.

### (b) The American Cyanamid principles and CPR case management

15–9 At bottom, the principles are based on the "great object" of the court when hearing an application for an interlocutory injunction; which is, "to abstain from expressing any opinion on the merits of the case until the hearing". The objective is to prevent the court from being bogged down with complex, highly contentious issues, not suitable for determination in interlocutory proceedings, in circumstances where the date of trial cannot be predicted and is likely to be a long way off. In a sense the principles are crude case management rules designed to reduce costs and delays and, in particular, to avoid a case being tried twice, whilst preserving the status quo insofar as this is just in cases where the prospects of ultimate success in the proceedings of either side cannot reasonably be assessed. The *American Cyanamid Co* case was decided in 1975 when concerns about pre-trial delays in civil cases were rising and when "interlocutory warfare" was seen as a prime cause for delays.

The coming into effect in 1998 of the CPR heralded a new, more flexible approach to case management. As a result, the context within which the *American Cyanamid* principles were designed to operate was altered significantly. Under the CPR, the early identification and resolution of issues likely to be dispositive of proceedings (whether by application for summary judgment or otherwise) is encouraged and the tests according to which early disposal may be achieved are different to those that applied previously. Further, in the bulk of cases delays between the issue of proceedings and trial are much reduced. However, there are tensions within the modern law of civil procedure, arising from the conflicting policies that underlie the law. Some of those policies are in accord with the policy considerations underlying the *American Cyanamid* rules (and to that extent there is no conflict with the rules), but some are not (and to that extent there is). There may come a time when the principle that, on an interlocutory application, the court should simply determine whether there is a serious question to be tried, and not enter into an investigation of the prospects of success of either party, should be re-assessed by the House of Lords (*SmithKline Beecham v Generics UK Ltd* October 23, 2001, unrep., Jacob J.).

## 3. GUIDELINES—ADEQUACY OF DAMAGES AS A REMEDY AND THE BALANCE OF CONVENIENCE

After stating the principles enumerated above, Lord Diplock gave guidance on how the balance of convenience should be determined in individual cases. In *R. v Secretary of State for Transport, Ex p. Factortame Ltd (No.2)* [1991] 1 A.C. 603, HL, Lord Goff said that the points made by Lord Diplock in the *American Cyanamid* case on this matter may properly be described as "guidelines" because his Lordship's speech should not be read as intending to fetter the broad discretion conferred on the court by the Senior Courts Act 1981 s.37 (see also *Cayne v Global Natural Resources Plc* [1984] 1 All E.R. 225 at 237, CA, per May L.J. where the tendency to construe them as if they were provisions in an Act of Parliament is deprecated, and *Lansing Linde Ltd v Kerr* [1991] 1 W.L.R. 251, CA, at p.269 per Butler-Sloss, L.J.). **15–10**

In *Fellowes & Son v Fisher* [1976] 1 Q.B. 122, CA, at p.137, CA, Browne L.J. set out Lord Diplock's guidelines in an enumerated series (much relied upon by judges in subsequent cases) as follows.

(1) The governing principle is that the court should first consider whether, if the claimant succeeds at the trial, he would be adequately compensated by damages for any loss caused by the refusal to grant an interlocutory injunction. If damages would be adequate remedy and the defendant would be in a financial position to pay them, no interlocutory injunction should normally be granted, however strong the claimant's claim appeared to be at that stage.

(2) If, on the other hand, damages would not be an adequate remedy, the court should then consider whether, if the injunction were granted, the defendant would be adequately compensated under the claimant's undertaking as to damages. If damages in the measure recoverable under such an undertaking would be an adequate remedy and the claimant would be in a financial position to pay them, there would be no reason upon this ground to refuse an interlocutory injunction.

(3) It is where there is doubt as to the adequacy of the respective remedies in damages that the question of balance of convenience arises. It would be unwise to attempt even to list all the various matters which may need to be taken into consideration in deciding where the balance lies, let alone to suggest the relative weight to be attached to them. These will vary from case to case.

(4) Where other factors appear to be evenly balanced it is a counsel of prudence to take such measures as are calculated to preserve the status quo.

(5) The extent to which the disadvantages to each party would be incapable of being compensated in damages in the event of his succeeding at the trial is always a significant factor in assessing where the balance of convenience lies.

(6) If the extent of the uncompensatable disadvantage to each party would not differ widely, it may not be improper to take into account in tipping the balance the relative strength of each party's case as revealed by the written evidence adduced on the hearing of the application. This, however, should be done only where it is apparent upon the facts disclosed by evidence as to which there is no credible dispute that the strength of one party's case is disproportionate to that of the other party.

(7) In addition to the factors already mentioned, there may be many other special factors to be taken into consideration in the particular circumstances of individual cases.

### *(a) Stage 1—adequacy as a remedy of damages awarded at trial or payable under undertaking*

In *R. v Secretary of State for Transport, Ex p. Factortame Ltd (No.2)*, supra, Lord Goff **15–11**

***Paragraph numbers marked with a "+" can be found online and on CD.***

explained that Lord Diplock approached the matter in two stages, the first stage consisting of guidelines (1) and (2) as outlined by Browne L.J. and the second consisting of the remainder of those guidelines. That is to say, Lord Diplock said the relevance of the availability of an adequate remedy in damages, either to the claimant seeking the injunction or to the defendant in the event that an injunction is granted against him should be considered first. As far as the claimant is concerned, the availability to him of such a remedy will normally preclude the grant to him of an interim injunction. If that is not so, then the court should consider whether, if an injunction is granted against the defendant, there will be an adequate remedy in damages available to him under the claimant's undertaking in damages; if so, there will be no reason on this ground to refuse to grant the claimant an interim injunction.

It has been said that, as a practical matter, the nature and degree of harm and inconvenience for which an award of money can provide no adequate recompense that are likely to be sustained by the defendant (if an interlocutory injunction is granted) and by the claimant (if it is not) respectively "are generally sufficiently disproportionate to bring down by themselves the balance on one side or the other" (*N.W.L. Ltd v Woods* [1979] 1 W.L.R. 1294, HL, at p.1307 per Lord Diplock).

A literal application of guideline (2) would lead to the result that whenever a claimant puts forward a serious issue to be tried, and whenever he is also able to show that any inconvenience, let alone injustice, to the defendant by the grant of an injunction is capable of being compensated in damages against the claimant's cross-undertaking, the court would be bound to grant an injunction. This cannot possibly have been Lord Diplock's intention (*Cayne v Global Natural Resources Plc* [1984] 1 All E.R. 225, CA, at p.234 per Kerr L.J.).

### *(b) Stage 2—balance of convenience*

**15–12** As Lord Goff further explained in *R. v Secretary of State for Transport, Ex p. Factortame Ltd (No.2)*, op cit, if there is doubt as to the adequacy of either or both of the respective remedies in damages (see guideline (2)), then the court proceeds to the second stage, that is to say, to the "balance of convenience" and asks the question "where does the balance of convenience lie?" In practice, it is often hard to tell whether either or both of the respective remedies will be adequate. Consequently, it is frequently the case that the court is enjoined (by guideline 3) to proceed to this stage and to consider the balance of convenience issue. The use of the word "convenience" here reflects s.37(1) of the Senior Courts Act 1981, where it is stated that an injunction may be granted if it appears to the court "just and convenient to do so". In some cases, it has been said that the balance to be struck is more fundamental, more weighty, than mere "convenience", and is better described as the "balance of the risk of doing an injustice" raising the question: "which course caries the lower risk of injustice" (*N.W.L. Ltd v Woods* [1979] 1 W.L.R. 1294, HL, at p.1306 per Lord Diplock; *Cayne v Global Natural Resources Plc* [1984]1 All E.R. 225, CA, at p.237 per May L.J.; *Zockoll Group Ltd v Mecury Communications Ltd* [1998] F.S.R. 354, CA., at 371 per Simon Brown L.J.).

For the purpose of determining the balance of convenience, the court will consider all the circumstances of the case. In relation to this second stage Lord Goff said he had no wish to place any gloss on what Lord Diplock said but drew attention to the points made by his lordship in guidelines (3) and (7) as set forth by Browne L.J. in *Fellowes & Son v Fisher*. Guideline (3) emphasises that, it would be unwise (if not impossible) for appellate courts (1) to attempt to list all the various matters which may need to be taken into consideration in deciding where the balance of convenience lies, or (2) to suggest the relative weight to be attached to them. Necessarily, these will vary from case to case. The court "has to engage in trying to predict whether granting or withholding an injunction is more or less likely to cause irremediable prejudice (and to what extent) if it turns out that the injunction should not have been granted or withheld (as the case may be)" (*National Commercial Bank Jamaica Ltd v Olint Corp Ltd (Practice Note)* [2009] UKPC 16; [2009] 1 W.L.R. 1405; [2009] Bus. L.R. 1110, PC.). The basic principle is that the court "should take whatever course seems likely to cause the least irremediable prejudice to one party or the other" (ibid).

The willingness of the applicant to give the respondent a cross-undertaking in damages is a very material consideration for the court in determining whether or not the interim injunction should be ordered. The fact that an ultimately unsuccessful claimant will have to compensate the defendant for losses suffered by him through his complying with the interim remedy for the duration of the period during which it took effect is a major factor in assessing the balance of convenience (*SmithKline Beecham Plc v Apotex Europe Ltd* [2006] EWCA Civ 658; [2007] Ch. 71, CA, at para.26 per Jacob L.J.).

## 4. PARTICULAR GUIDELINES

Three of the guidelines as formulated by Browne L.J. in *Fellowes & Son v Fisher* [1976] 1 Q.B. 122, CA, at p.137, CA, (see para.15–8 above) can be considered separately. **15–13**

### (a) Preserving the status quo ante

Guideline (4) states that where other factors appear to be evenly balanced it is "a counsel of prudence" to take such measures as are calculated to preserve the status quo. Sometimes it is said that the principal function of the interlocutory injunction is to preserve the status quo (*Siskina v Distos Compania Naviera SA* [1979] A.C. 210, HL, at p.256 per Lord Diplock; see also *Daniel v Ferguson* [1891] 2 Ch. 27, CA). However, in a given case the preservation of the status quo may on balance clearly incur the greater risk of injustice. Further, parties should not be encouraged to believe that the court will be unwilling to undo by interlocutory injunction what would otherwise be a fait accompli (*Thompson v Park* [1944] 1 K.B. 408, CA), especially where one party, by conduct that reflects little credit on them, has "stolen a march" on the other (*Zockoll Group Ltd v Mercury Communication Ltd*, op cit, at p.371 per Simon Brown L.J.). The relevant point of time for the purpose of "status quo" may be difficult to determine and may vary (*Alfred Dunhill Ltd v Sunoptic SA* [1977] F.S.R. 337, CA, at p.376 per Megaw L.J.). **15–14**

### (b) "relative strength of each party's case"

Guideline (6) is cast in terms designed to restrict a consideration of the "relative strength of each party's case". This factor has to be disregarded except as a last resort when the balance of convenience is otherwise even in the circumstances stated in guideline (6) and even then it should not be taken into account unless it is apparent upon the facts disclosed by evidence as to which there is no credible dispute that the strength of one party's case is disproportionate to that of the other party. This is consistent with the whole object of the guidelines (see principle (9), supra) which is to avoid trying to resolve conflicts on affidavit and to avoid dealing with matters of fact or law which are for mature consideration at the trial (*Entec (Pollution Control) Ltd v Abacus Mouldings* [1992] F.S.R. 332, CA, at p.345 per Dillon L.J.). However, where the court has felt able to reach, and has reached, a firm conclusion as to the applicant's prospects of success it may be a counsel of perfection to expect the court to put that conclusion firmly on one side except for the limited purposes permitted by guideline (6). **15–15**

Not surprisingly therefore, in many cases it has been argued that, in assessing the balance of convenience, the court should be able to give greater prominence to its view of the relative strength of each party's case than that apparently allowed by guideline (6) (see, e.g. *Fellowes & Son v Fisher* [1976] Q.B. 122, CA, at p.141 per Sir John Pennycuick) and it has been said that in practice this guideline is not always followed strictly (*Series 5 Software v Clarke* [1996] 1 All E.R. 853, at p.856). If the guideline is put in context and in positive terms, some room for manoeuvre is apparent. Put this way the guideline states that, (1) where the uncompensatable disadvantage to each party does not differ widely and (2) there is no credible dispute as to the facts, and (3) without attempting to resolve difficult issues of fact or law, the court can come to the conclusion that "the strength of one party's case is disproportionate to that of the other party", then (4) the court may take that relative strength into account. It is not necessary that there should be no issues of fact or law to be resolved. What is necessary is that (1) there should be no credible dispute as to the facts, (2) the court should not embark on anything resembling a trial of the action on conflicting affidavits in order to evaluate the strength of each party's case, and (3) the court should be of the clear view that one party's case is much stronger than the other's. It can be argued that the first of these three conditions is unduly restrictive and, indeed, that it is subsumed by the second. That is to say, it could be contended that, even where there is a credible dispute as to the facts, the court may, without holding anything resembling a trial, be able to come to a clear view that one party's case is much stronger than the other's and should be able to take that factor into account. Support for this approach is found in the first instance case of *Series 5 Software v Clarke*, op cit.

The desire to give greater prominence to the relative strength of each party's case has led to the argument that in certain circumstances the question whether an injunction should be granted should be decided "without" the *American Cyanamid* guidelines, thereby circumventing the restrictive terms of guideline (6) completely. On the whole, that argument has been resisted. However, it has been deployed to some effect in cases where the grant or refusal of an interlocutory injunction would have the effect of disposing of the action finally (see para.15–17 et seq. below).

### (c) "other special factors"

15–16 It was suggested that guideline (7) indicated that the guidelines as a whole were not to be regarded as of general application and, therefore, the strength of either party's case could be taken into account whenever a case exhibited "other special factors" (see Lord Denning M.R. in *Fellowes & Son v Fisher* [1976] Q.B. 122, CA, and *Hubbard v Pitt* [1976] Q.B. 142, CA, but this view has not prevailed. It seems clear that guideline (7) refers only to special factors affecting the balance of convenience (see *Hubbard v Pitt*, *ibid*. at p.185 per Stamp L.J.).

## 5. INTERLOCUTORY RULING IN EFFECT DISPOSING OF ACTION FINALLY

15–17 In a given case, an application for an interlocutory injunction may be successful; on the other hand, it may not. The disposition of the application one way or the other is likely to have a bearing on the subsequent progress of the proceedings.

### (a) Likelihood of claimant succeeding at trial

15–18 Cases can arise in which, as a practical matter, the grant or refusal of an injunction at the interlocutory stage will, in effect, dispose of the action finally in favour of whichever party was successful in the application, because there would be nothing left on which it was in the unsuccessful party's interest to proceed to trial. Clearly, the *American Cyanamid* case was not such a case. However, in *N.W.L. Ltd v Woods* [1979] 1 W.L.R. 1294, HL, which was such a case, Lord Diplock said (at p.1306) that in these circumstances "the degree of likelihood that the plaintiff would have succeeded in establishing his right to an injunction if the action had gone to trial" is a factor which should be brought into the balance by the judge in weighing the risks that injustice may result from his deciding the application one way rather than the other. In Lord Diplock's view this is not inconsistent with the *American Cyanamid* case because there was nothing in the decision in that case to suggest that the judge ought not to give "full weight to all the practical realities of the situation to which the injunction will apply".

So, the position is that where the grant or refusal of an interlocutory injunction will effectively end the action, it is appropriate for the court in assessing the balance of convenience to investigate "the degree of likelihood" of the claimant succeeding at trial. However, such investigation need not, and perhaps should not, amount to a trial of the action. It is for the judge to control the extent of the inquiry undertaken (*Lansing Linde Ltd v Kerr* [1991] 1 W.L.R. 251; [1991] 1 All E.R. 418, CA, at p.258 and p.424, CA, per Staughton L.J., see also p.270 and p.435, per Butler-Sloss L.J.).

In some instances, the hearing of the application for interlocutory relief may well, in practice, be determinative of the dispute between the parties, not because the interim decision leaves nothing left on which it is in the unsuccessful party's interest to proceed to trial (as in *N.W.L. Ltd v Woods*, supra), but because, taking a commercial view, the court's decision at the hearing renders it not worthwhile for the unsuccessful party to continue to prosecute or defend (as the case may be) the action. Where the court, in determining whether to grant the interlocutory injunction, has faithfully applied the *American Cyanamid* principles and confined its attention to the question whether there is "a serious question to be tried", the unsuccessful party's decision in this respect will be based purely on the commercial realities (*R.H.M. Foods Ltd v Bovril Ltd* [1982] 1 W.L.R. 661; [1982] 1 All E.R. 673, CA, at p.666 and p.678, per Oliver

L.J.). However, if (contrary to the *American Cyanamid* principles) the court considered the degree of likelihood that the claimant would have succeeded in establishing his right to an action were the action to go to trial the court's view on the merits, in addition to the commercial realities, is likely to influence the unsuccessful party's decision.

Where it is clear that, whatever decision the court reaches as to the granting of an injunction, the commercial realities are likely to weigh very heavily on either or both parties, with the result that almost inevitably the proceedings will be at an end, it may be asking too much to expect the court to reach a decision purely on the basis of whether there is a serious question to be tried. It is perhaps for this reason that (contrary to the *American Cyanamid* principles) a consideration of the claimant's prospects of success has been regarded as of particular importance in passing-off actions (see, for contrasting examples, *Alfred Dunhill Ltd v Sunoptic SA* [1979] F.S.R. 337, CA, and *Newsweek Inc v British Broadcasting Corp.* [1977] R.P.C. 441, CA, where the strength or weakness of the parties' cases turned the day). However, it must be remembered that passing-off actions are not exempt from the rule that if the applicant fails to demonstrate that there is a serious question to be tried (see principle (10)) consideration of the balance of convenience does not arise and interlocutory relief must be refused (*Advance Magazine Publishing v Redwood Publishing* [1993] F.S.R. 449).

A difference of approach is apparent in the authorities coming after *N.W.L. Ltd v Woods*. On the one hand it is said (following Lord Diplock) that the cases in which the court's decision will, as a practical mater, dispose of the claim can be handled within the *American Cyanamid* guidelines without any modification of the principles established in that case as properly understood (see *Cambridge Nutrition Ltd v British Broadcasting Corporation* [1990] 3 All E.R. 523, CA, at p.539, CA, per Ralph Gibson L.J., and *Lawrence David Ltd v Ashton* [1989] I.C.R. 123, CA, sub nom. *David (Lawrence) v Ashton* [1991] 1 All E.R. 385, CA, at p.135 and p.396, per Balcombe L.J.), if only for the reason that the likely disposal of the whole action by the grant or refusal of the interlocutory injunction should be treated as a special factor to be taken into consideration in the particular circumstances of the case (guideline (7)).

On the other hand it has been said that a prerequisite to the application of the guidelines is that a trial is in fact likely to take place, in the sense that the claimant's case shows that they are genuinely concerned to pursue their claim to trial, and that they are seeking the injunction as a means of a holding operation pending the trial. Where this is not the case, so it is said, the court is not bound to apply the guidelines (see *Cayne v Global Natural Resources Plc* [1984] 1 All E.R. 225, CA, at p.234 and p.238 per Kerr and May L.JJ., and *Cambridge Nutrition Ltd v British Broadcasting Corporation* [1990] 3 All E.R. 523, CA, at p.534 per Kerr L.J.; note also *Byanston Finance v De Vries (No.2)* [1976] 2 W.L.R. 41, CA, at p.51, CA, Buckley L.J. and at p.55, per Sir John Pennycuick) and, indeed, may be entitled to approach the matter on a broad principle by asking "what can the court do to in its best endeavour to avoid injustice" (sometimes known as the "broad brush" approach) (see *Cayne v Global Natural Resources Plc, ibid.* at p.232 per Eveleigh L.J.). Note also *1st Choice Recruitment v Hancock* [2003] EWHC 2232 (QB), September 11, 2003, unrep. (McCombe J.), where, in a claim for an employee's breach of an employment contract covenant an injunction was bound to be dispositive of the proceedings, the judge held that the *American Cyanamid Co* principles could not realistically be applied.

In some cases, the courts have dealt with the problem by an admixture of the guidelines and the judgments given in *N.W.L. Ltd v Woods* and *Cayne v Global Natural Resources Plc*. and have found it unnecessary to decide whether the solution was to be found "within" or "without" the guidelines (the judgment of Dillon L.J. in *Entec (Pollution Control) Ltd v Abacus Mouldings* [1992] F.S.R. 332, CA, provides a good illustration). Quite commonly, *N.W.L. Ltd v Woods* is regarded as creating ""an exception" to American Cyanamid in the sense that it creates an exception to the rule that the relative strength of each party's case (or the claimant's prospects of success) generally should not be taken into account (see *Lawrence David Ltd v Ashton* [1989] I.C.R. 1234, CA, sub nom. *David (Lawrence) v Ashton* [1991] 1 All E.R. 385, CA, at p.135 and pp 395-396 per Balcombe L.J.).

### *(b) Likelihood of defendant establishing defence in labour dispute*

In a labour dispute, where an employer claimant applies for an interlocutory injunction, the balance of convenience will usually point in favour of granting the **15–19**

***Paragraph numbers marked with a "+" can be found online and on CD.***

injunction. Further, the granting of the injunction is likely to prove to be dispositive of the action in favour of the claimant. There is a risk that, in practice, the protection of the statutory immunities granted to trade unions will prove worthless. Shortly after the *American Cyanamid Co* case was decided, a provision designed to reduce this risk was inserted in the Trade Union and Labour Relation Act 1974 s.17 by the Employment Protection Act 1975 s.125, Sch.16, Pt III and is now found in the Trade Union and Labour Relations (Consolidation) Act 1992 s.221(2). That subsection provides that, where an application for an interlocutory injunction is made to a court pending the trial of an action and the party against whom it is sought claims that he acted in contemplation or furtherance of a trade dispute, the court shall, in exercising its discretion whether or not to grant the interlocutory injunction, have regard to the likelihood of the defendant's succeeding at the trial of the action in establishing any matter which would afford a defence to the action under s.219 (protection from certain tort liabilities) or s.220 (peaceful picketing) of the 1992 Act. This provision was discussed in *N.W.L. Ltd v Woods* [1979] 1 W.L.R. 1294; [1979] I.C.R. 867, HL, and *Associated British Ports v Transport and General Workers' Union* [1989] 3 All E.R. 796, CA.

### (c) Effect of delay to trial

15–20 In a given case, the question whether or not the grant or refusal of an interlocutory injunction will in effect dispose of the action finally may be affected by the length of delay to trial (*Lansing Linde Ltd v Kerr* [1991] 1 W.L.R. 251; [1991] 1 All E.R. 418, CA, at p.257 and p.423, CA, per Staughton L.J.). Although it may be true to say that, since the coming into effect of the CPR, generally speaking cases proceed more expeditiously to trial than before, cases can still arise in which delay to trial is an important factor.

The restraint of trade cases provide a good example. In such cases where the claimant, the former employer, seeks an interlocutory injunction preventing the defendant, the former employee, from taking up other employment for the remainder of the contractual period (whatever it is), the question whether damages would be an adequate remedy for one party or the other can be particularly difficult. Unless the defendant is a person of substance, the court may conclude that damages would not be an adequate remedy for the claimant if an injunction were not granted. If the claimant is financially sound the court may well conclude that the defendant would undoubtedly be compensated under the cross-undertakings if he was wrongly injuncted and kept out of work for a period. However, there may be a significant risk that the defendant, by being kept out of the employment market for the period of any injunction, will have difficulty in finding work subsequently and will therefore suffer long term damage beyond that period. This may not be easy to establish or, if established, to assess in monetary terms. Much will depend on the period for which the interlocutory injunction operates.

It has been said that it is only if the action cannot be tried before the period of the restraint has expired, or has run a large part of its course, that the grant of an interlocutory injunction should be regarded as effectively disposing of the action (*Lawrence David Ltd v Ashton* [1989] I.C.R. 123, sub nom. *David (Lawrence) v Ashton* [1991] 1 All E.R. 385, CA, at p.135 and p.395 per Balcombe L.J.).

Where the anticipated length of the delay before trial makes it likely that the grant or refusal of an interlocutory injunction would in effect dispose of the action finally, instead of taking up the time of the courts with contested applications for interlocutory injunctions, the parties might be better advised to use their best endeavours to cooperate in getting the case ready for trial quickly and applying for speedy trial (*Lawrence David Ltd v Ashton* [1989] I.C.R. 123, sub nom. *David (Lawrence) v Ashton* [1991] 1 All E.R. 385, CA, at p.134 and p.395 per Balcombe L.J.; see also *Dairy Crest Ltd v Pigott* [1989] I.C.R. 92, CA). Further, in a restraint of trade case the defendant should seriously consider, when the matter first comes before the court, offering an appropriate undertaking until the hearing of the action, provided that a speedy hearing of the action can then be fixed and the claimant is likely to be able to pay any damages on his cross-undertaking. It is only if a speedy trial should not be possible that it would be necessary to have a contest on the interlocutory application (*Lawrence David Ltd v Ashton* [1989] I.C.R. 123, sub nom. *David (Lawrence) v Ashton* [1991] 1 All E.R. 385, CA, at p.135 and pp.395–396 per Balcombe L.J.).

### (d) Risk of terminological confusion

15–21 There is a risk of terminological confusion. In the *American Cyanamid* case, the

House of Lords held that, as a threshold requirement to a consideration of the balance of convenience, the court must be satisfied on the material available to it that the claim is "not frivolous or vexatious"; in other words, that there is "a serious question to be tried" (principle (10)) or, put conversely, that such material "fails to disclose that the plaintiff has any real prospect of succeeding in his claim for a permanent injunction at the trial" (principle (11)).

In the limited circumstances permitted by guideline (6) only, in assessing the balance of convenience the court may take into account in tipping the balance a qualitatively different factor, that is "the relative strength of each party's case" as revealed by the written evidence. As noted above, in *N.W.L. Ltd v Woods* Lord Diplock said that in the circumstances under discussion here (interlocutory injunction disposing of action finally) "the degree of likelihood that the plaintiff would have succeeded in establishing his right to an injunction if the action had gone to trial" is a factor which should be brought into the balance. It would seem that this is but another way of saying that "the relative strength of each party's case" is a factor to be brought into the balance (see *Lawrence David Ltd v Ashton* [1989] I.C.R.123, CA, sub nom. *David (Lawrence) v Ashton* [1991] 1 All E.R. 385, CA, at pp.134–135 and pp.395–396 per Balcombe L.J.). However, in some later cases, the factor identified in *N.W.L. Ltd v Woods* has been described as the plaintiff's "prospects of success at trial" (see *Lansing Linde Ltd v Kerr* [1991] 1 All E.R. 418; [1991] 1 W.L.R. 251, CA, at p.422 and p.256 per Staughton L.J.). This may be an apt description in this context but it is submitted that there is a risk that it will be confused with the threshold requirement referred to in principle (11).

## 6. CASES EXCEPTED FROM GUIDELINES

The principles and guidelines derived from the *American Cyanamid Co* case are intended to be of general application. However, in certain circumstances they are subject to variations, and in some others the variations are so significant that it can reasonably be claimed that they do not apply. Further, cases can arise in which the circumstances are so highly unusual as to make the normal tests (or at least some of them) for the granting of interlocutory injunctions inappropriate (e.g. *R. v Secretary of State for Health, Ex p.Generics (UK) Ltd* [1998] Eu.L.R. 146; [1997] C.O.D. 294; *The Times*, February 25, 1997, CA, (both parties applying for interlocutory injunctions in judicial review proceedings challenging related decisions of authority as to drug-licensing). **15–22**

The aspect of the law derived from the *American Cyanamid*case that lawyers and judges appear to have had most difficulty in consistently applying in all circumstances is the principle that the threshold question is, not "whether the applicant has a prima facie case?", but the less onerous one of "is there a serious question to be tried?" The way in which this principle has come under strain in cases where, as a practical matter, the disposal of the application will result in the disposal of the claim, and the consequences of the lack of congruence between the "great object" which underpins the principle and modern case management principles, have been noted elsewhere in this commentary. It has also been noted elsewhere that the matter is complicated by the fact that it is clear that, once the threshold test has been applied and passed, and the court moves on to applying the appropriate guidelines, in certain circumstances the strengths of the parties' cases become relevant. (See further, the discussion of interim mandatory injunctions, para.15–24 below.)

## 7. STRENGTH OF APPLICANT'S CASE IN FREEZING INJUNCTION CASES

In *Rasu Maritima SA v Perusahaan Pertambangan Minyakdangas Bumi Negara (Pertamina)* [1978] Q.B. 644; [1977] 3 W.L.R. 518, CA, Lord Denning M.R. said that a freezing injunction (then known as a Mareva injunction) could be granted to freeze the assets within the jurisdiction of a defendant out of the jurisdiction whenever the claimant can show that he has "a good arguable case" (see also *Fary-Jones v I.F.M*, April 10, 1979, unrep., CA). His Lordship said that was an appropriate test because it was the test to be applied for service on a defendant out of the jurisdiction (under the rules of court applicable at the time) and he believed it was in conformity with the test as to the granting of interlocutory injunctions as laid down in the *American Cyanamid Co* case. **15–23**

***Paragraph numbers marked with a "+" can be found online and on CD.***

In *Ninemia Maritime Corporation v Trave Schiffahrtgesellschaft m.b.H und Co K.G. (The Niedersachsen)* [1983] 1 W.L.R. 1412; [1983] 2 Lloyd's Rep. 600, Mustill J. doubted the analogy with proceedings served out of the jurisdiction and said there were real difficulties in applying to freezing injunction cases the general principles governing the grant of interlocutory injunctions derived from the *American Cyanamid Co* case. A claimant seeks an ordinary interlocutory injunction for the purposes of holding until trial the substantive relief which he hopes to obtain on final judgment; the injunction is a direct reflection of his cause of action. A freezing injunction application, on the other hand, is of quite a different character; it bears no relation to the relief granted at trial. The claimant, however successful at the trial, will not obtain a perpetual injunction in terms of the interlocutory freezing injunction. The latter bears on assets which in the great majority of cases have no connection at all with the cause of action on which the injunction is founded. After referring to the *Rasu Maritima* case and later authorities (in particular *Z. Ltd v A.* [1982] Q.B. 558; [1982] 1 All E.R. 556, CA) Mustill J. said that, although they were not easy to reconcile, they establish that the claimant must have "a case of a certain strength" before the question of any freezing injunction relief can arise. In his lordship's opinion the claimant must show a case "which is more than barely capable of serious argument and yet not necessarily one which the judge believes to have a better than 50 per cent chance of success" (*ibid.* at p.404 and p.605). It would seem that this is not simply a substitute for the *American Cyanamid* "serious question to be tried" threshold test nor merely a test for evaluating the "relative strength of each party's case" in the limited circumstances permitted by guideline (6) when considering the "balance of convenience". It is a test to be applied in all cases before the question of any freezing injunction relief can arise.

The conclusion reached by Mustill J. in The *Niedersachsen* case was not disturbed on appeal and in subsequent freezing injunction cases the "good arguable case" test derived from it (together with other relevant considerations) has been habitually applied; e.g. *Aiglon Ltd v Gau Shan Co Ltd* [1993] 1 Lloyd's Rep. 164; see also *Polly Peck International Plc v Nadir (No.2)* [1992] 4 All E.R. 769, CA (injunction against co-defendant bank discharged on ground that the claimant's claim against it was no more than speculative); *Rowland v Gulfpac Ltd* [1999] Lloyd's Rep. Bank. 86 (although arguable that, on basis of articles of association, directors had claim for indemnity they had no good arguable case to that effect). In *Derby v Weldon* [1990] Ch. 48; [1989] 2 W.L.R. 276, CA, Parker L.J. said (at p.57 and p.283) that in freezing injunction cases the test is not whether there is "a serious question to be tried", but rather whether the applicant has shown "a good arguable case", and added that this difference "is incapable of definition").

In *Rowland v Gulfpac Ltd,* op cit, Rix J. stressed the importance of giving careful attention to the threshold question of whether the applicant has a good arguable case (and not proceeding on the basis of the "bona fide issue to be tried" test), especially in cases where the competing interests that will have to be taken into account upon the threshold being past on the question of the court's exercise of discretion are very powerful.

## 8. MANDATORY INJUNCTIONS

**15–24** A mandatory injunction directs that a positive act should be done to repair some omission or to restore the prior position by undoing some wrongful act. In certain circumstances, a mandatory injunction may be granted in a quia timet action; that is to say, to prevent an apprehended legal wrong where none has occurred at present and the applicant is without any remedy at law (*Morris v Redland Bricks ltd.* [1970] A.C. 652, HL). Traditionally, the power of the court to grant a positive injunction has been regarded as a more serious power than the power to grant a negative injunction, largely for the reason that it is one thing to order a respondent to refrain from doing something and another to order him to do something. Further, the power to grant a positive injunction has been regarded as a power that has to be exercised more carefully where it is sought to prevent an apprehended legal wrong than where it is sought to undo some wrongful act. Such distinctions may come sharply into focus or fade depending on the circumstances of the case.

The jurisdiction of the court to grant an injunction enshrined in s.37(1) of the Senior Courts Act 1981 is stated widely and in general terms. The court may by order "whether interlocutory or final" grant an injunction "in all cases in which it appears to the court to be just and convenient to do so". This has been regarded as quite sufficient to give the court jurisdiction to grant, not only prohibitory injunctions, but also mandatory injunctions. Further, it has been regarded as sufficient to give the court jurisdiction to grant a remedy in the form of a mandatory injunction, not only at a trial (as a final remedy), but also upon an interlocutory application (as an interim remedy).

Obviously, the question whether a mandatory injunction may be granted at all is quite distinct from the question whether it should be granted on an interlocutory application. The considerations relevant to the former question may largely overlap with those relevant to the latter, but they are distinct considerations nonetheless and are not exact.

In a number of cases decided since the principles and guidelines derived from the *American Cyanamid Co* case were formulated, questions have arisen as to the application of those principles and guidelines where the interim remedy sought is not a prohibitory injunction but a mandatory injunction (or, at least, has mandatory aspects). The particular significance of the *American Cyanamid Co* case was that it held there that it was not a necessary condition for the grant of an interim injunction that the applicant should show that he had a prima facie case; a showing of a serious question to be tried was sufficient. Before the *American Cyanamid Co* case, the authorities stated that, where a mandatory injunction was sought the court had to be satisfied, not only that the applicant had a prima facie case, but that his case was "unusually strong and clear" giving the court a "high degree of assurance" that at the trial it will appear that the injunction was rightly granted (*Shepherd Homes Ltd v Sandham* [1971] Ch. 340 (Megarry J.)). Inevitably, after the *American Cyanamid Co* case the question arose whether it was intended that the lower "serious question to be tried" standard should be applied, not only in cases of applications for prohibitory injunctions, but also in cases of applications for mandatory injunctions. A division of opinion emerged. In some cases it was said that, at least in certain circumstances where interim mandatory injunctions were sought, the *American Cyanamid* principles and guidelines were not relevant (see *Leisure Data v Bell* [1988] F.S.R. 367, CA, and the cases referred to there). In other cases courts proceeded on the assumption that they were relevant (see further below).

An investigation of this controversy reveals that the division of opinion was based, not only on lingering disagreement as to the wisdom of introducing the lower "serious question to be tried" standard, but on a lack of agreement (1) as to precisely what those principles (of which the lower standard test is but one) and guidelines actually say, (2) as to which of them bring into play as a consideration the likely result at the trial, and (3) as to the degree of flexibility with which they may be applied. As is explained immediately below, in modern cases it has been made clear that it is not right to say that applications for interim mandatory injunctions lie outwith the principles and guidelines derived from the *American Cyanamid Co* case. In particular, the proposition that where an interim mandatory injunction is sought the balance of convenience test requires that it should not be granted unless there is "a high degree of assurance" that at the trial it will appear that the injunction was rightly granted, has been rejected.

In *Nottingham Building Society v Eurodynamics Systems* [1993] F.S.R. 468, the claimants brought a contractual claim against their suppliers of computer services. The remedies sought by the claimants included an order requiring the defendants to deliver up certain computer software to which they claimed to be entitled upon termination of the agreements. The claimants applied for interlocutory relief in the form of a mandatory injunction to compel the defendants to deliver up before trial of the action such of the software as remained in their possession power or control. Chadwick J. applied the *American Cyanamid* principles and guidelines. Having determined that damages would not be an adequate remedy for either party, he went on to consider the balance of convenience. After considering the authorities referred to above (and, in addition, *Films Rover International Ltd v Cannon Film Sales Ltd* [1987] 1 W.L.R. 670), the judge said that the balance of convenience was to be determined in accordance with the following principles:

(1) The overriding consideration is which course is likely to involve the least risk of injustice if it turns out to be "wrong" in the sense of granting an interlocutory injunction to a party who fails to establish his right at trial (or would fail if there was a trial) or, alternatively, in failing to grant an injunction to a party who succeeds (or would succeed) at trial.

***Paragraph numbers marked with a "+" can be found online and on CD.***

(2) In considering whether to grant a mandatory injunction, the court must keep in mind that an order which requires a party to take some positive step at an interlocutory stage, may well carry a greater risk of injustice if it turns out to have been wrongly made than an order which merely prohibits action, thereby preserving the status quo.

(3) It is legitimate, where a mandatory injunction is sought, to consider whether the court does feel a high degree of assurance that the claimant will be able to establish this right at a trial. That is become the greater the degree of assurance the claimant will ultimately establish his right, the less will be the risk of injustice if the injunction is granted.

(4) But, even where the court is unable to feel any high degree of assurance that the claimant will establish his right, there may still be circumstances in which it is appropriate to grant a mandatory injunction at an interlocutory stage. Those circumstances will exist where the risk of injustice if this injunction is refused sufficiently outweigh the risk of injustice if it is granted.

In the circumstances (and without having to reach the fourth and last of these principles), Chadwick J. found that the risk of least injustice lay on the side of granting the claimant the interim mandatory injunction which it sought, rather than in leaving it to expend further time and money and then claim damages from an insolvent defendant. His lordship explained that this was a case in which he felt a high degree of assurance that the claimants would establish at trial that the contract was repudiated by the defendant. The Court of Appeal dismissed the defendant's appeal ([1995] F.S.R. 605, CA) (the principal issue on the appeal was whether the material wherein the judge found his "high degree of assurance" was inadequate because the evidence of the witnesses was in affidavit form and not the subject of cross-examination, and because discovery was not complete).

The fourth and last of the principles enunciated by Chadwick J., though not relied upon in this case, is perhaps the most important. There may be circumstances where the balance of convenience lies in granting the mandatory injunction for which the claimant applies, even though the court is unable to feel any high degree of assurance that he will establish his right at trial. This reflects the judgment of Hoffmann J. in *Films Rover International Ltd v Cannon Film Sales Ltd* in which his lordship said that, if it appears to the court that, exceptionally, the case is one in which withholding a mandatory interlocutory injunction would in fact carry a greater risk of injustice than granting it even though the court does not feel a "high degree of assurance" about the claimant's chances of establishing his right, there cannot be any rational basis for withholding the injunction. See further, and to same effect, *R. v Secretary of State for Transport, Ex p. Factortame Ltd (No.2)* [1991] 1 A.C. 603, HL, at 683, per Lord Jauncey; *National Commercial Bank Jamaica Ltd v Olint Corp Ltd (Practice Note)* [2009] UKPC 16, [2009] 1 W.L.R. 1405, [2009] Bus. L.R. 1110, PC, at [19] and [20].

In *Zockoll Group Ltd v Mercury Communications Ltd* [1998] F.S.R. 354, CA, a two-judge court of the Court of Appeal refused the claimant's application for an interim mandatory injunction made on the claimant's appeal from a judge's refusal to grant a prohibitory injunction. In this case Phillips L.J. (with whom Simon Brown L.J. agreed in the result) endorsed the principles enunciated by Chadwick J. in the Nottingham Building Society case (including the fourth and last of them) and commended his lordship's "concise summary" as being "all the citation that should in future be necessary" to guide the court on the question of the balance of convenience in cases where an interim mandatory injunction is sought. That summary is routinely referred to by judges at first instance (e.g. *Nikitenko v LeBoeuf Greene & Macrae,* December 16, 1998, unrep. (Richard McCombe Q.C.); *Norbrook Laboratories Ltd v National Office of Animal Health Ltd,* August 9, 2001, unrep., (Gray J.); *Getmapping Plc v Ordnance Survey* [2002] EWHC 1089 (Ch), May 31, 2002, unrep. (Laddie J.); *AAH Pharmaceuticals Ltd v Pfizer Ltd* [2007] EWHC 565 (Ch), March 5, 2007, unrep. (David Richards J.)). The approach of the court to applications of this type is illustrated by *Chambers v British Olympic Assoc* [2008] EWHC 2028 (QB), July 18, 2008, unrep. (Mackay J.), where an athlete brought proceedings for a declaration that a BOA bye-law was invalid, and applied for an interlocutory (and, in effect) mandatory injunction in circumstances in which, realistically, the disposal of that application would dispose of the substantive claim. The application was refused. The judge found (1) that he was not satisfied "to high degree of assurance" that the claimant would establish invalidity at trial, and (2) that the risk of injustice to the claimant in the event of the injunction being refused and his succeeding at trial, was not such as sufficiently to outweigh the risk of injustice if it was granted.

In *Astro Exito Navegacion SA v Southland Enterprise Co Ltd (No.2)* [1982] Q.B. 1248; [1982] 3 W.L.R. 296; [1982] 3 All E.R. 335, CA, on the defendants' application the judge stayed the claimants' action for specific performance pending arbitration on terms which included a mandatory injunction requiring the defendants to authorise the release by a bank of moneys secured by letter of credit, the money so released to be lodged in the joint names of the solicitors for the parties pending further order. In dismissing the defendants' appeal the Court of Appeal held (following *Smith v Peters* (1875) L.R. 20 Eq. 511) that the court has power, in an appropriate case, to grant an interlocutory mandatory order compelling the execution of a contractual obligation (this issue was not further pursued in the House of Lords, see [1983] A.C. 787; [1983] 2 All E.R. 725, HL).

In *Leisure Data v Bell* [1988] F.S.R. 367, CA, it was said that circumstances can arise (e.g. where there is "a salvage element" involved) where it is necessary that some form of mandatory order should be made to deal with a situation which cannot on the practical realities be left to wait until the trial. (In this case, various cases were cited illustrations.)

## 9. UNDERTAKING AS TO DAMAGES

Where a claimant is successful in an application for an order for an interim injunction restraining the defendant, normally the order will impose various undertakings on the claimant. (Generally they are called "cross-undertakings", to distinguish them from the undertakings that the defendant is required to give by the order.) **15–25**

### *(a) Introduction*

The Senior Courts Act 1981 s.37(2) states that an order granting an interlocutory injunction may be made either unconditionally or on such terms and conditions as the court thinks just. In *American Cyanamid Co v Ethicon Ltd* [1975] A.C. 396,HL, Lord Diplock explained (at p.406) that, where a claimant is granted relief by way of interlocutory injunction, the practice is (and has been since at least the middle of the nineteenth century) to make this subject to a condition in the form of the claimant's undertaking to pay damages to the defendant for any loss sustained by reason of the injunction if it subsequently transpires that it ought not to have been granted; for example, if the proceedings are discontinued, or if the injunction is discharged before trial, or "if it should be held at the trial that the claimant had not been entitled to restrain the defendant from doing what he was threatening to do". **15–26**

### *(b) Undertakings in interim injunctions generally*

Originally the undertaking was inserted only in ex parte orders for injunctions. The object was to protect the court as well as the defendant from improper applications for injunctions. By degrees the practice was extended to all cases of interlocutory injunction (*Smith v Day* (1882) 21 Ch.D. 421,CA, at p.424 per Jessel M.R.). At an early stage it was held that an undertaking ought to be a condition of every interlocutory injunction (*Graham v Campbell* (1878) 7 Ch.D. 490,, CA at p.484, CA, per James L.J.), though not where the order is in the nature of a final order (*Fenner v Wilson* [1893] 2 Ch. 656). **15–27**

A cross-undertaking is not given by the applicant to the respondent; it is given by the applicant to the court (*F. Hoffmann-La Roche & Co A.G. v Secretary of State for Trade and Industry* [1975] A.C. 295, HL, at p.361 per Lord Diplock; *Fletcher Sutcliffe Wild Ltd v Burch* [1982] F.S.R. 64). The terms of the cross-undertaking are for the court. Two things follow from this. First, where it is a matter for doubt, the proper interpretation of the cross-undertaking is not a matter if divining the mutual understanding of the parties to the proceedings. Secondly, it may be enforced by one who is not a party to the proceedings in those circumstances where it is given, not merely for the benefit of the respondent, but for his benefit as well (as to which, see further below) (*SmithKline Beecham Plc v Apotex Europe Ltd* [2005] EWHC 1655 (Ch); [2006] 1 W.L.R. 872; [2006] 2 All E.R. 53, at para.43 per Lewison J. (in this case the development and extent of undertakings generally is explained)).

***Paragraph numbers marked with a "+" can be found online and on CD.***

Such undertaking has been described as the "price" of an injunction (*Tucker v New Brunswick Trading Company of London*, (1890) 44 Ch.D. 249, CA, at p.253, per Lindley L.J.). Upon the respondent being required to undertake to conduct himself in accordance with the terms of the injunction, the applicant undertakes (cross-undertakes) to pay damages if, in the event, required to do so. If the applicant is unwilling to undertake to pay the price, he does not get the injunction. The cross-undertaking is the quid pro quo for the court making an interim order without having determined the facts or the claimant's entitlement to it. It is given, not to identified respondents, but to the court to enable the court, if it thinks fit, to compensate any innocent sufferer from an interim injunction which ought not to have been granted (*Harley Street Capital Ltd v Tchigirinski* [2005] EWHC 2471 (Ch), May 24, 2005, unrep. (Michael Briggs Q.C.)).

In *United States Securities & Exchange Commission v Manterfield* [2009] EWCA Civ 27; [2009] 1 Lloyd's Rep. 399; [2009] 2 All E.R. 1009, CA, where the applicant for a world-wide freezing order was a foreign public agency (C) and the application was made in support of proceedings abroad, the respondent's submission that, because C could offer no cross-undertaking, no freezing order ought to be made, was rejected by the Court of Appeal and it was held that the judge was right to start from the position that a cross-undertaking would not be given and to consider whether this was a case in which it should or should not be dispensed with.

The court cannot compel an applicant to give a cross-undertaking, but it can refuse to grant an injunction unless he does. Where the court is minded to impose such a condition it is a matter for the applicant to decide whether he is prepared to give it and, if it is insisted upon, to provide security. If he is not, the injunction does not go (*F. Hoffmann-La Roche & Co A.G. v Secretary of State for Trade and Industry*, op cit, at p.361 per Lord Diplock).

The willingness of the applicant to give the cross-undertaking is a very material consideration for the court in determining whether or not the interim injunction should be ordered. The fact that an ultimately unsuccessful claimant will have to compensate the defendant for losses suffered by him through his complying with the interim remedy for the duration of the period during which it took effect is a major factor in assessing the balance of convenience.

Since a cross-undertaking cannot be imposed, it follows that a fortiori it cannot be imposed retrospectively (*SmithKline Beecham Plc v Apotex Europe Ltd*, op cit, at para.41).

Usually, the cross-undertaking will be expressly given by the applicant and will be expressly incorporated in the court's order. Where it is not expressly given, the court may enforce an implied undertaking even if it had not been included in the order, unless the contrary had been agreed and expressed at the time (see *SmithKline Beecham Plc v Apotex Europe Ltd, op cit*, at paras 26 to 37 and cases cited there).

Where a limited cross-undertaking is offered and accepted by the court, there is in general no room for implying some further offer of an undertaking beyond that which was expressly offered and accepted (*ibid*).

The use of the word "damages" in this context is perhaps inappropriate because it might suggest that the grant of the injunction involved a breach of some legal or equitable rights of the defendant. The undertaking is given to the court and is not a matter of contract between the parties. At the time when it grants the injunction, the court has not finally determined the rights of the parties. The cross-undertaking is intended to provide a method of compensating the party enjoined if it subsequently appears that the injunction was wrongly granted (*Cheltenham and Gloucester Building Society v Ricketts* [1993] 1 W.L.R. 1545, CA; [1993] 4 All E.R. 276, CA at p.1551 and p.281 per Neill L.J.). A cross-undertaking is better described as providing for "compensation for loss", and this is the expression used in the standard cross-undertakings inserted in freezing injunctions and search orders (see further below). If the injunction is discharged at trial, the court has no power in its own hands to award damages to the successful defendant for any loss he may have suffered while it was in force. The cross-undertaking gives the defendant a means for redress, should he apply to enforce it.

As an extra condition, the claimant may be required to fortify the undertaking by giving security (see further para.15–32 below).

The point of a cross-undertaking in damages is to provide a means of compensation for loss if it occurs in relation to the injunction or undertaking. To that extent the court has, if necessary, to form a view as to the kind and degree of loss that may result in deciding whether an undertaking has sufficient value (with or without fortification) (*Re DPR Futures Ltd* [1989] 1 W.L.R. 778 (Millett J.); *Bhimji v Chatwani (No.2)* [1992] 1 W.L.R. 1158 (Knox J.); *Sinclair Investment Holdings S.A. v Cushnie* [2004] EWHC 218, (Ch), February 12, 2004, unrep. (Mann J.)).

An interlocutory injunction may be granted on terms that the claim form should be amended by adding a claimant in order that an undertaking as to damages might be given on his behalf (see, e.g. *Spanish General Agency Corp. v Spanish Corp.* (1891) 63 L.T. 161). In a case where it is determined subsequently that the injunction should not have been granted the undertaking is likely to be enforced, though the court retains a discretion not to do so (see further, "Application to enforce undertaking", para.15–34, below).

As amended by TSO CPR Update 42 (October 2006), para.5.1(1) of Practice Direction (Interim Injunctions) (i.e. 25PD supplementing CPR Pt 25) states that an injunction must contain "an undertaking by the applicant to the court to pay any damages which the respondent sustains which the court considers the applicant should pay", and para.5.1A states that, when the court makes an order for an injunction "it should consider whether to require an undertaking by the applicant to pay any damages sustained by a person other than the respondent, including another party to the proceedings or any other person who may suffer loss as a consequence of the order".

Where it is confined to damages suffered by the respondent, the usual form of undertaking is: "to abide by any order which this court may make as to damages in case this court shall be of the opinion that the respondent shall have suffered any by reason of this order which the applicant ought to pay".

### *(c) Undertakings in freezing injunctions and search orders*

As is the case with interim injunctions generally, freezing injunctions granted as interim remedies are granted on terms that the applicant gives an undertaking in damages to compensate the respondent should the court, in the event, find that the injunction caused the respondent loss for which he should be compensated. For explanation, see *Banco Nacional de Comercio Exterior SNC v Emprssa de Telecommunicaciones de Cuba SA* [2007] EWCA Civ 662; [2007] 2 Lloyd's Rep. 484, CA. **15–28**

In para.(1) of Sch.B of the example of a interim injunction in the form of a freezing injunction given in the Annex to Practice Direction (Interim Injunctions) (one of the practice directions supplementing CPR Pt 25) the undertaking to compensate the respondent is given as follows: "If the court later finds that this order has caused loss to the Respondent, and decides that the Respondent should be compensated for that loss, the Applicant will comply with any order the court may make." In an appropriate case the undertaking should be extended to include any other person who may suffer loss as a consequence of the order (see further para.15–29 below).

The applicant should put in a statement indicating his wealth or that he has sufficient adequately to cover the undertaking (*Staines v Walsh* ; [2003] EWHC 1486 *The Times* August 1, 2003, (Ch), (Laddie J.); *Sinclair Investment Holdings S.A. v Cushnie* [2004] EWHC 218, (Ch), February 12, 2004, unrep. (Mann J.)). Where a freezing injunction is granted after judgment it is the usual practice not to require such an undertaking. However, the practice is not immutable and undertakings may be required where the judge gives permission to appeal in a case where the substantive issue on which the injunction had been granted was a point of some difficulty upon which the Court of Appeal may take a different view (*Gwembe Valley Development Co Ltd (In Receivership) v Koshy (Injunction: Cross Undertaking in Damages)*, *The Times*, February 28, 2002 (Rimer J.)). It is important that undertakings given are complied with and, if they are not, that there is a good explanation as to why. The fact that there was a failure is a potentially serious matter that might justify the injunction being discharged (*Flightwise Travel Service Ltd v Gill* ; [2003] EWHC 3082 (Ch) *The Times*, December 5, 2003 (Neuberger J.)).

It is inherent in the freezing order jurisdiction that a claimant must disclose to the defendant any change in his financial position affecting his ability to honour his cross-undertaking (*Staines v Walsh* ; [2003] EWHC 1486 (Ch) *The Times*, August 1, 2003, (Laddie J.)). Other undertakings by the applicant may also be attached to a freezing injunction (whether made before or after judgment). For example, an undertaking not to use information obtained as a result of the order for the purpose of other legal proceedings or not to bring other proceedings. The purpose of such undertakings is to prevent the injunction from causing injustice or being used as a weapon of oppression (*Bates v Microstar Ltd* [2003] EWHC 661 (Ch) (Mr Bernard Livesey Q.C.) (claimant in breach of contract claim released from undertaking to permit his bringing of derivative claim in foreign jurisdiction)). Similar undertakings may be imposed on an order for the cross-examination of a defendant on his disclosure statement made in complying with a freezing injunction (as in *Motorola Credit Corp v Uzan (No.2)* [2002] EWHC 2187; October 18, 2002, unrep. (David Steel J.)).

Undertakings given by a claimant as a condition of the grant of a freezing injunction must be carried out to the letter; breach of such an undertaking may not necessarily be regarded as similar to a misrepresentation or non-disclosure of material facts, but, in an appropriate case, breach of an undertaking may result in discharge of the injunction (*Sabani v Economakis, The Times*, June 17, 1988).

In para.(1) of Sch.C of the example of a search order, also given in the Annex to Practice Direction (Interim Injunctions), the undertaking is given as follows: "If the court later finds that this order or carrying it out has caused loss to the Respondent, and decides that the Respondent should be compensated for that loss, the Applicant will comply with any order the court may make. Further if the carrying out of this order has been in breach of the terms of this order or otherwise in a manner inconsistent with the Applicant's solicitors' duties as officers of the court, the Applicant will comply with any order for damages the court may make."

As to undertakings by Crown, see para.15–53 below. As to the giving of security for undertakings in freezing injunctions and search orders, see para.15–32 below.

### *(d) Extent of undertaking as to damages*

**15–29** In a simple case, the cross-undertaking given by the claimant, as applicant for an interim injunction, extends to compensating losses suffered by the defendant restrained by the order. In a more complicated case there may be several defendants, and the question may arise whether the benefit of the undertaking extends to all of them. And in any case there may be the further question whether third parties, being persons affected in some way by the impact of the injunction, may also benefit. The question of the position of third parties has come to the fore since the development of the freezing injunction (Mareva injunction), a form of interim remedy that is unusual in a number of respects.

In *Berkeley Administration Inc v McClelland* [1996] I.L.P r.772, CA, the Court of Appeal concluded that, subject to any direction to the contrary a court may give in a particular case: (1) advantage can be taken of a cross-undertaking in damages by every defendant who was a party to the action when the undertaking was granted; (2) advantage cannot be taken of the cross-undertaking by persons who are not parties to the action, or, at least, do not become parties until after the order as been discharged. His lordship added that, in his opinion, the benefit of the injunction should extend to defendants who become parties while the undertaking is in force. Presumably, the benefit to such defendants runs from the time when they were joined, and is not restrospective (*SmithKline Beecham Plc v Apotex Europe Ltd* [2005] EWHC 1655 (Ch); [2006] 1 W.L.R. 872; [2006] 2 All E.R. 53, at para.49 per Lewison J.).

It is pointless, at the time of the grant of the injunction, to go into the question of which defendants will be affected if the injunction turns out to have been granted improperly, since damages will be payable only where damage is actually suffered (*Dubai Bank Ltd v Galadari (No.2)* [1990] 1 W.L.R. 731, CA). Within a few years of its being established that the court has jurisdiction to grant freezing injunctions, it became standard practice for the court to require cross-undertakings to be given by applicants in favour of banks and others who would be put to expense by execution of the order. It was held that an applicant for a freezing injunction should normally be required in addition to undertake, as a term of the order, to indemnify any third party (e.g. a bank) against any costs, expenses or fees reasonably incurred by the third party in seeking to comply with the order (*Searose v Seatrain (UK) Ltd* [1981] 1 W.L.R. 894; [1981] 1 All E.R. 806; *Clipper Maritime Co Ltd of Monravia v Mineralimportexport* [1981] 1 W.L.R. 1262; [1981] 3 All E.R. 664 and *Banco Nacional de Comercio Exterior SNC v Empresa de Telecommunicationes de Cuba SA* [2007] EWCA Civ 662; [2007] 2 Lloyd's Rep. 484, CA). The applicant may be obliged to make a broader undertaking in this respect and agree to indemnify the third party as well against all liabilities which may flow from such compliance (*Z Ltd v A-Z and AA-LL* [1982] 1 Q.B. 558; sub nom. *Z. Ltd v A.*

[1982] 1 All E.R. 556, CA). Whether a particular undertaking is of the narrower or broader type is a matter of construction (*Guinness Peat Aviation (Belgium) N.V. v Hispania Lineas Aereas SA* [1992] 1 Lloyd's Rep. 190). A form of the broader undertaking is included in the standard forms and should normally be used.

The recognition that, in that context, the cross-undertaking should be given in terms that would benefit third parties raised awareness of the fact that the court did not lack jurisdiction to require such terms in other forms of interim relief, if not routinely, then at least where this was just and convenient (e.g. *Allied Irish Bank v Ashford Hotels Ltd* [1997] 3 All E.R. 309, CA (application for cross-undertaking in favour of third parties as a condition for appointing a receiver refused)).

As was noted above, para.5.1A of Practice Direction (Interim Injunctions), para.5.1(1) (see para.25APD.5 below) states that, when the court makes an order for an injunction it should consider whether to require an undertaking by the applicant to pay any damages sustained by a person other than the respondent, including not only another party to the proceedings, but also "any other person who may suffer loss as a consequence of the order". The addition of "any other person who may suffer loss" was made by TSO CPR Update 42 (October 2006), and was made for the purpose of dealing with problems that had been identified (see *SmithKline Beecham Plc v Apotex Europe Ltd* [2006] EWCA Civ 658; [2007] Ch. 71, CA; [2006] 4 All E.R. 1078, CA, at para.29 per Jacob L.J.). The origins of the practice of requiring undertakings to the court in favour of third parties as part of the price of an interim injunction can be traced to the development of freezing orders, but is not confined to such orders (*SmithKline Beecham Plc v Apotex Europe Ltd*, op. cit.). Where a claimant seeks an interim injunction other than a freezing order, the court will not, as a matter of course, make the grant of an order conditional on the claimant undertaking to pay the reasonable costs of any third party incurred as a result of the order, but in appropriate circumstances the court may consider imposing a wider undertaking in damages than that normally extracted from an applicant for an interlocutory injunction (*Miller Brewing Co v Ruhi Enterprises Ltd* ; [2003] EWHC 1606 *The Times*, June 6, 2003 (Neuberger J.) (such undertaking to pay costs of one co-defendant, where freezing order made against another defendant, not imposed in trade mark claim)).

### *(e) Applicant unable to offer credible undertaking*

Where a claimant brings an action for a permanent injunction, normally, and for obvious reasons, he will apply for an interlocutory injunction. Where an applicant for an interim injunction is impecunious, or of limited means, he may be unable to give a credible undertaking, or unwilling to give an undertaking to the limit of his means. In *Allen v Jambo Holdings Ltd* [1980] 1 W.L.R. 1252; [1980] 2 All E.R. 502, CA, it was said that the court will not deny a legally aided claimant an interlocutory injunction (in this case, a freezing injunction), to which he would otherwise be entitled simply on the ground that his undertaking in damages would be of limited value, since questions of financial stability ought not to affect the position in regard to what is the essential justice of the case. In *Oxy Electric Ltd v Zainuddin* [1991] 1 W.L.R. 115; [1990] 2 All E.R. 902, the court rejected the argument that the action of a claimant of apparently limited means should be struck out unless he was willing to apply for an interlocutory injunction and to support an undertaking with adequate security (distinguishing *Blue Town Investments Ltd v Higgs & Hill Plc* [1990] 1 W.L.R. 696; [1990] 2 All E.R. 897, on the grounds that in that case the claimant's chances of obtaining a final injunction at trial were minimal). **15–30**

### *(f) Liquidated company applicant*

In *Rosling v Law Guarantee and Trust Co* (1903) 47 S.J. 255, the court rejected the argument that an insolvent company can only obtain an injunction on the condition that its liquidator gives a personal undertaking (not following *Westminster Association v Upward* (1880) 24 S.J. 690, where counsel for the claimant volunteered an undertaking on behalf of liquidator). **15–31**

In a case where proceedings are brought by the liquidators of a company against former directors to recover sums derived from the company's assets, the liquidators may be permitted to give a limited undertaking commensurate with the size of the company's assets; there is no requirement in such a case for the liquidators to provide

***Paragraph numbers marked with a "+" can be found online and on CD.***

an unlimited guarantee that the defendants will suffer no loss (*Re DPR Futures Ltd* [1989] 1 W.L.R. 778).

### (g) Fortifying undertaking

15–32 In a proper case, the court may impose a condition to the effect that the claimant's undertaking should be fortified by his giving security in a certain sum by the bond of an insurance company or by payment into court or by some other means, for example, by payment to the applicant's solicitor or to the solicitors for each party jointly to be held pending further order (*Baxter v Claydon* [1952] W.N. 376).

A defendant should apply for the security at the time when the injunction is granted and the undertaking is given. The court has no power subsequently to impose such an additional term on the grant of an injunction (*Commodity Ocean Transport Corp. v Basford Unicorn Industries Ltd (The Mito)* [1987] 2 Lloyd's Rep. 197).

Where an injunction has been granted, the respondent may apply to the court for the security to be fortified by further or additional security. Before an application to fortify an undertaking can succeed a likelihood of a significant loss arising as a result of the injunction and a sound basis for belief that the undertaking will be insufficient must be shown (*Bhimji v Chatwani; Chatwani v Bhimji (No.2)* [1992] 1 W.L.R. 1158; [1992] B.C.L.C. 387). For an explanation of the matters that the court should take into account where the defendant applies for an uplift by way of fortification of the security, see *Harley Street Capital Ltd v Tchigirinski* [2005] EWHC 2471 (Ch), May 24, 2005, unrep. (Mr Briggs Q.C.).

In the case of an application for a freezing injunction, the applicant should give security for the undertaking in damages. Paragraph (2) of Sch.B of the example of a interim injunction in the form of a freezing injunction given in the Annex to Practice Direction (Interim Injunctions) (one of the practice directions supplementing CPR Pt 25) contains a specimen clause having that effect. It states that the applicant will cause a written guarantee in a sum fixed by the order to be issued from a bank with a place of business in England and Wales.

In the case of an application for a search order the applicant should give security for the undertaking in damages. Paragraph (5) of Sch.C of the example of a search order given in the Annex to Practice Direction (Interim Injunctions) contains a specimen clause having that effect. It states that the applicant will maintain pending further order a sum fixed by the order in his solicitor's account.

### (h) Enforcement and assessment

15–33 The undertaking "in damages" (or to provide "compensation for loss") is given to the court and not to the party enjoined. However, if it should be held at the trial that the claimant had not been entitled by interlocutory injunction to restrain the defendant from doing what he was threatening to do, or if it is established before trial that the injunction ought not to have been granted in the first instance, the party enjoined may apply to the court for the undertaking to be enforced.

*(i) Application to enforce undertaking*

15–34 Sometimes, the status of the interim injunction in these circumstances mentioned immediately above is described as "wrongful", but this is not apt because it suggests that the court's decision to grant the injunction (now with hindsight seen to be unnecessary) was wrong or unjust when it was made. Old authorities on the subject established that an application to enforce an undertaking should be made promptly, and where the undertaking is dissolved at or before the trial should be then made; but this is not essential, and in a proper case damages may be awarded in a later application (*Re Hailstone, Hopkinson v Carter* (1910) 102 L.T. 877); but a long delay is fatal except in special circumstances (see *Ex p.Hall, Re Wood* (1883) 23 Ch.D. 644, and *Schlesinger v Bedford* [1893] W.N. 57). As a practical matter, in many cases injunctions will remain in being until the trial and in such cases the propriety of its original grant and the question of the enforcement of the undertaking will not be considered before the conclusion of the trial. Even then the court may occasionally wish to postpone the question of enforcement to a later date (see *Financiera Avenida v Shiblaq*, *The Times*, January 14, 1991, CA, per Lloyd L.J.).

When an application to enforce an undertaking as to damages is made there are two separate points to consider: first, as a matter of discretion, should the court order that the undertaking be enforced?, secondly, if so, what loss had the defendant suffered in terms of money, was it caused by the order and was it too remote? (*Balkanbank v Taher (No.2)* [1995] 1 W.L.R. 1056, CA). A judge may leave both questions to be determined at the same time, or, more probably, in an enquiry as to damages, or he may decide the first question himself. If he answers it in the sense that the undertaking should be enforced, he may then leave it to some other holder of judicial office to enquire into causation, remoteness and quantum.

An order made on an application for an inquiry into damages should spell out clearly what, if any, residual discretion is left to be exercised later and it should, for example, be possible to tell on the face of the order whether the claimant is to pay the amount ascertained on the inquiry (*Balkanbank v Taher* [1994] 4 All E.R. 239, at p.260, per Clarke J.). The court has no jurisdiction to require the applicant to provide security for the claimant's costs in relation to the determination as to whether the undertaking should be enforced and to the inquiry as to damages if ordered (*C.T. Bowring & Co (Insurance) Ltd v Corsi & Partners Ltd* [1994] 2 Lloyd's Rep. 567, CA). For procedure where injunction is discharged before trial, see para.15–37 below.

### *(ii) Decision to enforce*

The question whether the undertaking should be enforced is a separate question from the question whether the injunction should be discharged or continued (*Cheltenham and Gloucester Building Society v Ricketts* [1993] 1 W.L.R. 1545, CA; [1993] 4 All E.R. 276, CA, at p.1551 and p.281 per Neill L.J.). The latter question comes before the former. In relation to the question whether an injunction should be discharged or continued there is a distinction to be drawn between (1) an order which, on the material before the judge at the time of the making of the order, ought not to have been made, and (2) an order which was properly made on such material but which was later shown on trial or on an application to set aside to have been made wrongly made on the true facts (*Southwark London Borough Council v Storrie*, December 3, 1997, CA, unrep.). In the first situation, evidence at trial cannot be relied upon to justify ex post facto the making of an ex parte order (*Columbia Picture Industries Inc v Robinson* [1986] 3 All E.R. 338; [1987] Ch. 38 at p.378 and p.85 per Scott J.). However, where an interlocutory injunction is set aside, either in the first or the second situation, in determining whether the undertaking in damages should be enforced, the court must consider all the circumstances of the case and in particular the threat or risk, if any, which faced the claimant when the injunction was made and the proved conduct of the defendant (*Cheltenham and Gloucester Building Society v Ricketts* [1993] 1 W.L.R. 1545, CA; [1993] 4 All E.R. 276, CA, at p.1554 and p.284, CA, per Neill L.J.;*Southwark London Borough Council v Storrie, December* December 3, 1997, CA, unrep. **15–35**

In a case where it is determined that the injunction should not have been granted, the undertaking is likely to be enforced, though the court retains a discretion not to do so (*Cheltenham and Gloucester Building Society v Ricketts* [1993] 1 W.L.R. 1545; [1993] 4 All E.R. 276, CA, at p.1551 and p.281 per Neill L.J., and *Ushers Brewery Ltd v P.S. King & Co (Finance) Ltd* [1972] 1 Ch. 148, and authorities cited in those cases; see also *Graham v Campbell* (1878) 7 Ch.D. 490, CA, at p.494 per James L.J., and Mem. by Jessel M.R. in [1879] W.N. 74). Further, an inquiry should be directed where the claimant discontinues his action (*Newcomer v Coulson* (1878) 7 Ch.D. 764). The law as to the discharge of freezing orders and the enforcement of undertakings where there has been material non-disclosure (whether innocent or not) was explained in *Dadourian Group International Inc v Simms* [2009] EWCA Civ 169; [2009] 1 Lloyd's Rep. 601, CA; see further Vol.1 para. 25.3.5.

As the power to enforce the undertaking is incidental to the power to grant an injunction (see *Re Hailstone* (1910) 102 L.T. 877, at p.880), the discretion will be exercised in accordance with ordinary equitable principles (*Cheltenham & Gloucester Building Society v Ricketts* [1993] 1 W.L.R. 1545; [1993] 4 All E.R. 276 at 284, CA, per Peter Gibson L.J.).

Where a claimant has obtained an interlocutory injunction restraining the defendant from doing something until trial, and the court decides at trial that a permanent injunction should not be granted, the defendant can normally expect, virtually as of right, to have an enquiry as to the damages to which he is entitled pursuant to the cross-undertaking which the claimant will have been required to give as a condition of obtaining the interlocutory injunction. However, there are plainly exceptions to this general rule. But it is clear that "special circumstances" are required before an enquiry can properly be refused (see *Lunn Poly Ltd v Liverpool & Lancashire Properties Ltd* [2006] EWCA Civ 430, March 15, 2006, unrep., CA, at para.42 per Neuberger L.J. and authorities cited there). The court retains a discretion not to enforce the undertaking:

> "if it considers that the conduct of the defendant in relation to the obtaining or continuing of the injunction or the enforcement of the undertaking makes it inequitable to do so" (*F. Hoffmann-La Roche & Co A.G. v Secretary of State for Trade and Industry* [1975] A.C. 295, HL, at p.361; [1974] 2 All E.R. 1128, HL, at p.1150 per Lord Diplock).

An inquiry as to damages should not be ordered unless there is at least some reasonably arguable case that the injunction has caused the complaining party some loss or damage for which compensation ought to be paid (*Direct Sea Enterprises Ltd v O'Connor* , October 14, 1997, unrep. (Sir Richard Scott, V.C.). Where an injunction is maintained in force for far longer than it ought to have been, prima facie the party subject to it is entitled to be compensated for any loss he may have been caused by the injunction being maintained in force for that excessive period (*ibid.*).

In *North Principal Investments Fund Ltd v Greenoak Renewable Energy Ltd* [2009] EWHC 985 (Ch), May 1, 2009, unrep. (David Richards J.) the judge reviewed the relevant authorities (in particular *Yukong Line Ltd v Rendsburg Investments Corporation* [2001] 2 Lloyd's Rep. 113, CA) and stated (1) that if it is established that the injunction was wrongly granted, albeit without fault on the claimant's part, the court will ordinarily order an inquiry as to damages in any case where it appears that loss may have been caused as a result, (2) that the applicant must adduce some credible evidence that he has suffered loss as the result of the making of the order, and (3) that if the defendant shows that he has suffered loss which was prima facie or arguably caused by the order, then the evidential burden of any contention that the relevant loss would have been suffered regardless of the making of the order in practice passes to the defendants and an inquiry will be ordered.

Enforcement has been refused where a local authority defendant acted high-handedly and unreasonably in dealing with a private claimant who brought an unsuccessful action in nuisance (*Great House at Sonning v Berkshire CC* December 18, 1996, unrep.).

Where the judge makes a consent order directing that there should be an inquiry, that order is not a decision, in the exercise of discretion, that the undertaking should be enforced (*Balkanbank v Taher* [1995] 1 W.L.R. 1056, CA).

### *(iii) Assessment or inquiry as to damages*

**15–36** Where the court determines that an undertaking should be enforced the next step is an assessment of the damages payable. (As to the measure of damages, see para.15–38 below.) Damages can only be obtained by an immediate assessment or by an order for an inquiry; an independent action will not lie (*Fletcher Sutcliffe Wild Ltd v Burch* [1982] F.S.R. 64).

Normally, the court will order an inquiry as to damages but, where appropriate, the court may instead proceed to an immediate assessment upon discharging the order (see, e.g. *Columbia Picture Industries Inc v Robinson* [1986] Ch. 38, CA; [1987] 3 All E.R. 338, CA, where the injunction was discharged at trial) and the court should always consider doing so where a search order or a freezing injunction is discharged on the return date (see below). Where an injunction was obtained without notice, but should neither have been sought nor granted, and the respondent's case for damages on the cross-undertaking was unanswerable, the circumstances may be such as to enable the trial judge to assess damages without sending the matter off to an inquiry with pleadings, disclosure, evidence, expert evidence and a stay of proceedings (*Econet Wireless Ltd v Vee Networks Ltd* [2006] EWHC 1829 (Comm), July 14, 2006, unrep. (Morison J.)).

The court may refuse an inquiry if the damage sustained is trivial or remote (*Smith v Day* (1882) 21 Ch.D. 421, CA). An inquiry may be directed though the claimant was not guilty of misrepresentation, suppression, or other default in obtaining the injunction (*Griffith v Blake*, (1884) 27 Ch.D. 474, CA). Where the claimant succeeds at trial, but only in part, it may be the case that the defendant was subjected to restraints under the injunction in excess of what the claimant was legitimately entitled to on the basis of his rights as determined at trial; in that event an inquiry as to the defendant's damages resulting from the excess restraints may be ordered (*Richardson (John) Computers Ltd v Flanders (No.2)* [1994] F.S.R. 144).

Although there is no specific provision to the effect, under the CPR and the inherent jurisdiction, the court has ample powers in appropriate circumstances to dismiss summarily an inquiry as to damages (*F.S.L. Services Ltd v Macdonald* [2001] EWCA Civ 1008; June 21, 2001, unrep., CA).

In both the Ch.D. and QBD the inquiry is usually held before a Master.

### (iv) Enforcement of undertaking where injunction discharged before trial

Where an interlocutory injunction is discharged before the trial the court at the **15–37** time of discharge is faced with a number of possibilities (the following is based on the judgments of Neill and Peter Gibson L.JJ. in *Cheltenham and Gloucester Building Society v Ricketts* [1993] 1 W.L.R. 1545; [1993] 4 All E.R. 276, CA).

(a) The court can determine forthwith that the undertaking as to damages should be enforced and can proceed at once to make an assessment of the damages. Save in the most straightforward of cases where all the relevant facts are known the court is unlikely to exercise its discretion in this way. It will only be in rare cases that the court can take this course because the relevant evidence of damages is unlikely to be available.

(b) The court can determine forthwith that the undertaking is not to be enforced and refuse the application; but, again, this will only be done in very straightforward cases, such as, for example, when it is clear that the applicant has suffered no loss by reason of the injunction.

(c) The court may determine that the undertaking should be enforced but then direct an inquiry as to damages in which issues of causation and quantum will have to be considered. It is likely that the order will include directions as to pleadings and discovery in the inquiry. The court should not order an inquiry as to damages and at the same time leave open for the tribunal at the inquiry to determine whether or not the undertaking should be enforced (*Norwest Holst Civil Engineering Ltd v Polysius Ltd*, *The Times*, July 23, 1987, CA; [1987] CA Transcript 644, cf., *Zygal Dynamics Plc v McNulty* [1989] CA Transcript 571, and *Barclays Bank Ltd v Rosenberg* (1985) 135 New L.J. 633, at p.634, per Evans J.). A decision that the undertaking should be enforced is a precondition for the making of an order of an inquiry as to damages.

(d) The court can adjourn the application for the enforcement of the undertaking to the trial or further order. Usually the application will be adjourned to the trial, especially in a case in which the question whether the interlocutory injunction was rightly granted in the first instance has not been determined (see *Ushers Brewery Ltd v P.S. King & Co (Finance) Ltd* [1971] 2 All E.R. 468; [1972] Ch. 148, and *Cheltenham and Gloucester Building Society v Ricketts* [1993] 1 W.L.R. 1545; [1993] 4 All E.R. 276, CA).

### (v) Measure of damages

On an inquiry as to damages, the measure of damages is not discretionary. The is- **15–38** sue is whether the party subject to the injunction can show that he has suffered loss as a result of giving undertakings and, if so, what that loss is (*Triodos Bank N.V. v Dobbs* [2005] EWHC 108 (Ch), February 8, 2005, unrep. (Lightman J.)). In *F. Hoffmann-La Roche & Co A.G. v Secretary of State for Trade and Industry* [1975] A.C. 295, HL, on the basis of old authority (in particular, *Smith v Day* (1882) 21 Ch.D. 421, CA) Lord Diplock expressed the view (at p.361) that quantification of compensation under a cross-undertaking should be on a breach of notional contract between the parties to the effect that the injunctor would not prevent the injunctee from doing the injuncted acts (see also *Cheltenham and Gloucester Building Society v Ricketts* [1993] 1 W.L.R. 1545; [1993] 4 All E.R. 276 at 285, CA, per Neill L.J.). On that basis, the paying party will pay only for such damage as he could reasonably foresee the injunction might cause, either from his general knowledge or from his knowledge of the particular circumstances of the injunctee. (This follows from the contractual principle of *Hadley v Baxendale*, (1854) 9 Exch. 341.) An injunctee cannot recover for any damage directly caused to him by the "wrongful" injunction if that damage could not be foreseen by the injunctor because he did not have enough knowledge of the injunctee's circumstances.

Although the matter has not been settled authoritatively, the contract basis for assessment seems to be the preferred approach. In *Triodos Bank N.V. v Dobbs*, op cit, Lightman J. ruled that the legal principles to be applied as to causation, remoteness and quantum are essentially contractual, and contractual principles regarding mitigation of damages must also apply. The date on which the party entitled to damages was released from the interim injunction may be highly relevant to the amount of damages to be recovered. Where that party was dilatory in perfecting the order discharging the injunction to which he was subject, and the delay aggravated his losses, his failure in that respect may amount to a failure to mitigate his loss (*ibid*).

In *Al-Rawas v Pegasus Energy Ltd* [2008] EWHC 617 (QB), April 8, 2008, unrep. (Jack J.) it was stated that general damages may be awarded where orders have been wrongly obtained for the purpose of compensating the defendant for the consequences of the orders which cannot be claimed as special damages, but unless the particular facts make it appropriate as an exception, damages for emotional distress are not recoverable. In addition, it was explained that, subject to an exception, the undertakings in the prescribed forms for search and seizure orders and for freezing orders require claimants to accept liability for compensatory damages only. The exception is where the claimant in carrying out a search order acted in breach of its terms or otherwise in a manner inconsistent with his solicitor's duties as an officer of the court.

It has been said that the contract basis for assessment is or may be too narrow in some cases, and a straightforward measure of "the loss which is the natural consequence of the injunction" should be preferred (*R. v Medicines Control Agency, Ex p.Smith & Nephew Pharmaceuticals Ltd* [1999] R.P.C. 705 (Jacob J.); *Apex Frozen Foods Ltd v Ali* [2007] EWHC 469 (Ch), March 9, 2007, unrep. (Warren J.)). Whatever the measure, the real point is that the court must look for the loss caused to the injunctee (or other party identified in the cross-undertaking) by the injunction, distinguishing, if necessary, any loss to the injunctee caused by the litigation itself (*ibid*). In *SmithKline Beecham Plc v Apotex Europe Ltd* [2006] EWCA Civ 658; [2007] Ch. 71, CA, the Court of Appeal rejected the submission that a party identified in the cross-undertaking as one whom the injunctor will compensate (in this case, a corporate defendant) can claim compensation, not only for having been himself prevented from doing the restrained acts, but also for others (in this case, corporate affiliates of the defendant) who were adversely affected by the injunction.

In a number of English cases, the judgment given at first instance and the judgments on appeal given by the High Court of Australia in *Air Express Ltd v Ansett Transport Industries (Operations) Ltd* (1979) 146 C.L.R. 249 have been quoted with approval (note particularly the first instance judgment of Aickin J. exhaustively reviewing the earlier authorities) in support of the view that the court in exercising its equitable jurisdiction should adopt similar principles to those relevant in a claim for breach of contract (see *Tharros Shipping Co Ltd v Bias Shipping Ltd* [1994] 1 Lloyd's Rep. 577, and cases cited therein, and *R. v Medicines Control Agency, Ex p.Smith & Nephew Pharmaceuticals Ltd*, op cit). In the *Air Express Ltd* case it was held (1) that there is a distinction drawn between damage caused by the grant of the injunction and damage which flows from the fact of the litigation itself (only in the former instance are damages recoverable) and (2) that it is for the party who seeks to enforce the undertaking to show that the damage claimed would not have been sustained but for the injunction.

The relevant authorities were extensively reviewed at first instance in *Lilly Icos LLC v 8PM Chemists Ltd* [2009] EWHC 1905 (Ch), July 31, 2009, unrep. (Arnold J.) where the principal issue was the impact of illegality on a claim under a cross-undertaking and where it was held that that the court will not award compensation for the loss sustained by an unlawful business or where the beneficiary of the cross-undertaking had to rely to a substantial extent upon his own illegality in order to establish the loss ([282] to [287]).

At an inquiry as to damages, the question may arise whether the injuncted party failed reasonably to mitigate his loss. It arose in *Al-Rawas v Pegasus Energy Ltd* [2007]

EWHC 2427 (QB), October 23, 2007, unrep. (Eady J.) where, for the purpose of avoiding the restrictions imposed by a freezing injunction, the defendants paid US$33m into court, taking out a loan in order to do so. Upon the injunction being discharged, an inquiry as to damages was ordered, and the money in court released. The defendants applied for summary judgment to recover the difference between the interest paid to service the loan and the interest earned whilst the money was in court (US$392,972.79 plus interest). In granting the application the judge rejected the claimant's submission that there were sufficient grounds to suppose that, at trial, the claimants would be able to show on a balance of probabilities that the defendants failed to discharge their obligation to mitigate their loss (it being suggested that there were alternative courses that they could and should have taken).

## 10. INTERIM INJUNCTIONS IN PARTICULAR PROCEEDINGS

The circumstances in which an interim injunction may be applied for are many and various. Special considerations arise in certain proceedings. **15–39**

### (a) Restricting freedom of expression

The law relating to the granting of injunctions, whether interim or final, affecting freedom of expression was significantly altered by the Human Rights Act 1998. By that Act, the European Convention for the Protection of Human Rights and Fundamental Freedoms was introduced into English law. (The Convention is set out in Pt of Sch.1 to the Act.) **15–40**

For commentary on freedom of expression in intellectual property cases, see para.15–47.4 below.

#### *(i) The right to freedom of expression*

The nature and extent of the impact of the Act in this respect has been considered in a number of cases concerned with the relationship between art.10 of the Convention, which establishes for everyone the right to freedom of expression, and art.8, which establishes for everyone the right to respect for his private and family life, his home and his correspondence. In these cases, for the purposes of preventing publication of information, claimants asserting art.8 rights have sought injunctions against defendants asserting art.10 rights. The cases include, in particular, decisions of the House of Lords in *Campbell v MGN Ltd* [2004] UKHL 22; [2004] 2 A.C. 457, HL; *Cream Holdings Ltd v Banerjee* [2004] UKHL 44; [2005] 1 A.C. 253, HL; *Re S (A Child) (Identification: Restrictions on Publication)* [2004] UKHL 47; [2005] 1 A.C. 593, HL. See also *McKennitt v Ash* [2006] EWCA Civ 1714; [2008] Q.B. 73, CA; *Murray v Express Newspapers Plc* [2008] EWCA Civ 446, May 7, 2008, unrep., CA **15–41**

The right to freedom of expression guaranteed by art.10 is a qualified right. Article 10(1) protects the right, but art.10(2) recognises the need to protect the rights and freedoms of others (including their rights and freedoms under art.8). The right to respect for private and family life etc is also a qualified right. Article 8(1) protects the right, but recognition is given in art.8(2) to the protection of the rights and freedoms of others (including their rights and freedoms under art.10).

The content of the law in relation to the circumstances in which injunctions (both final and interim) should be granted, thereby restricting freedom of expression, or should not be granted, thereby infringing respect for privacy, in some respects has been, and remains, a matter of controversy. In this commentary it is not necessary to give a comprehensive account of the substantive law involved in all of the circumstances in which it is relevant. In what follows particular attention is given to s.12 of the Human Rights Act 1998, in which provisions expressly directed at applications for interim remedies restricting freedom of expression are found and, which, as a practical matter, most frequently becomes relevant in claims for misuse of private information.

#### *(ii) Human Rights Act 1998 s.12*

Section 12 of the Human Rights Act 1998 applies if a court is considering whether to grant "any relief" which, if granted, might affect "the exercise of the Convention **15–42** right to freedom of expression" (s.12(1)). In this context, "any relief" includes any remedy or order (other than in criminal proceedings) (s.12(5)). The right to freedom of expression is contained in art.10 of the Convention. Section 12(4) stipulates that the court "must have particular regard to the importance of" that right. (Having "particular regard" means having regard to art.10(1) as qualified by art.10(2) (*Douglas v Hello! Ltd* [2001] Q.B. 967, CA, at para.133 per Sedley L.J.).) Further, where the proceedings relate to material which the respondent claims, or which appears to the court, to be journalistic, literary or artistic material (or to conduct connected with such material), the court must have particular regard to (a) the extent to which (i) the material has, or is about to, become available to the public, or (ii) it is, or would be, in the public interest for the material to be published, (b) any relevant privacy code (s.12(4)).

Section 12 may be engaged, not only where a court is trying a claim in which an injunction affecting the exercise of art.10 rights is sought as a final remedy, but also where it is dealing with a pre-trial application for an interim injunction having that effect.

As a practical matter s.12 is likely to be engaged in proceedings where a claimant, having commenced proceedings for an injunction having the effect of affecting the defendant's art.10 rights, applies for similar interim relief pending trial. However, the section (apart from subs.(3)) is not confined to such proceedings.

Section 12(3) is directed specifically to the situation where the court is dealing with an application for interim relief. It states that no such relief (as is described in s.12(1)) is to be granted "so as to restrain publication" before trial "unless the court is satisfied that the applicant is likely to establish that publication should not be allowed". The sub-section is concerned, not with court-imposed restrictions on the right to freedom of expression generally, but with one particular aspect of that right; that is to say, with restrictions on the right to impart information and ideas without interference. It seems to be readily assumed that "likely to establish" means likely to establish at trial; see further below. It has been held that there is no conflict between s.12(3) and the Convention (*Douglas v Hello! Ltd*, op cit, at para.150 per Keene L.J.).

Section 12(2), though not confined in its application to the situation where the court is dealing with an application for interim relief, is particularly relevant to it. It states that, if the person against whom the application for relief is made ("the respondent") is neither present nor represented, no such relief is to be granted unless the court is satisfied (a) that the applicant has taken all practicable steps to notify the respondent, or (b) that there are compelling reasons why the respondent should not be notified.

Section 12(3) was included in the 1998 Act for the purpose of meeting the concern that, whenever claimants alleged that a threatened publication would infringe their rights under art.8 (Right to respect for private and family life) and applied for interim orders imposing prior restraint on newspapers and other media to preserve the status quo until trial, the courts, in applying the conventional *American Cyanamid* approach, might readily grant such applications. By providing that that no such relief is to be granted "unless the court is satisfied that the applicant is likely to establish that publication should not be allowed" the sub-section sets a higher threshold for the grant of interlocutory injunctions against the media than the *American Cyanamid* guideline of a "serious question to be tried" or a "real prospect" of success at trial. The legislative intent is that freedom of speech should be strengthened by providing that restrictions on publication will be imposed by interlocutory injunctions in a narrower range of circumstances than would otherwise be the case.

It is established that the term "likely" in s.12(3) does not bear the meaning of "more likely than not" or "probably". In *Cream Holdings Ltd v Banerjee* [2004] UKHL 44; [2005] 1 A.C. 253, HL, the House of Lords held that, in determining whether an applicant seeking an injunction restraining publication "is likely to establish that publication should not be allowed", the court must be satisfied that his prospects of success at trial are sufficiently favourable to justify the order being made in the circumstances. In determining what degree of likelihood makes the prospects of success sufficiently favourable, generally the applicant must satisfy the court, not merely (as the judge and the Court of Appeal held) that he has a real prospect of success, but that he would probably succeed at trial. In *Emerson Developments v Avery* [2004] EWHC 194 (QB), January 26, 2004, unrep. (Field J.) a judge at first instance in an harassment case found that claimants' claim had a real prospect of success and granted a prohibitory interim injunction.

However, cases may arise where a lesser degree of likelihood will suffice. In *Cream Holdings Ltd v Banerjee*, Lord Nicholls explained (op cit at para.19):

> "Cases may arise where the adverse consequences of disclosure of information would be extremely serious, such as a grave risk of personal injury to a particular person. Threats may have been made against a person accused or convicted of a crime or a person who gave evidence at a trial. Disclosure of his current whereabouts might have extremely serious consequences. Despite the potential seriousness of the adverse consequences of disclosure, the applicant's claim to confidentiality may be weak. The applicant's case may depend, for instance, on a disputed question of fact on which the applicant has an arguable but distinctly poor case. It would be extraordinary if in such a case the court were compelled to apply a 'probability of success' test and therefore, regardless of the seriousness of the possible adverse consequences, refuse to restrain publication until the disputed issue of fact can be resolved at the trial".

Where the court is satisfied that the applicant is likely to establish at trial that publication should not be allowed, there remains a discretion in the court (*Douglas v Hello! Ltd*, op cit, at para.153 per Keene L.J.).

The flexible approach to the term "likely" in s.12(3), as derived from the *Cream Holdings Ltd* case, was applied by the Court of Appeal in *Böehringer Ingelheim Ltd v Vetplus Ltd* [2007] EWCA Civ 583; *The Times* June 27, 2007, CA, to a trade mark infringement claim of the "comparative advertising" variety. In *Oven Clean Ltd v Gilbert* [2007] EWHC 3483 (Ch), December 19, 2007, unrep. (Briggs J.) it was doubted whether the *Cream Holdings Ltd* test applies to trade mark or passing off cases beyond that variety.

Where confidential documents supplied to a newspaper by an M.P. were displayed on the newspaper's website for a short period, the court considered that the claimant had a sufficiently realistic chance of persuading the trial court that the dissemination so far had not destroyed the confidentiality of the material contained in the documents. The court could see no reason why the newspaper should not be able to use the contents of documents to inform opinions and to stimulate public debate (even by quoting from the documents themselves). Freedom of speech is a precious value in a democratic society that the courts must strive to protect and promote. But this did not mean that that journalists should have complete freedom to publish in full confidential documents leaked in breach of a fiduciary duty, in the exercise of the right to freedom of expression: responsible journalists must themselves consider whether publication of personal details, even about the affairs of corporations not alleged to have violated any laws, is appropriate (*Barclays Bank Plc v Guardian News and Media Ltd* [2009] EWHC 591 (QB), March 19, 2009, unrep. (Blake J.).

### *(iii) Claims for misuse of private information*

As a practical matter, applications of the type to which s.12(3) is directed are made **15–43** routinely in proceedings in which claims are made based upon alleged breaches of privacy or of obligations of confidence, said to arise either by implication of law or from express contractual provision. Since the coming into effect of the Human Rights Act 1998, the substantive law applicable to such proceedings has in some respects been a matter of controversy. It seems that a significant shift has occurred as between, on the one hand, freedom of expression for the media (and the corresponding interest of the public to receive information), and, on the other hand, the legitimate expectation of citizens to have their private lives protected. The values enshrined in art.8 (Right to respect for private and family life) and art.10 (Freedom of expression) are now part of the cause of action for breach of confidence (perhaps better described as an action for misuse of private information).

In *McKennitt v Ash* [2006] EWCA Civ 1714; [2008] Q.B. 73, CA, Buxton L.J. referred to the modern authorities and explained (at para.11) that, where the complaint is of the wrongful publication of private information, the court has to determine two questions. First, is the information private in the sense that it is in principle protected by art.8? (This question embraces the sub-question: in the particular circumstances of the case, does the applicant have "a reasonable expectation of privacy" in relation to the information?) If the answer to the first question is, "no", that is the end of the matter. If "yes", the second question (the "balancing exercise" or "parallel analysis") arises: in all the circumstances, must the interest of the owner of the private information yield to the right of freedom of expression conferred on the publisher by art.10? In terms, both rights are qualified and neither right takes precedence over the other. The art.8 right may be interfered with, and the art.10 right restricted, provided various conditions are fulfilled. Among them is the condition that the interference or restriction must be no greater than is proportionate to the legitimate aim pursued. In this respect the proportionately of interfering with one right has to be balanced against the proportionality of restricting the other (the "ultimate balancing test").

Where an application of the type to which s.12(3) is directed is made in a claim for misuse of private information, the task confronting the court is that of (1) determining the two questions framed by Buxton L.J. in *McKennitt v Ash*, and (2) determining, in the light if the guidance given in *Cream Holdings Ltd v Banerjee* (see above), the question whether or not the claimant's prospects of success in establishing at trial that publication should not be allowed are sufficiently favourable to justify the order being made in the circumstances. In *Browne v Associated Newspapers Ltd* [2007] EWCA Civ 295; [2007] 3 W.L.R. 289, CA, the Court of Appeal said (at para.23):

> "As we see it, the approach required by section 12 arises in this way. The court should first consider whether this is a case in which article 8 is engaged. It should then consider whether article 10 is engaged and, critically, whether the applicant for relief has shown that he is likely to establish at a trial that publication should not be allowed within the meaning of section 12(3)."

It should be stressed that the question for the court is not whether the applicant has established at the hearing of the application for interim relief that publication should not be allowed, but whether he is likely to do so at trial.

In *Browne v Associated Newspapers Ltd*, op cit, the Court of Appeal considered the submission that, where the claimant shows that there is a real expectation of privacy, but the question whether publication would satisfy the public interest (see s.12(4)) cannot be resolved until trial, then the interests of justice would require (other things being equal) that the claimant's expectation of privacy should be protected until trial. The court rejected the submission on the ground that it was contrary to s.12(3), which proceeds on the footing that, where there is uncertainty publication should be permitted unless the claimant can show that he is likely to succeed at trial, using the word "likely" in the flexible manner described by Lord Nicholls in the *Cream Holdings Ltd* case (*ibid* at para.43).

The general principle is that, before an injunction is granted restraining publication, there must be evidence that the defendant intends to publish the information and the claimant must establish with particularity what is alleged to be confidential. Such evidence is required so that the court can make a judgment as to the balance between art.8 and art.10 rights in the light of s.12(3), and so that the injunction can be framed in such a way that the party affected knows with certainty what he is or is not allowed to do (*Browne v Associated Newspapers Ltd*, op cit, at paras 63 and 64).

### *(iv) Dealing with applications "in a more proportionate manner"*

**15–44** Actions for misuse of private information are usually brought at short notice and are followed by an immediate application for an interim injunction restraining publication before trial which has to be heard urgently and dealt with quickly. As was explained above, the judge dealing with the application has to embark on the difficult task of giving effect to arts. 8 and 10 and to the requirements of s.12 of the 1998 Act. All this creates considerable practical problems.

In March 2002, in the case of *A v B Plc* [2002] EWCA Civ 337; [2003] Q.B. 195, CA, the Court of Appeal laid down guidelines intended to assist judges and parties "to deal with the majority of these applications in a more proportionate manner". The guidelines are extensive. (There are fifteen individual guidelines, explained in over 3,500 words.) It has to be said (with respect) that the extent to which the guidelines offered real assistance to the judge dealing with an interlocutory application for an injunction pending trial, as distinct from the judge trying a claim for a final injunction prohibiting publication, was limited. Their value has been diminished by significant developments in the law since March 2002, in particular the decision of the House of Lords in *Cream Holdings Ltd v Banerjee*, op cit (clarifying s.12(3)), and the decision of the European Court of Human Rights in *Von Hannover v Germany* (2004) 40 E.H.R.R. 1 (restating the rights and expectations of public figures with regard to their private lives). In *McKennitt v Ash*, op cit, the Court of Appeal said (at para.64) that it seems clear that these guidelines cannot be read as any sort of binding authority on the content of art.8 and art.10.

### (v) Sitting in private—public and private judgments

When dealing with an application to which s.12(3) applies, the court (whether sitting at first instance or on appeal) is likely to exercise its power (given by CPR r.39.2(1)) to sit in private. **15–45**

A judge, having heard an interlocutory application in private, may give judgment in open court (public judgment), but is not obliged to do so and may restrict the availability of the judgment to the parties (private judgment). However, in recognition of the imperative of public justice, the court (especially an appellate court) may give, in effect, two complementary judgments, one public and the other private. Whether this is done, and how it is done, will be affected by the rulings made on the application (see *Browne v Associated Newspaper Ltd* [2007] 1 W.L.R. 289, CA, at paras 4 and 5).

Obviously, where an application for an injunction restraining publication before trial succeeds the whole point of the application and the court's ruling would be undermined were the court to give a public judgment revealing the details of the information and, in effect, creating the mischief that the injunction was designed to prevent. The less obvious and more difficult question of practice arises where the court decides that the application should fail in whole or in part with the result that the respondent should not be restrained by the court from publishing in advance of trial (should he wish to do so) the material which the claimant unsuccessfully sought to protect. If the court gives a public judgment containing the details of the material in question it risks in effect itself publishing information that the claimant may subsequently succeed in restraining the defendant from publishing, either on an appeal against the interlocutory ruling, or at the trial of the claim.

### (vi) Defamation claims—prior restraint

In certain circumstances, the law of prior restraint operates to protect the defendant's freedom of speech rights, and can provide a basis for rejecting a claimant's application to prevent by interlocutory injunction the further publication of the alleged defamatory material. **15–46**

For further explanation, see para.15–48 below.

## (b) Patents and other intellectual property claims

Before the decision of the House of Lords in American *Cyanamid Co v Ethicon Ltd* [1975] A.C. 396, HL, resolved it, the question whether interim relief should be accorded only to very strong causes of action or refused only to the very weak in patents and other intellectual property claims (see CPR Pt 63) was controversial. It is interesting to note that *American Cyanamid Co* was a case in which the claimants sought an interlocutory injunction against the defendants restraining them from infringing their registered patent. **15–47**

The principles and guidelines governing the grant of interlocutory injunctions derived from that case (and not merely the main point just mentioned) apply to proceedings in which patents and other intellectual property claims are made. However, the view that such claims demand consideration of peculiar problems that make the application of the principles and guidelines less than straight-forward, even to the extent of requiring that they may have to be ignored in part in particular cases, has persisted.

### (i) Consideration of the merits on interim injunctions

A long-term controversy in respect of the grant of interim relief for alleged infringement of trade mark and passing-off has been the extent to which the merits of the action ought to be taken into account. There are two reasons that this issue is of particular importance in relation to such cases: the fact that the damage caused is often inextricably linked with the strength of the case; and the fact that the grant of an interim injunction will often dispose of the case (for example, once a name has to be **15–47.1** changed there may be little point in later incurring the cost and disruption of changing it back following a trial).

*American Cyanamid Co v Ethicon Ltd* [1975] A.C. 396; [1975] 1 All E.R. 504; [1975] R.P.C. 513 (and see generally the notes to CPR Part 25) has decided that interim relief should be prima facie refused only to very weak causes of action, and that if there is to be no refusal on grounds of strength of cause of action, the matter should be decided on the balance of convenience, which depends principally on likelihood and extent of damage.

In passing-off cases, damage is an essential element of the cause of action for the tort, so that it may not be logically possible to differentiate between the cause of action and the likelihood of damage. See for example, *The Financial Times Ltd v Evening Standard Co Ltd* [1991] F.S.R. 7. A case in which the likelihood of damage is small is one in which the balance of convenience is likely to favour the defendant, and yet it may undermine the cause of action itself. To what extent therefore should the court consider the merits both when considering whether or not there is a serious issue to be tried and when considering the balance of convenience?

Even in trade mark infringement actions, the unconditional monopoly given by registration is not invaded unless the alleged infringement too closely resembles the registered mark. But if it does the plaintiff may suffer damage which will never be known to him (*Alltransport International Group v Alltrans Express Ltd* [1976] F.S.R. 13). So that even in trade mark cases cause of action and likelihood of damage are likely to march together in many instances. Where E.C. regulations treat as critical the risk of confusion (here with reference to the word "Champagne") the absence of likelihood of substantial damage does not justify refusal of an injunction. However, erosion of distinctiveness of a trade name by its use on different goods may constitute substantial damage (*Tattinger S.V. v Allbev Ltd* [1993] F.S.R. 641, CA).

Further, interim injunctions granted in these cases are very apt to dispose of the whole action, for a defendant forced at an interim stage to change his mark is in practical reality unlikely to change back again even if successful at trial.

The question then arises whether for one or other of these reasons, in cases of infringement of trade mark or passing-off, the *American Cyanamid* principles should be modified by according greater weight to the relative strength of the rival cases.

### *(ii) Passing off—a special case?*

**15–47.2** The Court of Appeal in *County Sound Plc v Ocean Sound Ltd* [1991] F.S.R. 367, CA at 372) purports to give an emphatic negative to this question and asserts that "it has long been recognised at first instance and in this court that the American Cyanamid principles apply as much to passing-off cases as to any other" and that indeed "a passing-off action is especially suited to the application of the American Cyanamid principles". The analysis that followed failed to properly address the issue however. In reviewing the cases (and specifically disapproving one CA decision, *Newsweek Inc. v BBC* [1979] R.P.C. 441) the CA in *County Sound* gave examples only of cases where the plaintiffs had either unarguably strong or weak prima facie cases, leaving the only type of case where the old and the new principles reach different results, namely the cases where the plaintiff has an arguable but not strong prima facie case, unexemplified.

Furthermore, in *County Sound* the CA did not specifically address itself to the question whether in trade mark and passing-off cases, cause of action and balance of convenience marched together, though (*ibid.*, at 372) it did in passing re-affirm the principle that in passing-off cases if there is no damage there is no tort.

In *Series 5 Software Ltd v Clarke* [1996] F.S.R. 273, Laddie J. carefully analysed the House of Lords decision in American Cyanamid and concluded that it did not preclude a consideration of the merits, but merely any attempt to resolve difficult issues of fact or law at the interim application stage. By that analysis Laddie J. concluded as follows:

1. The grant of an interlocutory injunction is a matter of discretion and depends on all the facts of the case.
2. There are no fixed rules as to when an injunction should or should not be granted. The relief must be kept flexible.
3. Because of the practice adopted on the hearing of applications for interlocutory relief, the court should rarely attempt to resolve complex issues of disputed fact or law.

***Paragraph numbers marked with a "+" can be found online and on CD.***

4. Major factors the court can bear in mind are (a) the extent to which damages are likely to be an adequate remedy for each party and the ability of the other party to pay. (b) the balance of convenience. (c) the maintenance of the status quo. (d) any clear view the court may reach as to the relative strength of the parties' cases.

*Series 5 Software* is often cited by practitioners as putting a "gloss" on *American Cyanamid*, or modifying the appropriate test. In fact it does not go so far—it merely explains in practice how the test laid down in *American Cyanamid* ought to be applied, which would, where the occasion demands it involve a consideration of the merits. The case is also often cited for the principle that the merits should be more closely considered in IP cases (and particularly passing off and trade mark cases) than in other cases. Again this goes too far. Whilst it may be appropriate to consider the impact of the merits in passing off and trade mark cases for the reasons explained above), *Series 5* is not so limited. Indeed *Series 5* was not really an intellectual property case at all (although it involved confidential information).

It may be noted that in *County Sound*, the CA disapproved the principle expounded by Denning M.R. in *Newsweek v BBC* that passing off cases were special cases which should ordinarily be disposed of at the interim stage. At first instance in *Newsweek* the judge had merely pointed out that the facts were uncontroversial, and therefore the case was one in which it was appropriate to consider the merits based on those facts, which is what *Series 5* suggests should be done.

*Series 5* was followed by *Antec International Ltd v South Western Chicks (Warren) Ltd (Interlocutory Injunction)*, [1997] F.S.R. 278 (Ch D), in which injunctive relief was granted, and considered with approval by Walker J. in *Barnsley Brewery Co Ltd v RBNB*, [1997] F.S.R. 462 (Ch D) in which injunctive relief was refused. We note that in the latter case, Walker J. stated (in accordance with the conclusions above) as follows:

> "That decision is sometimes, it seems, regarded as surprising or even heretical. I do not see it that way. I see it as a valuable reminder of the background and context of *American Cyanamid* and indeed of its basic message. The basic message is that applications for interlocutory injunctions cannot be mini trials of disputed issues of fact and that the court has to do the best it can on a provisional basis, with the relatively modest aim of reducing so far as possible the risk of the provisional decision ultimately proving to have produced an unjust result."

In relation to passing off cases in particular it is necessary to sound a word of caution. The above may tend to suggest that passing off cases may be more amenable than others to reaching a preliminary view as to the merits of the case. In fact of course the opposite may be true. In the case of *Neutrogena Corporation v Golden Ltd* [1996] R.P.C. 473 Jacob J. noted as follows:

> "It was certainly my experience in practice that my own view as to the likelihood of deception was not always reliable. As I grew more experienced I said more and more "it depends on the evidence."

It is certainly not the case (as suggested by *County Sound* for example) that there will always be an obvious answer as to the strength of the case, and even if such an answer seems to present itself, it may be shown to be wrong on the evidence.

This does not mean however that there will be no cases in which the relative merits of the parties' cases show a stark disparity. Plainly this must be factored in to the assessment at the interim stage. The question is the extent to which they ought to be factored in before the balance of convenience stage. The strict approach to *American Cyanamid* would suggest they should not (assuming the case is seriously arguable), but *Series 5* would suggest a more flexible approach is more appropriate. It is arguable to what extent this is likely to have any significant effect on decisions in practice.

And of course as a matter of practice, rather than strict legal principle, it is usually the case at the hearing of interim applications that the court will take the merits into account, at least in situations where it is possible to reach any conclusion as to the relative strength of those merits at that stage.

Nevertheless, there is still support for the proposition that passing off cases are a special case. In the unreported case of *Guardian Media Group Plc, Greater Manchester Newspapers Ltd, Manchester Morning News Ltd v Associated Newspapers Ltd*, a passing off case the Judge at first instance, having dealt with the *American Cyanamid* principles, said as follows:

> "But in passing off the questions of damage and likelihood of damage are

***Paragraph numbers marked with a "+" can be found online and on CD.***

intimately bound up with the strength of the cause of action itself. The more that deception and confusion is likely the stronger the case but also the more the unquantifiable damage that the claimant is likely to suffer. So, as it seems to me, in the ordinary run of passing off cases—and to some extent this is the ordinary run of passing off case—an interlocutory injunction would only be granted where the claimant can show significant likelihood of damage to his goodwill, i.e. significant likelihood of deception or confusion. I approach this case on that basis."

Walker LJ, in the unreported judgment of the Court of Appeal dated January 20, 2000 held as follows:

> "The *American Cyanamid* principles have a degree of flexibility and they do not prevent the court from giving proper weight to any clear view which the court can form at the time of the application for interim relief (and without the need for a mini-trial on copious affidavit evidence) as to the likely outcome at trial. That is particularly so when the grant or withholding of interim relief may influence the ultimate commercial outcome. It is not necessary to consider today whether the court's entitlement to give effect to its provisional view of the merits goes quite so far as Laddie J. sought in *Series 5 Software v Clarke* [1996] 1 All ER 853. In the end, there was not any significant difference between counsel on that point."

It is not entirely clear how much further *Series 5 Software* sought to go than this statement of Walker L.J. that "proper weight" could be given by the court to any clear view of the merits. However it is difficult to see what practical effect any such distinction would have.

In considering the impact of freedom of expression in relation to passing off cases in *Boehringer Ingelheim v Vetplus Ltd* [2007] EWCA Civ 583, Jacob L.J. said at paragraph 38:

> "No one has ever suggested or reasonably could suggest that the rule in Bonnard could operate to prevent the granting of an interim injunction to restrain an ordinary passing off. It is no good the defendant saying 'The representation which I made is true and I intend to justify it at trial'. The Court normally considers who is actually likely to win and grants or refuses an interim injunction on that basis. For if the plaintiff is likely to win, damage will be irreparable, if not, not."

It is not clear whether this is support for the proposition that passing off cases are "special cases" in which the merits should be considered separately from the balance of convenience, or merely support for the proposition that the merits form part of the balance of convenience question. Briggs J. in *Oven Clean Ltd v Gilbert* [2007] EWHC 3483 (Ch) has suggested the latter. This accorded with his judgment in Riemann & Co v *Linco Care Ltd* [2007] E.C.C. 23, in which he held that the concession on the part of the defendants that there was an arguable (albeit weak) case meant that only the balance of convenience fell to be considered.

In many cases of course, there is no precise analysis of the way in which the merits fall to be considered.

### *(iii) American Cyanamid and trade mark cases*

**15–47.3** As noted above, there are also trade mark cases in which the cause of action and balance of convenience "march together". See for example *Sirdar Ltd v. Les Fils de Louis Mulliez* [1975] F.S.R. 309; (1975) 15 C.M.L.R. 378 (degree of deceptive resemblance); and *Mail Newspapers Plc v Insert Median Ltd* [1987] R.P.C. 521 at 527 (similarity of rival marks).

On one view, there is no reason why the same considerations that apply to passing off cases should not apply to such cases. Again whether the merits are considered separately to the balance of convenience or not is a matter of debate. The merits are often considered, usually at the balance of convenience stage. See, e.g. *O2 Holdings Ltd v Hutchison 3G UK Ltd (Application for Interim Injunction)* [2004] EWHC 2571 (Ch); [2005] E.T.M.R. 61 (injunction refused since inter alia claimant's case weak). In practice the stage at which the merits are considered may be of little import.

It has been suggested that although the lack of evidence of actual confusion is not fatal to an application for an interim injunction in a trade mark infringement action, such lack is a factor of very great significance, requiring the claimant to bring forwards other substantial grounds to make up for it (*Baywatch Production Co Inc. v The Home Video Channel* [1997] F.S.R. 22). Of course this approach is not appropriate where there are serious practical difficulties preventing the claimant from obtaining such evidence, e.g. where the defendant's product has not been launched, or has not been launched long enough for confusion to have arisen.

### *(iv) Interim injunctions and freedom of expression*

Different principles apply to the grant of interim relief where issues of freedom of expression arise as set out in *Cream Holdings v Banerjee* [2005] 1 A.C. 253. In cases involving freedom of expression the Human Rights Act 1998 demands that claimants show that they are "likely" (and the test is necessarily flexible—"likely" does not mean "more likely than not") to win at trial, not merely a real prospect of success. See also *Douglas v Hello! Ltd (No.1)* [2001] Q.B. 967; [2001] 2 W.L.R. 992; [2001] 2 All E.R. 289; [2001] E.M.L.R. 9. See further "Restricting freedom of expression" at para.15–40 *et seq.* above. **15–47.4**

Freedom of expression has been considered in relation to passing off cases—see for example *Red Bull GmbH v Mean Fiddler Music Group Plc (Application: Interim Injunction)* [2004] EWHC 991 and *Consorzio del Prosciutto di Parma* [1990] F.S.R. 530 in which Morritt J. (as he then was) held that the right of free speech was not an absolute bar to a prior restraining order but was to be taken into account in the general balance of convenience test under *American Cyanamid.*

*MacMillan Magazines Ltd v RCN Publishing Co Ltd* [1998] F.S.R. 9; (1997) 20(9) I.P.D. 20089 (Ch D) —Where an action for malicious falsehood was brought and the parties both had an arguable case, no injunctive relief would be granted unless the statements made were obviously untrue in circumstances where the defendant indicated that it intended to justify the statements.

The flexible probability requirement which arises where an interim injunction would affect freedom of expression, as explained in *Cream Holdings* has been applied by the Court of Appeal to a commercial trade mark dispute in *Boehringer Ingelheim v Vetplus Ltd* [2007] EWCA Civ 583. The court held that there is no complete bar (i.e. in accordance with *Bonnard v Perryman*) to injunctive relief when the defendant indicates that he intends to justify a comparative advertisement. *See also Red Dot Technologies Ltd v Apollo Fire Detectors Ltd* [2007] EWHC 1166 (Ch).

Threats of proceedings for infringement of patent are not to be equated with questions of trade libel, so that interim injunctions to restrain them are proper (*Johnson Electric Industrial Manufactory Ltd v Mabuchi-Motor K.K.* [1986] F.S.R. 280).

### *(v) Mandatory injunctions*

It was thought that a special application of the *American Cyanamid* principles is required in deciding cases where a mandatory injunction was sought (see *Zockoll Group Ltd v Mercury Communications Ltd (No.1)* [1998] F.S.R. 354, CA; *Aegis Defence Services Ltd v Stoner* [2006] EWHC 1515 (Ch); *AAH Pharmaceuticals Ltd v Pfizer Ltd* [2007] EWHC 565 (Ch). However, in the Privy Council case of *National Commercial Bank Jamaica Ltd v Olint Corp Ltd (Practice Note)* [2009] UKPC 16, [2009] 1 W.L.R. 1405, [2009] Bus. L.R. 1110, PC, it was explained (at [19]) that in the *American Cyanamid* case Lord Diplock was not intending to confine the principles to prohibitory rather than mandatory injunctions, and that the underlying principle is the same, namely, that the court should take whichever course seems likely to cause the least irremediable prejudice to one party or the other. It is a generalisation to say that the features which ordinarily justify describing an injunction as mandatory are often more likely to cause irremediable prejudice than cases in which a defendant is merely prevented from taking or continuing with some course of action (*Films Rover International Ltd v Cannon Film Sales Ltd* [1987] 1 W.L.R. 670, at 680). **15–47.5**

See further para.15–24 above.

### *(vi) Disposal of the entire case*

As to cases dealing with the point that a granted injunction may dispose of the whole action, see *Newsweek Inc v BBC* [1979] R.P.C. 441 at 446 at first instance; *Gala of London Ltd v Chandler Ltd* [1991] F.S.R. 294; *Management Publications Ltd v Blenheim Exhibitions Group* [1991] F.S.R. 348; [1991] F.S.R. 550 CA (and see also *Morgan-* **15–47.6**

*Grampian v Training Personnel Ltd* [1992] F.S.R. 267 as to status quo); *Alfred Dunhill Ltd v Sunoptic SA* [1979] F.S.R. 337; *Elan Digital Systems Ltd v Elan Computer Ltd* [1984] F.S.R. 373 (circumstance gives rise to no point of law but only a point of fact to be taken into account in balance of convenience); *Post Office v Interlink Express Parcels Ltd* [1989] 1 F.S.R. 369; *Boots Company Ltd v Approved Prescription Services Ltd* [1988] F.S.R. 45.

In a predominantly copyright case also involving names, the Vice Chancellor noted that the interim proceedings would be determinative of the case and looked at the relative strength of the parties' cases because he had found the balance of convenience so even; *Mirage Studios v Counter-Feat* [1991] F.S.R. 145 at 154. In another copyright case *Entec (Pollution Control) Ltd v Abacus Mouldings* [1992] F.S.R. 332, the CA refused an interim injunction because it would dispose of the case, although in that case the defendants were impecunious and if injuncted could fight no more.

### *(vii) Status quo*

**15–47.7** The preservation of the status quo is of course a factor which may be taken into account according to the *American Cyanamid* principles. Often the status quo will favour the grant of an injunction, since the injunction will prevent the defendant from bringing his goods to market. However this is not always the case, and indeed what the appropriate status quo is for the purposes of determining the interim application is not always easy to determine in intellectual property disputes. For example it is not always the case that preventing the use of the defendant's mark will preserve the status quo—see the reasoning of *Aldous J. in Blazer Plc v Yardley and Co Ltd* [1992] F.S.R. 501. NB that the grant of an injunction preventing the defendant from using a particular trade mark does not necessarily prevent him from selling his goods see *Tattinger v Allbev Ltd* [1992] F.S.R. 647, and *Fyffes v Chiquita Brands International Inc* [1993] F.S.R. 83. Furthermore a party may not be able to take advantage of a status quo which has resulted from its own unreasonable conduct—see *Leo-Pharma A/S v Sandoz* [2008] EWHC 541 (Pat).

### *(viii) Irreparable damage and claimant's cross-undertaking*

**15–47.8** It has been held to be essential that a plaintiff seeking an interim injunction to restrain infringement should show a likelihood of irreparable damage (Broad & Co. Ltd v. *Graham Building Supplies Ltd (No.2)* [1969] R.P.C. 295 where the court refused to go into the question of infringement because no such damage was shown); see also Broad & Co Ltd v *Cast Iron Drainage Co Ltd*, above and *Post Office v Interlink Express Parcels Ltd* [1989] 1 F.S.R. 369. However see *SmithKline Beecham Plc v Apotex Europe Ltd* [2003] EWCA Civ 137; [2003] F.S.R. 31, where it was held that whether damages are recoverable and the extent of any such damage may be very important considerations when deciding whether to grant an interlocutory injunction, but the court's jurisdiction to grant interlocutory injunctions is not so limited. In any case, the CA held, where use of a property right is in issue, damages may not be the main consideration.

For a consideration of the relevance of damage to related companies: see *Peaudouce SA v Kimberley Clark* [1996] F.S.R. 680, although NB *SmithKline Beecham Plc v Apotex Europe Ltd* [2003] EWCA Civ 137; [2003] F.S.R. 31 as to damage not being an essential pre-requisite for interim relief.

Reasonable conduct by the plaintiff over the years regarding settlements may result in the fact that the potential loss between motion and trial is not such as to justify interim relief (Smith Kline & French Ltd v *Higson* [1988] F.S.R. 115).

An interim injunction was refused in a passing-off case where grant would cause the defendant great damage but very little to the plaintiff: (*Management Publications Ltd v Blenheim Exhibitions Group* [1991] F.S.R. 348).

An inability on the part of the plaintiff to meet the cross-undertaking is not an end of the matter. The question is what course involves the least risk of injustice: see *Fleming Fabrications Ltd v Albion Cylinders Ltd* [1989] R.P.C. 47 CA, where an injunction was granted because the plaintiffs were at a crucial point in their exploitation of the patent.

NB on the effect of cross undertakings in damages against non-parties—see *SmithKline Beecham Plc v Apotex Europe Ltd* [2006] EWCA Civ 658 [2007] Ch. 71; [2006] 3 W.L.R. 1146; [2006] 4 All E.R. 1078; [2006] C.P. Rep. 39; [2007] F.S.R. 6. See also *SmithKline Beecham Plc v Apotex Europe Ltd* [2005] EWHC 1655 (Ch); [2006] 1 W.L.R.

872; [2006] 2 All E.R. 53; [2005] F.S.R. 44 for an unsuccessful attempt to introduce third parties into the cross undertaking in damages by the application of the slip rule.

### *(ix) Delay*

Delay by the claimant in seeking interim relief may be a "powerful" factor against the grant of such relief—see, e.g. *AAH Pharmaceuticals Ltd v Pfizer Ltd* [2007] EWHC 565 (Ch); [2007] U.K.C.L.R. 1561. **15–47.9**

However delay may be excused where the chances of the plaintiff succeeding in the action is high (*Cavendish House (Cheltenham) v Cavendish Woodhouse, Ltd* [1970] R.P.C. 234, CA). See also, as to delay, *Effluent Disposal Ltd v Midlands Effluent Disposal Ltd* [1970] R.P.C. 238, and Broad & Co Ltd v *Cast Iron Drainage Co Ltd* [1970] F.S.R. 363.

Delay will be of less significance in circumstances where the defendant's conduct has not changed as a result of any delay—see *Radley Gowns Ltd v Costas Spyrou (t/a Touch of Class and Fiesta Girl)* [1975] F.S.R. 455 Ch D, and *Handi-Craft Co v B Free World Ltd* [2005] EWHC 1307 (Pat).

NB the relationship between delay and the damage and merits in certain cases such as passing off and certain trade mark cases. See, e.g. Lyle & Scott Ltd v *Primark Stores Ltd* [2007] EWHC 1549 (Ch)—where large numbers of the defendant's products had been put on the market and the claimant had not noticed, this suggested that the chances of serious loss were remote.

Where a claimant in a trade mark case non-used his mark for many years and only told the defendant of a token continued use after delivery of a counterclaim to rectify the Register, interim relief was refused and previous judgments stayed: *Gala of London Ltd v Chandler Ltd* [1991] F.S.R. 294.

### *(x) Nature of relief*

For the purposes of interim relief the injunction should be confined wherever possible to a precise statement of what is not permitted (*Biro Swan Ltd v Tallon Ltd* [1961] R.P.C. 326; *Berkeley Hotel Co Ltd v Berkley International (Mayfair) Ltd* [1972] R.P.C. 237). An interim injunction to restrain passing off may be refused as unnecessary where an injunction to restrain infringement of registered trade mark is granted (*Bowater-Scott Corp. Ltd v Modo Consumer Products Ltd* [1969] F.S.R. 330). **15–47.10**

### *(xi) Stay pending appeal*

A stay may be granted pending appeal (see, e.g. *Peck (John) & Co Ltd v Zelker (R.) Ltd* [1963] R.P.C. 85). The CA granted a limited stay of an interim injunction in respect of passing off pending appeal, entirely suspending the injunction relating to goods but as to the injunction relating to the business only adding a proviso franking advertisements which were either already contracted for or to which the plaintiffs consented: *Elan Digital Systems Ltd v Elan Computer Ltd* [1984] F.S.R. 373. **15–47.11**

### *(xii) Interim injunctions in patent actions*

The principles governing the grant of an interim injunction in a patent infringement action are no different from the principles in other cases. The leading case is *American Cyanamid Co v Ethicon Ltd* [1975] A.C. 396; [1975] 1 All E.R. 504, discussed generally in the notes to CPR Part 25. The above discussion of *Series 5* is as relevant to patent cases as to others. In that regard however it is most unusual for a patent case to be one in which it is obvious where the merits lie in all but the most extreme cases. This is particularly so in cases where the case will turn (as is often the position) on obviousness. **15–47.12**

NB also *Abbott Laboratories v Ranbaxy Europe Ltd* [2004] EWHC 2723 (Ch); (2005) 28(1) I.P.D. 27111, in which Pumfrey J. held that, notwithstanding the apparent weakness of the claimant's patent, that weakness would not have prevented the court granting interim relief if the position of those affected could have been protected by cross undertakings. Had there been a real prospect that the claimant's main claim was valid, an interlocutory injunction would have been granted.

The grant of injunctive relief in patent cases turns on the unique facts of each case just as in any other type of case. Often similar issues arise however. In *Mayne Pharma (USA) Inc v Teva UK Ltd* [2004] EWHC 3248, Pumfrey J. said as follows:

"In a case in which a pharmaceutical previously on the market is challenged by a generic on price grounds, the risk of price erosion irrecoverable if the patentee is ultimately successful at trial, is frequently the dominant factor in considering the grant of an interlocutory injunction. To the extent that one can generalise in cases of this description, it is possible to say that in the ordinary course all the remaining factors tend to be more or less evenly balanced. It is not infrequently the case that, first of all, the risk of irrecoverable damage, coupled with another common feature of these cases which is a failure by the defendants to clear the ground before they start their course of activity, will, in the mind of the judge disposing of the application, take on a heavy significance. Where, however, one is considering a very brief period indeed, these factors have much less weight. I must be satisfied, before I interfere by injunction at this stage on incomplete evidence, that there is a real risk over the period between now and the hearing of the effective application that there will be a significant risk of irrecoverable price erosion or some other head of damage for which the claimants will not adequately be compensated in damages."

On the other hand, it may be said that in many cases in which an injunction is not granted some sort of estimate of the claimant's damage can be made by reference to the defendant's sales, whereas normally a defendant who is wrongly stopped will find it very difficult to form any reasonable estimate of what sales he would have made but for the injunction.

Of course many factors arise—each case must be considered individually. For discussion of many of the sorts of factors which may arise and fall for consideration in cases however, see the following non-exhaustive list: *Novartis AG v Dexcel-Pharma Ltd* [2008] EWHC 1266 (Pat); [2008] F.S.R. 31—injunction granted—short period until trial, and status quo was that there was no competing product on market; *Leo Pharma A/S v Sandoz Ltd* [2008] EWCA Civ 850—judge was entitled to conclude that entry of a generic into the marketplace might lead to price drops and thus incalculable damage, and therefore grant of injunction was within his discretion [c.f. *Merrell Dow Pharmaceuticals Inc v H.N. Norton and Co Ltd* [1994] R.P.C. 1—where a patentee might have to lower his price permanently as a result of infringement, nevertheless his loss is ascertainable, whilst the possible market share of the infringer is not ascertainable: injunction refused]; *Les Laboratoires Servier v KRKA Polska Sp ZoO* [2006] EWHC 2453 (Pat); (2007) 30(1) I.P.D. 30006 (Ch D (Patents Ct))—injunction granted where serious issue on patent infringement and counterclaim for invalidity not made out on summary judgment basis—launch of defendant's products was likely to lead to launches by other generic companies and price erosion which would continue after trial; *Wyeth Holdings Corp v Alpharma Ltd* [2003] EWHC 3196—injunction granted—most just course involved maintaining status quo in light of proximity of trial; *SmithKline Beecham v Generics UK Ltd* (2002) 25(1) I.P.D. 25005 (Ch D (Patents Ct)) injunction granted where new entrants to the marketplace would cause irreparable damage; *Improver Corp. v Remington Consumer Products Ltd* [1989] R.P.C. 82, CA—interim injunction granted to preserve the status quo where the defendant was thought to be not yet on the market and had gone ahead with its eyes open; *Monsanto v Stauffer* cases—([1984] F.S.R. 559 N.Z. and [1984] F.S.R. 598, CA)—defendant seeking to enter the plaintiffs' herbicide market was restrained lest he establish a bridgehead for the time when the patent monopoly expired; *T.J. Smith and Nephew Ltd v 3M United Kingdom Plc* [1983] R.P.C. 92—the amount of time, energy and money which the patentees put into the marketing of the patented article may justify the assertion that infringements would cause irreparable damage, and once a patentee is willing to negotiate royalty arrangements it necessarily follows that he is willing to give up his monopoly position in return for money, and if the defendants are good for the money, then damages are an adequate remedy; *Brupat Ltd v Sanford Marine Products Ltd* [1983] R.P.C. 61—where a patent infringement was a reliable article and its sales would not affect the patentee's goodwill it was held that damages were an adequate remedy for the patentee and could be more easily assessed than damages on the cross undertaking—an impecunious defendant can protect the plaintiff by paying a royalty into a joint account; Vernon & Co (Pulp Products) Ltd v *Universal Pulp Containers Ltd* [1980] F.S.R. 179—no injunction against poor defendant who undertook, pending trial, to pay into a safeguard account 5 per cent of his sales price); *E.A.R. Corp. v Protector Safety Products (UK) Ltd* [1980] F.S.R. 574—injunction granted to protect plaintiff at a critical time in his business which was being built up under the patent umbrella; *Corruplast Ltd v George Har-*

*rison (Agencies) Ltd* [1978] R.P.C. 761, CA—plaintiff's market just turning in their favour, impossible to assess loss of competitive strength of patents after expiry, patent shortly to expire, defendant an importer, wrong to allow him to establish bridgehead shortly before expiry, injunction granted; *Polaroid Corp. v Eastman Kodak Co Ltd* [1977] R.P.C. 379, CA—worldwide competition, no UK manufacture by plaintiffs, substantial investment by defendants in UK, injunction refused (NB the fact that the defendants had taken reasonable precautions to avoid infringing any valid patent was held irrelevant); *Roussel-Uclaf v G.D. Searle & Co Ltd* [1977] F.S.R. 125—a reasonably accurate assessment of the claimant's loss could be made and the drug the subject of the patent could be life saving and had no precise equivalent, injunction refused); *Catnic Components Ltd v Stressline Ltd* [1976] F.S.R. 157, CA—defendants substantial and had made a substantial investment, drastic and long-lasting damage to plaintiff unlikely, injunction refused; *Hovercraft Development Ltd v Sealand Hovercraft Ltd* [1976] R.P.C. 393—plaintiff exploited patent by licensing but defendant was in financial trouble, injunction granted; *Standex International Ltd v C.B. Blades Ltd* [1976] F.S.R. 114—defendants had insufficient assets to be able to pay damages, injunction granted; *Belfast Ropework Ltd v Pixdane* [1976] F.S.R. 337, CA—defendants, importers, had no sufficient assets to safeguard plaintiffs, injunction granted.

To defend an application for an interim injunction a defendant should show that he genuinely does intend to defend the plaintiff's claim at trial. How he does this will depend on the facts of each case. See *T.J. Smith and Nephew Ltd v 3M United Kingdom Plc* [1983] R.P.C. 92—since the court cannot go into elaborate matters of fact at the interim stage it is not necessary for defendants to reveal the details of their defence to a claim for infringement nor invalidity at the interim stage, though the defendants conceded they would have to give particulars of the grounds on which they contested validity. A genuine intention to defend the action may be present even though the same grounds are relied on as failed in an earlier action; see *Quantel Ltd v Shima Seiki Europe Ltd* [1990] R.P.C. 436 in which the defendants intended to call additional evidence and on their providing a bank guarantee in the sum of £2 million—the balance of convenience lay in favour of no injunction.

It is wrong to grant an interim injunction on a patent which is in limbo as a result of an unconditional offer to amend; on a motion to commit, a court cannot try what final form the claims are going to take. If an interim injunction was granted before an application to amend, it would be discharged (*Molnlycke AB v Procter and Gamble Ltd (No.2)* [1990] R.P.C. 487).

Various factors which were of importance in early pre-*Cyanamid* cases may still be relevant, e.g. *Fomento (Sterling Area) Ltd v Refill Improvements (Ri-Co) Co Ltd* [1963] R.P.C. 163 (patent due to expire shortly, injunction refused. But cf. *Corruplast* [1978] R.P.C. 761, CA, above); *Hoffman-la Roche & Co A.G. v Inter-Continental Pharmaceuticals Ltd* [1966] R.P.C. 265 (existence of an application for a compulsory licence irrelevant, injunction granted); *Pfizer Corp. v Inter-Continental Pharmaceuticals Ltd* [1966] R.P.C. 566 (wrong to suspend injunction pending determination of application for compulsory licence); *Zaidener v Barrisdale Engineers Ltd* [1968] R.P.C. 489 (non-manufacturing patentee who exploited by licensing, injunction refused).

Interim injunctions to restrain threats of proceedings for infringement of patent are a valuable remedy. In most cases they are the only practical remedy to avoid the mischief. See *H.V.E. (Electric) Ltd v Cufflin Holdings Ltd* [1964] R.P.C. 149. See also *Bowden Controls Ltd v Acco Cable Controls* [1990] R.P.C. 427 (as well as *American Cyanamid* itself).

### *(xiii) Injunction against non-infringer*

In certain cases, for the preservation of the patentee's rights, an injunction (generally of a temporary nature) may be awarded against a non-infringer. The principle has been expressed thus: **15–47.13**

> "If a man has in his possession or control goods, the dissemination of which, whether in the way of trade or, possibly, merely by way of gifts (see *Upmann v Forester* L.R. (1885) 24 Ch. D. 231) will infringe another's patent or trade mark, he becomes, as soon as he is aware of this fact, subject to a duty (an equitable duty) not to allow those goods to pass out of his possession or control at any rate in circumstances in which the proprietor of the patent or mark might be injured by infringement ensuring. The man having the goods in his possession or control

***Paragraph numbers marked with a "+" can be found online and on CD.***

> must not aid the infringement by letting the goods get into the hands of those who may use them or deal with them in a way which will invade the proprietor's rights. Even though by doing so he might not himself infringe the patent or trade mark, he would be in dereliction of this duty to the proprietor. This duty is one which will, if necessary, be enforced in equity by way of injunction"

per Buckley L.J. in *Norwich Pharmacal Co v Commrs. of Customs and Excise* [1974] A.C. 133 at 146; [1972] 3 All E.R. 813; [1972] R.P.C. 743 (reversed on other grounds by the HL at [1974] A.C. 133; [1973] 2 All E.R. 943; [1974] R.P.C. 101). See also, e.g. *Washburn & Moen Mfg Co v Cunard Steamship Co* (1889) 6 R.P.C. 398.

Because the defendant who is joined under the protective jurisdiction is innocent, the plaintiff will normally bear the costs as against him, but he is able to recover those from the infringer (*Smith, Kline & French Laboratories Ltd v R.D. Harbottle (Mercantile) Ltd* [1980] R.P.C. 363).

### *(xiv) Interim injunctions for infringements of design right*

**15–47.14** On the question of whether or not the grant of an injunction is appropriate in circumstances where a licence of right is available, see *Dyrlund Smith A/S v Turberville Smith Ltd* [1998] F.S.R. 774. There is no working rule that an injunction will not be granted except in special circumstances—the *American Cyanamid* principles apply.

Section 233(2) of the Copyright, Designs and Patents Act 1988 does not operate as a bar to interim relief—see *Badge Sales v PMS International Group Ltd* [2004] EWHC 3382 (Ch); [2006] F.S.R. 1.

### *(c) Defamation claims (serious issued to be tried and prior restraint)*

**15–48** The court's power to grant interlocutory relief in defamation cases seems to be guided by two associated notions, one of high principle and one of principle and practicality. The first is the importance of protecting the individual's right to free speech. The second is an acknowledgement that the court should not, save in the clearest case, usurp the jury's role by restraining at an interlocutory stage publication of a statement that the jury might later find to be no libel or true or otherwise defensible.

The first principle involves the law of "prior restraint". In *Herbage v Pressdram Ltd* [1984] 1 W.L.R. 1160, CA; [1994] 2 All E.R. 769, CA, the Court of Appeal referred to the law of prior restraint in defamation actions and explained (1) that no interim injunction restraining publication of material alleged by the claimant to be defamatory will be granted if the defendant raises the defence of justification (*Bonnard v Perryman* [1891] 2 Ch. 269), and (2) that, unless the evidence of malice is so overwhelming that the judge is driven to the conclusion that no reasonable jury could find otherwise, no such injunction will be granted if the defence raises privilege. In the interests of freedom of speech, the courts will not restrain the publication of a defamatory statement, whether a trade libel or a personal one, where the defendant says he is going to justify it at the trial of the action, except where the statement is obviously untruthful and libellous (*Boehringer Ingelheim Ltd v Vetplus Ltd* ; [2007] EWCA Civ 584 *The Times*, June 27, 2007, CA). Normally, neither the motive of the defendant in making the libel threat, nor the threatened manner of publication, nor the potential damage to the claimant provides an exception to this rule (*Holley v Smyth* [1998] Q.B. 726, CA; [1998] 1 All E.R. 853, CA; *J. Trevor & Sons v Solomon*, (1977) 248 E.G. 779).

In *Herbage v Pressdram Ltd*, op cit, the court confirmed that, in the face of this long-established practice, the principles enunciated by the House of Lords in the *American Cyanamid Co* case relating to interim injunctions are not applicable to interlocutory applications to restrain publication made in actions for defamation. Griffiths L.J. explained that if the courts were to accept that the *American Cyanamid Co* principles did apply, in very many cases the practical effect would be that the claimant would obtain an injunction, because he would often show a serious issue to be tried, that damages would not be realistic compensation, and that the balance of convenience favoured restraining repetition of the alleged libel until trial of the action. That would be a very considerable incursion into the prior restraint rule, which is based on freedom of speech.

After the Human Rights Act 1998 came into effect, and after the decision of the House of Lords in *Cream Holdings Ltd v Banerjee* [2004] UKHL 4; [2005] 1 A.C. 253,

HL, in the case of *Greene v Associated Newspapers Ltd* [2004] EWCA Civ 1462; [2005] 1 All E.R. 30, CA, the Court of Appeal held that there was nothing in s.12(3) of the Act that could properly be interpreted as weakening the rule that, in an action for defamation, a court would not impose a prior restraint on publication unless it was clear that no defence would succeed at trial. (The law of prior restraint in defamation cases and the effects thereon of the 1998 Act are extensively reviewed and explained in the judgment of the court in this case.)

In *Woodward v Hutchins* [1977] 1 W.L.R. 760, CA, where there were concurrent claims in breach of confidence and defamation, it was held that an interlocutory injunction restraining publication should be refused on the ground that to hold otherwise would undermine the prior restraint rule.

The rule against prior restraint extends to a claim for trade mark infringement where the claim is, in reality, a claim brought to protect the claimant's reputation; but it does not extend to a case where the claim is brought, not to protect reputation, but to protect a property right (*Boehringer Ingelheim Ltd v Vetplus Ltd* [2007] EWCA Civ 584, op cit).

## 11. PROCEEDINGS AGAINST THE CROWN

Where a claimant brings civil proceedings against the Crown, and applies for an interim remedy in the form of an interlocutory injunction, special considerations arise. **15–49**

### *(a) Senior Courts Act 1981 s.37 and Crown Proceedings Act 1947 s.21*

Section 37(1) of the Senior Courts Act 1981 states that the High Court may by order, whether interlocutory or final, grant an injunction "in all cases in which it appears to the Court to be just to do so". However, subss.(1) and (2) of s.21 of the Crown Proceedings Act 1947 restricts the circumstances in which injunctions may be granted, respectively, "against the Crown" and "against an officer of the Crown" in "civil proceedings" (as defined in s.23(2) of that Act). Sub-section (1) states that no injunction shall be granted in any civil proceedings "against the Crown", but provides that the court may in lieu thereof make a declaratory order. Sub-section (2) states that no injunction shall be granted in any civil proceedings "against an officer of the Crown" if the effect of doing so would be "to give any relief against the Crown that could not have been obtained in proceedings against the Crown". **15–50**

In broad terms, s.21 prevents an injunction being granted (in the exercise of the court's powers under s.37(1)) in those situations where, prior to the 1947 Act, no injunctive relief could be obtained. The construction and application of s.21(2) has occasioned some difficulty. One particular question which has arisen is whether s.31 of the Senior Courts Act 1981 (Application for judicial review) on its true construction confers a jurisdiction which did not exist before 1981 (and which therefore did not exist before 1947) to grant injunctions against the Crown. Further, problems have arisen because of doubts as to precisely the circumstances in which, before the 1947 Act, injunctions would lie and which, therefore, were not caught by the restriction imposed on s.37(1) by s.21(2).

### *(b) Judicial review proceedings against Crown*

In *Factortame Ltd v Secretary of State for Transport* [1990] 2 A.C. 85, HL, the applicants brought judicial review proceedings against "the Crown", that is to say, against a Secretary of State in his capacity as an officer representing the Crown. The court decided that a substantive question should be referred to the European Court of Justice for a preliminary ruling under the EC Treaty (at the time the appropriate article was Art.177). The question then arose as to whether the applicants were entitled to interim relief (in the form of a mandatory injunction) pending the outcome of the reference. In the proceedings in a Divisional Court (where interim relief against the Crown was granted) and the Court of Appeal (where the Crown's appeal was allowed) (for both judgments, see [1989] 2 C.M.L.R. 353), the Solicitor-General accepted that, in the light of *R. v Licensing Authority, Ex p.Smith Kline & French Laboratories* [1990] A.C. 574, CA, it was not open to him to argue that, although the court has no jurisdiction to grant an interim injunction against the Crown in proceedings begun by writ (see Crown Proceedings Act 1947 s.21), it has such a jurisdiction on an application for judicial **15–51** review. The point was kept open for argument in the House of Lords where Lord Bridge said that the views expressed in the Licensing Authority case were erroneous. It would seem that this conclusion did not form part of the ratio decidendi of the Factortame case as Lord Bridge appears to have regarded it merely as an additional reason for holding that the order made by the Divisional Court in the instant case could not be supported.

The House of Lords returned to the question in the case of In *re M.* [1994] 1 A.C. 377, HL (on appeal from *M. v Home Office* [1992] Q.B. 270, CA). The House held (1) that, even prior to the 1947 Act an action could be brought against an officer of the Crown personally in respect of a tort committed or authorised by him although he had been acting in his official capacity, and he had not been entitled to plead Crown immunity, (2) that injunctions, including, interlocutory injunctions, could be granted and that s.21 of the 1947 Act did not prevent an injunction being granted in a situation in which it could have been granted prior to that Act, (3) that, historically, orders of prohibition and mandamus had regularly been granted against the Crown or officers of the Crown acting in their official capacity, and (4) that s.31(2) of the 1981 Act, on its natural interpretation, gave jurisdiction to the court on applications for judicial review to grant injunctions, including interim injunctions, against ministers and other officers of the Crown, although that jurisdiction should only be exercised in limited circumstances. In *R. v Ministry of Agriculture Fisheries and Food, Ex p.Monsanto Plc* [1999] Q.B. 1161, D.C., a company applied in judicial review proceedings for a stay pending a decision of the ECJ of the operation of decisions made by the Ministry having the effect of permitting their competitors from marketing herbicides over which their patents had expired. It was common ground that the court had power to grant such interim relief and that in exercising its discretion the court must have regard to the principles enunciated in the *American Cyanamid Co* case, but it was a matter of contention as to precisely how those principles should be applied in a public law case. A Divisional Court said that the principles had to be applied in the context of the particular public law questions to which the judicial review proceedings gave rise. Generally, speaking, judicial review proceedings are intended to provide swift relief against abuse of executive power. Such proceedings are neither intended for, nor well suited to, inhibiting commercial activity, particularly over an indefinite, substantial period of time. Before 1999, the relevant rules of court provided that, on an application for judicial review, the court could grant "such interim relief as could be granted in an action" (RSC Ord.53, r.3(10)). CPR Pt 54 contains rules for claims for judicial review. Rule 54.6 states that the claim form must state (amongst other things) any remedy including any interim remedy claimed.

For information on procedure for granting a claim for interim relief in judicial review proceedings, see commentary following CPR r.54.3 and r.54.6.

### *(c) Proceedings involving reference to European Court of Justice*

**15–52** In *Factortame Ltd v Secretary of State for Transport*, op cit, the House of Lords held that, as a matter of English law, the courts have no jurisdiction to grant interim relief in terms which would involve either overturning an English statute in advance of any decision by the European Court of Justice that the statute infringed Community law or (as has been explained above) granting an injunction against the Crown. It then became necessary to seek a preliminary ruling from the ECJ as to whether Community law itself invested the English court with such jurisdiction. The applicants contended that, although they may not have been entitled under domestic law to interim injunctive relief pending the outcome of the reference to the ECJ of the substantive question, it was a requirement of Community law that such relief should be available to them.

On this reference, the ECJ held that the English court had jurisdiction under Community law, in the circumstances postulated, to grant interim relief for the protection of directly enforceable rights under Community law and that no limitation on the court's jurisdiction imposed by any rule of national law could stand as the sole obstacle to preclude the grant of such relief (see *R. v Secretary of State for Transport, Ex p.Factortame Ltd (Case C-213/89)* [1990] 2 A.C. 85; [1990] 3 C.M.L.R. 1, ECJ). In the light of this ruling as to jurisdiction, the House of Lords applied the guidelines derived from *American Cyanamid Co v Ethicon Ltd* [1975] A.C. 396, HL, and decided that interim injunctive relief against the Crown should be granted to the applicants (*R. v Secretary of State for Transport, Ex p.Factortame Ltd (No.2)* [1991] 1 A.C. 603, HL). Lord Goff said that he doubted whether there is any rule that a party challenging the validity of a law under Community law must (to resist an application for an interim injunction against him, or to obtain an interim injunction restraining the enforcement of the law) show a strong prima facie case that the law is invalid. In the end, the matter is one for the discretion of the court, taking into account all the circumstances of the case. Even so, the court should not restrain a public authority by interim injunction from enforcing an apparently authentic law unless it is satisfied, having regard to all the circumstances, that the challenge to the validity of the law is, prima facie, so firmly based as to justify so exceptional a course being taken.

The House of Lords held that in applying the *American Cyanamid Co* guidelines to these cases the position was as follows:

(1) the balance of convenience was likely to be the deciding factor as there was unlikely to be an adequate remedy in damages available to either side;

(2) generally, the court should not restrain a public authority from enforcing apparently authentic national legislation unless the court was satisfied, having regard to all the circumstances, that the challenge to the law is, prima facie, so firmly based as to justify so exceptional a course being taken; but it is always a matter of discretion; and

(3) on the facts of the instant case, the applicants' challenge was, prima facie, a strong one and the balance of convenience came down in favour of the grant of the interim injunction sought.

It should be noted that the effect of the ruling on interim relief given by the ECJ in the Factortame case is not confined to proceedings against the Crown arising on judicial review, or, indeed, to proceedings involving the Crown at all, but extends to proceedings to which the restriction on the granting of injunctive relief found in s.21 of the Crown Proceedings Act 1947 (supra) might apply. Consequently, if in proceedings commenced other than by a claim form for judicial review against the Crown a question of whether a statute infringed Community law was referred to the ECJ the English court, though lacking jurisdiction under domestic law, would have jurisdiction under Community law to grant interim relief for the protection of directly enforceable rights under Community law.

In the Factortame case, the claimant challenged domestic legislation on the ground that it contravened European Community law. The relevant European Community law itself was not challenged. Cases may arise in which, in English proceedings, the validity of EU legislation (such as a Directive or Regulation) is challenged and an application is made for an interim injunction, suspending the operation of the legislation pending a ruling by the ECJ on the issue of validity. The ECJ has ruled that the national court should only grant interim relief suspending the operation of the measure pending the preliminary ruling of the ECJ if they are satisfied that there are serious doubts as to its validity and there is an urgent need for interim relief in order to avoid serious and irreparable damage to the party seeking interim relief (*Atlanta Fruchthandelsgesellschaft mbH v Bundesamt fur Ernahrung und Forstwirtschaft (C-465/93)* [1996] All E.R. (E.C.) 31; [1995] E.C.R. I-3761 and see *R. (ABNA Ltd) v Secretary of State for Health* [2003] EWHC 2420; [2004] Eu. L.R. 88).

Where domestic legislation implementing EU legislation is challenged on the indirect ground that the EU legislation is invalid, and the question of the validity of the latter is referred to the ECJ for a ruling, it is likely that an application will be made for interim relief suspending the effect of the domestic legislation until the ruling is given. It could be argued that, in such circumstances, the application would be determined in accordance with the *American Cyanamid Co* guidelines as applied in the Factortame Ltd On the other hand, it could be argued that the matter should be determined in accordance with the ruling of the ECJ in the Atlanta case. Different views were expressed on this matter in the judgments given by the Court of Appeal and by the House of Lords in *R. v Secretary of State for Health, Ex p.Imperial Tobacco Ltd* [2001] 1 W.L.R. 127, HL (see commentary following CPR r.54.3).

### *(d) Undertakings by the Crown and public bodies*

Before the Crown Proceedings Act 1947, the Crown could obtain an interlocutory injunction without giving the usual undertakings as to damages (*Secretary of State for* **15–53**

***Paragraph numbers marked with a "+" can be found online and on CD.***

*War v Cope* [1919] 2 Ch. 339), apparently on the ground that it was not liable in tort. The question whether the courts would alter their practice in this respect in the light of the changes to Crown immunity brought about by the 1947 Act was not authoritatively answered until the decision of the House of Lords in *F. Hoffmann-La Roche & Co A.G. v Secretary of State for Trade and Industry* [1975] A.C. 295, HL; [1974] 2 All E.R. 1128, HL In this case it was decided that a distinction should be drawn between actions brought by the Crown (1) to enforce or protect its proprietary or contractual rights, and (2) to restrain a subject from breaking a law where the breach would be harmful to the public or a section of it. In an action of the first type the Crown should be in no different a position from the ordinary citizen and so should be required to give an undertaking in the usual way. However, in an action of the second type, a law enforcement action, different principles apply.

Law enforcement proceedings are of two types, so a further distinction has to be drawn. First, there is the relator action in which, once the Attorney-General's consent has been obtained, the relator stands in the shoes of the claimant in an ordinary suit between subject and subject (in practice, often the relator will be a public authority of some kind). In these circumstances, an undertaking in damages is required from the relator but not from the Attorney-General. The second is a law enforcement action brought by the Crown, for example (as was the position in the *Hoffmann-La Roche* case itself), an action brought under a statute which provides expressly for enforcement of a provision of the statute by civil proceedings by the Crown in the discharge of the Crown's duty to the public at large to secure that the law is not flouted. The House of Lords held that, in these circumstances (i.e. where the Crown sues without a relator), there was no rigid rule that the Crown should never be required to give the usual undertaking. However, the practice of exacting an undertaking from the Crown ought not to be applied as a matter of course (as it should be in action between subject and subject, in relator actions, and in actions by the Crown to enforce or to protect its proprietary or contractual rights). On the contrary the propriety of requiring such an undertaking from the Crown as a condition for the granting of an interlocutory injunction should be considered in the light of the particular circumstances of the case. Indeed, an undertaking should not be a condition unless the party injuncted can show very good reason why it should be. In cases where the defence is that the law sought to be enforced by the Crown is invalid (and not merely that the defendant's actions are not prohibited by law) it is for the defence to show a strong prima facie case and even then it may still be inappropriate for the court to impose an undertaking as a condition (see *ibid.*, at p.367, per Lord Diplock).

These constraints have made it possible to assert that when the Crown is seeking an interlocutory injunction in an action in which it is attempting to enforce the law "the usual practice is that no undertaking is required" (*Director General of Fair Trading v Tobyward Ltd* [1989] 1 W.L.R. 517; [1989] 2 All E.R. 266, at p.525 and p.272, per Hoffmann J.). The underlying principle seems to be that where the Crown, in the discharge of its duty to the public at large to secure that the law is not flouted, attempts to enforce the law by bringing civil proceedings it should not have to incur legal liability to the person alleged to be in breach of the law should those proceedings fail, particularly where the Crown had no alternative legal avenues open to it to secure compliance with the law. However, there is no rule of law that an emanation of the Crown is exempt from giving a cross-undertaking in damages in law enforcement proceedings. The court has a discretion, and the presence or absence of undertakings is a matter to be taken into account by the court when considering the balance of convenience (*Customs and Excise Commissioners v Anchor Foods Ltd* [1999] 1 W.L.R. 1139; [1999] 3 All E.R. 268 (Neuberger J.)). The relevant law was summarised in *Securities and Investments Board v Lloyd-Wright* [1993] 4 All E.R. 210 (Morritt J.), where a freezing injunction was granted to the claimants in proceedings brought under the Financial Services Act 1986 and the defendant's application for a cross-undertaking in damages was refused. The remedies sought in the proceedings were provided by the 1986 Act for the benefit of the public at large, or those who suffered from infringements of the legislation, and was a matter of law enforcement. In *Customs and Excise Commissioners v Anchor Foods Ltd*, op cit, a freezing injunction was granted to the claimants in proceedings to recover unpaid customs duty provided a cross-undertaking in damages was given. Neuberger J. said that, on the spectrum of types of cases where the Crown seeks relief, this was neither at the law enforcement extreme nor was it at the other proprietary right enforcement extreme, though it was significantly nearer the former than the latter.

The exercise by the Attorney-General of the Crown's power to act as protector of charity has much in common with law enforcement proceedings. Because the Crown in not asserting any proprietary or contractual claim of its own, an undertaking as to damages should not be demanded as of course but may be required in an appropriate case (see e.g. *Attorney-General v Wright* [1988] 1 W.L.R. 164; [1987] 3 All E.R. 579, where an undertaking limited to the funds of a charity were imposed on the Crown in a case where it sought to recover property and asserted proprietary rights on behalf of the charity).

In the *Hoffmann-La Roche* case, the House of Lords was concerned only with the position of the Crown in law enforcement actions. It was not concerned with the position of local authorities which have the function of enforcing the law in their districts in the public interest or other public authorities. Whether the same principle should be held to apply in the case of public authorities other than the Crown charged with the enforcement of the law fell to be considered by the House in *Kirklees Metropolitan BC v Wickes Building Supplies Ltd* [1993] A.C. 227, HL; [1992] 3 All E.R. 717, HL, where a local authority brought an action for an injunction to restrain a trader from persistently breaching the Sunday trading laws. The House held (reversing the Court of Appeal and following the reasoning in the *Hoffmann-La Roche* case) that the court had a discretion to grant the local authority an interlocutory injunction without requiring it to give an undertaking in damages and that it should be exercised in favour of the authority. It should be noted that, in this case (unlike the *Hoffmann-La Roche* case), proceedings by way of injunction were not the only form of proceedings open to the local authority but, in the circumstances, no other proceedings would have been effective to enforce the law (cf., the earlier case of *Rochdale Borough Council v Anders* [1988] 3 All E.R. 490, where the judge held that an undertaking by the local authority should be a condition). Where a local authority takes civil proceedings for law enforcement purposes there is no requirement for an undertaking in damages unless it can be shown that special circumstances justify it, and even then it remains a matter for the court's discretion (*Coventry City Council v Finnie*, (1997) 29 H.L.R. 658, D.C.).

It is conceivable that in law enforcement proceedings, brought by the Crown (without a relator) or by a public authority of some kind, the defendant may argue by way of defence that the national law sought to be enforced is contrary to Community law. The resolution of this issue may involve a reference to the European Court of Justice and considerable delay in the ultimate disposal of the case. In *Kirklees Metropolitan Borough Council v Wickes Building Supplies Ltd* [1993] A.C. 227, HL; [1992] 3 All E.R. 717, HL, the House of Lords rejected the argument that where in such proceedings the claimants are granted an interlocutory injunction they should under Community law be required to give an undertaking to protect any Community law right of direct effect which might possibly be affected. However, the House held that the question of undertakings in these circumstances is not simply a question of procedure to be left to the national law. (For the reasons given by the House for not requiring undertakings from the claimant local authority in this case, see *ibid*., at p.282 and pp.734–735, per Lord Goff.)

# B. FREEZING INJUNCTIONS

## 1. INTRODUCTION

Section 37(1) of the Senior Courts Act 1981 states that the High Court may by order (whether interlocutory or final) grant an injunction "in all cases in which it appears to the court to be just and convenient to do so", and s.37(3) of that Act, for a technical purpose (see further below) refers expressly to a particular form of interlocutory injunction, that is to say one that restrains a party to any proceedings "from removing from the jurisdiction of the High Court, or otherwise dealing with assets located within that jurisdiction". See further, para15–3 above. **15–54**

In CPR r.25.1(1) various interim remedies that may be granted by the court in proceedings to which the CPR apply are listed. Included among them, in r.25.1(1)(f), is an order restraining a party (i) from removing from the jurisdiction assets located there, or (ii) from dealing with any assets whether located within the jurisdiction or not. It is stated in r.25.1(1)(f) that "an order" to that effect, shall be referred to as "a freezing injunction". This is clumsy and gives the impression that an "order" and an "injunction" are one and the same when the true position is that a freezing injunction is a remedy which the court may by order grant. Not surprisingly, in practice (despite what r.25.1(1)(f)) says) such orders are routinely referred to as "freezing orders". For information on matters of practice and procedure relevant to applications for freezing orders, see the commentary in r.25.1(1)(f) in Vol.1 para.25.1.25. The definition of "freezing injunction" as given in r.25.1(1)(f) draws no distinction between the situation (a) where the applicant makes a proprietary claim over the assets frozen by the injunction, and (b) where he does not. Until the CPR came into effect, injunctions freezing assets over which the applicant had no proprietary claim were known as "Mareva injunctions". The explanation for that is as follows.

In an action in which the claimant seeks to recover his property, in the exercise of its equitable jurisdiction, the court has power to grant an interlocutory injunction restraining the disposal of property over which the claimant has a proprietary claim. The traditional attitude of courts of equity has been that an unsecured creditor (having no proprietary claim) cannot obtain an injunction restraining a debtor from removing his property from the forum or from otherwise disposing of or dealing with his property. However, in 1975 in *Mareva Compania Naviera SA v International Bulk Carriers SA ("The Mareva") [1980] 1 All E.R. 213; [1975] 2 Lloyd's Rep. 509,* CA, the Court of Appeal (distinguishing *Lister & Co v Stubbs,* (1890) 45 Ch. D. 1, CA) held that, in appropriate circumstances, an injunction could be granted for these purposes. Assets up to a value sufficient to satisfy the claimant's claim may be "frozen" by such an injunction.

The single most significant feature of this extended form of interim relief is that it enables the court to grant the claimant an interlocutory injunction restraining the defendant from disposing of, or even merely dealing with, his assets, being assets over which the claimant asserts no proprietary claim but which after judgment may be attached to satisfy a money judgment. One of the hazards facing a claimant in litigation is that, come the day of judgment, it may not be possible for him to obtain satisfaction of that judgment fully or at all. By a freezing (or Mareva) injunction a defendant may be prevented from artificially creating such a situation; a defendant is not to be permitted to thwart in advance orders which the court may make (*Derby & Co Ltd v Weldon (Nos 3 & 4)* [1990] Ch. 65 at 76, CA, per Lord Donaldson M.R.; *Atlas Maritime Co SA v Avalon Maritime Ltd (No.3) (The "Coral Rose")* [1991] 1 W.L.R. 917 at 929, per Nicholls L.J.).

There is a clear distinction between tracing and other remedies available where a claimant asserts that the assets in question belong to him and that the dealings with them should be enjoined in order to protect his proprietary rights and freezing injunctions granted where the claimant does not claim any interest in the assets and "seeks an inhibition of dealings with them simply in order to keep them available for a possible future execution to satisfy an unconnected claim" (*Mercedes-Benz A.G. v Leiduck* [1996] 1 A.C. 284; [1995] 3 W.L.R. 718; [1995] 3 All E.R. 929 at 939, PC, per Lord Mustill) and the distinction is brought out in the cases when it is necessary to do so (e.g. *A. v C. (Note)* [1981] Q.B. 956; [1980] 2 All E.R. 347; *Bankers Trust Co v Shapira* [1980] 1 W.L.R. 1274; [1980] 3 All E.R. 353, CA; and *A.J. Bekhor & Co Ltd v Bilton* [1981] Q.B. 923; [1981] 2 All E.R. 565 at 573, CA, per Ackner L.J.).

So, freezing injunctions are a modern addition to the court's range of interim remedies. Since the Mareva case, the jurisdiction has been developed in a vast number of important decisions handed down by the Court of Appeal and the House of Lords. Over the years, the jurisdiction has been significantly expanded and refined by case law, practice directions and legislation. This development has had an impact on the law and practice relating to ordinary (or "orthodox") interlocutory injunctions. Indeed, such has been the advance of this form of relief that it is not uncommon for an interlocutory injunction to be called a freezing (or Mareva) injunction when it is in fact not confined to preventing the removal or disposal of assets to defeat judgment, but also includes terms securing property over which the claimant asserts a proprietary or tracing claim. This development of the law and practice as to freezing injunctions has not always gone smoothly. The courts have had to resolve many issues, and on some differences of judicial opinion have emerged. Frequently, the courts have warned that, because the law and practice has not stood still, dicta in earlier cases should be approached with caution (see, e.g. *Ninemia Maritime Corporation v Trave Schiffahrtgesellschaft mbH. und Co K.G. (The Niedersachsen)* [1984] 1 All E.R. 398; [1983] 2 Lloyd's Rep.

600 at 606, CA, per Mustill J.). It has been said that it is important that the jurisdiction should be kept flexible, so that the court can continue to do what is "just and convenient" in any given case and that the discretion of the court should not be hedged about with too many rules (*S.C.F. Finance Co Ltd v Masri* [1985] 1 W.L.R. 876; [1985] 2 All E.R. 747 at 750, CA, per Lloyd, L.J.).

The practical problems that have arisen have included: how to frame an order which, on the one hand protects the claimant against the manipulations of a defendant who may prove to be unscrupulous, without strangling the working capital of a defendant at the instance of a claimant who may prove to be unscrupulous; how to form the necessary judgment at a time when every fact is hotly controverted; how to choose ancillary orders which are effective without being oppressive (*Mercedes-Benz A.G. v Leiduck* [1996] 1 A.C. 284; [1995] 3 W.L.R. 718; [1995] 3 All E.R. 929 at 939, PC, per Lord Mustill).

In most instances, if a freezing injunction is to be efficacious it must be swiftly granted ex parte, without notice to the defendant, and, usually, before substantive proceedings have been instituted. If granted unjustly a freezing injunction may do incalculable damage to the defendant (*Third Chandris Corp. v Unimarine SA* [1979] Q.B. 645; [1979] 2 All E.R. 972, at 653 and 978, CA, per Mustill J.). In many respects the development of the law (both substantive and procedural) has reflected the need to adjust the competing claims of efficacy and justice. Difficulties have arisen as to the position of third parties (in particular, wholly innocent third parties) with an interest of some kind in the frozen assets. See further para.15–60 below. The authorities on dispensing with cross-undertakings in interim injunctions in cases where public authorities are seeking to enforce the law were examined by the Court of Appeal in *United States Securities & Exchange Commission v Manterfield* [2009] EWCA Civ 27; [2009] 1 Lloyd's Rep. 399; [2009] 2 All E.R. 1009, CA.

An example of a freezing injunction is annexed to Practice Direction (Interim Injunctions), supplementing CPR Pt 25 (see Vol.1, para.25APD.13). A perusal of the detailed terms of that example, including those imposing restraints and duties on the respondent, on third parties, and on the applicant (and the exceptions thereto), gives a good indication of particular practical problems which the courts have had to settle. (Many of the provisions in the example can be traced to particular authoritative decisions of the Court of Appeal and House of Lords; see further Vol.1, para.25.1.25.6.)

## 2. NATURE AND SCOPE OF POWER – GENERALLY

The nature of this legal power, the purposes of an order made under it, and the assets that may be covered by an order, have been explained in numerous cases; see e.g. *Fourie v Le Roux* [2007] UKHL 1; [2007] 1 W.L.R. 320, HL, per Lord Scott at para.25 et seq, and the detailed account by Aikens J. in *C. Inc Plc v L.* [2001] 2 Lloyd's Rep. 459. **15–55**

The freezing injunction is a remedy which exists for the purpose of restraining a judgment debtor, or potential judgment debtor, from committing the abuse of dissipating or hiding assets that the judgment creditor might lawfully attach for the purpose of satisfying a judgment given, or likely to be given, in his favour (*A. v C. (Note)* [1981] Q.B. 956). It is an interim remedy granted to protect the efficacy of court proceedings (domestic or foreign), in particular, to prevent a defendant dissipating his assets with the intention or effect of frustrating enforcement of a prospective judgment. It is not granted to give a claimant advance security for his claim, though it may have that effect. The claimant applying for such a remedy cannot of course guarantee that he will recover judgment, but he must at least point to proceedings already brought or about to be brought so as to show where and on what basis he expects to recover judgment (*Fourie v Le Roux*, op cit, at para.3 per Lord Bingham). It is difficult to visualise a case where the grant of a freezing order, made without notice, could be said to be properly made in the absence of any formulation of the case for substantive relief that the applicant for the order intended to institute (*ibid* at para.35 per Lord Scott). Assets up to a value sufficient to satisfy the claimant's claim in the action, should he be successful in obtaining judgment, may be "frozen" by such an injunction.

A freezing injunction (though made before substantive proceedings have been instituted) is of immediate effect. It takes effect against the defendant in personam and is not an attachment of the assets. It has its legal operation, not on the property itself, but on the defendant who is subject to the jurisdiction of the court. It restrains the respondent from dealing with his assets, but it does not prevent him from borrowing money, thereby increasing his overall indebtedness (*Cantor Index Ltd v Lister*, November 22, 2001, unrep. (Neuberger J.); *Anglo Eastern Trust Ltd v Kermanshahchi* [2002] EWHC 1702 (Ch); July 5, 2002, unrep. (Neuberger J.)). It gives the applicant no proprietary rights in the assets seized and no advantage over other creditors of the defendant (*Cretanor Maritime Co Ltd v Irish Marine Management Ltd* [1978] 1 W.L.R. 966; [1978] 3 All E.R. 164, CA, *Iraqi Ministry of Defence v Arcepey Shipping Co* [1981] Q.B. 65; [1980] 1 All E.R. 480, *Derby & Co Ltd v Weldon (No.2)* [1990] Ch. 65; sub nom. Derby & Co Ltd Weldon (No.2) [1989] 1 All E.R. 1002, CA, and *A.J. Bekhor & Co Ltd v Bilton* [1981] Q.B. 923; [1981] 2 All E.R. 565, CA). The purpose of this particular form of injunction is not to provide a claimant with security for its claim but to restrain a defendant from evading justice by disposing of assets otherwise than in the ordinary course of business so as to make itself judgment proof; a claimant has no interest in the assets the subject of a freezing injunction (*Gangway Ltd v Caledonian Park Investments (Jersey) Ltd* [2001] 2 Lloyd's Rep. 715 (Colman J.); *Flightline Ltd v Edwards* [2003] EWCA Civ; [2003] 1 W.L.R. 1200, CA (agreement to discharge order on terms as to deposit of cash giving applicant no security rights)). Further, it is not granted to punish the defendant for his alleged misdeeds, or to enable the claimant to exert pressure on him to settle the action (*P.C.W. (Underwriting Agencies) Ltd v Dixon* [1983] 2 All E.R 158, CA), but rather to protect the applicant (*Flightwise Travel Service Ltd v Gill* [2003] EWHC 3082 (Ch); The Times December 5, 2003 (Neuberger J.)). If the claimant obtains judgment, a freezing injunction merely ensures that once the mechanisms of enforcement are set in motion, there is something physically available upon which they can work (*Mercedes-Benz A.G. v Leiduck* [1996] 1 A.C. 284; [1995] 3 All E.R. 929 at 941, PC, per Lord Mustill).

As to the protection afforded defendants by the claimant's undertakings in orders for interim injunctions in the form of freezing orders, see para.15–28 above.

## 3. JURISDICTION

15–56 The creation of this form of injunction was a judicial innovation based on the equitable jurisdiction of the High Court.

### *(a) Generally*

15–57 The remedy has been found to be particularly useful in shipping and commercial cases but is not confined to such proceedings. It may be ordered by the court in respect of a pending or anticipated arbitration reference (Arbitration Act 1996 s.44 (2)(e), *The Rena K* [1979] Q.B. 377), in aid of the enforcement of an arbitration award where it has been converted into a judgment (*Gidrxslme Shipping Co v Tantomar-Transportes Lda.* [1995] 1 W.L.R. 299; [1994] 4 All E.R. 507), and in aid of a statutory adjudication of a building disputes (*Pynes Three Ltd v Transco Ltd* [2005] EWHC 2445 (TCC), July 22, 2005, unrep.).

Generally, the injunction will be an aid to the enforcement of a judgment obtained, or expected to be obtained, in proceedings for substantive relief in an English court. However, in certain circumstances, a party who has obtained, or who expects to obtain, a judgment in a foreign court may be granted a freezing injunction by the court. (On the question whether an injunction obtained for the last-mentioned purpose may freeze assets which are outside the jurisdiction as well as those within, see para.15–80 below.)

Article 22(5) of the Judgments Regulation states that, in proceedings concerned with the enforcement of judgments, the courts of the Member State in which judgment has been or is to be enforced shall have exclusive jurisdiction (see para.5–270 above). A freezing order is not within art.22(5), as that provision is concerned with actual enforcement, and not with steps that might lead to enforcement (*Masri v Consolidated Contractors International Company SAL* [2008] EWCA Civ 303; [2008] 2 Lloyd's Rep. 128, CA).

The existence of the jurisdiction to grant freezing injunctions is acknowledged by the Senior Courts Act 1981 s.37(3) (a provision first enacted in 1981 and not derived from earlier legislation). The explanation for the significance of this is as follows.

One issue on which doubt emerged at an early stage was whether a freezing injunction could be granted against a defendant whether he was resident inside or outside the jurisdiction and whatever his domicile or nationality might be (*Chartered Bank v*

***Paragraph numbers marked with a "+" can be found online and on CD.***

*Daklouche* [1980] 1 W.L.R. 107, CA, and *Rahman (Prince Abdul) bin Turki al Sudairy v Abu-Taha* [1980] 1 W.L.R. 1268; [1980] 3 All E.R. 409, CA, approving *Barclay-Johnson v Yuill* [1980] 1 W.L.R. 1259), and could be used to restrain his disposal of assets within the jurisdiction as well as without (*Ninemia Maritime Corporation v Trave Schiffahrtgesellschaft m.b.H. und Co K.G. (The Niedersachsen)* [1983] 1 W.L.R. 1412; [1983] 1 All E.R. 398; [1983] 2 Lloyd's Rep. 600, CA). (The demise of exchange control regulations had justified the extension of the power to domestic defendants; see*Z Ltd v A-Z and AA-LL* [1982] 1 Q.B. 558, sub nom. *Z Ltd v A.* [1982] 1 All E.R. 556 at 571 and 584, CA, per Kerr L.J.) The point was put beyond doubt by the Senior Courts Act 1981 s.37(3) which states that the power to grant the injunction shall be exercisable in cases where the party to be restrained is, as well as in cases where he is not, domiciled, resident or present within the jurisdiction.

It is convenient to note here that, later on again, after a period of further doubt (*Ashtiani v Kashi* [1987] Q.B. 888, CA), it was held that, in certain circumstances, the court has jurisdiction to grant a freezing injunction restraining a party (whether domiciled, resident or present within the jurisdiction of the court or not) from dealing with his assets located abroad, perhaps within several foreign jurisdictions (*Babanaft International Co SA v Bassatne* [1990] 1 Ch. 13; [1989] 1 All E.R. 433; [1988] 2 Lloyd's Rep. 435, CA, *Republic of Haiti v Duvalier* [1990] 1 Q.B. 202; [1989] 2 W.L.R. 261; [1989] 1 All E.R. 456, CA). As a result of this development, a distinction came to be drawn between "domestic" and "worldwide" freezing injunctions, having effect, respectively, within the jurisdiction and extra-territorially (as to the latter, see further para.15–81 below).

Section 37(3) of the 1981 Act did not, as is sometimes said, turn the common law freezing injunction into a statutory remedy; rather it assumed that the remedy existed, and tacitly indorsed its validity (*Mercedes-Benz AG v Leiduck* [1996] A.C. 284, PC). Where the court has in personam jurisdiction over the person against whom a freezing order is sought the court has jurisdiction to grant it, and the question for the court then becomes (as it does where any injunctive relief is sought) whether, in the light of the restrictions and limitation which have been placed by a combination of judicial precedent and rules of court on the circumstances in which the power should be exercised, relief can properly be granted.

As is the case with ordinary interlocutory injunctions, a freezing injunction may be granted where it appears to the court "to be just and convenient to so do" and it may be granted at any time (Senior Courts Act 1981 s.37 (1)); consequently, it may be granted after judgment in aid of execution as well as before judgment.

Where a claimant recovers judgment on a claim and the defendant's counterclaim is dismissed, and the defendant satisfies the judgment by paying money to the claimant, in the event of the defendant appealing a freezing injunction may be granted by the court or by the Court of Appeal, restraining the claimant from dealing with that money pending the outcome of the appeal on the counterclaim (*Ketchum International Plc v Group Public Relations Holdings Ltd* [1996] 4 All E.R. 374, CA).

If costs are awarded against a party seeking an interlocutory injunction and made payable forthwith, a freezing injunction may be granted against the party in aid of execution of that order, *Jet West Ltd v Haddican* [1992] 1 T.L.R. 487; [1992] 2 All E.R. 545, CA. Where a claimant brings minority shareholders' proceedings by petition under the Companies Act 1985 s.459, the court has no jurisdiction to grant a freezing injunction unless the petition contains allegations which could be said to constitute a cause of action against the directors (*In re Premier Electronics (GB) Ltd* [2002] B.C.C. 911 (Pumfrey J.)).

The court has an inherent jurisdiction to issue a bench warrant for the arrest of a person who failed to comply with a condition of a freezing injunction requiring him to surrender his passport (*Zakaharov v White The Times*, November 13, 2003 (Ch); 153 New L.J. 1669 (2003) (Roderick Evans J.)).

As to the respective powers of judges, Masters, and district judges in relation to the granting of freezing injunctions, see Vol.1, para.25.1.25.1.

### *(b) Equitable quia timet freezing order where indemnity claimed*

A number of authorities following *Siskina v Distos Cia Naviera SA (The Siskina)* [1979] **15–58**
A.C. 210; [1977] 3 All E.R. 803, HL, established that a freezing injunction cannot be

granted as ancillary relief in respect of a merely contingent cause of action, no matter how close to fruition that cause of action may be or how just or convenient it may otherwise be to grant an injunction (see para.15–67 below, and note also para.15–4 above). These authorities were reviewed (obiter) by Rix J. in *Rowland v Gulfpac Ltd* [1999] 1 Lloyd's Rep. Bank. 86 (Rix J.), a case in which directors sought a declaration to the effect that they were entitled to be indemnified against (at least) the cost of defending claims against them in foreign proceedings. His lordship concluded that there is no right to a freezing order unless there is a pre-existing cause of action. However, equity will give relief where the common law will not, and will even give relief in a situation of quia timet before a loss has actually occurred. But equity will do so only where there is reasonably good, perhaps clear, evidence that a liability will fall on the party entitled to be indemnified and that the person obliged to indemnify clearly proposes to ignore his obligations. This decision was based on *In re Anderson-Berry* [1928] 1 Ch. 290, CA.

In *Papamichael v National Westminster Bank Plc* [2002] 1 Lloyd's Rep. 332 (Judge Chambers Q.C.), a bank defending a claim by a depositor for return of monies, brought a claim for indemnity against a third party and applied for a freezing order and obtained a freezing order against that party. At the hearing of an application to set that order aside, on the basis of the Gulfpac case the bank applied for the grant of a quia timet injunction over the third party's assets, in the event of the judge holding that the freezing order could not stand because no cause of action had yet arisen against him. The judge held that the bank was entitled to the freezing order and to the relief of a quia timet injunction. In doing so the judge said that the temptation to think of the quia timet injunction as a form of "parallel" freezing order should be resisted. It is founded upon the need to protect a party where his right to indemnity or similar relief is contingent upon an event that has not yet occurred. The person responsible for the event may or may not be the person against whom the relief is sought.

See also, *Director of the Assets Recovery Agency v Gerrard* [2007] EWHC 908 (QB), March 30, 2007, unrep. (Pitchers J.); *Director of Assets Recovery Agency v McCormack* [2007] EWHC 908 (QB), March 30, 2007, unrep. (Pitchers J.).

### *(c) County courts*

**15–59** The power of county courts to grant freezing injunctions is restricted by the County Court Remedies Regulations 1991 (see Vol.2, para.9B–77) made under the County Courts Act 1984 s.38 (as amended in 1990) (*ibid.* Vol.2, para.9B–468+). The general rule is that a county court may not grant a freezing injunction. Exemption from this restriction is enjoyed by nominated circuit judges sitting in patents county courts and mercantile courts and by High Court judges sitting as judges for any county court district (*ibid.* reg.3(2)). Further, a county court may grant such relief in the circumstances listed in reg.3(3) and these include (a) for the purpose of making an order for the preservation, custody or detention of property which forms or may form the subject matter of proceedings (i.e. where the property is subject to a proprietary claim), and (b) in aid of execution of a judgment or order made in proceedings in a county court to preserve assets until execution can be levied upon them. A county court may not vary or revoke a freezing injunction granted by the High Court but may vary (but not revoke) such an injunction where all the parties are agreed on the terms of the variation (reg.3(1) and (4)(b)).

Article 3 of the High Court and County Courts Jurisdiction Order 1991 provides that the High Court shall have jurisdiction to hear an application for an injunction made in the course of or in anticipation of proceedings in a county court where a county court may not, by virtue of regulations under s.38(3)(b) or otherwise, grant an injunction (see Vol.2, para.9B–933). Thus, the High Court has jurisdiction to grant freezing injunctions incidental to and in support of county court proceedings. In *Schmidt v Wong (Practice Note)* [2005] EWCA Civ 1506; [2005] 1 W.L.R. 561, CA, the Court of Appeal explained that in order to invoke the High Court's assistance in this respect the claimant in the county court proceedings should make an application to the High Court in accordance with Pt 23 (issuing the application at the RCJ or the appropriate District Registry and paying the higher court fee). The application should be made returnable before a judge. In the body of the application there should appear an explanation along the following lines:

***Paragraph numbers marked with a "+" can be found online and on CD.***

"This application is being made in the course of [in anticipation of] proceedings in the ... County Court pursuant to article 3 of the High Court and County Courts Jurisdiction Order 1991, The County Court has no jurisdiction to grant the relief sought by reason of regulation 3(1) of the County Court Remedies Regulations 1991."

The court explained that the High Court's assistance is not to be invoked by issuing a claim form in the High Court. This is because a freezing injunction cannot be extracted from the claim to which it relates and treated as a free-standing remedy.

CPR r.27.2(1)(a) states that Pt 25 does not apply to small claims "except as it relates to interim injunctions".

## 4. THIRD PARTIES

As was noted above, in the development of the law and practice of freezing injunctions, difficulties have arisen as to the position of third parties (in particular, wholly innocent third parties) with an interest of some kind in the frozen assets. Where the third party is holder of an asset of the defendant (e.g. his bankers), in many instances, the effectiveness of the injunction will depend as much on the restraining of the actions of the third party as those of the defendant, if not more so. (In an appropriate case, of course, and in accordance with the relevant rules, a third party may be joined as a party to the action.) The applicant is required to give third parties notice of the injunction and to notify them of their right to seek to vary an order (*Guinness Peat Aviation (Belgium) N.V. v Hispania Lineas Aereas SA* [1992] 1 Lloyd's Rep. 190) (see further para.15–62 below). **15–60**

The innocent third party should be told with as much certainty as possible what he is to do or not to do. For example, in the case of a third party bank the claimant should identify the bank account by specifying the branch and heading of the account or any other asset with as much precision as possible or by undertaking to pay the cost involved to request the bank or other party to conduct a search to ascertain whether he holds assets of the defendant.

The claimant should inform the judge of the names of the third parties to whom notice is to be given, but of course he may give information to others on further inquiry.

A claimant cannot possibly be entitled to obtain the advantage of a freezing injunction at the expense of the business rights of an innocent third party merely by proffering him an indemnity. The court must take into account, not merely the balance of convenience and justice as between the claimant and the defendant, but also that balance as between the claimant and the third party. The court will decline to grant the claimant a freezing injunction which will have the effect of substantially interfering with the business rights of a third party in order to secure the ultimate recovery of debts or damages from the defendant with which the third party is in no way concerned. In such circumstances the offer of an indemnity by the claimant is not sufficient (*Galaxia Maritime SA v Mineral Import-Export* [1982] 1 W.L.R. 539; [1982] 1 All E.R. 796 at 799, CA, per Kerr L.J.).

### *(a) Duties of third party*

A third party is bound by the terms of the injunction as soon as he has notice of it, even though the defendant himself has not yet been served and does not know that the order has been made. He must do what he reasonably can to preserve the assets otherwise he will be guilty of contempt of court as an act of interference with the course of justice if he assists in their disposal. In particular, a third party who holds assets to the order of the defendant must not do anything which would assist him in the removal or disposal of such assets (*Z Ltd v A-Z and AA-LL* [1982]1 Q.B. 558; sub nom.*Z. Ltd v A.* [1982] 1 All E.R. 556, CA). These propositions are reflected in the example of an order granting a freezing injunction annexed to Practice Direction (Interim Injunctions), supplementing CPR Pt 25 (see Vol.1 para.25APD.13). **15–61**

The receipt by a bank of notice of a freezing injunction affecting a customer's account may override the customer's instructions regarding that account and make it unlawful for the bank to honour the customer's cheques. The bank is obliged to comply so far as it possibly can with the court's order; but where the bank has a security interest in the frozen assets it is entitled to exercise its rights in accordance with its own commercial judgment, provided always that is does nothing inconsistent with the

***Paragraph numbers marked with a "+" can be found online and on CD.***

underlying purpose of the injunction (*Gangway Ltd v Caledonian Park Investments (Jersey) Ltd* [2001] 2 Lloyd's Rep. 715, (Colman J.). A bank has no choice but to comply with the court's order but does not assume any responsibility towards the applicant ; see also *Customs and Excise Commissioners v Barclays Bank Plc* [2006] UKHL 26; [2006] 2 Lloyd's Rep. 327, HL (bank no liable in negligence for failing to prevent defendant from making unauthorised withdrawals of frozen funds)). See further, "Protection of third party" para.15–62 below.

Where the defendant is owed an asset by a third party (e.g. a pension payable by an employer) prima facie the transfer of that asset to the defendant does not amount to assisting in removal or dissipation, but different considerations would arise where it is known that the sole purpose of the transfer is to facilitate dissipation (*The Law Society v Shanks* [1988] 1 F.L.R. 504, CA). Mere notice of the existence of the injunction cannot render it a contempt of court for a third party to make over an asset to the defendant direct. Otherwise it might be impossible, for example, for a debtor with notice to pay over to the defendant even the most trivial sum without seeking the directions of the court. A distinction must be drawn between notice of the injunction on the one hand and notice of a probability that the asset will be disposed of or dealt with in breach of it on the other. Where the evidence demonstrates that a defendant will, if he can, dispose of money owed to him by a third party in breach of a freezing injunction, the court may, with the approval of the third party, order that the money should be paid into court, or into a frozen bank account of the defendant at a bank which has notice of the injunction (*Bank Mellat v Kazmi* [1989] 1 Q.B. 541; [1989] 1 All E.R. 925, CA).

### (b) Protection of third party

**15–62** Care must be taken to ensure that freezing injunctions do not bear harshly upon innocent third parties. Otherwise, a procedure which was forged to prevent abuse may become an instrument of oppression (*Searose Ltd v Seatrain UK Ltd* [1981] 1 W.L.R. 894, at 897).

As to the effects of freezing injunctions on third parties, especially where the assets are held out of the jurisdiction, note Commercial Court Guide paras F15.10 and F15.11 (see Vol.2, para.2A–99), and *Bank of China v NBM LLC* [2002] EWCA Civ 1933; [2002] 1 W.L.R. 844, CA.

Provisions designed to protect third parties are included in the example of an order for a freezing injunction annexed to the Practice Direction. Lack of proper consideration of such provisions was criticised by the Court of Appeal in *Ghoth v Ghoth* [1992] 2 All E.R. 920, CA.

In *Z Ltd v A-Z and AA-LL* [1982] 1 Q.B. 558; sub nom. *Z. Ltd v A.* [1982] 1 All E.R. 556, CA, the Court of Appeal laid down guidelines for the protection of third parties (in particular, of banks). Routine banking transactions should not be interfered with by a freezing injunction unless an exceptionally strong case that the principles of banking law were inapplicable (*Lewis & Peat (Produce) Ltd v Almatu Properties Ltd, The Times*, May 14, 1992, CA. A bank holding funds which become the subject of a freezing injunction is entitled to a variation of the injunction so as to enable it to exercise any right of set-off it has in connection with facilities granted to the customer's account before it receives notice of the injunction and such right of set-off can be exercised in respect of interest accruing in the future as well as interest already accrued, and indeed a freezing injunction served on a bank should ordinarily contain such a proviso to avoid the need for an application to vary it (*Oceanica Castelana Armadora SA v Mineralimportexport, The Theotokos* [1983] 1 W.L.R. 1294; [1983] 2 All E.R. 65). Accordingly, in the example of an order granting a freezing injunction annexed to Practice Direction (Interim Injunctions), supplementing CPR Pt 25 it is expressly stated that the injunction does not prevent any bank form exercising any right to set off it may have in respect of any facility which it gave to the respondent before it was notified on the order.

Obviously, a third party may suffer loss as a consequence of the order.As a term of a freezing injunction, the claimant may be obliged to undertake to indemnify any third party affected by the order against all expenses reasonably incurred in complying with the order; see further paras 15–28 and 15–29 above.

### (c) The Chabra jurisdiction

**15–63** In *TSB Private Bank International SA v Chabra* [1992] 1 W.L.R. 231, it was held that,

***Paragraph numbers marked with a "+" can be found online and on CD.***

where the defendant is restrained from disposing of the assets of a company, the court has jurisdiction on its own motion to join the company (in effect, a third party) as a second defendant and to grant a freezing injunction against it to support the claimant's claim against the defendant, even though there is no cause of action against the company. Where the court exercises the *Chabra* jurisdiction and restrains a third party, in effect the court is granting ancillary relief in aid of, and as part of, the freezing relief granted against the defendant. The jurisdiction may be exercised where there is good reason to suppose that the assets of the third party are, in truth, the assets of the injuncted defendant (e.g. where the assets are held by the third party on a bare trust (or as nominee) for the defendant), but is not limited to such a case and may extend to a situation where the principal defendant, whilst having no legal or equitable right to the assets in question, has some right in respect of, or control over, or other rights of access to them (*Dadourian Group International Inc v Azuri Ltd* [2005] EWHC 1768 (Ch), July 13, 2005, unrep.). A petitioner in a creditors' petition for the winding up of a company may obtain freezing orders against persons whose only alleged liabilities are to the company (or to the liquidator under statutory claims arising only in the event of liquidation). But, in the absence of cogent reasons, if freezing orders are to be obtained against potential judgment debtors of a company pending the making of a winding up order, they should be made on the application of a provisional liquidator rather than of a petitioning creditor (*H.M. Revenue and Customs v Egleton* [2006] EWHC 2313, September 19, 2006, unrep. (Briggs J.)).

## 5. "DOMESTIC" FREEZING INJUNCTIONS

The assets "frozen" by freezing injunctions may be assets within the jurisdiction or without. For purposes of exposition "domestic" freezing injunctions may be dealt with first before considering the additional and different matters relevant to "worldwide" injunctions, such as they are (though that may involve a degree of repetition). **15–64**

For commentary on practice and procedure relating to applications for orders for freezing injunctions, see Vol.1 para.25.1.25.

### (a) Relevant factors

The granting of a freezing injunction is a matter for the discretion of the judge hearing the application. In the exercise of this discretion, the court may grant an application for an injunction freezing the respondent's assets within the jurisdiction where the following matters are established: **15–65**

(1) the claimant has a good arguable case on a substantive claim over which the court has jurisdiction;
(2) the defendant has assets within the jurisdiction;
(3) there is a real risk of dissipation or secretion of assets which would render the claimant's relief nugatory.

The court may also grant an application for an injunction freezing the respondent's assets outside the jurisdiction (a "worldwide" freezing injunction), but on such an application additional factors become relevant. See further, "Worldwide freezing injunctions", para.15–81 below.

#### *(i) Good arguable case*

*American Cyanamid Co v Ethicon Ltd* [1975] A.C. 396, HL, holds that an applicant for an interlocutory injunction need show only "a serious question to be tried". In applications for freezing injunctions, the formula "a good arguable case" has been preferred. For discussion on this point, see para.15–23 above. **15–66**

#### *(ii) Court's jurisdiction over substantive claim*

In the normal case, an application for a freezing injunction will be made by a claimant in proceedings, either commenced or about to be commenced, in which it is clear that the court has jurisdiction over the substantive claims made against the defendant by the claimant. **15–67**

In *Siskina v Distos Cia Naviera SA (The Siskina)* [1979] A.C. 210; [1977] 3 All E.R. 803, HL, Lord Diplock said (at 256) the power to grant an interlocutory injunction can

**_Paragraph numbers marked with a "+" can be found online and on CD._**

only be exercised "in protection or assertion of some legal or equitable right which it has jurisdiction to enforce by final judgment". On the basis of this proposition it has been concluded that an interlocutory injunction in the form of a freezing injunction will not be granted to an applicant who has no cause of action against the defendant at the time of the application (*Siporex Trade SA v Comdel Commodities Ltd* [1986] 2 Lloyd's Rep. 428 at 436, per Bingham J., Veracruz *Transportation Inc v V.C. Shipping Co Inc* [1992] 1 Lloyd's Rep. 353 at 358, CA, per Beldam L.J., *Mercedes-Benz A.G. v Leiduck* [1996] 1 A.C. 284; [1995] 3 All E.R. 929, PC (where Lord Mustill said "the order cannot simply be made in the air")). It can only be granted when there is an actual or threatened invasion of a legal right; it cannot be made in respect of a contract that has not been breached and is not threatened with breach (*Zucker v Tyndall Holdings Plc* [1992] 1 W.L.R. 1127; [1993] 1 All E.R. 124, CA, see also *A. v B.* [1989] 2 Lloyd's Rep. 423).

However, it has been argued that Lord Diplock's statement must be regarded as unduly restrictive and that the absence of some existing legal or equitable right is not a matter going to the existence of the court's equitable jurisdiction but to the exercise of discretion (*Mercedes-Benz A.G. v Leiduck*, op cit, per Lord Nicholls). (In *Morris v Murjani* [1996] 1 W.L.R. 848, CA, where an interlocutory injunction restraining a bankrupt from leaving the jurisdiction was granted, it was stated that the requirement of a pre-existing cause of action was limited to cases involving an ordinary dispute relating to the allege violation of private rights and did not apply to a claim brought by a trustee against a bankrupt.)

The matter was clarified by the House of Lords in *Fourie v Le Roux* [2007] UKHL 1; [2007] 1 W.L.R. 320, HL, where it was held that the requirement of an existing legal or equitable right was not matter going to jurisdiction in the strict sense (see para.15–4above). However, the House held that, in that case, a freezing injunction was rightly discharged as no claim for substantive relief had been formulated by the applicant and shown to the judge. An applicant must be able to point to proceedings already brought, or proceedings about to be brought, so as to show where and on what basis he expects to recover judgment against the defendant (op cit at para.3, per Lord Bingham). A freezing injunction cannot properly be granted otherwise. See further paras 15–3 and 15–55 above.

It is clear that, in certain circumstances, where an application is made to the English court for a foreign injunction in aid of proceedings which have been or are to be commenced in a foreign court, or in courts in Scotland or Northern Ireland, the English court may have jurisdiction to grant the injunction even though it does not have jurisdiction over the substantive claim (see further para.15-3 above). Note also para.15-56 above (Equitable quia timet freezing order where indemnity claimed).

Where a claimant (C) has obtained a judgment against a defendant (D1), for the purposes of enforcement another defendant (D2) may be joined and C may obtain a freezing injunction against him, even though (1) there was no substantive claim against D2, and (2) his assets were not even arguably beneficially owned by D1, provided C had a right against D1, being a right that gave rise to a right that D1 could enforce against D2 and his assets (*C. Inc v L.* [2001] 2 Lloyd's Rep. 459, (Aikens J.) (granting freezing injunctions against spouse of judgment debtor where latter wholly dependant on former)).

In certain circumstances, a party armed with a foreign judgment or arbitration award may seek to enforce it through the English court. In order to do so, the judgment creditor may require permission under r. 6.20 to serve proceedings on the judgment debtor out of the jurisdiction. (In *Tasarruf Mevduati Sigorta Fonu v Demirel* [2007] EWCA Civ 79; [2007] 1 W.L.R. 2508, CA, the Court of Appeal rejected the submission that jurisdiction to serve our in these circumstances only exists where, at the time when the application is made, there are assets in the jurisdiction against which the judgment can be enforced, or at least where the judgment is otherwise enforceable in England and Wales.) The court has jurisdiction to grant the judgment creditor a domestic freezing injunction in aid of the proceedings. (The court is unlikely to exercise its discretion to grant a worldwide freezing injunction in these circumstances; *Rosseel N.V. v Oriental Commercial and Shipping (UK) Ltd* [1990] 1 W.L.R. 1387; [1990] 3 All E.R. 545, CA; *Banco Nacional de Comercio Exterior SNC v Empresa de Telecommunicationes de Cuba SA* [2007] EWCA Civ 662; [2007] 2 Lloyd's Rep. 484, CA).

### *(iii) Assets within jurisdiction*

**15–68** In declaring the existence of the jurisdiction, the Senior Courts Act 1981 s.37(3)

***Paragraph numbers marked with a "+" can be found online and on CD.***

states that a party may be restrained by a freezing injunction from "removing ... or otherwise dealing with" assets located within the jurisdiction of the court.

The term "assets" has no limitation put upon it and it includes ships and aircraft, chattels such as motor vehicles, jewellery, objets d'art, and other valuables as well as choses in action (*C.B.S. (UK) Ltd v Lambert* [1983] Ch. 37; [1982] 3 All E.R. 237, CA).

In the first instance, unless the case is exceptional, the court should freeze the defendant's assets up to a sum level with the claimant's prima facie justifiable claim (a "maximum sum" order), and not generally (*Z Ltd v A-Z and AA-LL* [1982] 1 Q.B. 558; [1982] 2 W.L.R. 288; [1982] 1 All E.R. 556, at 574–575 and 589, CA, per Kerr L.J.). It may be necessary to make different provisions in relation to the defendant's assets generally and in relation to such of his assets as are known or believed to be in the hands of third parties (*ibid.*). In some instances, the claimant will be capable of identifying with particularity (nature, location, etc.) the defendant's assets to be "frozen" by the injunction. To the extent to which the assets are known or suspected to exist, these should be identified even if their value is unknown; and if it is known or suspected that they are in the hands of third parties, everything should be done to define their location to the greatest possible extent (*ibid*).

In the example of a freezing order annexed to Practice Direction (Interim Injunctions) terms reflecting s.37(3) and relevant case law (in particular *Z Ltd v A-Z and AA-LL*) are found in paras 5 to 8. Paragraph 5 states that the respondent must not "remove" from England and Wales or in any way "dispose of, deal with or diminish the value of" any of his assets which are in the jurisdiction up to the value stipulated by the order.

The words "deal with" should be given a wide meaning. They should not be construed eiusdem generis with "removing from the jurisdiction"; they include disposing of, selling or charging the asset (see *C.B.S. UK Ltd v Lambert* [1983] Ch. 37; [1982] 3 All E.R. 237, CA).

Paragraph 6 of the example of a freezing order annexed to Practice Direction states that the assets which a respondent may be restrained from removing or disposing of etc includes any asset jointly owned. Further, they include any asset which he has the power, directly or indirectly, to dispose of or deal with as if it were his own; for these purposes the respondent has such "power" if a third party holds or controls the asset in accordance with the respondent's direct or indirect instructions. (Parts of this paragraph may be seen as a response to the decision of the Court of Appeal in *Federal Bank of the Middle East Ltd v Hadkinson* [2000] 1 W.L.R. 1695, CA.)

Where there is a dispute as to the ownership of assets that may be subject to the injunction, the following principles apply (*S.C.F. Finance Co Ltd v Masri* [1985] 1 W.L.R. 876; [1985] 2 All E.R. 747, CA): (1) if the assets appear to belong to a third party they should not be included in the scope of the injunction without evidence that they are the defendant's, (2) the mere assertion of the defendant that a third party owns the assets need not be accepted without inquiry (and the same principle applies to claims by a third party to intervene to vary the injunction to exclude the assets), (3) the court must do its best to do what is just and convenient between all concerned, (4) in a proper case the court may direct an issue to be tried either before or after the main action as to the ownership of the assets.

### (iv) Risk of judgment being unsatisified

**15–69** The purpose of the injunction is to ensure that the court's judgment is not rendered valueless "by an unjustifiable disposal of assets" (*Ketchum International Plc v Group Public Relations Holdings Ltd* [1997] 1 W.L.R. 4, CA). What has to be shown is that there is, without an injunction, "a real risk that a judgment or award in favour of the claimants would go unsatisfied" (*Ninemia Maritime Corporation v Trave Schiffahrtsgesellschaft m.b.h und Co K.G.* [1983] 1 W.L.R. 1412, CA). That formulation cannot, however, be regarded as a complete statement of the law. A defendant may be likely to make perfectly normal dispositions, such as the payment of ordinary trading debts, the effect of which may be that, when any award is made, it is, in whole or in part, unsatisfied when, absent those payments, it might have been satisfied or satisfied to a greater extent (*TTMI Ltd of England v ASM Shipping Ltd of India* [2005] EWHC 2666 (Comm); [2006] 1 Lloyd's Rep. 560 (Christopher Clarke J.)). The claimant should depose to objective facts from which it may be inferred that the defendant is likely to move assets

***Paragraph numbers marked with a "+" can be found online and on CD.***

or dissipate them; unsupported statements or expressions of fear have little weight (*O'Regan v Iambic Productions* (1989) 139 N.L.J. 1378 (Sir Peter Pain).) It is a fundamental principle that a freezing order is not granted for the purpose of providing security for the claim. By procuring an order an applicant is not put in a better position than any other creditor. The mere fact that the defendant's creditworthiness is in doubt does not justify the making of an order (*Mobil Cerro Negro Ltd v Petroleos de Venezuela SA* [2008] 1 Lloyd's Rep. 684 (Walker J.) at para.36).

In summary, a claimant will demonstrate a sufficient "risk of dissipation" if it can show that (1) there is a real risk that a judgment or award will go unsatisfied, in the sense of a real risk that, unless restrained by injunction, the defendant will dissipate or dispose of his assets other than in the ordinary course of business, or (2) that unless the defendant is restrained, assets are likely to be dealt with in such a way as to make enforcement of any award or judgment more difficult, unless those dealings can be justified for normal and proper business purposes (*Congentra AG v Sixteen Thirteen Marine SA* [2008] EWHC 1615 (Comm), July 15, 2008, unrep. (Flaux J.) at para.49).

Great care should be taken in the presentation of the evidence to the court so that the court can see whether there is a real risk of dissipation of assets. Where the respondent is alleged to have been dishonest, the court should scrutinise with care whether what is alleged in this respect in itself really justifies the inference that he is likely to dissipate assets unless restrained (*Thane Investments Ltd v Tomlinson* [2003] EWCA Civ 1272, July 29, 2003, CA, unrep.).

### (b) Assets excepted

**15–70** In a given case, a freezing injunction preventing the defendant from dealing with assets up to a certain amount could have very serious consequences for him unless he had access to other funds. For example, it could have the effect of preventing him from running his business (and perhaps even force its collapse), from paying his living and other routine expenses, from meeting unexpected bills (e.g. medical costs), and from paying legal expenses incurred by the action. The purpose of a freezing injunction is to prevent the defendant evading the due process of execution by hiding assets or otherwise making himself judgment proof. Where the court is satisfied that the defendant requires money for a purpose which does not conflict with that underlying purpose, the court should qualify the injunction (by insertion of an appropriate order in the original order or on the defendant's subsequent application) to allow the defendant to deal with assets subject to restraint but which are not subject to a proprietary claim for such purpose. Clearly, where, in a given case, the respondent uses his assets for these purposes as permitted by the terms of the order, the effect may be to reduce the value of the assets remaining to a level below that required to meet the claimant's claim.

The circumstances in which such qualification may be appropriate are briefly outlined below. In the example of a freezing order annexed to Practice Direction (Interim Injunctions) terms reflecting these circumstances are found in para.11.

#### *(i) Payments in the ordinary course of business—Angel Bell orders*

**15–71** The authorities on this matter start with *Iraqi Ministry of Defence v Arcepey Shipping Co SA (The "Angel Bell")* [1981] Q.B. 65; [1980] 1 All E.R. 480, where Goff J. held, in determining an issue as between an intervener and a claimant, that a Mareva injunction granted against a defendant should be varied so as to permit the defendant to make a payment in good faith and in the ordinary course of business to the intervener. Subsequently, *Angel Bell* orders became common place; see *Atlas Maritime Co SA v Avalon Maritime Ltd (The "Coral Rose")* [1991] 4 All E.R. 769; [1991] 1 Lloyd's Rep. 563, CA, and the authorities referred to therein, and *Halifax Plc v Chandler* [2001] EWCA Civ 1750, November 13, 2001, CA, at para.16 et seq., per Clarke L.J. On the one hand the injunction must not be used so as to amount to an instrument of oppression which would bring about the cessation of trading. On the other hand, the court must have regard to the interests of the claimant and consider whether the variation would involve a real risk that a judgment in his favour would remain unsatisfied (*The Coral Rose*, op. cit., at 776 and 568, per Neill L.J.).

#### *(ii) Living expenses and ordinary debts*

**15–72** Freezing injunctions addressed to natural persons should always make provision for

***Paragraph numbers marked with a "+" can be found online and on CD.***

the defendant's living expenses and for the payment of ordinary debts as they become due unless there is reason to believe that the defendant has other assets to which the injunction does not attach which would be available for that purpose (*The Law Society v Shanks* [1988] 1 F.L.R. 504, CA; *Babanaft International Co SA v Bassatne* [1990] 1 Ch. 13; [1989] 1 All E.R. 433; [1988] 2 Lloyd's Rep. 435, CA; *Investment and Pensions Advisory Service v Gray* [1990] B.C.L.C. 38; *P.C.W. (Undertaking Agencies) Ltd v Dixon* [1983] 2 All E.R. 158 (Lloyd J.), and [1983] 2 All E.R. 697, CA).

Paragraph 11(1) of the example of a freezing order annexed to the Practice Direction states that the respondent shall not be prohibited from spending each week a sum fixed by the court, or a reasonable sum, on "ordinary living expenses" and indicates that it may be further ordered that, before spending any such money, the respondent must tell the applicant's legal representatives where the money is to come from.

### *(iii) Legal expenses*

If the court is satisfied that the defendant does not have other available funds, the injunction may be qualified by the insertion of an order permitting him to make drawings from the assets to cover his expenses on legal advice and representation in the proceedings (*A. v C. (No.2)* [1981] Q.B. 961). Prima facie, the payment of legal fees is not dissipation (*Cala Cristal SA v Al-Borno (Emran), The Times*, May 6, 1994). **15–73**

Paragraph 11(1) of the example of a freezing order annexed to Practice Direction makes provision for this exemption in a manner similar to that made for the exemption as to living expenses.

Where the freezing injunction restrains the defendant from dealing with assets to which the claimant asserts title, the defendant must establish on proper evidence that there are no funds or assets available to him which can be used by him to pay his legal expenses other than the assets in respect of which the claimant brings his proprietary claim. Once that hurdle is cleared, the court can make an order allowing the defendant to use part of the funds (the equitable ownership of which is claimed by the claimant) for the defendant's legal expenses. That power in the court is a discretionary power. The court, in deciding whether to exercise it, must weigh the potential injustice to the claimant of permitting the funds which may turn out to be the claimant's property to be diminished so that the defendant can be legally represented, against the possible injustice to the defendant of depriving him of the opportunity of having the assistance of professional lawyers in advancing what may, at the end of the day, turn out to be a successful defence (see *The Ostrich Farming Corporation Ltd v Ketchell* December 10, 1997, unrep., CA, and earlier Court of Appeal decisions referred to there; see also *Independent Trustee Services Ltd v G P Noble Trustees Ltd* [2009] EWHC 161 (Ch), January 26, 2009, unrep. (Lewison J.)).

In *United Mizrahi Bank Ltd v Doherty* [1998] 1 W.L.R. 435, a bank (C) brought a proprietary claim against its former employee (D) for breach of duty and obtained an order freezing D's assets at home and abroad. The order included certain specific proprietary injunctions relating to particular funds alleged to have been wrongfully obtained by D. The judge refused D's application for an order that, notwithstanding C's alleged proprietary claim to a particular residential property, he be permitted to sell it and to apply the proceeds to the discharge of past and future legal costs. D's concern was that, although such sale would not be a breach of the freezing order, without such an order it might be suggested that he was expending funds which might turn out to be C's property and could amount to a further breach of trust. The judge held that the legal expenses exemption in the freezing order provided no guarantee for the recipients of the proceeds of the sale (including D's solicitors) that they would be protected from a possible claim in constructive trust should C establish their claim.

## (c) Ancillary orders

For the purpose of rendering a freezing injunction effective (before judgment as well as after judgment), the court may make orders requiring the defendant (1) to make a statement disclosing his assets, (2) to give discovery of documents, and (3) to provide information. Such orders can assist (1) in determining the existence, nature and location of assets, (2) in clarifying questions of title concerning assets, and (3) in identifying third parties to whom notice of the injunction should be given for the purpose of ensuring that they do not advertently or inadvertently assist the defendant **15–74** in the removal or disposal of assets. Quite commonly the making of such ancillary orders or the defendant's responses to them can result in further applications to the court by one party or the other (or by a third party) for modification of the terms of the injunction, of the terms of the ancillary order itself, or for other orders. Indeed, the defendant's responses may lead to the joinder of further parties against whom, in turn, further orders requiring disclosures by them may be made (see e.g. *Arab Monetary Fund v Hashim (No.5)* [1992] 2 All E.R. 911). See further Vol.1 para.25.1.26.

Where a respondent applies to set a freezing order aside, or appeals against the court's refusal to set aside the order, the question may arise whether the ancillary disclosure order should be stayed pending the outcome of the application or the appeal. The problem is that, where the disclosure order has been made at the same time as a freezing order made without notice, and the freezing order is subsequently set aside there will be no proper basis for the disclosure order. By that time the defendant may have been irremediably prejudiced by the disclosure of assets which he should not have been required to disclose. On the other hand, if it is held after full argument that the freezing order should stand, then the claimant may be irremediably prejudiced if the order has not been capable of being policed in the meantime. There is no general rule that the defendant is entitled to a stay; a balance has to be struck; in a normal case, a stay is likely to be refused (see *Motorola Credit Corporation v Uzan* [2002] EWCA Civ 989; [2002] 2 All E.R.(Comm) 945, CA; *Raja v Van Hoogstraten* [2004] EWCA Civ 968; [2004] 4 All E.R. 793, CA). See also, *JSC BTA Bank v Ablyazov* [2009] EWCA Civ 1125, October 27, 2009, CA, unrep.

See further Vol.1 para.25.1.26.

### *(i) Asset disclosure pre-judgment*

**15–75** Where the claimant has established the existence of assets within the jurisdiction (being assets over which the claimant makes no proprietary claim), or at least established that it is highly probable that such assets exist, the court may add to an order for a freezing injunction granted before judgment a disclosure requiring the defendant to disclose to the claimant the precise form and whereabouts of his assets for the purpose of making it more difficult for the defendant surreptitiously to disobey the restraining order and to enable notice to be given to third parties who might have custody of the assets so as to bind them to the injunction; without such power it would be difficult, if not impossible, to operate the freezing injunction jurisdiction properly (*A.J. Bekhor & Co Ltd v Bilton* [1981] Q.B. 923; [1981] 2 All E.R. 565, CA, *A v C (Note)* [1981] Q.B. 956; [1980] 2 All E.R. 347; see also *Z Ltd v A-Z and AA-LL* [1982] 1 Q.B. 558; sub nom. *Z Ltd v A* [1982] 1 All E.R. 556, CA, and *Campbell Mussells v Thompson* (1984) 8 L.S.Gaz. 2140, CA). The jurisdiction to attach such an order is inherent in theSenior Courts Act 1981 s.37(1).

In an action in which the claimant makes a proprietary claim, the court has jurisdiction, not only to grant an ordinary interlocutory injunction restraining the disposal of that property, but may also make orders designed to ascertain the whereabouts of that property. In these circumstances, the power of the court to make the ancillary orders is not based on the court's jurisdiction to grant freezing injunctions (as developed since Mareva injunctions were created), but has a different provenance. For example, the court may make orders requiring the defendant to provide information. Further, it may order a bank (whether or not party to the proceedings) to give discovery of documents in relation to the bank account of a defendant who is alleged to have defrauded the claimant of his assets (*Bankers Trust Co v Shapira* [1980] 1 W.L.R. 1274; [1980] 3 All E.R. 353, CA, approving *A. v C. (Note)* [1981] Q.B. 956; [1980] 2 All E.R. 347).

Paragraph 9 of the example of a freezing order annexed to Practice Direction (Interim Injunctions) contains terms for an ancillary order (based on authority) requiring the defendant to inform the claimant in writing at once of all his assets in England and Wales, whether in his own name or not and whether solely or jointly owned, and giving the value, location and details of all such assets.

### *(ii) Asset disclosure post-judgment*

**15–76** Under English law, after judgment, but not before judgment, a claimant is able to attach assets of the defendant against whom he has obtained judgment. The judgment debtor may be required to give disclosure of his assets and the claimant may obtain an order for his examination as to his assets under CPR Pt 71. The judgment debtor may be required to give disclosure of his assets wherever situate (whether within and without the jurisdiction) (*Interpool Ltd v Galani* [1988] Q.B. 738; [1987] 2 All E.R. 981, CA). In a case outside Pt 71, such disclosure may be ordered under the Senior Courts Act 1981 s.37 (Maclaine Watson & Co Ltd v *International Tin Council (No.2)* [1989] Ch. 286; [1988] 3 All E.R. 257, CA).

Obviously, in a given case, the object of ordering the disclosure of assets could be defeated by an unscrupulous judgment debtor if he was not restrained from removing or dealing with assets which he should disclose in response to the disclosure order. Accordingly, after judgment an application may be made for a freezing injunction (or for the continuation of such an injunction made before judgment), with an ancillary order attached (with a scope as deemed appropriate by the court), for the purpose of providing such restraint. The ancillary order may require the defendant to disclose assets without as well as within the jurisdiction (*Gidrxslme Shipping Co v Tantomar-Transportes Lda.* [1995] 1 W.L.R. 299; [1994] 4 All E.R. 507).

### *(iii) Respondent resisting disclosure, etc. on ground of privilege*

Paragraph 9 of the example of a freezing order annexed to Practice Direction (Interim Injunctions) states that, if the respondent's providing of information as to his assets in compliance with the ancillary order "is likely to incriminate" him, he "may be entitled to refuse to provide it". Further, among the undertakings that the applicant may be required to give the court is one to the effect that he will not, without the permission of the court, "use any information obtained as a result of this order for the purpose of any civil or criminal proceedings, either in England and Wales or in any other jurisdiction, other than this claim" (*ibid* Sch.B para.(9)). It is not necessary here to explain the scope of this privilege (see further para.15–93 below, and Vol.1 para.31.3.31). It is sufficient to note that cases have arisen in which the courts have had to consider the manner in which account should be taken of the privilege when making ancillary orders in support of freezing injunctions (e.g. *Arab Monetary Fund v Hashim* [1989] 1 W.L.R. 565; [1989] 3 All E.R. 466; *Sociedade Nacional de Combustiveis de Angola U.E.E v Lundqvist* [1991] 2 Q.B. 310; [1990] 3 All E.R. 283, CA, *Sociedade Nacional de Combustiveis de Angola U.E.E v Lundqvist* [1991] 2 Q.B. 310; [1990] 3 All E.R. 283, CA; *JSC BTA Bank v Ablyazov* [2009] EWCA Civ 1125, October 27, 2009, CA., unrep.). In *Dadourian Group International Inc v Simms (No.2)* [2006] EWCA Civ 1745; [2007] 1 W.L.R. 2967, CA, the defendant (D) gave disclosure by affidavit and was cross-examined on it. At trial, on the claimant's (C) application, the judge released C from their undertaking permitting them to use D's affidavit and the transcript of D's cross-examination, not only at trial, but also in other proceedings, including committal proceedings against D. On appeal, the Court of Appeal rejected D's submission that the court should permit release from the undertaking only in exceptional circumstances and held that the principle is that permission may be given to use information so obtained in committal proceedings where it is just and convenient for the purpose of policing and enforcing the freezing order. The court outlined the procedure to be followed where a claimant applies for release from his undertaking in these circumstances and the matters particularly to be taken into account by the court in dealing with such application. **15–77**

### *(iv) Cross-examination on disclosure affidavit*

The court may order cross-examination of the defendant upon any affidavits filed by him in purported compliance with order made ancillary to an order for a freezing injunction, and may do so even though no further order is required from the court consequent upon the cross-examination (*House of Spring Gardens Ltd v Waite* [1985] F.S.R. 173, CA). The fact that such cross-examination will relate to matters which are relevant to the substantive issues in the action is a matter to which the court should have regard when considering whether to permit cross-examination because the court must be astute to guard against abuse of the freezing injunction process by claimants who are using it in an attempt to discover facts that will assist them in the action (*Yukong Line Ltd of Korea v Rendsburg Investments Corp of Liberia*, *The Times*, October 22, 1996, CA). **15–78**

***Paragraph numbers marked with a "+" can be found online and on CD.***

### (d) Freezing injunction in aid of proceedings in other jurisdictions

15–79 The decision of the House of Lords in *Siskina v Distos Cia Naviera SA (The Siskina)* [1979] A.C. 210; [1977] 3 All E.R. 803, HL, provides authority for the proposition that, unless the English court is properly seised of an action, it has no jurisdiction to grant a freezing injunction over assets in this country or, indeed, any interlocutory injunction, in aid of proceedings abroad. (As noted above, it has been argued that the absence of some existing legal or equitable right which the English court has jurisdiction to enforce by final judgment is not a matter going to the existence of the court's equitable jurisdiction, but to the exercise of discretion.)

On the face of it, the proposition derived from The Siskina in most cases would prohibit an English court from granting a freezing injunction in aid of proceedings in other jurisdictions. However, in certain circumstances the proposition is in effect superseded by legislation having the effect of granting the court such jurisdiction in certain circumstances. As was explained above (para.15–5), as a consequence of various provisions (in particular the Civil Jurisdiction and Judgments Act 1982 s.25), the position was reached where the High Court has power to grant interim relief in aid of substantive proceedings elsewhere of whatever kind and wherever taking place. That power includes power to grant interim relief in the form of a domestic freezing injunction.

In *United States Securities & Exchange Commission v Manterfield* [2009] EWCA Civ 27; [2009] 1 Lloyd's Rep. 399; [2009] 2 All E.R. 1009, CA, where the claimants (C) in foreign proceedings (a public agency) in which fraud was alleged applied for a worldwide freezing injunction, the respondent's submission that, on the grounds that C were seeking to enforce a foreign penal law, the English court should decline jurisdiction was rejected. It was held (1) that the substance of what C would seek to enforce (if they prevailed in the action), and in relation to which they sought to preserve assets, was the disgorgement of what they alleged to be the proceeds of fraud, and (2) that in the circumstances, the fact that a civil penalty might be imposed was not of such significance as to form a basis for characterising the proceedings as for the enforcement of a penal law.

### (e) Freezing injunction in aid of foreign judgment registered for enforcement

15–80 Chapter III of the Judgments Regulation deals with recognition and enforcement in one Member State of the judgment of another Member State. By art.38 a judgment shall be enforced in another Member State once it has been declared enforceable there. In England this means once it has been registered for enforcement. (Formalities for registration are contained in Arts 53 to 56 of the Judgments Regulation and in CPR Pt 74.) The court is required by art.41 to register the judgment immediately on completion of the formalities. Article 47 in effect states that where a judgment creditor applies to register such judgment in England, the English court may make orders for provisional, including protective, measures in accordance with English law. (Paragraphs (1) to (3) of art.47 deal respectively with (a) the time before registration, (b) the time after registration, and (c) the time after registration where there is an appeal pending.) Thus the court may grant the applicant a freezing injunction, freezing the respondent's assets within the jurisdiction. *Banco Nacional de Comercio Exterior SNC v Empresa de Telecommunicationes de Cuba SA* [2007] EWCA Civ 662; [2007] 2 Lloyd's Rep. 484, CA, provides a recent example of a domestic freezing injunction being granted on this basis. (In this case, the Court of Appeal rejected the submission that art.47(1) provided the English court with jurisdiction to grant a worldwide freezing order where the judgment was recognised; see further below.)

## 6. "WORLDWIDE" FREEZING INJUNCTIONS

15–81 It was noted above (para.15–64) that the assets "frozen" by freezing injunctions may be assets within the jurisdiction or without and that additional and different matters arise in relation to "worldwide" injunctions.

### (a) Introduction

15–82 The early authorities relating to freezing injunctions of the type recognised by the

Court of Appeal in *Mareva Compania Naviera SA v International Bulk Carriers SA ("The Mareva")* [1980] 1 All E.R. 213; [1975] 2 Lloyd's Rep. 509, CA, imposed three territorial limitations upon the scope of this form of interim remedy. The remedy was granted only for the purpose (a) of restraining the removal of property from within the jurisdiction, (b) by persons resident outside the jurisdiction, (c) who had property within the jurisdiction. All three limitations were subsequently abandoned. The later cases stressed that s.37(1) of the Senior Courts Act 1981 is expressed in wide terms and contains no territorial limitation. Further, s.37(3) does not restrict the territorial ambit of freezing injunctions; its purpose is to ensure that there should be no discrimination against parties not domiciled, resident or present within the jurisdiction (*Babanaft International Co SA v Bassatne* [1990] 1 Ch. 13; [1989] 1 All E.R. 433 at 440, CA, per Kerr L.J.). Furthermore, the existence of assets of the defendant within the jurisdiction is not a pre-condition to the granting of an injunction having extraterritorial effect (*Derby & Co Ltd v Weldon (Nos 3 & 4)* [1990] 1 Ch. 65, CA, sub nom. *Derby & Co Ltd v Weldon (No.2)* [1989] 1 All E.R. 1002, CA). Since these limitations were removed, freezing injunctions having extra-territorial effect have become common place. However, it has been recognised since *Ashtiani v Kashi* [1987] Q.B. 888, CA, that to grant an injunction freezing assets abroad is not an automatic step; special grounds have to be shown.

The example of an order for a freezing injunction annexed to Practice Direction (Interim Injunctions) (supplementing CPR Pt 25) contains clauses that are appropriate for an order freezing injunction not limited to the respondent's assets in England and Wales, but restraining the respondent from dealing with or disposing of his assets located outside England and Wales. In *JSC BTA Bank v Ablyazov* [2009] EWHC 3267, December 12, 2009, unrep. (Teare J.), the court found good reason for permitting a variation of those clauses, with the effect that the respondent was restrained from disposing of or dealing with such assets so long as the value of all his assets "in England and Wales" (rather than "whether in or outside England and Wales") remained above the maximum sum. The case law on orders for so-called "worldwide" freezing injunctions (WFOs) is extensive. Much of it is reflected in the terms of the example of an order annexed to the Practice Direction.

### *(b) Relevant factors*

The granting of a freezing injunction is a matter for the discretion of the judge hearing the application. In the exercise of this discretion, in the context of English proceedings the court may grant an application for a WFO where the following matters are established: **15–83**

(1) the claimant has a good arguable case;

(2) the claimant has satisfied the court—

  (a) that there are no assets or insufficient assets within the jurisdiction to satisfy his claim; and

  (b) that there are assets without the jurisdiction; and

(3) there is a real risk of dissipation or secretion of those assets so as to render any judgment which the claimant may obtain nugatory.

In addition, in exercising its discretion the court should consider whether undertakings or provisos, or a combination of both, should be requested or imposed for the purpose of protecting the defendant from oppression and for protecting the position of foreign third parties.

The English court's jurisdiction to grant applications for interim injunctions in support of foreign proceedings includes power to grant a WFO. Generally, the court will only be prepared to exercise its discretion to grant this relief in such circumstances if the respondent or the dispute has a sufficiently strong link with England and Wales; for detailed explanation of this point, see *Mobil Cerro Negro Ltd v Petroleos de Venezuela SA* [2008] 1 Lloyd's Rep. 684 (Walker J.) at paras 86 to 119 (refusing application for WFO in support of intended arbitration in New York). There will always need to be a careful examination of any proposed part of the order which would tend to run counter to principles of comity with courts in other jurisdictions (*ibid*).

### *(c) Persons outside jurisdiction not affected by WFO*

In the commentary above on domestic freezing injunctions it was explained that **15–84** third parties may be affected directly by an order for such an injunction. The position of third parties in orders for worldwide freezing injunctions is somewhat different.

In *Babanaft International Co SA v Bassatne* [1990] Ch. 13; [1989] 1 All E.R. 433, CA, it was stated that it would be improper for the court to grant an unqualified injunction freezing foreign assets because such an injunction would amount to an exorbitant assertion of extra-territorial jurisdiction over third parties resident abroad who were in no sense subject to the English court's jurisdiction (e.g. banks holding the judgment debtor's assets). The appropriate terms for a "Babanaft proviso" were considered in subsequent cases and are now found in para.19 of the example of an order for a freezing injunction annexed to Practice Direction (Interim Injunctions) is directed specifically at WFOs.

Paragraph 19(1) states that, except as provided in para.19(2), the terms of the WFO "do not affect or concern anyone outside the jurisdiction of this court". The exceptions provided for in para.19(2) include any person who (a) is subject to the jurisdiction of the English court, (b) has been given written notice of the WFO at his residence or place of business within the jurisdiction of the court, and (c) is able to prevent acts or omissions outside the jurisdiction of the court which constitute or assist in a breach of the terms of the WFO. Any other person is affected or concerned only to the extent that the WFO is declared enforceable by, or is enforced by, a court in a country or state outside the jurisdiction of the English court.

### (d) Post-judgment WFO

**15–85** After a judgment has been given by an English court, the judgment debtor may be required to give disclosure of his assets wherever situate. The object of ordering such disclosure is to render the judgment effective, by enabling the judgment creditor to discover whether there are sufficient assets within the jurisdiction which may be attached to satisfy the judgment and, if not, whether there are assets elsewhere that might be pursued by enforcement processes in foreign courts.

Obviously, in a given case, the object of ordering the disclosure of assets could be defeated by an unscrupulous judgment debtor if he was not restrained from dealing with assets which he should disclose in response to the disclosure order.Where the judgment debtor has assets located abroad an application may be made for a freezing injunction for the purpose of restraining him from dealing with those assets.

The arguments against granting an injunction extending to assets outside the jurisdiction are much weaker in a case where judgment has been obtained than in a case where an interlocutory order is sought before trial (*Babanaft International Co SA v Bassatne, op cit*, per Kerr L.J., and Neill L.J., and *Republic of Haiti v Duvalier* [1990]1 Q.B. 202; [1989] 1 All E.R. 456 at 465, CA, per Staughton L.J.). In the former situation the court is no longer so concerned to protect the defendant.

### (e) Pre-judgment WFO

**15–86** In *Babanaft International Co SA v Bassatne* [1990] Ch. 13; [1989] 1 All E.R. 433, CA, Kerr L.J. said (at 33 and 444) that:

> "some situations ... cry out—as a matter of justice to plaintiffs—for disclosure orders and Mareva injunction type injunctions covering foreign assets of defendants even before judgment".

This dictum has been much quoted. Each case must depend on its own facts (*Derby & Co Ltd v Weldon* [1990] 1 Ch. 48; [1989] 1 All E.R. 469 at 473, CA, per May L.J., and at 62 and 478, per Nicholls L.J.; in this case it was said that there is every justification for an injunction where "the defendants are clearly sophisticated operators who have amply demonstrated their ability to render assets untraceable and a determination not to reveal them" at 57, per Parker L.J.).

A pre-judgment WFO would clearly be unjustified if, for example, there were sufficient English assets to meet any judgment to which the claimant might ultimately be entitled (in the case of a non-proprietary claim) (*Derby & Co Ltd v Weldon* (Nos 3 & 4) [1990] 1 Ch. 65 at 79, CA, per Lord Donaldson M.R.), or if the court were not satisfied that there were foreign assets or that there was a real risk of disposal of the same, or if it would in all the circumstances be oppressive to make the order (*Derby & Co Ltd v Weldon* [1990] 1 Ch. 48; [1989] 1 All E.R. 469 at 474, CA, per May L.J., per Parker L.J.). The risk of prejudice to the claimant must be appropriately grave before it will

***Paragraph numbers marked with a "+" can be found online and on CD.***

be just and convenient to make such a draconian order and special factors, such as the defendant's capacity and propensity to hide assets to defeat creditors are important to the assessment of that risk (Derby & Co Ltd v Weldon [1990] 1 Ch. 48; [1989] 1 All E.R. 469 at 478, CA, per Nicholls L.J.).

### (f) Permission to enforce abroad

The making of an order in respect of foreign assets is a serious step and the risks of refusing this relief must justify it. There is an obvious risk of oppression to the defendant and third parties. Accordingly, a WFO will usually contain an undertaking by the party who obtained the order not to seek to enforce it in another jurisdiction without the English court's permission. In the example of a freezing injunction annexed to the Practice Direction (Interim Injunctions) this undertaking is found in para.(10) of Sch.B. This reflects the long-standing concern that care should be taken to ensure that a WFO is not enforced oppressively by a multiplicity of applications in different countries throughout the world (*In re Bank of Credit and Commerce International S.A.* [1994] 1 W.L.R. 708, CA). On an application to enforce abroad it is to be expected to have before him (what the court granting the original order would not) evidence of the law and practice in the country or countries in which the order is sought to be enforced (*Derby v Weldon (No.1)* [1990] Ch. 48, CA, at p.59 per Nicholls L.J.). **15–87**

In *Dadourian Group International Inc v Simms (Practice Note)* [2006] EWCA Civ 399; [2006] 1 W.L.R. 2499, CA, the Court of Appeal stated that the court has a discretion to grant an applicant permission to enforce a WFO abroad whenever it considers it just so to do. (In this case, the court expressly rejected the submission that the court should not give permission to enforce a WFO abroad if the party alleged to hold the assets can be brought before the English court.) The court said there is a range of factors which the court is likely to need to consider. For this purpose the court set out and explained guidelines to be applied by the court (enumerated 1 to 8) where a party applies to the court for such permission (the "Dadourian guidelines"). As summarised by the court the guidelines are as follows (as to guideline 8, see further Vol.1, para.23.10.2).

(1) The principle applying to the grant of permission to enforce a WFO abroad is that the grant of that permission should be just and convenient for the purpose of ensuring the effectiveness of the WFO, and in addition that it is not oppressive to the parties to the English proceedings or to third parties who may be joined to the foreign proceedings.
(2) All the relevant circumstances and options need to be considered. In particular consideration should be given to granting relief on terms, for example terms as to the extension to third parties of the undertaking to compensate for costs incurred as a result of the WFO and as to the type of proceedings that may be commenced abroad. Consideration should also be given to the proportionality of the steps proposed to be taken abroad, and in addition to the form of any order.
(3) The interests of the applicant should be balanced against the interests of the other parties to the proceedings and any new party likely to be joined to the foreign proceedings.
(4) Permission should not normally be given in terms that would enable the applicant to obtain relief in the foreign proceedings which is superior to the relief given by the WFO.
(5) The evidence in support of the application for permission should contain all the information (so far as it can reasonably be obtained in the time available) necessary to make the judge to reach an informed decision, including evidence as to the applicable law and practice in the foreign court, evidence as to the nature of the proposed proceedings to be commenced and evidence as to the assets believed to be located in the jurisdiction of the foreign court and the names of the parties by whom such assets are held.
(6) The standard of proof as to the existence of assets that are both within the WFO and within the jurisdiction of the foreign court are a real prospect; that is the applicant must show that there is a real prospect that such assets are located within the jurisdiction of the foreign court in question.
(7) There must be evidence of a risk of dissipation of the assets in question.

***Paragraph numbers marked with a "+" can be found online and on CD.***

(8) Normally the application should be made on notice to the respondent, but in cases of urgency, where it is just to do so, the permission may be given without notice to the party against whom relief will be sought in the foreign proceedings but that party should have the earliest practicable opportunity of having the matter reconsidered by the court at a hearing of which he is given notice.

Where, as a quid pro quo for the grant of a WFO, one party undertakes not to begin proceedings against another on the same subject matter in another jurisdiction, that undertaking takes effect as if it were an injunction against the party giving the undertaking (*Grupo Torras S.A. v Sheikh Fahad Mohamed al Sabah* [2001] EWCA Civ 1370, July 30, 2001, CA).

### (g) WFO in support of proceedings pending in a Member State

15–88 It was explained above (para.15–5) that, under s.25(1) of the Civil Jurisdiction and Judgments Act 1982 and art.31 of the Judgments Regulation, the High Court may grant interim relief when the substantive proceedings are pending in a Member State. (These provisions are designed to enable the court of one Member State to assist the court of another by providing such interim relief as would be available if its own courts were seised of the substantive proceedings.) The question whether a WFO could or should be granted in these circumstances was considered by the Court of Appeal in *Banco Nacional de Comercio Exterior SNC v Empresa de Telecommunicationes de Cuba SA* [2007] EWCA Civ 662; [2007] 2 Lloyd's Rep. 484, CA, a case in which the respondent was not resident in England. The court held that, in the circumstances of this case, the English court was obliged to disclaim or decline jurisdiction as a matter of principle, having regard to the restrictions and limitations imposed by a combination of the provisions of the 1982 Act, the Judgments Regulation, and judicial precedent (including ECJ decisions).

# C. SEARCH ORDERS

## 1. INTRODUCTION

15–89 Paragraph (h) of CPR r.25.1(1) recites that the court may grant an interim remedy in the form of an order requiring a party to admit another party to premises "for the purpose of preserving evidence, etc." Such an order, formerly known as an Anton Piller order (see further below), is now referred to in that provision as a "search order". Detailed provisions concerning search orders and their execution are found in para.7 of Practice Direction (Interim Injunctions), supplementing CPR Pt 25, and an example of search order is annexed to that practice direction.

Three major types of case are likely to attract applications for search orders. They are (1) cases involving infringement of rights in intellectual property (such as trade marks, copyright and trade secrets, and passing-off), (2) anti-competition cases brought by ex-employers against ex-employees), and (3) matrimonial proceedings where it is thought that a spouse has failed to make truthful disclosure of his or her assets.

For principal commentary on the jurisdiction of the court to grant search orders, and relevant practice and procedure, see commentary to r.25.1(1)(f) in Vol.1.

As to the protection afforded respondents by the claimant's undertakings in search orders, see para.15–28 above.

## 2. JURISDICTION

15–90 A search order requires the defendant or respondent to permit certain persons to enter his premises, to search for documents or other articles of moveable property, and to take them away and retain them for the time being. It is necessarily made without notice, because if it is thought that the defendant or respondent knew that the order was about to made he would conceal, remove or destroy the documents or articles in question. The granting of a search order is a matter for the discretion of the judge hearing the application. The court's jurisdiction in this respect developed as an adjunct to the powers of the court to make pre-trial orders for the detention, custody or preservation of property which is the subject-matter of proceedings (CPR r.25.1(1)(c), formerly RSC O.29, r.2).

The jurisdiction may be traced to a series of first instance decisions in intellectual

***Paragraph numbers marked with a "+" can be found online and on CD.***

property cases given in 1974 (before the decision of the House of Lords in *American Cyanamid Co v Ethicon Ltd* [1975] A.C. 396, HL). The first of these cases to be fully reported was *E.M.I. Ltd v Pandit* [1975] 1 W.L.R. 302; [1975] 1 All E.R. 418 (decided on December 4, 1974). That was an infringement of copyright case in which the claimants were granted an interlocutory injunction restraining the defendant from selling or parting with the infringing material and requiring him to swear an affidavit disclosing those persons from whom he had received or to whom he had supplied the material. On a subsequent ex parte application, the claimants produced evidence tending to show that the defendant's affidavit was a fabrication and sought an order for the inspection and removal of certain material with an authorisation attached to permit them to enter upon the defendant's premises for these purposes. The question for the judge was, not whether such an order could be granted, but whether it could be granted on an ex parte application. Templeman J. concluded that from the terms of (what is now) CPR r.25.1(1)(c), and from the authorities, in exceptional circumstances and on terms designed to safeguard the defendant, the court had jurisdiction to make (what was then called) "permit" orders as sought by the claimants. Shortly afterwards, in *Anton Piller K.G. v Manufacturing Processes Ltd* [1976] 1 Ch. 55; [1976] 1 All E.R. 779, CA, another copyright case, such orders received the imprimatur of the Court of Appeal and thereafter came to be known as "Anton Piller orders" (see also *Universal City Studios Inc v Mukhtar & Sons* [1976] 1 W.L.R. 568; [1976] 2 All E.R. 330). Subsequently, a difference of opinion emerged as to the source of the court's jurisdiction to grant such orders. The matter was clarified by the Civil Procedure Act 1997 s.7 (see further below). In the years following these cases, a vast body of case law emerged as the implications of the judicial innovation of ex parte permit orders became apparent. The jurisdiction of the High Court to grant a search order was put on a statutory basis by the Civil Procedure Act 1997 s.7 (Power of courts to make orders for preserving evidence) (see Vol.2, para.9A–756). That provision was enacted following recommendations concerning search orders made by a committee of judges appointed by the Judges' Council (see "Anton Piller Orders: A Consultation Paper" (LCD 1992), hereinafter "1992 Consultation Paper"). The jurisdiction of county courts to grant search orders is restricted; see commentary to r.25.1(1)(f) in Vol.1. In various respects, s.7 put into statutory form authoritative decisions of the courts handed down in the years following the *Anton Piller* case. For example, by expressly stating that a search order may secure the preservation, not only of property that is the subject-matter of proceedings, but also of evidence (which is or may be relevant), s.7(1) carries on the effect of *Yousif v Salama* [1980] 1 W.L.R. 1540; [1980] 3 All E.R. 405, CA.

Section 7(1) states that the High Court may make an order under this section for the purpose of securing, in the case of any existing or proposed proceedings in the court:

(a) the preservation of evidence which is or may be relevant, or
(b) the preservation of property which is or may be the subject-matter of the proceedings or as to which any question arises or may arise in the proceedings.

A person who is, or appears to the court likely to be, a party to proceedings in the court may make an application for such an order (s.7(2)).

The heart of a search order consists of the directions which may be included in the order by the court in the exercise of the powers referred to in subss.(4), (5) and (6) of s.7. The order may direct any person to permit any person described in the order, or secure that any person so described is permitted:

(a) to enter premises (or any vehicle, see s.7(8)) in England and Wales, and
(b) while on the premises, to take in accordance with the terms of the order any of the following steps.

Those steps are:

(a) to carry out a search for or inspection of anything described in the order, and
(b) to make or obtain a copy, photograph, sample or other record of anything so described.

The order may also direct the person concerned:

(a) to provide any person described in the order, or secure that any person so described is provided, with any information or article described in the order, and
(b) to allow any person described in the order, or secure that any person so

***Paragraph numbers marked with a "+" can be found online and on CD.***

described is allowed, to retain for safe keeping anything described in the order.

The order may describe anything generally, whether by reference to a class or otherwise (s.7(8)). The order is to have effect subject to such conditions as are specified in the order (s.7(6)).

It is specifically provided that s.7 does not affect any right of a person to refuse to do anything on the ground that to do so might tend to expose him or his spouse to proceedings for an offence or for the recovery of a penalty (s.7(7)) (see further para.15–93 below).

Under the terms of a such order, the respondent is required to permit "the search party" (viz., the supervising solicitor and others) to enter his premises and to search for, inspect and copy such evidence or property as may be listed in the order and to deliver it into safekeeping.

## 3. GROUNDS FOR MAKING ORDER

15–91 In the early cases, it was stressed that the jurisdiction to grant search orders was exceptional and should be exercised only when there is a paramount need to prevent a denial of justice to the claimant which cannot be met by an order for delivery up or preservation of the documents; it should be exercised in rare instances, and then with extreme caution (*Anton Piller K.G. v Manufacturing Processes Ltd*, *op cit*, *Lock International Plc v Beswick* [1989] 1 W.L.R. 1268; [1989] 3 All E.R. 373). In fact, the granting of these orders quickly became common place in courts of first instance and in later cases the Court of Appeal took pains to bring the practice under control. Much of this law is now reflected in the provisions in para.7 of Practice Direction (Interim Injunctions), supplementing CPR Pt 25, and in the terms of the example of a search order annexed to that practice direction (which are elaborate).

Although in the *Anton Piller* case Lord Denning spoke of "an extreme case", in practice orders are granted far too routinely for them to be regarded as exceptional. However, the court still insists on a clear showing of fraud, dishonesty, contumacy, or imminent removal or destruction of property or evidence. The overriding principle is that of necessity. No order ought to be made unless it is necessary in the interests of justice. The so-called "balance of convenience" test, which plays a leading role in most decisions to grant interlocutory injunctions, has little, if any role to play in an application to grant a search order. Consistent with the principle of necessity, the cases have established the following conditions for the making of an order (see 1992 Consultation Paper, paras 2.4, et seq., and the summary in *Indicii Salus Ltd v Chandrasekaran* [2006] EWHC 521 (Ch), February 15, 2006, unrep. (Warren J.)).

(1) There must be a strong prima facie case of a civil cause of action. Suspicion that there may be a cause of action should not be enough. A scrutiny of the merits of the claimant's case is an essential preliminary to the grant of a search order. It is not sufficient for the applicant to show merely a "serious question to be tried" (as is sufficient in applications for orthodox interlocutory injunctions).

(2) The danger to the claimant to be avoided by the grant of an order must be serious. If an order is sought in order to forestall the destruction of evidence, the evidence in question must be of major, if not critical, importance.

(3) There must be clear evidence that the defendants had in their possession incriminating documents or things.

(4) The risk of destruction or removal of evidence must be a good deal more than merely possible. (In *Booker McConnell v Plascow Plc* [1985] R.P.C. 425 at 441, CA, Dillon L.J. referred to "a real possibility", which he contrasted with "extravagant fears which seem to afflict all claimants who have complaints of breach of confidence, breach of copyright or passing-off".) The fact that a respondent can be shown to have behaved improperly will not always justify an order. There must be a real reason to believe that the respondent will disobey an injunction for the preservation of the evidence in question.

(5) The harm likely to be caused by the execution of the order to the respondent and his business affairs must not be excessive or out of proportion to the legitimate object of the order. This precondition is particularly relevant where the seizure of trading stock or the perusal by the claimant of confidential com-

***Paragraph numbers marked with a "+" can be found online and on CD.***

mercial documents will be the effect of execution of the order and is strongly analogous to the principle of proportionality as applied by the European Court of Human Rights.

If any of these pre-conditions is absent, the weight of judicial authority suggests that an application for the grant of a search order should be refused. If each of these preconditions appears to be present, an order will not necessarily be justified. The court will still have to weigh in the balance the claimant's need for the order against the injustice to the respondent in making the order ex parte without any opportunity for the respondent to be heard. The judge who hears the application for the order should keep in mind that, in as much as audi alteram partem is a requirement of natural justice, the making of an ex parte mandatory order always risks injustice to the absent and unheard respondent. The order should not be made unless it appears that, without the order, the claimant will be likely to suffer a greater injustice than that which the court, by making the order, will be inflicting on the respondent (see *Columbia Picture Industries v Robinson* [1987] Ch. 38; [1986] 3 W.L.R. 542; [1986] 3 All E.R. 338). The court requires proportionality between the perceived threat to the claimant's rights and the remedy granted. The fact that there is overwhelming evidence that the defendant has behaved wrongfully in his commercial relationships does not necessarily justify a search order. People whose commercial morality allows them to take a customer list will not necessarily disobey an order of the court requiring them to deliver it up. Not everyone who is misusing confidential information will destroy documents in the face of a court order requiring him to preserve them (*Lock International Plc v Beswick* [1989] 1 W.L.R. 1268, [1989] 3 All E.R. 373) (Hoffmann J.)).

## 4. LEGAL EFFECT OF ORDER

A search order is an in personam order directed to a named person. In the Anton Piller case, Lord Denning conceded that "this may seem to be a search warrant in disguise". The court has no power to authorise entry on and search of private premises, let alone power to authorise one party to an action to enter and search the premises of his opponent. (The Senior Courts Act 1981 s.33 enables the court in certain circumstances to authorise entry on to private premises, but the purposes for which such an order can be made do not include the carrying out of a search of the premises.) Lord Denning explained that the court circumvents this lack of power by ordering the respondent to permit the entry and search. His disobedience to the order leaves his premises inviolate but subjects him to the risk of proceedings for committal for contempt of court. The entry, for which consent is demanded, is an entry for persons who have no legal or equitable right of entry. The court's order grants no such right. The granting of consent in obedience to the order enables the party entering and searching to justify what otherwise would be a clear trespass by reliance on the permission given (see 1992 Consultation Paper, paras 2.11 and 2.12). **15–92**

The realisation that a search order may be but a search warrant in disguise has affected the development of the law and procedure; in particular, the rule that an order should not be made except where necessary (see below), and then only on conditions designed to safeguard the respondent.

Section 7 of the 1997 Act states that an order "may direct any person to permit any person described in the order, or secure that any person so described is permitted" to make entry and to take the steps stated in the order.Normally, the "any person" to whom the order is directed will be a person who is, or who is about to become, a defendant in proceedings brought by the applicant for the order. However, the order may have, and usually does have, a broader focus. In para.5 of the example of a search order annexed to the Practice Direction it is stated that the order must be complied with by (a) the respondent, (b) any director, officer, partner or responsible employee of the respondent, and (c) if the respondent is an individual, any other person having responsible control of the premises to be searched. These words are intended to cover the situation which arises when the defendant is not personally at the premises at the time when the claimant's search party arrives. As surprise and lack of advance warning are of the essence of search order tactics, an immediate entry and search is usually thought to be essential.

Although the grant of a search order is likely to fall within the scope of art.8 of the European Convention on Human Rights it may be justified under art.8(2) as necessary to protect the rights of others (*Chappell v United Kingdom* (1990) 12 E.H.R.R. 1, ECtHR).

Article 8 refers to a person's "home", but the protection of this provision extends to professional premises (*Niemietz v Germany* (1993) 16 E.H.R.R. 97, ECtHR) and applies to searches by private individuals carried out with court sanction, such as is envisaged by a search order. Where a search order is drafted in broad terms and where no supervising solicitor is present, art.8 may be breached (*Niemietz v Germany*, opit). The European Commission has held that ECHR art.6(1) does not apply to the interlocutory proceedings in which search orders are granted (*Noviflora Sweden Aktiebolag v Sweden No.14369/88*, decision of October 12, 1992, unreported, EComHR). The seizure of property pursuant to a search warrant is likely to be considered justified in the general interest (*ibid*).

### 5. SELF-INCRIMINATION

15–93 Provisions as to the conduct of the search and the securing of materials are found in para.7 of Practice Direction (Interim Injunction) (supplementing Pt 25). The example of a search order annexed to that practice direction recognises that the respondent may be entitled to withhold production of documents on the ground that they are privileged or incriminating, and casts duties upon the supervising solicitor as to the handling of such material accordingly. It is expressly stated in s.7 of the 1997 Act that the power given to the court by that section to make a search order does not affect any right to the self-incrimination which the respondent may have (s.7(7)). In certain civil proceedings (notably, intellectual property proceedings), by statute the privilege of self-incrimination is expressly withdrawn, and therefore may not be claimed by a respondent to a search order in such proceedings. For convenience these statutory provisions are listed in para.7(9) of the Practice Direction (see Vol.1 para.25APD.7).

From time to time it has been recommended (e.g. by the committee of judges referred to above) that the privilege against self-incrimination should be withdrawn in civil proceedings generally (see also *Tate Access Floors Inc v Boswell* [1991] Ch. 512, CA). The question of the scope of the self-incrimination privilege is itself a matter for doubt and this creates uncertainty as to the circumstances in which it may be claimed by a respondent to a search order (see *C. Plc v P* [2007] EWCA Civ 493; [2007] 3 W.L.R. 437, CA, and the authorities referred to there. Note also Senior Courts Act 1981 s.72 (Withdrawal of privilege against incrimination of self or spouse in certain proceedings), Vol.2 para.9A–337 above.

See further, para.15–77 above, and Vol.1 para.31.3.31.

## D. INTERIM PAYMENTS

### 1. JURISDICTION

15–94 The Senior Courts Act 1981 s.32 and the County Courts Act 1984 s.50 state that provision may be made by rules of court enabling the High Court and the county courts "to make an order requiring a party to the proceedings to make an interim payment of such amount as may be specified in the order".

For these purposes, "interim payment" is defined as "a payment on account of any damages, debt or other sum (excluding costs) which that party may be held liable to pay to or for the benefit of another party to the proceedings if a final judgment or order of the court in the proceedings is given or made in favour of that other party" (s.32(5) and s.50(5)).

It is a general principle that a defendant has a right not to be held liable to pay until liability has been established by a final judgment. The court has no inherent power to order payment on account (*Moore v Assignment Courier Ltd* [1977] 1 W.L.R. 638; [1977] 2 All E.R. 842, CA). The jurisdiction granted by this legislation and carried into effect by rules of court (see CPR r.25.6 to 25.9) to order an interim payment is an exception to that principle. The exception was first established by the Administration of Justice Act 1969 s.20, which implemented a recommendation made in the Report of the Committee on Personal Injuries Litigation (1968) (Cmnd. 3691) (the Winn Committee), and was regarded as a significant innovation at the time. Its purpose was to mitigate the hardship caused to claimants making well-founded personal injuries claims by the long delays then existing between commencement of proceedings and receipt of damages by way of compensation. The Committee envisaged that this exceptional power would be of particular use in personal injury cases where (a) the defendant has admitted full liability, (b) the liability of the defendant has been established by the entry of interlocutory judgment for damages to be assessed, (c) where the claimant sues two or more defendants who blame each other but do not allege contributory negligence against him, provided all the defendants are insured and substantial.

Draft rules of court designed to carry this recommendation into effect in the manner proposed by the Committee were given in Appendix 6 to the Report. The primary legislation was enacted in terms wide enough to enable the jurisdiction to be exercised in cases other than personal injury claims should rules of court so permit. In 1969, the draft rules, which were confined in their effect to claims for damages in respect of wrongful death and personal injuries, were enacted. In 1980, the rules were amended to enable orders to be made for the payment of "any damages, debt or other sum (excluding costs)", thereby enlarging considerably the scope of the power.

Interim payment orders must be distinguished from orders for provisional damages in personal injuries claims provided for by the Senior Courts Act 1981 s.32A and CPR Pt 41, Section I), and also from orders for periodical payments of awards of damages as provided for by the Damages Act 1996 s.2 and CPR r.41.8.

Before the CPR came into effect, rules of court made in exercise of the particular rule-making power granted by s.32 of the 1981 Act were found in RSC O.29, Pt II, and with minor modifications, those provisions were applied in county courts by CCR O.13, r.12. In the CPR, the relevant rules are found in Section I of Pt 25, that is to say, in rr.25.6 to 25.9. In those rules, the general procedure for interim payment applications is stated (r.25.6), then provision is made for the conditions to be satisfied and matters to be taken into account by the court (r.25.7), and for the powers of the court subsequent to the making of an order (r.25.8). In the former rules, the principal distinction drawn was between orders in respect of damages (especially in actions for personal injuries) and orders in respect of sums other than damages. That distinction was, and remains to be taken into account by the court (see r.25.7). It is expressly provided that these rules do not apply to cases on the small claims track (r.27.2(1)(a)).

Rule 25.9 states that the fact that a defendant has made an interim payment whether voluntarily of by court order, shall not be disclosed to the trial judge until all questions of liability and the amount of money to be awarded have been decided, unless the defendant agrees. For further information on the effect and consequences of this rule, see the commentary in CPR Pt 25 (Vol.1 para.25.9.1).

## 2. APPLICATION FOR AN ORDER (CPR R.25.6)

The general procedure is stated in r.25.6. For commentary on that provision, see **15–95** Vol.1 para.25.6.1.

Orders for interim payments can be sought in all proceedings, whether commenced under CPR Pt 7 or Pt 8.

Before the CPR came into effect, specific provisions as to the making of applications for interim payment were found in RSC O.29, r.10. Now they are found (with modifications) partly in r.25.6 and partly in Pt 23. Under the CPR, applications for court orders are made in accordance with the general rules contained in Pt 23. Particular rules relating to specific applications appear elsewhere in the CPR and amplify or modify the provisions found in Pt 23 according to need. The general rule is that a copy of the application notice must be served on each respondent (r.23.4(1)). The respondent is "the person against whom the order is sought" (r.23.1(a)). (In the case of an application for interim payment it is obvious who the respondent should be.) The copy notice of application must be served as soon as practicable after it is filed (r.23.7(1)(a)); however, an application for an order for interim payment cannot be made before the time stated in r.25.6(1). The general rule is that a copy notice of application must in any event be served at least three days before the court is to deal with the application (r.23.7(1)(b)); however, where the application is for an order for interim payment it should be served at least 14 days before the hearing (r.25.6(3)(a)). Part 6 contains the general rules about service of documents, including applications.

A defendant may make an interim payment on account of damages (or a series of such payments) without putting the claimant to the trouble of making an application to the court. Circumstances may arise where, although a voluntary payment is offered and there is no disagreement between the parties, one or the other of them will think it wise to have an order. Rule 25.9 provides that the fact that a defendant has made an interim payment, whether voluntarily or by court order, shall not be disclosed to the trial judge until all questions of liability and the amount of money to be awarded have been decided, unless the defendant agrees.

The interim payment procedure is not suitable where the factual issues are complicated or where difficult points of law arise which may take many hours and the citation of many authorities to resolve (*Schott Kem Ltd v Bentley* [1991] 1 Q.B. 61, CA; *Chiron Corporation v Murex Diagnostics Ltd (No.13)* [1996] F.S.R. 578 (Robert Walker J.); *Bovis Lend Lease Ltd v Braehead Glasgow Ltd* (2000) 71 Con. L.R. 208 (Dyson J.)).

## 3. CONDITIONS TO BE SATISFIED AND MATTERS TO BE TAKEN INTO ACCOUNT (CPR R.25.7)

### (a) Generally

**15–96** The court may make an order for an interim payment in the several circumstances listed in r.25.7(1), but not otherwise. The jurisdiction to order an interim payment is an exceptional (see above) and is subject to the strict restrictions stated in r.25.7 (*R. (Teleos Plc) v Commissioners of Customs and Excise* [2005] EWCA Civ 200; [2005] 1 W.L.R. 3007, CA (rejecting submission that claimants entitled to interim payment where Revenue had authority to make discretionary reimbursement pending outcome of proceedings over disputed input VAT credits)).

With effect from April 1, 2005, para.(1) of r.25.7 was amended for the purpose of revising the categories of defendant against whom an interim payment order may be made. As a consequence, paras (2) and (3) of the rule, which contained special conditions applicable where the claim was for personal injuries, were omitted (see now r.25.7(1)). One purpose of these amendments was to make it possible for the court to make an interim payment order against a defendant in all cases, including personal injury cases where the defendant is uninsured (see r.25.7(1(c)). (As to the relevance of the ability of an uninsured defendant to pay, see "Defendant's resources" below.) Another purpose was to apply to all cases conditions that previously only applied in personal injury cases where there are two or more defendants (see r.25.7(1)(e)).

#### *(i) Judgment obtained*

**15–97** The most obvious circumstance in which an application for an interim may be made and granted is where the claimant has obtained judgment against the defendant, either (1) for damages to be assessed, or (2) "for a sum of money to be assessed (other than costs)" (r.25.7(1)(b)). The first of these is based on former RSC O.29, r.11(1)(b) and the second on RSC O.29, r.12(a), which stated that an order could be made where the claimant had obtained "an order for an account to be taken as between himself and the defendant and for any amount certified due on taking the account to be paid".

#### *(ii) Liability admitted*

**15–98** Next there is the situation where the defendant has admitted liability to pay to the claimant either (1) damages (see former RSC O.29, r.11(1)(a)), or (2) "some other sum of money" (in neither event need the sum be substantial) (r.25.7(1)(a)). The second of these did not figure in the former rules.

#### *(iii) Judgment predicted*

**15–99** Finally, there is the situation where the court is satisfied that, if the case went to trial, either (1) the claimant would obtain judgment for "a substantial amount of money (other than costs)" or, (2) in a claim for possession, the defendant would be held liable "to pay the claimant a sum of money" for occupation and use whilst the claim was pending (r.25.7(1)(c)) (see, respectively, former RSC O.29, rr.11(1)(c) and 12(b)).

*(iv) Personal injuries claims*

In practice, many applications for interim payment orders are made in personal injuries cases. A given personal injuries case may fall within any one of the three categories mentioned above, with the claimant seeking an order on the basis (1) that he has obtained judgment on liability, or (2) that liability has been admitted, or (3) that, if the case went to trial, he would obtain judgment for substantial damages. Obviously, it is the third of these three situations which creates the greatest difficulty (especially where there are several defendants) and which has attracted the bulk of the case law. If progress can be made towards securing earlier admissions of liability, the difficulty will be reduced. **15–100**

## (b) Grounds for contesting payment

The defendant against whom an order for interim payment is sought may show cause against the making of the order in the following ways: **15–101**

(i) by a technical objection, e.g. that the application does not satisfy the conditions stipulated by r.25.7;

(ii) on the merits by showing that there is a serious doubt whether the claimant will recover anything. In a claim for a sum of money, the court must be "satisfied" that the claimant "would obtain judgment for a substantial amount of money". In determining whether it is so satisfied the court should apply the civil standard of proof; the Court is not required to be sure in the sense of being satisfied beyond reasonable doubt (*Shearson Lehman Brothers Inc v Maclaine Watson & Co Ltd* [1989] Q.B. 842; [1987] 2 All E.R. 181, CA; *Gibbons v Wall, The Times*, February 24, 1988, CA). It should be observed, however, that the test prescribed by r.25.7(1)(c) is whether the court is satisfied that the claimant will succeed in his claim against the defendant, rather than whether he is likely to succeed (*British & Commonwealth Holdings Plc v Quadrex Holdings Inc* [1989] Q.B. 842; [1989] 3 All E.R. 492, CA; *Andrews v Schooling* [1991] 1 W.L.R. 783; [1991] 3 All E.R. 723, CA);

(iii) on quantum, r.25.7(5) expressly provides that the court must take into account any set-off or counterclaim as well as any allegation of contributory negligence. Thus the court must be satisfied, whatever the description of the bar relief on in opposition that the claimant would obtain judgment for a substantial amount at trial (*Smallman Construction v Redpath Dorman Long* (1992) 47 B.L.R. 15; 25 Con.L.R. 105, CA). "Substantial" will mean different amounts in different situations and real need of the claimant may be taken into account in this context; however, to say that its meaning extends to sums that are, in absolute terms, trivial would be straining the flexibility of the Order. Applications for small sums are discouraged but if made should be coupled with an application to transfer to the appropriate county court.

## (c) Two or more defendants (CPR r.25.7(1)(e))

As originally enacted, r.25.7(1)(c) provided that the court must be satisfied that, if the claim proceeds to trial, the claimant will obtain judgment for a substantial amount of money (whether damages or some other sum of money) "against the defendant from whom he is seeking an order for interim payment". By the Civil Procedure (Amendment No.4) Rules 2004 (SI 2004/3419), it was made clear that such an order could be made "whether or not that defendant is the only defendant or one of a number of defendants to the claim" (cf. former RSC Ord. 29, r.11(1)(c)). Interim payment orders may be made against two or more defendants in respect of the same liability and in respect of the same sum, if the court is satisfied as to the liability of each of the defendants against whom the order is made (*Schott Kem Ltd v Bentley* [1991] 1 Q.B. 61; [1990] 3 All E.R. 850, CA). There is no objection in principle to the making of orders for interim payments against two or more defendants for different fractions of the total amount thought to be just, provided (a) it is made clear in the order that, if the aggregate of the fractions awarded against the defendants exceeds the "just amount," the sum actually recoverable by the claimant cannot exceed the "just amount"; (b) in the case of a claim for damages, it is made clear that the sum actually recoverable by the claimant cannot exceed the "reasonable proportion of the damages"; and (c) the order otherwise complies with the rules (*ibid.*). **15–102**

***Paragraph numbers marked with a "+" can be found online and on CD.***

Difficulties may arise where the court is satisfied that if a claim against two defendants proceeds to trial the claimant would obtain judgment for a substantial amount of money against one or other of the defendants but not against both. Cases on the former rules held that proof of success to the necessary standard against a particular defendant is required before an order can be made against him (*Breeze v R. McKennon & Son Ltd* (1985) 32 Build. L.R. 41; 135 New L.J. 1233 (1985), CA; *Ricci Burns Ltd v Toole* [1989] 1 W.L.R. 993; [1989] 3 All E.R. 478, CA). As a result of the amendments to r.25.7 brought about by the Civil Procedure (Amendment No.4) Rules 2004 (SI 2004/3419), it is expressly provided in r.25.7(1)(e) that, in certain circumstances, the court may make interim payment orders where it is satisfied that, if the claim went to trial, the claimant would obtain judgment against at least one of the defendants, but the court cannot determine which. In terms, that provision is not restricted to personal injury claims.

### (d) Judgment "for a substantial amount of money" (CPR r.25.7(1)(c))

**15–103** The court is empowered to have regard to all the circumstances of the case, including the statements of case, any documents disclosed or exhibited and any other relevant material and any admissions made by the defendant, and to determine on such material whether it is satisfied that the claimant will at the trial obtain judgment for a substantial sum of money. This could arise in a claim for a quantum meruit, where the defence is that the claim is excessive or for work done and materials supplied where the defence is that some of the work was defective or was not done, and situations of a like character.

The application should be considered by the court in two stages (*Schott Kem Ltd v Bentley* [1991] 1 Q.B. 61; [1990] 3 All E.R. 850, CA). The court must first be satisfied that, if the action proceeds to trial, the claimant will obtain judgment for a substantial sum, and, if so, the court should then consider whether, in its discretion, it should order an interim payment. At the first stage the claimant must satisfy the court on the balance of probabilities, but to a high standard, that he will obtain judgment for a substantial sum; the likelihood of a set-off or any other defence succeeding must be considered by the court. At the second stage the rules also require (r.25.7(5)) the court to take into account any set-off claimed by the defendant, and any counterclaim arising out of some other transaction and not available as a defence (*Shanning International Ltd v George Wimpey International Ltd* [1988] 1 W.L.R. 981; [1988] 3 All E.R. 475, CA).

### (e) Alternative claims in debt and damages (CPR r.25.7(1)(c))

**15–104** Rule 25.7(1)(a) states that the court may order an interim payment if it is satisfied that, if the claim went to trial, the claimant would obtain judgment for a substantial sum of money, whether (1) damages or (2) some other sum of money. Formerly, these two forms of money judgment were dealt with in quite separate provisions in RSC O.29, specifically, in r.11(1)(c) (damages) and in r.12(c) (apart from damages). In *Shearson Lehman Brothers Inc v Maclaine Watson & Co Ltd* [1989] Q.B. 842; [1987] 2 All E.R. 181, CA, it was held that the two provisions should be read together to permit the court to make an order for interim payment where it is satisfied that, if the action proceeded to trial, the claimant would obtain judgment either for substantial damages or for a substantial sum of money apart from damages, even though thought not to be certain which. It would seem, however, that if there is doubt whether the sum claimed will prove to be recoverable as damages or under some other heading the court should apply a discount when ordering an interim payment to take account of the provision as to "a reasonable proportion of the likely amount of the final judgment" in r.35.7(4) (*Schott Kem Ltd v Bentley* [1991] 1 Q.B. 61; [1990] 3 All E.R. 850, CA).

### (f) Claim for possession of land (CPR r.25.7(1)(d))

**15–105** The object of r.25.7(1)(d) (formerly RSC O.29, r.12(b)) is to enable the court, during the pendency of the action, to order the defendant to make an interim payment to the claimant in respect of his continued use and occupation of the land, whoever should ultimately succeed on the claim for possession of the land itself. This rule operates to negative the decision in *Moore v Assignment Courier Ltd* [1977] 1 W.L.R. 638; [1977] 2 All E.R. 842, CA. This rule applies to an action for possession of land, on whatever ground it is based. An application for interim payment in these circum-

***Paragraph numbers marked with a "+" can be found online and on CD.***

stances should be distinguished from an application to determine the amount of the interim rent under the Landlord and Tenant Act 1954 s.24A (see CPR r.56.3 and Practice Direction (Landlord and Tenant Claims and Miscellaneous Provisions about Land), para.3.7 (Vol.1 paras 56.3.1 and 56PD.7)).

## 4. AMOUNT OF INTERIM PAYMENT (CPR R.25.7(4))

Rule 25.7(4) consolidates provisions formerly found in the RSC and, as a result, some subtle changes emerge. In all cases, the court must not order an interim payment of more than "a reasonable proportion of the likely amount of the final judgment". Former RSC O.29, rr.11(1) and 12 stated that, if it thought fit, the court should order a payment "of such amount as it thinks just" and, in cases of damages (but not in cases of sums other than damages) the amount was not to exceed a reasonable proportion, etc. In the reported cases, the requirement that the court should award "such amount as it thinks just" figures prominently and, presumably, despite its omission from these rules will continue to do so. However, in considering whether to order an interim payment the court must specifically address the conditions of r.25.7(4) and must consider what is "the likely amount of the final judgment" and what would be "a reasonable proportion of that amount", as well as other matters that it thinks material to the exercise of its overall discretion (*Spillman v Bradfield Riding Centre* [2007] EWHC 89 (QB), February 6, 2007, unrep. (Langley J.)). The court should take into account contributory negligence and any relevant set-off or counterclaim (r.25.7(5)). Whether a relevant set-off or counterclaim exists is to be determined in the light of the state of the pleadings (*O2 UK Ltd v Dimension Data Network Services Ltd* [2007] EWCA Civ 1551, November 6, 2007, CA, unrep. (defence, when properly analysed, precluding counterclaim)).There is no judicial guidance on what is "a reasonable proportion", nor should there be as the matter is one for the judge's discretion (*Dolman v Rowe* [2005] EWCA Civ 715, May 19, 2005, CA, unrep.). The judge has to do his best to make a rough estimate of the likely award and in doing so is entitled to bring into account his general experience (*ibid*). 15–106

As to the exercise of the discretion in cases where a trial order to the effect that damages should be paid by periodical payments is to be anticipated, see para.15–111 below.

The amount payable as an interim award should not be such as to expose the defendant to the risk that the eventual damages will be les than the sum or sums paid out as interim awards. If it turns out that the claimant has been over-paid, the circumstances may be such that a final adjustment under r.25.8 made to rectify the matter will be ineffective. Thus the claimant's ability to repay is a factor that the court may take into account in fixing the sum to be paid, or in considering whether terms might be imposed to protect the money in the event of the claimant being unable to repay it. In *Ultraframe (UK) Ltd v Eurocell Building Plastics Ltd* [2005] EWHC 2111 (Ch), August 26, 2005, unrep. (Pumfrey J.), where the claimant's (having obtained an interim injunction) had succeeded on the liability issue in a patent claim but were in a deteriorating financial position, a condition was added requiring the claimant's holding company to join in the undertaking to repay. (In this case, in addition, the judge fortified the claimant's cross-undertaking in the interim injunction by requiring it to be given by the holding company as well.) Particular care has to be taken where the claimant is impecunious and a large interim payment is asked fo r.It has been said that, although a claimant's impecuniosity does not disentitle him from an order, the amount specified in the order should reflect the possibility that he may be unable to comply with any adjustment order subsequently made under rule 25.8 (*Harmon CFEM Facades (UK) Ltd v Corporate Officer of the House of Commons (Interim Payment)* [2001] C.P. Rep. 20).

In personal injury cases where the circumstances are that any interim payment will be paid, not to the claimant personally, but to the Court of Protection, which will hold the money and only pay out what is reasonable for the claimant's needs, the risk that the payment might be dissipated before trial with the result that the defendant would be unable to recoup any excess is avoided. In such circumstances the judge is entitled to exercise his discretion rather more generously that he otherwise might (*Dolman v Rowe, op cit*, *Goode v West Hertfordshire Hospitals NHS Trust* [2006] EWHC 3007 (QB), September 6, 2006, unrep. (Walker J.)).

If the sum applied for is well within "the likely amount of the final judgment", it

***Paragraph numbers marked with a "+" can be found online and on CD.***

will normally be awarded, but it is a relevant consideration (which may lead the court to decline to make the order) that the payment sought may prejudice the trial or the position of the defendant in the proceedings, or pre-judge an issue to be determined at trial (the so-called "level playing field" principle) (*Tinsley v Sarkar* [2004] EWCA Civ 1098, July 23, 2004, CA, unrep., at para.48 per Thorpe L.J.). For example, in a medical negligence claim in which the amount of damages which should be awarded for the future care for a severely disabled claimant was in issue, the fact that the interim payment sought might deplete the likely amount of the final judgment to a level where it would be extremely difficult for the judge of quantum to exercise powers under s.2 of the Damages Act 1996 to make a periodical payments order for future care, was treated as a relevant consideration (*Osunde v Guy's & St Thomas' Hospital* [2007] EWHC 2275 (Fam), September 27, 2007, unrep. (Calvert-Smith J.)). But level playing field principle can never be an absolute bar to interim payment (*Campbell v Mylchreest* [1999] P.I.Q.R. Q17, CA).

The question whether an interim payment might pre-judge an issue yet to be determined, and the weight to be given to that prospect in determining an application for an interim payment, has arisen in personal injury cases where severely disabled claimants sought damages for future care. In such a case, a dispute can arise between the parties as to the arrangements to be made (and for which the defendant should pay) to ensure that the claimant has the necessary support that he needs to be maintained in reasonable health. Where an interim payment is sought for the purposes of putting in place the arrangements preferred by the claimant (e.g. care at home), being arrangements that (arguably) may cost more to implement and maintain than those preferred by the defendant (e.g. institutional care), the question arises whether an order would pre-judge the disputed issue and prejudice the defendants accordingly (particularly where the defendant wishes to contend that the claimant's accommodation plans are extravagant). Generally, the courts have given the likelihood of such prejudice in these cases little weight (*Campbell v Mylchreest, op cit, Dolman v Rowe, op cit,Goode v West Hertfordshire Hospitals NHS Trust, op cit*). Indeed, it has been said that experience gained in implementing the claimant's preferred arrangements by funding provided by an interim payment may prove useful in resolving the disputed issue, and that that is a consideration which may be borne in mind by the court in exercising its discretion whether to order such payment (*Osunde v Guy's & St Thomas' Hospital, op cit*).

### Defendant's resources

**15–107** Before r.25.7 was amended by the Civil Procedure (Amendment No.4) Rules 2004 (SI 2004/3419), it was expressly provided that, in a claim for personal injuries, generally the court could not make an interim payment order against an uninsured defendant. By indirect means, this rule continued the effect of former RSC Ord. 29, r.11(2)(c), which stated that an interim payment order could not be made against a defendant in a personal injury claim who, assuming he was not insured, was not "a person whose means and resources are such as to enable him to make the interim payment". But the rule protected from interim payment orders, not only the defendant whose means and resources were not such as to enable him to make an interim payment, but also those whose means and resources were sufficient. By the amendment made to r.25.7 in 2004, the restriction protecting uninsured defendants was removed. In cases decided before the CPR came into effect, it was said that the means and resources of the defendant were a relevant consideration, not only in personal injury claims, but in other claims as well (*Jones v Tower Hamlets LBC* (1996) 19(11) I.P.D. 19103, CA). It has been held that, if the defendant's resources are such that an order for interim payment will cause irremediable harm which cannot be made good by eventual repayment, that is a very relevant factor to be taken into account in fixing the amount of any interim payment (*British & Commonwealth Holdings Plc v Quadrex Holdings Inc* [1989] Q.B. 842; [1989] 3 All E.R. 492, CA).

### "financial position of each party"

**15–108** Rule 1.1 states that the "overriding objective" of the CPR is to enable the court "to deal with cases justly" and dealing with a case justly includes, so far as is practicable, dealing with it in ways which inter alia are proportionate "to the amount of money involved" and "to the financial position of each party" (r.1.1(2)(c)). The question whether or not an interim remedy in the form of an order for interim payment should

***Paragraph numbers marked with a "+" can be found online and on CD.***

be made is not a mere matter of practice or procedure but a matter of substantive remedy. It may be doubted, therefore, whether r.1.1 strictly applies. However, well before the CPR came into effect the courts emphasised that the discretion to order an interim payment is extremely wide (see "Court's discretion" Section G below) and it has always been the case that the courts have taken into account the financial positions of each party. Certainly it is not necessary for the claimant to satisfy the court of his need for an interim payment, or that he will suffer prejudice if he does not obtain one (*Schott Kem Ltd v Bentley* [1991] 1 Q.B. 61, CA).

**Delay to trial**

The power to grant orders for interim payments was introduced by legislation at a time when delays before trial had become so significant that the injustice that could be inflicted on personal injury claimants was patent. Obviously, the length of time before a claim may be settled or tried is an important consideration. Under a procedural system in which cases are actively managed by the court it might be expected that the incidence of early settlements would be increased and delays to trial very much reduced with the results that the need for interim payment orders might decline and that the amounts awarded might be reduced. However, it remains the position that in personal injury cases where claimants seek damages for long-term care the time needed to assemble all of the expert evidence relevant to quantum issues can still be considerable. **15–109**

**Interest**

Where an order for an interim payment is made in respect of expenditure already incurred and paid for, the court has power to award interest in its discretion. If the court should think it desirable to award interest on the amount of the interim payment, e.g. where the amount awarded is substantial or the trial is unlikely to come on for a long time, it should clearly and precisely specify the rate of interest awarded and the period or periods for which it is awarded, so that if the trial judge should award a different rate or rates or for a different period or periods, the necessary adjustments can be made to determine the correct total amount of interest which the trial judge has awarded. The rates at which, and the periods for which, interest may have been awarded in respect of an interim payment ordered before trial are not binding on the trial judge. **15–110**

**Interim payments and periodical payments of quantum judgment**

Before April 1, 2005, in cases where the claimant sought damages and made an application for an interim payment order, the court could generally assume that any award for damages made at trial would be in the form of a lump sum payment. Since that date, in cases to which the Damages Act 1996 s.2 (as amended by the Courts Act 2005) applies, that cannot be assumed, as in those cases a court dealing with quantum has to consider whether the award (or part of it) should not be capitalised but should be made in the form of a periodical payments order (see CPR Pt 41, Sect II). The factors to be taken into account are stated in CPR r.41.7. This innovation made it necessary (in cases to which it applied) for the courts to consider what is meant, in this context, by the stipulation in r.25.7(4) to the effect that the court must not order an interim payment "of more than a reasonable proportion of the likely amount of the final judgment". It has been recognised that it is conceivable that (in a given case to which s.2 applied) the granting of an interim payment order might affect the judge's ability in giving final judgment at trial of quantum to get the balance right between the lump sum element of any damages award and the periodical payments orders that may be necessary. And it has been held at first instance that the correct approach on an application for an interim payment order is for the court (in addition to having regard to the principles taken from the authorities applicable to such applications generally) to identify what is likely to be awarded for general damages, past losses and interest, and then to predict the likely capitalisation of the remainder of the claims; in carrying out this task, the court must endeavour to ensure that the amount of the interim payment order does not fetter the trial judge's exercise of discretion under r.41.7 (see *Brewis v Heatherwood & Wrexham Park Hospitals NHS Trust* [2008] EWHC 2526 (QB), October 20, 2008, unrep. (Coulson J.), where other authorities are explained). In *Eeles v Cobham Hire Services Ltd* [2009] EWCA Civ 204 ; March 13, 2009, **15–110.1**

***Paragraph numbers marked with a "+" can be found online and on CD.***

unrep., CA, the Court of Appeal explained that, in a case where a periodical payments order (PPO) is made, the amount of the final judgment is the actual capital sum awarded and does not include the notional capitalised value of the PPO, and held that, because he did not consider what capital sum was likely to be awarded at trial, a judge dealing with an interim payment order (IPO) application was not in a position to decide upon a reasonable proportion of that sum, and had therefore erred in that respect. The court reviewed some of the first instance authorities and stated that, for the purposes of an IPO application, (1) a judge should not normally begin to speculate about how the trial judge will allocate the damages, and, as a rule, should stop at the figure which he is satisfied is likely to be awarded as a capital sum, however (2) where the judge is able confidently to predict that the trial judge will capitalise additional elements of the future loss so as to produce a greater lump sum award, for example, where the claimant can clearly demonstrate a need for an immediate capital sum (probably to fund the purchase of accommodation), he may award a reasonable proportion of that greater sum, but (3) before encroaching on the trial judge's freedom to allocate in this way the judge should have a high degree of confidence that the trial judge will endorse the capitalisation undertaken. For recent examples of the effect of the guidance given by the Court of Appeal in the *Eeles* case on applications for IPOs, see *Johnson v Chesterfield & Derbyshire Royal Hospital NHS Trust*, May 22, 2009, unrep. (Judge Bullimore); *FP v Taunton & Somerset NHS Trust* [2009] EWHC 1965 (QB), July 31, 2009, unrep. (Blair J.).

## 5. NEED FOR INTERIM PAYMENT

**15–111** Considerable uncertainty may exist as to the quantum of damages likely to be awarded in the event. The claimant does not have to demonstrate that a certain sum is required to cover any particular need over and above the general need that a claimant has to be paid his damages as soon as reasonably may be done.

Considerable uncertainty may exist as to the quantum of damages likely to be awarded in the event. The claimant does not have to demonstrate that a certain sum is required to cover any particular need over and above the general need that a claimant has to be paid his damages as soon as reasonably may be done (*Stringman v McArdle* [1994] 1 W.L.R. 1653, CA; cf. *Schott Kem Ltd v Bentley* [1991] 1 Q.B. 61; [1990] 3 All E.R. 850, CA). The court is not concerned with what the claimant proposes to do with the money received (*Campbell v Mylchreest* [1999] P.I.Q.R. Q17, CA). In the case of a child or patient, the money will normally be paid into court and then the litigation friend will apply to the Master or district judge for payment out as and when the money is required. Where the Court of Protection is concerned, it is for that court to decide how and when the money is to be spent (*Stringman v McArdle*, op. cit.).

In *Wright v Sullivan* [2005] EWCA Civ 656; [2006] 1 W.L.R. 172, CA, the claimant applied for an interim payment for the purpose of obtaining funds for meeting costs of clinical case manager, to be appointed to provide support for the claimant. The judge rejected the defendant's submission that the interim payment order should be made conditional on the proposed case manager receiving joint instructions from the parties and reporting to them jointly. However, the judge directed that, in preparing any witness statement for the assessment of damages hearing, the manager (though a witness as to fact) should regard himself as owing the same duties to the court as those owed by an expert witness. The Court of Appeal dismissed the defendant's appeal against the judge's refusal to make the order conditional, and allowed the claimant's appeal against the direction (holding that the Pt 35 regime did not apply).

## 6. INTERIM PAYMENT AND SUMMARY JUDGMENT

**15–112** The court may give summary judgment against a defendant on the whole of a claim or a particular issue (r.24.2). Summary judgment is not available in certain possession proceedings (r.24.3(2)) but otherwise may be granted in cases where an interim payment order may be made. Depending on the circumstances, an application for summary judgment and for an interim payment order may conveniently be made and dealt with together (*Associated Bulk Carriers Ltd v Koch Shipping Inc* [1978] 2 All E.R. 254, CA). Where, in a claim for unliquidated damages, no application is made for an interim payment but summary judgment is given on liability and there is a triable issue as to quantum, the court has no power to give judgment for part of the damages unless the court is satisfied that such part of the damages can be clearly identified and quantified and that such ascertained part of the damages is undisputedly due (*ibid.*, and *Sinclair Investment Holdings SA v Cushine* [2006] EWHC 219 (Ch), January 27, 2006, unrep. (Mr Thomas Ivory Q.C.)).

The court may now give a claimant summary judgment if it considers that the defendant has "no real prospect of successfully defending" the claim or issue (r.24.2). The court may make an interim payment order if it is satisfied that the claimant "would obtain judgment for a substantial amount of money", if the claim went to trial. If the court is so satisfied it is likely that it will also consider that the defendant has no real prospect of defending. Under the former law, a defendant could be granted unconditional leave to defend where the court was satisfied that he had an arguable defence. In *Andrews v Schooling* [1991] 1 W.L.R. 783; [1991] 3 All E.R. 723, CA, the Court of Appeal examined the earlier authorities (which were not ad idem) and said that it was inconsistent to order an interim payment at the same time as giving unconditional leave to defend and approved the practice of making such leave conditional on the making of an interim payment. There is authority for the proposition that the mere fact that the defendant lodges a bona fide appeal against an order for summary judgment is not, of itself, a sufficient ground for refusing to award the claimant an interim payment order (*Halvanon Insurance Co Ltd v Central Reinsurance Corp.* [1984] 2 Lloyd's Rep. 420).

## 7. COURT'S DISCRETION

Whether or not an order is made is a matter of discretion. In the former RSC rules, **15–113** it was said that the court could make an interim payment order "if it thinks fit" and the amount of the payment was expressed to be "of such amount as [the court] thinks just". It was these phrases which encouraged the courts to emphasise that the discretion is extremely wide (*Crimpfil Ltd v Barclays Bank Plc, The Times*, February 24, 1995, CA) and that no limitations on its exercise (over and above those imposed by the rules themselves) should be implied (*Schott Kem Ltd v Bentley* [1991] 1 Q.B. 61; [1990] 3 All E.R. 850, CA). These phrases do not appear in r.25.7 but no restriction on the wide discretion should be implied from their omission. The emphasis on the broadness of the discretion can be seen as simply reflecting the fact that the circumstances in which its exercise may be called into play can vary enormously (and may include, not only the nature of the substantive claim and the heads under which damages or money are claimed, but also the stage in the progress of the proceedings at which an application is made).

Generally, interim payment procedures are not suitable where factual issues are complicated, or where difficult points of law arise (*Schott Kem Ltd v Bentley*, op. cit.), but this does not prevent an award being made in respect of part of a complex claim where (without venturing too far into disputed areas of fact or law) there is evidence establishing with reasonable certainty the minimum sum likely to be recoverable (*Chiron Group v Murex Diagnostics Ltd (No.13)* [1996] F.S.R. 578 (Robert Walker J.)). Where, in the substantive area involved, the assessment of damages is inherently difficult (e.g. future loss of sales where patent infringed), it may well be appropriate simply to ignore certain heads of claim altogether while concentrating on those parts of the claim which can be assessed on established principles with some confidence (*Ultraframe (UK) Ltd v Eurocell Building Plastics Ltd* [2005] EWHC 2111 (Ch), August 26, 2005, unrep. (Pumfrey J.)).

Where the court makes an order, it may make it subject to conditions and may specify the consequence of failure to comply with the order or a condition (r.3.1(3)). Presumably, where the order made is an interim payment order, in certain circumstances it may be appropriate for the court to specify that the defendant should not be entitled to defend if he fails to comply with the order (*Casio Computer Co Ltd v Sayo*, January 28, 2000, unrep. (Rimer J.)).

## 8. FURTHER MATTERS RELEVANT TO CPR R.25.7

### (a) Defendant insured

In many instances, where an interim payment is ordered against a defendant, the **15–114** defendant will be insured in respect of the claim. Until r.25.7 was amended by the

***Paragraph numbers marked with a "+" can be found online and on CD.***

Civil Procedure (Amendment No.4) Rules 2004 (SI 2004/ 3419), sub-rules (2) and (3) of the rule stated that an interim payment order could be made in a personal injury claim only if the defendant (or one of them where there were two or more) was insured and therefore clearly had the ability to pay (this marked a departure from former RSC Ord. 29, r.11(2), which was not so restricting). By that statutory instrument, sub-rules (2) and (3) were revoked (with effect from April 1, 2005) and sub-rule (1) amended. The intention is that, subject to an exception, it should be possible to make an interim payment in all cases, even if the defendant is uninsured or not a public body. The exception is cases (not only personal injury cases) where the court is satisfied that one or more defendants will be liable but has not determined which (see r.25.7(1)(e)).

### (b) Motor Insurers' Bureau

**15–115** Rule 25.7(1)(e) states that an order for an interim payment may be made where the defendant's liability will be met by an insurer "acting under" the MIB agreement, as well as by the MIB "where it is acting for itself" (r.25.7(2)(b)). The drafting here is different to that found in former RSC O.29, r.11(2)(a) and is designed to implement the decision of the Court of Appeal in *Sharp v Pereira* [1999] 1 W.L.R. 195; [1998] 4 All E.R. 145, CA.

### (c) Recoverable benefits and interim payments

**15–116** The Social Security (Recovery of Benefits) Act 1997 replaces (with some modifications) the legislative scheme formerly found in the Social Security Administration Act 1992, Pt IV, providing for the recoupment by the Secretary of State from persons making compensation payments of certain benefits paid to the injured parties. An interim payment, whether made voluntarily or under a court order, appears to fall within the definition of a compensation payment under s.29 of this Act. Consequently, a person making an interim payment is liable to the Secretary of State for an amount equal to the total certified recoverable benefits (s.6(1)). (Certain payments are exempted and "small payments" as fixed by regulations may be disregarded.) In these circumstances, where an application for an interim payment is otherwise than by consent, the practice stated in Practice Direction (Interim Payments), paras 4.1 and 4.2 should be followed (see Vol.1 para.25BPD.1). The order will set out the amount by which the payment to be made has been reduced and the payment made to the claimant will be the net amount (*ibid.* paras 4.3 and 4.4). Following upon amendments to other CPR provisions, notably to r.36.15 (Deduction of benefits and lump sum payments), coming about as a consequence of modifications made to the 1997 Act by the Social Security (Recovery of Benefits) (Lump Sum Payments) Regulations 2008, paras 4.1 and 4.3 of this Practice Direction were substituted by TSO CPR Update 47 (with effect from October 1, 2008).

### (d) Costs

**15–117** An interim payment order is an order for payment on account of any sum which a party may be held liable to pay if final judgment is given against him. However, such an order cannot be made for the purpose of requiring a party to make a payment on account of any costs for which he may be required to indemnify his opponent by an order for costs made upon final judgment (see Senior Courts Act 1981 s.32(5)). (For interim payment rules as to costs, see CPR r.44.3(8).) In certain circumstances, a party may be required, not to make a payment on account of expected orders for costs, but to provide security for his opponent's costs. For example, where an application for summary judgment fails, the court may order that a party with a weak case should pay a sum of money into court as security for costs (see CPR rr.3.1(3) and 24.6).

### (e) Manner of payment

**15–118** Former RSC O.29, r.13 contained some express provisions as to the manner in which an interim payment should be paid. These provisions are not repeated in Pt 25 but the practice remains the same. The order should specify to whom the payment is to be made and fix a time for payment. If the claimant is a child or patient the money should be dealt with in accordance with directions given by the court under CPR r.21.11.

Former RSC O.29, r.13 stated that the court had power to order payment into court of an interim award. This power (which was seldom used) may now be derived from CPR r.3.1(3). Payment is usually in a lump sum, but the court may order payment by instalments. In the case of payments for the occupation of land, it is usual to order periodical payments as if they were of rent in arrea r.In personal injury cases the payment may, in appropriate cases, be expressly ordered to be made in respect of the special damages and loss of wages claimed; this may simplify the calculation of interest at the end of the day.

### *(f) Directions for further conduct of case*

Former RSC O.29, r.14 provided that, on an application for interim payment, whether or not an order was made, the court could give directions as to the further conduct of the case, particularly where the issue of liability still remained to be tried and the hearing of the application revealed that an early trial was desirable. Under the case management system introduced by the CPR, no express provision to that effect is required. The court has ample powers to adjust the management of the case in the light of any order as to interim payment. As to restrictions on disclosure of interim payment, see CPR r.25.9. **15–119**

### *(g) Enforcement*

An order for an interim payment is an "order for the payment of money" within CPR r.70.1 and, unless time has been given, may be enforced forthwith by the methods referred to in r.70.2 as provided. Doubtless, failure to satisfy an order may found winding-up proceedings. **15–120**

### *(h) Part 36 offer and interim payment*

CPR Pt 36 contains provisions relating to offers to settle. That Part was substituted by the Civil Procedure (Amendment No.3) Rules 2006 (S.I. 2006/3435) for the purpose of effecting substantial changes and the new provisions came into force on April 6, 2007 (subject to transitional provisions affecting offers made before that date). Rule 36.5(5), as it stood before the whole Part was substituted, stated that a Part 36 offer "may be made by reference to an interim payment". And, r.36.6(2)(d), as it stood, stated that where, after making an interim payment a defendant offered to settle a money claim by paying a sum into court under Pt 36, the notice of payment should state that the defendant had taken into account the interim payment. In Pt 36 as substituted, offers made under that Part are no longer made in the form of payments into court. As a consequence no such comparable provisions are to be found in that Part. **15–121**

There is no objection to the court being told, on an application for an interim payment order, of any payment into court (*Fryer v London Transport Executive*, *The Times*, December 4, 1982, CA). If money has been paid into court, and an interim payment order is made subsequently, it is usual for the payment to be made from that money.

## 9. POWERS OF COURT WHERE IT HAS MADE AN ORDER FOR INTERIM PAYMENT (CPR R.25.8)

### *(a) Discharge, variation, repayment*

The court has wide powers to discharge or vary an interim payment order, including the power to order any money paid repaid. Further, in certain circumstances the court may order a defendant to reimburse, either wholly or partly, another defendant who has made an interim payment (r.25.8(3)). The court may adjust an order that has been made but not yet paid. **15–122**

The court may make an order under this rule without an application by any party if it makes the order when it disposes of the claim or any part of it (r.25.8(4)) by final judgment or grant of leave to discontinue. Otherwise an application for the relief permitted under this rule may be made by any party at any time.

### *(b) Interest*

Former RSC O.29, r.17 contained no specific provisions as to interest; the matter **15–123**

***Paragraph numbers marked with a "+" can be found online and on CD.***

was dealt with by case law. It is clear that, where, following final judgment or order, the court orders that part of the interim payment should be repaid to the defendant, the court may award him interest on the overpaid amount from the date when he made the interim payment (r.25.8(5)); that is to say, when his "total liability" is less than the interim payment. Presumably, where a defendant is found not liable at all he would be entitled to interest on the full amount of the interim payment. The court may award interest on an interim payment made voluntarily as well as under an order of the court.

### (c) Adjustment on final judgment or order or on discontinuance

*(i) Final judgment*

**15–124** Where an action proceeds to trial either on the issue of liability or of damages or both after the defendant or one of two or more defendants has made an interim payment whether voluntarily or pursuant an order, the court may, before the final judgment or order is given or made, make such adjustments with respect to the interim payment as may be necessary, for the purpose of giving effect to its determination of that defendant's liability. Such adjustments may become necessary (a) as between the claimant and that defendant, and (b) as between that defendant and any co-defendant of his (r.25.8(2)(b) and (c)).

As between the claimant and the defendant, the first and obvious adjustment that needs to be made is that the amount of the interim payment should be deducted from the amount of the total award of damages, and subject to any further adjustment with regard to the interest on the damages (see para.25.8.3) judgment should be entered for the claimant only for the difference between these two amounts. The form of the judgment should recite the amount of the final judgment or the assessment of the damages and should further recite the order for interim payment and payment made thereunder or the amount paid voluntarily. The judgment or order should then provide for entry of judgment and payment of the balance (see Practice Direction (Interim Payments), paras 5.2 and 5.3 (para.25BPD.5) and, to same effect, Practice Direction (Judgments and Orders), paras 6.1 and 6.2 are to same effect (Vol.1 para.40BPD.6)).

Where the claimant has invested interim payments received from the defendant and earned interest, that accrued interest should not be deducted from the sum allowed for interest in the final determination of quantum (*Parry v North West Surrey Health Authority*, *The Times*, January 5, 2000).

In the unlikely event that the amount of the interim payment should exceed the amount of the final award for damages, debt or other sum, the court will order the claimant to repay the difference to the defendant who made the payment (see r.25.8(2)(c)). In addition, the court may award the defendant interest on the overpaid amount in accordance with r.25.8(5) (putting into legislative form *Mercers of the City of London v New Hampshire Insurance Co* [1991] 1 W.L.R. 1173; [1991] 4 All E.R. 542). For form of judgment in this event, see Practice Direction (Interim Payments), paras 6.3 and 6.4 (para.25BPD.5 below) and, to same effect, Practice Direction (Judgments and Orders), paras 5.4 and 5.5 (see Vol.1 para.40BPD.6).

*(ii) Discontinuance*

**15–125** The court's power to adjust an interim payment may also be exercised where the court grants leave to the claimant to discontinue his action or to withdraw the claim in respect of which the interim payment was made. Rule 38.2(2)(b) states that where the claimant has received an interim payment, whether voluntarily or pursuant to order, in relation to the whole or part of his claim he may discontinue that claim or that part of it only if (1) the defendant who has made the payment consents in writing, or (2) the court gives permission. It should be noted that leave to discontinue is required when the claimant "has received an interim payment", and not where such payment has been ordered but not paid, and leave may be dispensed with where the "defendant who has made the payment" consents, and the consent of all other parties is not required. In these two respects, r.38.2(2)(b) differs from former RSC O.21, r.2(2A). Presumably, "has received an interim payment" includes having received any instalment where the interim payment was to be paid by instalments.

***Paragraph numbers marked with a "+" can be found online and on CD.***

*(iii) Adjustment between co-defendants*

As between the defendant who makes the interim payment and his co-defendants, the court may order any defendant to pay the whole or part of the interim payment to the defendant who made it. **15–126**

The effect of r.25.8 in this context is as follows. Where (1) a defendant has been ordered to make an interim payment, or has in fact made an interim payment (either voluntarily or under an order), and (2) he made that payment in relation to a claim or part of a claim in respect of which he has made a claim against the co-defendant for a contribution, indemnity or other relief (former RSC O.29, r.17 added here "relating to or connected with the plaintiff's claim"), then (3) the court may order the co-defendant to reimburse him either wholly or partly. Obviously, such an order is likely to be made on or after final judgment or discontinuance of the claim or the part of the claim to which the interim payment related. However, subject to r.25.8(3)(b), such order for reimbursement may be made at an earlier stage in the proceedings.

# APPENDIX 1

## COURTS DIRECTORY

# APPENDIX 1 COURTS DIRECTORY

## *The Daily Cause List*

1. Copies of the Daily Cause List will be available in Room EO1, Royal Courts of Justice, at 4 pm on each sitting day during Term. The Daily Cause List is also available from the Court Service website: *www.hmcourts-service.gov.uk/cms/cause.htm*. **AP–1**
2. If an alteration has to be made in any list after 2.45 pm on any day the solicitors affected by the alteration will be notified by telephone by the appropriate official at the Royal Courts of Justice. Except in rare instances such alterations will be by way of deletion of cases appearing in the printed List published at 4 pm, as opposed to the insertion of cases not so appearing.

## *Areas and Regions*

On April 1, 2005 Her Majesty's Courts Service was set up as an executive agency of the Department of Constitutional Affairs, now the Ministry of Justice. The system of dividing the country into Circuits was replaced, and for the purposes of administration, the country is divided into seven Regions, namely, Midlands, North West, North East, Wales and Cheshire, South West, South East, London and Royal Courts of Justice. **AP–2**

Each Region is under the administrative control of a Regional Director who, subject to the overriding judicial control of the Presiding Judges assigned to each Region, is responsible to the Lord Chancellor and the Secretary of State for Justice for the efficient conduct of court business in his Region.

Each Region is further divided into a number of Areas for which an Area Director is responsible for the efficient conduct of business in all courts in his area. He will in practice act as a point of contact for all concerned, including judges, the legal profession and others to ensure the flexible arrangements for the disposal of court business, including the planning of court sittings, the allocation of judge-power and court accommodation.

The following is the list of Areas and Regions for the High Court, together with the addresses and telephone numbers of the Region and Area Directors. This is followed by a list of Trial Centres.

**For the list of Areas and Regions for the High Court see paragraphs AP–4+ on White Book on Westlaw UK or the Civil Procedure CD.** **AP–3**

## *List of Trial Centres*

**For the List of Trial Centres see paragraph AP–6+ on White Book on Westlaw UK or the Civil Procedure CD.** **AP–5**

## *List of District Registries*

[Civil Courts Order 1983 (SI 1983/713), as amended] **AP–7**

| District Registry | Districts defined by reference to County Court Districts | Designated Trial Centre |
|---|---|---|
| ABERYSTWYTH | Aberystwyth | Swansea |
| BARNSLEY | Barnsley | Sheffield |
| BARNSTAPLE | Barnstaple | Exeter |
| BARROW IN FURNESS | Barrow in Furness | Preston |
| BASINGSTOKE | Basingstoke | London |
| BATH | Bath<br>Trowbridge | Bristol |
| BEDFORD | Bedford | London |

## Appendix 1: Courts Directory

| District Registry | Districts defined by reference to County Court Districts | Designated Trial Centre |
|---|---|---|
| Birkenhead | Birkenhead | Liverpool |
| Birmingham (Chancery) | Birmingham<br>Redditch | Birmingham |
| Blackburn | Blackburn | Preston |
| Blackpool | Blackpool | Preston |
| Blackwood | Blackwood | Cardiff |
| Bolton | Bolton | Manchester |
| Boston | Boston<br>Skegness | Lincoln |
| Bournemouth | Bournemouth<br>Poole | Winchester |
| Bradford | Bradford | Leeds |
| Brecknock | Brecknock | Cardiff |
| Bridgend | Bridgend<br>Neath and Port Talbot | Cardiff |
| Brighton | Brighton<br>Haywards Heath<br>Lewes | Lewes |
| Bristol (Chancery) | Bristol<br>Weston super Mare | Bristol |
| Burnley | Accrington<br>Burnley<br>Nelson<br>Rawtenstall | Preston |
| Bury | Bury | Manchester |
| Bury St Edmunds | Bury St Edmunds | Norwich |
| Caernarfon | Caernarfon<br>Conwy and Colwyn | Caernarfon |
| Cambridge | Cambridge | London |
| Canterbury | Ashford<br>Canterbury | London |
| Cardiff (Chancery) | Cardiff | Cardiff |
| Carlisle | Carlisle<br>Penrith | Carlisle |
| Carmarthen | Carmarthen<br>Llanelli | Swansea |
| Chelmsford | Chelmsford | Chelmsford |
| Cheltenham | Cheltenham | Bristol |
| Chester | Chester<br>Runcorn | Chester/Mold |
| Chesterfield | Chesterfield<br>Worksop | Nottingham |
| Chichester | Chichester | Lewes |
| Colchester | Braintree<br>Colchester | Chelmsford |
| Coventry | Banbury<br>Coventry<br>Nuneaton<br>Stratford on Avon<br>Warwick | Birmingham |

| District Registry | Districts defined by reference to County Court Districts | Designated Trial Centre |
|---|---|---|
| Crewe | Crewe<br>Northwich | Chester/Mold |
| Croydon | Bromley<br>Croydon | London |
| Darlington | Darlington | Teesside |
| Derby | Burton upon Trent<br>Buxton<br>Derby | Nottingham |
| Dewsbury | Dewsbury | Leeds |
| Doncaster | Doncaster<br>Goole<br>Rotherham | Sheffield |
| Dudley | Dudley<br>Kidderminster<br>Stourbridge | Birmingham |
| Durham | Bishop Auckland<br>Durham | Newcastle |
| Eastbourne | Eastbourne | Lewes |
| Exeter | Exeter | Exeter |
| Gloucester | Gloucester | Bristol |
| Great Grimsby | Great Grimsby | Lincoln |
| Guildford | Aldershot and Farnham<br>Epsom<br>Guildford<br>Reigate | London |
| Halifax | Halifax | Leeds |
| Harlow | Bishop's Stortford<br>Harlow<br>Hertford | Chelmsford |
| Harrogate | Harrogate | Leeds |
| Hartlepool | Hartlepool | Teesside |
| Hastings | Hastings | Lewes |
| Haverfordwest | Haverfordwest | Swansea |
| Hereford | Hereford<br>Ludlow | Birmingham |
| Huddersfield | Huddersfield | Leeds |
| Ipswich | Ipswich | Norwich |
| Keighley | Keighley<br>Skipton | Leeds |
| Kendal | Kendal | Preston |
| King's Lynn | King's Lynn | Norwich |
| Kingston upon Hull | Kingston upon Hull | Leeds |
| Lancaster | Lancaster | Preston |
| Leeds (Chancery) | Leeds | Leeds |
| Leicester | Leicester<br>Loughborough<br>Melton Mowbray | Nottingham |
| Lincoln | Grantham<br>Lincoln<br>Newark | Lincoln |
| Liverpool (Chancery) | Liverpool | Liverpool |

| District Registry | Districts defined by reference to County Court Districts | Designated Trial Centre |
|---|---|---|
| LLANGEFNI | Llangefni | Caernarfon |
| LOWESTOFT | Lowestoft<br>Great Yarmouth | Norwich |
| LUTON | Hitchin<br>Luton | London |
| MACCLESFIELD | Macclesfield | Chester/Mold |
| MAIDSTONE | Maidstone | London |
| MANCHESTER (CHANCERY) | Altrincham<br>Manchester | Manchester |
| MANSFIELD | Mansfield | Nottingham |
| MEDWAY | Dartford<br>Gravesend<br>Medway | London |
| MERTHYR TYDFIL | Merthyr Tydfil | Cardiff |
| MIDDLESBROUGH | Middlesbrough | Teesside |
| MILTON KEYNES | Aylesbury<br>Milton Keynes | London |
| NEWCASTLE UPON TYNE (CHANCERY) | Alnwick<br>Berwick upon Tweed<br>Blyth<br>Morpeth<br>Newcastle upon Tyne | Newcastle |
| NEWPORT (SOUTH WALES) | Chepstow<br>Monmouth<br>Newport (Gwent)<br>Pontypool | Cardiff |
| NEWPORT (ISLE OF WIGHT) | Newport (Isle of Wight) | Winchester |
| NORTHAMPTON | Kettering<br>Northampton<br>Rugby<br>Wellingborough | London |
| NORWICH | Norwich | Norwich |
| NOTTINGHAM | Nottingham | Nottingham |
| OLDHAM | Oldham<br>Tameside | Manchester |
| OXFORD | Oxford | Oxford |
| PETERBOROUGH | Huntingdon<br>Peterborough | Nottingham |
| PLYMOUTH | Plymouth | Exeter |
| PONTEFRACT | Pontefract | Leeds |
| PONTYPRIDD | Aberdare<br>Caerphilly<br>Pontypridd | Cardiff |
| PORTSMOUTH | Portsmouth | Winchester |
| PRESTON (CHANCERY) | Chorley<br>Preston | Preston |
| READING | Newbury<br>Reading<br>Slough | London |
| RHYL | Rhyl | Chester/Mold |

| District Registry | Districts defined by reference to County Court Districts | Designated Trial Centre |
|---|---|---|
| Romford | Basildon<br>Grays Thurrock<br>Ilford<br>Romford | Chelmsford |
| St. Helens | St. Helens | Liverpool |
| Salford | Salford | Manchester |
| Salisbury | Salisbury | Winchester |
| Scarborough | Bridlington<br>Scarborough | Leeds |
| Scunthorpe | Scunthorpe | Lincoln |
| Sheffield | Sheffield | Sheffield |
| Shrewsbury | Shrewsbury<br>Telford | Stafford |
| Southampton | Southampton | Winchester |
| Southend-on-Sea | Southend-on-Sea | Chelmsford |
| Southport | Southport | Liverpool |
| South Shields | North Shields<br>South Shields | Newcastle |
| Stafford | Stafford | Stafford |
| Stockport | Stockport | Manchester |
| Stoke on Trent | Stoke on Trent | Stafford |
| Sunderland | Consett<br>Gateshead<br>Sunderland | Newcastle |
| Swansea | Swansea | Swansea |
| Swindon | Swindon | Bristol |
| Taunton | Taunton<br>Bridgewater | Bristol |
| Thanet | Thanet | London |
| Torquay and Newton Abbot | Torquay and Newton Abbot | Exeter |
| Truro | Bodmin<br>Penzance<br>Truro | Truro |
| Tunbridge Wells | Tunbridge Wells | Lewes |
| Wakefield | Wakefield | Leeds |
| Walsall | Lichfield<br>Tamworth<br>Walsall | Birmingham |
| Warrington | Warrington | Chester/Mold |
| Welshpool | Welshpool and Newtown | Chester/Mold |
| Weymouth | Weymouth | Winchester |
| Whitehaven | | |
| Wigan | Leigh<br>Wigan | Liverpool |
| Winchester | Winchester | Winchester |
| Wolverhampton | Wolverhampton | Stafford |
| Worcester | Evesham<br>Worcester | Birmingham |

| District Registry | Districts defined by reference to County Court Districts | Designated Trial Centre |
|---|---|---|
| WORTHING | Horsham<br>Worthing | Lewes |
| WREXHAM | Mold<br>Oswestry<br>Wrexham | Chester/Mold |
| YEOVIL | Yeovil | Exeter |
| YORK | York | Leeds |

AP–8 *Note* —Printed as amended by Civil Courts (Amendment No.2) Order 1993 (SI 1993/3120) and 1994 (SI 1994/1536); the Civil Courts (Amendment No.3) Order 1994 (SI 1994/2626); the Civil Courts (Amendment No.4) Order 1994 (SI 1994/2893); the Civil Courts (Amendment) Order 1995 (SI 1995/1897); the Civil Courts (Amendment No.2) Order 1995 (SI 1995/3173); the Civil Courts (Amendment) Order 1996 (SI 1996/68); the Civil Courts (Amendment) (No.2) Order 1995 (SI 1995/3173); the Civil Courts (Amendment) (No.2) Order 1996 (SI 1996/588); the Civil Courts (Amendment) (No.3) Order 1996 (SI 1996/2579); the Civil Courts (Amendment) Order 1997 (SI 1997/361) and the Civil Courts (Amendment) (No.2) Order 1997 (SI 1997/1085); the Civil Courts (Amendment) (No.2) Order 1998 (SI 1998/2910); the Civil Courts (Amendment) Order 1998 (SI 1998/1880); the Civil Courts (Amendment) Order 1999 (SI 1999/216).

## *County Court Directory*

AP–9 [Civil Courts Order 1983 (SI 1983/713), as amended, up to and including the Civil Courts (Amendment No.2) Order 1998 (SI 1998/2910).]

| *Court (Courts with Bankruptcy jurisdiction in bold)* | *Address* | *Contact Nos* |
|---|---|---|
| **ABERDARE AA** | The Court House<br>Cwmbach Road<br>Aberdare<br>Wales CF44 OJE | Tel: 01685 888575<br>Fax: 01685 883413<br>DX: 99600 Aberdare-2 |
| **ABERYSTWYTH AB** | Edleston House<br>Queens Road<br>Aberystwyth<br>Ceredigion SY23 2HP | Tel: 01970 636370<br>Fax: 01970 625985<br>DX: 99560<br>Aberystwyth-2 |
| ACCRINGTON AC | Bradshawgate House<br>1 Oak Street<br>Accrington<br>Lancashire BB5 1EQ | Tel: 01254 237490<br>Fax: 01254 393869<br>DX: 702645<br>Accrington-2 |
| ALDERSHOT & FARNHAM AF | 78–82 Victoria Rd<br>Aldershot<br>Hampshire GU11 1SS<br><br>Court House<br>84–86 Victoria Road<br>Aldershot<br>Hampshire GU11 1SS | Tel: 01252 796800<br>Fax: 01252 345705<br>DX: 98530 Aldershot-2 |
| ALTRINCHAM AL | Trafford Courthouse<br>Ashton Lane<br>Sale<br>Cheshire M33 7WX | Tel: 0161 975 4760<br>Fax: 0161 975 4761<br>DX: 708292 Sale-6 |

| *Court (Courts with Bankruptcy jurisdiction in bold)* | *Address* | *Contact Nos* |
|---|---|---|
| ASHFORD AS | Ground Floor<br>The Court House<br>Tufton Street<br>Ashford<br>Kent TN23 1QQ | Tel: 01233 632464<br>Fax: 01233 612786<br>DX: 98060 Ashford-3 (Kent) |
| **AYLESBURY AY** | Walton Street<br>Aylesbury<br>Buckinghamshire HP21 7QZ | Tel: 01296 554327<br>Fax: 01296 554320<br>DX: 97820 Aylesbury-10 |
| **BANBURY ZA** | The Court House<br>Warwick Road<br>Banbury<br>Oxfordshire OX16 2AW | Tel: 01295 452090<br>Fax: 01295 452051<br>DX: 701967 Banbury-2 |
| BARNET BT | Barnet Civil and Family Courts Centre<br>St Mary's Court<br>Regents Park Road<br>Finchley<br>London N3 1BQ | Tel: 020 8343 4272<br>Fax: 020 8343 1324<br>DX: 122570 Finchley (Church End) |
| **BARNSLEY BY** | 12 Regent Street<br>Barnsley<br>South Yorkshire S70 2EW | Tel: 01226 777550<br>Fax: 01226 779126<br>DX: 702080 Barnsley-3 |
| **BARNSTAPLE BP** | 7th Floor<br>Civic Centre<br>North Walk<br>Barnstaple<br>Devon EX31 1DY | Tel: 01271 372252<br>Fax: 01271 322968<br>DX: 98560 Barnstaple-2 |
| **BARROW-IN-FURNESS BW** | Barrow Law Courts<br>Abbey Road<br>Barrow in Furness<br>Cumbria LA14 5QX | Tel: 01229 840370<br>Fax: 01229 840371<br>DX: 65210 Barrow-in-Furness-2 |
| BASILDON BQ | Basildon Combined Court<br>The Gore<br>Basildon<br>Essex SS14 2BU | Tel: 01268 458000<br>Fax: 01268 458100<br>DX: 97633 Basildon–5<br>Email: e-filing@basildon.countycourt.gsi.gov.uk<br>Email: bailiffs@basildon.countycourt.gsi.gov.uk<br>Email: hearings@basildon.countycourt.gsi.gov.uk<br>Email: enquiries@basildon.countycourt.gsi.gov.uk |
| BASINGSTOKE BK | 3rd Floor<br>Grosvenor House<br>Basing View<br>Basingstoke<br>Hampshire RG21 4HG | Tel: 01256 318200<br>Fax: 01256 318225<br>DX: 98570 Basingstoke-3 |
| **BATH BA** | The Law Courts<br>North Parade Road<br>Bath<br>Somerset BA1 5AF | Tel: 01225 476730<br>Fax: 01225 476724<br>DX: 98580 Bath-2 |
| **BEDFORD BE** | Shire Hall<br>3 St Paul's Square<br>Bedford MK40 1SQ | Tel: 01234 319001<br>Fax: 01234 319026<br>DX: 97590 Bedford-11 |

| *Court (Courts with Bankruptcy jurisdiction in bold)* | *Address* | *Contact Nos* |
|---|---|---|
| **BIRKENHEAD BI** | 76 Hamilton Street<br>Birkenhead<br>Merseyside CH41 5EN | Tel: 0151 666 5800<br>Fax: 0151 666 5873<br>DX: 725000 Birken-head–10 |
| **BIRMINGHAM BM, ZB** | Birmingham Civil Justice Centre<br>The Priory Courts<br>33 Bull Street<br>Birmingham B4 6DS | Tel: 0121 681 4441<br>Fax: 0121 681 3001<br>DX: 701987 Birmingham-7<br>Email: e-filing@birmingham.countycourt.gsi.gov.uk<br>Email: bailiffs@birmingham.countycourt.gsi.gov.uk<br>Email: hearings@birmingham.countycourt.gsi.gov.uk<br>Email: enquiries@birmingham.countycourt.gsi.gov.uk<br>Email: birmingham.chancery@hmcourts-service.gsi.gov.uk<br>Email: birmingham.ccc@hmcourts-service.gsi.gov.uk<br>Email: birmingham.mercantile@hmcourts-service.gsi.gov.uk |
| BISHOP AUCKLAND ZH | Woodhouse Close<br>Bishop Auckland<br>Co Durham DL14 6LD | Tel: 01388 660251<br>Fax: 01388 660264<br>DX: 65100 Bishop Auckland-2 |
| **BLACKBURN BB** | 64 Victoria Street<br>Blackburn<br>Lancashire BB1 6DJ | Tel: 01254 299840<br>Fax: 01254 692712<br>DX: 702650 Blackburn-4 |
| **BLACKPOOL BC** | The Law Courts<br>Chapel Street<br>Blackpool<br>Lancashire FY1 5RJ | Tel: 01253 754020<br>Fax: 01253 295255<br>DX: 724900 Blackpool-10 |
| **BLACKWOOD ZJ** | Civil and Family Court<br>8 Hall Street<br>Blackwood<br>South Wales NP12 1NY | Tel: 01495 238200<br>Fax: 01495 238203<br>DX: 99470 Blackwood-2 |
| BODMIN BJ | The Law COurts<br>Launceston Road<br>Bodmin<br>Cornwall PL31 2AL | Tel: 01208 261580<br>Fax: 01208 77255<br>DX: 136846 Bodmin 2 |
| **BOLTON BL** | Bolton Combined Court Centre<br>The Law Courts<br>Blackhorse Street<br>Bolton<br>Greater Manchester BL1 1SU | Tel: 01204 392881<br>County Court Fax: 01204 373706<br>Crown Court Fax: 01204 303204<br>DX: 702610 Bolton-3 |

| *Court (Courts with Bankruptcy jurisdiction in bold)* | *Address* | *Contact Nos* |
|---|---|---|
| **BOSTON** | Boston Court House<br>55 Norfolk Street<br>Boston<br>Lincolnshire PE21 6PE | Tel: 01205 366080<br>Fax: 01205 311692<br>DX: 701922 Boston-2 |
| **BOURNEMOUTH BH** | The Courts of Justice<br>Deansleigh Road<br>Bournemouth<br>Dorset BH7 7DS | Tel: 01202 502800<br>Fax: 01202 502801<br>DX: 98420<br>Bournemouth-4<br>Email:<br>e-filing@bournemouth.<br>countycourt.gsi.gov.uk<br>Email:<br>bailiffs@bournemouth.<br>countycourt.gsi.gov.uk<br>Email:<br>hearings@bournemouth.<br>countycourt.gsi.gov.uk<br>Email:<br>enquiries@bournemouth.<br>countycourt.gsi.gov.uk<br>Email:<br>family@bournemouth.<br>countycourt.gsi.gov.uk |
| BOW BO | 96 Romford Road<br>Stratford<br>London E15 4EG | Tel: 020 8536 5200<br>Fax: 020 8503 1152<br>DX: 97490 Stratford<br>(London)-2 |
| **BRADFORD BD** | The Bradford Combined<br>Court Centre<br>Bradford Law Courts<br>Exchange Square<br>Drake Street<br>Bradford BD1 1JA | Tel: 01274 840274<br>Fax: 01274 840275<br>DX: 702083 Bradford-2 |
| BRECON ZM | Brecon Law Courts<br>Cambrian Way<br>Brecon<br>Powys LD3 7HR | Tel: 01874 622993<br>Fax: 01874 622441<br>DX:124340 Brecon 2 |
| BRENTFORD BF | Alexandra Road<br>High Street<br>Brentford<br>Middlesex TW8 0JJ | Tel: 020 8231 8940<br>Fax: 020 8568 2401<br>DX: 97840 Brentford-2 |
| **BRIDGEND BG** | The Law Courts<br>Sunnyside<br>Bridgend<br>South Wales CF31 4AJ | Tel: 01656 673833<br>Fax: 01656 647124<br>DX: 99750 Bridgend-2 |
| **BRIGHTON BN** | William Street<br>Brighton<br>East Sussex BN2 0RF | Tel: 01273 674421<br>Fax: 01273 602138<br>DX: 98070 Brighton-3 |
| Brighton County Court—Family Centre | 1 Edward Street<br>Brighton BN2 0JD | Tel: 01273 811333<br>Fax: 01273 607638<br>DX: 142600 Brighton-12 |
| **BRISTOL BS** | Lewins Place<br>Lewins Mead<br>Bristol BS1 2NR | Tel: 0117 910 6700<br>Fax: (General) 0117 910 6729<br>(Bailiffs) 0117 910 6730<br>(Diary Manager) 0117 910 6760<br>DX: 95903 Bristol-3 |

| *Court (Courts with Bankruptcy jurisdiction in bold)* | *Address* | *Contact Nos* |
|---|---|---|
| BROMLEY BR | Court House<br>College Road<br>Bromley<br>Kent BR1 3PX | Tel: 020 8290 9620<br>Fax: 020 8313 9624<br>DX: 98080 Bromley-2 |
| BULK CENTRE | County Court Bulk Centre<br>4th Floor<br>St Katharines House<br>21–27 St Katherines Street<br>Northampton NN1 2LH | DX: 702885 Northampton-7<br>Tel: 0845 408 5302<br>Fax: 0845 408 5304 |
| **BURNLEY** | The Law Courts<br>Hammerton Street<br>Burnley<br>Lancashire BB11 1XD | Tel: 01282 855300<br>Fax: 01282 414911<br>DX: 724940 Burnley-4 |
| **BURTON-UPON-TRENT BX** | 165 Station Street<br>Burton-upon-Trent<br>Staffordshire DE14 1BP | Tel: 01283 568241<br>Fax: 01283 517245<br>DX: 702044 Burton-upon-Trent-3 |
| BURY BU | Tenters Street<br>Bury<br>Greater Manchester<br>BL9 0HX | Tel: 0161 447 8699<br>Fax: 0161 763 4995<br>DX: 702615 Bury-2 |
| **BURY ST EDMUNDS BV** | Triton House<br>Entrance B<br>St Andrews Street North<br>Bury St Edmunds<br>Suffolk IP33 1TR | Tel: 0844 892 4000<br>Fax: 01284 702687<br>DX: 97640 Bury St Edmunds-3 |
| BUXTON ZQ | Peak Buildings<br>Terrace Road<br>Buxton<br>Derbyshire SK17 6DY | Tel: 01298 23734<br>Fax: 01298 28035<br>DX: 701970 Buxton-2 |
| **CAERNARFON CJ** | The Court House<br>Llanberis Road<br>Caernarfon<br>Gwynedd LL55 2DF | Tel: 01286 684600<br>Fax: 01286 678965<br>DX: 702483 Caernarfon-2 |
| **CAMBRIDGE CB** | 197 East Road<br>Cambridge<br>Cambridgeshire CB1 1BA | Tel: 01223 224500<br>Fax: 01223 224590<br>DX: 97650 Cambridge-3 |
| **CANTERBURY CT** | Canterbury Combined Court<br>The Law Courts<br>Chaucer Road<br>Canterbury<br>Kent CT1 1ZA | Tel: 01227 819200<br>Fax: 01227 819283<br>DX: 99710 Canterbury-3 |
| **CARDIFF CF** | Cardiff Civil Justice Centre<br>2 Park Street<br>Cardiff<br>Wales CF10 1ET | Tel: 029 2037 6400<br>Fax: 029 2037 6475<br>DX: 99500 Cardiff-6 |
| **CARLISLE CA** | Carlisle Combined Court Centre<br>Courts of Justice<br>Earl Street<br>Carlisle<br>Cumbria CA1 1DJ | Tel: 01228 882140<br>Fax: 01228 590588<br>DX: 65331 Carlisle-2 |

| *Court (Courts with Bankruptcy jurisdiction in bold)* | *Address* | *Contact Nos* |
|---|---|---|
| **CARMARTHEN CX** | The Old Vicarage<br>Picton Terrace<br>Carmarthen<br>Wales SA31 1BJ | Tel: 01267 228010<br>Fax: 01267 221844<br>DX: 99570<br>Carmarthen-2 |
| CENTRAL LONDON CL<br>Business List<br>*For Patents County Court see under "P"* | 13–14 Park Crescent<br>London W1B 1HT | Tel: 020 7917 5000<br>Fax: 020 7917 5014<br>DX: 97325 Regents Park-2 |
| **CHELMSFORD CM** | Chelmsford County and Family Proceedings Court<br>Priory Place<br>New London Road<br>Chelmsford<br>Essex CM2 0PP | Tel: 01245 264670<br>Fax: 01245 295395<br>DX: 97660 Chelmsford-4 |
| **CHELTENHAM CN**<br>For County Court administration office | Gloucestershire Family and Civil Courts<br>Kimbrose Way<br>Gloucester GL50 3PF | Tel: 01452 834991<br>Fax: 01452 834923<br>DX: 98660 Gloucester-5 |
| For the Courtroom for Cheltenham County Court | Cheltenham Court House<br>St Georges Road<br>Cheltenham<br>Gloucester GL1 2DE | |
| **CHESTER CH** | Chester Civil Justice Centre<br>Trident House<br>Little St John Street<br>Chester CH1 1SN | Tel: 01244 404200<br>Fax: 01244 404300<br>DX: 702460 Chester-4 |
| **CHESTERFIELD CD** | St Mary's Gate<br>Chesterfield<br>Derbyshire S41 7TD | Tel: 01246 501200<br>Fax: 01246 501205<br>DX: 703160 Chesterfield 3 |
| CHICHESTER CI | Chichester Combined Court Centre<br>The Law Courts<br>Southgate<br>Chichester<br>West Sussex PO19 1SX | Tel: 01243 520700<br>Fax: 01243 533756<br>DX: 97460 Chichester-2 |
| CHORLEY CY | 59 St Thomas's Road<br>Chorley<br>Lancashire PR7 1JE | Tel: 01257 262778<br>Fax: 01257 232843<br>DX: 702655 Chorley-3 |
| CLERKENWELL & SHOREDITCH Ck | The Gee Street Courthouse<br>29–41 Gee Street<br>London EC1V 3RE | Tel: 020 7250 7200<br>Fax: 020 7250 7250<br>DX: 121000 Shoreditch–2 |
| **COLCHESTER CO** | Falkland House<br>25 Southway<br>Colchester<br>Essex CO3 3EG | Tel: 0844 892 4000<br>Fax: 01206 717250<br>DX: 97670 Colchester-3 |
| CONSETT CZ | Victoria Road<br>Consett<br>Co Durham DH8 5AU | Tel: 01207 502854<br>Fax: 01207 582626<br>DX: 65106 Consett-2 |
| CONWY AND COLWYN CC | 36 Princes Drive<br>Colwyn Bay<br>Conwy LL29 8LA | Tel: 01492 530807<br>Fax: 01492 533591<br>DX: 702492 Colwyn Bay |

| *Court (Courts with Bankruptcy jurisdiction in bold)* | *Address* | *Contact Nos* |
|---|---|---|
| **COVENTRY CV** | Coventry Combined Court Centre<br>140 Much Park Street<br>Coventry<br>West Midlands CV1 2SN | Tel: 024 7653 6166<br>Fax: 024 7652 0443<br>DX: 701580 Coventry-5 |
| **CREWE CW** | The Law Courts<br>Civic Centre<br>Crewe<br>Cheshire CW1 2DP | Tel: 01270 539300<br>Fax: 01270 216344<br>DX: 702504 Crewe-2 |
| **CROYDON CR** | The Law Courts<br>Altyre Road<br>Croydon<br>Surrey CR9 5AB | Tel: 020 8410 4797<br>Fax: 020 8760 0432<br>DX: 97470 Croydon-6 |
| **DARLINGTON DL** | 4 Coniscliffe Road<br>Darlington<br>County Durham DL3 7RL | Tel: 01325 463224<br>Fax: 01325 362829<br>DX: 65109 Darlington-3 |
| DARTFORD DA | Court House<br>Home Gardens<br>Dartford<br>Kent DA1 1DX | Tel: 01322 627600<br>Fax: 01322 270902<br>DX: 98090 Dartford-2 |
| **DERBY DE** | Derby Combined Court Centre<br>The Morledge<br>Derby DE1 2XE | Tel: 01332 622600<br>Fax: 01332 622543<br>DX: 724060 Derby 21 |
| **DEWSBURY DW** | County Court House<br>Eightlands Road<br>Dewsbury<br>West Yorkshire WF13 2PE | Tel: 01924 466860<br>Fax: 01924 456419<br>DX: 702086 Dewsbury-2 |
| **DONCASTER DN** | 74 Waterdale<br>Doncaster<br>South Yorkshire DN1 3BT | Tel: 01302 381730<br>Fax: 01302 768090<br>DX: 702089 Doncaster-4 |
| **DUDLEY DD** | Harbour Buildings<br>Waterfront West<br>Brierley Hill<br>Dudley<br>West Midlands DY5 1LN | Tel: 01384 480799<br>Fax: 01384 482799<br>DX: 701949 Dudley-2 |
| **DURHAM DH** | Durham Civil and Family Centre<br>Green Lane<br>Old Elvet<br>Durham DH1 3RG | Tel: 0191 375 1840<br>Fax: 0191 375 1844<br>DX: 65115 Durham-5 |
| **EASTBOURNE EA** | The Law Courts<br>Old Orchard Road<br>Eastbourne<br>East Sussex BN21 4UN | Tel: 01323 727518<br>Fax: 01323 649372<br>DX: 98110 Eastbourne-2 |
| EDMONTON ED | Court House<br>59 Fore Street<br>Edmonton<br>London<br>N18 2TN | Tel: 020 8884 6500<br>Fax: 020 8803 0564<br>DX: 136686 Edmonton-3 |
| EPSOM EP | Epsom Point<br>84–90 East Street<br>Epsom<br>Surrey KT17 1DN | Tel: 01372 721801<br>Fax: 01372 734229<br>DX: 97850 Epsom-3 |

| *Court (Courts with Bankruptcy jurisdiction in bold)* | *Address* | *Contact Nos* |
|---|---|---|
| EVESHAM EV | 1st Floor<br>87 High Street<br>Evesham<br>Worcestershire WR11 4EE | Tel: 01386 442287<br>Fax: 01386 49203<br>DX: 70910 Evesham-3 |
| **EXETER EX** | Exeter Combined Court Centre<br>Southernhay Gardens<br>Exeter<br>Devon EX1 1UH | Tel: 01392 415300<br>Fax: 01392 415642<br>DX: 98440 Exeter-2 |
| GATESHEAD GH | Gateshead Law Courts<br>Warwick Street<br>Gateshead<br>Tyne and Wear NE8 1DT | Tel: 0191 477 5821<br>Fax: 0191 440 7209<br>DX: 742120 Gateshead-6 |
| **GLOUCESTER GL** | Gloucester Family and Civil Courts<br>Kimbrose Way<br>Gloucester GL1 2DE | Tel: 01452 834900<br>Fax: 01452 834923<br>DX: 98660 Gloucester-5 |
| GRANTHAM GR | Harlaxton Road<br>Grantham<br>Lincolnshire NG31 7SB | Tel: 01476 539030<br>Fax: 01476 539040<br>DX: 711100 Grantham-4 |
| **GREAT GRIMBSY GG** | Great Grimsby Combined Court Centre<br>Town Hall Square<br>Great Grimsby<br>Lincolnshire DN31 1HX | Tel: 01472 265200<br>Fax : 01472 265201<br>DX: 702007 Grimsby-3 |
| **GUILDFORD GU** | The Law Courts<br>Mary Road<br>Guildford<br>Surrey GU1 4PS | Tel: 01483 405300<br>Fax: 01483 300031<br>DX: 97860 Guildford-5 |
| **HALIFAX HX** | Prescott Street<br>Halifax<br>West Yorkshire HX1 2JJ | Tel: 01422 344700<br>Fax: 01422 360132<br>DX: 702095 Halifax-2 |
| HARLOW HA | Gate House<br>The High<br>Harlow<br>Essex CM20 1UW | Tel: 01279 443291<br>Fax: 01279 451110<br>DX: 97700 Harlow-2 |
| **HARROGATE HG** | 2 Victoria Avenue<br>Harrogate<br>North Yorkshire HG1 1EL | Tel: 01423 503921<br>Fax: 01423 528679<br>DX: 702098 Harrogate-3 |
| HARTLEPOOL HL | Law Courts<br>Victoria Road<br>Hartlepool<br>Cleveland TS24 8BS | Tel: 01429 268198<br>Fax: 01429 862550<br>DX: 65121 Hartlepool-2 |
| **HASTINGS HS** | The Law Courts<br>Bohemia Road<br>Hastings<br>East Sussex TN34 1QX | Tel: 01424 710280<br>Fax: 01424 421585<br>DX: 98150 Hastings-2 |
| **HAVERFORDWEST HV** | Penffynnon<br>Hawthorn Rise<br>Haverfordwest<br>Dyfed SA61 2AX | Tel: 01437 772060<br>Fax: 01437 769222<br>DX: 99610 Haverfordwest-2 |
| HAYWARDS HEATH HH | The Law Courts<br>Bolnore Road<br>Haywards Heath<br>West Sussex RH16 4BA | Tel: 01444 417611<br>Fax: 01444 472639<br>DX: 135596 Haywards Heath-6 |

| *Court (Courts with Bankruptcy jurisdiction in bold)* | *Address* | *Contact Nos* |
|---|---|---|
| **HEREFORD HR** | First Floor<br>Barclays Bank Chambers<br>1/3 Broad Street<br>Hereford<br>Herefordshire HR4 9BA | Tel: 01432 357233<br>Fax: 01432 352593<br>DX: 701904 Hereford-2 |
| **HERTFORD HF** | 4th Floor<br>Sovereign House<br>Hale Road<br>Hertford<br>Hertfordshire SG13 8DY | Tel: 0844 892 0550<br>Fax: 01992 501274<br>DX: 97710 Hertford-2 |
| HIGH WYCOMBE HW | The Law Courts<br>Ground Floor<br>Easton Street<br>High Wycombe<br>Buckinghamshire HP11 1LR | Tel: 0118 987 0508<br>Fax: 01494 651030<br>DX: 98010 Reading-6 |
| HITCHIN HI | Park House<br>1–12 Old Park Road<br>Hitchin<br>Hertfordshire SG5 2JR | Tel: 0844 8920550<br>Fax: 01462 445444<br>DX: 97720 Hitchin-2 |
| HORSHAM HM | The Law Courts<br>Hurst Road<br>Horsham<br>West Sussex RH12 2EU | Tel: 01403 252474<br>Fax: 01403 258844<br>DX: 98170 Horsham-2 |
| **HUDDERSFIELD HD** | Queensgate House<br>Queensgate<br>Huddersfield<br>West Yorkshire HD1 2RR | Tel: 01484 421043<br>Fax: 01484 426366<br>DX: 703013<br>Huddersfield-2 |
| HUNTINGDON HN<br>For County Court postal address see Peterborough Combined Courts Centre | Huntingdon Trial Centre<br>Walden Road<br>Huntingdon<br>Cambridgeshire PE29 3DW | Tel: 01733 349161<br>Fax: 01733 557348 |
| ILFORD IG | Buckingham Road<br>Ilford<br>Essex IG1 1TP | Tel: 020 8477 1920<br>Fax: 020 8553 2824<br>DX: 97510 Ilford-3 |
| **IPSWICH IP** | 8 Arcade Street<br>Ipswich<br>Suffolk IP1 1EJ | Tel: 01473 214256<br>Fax: 01473 251 797<br>DX: 97730 Ipswich-3 |
| KEIGHLEY KE | County Court House<br>North Street<br>Keighley<br>West Yorkshire BD21 3SH | Tel: 01535 602803<br>Fax: 01535 610549 |
| **KENDAL KN** | The Courthouse<br>Burneside Road<br>Kendal<br>Cumbria LA9 4NF | Tel: 01539 721218<br>Fax: 01539 733840<br>DX: 63450 Kendal-2 |
| KETTERING KG | Dryland Street<br>Kettering<br>Northamptonshire NN16 0BE | Tel: 01536 512471<br>Fax: 01536 416857<br>DX: 701886 Kettering-2 |
| **KIDDERMINSTER KI** | Comberton Place<br>Kidderminster<br>Worcestershire DY10 1QT | Tel: 01562 514000<br>Fax: 01562 514084 |

| *Court (Courts with Bankruptcy jurisdiction in bold)* | *Address* | *Contact Nos* |
|---|---|---|
| **KING'S LYNN KL** | Chequer House<br>12 King Street<br>King's Lynn<br>Norfolk PE30 1ES | Tel: 01553 772067<br>Fax: 01553 769824<br>DX: 97740 King's Lynn-2 |
| **KINGSTON-UPON-HULL KH** | Kingston-upon-Hull Combined Court Centre<br>Lowgate<br>Humberside<br>HU1 2EZ | Tel: 01482 586161<br>Fax: 01482 588527<br>DX: 703010 Hull-5 |
| **KINGSTON-UPON-THAMES KT** | St James Road<br>Kingston-upon-Thames<br>Surrey<br>KT1 2AD | Tel: 020 8972 8700<br>Fax: 020 8547 1426<br>DX: 97890 Kingston-upon-Thames-3 |
| LAMBETH LB | Court House<br>Cleaver Street<br>Kennington Road<br>London SE11 4DZ | Tel: 020 7091 4410<br>Fax: 020 7587 1951<br>DX: 145020 Kennington-2 |
| **LANCASTER LA** | 2nd Floor<br>Mitre House<br>Church Street<br>Lancaster<br>Lancashire LA1 1UZ | Tel: 01524 68112<br>Fax: 01524 846478<br>DX: 145880 Lancaster-2 |
| **LEEDS LS** | Leeds Combined Court Centre<br>The Courthouse<br>1 Oxford Row<br>Leeds<br>West Yorkshire LS1 3BG | Tel: 0113 306 2800<br>Issue–0113 306 2401<br>Listings–0113 306 2393<br>Enforcement–0113 306 2471<br>Family–0113 306 2394<br>Chancery–0113 306 2461<br>DX: 703016 Leeds-6 |
| **LEICESTER LE** | 90 Wellington Street<br>Leicester<br>Leicestershire LE1 6HG | Tel: 0116 222 5700<br>Fax: 0116 222 5763<br>DX: 17401 Leicester-3 |
| LEIGH LG | Darlington Street<br>Wigan<br>Greater Manchester WN1 1DW | Tel: 01942 405405<br>Fax: 01942 405459 |
| LEWES LW | Lewes Combined Court Centre<br>The Law Courts<br>High Street<br>Lewes<br>East Sussex BN7 1YB<br><br>Sittings also at:<br>Hove Trial Centre<br>The Court House<br>Lansdowne Rd<br>Hove BN3 3BN | Tel: 01273 480400<br>Fax: 01273 485269<br>DX: 97395 Lewes-4<br><br><br>Tel: 01273 229200<br>Fax: 01273 229229<br>DX 99402 Hove-3 |
| **LINCOLN LN** | 360 High Street<br>Lincoln LN5 7PS | Tel: 01522 551500<br>Fax: 01522 551551<br>DX: 703231 Lincoln-6 |
| **LIVERPOOL LV** | Liverpool Civil & Family Courts<br>35 Vernon Street<br>Liverpool L2 2BX | Tel: 0151 296 2200<br>Fax: 0151 296 2201<br>Bailiff fax: 0151 296 2608<br>DX: 702600 Liverpool-5 |

| *Court (Courts with Bankruptcy jurisdiction in bold)* | *Address* | *Contact Nos* |
|---|---|---|
| LLANELLI LI | 2nd Floor<br>Court Buildings<br>Town Hall Square<br>Llanelli<br>Carmarthenshire SA15 3AL | Tel: 01554 757171<br>Bailiff tel: 01554 776282<br>Fax: 01554 758079<br>DX: 99510 Llanelli-2 |
| LLANGEFNI LL | County Court Buildings<br>Glanhwfa Road<br>Llangefni<br>Anglesey LL77 7EN | Tel: 01248 750225<br>Fax: 01248 750778<br>DX: 702480 Llangefni-2 |
| LONDON | *See* BARNET<br>BOW<br>CENTRAL LONDON<br>CLERKENWELL<br>EDMONTON<br>LAMBETH<br>MAYOR'S AND CITY OF LONDON<br>SHOREDITCH<br>WANDSWORTH<br>WEST LONDON<br>WILLESDEN<br>WOOLWICH | |
| LOWESTOFT LO | Old Nelson Street<br>Lowestoft<br>Suffolk NR32 1HJ | Tel: 01502 501060<br>Fax: 01502 513875<br>DX: 97750 Lowestoft-2 |
| LUDLOW LD | Guild Hall<br>Mill Street<br>Ludlow<br>Shropshire SY8 1BB | (All enquiries to Telford County Court)<br>DX: 702013 Ludlow-2 |
| **LUTON LU** | 2nd Floor<br>Cresta House<br>Alma Street<br>Luton<br>Bedfordshire LU1 2PU | Tel: 01582 506700<br>Fax: 01582 506701<br>DX: 97760 Luton-4 |
| **MACCLESFIELD MC** | 2nd Floor<br>Silk House<br>Park Green<br>Macclesfield<br>Cheshire SK11 7NA | Tel: 01625 412800<br>Fax: 01625 501262<br>DX: 702498 Macclesfield-3 |
| **MAIDSTONE MS** | Maidstone Combined Court Centre<br>The Law Courts<br>Barker Road<br>Maidstone<br>Kent ME16 8EQ | Tel: 01622 202000<br>Fax: 01622 202002 (County)<br>Fax: 01622 202001 (Crown)<br>DX: 130065 Maidstone-7 |
| **MANCHESTER** | Manchester Civil Justice Centre<br>1 Bridge Street West<br>Manchester<br>Greater Manchester M60 9DJ | Tel: 0161 240 5000<br>Fax: 0161 240 5050<br>Bailiffs fax: 0161 240 5480<br>DX: 724783 Manchester-44 |
| MANSFIELD MF | Beech House<br>58 Commercial Gate<br>Mansfield<br>Nottinghamshire NG18 1EU | Tel: 01623 656406<br>Fax: 01623 626561<br>DX: 702180 Mansfield-3 |

| *Court (Courts with Bankruptcy jurisdiction in bold)* | *Address* | *Contact Nos* |
|---|---|---|
| MAYOR'S AND CITY OF LONDON MY | Guildhall Buildings<br>Basinghall Street<br>London EC2V 5AR | Tel: 020 77965400<br>Fax: 020 77965424<br>DX: 97520 Moorgate-EC2 |
| **MEDWAY ME** | Anchorage House<br>47–67 High Street<br>Chatham<br>Kent ME4 4DW | Tel: 01634 810720<br>Fax: 01634 811332<br>DX: 98180 Chatham-4 |
| MELTON MOWBRAY MM | The Court House<br>Norman Way<br>Melton Mowbray<br>Leicestershire LE13 1NH | Tel: 01664 485100<br>Fax: 01664 501869<br>DX: 701937 Melton Mowbray-2 |
| **MERTHYR TYDFIL MT** | Merthyr Tydfil Combined Court Centre<br>The Law Courts<br>Glebeland Place<br>Merthyr Tydfil<br>Mid Glamorgan CF47 8BH | Tel: 01685 727600<br>Fax: 01685 727703<br>DX: 99582 Merthyr Tydfil-2 |
| **MIDDLESBROUGH MB** | Middlesborough County Court at<br>Teeside Combined Court<br>The Law Courts<br>Russell Street<br>Middlesbrough TS1 2AE | Tel: 01642 340000<br>Fax: 01642 340002<br>DX: 65152 Middlesbrough-2 |
| **MILTON KEYNES MK** | 351 Silbury Boulevard (Rear)<br>Witan Gate East<br>Central Milton Keynes<br>Buckinghamshire<br>MK9 2DT | Tel: 01908 302800<br>Fax: 01908 230063<br>DX: 136266 Milton Keynes 6 |
| MOLD ML | Law Courts<br>Civic Centre<br>Mold<br>Flintshire CH7 1AE | Tel: 01352 707330<br>Fax: 01352 707333<br>DX: 702521 Mold-2 |
| MORPETH and BERWICK MP | Fountain House<br>Newmarket<br>Morpeth<br>Northumberland NE61 1LA | Tel: 01670 512221<br>Fax: 01670 504188<br>DX: 65124 Morpeth-2 |
| **NEATH & PORT TALBOT NT** | Forster Road<br>Neath<br>South Wales SA11 3BN | Tel: 01639 642267<br>Fax: 01639 633505<br>DX: 99550 Neath-2 |
| NELSON NL | Phoenix Chambers<br>9/13 Holme Street<br>Nelson<br>Lancashire BB9 9SU | Tel: 01282 601177<br>Fax: 01282 619557<br>DX: 702560 Nelson-2 |
| NEWARK NK | Newark Court House<br>Beech House<br>58 Commercial Gate<br>Mansfield<br>Nottinghamshire NG18 1EU | Tel: 01636 656406<br>DX: 702180 Mansfield-3 |
| **NEWBURY NB** | The Court House<br>Mill Lane<br>Newbury<br>Berkshire RG14 5QS | Tel: 01635 642210<br>Fax: 01635 529580<br>DX: 30816 Newbury-1 |

| *Court (Courts with Bankruptcy jurisdiction in bold)* | *Address* | *Contact Nos* |
|---|---|---|
| **NEWCASTLE UPON TYNE NE** | Newcastle upon Tyne<br>Combined Court Centre<br>The Law Courts<br>Quayside<br>Newcastle upon Tyne<br>NE1 3LA | Tel: 0191 201 2000<br>Fax: 0191 201 2001<br>DX: 65127 Newcastle-upon-Tyne-2 |
| **NEWPORT (GWENT) NP** | Clarence House<br>5th Floor<br>Clarence Place<br>Newport<br>Gwent<br>South Wales NP19 7AA<br><br>Court House<br>The Magistrates' Court<br>Pentonville<br>Newport<br>Gwent NP20 5HZ | Tel: 01633 245040<br>Fax: 01633 245041<br>Tel: 01633 258920<br>(telephone conference arrangements)<br>Tel: 01633 258940<br>(video conference arrangements)<br>DX: 99480 Newport (South Wales)-4 |
| **NEWPORT (I.O.W.) NI** | 1 Quay Street<br>Newport<br>Isle of Wight PO30 5YT | Tel: 01983 535100<br>Fax: 01983 821039<br>DX: 98460 Newport-IW2 |
| **NORTHAMPTON NN** | Northampton Combined Court<br>85–87 Lady's Lane<br>Northampton NN1 3HQ<br>N.B. See Bulk Centre for bulk issue | Tel: 01604 470400<br>Fax: 01604 232398<br>DX: 725380<br>Northampton-21 |
| NORTH SHIELDS NS | Kings Court<br>Earl Grey Way<br>Royal Quays<br>North Shields NE29 6AR | Tel: 0191 298 2339<br>Fax: 0191 298 2337<br>DX: 65137 North Shields-2 |
| NORTHWICH MAGISTRATES' AND COUNTY COURT HN | The Court House<br>Chester Way<br>Northwich<br>Cheshire CW9 5ES | Tel: 01606 338508<br>Fax: 01606 48740<br>DX: 702515<br>Northwich-3 |
| **NORWICH NR** | Norwich Combined Court<br>The Law Courts<br>Bishopgate<br>Norwich<br>Norfolk NR3 1UR | Tel: 01603 728200<br>Fax: 01603 760863<br>DX: 97385 Norwich-5 |
| **NOTTINGHAM NG** | 60 Canal Street<br>Nottingham<br>NG1 7EJ | Tel: 0115 910 3500<br>Fax: 0115 910 3510<br>DX: 702380<br>Nottingham-7 |
| NUNEATON NU | Warwickshire Justice Centre<br>PO Box 3878<br>Vicarage Street<br>Nuneaton<br>Warwickshire CV11 4JJ | Tel: 024 7648 2970<br>Fax: 024 7635 2835<br>DX: 701940 Nuneaton-2 |
| **OLDHAM OL** | New Radcliffe Street<br>Oldham<br>Greater Manchester<br>OL1 1NL | Tel: 0161 290 4200<br>Fax: 0161 290 4222<br>Bailiff: 0161 290 4229<br>DX: 702595 Oldham-2 |

| *Court (Courts with Bankruptcy jurisdiction in bold)* | *Address* | *Contact Nos* |
|---|---|---|
| **OSWESTRY OS** | The Court House<br>Holbache Road<br>Oswestry<br>Shropshire SY11 1RP | Tel: 01691 652127<br>Fax: 01691 658902<br>Tel: 01952 238325<br>(Bailiff's office)<br>DX: 701958 Oswestry-2 |
| **OXFORD OX** | Oxford Combined Court Centre<br>St Aldates<br>Oxford<br>Oxfordshire OX1 1TL | Tel: 01865 264200<br>Fax: 01865 790773<br>DX: 96450 Oxford-4 |
| PATENTS | Patents County Court<br>15–25 Breams Buildings<br>London EC4A 1DZ | Tel: 020 7073 4251 (for enquiries re. existing cases)<br>Tel: 020 7917 7821<br>020 7917 7953 (for general enquiries<br>Tel: 020 7947 7717<br>Fax: 020 7947 7345<br>(Listing) |
| PENRITH PN | The Court House<br>Lowther Terrace<br>Penrith<br>Cumbria CA11 7QL | Tel: 01768 862535<br>Fax: 01768 899700<br>DX: 65207 Penrith |
| PENZANCE PZ | Trevear<br>Alverton Terrace<br>Penzance<br>Cornwall TR18 4GH | Tel: 01872 267460<br>Fax: 01872 222348<br>DX: 135396 Truro-2 |
| **PETERBOROUGH PE** | Peterborough Combined Courts Centre<br>Crown Buildings<br>Rivergate<br>Peterborough<br>Cambridgeshire PE1 1EJ | Tel: 01733 349161<br>Fax: 01733 557348<br>DX: 702302<br>Peterborough-8 |
| **PLYMOUTH PL** | Plymouth Combined Court<br>The Law Courts<br>10 Armada Way<br>Plymouth<br>Devon PL1 2ER | Tel: 01752 677400<br>Fax: 01752 208286<br>(Enforcement)/01752 677455 (Civil)<br>DX: 98470 Plymouth-7 |
| PONTEFRACT PF | Horsefair House<br>Horsefair<br>Pontefract<br>West Yorkshire WF8 1RJ | Tel: 01977 702357<br>Fax: 01977 600204<br>DX: 703022 Pontefract-2 |
| PONTYPOOL PP | Park Road<br>Riverside<br>Pontypool<br>Torfaen NP4 6NZ | Tel: 01495 762248<br>Fax: 01495 762467<br>DX: 117500 Pontypool 2 |
| **PONTYPRIDD PD** | The Court House<br>Courthouse Street<br>Pontypridd<br>Rhondda Cynon Taf<br>CF37 1JR | Tel: 01443 490800<br>Fax: 01443 480305<br>DX: 99620 Pontypridd-2 |
| POOLE PH | The Law Courts<br>Civic Centre<br>Park Road<br>Poole<br>Dorset BH15 2NS | Tel: 01202 741150<br>Fax: 01202 747245<br>DX: 98700 Poole-4 |

| *Court (Courts with Bankruptcy jurisdiction in bold)* | *Address* | *Contact Nos* |
|---|---|---|
| **PORTSMOUTH PO** | Portsmouth Combined Court<br>The Courts of Justice<br>Winston Churchill Avenue<br>Portsmouth<br>Hampshire<br>PO1 2EB | Tel: 023 9289 3000<br>Fax: 023 9282 6385<br>DX: 98490 Portsmouth 5 |
| **PRESTON PR** | The Law Courts<br>Ring Way<br>Preston<br>Lancashire PR1 2LL | Tel: (General): 01772 844700<br>Tel: (Bailiffs): 01772 844880<br>Fax: (County Court): 01772 844710<br>DX: 702660 Preston-5 |
| RAWTENSTALL RA | 1 Grange Street<br>Rawtenstall<br>Lancashire BB4 7RT | Tel: 01706 214614<br>Fax: 01706 219814<br>DX: 702565 Rawtenstall-2 |
| **READING RG** | 160–163 Friar Street<br>Reading<br>Berkshire RG1 1HE | Tel: 0118 987 0500<br>Fax: 0118 987 0555<br>DX: 98010 Reading-6 |
| REDDITCH RD | 13 Church Road<br>Redditch<br>Worcestershire B97 4AB | Tel: 01527 67822<br>Fax: 01527 65791<br>DX: 701880 Redditch-2 |
| REIGATE RH | Law Courts<br>Hatchlends Rd<br>Redhill<br>Surrey RH1 6BL | Tel: 01737 763637<br>Fax: 01737 766917<br>DX: 98020 Redhill West |
| **RHYL RI** | The Court House<br>Clwyd Street<br>Rhyl<br>Denbighshire LL18 3LA | Tel: 01745 352940<br>Fax: 01745 336726<br>DX: 702489 Rhyl-2 |
| **ROMFORD RM** | 2a Oaklands Avenue<br>Romford<br>Essex RM1 4DP | Tel: 01708 775353<br>Fax: 01708 756653<br>DX: 97530 Romford-2 |
| ROTHERHAM RT | Rotherham Law Courts<br>The Statutes<br>PO Box 15<br>Rotherham<br>South Yorkshire S60 1YW | Tel: 01709 839339<br>Fax: 01709 370082<br>DX: 703025 Rotherham-4 |
| RUGBY RU | The New Courthouse<br>Newbold Road<br>Rugby<br>Warwickshire CV21 2LQ | Tel: 01788 542543<br>Fax: 01788 866004<br>DX: 701934 Rugby-2 |
| **ST ALBANS SI** | The Court Building<br>Bricket Road<br>St Albans<br>Hertfordshire AL13 3JW | Tel: 0844 892 0550<br>Fax: 01727 753234<br>DX: 97770 St Albans-2 |
| St HELENS HW | 1st Floor<br>Rexmore House<br>Cotham Street<br>St Helens<br>Merseyside WA10 1SE | Tel: 01744 27544<br>Fax: 01744 20484<br>DX: 725020 St Helens-4 |

| Court (Courts with Bankruptcy jurisdiction in bold) | Address | Contact Nos |
|---|---|---|
| **SALFORD SF DB** | Prince William House<br>Peel Cross Road (off Eccles New Road)<br>Salford<br>Greater Manchester M5 4RR | Tel: 0161 745 7511<br>Fax: 0161 745 7202<br>DX: 702630 Salford-5 |
| **SALISBURY LAW COURT SB** | Wilton Road<br>Salisbury<br>Wiltshire SP2 7EP | Tel: 01722 345200<br>Fax: 01722 345201<br>DX: 98500 Salisbury-2 |
| **SCARBOROUGH SZ** | Pavilion House<br>Valley Bridge Rd<br>Scarborough<br>North Yorkshire<br>YO11 2JS | Tel: 01723 366361<br>Fax: 01723 501992<br>DX: 65140<br>Scarborough-2 |
| **SCUNTHORPE SC** | Scunthorpe Court Centre<br>Laneham Street<br>Scunthorpe<br>Lincolnshire DN15 6JY | Tel: 01724 281100<br>Fax: 01724 281890<br>DX: 742212<br>Scunthorpe-10 |
| **SHEFFIELD SE** | Sheffield Combined Court Centre<br>The Law Courts<br>50 West Bar<br>Sheffield<br>South Yorkshire S3 8PH | Tel: 0114 281 2400<br>Fax: 0114 281 2425<br>DX: 703028 Sheffield-6 |
| **SHREWSBURY SY** | 4th Floor Cambrian Business Centre<br>Chester Street<br>Shrewsbury<br>Shropshire SY1 1NA | Tel: 01743 289069<br>Fax: 01743 237954<br>DX: 702047<br>Shrewsbury-3 |
| SKEGNESS | 55 Norfolk Street<br>Boston<br>Lincolnshire PE21 6PE | Tel: 01205 366080<br>Fax: 01205 311692<br>DX: 701922 Boston-2 |
| SKIPTON SP | The Court House<br>Otley Street<br>Skipton<br>North Yorkshire BD23 1RH | Tel: 01756 692650<br>Fax: 01756 692655<br>DX: 703031 Skipton-2 |
| **SLOUGH** | The Law Courts<br>Windsor Road<br>Slough<br>Berkshire SL1 2HE | Tel: 01753 690300<br>Fax: 01753 575990<br>DX: 98030 Slough-3 |
| **SOUTHAMPTON SO** | Southampton Combined Court Centre<br>The Courts of Justice<br>London Road<br>Southampton<br>Hampshire SO15 2XQ | Tel: 023 8021 3200<br>Fax: 023 8021 3222/023 8021 3227 (Bailiffs)<br>DX: 111000<br>Southampton-11 |
| **SOUTHEND SS** | Tylers House<br>Tylers Avenue<br>Southend<br>Essex SS1 2AW | Tel: 01702 601991<br>Fax: 01702 603090<br>DX: 97780 Southend-on-Sea-2 |
| SOUTHPORT DC | Duke's House<br>34 Hoghton Street<br>Southport<br>Merseyside PR9 0PU | Tel: 01704 531541<br>Fax: 01704 542487<br>DX: 702580 Southport-2 |

| *Court (Courts with Bankruptcy jurisdiction in bold)* | *Address* | *Contact Nos* |
|---|---|---|
| SOUTH SHIELDS SH | Millbank<br>Secretan Way<br>South Shields<br>Tyne & Wear NE33 1RG | Tel: 0191 456 3343<br>Fax: 0191 427 9503<br>DX: 65143 South Shields-3 |
| **STAFFORD ST** | Stafford Combined Court Centre<br>Victoria Square<br>Stafford<br>Staffordshire ST16 2QQ | Tel: 01785 610730<br>Fax: 01785 213250<br>DX: 703190 Stafford-4 |
| STAINES SM | The Law Courts<br>Knowle Green<br>Staines<br>Middlesex TW18 1XH | Tel: 01784 459175<br>Fax: 01784 460176<br>DX: 98040 Staines-2 |
| **STOCKPORT SK** | 5th Floor<br>Heron House<br>Wellington Street<br>Stockport<br>Greater Manchester SK1 3DJ | Tel: 0161 474 7707<br>Fax: 0161 476 3129<br>DX: 702620 Stockport-4 |
| **STOKE-ON-TRENT SQ** | Stoke on Trent Combined Court<br>Bethesda Street<br>Hanley<br>Stoke-on-Trent<br>Staffordshire ST1 3BP | Tel: 01782 854000<br>Fax: 01782 854046<br>DX: 703360 Hanley-3 |
| **STOURBRIDGE SX** | 7 Hagley Road<br>Stourbridge<br>West Midlands DY8 1QL | Tel: 01384 394232<br>Fax: 01384 441736<br>DX: 701889 Stourbridge-2 |
| STRATFORD-UPON-AVON SV | 5 Elm Court<br>Arden Street<br>Stratford-upon-Avon<br>Warwickshire CV37 6PA | Tel: 01789 293056<br>Fax: 01789 414973<br>DX: 701998 Stratford-u-Avon-3 |
| **SUNDERLAND SR** | 44 John Street<br>Sunderland<br>Tyne and Wear SR1 1RB | Tel: 0191 5680750<br>Fax: 0191 514 3028<br>DX: 65149 Sunderland-2 |
| **SWANSEA SA** | Swansea Civil Justice Centre<br>Caravella House<br>Quay West<br>Quay Street<br>Swansea<br>West Glamorgan SA1 1SP | Tel: 01792 485800<br>Fax: 01792 485810<br>DX: 99740 Swansea-5 |
| **SWINDON SN** | Swindon Combined Courts<br>The Law Courts<br>Islington Street<br>Swindon<br>Wiltshire SN1 2HG | Tel: 01793 690500 (Switchboard)<br>Fax: 01793 690555<br>01793 690514 (Listing)<br>DX: 98430 Swindon-5 |
| **TAMESIDE TS** | PO Box 166<br>Henry Square<br>Ashton-under-Lyne<br>Lancashire OL6 7TP | Tel: 0161 331 5614<br>Fax: 0161 331 5649<br>DX: 702625 Ashton-under-Lyne 2 |
| TAMWORTH TM | The Court House<br>Spinning School Lane<br>Tamworth<br>Staffordshire B79 7AN | Tel: 01827 305910<br>Fax: 01827 303823<br>DX: 702016 Tamworth 2 |

| *Court (Courts with Bankruptcy jurisdiction in bold)* | *Address* | *Contact Nos* |
|---|---|---|
| **TAUNTON TA** | Shire Hall<br>Taunton<br>Somerset TA1 4EU | Tel: 01823 281110<br>Fax: 01823 351337<br>DX: 98410 Taunton-2 |
| TEESSIDE | *See* MIDDLESBROUGH | |
| TELFORD TF | Telford Square<br>Malinsgate<br>Town Centre<br>Telford<br>Shropshire TF3 4JP | Tel: 01952 238280<br>Fax: 01952 291601<br>DX: 701976 Telford-3 |
| THANET TT | The Court House<br>2nd Floor<br>Cecil Square<br>Margate<br>Kent CT9 1RL | Tel: 01843 221722<br>Fax: 01843 222730<br>DX: 98210 Cliftonville-2 |
| **TORQUAY TQ** | Torquay & Newton Abbott County Court<br>The Willows<br>Nicholson Road<br>Torquay TQ2 7AZ | Tel: 01803 616791<br>Fax: 01803 616795<br>DX: 98740 Torquay-4 |
| TROWBRIDGE TW | Ground Floor<br>Clark's Mill<br>Stallard Street<br>Trowbridge<br>Wiltshire BA14 8DB | Tel: 01225 752101<br>Fax: 01225 776638<br>DX: 98750<br>Trowbridge-2 |
| **TRURO TR** | The Courts of Justice<br>Edward Street<br>Truro<br>Cornwall TR1 2PB | Tel: 01872 267460<br>Fax: 01872 222348<br>DX: 135396 Truro-2 |
| **TUNBRIDGE WELLS TN** | Merevale House<br>42/46 London Road<br>Tunbridge Wells<br>Kent TN1 1DP | Tel: 01892 700150<br>Fax: 01892 513676<br>DX: 98220 Tunbridge Wells-3 |
| UXBRIDGE UB | 501 Uxbridge Road<br>Hayes<br>Middlesex UB4 8HL | Tel: 020 8756 3520<br>Fax: 020 85612020<br>DX: 44658 Hayes (Middlesex) |
| **WAKEFIELD WF** | Crown House<br>127 Kirkgate<br>Wakefield<br>West Yorkshire WF1 1JW | Tel: 01924 370268<br>Fax: 01924 200818<br>DX: 703040 Wakefield-3 |
| **WALSALL WJ** | Walsall Hearing Centre<br>Bridge House<br>Bridge Street<br>Walsall<br>West Midlands WS1 1JQ | General enquiries:<br>Tel: 01922 728855<br>Fax: 01922 728891<br>DX: 701943 Walsall-2<br>Email: enquiries@walsall countycourt.gsi.gov.uk<br><br>Family enquiries:<br>Email: family@walsall countycourt.gsi.gov.uk<br><br>Bailiffs enquiries:<br>Email: bailiffs@walsall countycourt.gsi.gov.uk<br><br>Listing enquiries:<br>Email: hearings@walsall countycourt.gsi.gov.uk |

| *Court (Courts with Bankruptcy jurisdiction in bold)* | *Address* | *Contact Nos* |
|---|---|---|
| WANDSWORTH WT | 76/78 Upper Richmond Road<br>Putney<br>London SW15 2SU | Tel: 020 8333 4351<br>Fax: 020 8877 9854<br>DX: 97540 Putney-2 |
| **WARRINGTON and RUNCORN COUNTY COURTS WA** | Legh Street<br>Warrington<br>Cheshire WA1 1UR | Tel: 01925 256700<br>Fax: 01925 413335<br>DX: 702501 Warrington-3 |
| **WARWICK WW** | Warwick Combined Court Centre<br>Northgate<br>South Side<br>Warwick CV34 4RB | Tel: 01926 492276<br>Fax: 01926 411855<br>DX: 701964 Warwick-2 |
| WATFORD WD | 3rd Floor<br>Cassiobury House<br>11/19 Station Road<br>Watford<br>Hertfordshire WD17 1EZ | Tel: 01923 699400/ 01923 699401<br>Fax: 01923 251317<br>DX: 122740 Watford-5 |
| WELLINGBOROUGH WE | Lothersdale House<br>West Villa Road<br>Wellingborough<br>Northamptonshire NN8 4NF | Tel: 01933 226168<br>Fax: 01933 272977<br>DX: 701883 Wellingborough-2 |
| **WELSHPOOL AND NEWTOWN WP** | The Mansion House<br>24 Severn Street<br>Welshpool<br>Powys SY21 7UX | Tel: 01938 552004<br>Fax: 01938 555395<br>DX: 702524 Welshpool-2 |
| WEST LONDON WL | West London Courthouse<br>Magistrates, County and Youth Courts<br>181 Talgarth Road<br>Hammersmith<br>London W6 8DN | Tel: 020 8600 6868<br>Fax: 020 8600 6860<br>DX: 97550 Hammersmith 8 |
| WESTON-SUPER-MARE WM | North Somerset Courthouse<br>The Hedges<br>St Georges<br>Weston-Super-Mare<br>Avon BS22 7BB | Tel: 01934 528686<br>Fax: 01934 528594<br>DX: 152361 Weston-Super-Mare-5 |
| **WEYMOUTH AND DORCHESTER WY** | Weymouth and Dorchester Combined Court Centre<br>Westwey House<br>Westwey Road<br>Weymouth<br>Dorset DT4 8TE | Tel: 01305 752510<br>Fax: 01305 788293<br>DX: 98820 Weymouth-3 |
| WHITEHAVEN WH | Old Town Hall<br>Duke Street<br>Whitehaven<br>Cumbria CA28 7NU | Tel: 01946 67788<br>Fax: 01946 691219<br>DX: 63990 Whitehaven-2 |
| **WIGAN WN** | Wigan and Leigh Courthouse<br>Darlington Street<br>Wigan<br>Greater Manchester WN1 1DW | Tel: 01942 405405<br>Fax: 01942 405499<br>DX: 724820 Wigan-9 |

| *Court (Courts with Bankruptcy jurisdiction in bold)* | *Address* | *Contact Nos* |
|---|---|---|
| WILLESDEN WI | 9 Acton Lane<br>Harlesden<br>London NW10 8SB | Tel: 020 8963 8200<br>Fax: 020 8453 0946<br>DX: 97560 Harlesden-2 |
| **WINCHESTER WC** | Winchester Combined Court Centre<br>The Law Courts<br>Winchester<br>Hampshire SO23 9EL | Tel: 01962 814100<br>Fax: 01962 853821<br>DX: 98520 Winchester-3 |
| **WOLVERHAMPTON WV** | Wolverhampton Combined Court Centre<br>Pipers Row<br>Wolverhampton<br>West Midlands WV1 3LQ | Tel: 01902 481000<br>Fax: 01902 481001<br>DX: 702019 Wolverhampton-4 |
| WOOLWICH WO | The Court House<br>165 Powis Street<br>Woolwich<br>London SE18 6JW | Tel: 020 8301 8700<br>Fax: 020 8316 4842<br>DX: 123450 Woolwich-8 |
| **WORCESTER WR** | Worchester Combined Court<br>The Shirehall<br>Foregate Street<br>Worcester WR1 1EQ | Tel: 01905 730807<br>Fax: 01905 730801<br>DX: 721120 Worcester-11 |
| WORKSOP WS | 30 Potter Street<br>Worksop<br>Nottinghamshire S80 2AJ | Tel: 01623 656406<br>Fax: 01623 626561<br>DX: 743240 Worksop-4 |
| WORTHING WG | The Law Courts<br>Christchurch Road<br>Worthing<br>Sussex BN11 1JD | Tel: 01903 221920<br>Fax: 01903 235559<br>DX: 98230 Worthing-4 |
| **WREXHAM WX** | 2nd Floor Crown Buildings<br>31 Chester Street<br>Wrexham<br>Denbighshire LL13 8XN | Tel: 01978 296140<br>Fax: 01978 290677<br>DX: 721921 Wrexham-4 |
| **YEOVIL YE** | 22 Hendford<br>Yeovil<br>Somerset BA20 2QD | Tel: 01935 382150<br>Fax: 01935 410004<br>DX: 98830 Yeovil-2 |
| **YORK YO** | Piccadilly House<br>55 Piccadilly<br>York<br>North Yorkshire YO1 9WL | Tel: 01904 688550<br>Fax: 01904 679963<br>DX: 65165 York-4 |

## *Directory of High Court Enforcement Officers—Listed Alphabetically by Postal District*

**For the "Directory of High Court Enforcement Officers—Listed Alphabetically by Postal District" see paragraph AP–11+ on White Book on Westlaw UK or the Civil Procedure CD.** **AP–10**

## *Directory of High Court Enforcement Officers—Addresses and Contact Details for Appointed Enforcement Officers*

**For the "Directory of High Court Enforcement Officers—Addresses and Contact Details for Appointed Enforcement Officers"see paragraph AP–13+ on White Book on Westlaw UK or the Civil Procedure CD.** **AP–12**

# INDEX

LEGAL TAXONOMY

FROM SWEET & MAXWELL

This index has been prepared using Sweet and Maxwell's Legal Taxonomy. Main index entries conform to keyworks provided by the Legal Taxonomy except where references to specific documents or non-standard terms (denoted by quotation marks) have been included. These keywords provide a means of identifying similar concepts in other Sweet & Maxwell publications and online services to which keywords from the Legal Taxonomy have been applied. Readers may find some minor differences between terms used in the text and those which appear in the index. Suggestions to *taxonomy@sweetandmaxwell.co.uk*

**(All references are to paragraph number)**



***Paragraph numbers marked "+" denote electronic content; those within [...] refer to Volume 2***

*Paragraph numbers marked "+" denote electronic content; those within [...] refer to Volume 2*

INDEX

***Paragraph numbers marked "+" denote electronic content; those within [...] refer to Volume 2***

***Paragraph numbers marked "+" denote electronic content; those within [...] refer to Volume 2***

***Paragraph numbers marked "+" denote electronic content; those within [...] refer to Volume 2***

***Paragraph numbers marked "+" denote electronic content; those within [...] refer to Volume 2***

***Paragraph numbers marked "+" denote electronic content; those within [...] refer to Volume 2***

***Paragraph numbers marked "+" denote electronic content; those within [...] refer to Volume 2***



INDEX

***Paragraph numbers marked "+" denote electronic content; those within [...] refer to Volume 2***

*Paragraph numbers marked "+" denote electronic content; those within [...] refer to Volume 2*

***Paragraph numbers marked "+" denote electronic content; those within [...] refer to Volume 2***

***Paragraph numbers marked "+" denote electronic content; those within [...] refer to Volume 2***

***Paragraph numbers marked "+" denote electronic content; those within [...] refer to Volume 2***

***Paragraph numbers marked "+" denote electronic content; those within [...] refer to Volume 2***

*Paragraph numbers marked "+" denote electronic content; those within [...] refer to Volume 2*

***Paragraph numbers marked "+" denote electronic content; those within [...] refer to Volume 2***

*Paragraph numbers marked "+" denote electronic content; those within [...] refer to Volume 2*

***Paragraph numbers marked "+" denote electronic content; those within [...] refer to Volume 2***

*Paragraph numbers marked "+" denote electronic content; those within [...] refer to Volume 2*

***Paragraph numbers marked "+" denote electronic content; those within [...] refer to Volume 2***

***Paragraph numbers marked "+" denote electronic content; those within [...] refer to Volume 2***

***Paragraph numbers marked "+" denote electronic content; those within [...] refer to Volume 2***

***Paragraph numbers marked "+" denote electronic content; those within [...] refer to Volume 2***

***Paragraph numbers marked "+" denote electronic content; those within [...] refer to Volume 2***

*Paragraph numbers marked "+" denote electronic content; those within [...] refer to Volume 2*

*Paragraph numbers marked "+" denote electronic content; those within [...] refer to Volume 2*

***Paragraph numbers marked "+" denote electronic content; those within [...] refer to Volume 2***

***Paragraph numbers marked "+" denote electronic content; those within [...] refer to Volume 2***

*Paragraph numbers marked "+" denote electronic content; those within [...] refer to Volume 2*

*Paragraph numbers marked "+" denote electronic content; those within [...] refer to Volume 2*

***Paragraph numbers marked "+" denote electronic content; those within [...] refer to Volume 2***

***Paragraph numbers marked "+" denote electronic content; those within [...] refer to Volume 2***

***Paragraph numbers marked "+" denote electronic content; those within [...] refer to Volume 2***

***Paragraph numbers marked "+" denote electronic content; those within [...] refer to Volume 2***

*Paragraph numbers marked "+" denote electronic content; those within [...] refer to Volume 2*

***Paragraph numbers marked "+" denote electronic content; those within [...] refer to Volume 2***

***Paragraph numbers marked "+" denote electronic content; those within [...] refer to Volume 2***

INDEX

***Paragraph numbers marked "+" denote electronic content; those within [...] refer to Volume 2***

*Paragraph numbers marked "+" denote electronic content; those within [...] refer to Volume 2*

***Paragraph numbers marked "+" denote electronic content; those within [...] refer to Volume 2***

***Paragraph numbers marked "+" denote electronic content; those within [...] refer to Volume 2***

***Paragraph numbers marked "+" denote electronic content; those within [...] refer to Volume 2***

***Paragraph numbers marked "+" denote electronic content; those within [...] refer to Volume 2***

*Paragraph numbers marked "+" denote electronic content; those within [...] refer to Volume 2*

***Paragraph numbers marked "+" denote electronic content; those within [...] refer to Volume 2***

***Paragraph numbers marked "+" denote electronic content; those within [...] refer to Volume 2***

*Paragraph numbers marked "+" denote electronic content; those within [...] refer to Volume 2*

*Paragraph numbers marked "+" denote electronic content; those within [...] refer to Volume 2*

***Paragraph numbers marked "+" denote electronic content; those within [...] refer to Volume 2***

***Paragraph numbers marked "+" denote electronic content; those within [...] refer to Volume 2***

***Paragraph numbers marked "+" denote electronic content; those within [...] refer to Volume 2***

*Paragraph numbers marked "+" denote electronic content; those within [...] refer to Volume 2*

***Paragraph numbers marked "+" denote electronic content; those within [...] refer to Volume 2***

***Paragraph numbers marked "+" denote electronic content; those within [...] refer to Volume 2***

***Paragraph numbers marked "+" denote electronic content; those within [...] refer to Volume 2***

***Paragraph numbers marked "+" denote electronic content; those within [...] refer to Volume 2***

***Paragraph numbers marked "+" denote electronic content; those within [...] refer to Volume 2***

***Paragraph numbers marked "+" denote electronic content; those within [...] refer to Volume 2***

*Paragraph numbers marked "+" denote electronic content; those within [...] refer to Volume 2*

***Paragraph numbers marked "+" denote electronic content; those within [...] refer to Volume 2***

***Paragraph numbers marked "+" denote electronic content; those within [...] refer to Volume 2***

***Paragraph numbers marked "+" denote electronic content; those within [...] refer to Volume 2***

*Paragraph numbers marked "+" denote electronic content; those within [...] refer to Volume 2*

***Paragraph numbers marked "+" denote electronic content; those within [...] refer to Volume 2***

***Paragraph numbers marked "+" denote electronic content; those within [...] refer to Volume 2***

***Paragraph numbers marked "+" denote electronic content; those within [...] refer to Volume 2***

*Paragraph numbers marked "+" denote electronic content; those within [...] refer to Volume 2*

***Paragraph numbers marked "+" denote electronic content; those within [...] refer to Volume 2***

***Paragraph numbers marked "+" denote electronic content; those within [...] refer to Volume 2***

***Paragraph numbers marked "+" denote electronic content; those within [...] refer to Volume 2***

***Paragraph numbers marked "+" denote electronic content; those within [...] refer to Volume 2***

***Paragraph numbers marked "+" denote electronic content; those within [...] refer to Volume 2***

***Paragraph numbers marked "+" denote electronic content; those within [...] refer to Volume 2***

***Paragraph numbers marked "+" denote electronic content; those within [...] refer to Volume 2***

***Paragraph numbers marked "+" denote electronic content; those within [...] refer to Volume 2***



INDEX

INDEX

***Paragraph numbers marked "+" denote electronic content; those within [...] refer to Volume 2***

***Paragraph numbers marked "+" denote electronic content; those within [...] refer to Volume 2***

***Paragraph numbers marked "+" denote electronic content; those within [...] refer to Volume 2***

***Paragraph numbers marked "+" denote electronic content; those within [...] refer to Volume 2***

***Paragraph numbers marked "+" denote electronic content; those within [...] refer to Volume 2***

*Paragraph numbers marked "+" denote electronic content; those within [...] refer to Volume 2*

***Paragraph numbers marked "+" denote electronic content; those within [...] refer to Volume 2***

INDEX

***Paragraph numbers marked "+" denote electronic content; those within [...] refer to Volume 2***

*Paragraph numbers marked "+" denote electronic content; those within [...] refer to Volume 2*

*Paragraph numbers marked "+" denote electronic content; those within [...] refer to Volume 2*

*Paragraph numbers marked "+" denote electronic content; those within [...] refer to Volume 2*

***Paragraph numbers marked "+" denote electronic content; those within [...] refer to Volume 2***

*Paragraph numbers marked "+" denote electronic content; those within [...] refer to Volume 2*

***Paragraph numbers marked "+" denote electronic content; those within [...] refer to Volume 2***

***Paragraph numbers marked "+" denote electronic content; those within [...] refer to Volume 2***

***Paragraph numbers marked "+" denote electronic content; those within [...] refer to Volume 2***

***Paragraph numbers marked "+" denote electronic content; those within [...] refer to Volume 2***



INDEX

***Paragraph numbers marked "+" denote electronic content; those within [...] refer to Volume 2***

*Paragraph numbers marked "+" denote electronic content; those within [...] refer to Volume 2*



INDEX

***Paragraph numbers marked "+" denote electronic content; those within [...] refer to Volume 2***

***Paragraph numbers marked "+" denote electronic content; those within [...] refer to Volume 2***

***Paragraph numbers marked "+" denote electronic content; those within [...] refer to Volume 2***

***Paragraph numbers marked "+" denote electronic content; those within [...] refer to Volume 2***

*Paragraph numbers marked "+" denote electronic content; those within [...] refer to Volume 2*

*Paragraph numbers marked "+" denote electronic content; those within [...] refer to Volume 2*

***Paragraph numbers marked "+" denote electronic content; those within [...] refer to Volume 2***

***Paragraph numbers marked "+" denote electronic content; those within [...] refer to Volume 2***

***Paragraph numbers marked "+" denote electronic content; those within [...] refer to Volume 2***

***Paragraph numbers marked "+" denote electronic content; those within [...] refer to Volume 2***

*Paragraph numbers marked "+" denote electronic content; those within [...] refer to Volume 2*

***Paragraph numbers marked "+" denote electronic content; those within [...] refer to Volume 2***

***Paragraph numbers marked "+" denote electronic content; those within [...] refer to Volume 2***

***Paragraph numbers marked "+" denote electronic content; those within [...] refer to Volume 2***

***Paragraph numbers marked "+" denote electronic content; those within [...] refer to Volume 2***

*Paragraph numbers marked "+" denote electronic content; those within [...] refer to Volume 2*

***Paragraph numbers marked "+" denote electronic content; those within [...] refer to Volume 2***

***Paragraph numbers marked "+" denote electronic content; those within [...] refer to Volume 2***

*Paragraph numbers marked "+" denote electronic content; those within [...] refer to Volume 2*

*Paragraph numbers marked "+" denote electronic content; those within [...] refer to Volume 2*

***Paragraph numbers marked "+" denote electronic content; those within [...] refer to Volume 2***

***Paragraph numbers marked "+" denote electronic content; those within [...] refer to Volume 2***

***Paragraph numbers marked "+" denote electronic content; those within [...] refer to Volume 2***

***Paragraph numbers marked "+" denote electronic content; those within [...] refer to Volume 2***

***Paragraph numbers marked "+" denote electronic content; those within [...] refer to Volume 2***

***Paragraph numbers marked "+" denote electronic content; those within [...] refer to Volume 2***

***Paragraph numbers marked "+" denote electronic content; those within [...] refer to Volume 2***

INDEX

*Paragraph numbers marked "+" denote electronic content; those within [...] refer to Volume 2*

***Paragraph numbers marked "+" denote electronic content; those within [...] refer to Volume 2***

INDEX

***Paragraph numbers marked "+" denote electronic content; those within [...] refer to Volume 2***

*Paragraph numbers marked "+" denote electronic content; those within [...] refer to Volume 2*

***Paragraph numbers marked "+" denote electronic content; those within [...] refer to Volume 2***

***Paragraph numbers marked "+" denote electronic content; those within [...] refer to Volume 2***

***Paragraph numbers marked "+" denote electronic content; those within [...] refer to Volume 2***

***Paragraph numbers marked "+" denote electronic content; those within [...] refer to Volume 2***

***Paragraph numbers marked "+" denote electronic content; those within [...] refer to Volume 2***

***Paragraph numbers marked "+" denote electronic content; those within [...] refer to Volume 2***

***Paragraph numbers marked "+" denote electronic content; those within [...] refer to Volume 2***

***Paragraph numbers marked "+" denote electronic content; those within [...] refer to Volume 2***

***Paragraph numbers marked "+" denote electronic content; those within [...] refer to Volume 2***

***Paragraph numbers marked "+" denote electronic content; those within [...] refer to Volume 2***

***Paragraph numbers marked "+" denote electronic content; those within [...] refer to Volume 2***

*Paragraph numbers marked "+" denote electronic content; those within [...] refer to Volume 2*

*Paragraph numbers marked "+" denote electronic content; those within [...] refer to Volume 2*

***Paragraph numbers marked "+" denote electronic content; those within [...] refer to Volume 2***

*Paragraph numbers marked "+" denote electronic content; those within [...] refer to Volume 2*

***Paragraph numbers marked "+" denote electronic content; those within [...] refer to Volume 2***

***Paragraph numbers marked "+" denote electronic content; those within [...] refer to Volume 2***

*Paragraph numbers marked "+" denote electronic content; those within [...] refer to Volume 2*

***Paragraph numbers marked "+" denote electronic content; those within [...] refer to Volume 2***

***Paragraph numbers marked "+" denote electronic content; those within [...] refer to Volume 2***

***Paragraph numbers marked "+" denote electronic content; those within [...] refer to Volume 2***

***Paragraph numbers marked "+" denote electronic content; those within [...] refer to Volume 2***

# 2009

**JANUARY**

| M | T | W | Th | F | Sa | Su |
|---|---|---|---|---|---|---|
| | | | 1 | 2 | 3 | 4 |
| 5 | 6 | 7 | 8 | 9 | 10 | 11 |
| 12 | 13 | 14 | 15 | 16 | 17 | 18 |
| 19 | 20 | 21 | 22 | 23 | 24 | 25 |
| 26 | 27 | 28 | 29 | 30 | 31 | |

**FEBRUARY**

| M | T | W | Th | F | Sa | Su |
|---|---|---|---|---|---|---|
| | | | | | | 1 |
| 2 | 3 | 4 | 5 | 6 | 7 | 8 |
| 9 | 10 | 11 | 12 | 13 | 14 | 15 |
| 16 | 17 | 18 | 19 | 20 | 21 | 22 |
| 23 | 24 | 25 | 26 | 27 | 28 | |

**MARCH**

| M | T | W | Th | F | Sa | Su |
|---|---|---|---|---|---|---|
| | | | | | | 1 |
| 2 | 3 | 4 | 5 | 6 | 7 | 8 |
| 9 | 10 | 11 | 12 | 13 | 14 | 15 |
| 16 | 17 | 18 | 19 | 20 | 21 | 22 |
| 23 | 24 | 25 | 26 | 27 | 28 | 29 |
| 30 | 31 | | | | | |

**APRIL**

| M | T | W | Th | F | Sa | Su |
|---|---|---|---|---|---|---|
| | | 1 | 2 | 3 | 4 | 5 |
| 6 | 7 | 8 | 9 | 10 | 11 | 12 |
| 13 | 14 | 15 | 16 | 17 | 18 | 19 |
| 20 | 21 | 22 | 23 | 24 | 25 | 26 |
| 27 | 28 | 29 | 30 | | | |

**MAY**

| M | T | W | Th | F | Sa | Su |
|---|---|---|---|---|---|---|
| | | | | 1 | 2 | 3 |
| 4 | 5 | 6 | 7 | 8 | 9 | 10 |
| 11 | 12 | 13 | 14 | 15 | 16 | 17 |
| 18 | 19 | 20 | 21 | 22 | 23 | 24 |
| 25 | 26 | 27 | 28 | 29 | 30 | 31 |

**JUNE**

| M | T | W | Th | F | Sa | Su |
|---|---|---|---|---|---|---|
| 1 | 2 | 3 | 4 | 5 | 6 | 7 |
| 8 | 9 | 10 | 11 | 12 | 13 | 14 |
| 15 | 16 | 17 | 18 | 19 | 20 | 21 |
| 22 | 23 | 24 | 25 | 26 | 27 | 28 |
| 29 | 30 | | | | | |

**JULY**

| M | T | W | Th | F | Sa | Su |
|---|---|---|---|---|---|---|
| | | 1 | 2 | 3 | 4 | 5 |
| 6 | 7 | 8 | 9 | 10 | 11 | 12 |
| 13 | 14 | 15 | 16 | 17 | 18 | 19 |
| 20 | 21 | 22 | 23 | 24 | 25 | 26 |
| 27 | 28 | 29 | 30 | 31 | | |

**AUGUST**

| M | T | W | Th | F | Sa | Su |
|---|---|---|---|---|---|---|
| | | | | | 1 | 2 |
| 3 | 4 | 5 | 6 | 7 | 8 | 9 |
| 10 | 11 | 12 | 13 | 14 | 15 | 16 |
| 17 | 18 | 19 | 20 | 21 | 22 | 23 |
| 24 | 25 | 26 | 27 | 28 | 29 | 30 |
| 31 | | | | | | |

**SEPTEMBER**

| M | T | W | Th | F | Sa | Su |
|---|---|---|---|---|---|---|
| | 1 | 2 | 3 | 4 | 5 | 6 |
| 7 | 8 | 9 | 10 | 11 | 12 | 13 |
| 14 | 15 | 16 | 17 | 18 | 19 | 20 |
| 21 | 22 | 23 | 24 | 25 | 26 | 27 |
| 28 | 29 | 30 | | | | |

**OCTOBER**

| M | T | W | Th | F | Sa | Su |
|---|---|---|---|---|---|---|
| | | | 1 | 2 | 3 | 4 |
| 5 | 6 | 7 | 8 | 9 | 10 | 11 |
| 12 | 13 | 14 | 15 | 16 | 17 | 18 |
| 19 | 20 | 21 | 22 | 23 | 24 | 25 |
| 26 | 27 | 28 | 29 | 30 | 31 | |

**NOVEMBER**

| M | T | W | Th | F | Sa | Su |
|---|---|---|---|---|---|---|
| | | | | | | 1 |
| 2 | 3 | 4 | 5 | 6 | 7 | 8 |
| 9 | 10 | 11 | 12 | 13 | 14 | 15 |
| 16 | 17 | 18 | 19 | 20 | 21 | 22 |
| 23 | 24 | 25 | 26 | 27 | 28 | 29 |
| 30 | | | | | | |

**DECEMBER**

| M | T | W | Th | F | Sa | Su |
|---|---|---|---|---|---|---|
| | 1 | 2 | 3 | 4 | 5 | 6 |
| 7 | 8 | 9 | 10 | 11 | 12 | 13 |
| 14 | 15 | 16 | 17 | 18 | 19 | 20 |
| 21 | 22 | 23 | 24 | 25 | 26 | 27 |
| 28 | 29 | 30 | 31 | | | |

# 2010

**JANUARY**

| M | T | W | Th | F | Sa | Su |
|---|---|---|---|---|---|---|
| | | | | 1 | 2 | 3 |
| 4 | 5 | 6 | 7 | 8 | 9 | 10 |
| 11 | 12 | 13 | 14 | 15 | 16 | 17 |
| 18 | 19 | 20 | 21 | 22 | 23 | 24 |
| 25 | 26 | 27 | 28 | 29 | 30 | 31 |

**FEBRUARY**

| M | T | W | Th | F | Sa | Su |
|---|---|---|---|---|---|---|
| 1 | 2 | 3 | 4 | 5 | 6 | 7 |
| 8 | 9 | 10 | 11 | 12 | 13 | 14 |
| 15 | 16 | 17 | 18 | 19 | 20 | 21 |
| 22 | 23 | 24 | 25 | 26 | 27 | 28 |

**MARCH**

| M | T | W | Th | F | Sa | Su |
|---|---|---|---|---|---|---|
| 1 | 2 | 3 | 4 | 5 | 6 | 7 |
| 8 | 9 | 10 | 11 | 12 | 13 | 14 |
| 15 | 16 | 17 | 18 | 19 | 20 | 21 |
| 22 | 23 | 24 | 25 | 26 | 27 | 28 |
| 29 | 30 | 31 | | | | |

**APRIL**

| M | T | W | Th | F | Sa | Su |
|---|---|---|---|---|---|---|
| | | | 1 | 2 | 3 | 4 |
| 5 | 6 | 7 | 8 | 9 | 10 | 11 |
| 12 | 13 | 14 | 15 | 16 | 17 | 18 |
| 19 | 20 | 21 | 22 | 23 | 24 | 25 |
| 26 | 27 | 28 | 29 | 30 | | |

**MAY**

| M | T | W | Th | F | Sa | Su |
|---|---|---|---|---|---|---|
| | | | | | 1 | 2 |
| 3 | 4 | 5 | 6 | 7 | 8 | 9 |
| 10 | 11 | 12 | 13 | 14 | 15 | 16 |
| 17 | 18 | 19 | 20 | 21 | 22 | 23 |
| 24 | 25 | 26 | 27 | 28 | 29 | 30 |
| 31 | | | | | | |

**JUNE**

| M | T | W | Th | F | Sa | Su |
|---|---|---|---|---|---|---|
| | 1 | 2 | 3 | 4 | 5 | 6 |
| 7 | 8 | 9 | 10 | 11 | 12 | 13 |
| 14 | 15 | 16 | 17 | 18 | 19 | 20 |
| 21 | 22 | 23 | 24 | 25 | 26 | 27 |
| 28 | 29 | 30 | | | | |

**JULY**

| M | T | W | Th | F | Sa | Su |
|---|---|---|---|---|---|---|
| | | | 1 | 2 | 3 | 4 |
| 5 | 6 | 7 | 8 | 9 | 10 | 11 |
| 12 | 13 | 14 | 15 | 16 | 17 | 18 |
| 19 | 20 | 21 | 22 | 23 | 24 | 25 |
| 26 | 27 | 28 | 29 | 30 | 31 | |

**AUGUST**

| M | T | W | Th | F | Sa | Su |
|---|---|---|---|---|---|---|
| | | | | | | 1 |
| 2 | 3 | 4 | 5 | 6 | 7 | 8 |
| 9 | 10 | 11 | 12 | 13 | 14 | 15 |
| 16 | 17 | 18 | 19 | 20 | 21 | 22 |
| 23 | 24 | 25 | 26 | 27 | 28 | 29 |
| 30 | 31 | | | | | |

**SEPTEMBER**

| M | T | W | Th | F | Sa | Su |
|---|---|---|---|---|---|---|
| | | 1 | 2 | 3 | 4 | 5 |
| 6 | 7 | 8 | 9 | 10 | 11 | 12 |
| 13 | 14 | 15 | 16 | 17 | 18 | 19 |
| 20 | 21 | 22 | 23 | 24 | 25 | 26 |
| 27 | 28 | 29 | 30 | | | |

**OCTOBER**

| M | T | W | Th | F | Sa | Su |
|---|---|---|---|---|---|---|
| | | | | 1 | 2 | 3 |
| 4 | 5 | 6 | 7 | 8 | 9 | 10 |
| 11 | 12 | 13 | 14 | 15 | 16 | 17 |
| 18 | 19 | 20 | 21 | 22 | 23 | 24 |
| 25 | 26 | 27 | 28 | 29 | 30 | 31 |

**NOVEMBER**

| M | T | W | Th | F | Sa | Su |
|---|---|---|---|---|---|---|
| 1 | 2 | 3 | 4 | 5 | 6 | 7 |
| 8 | 9 | 10 | 11 | 12 | 13 | 14 |
| 15 | 16 | 17 | 18 | 19 | 20 | 21 |
| 22 | 23 | 24 | 25 | 26 | 27 | 28 |
| 29 | 30 | | | | | |

**DECEMBER**

| M | T | W | Th | F | Sa | Su |
|---|---|---|---|---|---|---|
| | | 1 | 2 | 3 | 4 | 5 |
| 6 | 7 | 8 | 9 | 10 | 11 | 12 |
| 13 | 14 | 15 | 16 | 17 | 18 | 19 |
| 20 | 21 | 22 | 23 | 24 | 25 | 26 |
| 27 | 28 | 29 | 30 | 31 | | |